PUBLIC LIBRARY CORE COLLECTION: NONFICTION

CORE COLLECTION SERIES

FORMERLY
STANDARD CATALOG SERIES

SHAUNA GRIFFIN, MLIS, GENERAL EDITOR

CHILDREN'S CORE COLLECTION
FICTION CORE COLLECTION
GRAPHIC NOVELS CORE COLLECTION
MIDDLE AND JUNIOR HIGH CORE COLLECTION
PUBLIC LIBRARY CORE COLLECTION: NONFICTION
SENIOR HIGH CORE COLLECTION
YOUNG ADULT FICTION CORE COLLECTION

PUBLIC LIBRARY CORE COLLECTION: NONFICTION

Twentieth Edition

Volume 1

EDITED BY
KENDAL SPIRES

H. W. Wilson
A Division of EBSCO Information Services, Inc.
Ipswich, Massachusetts
2025

GREY HOUSE PUBLISHING

Cover: iStock

Copyright © 2025 by H. W. Wilson, A Division of EBSCO Information Services, Inc. All rights reserved. No part of this work may be used or reproduced in any manner whatsoever or transmitted in any form or by any means, electronic or mechanical, including photocopy, recording, or any information storage and retrieval system, without written permission from the copyright owner. For permissions requests, contact proprietarypublishing@ebsco.com.

ISBN 979-8-89179-060-5

The Dewey Decimal Classification is © 2003-2017 OCLC Online Computer Library Center, Inc. Used with Permission. DDC, Dewey, Dewey Decimal Classification and WebDewey are registered trademarks/service marks of OCLC Online Computer Library Center, Inc.

Public Library Core Collection: Nonfiction, Twentieth Edition, published by Grey House Publishing, Inc., Amenia, NY, under exclusive license from EBSCO Information Services, Inc.

CONTENTS

Preface vii
Purpose and Organization xi
Acknowledgments... xv
Volume 1. Essential and Recommended Titles 1
Volume 2. Author, Title, Series, and Subject Index 1553

PREFACE

PUBLIC LIBRARY CORE COLLECTION: NONFICTION is a curated list of nonfiction titles for adults that may be used to develop a collection serving general readers in public libraries of all sizes. It also includes professional materials for librarians, including titles focusing on collection development, readers' advisory, reference, and managing a public library.

This Core Collection is an abridgment of the database available from EBSCO Information Services, which has an additional two recommendation levels, Lexile measures, book reviews and articles, and expanded metadata. It is updated weekly. Contact your EBSCO or NoveList sales rep for a free trial, or visit https://www.ebscohost.com/novelist/our-products/core-collections for more information. EBSCO also invites feedback from Core Collections customers at novelist@ebsco.com.

What's in this Edition?

This edition continues to emphasize equity, diversity, and inclusion, representing and reflecting a varied community in which many voices can be heard. Significant weeding is undertaken to ensure that older, outdated books are removed in favor of more relevant recommendations.

With more than 11,000 nonfiction titles appropriate to general adult readers as well as a selection of professional materials of use to librarians and library administrators, this 20th edition contains both new titles that reflect new topics of interest or new interpretations of traditional knowledge as well as older titles—sometimes in updated versions—that remain the best in their field.

As always, a star (★) at the start of an entry indicates that a book is an *Essential* title, our highest recommendation level. These titles are the essential books in a given category or on a given subject; while there are often a number of recommended titles, this designation helps users who want only a small selection. Non-starred entries represent *Recommended* titles, which provide a fuller list of recommended books. This is reflected in both the Classified section and, for the first time, in the Index as well.

History

The first of several installments of the "Standard Catalog" for the general library was published in 1918. It was called STANDARD CATALOG: SOCIOLOGY SECTION. Additional installments were issued over the next fourteen years, covering Biography; Fiction; Fine Arts; History and Travel; Science and Useful Arts; Literature and Philology; and Philosophy, Religion, and General Works. Finally, a fully integrated first edition of the STANDARD CATALOG FOR PUBLIC LIBRARIES was assembled and published in 1934. The contents were displayed in classified order, according to the Dewey Decimal Classification. The name was changed to PUBLIC LIBRARY CATALOG with the publication of the fifth edition in 1969, and then to PUBLIC LIBRARY CORE COLLECTION: NONFICTION with the thirteenth edition in 2008.

The collection subsequently evolved, along with other Core Collections, into an online resource called WilsonWeb. EBSCO Information Services acquired H.W. Wilson in 2011, and the collections became EBSCO*host* databases in 2012. In 2020, the readers' advisory experts at NoveList applied their expertise: while Core Collections continues to provide impartial collection development guidance by experts in their fields, this marriage of

PUBLIC LIBRARY CORE COLLECTION: NONFICTION
Twentieth Edition

readers advisory and collection development expertise strengthened the application of genre and subject headings, expanded awards content, and improved search and browse capabilities in the online Core Collections databases.

Scope

PUBLIC LIBRARY CORE COLLECTION: NONFICTION is a guide to nonfiction books published in the United States or published in other countries and distributed in the United States. It excludes non-print materials; periodicals; non-English items (with the exception of dictionaries); and works of an ephemeral nature. Original paperback materials are included. Multiple subjects provide access points via the subject index.

The Core Collection is intended to serve the needs of public and undergraduate libraries and stands as a basic or "opening day" collection. The newer titles help in identifying areas in a collection that can be updated or strengthened, while the retention of useful material from the previous edition enables the librarian to make informed decisions about weeding a collection. With its classified arrangement, complete bibliographical data, and descriptive and evaluative annotations, the Core Collection provides useful information for the acquisitions librarian, the reference librarian, and the cataloger.

Although a Fiction Section was issued in 1923, followed by supplements in 1928 and 1931, fiction was omitted from the first edition of the complete Catalog in 1934. A new expanded edition of the Fiction Section was published as FICTION CATALOG in 1942. In its preface, that Catalog was referred to as a "companion volume to the Standard Catalog for Public Libraries." This complementary relationship has continued to the present: PUBLIC LIBRARY COLRE COLLECTION: NONFICTION has always listed works of literary criticism and literary history, as well as books about literary technique.

Books are listed with an ISBN—most frequently for a hardcover edition published in the United States, or published in Canada or the United Kingdom and distributed in the U.S. Out-of-print titles are retained in the belief that good books are not obsolete simply because they happen to go out of print.

The Database

This Core Collection is derived from the database available from EBSCO Information Services. Metadata for the titles in this volume is provided by the metadata librarians at NoveList, who manage and apply a controlled vocabulary that adapts as terms come in and out of style, or as events require new ones. There are additional, browsable access points, plus full-text book reviews and articles, full-color cover art, Lexile measures, and all of the *Supplemental* book recommendations and *Weeded* titles. It is updated weekly. For more information or for a free trial, contact your EBSCO or NoveList sales rep, or visit https://www.ebscohost.com/novelist/our-products/core-collections. EBSCO also invites feedback from Core Collections customers at novelist@ebsco.com.

In 2017, EBSCO renamed the PUBLIC LIBRARY CORE COLLECTION: NONFICTION database. Now called NONFICTION CORE COLLECTION, it is in line with the other database names, is less cumbersome, and signifies its applicability to general readers in libraries of all types. Although the title of this edition is different from the database from which it is derived, it contains the same content, and is not a separate set of book recommendations.

PREFACE

Preparation

Books included in Core Collections are selected by experienced librarians representing public library systems, school libraries, and academic libraries across the United States and Canada, as well as NoveList staff. These librarians also act as advisors on library policy, trends, and special projects. The names of participating librarians and their affiliations are listed in the Acknowledgements.

Core Collections Products

For recommendations for children's books, librarians are encouraged to investigate the following databases and their associated print versions:

CHILDREN'S CORE COLLECTION
MIDDLE AND JUNIOR HIGH CORE COLLECTION
SENIOR HIGH CORE COLLECTION

For young adult fiction specifically, consult the YOUNG ADULT FICTION CORE COLLECTION, available only in print.

For adult nonfiction for the general reader, try the database NONFICTION CORE COLLECTION or the associated print volume PUBLIC LIBRARY CORE COLLECTION: NONFICTION. For fiction, please use FICTION CORE COLLECTION, either as a database or the associated print version.

For Graphic Novels for all ages, try the GRAPHIC NOVELS CORE COLLECTION in print or database form, which includes both fiction and nonfiction recommendations.

In 2023, the CORE COLLECTION EN ESPAÑOL was launched, which includes titles for a Spanish-speaking audience at all levels, available only as a database.

PURPOSE AND ORGANIZATION

PURPOSE

CORE COLLECTIONS is designed to serve a number of purposes:

As an aid in purchasing. Core Collections is designed to assist in the selection and ordering of titles. Summaries and evaluative excerpts are provided for each title along with information regarding the publisher, ISBN, page count, and publication year. In evaluating the suitability of a work, each library will want to consider the needs of the unique patron base it serves.

As an aid in verification of information. For this purpose, bibliographical information is provided in the list of works. Entries also include recommended subject headings based on NoveList's proprietary subject vocabulary. Notes may describe editions available and other content; for the most up-to-date metadata, please consult the EBSCO*host* database.

As an aid in curriculum or programming support. The classified approach, subject indexing, annotations, and evaluative excerpts are helpful in identifying materials appropriate for classroom support, for book discussions, and other programming.

As an aid in collection maintenance. Information about titles available on a subject facilitates decisions to rebind, replace, or discard items. If a book has been demoted to the Supplemental or Weeded recommendation levels and therefore no longer appears in the print abridgement of the database, that demotion is not intended as a sign that the book is no longer valuable or that it should necessarily be weeded from your library's collection.

As an aid in professional development or instruction. The Core Collection is useful in courses or professional training that deal with collection development and readers' advisory; it may also be used in course that deal with literature and book selection, especially in the creation of bibliographies and reading lists.

As an aid to readers' advisory. Every title in this Core Collection is a recommended work and can be given with confidence to a user who expresses a need based on topic, genre, etc. Readers' advisory and user service are further aided by series and awards information, by the descriptive summaries and evaluative excerpts from trusted review sources, and by the subject headings in the Title and Subject Index applied by professional metadata librarians at NoveList.

ORGANIZATION

This Core Collection consists of two parts: a list of Essential and Recommended Titles, found in Volume 1, and a Title, Author, Series, and Subject Index, found in Volume 2.

Volume 1. Essential and Recommended Titles

The list of Essential and Recommended Titles is arranged and classified according to the Dewey Decimal Classification in numerical order from 000 to 999. The exception is individual biographies, which are classed at 92 and

PUBLIC LIBRARY CORE COLLECTION: NONFICTION
Twentieth Edition

close out the collection. These will have a subject heading B and are organized by author. Locate biographies by subject by using the Author, Title, Series, and Subject Index.

An Outline of Classification, which serves as a table for contents for the list of Essential and Recommended Titles, is reproduced following this section. It should be noted that many topics can be classified in more than one discipline. If a particular title is not found where it might be expected, the Index should be consulted to determine if it is classified elsewhere.

Within classes, works are arranged alphabetically under main entry, first by author, then by title.

Each listing consists of a bibliographic description, suggested subject headings derived from NoveList, series and awards information where relevant, a suggested classification number from the *Abridged Dewey Decimal Classification and Relative Index*, a brief description of the contents of the book, and where possible an evaluative excerpt from a notable source. The following is an example of a typical entry and a description of its components.

> **Roach, Mary**
> ★ *Stiff: The Curious Lives of Human Cadavers*. Mary Roach.
> W.W. Norton & Co., 2003. 303 p. : Illustration
> ISBN 0393050939
> Grades: 11 12 Adult   611
> 1. Human experimentation in medicine 2. Dead 3. Human dissection 4. Medical research 5. Forensic sciences 6. Forensic scientists 7. Forensic medicine 8. Cannibalism 9. Transplantation of organs, tissues, etc. 10. True Crime—Forensic sciences 11. Science Writing—Biology 12. Adult books for young adults 13. Nonfiction that reads like fiction
> LC 2002152908
> Alex Award, 2004 ; Booklist Editors' Choice: Adult Books for Young Adults, 2003 ; Garden State Teen Book Award (New Jersey), Nonfiction, 2006 ; School Library Journal Best Books: Best Adult Books 4 Teens, 2003 ; YALSA Best Books for Young Adults, 2004.
> A look inside the world of forensics examines the use of human cadavers in a wide range of endeavors, including research into new surgical procedures, space exploration, and a Tennessee human decay research facility.
> "Roach writes in an insouciant style and displays her metier in tangents about bizarre incidents in pathological history. Death may have the last laugh, but, in the meantime, Roach finds merriment in the macabre." —*Booklist*
> Includes bibliographical references (p.[295]-303).

The name of the author, Mary Roach, is given in conformity with Library of Congress Authorities. The star at the start of the title indicates that this is an Essential title. The title of the book is Stiff: The Curious Lives of Human Cadavers. The book was published by W.W. Norton & Co. in 2003. It has 303 pages, and illustrations. If it were part of a series, the series name would follow this information.

PURPOSE AND ORGANIZATION

An ISBN (International Standard Book Number) is included to facilitate ordering; however, there will often be many editions and formats of a given title; due to space constraints these ISBNs are not provided in the print edition, though many can be found in the corresponding database.

This book is recommended for older teens (11th and 12th graders) and adutls, At the end of the last line of type in the body entry is 611 in boldface type. This is the classification number or category derived from the fifteenth edition of the *Abridged Dewey Decimal Classification*.

The numbered terms "1. Human experimentation in medicine. 2. Dead. 3. Human dissection. 4. Medical research." are recommended subject headings for this book.

The Library of Congress control number is provided when available.

Any awards the book has won, or notable lists the book has landed on, follows. In this case, the Alex Award, the Garden State Awards, and several lists. These are followed by a brief summary and an evaluative excerpt from a critical reviewing source, in this case Booklist. Such summaries and excerpts are useful in evaluating books for selection and in determining which of several books on the same subject is best suited for the individual reader or purchasing library.

Notes are also made to describe special features, such as a bibliography, if applicable. or to describe series order and companion volumes, editions available, awards, and publication history.

Volume 2. Author, Title, Series, and Subject Index

The Index is a single alphabetical list of all the books entered in the Core Collection. Each book is entered under author, title, series, and subject. The classification number, displayed in boldface type, is the key to the location of the main entry for the book in the list of Essential and Recommended titles. Biographies will have the subject indicator B.

The following are examples of index entries for the book cited above:

Author	**Roach, Mary**	
	★ *Stiff*	611
Title	★ *Stiff*. Roach, Mary	611
Subject	**HUMAN EXPERIMENTATION IN MEDICINE**	
	Roach, Mary. ★ *Stiff*	611

ACKNOWLEDGMENTS

H.W. Wilson, NoveList, and EBSCO Information Services express special gratitude to the following librarians who advised on editorial matters and assisted in the selection and weeding of titles for this Core Collection.

Steven Ashley
Librarian
Carrboro, North Carolina

Manda Carr
Librarian
Troy Public Library
Troy, MI

Cassidy Charles
Legislative Data Analysis Librarian
Library of Congress
Washington, DC

Laura Cohen
Readers & Information Services Librarian
Vernon Area Public Library District
Lincolnshire, IL

Heather Cover
Special Projects Librarian
Homewood Public Library
Homewood, AL

Andrienne Cruz
Librarian
Azusa City Library
Azusa, CA

Gail de Vos
Storyteller & Adjunct Instructor, SLIS
University of Alberta, Edmonton
Canada

Brian Flota
Humanities Librarian
James Madison University
Harrisonburg, VA

Francisca Goldsmith
Library and Media Consultant
Worcester, MA

Patrick Holt
Graphic Designer and Former Librarian
Durham, NC

Malia Jackson
Freelance librarian
Bloomington, IN

Jane Jorgenson
Library Supervisor
Madison Public LIbrary
Madison, WI

Angela Leeper
Director, Curricular Materials Center
University of Richmond
Richmond, Virginia

Marcela Peres
Director
Lewiston Public Library
Lewiston, Maine

Stephanie Sendaula
Programming & Outreach Specialist
LibraryLinkNJ
Ewing, NJ

Sara Shiver McBride
Librarian
Richland Library
Columbia, SC

Jennie Stevens
Teen Librarian
Naperville Public Library
Naperville, IL

Sarah Bean Thompson
Youth Services Manager
Springfield-Green County
Springfield, Missouri

PUBLIC LIBRARY CORE COLLECTION: NONFICTION
Twentieth Edition

Rebecca Vargha
Head Librarian
School of Information and Library Science
UNC-Chapel Hill
Chapel Hill, NC

Basia Wilson
Poet & NoveList Advisor
Collingswood, New Jersey

PUBLIC LIBRARY CORE COLLECTION: NONFICTION
Twentieth Edition

001 Knowledge

Bogdanich, Walt
When McKinsey Comes to Town: The Hidden Influence of the World's Most Powerful Consulting Firm. Walt Bogdanich and Michael Forsythe. Doubleday 2022. 352 p.
ISBN 9780385546232
Grades: Adult **001**
1. Consulting firms 2. Corruption 3. Inequality 4. Business consultants 5. Business 6. Business and economics — Industries 7. Business and economics — Economics — History 8. Business and economics — Corruption and scandal

Conducting hundreds of interviews, obtaining tens of thousands revelatory documents and following the money, two prizewinning investigative journalists expose how the prestigious international consulting firm that advises corporations and governments has often made the world more unequal, more corrupt and more dangerous.

"Thanks to their unprecedented level of access to crucial records and key insider accounts, this monumental corporate exposé will do for management consulting what Patrick Radden Keefe's Empire of Pain (2021) did for the opioid epidemic and the Sacklers." —*Booklist*

001.4 Research statistical methods

Booth, Wayne C.
The Craft of Research. Wayne C. Booth, Gregory G. Colomb, Joseph M. Williams, Joseph Bizup, William T. FitzGerald. The University of Chicago Press 2016. xvi, 316 p. : Illustration
ISBN 9780226239569
Grades: Adult **001.4**
1. Research 2. Nonfiction writing 3. Reference — Writing
LC 2016000143

This fundamental work explains how to find and evaluate sources, anticipate and respond to reader reservations, and integrate these pieces into an argument that stands up to reader critique.
Includes bibliographical references and index.

Page, Scott E
The Model Thinker: What You Need to Know to Make Data Work for You. Scott E. Page. Basic Books 2018. xiii, 427 pages : Illustration
ISBN 9780465094622
Grades: Adult **001.4**
1. Information visualization 2. Data mining 3. Science writing — Computing, the Internet, and Technology 4. Science writing — Mathematics
LC Bl2018193882

A University of Michigan social scientist demonstrates the mathematical, statistical and computational models that can organize raw data into more robust and informative designs for more accurate predictions and decision-making.
Includes bibliographical references (pages 357-409) and index.

Stone, Deborah A.
Counting: How We Use Numbers to Decide What Matters. Deborah Stone. Liveright Publishing 2020. xvi, 291 pages : Illustration
ISBN 9781631495922
Grades: Adult **001.4**
1. Statistics 2. Counting 3. Measurement 4. Perception 5. Misconceptions 6. Psychology 7. Demography 8. Social policy 9. Society and culture — Psychology and human behavior 10. Science Writing — Mathematics

LC 2020014990

Most of us think of counting as a skill so basic that we see numbers as objective, indisputable facts. Not so, says scholar Deborah Stone. In this playful-yet-probing work, Stone reveals the inescapable link between quantifying and classifying, and explains how counting determines almost every facet of our lives—from how we are evaluated at work to how our political opinions are polled to whether we get into college or even out of prison. But numbers, Stone insists, need not rule our lives.

"A delightful takedown of our unreasonable worship of numbers. . . . As Stone lays out her examples of irrational faith in numbers, readers will squirm, but not with disbelief." —*Kirkus*
Includes bibliographical references (pages 247-274) and index.

Tufte, Edward R.
The Visual Display of Quantitative Information. Edward R. Tufte. Graphics Press 2001. 197 p. : Illustration; Color; Map
ISBN 9780961392147
Grades: Adult **001.4**
1. Statistics 2. Science writing — Mathematics 3. Society and culture — Sociology
LC 2001271866

The classic book on statistical graphics, charts, tables.
Includes index.

Whitby, Andrew
The Sum of the People: How the Census Has Shaped Nations, from the Ancient World to the Modern Age. Andrew Whitby. Basic Books 2020. 356 p.
ISBN 9781541619340
Grades: Adult **001.4**
1. Census 2. Demography 3. Social control 4. Social change 5. Political science 6. Statistics 7. United States 8. Politics and global affairs — General 9. History writing — General
LC Bl2020007460

In April 2020, the United States will embark on what has been called "the largest peacetime mobilization in American history": the decennial population census. It is part of a tradition of counting people that goes back at least three millennia and now spans the globe. In The Sum of the People, data scientist Andrew Whitby traces the remarkable history of the census, from ancient China and the Roman Empire, through revolutionary America and Nazi-occupied Europe, to the steps of the Supreme Court. Marvels of democracy, instruments of exclusion, and, at worst, tools of tyranny and genocide, censuses have always profoundly shaped the societies we've built.

"An important, accessible, and engaging book that will find a varied audience from readers of political science, history, economics, and national security." —*Library Journal*
Includes bibliographical references and index.

001.9 Controversial knowledge

Beres, Derek
Conspirituality: How New Age Conspiracy Theories Became a Health Threat. Derek Beres, Matthew Remski, Julian Walker. Public Affairs 2023. 368 p.
ISBN 9781541702981
Grades: Adult **001.9**
1. Public health 2. Conspiracies 3. Health 4. Alternative medicine 5. New Age 6. Spirituality 7. Misinformation 8. History Writing — Conspiracy theories

PUBLIC LIBRARY CORE COLLECTION: NONFICTION
Twentieth Edition

9. Spirituality and religion — General 10. Politics and global affairs — Public health

Using their Conspirituality podcast to expose alt-health practitioners and the politics of paranoia, the authors, in this expansive and eye-opening book, help readers recognize wellness grifts, engage with loved ones who've fallen under the influence and counter lies and distortions with insight and empathy.

"Packed with surprising insights and no-holds-barred takedowns, this is a forceful exposé." —*Publishers Weekly*

Bowlin, Ben
Stuff They Don't Want You to Know. Ben Bowlin, with Matthew Frederick and Noel Brown, hosts of the hit podcast. Stuff You Should Read/An iHeart Book, Flatiron Books 2022. xv, 224 pages : Illustration; Color
ISBN 9781250268563
Grades: Adult   **001.9**
1. Conspiracy theories 2. Conspiracies 3. Misinformation 4. Society and culture — General 5. Reference — General
LC 2022009366

With open minds and extensive research, the hosts of the podcast Stuff They Don't Want You to Know separate conspiracy fact from conspiracy fiction, helping readers to understand the unexplainable and use truth as a powerful weapon against ignorance, misinformation and lies.

"This is a valuable resource for understanding how conspiracy thinking gained its current grip on American politics and culture." —*Publishers Weekly*
Includes bibliographical references.

Weill, Kelly
Off the Edge: Flat Earthers, Conspiracy Culture, and Why People Will Believe Anything. Kelly Weill. Algonquin Books of Chapel Hill 2022. 320 p.
ISBN 9781643750682
Grades: Adult   **001.9**
1. Pseudoscience 2. Scientific errors 3. Conspiracy theories 4. Dimensions 5. Earth 6. United States 7. History writing — General 8. Science Writing — General
LC 2021035867

Drawing a straight line from today's conspiratorial moment back to the early days of Flat Earth theory in the 1830s, a journalist introduces us to a cast of larger-than-life characters as she attends Flat Earther conferences, in this powerful story about belief.

"An illuminating study that locates the common human psychological impulses behind conspiracy culture." —*Library Journal*
Includes bibliographical references.

001.94 Mysteries

Prothero, Donald R.
UFOs, Chemtrails, and Aliens: What Science Says. Donald R. Prothero and Timothy D. Callahan; foreword by Michael Shermer. Indiana University Press 2017. 448 p.
ISBN 9780253026927
Grades: Adult   **001.94**
1. Conspiracy theories 2. UFOs 3. Aliens 4. Curiosities and wonders 5. Pseudoscience 6. Paranormal phenomena 7. Human-alien encounters 8. Society and culture — Pop culture 9. Science writing — General
LC 2017006388

"With their book's brisk pace and energetic writing, Prothero and Callahan offer entertainment as well as wisdom for everyone who's ever wondered what's behind so many conspiracy theories and paranormal phenomena." —*Publishers Weekly*
Includes bibliographical references and index.

001.942 Unidentified flying objects (UFOs)

Graff, Garrett M.
UFO: The Inside Story of the US Government's Search for Alien Life Here - and Out There. Garrett M. Graff. Avid Reader Press 2023. 368 p.
ISBN 9781982196776
Grades: Adult   **001.942**
1. UFOs 2. Conspiracy theories 3. Curiosities and wonders 4. Government information 5. Science Writing — Weird science

This thrilling story of science, the Cold War, Nazi research, atomic anxieties, secret spy planes and the space race draws on original archival research, declassified documents and interviews to present a narrative history of humanity's hunt for alien life, including the military and CIA's secret, decades-long quest to study UFOs.

"The UFO history is loads of fun, and Graff's agnosticism has the potential to appeal to skeptics and believers alike. It's a fascinating dive down the rabbit hole." —*Publishers Weekly*

Mezrich, Ben
The 37th Parallel: The Secret Truth Behind America's UFO Highway. Ben Mezrich. Atria Books 2016. 288 p.
ISBN 9781501135521
Grades: Adult   **001.942**
1. Zukowski, Chuck 2. UFOs 3. UFO abductions 4. Paranormal phenomena 5. Human-alien encounters 6. Science Writing — Weird science
LC 2016021639

Documents the true story of the author's investigations into paranormal UFO events in America's heartland, detailing a baffling case involving mutilated and exsanguinated livestock and how it was tied to unexplained sightings in Roswell, Area 51 and other regions associated with alien activity.

"Mezrich probably won't sway the skeptical, but fans of Art Bell and company will find all the affirmation they need." —*Kirkus*

Scoles, Sarah
They Are Already Here: UFO Culture and Why We See Saucers. Sarah Scoles. Pegasus Books 2020. 248 pages
ISBN 9781643133058
Grades: Adult   **001.942**
1. UFOs 2. Belief and doubt 3. Curiosities and wonders 4. Life on other planets 5. Aliens 6. Human-alien encounters 7. Impartial writing 8. Science Writing — Weird science
LC Bl2020005217

Explores the history of human encounters with unidentified flying objects and the skepticism of some people within the UFO community.

"More general insights into the mercurial quality of memory and belief add considerable heft to this take on an admittedly well-worn topic. Through it all, Scoles remains an open-minded skeptic, and it's this objectivity that makes her buoyant survey so delightful to read." —*Publishers Weekly*
Includes bibliographical references (pages 231-240) and index.

001.944 Monsters and related phenomena

Loxton, Daniel
Abominable Science!: Origins of the Yeti, Nessie, and Other Famous Cryptids. Daniel Loxton and Donald R. Prothero. Columbia University Press 2013. 368 p.
ISBN 9780231153201
Grades: Adult   **001.944**
1. Cryptozoology 2. Mythical creatures 3. Pseudoscience 4. Science Writing — Weird science
LC 2013008424

A look at mythic beasts and legendary creatures and the arguments both for and against their existence.
Includes bibliographical references and index.

ESSENTIAL AND RECOMMENDED TITLES
002 The book

O'Connor, John
The Secret History of Bigfoot: Field Notes on a North American Monster. John O'Connor. Sourcebooks Inc 2024. 304 p.
ISBN 9781464216633
Grades: Adult   **001.944**
1. Sasquatch 2. Cryptozoology 3. Expeditions 4. Monsters 5. Mythical creatures 6. Mythology 7. Popular culture 8. Supernatural 9. Pacific Northwest 10. Science Writing — Weird science 11. Society and culture — Pop culture

From the shrouded forests of the Pacific Northwest to off-the-wall cryptozoological conventions, one man searches high and low for the answer to the question: Real or not, why do we want to believe? Bigfoot is an instantly recognizable figure. Through the decades, this elusive primate has been featured in movies and books, and on coffee mugs, beer koozies, car polish, and CBD oil. Which begs the question: What is it about Bigfoot that's caught hold of our imaginations?

"What does it mean that so many Americans believe a large ape-like creature roams the country's forests? Journalist O'Connor attempts to answer this question in an amusing and thoughtful debut that focuses on 'Bigfooters' as much as on the legendary beast itself." —*Publishers Weekly*

002 The book

Lansky, Aaron
Outwitting History: The Amazing Adventures of a Man Who Rescued a Million Yiddish Books. by Aaron Lansky. Algonquin Books of Chapel Hill 2004. 316 p.
ISBN 9781565124295
Grades: 11 12 Adult   **002**
1. Lansky, Aaron, 1955- 2. Book collecting 3. Language revival 4. Yiddish language 5. Books 6. Jewish men 7. Arts and Entertainment — Writing and Publishing 8. Adult books for young adults
LC 2004051587

ALA Notable Book, 2005; Library Journal Best Books, 2004; Massachusetts Book Awards, Nonfiction Award, 2005.

In 1980 an entire body of Jewish literature—the physical remnant of Yiddish culture—was on the verge of extinction. Precious volumes that had survived Hitler and Stalin were being passed down from older generations of Jewish immigrants to their non-Yiddish-speaking children only to be discarded or destroyed. So Aaron Lansky, just twenty-three, issued a worldwide appeal for unwanted Yiddish works.

"Part memoir and part history, this is the . . . tale of how Lansky retrieved thousands of books from dumpsters and abandoned buildings across America, He also rescued books from the aftermath of the 1994 terrorist bombing of the Jewish Community Center in Buenos Aires and went to Havana to save the few remaining Yiddish books of a vestigial Jewish community there." —*Library Journal*

Includes bibliographical references (p. [313]-316).

Smith, Emma
Portable Magic: A History of Books and Their Readers. Emma Smith. Alfred A. Knopf 2022. 352 pages
ISBN 9781524749095
Grades: Adult   **002**
1. Books and reading 2. Literary criticism 3. Publishers and publishing 4. Books 5. Arts and Entertainment — Writing and publishing 6. History writing — Arts and culture

An effervescent and excitingly revisionist history of bibliophilia, from a globally respected Shakespeare scholar Most of what we say about books is really about their contents, the rosy nostalgic glow for childhood reading, the lifetime companionship of a much-loved novel. But books are things as well as words, objects in our lives as well as worlds in our heads. And just as we crack their spines, loosen their leaves and write in their margins, so they disrupt and disorder us in turn. All books are, as Stephen King put it, 'A uniquely portable magic'. In this thrilling new history, Emma Smith shows us why.

"Readers should make space on their shelves for this dazzling and provocative study." —*Publishers Weekly*

Originally published in by Allen Lane, an imprint of Penguin Random House UK, in London in 2022; Includes bibliographical references and index.

002.03 The book — Dictionaries

Berger, Sidney E
The Dictionary of the Book: A Glossary for Book Collectors, Booksellers, Librarians, and Others. Sidney E. Berger. Rowman & Littlefield 2016. xiv, 319 pages : Illustration
ISBN 9781442263390
Grades: Adult Professional   **002.03**
1. Book collecting 2. Library science 3. Professional materials — General 4. Reference — Dictionaries
LC 2016013533

"A former museum library director and curator of manuscripts at different institutions, Berger is highly qualified to compile this informative and important work." —*Booklist*

Includes bibliographical references (pages 303-317) and index.

002.09 The book — History

Houston, Keith
The Book: A Cover-to-Cover Exploration of the Most Powerful Object of Our Time. Keith Houston. W W Norton & Co. Inc 2016. 400 p.
ISBN 9780393244793
Grades: Adult   **002.09**
1. Books 2. Books and reading 3. Fiction and culture 4. Reading 5. Printing 6. Publishers and publishing 7. Writing 8. History writing — Microhistory 9. Arts and entertainment — Writing and publishing
LC 2016002842

The author of Shady Characters reveals how books and the materials that make them reflect the rich history and culture of human civilization, tracing the development of writing, printing, illustrating and binding to demonstrate the transition from cuneiform tablets and papyrus scrolls to the mass-distributed books of today.

"Pulling together aspects of archaeology, history, literature, and biography, the author reveals the facts, conjecture, and educated guesses experts have made about how and when the first modern tome came to be, which is surprisingly difficult to pin down." —*Library Journal*

McIlwaine, Catherine
Tolkien: Maker of Middle-Earth. Catherine McIlwaine. Bodleian Library, University of Oxford 2018. 416 pages : Illustration; Color; Map
ISBN 9781851244850
Grades: Adult   **002.09**
1. Tolkien, J. R. R. (John Ronald Reuel), 1892-1973 2. Authors, English 3. Creation (Literary, artistic, etc.) 4. Characters and characteristics in literature 5. Writing 6. Authors 7. Creativity 8. Fantasy fiction writing 9. Middle Earth (Imaginary place) 10. Illustrated books 11. Arts and Entertainment — Writing and Publishing
LC 2018411739

This richly illustrated book explores the huge creative endeavour behind Tolkien's enduring popularity. Lavishly illustrated with over 300 images of his manuscripts, drawings, maps and letters, the book traces the creative process behind his most famous literary works—The Hobbit, The Lord of the Rings, and The Silmarillion—and reproduces personal photographs and private papers (some of which have never been seen before in print).

"Richly illustrated and dense with information: Tolkien fans could have no better companion." —*Kirkus*

Catalogue published for the exhibition at the Bodleian Library, University of Oxford (2018), and at the Morgan Library & Museum, New York (2019); Includes bibliographical references (pages 405- 409) and index.

PUBLIC LIBRARY CORE COLLECTION: NONFICTION
Twentieth Edition

004 Computer science; computer programming, programs, data; special computer methods

Dyson, George
Turing's Cathedral: The Origins of the Digital Universe. George Dyson. Pantheon Books 2012. 512 p.
ISBN 9780375422775
Grades: Adult **004**
1. Von Neumann, John, 1903-1957 2. Turing, Alan Mathison, 1912-1954 3. Computers 4. Computer technology 5. Science Writing — Computing, the Internet, and Technology
LC 2011030265
ALA Notable Book, 2013.
Legendary historian and philosopher of science George Dyson vividly re-creates the scenes of focused experimentation, incredible mathematical insight, and pure creative genius that gave us computers, digital television, modern genetics, models of stellar evolution—in other words, computer code.
Includes index.

4.092 Computer science — biography

Kleiman, Kathy
Proving Ground: The Untold Story of the Six Women Who Programmed the World's First Modern Computer. Kathy Kleiman. Grand Central Publishing 2022. 432 p.
ISBN 9781538718285
Grades: Adult **4.092**
1. Women computer programmers 2. ENIAC (Computer) 3. Women mathematicians 4. Technological innovations 5. World War II home front 6. Computer programming 7. Sexism 8. Collective biographies 9. Life stories — Science, technology, and medicine 10. Life stories — Identity — Gender 11. Science Writing — Computing, the Internet, and Technology 12. History writing — Women's history 13. History writing — Technological innovations 14. Nonfiction that reads like fiction 15. Debut title
LC 2022004309
This untold, WWII-era story restores the six women who programmed the world's first modern computer to their rightful place as technological revolutionaries.
"An important and inspiring little-known narrative in modern computing history." —*Kirkus*
Includes bibliographical references and index.

004.67 Wide-area networks

Goodin, Tanya
Stop Staring at Screens: A Digital Detox for the Entire Family. Tanya Goodin; foreword by Dr Mark Griffiths. Ilex 2018. 144 pages : Color; Illustration
ISBN 9781781575765
Grades: Adult **004.67**
1. Internet addiction 2. Internet and children 3. Stress management 4. Technology 5. Family and Relationships — General 6. Family and Relationships — Parenting 7. Science writing — General
LC Bl2019007442
Guides readers with how to find a balance between screen time and family time, identifies key triggers to avoid arguments, and offers diagnostic quizzes to address common issues.
"The author is not antitechnology but does stress that families enjoy more balanced lives when they engage in face-to-face communication. Her suggestions range from establishing screen-free zones to planning enjoyable outdoor activities." —*Library Journal*

005.1092 Computer software developers

Thompson, Clive
Coders: The Making of a New Tribe and the Remaking of the World. Clive Thompson. Penguin Press 2019. 448 p.
ISBN 9780735220560
Grades: Adult **005.1092**
1. Computer programmers 2. Computer programming 3. Interpersonal relations 4. Information technology 5. Social groups 6. Computers and civilization 7. Canadian literature 8. Science Writing — Computing, the Internet, and Technology 9. Society and culture — Media and technology
LC 2018051657
We live in a world constructed of code—and coders are the ones who built it for us. From acclaimed tech writer Clive Thompson comes a brilliant anthropological reckoning with the most powerful tribe in the world today, computer programmers, in a book that interrogates who they are, how they think, what qualifies as greatness in their world, and what should give us pause. They are the most quietly influential people on the planet, and Coders shines a light on their culture.
"This engaging work will appeal to readers who wish to learn more about the intersection of technology and culture, and the space in which they blur together." —*Library Journal*
Includes bibliographical references and index.

005.7 Data in computer systems

Malone, Thomas W.
Superminds: The Surprising Power of People and Computers Thinking Together. Thomas W. Malone. Little, Brown and Company 2018. 288 p.
ISBN 9780316349130
Grades: Adult **005.7**
1. Computers and civilization 2. Swarm intelligence 3. Thought and thinking 4. Artificial intelligence 5. Business communication 6. Business psychology 7. Collaboration 8. Brainstorming 9. Human-computer interaction 10. Science Writing — Computing, the Internet, and Technology 11. Society and culture — Media and technology 12. Business and economics — Business advice — Leadership and management
LC Bl2018080009
The founding director of the MIT Center for Collective Intelligence demonstrates through examples and case studies how artificially intelligent computers can and will amplify the power of groups of people working together collectively in "superminds."

O'Neil, Cathy
Weapons of Math Destruction: How Big Data Increases Inequality and Threatens Democracy. Cathy O'Neil. Crown Publishers 2016. 272 p.
ISBN 9780553418811
Grades: Adult **005.7**
1. Big data 2. Social indicators 3. Democracy 4. Mathematical models 5. Inequality 6. United States 7. 21st century 8. Politics and global affairs — General 9. Society and culture — Media and technology
LC 2016003900
New York Times Notable Book, 2016.
A former Wall Street quantitative analyst sounds an alarm on mathematical modeling, a pervasive new force in society that threatens to undermine democracy and widen inequality.

005.8 Data security

Mitnick, Kevin D.
The Art of Invisibility: The World's Most Famous Hacker Teaches You How to Be Safe in the Age of Big Brother and Big Data. Kevin Mitnick with Robert Vamosi. Little, Brown and Company 2017. 320 p.
ISBN 9780316380508

ESSENTIAL AND RECOMMENDED TITLES
006.2 Special-purpose systems

Grades: Adult **005.8**
1. Internet security 2. Computer security 3. Data protection 4. Privacy rights 5. Computer crimes 6. Society and culture — Media and technology 7. Science Writing — Computing, the Internet, and Technology
LC 2016024302

A world-famous hacker reveals unsettling truths about information vulnerability while outlining affordable online and offline strategies for maximizing privacy and computer security.
Includes bibliographical references and index.

006.2 Special-purpose systems

Hill, Kashmir
★ *Your Face Belongs to Us: A Secretive Startup's Quest to End Privacy as We Know It.* Kashmir Hill. Random House 2023. 320 p.
ISBN 9780593448564
Grades: Adult **006.2**
1. Artificial intelligence 2. Corporations 3. Investors 4. Computer software 5. Identity 6. Identification 7. Surveillance 8. Big data 9. Privacy 10. Business ethics 11. High technology 12. Business and economics — Industries — Technology 13. Politics and global affairs — Civil and human rights 14. Science Writing — Computing, the Internet, and Technology 15. Debut title
LC 2023008999

A tech reporter at the New York Times presents this gripping true story about a mysterious app called Clearview AI that could identify anyone based on just one snapshot of their face, which would be the ultimate surveillance tool—and which would end privacy as we know it.

"Hill's thorough and revealing investigation should be read by everyone who values privacy and holding the powerful accountable for infringing on our rights." —*Booklist*
Includes bibliographical references and index.

006.3 Artificial intelligence and natural computing

Favro, Terri
Generation Robot: A Century of Science Fiction, Fact, and Speculation. Terri Favro. Skyhorse Publishing 2018. 300 p.
ISBN 9781510723108
Grades: Adult **006.3**
1. Favro, Terri 2. Technology and civilization 3. Popular culture 4. Technological innovations 5. Scientific forecasting 6. Nostalgia 7. Literary criticism 8. Autobiographies and memoirs 9. Canadian literature 10. Science fiction 11. Life stories — People in history — Witness to history 12. Science Writing — Computing, the Internet, and Technology 13. Society and culture — Pop culture 14. History writing — Science, technology, and medicine
LC Bl2018002037

Covering a century of science fiction, fact and speculation, from the 1950 publication of Isaac Asimov's I, Robot, to the 2050 Singularity when artificial intelligence are predicted to merge, a nostalgic and fascinating book shows how our relationship with robotics and futuristic technologies has shifted over time.

"In every chapter, Favro shows how different actual robots are from many of their counterparts in science fiction. Her book's greatest achievement may be to get readers looking at their cell phones, computers, prosthetics, and other gadgets as robots in the real world." —*Publishers Weekly*

Kaku, Michio
Quantum Supremacy: How the Quantum Computer Revolution Will Change Everything. Dr. Michio Kaku, Professor of Theoretical Physics, City University of New York. Doubleday 2023. 368 p.
ISBN 9780385548366
Grades: Adult **006.3**
1. Quantum computers 2. Quantum theory 3. Atomic theory 4. Computers and civilization 5. Problem solving 6. Biotechnology 7. Energy production 8. Technological innovations 9. Technological forecasting 10. Science Writing — Computing, the Internet, and Technology 11. Science Writing — Great Engineering Feats 12. Society and culture — Media and technology
LC 2022046826

The runaway success of the microchip processor may be reaching its end. Running up against the physical constraints of smaller and smaller sizes, traditional silicon chips are not likely to prove useful in solving humanity's greatest challenges, from climate change, to global starvation, to incurable diseases. But the quantum computer, which harnesses the power and complexity of the atomic realm, already promises to be every bit as revolutionary as the transistor and microchip once were. Its unprecedented gains in computing power herald advancements that could change every aspect of our daily lives.

"An informative and highly entertaining read about the computing revolution already underway." —*Kirkus*
Includes bibliographical references and index.

Kasparov, G. K.
Deep Thinking: Where Machine Intelligence Ends and Human Creativity Begins. Garry Kasparov, with Mig Greengard. Public Affairs 2017. VII, 287 pages
ISBN 9781610397865
Grades: Adult **006.3**
1. Kasparov, G. K. (Garri Kimovich) 2. Chess players 3. Computers 4. Artificial intelligence 5. Cooperation 6. Intelligence 7. Critical thinking 8. Chess 9. Robotics 10. Decision-making 11. Human-computer interaction 12. Science Writing — Computing, the Internet, and Technology 13. Sports and Competition — Games 14. History writing — Technological innovations
LC 2017304768

The former world chess champion who played, and lost, against Deep Blue, a supercomputer, in 1997 discusses why he thinks humans should embrace the competition between themselves and machine intelligence and how it can open us up to exploring new challenges.

"Thoughtful reading for anyone interested in human and machine cognition and a must for chess fans." —*Kirkus*
Includes bibliographical references and index.

Lee, Kai-Fu
AI 2041: Ten Visions for Our Future. by Kai-Fu Lee and Chen Qiufan. Currency 2021. 336 p.
ISBN 9780593238295
Grades: Adult **006.3**
1. Artificial intelligence 2. Social forecasting 3. Technology 4. Science Writing — Computing, the Internet, and Technology 5. Society and culture — Media and technology
LC 2021012928

In a groundbreaking blend of science and imagination, the former president of Google China and a leading writer of speculative fiction join forces to answer an urgent question: How will artificial intelligence change our world over the next twenty years?
Includes index.

Scharre, Paul
Four Battlegrounds: Power in the Age of Artificial Intelligence. Paul Scharre. W W Norton & Company 2023. 448 p.
ISBN 9780393866865
Grades: Adult **006.3**
1. Artificial intelligence 2. Power 3. Technological innovations 4. Military engineering 5. National security 6. International relations 7. China 8. United States 9. Politics and global affairs — World politics 10. Politics and global affairs — National security 11. History Writing — Military

"This study of the struggle over AI is well-written, impeccably sourced, and densely detailed." —*Booklist*

PUBLIC LIBRARY CORE COLLECTION: NONFICTION
Twentieth Edition

006.301 Artificial intelligence — Philosophy

Russell, Stuart J.
Human Compatible: Artificial Intelligence and the Problem of Control. Stuart Russell. Viking 2019. 352 pages
ISBN 9780525558613
Grades: Adult   **006.301**
1. Artificial intelligence 2. Automation 3. Risk management 4. Risk analysis 5. Computer errors 6. Technological forecasting 7. Computers and civilization 8. Computers 9. Technology 10. Control 11. Human-computer interaction 12. Science Writing — Computing, the Internet, and Technology 13. Society and culture — Media and technology
LC 2019029688
A leading artificial intelligence researcher lays out a new approach to AI that will enable us to coexist successfully with increasingly intelligent machines.
Includes bibliographical references and index.

Tegmark, Max
Life 3.0: Being Human in the Age of Artificial Intelligence. Max Tegmark. Alfred A. Knopf 2017. 336 p.
ISBN 9781101946596
Grades: Adult   **006.301**
1. Artificial intelligence 2. Robotics 3. Forecasting 4. Technology 5. Machines and labor 6. Automation 7. Society and culture — Media and technology 8. Science Writing — Computing, the Internet, and Technology
LC 2017006248
An MIT professor of physics and co-founder of the Future of Life Institute explores key questions related to a near-future world of increasing digital autonomy, exploring the likeliness of suprahuman intelligence, the role of AI in replacing human jobs and how legal systems might handle autonomous issues.
"Stretching the superhuman AI idea to intergalactic proportions by envisioning its colonization of the universe, Tegmark enthusiastically lays out concepts of AI, to the delight or disturbance of readers." —*Booklist*

006.7 Multimedia systems

Bilton, Nick
Hatching Twitter: A True Story of Money, Power, Friendship, and Betrayal. Nick Bilton. Portfolio 2013. 288 p.
ISBN 9781591846017
Grades: Adult   **006.7**
1. Dorsey, Jack, 1976- 2. Williams, Evan, 1972- 3. Stone, Biz 4. Glass, Noah 5. Internet industry and trade 6. Online social networks 7. Internet 8. Instant messaging 9. Social networks 10. Friendship 11. Science Writing — Computing, the Internet, and Technology 12. Business and economics — Industries — Technology
LC 2013037924
A behind-the-scenes portrait of the influential news and networking company traces its rise from a failed podcasting business to a multi-billion-dollar giant, recounting the high-stakes power struggles, betrayed friendships and global influences that shaped its evolution.

Maxwell, Lucas
Podcasting with Youth: A Quick Guide for Librarians and Educators. Lucas Maxwell. Libraries Unlimited 2020. 90 p.
ISBN 9781440870354
Grades: Professional   **006.7**
1. Children's libraries 2. Podcasting 3. Activity programs in education 4. Professional materials — Programming
LC 2020003262
Learn how to set up a student-led podcast in your library, involve staff from several subject areas, market effectively, what challenges you are likely to face, and how podcasting will benefit the students and school overall.
Includes bibliographical references and index.

011.62 Works for young people

Chance, Rosemary
Young Adult Literature in Action: A Librarian's Guide. Rose Brock. Libraries Unlimited 2019. xvii, 219 pages
ISBN 9781440866937
Grades: Professional   **011.62**
1. Teenagers 2. Books and reading 3. Young adults 4. Young adult literature 5. High school libraries 6. United States 7. Professional materials — Collection development
LC 2019018612
Taking a genre approach, this overview of young adult literature shows new librarians and library science students the criteria to use for selecting quality books, including recommended titles.
Includes bibliographical references (pages 185-193) and index.

016 Bibliographies and catalogs of works on specific subjects

Morton, Brian
★ *The Penguin Jazz Guide: The History of the Music in the 1,001 Best Albums.* Brian Morton. Penguin Group 2010. 730 p.
ISBN 9780141048314
Grades: Adult   **016**
1. Jazz music 2. Music history and criticism 3. Sound recording industry and trade 4. Arts and Entertainment — Music — Jazz and the Blues
Offers a chronologically arranged survey of jazz recordings, including biographical details and lineups.
"This guide's cover touts the contents as the "1001 best" recordings, although the authors' introduction indicates that these selections tend to be representative over the broad swath of jazz's history." —*Choice*

Ottemiller, John H.
Ottemiller's Index to Plays in Collections: An Author and Title Index to Plays Appearing in Collections Published Since 1900. Denise L. Montgomery. Scarecrow Press, Inc. 2011. xlix, 781 p.
ISBN 9780810877207
Grades: 11 12 Adult   **016**
1. Drama 2. Arts and Entertainment — Theater 3. Reference — Bibliographies and indexes
LC 2010053010
"Returning after some 20 years, this volume (7th ed, 1988) remains the classic index to plays in collections and anthologies... Plays are indexed by title, author, and anthology title. Montgomery adds more than 2,300 new authors and 3,593 new plays, expanding the work's focus to include works from 103 countries and making works by women and LGBT authors more discoverable." —*Choice*

016.74 Graphic arts — Bibliographies

Pawuk, Michael
Graphic Novels: A Guide to Comic Books, Manga, and More. Michael Pawuk and David S. Serchay. Libraries Unlimited 2017. xxxv, 719 pages : Illustration
ISBN 9781598847000
Grades: Adult   **016.74**
1. Comic books, strips, etc. 2. Professional materials — Collection development 3. Professional materials — Readers' advisory
LC 2017002418
An annotated bibliographic guide to graphic novels and comics contains over three thousand titles listed by genre and sub-genre.
Includes bibliographical references (pages 643-648) and indexes.

ESSENTIAL AND RECOMMENDED TITLES
016.78 Music — Bibliographies

016.78 Music — Bibliographies

Friedwald, Will
The Great Jazz and Pop Vocal Albums. Will Friedwald. Pantheon Books 2017. xxv, 402 pages : Illustration; Color
ISBN 9780307379078
Grades: Adult   016.78
1. Popular music 2. Singers 3. Sound recordings 4. Arts and Entertainment — Music — Jazz and the Blues 5. Arts and Entertainment — Music — Pop
LC 2016027178

A deeply personal survey of 57 of the greatest 20th-century jazz and pop albums considers how singers and musicians shaped and organized their extraordinary collections of songs, revealing personal stories of the singers' successes and failures.

Surveys fifty-seven of the greatest twentieth-century jazz and pop albums, including Fred Astaire's "The Astaire Story," Ella Fitzgerald's "Lullabies of Birdland," and Della Reese's "Della Della Cha Cha Cha."

"This absolutely indispensable compendium of essential jazz and pop vocal albums is a testament to the ongoing vibrancy of jazz music and the Great American Songbook." —*Booklist*

016.8223 Shakespeare, William, 1564-1616 — Bibliographies

Collins, Paul
The Book of William: How Shakespeare's First Folio Conquered the World. Paul Collins. Bloomsbury USA 2009. 288 p.
ISBN 9781596911956
Grades: Adult   016.8223
1. Shakespeare, William, 1564-1616 2. Manuscripts, English 3. Manuscripts 4. Book collecting 5. Rare books 6. Books 7. Collectors and collecting 8. 17th century 9. Arts and Entertainment — Writing and Publishing 10. Travel Writing — Retracing Historic Journeys 11. Adult books for young adults
LC 2009006722

A history of the Bard's competitively pursued First Folio traces the author's travels from the site of a Sotheby auction to regions in Asia, throughout which he investigated the roles played by those who have sought and owned the Folios.

---

020 Library and information sciences

Anderson, Jimmeka
Power Lines: Connecting with Teens in Urban Communities Through Media Literacy. Jimmeka Anderson and Kelly Czarnecki. ALA Editions 2022. 246 p.
ISBN 9780838937907
Grades: Professional   020
1. Teenagers' library services 2. Media literacy 3. Libraries and community 4. Libraries and schools 5. Marginalized people 6. Marginalized teenagers 7. Libraries 8. Public libraries 9. Metropolitan areas 10. Library outreach programs 11. United States 12. Professional materials — Programming

The book provides strategic and practical approaches towards building relationships and making a space for teens to engage and learn media literacy skills.

"The writers' tone is both personal and conversationally professional...All librarians can benefit from the book's insights and practices; the media literacy lens is particularly relevant now." —*Booklist*
Includes bibliographical references and index.

Bignoli, Callan
★ *Responding to Rapid Change in Libraries: A User Experience Approach.* Callan Bignoli and Lauren Stara. ALA Editions 2021. 136 p.
ISBN 9780838948354
Grades: Professional   020
1. Libraries 2. Library administration 3. Library users 4. Librarians 5. Public libraries 6. Organizational change 7. Information services 8. Information technology 9. United States 10. Professional materials — General

Libraries can stay ahead of rapid technological change and increasing service expectations with the strategies, tools, and holistic understanding presented in this book.

"A quick read that encourages accepting uncertainty and imperfect results to build resilience. Will appeal broadly to librarians, particularly those in management and leadership positions." —*Library Journal*
Includes bibliographical references and index.

020.9 Library and information sciences — History, geographic treatment, biography

Gleick, James
The Information: A History, a Theory, a Flood. James Gleick. Pantheon Books 2011. 416 p.
ISBN 9780375423727
Grades: Adult   020.9
1. Information science 2. Information society 3. Technological innovations 4. Civilization 5. Science Writing — Computing, the Internet, and Technology
LC 2010023221

ALA Notable Book, 2012; Booklist Editors' Choice, 2011; New York Times Notable Book, 2011; Royal Society General Prizes for Science Books, 2012; National Book Critics Circle Award for Nonfiction finalist, 2011; Andrew Carnegie Medal for Excellence in Non-Fiction finalist, 2012.

The best-selling author of Chaos analyzes how information has become a defining quality of the modern era, tracing the evolutions of pivotal information technologies while profiling key contributors from Charles Babbage and Ada Byron to Samuel Morse and Claude Shannon.

"As he traces the evolution of intertwined ideas, [Gleick] provides vivid portraits of [Claude] Shannon and other pioneers of our Information Age, including Charles Babbage, whose unbuilt 19th-century Analytical Engine anticipated modern computers, and Alan Turing, whose machines helped the Allies crack German codes during World War II." —*Wall Street Journal*
Includes bibliographical references and index.

Wright, Alex
Cataloging the World: Paul Otlet and the Birth of the Information Age. Alex Wright. Oxford University Press 2014. 384 p.
ISBN 9780199931415
Grades: Adult Professional   020.9
1. Otlet, Paul, 1868-1944 2. Librarians 3. Information organization 4. Knowledge 5. Information management 6. Visionaries 7. World Wide Web 8. Belgium 9. Biographies 10. Life stories — Science, technology, and medicine
LC 2013035233

In 1934, a Belgian entrepreneur named Paul Otlet sketched out plans for a worldwide network of computers—or "electric telescopes," as he called them—that would allow people anywhere in the world to search and browse through millions of books, newspapers, photographs, films and sound recordings, all linked together in what he termed a râeseau mondial: a "worldwide web." Today, Otlet and his visionary proto-Internet have been all but forgotten, thanks to a series of historical misfortunes—not least of which involved the Nazis marching into Brussels and destroying most of his life's work. In the years since Otlet's death, however, the world has witnessed the emergence of a global network that has proved him right about the possibilities—and the perils—of networked information. In Cataloging the World, Alex Wright brings to light the forgotten genius of Paul Otlet, an introverted librarian who harbored a bookworm's dream to organize all the world's information. Recognizing the limitations of traditional libraries and archives, Otlet began to imagine a radically new way of organizing information, and undertook his life's great work: a universal bibliography of all the world's published knowledge that ultimately totaled more than 12 million individual entries. That effort eventually evolved into the Mundaneum, a vast "city of knowledge" that opened its doors to the public in 1921 to widespread attention. Like many ambitious dreams, however, Otlet's eventually faltered, a victim to technological constraints and political upheaval in Europe on the eve of World War II. "

PUBLIC LIBRARY CORE COLLECTION: NONFICTION
Twentieth Edition

"Wright ends his illuminating story in the present, where Otlet's thoughts about the connection of information to knowledge, and knowledge to insight, are still urgent." —*Kirkus*

020.92 Information scientists, librarians, archivists

Crowley, Bill
Defending Professionalism: A Resource for Librarians, Information Specialists, Knowledge Managers, and Archivists. Bill Crowley, editor. Libraries Unlimited, an imprint of ABC-CLIO, LLC 2012. xiii, 235 pages
ISBN 9781598848694
Grades: Adult Professional   **020.92**
1. Archivists 2. Librarians 3. Libraries and society 4. Professional materials — Library management
LC 2012006410

This book provides overdue guidance for demonstrating and preserving library, information, knowledge, and archival professionalism in American, British, and Canadian communities and organizations.
Includes bibliographical references and index.

021.2 Relationships with the community

Damon-Moore, Laura C.
The Artist's Library: A Field Guide from the Library as Incubator Project. Laura Damon-Moore, Erinn Batykefer. Coffee House Press 2014. 217 pages : Illustration
ISBN 9781566893534
Grades: Professional   **021.2**
1. Libraries and community 2. Libraries 3. Arts 4. Creation (Literary, artistic, etc.) 5. Library users 6. Professional materials — General 7. Language arts and studies — Writing skills 8. Arts and Entertainment — Crafts and hobbies
LC 2013035168

Creativity, like information, is free to everyone who steps into a library. The Artist's Library offers the idea that an artist is any person who uses creative tools to make new things, and the guidance and resources to make libraries of all sizes and shapes come alive as spaces for art-making and cultural engagement. Case studies included in the book range from the crafty (pop-up books) to the community-minded (library galleries) to documentary (photo projects) to the technically complex ('listening' to libraries via Dewey Decimal frequencies). The Library as Incubator Project was created by Erinn Batykefer, Laura Damon-Moore, and Christina Endres. It highlights the ways that libraries and artists can work together, and works to strengthen these partnerships. By calling attention to one of the many reasons libraries are important to our communities and our culture, it provides a dynamic online forum for sharing ideas.

Maddigan, Beth
Community Library Programs That Work: Building Youth and Family Literacy. Beth Maddigan and Susan Bloos. Libraries Unlimited 2014. xiii, 215 pages
ISBN 9781610692632
Grades: Professional   **021.2**
1. Libraries and community 2. Libraries 3. Communities 4. Activity programs in education 5. Professional materials — Library management 6. Language arts and studies — Reading skills
LC 2013029493

A collection of engaging best practices for promoting literacy development by utilizing local community connections in school and public libraries.
Includes bibliographical references (pages 201-204) and index.

021.7 Promotion of libraries, archives, information centers

Thenell, Jan
The Library's Crisis Communications Planner: A PR Guide for Handling Every Emergency. Jan Thenell. American Library Association 2004. VII, 77 p. : Illustration
ISBN 9780838908709
Grades: Adult   **021.7**
1. Archives 2. Crisis management 3. Libraries 4. Buildings 5. Educator resources — General 6. Reference books — Handbooks, manuals, etc.
LC 2004010891

"Offering advice, firsthand experience, scenarios, and guidelines for communicating effectively before, during, and after a crisis or crisis-producing events, . [the author's] guide is a ready-made workshop on how to establish and maintain relationships with the media, including how to write a press release, how to keep all staff informed and aware of what to do when an emergency occurs, and how to make sure library board members and other community stakeholders are notified and/or involved. Whether or not you have a public relations office or officer, this slim volume is a must for your professional shelf." —*Library Journal*
Includes bibliographical references (p. 73-74) and index.

023 Personnel management (Human resource management)

Boland, Becca
Making the Most of Teen Library Volunteers: Energizing and Engaging Community. Becca Boland. Libraries Unlimited, an imprint of ABC-CLIO, LLC 2020. xix, 150 pages
ISBN 9781440865626
Grades: Professional   **023**
1. Volunteers 2. Libraries 3. Teenagers 4. Teenage volunteers 5. Teenagers' library services 6. United States 7. Professional materials — General
LC 2019051212

The book begins with the big picture, discussing benefits to teens, libraries, and communities; it then reviews volunteer types and volunteer possibilities for teens, including the traditional roles of shelving and programming as well as passion-led projects, programming opportunities, and special initiatives and drives. Specific volunteer roles are described in depth, with instructions for practical applications, and concrete examples and experiences from various types of libraries illustrate principles discussed.
Includes bibliographical references (pages 139-145) and index.

Henry, Jo
Cultivating Civility: Practical Ways to Improve a Dysfunctional Library. Jo Henry, Joe Eshleman, and Richard Moniz. ALA Editions 2020. xiii, 216 pages : Illustration
ISBN 9780838947166
Grades: Professional   **023**
1. Library personnel management 2. Communication 3. Library administration 4. Library employees 5. Conflict resolution 6. Organizational behavior 7. Professional materials — Library management
LC 2019954457

Following up their acclaimed examination of the dysfunctional library…here the authors present a book of proactive solutions and guidance culled from their own research, including interviews with library administrators and staff. Sharing valuable insights that will stimulate thought and discussion towards the goal of a healthier and more harmonious workplace, this book addresses the subject from four viewpoints—individual, team, leader, and organization—focusing on solutions and practical steps in each area.

"All the chapters are well written and include boxes of information that break up the text and very useful discussion questions. This book can be used as a textbook, as a professional development tool, or as background to discuss issues in the library organization." —*Choice*
Includes bibliographical references and index.

ESSENTIAL AND RECOMMENDED TITLES
025 Operations of libraries, archives, information centers

McNeil, Beth
Fundamentals of Library Supervision. Beth McNeil. ALA Neal-Schuman, an imprint of the American Library Association 2017. xi, 242 pages
ISBN 9780838915547
Grades: Professional　　　　　　　　　　　　　　　　023
1. Library personnel management 2. Library administration 3. Management 4. Supervision of employees 5. Professional materials — Library management
LC 2017002509

Guiding supervisors through the intricate process of managing others, this to-the-point handbook addresses the fundamental issues facing those taking on this position.

"Clear and concise, this classic text is recommended for new and seasoned library managers." —*Library Journal*

Previous edition authored by Joan Giesecke and Beth McNeil; Includes bibliographical references and index.

Newman, Bobbi L.
★ *Fostering Wellness in the Workplace: A Handbook for Libraries.* Bobbi L. Newman. ALA Editions 2022. 82 p.
ISBN 9780838937914
Grades: Professional　　　　　　　　　　　　　　　　023
1. Library personnel management 2. Work environment 3. Health 4. Professional materials — Library management
LC 2022018874

The good news is that by turning inward, libraries can foster wellness in their workplace and make a real difference in the day-to-day lives of their staff. Newman, who has led a popular course on the subject attended by workers from many types of different libraries, here takes a holistic approach to examine why and how libraries should focus on improving the health and wellness of employees.

"This well-researched guide concludes with a list of multiple references for further study. Newman acknowledges the challenges in implementing these changes but emphasizes that they are worth it, not just for the health of staff but for the library overall." —*Library Journal*

Includes bibliographical references and index.

Stanley, Mary J.
Managing Library Employees: A How-To-Do-It Manual. Mary J. Stanley. Neal-Schuman Publishers 2008. xi, 247 p.
ISBN 9781555706289
Grades: Adult Professional　　　　　　　　　　　　　023
1. Library personnel management 2. Business and economics — Business advice 3. Professional materials — General 4. Reference books — Handbooks, manuals, etc.
LC 2007051961

"Oriented to librarians who do not have a human resources department in the library, Managing Library Employees is for the nonexpert trying to come to terms with managing a library's largest expenditure and assetits employees. The chapters are divided into subtopics posed as questions. The chapters also provide information on writing an effective job description, designing a disciplinary procedure, and identifying potential issues that might lead to a lawsuit. This useful guide for everyday situations should be on any library director or manager's professional reference shelf." —*Booklist*

Includes bibliographical references (p. 225-240) and index.

Tucker, Dennis C.
Crash Course in Library Supervision: Meeting the Key Players. Dennis C. Tucker and Shelley Elizabeth Mosley. Libraries Unlimited 2008. IX, 139 p.
ISBN 9781591585640
Grades: Professional　　　　　　　　　　　　　　　　023
1. Library personnel management 2. Library administration 3. Supervision of employees 4. Reference books 5. Professional materials — General
LC 2007030131

Provides information on becoming an effective leader in a library, covering such topics as getting to know the staff, evaluating staff, personnal laws, hiring and firing employees, finding volunteers, and working with a library board.

Includes bibliographical references (p. 123-129) and index.

025 Operations of libraries, archives, information centers

Johnson, Peggy
★ *Fundamentals of Collection Development and Management.* Peggy Johnson. ALA Editions, an imprint of the American Library Association 2018. xiii, 418 pages
ISBN 9780838916414
Grades: Professional　　　　　　　　　　　　　　　　025
1. Collection management (Libraries) 2. Materials selection (Libraries) 3. Library materials 4. Professional materials — Collection development
LC 2017051474

Johnson has revised and freshened this resource to ensure its timeliness and continued excellence. Consideration is given to traditional management topics, cooperative collection development and management, licenses, negotiation, and other purchasing and budgeting topics, and the ways that changes in information delivery and access technologies continue to reshape the discipline.

Includes bibliographical references (pages 375-381) and index.

025.04 Information storage and retrieval systems

Brown, Christopher C.
Librarian's Guide to Online Searching: Cultivating Database Skills for Research and Instruction. Christopher C. Brown and Suzanne S. Bell. Libraries Unlimited 2018. xxiii, 374 p. : Illustration
ISBN 9781440861567
Grades: Professional　　　　　　　　　　　　　　　025.04
1. Professional materials — General
LC 2018011054

This book describes the background of how databases work; how they are constructed and in the case of some databases; how they transitioned from the legacy print world to an online environment; how technologies within databases can interact with other products like bibliography citation services, outbound linking to full text content, and social media mentions; and the methods used by libraries to provide access to licensed content from anywhere in the world.

Includes bibliographical references and index.

025.06 Information storage and retrieval systems devoted

Sankey, Michael L.
The Manual to Online Public Records: The Researcher's Tool to Online Resources of Public Records and Public Information. Sankey & Hetherington. Facts on Demand Press 2017. II, 620 p. : Illustration
ISBN 9781889150628
Grades: Adult　　　　　　　　　　　　　　　　　025.06
1. Public records 2. Reference books — Directories
LC BI2017002725

Shares strategies for using the Internet to conduct research and access online resources, in a guide that provides the public records available for each state, along with advice on evaluating online data for reliability.

025.1 Administration

Curzon, Susan Carol
What Every Library Director Should Know. Susan Carol Curzon. Rowman & Littlefield 2023. 179 p.
ISBN 9781538172698
Grades: Professional　　　　　　　　　　　　　　　　025.1

PUBLIC LIBRARY CORE COLLECTION: NONFICTION
Twentieth Edition

1. Library administration 2. Libraries 3. Professional materials — Library management

LC 2022056527

In this unconventional management book, author Susan Carol Curzon presents a different take on traditional library management tools. Through personal narrative and anecdotes from other working professionals, Curzon presents the many everyday challenges one meets as a library manager.

"Although the book will be especially valuable for new or aspiring directors, experienced administrators will gain insight in handling the unexpected, such as a death in the library family, changes in a Friends group, staff relationships, press interviews, union relations, and outside factors that can impact a library's operations." —*Booklist*

Includes bibliographical references and index.

Johnson, Doug
The **Indispensable** Librarian: Surviving and Thriving in School Libraries in the Information Age. Doug Johnson; illustrations by Brady Johnson. Linworth, an imprint of ABC-CLIO, LLC 2013. xix, 207 pages : Illustration
ISBN 9781610692397
Grades: Professional 025.1
1. School librarians 2. School libraries 3. Professional materials — Library management 4. Professional materials — School media centers

LC 2012051394

"Johnson offers both theory and practical suggestions on ways to embed [librarians] and [their] jobs into the fabric of a school's culture and curriculum." —*Library Media Connection*

Includes bibliographical references and index.

Landau, Herbert B.
The **Small** Public Library Survival Guide: Thriving on Less. Herbert B. Landau. American Library Association 2008. VIII, 159 p.
ISBN 9780838935750
Grades: Adult Professional 025.1
1. Libraries and community 2. Libraries 3. Public libraries 4. Marketing 5. Professional materials — General

LC 2008007425

Details the author's move from the corporate world to running a small rural library, discussing the challenges of dramatic funding cuts and the unorthodox solutions that he used to keep the library afloat.

"This volume covers many topics of interest to staff in small public libraries. Written in a conversational, accessible style, information is presented in short chapters with relevant examples and sample documents. Covering topics from low-budget programming to building noncash support from the community, this text has something for almost everyone involved in the operations of a small public library. Easy and enjoyable to read." —*Voice of Youth Advocates*

Includes bibliographical references (p. 149-152) and index.

Larson, Jeanette
The **Public** Library Policy Writer: A Guidebook with Model Policies on Cd-rom. Jeanette C. Larson and Herman L. Totten. Neal-Schuman Publishers 2008. xxi, 280 p.
ISBN 9781555706036
Grades: Professional 025.1
1. Public libraries 2. Professional materials — Library management

LC 2008017622

"The guidebook is written mainly for small to medium-sized public library directors who need to analyze current policies, revise or update those still in use, and develop new ones. The book is organized by administrative and service areas such as employment practices, staff and patron conduct, use of materials, collection development, and access to facilities." —*Booklist*

Includes bibliographical references (p. 265-268) and index.

Laughlin, Sara
The **Quality** Library: A Guide to Staff-driven Improvement, Better Efficiency, and Happier Customers. Sara Laughlin and Ray W. Wilson. American Library Association 2008. xiv, 144 p. : Illustration
ISBN 9780838909522
Grades: Professional 025.1
1. Library administration 2. Business and economics — General 3. Professional materials — General

LC 2007030710

Based on more than 50 years of author expertise in organizational improvement, the Quality Library offers a methodology to pinpoint trouble areas and improve processes.

"This can be a useful guide for libraries whose governing bodies are looking for businesslike solutions and for managers who want to heed input from those who do the job." —*Booklist*

Includes bibliographical references (p. 137-139) and index.

MacKellar, Pamela H.
★ **Winning** Grants: A How-to-Do-It Manual for Librarians. Stephanie K. Gerding and Pamela H. MacKellar; foreword by Susan Hildreth. ALA Neal-Schuman, an imprint of the American Library Association 2017. xxi, 224 pages : Illustration
ISBN 9780838914731
Grades: Professional 025.1
1. Proposal writing for grants 2. Business and economics — General 3. Professional materials — Library management 4. Reference books — Handbooks, manuals, etc.

LC 2016025285

Written by two librarians who are experts in grantsmanship, this all-in-one toolkit for winning grants is a must-have for library directors, grant writers, board members, consultants, and anyone else involved in planning library programs and services.

"Overall, the resources are valuable and will facilitate streamlining and refining the process of grant winning while teaching grant seekers how to achieve the results they desire." —*VOYA*

Includes bibliographical references (pages 207-210) and index.

Smith, G. Stevenson
Cost Control for Nonprofits in Crisis. G. Stevenson Smith. American Library Association 2011. VIII, 133 p. : Illustration
ISBN 9780838910986
Grades: Adult Professional 025.1
1. Libraries 2. Library administration 3. Nonprofit organizations 4. Finance 5. Professional materials — General

LC 2011025285

Libraries, like many other cultural institutions such as museums, art councils, and theater groups, are looking for answers to the pressing problem of financial stability, and ultimately survival. Cost Control for Nonprofits in Crisis helps managers and directors tackle the harsh realities before them.

"The strategies and methods outlined here will assist managers who want to ensure that the decisions they must make during challenging financial times will keep their organizations vibrant, relevant, and lasting." —*VOYA*

Includes bibliographical references and index.

VanDuinkerken, Wyoma
The **Challenge** of Library Management: Leading with Emotional Engagement. Wyoma vanDuinkerken and Pixey Anne Mosley. American Library Association 2011. 169 p.
ISBN 9780838911020
Grades: Professional 025.1
1. Library administration 2. Organizational change 3. Leadership 4. Management 5. Professional materials — General

LC 2011011349

Peppered with short narratives that use real-life examples of change principles, this book helps managers reassure their staff that change can be an opportunity for reflection and personal growth.

"While the authors tailor the advice to librarians by using example specific to libraries, the advice could be applied to any organizational setting. All in all, the suggestions contained here are helpful when planning change in a library." —*VOYA*

Includes bibliographical references (p. 155-163) and index.

ESSENTIAL AND RECOMMENDED TITLES
025.2 Acquisitions and collection development

025.2 Acquisitions and collection development

Alabaster, Carol
Developing an Outstanding Core Collection: A Guide for Libraries. Carol Alabaster. American Library Association 2010. x, 191 p. : Illustration
ISBN 9780838910405
Grades: Professional   025.2
1. Public libraries 2. Professional materials — Collection development
LC 2009040342

Presents guidelines to developing a high-quality core library collection, and includes discussions on the philosophy behind core collections, strategies for their implementation, and lists containing selection criteria.

"The author suggests that the general public needs materials beyond current best-sellers and ready-reference works; that those materials should be high-quality, enduring pieces; and that librarians are the best persons to decide what constitutes appropriate core collections for their communities. [She also] addresses the technological changes that drastically affect reading habits and our ability to satisfy the needs of the people's university. [This book is] required reading for all those charged with the task of adult collection development." —*Booklist*
Includes bibliographical references and index.

Bartlett, Wendy K.
Floating Collections: A Collection Development Model for Long-Term Success. Wendy K. Bartlett. Libraries Unlimited, an imprint of ABC-CLIO, LLC 2014. xix, 128 pages
ISBN 9781598847437
Grades: Adult   025.2
1. Public libraries 2. Professional materials — Collection development
LC 2013033820

This easy-to-use, comprehensive guide shows how to establish a floating collection in any library—regardless of type or size.

"Chapters include tips on how to approach the practice with staff, how to ready facilities and collections, and, most importantly, how to manage new collections. Also offered are practical evaluations, FAQs, and a list of larger systems in the United States that offer floating collections." —*School Library Journal*
Includes bibliographical references and index.

Bradford, Robin
★ *The Readers' Advisory Guide to Romance.* Robin Bradford. ALA Editions 2023. 89 p.
ISBN 9780838938676
Grades: Professional   025.2
1. Fiction in libraries 2. Romance authors 3. Libraries 4. Library materials 5. Books 6. Professional materials — Readers' advisory 7. Reference — Bibliographies and indexes
LC 2022051830

This vital resource provides everything you need to know about the Romance genre from collection development tips and readers' advisory know-how to program planning ideas.

"Readers' advisors, whether they are new to the genre or seasoned citizens of Romancelandia, will find the Readers' Advisory Guide to Romance to be a supremely useful guide for helping romance readers in their communities." —*Booklist*
Includes bibliographical references and index.

Disher, Wayne
Crash Course in Collection Development. Wayne Disher. Libraries Unlimited 2014. xii, 139 pages
ISBN 9781610698139
Grades: Adult   025.2
1. Materials selection (Libraries) 2. Libraries 3. Professional materials — Collection development
LC 2014018813

This indispensable resource provides tools for collection management in public libraries, featuring essential strategies for inventory assessment, market analysis, budgeting, marketing, and customer service. This book is a must-have for those just entering the field or professionals in need of a refresher in effective library operations.

"Disher, a seasoned practitioner and part-time instructor in San Jose State Universitys School of Library and Information Science, speaks primarily to public library staff with little, if any, experience in collection development. Short on theory but long on practicality, the book provides the reader with basic definitions and step-by-step outlines... Recommended for all public library collections." —*Booklist*
Includes bibliographical references and index.

Evans, G. Edward
Collection Management Basics. G. Edward Evans and Margaret Zarnosky Saponaro. Libraries Unlimited, an imprint of ABC-CLIO, LLC 2012. xvi, 343 pages
ISBN 9781598848632
Grades: Adult Professional   025.2
1. Collection management (Libraries) 2. Libraries 3. Electronic information resources 4. Professional materials — Collection development
LC 2012008872

Now thoroughly revised for today's 21st-century library environment, this title provides a complete update of the classic Developing Library and Information Center Collections—the standard text and authority on collection development for all types of libraries and library school students since 1979.
Includes bibliographical references and index.

Goldsmith, Francisca
The Readers' Advisory Guide to Graphic Novels. Francisca Goldsmith. ALA Editions, an imprint of the American Library Association 2017. xvi, 215 pages
ISBN 9780838915097
Grades: Professional   025.2
1. Comics and graphic novel writing 2. United States 3. Professional materials — Readers' advisory
LC 2016042034

"This is a book to spend time with, not flip through, although a strong index and table of contents make it easily consultable for patron interactions as well." —*Voice of Youth Advocates*
Includes bibliographical references and index.

Goodridge, Michelle
Librarian's Guide to Games and Gamers: From Collection Development to Advisory Services. Michelle Goodridge, Matthew J. Rohweder. Libraries Unlimited, an imprint of ABC-CLIO, LLC 2022. xii, 247 pages : Illustration
ISBN 9781440867316
Grades: Professional   025.2
1. Libraries 2. Games 3. Library materials 4. Video games 5. Board games 6. Role playing games 7. Virtual reality games 8. Collection management (Libraries) 9. United States
LC 2021026454

This book maps all types of games—board, roleplaying, digital, and virtual reality—providing all the information needed to understand and appropriately recommend games to library users. Organized by game type, hundreds of descriptions offer not only bibliographic information (title, publication date, series, and format/platform), but genre classifications, target age ranges for players, notes on gameplay and user behavior type, and short descriptions of the game's basic premise and appeals.

"A superb book for early-career librarians, librarians who are new to games and gaming, academic librarians hoping to install games into the collection, and anyone looking for a fresh perspective on gaming." —*Library Journal*
Includes bibliographical references and index.

Hughes-Hassell, Sandra
★ *Collection Management for Youth: Equity, Inclusion, and Learning.* Sandra Hughes-Hassell. ALA Editions 2020. 164 p.
ISBN 9780838947500
Grades: Professional   025.2

PUBLIC LIBRARY CORE COLLECTION: NONFICTION
Twentieth Edition

1. Instructional materials centers 2. School libraries 3. School librarians 4. Curriculum planning 5. Educational innovations 6. Professional materials — Collection development

LC 2020000768

Hughes-Hassell provides models and tools for collection managers that will enable library staff who serve youth to put in place, demonstrate, and create learner-centered collections that are inclusive and provide equitable access to all youth.

Includes bibliographical references and index; Previously published under title: Collection management for youth: Responding to the needs of learners.

LaRue, James
★ *On Censorship: A Public Librarian Examines Cancel Culture in the US*. James LaRue. Fulcrum Publishing 2023. 144 p.
ISBN 9781682753477
Grades: Adult 025.2
1. Libraries 2. Censorship 3. Intellectual freedom 4. Democracy 5. Books and reading 6. Banned books 7. Political culture 8. United States 9. Essays 10. Politics and global affairs — Civil and human rights 11. Society and culture — Gender

LC 2023011514

In America today, more books are being banned than ever before. This censorship is part of a larger assault on such American institutions as schools, public libraries, and universities. In On Censorship: A Public Librarian Examines Cancel Culture in the US, respected long-time public librarian James LaRue issues a balanced and reasonable call to action for all citizens. Synthesizing his more than twenty-five years of experience on the front lines of these issues, he takes the reader through attempts he encountered to remove or restrict access to ideas, while placing the debate in the greater context about the role of libraries and free expression in a democratic society.

"This is a worthy addition to the intellectual-freedom canon." —*Booklist*

Pinnell-Stephens, June
Protecting Intellectual Freedom in Your Public Library: Scenarios from the Front Lines. June Pinnell-Stephens for the Office for Intellectual Freedom. American Library Association 2012. xi, 148 p. : Illustration
ISBN 9780838935835
Grades: Adult Professional 025.2
1. Intellectual freedom 2. Public libraries 3. Professional materials — General

LC 2011029691

"Packed with current legal information and practical suggestions, this book is a "must-read" for all levels of library staff." —*Library Journal*

Includes bibliographical references and index.

Verminski, Alana
★ *Fundamentals of Electronic Resources Management*. Alana Verminski, Kelly Marie Blanchat. Neal-Schuman, an imprint of the American Library Association 2017. VIII, 251 pages : Illustration
ISBN 9780838915417
Grades: Professional 025.2
1. Electronic information resources 2. Libraries and electronic publishing 3. Libraries 4. Professional materials — Library management

LC 2016044178

This guide to ERM fundamentals will prove invaluable, both as a primer for those preparing to enter the field as well as a ready reference for current practitioners.

Includes bibliographical references and index.

Vnuk, Rebecca
The Weeding Handbook: A Shelf-by-Shelf Guide. Rebecca Vnuk, Booklist collection management editor. ALA Editions, an imprint of the American Library Association 2015. xix, 196 pages : Illustration; Charts
ISBN 9780838913277
Grades: Adult 025.2

1. Public libraries 2. Professional materials — Collection development 3. Reference books — Handbooks, manuals, etc.

LC 2015008707

Filled with field-tested, no nonsense strategies, this handbook will enable libraries to bloom by maintaining a collection that users actually use.

Includes index.

Wilkinson, Frances C.
The Complete Guide to Acquisitions Management. Frances C. Wilkinson, Linda K. Lewis, and Rebecca L. Lubas. Libraries Unlimited 2015. xiv, 200 pages
ISBN 9781610697132
Grades: Adult 025.2
1. Professional materials — Library management 2. Professional materials — Collection development

LC 2015007852

Updated and enhanced, the second edition of this text provides both library students and practitioners with a thorough understanding of procedural and philosophical approaches in acquisitions management.

Includes bibliographical references and index.

025.3 Bibliographic analysis and control

Duncan, Dennis
Index, a History of The: A Bookish Adventure from Medieval Manuscripts to the Digital Age. Dennis Duncan. W.W. Norton & Company 2022. 336 p.
ISBN 9781324002543
Grades: Adult 025.3
1. Books 2. Digital communications 3. Information access 4. Publishers and publishing 5. Arts and Entertainment — Writing and Publishing 6. History writing — Arts and culture

LC 2021050496

A playful history of the humble index and its outsized effect on our reading lives. Charting its curious path from the monasteries and universities of thirteenth-century Europe to Silicon Valley in the twenty-first, Duncan uncovers how it has saved heretics from the stake, kept politicians from high office, and made us all into the readers we are today. We follow it through German print shops and Enlightenment coffee houses, novelists' living rooms and university laboratories, encountering emperors and popes, philosophers and prime ministers, poets, librarians and—of course—indexers along the way.

"Duncan (coeditor, Book Parts), a lecturer in English at University College London, mixes humor and scholarship to brilliant effect in this accessible deep dive into the history of indexes.... Readers of this enlightening and entertaining survey won't take the humble index for granted again." —*Publishers Weekly*

Originally published in the UK under the title Index, a history of the : a bookish adventure by Allen Lane, London, in 2021; Includes bibliographical references and index.

Maxwell, Robert L.
Maxwell's Handbook for RDA, Resource Description & Access: Explaining and Illustrating RDA: Resource Description and Access Using Marc21. Robert L. Maxwell. ALA Editions 2013. x, 900 pages
ISBN 9780838911723
Grades: Adult 025.3
1. Professional materials — General

LC 2013035124

A guided tour of the new standard from a respected authority, this essential handbook will help catalogers, LIS students, and cataloging instructors navigate RDA smoothly and find the information they need efficiently.

Includes bibliographical references and index.

ESSENTIAL AND RECOMMENDED TITLES
025.5 Services and programs for users

025.5 Services and programs for users

Goldsmith, Francisca
Crash Course in Contemporary Reference. Francisca Goldsmith. Libraries Unlimited 2017. xii, 183 pages
ISBN 9781440844812
Grades: Adult Professional   025.5
1. Reference services (Libraries) 2. Professional materials — General
LC 2016030068

A fresh, detailed, and thoughtful examination of reference services in the context of evolving community information needs and habits, a changing technological landscape, and new search strategies.
Includes bibliographical references and index.

Hernon, Peter
Assessing Service Quality: Satisfying the Expectations of Library Customers. Peter Hernon + Ellen Altman. American Library Association 2010. xi, 206 p. : Illustration
ISBN 9780838910214
Grades: Professional   025.5
1. Professional materials — General
LC 2009040332

This classic book is brought fully up to date as Hernon and Altman integrate the use of technology into the customer experience. They offer solid, practical ideas for developing a customer service plan that meets the library's customer-focused mission, vision, and goals, challenging librarians to think about customer service in new ways.
Includes bibliographical references and index.

Mulac, Carolyn
Fundamentals of Reference. Carolyn M. Mulac. American Library Association 2012. xii, 131 pages
ISBN 9780838910870
Grades: Professional   025.5
1. Reference services (Libraries) 2. Reference sources 3. Professional materials — General 4. Reference — Bibliographies and indexes
LC 2012010058

An excellent training tool for both new and experienced staff, Fundamentals of Reference will quickly become your fundamental reference!
Includes bibliographical references and index.

Orr, Cynthia
★ *Crash Course in Readers' Advisory.* Cynthia Orr. Libraries Unlimited, an imprint of ABC-CLIO, LLC 2015. xiv, 173 pages
ISBN 9781610698252
Grades: Adult Professional   025.5
1. Professional materials — Collection development 2. Professional materials — Readers' advisory
LC 2014027064

One of the key services librarians provide is helping readers find books they'll enjoy. This "crash course" will furnish you with the basic, practical information you need to excel at readers' advisory (RA) for adults and teens.
Includes bibliographical references and index.

Ross, Catherine Sheldrick
Conducting the Reference Interview: A How-To-Do-It Manual for Librarians. Catherine Sheldrick Ross, Kirsti Nilsen, and Marie L. Radford. Neal-Schuman Publishers Inc. 2009. xiv, 290 p. : Illustration
ISBN 9781555706555
Grades: Professional   025.5
1. Reference services (Libraries) 2. Interviewing 3. Electronic information resources 4. Professional materials — General
LC 2009017660

"This outstanding work is highly recommended for all libraries and is essential reading for all LIS educators and librarians involved in staff training." —*Booklist*
Includes bibliographical references and index.

Spratford, Becky Siegel
The Readers' Advisory Guide to Horror. Becky Siegel Spratford. ALA Editions 2021. xv, 182 pages : Illustration
ISBN 9780838948767
Grades: Professional   025.5
1. Fiction in libraries 2. Horror in literature 3. Horror authors 4. Library materials 5. Books 6. Libraries 7. United States 8. Professional materials — Readers' advisory 9. Reference — Bibliographies and indexes
LC 2021017435

Covering the latest in monsters and the macabre, horror expert Spratford's resource is ideal as both an introductory guide for novices and a fount of new ideas for horror-aware reference staff.

"Librarians will appreciate the updated recommendations and accessible organization. Those interested in a more complete history of horror fiction will find within a thoughtful exploration of previously excluded authors and emerging talent." —*Library Journal*
Includes bibliographical references and index.

025.8 Maintenance and preservation of collections

Flaherty, Mary Grace
★ *The Disaster Planning Handbook for Libraries.* Mary Grace Flaherty with Katherine R. Greene and Michelle Runyon. ALA Editions 2022. xii, 151 pages : Illustration
ISBN 9780838937990
Grades: Professional   025.8
1. Libraries 2. Buildings 3. Safety 4. Library materials 5. Emergency planning 6. Professional materials — Library management
LC 2021031229

Libraries are in a unique position to aid communities during times of adversity, and this comprehensive handbook's practical tools and expert guidance will help ensure that your library is thoroughly prepared for emergency response and recovery.
Includes bibliographical references and index.

Halsted, Deborah D.
★ *Disaster Planning: A How-To-Do-It Manual for Librarians with Planning Templates on CD-Rom.* Deborah D. Halsted, Richard P. Jasper, and Felicia M. Little. Neal-Schuman Publishers 2005. xx, 267 p. : Illustration
ISBN 9781555704865
Grades: Professional   025.8
1. Library materials 2. Emergency planning 3. Professional materials — Library management
LC 2003065152

"Whether a disaster is caused by avalanche, hurricane, computer hackers, explosion, flood, terrorist attack, or other event, this guide will help readers develop a precise, logical, and flexible plan for being prepared." —*Booklist*
Includes bibliographical references (p. 245-255) and index.

Hammer, Joshua
The Bad-Ass Librarians of Timbuktu: And Their Race to Save the World's Most Precious Manuscripts. Joshua Hammer. Simon & Schuster 2016. 278 p.
ISBN 9781476777405
Grades: Adult   025.8
1. Libraries 2. Manuscripts 3. Cultural property 4. Islam 5. Librarians 6. Pillage 7. African history 8. Mali 9. Tombouctou, Mali 10. History writing — Arts and culture 11. Politics and global affairs — World politics — Africa
LC 2015030396
LibraryReads Favorites, 2016.

PUBLIC LIBRARY CORE COLLECTION: NONFICTION
Twentieth Edition

Describes how an average, mild-mannered archivist and historian became an expert smuggler when she organized a dangerous operation to sneak 350,000 precious manuscripts out of Timbuktu in the face of the 2012 al Qaeda takeover.

"Hammer's clearly written and engaging chronicle of the achievements of Timbuktu, the risks presented to this area, and the portraits of several brave and dedicated individuals brings to light an important and unfamiliar story." —*Library Journal*

Lavender, Kenneth
Book Repair: A How-to-Do-It Manual. Kenneth Lavender. Neal-Schuman Publishers Inc. 2011. xiv, 265 p. : Illustration
ISBN 9781555707477
Grades: Professional   **025.8**
1. Books 2. Bookbinding 3. Professional materials — General
LC 2011022636

Covering both basic book repair techniques and sound preservation practices, this practical, step-by-step manual offers illustrated sections on cleaning, mending, hinge and spine repair, strengthening paperbacks, and more.
Includes bibliographical references and index.

026 Specific kinds of institutions

Phoenix, Jack
Maximizing the Impact of Comics in Your Library: Graphic Novels, Manga, and More. Jack Phoenix. Libraries Unlimited 2020. 248 p.
ISBN 9781440868856
Grades: Professional   **026**
1. Libraries 2. Activity programs in education 3. Professional materials — Programming 4. Professional materials — Collection development
LC 2019056103

This unique guide offers fresh insights on how graphic novels and comics differ from traditional books and require different treatment in the library-from purchasing, shelving, and cataloging to readers' advisory services, programs, and curriculum.

"Marrying in-depth knowledge of comics and libraries, Phoenix has produced a practical, user-friendly read that's essential book for school and public librarians." —*School Library Journal*

"Marrying in-depth knowledge of comics and libraries, Phoenix has produced a practical, user-friendly read that's an essential book for school and public librarians." —*School Library Journal*
Includes bibliographical references and index.

027 General libraries, archives, information centers

Ryback, Timothy W.
Hitler's Private Library: The Books That Shaped His Life. by Timothy W. Ryback. Alfred A. Knopf 2008. xx, 278 p. : Illustration; Map
ISBN 9781400042043
Grades: Adult   **027**
1. Hitler, Adolf, 1889-1945 2. Books and reading 3. Home libraries 4. Nazis 5. Political leadership 6. Third Reich, 1933-1945 7. History writing — Europe — Germany
LC 2008022010

A study of Hitler's emotional and intellectual world traces the evolution of his life and political philosophy as it examines the books that shaped his life, analyzing key phrases and ideas from his personal books as revealed in his own writings, speeches, conversations, philosophy, and actions.
Includes bibliographical references and index.

Rydell, Anders
The Book Thieves: The Nazi Looting of Europe's Libraries and the Race to Return a Literary Inheritance. Anders Rydell. Penguin Group USA 2017. 352 p.
ISBN 9780735221222
Grades: Adult   **027**
1. Nazis 2. Book thefts 3. Nazi plunder 4. Pillage 5. Stealing 6. Libraries 7. Antisemitism 8. Translations — Swedish to English 9. History writing — Wars and conflicts — Holocaust — World War II
LC 2016044051

An account of the Nazis' systematic pillaging of Europe's libraries, and the heroic efforts of librarians working today to return the books to their owners, explores how stolen books were used as part of a campaign to rewrite history in accordance with Third Reich views.

"An engrossing, haunting journey for bibliophiles and World War II historians." —*Kirkus*

Originally published as Boktjuvarna: Jakten pa de forsvunna biblioteken in 2015 by Norstedts; Translated from the Swedish by Henning Koch.

027.4 Public libraries

Gunnels, Claire B.
Joint Libraries: Models That Work. Claire B. Gunnels, Susan E. Green, and Patricia M. Butler. American Library Association 2012. xi, 220 pages : Illustration
ISBN 9780838911389
Grades: Professional   **027.4**
1. Professional materials — General
LC 2011044057

The joint-use college/Public library can be an ideal solution to serving patrons while managing overextended resources, and this illuminating book scrutinizes successes and failures of the joint-use model.
Includes bibliographical references (pages 201-209) and index.

Orlean, Susan
★ *The Library Book*. Susan Orlean. Simon & Schuster 2018. 319 p.
ISBN 9781476740188
Grades: Adult   **027.4**
1. Libraries 2. Fires 3. Librarians 4. Arson 5. Library science 6. Arson investigation 7. Fire prevention 8. United States history 9. Los Angeles, California 10. History writing — Regional history — United States 11. History writing — Arts and culture 12. Book club best bets
LC 2018022454

Booklist Editors' Choice, 2018; LibraryReads Favorites, 2018; New York Times Notable Book, 2018.

The author reopens the unsolved mystery of the most catastrophic library fire in American history, and delivers a dazzling love letter to a beloved institution: Our libraries.

"Bibliophiles will love this fact-filled, bookish journey." —*Kirkus*

Pettegree, Andrew
The Library: A Fragile History. Andrew Pettegree and Arthur der Weduwen. Basic Books 2021. 518 p.
ISBN 9781541600775
Grades: Adult   **027.4**
1. Libraries 2. Books 3. Collectors and collecting 4. Book collecting 5. Rare books 6. Manuscripts 7. Books and reading 8. Public libraries 9. Electronic information resources 10. History writing — Microhistory 11. History writing — Arts and culture

Famed across the known world, jealously guarded by private collectors, built up over centuries, destroyed in a single day, ornamented with gold leaf and frescoes, or filled with bean bags and children's drawings—the history of the library is rich, varied, and stuffed full of incident. In The Library, historians Andrew Pettegree and Arthur der Weduwen introduce us to the antiquarians and philanthropists who shaped the world's great collections, trace the rise and fall of literary tastes, and reveal the high crimes and misdemeanors committed in pursuit of rare manuscripts. In doing so, they reveal that while collections themselves are fragile, often falling into ruin within a few decades, the idea of the library has been remarkably resilient as each generation makes—and remakes—the institution anew.

ESSENTIAL AND RECOMMENDED TITLES
027.5 Government libraries

"Historians Pettegree and der Weduwen (The Bookshop of the World) take a comprehensive and fascinating deep dive into the evolution of libraries.... Bibliophiles should consider this a must-read." —*Publishers Weekly*

Includes bibliographical references and index.

Snow, Jess
★ *Outreach Services for Teens: A Starter Guide.* Jess Snow; foreword by Anthony Bernier. ALA Editions 2021. 89 p.

ISBN 9780838948156

Grades: Professional   **027.4**

1. Teenagers' library services 2. Library outreach programs 3. Libraries and community 4. Young adults' libraries 5. Libraries 6. Teenagers 7. United States 8. Professional materials — Programming

LC 2020019296

This book provides readers with a working definition of outreach services, shares tools to create successful partners, explores what successful outreach service looks like, and examines ways to evaluate outreach services.

Includes bibliographical references and index.

027.5 Government libraries

Conaway, James
America's Library: The Story of the Library of Congress, 1800-2000. James Conaway; foreword by James H. Billington; introduction by Edmund Morris. Yale University Press in association with the Library of Congress 2000. xiii, 226 p. : Illustration; Color

ISBN 9780300083088

Grades: 11 12 Adult   **027.5**

1. 19th century 2. 20th century 3. History writing — United States

LC 99058751

Traces the history of the Library of Congress under the leadership of each of the men who have been appointed as Librarian of Congress and discusses how the Library's collections have reflected American political and intellectual developments.

"This history of the Library of Congress is organized around that tiny, hardy band of men and women who have used both political acumen and intellectual vision to build the library's collections and establish those services that make the LC library to both Congress and nation. Richly supplemented with photographs, this history reaches out to touch all who love libraries." —*Booklist*

Includes bibliographical references (p. 211-217) and index.

027.6 Libraries for special groups and organizations

Anderson, Amelia
Library Programming for Autistic Children and Teens. Amelia Anderson; foreword by Barbara Klipper. ALA Editions 2021. xvi, 190 pages : Illustration

ISBN 9780838994856

Grades: Professional   **027.6**

1. Libraries 2. Autism spectrum disorders 3. Autistic children 4. Autistic teenagers 5. Autistic people 6. Children with disabilities 7. People with disabilities 8. Professional materials — Programming

LC 2020053383

This edition reflects the new knowledge that has been learned about autism since the publication of the first edition, amplifies the voices of autistic self-advocates, and provides new, easy-to-replicate programming ideas for successfully serving autistic children and teens.

"Anderson's guidance is helpful and practical. Libraries that own the first edition and have already commenced programming will welcome this enhanced version. Librarians considering their first steps will find ample professional and personal support." —*Booklist*

Includes bibliographical references (pages 171-172) and index.

Kowalsky, Michelle
Creating Inclusive Library Environments: A Planning Guide for Serving Patrons with Disabilities. Michelle Kowalsky, John Woodruff. ALA Editions, an imprint of the American Library Association 2017. x, 218 pages

ISBN 9780838914854

Grades: Professional   **027.6**

1. Business and economics — General 2. Professional materials — Library management

LC 2016026241

This planning guide will enable libraries to create and maintain a truly inclusive environment for all patrons.

Includes bibliographical references and index.

Rogers-Whitehead, Carrie
★ *Serving Teens and Adults on the Autism Spectrum: A Guide for Libraries.* Carrie Rogers-Whitehead. Libraries Unlimited 2020. xviii, 148 pages : Illustration

ISBN 9781440874819

Grades: Professional   **027.6**

1. Libraries 2. Library outreach programs 3. Autistic teenagers 4. Autistic people 5. Autism spectrum disorders 6. People with disabilities 7. Teenagers' library services 8. Professional materials — Programming

LC 2020011233

Relying on feedback and help from the autism community in her area, Carrie Rogers-Whitehead created programs for children, teens, and young adults on the autism spectrum. In this book, she shares advice on developing programs that focus on teamwork, transitions, and social skills. She explains best practices for reference interviews and teaches readers how their libraries can partner with nonprofit and government entities to develop workforce skills and connect adults with autism to jobs. Ready-made program activities for teens and adults with autism make it easy for libraries to better serve this often misunderstood group.

Includes bibliographical references and index.

027.62 Libraries for specific age groups

Bratt, Jessica Anne
Let's Talk About Race in Storytimes. Jessica Anne Bratt, foreword by Kirby McCurtis. ALA Editions 2021. xxvi, 86 pages : Illustration

ISBN 9780838937891

Grades: Professional   **027.62**

1. Storytimes 2. Race (Social sciences) 3. Children's libraries 4. Libraries 5. Marginalized people 6. Children's library services 7. Books and reading 8. Multicultural education 9. United States 10. Professional materials — Programming

LC 2021043149

With the help of this book's adaptable storytime activities, tools for self-reflection, and discussion starters, children's librarians will learn how to put anti-racism work into their professional practice while fostering an environment that celebrates all identities.

Includes bibliographical references (pages 81-82) and index.

Del Negro, Janice
Folktales Aloud: Practical Advice for Playful Storytelling. Janice M. Del Negro. ALA editions 2014. x, 212 pages

ISBN 9780838911358

Grades: Adult Professional   **027.62**

1. Children's libraries 2. Elementary school libraries 3. Storytelling 4. Activity programs in education 5. Professional materials — School media centers 6. Professional materials — Programming 7. Reference books — Library science

LC 2013028036

Offers advice for storytelling that promotes reading and fosters the imagination of the listeners.

PUBLIC LIBRARY CORE COLLECTION: NONFICTION
Twentieth Edition

"Folktales are an integral part of children's literature and are the basis for many classic books librarians use daily in their work. These much loved tales are also the backbone of the art of storytelling…Del Negro leads novice tellers through the nuances of successful storytelling…Advice is offered in a very practical way on how to approach this group and suggestions are made as to how to grab and hold their interest with pacing, movement and suspense. If you have even a passing interest in the art of storytelling, this guide is not to be missed." —*School Library Journal*

Includes bibliographical references and index.

Flowers, Sarah
Evaluating Teen Services and Programs. Sarah Flowers. Neal-Schuman, an imprint of the American Library Association 2012. xv, 119 pages : Illustration
ISBN 9781555707934
Grades: Adult Professional   027.62
1. Young adults' libraries 2. Teenagers' library services 3. Professional materials — General
     LC 2012015105

Flowers offers guidance for librarians in examining all aspects of teen programming and services to determine where improvement is needed.

"Overall these resources are beneficial to have on hand. We may know that teen services are a valuable and necessary resource, but these materials can help librarians prove and promote the reasons." —*VOYA*

Includes bibliographical references and index.

Ghoting, Saroj Nadkarni
Step into Storytime: Using Storytime Effective Practice to Strengthen the Development of Newborns to Five-Year-Olds. Saroj Nadkarni Ghoting and Kathy Fling Klatt. ALA Editions, an imprint of the American Library Association 2014. xii, 356 pages : Illustration
ISBN 9780838912225
Grades: Professional   027.62
1. Children's libraries 2. Storytelling 3. Preschool children 4. Early childhood education 5. Books and reading 6. Activity programs in education 7. Libraries 8. Professional materials — General
     LC 2014004162

"It is a rare volume that could serve as both pleasure reading or as a textbook, but Step into Storytime walks that fine line…The majority of children's librarians have studied childhood development and early literacy best practices; consider this book required reading to keep this knowledge fresh while reminding us of the importance—and delightful fun—of our work." —*Booklist*

Includes bibliographical references (pages 335-340) and index.

Knoll, Debra J.
Engaging Babies in the Library: Putting Theory into Practice. Debra J. Knoll. ALA Editions, an imprint of the American Library Association 2016. xvi, 115 pages
ISBN 9780838914342
Grades: Professional   027.62
1. Children's libraries 2. Babies 3. Toddlers 4. Professional materials — School media centers
     LC 2015049312

With Knoll's guidance, children's librarians will be informed and inspired to rise to the challenge of providing quality service to babies, toddlers, and care providers.

Includes bibliographical references and index.

Pattee, Amy
Developing Library Collections for Today's Young Adults. Amy S. Pattee. The Scarecrow Press, Inc. 2014. xiii, 267 pages
ISBN 9780810887343
Grades: Adult Professional   027.62
1. Libraries 2. Young adults' libraries 3. Teenagers' library services 4. Family and Relationships — Growing up 5. Professional materials — Collection development
     LC 2013018596

A guide to developing a young adult collection, offers information on assessing, selecting, and maintaining materials.

Includes bibliographical references and index.

Reid, Rob
★ *200+ Original and Adapted Story Program Activities.* Rob Reid. ALA Editions 2018. xiii, 266 pages
ISBN 9780838917381
Grades: Professional   027.62
1. Children's libraries 2. Storytelling 3. Activity programs in education 4. Libraries 5. Preschool children 6. Professional materials — General 7. Educator resources — Primary education 8. Educator resources — General
     LC 2018024987

200+ Original and Adapted Story Program Activities is Rob Reid's Greatest Hits concept. It gathers over 200 storytime activities (original fingerplays, movement activities, songs and musical activities, poems, and sound effect stories for preschool story programs) from previous ALA Editions books, Upstart books, and LibrarySparks magazine articles and shares them in one package. It also includes a dozen or so new (and previously unpublished) activities.

"An experienced children's librarian presents storytime activities aimed at preschoolers and early elementary school students: finger plays, movement and sound effects, imagination exercises, felt stories, spoonerisms, raps, and even drama presentations." —*School Library Journal*

Includes bibliographical references and index.

Sweeney, Jennifer
Literacy: A Way Out for At-Risk Youth. Jennifer Sweeney. Libraries Unlimited 2012. xx, 133 pages : Illustration
ISBN 9781598846744
Grades: Adult   027.62
1. Juvenile corrections 2. Juvenile delinquents 3. Literacy 4. Prison libraries 5. At-risk youth 6. Rehabilitation 7. Education 8. United States 9. Educator resources — General 10. Professional materials — General
     LC 2011042804

This exploration of juvenile corrections librarianship provides a complete description of these specialized services, addresses unique challenges in this library environment, and promotes intellectual and social growth for at-risk youth.

Includes bibliographical references (pages [123]- 128) and index.

028 Reading and use of other information media

Basbanes, Nicholas A.
Every Book Its Reader: The Power of the Printed Word to Stir the World. Nicholas A. Basbanes. Harper Collins 2005. xviii, 360 p. : Illustration
ISBN 9780060593230
Grades: Adult   028
1. Books and reading 2. Arts and Entertainment — Writing and Publishing
     LC 2005046164

In celebration of five eventful centuries of the printed word, Basbanes considers of writings that have "made things happen" in the world, works that have both nudged the course of history and fired the imagination of influential people. Basbanes asks what we can know about such figures as Milton, Gibbon, Locke, Newton, Coleridge, John Adams, Frederick Douglass, Abraham Lincoln, Henry James, Thomas Edison, Helen Keller—even the Marquis de Sade and Hitler—by knowing what they read. He shows how books that these people have consulted, in some cases annotated with their marginal notes, can offer clues to the development of their thought. He then profiles some of the most articulate readers of our time, who discuss such concepts as literary canons, classic works in translation, the timelessness of poetry, the formation of sacred texts, and the power of literature to train physicians, nurture children, and rehabilitate criminal offenders.

"The author focuses on peoples' reading habits and on the books they have read, both obscure and renowned, as well as on the importance of particular books in specific contexts. Basbanes begins by interviewing some of the best-read people alive, among them David McCullough, Harold Bloom, Helen

ESSENTIAL AND RECOMMENDED TITLES
028.5 Reading and use of other information media by young people

Vendler, and Elaine Pagels; he also mentions a wide variety of contemporary and historical personages. The loosely related stories are often inspirational, making this an engrossing read." —*Library Journal*

Includes bibliographical references (p. [333]-343) and index.

Cole, Natalie
★ *Transforming Summer Programs at Your Library: Outreach and Outcomes in Action.* Natalie Cole, Virginia A. Walter. ALA editions, an imprint of the American Library Association 2018. xv, 160 pages

ISBN 9780838916285

Grades: Professional   028

1. Library outreach programs 2. Reading promotion 3. Professional materials — General

LC 2017052415

Traditional summer reading programs need to be reimagined. Working groups of librarians, in partnership with the California Library Association and the California State Library, have done just that, creating and implementing outcomes- and outreach-based summer reading programs that speak directly to diverse and changing communities.

Includes bibliographical references (pages 141-147) and index.

Kakutani, Michiko
Ex Libris: 100+ Books to Read and Reread. Michiko Kakutani; illustrations by Dana Tanamachi. Clarkson Potter 2020. 301 p.

ISBN 9780525574972

Grades: Adult   028

1. Kakutani, Michiko 2. Reading 3. Literature 4. Critics 5. Best books 6. Books and reading 7. Literary criticism 8. United States 9. Autobiographies and memoirs 10. Essays 11. Biographies 12. Life stories — Arts and culture — Writing 13. Arts and Entertainment — Writing and Publishing

LC 2020007615

The Pulitzer Prize-winning literary critic shares 100 personal, thought-provoking essays on the life-changing works of fiction, nonfiction and poetry she most recommends for the establishment of well-read world citizenship, from the Federalist Papers to the Harry Potter novels.

"Kakutani's recommendations and her 'sense of the shared joys and losses of human experience' are revelations." —*Publishers Weekly*

Mustich, James
★ *1,000 Books to Read: A Life-Changing List Before You Die.* James Mustich; with Margot Greenbaum Mustich, Thomas Meagher, and Karen Templer. Workman Publishing 2018. xii, 948 pages : Color; Illustration

ISBN 9781523504459

Grades: Adult   028

1. Books and reading 2. Arts and Entertainment — Writing and Publishing

LC 2018036090

A celebration of the reading life presents a cross-genre, historically representative compendium of one thousand works of literature, complemented by essays on each book's particular relevance.

Includes indexes.

Prose, Francine
What to Read and Why. Francine Prose. HarperCollins 2018. 336 p.

ISBN 9780062397867

Grades: Adult   028

1. Literary criticism 2. Books and reading 3. Fiction writing 4. Authors 5. Reading 6. Literature 7. Essays 8. Arts and Entertainment — Writing and Publishing 9. Arts and Entertainment — Writing and Publishing — Literary criticism

LC 2019296611

In this brilliant collection, the follow-up to her New York Times bestseller Reading Like a Writer, the distinguished novelist, literary critic, and essayist celebrates the pleasures of reading and pays homage to the works and writers she admires above all others, from Jane Austen and Charles Dickens to Jennifer Egan and Roberto Bolano.

Reed, Shannon
Why We Read: On Bookworms, Libraries, and Just One More Page Before Lights Out. Shannon Reed. Harlequin Books 2024. 274 p.

ISBN 9781335007964

Grades: Adult   028

1. Reed, Shannon 2. Books and reading 3. Reading 4. Books 5. Readers 6. Teachers 7. Book collectors 8. Autobiographies and memoirs 9. Essays 10. Arts and Entertainment — Writing and publishing 11. Life stories — General

LibraryReads Favorites, 2024.

A humorous and incisive exploration of the joys of reading from a teacher, bibliophile and Thurber Prize finalist.

"In this loving ode, Reed serves up witty reflections on the joys of books…Bibliophiles will find much to love." —*Publishers Weekly*

028.5 Reading and use of other information media by young people

Brown, Noah
Reading Together: Share in the Wonder of Books with a Parent-Child Book Club. by Noah Brown, Dominic De Bettencourt, Luci Doherty, Owen Lowe-Rogstad, and Ronan McCann (with their moms).. Chronicle Books 2022. 208 p.

ISBN 9781797205151

Grades: Adult Professional   028.5

1. Book clubs 2. Parent and child 3. Books and reading 4. Children 5. Reading 6. Parenting 7. Family and Relationships — Parenting 8. Arts and Entertainment — Writing and Publishing

Reading Together is the essential guide for parents interested in starting a book club with their kids and raising their children to become book-loving adults.

"Five mothers who formed a 'neighborhood parent-kid book club' in 2008 hold forth on how readers can start their own child-focused reading group in this spot-on guide….The book's bright graphic design…is a plus, as is the authors' mindfulness toward diversity and inclusion." —*Publishers Weekly*

Dorr, Christina H.
★ *Profiles in Resilience: Books for Children and Teens That Center the Lived Experience of Generational Poverty.* Christina H. Dorr; foreword by Rudine Sims Bishop. ALA Editions 2022. 190 p.

ISBN 9780838937884

Grades: Professional   028.5

1. Books 2. Children 3. Teenagers 4. Poverty 5. Poor children 6. Poor people 7. Library materials 8. Professional materials — Readers' advisory 9. Professional materials — Collection development 10. Reference — Bibliographies and indexes

LC 2021016610

In this book, Dorr discusses the needs of children and teens living in generational poverty; suggests authors, illustrators, and books that depict the struggles and joys of this population; and shares compelling biographies and memoirs of inspirational authors, illustrators, and individuals who were raised in generational poverty.

Includes bibliographical references and index.

028.7 Use of books and other information media as sources of information

Breitenbach, Kathleen
★ *LGBTQIA+ Books for Children and Teens.* Kathleen Breitenbach and Liz Deskins. ALA Editions 2023. xii, 208 pages : Illustration

ISBN 9780838938577

Grades: Professional   028.7

1. LGBTQIA+ children 2. LGBTQIA+ teenagers 3. LGBTQIA+ people 4. Library materials 5. Books 6. Children's library services 7. Teenagers' library

services 8. Books and reading 9. Libraries 10. United States 11. Professional materials — Collection development
LC 2022057355

This resource discusses the best titles in LGBTQIA+ literature for children and teens and offers guidance on how to share this literature in ways that encourage understanding and acceptance among parents, administrators, and the wider community.

Includes bibliographical references and indexes.

Turnbow, Dominique
★ *Demystifying* Online Instruction in Libraries: People, Process, and Tools. Dominique Turnbow, Amanda Roth. ALA Editions 2020. VIII, 104 pages : Illustration; Footnotes
ISBN 9780838919378
Grades: Professional   028.7
1. Information literacy 2. Internet literacy 3. Learning 4. Internet 5. Distance education 6. Academic libraries 7. Libraries 8. Educational technology 9. Professional materials — Technology
LC 2019026650

The design of information literacy instruction and the building of it are two distinct skillsets and processes; yet all too often everything gets mashed together, creating needless confusion and stress. In this book Turnbow, an instructional designer, and Roth, an instructional technologist, suggest a better way to organize the work.

"While the title highlights online instruction specifically, colleagues who are primarily teaching in face-to-face settings will also find this volume incredibly helpful…An invaluable primer." —*Library Journal*

Includes bibliographical references and index.

028.9 Reading interests and habits

Spence, Annie
Dear Fahrenheit 451: Love and Heartbreak in the Stacks. Annie Spence. Flatiron Books 2017. 224 p.
ISBN 9781250106490
Grades: Adult   028.9
1. Books and reading 2. Reading 3. Libraries 4. Books 5. Librarians 6. Essays 7. Arts and Entertainment — Writing and Publishing 8. Humor writing — General 9. Arts and Entertainment — Writing and Publishing — Literary criticism
LC 2017027324

LibraryReads Favorites, 2017.

A deeply personal collection of love letters and break-up notes to the books in the librarian author's life explains the complicated reasons why libraries are keeping or removing books that either are no longer checked out by readers or have poor literary value.

"A librarian delivers a charming epistolary volume that begs to be read with pencil in hand." —*Kirkus*

Young, Damon
The Art of Reading. Damon Young. Scribe 2018. 176 p.
ISBN 9781947534025
Grades: Adult   028.9
1. Books and reading 2. Reading interests 3. Reading promotion 4. Popular culture 5. Reading 6. Australian literature 7. Arts and Entertainment — Writing and Publishing

"This literary study is serious but also witty and fun—a tough balance to strike, but Young nails it." —*Publishers Weekly*

Originally published: Carlton, Vic. : Melbourne University Publishing, 2016.

030.9 General encyclopedic works — History, geographic treatment, biography

Garfield, Simon
★ *All the Knowledge in the World: The Extraordinary History of the Encyclopedia.* Simon Garfield. William Morrow and Company 2023. 400 p.
ISBN 9780063292277
Grades: Adult   030.9
1. Information 2. Information science 3. Knowledge 4. Knowledge management 5. Encyclopedias 6. Society and culture — General 7. Arts and Entertainment — Writing and publishing 8. History Writing — Microhistory

The New York Times best-selling author of Just My Type delves into the history of the encyclopedia from Ancient Greece to today and examines what we have lost in the digital age of infinite information.

"Fast-paced and fact-filled, this entertaining compendium is a worthy tribute to the pursuit of knowledge." —*Publishers Weekly*

Originally published in the UK by Orion, London, in 2022.

031 General encyclopedic works in specific languages and language families

Carlsen, Spike
A Walk Around the Block: Stoplight Secrets, Mischievous Squirrels, Manhole Mysteries & Other Stuff You See Every Day (and Know Nothing About). Spike Carlsen. HarperOne 2020. 328 p.
ISBN 9780062954756
Grades: Adult   031
1. Curiosities and wonders 2. Inventions 3. Material culture 4. Everyday life 5. Questions and answers 6. Recreation 7. Nature 8. Science Writing — Great Engineering Feats 9. History writing — Technological innovations
LC 2020025829

On his regular walk one morning, Spike Carlsen realized there was an entire world outside his front door that he knew nothing about. How does that fire hydrant work, he wondered? Why are street lights shining more brightly than ever before? And, on a more personal level, why does an easy stroll around the neighborhood always leave him feeling more creative and spry, better able to take on the day? A simple walk around the block set Carlsen off on an investigative journey to discover everything he could about every thing we take for granted in our everyday life, from manhole covers and recycling bins to pedestrian crossings and bike lanes.

"Writing in the mode of Edward Humes, David Owen, and Mary Roach, Carlsen offers an eye-opening and exuberantly informative walk-around-the-block tour that is made-to-order for this time of necessary at-homeness." —*Booklist*

Includes bibliographical references.

031.02 Books of miscellaneous facts

Iggulden, Conn
The Double Dangerous Book for Boys. Conn Iggulden. HarperCollins 2019. 304 pages
ISBN 9780062857972
Grades: Adult   031.02
1. Life skills 2. Amusements 3. Recreation 4. Boys 5. Sports and recreation — General
LC Bl2019032101

This long-awaited sequel to the bestselling Dangerous Book for Boys, which became an instant classic, is designed for boys from eight to eighty and includes more than 70 new chapters and important skills, historical information and essential stories.

ESSENTIAL AND RECOMMENDED TITLES
069 Museology (Museum science)

069 Museology (Museum science)

Conniff, Richard
House of Lost Worlds: Dinosaurs, Dynasties, and the Story of Life on Earth. Richard Conniff. Yale University Press 2016. 320 p.
ISBN 9780300211634
Grades: Adult   069
1. Museums 2. Natural history museums 3. Science 4. History writing — Science, technology, and medicine
LC Bl2016013886

Tells the story of how one museum changed ideas about dinosaurs, dynasties, and even the story of life on earth. The Yale Peabody Museum of Natural History, now celebrating its 150th anniversary, has remade the way we see the world.

"Colored, boxed sections highlighting people and events and over 100 illustrations and photos provide a pleasant coffee table-book feel, and 23 pages of footnotes attest to Conniff's exhaustive research." —*Kirkus*

Wilkins, Robert L.
Long Road to Hard Truth: The 100-year Mission to Create the National Museum of African American History and Culture. Robert L. Wilkins. Proud Legacy Publishing 2016. 155 p.
ISBN 9780997910407
Grades: Adult   069
1. Museums 2. Race relations 3. African Americans 4. Historical museums 5. African American history 6. Civil rights 7. History writing — African American — United States
LC 2016950268

In Long Road to Hard Truth: The 100 Year Mission to Create the National Museum of African American History and Culture, Robert L. Wilkins tells the story of how his curiosity about why there wasn't a national museum dedicated to African American history and culture became an obsession-eventually leading him to quit his job as an attorney when his wife was seven months pregnant with their second child, and make it his mission to help the museum become a reality.

"Given all the historical minutiae that Wilkins provides, its a surprisingly gripping historical drama. A delightful, edifying tale written with intelligence and emotional sensitivity." —*Kirkus*

070 Documentary media, educational media, news media; journalism; publishing

Van Agtmael, Peter
Look at the USA: A Diary of War and Home. Peter Van Agtmael. Thames and Hudson Ltd (ADS) 2024. 352 pages : Illustration
ISBN 9780500027028
Grades: Adult   070
1. United States history 2. War on Terrorism, 2001-2009 3. Afghan War, 2001-2021 4. Iraq War, 2003-2011 5. Photojournalism 6. War photography 7. Photography 8. Nationalism 9. United States 10. Afghanistan 11. Iraq 12. Visual nonfiction 13. History writing — Early 21st century — United States 14. Arts and Entertainment — Photography

A chronicle of post-9/11 America, at war and at home, as seen through the lens of one of Magnum Photos' leading photographers: a compelling and ground-shaking meditation on war and society. Through reportage and memoir, in photographs and words, Look at the U.S.A. documents the major fault lines that have defined post-9/11 America at home and abroad, beginning with the war in Iraq and ending with the Taliban takeover of Afghanistan.

"[This] collection succeeds in viscerally exposing the often 'ridiculous and obscene' narratives of American 'triumphs' and their costs. This is hard to look away from." —*Publishers Weekly*

070.1 Documentary media, educational media, news media

Fager, Jeffrey
Fifty Years of 60 Minutes: The Inside Story of Television's Most Influential News Broadcast. Jeff Fager. Simon & Schuster 2017. 320 p.
ISBN 9781501135804
Grades: Adult   070.1
1. Broadcast journalism 2. Television news 3. Television newscasters and commentators 4. Journalism 5. Arts and entertainment — Movies and television
LC 2017025966

A history of 60 Minutes—the iconic American TV news broadcast—going behind the scenes of the most famous breakthrough stories of its remarkable fifty-year run to reveal the secrets of the program's success.

"This insider perspective gives a behind-the-scenes view of how stories were developed, along with the complex interactions of the talented and competitive staff." —*Library Journal*

Includes bibliographical references and index.

Thompson, Hunter S.
Fear and Loathing at Rolling Stone: The Essential Writing of Hunter S. Thompson. Edited and with a foreword by Jann S. Wenner and with an introduction by Paul Scanlon. Simon & Schuster 2011. 320 p.
ISBN 9781439165959
Grades: Adult   070.1
1. Thompson, Hunter S. 2. Wenner, Jann 3. Gonzo journalism 4. Journalism 5. Periodical writing 6. Arts and Entertainment — Writing and Publishing
LC 2011032312

An anthology of "Rolling Stone" articles offers insight into both the late Thompson's early career and the magazine's fledgling years, and includes selected correspondence between Thompson and editor Jann Wenner.

"Thompson published his first article in Rolling Stone in 1970, documenting his campaign for sheriff and the rise of what he called freak power in Aspen, CO. He would continue to be a prolific contributor to the magazine throughout the 1970s from his infamous Fear and Loathing in Las Vegas (1971) to his political journalism beginning with his coverage of the Nixon-McGovern presidential campaign in 1972 and lasting until 2004, a year before his death. Rolling Stone's cofounder and publisher, Wenner, edits this collection of Thompson's Rolling Stone pieces. It includes not only Thompson's writings for the magazine but the two men's correspondence, deepening our understanding of how they worked together. Thompson's iconic voice remains fresh, vibrant, and relevant, also enabling today's readers to gain perspective on over 30 years of political and cultural change." —*Library Journal*

Wenger, Debora Halpern
Advancing the Story: Broadcast Journalism in a Multimedia World. Debora Halpern Wenger and Deborah Potter. CQ Press/SAGE 2018. xxxi, 380 p. : Illustration
ISBN 9781544332451
Grades: Adult   070.1
1. Broadcast journalism 2. Language arts — Journalism
LC 2018010986

It's a multimedia world, and today's journalists must develop a multimedia mindset. How does this way of thinking change the newsgathering and news production processes? Having conceived of and written their book in this changed media landscape, broadcast veterans Debora Halpern Wenger and Deborah Potter seamlessly build on the fundamentals of good news reporting while teaching students to use depth, interactivity and immediacy as they maximize the advantages of each platform.

Includes bibliographical references and index.

Wilkman, Jon
Screening Reality: How Documentary Filmmakers Reimagined America. Jon Wilkman. Bloomsbury Publishing 2020. 400 p.
ISBN 9781635571035
Grades: Adult   070.1

PUBLIC LIBRARY CORE COLLECTION: NONFICTION
Twentieth Edition

1. Filmmaking 2. Historical research 3. Truth 4. Propaganda 5. Documentary films 6. Film history and criticism 7. United States history 8. Arts and Entertainment — Movies and Television 9. History writing — United States 10. History writing — Arts and culture

LC 2019019146

Screening Reality is a widescreen view of the rarely examined relationship between nonfiction movies and American history—how 'reality' has been discovered, defined, projected, televised, and streamed during more than one hundred years of dramatic change, through World Wars I and II, the dawn of mass media, the social and political turmoil of the sixties and seventies, and the communications revolution that led to a twenty-first century of empowered yet divided Americans.

Includes bibliographical references and index.

070.4 Journalism

Baron, Martin
★ *Collision* of Power: Trump, Bezos, and the Washington Post. Martin Baron. Flatiron Books 2023. 352 p.

ISBN 9781250844200

Grades: Adult 070.4

1. Baron, Martin, 1954- 2. Trump, Donald, 1946- 3. Bezos, Jeffrey 4. Journalists 5. Newspapers 6. Newspaper editors 7. Presidents 8. Mass media executives 9. Power 10. Freedom of the press 11. Political journalism 12. Press and politics 13. Politics and government 14. United States 15. Life stories — Arts and culture — Writing — Journalists 16. Arts and Entertainment — Writing and Publishing 17. Politics and global affairs — Mass media and politics 18. Debut title

LC 2023006383

Marty Baron took charge of the Washington Post newsroom in 2013, after nearly a dozen years leading the Boston Globe. Just seven months into his new job, Baron received explosive news: Jeff Bezos, the founder of Amazon, would buy the Post, marking a sudden end to control by the venerated family that had presided over the paper for 80 years. Just over two years later, Donald Trump won the presidency. Pressures on Baron and his colleagues were immense and unrelenting, having to meet the demands of their new owner while contending with a president who waged a war of unprecedented vitriol and vengeance against the media.

"A newspaper resists manipulation and lies…An impassioned argument for objective journalism." —*Kirkus*

Includes bibliographical references and index.

Berkow, Ira
How Life Imitates Sports: A Sportswriter Recounts, Relives, and Reckons with 50 Years on the Sports Beat. Ira Berkow. Sports Publishing 2020. 379 p.

ISBN 9781683583790

Grades: Adult 070.4

1. Berkow, Ira 2. Sports 3. Sportswriters 4. Sports history 5. Athletes 6. 21st century 7. 20th century 8. Essays 9. Sports and Competition — Sports History 10. Life stories — Sports

For the last half century, Pulitzer Prize-winning sportswriter Ira Berkow has been at the center of some of the most memorable moments in sports history. From the World Series, NBA Finals, and Super Bowl, to Heavyweight Title Fights, the Olympics, and the Masters, he has seen and covered them all. How Life Imitates Sports shares how these events, and their participants, have significantly shaped how we as a nation have come to understand and perceive our culture (and even our politics). They are a historical record of one significant sphere of our life and times: sports.

"A New York Times sports reporter and columnist for more than 25 years and the author of numerous books, Berkow offers a wide-ranging collection of pieces on athletes and sports events from 1970 forward. . . . For those who value sports journalism, Berkow's work is certain to endure." —*Booklist*

Buell, Hal
Moments: The Pulitzer Prize Photographs : A Visual Chronicle of Our Time. Hal Buell; foreword by David Halberstam. Black Dog & Leventhal Publishers 2015. 336 p. : Illustration; Color

ISBN 9781631910081

Grades: Adult 070.4

1. Photojournalism 2. Pulitzer Prizes 3. Arts and Entertainment — Photography 4. History writing — General

LC Bl2015036668

Presents dozens of Pulitzer Prize-winning photographs that capture unforgettable moments in twentieth-century history, including the Marines raising the flag at Iwo Jima and Babe Ruth's final salute at Yankee Stadium.

Includes index.

Cronkite, Walter
Cronkite's War: His World War II Letters Home. Walter Cronkite IV and Maurice Isserman. National Geographic Society 2013. 352 p.

ISBN 9781426210198

Grades: Adult 070.4

1. Cronkite, Walter 2. Cronkite, Betsy, -2005 3. War correspondents 4. World War II 5. Journalists 6. London, England 7. Love letters 8. Letters 9. History writing — Wars and conflicts — World War II — European Theater 10. Family and Relationships — Dating and Marriage 11. Arts and Entertainment — Writing and Publishing

LC 2012045334

The iconic American journalist shares the story of his World War II experiences as a then-obscure United Press wire service reporter, tracing his two convoys across the dangerous North Atlantic to assignments in England and North Africa, which he documented in long, detailed letters to his beloved wife, Betsy.

Includes bibliographical references and index.

Kroeger, Brooke
Undaunted: How Women Changed American Journalism. Brooke Kroeger. Alfred A. Knopf 2023. 304 p.

ISBN 9780525659143

Grades: Adult 070.4

1. Women journalists 2. Women television newscasters and commentators 3. Women periodical writers 4. Women photojournalists 5. Women war correspondents 6. Investigative journalism 7. Male domination (Social structure) 8. Women's rights 9. United States history 10. Life stories — Arts and culture — Writing — Journalists 11. Life stories — Identity — Gender 12. Arts and Entertainment — Writing and Publishing 13. History writing — Women's history

LC 2022031484

Undaunted is a representative history of the American women who surmounted every impediment put in their way to do journalism's most valued work. From Margaret Fuller's improbable success to the highly paid reporters of the mid-nineteenth century to the breakthrough investigative triumphs of Nellie Bly, Ida Tarbell, and Ida B. Wells, Brooke Kroeger examines the lives of the best-remembered and long-forgotten woman journalists. She also celebrates those exceptional careers up to the present, including those of Martha Gellhorn, Rachel Carson, Janet Malcolm, Joan Didion, Cokie Roberts, and Charlayne Hunter-Gault.

"Merging feminist struggles with journalistic triumphs, Kroeger sheds an important light on both spheres." —*Booklist*

Includes bibliographical references and index.

MacKrell, Judith
The Correspondents: Six Women Writers on the Front Lines of World War II. Judith MacKrell. Doubleday 2021. 496 p.

ISBN 9780385547666

Grades: Adult 070.4

1. Women journalists 2. War correspondents 3. Women and war 4. World War II 5. Journalists 6. Military journalism 7. Women's participation in wars 8. Second World War era (1939-1945) 9. Collective biographies 10. Life stories — Arts and culture — Writing — Journalists 11. History writing — Wars and conflicts — World War II 12. History writing — Women's history

ESSENTIAL AND RECOMMENDED TITLES
070.449796 Sports — Journalism

Following six remarkable woman as their lives and careers intertwine, this riveting, untold history of a group of heroic women reporters who revolutionized the narrative of WW II reveals how they were forced to fight for the right to work on equal terms with men.

"In this rich and evocative history, journalist Mackrell (The Unfinished Palazzo) profiles six women who reported on World War II.... A must-read for those interested in women's history and the Second World War." —*Library Journal*

Schieffer, Bob
Overload: Finding the Truth in Today's Deluge of News. Bob Schieffer, with H. Andrew Schwartz. Rowman & Littlefield 2017. 204 pages
ISBN 9781538107218
Grades: Adult   070.4
1. Journalism 2. Mass media 3. Press and politics 4. Political journalism 5. Information technology 6. Electronic newspapers 7. Elections 8. Political campaigns 9. Presidential election, 2016 10. Politics and global affairs — Mass media and politics 11. Society and culture — Media and technology
LC 2017021959

In Overload, legendary television journalist Bob Schieffer examines today's journalism and those who practice it. Based on interviews with over 40 media leaders from television, print media, and the internet, Schieffer surveys the perils and promises of journalism's rapidly changing landscape.

"Succinct, savvy, and shrewd, this read-in-one-seating treatise on the Fourth Estate provides a crucial tool for critical analysis." —*Booklist*
Includes index.

Smith, Ben
Traffic: Genius, Rivalry, and Delusion in the Billion-Dollar Race to Go Viral. Ben Smith. Penguin Press 2023. 352 p.
ISBN 9780593299753
Grades: Adult   070.4
1. Peretti, Jonah 2. Denton, Nicholas 3. News media 4. Current events 5. Competition 6. Mass media 7. Digital media 8. Internet industry and trade 9. United States 10. Society and culture — Media and technology 11. Society and culture — Pop culture 12. Business and economics — Industries — Entertainment and media
LC 2022028861

The origin story of the Age of Disinformation: the candid inside tale of two online media rivals, Jonah Peretti of HuffPost and BuzzFeed and Nick Denton of Gawker Media, whose delirious pursuit of attention at scale helped release the dark forces that would overtake the internet and American society.

"There's no better history of the Wild West days of early social media than this one." —*Kirkus*
Includes bibliographical references and index.

Stelter, Brian
Hoax: Donald Trump, Fox News, and the Dangerous Distortion of Truth. Brian Stelter. Signal Press 2020. 320 p.
ISBN 9781982142445
Grades: Adult   070.4
1. Trump, Donald, 1946- 2. Hannity, Sean, 1961- 3. Television networks 4. Television journalists 5. Mass media bias 6. Journalism 7. Conservatism 8. New right 9. Propaganda 10. Misinformation 11. Journalistic ethics 12. Mass media 13. Television news 14. Presidents 15. United States 16. Liberal writing 17. Politics and global affairs — Political figures 18. Politics and global affairs — Mass media and politics 19. Life stories — Arts and culture — Writing — Journalists

Brian Stelter, CNN correspondent, subject of the Page One documentary and author of Top of the Morning examines the 45th President's complicated relationship with the media and his controversial relationship with the Fox News network. Over the course of two years, Stelter spoke with over 250 current and former Fox insiders in an effort to understand the inner workings of Rupert Murdoch's multibillion-dollar media empire.

"A deep, dispiriting dive into the nefarious intersection of politics, conspiracy, lies, and money as served up by Donald Trump and Fox News." —*Kirkus*

070.449796 Sports — Journalism

Ribowsky, Mark
Howard Cosell: The Man, the Myth, and the Transformation of American Sports. Mark Ribowsky. W.W. Norton & Co. 2012. 496 p.
ISBN 9780393080179
Grades: Adult   070.449796
1. Cosell, Howard, 1918-1995 2. Sportscasters 3. Sports history 4. Social life and customs 5. United States 6. 20th century 7. Biographies 8. Life stories — Arts and culture — Writing — Journalists 9. Arts and Entertainment — Movies and Television 10. Sports and Competition — General
LC 2011027501

Describes the life of one of the most recognizable, colorful figures in American sports history and offers a behind-the-scenes look at Monday Night Football and the commercialization of sports based on more than forty interviews with colleagues and athletes.

"The sportscaster Howard Cosell erupted onto the national stage in the 1960s and quickly became a pop-culture icon. His raspy, heavily New York-accented voice, a sharp mind, an expansive vocabulary and a photographic memory were packaged into a larger-than-life and sometimes abrasive figure. Whether his audience loved him, hated him or loved to hate him, they tuned in, and he turned them on. He was impossible to ignore. Mr. Ribowsky's book is an entertaining read and a thought-provoking portrayal of the multifaceted Howard Cosell in all his glory and enmity. It is based on voluminous, well-sourced research into print and electronic material, coupled with numerous interviews with Cosell's contemporaries." —*Wall Street Journal*
Includes bibliographical references and index.

070.5 Publishing

Brunsting, Karen
★ *Open Access Literature in Libraries:* Principles and Practices. Karen Brunsting, Caitlin Harrington, and Rachel E. Scott in collaboration with Core Publishing. ALA Editions 2023. 118 p.
ISBN 9780838939543
Grades: Professional   070.5
1. Publishers and publishing 2. Periodical publishers and publishing 3. Research 4. Library research 5. Materials selection (Libraries) 6. Collection management (Libraries) 7. Professional materials — General
LC 2022045249

Open Access has evolved into the most complex challenge of the scholarly publishing landscape and something libraries grapple with on a regular basis. But although librarians hold increasingly positive perceptions about OA, including its richness of unique content and immediacy of access, many lack the understanding, training, documentation, and knowledge of best practices that would allow them to engage with it confidently. This book helps to fill that gap, using a holistic approach that walks readers through the steps of integrating OA resources into library collections and supporting OA initiatives irrespective of budget, institution type, collection size, and staffing.
Includes bibliographical references and index.

Miller, Adrienne
In the Land of Men: A Memoir. Adrienne Miller. HarperCollins 2020. 336 pages
ISBN 9780062682413
Grades: Adult   070.5
1. Miller, Adrienne 2. Wallace, David Foster 3. Periodical editors 4. Women periodical editors 5. Periodicals 6. Women editors 7. Patriarchy 8. Gender role 9. Identity 10. Sexism 11. Sexism in employment 12. Authors and editors 13. Publishers and publishing 14. Men-women relations 15. New York City 16. Autobiographies and memoirs 17. Life stories — Arts and culture — Writing 18. Life stories — Identity — Gender 19. Arts and Entertainment — Writing and Publishing 20. Society and culture — Gender — Women
LC 2019028856

PUBLIC LIBRARY CORE COLLECTION: NONFICTION
Twentieth Edition

The author of The Coast of Akron traces her coming of age in the male-dominated 1990s literary world, discussing her relationship with David Foster Wallace and her achievements as the first female literary editor of Esquire.

"This intriguing memoir about the literary life of a female editor working in the 'last-hurrah days' of print magazine publishing will appeal to book nerds and fans of David Foster Wallace." —Publishers Weekly

Pettegree, Andrew
The Book in the Renaissance. Andrew Pettegree. Yale University Press 2010. 421 p.
ISBN 9780300110098
Grades: Adult   070.5
1. Book industry and trade 2. Books 3. European Renaissance 4. Reformation 5. Printing 6. Europe 7. Renaissance (1300-1600) 8. 16th century 9. Arts and Entertainment — Writing and Publishing 10. History writing — Renaissance — Europe 11. Arts and Entertainment — Writing and Publishing — Literary criticism
LC 2009026513
New York Times Notable Book, 2010.
Surveys Europe's printing industry, from Gutenberg's invention to the seventeenth century, discussing topics such as the challenges of early publishers and the political and religious conflicts that arose as more secular material entered the market.

"The author's treatment is both thorough and engaging, ably situating the social, economic, and historical within the stories of individuals involved." —Library Journal

Includes bibliographical references and index.

Prothero, Stephen R.
God the Bestseller: How One Editor Transformed American Religion a Book at a Time. Stephen Prothero. HarperOne, an imprint of HarperCollinsPublishers 2023. 352 p.
ISBN 9780062464040
Grades: Adult   070.5
1. Exman, Eugene 2. Literature 3. Editors 4. Publishers and publishing 5. Religious pluralism 6. National characteristics, American 7. Religions 8. United States 9. 20th century 10. Biographies 11. Life stories — Arts and culture — Writing — Journalists 12. Spirituality and religion — General 13. History Writing — United States 14. Arts and entertainment — Writing and Publishing
LC 2022041749
The compelling and unique saga of twentieth-century America on an identity quest through the eyes and books of one of the most influential editors of the day—a search, born of two world wars, for resolution of our divided identity as a Christian nation and a nation of religions.

"Prothero introduces readers to both a surprisingly important figure and to a number of books worth rediscovering." —Booklist

Includes bibliographical references.

Suber, Peter
Open Access. Peter Suber. MIT Press 2012. xii, 242 p.
ISBN 9780262517638
Grades: Adult Professional   070.5
1. Professional materials — General
LC 2011038297
A concise introduction to the basics of open access, describing what it is (and isn't) and showing that it is easy, fast, inexpensive, legal, and beneficial.
Includes bibliographical references (p. [177]-221) and index.

Yager, Jan
How to Self Publish Your Book: A Complete Guide to Writing, Editing, Marketing & Selling Your Own Book. Dr. Jan Yager. Square One Publishers 2019. 257 pages : Illustration
ISBN 9780757004650
Grades: Adult   070.5
1. Arts and Entertainment — Writing and publishing 2. Reference — Writing
LC 2018045394

"Choosing to self-publish a book means the author has full control of every step of the process and responsibility for everything. Yager, who has been both traditionally and self-published, breaks it all down in this realistic, accessible, and thorough guide." —Booklist

Includes bibliographical references and index.

070.92 Biography regardless of area, region, place

Cohen, Deborah
Last Call at the Hotel Imperial: The Reporters Who Took on a World at War. Deborah Cohen. Random House 2022. 304 p.
ISBN 9780525511199
Grades: Adult   070.92
1. Knickerbocker, H. R. (Hubert Renfro), 1898-1949 2. Sheean, Vincent, 1899-1975 3. Thompson, Dorothy, 1893-1961 4. Gunther, John, 1901-1970 5. Gunther, Frances 6. Foreign correspondents 7. Journalism 8. Journalists 9. Social life and customs 10. United States history 11. United States 12. 20th century 13. Collective biographies 14. Life stories — Arts and culture — Writing — Journalists 15. Arts and Entertainment — Writing and publishing 16. History writing — Wars and conflicts — World War II
LC 2021035621
Mark Lynton History Prize, 2023.
Married foreign correspondents John and Frances Gunther intimately understood that it isn't only impersonal, economic forces that propel history, bringing readers so close to the front lines of history that they could feel how personal pathologies became the stuff of geopolitical crises. Together with other reporters of the Lost Generation—American journalists H.R. Knickerbocker, Vincent Sheean, and Dorothy Thompson—the Gunthers slipped through knots of surveillance and ignored orders of expulsion in order to expose the mass executions in Badajoz during the Spanish Civil War, the Nazi-Soviet Non-Aggression Pact, the millions of dollars that Joseph Goebbels salted away abroad, and the sexual peccadillos of Hitler's brownshirts. They conjured what it was like to ride with Hitler in an airplane ("not a word did he say to any soul"); broke the inside story about Mussolini's claustrophobia and superstitions (he "took fright" at an Egyptian mummy that had been given to him); and verified the hypnotic impression Stalin made when he walked into a room ("You felt his antennae"). But just as they were transforming journalism, it was also transforming them: who they loved and betrayed, how they raised their children and coped with death. Over the course of their careers they would popularize bringing the private life into public view, not only in their reporting on the outsized figures of their day, but in what they revealed about their own (and each other's) intimate experiences as well. What were intimate relationships, after all, but geopolitics writ small?

"Northwestern University historian Cohen (Family Secrets) delivers an evocative portrait of a tight-knit coterie of American journalists who reported from the world's hot spots from the 1920s through the 1940s....Striking a masterful balance between the personal and the political, this ambitious and eloquent account brings a group of remarkable people—and their tumultuous era—to vivid life." —Publishers Weekly

Includes bibliographical references and index.

Green, Robin
The Only Girl: My Life and Times on the Masthead of Rolling Stone. Robin Green. Little Brown & Co. 2018. 304 p.
ISBN 9780316440028
Grades: Adult   070.92
1. Green, Robin 2. Women journalists 3. Periodicals 4. Sexism in employment 5. Women 6. Journalists 7. Work 8. Popular culture 9. 1970s 10. 20th century 11. Autobiographies and memoirs 12. Life stories — Arts and culture — Writing — Journalists
LC 2018935533
The only woman writer on the masthead of Rolling Stone magazine in the early 70s provides a raucous and vividly dishy memoir.

"Reading like a real-life road novel, Green's memoir is a must for aspiring writers." —Library Journal

ESSENTIAL AND RECOMMENDED TITLES
071 Geographic treatment of journalism and newspapers

Ressa, Maria
★ *How to Stand up to a Dictator: The Fight for Our Future.* Maria Ressa. HarperCollins 2022. 336 p.
ISBN 9780063257511
Grades: Adult   070.92
1. Political corruption 2. Authoritarianism 3. Women investigative journalists 4. Social media 5. Investigative journalists 6. Filipino people 7. Filipino Americans 8. American people 9. Philippines 10. Life stories — Facing adversity 11. Politics and global affairs — Political philosophy 12. Politics and global affairs — Mass media and politics

A Philippine Journalist who received the 2021 Nobel Peace Prize presents strategies for speaking truth to power, challenging corruption and standing up against authoritarians to battle information and lies.

"In this impassioned warning and inspirational call to arms, Ressa identifies and illuminates her core values of empathy, honesty, and faith in humanity to illustrate how a strong commitment to such foundational beliefs can provide the key to democracy's survival." —*Booklist*

Sullivan, Margaret
Newsroom Confidential: Lessons (and Worries) from an Ink-Stained Life. Margaret Sullivan. St. Martin's Press 2022. 320 p.
ISBN 9781250281906
Grades: Adult   070.92
1. Sullivan, Margaret, 1957- 2. Women journalists 3. Journalism 4. United States 5. Autobiographies and memoirs 6. Life stories — Arts and culture — Writing — Journalists 7. Arts and Entertainment — Writing and publishing
LC 2022020121

A trusted champion and critic of the American news media recounts her four decades of working in newsrooms big and small, taking us behind the scenes of the nation's most influential news outlets to explore how Americans lost trust in the news and what it will take to regain it.

"A veteran journalist recounts her life in the newsroom while prescribing cures for the media's current woes." —*Kirkus*

---

071 Geographic treatment of journalism and newspapers

Baker, Nicholson
The World on Sunday: Graphic Art in Joseph Pulitzer's Newspaper (1898-1911). Nicholson Baker and Margaret Brentano. Bulfinch Press 2005. xii, 131 p. : Illustration; Color
ISBN 9780821261934
Grades: Adult   071
1. Arts and Entertainment — General 2. Language arts and studies — Journalism
LC 2005000224

Celebrates the artistry and graphic design that transformed Joseph Pulitzer's New York World at the turn of the twentieth century, presenting a wide array of cartoons, caricatures, typography, photography, drawings, maps, and other artwork from a variety of legendary illustrators.

Includes bibliographical references and index.

Burns, Eric
Infamous Scribblers: The Founding Fathers and the Rowdy Beginnings of American Journalism. Eric Burns. Public Affairs 2006. x, 467 p.
ISBN 9781586483340
Grades: 11 12 Adult   071
1. Journalism 2. Newspapers 3. Press 4. Social life and customs 5. United States history 6. United States 7. 18th century 8. Arts and Entertainment — Writing and Publishing 9. Adult books for young adults
LC 2005053542

Discusses the raucous journalism of the Revolutionary era, showing how it helped build a nation that endured and offering new perspectives on today's media wars.

"From the sniping feuds among Boston's first papers to sex scandals involving Alexander Hamilton and Thomas Jefferson, the snappy patter gives clear indication of how much Burns relishes telling his story." —*Publishers Weekly*

Includes bibliographical references (p. [441]-449) and index.

Cohen, Roger
An Affirming Flame: Meditations on Life and Politics. Roger Cohen. Alfred A. Knopf 2023. 288 p.
ISBN 9780593321522
Grades: Adult   071
1. World politics 2. Civilization 3. Journalism 4. Democracy 5. United States 6. Essays 7. Politics and global affairs — World politics — United States
LC 2022027151

The collection from the former New York Times columnist traces America's fight to defend America's openness, democratic institutions and ideals in the face of foreign crises, creeping authoritarianism and assault on truth.

"A collection of perceptive, astute journalism from a master at the craft." —*Kirkus*

This is a Borzoi Book published by Alfred A. Knopf.

Nagourney, Adam
The Times: How the Newspaper of Record Survived Scandal, Scorn, and the Transformation of Journalism. Adam Nagourney. Crown 2023. 576 p.
ISBN 9780451499363
Grades: Adult   071
1. Newspapers 2. Newspaper editors 3. Publishers and publishing 4. News media 5. Journalism 6. Online journalism 7. Scandals 8. Public opinion 9. Social change 10. Arts and Entertainment — Writing and Publishing 11. Life stories — Arts and culture — Writing — Journalists
LC 2023012060

Drawing on hundreds of interviews and thousands of documents and letters from its archives, this firsthand account of four decades of the New York Times, from the final years of Arthur "Punch" Sulzberger's reign as publisher to the election of Donald Trump in 2016, recounts the newspaper's triumphs and failures.

"An exemplary work of journalism about journalism, of surpassing interest to any serious consumer of the news." —*Kirkus*

Includes bibliographical references and index.

Ostertag, Bob
People's Movements, People's Press: The Journalism of Social Justice Movements. Bob Ostertag. Beacon Press 2006. 232 p. : Illustration
ISBN 9780807061640
Grades: Adult   071
1. Newspapers 2. Underground press publications 3. Journalism 4. Social problems 5. Social justice 6. Social life and customs 7. United States 8. 20th century 9. Arts and Entertainment — Writing and Publishing 10. History writing — General
LC 2005031735

An insightful analysis of five social justice movements and their relationship with the newspapers and journals produced by the activists traces the history of the alternative print media and their influence on the forces of abolition, women's suffrage, environmental awareness, gay liberation, and the Vietnam anti-war movement, as well as on public opinion as a whole.

Includes bibliographical references (p. 196-218) and index.

Trillin, Calvin
The Lede: Dispatches from a Life in the Press. Calvin Trillin. Random House 2024. 320 p.
ISBN 9780593596449
Grades: Adult   071
1. Trillin, Calvin 2. Journalism 3. News agencies 4. Journalists 5. American wit and humor 6. United States 7. Essays 8. Arts and Entertainment — Writing and publishing 9. History Writing — United States 10. Society and culture — Media and technology
LC 2023015611

Drawing on his six-decade career, the best-selling author and beloved New Yorker writer, in this fascinating, opinionated portrait of journalism, uses his unique combination of reportage and humor to take on his own professional environment: the American press.

"An invaluable collection of observations about journalism authored by a beloved American reporter and humorist." —*Kirkus*

071.3 Journalism — United States

LaFollette, Marcel C.
Writing for Their Lives: America's Pioneering Female Science Journalists. Marcel Chotkowski LaFollette. The MIT Press 2023. 296 p.
ISBN 9780262048163
Grades: Adult   071.3
1. Women journalists 2. Science journalism 3. Sexism 4. Journalism 5. Women 6. Press 7. United States history 8. Arts and Entertainment — Writing and publishing 9. Life stories — Arts and culture — Writing — Journalists 10. History Writing — Women's history
LC 2022038709

Based on extensive archival research in the voluminous Science Service records at the Smithsonian Institution, Writing for Their Lives focuses on a remarkable group of women whose contributions to science and journalism deserve greater recognition.

"Readers interested in science, journalism history, and women's studies will find inspiration in learning more about these talented pioneers." —*Library Journal*

Includes bibliographical references and index.

071.7 Journalism and newspapers in the United States

Cullen, Art
Storm Lake: A Chronicle of Change, Resilience, and Hope from a Heartland Newspaper. Art Cullen. Viking 2018. 336 p.
ISBN 9780525558873
Grades: Adult   071.7
1. Cullen, Art 2. Newspapers 3. Small towns 4. Agribusiness 5. Journalism 6. Immigrants 7. Farms 8. Environmental degradation 9. Social advocacy 10. Environmentalism 11. Blue collar workers 12. Rural life 13. Iowa 14. Liberal writing 15. Life stories — Arts and culture — Writing — Journalists 16. Society and culture — Social activism and philanthropy 17. Society and culture — Urban and regional studies 18. Politics and global affairs — Environmental issues and policies
LC 2018025006

The Pulitzer Prize-winning owner of a small, twice-weekly Iowa newspaper that took on a big agri-industry corporation for poisoning their local rivers takes a candid look at the changing politics, environment, economics and demographics of his farming and meatpacking town.

081 General collections in American English

Einstein, Albert
Ideas and Opinions. Albert Einstein; with an introduction by Alan Lightman; new translations and revisions by Sonja Bargmann. Modern Library 1994. xix, 418 p. : Illustration
ISBN 9780679601050
Grades: 11 12 Adult   081
1. Physics 2. Peace 3. Science 4. Philosophy 5. Essays 6. Science writing — General
LC 94002115

A survey of Einstein's scientific achievements follows excerpts from letters, speeches, and interviews that reveal his thoughts on religious, political, cultural, social, and economic issues.

Based on Mein Weltbild, edited by Carl Seelig, and other sources; Originally published: New York : Crown Publishers, 1954.

Ferriss, Timothy
Tools of Titans: The Tactics, Routines, and Habits of Billionaires, Icons, and World-class Performers. Tim Ferriss; foreword by Arnold Schwarzenegger; illustrations by Remie Geoffroi. Houghton Mifflin Harcourt 2016. xxvii, 673 pages : Illustration
ISBN 9781328683786
Grades: Adult   081
1. Change (Psychology) 2. Physical fitness 3. Self-actualization 4. Self-fulfillment 5. Successful people 6. Wealth 7. Wisdom 8. Success (Concept) 9. Personal conduct 10. Interviews 11. Business and economics — General 12. Self-Help — Personal growth
LC 2016304630

Fitness, money, and wisdom—here are the tools. Over the last two years, Tim Ferriss has collected the routines and tools of world-class performers around the globe while interviewing them for his self-titled podcast. Now the distilled notebook of tipsand tricks that helped him double his income, flexibility, happiness, and more is available as Tools of Titans.

The #1 New York Times best-selling author of The 4-Hour Workweek collects the best tools and tactics that he's learned from the top celebrities and thinkers that he's had on his popular podcast.

Includes bibliographical references.

Pauling, Linus
Linus Pauling: In His Own Words : Selected Writings, Speeches, and Interviews. Edited by Barbara Marinacci; introduction by Linus Pauling. Simon & Schuster 1995. 320 p.
ISBN 9780684813875
Grades: Adult   081
1. Pauling, Linus, 1901-1994 2. Scientists 3. Science 4. Biographies 5. Life stories — Science, technology, and medicine
LC 95031123

Selected writings share the late scientist's views on chemistry, education, the structure of matter, proteins, nuclear politics, fallout, and nutritional medicine.

"This book attempts to follow the life and career of Dr. Pauling through his own writings, interspersed with narrative by the editor. The book succeeds wonderfully. Linus Pauling is unique among modern scientists, both for winning two Nobel Prizes and for his political and social views. Through his writings, the breadth and depth of his work become clear to the reader." —*Science Books & Films*

A Touchstone book; Includes bibliographical references (p. [291]-302) and index.

Scalia, Antonin
Scalia Speaks: Reflections on Law, Faith, and Life Well Lived. Antonin Scalia, Christopher J. Scalia, Edward Whelan; foreword by Ruth Bader Ginsburg. Crown Forum 2017. 384 p.
ISBN 9780525573326
Grades: Adult   081
1. Scalia, Antonin, 1936-2016 2. Judicial opinions 3. Judges 4. Judicial system 5. Speeches, addresses, etc. 6. Politics and global affairs — Judicial politics
LC 2017034660

This definitive collection of beloved Supreme Court Justice Antonin Scalia's finest speeches covers topics as varied as the law, faith, virtue, pastimes, and his heroes and friends. Featuring a foreword by longtime friend Ruth Bader Ginsburg and an intimate introduction by his youngest son, this volume includes dozens of speeches, some deeply personal, that have never before been published.

"This fine representative assemblage of Supreme Court Justice Scalia's speeches pays tribute to his ready wit and facility with language." —*Library Journal*

Includes bibliographical references and index.

ESSENTIAL AND RECOMMENDED TITLES
091 Manuscripts

091 Manuscripts

De Hamel, Christopher
*The **Manuscripts** Club: The People Behind a Thousand Years of Medieval Manuscripts.* Christopher de Hamel. Penguin Press 2023. 640 p.
ISBN 9780525559412
Grades: Adult **091**
1. Illumination of books and manuscripts, Medieval 2. Book industry and trade 3. Manuscripts, Medieval 4. Collectors and collecting 5. Illustrators 6. Social life and customs 7. Art history 8. European history 9. Medieval period (476-1492) 10. Collective biographies 11. Life stories — Arts and culture — Writing
LC 2022058165

Illuminates the extraordinary people who have spent their lives making, collecting and preserving manuscripts of the Middle Ages, which are among the greatest works of European art and literature, through the centuries, revealing how manuscripts have survived and been used by very different kinds of people in many different circumstances.

"This tour through manuscript history is dense with facts and dates but never dry. De Hamel…is a charming and knowledgeable guide, and his 'Visits' with his subjects—tours of their residences or libraries—brings their obsessions to vivid life." —*Kirkus*

Includes bibliographical references and index.

★ ***Meetings** with Remarkable Manuscripts: Twelve Journeys into the Medieval World.* Christopher de Hamel. Penguin Press 2017. 640 p. : Color; Illustration
ISBN 9781594206115
Grades: Adult **091**
1. Manuscripts 2. Material culture 3. Civilization, Medieval 4. Social life and customs 5. European history 6. Europe 7. Medieval period (476-1492) 8. History writing — Medieval — Europe
LC 2017031392

In a full-color exploration of the medieval world through 12 manuscripts, a leading expert travels the globe to visit these hand-made treasures and unlocks their mysteries, telling a story of intellectual culture and art over the course of a millennium.

"A rare, erudite, and delightfully entertaining history." —*Kirkus*

093 Manuscripts & rare books — Incunabula

Davis, Margaret Leslie
*The **Lost** Gutenberg: The Astounding Story of One Book's Five-Hundred-Year Odyssey.* Margaret Leslie Davis. TarcherPerigee 2019. 304 p.
ISBN 9781592408672
Grades: Adult **093**
1. Doheny, Estelle, 1875-1958 2. Rare books 3. Book collectors 4. Lost books 5. Collectors and collecting 6. History writing — Arts and culture 7. Arts and Entertainment — Writing and Publishing
LC 2018049581

Recounting five centuries in the life of one copy of the extremely rare Gutenberg Bible, a never-before-told story reveals its impact on the lives of the fanatical few who were lucky enough to own it.

"Davis does a fine job telling a fascinating story that touches on the origin of books, the passion of collectors, the unseen world of rare-book dealers, and the lives of the super-rich, past and present." —*Kirkus*

Includes bibliographical references and index.

098 Prohibited works, forgeries, hoaxes

Baez, Fernando
Universal History of the Destruction of Books: From Ancient Sumer to Modern-day Iraq. Fernando Baez. W. W. Norton & Co. Inc. 2008. 272 p.
ISBN 9781934633014
Grades: Adult **098**
1. Censorship 2. Book burning 3. Banned books 4. Libraries 5. History writing — General 6. Arts and Entertainment — Writing and Publishing — Literary criticism
LC Bl2008025448

Booklist Editors' Choice, 2008.

An investigation into the practice of book destruction and censorship explores such historical examples as the smashed tablets of ancient Sumer, the decimation of the Library of Alexandria, and the looting of libraries in post-war Iraq, in a chronicle that evaluates the political and human motives behind the practice.

"This is a horrific chronicle of the centuries-long assault on human memory. A sobering reminder of just how deep-seated is the instinct to destroy other people's truths." —*Kirkus*

Tigay, Chanan
*The **Lost** Book of Moses: The Hunt for the World's Oldest Bible.* Chanan Tigay. Ecco 2016. 352 p.
ISBN 9780062206411
Grades: Adult **098**
1. Shapira, Mozes Vilhelm, 1830?-1884 2. Forgers 3. Forgery 4. Archaeology 5. History writing — Archaeology
LC Bl2016003507

In this combination of biography, memoir, travelogue, and scriptural history, author Chanan Tigay explores the life of a 19th-century antiquities dealer who claimed to have discovered the oldest manuscript of Deuteronomy. The dealer, Moses Shapira, was denounced as a fraud, and the scroll disappeared, but 64 years later the Dead Sea Scrolls were discovered, transforming the field of biblical archaeology. Could Shapira's find have been genuine? In The Lost Book of Moses, Tigay traces his efforts to find the lost manuscript while chronicling Shapira's life. Fans of archaeology and scriptural history won't want to miss this thrilling account.

"A work of broad appeal, for the history buff and mystery lover alike." —*Kirkus*

100 Philosophy, parapsychology and occultism, psychology

Blackburn, Simon
***Think:** A Compelling Introduction to Philosophy.* Simon Blackburn. Oxford University Press 1999. VII, 312 p.
ISBN 9780192100245
Grades: 11 12 Adult **100**
1. Philosophy 2. Spirituality and Religion — General 3. Science writing — Physics
LC 00265286

An introduction to philosophy explores basic themes and the work of major philosophers.

"The author explores such areas as knowledge, mind, free will, identity, God, goodness and justice. His method is to introduce what other philosophers—primarily Plato, Descartes, Locke, Berkeley, Leibniz, Hume, and Kant—have had to say about these themes. Readers new to the subject could very well be captivated." —*Library Journal*

Includes bibliographical references (p. 307-310) and index.

Gutting, Gary
What Philosophy Can Do. Gary Gutting. W.W. Norton & Company 2015. 320 p.
ISBN 9780393242270
Grades: Adult **100**
1. Philosophy 2. Thought and thinking 3. Essays 4. Society and culture — Philosophy
LC 2015013783

How can we have meaningful debates with political opponents? How can we distinguish reliable science from over-hyped media reports? How can we talk sensibly about God? In What Philosophy Can Do, Gary Gutting takes a philosopher's scalpel to modern life's biggest questions and the most powerful forces in our society—politics, science, religion, education, and capitalism—to show how we can improve our discussions of contentious contemporary issues.

"While Gutting applies complex philosophical and logical principles in his essays, he does so in an accessible way. The range of essays makes this work appealing to anyone with an interest in philosophy." —*Library Journal*

Includes bibliographical references and index.

Weiner, Eric
The *Socrates Express: In Search of Life Lessons from Dead Philosophers*. Eric Weiner. Avid Reader Press 2020. 352 p.
ISBN 9781501129018
Grades: Adult   **100**
1. Philosophy 2. Purpose in life 3. Society and culture — Philosophy
LC Bl2020019383

The New York Times best-selling author follows in the footsteps of history's greatest thinkers and shows us how each—from Epicurus to Gandhi, Thoreau to Beauvoir—offers practical and spiritual lessons for today's unsettled times.

"Journalist Weiner (The Geography of Bliss) makes a convincing and winningly presented case for the practical applications of philosophy to everyday existence in the 21st century. With humor and thoughtfulness, he distills the wisdom of thinkers from throughout history." —*Publishers Weekly*

101 Theory of philosophy

Ortega Y Gasset, Jose
What Is Philosophy? Translated from the Spanish by Mildred Adams. Norton 1961. 252 p.
ISBN 9780393001266
Grades: Adult   **101**
1. Philosophy 2. Society and culture — Philosophy
LC 61005621

A work powerful and pervading in its implications not only for metaphysics but also for art, political science, and the philosophy of history.

Lectures given in Madrid and Buenos Aires.

103 Dictionaries, encyclopedias, concordances of philosophy

Blackburn, Simon
The *Oxford Dictionary of Philosophy*. Simon Blackburn. Oxford University Press 2005. VIII, 407 p. : Illustration
ISBN 9780198610144
Grades: Adult   **103**
1. Philosophy 2. Reference books — Humanities 3. Reference — Dictionaries
LC 2006271895

More than four hundred new entries are contained in the revised and updated edition of this wide-ranging and authoritative reference that covers every aspect of philosophy, from Aristotle to Zen, and contains more than three thousand alphabetical entries that encompasses world philosophical traditions, hundreds of influential philosophers, terms and concepts, and more.

Includes bibliographical references.

109 History and collected biography

Grayling, A. C.
The *History of Philosophy*. A.C. Grayling. Penguin Press 2019. 704 pages
ISBN 9781984878748
Grades: Adult   **109**
1. Philosophy 2. Philosophers 3. Philosophy, Ancient 4. Philosophy, Medieval 5. Philosophy, Asian 6. Philosophy, Western 7. Philosophy, Modern 8. Society and culture — Philosophy 9. History writing — General
LC 2019035983

The first authoritative and accessible single-volume history of philosophy to cover both Western and Eastern traditions, from one of the world's most eminent thinkers the story of philosophy is the story of who we are and why. An epic tale, spanning civilizations and continents, it explores some of the most creative minds in history. But not since the long-popular classic Bertrand Russell's a History of Western Philosophy, published in 1945, has there been a comprehensive and entertaining single-volume history of this great, intellectual, world-shaping journey. With characteristic clarity and elegance, A. C. Grayling takes the reader from the worldviews and moralities before the age of the Buddha, Confucius and Socrates through Christianity's capture of the European mind, from the Renaissance and Enlightenment on to Mill, Nietzsche, Sartre and, finally, philosophy today. Bringing together these many threads that all too often run parallel, he surveys in tandem the great philosophical traditions of India, China and the Persian-Arabic world.

Includes bibliographical references and index.

Russell, Bertrand
A *History* of Western Philosophy, and Its Connection with Political and Social Circumstances from the Earliest Times to the Present Day. Bertrand Russell. Simon and Schuster 1945. xxiii, 895 p.
ISBN 9780671314002
Grades: Adult   **109**
1. Philosophy 2. Society and culture — Philosophy
LC 45008884

Describes and analyzes the major philosophers and philosophical issues from the pre-Socratics to the philosphy of logical analysis.

Originally designed and partly delivered as lectures at the Barnes foundation in Pennsylvania.—Pref.

110 Metaphysics

Hagglund, Martin
This Life: Secular Faith and Spiritual Freedom. Martin Hagglund. Pantheon Books 2019. 450 pages
ISBN 9781101870402
Grades: Adult   **110**
1. Faith 2. Purpose in life 3. Human behavior 4. Philosophers 5. Freedom 6. Semantics 7. Free will and determinism 8. Secularism 9. Social values 10. Democratic socialism 11. Interpersonal relations 12. Caring 13. Commitment (Psychology) 14. Religious psychology 15. Faith and reason 16. Society and culture — Philosophy 17. Society and culture — Psychology and human behavior 18. Spirituality and Religion — General
LC 2018029429

Challenging our preconceived notions of faith and freedom, and engaging with great philosphers, the author presents a critique of religion that takes readers to the heart of what it means to mourn our loved ones, be committed and care about a sustainable world.

"In a densely argued critique of religion and capitalism, philosopher Hgglund tackles thorny questions of value, freedom, and responsibility." —*Kirkus*

Includes bibliographical references and index.

Russell, Bertrand
The *Problems of Philosophy*. Bertrand Russell. Gray Cadence 2011. IX, 189 p.
ISBN 9780983360612
Grades: Adult   **110**
1. Philosophy 2. Intellectual life 3. Ideas (Philosophy) 4. Society and culture — Philosophy
LC 2011926546

Cited in Books for College Libraries, 3d ed. Accenting theory of knowledge issues over metaphysics in this classic, Russell's ability to make philosophy accessible clinches his case for students reading great philosophers' works rather than secondary texts. Originally published by Williams and Norgate.

ESSENTIAL AND RECOMMENDED TITLES
111 Ontology

"The work is concise, free from technical terms and perfectly clear to the general reader with no prior knowledge of the subject." —*Booklist*

Includes bibliographical references (p. 189); Originally published: London : Williams and Norgate, 1912.

111 Ontology

Barrow, John D.
The Infinite Book: A Short Guide to the Boundless, Timeless, and Endless. John D. Barrow. Pantheon Books 2005. xvi, 328 p. : Illustration
ISBN 9780375422270
Grades: Adult　　　　　　　　　　　　　　　　　　　111
1. Infinity 2. Metaphysics 3. Mathematics 4. Science Writing — Mathematics 5. Adult books for young adults
LC 2004060206

Explores the concept of infinity, tracing the history and meaning of infinity from ancient times to the present day, and examining the diverse permutations of the infinite and their influence on the human sense of the world around.

"The author approaches the subject [of infinity] from the viewpoints of mathematics, physics, and scientific cosmology and also delves into philosophers' and theologians' reflections concerning infinity. Well suited to a general audience, this book requires no specialized knowledge of mathematics or science." —*Library Journal*

Includes bibliographical references (p. [277]-316) and index.

Eco, Umberto
History of Beauty. Edited by Umberto Eco; translated by Alastair McEwen. Rizzoli 2005. 438 p. : Illustration; Color
ISBN 9780847826469
Grades: Adult　　　　　　　　　　　　　　　　　　　111
1. Aesthetics 2. Art 3. Art and philosophy 4. Philosophy 5. Arts and Entertainment — General

A study of the idea of beauty explores the ever-changing concept of beauty from the ancient Greeks to today.

"The editor traces the protean subject of beauty in art, literature, philosophy, the mass media, and other humanities from ancient times to the present, setting forth various Western cultural aesthetic ideals ranging from ancient Greek to modern American. This is not a quick, one-time coffee-table read but a nearly flawless presentation of the history of a fascinating and elusive idea that will delight and enlighten general readers as well as scholars." —*Library Journal*

Includes bibliographical references (p. 431) and indexes.

On Ugliness. Umberto Eco; translated by Alastair McEwen. Rizzoli International Publications 2007. 456 p.
ISBN 9780847829866
Grades: Adult　　　　　　　　　　　　　　　　　　　111
1. Ugliness 2. Taboo 3. Aesthetics 4. Art 5. Art and philosophy 6. Arts and Entertainment — General
LC 2007930249

In a companion volume to his History of Beauty, the renowned philosopher and cultural critic analyzes our attraction to the gruesome, horrific, and repellant in visual culture and the arts, drawing on abundant examples of painting and sculpture, ranging from antiquity to the works of Bosch, Goya, and others, complemented by quotations by celebrated writers and thinkers.

"In this collection of images and written excerpts from ancient times to the present, all woven together with a provocative commentary and translated by Alastair McEwen, [the editor] asks: is repulsiveness, too, in the eye of the beholder? And what do we learn about that beholder when we delve into his aversions? Selecting stark visual images of gore, deformity, moral turpitude and malice, and quotations from sources ranging from Plato to radical feminists, Eco unfurls a taxonomy of ugliness. As gross-out contests go, it's both absorbing and highbrow." —*New York Times Book Review*

Heidegger, Martin
★ *Being and Time.* Martin Heidegger; translated by John MacQuarrie and Edward Robinson; foreword by Taylor Carman. Harpercollins 2008. 589 p.
ISBN 9780061575594
Grades: Adult　　　　　　　　　　　　　　　　　　　111
1. God 2. Existentialism 3. Philosophy 4. Ontology 5. Metaphysics 6. Religions 7. Society and culture — Philosophy
LC 2009293338

The fundamental philosophy of the existentialist movement is revealed in Heidegger's discussion of human existence, nonhuman presence, personal consciousness, and angst.

Magsamen, Susan
Your Brain on Art: How the Arts Transform Us. Susan Magsamen and Ivy Ross. Random House 2023. 240 p.
ISBN 9780593449233
Grades: Adult　　　　　　　　　　　　　　　　　　　111
1. Art 2. Neuroscience 3. Brain 4. Mental health 5. Health 6. Science Writing — Biology 7. Arts and Entertainment — General

Combining breakthrough research, insights from multidisciplinary pioneers and real-life stories, this authoritative guide to the new science of neuroaesthetics shows how the arts, from painting and dancing to expressive writing, architecture and more, are essential for improving physical and mental health.

"A useful guide to the science behind why the arts are fundamental to our physical and emotional health….Regularly engaging with the arts can make you live longer, and this absorbing book explains how." —*Kirkus*

Sartre, Jean-Paul
★ *Being and Nothingness.* Jean-Paul Sartre; translated and with an introduction by Hazel E. Barnes. Gramercy Books 1994. LXVII, 636 p.
ISBN 9780517101858
Grades: Adult　　　　　　　　　　　　　　　　　　　111
1. Existentialism 2. Society and culture — Philosophy
LC 94011808

An informative introduction to Sartre and his philosophy and a key to special terminology enhance a handsome edition of Sartre's classic study of modern existentialism.

Includes index; Originally published: New York : Philosophical Library, 1956.

Existentialism and Human Emotions. Philosophical Library 1967. 96 p.
ISBN 9780806509020
Grades: Adult　　　　　　　　　　　　　　　　　　　111
1. Existentialism 2. Society and culture — Philosophy
LC 57004372

In this provocative philosophical analysis, Jean-Paul Sartre refutes the idea that existentialism drains meaning from human life, by claiming that the philosophy instead gives man total freedom to achieve his own significance.

The section on 'Existentialism' is taken from the book of that name, translated by Bernard Frechtman; all other selections are from Being and nothingness, translated by Hazel E. Barnes.

Whitefield-Madrano, Autumn
Face Value: The Hidden Ways That Beauty Shapes Women's Lives. Autumn Whitefield-Madrano. Simon & Schuster 2016. 288 p.
ISBN 9781476754000
Grades: Adult　　　　　　　　　　　　　　　　　　　111
1. Feminism 2. Feminine beauty (Aesthetics) 3. Women 4. Aesthetics 5. Beauty 6. Beauty care 7. Psychology 8. Body image 9. Self-perception 10. Society and culture — Gender — Women
LC 2015038730

Part social commentary, part cultural analysis, part careful investigation and part powerful personal anecdotes, a provocative book explores the relationship between appearance and science, social media, sex, friendship, language and advertising to show how beauty actually affects us day to day.

"This is a valuable addition to contemporary feminist writing, providing much-needed perspective to a pervasive issue that young women and staunch feminists will glean much from, whether they agree with the author's findings or not." —*Library Journal*

PUBLIC LIBRARY CORE COLLECTION: NONFICTION
Twentieth Edition

113 Cosmology (Philosophy of nature)

Holt, Jim
Why Does the World Exist?: An Existential Detective Story. Jim Holt. Liveright Pub. Corp. 2012. VI, 309 p. : Illustration
ISBN 9780871404091
Grades: Adult   113
1. Cosmology 2. Philosophy 3. Science Writing — General 4. Spirituality and Religion — General
LC 2012015177
ALA Notable Book, 2013; New York Times Notable Book, 2012; National Book Critics Circle Award for Nonfiction finalist, 2012.

Expands the search for the origins of the universe beyond God and the Big Bang theory, exploring more bizarre possibilities inspired by physicists, theologians, mathematicians, and even novelists.

Includes bibliographical references (p. 283-294) and index.

Volf, Miroslav
Life Worth Living: A Guide to What Matters Most. Miroslav Volf, Matthew Croasmun, and Ryan McAnnally-Linz. The Open Field/Penguin Life 2023. xxxiv, 315 pages : Illustration
ISBN 9780593489307
Grades: Adult   113
1. Purpose in life 2. Personal conduct 3. Desire 4. Goals and objectives 5. Philosophy 6. Religions 7. Questions and answers 8. Self-fulfillment 9. Society and culture — Philosophy 10. Society and culture — Psychology and human behavior
LC 2022030876

What makes a good life? the question is inherent to the human condition, asked by people across generations, professions, and social classes, and addressed by all schools of philosophy and religions. In A Life Worth Living, named after its authors' highly sought-after undergraduate course at Yale, Volf, Croasmun, and McAnnally-Linz chart out this question, providing readers with jumping-off points, road maps, and habits of reflection for figuring out where their lives hold meaning and where things need to change.

"Individuals will find more than one answer to every question posed, and a final, valuable encomium…A must-read for any age." —*Booklist*

Includes bibliographical references (pages 291-315).

Wilson, Edward O.
In Search of Nature. Edward O. Wilson. Island Press 1996. x, 214 p. : Illustration
ISBN 9781559632157
Grades: Adult   113
1. Human ecology 2. Philosophy of nature 3. Philosophy 4. Nature writing — Environmental Issues 5. Nature writing — General 6. Science writing — General
LC 96011226

Focusing on the interrelationship of wild nature and human nature, a collection of short writings and essays explores "Animal Nature, Human Nature," "The Patterns of Nature," and "Nature's Abundance."

Focusing on the interrelationship of wild nature and human nature, a three-part collection of seminal short writings and essays by the renowned naturalist explores "Animal Nature, Human Nature," "The Patterns of Nature," and "Nature's Abundance."

"Concerned people of all ages should enjoy the reasoning provided by the dedicated scientific writing presented in this attractive book." —*Science Books & Films*

A Shearwater book; Includes bibliographical references (p. 201-202) and index.

121 Epistemology (Theory of knowledge)

Dennett, D. C.
Intuition Pumps and Other Tools for Thinking. Daniel C. Dennett. W. W. Norton & Company 2013. xiv, 496 pages : Illustration; Color
ISBN 9780393082067
Grades: Adult   121
1. Philosophy 2. Thought and thinking 3. Spirituality and Religion — General
LC 2013000930

A philosophy professor offers exercises and tools to stretch the mind, offering new ways to consider, discuss, and argue positions on dangerous subject matter including evolution, the meaning of life, and free will.

The philosophy professor behind Breaking the Spell and Consciousness Explained offers exercises and tools to stretch the mind, offering new ways to consider, discuss and argue positions on dangerous subject matter including evolution, the meaning of life and free will.

Includes bibliographical references (pages 445-460) and index.

Hecht, Jennifer Michael
Doubt: A History : The Great Doubters and Their Legacy of Innovation, from Socrates and Jesus to Thomas Jefferson and Emily Dickinson. Jennifer Michael Hecht. Harper San Francisco 2003. xxi, 551 p. : Illustration
ISBN 9780060097721
Grades: Adult   121
1. Belief and doubt 2. Skepticism 3. Reasoning 4. Religions 5. History writing — Microhistory
LC 2004266061

In this sweeping history, Jennifer Michael Hecht celebrates doubt as an engine of creativity and as an alternative to the political and intellectual dangers of certainty—Just as belief has its own history featuring people whose unique expressions of faith have forever changed the world, doubt has a vibrant story and tradition with its own saints martyrs, and sages.

"The author's brief but splendid study of the great Renaissance skeptic Montaigne is alone worth the price of the book. Hecht's warm prose, lucid insights, and impeccable research combine for a lively, thoughtful, and first-rate study of a neglected idea." —*Library Journal*

Includes bibliographical references (p. [521]-528) and index.

Hoffman, Donald D.
The Case Against Reality: Why Evolution Hid the Truth from Our Eyes. Donald D. Hoffman. W. W. Norton & Company 2019. 272 p.
ISBN 9780393254693
Grades: Adult   121
1. Reality 2. Perception 3. Evolution 4. Philosophy of mind 5. Cognitive science 6. Observing things 7. Science Writing — Biology
LC 2019006962

Challenging leading scientific theories that claim our senses are objective, a groundbreaking examination of human perception reveals its evolutionary importance and how it is used today in marketing, design, and personal safety.

"A dense, lucid, and often unsettling exploration of how our brains interpret the world." —*Kirkus*

Includes bibliographical references and index.

Locke, John
An Essay Concerning Human Understanding. John Locke; edited by Roger Woolhouse. Penguin Books 1997. xxvii, 784, 1 p.
ISBN 9780140434828
Grades: Adult   121
1. Spirituality and Religion — General
LC 98175907

This new, complete, and unabridged edition represents the very latest in critical thinking on Locke's pioneering work, which set the groundwork for modern philosophy.

Includes bibliographical references (p. 750-785) and index.

ESSENTIAL AND RECOMMENDED TITLES
123 Determinism and indeterminism

Schulz, Kathryn
Being Wrong: Adventures in the Margin of Error. Kathryn Schulz. Harpercollins 2010. 416 p.
ISBN 9780061176043
Grades: Adult   **121**
1. Errors 2. Right and wrong 3. Human behavior 4. Misconceptions 5. Psychology 6. Science Writing — Medicine and health — Mental health 7. Society and culture — Psychology and human behavior
LC 2010282589

The author explains what in means to be right or wrong and why it matters so much to people, arguing that humans' tendency to make mistakes is an essential part of our intelligence."

"The author discusses how we make mistakes, how we behave when we find we have been wrong, and how our errors change us. Schulz writes with such lucidity and wit that her philosophical enquiry becomes a page-turner." —*Publishers Weekly*

Wilson, Edward O.
Consilience: The Unity of Knowledge. Edward O. Wilson. Knopf 1998. 332 p. : Illustration
ISBN 9780679450771
Grades: Adult   **121**
1. Philosophy 2. Order (Philosophy) 3. Philosophy and science 4. Semantics 5. Society and culture — Philosophy
LC 97002816

Booklist Editors' Choice, 1998; New York Times Notable Book, 1998.

An expert on sociobiology and biodiversity argues for the fundamental unity of all knowledge in the face of the increasing fragmentation and specialization of knowledge over the past two centuries.

"As human population burgeons and its environment deteriorates, continued human success depends on making the wise choices that sound knowledge makes possible. Wilson dazzlingly reaffirms the cogency and the power of scientific materialism." —*Booklist*

Includes bibliographical references (p. 299-319) and index.

123 Determinism and indeterminism

Sapolsky, Robert M.
Determined: A Science of Life Without Free Will. Robert M. Sapolsky. Penguin Press 2023. 511 p.
ISBN 9780525560975
Grades: Adult   **123**
1. Human behavior 2. Ethics 3. Free will and determinism 4. Decision-making 5. Options, alternatives, choices 6. Consciousness 7. Philosophy 8. Physics 9. Science Writing — Biology 10. Society and culture — Psychology and human behavior 11. Science Writing — Physics 12. Society and culture — Philosophy
LC 2023023790

An acclaimed behavioral scientist tackles major arguments of free will and takes them out, navigating through the chaos and complexity of science, quantum physics, and philosophy to apply a new understanding of life beyond free will to some of our most essential questions around punishment, morality and living well together.

"Acclaimed behavioral scientist Sapolsky (Behave, 2017) presents in his inimitable style a cogent argument explaining that free will is an illusion." —*Booklist*

Includes bibliographical references and index.

128 Humankind

Becker, Ernest
★ *The* **Denial** *of Death*. Ernest Becker. Free Press 1997. xxii, 314 p.
ISBN 9780684832401
Grades: Adult   **128**
1. Death 2. Mortality 3. Motivation 4. Life 5. Denial (Psychology) 6. Mythology 7. Heroes and heroines 8. History writing — Microhistory
LC 73001860

Pulitzer Prize for General Nonfiction, 1974.

Drawing from religion and the human sciences, particularly psychology after Freud, the author attempts to demonstrate that the fear of death is man's central concern.

Companion vol.: Escape from evil; Includes bibliographical references (p. 286-304) and index; Originally published: New York : Free Press, 1973.

Goodall, Jane
★ *The* **Book** *of Hope: A Survival Guide for Trying Times*. Jane Goodall and Doug Abrams, with Gail Hudson. Celadon Books 2021. 320 p.
ISBN 9781250784094
Grades: Adult   **128**
1. Goodall, Jane, 1934- 2. Hope 3. Women naturalists 4. Human nature 5. Persistence 6. Nature 7. Social advocates 8. Influence (Literary, artistic, etc.) 9. Environmentalism 10. Life stories — Politics — Activists and reformers 11. Spirituality and Religion — General 12. Life stories — Science, technology, and medicine — Scientists and inventors

A famous naturalist and a best-selling author explore how do we hold on to hope in a world that seems so troubled.

"An inspiring, personal, hopeful look at ways in which people can work towards solutions to serious problems to prevent further environmental disaster." —*Library Journal*

Heath, Chip
The **Power** *of Moments: Why Certain Experiences Have Extraordinary Impact*. Chip Heath, and Dan Heath. Simon & Schuster 2017. 288 p.
ISBN 9781501147760
Grades: Adult   **128**
1. Personal conduct 2. Interpersonal relations 3. Life change events 4. Society and culture — Psychology and human behavior
LC BI2017035688

The best-selling authors of Made to Stick explore why certain defining moments can be elevating and transforming, sharing the stories of people who have created and experienced such moments and how readers can facilitate meaningful, powerful moments of positive change themselves.

"Brothers Chip and Dan Heath—coauthors of Decisive and business school professors at, respectively, Stanford and Duke—take on the challenge of teaching readers how to foster memorable moments, for themselves and others, but fail to address the question of authenticity that their prescriptions raise." —*Publishers Weekly*

Paul, Annie Murphy
The **Extended** *Mind: The Power of Thinking Outside the Brain*. Annie Murphy Paul. Houghton Mifflin Harcourt 2021. 256 p.
ISBN 9780544947665
Grades: Adult   **128**
1. Brain 2. Neuroscience 3. Intelligence 4. Creativity 5. Thought and thinking 6. Science Writing — Biology 7. Society and culture — Psychology and human behavior
LC 2020039127

Reveals how we can tap the intelligence that exists beyond our brains—in our bodies, our surroundings, and our relationships.

"Science journalist Paul (Brilliant: The New Science of Smart) pushes back against the idea that brains are 'A cordoned-off space where cognition happens' in this thoroughly reported look at myriad types of thinking." —*Publishers Weekly*

Sagan, Carl
Broca's **Brain**: *Reflections on the Romance of Science*. Carl Sagan. Presidio Press 1993. xiii, 398 p.
ISBN 9780345336897
Grades: 11 12 Adult   **128**

1. Broca, Paul, 1824-1880 2. Physicians 3. Intelligence 4. Brain 5. Cosmology 6. Space sciences 7. Science 8. Research 9. Philosophy 10. Science Writing — General

LC Bl 99789926

Sagan speculates on the primitive elements of the human mind and the ways the human brain today is coping with new discoveries about the cosmos.

"The author is a lucid, logical writer with a gift for explaining science to the layman and infecting the reader with his own boundless enthusiasm and curiosity." —*National Review*

Originally published: New York : Random House, c1979; Includes bibliographical references (p. 369-372) and index.

Setiya, Kieran
Life Is Hard: How Philosophy Can Help Us Find Our Way. Kieran Setiya. Riverhead Books 2022. xii, 222 pages
ISBN 9780593538210
Grades: Adult   128
1. Suffering 2. Hope 3. Personal conduct 4. Philosophy 5. Self-Help — Personal growth — Happiness 6. Society and culture — Philosophy

LC 2022008948

Deeply personal and thought-provoking, this book, drawing on ancient and modern philosophy, as well as fiction, history, memoir, film, comedy, social science and stories from the author's own experience, offers a map for navigating rough terrain, from personal trauma to the injustice and absurdity of the world.

"Libraries that serve those interested in philosophy will want to make this a first purchase." —*Library Journal*

Includes bibliographical references (pages 185-214) and index.

Terkel, Studs
Will the Circle Be Unbroken?: Reflections on Death, Rebirth, and Hunger for a Faith. Studs Terkel. New Press 2001. xxiv, 407 p.
ISBN 9781565846920
Grades: 11 12 Adult   128
1. Death 2. Life after death 3. Rebirth (Psychology) 4. Faith 5. Oral histories 6. Spirituality and Religion — General 7. Family and Relationships — Aging and Death

LC 2001030781

Booklist Editors' Choice, 2001.

Interviews with emergency room doctors, Hiroshima survivors, AIDS co-workers, and death-row parolees express the beliefs, hopes, fears, and expectations of people confronted with death and life's ultimate experience.

"Terkel talks to 60 people about their encounters with death. His subjects range from emergency room doctors and paramedics to public figures such as author Kurt Vonnegut and guitarist Doc Watson. A stirring celebration of life and exploration of death." —*Booklist*

Includes bibliographical references.

Wilson, Edward O.
The Meaning of Human Existence. Edward O. Wilson. Liveright Publishing Corporation, a Division of W.W. Norton & Company 2014. 192 p.
ISBN 9780871401007
Grades: Adult   128
1. Humans 2. Sociobiology 3. Social evolution 4. Human evolution 5. Human ecology 6. Human nature 7. Philosophy 8. Philosophical anthropology 9. Society and culture — Philosophy

LC 2014016707

National Book Award for Nonfiction finalist, 2014.

A 21st-century philosophical argument against mechanistic views of human life outlines expansive and advanced theories on human behavior to consider how humans are supremely different from all other species. By the Pulitzer Prize-winning author of on Human Nature.

"Wilson's suggested solutions to our paradoxical predicaments are firmly rooted in science and finely crafted with tonic common sense, unusual directness, and no small measure of valor." —*Booklist*

Zorn, Justin
Golden: The Power of Silence in a World of Noise. Justin Zorn and Leigh Marz. Harper Wave 2022. 320 p.
ISBN 9780063027602
Grades: Adult   128
1. Silence and silent things 2. Noise 3. Tranquility 4. Mindfulness 5. Meditation 6. Philosophy 7. Distraction (Psychology) 8. Spirituality and Religion — Body, mind, and spirit 9. Society and culture — Psychology and human behavior

LC 2021062983

Looks at the science, psychology, philosophy, and spirituality of silence by giving new context to the noise all around us—physical and metaphorical—to change the way we hear and experience the world.

"This book fits at the nexus of spirituality, behavioral sciences, psychology, and self-help, making it a natural fit for readers looking for help navigating a world that's drowning in constant noise and distraction." —*Booklist*

Includes bibliographical references and index.

129 Origin and destiny of individual souls

Roach, Mary
★ *Spook:* Science Tackles the Afterlife. Mary Roach. W.W. Norton 2005. 311 p. : Illustration
ISBN 9780393059625
Grades: 11 12 Adult   129
1. Life after death 2. Soul 3. Religion and science 4. Near-death experience 5. Astral projection 6. Paranormal phenomena 7. Research 8. Science Writing — General 9. Adult books for young adults

LC 2005014450

New York Times Notable Book, 2005.

Draws on the achievements of scientists, engineers, and mediums to consider the feasibility of life after death, from a reincarnation researcher's experimentation with out-of-body experiences to laboratory investigations into ghosts.

"Roach perfectly balances her skepticism and her boundless curiosity with a sincere desire to know. . . . She is an original who can enliven any subject with wit, keen reporting and a sly intelligence." —*Publishers Weekly*

Includes bibliographical references (p. [299]-311).

130 Parapsychology and occultism

Dell, Christopher
The Occult, Witchcraft & Magic: An Illustrated History. Christopher Dell. Thames & Hudson 2016. 399 pages : Illustration; Color
ISBN 9780500518885
Grades: Adult   130
1. Occultism 2. Witchcraft 3. Magic 4. History writing — Medieval — Europe

LC Bl2016045815

Shares a history of magic, the occult, witchcraft, and ritual, from their earliest appearances to modern times.

"A stunning treasury for anyone interested in the history of magic." —*Booklist*

Includes bibliographical references (pages 390-391) and index.

Dickey, Colin
The Unidentified: Mythical Monsters, Alien Encounters, and Our Obsession with the Unexplained. Colin Dickey. Viking 2020. 307 p.
ISBN 9780525557562
Grades: Adult   130
1. Occultism 2. Paranormal phenomena 3. Curiosities and wonders 4. Belief and doubt 5. Cryptozoology 6. Imaginary creatures 7. Conspiracy theories 8. Science Writing — Weird science 9. Society and culture — Pop culture

LC 2019043380

In a world where rational, scientific explanations are more available than ever, belief in the unprovable and irrational—in fringe—is on the rise. It seems

ESSENTIAL AND RECOMMENDED TITLES
131 Parapsychological and occult methods for achieving well-being, happiness, success

the more our maps of the known world get filled in, the more we crave mysterious locations full of strange creatures. Colin Dickey, co-editor of the Morbid Anatomy Anthology and author of Ghostland, examines the world's most persistent unexplained phenomena, from Atlantis and alien encounters to Flat Earth and the Loch Ness monster, to explore their origins and historical endurance.

"Readers will find this to be a thought-provoking and deliciously unsettling guide into the stranger corners of American culture." —*Publishers Weekly*

Includes bibliographical references.

Smith, Richard MacLean
Unexplained: Real-Life Supernatural Stories for Uncertain Times. Richard MacLean Smith. Sourcebooks 2019. xvii, 349 p.
ISBN 9781492697718
Grades: Adult   130
1. Paranormal phenomena 2. Supernatural 3. Curiosities and wonders 4. Perception 5. Media tie-ins 6. Science Writing — Weird science 7. History writing — Historical mysteries 8. True Crime — Cold Cases and Unsolved Mysteries 9. Adult books for young adults
LC 2019023946

In every corner of this earth there are secrets. They are hidden in the dark edge of the woods, nestled in the cold stars, and staring out from a stranger's eyes. And whether they be demonic possession or an unsolved murder, the unknown has always haunted our dreams. From the hit podcast Unexplained comes a volume perfectly crafted for the curious, the cynical, and the not-easily-frightened. Richard Maclean Smith is the expert in the unknown, and humbly offers up ten tales of real-life events that continue to evade explanation.

Based on a podcast; Includes bibliographical references.

131 Parapsychological and occult methods for achieving well-being, happiness, success

Dale, Cyndi
Llewellyn's Complete Book of Chakras: Your Definitive Source of Energy Center Knowledge for Health, Happiness, and Spiritual Evolution. Cyndi Dale. Llewellyn Publications 2016. xlviii,1006 pages : Illustration
ISBN 9780738739625
Grades: Adult   131
1. Chakras 2. Spirituality and Religion — Body, mind, and spirit
LC 2015026134

A comprehensive guide to chakras and energy healing explores the science, history, practices, and structures of energy systems.

One of the world's foremost experts on chakras and energy healing explores the science, history, practices and structures of subtle energy systems, with chakras as the center point, distilling and synthesizing 12,000 years of cross-cultural knowledge, in an entertaining and highly readable encyclopedia.

Includes bibliographical references and index.

133 Specific topics in parapsychology and occultism

Shermer, Michael
Why People Believe Weird Things: Pseudoscience, Superstition, and Other Confusions of Our Time. Michael Shermer; foreword by Stephen Jay Gould. A.W.H. Freeman/Owl Book 2002. xxvi, 349 p. : Illustration
ISBN 9780805070897
Grades: 11 12 Adult   133
1. Pseudoscience 2. Creativity in science 3. Science 4. Science Writing — General
LC 2002068784

Argues that the search for meaning and spiritual fulfillment often results in the embracing of extraordinary claims and controversial ideas.

"Dedicated to Carl Sagan, with a foreword by Stephen Jay Gould, this book by the publisher of Skeptic magazine and the Director of the Skeptics Lecture Series at California Institute of Technology, has the pedigree to be accepted as a work of scholarly value. Fortunately, it is also readable, interesting, and well indexed and provides an extensive bibliography." —*School Library Journal*

First Owl Books edition—T.P. verso; Includes bibliographical references (p. 315-332) and index.

Sollee, Kristen J.
Witch Hunt: A Traveler's Guide to the Power and Persecution of the Witch. Kristen J. Sollee. Red Wheel/Weiser 2020. 256 p.
ISBN 9781578636990
Grades: Adult   133
1. Witchcraft 2. Trials (Witchcraft) 3. History writing — Women's history 4. Society and culture — Gender — Women

Part history, part feminist memoir, part travelogue, Witch Hunt provides a personal guide to the witch trials in western Europe and America and explores how their legacy continues to affect women today."

"This is clearly written for a general audience, but Sollee's judicious use of scholarly sources adds weight to the text and serves as a guide to readers who want to learn more. A valuable resource for planning a magical itinerary—or exploring the landscape of witchcraft from the couch." —*Kirkus*

133.1 Apparitions

Aykroyd, Peter
A History of Ghosts: The True Story of Seances, Mediums, Ghosts, and Ghostbusters. by Peter Aykroyd, with Angela Narth; introduction by Dan Aykroyd. Rodale : 2009. 256 p.
ISBN 9781605298757
Grades: Adult   133.1
1. Spiritualism 2. Ghosts 3. Paranormal phenomena 4. Supernatural 5. History writing — General 6. Science Writing — Weird science
LC 2009018360

Introduces the reader to notable mediums while telling the story of the development of spiritualism, interweaving the author's personal history—which includes the inspiration for his son's film Ghostbusters—with a larger narrative about the role the paranormal has played in American culture.

"The author's grandfather was a spiritualist: he believed the human personality survives after bodily death, and practiced regular communication with ghosts—much of which he documented in journals. Aykroyd broadens the discussion with historical figures like Sir Arthur Conan Doyle, creator of Sherlock Holmes, who joined the Society of Psychical Research three weeks after his father's death. This is a smart consideration of the paranormal and a curious artifact of the Aykroyd legacy." —*Publishers Weekly*

Includes bibliographical references and index.

Dickey, Colin
Ghostland: An American History in Haunted Places. Colin Dickey. Viking 2016. xiii, 320 p.
ISBN 9781101980194
Grades: Adult   133.1
1. Paranormal phenomena 2. Haunted places 3. Curiosities and wonders 4. Supernatural 5. United States 6. Science writing — Weird Science
LC 2016044006

Takes readers on a road trip through some of the United States' most infamously haunted places—and deep into the dark side of American history.

"His book is a fascinating, measured assessment of phenomena more often exploited for sensationalism." —*Publishers Weekly*

Includes bibliographical references and index.

Guiley, Rosemary
★ *The Encyclopedia of Ghosts and Spirits.* Rosemary Ellen Guiley; foreword by Troy Taylor. Facts on File 2007. xii, 564 p. : Illustration
ISBN 9780816067374
Grades: 11 12 Adult   133.1
1. Ghosts 2. Spirits 3. Spirituality and Religion — Body, mind, and spirit 4. Reference — Encyclopedias

PUBLIC LIBRARY CORE COLLECTION: NONFICTION
Twentieth Edition

LC 2006103302

Covers the realm of ghost folklore and mythology with over six hundred entries on historical sightings, paranormal research, and supernatural hauntings.

Includes bibliographical references and index.

Jones, Marie D.
Celebrity Ghosts and Notorious Hauntings. Marie D. Jones. Visible Ink Press 2019. xi, 388 pages
ISBN 9781578596898
Grades: Adult   133.1
1. Celebrities 2. Ghosts 3. Spirituality and Religion — Body, mind, and spirit

LC 2019016565

"Lightly illustrated with photographs and art, Jones's well-researched guide will be a treasure trove for amateur ghost hunters." —*Publishers Weekly*

Stories of fame, death, and ghostly immortality. —Cover; Includes bibliographical references (pages 369-370) and index.

Norman, Michael
Haunted America. Michael Norman and Beth Scott. Tor 1995. xvii, 556 p.
ISBN 9780812550542
Grades: 11 12 Adult   133.1
1. Haunted houses 2. Ghosts 3. United States 4. Canada 5. Spirituality and Religion — Body, mind, and spirit

LC Bl 99766422

A compendium of seventy American true ghost legends includes battlefield specters at Little Big Horn, ghostly apparitions in President Garfield's home in Ohio, and hauntings in the White House.

"This collection of chilling tales of the supernatural includes at least one story from each state and from the English-speaking Canadian provinces. The stories recount sightings of ghostly apparitions and mysterious happenings, and their history and evolution is documented." —*Library Journal*

Authors' names in reverse order in original ed; Reprint. Originally published: 1994; a Tom Doherty Associates book; Includes bibliographical references (p. [507]-556).

Ramsland, Katherine M.
Ghost: Investigating the Other Side. Katherine Ramsland. Thomas Dunne Books/St. Martin's Press 2001. xiii, 322 p, 16 p. of plates : Illustration
ISBN 9780312261641
Grades: Adult   133.1
1. Ramsland, Katherine M, 1953- 2. Ghosts 3. United States 4. Spirituality and Religion — Body, mind, and spirit

LC 2001041725

Takes readers into the world of real-life ghost hunters, revealing their high- and low-tech methods for rooting out spirits.

The author of Prism of the Night takes readers into the world of real-life ghost hunters, revealing their high- and low-tech methods for rooting out spirits.

"Although prepared to dismiss many so-called paranormal occurrences in favor of natural explanations, {the author nevertheless encounters, experiences, and investigates a variety of inexplicable visual, photographic, and verbal manifestations. Both skeptics and believers will be intrigued by this first-person exploration of ghostly visitations." —*Booklist*

Includes bibliographical references (p. [303]-305) and index.

Whitmer, Jamie Davis
America's Most Haunted Hotels: Checking in with Uninvited Guests. by Jamie Davis Whitmer. Llewellyn Worldwide 2016. 264 p.
ISBN 9780738748009
Grades: Adult   133.1
1. Haunted hotels 2. Ghosts 3. United States 4. Travel Writing — United States 5. Science Writing — Weird science

LC 2016024296

"Though readers must decide just how much to believe in Whitmer's accounts of ghostly contact, everyone can enjoy the more straightforward travelogue aspects of the book, which provide handy contact information for the hotels

and potential itineraries as part of its overview. Perhaps it'll help you plan your next trip." —*Publishers Weekly*

Includes bibliographical references.

133.3 Divinatory arts

Crispin, Jessa
★ *The Creative Tarot: A Modern Guide to an Inspired Life.* Jessa Crispin. Touchstone 2016. xxi, 327 pages : Illustration; Color
ISBN 9781501120237
Grades: Adult   133.3
1. Tarot 2. Spirituality and Religion — Body, mind, and spirit 3. Self-Help — Personal growth — Creativity

LC 2015038927

A reference for artists who would use tarot for guidance adapts readings to promote the creative process and help overcome blocks, sharing engaging anecdotes about how famous artists pursued inspiration.

A stylish, accessible reference for artists who would use tarot for guidance adapts readings to promote the creative process and help overcome blocks, sharing engaging anecdotes about how famous artists pursued inspiration.

"Even readers with no previous interest in the tarot will be intrigued and delighted by Crispin's ardently researched, spirited, creative, and inspiring elucidation." —*Booklist*

133.4 Demonology and witchcraft

Abrev, Ileana
The Little Big Book of White Spells. Ileana Abrev. Llewellyn Publications 2017. IX, 396 pages
ISBN 9780738751696
Grades: Adult   133.4
1. Charms 2. Incantations 3. Magic 4. Occultism 5. Spirituality and Religion — Body, mind, and spirit

LC Bl2017003810

Offers over two hundred spells that will create transformation in the lives of the spell casters.

"For readers wishing to experiment with white magic, this book of mini recipes is a great starting point." —*Publishers Weekly*

Feldmann, Erica
Hausmagick: Transform Your Home with Witchcraft. Erica Feldmann. HarperOne 2019. 254 pages : Illustration; Color
ISBN 9780062906151
Grades: Adult   133.4
1. Houses 2. Design and construction 3. Magic 4. Witchcraft 5. Occultism 6. Spirituality and Religion — Body, mind, and spirit 7. House and Home — Interior Decorating and Furnishings

LC 2018036758

An illustrated guide from the HausWitch store and brand founder explains how to create a beautiful, healing living space using earth magic, meditation, herbalism, self-awareness, tarot, astrology, feminist spirituality, and interior decoration.

"Blending interior design with tools for spiritual health, the book explores ways that the physical environment can influence and access the magical realm." —*Publishers Weekly*

Includes bibliographical references (pages 240-241) and index.

Gibson, Marion
Witchcraft: A History in Thirteen Trials. Marion Gibson. Simon & Schuster 2024. 320 p.
ISBN 9781668002421
Grades: Adult   133.4
1. Trials (Witchcraft) 2. Social history 3. Witch hunting 4. Hysteria (Social psychology) 5. Witchcraft 6. Witches 7. Spirituality 8. Colonialism 9. Misogyny

ESSENTIAL AND RECOMMENDED TITLES
133.4 Demonology and witchcraft

10. History writing — General 11. Society and culture — Psychology and human behavior

A fascinating, vivid global history of witch trials across Europe, Africa, and the Americas, told through thirteen distinct trials that illuminate the pattern of demonization and conspiratorial thinking that has profoundly shaped human history.

"A thought-provoking, sweeping work of social history." —*Kirkus*

Originally published in the UK by Simon & Schuster, London, in 2023.

Gosden, Chris
Magic: A History : From Alchemy to Witchcraft, from the Ice Age to the Present. Chris Gosden. Farrar, Straus and Giroux 2020. xix, 482 p. : Illustration
ISBN 9780374200121
Grades: Adult   **133.4**
1. Occultism 2. Witchcraft 3. Mythology 4. Literary criticism 5. Religions 6. Illustrated books 7. Spirituality and Religion — General 8. Society and culture — Psychology and human behavior 9. History writing — General
LC 2020013393

An Oxford professor of archaeology explores the history of magic and the propaganda campaigns behind the practice's current notoriety while describing the magic-themed traditions of historical cultures and magic's less-recognized role in modern civilization.

"Magic is an authoritative history of humanity's engagement with the supernatural." —*Booklist*

Includes bibliographical references and index; Originally published in 2020 by Viking, Great Britain, as The History of Magic: From Alchemy to Witchcraft, from the Ice Age to the present.

Grimassi, Raven
What We Knew in the Night: Reawakening the Heart of Witchcraft. Raven Grimassi. Weiser Books, an imprint of Red Wheel/Weiser, LLC 2019. xvi, 252 pages
ISBN 9781578636518
Grades: Adult   **133.4**
1. Witchcraft 2. Spirituality and Religion — Body, mind, and spirit 3. Spirituality and Religion — General
LC 2019021665

A cohesive and complete system of witchcraft based on traditional sources, assembling and integrating key components from the past and present. Also offers practical instructions and a clear five-step process of empowerment for anyone who wants to walk the path of witchcraft.

Includes bibliographical references.

Grossman, Pam
Waking the Witch: Reflections on Women, Magic, and Power. Pam Grossman. Gallery Books 2019. 288 p.
ISBN 9781982100704
Grades: Adult   **133.4**
1. Grossman, Pam 2. Witches 3. Witchcraft 4. Archetype (Psychology) 5. Occultism 6. Feminism 7. Women 8. Media tie-ins 9. Society and culture — Gender — Women 10. Society and culture — Pop culture
LC 2018054467

When you think of a witch, what do you picture? Pointy black hat, maybe a broomstick. But witches in various guises have been with us for millennia. In Waking the Witch, Pam Grossman explores the cultural and historical impact of the world's most magical icon. In this fascinating read that is part cultural analysis, part memoir, Pam opens up about her own journey on the path to witchcraft, and how her personal embrace of the witch helped her find strength, self-empowerment, and a deeper purpose.

Based on a podcast.

Guiley, Rosemary
The Encyclopedia of Demons and Demonology. Rosemary Ellen Guiley; foreword by John Zaffis. Facts on File 2009. xv, 302 p. : Illustration
ISBN 9780816073146
Grades: 11 12 Adult   **133.4**
1. Demonic possession 2. Demons 3. Paranormal phenomena 4. Encyclopedias 5. Curiosities, marvels, and wonders — Mythical places and beings
LC 2008052488

Brief entries and illustrations introduce topics including individually named demons from a variety of cultures, historical figures, films, and cases of possession.

Includes bibliographical references and index.

The Encyclopedia of Witches, Witchcraft and Wicca. Rosemary Ellen Guiley. Facts on File 2008. xii, 436 p. : Illustration
ISBN 9780816071036
Grades: 11 12 Adult   **133.4**
1. Witchcraft 2. Witches 3. Spirituality and Religion — Body, mind, and spirit 4. Reference — Encyclopedias
LC BI2008030438

More than 480 entries identify famous witches, explains terms dealing with witchcraft, and describes related churches and organizations.

Presents encyclopedic information on witches, witchcraft, and wicca, including the history of witchcraft and notable witches and wizards throughout history.

"Spanning centuries and continents, the book defines 480 of witchcraft's and wizardry's major historical events, figures, tools, sites, symbols, and abstract terms. The highly engaging, alphabetically organized entries run several paragraphs in length and deftly clarify a term's etymology as well as its spiritual, historical, or spell-making significance." —*Library Journal*

Rev. ed. : The encyclopedia of witches and witchcraft. 1999; Includes bibliographical references (p. 407-413) and index.

Hutton, Ronald
The Triumph of the Moon: A History of Modern Pagan Witchcraft. Ronald Hutton. Oxford University Press 1999. xv, 486 p.
ISBN 9780198207443
Grades: Adult   **133.4**
1. Witchcraft 2. Neopaganism 3. Religions 4. Great Britain 5. 19th century 6. 20th century 7. Spirituality and Religion — General
LC 99031586

Presents a history of witchcraft as a religion, offering profiles of key figures and chronicling actual wiccan practices.

"This history of paganism in 19th- and 20th-century Britain centers on Wicca, the system of witchcraft Gerald B. Gardner introduced to a startled public in the 1950s. Hutton's exceptional work is by far the most scholarly, comprehensive and judicious analysis of the subject yet published." —*Publishers Weekly*

Includes bibliographical references (p. 417-470) and index.

Jones, Marie D.
Demons, the Devil, and Fallen Angels. Marie D. Jones and Larry Flaxman. Visible Ink 2017. xv, 368 p.
ISBN 9781578596133
Grades: Adult   **133.4**
1. Occultism 2. Spirituality and Religion — General
LC 2017022073

"An image-packed compendium on embodiments of evil, this overview incorporates significant historical events and modern phenomena. By salting pages with a portrait of mystic Antoinette Bourignon, photos of Santeria practitioners, and the title page of Malleus Maleficarum, the authors add weight to their entries on the impact of witch hunts in previous eras as well as current strands of the occult, including haunted dolls and the alleged satanic influence on rock and roll." —*Booklist*

Karlsen, Carol F.
★ *The Devil in the Shape of a Woman: Witchcraft in Colonial New England.* Carol F. Karlsen. Norton 1987. xvii, 360 p.
ISBN 9780393024784
Grades: Adult   **133.4**
1. Witchcraft 2. New England 3. History writing — Colonial America — United States
LC 87016615

PUBLIC LIBRARY CORE COLLECTION: NONFICTION
Twentieth Edition

Analyzes the belief in witchcraft in colonial times, looks at the characteristics of those charged and their accusers, and discusses Puritan attitudes toward women.

Includes index; Bibliography: P. 265-342.

Levack, Brian P.
The Devil Within: Possession & Exorcism in the Christian West. Brian Levack. Yale University Press 2013. xii, 346 pages : Illustration
ISBN 9780300114720
Grades: Adult   133.4
1. Exorcism 2. Spirituality and Religion — Christianity 3. Spirituality and Religion — Christianity — History 4. Spirituality and Religion — General
LC 2012042933

A fascinating, wide-ranging survey examines the history of possession and exorcism through the ages.

"In this riveting, readable study, Levack...offers readers a comprehensive view of reports of demon possession and efforts to rid victims of it." —*Publishers Weekly*

Includes bibliographical references (pages 314-335) and index.

Rajchel, Diana
Urban Magick: A Guide for the City Witch. Diana Rajchel. Llewellyn Publications 2020. x, 296 pages
ISBN 9780738752747
Grades: Adult   133.4
1. Witchcraft 2. Magic 3. City life 4. Spirituality 5. Cities and towns 6. City dwellers 7. Neopaganism 8. Rites and ceremonies 9. Occultism 10. Spirituality and Religion — General 11. Society and culture — Urban and regional studies
LC 2019055224

Engage with the urban landscape around you and harness its boundless possibilities for a thriving magickal practice. Urban Magick shows you how to connect with your city's diverse spiritual ecosystem and channel the powerful energy running through it.

"Presents an informative, socially conscious guide for magic practitioners." —*Publishers Weekly*

Includes bibliographical references and index.

Roth, Harold
The Witching Herbs: 13 Essential Plants and Herbs for Your Magical Garden. Harold Roth. Weiser Books 2017. xviii, 263 p. : Illustration
ISBN 9781578635993
Grades: Adult   133.4
1. Witchcraft 2. Herbs 3. Spirituality and Religion — Body, mind, and spirit
LC 2018137761

"Connecting with plant spirits by growing magical plants yourself is the ultimate in herbal magic, according to this debut. Roth leans heavily on a modernized version of the ancient Doctrine of Signatures that teaches practitioners to look to a plant's morphology to understand its use, adding clues from growth patterns, traditional medicine, and chemistry as well as from traditional lore and personal gnosis." —*Publishers Weekly*

Includes bibliographical references.

133.42 Demonology

Gallagher, Richard E.
Demonic Foes: My Twenty-Five Years as a Psychiatrist Investigating Possessions, Diabolic Attacks, and the Paranormal. Richard, M.D. Gallagher. HarperOne 2020. 255 p.
ISBN 9780062876478
Grades: Adult   133.42
1. Demonic possession 2. Exorcism 3. Spirituality and Religion — General 4. Society and culture — Psychology and human behavior
LC Oc2020002129

A board-certified psychiatrist and active member of the International Association of Exorcists describes his path from cynic to believer after spending the last 25 years studying and witnessing demonic activity as he recalls his most famous cases.

"Believers will love it, unbelievers will relish an argument with its premises, and even the most skeptical will marvel at the mysteries of human behavior it investigates. An unsettling, absorbing account of the phenomenon of demonic possession by a medical expert." —*Kirkus*

133.5 Astrology

Brown, Maressa
Raising Baby by the Stars: A New Parent's Guide to Astrology. Maressa Brown. Artisan 2023. 351 pages : Color; Illustration
ISBN 9781648290954
Grades: Adult   133.5
1. Astrology 2. Babies 3. Parenting 4. Zodiac 5. Family and Relationships — Parenting 6. Spirituality and Religion — General
LC 2022033376

This book is meant as introduction to a time-honored, powerful tool: your baby's astrological blueprint, known as their natal, or birth, chart."

"This thoroughness paired with the gentle advice makes for an ideal reference for the new age set. Open-minded parents will find this a fun resource." —*Publishers Weekly*

Includes index.

Crawford, Saffi
The Power of Birthdays, Stars & Numbers: The Complete Personology Reference Guide. Saffi Crawford and Geraldine Sullivan. Ballantine 1998. 831 p. : Illustration
ISBN 9780345418197
Grades: Adult   133.5
1. Birthdays 2. Astrology 3. Numerology 4. Personality 5. Spirituality and Religion — Body, mind, and spirit
LC 98013941

An introduction to astrology includes a zodiac reading for each day of the year.

"This browser's dream begins with an introduction that briefly explains astrology, the affect of the planets on personality, decantes, fixed stars, and numerology. Then, each day of the calendar is described in terms of the zodiac, fixed star-signs, and numerology." —*School Library Journal*

Goldschneider, Gary
★ *The Secret Language of Birthdays: Personology Profiles for Each Day of the Year.* Gary Goldschneider; Aron Goldschneider, editor. Penguin Studio 2013. 832 pages : Illustration
ISBN 9780525426882
Grades: Adult   133.5
1. Birthdays 2. Astrology 3. Personality 4. Spirituality and Religion — Body, mind, and spirit
LC 2013372244

Previously published: 2004; a Joost Elffers Production; Includes index.

Goodman, Linda
Linda Goodman's Star Signs: The Secret Codes of the Universe: Forgotten Rainbows and Forgotten Melodies of Ancient Wisdom. Griffin 1998. xli, 477 p. : Illustration
ISBN 9780312192037
Grades: Adult   133.5
1. Astrology 2. Self-help psychology 3. Self-Help — Personal growth
LC 87-28375

Discusses a wide variety of matters relating to spiritual and physical well-being, including the Karmic Wheel, reincarnation, holistic health, spiritual advisors, channelers, crystals, and the third eye.

"Goodman explains numerology, lexigrams (secret codes of words, names, and titles), the power of sound, and the power of color. Along with explanations of karma and other modes of spiritual growth, she interweaves her own experi-

ESSENTIAL AND RECOMMENDED TITLES
133.8 Psychic phenomena

ences with avatars and gurus, as well as common folk who are on their own spiritual path." —*Booklist*

Linda *Goodman's Sun Signs*. Taplinger Pub. Co. 1968. xxiii, 549 p.
ISBN 9780800849009
Grades: Adult   133.5
1. Astrology 2. Self-help psychology 3. Self-Help — Personal growth
LC 68031737

"This book is part astrology, part psychology, and always entertaining." —*Library Journal*

Miller, Susan
Planets and Possibilities: Explore the Worlds Beyond Your Sun Sign. Susan Miller. Warner Books 2001. x, 418 p. : Illustration
ISBN 9780446524346
Grades: 11 12 Adult   133.5
1. Astrology 2. Spirituality and Religion — Body, mind, and spirit
LC 00109235

Provides advice based on how the planets, the sun, and the moon work together to influence lives, with a separate chapter exploring each sun sign.

The creator of the "Astrology Zone" Web site shares her advice and wisdom with readers hungry to find solace and satisfaction in the stars as she explains how the planets, the sun, and the moon work together to influence one's life.

"The author provides character analysis of each sign. The cosmic gifts, relationship trends, financial tendencies, and career tendencies associated with each sign are all described in detail. The mythology of each sign is included as well, nicely rounding out the book." —*Library Journal*

Includes bibliographical references (p. 416-418).

Snodgrass, Mary Ellen
Signs of the Zodiac: A Reference Guide to Historical, Mythological, and Cultural Associations. Mary Ellen Snodgrass; illustrated by Raymond Miller Barrett, Jr. Greenwood Press 1997. xiv, 243 p. : Illustration
ISBN 9780313302763
Grades: 11 12 Adult   133.5
1. Astrology 2. Zodiac 3. Society and culture — Pop culture
LC 97005598

A historical look at astrology examines each zodiac sign, discussing its mythological background and traits associated with those born under it.

"After brief descriptions of zodiacal variants from other parts of the world, plus chapters on the historical foundations of astrology and its pervasiveness in the arts and sciences, Snodgrass treats each sign to a full workover: major stars in each, mythological background and symbology, commonly accepted character traits of those born under its influence, and thumbnail biographies of select prominent people who exemplify those traits." —*School Library Journal*

Includes bibliographical references (p. [225]-232) and index.

133.8 Psychic phenomena

Clegg, Brian
Extra Sensory: The Science and Pseudoscience of Telepathy and Other Powers of the Mind. Brian Clegg. St. Martin's Press 2013. 320 p.
ISBN 9781250019066
Grades: Adult   133.8
1. Psychic ability 2. Extrasensory perception 3. Mind and body 4. Paranormal phenomena 5. Science and paranormal phenomena 6. Science Writing — Weird science
LC 2013004038

A pop-science tour of legitimate modern studies in the areas of ESP, telekinesis and other seemingly supernatural abilities considers whether they are actual talents or manifestations of fantasy, documenting the question-raising research of serious scientists while assessing the possible physical mechanisms for ESP.

Jacobsen, Annie
Phenomena: The Secret History of the U.S. Government's Investigations into Extrasensory Perception and Psychokinesis. Annie Jacobsen. Little, Brown & Company 2017. 544 pages
ISBN 9780316349369
Grades: Adult   133.8
1. Paranormal phenomena 2. Military research 3. Secrecy in government 4. Psychics 5. Extrasensory perception 6. Precognition 7. Psychokinesis 8. Telepathy 9. National security 10. Conspiracy theories 11. Politics and government 12. Armed Forces 13. United States 14. History writing — Conspiracy theories 15. History writing — United States
LC Bl2017003679

The author presents a history of the military's controversial, decades-long investigation into boundary-pushing mental phenomena, sharing inside information about how the program has involved strategic experiments in the name of national security.

Knight, Sam
The *Premonitions* Bureau: A True Account of Death Foretold. Sam Knight. Penguin Books 2022. 288 p.
ISBN 9781984879592
Grades: Adult   133.8
1. Psychiatrists 2. Landslides 3. Precognition 4. Warnings 5. Dreams 6. Visions 7. Psychic ability 8. Women psychics 9. Supernatural 10. Newspapers 11. Disasters 12. Skepticism 13. Humiliation 14. Purpose in life 15. British history 16. 20th century 17. Science Writing — Weird science 18. History writing — Natural disasters and tragedies 19. History writing — Europe — United Kingdom 20. Life stories — Science, technology, and medicine — Scientists and inventors

On the morning of October 21, 1966, Kathleen Middleton, a music teacher in suburban London, awoke choking and gasping, convinced disaster was about to strike. An hour later, a mountain of rubble containing waste from a coal mine collapsed above the village of Aberfan, swamping buildings and killing 144 people, many of them children. Among the doctors and emergency workers who arrived on the scene was John Barker, a psychiatrist from Shelton Hospital, in Shrewsbury. At Aberfan, Barker became convinced there had been supernatural warning signs of the disaster, and decided to establish a "premonitions bureau," in conjunction with the Evening Standard newspaper, to collect dreams and forebodings from the public, in the hope of preventing future calamities. In Sam Knight's crystalline telling, this astonishing true story comes to encompass the secrets of the world. Our lives are full of collisions and coincidence: the question is how we perceive these implausible events and therefore make meaning in our lives.

"A British psychiatrist's inquiries into 'the problem of precognition' are recounted in New Yorker contributor Knight's mesmerizing debut....The result is a captivating study of the uncanny." —*Publishers Weekly*

Shumsky, Susan G.
Earth Energy Meditations: Awaken Your Root Chakra — the Foundation of Well-being. Susan Shumsky, DD.. Weiser Books 2021. xviii, 202 pages : Illustration
ISBN 9781578637034
Grades: Adult   133.8
1. Psychic ability 2. Chakras 3. Meditation 4. Spirituality and Religion — Body, mind, and spirit — Meditation and mindfulness
LC 2020048572

The energy center known in Sanskrit as "muladhara" is called the "root chakra." It is located in a layer of our subtle body called "pranamaya kosha" at the base of our spine in the tailbone area. The root chakra is our connection to the earth and to humanity at large. When this chakra is closed, muddied, and unhealthy, we experience many negative emotions, and we manifest unhealthy habits, addictions, and behaviors. This book provides an answer to these maladies. It helps us reconnect with the earth and primal energies with powerful, easy-to-use methods of guided meditation, affirmation, visualization, breathing, and physical movements.

"Meditators of all experience and skill level, metaphysical thinkers and seekers, and those who take issue with the distractions of media hype will find this collection of meditations to be both practical and inspiring." —*Library Journal*
Includes bibliographical references (pages 193-194).

133.9 Spiritualism

Blum, Deborah
Ghost Hunters: William James and the Search for Scientific Proof of Life After Death. Deborah Blum. Penguin Press 2006. 370 p.
ISBN 9781594200908
Grades: 11 12 Adult   133.9
1. James, William, 1842-1910 2. Paranormal phenomena 3. Spiritualism 4. Ghosts 5. 19th century 6. Adult books for young adults 7. Science Writing — Weird science
LC 2006044948
Traces how the respected psychologist brother of Henry James set out to gather scientific data proving the existence of ghosts at the end of the nineteenth century, forming the American Society for Psychical Research.
"In this book, the author examines the Victorian era conflict between science and religion by reviewing the history of the British Society for Psychical Research and its U.S. counterpart, the American Society for Psychical Research, both of which aimed to find scientific proof of the existence of the supernatural. . . . Her clearly written presentation of the history, frauds, and personalities involved in this unique slice of Victorian life is recommended for all history of science collections." —*Library Journal*
Includes bibliographical references and index.

Moody, Raymond A.
Life After Life: The Investigation of a Phenomenon-Survival of Bodily Death. Raymond A. Moody, Jr; with a new preface by Melvin Morse and a foreword by Elizabeth Kubler-Ross. HarperSanFrancisco 2001. xxviii, 175 p.
ISBN 9780062517395
Grades: Adult   133.9
1. Near-death experience 2. Life after death 3. Spirituality and Religion — Body, mind, and spirit 4. Self-Help — Personal growth
LC 00046156
Reports on and draws careful conclusions from the out-of-the-body experiences of people who, revived from clinical death or from near-death, regained consciousness, in a twenty-fifth anniversary edition of the pioneering study of the afterlife.
Originally published in 1975 by MBB.Inc. and later published by Bantam Books.

Rasmussen, Christina
Where Did You Go?: A Life-Changing Journey to Connect with Those We've Lost. Christina Rasmussen. HarperOne 2018. 229 pages
ISBN 9780062689627
Grades: Adult   133.9
1. Spiritualism 2. Life after death 3. Spirituality and Religion — Body, mind, and spirit 4. Family and Relationships — Aging and Death 5. Self-Help — Mental health — Grief and loss
LC 2018035459
An internationally recognized grief educator reveals how to connect with loved ones who have passed on and provides practical exercises and a step-by-step guide to travel to the other side to find answers and discover peace.
Includes bibliographical references.

142 Critical philosophy

Barrett, William
Irrational Man: A Study in Existential Philosophy. William Barrett. Anchor Books, Doubleday 1990. 305 p.
ISBN 9780385031387

Grades: Adult   142
1. Existentialism 2. Society and culture — Philosophy
LC 90033388
Examines the sources, major proponents, and widespread influence of twentieth-century existentialism.
Includes index; Originally published: New York : Doubleday, 1958.

146 Naturalism and related systems and doctrines

Dennett, D. C.
Darwin's Dangerous Idea: Evolution and the Meanings of Life. Daniel C. Dennett. Simon & Schuster 1996. 586 p. : Illustration
ISBN 9780684824710
Grades: Adult   146
1. Darwin, Charles, 1809-1882 2. Natural selection 3. Evolution 4. Human evolution 5. Philosophy 6. Science Writing — Biology
LC BL 99774686
Pulitzer Prize for General Nonfiction finalist; National Book Award for Nonfiction finalist, 1995.
Offers a wider perspective on Darwin's scientific theory of natural selection, explaining how it extends beyond biology, analyzing current controversies over the origins of life and inherent biases, and challenging popular philosophies.
"Current controversies associated with the origin of life, sociobiology, punctuated equilibrium, the evolution of culture and language, and evolutionary ethics are investigated rigorously within the context of Darwinian science and philosophy. Dennett challenges the ideas of several imminent scientists, including Roger Penrose and Stephen Jay Gould, who, Dennett asserts, tend to limit the power or implications of Darwin's dangerous ideas." —*Library Journal*
Reprint. Originally published: C1995; a Touchstone book; Includes bibliographical references (p. [525]-550) and index.

149 Other philosophical systems and doctrines

Rand, Ayn
★ *The Virtue of Selfishness: A New Concept of Egoism.* Ayn Rand; with additional articles by Nathaniel Branden. Signet 2014. xii, 173 pages
ISBN 9780451163936
Grades: Adult   149
1. Objectivism (Philosophy) 2. Selfishness 3. Egotism 4. Spirituality and Religion — General
LC Bl2017014665
Presents a collection of essays that sets forth the moral principles of the author's philosophy, Objectivism.
Includes index.

150 Psychology

Bloom, Paul
Psych: The Story of the Human Mind. Paul Bloom. Ecco 2023. 368 p.
ISBN 9780063096356
Grades: Adult   150
1. Freud, Sigmund, 1856-1939 2. Descartes, Rene, 1596-1650 3. Skinner, B. F, 1904-1990 4. Piaget, Jean, 1896-1980 5. Psychology 6. Cognitive science 7. Consciousness 8. Perception 9. Brain 10. Emotions 11. Intelligence 12. Society and culture — Psychology and human behavior
LC 2022035484
Filled with humor, insight and memorable stories, this riveting new book about the science of the mind—and the story of us, based on one of Yale's most popular courses of all time, reveals what psychology can tell us about the most pressing moral and political issues of our time.
"Illuminating reading for anyone interested in the human brain." —*Kirkus*
Includes bibliographical references and index.

ESSENTIAL AND RECOMMENDED TITLES
150.19 Systems, schools, viewpoints

Glasser, William
Choice Theory: A New Psychology of Personal Freedom. William Glasser. HarperCollinsPublishers 1998. xii, 340 p. : Illustration
ISBN 9780060191092
Grades: Adult **150**
1. Psychology 2. Science writing — Medicine and health — Psychology
LC 97036025

A world-renowned psychiatrist, the author of Reality Therapy, calls for a complete overhaul of traditional psychology based on the goal of strengthening relationships by appealing to each individual's basic needs for love, power, freedom, and pleasure.

Calls for a complete overhaul of traditional psychology based on the goal of strengthening relationships by appealing to each individual's basic needs for love, power, freedom, and pleasure.

"Choice theory helps its users avoid confrontation and ask pertinent questions. It sees conscious or unconscious desire for external control as the main problem in the four major personal relationships: Husband-wife, parent-child, teacher-student, and manager-worker. Combining choice theory and reality therapy in his practice, Glasser has been able to shorten the durations of his treatment programs substantially. As he presents them here, his theories and approaches can be applied in education and business as well as for self-help." —*Booklist*

150.19 Systems, schools, viewpoints

Frankl, Viktor E.
Yes to Life: In Spite of Everything. Viktor E. Frankl; introduction by Daniel Goleman; afterword by Franz Vesely; translated from the German by Joelle Young. Beacon Press 2020. 127 p.
ISBN 9780807005552
Grades: Adult **150.19**
1. Purpose in life 2. Resilience 3. Science writing — Medicine and health — Psychology 4. Spirituality and Religion — Judaism 5. History writing — Wars and conflicts — Holocaust — World War II
LC 2019059317

Eleven months after his liberation from Auschwitz, Viktor E. Frankl held a series of public lectures in Vienna, published here for the first time. The psychologist, who was to become world famous, explained his central thoughts on meaning, resilience and the importance of embracing life even in the face of great adversity.

Includes bibliographical references (pages 125-127).

Freud, Sigmund
★ *The Basic Writings of Sigmund Freud.* Translated and edited by A.A. Brill. Modern Library 1995. xii, 973 p.
ISBN 9780679601661
Grades: Adult **150.19**
1. Psychoanalysis 2. Science writing — Medicine and health — Psychology
LC 95013411

Presents a selection of the important writings of the nineteenth-century psychiatrist, including "Psychopathology of Everyday Life," "The Interpretation of Dreams," and "Totem and Taboo."

Includes index; Originally published: New York : Modern Library, c1938.

Civilization and Its Discontents. Sigmund Freud; introduction by Christopher Hitchens; translated and edited by James Strachey; biographical afterword by Peter Gay. W.W. Norton & Company 2010. 186 p.
ISBN 9780393304510
Grades: Adult **150.19**
1. Psychoanalysis 2. Civilization 3. Behavior 4. Human behavior 5. Heredity and environment (Psychology) 6. Instinct 7. Oppression (Psychology) 8. Science Writing — Medicine and health — Mental health
LC 2004027112

Presents the eminent Austrian psychoanalyst's views on the irreconcilable antagonism between instinctual drives and the repressive attitudes of civilization.

Includes bibliographical references and index.

Gay, Peter
A Godless Jew: Freud, Atheism, and the Making of Psychoanalysis. Peter Gay. Yale University Press 1987. xvii, 182 p.
ISBN 9780300040081
Grades: Adult **150.19**
1. Freud, Sigmund, 1856-1939 2. Psychoanalysis and religion 3. Atheism 4. Life stories — Science, technology, and medicine
LC 87008267

Argues that Freud was an atheist and that atheism was an important prerequisite for his development of psychoanalysis.

Includes index; Bibliography: P. 157-177.

Jung, C. G.
★ *The Basic Writings of C.G. Jung.* Edited, with an introduction by Violet Staub de Laszlo. Modern Library 1993. xxxiii, 691 p.
ISBN 9780679600718
Grades: 11 12 Adult **150.19**
1. Psychoanalysis 2. Spirituality and Religion — Body, mind, and spirit 3. Science writing — Medicine and health — Psychology
LC 93017801

Presents selected writings for Jung's major studies on the nature and functioning of the human psyche.

Includes bibliographical references (p. 675-681) and index; Originally published: New York : Random House, 1959.

Memories, Dreams, Reflections. C.G. Jung; recorded and edited by Aniela Jaffe; translated from the German by Richard and Clara Winston. Vintage Books 1989. xiii, 430 p.
ISBN 9780679723950
Grades: Adult **150.19**
1. Jung, C. G. (Carl Gustav), 1875-1961 2. Psychoanalysts 3. Life stories — Science, technology, and medicine 4. Science writing — Medicine and health — Psychology
LC 88037040

The Swiss psychologists shares the visions, inner experiences, and dreams that have shaped his work and thought.

Translation of: Erinnerungen, Traume, Gedanken; Includes index; Bibliography: P. 403-410.

May, Rollo
The Discovery of Being: Writings in Existential Psychology. Rollo May. Norton 1983. 192 p.
ISBN 9780393017908
Grades: Adult **150.19**
1. Psychotherapy 2. Self-discovery 3. Philosophy, Modern 4. Self-Help — Mental health
LC 83004282

"The author provides the reader with principles of his existential psychotherapy; delineates his view of the cultural-historical context that gave rise to both psychoanalysis and existentialism; and sets forth what he considers to be the contributions to therapy of an existential approach." —*Choice*

Includes bibliographical references and index.

150.92 Psychologists

Spofford, Tim
What the Children Told Us: The Untold Story of the Famous. Tim Spofford. Sourcebooks 2022. 336 p.
ISBN 9781728248073
Grades: Adult **150.92**
1. Clark, Mamie Phipps 2. Clark, Kenneth Bancroft, 1914-2005 3. Psychologists 4. African American psychologists 5. Social advocates 6. African American civil rights 7. Child psychology 8. Segregation 9. Civil rights 10. Collective biographies 11. Society and culture — Psychology and human behavior 12. Life

stories — Science, technology, and medicine — Healthcare professionals 13. Science Writing — Medicine and health — Doctors and nurses

LC 2021055924

For readers of the Immortal Life of Henrietta Lacks and Hidden Figures, What the Children Told Us tells the story of the towering intellectual and emotional partnership between the two Black psychologists who pioneered the groundbreaking "doll test," paving the way for the landmark Brown v. Board of Education case and decades of impactful civil rights activism.

"This detailed and sympathetic biography shines a well-deserved spotlight on two racial justice pioneers." —*Publishers Weekly*

Includes bibliographical references and index.

152.1 Sensory perception

Ackerman, Diane

A Natural History of the Senses. Diane Ackerman. Random House 1990. xix, 331p.

ISBN 9780679735663

Grades: 11 12 Adult   152.1

1. Senses and sensation 2. Social life and customs 3. Human behavior 4. Smell 5. Taste 6. Vision 7. Touch 8. Hearing 9. Science Writing — Biology

LC 89043416

ALA Notable Book, 1991.

A perceptive celebration of the sensory world offers a poetic tour of the human senses and explains how human beings absorb and savor the wonders of the world around.

"Ackerman celebrates the senses by examining their biological bases and the various and bizarre ways we have come to indulge them. Her catalog of the senses is itself a sensuous journey, with prose rich in imagery and rhythm. Ackerman's book is a provocative and entertaining treat whose details will bestir the reader's imagination." —*Library Journal*

Includes bibliographical references (p. [311]-315) and index.

Dooner, Caroline

Tired as F*ck: Burnout at the Hands of Diet, Self-Help, and Hustle Culture. Caroline Dooner. Harper Wave 2022. 304 p.

ISBN 9780063052970

Grades: Adult   152.1

1. Diet 2. Women 3. Self-help psychology 4. Mental health 5. Burn out (Psychology) 6. Self-care 7. Health 8. Self-Help — Mental health

"By boldly sharing vulnerabilities, Dooner's account should go a long way in helping others accept their own. It's a brave and bracing manifesto that will be welcomed by any reader living in the aftermath of burnout—or trying to avoid it." —*Publishers Weekly*

Keyes, Corey L. M.

★ *Languishing: How to Feel Alive Again in a World That Wears Us Down.* Corey Keyes. Crown 2024. xxiii, 271 pages

ISBN 9780593444627

Grades: Adult   152.1

1. Mental health 2. Fatigue 3. Motivation 4. Success (Concept) 5. Happiness 6. Self-Help — Mental health 7. Science Writing — Medicine and health — Psychology

LC 2023048676

Building on decades of research, a sociologist explores the concept of languishing, which wears away our sense of purpose, its impact on our well-being and its societal roots, offering a comprehensive guide to understanding and addressing this pervasive condition.

"Supported by research, this book is a valuable resource for those who may be languishing or who want to find more meaning in their life. Action plans are included." —*Library Journal*

Includes bibliographical references (pages 231-255) and index.

Rubin, Gretchen Craft

★ *Life in Five Senses: How Exploring the Senses Got Me Out of My Head and into the World.* Gretchen Rubin. Crown 2023. xiii, 250 pages : Illustration

ISBN 9780593442746

Grades: Adult   152.1

1. Rubin, Gretchen Craft 2. Women authors 3. Senses and sensation 4. Perception 5. Awareness 6. Mindfulness 7. Happiness 8. Self-fulfillment 9. Effect of environment on humans 10. Psychology 11. Society and culture — Psychology and human behavior 12. Life stories — Personal growth

LC 2022052223

For more than a decade, Gretchen Rubin had been studying happiness and human nature. Then, one day, a visit to her eye doctor made her realize that she'd been overlooking a key element of happiness: her five senses. She'd spent so much time stuck in her head that she'd allowed the vital sensations of life to slip away, unnoticed. In this journey of self-experimentation, Rubin explores the mysteries and joys of the five senses as a path to a happier, more mindful life. Drawing on cutting-edge science, philosophy, literature, and her own efforts to practice what she learns, she investigates the profound power of tuning in to the physical world.

"This inspiring book will prompt readers to open themselves to the world around them." —*Booklist*

Includes bibliographical references (pages 235-250).

152.109 Sensory perception — History, geographic treatment, biography

Purnell, Carolyn

The Sensational Past: How the Enlightenment Changed the Way We Use Our Senses. Carolyn Purnell. W. W. Norton & Company 2017. 304 pages

ISBN 9780393249378

Grades: Adult   152.109

1. Senses and sensation 2. Enlightenment (European intellectual movement) 3. Social influence 4. Philosophy, Modern 5. Essay writing 6. 18th century 7. History writing — Enlightenment — Europe 8. Society and culture — Philosophy

LC 2016031574

A lively exploration of the eccentric ways that human senses were perceived throughout the Enlightenment reveals how the way we think about the senses has dramatically changed throughout history and how today's sensory experiences are representative of the beliefs of earlier times.

Includes bibliographical references and index.

152.14 Visual perception

Grandin, Temple

★ *Visual Thinking: The Hidden Gifts of People Who Think in Pictures, Patterns, and Abstractions.* Temple Grandin. Riverhead Books 2022. 320 p.

ISBN 9780593418369

Grades: Adult   152.14

1. Visual perception 2. Art 3. Thought and thinking 4. Education 5. Parenting 6. Society and culture — Education 7. Society and culture — Psychology and human behavior 8. Science Writing — Medicine and health — Disabilities and disorders

LC 2022006436

Temple Grandin, who forever changed how the world understood autism, draws on cutting-edge research to take us inside visual thinking, proposing new approaches to education, parenting, employing and collaborating with the special minds and contributions of visual thinkers.

"There is much to like about and learn from Grandin's thoughtful book. Readers will seek out the latest from Grandin, a leader in illuminating the meaning and value of neurodiversity." —*Booklist*

Includes index.

ESSENTIAL AND RECOMMENDED TITLES
152.3 Movements and motor functions

Herman, Amy
Visual Intelligence: Sharpen Your Perception, Change Your Life. Amy E. Herman. Houghton Mifflin Harcourt 2016. xx, 316 pages : Color; Illustration
ISBN 9780544381056
Grades: Adult   152.14
1. Visual perception 2. Observation (Psychology) 3. Self-Help — Personal growth 4. Science writing — General
LC 2015037245

A guide to seeing and communicating more clearly in accordance with the guidelines taught to FBI agents, police officers, CEOs, ER doctors and other professionals draws on the seminars of art historian Amy Herman to explain how to become more observant to recognize and convey important information.

"Sharp and original, this book should alter how readers look at the world." —*Kirkus*

An Eamon Dolan Book; Includes index.

Hoffman, Donald D.
Visual Intelligence: How We Create What We See. Donald D. Hoffman. W.W. Norton 1998. xv, 294 p. : Illustration; Color
ISBN 9780393046694
Grades: Adult   152.14
1. Visual perception 2. Vision 3. Human information processing 4. Neuropsychology 5. Science Writing — Biology
LC 98006181

Reveals the way the human eye acts on the visual world not just to represent but to actively construct the things we see, outlining the rules of vision and their application in art and technology.

"Not only is this book an outstanding example of creative popular science but, given the many optical illusions it presents, it's also the rare book that, in line with its subject, can be thoroughly enjoyed both right side up and upside down." —*Publishers Weekly*

Includes bibliographical references (p. [223]-276) and index.

Rogers, Adam
Full Spectrum: How the Science of Color Made Us Modern. Adam Rogers. Houghton Mifflin Harcourt 2021. 288 p.
ISBN 9781328518903
Grades: Adult   152.14
1. Color 2. Perception 3. Science 4. Color in art 5. Physics 6. History writing — Microhistory 7. History writing — Arts and culture 8. Science Writing — General 9. Arts and Entertainment — General
LC 2020039337

A lively account of our age-old quest for better and newer colors, which changed the way we see the world.

"In this entertaining and effective account, Rogers explores the nature of color and exactly how we perceive, create, and utilize colors via an appealing mix of neuroscience, chemistry, physics, and culture." —*Booklist*

152.3 Movements and motor functions

Provine, Robert R.
Curious Behavior: Yawning, Laughing, Hiccupping, and Beyond. Robert R. Provine. Belknap Press of Harvard University Press 2012. 246 p.
ISBN 9780674048515
Grades: Adult   152.3
1. Human behavior 2. Human biology 3. Neuropsychology 4. Genetic psychology 5. Science Writing — Biology
LC 2012007754

Library Journal Best Books, 2012.

Explores the quirks of human behavior, looking at why such reflexive acts as yawning, sneezing, and hiccupping can explain how the human brain works and may shed light on the instinctual range of behavior.

Includes bibliographical references.

Wood, Wendy
Good Habits, Bad Habits: The Science of Making Positive Changes That Stick. Wendy Wood. Farrar, Straus and Giroux 2019. 303 pages : Color; Illustration
ISBN 9781250159076
Grades: Adult   152.3
1. Change (Psychology) 2. Social psychology 3. Cognitive neuroscience 4. Habit breaking 5. Habit 6. Society and culture — Psychology and human behavior
LC 2018060812

Revealing how a high percentage of everyday life is spent performing unconscious habits, a report based on extensive research into behavioral science reveals how to transition to better habits without exclusive reliance on willpower.

Includes bibliographical references and index.

152.4 Emotions

Barrett, Lisa Feldman
★ *How Emotions Are Made: The New Science of the Mind and Brain.* Lisa Feldman Barrett. Houghton Mifflin Harcourt 2017. 304 p.
ISBN 9780544133310
Grades: Adult   152.4
1. Neuroscience 2. Brain 3. Emotions 4. Emotions and cognition 5. Thought and thinking 6. Research 7. Science Writing — Medicine and health
LC 2016038354

Outlines new theories about how the brain constructs emotions to evaluate a growing potential for revolutionizing psychology, health care, law enforcement and modern understandings about the human mind.

"The book is a challenging read and will offer the most rewards to researchers already familiar with the longstanding and apparently still unresolved arguments about what emotions are." —*Publishers Weekly*

Berry, Erica
Wolfish: Wolf, Self, and the Stories We Tell About Fear. Erica Berry. Flatiron Books 2023. 336 p.
ISBN 9781250821621
Grades: Adult   152.4
1. Berry, Erica (Writer) 2. Fear 3. Gray wolves 4. Wolves 5. Violence 6. Predatory animals 7. Identity 8. Femininity 9. Courage 10. Human-animal relationships 11. Essays 12. Life stories — Identity 13. Nature Writing — Personal responses 14. Debut title
LC 2022035473

Oregon Book Awards, Sarah Winnemucca Award for Creative Nonfiction, 2024.

An original and probing debut work of nonfiction by a brilliant new writer, rooted in her years-long quest to study the cultural legacy of the wolf in this enthralling, kaleidoscopic exploration of wolves both real and symbolic, Erica Berry weaves historic and scientific findings alongside criticism, journalism, and memoir to illuminate the strands of our cultural constructions of predator and prey, and what it means to navigate a world in which we can be both.

"A fascinating read, perfect for fans of Mary Roach's Fuzz, or anyone who enjoys learning about wolves and what they can teach about human nature." —*Library Journal*

Includes bibliographical references.

Boone, Matthew S.
Stop Avoiding Stuff: 25 Microskills to Face Your Fears and Do It Anyway. Matthew S. Boone, Jennifer Gregg, and Lisa Coyne. New Harbinger Publications, Inc. 2020. 176 p.
ISBN 9781684036059
Grades: Adult   152.4
1. Fear 2. Anxiety 3. Avoidance (Psychology) 4. Acceptance and commitment therapy 5. Behavior therapy 6. Self-fulfillment 7. Self-Help — Personal growth
LC 2020022628

To fear is to be human. But fear can also keep us stuck living lives that are stale, stagnant, or downright miserable. In Stop Avoiding Stuff, three psychologists offer 25 "microskills" to help readers identify how their fears are holding them back. Drawing on proven-effective acceptance and commitment therapy (ACT), readers will learn how to get comfortable with discomfort, do the very things that scare them, and use values-based action to live their very best lives.

"This delightful, information-packed guide will appeal to self-help readers of all types." —Publishers Weekly

Includes bibliographical references (pages 172-176).

Brackett, Marc A
Permission to Feel: Unlocking the Power of Emotions to Help Our Kids, Ourselves, and Our Society Thrive. Marc Brackett, Ph.D, director, Yale Center for Emotional Intelligence, professor, Yale Child Study Center. Celadon Books 2019. 292 pages
ISBN 9781250212849
Grades: Adult   152.4
1. Emotional intelligence 2. Science writing — Medicine and health — Psychology 3. Society and culture — Children's studies 4. Family and Relationships — Parenting
LC Bl2019021303

The founding director of the Yale Center for Emotional Intelligence outlines a blueprint for understanding human emotions and using them wisely so that they can help, rather than hinder, personal success and well-being.

Includes bibliographical references (pages 243-285).

Breggin, Peter Roger
Guilt, Shame, and Anxiety: Understanding and Overcoming Negative Emotions. Peter R. Breggin, MD.. Prometheus Books 2014. 317 p.
ISBN 9781616141493
Grades: Adult   152.4
1. Emotions 2. Guilt 3. Shame 4. Anxiety 5. Science writing — Medicine and health — Psychology 6. Self-Help — Mental health
LC 2014023875

Dr. Breggin shows how guilt, shame, and anxiety eventually became self-defeating and demoralizing legacies from our primitive past that no longer play any useful or positive role in mature adult life. He then guides the reader through the Three Steps to Emotional Freedom.

"Breggin conveys empathy and maintains a clear, conversational tone while spelling out his prescriptions for overriding destructive impulses in a variety of real-world situations." —Publishers Weekly

Includes bibliographical references and index.

Damasio, Antonio R.
Looking for Spinoza: Joy, Sorrow, and the Feeling Brain. Antonio Damasio. Harcourt 2003. x, 355 p. : Illustration
ISBN 9780151005574
Grades: Adult   152.4
1. Spinoza, Benedictus de, 1632-1677 2. Emotions 3. Neuropsychology 4. Joy and sorrow 5. Science Writing — Biology 6. Science Writing — Medicine and health — Mental health
LC 2002011347

Investigates the cerebral mechanisms behind emotions and feelings to explain the role between emotion, survival, and cultural accomplishment.

"This is a discussion of the difference between emotions (of the body) and feelings (of the mind), various sites in the brain that trigger these states, and the…synthesis of the homeostatic process, memory, sensory input, imagination, and foresight that links the unconscious to consciousness and feelings to reasoning." —Booklist

Includes bibliographical references and index.

Gardner, Dan
The Science of Fear: Why We Fear the Things We Shouldn't — and Put Ourselves in Greater Danger. Daniel Gardner. Dutton 2008. 320 p.
ISBN 9780525950622
Grades: Adult   152.4
1. Psychology 2. Risk 3. Fear 4. Risk analysis 5. Decision-making 6. Reason 7. Phobias 8. Anxiety 9. Human behavior 10. Science Writing — Biology
LC 2008003024

Science in Society Book Award (Canadian Science Writers' Association), for Adult Nonfiction, 2008.

An analysis of the scientific causes of irrational fear offers insight into the brain's role in causing people to experience and react to fear, in a report that explains how heightened fear in the post-9/11 world is dangerously intersecting with biologically driven responses.

"Gardner analyses everything from the media's predilection for irrational scare stories to the cynical use of fear by politicians pushing a particular agenda. [He] never falls into the trap of becoming frustrated and embittered by the waste and needless worry that he is documenting. A personal anecdote about an unwise foray into a Nigerian slum in search of a stolen wallet disposes of the idea that the author is immune to the foibles he describes. What could easily have been a catalogue of misgovernance and stupidity instead becomes a cheery corrective to modern paranoia." —The Economist

Reprinted 2015; aOriginally published under the title Risk: the science and politics of fear (Toronto: McClelland & Stewart, 2008).

Goleman, Daniel
Emotional Intelligence. Daniel Goleman. Bantam Books 2005. xxiv, 358 p. : Illustration
ISBN 9780553383713
Grades: 11 12 Adult   152.4
1. Emotional intelligence 2. Science writing — Medicine and health — Psychology
LC 2005282310

Draws on the latest research in psychology and neuroscience to show how the rational and the emotional faculties of the mind work together to shape the fate of each individual and how they shape everything from personal success to physical well-being, in an updated, tenth anniversary edition of the best-selling study.

"The author explains how to develop our emotional intelligence in ways that can improve our relationships, our parenting, our classrooms, and our workplaces. Goleman assures us that our temperaments may be determined by neurochemistry, but they can be altered." —Booklist

Includes bibliographical references and index.

Havrilesky, Heather
What If This Were Enough?: Essays. by Heather Havrilesky. Doubleday 2018. 240 p.
ISBN 9780385542883
Grades: Adult   152.4
1. Havrilesky, Heather 2. Happiness 3. Everyday life 4. Personal conduct 5. Awareness 6. Interpersonal relations 7. Social pressure 8. Authors 9. Essays 10. Biographies 11. Life stories — Arts and culture — Writing — Authors 12. Society and culture — General
LC 2018001398

Through her incisive and witty inquiries, Havrilesky urges us to reject the pursuit of a shiny, shallow future that will never come. These timely, provocative, and often hilarious essays suggest an embrace of the flawed, a connection with what already is, who we already are, what we already have. She asks us to consider: What if this were enough? Our salvation, Havrilesky says, can be found right here, right now, in this imperfect moment.

Ignatieff, Michael
On Consolation: Finding Solace in Dark Times. Michael Ignatieff. Metropolitan Books 2021. 288 p.
ISBN 9780805055214
Grades: Adult   152.4
1. Consolation 2. Grief 3. Tragedy 4. Philosophers 5. Philosophy 6. Resilience 7. Personal conduct 8. Literary criticism 9. Religions 10. Canadian literature 11. Society and culture — Philosophy 12. Life stories — Facing adversity 13. Arts and Entertainment — Writing and Publishing — Literary criticism
LC 2021021338

ESSENTIAL AND RECOMMENDED TITLES
152.4 Emotions

When we lose someone we love, when we suffer loss or defeat, when catastrophe strikes—war, famine, pandemic—we go in search of consolation. Rejecting the solace of ancient religious texts, humanity since the sixteenth century has increasingly placed its faith in science, ideology, and the therapeutic. How do we console each other and ourselves in an age of unbelief? Esteemed writer and historian Michael Ignatieff shows how men and women in extremity have looked to each other across time to recover hope and resilience.

"Readers interested in history or philosophy (whether or not they are religious), will find Ignatieff's blend of spirituality and self-help to be particularly significant." —*Library Journal*

Includes bibliographical references and index.

Jeffers, Susan J.
Feel the Fear— and Do It Anyway. Susan Jeffers. Ballantine Books 2007. 214 p. : Illustration
ISBN 9780345487421
Grades: Adult   152.4
1. Fear 2. Self-Help — Personal growth
LC 2007271292

A psychotherapist shows how to identify the fears that are inhibiting one's life, ranging from public speaking and intimacy to aging and rejection, and how to transform frustration and helplessness into power to create success in every aspect of life, in a twentieth anniversary edition of the best-selling guide. Reissue.

20th anniversary edition—Cover; Includes bibliographical references (p. 211-214).

Keltner, Dacher
★ *Awe: The New Science of Everyday Wonder and How It Can Transform Your Life.* Dacher Keltner. Penguin Books 2023. 352 p.
ISBN 9781984879684
Grades: Adult   152.4
1. Sense of wonder 2. Elation 3. Surprise 4. Emotions 5. Change (Psychology) 6. Inspiration 7. Mental health 8. Society and culture — Psychology and human behavior 9. Science Writing — Medicine and health — Mental health
LC 2022002707

Awe is mysterious. How do we begin to quantify the goose bumps we feel when we see the Grand Canyon, or the utter amazement when we watch a child walk for the first time? How do you put into words the collective effervescence of standing in a crowd and singing in unison, or the wonder you feel while gazing at centuries-old works of art? Up until fifteen years ago, there was no science of awe, the feeling we experience when we encounter vast mysteries that transcend our understanding of the world. In Awe, Dacher Keltner presents a radical investigation and deeply personal inquiry into this elusive emotion.

"Eye-opening science and Keltner's appropriate sense of wonder add up to an enlightening take on the importance and potency of awe. Readers will be enchanted." —*Publishers Weekly*

Includes bibliographical references and index.

Lembke, Anna
Dopamine Nation: Finding Balance in the Age of Indulgence. Anna Lembke, M.D.. E.P. Dutton 2021. 320 p.
ISBN 9781524746728
Grades: Adult   152.4
1. Pleasure 2. Pain 3. Psychotherapist and patient 4. Addiction 5. Compulsive behavior 6. Internet 7. Drug abuse 8. Balance 9. Human behavior 10. Society and culture — Illness and disease — Addiction 11. Society and culture — Psychology and human behavior 12. Life stories — Facing adversity — Medical issues — Addiction
LC 2020041077

We're living in a time of unprecedented access to high-reward, high-dopamine stimuli: drugs, food, news, gambling, shopping, gaming, texting, sexting, Facebooking, Instagramming, YouTubing, tweeting… the increased numbers, variety, and potency is staggering. The smartphone is the modern-day hypodermic needle, delivering digital dopamine 24/7 for a wired generation. As such we've all become vulnerable to compulsive overconsumption. In Dopamine Nation, Dr. Anna Lembke, psychiatrist and author, explores the exciting new scientific discoveries that explain why the relentless pursuit of pleasure leads to pain… and what to do about it.

"Finding a balance between pain and pleasure is 'essential for a life well lived,' writes psychiatrist Lembke (Drug Dealer MD) in this eye-opening survey on pleasure-seeking and addiction." —*Publishers Weekly*

Includes bibliographical references and index.

Lerner, Harriet Goldhor
★ *The Dance of Anger: A Woman's Guide to Changing the Patterns of Intimate Relationships.* Harriet Lerner. Perennial Currents 2005. xvi, 239 p. : Illustration
ISBN 9780060741044
Grades: Adult   152.4
1. Anger 2. Interpersonal relations 3. Women 4. Psychology 5. Self-Help — Mental health — Anger 6. Self-Help — Personal growth — Happiness
LC 2004060074

Based on the author's clinical experience and workshops she has introduced, a twentieth anniversary edition of the classic guide helps women understand the causes and patterns of their anger while providing specific alternatives for forging more powerful relationships.

Includes bibliographical references (p. 225-232) and index; Originally published: 1st ed. New York : Harper & Row, c1985. With new introd.

Lieberman, David J
Never Get Angry Again: The Foolproof Way to Stay Calm and in Control in Any Conversation or Situation. David J. Lieberman, Ph.D.. St. Martin's Press 2018. VII, 225 pages
ISBN 9781250154392
Grades: Adult   152.4
1. Adjustment 2. Anger 3. Family and Relationships — General 4. Science writing — Medicine and health — Psychology 5. Self-Help — Mental health — Anger
LC 2017037537

A comprehensive, holistic look at the underlying emotional, physical and spiritual causes of anger cites the shortcomings of traditional anger-management techniques while explaining how readers can shift their perspectives to maintain a state of calm and prevent angry feelings.

A holistic look at the underlying emotional, physical, and spiritual causes of anger cites the shortcomings of traditional anger-management techniques while explaining how to shift one's perspective to maintain a state of calm.

Includes bibliographical references.

Manson, Mark
*Everything Is F*cked: A Book About Hope.* Mark Manson. HarperCollins 2019. 224 p.
ISBN 9780062888433
Grades: Adult   152.4
1. Hope 2. Optimism 3. Despair 4. Global warming 5. Self-help psychology 6. Political culture 7. United States 8. 21st century 9. Humor writing — General
LC BI2019004875

From the New York Times best-selling author of The Subtle Art of Not Giving a F*ck comes a new unorthodox self-help book.

"The popular blogger and author delivers an entertaining and thought-provoking third book about the importance of being hopeful in terrible times. Clever and accessibly conversational, Manson reminds us to chill out, not sweat the small stuff, and keep hope for a better world alive." —*Kirkus*

Mlodinow, Leonard
Emotional: How Feelings Shape Our Thinking. Leonard Mlodinow. Pantheon Books 2022. 256 p.
ISBN 9781524747596
Grades: Adult   152.4
1. Emotions 2. Thought and thinking 3. Reason 4. Logic 5. Decision-making 6. Subconsciousness 7. Emotional intelligence 8. Human behavior 9. Neuroscience 10. Society and culture — Psychology and human behavior 11. Science Writing — Medicine and health — Mental health

PUBLIC LIBRARY CORE COLLECTION: NONFICTION
Twentieth Edition

LC 2021005986

For millennia, we have viewed thinking and feeling as fundamentally opposed processes. According to this persistent, age-old belief, to truly live well we must marshal our logical and rational capacities to master our emotions. This perceived dichotomy lies at the heart of our historical pursuits in theology, philosophy, and psychology. But extraordinary advances in psychology and neuroscience, including neuroimaging and other related technologies, have cast doubt upon this traditional conception and led to a revolution in the science of emotions. In Emotion, Leonard Mlodinow takes us on a captivating journey to the frontier of this new field. Contrary to ancient wisdom, we begin to see that emotions aren't an obstacle to our incredible human ability to reason, but are an integral component of it.

"A readable work of popular science that reveals little-known facets of our worried, weary minds." —*Kirkus*

Includes index.

O'Neil, Cathy
*The **Shame** Machine: Who Profits in the New Age of Humiliation.* Cathy O'Neil. Crown 2022. 304 p.
ISBN 9781984825452
Grades: Adult   152.4
1. O'Neil, Cathy 2. Shame 3. Blame 4. Discrimination 5. Social problems 6. Social responsibility 7. Social control 8. Society and culture — Psychology and human behavior

LC 2021052960

Shame is a powerful and sometimes useful tool: When we publicly shame corrupt politicians, abusive celebrities, or predatory corporations, we reinforce values of fairness and justice. But as Cathy O'Neil argues in this revelatory book, shaming has taken a new and dangerousturn. It is increasingly being weaponized—used as a way to shift responsibility for social problems from institutions to individuals. Shaming children for not being able to afford school lunches or adults for not being able to find work lets us off the hook as a society. O'Neil explores the machinery behind all this shame, showing how governments, corporations, and the healthcare system capitalize on it. With clarity and nuance, O'Neil dissects the relationship between shame and power.

"Readers will be taken on a broad and meaningful survey of the 'Shamescape' from incels to Google AI to masking and vaxxing to addiction recovery." —*Booklist*

Includes bibliographical references and index.

Owens, Lama Rod
Love and Rage: The Path of Liberation Through Anger. Lama Rod Owens. North Atlantic Books 2020. xviii, 280 p.
ISBN 9781623174095
Grades: Adult   152.4
1. Love 2. Anger 3. Self-fulfillment 4. Social change 5. Self-Help — Mental health — Anger 6. Spirituality and Religion — Body, mind, and spirit

LC 2020003934

Reconsidering the power of anger as a positive and necessary tool for achieving spiritual liberation and social change.

"Highly recommended for Eastern philosophy/Buddhism collections; a wonderful resource for social justice advocates." —*Library Journal*

Ronson, Jon
So You've Been Publicly Shamed: A Journey Through the World of Public Humiliation. Jon Ronson. Riverhead Hardcover 2015. 304 p.
ISBN 9781594487132
Grades: Adult   152.4
1. Social control 2. Shame 3. Social media 4. Interpersonal relations 5. Internet 6. Honor 7. Human behavior 8. Public shaming 9. Adult books for young adults 10. Society and culture — Psychology and human behavior

LC 2014038382

We've all seen it happen—someone makes a bad decision in the public eye and people pile on in judgment. His interest piqued by a takeover of his own Twitter account, journalist Jon Ronson dove deep into an exploration of human nature, technology, and humiliation via social media. Interviewing both those famous for being shamed and those doing the shaming, Ronson discusses motivations, consequences, and recoveries.

Tallis, Frank
*The **Incurable** Romantic: And Other Tales of Madness and Desire.* Frank Tallis. Perseus Books Group 2018. 304 p.
ISBN 9781541617551
Grades: Adult   152.4
1. Obsession 2. Love 3. Desire 4. People with mental illnesses 5. Mental illness 6. Psychology 7. Society and culture — Psychology and human behavior

LC 2017056452

A psychologist describes the amazing stories of patients who were literally crazy in love, including a man who tries to make over 3,000 prostitutes fall in love with him and a woman who stalks her dentist.

Zhu, Mimi
Be Not Afraid of Love: Lessons on Fear, Intimacy, and Connection. Mimi Zhu. Penguin Life 2022. 224 p.
ISBN 9780143137122
Grades: Adult   152.4
1. Zhu, Mimi 2. Chinese Australians 3. Authors 4. Partner abuse 5. Love 6. Fear 7. Intimacy 8. Interpersonal relations 9. Essays 10. Australian literature 11. Autobiographies and memoirs 12. Life stories — Arts and culture — Artists 13. Life stories — Facing adversity — Abuse survivors 14. Family and relationships — Abuse

LC 2022002725

This collection of interconnected essays and affirmations traces the Chinese-Australian writer and artist's journey through recovery from a violent romantic relationship and explores the intersections of love and fear.

"Powerful and unique, this offers a nuanced perspective on what it means to love others and oneself has inspired many to acknowledge and even pursue dreams of more laid-back existences, readers will appreciate this very personal glimpse into a redirected, well-channeled life." —*Publishers Weekly*

Includes bibliographical references.

153 Conscious mental processes and intelligence

Clark, Andy
*The **Experience** Machine: How Our Minds Predict and Shape Reality.* Andy Clark. Pantheon Books 2023. 320 p.
ISBN 9781524748456
Grades: Adult   153
1. Cognitive science 2. Neuroscience 3. Brain 4. Consciousness 5. Experience 6. Expectation 7. Mental suggestion 8. Forecasting 9. Prediction (Psychology) 10. Society and culture — Psychology and human behavior 11. Science Writing — Medicine and health

LC 2022037742

Widely acclaimed philosopher and cognitive scientist Andy Clark unpacks this provocative new theory that the brain is a powerful, dynamic prediction engine, mediating our experience of both body and world. From the most mundane experiences to the most sublime, reality as we know it is the complex synthesis of sensory information and expectation. Exploring its fascinating mechanics and remarkable implications for our lives, mental health, and society, Clark nimbly illustrates how the predictive brain sculpts all human experience.

"Drawing on insights from psychology, neuroscience, and philosophy, Clark, a professor of cognitive philosophy, examines how our understanding of the world is fundamentally informed by cognitive forecasting….A startling, profoundly illuminating account of our mind's predictive abilities." —*Kirkus*

Includes index.

Damasio, Antonio R.
*The **Feeling** of What Happens: Body and Emotion in the Making of Consciousness.* Antonio R. Damasio. Harcourt Brace 1999. xii, 386 p. : Illustration
ISBN 9780151003693
Grades: Adult   153

ESSENTIAL AND RECOMMENDED TITLES
153.1 Memory and learning

1. Consciousness 2. Emotions 3. Mind and body 4. Neuroscience 5. Science Writing — Biology

LC 99026357

Booklist Editors' Choice, 1999; Library Journal Best Books, 1999.

A new theory of consciousness and the construction of identity focuses on the body's reaction to its world, postulating that a complex relationship between body, emotion, and mind is required to configure the self.

"The author contends that consciousness arises from our ability to map relations between the self and others through our emotions. This bold attempt to mend the classical breach between emotion and reason is all the more compelling for its poetic expression." —*Publishers Weekly*

Includes bibliographical references (p. 336-365) and index.

Eagleman, David
Incognito: The Secret Lives of the Brain. David Eagleman. Pantheon 2011. 288 p.
ISBN 9780307377333
Grades: Adult   153
1. Subconsciousness 2. Brain 3. Consciousness 4. Neurology 5. Neuroscience 6. Decision-making 7. Science Writing — Biology

LC 2010053184

A leading neuroscientist reveals the functions of the unconscious regions of the brain, drawing on up-to-the-minute research to identify the significance of brain areas outside of our awareness and their roles in such areas as mate selection, the perception of beauty and the future of criminal law.

"Eagleman's main theme is that what one calls me, the conscious mind, is only the tip of the iceberg, and that most of the interesting and important things the brain does are inaccessible to the brain's owner. What Eagleman does is explain the idea to the neophyte through discussion of dozens of fascinating, engaging examples. Eagleman's prose is vivid and, more important, accessible." —*Choice*

Includes bibliographical references and index.

Hallinan, Joseph T.
Why We Make Mistakes: How We Look Without Seeing, Forget Things in Seconds, and Are All Pretty Sure We Are Way Above Average. Joseph T. Hallinan. Broadway Books 2009. 283 p. : Illustration
ISBN 9780767928052
Grades: 11 12 Adult   153
1. Failure 2. Errors 3. Human behavior 4. Consequences 5. Brain 6. Science — Human body — Nervous system

LC 2008030818

Surveys the workings of the human mind to examine the science behind the brain's ability to see, think, remember, and forget, accompanied by anecdotes, visual puzzles, informational sidebars, and simple solutions for overcoming imperfections.

Includes bibliographical references (p. [239]-273) and index.

Hofstadter, Douglas R.
I Am a Strange Loop. Douglas Hofstadter. Basic Books 2007. xix, 412 p, 4 p. of plates : Illustration; Color
ISBN 9780465030781
Grades: Adult   153
1. Self 2. Consciousness 3. Intelligence 4. Soul 5. Self-awareness 6. Spirituality and Religion — General

LC 2007310563

Los Angeles Times Book Prize for Science and Technology, 2007.

Argues that the key to understanding selves and consciousness is a special kind of abstract feedback loop inhabiting our brains, which include a network of abstractions that we call "symbols," the most central and complex symbol in our brains is the one we call "I." but how can such a mysterious abstraction be real—or is our "I" merely a convenient fiction?

"The author's model of self is neither spiritual he's not a religious mannor is it locked into the cold neurological materialism of cellular mechanics. [The book] scales some lofty conceptual heights, but it remains very personal, and it's deeply colored by the facts of Hofstadter's later life." —*Time*

Includes bibliographical references (p. [377]-382) and index.

Medina, John
Brain Rules: 12 Principles for Surviving and Thriving at Work, Home, and School. John Medina. Pear Press 2014. I, 288 p. : Illustration
ISBN 9780983263371
Grades: Adult   153
1. Human information processing 2. Perception 3. Senses and sensation 4. Brain 5. Science writing — General

LC Bl2014015978

Presents twelve scientifically proven facts about how the human brain works and explains how to apply each on a daily basis, discussing such concepts as attention, memory, and sleep.

Includes index.

Pinker, Steven
How the Mind Works. Steven Pinker. Norton 1997. xii, 660 p.
ISBN 9780393045352
Grades: 11 12 Adult   153
1. Cognitive neuroscience 2. Neuropsychology 3. Natural selection 4. Human evolution 5. Psychology 6. Science Writing — Biology

LC 97001855

Los Angeles Times Book Prize for Science and Technology, 1997; New York Times Notable Book, 1997; National Book Critics Circle Award for Nonfiction finalist, 1997; Pulitzer Prize for General Nonfiction finalist, 1998.

A prominent cognitive scientist explains how the brain evolved to store and use information, allowing our ancestors to control their environment, and why we think and act as we do.

"Pinker has a gift for making enormously complicated mechanisms—and human foibles—accessible." —*Publishers Weekly*

Includes bibliographical references (p. 589-625) and index.

Sagan, Carl
The Dragons of Eden: Speculations on the Evolution of Human Intelligence. Carl Sagan. Random House 1977. 263 p. : Illustration
ISBN 9780345346292
Grades: 11 12 Adult   153
1. Intelligence 2. Brain 3. Genetic psychology 4. Science Writing — Biology

LC 76053472

Pulitzer Prize for General Nonfiction, 1978; National Book Critics Circle Award for Nonfiction finalist, 1977.

The well-known astronomer and astrobiologist surveys current knowledge of the development of intelligence on Earth in various forms of life and explains his persuasion that intelligence must have developed along similar paths throughout the universe.

"In this study of human intellect Sagan is principally preoccupied with the neocortex, with its left hemisphere, responsible for language and logic, a right hemisphere in charge of intuition and spatial dimension, and a corpus callosum that mediates and synthesizes the two." —*The Atlantic*

Includes Bibliographical references (p. 241-249) and index.

153.1 Memory and learning

Boser, Ulrich
Learn Better: Mastering the Skills for Success in Life, Business, and School, Or, How to Become an Expert in Just About Anything. Ulrich Boser. Rodale 2017. xxvi, 277 pages : Illustration
ISBN 9781623365264
Grades: Adult   153.1
1. Educator resources — General 2. Science writing — Medicine and health — Psychology 3. Self-Help — Personal growth

LC Bl2017004372

An education researcher maps out the new science of learning, showing how simple techniques like comprehension check-ins and making material personally relatable can help people gain expertise in dramatically better ways than simple rote memorization.

PUBLIC LIBRARY CORE COLLECTION: NONFICTION
Twentieth Edition

Shakes up the conventional wisdom on how humans learn, mapping out a new science of learning that shows how simple techniques like comprehension check-ins and making material personally relatable can help people gain expertise in dramatically better ways. By the senior fellow at the Center for American Progress.

"This work infuses a sense of fresh excitement and accessibility into a topic sometimes considered stodgy or overly cerebral. Readers will be left craving something new to learn." —*Publishers Weekly*

Includes bibliographical references (pages 229-263) and index.

Carey, Benedict
How We Learn: The Surprising Truth About When, Where, and Why It Happens. Benedict Carey. Random House 2014. 272 p.
ISBN 9780812993882
Grades: Adult   153.1
1. Learning 2. Memory 3. Society and culture — Education
LC 2013049850

A leading New York Times neuroscientist presents a lighthearted exploration of what is known about learning and memory today that considers how to adapt negative characteristics, like ignorance and laziness, to expand learning potential.

"A totally fascinating look at learning, with helpful insights for students and any reader interested in learning everything from a new language to flying to playing chess." —*Booklist*

Foer, Joshua
Moonwalking with Einstein: The Art and Science of Remembering Everything. Joshua Foer. Penguin Press 2011. 307 p.
ISBN 9781594202292
Grades: Adult   153.1
1. Mnemonics 2. Memory 3. Neuroscience 4. Learning 5. Memories 6. Science Writing — Biology
LC 2010030265

Moonwalking with Einstein draws on cutting-edge research, a surprising cultural history of memory, and venerable tricks of the mentalist's trade to transform our understanding of human remembering. Under the tutelage of top "mental athletes," Foer learns ancient techniques once employed by Cicero to memorize his speeches and by medieval scholars to memorize entire books. Using methods that have been largely forgotten, he discovers that we can all dramatically improve our memories.

"Mr. Foer writes in these pages with fresh enthusiasm. His narrative is smart and funny and . it's informed by a humanism that enables its author to place the mysteries of the brain within a larger philosophical and cultural context." —*New York Times*

Includes bibliographical references (p. [289]-297) and index.

Fogler, Janet
Improving Your Memory: How to Remember What You're Starting to Forget. Janet Fogler and Lynn Stern. Johns Hopkins University Press 2014. VIII, 153 pages : Illustration
ISBN 9781421415703
Grades: Adult   153.1
1. Seniors' memory 2. Memory 3. Mnemonics 4. Self-Help — Personal growth
LC 2014008681

University of Michigan social workers Janet Fogler and Lynn Stern have completely updated their friendly and usable guide to memory improvement techniques. Recognizing that people worry something is wrong with them when they forget things, Fogler and Stern suggest that the antidote to worry is taking positive actions to help us remember what we want to remember. They provide readers with tools for understanding and improving memory, including sixteen helpful exercises. Simple techniques like writing information down, creating a catch word or phrase, altering something in your environment, and reviewing details in advance can put you actively in charge of retrieving information more easily.

Pink, Daniel H.
Drive: The Surprising Truth About What Motivates Us. Daniel H. Pink. Riverhead Books 2009. 242 p.
ISBN 9781594488849
Grades: Adult   153.1
1. Motivation 2. Psychological growth 3. Goals and objectives 4. Success (Concept) 5. Leadership in business 6. Leadership 7. Cognition 8. Business and economics — Business Advice 9. Society and culture — Psychology and human behavior
LC 2009040651

Pink argues that the secret to high performance and satisfaction in today's world is the deeply human need to direct our own lives, to learn and create new things, and to do better by ourselves and our world. Challenges popular misconceptions to reveal what actually motivates people and how to harness that knowledge to promote personal and professional fulfillment.

"The author presents an integral addition to a growing body of literature that argues for a radical shift in how businesses operate in a world dominated by technology, and soon to be led by a generation that doesn't necessarily equate money with happiness. Important reading for frustrated but open-minded business leaders struggling to connect with stressed-out workers." —*Kirkus*

Ranganath, Charan
★ *Why We Remember: Unlocking Memory's Power to Hold on to What Matters*. Charan Ranganath. Doubleday 2024. 304 p.
ISBN 9780385548632
Grades: Adult   153.1
1. Memory 2. Cognition 3. Neuroscience 4. Memories 5. Science Writing — Medicine and health — Mental health 6. Society and culture — Psychology and human behavior
LC 2023031694

Combining accessible language with cutting-edge research, eye-opening studies and examples from pop culture, a pioneering neuroscientist and psychologist unveils the hidden role memory plays throughout our lives and how once we understand its power, we can cut through the clutter to remember the things we want to remember.

"Approachable and enlightening, this is worth seeking out." —*Publishers Weekly*

Includes bibliographical references and index.

Schacter, Daniel L.
The Seven Sins of Memory: How the Mind Forgets and Remembers. Daniel L. Schacter. Houghton Mifflin 2001. x, 272 p. : Illustration
ISBN 9780618040193
Grades: 11 12 Adult   153.1
1. Memory disorders 2. Memory 3. Memories 4. Absent-mindedness 5. Persistence 6. Science Writing — Medicine and health — Illness and disease
LC 00053885

New York Times Notable Book, 2001.

A respected expert on memory describes how the brain stores and recalls information as he describes seven key problems with memory—transience, absent-mindedness, blocking, misattribution, suggestibility, bias, and persistence.

Includes bibliographical references (p. 230-257) and index.

Wiking, Meik
The Art of Making Memories: How to Create and Remember Happy Moments. Meik Wiking. William Morrow 2019. 288 p. : Color; Illustration
ISBN 9780062943385
Grades: Adult   153.1
1. Happiness 2. Memory 3. Neuroscience 4. Memories 5. Human behavior 6. Nostalgia 7. Psychological growth 8. Society and culture — Psychology and human behavior 9. Science Writing — Biology

The author shares advice for creating positive memories for overall lasting happiness, drawing on extensive research to explain how to forge positive memories and let go of negative experiences.

ESSENTIAL AND RECOMMENDED TITLES
153.3 Imagination, imagery, creativity

"Wiking's focus on the pleasure and solace created by happy memories will make this accessible book great for deep study and casual perusal alike." —*Publishers Weekly*

153.3 Imagination, imagery, creativity

Brandt, Anthony K.
The Runaway Species: How Human Creativity Remakes the World. Anthony Brandt and David Eagleman. Catapult 2017. 200 p.
ISBN 9781936787524
Grades: Adult   153.3
1. Creativity 2. Social psychology 3. Page to screen 4. Society and culture — Psychology and human behavior
LC Bl2017040997

David Eagleman, a neuroscientist and New York Times best-selling author, teams up with composer Anthony Brandt in this powerful, wide-ranging exploration of human creativity. Taking inspiration from the arts, business, education, the space program, architecture, and even hairstyles, Eagleman and Brandt discover the principles guiding human creativity. They incisively explore how individuals, organizations, and education can benefit from increased creativity, and celebrate humanity's spirit and unique ability to remake the world.

"Packed with vivid images, countless examples, and fun facts that will leave readers eager to discuss it with friends, this is a refreshing and thought-provoking book that captures both the wonder of science and the beauty of the human spirit." —*Booklist*

Adapted into a film entitled the Creative Brain in 2019.

Cameron, Julia
Living the Artist's Way: An Intuitive Path to Greater Creativity : A Six-week Artist's Way Program. Julia Cameron. 2024. Pages cm
ISBN 9781250897589
Grades: Adult   153.3
1. Creativity 2. Creation (Literary, artistic.) 3. Self-actualization 4. Writing 5. Self-Help — Personal growth — Creativity 6. Language arts and studies — Writing skills
LC 2023033040

In the thirty years following the publication of the Artist's Way, Julia Cameron relied on an essential tool to help her through every juncture in life: Writing for guidance. Now, in Living the Artist's Way, Cameron finally shares this method with the world as the fourth main Artist's Way tool. Over the course of six weeks, readers learn how to ask for guidance from a higher power within themselves, and trust the answers they receive.

Includes index.

Ellenhorn, Ross D.
★ *Purple Crayons: The Art of Drawing a Life*. Ross Ellenhorn. Harper Wave, an imprint of HarperCollinsPublishers 2022. 214 pages : Color; Illustration
ISBN 9780063143807
Grades: Adult   153.3
1. Originality 2. Resilience 3. Self-reliance 4. Self-Help — Personal growth
LC 2022021828

Drawing on the beloved children's book Harold and the Purple Crayon, the author, as he traces Harold's journey, offers insights into our "sacred originality"—the idea that each of our unique inner lives are worth nurturing and protecting, and perseverance, courage, connection and community necessary to sustain them.

"This children's book is a classic for a variety of reasons. Now Ellenhorn's thoughtful approach turns the seemingly simple text and line drawings into a celebration of originality, creativity, and spontaneity and a guide to living more fully." —*Booklist*

Gawain, Shakti
★ *Creative Visualization: Use the Power of Your Imagination to Create What You Want in Your Life*. Shakti Gawain. Nataraj Pub./New World Library 2002. xvi, 175 p. : Illustration
ISBN 9781577312291
Grades: Adult   153.3
1. Affirmations 2. Self-actualization 3. Visualization 4. Spirituality and Religion — Body, mind, and spirit 5. Self-Help — Personal growth — Meditation
LC 2003265316

Explains how to use mental imagery and affirmations to produce positive change, offering meditation suggestions and exercises designed to strengthen self-esteem, improve health, and promote relaxation.

"The author asserts that people can achieve an ideal existence simply through mental visualization." —*Library Journal*

25th anniversary edition—Cover; Includes bibliographical references (p. 172-174).

Gilbert, Elizabeth
★ *Big Magic: Creative Living Beyond Fear*. Elizabeth Gilbert. Riverhead Books 2015. 276 pages
ISBN 9781594634710
Grades: Adult   153.3
1. Courage 2. Inspiration 3. Magical thinking 4. Personal conduct 5. Creativity 6. Spirituality and Religion — Body, mind, and spirit 7. Self-Help — Personal growth — Creativity 8. Self-Help — Personal growth — Motivation
LC 2015010717

The best-selling author of Eat Pray Love builds on her personal generative process to counsel readers on how to let go of needless suffering while learning to understand the mysterious nature of inspiration and creativity.

"Gilbert serves as an enthusiastic coach for readers who want more out of life. Highly recommended." —*Library Journal*

Godin, Seth
The Practice: Shipping Creative Work. Seth Godin. Portfolio 2020. 272 p.
ISBN 9780593328972
Grades: Adult   153.3
1. Creativity in business 2. Leadership in business 3. Creation (Literary, artistic, etc.) 4. Entrepreneurship 5. Desire 6. Job satisfaction 7. Advice 8. Business and economics — Business advice — Leadership and management 9. Business and economics — Popular psychology 10. Arts and Entertainment — General
LC 2020025982

Creative work doesn't come with a guarantee. But there is a pattern to who succeeds and who doesn't. And engaging in the consistent practice of its pursuit is the best way forward. Based on the breakthrough Akimbo workshop pioneered by legendary author Seth Godin, the Practice will help you get unstuck and find the courage to make and share creative work. Godin insists that writer's block is a myth, that consistency is far more important than authenticity, and that experiencing the imposter syndrome is a sign that you're a well-adjusted human. Most of all, he shows you what it takes to turn your passion from a private distraction to a productive contribution, the one you've been seeking to share all along.

Grant, Adam M.
Originals: How Non-Conformists Move the World. Adam Grant; foreword by Sheryl Sandberg. Viking 2016. 320 p.
ISBN 9780525429562
Grades: Adult   153.3
1. Creative thinking 2. Creativity in business 3. Creativity 4. Organizational change 5. New products 6. Entrepreneurship 7. Success in business 8. Business and economics — Business Advice
LC 2015041287

Examines how provocative thought leaders can champion originality in their organizations, drawing on illustrative studies and stories spanning a range of disciplines to explain how to recognize a good idea, speak up, build allies, choose a time to act and manage doubts.

PUBLIC LIBRARY CORE COLLECTION: NONFICTION
Twentieth Edition

"No matter whether the reader is an original or a wannabe, this book is enjoyable and full of useful information." —*Library Journal*

Greenberg, Sarah Stein
Creative Acts for Curious People: How to Think, Create, and Lead in Unconventional Ways. Sarah Stein Greenberg; foreword by David M. Kelley; illustrations by Michael Hirshon. Ten Speed Press 2021. VII, 295 pages : Color; Illustration
ISBN 9781984858160
Grades: Adult 153.3
1. Creativity 2. Creative thinking 3. Business and economics — Business advice 4. Self-Help — Personal growth — Creativity
LC Bl2021023463

Perfect for people who choose curiosity in the face of uncertainty, this thought-provoking and highly visual manual from Stanford University's world-renowned school presents more than 80 innovative assignments that are at once lighthearted, surprising, tough and impactful.

"An inspiring, thought-provoking, and highly recommended work with a multitude of exercises to heighten creativity in management." —*Library Journal*
A Stanford d.School book—Cover; Includes index.

Harford, Tim
Messy: The Power of Disorder to Transform Our Lives. Tim Harford. Riverhead Books 2016. 288 p.
ISBN 9781594634796
Grades: Adult 153.3
1. Neatness and messiness 2. Chaos 3. Social values 4. Creativity 5. Business and economics — Popular psychology
LC Bl2016043057

From the award-winning columnist and author of the national best-seller The Undercover Economist comes a provocative big idea book about the genuine benefits of being messy at home, at work, in the classroom and beyond.

"Weaving together lessons from history, art, technology, and social and scientific research, Harford's theories have many potential benefits for individuals and businesses seeking to remain on the creative cutting edge, as well as profound implications for society." —*Publishers Weekly*

Livio, Mario
Why?: An Exploration of Human Curiosity. by Mario Livio. Simon & Schuster 2017. 288 p.
ISBN 9781476792095
Grades: Adult 153.3
1. Curiosity 2. Learning 3. Neuroscience 4. Knowledge 5. Thought and thinking 6. Perception 7. Creativity 8. Science Writing — General 9. Society and culture — Philosophy 10. Society and culture — Psychology and human behavior
LC 2016040604

An internationally respected astrophysicist explores the science behind curiosity to evaluate its role in human creativity, ambition and culture, drawing on interviews with scientists and students while examining the lives of forefront intellectuals to identify how curiosity manifests in the brain.

"The information presented is accessible to all readers and the tone is engaging, sometimes even playful." —*Library Journal*
Includes bibliographical references and index.

Okorafor, Nnedi
Broken Places & Outer Spaces: Finding Creativity in the Unexpected. Nnedi Okorafor. Simon & Schuster 2019. 128 p.
ISBN 9781501195471
Grades: Adult 153.3
1. Science fiction authors 2. Storytelling 3. College athletes 4. Creativity 5. Track and field 6. Scoliosis 7. People with paraplegia 8. Surgery 9. Dreams 10. Paralysis 11. Racism 12. Autobiographies and memoirs 13. Life stories — Facing adversity — Medical issues 14. Life stories — Arts and culture — Writing — Authors 15. Arts and Entertainment — Writing and Publishing
LC Bl2019017586

Following her journey from star athlete to sudden paralysis to creative awakening, acclaimed sci-fi writer Nnedi Okorafor reveals that what we perceive as limitations have the potential to become our greatest strengths, and that creativity often springs from the broken places.

"A brief but arresting memoir draped with colors of hope and resilience." —*Library Journal*

Rubin, Rick
★ *The Creative Act: A Way of Being.* Rick Rubin. Penguin Books 2023. 404 p.
ISBN 9780593652886
Grades: Adult 153.3
1. Creation (Literary, artistic, etc.) 2. Creativity 3. Creative thinking 4. Advice 5. Learning 6. Self-discovery 7. Psychology 8. Philosophy 9. Arts and Entertainment — General 10. Society and culture — Psychology and human behavior

Many famed music producers are known for a particular sound that has its day and then ages out. Rick Rubin is known for something else: Creating a space where artists of all different genres and traditions can home in on who they really are and what they really offer. He has made a practice of helping people transcend their self-imposed expectations in order to reconnect with a state of innocence from which the surprising becomes inevitable. The Creative Act is a beautiful and generous course of study that illuminates the path of the artist as a road we all can follow.

"Grammy-winning music producer Rubin debuts with a meditative manual on how to boost one's creativity….Rubin stresses that readers should find what works for them." —*Publishers Weekly*

Sonenshein, Scott
Stretch: Unlock the Power of Less— and Achieve More Than You Ever Imagined. Scott Sonenshein. HarperBusiness 2017. xi, 283 pages
ISBN 9780062457226
Grades: Adult 153.3
1. Resourcefulness 2. Creativity 3. Adaptability 4. Success (Concept) 5. Self-help techniques 6. Self-Help — Personal growth
LC 2016028800

A guide to driving achievement and promoting creativity and innovation at work explains how to do more with your existing resources through a four-part framework that explains how different mindsets can diversify experiences, act without over-planning and expect positive outcomes.

Includes bibliographical references (pages 233-268) and index.

Zomorodi, Manoush
Bored and Brilliant: How Spacing Out Can Unlock Your Most Productive and Creative Self. Manoush Zomorodi. Picador, St. Martin's Press 2018. IX, 192 pages
ISBN 9781250126658
Grades: Adult 153.3
1. Boredom 2. Creativity 3. Labor productivity 4. Self-Help — Personal growth — Creativity
LC Bl2018185119

The podcaster and radio host argues that boredom is essential in making lives happier and more productive, and includes exercises for bringing about critical thinking.

"In this age of information, Zomorodi's book seems revolutionary, almost subversive. Sprinkled liberally with research and insights from some of the leading minds in technology and futurism, Bored and Brilliant is an important reminder that we are not beholden to our devices." —*BookPage*
Includes index.

153.4 Thought, thinking, reasoning, intuition, value, judgment

Brotherton, Rob
Suspicious Minds: Why We Believe Conspiracy Theories. Rob Brotherton. St. Martin's Press 2015. 288 p.

ESSENTIAL AND RECOMMENDED TITLES
153.4 Thought, thinking, reasoning, intuition, value, judgment

ISBN 9781472915610
Grades: Adult **153.4**
1. Conspiracies 2. Conspiracy theories 3. Belief and doubt 4. Human behavior 5. Society and culture — Psychology and human behavior
LC Bl2015046771

Looks at the psychology behind conspiracy theories and explains why everyone can be prone to them, revealing the consequences they can have—from discouraging parents from vaccinating their children against deadly diseases to hampering political policies to combat climate change.

"Clearly written and with liberal use of humor and numerous examples from scholarly research, this title provides a valuable look at why conspiracy theories abound and why we should continually assess our thinking."—*Library Journal*

Christian, Brian
Algorithms to Live By: The Computer Science of Human Decisions. Brian Christian and Tom Griffiths. Henry Holt and Company 2016. x, 351 pages
ISBN 9781627790369
Grades: Adult **153.4**
1. Human behavior 2. Computer simulation 3. Computer algorithms 4. Problem solving 5. Science writing — Mathematics 6. Society and culture — Psychology and human behavior
LC 2015032177

Explores how computer algorithms can be applied to everyday life, drawing on myriad disciplines to explain how computers have proven adept at making decisions and taking chances.

Includes bibliographical references and index.

Dobelli, Rolf
The Art of Thinking Clearly. Rolf Dobelli; translated from the Germa by Nicky Griffin. HarperBusiness 2013. 384 p.
ISBN 9780062219701
Grades: Adult **153.4**
1. Cognition 2. Decision making 3. Errors 4. Science writing — Medicine and health — Psychology
LC Oc2013033342

This insightful exploration into human reasoning, filled with practical examples and anecdotes, reveals how to recognize and avoid the simple errors we make in our day-to-day thinking so that we can change the way we think and transform our decision-making process.

Translation of the author's Die Kunst des klaren Denkens, published by Hanser in 2012.

Gladwell, Malcolm
Blink: The Power of Thinking Without Thinking. Malcolm Gladwell. Little, Brown and Co. 2005. VIII, 277 p. : Portrait
ISBN 9780316172325
Grades: 11 12 Adult **153.4**
1. Decision making 2. Intuition 3. Thought and thinking 4. Knowledge 5. Consciousness 6. Canadian literature 7. Business and economics — Popular psychology

Utilizing case studies as diverse as speed dating, pop music, and the shooting of Amadou Diallo, Gladwell reveals that what we think of as decisions made in the blink of an eye are much more complicated than assumed. Drawing on cutting-edge neuroscience and psychology, he shows how the difference between good decision-making and bad has nothing to do with how much information we can process quickly, but on the few particular details on which we focus.

"Gladwell has a dazzling ability to find commonality in disparate fields of study. . . . Each case study is satisfying, and Gladwell imparts his own evident pleasure in delving into a wide range of fields and seeking an underlying truth." —*Publishers Weekly*

Includes bibliographical references (p. [255]-262) and index.

Grant, Adam M.
★ *Think Again: The Power of Knowing What You Don't Know.* Adam Grant. Viking 2021. 320 p.
ISBN 9781984878106

Grades: Adult **153.4**
1. Thought and thinking 2. Critical thinking 3. Questioning 4. Theory of knowledge 5. Belief and doubt 6. Social psychology 7. Human behavior 8. Business and economics — Popular psychology 9. Society and culture — Psychology and human behavior
LC 2020035237

The Wharton organizational psychologist and best-selling author examines the critical art of rethinking, explaining how questioning one's opinions and opening the minds of others can promote personal and professional excellence.

"Readers with an interest in psychology, as well as the proverbial 'General reader,' will enjoy this fast-paced account by a leading authority on the psychology of thinking." —*Library Journal*

Includes bibliographical references and index.

Gupta, Sanjay
★ *Keep Sharp: Build a Better Brain at Any Age.* Sanjay Gupta, MD.. Simon & Schuster 2020. 352 p.
ISBN 9781501166730
Grades: Adult **153.4**
1. Cognition 2. Human information processing 3. Brain 4. Aging 5. Preventive medicine 6. Science writing — Medicine and health — Aging and longevity
LC 2019057039

The Emmy Award-winning CNN chief medical correspondent and best-selling author draws on cutting-edge scientific research to outline strategies for protecting brain function and maintaining cognitive health at any age.

"A genuine source of practical knowledge and sympathy to those struggling with dementia and the family members who are primary caregivers—to whom he tenders a wealth of resources. Inclusive and recognizably sturdy advice on building a healthy brain."—*Kirkus*

Includes bibliographical references and index.

Jacobs, Alan
How to Think: A Survival Guide for a World at Odds. Alan Jacobs. Convergent Books 2017. 192 p.
ISBN 9780451499608
Grades: Adult **153.4**
1. Thought and thinking 2. Reasoning 3. Decision-making 4. Human behavior 5. Society and culture — Psychology and human behavior
LC 2016052795

A distinguished professor and long-time writer for the Atlantic and Christian Century diagnoses the forces that prevent modern people from thinking, including distraction, social bias and fear of rejection and offers hope and tips to regain our mental lives.

"Witty, engaging, and ultimately hopeful, Jacobss guide is sorely needed in a society where partisanship too often trumps the pursuit of knowledge." —*Publishers Weekly*

Kahneman, Daniel
★ *Thinking, Fast and Slow.* Daniel Kahneman. Farrar, Straus and Giroux 2011. 499 p. : Illustration
ISBN 9780374275631
Grades: Adult **153.4**
1. Thought and thinking 2. Decision making 3. Intuition 4. Reasoning 5. Science Writing — Medicine and health — Mental health 6. Business and economics — Popular psychology
LC 2011027143

ALA Notable Book, 2012; Los Angeles Times Book Prize for Current Interest, 2011; National Academies Communication Award, 2012; New York Times Notable Book, 2011.

A Nobel Prize-winning psychologist draws on years of research to introduce his "machinery of the mind" model on human decision making to reveal the faults and capabilities of intuitive versus logical thinking, providing insights into such topics as optimism, the unpredictability of happiness and the psychological pitfalls of risk-taking.

Includes bibliographical references and index.

PUBLIC LIBRARY CORE COLLECTION: NONFICTION
Twentieth Edition

Konnikova, Maria
Mastermind: How to Think Like Sherlock Holmes. Maria Konnikova. Viking Adult 2013. 320 p.
ISBN 9780670026579
Grades: Adult   153.4
1. Logic 2. Reasoning 3. Brain 4. Characters and characteristics in literature 5. Holmes, Sherlock (Fictitious character) 6. Science Writing — Biology 7. Arts and Entertainment — Writing and Publishing
LC 2012035455
The "Literally Psyched" columnist for Scientific American draws on neuroscience and psychology studies while analyzing the deductive strategies used by the character of Sherlock Holmes to counsel readers on how to promote mental strength, clearer observation and effective problem-solving.
Includes index.

Levitin, Daniel J.
★ *A Field* Guide to Lies: Critical Thinking in the Information Age. Daniel J. Levitin. Dutton 2016. 304 p.
ISBN 9780525955221
Grades: Adult   153.4
1. Critical thinking 2. Misinformation 3. Reasoning 4. Online journalism 5. Internet 6. Technology 7. Fake news 8. Mass media bias 9. Fallacies (Logic) 10. Propaganda 11. Science Writing — Computing, the Internet, and Technology
LC 2016007356
Quebec Writers' Federation Literary Awards, Mavis Gallant Prize for Non-fiction, 2016.
Outlines recommendations for critical thinking practices that meet the challenges of the digital age's misinformation, demonstrating the role of science in information literacy while explaining the importance of skeptical reasoning in making decisions based on online information.
Includes bibliographical references and index; Updated and reprinted with a new introduction in 2017 as Weaponized lies : How to think critically in the post-truth era. ISBN 9781101983829.

Montell, Amanda
★ *The Age* of Magical Overthinking: Notes on Modern Irrationality. Amanda Montell. Signal Press 2024. 320 p.
ISBN 9781668007976
Grades: Adult   153.4
1. Power 2. Unconscious bias 3. Irrationality (Psychology) 4. Cynicism 5. Thought and thinking 6. Visualization 7. Culture 8. Psychology 9. Essays 10. Society and culture — Pop culture 11. Society and culture — Psychology and human behavior
A blend of cultural criticism and personal narrative explores our cognitive biases and the power, disadvantages and highlights of magical thinking.
"This seamless tie-in to Montell's Cultish (2021) and her podcast, Sounds Like a Cult, examines the recent upsurge in cults, conspiracies, extreme fandom, and distorted nostalgia." —*Booklist*

Nisbett, Richard E.
Mindware: Tools for Smart Thinking. Richard E. Nisbett. Farrar, Straus and Giroux 2015. 320 p.
ISBN 9780374112677
Grades: Adult   153.4
1. Reasoning 2. Thought and thinking 3. Society and culture — Psychology and human behavior
LC 2015005007
A renowned psychology expert offers a tool kit for thinking more clearly and making better decisions, explaining how to reframe problems using simplified concepts from science and statistics including the law of large numbers, statistical regression, cost-benefit analysis and causation and correlation.
"Nisbett's goal is to help us look at problems and choices in new ways, to attack them from new analytic angles, to find clarity out of chaos. No psychological self-help book succeeds completely, but this one comes close." —*Booklist*
Includes bibliographical references and index.

Nye, Bill
Everything All at Once: How to Unleash Your Inner Nerd, Tap into Radical Curiosity and Solve Any Problem. by Bill Nye; edited by Corey S. Powell. Rodale Books 2017. 384 p.
ISBN 9781623367916
Grades: Adult   153.4
1. Nye, Bill 2. Critical thinking 3. Science 4. Misfits (People) 5. Social change 6. Belief and doubt 7. Skepticism 8. Essays 9. Autobiographies and memoirs 10. Life stories — Science, technology, and medicine — Scientists and inventors 11. Society and culture — Philosophy
LC 2017022105
Everyone has an inner nerd just waiting to be awakened by the right passion. In Everything All at Once, Bill Nye will help you find yours. With his call to arms, he wants you to examine every detail of the most difficult problems that look unsolvable—that is, until you find the solution. Bill shows you how to develop critical thinking skills and create change, using his "everything all at once" approach that leaves no stone unturned.
"Bow-tied nerd superhero Nye (Unstoppable: Harnessing Science to Change the World, 2015, etc.) serves up a tasty combination of memoir and manifesto." —*Kirkus*

Pinker, Steven
Rationality: What It Is, Why It Seems Scarce, Why It Matters. Steven Pinker. Viking 2021. 400 p.
ISBN 9780525561996
Grades: Adult   153.4
1. Critical thinking 2. Reason 3. Logic 4. Probabilities 5. Causation 6. Irrationality (Psychology) 7. Errors 8. Misconceptions 9. Decision-making 10. Cognition 11. Psychology 12. Society and culture — Psychology and human behavior 13. Science Writing — Biology
LC 2021003592
Discusses the benchmarks of rationality, that help us understand the basics of logic, critical thinking, probability, correlation and causation.
"The result is both a celebration of humans' ability to make things better with careful thinking and a penetrating rebuke to muddleheadedness." —*Publishers Weekly*
Includes bibliographical references and index.

Shermer, Michael
The Believing Brain: From Ghosts and Gods to Politics and Conspiracies—How We Construct Beliefs and Reinforce Them as Truths. by Michael Shermer. Times Books 2011. 400 p.
ISBN 9780805091250
Grades: Adult   153.4
1. Belief and doubt 2. Theory of knowledge 3. Cognitive neuroscience 4. Neurology 5. Science Writing — Biology
LC 2010030706
Draws on three decades of research to outline a provocative theory about how humans form beliefs about the world, tracing the ways in which the brain finds patterns in sensory data that are then reinforced with meaning, in a report that explains how the author's findings apply to politics, economics and religion.
Includes bibliographical references and index.

Vedantam, Shankar
Useful Delusions: The Power and Paradox of the Self-Deceiving Brain. Shankar Vedantam and Bill Mesler. W. W. Norton & Company 2021. 264 p.
ISBN 9780393652208
Grades: Adult   153.4
1. Deception 2. Self-deception 3. Truthfulness and falsehood 4. Psychology 5. Human behavior 6. Delusions 7. Society and culture — Psychology and human behavior 8. Book club best bets
LC 2020028515
The lies we tell ourselves sustain our daily interactions with friends, lovers, and coworkers. They can explain why some people live longer than others, why some couples remain in love and others don't, why some nations hold together while others splinter.

ESSENTIAL AND RECOMMENDED TITLES
153.6 Communication

"This excellent narrative nonfiction work will engage a variety of readers, and is a solid choice for book clubs who like to discuss current events." —*Library Journal*

Includes bibliographical references and index.

153.6 Communication

Alda, Alan
If I Understood You, Would I Have This Look on My Face?: My Adventures in the Art and Science of Relating and Communicating. Alan Alda. Random House 2017. 224 p.
ISBN 9780812989144
Grades: Adult   **153.6**
1. Interpersonal communication 2. Interpersonal relations 3. Communication 4. Intuition 5. Empathy 6. Listening 7. Society and culture — Psychology and human behavior
LC 2016045922

The Emmy Award-winning actor and founder of the Alan Alda Center for Communicating Science traces his personal quest to understand and teach others how to relate and communicate better, from practicing empathy and using improv games to storytelling and developing better intuitive skills.

"A sharp and informative guide to communication."—*Kirkus*

Cameron, Julia
★ *The Listening Path: The Creative Art of Attention.* Julia Cameron. St. Martin's Essentials 2021. 190 pages
ISBN 9781250799746
Grades: Adult   **153.6**
1. Creativity 2. Listening 3. Attention 4. Mindfulness 5. Arts and Entertainment — General 6. Self-Help — Personal growth — Creativity
LC 2020035330

The Listening Path offers a new method of creative and personal transformation. Each week, readers will be challenged to expand their ability to listen in a new way, beginning by listening to their environment and culminating in learning to listen to silence. These weekly practices open up a new world of connection and fulfillment. In a culture of bustle and constant sound, The Listening Path is a deeply necessary reminder of the power of truly hearing.

"Cameron writes beautifully and sincerely. Although some readers may need to expand their belief systems, this is nevertheless a much-needed primer on opening ourselves to listening to others at a time when that is so badly needed." —*Booklist*

Includes index.

Corrigan, Kelly
Tell Me More: Stories About the 12 Hardest Things I'm Learning to Say. Kelly Corrigan. Random House 2018. 240 p.
ISBN 9780399588389
Grades: Adult   **153.6**
1. Corrigan, Kelly, 1967- 2. Interpersonal communication 3. Conversation 4. Interpersonal relations 5. Personal conduct 6. Autobiographies and memoirs 7. Life stories — Personal growth 8. Society and culture — Psychology and human behavior
LC BI2017045653

The best-selling author of Glitter and Glue assesses seven phrases that can lead to more qualitative adult lives, sharing poignant and whimsical stories of growth surrounding such expressions as "I don't know," "You got this" and "I was wrong."

"Moving and deeply personal, Corrigan's portraits of love and loss urge readers to speak more carefully and hold on tighter to the people they love." —*Kirkus*

Duhigg, Charles
★ *Supercommunicators: How to Unlock the Secret Language of Connection.* Charles Duhigg. Random House 2024. xviii, 299 p.
ISBN 9780593243916
Grades: Adult   **153.6**
1. Communication 2. Interpersonal communication 3. Interpersonal conflict 4. Conversation 5. Emotions 6. Listening 7. Problem solving 8. Social interaction 9. Social psychology 10. Society and culture — Psychology and human behavior 11. Business and economics — Popular psychology

Come inside a jury room as one juror leads a starkly divided room to consensus. Join a young CIA officer as he recruits a reluctant foreign agent. And sit with an accomplished surgeon as he tries, and fails, to convince yet another cancer patient to opt for the less risky course of treatment. In Supercommunicators, Charles Duhigg blends deep research and his trademark storytelling skills to show how we can all learn to identify and leverage the hidden layers that lurk beneath every conversation.

"A how-to-guide and useful overview for readers wanting to communicate more effectively…A timely primer for creating deeper connections with others." —*Library Journal*

Includes bibliographical references and index.

Headlee, Celeste Anne
We Need to Talk: How to Have Conversations That Matter. Celeste Headlee. Harper Wave 2017. xix, 244 pages
ISBN 9780062669018
Grades: Adult   **153.6**
1. Interpersonal communication 2. Conversation 3. Self-Help — Personal growth 4. Family and Relationships — General
LC 2017013596

From NPR veteran Celeste Headlee, an informative, timely, and practical guide to the lost art of conversation.

Includes bibliographical references (pages 237-244).

Murphy, Kate
You're Not Listening: What You're Missing and Why It Matters. Kate Murphy. Celadon Books 2020. VIII, 278 pages
ISBN 9781250297198
Grades: Adult   **153.6**
1. Listening 2. Interpersonal communication 3. Self-Help — Relationships 4. Society and culture — Sociology
LC 2019034095

A reporter exposes why our ultra-connected modern world leaves so many people feeling alone and suicidal, blaming it on a worldwide epidemic of not listening and describes how to re-learn this important skill.

Includes bibliographical references and index.

Pease, Allan
The Definitive Book of Body Language. Allan & Barbara Pease. Bantam Books 2006. 386 p.
ISBN 9780553804720
Grades: Adult   **153.6**
1. Body language 2. Communication 3. Sex differences 4. Family and Relationships — General

A guide to human body language explains how to decipher nonverbal communication, how to read other people's thoughts and emotions through their gestures, and how to insure that one's own gestures are sending the right message.

Sale, Anna
★ *Let's Talk About Hard Things.* Anna Sale. Simon & Schuster 2021. 352 p.
ISBN 9781501190247
Grades: Adult   **153.6**
1. Sale, Anna 2. Communication 3. Podcasters 4. Interpersonal relations 5. Reconciliation 6. Death 7. Desire 8. Money 9. Podcasts 10. Families 11. Identity 12. Autobiographies and memoirs 13. Society and culture — Psychology and human behavior 14. Life stories — Relationships 15. Life stories — Arts and Culture 16. Life stories — Personal growth

Sale uses the best of what she's learned from her podcast to reveal that when we have the courage to talk about hard things, we learn about ourselves, others, and the world that we make together. Diving into five of the most fraught conversation topics—death, sex, money, family, and identity—she moves between memoir, fascinating snapshots of a variety of Americans opening up about their lives, and expert opinions to show why having tough conversations is important and how to do them in a thoughtful and generous way.

"Not to be mistaken for a self-help guide, Sale's book also analyzes the structural and cultural dynamics that impede meaningful conversations. Besides listeners of her podcast, this will appeal to any adult struggling to broach these topics." —*Library Journal*

153.7 Perceptual processes

Ellard, Colin
You Are Here: Why We Can Find Our Way to the Moon but Get Lost in the Mall. Colin Ellard. Doubleday 2009. 240 p.
ISBN 9780385528061
Grades: Adult   153.7
1. Space perception 2. Geographical perception 3. Senses and sensation 4. Navigation 5. Science Writing — General 6. Travel Writing — General
LC 2009007822

Psychologist Colin Ellard explains how, over centuries of innovation, we have lost our instinctive ability to find our way and suggests that architects and city planners need to consider human behavior when designing human environments, and we all need to recognize that we are part of, not isolated from, the space around us.

"If you're looking for an eye-opening, if somewhat embarrassing, book to help understand why you keep getting lost when you know you shouldn't and what you can do about it well, here you are." —*Booklist*

Published in Canada as Where am I? : Why we can find our way to the moon but get lost in the mall: Toronto : HarperCollins Canada, 2009.

Goleman, Daniel
Focus: The Hidden Driver of Excellence. Daniel Goleman. Harper 2013. 256 p.
ISBN 9780062114860
Grades: Adult   153.7
1. Attention 2. Self-control 3. Success (Concept) 4. Thought and thinking 5. Distractions 6. Will 7. Science Writing — Medicine and health — Mental health
LC 2013007290

Drawing on cutting-edge research along with practical findings, this landmark book on the science of attention reveals what distinguishes experts from amateurs and stars from average performers, and urges readers to pay attention to what matters to them most.
Includes index.

Greenspan, Stanley I.
The First Idea: How Symbols, Language, and Intelligence Evolved from Our Primate Ancestors to Modern Humans. Stanley I. Greenspan, Stuart G. Shanker. Da Capo Press 2004. VIII, 504 p.
ISBN 9780738206806
Grades: Adult   153.7
1. Language arts and studies — Linguistics 2. Science writing — Medicine and health — Psychology
LC 2004010658

A noted child psychiatrist and a philosopher trace the evolution of thinking, language, and social skills among ancient primates and humans, linking these abilities not to genes and natural selection but to the development of cultural practices learned and relearned by each generation over the course of millions of years.

A Merloyd Lawrence book; Includes bibliographical references (p. 471-488) and index.

Odell, Jenny
★ *Saving Time: Discovering a Life Beyond the Clock*. Jenny Odell. Random House 2023. 384 p.
ISBN 9780593242704
Grades: Adult   153.7
1. Time 2. Work life balance 3. Time perception 4. Work 5. Leisure 6. Time management 7. Philosophy 8. Society and culture — Psychology and human behavior

In this thought-provoking, deeply hopeful reframing of time, the author takes us on a journey through other temporal habitats, urging us to become stewards of different rhythms of life, to imagine an existence, identity and source of meaning outside the world of work and profit.

"Saving Time is the rare book that does more than meet the current moment, it defines it. This will find a long life on any library's shelves." —*Booklist*

Pink, Daniel H.
When: The Scientific Secrets of Perfect Timing. Daniel H. Pink. Riverhead Books 2017. 256 p.
ISBN 9780735210622
Grades: Adult   153.7
1. Time 2. Time perception 3. Time management 4. Success (Concept) 5. Business and economics — Popular psychology
LC 2017033061

Illuminates the scientific factors that shape the hidden patterns of a day and challenge scheduled activities, drawing on research in the disciplines of psychology, biology, and economics to share practical advice and anecdotes for promoting a richer, more engaged life.

"Both those seeking this as a business resource and general readers interested in social psychology, time management, personal development, and decision making will find helpful, inspiring, and thoughtful advice from Pink." —*Booklist*

Smil, Vaclav
Size: How It Explains the World. Vaclav Smil. William Morrow & Co. 2023. 384 p.
ISBN 9780063324091
Grades: Adult   153.7
1. Size 2. Appearances 3. Mathematics 4. Physics 5. Engineering 6. Technology 7. Biological systems 8. Astrophysics 9. Society and culture — Psychology and human behavior 10. Science Writing — Physics 11. Science Writing — Biology 12. Science Writing — General

Size is the most fundamental structural variable of the universe. Neither bacteria nor empires are immune to its laws. Grounded in history and drawing on the latest science, with much recourse to art and classic literature, Size explains the regularities—and peculiarities—of the key processes shaping life (from microbes to whales), the Earth (from asteroids to volcanic eruptions), technical advances (from architecture to transportation), and societies and economies (from cities to wages). Vaclav Smil tackles a goliath subject and it is no exaggeration to say that this tour de force will change the way you look at absolutely everything.

"In this meandering investigation, Smil (Grand Transitions), a geography professor at the University of Manitoba, Canada, meditates on size and its relation to status, intelligence, wealth, and beauty." —*Publishers Weekly*

153.8 Will (Volition)

Ariely, Dan
Predictably Irrational: The Hidden Forces That Shape Our Decisions. Dan Ariely. Harper 2008. xxii, 280 p. : Illustration
ISBN 9780061353239
Grades: Adult   153.8
1. Reason 2. Human behavior 3. Decision-making 4. Practical reason 5. Logic 6. Consumer behavior 7. Irrationalism (Philosophy) 8. Personal conduct 9. Page to screen 10. Business and economics — Business Advice
New York Times Notable Book, 2008.

Ever wonder why something free is so hard to pass up, even if you don't need it and you have to stand in line to get it? It's this sort of odd behavior that author and professor Dan Ariely assesses in Predictably Irrational, using scientific stud-

ESSENTIAL AND RECOMMENDED TITLES
153.8 Will (Volition)

ies and behavioral economics to explain some of the reasons why we act and spend our money the way we do.

Made into a television show called the Irrational on Peacock, 2023; Includes bibliographical references (p. [259]-267) and index.

Cialdini, Robert B.
Influence: The Psychology of Persuasion. Robert B. Cialdini. Collins 2007. xiv, 320 p. : Illustration
ISBN 9780061241895
Grades: Adult   153.8
1. Influence (Psychology) 2. Persuasion (Psychology) 3. Science writing — Medicine and health — Psychology
LC Bl2007025274

"Cialdini's fascinating look into how opinions and behaviors are swayed by outside influence can help readers develop their own powers of persuasion. For all areas of life where influence is needed." —*Library Journal*

Includes bibliographical references (p. [281]-309) and index.

Dutton, Kevin
Split-Second Persuasion: The Ancient Art and New Science of Changing Minds. Kevin Dutton. Houghton Mifflin Harcourt 2011. 288 p.
ISBN 9780151012794
Grades: Adult   153.8
1. Persuasion (Psychology) 2. Change (Psychology) 3. Influence (Psychology) 4. Decision-making 5. Business and economics — Popular psychology
LC 2010005739

A respected psychologist presents an anecdotal analysis of the role of coercion in today's culture while introducing the tactics of leading persuasion experts, from magicians and religious leaders to advertisers and con men.

"This is a well-researched, wide-ranging treatise on the psychology of persuasion. The first section reviews research from an impressive variety of disciplines, from neuroscience to the biological and social sciences. The second section focuses on the author's main themes—split-second persuasion—a powerful superstrain of persuasion that occurs quickly. Written for a less-experienced audience, the book is clear and nontechnical." —*Choice*

First published in Great Britain in 2010 by William Heinemann—; Includes bibliographical references and index.

Dweck, Carol S.
★ *Mindset:* The New Psychology of Success. Carol S. Dweck. Random House 2006. x, 276 p.
ISBN 9781400062751
Grades: Adult   153.8
1. Belief and doubt 2. Success (Concept) 3. Science writing — Medicine and health — Psychology 4. Self-Help — Personal growth — Happiness
LC 2005046454

An authority in the fields of motivation and developmental psychology reveals how one's personal mindsets affect one's life, identifying two basic mindsets—the fixed and the growth—and how they control every aspect of one's life and explaining how to use the growth mindset at any stage of life to promote success and personal fulfillment.

Includes bibliographical references (p. [241]-266) and index.

Grant, Adam M.
Hidden Potential: The Science of Achieving Greater Things. Adam Grant. Viking 2023. 320 p.
ISBN 9780593653142
Grades: Adult   153.8
1. Achievement motivation 2. Motivation 3. Success (Concept) 4. Human behavior 5. Ability 6. Learning 7. Character 8. Self-actualization 9. Business and economics — Popular psychology 10. Society and culture — Psychology and human behavior
LC 2023020778

The #1 New York Times bestselling author of Think Again illuminates how we can elevate ourselves and others to unexpected heights.

"Writing with authority and clarity, Grant examines how talents can be discovered, developed, and turned into achievement." —*Kirkus*

Includes bibliographical references and index.

Iyengar, Sheena
The Art of Choosing. Sheena Iyengar. Twelve 2010. xiii, 329 p. : Illustration
ISBN 9780446504102
Grades: Adult   153.8
1. Options, alternatives, choices 2. Decision making 3. Human behavior 4. Psychology 5. Cognition 6. Society and culture — Psychology and human behavior
LC 2009037664

Discusses the cultural and biological factors that influence free will, addressing such issues as whether the desire for choice is innate or created by culture and how much control people have over their choices.

"In the Art of Choosing, a broad and fascinating survey of current research on the subject, Iyengar stitches together personal anecdotes, examples from popular culture, and scientific evidence to explain the complex calculus that goes into our everyday choices, from picking our favorite soda to choosing our medical insurance. She also writes about the ways in which her blindness Iyengar lost her sight as a teenager has given her a unique perspective on the subject." —*Salon*

Includes bibliographical references (p. [299]-315) and index.

Johnson, Steven
Farsighted: How We Make the Decisions That Matter the Most. Steven Johnson. Riverhead Books 2018. 272 p.
ISBN 9781594488214
Grades: Adult   153.8
1. Cognition 2. Decision-making 3. Thought and thinking 4. Reason 5. Science Writing — General
LC 2017060305

Draws on lessons from cognitive science, social psychology, military strategy, and other disciplines to discuss how to take a deliberative approach to making consequential, long-term decisions.

"Science writer Johnson (Wonderland: How Play Made the Modern World) looks at decision-making, on both the individual and collective level, persuasively arguing that it should be approached not intuitively, but deliberately, rationally, and even scientifically." —*Publishers Weekly*

Includes bibliographical references and index.

McGinnis, Patrick J.
Fear of Missing Out: Practical Decision-making in a World of Overwhelming Choice. Patrick J. McGinnis. Sourcebooks 2020. xvii, 236 pages : Illustration
ISBN 9781492694946
Grades: Adult   153.8
1. Decision making 2. Time management 3. Stress management 4. Self-Help — Personal growth — Happiness
LC 2019053664

A venture capitalist and private equity investor shares the scientific secrets to make any decision simple—while simultaneously eliminating your stress.

"This is a useful one-stop shop for those looking to take a decisive stand against the fear of what could have been." —*Publishers Weekly*

Includes bibliographical references (pages 217-226) and index.

McKeown, Greg
Essentialism: The Disciplined Pursuit of Less. Greg McKeown. Crown Business 2014. 260 pages : Illustration
ISBN 9780804137386
Grades: Adult   153.8
1. Decision making 2. Options, alternatives, choices 3. Business and economics — General 4. Self-Help — Personal growth
LC 2013038729

Outlines a systematic framework for enabling greater productivity without overworking, sharing strategies on how to eliminate unnecessary tasks while streamlining essential employee functions. By the co-author of the best-selling Multipliers.

Punctuated with zippy, thoughtful one-liners, this guide to doing 'less but better' offers strategies for determining what is truly necessary, and shedding what is not. Too many people fall for the having-it-all myth, and would benefit from shifting from a non-essentialist mindset (unable to distinguish and parse out the truly important) to an essentialist one (capable of identifying the goal), contends McKeown. Instead of attempting to achieve everything, readers need to figure out how to do the 'right thing the right way at the right time.' —*Publishers Weekly*

Includes bibliographical references and index.

Pryor, Karen
★ *Don't Shoot the Dog: The Art of Teaching and Training.* Karen Pryor. Simon & Schuster 2019. 213 p.
ISBN 9781982106461
Grades: Adult   153.8
1. Behavior modification 2. Behavior therapy 3. Animal behavior 4. Human behavior 5. Psychology 6. Animal training 7. Society and culture — Psychology and human behavior 8. Self-Help — General

Karen Pryor's clear and entertaining explanation of behavioral training methods made Don't Shoot the Dog a bestselling classic with revolutionary insights into animal—and human—behavior.... Pryor clearly explains the underlying principles of behavioral training and reveals how this art can be applied to virtually any common situation.... From the eight methods for putting an end to all kinds of undesirable behavior to the ten laws of "shaping" behavior, Pryor helps you combat your own addictions and deal with such difficult problems as a moody spouse, an impossible teen, or an aged parent.

Includes index.

Vanderbilt, Tom
You May Also Like: Taste in an Age of Endless Choice. by Tom Vanderbilt. Alfred A. Knopf 2016. 368 p.
ISBN 9780307958242
Grades: Adult   153.8
1. Options, alternatives, choices 2. Consumers' preferences 3. Social media 4. Brand choice 5. Public opinion 6. Business and economics — Popular psychology 7. Business and economics — Economics — Consumerism
LC 2015026997

From the best-selling author of Traffic, a brilliant and entertaining exploration of our personal tastes—why we like the things we like, and what it says about us.

"Essential for readers who are interested in getting a glimpse of the decision-making process at influential online media companies, as well as those who are interested in the processes that govern individual preferences and taste making." —*Library Journal*

Includes bibliographical references.

Weber, Charlotte Fox
Tell Me What You Want: A Therapist and Her Clients Explore Our 12 Deepest Desires. Charlotte Fox Weber. Atria Books 2023. 288 p.
ISBN 9781982170660
Grades: Adult   153.8
1. Purpose in life 2. Psychotherapist and patient 3. Desire 4. Emotions 5. Life 6. Interpersonal relations 7. Self-awareness 8. Personal conduct 9. Psychology 10. Psychotherapy 11. Society and culture — Psychology and human behavior 12. Debut title

Explores the 12 fundamental psychological needs we all share and goes behind the closed doors of therapy to guide us in navigating our deepest longings.

"Readers who enjoy pondering emotional intelligence and learning through storytelling will appreciate this book." —*Booklist*

153.9 Intelligence and aptitudes

Bloom, Harold
Genius: A Mosaic of One Hundred Exemplary Creative Minds. Harold Bloom. Warner Books 2002. xviii, 814 p. : Illustration
ISBN 9780446527170
Grades: Adult   153.9
1. Genius 2. Gifted people 3. Arts and Entertainment — General
LC 2002016808

Booklist Editors' Choice, 2002; New York Times Notable Book, 2002.

In a celebration of the greatest creative writers of all time, the literary critic explores the mysteries of genius as expressed in one hundred of the most creative minds in history, including Milton, Dante, and Whitman.

"Although the book is a delight to read, its real value lies in the author's ability to provoke the reader into thinking about literature, genius, and related topics. No similar work discusses literary genius in this way or covers this many writers." —*Library Journal*

Epstein, David J.
★ *Range: Why Generalists Triumph in a Specialized World.* David Epstein. Riverhead Books 2019. 352 pages
ISBN 9780735214484
Grades: Adult   153.9
1. Success (Concept) 2. Ability 3. Learning 4. Successful people 5. Creativity 6. Expertise 7. Skills 8. Doing things 9. Multiple intelligences 10. Learning by discovery 11. Self-discovery 12. Human behavior 13. High achievement 14. Achievement motivation 15. Society and culture — Psychology and human behavior 16. Business and economics — Popular psychology
LC 2018051571

Shares counterintuitive advice on the most effective path to success in any domain while revealing the essential contributions of generalist, not specialist, team members.

"Epstein follows up The Sports Gene, which explored the roots of elite sport performance, with this intriguing analysis of successful artists, musicians, inventors, forecasters, scientists, and athletes. The author's revelation is that generalists, not specialists, are more primed to excel, with generalists often finding their path late and participating in many interests." —*Library Journal*

Includes bibliographical references and index.

Ericsson, K. Anders
Peak: Secrets from the New Science of Expertise. Anders Ericsson and Robert Pool. Houghton Mifflin Harcourt 2016. xxiii, 307 pages
ISBN 9780544456235
Grades: Adult   153.9
1. Ability 2. Expertise 3. Performance 4. Science writing — Medicine and health — Psychology 5. Self-Help — Personal growth 6. Sports and Competition — General
LC 2015042796

Draws on the examples of chess champions, violin virtuosos, star athletes and memory mavens to outline a powerful approach to learning that enables readers to develop proficiency through strategic goal setting, self-motivation and feedback exercises.

An Eamon Dolan book; Includes index.

Gopnik, Adam
The Real Work: On the Mystery of Mastery. Adam Gopnik. Liveright Publishing Corporation 2023. 256 p.
ISBN 9781324090755
Grades: Adult   153.9
1. Gopnik, Adam 2. Art 3. Expertise 4. Creation (Literary, artistic, etc.) 5. Experts 6. Skills 7. Essays 8. Arts and entertainment — General 9. Society and culture — Psychology and human behavior

"In top form, Gopnik makes his subject intellectually and viscerally thrilling." —*Kirkus*

ESSENTIAL AND RECOMMENDED TITLES
154.2 The subconscious

Gould, Stephen Jay
The Mismeasure of Man. Stephen Jay Gould. Norton 1981. 352 p. : Illustration
ISBN 9780393314250
Grades: Adult   153.9
1. Intelligence tests 2. Intelligence 3. Personality tests 4. Science Writing — Biology
LC 81038430
National Book Critics Circle Award for Non-Fiction, 1981.
Exposes the fatal flaws in the ranking of people according to their supposed gifts and limits by discussing the development of the theory of limits and by reanalyzing the data on which it is based.
Includes bibliographical references (p. 337-344) and index.

Kurzweil, Ray
★ *The Singularity Is Near: When Humans Transcend Biology.* Ray Kurzweil. Viking 2005. xvii, 652 p. : Illustration
ISBN 9780670033843
Grades: Adult   153.9
1. Brain 2. Human evolution 3. Genetics 4. Nanotechnology 5. Robotics 6. Evolution 7. Science Writing — Biology
LC 2004061231
A controversial scientific vision predicts a time in which humans and machines will merge and create a new form of non-biological intelligence, explaining how the occurrence will solve such issues as pollution, hunger, and aging.
"Anyone can grasp Mr. Kurzweil's main idea: that mankind's technological knowledge has been snowballing, with dizzying prospects for the future. The basics are clearly expressed. But for those more knowledgeable and inquisitive, the author argues his case in fascinating detail." —*New York Times*
Includes bibliographical references and index.

Murdoch, Stephen
IQ: A Smart History of a Failed Idea. Stephen Murdoch. J. Wiley and Sons 2007. xiv, 269 p.
ISBN 9780471699774
Grades: 11 12 Adult   153.9
1. Intelligence 2. Intelligence tests 3. Standardized tests 4. Educational tests and measurements 5. History writing — Microhistory 6. Society and culture — Education
LC 2006032488
A thought-provoking study examines the history, politics, and implications of intelligence testing, from its origins to the present day, and discusses its powerful impact on both public policy and private lives, the well-documented shortcomings of testing, and suggestions for developing an entire new model for measuring intelligence.
Includes bibliographical references (p. 235-258) and index.

154.2 The subconscious

Bargh, John A
Before You Know It: The Unconscious Reasons We Do What We Do. John Bargh. Touchstone 2017. 320 p.
ISBN 9781501101212
Grades: Adult   154.2
1. Subconsciousness 2. Cognition 3. Motivation 4. Human behavior 5. Society and culture — Psychology and human behavior
LC 2017008149
A leading expert on the unconscious human mind draws on 20 years of research to present a tour of the influences that shape everyday behavior, combining engaging anecdotes with the stories of remarkable discoveries about the role of science in everything from relationships and parenting to consumer behavior and business.
"In this impressive debut, Bargh, a professor of social psychology at Yale University, dives deep into human behavior and social psychology to unlock the enigmatic human unconscious." —*Publishers Weekly*

Kandel, Eric R.
The Age of Insight: The Quest to Understand the Unconscious in Art, Mind, and Brain : From Vienna 1900 to the Present. Eric R. Kandel. Random House 2011. 448 p.
ISBN 9781400068715
Grades: Adult   154.2
1. Subconsciousness 2. Perception 3. Science and art 4. Neuroscience 5. Art history 6. European history 7. Vienna, Austria 8. 20th century 9. Arts and Entertainment — Painting, Drawing, and Sculpture 10. Science Writing — Biology 11. Arts and Entertainment — Writing and Publishing — Literary criticism
LC 2011025274
Booklist Editors' Choice 2011.
A Nobel Prize-winning neuroscientist and author of in Search of Memory documents the work of five leading minds including Sigmund Freud and Gustave Klimt in 1900 Vienna, revealing how their critical breakthroughs in science, medicine and art laid the groundwork for present-day discoveries in brain science.

154.6 Sleep phenomena

Freud, Sigmund
★ *The Interpretation of Dreams.* Sigmund Freud; translated by Joyce Crick; with an introduction and notes by Ritchie Robertson. Oxford University Press 2008. Liv, 458 p. : Illustration
ISBN 9780199537587
Grades: Adult   154.6
1. Dream interpretation 2. Psychoanalysis 3. Science writing — Medicine and health — Sleep 4. Science writing — Medicine and health — Psychology
LC Bl2010001661
Based on the original text, unmodified by Freud's later additions, presents a new translation of his psychoanalytic study of the function, sources, nature, and characteristics of dreams.
Includes bibliographic references (p. [xlviii]-li) and indexes; Reprint. Originally published: 1999.

155.2 Individual psychology

Aktipis, Athena
★ *A Field Guide to the Apocalypse: A Mostly Serious Guide to Surviving Our Wild Times.* Athena Aktipis; Illustrations by Neil Smith. Workman Publishing 2024. 256 p.
ISBN 9781523518258
Grades: Adult   155.2
1. Resilience 2. Fear 3. Survival 4. Preparedness 5. Safety 6. Cooperation 7. Natural disasters 8. Disasters 9. Security 10. Adventure writing — Natural disaster
LC 2023048964
Drawing on evolutionary psychology, history, brain science, game theory, and more, cooperation theorist (and, coincidentally, zombie expert) Athena Aktipis reassuringly explains how we, as a species, are hardwired to survive big existential crises. And how we can do so again by leveraging our innate abilities to communicate and cooperate. Pack a ukulele in your prep kit. Practice your risk-management skills. Enlist your crew into a survival team. And embrace the apocalypse. You might just enjoy it. Plus, it will help us build a better and more resilient future for all humankind.—.
"This feel-good book about the end of human existence comes just in time to remedy the winter doldrums…Aktipis' advice seems a sensible response to it all." —*Booklist*
Includes bibliographical references and index.

Bluestein, Jane
The Perfection Deception: Why Trying to Be Perfect Is Sabotaging Your Relationships, Making You Sick, and Holding Your Happiness Hostage. Jane Bluestein. Health Communications, Inc. 2015. xii, 299 pages

PUBLIC LIBRARY CORE COLLECTION: NONFICTION
Twentieth Edition

ISBN 9780757318252
Grades: Adult   155.2
1. Psychology 2. Self-help techniques 3. Perfectionism 4. Self-Help — Personal growth — Self-esteem

LC 2015027944

"According to educator and author Bluestein (Creating Emotionally Safe Schools), striving for excellence and striving for perfection are two very different animals. While the former means dedicating oneself to doing one's best, the latter involves being motivated by something artificial and unrealistic." —*Publishers Weekly*

Includes bibliographical references (pages 265-299) and index.

Cain, Susan
★ *Bittersweet: How Sorrow and Longing Make Us Whole.* by Susan Cain. Crown 2022. 288 p.
ISBN 9780451499783
Grades: Adult   155.2
1. Sadness 2. Melancholy 3. Emotions 4. Interpersonal relations 5. Grief 6. Desire 7. Intergenerational trauma 8. Book club best bets 9. Society and culture — Psychology and human behavior

LC 2021053380

The author of the best-selling Quiet discusses how a bittersweet state of mind can actually be a kind of silent energy that aids us in overcoming our personal and societal suffering.

"Timely in its focus, this latest work by Cain delivers an eloquent and compelling case supporting the transformative possibilities of embracing sorrow. Highly recommended." —*Library Journal*

Includes bibliographical references and index.

Quiet: The Power of Introverts in a World That Can't Stop Talking. Susan Cain. Crown 2012. 320 p.
ISBN 9780307352149
Grades: Adult   155.2
1. Interpersonal relations 2. Introversion 3. Introverts 4. Science Writing — General 5. Family and Relationships — General

LC 2010053204

Goodreads Choice Award, 2012; Library Journal Best Books, 2012; ALA Notable Book, 2013.

Demonstrates how introverted people are misunderstood and undervalued in modern culture, charting the rise of extrovert ideology while sharing anecdotal examples of how to use introvert talents to adapt to various situations.

Includes bibliographical references.

Crawford, Matthew B.
The World Beyond Your Head: On Becoming an Individual in an Age of Distraction. Matthew B. Crawford. Farrar Straus & Giroux 2015. 288 p.
ISBN 9780374292980
Grades: Adult   155.2
1. Skills 2. Philosophy 3. Individualism 4. Attention 5. Handicraft 6. Quality of life 7. Consumerism 8. Personal conduct 9. Commercialization 10. Common good 11. Business and economics — Popular psychology

LC 2014043840

Investigates the challenge of mastering one's own mind by showing that our current crisis of attention is only superficially the result of digital technology, and certain assumptions at the root of Western culture are the root of the cause.

"This illuminating work will appeal to students of philosophy and sociology, as well as fans of good cultural analysis." —*Library Journal*

Dimitrius, Jo-Ellan
Reading People: How to Understand People and Predict Their Behavior— Anytime, Anyplace. Jo-Ellan Dimitrius and Mark Mazzarella. Random House 1998. xiv, 281 p.
ISBN 9780345425874
Grades: Adult   155.2
1. Body language 2. Physiognomy 3. Science writing — Medicine and health — Psychology

LC 98004934

In a New York Times best-seller, the nation's leading jury consultant shows readers how to analyze others' true thoughts and predict their behavior by deciphering the hidden signals they give off.

"Dimitrius shares the people-reading techniques she developed over 15 years as a jury consultant. In so doing, she provides a wealth of tips and strategies for ferreting out people's real viewpoints, motives and character traits." —*Publishers Weekly*

Durvasula, Ramani
★ *It's Not You: Identifying and Healing from Narcissistic People.* Ramani Durvasula, PhD.. The Open Field/Penguin Life 2024. xxviii, 333 pages
ISBN 9780593492628
Grades: Adult   155.2
1. Narcissism 2. Autonomy 3. Emotional abuse 4. Self-Help — Mental health 5. Family and Relationships — Abuse 6. Society and culture — Psychology and human behavior

LC 2023040075

A clinical psychologist and professor examines how the narcissists in your life can hijack your wellbeing and demonstrates how to become gaslight resistant, create realistic boundaries, learn discernment and protect yourself from their toxic influence.

"Helpful counsel for emotional survival." —*Kirkus*

Includes bibliographical references (pages 313-317)and index.

Ehrenreich, Barbara
Bright-Sided: How the Relentless Promotion of Positive Thinking Has Undermined America. Barbara Ehrenreich. Henry Holt and Company 2009. 256 p.
ISBN 9780805087499
Grades: Adult   155.2
1. Optimism 2. Happiness 3. Self-confidence 4. Success in business 5. Motivation 6. United States 7. Society and culture — Psychology and human behavior

LC 2009023588

The best-selling author of Bait and Switch exposes the downside of America's penchant for positive thinking, which she believes leads to self-blame and a preoccupation with stamping out "negative" thoughts on a personal level, and, on a national level, has brought on economic disaster.

"The author's tough-minded and convincing broadside raises troubling questions about many aspects of contemporary American life. Bright, incisive, provocative thinking." —*Kirkus*

Includes bibliographical references and index.

Gladwell, Malcolm
David and Goliath: Underdogs, Misfits, and the Art of Battling Giants. Malcolm Gladwell. Little Brown & Co. 2013. 304 p.
ISBN 9780316204361
Grades: Adult   155.2
1. Success (Concept) 2. Goals and objectives 3. Strength and weakness 4. Business and economics — Popular psychology 5. Society and culture — Psychology and human behavior

LC 2013941807

Booklist Editors' Choice, 2013.

The best-selling author of Outliers uncovers the hidden rules that shape the balance between the weak and the mighty, the powerful and the dispossessed.

"Gladwell rewards readers with moving stories, surprising insights and consistently provocative ideas." —*Kirkus*

Goldsmith, Marshall
Triggers: Creating Behavior That Lasts— Becoming the Person You Want to Be. Marshall Goldsmith and Mark Reiter. Crown Business 2015. xix, 244 pages : Illustration
ISBN 9780804141239
Grades: Adult   155.2
1. Adjustment 2. Change (Psychology) 3. Positive psychology 4. Self-Help — Personal growth

LC Bl2015018578

ESSENTIAL AND RECOMMENDED TITLES
155.2 Individual psychology

Demonstrates how to recognize and overcome the emotional and psychological triggers that set off a reaction or a behavior that often is detrimental in order to achieve meaningful and sustained change.

Includes index.

Greitens, Eric
Resilience: Hard-Won Wisdom for Living a Better Life. Eric Greitens. Mariner Books / Houghton Mifflin Harcourt 2016. xii, 301 pages : Illustration
ISBN 9780544705265
Grades: Adult 155.2
1. Resilience 2. Life skills 3. Self-help techniques 4. Personal conduct 5. Friendship 6. Coping 7. Veterans 8. Post-traumatic stress disorder 9. Autobiographies and memoirs 10. Life stories — Law and order — Armed forces personnel 11. Life stories — Personal growth

A masterpiece of warrior wisdom that shows how to overcome obstacles with positive action. The best-selling author, Navy SEAL, and humanitarian Eric Greitens offers a self-help book unlike any other. Two years ago, Eric Greitens unexpectedly heard from a former SEAL comrade, a brother-in-arms he hadn't seen in a decade. Drew Sheets had been one of the toughest of the tough. But ever since he returned home from war to his young family in a small logging town, he'd been struggling. Without a sense of purpose, plagued by PTSD, and masking his pain with heavy drinking, he needed help. Drew and Eric started writing and talking nearly every day, and Eric set down his thoughts on what it takes to build resilience in our lives. Eric's letters—drawing on both his own experience and wisdom from ancient and modern thinkers—are now gathered and edited into a timeless handbook. They explain how we can build purpose, confront the pain in our lives, practice compassion, develop our vocations, find a mentor, create happiness, follow a role model, think about the story of our lives, and much more. Resilience grapples with real hardship. The lessons are deep, yet practical, and the advice leads to clear solutions. This is a profoundly hopeful book: We all face pain, difficulty, and doubt. But with resilience, we can lead vital, flourishing lives.

"Based on the practices he suggests to build compassion, confront pain and create happiness, readers can move beyond their fears and create creative, energized lives rich in wisdom and filled with friendships and mentorships. Robust, heart-to-heart lessons for moving beyond obstacles to create a better life." —*Kirkus*

Includes bibliographical references (pages 281-301).

Helgoe, Laurie A.
Introvert Power: Why Your Inner Life Is Your Hidden Strength. Laurie Helgoe. Sourcebooks 2008. xxiv, 256 p. : Illustration
ISBN 9781402211171
Grades: Adult 155.2
1. Introversion 2. Introverts 3. Self-Help — Personal growth
LC 2008004967

Shows readers how to use introversion not as a weakness but as a source of power.

"The author's voice is vivid and engaging, and she skillfully draws real-life examples of awkward scenarios introverts find themselves in when forced to play a role in society or the workplace. Readers will find much insight, as well as a comforting sense of being understood and validated." —*Publishers Weekly*

Includes bibliographical references (p. [240]-245) and index.

Keltner, Dacher
Born to Be Good: The Science of a Meaningful Life. Dacher Keltner. W. W. Norton 2009. 352 p.
ISBN 9780393065121
Grades: Adult 155.2
1. Emotions 2. Helpfulness 3. Altruism 4. Cooperation 5. Interpersonal relations 6. Personal conduct 7. Good and evil 8. Science Writing — Biology
LC 2008042492

An optimistic assessment of humanity's biological predisposition for goodness draws on scientific findings, personal narrative, and eastern philosophy to explain how positive emotions are a key component of ethical action, the establishment of cooperative societies, and living a happy life."

"A landmark book in the science of emotion and its implications for ethics and human universals, this is essential for all libraries." —*Library Journal*

Lifford, Tina
The **Little** *Book of Big Lies: A Journey into Inner Fitness.* Tina Lifford. Amistad 2019. 224 pages
ISBN 9780062930286
Grades: Adult 155.2
1. Self-awareness 2. Self-acceptance 3. Self-care 4. Emotions 5. Dishonesty 6. Mental health 7. Self-esteem 8. African Americans 9. Actors and actresses 10. Autobiographies and memoirs 11. Book club best bets 12. Life stories — Personal growth 13. Life stories — Facing adversity — Personal transformation 14. Life stories — Arts and culture — Performing arts — Actors and actresses 15. Society and culture — Psychology and human behavior 16. Adult books for young adults
LC 2019015110

An actress, playwright and CEO of a personal development network offers insights and practical advice for nurturing our inner selves and building emotional strength so that old pain can be turned into power and we can thrive.

Lowery, Brian S.
Selfless: The Social Creation of You. Brian Lowery. HarperCollins 2023. 400 p.
ISBN 9780062913005
Grades: Adult 155.2
1. Identity 2. Social psychology 3. Interpersonal relations 4. Social groups 5. Collective behavior 6. Society and culture — Pop culture 7. Society and culture — Psychology and human behavior 8. Society and culture — Philosophy

Social psychologist and Stanford professor Brian Lowery presents a provocative, powerful theory of identity, arguing that there is no essential "self"—our selves are social creations of those with whom we interact—exploring what that means for who we can be and who we allow others to be.

"An informed, thought-provoking consideration of the relational dimensions of our lives." —*Kirkus*

McKay, Matthew
Self-Esteem: A Proven Program of Cognitive Techniques for Assessing, Improving, & Maintaining Your Self-Esteem. Matthew McKay, PHD, Patrick Fanning. New Harbinger Publications, Inc. 2016. VII, 358 pages : Illustration
ISBN 9781626253933
Grades: Adult 155.2
1. Acceptance and commitment therapy 2. Behavior therapy 3. Self-esteem 4. Self-help psychology 5. Self-Help — Personal growth — Self-esteem
LC 2016461087

The go-to guide for those seeking to increase their sense of self-worth. This fully revised new edition features an innovative application of acceptance and commitment therapy (ACT) to self-esteem and utilizes updated cognitive behavioral therapy (CBT) to help readers create positive change and thrive.

Includes bibliographical references (pages 357-358).

Moran, Joe
Shrinking Violets: The Secret Life of Shyness. Joe Moran. Yale University Press 2017. 272 pages
ISBN 9780300222821
Grades: Adult 155.2
1. History writing — General 2. Life stories — Identity 3. Science writing — Medicine and health — Psychology
LC 2016948565

A deeply perceptive and beautifully written cultural history of shyness, from one of our most astute observers of the everyday.

First published in the English language in a different form by Profile Books.—Title page verso; Includes bibliographical references (pages 237-254) and index.

PUBLIC LIBRARY CORE COLLECTION: NONFICTION
Twentieth Edition

Myers, David G.
How Do We Know Ourselves?: Curiosities and Marvels of the Human Mind. David G. Myers. Farrar, Straus and Giroux 2022. 160 p.
ISBN 9780374601959
Grades: Adult   **155.2**
1. Psychology 2. Human behavior 3. Self 4. Everyday life 5. Interpersonal relations 6. Essays 7. Society and culture — Psychology and human behavior
LC 2022023782

A delightful tour of the wonders of our humanity from David G. Myers, the award-winning professor and author of psychology's bestselling textbook.

"Myers's bite-size treatment of the current state of social psychology research makes for a quick and illuminating overview of the human mind." —*Publishers Weekly*

Includes bibliographical references.

Myers, Isabel Briggs
Gifts Differing: Understanding Personality Type. Isabel Briggs Myers with Peter B. Myers. Davies-Black Pub. 1995. xv, 228 p.
ISBN 9780891060741
Grades: Adult   **155.2**
1. Typology (Psychology) 2. Science writing — Medicine and health — Psychology
LC 95004184

The classic work on the 16 major personality types as identified in the Myers-Briggs Type Indicator.

Includes bibliographical references and index; Originally published: Palo Alto, CA : Consulting Psychologists Press, c1980.

Northrup, Christiane
Dodging Energy Vampires: An Empath's Guide to Evading Relationships That Drain You and Restoring Your Health and Power. Christiane Northrup, M.D.. Hay House, Inc. 2018. xii, 230 pages
ISBN 9781401954772
Grades: Adult   **155.2**
1. Empathy 2. Mental health 3. Well-being 4. Sensitivity (Personal quality) 5. Spirituality and Religion — Body, mind, and spirit 6. Self-Help — General 7. Self-Help — Personal growth
LC 2017048779

A guide to identifying and avoiding the most common types of "energy vampires," offers tactics for leaving harmful relationships behind, regaining energy, and becoming happier, wealthier, and more vibrant.

This guide for highly sensitive, empathic people helps them identify and avoid the most common types of "energy vampires" who will feed off their energy to fuel their dysfunctional lives, resulting in health, emotional and financial problems.

Includes bibliographical references (pages 211-214) and index.

Pinker, Steven
The Blank Slate: The Modern Denial of Human Nature. Steven Pinker. Viking 2002. xvi, 509 p. : Illustration
ISBN 9780670031511
Grades: Adult   **155.2**
1. Heredity and environment (Psychology) 2. Human nature 3. Genetic psychology 4. Evolution 5. Cognition 6. Science Writing — Biology
LC 2002022719

New York Times Notable Book, 2002; Pulitzer Prize for General Nonfiction finalist.

In a study of the nature versus nurture debate, one of the world's foremost experts on language and the mind explores the modern self-denial of our basic human natures.

"The author attacks the notion that an infant's mind is a blank slate, arguing instead that human beings have an inherited universal structure shaped by the demands made upon the species for survival, albeit with plenty of room for cultural and individual variation." —*Publishers Weekly*

Includes bibliographical references (p.461-489) and index.

Seligman, Martin E. P.
★ *Learned Optimism: How to Change Your Mind and Your Life.* Martin E.P. Seligman. Vintage Books 2006. x, 319 p.
ISBN 9781400078394
Grades: Adult   **155.2**
1. Optimism 2. Self-fulfillment 3. Science writing — Medicine and health — Psychology 4. Self-Help — Personal growth — Happiness
LC 2006277713

An authority on cognitive psychology and motivation documents the positive effects of optimism on the quality of life and provides a program of specific exercises designed to break the pessimism habit while developing an optimistic outlook.

Includes bibliographical references (p. [293]-303) and index; Originally published: Pocket Books, 1998.

Storr, Will
Selfie: How We Became so Self-Obsessed and What It's Doing to Us. Will Storr. Overlook Press 2018. 416 p.
ISBN 9781468315899
Grades: Adult   **155.2**
1. Self 2. Identity 3. Perfectionism 4. Self-fulfillment 5. Individualism 6. Self-reliance 7. Society and culture — Psychology and human behavior
LC Bl2017052046

The Amnesty International Award-winning investigative journalist and author of the Unpersuadables examines how our world's establishment of an impossible standard of perfection is leading to unprecedented levels of depression and suicide, tracing the sources of unrealistic human ideals from the ancient world to the present realities of hyper-individualism.

Includes index.

Stout, Martha
Outsmarting the Sociopath Next Door: How to Protect Yourself Against a Ruthless Manipulator. Martha Stout, Ph.D.. Harmony Books 2020. 294 p.
ISBN 9780307589071
Grades: Adult   **155.2**
1. Psychopaths 2. Control 3. Science writing — Medicine and health — Psychology 4. Self-Help — General
LC 2019024151

From Dr. Martha Stout's influential work The Sociopath Next Door, we learned how to identify a sociopath. Now she tells us what to actually do about it. Using the many chilling and often heartbreaking emails and letters she has received over the years, Dr. Stout uncovers the psychology behind the sociopath's methods and provides concrete guidelines to help navigate these dangerous interactions.

Includes bibliographical references (pages 265-279) and index.

Van Bavel, Jay J.
The Power of Us: Harnessing Our Shared Identities to Improve Performance, Increase Cooperation, and Promote Social Harmony. Jay J. Van Bavel, PhD, and, Dominic J. Packer, PhD.. Little Brown Spark 2021. 272 p.
ISBN 9780316538411
Grades: Adult   **155.2**
1. Identity 2. Social psychology 3. Group identity 4. Human behavior 5. Society and culture — Psychology and human behavior

A revolutionary new understanding of identity, showing how our groups have a powerful influence on our feelings, beliefs, and behavior—and how these shared identities can inspire both personal change and social movements.

"Providing a wealth of insight in a page-turning package, this timely survey hits the mark." —*Publishers Weekly*

Includes bibliographical references and index.

ESSENTIAL AND RECOMMENDED TITLES
155.24 Adaptability and adjustment

155.24 Adaptability and adjustment

Clear, James
★ *Atomic* Habits: An Easy & Proven Way to Build Good Habits & Break Bad Ones. James Clear. Avery 2018. 352 p.
ISBN 9780735211292
Grades: Adult 155.24
1. Human behavior 2. Personal conduct 3. Success (Concept) 4. Behavior modification 5. Business and economics — Popular psychology 6. Self-Help — General
One of the world's leading experts on habit formation reveals practical strategies that will teach readers exactly how to form good habits, break bad ones and master the tiny behaviors that lead to remarkable results.

155.3 Sex psychology; psychology of people by gender or sex, by sexual orientation

Brodeur, Michael Andor
★ *Swole:* The Making of Men and the Meaning of Muscle. Michael Andor Brodeur. Beacon Press 2024. 224 p.
ISBN 9780807059364
Grades: Adult 155.3
1. Masculinity 2. Body image 3. Bodybuilding 4. Weight lifting 5. Society and culture — Gender — Men 6. Sports and Competition — General
LC 2023051016
From a Washington Post critic and self-described meathead: a witty, incisive, poignant exploration of male body image, from the history of the gym to the politics of superheroes to the world of manfluencers.
"Brodeur debuts with a winsome and insightful blend of cultural history and memoir…Punchy, entertaining, and perceptive, this delivers." —*Publishers Weekly*
Includes bibliographical references.

Chemaly, Soraya L.
Rage Becomes Her: The Power of Women's Anger. Soraya Chemaly. Atria Books 2018. 416 p.
ISBN 9781501189555
Grades: Adult 155.3
1. Feminism 2. Social change 3. Sexism 4. Sex discrimination 5. Women's rights 6. Gender equity 7. Anger 8. Society and culture — Gender — Women 9. Society and culture — Social activism and philanthropy 10. Adult books for young adults
LC 2018010867
The director of the Women's Media Center Speech Project urges 21st-century women to embrace their anger and harness it as a tool for lasting personal and societal change.

Eldredge, Niles
Why We Do It: Rethinking Sex and the Selfish Gene. Niles Eldredge. Norton 2004. 269 p; Illustration
ISBN 9780393050820
Grades: Adult 155.3
1. Sex (Biology) 2. Sociobiology 3. Human evolution 4. Science Writing — Biology
LC 2003027564
An evolutionary biologist argues against the belief that sexual behavior is governed by genes, identifying an intricate interplay among humans that involves day-to-day survival, reproduction, and learned cultural factors.
"This book, while written for the lay reader, is appropriate for a scientific audience as well. It could be used as supplementary reading in college courses in animal behavior." —*Science Books & Films*
Includes bibliographical references (p. [237]-258) and index.

Filipovic, Jill
The H-Spot: The Feminist Pursuit of Happiness. Jill Filipovic. Nation Books 2017. 288 p.
ISBN 9781568585475
Grades: Adult 155.3
1. Women 2. Feminist theory 3. Happiness 4. Gender role 5. Feminism 6. Gender wars 7. Social norms 8. Intersectionality 9. Psychology 10. Society and culture — Gender — Women
LC 2016050782
Challenging misperceptions about how today's feminists must work harder or make difficult compromises to achieve fulfillment and happiness, a former Guardian columnist and senior political writer for Cosmopolitan.Com identifies irregular cultural and professional expectations that continue to enforce gender divides.
"A timely, enlightening exploration of what American women truly want and need to live purposeful, fulfilling, happy lives." —*Kirkus*
Includes bibliographical references.

Fine, Cordelia
Testosterone Rex: Myths of Sex, Science, and Society. Cordelia Fine. W.W. Norton & Company 2017. 320 p.
ISBN 9780393082081
Grades: Adult 155.3
1. Brain 2. Gender role 3. Sex differences 4. Cognitive science 5. Sex (Biology) 6. Neuropsychology 7. Men 8. Women 9. Science Writing — Biology 10. Society and culture — Gender
LC 2016031608
Royal Society General Prizes for Science Books, 2017.
The acclaimed author of Delusions of Gender challenges conventional beliefs about evolutionary factors that are used to justify gender politics, outlining lively arguments against cultural stereotypes, in a call for a more equal society that recognizes the potential of both sexes.
Includes bibliographical references and index.

Hackman, Rose
★ *Emotional* Labor: The Invisible Work Shaping Our Lives and How to Claim Our Power. Rose Hackman. Flatiron Books 2023. 304 p.
ISBN 9781250777355
Grades: Adult 155.3
1. Women 2. Psychology 3. Work 4. Mental health 5. Emotions 6. Feminism 7. Society and culture — Gender — Women 8. Family and relationships — General
LC 2022033809
A groundbreaking and deeply researched into the history and current state of "emotional labor"—the invisible, uncompensated work women and minorities are expected to perform every day.
Expertly blending case studies and statistics, this is a profound call for reorienting 'Our fundamental value systems.' —*Publishers Weekly*
Includes bibliographical references.

Hartley, Gemma
Fed Up: Emotional Labor, Women, and the Way Forward. Gemma Hartley. HarperOne 2018. 272 p.
ISBN 9780062855985
Grades: Adult 155.3
1. Emotions 2. Division of labor 3. Sex differences 4. Sexism 5. Feminism 6. Gender role 7. Stress 8. Society and culture — Gender — Women
LC 2018033285
Asserts that carrying the thankless day-to-day anticipating of needs and solving of problems large and small is adversely affecting women's lives and feeding gender inequality, and shows the way forward for better balancing their lives.
Includes bibliographical references.

Jamieson, Alexandra
Women, Food, and Desire: Embrace Your Cravings, Make Peace with Food, Reclaim Your Body. Alexandra Jamieson. Gallery Books 2015. IX, 243 pages

ISBN 9781476765044
Grades: Adult   155.3
1. Body image 2. Self-actualization 3. Women 4. Psychology 5. Nutrition 6. Science writing — Medicine and health 7. Science writing — Medicine and health — Women's health 8. Self-Help — Personal growth — Happiness
LC 2014016467

A transformational health expert and co-star of the documentary Super Size Me describes how actually listening to our body's cravings can help cleanse the nutritional, emotional, physical and mental blocks that are preventing happiness.

Moran, Caitlin

What About Men?: A Feminist Answers the Question. Caitlin Moran. HarperCollins 2023. 320 p.
ISBN 9780062893741
Grades: Adult   155.3
1. Men 2. Masculinity 3. Gender role 4. Gender identity 5. Society and culture — Gender — Men

Attempting to answer society's weirdly unasked question: What About Men?, the New York Times best-selling author, interviewing men in her orbit, bringing up very difficult and candid topics and receiving vulnerable and honest responses about perceptions and expectations, opens a genuinely new debate about how to reboot masculinity for the 21st century.

"Insightful nuggets of truth and practical wisdom mix with the snorts and sputters of laughter, making this a worthwhile, enjoyable, and timely read." —*Booklist*

Strings, Sabrina

The End of Love: Racism, Sexism, and the Death of Romance. Sabrina Strings. Beacon Press 2023. 256 p.
ISBN 9780807008621
Grades: Adult   155.3
1. Masculinity 2. Men 3. Identity 4. Psychology 5. African American women 6. Interpersonal relations 7. Love 8. Racism 9. Sexism 10. Society and culture — General 11. Family and relationships — Dating and Marriage
LC 2023028250

From Playboy to Jay Z, the racial origins of toxic masculinity and its impact on women, especially Black and "insufficiently white" women.

"Strings's personal testimonies about terrible dating situations and experiences of sexual assault are impactful, but her solutions—embracing queerness and nonromantic love—feel underdeveloped. The results are more provocative that persuasive." —*Publishers Weekly*

Includes bibliographical references and index.

Zimmerman, Jess

Women and Other Monsters: Building a New Mythology. Jess Zimmerman. Beacon Press 2020. 224 p.
ISBN 9780807054932
Grades: Adult   155.3
1. Zimmerman, Jess 2. Misogyny 3. Femininity 4. Monsters 5. Mythology, Greek 6. Characters and characteristics in mythology 7. Gender role 8. Expectation 9. Feminism 10. Men-women relations 11. Self-esteem 12. Society and culture — Gender — Women 13. Mythology, folklore, and legends
LC 2020045208

The folklore that has shaped our dominant culture teems with frightening female creatures. In our language, in our stories (many written by men), we underline the idea that women who step out of bounds—who are angry or greedy or ambitious, who are overtly sexual or not sexy enough—aren't just outside the norm. They're unnatural. Monstrous. But maybe, the traits we've been told make us dangerous and undesirable are actually our greatest strengths. Through fresh analysis of eleven female monsters, including Medusa, the Harpies, the Furies, and the Sphinx, Jess Zimmerman takes us on an illuminating feminist journey through mythology. She guides women (and others) to reexamine their relationships with traits like hunger, anger, ugliness, and ambition, teaching readers to embrace a new image of the female hero: one that looks a lot like a monster, with the agency and power to match.

"Zimmerman's wit and eloquence, as well as her understanding of these myths, make for persuasive and empowering reading that will have women embracing their inner monsters." —*Library Journal*

Includes bibliographical references and index.

155.4 Psychology of specific ages

Asika, Uju

Bringing up Race: How to Raise a Kind Child in a Prejudiced World. Uju Asika. Sourcebooks 2021. 339 p.
ISBN 9781728238562
Grades: Adult   155.4
1. Antiracism 2. Parenting 3. Child rearing 4. Empathy 5. Race awareness in children 6. Kindness 7. Social justice 8. Antiracist literature 9. Family and relationships — Parenting 10. Society and culture — Race
LC 2020058262

Bringing up Race is an important book, for all families, whatever their race or ethnicity. It's for everyone who wants to instill a sense of open-minded inclusivity in their kids, and those who want to discuss difference instead of shying away from tough questions.

"This is a must-read for parents, educators, and anyone looking to raise kinder children." —*Publishers Weekly*

Includes bibliographical references (pages 295-311) and index.

Carey, Tanith

What's My Child Thinking?: Practical Child Psychology for Modern Parents. Tanith Carey; contributing editor, Eileen Kennedy-Moore, PhD... DK 2019. 256 p. : Illustration; Color
ISBN 9781465479372
Grades: Adult   155.4
1. Child psychology 2. Parenting 3. Parent and child 4. Science writing — Medicine and health — Psychology 5. Family and Relationships — Growing up 6. Family and Relationships — Parenting
LC 2018287451

Find out what your child really means when he says "Look what I did," "But I'm not tired," or "You're embarrassing me," and discover what's really going on when he can't express himself at all. Using more than 100 everyday scenarios, the book leads you through each one step by step, explaining not only your child's behavior and the psychology behind it but also your own feelings as a parent. It then gives instant recommendations for what you could say and do in response to best resolve the situation. Covering all your child's developmental milestones from ages 2 to 7 years, What's My Child Thinking? covers important issues, such as temper tantrums, friendships (real and imaginary), sibling rivalry, aggressive behavior, and peer pressure. There's also a bank of practical "survival guides" for critical times, such as traveling in the car, eating out, and going online safely. Rooted in evidence-based clinical psychology and championing positive parenting, What's My Child Thinking? will help you tune in to your child's innermost thoughts and be the parent you want to be.

For ages 2 to 7 — on cover; Includes bibliographical references (pages 246-249) and index.

Elkind, David

The Power of Play: How Spontaneous, Imaginative Activities Lead to Happier, Healthier Children. David Elkind. Da Capo Lifelong 2007. xii, 240 p.
ISBN 9780738210537
Grades: Adult   155.4
1. Play 2. Family and Relationships — Parenting 3. Science writing — Medicine and health — Psychology
LC 2006035592

"With clarity and insight, Elkind calls for society to bring back long recesses, encourage imagination and let children develop their minds at a natural pace." —*Publishers Weekly*

Includes bibliographical references (p. 221-227) and index.

ESSENTIAL AND RECOMMENDED TITLES
155.4 Psychology of specific ages

Galanti, Regine
★ *Parenting* Anxious Kids: Understanding Anxiety in Children by Age and Stage. Regine Galanti, PhD.. Sourcebooks 2024. xvii, 295 pages : Illustration
ISBN 9781728273020
Grades: Adult   155.4
1. Anxiety in children 2. Anxiety 3. Teenagers 4. Parenting 5. Family and Relationships — Parenting 6. Science Writing — Medicine and health — Children's health 7. Science Writing — Medicine and health — Psychology
LC 2023028425

In this complete guide for parenting kids with anxiety, a licensed clinical psychologist provides research-based tips and actionable steps for raising resilient, independent and healthy children despite childhood anxieties.
"This very practical, accessible book will be welcomed by parents trying to help their children ease into independence at any age." —*Booklist*
Includes bibliographical references (pages 273-280) and index.

Gopnik, Alison
The Gardener and the Carpenter: What the New Science of Child Development Tells Us About the Relationship Between Parents and Children. Alison Gopnik. Farrar, Straus and Giroux 2016. 224 p.
ISBN 9780374229702
Grades: Adult   155.4
1. Developmental psychology 2. Child psychology 3. Parenting 4. Parent and child 5. Child rearing 6. Family and Relationships — Parenting 7. Society and culture — Psychology and human behavior
LC 2015048667

A developmental psychologist uses natural history and the latest scientific research to demonstrate how the modern style of parenting, one of obsessively controlling offspring with goal-oriented labor, is bad for both the child and the parents.
"A highly thoughtful and entertaining treatment of a subject that merits serious consideration." —*Kirkus*
Includes bibliographical references and index.

Kennedy-Moore, Eileen
★ *Kid Confidence: Help Your Child Make Friends, Build Resilience, and Develop Real Self-Esteem.* Eileen Kennedy-Moore, PhD.. New Harbinger Publications 2019. IX, 220 p.
ISBN 9781684030491
Grades: Adult   155.4
1. Self-esteem in children 2. Self-actualization 3. Interpersonal relations 4. Parenting 5. Family and Relationships — Parenting 6. Self-Help — Personal growth — Self-esteem
LC 2018031430

In Kid Confidence, a licensed clinical psychologist and parenting expert offers practical, evidence-based parenting strategies to help kids foster satisfying relationships, develop competence, and makechoices that fit who they are and want to become.
Includes bibliographical references (pages 202-220).

Lancaster, Jen
Welcome to the United States of Anxiety: Observations from a Reforming Neurotic. Jen Lancaster. Little a 2020. 239 p.
ISBN 9781542007948
Grades: Adult   155.4
1. Lancaster, Jen, 1967- 2. Anxiety 3. Social media 4. Happiness 5. Social interaction 6. Insecurity 7. Well-being 8. Social life and customs 9. United States 10. Society and culture — Media and technology 11. Humor Writing — Social humor
LC Bl2020033423

Jen Lancaster is here to take a hard look at our elevating anxieties, and with self-deprecating wit and levelheaded wisdom, she charts a path out of the quagmire that keeps us frightened of the future and ashamed of our imperfectly perfect human lives. Take a deep breath,andher advice, and you just might get through a holiday dinner without wanting to disown your uncle.

"Lancaster is very funny, and her insightful, always entertaining critique may motivate readers to back away from social media, if only a little bit." —*Publishers Weekly*

Shankar, Shalini
Beeline: What Spelling Bees Reveal About Generation Z's New Path to Success. Shalini Shankar. Basic Books 2019. 336 p.
ISBN 9780465094523
Grades: Adult   155.4
1. Generation Z. 2. Spelling bees 3. Performance in children 4. Spelling ability 5. Achievement motivation 6. Childhood 7. Growing up 8. Tournaments 9. Immigrants 10. Words 11. Generations 12. Success (Concept) 13. Society and culture — Education 14. Society and culture — Ethnic studies 15. Sports and Competition — Games
LC 2018043156

Uses spelling bees as a window into the diverse traits of Generation Z, arguing that the generation displays a sophisticated understanding of self-promotion, self-direction, and social mobility.
"In this revealing look at how the youngest generation is adapting to face an exceptionally competitive world, Shankar shows that these bright, dedicated competitors give us many reasons to feel hopeful." —*Booklist*
Includes bibliographical references and index; School Library Journal (March 2019).

Siegel, Daniel J.
★ *The Yes Brain: How to Cultivate Courage, Curiosity, and Resilience in Your Child.* Daniel J. Siegel, M.D. and Tina Payne Bryson, Ph.D.. Bantam 2018. xii, 184 p. : Illustration
ISBN 9780399954663
Grades: Adult   155.4
1. Resilience in children 2. Child rearing 3. Parenting 4. Family and Relationships — Parenting 5. Science writing — Medicine and health — Psychology
LC 2017037802

The authors counsel caregivers and educators on how to help children reach their full potential by cultivating mental receptivity, sharing scripts, ideas and activities for transitioning resistant children away from reactive states and into mindsets that are more curious, creative and resilient.

Stixrud, William R.
The Self-Driven Child: The Science and Sense of Giving Your Kids More Control Over Their Lives. William Stixrud, PhD, and Ned Johnson. Viking 2018. VIII, 367 p.
ISBN 9780735222519
Grades: Adult   155.4
1. Child rearing 2. Parenting 3. Self-reliance in children 4. Stress management for children 5. Educator resources — General 6. Family and Relationships — Parenting 7. Science writing — Medicine and health — Psychology
LC Bl2018064074

A clinical psychologist and a test-prep expert combine cutting-edge brain science with insights from their work with families to outline a case for giving children more freedom to unleash their full potential.
Includes bibliographical references (pages 327-351) and index.

★ *What Do You Say?: How to Talk with Kids to Build Motivation, Stress Tolerance, and a Happy Home.* William Stixrud, PhD, and Ned Johnson. Viking 2021. 322 pages
ISBN 9781984880369
Grades: Adult   155.4
1. Parent and child 2. Stress management for children 3. Self-reliance in children 4. Family and Relationships — Parenting 5. Self-Help — Relationships
LC 2021012465

If you're a parent, you've had a moment—maybe many of them—when you've thought, "How did that conversation go so badly?" At some point after the sixth grade, the same kid who asked "why" non-stop at age four suddenly stops talking to you. And the conversations that you wish you could have—ones fueled by your desire to see your kid not just safe and healthy, but passionately engaged—suddenly feel nearly impossible to execute. The good news is that effective communication can be cultivated, learned, and taught. And as you get better at this, so will your kids."

"What Do You Say? could not have arrived at a better time and is essential reading for today's parents." —*Booklist*

Includes bibliographical references (pages 279-307) and index.

155.43 Children by gender or sex

Parker, Kate T.
Strong Is the New Pretty: A Celebration of Girls Being Themselves. Kate T. Parker. Workman Publishing 2017. V, 250 pages : Illustration; Color
ISBN 9780761189138
Grades: Adult 155.43
1. Girls 2. Resilience 3. Creativity 4. Kindness 5. Psychology 6. Self-confidence in children 7. Independence 8. Books for browsing 9. Growing up — Character building
LC 2017007862

A visual celebration of strong girls presents photographs ranging from yogis and skateboarders to cancer survivors and valedictorians that demonstrate how female power is about confidence, creativity, kindness, and independence as much as muscle.

"Parker shows how, whether smiling, looking tough, or helping one another out, these girls of various ages, pasts, and abilities are strong. Positively moving and totally glorious." —*Booklist*

Reiner, Andrew
Better Boys, Better Men: The New Masculinity That Creates Greater Courage and Emotional Resiliency. Andrew Reiner. HarperOne 2020. VIII, 264 pages
ISBN 9780062854940
Grades: Adult 155.43
1. Masculinity 2. Young men 3. Child development 4. Psychology 5. Personal conduct 6. Boys 7. Society and culture — Gender — Men
LC 2020003439

How modern forms of masculinity are harming men—and what we can do about it.

"Parents, educators, coaches, counselors, and scholars of gender studies will want to take a look at this humane and inspirational portrait of an emotionally grounded, resilient masculinity." —*Publishers Weekly*

Includes index.

155.44 Children by status and relationships

De Bres, Helena
How to Be Multiple: The Philosophy of Twins. Helena De Bres; illustrations by Julia De Bres. Bloomsbury Publishing Place USA 2023. 272 p. : Illustration
ISBN 9781639730346
Grades: Adult 155.44
1. Twins 2. Families 3. Philosophy 4. Identical twins 5. Identity 6. Self 7. Culture 8. Social psychology 9. Twin sisters 10. Essays 11. Society and culture — Philosophy 12. Family and Relationships — Siblings

A professor of philosophy discusses the unique place of twins in the world, including their representations in art, myth and popular culture, with illustrations by her identical twin sister.

"An exploration of selfhood and twinship…A thoughtful, well-rendered collection of musings on identity." —*Publishers Weekly*

155.45 Exceptional children; children by social and economic levels, by ethnic or national group

Ruthsatz, Joanne
The Prodigy's Cousin: The Family Link Between Autism and Extraordinary Talent. Joanne Ruthsatz and Kimberly Stephens. Current 2016. x, 273 pages
ISBN 9781617230189
Grades: Adult 155.45
1. Child prodigies 2. Autistic children 3. Heredity and environment (Psychology) 4. Savant syndrome 5. Child psychology 6. Child development 7. Autism spectrum disorders 8. Neurodivergent people 9. Science Writing — Medicine and health — Disabilities and disorders

In a scientific detective story, the author, along with a reporter, investigates more than 30 child prodigies, all of whom had extraordinary memories and a keen eye for detail, and discovers a genetic link between prodigy and autism, confirming her long-held hunch and an important piece of the puzzle.

"People with an interest in autism or prodigies will be intrigued by the interesting hypothesis posed by this psychologist-journalist duo, who provide a lovely epilogue about what their young prodigies are doing today." —*Booklist*

Includes bibliographical references and index.

155.5 Psychology of young people twelve to twenty

Damour, Lisa
The Emotional Lives of Teenagers: Raising Connected, Capable, and Compassionate Adolescents. Lisa Damour, Ph.D… Ballantine Books 2023. xxiv, 226 pages : Illustration
ISBN 9780593500019
Grades: Adult 155.5
1. Emotions in teenagers 2. Teenagers 3. Parent and teenager 4. Family and Relationships — Parenting
LC 2022032622

With clear, research-informed explanations alongside illuminating, real-life examples, this must-have guide provides parents of teens dealing with academic pressure, social media stress, worries about the future and their own mental health with the essential information for supporting them through the transformational journey into adulthood.

"Comprehensive and encompassing of the many of the struggles teens face today, this book is a must for libraries looking for mental health resources for parents of teens." —*Library Journal*

Includes bibliographical references (pages 187-215) and index.

★ *Under Pressure: Confronting the Epidemic of Stress and Anxiety in Girls.* Lisa Damour. Ballantine Books 2019. xxi, 261 pages
ISBN 9780399180057
Grades: 9 10 11 12 Adult 155.5
1. Stress management 2. Teenage girls 3. Psychology 4. Family and Relationships — Growing up 5. Family and Relationships — Parenting
LC 2018039456

An urgent guide by the clinical psychologist shares anecdotal reassurance about how to protect today's girls from rising rates of unhealthy anxiety and stress, sharing critical steps for safeguarding against toxic cultural pressure.

"Damour offers practical suggestions for heading off stressful encounters and counteracting their influences. Although aimed at parents, Damour's sensible and empathetic approach will also be reassuring for teens seeking guidance." —*Booklist*

Includes bibliographical references and index.

Kline, Emily
★ *The School of Hard Talks: How to Have Real Conversations with Your (Almost Grown) Kids.* Emily Kline, PhD.. Sasquatch Books 2023. 167 pages : Color; Illustration
ISBN 9781632174703
Grades: Adult 155.5
1. Children and adults 2. Parent and teenager 3. Parent and adult child 4. Parenting 5. Interpersonal relations 6. Intergenerational communication 7. Motivation 8. Teenagers 9. Family and Relationships — Parenting
LC 2022038686

Clinical psychologist and parent-child relationship specialist Dr. Emily Kline offers a set of five easy-to-learn, clinically proven techniques to improve communication between young adults and their parents. Based in based a methodology known as Motivational Interviewing, these techniques focus on eluci-

ESSENTIAL AND RECOMMENDED TITLES
155.6 Psychology of adults

dating young people's own thoughts and motivations, rather than trying to impose parental views upon them.".

"The book may appear disarmingly short, but to any parent or grandparent scrambling to talk to their teens, its brevity—and Kline's informal, engaging, and inspiring tone—is a strength. It belongs in every public library." —*Booklist*

Includes bibliographical references (pages 157-161) and index.

Siegel, Daniel J.
Brainstorm: The Power and Purpose of the Teenage Brain. Daniel J. Siegel, M.D.. Tarcher/Penguin 2013. 321 pages : Illustration
ISBN 9781585429356
Grades: 11 12 Adult   **155.5**
1. Adolescence 2. Child development 3. Brain 4. Biological growth 5. Society and culture — Psychology and human behavior
LC 2013029724

The best-selling author, drawing on important new research in the field of interpersonal neurobiology, helps parents understand how the brain functions between the ages of 12 and 24 so that they can turn one of the most challenging periods in their children's lives into one of the most rewarding.

Includes index.

Simmons, Rachel
★ *Enough as She Is: How to Help Girls Move Beyond Impossible Standards of Success to Live Healthy, Happy, and Fulfilling Lives.* Rachel Simmons. Harper 2018. xxiv, 270 pages
ISBN 9780062438393
Grades: Adult   **155.5**
1. Teenage girls 2. Psychology 3. Family and Relationships — Growing up 4. Family and Relationships — Parenting 5. Society and culture — Gender — Women
LC Bl2017051385

Offers advice to help parents guide teenage girls to recognize and reject perfectionist messages that lead to self-doubt, unfulfilling relationships, and fears of failure, and teach them self-compassion, how to take healthy risks, and the importance of finding support.

The best-selling author of Odd Girl Out counsels today's young women on how to recognize and reject perfectionist messages that lead to self-doubt, unfulfilling relationships and fears of failure, drawing on two decades of research to share practical counsel on healthy risk-taking and finding support.

"A fascinating read that provides ideas for combatting the 'Not enough' ideals that are devastating young girls." —*Library Journal*

Includes bibliographical references (pages 241-255) and index.

155.6 Psychology of adults

Hagerty, Barbara Bradley
Life Reimagined: The Science, Art, and Opportunity of Midlife. Barbara Bradley Hagerty. Riverhead Books 2016. 400 p.
ISBN 9781594631702
Grades: Adult   **155.6**
1. Middle-age 2. Middle-aged women 3. Aging 4. Midlife crisis 5. Science Writing — General 6. Family and relationships — Aging and death
LC 2016006516

An award-winning journalist exposes the myth of the midlife crisis, drawing on emerging information from the fields of neurology, psychology, biology, genetics and sociology and explains that it should instead be about fresh possibilities, transformation and plotting new courses.

"This work is a joyous reminder that the middle years can be satisfying, resilient, and significant." —*Library Journal*

Kim, John
Single on Purpose: Redefine Everything. Find Yourself First. John Kim. HarperOne 2021. 256 p.
ISBN 9780062980731
Grades: Adult   **155.6**
1. Self-fulfillment 2. Single people 3. Personal conduct 4. Self-Help — Personal growth
LC 2020021750

From The Angry Therapist and author of I Used to Be a Miserable F*ck comes a guide to prioritizing your relationship with yourself and living a more meaningful life, regardless of your relationship status."

"Kim's wry humor and approachable lessons will appeal to any single reader looking for encouragement." —*Publishers Weekly*

Lerner, Harriet Goldhor
The Dance of Intimacy: A Woman's Guide to Courageous Acts of Change in Key Relationships. Harriet Goldhor Lerner. Perennial Library 1990. 25 p.
ISBN 9780060916466
Grades: Adult   **155.6**
1. Women 2. Intimacy 3. Interpersonal relations 4. Change (Psychology) 5. Psychology 6. Science writing — Medicine and health — Psychology 7. Family and Relationships — Dating and Marriage
LC BL 99705951

Focuses on the anxiety that is born of unhappy relationships—with a loved one, best friend, or family member—and offers advice on how to improve relations.

Includes bibliographical references; Originally published: New York : Harper & Row, c1989.

McConville, Mark
Failure to Launch: Why Your Twentysomething Hasn't Grown Up...and What to Do About It. Mark McConville, Ph.D.. G.P. Putnam's Sons 2020. 320 p.
ISBN 9780525542186
Grades: Adult   **155.6**
1. Parent and adult child 2. Adult children living with parents 3. Adulthood 4. Young adults 5. Purpose in life 6. Responsibility 7. Growing up 8. Intergenerational relations 9. Family relationships 10. Independence 11. Family and Relationships — Families 12. Family and Relationships — Growing up 13. Society and culture — Psychology and human behavior
LC 2019021470

From an expert in adolescent psychology comes a groundbreaking, timely, and necessary guide for parents of the 2.2 million young adults in America who are struggling to find their way in the world.

"A valuable go-to resource for parents and teens alike." —*Library Journal*

Includes bibliographical references and index.

Rauch, Jonathan
The Happiness Curve: Why Life Gets Better After 50. Jonathan Rauch. Picador 2019. xiv, 257 pages
ISBN 9781250080912
Grades: Adult   **155.6**
1. Middle-age 2. Midlife crisis 3. Depression 4. Anxiety 5. Happiness 6. Mental health 7. Psychology 8. Science Writing — Medicine and health — Mental health 9. Society and culture — Psychology and human behavior
LC 2020304096

Draws on cutting-edge scientific studies to discuss the U-shaped trajectory of happiness, which declines from the optimism of youth before surging upward again after age fifty, and offers ways to endure the slump during midlife.

Includes bibliographical references and index.

155.67 People in late adulthood

Applewhite, Ashton
This Chair Rocks: A Manifesto Against Ageism. Ashton Applewhite. Celadon Books 2019. 285 p.
ISBN 9781250311481
Grades: Adult   **155.67**
1. Ageism 2. Aging 3. Seniors 4. Prejudice 5. Social problems 6. Stereotypes 7. Public opinion 8. Family and Relationships — Aging and Death 9. Society and culture — General

PUBLIC LIBRARY CORE COLLECTION: NONFICTION
Twentieth Edition

LC Bl2019001375

An author, activist, and TED-Talk speaker has written a manifesto calling for an end to discrimination and prejudice on the basis of age.

"This enjoyable read provides a positive view of aging that is sorely missing in today's popular culture. Appealing to a wide audience, it might even serve as a spark for positive social change." —*Library Journal*

Cameron, Julia

It's Never Too Late to Begin Again: Discovering Creativity and Meaning at Midlife and Beyond. Julia Cameron, with Emma Lively. TarcherPerigee 2016. xxxii, 265 p.

ISBN 9780399174216

Grades: Adult   155.67

1. Aging 2. Creativity 3. Self-Help — Personal growth — Creativity 4. Family and Relationships — Growing up 5. Self-Help — Personal growth — Aging

LC 2015050216

Julia Cameron has inspired millions with her bestseller The Artist's Way. Now at the age of sixty-five, she shows her contemporaries how retirement can be the most creative and fulfilling stage of life yet. For some, retirement is a day to work toward with anticipation. Others approach retirement with greater ambivalence. While the newfound freedom is exciting and filled with possibility, the idea of retirement can also be very daunting. You are in a unique position to explore yourself and your desiresfrom a place of experience. But the line has been drawn in the sand: The life that you have known has changed, and the life to come is yet to be defined. This book is a twelve-week course aimed at defining—and creating—the life you want to have as you redefine—and re-create—yourself. Filled with essays, tools, and exercises to be done alone or in groups, this toolkit will guide and inspire retirees wishing to expand their creativity. This fun, gentle, step-by-step process will help you explore your creative dreams, wishes, and desires—and quickly find that it's never too late to begin anything.

Includes bibliographical references and index.

Moore, Thomas

Ageless Soul: The Lifelong Journey Toward Meaning and Joy. Thomas Moore. St. Martins Press 2017. VIII, 294 pages

ISBN 9781250135810

Grades: Adult   155.67

1. Seniors 2. Aging 3. Spiritual life 4. Religious psychology 5. Religious life 6. Family and Relationships — Aging and Death 7. Spirituality and Religion — General

LC 2017018867

Offers advice on how to embrace healthier perspectives on aging through a rich spiritual life, covering subjects ranging from depression and mentorship to sexuality and the spiritual paths that open later in life.

"This gentle book, filled with specific suggestions and thought-provoking examples, will be inspiring to older readers and a comfort to their caregivers." —*Booklist*

Includes index.

155.7 Evolutionary psychology

Dunbar, R. I. M.

Human Evolution: Our Brains and Behavior. Robin Dunbar. Oxford University Press 2016. 272 p.

ISBN 9780190616786

Grades: Adult   155.7

1. Genetic psychology 2. Evolution 3. Cognition 4. Heredity and environment (Psychology) 5. Human nature 6. Science Writing — Biology

LC 2016009401

This book covers the psychological aspects of human evolution with a table of contents ranging from prehistoric times to modern days. Dunbar focuses on an aspect of evolution that has typically been overshadowed by the archaeological record: the biological, neurological, and genetic changes that occurred with each "transition" in the evolutionary narrative.

"Readers who pay attention and do not skim the many graphs, tables, and statistics will discover a rich trove of discoveries on how primitive primates became modern humans." —*Kirkus*

Includes bibliographical references and index.

Foster, Charles

Being a Human: Adventures in Forty Thousand Years of Consciousness. Charles Foster. Metropolitan Books 2021. 379 p.

ISBN 9781250783714

Grades: Adult   155.7

1. Foster, Charles, 1962- 2. Human behavior 3. Consciousness 4. Genetic psychology 5. Human evolution 6. Senses and sensation 7. Survival 8. Intelligence 9. Culture 10. Anthropology 11. Evolution 12. Science Writing — Biology 13. Society and culture — Psychology and human behavior

LC 2021019046

How did humans come to be who we are? In his marvelous, eccentric, and widely lauded book Being a Beast, legal scholar, veterinary surgeon, and naturalist extraordinaire Charles Foster set out to understand the consciousness of animal species by living as a badger, otter, fox, deer, and swift. Now, he inhabits three crucial periods of human development to understand the consciousness of perhaps the strangest animal of all—the human being. Drawing on psychology, neuroscience, natural history, agriculture, medical law and ethics, Being a Human is one man's audacious attempt to feel a connection with 45,000 years of human history. This glorious, fiercely imaginative journey from our origins to a possible future ultimately shows how we might best live on earth—and thrive.

"An expansion of mind and soul, wonderment for the natural world, and intense self-examination all flash in this unusual exploration of three crucial periods of human history, the early Upper Paleolithic, the Neolithic, and the Enlightenment. . . . A thought-provoking fusion of anthropology, archaeology, environmentalism, and much more, Foster's heady narrative swerves between dizzying and dazzling." —*Booklist*

Includes bibliographical references.

Miller, Kenneth R.

The Human Instinct: How We Evolved to Have Reason, Consciousness, and Free Will. Kenneth Miller. Simon & Schuster 2018. 304 p.

ISBN 9781476790268

Grades: Adult   155.7

1. Human evolution 2. Genetic psychology 3. Consciousness 4. Behavior evolution 5. Free will and determinism 6. Natural selection 7. Human behavior 8. Science Writing — Biology 9. Society and culture — Psychology and human behavior

LC 2017006770

Explores how humans evolved to develop reason, consciousness, and free will, achieving a level of self-awareness and understanding unrivaled by the creatures they evolved alongside.

"Miller's latest work seamlessly crosses between science and philosophy, appealing to readers of both subjects. Those interested in the human condition or wishing to delve into an introspective text on the self and mind will appreciate the depth and thought." —*Booklist*

Includes bibliographical references and index.

155.8 Ethnopsychology and national psychology

Levi-Strauss, Claude

★ *The Savage Mind.* Claude Levi-Strauss; translated from the French by John Weightman and Doreen Weightman. University of Chicago Press 1966. xii, 290 p. Illustration; Portrait

ISBN 9780226474847

Grades: Adult   155.8

1. Ethnopsychology 2. Society and culture — General

LC 66028197

Discusses the significance of totemism among primitive peoples and its interpretation by anthropologists and philosophies.

Bibliography: P. 271-282.

ESSENTIAL AND RECOMMENDED TITLES
155.9 Environmental psychology

155.9 Environmental psychology

Adichie, Chimamanda Ngozi
Notes on Grief. Chimamanda Ngozi Adichie. Alfred A. Knopf 2021. 80 pages
ISBN 9780593320808
Grades: Adult   **155.9**
1. Adichie, Chimamanda Ngozi, 1977- 2. Death of fathers 3. Grief 4. Death 5. Igbo (African people) 6. Loss 7. Women authors 8. Family relationships 9. Nigeria 10. 2020s 11. Autobiographies and memoirs 12. Life stories — Facing adversity — Coping with death 13. Family and Relationships — Aging and death
Presents a deeply personal work of meditation, hope, and remembrance recounting the death of the author's beloved father in the summer of 2020.
"Adichie's exquisitely forthright chronicle of grief generously articulates the harrowing amplification of sorrow, helplessness, and loss during the COVID-19 pandemic, making this an intimate and essential illumination of a tragic time." —*Booklist*

Benson, Herbert
The Relaxation Response. Herbert Benson, with Miriam Z. Klipper. Quill 2001. Liv, 179 p. : Illustration
ISBN 9780380815951
Grades: Adult   **155.9**
1. Relaxation 2. Stress management 3. Preventive medicine 4. Self-Help — General
LC 2003269877
An updated health handbook outlines techniques of concentration designed to reduce physiological stress and presents scientific data indicating the effectiveness of similar systems of relaxation.
"This guide to relieving stress is recommended for patients suffering from heart conditions, hypertension, chronic pain, and other ailments. A classic." —*Library Journal*
Includes bibliographical references (p. 146-170) and index; Originally published: New York, Morrow, 1975.

Cacciatore, Joanne
Bearing the Unbearable: Love, Loss, and the Heartbreaking Path of Grief. Joanne Cacciatore, PhD; foreword by Jeffrey B. Rubin, PhD.. Wisdom Publications 2017. 222 pages
ISBN 9781614292968
Grades: Adult   **155.9**
1. Adjustment 2. Grief 3. Loss 4. Love 5. Family and Relationships — Aging and Death 6. Science writing — Medicine and health — Psychology 7. Self-Help — Mental health — Grief and loss
LC 2016044492
"Cacciatore . has taken a unique, straightforward approach that will enlighten those who have not made this journey, offer guidance to those who are navigating loss, and provide validation for those who failed to meet society's expectations of how they should respond to their lives being forever changed." —*Choice*
Includes index.

Dugdale, Lydia S.
The Lost Art of Dying: Reviving Forgotten Wisdom. L.S. Dugdale; artwork by Michael W. Dugger. HarperOne 2020. VIII, 259 p.: Illustration
ISBN 9780062932631
Grades: Adult   **155.9**
1. Death 2. Terminal care 3. Loss 4. Family and Relationships — Aging and Death 5. Self-Help — Mental health — Grief and loss
LC 2019031054
A Yale physician's fascinating and wise exploration of why so many people die poorly and how a medieval bestseller on the art of dying well holds important lessons for today.
A Columbia University physician shares uplifting prescriptive advice on how to rethink death and the art of dying well, drawing on specialist insights in medical ethics and elder care to outline more qualitative, holistic approaches.

"This illuminating and thought-provoking book will convince many readers to reexamine their assumptions about death and dying." —*Publishers Weekly*
Includes bibliographical references (pages 245-256).

Edelman, Hope
The AfterGrief: Finding Your Way Along the Long Arc of Loss. Hope Edelman. Ballantine Books 2020. xxix, 288 pages : Illustration
ISBN 9780399179785
Grades: Adult   **155.9**
1. Grief 2. Loss 3. Sadness 4. Self-Help — Mental health — Grief and loss
LC 2020028125
Because of the common assumption that grief should be time-limited, too many of us believe we've done it 'wrong' when sadness reemerges months or even years after a major loss. In The AfterGrief, Hope Edelman offers a new and reality-affirming paradigm: Grief is not an emotion to pass through on the way to 'feeling better,' but a state that we repeatedly return to as we experience important life transitions and new crises. Drawing from her own encounters with the ripple effects of early loss, as well as interviews with more than seventy-five people, Edelman offers profound advice for reassessing loss and adjusting the stories we tell ourselves about its impact on our identities. With guidance for reframing astory of loss, finding equilibrium within it, and experiencing renewed growth and purpose, The AfterGrief shows that though grief may be a lifelong process, it doesn't have to be a lifelong struggle.
"A timelessly relevant chronicle on enduring grief." —*Kirkus*
Includes bibliographical references (pages 267-283).

Motherless Daughters: The Legacy of Loss. Hope Edelman. Da Capo Lifelong 2014. 400 pages
ISBN 9780738217734
Grades: Adult   **155.9**
1. Mothers and daughters 2. Mother-separated children 3. Grief 4. Deprivation (Psychology) 5. Loss 6. Family and relationships — Aging and death
LC 2013044875
The author joins with other women whose mothers died when they were young to discuss the lasting effects of this loss on their identity, family, relationships with others, and decisions in life.
"Writing of her own experiences of losing her mother when she was 17, and the grief of hundreds of women she interviewed who lost their mothers through death, abandonment or another form of separation . Edelman marshals a wealth of anecdotal evidence, supplemented with psychological research about bereavement, that indicates that one's longing for a mother never disappears." —*Publishers Weekly*
Includes bibliographical references (pages 317-346) and index; Originally published by addison-Wesley in 1994.

Emswiler, Mary Ann
Guiding Your Child Through Grief. Mary Ann Emswiler & James P. Emswiler. Bantam Books 2000. 286 p. : Portrait
ISBN 9780553380255
Grades: Adult   **155.9**
1. Child rearing 2. Children and death 3. Grief in teenagers 4. Grief in children 5. Loss in teenagers 6. Loss in children 7. Teenagers and death 8. Family and Relationships — Aging and Death 9. Family and Relationships — Parenting
LC 00023645
The founders of The Cove, a program for grieving children and their families, offer advice to help children and teenagers cope with the death of a parent or sibling and effective ways to ease family members through a time of difficult transition.
The founders of the New England Center for Loss & Transition introduce the Cove, their acclaimed program designed to help grieving children, offering compassionate advice on how to help youngsters cope with the death of a parent or sibling and effective ways to ease family members through a time of difficult transition.
"Thoroughly researched and bolstered with the wisdom of bereavement experts nationwide, this fine guide does those working through the loss of loved

ones an enormous service. It should rank amongst the first line of defense and support for those facing a death in the family." —*Publishers Weekly*

Includes bibliographical references and index.

Fletcher, Emily
Stress Less, Accomplish More: Meditation for Extraordinary Performance. Emily Fletcher. William Morrow 2019. 252 pages : Illustration

ISBN 9780062747501

Grades: Adult   155.9

1. Meditation 2. Stress management 3. Spirituality and Religion — Body, mind, and spirit 4. Spirituality and Religion — Body, mind, and spirit — Meditation and mindfulness 5. Self-Help — Personal growth

LC Bl2019004921

Teaching the powerful trifecta of mindfulness, meditation and manifesting, a leading expert in meditation for high performance shares her 15-minute twice-daily plan called the Z Technique for improving focus and increasing productivity levels.

Outlines the author's fifteen-minute, twice a day plan to improve focus and increase productivity levels through meditation, mindfulness, and manifestation.

Includes bibliographical references (pages 235-239) and index.

Foster, Craig
★ *Amphibious* Soul: Finding the Wild in a Tame World. Craig Foster. HarperOne 2024. 256 p.

ISBN 9780063289024

Grades: Adult   155.9

1. Foster, Craig (Filmmaker) 2. Nature 3. Humans and nature 4. Wilderness areas 5. Effect of environment on humans 6. Earth 7. Autobiographies and memoirs 8. Life stories — Nature and outdoors 9. Life stories — Facing adversity

One of the world's leading natural history filmmakers shows how we can reinvigorate our lives by developing a deep connection to the Earth, nurture our individual wildness and deepen our love for all living things.

"Candid, transporting, and philosophical, Foster pays tribute to his teachers animal and human and discerns lessons within his adventures harrowing and ecstatic." —*Booklist*

Gerson, Merissa Nathan
Forget Prayers, Bring Cake: A Single Woman's Guide to Grieving. Merissa Nathan Gerson. Mandala 2021. 240 p.

ISBN 9781647224196

Grades: Adult   155.9

1. Gerson, Merissa Nathan 2. Single women 3. Loss 4. Grief 5. Self-acceptance 6. Friendship 7. Death of fathers 8. Self-care 9. Communities 10. Intergenerational trauma 11. Autobiographies and memoirs 12. Life stories — Relationships 13. Life stories — Facing adversity — Coping with death 14. Life stories — Personal growth

Though at times it may seem impossible, we can heal with help from our friends and community, if we know how to ask. This heartrending, relatable account of one woman's reckoning with loss is a guide to the world of self-recovery, self-love, and the skills necessary to meeting one's own needs in these times of pain, especially when that pain is suffered alone.

"An excellent resource for readers dealing with grief or trauma on their own." —*Library Journal*

Gilbert, Sandra M.
Death's Door: Modern Dying and the Ways We Grieve. Sandra M. Gilbert. W.W. Norton 2006. xxv, 580 p. : Illustration

ISBN 9780393051315

Grades: Adult   155.9

1. Grief 2. Mourning customs 3. Death 4. Family and Relationships — Aging and Death

LC 2004065430

Explores modern humanity's relationship with death as reflected in literature, history, and society, evaluating how perceptions about death and the experience of grief have changed, citing the influence of such events as Hiroshima, the Holocaust, and the September 11 attacks.

"Those who have experienced the death of a loved one will recognize themselves in this meticulously researched, comprehensively organized, and exceptionally caring examination of society's attitudes about mortality and mourning." —*Booklist*

Includes bibliographical references (p. [525]-553) and index.

Greene, Jayson
Once More We Saw Stars: A Memoir. Jayson Greene. Alfred A. Knopf 2019. 256 p.

ISBN 9781524733537

Grades: Adult   155.9

1. Greene, Jayson 2. Death of children 3. Grief 4. Fathers 5. Families 6. Grief therapy 7. Spiritual journeys 8. Loss 9. Accidental death 10. Manhattan, New York City 11. New York City 12. Autobiographies and memoirs 13. Life stories — Facing adversity — Coping with death 14. Family and Relationships — Families

LC 2018013866

Devastated by his 2-year-old daughter's accidental death, a father in Upper West Side Manhattan navigates unendurable pain and taps the healing power of love to rebuild his shattered family.

"After suffering an unimaginable loss, the author's ability to pursue fatherhood again while still honoring the daughter he lost is a testament to the resilience of the human spirit and its capacity to love. Heartbreaking and inspiring." —*Library Journal*

This is a Borzoi book.

James, John W.
★ *The Grief* Recovery Handbook: The Action Program for Moving Beyond Death, Divorce, and Other Losses Including Health Career, and Faith. John W. James and Russell Friedman. Collins Living 2009. xvi, 208 p. : Illustration

ISBN 9780061686078

Grades: Adult   155.9

1. Grief 2. Loss 3. Self-Help — Mental health — Grief and loss 4. Family and Relationships — Aging and Death

LC 2010455458

Presents a step-by-step program for recovering from loss, discussing the concepts of grief and recovery, the extent to which people are prepared to deal with loss, and the active decision to recover.

Johnson, Earl
Finding Comfort During Hard Times: A Guide to Healing After Disaster, Violence, and Other Community Trauma. Earl Johnson. Rowman & Littlefield 2020. IX, 166 p.

ISBN 9781538127094

Grades: Adult   155.9

1. Disasters 2. Psychic trauma 3. Healing 4. Self-Help — Mental health 5. Science writing — Medicine and health — Psychology

LC 2019046265

Finding Comfort is about providing emotional and spiritual care following a mass fatality incident like a mass shooting, terrorist act or catastrophic natural disaster. Through examples and practical suggestions, it explores the needs of those who are suffering and how those needs can be met.

Includes bibliographical references and index.

Kerr, Christopher
Death Is but a Dream: Finding Hope and Meaning at Life's End. Christopher Kerr, MD, PhD, with Carine Mardorossian, PhD.. Avery 2020. 272 p.

ISBN 9780525542841

Grades: Adult   155.9

1. Dream interpretation 2. Death 3. Mortality 4. Lucid dreams 5. Hospice care 6. People with terminal illnesses 7. Peace of mind 8. Family and Relationships — Aging and Death 9. Science Writing — Medicine and health

LC 2019038405

Christopher Kerr is a hospice doctor. All of his patients die. Yet he has cared for thousands of patients who, in the face of death, speak of love and grace. Beyond the physical realities of dying are unseen processes that are remarkably

ESSENTIAL AND RECOMMENDED TITLES
155.9 Environmental psychology

life-affirming. These include dreams that are unlike any regular dream. Described as "more real than real," these end-of-life experiences resurrect past relationships, meaningful events and themes of love and forgiveness; they restore life's meaning and mark the transition from distress to comfort and acceptance.

"This comforting guide will reassure the dying and their loved ones while providing instructive portraits of end-of-life patients for those who work in medical and healing professions." —*Publishers Weekly*

Includes bibliographical references and index.

Kessler, David
Finding Meaning: The Sixth Stage of Grief. David Kessler; written with support of the Elisabeth Kubler-Ross Family and the Elisabeth Kubler-Ross Foundation. Scribner 2019. 272 pages
ISBN 9781501192739
Grades: Adult **155.9**
1. Death 2. Grief 3. Purpose in life 4. Healing 5. Family and Relationships — Aging and Death 6. Life stories — Facing adversity — Coping with death
LC 2019028917

Drawing on hard-earned experiences, as well as wisdom garnered from decades of work, an expert on grief and the coauthor of the iconic on Grief and Grieving introduces the stages of grief with the same transformative pragmatism and compassion.

Kubler-Ross, Elisabeth
★ *On Death and Dying.* Elisabeth Kübler-Ross. Scribner Classics 1997. 286 p. : Illustration
ISBN 9780684842233
Grades: 9 10 11 12 Adult **155.9**
1. Death 2. People with terminal illnesses 3. Grief 4. Coping 5. Psychology 6. Family and Relationships — Aging and Death 7. Science Writing — Medicine and health — Mental health

Explains the attitudes of the dying toward themselves and others and presents a humane approach to relieving the psychological suffering of the terminally ill and their families.

Includes bibliographical references (p. 277-286); Originally published: New York : Macmillan, 1969.

Mariani, Mike
★ *What Doesn't Kill Us Makes Us: Who We Become After Tragedy and Trauma.* Mike Mariani. Ballantine Books 2022. 384 p.
ISBN 9780593236949
Grades: Adult **155.9**
1. Life change events 2. Psychic trauma 3. Adjustment 4. Survival 5. Suffering 6. Identity 7. Transformations, Personal 8. Resilience 9. Life stories — Facing adversity 10. Society and culture — General
LC 2021041264

Tracing the lives of six people who have experienced catastrophic, life-changing events, a journalist, using his own experience and the lessons of psychology, literature, mythology and religion, explores the nuances and largely uncharted territory of what happens after one's life is cleaved into a before and after.

"The author's superior storytelling abilities shine throughout and portray his subjects with compassion and nuance. The result captivates, offering a poignant exploration of how humans make meaning out of tragedy." —*Publishers Weekly*

Includes bibliographical references.

May, Katherine
Wintering: The Power of Rest and Retreat in Difficult Times. Katherine May. Riverhead Books 2020. 256 p.
ISBN 9780593189481
Grades: Adult **155.9**
1. May, Katherine 2. Rest 3. Self-acceptance 4. Natural healing 5. Healing 6. Family relationships 7. Diseases 8. Life change events 9. Solitude 10. Transformations, Personal 11. Autobiographies and memoirs 12. Life stories — Facing adversity — Medical issues 13. Life stories — Relationships — Family 14. Family and Relationships — Illness and the Family

LC 2020001772

Sometimes you slip through the cracks: Unforeseen circumstances like an abrupt illness, the death of a loved one, a break up, or a job loss can derail a life. These periods of dislocation can be lonely and unexpected. For May, her husband fell ill, her son stopped attending school, and her own medical issues led her to leave a demanding job. Wintering explores how she not only endured this painful time, but embraced the singular opportunities it offered.

"In this introspective, beautifully written mix of memoir and philosophy, May explores life's hardest season and the lessons of acceptance. With a pandemic keeping us isolated in so many ways, May offers much-needed solace and comfort and a reminder that seasons eventually turn." —*Booklist*

McInerny, Nora
The Hot Young Widows Club: Lessons on Survival from the Front Lines of Grief. Nora McInerny. TED Books/Simon & Schuster 2019. 128 p.
ISBN 9781982109981
Grades: Adult **155.9**
1. McInerny, Nora 2. Death 3. Grief 4. Loss 5. Life change events 6. Widows 7. Widowers 8. Autobiographies and memoirs 9. Life stories — Facing adversity — Coping with death 10. Family and Relationships — General 11. Society and culture — Psychology and human behavior
LC Bl2019011698

The author, whose husband died young of brain cancer, provides wise, heartfelt, and humorous advice for those grieving the loss of a loved one, and offers suggestions for how to help people who are grieving.

Ripley, Amanda
The Unthinkable: Who Survives When Disaster Strikes and How We Can Do Better. Amanda Ripley. Harmony 2024. 288 p.
ISBN 9780593796726
Grades: Adult **155.9**
1. Resilience 2. Disaster relief 3. Preparedness 4. Risk management 5. Risk analysis 6. Emergency planning 7. Crisis intervention 8. Disaster victims 9. Disasters 10. Mental health 11. Adventure writing — Survival 12. Science Writing — Medicine and health — Mental health
LC 2007040315

Offers a glimpse at disasters and their aftermath, describing the three stages of disaster response, how we react—or do not react—in moments of catastrophe, and how we can train ourselves and other victims to survive in the event of a disaster.

"Ripley offers an elementary discussion of disaster and survival, drawing on both survivors' personal accounts and scientific studies that reveal how the human brain functions under duress. She shows how individuals and groups react when such disasters as shipwrecks, fires, terrorist attacks, and tsunamis occur, detailing the traits survivors demonstrate that help them respond effectively. Offering tips on how we can boost our odds, her self-help approach to survival will attract readers." —*Library Journal*

Originally published by Crown, New York, in 2008; Includes bibliographical references.

Rosenblatt, Roger
Kayak Morning: Reflections on Love, Grief, and Small Boats. Roger Rosenblatt. HarperCollins 2012. 160 p.
ISBN 9780062084033
Grades: Adult **155.9**
1. Grief 2. Loss 3. Healing 4. Death 5. Family and Relationships — Aging and Death
LC 2012374546

New York Times Notable Book, 2012.

A meditation on the stages of grief documents the period after the wrenching death of the author's adult daughter and describes a kayak journey he took years later that metaphorically represented his journey of loss and healing.

"The lyrical nature of the piece, which combines short vignettes, poetic verses, snippets of conversations and meaningful quotations, allows Rosenblatt's masterful writing skills to shine. In one instance, he describes how his two sons still stand as if their deceased sister is between them, and his words

connect in a way that conveys his sadness but also affirms the goodness of life."
—*Publishers Weekly*

Rosling, Hans
Factfulness: Ten Reasons We're Wrong About the World—and Why Things Are Better Than You Think. Hans Rosling with Ola Rosling and Anna Rosling Ronnlund. Flatiron Books 2018. 288 p.
ISBN 9781250107817
Grades: Adult   155.9
1. Decision making 2. Human behavior 3. Possibilities 4. Cognition 5. Psychology 6. Options, alternatives, choices 7. Information 8. Society and culture — Psychology and human behavior 9. Business and economics — Popular psychology

LC 2018000167

Inspiring and revelatory, this is a book of stories by a late legend, for anyone who wants to really understand the world. It is based on a lifetime trying to teach a fact-based worldview, and of listening to how people misinterpret and overdramatize the facts even when they are right there in front of them. Written by Hans Rosling as he approached death, it features surprising, shocking, funny and poignant stories from Hans' life—from his difficult childhood in Sweden, through his work in Mozambique as a junior doctor, to his later work wowing audiences of millions around the world.

Samuel, Julia
Grief Works: Stories of Life, Death and Surviving. Julia Samuel. Scribner 2018. 288 pages
ISBN 9781501181535
Grades: Adult   155.9
1. Grief 2. Death 3. Grief therapy 4. Loss 5. Family and Relationships — Aging and Death

LC Bl2017046393

Shares optimistic and compassionate counsel for anyone suffering a loss and shares uplifting case studies from survivors who have journeyed through the process of grief to achieve healing, self-awareness, and confidence.

"As a guide for the newly grieving, the book succeeds on many levels, and the author's compassionate storytelling skills provide even broader appeal. Though often touching on profoundly sad situations, Samuel's stories and reflections consistently hit an authentically inspiring note." —*Kirkus*

Includes bibliographical references.

Sandberg, Sheryl
Option B: Facing Adversity, Building Resilience, and Finding Joy. Sheryl Sandberg and Adam Grant. Alfred A. Knopf 2017. 240 p.
ISBN 9781524732684
Grades: Adult   155.9
1. Coping 2. Psychology 3. Loss 4. Grief 5. Survival 6. Resilience 7. Life stories — Facing adversity 8. Society and culture — Psychology and human behavior

LC 2016057738

From the Facebook COO and #1 New York Times best-selling author of Lean In, and the #1 New York Times best-selling author of Originals comes a book about finding resilience and moving forward after life's inevitable setbacks.

"Option B is not simply a self-help book for those who are suffering; rather, it is a richly informed, engaging read that will broaden readers understanding of empathy and reveal the strength of the human spirit." —*Booklist*

Sife, Wallace
The Loss of a Pet. Wallace Sife. Howell Book House 2005. xii, 260 p. : Illustration
ISBN 9780764579301
Grades: Adult   155.9
1. Grief 2. Pet owners 3. Death of pets 4. Psychology 5. Nature writing — Animal studies — Pet care

LC 2005012603

"The author addresses the pet owner whose grief at a pet's death is largely misunderstood or even ridiculed by friends, associates and society in general. Sife is to be commended for offering information that is not only compassionate but concise, wide-ranging and, above all, practical." —*Publishers Weekly.* {review of 1993 edition

Includes index.

Soep, Elisabeth
Other People's Words: Friendship, Loss, and the Conversations That Never End. Lissa Soep. Spiegel & Grau 2024. 160 p.
ISBN 9781954118355
Grades: Adult   155.9
1. Soep, Elisabeth 2. Women authors 3. Couples 4. Friendship 5. Interpersonal relations 6. Death 7. Loss 8. Memory 9. Philosophers 10. Words 11. Speech 12. Communication 13. Conversation 14. Language and languages 15. Memorials 16. Life stories — Facing adversity — Coping with death 17. Life stories — Relationships 18. Society and culture — General

In the wake of the loss of two close friends, Lissa Soep remembered the work of a Russian critic she had studied in graduate school. Suddenly, Mikhail Bakhtin's theory that our language is "filled to overflowing with other people's words" came to life. Other People's Words shows us how we carry within us the language of loved ones who are gone, and how their words can be portals to other times and places. Language—as with love—is boundless, and Other People's Words is an intimate, original, and profoundly generous look at its power to nurture life amid the wreckage of grief.

"Soep writes poignantly of her friendships and deep grief, intertwining them with Bakhtin's life and work. Anyone who has lost a loved one and still seeks their voice will appreciate this pensive book." —*Booklist*

Williams, Florence
The Nature Fix: Why Nature Makes Us Happier, Healthier, and More Creative. Florence Williams. W. W. Norton & Company 2017. 304 pages
ISBN 9780393242713
Grades: Adult   155.9
1. Nature 2. Effect of environment on humans 3. Environmental psychology 4. Creativity 5. Health 6. Well-being 7. Nature Writing — Personal Responses 8. Science Writing — Medicine and health

LC 2016040709

An investigation into the restorative benefits of nature draws on cutting-edge research and the author's explorations with international nature therapy programs to examine the relationship between nature and human cognition, mood and creativity.

"This powerful environmental call to arms proposes that for optimal well-being, regular doses of nature are not only recommended but required." —*Publishers Weekly*

Includes bibliographical references.

Winch, Guy
How to Fix a Broken Heart. Guy Winch. TED Books 2018. 120 p.
ISBN 9781501120121
Grades: Adult   155.9
1. Emotions 2. Love 3. Interpersonal relations 4. Coping 5. Society and culture — Psychology and human behavior

LC Bl2018003809

A licensed psychologist and author explains how heartbreak works, how it impacts the human brain and behavior in dramatic and unexpected ways and offers a toolkit on how to handle the emotion and learn to move on.

"Most importantly, he preaches self-compassion. This tender book reminds readers to be kind to others and themselves." —*Publishers Weekly*

Wray, Britt
Generation Dread: Finding Purpose in an Age of Climate Crisis. Britt Wray. Knopf Canada 2022. 336 p.
ISBN 9780735280724
Grades: Adult   155.9

ESSENTIAL AND RECOMMENDED TITLES
156 Comparative psychology

1. Climate change 2. Stress management 3. Anxiety 4. Mental health 5. Society and culture — Psychology and human behavior 6. Nature Writing — Environmental Issues

Finalist for the Governor General's Literary Award for English-Language Nonfiction, 2022.

Climate and environment-related fears and anxieties are on the rise everywhere. As with any type of stress, eco-anxiety can lead to lead to burnout, avoidance, or a disturbance of daily functioning. Britt Wray seamlessly merges scientific knowledge with emotional insight to show how these intense feelings are a healthy response to the troubled state of the world.

"Climate activists feeling near the end of their rope will find this full of wisdom." —*Publishers Weekly*

Finalist for the Governor General's Literary Award for English-Language Nonfiction, 2022.

Yalom, Irvin D.
Staring at the Sun: Overcoming the Terror of Death. Irvin D. Yalom. Jossey-Bass 2008. VIII, 306 p.
ISBN 9780787996680
Grades: Adult   155.9
1. Death 2. Aging 3. Fear of death 4. Mortality 5. Existentialism 6. Self-fulfillment 7. Family and Relationships — Aging and Death 8. Science Writing — Medicine and health — Mental health
LC 2007027048

Irvin D. Yalom is an author whose best-selling trade books and novels tell compelling, dramatic, and illuminating stories with which readers can identify. At 74, Yalom has penned a book that is the climax of his lifework, focusing on the universal human issues of mortality and death. He suggests that what he calls the "awakening experience" can help us acknowledge, accept, and utilize our fear of death in a very positive manner. Such an awakening experience can be as simple as a dream, or quick as a sudden insight. It is often a loss, a trauma, or just plain aging that can prompt an awakening experience that is a turning point for a more meaningful life. He discusses how people can make lasting changes in their lives, rearrange their priorities, communicate more deeply with those they love, eliminate interpersonal fears of rejection, and increase a willingness to take risks for personal fulfillment and a life filled with love.

Includes bibliographical references and index.

Zimbardo, Philip G.
The Lucifer Effect: Understanding How Good People Turn Evil. Philip Zimbardo. Random House 2007. xx, 551 p. : Illustration
ISBN 9781400064113
Grades: Adult   155.9
1. Good and evil 2. Mental health 3. Applied psychology 4. Social behavior 5. Social psychology 6. Human experimentation in psychology 7. Human rights 8. Peer pressure 9. Science Writing — Medicine and health — Mental health
LC 2006050388

Discusses why people are susceptible to the power of evil, the ability of group dynamics and situational pressures to transform human behavior, the significance of disobedience, and the true nature of heroism.

"Combining a dense but readable and often engrossing exposition of social psychology research with an impassioned moral seriousness, Zimbardo challenges readers to look beyond glib denunciations of evil-doers and ponder our collective responsibility for the world's ills." —*Publishers Weekly*

Includes bibliographical references (p. [491]-533) and index.

---

156 Comparative psychology

Fouts, Roger
Next of Kin: What Chimpanzees Have Taught Me About Who We Are. Roger Fouts with Stephen Tukel Mills; introduction by Jane Goodall. William Morrow 1997. xi, 420 p, 16 p. of plates : Illustration
ISBN 9780688148621
Grades: 11 12 Adult   156

1. Fouts, Roger 2. American Sign Language 3. Animal communication 4. Primatologists 5. Chimpanzees 6. Animal behavior 7. Human-animal communication 8. Human-animal relationships 9. Nature Writing — Animal Studies — Primates 10. Language arts and studies — Sign language
LC 97015144

ALA Notable Book, 1998; Booklist Editors' Choice: Adult Books for Young Adults, 1997.

Presents the story of Roger Fouts, a pioneer in the study of communication with chimpanzees through sign language, and his thirty-year realationship with Washoe, the clever and rambunctious matriarch of a clan of chimpanzees.

"What makes this book an exceptional popularization of scientific research is the authors' ability to charm with a fascinating story while also teaching why the story is so fascinating." —*Booklist*

A living planet book; Includes bibliographical references (p. [392]-407) and index.

Peterson, Dale
The Moral Lives of Animals. Dale Peterson. Bloomsbury Press 2010. 352 p.
ISBN 9781596914247
Grades: 11 12 Adult   156
1. Animal behavior 2. Ethics 3. Motivation 4. Zoology 5. Nature Writing — Animal Studies 6. Adult books for young adults
LC 2010024662

Challenges popular beliefs to reveal the animal kingdom's impulses toward cooperation, generosity and fairness, citing numerous examples of animals who have compromised their own safety to protect each other and what humans can learn from animal codes of behavior.

Includes bibliographical references .

Suddendorf, Thomas
The Gap: The Science of What Separates Us from Other Animals. Thomas Suddendorf. Basic Books 2013. 368 pages
ISBN 9780465030149
Grades: Adult   156
1. Comparative psychology 2. Animal behavior 3. Human nature 4. Human behavior 5. Imagination 6. Psychology 7. Human-animal relationships 8. Science Writing — Biology 9. Nature Writing — Animal Studies
LC 2013017538

An award-winning psychologist argues that a capacity for fiction distinguishes humans from animals, explaining how the human mind has a unique ability to imagine, reflect and connect with other minds to consider real and imagined scenarios.

"A reader-friendly examination of the great gap that exists between human beings and the rest of the animal world and an explanation of how our minds came to be unique." —*Kirkus*

Includes bibliographical references and index.

Waal, F. B. M. de
Our Inner Ape: A Leading Primatologist Explains Why We Are Who We Are. Frans de Waal; photographs by the author. Riverhead Books 2005. 274 p. : Illustration
ISBN 9781573223126
Grades: 11 12 Adult   156
1. Chimpanzees 2. Bonobos 3. Human behavior 4. Comparative psychology 5. Animal behavior 6. Nature Writing — Animal Studies — Primates
LC 2005042768

Booklist Editors' Choice, 2005; New York Times Notable Book, 2005.

Why we are who we are through vivid, entertaining stories of politics, sex, violence and kindness. An engrossing discourse that proposes thought-provoking and sometimes shocking connections among chimps, bonobos, and those most paradoxical of apes, human beings.

"Readers might be surprised at how much these apes and their stories resonate with their own lives, and may well be left with an urge to spend a few hours watching primates themselves at the local zoo." —*Publishers Weekly*

Includes bibliographical references (p. [239]-257) and index.

PUBLIC LIBRARY CORE COLLECTION: NONFICTION
Twentieth Edition

158 Applied psychology

Ashley, Maurice
Move by Move: Life Lessons on and off the Chessboard. Maurice Ashley, chess grandmaster. Chronicle Prism 2024. 176 p.
ISBN 9781797223650
Grades: Adult   158
1. Ashley, Maurice 2. Chess players 3. African American men 4. Chess 5. Advice 6. Personal conduct 7. Jamaican people 8. American people 9. United States 10. Autobiographies and memoirs 11. Self-Help — Personal growth — Motivation 12. Sports and Competition — Games

At age thirty-three, Maurice Ashley became the first African American to attain the rank of International Grand Master of Chess. Since that historic moment, he has brought his love of the game to a wide audience as an educator, innovator, and motivational speaker. In Move by Move, Ashley guides readers through the essential lessons that chess has taught him about life, using both personal examples from his rise from an immigrant kid playing matches in Brooklyn parks to the most rarefied levels of competition, as well as insights and anecdotes from fellow notable chess players.

"Readers need not be chess players to benefit from Ashley's solid wisdom and inspiring dedication to the game." —*Publishers Weekly*

Includes bibliographical references.

Bennett, Michael
*F*ck Feelings: One Shrink's Practical Advice for Managing All Life's Impossible Problems.* Michael Bennett, MD, Sarah Bennet. Simon & Schuster 2015. xi, 370 pages
ISBN 9781476789996
Grades: Adult   158
1. Interpersonal relations 2. Problem solving 3. Self-actualization 4. Self-help techniques 5. Self-Help — Personal growth — Happiness 6. Science writing — Medicine and health — Psychology
LC 2014048966

In a book filled with no-nonsense advice, a board-certified, Harvard-educated psychiatrist and his comedy-writer daughter, using humor and common sense, open the shrinks' secret solution manual to show readers how to find a new kind of freedom by working toward realistic goals and doing the best with what one can control.

In the title, the [u] is represented by an asterick.

Bernstein, Gabrielle
Judgment Detox: Release the Beliefs That Hold You Back from Living a Better Life. Gabrielle Bernstein. North Star Way 2018. 229 pages
ISBN 9781501168963
Grades: Adult   158
1. Happiness 2. Judgment 3. Self-actualization 4. Spirituality and Religion — Body, mind, and spirit 5. Self-Help — Personal growth — Happiness 6. Self-Help — Personal growth — Motivation
LC 2017021778

The best-selling author of The Universe Has Your Back outlines a proactive, step-by-step program for eliminating judgmental habits and achieving oneness, citing judgment as the source of most discomforts while drawing on principles ranging from yoga and meditation to EFT and metaphysical teachings to explain how to release negative beliefs.

"Readers concerned about the downsides of judgement—for both the judge and the accused—will find relief in Bernstein's comforting words and concrete plans for action." —*Publishers Weekly*

Brown, Brene
The Gifts of Imperfection: Let Go of Who You Think You're Supposed to Be and Embrace Who You Are. Brene Brown. Random House 2020. 160 p.
ISBN 9780593133583
Grades: Adult   158
1. Self-acceptance 2. Identity 3. Transformations, Personal 4. Change (Psychology) 5. Insecurity 6. Life stories — Relationships 7. Society and culture — Psychology and human behavior
LC Bl2020033635

Brown explores the psychology of releasing our definitions of an 'imperfect' life and embracing living authentically. In a world where insults, criticisms, and fears are spread too generously alongside messages of unrealistic beauty, attainment, and expectation, she provides ten 'guideposts' that can help anyone establish a practice for a life of honest beauty—a perfectly imperfect life.

"Brown offers exercises for readers to plumb their own emotions and begin to develop the kind of resilience needed to stand up to unrealistic expectations of others and ourselves." —*Booklist*

Originally published: Center City, MN : Hazelden Publishing, 2010.

Canfield, Jack
The Success Principles: How to Get from Where You Are to Where You Want to Be. Jack Canfield with Janet Switzer. Harper Resource Book 2005. xxxiii, 473 p. : Illustration
ISBN 9780060594886
Grades: Adult   158
1. Success (Concept) 2. Psychological growth 3. Spirituality and Religion — Body, mind, and spirit 4. Self-Help — Personal growth 5. Self-Help — Personal growth — Motivation
LC 2004054259

A self-improvement guide for business professionals, teachers, students, parents, or anyone interested in promoting themselves within today's success-oriented culture shares sixty-four practical or inspiring principles on how to reach desired goals.

"The author has an easy style and talks directly to readers, responding to potential what ifs and buts with encouragement and sound advice. The book's layout is superb—small paragraphs are punctuated by italicized quotes, questions for self-study, and several appropriate cartoons." —*Library Journal*

Includes bibliographical references (p. [441]-451) and index.

Carnegie, Dale
★ *How to Win Friends and Influence People.* Dale Carnegie; editorial consultant, Dorothy Carnegie, editorial assistance, Arthur R. Pell. Pocket Books 1982. xxv, 276 p.
ISBN 9780671723651
Grades: Adult   158
1. Success (Concept) 2. Business and economics — Business advice 3. Science writing — Medicine and health — Psychology 4. Self-Help — Personal growth
LC 94176452

Provides suggestions for successfully dealing with people both in social and business situations.

Includes bibliographical references and index.

Covey, Stephen R.
★ *The 7 Habits of Highly Effective People: Powerful Lessons in Personal Change.* Stephen R. Covey. Free Press 2004. 384 p.
ISBN 9780743272452
Grades: Adult   158
1. Success (Concept) 2. Character 3. Self-fulfillment 4. Personal conduct 5. Contentment 6. Vocation 7. Business and economics — Business advice 8. Adult books for young adults
LC 2004057494

A leading management consultant outlines seven organizational rules for improving effectiveness and increasing productivity at work and at home.

Includes index.

The 8th Habit: From Effectiveness to Greatness. Stephen R. Covey. Free Press 2004. xvi, 409 p.: Illustration
ISBN 9780684846651
Grades: Adult   158
1. Leadership 2. Self-fulfillment 3. Success (Concept) 4. Contentment 5. Vocation 6. Business and economics — Business Advice
LC 2004056371

ESSENTIAL AND RECOMMENDED TITLES
158 Applied psychology

A leading management consultant draws on his seven organizational rules for improving effectiveness to present an eighth principle, voice, that is based on the right balance of talent, need, conscience, and passion.

"Though conceived for individuals, Covey's book will be of tremendous importance to organizations and businesses." —*Library Journal*

Includes bibliographical references and index.

Duhigg, Charles
Smarter Faster Better: The Secrets of Productivity in Life and Business. Charles Duhigg. Random House 2016. x, 380 pages : Illustration
ISBN 9780812993394
Grades: Adult   158
1. Performance 2. Motivation 3. Decision making 4. Industrial productivity 5. Success (Concept) 6. Business and economics — Popular psychology
LC 2015034214

Explores the science of productivity, and why, in today's world, managing how you think—rather than what you think—can transform your life.

"Duhigg shows an uncanny ability to find just the right exciting example of productivity-boosting methods, leaving readers to nod in recognition that they might act in the same way to improve their lives and work." —*Kirkus*

Includes bibliographical references (pages 293-368) and index.

Fabritius, Friederike
The Leading Brain: Powerful Science-Based Strategies for Achieving Peak Performance. Friederike Fabritius, MS, and Hans W. Hagemann, PhD.. TarcherPerigee, Book 2017. xii, 324 pages
ISBN 9780143129356
Grades: Adult   158
1. Leadership 2. Performance 3. Business and economics — General 4. Science writing — Medicine and health — Psychology
LC 2016038838

Describes how neuroscience affects leadership and performance in the workplace, discussing how data can be applied in such areas as decision making, focus, teambuilding, and retaining information.

Two partners at a global leadership consultancy use their combined expertise in neuropsychology and management consulting to help readers advance their performance, retain information more efficiently, improve decision-making and build stronger teams on the job.

Includes bibliographical references (pages 285-304) and index.

Fisher, Roger
★ *Getting to Yes: Negotiating Agreement Without Giving In.* Roger Fisher and William Ury, with Bruce Patton, editor. Penguin 2011. xxix, 204 p. : Illustration
ISBN 9780143118756
Grades: Adult   158
1. Negotiation 2. Business and economics — General
LC 2011006319

Since it was first published in 1981 Getting to Yes has become a central book in the Business Canon: the key text on the psychology of negotiation. Its message of "principled negotiations"—finding acceptable compromise by determining which needs are fixed and which are flexible for negotiating parties—has influenced generations of businesspeople, lawyers, educators and anyone who has sought to achieve a win-win situation in arriving at an agreement. It has sold over 8 million copies worldwide in 30 languages, and since it was first published by Penguin in 1991 (a reissue of the original addition with Bruce Patton as additional coauthor) has sold over 2.5 million copies—which places it as the #10 bestselling title overall in Penguin Books, and #3 bestselling nonfiction title overall. We have recently relicensed the rights to Getting to Yes, and will be doing a new revised edition—a 30th anniversary of the original publication and 20th the of the Penguin edition. The authors will be bringing the book up to date with new material and a assessment of the legacy and achievement of Getting to Yes after three decades.

Includes bibliographical references.

Fogg, B. J.
Tiny Habits: The Small Changes That Change Everything. BJ Fogg, PhD.. Houghton Mifflin Harcourt 2019. 320 pages
ISBN 9780358003328
Grades: Adult   158
1. Fogg, B. J. 2. Habit 3. Change (Psychology) 4. Motivation 5. Behavior 6. Self-improvement 7. Society and culture — Psychology and human behavior 8. Life stories — Personal growth
LC 2019023920

An expert of habit formation and behavior science describes how to harness the power of transformation, whether it be to lose weight, exercise more or de-stress, through making tiny changes that we can feel good about.

Gilbert, Daniel Todd
★ *Stumbling on Happiness.* Daniel Gilbert. A.A. Knopf 2006. xvii, 277 p. : Illustration
ISBN 9781400077427
Grades: Adult   158
1. Happiness 2. Psychology 3. Decision-making 4. Society and culture — Psychology and human behavior
LC 2005044459

Royal Society General Prizes for Science Books, 2007.

A reflection on human nature brilliantly describes all that science has to tell us about the uniquely human ability to envision the future, and how likely we are to enjoy it when we get there.

"The book is a sly, irresistible romp down, or through, memory lanepast, present, and future. It is not only wildly entertaining but also hilarious . and yet full of startling insight, imaginative conclusions, and even bits of wisdom." —*Booklist*

Includes bibliographical references and index.

Gillard, Julia
★ *Women and Leadership: Real Lives, Real Lessons.* Julia Gillard, Ngozi Okonjo-Iweala. The MIT Press 2021. 336 p.
ISBN 9780262045742
Grades: Adult   158
1. Women politicians 2. Mentoring 3. Role models 4. Sexism 5. Misogyny 6. Women 7. Work 8. Ambition 9. Leadership 10. Politics and global affairs — Political figures 11. Politics and global affairs — World politics 12. Society and culture — Gender — Women 13. Business and economics — Business advice — Leadership and management
LC 2020041703

In conversation with some of the world's most powerful and interesting women, Women and Leadership explores gender bias and explores the barriers to women's participation in politics.

"A thought-provoking study of women and leadership and an outstanding contribution to this topic." —*Library Journal*

Includes bibliographical references and index; Originally published: North Sydney, N.S.W. : Random House Australia, 2020.

Hardy, Benjamin
Willpower Doesn't Work: Discover the Hidden Keys to Success. Benjamin Hardy. Hachette Books 2018. xviii, 235 pages
ISBN 9780316441322
Grades: Adult   158
1. Identity 2. Self 3. Self-Help — Personal growth 4. Self-Help — Personal growth — Happiness 5. Self-Help — Personal growth — Motivation
LC 2017042668

An organizational psychologist and Medium.Com's most-read writer, building on existing research as well as his own experiences, explains how people can change their lives on every level by making small, impactful changes in their environment that will help them to evolve into the person they want to become.

Includes index.

PUBLIC LIBRARY CORE COLLECTION: NONFICTION
Twentieth Edition

King, Vanessa
10 Keys to Happier Living: A Practical Handbook for Happiness. Vanessa King. Headline 2016. 336 pages : Illustration
ISBN 9781472233424
Grades: Adult   158
1. Happiness 2. Mental health 3. Well-being 4. Self-Help — Personal growth — Happiness
LC Bl2018037281

A practical guide to understanding happiness and how to be happier—at home, in the office and in your community.
Action for happiness—Cover; Includes bibliographical references (pages 322-332) and index.

Kishimi, Ichiro
The Courage to Be Disliked: The Japanese Phenomenon That Shows You How to Change Your Life and Achieve Real Happiness. Ichiro Kishimi and Fumitake Koga. Atria Books 2018. xviii, 270 pages
ISBN 9781501197277
Grades: Adult   158
1. Adler, Alfred, 1870-1937 2. Self-actualization 3. Psychology 4. Personal conduct 5. Thought and thinking 6. Philosophy 7. Translations — Japanese to English 8. Self-Help — Personal growth — Self-esteem 9. Self-Help — Personal growth — Happiness
LC 2018002432

Using the theories of Alfred Adler, one of the three giants of twentieth century psychology, the Courage to Be Disliked follows an illuminating conversation between a philosopher and a young man. The philosopher explains to his pupil how each of us is able to determine our own life, free from the shackles of past experiences, doubts, and the expectations of others. It's a way of thinking that is deeply liberating, allowing us to develop the courage to change, and to ignore the limitations that we and other people have placed on us. The result is a book thatis both highly accessible and profound in its importance.

"For those seeking a discourse that helps explain who they are in the world, Kishimi and Koga provide an illuminating conversation." —*Library Journal*

Langshur, Eric
Start Here: Master the Lifelong Habit of Wellbeing. Eric Langshur and Nate Klemp, PhD; foreword by Dr. Richard J. Davidson. North Star Way 2016. xi, 320 pages
ISBN 9781501129087
Grades: Adult   158
1. Happiness 2. Stress management 3. Mental health 4. Contentment 5. Well-being 6. Self-Help — Personal growth — Happiness
LC 2015043325

This revolutionary work outlines the first and only cross-training system for mastering the skill of happiness. Think P90x for the soul.

"Personal anecdotes add interest to the nuts-and-bolts format. Other books have touched on these same principles, but this book does an especially good job, walking readers step-by-step through the practices, presenting achievable goals, and encouraging readers to take charge of their emotional lives." —*Booklist*

Includes bibliographical references and index.

Lyubomirsky, Sonja
The How of Happiness: A Scientific Approach to Getting the Life You Want. Sonja Lyubomirsky. Penguin Press 2008. 366 p. : Illustration
ISBN 9781594201486
Grades: Adult   158
1. Happiness 2. Science writing — Medicine and health — Psychology
LC 2007039942

An easy-to-follow, life-changing approach designed to increase happiness and fulfillment in everyday life furnishes a comprehensive guide that redefines what happiness and what it is not and introduces activities, including exercises in practicing optimism, tips on how to savor life's pleasures, and an emphasis on staying active to achieve a happier life.

Includes bibliographical references (p. [313]-357) and index.

McGraw, Phillip C.
Life Strategies: Doing What Works, Doing What Matters. Phillip C. McGraw. Hyperion Books 2000. xiii, 304 p. : Illustration
ISBN 9780786884599
Grades: Adult   158
1. Change (Psychology) 2. Psychological growth 3. Success (Concept) 4. Self-Help — Personal growth
LC BL 00001109

A behavioral specialist and trail expert explains how to analyze one's life, identify barriers to success, and take practical steps to make life more rewarding, meaningful, and satisfying.

"McGraw claims that people in dire situations have serious problems, including denial and choosing initial assumptions without testing them for accuracy. To create a life strategy that works, McGraw lays out his ten 'Life Laws' along with checklists and 18 assignments." —*Library Journal*

Reprint. Originally published: 1999.

Palmieri, Jennifer
Dear Madam President: An Open Letter to the Women Who Will Run the World. Jennifer Palmieri. Grand Central Pub. 2018. 208 p.
ISBN 9781538713457
Grades: Adult   158
1. Women presidents 2. Women heads of state 3. Women politicians 4. Women 5. Leadership 6. Biographies 7. Business and economics — Women and the workplace
LC Bl2018000897

A former Hillary Clinton Communications Director presents an open letter to the future first woman president—and by extension, to all women working to succeed in any field—creating a forward-thinking framework of inspirational and practical advice for all women everywhere who are determined to seize control of their lives, their workplaces and their country.

Rubin, Gretchen
Outer Order, Inner Calm: Declutter & Organize to Make More Room for Happiness. Gretchen Rubin. Harmony 2019. 215 p.
ISBN 9781984822802
Grades: Adult   158
1. Self-actualization 2. Happiness 3. Orderliness 4. Success (Concept) 5. Self-Help — Personal growth — Happiness 6. Self-Help — Personal growth 7. House and Home — Cleaning, caretaking, and organizing
LC 2018029854

In this easy-to-read but hard-to-put-down book, Gretchen Rubin suggests more than 150 short, concrete clutter-clearing ideas so each reader can choose the ones that resonate most. The fact is, when we tailor our approach to suit our own particular challenges and habits, we're far more likely to be able to create the order that will make our lives happier, healthier, more productive, and more creative. With a sense of fun, and also a clear idea of what's realistic for most people, Gretchen Rubin suggests dozens of manageable steps for creating a more serene, orderly environment—one that helps us to create the lives we yearn for.

Schwartz, David Joseph
★ *The Magic of Thinking Big.* David Joseph Schwartz. Simon & Schuster 1987. 192 p.
ISBN 9780671646783
Grades: Adult   158
1. Success (Concept) 2. Self-Help — Personal growth 3. Family and Relationships — Dating and Marriage
LC 87008516

The Magic of Thinking Big gives you useful methods, not empty promises. Dr. Schwartz presents a carefully designed program for getting the most out of your job, your marriage and family life, and your community. He proves that you don't need to be an intellectual or have innate talent to attain great success and satisfaction—but you do need to learn and understand the habit of thinking and behaving in ways that will get you there. This book gives you those secrets!

A Fireside book; Includes index.

ESSENTIAL AND RECOMMENDED TITLES
158.1 Personal improvement and analysis

158.1 Personal improvement and analysis

Allen, Cory
Now Is the Way: An Unconventional Approach to Modern Mindfulness. Cory Allen. A TarcherPerigee Book 2019. xix, 185 pages
ISBN 9780525538042
Grades: Adult   158.1
1. Distraction (Psychology) 2. Mindfulness 3. Self-Help — Mental health — Anxiety and stress 4. Self-Help — Personal growth — Happiness 5. Self-Help — Personal growth — Meditation
LC 2019010666
From the popular host of the Astral Hustle, an accessible guide to hacking your mind—and life—to feel more fully present and alive, even if you're not the "the meditating type."

Alter, Adam L.
Anatomy of a Breakthrough: How to Get Unstuck When It Matters Most. Adam Alter. Simon & Schuster 2023. xxvi, 289 pages
ISBN 9781982182960
Grades: Adult   158.1
1. Self-actualization 2. Achievement motivation 3. Success (Concept) 4. Persistence 5. Self-Help — Personal growth — Motivation
LC Bl2023016410
A guide to escaping the negative thoughts, habits, jobs and relationships that keep us stuck in life offers a proven path to overcoming these factors in order to achieve our full potential.
"Alter's work will strike a chord with many looking to break out in their fields." —*Booklist*
Includes bibliographical references (pages 251-277) and index.

Asprey, Dave
Game Changers: What Leaders, Innovators, and Mavericks Do to Win at Life. Dave Asprey. Harper Wave 2018. xvii, 331 pages : Illustration
ISBN 9780062652447
Grades: Adult   158.1
1. Happiness 2. Success (Concept) 3. Personal conduct 4. Science writing — Medicine and health 5. Self-Help — Personal growth 6. Self-Help — Personal growth — Happiness
LC Bl2018188992
The Bulletproof Radio podcaster and best-selling author of the Bulletproof Diet outlines proven techniques for promoting personal happiness, health and success in accordance with the examples of today's game changers, from David Perlmutter to Arianna Huffington.
Includes bibliographical references (pages 307-317) and index.

Barry, Harry
Emotional Healing: How to Put Yourself Back Together Again. Harry, Ph.D. Barry. Pegasus Books 2021. 299 p.
ISBN 9781643136646
Grades: Adult   158.1
1. Grief 2. Loss 3. Healing 4. Emotions 5. Self-Help — Mental health — Grief and loss
In this instructive and uplifting narrative, Dr. Barry explores how to recover from loss, trauma, grief, and loneliness by helping readers identify their emotions and providing the steps to emotionally heal yourself.
"Barry offers hope to anyone willing to face their fears and do the work. Much-needed guidance in today's turbulent world." —*Booklist*

Beck, Martha Nibley
The Way of Integrity: Finding the Path to Your True Self. Martha Beck. The Open Field-Penguin Life 2021. xxiv, 327 pages; Illustration
ISBN 9781984881489
Grades: Adult   158.1
1. Self-confidence 2. Purpose in life 3. Happiness 4. Self-Help — Personal growth — Happiness 5. Book club best bets
LC 2020038463

The best-selling author and life coach draws inspiration from Dante's classic hero's journey as depicted in The Divine Comedy to outline a four-stage process for using integrity and purpose for emotional healing and relief from suffering.
"Frequent quizzes and questions help steer readers through the work needed to find their true selves, and many will be moved by Beck's sincerity and lucid techniques." —*Booklist*

Brooks, Arthur C.
Build the Life You Want: The Art and Science of Getting Happier. Arthur C. Brooks and Oprah Winfrey. Portfolio/Penguin 2023. xxvi, 242 pages
ISBN 9780593545409
Grades: Adult   158.1
1. Happiness 2. Emotions 3. Change (Psychology) 4. Self-fulfillment 5. Self-Help — Personal growth — Happiness
LC 2023019086
Offering practical research-based practices, this blueprint for a better life equips you with the emotional self-management tools needed for taking control of your present and future rather than hoping and waiting for your circumstances to improve.
"A quick read, this hopeful book will benefit readers searching for enriched well-being." —*Kirkus*
Includes bibliographical references (pages 209-242).

Brown, Tabitha
I Did a New Thing: 30 Days to Living Free. Tabitha Brown. William Morrow, an imprint of HarperCollinsPublishers 2024. xi, 241 pages
ISBN 9780063286115
Grades: Adult   158.1
1. Self-actualization 2. Inspiration 3. Habit 4. Success (Concept) 5. Change (Psychology) 6. Self-Help — Personal growth — Motivation
LC Bl2024001900
Presents an inspirational guide for encouraging positive changes in your life—one day and one challenge at a time.
"Brown's guidebook is a beacon of hope and positive changes." —*Booklist*

Cuddy, Amy
Presence: Bringing Your Boldest Self to Your Biggest Challenges. Amy Cuddy. Little, Brown & Co. 2015. 304 p.
ISBN 9780316256575
Grades: Adult   158.1
1. Self-confidence 2. Influence (Psychology) 3. Human behavior 4. Psychology 5. Society and culture — Psychology and human behavior
LC 2015952382
A Harvard psychologist and TED star shares strategic advice on how to live in accordance with one's inner resources to overcome social fears and self-doubt while heightening confidence, productivity and influence.
"Given the popularity of Cuddy's TED Talk, one would expect that this book will be in demand, and readers will not be disappointed." —*Library Journal*

Daley-Ward, Yrsa
The How: Notes on the Great Work of Meeting Yourself. Yrsa Daley-Ward. Penguin Books 2021. xxxi, 155 pages
ISBN 9780143135609
Grades: Adult   158.1
1. Self-fulfillment 2. Mind and body 3. Self-Help — Personal growth — Self-esteem 4. Poetry
LC 2021010716
Mixing together short lyrical musings with beautiful poetry, the author encourages us to meet with our most intimate self, showing us how we can remove our filters and see and feel more of who we really are behind the preconceived notions of propriety and manners,.
"Amid her musings, Daley-Ward also weaves in affirmations and prompts for self-reflection. This is a tender, hopeful meditation." —*Publishers Weekly*

PUBLIC LIBRARY CORE COLLECTION: NONFICTION
Twentieth Edition

Davis, Pete
Dedicated: The Case for Commitment in an Age of Infinite Browsing. Pete Davis. Avid Reader Press 2021. 258 p.
ISBN 9781982140908
Grades: Adult   158.1
1. Commitment (Psychology) 2. Options, alternatives, choices 3. Decision making 4. Self-Help — Personal growth
LC Bl2021010406

In a culture of restlessness and indecision, which causes tension in our lives, a civic advocate, using examples from history, personal stories and applied psychology, shows how purposeful commitment can be a powerful force.

"Well-versed in the current zeitgeist, Davis is insightful without being preachy, and his wise guide to commitment should be on everyone's reading list." —*Booklist*

Delaney, Brigid
Reasons Not to Worry: How to Be Stoic in Chaotic Times. Brigid Delaney. HarperCollins,c2023, c2022 2023. 293 p.
ISBN 9780063314825
Grades: Adult   158.1
1. Stoics 2. Philosophy 3. Psychological growth 4. Coping 5. Worry 6. Society and culture — Philosophy

In this soul-searching work, a journalist decides to let the Stoics, ancient philosophers who pondered the deepest questions of existence, be her guide, following the wisdom of Seneca, Epictetus and Marcus Aurelius to provide compelling and sensible reasons not to worry while navigating life in the modern world.

"To navigate our troubled times, Delaney turns to the work of the Stoics...She shares personal experiences along with quotes from the ancients to assess our world and the sense of desperation that seems so pervasive." —*Booklist*

Originally published in Australia by Allen & Unwin, Sydney, in 2022.

Duckworth, Angela
Grit: The Power of Passion and Perseverance. Angela Duckworth. Scribner 2016. 320 p.
ISBN 9781501111105
Grades: Adult   158.1
1. Success (Concept) 2. Persistence 3. Expectation 4. Diligence 5. Personality 6. Society and culture — Psychology and human behavior
LC 2015042880

Why do some people succeed and others fail? Sharing new insights from her landmark research on grit, MacArthur "genius" Angela Duckworth explains why talent is hardly a guarantor of success. Rather, other factors can be even more crucial such as identifying our passions and following through on our commitments. Drawing on her own powerful story as the daughter of a scientist who frequently bemoaned her lack of smarts, Duckworth describes her winding path through teaching, business consulting, and neuroscience, which led to the hypothesis that what really drives success is not "genius" but a special blend of passion and long-term perseverance. As a professor at the University of Pennsylvania, Duckworth created her own "character lab" and set out to test her theory.

"Not your grandpa's self-help book, but Duckworth's text is oddly encouraging, exhorting us to do better by trying harder, and a pleasure to read." —*Kirkus*

Includes bibliographical references and index.

Duhigg, Charles
★ *The* **Power** *of Habit: Why We Do What We Do in Life and Business.* Charles Duhigg. Random House 2012. xx, 371 p. : Illustration
ISBN 9781400069286
Grades: Adult   158.1
1. Habit 2. Change (Psychology) 3. Social psychology 4. Organizational behavior 5. Science Writing — General 6. Business and economics — Popular psychology

Identifying the neurological processes behind behaviors while explaining that self-control and success are largely driven by habits, a guide by a Yale-educated investigative reporter for the New York Times shares scientifically based guidelines for achieving personal goals and overall well-being by adjusting specific habits.

"Broad in scope and always interesting, the book should surprise and educate readers, not to mention telling them perhaps a bit more than they're comfortable knowing about the way their minds work." —*Booklist*

Includes bibliographical references (p. [293]-353) and index.

Dunne, Linnea
Lagom: The Swedish Art of Balanced Living. Linnea Dunne. Running Press 2017. 160 pages : Color; Illustration
ISBN 9780762463756
Grades: Adult   158.1
1. Self-actualization 2. Well-being 3. Work-life balance 4. Spirituality and Religion — Body, mind, and spirit 5. Self-Help — General 6. Self-Help — Personal growth — Fashion and style
LC Bl2017042018

Explains how to live "lagom," or a balanced life, by cherishing relationships, improving work-life balance, freeing the home from clutter, and savoring good food.

Includes index.

Dyer, Wayne W.
★ *The* **Power** *of Intention: Learning to Co-Create Your World Your Way.* Wayne W. Dyer. Hay House 2004. IX, 259 p.
ISBN 9781401902155
Grades: Adult   158.1
1. Spirituality and Religion — Body, mind, and spirit
LC 2003014622

Argues that intention is a force found in the universe that propels an individual into action and includes stories and examples of the prinicples of intention and ways to apply intention to everyday life.

"The author argues that there are seven faces, or energy fields, of intention: creativity, kindness, love, beauty, expansion, abundance and receptivity. Drawing on a variety of spiritual traditions and gurus, Dyer describes how to surmount the barriers that may get in the way of connecting to this power, such as negative thinking, relying on the opinion of others or retaining a controlling ego." —*Publishers Weekly*

Edmondson, Amy C.
The **Right** *Kind of Wrong: The Science of Failing Well.* Amy Edmondson. Atria Books 2023. 368 p.
ISBN 9781982195069
Grades: Adult   158.1
1. Failure 2. Industrial psychology 3. Psychology 4. Resilience 5. Business and economics — Popular psychology 6. Society and culture — Psychology and human behavior
LC 2022061950

Award-winning Harvard Business School professor Amy Edmondson has influenced legion MBA grads as well as Big Think authors from Brené Brown to Adam Grant with her pioneering work on psychological safety. Now, Amy is bringing her work to the wider world, upending our entire cultural notion of failure with this guide to the science of failing well, which actualizes the potential of psychological safety for both individuals and organizations alike.

"Perfect for readers more interested in evidence-based research than vision boards, this is a recommended addition to any self-help shelf." —*Library Journal*

Includes bibliographical references and index.

Fall, Jeremy
Falling Upwards: Living the Dream, One Panic Attack at a Time. Jeremy Fall. Hachette Go 2023. VII, 207 p.
ISBN 9780306830952
Grades: Adult   158.1
1. Fall, Jeremy, 1990- 2. Restaurateurs 3. Entrepreneurs 4. Celebrity chefs 5. Growing up 6. Anxiety 7. OCD 8. Neurodivergent people 9. Restaurants 10. Nightclubs 11. Creativity 12. Success (Concept) 13. Psychotherapy 14. Mas-

ESSENTIAL AND RECOMMENDED TITLES
158.1 Personal improvement and analysis

culinity 15. Mental health 16. North American people 17. American people 18. Autobiographies and memoirs 19. Life stories — Arts and culture — Culinary arts 20. Life stories — Facing adversity — Medical issues — Living with disabilities 21. Food writing — Memoirs and biographies 22. Science Writing — Medicine and health — Mental health 23. Debut title

LC 2023001357

Jeremy Fall grew up blocks away from LA's infamous Skid Row with a single mom who managed a restaurant to make ends meet. At night, he'd go into the kitchen and prepare elaborate and comforting snacks—the only way he knew to calm his anxious, OCD mind. As an adult, Jeremy opened fourteen restaurants around the country, collaborated with Quincy Jones, and became the first restaurateur to be represented by Jay Z's Roc Nation. Determined to destigmatize mental health for men, Falling Upwards blends Jeremy's personal narrative with practical takeaways designed to help us harness our craziest ideas and make them work—without giving up on our own mental health.

"With unvarnished honesty, Fall renders his attempts to heal amid a pressure-cooker service industry culture…which can leave little space for emotional vulnerability. It's a raw and riveting account." —*Kirkus*

Fallon, Allison
The Power of Writing It Down: A Simple Habit to Unlock Your Brain and Reimagine Your Life. Allison Fallon. Zondervan Thrive 2021. 209 pages
ISBN 9780310359340
Grades: Adult **158.1**
1. Writing 2. Behavior modification 3. Self-Help — Personal growth

LC 2020029304

For anyone feeling stuck and looking to make sense of life, author and writing coach Allison Fallon shares a simple practice and proven method to reclaiming your narrative, increasing your emotional and spiritual health, and discovering more clarity and freedom in the Power of Writing It Down.

"Any self-help reader will find comfort and clarity in Fallon's simple tips for improvement through self-expression." —*Publishers Weekly*

Includes bibliographical references (pages 205-209).

Fenet, Lydia
Claim Your Confidence: Unlock Your Superpower and Create the Life You Want. Lydia Fenet. Gallery Books 2023. VII, 280 pages
ISBN 9781982196684
Grades: Adult **158.1**
1. Self-confidence 2. Self-actualization 3. Fear 4. Self-Help — Personal growth

LC 2022018002

The author of The Most Powerful Woman in the Room Is You returns with a guide to overcoming fear and finding confidence, with insights and advice on getting out of your comfort zone and taking control of your own life.

"This book is both inspiring and invigorating, and readers will certainly respond to her challenges." —*Booklist*

Fredrickson, Barbara
Positivity: Groundbreaking Research Reveals How to Embrace the Hidden Strength of Positive Emotions, Overcome Negativity, and Thrive. Barbara Fredrickson. Crown Publishers 2009. 277 p. : Illustration
ISBN 9780307393739
Grades: Adult **158.1**
1. Positive psychology 2. Science writing — Medicine and health — Psychology

LC 2008027683

A psychologist explains how to create a richer, healthier, more fulfilling life through a process called the upward spiral that incorporates innovative techniques for using positivity to influence relationships, health, and work.

Includes bibliographical references (p. 235-266) and index.

Gardner, Chris
★ *Permission to Dream.* Christopher Gardner with Mim Eichler Rivas. Amistad 2021. 208 p.
ISBN 9780063031562

Grades: Adult **158.1**
1. Goals and objectives 2. Grandfather and granddaughter 3. Self-fulfillment 4. Harmonica 5. Death of girlfriends 6. Ambition 7. Success (Concept) 8. Autobiographies and memoirs 9. Life stories — Personal growth

LC 2020039196

Inspired by a girlfriend's death to make the most of his remaining time, Chris assists his granddaughter's search for the harmonica of her dreams while revisiting an old ambition.

"This fable-like tale, which blends biography and self-help, is an inspirational reminder to dream big and dream often. Gardner's latest memoir will especially resonate with readers of Mitch Albom and Paulo Coelho." —*Library Journal*

Goleman, Daniel
Why We Meditate: The Science and Practice of Clarity and Compassion. Daniel Goleman and Tsoknyi Rinpoche with Adam Kane. Atria Books 2022. 212 pages
ISBN 9781982178451
Grades: Adult **158.1**
1. Meditation 2. Mind and body 3. Mindfulness 4. Spirituality and Religion — Body, mind, and spirit — Meditation and mindfulness 5. Self-Help — Personal growth — Meditation 6. Self-Help — Personal growth — Happiness

LC 2022001560

Based on groundbreaking neuroscience, this practical and soul-stirring guide to meditation helps you break free from negative patterns of thought and behavior to radically embrace your very being.

"As valuable for skeptical or reluctant meditative practitioners as it is for experienced ones, this book is actionable, intentional, personal, and practical." —*Library Journal*

Includes bibliographical references (pages 197-202) and index.

Gopnik, Adam
All That Happiness Is: Some Words on What Matters. Adam Gopnik. W.W. Norton & Company 2024. 96 p.
ISBN 9781324094852
Grades: Adult **158.1**
1. Gopnik, Adam 2. Authors 3. Happiness 4. Doing things 5. Hobbies 6. Passion 7. Imagination 8. Inspiration 9. Contentment 10. Self-fulfillment 11. Arts and Entertainment — General 12. Life stories — Personal growth 13. Society and culture — Philosophy

"The result is a thought-provoking look at an eternally fascinating topic." —*Publishers Weekly*

Grover, Joanna
The Choice Point: The Scientifically Proven Method to Push Past Mental Walls and Achieve Your Goals. Joanna Grover, LCSW, and Jonathan Rhodes, PhD.; Hachette Go, an imprint of Hachette Books, Hachette Book Group 2023. xi, 256 pages : Illustration
ISBN 9780306830273
Grades: Adult **158.1**
1. Self-actualization 2. Cognitive therapy 3. Motivation 4. Goals and objectives 5. Options, alternatives, choices 6. Self-Help — Personal growth — Motivation

LC Bl2023021668

Using Functional Imagery Training (FIT), which is grounded in science, this step-by-step guide from the British psychologist who helped develop FIT and an experienced therapist and coach provides tools to achieve peak performance by helping us get to the root of our motivation and become drivers of our own minds.

"Readers looking to get off the couch and make some changes will benefit." —*Publishers Weekly*

Includes bibliographical references (pages 251-256).

Gupta, Suneel
Everyday Dharma: 8 Essential Practices for Finding Success and Joy in Everything You Do. Suneel Gupta. HarperOne 2023. 178 p.

ISBN 9780063143876
Grades: Adult 158.1
1. Dharma (Buddhism) 2. Purpose in life 3. Chakras 4. Self-actualization 5. Self-Help — Personal growth — Happiness

We've been lead to believe that if you work hard and achieve success, happiness will follow. What do we do when this formula leaves us feeling lost, exhausted, and empty inside? Gupta delivers breakthrough habits and actionable tools that will help you rediscover your calling, follow your wildest dreams, and find the fulfillment you've been searching for all along.

"Those seeking purpose amid the rigors of the everyday will find inspiration aplenty." —*Publishers Weekly*

Includes bibliographical references.

Harris, Dan

★ *10% Happier: How I Tamed the Voice in My Head, Reduced Stress Without Losing My Edge, and Found Self-Help That Actually Works—a True Story.* Dan Harris. It Books 2014. 256 pages

ISBN 9780062265425
Grades: Adult 158.1
1. Mind and body 2. Stress management 3. Meditation 4. Buddhism 5. Mindfulness 6. Buddhist meditation 7. Autobiographies and memoirs 8. Spirituality and Religion — Body, mind, and spirit — Meditation and mindfulness 9. Life stories — Religion and spirituality — Personal faith

LC 2013043037

The Nightline anchor, who had a nationally televised panic attack on Good Morning America, takes readers on a rollicking ride through the outer reaches of neuroscience to the inner sanctum of network news during which he discovered a way to get happier that is truly achievable.

Meditation for Fidgety Skeptics: A 10% Happier How-to Book. Dan Harris and Jeff Warren, with Carlye Adler. Spiegel & Grau 2017. xi, 286 pages

ISBN 9780399588945
Grades: Adult 158.1
1. Happiness 2. Meditation 3. Self-Help — Personal growth 4. Self-Help — Personal growth — Happiness 5. Self-Help — Personal growth — Meditation

LC 2017037570

Presents a practical guide to meditation that debunks the myths, misconceptions, and self-deceptions that make many people reluctant to try it, and suggests a range of meditation practices.

The co-anchor of Nightline and author of the best-selling 10% Happier presents a lighthearted, practical guide to meditation that debunks the myths, misconceptions and self-deceptions that make everyday people reluctant to participate.

Hase, Craig

How Not to Be a Hot Mess: A Survival Guide for Modern Life. Craig Hase & Devon Hase. Shambhala 2020. IX, 164 p.

ISBN 9781611807981
Grades: Adult 158.1
1. Personal conduct 2. Buddhism 3. Meditation 4. Mindfulness 5. Spiritual life 6. Spirituality and Religion — Body, mind, and spirit 7. Self-Help — Personal growth — Happiness 8. Spirituality and Religion — Buddhism

LC 2019022861

The dumpster fire of life rages on, but you got this. Six good rules to keep you grounded, weather the sh*tstorm, and actually be a decent person. It may seem like the world's going to hell in a handbasket right now. Whether it's the big stuff like politics, family dynamics, and climate change, or the little stuff like paying your bills, getting to work on time, and fending off social media trolls, we can all admit, life's no cakewalk. And yet, we all really want to at least try to show up and do the best we can (even though there's a 100% chance of f*ck-ups along the way). Here are six really good guiding principles, inspired from the ancient wisdom of Buddhism and mindfulness practice, to keep you anchored and steady as the winds of life toss you to and fro.

Includes bibliographical references (pages 153-162) and index.

Heller, Rick

Secular Meditation: 32 Practices for Cultivating Inner Peace, Compassion, and Joy. Rick Heller; foreword by Greg Epstein. New World Library 2015. xvi, 287 pages

ISBN 9781608683697
Grades: Adult 158.1
1. Meditation 2. Happiness 3. Relaxation 4. Secularism 5. Self-Help — Personal growth — Meditation 6. Spirituality and Religion — Body, mind, and spirit — Meditation and mindfulness

LC 2015027201

Meditation is an age-old secular practice with numerous scientifically verified physical and psychological benefits. As longtime meditation teacher Rick Heller here shows, meditation's benefits extend beyond the personal to enrich relationship with others, with community, and with the world. Step-by-step instructions, personal stories, and provocative questions teach empathy for others, stress reduction and inner peace, and the kind of in-the-moment living that fosters appreciation for life and resilience in the face of adversity.

"This book is an ideal guide for those who want to study meditation and mindfulness but are put off by the focus on Buddhism or religion in general." —*Library Journal*

A guide from the humanist community at Harvard; Includes bibliographical references and index.

Hendricks, Gay

Conscious Luck: Eight Secrets to Intentionally Change Your Fortune. Gay Hendricks and Carol Kline. St. Martin's Essentials 2020. x, 180 p.

ISBN 9781250622945
Grades: Adult 158.1
1. Attitude 2. Success (Concept) 3. Self-Help — Personal growth — Motivation

LC 2019054418

Two New York Times bestselling authors explain how you can Change Your Luck and Create the Life You Want. Many of us believe that luck-that mysterious force that makes life run smoothly-is somehow beyond our control. But what if you could make your own luck? What if luck, like your health and your happiness, is something that you can consciously create for yourself? In Conscious Luck, New York Times bestselling authors Gay Hendricks and Carol Kline share eight secrets-four core shifts and four daily practices-that will allow anyone to intentionally change their fortune. Instead of living at the whim of luck, waiting for the winds of chance to offer opportunities and success, Conscious Luck shows you how to seize control of your destiny, cultivate your own luck, and create the life you want to live. This step-by-step program, which includes practical techniques, inspiring true stories, and the authors' personal journeys, will lead you on the path towards freedom and abundance. From creating a luck mind-set and setting "luck-worthy" goals to learning how to be in the right place at the right time, the secrets are insightful and practical. Supported by the authors' many years of experience, this unique and highly effective toolkit offers a revolutionary way to transform your life.

Holiday, Ryan

Ego Is the Enemy. Ryan Holiday. Portfolio, Penguin 2016. xxv, 226 pages

ISBN 9781591847816
Grades: Adult 158.1
1. Ambition 2. Success (Concept) 3. Personal conduct 4. Egotism 5. Self-Help — Personal growth 6. Self-Help — Personal growth — Motivation

LC 2016017401

The best-selling author of The Obstacle is the Way, drawing on numerous stories and examples, from literature to philosophy to history to his own experience advising many high-profile clients, offers a brutally honest portrait of how we let our egos seduce us, and offers valuable advice for how we can overcome them.

Includes bibliographical references (pages 221-224).

ESSENTIAL AND RECOMMENDED TITLES
158.1 Personal improvement and analysis

Holmes, Cassie
Happier Hour: How to Beat Distraction, Expand Your Time, and Focus on What Matters Most. Cassie Holmes. Gallery Books 2022. VIII, 308 pages : Illustration
ISBN 9781982148805
Grades: Adult   158.1
1. Self-actualization 2. Time management 3. Contentment 4. Self-Help — Personal growth
LC 2021062259

A professor at UCLA's Anderson School of Management discusses ways we can maximize our limited time, with easy-to-implements tips for sidestepping distractions, designing a schedule with purpose and optimally spending the hours in the day.

"As thorough as it is practical, this one's well worth readers' time." —*Publishers Weekly*

Includes bibliographical references (pages 241-287) and index.

Jamie, Poppy
Happy Not Perfect: Upgrade Your Mind, Challenge Your Thoughts, and Free Yourself from Anxiety. Poppy Jamie. Harmony Books 2021. 298 p.
ISBN 9780593231685
Grades: Adult   158.1
1. Mindfulness 2. Self-help techniques 3. Mind and body 4. Happiness 5. Well-being 6. Mental health 7. Self-Help — Personal growth
LC Bl2021013015

An entrepreneur and influencer in mental health and mindfulness social media describes how you can create new neural pathways in your brain to upgrade your headspace and leave behind thoughts of failure, patterns of avoidance and fears of unworthiness.

"Jamie's popularity provides this self-help plan with a ready audience, and her solid, commonsense advice makes this a worthy read." —*Booklist*

Kelly, Kevin
★ *Excellent* Advice for Living: Wisdom I Wish I'd Known Earlier. Kevin Kelly. Viking 2023. 212 pages
ISBN 9780593654521
Grades: Adult   158.1
1. Personal conduct 2. Advice 3. Goals and objectives 4. Parenting 5. Interpersonal relations 6. Self-Help — Personal growth
LC Bl2023014753

A writer who helped launch Wired magazine recorded for his children some things that he had learned in life, but wished he'd known sooner, and kept adding to it, creating this optimistic guide to navigating life with grace and creativity.

"In this insightful entry, Kelly collects pearls of wisdom for all stages of life…The result is an unapologetically upbeat offering." —*Publishers Weekly*

Kross, Ethan
★ *Chatter:* The Voice in Our Head, Why It Matters, and How to Harness It. Ethan Kross. Crown Publishing 2021. 272 p.
ISBN 9780525575238
Grades: Adult   158.1
1. Self-talk 2. Thought and thinking 3. Communication 4. Interpersonal communication 5. Conversation 6. Society and culture — Psychology and human behavior
LC 2020025201

An award-winning psychologist reveals the hidden power of our inner voice and shows how we can harness it to live healthier, more satisfying, and productive lives. Tell a stranger that you talk to yourself, and you're likely to get written off as eccentric. But the truth is that we all have a voice in our head. When we talk to ourselves, we often hope to tap into our inner coach but find our inner critic instead. When we're facing a tough task, our inner coach can buoy us up: Focus—you can do this. But just as often, our inner critic sinks us entirely. I'm going to fail. They'll all laugh at me. What's the use? In Chatter, acclaimed psychologist Ethan Kross explores the silent conversations we have with ourselves. Interweaving groundbreaking behavioral and brain research from his own lab with real-world case studies—from a pitcher who forgets how to pitch to a Harvard undergrad negotiating her double life as a spy—Kross explains how these conversations shape our lives, work, and relationships. He warns that giving in to negative and disorienting self-talk—what he calls "chatter"—can tank our health, sink our moods, strain our social connections, and cause us to fold under pressure. But the good news is that we're already equipped with the tools we need to make our inner voice work in our favor. These tools are often hidden in plain sight—in the words we use to think about ourselves, the technologies we embrace, the diaries we keep in our drawers, the conversations we have with our loved ones, and the cultures we create in our schools and workplaces. Brilliantly argued, expertly researched, and filled with compelling stories, Chatter gives us the power to change the most important conversation we have each day: the one we have with ourselves.

In this debut, psychologist Kross (Emotional & Self Control Lab, Univ. of Michigan) uses numerous examples and research to show that while positive self-talk ('great job!') can be good for us, negative self-talk ('chatter') can lead to a frightening, downward spiral that can 'harm our bodies, damage our social lives, and derail our careers.' —*School Library Journal*

Manson, Mark
The Subtle Art of Not Giving a F*ck: A Counterintuitive Approach to Living a Good Life. Mark Manson. HarperOne 2016. VII, 212 pages
ISBN 9780062457714
Grades: Adult   158.1
1. Personal conduct 2. Self-fulfillment 3. Psychological growth 4. Success (Concept) 5. Failure 6. Bloggers 7. Self-help psychology 8. Page to screen 9. Humor writing — General
LC 2016011724

Filled with entertaining stories and profane, ruthless humor, a generation-defining self-help guide, written by a blogger who is read by more than 2 million people each month, helps readers figure out the things that they should care about to lead contented, grounded lives.

"This book, full of counterintuitive suggestions that often make great sense, is a pleasure to read and worthy of rereading. A good yardstick by which self-improvement books should be measured." —*Kirkus*

Made into a VOD movie, 2023.

Marriott, Sue
Secure Relating: Holding Your Own in an Insecure World. Sue Marriott, LCSW, CGP & Ann Kelley, PhD.. Harper, an imprint of HarperCollinsPublishers 2024. xx, 327 pages : Illustration; Color
ISBN 9780063334557
Grades: Adult   158.1
1. Attachment behavior 2. Interpersonal relations 3. Self-actualization 4. Mental health 5. Psychology 6. Neurobiology 7. Self-Help — Relationships 8. Self-Help — Personal growth 9. Science Writing — Medicine and health — Psychology
LC Bl2024008746

Integrating modern attachment theory, relational neuroscience and depth psychology into practical tools, two experienced mental health professionals and hosts of the Therapist Uncensored podcast offer a fresh and innovative approach to understanding and improving relationships in today's increasingly polarized world.

"An encouraging guide to a healthy mindset." —*Kirkus*

Includes bibliographical references (pages 309-318) and index.

May, Katherine
Enchantment: Awakening Wonder in an Anxious Age. Katherine May. Riverhead Books 2023. 224 p.
ISBN 9780593329993
Grades: Adult   158.1
1. May, Katherine 2. Self-actualization 3. Sense of wonder 4. Happiness 5. Self-care 6. Burn out (Psychology) 7. Self-discovery 8. Autobiographies and memoirs 9. Life stories — Personal growth
LC 2022023376

In Enchantment, May invites the reader to come with her on a journey to reawaken our innate sense of wonder and awe. With humor, candor, and warmth, she shares stories of her own struggles with work, family, and the aftereffects of

PUBLIC LIBRARY CORE COLLECTION: NONFICTION
Twentieth Edition

pandemic, particularly feelings of overwhelm as the world rushes to reopen. Enchantment invites each of us to open the door to human experience in all its sensual complexity, and to find the beauty waiting for us there.

"May's pursuit of enchantment will resonate with anyone feeling burned out or disconnected." —*Kirkus*

McGovern, Anna
Pottering: A Cure for Modern Life. Anna McGovern; illustrations by Charlotte Ager. Laurence King Publishing, Ltd 2020. 128 pages
ISBN 9781786277275
Grades: Adult   158.1
1. Personal conduct 2. Well-being 3. Resourcefulness 4. Stress management 5. Relaxation 6. Quality of life 7. Stress 8. Nothing 9. Self-Help — General

This little book is both a discussion and practical guide to one of the most British of pastimes, pottering. Author Anna McGovern writes with charm about the joy & practicality of living in the meandering moment, not asking too much of yourself and yet still getting things done in the gentlest of ways. This is the book for people who want to discover productivity at an easier pace, and above all the contentment you achieve when accepting that you can only do what you can do. Pottering is a true ode to slow living and an antidote to the stresses of modern life.

"This is a natural next-step for followers of notions like Danish hygge and Marie Kondo's tidying up." —*Booklist*

McHargue, Mike
You're a Miracle (and a Pain in the Ass): Embracing the Emotions, Habits and Mystery That Make You You. Mike McHargue. Convergent 2020. xii, 226 p. : Illustration
ISBN 9781984823243
Grades: Adult   158.1
1. Self-acceptance 2. Self-fulfillment 3. Self-management 4. Self-Help — Personal growth — Happiness 5. Self-Help — Personal growth — Motivation
LC 2019048567

Why is there such a gap between what you want to do and what you actually do? the co-host of The Liturgists Podcast and Ask Science Mike explains why our desires and our real lives are so wildly different—and what you can do to close the gap.

Includes bibliographical references (pages 209-215) and index.

Miller, Caroline Adams
Creating Your Best Life: The Ultimate Life List Guide. Caroline Adams Miller and Michael B. Frisch. Sterling 2009. xi, 276 p. : Illustration
ISBN 9781402762598
Grades: Adult   158.1
1. Self-actualization 2. Self-fulfillment 3. Happiness 4. Behavior modification 5. Change (Psychology) 6. Success (Concept) 7. Self-Help — Personal growth — Happiness
LC 2010275766

Designed to help you understand how to set and achieve clear-cut goals while also learning how and why this process can contribute to greater contentment.
Includes bibliographical references (p. [255]-268) and index.

Minami, Jikisai
It's Okay Not to Look for the Meaning of Life: A Zen Monk's Guide to Living Stress-free One Day at a Time. Jikisai Minami. Tuttle Publishing 2023. 190 pages : Illustration
ISBN 9784805317785
Grades: Adult   158.1
1. Self-actualization 2. Stress 3. Self 4. Interpersonal relations 5. Death 6. Zen Buddhism 7. Zen priests 8. Essays 9. Spirituality and Religion — Body, mind, and spirit 10. Spirituality and Religion — Buddhism 11. Self-Help — Personal growth
LC Bl2024005692

Zen monk Jikisai Minami takes the things we are supposed to strive for and turns them on their head. The 35 short, thought-provoking essays in this book are divided into four chapters about our sense of self, our hopes and dreams, our personal relationships and how to face death. Each essay begins with a deliberately controversial point of view to help us look at life's problems through fresh eyes.

"The result is an invigorating perspective on what gives life meaning and the value of focusing on the here and now." —*Publishers Weekly*

Morin, Amy
13 Things Mentally Strong Women Don't Do: Own Your Power, Channel Your Confidence, and Find Your Authentic Voice for a Life of Meaning and Joy. Amy Morin. William Morrow 2019. 335 pages
ISBN 9780062847621
Grades: Adult   158.1
1. Fortitude 2. Mental discipline 3. Business and economics — General 4. Self-Help — Personal growth — Happiness 5. Society and culture — Gender — Women
LC Bl2018197574

Describes how to foster the vital quality of mental toughness by avoiding behaviors such as insisting on perfection, comparing oneself to others, seeing vulnerability as a weakness, and letting self-doubt get in the way of goals.

"More than lists of feelings and behaviors to avoid, each of Morin's points leads into a good examination of the whys and the issues, along with common-sense alternatives." —*Booklist*

Includes bibliographical references (pages 321-335).

Oyeneyin, Tunde
Speak: Find Your Voice, Trust Your Gut, and Get from Where You Are to Where You Want to Be. Tunde Oyeneyin with Hilary Liftin. Avid Reader Press 2022. xiv, 218 pages
ISBN 9781982195441
Grades: Adult   158.1
1. Oyeneyin, Tunde 2. Self-actualization 3. Bicycling 4. Training 5. Nigerian Americans 6. Self-Help — Personal growth — Motivation
LC Bl2022013075

The hugely popular Peloton instructor, fitness star and founder of Speak shares her transformative personal journey during which she learned lessons about loss, love, body image and self-confidence, offering an accessible blueprint for anyone looking to make a positive change in their lives.

"Fans of Oyeneyin will appreciate her guidance and find pieces of solid advice from her personal experiences." —*Kirkus*

Parker, James
★ *Get Me Through the Next Five Minutes: Odes to Being Alive.* James Parker. W W Norton & Co. Inc 2024. 288 p.
ISBN 9781324091639
Grades: Adult   158.1
1. Gratitude 2. Everyday life 3. Psychological growth 4. Memories 5. Essays 6. Anthologies 7. Humor writing — Social humor 8. Arts and Entertainment — General

Our politics are broken; our world is melting; the next catastrophe looms. Enter James Parker, who for years now has been writing odes of appreciation on subjects from the seemingly minor ("Ode to Naps") to the unexpected ("Ode to Giving People Money") to the seemingly minor, unexpected, and hyperspecific ("Ode to Running in Movies"). Collecting Parker's beloved and much-lauded odes in one place, this volume demonstrates the profound power of the form. The odes range across music, movies, literature, psychology, and more, all through the lens of Parker's personal history. Together, they form an accidental how-to guide to honoring your own experience—and to finding your own odes.

"An entertaining book that exudes style, it can be dabbled in and read in short bursts." —*Booklist*

Patrick, Vanessa M.
The Power of Saying No: The New Science of How to Say No That Puts You in Charge of Your Life. Vanessa Patrick, PhD.. Sourcebooks 2023. xviii, 315 pages : Illustration
ISBN 9781728251523
Grades: Adult   158.1

ESSENTIAL AND RECOMMENDED TITLES
158.1 Personal improvement and analysis

1. Assertiveness 2. Respect 3. Personal conduct 4. Self-Help — Personal growth

LC 2022047817

Everyone has a hard time saying no, but doing so can vastly improve our lives and relationships. Enter the art of empowered refusal: the skill of strategically saying no from a place of personal power that gives voice to your principles, values, and priorities while protecting your relationships and reputations. In Power of Saying No, Professor and researcher Vanessa Patrick explains that empowered refusal is a much-needed framework that can be mastered with thoughtful practice. By setting boundaries and being respectful to others (and yourself!) saying no can help you live your happiest, most successful life.".

"Filled with personal anecdotes, case studies, and quotes from literature, this persuasive book will set readers on the path to self-awareness and empowerment." —Booklist

Includes bibliographical references (pages 279-300) and index.

Peck, M. Scott
★ The Road Less Traveled: A New Psychology of Love, Traditional Values, and Spiritual Growth. M. Scott Peck. Simon & Schuster 2002. 315 p.
ISBN 9780743238250
Grades: Adult   158.1

1. Self-fulfillment 2. Psychological growth 3. Interpersonal relations 4. Love 5. Values 6. Spirituality 7. Spirituality and Religion — General

LC 2002075858

A psychiatrist suggests ways in which confronting and resolving problems, a painful process most people try to avoid, can lead to greater self-understanding and spiritual growth.

"This book proved a smash when it debuted in 1978, selling several million copies. This 25th-anniversary edition includes a new introduction in which the publisher claims the author "explains the ideas that shaped this book and continue to influence an expanding audience of readers." That might sound like PR, but this truly was one of the first books dealing with the psychology of spirituality and paved the way for numerous others that followed in its wake." —Library Journal

Power, Marianne
Help Me!: One Woman's Quest to Find Out If Self-Help Really Can Change Your Life. Marianne Power. Grove Press 2019. 384 p.
ISBN 9780802129062
Grades: Adult   158.1

1. Power, Marianne 2. Women 3. Self-help psychology 4. Self-improvement 5. Self-fulfillment 6. Personal finance 7. Women journalists 8. Interpersonal relations 9. Psychology 10. Autobiographies and memoirs 11. Life stories — Personal growth

LC 2018045957

Offers a humorous and honest account of the author's year-long quest to remake her life using the advice from some of the best known and acclaimed self-help books.

"Some of her plights are hilarious; others are almost unbearably poignant. Self-help seekers will be moved and entertained by Power's over-the-top exploits." —Booklist

Originally published in the UK by Pan Macmillan, 2018.

Price, Devon
★ Laziness Does Not Exist. Devon Price. Atria Books 2021. 256 p.
ISBN 9781982140106
Grades: Adult   158.1

1. Laziness 2. Labor productivity 3. Work-life balance 4. Success (Concept) 5. Work 6. Corporate culture 7. Social psychology 8. Psychology 9. Business and economics — Popular psychology 10. Society and culture — Psychology and human behavior

A social psychologist uncovers the psychological basis of the "laziness lie," which originated with the Puritans and has ultimately created blurred boundaries between work and life with modern technologies and offers advice for not succumbing societal pressure to "do more."

"With particular impact for those in managerial positions, Price's important and eye-opening book will benefit every reader." —Booklist

Rinaldi, Karen
It's Great to Suck at Something: The Unexpected Joy of Wiping Out and What It Can Teach Us About Patience, Resilience, and the Stuff That Really Matters. Karen Rinaldi. Atria Books, c2019. 2019. 238 pages
ISBN 9781501195761
Grades: Adult   158.1

1. Failure 2. Resilience 3. Life skills 4. Play 5. Imperfection 6. Enjoyment 7. Happiness 8. Motivation 9. Self-acceptance 10. Self-fulfillment 11. Society and culture — Psychology and human behavior

LC Bl2019006313

Citing the inherent shortcomings of today's prioritization of productivity over play, a guide to building resilience through imperfection shares counsel on how to have fun trying new things without the expectation of being good at them.

"For Rinaldi, current trends that elevate hyperspecialization have created a culture of imbalance and stress. To make her points, she brings in ideas of others writers, such as Thich Nhat Hanh, Anthony Bourdain, and Edward Lorenz, to support the suck at something ethos. Rinaldi's seductive lessons and embrace of messiness and incompleteness will inspire readers looking to spark personal change." —Publishers Weekly

Robbins, Anthony
Unlimited Power: The New Science of Personal Achievement. Anthony Robbins. Simon & Schuster 1997. xix, 425 p. : : Illustration
ISBN 9780684845777
Grades: Adult   158.1

1. Success (Concept) 2. Psychological growth 3. Self-Help — Personal growth

LC 97035403

Reveals the secrets of neurolinguistic programming and explains how to master both mind and body while gaining emotional and financial freedom and increasing self-confidence.

Originally published: 1986.

Rodsky, Eve
Find Your Unicorn Space: Reclaim Your Creative Life in a Too-Busy World. Eve Rodsky. G.P. Putnam's Sons 2021. xvii, 316 pages : Illustration
ISBN 9780593328019
Grades: Adult   158.1

1. Goals and objectives 2. Creativity 3. Self-fulfillment 4. Self-Help — Personal growth — Creativity

LC 2021046693

The New York Times bestselling author of Fair Play presents an inspirational guide for setting personal goals, cultivating creativity, and reclaiming your "Unicorn Space"—the personal time we all need to discover our gifts, interests and talents.

"Rodsky's friendly tone is encouraging and reassuring to readers trying to relocate their life's spark and the time to pursue it." —Booklist

Includes bibliographical references (pages 301-308) and index.

Roth, Robert
Strength in Stillness: The Power of Transcendental Meditation. Bob Roth, with Kevin Carr O'Leary. Simon & Schuster 2018. 214 p.
ISBN 9781501161216
Grades: Adult   158.1

1. Transcendental Meditation 2. Self-Help — Personal growth — Meditation 3. Spirituality and Religion — General 4. Self-Help — Personal growth

LC 2017035499

A practical guide to meditation by a leading authority shares insights into the scientific principles behind why and how Transcendental Meditation works to reduce stress, access inner power, and build resilience.

"A thorough explanation of what transcendental meditation is and is not that will appeal to readers of mindfulness and seekers of stress reduction and mental composure." —Library Journal

PUBLIC LIBRARY CORE COLLECTION: NONFICTION
Twentieth Edition

Sharot, Tali
Look Again: The Power of Noticing What Was Always There. Tali Sharot and Cass R. Sunstein. Signal Press 2024. 288 p.
ISBN 9781668008201
Grades: Adult   158.1
1. Observing things 2. Self-fulfillment 3. Everyday life 4. Options, alternatives, choices 5. Life 6. Society and culture — Psychology and human behavior

For fans of Thinking Fast and Slow and the Power of Habit, a groundbreaking new study of how disrupting our well-worn routines, both good and bad, can rejuvenate our days and reset our brains to allow us to live happier and more fulfilling lives.

"If your world is starting to look gray and dull, this book might be your road map out of the comfort zone." —Kirkus

Shlain, Tiffany
24/6: The Power of Unplugging One Day a Week. Tiffany Shlain. Gallery Books 2019. 246 pages
ISBN 9781982116866
Grades: Adult   158.1
1. Time management 2. Technology 3. Quality of life 4. Work-life balance 5. Rest 6. Distraction (Psychology) 7. Creativity 8. Compassion 9. Family relationships 10. Interpersonal relations 11. Interpersonal communication 12. Society and culture — Media and technology 13. Family and Relationships — Families 14. Business and economics — Popular psychology
LC 2019943854

The award-winning Internet pioneer and filmmaker chronicles the past, present and future of ideas about time and technology, outlining a strategy for clarity and life-quality based on disconnecting from technology for one restful day of the week.

Siegel, Daniel J.
Aware: The Science and Practice of Presence : The Groundbreaking Meditation Practice. Daniel J. Siegel, M.D.. TarcherPerigee, a imprint of Penguin Random House LLC 2018. xiii, 379 pages : Illustration
ISBN 9781101993040
Grades: Adult   158.1
1. Meditation 2. Mindfulness 3. Self-actualization 4. Spirituality and Religion — Body, mind, and spirit — Meditation and mindfulness 5. Science writing — Medicine and health — Psychology 6. Self-Help — Personal growth
LC 2018016987

The New York Times best-selling author of Brainstorm and Mindsight introduces readers to his science-based Wheel of Awareness meditation discipline, demonstrating how a practice of focused attention and kindness can promote brain health and psychological wellness.

Includes bibliographical references (pages 367-368) and index.

Sincero, Jen
You Are a Badass. Jen Sincero. Running Press 2017. 269 pages
ISBN 9780762490547
Grades: Adult   158.1
1. Self-actualization 2. Self-help techniques 3. Self-Help — Personal growth — Happiness 4. Self-Help — Personal growth — Motivation
LC Bl2017041242

A special hardcover edition of the #1 New York Times best-selling self-help classic, which empowers readers to create positive changes in their lives, and is filled with unforgettable lessons, features a new foreword from the author, who reflects on the book's almost-five-year span of incredible success.

Offers a blunt and irreverent guide to achieving the money, relationships, career, and happiness that one desires through recognizing and doing away with self-sabotaging beliefs and behaviors.

"Sincero writes with candor about her own struggles, heightening the message's accessibility, particularly among a younger set." —Publishers Weekly

Includes bibliographical references (pages 257-267).

You Are a Badass Every Day: How to Keep Your Motivation Strong, Your Vibe High, and Your Quest for Transformation Unstoppable. Jen Sincero. Viking 2018. 216 pages
ISBN 9780525561644
Grades: Adult   158.1
1. Motivation 2. Success (Concept) 3. Spirituality and Religion — Body, mind, and spirit 4. Self-Help — Personal growth — Creativity 5. Self-Help — Personal growth — Motivation
LC 2018045770

An empowering collection of edgy, bite-sized daily mantras and meditations counsels readers on how to make the most of personal resources and opportunities while embracing the courage to let go of mistakes, take responsibility and enjoy one's successes.

An empowering collection of edgy, bite-sized daily mantras and meditations offers advice on how to make the most of personal resources and opportunities while embracing the courage to let go of mistakes, take responsibility, and enjoy success.

Includes index.

Stulberg, Brad
Peak Performance: Elevate Your Game, Avoid Burnout, and Thrive with the New Science of Success. Brad Stulberg, Steve Magness. Rodale 2017. IX, 230 p.
ISBN 9781623367930
Grades: Adult   158.1
1. Self-actualization 2. Self-Help — Personal growth 3. Business and economics — General 4. Science writing — Medicine and health — Psychology
LC 2017021865

A few common principles drive performance, regardless of the field or the task at hand. Whether someone is trying to qualify for the Olympics, break ground in mathematical theory or craft an artistic masterpiece, many of the practices that lead to greatsuccess are the same. In Peak Performance, Brad Stulberg, a former McKinsey and Company consultant and writer who covers health and the science of human performance, and Steve Magness, a performance scientist and coach of Olympic athletes, team up to demystify these practices and demonstrate how everyone can achieve their best. The first book of its kind, Peak Performance combines the inspiring stories of top performers across a range of capabilities—from athletic, to intellectual, to artistic—with the latest scientific insights into the cognitive and neurochemical factors that drive performance in all domains. In doing so, Peak Performance uncovers new linkages that hold promise as performance enhancers but have been overlooked in our traditionally-siloed ways of thinking. The result is a life-changing book in which readers learn how to enhance their performance via myriad ways including: optimally alternating between periods of intense work and rest; priming the body and mind for enhanced productivity; and developing and harnessing the power of a self-transcending purpose. In revealing the science of great performance and the stories of great performers across a wide range of capabilities, Peak Performance uncovers the secrets of success, and coaches readers on how to use them. If you want to take your game to the next level, whatever "your game" may be, Peak Performance will teach you how.

Includes bibliographical references (pages 203-216) and index.

Stutz, Phil
Lessons for Living: What Only Adversity Can Teach You. Phil Stutz. Random House 2023. xiii, 183 pages
ISBN 9780593731086
Grades: Adult   158.1
1. Resilience 2. Life change events 3. Happiness 4. Self-Help — Personal growth
LC 2023032649

In this profound collection of short essays he's been writing since the late 1990s, the famed therapist and subject of the Netflix documentary Stutz addresses real-world circumstances and offers a new way to think about life itself in a culture that denies the nature of reality.

"Stutz lays a clear path to self-acceptance and self-love. The essays are not grouped by topic, but there is a natural flow that makes for compelling reading." —Booklist

ESSENTIAL AND RECOMMENDED TITLES
158.1 Personal improvement and analysis

Suh, Krista
DIY Rules for a WTF World: How to Speak Up, Get Creative, and Change the World. Krista Suh. Grand Central Publishing 2018. 248 pages : Color; Illustration
ISBN 9781538712337
Grades: Adult **158.1**
1. Feminism 2. Creativity 3. Self-fulfillment 4. Business and economics — Business advice — Leadership and management 5. Self-Help — Personal growth — Creativity 6. Self-Help — Personal growth — Self-esteem
LC Bl2018000296

Offers advice, personal experiences, and inspiration from the creator of the Pussyhat Project intended to help readers live life purposefully and make the world better though creativity, self confidence, and overcoming obstacles and negativity.

The artist, feminist and screenwriter behind the Pussyhat Project offers her proclamation and guide for women everywhere to use to create their own personal paths to joy and success while making the world a safer place for others on similar journeys.

Includes bibliographical references (page 247).

Tatum, Scott
Friendly Reminders: Lessons from a Self-Care Savage. Scott Tatum. Rock Point 2023. 191 p.
ISBN 9781631069338
Grades: Adult **158.1**
1. Self-actualization 2. Happiness 3. Self-fulfillment 4. Self-help techniques 5. Self-Help — Personal growth — Self-esteem

Scott Tatum is here to help you find your way back to yourself. In Friendly Reminders, Scott reminds us that life is tough, but meeting challenges with discipline, determination, a positive attitude, and mindfulness can lead you to a meaningful life that will inspire others. With 140 friendly reminders and practical advice, you'll learn how to prioritize yourself and your well-being by entering the Self-Care Savage journey of self-healing.

"Those seeking motivation will find it here." —*Publishers Weekly*

Tierney, John
The Power of Bad: How the Negativity Effect Rules Us and How We Can Rule It. John Tierney and Roy F. Baumeister. Penguin Press 2019. 304 p.
ISBN 9781594205521
Grades: Adult **158.1**
1. Negativism 2. Interpersonal conflict 3. Personal conduct 4. Self-management 5. Society and culture — Psychology and human behavior
LC 2019017303

The best-selling authors present a revelatory analysis of the negativity bias to explain its inherent role in social, political and professional conflicts, sharing recommendations for balancing phobias with rational strategies.

Includes bibliographical references and index.

Tippett, Krista
★ *Becoming Wise: An Inquiry into the Mystery and Art of Living.* Krista Tippett. Penguin Group USA 2016. 384 p.
ISBN 9781594206801
Grades: Adult **158.1**
1. Personal conduct 2. Spirituality 3. Faith 4. Psychological growth 5. Media tie-ins 6. Spirituality and religion — General
LC Bl2016007662

From the best-selling author and host of NPR's On Being comes a master class in living drawn from the inspiring stories of extraordinary individuals who possess what she calls "spiritual genius."

"A hopeful consideration of the human potential for enlightenment." —*Kirkus*

Based on a podcast.

Toussaint, Alex
★ *Activate Your Greatness.* Alex Toussaint. Henry Holt and Company 2023. 245 pages
ISBN 9781250852038
Grades: Adult **158.1**
1. Personal conduct 2. Success (Concept) 3. Achievement motivation 4. Personal trainers 5. Autobiographies and memoirs 6. Self-Help — Personal growth — Motivation 7. Life stories — Personal growth
LC 2023017112

Drawing on his mantra of "Feel good, Look Good, Do Better," the Senior Peloton Instructor gives readers the inspiration and motivation to excel in every aspect of their lives both on and off the bike.

"Told with humility and gratitude, Toussaint's mix of memoir and self-help is sure to inspire a wide range of readers." —*Booklist*

Turner, Tina
★ *Happiness Becomes You: A Guide to Changing Your Life for Good.* Tina Turner. Atria Books 2020. 240 pages
ISBN 9781982152154
Grades: Adult **158.1**
1. Turner, Tina, 1939-2023 2. Buddhist women 3. Buddhism 4. Spiritual life 5. Buddhists 6. Women singers 7. African American women musicians 8. Loss 9. Rock musicians 10. United States 11. Autobiographies and memoirs 12. Biographies 13. Life stories — Religion and spirituality 14. Spirituality and religion — Buddhism 15. Arts and Entertainment — Music — Rock 16. Life stories — Arts and culture — Performing arts — Musicians and composers

The iconic performing artist provides spiritual tools and advice for self-empowerment and fulfillment while examining the role of her enduring Buddhist faith in helping her overcome poverty, loss, and other personal and professional obstacles.

"This is a quasi-biography wrapped around an exploration of Buddhism, with roughly equal emphasis on personal anecdotes and devotional practices.... Acessible explanations of Buddhist principles are neatly integrated into the narrative." —*Booklist*

Vollmer, Becky
You Are Not Stuck: How Soul-Guided Choices Transform Fear into Freedom. Becky Vollmer. St. Martin's Essentials 2023. xxv, 214 pages : Illustration
ISBN 9781250864369
Grades: Adult **158.1**
1. Change (Psychology) 2. Options, alternatives, choices 3. Contentment 4. Self-fulfillment 5. Self-Help — Personal growth — Happiness 6. Self-Help — Personal growth — Self-esteem
LC 2022040409

Becky Vollmer's You Are Not Stuck…is a unique blend of permission and spirituality that will help you excavate your divine inner badass, close the gap between intention and action, and develop a strategic path forward that's as unique as your thumbprint. Through warm and straightforward wisdom, a modern and approachable take on ancient yoga philosophy, a series of practical and insightful grounding exercises, and a healthy dose of laugh-out-loud humor, you'll learn how to make soul-guided choices in support of the life you've desired all along."

"Vollmer's candid reflections about disliking the person she was before she quit her job add gravitas to the spirited prose. The result is an earnest exhortation to pursue one's passions." —*Publishers Weekly*

Includes bibliographical references (pages 205-214).

Waldinger, Robert J.
★ *The Good Life: Lessons from the World's Longest Scientific Study of Happiness.* Robert Waldinger, MD, and Marc Schulz, PhD.. Simon & Schuster 2023. 352 p.
ISBN 9781982166694
Grades: Adult **158.1**
1. Psychology 2. Research 3. Data mining 4. Generations 5. Happiness 6. Contentment 7. Interpersonal relations 8. Purpose in life 9. Society and culture — Psychology and human behavior 10. Science Writing — Medicine and health — Mental health 11. Life stories — General

What makes a life fulfilling and meaningful? The simple but surprising answer is: relationships. The stronger our relationships, the more likely we are to live happy, satisfying, and overall healthier lives. The invaluable insights in this book emerge from the revealing personal stories of hundreds of participants in the Harvard Study of Adult Development as they were followed year after year for their entire adult lives, and this wisdom is bolstered by research findings from this and many other studies.

"Combining intensive research with actionable steps, this penetrating testament to the power of human connection offers gems for almost anyone looking to improve their happiness." —*Publishers Weekly*

Includes bibliographical references and index.

Wan, Bonnie
The Life Brief: A Playbook for No-Regrets Living. Bonnie Wan. Simon Element 2024. xxv, 227 pages
ISBN 9781982195502
Grades: Adult **158.1**
1. Self-actualization 2. Self-fulfillment 3. Decision making 4. Personal conduct 5. Self-Help — Personal growth
LC Bl2024000938

Based on the business world's most-used organizational tool, this essential guide for aligning life with your personal, professional, cultural and spiritual dreams features three phases to help you identify your core values and align every are of your life with them so you can feel fulfilled every day.

"Readers willing to put in the work will be rewarded with true insights." —*Booklist*

Includes bibliographical references (pages 213-216) and index.

Wiking, Meik
The Little Book of Hygge: Danish Secrets to Happy Living. Meik Wiking. William Morrow 2017. IX, 221 pages : Color; Illustration
ISBN 9780062658807
Grades: Adult **158.1**
1. Happiness 2. Self-actualization 3. Personal conduct 4. Spirituality and Religion — Body, mind, and spirit — Meditation and mindfulness 5. Science writing — Medicine and health 6. Self-Help — Personal growth — Happiness
LC Bl2016052564

A guide to the Danish philosophy of well-being shares advice and ideas for taking healthy breaks, living in the moment, creating positive atmospheres, building relationships and finding the richness of life in everyday small comforts.

"An exciting and intriguing guide, full of ideas for making everyday life more cozy." —*Library Journal*

Willink, Jocko
Discipline Equals Freedom: Field Manual. Jocko Willink. St. Martin's Press 2017. 199 pages : Illustration
ISBN 9781250156945
Grades: Adult **158.1**
1. Discipline 2. Mental discipline 3. Self-control 4. Business and economics — General 5. Self-Help — Personal growth 6. Self-Help — Personal growth — Motivation
LC Bl2017034739

An ex-Navy SEAL presents a guide on how to achieve freedom through discipline, outlining the mental and physical practices that shaped his career and continue to help him reach fulfilling goals while outmaneuvering common pitfalls.

The former Navy SEAL and host of the top-rated "Jocko Podcast" presents a motivational guide on how to achieve freedom through discipline, outlining the mental and physical practices that shaped his career and continue to help him reach fulfilling goals while outmaneuvering common pitfalls in the areas of procrastination, fitness and lifestyle habits.

Wilson, A'ja
★ *Dear Black Girls: How to Be True to You.* A'ja Wilson. Flatiron Books 2024. 208 p.
ISBN 9781250290045
Grades: Adult **158.1**
1. African American women 2. Racism 3. Sexism 4. Success (Concept) 5. Self-esteem 6. Black people 7. Women basketball players 8. Women Olympic athletes 9. American people 10. North American people 11. United States 12. Autobiographies and memoirs 13. Life stories — Identity — Race and ethnicity
LC 2023037609

In this empowering and deeply personal collection—adapted from and expanded upon the piece of the same name in the Players' Tribune—WNBA star A'ja Wilson shares stories from her life. Despite gold medals, championships, and a list of accolades, Wilson knows how it feels to be swept under the rug. To not be heard, to not feel seen, to not be taken seriously. One remarkable author's necessary and meaningful exploration of what it means to be a Black woman in America today—and an of-the-moment rally cry to lift up women and girls everywhere.

"Her book is a powerful and crucial call to support women and girls worldwide and a source of encouragement for everyone seeking to embrace their authentic self and overcome obstacles." —*Booklist*

158.2 Interpersonal relations

Bradford, Joy Harden
Sisterhood Heals: The Transformative Power of Healing in Community. Joy Harden Bradford, PhD.. Ballantine Books 2023. 240 p.
ISBN 9780593497241
Grades: Adult **158.2**
1. Female friendship 2. African American women 3. Sisterhood 4. Healing 5. Psychological growth 6. Friendship 7. Interpersonal relations 8. Communities 9. Debut title 10. Family and relationships — Friendship 11. Society and culture — Psychology and human behavior
LC 2023001241

A licensed psychologist and host of the award-winning mental health podcast Therapy for Black Girls helps us foster relationships that are not only positive, but transformative, bringing the warmth, wisdom, empathy and levity to remind us that during difficult times, sisterhood is often a much-needed lifeline.

"Bradford's celebration of friendship is moving, backed with psychological depth, and especially welcome in a culture that sometimes downplays nonromantic bonds. This is food for the soul." —*Publishers Weekly*

Includes bibliographical references.

Brooks, David
★ *How to Know a Person: The Art of Seeing Others Deeply and Being Deeply Seen.* David Brooks. Random House 2023. 352 p.
ISBN 9780593230060
Grades: Adult **158.2**
1. Interpersonal communication 2. Interpersonal relations 3. Social behavior 4. Listening 5. Respect 6. Mutualism 7. Understanding (Personal quality) 8. Ethics 9. Self-fulfillment 10. Psychology 11. Social psychology 12. Society and culture — Psychology and human behavior 13. Family and Relationships — General

As David Brooks observes, "There is one skill that lies at the heart of any healthy person, family, school, community organization, or society: the ability to see someone else deeply and make them feel seen—to accurately know another person, to let them feel valued, heard, and understood." and yet we humans don't do this well. All around us are people who feel invisible, unseen, misunderstood. Here Brooks sets out to help us do better, posing questions that are essential for all of us: If you want to know a person, what kind of attention should you cast on them? What kind of conversations should you have? What parts of a person's story should you pay attention to?

"His advice may not be revolutionary, but it's certainly down-to-earth and entertaining." —*Booklist*

Coel, Michaela
★ *Misfits: A Personal Manifesto.* Michaela Coel. Henry Holt & Company 2021. 80 p.
ISBN 9781250843449
Grades: Adult **158.2**

ESSENTIAL AND RECOMMENDED TITLES
158.2 Interpersonal relations

1. Coel, Michaela 2. Actors and actresses 3. Black British women 4. Women playwrights 5. Growing up 6. Misfits (People) 7. Sexual violence victims 8. Psychic trauma 9. Identity 10. Advice 11. Personal conduct 12. Honesty 13. Self-discovery 14. Life stories — Arts and culture — Performing arts 15. Life stories — Identity — Race and ethnicity 16. Life stories — Personal growth

When invited to deliver the MacTaggart Lecture at the Edinburgh International Television Festival, Michaela Coel touched a lot of people with her striking revelations about race, class and gender, but the person most significantly impacted was Coel herself. Building on her celebrated speech, Misfits immerses readers in her vision through powerful allegory and deeply personal anecdotes—from her coming of age in London public housing to her discovery of theater and her love for storytelling. And she tells of her reckoning with trauma and metamorphosis into a champion for herself, inclusivity, and radical honesty.

"Coel is a gifted storyteller, and her meditations on not fitting in will resonate and be welcomed by an audience of new and longtime fans." —*Library Journal*

Dahl, Melissa
Cringeworthy: A Theory of Awkwardness. Melissa Dahl. Portfolio 2018. xii, 286 pages
ISBN 9780735211636
Grades: Adult   158.2
1. First impressions 2. Self-perception 3. Social phobia 4. Human behavior 5. Self 6. Psychology 7. Shyness 8. Introverts 9. Embarrassment 10. Identity 11. Interpersonal relations 12. Society and culture — Psychology and human behavior 13. Family and Relationships — General
LC 2017052219

The editor of New York magazine's "Science of Us" website explores the compelling psychology of awkwardness, sharing scientific insights into how truly embarrassing moments are actually perceived by others and how learning to accept one's cringe-worthy gaffes can be socially advantageous.

Includes bibliographical references (pages 257-276) and index.

Darling, Daniel
Agents of Grace: How to Bridge Divides and Love as Jesus Loved. Daniel Darling. Zondervan 2023. 240 p.
ISBN 9780310366324
Grades: Adult   158.2
1. Faith (Christianity) 2. Love 3. Christian life 4. Spirituality and Religion — Christianity

For each of us who feels discouraged about the divisions in our country, our churches, and our families, Daniel Darling offers a hope-filled way forward in this practical, compelling call to obey Jesus's command to love one another.

"Those looking for common ground with other believers will find this a useful place to start." —*Publishers Weekly*

Denworth, Lydia
Friendship: The Evolution, Biology, and Extraordinary Power of Life's Fundamental Bond. Lydia Denworth. W.W. Norton & Company 2020. 297 p.
ISBN 9780393651546
Grades: Adult   158.2
1. Friendship 2. Neuropsychology 3. Mind and body 4. Evolution 5. Biology 6. Companionship 7. Social interaction 8. Human behavior 9. Science Writing — Biology 10. Society and culture — Psychology and human behavior
LC 2019032111

In Friendship, journalist Lydia Denworth visits the front lines of the science of friendship in search of its biological, psychological, and evolutionary foundations. Denworth weaves together past and present, field biology and cutting-edge neuroscience, to show how our bodies and minds are designed to make friends, the process by which social bonds develop, and how a drive for friendship underpins human (and nonhuman) society.

"Denworth's work achieves the best of science writing by making complicated concepts clear. She uses intelligent observation, empathy, and curiosity to offer a friendship manifesto that will absolutely affect readers' own personal approaches to friendship." —*Booklist*

Includes bibliographical references and index.

Goleman, Daniel
★ *Social Intelligence: The New Science of Human Relationships*. Daniel Goleman. Bantam Books 2006. 403 p. : Illustration
ISBN 9780558303525
Grades: 9 10 11 12 Adult   158.2
1. Interpersonal relations 2. Emotions 3. Social intelligence 4. Neuroscience 5. Society and culture — Psychology and human behavior

Explores the nature of human relationships, finding that humans are "wired to connect," and bringing together the latest research in biology and neuroscience to reveal how one's daily encounters shape the brain and affect the body.

"The author argues for a new social model of intelligence drawn from the emerging field of social neuroscience. Goleman illuminates new theories about attachment, bonding, and the making and remaking of memory as he examines how our brains are wired for altruism, compassion, concern and rapport." —*Publishers Weekly*

Includes bibliographical references (p. [337]-391) and index.

Goulston, Mark
Talking to Crazy: How to Deal with the Irrational and Impossible People in Your Life. Mark Goulston. American Management Association 2015. 259 pages : Illustration
ISBN 9780814436363
Grades: Adult   158.2
1. Interpersonal conflict 2. Interpersonal relations 3. Science writing — Medicine and health — Psychology 4. Self-Help — Relationships
LC 2015012549

Provides a range of techniques for communicating with unreasonable people by empathizing with their "crazy," using this counterintuitive method to change the dynamic of the conversation and become an ally rather than a threat.

Includes index.

Grant, Adam M.
Give and Take: A Revolutionary Approach to Success. Adam M. Grant. Viking Press 2013. 320 p.
ISBN 9780670026555
Grades: Adult   158.2
1. Generosity 2. Success (Concept) 3. Goals and objectives 4. Altruism 5. Motivation 6. Social psychology 7. Human behavior 8. Business and economics — Business Advice
LC 2012039995

An award-winning researcher and consultant explains how effective networking, influence and leadership skills are subject to the professional interaction styles of takers, matchers and givers that dramatically shape success rates, citing the essential roles of behind-the-scenes contributors to famous organizations while outlining a revolutionary approach to networking and productivity.

Howes, Molly
A Good Apology: Four Steps to Make Things Right. Molly Howes. Grand Central Publishing 2020. 304 pages
ISBN 9781538701317
Grades: Adult   158.2
1. Apologizing 2. Emotions 3. Self-Help — Personal growth 4. Self-Help — Relationships
LC 2019050663

"Those looking for a way to say sorry and mean it will learn much from Howe's approachable demystification of the art of the apology." —*Publishers Weekly*

Includes bibliographical references and index.

Ingall, Marjorie
Sorry, Sorry, Sorry: The Case for Good Apologies. Marjorie Ingall and Susan McCarthy. Gallery Books 2023. x, 355 pages : Illustration
ISBN 9781982163495
Grades: Adult   158.2
1. Apologizing 2. Remorse 3. Communication 4. Personal conduct 5. Society and culture — Psychology and human behavior 6. Self-Help — General

LC 2022020890

Drawing on a deep well of research in psychology, sociology, law, and medicine, [Ingall and McCarthy] explain why a good apology is hard to find and why it doesn't have to be. Alongside their six (and a half)-step formula for apologizing beautifully, Ingall and McCarthy also delve into how to respond to a bad apology; why corporations, celebrities, and governments seldom apologize well; how to teach children to apologize; how gender and race affect both apologies and forgiveness; and most of all, why good apologies are essential, powerful, and restorative."

"Useful, helpful, and full of relevant examples to illustrate how to improve one's apology skills." —*Library Journal*

Includes bibliographical references (pages 317-355).

Murthy, Vivek Hallegere

Together: The Healing Power of Human Connection in a Sometimes Lonely World. Vivek H. Murthy, MD.. Harper Wave 2020. 352 p.
ISBN 9780062913296
Grades: Adult **158.2**
1. Communities 2. Loneliness 3. Mental health 4. Public health 5. Communication 6. Science writing — Medicine and health — Mental health

LC 2020002242

In Together, the former Surgeon General addresses the overlooked epidemic of loneliness as the underpinning to the current crisis in mental wellness and offers solutions to create connection and stresses the importance of community to counteract the forces driving us to depression and isolation.

"A touch too pat at times but, overall, a well-considered diagnosis of a real and overlooked crisis in public health." —*Kirkus*

Includes bibliographical references and index.

Phillips, Adam

On Giving Up. Adam Phillips. Farrar, Straus, and Giroux 2024. 160 p.
ISBN 9780374614140
Grades: Adult **158.2**
1. Self-sacrifice 2. Addiction 3. Change 4. Lifestyle change 5. Failure 6. Transformations, Personal 7. Personal conduct 8. Ethics 9. Psychoanalysis 10. Society and culture — Psychology and human behavior 11. Society and culture — Philosophy

LC 2023040929

Giving up our supposed vices is one thing; giving up on life itself is quite another. One form of self-sacrifice feels positive, something to admire and aspire to, while the other is profoundly unsettling, if not actively undesirable. There are always, it turns out, both good and bad sacrifices, but it is not always clear beforehand which is which. We give something up because we believe we can no longer go on as we are. In On Giving Up, the acclaimed psychoanalyst Adam Phillips illuminates both the gaps and the connections between the many ways of giving up and helps us to address the central question: What must we give up in order to feel more alive?

"If this collection marks the beginning of Phillips' late style, we have a lot to look forward to." —*Booklist*

Rollag, Keith

What to Do When You're New: How to Be Comfortable, Confident, and Successful in New Situations. Keith Rollag. AMACOM—American Management Association 2015. x, 230 pages
ISBN 9780814434895
Grades: Adult **158.2**
1. Interpersonal relations 2. Self-confidence 3. Success (Concept) 4. Business and economics — Business advice

LC 2015011043

Provides strategies for becoming more comfortable and achieving success in new situations, explaining how to overcome anxieties in order to make great first impressions, fearlessly perform tasks, and confidently interact with others.

Includes bibliographical references (pages 217-223) and index.

Schafer, John R.

The Like Switch: An Ex-FBI Agent's Guide to Influencing, Attracting, and Winning People Over. Jack Schafer, Ph.D, with Marvin Karlins, Ph.D.. Simon & Schuster 2015. xv, 270 pages : Illustration
ISBN 9781476754482
Grades: Adult **158.2**
1. Friendship 2. Interpersonal attraction 3. Influence (Psychology) 4. Interpersonal relations 5. Self-Help — Personal growth

LC 2014009121

Offers advice and strategies for readers to get others to like them, assess truthfulness, and read the body behavior of others.

Includes bibliographical references (pages 257- 261) and index.

Shapiro, Susan

The Forgiveness Tour: How to Find the Perfect Apology. Susan Shapiro. Skyhorse Publishing 2021. x, 238 pages
ISBN 9781510762718
Grades: Adult **158.2**
1. Shapiro, Susan 2. Apologizing 3. Forgiveness 4. Self-Help — Personal growth

In her entrancing, heartfelt new memoir the Forgiveness Tour: How to Find the Perfect Apology, Shapiro wrestles with how to exonerate someone who can't cough up a measly 'My bad' or mumble 'Mea culpa.' Seeking wisdom, she explores the billion-dollar Forgiveness Industry touting the personal benefits of absolution, where the only choice on every channel is: Radical forgiveness. She fears it's all bullshit."

"By blending these stories with her own experiences and writing with insight, humor, and grace, Shapiro's elegant survey becomes one largely about plumbing the boundless depths of the human heart. This is essential reading." —*Publishers Weekly*

Stone, Douglas

Difficult Conversations: How to Discuss What Matters Most. Douglas Stone, Bruce Patton, Sheila Heen. Viking 1999. xxi, 250 p. : Illustration
ISBN 9780670883394
Grades: Adult **158.2**
1. Communication 2. Interpersonal relations 3. Interpersonal communication 4. Confrontation (Interpersonal relations) 5. Family and Relationships — General

LC 98033346

Offers advice on working gracefully and effectively through such confrontational situations as ending relationships and asking for a raise, identifying key adjustments necessary to the dialogue process.

Waxman, Jamye

How to Break up with Anyone: Letting Go of Friends, Family, and Everyone In-Between. Jamye Waxman. Seal Press 2015. 228 p.
ISBN 9781580055970
Grades: Adult **158.2**
1. Friendship 2. Conflict resolution 3. Self-fulfillment 4. Interpersonal relations 5. Self-help techniques 6. Self-Help — Personal growth 7. Family and Relationships — General

LC 2015019613

Offers advice to deal with every step of a non-romantic breakup, and provides strategies for disengaging from a friend, family member, or community.

"Sound guidance for those involved in toxic relationships and looking for a way out." —*Library Journal*

Includes bibliographical references.

---

160 Philosophical logic

Copi, Irving M.

★ *Introduction* to Logic. Irving M. Copi, Carl Cohen. Pearson/Prentice Hall 2019. xvii, 670 p. : Illustration
ISBN 9781138500860

ESSENTIAL AND RECOMMENDED TITLES
169 Analogy

Grades: Adult **160**
   1. Logic 2. Society and culture — Philosophy
                                                   LC 2018056876

For more than six decades, and for thousands of students, Introduction to Logic has been the gold standard in introductory logic texts. In this 15th Edition, Carl Cohen and Victor Rodych update Irving M. Copi's classic text, improving on its many strengths and introducing new and helpful material that will greatly assist both students and instructors.

Includes bibliographical references and index.

169 Analogy

Hofstadter, Douglas R.
Surfaces and *Essences*. Douglas Hofstadter and Emmanuel Sander. Basic Books 2010. 512 p.
   ISBN 9780465018475
Grades: Adult **169**
   1. Thought and thinking 2. Psychology 3. Cognitive science 4. Reasoning 5. Science Writing — General 6. Society and culture — Psychology and human behavior
                                                   LC BI2010009678

Shows how analogy-making pervades human thought at all levels, choosing our words and phrases for us when we speak, framing how we understand even the most boring everyday situation, guiding us in unfamiliar situations, and giving rise to great acts of imagination.

170 Ethics (Moral philosophy)

Coles, Robert
Lives of Moral Leadership. Robert Coles. Random House 2000. xvii, 247 p.
   ISBN 9780375501081
Grades: 9 10 11 12 Adult **170**
   1. Personal conduct 2. Leadership 3. Ethics 4. Role models 5. History writing — General
                                                   LC 00027858

In an incisive study of moral leadership and its implications, the best-selling author of the Moral Life of Children profiles individuals who have had a profound influence on contemporary American life and examines those qualities that allow people to become moral leaders in their homes, communities, and nation.

Dalai Lama
An Appeal to the World: The Way to Peace in a Time of Division. Dalai Lama XIV. William Morrow & Company 2017. 128 p.
   ISBN 9780062835536
Grades: Adult **170**
   1. Peace-building 2. Political science 3. Philosophy, Buddhist 4. Buddhist doctrines 5. Buddhism 6. Spiritual life 7. Spirituality and Religion — Buddhism 8. Politics and global affairs — World politics
                                                   LC 2017278828

A noted religious leader addresses the world's time of division, calling on us to draw upon the innate goodness of our shared humanity to overcome the rancor, mistrust and divisiveness that threaten world peace and sustainability.

"Always inspiring and accessible, this lovely book is, itself, readers will discover, worth meditation and contemplation." —*Booklist*

Egan, Kerry
On Living. Kerry Egan. Riverhead Books 2016. 208 pages :
   ISBN 9781594634819
Grades: Adult **170**
   1. Death 2. Regret 3. Terminal care 4. Physicians 5. Life 6. Autobiographies and memoirs 7. Life stories — Facing adversity — Coping with death
                                                   LC 2016026365

A hospice chaplain shares the meaning the dying make of their lives, to help us understand what is ultimately important and to make the most of our own still-being-lived lives.

"As the title suggests, this is not just a book about dying. Its one that will inspire readers to make the most of every day." —*Publishers Weekly*

Kubler-Ross, Elisabeth
Life Lessons: Two Experts on Death and Dying Teach Us About the Mysteries of Life and Living. Elisabeth Kubler-Ross and David Kessler. Scribner 2000. 224 p.
   ISBN 9780684870748
Grades: Adult **170**
   1. Personal conduct 2. Death 3. Life 4. Fear 5. Anger 6. Love 7. Forgiveness 8. Family and Relationships — Aging and Death
                                                   LC 00057387

A guide to living life in the moment uses lessons learned from the dying to help the living find the most enjoyment and happiness.

"As in each of their previous individual works, the authors provide useful and accessible information." —*Library Journal*

Lamott, Anne
Almost Everything: Notes on Hope. Anne Lamott. Riverhead Books 2018. 192 p.
   ISBN 9780525537441
Grades: Adult **170**
   1. Lamott, Anne 2. Spirituality 3. Hope 4. Life 5. Anxiety 6. Self-esteem 7. Autobiographies and memoirs 8. Spirituality and Religion — Christianity 9. Life stories — Religion and spirituality — Personal faith
                                                   LC 2018013899

Presents an inspirational guide to the role of hope in everyday life and explores essential truths about how to overcome burnout and suffering by deliberately choosing joy.

Lavery, Daniel M.
Dear Prudence: Liberating Lessons from Slate.Com's Beloved Advice Column. Daniel M. Lavery. HarperOne 2023. 368 p.
   ISBN 9780063140363
Grades: Adult **170**
   1. Personal conduct 2. Lifestyles 3. Advice columns 4. Advice columnists 5. Interpersonal relations 6. Anthologies 7. Essays 8. Society and culture — Psychology and human behavior 9. Society and culture — Media and technology
                                                   LC 2022047770

Based on the long-running SLATE advice column, a collection of the most eye-opening, illuminating, and provocative installments during Daniel M. Lavery's tenure as the titular Prudence.—.

"Lavery's wit is on full display and his biting responses satisfyingly pull no punches." —*Booklist*

Shahvisi, Arianne
Arguing for a Better World: How Philosophy Can Help Us Fight for Social Justice. Arianne Shahvisi. Penguin 2023. 293 p.
   ISBN 9780143136835
Grades: Adult **170**
   1. Philosophy 2. Ideology 3. Ethics 4. Argumentation 5. Social justice 6. Social change 7. Society and culture — Philosophy 8. Society and culture — Social activism and philanthropy

Philosopher Arianne Shahvisi shows us how to work through thorny moral questions by examining their parts in broad daylight, equipping us to not only identify our own positions but to defend them as well. This book demonstrates the relevance of philosophy to our everyday lives, and offers some clear-eyed tools to those who want to learn how to better fight for justice and liberation for all.

"This is a fascinating, pragmatic resource for those who want to make a difference but don't know where to start." —*Publishers Weekly*

Includes bibliographical references (pp. 235-282) and index.

PUBLIC LIBRARY CORE COLLECTION: NONFICTION
Twentieth Edition

Shriver, Maria
I've Been Thinking ...: Reflections, Prayers, and Meditations for a Meaningful Life. Maria Shriver. Pamela Dorman Books/Viking 2018. xi, 225 pages
ISBN 9780525522607
Grades: Adult **170**
1. Spiritual life 2. Purpose in life 3. Optimism 4. Spirituality and religion — General
LC 2018300874

Presents a book of reflections for those seeking wisdom, guidance, encouragement, and inspiration on the road to a meaningful life.

"Among the topics she covers are kindness, mental health, peace, time to reflect, grief, and power of the mind, of women, of the pause, of empathy. The honesty of this uplifting book will please Shrivers established readership as well as new readers looking for inspiration." —*Publishers Weekly*

Sullivan, Meghan
The Good Life Method: Reasoning Through the Big Questions of Happiness, Faith, and Meaning. Meghan Sullivan and Paul Blaschko. Penguin Press 2022. 304 p.
ISBN 9781984880307
Grades: Adult **170**
1. Virtue 2. Ethics 3. Personal conduct 4. Society and culture — Philosophy
LC 2020054704

Notre Dame Philosophy professors Meghan Sullivan and Paul Blaschko have gone deep with that work in their wildly popular and influential undergraduate course GOD AND THE GOOD LIFE, in which they wrestle with the big questions about how to live and what makes life meaningful. Now they invite us into the classroom to tackle such issues as what justifies your beliefs, whether you should practice a religion, and what sacrifices you should make for others—as well as to investigate what Aristotle, Plato, Descartes, Kant, and Murdoch have to say about how to live well. Sullivan and Blaschko teach us how to reason through real-world case studies by doing the timeless work of philosophy like escaping our own caves, learning to doubt everything, asking strong questions, grasping our own purpose, and wrestling with the problem of evil and the existence of God.

"Recommended for those interested in improving their lives through an intellectual approach grounded in the realities of life in today's challenging world." —*Library Journal*

Includes bibliographical references and index.

Tutu, Desmond
Made for Goodness: And Why This Makes All the Difference. Desmond Tutu and Mpho Tutu. Harpercollins 2010. 256 p.
ISBN 9780061706592
Grades: Adult **170**
1. Hope 2. Virtue 3. Common good 4. Optimism 5. Joy and sorrow 6. Forgiveness 7. Prayer 8. Spirituality and Religion — Christianity 9. Adult books for young adults
LC 2010003774

In his most personal and inspirational book to date, a beloved Nobel Prize-winner joins his daughter, an Anglican minister, to share a powerful vision on why each of us can find hope and joy even in troubled times—because we are all made for goodness."

"The book is founded on the broad notion that we are created with the freedom to choose good or evil but also incline fundamentally to the good. A crucially important book from the Nobel Peace Prize winner; a witness to our tumultuous times." —*Library Journal*

Winkler, Kyle
Permission to Be Imperfect: How to Strive Less, Stress Less, Sin Less. Kyle Winkler. Chosen, a division of Baker Publishing Group 2024. 219 pages
ISBN 9780800763695
Grades: Adult **170**
1. Personal conduct 2. Christian life 3. Peace of mind 4. Happiness 5. God (Christianity) 6. Spirituality and Religion — Christian living 7. Self-Help — Personal growth — Spirituality

LC 2023036796

Popular Bible teacher Kyle Winkler shares the keys to lasting peace, joy, and healing, helping you win the war against toxic emotions and behaviors, spark growth fueled by God's love and grace—not rules and performance—and experience a powerful new way of living. God designed the abundant, victorious life to happen more effortlessly than you imagined!

"Winkler recalls in this candid guide how…he felt tormented by unfulfilled promises of inner peace and pressures to display flawless religious devotion…Self-critical Christians will find Winkler's assurances a breath of fresh air." —*Publishers Weekly*

Includes bibliographical references (pages 215-219).

171 Ethical systems

Aristotle
★ *Nicomachean Ethics.* Aristotle; translation (with historical introduction) by Christopher Rowe; philosophical introduction and commentary by Sarah Broadie. Oxford University Press 2002. x, 468 p.
ISBN 9780198752714
Grades: Adult **171**
1. Ethics 2. Society and culture — Philosophy
LC 2002283430

This work presents the Nicomachean Ethics in a fresh English translation by Christopher Rowe that strives to be meticulously accurate yet also accessible. The translation is accompanied by Sarah Broadie's detailed line-by-line commentary, which brings out the subtlety of Aristotle's thought as it develops from moment to moment.

Includes bibliographical references (p. 457-462) and indexes.

172 Political ethics

Sandel, Michael J.
Justice: What's the Right Thing to Do? Michael J. Sandel. Farrar Straus & Giroux 2009. 288 p.
ISBN 9780374180652
Grades: Adult **172**
1. Justice 2. Values 3. Ethics 4. Common good 5. Personal conduct 6. Social change 7. Social life and customs 8. United States 9. 21st century 10. Society and culture — Violence and crime — Criminal justice system
LC 2009025438

A Harvard professor assesses the role of justice in modern society as well as the moral responsibilities faced by ordinary citizens, weighing a range of issues from euthanasia and abortion to affirmative action and tax structuring.

"The author has a talent for making the difficult—Kant's categorical imperative or Rawls's difference principle—readily comprehensible, and his relentless, though often unoppressive, reason shines throughout the narrative. Sparkling commentary from the professor we all wish we had." —*Kirkus*

174 Occupational ethics

Callahan, David
The Cheating Culture: Why More Americans Are Doing Wrong to Get Ahead. David Callahan. Harcourt 2004. IX, 366 p.
ISBN 9780156030052
Grades: 11 12 Adult **174**
1. Business ethics 2. Professional ethics 3. Social ethics 4. Moral conditions 5. United States 6. Adult books for young adults 7. Business and economics — Popular psychology 8. Society and culture — Pop culture
LC Bl2005009403

A look at cheating in modern-day society places the blame on the highly competitive economic climate of the past two decades, explaining why an unfettered market and unprecedented economic inequities have eroded American values.

ESSENTIAL AND RECOMMENDED TITLES
174.2 Medical and health professions

"If all business school students could be required to read one book, this should be it." —*Choice*

A Harvest book; Includes bibliographical references and index.

Gentile, Mary C.
Giving Voice to Values: How to Speak Your Mind When You Know What's Right. Mary C. Gentile. Yale University Press 2010. xliv, 273 p.
ISBN 9780300161182
Grades: Adult   174
1. Business ethics 2. Leadership 3. Values 4. Business and economics — Business advice 5. Business and economics — Business advice — Leadership and management
LC 2010011905

"Gentile offers a powerful action-oriented manifesto for living with integrity, fighting for one's convictions, and building a more ethical workplace." —*Publishers Weekly*

Includes bibliographical references (p. 259-268) and index.

Oreskes, Naomi
Merchants of Doubt: How a Handful of Scientists Obscured the Truth on Issues from Tobacco Smoke to Global Warming. Naomi Oreskes and Erik M. Conway. Bloomsbury Press 2010. 368 p.
ISBN 9781596916104
Grades: Adult   174
1. Scientists 2. Science news 3. Environmental sciences 4. Science Writing — General
LC 2009043183

Documents the troubling influence of a small group of scientists who the author contends misrepresent scientific facts to advance key political and economic agendas, revealing the interests behind their detractions on findings about acid rain, DDT and other hazards."

Includes bibliographical references and index.

Romeo, Nick
The Alternative: How to Build a Just Economy. Nick Romeo. Public Affairs Books 2024. 384 p.
ISBN 9781541701595
Grades: Adult   174
1. Economic policy 2. Economics 3. Success in business 4. Income inequality 5. Business ethics 6. Fairness 7. Social justice 8. Private equity 9. Anthologies 10. Business and economics — Economics — Socioeconomics 11. Business and economics — Economics

Covering the world's most innovative economic and policy ideas for the New Yorker, a journalist presents unforgettable stories and successes of people working to build economies that are more equal, just and livable, and, combining in-depth reporting with expert analysis, explores the structure of a system that could actually work for everyone.

"This is an eye-opening handbook for a better world." —*Publishers Weekly*

Sandel, Michael J.
What Money Can't Buy: The Moral Limits of Markets. Michael J. Sandel. Farrar, Straus and Giroux 2012. 256 p.
ISBN 9780374203030
Grades: Adult   174
1. Economics 2. Capitalism 3. Wealth 4. Value 5. Business and economics — Economics — Socioeconomics
LC 2011052182

The political philosopher shares a revisionist view of the roles of markets and money in a democratic society, assessing the moral limits of markets in private life and how the market economy has encroached on private and societal values.

Includes bibliographical references and index.

174.2 Medical and health professions

Elliott, Carl
★ *The Occasional Human Sacrifice: Medical Experimentation and the Price of Saying No.* Carl Elliott. W.W. Norton & Company 2024. 320 p.
ISBN 9781324065500
Grades: Adult   174.2
1. Elliott, Carl, 1961- 2. Medical research 3. Experimental medicine 4. Human experimentation in medicine 5. Patients 6. Patient advocacy 7. Risk 8. Medical malpractice 9. Whistle blowers 10. Scandals 11. Medical ethics 12. Science Writing — Medicine and health 13. History writing — Scandals 14. History writing — Science, technology, and medicine 15. Life stories — Science, technology, and medicine

Carl Elliott is a bioethicist at the University of Minnesota who was trained in medicine as well as philosophy. For many years he fought for an external inquiry into a psychiatric research study at his own university in which an especially vulnerable patient lost his life. Elliott's efforts alienated friends and colleagues. The university stonewalled him and denied wrongdoing until a state investigation finally vindicated his claims. His experience frames the six stories in this book of medical research in which patients were deceived into participating in experimental programs they did not understand, many of which had astonishing and well-concealed mortality rates.

"Elliot's exposé of unconscionable medical experiments pays tribute to the often wounded truth tellers who unmask these appalling practices." —*Booklist*

Reverby, Susan M.
Examining Tuskegee: The Infamous Syphilis Study and Its Legacy. Susan M. Reverby. University of North Carolina Press 2009. 384 pages : Illustration
ISBN 9780807833100
Grades: Adult   174.2
1. Racism in medical care 2. Medical ethics 3. Human experimentation in medicine 4. Medical research 5. Syphilis 6. Alabama 7. Science Writing — Medicine and health — Illness and disease 8. History writing — Plague and famine 9. History writing — African American — Civil rights — United States

"The 'What' and the 'Why' of the Tuskegee Study are surrounded by conflicting accounts and complex agendas, giving it at least two lives: That of the study itself and that of the telling and retelling of the story of the study." —*Choice*

Includes bibliographical references and index.

Tucker, Todd
The Great Starvation Experiment: The Heroic Men Who Starved so That Millions Could Live. Todd Tucker. Free Press 2006. xi, 270 p. : Illustration
ISBN 9780743270304
Grades: 11 12 Adult   174.2
1. Keys, Ancel Benjamin, 1904- 2. Hunger 3. Human experimentation in medicine 4. Conscientious objectors 5. World War II 6. United States 7. 20th century 8. History writing — Wars and conflicts — World War II 9. Adult books for young adults
LC 2006278255

An account of a six-month, late-World War II experiment on thirty-six American conscientious objectors assigned to the Civilian Public Service corps traces how Dr. Ancel Keys, the inventor of the K-ration, studied the effects of extreme food rationing practices in Europe.

"As WWII neared an end, 36 idealistic conscientious objectors, members of the Civilian Public Service, volunteered to be systematically starved. The project, headed by Dr. Ancel Keys, was designed to develop an understanding of the physiology and psychology of starvation and to provide strategies to manage the mass starvation that might follow the war's end in Europe. Tucker . . . provides a fascinating and moving history of the experiment, centering on the lives and experiences of the volunteers and the formidable obstacles they overcame." —*Publishers Weekly*

Includes bibliographical references (p. 233-258) and index.

PUBLIC LIBRARY CORE COLLECTION: NONFICTION
Twentieth Edition

176 Ethics of sex and reproduction

Chavez Perez, Inti
Respect: Everything a Guy Needs to Know About Sex, Love, and Consent. Inti Chavez Perez; translated from the Swedish by Stuart Tudball. Penguin Books 2019. 206 p.
ISBN 9780143134251
Grades: Adult 176
1. Respect 2. Young men 3. Interpersonal relations 4. Men-women relations 5. Science writing — Medicine and health — Men's health 6. Family and Relationships — Growing Up
LC 2019018370

Citing the serious issues revealed by the #MeToo movement, an all-encompassing guide counsels male readers on sex and consent in the 21st century, covering topics ranging from body image and relationships to gender identity and sexual orientation.

Translation of author's book Respekt; Includes bibliographical references.

177 Ethics of social relations

Agarwal, Pragya
Sway: Unravelling Unconscious Bias. Pragya Agarwal. Bloomsbury Sigma 2020. 448 pages
ISBN 9781472971357
Grades: Adult 177
1. Unconscious bias 2. Subliminal perception 3. Prejudice 4. Discrimination 5. Sex discrimination 6. Gender equity 7. Race relations 8. Racism 9. Stereotypes 10. Society and culture — General

Using real-world stories underpinned by scientific theories and research, one of the top 100 most influential women in social enterprise in the UK unravels the way our unconscious bias affects the way we communicate and perceive the world.

"Despite a generally scholarly tone, this relevant work accessibly reveals the insidious nature of stereotyping and does much to encourage readers to examine—and take responsibility for—their own implicit biases." —*Publishers Weekly*

Includes bibliographical references (pages 416-441) and index.

Ariely, Dan
The Honest Truth About Dishonesty: How We Lie to Everyone—especially Ourselves. Dan Ariely. Harper 2012. xiii, 285 pages
ISBN 9780062183590
Grades: Adult 177
1. Dishonesty 2. Truth 3. Human behavior 4. Behavioral economics 5. Honesty 6. Personal conduct 7. Decision-making 8. Psychology 9. Society and culture — Psychology and human behavior 10. Science Writing — General
LC 2012015990

From Washington to Wall Street, the classroom to the workplace, an award-winning, bestselling author and behavior economist explores the question of dishonesty to help us understand why cheating is so prevalent and what we can do about it.

Includes bibliographical references (pages 267-273) and index.

Armstrong, Karen
Twelve Steps to a Compassionate Life. Karen Armstrong. Alfred A. Knopf 2010. 240 p.
ISBN 9780307595591
Grades: Adult 177
1. Compassion 2. Virtues 3. Ethics 4. Christian ethics 5. Christianity 6. Twelve-step programs 7. Mindfulness 8. Spirituality and Religion — Christianity
LC 2010036870

The award-winning author shares practical recommendations for promoting world peace by cultivating one's intrinsic tendencies for compassion, outlining a program for achieving mindfulness and engaging in acts of kindness.

A Borzoi book; Includes bibliographical references.

Baker, Billy
We Need to Hang Out: A Memoir of Making Friends. Billy Baker. Avid Reader Press 2021. 288 p.
ISBN 9781982111083
Grades: Adult 177
1. Baker, Billy (Journalist) 2. Journalists 3. Married men 4. Male friendship 5. Loneliness 6. Solitude 7. Social interaction 8. College friends 9. Childhood friends 10. Friendship 11. Social life and customs 12. Social psychology 13. United States 14. Autobiographies and memoirs 15. Life stories — Personal growth 16. Family and Relationships — Friendship 17. Society and culture — Gender — Men 18. Society and culture — Psychology and human behavior

At the age of forty, having settled into his busy career and active family life, Billy Baker discovers that he's lost something crucial along the way: His friends. Other priorities always seemed to come first, until all his close friendships had lapsed into distant memories. In We Need to Hang Out, Baker embarks on an entertaining and relatable quest to reprioritize his ties with his buddies and forge more connections, all while balancing work, marriage, and kids. Along the way, Baker talks to experts in sociology and psychology to investigate how such naturally social creatures as humans could become so profoundly isolated today.

"Baker's evolution from the start of his project to the end of the book is gratifying, and he also discusses the effects of the pandemic on his experiences, providing readers with an up-to-date viewpoint on the necessity of strong male friendships, especially during times of crisis." —*Kirkus*

Campbell, Jeremy
The Liar's Tale: A History of Falsehood. Jeremy Campbell. Norton 2001. 363 p.
ISBN 9780393025590
Grades: Adult 177
1. Truthfulness and falsehood 2. Society and culture — Philosophy
LC 2001030286

Inquires into the nature of deception and debates the nature of truth and ethics, the diverse faces and devices of falsehood, and the postmodern emphasis on meaning at the expense of truth.

"This challenging romp through the underbelly of intellectual history ... is fascinating and troublesome." —*New York Times Book Review*

Includes bibliographical references (p. 315-344) and index.

Cohen, Rhaina
★ *The Other Significant Others: Reimagining Life with Friendship at the Center.* Rhaina Cohen. St. Martin's Press 2024. 304 p.
ISBN 9781250280916
Grades: Adult 177
1. Friendship 2. Single people 3. Platonic love 4. Devotedness 5. Personal conduct 6. Expectation 7. Social norms 8. Alternative lifestyles 9. Happiness 10. Family and Relationships — Friendship 11. Life stories — Relationships — Friendship 12. Society and culture — General 13. Debut title
LC 2023036060

Inviting us into the lives of people who have defied convention by choosing a friend as a life partner, a producer and editor for NPR offers a powerful narrative on platonic partnerships and how the thrill, intimacy and commitment we seek is often found through meaningful friendship.

"This inspiring book disrupts traditional perspectives on relationships, making it a captivating read for those intrigued by alternative models and seeking a more expansive comprehension of a fulfilling life." —*Booklist*

Includes bibliographical references and index.

Sow, Aminatou
Big Friendship: How We Keep Each Other Close. Aminatou Sow and Ann Friedman. Simon & Schuster 2020. 288 p.
ISBN 9781982111908

ESSENTIAL AND RECOMMENDED TITLES
179 Other ethical norms

Grades: Adult   177

1. Sow, Aminatou 2. Friedman, Ann 3. Friendship 4. Female friendship 5. Interpersonal relations 6. Long distance friendship 7. Interracial friendship 8. Media tie-ins 9. Life stories — Relationships — Friendship 10. Family and Relationships — Friendship 11. Society and culture — Psychology and human behavior

LC 2020002283

The feminist hosts of the Call Your Girlfriend podcast argue that close friendship is the most influential and important relationship a human life can have, sharing strategies for creating fulfilling, long-term relationships with friends.

"A soul-searching reflection that delivers an emotional journey to amplify the self-help tips." —*Kirkus*

Includes index; Based on a podcast.

Velasquez, Lizzie
Dare to Be Kind: How Extraordinary Compassion Can Transform Our World. Lizzie Velasquez, with Catherine Avril Morris. Hachette Books 2017. 192 pages
ISBN 9780316272438
Grades: Adult   177

1. Bullies and bullying 2. Kindness 3. Family and Relationships — General 4. Life stories — Arts and culture — Performing arts 5. Self-Help — Personal growth — Motivation

LC 2017002974

A motivational speaker and YouTube sensation shows readers how they can learn to accept all parts of themselves and others, and in doing so create a "culture of kindness" and a more compassionate world.

The author shares her experiences in being bullied because of her unusual appearance caused by a medical condition, and uses them to explore the causes behind cruelty and how they can be redirected to produce kindness and improve the world.

"This is a wonderful and fast read, full of vitality that captures the luminous spirit of kindness that Velasquez so beautifully embodies." —*Booklist*

Young, Kevin
Bunk: The Rise of Hoaxes, Humbug, Plagiarists, Phonies, Post-facts, and Fake News. Kevin Young. Graywolf Press 2017. 480 p.
ISBN 9781555977917
Grades: Adult   177

1. Hoaxes 2. Race (Biology) 3. Stereotypes 4. Deception 5. Fraud 6. Truth 7. Society and culture — Pop culture 8. Society and culture — Race 9. History writing — Microhistory 10. Arts and Entertainment — Writing and Publishing — Literary criticism

LC Bl2017037554

New York Times Notable Book, 2017; Booklist Editors' Choice, 2017; Longlisted for the Andrew Carnegie Medal for Excellence in Non-Fiction, 2018; Longlisted for the National Book Award for Nonfiction, 2017.

The award-winning author traces the history of the hoax as a distinct American phenomenon, exploring the roles of stereotype, suspicion and racism as factors that have shaped fraudulent activities from the heyday of P. T. Barnum through the "fake news" activities of Donald Trump.

"Young presents a rogue's gallery, including Grey Owl, Bernie Madoff, and Lance Armstrong, paying particular attention to the especially heinous frauds of journalists, including Stephen Glass and Jayson Blair. Young closes with an examination of today's constant bombardment of intertwined facts and factoids and the need for each of us to try to suss out the truth. Compelling and eye-opening." —*Booklist*

179 Other ethical norms

Batterson, Mark
Please, Sorry, Thanks: The Three Words That Change Everything. Mark Batterson. Multnomah 2023. xvi, 163 pages
ISBN 9780593192795
Grades: Adult   179

1. Gratitude 2. Forgiveness 3. Christian life 4. Spirituality and Religion — Christian living 5. Self-Help — Personal growth

LC 2022055934

The best predictor of success in life, in love, and in leadership is your proficiency at please, sorry, and thanks. Those three words are the foundation of all healthy relationships and successful careers. Those three words are the only ceiling on achieving your dreams. Those three words will determine how happy you are."

"This earnest entry offers believers abundant inspiration." —*Publishers Weekly*

Includes bibliographical references (pages 143-163).

Baur, Gene
Farm Sanctuary: Changing Hearts and Minds About Animals and Food. Gene Baur. Simon & Schuster 2008. xv, 286 p. : Illustration
ISBN 9780743291583
Grades: 11 12 Adult   179

1. Livestock 2. Animal industry and trade 3. Animal welfare 4. Nature Writing — Animal Studies 5. Adult books for young adults

A founder of an organization dedicated to promoting the compassionate treatment of animals and combating factory farming addresses key questions about the ethics of breeding animals for food, exposing inhumane practices utilized by typical food-production companies.

"Baur's report is not for the faint of heart, but it is critical reading for anyone willing to ask about the origin of their food, and readers are rewarded with tales of animals who have been saved, and the surprising things that have been learned about farm animals from close observation of their habits. A life-altering read." —*Booklist*

A Touchstone book; Includes bibliographical references (p. [251]-252) and index.

Beers, Diane L.
★ *For the Prevention of Cruelty: The History and Legacy of Animal Rights Activism in the United States.* Diane L. Beers. Swallow Press/Ohio University Press 2006. xvi, 312 p. : Illustration
ISBN 9780804010870
Grades: 11 12 Adult   179

1. Animal rights movement 2. Animal welfare 3. Animal rights 4. Animal rights advocates 5. United States 6. Nature Writing — Animal Studies

LC 2006004294

Provides an organized history of advocacy on the behalf of animals in the United States.

Includes bibliographical references (p. 267-294) and index.

Greek, C. Ray
Sacred Cows and Golden Geese: The Human Cost of Experiments on Animals. C. Ray Greek and Jean Swingle Greek; foreword by Jane Goodall. Continuum 2000. 256 p.
ISBN 9780826412263
Grades: 11 12 Adult   179

1. Animal experimentation 2. Animal rights 3. Animals 4. Nature Writing — Animal Studies 5. Adult books for young adults

LC 99057157

"This covers the history of animal experimentation, legislation that promulgates it, the real cost to humans, and alternatives. It is a well-written, if disturbing, book." —*Library Journal*

Includes bibliographical references (p. [227]-251) and index.

Kohan, Rafi
★ *Trash Talk: The Only Book About Destroying Your Rivals That Isn't Total Garbage.* Rafi Kohan. PublicAffairs 2023. 336 p.
ISBN 9781541788916
Grades: Adult   179

1. Insults 2. Epithets 3. Sportsmanship 4. Competition 5. Rudeness 6. Interpersonal relations 7. Sports rivalry 8. Athletes 9. Sports and competition — General 10. Society and culture — General

LC 2023018367

In this entertaining history of trash talking, the author interviews some of the world's top competitors who reveal the petty rivalries and mind games that fuel them, which helps him form a theory about the surprising and influential role name-calling plays in our world.

"In this thoroughly reported, example-laden look at 'Trash talk,' Kohan makes a compelling case for the power of words...Good advice for anyone under any circumstances." —Booklist

McCubbin, Tracy

Make Space for Happiness: How to Stop Attracting Clutter and Start Magnetizing the Life You Want. Tracy McCubbin. Sourcebooks 2022. 216 pages : Illustration
ISBN 9781728263816
Grades: Adult 179
1. Simplicity 2. Orderliness 3. Clutter 4. Self-Help — Personal growth — Happiness 5. House and Home — Cleaning, caretaking, and organizing

LC 2022006670

We've all done it: Looked around and thought, "How did I get so much stuff I don't really need?" in Make Space for Happiness, Tracy McCubbin addresses that burning question, and offers a solution. What she's found is that people who suffer from chronic clutter want, above all, to attract the feeling their "stuff" represents. In this exciting decluttering book with Gretchen Rubin appeal, Tracy presents the 7 emotional magnets, and how you can recognize your magnet to attract more of what you really want:love, self-confidence, time, and ease."

"An empowering, accessible guide to decluttering for emotional fulfillment." —Library Journal

Includes bibliographical references (pages 203-207) and index.

Plantinga, Cornelius

Gratitude: Why Giving Thanks Is the Key to Our Well-Being. Cornelius Plantinga. Brazos Press, a division of Baker Publishing Group 2024. 176 p.
ISBN 9781587436222
Grades: Adult 179
1. Gratitude 2. Optimism 3. Hope 4. Suffering 5. Well-being 6. Faith (Christianity) 7. Spirituality and Religion — Christianity

LC 2023028481

This book explores gratitude in a theologically informed and pastorally sensitive way. Going deeper than mindfulness and positive psychology, seasoned author Cornelius Plantinga shows that being grateful to God is not only our righteous duty but also the single best predictor of our well-being. Gratitude makes us more faithful, joyful, generous, healthy, and content. While it's easy to focus on the suffering, fear, and worries that surround us, Plantinga places all of that in the larger context of provision, abundance, and delight, empowering us to experience the deep joy of giving thanks.

"This worthy meditation on an essential state of being uplifts without sugarcoating." —Publishers Weekly

Includes bibliographical references.

Singer, Peter

★ *Animal* Liberation. Peter Singer. Ecco Book/Harper Perennial 2001. xiii, 311, 32 p. : Illustration
ISBN 9780061711305
Grades: Adult 179
1. Animal rights 2. Animal welfare 3. Vegetarianism 4. Nature Writing — Animal Studies

LC 2001040903

An updated edition of the groundbreaking study of animal rights describes the shocking abuse of animals—including laboratory experimentation, the fur industry, and product testing procedures—and argues that those who oppose human suffering must also oppose inflicting suffering on animals.

Includes bibliographical references and index; Includes bibliographical references (p. [251]-298, 2nd group) and index.

Tillich, Paul

★ *The* Courage to Be. Paul Tillich; with an introduction by Peter J. Gomes. Yale University Press 2000. 197 p.
ISBN 9780300188790
Grades: Adult 179
1. Courage 2. Ontology 3. Anxiety 4. Existentialism 5. Society and culture — Philosophy

LC 00102364

Originally published more than fifty years ago, the Courage to Be has become a classic of twentieth-century religious and philosophical thought. The great Christian existentialist thinker Paul Tillich describes the dilemma of modern man and points a way to the conquest of the problem of anxiety.

Includes index; Originally published: New Haven, CT : Yale University Press, 1952.

Tutu, Desmond

The Book of Forgiving: The Fourfold Path for Healing Ourselves and Our World. Desmond Tutu and Mpho A. Tutu; edited by Douglas C. Abrams. HarperOne 2014. 240 p.
ISBN 9780062203564
Grades: Adult 179
1. Forgiveness 2. Revenge 3. Victims 4. Reconciliation 5. Christianity 6. Spirituality and Religion — Christianity 7. Adult books for young adults 8. History writing — Africa

LC 2013033890

The Nobel Peace Prize winner and international cultural icon reveals, after much reflection on the process of forgiveness, the four important steps of healing that will allows us to free ourselves of the ties that bind perpetrator to victim in an endless and unyielding cycle of pain and retribution.

"The book is almost entirely practical in focus, geared toward helping people come to grips with issues of anger, grief and loss. It includes meditations, rituals and journal exercises after each chapter." —Kirkus

Includes bibliographical references.

Wasik, Bill

★ *Our* Kindred Creatures: How Americans Came to Feel the Way They Do About Animals. Bill Wasik and Monica Murphy. Alfred A. Knopf 2024. 464 p.
ISBN 9780525659068
Grades: Adult 179
1. Animal rights 2. Animal welfare 3. Ethics 4. Animals 5. United States 6. 19th century 7. Nature Writing — Animal studies 8. History Writing — United States

LC 2023003995

This fascinating history of the moral revolution on behalf of animals and the battles it sparked in American life discusses the leaders of the reform as well as those caught in the movement's crosshairs and challenges us to consider the obligations we still have to all our kindred creatures.

"Of obvious appeal to animal lovers, this engaging account will also resonate with readers who enjoy in-depth looks at the history and shaping of contemporary American values." —Booklist

Includes bibliographical references and index.

179.7 Respect and disrespect for human life

Engelhart, Katie

The Inevitable: Dispatches on the Right to Die. Katie Engelhart. St. Martin's Press 2021. 304 p.
ISBN 9781250201461
Grades: Adult 179.7
1. Euthanasia 2. Right to die 3. Assisted suicide 4. Physician-assisted suicide 5. People with terminal illnesses 6. Ethics 7. Debates and debating 8. Human rights 9. Civil rights 10. Impartial writing 11. Life stories — Facing adversity — Medical issues 12. Life stories — Science, technology, and medicine — Healthcare professionals 13. Science Writing — Medicine and health

LC 2020040116

ESSENTIAL AND RECOMMENDED TITLES
179.7 Respect and disrespect for human life

As much of the world's population grows older, the quest for a "good death," has become a significant issue. For many, the right to die often means the right to die with dignity. The Inevitable moves beyond margins of the law to the people who are meticulously planning their final hours—far from medical offices, legislative chambers, hospital ethics committees, and polite conversation—and the people who help them, loved ones or clandestine groups on the Internet known as the "euthanasia underground." Katie Engelhart, a veteran journalist, focuses on six people representing different aspects of the debate. Spanning Australia, North America, and Europe, Engelhart presents a deeply reported portrait of everyday people struggling to make hard decisions, and wrestling back a measure of authenticity and dignity to their lives.

"A must-read for anyone concerned about quality of life at the end of life." —Library Journal

Includes bibliographical references.

Gandhi
★ *Gandhi on Non-violence: Selected Texts from Mohandas K. Gandhi's Non-violence in Peace and War.* Edited with an introduction by Thomas Merton; preface by Mark Kurlansky. New Directions Pub. 2007. xviii, 101 p.
ISBN 9780811216869
Grades: Adult   179.7
1. Nonviolence 2. Politics and global affairs — Political philosophy 3. History writing — Asia — South Asia 4. Society and culture — Philosophy
LC 2007032262

Originally published in 1965, a compendium of excerpts offers insight into the spiritual leader's beliefs about action as a central component of non-violent resistance, his opposition to the caste system, and legacy as a proponent of spiritual integrity.

A New Directions Paperbook; Includes bibliographical references and index; Originally published: New York : New Directions, 1965.

Rehm, Diane
★ *When My Time Comes: Conversations About Whether Those Who Are Dying Should Have the Right to Determine When Life Should End.* Diane Rehm; foreword by John Grisham. Alfred a Knopf 2020. 224 pages
ISBN 9780525654759
Grades: Adult   179.7
1. Right to die 2. Assisted suicide 3. Terminal care 4. Media tie-ins 5. Life stories — Facing adversity — Coping with death 6. Family and relationships — Aging and death
LC 2019033872

A renowned radio host and best-selling author addresses the hotly contested cause of the right-to-die movement, of which she is one of the strongest voices.

"Rehm and her subjects offer practical information, nuanced perspectives, and poignant stories of peaceful final moments achieved through end-of-life care. Readers faced with similar decisions will cherish this thoughtful account." —Publishers Weekly

Sanger, Carol
About Abortion: Terminating Pregnancy in Twenty-first-century America. Carol Sanger. The Belknap Press of Harvard University Press 2017. xv, 304 pages
ISBN 9780674737723
Grades: Adult   179.7
1. Abortion 2. Unplanned pregnancy 3. Legislation 4. Law — General 5. Society and culture — Gender — Women — Reproductive rights
LC 2016041934

One of the most private decisions a woman can make, abortion is also one of the most contentious topics in American civic life. Protested at rallies and politicized in party platforms, terminating pregnancy is often characterized as a selfish decision by women who put their own interests above those of the fetus. This background of stigma and hostility has stifled women's willingness to talk about abortion, which in turn distorts public and political discussion. To pry open the silence surrounding this public issue, Sanger distinguishes between abortion privacy, a form of nondisclosure based on a woman's desire to control personal information, and abortion secrecy, a woman's defense against the many harms of disclosure. Laws regulating abortion patients and providers treat abortion not as an acceptable medical decision—let alone a right—but as something disreputable, immoral, and chosen by mistake. Exploiting the emotional power of fetal imagery, laws require women to undergo ultrasound, a practice welcomed in wanted pregnancies but commandeered for use against women with unwanted pregnancies. Sanger takes these prejudicial views of women's abortion decisions into the twenty-first century by uncovering new connections between abortion law and American culture and politics. New medical technologies, women's increasing willingness to talk online and off, and the prospect of tighter judicial reins on state legislatures are shaking up the practice of abortion. As talk becomes more transparent and acceptable, women's decisions about whether or not to become mothers will be treated more like those of other adults making significant personal choices.—.

Includes bibliographical references and index.

Wanzer, Sidney H.
★ *To Die Well: Your Right to Comfort, Calm, and Choice in the Last Days of Your Life.* Sidney H. Wanzer with Joseph Glenmullen. Da Capo Press 2007. xii, 209 p.
ISBN 9780738210834
Grades: Adult   179.7
1. Right to die 2. Assisted suicide 3. Euthanasia 4. Self-Help — Mental health — Grief and loss 5. Family and Relationships — Aging and Death
LC BI2007006665

Provides clear legal and medical guidelines for the terminally ill and their loved ones who are facing end-of-life decisions, covering such topics as how to appoint a health care proxy, refuse unwanted treatments, and the controversial issue of hastening the death of terminally ill patients.

Warraich, Haider
Modern Death: How Medicine Changed the End of Life. Haider Warraich. St. Martin's Press 2017. 336 p.
ISBN 9781250104588
Grades: Adult   179.7
1. Terminal Care 2. Right to die 3. Death education 4. Quality of Life 5. Aging 6. Science Writing — Medicine and health 7. Family and relationships — Aging and death 8. Society and culture — Illness and disease
LC 2016038746

A contemporary exploration of death and dying by a young Duke Fellow investigates the hows, whys, wheres and whens of modern death and their cultural significance as they have changed through technological advances and evolving trends.

"An important contribution to a serious discussion of profound life-and-death issues." —Kirkus

Wiesenthal, Simon
★ *The Sunflower: On the Possibilities and Limits of Forgiveness.* Simon Wiesenthal; with a symposium edited by Harry James Cargas and Bonny V. Fetterman. Schocken Books 1998. xii, 289 p.
ISBN 9780805210606
Grades: Adult   179.7
1. Wiesenthal, Simon 2. World War II 3. Concentration camps 4. Genocide 5. Forgiveness 6. Autobiographies and memoirs 7. History writing — Wars and conflicts — Holocaust — World War II 8. History writing — Wars and conflicts — World War II — European Theater 9. Life stories — General
LC 99198049

Author Simon Wiesenthal inquires into the possibilities and limits of compassion, forgiveness, justice, and human responsibility among a diverse group of fifty-three men and women, including Holocaust survivors, victims of attempted genocide, psychiatrists, political leaders, and more.

"The responses to the author's question are as varied as their authors. The mystery of evil and atonement remain, and the reader is left challenged on these most basic issues of meaning in human life." —Publishers Weekly

PUBLIC LIBRARY CORE COLLECTION: NONFICTION
Twentieth Edition

179.9 Virtues

Chayka, Kyle
The Longing for Less: Living with Minimalism. Kyle Chayka. Bloomsbury Publishing 2020. 258 p. : Illustration
ISBN 9781635572100
Grades: Adult 179.9
1. Simplicity 2. House and Home — Cleaning, caretaking, and organizing 3. Arts and Entertainment — General 4. House and Home — Interior Decorating and Furnishings
LC Bl2020005914
One of our keenest social observers examines the deep roots—and untapped possibilities—of our newfound, all-consuming drive to reduce.
Includes bibliographical references (pages 235-247) and index.

180 Ancient, medieval, eastern philosophy

Gottlieb, Anthony
The Dream of Reason: A History of Western Philosophy from the Greeks to the Renaissance. Anthony Gottlieb. W.W. Norton 2000. IX, 468 p.
ISBN 9780393049510
Grades: 11 12 Adult 180
1. Philosophy 2. Philosophy, Western 3. Philosophy, Ancient 4. Society and culture — Philosophy
LC 00049012
New York Times Notable Book, 2001.
The author re-examines the basic assumptions of philosophical thought from the pre-Socratic philosophers to Erasmus.
"This eloquent book offers a lively chronicle of the evolution of Western philosophy." —*Publishers Weekly*
Includes bibliographical references (p. 432-456) and index.

Nicolson, Adam
How to Be: Life Lessons from the Early Greeks. Adam Nicolson. Farrar, Straus and Giroux 2023. 356 p.
ISBN 9780374610104
Grades: Adult 180
1. Ancient philosophers 2. Philosophy, Ancient 3. Existentialism 4. Influence (Psychology) 5. Intellectual life 6. Seafaring life 7. Thought and thinking 8. Personal conduct 9. Purpose in life 10. Civilization, Ancient 11. Ancient Greece 12. Ancient Greece (800 B.C.E.-640 C.E.) 13. History writing — Ancient — Greece 14. Society and culture — Philosophy 15. Life stories — Education — Philosophers 16. Life stories — People in history
LC 2023014917
Before the Greeks, the idea of the world was dominated by god-kings and their priests. Twenty-five hundred years ago, in a succession of small eastern Mediterranean harbor cities, a few heroic men and women decided to cast off mental subservience and apply their own thinking minds to the conundrums of life. The award-winning writer Adam Nicolson travels with us through this transforming world and asks what light these ancient thinkers can throw on our deepest preconceptions. Nicolson takes us to the dawn of investigative thought and makes the fundamental questions of the ancient philosophers new again.
"Historian Nicolson (The Life Between the Tides) illuminates in this meditative account the vital influence geography had on the evolution of Greek philosophy from the 11th to the 5th centuries BCE, arguing that places gave rise to frames of mind that served as wellsprings of new ideas." —*Publishers Weekly*
Includes bibliographical references and index.

183 Sophistic, Socratic, related Greek philosophies

Johnson, Paul
Socrates: A Man for Our Times. Paul Johnson. Viking 2011. 240 p.
ISBN 9780670023035
Grades: Adult 183
1. Socrates, 469-399 B.C.E 2. Philosophy, Ancient 3. Ancient philosophers 4. Philosophers 5. Philosophy 6. Ancient Greece 7. Ancient Greece (800 B.C.E.-640 C.E.) 8. Biographies 9. History writing — Ancient — Greece 10. Life stories — Education — Philosophers 11. Society and culture — Philosophy
LC 2011019767
Illuminates key tenets in the influential philosopher's beliefs through the story of his life, tracing his middle-class existence against a vibrant backdrop of fifth century B.C. Athens while sharing intimate analyses of specific aspects of his personality.
Includes bibliographical references and index.

Kreeft, Peter
★ *Philosophy 101 by Socrates: An Introduction to Philosophy Via Plato's Apology : Forty Things Philosophy Is According to History's First and Wisest Philosopher.* Peter Kreeft. Ignatius Press 2002. 149 p.
ISBN 9780898709254
Grades: Adult 183
1. Plato, 428-347 B.C.E 2. Socrates, 469-399 B.C.E 3. Philosophy 4. Spirituality and Religion — General
LC 2001098029
Philosophy means "the love of wisdom." Kreeft uses the dialogues of Socrates to help the reader grow in that love. He says that no master of the art of philosophizing has ever been more simple, clear, and accessible to beginners as has Socrates. He focuses on Plato's dialogues, The Apology of Socrates, as a lively example to imitate, and a model partner for the reader for dialogue.

Stone, I. F.
The Trial of Socrates. I.F. Stone. Little, Brown 1988. xi, 282 p.
ISBN 9780316817585
Grades: Adult 183
1. Socrates, 469-399 B.C.E 2. Civilization, Ancient 3. Philosophers 4. Trials (Blasphemy) 5. Trials (Sedition) 6. Social life and customs 7. Civilization 8. Athens, Ancient Greece 9. History writing — Ancient — Greece
LC 87022855
Combines classical scholarship with techniques of modern investigative journalism in an attempt to unravel the mystery behind the trial and conviction of Athens' most prominent philosopher.
Includes index; Bibliography: P. [249]-267.

184 Platonic philosophy

Hare, R. M.
★ *Plato.* R.M. Hare. Oxford University Press 1982. VI, 82 p.
ISBN 9780192875853
Grades: 11 12 Adult 184
1. Plato, 428-347 B.C.E 2. Philosophy, Ancient 3. Life stories — Education — Philosophers 4. Society and culture — Philosophy
LC 83159441
Offers a look at Plato's life and discusses his philosophy and teachings.
Includes bibliographical references and index.

Plato
★ *The Collected Dialogues of Plato, Including the Letters.* Edited by Edith Hamilton and Huntington Cairns. With introd. and prefatory notes. [Translators: Lane Cooper and others]. Pantheon Books 1961. xxv, 1743 p.
ISBN 9780691097183
Grades: Adult 184
1. Philosophy, Ancient 2. Society and culture — Philosophy
LC 61011758
Presents outstanding translations of the Greek philosopher's works by leading British and American scholars of the last century.

ESSENTIAL AND RECOMMENDED TITLES
185 Aristotelian philosophy

185 Aristotelian philosophy

Adler, Mortimer Jerome
Aristotle for Everybody: Difficult Thought Made Easy. Mortimer J. Adler. Simon & Schuster 1997. xiv, 206 p.
ISBN 9780684838236
Grades: Adult   185
1. Aristotle 2. Society and culture — Philosophy 3. History writing — Ancient — Greece
LC Oc2007014723

Offers an imaginative perspective on Aristotelian logic, presenting an exploration of nature, society, and man in light of commonplace events and reexamining concepts of body, mind, change, cause, part, whole, one, and many.

A Touchstone book; Includes bibliographical references (p. 193-206); Originally published: New York : Macmillan, c1978.

Aristotle
★ *The Basic Works of Aristotle.* Edited by Richard McKeon; introduction by C.D.C. Reeve. Modern Library 2001. xxi, 1487 p; (The Modern Library classics)
ISBN 9780375757990
Grades: Adult   185
1. Philosophy 2. Arts and Entertainment — Writing and Publishing 3. Society and culture — Philosophy
LC 2001030607

Examines the pervading influence of this eminent Greek philosopher through a collection of his major works.

Includes bibliographical references; Originally published: New York : Random House, c1941. With new introd.

Shields, Christopher John
Aristotle. Christopher Shields. Routledge, Taylor & Francis Group 2014. xviii, 505 pages
ISBN 9780415622493
Grades: Adult   185
1. Aristotle 2. Society and culture — Philosophy
LC 2013021013

In this extensively revised new edition of his excellent guidebook, Christopher Shields introduces the whole of Aristotle's philosophy, showing how his powerful conception of human nature shaped much of his thinking on the nature of the soul and the mind, ethics, politics, and the arts.

Includes bibliographical references (pages 495-501) and index.

187 Epicurean philosophy

Lucretius Carus, Titus
On the Nature of Things =: De Rerum Natura. Lucretius; edited and translated by Anthony M. Esolen. Johns Hopkins University Press 1995. IX, 296 p.
ISBN 9780801850554
Grades: Adult   187
1. Philosophy, Ancient 2. Spirituality and Religion — General
LC 94025165

"Ensolen has focused on the poet, translating the Latin hexameters into accented pentameter in order to capture the dynamics, rhythms, and syntax of the original. The results are both satisfying and readable. Ensolen includes an elegant introduction to Lucretius, as well as useful notes. A valuable contribution to students of literature as well as philosophy." —*Library Journal*

Includes bibliographical references (p. 287) and index.

188 Stoic philosophy

Holiday, Ryan
Lives of the Stoics: The Art of Living from Zeno to Marcus Aurelius. Ryan Holiday and Stephen Hanselman, authors of The Daily Stoic. Portfolio/Penguin 2020. xv, 329 pages : Illustration
ISBN 9780525541875
Grades: Adult   188
1. Stoics 2. Philosophy 3. Self-Help — Personal growth 4. Society and culture — Philosophy
LC 2020011797

From the bestselling authors of The Daily Stoic comes an inspiring guide to the lives of the Stoics, and what the ancients can teach us about happiness, success, resilience and virtue. Nearly 2,300 years after a ruined merchant named Zeno first established a school on the Stoa Poikile of Athens, Stoicism has found a new audience among those who seek greatness, from athletes to politicians and everyone in between. It's no wonder; the philosophy and its embrace of self-mastery, virtue, and indifference tothat which we cannot control is as urgent today as it was in the chaos of the Roman Empire. In Lives of the Stoics, Holiday and Hanselman present the fascinating lives of the men and women who strove to live by the timeless Stoic virtues of Courage. Justice. Temperance. Wisdom. Organized in digestible, mini-biographies of all the well-known—and not so well-known—Stoics, this book vividly brings home what Stoicism was like for the people who loved it and lived it, dusting off powerful lessons to be learned from their struggles and successes. More than a mere history book, every example in these pages, from Epictetus to Marcus Aurelius—slaves to emperors—is designed to help the reader apply philosophy in their own lives. Holiday and Hanselman unveil the core values and ideas that unite figures from Seneca to Cato to Cicero across the centuries. Among them are the idea that self-rule is the greatest empire, that character is fate; how Stoics benefit from preparing not only for success, but failure; and learn to love, not merely accept, the hand they are dealt in life. A treasure of valuable insights and stories, this book can be visited again and again by any reader in search of inspiration from the past."

"This illuminating collection of biographies makes great use of Stoic wisdom to demonstrate the tradition's values for any reader interested in ancient philosophy." —*Publishers Weekly*

Includes bibliographical references (pages 321-326) and index.

Marcus Aurelius
★ *Meditations.* Marcus Aurelius; a new translation, with an introduction, by Gregory Hays. Modern Library 2002. LVII, 191 p.
ISBN 9780679642602
Grades: Adult   188
1. Ethics 2. Life 3. Stoics 4. Spirituality and Religion — Body, mind, and spirit 5. Spirituality and Religion — General
LC 2001057947

An incisive introduction to the life and times of the Roman philosopher and emperor, the fundamental principles and concepts of Stoicism, the recurring themes and structure of the Meditations, and the work's impact preface a new translation of the influential and admired journal.

Presents an introduction to the life and times of the Roman philosopher and emperor, the fundamental principles and concepts of Stoicism, the recurring themes and structure of the Meditations, and the work's impact.

Includes bibliographical references (p. [171]-180) and index.

190 Modern western and other noneastern philosophy

Durant, Will
★ *The Story of Philosophy: The Lives and Opinions of the Great Philosophers of the Western World.* Will Durant. Simon and Schuster 1983. xvi, 412 p.
ISBN 9780671201593
Grades: Adult   190
1. Philosophy 2. Philosophers 3. Society and culture — Philosophy 4. History writing — General 5. Life stories — Education — Philosophers
LC 83171619

Examines the history of speculative thought by focusing on such dominant personalities as Plato, Bacon, Spinoza, Kant, Schopenhauer, and Nietzsche.

Includes index; Bibliography: P. 403-404.

PUBLIC LIBRARY CORE COLLECTION: NONFICTION
Twentieth Edition

Gay, Peter

*The **Enlightenment**: An Interpretation : The Science of Freedom.* Peter Gay. W.W. Norton 1996. xviii, 705, xviii p.
ISBN 9780393313666
Grades: Adult   **190**
1. Philosophy 2. 18th century 3. History writing — Enlightenment — Europe 4. Society and culture — Philosophy
LC BL 99780253

The Science of Freedom completes Peter Gay's brilliant reinterpretation begun in the Enlightenment: The Rise of Modern Paganism. In the present book, he describes the philosophes' program and their views of society. His masterful appraisal opens a new range of insights into the Enlightenment's critical method and its humane and libertarian vision.

Includes bibliographical references and index; Originally published: The enlightenment: an interpretation. Volume 2: The science of freedom. New York : Knopf, 1966-69.

*The **Enlightenment**: The Rise of Modern Paganism.* Peter Gay. W.W. Norton 1995. 2 vol.
ISBN 9780393313024
Grades: Adult   **190**
1. Philosophy 2. 18th century 3. Spirituality and Religion — General
LC BL 99766232

The eighteenth-century Enlightenment marks the beginning of the modern age, when the scientific method and belief in reason and progress came to hold sway over the Western world. In the twentieth century, however, the Enlightenment has often been judged harshly for its apparently simplistic optimism. Now a master historian goes back to the sources to give a fully rounded account of its true accomplishments.

Includes bibliographical references and index; Originally published: New York : Knopf, c1966.

Gottlieb, Anthony

★ *The **Dream** of Enlightenment: The Rise of Modern Philosophy.* Anthony Gottlieb. Liveright Publishing Corporation, a division of W. W. Norton & Company 2016. 384 p.
ISBN 9780871404435
Grades: Adult   **190**
1. Philosophy 2. Intellectual life 3. Enlightenment (European intellectual movement) 4. Philosophy, Modern 5. Society and culture — Philosophy 6. History writing — Enlightenment — Europe
LC 2016015063

Presents a chronicle of modern thought from Descartes to Rousseau, detailing the role of then-amateur philosophers in shaping Western intellectual pursuits against a backdrop of religious upheaval and the rise of Galilean science.

"Accessibly written philosophical studies can be surprisingly popular as evidenced by the current success of Sarah Bakewell's At the Existentialist Cafe. Don't miss." —*Library Journal*

Includes bibliographical references and index.

Magee, Bryan

*The **Story** of Philosophy.* Bryan Magee. DK Pub. 1998. 240 p. : Illustration; Color; Map
ISBN 9780789435118
Grades: 11 12 Adult   **190**
1. Philosophy 2. Books for browsing
LC 98003780

"Writing with a clear and lively style, Magee provides an excellent introduction to the topic." —*School Library Journal*

Includes bibliographical references (p. 232-233) and index.

Robertson, Ritchie

*The **Enlightenment**.* Ritchie Robertson. HarperCollins 2021. 576 p.
ISBN 9780062410658
Grades: Adult   **190**
1. Enlightenment (European intellectual movement) 2. Philosophy 3. Intellectual life 4. Humanism 5. Reason 6. Empiricism 7. 18th century 8. History writing — Enlightenment — Europe

A magisterial history that recasts the Enlightenment as a period not solely consumed with rationale and reason, but rather as a pursuit of practical means to achieve greater human happiness.

"This massive and deeply erudite work serves as a stimulating and accessible introduction to a watershed period in the intellectual development of the West." —*Library Journal*

190.82 Women philosophers — Modern

Penaluna, Regan

★ *How to Think Like a Woman: Four Women Philosophers Who Taught Me How to Love the Life of the Mind.* Regan Penaluna. Grove Press 2023. 320 p.
ISBN 9780802158802
Grades: Adult   **190.82**
1. Penaluna, Regan 2. Masham, Damaris, Lady, 1658-1708 3. Astell, Mary, 1666-1731 4. Trotter, Catharine, 1679-1749 5. Wollstonecraft, Mary, 1759-1797 6. Women scholars and academics 7. Women philosophers 8. Intellectual life 9. Misogyny 10. Sexism in universities and colleges 11. Social criticism 12. Society and culture — Philosophy 13. Society and culture — Gender — Women 14. Life stories — Education — Philosophers 15. Life stories — Identity — Gender 16. Debut title
LC 2022044376

As a young woman, Regan Penaluna fell in love with philosophy and chose to pursue it as an academician, the first step, she believed, to becoming a self-determined person living a life of the mind. What Penaluna didn't realize was that the Western philosophical canon taught in American universities would slowly grind her down through its misogyny, its harassment, its devaluation of women and their intellect. In How to Think Like a Woman, Regan Penaluna blends memoir, biography, and criticism to tell the stories of four women philosophers, weaving throughout an alternative history of philosophy as well as her own search for love and truth.

"Lucid and frank, this blend of memoir, biography, and criticism makes a solid case for why representation matters." —*Publishers Weekly*

Includes bibliographical references.

191 Philosophy of United States and Canada

Kaag, John J.

American Philosophy: A Love Story. John Kaag. FSG 2016. 240 p.
ISBN 9780374154486
Grades: Adult   **191**
1. Kaag, John J, 1979- 2. Philosophy 3. Scholars and academics 4. Intellectual life 5. Book collectors 6. Intellectuals 7. Disillusionment 8. Rare books 9. Cataloging 10. Books and reading 11. Autobiographies and memoirs 12. Life stories — Personal growth 13. Society and culture — Philosophy 14. Life stories — Education — Scholars and educators
LC 2016001908

When he stumbles upon a treasure trove of rare books that once belonged to the Harvard philosopher William Ernst Hocking, the author, a disillusioned philosopher at sea in his marriage and career, begins to catalog and preserve this collection and rediscovers the very tenets of American philosophy, seeing them within a 21st-century context.

"Kaag's lively prose, acute self-examination, unfolding romance, and instructive history of philosophy as a discipline make for a surprisingly absorbing book." —*Kirkus*

Includes bibliographical references and index.

Rand, Ayn

*The **Voice** of Reason: Essays in Objectivist Thought.* Ayn Rand; edited and with an introduction by Leonard Peikoff; and with additional essays by Leonard Peikoff and Peter Schwartz. New American Library 1989. xii, 353 p.

ESSENTIAL AND RECOMMENDED TITLES
192 Philosophy of British Isles

ISBN 9780453006347
Grades: Adult **191**
1. Rand, Ayn 2. Philosophy 3. Political science 4. Society and culture — Philosophy
LC 88018192
Essays discuss Objectivism, Apollo II, the quota system, public TV, foreign aid, socialized medicine, religion, and Vietnam.
Includes bibliographical references.

Romano, Carlin
America the Philosophical. Carlin Romano. Knopf 2012. 672 p.
ISBN 9780679434702
Grades: Adult **191**
1. Philosophy 2. Intellectual life 3. Philosophy, Modern 4. History writing — Arts and culture 5. History writing — United States
LC 2011034753
A former president of the National Book Critics Circle and finalist for the Pulitzer Prize in criticism argues that America is a leading philosophical culture in the history of the world, outlining a rich overview of thought to explain that Americans demonstrate a high capacity for intellectual enterprises in the spirit of the less-remembered Greek philosopher, Isocrates.
Includes bibliographical references and index.

Stewart, Jeffrey C.
★ *The New Negro: The Life of Alain Locke*. Jeffrey C. Stewart. Oxford University Press 2018. 962 p.
ISBN 9780195089578
Grades: Adult **191**
1. Locke, Alain LeRoy, 1886-1954 2. Harlem Renaissance 3. Intellectual life 4. African American intellectuals 5. African Americans 6. New York City 7. Harlem, New York City 8. Biographies 9. Life stories — Education — Philosophers 10. History writing — African American — United States
LC 2017026626
BCALA Literary Award for Nonfiction, 2019; Booklist Editors' Choice, 2018; National Book Award for Nonfiction, 2018; Pulitzer Prize for Biography or Autobiography, 2019.
In the New Negro: The Life of Alain Locke, Jeffrey C. Stewart offers the definitive biography of the father of the Harlem Renaissance, based on the extant primary sources of his life and on interviews with those who knew him personally. He narrates the education of Locke, including his becoming the first African American Rhodes Scholar and earning a PhD in philosophy at Harvard University, and his long career as a professor at Howard University.
"Those who love biographies or reading about important yet undercelebrated Americans will enjoy Stewart's comprehensive, richly contextualized portrait of a key writer, educator, philosopher, and supporter of the arts." —*Booklist*
Includes bibliographical references and index.

192 Philosophy of British Isles

Edmonds, David
Wittgenstein's Poker: The Story of a Ten-Minute Argument Between Two Great Philosophers. David Edmonds and John Eidinow. Ecco 2001. x, 340 p. : Illustration
ISBN 9780066212449
Grades: Adult **192**
1. Wittgenstein, Ludwig, 1889-1951 2. Popper, Karl, 1902-1994 3. Debates and debating 4. College teachers 5. 1940s 6. Spirituality and Religion — General
LC 2002276301
Booklist Editors' Choice, 2001; New York Times Notable Book, 2002.
A blend of philosophy, history, biography, and literary detection brings to life the meeting of two great philosophers—Ludwig Wittgenstein and Karl Popper—on October 25, 1946 in Cambridge, England.
"On the Cambridge University campus in 1946, two of the twentieth-century's most notable philosophers, Ludwig Wittgenstein and Karl Popper, squared off in an intense 10-minute clash rumored to have culminated with Wittgenstein brandishing a red-hot poker. The authors explain what the fight was about and how it reflects the development of philosophy. Ivory-tower drama at its crackling best." —*Booklist*
Includes bibliographical references (p. [317]-327) and index.

193 Philosophy of Germany and Austria

Heidegger, Martin
Basic Writings: From Being and Time (1927) to the Task of Thinking (1964). Martin Heidegger; edited, with general introduction and introductions to each selection by David Farrell Krell. HarperSanFrancisco 1993. xii, 452 p.
ISBN 9780060637637
Grades: Adult **193**
1. Society and culture — Philosophy 2. Spirituality and Religion — General
LC 91058187
Heidegger's most popular collection of essential writings, now revised and expanded, includes the 10 key essays plus the introduction to Being and Time.
Includes bibliographical references (p. [450]-452).

Kaag, John J.
Hiking with Nietzsche: On Becoming Who You Are. John Kaag. Farrar, Straus, and Giroux 2018. 256 p.
ISBN 9780374170011
Grades: Adult **193**
1. Nietzsche, Friedrich Wilhelm, 1844-1900 2. Hiking 3. Philosophy 4. Mountaineering 5. Self 6. Men and nature 7. Nature 8. Swiss Alps 9. Autobiographies and memoirs 10. Sports and Competition — Mountaineering 11. Society and culture — Philosophy
LC 2017057604
In an illuminating Alpine trek though the Swiss peaks, the author, drawing on two separate journeys—one when he was 19 and one 17 years later—channels the spirit of Friedrich Nietzche as he searches for meaning.
"A wonderful introduction to Nietzsche set against the unique backdrop of the landscape and cities he experienced. The tone and writing style make it accessible to general readers, while the content will reward those familiar with Nietzsche as well." —*Library Journal*
Includes bibliographical references and index.

Kant, Immanuel
★ *Basic Writings of Kant*. Edited and with an introduction by Allen W. Wood. Modern Library 2001. xxv, 478 p; (The Modern Library classics)
ISBN 9780375757334
Grades: Adult **193**
1. Philosophy 2. Arts and Entertainment — Writing and Publishing
LC 2001018303
Presents the essential works of the philosopher, including "Critique of Pure Reason" and "Eternal Peace."
Includes bibliographical references (p. [477]-478).

Nietzsche, Friedrich Wilhelm
★ *Basic Writings of Nietzsche*. Introduction by Peter Gay; translated and edited by Walter Kaufmann. Modern Library 2000. xxiv, 862 p.
ISBN 9780679783398
Grades: Adult **193**
1. Philosophy 2. Arts and Entertainment — Writing and Publishing
LC 00064578
Six works selected from Nietzsche's writings, including "The Birth of Tragedy," "Beyond Good and Evil," and "On the Genealogy of Morals" reflect the philosopher's critique of Western morality and insights into Christianity and art.
Includes indexes; Includes bibliographical references and indexes; Originally published: New York : Modern Library, 1968. With new commentary.

★ *Thus Spoke Zarathustra: A Book for Everyone and Nobody*. Friedrich Nietzsche; translated with an introduction and notes by Graham Parkes. Oxford University Press 2005. xliii, 335 p; 20
ISBN 9780192805836

Grades: Adult **193**
1. Philosophy 2. Spirituality and Religion — General
LC 2005019431

Thus Spake Zarathustra is a masterpiece of literature as well as philosophy. It was Nietzsche's own favorite and has proved to be his most popular. In this book he addresses the problem of how to live a fulfilling life in a world without meaning, in the aftermath of 'the death of God.' His solution lies in the idea of eternal recurrence, which he calls 'the highest formula of affirmation that can ever be attained.' a successful engagement with this profoundly Dionysian idea enables us to choose clearly among the myriad possibilities that existence offers, and thereby to affirm every moment of our lives with others on this 'sacred' earth.

Includes bibliographical references (p. [288]- 321) and index.

The Will to Power. a new translation by Walter Kaufmann and R. J. Hollingdale; edited, with commentary, by Walter Kaufmann, with facsims. of the original manuscript. Random House 1967. xxxii, 576 p. Facsimile
ISBN 9780394704371
Grades: Adult **193**
1. Society and culture — Philosophy
LC 66021465

Offers a selection from the author's notebooks, chosen by his sister, that reveals his views on nihilism, art, morality, religion, the theory of knowledge, and other subjects.

Translation of Der Wille zur Macht.

194 Philosophy of France

Curran, Andrew S.
Diderot and the Art of Thinking Freely. Andrew S. Curran. Other Press 2019. 320 p.
ISBN 9781590516706
Grades: Adult **194**
1. Diderot, Denis, 1713-1784 2. Philosophers 3. Enlightenment (European intellectual movement) 4. Intellectual freedom 5. Intellectual life 6. Thought and thinking 7. Social life and customs 8. France 9. Europe 10. 18th century 11. Biographies 12. History writing — Enlightenment — Europe 13. Life stories — Education — Philosophers
LC 2018019273

A biography of the prescient philosopher who was jailed in 1749 for atheism describes how he thought about natural selection before Darwin did, mused about the Oedipus complex before Freud and wondered about genetic manipulation centuries before Dolly the Sheep.

Includes bibliographical references and index.

Descartes, Rene
★ *Descartes:* Selected Philosophical Writings. Translated by John Cottingham, Robert Stoothoff, Dugald Murdoch; with an introduction by John Cottingham. Cambridge University Press 1988. xii, 249 p. : Illustration
ISBN 9780521352642
Grades: Adult **194**
1. Descartes, Rene, 1596-1650 2. Philosophy 3. Philosophy, French 4. 17th century 5. Society and culture — Philosophy
LC 87026799

Based on the new and much acclaimed two volume Cambridge edition of the Philosophical Writings of Descartes by Cottingham, Stoothoff, and Murdoch, this anthology of essential texts contains the most important and widely studied of those writings, including the Discourse and Meditations and substantial extracts from the Regulae, Optics, Principles, Objections and Replies, Comments on a Broadsheet, and Passions of the Soul.

Includes index.

199 Philosophy in other geographic areas

Moore, Peter
Life, Liberty, and the Pursuit of Happiness: Britain and the American Dream. Peter Moore. Farrar, Straus and Giroux 2023. 544 p.
ISBN 9780374600594
Grades: Adult **199**
1. Franklin, Benjamin, 1706-1790 2. Paine, Thomas, 1737-1809 3. Johnson, Samuel, 1709-1784 4. Wilkes, John, 1725-1797 5. Macaulay, Catharine, 1731-1791 6. Strahan, William, 1715-1785 7. Enlightenment (European intellectual movement) 8. Political science 9. Politicians 10. American dream 11. Freedom 12. Philosophers 13. British people 14. British history 15. United States history 16. 18th century 17. Colonial America (1600-1775) 18. Collective biographies 19. Life stories — People in history 20. History writing — Europe — United Kingdom 21. History writing — Colonial America — United States 22. Nonfiction that reads like fiction
LC 2023001279

The true story of what may be the most successful import in US history: the "American dream." Centered on the friendship between Benjamin Franklin and the British publisher William Strahan, and featuring figures including the cultural giant Samuel Johnson, the ground-breaking historian Catharine Macaulay, the firebrand politician John Wilkes, and revolutionary activist Thomas Paine, this book looks at the generation that preceded the Declaration in 1776. Everyone, it seemed, had "life, liberty, and the pursuit of happiness" on their minds; Moore shows why, and reveals how these still-nascent ideals made their way across an ocean and started a revolution.

"Historian Moore (Endeavour) offers a rich and immersive intellectual history of the American Revolution focused on its roots in Enlightenment era Britain." —*Publishers Weekly*

Includes bibliographical references and index.

200 Religion

Armstrong, Karen
The Battle for God. Karen Armstrong. Alfred A. Knopf 2000. xvi, 442 p.
ISBN 9780679435976
Grades: 11 12 Adult **200**
1. God 2. Fundamentalism 3. Orthodox Judaism 4. Christianity 5. Judaism 6. Islam 7. Israel 8. Spirituality and Religion — Christianity 9. Spirituality and Religion — Islam 10. Spirituality and Religion — Judaism
LC 99034022

Booklist Editors' Choice, 2000; New York Times Notable Book, 2000.

Focusing on the rise of fundamentalism in three major religions reveals how these movements in Christianity, Judaism, and Islam were born out of a dread of modernity.

"The author is sympathetic to the human need for spiritual meaning, but she points out that the intellectual flaws of fundamentalist beliefs are customarily accompanied by paranoia, anger, and aggression—which, in turn, frequently betray the message of the faith." —*The New Yorker*

Includes bibliographical references (p. [409]-424) and index.

Chittister, Joan
The Gift of Years: Growing Older Gracefully. Joan Chittister. BlueBridge 2008. xvi, 222 p.
ISBN 9781933346106
Grades: Adult **200**
1. Seniors 2. Aging 3. Personal conduct 4. Psychology 5. Christianity 6. Family and Relationships — Aging and Death 7. Spirituality and Religion — General
LC 2008000332

Author Joan Chittister examines the aging process from a Christian perspective. Urging listeners to celebrate their growing older, Chittister highlights the rewards of old age and also addresses key issues facing the elderly.

ESSENTIAL AND RECOMMENDED TITLES
200.1 Systems, scientific principles, psychology of religion

"This collection of inspirational reflections, not meant to be read in one sitting, or even in order, but one topic at a time, abounds in gentle insights and arresting aphorisms." —*Publishers Weekly*
Includes bibliographical references.

De Botton, Alain
Religion for Atheists: A Non-Believer's Guide to the Uses of Religion. Alain de Botton. Pantheon Books 2012. 320 p.
ISBN 9780307379108
Grades: Adult   **200**
1. Atheists 2. Religious life 3. Atheism 4. Spirituality and Religion — General
LC 2011021286
An atheist's provocative argument for how everyone can benefit from the wisdom and power of religion regardless of beliefs explains how the secular world can glean insights from religious stories about how to live, structure societies and achieve a greater appreciation for culture.

Dennett, D. C.
Breaking the Spell: Religion as a Natural Phenomenon. Daniel C. Dennett. Viking 2006. xvi, 448 p.
ISBN 9780670034727
Grades: Adult   **200**
1. Spirituality 2. Faith 3. Religions 4. Spirituality and Religion — General
LC 2005042415
Explores the nature of faith and how religion shapes everyday life, addressing controversial issues about the relevance of faith, while tracing the history of organized religion from its roots in folk beliefs to its key role in modern issues.
Includes bibliographical references (p. 413-426) and index.

Hexham, Irving
Understanding World Religions: An Interdisciplinary Approach. Irving Hexham. Zondervan 2011. 512 p. : Illustration; Map
ISBN 9780310259442
Grades: Adult   **200**
1. Religions 2. Spirituality and Religion — General
LC 2010013103
Irving Hexham's introductory world religions text explores various religions under the broad categories of African Religions, the Yogic Traditions (including Buddhism), and the Abrahamic traditions. He presents an appreciative yet realistic approach, noting both the strengths and inherent problems of various world religions.
Cover subtitle: An interdisciplinary approach; Includes bibliographical references and index.

Lewis, James R.
Legitimating New Religions. James R. Lewis. Rutgers University Press 2003. VIII, 272 p. : Illustration
ISBN 9780813533247
Grades: Adult   **200**
1. Cults 2. Religious psychology 3. Authority 4. Religious pluralism 5. Religions 6. Spirituality and Religion — General
LC 2003005987
Lewis (U. of Wisconsin-Stevens Point) first explores the methods by which new religions legitimate themselves to the larger society, with case studies of the Raelian Movement, Native American prophet religions, spiritualism, Scientology, the Church of Satan, Heaven's Gate, Unitarianism, and others. Then he looks at how repression of them is legitimated through atrocity tales, charges of insanity, cult stereotypes, and scholarship.
"Lewis's work is a valuable contribution. Recommended for academic libraries with religious studies collections." —*Library Journal*
Includes bibliographical references (p. 249-259) and index.

Marty, Martin E.
Pilgrims in Their Own Land: 500 Years of Religion in America. Martin E. Marty. Little, Brown 1984. xii, 500 p. : Illustration
ISBN 9780316548670
Grades: Adult   **200**
1. Christianity 2. Religions 3. Church history 4. United States 5. Spirituality and Religion — General 6. History writing — United States
LC 84000821
An eminent historian of religion offers candid accounts of the lives of America's leading religious leaders and of the movements, spiritual forces, and groups that shaped religion in the United States.
Includes bibliographical references (p. 478-488) and index.

Minois, Georges
The Atheist's Bible: The Most Dangerous Book That Never Existed. Georges Minois; translated by Lys Ann Weiss. The University of Chicago Press 2012. xii, 249 p. : Map
ISBN 9780226530291
Grades: Adult   **200**
1. Rationalism 2. Books 3. Heresy 4. Popes 5. Scandals 6. Atheism 7. Blasphemy 8. Spirituality and Religion — General 9. History writing — General
LC 2012011212
Like a lot of good stories, this one begins with a rumor: in 1239, Pope Gregory IX accused Frederick II, the Holy Roman Emperor, of heresy. Without disclosing evidence of any kind, Gregory announced that Frederick had written a supremely blasphemous book—De tribus impostoribus, or The Treatise of the Three Impostors—in which Frederick denounced Moses, Jesus, and Muhammad as impostors. Of course, Frederick denied the charge, and over the following centuries the story played out across Europe, with libertines, freethinkers, and other 'strong minds' seeking a copy of the scandalous text.
Includes bibliographical references (pages [209]-223) and index.

Prothero, Stephen R.
God Is Not One: The Eight Rival Religions That Run the World—and Why Their Differences Matter. Stephen Prothero. HarperOne 2010. 400 p.
ISBN 9780061571275
Grades: Adult   **200**
1. Religions 2. 21st century 3. Spirituality and Religion — General
LC 2009053372
Argues that the differences between the world's religions are far greater than previously acknowledged, and presents cautionary advice against underestimating these differences.
"Provocative, thoughtful, fiercely intelligent and, for both believing and nonbelieving, formal and informal students of religion, a must-read." —*Booklist*

Williams, Juan
This Far by Faith: Stories from the African-American Religious Experience. Juan Williams and Quinton Dixie. William Morrow 2003. 326 p. : Illustration
ISBN 9780060188634
Grades: Adult   **200**
1. African Americans 2. African American history 3. Religions 4. Spirituality and Religion — General
LC 2002071884
A detailed examination of African-American religious life and its relationship with the Black American experience brings together historical research, photographs, contemporary interviews, and commentary by top clergy.
Includes bibliographical references (p. [305]-310) index.

200.1 Systems, scientific principles, psychology of religion

DeSteno, David
How God Works: The Science Behind the Benefits of Religion. David DeSteno. Simon & Schuster 2021. 288 p.
ISBN 9781982142315
Grades: Adult   **200.1**
1. Religious psychology 2. Religious life 3. Faith 4. Empathy 5. Spirituality and Religion — General
LC 2021020294

A psychology professor explains how religious practices are rewarding and beneficial to those who follow them, regardless of faith, citing as examples Japanese Shinto rituals that help with postpartum depression and Christians saying grace before a meal increasing empathy.

"Parents, teachers, and religious leaders will appreciate DeSteno's work, which is accompanied by copious endnotes." —*Booklist*

Includes bibliographical references and index.

McLaren, Brian D.

Life After Doom: Wisdom and Courage for a World Falling Apart. Brian D. McLaren. St. Martin's Essentials 2024. 272 p.

ISBN 9781250893277

Grades: Adult **200.1**

1. Climate change 2. Uncertainty 3. Resilience 4. Civilization, Western 5. 21st century 6. Spirituality and Religion — Christianity

LC 2023058064

A deeply insightful exploration of how to live with wisdom, resilience and love in our turbulent times.

"These are not easy conditions to face, but McLaren's candor, insights, and guidance will inspire readers to speak out and make positive changes." —*Booklist*

200.71 Education

Prothero, Stephen R.

Religious Literacy: What Every American Needs to Know—and Doesn't. Stephen Prothero. Harper San Francisco 2007. VIII, 296 p.

ISBN 9780060846701

Grades: Adult **200.71**

1. Religious education 2. Religions 3. Religion in the public schools 4. Spirituality and Religion — General

LC 2006041310

A religious primer serves as an argument for why religion should become a mandatory subject in American public schools, contending that most Americans are not able to identify basic tenets of their faith and that key political challenges can be better met with faith-based resolutions.

"In this book, the author combines a lively history of the rise and fall of American religious literacy with a set of proposed remedies based on his hope that the Fall into religious ignorance is reversible. He also includes a useful multicultural glossary of religious definitions and allusions, in which religious illiterates can find the prodigal son, the promised land, the Quakers and the Koran." —*Washington Post Book World*

Includes bibliographical references (p. [245]-279) and index.

200.9 Religion — History, geographic treatment, biography

Armstrong, Karen

★ *The Great Transformation: The Beginning of Our Religious Traditions.* Karen Armstrong. Knopf 2006. xviii, 469 p. : Illustration; Map

ISBN 9780375413179

Grades: Adult **200.9**

1. Monotheism 2. Philosophy, Ancient 3. Ancient history 4. Confucianism 5. Taoism 6. Hinduism 7. Buddhism 8. Religions 9. Chinese history 10. Indian history 11. Southwest Asia and North Africa (Middle East) history 12. China 13. India 14. Israel 15. Greece 16. Spirituality and Religion — General 17. History writing — General

LC 2005047536

Examines the origins of the religious traditions of the world during the ninth century B.C.E. in four distinct regions—Confucianism and Daoism in China, Hinduism and Buddhism in India, monotheism in Israel, and philosophical rationalism in Greece.

"This could very possibly be one of the greatest intellectual histories ever written." —*Library Journal*

Includes bibliographical references and index.

Miles, Jack

Religion as We Know It: An Origin Story. Jack Miles. W. W. Norton & Company, Inc. 2020. 128 pages

ISBN 9781324002789

Grades: Adult **200.9**

1. Civilization, Western 2. Western religions 3. Christianity 4. Religion and culture 5. Religions 6. Western Hemisphere 7. Spirituality and Religion — General

LC 2019026444

In his new book, acclaimed scholar Jack Miles poses a question: How did our forebears begin to think about religion as a distinct domain, separate from other activities that were once inseparable from it? Starting at the birth of Christianity—a religion inextricably bound to Western thought—Miles reveals how we in the West have come to isolate religion as an object of study, and how drastically our perception has changed over time and across societies.

Includes bibliographical references and index.

200.951 Religion — China

Johnson, Ian

The Souls of China: The Return of Religion After Mao. Ian Johnson. Pantheon Books 2017. 384 p.

ISBN 9781101870051

Grades: Adult **200.951**

1. Communism and Christianity 2. Communism and religion 3. Religions 4. China 5. Spirituality and Religion — General 6. History writing — Asia — China

LC 2016036412

A Pulitzer Prize-winning journalist—who lived for extended periods with underground church members, rural Daoists and Buddhist pilgrims—uses his experiences to paint a revelatory portrait of religion in China today—its history, the spiritual traditions of its Eastern and Western faiths and the ways in which it is influencing China's future.

"Johnson provides a fascinating account of how traditional activities recovered after enduring severe repression during China's Cultural Revolution (1966-76)." —*Library Journal*

200.973 Religion — United States

Olson, Roger E.

★ *Handbook of Denominations in the United States.* Roger E. Olson, Frank S. Mead, Samuel S. Hill & Craig D. Atwood. Abingdon Press 2018. 384 p. : Illustration

ISBN 9781501822513

Grades: Adult **200.973**

1. Sects 2. Christian sects 3. Religions 4. United States 5. Spirituality and Religion — Christianity

LC 2010007092

The 14th edition is completely updated with current statistics, new denominations, and recent trends. The book has been made more useful and manageable by moving very small groups into broader articles while giving more detail and description to the large and influential denominations.

Includes bibliographical references and index.

Ozment, Katherine

Grace Without God: The Search for Meaning, Purpose, and Belonging in a Secular Age. Katherine Ozment. Harper Wave, HarperCollins Publishers 2016. 256 p.

ISBN 9780062305114

Grades: Adult **200.973**

1. Irreligion 2. Spirituality 3. Spiritual life 4. Religions 5. Spirituality and Religion — General 6. Society and culture — General

LC 2016004086

ESSENTIAL AND RECOMMENDED TITLES
201 Specific aspects of religion

Looks at the trends and ramifications of a country increasingly leaving organized religion behind, focusing on how this growing number of nonreligious Americans find meaning, purpose, and community.

"Ozment successfully writes an informative and relatable discussion on the changing landscape of religion, society, and identity." —*Library Journal*

Includes bibliographical references and index.

201 Specific aspects of religion

Armstrong, Karen
Fields of Blood: Religion and the History of Violence. Karen Armstrong. Knopf 2014. 512 p.
ISBN 9780307957047
Grades: Adult   201
1. Violence 2. Religious terrorism 3. Ethics 4. Canadian literature 5. Spirituality and religion — General 6. History writing — Microhistory
LC 2014011057

Provides a sweeping exploration of religion's connection to violence, from the agrarian societies of early civilized man to the growing post-9/11 disillusionment with religion.

★ *A Short History of Myth*. Karen Armstrong. Canongate 2006. 159 p.
ISBN 9781841958002
Grades: 11 12 Adult   201
1. Mythology 2. Civilization, Stone age 3. Civilization, Western 4. Spirituality and Religion — General 5. History writing — General
LC Bl2006026966

The author of The History of God and In the Beginning: A New Reading of Genesis offers a useful, well-written introduction to mythology from the Paleolithic period to the "Great Western Transformation" that used science to discredit myth.

"This is an overview of the ever-evolving partnership between myth and man from Paleolithic times to the present. Succinct and cleanly written, it is hugely readable and, in its journey across the epochs of human experience, often moving. . . . Armstrong's exposition is streamlined and uncluttered without being simplistic." —*New York Times Book Review*

Includes bibliographical references (p. 151-159); Reprint. Originally published: 2005.

Carroll, Georgie
The Mythology Book. Philip Wilkinson, consultant; contributors Georgie Carroll, Dr. Mark Faulkner, Dr. Jacob F. Field, Dr. John Haywood, Michael Kerrigan, Neil Philip, Dr. Nicholaus Pumphrey, Juliette Tocino-Smith. DK 2018. 351 pages : Illustration; Color
ISBN 9781465473370
Grades: Adult   201
1. Mythology 2. Mythology, folklore, and legends 3. Reference — Encyclopedias
LC Bl2018080006

Explores the mythology of different cultures throughout history and around the world, through retellings and explanations of over eighty traditional stories, presented in an accessible, visual style.

Includes index.

Grant, Edward
Science and Religion, 400 B.C. To A.D. 1550: From Aristotle to Copernicus. Edward Grant. Greenwood Press 2004. xxvi, 307 p. : Illustration
ISBN 9780313328589
Grades: 11 12 Adult   201
1. Religion and science 2. Science writing — General 3. Spirituality and Religion — General
LC 2004017429

Explores the relationship between science and religion during the Middle Ages and argues that theologians did not discourage science, but embraced it, which ultimately led to the Scientific Revolution.

Includes bibliographical references (p. [279]-294) and index.

Harman, Oren Solomon
Evolutions: Fifteen Myths That Explain Our World. Oren Harman. Farrar, Straus and Giroux 2018. 240 p.
ISBN 9780374150709
Grades: Adult   201
1. Evolution 2. Science 3. Philosophy 4. Society and culture — Philosophy 5. Science writing — General
LC 2017047954

A lyrical exploration of how modern science illuminates what it means to be human shares the latest understandings about the birth of the universe and the evolution of the mind to create new mythologies connecting science to our existential questions.

Sacks, Jonathan
The Great Partnership: God, Science and the Search for Meaning. Jonathan Sacks. Schocken Books 2012. 384 p.
ISBN 9780805243017
Grades: 10 11 12 Adult   201
1. Religion and science 2. Purpose in life 3. Science 4. Spirituality and Religion — General 5. Science Writing — General
LC 2012006601

A renowned author and rabbi discusses the relationship between science and religion and the importance of the coexistence of both in that religion is the search for meaning and science is the search for explanation.

Includes bibliographical references.

Sheldrake, Rupert
Science and Spiritual Practices: Transformative Experiences and Their Effects on Our Bodies, Brains, and Health. Rupert Sheldrake. Counterpoint 2018. 256 p.
ISBN 9781640091177
Grades: Adult   201
1. Medicine 2. Health 3. Spiritual life 4. Religion and science 5. Thought and thinking 6. Meditation 7. Science Writing — General 8. Spirituality and Religion — General
LC 2018002867

Describes how science helps validate seven practices on which many religions are built, including meditation, gratitude, connecting with nature, rituals, relating to plants, singing, and pilgrimage.

Includes bibliographical references and index.

201.3 Mythology and mythological foundations

Campbell, Joseph
The Masks of God. Joseph Campbell. Arkana 1991. 4 v. : Illustration
ISBN 9780140194432
Grades: 11 12 Adult   201.3
1. Mythology 2. Heroes and heroines 3. Gods and goddesses 4. Human behavior 5. Archetype (Psychology) 6. Literary criticism 7. Church history 8. Religions 9. Spirituality and Religion — General
LC 91214960

Studies the development of man's philosophical views of supreme beings in primitive, Eastern, and Western culture.

Includes bibliographical references (p. 681-710) and index; Originally published: New York : Viking Press, 1959.

The Power of Myth. Joseph Campbell, with Bill Moyers; Betty Sue Flowers, editor. Doubleday 1988. xix, 231 p, 16 p. of plates : Illustration; Color
ISBN 9780385247740
Grades: 11 12 Adult   201.3
1. Campbell, Joseph, 1904-1987 2. Mythology 3. Heroes and heroines 4. Human behavior 5. Literary criticism 6. Religions 7. Spirituality and Religion — General
LC 88004218

Explores the common themes that underlie diverse religions of Eastern and Western cultures.

"Campbell is the hero on his own voyage of discovery. This well-bound book on lovely paper with helpful illustrations from art is highly recommended for all libraries." —*Choice*

201.723 Civil rights

Nussbaum, Martha Craven
The New Religious Intolerance: Overcoming the Politics of Fear in an Anxious Age. Martha C. Nussbaum. Belknap Press of Harvard University Press 2012. 304 p.
ISBN 9780674065901
Grades: Adult 201.723
1. Freedom of religion 2. Religious tolerance 3. Religious discrimination 4. Fear 5. Discrimination 6. Prejudice 7. Spirituality and Religion — General
LC 2011051712

Examines the new religious intolerance of Islam—from protests against a proposed Manhattan Islamic center to the banning of minarets in Switzerland—and offers a way back to an equal and free global society.

"This powerful and profound book is useful to anyone seriously concerned with religious pluralism and civil liberty." —*Library Journal*

Includes bibliographical references and index.

202 Doctrines

Armstrong, Karen
A History of God: The 4000-Year Quest of Judaism, Christianity, and Islam. by Karen Armstrong. Gramercy Books 2004. xxiii, 460 p. : Illustration; Map
ISBN 9780517223123
Grades: Adult 202
1. God 2. God (Christianity) 3. God (Islam) 4. God (Judaism) 5. Monotheism 6. Christian doctrines 7. Judaic doctrines 8. Islamic doctrines 9. Christianity 10. Judaism 11. Islam 12. Biblical teaching 13. Theology 14. Religions 15. Spirituality and Religion — Christianity 16. Spirituality and Religion — Islam 17. Spirituality and Religion — Judaism
LC 2003062755

One of England's foremost religious commentators, the author of Beginning the World explores the evolution of the idea and experience of God, from Abraham to the present.

"Public librarians should be aware that conservative readers may be offended by this book, and even religious scholars may find Armstrong's rather one-sided 'death of God' optimism about humanity a bit passe. Otherwise, this is an excellent and informative book." —*Library Journal*

Includes bibliographical references (p. [427]-436) and index; Originally published: New York : Ballantine Books, 1993.

Bartlett, Sarah
A Brief History of Angels and Demons. Sarah Bartlett. Running Press 2011. xii, 259 p.
ISBN 9780762442782
Grades: Adult 202
1. Angels 2. Demons 3. Spirituality 4. Spirituality and Religion — General
LC Bl2012029693

Looks at the history of angels and demons and their depiction in literature, myth, religion, and art through the ages.

Holloway, Richard
Waiting for the Last Bus: Reflections on Life and Death. Richard Holloway. Canongate Books 2018. 368 p.
ISBN 9781786890214
Grades: Adult 202
1. Death 2. Coping 3. Spiritual life 4. Loss 5. Life after death 6. Grief 7. Spirituality and Religion — Christianity
LC Bl2018053415

Now in his ninth decade, former Bishop of Edinburgh Richard Holloway has spent a lifetime at the bedsides of the dying, guiding countless men and women towards peaceful deaths. In The Last Bus, he presents a positive, meditative and profound exploration of the many important lessons we can learn from death: facing up to the limitations of our bodies as they falter, reflecting on our failings, and forgiving ourselves and others.

"This powerful volume abounds with thoughtful guidance for soothing the dying, comforting the grieving, and preparing for ones own death." —*Publishers Weekly*

Jennings, Ken
★ *100 Places to See After You Die: A Travel Guide to the Afterlife.* Ken Jennings. Scribner 2023. 320 p.
ISBN 9781501131585
Grades: Adult 202
1. Life after death 2. Eternity 3. Heaven 4. Hell 5. Religions 6. Gods and goddesses 7. Mythical creatures 8. Popular culture 9. Tourism 10. Humorous writing 11. Humor writing — General 12. Spirituality and Religion — General 13. Society and culture — Pop culture
LC 2022037903

From a New York Times best-selling author and Jeopardy! champion and host comes a humorous travel guide to the afterlife, exploring destinations to die for from literature, mythology, and pop culture ranging from Dante's Inferno to Hadestown to NBC's The Good Place.

"An entertaining, amusing collection of a wide variety of visions of the afterlife." —*Kirkus*

Includes index.

Jordan, Michael
Dictionary of Gods and Goddesses. Michael Jordan. Facts on File 2004. xi, 402 p. : Illustration
ISBN 9780816059232
Grades: Adult 202
1. Gods and goddesses 2. Spirituality and Religion — Body, mind, and spirit 3. Reference — Dictionaries
LC 2004013028

Provides information on both significant and minor deities of cultures from around the world, discussing the role of the god in each culture and the characteristics and symbols associated with each god.

"The author's alphabetical list includes gods and goddesses from a variety of religions. Each entry provides a brief description with cross-references where appropriate; some supply translations of the names. Longer entries include origin, dates of observance, synonyms, geographic location of the cult center, art references by type (e.g., stone carvings), and literary sources. This [is] a usable, well-written resource for short descriptions of cross-cultural deities." —*Choice*

Rev. ed. of: Encyclopedia of gods. c1993; Includes bibliographical references (p. 361-366) and index.

Ruttenberg, Danya
On Repentance and Repair: Making Amends in an Unapologetic World. Danya Ruttenberg. Beacon Press 2022. x, 243 pages
ISBN 9780807010518
Grades: Adult 202
1. Maimonides, 1135-1204 2. Philosophers 3. Philosophy 4. Judaic doctrines 5. Repentance 6. Guilt 7. Responsibility 8. Social responsibility 9. Atonement 10. Ethics 11. Empathy 12. Reconciliation 13. Freedom 14. Social justice 15. Society and culture — Philosophy 16. Spirituality and Religion — Judaism — History
LC Oc2022002043

A crucial new lens on repentance, atonement, forgiveness, and repair from harm-from personal transgressions to our culture's most painful and unresolved issues. American culture focuses on letting go of grudges and redemption narratives instead of the perpetrator's obligations or recompense for harmed parties. As survivor communities have pointed out, these emphases have too often only caused more harm. But Danya Ruttenberg knew there was a better model, rooted in the work of the medieval philosopher Maimonides.

ESSENTIAL AND RECOMMENDED TITLES
203 Public worship and other practices

"Ruttenberg's book sets out guidelines for full-hearted repentance—the kind of atonement that people should do, but often don't." —*Library Journal*
Includes bibliographical references (pages 205-234) and index.

Speerstra, Karen
The **Divine** *Art of Dying: How to Live Well While Dying*. Karen Speerstra + Herbert Anderson; foreword by Ira Byock, MD.. DIVINE ARTS 2014. xviii, 268 pages
ISBN 9781611250237
Grades: Adult **202**
1. Death 2. Palliative treatment 3. Hospice care 4. Family and Relationships — Aging and Death
LC 2013047709
A guide to end-of-life decisions combines personal stories with research on palliative and hospice care.
"A valuable resource; this books brims with wisdom and grace." —*Publishers Weekly*
Includes bibliographical references (pages 264-267).

203 Public worship and other practices

Iyer, Pico
★ *The* **Half** *Known Life: In Search of Paradise*. Pico Iyer. Riverhead Books 2023. 240 p.
ISBN 9780593420256
Grades: Adult **203**
1. Spiritual life 2. Paradise 3. Psychological growth 4. Interethnic conflict 5. Cross-cultural studies 6. Voyages and travels 7. Travel Writing — General 8. Spirituality and Religion — General
LC 2022002855
A journey through competing ideas of paradise to see how we can live more peacefully in an ever more divided and distracted world.—.
"With keen observation and beautiful language, Iyer shows us the essential truths of places, people, and ideas." —*Kirkus*

Mendelson, Cheryl
★ **Vows:** *The Modern Genius of an Ancient Rite*. Cheryl Mendelson. Simon & Schuster 2024. 256 p.
ISBN 9781668021569
Grades: Adult **203**
1. Marriage 2. Marriage customs and rites 3. Promises 4. Contracts 5. Tradition (Philosophy) 6. Gender equity 7. Romantic love 8. History 9. Social life and customs 10. Family and Relationships — Dating and Marriage 11. Society and culture — Philosophy 12. History writing — Microhistory
In the West, marrying is so thoroughly identified with ceremonial promises that "taking vows" is a synonym for getting married. So, it's a surprise to realize that this custom is actually a historical and anthropological oddity. Most of the world, for most of history, married without making promises. And there's a reason for that. Marriage by vow presupposes free choice, and free choice makes a love-match possible. It is a very modern arrangement. Vows is both a moving memoir of two marriages and a thoughtful meditation on marriage itself. Cheryl Mendelson tackles the sociology of commitment through our most traditional promises and shows why they endure.
"The wide-ranging narrative draws on an impressive array of sources, from Ovid to the polyamorous Oneida community in 19th-century New York. It's a hugely informative history of the very idea of what makes a marriage." —*Publishers Weekly*
Includes bibliographical references and index.

204 Religious experience, life, practice

Briggs, Lyvonne
★ **Sensual** *Faith: The Art of Coming Home to Your Body*. Lyvonne Briggs; foreword by Briana Boyd. Convergent 2023. 208 p.
ISBN 9780593443217
Grades: Adult **204**
1. Body image 2. African American women 3. Body awareness 4. African American feminism 5. Spirituality 6. Faith 7. Christianity 8. Sexuality 9. Spirituality and religion — Christianity 10. Society and culture — Gender — Women 11. Debut title
"Black women looking to love themselves while loving God will find much to gain." —*Publishers Weekly*

Chopra, Deepak
Metahuman: *Unleashing Your Infinite Potential*. Deepak Chopra, M.D.. Harmony Books 2019. 354 pages
ISBN 9780307338334
Grades: Adult **204**
1. Mind and body 2. Self-fulfillment 3. Spiritual life 4. Self-Help — Personal growth 5. Self-Help — Personal growth — Motivation 6. Self-Help — Personal growth — Spirituality
LC 2019004165
The best-selling author of You Are the Universe draws on wisdom traditions and the latest research into the human brain, artificial intelligence and biometrics to explain what higher consciousness is and its role in health and spirituality. Illustrations.
Includes bibliographical references and index.

James, William
★ *The* **Varieties** *of Religious Experience: A Study in Human Nature*. William James; introduction by Reinhold Niebuhr. Simon & Schuster 2004. xiii, 398 p.
ISBN 9780743257879
Grades: Adult **204**
1. Experience (Religion) 2. Religious psychology 3. Religious conversion 4. Philosophy and religion 5. Religions 6. Spirituality and Religion — General
LC 2004042870
In a series of twenty lectures, the philosopher explores conversion, mysticism, repentence, prayer, saintliness, hopes of reward, and fears of punishment with sympathy and boldness. Religious phenomena are documented by various case histories. Both the believer and the non-believer will find a great deal of food for thought.
A Touchstone book; Includes bibliographical references and index.

208 Sources

Armstrong, Karen
The **Lost** *Art of Scripture: Rescuing the Sacred Texts*. by Karen Armstrong. Alfred A. Knopf 2019. 448 p.
ISBN 9780451494863
Grades: Adult **208**
1. Sacred books 2. Religion and culture 3. Semantics 4. Fundamentalism 5. Religions 6. Spirituality and Religion — General 7. History writing — General
LC 2019009391
New York Times Notable Book, 2019.
A history of the holy texts from a number of the world's religions and how in our secular world they are at best seen as irrelevant and at worst as a reason to incite violence, hatred, and division.
Includes bibliographical references and index.

211 Concepts of God

The **Case** *for God*. Karen Armstrong. Knopf 2009. 432 p.
ISBN 9780307269188
Grades: Adult **211**
1. God 2. God (Christianity) 3. Religious life 4. Monotheism 5. Christian life 6. Christian apologetics 7. Theology 8. Spirituality and Religion — Christianity
LC 2009014044

New York Times Notable Book, 2009.

Evaluates the role of religion in history, stating that modern expressions of faith are considerably removed from those of previous generations while arguing that an increased awareness of past insights may build a faith that speaks to an increasingly polarized society.

"Magisterial is the adjective of choice to describe Armstrong's work; her usual confident sweep across times and cultures rises above the answer-the-atheists tired angle to make a passionate footnoted argument for the human need for a God." —*Publishers Weekly*

Includes bibliographical references and index.

Aslan, Reza

God: A Human History. Reza Aslan. Random House 2017. 240 p.
ISBN 9780553394726

Grades: Adult   211

1. God 2. Monotheism 3. Philosophy and religion 4. Western religions 5. Church history 6. Religions 7. Spirituality and Religion — General 8. History writing — General

LC 2017034711

The best-selling author of Zealot and host of Believer explores how different ideas about religion have united, divided and propelled humanity forward for millennia.

"Written in language accessible to the layperson but based on wide reading in the relevant literature, Aslan's work will appeal to anyone interested in the history of religion." —*Library Journal*

Includes bibliographical references and index.

Hazleton, Lesley

Agnostic: A Spirited Manifesto. Lesley Hazleton. Riverhead Books 2016. 240 p.
ISBN 9781594634130

Grades: Adult   211

1. Agnostics 2. Belief and doubt 3. Agnosticism 4. Spirituality and religion — General

LC 2016006449

One in four Americans reject any affiliation with organized religion, and nearly half of those under thirty describe themselves as "spiritual but not religious." but as the airwaves resound with the haranguing of preachers and pundits, who speaks for the millions who find no joy in whittling the wonder of existence to a simple yes/no choice?

"This engaging and highly accessible read will satisfy those who puzzle over the idea of infinity, question theological truth or what death means for the mind and body, and who wish to delve deeper into our belief system." —*Library Journal*

Hitchens, Christopher

The Four Horsemen: The Conversation That Sparked an Atheist Revolution. Christopher Hitchens, Richard Dawkins, Sam Harris, Daniel Dennett; introduction by Stephen Fry. Random House Inc 2019. 128 p.
ISBN 9780525511953

Grades: Adult   211

1. Atheism 2. Belief and doubt 3. Existentialism 4. Faith 5. Humans 6. Intellectual life 7. Thought and thinking 8. Spirituality 9. Ethics 10. Philosophy 11. Purpose in life 12. Religions 13. Essays 14. Spirituality and Religion — General 15. Society and culture — Philosophy

LC 2019004626

A transcript of the 2007 viral documentary features intellectual responses to the fundamental questions of faith, human existence and the new atheism, in a volume that is complemented by new, contextualized essays by the group's three surviving members.

"Spanning religion and philosophy, this work will appeal to readers of both, especially those interested in atheism and apologetics." —*Library Journal*

Pinn, Anthony B.

The Black Practice of Disbelief: An Introduction to the Principles, History, and Communities of Black Nonbelievers. Anthony B. Pinn. Beacon Press 2024. 144 p.
ISBN 9780807045220

Grades: Adult   211

1. African Americans 2. Religious life 3. Humanism 4. Secular humanism 5. Skepticism 6. Philosophy 7. Identity 8. Communities 9. African American history 10. History writing — African American — United States 11. Society and culture — Philosophy 12. Society and culture — Race

In the United States, to be a Black American is to be a Black Christian. And there's something to this assumption in that the vast majority of African Americans are Christian. However, in recent years a growing number of African Americans have said they claim no particular religious affiliation—they are Black "nones." and of these Black "nones," the most public and vocal are those who claim to be humanists. Animated by six central principles, and discussed in terms of its history, practices, formations, and community rituals, this book argues that Black humanism can be understood as a religious movement.

"It's a perceptive window into an often-overlooked—yet increasingly important—system of thought." —*Publishers Weekly*

Includes bibliographical references and index.

Zuckerman, Phil

Living the Secular Life: New Answers to Old Questions. Phil Zuckerman. Penguin Press 2014. 240 p.
ISBN 9781594205088

Grades: Adult   211

1. Secularism 2. Irreligion 3. Ethics 4. Atheism 5. Humanism 6. Agnosticism 7. Free thought 8. Personal conduct 9. Secular humanism 10. Religions 11. United States 12. Spirituality and Religion — General 13. Society and culture — Philosophy

LC 2014009785

A sociology professor examines the demographic shift that has led more Americans than ever before to embrace a nonreligious life and highlights the inspirational stories and beliefs that empower modern-day secular culture.

"Highly recommended for all readers, both religious and nonreligious, seeking a more accurate understanding of this ever-growing segment of the American population." —*Library Journal*

Includes bibliographical references and index.

215 Science and religion

Collins, Francis S.

The Language of God: A Scientist Presents Evidence for Belief. Francis S. Collins. Free Press 2006. VIII, 294 p. : Illustration
ISBN 9780743286398

Grades: 11 12 Adult   215

1. Religion and science 2. Christian apologetics 3. Religions 4. Spirituality and Religion — General

LC 2006045316

A head of the Human Genome Project and former atheist presents a scientific argument for the existence of God, revealing how science can support faith by citing the areas of nature that can and cannot be fully explained by Darwinian evolution.

"The author entertains propositions both for and against the existence of God and biblical authority, as well as the moral implications of bioethics. He personalizes the narrative by recounting his own journey from atheism to faith, portraying it as much an intellectual quest as a spiritual one. . . . An essential read, equally for readers of religious or secular persuasions." —*Library Journal*

Includes bibliographical references (p. 273-280) and index.

Lightman, Alan P.

The Transcendent Brain: Spirituality in the Age of Science. Alan P. Lightman. Pantheon Books 2023. 208 p.
ISBN 9780593317419

ESSENTIAL AND RECOMMENDED TITLES
220.09 Bible — History, geographic treatment, biography

Grades: Adult **215**
1. Religion and science 2. Spirituality 3. Science 4. Spirituality and religion — General 5. Science Writing — General
LC 2022010019

From the acclaimed author of Einstein's Dreams comes a rich, fascinating answer to the question, Can the scientifically inclined still hold space for spirituality?

"Physicist Lightman (Probable Impossibilities) contends that 'Some human experiences are simply not reducible to zeros and ones' and draws on philosophy and science to suggest that materialism and spirituality are compatible….Lightman's arguments succeed in walking the fine line between honoring spiritual experiences without lapsing into pseudoscience." —*Publishers Weekly*

Includes bibliographical references.

220.09 Bible — History, geographic treatment, biography

Armstrong, Karen
The *Bible*: A Biography. Karen Armstrong. Atlantic Monthly Press 2007. 192 p.
ISBN 9780871139696
Grades: Adult **220.09**
1. Bible as literature 2. Religions 3. Spirituality and Religion — Christianity

Examines the Bible's complex history, the social and political environment in which oral history became written scripture, how the various books were collected into a single volume, and its acceptance as Christianity's sacred text.

Barton, John
A *History* of the Bible: The Story of the World's Most Influential Book. John Barton. Viking 2019. xix, 613 pages : Illustration; Map
ISBN 9780525428770
Grades: Adult **220.09**
1. Judaism 2. Christianity 3. Jewish people 4. Impartial writing 5. Spirituality and Religion — Christianity — History 6. Spirituality and Religion — Judaism
LC 2019022727

An Oxford scholar and Anglican priest discusses the Bible in its historical context, from its beginnings as myth and folklore through the additions of narratives, laws, proverbs, prophesies, poems and letters to its interpretations through the centuries.

Includes bibliographical references (pages 547-565) and index.

220.5 Modern versions and translations

Ruden, Sarah
The *Face* of Water: A Translator on Beauty and Meaning in the Bible. Sarah Ruden. Pantheon Books 2017. xxxviii, 232 pages
ISBN 9780307908568
Grades: Adult **220.5**
1. Spirituality and Religion — Religious texts 2. Arts and Entertainment — Writing and Publishing — Literary criticism
LC 2016014872

Offers an exploration of the original languages and texts of the Bible, with examinations and retranslations of some of its most famous passages as well as inquiries into the historical development of the work and the purposes of translation.

"This combination of casual ease and serious scholarship allows Ruden to bring fresh insights into even the most familiar stories and will make the book a true pleasure for anyone with an interest in translation or the Bible." —*Publishers Weekly*

Includes bibliographical references and indexes.

Strong, James
The *New* Strong's Expanded Exhaustive Concordance of the Bible. James Strong. Thomas Nelson 2010. 1 volume (various pagings)
ISBN 9781418541682

Grades: Adult **220.5**
1. Hebrew language 2. Greek language 3. Spirituality and Religion — Christianity 4. Reference books — Religion
LC Bl2010015608

An index to every word of the King James Version of the Bible includes a dictionary of Greek and Hebrew words, Strong's numbering system, and the words of Christ emphasized.

Expanded with the best of Vine's dictionary of Old & New Testament words.

220.6 Interpretation and criticism (Exegesis)

Levine, Amy-Jill
The *Bible* with and Without Jesus: How Jews and Christians Read the Same Stories Differently. Amy-Jill Levine, Marc Zvi Brettler. HarperOne 2020. 448 p.
ISBN 9780062560155
Grades: Adult **220.6**
1. Christianity 2. Theology 3. Interfaith relations 4. Judaism 5. Religions 6. Spirituality and Religion — Christianity 7. Spirituality and Religion — Judaism
LC 2020003441

The editors of the Jewish Annotated New Testament, Amy-Jill Levine and Marc Brettler, explore how Jews and Christians can learn from and understand each other better by exploring how they read many of the same Bible stories through different lens.

"The chapter on the original meanings of sections of the Sermon on the Mount is alone worth the price of admission. A rich and important offering." —*Booklist*

220.8 Nonreligious subjects treated in Bible

Murphy, Cullen
The *Word* According to Eve: Women and the Bible in Ancient Times and Our Own. Cullen Murphy; foreword by Karen Armstrong. Houghton Mifflin 1999. xxv, 302 p.
ISBN 9780618001927
Grades: Adult **220.8**
1. Bible and feminism 2. Spirituality and Religion — Religious texts
LC 99040646

"This is an examination of feminist Biblical scholarship. Murphy divides his study into Old Testament scholarship and New Testament and early church history." —*New York Times Book Review*

A Mariner book; a Peter Davison book; Includes bibliographical references (p. 260-275) and index; Originally published: Boston : Houghton Mifflin, 1998. With new foreword.

222 Historical books of Old Testament

Feiler, Bruce
The *First* Love Story: Adam, Eve, and Us. Bruce Feiler. Penguin Group USA 2017. 368 p.
ISBN 9781594206818
Grades: Adult **222**
1. Adam (Biblical figure) 2. Eve (Biblical figure) 3. Interpersonal relations 4. Gender wars 5. Love 6. Romantic love 7. Marriage 8. Popular culture 9. Men-women relations 10. Society and culture — Gender 11. Family and Relationships — Dating and Marriage 12. Spirituality and Religion — Christianity
LC 2016043490

The PBS host and best-selling author of Walking the Bible and Abraham presents a revelatory account of Adam and Eve's symbolism as central figures in Western imagination and their role in shaping humanity's deepest feelings about relationships, family and togetherness.

"Part travelogue, part historical survey, the book presents an impressive array of perspectives and a broad archive." —*Booklist*

PUBLIC LIBRARY CORE COLLECTION: NONFICTION
Twentieth Edition

Robinson, Marilynne
★ *Reading* Genesis. Marilynne Robinson. Farrar, Straus and Giroux 2024. 192 p.
ISBN 9780374299408
Grades: Adult **222**
1. Christianity 2. Literary criticism 3. Theology 4. Spirituality and religion — Christianity
LC 2023038966

A noted novelist and thinker presents an interpretation of the book of Genesis.

"Like the biblical book it explicates, Robinson's offering is demanding, intense, and best read slowly. Patient readers will be rewarded." —*Publishers Weekly*

223 Poetic books of Old Testament

Bernstein, Ellen
Toward a Holy Ecology: Reading the Song of Songs in the Age of Climate Crisis. Rabbi Ellen Bernstein, forward by Bill McKibben. Monkfish Book Publishing Company 2024. 160 p.
ISBN 9781958972199
Grades: Adult **223**
1. Biblical teaching 2. Human ecology 3. Effect of humans on nature 4. Effect of environment on humans 5. Environmentalism 6. Nature and culture 7. Nature 8. Judaism 9. Translations — Hebrew to English 10. Nature Writing — General 11. Spirituality and Religion — Judaism
LC 2023006978

Song of Songs is known as the erotic part of the Bible, but Ellen Bernstein shows how it is also an ancient source of deep ecological wisdom. Toward a Holy Ecology is a new translation of this Hebrew text, illuminating the place of humans in the natural world and inviting you to develop a holy, ecological language for life. This book sets the natural world before you with intensity and beauty, inviting you to savor it with all your senses. Then you are able to return to the world with a renewed clarity, love, and energy necessary for creating a healthier future for the earth and all her inhabitants.

"A well-researched and engaging exploration of a classic text through an ecological lens." —*Kirkus*

Includes bibliographical references.

Greenstein, Edward L.
Job: A New Translation. Edward L. Greenstein. Yale University Press 2019. xxxvii, 206 pages
ISBN 9780300162349
Grades: Adult **223**
1. Spirituality and Religion — Judaism 2. Spirituality and Religion — Religious texts
LC Bl2019023158

This revelatory new translation of Job by one of the world's leading biblical scholars will reshape the way we read this canonical text.

Includes bibliographical references (pages 189-199) and index.

Smith, James K. A.
How to Inhabit Time: Understanding the Past, Facing the Future, Living Faithfully Now. James K. A. Smith. Brazos Press 2022. 208 p.
ISBN 9781587435232
Grades: Adult **223**
1. Christian values 2. Mindfulness 3. Idealism 4. Christianity 5. Spirituality and Religion — Christianity

Popular speaker and award-winning author James K. A. Smith helps Christians and the church develop a sense of "temporal awareness" that is attuned to the texture of history, the vicissitudes of life, and the tempo of the Spirit. Smith shows that awakening to the spiritual significance of time is crucial for orienting faith in the 21st century.

"Smith delivers a lyrical exploration of how faith intersects with history and time....This incisive and eloquent volume will expand readers' minds." —*Publishers Weekly*

226.8 Parables

Levine, Amy-Jill
Short Stories by Jesus: The Enigmatic Parables of a Controversial Rabbi. Amy-Jill Levine. HarperOne 2014. 320 p.
ISBN 9780061561016
Grades: Adult **226.8**
1. Jesus Christ 2. Christianity 3. Philosophy, Jewish 4. Spirituality and Religion — Christianity
LC 2014012012

Examines Jesus' most popular parables and looks at how they have been misinterpreted and misunderstood, seeking to make them more relevant to today's readers.

228 Revelation (Apocalypse)

Peterson, Eugene H.
This Hallelujah Banquet: How the End of What We Were Reveals Who We Can Be. Eugene H. Peterson. WaterBrook 2021. IX, 181 pages
ISBN 9781601429858
Grades: Adult **228**
1. Spirituality and Religion — Christian living
LC 2020020781

In this powerful new interpretation of the Book of Revelation, the late, revered author and translator of the Message Bible shows us how to live with profound joy and faithfulness—even when it feels like the end of the world.

"A new interpretation of the Book of Revelation for Christians seeking spiritual maturity." —*Library Journal*

229 Apocrypha, pseudepigrapha, intertestamental works

Pagels, Elaine H.
Beyond Belief: The Secret Gospel of Thomas. Elaine Pagels. Random House 2003. 241 p.
ISBN 9780375501562
Grades: Adult **229**
1. Jesus Christ 2. Christianity 3. Gnosticism 4. Spirituality and Religion — Christianity
LC 2002036840

New York Times Notable Book, 2003.

Spurred by personal tragedy, Elaine Pagels turns to a consideration of the Gnostic Gospels—in particular, the Gospel of Thomas. Pagels believes that Thomas's words lead to a more open, welcoming, and equitable kind of Christianity. If Beyond belief is at odds with conservative theological certainties, it nonetheless speaks to Jesus's humanity—and to our own.

"Even those who possess only a nodding acquaintance with Gnostic writings will find themselves stimulated by the author's arguments and perhaps transformed by her conclusions. A fresh and exciting work of theology and spirituality." —*Booklist*

Includes bibliographical references and index.

230 Christianity

Carranca, Adriana
Soul by Soul: The Evangelical Mission to Spread the Gospel to Muslims. Adriana Carranca. Columbia Global Reports 2023. 190 pages
ISBN 9798987053522
Grades: Adult **230**

ESSENTIAL AND RECOMMENDED TITLES
231 Christian doctrinal theology

1. Evangelicalism 2. Muslims 3. Religious converts 4. Christian missionaries 5. Converts to Christianity from Islam 6. Southwest Asia and North Africa (Middle East) 7. Spirituality and Religion — Christianity — Political Aspects 8. Spirituality and Religion — Islam — Political Aspects

LC 2022060267

A journey through the fault lines of contemporary religious wars.
"An eye-opening look at a hidden reality of Evangelical missions." —*Kirkus*
Includes bibliographical references.

Davies, Brian
The Thought of Thomas Aquinas. Brian Davies. Clarendon Press; 1992. xv, 391 p.
ISBN 9780198264583
Grades: Adult   230
1. Thomas, Aquinas, Saint, 1225?-1274 2. Catholic theology 3. Theology, Doctrinal 4. Medieval period (476-1492) 5. Spirituality and Religion — Christianity

LC 91035671

"Davies aims to cover the whole programme of the Summa in 370 pages. This necessarily means that, though his writing is admirably clear and never cryptic, much of what he says is extremely concise, and some topics get less airing than others." —*Times Literary Supplement*
Includes bibliographical references (p. [377]-383) and index.

Douthat, Ross Gregory
To Change the Church: Pope Francis and the Future of Catholicism. Ross Douthat. Simon & Schuster 2018. 224 p.
ISBN 9781501146923
Grades: Adult   230
1. Francis, Pope, 1936- 2. Popes 3. Social change 4. Christian doctrines 5. Church history 6. Change 7. Religion and politics 8. Conservative writing 9. Spirituality and Religion — Christianity — Catholicism

The New York Times columnist, author of Grand New Party and influential conservative assesses the efforts of Pope Francis to change today's Roman Catholic Church, sharing insights into why the author disagrees with Francis' increasingly popular willingness to include and share communion with formerly excluded segments of the population.

Edman, Elizabeth M.
Queer Virtue: What LGBTQ People Know About Life and Love and How It Can Revitalize Christianity. the Reverend Elizabeth M. Edman. Beacon Press 2016. 216 p.
ISBN 9780807061343
Grades: Adult   230
1. Christianity and sexuality 2. Queer theory 3. Christianity 4. Society and culture — LGBTQIA+ 5. Spirituality and religion — Christianity

LC 2015027701

Frustrated by the notion that "Christian love = tolerance," Edman argues that Christianity, at its scriptural core, is not a tradition that is hostile to queer people but is, in fact, itself inherently queer. Edman reveals how "queering" Christianity—that is, disrupting simplistic ways of thinking about gender and sexuality—can illuminate contemporary Christian faith and shows why queer Christians are gifts to the Church.
"An intellectual and provocative perspective challenging Christians and others to reconsider the confines of spiritual interconnection, harmony, and progressive inclusion in modern religion." —*Kirkus*
Includes bibliographical references.

Holifield, E. Brooks
Theology in America: Christian Thought from the Age of the Puritans to the Civil War. E. Brooks Holifield. Yale University Press 2003. IX, 617 p.
ISBN 9780300095746
Grades: Adult   230
1. Theology, Doctrinal 2. Christian history 3. Religions 4. United States 5. 19th century 6. Spirituality and Religion — Christianity — History

LC 2003042289

"In this majestic achievement, Holifield provides a first-rate, richly evocative and unrivaled history of theology in America. This masterfully narrated, splendid book will become the definitive study of the development of American theology." —*Publishers Weekly*
Includes bibliographical references (p. 513-595) and index.

Kung, Hans
Great Christian Thinkers: Paul, Origen, Augustine, Aquinas, Luther, Schleiermacher, Barth. Hans Kung. Continuum 1995. 235 p.
ISBN 9780826408488
Grades: Adult   230
1. Theologians 2. Theology 3. Spirituality and Religion — General

LC Bl 99779007

An introduction to theologians who greatly affected Christian thought includes portraits of Paul, Origen, Augustine, Thomas Aquinas, Martin Luther, Friedrich Schleiermacher, and Karl Barth.
Includes bibliographical references (p. 217-235); Reprint. Originally published: C1994.

Lewis, C. S.
Mere Christianity: A Revised and Amplified Edition, with a New Introduction, of the Three Books, Broadcast Talks, Christian Behaviour, and Beyond Personality. C.S. Lewis. Harper San Francisco 2001. xx, 227 p.
ISBN 9780060652883
Grades: Adult   230
1. Theology, Doctrinal 2. Christian apologetics 3. Christian ethics 4. Christianity 5. Ethics 6. Compassion 7. Spirituality and Religion — Christianity

LC 00049862

Discusses the essence of Christian faith and the doctrine of the Trinity.
Includes bibliographical references; Originally published: London : G Bles, 1952.

Thomas
Selected Writings. Thomas Aquinas; edited and translated with an introduction and notes by Ralph McInerny. Penguin Books 1998. xxxviii, 841 p.
ISBN 9780140436327
Grades: Adult   230
1. Theology, doctrinal 2. Spirituality and Religion — General

LC 99180304

Brings together sermons, commentary responses to criticism, and substantial extracts from the "Summa Theologiae," arranged chronologically.
Includes bibliographical references.

231 Christian doctrinal theology

Cairns, Scott
The End of Suffering: Finding Purpose in Pain. Scott Cairns. Paraclete Press 2009. xi, 126 p.
ISBN 9781557255631
Grades: Adult   231
1. Suffering 2. Christian life 3. Christianity 4. Spirituality and Religion — Christian living

LC 2009018728

A poet and essayist examines ancient Christian wisdom for the meaning of suffering and grief and finds hope in life's trials and afflictions.
"The author offers a profoundly touching and deeply considered treatment of the notion of suffering, especially grief, in a Christian's life. For Cairns, suffering is not about the presence of evil; instead, it provides occasions where God can be known more intimately. Eloquent in its simplicity, Cairns's brief book is a superb treatment of the thorny issues of suffering and grief." —*Library Journal*
Includes bibliographical references.

Stavrakopoulou, Francesca
God: An Anatomy. Francesca Stavrakopoulou. Alfred A. Knopf 2022. 304 p.
ISBN 9780525520450

Grades: Adult **231**
1. God 2. Christianity 3. Theology 4. Spirituality and Religion — Christianity — History

LC 2021026356

An astonishing and revelatory history that re-presents God as he was originally envisioned by ancient worshippers—with a distinctly male body, and with superhuman powers, earthly passions, and a penchant for the fantastic and monstrous. The scholarship of theology and religion teaches us that the God of the Bible was without a body, only revealing himself in the Old Testament in words mysteriously uttered through his prophets, and in the New Testament in the body of Christ. The portrayal of God as corporeal and masculine is seen as merely metaphorical, figurative, or poetic. But, in this revelatory study, Francesca Stavrakopoulou presents a vividly corporeal image of God: a human-shaped deity who walks and talks and weeps and laughs, who eats, sleeps, feels, and breathes, and who is undeniably male. Here is a portrait—arrived at through the author's close examination of and research into the Bible—of a god in ancient myths and rituals who was a product of a particular society, at a particular time, made in the image of the people who lived then, shaped by their own circumstances and experience of the world. From head to toe—and every part of the body in between—this is a god of stunning surprise and complexity, one we have never encountered before.

Re-examines the original depiction of God by ancient worshippers with a distinctly male body and superhuman powers and instead presents a more corporeal image of a deity who walks, talks, weeps and laughs. Maps.

"Stavrakopoulou writes with the fluidity of a seasoned storyteller, using ample footnotes, but never getting weighed down by academic jargon. This is a provocative tour de force." —*Publishers Weekly*

This is a Borzoi book published by Alfred A. Knopf; Includes bibliographical references and index.

Whittle, Lisa
God Knows: When Your Worries and Whys Need More Than Temporary Relief. Lisa Whittle. 2023. xviii, 201 pages
ISBN 9780785290186
Grades: Adult **231**
1. God (Christianity) 2. Theology 3. Biblical teaching 4. Spirituality and Religion — Christian living

LC 2022944346

Based on the seldom-studied book of Nahum, God Knows details what His great knowing entails and how his omniscience provides the healing and peace we are all desperate to find.

"While Whittle hammers home her message of trust in God's power, the advice that comes along with it…tends to be useful. Believers will appreciate Whittle's wisdom." —*Publishers Weekly*

Includes bibliographical references.

231.7 Relation to the world

Grabbe, Lester L
Faith and Fossils: The Bible, Creation, and Evolution. Lester L. Grabbe. William B. Eerdmans Publishing Company 2018. xiii, 182 pages
ISBN 9780802869104
Grades: Adult **231.7**
1. Creation 2. Science writing — Biology 3. Spirituality and Religion — General 4. Spirituality and Religion — Religious texts

LC 2017050292

"Grabbe asserts that religion and science are not necessarily incompatible and they can exist side by side harmoniously so long as the respective adherents do not poach on the others territory. His illuminating work will doubtless invite thought and serious discussion by both camps." —*Booklist*

Includes bibliographical references (pages 160-170).

Lewis, C. S.
Miracles: A Preliminary Study. C.S. Lewis. Harper San Francisco 2001. 294 p.
ISBN 9780060653019
Grades: Adult **231.7**
1. Miracles 2. Christianity 3. Spirituality 4. Faith 5. Spirituality and Religion — Christianity

LC 00049863

British author C. S. Lewis discusses the possibility that supernatural occurrences have taken place throughout history. Centering his argument on the Incarnation, the moment where God and man became one, Lewis challenges skeptics and non-believers with sound evidence.

"Mr. Lewis casts his net fairly wide and, under the guise of a book on miracles, offers a rational justification both of theism and of doctrinal Christianity." —*Times Literary Supplement*

Originally published: London : G. Bles, 1947.

Wintz, Jack
Will I See My Dog in Heaven?: God's Saving Love for the Whole Family of Creation. Jack Wintz. Paraclete Press 2009. 153 p.
ISBN 9781557255686
Grades: Adult **231.7**
1. Animals 2. Life after death 3. Catholic theology 4. Christian doctrines 5. Christianity 6. Religions 7. Spirituality and Religion — Christianity

LC 2009000259

A Franciscan friar uses the words of the Bible and the life and words of St. Francis to support his view that God's promise of a new creation at the end of time extends to the companion animals we have known and loved in this life.

"The author, a Franciscan friar, argues that God's promise of a new creation at the end of time extends to the animal companions we have known and loved in this life. Strongly recommended." —*Library Journal*

Includes bibliographical references.

Woodward, Kenneth L.
The **Book** *of Miracles: The Meaning of the Miracle Stories in Christianity, Judaism, Buddhism, Hinduism, Islam.* Kenneth L. Woodward. Simon & Schuster 2001. 429 p.
ISBN 9780743200295
Grades: Adult **231.7**
1. Miracles 2. Spirituality and Religion — General

LC BL2001011232

A collection of stories about miracle workers explores scriptural contexts of each religious tradition and discusses traditions relating to the Sufi mystics, Hindu and Buddhist saints, Christian hermits, Talmudic wonder-workers, and Muslim ascetics.

"A great resource for studies in comparative religions and interfaith dialog." —*Library Journal*

A Touchstone book; Includes bibliographical references (p. [387]-419) and index; Originally published: 2000.

232 Jesus Christ and his family

Blum, Edward J.
The **Color** *of Christ: The Son of God and the Saga of Race in America.* Edward J. Blum and Paul Harvey. University of North Carolina Press 2012. 336 p.
ISBN 9780807835722
Grades: Adult **232**
1. Jesus Christ 2. Racism 3. Race relations 4. Interethnic relations 5. African Americans 6. Indigenous peoples of North America 7. Christianity 8. Religions 9. Church history 10. United States 11. Spirituality and Religion — Christianity 12. History writing — United States 13. Society and culture — Race

LC 2012004088

Explores the dynamic nature of Christ worship in the U.S., addressing how his image has been visually remade to champion the causes of white supremacists and civil rights leaders alike, and why the idea of a white Christ has endured.

ESSENTIAL AND RECOMMENDED TITLES
232.9 Family and life of Jesus

"A must-read for those interested in American religious history, this book will forever change the way you look at images of Jesus." —*Publishers Weekly*
Includes bibliographical references and index.

Rohr, Richard
The Universal Christ: How a Forgotten Reality Can Change Everything We See, Hope For, and Believe. Richard Rohr. Convergent Books 2019. 240 p.
ISBN 9781524762094
Grades: Adult 232
1. Jesus Christ 2. Faith (Christianity) 3. Christian life 4. Religion and culture 5. Spirituality 6. Philosophy 7. Christianity 8. Martyrs 9. Religions 10. Spirituality and Religion — Christianity — History
LC 2018056812

From one of the world's most influential spiritual thinkers, a long-awaited book exploring what it means that Jesus was called "Christ," and how this forgotten truth can restore hope and meaning to our lives.
Includes bibliographical references and index.

232.9 Family and life of Jesus

Girzone, Joseph F.
A Portrait of Jesus. Joseph F. Girzone. Image Books 1999. 179 p.
ISBN 9780385484770
Grades: Adult 232.9
1. Jesus Christ 2. Christian life 3. Life stories — Religion and spirituality 4. Spirituality and Religion — Christian living 5. Spirituality and Religion — Christianity
LC BL 99012297

An acclaimed religious author offers a study of Jesus as he was perceived by those around him, in an effort to place the man in the historical context of his time and to make him palpably real.
"This is popular liberal Catholic theology, more filled with forgiveness and fellowship than shaming and hierarchy. Many a non-Catholic and even non-Christian may embrace it, too." —*Booklist*
Originally published: New York : Doubleday, 1998.

Villodas, Rich
Good and Beautiful and Kind: Becoming Whole in a Fractured World. Rich Villodas. WaterBrook 2022. xxiii, 214 pages : Illustration
ISBN 9780525654414
Grades: Adult 232.9
1. Jesus Christ 2. Christian life 3. Spirituality and Religion — Christian living
LC 2021061658

An invitation to love like Jesus and step beyond distraction and division into the joy we long to experience—from the author of The Deeply Formed Life, winner of the Christianity Today Book Award."
"Villodas's work, which presents the Christian God as one who seeks to forgive, not punish, and calls on disciples to do the same, will appeal to readers who appreciate a down-to-earth Christianity that is not solely focused on itself." —*Library Journal*
Includes bibliographical references (pages 209-214).

232.91 Mary, mother of Jesus

Pelikan, Jaroslav
Mary Through the Centuries: Her Place in the History of Culture. Jaroslav Pelikan. Yale University Press 1996. x, 267 p, 16 p. of plates : Illustration; Color
ISBN 9780300069518
Grades: Adult 232.91
1. Mary, Blessed Virgin, Saint 2. Spirituality and Religion — General
LC 96024726

Explores how Mary has been represented in theology, art, music, and literature throughout the ages.

An illustrated analysis of the diverse ways in which the Virgin Mary has been depicted and venerated throughout the ages examines the biblical portrait of Mary; Orthodox, Protestant, Catholic, and Islamic views of her; and literary and artistic renditions of Mary.
"Although volumes have been written about the Virgin Mary from a wide variety of perspectives, it is rare to find a scholarly work that is easily accessible to the general, educated reader." —*Choice*
Includes bibliographical references (p. 231-258) and indexes.

233 Humankind

Greenblatt, Stephen
The Rise and Fall of Adam and Eve. Stephen Greenblatt. W. W. Norton & Company 2017. 719 p.
ISBN 9780393240801
Grades: Adult 233
1. Adam (Biblical figure) 2. Eve (Biblical figure) 3. Parents 4. Humans 5. Creation 6. Garden of Eden (Biblical place) 7. Theology 8. Misogyny 9. Religion and literature 10. Art and religion 11. Literary criticism 12. Evolution 13. Spirituality and Religion — General 14. History writing — Arts and culture

Longlisted for the Andrew Carnegie Medal for Excellence in Non-Fiction, 2018.
Explores the biblical story of human origins, drawing on theological, artistic, and cultural influences to discuss how the story of Adam and Eve reflects the fears, desires, and problems of humanity through the ages.
"Greenblatt has shaped an enjoyable and well-paced narrative that effectively draws from many disciplines." —*Library Journal*
Includes bibliographical references (pages 367-391) and index.

Jacobs, Alan
Original Sin: A Cultural History. Alan Jacobs. Harper Collins 2008. 304 p.
ISBN 9780060783402
Grades: Adult 233
1. Sin 2. Original sin (Christian theology) 3. Good and evil 4. Free will and determinism 5. Spirituality and Religion — General
LC 2008006582

A cultural history of the controversial idea that people are born with a predisposition to evil shares the stories of the philosophy's proponents and disclaimers, in an account that cites the contributions of such figures as St. Augustine, G. K. Chesterton, and Blaise Pascal.

Teilhard de Chardin, Pierre
★ *The Divine Milieu.* Pierre Teilhard de Chardin. Perennial 2001. xlvii, 140 p.
ISBN 9780060937256
Grades: Adult 233
1. Christian philosophy 2. Spiritual life 3. Philosophy and religion 4. Christianity 5. Spirituality and Religion — General
LC 2001039440

Teilhard de Chardin—geologist, priest, and major voice in twentieth-century Christianity—probes the ultimate meaning of all physical exploration and the fruit of his own inner life. The Divine Milieu is a spiritual treasure for every religion bookshelf.
Includes index.

Zahl, David
Low Anthropology: The Unlikely Key to a Gracious View of Others (and Yourself). David Zahl. Brazos Press, a division of Baker Publishing Group 2022. 203 pages : Illustration
ISBN 9781587435560
Grades: Adult 233
1. Humankind (Christian theology) 2. Sin 3. Christianity 4. Spirituality and Religion — Christian living
LC 2022004877

The founder of Mockingbird Ministries argues that having an accurate view of humans helps us avoid the temptation to divide the world into good and bad people, provides the foundation for real relationships rooted in vulnerability, and leads us to a more liberating view of human nature, sin, and grace."

"The fresh and unexpectedly positive take on sin and pride makes for a light-hearted yet high-minded exploration of failure's ability to serve as a gateway to grace." —*Publishers Weekly*

Includes bibliographical references.

234 Salvation and grace

Carter, Jimmy
Faith: A Journey for All. Jimmy Carter. Simon & Schuster 2018. 208 pages
ISBN 9781501184413
Grades: Adult 234
1. Faith 2. Christianity and culture 3. History 4. Faith (Christianity) 5. Christianity 6. Spirituality and Religion — Christianity
LC 2018003986

Explores the meaning of faith and its profound effects on people's lives and the world, as well as how the author's own religious faith has guided, sustained, and challenged him throughout his life.

Includes index.

McLaren, Brian D.
Faith After Doubt: Why Your Beliefs Stopped Working and What to Do About It. Brian D. McLaren. St. Martin's Essentials 2021. 256 pages
ISBN 9781250262776
Grades: Adult 234
1. Spiritual journeys 2. Belief and doubt 3. Faith (Christianity) 4. Christian life 5. Psychological growth 6. Spiritual growth 7. Christianity 8. Spirituality and Religion — Christianity
LC 2020035306

Sixty-five million adults in the U.S. have dropped out of active church attendance and about 2.7 million more are leaving every year. This book is for the millions of people around the world who feel that their faith is falling apart.

"A helpful, non-judgmental resource for readers questioning their Christian faith, and looking for guidance on living with doubt." —*Library Journal*

Includes bibliographical references.

Rush, Charaia
Courageously Soft: Daring to Keep a Tender Heart in a Tough World. Charaia Rush. Baker Books, a division of Baker Publishing Group 2024. 176 p.
ISBN 9781540903860
Grades: Adult 234
1. Rush, Charaia, 1991- 2. Christian women 3. Marriage 4. Motherhood 5. Divorce 6. Psychic trauma 7. Suffering 8. Faith (Christianity) 9. Spirituality 10. Resilience 11. Hope 12. Vulnerability 13. Forgiveness 14. Healing 15. Life stories — Personal growth 16. Life stories — Religion and spirituality — Personal faith 17. Spirituality and Religion — Christianity 18. Debut title
LC 2023032419

In a world that gives us plenty of reasons to armor up, shut down, or numb out comes this invitation to stay soft-hearted and live awake to the authentic hope, healing, and transformation only God can bring about.

"Believers seeking the strength to surmount their own obstacles will find comfort in Rush's hard-earned wisdom." —*Publishers Weekly*

Includes bibliographical references.

Strobel, Lee
The Case for Grace: A Journalist Explores the Evidence of Transformed Lives. Lee Strobel. Zondervan, Willow Creek Resources 2015. 230 pages
ISBN 9780310259176
Grades: Adult 234
1. God (Christianity) 2. Grace (Christian theology) 3. Christian life 4. Essays 5. Collective autobiographies and memoirs 6. Life stories — Religion and spirituality — Spiritual journeys 7. Spirituality and religion — Christianity
LC Bl2015003220

ECPA Christian Book Awards, Non-Fiction, 2016.

Shares inspiring stories and experiences from the author's own life that illustrate the ways that God can radically transform the lives of spiritually wayward people.

"This eloquent and honest book should appeal to those who have found grace, as well as those seeking it." —*Publishers Weekly*

Includes bibliographical references.

Teresa
A Call to Mercy: Hearts to Love, Hands to Serve. Mother Teresa. Image 2016. xx, 364 pages
ISBN 9780451498205
Grades: Adult 234
1. Spiritual life 2. Compassion 3. Spirituality 4. Faith 5. Spirituality and Religion — Body, mind, and spirit — Meditation and mindfulness
LC Bl2016027911

A collection of unpublished material from the Nobel Peace Prize-winning holy woman who was canonized as a Saint by the Vatican in September 2016 offers her wisdom on showing compassion in our daily lives and working to create a heaven on earth.

"These reflections, stories, and testimonials will challenge and inspire readers to bear witness to a venerable spiritual legacy." —*Publishers Weekly*

Includes bibliographical references (pages 333-364).

235 Spiritual beings

Pagels, Elaine H.
The Origin of Satan. Elaine Pagels. Random House 1995. xxiii, 214 p.
ISBN 9780679731184
Grades: Adult 235
1. Devil 2. Antisemitism in Christianity 3. Paganism 4. Biblical teaching 5. Spirituality and Religion — Christianity
LC 95007983

A study of the role of the devil in biblical and modern times theorizes that dissident social groups that resisted Christianity were typically portrayed as demons and therefore established as threats.

"Pagels shows herself to be a masterful guide through the risk-laden complexities of biblical studies." —*Publishers Weekly*

Includes bibliographical references and index.

Sullivan, Randall
The Devil's Best Trick: How the Face of Evil Disappeared. Randall Sullivan. Atlantic Monthly Press 2024. 432 p.
ISBN 9780802119131
Grades: Adult 235
1. Devil 2. Good and evil 3. Violence 4. Murder 5. Satanism 6. Exorcism 7. Human behavior 8. Psychopathology 9. Superstition 10. Belief and doubt 11. True Crime — General 12. Society and culture — Violence and crime 13. Society and culture — Philosophy
LC 2023056567

How we explain the evils of the world—and the darkest parts of ourselves—has preoccupied humans throughout history. A sweeping and comprehensive search for the origins of belief in a Satanic figure across the centuries, The Devil's Best Trick is a keen investigation into the inescapable reality of evil and the myriad ways we attempt to understand it. Journalist Randall Sullivan melds historical, religious, and cultural conceptions of evil to present an instructive and unnerving rumination on crime, violence, and the darkness in all of us.

"It's a dizzying plunge into darkness in search of moral clarity." —*Publishers Weekly*

Includes bibliographical references and index.

Wray, T. J.
The Birth of Satan: Tracing the Devil's Biblical Roots. T.J. Wray, Gregory Mobley. Palgrave Macmillan 2005. xix, 211 p.

ESSENTIAL AND RECOMMENDED TITLES
235.24 Beatification and canonization

ISBN 9781403969330
Grades: Adult **235**
1. Devil 2. Good and evil 3. Faith 4. Biblical teaching 5. Theology 6. Religions 7. Spirituality and Religion — Christianity 8. Spirituality and Religion — Judaism
LC 2005043046

A groundbreaking search for the origins of the Prince of Darkness.
Includes bibliographical references (p. [198]-203) and index.

235.24 Beatification and canonization

Woodward, Kenneth L.
Making Saints: How the Catholic Church Determines Who Becomes a Saint, Who Doesn't, and Why. Kenneth L. Woodward. Simon & Schuster 1996. xv, 462 p. : Illustration
ISBN 9780684815305
Grades: Adult **235.24**
1. Canonization 2. Christian saints 3. Catholic theology 4. 20th century 5. Spirituality and Religion — Christianity — Catholicism
LC 97126222

A pioneering work of investigative journalism penetrates the Vatican to explain the canonization process and describes the political in-fighting, the medical questions, and the costs of canonization.

"This is the most comprehensive, critical and up-to-date look at saint making so far written." —*New York Times Book Review*

A Touchstone book; Includes bibliographical references (p. [431]-442) and index.

236 Eschatology

Ehrman, Bart D.
★ *Armageddon: What the Bible Really Says About the End.* Bart D. Ehrman. Simon & Schuster 2023. 288 p.
ISBN 9781982147990
Grades: Adult **236**
1. Armageddon (Christian theology) 2. End of the world (Christian theology) 3. Christianity 4. Spirituality and religion — Christianity — History
LC 2022043682

In Armageddon, acclaimed New Testament authority Bart D. Ehrman delves into the most misunderstood—and possibly the most dangerous—book of the Bible, exploring the horrifying social and political consequences of expecting an imminent apocalypse and offering a fascinating tour through three millennia of Judeo-Christian thinking about how our world will end.

"Lucid and compelling, Ehrman challenges readers to encounter the ancient Book of Revelation once again. This title makes it worthwhile." —*Library Journal*

Includes bibliographical references and index.

Eire, Carlos M. N.
A Very Brief History of Eternity. Carlos Eire. Princeton University Press 2010. xv, 268 p. : Illustration
ISBN 9780691133577
Grades: Adult **236**
1. Eternity 2. Theology 3. Christian doctrines 4. Christianity 5. Civilization, Western 6. Spirituality and Religion — Christianity
LC 2009022951

Examines the rise and fall of five different conceptions of eternity, exploring how they developed and how they have helped shape individual and collective self-understanding.

"The author's skill at engaging readers conceals the rigorous, thoughtful research and methodology that went into this volume. This thought-provoking book is sure to be a classic." —*Choice*

Includes bibliographical references and index.

Spong, John Shelby
Eternal Life: Pious Dream or Realistic Hope? by John Shelby Spong. Harper One 2009. 288 p.
ISBN 9780060762063
Grades: Adult **236**
1. Death 2. Life after death 3. Fear of death 4. Eternity 5. Life 6. Christianity 7. Spirituality and Religion — Christianity
LC 2008051443

A best-selling author and controversial bishop continues to challenge traditional Christian theology with his thoughts on one of the most profound issues of all: God and life after death.
Includes bibliographical references.

Turner, Alice K.
The History of Hell. Alice K. Turner. Harcourt Brace 1993. VI, 275 p, 22 p. of plates : Illustration; Color; Map
ISBN 9780151409341
Grades: Adult **236**
1. Hell 2. Life after death 3. Spirituality and Religion — General
LC 93009909

A survey of four thousand years of belief in Hell reveals how religious leaders, poets, painters, and ordinary people—including Homer, Dante, Blake, and Freud—have visualized the den of the Devil.

"Belief in a hell or some sort of afterlife has been intrinsic to the religions of the world ever since the first stories were shared aloud and incised in clay tablets. Turner's richly illustrated history surveys the myriad forms hell has taken in the West from Sumer to Rome and beyond." —*Booklist*

Includes bibliographical references (p. 246-255) and index.

239 Apologetics and polemics

Augustine
Concerning the City of God Against the Pagans. St. Augustine; translated by Henry Bettenson; with a new introduction by G.R. Evans. Penguin Books 2003. LXXI, 1097 p.
ISBN 9780140448948
Grades: Adult **239**
1. Christian apologetics 2. Kingdom of God 3. History writing — Ancient — Rome 4. Spirituality and Religion — Christianity — History
LC 2004269353

St Augustine, bishop of Hippo, was one of the central figures in the history of Christianity, and City of God is one of his greatest theological works. Written as an eloquent defence of the faith at a time when the Roman Empire was on the brink of collapse, it examines the ancient pagan religions of Rome, the arguments of the Greek philosophers and the revelations of the Bible. Pointing the way forward to a citizenship that transcends the best political experiences of the world and offers citizenship that will last for eternity, City of God is one of the most influential documents in the development of Christianity.

Includes bibliographical references (p. [lviii]-lix) and index; Originally published: 1972.

Bignon, Guillaume
Confessions of a French Atheist: How God Hijacked My Quest to Disprove the Christian Faith. Guillaume Bignon; foreword by Lee Strobel. Tyndale Momentum 2022. 250 p.
ISBN 9781496443021
Grades: Adult **239**
1. Bignon, Guillaume 2. Ethics 3. Spirituality 4. Belief and doubt 5. Science 6. God 7. Faith 8. Atheists 9. Atheism 10. Religions 11. Autobiographies and memoirs 12. Spirituality and religion — Christianity 13. Life stories — Religion and spirituality — Spiritual journeys

"Part memoir, part spiritual and intellectual treatise, this book has the power to change minds." —*Publishers Weekly*

PUBLIC LIBRARY CORE COLLECTION: NONFICTION
Twentieth Edition

Keller, Timothy J.
*The **Reason** for God: Belief in an Age of Skepticism.* Timothy Keller. Dutton 2008. 320 p.
ISBN 9780525950493
Grades: Adult **239**
1. Christian apologetics 2. Christianity 3. Faith 4. Skepticism 5. Spirituality and Religion — Christianity
LC 2007043745

Arguing that most Americans are members of the Christian faith, a response to promoters of science and secularism addresses key questions about suffering, exclusivity, and the belief that Christianity is the only true religion.

"It is refreshing to read a book that presents a religious view without being overly critical of the secular side presented in other books. An excellent conversation starter, this book presents a valid, well-written, and well-researched argument and should be considered for public libraries." —*Library Journal*

241 Christian ethics

Bass, Diana Butler
Grateful: The Transformative Power of Giving Thanks. Diana Butler Bass. HarperCollins 2018. 256 p.
ISBN 9780062659477
Grades: Adult **241**
1. Gratitude 2. Personal conduct 3. Faith (Christianity) 4. Spirituality and religion — Christianity
LC 2017047233

Library Journal Best Books, 2018.

The author of the multiple award-winning Grounded and leading trend spotter in contemporary Christianity explores why gratitude is missing as a modern spiritual practice, offers practical suggestions for reclaiming it, and illuminates how the shared practice of gratitude can lead to greater connection with God, our world, and our own souls.

Becker, Joshua
*The **Minimalist** Home: A Room-by-Room Guide to a Decluttered, Refocused Life.* Joshua Becker, with Eric Stanford. WaterBrook 2018. xii, 239 pages
ISBN 9781601427991
Grades: Adult **241**
1. House cleaning 2. Orderliness 3. Personal belongings 4. Simplicity 5. Christianity 6. House and Home — Cleaning, caretaking, and organizing 7. Self-Help — Personal growth — Happiness 8. Self-Help — Personal growth — Motivation
LC 2018014041

The popular blogger and author of The More of Less outlines practical guidelines for simplifying a home lifestyle and rendering spaces both peaceful and purposeful while addressing the underlying issues that contribute to home clutter problems.

"For readers seeking a no excuses approach to minimizing their living spaces." —*Booklist*

Includes bibliographical references.

*The **More** of Less: Finding the Life You Want Under Everything You Own.* Joshua Becker. WaterBrook Press 2016. 230 pages
ISBN 9781601427960
Grades: Adult **241**
1. Simplicity 2. Christianity 3. Business and economics — General 4. Self-Help — Personal growth — Motivation 5. Spirituality and Religion — Christian living
LC 2015042586

Offers a guide to adopting a minimalist lifestyle, offering practical advice and encouraging readers to find contentment by divesting themselves of nonessential possessions.

"With action plans, lists, and appeals to the reader's quiet nature, Becker successfully presents a well-rounded argument that a journey toward minimalism is possible and even enjoyable." —*Publishers Weekly*

Chapman, Gary D.
Love as a Way of Life: Seven Keys to Transforming Every Aspect of Your Life. Gary Chapman. Doubleday 2008. xiv, 239 p.
ISBN 9780385518581
Grades: Adult **241**
1. Interpersonal relations 2. Christianity 3. Love 4. Spirituality and Religion — Christian living
LC 2007050546

A follow-up to the best-selling The Five Love Languages reveals the seminal role of spiritual insight and understanding in our daily lives and sheds new light on the qualities that help us express and respond to love—kindness, patience, forgiveness, humility, courtesy, giving, and honesty—as well as the obstacles and misunderstandings that undermine relationships.

Reveals the seminal role of spiritual insight and understanding in our daily lives while examining the qualities that help us express and respond to love, as well as the obstacles and misunderstandings that undermine relationships.

"All self-help books run the risk of clich, but Chapman manages to make tried-and-true material feel fresh through carefully chosen examples from his pastoral counseling practice and his own life. Although Christian faith provides the scaffolding for his program and a concluding chapter makes the need for God's help explicit, Chapman's judicious counsel can be implemented by people of many religious traditions." —*Publishers Weekly*

Includes bibliographical references (p. [231]-235) and index.

Cobbs-Leonard, Tasha
Do It Anyway: Don't Give up Before It Gets Good. Tasha Cobbs Leonard, with Travis Thrasher. WaterBrook Press 2024. 224 p.
ISBN 9780593600870
Grades: Adult **241**
1. Cobbs-Leonard, Tasha, 1981- 2. Women gospel singers 3. African American women 4. Clergywomen 5. People with depression 6. Infertility 7. Adoption 8. Interracial families 9. Persistence 10. Faith (Christianity) 11. American people 12. Autobiographies and memoirs 13. Life stories — Facing adversity 14. Life stories — Personal growth 15. Life stories — Religion and spirituality — Personal faith 16. Spirituality and Religion — Christianity 17. Debut title
LC 2023046527

Pastor, entrepreneur, and gospel music icon Tasha Cobbs Leonard tells of journeying through moments of unforeseen challenges while holding to an unshakable God and discovering that our greatest breakthroughs come when we make the courageous choice to show up and do hard things anyway. Tasha tells remarkable stories of experiencing this firsthand when she committed to dreams even when they seemed unrealistic, pursued adoption though it looked impossible, navigated the dynamics of a blended family despite challenges, and watched God move in each step of endurance through infertility and depression.

"For gospel music fans, this hits all the right notes." —*Publishers Weekly*

Includes bibliographical references.

Curry, Michael B.
Love Is the Way: Holding Onto Hope in Troubling Times. Bishop Michael Curry and Sara Grace. Avery 2020. 264 p.
ISBN 9780525543039
Grades: Adult **241**
1. Curry, Michael B. 2. Hope (Christianity) 3. Love 4. Resilience 5. African American clergy 6. Grace (Christian theology) 7. Christianity 8. Spirituality and Religion — Christianity 9. Life stories — Religion and spirituality — Religious and spiritual leaders
LC 2020008843

An Episcopal bishop, descended from slaves and the son of a civil rights activist, who delivered the sermon at the royal wedding of Prince Harry and Meghan Markle expands on his inspirational message of hope, love, wisdom and resilience.

"A powerful meditation on social justice and religion that will engage a variety of readers." —*Library Journal*

ESSENTIAL AND RECOMMENDED TITLES
242 Devotional literature

Lamott, Anne
★ *Hallelujah Anyway: Rediscovering Mercy.* Anne Lamott. Riverhead Books 2017. 176 p.
ISBN 9780735213586
Grades: Adult   241
1. Mercy 2. Kindness 3. Compassion 4. Faith (Christianity) 5. Personal conduct 6. Christian ethics 7. Christian life 8. Spirituality and Religion — Christianity
LC 2016036301

An impassioned exploration of mercy, its elusive presence and why people ignore or embrace it, shares advice for forging deeper self-understanding and how to pursue an honest, meaningful life that involves kindness to others.

"As in previous works, Lamott's courageous honesty and humility, laced with wit and compassion, offer wisdom and hope for difficult times." —*Publishers Weekly*

Meyaard-Schaap, Kyle
Following Jesus in a Warming World: A Christian Call to Climate Action. Kyle Meyaard-Schaap. Intervarsity Press 2023. 192 p.
ISBN 9781514004456
Grades: Adult   241
1. Christianity 2. Environmentalism 3. Global warming 4. Environmental protection 5. Political participation 6. Creation (Christianity) 7. Christian ethics 8. Nature Writing — Environmental Issues 9. Spirituality and Religion — Christianity — Political Aspects 10. Debut title
LC 2022046253

Many young Christians are waking up to the realities of climate change but just don't know how to help. Through stories from the field, theological and scriptural exploration, and practical advice, this field guide from Christian climate activist Kyle Meyaard-Schaap helps us take meaningful action grounded in the joy of caring for creation.

"Christians will welcome this definitive faith-driven take on climate change." —*Publishers Weekly*

Includes bibliographical references.

Price, Reynolds
A Serious Way of Wondering: The Ethics of Jesus Imagined. Reynolds Price. Scribner 2003. 146 p.
ISBN 9780743230087
Grades: Adult   241
1. Jesus Christ 2. Ethics 3. Christian ethics 4. Religious ethics 5. Homosexuality 6. Suicide 7. Women's role 8. Spirituality and Religion — Christianity
LC 2003041506

A collection of literary and analytical writings, based on the author's lectures at the National Cathedral and Auburn Seminary, considers the ethics of Jesus Christ and presents fictional situations where He confronts such issues as suicide, homosexuality, and misogyny.

"In three brilliant and moving apocryphal gospel stories, Price's Jesus engages in conversations about homosexuality, suicide and the plight of women in male-dominated societies. Elegant and passionate, Price's provocative parables provide no simple answers to the saccharine question What would Jesus do? Rather, they compel us to imagine creatively our engagements with Jesus' teachings and the impact of those teachings on our lives." —*Publishers Weekly*

Includes bibliographical references.

242 Devotional literature

Karon, Jan
Bathed in Prayer. Jessica Fellowes. G. P. Putnam's Sons 2018. 226 p. (Mitford years)
ISBN 9780525537564
Grades: Adult   242
1. Sermons, American 2. Faith (Christianity) 3. Prayers 4. Spirituality 5. Kavanaugh, Timothy (Fictitious character) 6. Christian life 7. Mitford, North Carolina (Imaginary place) 8. Spirituality and Religion — Christianity
LC 2018289308

A fan's collection of prayers, sermons, and inspirational quotes from the Mitford series' beloved fictional religious leader is complemented by new essays and author reflections on faith.

King, Martin Luther
"Thou, Dear God": Prayers That Open Hearts and Spirits. Martin Luther King, Jr; foreword by the Julius R. Scruggs; edited and introduced by Lewis V. Baldwin. Beacon Press 2012. 245 p.
ISBN 9780807086032
Grades: Adult   242
1. Prayers 2. Politics and global affairs — Civil and human rights 3. Spirituality and Religion — Christianity
LC 2011031431

Collects sixty-eight prayers by Martin Luther King, Jr, covering such situations as spiritual guidance, special occasions, times of adversity, times of trial, uncertain times, and social justice.

Includes bibliographical references (p. 239-245).

Lewis, C. S.
★ *A Grief Observed.* C.S. Lewis. Harper San Francisco 2001. xxxi, 76 p.
ISBN 9780060652388
Grades: Adult   242
1. Davidman, Joy, 1915-1960 2. Lewis, C. S. (Clive Staples), 1898-1963 3. Consolation 4. Grief 5. Christianity 6. Faith 7. Spirituality and Religion — Christianity 8. Family and Relationships — Aging and Death
LC 00063227

The author recounts his grief over the death of his wife, and explains how he reexamined his religious beliefs.

Originally published: 1961.

248 Christian experience, practice, life

Joyce, Russell W.
His Face Like Mine: Finding God's Love in Our Wounds. Russell W. Joyce. Intervarsity Press 2024. 224 p.
ISBN 9781514009086
Grades: Adult   248
1. Spiritual growth 2. Faith (Christianity) 3. Christian life 4. Birth defects 5. Scars 6. Face 7. Surgery 8. Healing 9. Autobiographies and memoirs 10. Life stories — Facing adversity — Medical issues

Born with a rare craniofacial disorder, Russell Joyce endured years of patchwork surgeries that left him with deep pain and physical and emotional scars. But a life-changing encounter set him on a journey where he learned how God doesn't love us despite our wounds but through them. We can find freedom in Christ, scars and all.

"Sensitive and nuanced, this lingers in the mind." —*Publishers Weekly*

Jun, Tasha
★ *Tell Me the Dream Again: Reflections on Family, Ethnicity, and the Sacred Work of Belonging.* Tasha Jun; foreword by Alia Joy. Tyndale Momentum 2023. 211 p.
ISBN 9781496459572
Grades: Adult   248
1. Jun, Tasha 2. Christian women 3. Korean Americans 4. Multiracial people 5. Ethnic identity 6. Social marginality 7. Culture 8. Belief and doubt 9. Self-discovery 10. Belonging 11. Faith (Christianity) 12. North American people 13. American people 14. East Asian people 15. Korean people 16. Essays 17. Autobiographies and memoirs 18. Life stories — Identity — Race and ethnicity 19. Life stories — Religion and spirituality — Personal faith 20. Society and culture — Race 21. Spirituality and Religion — Christianity

Tasha Jun has always been caught between worlds: American and Korean, faith and doubt, family devotion and fierce independence. The world taught Tasha that her Korean normal was a barrier to belonging—that assimilation was the only way she would ever be truly accepted. But if that were true, did that mean God had made a mistake in knitting her together? *Tell Me the Dream Again* is a memoir-in-essays exploring what it means to be biracial in America today, the joy and healing that comes with embracing every part of who we are, and how our identity in Christ is tightly woven with the unique colors, scents, and culture he's given us.

"Jun writes in lyrical prose, with longing simmering below the surface on almost every page…This mesmerizes." —*Publishers Weekly*

Includes bibliographical references.

Kierkegaard, Soren

Fear and Trembling. Soren Kierkegaard; translated from the Danish by Alastair Hannay. Penguin Books 2006. 151 p.

ISBN 9780143037576

Grades: Adult   **248**

1. Christianity 2. Society and culture — Philosophy

LC OC2012121048

Uses the story of Abraham and Isaac to discuss the "theological suspension of ethics," a philosophical concept that claims when one acts out of direction from God, one is not necessarily subject to the ethical laws of the universe.

This ed. originally published: London : Penguin Books (UK), 2005.

Lamott, Anne

Small Victories: Spotting Improbable Moments of Grace. Anne Lamott. Riverhead Books, a member of Penguin Group (USA) 2014. 256 p.

ISBN 9781594486296

Grades: Adult   **248**

1. Lamott, Anne 2. Christian life 3. Hope 4. Grace (Christian theology) 5. Christianity 6. Happiness 7. Essays 8. Autobiographies and memoirs 9. Life stories — Religion and spirituality — Personal faith 10. Spirituality and religion — Christianity

LC 2014026967

Anne Lamott writes about community, family and faith in essays that are wise, irreverent, funny and poignant—a style that has become her trademark. Now in Small Victories, Lamott has once again written a brilliant and insightful book that offers a message of hope that celebrates the triumph of light over the darkness in our lives. Our victories over hardships and pain may be small, they may be infrequent, but they keep us going and they often come from the most unexpected places: Within ourselves. Lamott shows how we can forgive thoughtless family members; spotlights the value of turning toward love even in the most hopeless situations (the death of a loved one, a cancer diagnosis), and shows how to find the joy in getting lost in traffic while racing to the aid of a sick friend.

"Lamott confronts each situation with humor and rectitude and shows readers how she found something redeeming in each one. Sage advice on finding beauty and happiness in life despite bad circumstances." —*Kirkus*

Seiffert, Amy

Starved: Why We Need a Spiritual Diet Change to Move Us from Tired, Anxious, and Overwhelmed to Fulfilled, Whole, and Free. Amy Seiffert. Tyndale Momentum, an imprint of Tyndale House Publishers 2023. 253 p.

ISBN 9781496460295

Grades: Adult   **248**

1. Christianity 2. Spiritual life 3. Virtues (Christianity) 4. Spirituality and Religion — Christian living 5. Self-Help — Personal growth — Spirituality

In Starved, popular author and teacher Amy Seiffert shows readers how to stop ingesting spiritual junk food and offers simple and replenishing practices like silence, service, and Sabbath that can bring us closer to Jesus. She encourages us to put down our phones, set aside our pride, and let go of the hustle so that we can receive a spiritual diet change that will leave us delightfully content, spiritually healthy, and free to experience the goodness of Jesus.

"Fans of Christian self-help will appreciate this." —*Publishers Weekly*

248.3 Worship

Lewis, C. S.

Letters to Malcolm: Chiefly on Prayer : Reflections on the Intimate Dialogue Between Man and God. C.S. Lewis. Harcourt 1992. 124 p.

ISBN 9780156027663

Grades: Adult   **248.3**

1. Prayer (Christianity) 2. Christian life 3. Spirituality and Religion — Christianity

LC Bl2012030463

The British scholar discusses many aspects of the private dialogue between man and God in these informal letters to a close friend.

A Harvest book.

Lucado, Max

Before Amen: The Power of a Simple Prayer. Max Lucado. Thomas Nelson 2014. 192 p.

ISBN 9780849948480

Grades: Adult   **248.3**

1. Prayer (Christianity) 2. Christian life 3. Faith (Christianity) 4. Christianity 5. Spirituality and Religion — Christianity

LC 2014007855

Distilling prayers in the Bible down to one pocket-sized prayer, a best-selling author reminds readers that prayer is not a privilege for the pious nor the art of a chosen few but simply a heartfelt conversation between God and his child.

"The concept that there is power in a simple prayer normally wouldnt take a whole book to convey, but Lucado (You'll Get Through This), a prolific author with 92 million books in print, succeeds in getting readers to approach communication with God in a whole new way." —*Publishers Weekly*

Includes bibliographical references.

Martin, James

Learning to Pray: A Guide for Everyone. James Martin, SJ.. HarperOne, an imprint of HarperCollinsPublishers 2021. xii, 386 pages

ISBN 9780062643230

Grades: Adult   **248.3**

1. Prayer (Christianity) 2. Prayers 3. Christian life 4. Spirituality and Religion — Christian living 5. Self-Help — Personal growth — Spirituality

LC Bl2020073384

Explains what prayer is, what to expect from praying, how to do it, and how it can transform lives when it becomes a regular practice, discussing different styles and traditions of prayer throughout Christian history and encouraging readers to experimentand discover which works best for them.

"With Martin's guidance, interested readers may see prayer as both the most natural yet transcendent thing in the world." —*Booklist*

Includes bibliographical references (pages 373-386).

248.4 Christian life and practice

Bragg, Sarah

Is Everyone Happier Than Me?: An Honest Guide to the Questions That Keep You up at Night. Sarah Bragg. Zondervan Books 2024. xxi, 200 pages

ISBN 9780310361374

Grades: Adult   **248.4**

1. Happiness 2. Christian life 3. Personal conduct 4. Self-Help — Personal growth — Happiness 5. Spirituality and Religion — Christian living

LC 2023039007

In hard seasons, it's easy to feel lonely, lost, unsure, stuck, and even flat-out unhappy. Is Everyone Happier Than Me? by Sarah Bragg provides practical and relatable answers to the questions you've likely been asking about your life, and poses a few more, to help you figure out what's standing in the way of your happiness, peace, and connection.

"This frank and chatty offering will go a long way toward helping believers feel less alone." —*Publishers Weekly*

Includes bibliographical references (pages 199-200).

ESSENTIAL AND RECOMMENDED TITLES
248.4 Christian life and practice

Carter, Jimmy
Sources of Strength: Meditations on Scripture for a Living Faith. Jimmy Carter. Times Books 1999. xvii, 252 p.
ISBN 9780812932362
Grades: Adult   **248.4**
1. Christian life 2. Baptists 3. Spirituality and Religion — Christian living
LC BL 99012849

In the sequel to Living Faith, the former president shares his favorite readings from the Bible, presenting scriptural texts, dealing with themes ranging from family to reconciliation to the transforming power of God's love, accompanied by his personal reflections on their meaning in terms of the challenges of modern life.

"This is a collection of 52 brief Bible lessons—one for each week of the year—written by former president Jimmy Carter. All were used in adult Sunday school classes he taught himself. Carter's lessons are open-minded and socially progressive while remaining unapologetically conservative and Christian theologically. The lessons are grouped in nine categories, such as 'What We Believe' and 'Christians in the World,' but each lesson stands well on its own." —*Library Journal*

Includes indexes; Originally published in hardcover by Times Books, in 1977 [i.e. 1997]—T.P. verso.

Chaput, Charles J.
Things Worth Dying For: Thoughts on a Life Worth Living. Charles J. Chaput. Henry Holt and Company 2021. 288 p.
ISBN 9781250239785
Grades: Adult   **248.4**
1. Catholic theology 2. Christianity 3. Faith (Christianity) 4. Life 5. Purpose in life 6. Christian life 7. Spiritual life 8. Christian apologetics 9. Spirituality and Religion — Christianity — Catholicism
LC 2020034254

With a balance of wisdom, candor, and scholarly rigor the beloved Archbishop Emeritus of Philadelphia takes on life's central questions: Why are we here, and how can we live and die meaningfully?

"Written with passion and erudition, this title will appeal to Catholics and Christians searching for meaning during this time." —*Library Journal*

Includes bibliographical references.

Chittister, Joan
Following the Path: The Search for a Life of Passion, Purpose, and Joy. Joan, Sister Chittister. Image 2012. 188 p.
ISBN 9780307953988
Grades: Adult   **248.4**
1. Jesus Christ 2. God (Christianity) 3. Ability 4. Christian life 5. Purpose in life 6. Charity 7. Vocation 8. Belonging 9. Happiness 10. Decision-making 11. Achievement motivation 12. Self-fulfillment 13. Religions 14. United States 15. 21st century 16. Autobiographies and memoirs 17. Spirituality and Religion — Christianity 18. Life stories — Religion and spirituality — Personal faith
LC Bl2012013838

The author of The Gift of Years aims to help readers find purpose, happiness and fulfillment in their lives.

Evans, Rachel Held
Wholehearted Faith. Rachel Held Evans, with Jeff Chu. HarperOne 2021. 196 p.
ISBN 9780062894472
Grades: Adult   **248.4**
1. Evans, Rachel Held, 1981-2019 2. Christian women 3. Faith (Christianity) 4. Kindness 5. Questioning 6. Humility 7. Conversation 8. Belief and doubt 9. Christian life 10. Christianity 11. Essays 12. Spirituality and Religion — Christianity 13. Life stories — Religion and spirituality — Personal faith

Rachel Held Evans is widely recognized for her theologically astute, profoundly honest, and beautifully personal books, which have guided, instructed, edified, and shaped Christians as they seek to live out a just and loving faith. At the time of her tragic death in 2019, Rachel was working on a new book about wholeheartedness. With the help of her close friend and author Jeff Chu, that work-in-progress has been woven together with some of her other unpublished writings into a rich collection of essays that ask candid questions about the stories we've been told—and the stories we tell—about our faith, our selves, and our world.

"Even readers unfamiliar with Evans' previous work will find much to appreciate." —*Booklist*

Francis
Happiness in This Life: A Passionate Meditation on Earthly Existence. Pope Francis; translated from the Italian by Oonagh Stransky. Random House Inc 2017. 272 pages
ISBN 9780525510970
Grades: Adult   **248.4**
1. Christian life 2. Happiness 3. Civil rights 4. Mercy 5. Faith (Christianity) 6. Toleration 7. Christianity 8. Spirituality and Religion — Christianity — Catholicism

Presents a collection of homilies, speeches and "messages of the day" that brings together Pope Francis' wisdom on finding happiness in the here and now.

Fusco, Daniel
Crazy Happy: Nine Surprising Ways to Live the Truly Beautiful Life. Daniel Fusco with Lindsey Ponder. WaterBrook 2021. xiv, 202 pages
ISBN 9780593192665
Grades: Adult   **248.4**
1. Beatitudes 2. Happiness 3. Life 4. Christianity 5. Self-Help — Personal growth — Happiness 6. Spirituality and Religion — Christian living
LC 2020006516

Blessed are the meek..." and "The fruit of the Spirit is love..." so begin the Beatitudes and the Fruit of the Spirit, two of the most beloved passages in the Bible. Each provides incredible wisdom about what makes for a good life. But what happens when we bring these nine teachings and nine fruit together? An incredible biblical synergy that forms a beautiful and surprising invitation to the deep happiness we desire. It's so simple and so profound we might even be tempted to call it "crazy." with wit and wisdom, clarity and conviction, Pastor Daniel Fusco unpacks these key teachings of Jesus and Paul for everyday readers with a fresh, redemptive arc toward a blessed future. He shows us nine countercultural ways our lives change for good when we learn to see the world like Jesus does, making fresh spiritual connections that can transform our lives for the healthier and happier. Spiritually rich and practically accessible, Crazy Happy will change the way you see yourself, your family, your neighbors, your enemies, and yes, even God.

"Fusco's enthusiasm for his topic is on full display and will certainly charm like believers." —*Library Journal*

Girzone, Joseph F.
Never Alone: A Personal Way to God by the Author of Joshua. Joseph F. Girzone. Image Books 1995. 115 p. : Illustration
ISBN 9780385476836
Grades: Adult   **248.4**
1. Girzone, Joseph F. 2. Spiritual life 3. Love (Christianity) 4. Forgiveness 5. Spiritual growth 6. Former priests 7. Inspiration 8. Christian life 9. Christianity 10. Religious life 11. United States 12. 20th century 13. Spirituality and Religion — Christianity — Catholicism
LC BL 99760988

The author unveils his personal way to God, describing a God who is neither silent nor condemning with words of wisdom, sympathy, and generosity.

"Girzone's empathy for the loneliness and insecurity of being human guides readers toward a more satisfying religious experience than that provided by organized religions, which he continues to criticize for not sufficiently following the living message of Jesus' life." —*Booklist*

Originally published: New York : Doubleday, 1994.

Guthrie, Savannah
Mostly What God Does: Reflections on Seeking and Finding His Love Everywhere. Savannah Guthrie. Thomas Nelson 2024. xiii, 302 p.
ISBN 9781400341122
Grades: Adult   **248.4**

1. Guthrie, Savannah 2. Women television personalities 3. Women television talk show hosts and guests 4. Christian women 5. God (Christianity) 6. Faith (Christianity) 7. Love (Christianity) 8. Prayer 9. Self-acceptance 10. Imperfection 11. Advice 12. Life stories — Religion and spirituality — Personal faith 13. Spirituality and Religion — Christianity

Savannah Guthrie, coanchor of the Today show, shares reflections on faith and life and offers inspiration for all of us to do what God does—love. The author persuasively renders the evolution of a hard-won religious belief that makes room for imperfection.

"Guthrie makes her adult debut with a poignant account of the role that religious faith has played in her life…This openhearted offering inspires." —*Publishers Weekly*

Jakes, T. D
Destiny: Step into Your Purpose. T.D. Jakes. Faithwords Large Print 2015. xiii, 349 pages
ISBN 9781455589630
Grades: Adult   248.4
1. Christian life 2. Fate and fatalism 3. Vocation 4. Spirituality and Religion — Christian living
LC Bl2015030474

The #1 New York Times best-selling author of Instinct outlines steps for recognizing and accepting one's personal destiny in the face of apparent setbacks. Also published in large print format.

Lewis, C. S.
★ *The Screwtape Letters: With Screwtape Proposes a Toast.* by C. S. Lewis. HarperSanFrancisco 2001. x, 209 p.
ISBN 9780060652890
Grades: 11 12 Adult   248.4
1. Christianity 2. Devil 3. Temptation 4. Good and evil 5. Uncles 6. Uncle and nephew 7. Personal letters 8. 20th century 9. Epistolary novels 10. Christian fiction

In a series of letters, one of Satan's more experienced tempters writes to a junior agent in the field, instructing him in the finer points of capturing souls.
Originally published: New York : Macmillan, 1961.

Lucado, Max
Unshakable Hope: Building Our Lives on the Promises of God. Max Lucado. Thomas Nelson 2018. xiv, 216 pages
ISBN 9780718096144
Grades: Adult   248.4
1. Christian life 2. Self-Help — Mental health — Depression 3. Self-Help — Personal growth — Motivation 4. Spirituality and Religion — Christian living
LC Bl2018100083

Citing a dramatic rise in suicide in the past 20 years, a New York Times best-selling author draws on favorite scriptural passages to inspire readers to find encouragement in the promises of God and the Christian faith.

Offers encouraging, practical advice for overcoming difficult circumstances and creating a better future, focusing on twelve of God's promises and how considering them can help one meet challenges, find security, and make wise decisions.

You Are Never Alone: Trust in the Miracle of God's Presence and Power. Max Lucado. Thomas Nelson 2020. xii, 219 pages
ISBN 9781400217342
Grades: Adult   248.4
1. Christian life 2. Spirituality and Religion — Christian living
LC Bl2020018068

Offers a guide to finding biblical inspiration, strength, and comfort in the face of life's more daunting challenges.

"Christians looking for strength and direction in prayer will love this faith-affirming, impassioned work." —*Publishers Weekly*
Includes bibliographical references (pages 215-219).

Martin, James
The Jesuit Guide to (Almost) Everything: A Spirituality for Real Life. James Martin. HarperCollins Publishers 2010. VII, 420 p. : Illustration
ISBN 9780061981401
Grades: Adult   248.4
1. Ignatius, of Loyola, Saint, 1491-1556 2. Spiritual life 3. Spirituality and Religion — Christian living 4. Spirituality and Religion — Christianity — Catholicism 5. Spirituality and Religion — General
LC Oc2012193217

A practical, spiritual guidebook based on the life and teachings of St. Ignatius of Loyola shows readers how to manage relationships, money, work, prayer and decision making, while keeping a sense of humor about it all.

"In this digestible account of all things Jesuit, James Martin, S.J, encapsulates the uniquely Ignatian concept of spirituality. Translating the essence of the Jesuit philosophy into layman's terms, he uses both traditional stories and personal anecdotes to vividly illustrate the Jesuit approach to God, friendship, social justice, decision-making, prayer, simplicity, obedience, and self-actualization. Martin's engaging, intimate tone will appeal to anyone interested in understanding the history, the efficacy, and the universality of the Jesuit mission and way of life." —*Booklist*

Includes bibliographical references (p. 401-406) and index.

Meyer, Joyce
Seize the Day: Living on Purpose and Making Every Day Count. Joyce Meyer. Faith Words 2016. 234 pages
ISBN 9781455559893
Grades: Adult   248.4
1. Christian life 2. Spirituality and Religion — Christian living
LC 2016015536

A guide to living a purposeful, urgent life spent in daily commitment to God shares personal stories and biblical insights to explain how to discover one's purpose in order to achieve greater happiness and blessings.

Encourages readers to adopt a purposeful approach to everyday living by asking God to help them discover the blessings and value available in every day life, allowing them to stop wasting time and live the life God intends for them.

"Meyer advocates seizing control of one's schedule to focus on life's purpose, but also recommends being flexible, finding a system that fits one's style, and taking time to laugh." —*Publishers Weekly*
Also published in large print format.

Osteen, Joel
The Power of I Am: Two Words That Will Change Your Life Today. Joel Osteen. Faith Words 2015. x, 269 pages
ISBN 9780892969968
Grades: Adult   248.4
1. Affirmations 2. Self-confidence 3. Self-talk 4. Spirituality and Religion — Christian living
LC 2015025973

A #1 New York Times best-selling author shares a principle that he hopes will give the readers the confidence they need to face life's challenges.

Offers a technique for leading a more productive and happy life based on affirming of oneself "I am" followed by the desired trait.

"Directing believers to look beyond their own needs and wants, Osteen advances his message to a higher plane, advocating a life of reaching out and sharing your blessings." —*Publishers Weekly*

Riess, Jana
Flunking Sainthood: A Year of Breaking the Sabbath, Forgetting to Pray, and Still Loving My Neighbor. Jana Riess. Paraclete Press 2011. x, 179 p.
ISBN 9781557256607
Grades: Adult   248.4
1. Riess, Jana 2. Spiritual life 3. Perfection 4. Failure 5. Success (Concept) 6. Women authors 7. Christianity 8. Autobiographies and memoirs 9. Biographies 10. Life stories — Religion and spirituality 11. Life stories — Personal growth
LC 2011022595

ESSENTIAL AND RECOMMENDED TITLES
248.8 Guides to Christian life for specific groups of people

The author chronicles a year of her life in which she tried to act saintly by engaging in twelve practices, including fasting, Sabbath-keeping, and generosity, and how she failed miserably in doing so.

"The author intended to devote an entire year (a year-long experiment) to mastering 12 different spiritual challenges, including praying at fixed times during the day, exhibiting gratitude, observing the Sabbath, practicing hospitality according to the rules set by St. Benedict, abstaining from eating meat, and amply demonstrating her generosity. But nothing turned out as planned. Although her spiritual quest falls far short, she can still proffer spiritual lessons. Anyone who has failed to live up to expectations, which means most everyone, will love this book." —*Booklist*

Includes bibliographical references.

Villodas, Rich
The Deeply Formed Life: Five Transformative Values to Root Us in the Way of Jesus. Rich Villodas; foreword by Pete Scazzero. WaterBrook 2020. xxviii, 230 pages
ISBN 9780525654384
Grades: Adult **248.4**
1. Spiritual life 2. Christian life 3. Spiritual growth 4. Christianity 5. Spirituality and Religion — Christian living
LC 2020010606

The world is faster and busier than it's ever been, with more noise and distraction unsettling our already restless souls. We are a people out of rhythm. For Christians who are frustrated with churches that only add to the hustle and bustle, there must be an answer in our interior spiritual life. We long for deeper, more meaningful faith. Author and pastor Rich Villodas's The Deeply Formed Life offers an expansive, interconnected vision of spiritual formation comprised of five key pathways."

"Christians looking to bring more intention and emotion into their religious life will love this." —*Publishers Weekly*

Includes bibliographical references (pages 223-230).

248.8 Guides to Christian life for specific groups of people

Armas, Kat
Abuelita Faith: What Women on the Margins Teach Us About Wisdom, Persistence, and Strength. Kat Armas. Brazos Press, a division of Baker Publishing Group 2021. 224 p.
ISBN 9781587435300
Grades: Adult **248.8**
1. Christianity and women 2. Christian women 3. Cuban Americans 4. Grandmothers 5. Immigrants 6. Faith (Christianity) 7. Women in the Bible 8. Marginalized people 9. Spirituality and Religion — Christianity
LC 2020052198

Combining personal storytelling with biblical reflection, a Cuban American writer tells the story of unnamed and overlooked theologians-mothers, grandmothers, sisters, and daughters-whose survival, resistance, and persistence teach us the true power of faith and love.

"Armas's gift for storytelling and in-depth research in Latine theology make for an account that's accessible for lay readers as well as religion scholars interested in Christian theology through the lens of Indigenous knowledge systems."
—*Library Journal*

Includes bibliographical references.

Baskette, Molly Phinney
How to Begin When Your World Is Ending: A Spiritual Field Guide to Joy Despite Everything. Molly Phinney Baskette. Broadleaf Books 2022. 215 p.
ISBN 9781506481609
Grades: Adult **248.8**
1. Baskette, Molly Phinney, 1970- 2. Clergywomen 3. Churches 4. Cancer survivors 5. Spiritual growth 6. Grief 7. Anxiety 8. Life change events 9. Advice 10. Healing 11. Resilience 12. Community life 13. Faith (Christianity) 14. Life stories — Religion and spirituality — Religious and spiritual leaders 15. Life stories — Facing adversity 16. Spirituality and Religion — Christianity

"Pastor Baskette delivers a sincere and funny guide to surviving hardships....Anne Lamott fans will find in Baskette a kindred spirit." —*Publishers Weekly*

Billings, J. Todd
Rejoicing in Lament: Wrestling with Incurable Cancer and Life in Christ. J. Todd Billings. Brazos Press 2015. 224 p.
ISBN 9781587433580
Grades: Adult **248.8**
1. Billings, J. Todd 2. People with cancer 3. Cancer 4. Suffering 5. Clergy 6. Christian life 7. Faith (Christianity) 8. Psychology 9. Christianity 10. Autobiographies and memoirs 11. Life stories — Religion and spirituality — Personal faith 12. Life stories — Facing adversity — Medical issues — Physical illness
LC 2014040099

A theologian who was diagnosed with incurable cancer shares his journey as well as reflections on Christ and providence.

"His poignant insight into the role of lament in faithful Christian living makes this a work of both astute scholarship and powerful testimony." —*Publishers Weekly*

Includes bibliographical references and index.

Boa, Kenneth D.
Recalibrate Your Life: Navigating Transitions with Purpose and Hope. Kenneth Boa and Jenny Abel. Intervarsity Press 2023. 256 p.
ISBN 9781514000724
Grades: Adult **248.8**
1. Middle age 2. Change 3. Aging 4. Faith (Christianity) 5. Spirituality 6. Self-evaluation 7. Life change events 8. Purpose in life 9. Advice 10. Family and Relationships — Aging and Death 11. Spirituality and Religion — Christianity

Times of transition, especially in midlife or later life, are ideal moments for recalibrating our priorities and habits. Ken Boa and Jenny Abel give us the practical tools and eternal perspective needed to evaluate our God-given gifts, skills, wisdom, resources, and opportunities in order to live meaningfully now and into the future.

"Believers eager to take a fresh look at their lives will find this a welcome resource." —*Publishers Weekly*

Brownback, Lydia
Finding God in My Loneliness. Lydia Brownback. Crossway 2017. 174 pages
ISBN 9781433553936
Grades: Adult **248.8**
1. Christian women 2. Loneliness 3. Encouragement 4. Faith healing 5. Prayer 6. Christianity 7. Self-Help — Personal growth — Spirituality 8. Spirituality and Religion — Christianity
LC 2016031222

"Brownback's encouraging book is a sharp, thoroughly readable entreaty to readers looking for grace in loneliness." —*Publishers Weekly Annex*

Includes bibliographical references and indexes.

Chittister, Joan
The Monastic Heart: 50 Simple Practices for a Contemplative and Fulfilling Life. Joan Chittister. Convergent 2021. xviii, 264 pages
ISBN 9780593239407
Grades: Adult **248.8**
1. Benedict, Saint, Abbot of Monte Cassino 2. Monasticism and religious orders 3. Spiritual life 4. Spirituality and Religion — Christian living 5. Self-Help — Personal growth — Spirituality
LC 2021012932

The activist, nun, and esteemed spiritual voice who has twice appeared on Oprah's Super Soul Sunday sounds the call to create a monastery within ourselves—to cultivate wisdom and resilience so that we may join God in the work of renewal, restoration, and justice right where we are."

DiFelice, Bekah
Almost There: Searching for Home in a Life on the Move. Bekah DiFelice. NavPress 2017. 208 pages
ISBN 9781631464713
Grades: Adult   248.8
1. DiFelice, Bekah 2. Moving to a new home 3. Wanderers and wandering 4. Christian life 5. Life change events 6. Military spouses 7. Coping 8. Loneliness 9. Faith (Christianity) 10. Family relationships 11. Autobiographies and memoirs 12. Life stories — Religion and spirituality — Personal faith 13. Spirituality and Religion — Christianity
LC Bl2017026896

Almost There is for those on the move and those who feel restless right where they are. It's for those who struggle with not belonging, with feeling unsettled, with believing that home is out of their reach, at least for the moment. And Almost There is for those who find themselves in a transient lifestyle they didn't expect—say, moving across the country for a new job or the military or an opportunity to begin again.

"This book will appeal broadly to those who have lived a wandering existence, and Christian readers in particular will appreciate DiFelices tangents on the lives of biblical characters ." —*Publishers Weekly*

Dokun, Chanel
Life Starts Now: How to Create the Life You've Been Waiting for. Chanel Dokun. Nelson Books, an imprint of Thomas Nelson 2022. IX, 213 pages
ISBN 9781400231294
Grades: Adult   248.8
1. Christian women 2. Religious life 3. Self-actualization 4. Vocation 5. Christianity 6. Spirituality and Religion — Christian living 7. Self-Help — Personal growth — Happiness
LC 2022003321

Certified Life Planner and Relationship Expert Chanel Dokun shows women how to leave behind the stress and disappointment of a life spent chasing external significance and success and find profound joy and fulfillment in building a new one rooted in living out your unique purpose."

"Readers will be heartened by this affirming volume." —*Publishers Weekly*
Includes bibliographical references (pages 207-211).

Evans, Jimmy
Strengths Based Marriage: Build a Stronger Relationship by Understanding Each Other's Gifts. Jimmy Evans & Allan Kelsey. Nelson Books 2016. xvii, 181 pages
ISBN 9780718083625
Grades: Adult   248.8
1. Marriage 2. Christian marriage 3. Christian life 4. Christianity 5. Spirituality and Religion — Christian living
LC 2016017800

"A superb tool for those wanting to understand and be understood by others." —*Library Journal*
Includes bibliographical references (pages 179-180).

Hatmaker, Jen
Of Mess and Moxie: Wrangling Delight Out of This Wild and Glorious Life. Jen Hatmaker. Thomas Nelson 2017. 224 pages
ISBN 9780718031848
Grades: Adult   248.8
1. Christian life 2. Gender role 3. Faith (Christianity) 4. Motherhood 5. Women's role 6. Everyday life 7. Self-acceptance 8. Resilience 9. Happiness 10. Spirituality and Religion — Christianity 11. Family and Relationships — General 12. Humor writing — Family and relationship humor
LC Bl2017028740

Author Jen Hatmaker, with playful hilarity, shameless honesty, and refreshing insight, assures readers they have all the pluck they need for vibrant, courageous, grace-filled lives.

"Hatmaker shares the importance of reaching beyond comfort zones and extending welcomes. She owns the moxie shes writing about." —*Booklist*

Nockels, Christy
The Life You Long For: Learning to Live from a Heart of Rest. Christy Nockels. Multnomah 2021. VIII, 220 pages
ISBN 9780593192542
Grades: Adult   248.8
1. Christian women 2. Trust in God 3. Rest 4. Christianity 5. Religious life 6. Spirituality and Religion — Christian living 7. Self-Help — Personal growth — Spirituality
LC 2020011868

A beloved worship leader and music artist invites women to let go of the striving for control that leaves them exhausted and instead learn to trust God with their deepest dreams and desires.

"Christians looking to slow down and form more intimate relationships will enjoy Nockels's impassioned reminder that God provides a community and love to those who ask." —*Publishers Weekly*
Includes bibliographical references (pages 213-220).

Norris, Kathleen
Acedia & Me: A Marriage, Monks, and a Writer's Life. Kathleen Norris. Riverhead Books 2008. 352 p.
ISBN 9781594489969
Grades: Adult   248.8
1. Norris, Kathleen, 1947- 2. Soul (Christianity) 3. Melancholy 4. Unhappiness 5. Depression 6. Apathy 7. Monasticism and religious orders 8. Joy and sorrow 9. Christianity 10. Spirituality and Religion — General 11. Family and Relationships — Aging and Death
LC 2008010150

Discusses the ancient concept of "soul weariness" and explores the phenomenon's relevance in modern culture, meditating on the ways in which depression-like acedia influenced the author's experiences as a writer, a family member, and a patient.
Includes bibliographical references.

Park, J. S.
★ *As Long as You Need: Permission to Grieve.* J. S. Park. Thomas Nelson 2024. 240 p.
ISBN 9781400336845
Grades: Adult   248.8
1. Park, J. S. (Hospital chaplain) 2. Hospital chaplains 3. Grief 4. Death 5. Loss 6. Counseling 7. Spirituality 8. Faith (Christianity) 9. Suffering 10. Patience 11. Family and Relationships — Aging and Death 12. Life stories — Facing adversity — Disasters and tragedies 13. Spirituality and Religion — Christianity

In As Long as You Need, J.S. Park offers an honest and unrushed engagement with grief, decoding four types of grieving—spiritual, mental, physical, and relational—and offering compassionate self-care and soul-care along the way. While the DNA of grief might be universal to the human condition, how you experience and process grief is unique to you.

"It's an excellent resource for those working their way through loss." —*Publishers Weekly*

Sauls, Scott
Beautiful People Don't Just Happen: How God Redeems Regret, Hurt, and Fear in the Making of Better Humans. Scott Sauls. Zondervan Books 2022. xvi, 207 pages
ISBN 9780310363446
Grades: Adult   248.8
1. Suffering 2. Pain 3. Fear 4. Regret 5. Christianity 6. Spirituality and Religion — Christian living
LC 2022005008

ESSENTIAL AND RECOMMENDED TITLES
248.8086 People by miscellaneous social attributes

Regret, hurt, and fear are familiar to us all. Often we feel trapped in their grip, but it doesn't have to be that way. Scott Sauls is our empathetic guide to the freedom that is found in God—freedom that unburdens us from regret, hurt, and fear and opens the door to a new life of relief, contentment, and hope.

"This is a soothing guide for weary souls." —*Publishers Weekly*

Includes bibliographical references.

Shankle, Melanie
Church of the Small Things: The Million Little Pieces That Make up a Life. Melanie Shankle; foreword by Ree Drummond. Zondervan 2017. 224 pages
ISBN 9780310348870
Grades: Adult   248.8
1. Shankle, Melanie 2. Everyday life 3. Purpose in life 4. Family relationships 5. Simplicity 6. Faith (Christianity) 7. Essays 8. Family and Relationships — Families 9. Family and Relationships — Friendship
LC 2017003557

In Church of the Small Things, New York Times bestselling author Melanie Shankle celebrates, with her trademark stories and humor, the wonder of the many small moments in life that add up to make a big difference and ultimately shape the person we become.

"Shankle's winsome book will be well-received by Christian readers looking to be more conscientious in everyday life." —*Publishers Weekly*

248.8086 People by miscellaneous social attributes

Hays, Katie
Family of Origin, Family of Choice: Stories of Queer Christians. Katie Hays and Susan A. Chiasson; foreword by Paula Stone Williams. William. B. Eerdmans Publishing Company 2021. 162 p.
ISBN 9780802878571
Grades: Adult   248.8086
1. LGBTQIA+ people 2. Families 3. Christians 4. Love 5. Family relationships 6. Religious life 7. Christianity and homosexuality 8. Christianity and sexuality 9. Oral histories 10. Life stories — Identity — LGBTQIA+ 11. Life stories — Relationships — Family 12. Family and Relationships — LGBTQIA+ 13. Spirituality and Religion — Christianity 14. Life stories — Religion and spirituality
LC 2020049006

A collection of first-person narratives from LGBTQ+ Christians about navigating their family relationships after coming out.

"These moving narratives, offering firsthand perspectives from a racially diverse group of LGBTQ Christians and their families, will resonate with many." —*Library Journal*

252 Texts of sermons

Francis
The Church of Mercy. Pope Francis. Loyola Press 2014. 200 p.
ISBN 9780829441680
Grades: Adult   252
1. Mercy 2. Charity 3. Hope 4. Catholic Church renewal 5. Poverty 6. Essays 7. Spirituality and Religion — Christianity — Catholicism
LC 2014934036

Designed for a broad readership, the Church of Mercy is a compilation of essays, speeches, and homilies by Pope Francis since his election on being a church that exists among and for the people, solidarity with the poor, and the need to demolish the idols of power and money.

"Refreshingly humane, focusing on people rather than institutions. Admirers of Francis and students of church history alike will find this a useful introduction to the pontiff's thought." —*Kirkus*

254 Local church administration

Nagassar, Rohadi
When We Belong: Reclaiming Christianity on the Margins. Rohadi Nagassar. Herald Press 2022. 215 p.
ISBN 9781513810362
Grades: Adult   254
1. Marginalized people 2. Social marginality 3. Racism in Christianity 4. Church membership 5. Church and social problems 6. Belonging 7. Love (Christianity) 8. Multiculturalism 9. Social integration 10. Social justice 11. Religions 12. Spirituality and Religion — Christianity — Political Aspects 13. Society and culture — Race
LC 2022007490

Step into a journey toward liberation, belonging, and a faith that fits your skin. We need belonging to survive and thrive. For Christians in marginalized communities who know the pain, isolation, and loss of identity that come with the ongoing struggle to be seen in churches and institutions full of barriers to belonging, it can feel easier to walk away from faith completely. But there is another way. When it feels as though there's no place left to belong, Jesus invites us into a love that knows no bounds and a community that truly liberates. In this hope-filled book, author Rohadi Nagassar brings the margins to the center to help readers rediscover a reality of love, belonging, and beauty through the journey of deconstructing, decolonizing, and reclaiming faith.

"Well researched and passionately argued, this should be required reading for justice-minded churchgoers." —*Publishers Weekly*

Includes bibliographical references.

255 Religious congregations and orders

Norris, Kathleen
The Cloister Walk. Kathleen Norris. Riverhead Books 1996. xv, 384 p.
ISBN 9781573225847
Grades: Adult   255
1. Norris, Kathleen, 1947- 2. Monasticism and religious orders 3. Spiritual life 4. Monasteries 5. Catholics 6. Christianity 7. Faith 8. Spirituality and Religion — Christianity — Catholicism
LC 96000863

A reverent study of the monastic world assesses the meaning of the cloistered life in modern times, journeying through a liturgical year to capture the relevance and spiritual significance of the religious life.

261 Social theology and interreligious relations and attitudes

Beaty, Katelyn
Celebrities for Jesus: How Personas, Platforms, and Profits Are Hurting the Church. Katelyn Beaty. Brazos Press, a division of Baker Publishing Group 2022. 224 p.
ISBN 9781587435188
Grades: Adult   261
1. Christianity and culture 2. Fame 3. Evangelicalism 4. Celebrities 5. Greed 6. Faith (Christianity) 7. Christian life 8. Spirituality and religion — Christianity
LC 2022003445

An award-winning writer shows how and why celebrity is woven into the fabric of the evangelical movement, identifies many ways fame goes awry, shows us how we all unwittingly foster a celebrity culture, and offers a vision of faithfulness to the Messiah who was despised and rejected.

"This is a must-read for anyone invested in the fate of evangelicalism." —*Publishers Weekly*

Includes bibliographical references.

Carroll, James
Constantine's Sword: The Church and the Jews : A History. James Carroll. Houghton Mifflin 2001. xii, 756 p.
ISBN 9780395779279

PUBLIC LIBRARY CORE COLLECTION: NONFICTION
Twentieth Edition

Grades: Adult **261**

1. Former priests 2. Antisemitism in Christianity 3. Judaism 4. Interfaith relations 5. Biographies 6. Spirituality and Religion — Judaism 7. Spirituality and Religion — Christianity

LC 00061329

Library Journal Best Books, 2001; National Jewish Book Award, 2001; New York Times Notable Book, 2001.

Examines the two-thousand-year relationship between Christianity and Judaism, examining the long entrenched tradition of anti-Semitism that culminated in the Church's failure to protest the Holocaust during World War II.

"This magisterial work will satisfy Jewish and Christians readers alike, challenging both to a renewed conversation with one another." —*Publishers Weekly*

Includes bibliographical references (p. [696]-719) and index.

Griffin, Chante
Loving Your Black Neighbor as Yourself: A Guide to Closing the Space Between Us. Chanté Griffin. WaterBrook 2024. 240 p.

ISBN 9780593445594

Grades: Adult **261**

1. Jesus Christ 2. Race relations 3. African Americans 4. European Americans 5. Christianity 6. Interpersonal relations 7. Humility 8. Honesty 9. Love (Christianity) 10. Reconciliation 11. Christian doctrines 12. Golden rule 13. Spirituality and Religion — Christianity 14. Society and culture — Race

LC 2023039945

Jesus calls you to love your neighbor, and in the fight against racial injustice, that call includes your Black Neighbor: Your Black colleagues, the Black congregants at church, the Black family in your neighborhood. Yet maybe you're unsure of how best to show your love, or maybe you fear either saying or doing the wrong thing. In Loving Your Black Neighbor as Yourself, Chanté Griffin equips you to see and love your Black Neighbor with God's deep, holistic love.

"The result is an actionable resource for believers looking to build a more equitable world, starting from within." —*Publishers Weekly*

Includes bibliographical references.

Holland, Tom
Dominion: How the Christian Revolution Remade the World. Tom Holland. Basic Books 2019. 496 p.

ISBN 9780465093502

Grades: Adult **261**

1. Civilization, Christian 2. Civilization, Western 3. Religion and culture 4. Christian history 5. Moral conditions 6. Ethics 7. Christianity and culture 8. Religion and civilization 9. Spirituality and Religion — Christianity — History 10. History writing — Ancient

LC BI2019024758

Shows how the Christian Revolution forged the Western imagination.

261.2 Christianity and other systems of belief

Bidwell, Duane R.
When One Religion Isn't Enough: The Lives of Spiritually Fluid People. Duane R. Bidwell. Beacon Press 2018. 200 p.

ISBN 9780807091241

Grades: Adult **261.2**

1. Social change 2. Faith 3. Religions 4. Religious adherents 5. Options, alternatives, choices 6. Pluralism (Social sciences) 7. Identity 8. Impartial writing 9. Spirituality and Religion — General 10. Life stories — Religion and spirituality — Personal faith

LC 2018018026

Library Journal Best Books, 2018.

Through in-depth conversations with spiritually fluid people, renowned scholar Duane Bidwell explores how people come to claim and be claimed by multiple religious traditions, how spiritually fluid people engage radically opposed truth claims, and what this growing population tells us about change within our communities.

"Will appeal to spiritual readers seeking an understanding and affirmation of the growing multireligious movement. Strongly recommended for libraries of all types." —*Library Journal*

Includes bibliographical references and index.

261.5 Christianity and secular disciplines

Baraka, Sho
He Saw That It Was Good: Reimagining Your Creative Life to Repair a Broken World. Sho Baraka. WaterBrook Press 2021. xxix, 189 p.

ISBN 9780593193044

Grades: Adult **261.5**

1. Baraka, Sho 2. Christian African Americans 3. Rap musicians 4. Creativity 5. Creation (Literary, artistic, etc.) 6. Christian life 7. Social justice 8. Identity 9. Self-discovery 10. Grace (Christian theology) 11. Christianity and the arts 12. Christianity 13. Life stories — Arts and culture — Performing arts — Musicians and composers 14. Life stories — Religion and spirituality — Personal faith 15. Spirituality and Religion — Christianity 16. Arts and Entertainment — General 17. Society and culture — General

LC 2020054693

We were made to create. But our troubled world doesn't make it easy. Few people understand this better than acclaimed hip-hop artist and creative polymath Sho Baraka. With unforgettable prose and crisp storytelling, Sho will inspire you to speak truth, chase beauty, and live out the deep satisfaction of your life's true work.

"Relevant from both a Christian and a secularly political perspective, this timely book is a must-read." —*Booklist*

Includes bibliographical references.

261.55 Science

Wilson, Derek K.
A Magical World: Superstition and Science from the Renaissance to the Enlightenment. Derek K. Wilson. Pegasus Books 2017. 320 p.

ISBN 9781681776453

Grades: Adult **261.55**

1. Religion and science 2. Science 3. Ideas (Philosophy) 4. Superstition 5. Enlightenment (European intellectual movement) 6. Intellectual life 7. Theory of knowledge 8. Philosophy 9. European history 10. Renaissance (1300-1600) 11. History writing — Enlightenment — Europe 12. History writing — Renaissance — Europe

LC 2018303384

A rich and multi-faceted history of heroes and villains interwoven with the profound changes in human knowledge that took place between the Renaissance and the Enlightenment.

"A dazzling chronicle, a bracing challenge to modernitys smug assumptions." —*Booklist*

261.7 Christianity and political affairs

Rashid, Jonny
Jesus Takes a Side: Embracing the Political Demands of the Gospel. Jonny Rashid. Herald Press 2022. 192 p.

ISBN 9781513810447

Grades: Adult **261.7**

1. Christianity and politics 2. Christianity 3. Political culture 4. LGBTQIA+ rights 5. Politics and global affairs — Religion and politics 6. Spirituality and Religion — Christianity — Political Aspects

In a world divided by left and right, red and blue, many Christians have upheld a "third way" approach in pursuit of moderation, harmony, and unity. But if Christians are more concerned with divisiveness than with faithfulness, we have failed to grasp the gospel's political demands. We do not see Jesus taking a "third

ESSENTIAL AND RECOMMENDED TITLES
261.8 Christianity and socioeconomic problems

way" between oppressor and oppressed. And as followers of Jesus, neither should we.

"The parallels Rashid draws between the gospels and contemporary American politics are original and persuasive, making accessible for today's Christians the moral implications of ancient political conflicts. The result is a bold reappraisal of what it means to follow Jesus in the current political climate." —*Publishers Weekly*

Volf, Miroslav
Public Faith in Action: How to Think Carefully, Engage Wisely, and Vote with Integrity. Miroslav Volf and Ryan McAnnally-Linz. Brazos Press 2016. xiii, 240 pages
ISBN 9781587433849
Grades: Adult 261.7
1. Christianity and politics 2. Christians 3. Church and social problems 4. Political participation 5. Spirituality and Religion — Christian living 6. Spirituality and Religion — Christianity
LC 2016003425

This nonpartisan handbook offers Christians practical guidance for thinking through complicated public issues and faithfully following Jesus as citizens of their countries.

"Working on the premise that Christian faith must naturally spill over into public discussion, they offer insight into making informed decisions around candidates and political issues. Aptly subtitled, the book asks readers to consider issues from a biblical perspective and then to take action in a courageous but respectful and humble manner, working to influence society while representing Christ well." —*Publishers Weekly*

Includes index.

Wallis, Jim
The False White Gospel: Rejecting Christian Nationalism, Reclaiming True Faith, and Refounding Democracy. Jim Wallis. St Martins Essentials 2024. 304 p.
ISBN 9781250291899
Grades: Adult 261.7
1. Faith (Christianity) 2. Nationalism 3. New Right 4. Christianity 5. Democracy 6. Religion and politics 7. United States 8. Spirituality and religion — Christianity 9. Politics and global affairs — Religion and politics

"In this ardent manifesto, Wallis urges readers to…reclaim core biblical principles…This promises to be a conversation starter in church groups and beyond." —*Publishers Weekly*

261.8 Christianity and socioeconomic problems

Bailey, Jennifer
To My Beloveds: Letters on Faith, Race, Loss, and Radical Hope. Jennifer Bailey. Chalice Press 2021. 128 p.
ISBN 9780827237278
Grades: Adult 261.8
1. Bailey, Jennifer 2. African American clergywomen 3. Faith 4. Loss 5. Hope 6. Christian life 7. African American women 8. Memory 9. Grief 10. Racism 11. Essays 12. Autobiographies and memoirs 13. Life stories — Religion and spirituality — Personal faith 14. Spirituality and religion — Christianity

How do we heal our grief and loss to become the leaders the world needs today? in this unique collection love letters to her fellow activists and faith leaders, Jennifer Bailey offers comfort, wisdom, encouragement, support, and hope for young activistsand emerging faith leaders aspiring to build a better world amidst its violence, trauma, and loss—and who may wonder if they're up to the task or unsure if they'll ever see the change they seek. Considering three central questions—what is dying, what wants to emerge, and what is already blooming beautifully—Bailey's poignant letters inspire us to imagine how our grief and despair can be composted into new life filled with courage, hope, and purpose for our shared future.

"Bailey's new book breathes new life into epistolary nonfiction in a poignant collection about remembrance, gratitude, grief, and hope." —*Library Journal*

Barber, William J.
We Are Called to Be a Movement. Reverend Dr. William J. Barber II.. Workman Publishing Company 2020. 96 pages
ISBN 9781523511242
Grades: Adult 261.8
1. Democracy 2. Ethics 3. Poor people 4. Poverty 5. Equality 6. Social movements 7. Social action 8. Social justice 9. Church and social problems 10. Protests, demonstrations, vigils, etc. 11. Christianity and politics 12. Moral conditions 13. United States 14. Speeches, addresses, etc. 15. Spirituality and Religion — Christianity — Political Aspects 16. Society and culture — Wealth and class — Poverty
LC 2020937934

The text of a sermon given by Dr. William J. Barber II, on June 3, 2018, at the National Cathedral in Washington, D.C, asking people to come together to renounce the politics of rejection, division, and greed.

"Christians looking for inspiration toward collective action will love this." —*Publishers Weekly*

Bolz-Weber, Nadia
Shameless: A Sexual Reformation. Nadia Bolz-Weber. Convergent 2019. 224 p.
ISBN 9781601427588
Grades: Adult 261.8
1. Bolz-Weber, Nadia 2. Sexuality 3. Christianity and sexuality 4. Shame 5. Judgment 6. Sexual freedom 7. Sex discrimination 8. Biblical teaching 9. Spirituality and Religion — Christianity 10. Society and culture — Sex and sexuality
LC 2018021697

Christians are obsessed with sex. But not in a good way. For generations countless people have suffered pain, guilt, and judgment as a result of this toxic fixation on sex, the body, and physical pleasure. In the follow-up to her celebrated New York Times bestseller Accidental Saints, Bolz-Weber unleashes her critical eye, her sharp pen, and her vulnerable but hopeful soul on the caustic, fear-riddled, and religiously inspired messages about sex that have fed our shame.

Chu, Jeff
Does Jesus Really Love Me?: A Gay Christian's Pilgrimage in Search of God in America. Jeff Chu. Harper 2013. 256 p.
ISBN 9780062049735
Grades: Adult 261.8
1. Chu, Jeff 2. Christianity and homosexuality 3. Christianity 4. Homosexuality 5. Christian gay men and lesbians 6. Gay men 7. Christians 8. Autobiographies and memoirs 9. Spirituality and Religion — Christianity 10. Life stories — Religion and spirituality — Personal faith 11. Society and culture — LGBTQIA+
LC Bl2013011143

Tired of the homophobic image of Christianity in America, writer and editor Jeff Chu (a gay man, raised Southern Baptist) went on the road to talk to Christians about their views on whether God loves homosexuals. Most of the people he interviewed expressed accepting—even welcoming—attitudes on topics like same-sex marriage and the full inclusion of gay church members. Even those less accepting still didn't express hostility. This word-on-the-street memoir offers informative reading at the intersection of Christianity and American culture today.

"[T]he book brings complexity and humanity to a discourse often lacking in both." —*Publishers Weekly*

Gilliard, Dominique Dubois
Rethinking Incarceration: Advocating for Justice That Restores. Dominique Dubois Gilliard. InterVarsity Press 2018. 240 p.
ISBN 9780830845293
Grades: Adult 261.8
1. Prisons 2. Criminal justice system 3. Christian life 4. Imprisonment 5. United States 6. Society and culture — Violence and crime — Criminal justice

system 7. Society and culture — Race 8. Spirituality and religion — Christianity 9. Antiracist literature

LC 2018005769

The United States has more people locked up in jails, prisons, and detention centers than any other country in the history of the world. Exploring the history and foundations of mass incarceration, Dominique Gilliard examines Christianity's role in its evolution and expansion, assessing justice in light of Scripture, and showing how Christians can pursue justice that restores and reconciles.

"In his debut, Gilliard, an Evangelical Covenant Church pastor, builds on the work of Michelle Alexander (The New Jim Crow), Bryan Stevenson (Just Mercy), and Christopher D. Marshall (Compassionate Justice) to create a readable narrative history of racialized incarceration in the U.S." —*Publishers Weekly*

Gonzalez, Karen

Beyond Welcome: Centering Immigrants in Our Christian Response to Immigration. Karen Gonzalez. Brazos Press, a division of Baker Publishing Group 2022. 176 p.

ISBN 9781587435867

Grades: Adult   261.8

1. Christianity 2. Church and social problems 3. Immigrants 4. Immigration and emigration 5. Society and culture — Immigration 6. Spirituality and religion — Christianity

Challenging many common assumptions, a Guatemalan immigrant and advocate with World Relief examines the racial, social, political, and theological implications of centering immigrants themselves in our advocacy and care.

"The author's biblical analysis achieves the difficult task of drawing fresh conclusions from familiar stories and finding wisdom in those less discussed….The result is a top-notch Christian look at immigration, humane and full of heart." —*Publishers Weekly*

Griffith, R. Marie

Moral Combat: How Sex Divided American Christians and Fractured American Politics. R. Marie Griffith. Basic Books 2017. 384 p.

ISBN 9780465094752

Grades: Adult   261.8

1. Religion and politics 2. Christianity and politics 3. Fundamentalism 4. Gender role 5. Women's rights 6. Ethics 7. Christianity and democracy 8. Christian conservatism 9. Christians 10. Protestant churches 11. Political participation 12. Interfaith relations 13. Religions 14. United States history 15. Spirituality and Religion — Christianity — Political Aspects 16. Politics and global affairs — Religion and politics

LC 2017037768

A scholar of American religion and sexuality chronicles the century of religious conflict behind many of today's most contentious issues, exploring how the Christian consensus about gender roles and sexual morality has changed throughout recent decades.

"Griffiths remarkably comprehensive book will be of interest to scholars and lay readers alike." —*Publishers Weekly*

Includes bibliographical references and index.

Hardwick, Lamar

How Ableism Fuels Racism: Dismantling the Hierarchy of Bodies in the Church. Lamar Hardwick. Brazos Press, a division of Baker Publishing Group 2024. 192 p.

ISBN 9781587436284

Grades: Adult   261.8

1. Disabilities 2. Christianity 3. Ableism 4. Racism 5. Discrimination 6. Social change 7. Race relations 8. Spirituality and religion — Christianity 9. Society and culture — Race

LC 2023028482

An autistic pastor and disability scholar helps the contemporary church understand the connections between ableism and racism and how to dismantle both in attitudes and practices.

"Hardwick delivers a searing indictment of the ableist theology that has fueled racial bias in the American church and society…Marshaling fine-grained historical detail and scrupulous analysis, Hardwick persuades." —*Publishers Weekly*

Includes bibliographical references.

Rowan, Barry L.

The Spiritual Art of Business: Connecting the Daily with the Divine. Barry L. Rowan. IVP, an imprint of InterVarsity Press 2023. 167 pages : Illustration

ISBN 9781514007624

Grades: Adult   261.8

1. Work 2. Christian life 3. Christianity 4. Employees 5. Religious life 6. Spirituality and Religion — Christian living 7. Business and economics — Business advice — Leadership and management

LC 2023006610

How do we bring meaning to our work, instead of being defined by what we do? "Corporate mystic" Barry Rowan invites us to see our work as a chance to serve God by contributing to a better society. With forty short chapters, this book beckons us into a connection with God that will infuse our lives, our offices, and our world with meaning.

"Christian professionals will be inspired." —*Publishers Weekly*

262 Ecclesiology

Duffy, Eamon

Saints & Sinners: A History of the Popes. Eamon Duffy. Yale University Press, in association with S4C 1997. 326 p. : Color illustration

ISBN 9780300206128

Grades: Adult   262

1. Papacy 2. Popes 3. Spirituality and Religion — Christianity — Catholicism

LC 97060897

Traces the history of the Papacy from its development after the execution of Peter to the reign of Pope John Paul II. This 4th edition also covers the unprecedented resignation of Benedict XVI and the election of the first Argentinian pope.

Published in conjunction with the TV production of the same title; Includes bibliographical references (p. [307]-317) and index.

Roberts, Matthias

Holy Runaways: Rediscovering Faith After Being Burned by Religion. Matthias Roberts. Broadleaf Books 2023. xiv, 270 p.

ISBN 9781506485652

Grades: Adult   262

1. Roberts, Matthias 2. Christians 3. Gay men 4. Former church members 5. Alienation 6. Spirituality 7. Self-fulfillment 8. Love (Christianity) 9. Toleration 10. Christian doctrines 11. Encouragement 12. Faith (Christianity) 13. Spirituality and Religion — Christianity 14. Life stories — Religion and spirituality — Leaving religion 15. Life stories — Religion and spirituality — Personal faith

LC 2023005208

Psychotherapist Matthias Roberts speaks with empathy and compassion to people who have left their faith community after experiencing trauma, hypocrisy, or resistance to change. Blending personal stories, new interpretations of Christian parables, and research on religious trauma, Roberts guides "holy runaways" toward new and loving spiritual homes.

"Christians who feel alienated from their church communities will find plenty of food for thought." —*Publishers Weekly*

Includes bibliographical references.

262.001 Philosophy and theory, ecumenism, church renewal

Smietana, Bob

Reorganized Religion: The Reshaping of the American Church and Why It Matters. Bob Smietana. Worthy 2022. 256 p.

ISBN 9781546001614

Grades: Adult   262.001

ESSENTIAL AND RECOMMENDED TITLES
263 Days, times, places of religious observance

1. Christian church renewal 2. Spirituality 3. Faith 4. Christian life 5. Christianity 6. Churches 7. Church attendance 8. Social life and customs 9. Church history 10. United States 11. Spirituality and religion — Christianity

LC 2022009847

Reorganized Religion is an in-depth and critical look at why people are leaving American churches and what we lose as a society as it continues. But it also accepts the dismantling of what has come before and try to help readers reinvent the path forward. This book looks at the future of organized religion in America and outline the options facing churches and other faith groups. Will they retreat? Will they become irrelevant? or will they find a new path forward?

"Telling rich stories about people and communities across a vast religious spectrum, Smietana delivers his insights on reimagining American Christianity and organized religion more broadly." —*Library Journal*

Includes bibliographical references.

263 Days, times, places of religious observance

Egan, Timothy
A Pilgrimage to Eternity: From Canterbury to Rome in Search of a Faith. Timothy Egan. Viking 2019. 384 p.
ISBN 9780735225237
Grades: Adult   263
1. Pilgrims and pilgrimages 2. Faith (Christianity) 3. Walking 4. Catholic families 5. Belief and doubt 6. Voyages and travels 7. Europe 8. Travel writing — Modes of transportation — on foot 9. Travel writing — Retracing historic journeys 10. Spirituality and religion — Christianity

LC 2019015599

New York Times Notable Book, 2020.

The Pulitzer Prize-winning reporter and author of The Immortal Irishman traces an ancient pilgrimage route from Canterbury to Rome, visiting some of Christianity's most important shrines to explore the faith's past, present and future.

Includes bibliographical references and index.

Mullins, Edwin
The Four Roads to Heaven: France and the Santiago Pilgrimage. Edwin Mullins. Interlink Books 2018. x, 254 pages, 12 unnumbered pages of plates : Illustration; Color; Map
ISBN 9781623719913
Grades: Adult   263
1. Pilgrims and pilgrimages 2. Walking 3. Travelers 4. Voyages and travels 5. Camino de Santiago de Compostela 6. Spain 7. History writing — Europe 8. Spirituality and religion — General

"Essential for potential pilgrims and an excellent European history for others." —*Library Journal*

Includes bibliographical references and index; Originally published: Oxford, UK : Signal Books, 2017.

269 Spiritual renewal

Garcia, Damon
The God Who Riots: Taking Back the Radical Jesus. Damon Garcia. Broadleaf Books 2022. 200 p.
ISBN 9781506480374
Grades: Adult   269
1. Social justice 2. Christianity 3. Christianity and culture 4. Christianity and politics 5. Spirituality and Religion — Christianity

In his his frank, tell-it-like-it-is style to connect us with the Jesus who flipped tables in the temple and led an empire-destabilizing movement for liberation. The spirit of this God is embodied in today's protests, riots, and strikes. As we join this struggle for liberation, we are joining the God who riots alongside us, within us, and through us.

"Tackling issues often charged with high emotions, Garcia offers a guide to social change with an accessible and easy-to-understood model. Suited for readers interested in religious studies and social justice." —*Library Journal*

270 History, geographic treatment, biography of Christianity

Farmer, David Hugh
The Oxford Dictionary of Saints. David Hugh Farmer. Oxford University Press 2004. xxiv, 579 p. : Map
ISBN 9780198609490
Grades: Adult   270
1. Christian saints 2. Saints 3. Reference — General 4. Spirituality and Religion — Christianity — History

LC 2005272790

"Even those who do not believe in the saints . will be able to enjoy and to profit from this splendid book." —*The Economist*

Reissued with new covers 2004—T.P. verso; Includes bibliographical references and index.

MacCulloch, Diarmaid
Christianity: The First Three Thousand Years. Diarmaid MacCulloch. Viking 2010. xvii, 1161 p, 32 p. of plates : Illustration; Color; Map
ISBN 9780670021260
Grades: Adult   270
1. Church history 2. Christian history 3. Evangelicalism 4. Christians 5. Spirituality and Religion — Christianity — History

LC 2009040184

Cundill Prize in History, 2010; New York Times Notable Book, 2010.

Conveyed with compelling skill and scholarship, this groundbreaking work ranges back to the origins of the Hebrew Bible and follows the three mains strands of the Christian faith.

"It is difficult to imagine a more comprehensive and surprisingly accessible volume on the subject than MacCulloch's. Want a refresher on the rise of the papacy? It is here. On Charlemagne and Carolingians? That is here, too. On the Fourth Crusade and its aftermath? Look no farther." —*New York Times Book Review*

Includes bibliographical references (p. [1017]-1112) and index; Originally published as: A history of Christianity: the first three thousand years. London : Allen Lane, 2009.

270.1 Historical periods

Ehrman, Bart D.
The Triumph of Christianity: How a Forbidden Religion Swept the World. Bart D. Ehrman. Simon & Schuster 2018. 352 p.
ISBN 9781501136702
Grades: Adult   270.1
1. Constantine I, Emperor of Rome, died 337 2. Church history 3. Christianity 4. Religions 5. Medieval period (476-1492) 6. Spirituality and Religion — Christianity — History

LC 2016056895

Looks at how Christianity went from being an obscure sect of Judaism followed by a small group of rural peasants to being the dominant religion in the west in less than four hundred years.

"The author maps out the early growth of Christianity against a detailed background of Roman society and history…He not only brings a clear presentation of his own views but also gives alternative interpretations a fair hearing." —*Library Journal*

Includes bibliographical references.

Riley, Gregory J.
The River of God: A New History of Christian Origins. Gregory J. Riley. Harper San Francisco 2001. III, 252 p.
ISBN 9780060669799

Grades: Adult **270.1**
1. Christianity 2. Church history 3. Spirituality and Religion — Christianity
LC 2001016888

Argues that true Christianity is pluralistic and receptive to diverse beliefs, presents a new understanding of the early churches, and communicates a critical message regarding the true nature of Christian faith in today's society.

"This volume will become one of the most important books on the subject." —*Library Journal*

Includes bibliographical references (p. 239-243) and index.

270.2 Period of ecumenical councils, 325-787

Brown, Peter
Through the Eye of a Needle: Wealth, the Fall of Rome, and the Making of Christianity in the West, 350-550 AD. Peter Brown. Princeton University Press 2012. xxx, 759 p, 16 p. of plates : Illustration; Color; Map
ISBN 9780691152905
Grades: Adult **270.2**
1. Church history 2. Wealth 3. Ancient history 4. Politics and government 5. Ancient Rome 6. Medieval period (476-1492) 7. Roman Empire (27 B.C.E.-476 C.E.) 8. Spirituality and Religion — Christianity — History 9. History writing — Ancient — Rome
LC 2011045697

Traces the intellectual and social history of wealth in the early Christian church, examining the financial rise of the church and its effects on the waning Roman empire as well as the church's own beliefs on poverty.

Map on lining papers; Includes bibliographical references and index.

270.6 Period of Reformation and Counter-Reformation, 1517-1648

MacCulloch, Diarmaid
The Reformation. Diarmaid MacCulloch. Viking 2004. xxiv, 792 p. : Illustration; Map
ISBN 9780670032969
Grades: Adult **270.6**
1. Reformation 2. Protestantism 3. Christian history 4. 16th century 5. Renaissance (1300-1600) 6. History writing — Renaissance — Europe 7. Spirituality and Religion — Christianity — History
LC 2003061607

National Book Critics Circle Award for Non-Fiction, 2004.

A history of the Reformation and Counter-Reformation examines the lasting implications of this period, providing profiles of the individuals involved and discussing the impact of the Reformation on everyday lives.

"The author has produced the definitive survey for this generation. This well-written book is a joy to read, with new facts and interpretations on nearly every page." —*Library Journal*

Includes bibliographical references and index.

270.8 Modern period, 1789-

Alberta, Tim
The Kingdom, the Power, and the Glory: American Evangelicals in an Age of Extremism. Tim Alberta. Harper 2023. 400 p.
ISBN 9780063226883
Grades: Adult **270.8**
1. Christianity 2. Christians 3. Evangelicalism 4. Conservatism 5. Political culture 6. Extremism 7. New Right 8. Nationalism 9. Social change 10. Polarization (Social sciences) 11. United States 12. Spirituality and Religion — Christianity — Political Aspects 13. Politics and global affairs — Religion and politics 14. Life stories — Religion and spirituality

Evangelical Christians are perhaps the most polarizing—and least understood—people living in America today. In his seminal new book, The Kingdom, the Power, and the Glory, journalist Tim Alberta, himself a practicing Christian and the son of an evangelical preacher, paints an expansive and profoundly troubling portrait of the American evangelical movement. Through the eyes of televangelists and small-town preachers, celebrity revivalists and everyday churchgoers, Alberta tells the story of a faith cheapened by ephemeral fear, a promise corrupted by partisan subterfuge, and a reputation stained by perpetual scandal.

"Sometimes overly personal yet well researched and comprehensive." —*Kirkus*

McLaren, Brian D.
Do I Stay Christian?: A Guide for the Doubters, the Disappointed, and the Disillusioned. Brian D. McLaren. St. Martin's Essentials 2022. 256 p.
ISBN 9781250262790
Grades: Adult **270.8**
1. Christian apologetics 2. Faith (Christianity) 3. Ethics 4. Argumentation 5. Philosophy 6. Identity 7. Religions 8. Spirituality and Religion — Christianity — Political Aspects 9. Society and culture — Philosophy
LC 2022000928

Do I Stay Christian? addresses in public the powerful question that surprising numbers of people—including pastors, priests, and other religious leaders—are asking in private. Picking up where Faith After Doubt leaves off, Do I Stay Christian? is not McLaren's attempt to persuade Christians to dig in their heels or run for the exit. Instead, he combines his own experience with that of thousands of people who have confided in him over the years to help readers make a responsible, honest, ethical decision about their religious identity.

"This earnest inquiry solidifies McLaren's place as one of the more thoughtful interrogators of modern Christianity." —*Publishers Weekly*

Includes bibliographical references.

Stanley, Brian
Christianity in the Twentieth Century: A World History. Brian Stanley. Princeton University Press 2018. 472 p.
ISBN 9780691157108
Grades: Adult **270.8**
1. Church history 2. Christianity 3. Christianity and culture 4. Social change 5. Multiculturalism 6. Faith 7. Ethics 8. Religion and culture 9. Religion and civilization 10. Human rights 11. Religions 12. Political science 13. 20th century 14. Spirituality and Religion — Christianity
LC 2017039619

Offers a history of world Christianity in the twentieth century, documenting its profound transformation during a period of political and cultural upheavals, accompanied by case studies intended to shed light on themes important for understanding modern Christianity.

"A finely crafted exploration of Christianity in the 20th century." —*Kirkus*

Includes bibliographical references and index.

Tickle, Phyllis
The Great Emergence: How Christianity Is Changing and Why. Phyllis Tickle. Baker Books 2008. 172 p.
ISBN 9780801013133
Grades: Adult **270.8**
1. Christianity 2. Church history 3. Religions 4. United States 5. 21st century 6. Spirituality and Religion — Christianity
LC 2008021706

From the church's birth to the reign of St. Gregory the great, to the Great Schism and through the Reformation, Phyllis Tickle notes that every 500 years the church has been rocked by massive transitions. Remarkably enough, Tickle suggests to us that we live in such a time right now. The Great Emergence Examines history, social upheaval, and current events, showing how a new form of Christianity is rising within postmodern culture. Anyone interested in the future of the church in America, no matter what their personal affiliation, will find this book a fascinating exploration.

"This is a must-read for anyone seeking to understand the face and future of Christianity." —*Publishers Weekly*

ESSENTIAL AND RECOMMENDED TITLES
271 Religious congregations and orders in church history

271 Religious congregations and orders in church history

Grathwohl, Marya
This Wheel of Rocks: An Unexpected Spiritual Journey. Sister Marya Grathwohl. Riverhead Books 2023. 320 p.
ISBN 9781594487309
Grades: Adult   271
1. Grathwohl, Marya, Sister 2. Nuns 3. Effect of environment on humans 4. Nature and culture 5. Indigenous reservations 6. Cheyenne (North American people) 7. Crow (Apsáalooke) (North American people) 8. Indigenous peoples of North America 9. United States 10. Montana 11. Autobiographies and memoirs 12. Life stories — Religion and spirituality — Personal faith
LC 2023008409

In this deeply personal, revelatory memoir, a Catholic nun recounts her own spiritual journey and how she became embraced by the Crow and Northern Cheyenne, and how their traditions prompted in her an expanding devotion to the land, its resources and its connections to faith and God.

"Catholic readers will especially appreciate this nuanced exploration of a deep-rooted faith and well-lived life." —*Publishers Weekly*

Jones, Dan
The Templars: The Rise and Spectacular Fall of God's Holy Warriors. Dan Jones. Viking Press 2017. 384 p.
ISBN 9780525428305
Grades: Adult   271
1. Crusades 2. Heresy 3. Military religious orders 4. Armies 5. Crusaders (Middle Ages) 6. Secret societies 7. Medieval period (476-1492) 8. History writing — Medieval — Europe
LC 2017025385

A narrative history of the Knights Templar draws on extensive original sources to separate fact from myth, exploring their actual work and influence, the reasons they fell out of favor, and whether or not they were guilty of heresy.

"This is an engrossing examination of a period whose conflicts are still reverberating today." —*Publishers Weekly*

271.7913 Knights Templars

Haag, Michael
The Tragedy of the Templars: The Rise and Fall of the Crusader States. Michael Haag. Harper 2013. 433 pages, 16 unnumbered pages of plates : Illustration; Color; Map
ISBN 9780062059758
Grades: Adult   271.7913
1. Saladin, Sultan of Egypt and Syria, 1137-1193 2. Military religious orders 3. Crusades 4. Secret societies 5. Civilization, Medieval 6. Crusaders (Middle Ages) 7. Orders of knighthood and chivalry 8. Islamic Empire 9. Medieval period (476-1492) 10. Spirituality and Religion — Christianity — History 11. History writing — Southwest Asia and North Africa (Middle East)
LC 2014397588

In this companion to The Templars: The History & the Myth, a noted historian expertly recounts the clashes and crashes that sent the religious order of fighter knights, who were dedicated to defending the Holy Land and Christian pilgrims, from domination and power to condemnation.

Includes bibliographical references (pages [393]-401) and index; Originally published: London : Profile, 2012.

272 Persecutions in general church history

Kamen, Henry
The Spanish Inquisition: A Historical Revision. Henry Kamen. Yale University Press 1998. xii, 369 p. : Illustration
ISBN 9780300075229
Grades: Adult   272
1. Church and state 2. Inquisition 3. Religions 4. Church history 5. Spain 6. Renaissance (1300-1600) 7. History writing — Renaissance — Europe 8. Spirituality and Religion — Christianity — History
LC 97032451

New York Times Notable Book, 1998.

In this completely updated edition of Henry Kamen's classic survey of the Spanish Inquisition, the author incorporates the latest research in multiple languages to offer a new-and thought-provoking-view of this fascinating period. Kamen sets the notorious Christian tribunal into the broader context of Islamic and Jewish culture in the Mediterranean, reassesses its consequences for Jewish culture, measures its impact on Spain's intellectual life, and firmly rebuts a variety of myths and exaggerations that have distorted understandings of the Inquisition. He concludes with disturbing reflections on the impact of state security organizations in our own time.

"In this revision of his 1965 study, the author restates his original argument. He reaffirms his contention that an all-powerful, torture-mad Inquisition is largely a 19th-century myth. In its place he portrays a poor, understaffed institution whose scattered tribunals had only a limited reach and whose methods were more humane than those of most secular courts. As for the Inquisition's much-vaunted role as Big Brother and its responsibility for intellectual decline, Kamen rejects this hypothesis out of hand. {He also dismisses the notion that the Inquisition enjoyed widespread popular support." —*New York Times Book Review*

Includes bibliographical references (p. 353-356) and index.

Perez, Joseph
★ *The Spanish Inquisition: A History.* Joseph Perez; translated from the French by Janet Lloyd. Yale University Press 2005. VII, 248 p.
ISBN 9780300107906
Grades: 11 12 Adult   272
1. Inquisition 2. Spain 3. History writing — Europe — Spain 4. Spirituality and Religion — Christianity — History
LC 2004114614

A new history of the Spanish Inquisition—a terrifying battle for a unified faith.

"Perez, a noted historian of early modern Spain (emer, Univ. of Bordeaux), has produced an objective, scholarly, and eminently usable overview of the origins, administration, operations, and impact of the Spanish Inquisition." —*Choice*

Includes bibliographical references (p. 239-242) and index; Translated from the French.

Rounding, Virginia
The Burning Time: Henry VIII, Bloody Mary, and the Protestant Martyrs of London. Virginia Rounding. St. Martin's Press 2017. 432 p.
ISBN 9781250040640
Grades: Adult   272
1. Mary I, Queen of England, 1516-1558 2. Henry VIII, King of England, 1491-1547 3. Edward VI, King of England, 1537-1553 4. Henry VII, King of England, 1491-1547 5. Religious persecution 6. Church and state 7. Christian martyrs 8. Christian heretics 9. Martyrdom (Christianity) 10. Church history 11. British history 12. England 13. Tudor period (1485-1603) 14. Renaissance (1300-1600) 15. 16th century 16. History writing — Europe — United Kingdom 17. Spirituality and Religion — Christianity — History 18. History writing — Renaissance — Europe
LC 2017023617

Offers an account of the religious persecutions in England under Henry VIII and his daughter, Mary, with a focus on the lives of Baron Richard Rich, who played a role in the persecutions, and John Deane, who managed to avoid them throughout the period.

"An excellent account of 16th-century religious persecution and martyrdom." —*Publishers Weekly*

Includes bibliographical references and index.

273 Doctrinal controversies and heresies in general church history

Pagels, Elaine H.
★ *The Gnostic Gospels.* Elaine Pagels. Vintage Books 1979. xxxvi, 182 p.
ISBN 9780679724537
Grades: 11 12 Adult   273
1. Gnosticism 2. Christianity 3. Apocryphal books (New Testament) 4. Spirituality and Religion — Christianity

LC 79004764

A study of the Gnostic texts, which describe the same people and events portrayed in the New Testament but from a different perspective, reveals why their suppression was essential to the development of the Christian church.

"Pagels writes for the layman, which is refreshing, and she does so lucidly, which is a challenge, especially when gnosticism was regarded by its own adherents to be for the initiated only." —*Christian Science Monitor*

Includes bibliographical references and index; Originally published: New York : Random House, 1979.

275 Christianity in Asia

Liao, Yiwu
God Is Red: The Secret Story of How Christianity Survived and Flourished in Communist China. Liao Yiwu; translated by Wen Huang. HarperOne 2011. 256 p.
ISBN 9780062078469
Grades: Adult   275
1. Communism and Christianity 2. Communism and religion 3. Christianity and politics 4. Communism 5. Christianity 6. Religions 7. Chinese history 8. Spirituality and Religion — Christianity — Political Aspects 9. Politics and global affairs — Religion and politics

LC 2010051154

Profiling the remarkable lives of ordinary Chinese believers, the author, a celebrated Chinese dissident who was imprisoned, provides a rare glimpse into the thriving—and secret—underground Christian movement in China.

"The author examines Christianity, which survived under China's Cultural Revolution despite attempts to eradicate it as a lackey of the imperialists. In an attempt to understand why a foreign religion gained such popularity, Liao interviews a wide range of Chinese Christians, from an elderly nun who witnessed both the closing and eventual reopening of her church by the Communist regime, to a missionary doctor treating impoverished villagers in lieu of working in a government-run hospital, to a dying tailor who finds meaning in his recent conversion to the faith. Will appeal to both Christian and secular readers interested in the cultural realities of China's Great Leap Forward." —*Kirkus*

277 Christianity in North America

Boyle, Greg
Tattoos on the Heart: The Power of Boundless Compassion. Gregory Boyle. Free Press 2010. xv, 217 p.
ISBN 9781439153024
Grades: Adult   277
1. Boyle, Greg 2. Christian life 3. Church work 4. Christian men 5. Spirituality and Religion — Christianity

LC 2009032970

A Jesuit priest shares anecdotes from his life of working in broken-down urban areas with underprivileged children, describing how he helped them to find faith and embrace such values as patience, self-worth, and kinship.

FitzGerald, Frances
The Evangelicals: The Struggle to Shape America. Frances FitzGerald. Simon & Schuster 2017. 848 p.
ISBN 9781439131336
Grades: Adult   277
1. Fundamentalism 2. Religion and politics 3. Evangelical theology 4. Conservatism 5. Protestantism 6. Evangelicalism 7. Christianity and politics 8. Church history 9. United States 10. Impartial writing 11. Politics and global affairs — Religion and politics 12. Spirituality and Religion — Christianity — Political Aspects 13. History writing — United States

LC 2016025851

New York Times Notable Book, 2017; National Book Critics Circle Award for Non-Fiction, 2017; National Book Award for Nonfiction finalist, 2017.

A dramatic history of the Evangelical movement in America traces the revivals of the 18th and 19th centuries that rendered evangelism a dominant religious force, describing the rise and fall of denominations and how they influenced American agendas ranging from civil rights and gender equality to climate change and immigration reform.

"This is a timely and accessible contribution to the rapidly growing body of literature on Christianity in modern America." —*Publishers Weekly*

Includes bibliographical references and index.

Francois, Willie Dwayne
Silencing White Noise: Six Practices to Overcome Our Inaction on Race. Willie Dwayne Francois, III.. Brazos Press, a division of Baker Publishing Group 2022. 192 p.
ISBN 9781587435652
Grades: Adult   277
1. Race relations 2. Racism 3. Christianity 4. Spirituality and Religion — Christianity 5. Society and culture — Race 6. Antiracist literature

LC 2021057275

A prominent Black church leader calls people of all races to engage six "rhythms of reparative intercession" to silence White Noise—the racist speech, ideas, and policies that lull us into inaction on racial injustice—and to develop lifelong Christian antiracist practices.

"This is a superior volume on Christian antiracism." —*Publishers Weekly*

Gates, Henry Louis
★ *The Black Church: This Is Our Story, This Is Our Song.* Henry Louis Gates, Jr. Penguin Press 2021. 304 p.
ISBN 9781984880338
Grades: Adult   277
1. African Americans 2. Christianity 3. African American churches 4. Political participation 5. Religions 6. United States history 7. United States 8. Page to screen 9. History writing — African American — United States 10. Spirituality and Religion — Christianity — History 11. Society and Culture — Race 12. Antiracist literature

LC 2020042098

A history of the Black church in America that illuminates its essential role in culture, politics and resistance to white supremacy.

In a companion book to a PBS documentary, renowned historian Gates delves into the history of the Black Church, which Harvard historian Evelyn Brooks Higginbotham called 'the single most important institution in the Black community.' —*Kirkus*

Made into a TV series on PBS in 2021; Includes bibliographical references and index.

Hartke, Austen
Transforming: The Bible and the Lives of Transgender Christians. Austen Hartke. Westminster John Knox Press 2018. 198 p.
ISBN 9780664263102
Grades: Adult   277
1. Hartke, Austen 2. Trans men 3. Christian men 4. Transgender people 5. Gender nonconformity 6. Gender identity 7. Transphobia 8. Christianity 9. Toleration 10. Gender-nonconforming people 11. Autobiographies and memoirs 12. Life stories — Identity — LGBTQIA+ 13. Life stories — Religion and spirituality — Personal faith 14. Spirituality and Religion — Christianity 15. Society and culture — LGBTQIA+

LC 2017050167

ESSENTIAL AND RECOMMENDED TITLES
277.308 Christianity — United States

"Its an informative and illuminating quest, supplemented by an extensive appended list of further reading and resources. This is an important book that fills an urgent need." —*Booklist*
Includes bibliographical references.

Jones, Robert P.
White Too Long: The Legacy of White Supremacy in American Christianity. Robert P. Jones. Simon & Schuster 2020. 288 p.
ISBN 9781982122867
Grades: Adult   277
1. Jones, Robert P. (Robert Patrick) 2. Christians 3. White privilege 4. Christian church and race relations 5. Racism 6. Christianity 7. Church history 8. United States 9. Spirituality and Religion — Christianity 10. Society and culture — Race
LC 2019049393
White Too Long draws on history, statistics, and memoir to urge that white Christians reckon with the racism of the past and the amnesia of the present to restore a Christian identity free of the taint of white supremacy.
"An indispensable study of Christianity in America.... a concise yet comprehensive combination of deeply documented religious history, social science research about contemporary religion, and heartfelt memoir." —*Kirkus*
Includes bibliographical references and index.

Manseau, Peter
Objects of Devotion: Religion in Early America. Peter Manseau. Smithsonian Books 2017. VII, 251 pages
ISBN 9781588345929
Grades: Adult   277
1. Material culture 2. Religious articles 3. Americana 4. Religions 5. Church history 6. United States 7. Arts and Entertainment — Antiques and collectibles 8. History writing — United States 9. Spirituality and Religion — General
LC 2016038040
Explores the wide range of religions vying for a prominent place in the early American public square, focusing on such Christian sects as Anglicans, Baptists, and Methodists, as well as faiths ranging from Judaism to Native American beliefs.
"This landmark study of the role of religion in the early history of the U.S.From the mid-17th century to the mid-19th centurydemonstrates how deeply religion influenced Americas founders and their descendants." —*Publishers Weekly*
Includes bibliographical references (pages 234-243) and index.

277.308 Christianity — United States

Brennan, Chad
Faithful Antiracism: Moving Past Talk to Systemic Change. Chad Brennan and Christina Edmondson. InterVarsity Press 2021. 248 p.
ISBN 9780830847235
Grades: Adult   277.308
1. Christian church and race relations 2. Christian life 3. Social justice 4. Racism 5. Christianity 6. Race relations 7. United States 8. Spirituality and Religion — Christianity 9. Society and culture — Race 10. Antiracist literature
LC 2021041934
Racism presents itself as an undefeatable foe-a sustained scourge on the reputation of the church. Drawing on brand-new research, Chad Brennan and Christina Edmondson remind us that Christ has overcome the world and offer clear analysis and interventions to challenge and resist racism's pernicious power, equipping readers to move past talk and enter the fight in practical and hopeful ways.
"While it has an unmistakable Christian perspective, much here will resonate with people of all faiths who are dedicated to racial justice." —*Publishers Weekly*
Includes bibliographical references.

Du Mez, Kristin Kobes
Jesus and John Wayne: How White Evangelicals Corrupted a Faith and Fractured a Nation. Kristin Kobes Du Mez. Liveright Publishing Corporation 2020. 365 p.
ISBN 9781631495731
Grades: Adult   277.308
1. Trump, Donald, 1946- 2. Christianity and politics 3. Evangelicalism 4. New Right 5. Christianity and culture 6. Religion and politics 7. Democracy 8. Masculinity 9. Ideology 10. Religions 11. United States 12. 21st century 13. Liberal writing 14. Spirituality and Religion — Christianity — Political Aspects 15. Politics and global affairs — Religion and politics
LC 2019059451
A scholar of American Christianity presents a seventy-five-year history of evangelicalism that identifies the forces that have turned Donald Trump into a hero of the Religious Right.
"This lucid, potent history adds a much needed religious dimension to understanding the current American right and the rise of Trump." —*Publishers Weekly*

McCammon, Sarah
★ *The Exvangelicals: Loving, Living, and Leaving the White Evangelical Church.* Sarah McCammon. St Martins Press 2024. 304 p.
ISBN 9781250284471
Grades: Adult   277.308
1. Evangelicalism 2. Church attendance 3. Church membership 4. Disillusionment 5. Faith (Christianity) 6. Religion and politics 7. Autobiographies and memoirs 8. Life stories — Religion and spirituality — Leaving religion
A work of memoir and investigative journalism on the evangelical movement: Its origins; stories of its members; and massive social, cultural and political impact.
"A much-needed look at evangelicalism from a perspective that's both investigative and personal. It offers intriguing, compelling insight with expert reporting." —*Library Journal*

Ward, Jon
Testimony: Inside the Evangelical Movement That Failed a Generation. Jon Ward. Brazos Press, a division of Baker Publishing Group 2023. 240 p.
ISBN 9781587435775
Grades: Adult   277.308
1. Ward, Jon (Writer of politics) 2. Christian men 3. Growing up 4. Children of clergy 5. Evangelicalism 6. Christian conservatism 7. Religion and politics 8. Alienation 9. Disillusionment 10. Family relationships 11. Church and the world 12. North American people 13. American people 14. Autobiographies and memoirs 15. Life stories — Arts and culture — Writing — Journalists 16. Life stories — Religion and spirituality — Leaving religion 17. Spirituality and Religion — Christianity — Political Aspects
LC 2022034464
A journalist recounts his upbringing and eventual break from an influential evangelical church to diagnose broader political and cultural issues.
"This will resonate especially with Christians wondering about faith's place in modern American society." —*Publishers Weekly*
Includes bibliographical references.

280 Denominations and sects of Christian church

Ryrie, Alec
Protestants: The Faith That Made the Modern World. Alec Ryrie. Viking Press 2017. 464 pages
ISBN 9780670026166
Grades: Adult   280
1. Protestantism 2. Reformation 3. Fundamentalism 4. Christianity 5. Spirituality and Religion — Christianity — History
LC 2016056692
Five hundred years ago an obscure monk challenged the authority of the pope with a radical vision of what Christianity could be. The revolution he set in motion inspired one of the most creative and destructive movements in human

history. In this global history that charts five centuries of innovation and change, Alec Ryrie makes the case that Protestants made the modern world.

"Rarely has an author of such deep faith offered such a tolerant, engaging history of any religion." —*Kirkus*

281.9 Orthodox churches

Mathewes-Green, Frederica
Welcome to the Orthodox Church: An Introduction to Eastern Christianity. Frederica Mathewes-Green. Paraclete Press 2015. xviii, 361 pages
ISBN 9781557259219
Grades: Adult   281.9
1. Spirituality and Religion — Christianity
LC 2014041905

There are other introductory books about Orthodoxy, but they are all somewhat academic. This one comprehensively covers the history, theology, and practice without talking over your head. Mathewes-Green takes the original approach of bringing you into a typical church for a series of visits. That is how Christians learned the faith for most of history, by coming into a community and keeping their eyes and ears open. Designed primarily for newcomers to come to understand Orthodoxy and Orthodox Christians, this guide to the faith is also a non-threatening and accessible introduction to people already "in the pews."

Includes bibliographical references and index.

281.909 Orthodox churches — History, geographic treatment, biography
---

McGuckin, John Anthony
★ *The Eastern Orthodox Church: A New History.* John Anthony McGuckin. Yale University Press 2020. 352 p.
ISBN 9780300218763
Grades: Adult   281.909
1. Christian sects 2. Faith (Christianity) 3. Theology 4. Spirituality and Religion — Christianity — History
LC 2019948578

In this short, accessible account of the Eastern Orthodox Church, John McGuckin begins by tackling the question "What is the Church?" His answer is a clear, historically and theologically rooted portrait of what the Church is for Orthodox Christianity and how it differs from Western Christians' expectations.

"McGuckin presents another well-written and well-researched work in this fantastic introduction to the Eastern Orthodox Church." —*Library Journal*

Includes bibliographical references and index.

282.09 Roman Catholic Church — History, geographic treatment, biography
---

Francis
Walking with Jesus: A Way Forward for the Church. Pope Francis. Loyola Press 2015. 160 p.
ISBN 9780829442489
Grades: Adult   282.09
1. Jesus Christ 2. Christian doctrines 3. Sacraments 4. Catholics 5. Spirituality and Religion — Christianity — Catholicism
LC Bl2015028437

Two thousand years ago Jesus said, "follow me." What if the twenty-first-century church actually heeded that call? What would the world look like if the church were truly on the move? Simply put, very different. But these ponderings beg one more critical question: What exactly should the church be moving toward? In Walking with Jesus: A Way Forward for the Church, with a foreword by Archbishop of Chicago, Blase J. Cupich, Pope Francis' first major appointment in the United States, Walking with Jesus offers the church a much-needed way forward, past its inner and outer walls, as it fearlessly follows Christ toward the future.

"Perhaps no one has as much potential to buoy the human spirit through his words as Francis, whose life and public speeches are closely watched by so many. The book's foreword is by Archbishop Blase J. Cupich of Chicago, the pope's first major U.S. appointment." —*Publishers Weekly*

McGreevy, John T.
★ *Catholicism: A Global History from the French Revolution to Pope Francis.* John T. McGreevy. W.W. Norton & Company 2022. 512 p.
ISBN 9781324003885
Grades: Adult   282.09
1. Catholic theology 2. Papacy 3. Catholic Church renewal 4. Tradition (Philosophy) 5. Social change 6. Scandals 7. Multiculturalism 8. Spirituality and Religion — Christianity — Catholicism 9. Spirituality and Religion — Christianity — History

The story of Roman Catholicism has never followed a singular path. In no time period has this been more true than over the last two centuries. Beginning with the French Revolution, extending to the Second Vatican Council in the 1960s, and concluding with present-day crises, John T. McGreevy chronicles the dramatic upheavals and internal divisions shaping the most multicultural, multilingual, and global institution in the world.

"Throughout the text, McGreevy provides a wealth of detail about the church and the changing world to which it has been reacting for the past 200 years. A must-read for practicing Catholics and anyone interested in religious studies." —*Kirkus*

Wills, Garry
The Future of the Catholic Church with Pope Francis. Garry Wills. Viking 2015. xxi, 263 pages
ISBN 9780525426967
Grades: Adult   282.09
1. Francis, Pope, 1936- 2. Popes 3. Church history 4. Christian doctrines 5. Change 6. Social change 7. Religion and politics 8. Church and state 9. Antisemitism in the Catholic Church 10. Ordination of women 11. Birth control 12. Sexism 13. Spirituality and Religion — Christianity — Catholicism 14. Spirituality and Religion — Christianity — Political Aspects

The Pulitzer Prize-winning historian considers Pope Francis's potential for enabling change in the Catholic Church, analyzing seven key examples of profound change within the past century that have not been advanced by the papacy.

"Highly recommended for all interested in a fact-based study of the church's evolution." —*Library Journal*

Includes index.

282.092 Roman Catholics — Biography

Eisner, Peter
The Pope's Last Crusade: How an American Jesuit Helped Pope Pius XI's Campaign to Stop Hitler. Peter Eisner. William Morrow 2013. 292 p. : Illustration; Map
ISBN 9780062049148
Grades: Adult   282.092
1. Pius XI, Pope, 1857-1939 2. Hitler, Adolf, 1889-1945 3. Nazism 4. Catholic Church and Nazism 5. Popes 6. Ideology 7. Religion and politics 8. World War II 9. Third Reich, 1933-1945 10. Politics and government 11. Germany 12. 20th century 13. History writing — Wars and conflicts — World War II 14. Spirituality and Religion — Christianity — Catholicism 15. History writing — Europe — Germany

In 1939, American Jesuit priest, John LaFarge, worked with Pope Pius XI on a an encyclical (a formally stated Vatican policy) that condemned anti-Semitism in general and Nazi oppression in particular. Sadly, Pius XI died before its completion, and his successor (Pope Pius XII) saw Communism as more dangerous than Nazism and took a course that tended toward anti-Semitism. The Pope's Last Crusade reveals LaFarge's draft encyclical and explores the forces that pre-

ESSENTIAL AND RECOMMENDED TITLES
284.1 Lutheran churches

vented its release—begging the poignant question: How might this have changed history, had it been released?

Also published in large print format; Includes bibliographical references (p. [245]-277) and index.

Francis
Let Us Dream: The Path to a Better Future. Pope Francis. Simon & Schuster 2020. 160 p.
ISBN 9781982171865
Grades: Adult — 282.092
1. Francis, Pope, 1936- 2. Christianity and justice 3. Christian life 4. Inequality 5. COVID-19 (Disease) 6. Life change events 7. Social problems 8. Social justice 9. Spirituality and Religion — Christianity — Catholicism 10. Spirituality and Religion — Christianity — Political Aspects 11. Life stories — Religion and spirituality — Religious and spiritual leaders

A spiritual leader explains why we must—and how we can—make the world safer, fairer, and healthier for all people now.

"Informed by spiritual sources and the thinking of some of the world's foremost scientists, economists, and activists, Pope Francis offers tools for creating a better, more just world." —*Library Journal*

Kertzer, David I.
The Pope Who Would Be King: The Exile of Pius IX and the Emergence of Modern Europe. David I. Kertzer. Random House 2018. 304 p.
ISBN 9780812989915
Grades: Adult — 282.092
1. Pius IX, Pope, 1792-1878 2. Popes 3. Church history 4. Power 5. Exiles 6. Papacy 7. Politics and government 8. Europe 9. 19th century 10. History writing — Europe 11. Spirituality and Religion — Christianity — Political Aspects
LC 2017038825

The Pulitzer Prize-winning author documents the lesser-known story of the violent revolution that established the end of the papacy as a political power and signaled the birth of modern Europe.

"A consummate storyteller, Kertzer blends academic rigor with fluid, energetic prose, and the result will satisfy specialists while entertaining those who might otherwise expect to be bored stiff by a volume of church history." —*Publishers Weekly*

Includes bibliographical references and index.

Nouwen, Henri J. M.
Love, Henri: Letters on the Spiritual Life. Henri J.M. Nouwen; edited and with a preface by Gabrielle Earnshaw; foreword by Brene Brown. Convergent 2016. xxiv, 351 pages
ISBN 9781101906354
Grades: Adult — 282.092
1. Nouwen, Henri J. M. 2. Spirituality and Religion — Christian living 3. Spirituality and Religion — Christianity
LC 2016034448

Presents over one hundred letters throughout Nouwen's career, highlighting such themes in his work and life as vocation, solitude, prayer, suffering, and perseverance in difficult times.

Includes bibliographical references.

Politi, Marco
Pope Francis Among the Wolves: The Inside Story of a Revolution. Marco Politi, translated by William McCuaig. Columbia University Press 2015. 288 p.
ISBN 9780231174145
Grades: Adult — 282.092
1. Francis, Pope, 1936- 2. Popes 3. Biographies 4. Translations — Italian to English 5. Life stories — Religion and spirituality — Religious and spiritual leaders 6. Spirituality and religion — Christianity — Catholicism
LC 2014046193

Marco Politi takes us deep inside the power struggle roiling the Roman Curia and the Catholic Church worldwide, beginning with Benedict XVI, the pope who famously resigned in 2013, and intensifying with the contested and unexpected election of Jorge Mario Bergoglio, archbishop of Buenos Aires, now known as Pope Francis. Politi's account balances the perspectives of Pope Francis's supporters, Benedict's sympathizers, and those disappointed members of the Catholic laity who feel alienated by the institution's secrecy, financial corruption, and refusal to modernize.

"This book is well translated and accessible to a wide audience of Francis's admirers and opponents, both inside and outside of the Catholic Church." —*Library Journal*

Originally published in Italian as Francesco tra i lupi, 2014.

284.1 Lutheran churches

Bolz-Weber, Nadia
Accidental Saints: Finding God in All the Wrong People. Nadia Bolz-Weber. Convergent Books 2015. 224 p.
ISBN 9781601427557
Grades: Adult — 284.1
1. Bolz-Weber, Nadia 2. Lutheran Church 3. Toleration 4. God (Christianity) 5. Faith (Christianity) 6. Grace (Christian theology) 7. Christian life 8. Christian values 9. Christian doctrines 10. Autobiographies and memoirs 11. Life stories — Religion and spirituality — Personal faith 12. Spirituality and Religion — Christianity
LC 2015012506

A standup comic-turned-pastor describes her experiences with "accidental saints"—individuals with whom she has found the meaning of grace—including a drag queen, a felonious bishop, and a gun-toting member of the NRA.

"Recommended for readers who enjoyed Bolz-Weber's previous books or authors such as Anne Lamott and Brian McClaren. An entertaining, reality-based alternative to the polished professional Christian memoir." —*Library Journal*

289 Other denominations and sects

Stein, Stephen J.
The Shaker Experience in America: A History of the United Society of Believers. Stephen J. Stein. Yale University Press 1992. xx, 554 p. : Illustration; Map
ISBN 9780300051391
Grades: Adult — 289
1. Spirituality and Religion — Christianity
LC 91030836

Draws on oral and written testimony to trace the history and evolution of the Shakers, set within the broader context of American life.

Includes bibliographical references (p. [521]-523) and index.

289.3 Latter-Day Saints (Mormons)

Brown, Samuel Morris
In Heaven as It Is on Earth: Joseph Smith and the Early Mormon Conquest of Death. Samuel Morris Brown. Oxford University Press 2011. 400 p.
ISBN 9780199793570
Grades: Adult — 289.3
1. Smith, Joseph, 1805-1844 2. Death 3. Mormon theology 4. Theology 5. Spirituality and Religion — Christianity — Mormonism
LC 2011002848

Discusses the foundational beliefs of the Mormon Church by focusing on early Mormon conceptions of death.

Includes bibliographical references and index.

Bushman, Richard L.
Mormonism: A Very Short Introduction. Richard Lyman Bushman. Oxford University Press 2008. 144 p.
ISBN 9780195310306
Grades: 11 12 Adult — 289.3

1. Mormon theology 2. Spirituality and Religion — Christianity — Mormonism

LC 2007044444

Looks at the history and teachings of the Church of Jesus Christ of Latter-day Saints.

Includes bibliographical references and index.

Gutjahr, Paul C.
The Book of Mormon: A Biography. Paul C. Gutjahr. Princeton University Press 2012. xix, 255 pages : Illustration; Map
ISBN 9780691144801
Grades: Adult 289.3
1. Smith, Joseph, 1805-1844 2. Mormons 3. Spirituality and Religion — Christianity — Mormonism

LC 2011044063

Shows how Joseph Smith, Jr.'s influential Book of Mormon launched one of the fastest growing new religions on the planet.

Includes bibliographical references (pages 209-246) and index.

Hardy, Grant
Understanding the Book of Mormon: A Reader's Guide. Grant Hardy. Oxford University Press 2010. xxi, 346 p.
ISBN 9780199731701
Grades: Adult 289.3
1. Spirituality and Religion — Christianity — Mormonism

LC 2009026675

Examines the Book of Mormon not as scripture or fraud, but as a highly influential work of literature, with an emphasis on the distinctive voices of its three main narrators, Nephi, Mormon, and Moroni.

Includes bibliographical references (p. [275]-327) and indexes.

Park, Benjamin E.
American Zion: A New History of Mormonism. Benjamin E. Park. Liveright Publishing Corporation, a division of W.W. Norton & Company 2024. 480 p.
ISBN 9781631498657
Grades: Adult 289.3
1. Mormons 2. Mormon theology 3. Christianity 4. United States 5. Spirituality and Religion — Christianity — Mormonism 6. History Writing — United States

The first major history of Mormonism in a decade, drawing on newly available sources to reveal a profoundly divided faith that has nevertheless shaped the nation.

"A welcome updating of earlier studies, and a readable, engaging work of religious history." —*Kirkus*

289.5 Church of Christ, Scientist (Christian Science)

Eddy, Mary Baker
★ *Mary Baker Eddy: Speaking for Herself.* by Mary Baker Eddy. Writings of Mary Baker Eddy 2002. xlv, 183 p. : Illustration
ISBN 9780879522759
Grades: Adult 289.5
1. Eddy, Mary Baker, 1821-1910 2. Christian Scientists 3. Faith healing 4. Autobiographies and memoirs 5. Spirituality and Religion — Christianity 6. Life stories — Religion and spirituality

LC 2002111766

"Provide[s] a fresh glimpse of the founder of Christian Science." —*Publishers Weekly*

Includes bibliographical references (p. 147-165) and index.

289.6 Society of Friends (Quakers)

Hamm, Thomas D.
★ *The Quakers in America.* Thomas D. Hamm. Columbia University Press 2003. VIII, 293 p. : Illustration; Map
ISBN 9780231123624
Grades: Adult 289.6
1. Quakers 2. Spirituality and Religion — Christianity

LC 2002041422

In tracing the history of Quakerism in the US, Hamm (history, Earlham College), an archivist for the Friends Collection, discusses the movement's roots, George Fox's early role, growth, persecution, diversity, worldviews, beyond-their-numbers influence, and current debates on such issues as homosexuality. He includes biographical sketches of 15 notable historical and contemporary Quakers, plus a movement chronology. Illustrations feature key Friends, meetings houses, and antiwar protests.

"The author provides an introduction to Quaker origins abroad, their influences on American politics and culture, as well as their beliefs and traditions as they are played out on American soil. Though this is a serious history with a glossary, chronology, and 40 pages of notes, cartoons and anecdotes leaven the text. For both public and academic libraries." —*Library Journal*

Includes bibliographical references and index.

289.7 Mennonite churches

Kraybill, Donald B.
Concise Encyclopedia of Amish, Brethren, Hutterites, and Mennonites. Donald B. Kraybill. Johns Hopkins University Press 2010. xvii, 302 p. : Illustration; Map
ISBN 9780801896576
Grades: Adult 289.7
1. Anabaptists 2. Reference — Encyclopedias 3. Spirituality and Religion — Christianity

LC 2009046015

Donald B. Kraybill has spent his career among Anabaptist groups, gaining an unparalleled understanding of these traditionally private people. Kraybill shares that deep knowledge in this succinct overview of the beliefs and cultural practices of Amish, Brethren, Hutterites, and Mennonites in North America. Found throughout Canada, Central America, Mexico, and the United States, these religious communities include more than 200 different groups with 800,000 members in 17 countries. Through 340 short entries, Kraybill offers readers information on a wide range of topics related to religious views and social practices. With thoughtful consideration of how the diverse communities are related, this compact reference provides a brief and accurate synopsis of these groups in the twenty-first century. No other single volume provides such a broad overview of Amish, Brethren, Huterites, and Mennonites in North America. Organized for ease of searching—with a list of entries, a topic finder, an index of names, and ample cross-references—the volume also includes abundant resources for accessing additional information. Wide in scope, succinct in content, with directional markers along the way, The Concise Encyclopedia of Amish, Brethren, Hutterites, and Mennonites is a must-have reference for anyone interested in Anabaptist groups.

Includes bibliographical references (p. 259-285) and indexes.

★ *On the Backroad to Heaven: Old Order Hutterites, Mennonites, Amish, and Brethren.* Donald B. Kraybill, Carl F. Bowman. Johns Hopkins University Press 2001. xvi, 330 p. : Illustration; Map
ISBN 9780801865657
Grades: Adult 289.7
1. Old Order Mennonites 2. Amish 3. Plain People 4. Spirituality and Religion — Christianity

LC 00010406

Kraybill (sociology and Anabaptist studies, Messiah College) and Bowman (sociology, Bridgewater College) describe Old Order Anabaptist culture and the contemporary communities that continue variations of that tradition. They discuss the beliefs and practices of Hutterites, Mennonites, the Amish, and the

ESSENTIAL AND RECOMMENDED TITLES
289.9 Denominations and sects not provided for elsewhere

Brethren. Each group's strategy for preserving its own unique identity is examined and the commonalties and differences between the groups are described. The lessons of Anabaptist culture for modern America are also discussed.

"The authors give the general reader an excellent basic understanding of the beliefs and practices shared by all of these separatists while making the uniqueness of each group clear. One of the best single-volume works on this subject; highly recommended for academic and public libraries." —*Library Journal*

Includes bibliographical references (p. [309]-322) and index.

Mackall, Joe
Plain Secrets: An Outsider Among the Amish. Joe Mackall. Beacon Press 2007. xxxiv, 208 p.
ISBN 9780807010648
Grades: Adult **289.7**
1. Amish 2. Rumspringa 3. Religions 4. Ohio 5. Spirituality and Religion — Christianity
LC Oc2007129864

The author describes his relationship with a neighboring Swartzentruber Amish family, the Shetlers, over sixteen years, using the example of the Shetlers to look at the lives and customs of the Swartzentruber Amish in general.

"This is a loving portrait, warts and all, of an often-misunderstood people." —*Booklist*

Includes bibliographical references (p. 205-208).

289.9 Denominations and sects not provided for elsewhere

Guinn, Jeff
The Road to Jonestown: Jim Jones and Peoples Temple. Jeff Guinn. Simon & Schuster 2017. 416 p.
ISBN 9781476763828
Grades: Adult **289.9**
1. Jones, Jim, 1931-1978 2. Jonestown Mass Suicide, Jonestown, Guyana, 1978 3. Cults 4. Suicide 5. Murder 6. Scandals 7. Poisoning 8. Socialists 9. 1970s 10. Biographies 11. True crime — Murder 12. Life stories — Religion and spirituality — Religious and spiritual leaders
LC 2016051471

A portrait of the influential cult leader behind the Jonestown Massacre examines his personal life, from his extramarital affairs and drug use to his fraudulent faith healing practices and his decision to move his followers to Guyana, sharing astonishing new details about the events leading to the 1978 tragedy.

"A vivid, fascinating revisitation of a time and series of episodes fast receding into history even as their forgotten survivors still walk among us." —*Kirkus*

292 Classical religion (Greek and Roman religion)

Hughes, Bettany
Venus and Aphrodite: A Biography of Desire. Bettany Hughes. Basic Books 2020. 224 p.
ISBN 9781541674233
Grades: Adult **292**
1. Aphrodite (Greek deity) 2. Venus (Roman deity) 3. Gods and goddesses 4. Women warriors 5. Symbolism 6. Sexuality 7. Fertility 8. Violence 9. Power 10. Art and mythology 11. Mythology in literature 12. Characters and characteristics in mythology 13. History writing — Ancient 14. History writing — Women's history 15. History writing — Arts and culture
LC 2020013390

Aphrodite was said to have been born from the sea, rising out of a froth of white foam. But long before the Ancient Greeks conceived of this voluptuous blonde, she existed as an early spirit of fertility on the shores of Cyprus—and thousands of years before that, as a ferocious warrior-goddess in the Middle East. Proving that this fabled figure is so much more than an avatar of commercialized romance, historian Bettany Hughes reveals the remarkable lifestory of one of antiquity's most potent myths.

"British historian Hughes (Istanbul: A Tale of Three Cities) presents a brisk and incisive cultural history of the mythological goddess of sexual love." —*Publishers Weekly*

Includes bibliographical references and index.

292.1 Specific elements

Hamilton, Edith
★ *Mythology: Timeless Tales of Gods and Heroes.* Edith Hamilton; illustrated by Jim Tierney. Black Dog & Leventhal Publishers 2017. 371 pages : Illustration; Color
ISBN 9780316438520
Grades: Adult **292.1**
1. Gods and goddesses 2. Heroes and heroines in mythology 3. Mythology, folklore, and legends
LC Bl2017036579

A collection of Greek and Roman myths arranged in sections on the gods and early heroes, love and adventure stories, the Trojan War, and a brief section on Norse mythology.

Includes index.

293 Germanic religion

Larrington, Carolyne
The Norse Myths: A Guide to the Gods and Heroes. Carolyne Larrington. Thames & Hudson 2017. 208 pages
ISBN 9780500251966
Grades: Adult **293**
1. Mythology, Norse 2. Gods and goddesses, Norse 3. Characters and characteristics in mythology 4. Odin (Norse deity) 5. Loki (Norse deity) 6. Thor (Norse deity) 7. Mythical creatures 8. Scandinavia 9. Northern Europe 10. History writing — Medieval — Europe 11. Mythology, folklore, and legends
LC 2016941839

Introduces the gods and goddesses of the Norse tradition and describes the cosmos they inhabit, their escapades, and their cultural legacy.

Includes bibliographical references and index.

294 Religions of Indic origin

Dalrymple, William
Nine Lives: In Search of the Sacred in Modern India. William Dalrymple. Alfred A. Knopf 2010. xvii, 275 p. : Illustration; Map
ISBN 9780307272829
Grades: Adult **294**
1. Religious life 2. Social life and customs 3. India 4. Spirituality and Religion — General

A study of the ways in which traditional forms of religious life in India have been transformed in the vortex of the region's rapid change.

"Throughout the book, Dalrymple showcases his knowledge of the breadth of India and his fearless willingness to penetrate its sometimes unsavory nooks and crannies, rendering this a truly heartfelt work for readers craving a deeper connection to India and its rich spiritual heritage. A remarkable feat of journalism." —*Kirkus*

Includes bibliographical references (p. [263]-267) and index; First published: London : Bloomsbury, 2009.

294.3 Buddhism

Chodron, Pema
How We Live Is How We Die. Pema Chodron; edited by Joseph Waxman. Shambhala Publications, Inc. 2022. 224 p.
ISBN 9781611809244

PUBLIC LIBRARY CORE COLLECTION: NONFICTION
Twentieth Edition

Grades: Adult   **294.3**
1. Change (Psychology) 2. Buddhism 3. Spirituality and Religion — Buddhism

LC 2022003735

Discover newfound freedom in life's ever-constant flow of endings and beginnings with the wise words of Pema Chodron, beloved Buddhist nun and best-selling author of When Things Fall Apart.

"Chodron's straightforward prose grounds the thoughtful examination of what the bardo can teach readers about meeting suffering with kindness and compassion. This wise volume shines." —*Publishers Weekly*

Includes index.

Practicing Peace. Pema Chodron; based on talks edited by Sandy Boucher. Shambhala 2018. x, 88 pages
ISBN 9781611806137

Grades: Adult   **294.3**
1. Dharma (Buddhism) 2. Peace of mind 3. Peace 4. Spiritual life 5. Buddhism 6. Spirituality and Religion — Body, mind, and spirit — Meditation and mindfulness 7. Self-Help — Personal growth — Meditation 8. Spirituality and Religion — Buddhism

LC Bl2018180023

Draws on Buddhist teachings to explore the origins of anger, aggression, hatred, and war, and offers practical techniques that are used to find genuine, lasting peace.

"Chodron teaches readers how to pause and let experiences pierce the heart so that the sparks of aggression may burn themselves out, leaving a positive sense of groundlessness and insecurity. These are familiar teachings to those acquainted with her work, but her approach remains invaluable for guidance on working with hatred and anger." —*Publishers Weekly*

Connelly, Ben

Inside Vasubandhu's Yogacara: A Practitioner's Guide. Ben Connelly; with a new translation from Sanskrit by Ben Connelly and Weijen Teng; foreword by Norman Fischer. Wisdom Publications 2016. xi, 231 pages
ISBN 9781614292845

Grades: Adult   **294.3**
1. Vasubandhu 2. Spirituality and Religion — Buddhism 3. Spirituality and Religion — Body, mind, and spirit

LC 2016008752

Ben Connelly guides us through the intricacies of Yogacara and the richness of the "Thirty Verses," dedicating a chapter of the book to each line of the poem. His warm and wise voice unpacks and contextualizes its wisdom, showing us how we can apply its ancient insights to our own modern lives, to create a life of engaged peace, harmony, compassion, and joy. In fourth-century India one of the great geniuses of Buddhism, Vasubandhu, sought to reconcile the diverse ideas and forms of Buddhism practiced at the time and demonstrate how they could be effectively integrated into a single system. This was the Yogacara movement, and it continues to have great influence in modern Tibetan and Zen Buddhism. This is a great introduction to a philosophy, a master, and a work whose influence reverberates throughout modern Buddhism.

"Newcomers and adherents to this lesser-known Buddhist school alike are lucky to have Connelly as an exceptional guide to the central themes of Yogacara." —*Publishers Weekly*

Includes bibliographical references (pages [205]-206) and index.

Dalai Lama

Approaching the Buddhist Path. the Dalai Lama and Thubten Chodron. Wisdom Publications 2017. 384 pages
ISBN 9781614294412

Grades: Adult   **294.3**
1. Gautama Buddha 2. Buddhism 3. Spiritual life 4. Enlightenment (Buddhism) 5. Spiritual growth 6. Dharma (Buddhism) 7. Spirituality and Religion — Buddhism

LC 2016053409

The Dalai Lama has been publicly teaching Buddhism for decades. This series collects his presentations of every step of the path to enlightenment.

"An excellent and intellectually stimulating introduction to the Buddhist way of life." —*Publishers Weekly*

Includes bibliographical references and index.

The Book of Joy: Lasting Happiness in a Changing World. His Holiness the Dalai Lama and Archbishop Desmond Tutu, with Douglas Abrams. Avery 2016. 288 p.
ISBN 9780399185045

Grades: Adult   **294.3**
1. Happiness 2. Spiritual life 3. Spiritual growth 4. Hope 5. Spirituality 6. Spirituality and Religion — General

LC 2016026669

Two leading spiritual masters share their hard-won wisdom about living with joy even in the face of adversity, sharing personal stories and teachings about the science of profound happiness and the daily practices that anchor their emotional and spiritual lives.

How to Be Compassionate: A Handbook for Creating Inner Peace and a Happier World. Dalai Lama XIV, translated and edited by Jeffrey Hopkins. Atria Books 2011. 224 p.
ISBN 9781451623901

Grades: Adult   **294.3**
1. Compassion 2. Happiness 3. Transformations, Personal 4. Spirituality 5. Peace 6. Buddhism 7. Spirituality and Religion — Buddhism

LC Bl2011001885

Through practical exercises and personal anecdotes, a revered spiritual leader shows how individuals' compassion can lead to global changes.

"Light on politics and even lighter on the more abstruse points of Tibetan Buddhism, this is a fine and accessible book for the everyday reader." —*Library Journal*

Includes bibliographical references (p. [145]-147).

The Second Dalai Lama: His Life and Teachings. Translated, edited, introduced, and annotated by Glenn H. Mullin. Snow Lion Publications 2005. xvii, 270 p.
ISBN 9781559392334

Grades: 9 10 11 12   **294.3**
1. Dalai Lama II, 1476-1542 2. Dge-lugs-pa doctrines 3. Buddhism 4. Dalai lamas 5. Religions 6. Spirituality and Religion — Buddhism

LC 2005281580

Illuminating one of the great Lamas in the Tibetan Buddhist tradition, the author offers a rare look at the life and work of teachers who influenced the current Dalai Lama.

Includes bibliographical references (p. 253-265); Previously published under the title: Mystical verses of a mad Dalai Lama. Wheaton, Ill. : Theosophical Pub. House, 1994.

Emet, Joseph

Finding the Blue Sky: A Mindful Approach to Choosing Happiness Here and Now. Joseph Emet. TarcherPerigee,, LLC 2016. xiii, 193 pages
ISBN 9780143109631

Grades: Adult   **294.3**
1. Happiness 2. Spiritual life 3. Buddhism 4. Spirituality and Religion — Body, mind, and spirit — Meditation and mindfulness 5. Self-Help — Personal growth — Happiness 6. Spirituality and Religion — Buddhism

LC 2016022074

Examines the principles of Buddhism and discusses how they correlate with the latest research into happiness outlined in positive psychology.

Includes bibliographical references.

Epstein, Mark

Advice Not Given: A Guide to Getting Over Yourself. Mark Epstein, MD.. Penguin Press 2018. 224 p.
ISBN 9780399564338

Grades: Adult   **294.3**
1. Buddhism 2. Psychotherapy 3. Psychology 4. Egotism 5. Buddhist doctrines 6. Autobiographies and memoirs 7. Science writing — Medicine and health — Psychology 8. Spirituality and Religion — Buddhism

ESSENTIAL AND RECOMMENDED TITLES
294.3 Buddhism

LC 2017037517

The Harvard-trained psychologist and author of the Trauma of Everyday Life explores how the traditions of Buddhism and Western psychotherapy can complement each other to promote a healthier ego and maximize the human potential for living a better life.

"Epsteins book of practical suggestions will leave readers educated, inspired, and equipped with new tools for psychological health." —*Publishers Weekly*

Includes bibliographical references and index.

The Zen of Therapy: Uncovering a Hidden Kindness in Life. Mark Epstein. Penguin Press 2022. 288 p.

ISBN 9780593296615

Grades: Adult   294.3

1. Epstein, Mark, 1953- 2. Psychotherapists 3. Psychotherapy 4. Buddhism 5. Meditation 6. Buddhists 7. Self-awareness 8. Psychotherapy patients 9. Psychotherapist and patient 10. Spirituality 11. Life stories — Science, technology, and medicine — Healthcare professionals 12. Spirituality and Religion — Buddhism 13. Society and culture — Psychology and human behavior 14. Science Writing — Medicine and health

A remarkable exploration of the therapeutic relationship, Dr. Mark Epstein reflects on one year's worth of therapy sessions with his patients to observe how his training in Western psychotherapy and his equally long investigation into Buddhism, in tandem, led to greater awareness—for his patients, and for himself.

"Meditation has become increasingly popular in self-help in recent years; Epstein's book is recommended for anyone interested in exploring the potential benefits of a meditation practice." —*Library Journal*

Gunaratana, Henepola

Start Here, Start Now: A Short Guide to Mindfulness Meditation. Bhante Gunaratana. Wisdom Publications 2019. VI, 155 pages

ISBN 9781614296270

Grades: Adult   294.3

1. Meditation 2. Buddhism 3. Buddhist meditation 4. Spirituality and Religion — Body, mind, and spirit — Meditation and mindfulness 5. Spirituality and Religion — Buddhism

LC 2019014015

"Gunaratana (Mindfulness in Plain English) offers a straightforward and informative introduction to mindfulness meditation, walking a fine line between familiar secularized instructions and careful guidance through difficult experiences that may challenge one's worldview." —*Publishers Weekly*

Han, Chenxing

Be the Refuge: Raising the Voices of Asian American Buddhists. Chenxing Han. North Atlantic Books 2021. 256 p.

ISBN 9781623175238

Grades: Adult   294.3

1. Han, Chenxing, 1986- 2. Buddhism 3. Buddhists 4. Asian Americans 5. Race (Social Sciences) 6. Representation (Philosophy) 7. Racism 8. Identity 9. United States 10. Interviews 11. Society and culture — Race 12. Spirituality and Religion — Buddhism 13. Life stories — Religion and spirituality

Championing nuanced representation over stale stereotypes, Han and the 89 interviewees in Be the Refuge push back against false narratives like the Oriental monk, the superstitious immigrant, and the banana Buddhist—typecasting that collapses the multivocality of Asian American Buddhists into tired, essentialized tropes. Encouraging frank conversations about race, representation, and inclusivity among Buddhists of all backgrounds, Be the Refuge embodies the spirit of interconnection that glows at the heart of American Buddhism.

"Han's contribution to this overlooked aspect of the Asian American experience is an important one as it gives a voice to many invisible people in American society." —*Library Journal*

Keown, Damien

★ *A Dictionary of Buddhism.* Damien Keown; contributors, Stephen Hodge, Charles Jones, Paoli Tinti. Oxford University Press 2003. VIII, 357 p. : Illustration; Map

ISBN 9780198605607

Grades: Adult   294.3

1. Buddhism 2. Reference — Dictionaries 3. Spirituality and Religion — Buddhism

LC 2003276701

A wide-ranging, comprehensive, and accessible guide to Buddhism includes more than two thousand entries covering the history, beliefs, and practices of Buddhists worldwide.

"The entries are short...but such accessibility is the very reason why this should be on the bookshelf of every student of Buddhism." —*Publishers Weekly*

Kerouac, Jack

★ *Some of the Dharma.* Jack Kerouac. Penguin Books 1999. 419 p.

ISBN 9780140287073

Grades: Adult   294.3

1. Buddhism 2. Arts and Entertainment — Writing and Publishing

LC BL 00001221

Jack Kerouac's earliest foray into Buddhism is captured in a volume that includes poems, haiku, prayers, journal entries, meditations, letter fragments, ideas, and much more, all assembled in the visually daring format Kerouac originally envisioned.

Offers a collage of poems, haiku, journal entries, letters, meditations, ideas on writing, notes on Buddhism, prayers, blues, and sketches.

"Begun in December 1951 as a notebook for his Buddhist studies, this work records Kerouac's reactions to a variety of Buddhist texts. Over the course of five years, it grew to include poems, prayers, dialogs, meditations, and notes on his reading, as well as commentary on family, friends, and meaningful concerns in his life. Long anticipated by Kerouac scholars, this major work belongs in all literature collections." —*Library Journal*

Originally published: New York : Viking, 1997.

Kongtrul, Dzigar

Peaceful Heart: The Buddhist Practice of Patience. Dzigar Kongtrul; edited by Joseph Waxman; foreword by Pema Chödrön. Shambhala 2020. x, 219 pages

ISBN 9781611804645

Grades: Adult   294.3

1. Santideva, active 7th century 2. Patience 3. Buddhist doctrines 4. Spirituality and Religion — Buddhism 5. Spirituality and Religion — Body, mind, and spirit

LC 2020017030

An introductory guide to cultivating patience and opening your heart to difficult circumstances from leading Buddhist teacher, Dzigar Kongtrul Rinpoche. Patience is one of the most important qualities we can develop, as it represents our mind's ability to work positively with anything that bothers us, including anger, loss, jealousy, and helplessness. We are consistently confronted with situations or outcomes we weren't expecting or didn't want, and our default response is to reject what happened with feelings of mild irritation, inward complaining, self-aggression, or seething resentment. Patience is an antidote to all these forms of rejection. Those who have mastered patience have learned to welcome all challenging situations, people, and emotions as opportunities to open their hearts rather than close them. Based on the teachings of the sixth chapter of Shantideva's the Way of the Bodhisattva, Peaceful Heart explores how Buddhist teachings on patience can help you work with whatever disturbances arise in your life and in your mind. Dzigar Kongtrul provides practices and examples throughout the book to challenge readers on the path to developing a more patient heart.

"Buddhists will appreciate Kongtrul's ode to Shantideva, but even non-Buddhist readers will enjoy this powerful work's vivid writing and wise instruction." —*Publishers Weekly*

Kornfield, Jack

The Wise Heart: A Guide to the Universal Teachings of Buddhist Psychology. Jack Kornfield. Bantam Books 2008. x, 429 p.

ISBN 9780553803471

Grades: Adult   294.3

1. Buddhism 2. Psychology 3. Science writing — Medicine and health — Alternative medicine 4. Spirituality and Religion — Buddhism 5. Science writing — Medicine and health — Psychology

LC 2008005916

Presents a guide to Buddhist psychology, concepts, and practices, offering techniques for healing, training, and transforming the mind.
Includes bibliographical references (p. [403]-407) and index.

Lahn, Bussho
Singing and Dancing Are the Voice of the Law: A Commentary on Hakuin's. Bussho Lahn; introduction by Tim Burkett. Monkfish Book Publishing Company 2022. 220 p.
ISBN 9781948626781
Grades: Adult 294.3
1. Hakuin, 1686-1769 2. Meditation 3. Zen Buddhism 4. Buddhism 5. Spiritual life 6. 18th century 7. Spirituality and Religion — Buddhism
LC 2022019732

Singing and Dancing Are the Voice of the Law introduces us to one of the great works of Zen literature, the Song of Zazen.
"Engaging and profound, Lahn's insights will be much welcomed by readers looking to deepen their meditation practice....The essence of his teachings will resonate with people of a variety of backgrounds." —*Library Journal*

Masuno, Shunmy
The Art of Simple Living: 100 Daily Practices from a Japanese Zen Monk for a Lifetime of Calm and Joy. Shunmy Masuno; translated by Allison Markin Powell; artwork by Harriet Lee-Merrion. Penguin Books 2019. xvi, 207 pages : Illustration
ISBN 9780143134046
Grades: Adult 294.3
1. Religious life 2. Simplicity 3. Spiritual life 4. Zen Buddhism 5. Spirituality and Religion — Body, mind, and spirit — Meditation and mindfulness 6. Spirituality and Religion — General 7. Self-Help — Personal growth — Happiness
LC 2018051572

Relax and find happiness amid the swirl of the modern world with this internationally best-selling guide to simplifying your life by a Japanese monk who embodies the wisdom of Zen. Illustrations.
A Japanese monk who embodies the wisdom of Zen provides daily lessons to make small changes to one's life in order to open up to a renewed sense of peace and calm.

Nhat Hanh
The Art of Living: Peace and Freedom in the Here and Now. Thich Nhat Hanh. HarperOne 2017. IX; 206 pages
ISBN 9780062434661
Grades: Adult 294.3
1. Nhat Hanh, Thich 1926-2022 2. Spiritual life 3. Meditation 4. Everyday life 5. Awareness 6. Happiness 7. Mindfulness 8. Buddhist meditation 9. Buddhism 10. Spirituality and Religion — Buddhism 11. Life stories — Religion and spirituality — Religious and spiritual leaders
LC 2017013611

Offers a guide to the art of living in mindfulness, consisting of seven meditations intended to help readers live lives that are happy, peaceful, active, and free of fear in the face of death.

Zen and the Art of Saving the Planet. Thich Nhat Hanh; edited and with commentary by Sister True Dedication. HarperOne 2021. 304 p.
ISBN 9780062954794
Grades: Adult 294.3
1. Environmental protection 2. Buddhism 3. Zen Buddhism 4. Social change 5. Climate change 6. Spirituality 7. Spiritual life 8. Spirituality and Religion — Buddhism 9. Society and culture — Philosophy
LC 2021016330

One of the most revered spiritual leaders in the world today, Thich Nhat Hanh's masterful work on how to be the change we want to see in the world.
"General readers will benefit from Nhat Hanh's focus on mindfulness and positive at the individual level. Recommended for anyone wanting a better world for future generations." —*Library Journal*

Nichtern, David
Creativity, Spirituality & Making a Buck. David Nichtern. Wisdom Publications 2019. xviii, 225 p.
ISBN 9781614294986
Grades: Adult 294.3
1. Spiritual life 2. Creation (Literary, artistic, etc.) 3. Success in business 4. Creativity 5. Self-Help — Personal growth — Creativity
LC 2019016594

"In this profound, delightful work, Nichtern (Awakening from the Daydream), a Buddhist teacher and professional guitarist, humorously explores balancing one's spirituality with earning a living." —*Publishers Weekly*

Oliver, Joan Duncan
Buddhism: An Introduction to the Buddha's Life, Teachings, and Practices. Joan Duncan Oliver. St. Martins Essentials 2019. 205 p.
ISBN 9781250313683
Grades: Adult 294.3
1. Gautama Buddha 2. Buddhism 3. Buddhist doctrines 4. Buddhist meditation 5. Spirituality and Religion — Buddhism
LC 2018050710

Buddhism: An Introduction to the Buddha's Life, Teachings, and Practices is an indispensable guide to a 2,600-year-old wisdom tradition that has transformed the lives of millions across centuries and around the world. Readers will learn how Siddhartha Gautama became the Buddha, one of the most influential spiritual leaders of all time, and discover how they too can follow his revolutionary methods to attain happiness and inner freedom.
"She begins her guidance with a biography of the Buddha, followed by a history of the evolution of Buddhism and its teachings after the Buddhas death, bringing her coverage up to the current day to include the presence of cyber-sanghas (communities of followers) using such new methods of delivery of the Dharma (teachings and practices taught by the Buddha) as podcasts and social media." —*Booklist*
Includes bibliographical references and index.

Olson, Carl
Historical Dictionary of Buddhism. Carl Olson. Scarecrow Press 2009. xxix, 327 p, 11 p. of plates : Illustration; Map
ISBN 9780810857711
Grades: Adult 294.3
1. Buddhism 2. Reference — Dictionaries 3. Reference books — Religion 4. Spirituality and Religion — Buddhism
LC 2009007383

The Historical Dictionary of Buddhism covers and clarifies Buddhist concepts, significant figures, movements, schools, places, activities, and periods. This is done through a chronology, an introductory essay, a bibliography, and over 700 cross-referenced dictionary entries.
Rev. ed. of: Historical dictionary of Buddhism / Charles S. Prebish. 1993; Includes bibliographical references (p. 247-326).

Rinzler, Lodro
The Buddha Walks into a Bar: A Guide to Life for a New Generation. Lodro Rinzler. Shambhala 2012. 211 p.
ISBN 9781590309377
Grades: Adult 294.3
1. Spiritual life 2. Buddhism 3. Buddhists 4. Spirituality 5. Spirituality and Religion — Buddhism
LC 2011014498

Presents Buddhism in easy-to-understand terms aimed at people under thirty years old.
"A fine beginning resource for younger adults ready to try the approaches of Buddhism; this is Eastern spirituality for the Harry Potter generation." —*Library Journal*

Love Hurts: Buddhist Advice for the Heartbroken. Lodro Rinzler. Shambhala 2016. xii, 170 pages
ISBN 9781611803549

ESSENTIAL AND RECOMMENDED TITLES
294.3 Buddhism

Grades: Adult   294.3
1. Consolation 2. Suffering 3. Buddhism 4. Family and Relationships — Dating and Marriage 5. Self-Help — Personal growth 6. Spirituality and Religion — Buddhism

LC 2016013202

Shares Buddhist wisdom on how to deal with emotional suffering, and includes practical advice for self-care.

"Rinzler melds his Shambhala training with sharp humor, an eye for detail, and deep empathy in this superb book for any heartbroken reader." —*Publishers Weekly*

Includes bibliographical references (pages 166-170).

Salguero, C. Pierce
★ *Buddhish: A Guide to the 20 Most Important Buddhist Ideas for the Curious and Skeptical.* C. Pierce Salguero. Beacon Press 2022. 192 p.
ISBN 9780807064566

Grades: Adult   294.3
1. Buddhism 2. Spirituality and Religion — Buddhism

LC 2021047964

Finally, a balanced and readable introduction to Buddhism for open minded readers who have no interest in professing faith in a new religion or adopting a new ideology.

"Those new to Buddhism will find this a nuanced and approachable explanation of its essential concepts." —*Publishers Weekly*

Sawaki, Kodo
Discovering the True Self: Kodo Sawaki's Art of Zen Meditation. Translated, edited, and with an introduction by Arthur Braverman. Counterpoint Press 2020. 272 p.
ISBN 9781640093775

Grades: Adult   294.3
1. Sawaki, Kodo, 1880-1965 2. Zen priests 3. Orphans 4. Men 5. Spiritual life 6. Buddhist meditation 7. Self 8. Self-discovery 9. Zen Buddhism 10. Translations — Japanese to English 11. Spirituality and Religion — Buddhism 12. Spirituality and Religion — Body, mind, and spirit — Meditation and mindfulness 13. Life stories — Religion and spirituality — Religious and spiritual leaders

LC 2020000997

Having come of age as an orphan in the slums of Tsu City, Japan, Kodo Sawaki had to fight his way to adulthood, and became one of the most respected Zen masters of the 20th century. He had a great understanding of Dogen Zenji's teaching and he knew how to express Dogen's philosophy in clear, easily-understood language. Sawaki's primary mission was to bring all people to an awareness of the Self, which he believed came through Zen meditation. One of a few collections of Sawaki's teachings published in English, this anthology of his life and work brackets the most intriguing and influential period of modern Zen practice in Japan and America.

"This is an essential resource for those interested in Zen meditation." —*Publishers Weekly*

Siff, Jason
Thoughts Are Not the Enemy: An Innovative Approach to Meditation Practice. Jason Siff. Shambhala 2014. x, 212 pages
ISBN 9781611800432

Grades: Adult   294.3
1. Meditation 2. Buddhism 3. Buddhist meditation 4. Spirituality and Religion — Body, mind, and spirit 5. Spirituality and Religion — Body, mind, and spirit — Meditation and mindfulness

LC 2013046153

A revolutionary new approach to meditation: a mindfulness of thinking that accepts and investigates the thoughts that arise as you meditate—from the author of Unlearning Meditation. In most forms of meditation, the meditator is instructed to let go of thoughts as they arise. As a result, thinking is often taken, unnecessarily, to be something misguided or evil. This approach is misguided, says Jason Siff. In fact, if we allow thoughts to arise and become mindful of the thoughts themselves, we gain tranquillity and insight just as in other methods without having to reject our natural mental processes. And by observing the thoughts themselves with mindfulness and curiosity, we can learn a good deal about ourselves in the process.

"Though Siff emphasizes open and unstructured exploration, some instructions veer toward technical, which may leave inexperienced meditators behind. Meditation scenarios, in which he presents fictionalized accounts of practitioners using different methods, often serve as awkward detours in this otherwise excellent work. Unafraid to go against the grain, Siff teaches readers how to adequately approach conceptual thought, the everyday state of existence, in all of its messiness." —*Publishers Weekly*

Includes bibliographical references and index.

Sogyal
The Tibetan Book of Living and Dying. Sogyal Rinpoche; edited by Patrick Gaffney and Andrew Harvey. Harper San Francisco 1992. xiv, 425 p. : Illustration
ISBN 9780062507938

Grades: Adult   294.3
1. Buddhist doctrines 2. Religious life 3. Death 4. Life after death 5. Buddhism 6. Spirituality and Religion — Buddhism

LC 90056214

A discussion of the age-old techniques on which the classic "Tibetan Book of the Dead" is based examines the possibility for healing that can be released when people begin to view death as another chapter of life.

"The author is well qualified to pass on his tradition. He does this beautifully, in limpid prose free of the scholastic list making that deadens many Tibetan Buddhist primers." —*New York Times Book Review*

Includes bibliographical references (p. 406-408) and index.

Suzuki, Shunryu
Zen Mind, Beginner's Mind. Shunryu Suzuki; edited by Trudy Dixon, with a preface by Huston Smith, an introduction by Richard Baker, and an afterword by David Chadwick. Shambhala 2020. xx, 148 pages
ISBN 9781611808414

Grades: Adult   294.3
1. Meditation 2. Zen Buddhism 3. Spirituality and Religion — Buddhism 4. Spirituality and Religion — Body, mind, and spirit — Meditation and mindfulness

LC 2019051711

A 50th Anniversary edition of the bestselling Zen classic on meditation, maintaining a curious and open mind, and living with simplicity."

Thondup
Enlightened Journey: Buddhist Practice as Daily Life. Tulku Thondup; edited by Harold Talbott. Shambhala; 1995. xix, 268 p.
ISBN 9781570620218

Grades: Adult   294.3
1. Spiritual life 2. Rdzogs-chen 3. Spirituality and Religion — Buddhism

LC 94036154

Collects fifteen articles and talks by a Tibetan Buddhist scholar on the principles of Buddhism, the Buddhist way of life, and Buddhist forms of meditation.

Includes bibliographical references (p. [265]-268).

Thubten Zopa
The Four Noble Truths: A Guide for Everyday Life. Lama Zopa Rinpoche; edited by Yeo Puay Huei. Wisdom 2018. VIII, 293 p.
ISBN 9781614293941

Grades: Adult   294.3
1. Four Noble Truths 2. Spirituality and Religion — Buddhism

LC 2017048508

The Buddha's profound teachings on the four noble truths are illuminated by a Tibetan master simply and directly, so that readers gain an immediate and personal understanding of the causes and conditions that give rise to suffering as well as the spiritual life as the path to liberation.

"Using a mix of personal stories, familiar fables, simple analogies, and a touch of gentle humor, Zopa (How to Enjoy Death), a Tibetan Buddhist scholar, skillfully explains how Buddhism's four noble truths (suffering, the cause of suf-

fering, the cessation of suffering, and the path to end suffering) offer hope for genuine happiness." —*Publishers Weekly*
Includes index.

Van Buren, Mark
A Fool's Guide to Actual Happiness. Mark Van Buren. Wisdom 2018. xiii, 244 p.
ISBN 9781614294481
Grades: Adult   294.3
1. Buddhism 2. Happiness 3. Psychology 4. Self-Help — Personal growth — Happiness 5. Spirituality and Religion — Body, mind, and spirit
LC 2017048415

Presents advice on cultivating empathy, self-acceptance, and wisdom in facing life's challenges and finding inner peace through a practice of mindfulness.

Watts, Alan
The Way of Zen. Alan Watts. Vintage Books 1999. xv, 236 p. : Illustration
ISBN 9780375705106
Grades: 11 12 Adult   294.3
1. Zen Buddhism 2. Spirituality and Religion — General
LC Bl2012026394

Traces the origin of Zen and discusses the Zen way of life against its historical and cultural background.
Includes bibliographical references (p. 203-210) and index; Originally published: New York : Pantheon, 1957.

Wright, Robert
Why Buddhism Is True: The Science and Philosophy of Meditation and Enlightenment. Robert Wright. Simon & Schuster 2017. 336 p.
ISBN 9781439195451
Grades: Adult   294.3
1. Philosophy, Buddhist 2. Personal conduct 3. Buddhism 4. Cognitive neuroscience 5. Society and culture — Psychology and human behavior 6. Society and culture — Philosophy 7. Spirituality and religion — Buddhism
LC 2016041766

The best-selling author of The Evolution of God philosophically explains how the human mind evolved to channel anxiety, depression, anger and greed and how a healthy practice of Buddhist meditation can promote clarity and alleviate suffering.
"Wright's joyful and insightful book is both entertaining and informative, equally accessible to general audiences and more experienced practitioners." —*Publishers Weekly*

294.309 Buddhist fundamentalism, . . .

Sutin, Lawrence
★ *All Is Change: The Two-Thousand-Year Journey of Buddhism to the West.* Lawrence Sutin. Little, Brown and Co. 2006. x, 403 p. : Illustration
ISBN 9780316741569
Grades: Adult   294.309
1. Buddhism 2. Spirituality and Religion — Buddhism — History
LC 2006040824

A history of Buddhism's journey and entry into the western world explores such topics as the early exchanges between the classical Greeks and the Buddhists of India, the influence of Buddhism on western philosophers, and the current fascination with the Dalai Lama.
"Greeks and Buddhists in India found common metaphysical ground 2,000 years ago, and Sutin also documents parallels between Buddist and Gnostic teachings in this vital study of a remarkable spiritual migration." —*Booklist*
Includes bibliographical references (p. [369]-392) and index.

294.5 Hinduism

Calasso, Roberto
Ardor. Roberto Calasso; translated from the Italian by Richard Dixon. Farrar, Straus and Giroux 2014. 420 pages : Illustration; Color
ISBN 9780374182311
Grades: Adult   294.5
1. Translations — Italian to English 2. Spirituality and Religion — Hinduism
LC 2013044345

A meditation on the ancient wisdom of the Vedas, in which Calasso brings ritual and sacrifice to bear on the modern world.
"Richard Dixon's supple and elegant translation brings Calasso's poetic meditations to life. Readers will return again and again for wisdom and insight." —*Publishers Weekly*
Includes bibliographical references and index.

Das, Gaur Gopal
The Way of the Monk: How to Find Purpose, Balance, and Lasting Happiness. Gaur Gopal Das. Sounds True 2020. xi, 209 pages : Illustration
ISBN 9781683646624
Grades: Adult   294.5
1. Spiritual life 2. Self-Help — Personal growth — Spirituality 3. Spirituality and Religion — Body, mind, and spirit
LC 2019052848

In The Way of the Monk, Gopal Das presents a guide to navigating some of the contemporary world's most fundamental questions. How can we achieve peace when the world is so full of noise and conflict? How do we learn to let go of attachment when consumerculture constantly tells us that we are unfulfilled? How can we embody love when our interactions with others are so fraught with old wounds and misunderstanding?
"Krishna monk Das follows up Life's Amazing Secrets with this delightful collection of spiritual and life tools. . . . Das's sharp methods for discovering one's purpose will be appreciated by readers who enjoyed Zen and the Art of Motorcycle Maintenance." —*Publishers Weekly*

Davis, Richard H.
The Bhagavad Gita: A Biography. Richard H. Davis. Princeton University Press 2015. x, 243 pages : Illustration
ISBN 9780691139968
Grades: Adult   294.5
1. Hinduism 2. Spirituality and Religion — Hinduism
LC 2014023890

An essential biography of a timeless masterpiece, this book is an ideal introduction to theGita and its insights into the struggle for self-mastery that we all must wage.
"Davis neatly organizes a great deal of material, and he presents it in utterly accessible prose." —*Choice*
Includes bibliographical references (pages 233-235) and index.

Doniger, Wendy
On Hinduism. Wendy Doniger. Oxford University Press 2014. 680 pages
ISBN 9780199360079
Grades: Adult   294.5
1. Hinduism 2. Polytheism 3. Religions 4. Essays 5. Spirituality and Religion — Hinduism
LC 2013038952

On Hinduism is a penetrating analysis of many of the most crucial and contested issues in Hinduism, from the Vedas to the present day. In a series of 63 connected essays, it discusses Hindu concepts of polytheism, death, gender, art, contemporary puritanism, non-violence, and much more.
"This book assumes some basic knowledge of the subject, but [Doniger's] writing is clear and direct and will be intelligible to readers unacquainted with the technicalities of Hindu doctrine and literature." —*Library Journal*

ESSENTIAL AND RECOMMENDED TITLES
294.509 Hinduism — History, geographic treatment, biography

Narayan, R. K.
★ *The Ramayana: A Shortened Modern Prose Version of the Indian Epic (suggested by the Tamil Version of Kamban)*. R.K. Narayan; introduction by Pankaj Mishra. Penguin Books 2006. xviii, 157 p.
ISBN 9780143039679
Grades: 11 12 Adult   294.5
1. Rama (Hindu deity) 2. Kidnapping 3. Courtship 4. Translations — Tamil to English 5. Epics and hero tales — Asia
LC 2006045201
A sweeping tale of abduction, battle, and courtship played out in a universe of deities and demons.

Sengupta, Hindol
Being Hindu: Understanding a Peaceful Path in a Violent World. Hindol Sengupta. Rowman & Littlefield 2017. IX, 189 pages
ISBN 9781442267459
Grades: Adult   294.5
1. Hinduism 2. Hindus 3. Religions 4. Spirituality and religion — Hinduism
LC 2017023126
Told from the frank and refreshing perspective of a practicing Hindu, this book analyses the importance of Hinduism as the secular, plural middle path in the battle between Islam and Christianity that is playing out across the globe. Being Hindu presents a faith of peace, liberation, and understanding in an increasingly violent world.
"Sengupta's enlightening elucidation is invaluable for understanding Hinduism, India, and the growing Hindu community in the U.S." —*Booklist*
Originally published: Haryana, India : Penguin Books, 2015; Includes bibliographical references (pages 169-181) and index.

294.509 Hinduism — History, geographic treatment, biography

Goldberg, Philip
American Veda: From Emerson and the Beatles to Yoga and Meditation : How Indian Spirituality Changed the West. Philip Goldberg. Harmony Books 2010. xv, 398 p, 8 p. of plates : Illustration
ISBN 9780385521345
Grades: Adult   294.509
1. Hinduism 2. Yoga 3. Religions 4. United States 5. Spirituality and Religion — Hinduism — History
LC 2010011040
Traces the history and influence of Indian spirituality in the United States while explaining how Hinduism and Vedic tradition have shaped American practices, ranging from prayer and pop culture to relationships and meditation.
"From meditating movie stars, scandalous gurus, and psychedelic drugs to genuine spiritual breakthroughs and devotion to helping others, Goldberg's history of American Veda takes measure of a powerful, if underappreciated, force." —*Booklist*
Includes bibliographical references (p. 349-385) and index.

296 Judaism

Belser, Julia Watts
★ *Loving Our Own Bones: Disability Wisdom and the Spiritual Subversiveness of Knowing Ourselves Whole*. Julia Watts Belser. Beacon Press 2023. 288 p.
ISBN 9780807006757
Grades: Adult   296
1. Belser, Julia Watts, 1978- 2. Women rabbis 3. People with disabilities 4. LGBTQIA+ people 5. Disabilities 6. Religions 7. Christianity 8. Judaism 9. Spirituality 10. Theology 11. Belonging 12. Social marginality 13. Social advocacy 14. Science Writing — Medicine and health — Disabilities and disorders 15. Spirituality and Religion — General 16. Life stories — Religion and spirituality — Personal faith 17. Life stories — Facing adversity — Medical issues — Living with disabilities
LC 2023013079

"What's wrong with you?" Activist and rabbi Julia Watts Belser is all too familiar with this question. What's wrong isn't her wheelchair, though—it's exclusion, objectification, pity, and disdain. Our attitudes about disability have such deep cultural roots that we almost forget their sources. But open the Bible and disability is everywhere. For centuries, these stories have been told and retold in ways that treat disability as a metaphor for spiritual incapacity or as a challenge to be overcome. Through fresh and unexpected readings of the Bible, Loving Our Own Bones instead paints a luminous portrait of what it means to be disabled and one of God's beloved.
"An excellent, impressive addition to the conversation around theology and disability that shines on many levels." —*Library Journal*
Includes bibliographical references and index.

Bronfman, Edgar M.
Why Be Jewish?: A Testament. Edgar M. Bronfman. Twelve 2016. 256 p.
ISBN 9781455562893
Grades: Adult   296
1. Judaism 2. Jewish way of life 3. Jewish people 4. Identity 5. Spirituality and religion — Judaism
LC 2015039135
A former CEO of the Seagram Company and a renowned philanthropist offers a passionate testimonial to his own personal Jewish journey and the story of the Jewish people.
"Excellent for nontheistic and unaffiliated readers, Jewish or not, who want to better understand this religion." —*Library Journal*
Includes bibliographical references and index.

Freedman, Samuel G.
Jew vs. Jew: The Struggle for the Soul of American Jewry. Samuel G. Freedman. Simon & Schuster 2000. 397 p.
ISBN 9780684859446
Grades: Adult   296
1. Jewish Americans 2. Orthodox Judaism 3. Reform Judaism 4. Judaism 5. Identity 6. Interethnic relations 7. United States 8. 20th century 9. Spirituality and Religion — Judaism
LC 00033907
New York Times Notable Book, 2000.
Explores the meaning of Judaism in America today, concluding that beneath its prosperous exterior, American Jews are bitterly divided along sectarian and political lines.
"The author describes the paradoxical situation faced by today's American Jews, living in a country where religious freedom has yielded unreconcilable devisiveness. This is a helpful guide for anyone seeking an understanding of intra-Jewish conflicts in contemporary America." —*Library Journal*
Includes bibliographical references (p. 360-371) and index.

Sarna, Jonathan D.
★ *American Judaism: A History*. Jonathan D. Sarna. Yale University Press 2004. xx, 490 p. : Illustration
ISBN 9780300101973
Grades: Adult   296
1. Judaism 2. Jewish Americans 3. Religions 4. Interethnic relations 5. United States 6. History writing — Jewish history 7. Society and culture — Ethnic studies 8. Spirituality and Religion — Judaism — History 9. History writing — United States
LC 2003014464
Provides a 350 year history of the Jewish religion, discussing key events, personalities, and struggles pertaining to Jews and the Jewish religion in the United States.
"This comprehensive and insightful study of the American Jewish experience is much more than just a record of events. It is an account of how people shaped events: Establishing and maintaining communities, responding to challenges, and working for change. It is compelling reading for Jews and non-Jews alike." —*Booklist*
Includes bibliographical references (p. 441-465) and index.

296.09 Judaism — History, geographic treatment, biography

Goodman, Martin
★ *A History of Judaism: From Its Origins to the Present.* Martin Goodman. Princeton University Press 2018. 736 p.
ISBN 9780691181271
Grades: Adult 296.09
1. Judaism 2. Judaic doctrines 3. Religions 4. Spirituality and Religion — Judaism
LC Bl2018003616
Library Journal Best Books, 2018.
A History of Judaism is a spellbinding chronicle of a vibrant and multifaceted religious tradition that has shaped the spiritual heritage of humankind like no other.
"While dense and detailed, this volume is ideal for anyone looking for a comprehensive history of Judaism. Even experts will find something new to consider." —*Library Journal*

Hoffman, Adina
Sacred Trash: The Lost and Found World of the Cairo Geniza. Adina Hoffman and Peter Cole. Schocken 2010. 288 p.
ISBN 9780805242584
Grades: Adult 296.09
1. Judaism 2. Jewish people 3. Manuscripts 4. Intellectual life 5. Spirituality and Religion — Judaism — History 6. History writing — Jewish history
LC 2010016751
Sophie Brody Medal, 2012.
Traces the efforts of two women scholars who in 1896 traveled throughout multiple countries to recover what has become the most vital cache of Hebrew manuscripts ever discovered, in an account that profiles key contributors and explains what the findings reveal about Mediterranean Judaism throughout the past millennium.
"An accessible, neatly narrated story of hallowed detritus and the resurrection of nearly 1,000 years of culture and learning." —*Kirkus*
Includes bibliographical references.

296.0973 Judaism — United States

Weisman, Steven R.
The Chosen Wars: How Judaism Became an American Religion. Steven R. Weisman. Simon & Schuster 2018. 368 p.
ISBN 9781416573265
Grades: Adult 296.0973
1. Religion and culture 2. Jewish Americans 3. Social history 4. Social change 5. Judaic doctrines 6. Immigrants, Jewish 7. Judaism 8. Religions 9. United States 10. 18th century 11. 19th century 12. Spirituality and Religion — Judaism — History 13. History writing — United States
LC 2017058478
The award-winning author traces the redefinition of Judaism throughout the 18th and 19th centuries, citing the roles of key contributors and the dynamic influence of western culture.
Includes bibliographical references and index.

296.1 Sources

Freedman, H.
★ *The Talmud:* A Biography : Banned, Censored and Burned, the Book They Couldn't Suppress. Harry Freedman. Bloomsbury 2014. x, 243 pages
ISBN 9781472905949
Grades: Adult 296.1
1. Judaism 2. Judaic doctrines 3. Judaic law 4. Tradition (Judaism) 5. Jewish history 6. Faith (Judaism) 7. Spirituality and Religion — Judaism
LC Bl2014033550
Discusses the history of the Talmud, tracing its path from a record of discussions among scholars in towns and villages close to modern-day Baghdad, its role during the Enlightenment, and its influence over traditional Judaism.
"Freedman (independent scholar) makes clear that this is no academic volume; his goal is to make the Talmud's story interesting and perhaps even inspiring to the unacquainted reader." —*Choice*
Includes bibliographical references and index.

Leibovitz, Liel
★ *How* the Talmud Can Change Your Life: Surprisingly Modern Advice from a Very Old Book. Liel Leibovitz. W.W. Norton & Company 2023. 320 p.
ISBN 9781324020820
Grades: Adult 296.1
1. Ethics, Jewish 2. Judaic law 3. Judaic doctrines 4. Judaism 5. Spirituality and Religion — Judaism
"Meticulously analyzed and surprisingly accessible, this is a worthy complement to Jonathan Rosen's the Talmud and the Internet." —*Publishers Weekly*

Schiffman, Lawrence H.
Reclaiming the Dead Sea Scrolls: The History of Judaism, the Background of Christianity, the Lost Library of Qumran. Lawrence H. Schiffman; with a foreword by Chaim Potok. Doubleday 1995. xxvii, 529 p. : Illustration; Map (The Anchor Bible reference library)
ISBN 9780385481212
Grades: Adult 296.1
1. Dead Sea scrolls 2. Qumran community 3. Spirituality and Religion — Judaism — History
LC 95017280
"Schiffman provides a description and evaluation of the scrolls, the archeology of Qumran (the site near the Dead Sea from which the scrolls originated), the history and nature of the Jewish community that lived at Qumran and the setting of the scrolls in Jewish history and thought from the second century B.C. through the first century A.D." —*New York Times Book Review*
Includes bibliographical references (p. 471-511) and index; Previously published: 1st ed. Philadelphia : Jewish Publication Society, 1994.

296.3 Theology, ethics, views of social issues

Brous, Sharon
★ *The Amen* Effect: Ancient Wisdom to Mend Our Broken Hearts and World. Sharon Brous. Avery, an imprint of Penguin Random House 2024. xxi, 218 pages
ISBN 9780593543313
Grades: Adult 296.3
1. Judaism 2. Solidarity 3. Compassion 4. Caring 5. Interpersonal relations 6. Helpfulness 7. Loneliness 8. Communities 9. Spirituality and Religion — Judaism
LC 2023023298
Based on one of her most impactful sermons, a leading American rabbi pairs anecdotes from building and pastoring a leading-edge faith community with ancient Jewish wisdom and contemporary science to offer a blueprint for a more meaningful life and a more connected, caring world.
"Rabbi Brous explores in her compassionate debut how to better connect with others in a social climate of widespread division…This inspires." —*Publishers Weekly*
Includes bibliographical references (pages 197-210) and index.

Epstein, Lawrence J.
The Basic Beliefs of Judaism: A Twenty-First-Century Guide to a Timeless Tradition. Lawrence J. Epstein. Jason Aronson 2013. xxii, 201 pages
ISBN 9780765709691
Grades: Adult 296.3
1. Jewish way of life 2. Judaism 3. Spirituality and Religion — Judaism — History
LC 2013015985

ESSENTIAL AND RECOMMENDED TITLES
296.4 Traditions, rites, public services

One of the oldest monotheistic religions known to humankind, Judaism has withstood the tests of time. So what exactly are the tenets of this ancient faith that have been passed down over the millennia, and how do they apply to our lives in the 21st century? The Basic Beliefs of Judaism gives an updated overview of the belief system on which the Jewish faith is based.

Includes bibliographical references (pages 185-197) and index.

Feldman, Noah
★ *To Be a Jew Today: A New Guide to God, Israel, and the Jewish People.* Noah Feldman. Farrar, Straus and Giroux 2024. 336 p.
ISBN 9780374298340
Grades: Adult **296.3**
1. Judaism 2. Jewish people 3. Spirituality 4. Theology 5. God (Judaism) 6. Culture 7. Nationalism 8. Identity 9. Belonging 10. Israel 11. Spirituality and Religion — Judaism 12. Society and culture — Ethnic studies
LC 2023038955

What does it mean to be a Jew? At a time of worldwide crisis, venerable answers to this question have become unsettled. In To Be a Jew Today, the legal scholar and columnist Noah Feldman draws on a lifelong engagement with his religion to offer a wide-ranging interpretation of Judaism in its current varieties. Written with learning, empathy and clarity, To Be a Jew Today is a critical resource for readers of all faiths.

"A multifaceted exploration of Jewish identity in the modern world and the place Israel has come to hold in it…An eloquent, accessible, well-written reflection on the significance of being a Jew." —*Kirkus*

Includes bibliographical references and index.

Held, Shai
★ *Judaism Is About Love: Recovering the Heart of Jewish Life.* Shai Held. Farrar, Straus and Giroux 2024. 560 p.
ISBN 9780374192440
Grades: Adult **296.3**
1. God (Judaism) 2. Love 3. Worship 4. Spirituality 5. Theology 6. Ethics 7. Personal conduct 8. Jewish way of life 9. Spirituality and Religion — Judaism 10. Society and culture — Ethnic studies
LC 2023040928

A dramatic misinterpretation of the Jewish tradition has shaped the history of the West: Christianity is the religion of love, and Judaism the religion of law. In the face of centuries of this widespread misrepresentation, Rabbi Shai Held—one of the most important Jewish thinkers in America today—recovers the heart of the Jewish tradition, offering the radical and moving argument that love belongs as much to Judaism as it does to Christianity.

"A relevant and useful title that's perfect for readers interested in Judaism, theology, religious ethics, or social justice." —*Library Journal*

Includes bibliographical references and index.

Kugel, James L.
The Great Shift: Encountering God in Biblical Times. James L. Kugel. Houghton Mifflin Harcourt 2017. 288 p.
ISBN 9780544520554
Grades: Adult **296.3**
1. Belief and doubt 2. Religion and culture 3. Theology 4. God 5. Individualism 6. Religions 7. Spirituality and Religion — General
LC 2017019809

One of the world's leading Bible scholars summarizes a career of study to ask the biggest questions: How has the nature of God changed over time? What are the origins of belief and religion? Why is the modern West so unusual in its worldview?

"Biblical exegesis at its best: a brilliant and sensitive reading of ancient texts, all with an eye to making them meaningful to our time by making sense of what they meant in their own." —*Kirkus*

Kushner, Harold S.
When Bad Things Happen to Good People. Harold S. Kushner. Schocken Books 2001. VII, 202 p.
ISBN 9780805241938
Grades: Adult **296.3**
1. Providence and government of God (Judaism) 2. Theodicy 3. Suffering 4. Spiritual life 5. Spirituality and Religion — Judaism
LC 81040411

A twentieth anniversary edition of the classic self-help guide by the respected rabbi explains how to find comfort and strength in the face of tragedy and the challenges of life and how to understand God's role in recovery.

"A bright and happy infant, Rabbi Kushner's first-born son gradually succumbed to progeria, 'rapid aging': he never grew beyond three feet tall, looked like a hairless, wizened old man, and died in his teens. This book is his father's attempt to make sense out of his son's fate, his own pain, and the pain of others enduring undeserved misfortunes." —*Library Journal*

Telushkin, Joseph
Jewish Wisdom: Ethical, Spiritual, and Historical Lessons from the Great Works and Thinkers. Rabbi Joseph Telushkin. W. Morrow 1994. xxiv, 663 p.
ISBN 9780688129583
Grades: Adult **296.3**
1. Jewish people 2. Quotations 3. Judaism 4. Spirituality and Religion — Judaism
LC 94009186

A companion volume to Jewish Literacy sets texts from chosen Jewish passages, ranging from the Talmud to modern writings, in a historical perspective while explaining why they are vital and challenging to contemporary Jews.

"Organized by subject, this is a collection of teachings and quotations from the Talmud, the Bible, rabbinical commentaries, and ancient and modern religious and secular writings. Writers include Elie Wiesel, Isaac Bashevis Singer, Hebrew poet Hayim Bialik, Cynthia Ozick, Emile Zola, Albert Einstein, Bruno Bettelheim, Gertrude Stein, Irving Howe, and Maimonides. Jews—and even non-Jews—will find the book a treasure." —*Booklist*

Includes bibliographical references (p. 619-634) and index.

296.4 Traditions, rites, public services

Ashton, Dianne
Hanukkah in America: A History. Dianne Ashton. New York University Press 2013. 368 p.
ISBN 9780814707395
Grades: Adult **296.4**
1. Hanukkah 2. Judaism 3. Jewish Americans 4. Spirituality and Religion — Judaism — History 5. History writing — Jewish history
LC 2013014009

Provides a comprehensive history of the Jewish holiday, from its roots in ancient history through its rise to prominence in the United States.

Includes bibliographical references and index.

Axelrod, Matt
Your Guide to the Jewish Holidays: From Shofar to Seder. Cantor Matt Axelrod. Jason Aronson 2014. 203 pages
ISBN 9780765709899
Grades: Adult **296.4**
1. Fasts and feasts 2. Spirituality and Religion — Judaism
LC 2013033886

Presents a light-hearted look at eleven of the most important Jewish holidays, including Yom Kippur, Purim, and Passover, describing each holiday's rituals in a historical context.

Includes index.

Bolsta, Hyla Shifra
The Illuminated Kaddish: Interpretations of the Mourner's Prayer. Paintings, calligraphy, and interpretations by Hyla Shifra Bolsta. KTAV Pub. House, Inc. 2012. 108 p. : Color illustration
ISBN 9781602801912
Grades: Adult **296.4**

1. Kaddish 2. Judaism 3. Rites and ceremonies 4. Spirituality and Religion — Judaism 5. Spirituality and Religion — Religious texts

LC 2011033483

"The kaddish is the Jewish prayer of mourning, though the word death is never mentioned. In fact, the prayer is a sanctification of God's name, spoken even (or especially) in the midst of grief. This compelling illustrated volume looks at the kaddish from many different angles." —Booklist

Includes bibliographical references; Text of Kaddish in Aramaic, romanized Aramaic, with translation into English; commentary in English.

Diamant, Anita
The Jewish Wedding Now. Anita Diamant. Scribner 2017. xxi, 224 pages : Illustration

ISBN 9781501153945

Grades: Adult   296.4

1. Jewish weddings 2. Wedding planning 3. Reference — Weddings 4. Spirituality and Religion — Judaism

LC Bl2017051420

Presents suggestions for ceremonies and celebrations that are true to contemporary values as well as time-honored Jewish customs.

Includes bibliographical references (pages 193-197) and index.

Goldman, Ari L.
Being Jewish: The Spiritual and Cultural Practice of Judaism Today. Ari L. Goldman. Simon & Schuster 2000. 286 p. : Illustration

ISBN 9780684823898

Grades: Adult   296.4

1. Judaism 2. Religious holidays 3. Jewish way of life 4. Rites and ceremonies 5. Spirituality and Religion — Judaism

LC 00044047

Discussing the practice of Judaism from both a contemporary and a historical perspective, an exploration of the nature of Judaism, its spiritual heritage, and its rituals offers a non-ideological framework for its viewpoint.

"An excellent resource." —Booklist

Includes bibliographical references (p. 267-269) and index.

Pogrebin, Abigail
My Jewish Year: 18 Holidays, One Wondering Jew. Abigail Pogrebin; foreword by A. J. Jacobs. Fig Tree Books 2017. 225 pages

ISBN 9781941493205

Grades: Adult   296.4

1. Pogrebin, Abigail 2. Judaism 3. Faith (Judaism) 4. Jewish holidays 5. Jewish families 6. Rosh ha-Shanah 7. Yom Kippur 8. Rites and ceremonies 9. Autobiographies and memoirs 10. Spirituality and Religion — Judaism 11. Life stories — Religion and spirituality — Personal faith 12. Life stories — Personal growth

LC Bl2017009327

Although she grew up following some holiday rituals, Pogrebin realized how little she knew about their foundational purpose and contemporary relevance; she wanted to understand what had kept these holidays alive and vibrant, some for thousands of years. Her curiosity led her to embark on an entire year of intensive research, observation, and writing about the milestones on the religious calendar.

"A sentimental journey through Judaic practice and thought." —Kirkus

Shulevitz, Judith
The Sabbath World: Glimpses of a Different Order of Time. Judith Shulevitz. Random House 2010. 352 p.

ISBN 9781400062003

Grades: Adult   296.4

1. Shulevitz, Judith, 1963- 2. Sabbath 3. Sunday 4. Rest 5. Time 6. Christianity 7. Spirituality and Religion — Judaism 8. Spirituality and Religion — Christianity

LC 2009026417

New York Times Notable Book, 2010; Sophie Brody Medal, 2011.

Questions the origin, meaning and cultural importance of keeping one day a week holy through an exploration of ritual, religious law and the communitarian way of life in our modern, workaholic, increasingly secular world.

"In personal terms, and without sanctimony, [the author] explores the history of the Sabbath, its philosophical foundations, its consolations, its purposes, and, in doing so, writes a swift, penetrating book intent on shattering the habits of mindless workaholism and the inability to recognize the blessings of rest, reflection, spirit, and family." —The New Yorker

Includes bibliographical references and index.

Wagner, Jordan Lee
The Synagogue Survival Kit: A Guide to Understanding Jewish Religious Services. Jordan Lee Wagner. Rowman & LIIttlefield Publishers, Inc. 2013. xviii, 347 pages : Illustration

ISBN 9780765709684

Grades: Adult   296.4

1. Judaism 2. Prayer (Judaism) 3. Synagogues 4. Spirituality and Religion — Judaism

LC Bl2014000876

Explains synagogue services, etiquette, and the prayer cycle, including Orthodox, Conservative, Reform, and Reconstructionist traditions.

"Extensive notes follow each chapter, and a cross-reference to selections in the most commonly used prayer books fleshes out this carefully crafted primer, which is perfect for Jews rediscovering their own traditions, Jews by choice and others who wish to participate in Jewish events." —Publishers Weekly

A guide to understanding Jewish religious services—Cover; a Jason Aronson book; Includes index.

Wieseltier, Leon
Kaddish. Leon Wieseltier. Knopf 1998. xi, 588 p.

ISBN 9780375403897

Grades: Adult   296.4

1. Wieseltier, Leon 2. Kaddish 3. Judaism 4. Jewish mourning customs 5. Death of fathers 6. Rites and ceremonies 7. Grief 8. Spirituality and Religion — Judaism

LC 98015881

New York Times Notable Book, 1998.

The author recounts his traditional year of mourning after the death of his father, and his pursuit of meaning in ancient Hebrew texts.

"When his father died in 1996 . Wieseltier began to observe the Jewish rituals of the traditional year of mourning. His own mourning led him to an in-depth study of the history and meaning of Kaddish in Judaism. Wieseltier provides a work of history, philosophy and spiritual memoir that demonstrates how the practice of religion meets the needs of a troubled soul." —Publishers Weekly

296.7 Religious experience, life, practice

Diamant, Anita
Pitching My Tent: On Marriage, Motherhood, Friendship, and Other Leaps of Faith. Anita Diamant. Scribner 2005. xiii, 223 p.

ISBN 9780743246170

Grades: Adult   296.7

1. Diamant, Anita 2. Jewish women 3. Judaism 4. Jewish people 5. United States 6. Autobiographies and memoirs 7. Family and Relationships — Growing up 8. Spirituality and Religion — Judaism

LC Bl2005020665

A collection of essays by the author of The Red Tent and Good Harbor, written during her pre-novelist years as an columnist, considers such themes as the nature of family, the relationship between parents and children, and embracing Judaism in today's culture.

A collection of essays written by the author during her pre-novelist years as a columnist considers such themes as the nature of family, the relationship between parents and children, and embracing Judaism in today's culture.

"This collection of short essays, culled primarily from the Boston Globe Sunday Magazine and then reworked [are] organized around such themes as love

ESSENTIAL AND RECOMMENDED TITLES
296.833 Mystical Judaism

and marriage, child rearing, friendship and living a religious life. The book's strength lies in its woman-to-woman conversational tone, especially in the opening section about married life and its dark side. These morsels will make a tasty snack for Diamant's admirers." —*Publishers Weekly*

Reprint. Originally published: 2003.

Isaacs, Ronald H.
★ *Kosher Living: It's More Than Just the Food*. Ron Isaacs. Jossey-Bass 2005. xlvii, 286 p.
ISBN 9780787976422
Grades: Adult   **296.7**
1. Jewish way of life 2. Judaism 3. Spirituality and Religion — Judaism
LC 2004026727

"The book not only covers the expected Jewish topics circumcision, marriage, prayer, Shabbat, synagogue behavior and morebut also intriguing items of general interest, such as employer-employee relations, shopping and even war. This resource offers timeless wisdom through a contemporary lens." —*Publishers Weekly*

An Arthur Kurzweil book; Includes bibliographical references and index.

Kushner, Harold S.
How Good Do We Have to Be?: A New Understanding of Guilt and Forgiveness. Harold S. Kushner. Little, Brown & Co. 1996. IX, 181 p.
ISBN 9780316507417
Grades: Adult   **296.7**
1. Good and evil 2. Eden 3. Self-esteem 4. Perfection 5. Guilt 6. Forgiveness 7. Spirituality and Religion — General
LC 95025350

Drawing on the Bible, modern literature, psychology, theology, and his own thirty years as a congregational rabbi, Harold Kushner reveals why we should not fear the loss of God's love when we make mistakes and shows how acceptance and forgiveness can enhance our lives.

"This is one psychological self-help book that deserves the popularity it is likely to achieve." —*Booklist*

Also published in large print format.

Overcoming Life's Disappointments. Harold S. Kushner. A. A. Knopf 2006. x, 174 p.
ISBN 9781400040575
Grades: Adult   **296.7**
1. Moses (Biblical leader) 2. Disappointment 3. Faith 4. Adjustment 5. Self-fulfillment 6. Forgiveness 7. Spirituality and Religion — Religious Leaders
LC 2005044752

Draws on the life, teachings, and example of Moses to present a series of principles designed to help cope with the problems of everyday life, offering guidelines for dealing with disillusionment of an unfulfilled life, the loss of a job, and other trials.

Who Needs God. Harold Kushner. Summit Books 1989. 208 p.
ISBN 9780671680268
Grades: Adult   **296.7**
1. God (Judaism) 2. God 3. Jewish way of life 4. Spiritual life 5. Faith (Judaism) 6. Spirituality and Religion — Judaism
LC 89035140

The author calls for a return to religious commitment in people's lives in order to fulfill a need for connection, joy, and community, and explains what religion can offer.

Reuben, Steven Carr
★ *Becoming Jewish: The Challenges, Rewards, and Paths to Conversion*. Steven Carr Reuben and Jennifer S. Hanin. Rowman & Littlefield 2011. xvi, 256 p.
ISBN 9781442208483
Grades: Adult   **296.7**
1. Conversion to Judaism 2. Converts to Judaism 3. Spirituality and Religion — Judaism
LC 2011014083

"Converting to Judaism is a long, involved process. This guide by a Reconstructionist rabbi and a freelance writer who converted is a welcome resource. The authors explain such details as finding the right denomination, choosing a rabbi, selecting a Hebrew name, and the need to learn Hebrew." —*Booklist*

Includes index.

296.833 Mystical Judaism

Telushkin, Joseph
Rebbe: The Life and Teachings of Menachem M. Schneerson, the Most Influential Rabbi in Modern History. Joseph Telushkin. HarperWave 2014. 544 p.
ISBN 9780062318985
Grades: Adult   **296.833**
1. Schneerson, Menachem Mendel, 1902-1994 2. Rabbis 3. Religious leaders 4. Jewish leadership 5. Hasidism 6. Orthodox Judaism 7. Judaism 8. Scholars and academics 9. Messiahs 10. Lubavitcher Hasidism 11. Religious life 12. Brooklyn, New York City 13. United States 14. 20th century 15. Biographies 16. Spirituality and Religion — Judaism 17. Life stories — Religion and spirituality — Religious and spiritual leaders
LC 2015370576

The inspiring story of the prominent yet deeply modest leader who rebuilt a dwindling post-holocaust community into the most influential Jewish organization in the world, the late Rebbe Menachem Mendel Schneerson.

"The book is rich with accounts of encounters with the Rebbe, including, besides his own followers, Jews of many denominations, secular Israeli leaders, American politicians, students of philosophy, and non-Jews. What stands out is Schneerson's engagement with the principles by which he managed to wield a considerable and controversial influence upon the American cultural scene and the Jewish world." —*Publishers Weekly*

297 Islam, Babism, Bahai Faith

Abdul Rauf, Feisal
Moving the Mountain: Beyond Ground Zero to a New Vision of Islam in America. Feisal Abdul Rauf. Free Press 2012. 240 p.
ISBN 9781451656008
Grades: Adult   **297**
1. Religion and culture 2. Muslims 3. Interfaith relations 4. Islam 5. Religions 6. United States 7. Spirituality and Religion — Islam
LC 2011050797

The Muslim leader best known for his contributions to the establishment of an interfaith community center near Manhattan's Ground Zero offers insight into his progressive beliefs, ambassador service and advocacy of tolerance and equal rights.

Includes bibliographical references.

Armstrong, Karen
★ *Islam: A Short History*. Karen Armstrong. Modern Library 2000. xxxiv, 222 p. : Map
ISBN 9780679640400
Grades: 11 12 Adult   **297**
1. Islam 2. Muslims 3. Monotheism 4. Religions 5. Islamic Empire 6. Spirituality and Religion — Islam — History 7. Adult books for young adults 8. History writing — Southwest Asia and North Africa (Middle East)
LC 00025285

A concise summation of years of thinking and writing about the world's fastest growing religion, by one of the foremost international scholars on religious affairs.

"The author does an admirable job of presenting Islamic history from an objective, unbiased point of view." —*Library Journal*

Includes bibliographical references (p. [205]-211) and index.

PUBLIC LIBRARY CORE COLLECTION: NONFICTION
Twentieth Edition

Aslan, Reza
★ *No God but God: The Origins, Evolution, and Future of Islam.* Reza Aslan. Random House 2005. xxxii, 310 p.
ISBN 9780812971897
Grades: 11 12 Adult   297
1. Islam 2. Spirituality and Religion — Islam
LC 2006272556

An authoritative study of the Islamic faith in relation to the other world religions sheds new light on its origins and history, from the social reformation role of Muhammad to the impact of fundamentalism and terrorism on Islam.

"Beginning with an exploration of the religious climate in the years before the Prophet's Revelation, Aslan traces the story of Islam from the Prophet's life and the so-called golden age of the first four caliphs all the way through European colonization and subsequent independence. This is an excellent overview that doubles as an impassioned call to reform." —*Booklist*

Includes bibliographical references (p. [289]-294) and index; Originally published: New York : Random House, 2005. With new introd. by the author.

Ben Jelloun, Tahar
Islam Explained. Tahar Ben Jelloun. New Press 2002. 120 p.
ISBN 9781565847811
Grades: 11 12 Adult   297
1. Muhammad, Prophet, d. 632 2. Islamic doctrines 3. Islam 4. Questions and answers 5. Spirituality and Religion — Islam
LC 2002030500

Booklist Editors' Choice: Adult Books for Young Adults, 2002.

Uses a question and answer format to explain the origins of Islam and its contributions to world science and philosophy.

"Cast in the form of an extended conversation between Ben Jelloun and his young daughter. Father and child discuss the history of Islam, what it means to be a Muslim today, the challenges facing the Islamic world, and terrorism. Its openness and emotional honesty, particularly when discussing the tragedy of 9/11, make it a valuable addition to a growing public discourse. As an introduction to the religion, it is spotty, but as a liberal Muslim voice of reconciliation, heartbreak, and compassion, it is priceless." —*Booklist*

Includes index; Originally published in French as Islam explique aux enfants: New York : New Press, 2002.

Gordon, Matthew
Understanding Islam: Origins, Beliefs, Practices, Holy Texts, Sacred Places. Matthew S. Gordon. Watkins Pub. 2010. 112 p. : Color illustration
ISBN 9781907486166
Grades: 8 9 10 11 12 Adult   297
1. Islam 2. Spirituality and Religion — Islam
LC 2010002376

In a thoughtful exploration of Islam's history, beliefs, and practices, this enlightening book corrects many common misconceptions. Issues such as political Islam, Islam and Israel, and Islamic fundamentalism are addressed with intelligence, skill, and sensitivity.

Includes bibliographical references and index.

Grieve, Paul
A Brief Guide to Islam: History, Faith and Politics : The Complete Introduction. Paul Grieve. Carroll and Graf Publishers 2006. IX, 433 p. : Illustration; Map
ISBN 9780786718047
Grades: Adult   297
1. Islam 2. Christianity 3. Islamic doctrines 4. Islam and politics 5. Judaism 6. Religions 7. 21st century 8. Spirituality and Religion — Christianity 9. Spirituality and Religion — Islam 10. Spirituality and Religion — Judaism
LC 2006282191

Looks at the similarities and differences among the three major world religions—Judaism, Christianity, and Islam—and explores the history of Islam and the foundations of the culture that grew out of the Islamic faith.

Includes index; Originally published: London : Robinson, 2006.

Husain, Ed
★ *The House of Islam: A Global History.* Ed Husain. Bloomsbury USA 2018. 320 p.
ISBN 9781632866394
Grades: Adult   297
1. Islam 2. Muslims 3. Ethics 4. Faith 5. Art, Islamic 6. Mysticism 7. Cultural relations 8. Monotheism 9. Sacred books 10. Sunni Islam 11. Shiah Islam 12. Spirituality and Religion — Islam 13. Politics and global affairs — Religion and politics
LC 2018023581

Authoritative and engaging, Ed Husain leads us clearly and carefully through the nuances of Islam and its people, taking us back to basics to contend that the Muslim world need not be a stranger to the West, nor our enemy, but our peaceable allies.

"By explaining the contours of global Islam, Husain ends up making a strong case against Koranic textual literalism that readers of all backgrounds will appreciate." —*Publishers Weekly*

Kugle, Scott Alan
Living Out Islam: Voices of Gay, Lesbian, and Transgender Muslims. Scott Siraj al-Haqq Kugle. NYU Press 2014. x, 265 pages
ISBN 9780814744482
Grades: Adult   297
1. Islam 2. Muslims 3. Gay activists 4. Lesbian activists 5. Transgender people 6. Gay men 7. Lesbians 8. Spirituality and Religion — Islam 9. Society and culture — LGBTQIA+
LC 2013023734

Stonewall Book Awards: Israel Fishman Non-fiction Award, 2015.

Living Out Islam documents the rarely-heard voices of Muslims who live in secular democratic countries and who are gay, lesbian, and transgender. It weaves original interviews with Muslim activists into a compelling composite picture which showcases the importance of the solidarity of support groups in the effort to change social relationships and achieve justice. This nascent movement is not about being "out" as opposed to being "in the closet." Rather, as the voices of these activists demonstrate, it is about finding ways to live out Islam with dignity and integrity, reconciling their sexuality and gender with their faith and reclaiming Islam as their own.

Includes bibliographical references and index.

Nasr, Seyyed Hossein
Islam: Religion, History, and Civilization. Seyyed Hossein Nasr. HarperSanFrancisco 2003. xxv, 198 p.
ISBN 9780060507145
Grades: Adult   297
1. Islam 2. Religion and culture 3. Civilization, Islamic 4. Spiritual life 5. Muslims 6. Islamic doctrines 7. Spirituality and Religion — Islam
LC 2002032810

Explores the doctrines and beliefs of Islam, its practices and institutions, the history of the religion, schools of thought, its place in contemporary society, its relationship to other religions, and its spiritual significance.

"Provides compelling analysis of contemporary Islam and its conflicts without overwhelming the reader with information." —*Booklist*

Includes bibliographical references and index.

Ramadan, Tariq
★ *Introduction to Islam.* Tariq Ramadan. Oxford University Press 2017. 256 p.
ISBN 9780190467487
Grades: Adult   297
1. Islam 2. Muslims 3. Pillars of Islam 4. Faith (Islam) 5. Islamic doctrines 6. Spirituality and religion — Islam
LC 2017004515

Whether the issue is violence, terrorism, women's rights, or slavery, Muslims today are expected to provide answers and to justify what Islam is—or is not. But little opportunity exists, either in the media or in society as a whole, to describe

ESSENTIAL AND RECOMMENDED TITLES
297.03 Islam — Encyclopedias, ...

Islam. In simple, direct language, Introduction to Islam introduces readers to Islam and to its principles, rituals, diversity, and evolution.

"For non-Muslims, it is an invitation to understand the basics of Islam as well as to dive a bit deeper into its history, theology, and various manifestations over time and across the globe." —*Publishers Weekly*

Renard, John
  The *Handy Islam Answer Book*. John Renard, Ph.D. Visible Ink Press 2015.
  xii, 435 p. : Illustration
  ISBN 9781578595105
  Grades: Adult   297
  1. Islam 2. Spirituality and Religion — Islam
                                                                   LC 2014033780

A comprehensive set of questions and answers regarding Islam includes such topics as history, beliefs, symbols, rituals, art and literature, customs, leadership, traditions, and ethnic diversity.

Zafar, Harris
  Demystifying Islam: Tackling the Tough Questions. Harris Zafar. Rowman & Littlefied 2014. 248 p.
  ISBN 9781442223271
  Grades: 10 11 12 Adult   297
  1. Muhammad, Prophet, d. 632 2. Islam 3. Islamic doctrines 4. Spirituality and Religion — Islam
                                                                   LC 2014004827

Demystifying Islam is a concise guide to what Islam really teaches about provocative topics, from the burqa to Shariah law. After a short introduction to basic beliefs and practices, each chapter boldly tackles a challenging topic about Islam today. The book is forthright about issues where Muslims disagree, and provides a single, engaging source where readers can turn for answers to these important topics.
  Includes index.

297.03 Islam — Encyclopedias, ...

Glasse, Cyril
  The New Encyclopedia of Islam. Cyril Glasse. Rowman & Littlefield 2013.
  VIII, 736 pages : Illustration
  ISBN 9781442223486
  Grades: Adult   297.03
  1. Islam 2. Reference — Encyclopedias 3. Spirituality and Religion — Islam
                                                                   LC BI2013055985

A comprehensive reference work covering the different aspects of Islamic civilization, with maps showing the faith's spread over the centuries, and charts of the different branches of Islam.

"This beautifully illustrated and clearly written book provides a myriad of facts and insights about Islam that many readers—novices and scholars alike—will find informative, interesting, and enlightening." —*Choice*
  Includes bibliographical references.

297.09 Islam, Babism, Bahai Faith — History, geographic treatment, biography
---

Abou El Fadl, Khaled
  The Great Theft: Wrestling Islam from the Extremists. Khaled Abou El Fadl. Harper San Francisco 2005. VIII, 308 p.
  ISBN 9780060563394
  Grades: Adult   297.09
  1. Islamic doctrines 2. Wahhabiyah 3. Fundamentalism 4. Islam 5. Spirituality and Religion — Islam — Political Aspects 6. Politics and global affairs — World politics — Southwest Asia and North Africa (Middle East)
                                                                   LC 2005283877

A passionate defense of Islam against the influence of fundamentalism defines moderate Islam as a religion that opposes extremism and is based on moral tradition, in a volume that discusses the importance of reconnecting with past beliefs in order to safeguard the faith from radical practices.

"This book is a fulfilling read for moderate Muslims concerned about conservative leadership and any non-Muslims who want to inform themselves about the extremists' misuse of Islam." —*Publishers Weekly*
  Includes bibliographical references.

Akyol, Mustafa
  ★ *Reopening Muslim Minds: A Return to Reason, Freedom, and Tolerance*. Mustafa Akyol. St. Martin's Essentials 2021. 304 p.
  ISBN 9781250256065
  Grades: Adult   297.09
  1. Islam 2. Civilization, Islamic 3. Muslims 4. Theology 5. Religious life 6. Spirituality and religion — Islam
                                                                   LC 2020045304

In Reopening Muslim Minds, Mustafa Akyol, senior fellow at the Cato Institute and opinion writer for the New York Times, both diagnoses "the crisis of Islam" in the modern world, and offers a way forward.

"This insightful book blends histories of religious belief, political change, and societal needs, to provide a coherent narrative outlining various undercurrents that shaped and ultimately determined predominant religious views." —*Library Journal*
  Includes bibliographical references and index.

Ghobash, Omar Saif
  Letters to a Young Muslim. Omar Saif Ghobash. Picador 2017. 272 pages
  ISBN 9781250119841
  Grades: Adult   297.09
  1. Ghobash, Omar Saif, 1971- 2. Islam 3. Advice 4. Muslim youth 5. Fundamentalism 6. Social change 7. Multiculturalism 8. Ambassadors 9. Fathers and sons 10. Spiritual life 11. Faith (Islam) 12. 21st century 13. Letters 14. Spirituality and Religion — Islam 15. Life stories — Identity 16. Life stories — Religion and spirituality — Personal faith
                                                                   LC 2016039168

In a series of personal letters to his sons, Omar Saif Ghobash offers a short and highly readable manifesto that tackles our current global crisis with the training of an experienced diplomat and the personal responsibility of a father.

"He urges them to pursue a middle path that is simultaneously true to Islam and yet effectively and energetically engaged in the modern world. This is a fantastic book for Muslims and non-Muslims alike." —*Publishers Weekly*

Kennedy, Hugh
  ★ *The Great Arab Conquests: How the Spread of Islam Changed the World We Live in*. Hugh Kennedy. Da Capo Press 2007. VIII, 421 p. : Illustration; Map
  ISBN 9780306815850
  Grades: Adult   297.09
  1. Conquerors 2. Islam 3. Conversion to Islam 4. Religion and culture 5. Religions 6. Southwest Asia and North Africa (Middle East) history 7. Islamic Empire 8. Spirituality and Religion — Islam — History 9. History writing — Southwest Asia and North Africa (Middle East)
                                                                   LC BI2007021158

Examines the history of the great Islamic expansion, reveals how the Arab armies were able to overcome almost everything in their path, and brings to light the unique characteristics of Islamic settlement in new lands and the conversion to Islam of vast populations.

"The author has produced an extremely readable work chronicling the early Arab conquests to 750 CE. In the flowing narrative style for which he has become known, Kennedy brings together Arab, Byzantine, Armenian, Coptic, and Persian histories, legends, and anecdotes related to Arab expansion into the lands stretching from the Iberian Peninsula to the Sind. Each chapter details the conquest of a given region, intertwining historic reality with legendary tales to provide for very colorful reading." —*Choice*

Originally published: London : Weidenfeld & Nicolson, 2007; Includes bibliographical references (p. [377]-408) and index.

297.122 Qur'an

Cook, M. A.
The Koran: A Very Short Introduction. Michael Cook. Oxford University Press 2000. 162 p. : Illustration; Map
ISBN 9780192853448
Grades: Adult   297.122
1. Islam 2. Spirituality and Religion — Islam
LC 99057686

The Koran has constituted a remarkably resilient core of identity and continuity for a religious tradition that is now in its fifteenth century. In this Very Short Introduction, Michael Cook provides a lucid and direct account of the significance of the Koran both in the modern world and in that of traditional Islam. He gives vivid accounts of its role in Muslim civilization, illustrates the diversity of interpretations championed by traditional and modern commentators, discusses the processes by which the book took shape, and compares it to other scriptures and classics of the historic cultures of Eurasia.

Includes bibliographical references (p. 149-151) and indexes.

Haleem, M. A. S. Abdel
★ *The Qur'an: English Translation and Parallel Arabic Text.* Translated with an introduction and notes by M.A.S. Abdel Haleem. Oxford University Press 2010. xxxix, 624 p. : Map
ISBN 9780199570713
Grades: Adult   297.122
1. Spirituality and Religion — Islam
LC 2010281328

One of the most influential books in the history of literature, recognized as the greatest literary masterpiece in Arabic, the Qur'an is the supreme authority and living source of all Islamic teaching, the sacred text that sets out the creed, rituals, ethics, and laws of Islam. First published in 2004, M. A. S. Abdel Haleem's superb English translation has been acclaimed for both its faithfulness to the original and its supreme clarity. Now Haleem's translation is published side-by-side with the original Arabic text, to give readers a greater appreciation and understanding of the holy book.

Approved by Al-Azhar—P. [4] of cover; Edition statement from front jacket flap; Prev. ed. published in 2004; Includes bibliographical references and index; Translated from the Arabic.

Jebara, Mohamad
★ *The Life of the Qur'an: From Eternal Roots to Enduring Legacy.* Mohamad Jebara. St. Martin's Essentials 2024. 272 p.
ISBN 9781250282361
Grades: Adult   297.122
1. Islam 2. Sacred books 3. Prophets 4. History 5. Historiography 6. Language and languages 7. Translating and interpreting 8. Culture 9. Spirituality and Religion — Islam — History 10. Society and culture — General
LC 2023045085

Over a billion copies of the Qur'an exist, yet it remains an enigma. Its classical Arabic language resists simple translation, and its non-linear style of abstract musings defies categorization. Moreover, those who champion its sanctity and compete to claim its mantle offer widely diverging interpretations of its core message at times with explosive results. Building on his intimate portrait of the Qur'an's prophet in Muhammad the World-Changer, Mohamad Jebara returns with a vivid profile of the book itself. The Life of the Qur'an recounts this vivid drama as a biography examining the book's obscured heritage, complex revelation, and contested legacy.

"An extensively researched look at the text of the Qur'an. It is sure to appeal to Muslims, religious scholars, and any readers interested in learning more about the sacred scripture of Islam." —*Library Journal*

Includes index.

Mattson, Ingrid
★ *The Story of the Qur'an: Its History and Place in Muslim Life.* Ingrid Mattson. Wiley-Blackwell 2013. xiii, 298 p. : Illustration; Map
ISBN 9780470673492
Grades: Adult   297.122
1. Islamic values 2. Islamic doctrines 3. Muslims 4. Islamic law 5. Canadian literature 6. Spirituality and Religion — Islam — History
LC 2012042779

Acclaimed Islamic scholar, Ingrid Mattson now updates her authoritative and comprehensive introduction through the addition of expanded sections on the Qur'an in art and architecture, in the life cycle of Muslims, and in Islamic ethics and law. Through a close examination of the doctrines in the Qur'an, Mattson reveals their significance to individual Muslims and the societies in which they live. Combining scholarly precision with an engaging style, the Story of the Qur'an, 2nd Edition, offers a fascinating and unique account of the history and current place of the Qur'an in Muslim life.

"An excellent companion resource for study and understanding of the Qur'an." —*Library Journal*

Includes bibliographical references (p. [271]-286), Internet addresses and index.

Wagner, Walter H.
Opening the Qur'an: Introducing Islam's Holy Book. Walter H. Wagner. University of Notre Dame Press 2008. xix, 547 p.
ISBN 9780268044152
Grades: Adult   297.122
1. Spirituality and Religion — Islam
LC 2008027221

"This work, premised on the conviction that understanding the Qur'an is the key to understanding Islam, insists on the importance of approaching the Qur'an in an open, critically informed manner, yet one that is sensitive to Muslim perspectives." —*Choice*

Includes bibliographical references (p. 502-515) and indexes.

Wills, Garry
What the Qur'an Meant and Why It Matters: And Why It Matters. Garry Wills. Viking 2017. 240 p.
ISBN 9781101981023
Grades: Adult   297.122
1. Islamic doctrines 2. Islam 3. Islam and women 4. Islam and politics 5. Islamic law 6. Spirituality and Religion — Islam
LC 2017025389

A Pulitzer Prize-winning historian and religious scholar redirects his lifelong focus on Christianity and takes open-minded look at the Qur'an, finding the original meaning of the sacred text and showing numerous parallels between it and the Old and New Testaments.

Includes index.

297.2 Islamic doctrinal theology (Aqaid and Kalam) Islam and secular disciplines Islam and other

Akyol, Mustafa
The Islamic Jesus: How the King of the Jews Became a Prophet of the Muslims. Mustafa Akyol. St. Martins Press 2017. 256 p.
ISBN 9781250088697
Grades: Adult   297.2
1. Jesus Christ 2. Interfaith relations 3. Prophets 4. Religions 5. Faith 6. Christianity 7. Islam 8. Judaism 9. Spirituality and Religion — Islam 10. Spirituality and Religion — Christianity
LC 2016038747

An exploration of the connection between Christianity and Islam through the lost "heresy" of Jewish Christianity reveals new truths about Islam in the context of the first Muslims and the early origins of Christianity, explaining how key differences in early beliefs diverged and evolved.

"A fascinating bridge text between Islam and Christianity." —*Kirkus*

Includes bibliographical references and index.

ESSENTIAL AND RECOMMENDED TITLES
297.4 Sufism (Islamic mysticism)

Bhutto, Benazir
Reconciliation: Islam, Democracy, and the West. Benazir Bhutto. Harper Collins 2008. VIII, 328 p.
ISBN 9780061567582
Grades: Adult   **297.2**
1. Bhutto, Benazir, 1953-2007 2. Women prime ministers 3. Islam 4. International relations 5. Islam and politics 6. Elections 7. Democracy 8. Politics and government 9. Southwest Asia and North Africa (Middle East) 10. Asia 11. United States 12. Pakistan 13. 21st century 14. Biographies 15. Politics and global affairs — World politics — Asia 16. Spirituality and Religion — Islam — Political Aspects 17. Politics and global affairs — Religion and politics 18. Politics and global affairs — World politics
LC 2008273737

A former prime minister of Pakistan offers a provocative assessment of the growing tensions between Islam and the western world, in an assessment that shares historical information that traces the roots of international terrorism to American support for former dictator Zia ul Haq and reveals how democracy and Islam can be compatible.

"This is a book of enormous intelligence, courage and clarity. Washington should arrange to have the portions of the book about Islam republished as a separate volume and translated into several languages. It would do more to win the battle of ideas within Islam than anything an American president could ever say."
—*New York Times Book Review*

Griswold, Eliza
The Tenth Parallel: Dispatches from the Fault Line Between Christianity and Islam. Eliza Griswold. Farrar, Straus and Giroux 2010. xi, 317 p. : Map
ISBN 9780374273187
Grades: Adult   **297.2**
1. Islam 2. Christianity 3. Interfaith relations 4. Faith 5. Religions 6. Spirituality and Religion — Christianity 7. Spirituality and Religion — Islam
LC 2010001480

J. Anthony Lukas Book Prize, 2011; New York Times Notable Book, 2010.

Uses stories about the region where Islam and Christianity collide to examine the complex relationships of religion, land, and oil, among other resources; local conflicts and global ideology; and politics and contemporary martyrdom, both Islamic and Christian.

"This is a beautifully written book, full of arresting stories woven around a provocative issuewhether fundamentalism leads to violencewhich Griswold investigates through individual lives rather than caricatures or abstractions."
—*New York Times Book Review*
Includes bibliographical references and index.

Harris, Sam
Islam and the Future of Tolerance: A Dialogue. Sam Harris, Maajid Nawaz. Harvard University Press 2015. 120 p.
ISBN 9780674088702
Grades: Adult   **297.2**
1. Toleration 2. Islam 3. Extremism 4. Extremists 5. Secularism 6. Spirituality and religion — Islam
LC 2015009535

A famous atheist and a former radical discuss the nature of Islam as it relates to tolerance, including such topics as why so many Muslims are drawn to extremism and if reformation of the religion is possible.

Miles, Jack
God in the Qur'an. Jack Miles. Alfred A. Knopf 2018. 256 p.
ISBN 9780307269577
Grades: Adult   **297.2**
1. God (Islam) 2. Islam 3. Religions 4. Comparison 5. Theology 6. Spirituality and Religion — Islam
LC 2018005105

Who is Allah? What makes Him unique? And what does He ask of those who submit to His teachings? in the spirit of his Pulitzer Prize-winning *God, a trailblazing "biography" of the protagonist of the Old Testament, and *Christ*, his brilliant portrait of biblical Jesus, acclaimed religious scholar Jack Miles undertakes to answer these questions with his characteristic perspicacity, intelligence, and command of the subject.

"Readers will discover that writings in the Qur'an have less literary complexity but consistently show God (Allah) as full of forgiveness and compassion. Miles concludes by urging Christians to rethink their ideas about Islam and to respond with charity and tolerance." —*Library Journal*
Includes bibliographical references and index.

297.4 Sufism (Islamic mysticism)

Ernst, Carl W.
The Shambhala Guide to Sufism. Carl W. Ernst. Shambhala 1997. xxi, 264 p. : Illustration
ISBN 9781570621802
Grades: Adult   **297.4**
1. Sufism 2. Spirituality and Religion — Islam
LC 97010189

"This guide to Sufism covers its beginnings, its basic philosophies, and its place in Islam." —*Library Journal*
Discography: P. 247-249; Includes bibliographical references (p. 243-245) and index.

297.8 Islamic sects and reform movements

Hazleton, Lesley
After the Prophet: The Epic Story of the Shia-Sunni Split in Islam. Lesley Hazleton. Doubleday 2009. 239 p. : Map
ISBN 9780385523936
Grades: 9 10 11 12 Adult   **297.8**
1. Muhammad, Prophet, d. 632 2. Aishah, ca. 614-678 3. Ali ibn Abi Talib, Caliph, ca. 600-661 4. Islam 5. Caliphate 6. Shiah Islam 7. Sunni Islam 8. Spirituality and Religion — Islam — History 9. Adult books for young adults
LC 2009006498

A narrative history of the origins of the Shia and Sunni conflict describes how a seventh-century struggle between the supporters of the late Muhammad's surviving family members erupted in a massacre at Karbala that would become a central component of Shia Islam.

Nasr, Seyyed Vali Reza
The Shia Revival: How Conflicts Within Islam Will Shape the Future. Vali Nasr. W. W. Norton 2006. 287 p. : Map
ISBN 9780393062113
Grades: Adult   **297.8**
1. Sunni Islam 2. Social conflict 3. Shiites 4. Islam and politics 5. Politics and government 6. Southwest Asia and North Africa (Middle East) 7. 20th century 8. Spirituality and Religion — Islam — Political Aspects 9. Politics and global affairs — World politics — Southwest Asia and North Africa (Middle East) 10. History writing — Nationalism — Southwest Asia and North Africa (Middle East)
LC 2006012361

Considers the ways in which struggles between the Shia and Sunni in the Middle East will affect the region's future, offering insight into the power conflicts between Iran and Saudi Arabia for political and spiritual leadership of the Muslim world.
Includes bibliographical references (p. 255-268) and index.

299 Religions not provided for elsewhere

Adler, Margot
Drawing Down the Moon: Witches, Druids, Goddess-Worshippers, and Other Pagans. Margot Adler. Penguin 2006. 672 p.
ISBN 9780143038191
Grades: Adult   **299**

PUBLIC LIBRARY CORE COLLECTION: NONFICTION
Twentieth Edition

1. Neopaganism 2. Witchcraft 3. Paganism 4. United States 5. Spirituality and Religion — General

LC 2006043786

Explores the current Neo-Pagan movement in the United States through discussions with various groups whose rituals, festivals, beliefs, religious experiences, and lifestyles are inspired by ancient dieties, visions from science fiction, Wicca, or witchcraft. Reprint. 10,000 first printing.

"Despite its clear anti-Judaic and anti-Christian bias, this book is recommended for general and college audiences interested in religion, the occult, and modern social phenomena." —*Choice*. {review of 1979 edition

Castaneda, Carlos
*The **Teachings** of Don Juan: A Yaqui Way of Knowledge.* Carlos Castaneda. University of California Press 1968. VIII, 196 p.
ISBN 9780520217553
Grades: Adult   299

1. Juan, Don, 1891-1973 2. Indigenous peoples of North America — Religion 3. Yaqui (North American people) 4. Hallucinogenic drugs and religious experience 5. Society and culture — General

LC 68017303

An anthropologist records his corversations with the Yaqui Indian sorcerer and offers a structural analysis of Don Juan's teachings.

Chevannes, Barry
Rastafari: Roots and Ideology. Barry Chevannes. Syracuse University Press 1994. xiv, 298 p.
ISBN 9780815626381
Grades: Adult   299

1. Rastafarians 2. Religions 3. Kingston, Jamaica 4. Spirituality and Religion — General

LC 94018608

Traces the cultural development of the Rastafari movement from the slave trade in the sixteenth century, when it developed as a resistance reaction.

"Vital for students of African American religions and Caribbean religions, but also of interest to anthropologists, sociologists, and historians." —*Choice*

Includes bibliographical references (p. 283-289) and index.

Cook, Kevin
Waco Rising: David Koresh, the FBI, and the Birth of America's Modern Militias. Kevin Cook. Henry Holt and Company 2023. 288 p.
ISBN 9781250840523
Grades: Adult   299

1. Koresh, David, 1959-1993 2. Militia movement 3. Waco Massacre, 1993 4. Cults 5. Cult leaders 6. Raids (Military science) 7. Waco, Texas 8. True Crime — General 9. History writing — 1990s — United States 10. Life stories — Law and order

LC 2022036184

A news-making account of the war between David Koresh's Branch Davidians and the FBI, and how their standoff launched today's militias.

"Former sports journalist Cook augments his track record of producing thrilling exposés of recent phenomena (Kitty Genovese; The Burning Blue) with this fast-paced, vivid retelling of the U.S. law enforcement siege of the Branch Davidian millenarian sect's compound in Waco, Texas, in 1993." —*Library Journal*

Includes bibliographical references and index.

Crosson, Monica
*The **Magikal** Family: Pagan Living in Harmony with Nature.* Monica Crosson. Llewellyn Worldwide, Ltd. 2017. xv, 300 pages : Illustration
ISBN 9780738750934
Grades: Adult   299

1. Families 2. Magic 3. Occultism 4. Spirituality and Religion — Body, mind, and spirit 5. House and Home — Sustainable living 6. Spirituality and Religion — General

LC 2017025403

"In this delightful mix of memoir and Wiccan ritual advice guide, Crosson (Summer Sage) relates anecdotes of her children's spiritual awakening and celebrations of the pagan lifestyle. Crosson, a resident of the Pacific Northwest and member of the Blue Moon Coven, explores how families can live holistically and spiritually year-round by following the Goddess's teachings." —*Publishers Weekly*

Includes bibliographical references and index.

Mar, Alex
Witches of America. Alex Mar. Sarah Crichton Books- Farrar, Straus and Giroux 2015. 368 p.
ISBN 9780374291372
Grades: Adult   299

1. Neopaganism 2. Witchcraft 3. Paganism 4. United States 5. Spirituality and Religion — General

LC 2015010897

New York Times Notable Book, 2015.

Examines paganism and the occult, from its roots in 1950s England to its current American mecca in the Bay Area, and from a gathering of more than a thousand witches in the Illinois woods to the New Orleans branch of one of the world's most influential magical societies.

"A top-notch read for pagans and open-minded seekers curious about the fascinating beginnings of American witchcraft and some of the various directions its form is taking." —*Library Journal*

Reitman, Janet
Inside Scientology: The Story of America's Most Secretive Religion. Janet Reitman. Houghton Mifflin Harcourt 2011. 400 p.
ISBN 9780618883028
Grades: Adult   299

1. Dianetics 2. Secrets 3. Western religions 4. Religions 5. United States 6. Impartial writing 7. Spirituality and Religion — General

LC 2010049837

ALA Notable Book, 2012; New York Times Notable Book, 2011.

Traces the story of the fast-growing religion while addressing such controversies as the organization's attacks on psychiatry, its celebrity support, and its steep tithing requirements.

"An expose culled from hundreds of interviews with active Scientologists and defectors alike. Reitman brings an almost clinical detachment to the religion's story, from its birth in the sci-fi imagination of founder L. Ron Hubbard to its current Hollywood heyday. Her revelations—including abuse allegations against church leader David Miscavige and details about the organization's aggressive courtship of Tom Cruise—come with impressive backup." —*Entertainment Weekly*

Includes bibliographical references and index.

Wilkinson, Richard H.
★ *The **Complete** Gods and Goddesses of Ancient Egypt.* Richard H. Wilkinson. Thames & Hudson 2017. 256 pages : Illustration; Color
ISBN 9780500284247
Grades: Adult   299

1. Gods and goddesses, Egyptian 2. Mythology, Egyptian 3. Religions 4. Egypt 5. History writing — Ancient — Egypt 6. Mythology, folklore, and legends

LC Bl2017006370

Presents a guide to Egyptian religion, describing the mythology, iconography, and forms of worship associated with each god and goddess.

Includes bibliographical references (pages 244-248) and index.

Williamson, Marianne
Tears to Triumph: The Spiritual Journey from Suffering to Enlightenment. Marianne Williamson. HarperLuxe 2016. xx, 275 pages
ISBN 9780062441591
Grades: Adult   299

1. Suffering 2. Self-Help — Personal growth 3. Self-Help — Personal growth — Spirituality

ESSENTIAL AND RECOMMENDED TITLES
299.5 Religions of East and Southeast Asian origin

LC Bl2016024499

Argues that avoiding pain and hurt denies people opportunities to gain wisdom, personal growth, and enlightenment and encourages readers to face pain and become aware of what it can teach.

Wright, Lawrence
Going Clear: Scientology, Hollywood, and the Prison of Belief. Lawrence Wright. Alfred A. Knopf 2013. xiii, 430 p. : Illustration
ISBN 9780307700667
Grades: Adult 299

1. Hubbard, L. Ron (La Fayette Ron), 1911-1986 2. Scientologists 3. Philosophy and religion 4. Dianetics 5. Secrets 6. Western religions 7. Authors, American 8. Religions 9. Religious life 10. United States 11. 20th century 12. Page to screen 13. Biographies 14. Spirituality and Religion — General

Booklist Editors' Choice, 2013; New York Times Notable Book, 2013; National Book Award for Nonfiction finalist, 2013; National Book Critics Circle Award for Nonfiction finalist, 2013.

Examines the Church of Scientology; discusses the esoteric cosmology, the auditing process for determining an inductee's state of being, and the Bridge for Total Freedom; and details how the church pursues celebrities.

Adapted into a film by HBO in 2015; Includes bibliographical references (p. [373]-418) and index.

299.5 Religions of East and Southeast Asian origin

Hardacre, Helen
Shinto: A History. Helen Hardacre. Oxford University Press 2016. 720 pages
ISBN 9780190621711
Grades: Adult 299.5

1. Rites and ceremonies 2. Spirituality 3. Shinto 4. Religions 5. Social life and customs 6. Politics and government 7. Japanese history 8. Japan 9. Impartial writing 10. Spirituality and Religion — General 11. History writing — Asia — Japan

LC 2016021265

Often called "the indigenous religion of Japan," Shinto's institutions, rituals, and symbols are omnipresent throughout the island nation. But, perhaps surprisingly, both its religiosity and its Japanese origins have been questioned. Hardacre investigates the claims about Shinto as the embodiment of indigenous tradition, and about its rightful place in the public realm.

"Hardacre, a professor of Japanese religions and society at Harvard, surveys the history of Shinto from ancient Japan to the present in this even-handed and detailed treatment of the topic." —*Publishers Weekly*

Includes bibliographical references (p. 659-680) and index.

Yang, Lihui
★ *Handbook of Chinese Mythology.* Lihui Yang and Deming An, with Jessica Anderson Turner. ABC-CLIO 2005. xiii, 293 p. : Illustration; Map
ISBN 9781576078068
Grades: Adult 299.5

1. Mythology, Chinese 2. Reference books 3. Society and culture — Pop culture

LC 2005013851

An informative work of historical and contemporary Chinese myths, including a useful collection of historical documents, detailing myths as they live and change in China today.

Includes bibliographical references (p. 251-260) and index.

299.7 Religions of North American native origin

Nabokov, Peter
Where the Lightning Strikes: The Lives of American Indian Sacred Places. Peter Nabokov. Viking 2006. xvii, 350 p.
ISBN 9780670034321
Grades: 11 12 Adult 299.7

1. Indigenous peoples of North America — Religion 2. Sacred space 3. Geographical perception 4. Mythology 5. Literary criticism 6. United States history 7. Spirituality and Religion — General

LC 2005042227

Profiles sixteen locations of sacred relevance to Native Americans, explaining how each site reflects the diversity of a unique Native American culture, including the Rainbow Canyon in Arizona and the high country of northwestern California.

"The author's careful documentation of unbroken reverence for these sacred places powerfully illuminates Native American attachment to the earth itself." —*Booklist*

Includes bibliographical references (p. [303]-335) and index.

301 Sociology and anthropology

Cottom, Tressie McMillan
Thick: And Other Essays. Tressie McMillan Cottom. The New Press 2019. 224 p.
ISBN 9781620974360
Grades: Adult 301

1. Cottom, Tressie McMillan 2. African American women college teachers 3. Feminism 4. Beauty 5. Intersectionality 6. African Americans 7. Political culture 8. Social life and customs 9. United States 10. 21st century 11. Essays 12. Book club best bets 13. Society and culture — Gender — Women 14. Society and culture — Race 15. Life stories — Identity

LC 2018042930

ALA Notable Book, 2020; New York Times Notable Book, 2019; National Book Award for Nonfiction finalist, 2019.

In these eight piercing explorations on beauty, media, money, and more, Tressie McMillan Cottom—award-winning professor and acclaimed author of Lower Ed—embraces her venerated role as a purveyor of wit, wisdom, and Black Twitter snark about all that is right and much that is wrong with this thing we call society.

"Sociology and personal experience blend in a concise collection of essays about contemporary Black American women." —*Kirkus*

Includes bibliographical references.

302 Specific topics in sociology and anthropology

Benjamin, Ruha
★ *Imagination: A Manifesto.* Ruha Benjamin. W.W. Norton & Company 2024. 192 p.
ISBN 9781324020974
Grades: Adult 302

1. Imagination 2. Collective memory 3. Group identity 4. Creativity 5. Curiosity 6. Cooperation 7. Collaboration 8. Social change 9. Social justice 10. Humanitarianism 11. Society and culture — Social activism and philanthropy

"Benjamin posits in this wide-ranging treatise that 'collective imagination' will be a key force behind the creation of an emerging new social order…It's a powerful exhortation for society to point its dreams toward the collective good." —*Publishers Weekly*

Brooks, David
★ *The Second Mountain: The Quest for a Moral Life.* David Brooks. Random House 2019. 240 p.
ISBN 9780812993264
Grades: Adult 302

1. Commitment (Psychology) 2. Happiness 3. Responsibility 4. Ethics 5. Purpose in life 6. Personal conduct 7. Character 8. Society and culture — Philosophy

LC 2019004624

In The Second Mountain, David Brooks explores the four commitments that define a life of meaning and purpose: to a spouse and family, to a vocation, to a philosophy or faith, and to a community. Our personal fulfillment depends on

PUBLIC LIBRARY CORE COLLECTION: NONFICTION
Twentieth Edition

how well we choose and execute these commitments. In The Second Mountain, Brooks looks at a range of people who have lived joyous, committed lives, and who have embraced the necessity of dependence. He gathers their wisdom on how to choose a partner, how to pick a vocation, how to live out a philosophy, and how we can begin to integrate our commitments into one overriding purpose.

"A thoughtful work that offers an uplifting message to those struggling in the wilderness of career and existential challenge." —*Kirkus*

Field, Andy
Encounterism: The Neglected Joys of Being in Person. Andy Field. W.W. Norton & Company 2023. 304 p.

ISBN 9781324036586

Grades: Adult   302

1. Interpersonal relations 2. Interpersonal communication 3. Social interaction 4. Communities 5. Society and culture — Psychology and human behavior

A playful, analytical, informed, and poetic exploration of the delight and transformative power of real-life encounters.

"A poetic, insightful examination of human connections and unexpected intimacy." —*Kirkus*

Gladwell, Malcolm
Outliers: The Story of Success. Malcolm Gladwell. Little, Brown and Co. 2008. 320 p.

ISBN 9780316017930

Grades: Adult   302

1. Successful people 2. Success (Concept) 3. Success in business 4. High achievement 5. Achievement motivation 6. Intellectuals 7. Personal conduct 8. Human behavior 9. Canadian literature 10. Business and economics — Popular psychology

LC 2008032824

Identifies the qualities of successful people, posing theories about the cultural, family, and idiosyncratic factors that shape high achievers, in a resource that covers such topics as the secrets of software billionaires and why the Beatles earned their fame.

"Gladwell's subject is success—an outlier is a superachiever, like Bill Gates or the four Beatles, and Gladwell wants to know what sets these titans apart. It's not mere talent, he insists, offering up instead one thrilling, exquisitely unfurled counterargument after another. There are both brilliant yarns and life lessons here: Outliers is riveting science, self-help, and entertainment, all in one book." —*Entertainment Weekly*

Includes bibliographical references and index.

★ *Talking to Strangers: What We Should Know About the People We Don't Know.* Malcolm Gladwell. Little, Brown & Company 2019. 304 p.

ISBN 9780316478526

Grades: Adult   302

1. Interpersonal relations 2. Interpersonal communication 3. Mass media 4. Strangers 5. Personal conduct 6. Social conflict 7. Social psychology 8. Human behavior 9. Society and culture — Psychology and human behavior 10. Society and culture — Media and technology

LC 2019935109

Talking to Strangers is a classically Gladwellian intellectual adventure, a challenging and controversial excursion through history, psychology, and scandals taken straight from the news. Something is very wrong, Gladwell argues, with the tools and strategies we use to make sense of people we don't know. And because we don't know how to talk to strangers, we are inviting conflict and misunderstanding in ways that have a profound effect on our lives and our world.

"This work should stimulate further research that could serve as control for these variables and more directly link how the factor of strangeness might influence certain reactions, providing a valuable contribution to psychology and psychiatry collections in larger university libraries." —*Library Journal*

The Tipping Point: How Little Things Can Make a Big Difference. Malcolm Gladwell. Little, Brown 2000. VIII, 279 p.

ISBN 9780316316965

Grades: 10 11 12 Adult   302

1. Social psychology 2. Contagion (Social psychology) 3. Causation 4. Human behavior 5. Memetics 6. Information science 7. Theory of knowledge 8. Social change 9. Context effects (Psychology) 10. Canadian literature 11. Society and culture — Psychology and human behavior

LC 99047576

New York Times Notable Book, 2000.

Explains why major changes in society often happen suddenly and unexpectedly. Also describes the personality types who are natural originators of new ideas and trends.

Includes bibliographical references and index.

Killam, Kasley
The Art and Science of Connection: Why Social Health Is the Missing Key to Living Longer, Healthier, and Happier. Kasley Killam, MPH.. HarperOne, an imprint of HarperCollinsPublishers 2024. VIII, 278 pages

ISBN 9780063289116

Grades: Adult   302

1. Social interaction 2. Interpersonal relations 3. Friendship 4. Well-being 5. Self-care 6. Psychology 7. Health 8. Self-Help — Personal growth — Happiness 9. Science Writing — Medicine and health — Psychology 10. Society and culture — Psychology and human behavior

LC Bl2024013088

In this groundbreaking redefinition of health and wellbeing, an internationally recognized expert in social health argues that the definition of wellbeing is missing a major component: social connection, proving that relationships not only make us happy, but they are also critical to our overall health and longevity.

"Upbeat and informative, this book will spark an interest in building and strengthening vital relationships." —*Booklist*

Includes bibliographical references (pages 209-227) and index.

Stryker, Kitty
Ask: Building Consent Culture. Kitty Stryker; afterword by Carol Queen; foreword by Laurie Penny. Thorntree Press 2017. 224 p.

ISBN 9781944934255

Grades: Adult   302

1. Feminism 2. Power 3. Feminist theory 4. Boundaries (Interpersonal relations) 5. Life skills 6. Self-acceptance 7. People with mental illnesses 8. Crimes against people 9. Interpersonal relations 10. Society and culture — Psychology and human behavior 11. Family and relationships — General

LC 2017022470

Assembles writers, journalists, and activists to examine how a culture based on consent can empower us outside the bedroom, from the doctor's office to the justice system to schools and families.

"A vibrant treatise from the very first page, this radical collection provides a multifaceted view of consent as an essential concept in not only the bedroom but in the realms of politics, technology, education, and society overall." —*Library Journal*

302.2 Communication

Cairo, Alberto
How Charts Lie: Getting Smarter About Visual Information. Alberto Cairo. W.W. Norton & Company 2019. 221 p.

ISBN 9781324001560

Grades: Adult   302.2

1. Charts 2. Visual communication 3. Misinformation 4. Information visualization 5. Propaganda 6. Errors 7. Graphic methods 8. Science Writing — Mathematics 9. Society and culture — Media and technology

LC Bl2019027913

We've all heard that a picture is worth a thousand words, but what if we don't understand what we're looking at? Social media has made charts, infographics, and diagrams ubiquitous—and easier to share than ever. We associate charts with science and reason; the flashy visuals are both appealing and persuasive. However, they can also lead us astray. Charts lie in a variety of ways—displaying incomplete or inaccurate data, suggesting misleading patterns, and concealing

ESSENTIAL AND RECOMMENDED TITLES
302.23 Media (Means of communication)

uncertainty—or are frequently misunderstood. To make matters worse, many of us are ill-equipped to interpret the visuals that politicians, journalists, advertisers, and even our employers present each day, enabling bad actors to easily manipulate them to promote their own agendas.

Includes bibliographical references and index.

Kinzler, Katherine D.
How You Say It: Why You Talk the Way You Do and What It Says About You. Katherine D. Kinzler. Houghton Mifflin Harcourt 2020. 272 p.
ISBN 9780544986558
Grades: Adult   302.2
1. Language and languages 2. Linguistic change 3. Second language acquisition 4. Sociolinguistics 5. Social psychology 6. Perception 7. Prejudice 8. Society and culture — Psychology and human behavior
LC 2019049915

A pioneering psychology professor explains how we are hardwired to prejudge others by the way they speak and discusses how accents can even determine the economic opportunity and discrimination one might face in life.

"Writing informally and concisely, Kinzler aims to raise our awareness of this unnoticed prejudice so that we can put an end to it. An articulate examination of an underrecognized aspect of human communication." —*Kirkus*

Includes bibliographical references and index.

Klein, Naomi
★ *Doppelganger: A Trip into the Mirror World.* Naomi Klein. Farrar, Straus and Giroux 2023. 416 p.
ISBN 9780374610326
Grades: Adult   302.2
1. Klein, Naomi, 1970- 2. Women authors 3. Doppelgangers 4. Mistaken identity 5. Ideology 6. Polarization (Social sciences) 7. Culture 8. Social advocacy 9. Social media 10. Collective memory 11. Public opinion 12. Canadian literature 13. Life stories — Arts and culture — Writing — Journalists 14. Life stories — Identity 15. Society and culture — Media and technology

Women's Prize for Non-Fiction, 2024.

What if you woke up one morning and found you'd acquired another self—a double who was almost you and yet not you at all? Not long ago, activist and intellectual Naomi Klein had just such an experience—she was confronted with a doppelganger whose views she found abhorrent but whose name and public persona were sufficiently similar to her own that many people got confused about who was who. Klein here turns her gaze inward to our psychic landscapes, and outward to the possibilities for building hope amid intersecting economic, medical, and political crises, asking, is there a cure for our moment of collective vertigo?

"[Klein's] provocative thought exercise illuminates the myriad ways taken-for-granted balances can be upended and calls for heightened awareness of the dangers of identity erosion on both large and small scales." —*Booklist*

Lyons, Daniel
STFU: The Power of Keeping Your Mouth Shut in an Endlessly Noisy World. Dan Lyons. Henry Holt and Company 2023. 252 pages
ISBN 9781250850348
Grades: Adult   302.2
1. Silence and silent things 2. Conversation 3. Social media 4. Personal conduct 5. Communication 6. Critical thinking 7. Self-Help — Personal growth
LC 2022047772

Combining leading behavioral science with actionable advice, a New York Times bestselling author shows how to communicate with intent, think critically and open your mind and ears to the world around you by shutting the f*ck up and quietly changing your life.

"Every library should get a copy. Readers, especially Lyons's fans, will look forward to this witty, well-researched book." —*Library Journal*

Includes bibliographical references (pages 219-252).

Postman, Neil
Amusing Ourselves to Death: Public Discourse in the Age of Show Business. Neil Postman; new introduction by Andrew Postman. Penguin Books 2006. xx, 184 p.
ISBN 9780143036531
Grades: 11 12 Adult   302.2
1. Television 2. Mass media 3. United States 4. Arts and Entertainment — Movies and Television
LC 2006275381

Examines the ways in which television has transformed public discourse—in politics, education, religion, science, and elsewhere—into a form of entertainment that undermines exposition, explanation and knowledge.

"A sustained, withering and thought-provoking attack on television and what it is doing to us." —*Publishers Weekly*

Includes bibliographical references (p. 173-175) and index.

Schein, Edgar H.
Humble Inquiry: The Gentle Art of Asking Instead of Telling. Edgar H Schein. Berrett-Koehler Publishers, Inc. 2013. 123 pages : Illustration
ISBN 9781609949815
Grades: Adult   302.2
1. Humility 2. Interpersonal communication 3. Interpersonal relations 4. Organizational behavior 5. Business and economics — Business advice 6. Business and economics — General 7. Science writing — Medicine and health — Psychology
LC 2013016855

From one of the true giants in organizational development, career development and organizational psychology comes a simple and effective technique for building more positive relationships—particularly between people of different status—that will lead to more honest and open interactions and stronger organizations.

We live, says Ed Schein, in a culture of Tell. Rather than trying to genuinely relate to other people we tell them what we think they need to know or should do based on assumptions we've made about them. But telling makes people feel inferior—it shuts them down. This is particularly true of interactions between superiors and subordinates, and that's where it's particularly problematic. In today's complex, interconnected, rapidly changing world hierarchy means nothing—anybody anywhere could have that vital fact or insight that could mean the difference between success or disaster. A free flow of information is crucial. Humble Inquiry builds the kinds of positive, trusting, balanced relationships that encourage honest and open interactions in both our professional and personal lives. Schein defines Humble Inquiry as "the fine art of drawing someone out, of asking questions to which you do not know the answer, of building a relationship based on curiosity and interest in the other person." in this seminal work he explores the concept of humility, looks at how Humble Inquiry differs from other kinds of inquiry, offers examples of Humble Inquiry in action in many different settings, and shows how to overcome the cultural, organizational and psychological barriers that keep us from practicing it. This is a major new contribution to how we see human dynamics and relationships, presented in a compact, personal, eminently practical way.

Includes bibliographical references and index.

302.23 Media (Means of communication)

Lorenz, Taylor
★ *Extremely Online: The Untold Story of Fame, Influence, and Power on the Internet.* Taylor Lorenz. Simon & Schuster 2023. 352 p.
ISBN 9781982146863
Grades: Adult   302.23
1. Social media 2. Influencers 3. Influence (Psychology) 4. Power 5. Internet 6. Fame 7. Culture 8. 21st century 9. Society and culture — Media and technology 10. Society and culture — Pop culture

An acclaimed Washington Post reporter and leading authority on internet culture reveals how online influence came to upend the world, showing how this phenomenon become one of the most disruptive changes in modern capitalism, forming an unappreciated and insurgent digital dynamic resulting in new approaches to work, entertainment, fame and ambition.

"This socioeconomics docudrama is both fun and terrifying…just like the internet." —*Booklist*

Phillips, Maya
Nerd: Adventures in Fandom from This Universe to the Multiverse. Maya Phillips. Atria Books 2022. 288 p.
ISBN 9781982165772
Grades: Adult   302.23
1. Phillips, Maya, 1990- 2. Fans (People) 3. Media fandom 4. Television programs 5. Films 6. Comic book characters 7. Popular culture 8. Race (Social sciences) 9. Gender identity 10. Social criticism 11. Religions 12. Essays 13. Society and culture — Pop culture 14. Life stories — Identity 15. Arts and Entertainment — General
LC 2022020256

Spanning from the 90s through today, this humorous and insightful essay collection from the New York Times critic at large explores race, gender expression, religion and more through the lens of her favorite pop culture fandoms, analyzing the mark these beloved intellectual properties leave on young and adult minds.

"These sparkling essays demolish the boundaries between high and low art." —*Publishers Weekly*
Includes bibliographical references.

302.3 Social interaction within groups

Horwitz, Jeff
★ *Broken* Code: Inside Facebook and the Fight to Expose Its Harmful Secrets. Jeff Horwitz. Doubleday 2023. 384 p.
ISBN 9780385549189
Grades: Adult   302.3
1. Social media 2. Corruption 3. Leaks (Disclosure of information) 4. Business and economics — Industries — Technology 5. Business and economics — Corruption and scandal 6. Society and culture — Media and technology
LC 2023016222

An award-winning Wall Street Journal technology reporter provides an inside look into the ways Facebook used manipulative tactics to grow its business while ignoring the warnings from its own employees about the dangers of such methods.

"This convincingly makes the case that Facebook's pursuit of growth at any cost has had disastrous offline consequences." —*Publishers Weekly*
Includes bibliographical references.

van der Linden, Sander
★ *Foolproof:* Why Misinformation Infects Our Minds and How to Build Immunity. Sander van der Linden. W W Norton & Co. Inc 2023. 336 p.
ISBN 9780393881448
Grades: Adult   302.3
1. Misinformation 2. Fake news 3. Social psychology 4. Social networks 5. Political corruption 6. Society and culture — Media and technology 7. Politics and global affairs — Mass media and politics

With remarkable clarity, Sander van der Linden explains why our brains are so vulnerable to misinformation, how it spreads across social networks, and what we can do to protect ourselves and others. Like a virus, misinformation infects our minds, exploiting shortcuts in how we see and process information to alter our beliefs, modify our memories, and replicate at astonishing rates. Once the virus takes hold, it's very hard to cure.

"Thoroughly researched and lucidly written, this is a standout guide to one of the world's most pressing social issues." —*Publishers Weekly*

302.34 Social interaction in primary groups

Bazelon, Emily
Sticks and Stones: Defeating the Culture of Bullying and Rediscovering the Power of Character and Empathy. Emily Bazelon. Random House 2013. 256 p.
ISBN 9780812992809
Grades: Adult Professional   302.34
1. Bullies and bullying 2. Schools 3. Aggressiveness 4. Interpersonal relations 5. Society and culture — Education
LC 2012022773

Offers insights into teen bullying in the Internet era, counseling parents, educators, advocates, and kids on how to understand its dynamics and consequences and take appropriate protective measures.

"While less prescriptive than other books on the topic, very useful FAQs are included, as are resource lists for readers. Masterfully written, Bazelon's book will increase understanding, awareness, and action." —*Publishers Weekly*
Includes bibliographical references and index.

Franco, Marisa G.
Platonic: How the Science of Attachment Can Help You Make and Keep Friends as an Adult. Marisa G. Franco, PhD.. G. P. Putnam's Sons 2022. 288 p.
ISBN 9780593331897
Grades: Adult   302.34
1. Friendship 2. Human behavior 3. Psychology 4. Psychological growth 5. Society and culture — Psychology and human behavior
LC 2022019244

Drawing on the latest scientific research on friendship, an acclaimed psychologist helps us understand our attachment style by providing a blueprint for forging strong, lasting connections with others to become our happiest, most fulfilled selves in the process.

"A pleasing mix of research, advice, and humor, this book is a useful tonic to a key social ailment." —*Kirkus*
Includes bibliographical references and index.

Jackson, Danielle Bayard
Fighting for Our Friendships: The Science and Art of Conflict and Connection in Women's Relationships. Danielle Bayard Jackson. Hachette Go, an imprint of Hachette Books 2024. xi, 256 pages
ISBN 9780306830617
Grades: Adult   302.34
1. Female friendship 2. Interpersonal relations 3. Communication 4. Conflict resolution 5. Women 6. Friendship 7. Family and Relationships — Friendship 8. Self-Help — Relationships
LC Bl2024012636

Based on the most recent studies on women's collaboration and communication, a friendship coach and educator offers practical tactics for maintaining and enhancing these connections with real-life solutions for the most common conflicts.

"Readers will be encouraged to examine and appreciate their own relationships." —*Booklist*
Includes bibliographical references (pages 241-246) and index.

302.5 Relation of individual to society

Kim, Anne
★ *Poverty* for Profit: How Corporations Get Rich off America's Poor. Anne Kim. The New Press 2024. 304 p.
ISBN 9781620977811
Grades: Adult   302.5
1. Poverty 2. Ethics 3. Poor people 4. Corporations 5. Inequality 6. Institutional racism 7. Business ethics 8. Antipoverty programs 9. Social policy 10. Corporations, American 11. Welfare 12. United States 13. Society and culture — Wealth and class — Poverty 14. Politics and global affairs — General
LC 2023055173

ESSENTIAL AND RECOMMENDED TITLES
303.3 Coordination and control

A veteran journalist investigates the multiple industries that infiltrate—and profit from—almost every aspect of the lives of the poor—health care, housing, criminal justice, and nutrition, adding a crucial dimension to our understanding of how structural inequality and structural racism function today.

"Readers will be intrigued by this well-researched book and will develop an understanding of how the infrastructure of poverty is a big business." —*Booklist*

Includes bibliographical references and index.

Simmons, Rachel
Odd Girl Out: The Hidden Culture of Aggression in Girls. Rachel Simmons. Mariner Books 2011. xix, 412 p.
ISBN 9780547520193
Grades: Adult **302.5**
1. Aggressiveness in children 2. Girls 3. Psychology 4. Educator resources — General 5. Science writing — Medicine and health — Psychology
LC Bl2011020952

Identifies the subtle means by which girls behave aggressively toward one another and examines specific behaviors while explaining the importance of enabling girls to express anger and resolve conflicts.

Includes bibliographical references (p. 369-386) and index.

303.3 Coordination and control

Eberhardt, Jennifer L.
★ *Biased: Uncovering the Hidden Prejudice That Shapes What We See, Think, and Do.* Jennifer L. Eberhardt. PhD.. Viking 2019. 352 p.
ISBN 9780735224933
Grades: Adult **303.3**
1. Prejudice 2. Discrimination 3. Race relations 4. Racism 5. Criminal justice system 6. Unconscious bias 7. Education 8. Discrimination in employment 9. Psychology 10. Problem solving 11. Society and culture — Race 12. Society and culture — Psychology and human behavior 13. Adult books for young adults 14. Antiracist literature
LC 2018051011

A leading expert on unconscious racial bias examines the manifestations of automatic racism in contemporary society and how they influence race relations and criminal justice.

"Though there's no easy answer, Eberhardt posits the key to change is confronting bias head-on rather than trying to pretend it doesnt exist, and to question and challenge our own snap judgments and their sources. This is a seminal work on a topic that necessitates wide and frank discussion." —*Booklist*

Includes index.

Hill, Marc Lamont
Seen and Unseen: Technology, Social Media, and the Fight for Racial Justice. Marc Lamont Hill and Todd Brewster. Atria Books 2022. 288 p.
ISBN 9781982180393
Grades: Adult **303.3**
1. Violence against African Americans 2. Violence against marginalized people 3. Videos 4. Internet videos 5. Digital media 6. Racism 7. Racism in law enforcement 8. Social justice 9. Race relations 10. United States 11. Society and culture — Race 12. Society and culture — Violence and crime 13. Society and culture — Media and technology

Marc Lamont Hill and Todd Brewster weave some of the most pivotal recent moments in the country's racial divide—the killings of George Floyd and Ahmaud Arbery and the harassment of Christian Cooper—into their historical context. In doing so, they reveal the common thread between these harrowing incidents: Video recordings and the immediacy of technology has irrevocably changed our conversations about race and in many instances tipped the levers of power in favor of the historically disadvantaged. Drawing on the powerful role of technology as a driver of history, identity, and racial consciousness, Seen and Unseen asks why, after so much video confirmation of police violence on people of color, it took the footage of George Floyd to trigger an overwhelming response of sympathy and outrage?

"Packed with relevant history lessons and sharp analysis, this offers a fresh angle on an issue of vital importance." —*Publishers Weekly*

Imani, Blair
Read This to Get Smarter: About Race, Class, Gender, Disability & More. Blair Imani. Ten Speed Press 2021. 181 pages
ISBN 9781984860545
Grades: Adult **303.3**
1. Social justice 2. Social problems 3. Social classes 4. Gender identity 5. Race (Social sciences) 6. Antiracist literature 7. Society and culture — General
LC Bl2021026545

A critically acclaimed historian and outspoken advocate and activist helps readers become informed, compassionate, and socially conscious through discussions on race, gender, and sexual orientation to disability, class, and beyond.

"Through openness and strategic brevity, Imani's work is sure to make positive change." —*Booklist*

Includes bibliographical references (pages 153-169) and index.

Kissinger, Henry
Leadership: Six Studies in World Strategy. Henry Kissinger. Penguin 2022. 400 p.
ISBN 9780593489444
Grades: Adult **303.3**
1. Adenauer, Konrad, 1876-1967 2. Gaulle, Charles de, 1890-1970 3. Sadat, Anwar, 1918-1981 4. Nixon, Richard M. (Richard Milhous), 1913-1994 5. Thatcher, Margaret 6. Lee, Kuan Yew, 1923-2015 7. World leaders 8. Political leadership 9. Strategy 10. Power 11. Democracy 12. Geopolitics 13. Political science 14. Collective biographies 15. Life stories — Politics — Politicians 16. Politics and global affairs — Political figures 17. Politics and global affairs — World politics

Drawing on his deep study of history as well as his distinguished career in government, the consummate diplomat and statesman studies six impactful leaders in modern history, including Anwar Sadat, Margaret Thatcher and Lee Kuan Yew, revealing the masterful strategies and leadership of these great geopolitical minds.

"Former National Security Advisor and Secretary of State Kissinger (Diplomacy; World Order) fulfills expectations with a reflective, contextual analysis of 20th century political leaders he knew." —*Library Journal*

Owens, Ernest
★ *The Case for Cancel Culture: How This Democratic Tool Works to Liberate Us All.* Ernest Owens. St. Martin's Press 2023. 256 p.
ISBN 9781250280930
Grades: Adult **303.3**
1. Political culture 2. Public opinion 3. Social media 4. Mass media 5. Polarization (Social sciences) 6. Protests, demonstrations, vigils, etc. 7. Social responsibility 8. Democracy 9. Social change 10. Society and culture — Media and technology 11. Society and culture — Social activism and philanthropy 12. Politics and global affairs — Mass media and politics
LC 2022045420

"___ is canceled." Chances are, you've heard this a lot lately. What might've once been a niche digital term has been legitimized in the discourse of presidents, politicians, and lawmakers, and equated with censorship. But it's time to raise the bar on our definition—to think of cancel culture less as scandal or suppression, and more as an essential means of democratic expression and accountability. Why should we care? Because in a world where protest and free speech are being challenged by the most powerful institutions, those without power deserve to understand the nuance and importance of this democratic tool available to them.

"This is a provocative and important book that enables readers to gain a deep appreciation for the nuanced meaning of cancel culture." —*Library Journal*

Includes bibliographical references.

Solnit, Rebecca
Call Them by Their True Names: American Crises (and Essays). Rebecca Solnit. Haymarket Books 2018. 188 p.

PUBLIC LIBRARY CORE COLLECTION: NONFICTION
Twentieth Edition

ISBN 9781608463299
Grades: Adult 303.3
1. Feminism 2. Environmentalism 3. Hypocrisy 4. Hope 5. Political culture 6. Social problems 7. United States 8. Essays 9. Liberal writing 10. Politics and global affairs — General 11. Society and culture — Social activism and philanthropy
LC BI2018184189
Kirkus Prize for Nonfiction, 2018.
Rebecca Solnit unearths the roots of our contemporary crises, countering the despair of our age with a dose of solidarity, creativity, and hope.
"Solnit is careful with her words (she always is) but never so much that she mutes the infuriated spirit that drives these essays." —*Kirkus*

Wills, Garry
Certain Trumpets: The Call of Leaders. Garry Wills. Simon & Schuster 1994. 336 p. : Illustration
ISBN 9780671657024
Grades: 11 12 Adult 303.3
1. Leadership 2. Social participation 3. Power 4. Essays 5. Business and economics — Business leaders and entrepreneurs 6. Business and economics — Popular psychology
LC 94006526
Booklist Editors' Choice, 1994.
An examination of leadership that analyzes modes of leadership to better understand society offers profiles of a variety of leaders, including Harriet Tubman, Napoleon, Ross Perot, and Martha Graham.
"A wise, witty, entertaining look at the psychology of leaders and their followers." —*Publishers Weekly*
Includes bibliographical references and index.

303.4 Social change

Diamond, Jared M.
Guns, Germs, and Steel: The Fates of Human Societies. Jared Diamond. Norton 2005. 518 p. : Illustration; Map
ISBN 9780393061314
Grades: 11 12 Adult 303.4
1. Social evolution 2. Civilization 3. Ethnology 4. Effect of environment on humans 5. Cultural diffusion 6. Geography 7. Demography 8. History writing — General 9. Adult books for young adults
LC 2005284261
New York Times Notable Book, 1997; Pulitzer Prize for General Nonfiction, 1998; Royal Society General Prizes for Science Books, 1998.
The author dismantles racially based theories of human history by revealing the environmental factors he feels are responsible for history's broadest patterns.
"This book poses a simple but profound question about the distribution of wealth and power in the modern world: Why weren't Native Americans, Africans, and Aboriginal Australians the ones who decimated, subjugated, or exterminated Europeans and Asians? . . To explore the discrepancies in technological and cultural development he looks not at peoples but at places, and at the natural resources available to different indigenous populations since 11,000 B.C. The scope and the explanatory power of this book are astounding." —*The New Yorker*
Includes bibliographical references (p. 466-496) and index; Originally published: New York : W.W. Norton, 1997.

Shah, Rajiv Janardan
Big Bets: How Large-Scale Change Really Happens. Rajiv Shah. Simon Element 2023. 320 p.
ISBN 9781668004388
Grades: Adult 303.4
1. Social change 2. Social action 3. Leadership 4. Decision-making 5. Society and culture — General 6. Business and economics — Business advice — Leadership and management
LC 2023020668

Rajiv J. Shah, president of the Rockefeller Foundation and former administrator of President Barack Obama's United States Agency for International Development, shares a dynamic new model for creating large scale change, inspired by his own involvements with some of the largest humanitarian projects of our time.
"Readers who are curious about how to make big impacts will find this book inspiring." —*Booklist*
Includes bibliographical references and index.

303.44 Growth and development

Pinker, Steven
★ *Enlightenment Now: The Case for Reason, Science, Humanism, and Progress.* Steven Pinker. Viking Press 2018. 528 p.
ISBN 9780525427575
Grades: Adult 303.44
1. Quality of life 2. Social indicators 3. Social behavior 4. Social psychology 5. Attitude 6. Society and culture — Psychology and human behavior
LC 2017301147
New York Times Notable Book, 2018.
A follow-up to The Better Angels of Our Nature challenges the doom-and-gloom outlooks of today's media to present dozens of graphs and charts demonstrating that life quality, health, prosperity, safety, peace, knowledge and happiness are actually on the rise throughout the world as a result of the philosophies about an Enlightenment era that uses science to improve human existence.
"Pinker's sober, lucid, and meticulously researched vision of human progress is heartening and important." —*Publishers Weekly*

303.48 Causes of change

Acemoglu, Daron
Power and Progress: Our Thousand-Year Struggle Over Technology and Prosperity. Daron Acemoglu and Simon Johnson. PublicAffairs 2023. 560 p.
ISBN 9781541702530
Grades: Adult 303.48
1. Cyberculture 2. Technology and economic development 3. Progress 4. Technological forecasting 5. Technological innovations 6. Prosperity 7. Work 8. Business and economics — Economics — History
LC 2022059230
Two bestselling authors overturn conventional wisdom about how economies work, revealing the untold story of who wins and who loses the rewards of prosperity, in a work that fundamentally transforms how we look at and understand the world.
"A convincing attack on today's dysfunctional economy plus admirable suggestions for correcting matters." —*Kirkus*
Includes bibliographical references and index.

Albert, Daniel M.
Are We There Yet?: The American Automobile, Past, Present, and Driverless. Dan Albert. W. W. Norton & Company 2019. 304 p.
ISBN 9780393292749
Grades: Adult 303.48
1. Automobile driving 2. Automobiles 3. Autonomous vehicles 4. Automobile industry and trade 5. Business and economics — Industries — Transportation 6. History writing — Technological innovations 7. History writing — Microhistory
LC 2019014088
Tech giants and automakers have been teaching robots to drive. In Are We There Yet?, Dan Albert combines historical scholarship with personal narrative to explore how car culture has suffused America's DNA. The plain, old-fashioned, human-driven car built our economy, won our wars, and shaped our democratic creed as it moved us about. Since the 1980s, the car culture has triumphed

ESSENTIAL AND RECOMMENDED TITLES
303.48 Causes of change

and we now drive more miles than ever before. Have we reached the end of the road this time?
Includes bibliographical references and index.

Arce, Julissa
You Sound Like a White Girl: The Case for Rejecting Assimilation. Julissa Natzely Arce Raya. Flatiron Books 2022. 240 p.
ISBN 9781250787019
Grades: Adult   303.48
1. Assimilation (Sociology) 2. Americanization 3. Immigrants, Mexican 4. Identity 5. Marginalized people 6. Interethnic relations 7. United States 8. Life stories — Identity — Immigrants 9. Life stories — Identity — Race and ethnicity 10. Society and culture — Ethnic studies
LC 2021041591

Combing through history and her own story, this powerful cultural commentary delves into and tears apart the lie that assimilation leads to belonging, offering a bold new promise: Belonging only comes through celebrating yourself, your history, your culture, and everything that makes you uniquely you.

In this persuasive polemic, journalist Arce (Someone Like Me) draws on her experiences as an undocumented Mexican immigrant to encourage Latinx people to 'dismantl the lie of assimilation to reclaim the most essential and beautiful parts of ourselves, our history, and our culture.' —*Publishers Weekly*
Includes bibliographical references.

Bingham, Clara
Witness to the Revolution: Radicals, Resisters, Vets, Hippies, and the Year America Lost Its Mind and Found Its Soul. Clara Bingham. Random House 2016. 384 p.
ISBN 9780812993189
Grades: Adult   303.48
1. Social movements 2. Student movements 3. Vietnam War, 1961-1975 4. Radicalism 5. Public opinion 6. Student protesters 7. Peace movements 8. Protests, demonstrations, vigils, etc. 9. Protest movements 10. United States 11. 1960s 12. 1970s 13. Oral histories 14. History writing — Wars and conflicts — Protests — Vietnam War 15. Adult books for young adults
LC 2015046134

Offers a riveting oral history of American society in the turbulent years of the Vietnam War as told by the people in the thick of it, including Jane Fonda, Daniel Ellsberg, Bill Ayers, and many more.

"While Bingham's is one of many retrospective looks at that period, it is one of the most immediate and personal." —*Booklist*
Includes index.

Burrough, Bryan
Days of Rage: America's Radical Underground, the FBI, and the Forgotten Age of Revolutionary Violence. Bryan Burrough. Penguin 2015. 464 p.
ISBN 9781594204296
Grades: Adult   303.48
1. Guerrillas 2. Political violence 3. Radical organizations 4. Domestic terrorism 5. Revolutionaries 6. Counterculture 7. Bombings 8. Terrorism 9. Radicalism 10. United States 11. 1970s 12. History writing — 1970s — United States
LC 2014036663

An account of the decade-long battle between the FBI and America's revolutionary counterculture documents terrorist activities stemming from radical period beliefs, tracing the stories of such groups as the Weathermen and the Black Liberation Army.

"The author's history is thoroughgoing and fascinating, though with a couple of curious notes—e.g., the likening of the Weathermen et al. to the Nazi Werewolf guerrillas 'who briefly attempted to resist Allied forces after the end of World War II.' a superb chronicle, long—but no longer than needed—and detailed, that sheds light on how the war on terror is being waged today." —*Kirkus*
Includes bibliography and index.

Diamond, Jared M.
Upheaval: Turning Points for Nations in Crisis. Jared Diamond. Little Brown & Co. 2019. 512 pages

ISBN 9780316409131
Grades: Adult   303.48
1. Social evolution 2. Crisis management 3. Sociocultural anthropology 4. Psychic trauma 5. Coping 6. Comparative civilization 7. Social history 8. History of civilization 9. Social change 10. History writing — General 11. Society and culture — Psychology and human behavior
LC 2018952825

The Pulitzer Prize-winning author of Guns, Germs, and Steel and Collapse offers a new theory of how and why some nations recover from national trauma and others don't.

"Diamond is a master at explicating matters of pressing importance. His earlier books garnered a vast readership, and there will be equal demand for this one, too." —*Library Journal*
Includes bibliographical references and index.

Friedman, Thomas L.
★ *Thank You for Being Late: An Optimist's Guide to Thriving in the Age of Accelerations.* Thomas L. Friedman. Farrar Straus & Giroux 2016. 320 p.
ISBN 9780374273538
Grades: Adult   303.48
1. Information technology 2. Globalization 3. Climate change 4. Social change 5. World politics 6. International relations 7. Educational policy 8. Human-computer interaction 9. Politics and government 10. United States 11. Politics and global affairs — World politics 12. Society and culture — Media and technology
LC 2016034910

A field guide to the 21st century by a three-time Pulitzer Prize recipient and author of The World Is Flat shares strategies for surviving today's hectic technological, environmental and economic challenges, contrasting present-day environments with the working model of an earlier generation.

Required reading for a generation thats 'Going to be asked to dance in a hurricane.' —*Kirkus*

Garza, Alicia
The Purpose of Power: How We Come Together When We Fall Apart. Alicia Garza. One World 2020. 336 p.
ISBN 9780525509684
Grades: Adult   303.48
1. Garza, Alicia, 1981- 2. Political participation 3. Social change 4. Black Lives Matter movement 5. Civil rights 6. Human rights activists 7. Social movements 8. Growing up 9. Social policy 10. Equality 11. African Americans 12. Civil rights workers 13. Autobiographies and memoirs 14. Life stories — Identity — Race and ethnicity 15. Life stories — Politics — Activists and reformers 16. Antiracist literature 17. Society and culture — Race 18. Politics and global affairs — Civil and human rights
LC 2020023583

A guide to building the type of movements that can address the challenges of our time, from one of the country's leading organizers—one of the creators of Black Lives Matter.

"Drawing on feminist theory, political and economic history, and the principles of organizing, Garza makes a spirited and persuasive case for rethinking community activism in the era of social media. Progressive policy makers, activists, and voters will be galvanized." —*Publishers Weekly*

Gray, Emma
A Girl's Guide to Joining the Resistance: A Feminist Handbook on Fighting for Good. Emma Gray; illustrated by Eva Hill. William Morrow 2018. xiii, 130 pages : Illustration
ISBN 9780062748089
Grades: Adult   303.48
1. Women 2. Women social reformers 3. Feminists 4. Women political activists 5. Social change 6. Social action 7. Political participation 8. United States 9. Politics and global affairs — General 10. Society and culture — Sociology
LC Bl2018028853

Ideally suited to gift-giving, a guide for prospective activists by the Executive Women's Editor at HuffPost shares background information on key issues affecting today's women, insights into how to recognize bogus news, advice for navigating critical friends and practical guidelines for how to get and stay involved.

Includes bibliographical references (pages 125-130).

McCourt, Frank H.

★ *Our* Biggest Fight: Reclaiming Liberty, Humanity, and Dignity in the Digital Age. Frank H. McCourt, Jr, with Michael J. Casey. Crown 2024. 206 pages
ISBN 9780593728512
Grades: Adult   303.48
1. Internet 2. Social media 3. Information technology 4. Social history 5. Internet literacy 6. Business and economics — Industries — Technology 7. Society and culture — Media and technology 8. Science writing — Computing, the Internet, and Technology

LC 2023056212

The internet as we know it is broken. Here's how we can seize back control of our lives from the corporate algorithms that have poisoned our digital information system and create a third-generation Internet that uplifts humanity—before it's too late.

"An illuminating, provocative, and disturbing analysis of our current digital age." —*Kirkus*

Merchant, Brian

Blood in the Machine: The Origins of the Rebellion Against Big Tech. Brian Merchant. Little, Brown & Company 2023. 465 p.
ISBN 9780316487740
Grades: Adult   303.48
1. Industrial revolution 2. Luddites 3. Social movements 4. Protests, demonstrations, vigils, etc. 5. Factories 6. Automation 7. Artificial intelligence 8. Industrial robots 9. Machines and labor 10. Computers and civilization 11. Technological innovations 12. 19th century 13. 21st century 14. History writing — Technological innovations 15. Science Writing — Computing, the Internet, and Technology 16. Society and culture — Media and technology

The most urgent story in modern tech begins not in Silicon Valley but two hundred years ago in rural England, when workers known as the Luddites rose up rather than starve at the hands of factory owners who were using automated machines to erase their livelihoods. The Luddites organized guerrilla raids to smash those machines—on punishment of death—and won the support of Lord Byron, enraged the Prince Regent, and inspired the birth of science fiction. Today, technology imperils millions of jobs, robots are crowding factory floors, and artificial intelligence will soon pervade every aspect of our economy. How will this change the way we live? and what can we do about it?

"As American unions gain power and support, this book is a welcome parable of worker solidarity and resistance." —*Booklist*

Includes bibliographical references and index.

Murgia, Madhumita

Code Dependent: Living in the Shadow of AI. Madhumita Murgia. Henry Holt and Company 2024. 304 p.
ISBN 9781250867391
Grades: Adult   303.48
1. Artificial intelligence 2. Social life and customs 3. Human-computer interaction 4. Decision making 5. Inequality 6. Data processing 7. Social media 8. Society and culture — Media and technology 9. Science Writing — Computing, the internet, and technology — Artificial intelligence and machine learning

LC 2024003683

Shortlisted for the Women's Prize for Non-Fiction, 2024.

An award-winning Indian-British journalist and commentator shows how artificial intelligence systems are shaping people's lives around the globe and explores the perils and inequities of the growing reliance on automated decision-making.

"Throughout, the author writes with clarity and compassion in equal measure. A fascinating, sobering, wide-ranging examination." —*Kirkus*

Includes bibliographical references and index.

Neiwert, David A.

★ *The Age* of Insurrection: The Radical Right's Assault on American Democracy. David Neiwert. Melville House Publishing 2023. 305 p.
ISBN 9781685890360
Grades: Adult   303.48
1. Radicals 2. Right-wing extremists 3. Extremism 4. Fascism 5. Totalitarianism 6. Authoritarianism 7. Patriotism 8. Domestic terrorism 9. Right and left (Political science) 10. Ideology 11. Democracy 12. Nationalism 13. Terrorism 14. Politics and government 15. United States 16. 21st century 17. Politics and global affairs — Terrorism 18. Society and culture — Violence and crime 19. Politics and global affairs — Political philosophy

An award-winning investigative journalist and leading expert on the far-right explores the nature of the insurgent radical right and its relentless violence and how it will continue to attack American democracy for the foreseeable future.

"Equal parts enlightening and terrifying, this is imperative reading for anyone in the United States." —*Library Journal*

Preston, Diana

Before the Fallout: From Marie Curie to Hiroshima. Diana Preston. Walker & Co. 2005. xiv, 400 p. : Illustration
ISBN 9780802714459
Grades: 11 12 Adult   303.48
1. Nuclear weapons development 2. Science 3. Weapons of mass destruction 4. Nuclear fission 5. Radioactivity 6. Nuclear weapons 7. Nuclear warfare 8. Atomic bomb 9. World War II 10. Hiroshima, Japan 11. 20th century 12. Second World War era (1939-1945) 13. Science Writing — Physics 14. History writing — Wars and conflicts — Atomic Bomb — World War II 15. Adult books for young adults

LC 2004061953

Los Angeles Times Book Prize for Science and Technology, 2005.

Describes the history of discoveries that led up to the dropping of the atomic bomb in 1945.

"Avidly researched and gracefully constructed, Preston's revelatory history is rich in telling moments, powerful personalities, intense confrontations, and indelible images of the devastation delivered by nuclear weapons, our Damoclean sword." —*Booklist*

Includes bibliographical references (p. 373-379) and index.

Solnit, Rebecca

A Paradise Built in Hell: The Extraordinary Communities and Strange Joys That Arise in Disasters. Rebecca Solnit. Viking 2009. 432 p.
ISBN 9780670021079
Grades: Adult   303.48
1. Altruism 2. Solidarity 3. Disasters 4. Helpfulness 5. Society and culture — General

LC 2009004101

New York Times Notable Book, 2009.

Explores the phenomenon through which people become resourceful and altruistic after a disaster and communities often reflect a shared sense of purpose, analyzing such events as the 1906 San Francisco earthquake, the September 11 attacks, and Hurricane Katrina.

Includes bibliographical references and index.

Suleyman, Mustafa

The Coming Wave: Technology, Power, and the Twenty-First Century's Greatest Dilemma. Mustafa Suleyman with Michael Bhaskar. Crown Publishers 2023. 320 p.
ISBN 9780593593950
Grades: Adult   303.48
1. Artificial intelligence 2. Technology 3. Technological innovations 4. Power 5. Technology policy 6. Ethics 7. Technological forecasting 8. Society and culture — Media and technology

"Amid the flood of optimism about artificial intelligence, the significant dangers must be understood and assessed…An informative yet disturbing study and a clear warning from someone whose voice cannot be ignored." —*Kirkus*

ESSENTIAL AND RECOMMENDED TITLES
303.6 Conflict and conflict resolution

Swisher, Kara
Burn Book: A Tech Love Story. Kara Swisher. Simon & Schuster 2024. 320 p.
ISBN 9781982163891
Grades: Adult   **303.48**
1. Swisher, Kara 2. Journalists 3. Technology 4. Computer industry and trade 5. Internet 6. Technological innovations 7. High technology industry and trade 8. Silicon Valley, California 9. Autobiographies and memoirs 10. Business and economics — Industries — Technology 11. Society and culture — Media and technology 12. Life stories — Arts and culture — Writing — Journalists

From an award-winning journalist comes a witty, scathing, but fair accounting of the tech industry and its founders who wanted to change the world but broke it instead.

"Swisher, the bad-ass journalist and OG chronicler of Silicon Valley and its denizens (almost all of them male because, well, tech world), takes no prisoners in this highly readable look at the evolution of the digital world." —*Booklist*

Young, Ralph F.
Dissent: The History of an American Idea. Ralph Young. New York University Press 2015. xi, 603 pages; Illustration
ISBN 9781479806652
Grades: Adult   **303.48**
1. Dissenters 2. Protest movements 3. Social reformers 4. Democracy 5. Social problems 6. Politics and government 7. United States 8. History writing — Arts and culture 9. History writing — United States

Examines the key role dissent has played in shaping the United States, focusing on those who, from colonial times to the present, dissented against the ruling paradigm of their time, responding to what they saw as the injustices that prevented them from fully experiencing their vision of America.

Includes bibliographical references and index.

303.6 Conflict and conflict resolution

Blattman, Christopher
Why We Fight: The Roots of War and the Paths to Peace. Christopher Blattman. Viking 2022. 384 p.
ISBN 9781984881571
Grades: Adult   **303.6**
1. War and society 2. Social conflict 3. Interethnic conflict 4. Violence 5. War 6. Peace 7. Peace-building 8. Compromise 9. Social sciences 10. Political science 11. Society and culture — Psychology and human behavior 12. Society and culture — Violence and crime 13. Politics and global affairs — World politics
LC 2021034646

An acclaimed expert on violence and seasoned peacebuilder explains the five reasons why conflict (rarely) blooms into war, and how to interrupt that deadly process. It's easy to overlook the underlying strategic forces of war, to see it solely as a series of errors, accidents, and emotions gone awry. It's also easy to forget that war shouldn't happen—and most of the time it doesn't. Around the world there are millions of hostile rivalries, yet only a tiny fraction erupt into violence. With a counterintuitive approach, Blattman reminds us that most rivals loathe one another in peace. That's because war is too costly to fight. Enemies almost always find it better to split the pie than spoil it or struggle over thin slices. So, in those rare instances when fighting ensues, we should ask: What kept rivals from compromise?

"Game theory shows why violent conflicts start and how to forestall them, according to this penetrating treatise....This stimulating discussion of violence illuminates a fraught subject with sober reason." —*Publishers Weekly*

Includes bibliographical references and index.

Camus, Albert
The Rebel: An Essay on Man in Revolt. Albert Camus; with a foreword by Herbert Read; a revised and complete translation of L'Homme revolte by Anthony Bower. Vintage Books 1991. xii, 306 p.
ISBN 9780679733843
Grades: Adult   **303.6**
1. Revolutions 2. Essays 3. Translations — French to English 4. Society and culture — Philosophy
LC 91050022

The author traces the ways in which the theories of philosophers such as Rousseau, Hegel and Marx have been misused.

Translated from the French.

Zakaria, Fareed
Age of Revolutions: Progress and Backlash from 1600 to the Present. Fareed Zakaria. W.W. Norton & Company 2024. 416 p.
ISBN 9780393239232
Grades: Adult   **303.6**
1. Revolutions 2. History 3. Political culture 4. Right and left (Political science) 5. Social movements 6. Populism 7. Nationalism 8. Social change 9. History writing — Wars and conflicts — Revolutions 10. Politics and global affairs — General

Populist rage, ideological fracture, economic and technological shocks, war, and an international system studded with catastrophic risk—the early decades of the twenty-first century may be the most revolutionary period in modern history. But it is not the first. Humans have lived, and thrived, through more than one great realignment. What are these revolutions, and how can they help us to understand our fraught world? Fareed Zakaria masterfully investigates the eras and movements that have shaken norms while shaping the modern world.

"A thought-provoking tour of recent history and its considerable discontents." —*Kirkus*

303.60973 Social conflict — United States

Murphy, Chris
★ *The Violence Inside Us: A Brief History of an Ongoing American Tragedy.* by Chris Murphy. Random House 2020. 256 pages
ISBN 9781984854575
Grades: Adult   **303.60973**
1. Violence 2. Violence and guns 3. Gun control 4. Gun ownership 5. Political rights 6. Right to bear arms 7. Legislation 8. Politics and government 9. United States 10. Society and culture — Violence and crime 11. Politics and global affairs — World politics — United States
LC 2019030481

The youngest-elected U.S. Senator presents a sweeping history of the origins of humanity's violent impulses and obsession with firearms while exposing the national mythologies that block action against violence in today's America.

"Murphy's clear-eyed assessment of the nature of violence in America is destined to provoke meaningful, urgently needed discussions." —*Booklist*

Includes bibliographical references and index.

304.2 Human ecology

Ackerman, Diane
The Human Age: The World Shaped by Us. Diane Ackerman. W.W. Norton & Company 2014. 352 p.
ISBN 9780393240740
Grades: Adult   **304.2**
1. Effect of environment on humans 2. Environmental engineering 3. Environmental ethics 4. Environmental degradation 5. Nature Writing — Environmental Issues
LC 2014027691

Booklist Editors' Choice, 2014; National Outdoor Book Award for Natural History Literature, 2015; New York Times Notable Book, 2014.

Explores how human beings have become the dominant force shaping Earth's future by subduing three-quarters of the planet's surface, tinkering with nature, and altering the climate.

PUBLIC LIBRARY CORE COLLECTION: NONFICTION
Twentieth Edition

Diamond, Jared M.
Collapse: How Societies Choose to Fail or Succeed. Jared Diamond. Viking 2005. xi, 575 p, 24 p. of plates : Illustration; Map
ISBN 9780670033379
Grades: 11 12 Adult   **304.2**
1. Social history 2. Environmental policy 3. Environmental degradation 4. Social change 5. History writing — General 6. Nature Writing — Environmental Issues 7. Adult books for young adults

LC 2004057152

ALA Notable Book, 2006; Library Journal Best Books, 2005; New York Times Notable Book, 2005; School Library Journal Best Books: Best Adult Books 4 Teens, 2005.

A study of the downfall of some of history's greatest civilizations discusses the Anasazi, the Maya, and the Viking colony on Greenland, tracing patterns of environmental damage, poor political choices, and other factors in their demise.

"The author ... explores patterns of population growth, overfarming, overgrazing and overhunting, often abetted by drought, cold, rigid social mores and warfare, that lead inexorably to vicious circles of deforestation, erosion and starvation prompted by the disappearance of plant and animal food sources. . . . Readers will find his book an enthralling, and disturbing, reminder of the indissoluble links that bind humans to nature." —*Publishers Weekly*

Includes bibliographical references (p. [529]-560) and index.

Fagan, Brian M.
Climate Chaos: Lessons on Survival from Our Ancestors. Brian Fagan and Nadia Durrani. PublicAffairs 2021. 320 p.
ISBN 9781541750876
Grades: Adult   **304.2**
1. Paleoclimatology 2. Climate change 3. Civilization, Ancient 4. Natural disasters 5. Pollution 6. Effect of humans on nature 7. Droughts 8. Floods 9. Survival 10. Adaptability 11. Emergency planning 12. Immigration and emigration 13. History writing — Ancient 14. Nature Writing — Environmental Issues 15. Science Writing — Weather

LC 2021016383

Man-made climate change may have began in the last two hundred years, but humankind has witnessed many eras of climate instability. The results have not always been pretty: once-mighty civilizations felled by pestilence and glacial melt and drought. Butwe have one powerful advantage as we face our current crisis: history. The study of ancient climates has advanced tremendously in the past ten years, to the point where we can now reconstruct seasonal weather going back thousands of years, and see just how civilizations and nature interacted. The lesson is clear: the societies that survive are the ones that plan ahead. Climate Chaos is thus a book about saving ourselves. Brian Fagan and Nadia Durrani show in remarkable detail what it was like to battle our climate over centuries, and offer us a path to safer and healthier future.

"In this latest book, Fagan and Durrani (who previously collaborated on What We Did in Bed and Bigger Than History) seek to answer one question: why is history relevant to the way societies will handle future climate chaos? The result is a thorough study of human history, as seen entirely through the impact of climate." —*Library Journal*

Includes bibliographical references and index.

Frankopan, Peter
The Earth Transformed: An Untold History. Peter Frankopan. Random House Inc 2023. 656 p.
ISBN 9780525659167
Grades: Adult   **304.2**
1. Climate change 2. Global environmental change 3. Climate and civilization 4. Crops and climate 5. Climatic extremes 6. Impartial writing 7. Nature writing — Environmental issues 8. History writing — General

Spanning centuries and continents, this groundbreaking book, blending brilliant historical writing and cutting-edge research, reveals how climate change has dramatically shaped the development—and demise—of civilizations across time. Map(s).

"In this sweeping history, Oxford historian Frankopan (The New Silk Roads) explores how climate has shaped human history, and how humans have shaped the climate in return....Elegant and cogently argued, this illuminates an age-old and urgently important dynamic." —*Publishers Weekly*

Hayhoe, Katharine
Saving Us: A Climate Scientist's Case for Hope and Healing in a Divided World. Katharine Hayhoe. Signal Press 2021. 224 p.
ISBN 9781982143831
Grades: Adult   **304.2**
1. Hayhoe, Katharine 2. Climatologists 3. Climate change 4. Environmentalism 5. Argumentation 6. Discussion 7. Disagreement 8. Interpersonal relations 9. Polarization (Social sciences) 10. Consensus (Social sciences) 11. Social values 12. Canadian literature 13. Nature Writing — Environmental Issues 14. Society and culture — General 15. Politics and global affairs — Environmental issues and policies

Argues that when it comes to changing hearts and minds in regard to climate change,, facts are only one part of the equation. We need to find shared values in order to connect our unique identities to collective action. This is not another doomsday narrative about a planet on fire. It is a multilayered look at science, faith, and human psychology.

"Practical advice abounds in this compassionate guide to conducting meaningful discussions about the environment from climate scientist Hayhoe (All We Can Save). . . . While some may find her outlook a bit rose-tinged—'We can fix it. There are solutions'—those in search of a hope-filled approach will find plenty of encouragement." —*Publishers Weekly*

Kimmerer, Robin Wall
★ *Braiding Sweetgrass: Indigenous Wisdom, Scientific Knowledge and the Teachings of Plants.* Robin Wall Kimmerer. Milkweed Editions 2013. 320 p.
ISBN 9781571311771
Grades: Adult   **304.2**
1. Kimmerer, Robin Wall 2. Philosophy, Indigenous 3. Indigenous peoples 4. Nature 5. Philosophy of nature 6. Human ecology 7. Humans and plants 8. Botany 9. Potawatomi (North American people) 10. Indigenous peoples of North America — Social life and customs 11. Effect of humans on nature 12. Indigenous peoples of North America 13. Philosophy 14. Essays 15. Nature Writing — General

LC 2013012563

As a botanist, Robin Wall Kimmerer has been trained to ask questions of nature with the tools of science. As a member of the Citizen Potawatomi Nation, she embraces the notion that plants and animals are our oldest teachers. In Braiding Sweetgrass, Kimmerer brings these two lenses of knowledge together to take us on "a journey that is every bit as mythic as it is scientific, as sacred as it is historical, as clever as it is wise."

"Anyone who enjoys reading about natural history, botany, protecting nature, or Native American culture will love this book." —*Library Journal*

Kolbert, Elizabeth
★ *Under a White Sky: The Nature of the Future.* Elizabeth Kolbert. Crown 2021. 256 p.
ISBN 9780593136270
Grades: Adult   **304.2**
1. Effect of humans on nature 2. Human ecology 3. Environmental protection 4. Global environmental change 5. Sustainability 6. Technological innovations 7. Nature Writing — Environmental Issues 8. Science Writing — General

LC 2020047398

From her coverage in the New Yorker, Elizabeth Kolbert has become one of our most important writers on the environment. Now she investigates the immense challenges humanity faces as we scramble to reverse, in a matter of decades, the effects we've had on the atmosphere, the oceans, the world's forests and rivers—on the very topography of the globe. In her trademark persuasive and darkly comic prose, Kolbert introduces myriad innovations that offer ways to avert disaster—or may produce new disasters, ones that haven't been and perhaps cannot be anticipated. One way to look at human civilization, says Kolbert, is as a ten-thousand-year exercise in defying nature. Paradoxically, the very sorts of interventions that have imperiled our planet are increasingly seen as the only hope for its salvation.

ESSENTIAL AND RECOMMENDED TITLES
304.20973 Human ecology — United States

"This investigation of global change is brilliantly executed and urgently necessary." —*Publishers Weekly*
Includes bibliographical references and index.

Linden, Eugene
Fire and Flood: A People's History of Climate Change, from 1979 to the Present. Eugene Linden. Penguin Books 2022. 336 p.
ISBN 9781984882240
Grades: Adult   304.2
1. Climate change 2. Global environmental change 3. Environmental policy 4. Big business 5. Environmentalism 6. Anti-environmentalism 7. United States 8. 21st century 9. Politics and global affairs — Environmental issues and policies 10. Nature Writing — Environmental Issues 11. History writing — Early 21st century — United States

An award-winning science journalist looks at the last thirty years of climate change and the shocking failure by governments and key business interests to address the issue despite the evidence in front of our own eyes.

"Linden (Deep Past) has written a prescient book on the history of climate change initiatives, science and humanity's missed opportunities….Of the many books written on climate change and how humanity has gotten to where it is and where it needs to go, this is one of the most essential." —*Library Journal*

Lipsky, David
★ *The Parrot and the Igloo: Climate and the Science of Denial.* David Lipsky. W W Norton & Company 2022. 416 p.
ISBN 9780393866704
Grades: Adult   304.2
1. Climate change 2. Science 3. Denial (Psychology) 4. Nature Writing — Environmental issues 5. Science writing — General

LibraryReads Favorites, 2023.

The New York Times best-selling author explores how "anti-science" became so virulent in American life—through a history of climate denial and its consequences.

"This tome by award-winning author Lipsky takes the reader on a journey through the evolution of climate-change denial—including how cancer-denial strategies and lobbying by tobacco companies paved the way for its brand of scientific obfuscation—and how it has prevented legislative action…This can be considered the historical record to date on climate action and inaction." —*Booklist*

Miles, Tiya
★ *Wild Girls: How the Outdoors Shaped the Women Who Challenged a Nation.* Tiya Miles. W.W. Norton & Company 2023. 192 p.
ISBN 9781324020875
Grades: Adult   304.2
1. Women 2. Outdoor life 3. Rural life 4. African American women 5. Indigenous women 6. Social marginality 7. Gender role 8. Wilderness areas 9. Survival skills 10. Freedom 11. North American people 12. American people 13. Self-discovery 14. United States history 15. Society and culture — Gender — Women 16. Life stories — Nature and outdoors 17. Nature Writing — Personal Responses 18. History writing — Women's history

An award-winning historian shows how girls who found self-understanding in the natural world became women who changed America.

"With insight and imagination, Miles explores the ways in which the natural environment presented 'New possibilities' for 19th-century women and girls…It's an inventive take on what inspired people to challenge norms and agitate for change." —*Publishers Weekly*

Rich, Nathaniel
Second Nature: Scenes from a World Remade. Nathaniel Rich. MCD 2021. 304 p.
ISBN 9780374106034
Grades: Adult   304.2
1. Effect of humans on nature 2. Effect of environment on humans 3. Environmentalism 4. Climate change 5. Nature 6. Global warming 7. Pollution 8. Nature Writing — Environmental issues

LC 2020049011

From the author of Losing Earth, a deeply reported and beautifully told exploration of how we live in a post-natural world.

In this outstanding collection of pieces, some of which were published in different forms in the New York Times Magazine, the New Republic, Men's Journal, and other outlets, Rich provides vivid, often disturbing portraits of individuals and events contributing to 'The death rattle of the romantic idea that nature is innocent of human influence.' —*Kirkus*

Wallace-Wells, David
The Uninhabitable Earth: Life After Warming. David Wallace-Wells. Tim Duggan Books 2019. 256 p.
ISBN 9780525576709
Grades: Adult   304.2
1. Global warming 2. Climate change 3. Forecasting 4. Global environmental change 5. Nature Writing — Environmental Issues

LC 2018051268

ALA Notable Book, 2020; New York Times Notable Book, 2019.

It is worse, much worse, than you think. If your anxiety about global warming is dominated by fears of sea-level rise, you are barely scratching the surface of what terrors are possible. In California, wildfires now rage year-round, destroying thousands of homes. Across the US, "500-year" storms pummel communities month after month, and floods displace tens of millions annually. This is only a preview of the changes to come. And they are coming fast. Without a revolution in how billions of humans conduct their lives, parts of the Earth could become close to uninhabitable, and other parts horrifically inhospitable, as soon as the end of this century. In his travelogue of our near future, David Wallace-Wells brings into stark relief the climate troubles that await—food shortages, refugee emergencies, and other crises that will reshape the globe. But the world will be remade by warming in more profound ways as well, transforming our politics, our culture, our relationship to technology, and our sense of history. It will be all-encompassing, shaping and distorting nearly every aspect of human life as it is lived today. Like an Inconvenient Truth and Silent Spring before it, the Uninhabitable Earth is both a meditation on the devastation we have brought upon ourselves and an impassioned call to action. For just as the world was brought to the brink of catastrophe within the span of a lifetime, the responsibility to avoid it now belongs to a single generation.

"A well-organized, fully sourced, powerfully composed survey of the planetary changes happening now at shockingly rapid rates and their dire human consequences." —*Booklist*
Includes bibliographical references.

304.20973 Human ecology — United States

Hohn, Donovan
The Inner Coast: Essays. Donovan Hohn. W W Norton & Co. Inc 2020. 256 p.
ISBN 9781324005971
Grades: Adult   304.20973
1. Human ecology 2. Coastal towns 3. Effect of humans on nature 4. Essays

LC 2020008292

Prize-winning essays on our changing place in the natural world by the best-selling author of Moby-Duck.

"Settle in and savor a keen mind with a laudable moral compass." —*Kirkus*

304.209798 Human ecology — Alaska

Wohlforth, Charles P.
The Fate of Nature: Rediscovering Our Ability to Rescue the Earth. Charles Wohlforth. St. Martin's Press 2010. 434 p. : Map
ISBN 9780312377373
Grades: 11 12 Adult   304.209798

PUBLIC LIBRARY CORE COLLECTION: NONFICTION
Twentieth Edition

1. Human ecology 2. Conservation of natural resources 3. Environmental protection 4. Natural history 5. Environmental degradation 6. Alaska 7. Nature Writing — Environmental Issues

LC 2009045779

Draws on behavioral science to assess environmental protection activities in Alaska, in a partly philosophical analysis that cites the examples of such groups as evolutionary scientists, hippie activists, and oil tycoons.

"The author considers the consequences of Captain John Cook's hasty visit to the gulf in 1778, the Russian conquest of coastal Alaska, . . . the crash of the herring fisheries, and the cruel fates of the region's indigenous peoples. But Wohlforth believes that our consuming nature is balanced by the impulse to understand and cherish the living world, which is borne out in his compelling profiles of whale biologist Eva Saulitis; Geerat Vermeij, a blind evolutionary scientist who discovered an arms race among crustaceans; and various environmental heroes. . . . By analyzing competition and evolution, culture and economics, habits of living and of mind, science and suffering, Wohlforth brings a truly ecological perspective to the global debate over how to protect the biosphere." —Booklist

Thomas Dunne Books; Includes bibliographical references and index.

304.6 Population

Hitchens, Christopher
Mortality. Christopher Hitchens. Twelve 2012. 160 p.
ISBN 9781455502752
Grades: Adult   304.6
1. Hitchens, Christopher. 1949-2011 2. People with cancer 3. Mortality 4. Death 5. Authors, American 6. People with terminal illnesses 7. Men 8. Autobiographies and memoirs 9. Biographies 10. Life stories — Facing adversity — Medical issues 11. Science Writing — Medicine and health — Illness and disease

LC 2012014024

Traces the author's battle with esophageal cancer while he continued to write columns on politics and culture for "Vanity Fair," and describes his personal and philosophical view of life and death.

Junger, Sebastian
★ *In My Time of Dying: How I Came Face to Face with the Idea of an Afterlife*. Sebastian Junger. Simon & Schuster 2024. 160 p.
ISBN 9781668050835
Grades: Adult   304.6
1. Junger, Sebastian 2. Near-death experience 3. Life after death 4. Science 5. Philosophy 6. Death 7. Spirituality and religion — General 8. Science Writing — General 9. Life stories — Facing adversity — Coping with death

The New York Times best-selling author shares the story of how a near-death experience led him to question his own atheism and undertake a scientific and philosophical examination of mortality and what happens after we die.

"Ardently researched, consummately written, and boldly forthright, this an intensely moving and deeply provocative immersion." —Booklist

Mannix, Kathryn
With the End in Mind: Dying, Death, and Wisdom in an Age of Denial. Kathryn Mannix. Little, Brown and Company 2018. 304 p.
ISBN 9780316504485
Grades: Adult   304.6
1. Physician and patient 2. Death 3. Terminal care 4. Physicians 5. Dignity 6. Medical care 7. Grief 8. Society and culture — General

LC Bl2017046529

A palliative care physician draws on stories from her own practice to explain how to enable a gentle and peaceful death and how modern medicine, augmented by traditional palliative approaches, can restore dignity, humanity, and meaning to the end of life.

"Using case histories, Mannix provides poignant insight into the way people live when they know they are dying, and what those around them may be thinking and wishing to say." —Library Journal

Sciubba, Jennifer Dabbs
8 Billion and Counting: How Sex, Death, and Migration Shape Our World. Jennifer D. Sciubba. W.W. Norton & Company 2022. 288 p.
ISBN 9781324002703
Grades: Adult   304.6
1. Population 2. Demographic transition 3. Demography 4. Social change 5. Immigration and emigration 6. Society and culture — General

LC 2021052497

A provocative description of the power of population change to create the conditions for societal transformation.

"Sciubba (The Future Faces of War), an international studies professor at Rhodes College, looks at how population trends shape the world in this sobering survey….Comprehensive and full of incisive analysis, this is not to be missed." —Publishers Weekly

Includes bibliographical references and index.

304.8 Movement of people

Gatrell, Peter
The Unsettling of Europe: How Migration Reshaped a Continent. Peter Gatrell. Perseus Books Group 2019. 540 p.
ISBN 9780465093618
Grades: Adult   304.8
1. Immigrants 2. Refugees 3. Immigration and emigration 4. Immigration policy 5. European history 6. 20th century 7. History writing — Europe 8. Society and culture — Immigration

LC 2019006372

Migration is perhaps the most pressing issue of our time, and it has completely decentered European politics in recent years. But as we consider the current refugee crisis, acclaimed historian Peter Gatrell reminds us that the history of Europe has always been one of people on the move. Gatrell places migration at the center of post-war European history, and the aspirations of migrants themselves at the center of the story of migration. This is an urgent history that will reshape our understanding of modern Europe.

"Gatrell's detailed but lucid and accessible treatment balances close analysis of shifting policies with vivid, sympathetic sketches of migrants negotiating perilous border crossings and struggling to fit in. The result is a persuasive challenge to conventional wisdom that shows migration in Europe is nothing new." —Publishers Weekly

Includes bibliographical references and index.

Khakpour, Porochista
Brown Album: Essays on Exile and Identity. Porochista Khakpour. Vintage 2020. 226 p.
ISBN 9780525564713
Grades: Adult   304.8
1. Khakpour, Porochista 2. Iranian American women 3. Immigrants 4. Identity 5. Women authors 6. Refugees 7. Assimilation (Sociology) 8. Stereotypes 9. Intersectionality 10. Political culture 11. United States 12. Essays 13. Life stories — Identity — Race and ethnicity 14. Life stories — Identity — Immigrants 15. Society and culture — Race 16. Society and culture — Immigration

The award-winning author presents a collection of essays that draws on his personal experiences to explore the realities of the Iranian-American immigration experience in the post-9/11 era of Donald Trump.

"A triumphant entry in the personal essay canon." —Library Journal

Urrea, Luis Alberto
The Devil's Highway: A True Story. Luis Alberto Urrea. Little, Brown 2004. xii, 239 p.
ISBN 9780316746717
Grades: 11 12 Adult   304.8
1. Human smuggling 2. Desert survival 3. Undocumented immigrants 4. Undocumented workers 5. Crimes against undocumented workers 6. Survival 7. Immigration and emigration 8. Mexican-American Border Region 9. United

ESSENTIAL AND RECOMMENDED TITLES
304.80973 Emigration — United States

States 10. Mexico 11. Impartial writing 12. History writing — Immigration — United States 13. Adult books for young adults

LC 2003058930

Pulitzer Prize for General Nonfiction finalist.

Describes the attempt of twenty-six men to cross the Mexican border into the desert of southern Arizona, a region known as the Devil's Highway, detailing their harrowing ordeal and battle for survival against impossible odds.

Includes index.

304.80973 Emigration — United States

Wilkerson, Isabel
★ *The Warmth of Other Suns: The Epic Story of America's Great Migration.* Isabel Wilkerson. Random House 2010. 720 p.
ISBN 9780679444329
Grades: Adult   304.80973

1. Rural-urban migration 2. African American history 3. Migration, Internal 4. Immigration and emigration 5. Race relations 6. African Americans 7. Civilization 8. United States history 9. United States 10. 20th century 11. 19th century 12. History writing — African American — United States 13. Life stories — Identity — Race and ethnicity 14. Life stories — Facing adversity 15. Nonfiction that reads like fiction

LC 2009049753

ALA Notable Book, 2011; Booklist Editors' Choice, 2010; Hurston/Wright Legacy Award: Nonfiction, 2011; Library Journal Best Books, 2010; Mark Lynton History Prize, 2011; National Book Critics Circle Award for Non-Fiction, 2010; New York Times Notable Book, 2010.

In this epic, beautifully written masterwork, Pulitzer Prize-winning author Isabel Wilkerson chronicles one of the great untold stories of American history: the decades-long migration of Black citizens who fled the South for northern and western cities, in search of a better life. From 1915 to 1970, this exodus of almost six million people changed the face of America.

"An account of the Great Migration, the 55-year stretch (1915-70) during which 6 million Black Americans fled the Jim Crow South. Wilkerson, a Pulitzer Prize-winning journalist, uses the journeys of three of them—a Mississippi sharecropper, a Louisiana doctor, and a Florida laborer—to etch an indelible and compulsively readable portrait of race, class, and politics in 20th-century America. History is rarely distilled so finely." —*Entertainment Weekly*

Includes bibliographical references.

305 Groups of people

Bagby, Meredith E.
The New Guys: The Historic Class of Astronauts That Broke Barriers and Changed the Face of Space Travel. Meredith Bagby. William Morrow, an Imprint of HarperCollins Publishers 2023. 320 p.
ISBN 9780063141971
Grades: Adult   305

1. Astronauts 2. African American astronauts 3. Women astronauts 4. Space flight 5. Multiculturalism 6. United States 7. Science Writing — Space and Flight 8. Society and culture — General

LC 2022048599

Telling their stories for the first time ever, NASA's barrier-breaking Astronaut Class of 1978, dubbed "The New Guys," share their experiences pioneering the Shuttle program, which defined a generation of space travel, and helped build a dream of a new American century in space.

"In this exciting if speculative chronicle, Bagby (Rational Exuberance), a film and TV producer, presents the stories of NASA's class of 1978, the first to include women and people of color." —*Publishers Weekly*

Includes bibliographical references and index.

Marx, W. David
★ *Status and Culture: How Our Desire for Higher Social Rank Shapes Identity, Fosters Creativity, and Changes the World.* W. David Marx. Viking 2022. 304 p.
ISBN 9780593296707
Grades: Adult   305

1. Social status 2. Identity 3. Culture 4. Social success 5. Society and culture — Pop culture

LC 2022006836

W. David Marx weaves together the wisdom from history, psychology, sociology, anthropology, economics, philosophy, linguistics, semiotics, cultural theory, literary theory, art history, media studies, and neuroscience to demonstrate exactly how individual status seeking creates our cultural ecosystem. Marx examines three fundamental questions: why do individuals cluster around arbitrary behaviors and take deep meaning from them? How do distinct styles, conventions, and sensibilities emerge? Why do we change behaviors over time and why do some behaviors stick around?

"Hefty but compellingly readable—essential for anyone desiring a deeper understanding of status inequity." —*Kirkus*

Includes bibliographical references and index.

Norris, Michele
★ *Our Hidden Conversations: What Americans Really Think About Race and Identity.* Michele Norris. Simon & Schuster 2024. 528 p.
ISBN 9781982154394
Grades: Adult   305

1. Race relations 2. Identity 3. Ethnic identity 4. Social classes 5. Discrimination 6. Racism 7. Income inequality 8. Cultural differences 9. American people 10. North American people 11. United States 12. Anthologies 13. Society and culture — Race

A Peabody Award-winning journalist offers a transformative dialogue on race and identity in America, unearthed through her decade-long work at the Race Card Project.

"Norris offers crucial insight into how Americans think about race, combining the painful with the inspiring." —*Kirkus*

Piketty, Thomas
★ *Capital and Ideology.* Thomas Piketty, translated from the French by Arthur Goldhammer. Harvard University Press 2020. IX, 1093 p.
ISBN 9780674980822
Grades: Adult   305

1. Equality 2. Socialism 3. Ideology 4. Capitalism 5. Economics 6. International cooperation 7. Social change 8. Wealth redistribution 9. Property 10. Translations — French to English 11. Business and economics — Economics — Socioeconomics 12. Business and economics — Economics — World economy 13. Politics and global affairs — Political philosophy

LC 2019040839

The successor to the Capital in the Twenty-First Century is at once a retelling of global history, a scathing critique of contemporary politics and a bold proposal for a new and fairer economic system.

"A deftly argued case for a new kind of socialism that, while sure to inspire controversy, bears widespread discussion." —*Kirkus*

Includes bibliographical references and index; Originally published: Paris : Editions du Seuil, 2019; Translated from the French.

305.08 Sociology — Specific groups of people

Busby, Jill Louise
Unfollow Me: Essays on Complicity. Jill Louise Busby. Bloomsbury 2021. 208 p.
ISBN 9781635577112
Grades: Adult   305.08

1. Busby, Jill Louise 2. African American women 3. LGBTQIA+ people 4. Social media 5. Internet personalities 6. Fame 7. Identity 8. Inequality 9. Hypocrisy 10. Corporate culture 11. Liberalism 12. Race awareness 13. United

States 14. Essays 15. Society and culture — Race 16. Society and culture — Wealth and class 17. Life stories — Identity 18. Life stories — Business 19. Antiracist literature

Jill Louise Busby spent years in the nonprofit sector specializing in Diversity & Inclusion. She spoke at academic institutions, businesses, and detention centers on the topics of Race, Power, and Privilege and delivered over two-hundred workshops to nonprofit organizations all over the California Bay Area. In 2016, fed up with what passed as progressive in the Pacific Northwest, Busby uploaded a one-minute video about race, white institutions, and faux liberalism to Instagram. Busby's social commentary manages to be both wryly funny and achingly open-hearted as she recounts her shape-shifting moves among the subtle hierarchies of progressive communities.

"Busby's compelling writing elevates conversations on gender, race, and sexuality, drawing in readers from the very first page and setting this memoir-in-essays apart." —*Library Journal*

305.09 Social sciences — History

Piketty, Thomas
A Brief History of Equality. Thomas Piketty; translated from the French by Steven Rendall. The Belknap Press of Harvard University Press 2022. 320 p.
ISBN 9780674273559
Grades: Adult   305.09
1. Equality 2. History of civilization 3. Social classes 4. Income inequality 5. Wealth 6. Social justice 7. Translations — French to English 8. Society and culture — Wealth and class 9. Business and economics — Economics — Socioeconomics 10. Business and economics — Economics — History
LC 2021053186

A leading economist of inequality presents a short but sweeping and surprisingly optimistic history of human progress toward equality despite crises, disasters, and backsliding.

"Marked by Piketty's trademark lucidity, impressive multidisciplinary scholarship, and provocative progressivism, this is a vital introduction to his ideas." —*Publishers Weekly*

Originally published in French as UNE breve histoire de l'egalite by Editions du Seuil, Paris, in 2021; Includes bibliographical references and index.

305.2 Age groups

Twenge, Jean M.
Generations: The Real Differences Between Gen Z, Millennials, Gen X, Boomers, and Silents - and What They Mean for America's Future. Jean M. Twenge. Atria Books 2023. 400 p.
ISBN 9781982181611
Grades: Adult   305.2
1. Generations 2. Generation gap 3. Intergenerational relations 4. Interpersonal conflict 5. Communities 6. Social life and customs 7. United States 8. Society and culture — General 9. History Writing — United States

An expert on generational change looks at the six generations of Americans currently alive, from the Silents to the still-to-be-named generation born after 2012, and how they connect, conflict and compete with one another.

"Twenge (Generation Me), a professor of psychology at San Diego State University, takes a fascinating look at the six generations currently living in the U.S....It's an informative and insightful study of the dynamics at play in U.S. society today." —*Publishers Weekly*

305.23 Young people

Clinton, Hillary Rodham
It Takes a Village: And Other Lessons Children Teach Us. Hillary Rodham Clinton. Simon & Schuster 1996. 318 p. : Illustration
ISBN 9780684818436
Grades: Adult   305.23
1. Clinton, Hillary Rodham 2. Child development 3. Child welfare 4. Families 5. Presidents' spouses 6. Parenting 7. United States 8. Politics and global affairs — General
LC OC2014040133

The First Lady shares her observations on the needs of children and families in the modern, fragmented, fast-paced world and explores diverse ways in which we can improve family and community life.

Haidt, Jonathan
★ *The Anxious Generation: How the Great Rewiring of Childhood Is Causing an Epidemic of Mental Illness.* Jonathan Haidt. Penguin 2024. 320 p.
ISBN 9780593655030
Grades: Adult   305.23
1. Child internet users 2. Internet and children 3. Mental health 4. Smartphones 5. Social media 6. Digital media 7. Depression 8. Anxiety 9. Suicide 10. Children with mental illnesses 11. Child mental health 12. Child development 13. Safety 14. Child advocacy 15. Family and Relationships — Parenting 16. Family and Relationships — Growing up 17. Science Writing — Medicine and health — Mental health 18. Society and culture — Media and technology 19. Society and culture — Psychology and human behavior
LC 2023056736

In The Anxious Generation, social psychologist Jonathan Haidt lays out the facts about the epidemic of teen mental illness that hit many countries at the same time. He shows how the "play-based childhood" began to decline in the 1980s, and how it was finally wiped out by the arrival of the "phone-based childhood" in the early 2010s. He explains why social media damages girls more than boys and why boys have been withdrawing from the real world into the virtual world, with disastrous consequences for themselves, their families, and their societies.

"A vigorous contribution to the conversation and discourse about how to protect youths from psychological and neurological damage linked to technology. For parents, educators, and tech decision-makers." —*Library Journal*

Includes bibliographical references and index.

Wegner, Bobbi
Raising Feminist Boys: How to Talk to Your Child About Gender, Consent, & Empathy. Bobbi Wegner, PSYD.. New Harbinger Publications, Inc. 2021. VI, 202 pages
ISBN 9781684036677
Grades: Adult   305.23
1. Child rearing 2. Child development 3. Feminism 4. Character education 5. Personality development 6. Boys 7. Family and Relationships — Parenting
LC 2020052146

In a world steeped in gender inequality and sexual violence, it's become more and more clear that we can't just teach girls to protect themselves. We must also teach boys not to do harm. Written by a clinical psychologist with expertise in modern families, Raising Feminist Boys is a parent's guide to having developmentally appropriate conversations with boys about sexual responsibility, consent, gender, empathy, and identity.

"This timely manual will help parents understand what it takes to model good behavior and set a positive example." —*Booklist*

Includes bibliographical references (pages 191-202).

Whippman, Ruth
★ *Boymom: Reimagining Boyhood in the Age of Impossible Masculinity.* by Ruth Whippman. [Harmony] 2024. 288 p.
ISBN 9780593577639
Grades: Adult   305.23
1. Whippman, Ruth 2. Child rearing 3. Mothers and sons 4. Child development 5. Masculinity 6. Character education 7. Personality development 8. Boys 9. Psychology 10. Social life and customs 11. Autobiographies and memoirs 12. Family and relationships — Parenting 13. Life stories — Relationships — Parent and child
LC 2023039427

This deep dive into the complexities of raising boys in the face of the many cultural messages they face leave them anxious, emotionally repressed and socially isolated offers ways to help them overcome the confines of masculine expectations.

ESSENTIAL AND RECOMMENDED TITLES
305.23082 Girls

"It's an urgent call to reassess how boys are raised and socialized." —*Publishers Weekly*

Includes bibliographical references and index.

305.23082 Girls

Orenstein, Peggy
Cinderella Ate My Daughter: Dispatches from the Frontlines of the New Girlie-girl Culture. Peggy Orenstein. HarperCollins 2011. 288 p.
ISBN 9780061711527
Grades: Adult   305.23082
1. Girls 2. Femininity 3. Mothers and daughters 4. Popular culture 5. Gender role 6. Parenting 7. Intersectionality 8. Psychology 9. Family and Relationships — Parenting 10. Society and culture — Gender — Women
LC 2010028724

Reveals the dark side of pink and pretty and offers ways to prevent raising daughters who only care about image.

"The author finds today's pink and princess-obsessed girl culture grating when it threatens to lure her own young daughter, Daisy. In her quest to determine whether princess mania is merely a passing phase or a more sinister marketing plot with long-term negative impact, Orenstein travels to Disneyland, American Girl Place, the American International Toy Fair; visits a children's beauty pageant; attends a Miley Cyrus concert; tools around the Internet; and interviews parents, historians, psychologists, marketers, and others. With insight and biting humor, the author explores her own conflicting feelings as a mother as she protects her offspring and probes the roots and tendrils of the girlie-girl movement." —*Publishers Weekly*

Includes bibliographical references and index.

305.23086 Children by miscellaneous social attributes

Luiselli, Valeria
Tell Me How It Ends: An Essay in 40 Questions. Valeria Luiselli. Coffee House Press 2017. 119 pages
ISBN 9781566894951
Grades: Adult   305.23086
1. Undocumented immigrants 2. Child immigrants 3. Deportation 4. Citizenship 5. Naturalization 6. American dream 7. Latin American people 8. Immigration and emigration 9. United States 10. Essays 11. Society and culture — Immigration
LC 2017000414

Kirkus Prize for Nonfiction finalist, 2017.

Structured around the forty questions Luiselli translates and asks undocumented Latin-American children facing deportation, Tell Me How It Ends (an expansion of her 2016 Freeman's essay of the same name) humanizes these young migrants and highlights the contradiction of the idea of America as a fiction for immigrants with the reality of racism and fear—both here and back home.

"This is a vital document for understanding the crisis that immigrants to the U.S. Are facing, and a call to action for those who find this situation appalling." —*Publishers Weekly*

Includes bibliographical references and index.

305.231 Child development

Brookwood, Marilyn
The Orphans of Davenport: Eugenics, the Great Depression, and the War Over Children's Intelligence. Marilyn Brookwood. Liveright Publishing Corporation 2021. 336 p.
ISBN 9781631494680
Grades: Adult   305.231
1. Eugenics 2. People with disabilities 3. Child development 4. Developmental psychology 5. Developmental biology 6. Intelligence 7. Heredity and environment (Psychology) 8. Orphanages 9. Depressions, 1929-1941 10. Child psychology 11. Parent and child 12. United States history 13. United States 14. Iowa 15. Depression era (1929-1941) 16. 20th century 17. History writing — Regional history — United States 18. Society and culture — Psychology and human behavior
LC 2021005096

The fascinating-and eerily timely-tale of the forgotten Depression-era psychologists who overthrew long-accepted racist and classist views of childhood development. "Doomed from birth" was how psychologist Harold Skeels described two toddler girls at the Orphans' Home in Davenport, Iowa, in 1934. Following prevailing eugenic beliefs, Skeels and his colleague Marie Skodak assumed that the girls had inherited their parents' low intelligence and sent them to an institution. To their astonishment, under the women's care, the children's IQ scores became normal. This revolutionary finding infuriated leading psychologists, all eugenicists unwilling to accept that nature and nurture work together to decide our fates. Recasting Skeels and his team as intrepid heroes, Marilyn Brookwood weaves years of prodigious archival research to show how after decades of backlash, the Iowans finally prevailed.

"With this riveting history of an unsung scientific breakthrough in the 1930s, psychologist Brookwood tells how U.S. state and federal governments, backed by mainstream psychologists, had for decades enforced eugenicist policies.... A remarkable unsung history, told with empathy, nuance, and a knack for character-driven storytelling." —*Library Journal*

Includes bibliographical references and index.

305.232 Infants

Klein, Tovah P.
How Toddlers Thrive: What Parents Can Do Today for Children Ages 2-5 to Plant the Seeds of Lifelong Success. Tovah P. Klein, PhD.. Simon & Schuster 2014. xxii, 280 pages
ISBN 9781476735139
Grades: Adult   305.232
1. Child rearing 2. Toddlers 3. Family and Relationships — Growing up 4. Family and Relationships — Parenting 5. Science writing — Medicine and health — Psychology
LC 2013032839

A Sesame Street advisor and expert in toddler psychology argues that adult success is often established in the developmental preschool years, sharing advice for parents on how to promote such success-driving positive attributes as resilience, self-regulation and empathy.

Argues that adult success is often established in the developmental preschool years, sharing advice for parents on how to promote such success-driving positive attributes as resilience, self-regulation, and empathy.

A Touchstone Book; Includes bibliographical references (pages 263-269) and index.

Murkoff, Heidi Eisenberg
What to Expect the First Year. Heidi Murkoff and Sharon Mazel; foreword by Mark D. Widome, M.D, M.P.H, Professor of Pediatrics, Penn State Hershey Children's Hospital, Hershey, Pennsylvania. Workman Publishing 2014. xxv, 678 p. : Illustration
ISBN 9780761181507
Grades: Adult   305.232
1. Babies 2. Child rearing 3. Baby care 4. Reference books 5. Family and Relationships — Growing up 6. Family and Relationships — Parenting
LC 2014004520

An infant care guide describes monthly growth and development from infancy to toddler, discussing such topics as common childhood ailments, feeding, allergies, vaccinations, sleep strategies, and decoding crying.

PUBLIC LIBRARY CORE COLLECTION: NONFICTION
Twentieth Edition

305.233 Children three to five

Santomero, Angela C
Preschool Clues: Raising Smart, Inspired, and Engaged Kids in a Screen-filled World. Angela C. Santomero, M.A. with Deborah Reber. Touchstone 2018. xviii, 298 p. : Illustration
ISBN 9781501174339
Grades: Adult   305.233
1. Preschool children 2. Toddlers 3. Child development 4. Child rearing 5. Family and Relationships — Parenting 6. Educator resources — Primary education
LC 2017030842
The award-winning creator of Blue's Clues, Super Why!, and Daniel Tiger's Neighborhood shares the secret sauce behind her shows' powerful, transformative results in the form of eleven research-based, foundational "clues" to ensure that preschoolers flourish academically, socially, and emotionally during this critical time.

305.235 Young people twelve to twenty

Damour, Lisa
Untangled: Guiding Teenage Girls Through the Seven Transitions into Adulthood. Lisa Damour, Ph.D... Ballantine Books 2016. xix, 326 pages
ISBN 9780553393057
Grades: Adult   305.235
1. Adolescence 2. Adolescent psychology 3. Adulthood 4. Teenage girls 5. Psychology 6. Family and Relationships — Growing up 7. Family and Relationships — Parenting
LC 2015040046
A clinical psychologist offers guidance to parents of teenage girls, helping to demystify their erratic behavior and mood swings by describing the seven developmental passages that all girls go through as they transition to adulthood.

A clinical psychologist offers hope and guidance to parents of teenage girls, helping to demystify their erratic behavior and mood swings by describing the seven developmental passages that all girls go through as they transition to adulthood.

Includes bibliographical references (pages 283-309) and index.

Goodan, Chelsey
Underestimated: The Wisdom and Power of Teenage Girls. Chelsey Goodan. Gallery Books 2024. 256 p.
ISBN 9781668032688
Grades: Adult   305.235
1. Teenage girls 2. Adolescence 3. Growing up 4. Emotions 5. Honesty 6. Interpersonal communication 7. Femininity 8. Self-acceptance 9. Empowerment 10. Family and Relationships — Growing up 11. Family and Relationships — Parenting 12. Society and culture — Gender — Women 13. Debut title
LC 2023042576
Written with warmth and humor, Underestimated is the first book to invite us into a teenage girl's brain and heart, as told from the point of view of a beloved and trusted mentor. Chelsey Goodan is a highly sought-after academic tutor who has worked with hundreds of girls from all different backgrounds, earning their trust, confidence, and friendship. Rather than dismissing teenage girls based on our own fears or treating them as problems that need to be solved, Goodan encourages us as parents, and as a society, to help girls unleash their power and celebrate their intrinsic wisdom, creating more healing and connection for everyone.

"Goodan's...debut is a wise, well-articulated handbook to help adults listen to and hold space for teens." —*Booklist*

Orenstein, Peggy
★ *Boys & Sex: Young Men on Hookups, Love, Porn, Consent, and Navigating the New Masculinity.* Peggy Orenstein. Harper 2020. 320 p.
ISBN 9780062666970
Grades: Adult   305.235
1. Teenage boys 2. Young men 3. Masculinity 4. Sex education for children 5. Sexuality 6. Society and culture — Gender — Men 7. Society and culture — Sex and sexuality
LC 2019040572
The author of the groundbreaking, best-selling Girls & Sex turns her attention to young men, discussing and revealing how modern young men understand and navigate the new rules of physical and emotional intimacy.

"A highly constructive analysis that provides many topics for exploration and discussion by parents and others who interact with boys." —*Kirkus*

Includes bibliographical references and index.

Shachtman, Tom
★ *Rumspringa: To Be or Not to Be Amish.* Tom Shachtman. North Point Press 2006. 286 p.
ISBN 9780865476875
Grades: 11 12 Adult   305.235
1. Personal conduct 2. Amish 3. Rumspringa 4. Religions 5. Spirituality and Religion — Christianity 6. Adult books for young adults
LC 2006004329
An analysis of Amish youth culture profiles the coming-of-age ritual known as the rumspringa, during which sixteen-year-old Amish adolescents are permitted to venture outside of the bounds of their faith, experiment with alcohol and smoking, wear trendy clothes, and ultimately decide if they want to remain detached from the outside world.

"Shachtman is like a maestro, masterfully conducting an orchestra of history, anthropology, psychology, sociology, and journalism together in a harmonious and evocative symphony of all things Amish." —*Christian Science Monitor*

This book is based, in part, on research done for the Stick Figure Productions documentary the Devil's Playground—P. opposite tp; Includes bibliographical references (p. [281]-283).

Wiseman, Rosalind
Masterminds & Wingmen: Helping Our Boys Cope with Schoolyard Power, Locker-room Tests, Girlfriends, and the New Rules of Boy World. Rosalind Wiseman. Harmony Books 2013. 377 pages : Illustration
ISBN 9780307986658
Grades: Adult   305.235
1. Parent and teenager 2. Teenage boys 3. Psychology 4. Educator resources — General 5. Family and Relationships — Parenting 6. Science writing — Medicine and health — Psychology
LC 2013372427
Here is a landmark book that reveals how boys think, showing parents, educators, and coaches how to reach out and help boys overcome their most common yet difficult challenges. Do you constantly struggle to pull information from your son, student, or athlete, only to encounter evasive assurances like "It's nothing"? Do you sense that the boy you care about is being bullied, but that he'll do anything to avoid your "help?" Have you watched with frustration as your boy flounders with girls? Welcome to Boy World: a place where asking for help or showing emotional pain often feels impossible. Where sports and video games can mean everything, but working hard in school frequently earns ridicule. Where hiding problems from adults is the ironclad rule. Boy World is governed by social hierarchies and a powerful set of unwritten rules that have huge implications for your boy's relationships, his interactions with you, and the man he'll become. If you want what's best for him, you need to know what these rules areand how to work with them effectively.

The author of Queen Bees and Wannabees decodes the inner lives of boys to reveal how parents can forge stronger connections with their sons, explaining how boys are more likely to hide their feelings and resist adult support.

"Wiseman's sound and steady assistance provides a calm response to every twist and turn on the multifaceted road of parenthood. A wealth of sensible information for parents of boys." —*Kirkus*

Includes bibliographical references (pages 365-366) and index.

ESSENTIAL AND RECOMMENDED TITLES
305.2350973 Young people twelve to twenty — United States

305.2350973 Young people twelve to twenty — United States

Kim, Anne
★ *Abandoned: America's Lost Youth and the Crisis of Disconnection*. Anne Kim. The New Press 2019. 208 p.
ISBN 9781620975008
Grades: Adult   305.2350973
1. Young adults 2. At-risk youth 3. Adulthood 4. Teenagers 5. Counseling 6. Poverty 7. Unemployment 8. Homelessness 9. Lifestyle change 10. United States 11. Life stories — Relationships — Growing up 12. Society and culture — Wealth and class — Poverty
LC 2019034594

The director of domestic and social policy at the Progressive Policy Institute examines the 11.5 percent of sixteen- to twenty-four-year-olds who age out of foster care and the justice system and are forced to navigate early adulthood alone and impoverished.

"An outstanding book for policymakers and people who work with adrift young people." —*Kirkus*

Includes bibliographical references and index.

305.24 Adults

Friedman, Rachel
★ *And Then We Grew Up: On Creativity, Potential, and the Imperfect Art of Adulthood*. Rachel Friedman. Penguin Books 2019. 240 p.
ISBN 9780143132127
Grades: Adult   305.24
1. Friedman, Rachel, 1981- 2. Adulthood 3. Self-fulfillment 4. Ability 5. Hobbies 6. Creativity 7. Success (Concept) 8. Arts 9. Arts camps 10. Personal conduct 11. Self-discovery 12. Autobiographies and memoirs 13. Life stories — Personal growth 14. Arts and entertainment — General 15. Adult books for young adults
LC 2019019646

The author describes how her career in the arts was upended by unexpected challenges that compelled her to learn how the creative lives of her contemporaries shaped their relationships and identities.

Includes bibliographical references.

Lythcott-Haims, Julie
Your Turn: How to Be an Adult. Julie Lythcott-Haims. Henry Holt & Company 2021. 496 p.
ISBN 9781250137777
Grades: Adult   305.24
1. Adulthood 2. Adult children 3. Young adults 4. Expectation 5. Personal conduct 6. Advice 7. Growing up 8. Self-fulfillment 9. Psychology 10. Family and Relationships — Growing up 11. Life stories — Relationships — Growing up
LC 2020051626

Having tackled a far-reaching parenting crisis with her title How to Raise an Adult, Lythcott-Haims is back with an equally powerful and persuasive book for the adult children of those hovering parents—and for everyone who struggles to be a grown-up in these challenging times. Being an adult, it turns out, is not about any particular checklist; it is, instead, a process, one you can get progressively better at over time—becoming more comfortable with uncertainty and gaining the knowhow to keep going.

"With direct, encouraging, and heartfelt advice, Lythcott-Haims covers a lot of sensitive, relevant, and crucial territory." —*Booklist*

Includes index.

305.240973 Adults — United States

Caldwell, Christopher
The Age of Entitlement: America Since the Sixties. Christopher Caldwell. Simon & Schuster 2020. 352 p.
ISBN 9781501106897
Grades: Adult   305.240973
1. Progressivism (United States politics) 2. Right and left (Political science) 3. Polarization (Social sciences) 4. Entitlement attitudes 5. Social change 6. Social conflict 7. Political culture 8. Politics and government 9. United States 10. 20th century 11. 21st century 12. Conservative writing 13. Politics and global affairs — General 14. Society and culture — General 15. History writing — United States
LC 2019012957

An American intellectual argues that the reforms of the 1960s, reforms intended to make the nation more just and humane, instead left many Americans feeling alienated, despised, misled|and ready to put an adventurer in the White House.

"Liberals will find much to dispute, but Caldwell delivers the sharpest and most insightful conservative critique of mainstream politics in years." —*Publishers Weekly*

305.242 People in early adulthood

McGrath, Tom
Triumph of the Yuppies: America, the Eighties, and the Creation of an Unequal Nation. Tom McGrath. Grand Central Publishing 2024. 336 p.
ISBN 9781538725993
Grades: Adult   305.242
1. Young adults 2. Yuppies 3. Income inequality 4. Lifestyles 5. Equality 6. Inequality 7. Culture 8. Social classes 9. United States 10. 1980s 11. Society and culture — General 12. History writing — 1980s — United States
LC 2023052691

Filled with lively and nostalgic details, this first history of the Yuppie phenomenon chronicles the roots, rise and triumph of young urban professionals in the early 1980s, detailing how marketers, the media and politicians pivoted to appeal to this influential new group that helped create the largest income inequality in a century.

"It's a beguiling look at an era that inaugurated an ever-widening rift between a self-satisfied elite and a resentful working class." —*Publishers Weekly*

Includes index.

Petersen, Anne Helen
Can't Even: How Millennials Became the Burnout Generation. Anne Helen Petersen. Houghton Mifflin Harcourt 2020. xxvi, 276 p.
ISBN 9780358315070
Grades: Adult   305.242
1. Burn out (Psychology) 2. Group identity 3. Millennials 4. Capitalism 5. Work-life balance 6. Social media 7. Debt 8. Parenting 9. Society and culture — General 10. Adult books for young adults
LC 2020022439

An incendiary examination of burnout in millennials-the cultural shifts that got us here, the pressures that sustain it, and the need for drastic change.

"Petersen is more focused on bluntly describing her generation's many obstacles than offering solutions to burnout. By turns exasperated, indignant, and empathetic, she supports her claims with strong evidence and calls on millennials to be a force for widespread social change. The result is an incisive portrait of a generation primed for revolt." —*Publishers Weekly*

Includes bibliographical references and index.

Smith, Mychal Denzel
Invisible Man, Got the Whole World Watching: A Young Black Man's Education. Mychal Denzel Smith. Nation Books 2016. 320 p.
ISBN 9781568585284
Grades: Adult   305.242
1. Smith, Mychal Denzel, 1986- 2. African American men 3. Racism 4. Identity 5. African Americans 6. Race relations 7. Intersectionality 8. Black Lives Matter movement 9. Autobiographies and memoirs 10. Biographies 11. Life stories — Identity — Race and ethnicity 12. Society and culture — Race 13. Adult books for young adults

School Library Journal Best Books: Best Adult Books 4 Teens, 2016.

A prominent journalist and contributing writer to the Nation magazine describes his education and the experiences of Black masculinity against a backdrop of the Obama administration, the death of Trayvon Martin, the career of LeBron James and other pivotal influences that have shaped race relations in today's America.

"This is a commanding read that deserves a place in all libraries. It will make a great book group discussion, especially when paired with Coates's memoir."
—School Library Journal

305.244 People in middle adulthood

Calhoun, Ada
Why We Can't Sleep: Women's New Midlife Crisis. Ada Calhoun. Grove Press 2020. 288 p.
ISBN 9780802147851
Grades: Adult   305.244
1. Middle-aged women 2. Midlife crisis 3. Generation X 4. Self-fulfillment 5. Personal finance 6. Success (Concept) 7. Mental health 8. Psychology 9. People with depression 10. Women 11. Anxiety 12. Society and culture — Gender — Women 13. Society and culture — Wealth and class 14. Society and culture — Psychology and human behavior
LC 2019040577
The award-winning author presents a generation-defining exploration of the impossible standards being imposed on middle-aged Generation X women and what the author recommends to avoid burnout.

"Women of every generation will find much to relate to in this humorous yet pragmatic account." —*Publishers Weekly*

Includes bibliographical references.

Doust, Kelly
The Power Age. Kelly Doust; illustrated by Jessica Guthrie. Apollo Publishers 2020. 239 p.
ISBN 9781948062701
Grades: Adult   305.244
1. Middle-aged women 2. Senior women 3. Aging 4. Self-esteem 5. Australian literature 6. Self-Help — Personal growth — Aging

The Power Age is the ultimate guide to maturing with style, confidence, and influence. Like fine wine, women improve with age—growing in financial, sexual, and spiritual power every year. So why spend your second act collecting dust or invisible on thesidelines? with this exquisite full-color volume you'll learn how to age like a pro.

"Colorful profiles of prominent women, such as Ruth Bader Ginsberg, Yoko Ono, Helen Mirren, and Michelle Obama provide inspiration alongside the more clinical, professional advice on topics that include financial management, finding meaningful work, saving for retirement, and sexuality." —*Publishers Weekly*

Mann, Jen
★ *Midlife Bites: Anyone Else Falling Apart, or Is It Just Me?* Jen Mann. Ballantine Books 2022. 272 p.
ISBN 9780593158517
Grades: Adult   305.244
1. Mann, Jen 2. Women authors 3. Bloggers 4. Middle-aged women 5. Midlife crisis 6. Femininity 7. Women's role 8. Virtual community 9. Conversation 10. Self-care 11. Well-being 12. Society and culture — Gender — Women 13. Family and Relationships — Aging and Death 14. Humor writing — Social humor 15. Life stories — Personal growth

Jen Mann had what appeared to be the perfect life: a successful career as a bestselling author and award-winning blogger, a devoted husband, teenage kids who weren't total jerks, and a badass minivan. So imagine her surprise when, at forty-seven years old, a midlife crisis kicked her straight in the ladybits. Midlife Bites offers Jen's trademark wit and honesty when it comes to important conversations and observations about women in midlife. Jen Mann is leading the movement to create a new space where middle-aged women can share openly and honestly with one another. This no-BS collection of essays will help start the conversation and keep it going, because as women, we all have a right to be happy, fulfilled, and whole, no matter what stage of life.

"This is an entertaining and enjoyable complement to medicine-focused books on menopause and a refreshing change of pace from heavier self-help works. Recommended for collections where humorous nonfiction is in demand."
—*Library Journal*

305.26 Older people

Manly, Carla Marie
Aging Joyfully: A Woman's Guide to Optimal Health, Relationships, and Fulfillment for Her 50s and Beyond. Carla Marie Manly, PhD.. Familius LLC 2019. 254 pages
ISBN 9781641701419
Grades: Adult   305.26
1. Aging 2. Women 3. Psychology 4. Identity 5. Self-Help — Personal growth — Aging 6. Science writing — Medicine and health — Women's health 7. Science writing — Medicine and health — Psychology
LC Bl2020000982
"Psychologist Manly (Joy from Fear) guides women into their later years with wisdom and empathy in this touching work. Manly encourages those 50 and older to look at their life's experiences and celebrate them rather than to look back with regret about dreams not achieved." —*Publishers Weekly*

Includes bibliographical references (pages 247-252).

Pipher, Mary Bray
Women Rowing North: Navigating the Challenges to Our Selves as We Age. Mary Pipher. Bloomsbury Publishing 2019. 320 p.
ISBN 9781632869609
Grades: Adult   305.26
1. Senior women 2. Aging 3. Women 4. Psychology 5. Identity 6. Self-fulfillment 7. Society and culture — Psychology and human behavior 8. Society and culture — Gender — Women 9. Family and Relationships — Aging and Death
LC 2018015192
The best-selling author of Reviving Ophelia presents a guide to wisdom, authenticity and bliss for women as they age, exploring how the myriad roles and challenges of women can help promote balance and a transcendent sense of well-being.

"Attentive to varying experiences of class, race, gender, health, and marital status, even as she considers the deep 'Challenges of aging, including ageism and lookism, caregiving, loss, and loneliness,' Pipher offers practical, specific advice." —*Publishers Weekly*

Thomas, Elizabeth Marshall
Growing Old: Notes on Aging with Something Like Grace. Elizabeth Marshall Thomas. HarperOne 2020. 224 pages
ISBN 9780062956439
Grades: Adult   305.26
1. Thomas, Elizabeth Marshall, 1931- 2. Aging 3. Seniors 4. Memory 5. Old age assistance 6. Mortality 7. Death 8. Social life and customs 9. United States 10. 21st century 11. Autobiographies and memoirs 12. Life stories — Facing adversity — Coping with death 13. Family and relationships — Aging and death
LC 2019016989
Part memoir and part life-affirming map all of us may follow to embrace our later years with grace and dignity, this look at the social and historical traditions related to aging explores a wide range of issues connected with growing older.

"With wit and humor, Thomas thoughtfully conveys the realities of aging. This fully absorbing memoir will especially resonate with readers over 65 and those who work with geriatric populations, yet all readers should find much wisdom to be gained from this warm offering." —*Library Journal*

ESSENTIAL AND RECOMMENDED TITLES
305.3 People by gender or sex

305.3 People by gender or sex

Airton, Lee
★ *Gender:* Your Guide : A Gender-friendly Primer on What to Know, What to Say, and What to Do in the New Gender Culture. Lee Airton, PHD.. Adams Media 2018. 239 pages
ISBN 9781507209004
Grades: Adult   305.3
1. Gender identity 2. Parent and child 3. Parenting 4. Family and Relationships — Parenting 5. Society and culture — Gender 6. Society and culture — LGBTQIA+
LC 2018023274

An authentic and accessible guide to understanding—and engaging in—today's gender conversation. The days of two genders—male, female; boy, girl; blue, pink—are over, if they ever existed at all. Gender is now a global conversation, and one that is constantly evolving. More people than ever before are openly living their lives as transgender men or women, and many transgender people are coming out as neither men or women, instead living outside of the binary. From the differences among gender identity,gender expression, and sex, to the use of gender-neutral pronouns like singular they/Them, to thinking about your own participation in gender, Gender: Your Guide serves as a complete primer to all things gender. Guided by professor and gender diversity advocate Lee Airton, PhD, you will learn how gender works in everyday life, how to use accurate terminology to refer to transgender, non-binary, and/Or gender non-conforming individuals, and how to ask when you aren't sure what to do or say. It provides you with the information you need to talk confidently and compassionately about gender diversity, whether simply having a conversation or going to bat as an advocate.

"This guide is unlike anything else available today, and an obvious and necessary item for collections of all kinds."—*Library Journal*
Includes bibliographical references (pages 225-232) and index.

Bates, Laura
Men Who Hate Women: From Incels to Pickup Artists: The Truth About Extreme Misogyny and How It Affects Us All. Laura Bates. Sourcebooks 2021. 416 p.
ISBN 9781728236247
Grades: Adult   305.3
1. Bates, Laura, 1986- 2. Feminists 3. Misogyny 4. Sexism 5. Antifeminism 6. Extremists 7. Hate groups 8. Online hate speech 9. Influence (Psychology) 10. Misinformation 11. Stereotypes 12. Society and culture — Gender — Men
LC 2020047361

Women's rights activist Laura Bates is no stranger to misogynistic attacks online, but over time, the vitriol hinted at something widespread and toxic. Men Who Hate Women examines the rise of secretive extremist communities who despise women as Bates traces the roots of misogyny across a complex spiderweb of groups. Drawing parallels to other extremist movements around the world, Bates shows what attracts men to the movement, how it grooms and radicalizes boys, the structure in which it operates, and what can be done to stop it. Most urgently of all, she follows the pathways this extreme ideology has taken from the darkest corners of the internet to emerge covertly in our mainstream media, our playgrounds, and our government.

"Well-researched and meticulously documented, Bates's book on the power and danger of masculinity should be required reading for us all."—*Library Journal*
Includes bibliographical references and index.

Butler, Judith
★ *Who's Afraid of Gender?* Judith Butler. Farrar, Straus and Giroux 2024. 288 p.
ISBN 9780374608224
Grades: Adult   305.3
1. Gender identity 2. Sexuality 3. Fear 4. Society and culture — Gender
LC 2023040892

From a global icon comes a bold, essential account of how a fear of gender is fueling reactionary politics around the world. Index.

"A master class in how gender has been weaponized in support of conservative values and authoritarian regimes." —*Kirkus*
Includes bibliographical references and index.

Gottlieb, Iris
Seeing Gender: An Illustrated Guide to Identity and Expression. by Iris Gottlieb; foreword by Kacen Callender. Chronicle Books 2022. 204 p.
ISBN 9781797211978
Grades: 9 10 11 12   305.3
1. Gender identity 2. Gender expression 3. Identity 4. Sexual orientation 5. Gender-nonconforming people 6. Gender nonconformity 7. Books for browsing 8. Growing up — LGBTQIA+ 9. Social issues — Human rights — LGBTQIA+
LC 2018058585

Meticulously researched and fully illustrated, this examination into how we express and understand the complexities of gender today brings clarity and reassurance to the sometimes confusing process of navigating ones' identity.

"Readers will be immediately drawn to Gottlieb's colorful, detailed, and stylized artwork and will stay for the succinct text, made accessible in short passages set against plenty of white space." —*Booklist*
The 2022 revised edition contains a new forward by Kacen Callender; Includes bibliographical references (pages 196-199) and index.

Mangino, Kate
★ *Equal Partners: Improving Gender Equality at Home*. Kate Mangino. St. Martin's Press 2022. 288 p.
ISBN 9781250276117
Grades: Adult   305.3
1. Gender role 2. Gender equity 3. Inequality 4. Sexism 5. Homemakers 6. Househusbands 7. Society and culture — Gender
LC 2022002317

From gender expert and professional facilitator Kate Mangino comes Equal Partners, an informed guide about how we can all collectively work to undo harmful gender norms and create greater household equity.—.

"An enlightening read that offers tangible methods for families and community members interested in dismantling the gender binary." —*Booklist*
Includes bibliographical references and index.

Nordberg, Jenny
The Underground Girls of Kabul: In Search of a Hidden Resistance in Afghanistan. Jenny Nordberg. Crown 2014. 288 pages
ISBN 9780307952493
Grades: Adult   305.3
1. Gender Identity 2. Gender role 3. Male impersonators 4. Disguises 5. Girls 6. Afghanistan 7. Adult books for young adults 8. Society and culture — Gender — Women
LC 2014000295

Booklist Editors' Choice: Adult Books for Young Adults, 2014; J. Anthony Lukas Book Prize, 2015.

In Afghanistan, a culture ruled almost entirely by men, the birth of a son is cause for celebration and the arrival of a daughter is often mourned as misfortune. A bacha posh (literally translated from Dari as "dressed up like a boy") is a third kind of child ' a girl temporarily raised as a boy and presented as such to the outside world. Jenny Nordberg, the reporter who broke the story of this phenomenon for the New York Times, constructs a powerful and moving account of those secretly living on the other side of a deeply segregated society where women have almost no rights and little freedom.

"Nordbergs subtle, sympathetic reportage makes this one of the most convincing portraits of Afghan culture in print; through a small breach in the wall of gender apartheid, she reveals the harsh ironies of a system that so devalues women that it forces them to become men." —*Publishers Weekly*

Yoshino, Kenji
Say the Right Thing: How to Talk About Identity, Diversity, and Justice. Kenji Yoshino and David Glasgow. Atria Books 2023. 240 p.
ISBN 9781982181383

PUBLIC LIBRARY CORE COLLECTION: NONFICTION
Twentieth Edition

Grades: Adult 305.3

1. Identity 2. Gender identity 3. Ethnic identity 4. People with disabilities 5. LGBTQIA+ people 6. Social integration 7. Conversation 8. Respect 9. Social justice 10. Social psychology 11. Corporate culture 12. Organizational behavior 13. Business and economics — Popular psychology 14. Society and culture — Psychology and human behavior 15. Antiracist literature

LC 2022041564

In the current period of social and political unrest, conversations about identity are becoming more frequent and more difficult. On subjects like critical race theory, gender equity in the workplace, and LGBTQ-inclusive classrooms, many of us are understandably fearful of saying the wrong thing. Kenji Yoshino and David Glasgow are here to show potential allies that these conversations don't have to be so overwhelming. Through stories drawn from contexts as varied as social media posts, dinner party conversations, and workplace disputes, they offer seven user-friendly principles that help us better support people in our lives who experience bias.

"Readers interested in communications specifically related to equity, diversity, and inclusion will find lots of relevant advice in this timely book." —Booklist

Includes bibliographical references and index.

305.30973 Gender roles — United States

Lipman, Joanne
That's What She Said: What Men Need to Know and Women Need to Tell Them About Working Together. Joanne Lipman. William Morrow & Company 2018. 320 p.

ISBN 9780062437211

Grades: Adult 305.30973

1. Gender gap 2. Women executives 3. Inequality 4. Businesspeople 5. Leadership in business 6. Business and economics — Women and the workplace

LC Bl2017050883

An award-winning journalist and publisher outlines anecdotal solutions for harmonious working relationships between the sexes, citing the unique contributions of professional women and how their male counterparts can implement a healthier business culture that bridges gender gaps.

"A solid start to an essential, gender-inclusive conversation." —Kirkus

Talusan, Meredith
Fairest: A Memoir. Meredith Talusan. Penguin Group USA 2020. 320 p.

ISBN 9780525561309

Grades: Adult 305.30973

1. Talusan, Meredith 2. Gender identity 3. Passing (Identity) 4. Transgender people 5. Filipino Americans 6. Child immigrants 7. Self-discovery 8. Trans women 9. Asian Americans 10. Identity 11. Gay college students 12. Transitioning (Gender identity) 13. Self-fulfillment 14. Intersectionality 15. Albinism 16. White privilege 17. Southeast Asian Americans 18. Southeast Asian people 19. Autobiographies and memoirs 20. Life stories — Relationships — Growing up 21. Society and culture — Gender 22. Life stories — Identity

LC 2019031336

A heartrending immigrant memoir and a uniquely intersectional coming-of-age story of a life lived in duality and the in-between, and how one navigates through race, gender, and the search for love.

"This elegant memoir examining whiteness, womanhood, and the shaping of identity will resonate with readers of any community, LGBTQ or not." —Publishers Weekly

Tobia, Jacob
Sissy: A Coming-of-gender Story. Jacob Tobia. G. P. Putnam's Sons 2019. 320 p.

ISBN 9780735218826

Grades: 11 12 Adult 305.30973

1. Tobia, Jacob, 1991- 2. Gender identity 3. Genderqueer people 4. Nonbinary people 5. Coming out (Sexual or gender identity) 6. Growing up 7. Identity 8. Transgender people 9. Self-acceptance 10. Autobiographies and memoirs 11. Society and culture — LGBTQIA+ 12. Society and culture — Gender 13. Life stories — Relationships — Growing up 14. Life stories — Identity — LGBTQIA+ 15. Adult books for young adults

LC 2018041589

A gender-diverse cultural influencer on both the Forbes "30 Under 30" and "OUT 100" lists examines how their religious, political and educational experiences revealed the need for greater cultural inclusion and anti-discrimination legislation that acknowledges the gender spectrum.

"TV producer and performer Tobia, who uses the pronouns they/Them, recounts their journey from shy, closeted gender-nonconforming kid to out-and-proud young genderqueer LGBTQ activist in this hilarious and candid memoir. Tobia thoughtfully and accessibly captures the anguish of being placed inside boxes that dont fithow gender hurts us all by creating prisons of identity, with both kids and adults policing and bullying those who fail to conform." —Publishers Weekly

305.31 Men

Black, Michael Ian
A Better Man: A (mostly Serious) Letter to My Son. Michael Ian Black. Algonquin Books of Chapel Hill 2020. 304 pages

ISBN 9781616209117

Grades: Adult 305.31

1. Black, Michael Ian, 1971- 2. Personal conduct 3. Fathers and sons 4. Masculinity 5. Men 6. Gender role 7. Identity 8. Autobiographies and memoirs 9. Life stories — Relationships — Parent and child 10. Family and relationships — Families 11. Society and culture — Gender — Men 12. Life stories — Arts and culture — Performing arts — Entertainers and celebrities

LC 2019051609

The comedian, writer and actor discusses modern masculinity through a heartfelt letter to his college-bound son that will resonate with any parent looking to navigate complex gender issues and be or raise a better man.

"In this extended letter to his college-bound son, author and comedian Black (You're Not Doing Right) offers advice for navigating adulthood and masculinity, toxic or otherwise.... Both thoughtful and lighthearted, this work will appeal to anyone interested in masculinity and modern gender roles." —Library Journal

305.310973 Men — United States

Bly, Robert
★ *Iron John: A Book About Men.* Robert Bly. Da Capo Press 2015. xii, 292 pages

ISBN 9780306824265

Grades: Adult 305.310973

1. Men 2. Masculinity 3. Psychology 4. Society and culture — Gender — Men

LC 2004056137

In this timeless and deeply learned classic, poet and translator Robert Bly offers nothing less than a new vision of what it means to be a man. Bly's vision is based on his ongoing work with men, as well as on reflections on his own life. He addresses the devastating effects of remote fathers and mourns the disappearance of male initiation rites in our culture. Finding rich meaning in ancient stories and legends, Bly uses the Grimm fairy tale "Iron John"—in which a mentor or "Wild Man" guides a young man through eight stages of male growth-to remind us of ways of knowing long forgotten, images of deep and vigorous masculinity centered in feeling and protective of the young. At once down-to-earth and elevated, combining the grandeur of myth with the practical and often painful lessons of our own histories, Iron John is an astonishing work that will continue to guide and inspire men-and women-for years to come.

Includes bibliographical references (pages 281-291) and index; Originally published: Reading, Mass. : Addison-Wesley, 1990.

ESSENTIAL AND RECOMMENDED TITLES
305.4 Women

Oluo, Ijeoma
Mediocre: The Dangerous Legacy of White Male America. Ijeoma Oluo. Seal Press 2020. VII, 318 pages
ISBN 9781580059510
Grades: Adult   305.310973
1. European American men 2. Privilege (Social psychology) 3. White privilege 4. Power 5. Male domination (Social structure) 6. Mediocrity 7. Race relations 8. Identity 9. Racism 10. Sexism 11. National characteristics, American 12. United States history 13. Society and culture — Gender 14. Society and culture — Race 15. Politics and global affairs — Civil and human rights
LC 2020944625
Loan Stars Favourites, 2020.
Through the last 150 years of American history—from the post-reconstruction South and the mythic stories of cowboys in the West, to the present-day controversy over NFL protests and the backlash against the rise of women in politics—Ijeoma Oluo exposes the devastating consequences of white male supremacy on women, people of color, and white men themselves. Mediocre investigates the real costs of this phenomenon in order to imagine a new white male identity, one free from racism and sexism.
"Freelance writer Oluo (So You Want to Talk About Race) contends in this incisive treatise that American society revolves around 'Preserving white male power regardless of white male skill or talent.' . . . Erudite yet accessible, grounded in careful research as well as Oluo's personal experiences of racism and misogyny, this is an essential reckoning with race, sex, and power in America." —*Publishers Weekly*

305.4 Women

Beauvoir, Simone de
★ *The Second Sex.* Simone de Beauvoir; translated and edited by H.M. Parshley; with an introduction by Margaret Crosland. Alfred A. Knopf 1993. LV, 786 p.
ISBN 9780679420163
Grades: 11 12 Adult   305.4
1. Women 2. Gender role 3. Feminism 4. Feminists 5. Sexuality 6. Identity 7. Philosophy, Modern 8. Intersectionality 9. Society and culture — Gender — Women
LC 92054303
Presents a detailed analysis of womanhood that focuses on women's past and contemporary situation in Western culture.
Includes bibliographical references (p. xviii-xix) and index; Originally published: New York : Knopf, 1953.

Knight, Keltie
Lady Secrets: Real, Raw, and Ridiculous Confessions of Womanhood. Keltie Knight, Jac Vanek, and Becca Tobin. Rodale Press 2022. 256 p.
ISBN 9780593236338
Grades: Adult   305.4
1. Women 2. Podcasters 3. Secrets 4. Sharing 5. Embarrassment 6. Shame 7. Honesty 8. Life stories — Identity — Gender 9. Life stories — Facing adversity 10. Humor writing — Social humor
The authors of Act Like a Lady and hosts of the popular podcast LadyGang call on their many fans to bare their souls with their deepest and most tightly kept secrets, in this feminist manifesto for taking back un-ladylike behavior and owning it.
"The result makes for a rollicking and at times heartbreaking compendium of secrets." —*Publishers Weekly*

Saini, Angela
Inferior: How Science Got Women Wrong and the New Research That's Rewriting the Story. Angela Saini. Beacon Press 2017. 224 pages
ISBN 9780807071700
Grades: Adult   305.4
1. Women's studies 2. Sexism in science 3. Research 4. Feminism 5. Sex differences 6. Women and science 7. Women 8. Public opinion 9. Science 10. Society and culture — Gender — Women 11. Science Writing — General 12. Adult books for young adults
LC 2016048808
What science has gotten so shamefully wrong about women, and the fight, by both female and male scientists, to rewrite what we thought we knew.
"In admirably subtle prose, Saini questions, considers, and refuses to accept traditional generalizations. A brilliant approach to a long overlooked topic, Inferior is impossible to ignore and invaluable." —*Booklist*
Includes bibliographical references and index.

305.409 Women — History, geographic treatment, biography

Beard, Mary
★ *Women & Power:* A Manifesto. Mary Beard. Liveright 2017. 128 p.
ISBN 9781631494758
Grades: Adult   305.409
1. Power 2. Literature and society 3. Women in literature 4. Misogyny 5. Sexism 6. Gender role 7. Social classes 8. Society and culture — Gender — Women
LC 2017054169
At long last, Mary Beard addresses in one brave book the misogynists and trolls who mercilessly attack and demean women the world over, including, very often, Mary herself. In Women & Power, she traces the origins of this misogyny to its ancient roots, examining the pitfalls of gender and the ways that history has mistreated strong women since time immemorial.
"This slim and timely volume leaves readers to contemplate how women can reconfigure societys current perceptions of power." —*Publishers Weekly*

Davis, Lisa Selin
Tomboy: The Surprising History and Future of Girls Who Dare to Be Different. Lisa Selin Davis. Hachette Go 2020. 336 p.
ISBN 9780316458313
Grades: Adult   305.409
1. Tomboys 2. Gender identity 3. Gender nonconformity 4. Girls 5. Nonbinary people 6. Femininity 7. Sexuality 8. Transgenderism 9. Homosexuality 10. Social norms 11. Child development 12. Society and culture 13. Society and culture — Psychology and human behavior 14. Society and culture — LGBTQIA+ 15. Life stories — Identity — Gender
LC Bl2020017407
Inspired by her thought-provoking op-ed for the New York Times, Lisa Selin Davis's Tomboy explores the history and imagines the future of girls who defy societal expectations based on their gender. Tomboy is a revealing dive into the forces that have shifted and narrowed our ideas of what's normal for boys and girls, and for kids who don't fall neatly into either category. Davis talks to experts from clothing designers to psychologists, historians to neuroscientists, and tomboys from eight to eighty, to illuminate debates about what is masculine and feminine; what is biological versus socially constructed; what constitutes the categories of boy and girl; and the connection between tomboyism, gender identity, and sexuality.
"Davis's persuasive and deeply personal argument for moving beyond the gender binary will resonate with those curious about child rearing free of normative expectations." —*Publishers Weekly*
Includes bibliographical references and index.

305.40952 Women — Japan

Johnson, Akemi
Night in the American Village: Women in the Shadow of the U.S. Military Bases in Okinawa. Akemi Johnson. The New Press 2019. 224 p.
ISBN 9781620973318
Grades: Adult   305.40952
1. Military bases, American 2. Women and the military 3. Women 4. Soldiers 5. Prostitution 6. Sex crimes 7. Sexual violence 8. Culture conflict 9. Group identity 10. Okinawa 11. Japan 12. United States 13. Society and culture — General

14. Life stories — Identity — Race and ethnicity 15. Life stories — Identity — Gender 16. History writing — Military — Military Today

LC 2019004697

An examination of the complex relationship between the women living near the U.S. base in Okinawa and the servicemen who are stationed there."

"Johnson masterfully weaves historical details and current events into the interviews with her subjects, with each aspect enriching the broader tale. Highly recommended to readers with an interest in military history, women's studies, women's history, and Japanese-U.S. relations." —*Library Journal*

Includes bibliographical references.

305.409581 Women — Afghanistan

Badkhen, Anna
The World Is a Carpet: Four Seasons in an Afghan Village. Anna Badkhen. Penguin Group USA 2013. 288 p.
ISBN 9781594488320
Grades: Adult   305.409581
1. Villages 2. Rural families 3. Tradition (Philosophy) 4. Families 5. Carpets 6. Women weavers 7. Women 8. Poverty 9. Terrorism 10. Afghanistan 11. Central Asia 12. Islamic countries 13. History writing — Asia — South Asia — Afghanistan 14. Society and culture — Ethnic studies

LC 2013003827

Despite war and invasion, Turkoman weavers have created gorgeous carpets for centuries. In the tiny desert village of Oqa, Afghanistan, people still believe the world is flat; American fighter planes fly overheard, and hunger is common. An award-winning journalist traces the path of one beautifully intricate carpet woven here—from the purchase of its yarn, through months of intricate weavings that reflect the village's life, to its journey to market. This compelling read portrays fascinating people you won't soon forget, in a community bonded by rich traditions and tremendous hardships.

305.40973 Women — United States

Collins, Gail
When Everything Changed: The Amazing Journey of American Women from 1960 to the Present. Gail Collins. Little, Brown and CO 2009. 480 p.
ISBN 9780316059541
Grades: 11 12 Adult   305.40973
1. Women's history 2. Gender role 3. Women's role 4. Civil rights 5. Women 6. United States history 7. History writing — Women's history 8. History writing — United States 9. Adult books for young adults

LC 2008054933

New York Times Notable Book, 2009.

A follow-up to America's Women by a former New York Times editorial page editor chronicles the revolution of women's civil rights throughout the past half century, drawing on oral history and research in a variety of disciplines while celebrating Hillary Clinton's 2008 presidential campaign.

"Collins can be deadly serious and great fun to read at the same time. A revelatory book for readers of both sexes, and sure to become required reading for any American women's-studies course." —*Kirkus*

Includes bibliographical references and index.

Felder, Deborah G
The American Women's Almanac: 500 Years of Making History. Deborah G. Felder. Visible Ink 2019. 608 pages
ISBN 9781578596362
Grades: Adult   305.40973
1. Women 2. Women's history 3. Almanacs 4. Suffragist movement 5. Women's movement 6. Gender equity 7. Women scientists 8. Women entrepreneurs 9. Women artists 10. Women athletes 11. Women authors 12. Women politicians 13. Women social advocates 14. United States 15. 15th century 16. 16th century 17. 17th century 18. 18th century 19. 19th century 20. 20th century 21. 21st century 22. Biographies 23. Trivia and miscellaneous facts 24. Essays 25. History writing — Women's history 26. Society and culture — Gender — Women

LC 2019047814

Illustrates the history of women in America through biographies, historical facts and essays on legislation and movements highlighting both well- and lesser-known figures, including Susan B. Anthony, Clara Barton, Nellie Bly, Julie Ward, Dolley Madison, Pocahontas and many others. (U.S. history).

"An essential addition to reference or history collections in all public and academic libraries." —*Library Journal*

Includes bibliographical references and index.

305.42 Social role and status of women

Adichie, Chimamanda Ngozi
We Should All Be Feminists. Chimamanda Ngozi Adichie. Random House 2015. 64 p.
ISBN 9781101911761
Grades: Adult   305.42
1. Gender equity 2. Sex discrimination 3. Social change 4. Feminism 5. Gender role 6. Empowerment 7. Prejudice 8. Public opinion 9. Intersectionality 10. Essays 11. Society and culture — Gender — Women 12. Adult books for young adults

LC Bl2015005730

Amelia Bloomer List, 2016; School Library Journal Best Books: Best Adult Books 4 Teens, 2015.

Offers an updated definition of feminism for the twenty-first century, one rooted in inclusion and awareness.

"An eloquent, stirring must-read for budding and reluctant feminists." —*School Library Journal*

Based on the 2012 TED talk given by the author.

Ahmed, Sara
The Feminist Killjoy Handbook: The Radical Potential of Getting in the Way. Sara Ahmed. Seal 2023. 304 p.
ISBN 9781541603752
Grades: Adult   305.42
1. Feminism 2. Social change 3. Injustice 4. Marginalized people 5. Protests, demonstrations, vigils, etc. 6. Political participation 7. Radicalism 8. Liberal writing 9. Society and culture — Gender — Women 10. Society and culture — Social activism and philanthropy

LC 2023003929

Do you refuse to laugh at offensive jokes? Have you ever been accused of ruining dinner by pointing out your companion's sexist comment? Are you often told to stop being so "woke"? If so, you might be a feminist killjoy—and this book is for you. Feminist theorist Sara Ahmed shows how killing joy can be a radical world-making project. Presenting sharp analysis of literature, film, and influential feminist works, and drawing on her own experiences as a queer feminist scholar-activist of color, Ahmed offers an outstretched hand to feminist killjoys everywhere and an essential intellectual guide to the transformative power of getting in the way.

"This book arms readers with a sense of vital energy…Audiences curious about navigating the intersection between feminism and daily life, intellectualism, poetry, and activism will love this title." —*Library Journal*

Includes bibliographical references and index.

Bowen, Sesali
Bad Fat Black Girl: Notes from a Trap Feminist. Sesali Bowen. Amistad Press 2021. 272 p.
ISBN 9780063028708
Grades: Adult   305.42
1. Bowen, Sesali 2. African American women 3. Urban women 4. LGBTQIA+ people 5. Intersectionality 6. Feminism 7. Internet personalities 8. Hip-hop culture 9. Women 10. Identity 11. Self-acceptance 12. Body image 13. Society and culture — Gender — Women 14. Society and culture — Race 15. Society and culture — LGBTQIA+ 16. Life stories — Identity

ESSENTIAL AND RECOMMENDED TITLES
305.42 Social role and status of women

LC 2020056291

Growing up on the south side of Chicago, Sesali Bowen learned early on how to hustle, stay on her toes, and champion other Black women and femmes as she navigated Blackness, queerness, fatness, friendship, poverty, sex work, and self-love. Her love of trap music led her to the top of hip-hop journalism, profiling game-changing artists like Megan Thee Stallion, Lizzo, and Janelle Monae. But despite all the beauty, complexity, and general badassery she saw, Bowen found none of that nuance represented in mainstream feminism. Thus, she coined Trap Feminism, a contemporary framework that interrogates where feminism meets today's hip-hop. Bad Fat Black Girl offers a new, inclusive feminism for the modern world.

"Bowen's insight empowers the unapologetic women who culture loves to emulate and highlights the inspiration behind some of hip-hop's most memorable songs." —*Booklist*

Eltahawy, Mona
The Seven Necessary Sins for Women and Girls. Mona Eltahawy. Beacon Press 2019. 208 p.
ISBN 9780807013816
Grades: Adult   305.42
1. Feminism 2. Women's rights 3. Social action 4. Freedom of expression 5. Patriarchy 6. Leadership 7. Anger 8. Society and culture — Gender — Women 9. Society and culture — Social activism and philanthropy 10. Life stories — Politics — Activists and reformers

LC 2019006195

A bold and uncompromising feminist manifesto that shows women and girls how to defy, disrupt, and destroy the patriarchy by embracing the qualities they've been trained to avoid. Seizing upon the energy of the #MeToo movement, feminist activist Mona Eltahawy advocates a muscular, out-loud approach to teaching women and girls to harness their power through what she calls the "seven necessary sins" that women and girls are not supposed to commit: to be angry, ambitious, profane, violent, attention-seeking, lustful, and powerful. All the necessary "sins" that women and girls require to erupt.

Includes bibliographical references and index.

Friedan, Betty
★ *The Feminine Mystique.* by Betty Friedan; introduction by Gail Collins; afterword by Anna Quindlen. Norton 2013. xxxiv, 562 p.
ISBN 9780393322576
Grades: 9 10 11 12 Adult   305.42
1. Gender role 2. Sexism 3. Power 4. Women 5. Psychology 6. Feminism 7. United States 8. History writing — Women's history 9. Society and culture — Gender — Women

LC 2001044231

Views the distorted image of women that prevailed from the end of the Second World War through the early sixties and relects upon changes.

"A vastly significant book that has made a world of difference, much of it slowly acquired." —*Kirkus*

The 2013 edition (50th anniversary edition) includes a new intro by Gail Collins and an afterword by Anna Quindlen; Includes bibliographical references and index.

Gates, Melinda
★ *The Moment of Lift: How Empowering Women Changes the World.* Melinda Gates. Flatiron Books 2019. 224 p.
ISBN 9781250313577
Grades: Adult   305.42
1. Feminism 2. Women 3. Equality 4. Gender equity 5. Women's role 6. Society and culture — Gender — Women 7. Politics and global affairs — Civil and human rights

LC 2018051054

A timely call to action for women's empowerment by the influential co-chair of the Bill & Melinda Gates Foundation identifies the link between women's equality and societal health, sharing uplifting insights by international advocates in the fight against gender bias.

"At a time when beneficial globalization is being threatened by nationalism, and womens rights are in danger of being rolled back to nineteenth-century norms, Gates offers urgent reminders of why it's necessary to help women everywhere achieve their full potential." —*Booklist*

Griffith, Elisabeth
Formidable: American Women and the Fight for Equality, 1920-2020. Elisabeth Griffith. Pegasus Books 2022. 416 p.
ISBN 9781639361892
Grades: Adult   305.42
1. Women's history 2. Women 3. Women's Movement 4. Social movements 5. Women political activists 6. Equality 7. Gender equity 8. Feminism 9. Civil Rights 10. Race (Social sciences) 11. Social advocacy 12. Social change 13. United States history 14. History writing — Women's history 15. Life stories — Politics — Activists and reformers 16. Society and culture — Gender — Women 17. Society and culture — Social activism and philanthropy

The Nineteenth Amendment was an incomplete victory. Black and white women fought hard for voting rights and doubled the number of eligible voters, but the amendment did not enfranchise all women, or even protect the rights of those women who could vote. A century later, women are still grappling with how to use the vote and their political power to expand civil rights, confront racial violence, improve maternal health, advance educational and employment opportunities, and secure reproductive rights. In this riveting narrative, Dr. Elisabeth Griffith integrates the fight by white and Black women to achieve equality, providing a sweeping, century-long perspective, and an expansive cast of change agents.

"The history of women's rights in the U.S. Is messy, and historian Griffith's…book dives into the tangle of personalities, politics, and passions and surfaces with a great narrative….This is a fantastic and enjoyable book tracing 100 years of work and struggle for women's equality." —*Library Journal*

Hay, Carol
Think Like a Feminist: The Philosophy Behind the Revolution. Carol Hay. W.W. Norton & Company 2020. xvi, 222 p.
ISBN 9781324003090
Grades: Adult   305.42
1. Feminist theory 2. Feminism 3. Intersectionality 4. Gender role 5. Sexual violence 6. Femininity 7. Sexism 8. Feminism and racism 9. Classism 10. Society and culture — Gender — Women 11. History writing — Women's history 12. Society and culture — Philosophy

LC 2020010917

Think Like a Feminist is an irreverent yet rigorous primer that unpacks two hundred years of feminist ideas. Professor Carol Hay takes the long view on our current moment, framing it within the philosophical thinking that underlies the organization and activism that has transformed women's roles and lives. She delves into topics such as the role of oppression, gender roles, sexual violence, what it means to identify as a woman, and the intersections of sexism, racism, classism, and homophobia. Hay shatters common misconceptions about feminism as she sheds light on the social structures that continue to restrict women.

"Hay succeeds in clarifying abstract—and often sobering—concepts with straightforward terminology and a dash of irreverent humor. This crisp, well-informed primer on feminist theory will resonate with young women and experienced activists alike." —*Publishers Weekly*

Includes bibliographical references and index.

Hill, Anita
★ *Believing: Our Thirty-year Journey to End Gender Violence.* Anita Hill. Viking 2021. 336 p.
ISBN 9780593298299
Grades: Adult   305.42
1. Hill, Anita 2. Sexual harassment of women 3. Violence against women 4. Sexual violence 5. Sexual violence victims 6. Abused women 7. Violence 8. Violence against marginalized people 9. Social advocacy 10. Society and culture — Violence and crime 11. Politics and global affairs — Civil and human rights 12. Life stories — Facing adversity — Abuse survivors

LC 2021024489

From the woman who gave the landmark testimony against Clarence Thomas as a sexual menace, a new manifesto about the origins and course of gender violence in our society; a combination of memoir, personal accounts, law, and social analysis, and a powerful call to arms from one of our most prominent and poised survivors. In 1991, Anita Hill began something that's still unfinished work. The issues of gender violence, touching on sex, race, age, and power, are as urgent today as they were when she first testified. Believing is a story of America's three decades long reckoning with gender violence, one that offers insights into its roots, and paths to creating dialogue and substantive change. It is a call to action that offers guidance based on what this brave, committed fighter has learned from a lifetime of advocacy and her search for solutions to a problem that is still tearing America apart.

"With searing insight, Hill shows how much and how little things have changed since 1991. Her book gives hope, inspires activism, and discourages complacency." —*Library Journal*

Includes bibliographical references and index.

Hill, Katie
She Will Rise: Becoming a Warrior in the Battle for True Equality. Katie Hill. Grand Central Publishing 2020. x, 305 pages : Illustration
ISBN 9781538737002
Grades: Adult   305.42
1. Hill, Katie, (former Congressional representative) 2. Misogyny 3. Women politicians 4. Bisexual women 5. Women and politics 6. Feminism 7. Equality 8. Harassment 9. Women 10. Empowerment 11. Political participation 12. Politics and government 13. United States 14. Autobiographies and memoirs 15. Life stories — Politics — Politicians 16. Life stories — Identity — Gender 17. Society and culture — Gender — Women
LC 2020938825

Former Congresswoman Katie Hill shares her experience with misogyny and double standards in politics to help women topple the longstanding power structures that prevent them from achieving equality.

"Both thoughtful and thought-provoking, Hill unflinchingly takes responsibility for choices and actions that led to her political demise, while also offering sage advice for those fighting for women's rights in this straightforward and candid memoir-cum-manifesto." —*Booklist*

Includes bibliographical resources (pages 265-304).

Orenstein, Peggy
Don't Call Me Princess: Essays on Girls, Women, Sex, and Life. Peggy Orenstein. HarperCollins 2018. 336 p.
ISBN 9780062834058
Grades: Adult   305.42
1. Women in popular culture 2. Feminism 3. Sexuality 4. Women 5. Girls 6. Essays 7. Society and culture — Gender — Women
LC Bl2017052008

The best-selling author of Girls & Sex presents a first collection of essays, drawn from three decades of writing, that traces the progress and setbacks of feminism as reflected in areas ranging from princess culture and miscarriage to breast cancer and motherhood.

"Compelling and intelligent, Orenstein's book offers a powerful vision of the challenges of modern womanhood and of what it means to be female in 21st-century America. A sharp, timely collection of essays." —*Kirkus*

Palmieri, Jennifer
She Proclaims: Our Declaration of Independence from a Man's World. Jennifer Palmieri. Grand Central Publishing 2020. xi, 193 pages
ISBN 9781538750650
Grades: Adult   305.42
1. Feminism 2. Political participation 3. Women 4. patriarchy 5. Self-fulfillment 6. Society and culture — Gender — Women
LC 2020005491

An empowering guide to feminism by the best-selling author of Dear Madam President outlines a blueprint for activism while sharing lessons from her personal choice to live on her own terms instead of embracing toxic patriarchal norms.

"Feminists will be heartened by this inspirational guide to fighting for gender equality." —*Publishers Weekly*

Includes bibliographical references (pages 189-193).

Reese, Anney
★ *Stuff Mom Never Told You: The Feminist Past, Present, and Future.* Anney Reese & Samantha McVey. Flatiron Books 2023. 240 p. : Illustration
ISBN 9781250268600
Grades: Adult   305.42
1. Feminism 2. Women's rights 3. Civil rights 4. Society and culture — Gender 5. History Writing — Women's history

The hosts of the popular podcast Stuff Mom Never Told You explore today's major feminist issues.

"The popular podcast takes a deep dive into feminist issues, and this accessible book will reach fans of the show and more." —*Booklist*

Schuller, Kyla
The Trouble with White Women: A Counterhistory of Feminism. Kyla Schuller. Bold Type Books 2021. 320 p.
ISBN 9781645036890
Grades: Adult   305.42
1. White privilege 2. Marginalized women 3. Feminists 4. Racism 5. Women 6. Intersectionality 7. Gender equity 8. Feminism 9. United States 10. History writing — Women's history 11. Society and culture — Gender — Women
LC 2021008089

From suffragettes to sexuality, feminist history is often told as a narrative of women united in the fight against patriarchy. But there have always been limits and fault lines in the feminist movements that centered white women's rights at the expense of all others. As scholar Kyla Schuller argues in the Trouble with White Women, white women, across political classes, have used racism and other hierarchies of power to win their own rights and expand their personal opportunities. Their white feminist politics have come at a great cost, resulting in the sustained exploitation, oppression, and silencing of women of color. The Trouble with White Women details the history of white feminist icons and their counterparts from the 1840s to the present.

"Schuller's highly recommended feminist counterhistory is inspiring, and her arguments persuasive. She excels in letting the voices and lived experiences of women of color, trans women, and otherwise marginalized women come to the fore." —*Library Journal*

Includes bibliographical references.

Solnit, Rebecca
Men Explain Things to Me. Rebecca Solnit. Haymarket Books 2014. 160 p.
ISBN 9781608464968
Grades: Adult   305.42
1. Feminism 2. Control 3. Gender equity 4. Intersectionality 5. Men-women relations 6. Essays 7. Society and culture — Gender — Women
LC 2013427537

In her comic, scathing essay "Men Explain Things to Me," Rebecca Solnit took on what often goes wrong in conversations between men and women. This book features that now-classic essay with six perfect complements, including an examination of the great feminist writer Virginia Woolf's embrace of mystery, of not knowing, of doubt and ambiguity, a highly original inquiry into marriage equality, and a terrifying survey of the scope of contemporary violence against women.

"Sharp narratives that illuminate and challenge the status quo of women's roles in the world. Slim in scope, but yet another good book by Solnit." —*Kirkus*

The Mother of All Questions: Further Reports from the Feminist Revolutions. Rebecca Solnit. Haymarket Books 2017. 180 p.
ISBN 9781608467402
Grades: Adult   305.42
1. Feminism 2. Gender wars 3. Gender gap 4. Social justice 5. Women 6. Essays 7. Society and culture — Gender — Women
LC 2018418036

In this collection of essays, Solnit offers a timely commentary on gender and feminism. Her subjects include women who refuse to be silenced, misogynistic violence, the fragile masculinity of the literary canon, the recent history of rape jokes, and muchmore.

ESSENTIAL AND RECOMMENDED TITLES
305.42 Social role and status of women

"Solnit's voice is calm, clear, and unapologetic; each essay balances a warm wit with confident, thoughtful analysis, resulting in a collection that is as enjoyable and accessible as it is incisive." —*Booklist*

Spruill, Marjorie Julian
Divided We Stand: The Battle Over Women's Rights and Family Values That Polarized American Politics. Marjorie J. Spruill. Bloomsbury 2017. 368 p.
ISBN 9781632863140
Grades: Adult   305.42
1. Women's rights 2. Feminism 3. Women social advocates 4. Liberals 5. Conservatives 6. Radicalism 7. Politics and government 8. United States 9. Society and culture — Gender — Women 10. Politics and global affairs — World Politics — United States 11. History writing — Women's history
LC Bl2017007810

Forty years ago, two women's movements drew a line in the sand between liberals and conservatives. The legacy of that rift is still evident today in American politics and social policies.

"There are countless kernels of amazing achievement and courage throughout this jam-packed, engaging history." —*Kirkus*

Srinivasan, Amia
The Right to Sex: Feminism in the Twenty-first Century. Amia Srinivasan. Farrar, Straus & Giroux 2021. 208 p.
ISBN 9780374248529
Grades: Adult   305.42
1. Sexual ethics 2. Philosophy 3. Feminism 4. Intersectionality 5. Sexuality 6. Sexual violence 7. Sexuality and power (Social sciences) 8. Essays 9. Society and culture — Gender — Women 10. Society and culture — Sex and sexuality 11. Society and culture — Philosophy
LC 2021016449

Searching, trenchant and extraordinarily original, the Right to Sex is a landmark dismantling of the politics and ethics of sex in this world, animated by the hope of a different one.

"This exceptionally well-written collection . . . effectively merges academic analysis with lived experience in an accessible read that will interest readers from diverse professional and personal backgrounds." —*Library Journal*

Includes bibliographical references and index.

Steinem, Gloria
Outrageous Acts and Everyday Rebellions. Gloria Steinem; with a new foreword by Emma Watson and new material by the author. Picador 2019. xxii, 406 p.
ISBN 9781250204868
Grades: 11 12 Adult   305.42
1. Steinem, Gloria, 1934- 2. Feminists 3. Feminism 4. United States 5. Essays 6. Biographies 7. Society and culture — Gender — Women
LC 95031711

An updated, third edition of the renowned feminist's most diverse and timeless collection of essays.

Includes bibliographical references (p. xxi-xxii) and index.

The Truth Will Set You Free, but First It Will Piss You Off: Thoughts on Life, Love, and Rebellion. Gloria Steinem; illustrations by Samantha Dion Baker. Random House 2019. 304 p.
ISBN 9780593132685
Grades: Adult   305.42
1. Steinem, Gloria, 1934- 2. Life 3. Feminism 4. Inspiration 5. Quotations 6. Essays 7. Society and culture — Pop culture 8. Society and culture — Gender — Women
LC 2019029832

An illustrated collection of Gloria Steinem's most inspirational and outrageous quotes, with an introduction and essays by the feminist activist herself.

Turk, Katherine
The Women of Now: How Feminists Built an Organization That Transformed America. Katherine Turk. Farrar, Straus and Giroux 2023. 384 p.
ISBN 9780374601539
Grades: Adult   305.42
1. Hernandez, Aileen 2. Collins, Mary Jean 3. Burnett, Patricia Hill 4. Feminism 5. Political participation 6. Women's rights 7. United States 8. History Writing — Women's history 9. Society and culture — Gender — Women 10. Life stories — Identity — Gender
LC 2023003419

The story of the National Organization for Women-its structures, trials, and revolutionary mission-told through the work of three extraordinary, little-known members.

"Turk chronicles the founding, growth, and impact of the National Organization of Women by focusing on three key but lesser-known members." —*Library Journal*

Includes bibliographical references and index.

Vogelstein, Rachel B.
Awakening: #metoo and the Global Fight for Women's Rights. Rachel B. Vogelstein & Meighan Stone; foreword by Tarana Burke. Public Affairs 2021. 272 p.
ISBN 9781541758629
Grades: Adult   305.42
1. Me Too movement 2. Women's rights 3. Violence against women 4. Sexism 5. Social movements 6. Intersectionality 7. Women social advocates 8. Women's movement 9. Women 10. Society and culture — Gender — Women 11. Society and culture — Violence and crime 12. Politics and global affairs — Civil and human rights

Two advocates for women's rights chronicle the global impact of the #MeToo movement and how it uses technology to reach across borders, races and economic divides to fight against the violence and discrimination that women face.

"Complete with a broad selection of resources for advocacy, this call-to-action will spark the interest of aspiring activists." —*Library Journal*

Zakaria, Rafia
Against White Feminism: Notes on Disruption. Rafia Zakaria. W.W. Norton & Company 2021. x, 244 p.
ISBN 9781324006619
Grades: Adult   305.42
1. Feminism 2. Women's rights 3. Intersectionality 4. Marginalized women 5. Multiculturalism 6. Women's movement 7. Ethics 8. Power 9. Colonialism 10. Social justice 11. Social integration 12. Inclusive education 13. Society and culture — Gender — Women 14. Society and culture — Race 15. Society and culture — Ethnic studies
LC 2021011715

A radically inclusive, intersectional, and transnational approach to the fight for women's rights, covering such ground as the legacy of the British feminist imperialist savior complex and "the colonial thesis that all reform comes from the West," to the condescension of the white feminist?led "aid industrial complex" and the conflation of sexual liberation as the "sum total of empowerment." Rafia Zakaria follows in the tradition of intersectional feminist forebears Kimberle Crenshaw, Adrienne Rich, and Audre Lorde, ultimately refuting and reimagining the apolitical aspirations of white feminist empowerment in this staggering, radical critique, with Black and Brown feminist thought at the forefront.

"While Zakaria's argument is not the only one of its kind, her examination of current examples from politics and pop culture furnishes crucial evidence of the continued colonization of feminism by white women." —*Library Journal*

Includes bibliographical references and index.

Zoepf, Katherine
Excellent Daughters: The Secret Lives of Young Women Who Are Transforming the Arab World. Katherine Zoepf. Penguin Press 2016. 288 p.
ISBN 9781594203886
Grades: Adult   305.42
1. Women 2. Young women 3. Muslim women 4. Social change 5. Arab countries 6. Southwest Asia and North Africa (Middle East) 7. Society and culture — Gender — Women
LC 2015043395

A first-of-its-kind exploration of a new generation of Arab women who are questioning authority, changing societies and leading revolutions brings a new understanding of the changing Arab societies, from 9/11 to Tahrir Square to the rise of ISIS, and gives voice to the extraordinary women at the forefront of this change.

"In her absorbing, window-opening book, Zoepf reveals the variety of womens lives and interests away from political headlines and conventional stereotypes, and their power, often by small steps, to transform their world." —Publishers Weekly

305.4209 Feminism — History

Morris, Bonnie J.
★ *The Feminist Revolution: The Struggle for Women's Liberation.* Bonnie J. Morris, D-M Withers. Smithsonian Books 2018. 224 p.
ISBN 9781588346124
Grades: Adult   305.4209
1. Women's rights 2. Women's studies 3. Feminism 4. History writing — Women's history 5. Society and culture — Gender — Women 6. Adult books for young adults
LC 2017039814

Describes the political campaigns, protests, formation of women's publishing houses, groundbreaking magazines and other contributions that helped women around the world mobilize into the feminist revolution that began in 1966.

"Much like a museum exhibition, this collection uses accessible text and rich visual materials that invite readers to explore in a nonlinear fashion. It will appeal to both those deeply familiar with the topic as well as beginners of this influential moment in feminist history." —Library Journal

Includes bibliographical references and index.

305.420973 Feminism — United States

Hirshman, Linda R.
Reckoning: The Epic Battle Against Sexual Abuse and Harassment. Linda Hirshman. Houghton Mifflin Harcourt 2019. 304 p.
ISBN 9781328566447
Grades: Adult   305.420973
1. Sexual harassment of women 2. Trials (Sex crimes) 3. Sex crimes 4. Feminism 5. Women's rights 6. Social advocacy 7. Me Too movement 8. Women's Movement 9. Women 10. United States 11. 20th century 12. 21st century 13. History writing — Women's history 14. Society and culture — Gender — Women 15. Adult books for young adults
LC 2018051341

The best-selling author of Sisters in Law chronicles America's ongoing fight against sexual harassment, from the pivotal civil rights battles of the 1970s through the headline events of the #MeToo movement.

"An intense, harsh view of a long struggle; well worth a look for anyone curious about where #MeToo came fromand where it should go next." —Library Journal

Includes bibliographical references and index.

Kendall, Mikki
Hood Feminism: Notes from the Women That a Movement Forgot. Mikki Kendall. Viking Press 2020. 288 pages
ISBN 9780525560548
Grades: Adult   305.420973
1. Feminism 2. Marginalized women 3. Intersectionality 4. Women's rights 5. Essays 6. Society and culture — Gender — Women 7. History writing — Women's history 8. Antiracist literature
LC 2019033697

Rise: A Feminist Book Project List, 2021.

Insightful, incendiary and ultimately hopeful, Hood Feminism is both an irrefutable indictment of a movement in flux and also clear-eyed assessment of how to save it.

"This hard-hitting guide delivers crucial insights for those looking to build a more inclusive movement." —Publishers Weekly

Traister, Rebecca
Good and Mad: The Revolutionary Power of Women's Anger. Rebecca Traister. Simon & Schuster 2018. 352 p.
ISBN 9781501181795
Grades: Adult   305.420973
1. Women 2. Social change 3. Women's rights 4. Sexism 5. Sex discrimination 6. Gender equity 7. Political participation 8. Feminism 9. Anger 10. Society and culture — Gender — Women 11. History writing — Women's history 12. Adult books for young adults
LC 2018035975

Booklist Editors' Choice: Adult Books for Young Adults, 2018.

The New York Times best-selling author explores the transformative power of female anger and its ability to transcend into a political movement.

West, Lindy
The Witches Are Coming. Lindy West. Hachette Books 2019. 272 p.
ISBN 9780316449885
Grades: Adult   305.420973
1. Women 2. Women in popular culture 3. Women in mass media 4. Women in films 5. Sexism 6. Misogyny 7. Feminism 8. Public opinion 9. United States 10. Essays 11. Society and culture — Gender — Women
LC Bl2019030022

LibraryReads Favorites, 2019.

West unpacks the complicated, and sometimes tragic, journey and politics of not being a white man in the 21st century.

"Covering everything from the 2016 election and #metoo to abortion rights and fat-positive body representation to the climate crisis, West's latest will have progressive readers, especially longtime followers of her work, nodding along, quoting passages to friends. Hand to fans of Rebecca Traister, Ijeoma Oluo, and Roxane Gay." —Library Journal

305.48 Specific groups of women

Bernard, Emily
Black Is the Body: Stories from My Grandmother's Time, My Mother's Time, and Mine. by Emily Bernard. Alfred A. Knopf 2019. 192 p.
ISBN 9780451493026
Grades: Adult   305.48
1. Bernard, Emily, 1967- 2. African Americans 3. Ethnic identity 4. Growing up 5. Interracial marriage 6. African American women 7. Race relations 8. United States 9. 21st century 10. Essays 11. Autobiographies and memoirs 12. Biographies 13. Life stories — Identity — Race and ethnicity 14. Society and culture — Race 15. Arts and Entertainment — Writing and Publishing — Literary criticism 16. Antiracist literature
LC 2018022594

Los Angeles Times Book Prizes, Christopher Isherwood Prize for Autobiographical Prose, 2019.

A collection of personal essays explores the complexities and paradoxes of growing up Black in the South with a white surname as well as the author's experiences with interracial marriage, international adoption, and teaching at a Northern white college.

"Bernard's honesty and vulnerability reveal a strong voice with no sugarcoating, sharing her struggle, ambivalence, hopes, and fears as an individual within a web of relationships black and white. Highly recommended." —Library Journal

This is a Borzoi book.

ESSENTIAL AND RECOMMENDED TITLES
305.48 Specific groups of women

Berry, Daina Ramey
★ *A Black Women's History of the United States.* Daina Ramey Berry and Kali Nicole Gross. Beacon Press 2020. 288 p.
ISBN 9780807033555
Grades: Adult **305.48**
1. African American women 2. Intersectionality 3. Racism 4. Sexism 5. African American history 6. Social justice 7. Race relations 8. United States history 9. United States 10. History writing — African American — United States 11. History writing — Women's history 12. Life stories — Identity — Race and ethnicity 13. Life stories — Identity — Gender
LC 2019026852
Centering around Black women's stories, two award-winning historians offer an examination and celebration of Black womanhood, beginning with the first African women who arrived in what became the US to African American women of today.
"For anyone hoping to topple the remaining barriers, this book is a font of inspiration. A vital book for any library or classroom—and for foot soldiers in the fight for racial justice." —*Kirkus*
Includes bibliographical references and index.

Blay, Zeba
Carefree Black Girls: A Celebration of Black Women in Popular Culture. Zeba Blay. St. Martin's Griffin 2021. 240 p.
ISBN 9781250231567
Grades: Adult **305.48**
1. Blay, Zeba 2. African American women 3. Popular culture 4. Sex in mass media 5. African Americans 6. Essays 7. Society and culture — Race 8. Society and culture — Gender — Women 9. Society and culture — Pop culture 10. Book club best bets
LC 2021016071
A film and culture critic, who was one of the first people to coin the viral term #carefreeblackgirls on Twitter, presents essays in which she expands on this initial idea by delving into the work and lasting achievements of influential Black women in American culture.
"Calling for Black women (in and out of the public eye) to be treated with empathy, Blay's pivotal work will engage all readers, especially fans of Mikki Kendall's Hood Feminism." —*Library Journal*
Includes bibliographical references.

Brina, Elizabeth Miki
Speak, Okinawa: A Memoir. Elizabeth Miki Brina. Alfred A. Knopf 2021. 304 p.
ISBN 9780525657347
Grades: Adult **305.48**
1. Brina, Elizabeth Miki, 1981- 2. Growing up 3. Japanese American women 4. Belonging 5. Identity 6. Family relationships 7. Japanese Americans 8. Interracial marriage 9. East Asian Americans 10. Okinawa 11. New York State 12. Autobiographies and memoirs 13. Life stories — Relationships — Family 14. Family and Relationships — Families 15. Life stories — Relationships — Growing up 16. Family and Relationships — Growing up
LC 2020030710
A searing, deeply candid memoir about a young woman's journey to understanding her complicated parents—her father a Vietnam veteran, her mother an Okinawan war bride—and her own, fraught cultural heritage.
"In a debut memoir, the daughter of an Okinawan Vietnam War bride and an American soldier grapples with her complex familial roots." —*Kirkus*

Brooks, Geraldine
Nine Parts of Desire: The Hidden World of Islamic Women. Geraldine Brooks. Anchor Books 1995. 255 p.
ISBN 9780385475778
Grades: 11 12 Adult **305.48**
1. Muslim women 2. Islam and women 3. Women's role 4. Sexism 5. Sex discrimination 6. Sex discrimination against women 7. Women 8. Religions 9. Southwest Asia and North Africa (Middle East) 10. Spirituality and Religion — Islam
LC 94017496
ALA Notable Book, 1996.
An intimate portrait of the lives of modern Muslim women reveals how male pride and power have distorted the message of Islam to justify the subjugation of women and how a feminism of sorts has flowered in spite of repression.
"The author's revelations about these women's lives behind the veil are frank, enraging, and captivating." —*The New Yorker*
Includes bibliographical references (p. 245-247) and index.

Carruthers, Charlene A.
Unapologetic: A Black, Queer, and Feminist Mandate for Our Movement. Charlene A. Carruthers. Beacon Press 2018. 184 p.
ISBN 9780807019412
Grades: Adult **305.48**
1. African American lesbians 2. African American women 3. African American civil rights 4. Race relations 5. Feminism 6. Black power 7. Black Lives Matter movement 8. Social movements 9. Police brutality 10. Political participation 11. Politics and government 12. United States history 13. United States 14. 21st century 15. Autobiographies and memoirs 16. Book club best bets 17. Life stories — Identity — Race and ethnicity 18. Society and culture — Race 19. Politics and global affairs — Civil and human rights 20. Society and culture — LGBTQIA+ 21. History writing — African American — United States
LC 2017058987
Unapologetic is a 21st century guide to building a Black liberation movement through a Black queer feminist lens.
"Incantatory without being incendiary, strong but not strident, Carruthers argues for a world in which everyone is able to live with dignity and in right relationship with the land we inhabit. This handbook for the revolution is a rousing call for collective liberation." —*Publishers Weekly*
Includes bibliographical references and index.

Cho, Grace M.
Tastes Like War: A Memoir. Grace M. Cho. The Feminist Press at the City University of New York 2021. 296 p.
ISBN 9781952177941
Grades: Adult **305.48**
1. Cho, Grace M. 2. Korean American women 3. Children of people with mental illnesses 4. Mothers and daughters 5. Food habits 6. Cooking, Korean 7. Immigrant families 8. Multiracial women 9. Schizophrenia 10. War 11. Loss 12. Social life and customs 13. United States 14. South Korea 15. Life stories — Facing adversity — Medical issues — Mental illness 16. Life stories — Identity — Immigrants 17. Food writing — Memoirs and biographies 18. Life stories — Relationships — Parent and child 19. Family and relationships — Families
LC 2020051100
Asian Pacific American Award for Literature: Adult Nonfiction, 2022; National Book Award for Nonfiction finalist, 2021.
Grace M. Cho grew up in a small, rural American town as the daughter of a white American merchant marine and the Korean bar hostess he met abroad. When Grace was fifteen, her Korean mother experienced the onset of schizophrenia, a condition that would continue for the rest of her life. Part food memoir, part sociological investigation, TASTES LIKE WAR is a hybrid text about a daughter's search through intimate and global history to understand herself and the cultural roots of her mother's condition.
"A Korean immigrant and sociology professor reevaluates her mother's past and their fraught relationship." —*Kirkus*
Includes bibliographical references.

Dangarembga, Tsitsi
Black and Female: Essays. Tsitsi Dangarembga. Graywolf Press 2023. 128 p.
ISBN 9781644452110
Grades: Adult **305.48**
1. Identity 2. Women authors 3. Race (Social sciences) 4. Gender role 5. Racism 6. Postcolonialism 7. Essays 8. Society and culture — Gender 9. Society and culture — Race

This paradigm shifting essay collection weaves the personal and political in an illuminating exploration of internationally acclaimed novelist Tsitsi Dangarembga's complex relationship with race and gender.

"Dangarembga's candid reflections and lyrical prose bring urgency to this thought-provoking argument for political and social equality." —*Publishers Weekly*

Originally published in the UK by Faber & Faber, London, in 2022.

Flock, Elizabeth

★ *The Furies: Women, Vengeance, and Justice.* Elizabeth Flock. Harper 2024. 352 p.

ISBN 9780063048805

Grades: Adult   **305.48**

1. Women 2. Violence 3. Self-defense 4. Revenge 5. Marginalized women 6. Victims of crimes 7. Gangs 8. Militias and irregular armies 9. Feminism 10. Misogyny 11. Empowerment 12. Society and culture — Gender — Women 13. Society and culture — Violence and crime 14. Life stories — Identity — Gender 15. Life stories — Facing adversity

In The Furies, Elizabeth Flock examines how three real-life women have used violence to fight back, and how views of women who defend their lives are often distorted by their depictions in media and pop culture. Each woman chose to use lethal force to gain power, safety, and freedom when the institutions meant to protect them—government, police, courts—utterly failed to do so. Each woman has been criticized for their actions by those who believe that violence is never the answer.

"Flock's compelling narrative will resonate with those who seek to live in a more feminist, egalitarian society." —*Booklist*

Hong, Cathy Park

Minor Feelings: An Asian American Reckoning. Cathy Park Hong. Random House Inc 2020. 176 pages

ISBN 9781984820365

Grades: Adult   **305.48**

1. Hong, Cathy Park 2. Asian Americans 3. Asian American women 4. Poets, American 5. Identity 6. Children of immigrants 7. Korean American families 8. Race relations 9. Autobiographies and memoirs 10. Essays 11. Life stories — Identity — Race and ethnicity 12. Life stories — Arts and culture — Writing — Poets 13. Society and culture — Race 14. Book club best bets

LC 2019033869

National Book Critics Circle Award for Autobiography, 2020; Pulitzer Prize for General Nonfiction finalist, 2021.

An award-winning poet and essayist offers a ruthlessly honest, emotionally charged exploration of the psychological condition of being Asian American.

"An extraordinary blend of memoir, cultural criticism, and history that will invite readers from all backgrounds, though especially those who identify as Asian American, to consider the complex relationships between race, family, heritage, and society that shape American lives." —*Library Journal*

Hubbard, Shanita

★ *Ride-or-Die: A Feminist Manifesto for the Well-being of Black Women.* Shanita Hubbard. Legacy Lit 2022. 177 pages

ISBN 9780306874673

Grades: Adult   **305.48**

1. African American women 2. Identity 3. Feminism 4. Intersectionality 5. Hip-hop culture 6. Healing 7. Fatigue 8. Self-care 9. Interpersonal relations 10. Popular culture 11. Social change 12. Self-esteem 13. Society and culture — Race 14. Society and culture — Gender — Women 15. Society and culture — Psychology and human behavior

LC 2022019787

Melding entertaining conversations with black girlfriends and her personal experiences as a redeemed "ride-or-die" chick, an acclaimed writer urges black women to expel the myth that their self-worth is connected to how much labor they provide others, and guides them toward healing.

"Award-winning writer Hubbard pens a conflicted love letter to hip-hop, arguing that the 'Ride-or-die chick' cultural phenomenon is a double-edged sword….Perfect for fans of Brittney Cooper's Eloquent Rage and Mikki Kendall's Hood Feminism." —*Library Journal*

Includes bibliographical references.

Hunter-Gault, Charlayne

★ *My People: Five Decades of Writing About Black Lives.* Charlayne Hunter-Gault. HarperCollins 2022. 256 p.

ISBN 9780063135390

Grades: Adult   **305.48**

1. Civil rights movement 2. Journalism 3. African Americans 4. Racism 5. Race (Social sciences) 6. Marginalized people 7. African American civil rights 8. Race relations 9. United States 10. 20th century 11. 21st century 12. Essays 13. Society and culture — Race 14. History writing — African American — United States

Sharing her storied career spanning five decades, a legendary Emmy Award-winning journalist presents this collection of groundbreaking reportage, from the Civil Rights Movement through the election and inauguration of America's first Black president and beyond, chronicling the Black experience through trials, tragedies and triumphs and everyday lives.

"Y People is an inspirational collection and a must-read for aspiring writers interested in honing their craft and readers who want to become knowledgeable about Black lives past and present." —*Booklist*

Jackson, Jenn M.

★ *Black Women Taught Us: An Intimate History of Black Feminism.* Jenn M. Jackson. Random House 2024. 336 p.

ISBN 9780593243336

Grades: Adult   **305.48**

1. Jackson, Jenn M. 2. African American women political activists 3. African American feminism 4. Social justice 5. Race relations 6. Civil rights 7. Justice 8. Political activists 9. African American history 10. United States history 11. Community activism 12. Identity 13. Intersectionality 14. Black people 15. Feminism 16. African American women 17. United States 18. Essays 19. Society and culture — Gender — Women 20. Society and culture — Race

LC 2023012455

This collection of eleven original essays from Harriet Jacobs and Ida B. Wells to Audre Lorde explore the legacy of Black women writers and leaders and repositions their intellectual and political work at the center of today's liberation movements.

"Galvanizing appraisals of Black women's enduring search for freedom." —*Kirkus*

IIncludes bibliographical references and index.

Mojica Rodriguez, Prisca Dorcas

For Brown Girls with Sharp Edges and Tender Hearts: A Love Letter to Women of Color. Prisca Dorcas Mojica Rodriguez. Seal Press 2021. 304 p.

ISBN 9781541674875

Grades: Adult   **305.48**

1. Mojica Rodriguez, Prisca Dorcas, 1985- 2. Hispanic American women 3. Personal conduct 4. Marginalized women 5. Nicaraguan people 6. Teenage immigrants 7. Indigenous peoples 8. Ethnic identity 9. Hispanic Americans 10. Central American people 11. American people 12. Christian women 13. Growing up 14. Success (Concept) 15. Empowerment 16. Social advocacy 17. Racism 18. Race relations 19. United States 20. Society and culture — Social activism and philanthropy 21. Life stories — Identity — Race and ethnicity 22. Life stories — Identity — Gender 23. Life stories — Identity — Immigrants

LC 2021016112

For generations, Brown girls have had to push against powerful forces of sexism, racism, and classism, often feeling alone in the struggle. By founding Latina Rebels, Prisca Dorcas Mojica Rodríguez has created a community to help women fight together. In For Brown Girls with Sharp Edges and Tender Hearts, she offers wisdom and a liberating path forward for all women of color. She crafts powerful ways to address the challenges Brown girls face, from imposter syndrome to colorism. She empowers women to decolonize their worldview, and defy universal white narratives, by telling their own stories. Her book guides women of color toward a sense of pride and sisterhood and offers essential tools to energize a movement.

ESSENTIAL AND RECOMMENDED TITLES
305.5 People by social and economic levels

"Marked by its candidness and earnest commitment to the power of self-belief, this is an inspiring and well-informed call to action." —*Publishers Weekly*
Includes bibliographical references.

Roy, Jessica
American Girls: One Woman's Journey into the Islamic State and Her Sister's Fight to Bring Her Home. Jessica Roy. Scribner 2024. 352 p.
ISBN 9781982151317
Grades: Adult   305.48
1. Women radicals 2. American people 3. North American people 4. Radicalism 5. Jehovah's Witnesses 6. Sisters 7. Sex crimes 8. Family violence 9. Religious fanaticism 10. Families 11. Terrorist organizations 12. Arkansas 13. Syria 14. Life stories — Facing adversity — Victims of crime — Terrorism 15. Life stories — Relationships — Family 16. Family and Relationships — Abuse
LC 2023011337

A deeply reported narrative about religious extremism, radicalization and the bonds of family: the story of an American woman who traveled to ISIS-controlled Syria with her two children and extremist husband and the sister back home who worked tirelessly to help her escape.
"This is a thoughtful reframing of a sensational case." —*Publishers Weekly*

305.5 People by social and economic levels

Boo, Katherine
★ *Behind the Beautiful Forevers: Life, Death, and Hope in a Mumbai Undercity.* Katherine Boo. Random House 2011. 256 p.
ISBN 9781400067558
Grades: Adult   305.5
1. Urban poor people 2. Inequality 3. Poverty 4. Poor people 5. Mumbai, India 6. Travel Writing — Asia and the South Pacific 7. Adult books for young adults 8. Society and culture — Wealth and class — Poverty 9. Nonfiction that reads like fiction 10. Book club best bets
LC 2011019555

ALA Notable Book, 2013; Library Journal Best Books, 2012; Los Angeles Times Book Prize for Current Interest, 2012; National Book Award for Nonfiction, 2012; New York Times Notable Book, 2012; School Library Journal Best Books: Best Adult Books 4 Teens, 2012; National Book Critics Circle Award for Nonfiction finalist, 2012; Pulitzer Prize for General Nonfiction finalist, 2013.

Profiles everyday life in the settlement of Annawadi as experienced by a Muslim teen, an ambitious rural mother, and a young scrap metal thief, illuminating how their efforts to build better lives are challenged by religious, caste, and economic tensions.

Brooks, David
The Social Animal: A Story of Love, Character, and Achievement. David Brooks. Random House 2011. 224 p.
ISBN 9781400067602
Grades: Adult   305.5
1. Social mobility 2. Social status 3. Elite (Social sciences) 4. Character 5. Men-women relations 6. Family and Relationships — General 7. Society and culture — Psychology and human behavior
LC 2010045785

Booklist Editors' Choice, 2011.

Looks at current research from a variety of disciplines by following the lives and unconscious motivations of a hypothetical American couple as they grow, meet, and change throughout their lives.
"Brooks offers fictional characters Harold and Erica to illustrate how humans communicate, are educated, and succeedor don't. Synthesizing research on human unconsciousness, Brooks meshes sociology, psychology, and economics to show how character is formed and how we strive for happiness and success. [The author] offers a new look at the assumptions we make about life and a close, deep examination of the failure of social and economic policies that do not take into account the complexities of human behavior, treating us as if we were totally rational and guided by our thoughts rather than some combination of intellect and emotion." —*Booklist*

Gidla, Sujatha
Ants Among Elephants: An Untouchable Family and the Making of Modern India. Sujatha Gidla. Farrar, Straus and Giroux 2017. 400 p.
ISBN 9780865478114
Grades: Adult   305.5
1. Gidla, Sujatha, 1963- 2. Caste 3. Inequality 4. Pariahs 5. Dalits (Indian Scheduled Castes) 6. Families 7. Revolutionaries 8. Political corruption 9. Sexism 10. Poverty 11. India 12. 20th century 13. Autobiographies and memoirs 14. Life stories — Facing adversity — War and oppression 15. Society and culture — Ethnic studies 16. History writing — Asia — South Asia — India
LC 2016052857

A woman, born as an "untouchable" into the Indian caste system, describes how she was educated by Canadian missionaries in the 1930s and what it was like growing up in a world full of poverty and injustice but also full of incredible possibility.
"Gidla writes about the heavy topics of poverty, caste and gender inequality, and political corruption with grace and wit. an essential contribution to contemporary Indian literature." —*Publishers Weekly*

Goyal, Nikhil
★ *Live to See the Day: Coming of Age in American Poverty.* Nikhil Goyal. Metropolitan Books 2023. 320 p.
ISBN 9781250850065
Grades: Adult   305.5
1. Poverty 2. Poor people 3. Children 4. Marginalized people 5. United States 6. Philadelphia, Pennsylvania 7. Society and culture — Wealth and class — Poverty 8. History Writing — United States 9. Life stories — Facing adversity

Three children struggle to survive in the poorest neighborhood of the poorest city in America.
"Goyal's compelling writing and extensive research make this an excellent counterpart to Matthew Desmond's Poverty, by America (2023) and the works of Jonathan Kozol." —*Booklist*

Isenberg, Nancy
White Trash: The 400—year Untold History of Class in America. Nancy Isenberg. Viking 2016. 480 p.
ISBN 9780670785971
Grades: Adult   305.5
1. Social classes 2. Poor people 3. European Americans 4. Working class 5. Social history 6. Rednecks (Southern United States) 7. White privilege 8. History writing — Arts and culture 9. Society and culture — Wealth and class — Poverty 10. History writing — United States
LC 2016302095

New York Times Notable Book, 2016.

A history of the class system in America from Colonial times to the present illuminates the crucial legacy of the underprivileged white demographic, challenging popular notions about equality while citing the pivotal contributions of lower-class white workers in wartime, social policy and the rise of the Republican party. By the author of Fallen Founder.
"A riveting thesis supported by staggering research." —*Kirkus*

Jadhav, Narendra
Untouchables: My Family's Triumphant Journey Out of the Caste System in Modern India. Narendra Jadhav. Scribner 2005. 307 p.
ISBN 9780743270793
Grades: Adult   305.5
1. Jadhav, Narendra, 1953- 2. Economists 3. Dalits (Indian Scheduled Castes) 4. Caste 5. Social life and customs 6. India 7. 20th century 8. Autobiographies and memoirs 9. Life stories — Facing adversity — Personal transformation 10. Life stories — Facing adversity — War and oppression 11. Adult books for young adults 12. History writing — Asia — South Asia — India
LC 2005044166

Traces an Indian family's efforts to attain equality despite their nation's poor regard for the Dalit class, describing how the author's parents escaped a life of hunger, abuse, and fear by gaining acceptance into a higher caste.

"This moving story of perseverance from a sector of India rarely represented to American readers will be a standard text on Indian and Dalit themes for years to come." —*Library Journal*

First published in English in 2003 by Penguin Books as Outcaste.

Joyce, Patrick

Remembering Peasants: *A Personal History of a Vanished World*. Patrick Joyce. Scribner 2024. 352 p.

ISBN 9781668031087

Grades: Adult   **305.5**

1. Peasantry 2. Social history 3. Culture 4. Social classes 5. Civilization 6. Europe 7. History Writing — Europe 8. Society and culture — Ethnic studies 9. Life stories — People in history 10. Society and culture — Urban and regional studies

LC 2023046380

A landmark new history of the peasant experience, exploring a now neglected way of life that once encompassed most of humanity but is vanishing in our time. In this new history of peasantry, social historian Patrick Joyce aims to tell the story of this lost world and its people, and how we can commemorate their way of life.

"A historian laments the disappearance of rural European populations, and with it certain possibilities for people to connect with the land, the past, and each other." —*Booklist*

Includes bibliographical references.

Lewis, Michael

★ *Going Infinite: The Rise and Fall of a New Tycoon*. Michael Lewis. W W Norton & Company 2023. 288 p.

ISBN 9781324074335

Grades: Adult   **305.5**

1. Bankman-Fried, Sam 2. Billionaires 3. Capitalists and financiers 4. Cryptocurrencies 5. Digital currency 6. Bankruptcy 7. Finance 8. Business and economics — Corruption and scandal 9. Business and economics — Industries — Finance 10. Life stories — Business

The #1 best-selling author of the Big Short and Flash Boys tells the story of FTX's spectacular collapse and the enigmatic founder at its center.

Markovits, Daniel

The Meritocracy *Trap: How America's Foundational Myth Feeds Inequality, Dismantles the Middle Class, and Devours the Elite*. Daniel Markovits. Penguin Press 2019. 336 p.

ISBN 9780735221994

Grades: Adult   **305.5**

1. Middle class 2. Intellectuals 3. Elite (Social sciences) 4. Inequality 5. Ability 6. Wealth 7. Social policy 8. United States 9. 21st century 10. Society and culture — Wealth and class 11. Business and economics — Economics — Socioeconomics

LC 2019007519

An eminent Yale law professor challenges the myth of meritocracy to reveal its direct role in today's political, economic and psychological crises, outlining recommendations for ending and reversing the damage of current fraudulent practices.

"Bold proposals for a radical revision of contemporary society." —*Kirkus*

Includes bibliographical references and index.

Mechanic, Michael

Jackpot: How the Super-rich Really Live - and How Their Wealth Harms Us All. Michael Mechanic. Simon & Schuster 2021. 416 p.

ISBN 9781982127213

Grades: Adult   **305.5**

1. Wealth 2. Rich people 3. Income inequality 4. Social classes 5. United States 6. Impartial writing 7. Society and culture — Wealth and class 8. Business and economics — Economics — Socioeconomics

LC 2020046505

Have you ever fantasized about being ridiculously wealthy? Probably. Striking it rich is among the most resilient of American fantasies. But what is it actually like to be blessed with riches in an era of plagues, political rancor, and near-Dickensian economic differences? How mind-boggling are the opportunities and access, how problematic the downsides? Does the experience differ depending on whether the money is earned or unearned, where it comes from, and whether you are male or female, white or Black? Finally, how does our collective lust for affluence, and our stubborn belief in social mobility, explain how we got to the point where forty percent of Americans have literally no wealth at all? These are all questions that Michael Mechanic's Jackpot sets out to explore.

"Mother Jones senior editor Mechanic offers a harsh wake-up call for the millions of American dreamers who still believe that winning the lottery—or just simply having obscene wealth—will change their lives for the better. . . . A scathing but fair indictment of how the mindless worship of wealth makes us all poorer." —*Kirkus*

Includes index.

Neiman, Garrett

Rich White Men: What It Takes to Uproot the Old Boys' Club and Transform America. Garrett Neiman. Legacy Lit 2023. 256 p.

ISBN 9780306925566

Grades: Adult   **305.5**

1. Wealth 2. White privilege 3. European American men 4. Rich people 5. Social justice 6. Income inequality 7. Social classes 8. Race relations 9. Intersectionality 10. Power 11. Monopolies 12. Gender role 13. Segregation 14. Discrimination 15. American people 16. North American people 17. Economics 18. United States 19. Society and culture — Wealth and class 20. Society and culture — Gender — Men

LC 2022057863

It's no secret that our country has a serious problem when it comes to wealth inequality ? and systemic racism and patriarchy have only exacerbated the advantages of wealthy white men. Over the past three decades, America's richest white men have only become richer, while those suffering in poverty have only gotten poorer. The divide may seem too great to bridge, but Rich White Men exposes the hidden and insidious ways that white male elites inherit, increase, and preserve their status—and, in this book, we get clear on how to uproot their monopoly on power.—.

"This book will appeal to those who are interested in examining racial and socioeconomic segregation and looking to understand diverse viewpoints and how to combat inequality." —*Booklist*

Putnam, Robert D.

Our Kids: *The American Dream in Crisis*. Robert D. Putnam. Simon & Schuster 2015. 416 p.

ISBN 9781476769899

Grades: Adult   **305.5**

1. American Dream 2. Social mobility 3. Social policy 4. Middle class 5. Economics 6. United States 7. Politics and global affairs — World politics — United States

LC 2015001534

Booklist Editors' Choice, 2015.

In an authoritative, yet personal, examination of the growing inequality gap, a leading humanist and renowned scientist who has consulted for the last four U.S. Presidents, drawing on poignant life stories of rich and poor kids across the country, provides a disturbing account of the American dream. By the author of Bowling Alone. Includes 30 charts and graphs.

Quart, Alissa

Bootstrapped: Liberating Ourselves from the American Dream. Alissa Quart. Ecco Press 2022. 192 p.

ISBN 9780063028005

Grades: Adult   **305.5**

1. American dream 2. Self-reliance 3. Inequality 4. Survival 5. Individualism 6. United States 7. Society and culture — Wealth and class

ESSENTIAL AND RECOMMENDED TITLES
305.50973 Class — United States

An acclaimed journalist examines the American obsession with self-reliance, and how it has led to inequality, self-blame and shifted the responsibility for survival onto the backs of ordinary people.

"A provocative, important repudiation of gig-economy capitalism that proposes utopian rather than dystopian solutions." —*Kirkus*

Squeezed: *Why Our Families Can't Afford America.* Alissa Quart. Ecco 2018. 272 p.
ISBN 9780062412256
Grades: Adult   305.5
1. Middle class 2. Household finances 3. Cost and standard of living 4. Personal finance 5. Economic policy 6. Economics 7. United States 8. Business and economics — Economics — Contemporary U.S. economy
LC 2017056972

The executive editor of the journalism nonprofit, Economic Hardship Reporting Project, outlines counter-intuitive recommendations for meeting the challenges of today's high parenting costs and unstable job markets that are imposing difficult hardships on the middle class.

"Quart details sound policy-related solutions—an adjunct rights movement; free preschool; welfare-type assistance for elder care and childcare; an end to federal funding for sketchy, for-profit schools; and universal basic income. Her ambitious, top-tier reportage tells a powerful story of America today." —*Publishers Weekly*

Reeves, Richard V.
Dream Hoarders: How the American Upper Middle Class Is Leaving Everyone Else in the Dust, Why That Is a Problem, and What to Do About It. Richard V. Reeves. Brookings Institution Press 2017. 180 p.
ISBN 9780815729129
Grades: Adult   305.5
1. Middle class 2. Social mobility 3. Income inequality 4. Social change 5. Quality of life 6. Equality 7. Wealth 8. United States 9. Society and culture — Wealth and class
LC 2017010289

Shows how American society has become the very class-defined society that earlier Americans rebelled against, discussing how Americans can take effective action to reduce opportunity hoarding and thus provide ways to restore a more equitable society.

Veblen, Thorstein
★ *The Theory of the Leisure Class.* Theodore Veblen; edited with an Introduction and notes by Martha Banta. Oxford University Press 2007. xxxv, 263 p.
ISBN 9780192806840
Grades: Adult   305.5
1. Leisure class 2. Society and culture — Sociology
LC 2007008544

In his scathing the Theory of the Leisure Class, Thorstein Veblen produced a landmark study of affluent American society that exposes, with brilliant ruthlessness, the habits of production and waste that link invidious business tactics and barbaric social behavior.

Includes bibliographical references (p. [260]-263); Originally published: New York : Macmillan, 1899.

Warren, Elizabeth
This Fight Is Our Fight: The Battle to Save America's Middle Class. Elizabeth Warren. Henry Holt & Company 2017. 337 p.
ISBN 9781250120618
Grades: Adult   305.5
1. Middle class 2. Fiscal policy 3. Economic policy 4. Social policy 5. Politics and government 6. United States 7. Liberal writing 8. Politics and global affairs — World politics — United States 9. Business and economics — Economics — Contemporary U.S. economy
LC 2017007458

The senator shares stories of her battles in the Senate fighting for the working class, describing the experiences of middle class Americans struggling to survive.

"Warren's education in maneuvering through the powers that be is eye-opening, and she shares her experiences with grim frankness." —*Kirkus*

Wilkerson, Isabel
★ *Caste: The Origins of Our Discontents.* Isabel Wilkerson. Random House 2020. 400 p.
ISBN 9780593230251
Grades: Adult   305.5
1. Caste 2. Social classes 3. Ethnicity 4. Race relations 5. Power 6. Hierarchy (Social sciences) 7. Stigma (Social psychology) 8. United States 9. Page to screen 10. Society and culture — Wealth and class 11. Society and culture — Race 12. Society and culture — Ethnic studies 13. Book club best bets
LC 2020012794

ALA Notable Book, 2021; LibraryReads Favorites, 2020; Los Angeles Times Book Prize for Current Interest, 2020; New York Times Notable Book, 2020; Kirkus Prize for Nonfiction finalist, 2020; National Book Critics Circle Award for Nonfiction finalist, 2020.

The Pulitzer Prize-winning author of the Warmth of Other Suns identifies the qualifying characteristics of historical caste systems to reveal how a rigid hierarchy of human rankings, enforced by religious views, heritage and stigma, impact everyday American lives.

"In this outstanding work of social history, she explains how a rigid social order, or caste, is about power. . . . Similar to her previous book, the latest by Wilkerson is destined to become a classic, and is urgent, essential reading for all." —*Library Journal*

Made into a movie called Origin, 2023; Includes bibliographical references and index.

305.50973 Class — United States

Postel, Charles
Equality: An American Dilemma, 1866-1896. Charles Postel. Farrar, Straus and Giroux 2019. 464 p.
ISBN 9780809079636
Grades: Adult   305.50973
1. Oppression (Psychology) 2. Equality 3. Social movements 4. Reconstruction (United States history) 5. Working class 6. Race relations 7. Social classes 8. Discrimination 9. Social change 10. United States history 11. United States 12. Gilded Age (1865-1898) 13. 19th century 14. American Civil War era (1861-1865) 15. Impartial writing 16. Politics and global affairs — Civil and human rights 17. Society and culture — Wealth and class
LC 2019000171

Presents an in-depth study of the American social movements of the post-Civil War period, demonstrating their pivotal role in establishing anti-discrimination laws and informing today's world about approaches to inequality.

"With deep research and clear prose, Postel ably demonstrates that African-Americans were consistently excluded from these reformers' visions of a more equal America. Postel's broad and valuable study ably illuminates the era." —*Publishers Weekly*

Includes bibliographical references and index.

Stiglitz, Joseph E.
The Price of Inequality: How Today's Divided Society Endangers Our Future. Joseph E. Stiglitz. W.W. Norton & Co. 2012. 448 p.
ISBN 9780393088694
Grades: Adult   305.50973
1. Income inequality 2. Prosperity 3. Wealth 4. Inequality 5. Social problems 6. Social justice 7. Economics 8. United States 9. 21st century 10. Business and economics — Economics — Contemporary U.S. economy 11. Society and culture — Wealth and class
LC 2012014811

Robert F. Kennedy Book Award, 2013.

Examines how the wealthy classes have contributed to growing inequality in society and explains how the quest to increase wealth has hindered the country's economic growth as well as its efforts to solve its most pressing economic problems.

Includes bibliographical references and index.

305.6 Religious groups

Curtis, Edward E.
Muslims in America: A Short History. Edward E. Curtis IV.. Oxford University Press 2009. 168 p.
ISBN 9780195367560
Grades: 9 10 11 12 Adult 305.6
1. Muslims 2. Islam 3. Religions 4. Interethnic relations 5. Religious life 6. United States 7. History writing — United States 8. Spirituality and Religion — Islam
LC 2008047566

A history of the Muslim presence in the United States from slaves who managed to keep their religion to the varied communities of the twenty-first century covers the role of converts and immigrants in every stage of American history.

Includes bibliographical references and index.

Qureshi, Saqib Iqbal
Being Muslim Today: Reclaiming the Faith from Orthodoxy and Islamophobia. Dr. Saqib Iqbal Qureshi. Rowman & Littlefield 2024. 328 p.
ISBN 9781538189320
Grades: Adult 305.6
1. Islam 2. Muslims 3. Islam and culture 4. Islamophobia 5. Social history 6. Spirituality and religion — Islam

"Overall, Qureshi promotes a moderate and inclusive view of contemporary Islam, with the intellectual underpinnings to support it." —*Booklist*

305.8 Ethnic and national groups

Baldwin, James
★ *Notes of a Native Son.* James Baldwin. Beacon Press 2012. 179 p.
ISBN 9780807006115
Grades: Adult 305.8
1. Baldwin, James, 1924-1987 2. African American civil rights 3. Civil rights 4. Racism 5. Social classes 6. African Americans 7. Race relations 8. United States 9. 20th century 10. Essays 11. History writing — African American — Civil rights — United States
LC 90052598

A Black writer records his response to the conditions of Black life and white racism.

"The expression of so many insights enriches rather than clarifies, and behind every page stalks a man, an everyman, seeking his identity…and ours. Exceptional writing." —*Kirkus*

Originally published: New York : Dial Press, 1963.

Bell, W. Kamau
★ *Do the Work!: An Antiracist Activity Book.* W. Kamau Bell & Kate Schatz. Workman Publishing 2022. 160 pages : Illustration; Color
ISBN 9781523514281
Grades: Adult 305.8
1. Antiracism 2. Racism 3. Social justice 4. Race relations 5. United States 6. Society and culture — Race 7. Antiracist literature
LC Oc2022001616

Do the Work! is a hands-on workbook for anyone overwhelmed by racial injustice, who feels shocked by all the American histories they never learned, and who keeps asking the question "what can I DOOOOOO?!" Packed with humorous, thought-provoking activities-all are rooted in history and contemporary social justice concepts-the book helps readers move from "What can I do?" to… you know… actually doing the work.

"While the concepts covered will not be new for readers familiar with antiracism, the addition of activities and wry humor make for a unique and valuable compilation. Book clubs may take note." —*Library Journal*

Includes poster, stickers, paper doll, pop-out cards, and lift-the-flap pages; Packed with activities, games, illustrations, comics, and eye-opening conversation, Do the Work! challenges readers to think critically and act effectively—Page 4 of cover.

Boykin, Keith
Race Against Time: The Politics of a Darkening America. Keith Boykin. Bold Type Books 2021. 295 p.
ISBN 9781645037262
Grades: Adult 305.8
1. African Americans 2. Social change 3. Social justice 4. Political culture 5. Presidents 6. Racism 7. Political participation 8. Race relations 9. Politics and government 10. United States 11. 21st century 12. Society and culture — Race 13. Politics and global affairs — General 14. History writing — African American — United States 15. History writing — Early 21st century — United States 16. Antiracist literature
LC 2021006571

As the upheaval of 2020 has made clear, America has utterly failed to atone for its original sin of racism. In Race Against Time, national political commentator Keith Boykin offers a nuanced, in-depth account of political maneuverings from Washington to the streets, showing how Republicans, Democrats, and even populist movements have failed to address the dire realities that threaten the nation. Boykin details the effects of the emergence and persistence of the Black Lives Matter movement; Democrats' failed strategies of incrementalism during the Obama era and the legacies of Clinton-era policies; the minority, obstructionist policies of the Republicans; and the Bernie Sanders coalition's well-meaning but race-neutral economic reforms. With few exceptions, Boykin contends, we have refused to learn from the mistakes of these efforts, leaving us utterly unprepared for the future. Drawing on on-the-ground reporting and political analysis based on his years as a Washington insider, Boykin argues that the path forward is a race-based restructuring of the country where equality—not marginal improvement—is the goal.

"A must-read for anyone interested in the history of American politics and race, and a call-to-action for aspiring activists." —*Library Journal*

★ *Why Does Everything Have to Be About Race?: 25 Arguments That Won't Go Away.* Keith Boykin. Bold Type Books 2024. 224 p.
ISBN 9781541703315
Grades: Adult 305.8
1. Boykin, Keith 2. African Americans 3. Race (Social sciences) 4. Racism 5. Antiracism 6. Race relations 7. Misinformation 8. Argumentation 9. Debates and debating 10. Social justice 11. United States 12. Society and culture — Race 13. Life stories — Identity — Race and ethnicity 14. Antiracist literature
LC 2023019505

The most toxic racial arguments share one of five traits. They try to erase Black history, prioritize white victimhood, deny Black oppression, promote myths of Black inferiority, or rebrand racism as something else entirely. They're all designed to distract society from racial justice, but now we have the tools to debunk them. With a mixture of personal experience, reportage, and extensive research, Keith Boykin takes a wrecking ball to twenty-five of the most widespread deceptions about race, and shows us how to refute lies, myths, and misinformation with history, knowledge, and truth.

"Readers seeking books in Black Studies, civil rights, and issues of discrimination will find this one thought-provoking and crucial to understanding and dismantling the anti-Black consciousness that endures in American society." —*Booklist*

Includes bibliographical references and index.

Brown, Brene
Braving the Wilderness: The Quest for True Belonging and the Courage to Stand Alone. Brene Brown. Random House 2017. 208 p.
ISBN 9780812995848
Grades: Adult 305.8

ESSENTIAL AND RECOMMENDED TITLES
305.8 Ethnic and national groups

1. Belonging 2. Identity 3. Communities 4. Group identity 5. Individuality 6. Personal conduct 7. Interpersonal relations 8. Loneliness 9. Anxiety 10. Insecurity 11. Society and culture — Psychology and human behavior
LC 2017030221

The influential TED speaker and best-selling author of the Gifts of Imperfection draws on new research to challenge conventional beliefs about fitting in to counsel readers on the skills required to achieve actual belonging while being true to oneself.

"Grounded by moving interviews, case studies, her experience spearheading four educational companies, and a winning combination of perceptiveness and humor, Brown's enthusiastic narrative urges readers to discover their own 'Wilderness' by culling the strength and determination (and risk) necessary to truly live 'From our wild heart rather than our weary hurt.' Nothing truly groundbreaking, but an enthusiastic, practical guide to achieving a healthy sense of interconnectedness within one's culture and community." —*Kirkus*

DiAngelo, Robin J.
White Fragility: Why It's so Hard for White People to Talk About Racism. Robin DiAngelo; foreword by Michael Eric Dyson. Beacon Press 2018. 192 p.
ISBN 9780807047415
Grades: Adult   305.8

1. Racism 2. European Americans 3. Race relations 4. Interpersonal relations 5. Discussion 6. Multiculturalism 7. White privilege 8. Society and culture — Race 9. Antiracist literature
LC 2018003562

Groundbreaking book exploring the counterproductive reactions white people have when discussing racism that serve to protect their positions and maintain racial inequality.

"While especially helpful for those new to the critical analysis of whiteness, this work also offers a useful refresher to anyone committed to the ongoing process of self-assessment and antioppression work." —*Library Journal*

Includes bibliographical references.

Eddo-Lodge, Reni
Why I'm No Longer Talking to White People About Race. Reni Eddo-Lodge. Bloomsbury Circus 2017. xvii, 249 pages
ISBN 9781408870556
Grades: Adult   305.8

1. Racism 2. Social classes 3. Race relations 4. Multiculturalism 5. Classism 6. White privilege 7. Great Britain 8. Society and culture — Race 9. Antiracist literature
LC 2017431364

British Book Award for Narrative Nonfiction of the Year, 2018.

Exploring issues from eradicated Black history to the inextricable link between class and race, Reni Eddo-Lodge has written a searing, illuminating, absolutely necessary examination of what it is to be a person of colour in Britain today.

"With this thoughtful and direct book, Eddo-Lodge stokes the very conversation that the title rejects." —*Publishers Weekly*

Includes bibliographical references (pages 241-242) and index.

Gilliam, Fatimah
Race Rules: What Your Black Friend Won't Tell You. Fatimah Gilliam. Berrett-Koehler Publishers, Inc. 2024. 264 p.
ISBN 9781523004485
Grades: Adult   305.8

1. Race awareness 2. Race relations 3. Racism 4. Cultural appropriation 5. Behavior modification 6. Interpersonal relations 7. Interpersonal communication 8. Interpersonal conflict 9. Behavior and culture 10. White privilege 11. Stereotypes 12. Marginalized people 13. Rules 14. Etiquette 15. United States 16. Society and culture — Race 17. Society and culture — Psychology and human behavior
LC 2023028222

What if there were a set of rules to educate people against race-based social faux pas that damage relationships, perpetuate racist stereotypes, and harm people of color? This book provides just that in an effort to slow the malignant domino effect of race-based ignorance in American communities and workplaces to help address the vestiges of our nation's racist past.-.

"Those looking to move beyond performative allyship will find this an excellent resource." —*Publishers Weekly*

Includes bibliographical references and index.

Haitiwaji, Gulbahar
How I Survived a Chinese. Gulbahar Haitiwaji, Rozenn Morgat; translated by Edward Gauvin. Seven Stories Press 2022. 256 p.
ISBN 9781644211489
Grades: Adult   305.8

1. Haitiwaji, Gulbahar 2. Women internment camp inmates 3. Internment camp inmates 4. Violence 5. Survival 6. Concentration camps 7. Uighur (Turkic people) 8. Political refugees 9. XInjiang, China 10. China 11. France 12. Translations — French to English 13. Autobiographies and memoirs 14. Life stories — Facing adversity — War and oppression 15. History writing — Asia — China
LC 2021050222

The first Uyghur woman to escape from a Chinese re-education camp recalls how she endured hundreds of hours of interrogations, torture, hunger, police violence, brainwashing and forced sterilization and how she escaped with the help of her daughter.

"A viscerally affecting memoir from a Uyghur woman who 'Endured hundreds of hours of interrogation, torture, malnutrition, police violence, and brainwashing.' . . . A taut, moving, powerful account of an ongoing human rights disaster." —*Kirkus*

English translation; Translated from the French.

Hamad, Ruby
White Tears/Brown Scars: How White Feminism Betrays Women of Color. Ruby Hamad. Catapult 2020. xvii, 284 p.
ISBN 9781948226745
Grades: Adult   305.8

1. Antiracism 2. Sexism 3. Entitlement attitudes 4. Marginalized women 5. Sex discrimination 6. Race relations 7. White privilege 8. Society and culture — Gender — Women 9. Society and culture — Race 10. Antiracist literature 11. Debut title
LC 2020931161

Tells a charged story of white women's active participation in campaigns of oppression. It offers a long overdue validation of the experiences of women of color.

"This insistent and incisive call for change belongs in the contemporary feminist canon." —*Publishers Weekly*

Includes bibliographical references; Originally published: Carlton, Victoria : Melbourne University Publishing, 2019.

Headlee, Celeste Anne
Speaking of Race: Why We Need to Talk About Race—and How to Do It Effectively. Celeste Headlee. Harper Wave 2021. 272 p.
ISBN 9780063098152
Grades: Adult   305.8

1. Race (Social sciences) 2. Racism 3. Race relations 4. Interracial communication 5. Multiculturalism 6. Unconscious bias 7. Toleration 8. Interpersonal communication 9. Society and culture — Race 10. Antiracist Literature
LC 2021013730

Drawing on her experience as an award-winning journalist, and the latest research on bias, communication and neuroscience, the PBS host provides practical advice and insight for talking about race that will foster productive conversations that could bring us closer together.

"Headlee's personal-yet-proficient approach to potentially heated parlays is sure to inspire constructive, and perhaps life-changing, conversations." —*Publishers Weekly*

Includes bibliographical references.

Isen, Tajja
Some of My Best Friends: Essays on Lip Service. Tajja Isen. One Signal 2022. 256 p.

PUBLIC LIBRARY CORE COLLECTION: NONFICTION
Twentieth Edition

ISBN 9781982178420

Grades: Adult   305.8

1. Isen, Tajja 2. Multiracial women 3. Ethnic identity 4. Gender identity 5. Institutional racism 6. Prejudice 7. Inequality 8. Entertainment industry and trade 9. Animated film industry and trade 10. Publishers and publishing 11. Social criticism 12. Voice-overs 13. Actors and actresses 14. United States 15. Canada 16. Essays 17. Canadian literature 18. Society and culture — Gender 19. Society and culture — Race 20. Life stories — Identity 21. Arts and entertainment — General

Interlacing cultural criticism with her lived experiences, the editor-in-chief of Catapult and an award-winning voice actor, through nine daring essays, explores the gaps between what we say and what we do, what we do and what we value, what we value and what we demand.

"Catapult editor-in-chief Isen scrutinizes society's attempts to bandage over such issues as race and gender inequality in her powerful debut....Isen's voice is both wry and sensitive as she fearlessly lays out the limits of talk in solving inequality." —*Publishers Weekly*

Jackson, Regina

White Women: Everything You Already Know About Your Own Racism and How to Do Better. Regina Jackson, Saira Rao. Penguin Group USA 2022. 173 pages

ISBN 9780143136439

Grades: Adult   305.8

1. Women 2. Race relations 3. Antiracism 4. Social justice 5. Racism 6. Feminism 7. Discrimination 8. Misogyny 9. Antiracist literature 10. Society and culture — Race 11. Society and culture — Gender — Women

A no-holds-barred guidebook aimed at white women who want to stop being nice and start dismantling white supremacy.

"A must-read for all who have grown tired and weary of those who want to preserve the niceness of social interactions because of the way a situation looks instead of placing importance on what the reality is." —*Library Journal*

Jones, Robert P.

The Hidden Roots of White Supremacy: And the Path to a Shared American Future. Robert P. Jones. Simon & Schuster 2023. 416 p.

ISBN 9781668009512

Grades: Adult   305.8

1. Christianity 2. Church history 3. Racism 4. Colonialism 5. Genocide 6. Slavery 7. Violence against African Americans 8. Violence against Indigenous people 9. United States history 10. Minnesota 11. Oklahoma 12. Mississippi 13. History writing — United States 14. Spirituality and Religion — Christianity — History 15. Society and culture — Race

Beginning with contemporary efforts to reckon with the legacy of white supremacy in America, Robert P. Jones returns to the fateful year when a little-known church doctrine emerged that shaped the way five centuries of European Christians would understand the "discovered" world and the people who populated it. This reframing of American origins explains how the founders of the United States could build the philosophical framework for a democratic society on a foundation of mass racial violence—and why this paradox survives today in the form of white Christian nationalism.

"Jones...argues persuasively that the ideological origins of American racism are best understood in relation to religious edicts dating back to the late 15th century...A searing, stirring outline of the historical and contemporary significance of white Christian nationalism." —*Kirkus*

Kendi, Ibram X.

★ *How to Be an Antiracist*. Ibram X. Kendi. One World 2019. VIII, 305 pages

ISBN 9780525509288

Grades: Adult   305.8

1. Kendi, Ibram X. 2. Identity 3. Ethnic identity 4. Antiracism 5. Discrimination 6. Racism 7. Race relations 8. United States 9. Autobiographies and memoirs 10. Society and culture — Race 11. Antiracist literature

Library Journal Best Books, 2019; New York Times Notable Book, 2019.

From the National Book Award-winning author comes a bracingly original approach to understanding and uprooting racism and inequality in our society—and in ourselves. Ibram X. Kendi's concept of antiracism reenergizes and reshapes the conversation about racial justice in America—but even more fundamentally, points us toward liberating new ways of thinking about ourselves and each other.

"His prose is thoughtful, sincere, and polished. This powerful book will spark many conversations." —*Publishers Weekly*

Includes bibliographical references and index.

★ *Stamped from the Beginning: The Definitive History of Racist Ideas in America.* Ibram X. Kendi. Nation Books 2016. 464 p.

ISBN 9781568584638

Grades: Adult   305.8

1. Discrimination 2. Antiracism 3. Racism 4. Race relations 5. United States 6. Page to screen 7. Society and culture — Race 8. History writing — United States 9. Antiracist literature

LC 2015033671

National Book Award for Nonfiction, 2016; National Book Critics Circle Award for Nonfiction finalist, 2016.

A comprehensive history of anti-Black racism focuses on the lives of five major players in American history, including Cotton Mather and Thomas Jefferson, and highlights the debates that took place between assimilationists and segregationists and between racists and antiracists.

"Kendi's provocative egalitarian argument combines prodigious reading and research with keen insights into the manipulative power of racist ideologies that suppress the recognition of diversity." —*Library Journal*

Includes bibliographical references and index.

King, Martin Luther

Why We Can't Wait. Martin Luther King, Jr; introduction by Dorothy Cotton. Harper & Row 1964. xii, 178 p. : Illustration; Portrait

ISBN 9780451527530

Grades: 11 12 Adult   305.8

1. African American civil rights 2. Civil Rights Movement 3. Social justice 4. Nonviolence 5. 1960s 6. History writing — African American — Civil rights — United States 7. Society and culture — Race

LC 64019514

An impassioned work by Dr. Martin Luther King, Jr, shares a heartfelt argument for equality and an end to racial discrimination that explains why the civil rights struggle is vital to the United States.

Kuper, Adam

The Museum of Other People: From Colonial Acquisitions to Cosmopolitan Exhibitions. Adam Kuper. Pantheon Books 2024. 432 p.

ISBN 9780593700679

Grades: Adult   305.8

1. Science museums 2. Museum exhibits 3. Anthropology 4. Ethnic policy 5. Imperialism 6. Racism 7. Colonialism 8. Society and culture — Anthropology 9. Society and culture — Ethnic studies 10. Arts and Entertainment — Museums and Collections

In this meticulously researched, immersive history, one of the world's most distinguished anthropologists tells the story of how foreign and prehistoric peoples and cultures were represented in Western museums of anthropology, excavating a legacy of imperialism, colonialism and scientific racism in their creation.

"This highly recommended work about anthropological museums and creating culturally appropriate exhibits challenges preconceptions and encourages readers to think critically about this complex and important issue." —*Library Journal*

Originally published in the UK by Profile Books, London, in 2023.

Livingston, Robert W.

The Conversation: How Seeking and Speaking the Truth About Racism Can Radically Transform Individuals and Organizations. Robert Livingston. Currency 2021. 272 p.

ISBN 9780593238561

Grades: Adult   305.8

ESSENTIAL AND RECOMMENDED TITLES
305.8 Ethnic and national groups

1. Racism 2. Work environment 3. Unconscious bias 4. Racism in employment 5. Inequality 6. Discrimination 7. Social psychology 8. White privilege 9. Society and culture — Race 10. Business and economics — Business advice 11. Business and economics — Popular psychology 12. Antiracist Literature

LC 2020043497

A social psychologist discusses how businesses and other organizations can develop strategies to address racism in their ranks, identify and eliminate bias to make their workplaces and cultures more equitable and take steps to measure positive outcomes.

"Readers interested in workplace and organizational cultures and social psychology will find Livingston's work inspiring, and helpful in understanding the impact of racism on people, organizations, and communities at large." —*Booklist*

Includes bibliographical references and index.

Lowery, Wesley
★ *American Whitelash: A Changing Nation and the Cost of Progress.* Wesley Lowery. Mariner Books 2023. 288 p.
ISBN 9780358393269
Grades: Adult   305.8
1. Racism 2. African Americans 3. Political culture 4. Presidential elections 5. Violence against marginalized people 6. White supremacy movements 7. Race relations 8. United States history 9. United States 10. 21st century 11. Society and culture — Race 12. History writing — Early 21st century — United States 13. Antiracist literature

Interweaving deep historical analysis with gripping firsthand reporting on both victims and perpetrators of violence, a Pulitzer Prize-winning journalist charts the return of the American cycle of racial progress and white backlash and how the federal government has failed to intervene.

"A masterful blend of narrative history and empathetic reporting." —*Kirkus*

McGhee, Heather C.
★ *The Sum of US: What Racism Costs Everyone and How We Can Prosper Together.* Heather C. McGhee. One World 2021. 448 p.
ISBN 9780525509561
Grades: Adult   305.8
1. White privilege 2. Income inequality 3. Inequality 4. Racism 5. Race relations 6. United States history 7. United States 8. Society and culture — Race 9. Business and economics — Economics — Socioeconomics 10. Business and economics — Economics — Contemporary U.S. economy 11. Book club best bets

LC 2020044567

Robert F. Kennedy Book Award, 2022.

A powerful new exploration about the self-destructive bargain of white supremacy and its rising cost to all of us—including white people—from one of today's most insightful and influential thinkers.

"McGhee, uses her economic and social policy expertise to argue that structural racism and white supremacy harm everyone, not only people of color. . . . Essential reading for everyone working on incorporating more anti-racist thought leaders and perspectives into their collection." —*Library Journal*

Includes index.

McMillan, Tracie
★ *The White Bonus: Five Families and the Cash Value of Racism in America.* Tracie McMillan. Henry Holt & Co. 2024. 352 p.
ISBN 9781250619426
Grades: Adult   305.8
1. White privilege 2. United States history 3. Marginalized people 4. Income inequality 5. Family history 6. Social classes and family 7. Wealth 8. Money 9. Racism 10. Discrimination in education 11. Discrimination in employment 12. Discrimination in housing 13. Race relations 14. American people 15. United States 16. Autobiographies and memoirs 17. Society and culture — Wealth and class 18. Life stories — Relationships — Family

LC 2023042947

An award-winning journalist combines gripping memoir, top-notch original reporting and rigorous research to measure the cash value of being white in America.

"It all results in a fresh, urgent new look at the mechanisms of racism in America." —*Booklist*

Includes bibliographical references and index.

Meckler, Laura
★ *Dream Town: Shaker Heights and the Quest for Racial Equity.* Laura Meckler. Henry Holt and Company 2023. 352 p.
ISBN 9781250834416
Grades: Adult   305.8
1. African Americans 2. Equal education policy 3. Discrimination in housing 4. School integration 5. Race relations 6. Ohio 7. Society and culture — Education 8. History Writing — Regional history — United States 9. Society and culture — Race

LC 2023017026

The history of Shaker Heights, Ohio, which starting in the late 1950s became a national model for housing and school integration and the lessons it can offer to a nation still struggling with racial equity.

"Through detailed research and interviews, Meckler tells a remarkable story about a town that continuously strives to achieve the ideals it long ago set for itself." —*Booklist*

Includes bibliographical references and index.

Mukantabana, Yseult P.
★ *Real Friends Talk About Race: Bridging the Gaps Through Uncomfortable Conversations.* Yseult P. Mukantabana and Hannah Summerhill. Park Row Books 2023. 267 pages
ISBN 9780778387053
Grades: Adult   305.8
1. Race relations 2. Race (Social sciences) 3. Racism 4. Intercultural communication 5. Communication 6. Interracial friendship 7. Friendship 8. Unconscious bias 9. White privilege 10. Society and culture — Race 11. Self-Help — Relationships 12. Antiracist literature

LC Bl2023013322

Having conversations about race is uncomfortable. But for progress between individuals (and our communities) to happen, we need to be able to speak openly and honestly. Podcast hosts of the Kinswomen Yseult and Hannah use their own friendship and experiences from different racial backgrounds to offer guidance on navigating these layered conversations. In Real Friends Talk About Race, the duo share their two perspectives on the ways in which culture, history, and white supremacy have prevented us from having the skills to build trust and healthy relationships across race.

"Accessible and featuring helpful Q&As throughout, the book breaks down everything from communication, allyship, white supremacy, microaggressions, and newer concepts such as blackfishing. Essential for public libraries and book clubs." —*Booklist*

Includes bibliographical references.

Murray, Charles A.
Coming Apart: The State of White America, 1960-2010. Charles Murray. Crown 2012. 416 p.
ISBN 9780307453426
Grades: Adult   305.8
1. European Americans 2. Social mobility 3. Social classes 4. United States 5. Conservative writing 6. Society and culture — Wealth and class

LC 2011501987

Booklist Editors' Choice, 2012; New York Times Notable Book, 2012.

A critique of the white American class structure argues that the paths of social mobility that once advanced the nation are now serving to further isolate an elite upper class while enforcing a growing and resentful white underclass.

"Though it provides much to argue with, the book is a timely investigation into a worsening class divide no one can afford to ignore." —*Publishers Weekly*

Oluo, Ijeoma
★ *Be a Revolution: How Everyday People Are Fighting Oppression and Changing the World, and How You Can, Too.* Ijeoma Oluo. HarperOne, an imprint of HarperCollins 2024. 256 p.

PUBLIC LIBRARY CORE COLLECTION: NONFICTION
Twentieth Edition

ISBN 9780063140189
Grades: Adult   **305.8**
1. Racism 2. Oppression (Psychology) 3. Prejudice 4. Institutional racism 5. Social justice 6. Antiracism 7. Social advocacy 8. Race relations 9. United States 10. Society and culture — Race 11. Antiracist literature

From the #1 New York Times best-selling author of so You Want to Talk About Race and Mediocre comes an eye-opening and galvanizing look at the current state of anti-racist activism across America.

"Oluo affirms that 'Everyone has different roles in this revolution' in these enlightening profiles of people who've put their anti-racist values into action…Readers will find inspiration and clarity." —*Publishers Weekly*

Ortiz, Paul
An African American and Latinx History of the United States. Paul Ortiz. Beacon Press 2018. xi, 276 pages
ISBN 9780807013106
Grades: Adult   **305.8**
1. Hispanic Americans 2. African American history 3. Anti-imperialist movements 4. Working class 5. Intersectionality 6. International relations 7. Race relations 8. Interethnic relations 9. United States 10. Latin America 11. History writing — African American — United States 12. History writing — Latin America 13. Society and culture — Race 14. Antiracist literature
LC 2017020565

An intersectional history of the shared struggle for African American and Latinx civil rights.

A sleek, vital history that effectively shows how, 'From the outset, inequality was enforced with the whip, the gun, and the United States Constitution.' —*Kirkus*

Includes bibliographical references and index.

Phillips, Patrick
Blood at the Root: A Racial Cleansing in America. Patrick Phillips. W.W. Norton & Company 2016. 320 p.
ISBN 9780393293012
Grades: Adult   **305.8**
1. Hate crimes 2. Racism 3. Domestic terrorism 4. Violence against marginalized people 5. Violence against African-Americans 6. Prejudice 7. Lynching 8. Murder 9. White supremacists 10. Race relations 11. Georgia 12. 1910s 13. Society and culture — Race 14. True Crime — General 15. History writing — African American — Civil rights — United States
LC 2016018237

ALA Notable Book, 2017; Library Journal Best Books, 2016; LibraryReads Favorites, 2016; New York Times Notable Book, 2016; Andrew Carnegie Medal for Excellence in Non-Fiction Finalist, 2017.

A harrowing testament to the deep roots of racial violence in America chronicles acts of racial cleansing in early 20th-century Forsyth County, Georgia, where the murder of a young girl led to mob lynchings, acts of terror against Black workers and violent protests by night riders who would enforce whites-only citizenship.

"This is a gripping, timely, and important examination of American racism, and Phillips tells it with rare clarity and power." —*Publishers Weekly*

Includes bibliographical references and index.

Ray, Victor
On Critical Race Theory: Why It Matters & Why You Should Care. Victor Ray. Random House Inc 2022. 176 p.
ISBN 9780593446447
Grades: Adult   **305.8**
1. Race relations 2. Critical race theory 3. Race (Social sciences) 4. Inequality 5. Social justice 6. Essays 7. Society and culture — Race

Drawing on the radical thinking of Dr. Martin Luther King, Hr, Ida B. Wells and W.E.B. Du Bois, among others, a renowned scholar, through thoughtful essays, traces the foundations of Critical Race Theory, showing why it matters and why we all should car.

"Distinguished by its clarity of thought, purpose, and expression, this is a stirring defense of critical race theory as an 'Intellectual bulwark' against attempts to undermine multiracial democracy." —*Publishers Weekly*

Rehman, Sabeeha
Threading My Prayer Rug: One Woman's Journey from Pakistani Muslim to American Muslim. Sabeeha Rehman. Arcade Publishing 2016. 304 p.
ISBN 9781628726633
Grades: Adult   **305.8**
1. Rehman, Sabeeha 2. Pakistani Americans 3. Muslim women 4. Muslims 5. Interfaith relations 6. Culture conflict 7. Immigrants 8. South Asian Americans 9. South Asian people 10. Autobiographies and Memoirs 11. Life stories — Identity — Immigrants
LC 2016007676

This enthralling story of the making of an American is also a timely meditation on religion and culture. Threading My Prayer Rug is a richly textured reflection on what it is to be a Muslim in America today.

Roberts-Miller, Patricia
Speaking of Race: How to Have Antiracist Conversations That Bring Us Together. Patricia Roberts-Miller. The Experiment 2021. 131 pages
ISBN 9781615197323
Grades: Adult   **305.8**
1. Racism 2. Race (Social sciences) 3. Interpersonal communication 4. Antiracist literature 5. Society and culture — Race
LC 2020046571

From a scholar of communication, a guide to healing our fractured discourse on race and racism by infusing the topic with more constructive and enriching dialogue.

Packed with helpful examples and analogies, this lucid account takes a meaningful step toward 'Reducing racism in our world.' —*Publishers Weekly*

Rose, Tricia
★ *Metaracism: How Systemic Racism Devastates Black Lives and How We Break Free*. Tricia Rose. Basic Books 2024. 272 p.
ISBN 9781541602717
Grades: Adult   **305.8**
1. Racism 2. Institutional racism 3. Race relations 4. African Americans 5. Marginalized people 6. United States 7. Society and culture — Race

A pioneering scholar offers this new account of what systemic racism actually is, how it works and how we can fight back, revealing how hard-to-see systemic connections function to disproportionately contain, exploit and punish Black people and showing us how to create a more just America for us all.

"Marshalling extensive evidence into a lucid and powerful narrative, Rose provides an essential new look at American inequality. Even readers well versed in the topic will have their eyes opened by this cogent analysis." —*Publishers Weekly*

Ross, Dax-Devlon
Letters to My White Male Friends. Dax-Devlon Ross. St. Martin's Press 2021. 240 p.
ISBN 9781250276834
Grades: Adult   **305.8**
1. Ross, Dax-Devlon 2. Race awareness 3. African American men 4. European American men 5. White privilege 6. Antiracism 7. Racism 8. Race relations 9. United States 10. Essays 11. Society and culture — Race 12. Antiracist literature
LC 2020057563

Ross helps readers understand what it meant to be America's first generation raised after the civil rights era. He explains how we were all educated with colorblind narratives and symbols that typically, albeit implicitly, privileged whiteness and denigrated Blackness. He provides the context and color of his own experiences in white schools so that white men can revisit moments in their lives where racism was in the room even when they didn't see it enter. Ross shows how learning to see the harm that racism did to him, and forgiving himself, gave him the empathy to see the harm it does to white people as well. Ultimately, Ross offers white men direction so that they can take just action in their workplace, community, family, and, most importantly, in themselves, especially in the future when race is no longer in the spotlight.

ESSENTIAL AND RECOMMENDED TITLES
305.800973 Ethnic and national groups — United States

"Journalist and educator Ross (Make Me Believe) discusses in this astute and accessible account the challenges and double standards he faces as a Black man in America and what white people can do to help bring about change." —*Publishers Weekly*

Includes bibliographical references.

Wilkie, Curtis
When Evil Lived in Laurel: The. Curtis Wilkie. W. W. Norton & Company 2021. 400 p.
ISBN 9781324005759
Grades: Adult   305.8
1. Dahmer, Vernon Ferdinand, 1908-1966 2. Landrum, Tom, 1932- 3. Bowers, Samuel Holloway, 1924-2006 4. Crimes against African Americans 5. African American civil rights workers 6. Race relations 7. Mississippi 8. 1960s 9. History writing — Regional history — United States 10. History writing — African American — Civil rights — United States 11. True crime — Murder
LC 2021001786

The inside story of how a courageous FBI informant helped to bring down the KKK chapter responsible for a brutal civil rights-era killing. By early 1966, the civil rights work of Vernon Dahmer, head of the Forrest County chapter of the NAACP and a dedicated advocate for voter registration, was well-known in Mississippi. This put him in the crosshairs of the White Knights, one of the most violent sects of the KKK in the South-which carried out his murder in a raid that burned down his home and store.

"This real-life thriller is a worthy tribute to the courage of those who put everything on the line for civil rights." —*Publishers Weekly*

Includes bibliographical references and index.

Williams, Sophie
Anti-racist Ally: An Introduction to Activism and Action. Sophie Williams. Amistad 2021. 176 p.
ISBN 9780063081352
Grades: Adult   305.8
1. Antiracism 2. Racism 3. Discrimination 4. Unconscious bias 5. Social advocacy 6. Race relations 7. United States 8. Society and culture — Race 9. Antiracist literature

The creator of the popular @officialmillennialblack Instagram shares practical insights into active practices of anti-racism, covering subjects ranging from the terminology of today's world to the personal biases that shape inequality.

"Touching on issues from redlining to recognizing white privilege, Anti-Racist Ally provides a thoughtful entryway into the ongoing work of anti-racism." —*Booklist*

Wise, Tim J.
Dispatches from the Race War. Tim Wise. City Lights Publishers 2020. 352 p.
ISBN 9780872868090
Grades: Adult   305.8
1. Trump, Donald, 1946- 2. Racism 3. White supremacy movements 4. African Americans 5. Marginalized people 6. Violence against marginalized people 7. Social justice 8. Civil rights 9. Institutional racism 10. Injustice 11. White privilege 12. Race relations 13. United States history 14. 21st century 15. Essays 16. Society and culture — Race 17. History writing — Early 21st century — United States 18. Antiracist Literature
LC 2020036401

In this collection of essays, renowned social-justice advocate Tim Wise confronts racism in contemporary America. Seen through the lens of major flashpoints during the Obama and Trump years, Dispatches from the Race War faces the consequences of white supremacy in all its forms. This includes a discussion of the bigoted undertones of the Tea Party's backlash, the killing of Trayvon Martin, current day anti-immigrant hysteria, the rise of openly avowed white nationalism, the violent policing of African Americans, and more. Wise devotes a substantial portion of the book to explore the racial ramifications of COVID-19, and the widespread protests which followed the police murder of George Floyd.

"Still, he offers sound advice on how to promote antiracism and 'Solidarity and empathy across lines of identity.' the result is a bracing call to action in a moment of social unrest." —*Publishers Weekly*

Young, R. J.
Requiem for the Massacre: A Black History on the Conflict, Hope, and Fallout of the 1921 Tulsa Race Massacre. RJ Young. Counterpoint 2022. 318 p.
ISBN 9781640095021
Grades: Adult   305.8
1. Young, R. J. (Writer) 2. African American authors 3. African American history 4. Tulsa Race Massacre, Tulsa, Oklahoma, 1921 5. Violence against African Americans 6. Race riots 7. Massacres 8. Racism 9. History 10. Memory 11. Identity 12. Tulsa, Oklahoma 13. History writing — African American — United States 14. History writing — Natural disasters and tragedies 15. Society and culture — Race 16. Life stories — Identity — Race and ethnicity
LC 2022016663

In this cultural excavation of Tulsa 100 years after the most infamous act of racial violence in American history, the author reveals how things have changed and how they've stayed woefully stay the same, threading together his own reflections on a community and a nation trying to heal and trying to hope.

"Tulsa-raised Young digs deep into events surrounding the city's horrific 1921 massacre of Black residents while also considering how Tulsa deals with the legacy of the massacre and ongoing racial injustice today. Fox sportscaster Young has a big social media presence." —*Library Journal*

Includes bibliographical references.

305.800973 Ethnic and national groups — United States

Anderson, Carol
★ *White* Rage: The Unspoken Truth of Our Racial Divide. Carol Anderson. Bloomsbury 2016. 272 p.
ISBN 9781632864123
Grades: Adult   305.800973
1. Racism 2. Race (Social sciences) 3. African American civil rights 4. Civil rights 5. Opposition (Political science) 6. Black Lives Matter movement 7. White privilege 8. Race relations 9. United States 10. Society and culture — Race 11. History writing — African American — United States 12. Antiracist literature
LC 2015049398

New York Times Notable Book, 2016.

From the end of the Civil War to the tumultuous issues in America today, an acclaimed historian reframes the conversation about race, chronicling the powerful forces opposed to Black progress in America.

"Fitting together historical flash points from the aftermath of the Civil War to the current Black Lives Matter movement, historian Anderson (African American studies, Emory Univ; Bourgeois Radicals) displays how public policies have systematically discarded all attempts at a colorblind U.S. democracy." —*Library Journal*

Bailey, Issac J.
Why Didn't We Riot?: A Black Man in Trumpland. Issac J. Bailey. Other Press 2020. xi, 173 p.
ISBN 9781635420289
Grades: Adult   305.800973
1. African Americans 2. Discrimination in law enforcement 3. Police brutality 4. Crimes against African Americans 5. African Americans in mass media 6. Racism 7. Political participation 8. Race relations 9. United States history 10. United States 11. 21st century 12. Essays 13. Society and culture — Race 14. Society and culture — Violence and crime — Criminal justice system 15. Life stories — Identity — Race and ethnicity
LC 2020008891

South Carolina-based journalist Issac J. Bailey reflects on a wide range of complex, divisive topics—from police brutality and Confederate symbols to respectability politics and white discomfort—which have taken on a fresh urgency with the protest movement sparked by George Floyd's killing. Why Didn't We Riot? speaks to and for the millions of black and brown people throughout the United States who were effectively pushed to the back of the bus in the Trump era by a media that prioritized the concerns and feelings of the white working class and an administration that made white supremacists giddy, and explains why the country's fate in 2020 and beyond is largely in their hands.

"By no fault of Bailey's, die-hard Trumplandians aren't likely to be swayed; conscientious Americans will come away from this book further enraged by the pernicious, persistent pattern of racial injustice in this country. Brilliant, searing, and surprisingly vulnerable." —Kirkus

Baker, Calvin
A More Perfect Reunion: Race, Integration, and the Future of America. Calvin Baker. Bold Type Books 2020. 304 p.
ISBN 9781568589237
Grades: Adult   305.800973

1. Social integration 2. Democracy 3. Equality 4. Prejudice 5. Discrimination 6. Racism 7. African American history 8. Civil rights 9. Race relations 10. United States history 11. United States 12. Society and culture — Race 13. Politics and global affairs — Civil and human rights 14. History writing — African American — Civil rights — United States

LC 2019058186

A provocative case for integration as the single most radical, discomfiting idea in America, yet the only enduring solution to the racism that threatens our democracy. Americans have prided ourselves on how far we've come from slavery, lynching, and legal segregation—measuring ourselves by incremental progress instead of by how far we have to go. But fifty years after the last meaningful effort toward civil rights, the US remains overwhelmingly segregated and unjust. Our current solutions—diversity, representation, and desegregation—are not enough. At once a profound, masterful reading of US history from the colonial era forward and a trenchant critique of the obstacles in our current political and cultural moment, a More Perfect Reunion is also a call to action.

"Required reading for any American serious about dismantling systemic racism." —Kirkus

Includes bibliographical references and index.

Coates, Ta-Nehisi
★ *Between the World and Me*. Ta-Nehisi Coates. Spiegel & Grau 2015. 152 pages : Illustration
ISBN 9780812993547
Grades: 11 12 Adult   305.800973

1. African American men 2. African Americans 3. Racism 4. Race relations 5. Race (Social sciences) 6. Intersectionality 7. Black Lives Matter movement 8. Identity 9. Autobiographies and memoirs 10. Life stories — Identity — Race and ethnicity 11. Society and culture — Race 12. Adult books for young adults 13. Antiracist literature

ALA Notable Book, 2016; Alex Award, 2016; Booklist Editors' Choice, 2015; Booklist Editors' Choice: Adult Books for Young Adults, 2015; Indies' Choice Book Awards, Adult Nonfiction, 2016; Kirkus Prize for Nonfiction, 2015; Library Journal Best Books, 2015; National Book Award for Nonfiction, 2015; New York Times Notable Book, 2015; School Library Journal Best Books: Best Adult Books 4 Teens, 2015; Street Lit Book Award Medal: Adult Non-Fiction, 2016; Pulitzer Prize for General Nonfiction finalist, 2016.

Told through the author's own evolving understanding of the subject over the course of his life comes a bold and personal investigation into America's racial history and its contemporary echoes.

"In this brief book, which takes the form of a letter to the author's teenage son, Coates…comes to grips with what it means to be Black in America today….There is awesome beauty in the power of his prose and vital truth on every page." —Booklist

Currie, Elliott
A Peculiar Indifference: The Neglected Toll of Violence on Black America. Elliott Currie. Metropolitan Books 2020. 304 p.
ISBN 9781250769930
Grades: Adult   305.800973

1. Violence against African Americans 2. Crimes against African Americans 3. African Americans 4. Social justice 5. Social policy 6. Social marginality 7. White privilege 8. Racism 9. Race relations 10. United States history 11. United States 12. 21st century 13. History writing — African American — United States 14. Society and culture — Violence and crime 15. Antiracist literature

LC 2020013956

New York Times Notable Book, 2020.

Offers a devastating exploration of the racial disparities in violent death and injury in America and a blueprint for ending this fundamental social injustice.

"Meticulously researched and densely packed with stats and studies, Currie's book paints a heartbreaking picture, but it also makes an urgent case for bold measures to turn the tide in Black communities. A damning examination of violence in Black America and a call for intervention that is long overdue." —Kirkus

Includes bibliographical references and index.

Darby, Seyward
★ *Sisters in Hate: American Women on the Front Lines of White Nationalism*. Seyward Darby. Little, Brown & Company 2020. VII, 309 p.
ISBN 9780316487771
Grades: Adult   305.800973

1. White supremacy movements 2. Racism 3. European American women 4. Antifeminism 5. Right-wing extremists 6. Women executives 7. Influencers 8. Hate 9. Hate groups 10. Group identity 11. Social movements 12. Women 13. Race relations 14. United States 15. Life stories — Identity — Gender 16. Society and culture — Race 17. Society and culture — Gender — Women 18. Life stories — Politics

LC Bl2020016280

After the election of Donald J. Trump, journalist Seyward Darby went looking for the women of the so-called "alt-right"—really just white nationalism with a new label. The mainstream media depicted the alt-right as a bastion of angry white men, but was it? as women headlined resistance to the Trump administration's bigotry and sexism, Darby wanted to know why others were joining a movement espousing racism and anti-feminism. Darby researched dozens of women across the country before settling on three—Corinna Olsen, Ayla Stewart, and Lana Lokteff. Each was born in 1979, and became a white nationalist in the post-9/11 era. Their respective stories of radicalization upend much of what we assume about women, politics, and political extremism.

"Atavist editor-in-chief Darby describes women as a 'Sustaining feature' of white nationalism in her revelatory and harrowing debut focused on three women with ties to the 'Alt-right' movement. . . . The result is a disturbing and informative must-read." —Publishers Weekly

Includes bibliographical references and index.

Dyson, Michael Eric
The Black Presidency: Barack Obama and the Politics of Race in America. Michael Eric Dyson. Houghton Mifflin Harcourt 2016. 288 p.
ISBN 9780544387669
Grades: Adult   305.800973

1. Obama, Barack 2. Racism 3. Race (Social sciences) 4. African Americans 5. Political culture 6. Presidents 7. Race awareness 8. Identity 9. Race relations 10. United States 11. Politics and global affairs — Political figures 12. Society and culture — Race

LC 2015037026

Kirkus Prize for Nonfiction finalist, 2016.

Offers a deep-dive into the meaning of America's first Black presidency, and an analysis of how race and Blackness shape our understanding of Barack Obama's achievements, failures—and America's racial future.

Long Time Coming: Reckoning with Race in America. Michael Eric Dyson. St. Martin's Press 2020. 230 p.
ISBN 9781250276759
Grades: Adult   305.800973

1. African Americans 2. Black Lives Matter movement 3. Racial profiling 4. Racism in law enforcement 5. Protest movements 6. Social justice 7. Racism 8. Race relations 9. United States 10. Society and culture — Race 11. Society and

ESSENTIAL AND RECOMMENDED TITLES
305.800973 Ethnic and national groups — United States

culture — Violence and crime — Criminal justice system 12. Life stories — Facing adversity — War and oppression 13. Antiracist literature

LC 2020042056

Issues a passionate call to America to finally reckon with race and start the journey to redemption.

"In a series of profound and powerful letters written to Black martyrs to racial violence—Elijah McClain, Emmett Till, Breonna Taylor, Hadiya Pendleton, Sandra Bland, and Reverend Clementa Pinckney—and addressing many more along the way . . . distinguished professor, preacher, public intellectual, and best-selling author Dyson (Jay-Z, 2019; What Truth Sounds Like, 2018) offers both homage and history, emotion and analysis." —*Booklist*

Includes bibliographical references.

Tears We Cannot Stop: A Sermon to White America. Michael Eric Dyson. St. Martin's Press 2017. 160 p.
ISBN 9781250135995
Grades: Adult   305.800973
1. Racism 2. Police brutality 3. African Americans 4. Race (Social sciences) 5. Race relations 6. United States 7. Society and culture — Race 8. Antiracist literature

LC 2016049919

A call for change in the United States argues that racial progress can only be achieved after facing difficult truths, including being honest about how Black grievance has been ignored, dismissed, and discounted.

"With a reading list to encourage further learning, Dyson offers an intellectual framework for everyone to adopt in order to understand and embrace each others struggles to be united." —*Booklist*

What Truth Sounds Like: Robert F. Kennedy, James Baldwin, and Our Unfinished Conversation About Race in America. Michael Eric Dyson. St Martins Pr 2018. 288 p.
ISBN 9781250199416
Grades: Adult   305.800973
1. Baldwin, James, 1924-1987 2. Kennedy, Robert Francis, 1925-1968 3. Racism 4. African Americans 5. Social change 6. Race (Social sciences) 7. Race relations 8. United States 9. Society and culture — Race

LC 2018017174

Examines the sources of America's torturous racial politics, tracing the 1963 meeting that included James Baldwin, Robert Kennedy, and a host of expert activists, who transformed racial and political understandings and set the stage for national disputes that are still raging today.

"Dyson's much-recommended work puts forth the artists and activists who continue to celebrate Blackness, offering a welcome reminder of the power of art to maintain dialog with and within America." —*Library Journal*

Else, Jon
True South: Henry Hampton And. Jon Else. Viking Press 2017. 352 p.
ISBN 9781101980934
Grades: Adult   305.800973
1. Else, Jon 2. Hampton, Henry, 1940-1998 3. Television programs 4. civil rights movement 5. Social justice 6. Race (Social sciences) 7. Television in politics 8. Historical revisionism 9. Television producers and directors 10. African American history 11. Documentary television programs 12. Historiography 13. Autobiographies and memoirs 14. Essays 15. Society and culture — Race 16. Arts and Entertainment — Movies and Television 17. History writing — African American — Civil rights — United States 18. Life stories — Arts and culture — Performing arts — Directors and producers

LC 2016044049

Booklist Editors' Choice, 2017; Longlisted for the Andrew Carnegie Medal for Excellence in Non-Fiction, 2018.

Presents the inside story of the making of one of the most important and influential TV shows in history and of its legacy as the film that reframed of the entire history of the Civil Rights movement permanently.

"An illuminating look at racial strife and TV history." —*Kirkus*

Fleming, Crystal Marie
How to Be Less Stupid About Race: On Racism, White Supremacy and the Racial Divide. Crystal M. Fleming. Beacon Press 2018. 256 p.
ISBN 9780807050774
Grades: Adult   305.800973
1. Race awareness 2. Racism 3. Ignorance 4. Intersectionality 5. White supremacy movements 6. Race relations 7. United States 8. Society and culture — Race

LC 2018009257

Combining no-holds-barred social critique, humorous personal anecdotes, and analysis of the latest interdisciplinary scholarship on systemic racism, sociologist Crystal M. Fleming provides a fresh, accessible, and irreverent take on everything that's wrong with our "national conversation about race." Drawing upon critical race theory, as well as her own experiences as a queer Black millennial college professor and researcher, Fleming unveils how systemic racism exposes us all to racial ignorance—and provides a road map for transforming our knowledge into concrete social change.

"In this insightful and irreverent text, Fleming, a sociologist and self-described "Black bi girl from Tennessee," attempts to simplify critical race theory for the masses." —*Publishers Weekly*

Includes bibliographical references and index.

Glaude, Eddie S.
Begin Again: James Baldwin's America and Its Urgent Lessons for Our Own. Eddie S. Glaude. Crown Pub 2020. 304 pages
ISBN 9780525575320
Grades: Adult   305.800973
1. Baldwin, James, 1924-1987 2. Racism 3. Civil Rights Movement 4. African Americans 5. Presidential election, 2016 6. Black Lives Matter movement 7. Identity 8. Race relations 9. United States 10. Biographies 11. Society and culture — Race 12. Life stories — Arts and culture — Writing — Authors 13. History writing — African American — United States 14. Antiracist literature

LC 2019059122

BCALA Literary Award for Nonfiction, 2021.

James Baldwin grew disillusioned by the failure of the Civil Rights movement to force America to confront its lies about race; in the era of Trump, what can we learn from his struggle?

"A penetrating study of how the words of James Baldwin (1924-1987) continue to have (often painful) relevance today." —*Kirkus*

Hinton, Elizabeth Kai
★ *America on Fire: The Untold History of Police Violence and Black Rebellion Since the 1960s*. Elizabeth Hinton. Liveright Publishing 2021. 288 p.
ISBN 9781631498909
Grades: Adult   305.800973
1. Police 2. Police and African Americans 3. Racism in law enforcement 4. Police brutality 5. African American civil rights 6. Injustice 7. Riots 8. Civil disobedience 9. Protests, demonstrations, vigils, etc. 10. Race relations 11. United States history 12. United States 13. Society and culture — Race 14. Society and culture — Violence and crime — Criminal justice system 15. History writing — African American — United States

Drawing on new sources, a leading scholar presents a groundbreaking story of policing and "riots" that shatters our understanding of the post-civil rights era, arguing that we cannot understand the civil rights moment without coming to terms with the astonishing violence, and hugely expanded policing regime, that followed it.

"Readers interested in social movements in the United States, past or present, will not want to miss this illuminating work." —*Library Journal*

Johnson, Theodore R.
When the Stars Begin to Fall: Overcoming Racism and Renewing the Promise of America. Theodore R. Johnson. Atlantic Monthly Press 2021. 250 p.
ISBN 9780802157850
Grades: Adult   305.800973
1. Johnson, Theodore R. 2. American dream 3. African Americans 4. Racism 5. Solidarity 6. Equality 7. Multiculturalism 8. Political obligation 9. Race rela-

tions 10. United States 11. History writing — African American — United States 12. Society and culture — Race 13. Life stories — Identity — Race and ethnicity 14. Antiracist literature

When the Stars Begin to Fall makes a compelling, ambitious case for a pathway to the national solidarity necessary to mitigate racism. Weaving memories of his own and his family's multi-generational experiences with racism, alongside strands of history, into his elegant narrative, Johnson posits that a blueprint for national solidarity can be found in the exceptional citizenship long practiced in Black America. Understanding that racism is a structural crime of the state, he argues that overcoming it requires us to recognize that a color-conscious society—not a color-blind one—is the true fulfillment of the American Promise.

"Heartfelt and vividly written, this is a salient call for America to finally live up to its promise." —Publishers Weekly

Lee, Erika

America for Americans: A History of Xenophobia in the United States. Erika Lee. Basic Books 2019. VII, 416 p.

ISBN 9781541672604

Grades: Adult   305.800973

1. Xenophobia 2. History of immigrants 3. Marginalized people 4. Racism 5. National characteristics, American 6. Immigration policy 7. Nationalism 8. Race relations 9. Immigration and emigration 10. United States history 11. United States 12. History writing — Immigration — United States 13. Society and culture — Immigration 14. Society and culture — Race

LC 2019016168

Asian Pacific American Award for Literature: Adult Nonfiction, 2021.

The United States is known as a nation of immigrants. But it is also a nation of xenophobia. In America for Americans, Erika Lee shows that an irrational fear, hatred, and hostility toward immigrants has been a defining feature of our nation from the colonial era to the Trump era. Forcing us to confront this history, America for Americans explains how xenophobia works, why it has endured, and how it threatens America. It is a necessary corrective and spur to action for any concerned citizen.

Includes bibliographical references and index.

Lehr, Dick

★ *The* **Birth** *of a Nation: How a Legendary Director and a Crusading Editor Reignited America's Civil War.* Dick Lehr. PublicAffairs, a member of the Perseus Books Group 2014. 336 p.

ISBN 9781586489878

Grades: Adult   305.800973

1. Griffith, D. W. (David Wark), 1875-1948 2. Trotter, William Monroe, 1872-1934 3. Racism 4. Journalists 5. Censorship 6. Race relations 7. United States history 8. 1910s 9. 20th century 10. History writing — Early 20th century — United States

LC 2014029679

Documents the 1915 rivalry between a journalist agitator and a controversial filmmaker whose respective political views about a Civil War photoplay villainizing free slaves reignited the American debate between free speech and civil rights.

"The book culminates, as expected, with the highly publicized battle in Boston over the censorship of Griffith's film. However, the larger story for the reader is Lehr's fascinating portrait of simmering American racial tensions moving into the early 20th century, and his spotlight on men and women who, intentionally or not, helped galvanize painful and necessary conversations about civil rights, race relations, and the power of mass media for decades to come." —Library Journal

Includes bibliographical references and index.

Mehra, Nishta

Brown, White, Black: An American Family at the Intersection of Race, Gender, Sexuality, and Religion. Nishta Mehra. Picador 2019. 224 p.

ISBN 9781250133557

Grades: Adult   305.800973

1. Mehra, Nishta 2. Identity 3. Intersectionality 4. Interracial families 5. Interfaith families 6. Lesbian mothers 7. Indian Americans 8. Adoption 9. Motherhood 10. Immigration and emigration 11. Essay writing 12. White privilege 13. Race relations 14. United States 15. Autobiographies and memoirs 16. Life stories — Identity 17. Society and culture — Race 18. Society and culture — Gender 19. Family and Relationships — Families

LC 2018024338

Describes how the author's experiences as an Indian-American, the wife of a white Christian woman and the mother of an adopted Black son have been challenged by rigid cultural family norms.

"Mehra (The Pomegranate King) blends memoir and cultural analysis to dive into the complex realities of race, gender, ethnicity, sexuality, and the constructs that surround these topics." —Library Journal

Oluo, Ijeoma

★ *So You Want to Talk About Race.* Ijeoma Oluo. Seal Press 2018. V, 248 pages

ISBN 9781580056779

Grades: Adult   305.800973

1. Intercultural communication 2. Racism 3. Prejudice 4. Social justice 5. Intersectionality 6. Cultural appropriation 7. Black Lives Matter movement 8. African Americans 9. Microaggressions 10. White privilege 11. Race relations 12. United States 13. Society and culture — Race 14. Adult books for young adults 15. Antiracist literature

LC 2017041919

Library Journal Best Books, 2018.

A Seattle-based writer, editor and speaker tackles the sensitive, hyper-charged racial landscape in current America, discussing the issues of privilege, police brutality, intersectionality, micro-aggressions, the Black Lives Matter movement, and the "N" word.

"A clear and candid contribution to an essential conversation." —Kirkus School Library Journal (May 2018).

Pinckney, Darryl

Busted in New York and Other Essays. Darryl Pinckney; foreword by Zadie Smith. Farrar, Straus and Giroux 2019. 304 p.

ISBN 9780374117443

Grades: Adult   305.800973

1. Social history 2. Racism 3. Race (Social sciences) 4. African Americans 5. Race relations 6. United States 7. Essays 8. Society and culture — Race

LC 2019020214

A collection of 25 essays from the celebrated literary critic and novelist provides a view of our recent racial history that blends the social and personal and wonders how we arrived at our current moment.

"A deeply satisfying, beautifully crafted collection of work by a writer of uncommon excellence and humanity." —Kirkus

Porter, Eduardo

American Poison: How Racial Hostility Destroyed Our Promise. Eduardo Porter. Alfred A. Knopf 2020. 272 p.

ISBN 9780451494887

Grades: Adult   305.800973

1. Race awareness 2. Social policy 3. Inequality 4. Racism 5. Race relations 6. United States 7. Society and culture — Race 8. Politics and global affairs — Civil and human rights 9. History writing — United States

LC 2019030765

An economics reporter for the New York Times discusses how America's racism has stunted the country's development in organized labor, public education and the social safety net and offers a path towards hope, change and a better future.

"American Poison is a work for our times from a writer who has found his subject." —Booklist

Includes bibliographical references and index.

Ricketts, Rachel

★ *Do Better: Spiritual Activism for Fighting and Healing from White Supremacy.* Rachel Ricketts. Atria Books 2021. 384 p.

ISBN 9781982151270

Grades: Adult   305.800973

ESSENTIAL AND RECOMMENDED TITLES
305.800975 Ethnic groups — South Atlantic states

1. Antiracism 2. Social justice 3. Racism 4. Religion and social problems 5. Personal conduct 6. Discrimination 7. Social advocacy 8. Interpersonal relations 9. White privilege 10. Race relations 11. United States 12. Spirituality and Religion — General 13. Society and culture — Race 14. Antiracist literature

LC 2020045247

The racial justice educator and spiritual activist outlines mindfulness-based practices for dismantling racism at both personal and community levels, sharing actionable, sustainable recommendations for overcoming obstacles, healing and mitigating harm.

"Meticulously researched, compassionate, and bold, this book should be read immediately and frequently returned to as a textual companion for the ongoing, reiterative work of antiracism." —*Library Journal*

Rothstein, Richard

★ *The Color of Law: A Forgotten History of How Our Government Segregated America.* Richard Rothstein. Liveright Publishing Corporation 2017. 336 p.

ISBN 9781631492853

Grades: Adult   305.800973

1. Segregation 2. Discrimination 3. Racism 4. African Americans 5. Race relations 6. United States 7. 20th century 8. History writing — African American — Civil rights — United States 9. Society and culture — Race 10. Antiracist literature

LC 2017004962

New York Times Notable Book, 2017; Longlisted for the National Book Award for Nonfiction, 2017.

Richard Rothstein has painstakingly documented how American cities, from San Francisco to Boston, became so racially divided. Rothstein describes how federal, state, and local governments systematically imposed residential segregation: with undisguised racial zoning, public housing that purposefully segregated previously mixed communities, subsidies for builders to create whites-only suburbs, tax exemptions for institutions that enforced segregation, and support for violent resistance to African Americans in white neighborhoods. He demonstrates that such policies still influence tragedies in places like Ferguson and Baltimore.

"This is essential reading for anyone interested in social justice, poverty, American history, and race relations, and its narrative nonfiction style will also draw general readers." —*Booklist*

Signer, Michael

Cry Havoc: Charlottesville and American Democracy Under Siege. Michael Signer. Public Affairs 2020. 383 p.

ISBN 9781541736153

Grades: Adult   305.800973

1. Signer, Michael 2. Protests, demonstrations, vigils, etc. 3. Racism 4. Public safety 5. White nationalism 6. Freedom of speech 7. White supremacy movements 8. Riots 9. Murder 10. Mayors 11. Race relations 12. Politics and government 13. Charlottesville, Virginia 14. Virginia 15. United States 16. 21st century 17. Politics and global affairs — Civil and human rights 18. Society and culture — Race

LC Bl2020006703

The former mayor of Charlottesville, Virginia, describes the events of the August 2017 "Unite the Right" white supremacist rally that turned violent after protestors clashed with counter-protesters and calls for optimism and opportunities to bolster democracy.

"A complex, disturbing, valuable tale of racial disharmony, government failure, and one man's frantic attempts to save the day." —*Kirkus*

Tatum, Beverly Daniel

★ *"why Are All the Black Kids Sitting Together in the Cafeteria?": And Other Conversations About Race.* Beverly Daniel Tatum. Basic Books 2017. VI, 453 pages

ISBN 9780465060689

Grades: 11 12 Adult   305.800973

1. African Americans 2. Identity 3. African American children 4. African American teenagers 5. White privilege 6. Race awareness 7. Intercultural communication 8. Communication 9. Race relations 10. United States 11. Society and culture — Race 12. Antiracist literature

LC 2017014766

Walk into any racially mixed high school and you will see Black, White, and Latino youth clustered in their own groups. Is this self-segregation a problem to address or a coping strategy we should support? How can we get past our reluctance to discuss racial issues? Beverly Daniel Tatum, a renowned authority on the psychology of racism, argues that straight talk about our racial identities is essential if we are serious about enabling communication across racial and ethnic divides. These topics have only become more urgent as the national conversation about race is increasingly acrimonious. This fully revised and updated edition is essential reading for anyone seeking to understand the dynamics of race in America.

"In balanced sections, she considers understanding Blackness in a white context and the development of a white identity itself. There is also an examination of critical issues in Latino, American Indian, and Asian-Pacific American identity development." —*School Library Journal*

Fully revised and updated—Provided by publisher; Includes bibliographical references (pages 403-430) and index; Originally published in hardcover and ebook by Basic Books in September 1997—title page verso.

305.800975 Ethnic groups — South Atlantic states

Thompson, Tracy

The New Mind of the South: An Unconventional Portrait for the Twenty-first Century. Tracy Thompson. Simon & Schuster 2013. 320 p.

ISBN 9781439158036

Grades: Adult   305.800975

1. Group identity 2. Identity 3. Ethnic identity 4. Race relations 5. Southern States history 6. Southern States 7. Society and culture — Race

LC 2012021581

Challenges stereotypes and fallacies to reveal the true heart of the South today, explaining how traditions about adapting are responsible for key changes while assessing the influence of Latino immigrants throughout the past half century.

"Highly recommended for libraries of all types, especially those with Southern history collections and readers in American studies." —*Library Journal*

Includes bibliographical references and index.

305.8009756 Ethnic groups — North Carolina

Zucchino, David

Wilmington's Lie: The Murderous Coup of 1898 and the Rise of White Supremacy. David Zucchino. Atlantic Monthly Press 2020. 336 p.

ISBN 9780802128386

Grades: Adult   305.8009756

1. African American civil rights 2. Coups d'etat 3. Violence against African Americans 4. White supremacy movements 5. Racism 6. Injustice 7. Massacres 8. Voter suppression 9. Race relations 10. Politics and government 11. United States history 12. Wilmington, North Carolina 13. North Carolina 14. 19th century 15. History writing — African American — United States 16. History writing — Reconstruction — United States

LC 2019040587

Pulitzer Prize for General Nonfiction, 2021; ALA Notable Book, 2021.

The Pulitzer Prize-winning journalist documents the events of the 1898 Wilmington Insurrection and its unrecognized role in reversing the city's mixed-race advances, overthrowing local government and promoting white-supremacist agendas.

Includes bibliographical references and index.

PUBLIC LIBRARY CORE COLLECTION: NONFICTION
Twentieth Edition

305.8009763 Ethnic groups — Louisiana

Ball, Edward
Life of a Klansman: A Family History in White Supremacy. Edward Ball. Farrar Straus & Giroux 2020. 400 p.
ISBN 9780374186326
Grades: Adult   305.8009763
1. Lecorgne, Constant, 1832-1886 2. Lecorgne family 3. Reconstruction (United States history) 4. Racism 5. White supremacy movements 6. Creoles (Louisiana) 7. Race relations 8. New Orleans, Louisiana 9. 19th century 10. Autobiographies and memoirs 11. History writing — Reconstruction — United States 12. Life stories — People in history
LC 2020003403

Presents a trenchant exploration of a family's legacy of white supremacy, detailing how Louisiana carpenter Constant Lecorgne joined the KKK to promote fanatical racism in post-Civil War America.

"The result is a clear-eyed work of historical reclamation and an intimate, self-lacerating take on memory and collective responsibility." —*Publishers Weekly*

Includes bibliographical references and index.

305.8009794 Ethnic groups — California

Miranda, Deborah A.
Bad Indians: A Tribal Memoir. Deborah A. Miranda. Heyday 2013. xx, 217 p. : Illustration; Table
ISBN 9781597142014
Grades: Adult   305.8009794
1. Indigenous peoples of North America 2. Indigenous peoples of North America, Treatment of 3. Indigenous peoples of North America — History 4. Race relations 5. California 6. History writing — Indigenous peoples — United States 7. Family and Relationships — Families
LC 2012025266

This beautiful and devastating book—part tribal history, part lyric and intimate memoir—should be required reading for anyone seeking to learn about California Indian history, past and present. Deborah A. Miranda tells stories of her Ohlone Costanoan Esselen family as well as the experience of California Indians as a whole through oral histories, newspaper clippings, anthropological recordings, personal reflections, and poems. The result is a work of literary art that is wise, angry, and playful all at once, a compilation that will break your heart and teach you to see the world anew.

Includes bibliographical references.

305.809 Caucasian people

Berman, Ari
★ *Minority Rule: The Right-wing Attack on the Will of the People?and the Fight to Resist It.* Ari Berman. Farrar, Straus and Giroux 2024. 384 p.
ISBN 9780374600211
Grades: Adult   305.809
1. Conservatism 2. Right and left (Political science) 3. New right 4. Racism 5. Inequality 6. Electoral college 7. Voter suppression 8. Judicial power 9. Democracy 10. Politics and government 11. United States 12. Politics and global affairs — Elections 13. Politics and global affairs — Political parties
LC 2023045468

The mob that stormed the Capitol on January 6, 2021, represented an extreme form of the central danger facing American democracy today: a blatant disregard for the will of the majority. But this crisis didn't begin or end with Donald Trump's attempt to overturn the 2020 election. Through voter suppression, election subversion, gerrymandering, dark money, the takeover of the courts, and the whitewashing of history, reactionary white conservatives have strategically entrenched power in the face of a massive demographic and political shift. Ari Berman charts these efforts with sweeping historical research and incisive on-the-ground reporting.

"Readers concerned about the future of democracy in the U.S. will find considerable value in this holistic, historical approach to current threats." —*Library Journal*

Includes bibliographical references and index.

Saad, Layla F.
★ *Me and White Supremacy: Combat Racism, Change the World, and Become a Good Ancestor.* Layla F. Saad. Sourcebooks Inc 2020. 241 p.
ISBN 9781728209807
Grades: Adult   305.809
1. European Americans 2. Racism 3. Prejudice 4. Equality 5. Personal conduct 6. Unconscious bias 7. Race relations 8. Social movements 9. White privilege 10. Book club best bets 11. Society and culture — Race 12. Society and culture — Social activism and philanthropy 13. Antiracist literature
LC 2019031113

When Layla Saad began an Instagram challenge called #meandwhitesupremacy, she never predicted it would become a cultural movement. She encouraged people to own up and share their racist behaviors, big and small. Updated and expanded from the original edition, Me and White Supremacy teaches readers how to dismantle the privilege within themselves so that they can stop (often unconsciously) inflicting damage on people of color, and in turn, help other white people do better, too.

"This groundbreaking book should be required reading for people ready to acknowledge their behaviors, whether intentional or not. It will make a strong addition to both public and university libraries where it will equip scholars, activists, and allies with real tools to promote systemic change." —*Library Journal*

Includes bibliographical references.

305.868 Spanish Americans

Gomez, Laura E.
★ *Inventing Latinos: A New Story of American Racism.* Laura E. Gomez. The New Press 2020. 336 p.
ISBN 9781595589170
Grades: Adult   305.868
1. Hispanic Americans 2. Citizenship 3. Identity 4. Ethnic identity 5. White privilege 6. Racism 7. International relations 8. Race relations 9. Immigration and emigration 10. United States history 11. United States 12. Latin America 13. Society and culture — Race 14. History writing — United States
LC 2020010659

Part history, part guide for the future, the author, a professor of law, sociology and Chicana/Chicano studies at UCLA, presents a groundbreaking examination of how Latinos' new collective racial identity has changed the way race functions in this country.

"While not all Latinos agree with Gomez's call for censuses to treat 'Latino' as a race and not an ethnicity, she delivers a rigorous and provocative study of the liminal zone Latino/As inhabit in America's racial continuum. Required reading." —*Library Journal*

Includes bibliographical references and index.

Tobar, Hector
★ *Our Migrant Souls: A Meditation on Race and the Meanings and Myths Of.* Héctor Tobar. MCD / Farrar, Straus and Giroux 2023. 256 p.
ISBN 9780374609900
Grades: Adult   305.868
1. Hispanic Americans 2. Immigrants 3. Ethnic identity 4. Culture 5. Prejudice 6. Racism 7. Multiculturalism 8. Race relations 9. United States 10. Essays 11. Society and culture — Race 12. Life stories — Identity — Race and ethnicity 13. Life stories — Identity — Immigrants 14. History writing — United States 15. Antiracist literature
LC 2022055249

Kirkus Prize for Nonfiction, 2023.

Latino" is the most open-ended and loosely defined of the major race categories in the United States. Our Migrant Souls: A Meditation on Race and the Meanings and Myths of "Latino" assembles the Pulitzer Prize winner Héctor

ESSENTIAL AND RECOMMENDED TITLES
305.89 Other groups

Tobar's personal experiences as the son of Guatemalan immigrants and the stories told to him by his Latinx students to offer a spirited rebuke to racist ideas about Latino people. Investigating topics that include the US-Mexico border "wall," urban segregation, gangs, and queer Latino utopias, Tobar journeys across the country to expose something truer about the meaning of "Latino" in the twenty-first century.

"A pensive examination of the many ways there are to be Latinx in America....A powerful look at what it means to be a member of a community that, though large, remains marginalized." —*Kirkus*

305.89 Other groups

Aguon, Julian
No Country for Eight-spot Butterflies: A Lyric Essay. Julian Aguon. Astra House 2022. 128 p.
ISBN 9781662601637
Grades: Adult   **305.89**
1. Climate change 2. Indigenous peoples 3. Social justice 4. Environmental degradation 5. Environmental protection 6. Environmental responsibility 7. Environmental justice 8. Pacific Islander people 9. Civil rights lawyers 10. Guam 11. Autobiographies and memoirs 12. Essays 13. Life stories — General 14. Poetry 15. Nature Writing — Environmental Issues
LC 2022002991

Part memoir, part manifesto, Chamorro climate activist Julian Aguon's No Country for Eight-Spot Butterflies is a coming-of-age story and a call for justice—for everyone, but in particular, for Indigenous peoples. In bracing poetry and compelling prose, Aguon weaves together stories from his childhood in the villages of Guam with searing political commentary about matters ranging from nuclear weapons to global warming.

"An attorney and environmental activist from Guam turns a searching eye on the fate of his homeland in a time of undeniable climate change….A slender but meaningful call for justice." —*Kirkus*

Includes bibliographical references.

305.892 Semites

Aly, Gotz
Europe Against the Jews: 1880-1945. Gotz Aly; translated by Jefferson Chase. Metropolitan Books; 2019. 432 p.
ISBN 9781250170170
Grades: Adult   **305.892**
1. Racism 2. Genocide 3. Nationalism 4. Jewish people 5. Holocaust (1933-1945) 6. Antisemitism 7. European people 8. Religious persecution 9. Causes of war 10. European history 11. Europe 12. 19th century 13. 20th century 14. Translations — German to English 15. History writing — Jewish history 16. History writing — Europe 17. Society and culture — Violence and crime — Genocide
LC 2019038047

The Holocaust was perpetrated by the Germans, but it would not have been possible without the assistance of thousands of helpers in other countries: State officials, police, and civilians who eagerly supported the genocide. If we are to fully understand how and why the Holocaust happened, Götz Aly argues in this groundbreaking study, we must examine its prehistory throughout Europe. We must look at countries as far-flung as Romania and France, Russia and Greece, where, decades before the Nazis came to power, a deadly combination of envy, competition, nationalism, and social upheaval fueled a surge of anti-Semitism, creating the preconditions for the deportations and murder to come.

"This expertly researched account is destined to influence future histories of the Holocaust." —*Publishers Weekly*

Includes bibliographical references and index; Originally published: Bonn : Bundeszentrale fur politische Bildung, 2017; Translated from the German.

Bayoumi, Moustafa
How Does It Feel to Be a Problem?: Being Young and Arab in America. Moustafa Bayoumi. Penguin Press 2008. 304 p.
ISBN 9781594201769
Grades: 11 12 Adult   **305.892**
1. Arab Americans 2. Ethnic identity 3. Young adults 4. Teenagers 5. Race awareness 6. Race relations 7. United States history 8. United States 9. 21st century 10. Adult books for young adults 11. Society and culture — Race 12. Antiracist literature
LC 2007049272

A study of the Arab- and Muslim-American experience as reflected by the lives of seven young men and women in Brooklyn evaluates their daily encounters with such factors as prejudice, the Christian faith, and their relationships with friends and family members in the Middle East.

Includes bibliographical references and index.

Eggers, Dave
Zeitoun. Dave Eggers. McSweeney's 2009. 351 p. : Illustration
ISBN 9781934781630
Grades: Adult   **305.892**
1. Zeitoun, Abdulrahman, 1957- 2. Disaster victims 3. Muslims 4. Racism 5. Hurricane Katrina, 2005 6. Rescue work 7. Syrian Americans 8. Survival (after hurricanes) 9. Survival (after floods) 10. Crisis management 11. Arrest 12. New Orleans, Louisiana 13. United States 14. 21st century 15. Autobiographies and memoirs 16. Life stories — Facing adversity — Disasters and tragedies 17. Life stories — Identity — Race and ethnicity
LC 2010290452

Los Angeles Times Book Prize for Current Interest, 2009; ALA Notable Book, 2010; New York Times Notable Book, 2009.

In the wake of Hurricane Katrina, longtime New Orleans residents Abdulrahman and Kathy Zeitoun are cast into an unthinkable struggle with forces beyond wind and water. In the days after the storm, Abdulrahman traveled the flooded streets in a secondhand canoe, passing on supplies and helping those he could. A week later, on September 6, 2005, Zeitoun abruptly disappeared—arrested and accused of being an agent of al Qaeda.

"This book is a more powerful indictment of America's dystopia in the Bush era than any number of well-written polemics." —*New York Times Book Review*

Fersko, Diana
★ *We Need to Talk About Antisemitism.* Rabbi Diana Fersko. Seal Press 2023. VII, 239 p.
ISBN 9781541601949
Grades: Adult   **305.892**
1. Antisemitism 2. Jewish people 3. Identity 4. Religious communities 5. Religious discrimination 6. Violence against marginalized people 7. Awareness 8. Social justice 9. United States 10. Spirituality and Religion — Judaism — Political Aspects 11. Society and culture — Race 12. Society and culture — Ethnic studies 13. Antiracist literature
LC 2023002332

A millennial rabbi provides this ultimate guide to modern antisemitism in its many forms, exploring topics such as vile myths about Jewish people and the intersection of antisemitism with other forms of discrimination, and spreading a message of solidarity and hope in the fight for social justice.

"An essential read for anyone interested in any aspect of antiracism or diversity, equity, and inclusion, or who generally wants to understand the current climate for Jewish people." —*Library Journal*

Includes bibliographical references and index.

Keinan, Tal
God Is in the Crowd: Twenty-first-century Judaism. Tal Keinan. Spiegel & Grau 2018. 240 p.
ISBN 9780525511168
Grades: Adult   **305.892**
1. Jewish people 2. Jewish way of life 3. Judaism 4. Judaism and state 5. Identity 6. Israel 7. 21st century 8. Spirituality and Religion — Judaism
LC 2018000337

Argues that the concentration of Jewish people into two hubs, America and Israel, has threatened Jewish continuity by robbing it of the subtle code of governance of the diaspora, and argues for resurrecting this code through a virtual diaspora.

Includes bibliographical references and index.

305.893 Non-Semitic Afro-Asiatic peoples

Iftin, Abdi Nor
Call Me American: A Memoir. by Abdi nor Iftin with Max Alexander. Alfred A. Knopf 2018. 304 p.
ISBN 9781524732196
Grades: Adult   305.893
1. Iftin, Abdi nor 2. Somali Americans 3. Immigrants 4. Muslims 5. Radio broadcasters 6. Immigration policy 7. Immigration and emigration 8. Maine 9. United States 10. Autobiographies and memoirs 11. Life stories — Identity — Immigrants 12. Adult books for young adults
LC 2017043213
ALA Notable Book, 2019; Library Journal Best Books, 2018.

A young Somalian, who learned English through American pop culture uses his skills to post secret dispatches to the Internet and NPR after a radical Islamist group comes to power and until he finally wins a visa lottery to emigrate.

This is a Borzoi Book.

305.896 Africans and people of African descent

Alexander, Elizabeth
★ *The Trayvon Generation: Yesterday, Today, Tomorrow.* Elizabeth Alexander. Grand Central Publishing 2022. 144 p.
ISBN 9781538737897
Grades: Adult   305.896
1. Martin, Trayvon, 1995-2012 2. African Americans 3. Crimes against African Americans 4. Racism 5. Psychic trauma 6. Social justice 7. Race relations 8. Psychology 9. Intergenerational trauma 10. United States history 11. 21st century 12. Society and culture — Race
LC 2021041296

Originally published in the New Yorker, one of the great literary voices of our time shares her celebrated and moving reflection on the challenges facing young Black America, illuminating our nation's unresolved problem with race.

"By capturing the rich spectrum of Black culture in America, Alexander offers hope and instruction for younger generations. The result is a thought-provoking must-read." —*Publishers Weekly*

Asim, Jabari
We Can't Breathe: On Black Lives, White Lies, and the Art of Survival. Jabari Asim. Picador 2018. 208 p.
ISBN 9781250174536
Grades: Adult   305.896
1. African Americans 2. Survival 3. Resilience 4. Racism 5. Power 6. Race relations 7. United States history 8. United States 9. Essays 10. History writing — African American — United States 11. Society and culture — Race 12. Adult books for young adults
LC 2018022983

A critically acclaimed writer presents eight wide-ranging and powerful essays that tell the story of black survival and persistence through art and community in the face of centuries of racism.

"A sharp vision that challenges readers to shift perspective and examine conventional narratives." —*Kirkus*

Includes bibliographical references.

Baldwin, James
★ *The Fire Next Time.* James Baldwin; with connections. Modern Library 2021. 167 p.
ISBN 9780679601517
Grades: Adult   305.896
1. African Americans 2. Racism 3. Civil rights 4. Black Muslims 5. Intersectionality 6. Race relations 7. United States 8. History writing — African American — United States 9. Antiracist literature
LC 2001265860

A plea and a warning to citizens to examine the actual state of America after a century of emancipation.

Originally published: New York : Dial Press, 1963.

Bennett, Michael
Things That Make White People Uncomfortable. Michael Bennett and Dave Zirin; foreword by Martellus Bennett. Haymarket Books 2018. 220 p.
ISBN 9781608468935
Grades: Adult   305.896
1. Bennett, Michael, 1985- 2. Professional athletes 3. Football players 4. Social justice 5. Racism 6. Race relations 7. United States 8. Autobiographies and memoirs 9. Life stories — Sports — Athletes 10. Sports and Competition — Football 11. Society and culture — Race
LC Bl2018052748

Super Bowl Champion and two-time Pro Bowler Michael Bennett is an outspoken proponent for social justice and a man without a censor.

Blackmon, Douglas A.
Slavery by Another Name: The Re-Enslavement of Black People in America from the Civil War to World War II / Douglas A. Blackmon. Bantam Dell Pub Group 2008. 304 p.
ISBN 9780385506250
Grades: Adult   305.896
1. African Americans 2. Crimes against African-Americans 3. African American prisoners 4. Forced labor 5. Convict labor 6. Slavery 7. African American history 8. Civil rights 9. Work 10. Race relations 11. United States history 12. 19th century 13. 20th century 14. Page to screen 15. History writing — African American — Enslavement — United States
LC 2007034500

Pulitzer Prize for General Nonfiction, 2009.

Bringing to light a shameful chapter in American history, a shocking study reveals how, from the late 1870s through the mid-twentieth century, thousands of African-American men were arrested and forced to work off the outrageous fines by serving as unpaid labor to small-town businesses, provincial farmers, and even large corporations.

"The author gives a groundbreaking and disturbing account of a sordid chapter in American historythe lease (essentially the sale) of convicts to commercial interests between the end of the 19th century and well into the 20th. [The] book reveals in devastating detail the legal and commercial forces that created this neoslavery along with deeply moving and totally appalling personal testimonies of survivors." —*Publishers Weekly*

Coates, Ta-Nehisi
★ *We Were Eight Years in Power: An American Tragedy.* Ta-Nehisi Coates. One World 2017. 256 p.
ISBN 9780399590566
Grades: Adult   305.896
1. Obama, Barack 2. Racism 3. Race (Social sciences) 4. Race relations 5. Politics and government 6. United States 7. 2000s (Decade) 8. Essays 9. Society and culture — Race
LC 2017039343

New York Times Notable Book, 2017; Longlisted for the Andrew Carnegie Medal for Excellence in Non-Fiction, 2018.

A compelling portrait of the historic Barack Obama era, combining new and annotated essays from the National Book Award-winning author of Between the World and ME, includes the articles, "Fear of a Black President" and "The Case for Reparations" as well as two new pieces on the Obama administration and what is coming next.

"Biting cultural and political analysis from the award-winning journalist. Emotionally charged, deftly crafted, and urgently relevant essays." —*Kirkus*

ESSENTIAL AND RECOMMENDED TITLES
305.896 Africans and people of African descent

Du Bois, W. E. B.
The Oxford W.E.B. Du Bois Reader. Edited by Eric J. Sundquist. Oxford University Press 1996. IX, 680 p.
ISBN 9780195091786
Grades: 11 12 Adult   305.896
1. African Americans 2. Race relations 3. United States 4. Arts and Entertainment — Writing and Publishing
LC 95021307

The Oxford W.E.B. Du Bois Reader encompasses the whole of Du Bois's long and multifaceted writing career, from the 1890s through the early 1960s. The volume selects key essays and longer works that portray the range of Du Bois's thought on such subjects as African American culture, the politics and sociology of American race relations, art and music, Black leadership, gender and women's rights, Pan-Africanism and anti-colonialism, and Communism in the U.S. and abroad.
Includes bibliographical references (p. 676-680).

Gates, Henry Louis
And Still I Rise: Black America Since Mlk. Henry Louis Gates Jr. and Kevin M. Burke. Ecco 2015. 304 p.
ISBN 9780062427007
Grades: Adult   305.896
1. African Americans 2. Racism 3. Civil Rights Movement 4. Prejudice 5. Race awareness 6. Race relations 7. United States 8. Media tie-ins 9. Society and culture — Race
LC Bl2015035373

This companion book to the PBS series examines Black history from the passage of the Civil Rights Act to the election of Barack Obama and describes the contradictions in the modern African-American community.
"This is an amazing collection of images of achievement on the long road to equality in the U.S." —*Booklist*

The Future of the Race. by Henry Louis Gates, Jr. and Cornel West. A.A. Knopf : 1996. xvii, 196 p.
ISBN 9780679444053
Grades: 11 12 Adult   305.896
1. African Americans 2. African American leadership 3. African American intellectuals 4. Upper class 5. Race relations 6. United States 7. 20th century 8. History writing — African American — Civil rights — United States 9. Antiracist literature
LC 96014450

Draws on the ideas of W.E.B. Du Bois to study the hopes and fears of the African American community at the dawn of the twenty-first century.
"Gates and West explore the challenge of W.E.B. DuBois's famous essay the Talented Tenth and consider the future of African American society in light of it. The authors examine the responsibility of the successful and talented Black middle and upper classes to uplift the impoverished. The text includes DuBois's the Talented Tenth and, reprinted for the first time, his 1948 critique of it." —*Library Journal*
Includes bibliographical references (p. 179-196).

Henny, Ally
I Won't Shut Up: Finding Your Voice When the World Tries to Silence You. Ally Henny. Baker Books, a division of Baker Publishing Group 2023. 224 p.
ISBN 9781540902658
Grades: Adult   305.896
1. Henny, Ally, 1985- 2. African American women 3. Christian women 4. Racism 5. Injustice 6. Identity 7. Social advocacy 8. Social change 9. Society and culture — Gender — Women 10. Society and culture — Race 11. Spirituality and Religion — Christianity — Political Aspects 12. Life stories — Religion and spirituality — Personal faith 13. Antiracist literature 14. Debut title
LC 2022040931

Being Black in a society developed by white men to benefit white men means constantly pushing back against systems that were not constructed for your flourishing. You're made to feel that your life doesn't matter, your opinions aren't valid, and your entire existence is too loud. It can feel like the whole world is telling you to shut up. Ally Henny knows what it's like to navigate racism and racialized sexism. She's not taking it anymore, and she's calling you to join her in resisting racism by speaking the truth—no matter the cost.
"Throughout, Henny is candid about her own path to self-acceptance and her discussions of how racism can manifest in overt and subtle ways, from the church pew to the classroom, are smart and perceptive. Readers will be empowered." —*Publishers Weekly*
Includes bibliographical references.

Jefferson, Margo
Negroland: A Memoir. Margo Jefferson. Pantheon Books 2015. 288 p.
ISBN 9780307378453
Grades: Adult   305.896
1. Jefferson, Margo, 1947- 2. African American women 3. African Americans 4. Elite (Social sciences) 5. Racism 6. Upper class 7. Identity 8. Civil Rights Movement 9. Rich African Americans 10. Social classes and family 11. Middle class African Americans 12. Middle class African American families 13. Intersectionality 14. White privilege 15. Chicago, Illinois 16. Autobiographies and memoirs 17. Life stories — Identity — Race and ethnicity 18. Society and culture — Wealth and class 19. Society and culture — Race 20. Adult books for young adults 21. Book club best bets
LC 2015006843

National Book Critics Circle Award for Autobiography, 2015; New York Times Notable Book, 2015.

A highly personal meditation on race, sex and American culture by the Pulitzer Prize-winning critic traces her upbringing and education in upper-class African-American circles against a backdrop of the Civil Rights era and its contradictory aftermath.
"Jefferson swings the narrative back and forth through her life, exploring the tides of racism, opportunity, and dignity while also provocatively exploring the inherent contradictions for Jefferson and her family members in working so tirelessly to differentiate themselves." —*Kirkus*
Also published in large print format.

Jerkins, Morgan
Wandering in Strange Lands: A Daughter of the Great Migration Reclaims Her Roots. Morgan Jerkins. Harper 2020. 304 p.
ISBN 9780062873040
Grades: Adult   305.896
1. Jerkins, Morgan 2. African American women authors 3. Family history 4. Ancestors 5. Genealogy 6. Identity 7. Racism 8. Transcontinental journeys 9. Intersectionality 10. Immigration and emigration 11. African Americans 12. Voyages and travels 13. Self-discovery 14. United States history 15. United States 16. 20th century 17. Autobiographies and memoirs 18. Life stories — Identity — Race and ethnicity 19. History writing — African American — United States 20. Society and culture — Race 21. Society and culture — Ethnic studies 22. Travel Writing — United States
LC Bl2020016364

Between 1916 and 1970, six million Black Americans left their rural homes in the South for jobs in cities in the North, West, and Midwest in a movement known as the Great Migration. But while this event transformed the complexion of America and provided Black people with new economic opportunities, it also disconnected them from their roots, their land, and their sense of identity, argues Morgan Jerkins. In this fascinating and deeply personal exploration, she recreates her ancestors' journeys across America, following the migratory routes they took from Georgia and South Carolina to Louisiana, Oklahoma, and California.
"A thrilling, emotional, and engaging ride that almost commands the reader to turn the page. . . . [This] is required reading, accurately widening the lens of American history." —*Booklist*

King, Gilbert
★ *Devil in the Grove: Thurgood Marshall, the Groveland Boys, and the Dawn of a New America.* Gilbert King. Harper 2012. 352 p.
ISBN 9780061792281
Grades: Adult   305.896
1. Marshall, Thurgood, 1908-1993 2. Racism in the criminal justice system 3. Rape 4. African American civil rights 5. Innocence (Law) 6. Malicious accusa-

tion 7. Race relations 8. Florida 9. True Crime — Investigations and Trials 10. History writing — African American — Civil rights — United States

LC 2011033757

Pulitzer Prize for General Nonfiction, 2013.

Chronicles a little-known court case in which Thurgood Marshall successfully saved a Black citrus worker from the electric chair after the worker was accused of raping a white woman with three other Black men.

Lebron, Christopher J

The Making of Black Lives Matter: A Brief History of an Idea. Christopher J. Lebron. Oxford University Press 2017. xxii, 187 p.

ISBN 9780190601348

Grades: Adult   **305.896**

1. Black Lives Matter movement 2. Protest movements 3. African Americans 4. Equality 5. Racism 6. Politics and culture 7. Race relations 8. United States 9. 21st century 10. Society and culture — Race 11. Politics and global affairs — Civil and human rights 12. Antiracist literature

LC 2016042413

Started in the wake of George Zimmerman's 2013 acquittal in the death of Trayvon Martin, the #BlackLivesMatter movement has become a powerful and uncompromising campaign demanding redress for the brutal and unjustified treatment of Black bodies by law enforcement in the United States. The movement is only a few years old, but as Christopher J. Lebron argues in this book, the sentiment behind it is not; the plea and demand that "Black Lives Matter" comes out of a much older and richer tradition arguing for the equal dignity—and not just equal rights—of Black people.

"Throughout five brief essays, an introduction, and an afterword, Black scholars consider the persistent failure of the U.S. justice system to redress or remedy the white terrorism responsible for harming Black lives." —*Library Journal*

Includes bibliographical references and index.

Lemon, Don

This Is the Fire: What I Say to My Friends About Racism. Don Lemon. Little, Brown & Company 2021. 160 p.

ISBN 9780316257572

Grades: Adult   **305.896**

1. Lemon, Don 2. Race (Social sciences) 3. African Americans 4. Television newscasters and commentators 5. Race awareness 6. Social justice 7. Racism 8. Race relations 9. United States history 10. United States 11. Society and culture — Race 12. Life stories — Identity — Race and ethnicity 13. History writing — African American — United States 14. Antiracist literature

As America's only Black prime-time anchor, Don Lemon and his daily monologues on racism and antiracism, on the failures of the Trump administration and of so many of our leaders, and on America's systemic flaws speak for his millions of fans. Now, in an urgent, deeply personal, riveting plea, he shows us all how deep our problems lie, and what we can do to begin to fix them. As he writes to his young nephew: We must resist racism every single day. We must resist it with love.

"A thoughtful analysis which deserves a place on readers' anti-racist reading lists. Recommended for those interested in trying to enact systemic change." —*Library Journal*

Includes bibliographical references and index.

Mallory, Tamika D.

State of Emergency: How We Win in the Country We Built. Tamika D. Mallory. Black Privilege Publishing 2021. 224 p.

ISBN 9781982173463

Grades: Adult   **305.896**

1. Institutional racism 2. Social justice 3. Racism 4. Social change 5. African Americans 6. Civil rights workers 7. Race relations 8. United States 9. Society and culture — Social activism and philanthropy 10. Society and culture — Race 11. Life stories — Politics — Activists and reformers 12. Politics and global affairs — Civil and human rights 13. Antiracist literature

A globally recognized civil rights activist presents an unwavering history of American systemic racism, a first-hand view of what makes for effective activism today and a vision for lasting, positive change.

"Shifting between outrage, hope, and resolute determination, this call to action will resonate with readers already fighting for racial justice, as well as those looking to join the movement." —*Publishers Weekly*

Parker, Morgan

★ *You Get What You Pay For: Essays.* Morgan Parker. One World 2024. 288 p.

ISBN 9780525511441

Grades: Adult   **305.896**

1. Parker, Morgan 2. African Americans 3. Alienation 4. Race awareness 5. Social isolation 6. African American women 7. Safety 8. Loneliness 9. Race relations 10. Mental health 11. Culture 12. Social history 13. United States 14. Essays 15. Autobiographies and memoirs 16. Life stories — Identity — Race and ethnicity 17. Society and culture — Race

In this memoir-in-essays, the author, weaving unflinching criticism with intimate anecdotes, examines America's cultural history and relationship to black Americans through the ages, providing a deeper examination of racial consciousness and its effects on mental well-being today.

"The writing is captivating, rife with poetic turns of phrase and powerful insights. An absorbing, insightful collection from a multitalented writer." —*Booklist*

Rankine, Claudia

★ *Just Us: an American Conversation.* Claudia Rankine. Graywolf Press 2020. 342 pages : Illustration; Color

ISBN 9781644450215

Grades: Adult   **305.896**

1. Racism 2. Identity 3. Justice 4. African Americans 5. Violence 6. White privilege 7. Race relations 8. United States 9. Essays 10. Poetry 11. Society and culture — Race

LC 2019956891

ALA Notable Book, 2021; New York Times Notable Book, 2020; Andrew Carnegie Medal for Excellence in Non-Fiction Finalist, 2021.

As everyday white supremacy becomes increasingly vocalized with no clear answers at hand, how best might we approach one another? Claudia Rankine, without telling us what to do, urges us to begin the discussions that might open pathways through this divisive and stuck moment in American history. Just Us is an invitation to discover what it takes to stay in the room together, even and especially in breaching the silence, guilt, and violence that follow direct addresses of whiteness. Rankine's questions disrupt the false comfort of our culture's liminal and private spaces—the airport, the theater, the dinner party, the voting booth—where neutrality and politeness live on the surface of differing commitments, beliefs, and prejudices as our public and private lives intersect.

"Rankine presents another arresting blend of essays and images, perfectly attuned to this long-overdue moment of racial reckoning. In language all the more devastating for its simplicity, Rankine analyzes the overwhelming power of whiteness in everyday interactions." —*Booklist*

"A must-read to add to the conversation on racism, antiracism, and white fragility." —*Library Journal*

Ruffin, Amber

★ *The World Record Book of Racist Stories.* Amber Ruffin and Lacey Lamar. Grand Central Publishing 2022. 240 p.

ISBN 9781538724552

Grades: 9 10 11 12 Adult   **305.896**

1. Lamar, Lacey 2. Ruffin, Amber 3. Sisters 4. African Americans 5. African American families 6. Women comedians 7. Racism 8. Everyday life 9. Social interaction 10. American people 11. North American people 12. Race relations 13. United States 14. Society and culture — Race 15. Humor writing — Social humor 16. Life stories — Identity — Race and ethnicity 17. Antiracist literature

LC 2022026047

The host of the Amber Ruffin Show and writer/Cast member on NBC's Late Night with Seth Meyers and her sister present a hilarious, intergenerational look at the absurdity of everyday racism as experienced across age, gender and appearance.

"An excellent look at lived experiences of Black Americans that should be required reading for all Americans." —*Kirkus*

ESSENTIAL AND RECOMMENDED TITLES
305.896 Africans and people of African descent

"Having faced racism that will make readers' skin crawl, the authors offer humor in a riotous tangle of rage, disbelief, amusement, and frustration but never lose their underlying message: Racism is harmful, pervasive, and always wrong." —*Booklist*

You'll Never Believe What Happened to Lacey: Crazy Stories About Racism. Amber Ruffin and Lacey Lamar. Grand Central Publishing 2021. 240 p.
ISBN 9781538719367
Grades: Adult   305.896
1. Lamar, Lacey 2. Ruffin, Amber 3. Sisters 4. African American women 5. Women comedians 6. Racism 7. Everyday life 8. Social interaction 9. Humorous writing 10. Race relations 11. Omaha, Nebraska 12. New York City 13. United States 14. Page to screen 15. Society and culture — Race 16. Humor writing — Social humor 17. Life stories — Identity — Race and ethnicity 18. Antiracist literature

Now a writer and performer on Late Night with Seth Meyers and host of the Amber Ruffin Show, Amber Ruffin lives in New York, where she is no one's First Black Friend and everyone is, as she puts it, "stark raving normal." but Amber's sister Lacey? She's still living in their home state of Nebraska, and trust us, you'll never believe what happened to Lacey. From racist donut shops to strangers putting their whole hand in her hair, from being mistaken for a prostitute to being mistaken for Harriet Tubman, Lacey is a lightning rod for hilariously ridiculous yet all-too-real anecdotes. And now, Amber and Lacey share these entertainingly horrifying stories through their laugh-out-loud sisterly banter.

"There are many teen readers for this book: Ruffin's fans, late-night comedy fans, those who endure racism daily, and those who live unaware of racism's reach." —*Booklist*

"Featuring the authors' razor-sharp wit and limitless brilliance, these true tales of injustice are a gift to readers." —*Booklist*

Sanders, Chad
Black Magic: What Black Leaders Learned from Trauma and Triumph. Chad Sanders. Simon & Schuster 2021. 320 p.
ISBN 9781982104221
Grades: Adult   305.896
1. Sanders, Chad 2. African American leadership 3. African Americans 4. Identity 5. Leadership 6. Success (Concept) 7. Interviews 8. Essays 9. Life stories — Identity — Race and Ethnicity 10. Society and culture — Race

An evocative tribute to Black achievement in a discriminating world draws on interviews with Black leaders, scientists, artists, activists and champions while exploring the author's own experiences of being forced to emulate white culture.

"This mix of memoir, interviews, and motivation is for readers who have faced trauma and kept going and for individuals who have been underestimated because of their race, family, socioeconomic status, gender, sexuality, or any other target for mindless prejudice." —*Booklist*

Sharpe, Christina Elizabeth
Ordinary Notes. Christina Sharpe. Farrar Straus & Giroux 2023. 256 p.
ISBN 9780374604486
Grades: Adult   305.896
1. Loss 2. African Americans 3. Racism 4. Identity 5. Life 6. United States 7. Society and culture — Race 8. History Writing — African American — United States

Hilary Weston Writers' Trust Prize, 2023; National Book Award for Nonfiction finalist, 2023; National Book Critics Circle Award for Nonfiction finalist, 2023.

Told through a series of 248 notes, this brilliant volume explores profound questions about loss and the shapes of Black life that emerge in the wake, touching upon such themes as language, beauty, memory, history and literature.

"Sharpe (In the Wake), a Black studies professor at York University, Toronto, lays bare the brutality of anti-Black racism through 248 brief 'Notes' on history, art, and her personal life in this poignant and genre-defying triumph....Moving and profound, this is not to be missed." —*Publishers Weekly*

Nominated for the Hilary Weston Writers' Trust Prize for Nonfiction, 2023.

Tesfamariam, Rahiel
★ *Imagine* Freedom: Transforming Pain into Political and Spiritual Power. Rahiel Tesfamariam. Amistad Press 2024. 256 p.
ISBN 9780063253087
Grades: Adult   305.896
1. Freedom 2. African Americans 3. Self-discovery 4. Identity 5. Spirituality 6. Psychic trauma 7. Healing 8. Social change 9. Decolonization 10. American dream 11. United States 12. Africa 13. Society and culture — Race 14. Spirituality and religion — General 15. History Writing — African American — United States

A social activist, journalist, public theologian and international speaker offers a bold path to liberation and healing for people of African descent struggling in the shadows of the American Dream.

"Journalist and theologian Tesfamariam debuts with a bold vision for Black millennials living in Africa and across the diaspora...This has the power to move readers." —*Publishers Weekly*

Ward, Jesmyn
★ *The* Fire This Time: A New Generation Speaks About Race. Jesmyn Ward. Scribner 2016. 288 p.
ISBN 9781501126345
Grades: Adult   305.896
1. African Americans 2. Racism 3. Civil rights 4. Race relations 5. United States 6. Anthologies 7. Society and culture — Race 8. Adult books for young adults 9. Book club best bets
LC 2016005371

The National Book Award-winning author of Salvage the Bones presents a continuation of James Baldwin's 1963 the Fire Next Time that examines race issues from the past half century through essays, poems and memoir pieces by some of her generation's most original thinkers and writers.

"Wards remarkable achievement is the gift of freshly minted perspectives on a tale that may seem old and twice-told. Readers in search of conversations about race in America should start here." —*Publishers Weekly*

Whitaker, Mark
Smoketown: The Untold Story of the Other Great Black Renaissance. by Mark Whitaker. Simon & Schuster 2018. 432 p.
ISBN 9781501122392
Grades: Adult   305.896
1. African Americans 2. Intellectual life 3. African American athletes 4. Jazz musicians 5. Pittsburgh, Pennsylvania 6. 20th century 7. History writing — African American — United States
LC 2017019428

Chronicles the lesser-known African-American renaissance in Pittsburgh from the 1920s through the 1950s, assessing how it rivaled Harlem and Chicago as the site of the most widely read Black newspaper in the nation, the two leading Negro Leagues baseball teams and the childhood homes of forefront jazz pioneers.

"An expansive, prodigiously researched, and masterfully told history." —*Kirkus*

Includes bibliographical references and index.

Winters, Mary-Frances
Black Fatigue: How Racism Erodes the Mind, Body, and Spirit. Mary-Frances Winters. Berrett-Koehler Publishers 2020. xv, 234 p.
ISBN 9781523091300
Grades: Adult   305.896
1. Winters, Mary-Frances 2. Social justice 3. African Americans 4. Racism 5. Fatigue 6. Institutional racism 7. Inequality 8. Mental health 9. Health 10. Society and culture — Race 11. Antiracist literature
LC 2020941572

Presents information about the intergenerational impact of systemic racism on the physical and psychological health of African Americans and explains why and how society needs to collectively do more to combat its pernicious effects.

PUBLIC LIBRARY CORE COLLECTION: NONFICTION
Twentieth Edition

"An excellent entry-level resource on antiracism for anyone looking to begin but unsure of how to get started." —*Library Journal*

Includes bibliographical references and index.

Woodward, C. Vann

The Strange Career of Jim Crow. C. Vann Woodward; with a new afterword by William S. McFeely. Oxford University Press 2002. xvii, 245 p.

ISBN 9780195146899

Grades: 11 12 Adult   **305.896**

1. African Americans 2. Reconstruction (United States history) 3. African American history 4. Racism 5. Segregation 6. Race relations 7. Politics and government 8. United States 9. Southern States 10. 19th century 11. 20th century 12. History writing — Reconstruction — United States 13. History writing — African American — Civil rights — United States

LC 2001021668

Surveys the history of segregation in the United States, citing the changes, controversies, and leaders that have emerged from the Civil Rights movement.

Includes bibliographical references (p. 233-236) and index; Originally published: New York : Oxford University Press, 1955.

305.897 North American native peoples

Burns, Mike

The Only One Living to Tell: The Autobiography of a Yavapai Indian. Mike Burns; edited by Gregory McNamee. University of Arizona Press 2012. 179 p.

ISBN 9780816501205

Grades: Adult   **305.897**

1. Burns, Mike, 1865?-1934 2. Yavapai (North American people) 3. Indigenous peoples of North America 4. Orphans 5. United States history 6. Southwest (United States) 7. 19th century 8. Autobiographies and memoirs 9. History writing — Wars and conflicts — American Indigenous Wars 10. Life stories — Facing adversity — War and oppression — War survivors 11. Life stories — People in history — Indigenous peoples 12. History writing — Indigenous peoples — United States

LC 2011046513

Of interest to students of Southwestern American history and Indian history, this memoir of Arizona Yavapai Mike Burns' life provides a unique and unvarnished look at the atrocities and cultural genocide committed against the native peoples of the region, and presents one man's personal perspective, molded by his experiences living as an Indian in white society, of the travails of his people. The work is edited by Gregory McNamee, a researcher at the University of Arizona Southwest Center.

"Essential reading for anyone interested in the history of the Southwest and its native peoples as conveyed by a native writer." —*Library Journal*

Includes bibliographical references.

305.899 Oceanian native peoples

DeParle, Jason

★ *A Good Provider Is One Who Leaves: One Family and Migration in the 21st Century.* Jason DeParle. Viking 2019. 352 p.

ISBN 9780670785926

Grades: Adult   **305.899**

1. Comodas, Rosalie 2. Immigrants 3. Immigrant workers 4. Extended families 5. Discrimination in employment 6. Assimilation (Sociology) 7. Filipino people 8. Immigration and emigration 9. United States history 10. 21st century 11. Life stories — Identity — Immigrants 12. Society and culture — Immigration

LC 2019011071

ALA Notable Book, 2020; Library Journal Best Books, 2019.

An investigative reporter describes the lives of the Comodas family over several decades and three generations and shows the impact of global migration and how it has reordered economics, politics and culture around the world.

"A gorgeously written, uniquely insightful, and evenly critical volume that hits every talking point on immigration today." —*Kirkus*

Includes bibliographical references and index.

305.8994 Polynesian native peoples

Thompson, Christina

Sea People: The Puzzle of Polynesia. Christina Thompson. Harper 2019. xvi, 365 pages, 8 unnumbered pages of plates : Illustration; Color; Map

ISBN 9780062060877

Grades: Adult   **305.8994**

1. Polynesians 2. Maori (New Zealand people) 3. Polynesia 4. Islands of the Pacific 5. South Pacific Ocean 6. Oceania 7. Pacific Ocean 8. History writing — Maori — New Zealand

NSW Premier's History Awards, General History Prize, 2019; Prime Minister's Literary Awards: Nonfiction, 2020; Victorian Premier's Literary Awards, Nettie Palmer Prize for Non-Fiction, 2020.

Explores the origins of the Polynesian people, attempting to answer the questions about who founded and settled these remote Pacific islands in an era before writing or metal tools.

"A superb chronicler of the intellectual explorers of Polynesian history, Thompson writes with command and insight, enhancing this fascinating books rich appeal." —*Booklist*

Includes bibliographical references (pages 325-348) and index.

305.9 People by occupation and miscellaneous social statuses; people with disabilities and illnesses, gifted people

Blitzer, Jonathan

Everyone Who Is Gone Is Here: The United States, Central America, and the Lives in Between. Jonathan Blitzer. Penguin Press 2024. 496 p.

ISBN 9781984880802

Grades: Adult   **305.9**

1. Immigrants 2. Central American people 3. Immigration and emigration 4. Immigration policy 5. Immigration and emigration law 6. United States 7. Central America 8. History Writing — Regional history — United States 9. Society and culture — Immigration 10. Politics and global affairs — Immigration

LC 2023023980

A New Yorker staff writer examines the political factors in Central American countries such as El Salvador, Guatemala, and Honduras that have led to the humanitarian crises at American's southern border as told through the stories of these migrants.

"A sobering, well-reported history in which no one emerges a winner." —*Kirkus*

Includes bibliographical references and index.

Kushner, Jacob

Look Away: A True Story of Murders, Bombings, and a Far-right Campaign to Rid Germany of Immigrants. Jacob Kushner. Grand Central Publishing 2024. 288 p.

ISBN 9781538708118

Grades: Adult   **305.9**

1. Right-wing extremists 2. Racism 3. Fascism 4. Right and left (Political science) 5. Immigration and emigration 6. White supremacists 7. Violence against marginalized people 8. Violence against immigrants 9. Bank robberies 10. Hate crimes 11. Domestic terrorism 12. Anti-fascism 13. Frameups 14. Terrorism investigation 15. Germany 16. 2000s (Decade) 17. Life stories — Facing adversity — Victims of crime — Terrorism 18. Life stories — Law and order — Criminals and law-breakers 19. History writing — Europe — Germany

LC 2023051824

Not long after the Berlin Wall fell, three teenagers became friends in the East German town of Jena. It was a time of excitement, but also of economic crisis: Some four million East Germans found themselves out of jobs. The friends be-

ESSENTIAL AND RECOMMENDED TITLES
306 Culture and institutions

gan attending far-right rallies with people who called themselves National Socialists: Nazis. Like the Hitler-led Nazis before them, they blamed minorities for their ills. From 2000 to 2011, they embarked on the most horrific string of white nationalist killings since the Holocaust. Their target: Immigrants. Look Away documents a shocking spree of white supremacist violence, and how a nation and its government ignored them until it was too late.

"Kushner's penetrating insights into the terrorist fringe of the German right wing provide background to understanding the motives underlying the terrorists' horrific crimes. A gripping true crime story with deep historic undertones."
—*Booklist*

Includes index.

Ladau, Emily
Demystifying Disability: What to Know, What to Say, and How to Be an Ally. Emily Ladau. Ten Speed Press 2021. 167 pages : Color; Illustration
ISBN 9781984858979
Grades: Adult   305.9
1. People with disabilities 2. Disabilities 3. Science Writing — Medicine and health — Disabilities and disorders
LC 2020041583

A guide for how to be a thoughtful, informed ally to disabled people, with actionable steps for what to say and do (and what not to do) and how you can help make the world a more accessible place.

"Ladau has written an essential resource that readers can refer to at any time, browsing chapters individually or reading straight through. A must for libraries and fans of Disability Visibility, by Alice Wong." —*Library Journal*

Includes bibliographical references (pages 150-154) and index.

Oliva, Alejandra
Rivermouth: A Chronicle of Language, Faith, and Migration. Alejandra Oliva. Astra House 2023. 320 p.
ISBN 9781662601699
Grades: Adult   305.9
1. Oliva, Alejandra 2. Immigrants 3. Political refugees 4. Spanish Americans 5. Translating and interpreting 6. Language and languages 7. Faith 8. Bilingualism 9. Empathy 10. Immigration and emigration 11. United States 12. Autobiographies and memoirs 13. Book club best bets 14. Life stories — Identity — Immigrants 15. Society and culture — Immigration 16. Debut title
LC 2022057997

Rivermouth is a polemic arguing for porous borders, a decriminalization of immigration, a more open sense of what we owe one another, and a willingness to extend radical empathy.

"With uncut rage and breathtaking prose, Oliva edifies, infuriates, and moves readers all at once. This is required reading." —*Publishers Weekly*

Includes bibliographical references.

Olivares, Efren C.
My Boy Will Die of Sorrow: A Memoir of Immigration from the Front Lines. Efrén C. Olivares. Hachette Books 2022. 320 p.
ISBN 9780306847288
Grades: Adult   305.9
1. Olivares, Efren C. 2. Immigrants 3. Undocumented immigrants 4. Immigration and emigration 5. Separated friends, relatives, etc. 6. Punishment 7. Injustice 8. Family relationships 9. Loss 10. Identity 11. Immigration policy 12. Toleration 13. Compassion 14. Intergenerational trauma 15. Politics and global affairs — Immigration 16. Society and culture — Immigration 17. Life stories — Identity — Immigrants
LC 2021059948

Sharing gripping family separation stories alongside his own, a human rights lawyer gives voice to immigrants who have been punished and silenced for seeking safety and opportunity, discussing what nationhood means in America and challenging us to question our own empathy and compassion.

"Readers will appreciate this memoir as a moving firsthand account but also as a call to action to ensure that human rights prevail at America's borders." —*Library Journal*

Pipher, Mary Bray
The Middle of Everywhere: The World's Refugees Come to Our Town. Mary Pipher. Harcourt 2002. 390 p.
ISBN 9780151006007
Grades: Adult   305.9
1. Refugees 2. Immigrants 3. Assimilation (Sociology) 4. Americanization 5. Immigration and emigration 6. United States history 7. Nebraska 8. 21st century 9. 20th century 10. History writing — Immigration — United States 11. Adult books for young adults
LC 2001005863

Offers the tales of refugees who have escaped countries riddled by conflict and ripped apart by war to realize their dream of starting a new life in America, detailing their triumph over adversity.

"The author writes in rich, empathetic language and with a keen, observant eye for detail and nuance." —*Publishers Weekly*

Includes bibliographical references (p. [369]-371) and index.

Stephenson, Michael
The Last Full Measure: How Soldiers Die in Battle. Michael Stephenson. Crown Publishers 2012. xvi, 464 p.
ISBN 9780307395849
Grades: Adult   305.9
1. Battle casualties 2. Military history 3. Soldiers 4. Death 5. History writing — Wars and conflicts
LC 2011005874

Considers how soldiers through the ages have met their deaths in times of war, covering such subjects as weapons and battlefield strategies while offering insight into cultural differences and the nature of military combat.

Includes bibliographical references (p. [441]-452) and index.

306 Culture and institutions

Bossiere, Zoe
Cactus Country: A Boyhood Memoir. Zoe Bossiere. Harry N Abrams Inc 2024. 272 p.
ISBN 9781419773181
Grades: Adult   306
1. Bossiere, Zoe, 1992- 2. Growing up 3. Gender fluid 4. Genderqueer people 5. Sexism 6. Racism 7. Drug abuse 8. Violence 9. Childhood 10. Social classes 11. Masculinity 12. Self 13. Identity 14. Gender role 15. Tucson, Arizona 16. Southwest (United States) 17. Autobiographies and memoirs 18. Life stories — Identity — LGBTQIA+

This debut book chronicles the author's experiences growing up as a trans boy in a Tucson, Arizona trailer park and the challenges they faced living in world of sexism, racism, substance abuse and violence.

"Bossiere's concise prose style and gift for scene-setting draws readers in as they unpick the somewhat esoteric nuances of their gender identity." —*Publishers Weekly*

Chayka, Kyle
Filterworld: How Algorithms Flattened Culture. Kyle Chayka. Doubleday 2024. 288 p.
ISBN 9780385548281
Grades: Adult   306
1. Culture 2. Internet 3. Algorithms 4. Mathematical models 5. High technology industry and trade 6. Capitalism 7. Decision-making 8. Free will and determinism 9. Creativity 10. Consumer society 11. Social control 12. Society and culture — Media and technology 13. Science Writing — Computing, the Internet, and Technology
LC 2023020397

From trendy restaurants to city grids, to TikTok and Netflix feeds the world round, algorithmic recommendations dictate our experiences and choices. Over the last decade, this network of mathematically determined decisions has taken over, almost unnoticed—informing the songs we listen to, the friends with whom we stay in touch—as we've grown increasingly accustomed to our insipid new normal. What does it mean to make a choice when the options have been so carefully arranged for us? Is personal freedom possible on the Internet? This book argues yes—but to escape Filterworld, and even transcend it, we must first understand it.

"An important book about how to get out of the algorithmic box and make your own decisions." —*Kirkus*

Gies, Frances
Life in a Medieval Village. Frances and Joseph Gies. Harper Perennial 1991. IX, 257 p. : Illustration; Map
ISBN 9780060920463
Grades: 11 12 Adult   306
1. Peasantry 2. Social life and customs 3. Great Britain 4. England 5. Medieval period (476-1492) 6. Norman period (1066-1154) 7. Plantagenet period (1154-1485) 8. History writing — Medieval — Europe
LC BL 99714619

Focusing on the village of Elton, in the English East Midlands, this book describes the food and housing of the peasants, the tension between them and the lord of the manor, and the place of the Church in their lives.

"Elton, England, is the focal point of the authors' efforts to portray the everyday life and social structure of the High Middle Ages. After giving a brief summary of Elton's origins and development in the Roman and Anglo-Saxon periods, the book examines just how the residents lived and worked within the feudal structure at the beginning of the fourteenth century." —*Booklist*

Includes bibliographical references (p. 233-241) and index; Originally published: New York : Harper & Row, 1990.

Klinenberg, Eric
★ *2020: One City, Seven People, and the Year Everything Changed.* Eric Klinenberg. Alfred A. Knopf 2023. 432 p.
ISBN 9780593319482
Grades: Adult   306
1. Social history 2. Presidential election, 2020 3. COVID-19 Pandemic, 2020- 4. Equality 5. Life change events 6. 21st century 7. Collective biographies 8. Society and culture — Illness and disease — Epidemics 9. History Writing — United States 10. Society and culture — Urban and regional studies
LC 2023016554

The acclaimed sociologist and best-selling author tells the story of one of the most consequential years in history through profiles of seven New Yorkers, including 2020 an elementary school principal, a bar manager and a subway custodian.

"Scholarly but engrossing, this book captures the lingering uncertainty that has characterized the COVID pandemic, while assessing its global effects and likely future challenges. This vital title has breadth." —*Library Journal*

Includes index.

Lasch, Christopher
★ *The Revolt of the Elites: And the Betrayal of Democracy.* Christopher Lasch. W.W. Norton 1995. x, 276 p.
ISBN 9780393036992
Grades: Adult   306
1. Polarization (Social sciences) 2. Populism 3. Democracy 4. Elite (Social sciences) 5. Politics and government 6. United States 7. 20th century 8. Politics and global affairs — Political philosophy
LC 94037270

Argues that global mobility and a refusal to identify with one nation have caused America's professional and managerial elites to betray the ideal of democracy.

Taking aim at the values and beliefs of America's professional and managerial elites, a historian argues that global mobility and refusal to identify with one nation has caused them to betray the idea of democracy for all Americans.

Includes bibliographical references (p. 247-260) and index.

Mead, Margaret
Coming of Age in Samoa: A Psychological Study of Primitive Youth for Western Civilisation. Margaret Mead. Perennial Classics 2001. xxviii, 223 p.
ISBN 9780688050337
Grades: Adult   306
1. Samoan people 2. Girls 3. Children 4. Adolescence 5. Psychology 6. Samoan Islands 7. Society and culture — General
LC 00057528

The classic anthropological study describes what it was like in the 1920s for girls growing up in the primitive culture of the Samoan Islands, offering provocative insights into such topics as childhood, gender roles, and culture.

Includes index; Originally published: William Morrow and Co, 1930.

306.0952 Japan — culture

Alt, Matt
Pure Invention: How Japan's Pop Culture Conquered the World. Matt Alt. Crown 2020. 352 p.
ISBN 9781984826695
Grades: Adult   306.0952
1. Amusements 2. Toy industry and trade 3. Video games industry and trade 4. Recession (Economics) 5. Influence (Literary, artistic, etc.) 6. Animated films 7. Popular culture 8. Civilization 9. Japan 10. 20th century 11. Society and culture — Pop culture 12. Society and culture — Ethnic studies 13. History writing — Asia — Japan
LC 2020007250

The Walkman. Karaoke. Pikachu. Pac-Man. Akira. Emoji. We've all fallen in love with one or another of Japan's pop-culture creations, from the techy to the wild to the super-kawaii. But as Japanese media veteran Matt Alt proves in this brilliant investigation of Tokyo's pop-fantasy complex, we don't know the half of it. Japan's toys, gadgets, and imaginary worlds didn't merely entertain. They profoundly transformed the way we live.

"A nerd- and generalist-friendly look at how Japan shaped the post-World War II world, from toys to Trump." —*Kirkus*

Includes bibliographical references and index.

306.0956 Culture — Middle East

Shadid, Anthony
House of Stone: A Saga of Home, Family, and a Lost Middle East. Anthony Shadid. Houghton Mifflin Harcourt 2012. 256 p.
ISBN 9780547134666
Grades: Adult   306.0956
1. Home (Concept) 2. Building conservation and restoration 3. Immigrants 4. Identity 5. Family relationships 6. Houses 7. Lebanon 8. Southwest Asia and North Africa (Middle East) 9. Travel Writing — Living Abroad 10. Travel Writing — Southwest Asia and North Africa (Middle East) 11. History writing — Nationalism — Southwest Asia and North Africa (Middle East)
LC 2011036906

National Book Critics Circle Award for Autobiography/Memoir finalist; National Book Award for Nonfiction finalist, 2012.

A two-time Pulitzer Prize winner who was one of the four New York Times reporters to be captured and freed in Libya traces the story of his family's effort to rebuild an ancestral home in Lebanon amid political strife and how the work enabled a greater understanding of the emotions behind Middle East turbulence.

306.0973 Culture — United States

Brill, Steven
Tailspin: The People and Forces Behind America's Fifty-year Fall—and Those Fighting to Reverse It. Steven Brill. Alfred A. Knopf 2018. 352 p.
ISBN 9781524731632
Grades: Adult   306.0973
1. Social change 2. Political culture 3. Equality 4. Democracy 5. Politics and government 6. United States 7. 20th century 8. 21st century 9. Politics and global affairs — World politics — United States

ESSENTIAL AND RECOMMENDED TITLES
306.20951 Politics — China

LC 2017051857

The award-winning journalist and best-selling author of America's Bitter Pill explores the reasons why major American institutions are no longer able to function as intended and are triggering deep economic divides, in a sobering report that also traces the stories of individuals and organizations who are laying the foundations for sustainable change.

"He brings both detailed reporting and wide-ranging perspective to this insightful account of how America reached its current state."—*Publishers Weekly*

Includes bibliographical references.

Fallows, James M.
Our Towns: A 100,000-mile Journey into the Heart of America. James Fallows and Deborah Fallows. Pantheon 2018. 320 p.
ISBN 9781101871843
Grades: Adult   306.0973
1. Fallows, James M, 1949- 2. Fallows, Deborah 3. Social surveys 4. Voyages and travels 5. Politics and government 6. Public opinion 7. United States 8. Page to screen 9. Travel writing — United States

LC 2017052007

A portrait of the civil and economic renewal currently underway in American towns and under the radar of the media draws on the authors' visits with the nation's civic leaders, factory workers, recent immigrants and young entrepreneurs, who are observing and understanding the beginnings of important transitional dynamics and opportunities.

"With a commitment to observation and a sincere desire to understand each place on their journey, they offer a fascinating review of the many economic, environmental, educational, and cultural efforts taking place all over America. Far from the national narrative of crisis and decay, the authors suggest that a more hopeful renewal may be under way." —*Booklist*

Made into a movie of the same name in 2021.

Klein, Ezra
★ *Why We're Polarized.* Ezra Klein. Avid Reader Press 2020. xxiii, 312 pages : Illustration
ISBN 9781476700328
Grades: Adult   306.0973
1. Polarization (Social sciences) 2. Right and left (Political science) 3. Identity 4. Political culture 5. Political parties 6. Political participation 7. Politics and government 8. United States 9. 21st century 10. Politics and global affairs — Political parties

LC 2020276252

A journalist, political commentator and cofounder of VOX explains how today's rigidly partisan politics came to be, why we all participate in it and what it means for America's future.

"With YA crossover appeal, Klein's accessible work is for anyone wondering how we got here; it shows how understanding history can help us plan for the future." —*Library Journal*

Includes bibliographical references and index.

Klosterman, Chuck
★ *The Nineties: A Book.* Chuck Klosterman. Penguin Press 2022. 400 p.
ISBN 9780735217959
Grades: Adult   306.0973
1. Popular culture 2. Social change 3. Social life and customs 4. United States history 5. 1990s 6. 20th century 7. Essays 8. Society and culture — Pop culture 9. History writing — 1990s — United States

Discussing everything nineties, including film, music, sports, TV, politics, changes regarding race and class and sexuality, a New York Times bestselling author shows how this decade brought about a revolution in the human condition that we are still groping to understand.

"Wonderfully researched, compellingly written, and often very funny, this is a superb reassessment of an underappreciated decade from a stupendously gifted essayist." —*Booklist*

Kristof, Nicholas D.
★ *Tightrope: Americans Reaching for Hope.* Nicholas D. Kristof, Sheryl Wudunn. Alfred A. Knopf 2020. 304 pages : Illustration
ISBN 9780525655084
Grades: Adult   306.0973
1. Working class 2. Blue collar workers 3. Communities 4. Life expectancy 5. Poverty 6. United States 7. 21st century 8. Society and culture — Wealth and class

LC 2019014592

The Pulitzer Prize-winning authors draw on the true experiences of working-class Americans to outline possible solutions to governmental failures behind rising unemployment, poverty and opioid addiction.

"This essential, clear-eyed account provides worthy solutions to some of America|?'s most complex socioeconomic problems." —*Publishers Weekly*

Includes bibliographical references (pages 273-293) and index.

Menand, Louis
The Free World: Art and Thought in the Cold War. Louis Menand. Farrar, Straus & Giroux 2021. 880 p.
ISBN 9780374158453
Grades: Adult   306.0973
1. Cold War 2. Postwar life 3. Ideology 4. Subcultures 5. Art and society 6. Intellectual life 7. Popular culture 8. Civilization 9. United States history 10. United States 11. 20th century 12. History writing — Cold War 13. History writing — Arts and culture 14. Life stories — Arts and culture

LC 2020050736

A history of the thinkers, writers, and artists who shaped intellectual culture in Cold War Europe and America, this anticipated follow-up to the Metaphysical Club tells the story of American culture in the pivotal years from 1945 to 1970 that shaped our era.

"This sweeping intellectual history examines the flowering of European and American art and thought during the two decades after World War II." —*Library Journal*

Includes bibliographical references and index.

306.20951 Politics — China

Pan, Philip P.
Out of Mao's Shadow. Philip P. Pan. Simon & Schuster 2008. 368 p.
ISBN 9781416537052
Grades: 11 12 Adult   306.20951
1. Democracy 2. International relations 3. Capitalism 4. Politics and culture 5. Chinese history 6. China 7. 20th century 8. 21st century 9. Adult books for young adults 10. History writing — Asia — China

LC 2008011550

A vivid chronicle of the world's most successful authoritarian state. Pan, who reported from China for seven years, eluded the police and succeeded in going where few Western journalists have dared. From the rusting factories in the industrial northeast to a tabloid newsroom in the booming south, from a small-town courtroom to the plush offices of the nation's wealthiest tycoons, he takes us inside the battle for China's soul and into the lives of individuals struggling to come to terms with their nation's past and to take control of its future.

Includes bibliographical references and index.

306.20973 Politics — United States

Bryant, Howard
Full Dissidence: Notes from an Uneven Playing Field. Howard Bryant. Beacon Press 2020. 192 p.
ISBN 9780807019559
Grades: Adult   306.20973
1. Political culture 2. Civil rights 3. Power 4. Political corruption 5. Business and politics 6. Politics and government 7. United States 8. 2010s 9. 2020s 10. Essays 11. Liberal writing 12. Politics and global affairs — Civil and human rights

PUBLIC LIBRARY CORE COLLECTION: NONFICTION
Twentieth Edition

LC 2019026263

An impassioned meditation on injustice in America examines the fundamental inequities behind the country's most divisive issues, explaining how a normalizing of authoritarianism in today's political arenas is undermining freedom and democracy for everyday people.

"Bryant is a masterful writer and a voice of this generation. His passion and analysis on important topics is unparalleled." —*Library Journal*

Includes bibliographical references.

Kornacki, Steve

The Red and the Blue: The 1990s and the Birth of Political Tribalism. Steve Kornacki. Ecco Press 2018. 288 p.

ISBN 9780062438980

Grades: Adult   306.20973

1. Clinton, Bill, 1946- 2. Politicians 3. Political science 4. Political parties 5. Popular culture 6. Presidents 7. Politics and government 8. United States 9. 1990s 10. 20th century 11. 21st century 12. History writing — 1990s — United States 13. Politics and global affairs — Political parties

LC 2018016635

An MSNBC and NBC News national political correspondent presents a history of the 1990s twin paths of Bill Clinton and Newt Gingrich to argue that their rivalry triggered massive policy shifts that reverberate in today's political landscape.

"Now his journalistic prowess is on display in this sharp narrative tracking the steps and missteps over the last quarter-century that brought us to today's combative political stasis." —*Booklist*

Nussbaum, Martha Craven

The Monarchy of Fear: A Philosopher Looks at Our Political Crisis. Martha C. Nussbaum. Simon & Schuster 2018. xviii, 249 pages

ISBN 9781501172496

Grades: Adult   306.20973

1. Presidential election, 2016 2. Divided government 3. Fear 4. Political parties 5. Blame 6. Xenophobia 7. Polarization (Social sciences) 8. Pluralism (Social sciences) 9. Politics and government 10. United States 11. 21st century 12. Politics and global affairs — Political philosophy 13. Society and culture — Psychology and human behavior

The award-winning moral philosopher and author of Upheavals of Thought presents an examination of America's turbulent political environment since the 2016 election, outlining recommendations for how to mend partisan divides.

"Nussbaum's erudite but very readable investigation engages figures from Aristotle to Donald Trump in lucid and engaging prose, though some readers may feel she psychologizes politics without grappling sufficiently with positions' substance. Still, Nussbaum offers fresh, worthwhile insights into the animosities that roil contemporary public life." —*Publishers Weekly*

Includes bibliographical references and index.

Richardson, Heather Cox

★ *How the South Won the Civil War: Oligarchy, Democracy, and the Continuing Fight for the Soul of America.* Heather Cox Richardson. Oxford University Press 2020. xxix, 240 p.

ISBN 9780190900908

Grades: Adult   306.20973

1. Land settlement 2. Elite (Social sciences) 3. Conservatism 4. Inequality 5. Political culture 6. Politics and government 7. Territorial expansion 8. The West (United States) history 9. United States history 10. The West (United States) 11. United States 12. 19th century 13. American Civil War era (1861-1865) 14. History writing — Westward expansion — United States 15. Politics and global affairs — General

LC 2019036155

While in the short term—militarily—the North won the Civil War, in the long term—ideologically—victory went to the South. The continual expansion of the Western frontier allowed a Southern oligarchic ideology to find a new home and take root. Even with the abolition of slavery and the equalizing power of the 13th, 14th, and 15th Amendments, and the ostensible equalizing of economic opportunity afforded by Western expansion, anti-democratic practices were deeply embedded in the country's foundations, in which the rhetoric of equality struggled against the power of money. As the settlers from the East pushed into the West, so too did all of its hierarchies, reinforced by the seizure of Mexican lands at the end of the Mexican-American War and violence toward Native Americans.

"Though Richardson underemphasizes the prevalence of racism, sexism, and inequality in other parts of the country during and following the Civil War, she marshals a wealth of evidence to support the book's provocative title. Conservatives will cry foul, but liberal readers will be persuaded by this lucid jeremiad." —*Publishers Weekly*

Includes bibliographical references and index.

306.3 Economic institutions

Biss, Eula

Having and Being Had. Eula Biss. Riverhead Books 2020. 176 p.

ISBN 9780525537458

Grades: Adult   306.3

1. Leisure 2. Work 3. Quality of life 4. Social classes 5. Social mobility 6. Debt 7. Consumerism 8. Essays 9. Society and culture — Wealth and class 10. Business and economics — Economics — Socioeconomics

LC 2020010815

Having just purchased her first home, the author embarks on a self-audit of the value system she has bought into. The essays in this volume offer an interrogation of work, leisure, and the lived experience of capitalism.

"A typically thoughtful set of Biss essays: Searching, serious, and determined to go beyond the surface." —*Kirkus*

Includes bibliographical references.

Davies, Richard

Extreme Economies: What Life at the World's Margins Can Teach Us About Our Own Future. Richard Davies. Farrar, Straus & Giroux 2020. 304 p.

ISBN 9781250170484

Grades: Adult   306.3

1. Economics 2. Microeconomics 3. Economic forecasting 4. Adaptability 5. Technological innovations 6. Elasticity 7. Inequality 8. Business and economics — Economics — World economy 9. Business and economics — Economics — Socioeconomics

LC Bl2020001098

A leading expert in the field presents an accessible, story-driven look at the future of the global economy in which he revives a foundational idea from medical science to turn the logic of modern economics on its head.

"Highly recommended, sobering reading for anyone interested in the economic future, for good and bad." —*Kirkus*

De Botton, Alain

The Pleasures and Sorrows of Work. Alain de Botton. Pantheon Books 2009. 336 p.

ISBN 9780375424441

Grades: Adult   306.3

1. Work 2. Occupations 3. Human behavior 4. Personal conduct 5. Business 6. Business and economics — Economics — Socioeconomics

LC 2008046060

De Botton is an author of both fiction and non-fiction who has employed a philosophical perspective in this volume to discuss "the joys and perils of the modern workplace." Written for general readers, this volume examines a wide variety of occupations in the fields of art, finance, manufacturing, aviation and science to uncover what makes employment either fulfilling or "soul-destroying." Black-and-white photographs by Richard Baker provide an interesting counterpoint to the text.

"De Botton's sprightly mix of reportage and rumination expands beyond the workplace to investigate the broader meaning of life." —*Publishers Weekly*

Durkin, Hannah

★ *The Survivors of the Clotilda: The Lost Stories of the Last Captives of the American Slave Trade.* Hannah Durkin. [Amistad] 2024. 336 p.

ESSENTIAL AND RECOMMENDED TITLES
306.3 Economic institutions

ISBN 9780063072992
Grades: Adult **306.3**
1. Enslaved people 2. African Americans 3. Slave ships 4. Human trafficking 5. Slave trade 6. West African people 7. Alabama 8. Mobile, Alabama 9. 19th century 10. History writing — African American — Enslavement — United States 11. Society and culture — Race 12. Life stories — People in history 13. Life stories — Facing adversity — War and oppression — Enslaved people
LC 2023040988

Chronicles the history of the Clotilda, the last slave ship to land on U.S. soil, told through the stories of its survivors—the last documented survivors of any slave ship—whose lives diverged and intersected in profound ways.

"A highly recommended sweeping saga. Based on a rich archive that includes the survivors' own stories, this title provides a human history of enslaved people and a portrait of the postbellum South." —*Library Journal*

Includes bibliographical references.

Emberton, Carole
To Walk About in Freedom: The Long Emancipation of Priscilla Joyner. Carole Emberton. W. W. Norton & Company 2022. 256 p.
ISBN 9781324001829
Grades: Adult **306.3**
1. Joyner, Priscilla, 1858-1944 2. Joyner family 3. African American women 4. Multiracial women 5. Freed people 6. North Carolina 7. Virginia 8. Biographies 9. History writing — African American — United States 10. Life stories — People in history 11. Life stories — Facing adversity — War and oppression — Enslaved people
LC 2021050570

Giving us a kaleidoscopic look at the lived experiences of emancipation, and challenging the consequences of failing to reckon with the afterlife of slavery, this candid oral history recounts the story of Priscilla Joyner who embarked on a quest to define freedom after the Civil War.

"Drawing primarily on oral testimonies collected by the Federal Writers' Project in the 1930s, history professor Emberton examines Joyner's complex identity and its relevance to the social history of the Reconstruction and Jim Crow eras." —*Kirkus*

Includes bibliographical references and index.

Feiler, Bruce
★ *The Search: Finding Meaningful Work in a Post-career World.* Bruce Feiler. Penguin Press 2023. 368 p.
ISBN 9780593298916
Grades: Adult **306.3**
1. Quality of work life 2. Work-life balance 3. Personal conduct 4. Success (Concept) 5. United States 6. Business and economics — General 7. Society and culture — Psychology and human behavior
LC 2022049262

A bold new road map for finding meaning and purpose at work, based on insights drawn from hundreds of life stories of Americans from all backgrounds and vocations.

"A useful, insightful guide to anyone who is seeking a more satisfying way to live." —*Kirkus*

Includes bibliographical references and index.

Howard, Jennifer
Clutter: An Untidy History. Jennifer Howard. Belt Publishing 2020. 192 p.
ISBN 9781948742726
Grades: Adult **306.3**
1. Howard, Jennifer (Journalist) 2. Clutter 3. Consumer society 4. Orderliness 5. Organization 6. Materialism 7. Compulsive hoarding 8. Housekeeping 9. Consumerism 10. History writing — General 11. Society and culture — Pop culture 12. Society and culture — Psychology and human behavior

Sparked by the painful two-year process of cleaning out her mother's house in the wake of a devastating physical and emotional collapse, Howard sets her own personal struggle with clutter against a meticulously researched history of just how the developed world came to drown in material goods.

"Howard's exploration of one dark corner of consumer culture is quick-witted and insightful—and, appropriately for the subject, refreshingly concise. . . . A keen assessment of one of society's secret shames and its little-understood consequences." —*Kirkus*

Kars, Marjoleine
Blood on the River: The Untold Story of the Berbice Slave Rebellion: A Chronicle of Mutiny and Freedom on the Wild Coast. Marjoleine Kars. The New Press 2020. 336 p.
ISBN 9781620974599
Grades: Adult **306.3**
1. Enslaved people's resistance and revolts 2. Guerrilla warfare 3. Colonialism 4. Slave trade 5. Slavery 6. Colonists 7. Coffee plantations 8. Sugar plantations 9. Rain forests 10. Indigenous peoples of South America 11. Forced labor 12. Enslaved people 13. African history 14. Guyana 15. 18th century 16. History writing — Wars and conflicts — Revolutions 17. History writing — Latin America 18. History writing — Colonialism — Europe
LC 2019053892

Cundill Prize in History, 2021.

On Sunday, February 27, 1763, thousands of slaves in the Dutch colony of Berbice—in present-day Guyana—launched a massive rebellion which came amazingly close to succeeding. Surrounded by jungle and savannah, the revolutionaries (many of them African-born) and Europeans struck and parried for an entire year. In the end, the Dutch prevailed because of one unique advantage—their ability to get soldiers and supplies from neighboring colonies and from Europe. Blood on the River is the explosive story of this little-known revolution, one that almost changed the face of the Americas.

"A must-read for anyone interested in slave revolts and the history of Atlantic slavery." —*Library Journal*

Includes bibliographical references and index.

Orman, Suze
★ *The Ultimate Retirement Guide for 50+: Winning Strategies to Make Your Money Last a Lifetime.* Suze Orman. Hay House, Inc. 2020. 306 pages
ISBN 9781401959920
Grades: Adult **306.3**
1. Personal finance 2. Social security 3. Retirees 4. Self-help — Career and financial success
LC 2019058229

When you think about planning for retirement-whether it's years in the future or just around the corner-you're bound to have questions. Can I ever afford to stop working? Will Social Security be there for me when I need it? Is the market a safe place for my money? How can I make my money last? Have I waited too long to start saving? Suze Orman, America's most recognized expert on personal finance, answers all the questions that keep you up at night-starting with the biggest one: It is never too late to start planning for a next act that's fulfilling and secure. With her signature blend of compassion, insight, and expertise, Suze guides you toward a plan that will put you in control of your financial future and help you to create the retirement you deserve.

"Recommended reading for all and a solid addition to public library offerings." —*Library Journal*

Includes index.

Rae, Noel
★ *The Great Stain: Witnessing American Slavery.* Noel Rae. Overlook Pr 2018. 624 p.
ISBN 9781468315134
Grades: Adult **306.3**
1. Enslaved people 2. Slaveholders 3. Slavery 4. Slave trade 5. Freed people 6. Exploitation 7. African American history 8. United States history 9. 19th century 10. History books — African Americans — Slavery
LC BI2017051090

Comprising personal accounts from an intensely consequential chapter in human history, the transatlantic slave trade, the Great Stain takes readers from the depths of suffering to the heights of human dignity.

"Highly recommended for U.S. colonial, middle period, and Civil War scholars, and general readers." —*Library Journal*

Rothman, Joshua D.
*The **Ledger** and the Chain: How Domestic Slave Traders Shaped America.* Joshua D. Rothman. Basic Books 2021. 512 p. : Illustration

ISBN 9781541616615

Grades: Adult   306.3

1. Franklin, Isaac, 1789-1846 2. Armfield, John, 1797-1871 3. Ballard, Rice C. (Rice Carter), -1860 4. Slave traders 5. Slavery 6. Slave trade 7. Businesspeople 8. Southern States 9. United States 10. 19th century 11. Collective biographies 12. History writing — African American — Enslavement — United States 13. Life stories — People in history

LC 2020038845

This shocking story of the America's internal slave trade examines how over half a million enslaved people were trafficked by rich and respected businessmen using a combination of entrepreneurial ambition and brutal violence.

"University of Alabama history professor Rothman (Flush Times and Fever Dreams) delivers a harrowing portrait of how the domestic slave trade 'Helped define the financial, political, legal, cultural, and demographic contours' of 19th-century America.... This trenchant study deserves a wide and impassioned readership." —*Publishers Weekly*

Siler, Julia Flynn
*The **White** Devil's Daughters: The Fight Against Slavery in San Francisco's Chinatown.* Julia Flynn Siler. Alfred A. Knopf 2019. 352 p.

ISBN 9781101875261

Grades: Adult   306.3

1. Human trafficking 2. Social work 3. Chinese people in the United States 4. Forced labor 5. Human trafficking victims 6. Women abolitionists 7. Racism 8. Exploitation 9. Chinese people 10. Immigration and emigration 11. San Francisco, California 12. United States 13. History writing — United States

LC 2018039985

A revelatory history of the trafficking of young Asian girls throughout the first century of Chinese immigration in San Francisco shares insights into the activities of the Occidental Mission Home and its work as a refuge for freedom-seeking victims.

"An accessible, well-written, riveting tale of a dismal, little-known corner of American history." —*Kirkus*

This is a Borzoi Book; Includes bibliographical references.

306.36 Systems of labor

Raines, Ben
*The **Last** Slave Ship: The True Story of How Clotilda Was Found, Her Descendants, and an Extraordinary Reckoning.* Ben Raines. Simon & Schuster 2022. 304 p.

ISBN 9781982136048

Grades: Adult   306.36

1. Slavery 2. Slave trade 3. Shipwrecks 4. Ship captains 5. Slave traders 6. Enslaved people 7. African American history 8. Family history 9. Genealogy 10. Race relations 11. Reconciliation 12. United States history 13. Alabama 14. 19th century 15. History writing — African American — Enslavement — United States 16. History writing — Africa 17. Life stories — Facing adversity — War and oppression — Enslaved people 18. Life stories — People in history 19. Nonfiction that reads like fiction

LC 2021042307

The incredible true story of the last ship to carry enslaved people to America, the remarkable town its survivors founded after emancipation, and the complicated legacy their descendants carry with them to this day-by the journalist who discovered the ship's remains.

"Journalist Raines (Saving America's Amazon) unearths in this riveting chronicle the story of the last slave ship to arrive in the U.S.... The result is an evocative and informative tale of exploitation, deceit, and resilience." —*Publishers Weekly*

Includes bibliographical references and index.

306.362 Slavery

McGill, Joseph
Sleeping with the Ancestors: How I Followed the Footprints of Slavery. Joseph McGill, Jr. and Herb Frazier. Hachette Books 2023. 288 p.

ISBN 9780306829666

Grades: Adult   306.362

1. McGill, Joseph, Jr 2. Historians 3. African American history 4. Enslaved people 5. Slavery 6. Houses 7. Historic buildings 8. Historic sites 9. Social history 10. History writing — African American — Enslavement — United States 11. Life stories — Education — Scholars and educators 12. Travel Writing — United States

Joseph McGill Jr, a historic preservationist and Civil War reenactor, founded the Slave Dwelling Project in 2010 based on an idea that was sparked and first developed in 1999. Since founding the project, McGill has been touring the country, spending the night in former slave dwellings—throughout the South, but also the North and the West, where people are often surprised to learn that such structures exist. Events and gatherings are arranged around these overnight stays, and it provides a unique way to understand the often otherwise obscured and distorted history of slavery.

"A thoughtful, deeply humane addition to African American history." —*Kirkus*

Includes bibliographical references and index.

306.4 Specific aspects of culture

Chang, Jeff
Can't Stop, Won't Stop: A History of the Hip-Hop Generation. Jeff Chang; introduction by DJ Kool Herc. Picador 2006. xiii, 546 p. : Illustration

ISBN 9780312425791

Grades: 11 12 Adult   306.4

1. Rap music 2. Hip-hop culture 3. Music and society 4. Music history and criticism 5. Arts and Entertainment — Music — Rap and R&B 6. Adult books for young adults

LC Bl2006001087

A history of hip-hop cites its origins in the post-civil rights Bronx and Jamaica, drawing on interviews with performers, activists, gang members, DJs, and others to document how the movement has influenced politics and culture.

"A fascinating, far-reaching must for pop-music and pop-culture collections." —*Booklist*

Originally published: New York : St. Martin's Press, 2005; Includes bibliographical references, discography, filmography, and index.

Charnas, Dan
*The **Big** Payback: The History of the Business of Hip-Hop.* Dan Charnas. New American Library 2010. 352 p.

ISBN 9780451229298

Grades: Adult   306.4

1. Rap music 2. Sound recording industry and trade 3. Rap music industry and trade 4. Music industry and trade 5. Hip-hop culture 6. Arts and Entertainment — Music — Rap and R&B 7. Business and economics — Industries — Entertainment and media

LC 2010016062

Draws on the stories of three hundred industry veterans to chronicle hip-hop's rise from street culture to global industry, tallying who won, who lost, and who was on the cutting edge.

Includes index.

Ekirch, A. Roger
★ *At **Day's** Close: Night in Times Past.* A. Roger Ekirch. Norton 2005. xxxii, 447 p. : Illustration; Color

ISBN 9780393050899

Grades: Adult   306.4

1. Social history 2. Night 3. History writing — Microhistory

LC 2005002784

ESSENTIAL AND RECOMMENDED TITLES
306.4 Specific aspects of culture

A portrait of how people lived in the pre-industrial age describes how a lack of electric lighting separated daytime and evening into more contrasting worlds, explaining how superstition, work, fire, crime, religion, slavery, and other factors were different before the advent of electric lighting.

"This history finds Ekirch reminding us of how preindustrial Westerners lived during the nocturnal hours, when most were plunged into almost total darkness. A rich weave of citation and archival evidence, Ekirch's narrative is rooted in the material realities of the past, evoking a bygone world of extreme physicality and preindustrial survival stratagems." —*Publishers Weekly*

Includes bibliographical references (p. [341]-414) and index.

Fadiman, Anne
*The **Spirit** Catches You and You Fall Down: A Hmong Child, Her American Doctors, and the Collision of Two Cultures*. Anne Fadiman. Farrar, Straus, and Giroux 1997. xi, 339 p.
ISBN 9780374267810
Grades: 11 12 Adult   306.4
1. Cultural differences 2. Hmong Americans 3. Intercultural communication 4. Children with epilepsy 5. Medical care 6. California 7. 20th century 8. Science Writing — Medicine and health — Illness and disease
LC 97005175
Los Angeles Times Book Prize for Current Interest, 1997; National Book Critics Circle Award for Non-Fiction, 1997; New York Times Notable Book, 1997.

A study in the collision between Western medicine and the beliefs of a traditional culture focuses on a hospitalized child of Laotian immigrants, members of the Hmong tribe, whose belief that illness is a spiritual matter came into conflict with doctors' methods.

"Fadiman reveals the rigidity and weaknesses of these two ethnographically separated cultures. In a shrinking world, this painstakingly researched account of cultural dislocation has a haunting lesson for every healthcare provider." —*Library Journal*

Includes bibliographical references (p. [311]-324) and index.

King, Chrissy
*The **Body** Liberation Project: How Understanding Racism and Diet Culture Helps Cultivate Joy and Build Collective Freedom*. Chrissy King. Tiny Reparations Books 2023. x, 303 pages
ISBN 9780593187043
Grades: Adult   306.4
1. Body image 2. African American women 3. Self-acceptance 4. Racism 5. Social justice 6. Diet industry and trade 7. Autobiographies and memoirs 8. Self-Help — Personal growth 9. Society and culture — Gender — Women 10. Society and culture — Race
LC 2022040224

From an author and Instagram personality comes a narrative mix of memoir, inspiration and specific exercises and prompts, with timely messages about social and racial justice, and how the world needs to move beyond body positivity to something even more exciting and revolutionary—body liberation.

"Readers who are already familiar with these concepts may find the book too simplistic and repetitive, but many will likely find it interesting and helpful." —*Library Journal*

Includes bibliographical references (pages 293-303).

Kneeland, Jessi
Body Neutral: A Revolutionary Guide to Overcoming Body Image Issues. Jessi Kneeland. Penguin Books, an imprint of Penguin Random House LLC 2023. 421 pages
ISBN 9780593491768
Grades: Adult   306.4
1. Body image 2. Beauty 3. Self-esteem 4. Identity 5. Self-Help — Personal growth — Self-esteem
LC 2022051181

A coach, writer, and speaker dedicated to helping people overcome the suffering associated with body anxiety teaches readers how to develop the ability to accept and respect your body, even if it isn't the way you'd prefer it to be.

"Kneeland outlines an inclusive attitude toward self-acceptance aimed at readers of all races and gender identities, and the advice is informed without getting preachy." —*Publishers Weekly*

A Penguin Life book—Copyright page; Includes bibliographical references (pages 405-421).

Kugel, Seth
Rediscovering Travel: A Guide for the Globally Curious. Seth Kugel. Liveright Publishing Corporation 2018. 320 p.
ISBN 9780871408501
Grades: Adult   306.4
1. Kugel, Seth 2. Tourism 3. Vacations 4. Misadventures 5. Adventurers 6. Self-discovery 7. Recreation industry and trade 8. Voyages and travels 9. Travel Writing — General 10. Adult books for young adults

The former New York Times "Frugal Traveler" columnist and host of "Amigo Gringo" challenges the practices of the modern travel industry while sharing stories of memorable discoveries and misadventures that demonstrate how to enjoy a technology-balanced vacation.

Includes bibliographical references.

Langlands, Alex
Cræft: An Inquiry into the Origins and True Meaning of Traditional Crafts. Alexander Langlands. W. W. Norton & Company 2018. 336 p.
ISBN 9780393635904
Grades: Adult   306.4
1. Material culture 2. Artisans 3. Handicraft 4. Consumerism 5. Antiquities, Prehistoric 6. Arts and Entertainment — Crafts and hobbies 7. History writing — General
LC 2017047723

An archaeologist takes us into the ancient world of traditional crafts to uncover their deep, original histories.

"Langlands offers a fascinating history of whats setting trends today." —*Booklist*

Includes index.

Teng, Tara
★ *Your Body Is a Revolution: Healing Our Relationships with Our Bodies, Each Other, and the Earth*. Tara Teng. Broadleaf Books 2023. 208 pages
ISBN 9781506483788
Grades: Adult   306.4
1. Body image 2. Self-acceptance 3. Mind and body 4. Body awareness 5. Self-Help — Personal growth — Self-esteem 6. Spirituality and Religion — Body, mind, and spirit
LC Bl2023015106

Embodiment coach Tara Teng helps us untangle ourselves from centuries of body-based oppression built into our societal systems or masquerading as religion. When we embrace our relationship with our bodies, we come into alignment with all things: ourselves, each other, the earth, and our spirituality. When we embrace ourselves, we can take back what society says is too much—too loud, too feminine, too masculine, too gay, too worldly, too unique. Now is the time to journey back to our bodies and to celebrate our whole selves."

"Readers searching for a community-minded self-help title will enjoy this book, a refreshing, compassionate addition to the health and wellness space." —*Library Journal*

Includes bibliographical references (pages 203-208).

Winchester, Simon
Knowing What We Know: The Transmission of Knowledge: From Ancient Wisdom to Modern Magic. Simon Winchester. HarperCollins 2023. 464 p.
ISBN 9780063142886
Grades: Adult   306.4
1. Knowledge 2. Knowledge management 3. Civilization 4. Information management 5. History Writing — General

Examining such disciplines as education, journalist, encyclopedia creation, museum curation, photography and broadcasting, an award-winning writer explores how humans have attained, stored and disseminated knowledge and how continues to change our lives and our minds.

"Prolific historian Winchester brings his insatiable curiosity to a wide-ranging examination of how humans have acquired, retained, and passed on knowledge from ancient times to the information-saturated present." —*Kirkus*

306.43 Education

Kamenetz, Anya
The Stolen Year: How Covid Changed Children's Lives, and Where We Go Now. Anya Kamenetz. PublicAffairs 2022. 288 p.
ISBN 9781541700987
Grades: Adult   306.43
1. Education 2. COVID-19 Pandemic, 2020- 3. Children 4. Child welfare 5. Educational sociology 6. 21st century 7. Society and culture — Education
LC 2022001106

An NPR education reporter shows how the last true social safety net—the public school system—was decimated by the pandemic and how the roots of this crisis run far deeper than COVID, delving into the political history that brought us to this point.

"Striking an expert balance between the big picture and intimate profiles of students, teachers, parents, and school officials, this is an astute and vital first draft of history." —*Publishers Weekly*

306.44 Language

Perlin, Ross
★ *Language* City: The Fight to Preserve Endangered Mother Tongues in New York. Ross Perlin. Atlantic Monthly Press 2023. 432 p.
ISBN 9780802162465
Grades: Adult   306.44
1. Language and languages 2. Linguistics 3. Culture 4. Language policy 5. Immigrants 6. Language revival 7. New York City 8. History writing — Arts and culture 9. Society and culture — Urban and regional studies 10. Society and culture — Immigration

The linguist and co-director of the Endangered Language Alliance discusses his efforts to map little-known languages across the city of New York—the most linguistically diverse places that has ever existed—before they become extinct.

"The result is an immersive meander through N.Y.C.'s past and present that brings to the fore its multitudinous nature." —*Publishers Weekly*

306.7 Sexual relations

Cole, Samantha
How the Internet Changed Sex and Sex Changed the Internet: A History. Samantha Cole. Workman Pub. 2022. 256 p.
ISBN 9781523513840
Grades: Adult   306.7
1. Sexuality 2. Internet 3. Internet users 4. Dating 5. Online dating 6. Privacy rights 7. Data mining 8. Society and culture — Media and technology 9. Science Writing — Computing, the Internet, and Technology

This history of the development of sex and sexuality on the internet illustrates how it has informed issues we commonly face such as free speech, privacy, online banking, dating and data mining.

"This book is perfect for readers interested in how society reached the point it is at today with the internet and sex and the issues that have emerged." —*Library Journal*

Williams, Florence
Heartbreak: A Personal and Scientific Journey. Florence Williams. W.W. Norton & Company 2022. 320 p.
ISBN 9781324003489
Grades: Adult   306.7
1. Williams, Florence, 1967- 2. Journalists 3. Separation 4. Loss 5. Marriage 6. Divorce 7. Grief 8. Interpersonal relations 9. Women 10. Psychology 11. Men-women relations 12. Autobiographies and memoirs 13. Family and Relationships — General 14. Life stories — Relationships 15. Science Writing — Biology
LC 2021045264

After her 25-year marriage ends, a journalist reveals her personal insights and explores the cutting edge science of "social pain," including checking her blood for grief markers and receiving electrical shocks, to explain why heartbreak hurts so much.

"Much has been written about the science of falling in love, but very little about what happens on the other side,' writes journalist Williams (The Nature Fix) in this show-stopping, offbeat story about the science of heartbreak. . . . This is a courageous, whirlwind tale of healing and self-discovery." —*Publishers Weekly*

Includes bibliographical references.

306.7082 Women — Sexual relations

Taddeo, Lisa
Three Women. Lisa Taddeo. Avid Reader Press 2019. 306 p.
ISBN 9781451642292
Grades: Adult   306.7082
1. Desire 2. Intimacy 3. Women 4. Sexuality 5. Men-women relations 6. Social life and customs 7. United States 8. Society and culture — Sex and sexuality 9. Society and culture — Gender — Women 10. Book club best bets
LC 2018045846

British Book Award for Narrative Nonfiction of the Year, 2020; Loan Stars Favourites, 2019.

An account based on nearly a decade of reporting examines the sex lives of three American women, exploring the complexity and fragility of female desire.

"Dramatic, immersive, and wanting—much like desire itself." —*Kirkus*

306.73 General institutions

Hoffman, Damona
F the Fairy Tale: Rewrite the Dating Myths and Live Your Own Love Story. Damona Hoffman. Seal Press 2024. VIII, 295 pages
ISBN 9781541602250
Grades: Adult   306.73
1. Dating 2. Romantic love 3. Interpersonal relations 4. Self-Help — Relationships 5. Family and Relationships — Dating and Marriage
LC 2023027850

The celebrity dating coach and award-winning podcast coach dismantles long-held myths that can prevent finding lasting love and provides ways to escape ideas such as instant love and finding "the One."

"Those who've grown sick of aimlessly swiping will find hope." —*Publishers Weekly*

Includes bibliographical references (pages 275-278) and index.

Rallo, Eli
I Didn't Know I Needed This: The New Rules for Flirting, Feeling, and Finding Yourself. Eli Rallo. Harvest 2023. 288 p.
ISBN 9780063298460
Grades: Adult   306.73
1. Rallo, Eli 2. Dating 3. Flirtation 4. Couples 5. Men-women relations 6. Autobiographies and memoirs 7. Life stories — Relationships — Couples 8. Family and Relationships — Dating and Marriage
LC 2023033356

A social media star and podcaster presents a humorous and honest take on modern dating and offers tips and tricks for going on dates, falling in love and managing relationships from having sex to experience heartbreak.

"Rallo's assured voice and solid counsel carries this through. Those able to see the humor in heartache will be gratified." —*Publishers Weekly*

ESSENTIAL AND RECOMMENDED TITLES
306.74 Prostitution

306.74 Prostitution

Ditmore, Melissa Hope
★ *Unbroken* Chains: The Hidden Role of Human Trafficking in the American Economy. Melissa Hope Ditmore. Beacon Press 2023. xiv, 225 p.
ISBN 9780807006771
Grades: Adult   **306.74**
1. Human trafficking 2. Human trafficking victims 3. Forced labor 4. Labor exploitation 5. Immigration and emigration 6. Prostitution 7. Agriculture 8. Factories 9. Humanitarian assistance 10. Economics 11. United States 12. Society and culture — Violence and crime 13. Business and economics — Corruption and scandal 14. Business and economics — Economics — Contemporary U.S. economy
LC 2022053695

An urgent exposition of the pervasive human trafficking that lies just beneath the surface of the US economy—from the stories of its survivors.

The years of the COVID-19 pandemic have brought to light the exploitation of workers. In this moment of heightened visibility, Unbroken Chains demands that readers examine the hidden sector of American trafficked labor and understand its prevalence across our economy. Drawing from nearly two decades of research on US and international human trafficking, Melissa Hope Ditmore sets forth the harrowing stories of human trafficking survivors and grounds their accounts in the long history of US indentured servitude, looking to its iterations in chattel slavery, Chinese contract labor, and prison labor.

"Ditmore effectively shows how the stigma of sex work and an unwillingness to listen to survivors makes it harder for trafficked workers—including those trafficked into sex work—to get help. A stirring and compassionate book." —*Booklist*

Includes bibliographical references and index.

306.74082 Women

Moran, Rachel
Paid For: My Journey Through Prostitution. Rachel Moran. W.W. Norton & Company, Inc. 2015. 304 p.
ISBN 9780393351972
Grades: Adult   **306.74082**
1. Moran, Rachel 2. Prostitutes 3. Prostitution 4. Gender role 5. Ireland 6. Autobiographies and memoirs 7. Society and culture — Sex and sexuality — Sex industry 8. Life stories — Facing adversity
LC 2015009736

A former teen prostitute describes the fears she and others had working on the streets and in brothels and speaks to the psychological damage that accompanies prostitution and the estrangement from one's body.

"Moran's thoughtful, highly readable, and provocative treatise shines a necessary light on a dark and underdiscussed topic." —*Kirkus*

306.76 Sexual orientation, transgender identity, intersexuality

Arceneaux, Michael
I Finally Bought Some Jordans: Essays. Michael Arceneaux. HarperOne 2024. 304 p.
ISBN 9780063140417
Grades: Adult   **306.76**
1. African Americans 2. Creativity 3. Dating 4. Social media 5. Home (Concept) 6. African American gay men 7. COVID-19 Pandemic, 2020- 8. Family relationships 9. African American men 10. Millennials 11. City life 12. Social life and customs 13. Identity 14. Essays 15. Humor writing — General

A New York Times best-selling author returns with a humorous collection of essays about making your voice heard in an increasingly noisy and chaotic world.

"Arceneaux's (I Don't Want to Die Poor, 2020) third compendium of essays is his keenest and best yet, informed by the clarity of priorities that comes with making art in our era of public health disaster and racial reckoning." —*Booklist*

Bronski, Michael
A Queer History of the United States. by Michael Bronski. Beacon Press 2011. 288 p.
ISBN 9780807044391
Grades: Adult   **306.76**
1. Gay men 2. Lesbians 3. Homosexuality 4. Social life and customs 5. United States 6. History writing — LGBTQIA+ 7. History writing — United States 8. Society and culture — LGBTQIA+
LC 2010050225

Lambda Literary Award, 2011; Stonewall Book Award for the Israel Fishman Non-fiction Award, 2012.

A Queer History of the United States is groundbreaking and accessible. It looks at how American culture has shaped the LGBT, or queer, experience, while simultaneously arguing that LGBT people not only shaped but were pivotal in creating our country. Using numerous primary documents and literature, as well as social histories, Bronski's book takes the reader through the centuries—from Columbus' arrival and the brutal treatment the Native peoples received, through the American Revolution's radical challenging of sex and gender roles—to the violent, and liberating, 19th century—and the transformative social justice movements of the 20th. Bronski's book is filled with startling examples of often ignored or unknown aspects of American history: the ineffectiveness of sodomy laws in the colonies, the prevalence of cross-dressing women soldiers in the Civil War, the effect of new technologies on LGBT life in the 19th century, and how rock music and popular culture were, in large part, responsible for the great backlash against gay rights in the late 1970s. More than anything, a Queer History of the United States is not so much about queer history as it is about all American history—and why it should matter to both LGBT people and heterosexuals alike.

"This enthralling history spans 500 years of evolving perspectives on sexuality in Americafrom the European settlers' violent responses to the more fluid gender roles of Native Americans to how the birth control pill, which separated sex from reproduction, contributed to the cause of LGBT liberation. A savvy political, legal, literary (and even fashion) history, Bronski's narrative is as intellectually rigorous as it is entertaining." —*Publishers Weekly*

Includes bibliographical references and index.

Carter, David
Stonewall: The Riots That Sparked the Gay Revolution. David Carter. St. Martin's Griffin 2010. 336 p. : Illustration; Map
ISBN 9780312671938
Grades: Adult   **306.76**
1. Stonewall Riots, New York, N.Y, 1969 2. Gay and Lesbian Movement 3. Gay men 4. Lesbians 5. LGBTQIA+ rights 6. Organized crime 7. New York City history 8. Greenwich Village, New York City 9. New York City 10. United States 11. 20th century 12. History writing — 1960s — United States 13. History writing — LGBTQIA+ 14. Society and culture — LGBTQIA+

An examination of the 1969 series of riots over police action against the Stonewall Inn provides a background of the mob-controlled Greenwich Village gay bar, the political and social elements that contributed to the riots, and the event's impact on subsequent attitudes.

"The author depicts the Stonewall riots as a unique convergence of time, place, and circumstance and performs some gentle revisionism on the received version of events, emphasizing the contributions of lesbians and street youth while downplaying, but not discounting, the role of drag queens." —*Library Journal*

Includes bibliographical references (p. [277]-317) and index; Originally published: New York : St. Martin's Press, 2004.

Hester, Diarmuid
Nothing Ever Just Disappears: Seven Hidden Queer Histories. Diarmuid Hester. Pegasus Books 2024. 368 p.
ISBN 9781639365555
Grades: Adult   **306.76**
1. LGBTQIA+ people 2. Artists 3. Authors 4. Intellectuals 5. Place (Philosophy) 6. Queer theory 7. Social marginality 8. Gay men 9. Lesbians 10. Transgender people 11. Gender identity 12. Feminism 13. Freedom 14. Cre-

activity 15. History 16. 20th century 17. History writing — LGBTQIA+ 18. Society and culture — LGBTQIA+ 19. Life stories — Arts and culture 20. Life stories — Identity — LGBTQIA+

Nothing Ever Just Disappears brings to life the stories of seven remarkable figures and illuminates the connections between where they lived, who they loved, and the art they created. It shows that a queer sense of place is central to the history of the twentieth century and powerfully evokes how much is lost when queer spaces are forgotten. From the suffragettes in London and James Baldwin's home in Provence, to Kevin Killian's San Francisco and Derek Jarman's cottage in Kent, this is both a thrilling new literary history and a celebration of freedom, survival, and the hidden places of the imagination.

"The result is a scintillating investigation of the intersection between environment, creativity, and identity." —*Publishers Weekly*

Originally published in the UK by Allen Lane, London, in 2023.

Olsen, Craig

P.S. Burn This Letter Please: The Fabulous and Fraught Birth of Modern Drag, in the Queens' Own Words. Craig Olsen. Sphere 2023. 224 pages

ISBN 9780751585940

Grades: Adult **306.76**

1. Drag queens 2. Gay communities 3. Social life and customs 4. Social history 5. New York City 6. 1950s 7. 1960s 8. Letters 9. History writing — LGBTQIA+ 10. History writing — United States 11. Life stories — Identity — LGBTQIA+ 12. Society and culture — Gender 13. Society and culture — LGBTQIA+

In 1950s New York, a group of drag pioneers found work in a small number of Lower East Side clubs. They occupied the margins of society, determined to live authentically, despite the attentions of the police. These girls were unstoppable, fearless and fabulous, but their very existence was deemed a criminal threat to society. When a secret cache of their letters was discovered in 2014, these individuals were given a voice for the first time. The letters reveal personal triumphs and tragedies, and a fascinating world that has rarely been documented. Expertly weaving social, political and cultural history, Craig Olsen illuminates the lives and loves of our exceptional LGBTQ+ forebears.

"This charming account combines the poignancy of a coming-of-age narrative, the mordant humor of a gossip column, and the rigor of an archival investigation. It's an essential window into a long-hidden history." —*Publishers Weekly*

Shaw, Julia

Bi: The Hidden Culture, History, and Science of Bisexuality. Julia Shaw. Abrams Press 2022. 304 p.

ISBN 9781419744358

Grades: Adult **306.76**

1. Bisexuality 2. Bisexual people 3. Sexual orientation 4. Sexuality 5. Identity 6. Discrimination 7. Gender Identity 8. Nonconformity 9. Canadian literature 10. Society and culture — LGBTQIA+ 11. Society and culture — Sex and sexuality 12. History writing — LGBTQIA+

An internationally known pop-psychologist and vocal bisexual takes a provocative look at the science of sexuality and examines the culture of attraction beyond the binary choice of homosexuality vs. heterosexuality.

"Forthright and empowering, this is a call for understanding and supporting bisexuality." —*Booklist*

306.77 Sexual and related practices

Burke, Kelsy

The Pornography Wars: The Past, Present, and Future of America's Obscene Obsession. Kelsy Burke. Bloomsbury Publishing Place USA 2022. 304 p.

ISBN 9781635577365

Grades: Adult **306.77**

1. Pornography 2. Sex industry and trade 3. Pornography and society 4. Pornographic film industry and trade 5. Social life and customs 6. United States 7. Impartial writing 8. Society and culture — Sex and sexuality — Sex industry

An authoritative, big-think look at pornography in all its facets—historical, religious, and cultural.

"A mature, thoughtful book about a complex and divisive topic. No matter their personal opinions, readers will likely find observations here to inform their thoughts about pornography's creation and consumption." —*Library Journal*

306.81 Marriage and marital status

Havrilesky, Heather

Foreverland: On the Divine Tedium of Marriage. Heather Havrilesky. Ecco Press 2022. 304 p.

ISBN 9780062984463

Grades: Adult **306.81**

1. Havrilesky, Heather 2. Advice columnists 3. Married women 4. Marriage 5. Romantic love 6. Family relationships 7. Autobiographies and memoirs 8. Life stories — Relationships — Couples 9. Family and Relationships — Dating and Marriage 10. Book club best bets

LC 2021036814

If falling in love is the peak of human experience, then marriage is the slow descent down that mountain, on a trail built from conflict, compromise, and nagging doubts. Considering the limited economic advantages to marriage, the deluge of other mate options a swipe away, and the fact that almost half of all marriages in the United States end in divorce anyway, why do so many of us still chain ourselves to one human being for life? in Foreverland, Heather Havrilesky illustrates the delights, aggravations, and sublime calamities of her marriage over the span of fifteen years, charting an unpredictable course from meeting her one true love to slowly learning just how much energy is required to keep that love aflame. This refreshingly honest portrait of a marriage reveals that our relationships are not simply "happy" or "unhappy," but something much murkier—at once unsavory, taxing, and deeply satisfying.

"Havrilesky successfully provides ample opportunities for readers to laugh, commiserate, and critique, regardless of their phase in life or marital status. A welcome addition to memoir and women's studies collections." —*Library Journal*

306.85 Family

Berger, Lynn

Second Thoughts: On Having and Being a Second Child. Lynn Berger; Translated by Anna Asbury. Henry Holt & Company 2021. 208 p.

ISBN 9781250787866

Grades: Adult **306.85**

1. Berger, Lynn, 1984- 2. Second-born children 3. Pregnancy 4. Siblings 5. Families 6. Motherhood 7. Parenthood 8. Sibling rivalry 9. Family relationships 10. Parenting 11. Autobiographies and memoirs 12. Translations — Dutch to English 13. Life stories — Relationships — Parent and child 14. Family and Relationships — Parenting 15. Family and Relationships — Siblings

LC 2020039712

A lovely, searching meditation on second children-on whether to have one and what it means to be one-that seamlessly weaves pieces of art and culture on the topic with scientific research and personal anecdotes.

"Recommended for parents contemplating a second or third child, as well as readers interested in family dynamics." —*Library Journal*

Includes bibliographical references; Translated from the Dutch.

Lewis, Oscar

The Children of Sanchez: Autobiography of a Mexican Family. Oscar Lewis. Vintage Books 2011. xliii, 505 p.

ISBN 9780307744531

Grades: 11 12 Adult **306.85**

1. Families 2. Poor people 3. Family relationships 4. Poverty 5. Mexico City, Mexico 6. Autobiographies and memoirs 7. Family and Relationships — Families 8. Life stories — Relationships — Family 9. Society and culture — Wealth and class — Poverty

LC 2011292807

ESSENTIAL AND RECOMMENDED TITLES
306.850947 Family — Russia

If you want to know how the locals live, you hang out with them. To really get to know them, you hang out a lot. So, that's what author Oscar Lewis did. Though not a travelogue, his very readable the Children of Sanchez is an "anthropological classic" (The Los Angeles Times) that profiles a slum-dwelling Mexico City widower and his troubled adult children. Just seven years after this book was published, Mexico City became, in 1968, the first Spanish-speaking country to host the Summer Olympics.

O'Donnell Heffington, Peggy
Without Children: The Long History of Not Being a Mother. Peggy O'Donnell Heffington. Seal Press 2023. 304 p.
ISBN 9781541675575
Grades: Adult   306.85
1. Childlessness 2. Gender role 3. Women 4. Femininity 5. Motherhood 6. Interpersonal relations 7. History Writing — Women's history 8. Society and culture — Gender — Women
LC 2022045141

In an era of falling births, it's often said that millennials invented the idea of not having kids. But history is full of women without children: Some who chose childless lives, others who wanted children but never had them, and still others—the vast majority, then and now—who fell somewhere in between. Modern women considering how and if children fit into their lives are products of their political, ecological, and cultural moment. But history also tells them that they are not alone.

"A liberatingly perceptive work of sociology and cultural history." —*Kirkus*
Includes bibliographical references and index.

Streep, Abe
Brothers on Three: A True Story of Family, Resistance, and Hope on a Reservation in Montana. Abe Streep. Celadon Books 2021. VIII, 349 p.
ISBN 9781250210685
Grades: Adult   306.85
1. High school basketball players 2. Small towns 3. Indigenous reservations 4. Poverty 5. Addiction 6. Racism 7. Psychic trauma 8. Teenage boys 9. Indigenous teenagers 10. Family relationships 11. Salish (North American people) 12. Kootenai (Ktunaxa) (North American people) 13. Indigenous peoples of North America 14. Winning and losing 15. Basketball 16. Basketball players 17. Basketball teams 18. Intergenerational trauma 19. Montana 20. Sports and Competition — Basketball 21. Sports and Competition — Teams 22. Life stories — Identity — Race and ethnicity 23. Life stories — Sports 24. Society and culture — Urban and regional studies
LC 2021015634
Montana Book Award, 2021.

From journalist Abe Streep, the story of coming of age on a reservation in the American West and a team uniting a community. March 11, 2017, was a night to remember: in front of the hopeful eyes of thousands of friends, family members, and fans, the Arlee Warriors would finally bring the high school basketball state championship title home to the Flathead Indian Reservation. The game would become the stuff of legend, with the boys revered as local heroes. The team's place in Montana history was now cemented, but for starters Will Mesteth, Jr. and Phillip Malatare, life would keep moving on—senior year was only just beginning. In Brothers on Three, we follow Phil and Will, along with their teammates, coaches, and families, as they balance the pressures of adolescence, shoulder the dreams of their community, and chart their own individual courses for the future.

"In addition to being great sports journalism that will touch anyone who loves high school sports, Streep's book will appeal to readers interested in histories of generational trauma." —*Library Journal*
Includes bibliographical references.

306.850947 Family — Russia

Figes, Orlando
★ *The Whisperers: Private Life in Stalin's Russia.* Orlando Figes. Metropolitan Books 2007. 784 p.
ISBN 9780805074611
Grades: Adult   306.850947
1. Stalinism 2. Informers 3. Nationalism 4. City life 5. Communism 6. Soviet Union history 7. Soviet Union 8. 20th century 9. History writing — Communism — Europe — Russia
LC 2007024223
New York Times Notable Book, 2007.

Provides a portrait of everyday Russian life during the repression of the Stalin years, analyzing the regime's effect on people's personal lives as they struggled to survive in the middle of the fear, mistrust, betrayal, and compromise of the world in which they lived.

"This is a humbling monument to the evil and endurance of Russia's Soviet past and, implicitly, a guide to its present." —*The Economist*
Includes bibliographical references and index.

306.87 Intrafamily relationships

Berg, Anastasia
★ *What Are Children For?: On Ambivalence and Choice.* Anastasia Berg and Rachel Wiseman. St Martins Press 2024. 304 p.
ISBN 9781250276131
Grades: Adult   306.87
1. Parenthood 2. Pregnancy 3. Ambivalence 4. Uncertainty 5. Motherhood 6. Women's role 7. Options, alternatives, choices 8. Decision-making 9. Essays 10. Family and Relationships — Parenting 11. Society and culture — Gender — Women

A modern argument, grounded in philosophy and cultural criticism, about childbearing ambivalence and how to overcome it.

"Aptly highlights the paradoxes of parenting and gives readers grappling with the question of whether or not to have children an honest and balanced perspective that will help them decide what's right for them." —*Library Journal*

Farris, Grace
Mom Milestones: The True Story of the First Seven Years. Grace Farris. Workman Publishing 2022. 216 p. : Illustration
ISBN 9781523511471
Grades: Adult   306.87
1. Mothers 2. Motherhood 3. Mother and child 4. Childbirth 5. Child rearing 6. Humorous writing 7. Family and Relationships — Parenting 8. Humor writing — Family and relationship humor

Beginning with one-day-old mom, who may feel like she is learning a new language, Mom Milestones is a love letter to the myriad ways moms grow and adapt to motherhood. Here are significant firsts: First sleepless night. First walk with baby. First mom friend. Skills learned—how to soothe baby (sometimes); how to coax a preschooler into taking medicine. Mom's likes (adapting pop songs to lullaby format; gathering intelligence from other moms) and dislikes (emptying the lunch box with mystery smells; requests for video games). While there might not be a road map for motherhood, Mom Milestones tracks both the memorable and slightly forgettable guideposts along the way—sunrises, snack plates, cuddles, laughter, and astonishment—because, as the saying goes, the days are long, but the years are short.

"Readers will cozy up to calming, knowing comics-style illustrations and lap up the milk of compassion and solidarity in each mom milestone." —*Booklist*

Petersen, Sara
Momfluenced: Inside the Maddening, Picture-perfect World of Mommy Influencer Culture. Sara Petersen. Beacon Press 2023. 272 p.
ISBN 9780807006634
Grades: Adult   306.87
1. Motherhood 2. Social influence 3. Social media 4. Gender role 5. Mothers 6. Parenting 7. Family relationships 8. Women's role 9. Society and culture — Psychology and human behavior 10. Society and culture — Gender — Women — Reproductive rights
LC 2022053703

Drawing on her own fraught relationship to momfluencer culture, Sara Petersen incorporates pop culture analysis and interviews with prominent momfluencers and experts (psychologists, academics, technologists) to explore the glorification of the ideal mama online with both humor and empathy. Momfluenced argues that momfluencers don't simply sell mothers on the benefits of bamboo diapers, they sell us the dream of motherhood itself, a dream tangled up in whiteness, capitalism, and the heteronormative nuclear family.

"With an investigative eye and a sense of humor, Petersen sheds needed light on a key part of the social media landscape." —Kirkus

Includes bibliographical references.

306.874 Parent-child relationship

Apter, T. E.
The Teen Interpreter: A Guide to the Challenges and Joys of Raising Adolescents. Terri Apter. W.W. Norton & Company 2022. x, 292 pages
ISBN 9781324006510
Grades: Adult   306.874
1. Parent and teenager 2. Adolescent psychology 3. Teenagers 4. Parenting 5. Family and Relationships — Parenting
LC 2021052465

An insightful, revealing, and practical guide to adolescents' inner world, from a renowned psychologist. Once children hit adolescence, it seems as if overnight "I love you" becomes "leave me alone," and any question from a parent can be dismissed with one word: "fine." but while they may not show it, teens benefit from their parents' curiosity, delight, and connection. In The Teen Interpreter, psychologist Terri Apter looks inside teens' minds—minds that are experiencing powerful new emotions and awareness of the world around them—to show how parents can revitalize their relationship.

"Parents can't be perfect, but Apter offers welcome insights and strategies for living through these stressful years." —Booklist

Includes bibliographical references (pages 259-278) and index.

Berg, Elizabeth
I'll Be Seeing You: A Memoir. Elizabeth Berg. Random House 2020. 224 p.
ISBN 9780593134672
Grades: Adult   306.874
1. Berg, Elizabeth 2. Berg family 3. Children of aging parents 4. People with Alzheimer's disease 5. Husband and wife 6. Family relationships 7. Aging 8. Nursing home patients 9. Mothers and daughters 10. Loss 11. Change 12. Minnesota 13. Autobiographies and memoirs 14. Life stories — Relationships — Family 15. Life stories — Facing adversity — Medical issues — Physical illness 16. Family and Relationships — Aging and Death
LC 2019041943

The bestselling author shares her experiences caring for her parents in their final years, charting the passage from the anguish of loss to the understanding that even in the most fractious of times, love can heal.

"Berg's fans will be touched by her disclosures, and readers caring for an aging parent will see themselves in Berg's painfully honest, beautifully written account, and be comforted by her insights." —Booklist

Blackstone, Amy
Childfree by Choice: The Movement Redefining Family and Creating a New Age of Independence. Dr. Amy Blackstone. Dutton 2019. 304 pages
ISBN 9781524744090
Grades: Adult   306.874
1. Childlessness 2. Child-free lifestyle 3. Self-fulfillment 4. Family relationships 5. Options, alternatives, choices 6. Family and relationships — General 7. Society and culture — Gender — Women — Reproductive rights
LC 2018039378

The co-creator of the "We're (Not) Having a Baby" blog shares expert insights into the history and growing movement of adults choosing to forego parenthood, exploring its cultural, economic, and environmental significance.

"Though this books offerings are much more substantial than mere peer support, childfree readers will certainly feel affirmed, and possibly inspired to pass copies along to those who doubt their choices." —Publishers Weekly

Includes bibliographical references.

Brickman, Sophie
Baby, Unplugged: One Mother's Search for Balance, Reason, and Sanity in the Digital Age. Sophie Brickman. HarperOne 2021. 352 p.
ISBN 9780062966483
Grades: Adult   306.874
1. Brickman, Sophie 2. Mother and child 3. Mother and baby 4. Parenthood 5. Technological innovations 6. Information technology 7. Internet and children 8. Child rearing 9. Society and culture — Media and technology 10. Family and Relationships — Parenting 11. Life stories — Relationships — Parent and child
LC 2020051618

Combining a journalist's investigative eye with her unborn second child as an experimental guinea pig, Baby, Unplugged draws on Sophie Brickman's own experiences as a journalist and parent to try to discover what aspects of technology are actually helpful, which are making us crazy, and most importantly, how we might learn to trust ourselves and our instincts again when it comes to raising children.

"For parents wondering whether to bring gadgets into the nursery, this will be an invaluable tool." —Publishers Weekly

Chabon, Michael
Pops: Fatherhood in Pieces. Michael Chabon. HarperCollins 2018. 176 p.
ISBN 9780062834621
Grades: Adult   306.874
1. Chabon, Michael 2. Fathers 3. Fatherhood 4. Father and child 5. Growing up 6. Childhood 7. Essays 8. Autobiographies and memoirs 9. Life stories — Relationships — Parent and child 10. Family and Relationships — Parenting
LC 2017279681

The Pulitzer Prize-winning author of the Mysteries of Pittsburgh presents a full-length collection of essays on fatherhood, including his viral 2016 GQ piece about his 13-year-old son's immersion in Paris Men's Fashion Week.

"The author combines perfect pitch of tone with an acute eye for detail, whether reporting on his 13-year-old son's unlikely emergence as a fashion savant…or trying to navigate his way through reading Huckleberry Finn aloud to his children without repeating a word that makes him recoil. Even when he's driving at cruising speed, Chabon takes his readers for an enjoyable ride." —Kirkus

Conaboy, Chelsea
Mother Brain: How Neuroscience Is Rewriting the Story of Parenthood. Chelsea Conaboy. Henry Holt and Company 2022. 304 p.
ISBN 9781250762283
Grades: Adult   306.874
1. Motherhood 2. Parenthood 3. Neuroscience 4. Science Writing — Medicine and health 5. Family and Relationships — Parenting
LC 2022026985

In this powerful narrative, a journalist and mother delves into the major brain changes that come with being new parents, delving into the neuroscience to reveal unexpected upsides and how this science is mostly absent from the public conversation about parenthood.

"Conaboy's book isn't a parenting manual but rather a work of pop science jam-packed with neurobiological research; it's both fascinating and surprisingly readable." —Library Journal

Includes bibliographical references and index.

Cusk, Rachel
A Life's Work: On Becoming a Mother. Rachel Cusk. Picador USA 2002. 213 p.
ISBN 9780312269876
Grades: Adult   306.874
1. Motherhood 2. Parenting 3. New mothers 4. Mothers 5. Canadian literature 6. Family and Relationships — Parenting

ESSENTIAL AND RECOMMENDED TITLES
306.874 Parent-child relationship

LC 2001054894
New York Times Notable Book, 2002.

An account of a year of modern motherhood, set against the backdrop of sexual equality, details the author's many experiences during and after her transformation into a mother, all of which have taught her valuable lessons in life.

"This is not a happy guide; instead, it is a penetrating, sometimes joyful and amusing, sometimes frightening and disturbing look at pregnancy and motherhood." —*Booklist*

Originally published: Great Britain : Fourth Estate, 2001.

Dubin, Minna
★ *Mom Rage: The Everyday Crisis of Modern Motherhood*. Minna Dubin. Seal Press 2023. 256 p.
ISBN 9781541601307
Grades: Adult   **306.874**

1. Motherhood 2. Child rearing 3. Women caregivers 4. Psychology 5. Gender role 6. Identity 7. Equality 8. Division of labor 9. Sexism 10. Feminism 11. Social change 12. Shame 13. Anger 14. Society and culture — Gender — Women 15. Family and Relationships — Parenting

LC 2022059121

Mothers aren't supposed to be angry. Still, Minna Dubin was an angry mom: Exhausted by hard, thankless full-time parenting work and feeling her career slip away from her, she would find herself screaming at her child or exploding in anger at her husband. When Dubin pushed past her shame and talked with other mothers about how she was feeling, she realized that she was far from alone. Mom Rage is Dubin's groundbreaking work of reportage about an unspoken crisis of anger sweeping the country—and the world.

"This book represents a voice that belongs in every parenting collection, both for the information it provides and the validation it offers to families who struggle with the challenges of raising children." —*Booklist*

Includes bibliographical references and index.

Garbes, Angela
Essential Labor: Mothering as Social Change. Angela Garbes. Harper Wave 2022. 256 p.
ISBN 9780062937360
Grades: Adult   **306.874**

1. Garbes, Angela 2. Motherhood 3. Mothers 4. Filipino American women 5. Parenting 6. Caregivers 7. Work 8. Social marginality 9. Power 10. Value 11. Community development 12. Social change 13. Family and Relationships — Parenting 14. Society and culture — Gender — Women 15. Life stories — Relationships — Parent and child

LC 2021059766

The Covid-19 pandemic shed fresh light on a long-overlooked truth: Mothering is among the only essential work humans do. In response to the increasing weight placed on mothers and caregivers—and the lack of a social safety net to support them—writer Angela Garbes found herself pondering a vital question: How, under our current circumstances that leave us lonely, exhausted, and financially strained, might we demand more from American family life? Garbes contends that while the labor of raising children is devalued in America, the act of mothering offers the radical potential to create a more equitable society. In Essential Labor, Garbes reframes the physically and mentally draining work of meeting a child's bodily and emotional needs as opportunities to find meaning, to nurture a deeper sense of self, pleasure, and belonging. This is highly skilled labor, work that impacts society at its most foundational level.

"Garbes, a Filipina who describes herself as 'A woman of color, a writer, and a mother,' melds memoir with social, political, and cultural critique to offer a thoughtful analysis of the social and personal complexities of mothering." —*Kirkus*

Includes bibliographical references.

Grose, Jessica
Screaming on the Inside: The Unsustainability of American Motherhood. Jessica Grose. Mariner Books 2022. 304 p.
ISBN 9780063078352
Grades: Adult   **306.874**

1. Motherhood 2. Mothers 3. Family leave 4. Expectation 5. United States 6. Family and relationships — Parenting 7. Society and culture — Gender — Women

LC 2022021876

Weaving together her personal journey with scientific, historical and contemporary reporting, a New York Times opinion writer dismantles 200 years of unrealistic parenting expectations and empowers today's mothers to make choices that actually serve themselves, their children and their communities.

"A deeply researched and highly relatable analysis of American motherhood, past and present." —*Kirkus*

Includes bibliographical references and index.

Jones, Lucy
★ *Matrescence: On the Mind/Body/Spirit Transformations of Pregnancy, Childbirth, and Motherhood*. [by Lucy Jones]. Pantheon Books 2023. 320 p.
ISBN 9780593317310
Grades: Adult   **306.874**

1. Jones, Lucy (Journalist) 2. Motherhood 3. Pregnancy 4. Childbirth 5. Mothers 6. Psychology 7. Maternal love 8. Transformations, Personal 9. Autobiographies and memoirs 10. Life stories — Relationships — Parent and child 11. Life stories — Identity 12. Society and culture — Gender — Women 13. Family and relationships — Parenting

LC 2023033894

Part memoir, part scientific and health reporting, part social critique, ecological philosophy, eco-feminism and nature writing, the author discusses the physical and emotional changes in the maternal mind, body and spirit and shows us how these changes are far more profound, wild, and enduring than any that have been previously explored or written about before.

"In this probing meditation, Jones reflects on how becoming a mother physically and mentally transforms women…Elevated by inventive formal flourishes and searching reflection, this will resonate with mothers of all stripes." —*Publishers Weekly*

Includes bibliographical references and index.

Kalb, Bess
★ *Nobody Will Tell You This but Me: A True (as Told to Me) Story*. Bess Kalb. Alfred A. Knopf 2020. xiv, 199 pages : Illustration
ISBN 9780525654711
Grades: Adult   **306.874**

1. Kalb, Bess, 1987- 2. Bell, Bobby 3. Grandmothers 4. Grandmother and granddaughter 5. Women 6. Jewish women 7. Children of immigrants 8. Family relationships 9. Determination 10. Independence 11. Autobiographies and memoirs 12. Life stories — Relationships — Family

LC 2019026101

The award-winning television writer reflects on her relationship with her loving grandmother, the daughter of immigrants from 19th-century Belarus whose hardships, sacrifices and headstrong nature shaped the author's perspectives on family and career.

"An endearing, bittersweet, and entertainingly fresh take on the family memoir." —*Kirkus*

Kurcinka, Mary Sheedy
Raising Your Spirited Baby: A Breakthrough Guide to Understanding the Needs of Healthy Babies Who Are More Alert, Intense, and Energetic, and Struggle to Sleep. Mary Sheedy Kurcinka, EdD.. William Morrow 2020. xix, 325 p.
ISBN 9780062961525
Grades: Adult   **306.874**

1. Babies 2. Child rearing 3. Parent and baby 4. Baby psychology 5. Family and Relationships — Parenting

LC 2020002204

From the beloved bestselling author whose books have sold more than 1 million copies, comes Mary Sheedy Kurcinka's newest addition to her award-winning parenting books, this time turning the focus to babies."

"Sure to be a landmark book, Kurcinka's well-researched advice may just be a sanity and sleep saver for new parents." —*Library Journal*

Includes index.

Lemay, Mimi
What We Will Become: A Mother, a Son, and a Journey of Transformation. Mimi Lemay. Houghton Mifflin Harcourt 2019. 320 pages
ISBN 9780544965836
Grades: Adult   **306.874**
1. Lemay, Mimi 2. Parents of transgender children 3. Transgender children 4. Motherhood 5. Gender identity 6. Families 7. Faith 8. Gender role 9. Transgender people 10. Orthodox Jews 11. Identity 12. Human rights 13. Civil rights 14. Autobiographies and memoirs 15. Life stories — Relationships — Parent and child 16. Life stories — Identity 17. Society and culture — LGBTQIA+ 18. Spirituality and Religion — General 19. Family and Relationships — Parenting
LC 2019013136

A mother's memoir of her transgender child's odyssey, and her journey outside the boundaries of the faith and culture that shaped her.

"This is a vital and engrossing book about how to live an authentic life. Well suited for readers interested in gender and generational family dynamics." —*Library Journal*

Millwood, Molly
To Have and to Hold: Motherhood, Marriage, and the Modern Dilemma. Molly Millwood. HarperCollins 2019. 288 p.
ISBN 9780062838650
Grades: Adult   **306.874**
1. Motherhood 2. New mothers 3. Mothers 4. Marriage 5. Childbirth 6. Postpartum 7. Parents 8. Married people 9. Parenthood 10. Psychology 11. Family and Relationships — Parenting 12. Family and Relationships — Dating and Marriage
LC Bl2019008534

A clinical therapist and founding member of Vermont's Postpartum Wellness Project outlines practical recommendations for navigating the physical, professional and emotional complexities of early motherhood, including its impact on a marriage.

"Miller's resonant message is that everyone should acknowledge all facets of motherhood, including the negative. Mothers-to-be and parents of babies and young children may find it reassuring that it's typical to feel conflicted and even angry owing to the upheaval and transformation of their lives." —*Library Journal*

Senior, Jennifer
All Joy and No Fun: The Paradox of Modern Parenthood. Jennifer Senior. Ecco Press 2014. 384 p
ISBN 9780062072221
Grades: Adult   **306.874**
1. Parenting 2. Parent and child 3. Unhappiness 4. Child care 5. Responsibility 6. Family and Relationships — Parenting
LC 2013498720

Drawing on a vast array of sources in history, sociology, economics, psychology, philosophy and anthropology, an award-winning journalist challenges our culture's most basic beliefs about parenthood, while revealing the profound ways children deepen and add purpose to our lives.

"Full of fascinating ideas and information about the family structure and its history, this work is sure to be of strong interest to parents, in particular, as they look for meaning beyond the day to day." —*Library Journal*

Traig, Jennifer
Act Natural: A Cultural History of Misadventures in Parenting. Jennifer Traig. Ecco 2019. 320 p.
ISBN 9780062469809
Grades: Adult   **306.874**
1. Parenting 2. Child rearing 3. Social history 4. Humor writing — Family and relationship humor 5. Society and culture — Pop culture 6. Family and Relationships — Parenting
LC 2018022056

From ancient Rome to Puritan New England to the Dr. Spock craze of mid-century America, the author, in this entertaining history of Western parenting, explores parenting techniques ranging from the misguided, to the nonsensical, to the truly horrifying.

Tubbs, Anna Malaika
The Three Mothers: How the Mothers of Martin Luther King, Jr, Malcolm X, and James Baldwin Shaped a Nation. Anna Malaika Tubbs. Flatiron Books 2021. 272 p.
ISBN 9781250756121
Grades: 11 12 Adult   **306.874**
1. King, Alberta Williams, 1904-1974 2. Little, Louise Langdon, 1897-1989 3. Baldwin, Emma Berdis Jones, -1999 4. King, Martin Luther, Jr, 1929-1968 5. Malcolm X, 1925-1965 6. Baldwin, James, 1924-1987 7. African American mothers 8. Motherhood 9. African American families 10. Mothers and sons 11. African American women 12. Mothers 13. Racism 14. African American history 15. Civil rights 16. Race relations 17. United States history 18. United States 19. 20th century 20. Collective biographies 21. History writing — African American — United States 22. Life stories — Relationships — Parent and child 23. History writing — Women's history
LC 2020040974

In her groundbreaking and essential debut the Three Mothers, scholar Anna Malaika Tubbs celebrates Black motherhood by telling the story of the three women who raised and shaped some of America's most pivotal heroes: Martin Luther King, Jr, Malcolm X, and James Baldwin. Much has been written about Berdis Baldwin's son James, about Alberta King's son Martin Luther, and Louise Little's son Malcolm. But virtually nothing has been said about the extraordinary women who raised them, who were all born at the beginning of the 20th century and forced to contend with the prejudices of Jim Crow as Black women. Berdis, Alberta, and Louise passed their knowledge to their children with the hope of helping them to survive in a society that would deny their humanity from the very beginning-from Louise teaching her children about their activist roots, to Berdis encouraging James to express himself through writing, to Alberta basing all of her lessons in faith and social justice.

"Tubbs skillfully draws parallels between each woman's story, and vividly captures the early years of the civil rights movement. This immersive history gives credit where it's long overdue." —*Publishers Weekly*

"This heavily documented and unflinching look into the lives of early twentieth-century African American women is an extraordinary resource." —*Booklist*

Includes bibliographical references and index.

Warner, Judith
Perfect Madness: Motherhood in the Age of Anxiety. Judith Warner. Riverhead Books 2005. 327 p.
ISBN 9781573223041
Grades: Adult   **306.874**
1. Motherhood 2. Mothers 3. Guilt 4. Psychology 5. Family and Relationships — Parenting 6. Society and culture — Gender — Women
LC 2004056615

An exploration of the world of modern motherhood describes the author's early parenting experiences in Paris and how they contrasted with anxiety-marked parenting expectations in the United States.

"Writing from the perspective of her first few years of motherhood spent in France and her subsequent return to the U.S, Warner ponders the cultural factors driving the madness of pursuing perfect motherhood and the toll it is taking on American women." —*Booklist*

Includes bibliographical references and index.

306.8743 Mother-child relationship

Casares, Whitney
The Working Mom Blueprint: Winning at Parenting Without Losing Yourself. Whitney Casares, MD, MPH, FAAP.. American Academy of Pediatrics 2021. xxix, 240 pages
ISBN 9781610024860
Grades: Adult   **306.8743**

ESSENTIAL AND RECOMMENDED TITLES
306.8745 Grandparent-child relationship

1. Working mothers 2. Motherhood 3. Mother and child 4. Parenting 5. Family and Relationships — Parenting 6. Self-Help — Career and financial success
LC Oc2021002153

Sharing honest insights about her own challenges, a practicing pediatrician and mother of two young daughters presents this reassuring guide to navigating modern motherhood in which she provides a practical plan for setting priorities, cultivating self-care, delegating whenever appropriate and more.

"Casares's insights . . . don't feel especially novel. Still, millennial moms especially will appreciate Casare's encouragement and sensibility." —*Publishers Weekly*

Includes index.

306.8745 Grandparent-child relationship

Day, Marianne Waggoner
Camp Grandma: Next-Generation Grandparenting — Beyond Babysitting. Marianne Waggoner Day. She Writes Press 2019. xxiii, 228 p. : Illustration
ISBN 9781631525117
Grades: Adult   306.8745
1. Grandparenting 2. Grandparent and child 3. Child development 4. Family and Relationships — Parenting 5. Family and Relationships — Families
LC 2018958906

Camp Grandma reveals how a successful businesswoman merged her working career with her role as grandmother—and offers grandparents fun and creative ideas for enriching their relationships with their grandchildren while teaching the children valuable life skills that will help them grow strong and think critically. Readers will be introduced to a compelling, sometimes humorous, and totally unexpected twist on a role people often take for granted—as well as enter into the larger societal conversation we should be having about the possibilities and value of grandparenting, and how the women's movement has reinvigorated and reshaped not only women's approach to being grandmothers but also men's approach to the grandfather role. Warm cookies and milk are still okay, but what if they came with a workshop on goal setting or writing a business plan for the school year? Babysitting? Not even close.

Includes index.

306.875 Sibling relationships

Farley, Audrey Clare
★ *Girls and Their Monsters: The Genain Quadruplets and the Making of Madness in America.* Audrey Clare Farley. Grand Central Publishing 2023. 304 p.
ISBN 9781538724477
Grades: Adult   306.875
1. Quadruplets 2. Sisters 3. Fame 4. Schizophrenia 5. Child abuse victims 6. Social isolation 7. Psychic trauma 8. Hallucinations and illusions 9. Psychological research 10. Human experimentation in psychology 11. Genetics 12. Mental health 13. History writing — Science, technology, and medicine 14. Science Writing — Medicine and health — Mental health 15. Life stories — Facing adversity — Medical issues — Mental illness
LC 2022057896

A harrowing exploration of violence against children and its psychological and political consequences, from the author of the Unfit Heiress.

"As much a study of parenting as it is of what psychologists once thought of parents, Girls and Their Monsters follows Robert Kolker's Hidden Valley Road as another unsettling, behind-closed-doors look at families and mental illness." —*Booklist*

Includes index.

306.89 Separation and divorce

Blackstone-Ford, Jann
Co-Parenting Through Separation and Divorce: Putting Your Children First. Jann Blackstone, PsyD; David L. Hill, MD, FAAP.. American Academy of Pediatrics 2020. xx, 260 pages : Illustration
ISBN 9781610023801
Grades: Adult   306.89
1. Children of divorced parents 2. Divorce 3. Family and Relationships — Divorce 4. Family and Relationships — Parenting
LC Bl2020045694

Parents going through separation or divorce are understandably worried about how the change in the family will affect their children. This guide walks parents through all the factors they should consider and offers step-by-step guidance on how to work together to put their children first. From sharing the news with children in an age-appropriate way to handling the issue of custody, from concerns about affairs or abuse to embarking on remarriage and blending families, Co-Parenting Through Separation andDivorce offers a roadmap through one of life's most difficult challenges with the goal of healthy, happy kids informing every decision along the way.

Includes index.

Dais, Dawn
The Sh!t No One Tells You About Divorce: A Guide to Breaking Up, Falling Apart, and Putting Yourself Back Together. Dawn Dais. Hachette Go 2023. 272 p.
ISBN 9780306828546
Grades: Adult   306.89
1. Divorce 2. Family relationships 3. Dysfunctional families 4. Self-actualization 5. Coparenting 6. Lesbians 7. LGBTQIA+ people 8. Life stories — Relationships — Family 9. Life stories — Relationships — Couples
LC 2022042422

A bestselling author offers a refreshingly honest, compassionate guide to the sh!tstorm that is divorce: Falling apart, staying afloat, and new beginnings (whether you are ready for them or not).

"The guidance is largely geared toward separations in which both parents remain in the children's lives, but the author's animated style will appeal to anyone going through a divorce." —*Publishers Weekly*

Green, Janice
★ *Divorce After 50: Your Guide to the Unique Legal & Financial Challenges of a Gray Divorce, 5th Edition.* Attorney Janice Green. Nolo 2022. 418 pages
ISBN 9781413329551
Grades: Adult   306.89
1. Divorce 2. Middle-aged people 3. Reference books — Handbooks, manuals, etc. 4. Law — Family law 5. Family and Relationships — Divorce
LC 2018037647

Discusses the emotional, social, legal, and financial effects of late-life divorce.

Includes index; We recommend the newest edition of this book.

306.9 Institutions pertaining to death

Arthur, Alua
★ *Briefly Perfectly Human: Making an Authentic Life by Getting Real About the End.* Alua Arthur. Mariner Books 2024. 288 p.
ISBN 9780063240032
Grades: Adult   306.9
1. Arthur, Alua 2. Death 3. Terminal care 4. Purpose in life 5. Last days 6. Terminal illness 7. People with terminal illnesses 8. Mortality 9. Personal conduct 10. Autobiographies and memoirs 11. Life stories — Facing adversity — Coping with death 12. Society and culture — Illness and disease
LC 2023044130

A deeply transformative memoir that reframes how we think about death and how it can help us lead better, more fulfilling and authentic lives, from America's preeminent death doula.

"Arthur recalls in her elegant debut memoir how she became a death doula, providing emotional support and guidance to those who are nearing death...Readers of Caitlin Doughty and Lori Gottlieb will be fascinated." —*Publishers Weekly*

Doughty, Caitlin
Will My Cat Eat My Eyeballs?: Big Questions from Tiny Mortals About Death. Caitlin Doughty; illustrated by Diann Ruz. W. W. Norton & Co. 2019. 208 p.
ISBN 9780393652703
Grades: 9 10 11 12 Adult 306.9
1. Dead 2. Death 3. Undertakers 4. Biodegradation 5. Funerals 6. Mortality 7. Human biology 8. Science Writing — Biology 9. Adult books for young adults

Goodreads Choice Award, 2019; YALSA Quick Picks for Reluctant Young Adult Readers, 2020.

The creator of the "Ask a Mortician" web series and best-selling author provides comprehensive, science based answers to common questions about death, dead bodies and decomposition.

"An entertaining read, straightforward without being morbid. Of interest to anyone, young or old, who is curious about what happens to our bodies after we die." —*Library Journal*

Includes bibliographical references and index.

Leder, Steven Z.
The Beauty of What Remains: How Our Greatest Fear Becomes Our Greatest Gift. Steve Leder. Avery 2021. 240 p.
ISBN 9780593187555
Grades: Adult 306.9
1. Leder, Steven Z. 2. Death 3. Loss 4. Grief 5. Mortality 6. Personal conduct 7. Rabbis 8. Grief therapy 9. Death of fathers 10. Family and Relationships — Aging and Death 11. Life stories — Facing adversity — Coping with death
LC 2020026855

As the Senior Rabbi of one of the largest synagogues in the world, Steve Leder has learned over and over again the many ways death teaches us how to live and love more deeply by showing us not only what is gone, but also the beauty of what remains. This book takes us on a journey through the experience of loss that is fundamental to everyone. Yet even after having sat beside thousands of deathbeds, Steve Leder the rabbi was not fully prepared for the loss of his own father. It was only then that Steve Leder the son truly learned how loss makes life beautiful by giving it meaning and touching us with love that we had not felt before.

"Leder delivers insightful thoughts on death and the process of dying for the spiritual and secular alike.... Leder's elegant and compassionate rumination is a worthy addition to the literature on death and dying." —*Publishers Weekly*

Sacks, Oliver
Gratitude. Oliver Sacks. Alfred A. Knopf 2015. 45 p.
ISBN 9780451492937
Grades: Adult 306.9
1. Sacks, Oliver, 1933-2015 2. Death 3. Neurologists 4. Authors 5. Sick people 6. Gratitude 7. People with cancer 8. Essays 9. Life stories — Facing adversity — Coping with death 10. Life stories — Science, technology, and medicine — Scientists and inventors 11. Life stories — Arts and culture — Writing — Authors
LC Bl2015052034

No writer has succeeded in capturing the medical and human drama of illness as honestly and as eloquently as Oliver Sacks. During the last few months of his life, he wrote a set of essays in which he movingly explored his feelings about completing a life and coming to terms with his own death.

307.76 Urban communities

Currid-Halkett, Elizabeth
The Overlooked Americans: The Resilience of Our Rural Towns and What It Means for Our Country. Elizabeth Currid-Halkett. Basic Books 2023. 432 p.
ISBN 9781541646728
Grades: Adult 307.76
1. Cities and towns 2. Rural life 3. Small town life 4. Demography 5. Interviewing 6. Attitude 7. Social indicators 8. Perception 9. Prejudice 10. Stereotypes 11. Quality of life 12. United States 13. Society and culture — Urban and regional studies 14. Travel Writing — Small Town Life
LC 2022057988

In The Overlooked Americans, public policy expert Elizabeth Currid-Halkett breaks through stereotypes about rural America. She traces how small towns are doing as well as, or better than, cities by many measures. She also shows how rural and urban Americans share core values, from opposing racism and upholding environmentalism to believing in democracy. When we focus too heavily on the far-right fringe, we overlook the millions of rural Americans who are content with their lives.

"Idealistic yet well-grounded, this is a refreshing antidote to doom and gloom prognostications of where America is headed." —*Publishers Weekly*

Includes bibliographical references and index.

Green, Hardy
The Company Town: The Industrial Edens and Satanic Mills That Shaped the American Economy. Hardy Green. Basic Books 2010. 264 p.
ISBN 9780465018260
Grades: Adult 307.76
1. Company towns 2. Industries 3. Labor-management relations 4. Capitalism 5. Corporations, American 6. Business and economics — Industries — Manufacturing 7. History writing — United States
LC 2010013434

A history of how companies have created communities for their workers explores both the positive and negative effects the institution of "the company town" has had—on the one hand, companies have tried to take care of their workers and their families; on the other, they have also exploited the workers and tried to extract as much labor for as little compensation possible.

Includes bibliographical references and index.

Herold, Benjamin
Disillusioned: Five Families and the Unraveling of America's Suburbs. Benjamin Herold. Penguin Press 2024. 432 p.
ISBN 9780593298183
Grades: Adult 307.76
1. Suburbs 2. Suburban life 3. American Dream 4. Families 5. Marginalized people 6. Public schools 7. Inequality 8. Race relations 9. Social problems 10. United States 11. Society and culture — Education 12. Society and culture — Race 13. Society and culture — Wealth and class 14. Life stories — Facing adversity 15. Debut title
LC 2023016076

Told through the stories of five American families, a leading education journalist shows how the destructive legacy left behind by white suburban families has impacted the lives of the Black and brown families who have inherited it.

"Herold adeptly manages the sprawling storytelling and subtopics (albeit frequently focused on bureaucratic minutiae) with empathy, varied scenes, and well-rounded characterizations. A deeply valuable study of the decline of suburbia." —*Kirkus*

Includes bibliographical references and index.

Mumford, Lewis
The City in History: Its Origins, Its Transformations, and Its Prospects. Lewis Mumford. Harcourt, Brace & Co. 1989. xi, 657 p, 64 p. of plates : Illustration
ISBN 9780156180351
Grades: 11 12 Adult 307.76
1. Cities and towns 2. City life 3. History writing — General

ESSENTIAL AND RECOMMENDED TITLES
307.77 Self-contained communities

LC 61007689

National Book Award for Nonfiction, 1962.

An examination of cities of the Western world tracing their development from Egypt through the Middle Ages to the present.

Includes bibliographical references (p. 579-634) and index.

307.77 Self-contained communities

Stille, Alexander
The Sullivanians: Sex, Psychotherapy, and the Wild Life of an American Commune. Alexander Stille. Farrar Straus & Giroux 2023. 416 p.
ISBN 9780374600396
Grades: Adult   307.77
1. Collective settlements 2. Social control 3. Psychotherapy 4. Cults 5. Sexuality 6. Radical organizations 7. New York city 8. True Crime — General 9. History writing — United States

Explores the devolution of the Sullivan Institute, from psychoanalytic organization to insular, radical cult.

"This gripping tale of an attempted societal shift will entrance readers. Well-researched and accessible, its broad appeal makes it a necessary part of sociology and psychology collections." —*Library Journal*

Wayland-Smith, Ellen
Oneida: From Free Love Utopia to the Well-set Table. Ellen Wayland-Smith. Picado USA 2016. 336 p.
ISBN 9781250043085
Grades: Adult   307.77
1. Sexual freedom 2. Religious communities 3. Spiritual life 4. Gender equity 5. Business 6. New York (State) 7. History writing — Arts and culture 8. History writing — United States

LC 2015044336

Tells the uniquely American story of a community whose radical notions of equality, sex and religion transformed into a symbol of American middle-class respectability.

"This book is a fascinating look into the strange history of Oneida silverware and how its origins reflect an exhilarating period of American history." —*Publishers Weekly*

310 Collections of general statistics

Wiggins, Christopher L.
How Data Happened: A History from the Age of Reason to the Age of Algorithms. Chris Wiggins and Matthew L. Jones. W W Norton & Co. Inc 2023. 272 p.
ISBN 9781324006732
Grades: Adult   310
1. Computer technology 2. Information technology 3. Computer algorithms 4. Surveillance 5. Privacy rights 6. Big data 7. Machine learning 8. Statistics 9. Power 10. Society and culture — Media and technology 11. Politics and global affairs — Social issues and policies 12. Science Writing — Computing, the internet, and technology — Artificial intelligence and machine learning

From facial recognition to automated decision systems that inform who gets loans and who receives bail, each of us moves through a world determined by data-empowered algorithms. But these technologies didn't just appear: They are part of a history that goes back centuries, from the census enshrined in the US Constitution to the birth of eugenics in Victorian Britain to the development of Google search. Expanding on the popular course they created at Columbia University, Chris Wiggins and Matthew L. Jones illuminate the ways in which data has long been used as a tool and a weapon in arguing for what is true, as well as a means of rearranging or defending power.

"An informative dive into the history of statistics and data, providing context for the debate over information and who controls it." —*Kirkus*

320 Political science

Aristotle
★ *Politics.* Aristotle; translated by Ernest Barker; revised with an introduction and notes by R.F. Stalley. Oxford University Press 1998. xlvii, 423 p. : Map
ISBN 9780192833938
Grades: Adult   320
1. Political science 2. Politics and global affairs — Political philosophy

LC 98215869

The Politics is one of the most influential texts in the history of political thought, and it raises issues which still confront anyone who wants to think seriously about the ways in which human societies are organized and governed. By examining the way societies are run—from households to city states—Aristotle establishes how successful constitutions can best be initiated and upheld.

Includes bibliographical references (p. [xli]-xliv) and index.

★ *Politics, 2nd Ed.* Aristotle; translated and with an introduction by Carnes Lord. University of Chicago Press 2013. 265 p.
ISBN 9780226921839
Grades: Adult   320
1. Rulers 2. Comparative government 3. Philosophy 4. Democracy 5. City-states 6. Aristocracy 7. Constitutions 8. Political science 9. Translations — Greek to English 10. Politics and global affairs — Political philosophy

This new edition of the Politics retains and adds to Lord's already extensive notes, clarifying the flow of Aristotle's argument and identifying literary and historical references. A glossary defines key terms in Aristotle's philosophical-political vocabulary. Lord has made revisions to problematic passages throughout the translation in order to enhance both its accuracy and its readability. He has also substantially revised his introduction for the new edition. Further enhancing this new edition is an up-to-date selected bibliography.

Lord's translation is clearly the best available. Claremont Review of Books.
Original text written ca. 350 B.C.E.

DiResta, Renee
Invisible Rulers: The People Who Turn Lies into Reality. Renée Diresta. PublicAffairs 2024. 448 p.
ISBN 9781541703377
Grades: Adult   320
1. Social media 2. Digital media 3. Algorithms 4. Influencers 5. Misinformation 6. Rumor 7. Conspiracy theories 8. Deception 9. Polarization (Social sciences) 10. Political culture 11. Suspicion 12. Social conflict 13. Society and culture — Media and technology 14. Politics and global affairs — General

Renée DiResta's powerful, original investigation into the way power and influence have been profoundly transformed reveals how a virtual rumor mill of niche propagandists increasingly shapes public opinion. By revealing the machinery and dynamics of the interplay between influencers, algorithms, and online crowds, DiResta vividly illustrates the way propagandists deliberately undermine belief in the fundamental legitimacy of institutions that make society work. This alternate system for shaping public opinion, unexamined until now, is rewriting the relationship between the people and their government in profound ways.

"More detailed and insightful than most books in a crowded field, which makes it that much more disheartening." —*Kirkus*

Includes bibliographical references and index.

Kaplan, Robert D.
Warrior Politics: Why Leadership Demands a Pagan Ethos. Robert D. Kaplan. Random House 2002. xxii, 198 p.
ISBN 9780375505638
Grades: Adult   320
1. Leadership 2. Political ethics 3. International relations 4. United States 5. Politics and global affairs — Political philosophy

LC 2001031862

New York Times Notable Book, 2002.

PUBLIC LIBRARY CORE COLLECTION: NONFICTION
Twentieth Edition

The author draws on the historical wisdom of Sun-Tzu, Thucydides, Hobbes, Machiavelli, and other great thinkers to provide advice for modern-day world leaders confronted with the complex challenges of modern life.

"This is a provocative, smart and polemical work that will stimulate lively discussion." —*Publishers Weekly*

Includes bibliographical references (p. [157]-163) and index.

Lozada, Carlos
The Washington Book: How to Read Politics and Politicians. Carlos Lozada. Simon & Schuster 2024. 320 p.
ISBN 9781668050736
Grades: Adult   320

1. Presidents 2. Vice presidents 3. Presidential candidates 4. Politicians 5. Political leadership 6. Ambition 7. Identity 8. Power 9. History writing — Presidency — United States 10. Politics and global affairs — Political figures 11. Life stories — Politics — Politicians

As a long-time book critic and columnist in Washington, D.C, Carlos Lozada dissects all manner of texts: Commission reports, political reporting, Supreme Court decisions, congressional inquiries, and books by politicians and top officials. With this provocative essay collection, Lozada argues that no matter how carefully political figures sanitize their experiences, positions, and records, no matter how diligently they present themselves in the best light, they almost always let slip the truth. They show us their faults and blind spots, their ambitions and compromises, their underlying motives and insecurities. Whether they mean to or not, they tell us who they really are.

"More than just providing analysis, Lozada is willing to lay out criticisms up and down the political spectrum. His insights are piquant and enlightening, the result being an enhanced understanding of…American politics." —*Booklist*

320.01 Philosophy and theory

Acemoglu, Daron
The Narrow Corridor: States, Societies, and the Fate of Liberty. Daron Acemoglu, James A. Robinson. Penguin Press 2019. 496 p.
ISBN 9780735224384
Grades: Adult   320.01

1. Freedom 2. State (Political science) 3. Democracy 4. Representative government and representation 5. Decentralization in government 6. Executive power 7. Political violence 8. Power 9. Politics and global affairs — Political philosophy

LC 2019009146

A crucial new big-picture framework that answers the question of how liberty flourishes in some states but falls to authoritarianism or anarchy in others—and explains how it can continue to thrive despite new threats.

Includes bibliographical references and index.

Hobbes, Thomas
★ *Leviathan.* Thomas Hobbes; edited by J.C.A. Gaskin. Oxford University Press 2008. 508 p.
ISBN 9780199537280
Grades: 11 12 Adult   320.01

1. Political science 2. Philosophy 3. Politics and global affairs — Political philosophy

LC Oc2008095159

Leviathan is both a magnificent literary achievement and the greatest work of political philosophy in the English language. Permanently challenging, it has found new applications and new refutations in every generation. This new edition reproduces the first printed text, retaining the original punctuation but modernizing the spelling. It offers exceptionally thorough and useful annotation, an introduction that guides the reader through the complexities of Hobbes's arguments, and a substantial index.

Includes bibliographical references and index.

Ryan, Alan
On Politics: A History of Political Thought from Herodotus to the Present. Alan Ryan. W. W. Norton & Co. 2012. 2 v. (1120 p.)
ISBN 9780871404657
Grades: Adult   320.01

1. Political science 2. Political scientists 3. Thought and thinking 4. Ideology 5. World politics 6. Human behavior 7. Politics and global affairs — Political philosophy

LC 2012012351

Traces the origins of political philosophy and the lives of the great thinkers from the ancient Greeks to Machiavelli to Hobbes and to the present and illuminates the ideas and beliefs that helped shape each era.

Includes bibliographical references and index.

Turchin, Peter
End Times: Elites, Counter-elites, and the Path of Political Disintegration. Peter Turchin. Penguin 2023. xv, 352 p.
ISBN 9780593490501
Grades: Adult   320.01

1. Political stability 2. Elite (Social sciences) 3. Wealth 4. Power 5. Scarcity 6. Income inequality 7. Polarization (Social sciences) 8. Social classes 9. Social change 10. Revolutions 11. Social forecasting 12. Politics and government 13. United States 14. Impartial writing 15. Politics and global affairs — General 16. Business and economics — Economics — Socioeconomics 17. Society and culture — General

LC 2022044451

Peter Turchin, one of the most interesting social scientists of our age, has infused the study of history with approaches and insights from other fields for more than a quarter century. End Times is the culmination of his work to understand what causes political communities to cohere and what causes them to fall apart, as applied to the current turmoil within the United States. The lessons of world history are clear, Turchin argues: When the equilibrium between ruling elites and the majority tips too far in favor of elites, political instability is all but inevitable.

"It's a stimulating analysis of antagonisms past and present, and the crack-up they may be leading to." —*Publishers Weekly*

Includes bibliographical references and index.

320.082 Women in politics

Steinhauer, Jennifer
The Firsts: The Inside Story of the Women Reshaping Congress. Jennifer Steinhauer. Algonquin Books of Chapel Hill 2020. 262 pages
ISBN 9781616209995
Grades: 9 10 11 12 Adult   320.082

1. Women legislators 2. Women 3. Political participation 4. Politics and government 5. United States 6. 21st century 7. History writing — Politicians — United States 8. History writing — Early 21st century — United States 9. Politics and global affairs — Political figures 10. Politics and global affairs — Elections 11. Adult books for young adults

A lively, behind-the-scenes look at the historic cohort of diverse, young, and groundbreaking women newly elected to the House of Representatives in 2018 as they arrive in Washington, DC, and start working for change.

"A fine lesson in civics and political journalism and must reading for anyone contemplating working in electoral politics." —*Kirkus*

Includes bibliographical references and index.

320.1 The state

Cicero, Marcus Tullius
★ *The Republic: And the Laws.* Cicero; a new translation by Niall Rudd. Oxford University Press 2008. 288 p.
ISBN 9780199540112
Grades: Adult   320.1

ESSENTIAL AND RECOMMENDED TITLES
320.1092 Political philosophy — Biography

1. Political science 2. Utopias 3. Natural law 4. State (Political science) 5. Constitutions 6. Politics and government 7. Ancient Rome 8. Translations — Latin to English 9. History writing — Ancient — Rome 10. Politics and global affairs — Political philosophy

LC Oc2008018000

Cicero's the Republic is an impassioned plea for responsible government written just before the civil war that ended the Roman Republic in a dialogue following Plato. Drawing on Greek political theory, the work embodies the mature reflections of a Roman ex-consul on the nature of political organization, on justice in society, and on the qualities needed in a statesman. Its sequel, the Laws, expounds the influential doctrine of Natural Law, which applies to all mankind, and sets out an ideal code for a reformed Roman Republic, already half in the realm of utopia.

This translation originally published: 1998; Includes bibliographical references and index; Translated from the Latin De republica.

Fukuyama, Francis
Political Order and Political Decay: From the Industrial Revolution to the Globalization of Democracy. Francis Fukuyama. Farrar, Straus and Giroux 2014. 672 pages
ISBN 9780374227357
Grades: Adult   320.1

1. State (Political science) 2. Comparative government 3. Democracy 4. Order (Philosophy) 5. Political science 6. Politics and global affairs — Political philosophy

LC 2014016973

Taking up the essential question of how societies develop strong, impersonal, and accountable political institutions, Fukuyama follows the story from the French Revolution to the Arab Spring and the deep dysfunctions of contemporary American politics. He examines the effects of corruption on governance, and why some societies have been successful at rooting it out. He explores the different legacies of colonialism in Latin America, Africa, and Asia, and offers an account of why some regions have thrived and developed more quickly than others.

"A compelling historical overview of a useful template for the retooling of institutions in the modern state. Systematic, thorough and even hopeful fodder for reform-minded political observers." —*Kirkus*

Sequel to: The origins of political order : from prehuman times to the French Revolution; Includes bibliographical references and index.

Machiavelli, Niccolo
★ *The Prince*. Niccolo Machiavelli; translated by W.K. Marriott; with an introduction by Dominic Baker-Smith. Knopf 1992. xxxi, 190 p.
ISBN 9780679410447
Grades: 11 12 Adult   320.1

1. Political science 2. Political ethics 3. Politics and global affairs — Political philosophy

Records the Italian statesman's classic statement on the nature of government and the means by which political power is obtained.

Translation of: Principe, first published in 1532; This translation first published in Penguin Classics 1961—T.P. verso; Includes bibliographical references (p. 174-178) and index.

Marshall, Tim
The Power of Geography: Ten Maps That Reveal the Future of Our World. Tim Marshall. Scribner 2021. 320 p.
ISBN 9781982178628
Grades: Adult   320.1

1. Countries 2. Geography 3. Maps 4. Boundaries 5. Landforms 6. Geopolitics 7. International relations 8. International competition 9. Space exploration 10. Political forecasting 11. Political science 12. Politics and global affairs — World politics

Tim Marshall's global bestseller Prisoners of Geography offered us a "fresh way of looking at maps," showing how every nation's choices are limited by mountains, rivers, seas and concrete. Since then, the geography hasn't changed, but the world has. Now, in this revelatory new book, Marshall takes us into ten regions that are set to shape global politics and power. Find out why the Earth's atmosphere is the world's next battleground; why the fight for the Pacific is just beginning; and why Europe's next refugee crisis is closer than we think.

"Mountains, deserts, and distances still leave a deep mark on national character and international relations, according to this fascinating exploration of geopolitics. . . . Marshall offers an immersive blend of history, economics, and political analysis that puts geography at the center of human affairs." —*Publishers Weekly*

Rousseau, Jean-Jacques
★ *The Social Contract*. Jean-Jacques Rousseau; translated by Maurice Cranston. Penguin Books 2006. 167 p.
ISBN 9780143037491
Grades: 11 12 Adult   320.1

1. Political science 2. Social contract 3. Philosophy 4. Freedom 5. Citizen participation in government 6. Political ethics 7. Translations — French to English 8. Politics and global affairs — Political philosophy

LC 2006043772

Rousseau sought to ground his political theory in an understanding of human nature, which he believed to be basically good but corrupted by the conflicting interests within society. Here self-interest degenerated into a state of war from which humanity could only be extricated by the imposition of a contract. As a party to the compact, each individual would find his true interest served within the political expression of the community of man, or the general will.

Translation of : Du contrat social; Includes bibliographical references; Originally published in France in 1762.

320.1092 Political philosophy — Biography

Boucheron, Patrick
Machiavelli: The Art of Teaching People What to Fear. Patrick Boucheron; translated from the French by Willard Wood. Random House Inc 2020. 176 p.
ISBN 9781590519523
Grades: Adult   320.1092

1. Machiavelli, Niccolo, 1469-1527 2. Political scientists 3. Diplomats 4. Political ethics 5. Political science 6. Philosophy 7. Biographies 8. Translations — French to English 9. Life stories — Politics 10. Politics and global affairs — Political philosophy 11. History writing — Renaissance — Europe

LC 2019025723

In a series of poignant vignettes, a preeminent historian makes a compelling case for Machiavelli as an unjustly maligned figure with valuable political insights that resonate as strongly today as they did in his time. Whenever a tempestuous period in history begins, Machiavelli is summoned, because he is known as one for philosophizing in dark times. In fact, since his death in 1527, we have never ceased to read him to pull ourselves out of torpors. But what do we really know about this man apart from the term invented by his detractors to refer to that political evil, Machiavellianism? with verve and a delightful erudition, Patrick Boucheron sheds light on the life and works of this unclassifiable visionary, illustrating how we can continue to use him as a guide in times of crisis.

"Readers looking to learn more about the thinker, as well as those seeking an introduction, will find this creative work appealing." —*Library Journal*

Includes bibliographical references; Originally published in French as Un ete avec Machiavel in 2017 by Editions des Equateurs, Paris; Translated from the French.

320.473 Structure and functions of government — United States

Richardson, Heather Cox
Democracy Awakening: Notes on the State of America. Heather Cox Richardson. Viking 2023. xvii, 286 p.
ISBN 9780593652961
Grades: Adult   320.473

1. Democracy 2. Misconceptions 3. Elite (Social sciences) 4. Authoritarianism 5. Conservatism 6. Opposition (Political science) 7. Social movements 8. Equality 9. Pluralism (Social sciences) 10. Politics and government 11. United

States history 12. United States 13. Politics and global affairs — Civil and human rights 14. History writing — United States

LC 2023006034

A historian and author of the popular daily newsletter Letters from an American explains how America, once a beacon of democracy, now teeters on the brink of autocracy—and how we can turn back.

In Democracy Awakening, Richardson crafts a compelling and original narrative, explaining how, over the decades, a small group of wealthy people have made war on American ideals. By weaponizing language and promoting false history they have led us into authoritarianism—creating a disaffected population and then promising to recreate an imagined past where those people could feel important again. She argues that taking our country back starts by remembering the elements of the nation's true history that marginalized Americans have always upheld. Richardson sees this history as a roadmap for the nation's future.

Boston College historian Richardson (To Make Men Free) analyzes the history of the United States from its origins through the present day, reframing many of the nation's major internal conflicts as part of an ongoing clash between 'Liberal democracy' and emerging 'Authoritarianism.' —*Publishers Weekly*

Includes bibliographical references and index.

320.5 Political ideologies

Paine, Thomas
★ *Rights of Man: And, Common Sense*. Thomas Paine; with an introduction by Michael Foot. Knopf 1994. LI, 306 p.
ISBN 9780679433149
Grades: 11 12 Adult 320.5
1. Burke, Edmund, 1729-1797 2. Monarchy 3. Politics and government 4. France 5. Great Britain 6. United States 7. 18th century 8. 19th century 9. Revolutionary France (1789-1799) 10. Georgian era (1714-1837) 11. Politics and global affairs — Civil and human rights

LC 94005989

Collects Paine's political writings about the American and French revolutions.

Includes bibliographical references (xxx-xxxi).

Spencer, Kyle
Raising Them Right: The Untold Story of America's Ultraconservative Youth Movement and Its Plot for Power. Kyle Spencer. Ecco Press 2022. 368 p.
ISBN 9780063041363
Grades: Adult 320.5
1. Young adults 2. New Right 3. Right-wing extremists 4. Conservatism 5. Conservatives 6. Political action committees 7. Radicalism 8. Christianity and politics 9. Identity 10. Political participation 11. Social life and customs 12. Politics and government 13. United States 14. Politics and global affairs — Political parties

Using original reporting and unprecedented access, an award-winning journalist chronicles the people and organizations working to lure millions of unsuspecting young American voters into the far-right fold, harnessing social media in alarming ways and capitalizing on the democratization of celebrity culture.

"A dispiriting picture of deepening political polarization." —*Kirkus*

320.50973 Political ideologies — United States

Self, Robert O.
All in the Family: The Realignment of American Democracy Since the 1960s. Robert O. Self. Hill and Wang 2012. 512 p.
ISBN 9780809095025
Grades: Adult 320.50973
1. Family policy 2. Social policy 3. Families 4. Social values 5. Politics and government 6. United States 7. 20th century 8. 21st century 9. History writing — Politicians — United States

LC 2011051271

Analyzes the social and political movements that redefined the American family from 1964 to 2004, which saw the rise of feminist and gay rights causes, while allowing conservatives to brand liberalism as damaging to the nuclear family.

Includes index.

320.51 Liberalism

Brennan, Jason
Libertarianism: What Everyone Needs to Know. Jason Brennan. Oxford University Press 2012. xvi, 213 pages; (What everyone needs to know)
ISBN 9780199933891
Grades: Adult 320.51
1. Libertarianism 2. Politics and government 3. United States 4. Politics and global affairs — Political parties

LC 2012020049

Presents an introduction to libertarianism, describing how libertarians view such topics as human nature, government, democracy, civil rights, economics, social justice, and contemporary problems, including immigration, health care, and education.

Includes bibliographical references (p. [191]-198) and index.

Fukuyama, Francis
Liberalism and Its Discontents. Francis Fukuyama. Farrar, Straus and Giroux 2022. 192 p.
ISBN 9780374606718
Grades: Adult 320.51
1. Liberalism 2. Freedom 3. Individualism 4. Democracy 5. Right and left (Political science) 6. Philosophy 7. Political science 8. Impartial writing 9. Politics and global affairs — Political philosophy 10. Politics and global affairs — Civil and human rights

LC 2021059692

Classical liberalism is in a state of crisis. Developed in the wake of Europe's wars over religion and nationalism, liberalism is a system for governing diverse societies, which is grounded in fundamental principles of equality and the rule of law. It emphasizes the rights of individuals to pursue their own forms of happiness free from encroachment by government. As the renowned political philosopher Francis Fukuyama shows in Liberalism and Its Discontents, the principles of liberalism have, in recent decades, been pushed to new extremes by both the right and the left: Neoliberals made a cult of economic freedom, and progressives focused on identity over human universality as central to their political vision. The result, Fukuyama argues, has been a fracturing of our civil society and an increasing peril to our democracy.

"Essential reading for all students of political science. Fukuyama's scholarly, yet approachable work is highly recommended for any reader interested in understanding the current political environment." —*Library Journal*

Includes bibliographical references and index.

320.52 Conservatism

Arnsdorf, Isaac
★ *Finish What We Started: The MAGA Movement's Ground War to End Democracy*. Isaac Arnsdorf. Little, Brown and Company 2024. 256 p.
ISBN 9780316497510
Grades: Adult 320.52
1. Trump, Donald, 1946- 2. Presidents 3. Presidential candidates 4. Elections 5. Disagreement 6. Right-wing extremists 7. Grassroots movement 8. Political consultants 9. Strategy 10. Politics and government 11. United States 12. Politics and global affairs — Political parties 13. Politics and global affairs — Elections 14. Life stories — Politics 15. Debut title

Inspired by Donald Trump's election lies, a growing movement of grassroots activists mobilized around the country to pick up where the insurrection left off, laying the groundwork to succeed next time where Trump had failed to keep himself in power. Drawing on extensive on-the-ground reporting around the

ESSENTIAL AND RECOMMENDED TITLES
320.520973 Conservatism — United States

country, Washington Post reporter Isaac Arnsdorf has produced the defining journalistic account of the origins, evolution and future of the MAGA movement.

"This eye-opening, often terrifying debut work is rich with political history and recent case studies." —*Library Journal*

Includes bibliographical references and index.

Conason, Joe
*The **Longest** Con: How Grifters, Swindlers, and Frauds Hijacked American Conservatism.* Joe Conason; foreword by George T. Conway III.. St. Martin's Press 2024. 320 p.

ISBN 9781250621160

Grades: Adult   320.52

1. Conservatism 2. Conservatives 3. Political parties 4. Politicians 5. Political consultants 6. Corruption 7. Fraud 8. Deception 9. Politics and government 10. United States 11. Politics and global affairs — Political parties 12. Life stories — Politics 13. History writing — Scandals

The Longest Con tells the fascinating story of the partisan con artists who have corrupted conservative politics in our time, creating a toxic phenomenon that culminated in the election of Donald Trump. But long before he appeared, Trump's path to power was blazed by the motley horde of swindlers and quacks who preceded him. In an unsparing and often comic narrative, Joe Conason explores the right's long, steep descent into a movement whose principal aim is not to protect freedom or defend the Constitution, but merely to line the pockets of pretenders and blowhards whose malevolent tactics now endanger the nation.

"With disinformation run amok, unwavering investigations such as Conason's are essential reality checks on the duplicitous nature of money in politics." —*Booklist*

Includes bibliographical references and index.

Ganz, John
When the Clock Broke: Con Men, Conspiracists, and How America Cracked up in the Early 1990s. John Ganz. Farrar, Straus and Giroux 2024. 432 p.

ISBN 9780374605445

Grades: Adult   320.52

1. Conservatism 2. Populism 3. Extremism 4. New right 5. Politicians 6. Political consultants 7. Politics and government 8. United States history 9. United States 10. 1990s 11. Liberal writing 12. Politics and global affairs — Political figures 13. History writing — 1990s — United States 14. Life stories — Politics 15. Debut title

LC 2023051871

With the Soviet Union extinct, Saddam Hussein defeated, and U.S. power at its zenith, the early 1990s promised a "kinder, gentler America." Instead, it was a period of rising anger and domestic turmoil, anticipating the polarization and resurgent extremism we know today. In When the Clock Broke, the acclaimed political writer John Ganz tells the story of America's late-century discontents, immersing us in a time when what Philip Roth called the "indigenous American berserk" took new and ever-wilder forms.

"Ganz…debuts with a lucid and propulsive narrative of the failed right-wing populism at the fringe of the 1992 U.S. presidential election." —*Publishers Weekly*

Includes bibliographical references and index.

320.520973 Conservatism — United States

Allitt, Patrick
*The **Conservatives**: Ideas and Personalities Throughout American History.* Patrick Allitt. Yale University Press 2009. x, 325 p.

ISBN 9780300118940

Grades: Adult   320.520973

1. Conservatives 2. Politicians 3. Political science 4. Conservatism 5. Politics and government 6. United States 7. History writing — Politicians — United States

LC 2008042559

Argues how conservatism has taken various forms to combat percieved threats and challenges throughout American history.

"From present-day questions of taxation and big government, Allitt traces conservative principles to the earliest days of the republic. Cutting across the stereotypes of present-day conservatism, this nuanced, thoughtful history should educate the unaffiliated and help the disillusioned recover." —*Publishers Weekly*

Includes bibliographical references (p. 281-314) and index.

Will, George F.
*The **Conservative** Sensibility.* George F. Will. Hachette Books 2019. 736 pages

ISBN 9780316480932

Grades: Adult   320.520973

1. Founding Fathers of the United States 2. Constitutional history 3. Civics 4. Separation of powers 5. Civil rights 6. Freedom 7. Natural law 8. Conservatism 9. Political science 10. Politics and government 11. United States 12. Conservative writing 13. Politics and global affairs — Political philosophy 14. Politics and global affairs — Political parties 15. Politics and global affairs — World politics — United States 16. History writing — Politicians — United States

LC 2018048055

New York Times Notable Book, 2019.

A reflection on American conservatism, examining how the Founders' belief in natural rights created a great American political tradition—one that now finds itself under threat, both from progressives and elements inside the Republican Party.

"This is a timely and important book by one of the foremost contemporary conservative thinkers and writers. Recommended for most collections." —*Library Journal*

Includes bibliographical references and index.

320.53 Collectivism and fascism

Arendt, Hannah
*The **Origins** of Totalitarianism.* Hannah Arendt; intoduction by Samantha Power. Schocken Books 2004. xxvii, 674 p.

ISBN 9780805242256

Grades: 11 12 Adult   320.53

1. Totalitarianism 2. Imperialism 3. Antisemitism 4. Politics and culture 5. Social movements 6. 20th century 7. History writing — General 8. Politics and global affairs — Political philosophy

LC 2003060749

A political analysis of totalitarian societies traces the nineteenth-century rise of anti-Semitism in central and western Europe and considers the institutions and operations of Nazi Germany and Stalinist Russia, examining such phenomena as the transformation of classes into masses, the applications of propaganda, and the use of terror.

Includes bibliographical references (p. 633-656) and index; Originally published: 1st ed. New York : Harcourt, Brace, 1951.

Brown, Archie
★ *The **Rise** and Fall of Communism.* Archie Brown. Ecco 2009. 800 p.

ISBN 9780061138799

Grades: Adult   320.53

1. Communism 2. Ideology 3. Political science 4. Marxism 5. Class struggle 6. Philosophy 7. Politics and global affairs — Political philosophy

LC Bl2009012711

An in-depth history by the prize-winning Oxford professor author of the Gorbachev Factor traces the origins of the communist ideology through its collapse in many nations following perestroika, in an extensively researched volume that also explores communism's current incarnations.

"A seminal work from a distinguished scholar; highly recommended." —*Library Journal*

PUBLIC LIBRARY CORE COLLECTION: NONFICTION
Twentieth Edition

Maddow, Rachel
★ *Prequel: An American Fight Against Fascism.* Rachel Maddow. Crown 2023. 320 p.
ISBN 9780593444511
Grades: Adult 320.53
1. World War II 2. Politicians 3. Right-wing extremists 4. Nazism 5. Antisemitism 6. Fascism 7. Insurgency 8. Propaganda 9. Political corruption 10. Treason 11. United States history 12. Second World War era (1939-1945) 13. History writing — Scandals 14. History writing — United States 15. History writing — Wars and conflicts — World War II

An MSNBC anchor traces the fight to preserve American democracy back to World War II, when a handful of committed public servants and brave private citizens thwarted far-right plotters trying to steer our nation toward an alliance with the Nazis.

Paxton, Robert O.
The Anatomy of Fascism. Robert O. Paxton. Alfred A. Knopf 2004. xii, 321 p.
ISBN 9781400040940
Grades: Adult 320.53
1. Fascism 2. Europe 3. Politics and global affairs — Political philosophy 4. Adult books for young adults
LC 2004100489

Presents a detailed political analysis of how twentieth century fascism took hold and thrived in certain European countries, such as Italy and Germany, and not in others.

"While there are countless studies on fascism, readers will be hard pressed to find anything more in-depth from a scholar with Paxton's credentials." —*Library Journal*

Includes bibliographical references (p. 251-307) and index.

320.540973 Nationalism, regionalism, internationalism — United States

Brookhiser, Richard
Give Me Liberty: A History of America's Exceptional Idea. Richard Brookhiser. Basic Books 2020. IX, 292 p.
ISBN 9781541699137
Grades: Adult 320.540973
1. Freedom 2. National characteristics, American 3. Group identity 4. Social integration 5. Historic documents 6. Nationalism 7. Politics and government 8. United States history 9. United States 10. History writing — United States
LC 2019948392

Nationalism is inevitable: It supplies feelings of belonging, identity, and recognition. It binds us to our neighbors and tells us who we are. But increasingly—from the United States to India, from Russia to Burma—nationalism is being invoked for unworthy ends: to disdain minorities or to support despots. As a result, nationalism has become to many a dirty word. In Give Me Liberty, award-winning historian and biographer Richard Brookhiser offers up a truer and more inspiring story of American nationalism as it has evolved over four hundred years. He examines America's history through thirteen documents that made the United States a new country in a new world: a free country.

Includes bibliographical references and index.

320.56 Ideologies based on groups of people

Frank, Thomas
The People, No: A Brief History of Anti-populism. Thomas Frank. Metropolitan Books 2020. 307 p.
ISBN 9781250220110
Grades: Adult 320.56
1. Populism 2. Political culture 3. Social movements 4. Common good 5. Elite (Social sciences) 6. Plutocracy 7. Progressivism (United States politics) 8. Democracy 9. Politics and government 10. United States history 11. United States 12. History writing — United States 13. Politics and global affairs — Political philosophy
LC 2020009048

Today "populism" is seen as a frightening thing, a term pundits use to describe the racist philosophy of Donald Trump and European extremists. But this is a mistake. The real story of populism is an account of enlightenment and liberation; it is the story of American democracy itself, of its ever-widening promise of a decent life for all. Taking us from the tumultuous 1890s, when the radical left-wing Populist Party—the biggest mass movement in American history—fought Gilded Age plutocrats to the reformers' great triumphs under Franklin Roosevelt and Harry Truman, Frank reminds us how much we owe to the populist ethos.

"Frank's writing is notable for its clarity and its ability to make connections. His provocative conclusions, about elites and the people, sometimes turn common assumptions upside down—all the better for making readers think." —*Booklist*

Published in Australia under the title, People without power: the war on populism and the fight for democracy, Scribe, 2020; Includes bibliographical references and index.

320.943 Germany — Politics

Feigel, Lara
The Bitter Taste of Victory: In the Ruins of the Reich. Lara Feigel. Bloomsbury USA 2016. 384 p.
ISBN 9781632865519
Grades: Adult 320.943
1. World War II 2. Reconstruction (1939-1951) 3. Postwar life 4. German history 5. Germany 6. 20th century 7. History writing — Europe — Germany
LC Bl2016020710

When Germany surrendered in May 1945 it was a nation reduced to rubble. Immediately, America, Britain, Soviet Russia, and France set about rebuilding in their zones of occupation. Most urgent were physical needs—food, water, and sanitation—but from the start the Allies were also anxious to indoctrinate the German people in the ideas of peace and civilization.

"Many individuals had to come to terms with the evil they saw and with themselves, and Feigel does a masterful job in sorting it out. This is uniquely nuanced history." —*Booklist*

320.973 Politics — United States

Baer, Daniel Brooks
The Four Tests: What It Will Take to Keep America Strong and Good. Daniel Baer. Avid Reader Press 2023. VII, 257 p.
ISBN 9781668006580
Grades: Adult 320.973
1. International relations 2. International security 3. Political leadership 4. Democracy 5. Investments 6. Immigration and emigration 7. Fairness 8. Group identity 9. Cooperation 10. Politics and government 11. Policy sciences 12. United States 13. Politics and global affairs — General 14. History writing — Early 21st century — United States
LC 2023023288

The former US Ambassador to the Organization for Security and Cooperation in Europe sheds new light on America's future and the four "tests"—scale, investment, fairness and identity—we must face in the next ten years that will determine if we succeed over the next fifty.

"Policy wonks and activists will find much to ponder in Baer's lucidly argued platform." —*Kirkus*

Includes bibliographical references and index.

Bawer, Bruce
The Victims' Revolution: The Rise of Identity Studies and the Closing of the Liberal Mind. Bruce Bawer. Broadside Books 2012. 256 p.
ISBN 9780061807374

ESSENTIAL AND RECOMMENDED TITLES
321 Systems of governments and states

Grades: Adult   **320.973**
1. Higher education 2. Objectivity 3. Thought and thinking 4. Radicalism 5. Society and culture — Education — Higher education

A critique of the identity-based revolution in America's universities during the 1960s and 1970s, which impacted modern politics and society, explores how radical philosophies that denied aesthetic merit and objective truth came into being.

Giridharadas, Anand

★ *The Persuaders: At the Frontlines of the Fight for Hearts, Minds, and Democracy.* Anand Giridharadas. Alfred A. Knopf 2022. 304 p.
ISBN 9780593318997

Grades: Adult   **320.973**
1. Political culture 2. Persuasion (Psychology) 3. Political participation 4. Polarization (Social sciences) 5. Social change 6. Democracy 7. Social justice 8. Politics and government 9. United States 10. 21st century 11. Politics and global affairs — General 12. Society and culture — Social activism and philanthropy

LC 2022009611

Taking us inside movements and battles for justice, seeking out the dissenters who continue to champion persuasion in an age of polarization, the subjects of this book grapple with how to call out threats and injustices while calling in those who don't agree with them but just might one day.

"A welcome, revealing study of how political messages can be shaped positively to counter both enmity and disinformation." —*Kirkus*

Includes index.

Masciotra, David

Exurbia Now: The Battleground of American Democracy. David Masciotra. Melville House 2024. 320 p.
ISBN 9781685890896

Grades: Adult   **320.973**
1. Small towns 2. Rural life 3. Political culture 4. Conservatism 5. Polarization (Social sciences) 6. Urban-rural migration 7. Rural sociology 8. United States 9. Society and culture — Urban and regional studies 10. Politics and global affairs — General

Beyond a fanatical devotion to former president Donald Trump, one of the curious things that united the rank and file of the January 6 insurrectionist mob was that many of them were residents of one of America's fastest growing residential areas: Exurbia. Veteran political journalist David Masciotra provides a definitive account of what exurbia is, how it came to be, and how it's transforming American life. Exurbia, as it turns out, is ground zero for the fight over a democracy mightily beleaguered, yet still full of promise, and still worth fighting for.

"Masciotra brings his personal experience to his cogent and frightening analysis of the mindset that has taken hold in so many American small towns and rural communities, offering insight and a fresh perspective on the culture wars dividing the country." —*Booklist*

Tocqueville, Alexis de

★ *Democracy in America.* Alexis de Tocqueville; translated from the French by Arthur Goldhammer. Library of America 2004. xvi, 941 p. : Map
ISBN 9781931082540

Grades: Adult   **320.973**
1. American people 2. Political parties 3. Political culture 4. Sociology 5. Political institutions 6. French people in the United States 7. Democracy 8. Political science 9. Politics and government 10. United States 11. Translations — French to English 12. Politics and global affairs — Political philosophy

LC 2003061885

A study of our national government and character follows the author's concern about the effect of majority rule on the rights of individuals and provides insight into the rewards and responsibilities of a democratic government.

Translation of: De la democratie en Amerique (1835); Includes bibliographical references and index; Translated from the French.

321 Systems of governments and states

Plato

★ *The Republic.* Plato; edited by G.R.F. Ferrari; translated by Tom Griffith. Cambridge University Press 2000. xlviii, 382 p.
ISBN 9780521484435

Grades: 11 12 Adult   **321**
1. Justice 2. Political science 3. Utopias 4. Politics and global affairs — General

LC 00024471

Presents the most important of the Socratic dialogues as if it were a conversation; deals with the creation of an ideal commonwealth and ranks as one of the earliest Utopian works.

"Griffith's aim was to translate the Greek text as if it were a conversation, and he has succeeded admirably. The text does indeed flow like a conversation, with the entire back-and-forth interaction that such exchanges involve. [He] has also written a very useful introduction that places the work in a historical context and provides a glossary that will help readers identify individuals and places mentioned in the work." —*Library Journal*

Includes bibliographical references (p. xxxii-xxxvii) and index.

321.8 Democracy

Litt, David

Democracy in One Book or Less: How It Works, Why It Doesn't, and Why Fixing It Is Easier Than You Think. David Litt. Ecco 2020. 320 p.
ISBN 9780062879363

Grades: Adult   **321.8**
1. Political science 2. Voting 3. Practical politics 4. Political obligation 5. Voter registration 6. Citizen participation in government 7. Voter turnout 8. Democracy 9. Political participation 10. Politics and government 11. United States 12. Politics and global affairs — General

LC BL2020013829

What explains the gap between what We, the People want and what our elected leaders do? How can we fix our politics before it's too late? and how can we truly understand the state of our democracy without wanting to crawl under a rock? That's what former Obama speechwriter David Litt set out to answer. Citing the increased voting restrictions and fall in competitive Congressional districts behind major changes to democracy in America, the former White House speechwriter outlines strategies for reclaiming representation for all citizens.

"Both optimistic and clear-eyed, this quip-filled call to action will resonate strongly with young progressives." —*Publishers Weekly*

Also published in large print format.

Runciman, David

The Confidence Trap: A History of Democracy in Crisis from World War I to the Present. David Runciman. Princeton University Press 2013. 408 pages
ISBN 9780691148687

Grades: Adult   **321.8**
1. Democracy 2. World politics 3. Political science 4. History writing — General

LC 2013019899

Why do democracies keep lurching from success to failure? the current financial crisis is just the latest example of how things continue to go wrong, just when it looked like they were going right. In this wide-ranging, original, and compelling book, David Runciman tells the story of modern democracy through the history of moments of crisis, from the First World War to the economic crash of 2008.

Includes bibliographical references and index.

321.9 Authoritarian government

Applebaum, Anne
Twilight of Democracy: The Seductive Lure of Authoritarianism. Anne Applebaum. Doubleday 2020. 208 p.
ISBN 9780385545808
Grades: Adult   321.9
1. Authoritarianism 2. Democracy 3. Nationalism 4. New Right 5. World politics 6. 21st century 7. Politics and global affairs — Political philosophy 8. Politics and global affairs — World politics
LC 2020012450
A Pulitzer Prize-winning historian and journalist examines the current world-wide rise of authoritarianism and explains how it appeals to citizens by using conspiracy theory, political polarization, social media and nostalgia.
"Equal parts memoir, reportage, and history, this sobering account of the roots and forms of today's authoritarianism, by one of its most accomplished observers, is meant as a warning to everyone." —*Kirkus*
Also published in large print format; Includes bibliographical references.

Kalder, Daniel
The Infernal Library: On Dictators, Their Books, and Other Catastrophes of Literacy. Daniel Kalder. Henry Holt and Company 2018. 464 p.
ISBN 9781627793421
Grades: Adult   321.9
1. Dictatorship 2. Dictators 3. Propaganda 4. Language and power (Social sciences) 5. Knowledge 6. History writing — Wars and conflicts 7. Arts and Entertainment — Writing and Publishing — Literary criticism
LC 2017009633
A harrowing tour of "dictator literature" in the twentieth-century, featuring the soul-killing prose and poetry of Hitler, Mao, and many more, which shows how books have sometimes shaped the world for the worse.
"The author renders his highly compelling narrative in a cheeky yet erudite tone that will keep readers smirking despite the monstrousness of the book's protagonists. Dictators have never looked so educated." —*Kirkus*
Includes index.

Stanley, Jason
How Fascism Works: The Politics of Us and Them. Jason Stanley. Random House 2018. 208 p.
ISBN 9780525511830
Grades: Adult   321.9
1. Fascism 2. Polarization (Social sciences) 3. Political science 4. Nationalism 5. Philosophy 6. Politics and global affairs — Political philosophy
LC 2018013266
The Yale philosopher reveals the fascist politics behind today's ethnic, racial, and religious divides, identifying ten key examples of fascist politics that are used by political leaders to hold onto power.
Includes bibliographical references and index.

322 Relation of the state to organized groups and their members

Kertzer, David I.
The Pope and Mussolini: The Secret History of Pius XI and the Rise of Fascism in Europe. David I. Kertzer. Random House 2014. 576 pages
ISBN 9780812993462
Grades: Adult   322
1. Pius XI, Pope, 1857-1939 2. Mussolini, Benito, 1883-1945 3. Strategic alliances (Military) 4. Papacy 5. Fascism 6. Vatican City 7. Italy 8. History writing — Europe — Italy 9. History writing — Scandals
LC 2013019402
Pulitzer Prize for Biography or Autobiography, 2015.
Analyzes the relationship between Pius XI and the notorious Italian dictator, tracing how after coming into power in the same year they forged covert ties to one another to consolidate power and pursue political goals.

"Kertzer unravels the relationship between two of 20th-century Europes most important political figures and does so in an accessible style that makes for a fast-paced must-read." —*Publishers Weekly*
Includes bibliographical references and index.

Sharlet, Jeff
★ *The Undertow: Scenes from a Slow Civil War.* Jeff Sharlet. W.W. Norton & Company 2023. 302 p.
ISBN 9781324006497
Grades: Adult   322
1. Religious fanaticism 2. Misogyny 3. Conspiracy theories 4. Political culture 5. Right-wing extremists 6. Identity 7. Polarization (Social sciences) 8. United States 9. Essays 10. Society and culture — General 11. Politics and global affairs — Political parties 12. Life stories — People in history — Witness to history
National Book Critics Circle Award for Nonfiction finalist, 2023.
Lies, greed, and glorification of war boom through microphones at hipster megachurches that once upon a time might have preached peace and understanding. Political rallies are as aflame with need and giddy expectation as religious revivals. On the Far Right, everything is heightened—love into adulation, fear into vengeance, anger into white-hot rage. Here, in the undertow, our forty-fifth president, a vessel of conspiratorial fears and fantasies, continues to rise to sainthood. Framing this dangerous vision, Sharlet remembers and celebrates the courage of those who sing a different song of community, and of an America long dreamt of and yet to be fully born.
"This is a grim but necessary examination of democracy's potential assassins, leavened by Sharlet's incredible storytelling and acute observations." —*Booklist*

322.4 Political action groups

Chalmers, David Mark
Hooded Americanism: The History of the Ku Klux Klan. David M. Chalmers. Duke University Press 1987. xii, 477 p, 16 p. of plates : Illustration
ISBN 9780822307723
Grades: Adult   322.4
1. Hate groups 2. History writing — United States
LC 86029133
The nature and objectives of the Ku Klux Klan are revealed in a study of its development and members over one hundred years.
Includes index; Bibliography: P. [441]-463; Reprint. Originally published: New York : F. Watts, c1981.

Egan, Timothy
★ *A Fever in the Heartland: The Ku Klux Klan's Plot to Take Over America, and the Woman Who Stopped Them.* Timothy Egan. Viking 2023. 416 p.
ISBN 9780735225268
Grades: Adult   322.4
1. Stephenson, David Curtis, 1891-1966 2. Oberholtzer, Madge, 1896-1925 3. Hate groups 4. White supremacists 5. Swindlers and swindling 6. Rapists 7. Racism 8. Xenophobia 9. Violence 10. Power 11. Murder investigation 12. Women kidnapping victims 13. Witnesses 14. Criminal judgments 15. Indiana 16. 1920s 17. History writing — Roaring 20s — United States 18. History writing — Scandals 19. True Crime — Historical Crime
LC 2022029431
The Roaring Twenties—the Jazz Age—has been characterized as a time of Gatsby frivolity. But it was also the height of the uniquely American hate group, the Ku Klux Klan. Their domain was not the old Confederacy, but the Heartland and the West. And the man who set in motion their takeover of great swaths of America was a charismatic charlatan named D.C. Stephenson. But at the peak of his influence, it was a seemingly powerless woman— Madge Oberholtzer—who would reveal his secret cruelties, and whose deathbed testimony finally brought the Klan to their knees.

ESSENTIAL AND RECOMMENDED TITLES
323 Civil and political rights

"Dramatic twists of fate and vivid character sketches distinguish this harrowing look at a forgotten chapter of American history." —*Publishers Weekly*

Includes bibliographical references and index.

323 Civil and political rights

Honey, Michael K
To the Promised Land: Martin Luther King and the Fight for Economic Justice. Michael K. Honey. W.W. Norton & Company 2018. 224 p.
ISBN 9780393651263
Grades: Adult   323

1. King, Martin Luther, Jr, 1929-1968 2. Inequality 3. Income inequality 4. Civil Rights Movement 5. Equality 6. Social justice 7. Working class 8. Civil rights workers 9. African Americans 10. Discrimination in employment 11. United States 12. 20th century 13. Biographies 14. History writing — African American — Civil rights — United States 15. Life stories — Politics — Activists and reformers — Civil Rights leaders 16. Business and economics — Economics — Socioeconomics

LC 2017060268

Goes beyond popularized views of Martin Luther King, Jr, to explore his committed advocacy of the poor, the working class, and unions, as well as his views about nonviolent resistance to all forms of oppression, particularly economic inequality.

"Honey encourages the many who revere his memory to continue his work toward this goal. His book contains both insight and inspiration to activists of many stripes." —*Publishers Weekly*

Includes bibliographical references and index.

Kotz, Nick
Judgment Days: Lyndon Baines Johnson, Martin Luther King, Jr, and the Laws That Changed America. Nick Kotz. Houghton Mifflin 2005. xix, 522 p. : Illustration
ISBN 9780618088256
Grades: Adult   323

1. Johnson, Lyndon B, 1908-1973 2. King, Martin Luther, Jr, 1929-1968 3. African Americans 4. African American history 5. Civil rights 6. Legislation 7. Race relations 8. Politics and government 9. United States 10. 20th century 11. 1960s 12. History writing — African American — Civil rights — United States

LC 2004059852

Library Journal Best Books, 2005.

The first comprehensive account of the relationship between President Johnson and Martin Luther King uses FBI wiretaps, Johnson's taped telephone conversations, and previously undisclosed communications between the two to paint a fascinating portrait of this important relationship.

"This book is an informed political investigation of these two civil rights warriors and the cause for which they fought and, in King's case, died." —*Library Journal*

Includes bibliographical references (p. [480]-493) and index.

Laing, Olivia
Everybody: A Book About Freedom. Olivia Laing. W. W. Norton & Company 2021. 368 p.
ISBN 9780393608779
Grades: Adult   323

1. Reich, Wilhelm, 1897-1957 2. Human body 3. Psychoanalysts 4. Body image 5. Human rights 6. Sexuality 7. Repression (Psychology) 8. Freedom 9. History writing — General 10. Science Writing — Medicine and health — Mental health 11. Society and culture — Psychology and human behavior

LC 2021000768

The body is a source of pleasure and of pain, at once hopelessly vulnerable and radiant with power. In her ambitious, brilliant sixth book, Olivia Laing charts an electrifying course through the long struggle for bodily freedom, using the life of the renegade psychoanalyst Wilhelm Reich to explore gay rights and sexual liberation, feminism, and the civil rights movement.

"Laing's finely crafted blend of incisive memoir and biography vitalize this unique chronicle of the endless struggle 'To be free of oppression based on the kind of body' one inhabits, a work of fresh and dynamic analysis and revelation." —*Booklist*

Includes bibliographical references and index.

323.092 Civil rights leaders

Sokol, Jason
The Heavens Might Crack: The Death and Legacy of Martin Luther King, Jr. Jason Sokol. Basic Books 2018. 320 p.
ISBN 9780465055913
Grades: Adult   323.092

1. King, Martin Luther, Jr, 1929-1968 2. African American civil rights workers 3. Civil Rights Movement 4. Civil rights 5. Biographies 6. Life stories — Politics — Activists and reformers 7. History writing — African American — Civil rights — United States 8. History writing — 1960s — United States

LC 2017042658

On April 4, 1968, Martin Luther King Jr. Was fatally shot as he stood on the balcony of the Lorraine Motel in Memphis. At the time of his murder, King was a polarizing figure—scorned by many white Americans, worshipped by some African Americans and liberal whites, and deemed irrelevant by many Black youth. In The Heavens Might Crack, historian Jason Sokol traces the diverse responses, both in America and throughout the world, to King's death. Whether celebrating or mourning, most agreed that the final flicker of hope for a multiracial America had been extinguished. A deeply moving account of a country coming to terms with an act of shocking violence, the Heavens Might Crack is essential reading for anyone seeking to understand America's fraught racial past and present.

Includes bibliographical references and index.

Wexler, Stuart
Killing King: Racial Terrorists, James Earl Ray, and the Plot to Assassinate Martin Luther King Jr. Stuart Wexler and Larry Hancock. Counterpoint Press 2018. 304 pages
ISBN 9781619029194
Grades: Adult   323.092

1. King, Martin Luther, Jr, 1929-1968 2. Ray, James Earl, 1928-1998 3. African American civil rights workers 4. Civil Rights Movement 5. Civil rights 6. Conspiracies 7. United States 8. Biographies 9. Life stories — Politics — Activists and reformers 10. History writing — African American — Civil rights — United States 11. History writing — 1960s — United States

LC 2017054596

Uncovering previously unknown FBI files and sources, as well as new forensics, the authors of America's Secret Jihad convincingly make the case that Martin Luther King was assassinated by a clear and long simmering conspiracy orchestrated by the racial terrorists who were responsible for the Mississippi Burning murders.

Includes bibliographical references and index.

323.0975 Civil rights — Southeastern United States

Bond, Julian
★ *Julian Bond's Time to Teach: A History of the Southern Civil Rights Movement.* Julian Bond; edited by Pamela Horowitz and Jeanne Theoharis; photographs by Danny Lyon; afterword by Vann R. Newkirk II.. Beacon Press 2021. 416 p.
ISBN 9780807033203
Grades: Adult   323.0975

1. Civil Rights Movement 2. Civil rights demonstrations 3. Civil rights workers 4. Antiracism 5. Universities and colleges 6. African American history 7. Civil rights 8. 20th century 9. Speeches, addresses, etc. 10. History writing — African American — Civil rights — United States 11. Society and culture — Race 12. Life stories — Politics — Activists and Reformers — Civil Rights Leaders 13. Antiracist literature

PUBLIC LIBRARY CORE COLLECTION: NONFICTION
Twentieth Edition

LC 2020029089

Horace "Julian" Bond was an influential social justice activist, politician, and visionary who is best known as one of the founders of the Student Nonviolent Coordinating Committee (SNCC). For over two decades, he taught a popular class at the University of Virginia on the history of the civil rights movement. Compiled from his original lecture notes, Julian Bond's Time to Teach brings his invaluable teachings to a new generation of readers and provides a necessary toolkit for today's activists in the era of Black Lives Matter and #MeToo. Through his lectures, Bond detailed the ground-shaking disruption the movement caused, its immense unpopularity at the time, and the bravery of activists, some very young, who chose to disturb order to pursue justice.

"This authoritative testimony is bound to become a staple of American civil rights literature." —*Booklist*

Includes bibliographical references and index.

323.1 Civil and political rights of nondominant groups

Branch, Taylor
★ *Pillar of Fire: America in the King Years, 1963-65*. Taylor Branch. Simon & Schuster 1998. xiv, 746 p. : Illustration (America in the King years, 2)
ISBN 9780684808192
Grades: 11 12 Adult   323.1
1. King, Martin Luther, Jr, 1929-1968 2. African American civil rights 3. Civil Rights Movement 4. Freedom Riders (Civil rights movement) 5. March on Washington for Jobs and Freedom, 1963 6. Race relations 7. United States history 8. 1960s 9. 20th century 10. Biographies 11. History writing — African American — Civil rights — United States 12. History writing — 1960s — United States 13. Life stories — Politics — Activists and Reformers — Civil Rights Leaders

LC 97046076

ALA Notable Book, 1999; New York Times Notable Book, 1998.

Examines the jailing of Martin Luther King, jr, the end of segregation, and the growing rifts in the civil rights movement that led to calls for a more violent reaction to racism.

"Branch's research is impeccable and his knowledge of his material solid. The book is significant for marshaling so much information, particularly the profiles of all the many individuals involved in the race issues of that time." —*Booklist*

Sequel to: Parting the waters; Includes bibliographical references (p. [620]-716) and index.

Halberstam, David
★ *The Children*. David Halberstam. Random House 1998. 783 p, 16 p. of plates : Illustration
ISBN 9780679415619
Grades: Adult   323.1
1. African American students 2. Nonviolence 3. Civil Rights Movement 4. Civil rights workers 5. African American history 6. Civil rights 7. Race relations 8. Nashville, Tennessee 9. United States 10. 1950s 11. 1960s 12. 20th century 13. Biographies 14. History writing — African American — Civil rights — United States 15. Adult books for young adults

LC 97019974

Booklist Editors' Choice, 1998; New York Times Notable Book, 1998.

The Children is David Halberstam's brilliant and moving evocation of the early days of the civil rights movement, as seen through the story of the young people-the Children-who met in the 1960s and went on to lead the revolution. The Children is a story one of America's preeminent journalists has waited years to write, a powerful book about one of the most dramatic movements in American history.

"This is a recreation of the early days of the civil rights movement. The author focuses on a small group of young African Americans who attended the Reverend James Lawson's workshop for nonviolent demonstrators in Nashville in 1959, then went on to play active roles in the movement. A masterful achievement in reporting, research and understanding." —*Publishers Weekly*

Includes bibliographical references (p. [733]-736) and index.

King, Martin Luther
★ *A Testament of Hope: The Essential Writings and Speeches of Martin Luther King, Jr.* Edited by James Melvin Washington. HarperSanFrancisco 1991. xxvii, 702 p.
ISBN 9780060646912
Grades: Adult   323.1
1. African American civil rights 2. Race relations 3. United States 4. Spirituality and Religion — Christianity 5. Society and culture — Ethnic studies 6. History writing — United States

LC 90048203

Collects the civil rights leader's writings on nonviolence, social policy, integration, Black nationalism, and more.

Includes bibliographical references (p. 681-688) and index.

323.1196 African Americans — Civil and human rights

Baldwin, James
I Am Not Your Negro: A Major Motion Picture Directed by Raoul Peck. James Baldwin; film directed by Raoul Peck. Random House Inc 2017. 118 p.
ISBN 9780525434696
Grades: Adult   323.1196
1. African American civil rights 2. Racism 3. Social justice 4. Race relations 5. United States 6. Interviews 7. Essays 8. Media tie-ins 9. History writing — African American — United States

LC 2016053419

Transcript of the documentary film, I am not your negro, by Raoul Peck composed of unpublished and published writings, interviews, and letters by James Baldwin on the subject of racism in America.

Boyd, Herb
We Shall Overcome. Herb Boyd; narrated by Ossie Davis & Ruby Dee. Sourcebooks 2004. 263 p. : Illustration
ISBN 9781402202131
Grades: 11 12 Adult   323.1196
1. King, Martin Luther, Jr, 1929-1968 2. Till, Emmett, 1941-1955 3. Civil Rights Movement 4. Civil rights 5. Racism 6. Race relations 7. African American history 8. United States history 9. 20th century 10. Society and culture — Race 11. History writing — African American — Civil rights — United States

LC 2004012509

Chronicles the significant events and key figures from the civil right movement, including the assassination of Martin Luther King Jr, the murder of Emmet Till, and the Watts riots, with archival audio recordings on the accompanying CDs.

"Two audio CDs, narrated by actors Ossie Davis and Ruby Dee, offer everything from protests songs to the recollections of sit-in participants. Boyd's volume is a useful compilation of information arranged in an economical, accessible format, one sure to appeal to students, amateur historians and general readers." —*Publishers Weekly*

Includes bibliographical references (p. [252]-256) and index.

Branch, Taylor
★ *At Canaan's Edge: America in the King Years, 1965-68*. Taylor Branch. Simon & Schuster 2006. xiii, 1039 p. : Illustration (America in the King years, 3)
ISBN 9780684857121
Grades: 11 12 Adult   323.1196
1. King, Martin Luther, Jr, 1929-1968 2. Nonviolence 3. Civil Rights Movement 4. African American history 5. Civil rights 6. United States history 7. United States 8. 1960s 9. 20th century 10. Biographies 11. History writing — African American — Civil rights — United States 12. History writing — 1960s — United States 13. Life stories — Politics — Activists and Reformers — Civil Rights Leaders

LC 2005040177

New York Times Notable Book, 2006; National Book Award for Nonfiction finalist, 2006; National Book Critics Circle Award for Biography finalist, 2006.

ESSENTIAL AND RECOMMENDED TITLES
323.1196 African Americans — Civil and human rights

A comprehensive biography of the last three years of Martin Luther King's life describing the challenges to his leadership and his nonviolent philosophy.

"In this history that follows the life of Martin Luther King from the protest at Selma and the 1966 Meredith March through King's expanding political concern for the poor to his 1968 assassination in Memphis, Tenn, Branch gives us not only the civil rights leader's life but also the rapidly changing pulse of American culture and politics. This magisterial book is a fitting tribute to a magisterial man." —*Publishers Weekly*

Sequel to: Pillar of fire; Includes bibliographical references (p. 981-992) and index.

Gergel, Richard
Unexampled Courage: The Blinding of Sgt. Isaac Woodard and the Awakening of President Harry S. Truman and Judge J. Waties Waring. Richard Gergel. Sarah Crichton Books; 2019. 336 p.
ISBN 9780374107895
Grades: Adult   323.1196
1. Waring, Julius Waties, 1880-1968 2. Woodard, Isaac, 1919-1992 3. Violence against African Americans 4. African American civil rights 5. Police brutality 6. Hate crimes 7. Civil rights 8. Trials (Hate crimes) 9. Civil Rights Movement 10. Trials (Police misconduct) 11. Racism 12. African American World War II veterans 13. Legislation 14. 1940s 15. History writing — African American — Civil rights — United States
LC 2018021690

Documents the 1946 case of decorated African-American veteran Isaac Woodard, whose victimization by police brutality prompted Harry Truman to establish the first presidential commission on civil rights and order the desegregation in the U.S. armed forces.

Includes bibliographical references and index.

Jackson, Kellie Carter
We Refuse: A Forceful History of Black Resistance. by Kellie Carter Jackson. Seal Press 2024. 304 p.
ISBN 9781541602908
Grades: Adult   323.1196
1. African American civil rights 2. Politics and government 3. Resistance to government 4. Racism 5. White supremacy movements 6. Race relations 7. United States 8. Society and culture — Race 9. Politics and global affairs — Civil and human rights
LC 2023046379

Offering an unflinching examination of the breadth of Black responses to white oppression, particularly those pioneered by Black women, a noted historian presents a fundamental corrective to the historical record, a love letter to Black resilience and a path toward liberation.

"Black people have resisted white supremacy with many strategies other than nonviolent civil disobedience, yet these methods are chronically understudied, according to this enthralling account." —*Publishers Weekly*

Includes bibliographical references and index.

Jones, Doug
Bending Toward Justice: The Birmingham Church Bombing That Changed the Course of Civil Rights. U.S. Senator Doug Jones with Greg Truman. All Points Books 2019. 400 p.
ISBN 9781250201447
Grades: Adult   323.1196
1. Jones, Doug (G. Douglas), 1954- 2. Trials (Murder) 3. Bombings 4. Terrorism 5. Racism 6. Civil rights 7. Lawyers 8. African American civil rights 9. Race relations 10. United States history 11. Birmingham, Alabama 12. Alabama 13. 1960s 14. History writing — African American — Civil rights — United States 15. History writing — 1960s — United States 16. True Crime — Investigations and Trials
LC 2018039980

The story of the decades-long fight to bring justice to the victims of the 16th Street Baptist Church bombing, culminating in Sen. Doug Jones' prosecution of the last living bombers.

"This poignant and powerful story tracks changes in Southern life since the 1960s, uncovering hard truths to correct America's moral compass with an understanding of the need for activism and political discourse to achieve social justice." —*Library Journal*

Includes index.

Joseph, Peniel E.
Waiting 'Til the Midnight Hour: A Narrative History of Black Power in America. Peniel E. Joseph. Henry Holt and Co. 2006. 399 p. : Illustration
ISBN 9780805075397
Grades: Adult   323.1196
1. African American civil rights 2. Civil Rights Movement 3. African Americans 4. Black power 5. Political participation 6. Intellectual life 7. Race relations 8. United States 9. 20th century 10. History writing — African American — Civil rights — United States
LC 2005046765

A history of the Black Power movement in the United States traces the origins and evolution of the influential movement and examines the ways in which Black Power redefined racial identity and culture.

"Rather than simply detailing the history of radical organizations, Joseph…also profiles several famous leaders and uses their stories to spearhead a discussion of the intellectual and practical history of Black Power as a political movement. Enthusiastically recommended for public and academic libraries." —*Library Journal*

Includes bibliographical references (p. [351]-373) and index.

Masur, Kate
Until Justice Be Done: America's First Civil Rights Movement, from the Revolution to Reconstruction. Kate Masur. W. W. Norton & Company 2021. 480 p.
ISBN 9781324005933
Grades: Adult   323.1196
1. Civil rights 2. Free African Americans 3. African American history 4. Legislation 5. African Americans 6. Political participation 7. Race relations 8. United States history 9. 19th century 10. History writing — African American — Civil rights — United States 11. History writing — Wars and conflicts — American Civil War 12. History writing — Early America — United States 13. History writing — Antebellum America — United States
LC 2020045654

Pulitzer Prize for History finalist, 2022.

A groundbreaking history of the movement for equal rights that courageously battled racist laws and institutions, north and south, in the decades before the Civil War.

"This engrossing study goes beyond sectionalist accounts of the South's peculiar institution to show how racism and civil rights activism have shaped every corner of America." —*Publishers Weekly*

Includes bibliographical references and index.

Sorin, Gretchen Sullivan
Driving While Black: African American Travel and the Road to Civil Rights. Gretchen Sorin. W W Norton & Co. Inc 2020. 352 p.
ISBN 9781631495694
Grades: Adult   323.1196
1. African Americans 2. Tourism 3. Segregation in transportation 4. Automobile travel 5. Social change 6. Social mobility 7. Civil Rights Movement 8. Transportation, Automotive 9. Segregation 10. Race relations 11. United States history 12. 20th century 13. History writing — African American — United States 14. Travel Writing — Modes of Transportation — Road Trips 15. Society and culture — Race
LC 2019036574

The true story behind the award-winning film of the same name explores the role of travel in civil rights, the specific impact of the automobile on African-American life and the cultural importance of Victor and Alma Green's famous Green Book.

"The author also discusses how the car became a vehicle integral to the civil rights movement. A pleasing combination of terrific research and storytelling and engaging period visuals." —*Kirkus*

Includes bibliographical references and index.

Theoharis, Jeanne
A More Beautiful and Terrible History: The Uses and Misuses of Civil Rights History. Jeanne Theoharis. Beacon Press 2018. 288 pages
ISBN 9780807075876
Grades: Adult   323.1196
1. Civil Rights Movement 2. Social movements 3. Historiography 4. Historical revisionism 5. Social conflict 6. African American history 7. Civil rights 8. Race relations 9. United States history 10. 20th century 11. Liberal writing 12. History writing — African American — Civil rights — United States 13. Society and culture — Race 14. Society and culture — Social activism and philanthropy
LC 2017030979

Examines the accepted narrative of the civil rights movement to reveal the myths and fables that diminish its scope, and reveals the diversity of activists and the immense barriers and repression they faced.

"Chronicling the efforts of many activists, the author underscores her message that reform requires courage and hard work. An impassioned call for continued efforts for change." —*Kirkus*

Includes bibliographical references and index.

Watson, Bruce
Freedom Summer: The Savage Summer That Made Mississippi Burn and Made America a Democracy. Bruce Watson. Viking 2010. 384 p.
ISBN 9780670021703
Grades: 11 12 Adult   323.1196
1. Civil rights 2. African Americans 3. Civil rights workers 4. Freedom 5. Political rights 6. Equality before the law 7. Discrimination 8. Civil Rights Movement 9. Human rights 10. Suffrage 11. African American history 12. Race relations 13. United States history 14. Mississippi 15. United States 16. 20th century 17. History writing — African American — Civil rights — United States
LC 2009047211

Analyzes a critical shift in American race relations during the summer of 1964, documenting how civil rights demonstrations by hundreds of college students triggered African-American voter registries and violent uprisings.

Includes bibliographical references and index.

323.1197 Native Americans — Civil rights

Calloway, Colin G.
The Indian World of George Washington: The First President, the First Americans, and the Birth of the Nation. Colin G. Calloway. Oxford University Press 2018. 712 p.
ISBN 9780190652166
Grades: Adult   323.1197
1. Washington, George, 1732-1799 2. Government relations with indigenous peoples 3. Indigenous peoples of North America 4. American Revolution, 1775-1783 5. Presidents 6. French and Indian War, 1754-1763 7. United States history 8. United States 9. 18th century 10. Revolutionary America (1775-1783) 11. Biographies 12. History writing — Wars and conflicts — French and Indian War 13. Life stories — Politics — Politicians 14. History writing — Presidency — 18th century — United States
LC 2017028686

National Book Award for Nonfiction finalist, 2018.

An authoritative, sweeping, and fresh new biography of the nation's first president, Colin G. Calloway's book reveals fully the dimensions and depths of George Washington's relations with the First Americans.

Includes bibliographical references and index.

Hendricks, Steve
The Unquiet Grave: The FBI and the Struggle for the Soul of Indian Country. Steve Hendricks. Thunder Mouth Press 2006. 544 p.
ISBN 9781560257356
Grades: Adult   323.1197
1. Indigenous peoples of North America — History 2. Indigenous organizations 3. Red Power 4. Indigenous resistance and revolts 5. Indigenous activists 6. Trials (Murder) 7. 1970s 8. Impartial writing 9. History writing — Indigenous peoples — United States 10. True Crime — Investigations and Trials
LC Bl2006023860

Citing the 1976 murder of Native American activist Anna Mae Aquash, a history of the adversarial relationship between the FBI and Native Americans draws on the author's archival research into previously unreleased documents to reveal murderous conspiracies and cover-ups on both sides of the unofficial conflict.

Saunt, Claudio
Unworthy Republic: The Dispossession of Native Americans and the Road to Indian Territory. Claudio Saunt. W. W. Norton & Co. 2020. 288 pages
ISBN 9780393609844
Grades: Adult   323.1197
1. Indigenous peoples of North America — Forced removal 2. Indigenous peoples of North America — Land rights 3. Forced relocations 4. Deportation 5. Communities 6. Deception 7. Government relations with indigenous peoples 8. Indigenous peoples of North America, Treatment of 9. Land tenure 10. United States history 11. 1830s 12. 19th century 13. History writing — Indigenous peoples — United States

Robert F. Kennedy Book Award, 2021; National Book Award for Nonfiction finalist, 2020.

A history of the 1830s forced migration of indigenous populations to territories west of the Mississippi describes the government-driven fraud, intimidation and murder that were used to confiscate Native American homelands and property.

"This valuable addition to the scholarship of Native American dispossession and extermination should be read by scholars and general readers alike." —*Library Journal*

Includes bibliographical references and index.

323.3 Civil and political rights of other social groups

Mattlin, Ben
Disability Pride: Dispatches from a Post-ADA World. Ben Mattlin. Beacon Press 2022. 264 p.
ISBN 9780807036457
Grades: Adult   323.3
1. People with disabilities 2. Civil rights 3. Discrimination 4. Advocacy for people with disabilities 5. Community activism 6. Intersectionality 7. Ableism 8. Marginalized people 9. American people 10. North American people 11. United States 12. Science Writing — Medicine and health — Disabilities and disorders 13. Life stories — Facing adversity — Medical issues — Living with disabilities 14. Society and culture — Social activism and philanthropy
LC 2022024698

An eye-opening portrait of the diverse disability community as it is today and how attitudes, activism, and representation have evolved since the passage of the Americans with Disabilities Act (ADA).

"A sincere, thoughtful look at the advances made by the disabled community that deserve celebration and the improvements still to be made in all areas." —*Library Journal*

Includes bibliographical references and index.

323.4 Specific civil rights limitation and suspension of

McCoy, Alfred W.
A Question of Torture: CIA Interrogation, from the Cold War to the War on Terror. Alfred W. McCoy. Metropolitan Books/Henry Holt and Co. 2006. 290 p. : Illustration
ISBN 9780805080414
Grades: Adult   323.4
1. Torture 2. Military interrogation 3. Intelligence service 4. Politics and government 5. United States 6. History writing — Spies and spying
LC 2005051124

ESSENTIAL AND RECOMMENDED TITLES
323.44 Freedom of action (Liberty)

Describes the CIA's use of psychological torture, from the Cold War to the post-September 11th era, detailing the use of isolation, extremes of temperature, the manipulation of time, and assessing the implications of such inhumane practices.

"The author shows how, since 1950, the CIA and various nations have augmented traditional physical torture with psychological abuse techniques of sensory disorientation and self-inflicted pain, which he documents with some gruesome first-person accounts by victims and with stories of doctors who conducted horrific experiments." —*Library Journal*

Includes bibliographical references (p. [249]-270) and index.

Williams, Juan
Eyes on the Prize: America's Civil Rights Years, 1954-1965. Juan Williams; with the Eyes on the prize production team; introduction by Julian Bond. Viking 1987. xv, 300 p. : Illustration
ISBN 9780670814121
Grades: 7 8 9 10 11 12 Adult   323.4
1. Civil Rights Movement 2. African American history 3. Civil rights 4. Race relations 5. United States 6. 20th century 7. History writing — African American — Civil rights — United States 8. Adult books for young adults
LC 86040271

Traces the history of the civil rights movement, focusing on the unheralded activists who brought the movement to life.

"Highly recommended both as a socio-historical document and as a heartfelt, poignant remembrance of a movement and its activists." —*Booklist*

Includes index; Bibliography: P. [296]-297.

323.44 Freedom of action (Liberty)

McHangama, Jacob
★ *Free Speech: A History from Socrates to Social Media*. Jacob McHangama. Basic Books 2022. 496 p.
ISBN 9781541600492
Grades: Adult   323.44
1. Freedom of speech 2. Censorship 3. Freedom of expression 4. Communication 5. Ideas (Philosophy) 6. Intellectual life 7. Debates and debating 8. Power 9. Social control 10. Internet 11. Impartial writing 12. Politics and global affairs — Civil and human rights 13. Politics and global affairs — Political philosophy 14. History writing — Microhistory
LC 2021034456

Hailed as the "first freedom," free speech is the bedrock of democracy. But it is a challenging principle, subject to erosion in times of upheaval. Today, in democracies and authoritarian states around the world, it is on the retreat. In Free Speech, Jacob McHangama traces the riveting legal, political, and cultural history of this idea. Through captivating stories of free speech's many defenders—from the ancient Athenian orator Demosthenes and the ninth-century freethinker al-Razi, to the anti-lynching crusader Ida B. Wells and modern-day digital activists—McHangama reveals how the free exchange of ideas underlies all intellectual achievement and has enabled the advancement of both freedom and equality worldwide. Yet the desire to restrict speech, too, is a constant, and he explores how even its champions can be led down this path when the rise of new and contrarian voices challenge power and privilege of all stripes.

"A well-structured and compelling examination of the costs and benefits of free speech." —*Kirkus*

Includes bibliographical references and index.

Stone, Geoffrey R.
Perilous Times: Free Speech in Wartime from the Sedition Act of 1798 to the War on Terrorism. Geoffrey R. Stone. W.W. Norton & Co. 2004. xx, 730 p. : Illustration
ISBN 9780393058802
Grades: Adult   323.44
1. Freedom of speech 2. Political persecution 3. Civil rights 4. Dissenting opinions 5. National security 6. United States 7. History writing — Wars and conflicts
LC 2004017871

Los Angeles Times Book Prize for History, 2004; Robert F. Kennedy Book Award, 2005; New York Times Notable Book, 2004.

An investigation into how free speech and other civil liberties have been compromised in America by war in six historical periods describes how presidents, Supreme Court justices, and resistors contributed to the administration of civil freedoms, in an account complemented by rare photographs, posters, and historical illustrations. 20,000 first printing.

"The author delivers rich material in an engaging, character-based narrative. Stone offers deep insight into rhetorical history and the men and women who made it—resisters like Clement Vallandingham, Emma Goldman, Fred Korematsu and Daniel Ellsberg; presidents faced with wartime dilemmas; and the prosecutors, defenders and Supreme Court justices who shaped our understanding of the First Amendment today." —*Publishers Weekly*

Includes bibliographical references and index.

Strittmatter, Kai
We Have Been Harmonized: Life in China's Surveillance State. KAI Strittmatter. Custom House 2020. VI, 360 pages
ISBN 9780063027299
Grades: Adult   323.44
1. XI Jinping 2. Authoritarianism 3. Electronic surveillance 4. Censorship 5. Privacy rights 6. Civil rights 7. Technology 8. Propaganda 9. Politics and government 10. China 11. Politics and global affairs — World politics — Asia
LC 2020288922

ALA Notable Book, 2021.

The China correspondent for Germany's Sueddeutsche Zeitung national newspaper draws on in-depth investigative reporting to reveal how the chilling vision of authoritarianism in George Orwell's 1984 has come true in China's high-tech surveillance state.

"Strittmatter's accessible yet hard-hitting narrative will find an audience with policymakers and general readers alike." —*Kirkus*

Includes bibliographical references (pages 341-360); Originally published in Germany in 2018 by Piper Verlag GmbH; First English publication in Great Britain in 2019 by Old Street Publishing.

Weatherford, J. McIver
Genghis Khan and the Quest for God: How the World's Greatest Conqueror Gave Us Religious Freedom. Jack Weatherford. Penguin Group USA 2016. 304 p.
ISBN 9780735221154
Grades: Adult   323.44
1. Genghis Khan, 1162-1227 2. Conquerors 3. Religious tolerance 4. Religion and culture 5. Civilization 6. Religion and state 7. Freedom of religion 8. Religion and politics 9. Religions 10. Rulers 11. Mongolia 12. History writing — Asia
LC 2016039793

Reveals how Genghis Khan harnessed the power of religion to rule the largest empire the world has ever known. By the New York Times best-selling author of Genghis Khan and the Making of the Modern World.

"This sound examination of Khan, his methods of rule, and his views on religious tolerance presents a valid and welcome addition to scholarship on the subject." —*Library Journal*

323.6 Citizenship and related topics

Lekas Miller, Anna
Love Across Borders: Passports, Papers, and Romance in a Divided World. Anna Lekas Miller. Algonquin Books of Chapel Hill 2023. 272 p.
ISBN 9781643752334
Grades: Adult   323.6
1. Lekas Miller, Anna, 1990- 2. Border security 3. Love 4. Passports 5. Immigration and emigration 6. Couples 7. Interpersonal relations 8. Stateless people 9. Xenophobia 10. Life stories — Politics — Activists and reformers 11. Family

and relationships — General 12. Politics and global affairs — Immigration 13. Society and culture — Immigration

LC 2022061160

Love Across Borders takes readers through contentious frontiers around the world to reveal the widespread prejudicial laws intent on dividing us. Anna Lekas Miller tells her own gripping story of meeting Salem Rizk in Istanbul, where they were reportingon the Syrian civil war. But when Turkey started cracking down on refugees, Salem, who is Syrian, wasn't allowed to stay there, nor could he safely return to Syria. In this look at the global immigration crisis, Lekas Miller interweaves love stories similar to her own with a study of the history of passports, the legacy of colonialism, and the discriminatory laws shaping how people move through the world every day.

"Eye-opening reading that ably blends the personal and the universal." —*Kirkus*

Includes bibliographical references.

Rather, Dan

What Unites US: Reflections on Patriotism. Dan Rather & Elliot Kirschner. Algonquin Books 2017. 176 p.

ISBN 9781616207823

Grades: Adult   323.6

1. National characteristics, American 2. Patriotism 3. Citizenship 4. United States 5. Essays 6. Politics and global affairs — World politics — United States

LC 2017028401

The Emmy Award-winning veteran journalist shares passionate essays about what it means to be an American and the relevance of patriotism in today's world, exploring subjects ranging from the institutions that support the nation, major events from that past half century and how the country can better unite to secure a collective future.

"Rather has issued a stirring call for overcoming todays strident partisanship." —*Publishers Weekly*

Skach, C. L.

How to Be a Citizen: Learning to Be Civil Without the State. C. L. Skach. Basic Books 2024. 272 p.

ISBN 9781541605534

Grades: Adult   323.6

1. Civics 2. Citizenship 3. Quality of life 4. Law 5. Ethics 6. Human behavior 7. Polarization (Social sciences) 8. Cooperation 9. Social interaction 10. Social responsibility 11. Politics and global affairs — Political philosophy 12. Society and culture — Philosophy

LC 2023058426

In 2009, constitutional scholar C. L. Skach went to Iraq to help revise the constitution. She survived a missile barrage in the Green Zone—an event that proved a breaking point in her thinking about constitutions. In short: They don't really work. In How to Be a Citizen, Skach calls to move beyond constitutions. She argues that just as complex natural systems spontaneously generate order, we can, too. Looking to pandemic gardens, Reggio-Emilia schools, and community-driven safety patrols, she envisions not government by force, but society that is local, cultivated, and true.

"A constitutional scholar offers insights into why she believes that laws have become untenable 'Substitutes for our own judgement and collective action'…Necessary reading for those who wish to foster civil discourse and societal cooperation." —*Kirkus*

Includes bibliographical references and index.

323.60973 Citizenship — United States

Lalami, Laila

Conditional Citizens: On Belonging in America. Laila Lalami. Pantheon Books 2020. 208 p.

ISBN 9781524747169

Grades: Adult   323.60973

1. Lalami, Laila, 1968- 2. Citizenship 3. Discrimination 4. Naturalization 5. Immigrants, Arab 6. Muslim women 7. Racism 8. Sexism 9. Xenophobia 10. Immigration and emigration 11. United States history 12. United States 13. 21st century 14. Autobiographies and memoirs 15. Life stories — Identity — Immigrants 16. Life stories — Identity — Race and ethnicity 17. Politics and global affairs — Immigration

LC 2019037549

A Pulitzer Prize finalist recounts her unlikely journey from Moroccan immigrant to U.S. citizen, using it as a starting point for her exploration of the rights, liberties and protections that are traditionally associated with American citizenship.

"In this eloquent and troubling account, novelist and National Book Award?finalist Lalami (The Other Americans) draws on her personal history as 'An immigrant, a woman, an Arab, and a Muslim' to argue that becoming a U.S. citizen does not necessarily mean becoming 'An equal member of the American family'. . . . This profound inquiry into the American immigrant experience deserves to be widely read." —*Publishers Weekly*

Includes bibliographical references.

324 The political process

Sage, Sami

Democracy in Retrograde: How to Make Changes Big and Small in Our Country and in Our Lives. Sami Sage & Emily Amick. Gallery Books 2024. 246 pages

ISBN 9781668053485

Grades: Adult   324

1. Democracy 2. Political participation 3. Social change 4. Politics and government 5. Civics 6. United States 7. Politics and global affairs — General 8. Self-Help — General

LC Bl2024015126

In today's political climate, it's hard not to get discouraged. Isolated, doom scrolling, lacking a sense of purpose or community…it's easy to become overwhelmed by the dire state of American democracy and do nothing, because why try when the odds arenever in our favor? at this fragile moment in history, Emily Amick, lawyer and former counsel to Senate Majority Leader Chuck Schumer, alongside New York Times bestselling author and Betches Media cofounder Sami Sage, want to reframe civic engagement as a form of self-care: an assertion of one's values and self-respect. This book is not just about voting, but about claiming your singular place in your country and community.

"Two activists offer a comprehensive guide to regaining ownership of American civic life in an era of minoritarian rule…An uplifting and useful book of activism." —*Kirkus*

Includes bibliographical references (pages 242-246).

324.0973 Political process — United States

Plouffe, David

A Citizen's Guide to Beating Donald Trump. David Plouffe. Viking 2020. xxiii, 228 pages

ISBN 9781984879493

Grades: Adult   324.0973

1. Political campaigns 2. Presidential election, 2020 3. Citizen participation in government 4. Practical politics 5. Democrats 6. Elections 7. Political participation 8. United States 9. Liberal writing 10. Politics and global affairs — Elections

LC 2019052889

A voter's playbook on making a difference in the 2020 election and beyond, written by Barack Obama's campaign manager, outlines practical activities that everyday citizens can use to counter misinformation and garner voter support.

"For Democrats, liberals, and progressives . . . this is an invaluable map for political engagement." —*Booklist*

ESSENTIAL AND RECOMMENDED TITLES
324.2734 Republican Party

324.2734 Republican Party

Alberta, Tim
American Carnage: On the Front Lines of the Republican Civil War and the Rise of President Trump. Tim Alberta. HarperCollins 2019. 352 p.
ISBN 9780062896445
Grades: Adult   324.2734
1. Trump, Donald, 1946- 2. Presidential election, 2016 3. Polarization (Social sciences) 4. Republicans 5. Conservatism 6. Group identity 7. Political values 8. Political culture 9. Politics and government 10. United States 11. 21st century 12. Politics and global affairs — Political parties 13. History writing — Presidency — 21st century — United States 14. Politics and global affairs — World politics — United States
LC Bl2019014945

The Politico Magazine chief political correspondent reveals how a decade of cultural upheaval, populist outrage and ideological warfare made the GOP vulnerable to a hostile takeover by an unlikely presidential candidate.

Bordewich, Fergus M.
Congress at War: How Republican Reformers Fought the Civil War, Defied Lincoln, Ended Slavery, and Remade America. Fergus M. Bordewich. Alfred A. Knopf 2020. 464 p.
ISBN 9780451494443
Grades: Adult   324.2734
1. Legislators 2. War 3. Slavery 4. Social change 5. Politics and government 6. United States history 7. United States 8. 19th century 9. American Civil War era (1861-1865) 10. History writing — Wars and conflicts — American Civil War 11. History writing — Politicians — United States 12. Life stories — Politics — Politicians
LC 2019015354

Explains how Congress helped win the Civil War—a new perspective that puts the House and Senate, rather than Lincoln, at the center of the conflict.

"Bordewich contributes an entertaining, fresh perspective to our ever-evolving understanding and discussion of the Civil War. An important addition for both general readers of American history and scholars of the growing interpretations of Civil War studies." —*Library Journal*

A Borzoi Book; Includes bibliographical references and index.

Collins-Dexter, Brandi
Black Skinhead: Reflections on Blackness and Our Political Future. Brandi Collins-dexter. Celadon Books 2022. 352 p.
ISBN 9781250824073
Grades: Adult   324.2734
1. Political participation 2. African Americans 3. Race relations 4. Political science 5. Democrats 6. Ethnic identity 7. Identity 8. Voting 9. Politics and government 10. United states 11. Essays 12. Society and culture — Race 13. Politics and global affairs — Civil and human rights

A life-long fighter for racial justice and progressive politics presents a series of essays examining the breakdown of the bonds between Black voters and the Democratic party through both a political and a cultural lens.

"Political activist Collins-Dexter debuts with an immersive and insightful look at the Black community's fraying relationship with the Democratic Party….Seamlessly balancing the personal, political, and cultural, and enlivened with a sharp sense of wit, these standout pieces strike an essential note of warning for Democrats." —*Publishers Weekly*

Stevens, Stuart
The Conspiracy to End America: Five Ways My Old Party Is Driving Our Democracy to Autocracy. Stuart Stevens. Twelve 2023. 240 p.
ISBN 9781538765401
Grades: Adult   324.2734
1. Stevens, Stuart 2. Political Parties 3. Political consultants 4. Power 5. Democracy 6. Authoritarianism 7. Separation of powers 8. Political corruption 9. Politics and government 10. United States 11. Politics and global affairs — Political parties 12. Life stories — Politics

A former chief Republican strategist and best-selling author of It Was All a Lie offers an ominous warning that the GOP is dragging our country towards autocracy, and if we don't wake up to the crisis in our system, 2024 may well be our last free and fair election.

"This cautionary study makes it plain that so-called 'Trumpism' will survive its namesake since those five pillars have been building for decades, and this movement no longer needs the former president as its figurehead." —*Booklist*

It Was All a Lie: How the Republican Party Became Donald Trump. Stuart Stevens. Alfred A. Knopf 2020. 256 pages
ISBN 9780525658450
Grades: Adult   324.2734
1. Trump, Donald, 1946- 2. Goldwater, Barry M. 1909-1998 3. Reagan, Ronald 4. Racism 5. Classism 6. White supremacy movements 7. Elections 8. Conservatism 9. Nationalism 10. Political culture 11. Political parties 12. Race relations 13. Politics and government 14. United States 15. Politics and global affairs — Political parties 16. Politics and global affairs — Political philosophy 17. Politics and global affairs — Elections 18. History writing — United States 19. Society and culture — Race
LC 2019048755

A leading Republican political operative presents an unflinching expose of today's Republican party that argues that the Trump administration is a logical outcome for a morally bankrupt party still largely motivated by racism, political grandstanding and fiscal inequality.

"A one-time Republican operative recounts the transformation of the big-tent GOP into an organ of white nationalism. . . . [O]f interest to all politics junkies, for a formerly venerable party by a champion-turned-gravedigger." —*Kirkus*

This is a Borzoi book published by Alfred A. Knopf; Also published in large print format; Includes bibliographical references.

324.2734089 Republican Party — Ethnic groups

Cadava, Geraldo L.
The Hispanic Republican: The Shaping of an American Political Identity, from Nixon to Trump. Geraldo Cadava. Ecco Press 2020. 272 p.
ISBN 9780062946348
Grades: Adult   324.2734089
1. Hispanic Americans 2. Political participation 3. Conservatism 4. Impartial writing 5. History writing — United States 6. Politics and global affairs — World politics — United States 7. Politics and global affairs — Political parties 8. Society and culture — Ethnic studies 9. Society and culture — Race
LC Bl2020010968

A history of the growth of Hispanic-American Republican voters throughout the past half century discusses how the unlikely partnership between Latino voters and the Republican party has had a surprising impact on U.S. politics.

"A necessary acquisition for every nonfiction collection during this election year." —*Booklist*

324.2736 Democratic Party

Kazin, Michael
What It Took to Win: A History of the Democratic Party. Michael Kazin. Farrar, Straus and Giroux 2022. 400 p.
ISBN 9780374200237
Grades: Adult   324.2736
1. Political parties 2. Political science 3. Democrats 4. Politics and government 5. United States 6. History writing — United States 7. Politics and global affairs — Political parties
LC 2021044929

A history of the Democratic Party from Andrew Jackson to Joe Biden.

Georgetown University historian Kazin (War Against War) delivers a brisk and informative survey of the Democratic Party's evolution from its origins in the 1820s to the present. . . . The result is an insightful introduction to the complex history of the 'Oldest mass party in the world.' —*Publishers Weekly*

Includes bibliographical references and index.

PUBLIC LIBRARY CORE COLLECTION: NONFICTION
Twentieth Edition

Walker, Hunter
The Truce: Progressives, Centrists, and the Future of the Democratic Party. Hunter Walker and Luppe B. Luppen. W.W. Norton & Company 2024. x, 306 pages
ISBN 9781324020387
Grades: Adult 324.2736
1. Biden, Joseph R, 1942- 2. Trump, Donald, 1946- 3. Progressivism (United States politics) 4. Moderation 5. Polarization (Social sciences) 6. Political parties 7. Politics and government 8. United States history 9. United States 10. 20th century 11. 21st century 12. Interviews 13. Politics and global affairs — Political parties

LC Bl2024000293

Even before the cataclysmic 2016 election, the Democratic Party had long been at war with itself—yet Joe Biden's narrow victory in 2020 bridged the divide. Facing the dire threat of a second Trump administration, Democrats forged an unlikely but effective coalition that stalled Trumpism at the ballot box and enacted a raft of consequential legislation. But how long can the uneasy peace hold, and can Biden win again?

"The result is a revealing look at a seminal party transformation that has birthed the most potent left-wing politics in decades." —*Publishers Weekly*

Includes bibliographical references (page 299-306).

324.6 Election systems and procedures; suffrage

Anderson, Carol
★ *One Person, No Vote: How Voter Suppression Is Destroying Our Democracy.* Carol Anderson; foreword by Senator Dick Durbin. Bloomsbury Publishing 2018. 256 p.
ISBN 9781635571370
Grades: Adult 324.6
1. African Americans 2. Civil rights 3. Racism 4. Political activists 5. Elections 6. Marginalized people 7. Voter suppression 8. Gerrymandering 9. Voter fraud 10. Suffrage 11. Politics and government 12. United States 13. Politics and global affairs — Elections 14. History writing — Judicial branch — United States

LC 2018015633

Booklist Editors' Choice, 2018.

The New York Times best-selling author of White Rage presents a timely history of voter suppression that exposes America's insidious history of policies that have blocked African-American voting participation, placing particular focus on the Supreme Court's 2013 Shelby ruling.

Includes bibliographical references.

Berman, Ari
Give Us the Ballot: The Modern Struggle for Voting Rights in America. Ari Berman. Farrar, Straus and Giroux 2015. 320 p.
ISBN 9780374158279
Grades: Adult 324.6
1. Civil rights 2. Election law 3. Race relations 4. Marginalized people 5. Voter fraud 6. Suffrage 7. United States 8. Politics and global affairs — Civil and human rights 9. History writing — African American — Civil rights — United States 10. History writing — 1960s — United States 11. Antiracist literature

LC 2015004989

New York Times Notable Book, 2015; ALA Notable Book, 2016; National Book Critics Circle Award for Nonfiction finalist.

In 1965, the Voting Rights Act transformed election demographics in the United States. African Americans in the South began voting, running for office, and being elected for the first time since the Reconstruction period after the Civil War. Journalist Ari Berman compellingly details the act's history and also describes the recent "counterrevolution" against the VRA, in which dozens of state legislatures have passed measures making it more difficult to register and vote. Including views from different sides of the debate on voting restrictions, he presents a balanced but still revealing report on a wide variety of measures that have the potential to influence election results.

"General readers will appreciate the panoramic survey of the cases in which the VRA has been challenged and defended in federal and state courts and legislatures, and the fair inclusion of voices from both sides of the arguments. A timely and needed addition to the voting rights debate." —*Library Journal*

Includes index.

Cross, Tiffany D.
★ *Say It Louder!: Black Voters, White Narratives, and Saving Our Democracy.* Tiffany Cross. Amistad 2020. 176 pages
ISBN 9780062976772
Grades: Adult 324.6
1. African Americans 2. Elections 3. Democracy 4. Women journalists 5. Voter suppression 6. Voting 7. Police brutality 8. Demography 9. Discrimination 10. Racism 11. Social change 12. Political science 13. United States 14. Politics and global affairs — Elections 15. Society and culture — Race 16. Politics and global affairs — Mass media and politics 17. Society and culture — Media and technology

LC Bl2020016123

A political analyst discusses American Democracy and the role that African Americans have played in its shaping while exposing political forces aligned to subvert and suppress Black voters.

"An urgent plea for Black involvement in the political process, essential in this election year." —*Kirkus*

DuBois, Ellen Carol
Suffrage: Women's Long Battle for the Vote. Ellen Carol Dubois. Simon & Schuster 2020. 256 pages
ISBN 9781501165160
Grades: Adult 324.6
1. Voting 2. Women 3. African American women 4. Suffragist movement 5. Political rights 6. Suffrage 7. Politics and government 8. United States 9. 20th century 10. History writing — Women's history

LC Bl2020000218

Honoring the 100th anniversary of the 19th amendment to the Constitution, this exciting history explores the full scope of the movement to win the vote for women through portraits of its bold leaders and devoted activists.

"An authoritative, brisk, and sharply drawn history." —*Kirkus*

Jenkins, Jessica D.
Exploring Women's Suffrage Through 50 Historic Treasures. Jessica D. Jenkins. Rowman & Littlefield 2020. xxxvi, 305 pages : Illustration; Color
ISBN 9781538112793
Grades: Adult 324.6
1. Women's history 2. Suffrage 3. History writing — United States 4. Arts and Entertainment — Museums and Collections

LC 2019057194

Jenkins brings together a wide selection of cultural objects representing the milestones and legacy of the long fight for women's voting rights. Color photos and essays detailing each object's story placed readers in the action of a groundbreaking movement and transports them to the sites that are the keepers of our country's past.

Includes index.

Lichtman, Allan J.
The Embattled Vote in America: From the Founding to the Present. Allan J. Lichtman. Harvard University Press 2018. 336 p.
ISBN 9780674972360
Grades: Adult 324.6
1. Voting 2. Inequality 3. Elections 4. Discrimination 5. Voter turnout 6. Voter fraud 7. Suffrage 8. Politics and government 9. United States 10. Politics and global affairs — Elections 11. History writing — United States

LC 2018006882

Americans have died for the right to vote. Yet our democratic system guarantees no one, not even citizens, the opportunity to elect a government. Allan Lichtman calls attention to the founders' greatest error—leaving the franchise to

ESSENTIAL AND RECOMMENDED TITLES
324.60973 Election systems and procedures — United States

the discretion of individual states—and explains why it has triggered an unending struggle over voting rights.—.
Includes bibliographical references and index.

Quinn, Bridget
She Votes: How U.S. Women Won Suffrage, and What Happened Next. by Bridget Quinn; with a foreword by Nell Painter; with illustrations by 100 women artists. Chronicle Books 2020. 240 p.
ISBN 9781452173160
Grades: Adult   **324.6**
1. Women's history 2. Suffragists 3. Gender equity 4. Intersectionality 5. Women 6. Suffrage 7. Equality 8. Feminism 9. Illustrated books 10. History writing — Women's history 11. History writing — United States
LC 2019047183

She Votes is an intersectional story of the women who won suffrage, and those who have continued to raise their voices for equality ever since. From the first female Principal Chief of the Cherokee Nation to the first woman to wear pants on the Senate floor, author Bridget Quinn shines a spotlight on the women who broke down barriers.

"Art historian Quinn (Broad Strokes) commemorates the 100th anniversary of the ratification of the 19th Amendment in this vibrant and witty chronicle of women's rights in America. In 19 chapters illustrated by 100 female artists, Quinn profiles leaders of the women's suffrage and feminist movements, as well as groundbreaking women in the fields of art, politics, sports, and music.... This soaring movement history has something for neophytes and experts alike." —*Publishers Weekly*

Includes bibliographical references and index.

Weiss, Elaine F.
The *Woman's* Hour: The Great Fight to Win the Vote. Elaine F. Weiss. Viking Press 2018. 352 p.
ISBN 9780525429722
Grades: Adult   **324.6**
1. Suffragists 2. Women's rights 3. Suffragist movement 4. Women 5. Protests, demonstrations, vigils, etc. 6. Gender equity 7. Suffrage 8. 1920s 9. History writing — Women's history
LC 2018006746

Library Journal Best Books, 2018.

An uplifting account of the 1920 ratification of the constitutional amendment that granted voting rights to women traces the culmination of seven decades of legal battles and cites the pivotal contributions of famous suffragists and political leaders.

"Weiss brings to life the fascinating characters at the heart of one of the most pivotal events in U.S. history with striking similarity to the social and political tensions of today." —*Booklist*

324.60973 Election systems and procedures — United States

Abrams, Stacey
Our Time Is Now: Power, Purpose, and the Fight for a Fair America. Stacey Abrams. Henry Holt and Company 2020. 272 pages
ISBN 9781250257703
Grades: Adult   **324.60973**
1. Abrams, Stacey 2. Democracy 3. Political participation 4. Voter suppression 5. Voter registration 6. Racism 7. Suffrage 8. Presidential election, 2020 9. Identity 10. Absentee voting 11. Election corruption 12. Social change 13. Political science 14. Politics and government 15. United States 16. 2010s 17. 2020s 18. Politics and global affairs — Elections 19. Society and culture — Race
LC 2020005940

The award-winning House Democratic Leader and best-selling author of Lead from the Outside draws on extensive national research to outline an empowering blueprint for ending voter suppression, reclaiming identity and reshaping progressive politics in America.

"If you are feeling hopeless about politics, this well-informed blueprint for change may begin to restore your faith." —*Kirkus*
Includes bibliographical references and index.

Shimer, David
Rigged: America, Russia, and One Hundred Years of Covert Electoral Interference. David Shimer. Alfred A. Knopf 2020. 367 pages
ISBN 9780525659006
Grades: Adult   **324.60973**
1. Trump, Donald, 1946- 2. Election corruption 3. Diplomatic and consular service 4. Political corruption 5. Presidential election, 2020 6. Undercover operations 7. Political culture 8. Presidential election, 2016 9. International relations 10. Russia 11. United States 12. Politics and global affairs — Elections 13. History writing — Spies and spying
LC Bl2020013190

Presents a judicious history of covert foreign interference in world elections since the Cold War that discusses Russia's role in America's 2016 presidential election and why the threat is greater than ever in 2020.

"This incisive treatise lays bare the monumental task of countering foreign interference in the 2020 election." —*Publishers Weekly*

A Borzoi Book—Title page verso; Includes bibliographical references (pages 261-351) and index.

Wehle, Kim
What You Need to Know About Voting and Why. Kim Wehle. HarperCollins 2020. 304 p.
ISBN 9780062974785
Grades: Adult   **324.60973**
1. Voting 2. Suffrage 3. Voter registration 4. Election law 5. Voter suppression 6. Presidential elections 7. Gerrymandering 8. Political science 9. Voter turnout 10. Voter fraud 11. Absentee voting 12. Elections 13. Politics and government 14. United States 15. Politics and global affairs — Elections 16. Politics and global affairs — Civil and human rights
LC Bl2020013672

In What You Need to Know About Voting and Why, law professor and constitutional scholar Kimberly Wehle offers practical, useful advice on the mechanics of voting and an enlightening survey of its history and future. For new voters, would-be voters, young people and all of us looking ahead to the next election, here is a timely and informative guide, providing the background you need in order to make informed choices that will shape our shared destiny for decades to come.

"A probing and limpid explanation of an often misunderstood patchwork of systems, requirements, and mechanisms." —*Kirkus*

324.7 Conduct of election campaigns

Poniewozik, James
Audience of One: Donald Trump, Television, and the Fracturing of America. James Poniewozik. Liveright Publishing 2019. xxiii, 325 p.
ISBN 9781631494420
Grades: Adult   **324.7**
1. Trump, Donald, 1946- 2. Television 3. Mass media 4. Fame 5. Celebrities 6. Television industry and trade 7. Reality television programs 8. Television journalism 9. Presidents 10. United States 11. 21st century 12. Politics and global affairs — Political figures 13. Politics and global affairs — Mass media and politics 14. Society and culture — Media and technology 15. History writing — Presidency — 21st century — United States
LC 2019021970

New York Times Notable Book, 2019.

The New York Times chief television critic documents the history of mass media from the early 1980s through today, revealing how Donald Trump merged with America's most powerful medium to orchestrate his reinvention as a world leader.

PUBLIC LIBRARY CORE COLLECTION: NONFICTION
Twentieth Edition

Weissmann, Andrew
★ *Where Law Ends: Inside the Mueller Investigation.* Andrew Weissmann. Random House 2020. 402 p.
ISBN 9780593138571
Grades: Adult   **324.7**
1. Trump, Donald, 1946- 2. Mueller, Robert S, III, 1944- 3. Political campaigns 4. Corruption investigation 5. Investigations 6. Presidential election, 2016 7. Political corruption 8. Politicians 9. Election corruption 10. United States 11. 21st century 12. History writing — Presidency — 21st century — United States

In the first and only inside account of the Mueller investigation, one of the special counsel's most trusted prosecutors breaks his silence on the team's history-making search for the truth, their painstaking deliberations and costly mistakes, and Trump's unprecedented efforts to stifle their report.

"Weissmann provides valuable context behind the special counsel's most consequential decisions, though readers will wonder why he didn't speak up more forcefully as the investigation unfolded. Still, this is an essential record of what the Mueller investigation proved and why it failed to bring Trump down." —*Publishers Weekly*

324.70973 Election campaigns — United States

Harding, Luke
Collusion: Secret Meetings, Dirty Money, and How Russia Helped Donald Trump Win. Luke Harding. Vintage Books 2017. 354 p.
ISBN 9780525562511
Grades: Adult   **324.70973**
1. Trump, Donald, 1946- 2. Political culture 3. Political corruption 4. Presidential election, 2016 5. International relations 6. Russia 7. United States 8. Politics and global affairs — Elections
LC 2017470511

Argues that Russia has been trying to upend American democracy for more than a decade, and reveals the Trump administration's ties to Moscow, discussing such Russian figures as Aras Agalarov, Natalia Veselnitskaya, and Sergey Kislyak.

"One point not in dispute is Harding's ability to bring together diverse strands of a complicated story to make a book that is informative, accessible, and hard to put down." —*Publishers Weekly. Annex*

324.973 Elections — United States

Allen, Jonathan
Lucky: How Joe Biden Barely Won the Presidency. Jonathan Allen and Amie Parnes. Crown 2021. xxiii, 498 pages
ISBN 9780525574224
Grades: Adult   **324.973**
1. Biden, Joseph R, 1942- 2. Presidents 3. Political campaigns 4. Presidential candidates 5. Elections 6. Politics and government 7. United States 8. 21st century 9. Impartial writing 10. Politics and global affairs — Elections 11. Life stories — Politics — Politicians 12. History writing — Presidency — 21st century — United States
LC Bl2021005540

Presents the inside story of the historic 2020 presidential election and the string of chance events that resulted in Joe Biden's victory.

"Readers who enjoy political coverage of the election process and want to know more about Joe Biden's campaign will be well informed by this book." —*Library Journal*

Includes bibliographical references (pages 421-468) and index.

Shattered: Inside Hillary Clinton's Doomed Campaign. Jonathan Allen and Amie Parnes. Crown 2017. 288 p.
ISBN 9780553447088
Grades: Adult   **324.973**
1. Clinton, Hillary Rodham 2. Presidential election, 2016 3. Elections 4. Presidential candidates 5. Political campaigns 6. Campaigning 7. Politicians 8. Politics and government 9. United States 10. 21st century 11. Politics and global affairs — Elections
LC 2017010338

A dramatic analysis of the bitter 2016 election, told from the viewpoints of Hilary Clinton campaign insiders, reconstructs key decisions and missed opportunities that are being cited as the cause of the election upset.

"A top-notch campaign examination." —*Kirkus*

Farris, Scott
Almost President: The Men Who Lost the Race but Changed the Nation. Scott Farris. Lyons Press 2012. 336 p.
ISBN 9780762763788
Grades: 11 12 Adult   **324.973**
1. Presidential candidates 2. Presidential elections 3. Politicians 4. Politics and government 5. United States 6. History writing — Politicians — United States
LC 2011033001

Profiles individuals who ran for President but lost, describing each candidate's campaign and how, even in defeat, they revolutionized party ideologies, the election process, social barriers, and American democracy.

"When the author lost a 1998 race for Wyoming's at-large congressional district, he was prompted to examine the role losers play in democracy. Farris notes that some unsuccessful White House aspirants have had a far greater impact on American history than many who became president. . . . Documenting changes in the face of America and the impact of such issues as race, religion, and workplace reform on elections, Farris writes with a lively flair, skillfully illustrating his solid historical research with revelatory anecdotes and facts." —*Publishers Weekly*

Includes bibliographical references and index.

Hasen, Richard L.
Election Meltdown: Dirty Tricks, Distrust, and the Threat to American Democracy. Richard L. Hasen. Yale University Press 2020. xi, 187 pages : Illustration
ISBN 9780300248197
Grades: Adult   **324.973**
1. Manipulation (Social sciences) 2. Voting 3. Election corruption 4. Political corruption 5. Hacking 6. Voter suppression 7. Computer security 8. Propaganda 9. Fake news 10. Cyberterrorism 11. Presidential election, 2020 12. Voter fraud 13. Absentee voting 14. Democracy 15. Elections 16. Politics and government 17. United States 18. 2010s 19. 2020s 20. Impartial writing 21. Politics and global affairs — Elections
LC 2019945878

From the nation's leading expert, an indispensable analysis of key threats to the integrity of the 2020 American presidential election.

"A hard-hitting critique of the American election process as timely as it is frightening. . . . Required reading for legislators and voters." —*Kirkus*

Smith, Erin Geiger
★ *Thank You for Voting: The Maddening, Enlightening, Inspiring Truth About Voting in America.* Erin Geiger Smith. HarperCollins 2020. 208 p.
ISBN 9780062934826
Grades: Adult   **324.973**
1. Voting 2. Civics 3. Voter registration 4. Citizen participation in government 5. Democracy 6. Voter suppression 7. Misinformation 8. Social media 9. United States 10. Impartial writing 11. Politics and global affairs — Elections
LC Bl2020046592

A journalistic examination of the ongoing fight for voting equality shares insights into why so few Americans vote, citing the role of corporations in encouraging voter turnout while outlining innovative approaches to voter education and motivation.

"This is an excellent resource for first-time voters and activists hoping to motivate young people to get to the polls." —*Publishers Weekly*

ESSENTIAL AND RECOMMENDED TITLES
325.73 International migration — United States

325.73 International migration — United States

Cannato, Vincent
American Passage: The History of Ellis Island. Vincent J. Cannato. Harper 2009. 496 p.
ISBN 9780060742737
Grades: Adult   325.73
1. History of immigrants 2. Immigration and emigration 3. United States history 4. New York City history 5. Ellis Island, New York 6. 19th century 7. 20th century 8. History writing — Immigration — United States
LC 2008052245
Massachusetts Book Awards, Nonfiction Award, 2010.

A chronicle of the landmark port of entry's history documents its role as an execution site, immigration post, and deportation center that was profoundly shaped by evolving politics and ideologies.

"The author reaches back to the island's beginnings in the early 19th century, when, then named Gibbet Island, it served as a venue for hanging convicted pirates. Cannato then chronicles the many different peopleimmigrants, immigration officials, politicians and otherswho made Ellis Island what it was in the early 20th century. Ambitious in scope and rooted in solid storytelling." —*Kirkus*

Includes bibliographical references and index.

Ramos, Jorge
Stranger: The Challenge of a Latino Immigrant in the Trump Era. Jorge Ramos. Vintage Books 2018. 192 pages
ISBN 9780525563792
Grades: Adult   325.73
1. Ramos, Jorge, 1958- 2. Immigrants 3. Citizenship 4. Racism 5. Journalism 6. Deportation 7. Hispanic Americans 8. Immigration policy 9. Voter turnout 10. Public opinion 11. Identity 12. Immigration and emigration 13. United States 14. Autobiographies and memoirs 15. Life stories — Identity — Immigrants 16. Society and culture — Immigration 17. Adult books for young adults
LC Bl2018012491

In this personal manifesto, Ramos sets out to examine what it means to be a Latino immigrant, or just an immigrant, in present-day America. Using current research and statistics, with a journalist's nose for a story, and interweaving his own personal experience, Ramos shows us the changing face of America while also trying to find an explanation for why he, and millions of others, still feel like strangers in this country.

"An insightful read about prejudice against Latinx individuals in America. Readers of politics and culture will find Ramos's book enlightening." —*Library Journal*

Simultaneously published in Spanish by Vintage Espagñol.

Soboroff, Jacob
★ *Separated: Inside an American Tragedy.* Jacob Soboroff. Custom House 2020. xxii, 388 p.
ISBN 9780062992192
Grades: Adult   325.73
1. Immigrants 2. Parent-separated children 3. Immigration policy 4. Undocumented immigrants 5. Children of immigrants 6. Journalists 7. Child abuse 8. Child prisoners 9. Border patrol agents 10. Separated friends, relatives, etc. 11. Immigration and emigration 12. Mexican-American Border Region 13. United States 14. 21st century 15. Politics and global affairs — Immigration 16. History writing — Early 21st century — United States 17. Life stories — Identity — Immigrants
LC 2020014644

An NBC News correspondent lays bare the full truth behind the Trump administration's systematic separation of desperate migrant families at the US-Mexico border. In June 2018, Donald Trump's most notorious decision as president had secretly been in effect for months before most Americans became aware of the astonishing inhumanity being perpetrated by their own government. Jacob Soboroff was among the first journalists to expose this reality after seeing firsthand the living conditions of the children in custody.

"Soboroff's thoroughly engaging expose of the inner workings of a corrupt and unfeeling government is essential to understanding America's current immigration misery." —*Booklist*

Suarez, Ray
★ *We Are Home: Becoming American in the 21st Century: An Oral History.* Ray Suarez. Little Brown & Co. 2024. 320 p.
ISBN 9780316353762
Grades: Adult   325.73
1. Immigrants 2. Immigration and emigration 3. Citizenship 4. Identity 5. Belonging 6. Home (Concept) 7. United States 8. Oral histories 9. Society and culture — Immigration 10. History Writing — Immigration — United States 11. Life stories — Identity — Immigrants

From a veteran broadcaster and historian comes a richly reported portrait of the newest Americans, immigrants from all over the globe who are living all across the country, filled with their own voices.

"Without whitewashing the past and present ugliness of American prejudice, this generous and hopeful book reminds readers that the story of our nation, at its best, is one of opportunity for all." —*Booklist*

Yang, Jia Lynn
★ *One Mighty and Irresistible Tide: The Epic Struggle Over American Immigration, 1924-1965.* Jia Lynn Yang. W.W. Norton & Company 2020. 384 p.
ISBN 9780393635843
Grades: Adult   325.73
1. Immigration and emigration law 2. Immigrants 3. Immigration and emigration law reform 4. Immigration enforcement 5. Xenophobia 6. Racism 7. Immigration and emigration 8. United States history 9. 20th century 10. Society and culture — Immigration 11. History writing — Immigration — United States
LC 2019050475

A history of the 20th-century battle to reform the American immigration laws behind today's most contentious debates discusses the Congressional immigration restrictions of 1924, the 1965 Immigration and Nationality Act and the impact of transformative laws on nonwhite migration.

"The combination of meticulous research and captivating writing creates a beautiful surprise; a dark history that gleams under the spotlight of unvarnished truthtelling. Expect a lot of reader requests and award attention for this significant title." —*Booklist*

Includes bibliographical references and index.

326 Slavery and emancipation

Hochschild, Adam
Bury the Chains: Prophets and Rebels in the Fight to Free an Empire's Slaves. Adam Hochschild. Houghton Mifflin 2005. VIII, 468 p. : Illustration
ISBN 9780618104697
Grades: Adult   326
1. Clarkson, Thomas 1760-1846 2. Anti-slavery movements 3. Slavery 4. Slave trade 5. Abolitionists 6. Human rights 7. British history 8. Great Britain 9. 18th century 10. 19th century 11. History writing — Europe — United Kingdom
LC 2004054091
Lionel Gelber Prize (Canada), 2006; Los Angeles Times Book Prize for History, 2005; New York Times Notable Book, 2005; National Book Award for Nonfiction finalist, 2005.

Offers an account of the first great human rights crusade, which originated in England in the 1780s and resulted in the freeing of hundreds of thousands of slaves around the world.

"The author brings drama and incredible research to this thrilling look at the little-celebrated abolition movement in Britain and its reverberations throughout modern democracies." —*Booklist*

Includes bibliographical references (p. 409-427) and index.

PUBLIC LIBRARY CORE COLLECTION: NONFICTION
Twentieth Edition

Plant, Deborah G.
Of Greed and Glory: In Pursuit of Freedom for All. Deborah G. Plant. Amistad Press 2024. 277 p.
ISBN 9780062898494
Grades: Adult   326
1. Enslaved people 2. Marginalized people 3. Race relations 4. Civil rights 5. Justice 6. Slavery 7. Oppression (Psychology) 8. African American civil rights 9. Freed people 10. Freedom 11. African Americans 12. African American history 13. United States history 14. United States 15. Society and culture — Race 16. History writing — African American — Enslavement — United States

An active vigilance is required of those who would be and remain free; with of Greed and Glory, Deborah Plant reveals the many ways in which slavery continues in America today and charts our collective course toward personal sovereignty for all.

"A compelling argument against the systemic abuse of justice as a weapon of oppression." —*Kirkus*

Sinha, Manisha
The Slave's Cause: A History of Abolition. Manisha Sinha. Yale University Press 2016. 784 p.
ISBN 9780300181371
Grades: Adult   326
1. Abolitionists 2. Slavery 3. History of anti-slavery movements 4. African Americans 5. Enslaved people 6. Enslaved people's resistance and revolts 7. History writing — African American — Enslavement — United States
LC 2015948091

A groundbreaking history of abolition that recovers the largely forgotten role of African Americans in the long march toward emancipation from the American Revolution through the Civil War.

"Sinha's book is a tour de force that surpasses all previous works in scope, scale, and scholarship." —*Library Journal*

326.0973 Slavery and emancipation — United States

Rediker, Marcus
The Amistad Rebellion: An Atlantic Odyssey of Slavery and Freedom. Marcus Rediker. Viking 2012. 304 p.
ISBN 9780670025046
Grades: Adult   326.0973
1. Slave trade 2. Enslaved people 3. Slavery 4. Trials 5. Mutiny 6. Enslaved people's resistance and revolts 7. Anti-slavery movements 8. United States history 9. 19th century 10. History writing — African American — Enslavement — United States
LC 2012014810

Booklist Editors' Choice, 2012.

A scholarly account of the 19th-century slave ship rebellion is presented from the perspectives of the slaves and discusses their shared culture on another continent and their harrowing fight for freedom while placing their victory in a context of the great chain of resistance spanning the earliest slave revolts through the Civil Rights era.

"Spectacularly researched and fluidly composed, this latest study offers some much needed perspective on a critical yet oft-overlooked event in America's history." —*Publishers Weekly*

Includes bibliographical references and index.

327 International relations

Ghazvinian, John
America and Iran: A History, 1720 to the Present. John Ghazvinian. Alfred A. Knopf 2021. 688 p.
ISBN 9780307271815
Grades: Adult   327
1. World politics 2. International relations 3. Southwest Asia and North Africa (Middle East) history 4. Iran 5. United States 6. Impartial writing 7. History writing — Southwest Asia and North Africa (Middle East) 8. History writing — United States 9. Politics and global affairs — World politics — Southwest Asia and North Africa (Middle East) 10. Politics and global affairs — World politics — United States
LC 2019057328

A portrait of the two-centuries-long entwined histories of Iran and America, and the first book to examine, in all its aspects, the rich and fraught relations between these two powers—once allies, now adversaries.

"The result is a nuanced, illuminating, and much-needed corrective to one-sided vilifications of Tehran." —*Publishers Weekly*

Includes bibliographical references and index.

Kaplan, Robert D.
The Loom of Time: Between Empire and Anarchy from the Mediterranean to China. Robert D. Kaplan. Random House 2023. 400 p.
ISBN 9780593242797
Grades: Adult   327
1. Imperialism 2. Politics and government 3. Central Asia 4. Southwest Asia and North Africa (Middle East) 5. History Writing — Asia 6. History writing — Southwest Asia and North Africa (Middle East) 7. Politics and global affairs — World Politics — Asia 8. Politics and global affairs — World politics — Southwest Asia and North Africa (Middle East)
LC 2023001473

Exploring the Greater Middle East, which encompasses much of the Arab world, this book weaves together classic texts, immersive travel writing and voices from every country to reveal the impacts of history on the present state and make the case for classical realism as an approach to this vast region.

"The vast Muslim heartland of Afro-Eurasia is a tumult that might find stability and prosperity but rarely democracy, according to this sweeping geopolitical meditation." —*Publishers Weekly*

Includes bibliographical references and index.

327.12 Espionage and subversion

Anderson, Scott
★ *The Quiet Americans: Four CIA Spies at the Dawn of the Cold War — a Tragedy in Three Acts.* Scott Anderson. Doubleday 2020. 448 p.
ISBN 9780385540452
Grades: Adult   327.12
1. Burke, Michael, 1918-1987 2. Wisner, Frank, 1909-1965 3. Sichel, Peter M. F. 4. Lansdale, Edward Geary, 1908-1987 5. Cold War 6. Espionage 7. Intelligence officers 8. Spies 9. History writing — Spies and spying 10. Life stories — Law and order — Spies and secret agents
LC 2019054799

New York Times Notable Book, 2020.

From the best-selling author, a gripping history of the early years of the Cold War, the CIA's covert battles against communism, and the tragic consequences which still affect America and the world today.

"The roots of America's decline in international reputation since WWII lie in the government's confused and hypocritical actions during the first decade of the Cold War, according to this fascinating history by journalist Anderson (Fractured Lands)... Laced with vivid character sketches and vital insights into 20th-century geopolitics, this stand-out chronicle helps to make sense of the world today." —*Publishers Weekly*

Includes bibliographical references.

Blum, Howard
The Spy Who Knew Too Much: An Ex-cia Officer's Quest Through a Legacy of Betrayal. Howard Blum. HarperCollins 2022. 384 p.
ISBN 9780063054219
Grades: Adult   327.12
1. Former CIA agents 2. Reconciliation 3. CIA agents 4. Redemption 5. Betrayal 6. Spies 7. Fathers and daughters 8. True Crime — General 9. Life stories — Law and order — Spies and secret agents 10. Nonfiction that reads like fiction

ESSENTIAL AND RECOMMENDED TITLES
327.1209 Espionage and subversion — History

A retired spy gets back into the game to solve a perplexing case—and reconcile with his daughter, a CIA officer who married into the very family that derailed his own CIA career—in this compulsive true-life tale of vindication and redemption, filled with drama, intrigue, and mystery from the New York Times bestselling author of the Last Goodnight, It's a real-life thriller whose stunning conclusion will make headline news.

"Did the KGB have a mole with access to some of the CIA's most sensitive information who was never caught? That tantalizing question is at the heart of this nail-biting account from former New York Times investigative reporter Blum." —*Publishers Weekly*

Friedman, Matti
Spies of No Country: Secret Lives at the Birth of Israel. Matti Friedman. Algonquin Books of Chapel Hill 2019. 224 p.
ISBN 9781616207229
Grades: Adult   327.12
1. Spies 2. Espionage 3. Undercover operations 4. Mossad agents 5. Intelligence officers 6. Assassins 7. Sabotage 8. Betrayal 9. Israel-Arab War, 1948-1949 10. Southwest Asia and North Africa (Middle East) history 11. Palestine 12. Beirut, Lebanon 13. Israel 14. Lebanon 15. 1940s 16. 20th century 17. History writing — Southwest Asia and North Africa (Middle East) 18. History writing — Wars and conflicts — Arab-Israeli conflict
LC 2018026756

Canadian Jewish Book Award, 2019.
A meticulously researched chronicle of the Arab Section, Israel's first spy organization, details how undercover intelligence operatives in 1948 Beirut risked or lost their lives in support of Israeli statehood.
Includes bibliographical references.

Mundy, Liza
★ *The Sisterhood: The Secret History of Women at the CIA.* Liza Mundy. Crown 2023. 400 p.
ISBN 9780593238172
Grades: Adult   327.12
1. Espionage 2. Women intelligence officers 3. Women spies 4. Intelligence service 5. History Writing — Spies and spying 6. History Writing — Women's history 7. History Writing — United States 8. Politics and global affairs — National security
LC 2023021017

In this thrilling new perspective on history, the New York Times bestselling author of Code Girls turns her attention the women of the CIA who fought to become operatives, transformed spy craft and provided the data analysis that helped track down Bin Laden in his Pakistani compound.

"Every page is electric with revelations as Mundy vividly and perceptively portrays the remarkable women who covertly elevated this complicated, controversial, yet essential government agency." —*Booklist*

Includes bibliographical references and index.

Popkin, Jim
Code Name Blue Wren: The True Story of America's Most Dangerous Female Spy - and the Sister She Betrayed. Jim Popkin. Hanover Square Press 2023. 320 p.
ISBN 9781335449887
Grades: Adult   327.12
1. Montes, Ana 2. Women spies 3. Espionage 4. Intelligence service 5. Spies 6. American people 7. North American people 8. Sisters 9. Betrayal 10. Biographies 11. Life stories — Law and order — Spies and secret agents 12. True Crime — General 13. History Writing — Spies and Spying 14. History Writing — Women's History

Describes the true crime story of Ana Montes, a superstar of the US Intelligence community who had recently won a prestigious fellowship at the CIA was arrested and publicly exposed as a secret agent for Cuba.

"Investigative journalist Popkin's engrossing debut tells the story of Ana Montes, an intelligence analyst for the U.S. government who, probably before she joined the Defense Intelligence Agency in 1985, was spying for Cuba." —*Publishers Weekly*

Trahair, R. C. S.
Encyclopedia of Cold War Espionage, Spies, and Secret Operations 3rd Ed. Richard C.S. Trahair. Enigma Books 2012. 687 p.
ISBN 9781936274253
Grades: Adult   327.12
1. Cold War 2. Espionage 3. Spies 4. 20th century 5. History writing — United States 6. Reference — Biographical dictionaries

Previously unknown operations and new names continue to surface in the Encyclopedia of Cold War Espionage, Spies, and Secret Operations. This new edition contains updated information on Cold War spying, with over 350 A?Z main entries (over thirty of them new) biographical sketches, and an updated bibliography. In support of the entries the book includes useful tools: a complete chronology of significant espionage activities; a glossary of key terms and individuals; references to other sources, either in print or electronic formats; and a full index. The latest Russian deep cover spy cases of 2010 and the sequel are part of this edition.

327.1209 Espionage and subversion — History

Andrew, Christopher M.
The Secret World: A History of Intelligence. Christopher Andrew. Yale University Press 2018. 900 p.
ISBN 9780300238440
Grades: Adult   327.1209
1. Espionage 2. Intelligence service 3. Spies 4. Military intelligence 5. Counterintelligence 6. History writing — Spies and spying
LC 2018947154

The first-ever detailed, comprehensive history of intelligence, from Moses and Sun Tzu to the present day.

327.1247 Espionage — Russia

Walton, Calder
Spies: The Epic Intelligence War Between East and West. Calder Walton. Simon & Schuster 2023. xiii, 672 p.
ISBN 9781668000694
Grades: Adult   327.1247
1. Spies 2. Great powers 3. Intelligence service 4. Espionage 5. Cold War 6. Military intelligence 7. International competition 8. International intrigue 9. Electronic intelligence 10. Cyberterrorism 11. History 12. United States 13. Great Britain 14. Russia 15. China 16. History writing — Spies and spying 17. Politics and global affairs — National security 18. Politics and global affairs — World politics

Spies is the history of the secret war that Russia and the West have been waging for a century. The Cold War started long before 1945. But the West fought back after World War II, mounting its own shadow war, using disinformation, vast intelligence networks, and new technologies against the Soviet Union. This fresh reading of history, combined with practical takeaways for our current great power struggles, make Spies a unique and essential addition to the history of the Cold War and the unrolling conflict between the United States and China that will dominate the 21st century.

"This is an encyclopedic yet entertaining dossier on the people, organizations, and events that shaped one of the 20th century's defining ideological battles." —*Publishers Weekly*

Includes bibliographical references and index.

Wiehl, Lis W.
A Spy in Plain Sight: The Inside Story of the FBI and Robert Hanssen - America's Most Damaging Russian Spy. Lis W. Wiehl. Pegasus Books 2022. 336 p.
ISBN 9781639361717
Grades: Adult   327.1247
1. Hanssen, Robert 2. Espionage 3. Spies 4. Traitors 5. Moles (Spies) 6. Intelligence service 7. Computer security 8. Cyberterrorism 9. International relations

10. Russia 11. United States 12. Biographies 13. Life stories — Law and order — Spies and secret agents 14. History writing — Spies and spying

A Spy in Plain Sight reflects on the deeply sown divisions and paranoias of our present day and provides an unparalleled view into the functioning of the FBI, and will stand alongside pillars of the genre like Killers of the Flower Moon, The Spy and the Traitor, and No Place to Hide.

"Perhaps the best of the many books on Robert Hanssen (b. 1944), the agent who, for more than 20 years, sold American secrets to Russia....A superb account of a long-running intelligence disaster." —*Kirkus*

327.125694 Espionage — Israel and Palestine

Berg, Raffi
Red Sea Spies: The True Story of Mossad's Fake Diving Resort. Raffi Berg. Icon Books 2020. xxvii, 324 pages, 16 unnumbered pages of plates : Color; Illustration; Map
ISBN 9781785786006
Grades: Adult   327.125694
1. Intelligence service 2. Espionage 3. Jewish people 4. Ethiopian people 5. East African people 6. 20th century 7. History writing — Arab-Israeli relations — Southwest Asia and North Africa (Middle East) 8. History writing — Jewish history 9. History writing — Military — Special Forces
LC 2019467991

The little-known story of a daring Mossad operation and the holiday resort run by spies.
Includes bibliographical references and index.

327.1273 Espionage — United States

Cunningham, Benjamin
The Liar: How a Double Agent in the CIA Became the Cold War's Last Honest Man. Benjamin Cunningham. Public Affairs 2022. 320 p.
ISBN 9781541700796
Grades: Adult   327.1273
1. Koechner, Karel 2. Cold War 3. Espionage 4. Spies 5. Double agents 6. United States 7. 1970s 8. History writing — Spies and spying 9. True Crime — General

Using newly declassified documents, interrogation tapes and extraordinary first-hand accounts from the Koechers themselves, this thrilling novel recounts the shifting loyalties and over-the-top hedonism of Karel Koecher, who operated as a double agent at the height of the Cold War.

"Cunningham excels at his research, placing his story against a backdrop of political events through the 1980s as Karel and Hana reach their pinnacle in hedonistic, high society New York, until it all comes crashing down. An intriguing debut." —*Library Journal*

Jacobsen, Annie
Surprise, Kill, Vanish: The Secret History of CIA Paramilitary Armies, Operators, and Assassins. Annie Jacobsen. Little, Brown & Company 2019. 560 p.
ISBN 9780316441438
Grades: Adult   327.1273
1. Elite operatives 2. Paramilitary forces 3. Intelligence service 4. Assassination 5. Presidents 6. International relations 7. Undercover operations 8. United States 9. History writing — Spies and spying 10. Politics and global affairs — Terrorism
LC Bl2019008459

Tells the untold story of the CIA's Special Activities Division, a highly-classified branch of the CIA and the most effective black-operations force in the world.

"Similar to her previous treatments of the Pentagon's research division (The Pentagon's Brain) and paranormal activity (Phenomena), Jacobsen here presents a tour de force exploring the CIA's paramilitary activities. Highly recommended for those seeking a better understanding of American foreign policy in action." —*Library Journal*

Wilford, Hugh
The Cia: An Imperial History. Hugh Wilford. Basic Books 2024. 368 p.
ISBN 9781541645912
Grades: Adult   327.1273
1. Intelligence service 2. Cold War 3. Spies 4. History Writing — Spies and spying 5. Politics and global affairs — National security 6. History writing — Wars and conflicts

Drawing on decades of research to show the CIA as part of a larger picture, a celebrated intelligence historian tells the story of the birth of a new imperial order in the shadows that became the foremost defender of America's covert global empire.

"The book is full of such striking character portraits, as Wilford evocatively suggests that the CIA's tendency to overthrow foreign governments emerged from paranoia and personality defects among its leadership." —*Publishers Weekly*

327.1273009 Espionage — United States — History

Weiner, Tim
Legacy of Ashes: The History of the CIA. Tim Weiner. Doubleday 2007. 702 p, [8] p. of plates : Illustration
ISBN 9780385514453
Grades: 11 12 Adult   327.1273009
1. Intelligence officers 2. Secrecy in government 3. Spies 4. Espionage 5. Misadventures 6. Intelligence service 7. United States history 8. United States 9. 20th century 10. History writing — Spies and spying

Los Angeles Times Book Prize for History, 2007; National Book Award for Nonfiction, 2007; New York Times Notable Book, 2007; National Book Critics Circle Award for Nonfiction finalist, 2007.

Traces the history of the CIA from the end of World War II to Iraq, in a study that condemns the organization for its record, its inability to understand world affairs, the violence it has unleashed, and its undermining of American politics.
Includes bibliographical references and index.

327.1273043 Espionage — United States and Germany

Vogel, Steve
Betrayal in Berlin: The True Story of the Cold War's Most Audacious Espionage Operation. Steve Vogel. Custom House 2019. 464 p.
ISBN 9780062449627
Grades: Adult   327.1273043
1. Blake, George, 1922-2020 2. Tunnels 3. Cold War 4. Moles (Spies) 5. Surveillance 6. Espionage 7. Undercover operations 8. Betrayal 9. Tunneling 10. Spies 11. Intelligence service 12. German history 13. Berlin, Germany 14. East Berlin, Germany 15. West Berlin, Germany 16. Soviet Union 17. United States 18. Great Britain 19. 20th century 20. History writing — Spies and spying 21. History writing — Cold War 22. Life stories — Law and order — Spies and secret agents
LC Bl2019021002

Its code name was "Operation Gold," a wildly audacious CIA plan to construct a clandestine tunnel into East Berlin to tap into critical KGB and Soviet military telecommunication lines. Success would provide the CIA and the British Secret Intelligence Service access to a vast treasure of intelligence. Exposure might spark a dangerous confrontation with the Soviets. Yet as the Allies were burrowing into the German soil, a traitor, code-named Agent Diamond by his Soviet handlers, was burrowing into the operation itself. .

327.2 Diplomacy

Hill, Fiona
There Is Nothing for You Here: Finding Opportunity in the Twenty-first Century. Fiona Hill. Mariner Books 2021. 320 p.
ISBN 9780358574316

ESSENTIAL AND RECOMMENDED TITLES
327.41043 International relations — United Kingdom and Germany

Grades: Adult   **327.2**
1. Hill, Fiona, 1965- 2. International relations 3. Democracy 4. Populism 5. Income inequality 6. Growing up 7. Autobiographies and memoirs 8. Politics and global affairs — World politics 9. Politics and global affairs — Political figures 10. History writing — Europe — Russia 11. Life stories — Facing adversity — Personal transformation

A celebrated foreign policy expert and key impeachment witness reveals how declining opportunity has set America on the grim path of modern Russia—and draws on her personal journey out of poverty, and her unique perspectives as an historian and policy maker, to show how we can return hope to our forgotten places.

"This book by foreign policy expert Hill, combining memoir and political science, accounts for her 30-year career as a specialist in U.S.-Russia relations, provides insights on political divisions in the United States, and argues that declining economic opportunity can spark authoritarianism." —*Library Journal*

327.41043 International relations — United Kingdom and Germany

Bouverie, Tim
Appeasement: Chamberlain, Hitler, Churchill, and the Road to War. Tim Bouverie. Tim Duggan Books 2019. 416 pages
ISBN 9780451499844
Grades: Adult   **327.41043**
1. Chamberlain, Neville, 1869-1940 2. Churchill, Winston, 1874-1965 3. Hitler, Adolf, 1889-1945 4. World War II 5. Diplomacy 6. Causes of war 7. International relations 8. Politics and government 9. Great Britain 10. Germany 11. History writing — Wars and conflicts — World War II 12. History writing — Europe — United Kingdom
LC 2019000625

A narrative history of the British appeasement of the Third Reich before World War II draws on previously unseen archival resources to identify the indecision, failed diplomacy and parliamentary infighting that enabled Hitler's domination of Europe.
Includes bibliographical references and index.

Phillips, Adrian
Fighting Churchill, Appeasing Hitler: Neville Chamberlain, Sir Horace Wilson, & Britain's Plight of Appeasement, 1937-1939. Adrian Phillips. Pegasus Books 2019. xxxi, 448 pages, 8 unnumbered pages of plates : Illustration
ISBN 9781643132211
Grades: Adult   **327.41043**
1. Chamberlain, Neville, 1869-1940 2. Churchill, Winston, 1874-1965 3. Wilson, Horace, 1882-1972 4. Hitler, Adolf, 1889-1945 5. Political culture 6. World War II 7. Aggression (International relations) 8. Political science 9. Causes of war 10. International relations 11. Politics and government 12. Great Britain 13. Germany 14. 1930s 15. History writing — Wars and conflicts — World War II 16. History writing — Europe — United Kingdom
LC B12019032886

The author presents a controversial revisionist examination of the British policy of appeasement in the late 1930s to identify key miscalculations and fateful concessions that rendered World War II inevitable.
Includes bibliographical references (pages 389-433) and index.

327.73 Foreign relations — United States

Chomsky, Noam
Who Rules the World? Noam Chomsky. Metropolitan Books 2016. 320 p.
ISBN 9781627793810
Grades: Adult   **327.73**
1. September 11 Terrorist Attacks, 2001 2. Military power 3. Democracy 4. Politics and government 5. United States 6. Essays 7. Politics and global affairs — World politics — United States
LC 2016010018

Presents an examination of the waning American Century, the nature of U.S. policies in the post-9/11 world, and the dangers of prioritizing military power over democracy and human rights.

"Chomsky, fierce and unapologetic, has a strong fan base and continues to be an important voice." —*Booklist*

Farrow, Ronan
War on Peace: The End of Diplomacy and the Decline of American Influence. Ronan Farrow. W W Norton & Company 2018. 384 p.
ISBN 9780393652109
Grades: Adult   **327.73**
1. Diplomacy 2. International relations 3. United States 4. Politics and global affairs — World politics — United States
LC 2018006827

American diplomacy is under siege. Offices across the State Department sit empty, while abroad the military-industrial complex has assumed the work once undertaken by peacemakers. We're becoming a nation that shoots first and asks questions later. In an astonishing account ranging from Washington, D.C. to Afghanistan, Pakistan, and North Korea in the years since 9/11, acclaimed journalist and former diplomat Ronan Farrow illuminates one of the most consequential and poorly understood changes in American history.

"Excellent, wide-ranging reporting and sharp-edged analysis make this a book that's sure to be talked about inside the Beltway—and that deserves a wide audience beyond." —*Kirkus*
Includes index.

Ferreiro, Larrie D.
Brothers at Arms: American Independence and the Men of France and Spain Who Saved It. by Larrie D. Ferreiro. Knopf 2016. 416 p.
ISBN 9781101875247
Grades: Adult   **327.73**
1. American Revolution, 1775-1783 2. Alliances 3. International relations 4. French participation in wars 5. United States history 6. Spain 7. France 8. Great Britain 9. United States 10. 18th century 11. Revolutionary America (1775-1783) 12. History writing — Wars and conflicts — Revolutionary War (America)
LC 2016007136

Pulitzer Prize for History finalist, 2017.

The remarkable untold story of how the American Revolution's success depended on substantial military and financial assistance provided by France and Spain, and places the Revolution in the context of the global strategic interests of those nations in their fight against Great Britain.

"A largely untold, engrossing history of our nations fraught, and unlikely, path to liberty." —*Kirkus*

Indyk, Martin
Master of the Game: Henry Kissinger and the Art of Middle East Diplomacy. Martin Indyk. Alfred A. Knopf 2021. 512 p.
ISBN 9781101947548
Grades: Adult   **327.73**
1. Kissinger, Henry, 1923-2023 2. Diplomacy 3. International relations 4. Arab-Israeli relations 5. Arab-Israeli conflict 6. Israel-Arab War, 1973 7. Southwest Asia and North Africa (Middle East) 8. United States 9. 20th century 10. 1970s 11. History writing — Arab-Israeli relations — Southwest Asia and North Africa (Middle East) 12. History writing — Wars and conflicts — Arab-Israeli conflict
LC 2021001578

Based on newly available documents from American and Israeli archives, extensive interviews and the author's own interactions with some of the main players, this book returns to the origins of American-led peace efforts and to the man who created the Middle East peace process—Henry Kissinger.

"U.S. Secretary of State Henry Kissinger gave a 'Virtuoso' performance during and after the 1973 Yom Kippur War, according to this sweeping history.... This fascinating study illuminates both the cold logic of Kissingerian statecraft and the human factors that muddled it." —*Publishers Weekly*
Includes index.

Kennedy, Robert F.
Thirteen Days: A Memoir of the Cuban Missile Crisis. Robert F. Kennedy; foreword by Arthur Schlesinger, Jr. W.W. Norton 1999. 185 p.
ISBN 9780393318340
Grades: Adult   327.73
1. International relations 2. Cuba 3. Soviet Union 4. United States 5. History writing — United States 6. History writing — General
LC BL 00004822
Kennedy describes the moral dilemma the crisis posed and describes the attitudes and actions of President Kennedy and his advisory staff.
Reprint. Originally published: 1969. With a new foreword; Includes bibliographical references (p. 175-176) and index.

Kinzer, Stephen
★ *The* True *Flag: Theodore Roosevelt, Mark Twain, and the Birth of American Empire.* Stephen Kinzer. Henry Holt and Company 2016. 320 p.
ISBN 9781627792165
Grades: Adult   327.73
1. Roosevelt, Theodore, 1858-1919 2. Lodge, Henry Cabot, 1902-1985 3. Twain, Mark, 1835-1910 4. Spanish-American War, 1898 5. Imperialism 6. Imperialism, American 7. International relations 8. Nationalism 9. Politics and government 10. Territorial expansion 11. United States 12. 1910s 13. 20th century 14. History writing — Early 20th century — United States
LC 2016019840
The author of All the Shah's Men and the Brothers brings to life the forgotten political debate that set America's interventionist course in the world for the 20th century and beyond.
"A tremendously elucidating book that should be required reading for civics courses." —*Kirkus*
Includes bibliographical references and index.

Mead, Walter Russell
The Arc of a Covenant: The United States, Israel, and the Fate of the Jewish People. Walter Russell Mead. Alfred A. Knopf 2022. 288 p.
ISBN 9780375414046
Grades: Adult   327.73
1. Arab-Israeli conflict 2. Zionism 3. Religion and politics 4. International relations 5. Politics and government 6. Israel 7. United States 8. Politics and global affairs — World politics — United States 9. History writing — Arab-Israeli relations — Southwest Asia and North Africa (Middle East)
LC 2021037997
Citing examples from the earliest pilgrims to the present day, a Wall Street Journal columnist illuminates the place of Israel in American foreign policy, investigates the changing politics around the U.S.-Israel relationship, and unlocks the connection between that relationship and the upheavals reshaping American life.
"Mead (God and Gold), a professor of foreign affairs at Bard College, delivers a sweeping study of the relationship between the U.S. and Israel." —*Publishers Weekly*
This is a Borzoi Book published by Alfred A. Knopf; Includes bibliographical references and index.

327.73047 Foreign relations — United States and Russia

Budiansky, Stephen
Code Warriors: NSA's Codebreakers and the Secret Intelligence War Against the Soviet Union. by Stephen Budiansky. Alfred A. Knopf 2016. 384 p.
ISBN 9780385352666
Grades: Adult   327.73047
1. Cryptography 2. Codes (Communication) 3. Cold War 4. International relations 5. Soviet Union 6. United States 7. History writing — Cold War
LC 2015045330
A sweeping history of the NSA and its codebreaking achievements from World War II through the Cold War shares insights into the challenges faced by cryptanalysts and their role in some of the most complicated events of the twentieth century.
Includes bibliographical references and index.

Weiner, Tim
The Folly and the Glory: America, Russia, and Political Warfare, 1945-2020. Tim Weiner. Henry Holt and Company 2020. 320 p.
ISBN 9781627790857
Grades: Adult   327.73047
1. Trump, Donald, 1946- 2. Putin, Vladimir Vladimirovich, 1952- 3. Cold War 4. Secrecy in government 5. Espionage 6. Presidential election, 2016 7. Propaganda 8. Election corruption 9. Intelligence service 10. International relations 11. Soviet Union 12. Russia 13. United States 14. Politics and global affairs — World politics 15. History writing — Cold War
LC 2019057823
The Pulitzer Prize and National Book Award-winning author of One Man Against the World presents a contextual history of the development of political warfare between the U.S. and Russia from the Stalin era to today.
"Weiner offers a significant contribution to the literature of U.S.-Russia relations with a book that emphasizes the asymmetry of American capacity for political warfare, currently consisting of effective cyber counterespionage." —*Library Journal*
Includes bibliographical references and index.

328.3 Specific topics of legislative bodies

Seabrook, Nicholas R.
One Person, One Vote: A Surprising History of Gerrymandering in America, Where It Is Today and How We Got Here. Nick Seabrook. Pantheon Books 2022. 416 p.
ISBN 9780593315866
Grades: Adult   328.3
1. Gerrymandering 2. Apportionment (Election law) 3. State governments 4. Politics and government 5. United States 6. Politics and global affairs — Elections 7. Politics and global affairs — Political parties 8. History writing — United States
LC 2021050744
An authority on constitutional and election law, and an expert on gerrymandering, explores the rise of the most partisan gerrymanders in American history.
"Dense yet entertaining, this comprehensive survey is a worthy introduction to a high-stakes political issue." —*Publishers Weekly*
Includes bibliographical references and index.

328.73 Legislative process — United States

Cheney, Liz
Oath and Honor: A Memoir and a Warning. Liz Cheney. Little, Brown & Company 2023. 400 p.
ISBN 9780316572064
Grades: Adult   328.73
1. Cheney, Liz, 1966- 2. Women legislators 3. Women politicians 4. Republicans 5. Capitol Riot, Washington, D.C, 2021 6. Democracy 7. Political culture 8. Governmental investigations 9. Politics and government 10. North American people 11. American people 12. United States 13. Autobiographies and memoirs 14. Life stories — Politics — Politicians 15. Politics and global affairs — Political figures
In the aftermath of the 2020 presidential election, Donald Trump and many around him, including certain other elected Republican officials, intentionally breached their oath to the Constitution: They ignored the rulings of dozens of courts, plotted to overturn a lawful election, and provoked a violent attack on our Capitol. Liz Cheney, one of the few Republican officials to take a stand against these efforts, witnessed the attack first-hand, and then helped lead the Congressional Select Committee investigation into how it happened. Here she tells the story of this perilous moment in our history, and the risks we still face.

ESSENTIAL AND RECOMMENDED TITLES
330 Economics

"An earnest dissection of the threat Trump poses to our democracy." —*Kirkus*

Brazile, Donna
For Colored Girls Who Have Considered Politics. Donna Brazile, Yolanda Caraway, Leah Daughtry, and Minyon Moore with Veronica Chambers. St. Martin's Press 2018. 288 p.
ISBN 9781250137715
Grades: Adult **328.73**
1. African American women 2. Political planning 3. Political leadership 4. African American women politicians 5. African American politicians 6. Political science 7. Politicians 8. Political campaigns 9. Elections 10. Human rights 11. Civil rights 12. African American history 13. African Americans 14. Political participation 15. Politics and government 16. United States 17. 21st century 18. 20th century 19. Autobiographies and memoirs 20. Politics and global affairs — Elections 21. Life stories — Politics — Politicians 22. Life stories — Politics — Activists and reformers 23. History writing — African American — United States

LC 2018017175

Four of the most influential African-American women in politics share the story of their friendship and their behind-the-scenes public-service contributions during the careers of leaders ranging from Bill Clinton and Jesse Jackson to Coretta Scott King and Barack Obama.
Includes index.

Clinton, Hillary Rodham
What Happened. Hillary Rodham Clinton. Simon & Schuster 2017. 352 p.
ISBN 9781501175565
Grades: Adult **328.73**
1. Clinton, Hillary Rodham 2. Women presidential candidates 3. Presidential election, 2016 4. Political campaigns 5. Elections 6. Voter suppression 7. Politics and government 8. United States 9. 2010s 10. 2020s 11. Essays 12. Biographies 13. Life stories — Politics — Politicians 14. Politics and global affairs — Elections

LC Bl2017031097

Goodreads Choice Award, 2017; New York Times Notable Book, 2017.

A book of essays by the former secretary of state includes entries describing her experiences in the 2016 presidential campaign and incorporates hundreds of inspirational quotes that have shaped her life and work.

"Writing in her smart, sometimes self-deprecating voice, Clinton brings much-needed perspective to the election, especially for her millions of supporters, who also want to know what happened and why." —*Booklist*

Lewis, John
Carry On: Reflections for a New Generation. John Robert Lewis with Kabir Sehgal; foreword by Ambassador Andrew Young. Grand Central Publishing 2021. 192 p.
ISBN 9781538707128
Grades: Adult **328.73**
1. Lewis, John, 1940-2020 2. Wisdom 3. Courage 4. African American politicians 5. Faith 6. Forgiveness 7. Social justice 8. Hope 9. Inspiration 10. Speeches, addresses, etc. 11. Arts and Entertainment — Writing and Publishing 12. Life stories — Politics — Activists and Reformers — Civil Rights Leaders 13. Life stories — Politics — Politicians

The final reflections, words and wisdom of esteemed civil rights champion and late Congressman, John Lewis, who continued to offer inspiration and hope to millions even while he battled the cancer that ultimately ended his life.

"The book's conversational tone and brisk history lessons make it accessible to readers of all ages. The result is a winning introduction to the man and his philosophies of life." —*Publishers Weekly*

Zelizer, Julian E.
Burning Down the House: Newt Gingrich, the Fall of a Speaker, and the Rise of the New Republican Party. Julian E. Zelizer. Penguin Press 2020. 352 p.
ISBN 9781594206658
Grades: Adult **328.73**

1. Gingrich, Newt 2. Rhetoric 3. Politicians 4. Legislators 5. Political leadership 6. Communication in politics 7. Political culture 8. Power 9. Politics and government 10. Ruthlessness 11. United States 12. 20th century 13. 21st century 14. Politics and global affairs — Political figures 15. History writing — Politicians — United States 16. Politics and global affairs — Political parties 17. History writing — 1990s — United States

LC 2019044440

New York Times Notable Book, 2020.

Traces the story of how the former Speaker of the House and his allies orchestrated an era of ruthless GOP initiatives directly responsible for today's partisan divides.

"A masterfully written political road map for anyone wondering how we got to where we are." —*Kirkus*
Includes bibliographical references and index.

330 Economics

Chang, Ha-Joon
Economics: The User's Guide. Ha-Joon Chang. Bloomsbury 2014. 384 p.
ISBN 9781620408124
Grades: Adult **330**
1. Economics 2. Economic policy 3. Capitalism 4. Business and economics — Economics

LC 2014498623

The award-winning author of 23 Things They Don't Tell You About Capitalism outlines the real-world processes of the global economy while explaining how to better understand the strengths and weaknesses of key economics theories to better navigate today's interconnected world.

"A solid choice for those who want to learn more about economics without feeling like they are back in the classroom." —*Library Journal*

Hoffman, Liz
Crash Landing: The Inside Story of How the World's Biggest Companies Survived an Economy on the Brink. Liz Hoffman. Crown 2023. 352 p.
ISBN 9780593239018
Grades: Adult **330**
1. COVID-19 Pandemic, 2020- 2. Big Business 3. Corporations 4. Executives 5. Epidemics 6. Recession (Economics) 7. Panic 8. Business and politics 9. Bailouts (Government policy) 10. Decision-making 11. Crisis management 12. Economics 13. United States 14. 21st century 15. Business and economics — Economics — Contemporary U.S. economy 16. Business and economics — Business leaders and entrepreneurs 17. History writing — Early 21st century — United States

LC 2022039607

It was the ultimate test for CEOs, and almost none of them saw it coming. In early March 2020, with the Dow Jones flirting with 30,000, the world's biggest companies were riding an eleven-year economic high. By the end of the month, millions were out of work, iconic firms were begging for bailouts, and countless small businesses were in freefall. In Crash Landing, business journalist Liz Hoffman exposes the fear, grit, and gambles behind the pandemic economy, while probing its implications for the future of work, corporate leadership, and capitalism itself.

"Savvy analysis and colorful reportage make this an engrossing boardroom view of an economic cataclysm." —*Publishers Weekly*
Includes bibliographical references and index.

Kwak, James
Economism: Bad Economics and the Rise of Inequality. James Kwak. Pantheon Books 2016. 192 p.
ISBN 9781101871195
Grades: Adult **330**
1. Economics 2. Economic policy 3. United States 4. Business and economics — Economics — Contemporary U.S. economy

LC 2016024099

Outlines a deconstruction of the framework for understanding the world of classroom economics, clarifying assumptions and misleading teachings while sharing historical insights into how economism became a prevalent influence in the U.S.

"It should be companion reading to every introductory economics text." —*Publishers Weekly*

Includes bibliographical references and index.

Levitt, Steven D.
★ *Freakonomics: A Rogue Economist Explores the Hidden Side of Everything.* Steven D. Levitt and Stephen J. Dubner. William Morrow 2005. xii, 242 p.
ISBN 9780060731328
Grades: Adult   330
1. Causation 2. Social life and customs 3. Economics 4. United States 5. Page to screen 6. Business and economics — Economics
LC 2004065478

Book Sense Book of the Year Nonfiction, 2006; New York Times Notable Book, 2005.

Takes an unconventional look at how the economy really works, from cheating and crime to sports and child-rearing, offering a very different view on what really matters and what really drives the economy.

"This excellent, readable book will enlighten many library patrons."—*Booklist*

Includes bibliographical references and index.

Superfreakonomics: Global Cooling, Patriotic Prostitutes, and Why Suicide Bombers Should Buy Life Insurance. Steven D. Levitt and Stephen J. Dubner. William Morrow 2009. xvii, 270 p.
ISBN 9780060889579
Grades: Adult   330
1. Causation 2. Social life and customs 3. Economics 4. United States 5. Business and economics — Economics
LC 2009035852

In a follow-up to "Freakonomics," the authors offer a new analysis of how the economy really works.

"The authors assert that the unifying principle in the various topics they address is people responding to incentives in ways that are not necessarily predictable or manifest. Major themes are explored using a wide range of examples, e.g., life and death issues, terrorism, altruism, medical care, crime, and the environment. Levitt and Dubner succeed in applying economic analysis to timely topics with stimulation, wit, and humor. Best of all, their book will appeal to a broad segment of the population."—*Choice*

Includes bibliographical references (p. [221]-256) and index.

Schumacher, E. F.
Small Is Beautiful: Economics as If People Mattered. E.F. Schumacher; foreword by Bill McKibben. Harper Perennial 2010. xvi, 324 pages
ISBN 9780061997761
Grades: Adult   330
1. Economics 2. Business and economics — Economics
LC 2019300265

Small is Beautiful is Oxford-trained economist E.F. Schumacher's classic call for the end of excessive consumption. Schumacher inspired such movements as "Buy Locally" and "Fair Trade," while voicing strong opposition to "casino capitalism" and wastefulcorporate behemoths.... [It] presents eminently logical arguments for building our economies around the needs of communities, not corporations.

Includes bibliographical references (pages 319-324); This book was originally published by Blond & Briggs Ltd, London, in 1973—Title page verso.

Sowell, Thomas
Basic Economics: A Common Sense Guide to the Economy. Thomas Sowell. Basic Books 2015. IX, 689 pages
ISBN 9780465060733
Grades: Adult   330
1. Finance 2. Banks and banking 3. Commerce 4. Money 5. Economics 6. United States 7. Business and economics — Economics

An accessible, jargon-free resource outlines the principles behind each major type of economy including capitalist, socialist, and feudal, in terms of the incentives each creates.

"Sowell's volume does a fantastic job in cultivating the reader's economic imagination." —*Choice*

Includes bibliographical references and index.

Wheelan, Charles J.
Naked Economics: Undressing the Dismal Science. Charles Wheelan; foreword by Burton G Malkiel. Norton 2002. 260 p.
ISBN 9780393049824
Grades: Adult   330
1. World economy 2. Economic policy 3. Economics 4. Capitalism 5. Microeconomics 6. Macroeconomics 7. Banks and banking 8. Financial institutions 9. Federal reserve banks 10. Globalization (Economics) 11. Adult books for young adults 12. Business and economics — Economics
LC 2002023580

In Naked Economics, journalist Charles Wheelan does 'The impossible" he makes economic principles relevant, interesting and fun. Brimming with scores of down-to-earth examples and sprinkled with humorous anecdotes, this comprehensive overview will keep listeners smiling and wide awake.

"The author explains the essentials of economics, defining terms like GDP and inflation, explaining how they work and what the short- and long-term impact might be. This is a thoughtful, well-written introduction to economics, with the author projecting a genuine excitement for his material." —*Library Journal*

Includes bibliographical references and index.

Yunus, Muhammad
A World of Three Zeros: The New Economics of Zero Poverty, Zero Unemployment, and Zero Net Carbon Emissions. Muhammad Yunus, with Karl Weber. PublicAffairs 2017. 304 pages
ISBN 9781610397575
Grades: Adult   330
1. Capitalism 2. Free enterprise 3. Altruism 4. Entrepreneurship 5. Business innovations 6. Renewable energy sources 7. Small business 8. New businesses 9. Free trade 10. Economic development 11. Business and economics — Economics — World economy 12. Society and culture — Wealth and class
LC 2017017988

The co-winner of the 2006 Nobel Peace Prize describes why he feels that current capitalism is broken and leads to inequality, unemployment and environmental destruction and presents his ideas for a new capitalism that serves human needs in innovative ways.

Includes bibliographical references and index.

330.01 Philosophy and theory

Roth, Alvin E.
Who Gets What—and Why: The New Economics of Matchmaking and Market Design. Alvin E. Roth. Eamon Dolan/Houghton Mifflin Harcourt 2015. 320 p.
ISBN 9780544291133
Grades: Adult   330.01
1. Economics 2. Game theory 3. Markets 4. Business and economics — Economics
LC 2015010771

A Nobel laureate reveals the often surprising rules that govern a vast array of activities—both mundane and life-changing—where money plays little or no role.

Thaler, Richard H.
Misbehaving: The Making of Behavioral Economics. Richard H. Thaler. W.W. Norton & Company 2015. 336 p.
ISBN 9780393080940
Grades: Adult   330.01

ESSENTIAL AND RECOMMENDED TITLES
330.082 Women in economics

1. Economics 2. Human behavior 3. Decision-making 4. Business and economics — Economics — Socioeconomics

LC 2015004600

Argues that economical trends cannot be predicted as much as thought, mainly because humans are so unpredictable, and reveals how behavioral economic analysis opens up new ways to look at everything from household finance to assigning faculty offices in a new building. By the best-selling co-author of Nudge.

"Misbehaving chronicles Thalers participation in the development of behavioral economics, describes how it happened, and details some of what he and his colleagues learned along the way. This challenging book is written in an understandable manner and contains valuable insight for those interested in economics, psychology, other social sciences, public policy, and business." —Booklist

Includes bibliographical references and index.

330.082 Women in economics

Cox, Josie
Women Money Power: The Rise and Fall of Economic Equality. Josie Cox. Harry N Abrams Inc 2024. 288 p.
ISBN 9781419762987
Grades: Adult   330.082

1. Income inequality 2. Economic security 3. Financial literacy 4. Social justice 5. Discrimination in employment 6. Sex discrimination against women 7. Equality 8. Self-sufficiency 9. Freedom 10. Independence 11. Wages 12. Power 13. Women's history 14. Business and economics — Economics 15. Society and culture — Gender

From an experienced financial journalist, Women Money Power is the story of how women have fought for financial freedom, and the social and political hurdles that have kept them from equality.

Journalist Cox investigates American women's economic status from WWII through the present by telling stories of women 'Who dedicated their lives to female economic empowerment.' —Publishers Weekly

330.1 Systems, schools, theories

Hayek, Friedrich A. von
The Road to Serfdom: Text and Documents. F.A. Hayek; edited by Bruce Caldwell. University of Chicago Press 2007. xi, 283 p.
ISBN 9780226320540
Grades: Adult   330.1

1. Economic policy 2. Totalitarianism 3. Political science 4. Philosophy 5. Politics and government 6. Economics 7. United States 8. 20th century 9. History writing — Politicians — United States

Originally published in 1944, this book offers persuasive warnings against the dangers of central planning, along with what Orwell described as "an eloquent defense of laissez-faire capitalism." Hayek shows that the idea that "under a dictatorial government you can be free inside," is nothing less than a grievous fallacy. Such dictatorial governments prevent individual freedoms and they often use psychological measures to perform "an alteration of the character of the people." Gradually, the people yield their individuality to the point where they become part of the collectivist mass.

Includes bibliographical references (p. 239-241) and index.

Lanchester, John
How to Speak Money: What the Money People Say—and What It Really Means. John Lanchester. W W Norton & Co. Inc. 2014. 256 p.
ISBN 9780393243376
Grades: Adult   330.1

1. Economics 2. Personal finance 3. Banks and banking 4. Money 5. Language and languages 6. Business and economics — Economics

LC 2014028529

The award-winning author of I.O.U. presents a comprehensive and upbeat explanation of how the world of finance and economics really works, from the terms and conditions of personal checking accounts to the deliberate concealments of bankers.

"This entertaining, informative, useful reference, written in a lively style, is suitable for both practitioners and newcomers to the subject of economics." —Choice

Sowell, Thomas
Wealth, Poverty and Politics: An International Perspective. Thomas Sowell. Basic Books 2015. 320 p.
ISBN 9780465082933
Grades: Adult   330.1

1. Economics 2. Income inequality 3. Income 4. Wealth 5. Poverty 6. Conservative writing 7. Society and culture — Wealth and class 8. Politics and global affairs — World politics — United States

LC Bl2015035525

Drawing on accurate, empirical data, one of the foremost conservative public intellectuals in the U.S. argues that political and ideological struggles have led to dangerous confusion about income inequality in America.

330.12 Systems

Friedman, Benjamin M.
Religion and the Rise of Capitalism. Benjamin M. Friedman. Alfred A. Knopf 2021. 560 p.
ISBN 9780593317983
Grades: Adult   330.12

1. Religious thought 2. Christianity and capitalism 3. Capitalism 4. Protestantism 5. Economics 6. Christianity 7. Religions 8. Business and economics — Economics — History 9. Spirituality and Religion — Christianity

LC 2020010391

A leading expert on economic policy presents a major reassessment of the foundations of modern economic thinking to identify the historical religious influences behind today's fiercely defended beliefs about the free market.

"Friedman has made an important contribution to the literature on the intertwining of Western economic thought with religious beliefs. His detailed tracing of the roots of free market economics is well researched, well written, and well worth reading." —Library Journal

Gelles, David
The Man Who Broke Capitalism: How Jack Welch Gutted the Heartland and Crushed the Soul of Corporate America—and How to Undo His Legacy. David Gelles. Simon & Schuster 2022. 256 p.
ISBN 9781982176440
Grades: Adult   330.12

1. Welch, Jack, 1935-2020 2. Executives 3. Chief executive officers 4. Corporations 5. Profit 6. Business 7. Corporate downsizing 8. Employee termination 9. Corporate acquisitions 10. Middle class 11. Income inequality 12. Biographies 13. Life stories — Business — Business leaders 14. Business and economics — Business leaders and entrepreneurs 15. Business and economics — Economics 16. Business and economics — Industries — Manufacturing

In 1981, Jack Welch took over General Electric and quickly rose to fame as the first celebrity CEO. He golfed with presidents, mingled with movie stars, and was idolized for growing GE into the most valuable company in the world. But Welch's achievements didn't stem from some greater intelligence or business prowess. Rather, they were the result of a sustained effort to push GE's stock price ever higher, often at the expense of workers, consumers, and innovation. In this captivating, revelatory book, David Gelles argues that Welch single-handedly ushered in a new, cutthroat era of American capitalism that continues to this day. Gelles shows how Welch's celebrated emphasis on increasing shareholder value by any means necessary (layoffs, outsourcing, offshoring, acquisitions, and buybacks, to name but a few tactics) became the norm in American business generally. He demonstrates how that approach has led to the greatest socioeconomic inequality since the Great Depression and harmed many of the very companies that have embraced it.

"Full of color and vitriol, this is an incisive, eye-popping history." —*Publishers Weekly*

Levy, Jonathan
Ages of American Capitalism: A History of the United States. Jonathan Levy. Random House 2021. xxviii, 908 pages : Illustration; Map
ISBN 9780812995015
Grades: Adult   330.12
1. Capitalism 2. Social classes 3. Racism 4. Social Darwinism 5. Labor unions 6. Working class 7. Economics 8. United States 9. History writing — United States 10. Business and economics — Economics — History

A leading economic historian traces the evolution of American capitalism from the colonial era to the present and argues that we've reached yet another turning point that will define the era ahead.

"Levy makes a cohesive argument that provides a new perspective on the trajectory of the U.S. but will still feel familiar to any student of history." —*Library Journal*

Includes bibliographical references (pages 757-866) and index.

McMillan, John
Reinventing the Bazaar: A Natural History of Markets. John McMillan. Norton 2002. x, 278 p.
ISBN 9780393050219
Grades: Adult   330.12
1. Capitalism 2. Economic history 3. Free enterprise 4. World economy 5. Business and economics — Economics — History 6. Business and economics — Economics — World economy

LC 2002000521

New York Times Notable Book, 2002.

A high-energy tour of the history of markets features such examples as a camel trading fair in India, the twenty-million-dollar-per-day Aalsmeer flower market in the Netherlands, and the global trade in AIDS drugs. Reprint. 13,000 first printing.

"The author examines how markets in ancient times evolved and shows how countries experimented with markets, some successfully and some not. He takes a refreshingly commonsense approach to his subject, doesn't talk down to his readers, and refrains from excessive economic jargon." —*Library Journal*

Includes bibliographical references (p. [247]-262) and index.

Wolf, Martin
★ *The Crisis of Democratic Capitalism.* Martin Wolf. Penguin 2023. xxi, 474 p.
ISBN 9780735224216
Grades: Adult   330.12
1. World economy 2. World politics 3. Democracy 4. Capitalism 5. Compromise 6. Social change 7. Inequality 8. Authoritarianism 9. Business and economics — Economics — World economy 10. Politics and global affairs — World politics

LC 2022035909

Around the world, powerful voices argue that capitalism is better without democracy; others argue that democracy is better without capitalism. This book is a forceful rejoinder to both views. Even as it offers a deep, lucid assessment of why this marriage has grown so strained, it makes clear why a divorce of capitalism from democracy would be a calamity for the world. They need each other even if they find it hard to life together. For all its flaws, argues Martin Wolf, democratic capitalism remains far and away the best system for human flourishing.

"A vigorous defense of democratic capitalism worthy of the name." —*Kirkus*
Includes bibliographical references and index.

330.15 Schools of economic thought

Keynes, John Maynard
★ *The General Theory of Employment, Interest, and Money.* John Maynard Keynes. Harcourt, Brace, Jovanovich 1991. xii, 403 p. : Illustration

ISBN 9780156347112
Grades: Adult   330.15
1. Economics 2. Money 3. Monetary policy 4. Interest 5. Business and economics — Economics

LC 91006533

Keynes profoundly influenced the New Deal and created the basis for classic economic theory.

A Harvest/HBJ book; Includes bibliographical references and index; Originally published: 1953.

Smith, Adam
★ *The Wealth of Nations: Adam Smith; Introduction by Robert Reich; Edited, with Notes, Marginal Summary, and Enlarged Index by Edwin Cannan.* Adam Smith; introduction by Robert Reich; edited, with notes, marginal summary, and enlarged index by Edwin Cannan. Modern Library 2000. xxvi, 1154 p.
ISBN 9780679783367
Grades: 11 12 Adult   330.15
1. Economics 2. Business and economics — Economics 3. Arts and Entertainment — Writing and Publishing

LC 00064573

Presents the classic eighteenth-century treatise on political economics.

Includes bibliographical references and index; Originally published: An inquiry into the nature and causes of the wealth of nations / Adam Smith; edited ... by Edwin Cannan. 1994. With new introd. by Robert Reich.

330.9 Economic situation and conditions

Davidson, Adam
The Passion Economy: The New Rules for Thriving in the Twenty-first Century. Adam Davidson. Alfred A. Knopf 2020. 240 p.
ISBN 9780385353526
Grades: Adult   330.9
1. Economics 2. Businesspeople 3. Economic forecasting 4. Goals and objectives 5. Ambition 6. 21st century 7. Business and economics — Economics — World economy

LC 2019022771

The award-winning New Yorker staff writer and creator of NPR's Planet Money podcast explains the internal logic of today's dynamic economy while revealing its transformative potential for enabling millions to thrive.

"Fine inspiration for entrepreneurs that should be required reading in any business school curriculum." —*Kirkus*
Includes index.

De Long, J. Bradford
Slouching Towards Utopia: An Economic History of the Twentieth Century. J. Bradford DeLong. Basic Books 2022. 592 p.
ISBN 9780465019595
Grades: Adult   330.9
1. Economic history 2. Economic development 3. Wealth 4. Technological innovations 5. Capitalism 6. International trade 7. Globalization 8. Depressions 9. Social change 10. Income inequality 11. 20th century 12. Business and economics — Economics — History 13. Business and economics — Economics — World economy

One of the world's leading economists tells the story of the century that transformed the economy again and again, showing how this unprecedented explosion of material wealth occurred, how it changed the world and why it failed to deliver us to utopia.

"A sprawling but carefully argued, edifying account of modern economic history and its impact on global well-being." —*Kirkus*
Includes bibliographical references and index.

Hickel, Jason
The Divide: Global Inequality from Conquest to Free Markets. Jason Hickel. W. W. Norton & Company 2018. 344 p.
ISBN 9780393651362

ESSENTIAL AND RECOMMENDED TITLES
330.941 Economic conditions — Great Britain

Grades: Adult   **330.9**

1. Equality 2. Globalization 3. Poverty 4. Business and economics — Economics — History

LC 2017052787

An award-winning professor of anthropology examines global poverty and the growing divide between developed and developing countries as it relates to the global economy that has resulted from hundreds of years of conquest, colonialism, regime change, debt and trade deals.

"A sharply argued analysis of the traditional explanations for wealth and poverty in the world, offering a program for easing misery while addressing structural inequalities." —*Kirkus*

Includes bibliographical references and index; First published [in 2017] by the Random House Group Ltd in Great Britain under the title THE DIVIDE: A Brief Guide to Global Inequality and its Solutions.

Sharma, Ruchir
The Rise and Fall of Nations: Forces of Change in the Post-crisis World. Ruchir Sharma. W.W. Norton & Company 2016. xii, 466 pages
ISBN 9780393248890

Grades: Adult   **330.9**

1. Economic forecasting 2. Economic history 3. Social change 4. World economy 5. Political science 6. Economics 7. Developing countries 8. 21st century 9. Impartial writing 10. Business and economics — Economics — World economy

A reevaluation of economics as a practical art form by the Morgan Stanley economist and author of the best-selling Breakout Nations distills economics into 10 succinct rules while counseling readers on how to recognize political, economic and social changes that affect everyday life.

Includes bibliographical references (pages 417-445) and index.

Taplin, Jonathan
Move Fast and Break Things: How Facebook, Google, and Amazon Cornered Culture and Undermined Democracy. Jonathan Taplin. Little, Brown & Company 2017. 320 pages
ISBN 9780316275774

Grades: Adult   **330.9**

1. Internet 2. Monopolies 3. Intellectual property 4. Culture 5. Art 6. Digital media 7. Computer file sharing 8. Corporate greed 9. Inequality 10. Electronic commerce 11. Society and culture — Media and technology 12. Business and economics — Industries — Entertainment and media 13. Business and economics — Industries — Technology 14. Business and economics — Industries — Retail products and services

LC Bl2017013605

Describes the history of Facebook, Amazon and Google and the shift in power they presided over wherein more creative content is being devoured than ever before, but with less revenue flowing to the creators and owners of that content.

330.941 Economic conditions — Great Britain

Satia, Priya
Empire of Guns: The Violent Making of the Industrial Revolution. Priya Satia. Penguin Group USA 2018. 512 p.
ISBN 9780735221864

Grades: Adult   **330.941**

1. Gun ownership 2. Industrial Revolution 3. Weapons 4. Gun control 5. Industrialization 6. Manufacturing industry and trade 7. British history 8. 18th century 9. History writing — Europe — United Kingdom

LC 2018006181

A prizewinning historian's reframing of the Industrial Revolution, the expansion of British empire and the emergence of industrial capitalism presents them as inextricable from the gun trade and the story of disgraced Quaker gunmaker Samuel Galton, sharing insights into modern debates about gun control and the complex partnerships of government, the economy and the military.

330.973 Economic conditions — United States

Bruner, Robert F.
★ *The Panic of 1907, 2nd Ed.: Heralding a New Era of Finance, Capitalism, and Democracy.* Robert F. Bruner and Sean D. Carr. John Wiley & Sons 2023. 411 p.
ISBN 9781394180271

Grades: Adult   **330.973**

1. Depressions 2. Stock market 3. Bank failures 4. Banks and banking 5. Stocks 6. Financial crises 7. United States 8. 1900s (Decade) 9. 20th century 10. History writing — Early 20th century — United States

In this newly-revised second edition, offering 50% entirely new material, the Panic of 1907: Heralding a New Era of Finance, Capitalism, and Democracy, delivers a groundbreaking examination of one of the most consequential crises in financial history. Deftly weaving historical evidence, insightful analysis, and compelling narrative, the Panic of 1907 explains how and why a financial panic unfolds, with lessons that can be applied to our understanding of present-day financial and monetary systems.

Dayen, David
Chain of Title: How Three Ordinary Americans Uncovered Wall Street's Great Foreclosure Fraud. David Dayen. New Press 2016. 320 p.
ISBN 9781620971581

Grades: Adult   **330.973**

1. Financial crises 2. Foreclosure 3. Global Financial Crisis, 2008-2009 4. Banks and banking 5. Economic policy 6. Social advocates 7. Mortgages 8. Corruption 9. United States history 10. 21st century 11. Business and economics — Corruption and scandal 12. Business and economics — Industries — Finance 13. Politics and global affairs — General

LC 2016005544

In the depths of the Great Recession, a cancer nurse, a car dealership worker, and an insurance fraud specialist helped uncover the largest consumer crime in American history-a scandal that implicated dozens of major executives on Wall Street. They called it foreclosure fraud: Millions of families were kicked out of their homes based on false evidence by mortgage companies that had no legal right to foreclose. Lisa Epstein, Michael Redman, and Lynn Szymoniak did not work in government or law enforcement. They had no history of anticorporate activism. Instead they were all foreclosure victims, and while struggling with their shame and isolation they committed a revolutionary act: Closely reading their mortgage documents, discovering the deceit behind them, and building a movement to expose it. Fiscal Times columnist David Dayen recounts how these ordinary Floridians challenged the most powerful institutions in America armed only with the truth-and for a brief moment they brought the corrupt financial industry to its knees.

"Dayen relates how prosecutors, judges, and the Department of Justice have caved to powerful mortgage industry donors while illegal foreclosures continue. An inspiring, well-rendered, deeply reported, and often infuriating account." —*Kirkus*

Includes bibliographical references and index.

De Graaf, John
What's the Economy For, Anyway?: Why It's Time to Stop Chasing Growth and Start Pursuing Happiness. John de Graaf and David K. Batker. Bloomsbury Press 2011. 288 p.
ISBN 9781608195107

Grades: Adult   **330.973**

1. Economic development 2. Happiness 3. Economic policy 4. Economics 5. United States 6. Business and economics — Economics — Socioeconomics

LC 2011017438

Here, scholars John de Graaf (author of Affluenza) and David Batker tackle thirteen touchstone economic issues and challenge readers to consider just what the point of our economy is. Emphasizing powerful American ideals such as working together, pragmatism, and equality for all, de Graaf and Batker set forth a simple, powerful goal for any economic system: the greatest good for the greatest number, over the longest run.

PUBLIC LIBRARY CORE COLLECTION: NONFICTION
Twentieth Edition

"De Graaf and Batker examine new ways to think about economic processes, specifically as they relate to human happiness and well-being. The authors show that the indicators of performance developed during World War II—the Gross National Product—have become both obscurantist and counterproductive. They argue that human purposes and needs ought to provide the basis for much more broadly based measures of performance, which would consider what is the greatest good and benefit for the greatest number of people over the longest period of time. An entertaining presentation of important ideas and information about how lives could be improved." —*Kirkus*

Greenspan, Alan
Capitalism in America: A History. Alan Greenspan, Adrian Wooldridge. Penguin Group USA 2018. 512 p.
ISBN 9780735222441
Grades: Adult   330.973
1. Economics 2. Capitalism 3. Entrepreneurship 4. Business innovations 5. Wealth 6. United States history 7. Business and economics — Economics — History
LC 2018020397

The former Federal Reserve Chairman and the acclaimed Economist historian trace the epic story of America's evolution from a small patchwork of threadbare colonies to the world's most powerful engine of wealth and innovation.

Krugman, Paul R.
Arguing with Zombies: Economics, Politics, and the Fight for a Better Future. Paul Krugman. W. W. Norton & Company 2020. 480 pages
ISBN 9781324005018
Grades: Adult   330.973
1. Economic policy 2. Misconceptions 3. Economic history 4. Taxation 5. Health policy 6. Recession (Economics) 7. Social Security 8. Politics and government 9. Economics 10. United States 11. 21st century 12. Liberal writing 13. Business and economics — Economics — Contemporary U.S. economy 14. Business and economics — Economics
LC 2019032129

An introduction to today's major policy issues by the Nobel Prize-winning columnist clarifies widespread misunderstandings in basic economics while providing thematic explanations of subjects ranging from health care and housing bubbles to tax reform and social security.

"While Krugman's rousing, jargon-free writings will please progressive readers, they will be disconcerting to many conservative ones. An informative and controversial study combining business and political science." —*Library Journal*
Includes index.

Lemann, Nicholas
Transaction Man: The Rise of the Deal and the Decline of the American Dream. Nicholas Lemann. Farrar, Straus and Giroux 2019. 304 p.
ISBN 9780374277888
Grades: Adult   330.973
1. Corporations 2. Economic policy 3. Inequality 4. Economists 5. Big business 6. Working class 7. Middle class 8. American dream 9. Politics and government 10. Economics 11. United States 12. 20th century 13. Business and economics — Economics — History 14. Business and economics — Economics — Contemporary U.S. economy 15. Life stories — Business
LC 2019020255

The New Yorker writer chronicles how American strategists, financiers and politicians have influenced the perception of disruption strategies, creating a damaging culture of inequality and polarization that victimizes working-class families.
Includes index.

Leonhardt, David
★ *Ours Was the Shining Future: The Story of the American Dream.* David Leonhardt. Random House 2023. 384 p.
ISBN 9780812993202
Grades: Adult   330.973
1. American Dream 2. Economics 3. Capitalism 4. Sociology 5. United States 6. 20th century 7. 21st century 8. Business and economics — Economics — Socioeconomics
LC 2023008662

Drawing on decades of writing about the economy for the New York Times, a Pulitzer Prize-winning writer, in this definitive biography of American dream, offers an eye-opening account of how the U.S. built the most prosperous mass economy in history after the Depression, and how that economy gradually unraveled.

"Excellent, accessible overview of socioeconomic trends over the last decades and what they bode for the future." —*Kirkus*
Includes bibliographical references and index.

Lewis, Michael
The Big Short: Inside the Doomsday Machine. Michael Lewis. W. W. Norton 2010. 320 p.
ISBN 9780393072235
Grades: 11 12 Adult   330.973
1. Financial crises 2. World economy 3. Economics 4. United States 5. 21st century 6. Business and economics — Industries — Finance 7. Business and economics — Economics — Contemporary U.S. economy

Los Angeles Times Book Prize for Current Interest, 2010; Robert F. Kennedy Book Award, 2011.

Lewis examines the American economic collapse of the early 21st century, profiling very few heroes, numerous villains and several people who just should have known better. Lewis offers a biting rebuke to this motley band of financial "experts" with keen research and a sharp pen.

"The Big Short manages to give us the truest picture yet of what went wrong on Wall Street—and why. At times, it reads like a morality play, at other times like a modern-day farce. But as with any good play, its value lies in the way it reveals character and motive and explores the cultural context in which the plot unfolds." —*Washington Post*

McCraw, Thomas K.
★ *The Founders and Finance: How Hamilton, Gallatin, and Other Immigrants Forged a New Economy.* Thomas K. McCraw. Belknap Press of Harvard University Press 2012. VIII, 485 p. : Illustration
ISBN 9780674066922
Grades: Adult   330.973
1. Hamilton, Alexander, 1757-1804 2. Gallatin, Albert, 1761-1849 3. Public finance 4. Monetary policy 5. Revolutions 6. Economics 7. Finance 8. Banks and banking 9. American Revolution, 1775-1783 10. Economic policy 11. Politics and government 12. United States history 13. United States 14. Revolutionary America (1775-1783) 15. History writing — Early America — United States 16. Business and economics — Economics — History
LC 2012014006

Discusses how such immigrant founders as Alexander Hamilton, Albert Gallatin, and others were more financially savvy than native-born plantation owners Washington, Jefferson, and Madison, and how they carried the nation to prosperity.

"McCraw is a talented storyteller. His highly readable and fascinating work portrays the brilliance of Hamilton and Gallatin against the difficulty of their time and is strongly recommended to all readers interested in American and financial history." —*Library Journal*
Includes bibliographical references (p. 367-440) and index.

McLean, Bethany
All the Devils Are Here: The Hidden History of the Financial Crisis. Bethany McLean and Joe Nocera. Portfolio Penguin 2010. 496 p.
ISBN 9781591843634
Grades: Adult   330.973
1. Global Financial Crisis, 2008-2009 2. Financial crises 3. Mortgage backed securities 4. Financial institutions 5. Mortgages 6. Economic policy 7. Economics 8. United States 9. 21st century 10. Business and economics — Economics — Contemporary U.S. economy
LC 2010032893

ESSENTIAL AND RECOMMENDED TITLES
330.9747 Economic conditions — New York

New York Times Notable Book, 2010.

Before the dust even settled, competing theories emerged to explain the financial crisis. Should the blame fall on Wall Street, Main Street, or Pennsylvania Avenue? Bethany McLean and Joe Nocera, two of America's most acclaimed business journalists, offer the definitive answer. This surprising narrative goes back more than twenty years to reveal how Wall Street, the mortgage industry, and the government conspired to change the way Americans bought their homes.

"This is an account of the late financial meltdown, when, in the words of one analyst, we went from a collective belief in soundness to a collective belief in insolvency. Hard-hitting reporting and fluent writing bring the utter devastation of the Great Recession to life." —*Kirkus*

Includes bibliographical references and index.

Paulson, Henry M.
On the Brink: Inside the Race to Stop the Collapse of the Global Financial System. Henry M. Paulson. Grand Central Pub 2010. 288 p.
ISBN 9780446561938
Grades: Adult   **330.973**
1. Financial crises 2. Economic policy 3. Financial institutions 4. Global Financial Crisis, 2008-2009 5. Economics 6. United States 7. 2000s (Decade) 8. Business and economics — Economics — Contemporary U.S. economy
LC 2009939043

The Secretary of the Treasury during the final years of George W. Bush's presidency presents his side of the economic collapse that occurred in the waning days of his watch over America's banking system.

"This is the ultimate insider's account of the crisis, and, owing to its even-handed tone and penetrating insights into government actions, it will also remain an important contribution to the historical record of the crisis, essential reading for everyone interested in knowing what happened." —*Library Journal*

"Paulson, the former US treasury secretary, provides a day-by-day account of the worst financial crisis since the Great Depression. It also addresses the political implications of the crisis, revealing . conversations with President Obama, John McCain, Sarah Palin and Alistair Darling." —*New Statesman*

Perino, Michael A.
*The **Hellhound** of Wall Street: How Ferdinand Pecora's Investigation of the Great Crash Forever Changed American Finance.* Michael Perino. Penguin Press 2010. 352 p.
ISBN 9781594202728
Grades: Adult   **330.973**
1. Pecora, Ferdinand, 1882-1971 2. Stock market crash, October 1929 3. Stock market 4. Business corruption 5. Banks and banking 6. Government regulation 7. Financial crises 8. United States 9. History writing — Great Depression — United States 10. Business and economics — Economics — History
LC 2010019157

Chronicles the 1933 Senate committee hearings into the causes of the stock market crash of 1929, describing the rigorous questioning by former New York prosecutor Ferdinand Pecora that revealed shocking financial abuses and led to the economic reforms ofthe New Deal.

"The author recounts the 1933 investigation into Wall Street abuses by the Senate Committee on Banking and Currency, focusing on the 10-day interrogation by chief counsel Ferdinand Pecora of executives of National City Bank (precursor to Citigroup). Perino's book is a trenchant, entertaining study of the New Deal's heroic beginnings, one with obvious relevance to latter-day efforts to rein in Wall Street's excesses." —*Publishers Weekly*

Includes bibliographical references and index.

Sorkin, Andrew Ross
Too Big to Fail: The Inside Story of How Wall Street and Washington Fought to Save the Financial System from Crisis—and Themselves. Andrew Ross Sorkin. Viking 2009. xx, 600 p, [16] p. of plates : Illustration
ISBN 9780670021253
Grades: Adult   **330.973**
1. Financial crises 2. Economics 3. Business losses 4. World economy 5. Business failures 6. Bank failures 7. Global Financial Crisis, 2008-2009 8. United States history 9. 21st century 10. Page to screen 11. Business and economics — Industries — Finance 12. Business and economics — Economics — World economy
LC 2009036494

Presents a moment-by-moment account of the recent financial collapse that documents state efforts to prevent an economic disaster, offering insight into the pivotal consequences of decisions made throughout the past decade.

"Sorkin boasts of the hours spent interviewing, emailing, inspecting telephone call logs, billing time sheets and even expense reports [for this book], and his reward is the fullest and most convincing account of the Lehman debacle. Conversations are reconstructed, and an air of authenticity created by the accumulation of thousands of small facts." —*Times Literary Supplement*

Includes bibliographical references (p. 585-586) and index.

330.9747 Economic conditions — New York

Phillips-Fein, Kim
Fear City: New York's Fiscal Crisis and the Rise of Austerity Politics. Kimberly Phillips-Fein. Metropolitan Books 2017. 384 p.
ISBN 9780805095258
Grades: Adult   **330.9747**
1. Fiscal policy 2. Financial crises 3. Social policy 4. Budget deficits 5. Economic policy 6. Municipal services 7. Government spending policy 8. Economics 9. United States history 10. New York City 11. New York (State) 12. 1970s 13. 20th century 14. Business and economics — Economics — Socioeconomics 15. Business and economics — Economics — History 16. History writing — 1970s — United States
LC 2016033559

Pulitzer Prize for History finalist, 2018.

The author of Invisible Hands presents a history of an imperiled New York City while analyzing what the author terms the politics of austerity and how they are continuing to shape the world today.

"Paced like a thriller and extremely well written, the book chronicles the slow descent of the city into a fiscal abyss and its unlikely rescue by a group of hardened bureaucrats, altruistic investment bankers, and political power players ." —*Publishers Weekly. Annex*

Includes bibliographical references and index.

330.9775 Economic conditions — Wisconsin

Goldstein, Amy
Janesville: An American Story. Amy Goldstein. Simon & Schuster 2017. xiii, 351 pages
ISBN 9781501102233
Grades: Adult   **330.9775**
1. Automobile industry and trade 2. Plant closings 3. Blue collar workers 4. Automobile factories 5. Small towns 6. Manufacturing industry and trade 7. Factories 8. Economic policy 9. Industrial policy 10. Unemployment 11. Shrinking cities 12. Manufacturers 13. Mass production 14. Middle class 15. Automobiles 16. Economics 17. Wisconsin 18. United States 19. Middle West 20. Business and economics — Economics — Contemporary U.S. economy 21. Business and economics — Industries — Transportation 22. Society and culture — Wealth and class

J. Anthony Lukas Book Prize, 2018; New York Times Notable Book, 2017.

A Washington Post reporter provides an intimate account of the fallout from the closing of a General Motors' assembly plant in Janesville, Wisconsin—Paul Ryan's hometown—and a larger story of the hollowing of the American middle class.

"A simultaneously enlightening and disturbing look at working-class lives in America's heartland." —*Kirkus*

Includes bibliographical references (pages 317-341) and index.

PUBLIC LIBRARY CORE COLLECTION: NONFICTION
Twentieth Edition

331 Economics of labor, finance, land, energy

Murolo, Priscilla
From the Folks Who Brought You the Weekend: A Short, Illustrated History of Labor in the United States. Priscilla Murolo and A.B. Chitty; illustrations by Joe Sacco. New Press : 2001. xx, 364 p. : Illustration
ISBN 9781565847767
Grades: Adult 331
1. Labor movement 2. Working class 3. Work 4. United States 5. History writing — United States 6. Politics and global affairs — General
LC 2001030978

A history of labor in the United States explores the efforts of working people to win the rights one takes for granted—basic health and safety standards, fair on-the-job treatment, minimum wage, and weekend leisure.
Includes bibliographical references (p. [333]-344) and index.

331.0973 Labor — United States

Guendelsberger, Emily
On the Clock: What Low-wage Work Did to Me and How It Drives America Insane. Emily Guendelsberger. Little Brown & Co. 2019. 272 p.
ISBN 9780316509008
Grades: Adult 331.0973
1. Minimum wage 2. Employees 3. Work 4. Working class 5. Exploitation 6. Service industry and trade workers 7. Service industry and trade 8. Psychology 9. United States 10. Society and culture — Wealth and class — Poverty 11. Business and economics — Industries — Retail products and services
LC 2019930997

A college-educated young professional details his struggles to find a qualitative job, detailing the grueling realities of hourly labor for the fastest-growing segment of the American workforce while outlining strategies for more humane employment practices.
"This is a riveting window into minimum-wage work and the subsistence living it engenders." —*Publishers Weekly*

331.1 Labor force and market

Monforton, Celeste
On the Job: The Untold Story of Worker Centers and the New Fight for Wages, Dignity, and Health. Celeste Monforton and Jane M. Von Bergen. The New Press 2021. 288 p.
ISBN 9781620975015
Grades: Adult 331.1
1. Work 2. Employee ownership 3. Work environment 4. Employee rights 5. Labor movement 6. Labor organizers 7. Labor unions 8. Labor organizing 9. Occupational health and safety 10. Labor policy 11. Wages 12. United States history 13. 21st century 14. Business and economics — Economics — Socioeconomics
LC 2020049156

A noted public health expert and award-winning journalist traveled across the country, speaking with workers of all backgrounds and uncovering the stories of hundreds of new, worker-led organizations that have successfully achieved higher wages, safer working conditions and on-the-job dignity for their members.
"This timely and well-documented account offers hope for the future of the American labor movement." —*Publishers Weekly*
Includes bibliographical references and index.

331.11 Labor force

Pang, Amelia
★ *Made in China: A Prisoner, an Sos Letter, and the Hidden Cost of America's Cheap Goods.* Amelia Pang. Algonquin Books of Chapel Hill 2021. 288 p.
ISBN 9781616209179
Grades: Adult 331.11
1. Yi, Sun 2. Manufacturing industry and trade 3. Political prisoners 4. Products 5. Forced labor 6. Prisoners 7. Globalization (Economics) 8. Work environment 9. China 10. Business and economics — Industries — Manufacturing 11. Business and economics — Industries — Retail products and services 12. Politics and global affairs — World politics — Asia 13. Life stories — Facing adversity — War and oppression
LC 2020034508

After an Oregon mother finds an SOS letter in a box of Halloween decorations, a story unfolds about the man who wrote it: a Chinese political prisoner, sentenced without trial to work grueling hours at a "reeducation" camp-manufacturing the products sold in our own big-box stores.
"Readers will be drawn into this thoroughly researched narrative and will be awakened by the author's pleas for consumers to be more vigilant about the origin of their goods." —*Booklist*
Includes bibliographical references.

331.13 Discrimination in employment, labor shortages, unemployment

Taylor, Nick
American Made: The Enduring Legacy of the Wpa : When FDR Put the Nation to Work. Nick Taylor. Bantam Book 2008. 640 p.
ISBN 9780553802351
Grades: Adult 331.13
1. Job creation 2. Politics and government 3. United States 4. 20th century 5. History writing — Great Depression — United States
LC 2007034563

ALA Notable Book, 2009.
A history of FDR's New Deal looks at the origins of the Works Progress Administration in the dark days of the Great Depression, examining the politics and development of the WPA from 1935 to 1943 and assessing the legacy of the controversial program.
"Lavishly illustrated, the book also has a list of New Deal organizations, a partial list of construction projects, a New Deal chronology, and endnotes. It will be a boon to all 20th-century history collections." —*Library Journal*
Includes bibliographical references and index.

Urofsky, Melvin I.
The Affirmative Action Puzzle: A Living History from Reconstruction to Today. Melvin I. Urofsky. Pantheon Books 2020. 576 p.
ISBN 9781101870877
Grades: Adult 331.13
1. Affirmative action 2. Higher education 3. Civil rights 4. Marginalized people 5. Discrimination 6. Equality 7. Legislation 8. Affirmative action in education 9. Discrimination in education 10. United States 11. Impartial writing 12. History writing — African American — Civil rights — United States 13. Politics and global affairs — Civil and human rights
LC 2019016086

The legal historian examines the Supreme Court cases that upheld or struck down affirmative-action plans, exploring their impact on employment, education and the ongoing debates of today's world.
"A must-read for anyone interested in the history of affirmative action and its associated legal conundrums." —*Kirkus*
Includes bibliographical references and index.

331.25 Other conditions of employment

Auerbach, Annie
Flex: Reinventing Work for a Smarter, Happier Life. Annie Auerbach. HarperOne 2021. 192 p.
ISBN 9780063059641
Grades: Adult 331.25

ESSENTIAL AND RECOMMENDED TITLES
331.3 Labor force by personal attributes

1. Flex time 2. Work-life balance 3. Women employees 4. Work 5. Business and economics — General 6. Society and culture — General

LC 2020047001

The recent coronavirus outbreak has proven what Annie Auerbach has long championed: Working 9-5 in an office doesn't work for most us. It's time to change the rules. We can be efficient and productive when we're allowed the freedom of flexibility-to meet deadlines working during the hours and in the places we choose. But before the coronavirus pandemic, only 47 percent of American workers had access to flexible working options. As Auerbach makes clear, we reject "our toxic culture of presenteeism, time-pressure, and ultimately burnout. It helps us escape the army of octopus lady jugglers, crazed with the exhaustion of "having it all." It allows us to live longer lives more sustainably. It gives us self-worth.

"Informative, practical, and timely, this title is recommended for working women and contains sound advice about the effective use of Flex in the workplace and at home." —*Library Journal*

Includes bibliographical references.

331.3 Labor force by personal attributes

Bruder, Jessica
★ *Nomadland: Surviving America in the Twenty-first Century.* Jessica Bruder. W W Norton & Co. Inc 2017. 320 p.
ISBN 9780393249316
Grades: Adult   331.3
1. Migrant workers 2. Seniors 3. Retirement 4. Economic security 5. Survival (Economics) 6. Housing 7. Homeless people 8. Communities 9. Poor people 10. Retirees 11. Economics 12. United States 13. Page to screen 14. Society and culture — Wealth and class — Poverty 15. Book club best bets

LC 2017018056

New York Times Notable Book, 2017; Library Journal Best Books, 2017; Booklist Editors' Choice, 2017.

Author Jessica Bruder, who teaches at the Columbia School of Journalism, spent several years traveling with older Americans who have become itinerant workers in order to make ends meet. In Nomadland, she describes how they assume a "wheel estate" (instead of "real estate") existence as they travel from one seasonal job to the next, exchanging information on safe camping sites and enjoying the camaraderie of the road. Bruder vividly and sympathetically characterizes these "workampers" as she critiques the financial systems that have led them to adopt this solution.

"Engaging, highly relevant immersion journalism." —*Kirkus*

331.4 Women workers

Bravo, Reah
★ *Complicit: How Our Culture Enables Misbehaving Men.* Reah Bravo. Gallery Books 2024. 240 p.
ISBN 9781982154745
Grades: Adult   331.4
1. Sexual harassment 2. Sex crimes 3. Abused women 4. Sexism 5. Me Too movement 6. Society and culture — Gender

LC 2023043208

A former broadcast journalism producer presents a deeply researched and personal examination of how women unintentionally condone workplace abuse in a post-#MeToo world and offers suggestions on how we can all influence positive change.

"With examples from anthropological studies, contemporary children's books, the film Barbie, and more, Bravo offers scenarios that will resonate with readers…Her balanced and nuanced observations give readers much to think about." —*Booklist*

Includes bibliographical references and index.

Cahn, Naomi R.
★ *Fair Shake: Women and the Fight to Build a Just Economy.* Naomi Cahn, June Carbone, Nancy Levit. Simon & Schuster 2024. 240 p.
ISBN 9781982115128
Grades: Adult   331.4
1. Work 2. Women 3. Gender gap 4. Gender equity 5. Society and culture — Gender — Women

Three law professors look at the current state of women in the workplace and the ways in which systemic burdens hold them back, increase wage disparities and foster unhealthy competition between them.

"An account of the search for economic justice for women…Robust evidence for the need for systemic change." —*Kirkus*

Chang, Emily
Brotopia: Breaking up the Boys' Club of Silicon Valley. Emily Chang. Portfolio 2018. 288 p.
ISBN 9780735213531
Grades: Adult   331.4
1. Internet industry and trade 2. Sex discrimination in employment 3. Sex discrimination against women 4. Sexism in employment 5. Sexism 6. Discrimination in employment 7. Silicon Valley, California 8. Society and culture — Gender — Women 9. Business and economics — Industries — Technology 10. Nonfiction that reads like fiction 11. Book club best bets

LC Bl2017050241

Reveals how male-dominated Silicon Valley became sexist despite its utopian ideals and decades of companies claiming the moral high ground, and how women are finally starting to fight back against toxic workplaces and sexual harrassment.

Chang, Leslie T.
★ *Egyptian Made: Women, Work, and the Promise of Liberation.* Leslie T. Chang. Random House 2024. 320 p.
ISBN 9780525509219
Grades: Adult   331.4
1. Women employees 2. Businesspeople 3. Feminism 4. Egypt 5. Society and culture — Gender

LC 2023018287

The award-winning author of Factory Girls uses the centuries-old textiles industry in Egypt to deconstruct how globalization's promise of setting women free to start careers and earn money often sets them up for further repression.

"Chang's cogent analysis and lyric impressions…are threaded with insight into Egypt's political and economic history. It's an eye-opener." —*Publishers Weekly*

Includes index.

Factory Girls: From Village to City in a Changing China. Leslie T. Chang. Spiegel & Grau 2008. 420 p. : Map
ISBN 9780385520171
Grades: 11 12 Adult   331.4
1. Manufacturing industry and trade 2. Migrant workers 3. Blue collar women 4. Blue collar workers 5. Women 6. Young women 7. Work 8. Economics 9. China 10. Adult books for young adults 11. Society and culture — Gender — Women 12. Society and culture — Immigration

LC 2008012880

New York Times Notable Book, 2008.

Explores the world of the millions of female Chinese migrant workers who have left their homes in rural towns to find jobs in China's cities, as revealed through a two-year study of the lives of two young women.

"This is an exceptionally vivid and compassionate depiction of the day-to-day dramas, and the fears and aspirations, of the real people who are powering China's economic boom." —*New York Times Book Review*

Includes bibliographical references (p. [409]-416).

Davis, Lisa
★ *Housewife: Why Women Still Do It All and What to Do Instead.* Lisa Selin Davis. Legacy Lit 2024. 336 p.

ISBN 9781538722886
Grades: Adult 331.4
1. Women's role 2. Homemakers 3. Gender role 4. Society and culture — Gender

LC 2023020942

The notion of "housewife" evokes strong reactions. For some, it's nostalgia for a bygone era, simpler and better times when men were breadwinners and women remained home with the kids. For others, it's a sexist, oppressive stereotype of women's work. Either way, housewife is a long outdated concept—or is it? Discover the complete social history of the housewife archetype, from colonial America to the 20th century, and re-examine common myths about the "modern woman."

"Housewife provides both vindication and comfort for women tired of doing it all." —Booklist

Farrow, Ronan

★ *Catch and Kill: Lies, Spies and a Conspiracy to Protect Predators.* Ronan Farrow. Little, Brown and Company 2019. 448 p.

ISBN 9780316486637

Grades: Adult 331.4

1. Farrow, Ronan, 1987- 2. Lauer, Matt, 1957- 3. Weinstein, Harvey, 1952- 4. Sexual harassment 5. Threat (Psychology) 6. Investigative journalism 7. Surveillance 8. Investigative journalists 9. Harassment 10. Sexual violence victims 11. Coercion 12. Sex crimes 13. Me Too movement 14. Sexual harassment of women 15. Sex discrimination in employment 16. Film producers and directors 17. Hollywood, California 18. True Crime — Sex Crimes 19. Society and culture — Violence and crime

National Book Critics Circle Award for Autobiography/Memoir finalist, 2019.

Describes the author's investigation of sexual assault, sexual harassment, and rape accusations against Harvey Weinstein and Matt Lauer, and the many obstacles he faced, not only from Weinstein but also from his own employer, NBC.

"This chilling narrative reveals the unequal power dynamic between aspiring actors (and women in the media) and the dominant powerbrokers in Hollywood." —*Library Journal*

Includes bibliographical references (pages 420-441) and index.

Kessler-Harris, Alice

★ *Out to Work: A History of Wage-earning Women in the United States.* Alice Kessler-Harris. Oxford University Press 2003. xvi, 414 p. : Illustration

ISBN 9780195157093

Grades: Adult 331.4

1. Women's history 2. Working class women 3. Working class 4. Work 5. United States 6. History writing — Women's history

LC 2003267644

A history of American women and their work since colonial times focuses on society's changing expectations of women.

"This work remains a landmark in the field of analyzing the history of women's work in the United States from Colonial times to the Reagan era." —*Library Journal*

Includes bibliographical references and index; Originally published: New York : Oxford University Press, 1982.

McShane Wulfhart, Nell

The Great Stewardess Rebellion: How Women Launched a Workplace Revolution at 30,000 Feet. Nell McShane Wulfhart. Doubleday 2022. 288 p.

ISBN 9780385546454

Grades: Adult 331.4

1. Flight attendants 2. Airlines 3. Gender role in the work environment 4. Sex discrimination against women 5. Sexual harassment 6. Misogyny 7. Labor unions 8. Employee rights 9. Women's Movement 10. Labor laws and legislation 11. 1960s 12. 1970s 13. Business and economics — Industries — Transportation 14. Business and economics — Women and the workplace 15. History writing — Women's history 16. Life stories — Business — Working life 17. Life stories — Identity — Gender

LC 2021043017

In this rousing narrative of female empowerment and the paradigm-shifting '60s and '70s, a group of spirited stewardesses who, pushing back on unrealistic expectations, fought for their rights in the cabin and revolutionized the workplace for all American women.

"This engaging account describes how women flight attendants (or stewardesses, as they were known during the last half of the twentieth century) fought for decades for equal wages, an end to blatantly sexist work cultures, and the respect due to them as highly skilled professionals....This is an eye-opening chapter in the history of feminism and women's rights." —*Booklist*

Includes index.

Zernike, Kate

The Exceptions: Nancy Hopkins, Mit, and the Fight for Women in Science. Kate Zernike. Scribner 2023. 416 p.

ISBN 9781982131838

Grades: Adult 331.4

1. Sexism 2. Women scientists 3. Discrimination 4. Sexism in education 5. Sexism in science 6. History Writing — Women's history 7. History Writing — Science, technology, and medicine 8. Life stories — Science, technology, and medicine — Scientists and inventors

A Pulitzer Prize-winning journalist tells the powerful—and inspiring—story of Nancy Hopkins, a reluctant feminist who, in 1999, became the leader of sixteen female scientists who forced MIT to publicly admit it had been discriminating against its female faculty for years.

"Zernike offers an intriguing and often infuriating glimpse into the rarefied world of higher education." —*Publishers Weekly*

331.6 Workers by ethnic and national origin

Chang, Gordon H.

Ghosts of Gold Mountain: The Epic Story of the Chinese Who Built the Transcontinental Railroad. Gordon H. Chang. Houghton Mifflin Harcourt 2019. 304 p.

ISBN 9781328618573

Grades: Adult 331.6

1. Chinese people in the United States 2. Immigrant workers 3. Labor exploitation 4. Chinese Americans 5. Immigrants, Chinese 6. Railroads 7. Chinese people 8. East Asian Americans 9. Railroad workers 10. Immigration and emigration 11. Chinese history 12. The West (United States) history 13. 19th century 14. History writing — Immigration — United States

LC 2018042558

Asian Pacific American Award for Literature: Adult Nonfiction, 2020.

A history of the Chinese laborers who were pivotal to the construction of the American Transcontinental Railroad details the construction perils that cost innumerable lives before survivors were almost instantly lost to public memory.

"Successfully shedding light on the fascinating lives of the workers who completed a monumental task in the mountainous west, this is an essential read for anyone interested in the history of Chinese Americans, the American West, or the Transcontinental Railroad." —*Library Journal*

Includes bibliographical references and index.

Kelley, Blair Murphy

Black Folk: The Roots of the Black Working Class. Blair LM Kelley. Liveright Publishing 2023. 304 p.

ISBN 9781631496554

Grades: Adult 331.6

1. African Americans 2. History 3. Enslaved people 4. Working class 5. Blue collar workers 6. Labor supply 7. Inequality 8. Racism 9. Social history 10. Race relations 11. United States history 12. United States 13. History writing — African American — United States 14. Society and culture — Race

Robert F. Kennedy Book Award, 2024.

There have been countless books, articles, and televised reports in recent years about the almost mythic "white working class," a tide of commentary that has obscured the labor, and even the very existence, of entire groups of working people, including everyday Black workers. In this brilliant corrective, Black

ESSENTIAL AND RECOMMENDED TITLES
331.7 Labor by industry and occupation

Folk, acclaimed historian Blair LM Kelley restores the Black working class to the center of the American story.

"Full of persuasive insights into Black working-class life and the legacy of communal care spearheaded by Black women, this is a powerful reimagining of the history of labor in the U.S." —*Publishers Weekly*

Wingfield, Adia Harvey
Gray Areas: How the Way We Work Perpetuates Racism and What We Can Do to Fix It. Adia Harvey Wingfield. Amistad Press 2023. 320 p.
ISBN 9780063079816
Grades: Adult **331.6**
1. Work 2. Race (Social sciences) 3. African Americans 4. Professional employees 5. Institutional racism 6. Glass ceiling 7. Unconscious bias 8. Prejudice 9. Corporate culture 10. Organizational change 11. Society and culture — Race 12. Life stories — Business — Working life 13. Business and economics — Economics — Socioeconomics

A leading sociologist reveals why racial inequality persists in the workplace despite today's multibillion-dollar diversity industry—and provides actional solutions for creating a truly equitable, multiracial future.

"This vital and accessible study is a must-read for HR departments and managers, and will interest anyone concerned with workplace equality." —*Publishers Weekly*

331.7 Labor by industry and occupation

Press, Eyal
★ *Dirty Work: Essential Jobs and the Hidden Toll of Inequality in America.* Eyal Press. Farrar, Straus and Giroux 2021. 256 p.
ISBN 9780374140182
Grades: Adult **331.7**
1. Inequality 2. Work 3. Equality 4. Occupations 5. Economics 6. United States 7. Society and culture — Wealth and class
LC 2021011628

A groundbreaking, urgent report from the front lines of "dirty work"—the work that society considers essential but morally compromised.

"Americans might ignore dirty work, Eyal concludes, but we are all complicit in it. Essential reading for those interested in social justice issues." —*Library Journal*
Includes bibliographical references and index.

331.702 Choice of vocation

Morgan, Genevieve
Undecided: Navigating Life and Learning After High School. Genevieve Morgan. Zest Books 2020. 247 p.
ISBN 9781541597785
Grades: 9 10 11 12 Adult **331.702**
1. Vocational interests 2. Educational guidance 3. Vocational guidance 4. Vocational guidance for teenagers 5. Teenagers 6. Occupations 7. Career development 8. Career books — General
LC Bl2014012501

A comprehensive handbook for high school teens who have not yet established their post-graduation path outlines options ranging from training programs and the military to community colleges and universities to help students decide which course is best for them.

"A helpful guide full of good, sensible advice to teens feeling overwhelmed by the prospect of major life transitions." —*Kirkus*

"Some students know exactly what they want to do after graduating from high school, whether continuing their education or starting careers. Others aren't as sure. Morgan's book targets these readers, taking them through the many options available today—both traditional and nontraditional." —*School Library Journal*
Includes bibliographical references and index; Originally published: San Francisco, CA : Zest Books, 2014.

331.8 Labor unions, labor-management bargaining and disputes

Nolan, Hamilton
The Hammer: Power, Inequality, and the Struggle for the Soul of Labor. Hamilton Nolan. Hachette Books 2024. 304 p.
ISBN 9780306830921
Grades: Adult **331.8**
1. Nelson, Sara, 1973- 2. Labor movement 3. Labor unions 4. Labor leaders 5. Labor laws and legislation 6. Equality 7. Income inequality 8. Labor disputes 9. Labor policy 10. Flight attendants 11. United States history 12. United States 13. Politics and global affairs — Social issues and policies 14. Society and culture — Urban and regional studies
LC 2023037397

A long-time labor journalist presents this urgent on-the-ground excavation of the past, present and future of the American labor movement, drawing the line from forgotten workplaces in rural West Virgina to Washington's halls of power and showing how labor solidarity can transform American politics—if it can first transform itself.

"Labor journalist Nolan makes his book debut with a rousing look at union activities across the country and an impassioned argument for the protection of workers' rights…Spirited reporting on workers' lives." —*Kirkus*
Includes index.

331.88 Labor unions (Trade unions)

Zieger, Robert H.
American Workers, American Unions, 4th Ed.: The Twentieth Century. Robert H. Zieger & Gilbert J. Gall. Johns Hopkins University Press 2014. 334 p.
ISBN 9781421413433
Grades: Adult **331.88**
1. Labor unions 2. United States 3. History writing — United States

"His is the fourth edition of a book initially published in 1986 describing significant developments in the history of American workers and unions from the early 20th century through the first decade of 2000. Its authors are professional historians and labor leaders, and its nine chapters proceed chronologically." —*Choice*

Taking into account recent important work on the 1970s and the Reagan revolution, the fourth edition newly considers the stagflation issue, the rise of globalization and big box retailing, the failure of Congress to pass legislation supporting the right of public employees to collective bargaining, the defeat in Congress of legislation to revise the National Labor Relations Act, the emasculation of the Humphrey-Hawkins Act, and the changing dynamics of blue-collar politics.

331.880973 Labor unions — United States

Dubofsky, Melvyn
Labor in America: A History. Melvyn Dubofsky, Distinguished Professor Emeritus of History & Sociology, Binghamton University and Joseph A. McCartin, Professor of History, Georgetown University. Wiley Blackwell 2017. xix, 469 p.
ISBN 9781118976852
Grades: Adult **331.880973**
1. Labor unions 2. Working class 3. Labor movement 4. United States 5. History writing — United States
LC 2016043343

This book, designed to give a survey history of American labor from colonial times to the present, is uniquely well suited to speak to the concerns of today's teachers and students. As issues of growing inequality, stagnating incomes, declining unionization, and exacerbated job insecurity have increasingly come to define working life over the last 20 years, a new generation of students and teachers is beginning to seek to understand labor and its place and ponder seriously its future in American life. Like its predecessors, this ninth edition of our

classic survey of American labor is designed to introduce readers to the subject in an engaging, accessible way.
Includes bibliographical references and index.

331.890973 Collective bargaining — United States

McAlevey, Jane
A Collective Bargain: Unions, Organizing, and the Fight for Democracy. Jane McAlevey. Ecco 2019. 256 pages
ISBN 9780062908599
Grades: Adult   331.890973
1. Labor unions 2. Collective bargaining 3. Strikes 4. Democracy 5. Labor movement 6. Working class 7. United States 8. 21st century 9. Politics and global affairs — World politics — United States 10. Politics and global affairs — Political philosophy

LC 2019028863

A longtime labor, environmental and political organizer argues that unions are the only institution capable of fighting back against today's super-rich corporate class.

"After calling out Silicon Valley, with all its progressive veneer, for its anti-labor actions, McAlevey finishes with keen insights into creating a union and rebuilding a union from within. Another most-valuable book from McAlevey." —*Booklist*

Includes index.

332 Financial economics

O'Rourke, P. J.
None of My Business. P. J. O'Rourke. Atlantic Monthly 2018. 304 p.
ISBN 9780802128485
Grades: Adult   332
1. Finance 2. Social change 3. Technology and civilization 4. Economics 5. Wall Street, New York City 6. Conservative writing 7. Humor writing — General 8. Business and economics — Industries — Finance

LC 2018026530

In his latest book, P.J. O'Rourke takes forty-five years of experience making fun of terrible things in the most awful places in the world and applies it to a place that's even worse—Wall Street, and the whole wide world of finance.

Piketty, Thomas
★ *Capital in the Twenty-first Century.* Thomas Piketty; translated from the French by Arthur Goldhammer. The Belknap Press of Harvard University Press 2014. VIII, 685 pages : Illustration
ISBN 9780674430006
Grades: Adult   332
1. Income inequality 2. Wealth 3. Capitalism and inequality 4. Labor economics 5. Capital 6. Resource allocation 7. Translations — French to English 8. Business and economics — Economics — Socioeconomics 9. Business and economics — Economics — World economy 10. Business and economics — Economics — History

LC 2013036024

Kirkus Prize for Nonfiction finalist, 2014; National Book Critics Circle Award for Nonfiction finalist, 2014.

Analyzes a collection of data from twenty countries, ranging as far back as the eighteenth century, to uncover key economic and social patterns, transform debate, and set the agenda for the next generation of thought about wealth and inequality.

"Shows that plain language can be put to work explaining the most complex of ideas, foremost among them the fact that economic inequality is at an all-time high—and is only bound to grow worse." —*Kirkus*

Translation from the French of: Le capital au XXIe siecle; Includes bibliographical references (pages 579-655) and index; Originally published: Paris : Editions du Seuil, 2013.

332.024 Personal finance

Ariely, Dan
Dollars and Sense: How We Misthink Money and How to Spend Smarter. Dan Ariely and Jeff Kreisler. Harper, an imprint of HarperCollinsPublishers 2017. 256 p.
ISBN 9780062651204
Grades: Adult   332.024
1. Personal finance 2. Money 3. Credit cards 4. Budget 5. Household finances 6. Debt 7. Decision-making 8. Business and economics — Popular psychology 9. Business and economics — Economics — Consumerism

LC Bl2017036961

Shares anecdotal insight into the illogical influences behind poor financial decisions and how to outmaneuver them, covering topics ranging from credit-card debt and household budgeting to holiday spending and real estate sales.

"A user-friendly and often entertaining treatise on how to be a more discerning, vastly more aware handler of money." —*Kirkus*

De Leon, Paco
Finance for the People: Getting a Grip on Your Finances. Paco de Leon. Penguin Life 2022. xxxii, 349 pages : Illustration
ISBN 9780143136255
Grades: Adult   332.024
1. Personal finance 2. Money 3. Debt 4. Saving and thrift 5. Investments 6. Self-Help — Career and financial success

LC 2021026464

This practical and illustrated personal finance guide teaches readers to examine their beliefs and experiences about money in order to break out of the debt cycle and begin accumulating wealth.

"Often-funny drawings help to illustrate the points, and De Leon's breezy tone marries well with her practical advice. Readers beginning to tackle their personal finances will find a welcome guide in de Leon." —*Publishers Weekly*

Includes bibliographical references (pages 343-349).

Fagan, Chelsea
The Financial Diet: A Total Beginner's Guide to Getting Good with Money. Chelsea Fagan; designed by Lauren Ver Hage; illustrations by Eve Mobley. Henry Holt and Company 2018. 196 pages : Color; Illustration
ISBN 9781250176165
Grades: Adult   332.024
1. Personal finance 2. Women 3. Business and economics — Personal finance 4. Self-Help — Personal growth

LC 2017027973

Offers guidance on personal finance for readers who might be reluctant to bother with the subject, with easy-to-follow advice for budgeting, investing, handling credit, and living a satisfying lifestyle that is still budget conscious.

The founder of "The Financial Diet" blog outlines practical advice for securing a healthy financial life, explaining the basics of creating a budget, choosing worthwhile investments and managing credit responsibly while negotiating for raises and learning how to afford small luxuries.

"The breezy lifestyle-magazine-like writing style and easy-to-digest layout make this guide a useful and readable resource." —*Publishers Weekly*

A Holt Paperback.

Kobliner, Beth
Make Your Kid a Money Genius (even If You're Not): A Parents' Guide for Kids 3 to 23. Beth Kobliner. Simon & Schuster 2017. 256 pages : Illustration
ISBN 9781476766812
Grades: Adult   332.024
1. Children 2. Parenting 3. Personal finance 4. Business and economics — Personal finance 5. Family and Relationships — Parenting

LC 2016021573

The New York Times best-selling author of Get a Financial Life counsels parents on how to teach their children about smart money management, sharing jargon-free advice on subjects ranging from delayed gratification and living

ESSENTIAL AND RECOMMENDED TITLES
332.024 Personal finance

within one's means to getting a solid education and using credit cards responsibly.

"Best-selling financial author Kobliner (Get a Financial Life) here provides a step-by-step look at developing financial literacy skills throughout childhood." —*Library Journal*

Includes bibliographical references (pages 227-242) and index.

Kotlikoff, Laurence J.
Money Magic: An Economist's Secrets to More Money, Less Risk, and a Better Life. Laurence J. Kotlikoff. Little, Brown Spark 2022. VIII, 309 pages
ISBN 9780316541954
Grades: Adult   332.024
1. Personal finance 2. Self-Help — Career and financial success
LC Bl2021073751

One of our nation's premier personal finance experts harnesses the power of economics and advanced computation to provide a host of simple money magic tricks that will transform your financial future.

"Full of invaluable guidance, this is a must-read for anyone concerned about their financial future." —*Publishers Weekly*

Includes bibliographical references (pages 295-299) and index.

Lowry, Erin
★ *Broke Millennial Talks Money: Scripts, Stories, and Advice to Navigate Awkward Financial Conversations.* Erin Lowry. TarcherPerigee, Penguin Random House 2020. xvi, 280 pages
ISBN 9780143133650
Grades: Adult   332.024
1. Personal finance 2. Communication 3. Financial literacy 4. Negotiation 5. Millennials 6. Self-help — Career and financial success
LC 2020021204

The author of the Broke Millennial series shares user-friendly advice for a range of personal-finance scenarios, from salary negotiation and prenups to helping aging parents and telling friends you cannot afford their lifestyle.

"Any of the books in the 'Broke Millennial' series are strong guides for beginners, but this volume provides something unique: Scripts and walk-throughs on how to talk about money with coworkers, family, and partners." —*Library Journal*

Includes bibliographical references (pages 279-280).

Mecham, Jesse
You Need a Budget: The Proven System for Breaking the Paycheck-to-paycheck Cycle, Getting Out of Debt, and Living the Life You Want. Jesse Mecham. HarperBusiness 2017. 207 pages : Illustration
ISBN 9780062567581
Grades: Adult   332.024
1. Personal finance 2. Business and economics — Personal finance
LC Bl2017041802

A guide based on the tenets of the "You Need a Budget" financial platform argues that a well-planned budget can help to prioritize financial goals, reduce stress through strategic cash flow allocations, and meet the challenges of unplanned expenses.

A guide based on the tenets of the award-winning financial platform, "You Need a Budget," argues that a well-planned budget does not involve deprivation and counsels readers on how to prioritize financial goals, reduce stress through strategic cash flow allocations and meet the challenges of unplanned expenses.

"Mechams book is a handy guide for readers looking to increase their financial literacy and manage their money carefully and successfully." —*Booklist*

Includes index.

Morduch, Jonathan
The Financial Diaries: How American Families Cope in a World of Uncertainty. Jonathan Morduch and Rachel Schneider. Princeton Univ Pr 2017. 256 p.
ISBN 9780691172989
Grades: Adult   332.024
1. Personal finance 2. Household finances 3. Survival (Economics) 4. Cost and standard of living 5. Business and economics — Economics — Consumerism 6. Business and economics — Economics — Socioeconomics 7. Business and economics — Economics — Contemporary U.S. economy
LC 2016955128

Combining hard facts with the personal stories of 235 low- and middle-income families as they navigate through a year, the authors examine the economic stresses of today's families and offer fresh ideas for solving them.

"This is a must-read for anyone interested in causes of and potential solutions to American poverty." —*Publishers Weekly*

Quinn, Jane Bryant
★ *How to Make Your Money Last: The Indispensable Retirement Guide.* Jane Bryant Quinn. Simon & Schuster 2020. xviii, 412 pages
ISBN 9781982115838
Grades: Adult   332.024
1. Investments 2. Personal finance 3. Retirees 4. Retirement income 5. Planning 6. Business and economics — Personal finance
LC 2015007344

A strategic guide to turning retirement savings into a steady and lasting source of income shares strategic information for investing for growth and maximizing Social Security, pension, home equity and savings assets.

"Even though Quinn's key to financial success remains the same—manage your spending—readers, both Quinn's followers and anyone seeking a financial road map to retirement, will be drawn to the second edition's new information." —*Booklist*

Ramsey, Dave
The Total Money Makeover: A Proven Plan for Financial Fitness. Dave Ramsey. Nelson Books 2013. xxvii, 237 pages : Illustration
ISBN 9781595555274
Grades: Adult   332.024
1. Personal finance 2. Debt 3. Budget 4. Business and economics — Personal finance 5. Self-Help — Career and financial success
LC 2013431148

A strategy for changing attitudes about personal finances covers such topics as getting out of debt, the dangers of cash advances and keeping spending within income limits.

Includes index.

Rick, Scott
Tightwads and Spendthrifts: Navigating the Money Minefield in Real Relationships. Scott Rick. St. Martin's Press 2024. 230 pages
ISBN 9781250280077
Grades: Adult   332.024
1. Personal finance 2. Interpersonal relations 3. Self-Help — Relationships 4. Self-Help — Career and financial success 5. Business and Economics — Personal finance
LC 2023033037

In this science-based guide, the author, building on his original research, and surveying a vast body of interdisciplinary work, tells readers how to create a game plan for navigating financial decision-making that both Tightwads and Spendthrifts can rely on for a happy life together.

"This book is a compelling journey through the human psyche, shedding light on the intricacies of our financial choices and their far-reaching consequences. It's a must-read for anyone looking to unravel the mysteries of money and love." —*Booklist*

Includes bibliographical references (pages 179-220) and index.

Sabatier, Grant
Financial Freedom: A Proven Path to All the Money You Will Ever Need. Grant Sabatier; foreword by Vicki Robin. Avery 2019. 342 pages : Illustration
ISBN 9780525540885
Grades: Adult   332.024
1. Personal finance 2. Business and economics — Personal finance 3. Self-Help — Personal growth
LC 2018049617

The CNBC-declared "Millennial Millionaire" describes how he transitioned from being broke to wealthy in less than five years, revealing how today's financial rules are obsolete while outlining counterintuitive, step-by-step tips for making real-world fast money.

"Despite the ambitious premise, the strategies covered tend to be eminently practical, making this book a worthwhile purchase for anyone, not just aspiring millionaires, who feels overwhelmed by finances." —*Publishers Weekly*

Includes bibliographical references (pages 329-331) and index.

Simmons, Lauren

Make Money Move: A Guide to Financial Wellness. Lauren Simmons. Amistad, an imprint of HarperCollinsPublishers 2023. 231 pages
ISBN 9780063246539

Grades: Adult   332.024

1. Personal finance 2. Investments 3. Wealth 4. Money 5. Self-Help — Career and financial success 6. Business and economics — Personal finance

LC Bl2023174278

Driven by a passion for empowering women, the youngest full-time trader in the New York Stock Exchange brings a fresh perspective to personal finance based on her understanding of how to increase wealth and an awareness of generation and cultural barriers that hold people back from taking financial risks.

"Supplemented with charts and a glossary of financial terms, Make Money Move will be a valuable addition to general undergraduate, business-school, and public-library collections." —*Booklist*

Stanley, Thomas J.

The Next Millionaire Next Door: Enduring Strategies for Building Wealth. Thomas J. Stanley, PhD, and Sarah Stanley Fallaw, PhD.. Lyons Press 2018. xii, 260 pages : Illustration
ISBN 9781493035359

Grades: Adult   332.024

1. Personal finance 2. Wealth 3. United States 4. Business and economics — Personal finance

LC 2018030576

Twenty years after Thomas J. Stanley's groundbreaking work on self-made affluence, he and his daughter examine the changes in specific decisions, behaviors and characteristics, along with consumption, budgeting, careers and investing that have changed wealth-building in more recent years.

Includes bibliographical references (pages 251-260).

Tu, Vivian

Rich Af: The Winning Money Mindset That Will Change Your Life. Vivian Tu. Portfolio/Penguin, an imprint of Penguin Random House LLC 2023. 320 pages
ISBN 9780593714911

Grades: Adult   332.024

1. Personal finance 2. Saving and investment 3. Wealth 4. Self-Help — Career and financial success 5. Business and economics — Personal finance

From TikTok star and your (favorite) rich BFF Vivian Tu, the definitive book on personal finance for a new generation.

"This book will appeal to everyone who deals with money, especially younger readers who are starting their career journeys and looking to build financial strategies of their own." —*Booklist*

Includes bibliographical references and index.

332.0240082 Women — Personal finance

Orman, Suze

Women & Money. Suze Orman. Spiegel & Grau 2018. xiii, 206 pages
ISBN 9780812987614

Grades: Adult   332.0240082

1. Women 2. Wealth 3. Personal finance 4. United States 5. Business and economics — Personal finance 6. Self-Help — Career and financial success 7. Self-Help — Personal growth — Motivation

LC 2018019618

In a book that includes up-to-date tax information and economic data, a renowned personal-finance expert, TV host and best-selling author offers insights and compassion along with a clear and streamlined plan for women to attain durable financial security.

Revised edition of the author's Women & money, c2007; Includes index.

332.0240083 Young people — Personal finance

Lieber, Ron

The Opposite of Spoiled: Raising Kids Who Are Grounded, Generous, and Smart About Money. Ron Lieber. HarperCollins 2015. 320 p.
ISBN 9780062247018

Grades: Adult   332.0240083

1. Parenting 2. Personal finance 3. Generosity 4. Money 5. Parent and child 6. Children 7. Wealth 8. Family and Relationships — Parenting 9. Business and economics — Economics — Socioeconomics

LC 2014035600

A New York Times personal-finance columnist challenges popular taboos to explain how talking openly to children about money can help parents raise grounded, financially responsible young adults.

"Humble stories of kids raising money for Down syndrome research or creating kit bags to give to people living on the street offer inspiration for those who do have money to spend it wisely in the world and to teach their children to do the same. Sound advice on managing family finances but only if you have sufficient finances to manage." —*Kirkus*

332.0973 Finance — United States

Flitter, Emily

The White Wall: How Big Finance Bankrupts Black America. Emily Flitter. Signal Press 2022. 352 p.
ISBN 9781982183240

Grades: Adult   332.0973

1. Banks and banking 2. Institutional racism 3. Finance 4. African Americans 5. Racism 6. Wealth 7. Society and culture — Race 8. Business and economics — Economics — Socioeconomics 9. Society and culture — Wealth and class

An acclaimed New York Times finance reporter Looks at the systemic racism inside the American financial-services industry.

"A rousing body of evidence in favor of activist reform of financial practices, from ordinary loans to reparations." —*Kirkus*

Schulman, Daniel

The Money Kings: The Epic Story of the Jewish Immigrants Who Transformed Wall Street and Shaped Modern America. Daniel Schulman. Alfred A. Knopf 2023. 592 p.
ISBN 9780451493545

Grades: Adult   332.0973

1. Businesspeople 2. Investment bankers 3. Immigrants 4. Jewish people 5. German people 6. Banks and banking 7. Finance 8. Wall Street, New York City 9. Collective biographies 10. History writing — United States 11. Business and economics — Industries — Finance 12. Life stories — Business

LC 2023004044

The extraordinary saga of the German-Jewish immigrants who shaped the destiny of American finance—now familiar names like Goldman and Sachs, Warburg and Schiff and Lehman and Seligman—traces the interconnected origin stories of these financial dynasties, chronicling their paths to Wall Street dominance.

"A welcome, highly readable contribution to American financial and social history." —*Kirkus*

Includes bibliographical references and index.

ESSENTIAL AND RECOMMENDED TITLES
332.1 Banks

332.1 Banks

Bernanke, Ben
★ *21st Century Monetary Policy: The Federal Reserve from the Great Inflation to Covid-19.* Ben S. Bernanke. W. W. Norton & Company 2022. 512 p.
ISBN 9781324020462
Grades: Adult   332.1
1. Monetary policy 2. Economic policy 3. Federal Reserve banks 4. Inflation 5. Economics 6. United States 7. Business and economics — Economics — Contemporary U.S. economy
LC 2021055322

Former Federal Reserve Chair Ben S. Bernanke helps readers understand how the Federal Reserve, the steward of U.S. monetary policy, got to where it is today, what it has learned from the diverse challenges it has faced, and how it may evolve in the future.

"This impressive and accessible book will appeal to historians and educators as well as those who want to understand America's finances from a historical perspective." —*Booklist*

Includes bibliographical references and index.

Enrich, David
Dark Towers: Deutsche Bank, Donald Trump, and an Epic Trail of Destruction. David Enrich. Custom House 2020. 384 pages
ISBN 9780062878816
Grades: Adult   332.1
1. Trump, Donald, 1946- 2. Banking corruption 3. Corruption 4. International banking 5. Banks and banking 6. Scandals 7. Suicide 8. Fathers and sons 9. Investment banking 10. Germany 11. Business and economics — Industries — Finance
LC 2019034196

The New York Times finance editor and award-winning author presents a journalistic exposé of the scandalous activities of Deutsche Bank and its shadowy ties to Donald Trump's business empire.

"Part exposé, part mystery, Enrich's account is important because it illuminates Deutsche Bank's excesses and Trump's business practices. Readers of Andrew Sorkin's Too Big to Fail, which unveiled vulnerabilities in the financial industry, will find Enrich's more focused account equally compelling." —*Library Journal*

Includes bibliographical references and index.

Karabell, Zachary
Inside Money: Brown Brothers Harriman and the American Way of Power. Zachary Karabell. Penguin Press 2021. 448 p.
ISBN 9781594206610
Grades: Adult   332.1
1. Investment bankers 2. Banks and banking 3. Wealth 4. Capitalism 5. Economics 6. International relations 7. United States 8. History writing — United States 9. Business and economics — Industries — Finance
LC 2020019212

Using his complete access to the company's archives, an acclaimed historian, commentator and former financial executive offers a sweeping history of the legendary private investment firm Brown Brothers Harriman, exploring its central role in the story of American wealth and its rise to global power.

"A long overdue history offering a behind-the-scenes look at one of the world's leading financial institutions." —*Library Journal*

Includes bibliographical references and index.

Lowenstein, Roger
America's Bank: The Epic Struggle to Create the Federal Reserve. Roger Lowenstein. Penguin Group USA 2015. 368 p.
ISBN 9781594205491
Grades: Adult   332.1
1. Federal Reserve banks 2. Banks and banking 3. Central banking 4. 1910s 5. History writing — United States 6. Business and economics — Economics — History
LC 2015373201

Chronicles the tumultuous era and remarkable personalities that created the Federal Reserve, tracing the financial panic and widespread distrust of bankers that prompted the landmark 1913 Federal Reserve Act and launched America's first steps onto the world financial stage.

"Readers seeking a comprehensive history of the Federal Reserve from its conception to modern times will find this work especially appealing." —*Library Journal*

Meltzer, Allan H.
A History of the Federal Reserve: 1913-1951. Allan H. Meltzer; with a foreword by Alan Greenspan. University of Chicago, Ill. :Press 2003. 848 p; Illustration
ISBN 9780226519999
Grades: Adult   332.1
1. Federal Reserve banks 2. Business and economics — General
LC 2002072007

"The author provides a definitive history of the U.S. Federal Reserve from its founding in 1913 to its establishment as a separate, independent entity in 1951. Using meeting minutes, correspondence, and internal Federal Reserve documents, he traces the reasons behind Federal Reserves policy decisions, highlights the impact that individuals and events had on the Fed, and examines the Fed's influence on international affairs. This well-written and thoroughgoing account is recommended for academic, business, and public libraries." —*Library Journal*

Includes bibliographical references and index.

Smialek, Jeanna
★ *Limitless: The Federal Reserve Takes on a New Age of Crisis.* Jeanna Smialek. Alfred A. Knopf 2023. 352 p.
ISBN 9780593320235
Grades: Adult   332.1
1. Monetary policy 2. Economic policy 3. Federal Reserve banks 4. Economics 5. United States 6. Business and economics — Economics — Contemporary U.S. economy

This deep dive into the history and current state of the Federal Reserve focuses on its recent transformation from secrecy to the more transparent and activist institution we know today.

"The best book on the Fed in our time and a model of financial writing." —*Kirkus*

Wessel, David
In Fed We Trust: Ben Bernanke's War on the Great Panic. David Wessel. Crown Business 2009. xii, 323 p.
ISBN 9780307459688
Grades: Adult   332.1
1. Bernanke, Ben 2. Central banking 3. Financial crises 4. Monetary policy 5. Banks and banking 6. Economic policy 7. Economics 8. United States 9. 21st century 10. Business and economics — Economics — Contemporary U.S. economy

New York Times Notable Book, 2009.

Whatever it takes." That was Federal Reserve Chairman Ben Bernanke's vow as the worst financial panic in more than fifty years gripped the world and he struggled to avoid the once unthinkable: a repeat of the Great Depression. Brilliant but temperamentally cautious, Bernanke researched and wrote about the causes of the Depression during his career as an academic. Then when thrust into a role as one of the most important people in the world, he was compelled to boldness by circumstances he never anticipated. Believing that the economic catastrophe of the 1930s was largely the fault of a sluggish and wrongheaded Federal Reserve, Bernanke was determined not to repeat that epic mistake. In this penetrating look inside the most powerful economic institution in the world, David Wessel illuminates its opaque and undemocratic inner workings, while revealing how the Bernanke Fed led the desperate effort to prevent the world's financial engine from grinding to a halt.

"The author has written a gripping blow-by-blow account of how the top brass at the Federal Reserve and Treasury flailed against financial collapse. [The story] is a thrilling one, deftly told by a veteran journalist with access to those involved. Mr Wessel has an eye for enlivening detail…and he has a knack for making finance accessible to the layman without boring the specialist." —*The Economist*

How the federal reserve became the fourth branch of government—Dust jkt; Includes bibliographical references (p. [277]-302; [307]-308) and index.

332.10973 Banks (Finance) — United States

Servon, Lisa J.
The *Unbanking* of America: How the New Middle Class Survives. Lisa Servon. Houghton Mifflin Harcourt 2017. 288 p.
ISBN 9780544602311
Grades: Adult   332.10973
1. Middle class 2. Banks and banking 3. Personal finance 4. Bank regulation 5. Social classes 6. Social structure 7. Economics 8. United States 9. Society and culture — Wealth and class — Poverty
LC Bl2016055430

A gripping and incisive exposé of our broken banking system—why so many Americans on many rungs of the economic ladder are unable to efficiently get at their money, pay bills, or save for emergency expenses.

"This well-written book offers a fascinating read." —*Library Journal*

332.3 Credit and loan institutions

Grind, Kirsten
The *Lost Bank*: The Story of Washington Mutual—the Biggest Bank Failure in American History. Kirsten Grind. Simon & Schuster 2012. 384 p.
ISBN 9781451617924
Grades: Adult   332.3
1. Bank failures 2. Banks and banking 3. United States history 4. Seattle, Washington 5. Business and economics — Industries — Finance
LC 2011048587

An award-winning journalist best known for her coverage of the failure of Washington Mutual offers insight into the failings at the root of the recession, exploring how the bank was rendered vulnerable by destructive financial instruments and the well-intentioned practices of executives, customers, shareholders and regulators.

Includes bibliographical references.

Kardas-Nelson, Mara
We Are Not Able to Live in the Sky: The Seductive Promise of Microfinance. Mara Kardas-Nelson. Metropolitan Books : 2024. 384 p.
ISBN 9781250817228
Grades: Adult   332.3
1. Microlending 2. Women 3. Personal finance 4. Sierra Leone 5. Society and culture — Wealth and class 6. Business and economics — Economics — Socioeconomics 7. Society and culture — Social activism and philanthropy
LC 2023055945

A deeply reported work of journalism that explores the promise and peril of global microfinance, told through the eyes of those who work in microfinance and women borrowers in Sierra Leone.

"This thoughtful deep dive into the world of microfinance is both educative and heartbreaking." —*Kirkus*

Includes bibliographical references and index.

332.4 Money

Goldstein, Jacob
Money: The True Story of a Made-up Thing. Jacob Goldstein. Hachette Books 2020. xiii, 257 pages
ISBN 9780316417198
Grades: 9 10 11 12 Adult   332.4
1. Money 2. Monetary policy 3. Economic policy 4. Finance 5. Banks and banking 6. Business and economics — Economics — History 7. History writing — Microhistory 8. Society and culture — Wealth and class 9. Adult books for young adults
LC 2020011586

Money only works because we all agree to believe in it. In Money, Jacob Goldstein shows how money is a useful fiction that has shaped societies for thousands of years, from the rise of coins in ancient Greece to the first stock market in Amsterdam to the emergence of shadow banking in the 21st century.

"An informative primer from a genial guide." —*Kirkus*

"YAs curious about money's past and future will love Goldstein's approach." —*Booklist*

Includes bibliographical references and index.

Ledbetter, James
One Nation Under Gold: How One Precious Metal Has Dominated the American Imagination for Four Centuries. James Ledbetter. Liveright Pub Corp. 2017. 384 p.
ISBN 9780871406835
Grades: Adult   332.4
1. Gold 2. Gold standard 3. Monetary policy 4. Political science 5. Economics 6. United States 7. History writing — United States 8. Business and economics — Economics — History
LC 2017005139

An account of America's historical obsession with gold documents events ranging from the search for El Dorado to FDR's ban on private gold ownership, sharing insights into its current influences on the economy and human psyche.

"A vibrant and fascinating account of monetary golds volatile fortunes in the U.S." —*Booklist*

Small, Zachary
★ *Token* Supremacy: The Art of Finance, the Finance of Art, and the Great Crypto Crash of 2022. Zachary Small. Alfred A. Knopf 2024. 368 p.
ISBN 9780593536759
Grades: Adult   332.4
1. Cryptocurrencies 2. Recession (Economics) 3. Art 4. Digital art 5. Blockchains (Databases) 6. Ownership 7. Art auctions 8. Finance 9. Speculation 10. Money laundering 11. Arts and Entertainment — General 12. Society and culture — Media and technology 13. Business and economics — Economics — Contemporary U.S. economy
LC 2023014592

A New York Times investigative reporter traces the crypto economy back to its origins in the 2008 fiscal crisis, taking detours through art history to provide insight into the mythmaking tactics that drive stratospheric auction sales and help the wealthy launder their finances (and reputations) through art.

"A fascinating tale about NFTs, the art market, and investment for curious readers who have a solid understanding of how crypto and finance work." —*Library Journal*

Includes index.

332.401 Philosophy and theory

Hammond, Claudia
Mind Over Money: The Psychology of Money and How to Use It. Claudia Hammond. HarperCollins 2016. 368 p.
ISBN 9780062317001
Grades: Adult   332.401
1. Money 2. Personal finance 3. Wealth 4. Applied psychology 5. Social behavior 6. Social psychology 7. Neuroscience 8. Business and economics — Economics — Consumerism 9. Society and culture — Psychology and human behavior
LC 2017448126

An award-winning BBC Radio 4 host delves into the latest research in the fields of neuroscience, psychology and biology to show us that our relationship with money is more complex than we might think and reveals some simple and effective tricks that will help us use and save money better.

ESSENTIAL AND RECOMMENDED TITLES
332.6 Exchange of securities and commodities

332.6 Exchange of securities and commodities

Fabre, Cin
Wolf Hustle: A Black Woman on Wall Street. Cin Fabré.. Henry Holt and Company 2022. 320 p.
ISBN 9781250816856
Grades: Adult   332.6
1. Fabre, Cin 2. Women brokers 3. Brokers 4. Investment advisers 5. African American women 6. Stock market 7. African Americans 8. Autobiographies and memoirs 9. Life stories — Business 10. Business and economics — Industries — Finance
LC 2022026966

The author, who became one of the youngest Black female stockbrokers in the history of Wall Street, examines her years spent trading frantically—and hustling successfully—in a world where she had to endure sexual harassment and racism until she beat Wall Street at its own game.

"From hustling lunch tickets in the Bronx to being a successful investor, Fabré tells how she became one of Wall Street's youngest Black stockbrokers in the 1990s." —*Booklist*

Hagstrom, Robert G.
The Warren Buffett Way. Robert G. Hagstrom. Wiley 2014. xxxvii, 281 pages
ISBN 9781118503256
Grades: Adult   332.6
1. Buffett, Warren 2. Capitalists and financiers 3. Investments 4. Biographies 5. Business and economics — Industries — Finance
LC 2013023887

The bestselling book on Warren Buffett returns, with new insights on his continued success. Often described as the greatest investor of all time, Warren Buffett grew a $100 investment in the late 1950s into an investment empire. In the process, he has become one of the wealthiest individuals in the world, and the foremost authority on investing of our generation. With over one million copies sold, the Warren Buffett Way is the definitive book on "The Oracle of Omaha's" investment methods. Completely revised and updated, the Third Edition of the Warren Buffett Way focuses on the timeless principles and strategies behind Buffett's extraordinary investment success. This edition contains new chapters on the important distinctions between investing and trading, as well as an examination of the most successful disciples of Warren Buffett. Throughout the book, fresh examples and case studies are used and Buffett's successful formula is distilled in a way that will provide value to readers for decades to come. This edition represents the totality of Buffett's investment career and focuses on his timeless investing principles Companion website contains "Buffett Investment Calculators," which you can use to calculate the value and investment potential of companies Written by foremost Buffett expert Robert Hagstrom Engaging and informative, the Third Edition of the Warren Buffett Way is a must read—not just for avid Buffett fans, but for anyone who wants to know what it takes to make the best investment decisions possible.

Includes bibliographical references and index.

Morgenson, Gretchen
★ *These Are the Plunderers: How Private Equity Runs and Wrecks America.* Gretchen Morgenson and Joshua Rosner. Simon & Schuster 2023. 320 p.
ISBN 9781982191283
Grades: Adult   332.6
1. Private equity 2. Debt 3. Business corruption 4. Financial institutions 5. Middle class 6. Low-wage workers 7. American people 8. North American people 9. United States 10. Business and economics — Corruption and scandal 11. Business and economics — Economics — Contemporary U.S. economy

A Pulitzer Prize-winning and New York Times bestselling financial journalist and a policy analyst expose the greed and pillaging of a small group of celebrated Wall Street financiers who use excessive debt and dubious practices to undermine our nation's economy while enriching themselves: Private equity.

"It's a must-read for all for help in understanding a predacious side of capitalism." —*Booklist*

332.63 Specific forms of investment

Belfort, Jordan
★ *The Wolf of Investing: My Insider's Playbook for Making a Fortune on Wall Street.* Jordan Belfort. Gallery Books 2023. 323 pages : Illustration
ISBN 9781982197056
Grades: Adult   332.63
1. Belfort, Jordan 2. Investments 3. Stocks 4. Bonds 5. Mutual funds 6. Securities 7. Stock market 8. Securities industry and trade 9. Wall Street, New York City 10. New York City 11. United States 12. Business and economics — Industries — Finance 13. Business and economics — Personal finance
LC Oc2023002792

In his long-anticipated guide for mastering the stock market, the subject of the hit movie the Wolf of Wall Street teaches you everything you need to know about savvy investing while learning life's most profitable lessons for using Wall Street to your advantage.

"Whether readers know of Belfort from his previous books or the movie starring Leonardo DiCaprio, there is sure to be high demand for this book in both academic and public library collections." —*Booklist*

Hudson, Michael W.
The Monster: How a Gang of Predatory Lenders and Wall Street Bankers Fleeced America—and Spawned a Global Crisis. Michael W. Hudson. Times Books 2010. 320 p.
ISBN 9780805090468
Grades: Adult   332.63
1. Mortgages 2. Loans 3. Mortgage backed securities 4. Financial crises 5. Investment banking 6. Banking corruption 7. Business and economics — Corruption and scandal 8. Business and economics — Industries — Finance
LC 2010003223

An award-winning former staff reporter for the Wall Street Journal presents an inflammatory critique of the subprime-mortgage industry and its relationship with Wall Street that charges a group of maverick entrepreneurs with using high-pressure sales tactics and triggering the current economic crisis.

"The author exposes the source of the so-called toxic subprime mortgages that led to the 2008 financial crisis. He picks his way through a warren of mortgage brokers and lending companies that sat just outside banking regulations in the years following the savings and loan crisis. The book concentrates on the practices of mortgage lenders FAMCO and Ameriquest Mortgage, at one point the largest U.S. subprime lender. This is essential reading for anyone concerned with the mortgage crisis." —*Library Journal*

Includes bibliographical references and index.

Weatherall, James Owen
The Physics of Wall Street: A Brief History of Predicting the Unpredictable. James Owen Weatherall. Houghton Mifflin Harcourt 2013. 320 p.
ISBN 9780547317274
Grades: Adult   332.63
1. Securities industry and trade 2. Physics 3. Financial forecasting 4. Economics 5. Wall Street, New York City 6. Business and economics — Economics — History 7. Business and economics — Industries — Finance
LC 2012017323

A Harvard scholar challenges popular beliefs to argue that mathematical models can provide solutions to current economic challenges, citing the pivotal historical contributions of physicists to Wall Street while explaining that the economic meltdown of 2008 was based on a misunderstanding of scientific models rather than on the models themselves.

Includes bibliographical references and index.

332.64 Exchange of securities and commodities; speculation

Fox, Justin
The Myth of the Rational Market: A History of Risk, Reward, and Delusion on Wall Street. Justin Fox. Harper Business 2009. xvi, 382 p.
ISBN 9780060598990
Grades: Adult   332.64
1. Finance 2. Behavioral economics 3. Investments 4. Investors 5. Capitalism 6. Stock market 7. Wall Street, New York City 8. Business and economics — Economics — Contemporary U.S. economy
LC 2008052718
New York Times Notable Book, 2009.
Examines the rise and fall of the efficient markets theory, the development of modern finance, and the rise of behavioral economics, in an account that draws on interviews with top thinkers while demystifying the ideas that forged the modern market.
Includes bibliographical references (p. [334]-370) and index.

Russell, Rupert
Price Wars: How the Commodities Markets Made Our Chaotic World. Rupert Russell. Doubleday 2022. 256 p.
ISBN 9780385545853
Grades: Adult   332.64
1. Commodity exchanges 2. International finance 3. Price policy 4. 2010s 5. Business and economics — Economics — World economy 6. Business and economics — Economics — History
LC 2021031111
This groundbreaking expose of the power of the commodities markets to disrupt the world investigates what caused the wave of chaos that consumed the world in the 2010s.
"Deeply reported and thoroughly accessible, this investigation into the far-reaching consequences of economic speculation deserves a wide readership." —*Publishers Weekly*
Includes index.

332.645 Speculation

Buffett, Mary
Warren Buffett and the Art of Stock Arbitrage: Proven Strategies for Arbitrage and Other Special Investment Situations. Mary Buffett & David Clark. Scribner 2010. xviii, 153 p.
ISBN 9781439198827
Grades: Adult   332.645
1. Buffett, Warren 2. Investments 3. Business and economics — Personal finance
LC 2011280299
Analyzes Buffett's techniques for arbitrage and special situations investing and offers step-by-step instructions on how to take advantage of such events as spin-offs, liquidations, recapitalizations, and tender offers.
Includes glossary and index.

332.67 Investments in specific industries, in specific kinds of enterprise, by specific kinds of investors international

Graham, Benjamin
The Intelligent Investor: The Classic Text on Value Investing. Benjamin Graham. HarperBusiness 2005. xxvii, 269 p. : Illustration
ISBN 9780060752613
Grades: Adult   332.67
1. Securities 2. Investments 3. Business and economics — Personal finance 4. Business and economics — Industries — Finance
LC 2005282229

Analyzes the principles of stock selection and various approaches to investing, and compares the patterns and behavior of specific securities under diverse economic conditions.
Includes bibliographical references and index; Originally published: New York : Harper, 1949. Featuring a new foreword from John C. Bogle.

332.7 Credit

Davenport, Anthony
Your Score: An Insider's Secrets to Understanding, Controlling, and Protecting Your Credit Score. Anthony Davenport with Matthew Rudy. Houghton Mifflin Harcourt 2018. xvi, 202 pages
ISBN 9781328695277
Grades: Adult   332.7
1. Consumer credit 2. Personal finance 3. United States 4. Business and economics — Personal finance
LC 2017044246
A road map for how to navigate the confusing, secretive world of consumer credit, and how to upgrade and correct your score.
The most comprehensive insider's look at what every consumer needs to know about their credit score—and most importantly, how to fix it if you, like so many millions of Americans, are terrified by the daily headlines regarding Equifax and identity theft, and how all of this can directly affect your basic credit score, then this book should be considered as mandatory reading. Like it or not, a healthy credit score is essential if you want to participate in today's financial world. But very few people actually understand how their credit score is determined. Worse yet, most don't know how their score is used by all kinds of companies and banks to dictate financial terms that will strongly affect their daily lives. When consumers interact with the world of credit, they do so from a position of weakness. In Your Score, Anthony Davenport aims to change that. Finally, here is a road map for navigating the confusing world of consumer credit. Drawing on the real stories of his own firm's high-profile clients, as well as the stories of middle-class Americans, he reveals the hidden credit pitfalls that await even the most careful consumer and shares smart strategies to avoid them. An accessible but detailed manual, Your Score finally lets readers take control of their credit score, understand how to play the game, and gain an insider's knowledge of how to better navigate the most important financial decisions of their lives.
Presents a road map for how to navigate the confusing, secretive world of consumer credit, and how to upgrade and correct one's credit score.
"All readers who seek to better their knowledge of financial literacy, personal finance, and banking will find this a valuable resource." —*Booklist*
Includes bibliographical references and index.

Halpern, Jake
Bad Paper: Chasing Debt from Wall Street to the Underworld. Jake Halpern. Farrar, Straus and Giroux 2014. 256 pages
ISBN 9780374108236
Grades: Adult   332.7
1. Personal finance 2. Debt 3. Consumer credit 4. Bill collecting 5. Business and economics — Industries — Finance
LC 2014013576
Frequent New Yorker contributor Jake Halpern investigates the shadowy, unregulated world of consumer debt collection, focusing on an unlikely friendship between a former banking executive and former armed robber who go in search of "paper," spreadsheets of uncollected debt sold off by banks for pennies on the dollar.
"Colorful and chilling, this work is an important peek into the dark corner of consumer finance and recommended for all consumers and true crime aficionados." —*Library Journal*

Howard, Timothy
The Mortgage Wars: Inside Fannie Mae, Big-money Politics, and the Collapse of the American Dream. Timothy Howard. McGraw-Hill 2013. xvi, 288 pages
ISBN 9780071821094

ESSENTIAL AND RECOMMENDED TITLES
333.3 Private ownership of land

Grades: Adult   **332.7**
1. Mortgages 2. Global Financial Crisis, 2008-2009 3. Housing 4. Banks and banking 5. United States 6. Business and economics — Industries — Finance

LC 2013033450

The former Fannie Mae CFO's inside look at the war between the financial giants and government regulators. A provocative true-life thriller about the all-out fight for dominance of the mortgage industry—and how it nearly destroyed the global financial system.

333.3 Private ownership of land

Linklater, Andro
Owning the Earth: The Transforming History of Land Ownership. by Andro Linklater. Bloomsbury 2013. VIII, 482 pages, 16 pages of unnumbered plates : Illustration; Map
ISBN 9781620402894
Grades: Adult   **333.3**
1. Property rights 2. Land tenure 3. Landowners 4. Land use 5. Income inequality 6. Economics 7. Capitalism 8. Social responsibility 9. Representative government and representation 10. World politics 11. History writing — General

LC 2013011970

Library Journal Best Books, 2013.

Exploring the history and evolution of landownership, the author of Measuring America focuses on the idea of individual, exclusive ownership of land—a creative, yet destructive, cultural force that brought about the concept of individual freedom and a distinct form of democratic government.

"Many aspire to land ownership, taking the concept—that individuals may obtain a sliver of our planet as their own—for granted. Linklater's global study looks at land ownership—feudal, private, communal—through the lens of history and politics, rather than as merely a matter for economic study. The results are enlightening for our understanding not only of the past but of our future." —*Library Journal*

Includes bibliographical references and index.

333.33 Transfer of possession and of right to use

Brown, Eliot
The Cult of We: Wework, Adam Neumann, and the Great Startup Delusion. Eliot Brown and Maureen Farrell. Crown 2021. xiii, 446 p.
ISBN 9780593237113
Grades: Adult   **333.33**
1. Neumann, Adam, 1979- 2. New businesses 3. Chief executive officers 4. Business failures 5. Real estate business 6. Investments 7. High technology industry and trade 8. Venture capital 9. Greed 10. Scandals 11. Swindlers and swindling 12. Business and economics — Corruption and scandal 13. Life stories — Business — Business leaders

LC 2021011990

The definitive inside story of WeWork, its audacious founder, and what the company's epic unraveling exposes about Silicon Valley's delusions and the financial system's desperate hunger to cash in.

"This juicy cautionary tale, which complements the 2021 documentary WeWork: Or the Making and Breaking of a $47 Billion Unicorn, will appeal to fans of high drama in business and commerce." —*Library Journal*

Includes bibliographical references (pages 403-431) and index.

Wiedeman, Reeves
Billion Dollar Loser: The Epic Rise and Spectacular Fall of Adam Neumann and Wework. Reeves Wiedeman. Little Brown & Company 2020. 304 p.
ISBN 9780316461368
Grades: Adult   **333.33**
1. Neumann, Adam, 1979- 2. Businesspeople 3. Real estate business 4. Immigrants 5. Business failures 6. United States 7. Biographies 8. Life stories — Business — Business leaders 9. Business and economics — Business leaders and entrepreneurs 10. Nonfiction that reads like fiction

LC 2020940737

Moving between New York real estate, Silicon Valley venture capital, and the very specific force field of spirituality and ambition erected by Adam Neumann himself, Billion Dollar Loser lays bare the internal drama inside WeWork. Based on more than two hundred interviews, this book chronicles the breakneck speed at which WeWork's CEO built and grew his company along with Neumann's relationship to a world of investors, including Masayoshi Son of Softbank, who fueled its chaotic expansion into everything from apartment buildings to elementary schools.

"Readers will feel like they are in the room with Neumann and his beleaguered colleagues during every twist and turn of this fascinating corporate train wreck." —*Publishers Weekly*

Includes index.

333.7 Natural resources and energy

Conway, Edmund
Material World: The Six Raw Materials That Shape Modern Civilization. Ed Conway. Alfred A. Knopf 2023. 416 p.
ISBN 9780593534342
Grades: Adult   **333.7**
1. Materials 2. Materials science 3. Earth sciences 4. Sand 5. Salt 6. Oil 7. Lithium 8. Iron 9. Copper 10. Geology 11. Economics 12. Technology and civilization 13. Mines and mineral resources 14. Mining corporations 15. History writing — Microhistory 16. History writing — Technological innovations 17. Science Writing — Physics

LC 2023011293

Embarking on an epic journey across continents, cultures and time to reveal the underpinnings of modern life on Earth, the author celebrates the humans and human networks, the miraculous processes and the little-known companies that combine to turn raw materials into things of wonder.

"Wincott Foundation-winning British journalist Conway reveals how six materials in particular—sand, salt, iron, copper, oil, and lithium—have radically shaped human history." —*Library Journal*

Includes bibliographical references and index.

Goleman, Daniel
Ecological Intelligence: How Knowing the Hidden Impacts of What We Buy Can Change Everything. Daniel Goleman. Broadway Books 2009. x, 276 p.
ISBN 9780385527828
Grades: 11 12 Adult   **333.7**
1. Consumer behavior 2. Environmental responsibility 3. Industries 4. Environmentalism 5. Business and economics — General

LC 2008041811

Reveals the hidden environmental consequences of what societies make and buy, and how that knowledge can drive the changes necessary to save the planet.

The bestselling author of Emotional Intelligence and Primal Leadership reveals the hidden environmental consequences of what we make and buy, and shows how new market forces can drive the essential changes we all must make to save our planet.

Scheyder, Ernest
The War Below: Lithium, Copper, and the Global Battle to Power Our Lives. Ernest Scheyder. Atria/One Signal 2024. 384 p.
ISBN 9781668011805
Grades: Adult   **333.7**
1. Renewable energy sources 2. Alternative energy development 3. Green economics 4. Mines and mineral resources 5. Metals 6. Investments 7. International cooperation 8. Public opinion 9. Opposition (Political science) 10. Environmentalism 11. Options, alternatives, choices 12. Energy industry and trade 13. Clean energy industry and trade 14. Impartial writing 15. Nature Writing — Environmental Issues 16. Politics and global affairs — Environmental issues and policies 17. Business and economics — Industries — Energy

Tough choices loom if the world wants to go green. The United States and other countries must decide where and how to procure the materials that make our renewable energy economy possible. To build electric vehicles, solar panels, cell phones, and millions of other devices means the world must dig mines to extract lithium, copper, cobalt, rare earths, and nickel. But mines are deeply unpopular, even as they have a role to play in fighting climate change. Ernest Scheyder paints a nuanced picture of what is needed to fight climate change and secure energy independence, revealing how America and the rest of the world's hunt for the "new oil" directly affects us all.

"David vs. Goliath battles butt up against very real planetary perils in this evocative account of the energy transition's myriad complexities." —*Publishers Weekly*

333.703 Natural resources — Dictionaries, encyclopedias, concordances

Park, Chris C.
A Dictionary of Environment and Conservation. Chris Park, Michael Allaby. Oxford University Press 2013. 504 p. : Illustration
ISBN 9780199641666
Grades: Adult   333.703
1. Environmental sciences 2. Conservation of natural resources 3. Dictionaries 4. Nature writing — Environmental Issues
LC 2013387302

Thoroughly revised and updated to include the latest research in the field, a Dictionary of Environment and Conservation provides over 9,000 alphabetically arranged entries on scientific and social aspects of the environment, including concise and authoritative information on key thinkers, treaties, movements, organizations, concepts, and theories.

333.72 Conservation and protection

Freeman, Scott
Saving Tarboo Creek: One Family's Quest to Heal the Land. Scott Freeman, with illustrations by Susan Leopold Freeman. Timber Press 2018. 256 p.
ISBN 9781604697940
Grades: Adult   333.72
1. Freeman family 2. Leopold, Aldo, 1886-1948 3. Conservation of natural resources 4. Environmentalists 5. Effect of humans on nature 6. Streams 7. Washington (State) 8. Autobiographies and memoirs 9. Life stories — Nature and outdoors 10. Nature writing — Environmental issues
LC 2016055648

Examine the most pressing environmental issues of our time through one family's detailed account of creek restoration.

"Thought-provoking and unsettling, this highly readable book is made lovely by homey drawings sprinkled throughout." —*Booklist*

King, Dean
Guardians of the Valley: John Muir and the Friendship That Saved Yosemite. Dean King. Scribner 2023. 432 p.
ISBN 9781982144463
Grades: Adult   333.72
1. Muir, John, 1838-1914 2. Johnson, Robert Underwood, 1853-1937 3. Nature conservation 4. National parks and reserves 5. Environmentalists 6. Periodical editors 7. Naturalists 8. Yosemite National Park 9. Yosemite Valley 10. History Writing — United States 11. Nature Writing — Natural landscapes 12. Life stories — Nature and outdoors
LC 2022044155

The author of the best-selling Skeletons on the Zahara: A True Story of Survival returns with the story of how legendary outdoorsman and conservationist John Muir's fight to save Yosemite National Park from predatory mining, tourism and the logging industry.

"This comprehensively researched and compellingly readable history offers an intimate yet sweeping portrait of an inspirational friendship that literally altered the American landscape and enshrined the modern-day conservation movement." —*Booklist*
Includes bibliographical references and index.

Penniman, Leah
★ *Black Earth Wisdom: Soulful Conversations with Black Environmentalists.* Leah Penniman. Amistad Press 2023. 320 p.
ISBN 9780063160897
Grades: Adult   333.72
1. African Americans 2. Environmentalism 3. Environmentalists 4. Nature 5. Agriculture 6. Social justice 7. Racism in environmental policy 8. Nature Writing — Environmental issues 9. Life stories — Nature and outdoors

"The result is a potent look at the overlap between the environmental and racial justice movements." —*Publishers Weekly*

333.7209798 Conservation — Alaska

Heacox, Kim
★ *John Muir and the Ice That Started a Fire: How a Visionary and the Glaciers of Alaska Changed America.* Kim Heacox. Lyons Press 2014. 264 pages
ISBN 9780762792429
Grades: Adult   333.7209798
1. Muir, John, 1838-1914 2. Nature conservation 3. Glaciers 4. Geology 5. Climate change 6. Environmentalism 7. Alaska 8. Biographies 9. Life stories — People in history — Explorers 10. History writing — Regional history — United States 11. Adult books for young adults
LC 2013050235

John Muir and the Ice That Started a Fire takes two of the most compelling elements in the narrative of wild America, John Muir and Alaska, and combines them into a brisk and engaging biography.John Muir was a fascinating man who was many things: Inventor, scientist, revolutionary, druid (a modern day Celtic priest), husband, son, father and friend, and a shining son of the Scottish Enlightenment—both in temperament and intellect. Kim Heacox, author of the Only Kayak, bring us a story that evolves as Muir's life did, from one of outdoor adventure into one of ecological guardianship. Muir went from impassioned author to leading activist. He would popularize glaciers unlike anybody else, and be to glaciers what Jacques Cousteau would be to the oceans and Carl Sagan to the stars the book also offers an environmental caveat on global climate change and the glaciers' retreat alongside a beacon of hope: Muir shows us how one person changed America, helped it embrace its wilderness, and in turn, gave us a better world. Heacox takes us into how Muir changed our world, advanced the science of glaciology and popularized geology.

"The book is an engaging and informative look at Muir and his life's work, as well as a timely call to action that poses difficult questions to the reader and the philosophies that underpin modern life." —*Publishers Weekly*

333.73 Land

Biggers, Jeff
Reckoning at Eagle Creek: The Secret Legacy of Coal in the Heartland. Jeff Biggers. Nation Books 2010. 336 p.
ISBN 9781568584218
Grades: Adult   333.73
1. Coal mines and mining 2. Strip mining 3. Mountain life 4. Small town life 5. Mines and mineral resources 6. Illinois 7. History writing — Regional history — United States 8. Business and economics — Industries — Energy
LC 2009032686

Award-winning journalist and cultural historian Jeff Biggers takes us on a journey into the secret history of coal mining in the American heartland. Set in the ruins of his family's strip-mined homestead in the Shawnee National Forest in southern Illinois, Biggers delivers a deeply personal portrait of the largely overlooked human and environmental costs of our nation's dirty energy policy." "Reckoning at Eagle Creek digs deep into the tangled roots of the coal industry beginning with the policies of Thomas Jefferson and Andrew Jackson, chroni-

ESSENTIAL AND RECOMMENDED TITLES
333.75 Forest lands

cling the removal of Native Americans and the hidden story of legally sanctioned Black slavery in the land of Lincoln. It uncovers a century of regulatory negligence, vividly describing the epic mining wars for union recognition and workplace safety, and the devastating consequences of industrial strip-mining.

"Biggers takes a look at coal and its role in the history of southern Illinois as well as its human and environmental costs. Biggers also tells a personal story as he chronicles the saga of his family's strip-mined homestead in an area that one day would be a part of the Shawnee National Forest. A lot of history is presented here in a personal style by a cultural historian with a keen eye. A valuable read for followers of environmental history." —*Library Journal*

Flyn, Cal
★ *Islands of Abandonment: Nature Rebounding in the Post-human Landscape.* Cal Flyn. Viking 2021. 372 p.
ISBN 9781984878199
Grades: Adult   333.73
1. Restoration ecology 2. Nature conservation 3. Environmental disasters 4. Biotic communities 5. Wildlife recovery 6. Effect of humans on nature 7. Habitats 8. Landscape changes 9. Wilderness areas 10. Nature Writing — Natural Landscapes 11. Nature Writing — Environmental Issues 12. Science Writing — Biology
LC 2020041722

Cal Flyn visits the eeriest and most desolate places on Earth that due to war, disaster, disease, or economic decay, have been abandoned by humans. What she finds every time is an "island" of teeming new life: Nature has rushed in to fill the void faster and more thoroughly than even the most hopeful projections of scientists. Islands of abandonment is a tour through these new ecosystems, in all their glory, as sites of unexpected environmental significance, where the natural world has reasserted its wild power and promise. And while it doesn't let us off the hook for addressing environmental degradation and climate change, it's a case that hope is far from lost, and is ultimately a story of redemption. The most polluted spots on Earth can be rehabilitated through ecological processes, and in fact they already are.

"Through lush and poetic language, Flyn captures the vital forces at work in the natural world. This is nature writing at its most potent." —*Publishers Weekly*
Includes bibliographical references and index.

Lim, Audrea
Free the Land: How We Can Fight Poverty and Climate Chaos. Audrea Lim. St. Martin's Press 2024. 304 p.
ISBN 9781250275189
Grades: Adult   333.73
1. Land use 2. Landowners 3. Quality of life 4. Climate change 5. Discrimination 6. Race relations 7. Social justice 8. Inequality 9. Gentrification of cities 10. United States history 11. Canadian history 12. Canada 13. United States 14. Society and culture — Urban and regional studies
LC 2024003522

Free the Land is a captivating and beautifully rendered look at the ways that our relationship to the land is the core cause of the most pressing justice issues in North America. Lim expertly weaves together seemingly disparate themes into a unified theory of social justice, describes how the land ownership system developed over the centuries, and presents original reporting from a wide range of activists and policy makers to illustrate the profound impact it continues to have on our society today. An eye-opening examination of how treating land as a source of profit has a massive impact on racial inequality and the housing, gentrification, and environmental crises.

"A fascinating look at alternative landownership practices. Recommended for readers interested in economics, the environment, and issues of inequality." —*Library Journal*
Includes bibliographical references and index.

333.75 Forest lands

Hiss, Tony
★ *Rescuing the Planet: Protecting Half the Land to Heal the Earth.* Tony Hiss; introduction by E.O. Wilson. Alfred A. Knopf 2021. 288 p.
ISBN 9780525654810
Grades: Adult   333.75
1. Biodiversity conservation 2. Nature conservation 3. Conservation of natural resources 4. Climate change 5. Global warming 6. Greenhouse gases 7. Environmental policy 8. Wildlife refuges 9. Natural areas 10. Nature Writing — Environmental Issues
LC 2020026103

A former staff writer at the New Yorker makes a case for preserving 50 percent of the earth's land by 2050 to protect millions of species and highlights the important work being done by groups already engaged in the fight.

"Hiss creates a sense of hope with lyrical descriptions and immersive portrayals of various programs across the continent. This eye-opening survey will leave readers inspired." —*Publishers Weekly*

King, Greg
The Ghost Forest: Racists, Radicals, and Real Estate in the California Redwoods. Greg King. Public Affairs 2023. 528 p.
ISBN 9781541768673
Grades: Adult   333.75
1. King, Greg (Journalist) 2. Trees 3. Social advocates 4. Forests 5. Racism 6. Lumber industry and trade 7. Environmentalism 8. Autobiographies and memoirs 9. Life stories — Nature and outdoors 10. Nature Writing — Environmental issues 11. History writing — Regional history — United States

"[King's] haunting, sometimes inspiring narrative is sure to move anyone interested in trees and nature. A disheartening yet wholly engrossing, urgent account of redwood preservation." —*Kirkus*

333.77 Urban lands

Goldfarb, Ben
Crossings: How Road Ecology Is Shaping the Future of Our Planet. Ben Goldfarb. W.W. Norton & Company 2023. 384 p.
ISBN 9781324005896
Grades: Adult   333.77
1. Roads 2. Freeways 3. Traffic congestion 4. Ecology 5. Wildlife 6. Biotic communities 7. Habitats 8. Animal migration 9. Environmental degradation 10. Wildlife conservation 11. Problem solving 12. Nature Writing — Environmental Issues 13. Nature Writing — Animal Studies — Endangered Species 14. Science Writing — General

Some 40 million miles of roadways encircle the earth, yet we tend to regard them only as infrastructure for human convenience. While roads are so ubiquitous they're practically invisible to us, wild animals experience them as entirely alien forces of death and disruption, and as the new science of road ecology shows, the harms of highways extend far beyond roadkill. In Crossings, environmental journalist Ben Goldfarb travels throughout the United States and around the world to investigate how roads have transformed our planet.

"With vibrant and enlightening descriptions of the lives of deer, grizzlies, monarch butterflies, fish, and frogs, and striking insights into the culture and politics of roads, Goldfarb awakens readers to the ecological catastrophes roads cause and what we can do to ameliorate the damage and improve life on Earth." —*Booklist*

333.78 Recreational and wilderness areas

Bass, Rick
Why I Came West. Rick Bass. Houghton Mifflin Co. 2008. 288 p.
ISBN 9780618596751
Grades: Adult   333.78

1. Bass, Rick, 1958- 2. Writing 3. Authors, American 4. Montana 5. 20th century 6. Autobiographies and memoirs 7. Biographies 8. Arts and Entertainment — Writing and Publishing 9. Life stories — Arts and culture — Writing — Authors 10. Adult books for young adults

LC 2007030660

National Book Critics Circle Award for Autobiography/Memoir finalist.

A poignant look at the thirty-year journey of one of our country's great naturalist writers, Why I Came West explores how Rick Bass fell in love with the mystique of the West (and the Yaak Valley of northwestern Montana in particular) as a dramatic landscape, as an idea, and as a way of life. In a series of moving chapters, Bass describes his own transformation into the writer, hunter, and environmental activist that he is today. He profiles how the rugged, wild landscape smoothed out his own rough edges; attempts to define the appeal of the West that so transfixed him as a boy, a place of mountains and outlaws and continual rebirth, just beyond whatever was near it; and he describes his role as a reluctant environmental activist—sometimes at odds with his own neighbors—unable and unwilling to stand idly by and watch this treasured place disappear.

"Bass tells the tale of his apprenticeship to literature and the place that has defined his life for the past two decades, Montana's Yaak Valley. Bass looks back to his Houston childhood, Utah college years, and work as an oil geologist in Mississippi, searching for clues to his love-at-first sight response to the Yaak. As he describes his deep immersion in this bountiful land as a hunter, hiker, artist, and environmentalist, he . shares his anguish over the clear-cutting of woods, and chronicles the hard work of wilderness advocacy and the virulent hatred it arouses. Versed in paradox, Bass is bracing in his candor about how difficult it will be to change our destructive ways, and incandescent in his reasoned call to preserve the few remaining unspoiled places." —Booklist

Duncan, Dayton
The National Parks: America's Best Idea : An Illustrated History. Dayton Duncan, Ken Burns. Alfred A. Knopf 2009. 400 p.
ISBN 9780307268969
Grades: Adult   **333.78**
1. Natural areas 2. Parks 3. National parks and reserves 4. Nature conservation 5. Local history 6. United States 7. Nature Writing — Natural Landscapes

LC 2009020880

Presents a narrative history of the American national park system, examining the events and political battles that led to the establishment of each park while profiling each for its unique attributes.

333.79 Energy

Keefe, Bob
Clean Economy Now: Stories from the Frontlines of an American Business Revolution. Bob Keefe; foreword by Arnold Schwarzenegger. Rowman & Littlefield Publishers 2024. 296 p.
ISBN 9781538183045
Grades: Adult   **333.79**
1. Environmentalism 2. Clean energy industry and trade 3. Economics 4. Business 5. Renewable energy sources 6. Energy industry and trade 7. Energy policy 8. Renewable energy industry and trade 9. Business and economics — Industries — Energy 10. Politics and global affairs — Environmental issues and policies

"Keefe's insights will appeal to business leaders and climate activists alike." —Publishers Weekly

Vollmann, William T.
No Immediate Danger: Volume One of Carbon Ideologies. William T. Vollmann. Viking Press 2018. 704 p. (Carbon ideologies, 1)
ISBN 9780399563492
Grades: Adult   **333.79**
1. Fukushima Nuclear Disaster, Japan, 2011 2. Nuclear accidents 3. Climate change 4. Global warming 5. Nuclear power 6. Nuclear power industry and trade 7. Nature writing — Environmental issues 8. Politics and global affairs — Environmental issues and policies

LC 2018013155

A National Book Award-winning author presents a timely, eye-opening book about climate change and energy generation that focuses on the consequences of nuclear-power production.

Yergin, Daniel
The New Map: Energy, Climate, and the Clash of Nations. Daniel Yergin. Penguin Press 2020. xx, 492 p.
ISBN 9781594206436
Grades: Adult   **333.79**
1. Energy policy 2. Climate change 3. Geopolitics 4. Renewable energy sources 5. Fossil fuels 6. Effect of humans on nature 7. Politics and global affairs — Environmental issues and policies 8. Business and economics — Industries — Energy 9. Politics and global affairs — World politics

LC 2020002299

The global energy expert and Pulitzer Prize-winning author shares revelatory insights into how energy revolutions, climate battles and geopolitics are mapping a near future already complicated by the coronavirus pandemic and related economic fallout.

"Pulitzer Prize-winning energy expert Yergin shows us how the world has been remapped because of these major energy and geopolitical changes, even as climate change threatens further transformation." —Library Journal

Includes bibliographical references and index.

The Quest: Energy, Security and the Remaking of the Modern World. by Daniel Yergin. Penguin Press 2011. 704 p.
ISBN 9781594202834
Grades: Adult   **333.79**
1. Energy resources 2. Money 3. Oil industry and trade 4. Military strategy 5. World politics 6. Globalization 7. 20th century 8. History writing — Microhistory

LC 2011013100

New York Times Notable Book, 2011.

Demonstrates how the competition to solve pressing energy problems has become an engine of political and economic change and shares inside stories of current and developing energy sources from different world regions.

"This book is a masterly piece of work and, as a comprehensive guide to the world's great energy needs and dilemmas, it will be hard to beat." —The Economist

Includes bibliographical references and index.

333.7909 Energy — History, geographic treatment, biography

Rhodes, Richard
★ *Energy: A Human History.* Richard Rhodes. Simon & Schuster 2018. 384 p.
ISBN 9781501105357
Grades: Adult   **333.7909**
1. Energy development 2. Energy resources 3. Energy production 4. Energy 5. Technological innovations 6. History writing — Science, technology, and medicine 7. Science Writing — Computing, the Internet, and Technology

LC Bl2018045157

Booklist Editors' Choice, 2018.

A Pulitzer Prize- and National Book Award winning author describes five centuries of progress through the history of energy sources, from wood to coal to oil to electricity and beyond and highlights the successes and failures that led to each innovation.

"Pulitzer Prize-winning historian and author Rhodes . takes on entangled issues around the use of science and technology and makes complicated matters more approachable." —Library Journal

ESSENTIAL AND RECOMMENDED TITLES
333.7909748 Energy — Pennsylvania

333.7909748 Energy — Pennsylvania

McGraw, Seamus
The End of Country: Imagine a Small Farming Town Where Everybody Has Shared Hard Luck for as Long as They Can Remember, Scratching Out a Living from the Rocky Earth. Seamus McGraw. Random House Inc 2011. 224 p.
ISBN 9781400068531
Grades: Adult   333.7909748
1. Natural gas supply 2. Small towns 3. Greed 4. Natural gas 5. Homesteaders 6. Pennsylvania 7. Nature Writing — Environmental Issues 8. Society and culture — Social activism and philanthropy
LC Bl2012026563
Green Prize for Sustainable Literature: Adult Nonfiction, 2012.
Traces the 2007 rush to prospect Pennsylvania's Marcellus Shale natural gas deposits, drawing on the experiences of the author's mother and her neighbors to trace their efforts to defend their community and characters against the gas companies that would take over their lands.
"In 2006, in a hardscrabble part of Pennsylvania that had long lost its allure as a farming and industrial area, geologists began investigating the Marcellus Shale. It turned out to be the richest deposit of natural gas ever discovered anywhere. When his widowed mother was approached about permitting natural-gas exploration on their farm, journalist McGraw had to weigh their need for money against the future prospects of the farmland. Chronicling the impact of the find on his mother and her neighbors, McGraw's research led to this impressively detailed, highly engaging look at issues of energy policy, economics, and sociology that arose when a bucolic town was suddenly faced with the traveling circus of energy exploration. A completely engaging look at how energy policy affected a quiet, rural town." —*Booklist*

333.792 Primary forms of energy

Ferguson, Charles D.
Nuclear Energy: What Everyone Needs to Know. Charles D. Ferguson. Oxford University Press 2011. xvii, 222 p.
ISBN 9780199759460
Grades: 11 12 Adult   333.792
1. Science writing — General
LC 2010044449
"This compelling assembly of historical and scientific information deftly steps through the essential discoveries, definitions, and theory that led to the development of nuclear reactors and nuclear bombs…. After fully digesting the fundamentals of nuclear science in chapter 1, readers are well prepared to randomly select from the following chapters that cover safety, climate change, nuclear proliferation concerns, security, and the politically charged options for disposal of radioactive waste." —*Choice*
Includes bibliographical references (p. [209]-211) and index.

Mahaffey, James A.
Atomic Adventures: Secret Islands, Forgotten N-rays, and Isotopic Murder: A Journey into the Wild World of Nuclear Science. James Mahaffey. W W Norton & Co. Inc. 2017. 464 p.
ISBN 9781681774213
Grades: Adult   333.792
1. Nuclear physics 2. Science 3. Atoms 4. Scientists 5. Radioactivity 6. Atomic theory 7. Particles (Nuclear physics) 8. Nuclear weapons 9. Research 10. History writing — Science, technology, and medicine 11. Science Writing — Physics
LC Bl2017022514
The latest investigation from acclaimed nuclear engineer and author James Mahaffey unearths forgotten nuclear endeavors throughout history that were sometimes hair-brained, often risky, and always fascinating.
"His expertise and astonishing stories are matched by his writing skills, creating a sometimes humorous book that offers a valuable history of a deadly modern force and uncommonly clear, enjoyable explanations of related physics." —*Booklist*

333.793 Secondary forms of energy

Bakke, Gretchen Anna
The Grid: The Fraying Wires Between Americans and Our Energy Future. Gretchen Bakke. Bloomsbury USA 2016. 288 p.
ISBN 9781608196104
Grades: Adult   333.793
1. Electric power distribution 2. Clean energy 3. Power failures 4. Energy policy 5. Business and economics — Industries — Energy
LC 2016001376
A revelatory examination of America's national power grid traces how it developed while exposing its current vulnerabilities, making strategic recommendations for how it can be improved to meet the challenges of instability, security and sustainability.
"A lively analysis of the challenges renewables present to the production and distribution of electricity." —*Kirkus*

Blunt, Katherine
California Burning: The Fall of Pacific Gas and Electric — and What It Means for America's Power Grid. Katherine Blunt. Portfolio/Penguin 2022. 352 p.
ISBN 9780593330654
Grades: Adult   333.793
1. Corporations 2. Electric utilities 3. Electric power distribution 4. Wildfires 5. Natural disasters 6. Corporate negligence 7. Infrastructure 8. Deregulation 9. Profiteering 10. Energy industry and trade 11. California 12. Business and economics — Industries — Energy 13. Business and economics — Corruption and scandal 14. History writing — Natural disasters and tragedies 15. Debut title
LC 2022001979
Pacific Gas and Electric was a legacy company built by innovators and visionaries, establishing California as a desirable home and economic powerhouse. In California Burning, Wall Street Journal reporter and Pulitzer finalist Katherine Blunt examines how that legacy fell apart—unraveling a long history of deadly failures in which Pacific Gas and Electric endangered millions of Northern Californians, through criminal neglect of its infrastructure. As PG&E prioritized profits and politics, power lines went unchecked—until a rusted hook purchased for 56 cents in 1921 split in two, sparking the deadliest wildfire in California history.
"Diligent reporting and a clear focus make this a must-read for anyone interested in the future of energy." —*Publishers Weekly*
Includes bibliographical references and index.

333.91 Water and lands adjoining bodies of water

Dean, Cornelia
Against the Tide: The Battle for America's Beaches. Cornelia Dean. Columbia University Press 1999. xiv, 279 p. : Illustration
ISBN 9780231084185
Grades: 11 12 Adult   333.91
1. Coast changes 2. Erosion 3. Coastal towns 4. Science Writing — Geology 5. Adult books for young adults
LC 98050755
Library Journal Best Books, 1999; New York Times Notable Book, 1999.
The author warns beach lovers and environmentalists that U.S. beaches are vanishing, and traces the history and reviews the science of the Atlantic, Pacific, and Gulf coasts with a particular focus on hurricanes and other disasters.
"This thoroughly researched and thoughtful book is destined to become a classic of environmental science writing." —*Library Journal*
Includes bibliographical references (p. [251]-266) and index.

Doyle, Martin
The Source: How Rivers Made America and America Remade Its Rivers. Martin Doyle. W W Norton & Company 2018. 352 p.
ISBN 9780393242355
Grades: Adult   333.91

PUBLIC LIBRARY CORE COLLECTION: NONFICTION
Twentieth Edition

1. Rivers 2. Effect of environment on humans 3. River life 4. United States history 5. History writing — Regional history — United States 6. Nature writing — Natural landscapes 7. History writing — Microhistory

LC 2017051192

An environmental history of the role of rivers in shaping American politics, economics and society touches on subjects ranging from conservation and the New Deal to the Hoover Dam and Hurricane Katrina, drawing on experts from diverse backgrounds to explore how the natural and human transformations of rivers have made a significant impact on the nation.

"Doyle tackles the shifts in how America has viewed and used its extensive waterways, producing a comprehensive and enjoyable account." —*Publishers Weekly*

Gleick, Peter H.
The **Three** *Ages of Water: Prehistoric Past, Imperiled Present, and a Hope for the Future.* Peter Gleick. PublicAffairs 2023. 368 p.
ISBN 9781541702271
Grades: Adult   333.91
1. Water 2. Hydrology 3. Water-supply 4. Water use 5. Water consumption 6. History 7. Science 8. Civilization 9. Technological innovations 10. Climate change 11. Scarcity 12. Conservation of natural resources 13. Environmental protection 14. Sustainability 15. Science Writing — Geology 16. Nature Writing — Environmental Issues 17. History writing — Microhistory

From the very creation of the planet billions of years ago to the present day, water has always been central to existence on Earth. In The Three Ages of Water, Peter Gleick guides us through the long, fraught history of our relationship to this precious resource. Water has shaped civilizations and empires, and driven centuries of advances in science and technology—from agriculture to aqueducts, steam power to space exploration. But the achievements that have propelled humanity forward also brought consequences, including unsustainable water use, ecological destruction, and global climate change, that now threaten to send us into a new dark age.

"An invaluable introduction to hydrology with crucial recommendations for managing the world's water." —*Booklist*

Includes bibliographical references and index.

333.95 Biological resources

Alexander, Jane
Wild Things, Wild Places: Adventurous Tales of Wildlife and Conservation on Planet Earth. by Jane Alexander. Alfred A. Knopf 2016. 352 p.
ISBN 9780385354363
Grades: Adult   333.95
1. Alexander, Jane, 1939- 2. Environmentalists 3. Wildlife conservation 4. Rare and endangered animals 5. Effect of humans on nature 6. Animal welfare 7. Animal rights 8. Autobiographies and memoirs 9. Life stories — Nature and outdoors 10. Nature writing — Personal responses

LC 2016007803

The author writes of her steady and fervent immersion into the worlds of wildlife conservation, of her coming to know the scientists throughout the world and her travels with them to save many species from extinction.

"Highly recommended for all interested in travel, natural history, and environmental issues." —*Library Journal*

A Borzoi book; Includes bibliographical references and index.

Barrow, Mark V.
Nature's Ghosts: Confronting Extinction from the Age of Jefferson to the Age of Ecology. by Mark V. Barrow, Jr. The University of Chicago Press 2009. 512 p.
ISBN 9780226038148
Grades: Adult   333.95
1. Wildlife conservation 2. Rare and endangered animals 3. Extinction 4. Rare and endangered plants 5. Wildlife 6. United States 7. Nature Writing — Animal Studies — Endangered Species

LC 2008049085

Explores the early history of wildlife conservation in the United States, including early naturalists like John James Audubon and John Muir, and public reactions to such extinctions as the passenger pigeon.

"The author retraces the history of the earliest European and North American naturalists, from those who refused to believe that species comprising a perfect, stable world could go extinct, to the acceptance of extinction at the hands of humans and the legal mechanisms created to halt it. Professionals in ecology, conservation biology, and wildlife management and readers interested in natural history will find this book hard to put down." —*Choice*

Includes bibliographical references and index.

Ellis, Richard
Tuna: A Love Story. by Richard Ellis. Knopf 2008. xi, 334 p. : Illustration
ISBN 9780307267153
Grades: 11 12 Adult   333.95
1. Tuna 2. Rare and endangered fishes 3. Overfishing 4. Fisheries 5. Fish farming 6. Fishing 7. Social life and customs 8. Japan 9. 21st century 10. History writing — Microhistory 11. Food writing — History and microhistory 12. Nature Writing — Animal Studies — Fish and Fishing 13. Adult books for young adults

LC 2007052253

Examines the natural history of the tuna, one of the world's most endangered marine animals, revealing how the increasing demand for sushi has caused a devastating overfishing of the tuna and detailing the implications of its potential extinction.

Includes bibliographical references.

Goldfarb, Ben
Eager: The Surprising, Secret Life of Beavers and Why They Matter. Ben Goldfarb; foreword by Dan Flores. Chelsea Green Publishing 2018. 240 p.
ISBN 9781603587396
Grades: Adult   333.95
1. Beavers 2. Wildlife conservation 3. Ecology 4. Ecosystem management 5. Wetlands 6. Beaver lodges 7. Environmentalism 8. Biotic communities 9. Habitats 10. Erosion 11. North America 12. Nature Writing — Animal Studies

LC 2018004621

Booklist Editors' Choice, 2018.

An environmental journalist discusses why beavers are so important to the ecosystem and follows a growing number of passionate "Beaver Believers," including scientists, ranchers and regular citizens, who are working to help restore the helpful rodent to its habitat.

"Goldfarb traveled the country to observe researchers, beaver damage mitigators, county engineers, hydrologists, and wildlife biologists, all working with beavers and studying their positive effects on ecosystems from the western deserts to the replenishing forests of the east. Beavers are kind of magical, Goldfarb tells us: They can make wetlands appear." —*Booklist*

Includes bibliographical references and index.

Goodall, Jane
★ *The* **Ten** *Trusts: What We Must Do to Care for the Animals We Love.* Jane Goodall and Marc Bekoff. Harper San Francisco 2002. xx, 200 p.
ISBN 9780062517579
Grades: 11 12 Adult   333.95
1. Animal rights 2. Animal welfare 3. Wildlife conservation 4. Effect of humans on nature 5. Human-animal relationships 6. Nature Writing — Animal Studies 7. Adult books for young adults

LC 2002068717

The scientist who documented the lives of chimpanzees joins an animal behaviorist to present ten fundamental principles designed to show readers how to live in harmony with the animal kingdom.

"An accessible, compelling, and important expose." —*Booklist*

Includes bibliographical references (p. [187]-200).

Greenberg, Paul
American Catch: The Fight for Our Local Seafood. Paul Greenberg. The Penguin Press 2014. 320 p.

ESSENTIAL AND RECOMMENDED TITLES
333.95 Biological resources

ISBN 9781594204487
Grades: Adult   **333.95**
1. Seafood 2. Seafood industry and trade 3. Food habits 4. Imports 5. Salmon fisheries 6. Oysters 7. Food writing — Investigations
LC 2014005395

In 2005, the United States imported twelve billion dollars worth of seafood, nearly double what we had imported ten years earlier. During that same period, our seafood exports rose by a third. In American Catch, our foremost fish expert Paul Greenberg looks to New York oysters, gulf shrimp, and Alaskan salmon to reveal how it came to be that 91 percent of the seafood Americans eat is foreign.

Four Fish: The Future of the Last Wild Food. by Paul Greenberg. Penguin Press 2010. 284 p.
ISBN 9781594202568
Grades: Adult   **333.95**
1. Fish farming 2. Fishery management 3. Fishing 4. Fishing industry and trade 5. Salmon 6. Cod 7. Tuna 8. Nature Writing — Animal Studies — Fish and Fishing 9. Food writing — Investigations 10. Adult books for young adults
LC 2010001276

James Beard Foundation Book Awards, Writing and Literature, 2011; New York Times Notable Book, 2010.

Award-winning writer and lifelong fisherman Paul Greenberg takes us on a culinary journey, exploring the history of the fish that dominate our menus—salmon, sea bass, cod, and tuna—and investigating where each stands at this critical moment in time.

"The narrative is grounded in common sense and anchored by first-rate, on-scene reporting from the Yukon and Mekong Rivers, Lake Bardawil in the Sinai Peninsula and the waters off the coasts of Long Island, Greece, Hawaii and the Shetland Islands. Hugely informative, sincere and infectiously curious and enthusiastic." —*Kirkus*

Includes index.

Hanes, Stephanie

White Man's Game: Saving Animals, Rebuilding Eden, and Other Myths of Conservation in Africa. Stephanie Hanes. Metropolitan Books, Henry Holt and Company 2017. 288 p.
ISBN 9780805097160
Grades: Adult   **333.95**
1. Philanthropy 2. Culture conflict 3. Wildlife conservation 4. environmentalists 5. Philanthropists 6. Mozambique 7. Southern Africa
LC 2016034296

A behind-the-scenes account of the celebrated but troubled Gorongosa wildlife preserve cites the revival work of millionaire philanthropist Greg Carr and how Western conservation efforts are colliding with African culture.

In straightforward and fervent prose, Hanes gives readers 'A new way of thinking about nature, conservation, and the pitfalls of best intentions.' —*Publishers Weekly*

Includes bibliographical references and index.

Horwitz, Josh

War of the Whales: A True Story. Joshua Horwitz. Simon & Schuster 2014. 448 p.
ISBN 9781451645019
Grades: Adult   **333.95**
1. Reynolds, Joel 2. Military secrets 3. Whales 4. Military cover-ups 5. Marine mammals 6. Submarines 7. Nature Writing — Animal Studies — Fish and Fishing 8. History writing — Military
LC 2015301075

Green Prize for Sustainable Literature: Adult Nonfiction, 2015.

Documents the efforts of crusading lawyer Joel Reynolds and marine biologist Ken Balcolm to expose a covert U.S. Navy sub detection system that caused whales to beach themselves, an effort that challenged Ken's loyalties and pitted them against powerful military adversaries.

"Based on years of interviews and research, Horwitz delivers a powerful, engrossing narrative that raises serious questions about the unchecked use of secrecy by the military to advance its institutional power." —*Kirkus*

Kurlansky, Mark

Cod: A Biography of the Fish That Changed the World. Mark Kurlansky. Walker and Co. 1997. VIII, 294 p. : Illustration; Map; Color
ISBN 9780802713261
Grades: 11 12 Adult   **333.95**
1. Cod 2. Fisheries 3. Cod fishing 4. Fishing 5. Canada 6. North Atlantic Ocean 7. Food writing — History and microhistory 8. History writing — Microhistory
LC 97012165

Booklist Editors' Choice, 1997.

A history of the fish that has led to wars, stirred revolutions, sustained economies and diets, and helped in the settlement of North America features photographs, drawings, and recipes, as well as the natural history of this much sought after fish.

"This book offers maximum readability, plenty of handsome illustrations, and a 40-page appendix of superlatively annotated recipes." —*Booklist*

Colored maps on endpapers; Includes bibliographical references (p. [277]-282) and index.

Magdalena, Carlos

The Plant Messiah: Adventures in Search of the World's Rarest Species. Carlos Magdalena. Doubleday 2018. 272 p.
ISBN 9780385543613
Grades: Adult   **333.95**
1. Magdalena, Carlos 2. Horticulturists 3. Botanists 4. Rare and endangered plants 5. Plant conservation 6. Autobiographies and memoirs 7. Life stories — Nature and outdoors 8. Nature writing — Personal responses
LC 2017027303

In The Plant Messiah, Magdalena takes readers from the Amazon to the jungles of Mauritius to deep within the Australian Outback in search of the rare and the vulnerable. Back in the lab, we watch as he develops groundbreaking, left-field techniques for rescuing species from extinction, encouraging them to propagate and thrive once again. Along the way, he offers moving, heartfelt stories about the secrets contained within these incredible organisms.

"Magdalenas paean to flora is bound to enthrall readers and get them thinking more fully about plants." —*Publishers Weekly*

Mooallem, Jon

Wild Ones: A Sometimes Dismaying, Weirdly Reassuring Story About Looking at People Looking at Animals in America. Jon Mooallem. The Penguin Press 2013. 339 pages
ISBN 9781594204425
Grades: 11 12 Adult   **333.95**
1. Mooallem, Jon 2. Cultural property 3. Wildlife 4. Wildlife conservation 5. Animals 6. Rare and endangered animals 7. Polar bear 8. Butterflies 9. Rare and endangered insects 10. Whooping cranes 11. Environmentalists 12. Human-animal relationships 13. Nature Writing — Animal Studies 14. Adult books for young adults
LC Bl2013021689

New York Times Notable Book, 2013.

Tracks the dynamic relevance of America's animals throughout history to illuminate current extinction threats, tracing the author's tour of environmental regions with his young daughter to examine the conservation efforts for such species as the polar bear and the whooping crane.

Includes bibliographical references and index.

Orenstein, Ronald I.

Ivory, Horn and Blood: Behind the Elephant and Rhinoceros Poaching Crisis. Ronald Orenstein. Firefly Books 2013. 216 p. : Color illustration
ISBN 9781770852273
Grades: 9 10 11 12 Adult   **333.95**
1. Poaching 2. Elephants 3. Rhinoceros 4. Rare and endangered animals 5. Ivory poaching 6. Wild animal smuggling 7. Wildlife conservation 8. Ivory smuggling 9. African elephant 10. Indian elephant 11. Canadian literature 12. Nature Writing — Animal Studies — Endangered Species 13. Adult books for young adults

An in-depth look at the illegal ivory trade and the poaching crisis of African elephants and Vietnamese rhinoceroses.

Includes bibliographical references (p. [194]-211), Internet addresses and index.

Wilson, Edward O.
The Diversity of Life. Edward O. Wilson. W. W. Norton 1999. 424 p. : Illustration; Color; Map
ISBN 9780393319408
Grades: Adult   333.95
1. Biodiversity 2. Genetic resources conservation 3. Conservation of natural resources 4. Environmentalism 5. Effect of humans on nature 6. Science Writing — Biology

LC 00265625
National Book Critics Circle Award for Nonfiction finalist, 1992.

This classic by the distinguished Harvard entomologist tells how life on earth evolved and became diverse, and now, how diversity and life are endangered by us, truly. While Wilson contributed a great deal to environmental ethics by calling for the preservation of whole ecosystems rather than individual species, his environmentalism appears too anthropocentric: "We should judge every scrap of biodiversity as priceless while we learn to use it and come to understand what it means to humanity." And: "Signals abound that the loss of life's diversity endangers not just the body but the spirit." This reprint of the 1992 Belknap Press publication contains a new foreword.

"Identifying five natural events that have disrupted evolution and global diversity (climatic changes, meteorite strikes), Wilson maintains that the present sixth great extinction is being caused by human neglect and ignorance. This important book is highly recommended." —*Library Journal*

Includes bibliographical references and index; Originally published: Cambridge, MA : Belknap Press of Harvard University Press, 1992.

The Future of Life. Edward O. Wilson. Alfred A. Knopf 2002. xxiv, 229 p. : Illustration
ISBN 9780679450788
Grades: Adult   333.95
1. Rare and endangered animals 2. Rare and endangered plants 3. Extinction 4. Nature conservation 5. Environmental degradation 6. Nature Writing — Animal Studies — Endangered Species

LC 2001038316
ALA Notable Book, 2003; New York Times Notable Book, 2002.

Presents an impassioned call for urgent action to save the Earth's biological heritage, identifying essential species that are threatened with extinction while identifying ways they can be saved and exploring the importance of conservation.

"Wilson seeks to reconcile the tensions between capitalists and environmentalists. Whether he does so is debatable, but he undoubtedly contributes to the discussion." —*Library Journal*

Includes bibliographical references and index.

Half-Earth: Our Planet's Fight for Life. Edward O. Wilson. Liveright Publishing Corporation, a division of W. W. Norton & Company 2016. 256 p.
ISBN 9781631490828
Grades: Adult   333.95
1. Social evolution 2. Human evolution 3. Evolution 4. Biodiversity conservation 5. Biosphere reserves 6. Human ecology 7. Effect of humans on nature 8. Philosophy 9. Science Writing — Biology

LC 2015041784
A conclusion to the trilogy by the Pulitzer Prize-winning author of the National Book Award-finalistThe Meaning of Human Existence argues that humanity must consider the histories of millions of other Earth species and increase the planet's regions of natural reserves in order to prevent future mass extinctions.

"This startling, courageous, many will say wildly quixotic vision of a truly global preservation effort is guaranteed to stoke the fires of environmental debate." —*Booklist*

A Window on Eternity: Gorongosa and Biodiversity. Edward O. Wilson; photographs by Piotr Naskrecki. Simon & Schuster 2014. 228 p.
ISBN 9781476747415
Grades: Adult   333.95
1. Biodiversity 2. Nature conservation 3. Natural history 4. Restoration ecology 5. Mozambique 6. Nature Writing — General 7. Adult books for young adults

LC 2013032607
Featuring beautiful full-color photographs by two of the world's best wildlife photographers, a world-renowned biologist and Pulitzer Prize-winner tells the extraordinary story of how Gorongosa National Park in Mozambique was destroyed, restored and continues to evolve.

"Wilson (Letters to a Young Scientist) presents a lyrical ode to biodiversity within the framework of a memoir of his work in Mozambique's Gorongosa National Park, helping to rebuild it from the loss of nearly all of its megafauna as it was neglected, repurposed as a battleground, and destroyed by poachers during the 16-year civil war." —*Publishers Weekly*

Simon & Schuster nonfiction original hardcover—Title page verso; Includes index.

333.95822 Rare and endangered birds

Hirschfeld, Erik
The World's Rarest Birds. Erik Hirschfeld, Andy Swash & Robert Still; with contributions by Nick Langley … [et al.]; and illustrations by Tomasz Cofta. Princeton University Press 2013. 360 p. : Illustration; Color; Map
ISBN 9780691155968
Grades: Adult   333.95822
1. Rare and endangered birds 2. Extinct birds 3. Bird protection 4. Reference books 5. Nature writing — Animal Studies — Birds and Birding 6. Nature writing — Animal Studies — Endangered Species

LC 2012945960
This illustrated book vividly depicts the most threatened birds on Earth. It provides up-to-date information from BirdLife International on the threats each species faces, and the measures being taken to save them. Today, 590 birds species are classified as Endangered or Critically Endangered, or now only exist in captivity. This landmark publication features stunning photographs of 515 of these species—including the results of a prestigious international photographic competition organized specificallyfor this book. This is the first time that images of many of these birds have been published. It also showcases meticulously accurate illustrations by acclaimed wildlife artist Tomasz Cofta for the 75 speciies of which no photographs are known to exist.

Includes index.

335 Socialism and related systems

Bregman, Rutger
Utopia for Realists: How We Can Build the Ideal World. Rutger Bregman. Little, Brown & Company 2017. 272 pages
ISBN 9780316471893
Grades: Adult   335
1. Utopias 2. Social forecasting 3. Wealth 4. Income 5. Work 6. Boundaries 7. Politics and global affairs — Political philosophy 8. Society and culture — Philosophy

LC Bl2017009661
A noted Dutch journalist and economist proposes an outline for a new worldwide Utopia, with central tenets including a shortened work week, a guaranteed basic income for all, wealth redistribution, and open borders everywhere.

"A provocative pleasure to contemplate." —*Kirkus*

Butterworth, Alex
The World That Never Was: A True Story of Dreamers, Schemers, Anarchists & Secret Agents. Alex Butterworth. Pantheon Books 2010. 528 p.
ISBN 9780375425110
Grades: Adult   335

ESSENTIAL AND RECOMMENDED TITLES
335.4 Marxian systems

1. Anarchism 2. Anarchists 3. Revolutionaries 4. Radicalism 5. United States 6. History writing — Europe
LC 2009048115

A history of anarchism in the late 19th century is presented through the stories of violent revolutionaries, the secret police who tracked them and famous figures who played lesser-known roles, in a chronicle that traces the Paris Commune of 1871 through the 1905 Russian Revolution.

Includes bibliographical references and index.

Ghodsee, Kristen Rogheh
Everyday Utopia: What 2,000 Years of Wild Experiments Can Teach Us About the Good Life. Kristen R. Ghodsee. Simon & Schuster 2023. 352 p.
ISBN 9781982190217
Grades: Adult   335

1. Utopias 2. Everyday life 3. Happiness 4. Harmony 5. Feminism 6. Society and culture — Philosophy 7. Politics and global affairs — Political philosophy

A leading feminist thinker looks back on 2,000 years of utopian thinking and experiments and presents a vision for how to build more contented and connected societies and live the good life every day.

"Clear-eyed yet exuberant, wide-ranging yet intimate, this is an inspiring call for imagining a better future." —*Publishers Weekly*

Johnson, Steven
The Infernal Machine: A True Story of Dynamite, Terror, and the Rise of the Modern Detective. Steven Johnson. Crown 2024. xix, 346 p.
ISBN 9780593443958
Grades: Adult   335

1. Woods, Arthur, 1870-1942 2. Berkman, Alexander, 1870-1936 3. Goldman, Emma, 1869-1940 4. Police 5. Detectives 6. Anarchists 7. Women anarchists 8. Labor movement 9. Bombings 10. Assassination 11. Radicalism 12. Terrorism 13. Immigrants 14. Dynamite 15. Technology 16. Undercover operations 17. Law enforcement 18. Police surveillance 19. New York City history 20. New York City 21. First World War era (1914-1918) 22. History writing — Early 20th century — United States 23. Politics and global affairs — Terrorism 24. True Crime — Historical Crime 25. True Crime — Investigations and Trials 26. Nonfiction that reads like fiction
LC 2023047189

This engrossing account of the epic struggle between the anarchists who terrorized the streets of New York and the detectives who transformed policing to meet the threat reveals a mostly forgotten period of political conviction, scientific discovery, assassination plots, bombings, undercover operations and innovative sleuthing.

"Johnson's vivid, eye-opening history chronicles epic labor-movement battles, terrorist bombings failed and tragic, backlash against immigrants, love affairs, undercover operations, courtroom dramas, and prison life in a fast-paced narrative, rich in cinematic moments and resonance." —*Booklist*

Includes bibliographical references and index.

335.4 Marxian systems

Marx, Karl
★ *Capital: An Abridged Edition.* Karl Marx; edited with an introduction and notes by David McLellan. Oxford University Press 2008. xxxii, 499 p.
ISBN 9780199535705
Grades: 11 12 Adult   335.4

1. Capital 2. Economics 3. Politics and global affairs — General
LC 2008274361

A classic of early modernism, Capital combines vivid historical detail with economic analysis to produce a bitter denunciation of mid-Victorian capitalist society. It has proved to be the most influential work in twentieth-century social science; Marx did for social science what Darwin had done for biology. This is the only abridged edition to take into account the whole of Capital.

First issued as a World's Classic paperback 1995, reissued as an Oxford World's Classic paperback in 1999, reissued in 2008—T.P. verso; Includes indexes.

335.4092 Marxists

Hunt, Tristram
Marx's General: The Revolutionary Life of Friedrich Engels. Tristram Hunt. Metropolitan Books 2009. xii, 430 p, 16 p. of plates : Illustration; Portrait
ISBN 9780805080254
Grades: Adult   335.4092

1. Engels, Friedrich, 1820-1895 2. Communism 3. Communists 4. Ideology 5. Political science 6. Philosophy 7. Biographies 8. History writing — Europe — United Kingdom 9. Life stories — People in history
LC 2009003845

Elizabeth Longford Prize for Historical Biography, 2010.

A remarkable new biography from one of Britain's leading young historians that recovers the co-founder of communism from the shadows of history, portraying how one of the great "bon viveurs" of Victorian Britain reconciled his exuberant personal life with his radical political philosophy.

Includes bibliographical references (p. [369]-410) and index.

335.43 Communism

Lovell, Julia
Maoism: A Global History. Julia Lovell. Knopf 2019. 544 pages
ISBN 9780525656043
Grades: Adult   335.43

1. Mao, Zedong, 1893-1976 2. Ideology 3. Politics and culture 4. International relations 5. Communism 6. Economics 7. Chinese history 8. China 9. 20th century 10. Politics and global affairs — Political philosophy 11. History writing — Communist China — Asia — China
LC 2019010428

Cundill Prize in History, 2019.

An examination of the ideas and political legacy of Mao Zedong traces his role in such events as the Cold War, the Vietnam War and the Cambodian genocide, sharing insight into the violent reverberations that continue to shape today's world.

Includes bibliographical references and index.

Pipes, Richard
Communism: A History. Richard Pipes. Modern Library 2001. xi, 175 p.
ISBN 9780679640509
Grades: 11 12 Adult   335.43

1. Marxism 2. Communism 3. History writing — General 4. Adult books for young adults
LC 2001275458

Here is an exploration of a promising theory that, when put into practice, wreaked havoc on the world. An expert on communism, Richard Pipes follows the history of the Soviet Union from the 1917 revolution to the Cold War, and finally, to its deterioration and collapse.

"As a brief, polemical diatribe...this short account of communism should provoke and instruct." —*Library Journal*

Includes bibliographic references and index.

336.200973 Taxes — United States

Burman, Leonard
Taxes in America: What Everyone Needs to Know. Leonard E. Burman, Joel Slemrod. Oxford University Press 2020. 337 p. : Illustration
ISBN 9780190920852
Grades: Adult   336.200973

1. Taxation 2. Business and economics — General

Arguments about taxation are among the most heated- no other topic is as influential to the role of government and the distribution of costs and benefits in America. But while understanding of our tax system is of vital importance, the complexity can create confusion. Two of America's leading authorities on taxes, Leonard E. Burman and Joel Slemrod, bring clarity in this concise explanation of how our tax system works, how it affects people and businesses, and how it might be improved.

Includes bibliographical references and index.

Reid, T. R.
A Fine Mess: A Global Quest for a Simpler, Fairer, and More Efficient Tax System. T.R. Reid. Penguin Group USA 2017. 256 p.
ISBN 9781594205514
Grades: Adult   336.200973
1. Taxation 2. Tax policy 3. Public finance 4. Government spending policy 5. Economic policy 6. Income tax 7. Wealth 8. Budget 9. Economics 10. United States 11. 21st century 12. Business and economics — Economics — World economy 13. Politics and global affairs — World politics — United States
LC 2017301115
The Washington Post correspondent and best-selling author of the Healing of America presents an international investigation into America's failing tax code to share plainspoken assessments of current problems and what the author believes can be learned from other democratic nations.

"Washington Post correspondent Reid…examines taxation in countries around the world to find alternatives to the American system in this highly readable and informative book." —*Publishers Weekly*

336.3 Public debt and expenditures

Kirshner, Jodie Adams
★ *Broke: Hardship and Resilience in a City of Broken Promises.* Jodie Adams Kirshner. St. Martin's Press 2019. 352 pages
ISBN 9781250220639
Grades: Adult   336.3
1. Bankruptcy 2. Urban problems 3. Urban poor people 4. Urban economics 5. Cities and towns 6. Marginalized people 7. Racism 8. Poverty 9. Economics 10. Michigan 11. Detroit, Michigan 12. United States 13. 2010s 14. Society and culture — Wealth and class — Poverty 15. Society and culture — Urban and regional studies
LC 2019024268
Traces the experiences of seven Detroit residents throughout the city's 2013 bankruptcy, revealing the larger human ramifications of poor urban policies, restorative negligence and municipal distress for hundreds of thousands living below the poverty line.

Includes bibliographical references and index.

337 International economics

Daunton, M. J.
★ *The Economic Government of the World: 1933-2023.* Martin Daunton. Farrar Straus and Giroux 2023. 1024 p.
ISBN 9780374146412
Grades: Adult   337
1. Economic history 2. International economic relations 3. Globalization (Economics) 4. Economic policy 5. International finance 6. Economic development 7. International relations 8. Income inequality 9. Nationalism 10. Financial institutions 11. 20th century 12. 21st century 13. Business and economics — Economics — World economy
LC 2023021274
A distinguished economic historian pulls back the curtain on the institutions and individuals who have created and managed the global economy over the last 90 years while calling for a return to a more just and equitable form of globalization.

"The result is a robust history that elucidates the human impact of the machinery of global trade and finance." —*Publishers Weekly*

Includes bibliographical references and index.

Stiglitz, Joseph E.
Globalization and Its Discontents. Joseph E. Stiglitz. W. W. Norton 2002. xxii, 282 p.
ISBN 9780393051247
Grades: Adult   337
1. International economic integration 2. International trade regulation 3. International finance 4. Globalization (Economics) 5. Commercial policy 6. World economy 7. Politics and government 8. United States 9. History writing — General 10. Business and economics — Economics — Socioeconomics 11. Business and economics — Economics — World economy
LC 2002023148
Examines the effects of global economic policies on developing nations, discussing agencies and concepts including the International Monetary Fund, the East Asia crisis, trade laws, fair markets, and privatization.

"This smart, provocative study contributes significantly to the ongoing globalization debate." —*Publishers Weekly*

Includes bibliographical references and index.

337.09 International economics — History

Conway, Edmund
The Summit: Bretton Woods, 1944: J. M. Keynes and the Reshaping of the Global Economy. Ed Conway. Pegasus Books 2015. 480 p.
ISBN 9781605986814
Grades: Adult   337.09
1. Keynes, John Maynard, 1883-1946 2. White, Harry Dexter, 1892-1948 3. International economic relations 4. Economic development 5. Financial crises 6. Economic history 7. Monetary policy 8. International finance 9. 20th century 10. Business and economics — Economics — History
A narrative history of the World War II-era economic summit offers insight into its dramas and achievements, discussing such topics as John Maynard Keynes' heart attack, the corruption of Harry Dexter White and the machinations of the Russians and French.

"This is a gripping story for both general readers and scholars interested in World War II, the Cold War, and domestic and international political economy. The author knows how to write for those who are less informed about economics while telling the history of the turbulent conference through its leading characters and updating its legacy today. An essential purchase on this topic." —*Library Journal*

Includes bibliographical references and index.

338 Production

Clark, Taylor
Starbucked: A Double Tall Tale of Caffeine, Commerce, and Culture. Taylor Clark. Little, Brown 2007. 297 p.
ISBN 9780316013482
Grades: Adult   338
1. Coffee industry and trade 2. Coffee 3. Coffee shops 4. Corporate culture 5. Business 6. Multinational corporations 7. Social life and customs 8. United States history 9. United States 10. 20th century 11. 21st century 12. Business and economics — Industries — Agriculture and food 13. Food writing — Non-alcoholic beverages
LC 2007013074
Traces the meteoric rise of the Starbucks chain while evaluating the myriad ways in which the coffeehouse movement has impacted everyday life, in an investigative account that credits specific societal groups with the corporation's success.

"This is a breezily written business yarn with plenty of big-picture punch." —*Christian Science Monitor*

Includes bibliographical references (p. 275-289) and index.

ESSENTIAL AND RECOMMENDED TITLES
338.04 Entrepreneurship

Scott, Kevin
Reprogramming the American Dream: From Rural America to Silicon Valley—making Ai Serve Us All. Kevin Scott, with Greg Shaw; foreword by J. D. Vance. HarperBusiness 2020. 304 p.
ISBN 9780062879875
Grades: Adult   338
1. Artificial intelligence 2. Rural poor people 3. Technological innovations 4. Economic development 5. Economic policy 6. Technology policy 7. Job security 8. Rural sociology 9. Business and economics — Industries — Technology 10. Society and culture — Wealth and class — Poverty 11. Science Writing — Computing, the Internet, and Technology

There are two prevailing stories about AI: for heartland low- and middle-skill workers, a dystopian tale of steadily increasing job destruction; for urban knowledge workers and the professional class, a utopian tale of enhanced productivity and convenience. But there is a third way to look at this technology that will revolutionize the workplace and ultimately the world. Kevin Scott argues that AI has the potential to create abundance and opportunity for everyone and help solve some of our most vexing problems.

"Microsoft chief technology officer Scott offers a hopeful but not wholly convincing vision of how artificial intelligence might rescue America's rust belt." —*Publishers Weekly*

Waterhouse, Benjamin C.
One Day I'll Work for Myself: The Dream and Delusion That Conquered America. Benjamin C. Waterhouse. W W Norton & Co. 2024. 288 p.
ISBN 9780393868210
Grades: Adult   338
1. Entrepreneurs 2. Entrepreneurship 3. Ownership 4. Self-reliance 5. Business failures 6. Income inequality 7. Economic policy 8. Political culture 9. Popular culture 10. United States history 11. United States 12. Business and economics — Economics — Socioeconomics 13. Business and economics — Business leaders and entrepreneurs 14. Business and economics — Economics — History

The spirit of entrepreneurship runs deep in American culture and history, in the films we watch and the books we read, in our political rhetoric, and in the music piping through our speakers. What makes the dream of self-employment so alluring, so pervasive in today's world? Benjamin C. Waterhouse suggests the modern cult of the hustle is a direct consequence of economic failures—bad jobs, stagnant wages, and inequality—since the 1970s. Waterhouse traces a new narrative history of business in America, populated with vivid characters, from the activists, academics, and work-from-home gurus who hailed business ownership as our economic salvation to the upstarts who took the plunge.

"Readers will want to check this out before quitting their day job." —*Publishers Weekly*

338.04 Entrepreneurship

Stone, Brad
The Upstarts: How Uber, Airbnb, and the Killer Companies of the New Silicon Valley Are Changing the World. Brad Stone. Little, Brown & Co. 2017. 384 p.
ISBN 9780316388399
Grades: Adult   338.04
1. Entrepreneurship 2. Computer industry and trade 3. High technology 4. Technological innovations 5. Business innovations 6. Business 7. Silicon Valley, California 8. Business and economics — Industries — Technology
LC 2016958932

The world today is vastly different than it was even ten years ago, and it is due to the upstarts. In THE UPSTARTS, Brad Stone provides the rollicking narrative that shows the how our latest—and perhaps greatest—technological wave was born.

"Stone's account is illuminating reading for the business-minded." —*Kirkus*

338.1 Specific kinds of industries

Ackerman-Leist, Philip
Rebuilding the Foodshed: How to Create Local, Sustainable, and Secure Food Systems. Philip Ackerman-Leist. Post Carbon Institute; 2013. 304 p.
ISBN 9781603584234
Grades: Adult   338.1
1. Food supply 2. Local foods 3. Food security 4. Agriculture 5. Sustainable agriculture 6. Nature Writing — General 7. Society and culture — General 8. Food writing — Investigations
LC 2012043955

Showcasing some of the most promising, replicable models for growing, processing, and distributing sustainably grown food, this book points the reader toward the next stages of the food revolution. It also covers the full landscape of the burgeoning local-food movement, from rural to suburban to urban, and from backyard gardens to large-scale food enterprises.

"Dense with information and studded with numerous graphs and charts, this book provides a deeper understanding of what principles need to change in order to create local food environments." —*Kirkus*

Includes bibliographical references and index.

Faruqi, Sonia
Project Animal Farm: An Accidental Journey into the Secret World of Farming and the Truth About ... Our Food. Sonia Faruqi. Pegasus Books 2015. 336 p.
ISBN 9781605987989
Grades: Adult   338.1
1. Farms 2. Animal welfare 3. Organic farming 4. Factory farming 5. Livestock 6. Animal industry and trade 7. Food writing — Investigations
LC Bl2015024464

Traces the author's covert and sometimes life-risking tour of animal farms throughout the world to expose animal cruelty and identify ways to farm compassionately while promoting human health, economics, and environmental consciousness.

"Not for the fainthearted, but a good wake-up call for those concerned with decent treatment of animals and healthy food on the table." —*Kirkus*

Freeman, Andrea
★ *Ruin* Their Crops on the Ground: The Politics of Food in the United States, from the Trail of Tears to School Lunch. Andrea Freeman. Metropolitan Books 2024. 272 p.
ISBN 9781250871046
Grades: Adult   338.1
1. Food supply 2. Food security 3. Food habits 4. Food industry and trade 5. Agribusiness 6. Race (Social sciences) 7. Poverty 8. Diet and disease 9. Processed foods 10. Inequality 11. Food policy 12. United States history 13. United States 14. Food writing — History and microhistory 15. Business and economics — Industries — Agriculture and food 16. History writing — United States
LC 2023055948

From frybread to government cheese, Ruin Their Crops on the Ground draws on over fifteen years of research to argue that U.S. food law and policy have created and maintained racial and social inequality. In an epic, sweeping account, Andrea Freeman, who pioneered the term "food oppression," moves from colonization to slavery to the Americanization of immigrant food culture, to the commodities supplied to Native reservations, to milk as a symbol of white supremacy. This book will permanently upend the notion that we freely and equally choose what we put on our plates.

"This American history, rife with predation and injustice, leaves readers with plenty of challenges for both present and future." —*Booklist*

Includes bibliographical references and index.

Hewitt, Ben
★ *The Town* That Food Saved: How One Community Found Vitality in Local Food. Ben Hewitt. Rodale 2009. 256 p.
ISBN 9781605296869
Grades: 11 12 Adult   338.1

1. Food supply 2. Food industry and trade 3. Sustainable agriculture 4. Entrepreneurship 5. Sustainable societies 6. Local foods 7. Entrepreneurs 8. Small town life 9. 21st century 10. Food writing — General 11. Adult books for young adults

LC 2009034294

Relates how the farming community of Hardwick, Vermont, developed a sustainable, local food system with its own support network where entrepreneurs share advice, equipment, and business plans, and shows how the town is becoming a model for other communities.

"Adroitly balancing professional neutrality with personal commitment, Hewitt engagingly examines this paradigm shift in the way a community feeds its citizens." —*Booklist*

Monbiot, George
★ *Regenesis: Feeding the World Without Devouring the Llanet*. George Monbiot. Penguin Group USA 2022. 320 p.
ISBN 9780143135968
Grades: Adult   338.1
1. Environmental degradation 2. Food supply 3. Soil ecology 4. Agriculture 5. Food industry and trade 6. Farms 7. Climate change 8. Politics and global affairs — Environmental issues and policies 9. Nature Writing — Environmental Issues

Farming is the world's greatest cause of environmental destruction. We criticise urban sprawl, but farming sprawls across thirty times as much land. We have ploughed, fenced and grazed great tracts of the planet, felling forests, killing wildlife, and poisoning rivers and oceans to feed ourselves. Yet millions still go hungry. Now the food system itself is beginning to falter. This new book shows us that we can resolve the biggest of our dilemmas and feed the world without devouring the planet.

"Passionate and informative, this is a solid look at farming's effects on a changing planet." —*Publishers Weekly*

Rude, Emelyn
Tastes Like Chicken: A History of America's Favorite Bird. Emelyn Rude. Pegasus 2016. 272 p.
ISBN 9781681771632
Grades: Adult   338.1
1. Chickens 2. Domestic animals 3. Livestock 4. Food 5. Food writing — History and microhistory

LC Bl2016031510

From the domestication of the bird nearly ten thousand years ago to its current status as our go-to meat, the history of this seemingly commonplace bird is anything but ordinary.

"Readers of food histories such as Mark Kurlansky's Cod will appreciate this engaging, well-researched, and thorough history of America's changing food preferences." —*Library Journal*

Sorvino, Chloe
Raw Deal: Hidden Corruption, Corporate Greed, and the Fight for the Future of Meat. Chloe Sorvino. Atria Books 2022. 240 p.
ISBN 9781982172046
Grades: Adult   338.1
1. Meat industry and trade 2. Corporate greed 3. Corporate mergers 4. Labor exploitation 5. Animal welfare 6. Agribusiness 7. Environmental degradation 8. Meat substitutes 9. United States 10. Business and economics — Industries — Agriculture and food 11. Food writing — Investigations

LC 2022007638

Well before COVID-19 swept across the United States and the chairman of Tyson Foods infamously declared that the food supply chain was dangerously vulnerable, America's meat industry was reaching a breaking point. Years of consolidation, price-fixing, and power grabs by elite industry insiders have harmed consumers and caused environmental destruction. Americans have no idea where their meat comes from. And while that's hurting us, it's also making others rich. Now, financial journalist Chloe Sorvino presents an expansive view of the meat industry and its future as its fundamental weaknesses are laid bare for all to see.

"Though the book's arcane legal and financial discussions are best suited to those with a background in the subject, this is a deeply informed and eye-opening call for change." —*Publishers Weekly*
Includes bibliographical references and index.

Stuart, Andrea
Sugar in the Blood: A Family's Story of Slavery and Empire. Andrea Stuart. Knopf 2013. 448 p.
ISBN 9780307272836
Grades: Adult   338.1
1. Slavery 2. Enslaved people 3. Sugar 4. Sugar industry and trade 5. Agriculture 6. Family history 7. Barbados 8. 17th century 9. History writing — African American — Enslavement — United States 10. History writing — Latin America

LC 2012034259

Presents a history of the interdependence of sugar, slavery and colonial settlement in the New World through the story of the author's ancestors, exploring the myriad connections between sugar cultivation and her family's identity, genealogy and financial stability.

338.10973 Agricultural industries — United States

Berry, Wendell
The Art of Loading Brush: Last Agrarian Writings. Wendell Berry. Counterpoint 2017. 240 p.
ISBN 9781619020382
Grades: Adult   338.10973
1. Political science 2. Agriculture 3. Farm management 4. Environmentalism 5. Land reform 6. Essays 7. Nature Writing — Environmental Issues 8. Politics and global affairs — Environmental issues and policies

LC 2017034645

Wendell Berry's profound critique of American culture has entered its sixth decade, and in this new gathering he reaches with deep devotion toward a long view of Agrarian philosophy. Mr. Berry believes that American cultural problems are nearly always aligned with their agricultural problems, and recent events have shone a terrible spotlight on the divides between our urban and rural citizens. Our communities are as endangered as our landscapes. There is, as Berry outlines, still much work to do, and our daily lives—in hope and affection—must triumph over despair.

"About everything he loves and everything he regrets, he has never written better." —*Booklist*

Bittman, Mark
A Bone to Pick: The Good and Bad News About Food, Along with Wisdom, Insights, and Advice on Diets, Food Safety, Gmos Policy, Farming, and More. Mark Bittman. Clarkson Potter 2015. 256 p.
ISBN 9780804186544
Grades: Adult   338.10973
1. Food industry and trade 2. Agricultural policy 3. Nutrition 4. Diet 5. Essays 6. Food writing — Investigations

LC 2014044874

Mark Bittman made headlines three years ago when it was revealed that, for the first time, the New York Times opinion page would feature a food writer to help us make sense of the tangled webs of food, health, environment, politics, and culture. As an opinion columnist, Mark has delighted us, enraged us, and inspired us to do more for ourselves and our world with the same no-nonsense style. In the tradition of his NYT bestselling Food Matters, this book collects the best of his columns, updated to reflect the latest research, and tied together with new material to give context and show how far we've come in just a few years. What emerges is a collection that shows us the story of who we are as a nation of cooks, eaters, and voters right now.

"The author's keen analysis of the weakness of the Food and Drug Administration and its failures regarding food safety proves especially informative and enraging. Bittman successfully links a sound food system not just to the tastes of foodies (a word the author dislikes), but also to larger public health issues. An in-

ESSENTIAL AND RECOMMENDED TITLES
338.17361 Sugarcane — agricultural economics

telligent rallying cry for anyone seeking a safe and healthy food supply, and all that entails." —*Kirkus*
Collection of articles published in the New York times; Includes index.

Hamilton, Lisa M.
Deeply Rooted: Unconventional Farmers in the Age of Agribusiness. Lisa M. Hamilton. Counterpoint 2009. 230 p.
ISBN 9781593761806
Grades: Adult   338.10973
1. Agribusiness 2. Agriculture 3. Farmers 4. Food writing — Investigations 5. Adult books for young adults
LC 2008050526

A narrative report adds a critical perspective to the national discussion about where our food comes from, exploring key issues as perceived by everyday food growers from a Texas dairyman who battles agribusiness corporations to a tenth-generation rancher in New Mexico who struggles to restore his community's agriculture.

"Hamilton profiles farmers and ranchers who believe that agriculture is not an industry but, rather, a fundamental act that determines whether we as a society will live or die. Hamilton's in-depth portraits of independent farmers offer invaluable perspectives on American agriculture, past and present, while offering hope for a life-sustaining future." —*Booklist*

Logsdon, Gene
Letter to a Young Farmer: How to Live Richly Without Wealth on the New Garden Farm. Gene Logsdon. Chelsea Green Publishing 2017. 224 p.
ISBN 9781603587259
Grades: Adult   338.10973
1. Farm life 2. Agriculture 3. Sustainable agriculture 4. Sustainable living 5. Homesteading 6. Small farms 7. Rural life 8. Farmers 9. Nature 10. Business and economics — Industries — Agriculture and food 11. Nature Writing — Gardens
LC 2016050357

Discusses the author's vision of a nation filled with small-scale "garden farmers" creating a more sustainable, meaningful life for themselves.

"This work serves as a guiding light and lodestar for farmers facing the modern challenges of any farming operation, large or small." —*Publishers Weekly Annex*

338.17361 Sugarcane — agricultural economics

Walvin, James
Sugar: The World Corrupted, from Slavery to Obesity. James Walvin. Pegasus Books 2017. xxiv, 325 pages
ISBN 9781681776774
Grades: Adult   338.17361
1. Sugar 2. Sugar industry and trade 3. Slavery 4. Sugarcane 5. Sugar workers 6. Sugar plantations 7. Luxury 8. Culture 9. Food 10. Food habits 11. Food writing — History and microhistory 12. History writing — Microhistory

Documents the 500-year rise of sugar from a costly luxury to a staple thought to be the root of global health problems, tracing how the industry was established through plantation slavery and how it has shaped modern society.

338.2 Extraction of minerals

Briody, Blaire
The New Wild West: Black Gold, Fracking, and Life in a North Dakota Boomtown. Blaire Briody. St Martins Pr 2017. 384 p.
ISBN 9781250064929
Grades: Adult   338.2
1. Hydraulic fracturing 2. Rural development 3. Oil industry and trade 4. Effect of humans on nature 5. Cities and towns 6. Population 7. North Dakota 8. Nature Writing — Environmental Issues 9. Business and economics — Industries — Energy

An award-winning social justice reporter examines the negative impact of fracking on the sleepy farm community of Williston, North Dakota, tracing how the lure of the American Dream triggered the nation's biggest unregulated boom since the Gold Rush and gave way to regional violence, overcrowding and an impossibly high cost of living.

"Through intertwining disparate experiences, a comprehensive portrait is unveiled." —*Library Journal*

Burgis, Tom
The Looting Machine: Warlords, Oligarchs, Corporations, Smugglers, and the Theft of Africa's Wealth. Tom Burgis. Public Affairs 2015. 320 p.
ISBN 9781610394390
Grades: Adult   338.2
1. Economic development 2. Business 3. Economics 4. Africa 5. Business and economics — Economics — World economy
LC Bl2015011101

In his first book, the Looting Machine, Tom Burgis exposes the truth about the African development miracle: for the resource states, it's a mirage. The oil, copper, diamonds, gold and coltan deposits attract a global network of traders, bankers, corporate extractors and investors who combine with venal political cabals to loot the states' value. And the vagaries of resource-dependent economies could pitch Africa's new middle class back into destitution just as quickly as they climbed out of it. The ground beneath their feet is as precarious as a Congolese mine shaft; their prosperity could spill away like crude from a busted pipeline.

"Essential for understanding the colonial Africa of the past and, even more so, the diverse Africa of today." —*Library Journal*

Burrough, Bryan
The Big Rich: The Rise and Fall of the Greatest Texas Oil Fortunes. Bryan Burrough. Penguin Press 2008. 464 p.
ISBN 9781594201998
Grades: Adult   338.2
1. Oil industry and trade 2. Capitalism 3. Business 4. Money 5. Economics 6. United States history 7. Texas 8. History writing — Regional history — United States 9. Business and economics — Business leaders and entrepreneurs 10. Business and economics — Industries — Energy
LC 2008027043

An account of how Texas oil transformed wealth and power in America is presented through the stories of the state's four most influential oil families, tracing how they rose from modest backgrounds, shaped the government, and bankrolled the nation's largest rise of modern conservatism.

Includes bibliographical references and index.

Kara, Siddharth
Cobalt Red: How the Blood of the Congo Powers Our Lives. Siddharth Kara. St. Martin's Press 2023. 400 p.
ISBN 9781250284303
Grades: Adult   338.2
1. Miners 2. Human rights 3. Mineral industry and trade 4. Environmental degradation 5. Ethics 6. Mines and mineral resources 7. Congo (Democratic Republic) 8. Politics and global affairs — Civil and human rights 9. History Writing — Africa 10. Society and culture — Violence and crime
LC 2022043648

Pulitzer Prize for General Nonfiction finalist, 2024.

An unflinching investigation reveals the human rights abuses behind the Congo's cobalt mining operation—and the moral implications that affect us all.

"Teens researching companies, like Apple and Tesla, that rely on lithium batteries will learn a lot from this hard-charging book." —*Booklist*

"A penetrating exposé on the deliberate smoke screens created by powerful companies to obscure the realities behind the abysmal conditions of cobalt miners in the Congo....The author's well-written, forcefully argued report exposes the widespread, debilitating human ramifications of our device-driven global society." —*Kirkus*

Includes bibliographical references and index.

PUBLIC LIBRARY CORE COLLECTION: NONFICTION
Twentieth Edition

Maass, Peter
Crude World: The Violent Twilight of Oil. Peter Maass. Alfred A. Knopf 2009. 288 p.
ISBN 9781400041695
Grades: Adult   338.2
1. Oil industry and trade 2. Oil production 3. Energy production 4. Oil supply 5. Business and economics — Industries — Energy
LC 2009012303
A stunning and revealing examination of oil's indelible impact on the countries that produce it and the people who possess it, of the power of oil to exacerbate existing problems and create new ones.
This is a Borzoi book; Includes bibliographical references and index.

Maddow, Rachel
Blowout: Corrupted Democracy, Rogue State Russia, and the Richest, Most Destructive Industry on Earth. Rachel Maddow. Crown 2019. 304 p.
ISBN 9780525575474
Grades: Adult   338.2
1. Oil industry and trade 2. Oil executives 3. Business corruption 4. Business and politics 5. Fossil fuels 6. Democracy 7. Corporate power 8. Energy policy 9. Business and economics — Industries — Energy 10. Business and economics — Corruption and scandal 11. Politics and global affairs — World politics
LC 2019026915
The author explains how Big Oil and Gas adversely affect democracy.
Includes index.

Margonelli, Lisa
Oil on the Brain: Adventures from the Pump to the Pipeline. Lisa Margonelli. Nan A. Talese, Doubleday 2007. 324 p.
ISBN 9780385511452
Grades: 11 12 Adult   338.2
1. Oil industry and trade 2. Oil 3. Energy consumption 4. Social life and customs 5. United States 6. 21st century 7. Business and economics — Industries — Energy 8. Adult books for young adults
LC 2006020789
ALA Notable Book, 2008.
Looks at the economics of the petroleum industry and traces how crude oil from fields around the world eventually becomes the gasoline for automobiles.
"By giving voice to the people who are the links in the global oil chain, Margonelli invites us to leapfrog all the rhetoric, dry statistics, and dire pronouncements about oil in order to truly understand it." —*Fast Company*
Includes bibliographical references and index.

Rao, Maya
Great American Outpost: Dreamers, Mavericks, and the Making of an Oil Frontier. Maya Rao. Public Affairs 2018. 336 p.
ISBN 9781610396462
Grades: Adult   338.2
1. Oil industry and trade 2. Oil workers 3. Corruption 4. Eccentrics and eccentricities 5. Rural life 6. North Dakota 7. Society and culture — Urban and regional studies 8. Business and economics — Industries — Energy
LC 2017044028
A journalist, in response to an ad that you could earn $17,000 a month in the Bakken Oilfield of North Dakota, sets out in steel-toed boots to chronicle the largest oil boom since the 1968 discovery of oil in Prudhoe Bay, Alaska, and introduces the colorful cast of characters she encountered who would do just about anything to cash in.

Yergin, Daniel
★ *The Prize: The Epic Quest for Oil, Money, and Power.* Daniel Yergin. Simon & Schuster 1991. 877 p, 32 p. of plates : Illustration; Map
ISBN 9780671799328
Grades: Adult   338.2
1. Oil industry and trade 2. Military strategy 3. World War I 4. World War II 5. World politics 6. Causes of war 7. 20th century 8. History writing — Microhistory
LC 90047575
Pulitzer Prize for General Nonfiction, 1992.
Oil is the dominant player in world politics in this century. Yergin shows how and why oil is the biggest industry in the world and why it caused the two world wars.
"This is a history of the oil industry, from the first oil well ever drilled (near Titusville, Pennsylvania, in 1859) to the Iraqi invasion of Kuwait. It recalls advances in technology, innovations in salesmanship, and wars and truces among corporations and nations." —*The New Yorker*
Includes bibliographical references (p. [848]-873) and index.

338.3 Other extractive industries

Fagan, Brian M.
Fishing: How the Sea Fed Civilization. Brian Fagan. Yale University Press 2017. 352 pages
ISBN 9780300215342
Grades: Adult   338.3
1. Fishing 2. Humans and fish 3. Civilization 4. Fishing equipment 5. Fisheries 6. Food 7. Salt-water fishing 8. Archaeology 9. History writing — Microhistory 10. History writing — Ancient 11. Food writing — History and microhistory
LC 2017934016
Humanity's last major source of food from the wild, and how it enabled and shaped the growth of civilization.
"A much-needed volume for serious students of world history. Highly recommended for readers interested in archaeology, anthropology, ecology, and environmental science." —*Library Journal*

Hilborn, Ray
Overfishing: What Everyone Needs to Know. Ray Hilborn with Ulrike Hilborn. Oxford University Press 2012. xviii, 150 p; (What everyone needs to know)
ISBN 9780199798148
Grades: Adult   338.3
1. Overfishing 2. Sustainable fisheries 3. Fisheries 4. Environmental Policy 5. Science Writing — General 6. Nature Writing — Animal Studies — Fish and Fishing
LC 2011031308
A discussion of overfishing explores the scientific, political, ethical, and economic issues associated with harvesting the ocean's fish, using case studies of fisheries from around the world to answer the issue's most pressing questions.
Includes bibliographical references and index.

Smith, Bren
Eat Like a Fish: My Adventures as a Fisherman Turned Restorative Ocean Farmer. Bren Smith. Alfred A. Knopf 2019. 336 p.
ISBN 9780451494542
Grades: Adult   338.3
1. Smith, Bren 2. Aquaculture 3. Sustainable agriculture 4. Seaweed 5. Fishers 6. Food supply 7. Oceans 8. Shellfish 9. Environmentalism 10. Autobiographies and memoirs 11. Canadian literature 12. Life stories — Nature and outdoors 13. Nature Writing — Environmental Issues 14. Food writing — Memoirs and biographies 15. Adult books for young adults
LC 2018050112
James Beard Foundation Book Awards, Writing and Literature, 2020; Green Prize for Sustainable Literature: Adult Nonfiction, 2020.
Through tales that span from his childhood in Newfoundland to his early years on the high seas aboard commercial fishing trawlers, from pioneering new forms of ocean farming to surfing the frontiers of the food movement, Smith introduces the world of sea-based agriculture, and advocates getting ocean vegetables onto American plates. Here he shows how we can transform our food system while enjoying delicious, nutritious, locally grown food, and how restorative ocean farming has the potential to create millions of new jobs and protect

ESSENTIAL AND RECOMMENDED TITLES
338.4 Secondary industries and services

our planet in the face of climate change, rising populations, and finite food resources.

"Part memoir, part treatise on the life of a professional fisherman, part manual for the future of eating worldwide, this unique book cannot help but make readers think long and hard about the fate of the earth as it faces the challenges of global warming and the outlook for feeding the planet." —*Booklist*

Includes bibliographical references and index.

Strøksnes, Morten Andreas
Shark Drunk: The Art of Catching a Large Shark from a Tiny Rubber Dinghy in a Big Ocean Through Four Seasons. Morten Strøksnes; translated by Tiina Nunnally. Alfred A. Knopf 2017. 320 p.

ISBN 9780451493484

Grades: Adult · **338.3**

1. Fishing 2. Sailing 3. Oceans 4. Male friendship 5. Norway 6. Translations — Norwegian to English 7. Life stories — Nature and outdoors 8. Adventure writing — Adventure travel 9. Nature Writing — Animal Studies

LC 2016044185

Fishing trip! Topically wide-ranging, Shark Drunk documents the quest of award-winning journalist Morten Strøksnes and artist Hugo Aasjord to catch a massive Greenland Shark in the frigid waters near Norway's Lofoten islands. In a rubber dinghy over the course of four seasons, the two friends baited hooks in order to entice the massive shark while they sat, occasionally got wet, reeled in cod, ruminated, and talked. Covering ocean life, poetry, mythology, science, history, and more, this lyrical book reads like a novel and will hook fans of philosophical stories.

"Strksness erudition, salty humor, and unfussy prose yield a fresh, engrossing natural history." —*Publishers Weekly*

338.4 Secondary industries and services

Abramson, John
Sickening. John Abramson. Mariner Books 2022. 288 p.

ISBN 9781328957818

Grades: Adult · **338.4**

1. Drug industry and trade 2. Drugs 3. Prescription drugs 4. Medical care 5. Corruption 6. United States 7. Business and economics — Industries — Medical

Combining patient stories with his own experience serving as an expert in national drug litigation, the author, who has been on the faculty of Harvard Medical School for 20 years, shows how Big Pharma has corrupted American health care and presents a path toward reform.

"Readers interested in learning about the pharmaceutical industry (plus the ways drugs are introduced to healthcare providers, and the deceptions that get particular drugs into a patient's treatment regimen) may find themselves galvanized by what Abramson reveals." —*Library Journal*

Almond, Steve
★ *Candyfreak: A Journey Through the Chocolate Underbelly of America.* Steve Almond. Algonquin Books of Chapel Hill 2004. 266 p.

ISBN 9781565124219

Grades: 11 12 Adult · **338.4**

1. Almond, Steve 2. Candy industry and trade 3. Candy 4. Chocolate 5. Food writing — Investigations 6. History writing — Microhistory 7. Adult books for young adults

LC 2003070801

Alex Award, 2005; Booklist Editors' Choice: Adult Books for Young Adults, 2004; Library Journal Best Books, 2004.

Perhaps you remember the Marathon, Oompahs, Bit-O-Choc, or Kit Kat Dark. Where did they go? Driven by his obsession, stubborn idealism, and the promise of free candy, self-confessed candyfreak Steve Almond takes off on a quest to discover candy's origins in America, to explore little companies that continue to get by on pluck and perseverance, and to witness the glorious excess of candy manufacturing. Part candy porn, part candy polemic, part social history, part confession, Candyfreak explores the role candy plays in our lives as both source of pleasure and escape from pain. By turns ecstatic, comic, and bittersweet, Candyfreak is the story of how Steve Almond grew up on candy—and how, for better and worse, candy has grown up too.

"The author tells how candy shaped his childhood and continues to define his life in ways large and small. Once hundreds of American confectioners delivered regional favorites to consumers, but now the big three of candyHershey, Mars, and Nestlcontrol the market. To find out what happened to those candies of yesteryear, Almond talks to candy collectors and historians and visits a few of the remaining independent candy companies. Flavored with the author's amusingly tart sense of humor, Candyfreak is an intriguing chronicle of the passions that candy inspires and the pleasures it offers." —*Library Journal*

Becker, Elizabeth
Overbooked: The Exploding Business of Travel and Tourism. Elizabeth Becker. Simon & Schuster 2013. 320 p.

ISBN 9781439160992

Grades: Adult · **338.4**

1. Tourism 2. Recreation industry and trade 3. International relations 4. Globalization 5. Environmentalism 6. Travel Writing — General

LC 2012032848

Though the travel industry is relatively new, it's a trillion-dollar business, one of the largest in the world. Pulitzer Prize-winning journalist Elizabeth Becker presents a sobering assessment of what that means for the world economy, the environment, local cultures, historical sites, and individuals. From cruises to safaris—and traveling everywhere from Costa Rica to France—she unveils how the industry's shiny surfaces sometimes hide seedy underpinnings, including government corruption and sex trafficking.

Beckert, Sven
Empire of Cotton: A Global History. Sven Beckert. Knopf 2014. 512 p.

ISBN 9780375414145

Grades: Adult · **338.4**

1. Cotton manufacture 2. Cotton industry and trade 3. Slavery 4. Enslaved people 5. Textile workers 6. Capitalism 7. History writing — Microhistory

LC 2014009320

New York Times Notable Book, 2015; Pulitzer Prize for History finalist, 2015; Cundill Prize in Historical Literature finalist.

The epic story of the rise and fall of the empire of cotton, its centrality in the world economy, and its making and remaking of global capitalism. Sven Beckert's book tells the story of how, in a remarkably brief period, European entrepreneurs and powerful statesmen recast the world's most significant manufacturing industry combining imperial expansion and slave labor with new machines and wage workers to change the world.

"Both chronologically and geographically, this is a wide-ranging saga that examines the role of nation-states, politicians, entrepreneurs, and laborers on every continent. This is not a pretty story, since Beckert shows that this empire often depended upon coercion and violence for its growth and maintenance. This is a highly detailed, provocative work that combines history, economics, and sociology in an effort to show how cotton shaped the modern world." —*Booklist*

Campbell-Kelly, Martin
From Airline Reservations to Sonic the Hedgehog: A History of the Software Industry. Martin Campbell-Kelly. MIT Press 2003. xiv, 372 p. : Illustration

ISBN 9780262033039

Grades: Adult · **338.4**

1. Computer software industry and trade 2. Computers 3. Technology 4. Technological innovations 5. 20th century 6. Business and economics — Industries — Technology

LC 2002075351

Chronicles the software history's rise from its beginnings in the 1950s to America's fourth largest industrial sector, describing the different kinds of software, products, and markets that have developed.

"The author presents a history of the software industry from the 1950s to 1995. Dividing the business into three sectors (software contracting, corporate software precuts, and mass-market software products), he examines the key

DeBord, Matthew
Return to Glory: The Story of Ford's Revival and Victory in the Toughest Race in the World. Matthew Debord. Atlantic Monthly Press 2017. 272 pages
ISBN 9780802126504
Grades: Adult   338.4
1. Mulally, Alan R. 2. Automobile racing 3. Automobile industry and trade 4. Success in business 5. Business competition 6. Chief executive officers 7. Automobiles, Racing 8. Engineering design 9. Business and economics — Industries — Transportation 10. Sports and Competition — Racing — Cars 11. Business and economics — Business leaders and entrepreneurs
LC 2016046214

A veteran transportation journalist chronicles the development and racing achievement of the new 2015 Ford GT, exploring how the company has been returning to an era of success after implementing the decade-long "One Ford" plan of CEO Alan Mulally.

"DeBord, a senior correspondent for Business Insider, takes readers inside Ford before, during and after the 2016 Le Mans race and emerges with an upbeat, feel-good business story." —*Publishers Weekly*

Diaz, Tom
The Last Gun: How Changes in the Gun Industry Are Killing Americans and What It Will Take to Stop It. Tom Diaz. The New Press 2013. 319 p.
ISBN 9781595588302
Grades: Adult   338.4
1. Gun industry and trade 2. Guns 3. Gun control 4. Gun ownership 5. Gun accidents 6. Murder and guns 7. United States 8. Politics and global affairs — World politics — United States
LC 2012047230

Explores how the gun industry has changed and how the nature of gun violence has changed in step with industry trends and argues that a renewed political effort is necessary.

Includes bibliographical references.

Fabey, Michael
Heavy Metal: The Hard Days and Nights of the Shipyard Workers Who Build America's Supercarriers. Michael Fabey. William Morrow and Company 2022. 320 p.
ISBN 9780062996251
Grades: Adult   338.4
1. Aircraft carriers 2. Shipbuilders 3. Shipyard workers 4. Construction industry and trade 5. Working class 6. United States 7. History writing — Military — Naval history

An extraordinary story of American can-do, an inside look at the building of the most dangerous aircraft carrier in the world, the John F. Kennedy.

"Journalist Fabey (Crashback) chronicles the construction of the USS John F. Kennedy at a Newport News, Va, shipyard in this richly detailed account....This poignant portrait of working-class life will appeal to fans of Studs Terkel." —*Publishers Weekly*

Fine, Doug
Too High to Fail: Cannabis and the New Green Economic Revolution. Doug Fine. Gotham Books 2012. 368 p.
ISBN 9781592407095
Grades: Adult   338.4
1. Marijuana traffic 2. Drug industry and trade 3. Marijuana 4. True Crime — Drugs 5. Business and economics — Industries 6. Business and economics — Economics — Contemporary U.S. economy
LC 2012014437

An in-depth assessment of the legal cannabis industry and its potential role in today's evolving economy cites the lucrative proceeds generated by a small number of registered users and the underground revenues of illegal uses, providing a concise history of hemp and insider perspectives on a profitable growing season in Mendocino County.

Flannery, Kate
Strip Tees: A Memoir of Millennial Los Angeles. Kate Flannery. Henry Holt and company 2023. 240 p.
ISBN 9781250827289
Grades: Adult   338.4
1. Flannery, Kate 2. Charney, Dov, 1969- 3. Women college graduates 4. Moving to a new city 5. Corporations 6. Clothing industry and trade 7. Fashion 8. Women professional employees 9. Chief executive officers 10. Sexism 11. Sexual harassment 12. Misogyny 13. Corporate culture 14. Scandals 15. North American people 16. American people 17. Los Angeles, California 18. Autobiographies and memoirs 19. Life stories — Business — Working life 20. Business and economics — Corruption and scandal 21. Arts and Entertainment — Fashion 22. Debut title

Arriving in Los Angeles after graduating college for a new job at an upstart clothing company called American Apparel, the author slowly loses herself in rowdy sex-positivity, racy photo shoots and a cultlike devotion to the unorthodox CEO, leading her to question the company's ethics and wrestle with her own.

"This is an authentic portrait of the battle to remain true to oneself." —*Publishers Weekly*

Goldstone, Lawrence
Drive!: Henry Ford, George Selden, and the Race to Invent the Auto Age. Lawrence Goldstone. Ballantine Books 2016. 400 p.
ISBN 9780553394184
Grades: Adult   338.4
1. Ford, Henry, 1863-1947 2. Selden, George Baldwin, 1846-1922 3. Automobile industry and trade 4. Automobiles 5. 20th century 6. History writing — Early 20th century — United States 7. Business and economics — Industries — Transportation
LC 2016002581

From the acclaimed author of Birdmen comes another hidden history of entrepreneurship—a true tale of invention and competition that will forever change the way readers view the creation of the vehicle that forever changed America, and sets the record straight on Henry Ford.

"A splendid dissection of the Selden/Ford patent face-off and its place in automotive historiography." —*Library Journal*

Haag, Pamela
★ *The Gunning of America: Business and the Making of American Gun Culture.* Pamela Haag. Basic Books, a member of the Perseus Books Group 2016. 368 p.
ISBN 9780465048953
Grades: Adult   338.4
1. Gun industry and trade 2. Social history 3. Industries 4. Marketing 5. Advertising 6. Guns 7. United States 8. 19th century 9. History writing — United States 10. Business and economics — Economics — Consumerism
LC 2015036679

An acclaimed historian explodes the myth about the 'Special relationship' between Americans and their guns, revealing that savvy 19th century businessmen—not gun lovers—created American gun culture.

Includes bibliographical references and index.

Hardy, Alyssa
Worn Out: How Our Clothes Cover up Fashion's Sins. Alyssa Hardy. The New Press 2022. 256 p.
ISBN 9781620976944
Grades: Adult   338.4
1. Fashion 2. Clothing industry and trade 3. Clothing workers 4. Labor exploitation 5. Work environment 6. Solid waste management 7. Environmental degradation 8. Marketing 9. Consumer economics 10. Business ethics 11. Corporate accountability 12. Environmentalism 13. Labor unions 14. Social advocacy 15. Arts and Entertainment — Fashion 16. Business and economics —

ESSENTIAL AND RECOMMENDED TITLES
338.4 Secondary industries and services

Industries — Retail products and services 17. Business and economics — Corruption and scandal 18. Debut title

LC 2022020538

A former InStyle senior news editor examines the underside of our historic clothing binge and the fashion industry's fall from grace, exploring the lives of the millions of garment workers around the world and exposing the complicity of celebrities whose endorsements obscure the exploitation behind marquee brands.

"One of the book's most intriguing sections uses the case study of Nike's Air Jordan sneakers to analyze how celebrity marketers help companies distract consumers from 'Nefarious labor practices.'…This will have readers thinking twice before they make their next purchase." —*Publishers Weekly*

"This eye-opening account will almost certainly give fashion consumers pause." —*Booklist*

Includes bibliographical references.

Higham, Scott
American Cartel: Inside the Battle to Bring Down the Opioid Industry. Scott Higham and Sari Horwitz. Twelve 2022. 320 p.

ISBN 9781538737200

Grades: Adult **338.4**

1. Drug industry corruption 2. Opioid abuse 3. Opioid epidemic 4. Addiction 5. Drug overdoses 6. Drug enforcement agents 7. Lawyers 8. Corporate accountability 9. Justice 10. True Crime — Investigations and Trials 11. Business and economics — Corruption and scandal 12. Business and economics — Industries — Medical 13. Life stories — Law and order

LC 2021053699

A Pulitzer Prize-winning investigative reporter for the Washington Post offers a documented and unflinching dive into the complicity, culpability and corporate greed of the drug companies who enabled and promoted the opioid epidemic.

"This is a fast-paced and searing account of the astonishing corporate greed behind the opioid epidemic and the heroic efforts of those who fought against it. Expertly researched and a worthy addition to the growing canon of opioid literature." —*Booklist*

Includes index.

Hogge, Fred
Of Ice and Men: How We've Used Cold to Transform Humanity. Fred Hogge. Pegasus Books 2022. 352 p.

ISBN 9781639361830

Grades: Adult **338.4**

1. Ice 2. Cold 3. Cooling 4. Refrigeration and refrigerating machinery 5. Global warming 6. Science writing — General 7. History writing — Science, technology, and medicine

Ice tells a story. It writes it in rock. It lays it down, snowfall by snowfall at the ends of the earth where we may read it like the rings on a tree. It tells our planet's geological and climatological tale. Ice tells another story too: a story about us. It tells how our species has used ice to reshape the world according to our needs and our desires: How we have survived it, harvested it, traded it, bent science to our will to make it—and how in doing so we have created globe-spanning infrastructures that are entirely dependent upon it. And even after we have done all that, we take ice so much for granted that we barely notice it.

"Hogge, a British historian and filmmaker, contends that the use of cool air has been essential for humans to populate the whole planet and develop technological civilization….Hogge makes many fascinating points and digressions in this casual history about applications of cold." —*Library Journal*

Hughes, Evan
The Hard Sell: Crime and Punishment at an Opioid Startup. Evan Hughes. Doubleday 2022. 288 p.

ISBN 9780385544900

Grades: Adult **338.4**

1. Opioids 2. Fentanyl 3. Executives 4. Drug industry corruption 5. Physicians 6. Greed 7. Bribery 8. Medical ethics 9. Pain 10. Addiction 11. Opioid epidemic 12. Criminal investigation 13. Trials 14. Treatment 15. Page to screen 16. Science Writing — Medicine and health 17. True Crime — General 18. Life stories — Science, technology, and medicine 19. Nonfiction that reads like fiction

LC 2021018682

John Kapoor had amassed a small fortune in pharmaceuticals when he conceived of a new product. It was the 2000s, and opioids were big business. If Kapoor, an immigrant and the billionaire founder of Insys, could find a new way to administer the highly potent fentanyl, he could patent his invention and sell it to those in need—at a steep price. The only problem: There weren't enough people in need. Kapoor's drug was approved for breakthrough cancer pain. If Subsys was going to turn a profit, the company would need to persuade doctors to prescribe it "off-label," for other, lesser forms of pain. With executives leading the charge, Insys sales reps seduced doctors with charm, money, and sex. Its administrators lied to health care providers, claiming recipients had cancer when they did not. It pushed drugs onto patients that would have benefited from safer options, or no drugs at all. The strategy worked: When Insys went public, it notched the biggest IPO of its year. But several employees reached their limit and quietly blew the whistle, bringing the full force of the justice system upon the drug maker.

"Journalist Hughes (Literary Brooklyn) takes a revelatory deep dive into the ignominious history of the pharmaceutical manufacturer Insys Therapeutics, the leadership of which was convicted in 2019 of federal racketeering and conspiracy charges.... This is a powerful indictment of abhorrent industry practices." —*Publishers Weekly*

Made into a television show on Netflix, 2023; Includes bibliographical references.

Kurutz, Steven
American Flannel: How a Band of Entrepreneurs Are Bringing the Art and Business of Making Clothes Back Home. Steven Kurutz. Riverhead Books 2024. 256 p.

ISBN 9780593329610

Grades: Adult **338.4**

1. Clothing industry and trade 2. Entrepreneurs 3. Textile industry and trade 4. Textile fabrics 5. Manufacturing industry and trade 6. United States 7. 21st century 8. Business and economics — Industries — Manufacturing

LC 2023039150

The inspiring story of how a group of scrappy entrepreneur started a new company, American Giant, with the goal of reversing the trend of offshoring production and creating quality, affordable domestic clothing.

"Guaranteed to be of interest to anyone who appreciates bespoke and well-made goods, as well as artisan pride." —*Kirkus*

Lenzer, Jeanne
The Danger Within US: America's Untested, Unregulated Medical Device Industry and One Man's Battle to Survive It. Jeanne Lenzer. Little, Brown and Company 2017. 320 p.

ISBN 9780316343763

Grades: Adult **338.4**

1. Medical equipment 2. Corruption 3. Medical ethics 4. Medical accountability 5. Medical care 6. Medical fraud 7. Medicine 8. Business and economics — Corruption and scandal 9. Business and economics — Industries — Medical

LC 2017954610

An award-winning medical investigative journalist presents an unsettling exposé of the under-regulated medical-device industry, revealing the corruption, greed and deceit that have combined to render medical interventions a leading cause of death in America.

"An impassioned expose that uncovers a significant danger within the contemporary health care industry." —*Kirkus*

Loftus, Peter
The Messenger: Moderna, the Vaccine, and the Business Gamble That Changed the World. Peter Loftus. Harvard Business Review Press 2022. 272 p.

ISBN 9781647823191

Grades: Adult **338.4**

1. Vaccine industry and trade 2. Drug industry and trade 3. Covid-19 (Disease) 4. Vaccines 5. Biotechnology industry and trade 6. Business and economics — Industries — Medical

PUBLIC LIBRARY CORE COLLECTION: NONFICTION
Twentieth Edition

LC 2022001931

A Wall Street Journal reporter brings the inside story of how Moderna went all in on a single revolutionary idea; of quiet research with unknown consequence; of the evolution of a cutting-edge American innovation, industry, and economy that led to one of the great gambles in business history.

"This is a great look at the business of pandemic medicine." —*Publishers Weekly*

Includes index.

McClanahan, Paige

The New Tourist: Waking up to the Power and Perils of Travel. Paige McClanahan. Scribner 2024. 320 p.

ISBN 9781668011775

Grades: Adult   **338.4**

1. Tourism 2. Tourists 3. Ecotourism 4. Heritage tourism 5. Travelers 6. Voyages and travels 7. Travel Writing — General

Through deep and perceptive dispatches from tourist spots around the globe—from Hawaii to Saudi Arabia, Amsterdam to Angkor Wat—The New Tourist lifts the veil on an industry that accounts for one in ten jobs worldwide and generates nearly ten percent of global GDP. How did a once-niche activity become the world's most important means of contact across cultures? When does tourism destroy the soul of a city, and when does it offer a place a new lease on life? Is "last chance tourism" prompting a powerful change in perspective, or driving places we love further into the ground?

"Despite highlighting criticisms of tourism, the New Tourist remains optimistic…about developing a new travel sensibility that benefits the local community, making it suitable for readers interested in reflecting on their own excursions." —*Booklist*

McMillan, Tracie

The American Way of Eating: Undercover at Walmart, Applebee's, Farm Fields and the Dinner Table. Tracie McMillan. Simon & Schuster 2012. x, 319 p.

ISBN 9781439171950

Grades: Adult   **338.4**

1. Poverty 2. Investigative journalism 3. Nutrition 4. Food habits 5. California 6. Detroit, Michigan 7. New York City 8. United States 9. 21st century 10. Food writing — Investigations

An award-winning journalist traces her 2009 immersion into the national food system to explore issues about how working-class Americans can afford to eat as they should, describing how she worked as a farm laborer, Wal-Mart grocery clerk and Applebee's expediter while living within the means of each job.

"Full of personal stories of the daily struggle to put food of any kind on the table in today's economy, McMillan's book will force readers to question their own methods of purchasing and preparing food." —*Kirkus*

Includes bibliographical references (p. 295-318).

Miller, Chris

Chip War: The Fight for the World's Most Critical Technology. Chris Miller. Scribner 2022. 352 p.

ISBN 9781982172008

Grades: Adult   **338.4**

1. Microchips 2. Scarcity 3. Supply and demand 4. Computers and civilization 5. Technological innovations 6. International competition 7. Military engineering 8. Geopolitics 9. Defense industry and trade 10. Business and economics — Economics — World economy 11. Business and economics — Industries — Technology 12. Science Writing — Computing, the Internet, and Technology

An economic historian looks at the decades-old battle to control the microchip industry, which has emerged as the world's most critical resource, and how it will define the conflict between the United States and China in the upcoming decades.

"Well-researched and incisive, this is a noteworthy look at the intersection of technology, economics, and politics." —*Publishers Weekly*

Mitford, Jessica

★ *The American Way of Death Revisited.* Jessica Mitford. Alfred A. Knopf 1998. xix, 296 p.

ISBN 9780679450375

Grades: 11 12 Adult   **338.4**

1. Mitford, Jessica, 1917-1996 2. Undertakers 3. Funerals 4. Death 5. Economics 6. United States 7. 20th century 8. Family and Relationships — Aging and Death 9. Business and economics — Industries

LC 97049349

A revised version of an expose of the funeral industry includes new chapters on the practice of prepayment for funerals and other issues.

"Very interesting, informative, and easy to read, this book is written with wit, solid information, and refreshing bluntness." —*Library Journal*

Includes index; Originally published: New York : Simon and Schuster, 1963.

Pein, Corey

Live Work Work Work Die: A Journey into the Savage Heart of Silicon Valley. Corey Pein. Metropolitan Books 2018. 320 p.

ISBN 9781627794855

Grades: Adult   **338.4**

1. Internet industry and trade 2. High-technology industry and trade 3. Business competition 4. Technological innovations 5. Computer programmers 6. Entrepreneurship 7. New businesses 8. Silicon Valley, California 9. Business and economics — Industries — Technology 10. Society and culture — General

LC 2017040258

A journalist explores the true heart of Silicon Valley by becoming an entrepreneur and describes first-hand his experiences at gimmicky tech conferences, pitching his insane business ideas to investors and through interviews with quirky and outrageous characters including con artists, hackers and naive programmers.

Includes bibliographical references and index.

Posner, Gerald L.

★ *Pharma: Greed, Lies, and the Poisoning of America.* Gerald Posner. Avid Reader Press 2020. xi, 802 p.

ISBN 9781501151897

Grades: Adult   **338.4**

1. Drug industry and trade 2. Corruption 3. Corporate power 4. Corporations 5. Executives 6. Business corruption 7. Corporate greed 8. Prescription drugs 9. Government regulation 10. Addiction 11. Opioid epidemic 12. Business and economics — Industries — Medical 13. Business and economics — Corruption and scandal

LC Bl2020004435

The award-winning author of God's Bankers traces the rise of the Sackler family and the role of opioid addiction and soaring drug prices on healthcare, exposing the deadly consequences of industry corruption and profiteering.

"Explosively, even addictively, readable, Posner's meticulously documented investigation of the historical roots and contemporary state of Big Pharma examines everything from aspirin to Zantac." —*Booklist*

Includes bibliographical references and index.

Quigley, Fran

Prescription for the People: An Activist's Guide to Making Medicine Affordable for All. Fran Quigley. ILR Press, an imprint of Cornell University Press 2017. 341 pages

ISBN 9781501713750

Grades: Adult   **338.4**

1. Drug industry and trade 2. Health policy 3. Drug Prices 4. Prescription pricing 5. Medical care reform 6. Lobbying 7. Political participation 8. Business and economics — Industries — Medical 9. Politics and global affairs — Public health

LC 2017020499

In Prescription for the People, Fran Quigley diagnoses our inability to get medicines to the people who need them and then prescribes the cure. He delivers a clear and convincing argument for a complete shift in the global and U.S. approach to developing and providing essential medicines—and a primer on how to make that change happen.

"Quigley offers a focused analysis of the problem and advice for those who wish to help change the system." —*Library Journal*

Includes bibliographical references and index.

ESSENTIAL AND RECOMMENDED TITLES
338.5 General production economics

Rudacille, Deborah
Roots of Steel: The Boom and Bust of an American Mill Town. Deborah Rudacille. Pantheon Books 2010. 304 p.
ISBN 9780375423680
Grades: Adult 338.4
1. Steel industry and trade 2. Mill towns 3. Cities and towns 4. Metal industry and trade 5. Mills and millwork 6. United States history 7. Baltimore, Maryland 8. Maryland 9. History writing — Regional history — United States
LC 2009020962

The author of the Riddle of Gender traces the history of a Maryland steel mill town where she grew up as the daughter of a steelworker, a childhood during which she witnessed how the industry's decline and complicated social disputes put tens of thousands out of work."

Includes bibliographical references and index.

Sedgewick, Augustine
Coffeeland: One Man's Dark Empire and the Making of Our Favorite Drug. Augustine Sedgewick. Penguin Press 2020. 432 p.
ISBN 9781594206153
Grades: Adult 338.4
1. Coffee industry and trade 2. Colonialism 3. Consumerism 4. Coffee plantations 5. Plantation owners 6. Coffee 7. Inequality 8. Indigenous peoples 9. Wealth 10. Poverty 11. Labor exploitation 12. Central American history 13. United States 14. El Salvador 15. 20th century 16. History writing — Latin America 17. Business and economics — Industries — Agriculture and food 18. Food writing — Non-alcoholic beverages 19. Life stories — Business
LC 2019031332

The epic story of the rise of coffee in the Americas, and how it connected and divided the modern world. Sedgewick reveals how the growth of coffee production, trade, and consumption went hand in hand with the rise of the scientific idea of energy as a universal force, which transformed thinking about how the human body works as well as ideas about the relationship of one person's work to another's. In the process, both El Salvador and the United States earned the nickname "Coffeeland," though for radically different reasons, and with consequences that reach into the present. This history of how coffee came to be produced by the world's poorest people and consumed by its richest opens up a unique perspective on how the modern globalized world works, ultimately provoking a reconsideration of what it means to be connected to far-away people and places through the familiar things that make up our everyday lives.

"The breadth of Sedgewick's analysis of coffee's place in the world economy astonishes, as does his ability to bring historical figures to life. Coffee connoisseurs will relish this eye-opening history." —*Publishers Weekly*

Includes bibliographical references and index.

Slade, Rachel
American Hoodie: The Almost Impossible Quest to Make Things in Twenty-first Century America (and How It Got That Way). Rachel Slade. Pantheon Books 2024. 416 p.
ISBN 9780593316887
Grades: Adult 338.4
1. Businesspeople 2. Textile industry and trade 3. Clothing industry and trade 4. Free trade 5. Labor unions 6. United States 7. Business and economics — Industries — Manufacturing 8. Life stories — Business
LC 2023009052

Told through the experience of one young couple as they attempt to rebuild a lost industry ethically, this poignant and deeply personal account follows Ben and Whitney Waxman's quest to change the world as they attempt to do the impossible: Produce an American-made, union-made, all American-sourced sweatshirt.

"This galvanizing call...serves as both a sweeping report on a globalized industry and a practical road map for aspiring small-scale manufacturers. Readers will feel invigorated." —*Publishers Weekly*

Includes bibliographical references and index.

Vlasic, Bill
Once Upon a Car: The Fall and Revival of America's Big Three Auto Makers — Gm, Ford, and Chrysler. Bill Vlasic. Harpercollins 2011. 352 p.
ISBN 9780061845628
Grades: Adult 338.4
1. Automobile industry and trade 2. Business 3. Financial crises 4. Automobiles 5. Business and economics — Industries — Transportation
LC 2011020572

In this uniquely American story of success, failure and redemption, the Detroit bureau chief for the New York Times, covering events from 2005 to the present, documents the crumbling of the once-mighty car industry, revealing the impact of this crisis on workers and communities.

Williams, Bari A.
Seen yet Unseen: A Black Woman Crashes the Tech Fraternity. Bari A. Williams. Blackstone Publishing 2024. 290 p.
ISBN 9798212009881
Grades: Adult 338.4
1. Williams, Bari A. 2. African American women 3. Technology 4. Women 5. High technology 6. Multiculturalism 7. Identity 8. Belonging 9. Race relations 10. Work environment 11. Silicon Valley, California 12. Autobiographies and memoirs 13. Life stories — Business 14. Business and economics — Industries — Technology 15. Society and culture — Race

Part memoir, part searing revelation, Seen yet Unseen takes readers behind the scenes of some of the world's biggest tech companies and exposes the way their exclusion of and, at times, hostility toward Black women have lasting impacts on the technology we use every day.

"A revealing and intimate look at a Black woman's experiences in the technology industry." —*Library Journal*

338.5 General production economics

Derks, Scott
The Value of a Dollar: Colonial Era to the Civil War, 1600-1865. Scott Derks and Tony Smith. Grey House Pub. 2005. 436, 21 p. : Illustration
ISBN 9781592370948
Grades: Adult 338.5
1. Cost and standard of living 2. Prices 3. Wages 4. Business and economics — General 5. Reference — Business 6. Business and economics — Economics — Socioeconomics
LC 2006275331

"This source is an engaging statistical summary that looks at the history of the American people through the eyes of everyday workers and consumers. The 265 years it covers are presented in six chronological chapters: 1600-1749: The Development of the Colonies, 1750-1774: The Run up to the War of American Independence, and so on, ending with the close of the Civil War in 1865. [This book] will find a happy audience among students, researchers, and general browsers. It offers a fascinating and detailed look at early American history from the viewpoint of everyday people trying to make ends meet." —*Booklist*

[This is] the first edition of the Value of a Dollar, 1600-1865. This book both parallels and compliments its popular older brother the Value of a Dollar, 1860-2004—P. [i]; a Universal Reference Book; Includes bibliographical references (p. [437-442]) and index.

The Value of a Dollar: Prices and Incomes in the United States, 1860-2009. Scott Derks. Grey House Pub. 2009. xix, 690 p. : Illustration
ISBN 9781592374038
Grades: Adult 338.5
1. Cost and standard of living 2. Prices 3. Wages 4. Business and economics — Economics — Socioeconomics 5. Reference — Business
LC 2010286212

"Both great-grandparents and serious students in historical research will benefit from this book. It will be an especially valuable study to students of American history, economics, and even mathematics." —*Library Journal*

A universal reference book—Cover; Includes bibliographical references (p. 677]-685) and index.

PUBLIC LIBRARY CORE COLLECTION: NONFICTION
Twentieth Edition

Galbraith, John Kenneth
★ *The Great Crash, 1929.* John Kenneth Galbraith; with a new introduction by the author. Houghton Mifflin Co. 1997. xiv, 206 p. : Illustration
ISBN 9780395859995
Grades: 11 12 Adult   338.5
1. Depressions, 1929-1941 2. Stock market crash, October 1929 3. History writing — Great Depression — United States
LC 97022051

A study of the stock market crash of 1929 reveals the influential role of Wall Street on the economic growth of America.

Economic writings are seldom notable for their entertainment value, but this book is. Galbraith's prose has grace and wit, and he distills a good deal of sardonic fun from the whopping errors of the nation's oracles and the wondrous antics of the financial community. Atlantic Monthly.

A Mariner book; Includes bibliographical references and index.

Mullainathan, Sendhil
Scarcity: Why Having Too Little Means so Much. Sendhil Mullainathan and Eldar Shafir. Times Books, Henry Holt and Company 2013. 304 p.
ISBN 9780805092646
Grades: Adult   338.5
1. Supply and demand 2. Scarcity 3. Decision making 4. Psychology 5. Poverty 6. Science Writing — Medicine and health — Mental health 7. Society and culture — Psychology and human behavior
LC 2013004167

An examination of how scarcity—and our flawed responses to it—shapes our lives, our society, and our culture.

Includes bibliographical references and index.

Nations, Scott
A History of the United States in Five Crashes: Stock Market Meltdowns That Defined a Nation. Scott Nations. William Morrow & Company 2017. 304 p.
ISBN 9780062467270
Grades: Adult   338.5
1. Stock market 2. Financial crises 3. Recession (Economics) 4. Market indicators 5. Economic history 6. Economic indicators 7. Economics 8. Depressions 9. Business and economics — Economics — History
LC 2017033698

A financial executive and CNBC contributor examines the five most significant stock market crashes over the past century to reveal how they happened and shaped the present-day United States.

"An eye-opening examination of the many ways money can be madeand disappear." —*Kirkus*

Patterson, Scott
★ *Chaos Kings: How Wall Street Traders Make Billions in the New Age of Crisis.* Scott Patterson. Charles Scribner's Sons 2023. 288 p.
ISBN 9781982179939
Grades: Adult   338.5
1. Financial crises 2. Risk-taking 3. Chaos 4. Traders (Finance) 5. Financial forecasting 6. Prediction (Psychology) 7. Stock market 8. Investments 9. Securities 10. Climate change 11. Wall Street, New York City 12. Business and economics — Economics — World economy

Written by a veteran Wall Street Journal reporter, this is a fascinating deep dive into the world of billion-dollar traders and high-stakes crisis predictors who strive to turn extreme events into financial windfalls.

"Detailed yet accessible, this will appeal to fans of Michael Lewis's the Big Short." —*Publishers Weekly*

338.6 Organization of production

Foroohar, Rana
Homecoming: The Path to Prosperity in a Post-global World. Rana Foroohar. Crown 2022. 352 p.
ISBN 9780593240533
Grades: Adult   338.6
1. Regionalism 2. Nationalism 3. Business and economics — Economics — World economy
LC 2022016180

The Financial Times columnist and CNN analyst presents a vision of a new age of economic localization in the face of global trade and supply chain failures and how this trend can help keep investment and wealth closer to home.

"This astute survey provides a welcome measure of hope." —*Publishers Weekly*

Includes bibliographical references and index.

Freeman, Joshua Benjamin
★ *Behemoth: A History of the Factory and the Making of the Modern World.* Joshua B. Freeman. W W Norton & Co. 2018. 464 p.
ISBN 9780393246315
Grades: Adult   338.6
1. Factories 2. Technology and civilization 3. Industrialization 4. Industrial revolution 5. Economic history 6. History writing — Microhistory 7. Business and economics — Economics — History
LC 2017051960

A global history of the rise of the factory and its positive and negative effects on society traces the Industrial Revolution textile mills, through the massive steel and car plants of the 20th century, to the massive retail producers of today's world, offering insights into the views, debates and innovations of Alexander Hamilton, Henry Ford, Charlie Chaplin and others.

"Freeman has provided an ambitious, sweeping, and well-researched history of factories, which remains accessible and relevant to general readers." —*Library Journal*

338.7 Business enterprises

Auletta, Ken
Googled: The End of the World as We Know It. Ken Auletta. Penguin Press 2009. 400 p.
ISBN 9781594202353
Grades: Adult   338.7
1. Web search engines 2. Internet searching 3. Computers 4. Internet 5. Internet industry and trade 6. United States 7. Science Writing — Computing, the Internet, and Technology 8. Business and economics — Industries — Technology
LC 2009024770

Booklist Editors' Choice, 2009.

Critically examines the influence of Google on today's dynamic media landscape, profiling company founders Larry Page and Sergey Brin while offering insight into their lucrative business processes and assessing the internal and external threats that may inhibit the company's future prospects.

"The author's thorough reporting and declarative writing provide a crisp, informative read. Auletta displays the skill of a responsible journalist in both researching and crafting this snapshot of today's technological landscape." —*Christian Science Monitor*

Includes bibliographical references and index.

Bergen, Mark
Like, Comment, Subscribe: Inside Youtube's Chaotic Rise to World Domination. Mark Bergen. Viking Press 2022. 416 p.
ISBN 9780593296349
Grades: Adult   338.7
1. Internet broadcasting 2. Internet industry and trade 3. Popular culture 4. Technological innovations 5. Online social networks 6. Society and culture — Media and technology 7. Business and economics — Industries — Technology 8. Business and economics — Industries — Entertainment and media

In this first-of-its-kind book, a top technology reporter at Bloomberg reveals the inside story of YouTube's technology and business, detailing how it helped Google, its parent company, achieve unimaginable power, unleashing an outrage

ESSENTIAL AND RECOMMENDED TITLES
338.7 Business enterprises

Bissonnette, Zac
The Great Beanie Baby Bubble: Mass Delusion and the Dark Side of Cute. Zac Bissonnette. Portfolio 2015. 272 p.
ISBN 9781591846024
Grades: Adult   338.7
1. Warner, Ty, 1944- 2. Toy industry and trade 3. Page to screen 4. Business and economics — Industries 5. Business and economics — Economics — Consumerism
LC 2014038639
A classic American story of people winning and losing vast fortunes chasing what one dealer remembers as the most spectacular dream ever sold.
Includes bibliographical references and index.

Brenner, Joel Glenn
The Emperors of Chocolate: Inside the Secret World of Hershey and Mars. Joel Glenn Brenner. Random House 1999. xiv, 366 p. : Illustration
ISBN 9780679421900
Grades: Adult   338.7
1. Hershey, Milton Snavely, 1857-1945 2. Mars, Forrest, 1904-1999 3. Chocolate industry and trade 4. Candy industry and trade 5. Chocolate candy 6. Business competition 7. Food writing — History and microhistory 8. History writing — Microhistory 9. Adult books for young adults 10. Business and economics — Industries — Agriculture and food
LC 98021610
Examines one of the most bitter rivalries in American business.
"Brenner examines the candy industry, focusing on the rivalry between Hershey and Mars. Milton Hersey was and Forrest Mars is highly secretive and eccentric, and they both amassed huge fortunes. A wonderful inside look at successful businessmen." —*Booklist*
Includes bibliographical references (p. 325-343) and index.

Capparell, Stephanie
The Real Pepsi Challenge: The Inspirational Story of Breaking the Color Barrier in American Business. Stephanie Capparell. Free Press 2007. xvii, 349 p. : Illustration
ISBN 9780743265713
Grades: Adult   338.7
1. African American executives 2. Soft drinks 3. Marketing 4. Social life and customs 5. United States history 6. United States 7. 20th century 8. Business and economics — Industries — Agriculture and food 9. History writing — African American — United States
LC 2006041267
Describes the achievements of one dozen pioneering African-American Pepsi Cola businessmen who increased the company's post-World War II profits by effectively tapping African-American markets.
Also known as: The real Pepsi challenge: How one pioneering company broke color barriers in 1940s American business (2008); Includes bibliographical references (p. 289-329) and index.

Carreyrou, John
★ *Bad Blood: Secrets and Lies in a Silicon Valley Startup.* John Carreyrou. Knopf 2018. 352 p.
ISBN 9781524731656
Grades: Adult   338.7
1. New businesses 2. Fraud 3. Biotechnology 4. Business corruption 5. Business failures 6. Corruption investigation 7. United States 8. Business and economics — Corruption and scandal 9. True Crime — General 10. Business and economics — Industries — Medical 11. Nonfiction that reads like fiction 12. Book club best bets
LC 2018000263
New York Times Notable Book, 2018; Library Journal Best Books, 2018.

Recounts the story behind Theranos, the medical equipment company that misled investors to believe they developed a revolutionary blood testing machine, detailing how its CEO, Elizabeth Holmes, perpetuated the lie to bolster the value of the company by billions.
"Crime thriller authors have nothing on Carreyrou's exquisite sense of suspenseful pacing and multifaceted character development in this riveting, read-in-one-sitting tour de force. Investigative journalists are perhaps the country's last true protectors of truth and justice, and Carreyrou's commitment to unraveling Holmes' crimes has been literally of life-saving value." —*Booklist*

Cohan, William D.
Power Failure: The Rise and Fall of an American Icon. William D. Cohan. Portfolio/Penguin 2022. 512 p.
ISBN 9780593084168
Grades: Adult   338.7
1. Corporations 2. Big business 3. Chief executive officers 4. Electrical engineering 5. Manufacturing industry and trade 6. Transportation 7. Business and economics — Industries — Manufacturing 8. Business and economics — Corruption and scandal
LC 2022030569
No company embodied American ingenuity, innovation, and industrial power more spectacularly and more consistently than the General Electric Company. GE once developed and manufactured many of the inventions we take for granted today, nearly everything from the lightbulb to the jet engine. But even at the height of its prestige and influence, cracks were forming in its formidable foundation. In a masterful re-appraisal of a company that once claimed to "bring good things to life," journalist William D. Cohan argues that the incredible story of GE's rise and fall is not only a paragon, but also a prism through which we can better understand American capitalism.
"Cohan's thorough research and interviews with Jack Welch and others give readers a firsthand look at the rise and fall of an American institution." —*Library Journal*
Includes bibliographical references.

Coll, Steve
Private Empire: Exxonmobil and American Power. Steve Coll. Penguin Press 2012. 688 p.
ISBN 9781594203350
Grades: Adult   338.7
1. Oil industry and trade 2. Corporate power 3. Big business 4. Politics and government 5. United States 6. 21st century 7. Business and economics — Industries — Energy
LC 2011044722
National Book Critics Circle Award for Nonfiction finalist, 2012.
An investigation into the influential and fiercely private corporation traces the period between the Exxon Valdez accident and the Deepwater Horizion spill to profile chief executives Lee Raymond and Rex Tillerson as well as the company's role in violent international incidents. By the Pulitzer Prize-winning author of the Bin Ladens.
"Highly recommended for students of the energy economy as well as for motivated general readers." —*Library Journal*
Includes bibliographical references and index.

Doran, Peter B.
Breaking Rockefeller: The Incredible Story of the Ambitious Rivals Who Toppled an Oil Empire. Peter B. Doran. Viking Press 2016. 352 p.
ISBN 9780525427391
Grades: Adult   338.7
1. Rockefeller, John D. (John Davison), 1839-1937 2. Samuel, Marcus, 1853-1927 3. Deterding, Henri, 1866-1939 4. Oil industry and trade 5. Monopolies 6. Businesspeople 7. Media tie-ins 8. Business and economics — Economics — History 9. Business and economics — Industries — Energy
LC Bl2016012688
The author of the popular History of Oil podcast traces the early-20th-century rivalry between John D. Rockefeller's Standard Oil and Royal Dutch Shell, describing the origins of partners Marcus Samuel, Jr. and Henri Deterding and how they used respective talents to break Rockefeller's daunting monopoly.

PUBLIC LIBRARY CORE COLLECTION: NONFICTION
Twentieth Edition

"A readable popular history told largely through the actions of swashbuckling tycoons." —*Kirkus*

Based on a podcast.

Downs, Paul
Boss Life: Surviving My Own Small Business. Paul Downs. Blue Rider Press 2015. 368 p.

ISBN 9780399172335

Grades: Adult   **338.7**

1. Downs, Paul 2. Small business 3. New businesses 4. Cabinetmakers 5. Entrepreneurs 6. Management 7. Woodworking 8. Leadership 9. Autobiographies and memoirs 10. Business and economics — Business leaders and entrepreneurs 11. Life stories — Business — Business leaders

LC 2015016068

The author of the "You're the Boss" blog at NYTimes.Com details the development of his small furniture business and the challenges he has faced along the way.

"This is an invaluable look into operational details for anyone considering starting a business or caught up in the struggle of owning and running one." —*Booklist*

Ducharme, Jamie
Big Vape: The Incendiary Rise of Juul. Jamie Ducharme. Henry Holt & Company 2021. 320 p.

ISBN 9781250777539

Grades: Adult   **338.7**

1. Inventions 2. Smokers 3. Smoking 4. Nicotine addiction 5. Corporations 6. Entrepreneurs 7. Tobacco industry and trade 8. Health hazards 9. Business and economics — Industries — Agriculture and food 10. Business and economics — Corruption and scandal 11. Life stories — Business

LC 2021002301

It began with a smoke break. James Monsees and Adam Bowen were two ambitious graduate students at Stanford, and in between puffs after class they dreamed of a way to quit smoking. Their solution became the Juul, a sleek, modern device that could vaporize nicotine into a conveniently potent dosage. The company they built around that device, Juul Labs, would go on to become a $38 billion dollar company and draw blame for addicting a whole new generation of underage tobacco users. Author Jamie Ducharme follows Monsees and Bowen as they create Juul and, in the process, go from public health visionaries and Silicon Valley wunderkinds to two of the most controversial businessmen in the country.

"Fast-paced and impressively researched, this detailed account sings." —*Publishers Weekly*

Includes bibliographical references.

Elmore, Bartow J.
Citizen Coke: The Making of Coca-cola Capitalism. Bartow J. Elmore. W.W. Norton & Company 2014. 304 p.

ISBN 9780393241129

Grades: Adult   **338.7**

1. Soft drink industry and trade 2. International businesses 3. Soft drinks 4. Sustainable development 5. Corporate accountability 6. Business and economics — Industries — Agriculture and food

LC 2014022329

A critical history of Coca-Cola's business successes outlines the company's particularly effective strategies for production, cost control and franchising while citing Coke's role in world resource depletion and the obesity crisis.

"Without a doubt, Coke has been a good public citizen that stimulates economies and improves lives, writes the author, but the costs to taxpayersfor recycling systems, public pipes and subsidized farmsand the environment call into question how such unsustainable practices can continue in an age of scarcity. A superb, quietly devastating environmental and business history." —*Kirkus*

Includes bibliographical references and index.

Seed Money: Monsanto's Past and Our Food Future. Bartow J. Elmore. W.W. Norton & Company 2021. 464 p.

ISBN 9781324002048

Grades: Adult   **338.7**

1. Agricultural chemicals industry and trade 2. Seed industry and trade 3. Biotechnology 4. Genetically engineered plants 5. Biotechnology in agriculture 6. Genetically engineered food 7. Food crops 8. Business corruption 9. Agriculture 10. Business and economics — Industries — Agriculture and food 11. Science Writing — Biology 12. Food writing — Investigations

LC 2021022107

A deeply researched and eye-opening history that shows how Monsanto came to have outsized influence over our food system. This is the definitive history of Monsanto, a St. Louis chemical firm that became the world's largest genetically engineered seed enterprise. Monsanto merged with German pharma-biotech giant Bayer in 2018, but its Roundup Ready seeds, introduced twenty-five years ago, are still reshaping the farms that feed us. Incorporating global fieldwork, interviews with company employees, and untapped corporate and government records, award-winning historian Bartow J. Elmore traces Monsanto's astounding evolution from a scrappy chemical startup to a global agrobusiness powerhouse. Capitalizing on deals with customers like Coca-Cola, General Electric, and especially the US government, Monsanto used seed money derived from toxic products-including PCBs and Agent Orange-to build an agricultural empire, promising endless bounty through its genetically engineered technology. As new data emerges aboutits blockbuster Roundup system, and as Bayer faces a tide of lawsuits over Monsanto products past and present, Elmore's urgent history takes a penetrating look at the company's past.

"Combining elements of the film Erin Brockovich, Robert Bilott's Exposure, and Patrick Radden Keefe's Empire of Pain, Seed Money is a galvanizing achievement that will leave readers deeply impressed, impassioned, and infuriated." —*Booklist*

Includes bibliographical references and index.

Etter, Lauren
★ *The Devil's Playbook: Big Tobacco, Juul, and the Addiction of a New Generation.* Lauren Etter. Crown 2021. xxv, 465 pages

ISBN 9780593237984

Grades: Adult   **338.7**

1. Nicotine addiction 2. Drug abuse 3. Corporations 4. Executives 5. Business partnership 6. Greed 7. Tobacco industry and trade 8. High technology industry and trade 9. Product safety 10. Smoking 11. Teenagers 12. Health hazards 13. Business and economics — Corruption and scandal 14. Society and culture — Illness and disease — Addiction 15. Business and economics — Industries — Technology 16. Business and economics — Industries — Retail products and services

LC 2021004354

Howard Willard lusted after Juul. As the CEO of tobacco giant Philip Morris's parent company, and a veteran of the industry's long fight to avoid being regulated out of existence, he grew obsessed with a prize he believed could save his company—the e-cigarette, a product with all the addictive upside of the original without the same apparent health risks and bad press. Meanwhile, in Silicon Valley, Adam Bowen and James Monsees began work on a device meant to save lives and destroy Big Tobacco, only to end up baking the industry's DNA into their invention's science and marketing. Ultimately, Juul's e-cigarette was so effective, so market-dominating, that it put the company on a collision course with Philip Morris and sparked one of the most explosive public health crises in recent memory. Journalist Lauren Etter tells a riveting story of greed and deception in one of the biggest botched deals in business history.

"A well-told business story showing the unsurprising result when noble motives collide with corporate reality and the specter of large amounts of money." —*Library Journal*

Includes bibliographical references (pages 411-452) and index.

Ewing, Jack
Faster, Higher, Farther: The Volkswagen Scandal. Jack Ewing. W. W. Norton & Co. Inc 2017. 320 p.

ISBN 9780393254501

Grades: Adult   **338.7**

1. Automobile industry and trade 2. Business corruption 3. Greenhouse gas mitigation 4. Energy policy 5. Environmentalism 6. Business and economics —

ESSENTIAL AND RECOMMENDED TITLES
338.7 Business enterprises

Industries — Transportation 7. Business and economics — Corruption and scandal

LC 2017012672

In 2015, Volkswagen proudly reached its goal of surpassing Toyota as the world's largest automaker. Two months later, the EPA disclosed that Volkswagen had installed software that deceived emissions-testing mechanisms in 11 million cars. By August 2016, VW had settled with American regulators and car owners for $15 billion, with additional fines and suits still looming. In Faster, Higher, Farther, Jack Ewing rips the lid off the conspiracy.

"Capturing the public fascination with craven financial scandals, and with a movie in the works, Ewings sordid saga is the latest addition to the history of corporate fraud." —*Booklist*

Galloway, Scott
The Four: The Hidden DNA of Amazon, Apple, Facebook, and Google. Scott Galloway. Penguin 2017. 288 pages
ISBN 9780735213654
Grades: Adult   338.7

1. Success in business 2. Internet 3. Computers and civilization 4. Digital media 5. Entrepreneurship 6. Computers 7. Internet and identity 8. Virtual community 9. Social media 10. United States 11. Business and economics — Industries — Technology 12. Science Writing — Computing, the Internet, and Technology 13. Society and culture — Media and technology

LC 2017037152

An acclaimed NYU business professor examines the rise and influence of technology titans Apple, Amazon, Google and Facebook to reveal how they became successful by adapting the ideas of others in ways that reflect evolutionary psychology, outlining the likely path of a next possible major contender.

"Readers interested in innovation and strategies in technology and business management will find this book to be a provocative and insightful look at four powerful forces that dominate our social, psychological, and economic states today." —*Booklist*

Genoways, Ted
The Chain: Farm, Factory, and the Fate of Our Food. Ted Genoways. Harper 2014. 320 p.
ISBN 9780062288752
Grades: Adult   338.7

1. Meat industry and trade 2. Factory farming 3. Occupational health and safety 4. Agribusiness 5. Immigrant workers 6. Food industry and trade 7. Food writing — Investigations 8. Business and economics — Industries — Agriculture and food 9. Society and culture — General

LC 2014019018

An acclaimed journalist uses the story of Hormel Foods and soaring recession-era demand for its most famous product, Spam, to probe the state of the meatpacking industry, including the expansion of agribusiness and the effects of immigrant labor on Middle America, and expose such alarming trends as pollution, abused animals and more.

"Readers curious about meatpacking and agriculture as well as the social, economic, and environmental impacts of the food industry will find Genoways's nonfiction debut a valuable and stimulating read." —*Library Journal*

Includes bibliographical references.

Gryta, Thomas
Lights Out: Pride, Delusion, and the Fall of General Electric. Thomas Gryta and Ted Mann. Houghton Mifflin Harcourt 2020. IX, 353 p.
ISBN 9780358250418
Grades: Adult   338.7

1. Business and economics — Economics — History 2. Science writing — General 3. Business and economics — Business advice — Leadership and management

LC 2020005518

How could General Electric-perhaps America's most iconic corporation-suffer such a swift and sudden fall from grace?

Includes bibliographical references (pages 341-342) and index.

Harris, Blake J.
Console Wars: Sega, Nintendo, and the Battle That Defined a Generation. Blake J. Harris. It Books 2014. 320 p.
ISBN 9780062276698
Grades: Adult   338.7

1. Video games industry and trade 2. Video games 3. Nintendo video games 4. 1990s 5. Sports and Competition — Games 6. Business and economics — Industries — Entertainment and media

LC 2013050668

Chronicles how Sega|a small, scrappy gaming company led by an unlikely visionary and a team of rebels|took on the juggernaut Nintendo and revolutionized the video game industry.

"Harris defines the players immediately, honing in on their most notable characteristics, and puts the reader in the thick of the meetings and deal-making with a confidence stemming from hundreds of interviews." —*Booklist*

Hart, Matt
Win at All Costs: Inside Nike Running and Its Culture of Deception. Matt Hart. Dey Street Books 2020. 416 p.
ISBN 9780062917775
Grades: Adult   338.7

1. Salazar, Alberto, 1958- 2. Runners 3. Doping in sports 4. Sports equipment industry and trade 5. Track and field 6. Corruption 7. Track and field coaches 8. Olympic athletes 9. Sports 10. Whistle blowing 11. United States 12. Sports and Competition — Racing — Track and Field 13. Business and economics — Corruption and scandal

LC 2020021183

A behind-the-scenes journalistic exposé of the illicit activities of the Nike Oregon Project reveals how a company insider and two Olympic athletes risked their careers to expose cheating by Nike-sponsored runners, including top world athletes.

"A touch overlong, but a deeply reported and revealing look at the dire commercialization of American sports." —*Kirkus*

Includes bibliographical references and index.

Higgins, Tim
Power Play: Tesla, Elon Musk, and the Bet of the Century. Tim Higgins. Doubleday 2021. 400 p.
ISBN 9780385545457
Grades: Adult   338.7

1. Musk, Elon 2. Electric vehicles 3. Automobiles 4. Alternative fuels 5. Business competition 6. Success (Concept) 7. Automobile industry and trade 8. United States 9. Business and economics — Industries — Transportation 10. Business and economics — Industries — Energy 11. Business and economics — Business leaders and entrepreneurs

LC 2020048532

In this story of power, recklessness, struggle and triumph, a Wall Street Journal tech and auto reporter, who had a front-row seat for the drama, recounts the story of Elon Musk and Tesla's bid to build the world's greatest car.

"This book is a well-documented and comprehensive look at Tesla, Elon Musk, and the people involved with its creation and successes." —*Library Journal*

Includes bibliographical references.

Keefe, Patrick Radden
★ *Empire* of Pain: The Secret History of the Sackler Dynasty. Patrick Radden Keefe. Doubleday 2021. 560 p.
ISBN 9780385545686
Grades: Adult   338.7

1. Sackler, Arthur M. 2. Sackler family 3. Families 4. Opioids 5. Drug industry and trade 6. Rich families 7. Drugs 8. Drug industry corruption 9. Prescription drugs 10. Medical care 11. United States 12. Collective biographies 13. Life stories — People in history — Famous families 14. Business and economics — Industries — Medical 15. True Crime — Drugs

Baillie Gifford Prize for Non-Fiction, 2021; National Book Critics Circle Award for Nonfiction finalist, 2021.

A narrative account of how a prominent wealthy family sponsored the creation and marketing of one of the most commonly prescribed and addictive painkillers of the opioid crisis.

"History repeats itself and disaster ensues in this sweeping saga of the rise and fall of the family behind OxyContin, the painkiller widely credited with sparking the opioid epidemic in America. . . . Readers will be outraged and enthralled in equal measure." —*Publishers Weekly*

Knoedelseder, William
Bitter Brew: The Rise and Fall of Anheuser-busch and America's Kings of Beer. William Knoedelseder. HarperBusiness 2012. 400 p.
ISBN 9780062009265
Grades: Adult 338.7
1. Busch family 2. Brewing industry and trade 3. Name-brand products 4. Corporate mergers 5. Beer 6. Food writing — Investigations 7. Business and economics — Industries — Agriculture and food
LC 2012026942

Part cautionary tale, part business manual, this engrossing book, spanning three centuries, tells the story of how five generations of men took a small, bankrupt brewery on the banks of the Mississippi and turned it into an international empire until its downfall.

Leonard, Christopher
Kochland: The Secret History of Koch Industries and Corporate Power in America. Christopher Leonard. Simon & Schuster 2019. x, 687 pages : Illustration
ISBN 9781476775388
Grades: Adult 338.7
1. Koch, Charles G. (Charles de Ganahl), 1935- 2. Executives 3. Corporations 4. Corporate power 5. Business and politics 6. Interest groups 7. Energy industry and trade 8. Economic policy 9. Big business 10. Political participation 11. Impartial writing 12. Business and economics — General 13. Politics and global affairs — General 14. Life stories — Business — Business leaders
Library Journal Best Books, 2019; New York Times Notable Book, 2019.

A history of modern corporate America is presented through the story of the rise of Koch Industries, revealing how the Koch brothers operated as master disruptors and anti-union strategists for decades to become global billionaires.

"Based on six years of research and with a fast-paced writing style that interweaves multiple stories, this illuminating work on the exceedingly influential Koch and his company will be welcomed by all readers of business or politics. Leonard does for Koch what Andrew Sorkin's Too Big to Fail did for the 2008 financial crisis." —*Library Journal*

Includes bibliographical references (pages 593-660) and index.

Macy, Beth
★ *Factory Man:* How One Furniture Maker Battled Offshoring, Stayed Local—and Helped Save an American Town. Beth Macy. Little Brown & Co. 2014. 368 p.
ISBN 9780316231435
Grades: Adult 338.7
1. Globalization (Economics) 2. Furniture industry and trade 3. Family businesses 4. Company towns 5. Work 6. International relations 7. Virginia 8. China 9. United States 10. Business and economics — Industries — Manufacturing 11. Nonfiction that reads like fiction
LC 2014937343

ALA Notable Book, 2015; New York Times Notable Book, 2014.

Describes how the chairman of Vaughan-Bassett Furniture fought for his more than 700 employees in a small Virginia town using legal maneuvers, factory efficiencies and his wits and determination in the wake of sales losses to cheap Asian furniture imports.

"Macy's down-to-earth writing style and abundance of personal stories from manufacturing's beleaguered front lines make her work a stirring critique of globalization." —*Booklist*

Magner, Mike
Poisoned Legacy: The Human Cost of Bp's Rise to Power. Mike Magner. St. Martin's Press 2011. 384 p.
ISBN 9780312554941
Grades: Adult 338.7
1. Oil industry and trade 2. Oil 3. Oil workers 4. Corporations 5. Business ethics 6. Business and economics — Industries — Energy
LC 2010054461

An expose on British oil giant BP not only looks at the massive Deepwater Horizon explosion and oil spill but also the company's ongoing history of environmental and safety violations.

Mazzeo, Tilar J.
The Secret of Chanel No. 5: The Intimate History of the World's Most Famous Perfume. Tilar J. Mazzeo. Harper 2010. 304 p.
ISBN 9780061791017
Grades: Adult 338.7
1. Chanel, Coco, 1883-1971 2. Perfumes industry and trade 3. Perfumes 4. Fashion designers 5. Odors 6. France 7. Arts and Entertainment — General 8. History writing — Microhistory
LC 2010015284

Tilar Mazzeo shares her journey to discover the secret behind the creation, iconic status, and extraordinary success of Chanel No. 5, the world's most famous perfume.

"This unauthorized biography of a scent unearths the roots of the creation and fame of Coco Chanel's famous perfume. Mazzeo's lush prose covers relevant aspects of Coco Chanel's life, from the stark beauty of the orphanage where she was raised to the glamour and luxury of her adulthood, to the scents that wove through her life and shaped the development of her signature perfume. However, the book never bogs down in the detailsdespite the extensive research showcased in the bibliographyand a smooth pacing keeps it moving along at a fast clip." —*Library Journal*

Includes bibliographical references.

Mezrich, Ben
Breaking Twitter: Elon Musk and the Most Controversial Corporate Takeover in History. Ben Mezrich. Grand Central Publishing 2023. 288 p.
ISBN 9781538707593
Grades: Adult 338.7
1. Musk, Elon 2. Corporate acquisitions 3. Polarization (Social sciences) 4. Business 5. Social media 6. Technology 7. Internet 8. Ownership 9. Nonfiction that reads like fiction 10. Business and economics — Corruption and scandal 11. Business and economics — Industries — Technology

The New York Times best-selling author of the Accidental Billionaires tells the behind-the-scenes story of Elon Musk's controversial and polarizing acquisition of Twitter and its profound and continuing effects.

"This provides further proof of Mezrich's talent for chronicling the foibles of the tech elite." —*Publishers Weekly*

Micklethwait, John
The Company: A Short History of a Revolutionary Idea. John Micklethwait and Adrian Wooldridge. Modern Library 2003. xxiii, 227 p.
ISBN 9780679642497
Grades: Adult 338.7
1. Corporations 2. Incorporation 3. Entrepreneurship 4. Business 5. Commerce 6. Economic history 7. Business and economics — Economics — History
LC 2002026429

In The Company, the largely unknown history of the joint-stock company is presented by the editors of the Economist.

"In this history of the joint-stock company, Micklethwait and Wooldridge trace its progress from Assyrian partnership agreements through the 16th- and 17th-century European charter companies that opened trade with distant parts of the world, to today's multinationals. The authors' breadth of knowledge is impressive. They infuse their engaging prose with a wide range of cultural, historical and literary references, with quotes from poets to presidents. Moreover, the

ESSENTIAL AND RECOMMENDED TITLES
338.8 Combinations

authors argue that for all the change companies have engendered over time, their force has been for an aggregate good." —*Publishers Weekly*

Includes bibliographical references (p. [199]-212) and index.

Orbanes, Philip
The Game Makers: The Story of Parker Brothers from Tiddledy Winks to Trivial Pursuit. Philip E. Orbanes. Harvard Business School Press 2004. xvii, 245 p. : Illustration; Color

ISBN 9781591392699

Grades: Adult   338.7

1. Board games 2. Biographies 3. Sports and Competition — Games 4. Life stories — Business — Business leaders 5. Business and economics — Industries — Retail products and services

LC 2003010768

Presents a history of the toy industry, from the birth of board games with George S. Parker to how his successors built a family business empire and helped shape American culture.

"This is a study of the Parker Brothers, who developed such games as Monopoly, Clue and Risk. The author contends that the games reflect the American world view of the 20th century. Life is a ruthless struggle in which there are many losers, but it takes place within a framework of unbendable and fairminded rules." —*The Economist*

Includes bibliographical references (p. 221-232) and index.

Robertson, David C.
Brick by Brick: How Lego Rewrote the Rules of Innovation and Conquered the Global Toy Industry. David C. Robertson and Bill Breen. Crown Business 2013. 304 p.

ISBN 9780307951601

Grades: Adult   338.7

1. LEGO toys 2. Toy industry and trade 3. Toys 4. Business and economics — Industries — Retail products and services

LC 2013004798

The authors take you inside the LEGO you've never seen. By following the teams that are inventing some of the world's best-loved toys, it spotlights the company's disciplined approach to harnessing creativity and recounts one of the most remarkable business transformations in recent memory.

Robison, Peter
★ *Flying Blind: The 737 Max Tragedy and the Fall of Boeing.* Peter Robison. Doubleday 2021. 304 p.

ISBN 9780385546492

Grades: Adult   338.7

1. Commercial aviation 2. Airliners 3. Jet planes 4. Airplane accidents 5. Errors 6. Tragedy 7. Scandals 8. Corporate culture 9. Aircraft industry and trade 10. Accidents 11. United States 12. Business and economics — Corruption and scandal 13. Business and economics — Industries — Transportation

LC 2021006584

Boeing is a century-old titan of American industry, and remains a linchpin in the awesome routine of air travel today. But the two crashes of its 737 MAX 8, in 2018 and 2019, exposed a shocking pattern of malfeasance, leading to the biggest crisis in the company's history. How did things go so horribly wrong at Boeing? Flying Blind is the definitive expose of a corporate scandal that has transfixed the world. It reveals how a broken corporate culture paved the way for disaster, losses that were altogether avoidable. Drawing from aviation insiders, as well as exclusive interviews with senior Boeing staff, past and present, it shows how in its race to beat Airbus, Boeing skimped on testing, outsourced critical software to unreliable third-parties, and convinced regulators to put planes into service without properly equipping pilots to fly them.

"A remarkable look at corporate culture's impact on consumer safety, Flying Blind is a captivating and unsettling portrait of Boeing and American business." —*Booklist*

Includes bibliographical references and index.

338.8 Combinations

Bown, Stephen R.
Merchant Kings: When Companies Ruled the World, 1600-1900. Stephen R. Bown. Thomas Dunne Books 2010. 314 p. : Illustration

ISBN 9780312616113

Grades: Adult   338.8

1. Merchants 2. Monopolies 3. International businesses 4. Merchant ships 5. International trade 6. European history 7. Europe 8. Canadian literature 9. History writing — Europe 10. Business and economics — Economics — History

Traces the historically relevant contributions of six notorious merchant-adventurers who expanded their commercial enterprises to establish the world's first global monopolies, in a series of vignettes that includes profiles of such figures as Jan Pieterszoon Coen of the Dutch East India Company.

"The author has produced a magnificent description of the six great companies, and their leaders, that dominated the Heroic Age of Commerce. Bown demonstrates how the corporations served as stalking horses for kings and parliaments while enriching shareholders and the powerful managers themselves. Bown presents a fascinating look at the men who exploited resources and native peoples while laying the foundations of empires." —*Publishers Weekly*

Includes bibliographical references (p. 295-300) and index; Originally published: Vancouver, B.C. : Douglas & McIntyre, 2009.

Dayen, David
Monopolized: Life in the Age of Corporate Power. David Dayen. The New Press 2020. 336 p.

ISBN 9781620975411

Grades: Adult   338.8

1. Antitrust law 2. Corporations 3. Business ethics 4. Corporate power 5. Big business 6. Big business and politics 7. Business and economics — Corruption and scandal

LC 2019055148

Through vignettes and case studies, the editor of the American Prospect shows what it means to live in this new age of monopoly and how we might resist this corporate hegemony.

"A powerful, necessary call to arms to strengthen the antitrust movement and fight a system whose goal is complete control." —*Kirkus*

Includes bibliographical references and index.

Teachout, Zephyr
Break 'Em Up: Recovering Our Freedom from Big Ag, Big Tech, and Big Money. Zephyr Teachout; foreword by Senator Bernie Sanders. All Points Books 2020. 320 pages

ISBN 9781250200891

Grades: Adult   338.8

1. Monopolies 2. Antitrust law 3. Corporations 4. Wealth 5. Technology 6. Business ethics 7. Corporate power 8. Big business 9. Big business and politics 10. Business 11. World economy 12. Inequality 13. Business and mass media 14. Business and economics — economics — Contemporary U.S. economy 15. Politics and global affairs — General 16. Society and culture — Wealth and class 17. Business and economics — Industries

LC 2019058373

Teachout makes a compelling case that monopolies are the root cause of many of the issues that today's progressives care about; they drive economic inequality, harm the planet, limit the political power of average citizens, and historically-disenfranchised groups bear the brunt of their shameful and irresponsible business practices. In order to build a better future, we must eradicate monopolies from the private sector and create new safeguards that prevent new ones from seizing power. Through her expert analysis of monopolies in several sectors and their impact on courts, journalism, inequality, and politics, Teachout offers a concrete path toward thwarting these enemies of working Americans and reclaiming our democracy before it's too late.

"Attorney and political activist Teachout (Corruption in America) makes a passionate and persuasive case for a revitalized antitrust movement to strengthen democracy and improve the lives of middle- and working-class Americans ... Teachout delivers a forceful, clearly articulated vision of 'Moral markets' built on freedom, choice, and human dignity. Progressives will heed this clarion call for reform." —*Publishers Weekly*

Includes bibliographical references and index.

338.9 Economic development and growth

Ritchie, Hannah
Not the End of the World: How We Can Be the First Generation to Build a Sustainable Planet. Hannah Ritchie. Little Brown & CO 2024. 304 p.
ISBN 9780316536752
Grades: Adult 338.9
1. Sustainability 2. Climate change 3. Global environmental change 4. Climate change mitigation 5. Nature Writing — Environmental Issues

In this bold, radically hopeful book, a data scientist, drawing on the latest research, practical guidance and eye-opening graphics, gives us the tools for understanding our current environmental crisis and making lifestyle changes that actually have an impact.

"This energetic book argues that while humanity has significantly altered the natural world, surrendering to despair about that fact is not only counterproductive but unrealistic." —*Library Journal*

Sachs, Jeffrey
The Age of Sustainable Development. Jeffrey D. Sachs. Columbia University Press 2015. xvi, 543 pages : Illustration; Color; Map
ISBN 9780231173148
Grades: Adult 338.9
1. Sustainable development 2. Energy consumption 3. Economics 4. Renewable energy sources 5. Renewable resource management 6. World economy 7. Environmentalism 8. Business and economics — Economics — Socioeconomics 9. Politics and global affairs — Environmental issues and policies
LC 2014034070

Presents a practical framework to address the seemingly intractable worldwide problems of persistent extreme poverty, environmental degradation, and political-economic injustice: Sustainable development. Sachs explains how modern societies can develop economically, equitably, and sustainably.

"Overall, Sachs's book provides a basic but ambitious argument: to reverse current unsustainable trends, global warming must be mitigated, extreme poverty must end, gender imbalance must be corrected, and access to basic health care and education must be granted to all." —*Choice*

Includes bibliographical references (pages 513 - 519) and index.

338.91 International development and growth

Steil, Benn
★ *The Marshall Plan: Dawn of the Cold War.* Benn Steil. Simon & Schuster 2018. 592 p.
ISBN 9781501102370
Grades: Adult 338.91
1. Marshall Plan, 1948-1952 2. Economic assistance, American 3. Economic assistance 4. World politics 5. World economy 6. International relations 7. Economics 8. Europe 9. United States 10. 20th century 11. History writing — Post World War II - 1959 — United States
LC 2017301149

American History Book Prize, 2019.

The award-winning author of the Battle of Bretton Woods traces the dramatic history of the Marshall Plan and the ambitious efforts of Secretary of State George C. Marshall to reconstruct western Europe as a bulwark against communist authoritarianism, tracing a two-year period that shaped the collapse of postwar U.S.-Soviet relations and the beginning of the Cold War.

"Political history is often a tough slog, but Steil writes a vivid, opinionated narrative full of colorful characters, dramatic scenarios, villains, and genuine heroes, and the good guys won. It will be the definitive account for years to come." —*Kirkus*

339 Macroeconomics and related topics

Chatelain, Marcia
★ *Franchise: The Golden Arches in Black America.* Marcia Chatelain. Liveright Publishing 2020. 336 p.
ISBN 9781631493942
Grades: Adult 339
1. Fast food restaurants, chains, etc. 2. African American businesspeople 3. Restaurateurs 4. Chain restaurants 5. African American neighborhoods 6. African American-owned businesses 7. African American civil rights 8. Community activism 9. History writing — African American — United States 10. Business and economics — Industries — Agriculture and food 11. Society and culture — Race 12. Life stories — Business — Working life

Hurston/Wright Legacy Award: Nonfiction, 2021; Pulitzer Prize for History, 2021; James Beard Foundation Book Awards, Writing and Literature, 2022.

Traces the lesser-known history of how fast food became one of the greatest generators of Black wealth in America, revealing how unexpected collaborations among franchises, Black capitalists and civil rights leaders provided effective economic responses to racial inequality.

"This niche subject may not have wide-ranging appeal, but the research is invaluable for those studying the intersections of race, economics, and business in the United States." —*Library Journal*

339.2 Distribution of income and wealth

Milanovic, Branko
The Have and the Have-nots: A Short and Idiosyncratic History of Global Inequality. Branko Milanovic. Basic Books 2010. 236 p.
ISBN 9780465019748
Grades: Adult 339.2
1. Income inequality 2. Economic assistance 3. Rich people 4. Poor people 5. Poverty 6. Wealth 7. United States 8. Society and culture — Wealth and class
LC 2010029295

Booklist Editors' Choice, 2011.

A leading economist at the World Bank's research division traces the history of financial inequality as reflected in famous stories, analyzing such examples as the monetary disparities between Elizabeth Bennet and Mr. Darcy and the assets of wealthy ancient Romans compared to today's super-rich.

Includes bibliographical references and index.

Noah, Timothy
The Great Divergence: America's Growing Inequality Crisis and What We Can Do About It. Timothy Noah. Bloomsbury 2012. 264 p. : Illustration
ISBN 9781608196333
Grades: Adult 339.2
1. Economic policy 2. Inequality 3. Income inequality 4. Poverty 5. Wealth 6. Economics 7. United States 8. Business and economics — Economics — Contemporary U.S. economy 9. Society and culture — Wealth and class
LC 2011048447

Critically assesses income inequality in America and the ways it threatens democracy, tracing disturbing income ratio trends throughout the past three decades while outlining an urgent call for nonpartisan solutions.

Piketty, Thomas
The Economics of Inequality. Thomas Piketty, translated by Arthur Goldhammer. Belknap Press of Harvard University Press 2015. 144 p.
ISBN 9780674504806
Grades: Adult 339.2
1. Income inequality 2. Capitalism and inequality 3. Equality 4. Resource allocation 5. Social classes 6. Translations — French to English 7. Business and economics — Economics — Socioeconomics 8. Business and economics — Economics — History
LC 2015008813

Thomas Piketty—whose Capital in the Twenty-First Century pushed inequality to the forefront of public debate—wrote the Economics of Inequality as

ESSENTIAL AND RECOMMENDED TITLES
339.4 Factors affecting income and wealth

an introduction to the conceptual and factual background necessary for interpreting changes in economic inequality over time. This concise text has established itself as an indispensable guide for students and general readers in France, where it has been regularly updated and revised. Translated by Arthur Goldhammer, the Economics of Inequality now appears in English for the first time.

"Most readers will be better served by Capital in the Twenty-First Century, leaving students and economists as the likeliest audience for this title."—*Library Journal*

Originally published in French as Economie des inegalites, 1997.

Ridley, Matt
The Rational Optimist: How Prosperity Evolves. Matt Ridley. Harper 2010. 438 p. : Illustration
ISBN 9780061452055
Grades: Adult   339.2
1. Practical reason 2. Optimism 3. Prosperity 4. Wealth 5. History writing — General 6. Business and economics — Popular psychology
LC 2010004907

By looking at human history from its very beginning, the author argues disasters, downturns and setbacks are just part of a millenia-long cycle of increasing prosperity that will continue through the 21st century and beyond.

"The author posits that as long as civilization engages in exchange and specialization, we will be able to reinvent ourselves and responsibly use earthly resources ad infinitum. Ridley puts current perceptions about violence, wealth, and the environment into historical perspective, reaching back thousands of years to advocate global free trade, smaller government, and the use of fossil fuels. He confidently takes on the experts, from modern sociologists who fret over the current level of violence in the world to environmentalists who disdain genetically modified crops. An ambitious and sunny paean to human ingenuity, this is an argument for why ambitious optimism is morally mandatory."—*Publishers Weekly*

Includes bibliographical references and index.

Schwartz, Nelson
The Velvet Rope Economy: How Inequality Became Big Business. Nelson Schwartz. Doubleday 2020. 304 p.
ISBN 9780385543088
Grades: Adult   339.2
1. Classism 2. Inequality 3. Consumerism 4. Middle class 5. Class conflict 6. Rich consumers 7. Luxury 8. Working class 9. Income inequality 10. Economics 11. United States 12. 21st century 13. Impartial writing 14. Society and culture — Wealth and class 15. Business and economics — Economics — Consumerism
LC 2019021223

A New York Times business reporter investigates the invisible velvet rope that separates the rich from the middle- and working-class in America and how business innovators have exploited this divide catering to the wealthy while creating obstacles for everyone else.

"Economists and business professionals will be well-served by this insightful analysis, as will social activists and all those concerned by the growing separation between rich and poor." —*Library Journal*

339.4 Factors affecting income and wealth

Cohen, Lizabeth
A Consumers' Republic: The Politics of Mass Consumption in Postwar America. Lizabeth Cohen. Knopf 2003. 567 p. : Illustration
ISBN 9780375407505
Grades: Adult   339.4
1. Consumer economics 2. Equality 3. Consumer behavior 4. Economics 5. United States 6. 20th century 7. Business and economics — Economics — Consumerism
LC 2002141599

Booklist Editors' Choice, 2003.

An illuminating social and political history describes how mass consumption and the pursuit of prosperity transformed American life during the second half of the twentieth century, detailing the rise of political activism through the civil rights and consumer movements, the suburbanization of metropolitan areas, the changing relationship of Americans with government, and more.

"Without question, this is a difficult, demanding, and dense bookbut it is also a greatly significant contribution to business literature. Cohen submits a copiously researched, brilliantly conceived, and ultimately quite instructive study of American economics since the Depression."—*Booklist*

Includes bibliographical references and index.

Desmond, Matthew
★ *Evicted: Poverty and Profit in the American City.* Matthew Desmond. Crown 2016. 432 p.
ISBN 9780553447439
Grades: Adult   339.4
1. Low-income housing 2. Eviction 3. Poor families 4. Cities and towns 5. Poverty 6. Milwaukee, Wisconsin 7. United States 8. Society and culture — Wealth and class — Poverty
LC 2015027374

ALA Notable Book, 2017; Andrew Carnegie Medal for Excellence in Non-Fiction, 2017; Booklist Editors' Choice, 2016; Library Journal Best Books, 2016; National Book Critics Circle Award for Non-Fiction, 2016; New York Times Notable Book, 2016; PEN New England Award for Nonfiction, 2017; Pulitzer Prize for General Nonfiction, 2017; Robert F. Kennedy Book Award, 2017; Kirkus Prize for Nonfiction finalist, 2016.

A Harvard sociologist examines the under-represented challenge of eviction as a formidable cause of poverty in America, revealing how millions of people are wrongly forced from their homes and reduced to cycles of extreme disadvantage that are reinforced by dysfunctional legal systems.

Edin, Kathryn
$2.00 a Day: Living on Almost Nothing in America. Kathryn J. Edin, H. Luke Shaefer. Houghton Mifflin Harcourt 2015. 288 p.
ISBN 9780544303188
Grades: Adult   339.4
1. Poverty 2. Welfare 3. Poor people 4. Income inequality 5. Society and culture — Wealth and class — Poverty
LC 2015004337

New York Times Notable Book, 2015.

A revelatory assessment of poverty in America examines the survival methods employed by households with virtually no income to illuminate disturbing trends in low-wage labor and income inequality.

"An eye-opening account of the lives ensnared in the new poverty cycle." —*Kirkus*

★ *The Injustice of Place: Uncovering the Legacy of Poverty in America.* Kathryn J. Edin, H. Luke Shaefer, and Timothy J. Nelson. Mariner Books 2023. 352 p.
ISBN 9780063239494
Grades: Adult   339.4
1. Poverty 2. Rural poverty 3. Inequality 4. Cities and towns 5. Poor people 6. Economics 7. United States 8. Society and culture — Wealth and class — Poverty 9. Society and culture — Urban and regional studies 10. History Writing — United States
LC 2023009674

Through engaged ethnographic research, deep historical understanding and riveting storytelling, three of the nation's top researchers provide a sweeping and surprising new understanding of America's places of the most extreme poverty, shedding new light on deep disadvantage that must shape a new War on Poverty.

"This eye-opening account provides a powerful lens with which to view contemporary inequality in America." —*Publishers Weekly*

Includes bibliographical references and index.

Gerth, Karl
As China Goes, so Goes the World: How Chinese Consumers Are Transforming Everything. Karl Gerth. Hill and Wang 2011. 272 p.

ISBN 9780809026890

Grades: Adult   **339.4**

1. Consumerism 2. Consumer economics 3. Consumer behavior 4. Economic history 5. Economics 6. China 7. 21st century 8. Business and economics — Economics — Consumerism 9. Business and economics — Economics — World economy

LC Bl2013023456

Shares cautionary predictions about China's evolving consumer society and economy, revealing how the country's rapid development of a western-influenced consumer culture is resulting in a Chinese customer base that makes profoundly relevant, modern-world lifestyle choices.

Gordon, Robert J.

★ *The Rise and Fall of American Growth: The U.S. Standard of Living Since the Civil War.* Robert J. Gordon. Princeton University Press 2016. 776 p.

ISBN 9780691147727

Grades: Adult   **339.4**

1. Cost and standard of living 2. Economic history 3. Economics 4. United States 5. 20th century 6. Depression era (1929-1941) 7. Business and economics — Economics — History

LC 2015027560

New York Times Notable Book, 2016.

Discusses how the era of growth and innovations, which included the widespread affordability of amazing advances, from electricity to air travel, has ended and warns that the younger generation may be the first ever not to exceed their parents' standard of living.

"A masterful study to be read and reread by anyone interested in today's political economy." —*Kirkus*

Includes bibliographical references and index.

MacKinnon, J. B.

★ *The Day the World Stops Shopping: How Ending Consumerism Saves the Environment and Ourselves.* J.B. MacKinnon. Ecco 2021. 384 p.

ISBN 9780062856029

Grades: Adult   **339.4**

1. Consumer economics 2. Consumerism 3. Environmentalism 4. Green consumerism 5. Consumer society 6. Business and economics — Economics — Socioeconomics

LC 2021002621

Governor General's Literary Awards, English-language Non-fiction finalist.

Consuming less is our best strategy for saving the planet-but can we do it? In this thoughtful and surprisingly optimistic book, journalist J.B. MacKinnon investigates how we might achieve a world without shopping.

An award-winning journalist examines the effects of consumerism on the planet, looking towards a world without shopping and how it could help reduce carbon emissions and lead us to a closer relationship with our natural world and each other.

"MacKinnon's writing flows effortlessly and logically, incorporating solid research, relatable scenarios, and compelling arguments. Hopefully readers will stop and think the next time they're about to click Buy." —*Booklist*

Includes bibliographical references and index.

Rivlin, Gary

Broke, USA: From Pawnshops to Poverty, Inc. : How the Working Poor Became Big Business. by Gary Rivlin. Harper 2010. 358 p.

ISBN 9780061733215

Grades: Adult   **339.4**

1. Poor people 2. Poverty 3. Income 4. Social problems 5. Injustice 6. Low-wage workers 7. Pay equity 8. Pawnbroking 9. Social classes 10. Economics 11. United States 12. 21st century 13. Society and culture — Wealth and class — Poverty

LC 2010002874

Booklist Editors' Choice, 2010.

Delivers a shocking look at the under-reported poverty industry, which aims to mine the thin wallets of the country's poor through such ventures as subprime loans, pawn shops, check-cashing businesses, instant tax refunds, payday loans and more.

"A timely, important, and deeply disturbing look at the cycle of debt of the nation's most vulnerable." —*Publishers Weekly*

339.5 Macroeconomic policy

Steil, Benn

The Battle of Bretton Woods: John Maynard Keynes, Harry Dexter White, and the Making of a New World Order. Benn Steil. Princeton University Press 2013. 456 p.

ISBN 9780691149097

Grades: Adult   **339.5**

1. Keynes, John Maynard, 1883-1946 2. White, Harry Dexter, 1892-1948 3. Monetary policy 4. International finance 5. Economics 6. 20th century 7. Business and economics — Economics — History

LC 2012035709

Reveals how the blueprint for the post-World War II economic order was actually drawn.

A Council on Foreign Relations Book; Includes bibliographical references and index.

340.023 Law as a profession, occupation, hobby

Enrich, David

Servants of the Damned: Giant Law Firms, Donald Trump, and the Corruption of Justice. David Enrich. HarperCollins 2022. 416 p.

ISBN 9780063142176

Grades: Adult   **340.023**

1. Law firms 2. Corruption 3. Political corruption 4. White collar crime 5. United States 6. Politics and global affairs — World politics — United States

In this eye-opening new work of narrative nonfiction, the Business Investigations Editor at the New York Times focuses on Jones Day, one of the world's largest law firms who has become a highly effective enabler of the business world's worst behavior by protecting powerful bad actors in our society.

"Enrich's condemnations of corporations and their lawyers aren't always ironclad, but he delivers a vivid, crackling account of the law at its most bullying. Readers will be outraged." —*Publishers Weekly*

340.071 Law schools

Tamanaha, Brian Z.

Failing Law Schools. Brian Z. Tamanaha. The University of Chicago, Ill. :Press 2012. xvi, 235 pages

ISBN 9780226923611

Grades: Adult   **340.071**

1. Law schools 2. Law 3. Law — General

LC 2012006829

"Why does law school cost so much, and is it worth it? Tamanaha ... takes up these questions, recently subject to vigorous debate in the press and online." —*Library Journal*

340.072 Law — Research

Tucker, Virginia

Finding the Answers to Legal Questions. Virginia M. Tucker, Marc Lampson. ALA Neal-Schuman 2018. xxiv, 232 pages : Illustration; Footnotes

ISBN 9780838915691

Grades: Adult   **340.072**

1. Law 2. Legal research 3. United States 4. Law — General 5. Professional materials — General

LC 2017056093

This timely, clearly organized, and easy-to-use resource is an ideal text for LIS students preparing for careers as librarians. It provides an overview of the

ESSENTIAL AND RECOMMENDED TITLES
340.09 History, geographic treatment, biography of law

basic structure of the U.S. legal system; how-to instructions for finding primary law in printsources, free websites and pay-for-view databases; information on how to evaluate the trustworthiness of online and print resources; tips for conducting a legal reference interview; and guidance for handling common legal questions, such as lawsuits, family law, landlord-tenant disputes, and wills.

Includes bibliographical references and index.

340.09 History, geographic treatment, biography of law

Roffer, Michael H.
The Law Book: From Hammurabi to the International Criminal Court, 250 Milestones in the History of Law. Michael H. Roffer. Sterling 2015. 528 pages : Illustration; Color
ISBN 9781454901686
Grades: Adult   **340.09**
1. Law 2. Politics and global affairs — General
LC Bl2015050164

A visually stunning guide that is organized chronologically explores 250 of the most fundamental, far-reaching and often-controversial cases, laws and trials that have profoundly changed the world—for good or bad, presenting a comprehensive look at the rules by which people live their lives.

Explores over two hundred of the most fundamental and far-reaching cases, laws, and trials that have profoundly changed the world for good or bad, including the Justinian Code, the Nuremberg Trials, and the Affordable Care Act.

"This high quality and engaging book is recommended for most public libraries, where it will be appreciated more in a browsing collection than on a reference shelf." —*Booklist*

Includes bibliographical references (pages 511-524) and index.

340.092 Biography

Adams, Jarrett
Redeeming Justice: From Defendant to Defender, My Fight for Equity on Both Sides of a Broken System. Jarrett Adams. Convergent 2021. 272 p.
ISBN 9780593137819
Grades: Adult   **340.092**
1. Adams, Jarrett 2. Lawyers 3. African American lawyers 4. False imprisonment 5. Teenage prisoners 6. Defense attorneys 7. African American social advocates 8. African American defendants 9. Racism in the criminal justice system 10. Social justice 11. Autobiographies and memoirs 12. Life stories — Law and order — Judges and lawyers 13. Life stories — Law and order — Prisoners and inmates 14. Society and culture — Race 15. Society and culture — Violence and crime — Criminal justice system
LC 2021004332

Adam Jarrett was seventeen when an all-white jury sentenced him to prison for a crime he didn't commit. Now, in this unforgettable memoir, the pioneering lawyer recalls the journey that led to his exoneration—and inspired him to devote his life to fighting the many injustices in our legal system.

"There is rarely a minute when readers will not want to know what comes next, from prison to lawyering and fighting for not aspirational but equal justice, to how Adams handles each instance of anger, anxiety, guilt, and willpower in and out of prison. A consuming tale of a broken legal system, its trail of ruin, and the fortitude needed to overcome its scarring." —*Kirkus*

340.5 Legal systems

Ali-Karamali, Sumbul
Demystifying Shariah: What It Is, How It Works, and Why It's Not Taking Over Our Country. Sumbul Ali-Karamali. Beacon Press 2020. 256 p.
ISBN 9780807038000
Grades: Adult   **340.5**
1. Islamic law 2. Stereotypes 3. Islamophobia 4. Sharia (Islamic religious practice) 5. Islamic doctrines 6. Misinformation 7. Misconceptions 8. Muslims

9. Islam 10. Religions 11. United States 12. Spirituality and Religion — Islam — Political Aspects
LC 2019037396

A direct counterpoint to fear mongering headlines about shariah law tells the real story, eliminating stereotypes and assumptions with compassion, irony, and humor. Introducing us to the basic principles, goals and general development of shariah law, a Muslim American legal expert explains that shariah is religious rules and recommendations that provide Muslims with guidance in various aspects of life and describes the key lies and misunderstandings about shariah circulating in our public discourse.

"Taking something as complex as the Sharia and exploring it succinctly, lucidly, and without oversimplification is where this book excels. While a background in Islam is not required, some basic understanding of the faith will help readers. Well-suited—and highly recommended—for general readers (both Muslim and non-Muslim) with an interest in Sharia." —*Booklist*

Includes bibliographical references and index.

341.23 United Nations

Fasulo, Linda M.
An Insider's Guide to the Un, 4th Ed. Linda Fasulo. Yale University Press 2021. 335 p.
ISBN 9780300241259
Grades: 11 12 Adult   **341.23**
1. Diplomats 2. International relations 3. World politics 4. History writing — General 5. Adult books for young adults
LC 2003010668

School Library Journal Best Books: Best Adult Books 4 Teens, 2004.

Thoroughly revised and updated, a new edition of the most popular guide to the UN for students and interested readers.

4th edition; Includes bibliographical references and index.

341.4 Jurisdiction over physical space human rights

Waldman, Steven
Sacred Liberty: America's Long, Bloody, and Ongoing Struggle for Religious Freedom. Steve Waldman. HarperOne 2019. 288 pages
ISBN 9780062743145
Grades: Adult   **341.4**
1. Church and state 2. Freedom of religion 3. Religions 4. United States history 5. United States 6. History writing — United States 7. Spirituality and religion — General 8. Adult books for young adults
LC Bl2019006229

Argues that religious liberty is America's greatest innovation and the protection of religious minorities and the separation of church and state are at risk today.

341.48 Human rights

Sefarad, Mikhael
The Wall and the Gate: Israel, Palestine, and the Legal Battle for Human Rights. Michael Sfard; translated by Maya Johnston. Metropolitan Books, Henry Holt and Company 2017. 320 p.
ISBN 9781250122704
Grades: Adult   **341.48**
1. Israeli-Palestinian relations 2. Arab-Israeli conflict 3. Palestinian people 4. Human rights 5. Civil rights 6. Interethnic relations 7. West Bank (Jordan River) 8. Gaza strip 9. Israel 10. Palestine 11. Politics and global affairs — World politics — Southwest Asia and North Africa (Middle East) — Israel and Palestine 12. History writing — Arab-Israeli relations — Southwest Asia and North Africa (Middle East)
LC 2017000822

From renowned human rights lawyer Michael Sfard, an unprecedented exploration of the struggle for human rights in Israel's courts.
Includes bibliographical references and index.

341.5 Disputes and conflicts between states

Bass, Gary Jonathan
Freedom's Battle: The Origins of Humanitarian Intervention. by Gary J. Bass. Alfred A. Knopf 2008. 528 p.
ISBN 9780307266484
Grades: Adult   341.5
1. Intervention (International relations) 2. Intervention (International law) 3. Humanitarian assistance 4. Human rights policy 5. War 6. War and society 7. History writing — Wars and conflicts
LC 2007052252
New York Times Notable Book, 2008.
Traces the history of international humanitarian intervention, looking back over more than two hundred years to reveal the cultural and political factors that spawned early human rights activists and the role of a free press that exposed atrocities, from Greek oppression by the Ottoman Empire to the U.S. campaign against the 1915 Armenian genocide.
"This history of nineteenth-century campaigns to stop atrocities in Greece, Syria, and Bulgaria is a corrective to the idea that humanitarian interventions are a product of the dreamy interlude between 1989 and 9/11. The compelling narrative, rich with accounts of parliamentary debate and battlefield confrontation, presents a world of familiar political and military concerns, from the pressure of nonstop media coverage to the importance of a clear exit strategy. Bass's thesis that humanitarianism long preceded the crises of Bosnia and Rwanda is persuasive." —*The New Yorker*

341.6 Law of war

Lamb, Christina
Our Bodies, Their Battlefields: War Through the Lives of Women. Christina Lamb. Scribner 2020. 320 p.
ISBN 9781501199172
Grades: Adult   341.6
1. Women and war 2. Rape 3. Violence against women 4. Violence against marginalized women 5. War 6. Rape victims 7. Violent crimes 8. Sexual violence 9. War and society 10. Life stories — Facing adversity — War and oppression 11. Life stories — Facing adversity — Victims of crime 12. Society and culture — Violence and crime 13. Politics and global affairs — Civil and human rights
LC Bl2020052300
Lamb chronicles extraordinary tragedy and challenges in the lives of women in wartime. And none is more devastating than the increase of the use of rape as a weapon of war. Told as a journey, and structured by country, Our Bodies, Their Battlefields gives these women voice.
"A searing, absolutely necessary expose of the uses of rape in recent wars and of global injustices to the survivors." —*Kirkus*

Stern, Jessica
My War Criminal: Personal Encounters with an Architect of Genocide. Jessica Stern. Ecco 2020. 352 pages
ISBN 9780060889555
Grades: Adult   341.6
1. Stern, Jessica, 1958- 2. Karadzic, Radovan V, 1945- 3. War criminals 4. Genocide 5. White supremacists 6. War 7. Violence 8. Fear 9. War crimes 10. War crime trials 11. Yugoslav War, 1991-1995 12. Interviewing 13. White privilege 14. Atrocities 15. European history 16. Bosnia and Hercegovina 17. Biographies 18. Society and culture — Violence and crime — Genocide 19. History writing — Europe — Eastern Europe 20. History writing — Wars and conflicts — Civil Wars 21. Life stories — Politics — Politicians
LC Bl2019037365

An investigation into the nature of violence, terror, and trauma through conversations with a notorious war criminal and hero to white nationalists.
Includes bibliographical references.

341.69 War crimes

Rashke, Richard
Useful Enemies: John Demanjuk and America's Open-door Policy for Nazi War Criminals. Richard Rashke. HarperCollins 2013. xvii, 621 pages
ISBN 9781883285517
Grades: Adult   341.69
1. Nazis 2. War crimes 3. Immigration and emigration 4. History writing — United States
LC 2012285813
Examines the American government's campaign since 1940 to keep European Jews out of the U.S. and to secretly harbor Nazi war criminals, centering on the trial of John "Iwan" Demjanjuk, who was finally brought to justice in 2011.
"A richly researched, gripping narrative about war, suffering, survival, corruption, injustice and morality." —*Kirkus*

342.42 Law — England

Wise, Steven M.
Though the Heavens May Fall: The Landmark Trial That Led to the End of Human Slavery. Steven M. Wise. Da Capo Press 2005. xvi, 282 p. : Illustration
ISBN 9780738206950
Grades: Adult   342.42
1. Sommersett, James 2. Slavery 3. Enslaved people 4. Trials 5. Escapes 6. Politicians 7. Legislation 8. English history 9. 18th century 10. History writing — Colonialism — Europe 11. History writing — Colonization — Africa
LC 2004025346
Describes one of the most important and significant legal cases in history, the trial of James Somerset, which featured an incredible array of colorful figures fighting a landmark battle that would eventually lead to the end of slavery in the western world. 50,000 first prinitng.
"The author has an eye for evocative detail and an interest in the trappings and procedures of an 18th-century courtroom that do as much to engage the reader as the drama of the trials themselves." —*New York Times Book Review*
A Merloyd Lawrence book; Includes bibliographical references (p. 259-268) and index.

342.73 Constitutional law — United States

Amar, Akhil Reed
The Constitution Today: Timeless Lessons for the Issues of Our Era. Akhil Reed Amar. Basic Books 2016. 464 p.
ISBN 9780465096336
Grades: Adult   342.73
1. Constitutional history 2. Constitutional law 3. Essays 4. Society and culture — General 5. Politics and global affairs — Judicial politics
LC 2016023102
The Sterling Professor of Law and Political Science at Yale University considers the most bitterly contested debates of the last two decades—from gun control to gay marriage, affirmative action to criminal procedure, Bill Clinton's impeachment to Obamacare—helping readers to understand America's Constitution and its relevance today.
Includes bibliographical references and index.

Bade, Rachael
★ *Unchecked: The Untold Story Behind Congress's Botched Impeachments of Donald Trump.* Rachael Bade, Karoun Demirjian. William Morrow & Company 2022. 677 p.
ISBN 9780063040793

ESSENTIAL AND RECOMMENDED TITLES
342.73 Constitutional law — United States

Grades: Adult   **342.73**

1. Trump, Donald, 1946- 2. Presidents 3. Impeachments 4. Political parties 5. Misconduct in office 6. Capitol Riot, Washington, D.C, 2021 7. Separation of powers 8. Failure 9. Politics and government 10. United States 11. 21st century 12. Impartial writing 13. Politics and global affairs — Political figures 14. Politics and global affairs — Political parties 15. History writing — Presidency — 21st century — United States 16. History writing — Scandals

In a riveting account that flips the script on what readers think they know about the two impeachments of Donald Trump, Rachael Bade and Karoun Demirjian reveal how—and why—congressional oversight failed when it was needed most. Sourced from hundreds of interviews with all the key players, the authors of Unchecked pull back the curtain on how both parties pursued political expediency over fact-finding. The end result not only emboldened Trump, giving him room for a political comeback, but also undermined Congress by rendering toothless their most powerful check on a president: the power of impeachment.

"Though some of the political and legal headwinds faced by Democrats get short shrift, this is a thorough and often riveting account of why the efforts to impeach Trump failed." —*Publishers Weekly*

Barron, David J.
Waging War: The Clash Between Presidents and Congress, 1776 to Isis. David J. Barron. Simon & Schuster 2016. 496 p.
ISBN 9781451681970
Grades: Adult   **342.73**

1. War and emergency powers 2. War, Declaration of 3. Legislative power 4. Constitutional history 5. Decision-making 6. Politics and war 7. Public opinion 8. Executive power 9. Presidents 10. Politics and government 11. United States 12. History writing — Wars and conflicts 13. History writing — United States

A United States Circuit Judge describes the historical struggles that took place between sitting presidents and Congress over who has the power to start wars, including the American Revolution, the War of 1812 and the Civil War, all the way up through the fight against ISIS.

Includes bibliographical references and index.

Brettschneider, Corey Lang
The Oath and the Office: A Guide to the Constitution for Future Presidents. Corey Brettschneider. W.W. Norton & Company 2018. 224 p.
ISBN 9780393652123
Grades: Adult   **342.73**

1. Presidents 2. Constitutional law 3. Constitutional history 4. Separation of powers 5. Power 6. Elections 7. Political questions and judicial power 8. Executive power 9. Politics and government 10. United States 11. History writing — United States 12. Politics and global affairs — General

LC 2018016664

An essential guide to the presidential powers and limits of the Constitution answers timely questions about the checks and balances of government power and how the people of today's America can make informed voting and running decisions.

"The author offers a clear explanation of many complex issues, such as the provisions of the 14th Amendment, which guarantees equal protection under the law; and the process involved in impeachment, including the question of whether obstruction of justice is an impeachable offense. A cleareyed, accessible, and informative primer: Vital reading for all Americans." —*Kirkus*

Includes bibliographical references and index.

The Presidents and the People: Five Leaders Who Threatened Democracy and the Citizens Who Fought to Defend It. Corey Brettschneider. W. W. Norton 2024. 384 p.
ISBN 9781324006275
Grades: Adult   **342.73**

1. Presidents 2. Constitutional law 3. Executive power 4. Constitutional history 5. Separation of powers 6. Power 7. Politics and government 8. Civil rights 9. Crime 10. Elections 11. Democracy 12. United States 13. Politics and global affairs — Political figures 14. History writing — Presidency — United States

This meticulously researched account of assaults on democracy by five presidents who imprisoned critics, spread a culture of white supremacy and committed crimes with impunity shows how citizens like Frederick Douglass, Ida B. Wells and Daniel Ellsberg fought back against presidential abuses of power.

"A welcome reminder, in a time of growing repression, of the power of well-placed dissent." —*Kirkus*

Burnham, Margaret A.
★ *By Hands Now Known: Jim Crow's Legal Executioners.* Margaret A. Burnham. W W Norton & Company 2022. 352 p.
ISBN 9780393867855
Grades: Adult   **342.73**

1. Violence against African Americans 2. Racism 3. Law 4. Injustice 5. Race relations 6. United States 7. 20th century 8. History writing — United States 9. Politics and global affairs — Civil and human rights

Hurston/Wright Legacy Award: Nonfiction, 2023; Los Angeles Times Book Prize for History, 2022.

The director of Northeastern University's Civil Rights and Restorative Justice Project examines the legal apparatus that helped sustain Jim Crow-era violence, focusing on a series of harrowing cases from 1920 to 1960.

"Burnham, founding director of the Civil Rights and Restorative Justice Project at Northeastern University, debuts with a searing study of the 'Chronic, unpredictable violence that loomed over everyday Black life' in the Jim Crow South….The result is an essential reckoning with America's history of racial violence." —*Publishers Weekly*

Dennie, Madiba K.
The Originalism Trap: How Extremists Stole the Constitution and How We the People Can Take It Back. Madiba K. Dennie. Random House 2024. xii, 286 pages
ISBN 9780593729250
Grades: Adult   **342.73**

1. Constitutional law 2. Law and politics 3. Law 4. Reproductive rights 5. United States 6. History Writing — United States 7. Politics and global affairs — Civil and human rights 8. Politics and global affairs — Judicial politics

LC 2023059052

Discarding originalism in favor of a new approach that serves everyone: Inclusive constitutionalism, this thought-provoking book disentangles the Constitution's ideals from originalist ideology and emphasizes the power of the Reconstruction Amendments, showing readers the Constitution belongs to them and how they can use it to fight for their rights.

"A compelling case for considering the Constitution as palimpsest and not Mosaic tablet." —*Kirkus*

Includes index.

Finan, Christopher M.
How Free Speech Saved Democracy: The Untold History of How the First Amendment Became an Essential Tool for Securing Liberty and Social Justice. Christopher M. Finan; foreword by Randall Kennedy. Truth to Power Books 2022. 288 p. : Illustration
ISBN 9781586422981
Grades: Adult   **342.73**

1. Freedom of speech 2. Democracy 3. Social justice 4. Social change 5. Freedom 6. Politics and government 7. United States 8. History writing — United States 9. Politics and global affairs — Civil and human rights

Uncovering vivid and engaging stories about First Amendment pioneers, How Free Speech Saved Democracy shows how their struggle made possible the surging protests that aim to expand democracy today.

"Accessible, useful, and relevant." —*Booklist*

Foner, Eric
The Second Founding: How the Civil War and Reconstruction Remade the Constitution. Eric Foner. W.W. Norton & Company 2019. 288 p.
ISBN 9780393652574
Grades: Adult   **342.73**

1. Constitutional history 2. Reconstruction (United States history) 3. Constitutional law 4. Judicial process 5. Race relations 6. United States history 7. American Civil War era (1861-1865) 8. History writing — Reconstruction — United States 9. Politics and global affairs — General

LC 2019014793

The Declaration of Independence announced equality as an American ideal, but it took the Civil War and the subsequent adoption of three constitutional amendments to establish that ideal as American law. The author of the Fiery Trial presents a timely history of the constitutional changes that built or compromised equality within America's foundation, documenting alarming parallels between the Jim Crow era and the present day.

"Readers invested in social equality will find Foners guarded optimism about the possibility of judicial activism in this area inspiring, and both casual readers and those well-versed in American legal history will benefit from his clear prose and insightful exploration of constitutional history." —*Publishers Weekly*

Includes bibliographical references and index.

Jacobs, A. J.
★ *The Year of Living Constitutionally: One Man's Humble Quest to Follow the Constitution's Original Meaning.* A.J. Jacobs. Crown Publishing 2024. 240 p.

ISBN 9780593136744

Grades: Adult   342.73

1. Jacobs, A. J, 1968- 2. Constitutional law 3. Constitutional amendments 4. Constitutional history 5. United States 6. Autobiographies and memoirs 7. Life stories — Personal growth 8. Politics and global affairs — General 9. Humor writing — Political satire

LC 2023057911

A New York Times best-selling author chronicles his hilarious adventures as he attempts to live as closely as possible to the original meaning of the Constitution, and conducting interviews with constitutional experts from both sides, delves into originalism and living constitutionalism, the two rival ways of interpreting the document.

"Funny but not snarky, inventive but not obnoxious, learned but not pedantic, this book will make readers think about the nation's founding document more." —*Booklist*

Includes bibliographical references.

Rabban, David M.
Free Speech in Its Forgotten Years. David M. Rabban. Cambridge University Press 1997. xi, 404 p. : Illustration

ISBN 9780521620130

Grades: Adult   342.73

1. Freedom of speech 2. United States history 3. History writing — United States

LC 97015281

Offers evidence that between the Civil War and World War I, litigation over freedom of speech was quite common, with controversies over attempts to suppress labor unions, freethinkers, and sex reformers.

"Of particular note is Rabban's treatment of the tension between libertarian radicalism and American liberalism, especially in the context of the debate over the meaning and application of the free speech provision of the First Amendment. This enlightening work fills a void in First Amendment civil liberties studies." —*Library Journal*

Includes bibliographical references and index.

Rosenberg, Ian
The Fight for Free Speech: Ten Cases That Define Our First Amendment Freedoms. Ian Rosenberg. New York University Press 2021. 320 p.

ISBN 9781479801565

Grades: Adult   342.73

1. Freedom of speech 2. Freedom of expression 3. Freedom of the press 4. Constitutional law 5. Democracy 6. Politics and government 7. United States 8. Politics and global affairs — Civil and human rights 9. Politics and global affairs — Judicial politics 10. History writing — Judicial branch — United States

Americans today are confronted by a barrage of questions relating to their free speech freedoms. What are libel laws, and do they need to be changed to stop the press from lying? Does Colin Kaepernick have the right to take a knee? Can Saturday Night Live be punished for parody? The Fight for Free Speech answers this call with an accessible, engaging user's guide to free speech. Media lawyer Ian Rosenberg distills the spectrum of free speech law down to ten critical issues. Each chapter in this book focuses on a contemporary free speech question and then identifies, unpacks, and explains the key Supreme Court case that provides the answers. Together these fascinating stories create a practical framework for understanding where our free speech protections originated and how they can develop in the future.

"Rosenberg presents challenging, provocative material in an engaging manner that will have readers pondering these issues. Anyone interested in the history of free speech and the Supreme Court will enjoy this extensively researched book." —*Library Journal*

Simon, James F.
What Kind of Nation: Thomas Jefferson, John Marshall, and the Epic Struggle to Create a United States. James F. Simon. Simon & Schuster 2002. 348 p.

ISBN 9780684848709

Grades: Adult   342.73

1. Jefferson, Thomas, 1743-1826 2. Marshall, John, 1755-1835 3. Constitutional history 4. States' rights (American politics) 5. Political questions and judicial power 6. Executive power 7. Federal government 8. Politics and government 9. United States 10. 18th century 11. Early America (1784-1819) 12. 19th century 13. History writing — Presidency — 18th century — United States 14. History writing — Early America — United States 15. History writing — Presidency — 19th century — United States

LC 2001055027

New York Times Notable Book, 2002.

A re-creation of the battle between a President and a Chief Justice reveals how John Marshall's view that a strong federal government and an independent judiciary provide the best protection for the Constitution and the people still exists today.

"Simon's enlivening account proves that writing about constitutional law needn't be the dry preserve of academics." —*Booklist*

Includes bibliographical references (p. [303]-325) and index.

Smith, J. Douglas
On Democracy's Doorstep: The Inside Story of How the Supreme Court Brought. J. Douglas Smith. Hill and Wang 2014. 352 p.

ISBN 9780809074235

Grades: Adult   342.73

1. Apportionment (Election law) 2. Democracy 3. Voting 4. Politics and government 5. United States 6. Politics and global affairs — Judicial politics

LC 2013040784

The author of Managing White Supremacy shares the inside story of the Supreme Court rulings abolishing malapportionment, citing the crucial roles of Chief Justice Earl Warren and key lawyers, activists and Justice Department officials in establishing equality as a defining component of democracy.

Includes index.

Sullivan, Kevin
Trump on Trial: The Investigation, Impeachment, Acquittal and Aftermath. Kevin Sullivan and Mary Jordan. Scribner 2020. xxvi, 532 p.

ISBN 9781982152994

Grades: Adult   342.73

1. Trump, Donald, 1946- 2. Trials (Impeachment) 3. Abuse of administrative power 4. Politicians 5. Journalists 6. Mass media 7. Impeachments 8. Presidents 9. International relations 10. Politics and government 11. Ukraine 12. United States 13. 2010s 14. 2020s 15. 21st century 16. Politics and global affairs — Political figures 17. Politics and global affairs — Mass media and politics 18. History writing — Presidency — 21st century — United States 19. History writing — Scandals

LC Bl2020019453

In the spring of 2019, Speaker of the House Nancy Pelosi did not favor pursuing President Trump's impeachment. Her view was: "He's just not worth it." but by September, after a whistleblower complaint suggesting that Trump had used his office for his political benefit, Pelosi decided to risk it. The impeach-

ESSENTIAL AND RECOMMENDED TITLES
342.7302 Constitutions — United States

ment inquiry led to charges of abuse of power and obstruction of Congress, a gamble that ultimately meant Trump would be the first impeached president on the ballot in US history. Kevin Sullivan and Mary Jordan deftly illuminate the aims and calculations of key figures.

"Including 45 pages of footnotes and an exhaustive index, the granular detail of this history makes it a gift to posterity—and to news junkies—but any reader who does not support Trump will find plenty of useful material. Sets a standard for political storytelling with impeccable research and lively writing." —*Kirkus*

Includes bibliographical references and index.

Sunstein, Cass R.
Impeachment: A Citizen's Guide. Cass R. Sunstein. Harvard University Press 2017. 199 pages
ISBN 9780674983793
Grades: Adult   342.73
1. Political obligation 2. Responsibility 3. Trials (Impeachment) 4. Constitutional law 5. Impeachments 6. Presidents 7. United States 8. Impartial writing 9. Politics and global affairs — General

Cass Sunstein considers actual and imaginable arguments for a president's removal, explaining why some cases are easy and others hard, why some arguments for impeachment are judicious and others not. In direct and approachable terms, he dispels the fog surrounding impeachment so that all Americans may use their ultimate civic authority wisely.

"The resulting book is an essential guide to understanding impeachments function within the 'Constitutional system as a whole' and a persuasive argument that the impeachment clause places 'The fate of the republic' in the hands of its citizenry." —*Publishers Weekly*

Includes bibliographical references (pages 177-196) and index.

Tribe, Laurence H.
Uncertain Justice: The Roberts Court and the Constitution. Laurence Tribe, Joshua Matz. Henry Holt and Co. 2014. 352 p.
ISBN 9780805099096
Grades: Adult   342.73
1. Constitutional law 2. Politics and government 3. United States 4. Politics and global affairs — World politics — United States 5. Politics and global affairs — Judicial politics

LC 2014002845

An assessment of how the Supreme Court under Chief Justice John Roberts is significantly influencing the nation's laws and reinterpreting the Constitution includes in-depth analysis of recent rulings and their implications.

"A well-researched, unsettling investigation of recent trends in the nation's highest court." —*Kirkus*

Includes index.

342.7302 Constitutions — United States

Amar, Akhil Reed
★ *America's Constitution: A Biography.* Akhil Reed Amar. Random House 2005. xii, 657 p. : Illustration
ISBN 9781400062621
Grades: 11 12 Adult   342.7302
1. Constitutional history 2. Constitutional law 3. Politics and government 4. United States history 5. United States 6. Politics and global affairs — Political philosophy

LC 2004061464

Offers an analysis of the history and tenets of the U.S. Constitution, detailing the original intent of the creators of the document, answering questions about the text, and critically assessing the evolution of the Bill of Rights and all other amendments.

"Only rarely do you find a book that embodies scholarship at its most solid and invigorating; this is such a book." —*Publishers Weekly*

Includes bibliographical references and index.

The Words That Made US: America's Constitutional Conversation, 1760-1840. Akhil Reed Amar. Basic Books 2021. 592 p.
ISBN 9780465096350
Grades: Adult   342.7302
1. Constitutional history 2. Constitutional law 3. Law 4. Nation building 5. Literary criticism 6. United States history 7. History writing — Early America — United States

LC 2020046037

Constitutional scholar Akhil Reed Amar tells the story of America's constitutional conversation during its first eighty years—from the Constitution's birth in 1760 through the 1830s, when the last of America's early leaders died. Amar traces the threads of Constitutional discourse, uniting history and law in a narrative that seeks both to reveal this history anew and to make clear who was right and who was wrong on the biggest legal issues confronting early America. Amar provides an essential history of the Constitution's formative decades and an indispensable guide for anyone seeking to understand America's Constitution and its relevance today.

"Although sometimes dense in detail, Amar's original work offers general readers an accessible and often entertaining narrative and lessons to glean from the founding document of the United States." —*Library Journal*

Includes bibliographical references and index.

Beeman, Richard R.
★ *Plain, Honest Men: The Making of the American Constitution.* Richard Beeman. Random House 2009. 544 p.
ISBN 9781400065707
Grades: Adult   342.7302
1. Constitutional history 2. Conflict resolution 3. Common good 4. Separation of powers 5. Compromise 6. Consensus (Social sciences) 7. Executive power 8. United States history 9. United States 10. 18th century 11. History writing — Early America — United States

LC 2008028841

Demonstrates how the American Constitution was forged through conflict, compromise, and eventually fragile consensus as James Madison and his cohorts devised a plan to radically alter the balance of governmental power.

Includes bibliographical references.

Ellis, Joseph J.
The Quartet: Orchestrating the Second American Revolution, 1783-1789. Joseph J. Ellis. Alfred A. Knopf 2015. 320 p.
ISBN 9780385353403
Grades: Adult   342.7302
1. Washington, George, 1732-1799 2. Hamilton, Alexander, 1757-1804 3. Jay, John, 1745-1829 4. Madison, James, 1751-1836 5. Founding Fathers of the United States 6. American Revolution, 1775-1783 7. Revolutions 8. Politics and government 9. United States history 10. United States 11. Revolutionary America (1775-1783) 12. Early America (1784-1819) 13. 1780s 14. History writing — Early America — United States

LC 2014034503

The Pulitzer Prize-winning author of Founding Brothers shares historical insights into America's post-Revolution efforts for independence, citing key debates over the creations of the Articles of Confederation and the Bill of Rights.

"Ellis's approach employs deft characterizations and insights into these politicians and philosophers. With his usual skill, Ellis brings alive what otherwise might seem dry constitutional debates, with apt quotations and bright style." —*Publishers Weekly*

Klarman, Michael J.
The Framers' Coup: The Making of the United States Constitution. Michael J. Klarman. Oxford University Press 2016. 840 p.
ISBN 9780199942039
Grades: Adult   342.7302
1. Constitutional history 2. Historic documents 3. Constitutions 4. Founding Fathers of the United States 5. Politicians 6. 18th century 7. History writing — Early America — United States

LC 2016009496

Told largely through the voices of the participants, explains how the framers' interests shaped the American Constitution and argues that the document's sanctity should not go unchallenged today.

"A monumental project carried off to a high degree of excellence." —*Kirkus*

Madison, James
★ *The Constitutional Convention: A Narrative History : From the Notes of James Madison.* Edward J. Larson and Michael P. Winship. Modern Library 2005. x, 229 p.
ISBN 9780812975178
Grades: 11 12 Adult   **342.7302**
1. Constitutional history 2. Arts and Entertainment — Writing and Publishing 3. History writing — Early America — United States
LC 2005041649

Authoritative editions of great classics of world literature feature introductions by acclaimed writers, meticulous translations of foreign literature, commentary by distinguished writers and critics, biographical notes, and a comprehensive Reading Group Guide bound into each volume.

Presents the notes kept by James Madison at the Constitutional Convention and includes background information on all delegates and an overview of the times.

Includes bibliographical references p. ([217]-222) and index.

Maier, Pauline
Ratification: The People Debate the Constitution, 1787-1788. Pauline Maier. Simon & Schuster 2010. 544 p.
ISBN 9780684868547
Grades: Adult   **342.7302**
1. Constitutional history 2. Founding fathers of the United States 3. Civil rights 4. Politics and government 5. United States 6. 18th century 7. History writing — Early America — United States
LC 2010027709

New York Times Notable Book, 2010.

Draws on the speeches and letters of the United States' founders to recount the dramatic period after the Constitutional Convention and before the Constitution was finally ratified, describing the debates that took place in homes, taverns, and convention halls throughout the colonies.

"On Sept. 17, 1787, the convention that had been sitting in Philadelphia for four months to design a new form of government for the United States adjourned, offering its handiwork to the nation. Almost a year later, on Sept. 13, 1788, Congress declared that the Constitution had been duly ratified, and prescribed the rules for the first presidential election the following year. [This] book shows how America got from the first date to the secondand ultimately to today, since we still live with the same document, however modified." —*New York Times Book Review*

Meyerson, Michael
Liberty's Blueprint: How Madison and Hamilton Wrote the Federalist Papers, Defined the Constitution, and Made Democracy Safe for the World. Michael I. Meyerson. Basic Books 2008. 272 p.
ISBN 9780465002641
Grades: Adult   **342.7302**
1. Hamilton, Alexander, 1757-1804 2. Madison, James, 1751-1836 3. Founding fathers of the United States 4. Constitutional history 5. Constitutional law 6. Intellectuals 7. Intellectual life 8. 18th century 9. History writing — Early America — United States
LC 2007035376

Examines how the Federalist Papers were written and the philosophical thinking that shaped the Constitution, and explores how the wisdom of the Papers' main authors can illuminate current discussions of controversial issues.

Paulsen, Michael Stokes
The Constitution: An Introduction. Michael Stokes Paulsen and Luke Paulsen. Basic Books, a member of the Perseus Books Group 2015. 448 p.
ISBN 9780465053728
Grades: Adult   **342.7302**
1. Constitutional history 2. Constitutional law 3. Political science 4. Politics and government 5. United States 6. History writing — United States
LC 2014041943

Offers a lively introduction to the supreme law of the United States, covering the Constitution's history and meaning in clear, accessible terms.

"This is a highly accessible and scholarly but lively look at the nations guiding document." —*Booklist*

Includes bibliographical references and index.

Raphael, Ray
Constitutional Myths: What We Get Wrong and How to Get It Right. Ray Raphael. The New Press 2013. 316 p.
ISBN 9781595588326
Grades: Adult   **342.7302**
1. Constitutional history 2. Political science 3. Democracy 4. United States history 5. 18th century 6. Early America (1784-1819) 7. History writing — United States
LC 2012041849

Aims to dispel myths about the Constitution propagated by both the left and the right.

Includes bibliographical references and index.

Urofsky, Melvin I.
Dissent and the Supreme Court: Its Role in the Court's History and Nation's Constitutional Dialogue. Melvin I. Urofsky. Pantheon Books 2015. xiii, 528 pages : Illustration
ISBN 9780307379405
Grades: Adult   **342.7302**
1. Dissenting opinions 2. Judges 3. Constitutional law 4. Law 5. Literary criticism 6. Politics and government 7. United States 8. History writing — Judicial branch — United States 9. Politics and global affairs — Judicial politics
LC 2014048245

An examination of the role of dissent in the Supreme Court and interpretations of the Constitution examines key events throughout the Court's more than two-century history.

"This is an insightful look at dissents as dialogues between the justices that reflect broader dialogues among citizens on the controversial issues of our time." —*Kirkus*

342.730203 Constitutions — United States — Dictionaries and encyclopedias

Maddex, Robert L.
The U.S. Constitution A to Z. Robert L. Maddex. CQ Press 2008. xxix, 736 p. : Illustration; Map
ISBN 9780872897649
Grades: Adult   **342.730203**
1. Constitutional law 2. Constitutional history 3. Encyclopedias 4. Reference books 5. Law — General
LC 2008021902

Presents alphabetically arranged entries on topics related to the U.S. Constitution, ranging from abortion to zoning, and highlights current controversies and debates.

Includes bibliographical references (p. 693-702) and index.

Schultz, David A.
Encyclopedia of the United States Constitution. David Schultz. Facts on File 2009. 2 v. (xvii, 904 p.) : Illustration
ISBN 9780816067633
Grades: 9 10 11 12 Adult   **342.730203**
1. Constitutional law 2. History books — United States 3. Reference — Encyclopedias
LC 2008023349

Presents more than seven hundred alphabetically arranged entries on topics related to the U.S. Constitution, covering such areas as affirmative action, freedom of speech, privacy, and environmental regulations.

"This reference source can help high-school students, the general public, and other interested parties comprehend the fundamental concepts, evolutionary

ESSENTIAL AND RECOMMENDED TITLES
342.7303 Constitutional amendments — United States

character, and historic people and events that have shaped the [Constitution.]… the alphabetically arranged entries cover terms, events, people, landmark cases, and issues that help explain the Constitution's history. The appendix provides the Declaration of Independence, the Articles of Confederation, the Constitution, and the Bill of Rights as well as Other Amendments to the Constitution, a U.S. Constitution Time Line, and instructions on locating court cases." —*Booklist*
Includes bibliographical references (p. 858-864) and index.

342.7303 Constitutional amendments — United States

Vile, John R.
Encyclopedia of Constitutional Amendments, Proposed Amendments, and Amending Issues, 1789-2010. John R. Vile. ABC-CLIO 2010. 2 v. (xxxiv, 628, xiv, 28 p.)
ISBN 9781598843163
Grades: 10 11 12 Adult   342.7303
1. Constitutional amendments 2. Constitutional history 3. Encyclopedias 4. History writing — United States
LC 2010002113
"The author discusses the Constitution, its 27 ratified amendments, and the approximately 11,700 amendments proposed within the titular time frame to present a unique window into American history and politics. The alphabetical format and detailed index make information access a breeze, and the six appendixes provide a reprint of the Constitution along with charts of the number of proposals by decade, key events, and names of individuals submitting the proposals." —*Library Journal*
Includes bibliographical references and index.

342.7308 Constitutional law — United States — Groups of people

Carpenter, Dale
Flagrant Conduct: The Story of Lawrence V. Texas : How a Bedroom Arrest Decriminalized Gay Americans. Dale Carpenter. W. W. Norton & Company 2012. 352 p.
ISBN 9780393062083
Grades: Adult   342.7308
1. Lawrence, John Geddes 2. Sodomy (Law) 3. Homosexuality 4. LGBTQIA+ rights 5. Gay men 6. Legislation 7. Human rights 8. Civil rights 9. True Crime — Investigations and Trials 10. True Crime — Sex Crimes
LC 2011047245
Lambda Literary Award for LGBT Nonfiction; New York Times Notable Book, 2012.
Provides a detailed legal history and examines the motives of all players involved with the landmark Supreme Court gay rights case that protected consenting adults' rights, regardless of sexual preference, in the bedroom.
Includes bibliographical references and index.

Citron, Danielle Keats
The **Fight** *for Privacy: Protecting Dignity, Identity, and Love in the Digital Age*. Danielle Keats Citron. W.W. Norton & Company 2022. 320 p.
ISBN 9780393882315
Grades: Adult   342.7308
1. Privacy 2. High technology 3. Health 4. Interpersonal relations 5. Gender identity 6. Corporations 7. Manipulation (Social sciences) 8. Profit 9. Exploitation 10. High technology industry and trade 11. Civil rights 12. Social advocacy 13. Human-computer interaction 14. Society and culture — Media and technology 15. Business and economics — Industries — Technology 16. Politics and global affairs — Civil and human rights
The essential road map for understanding—and defending—your right to privacy in the twenty-first century.
"Accessible legal reasoning and galling case studies make this a cogent argument for reform." —*Publishers Weekly*

Davis, Lennard J.
Enabling Acts: The Hidden Story of How the Americans with Disabilities Act Gave the Largest Us Minority Its Rights. Lennard Davis. Beacon Press 2015. 296 p.
ISBN 9780807071564
Grades: Adult   342.7308
1. Discrimination 2. People with disabilities 3. Legislation 4. Society and culture — Illness and disease
LC 2014046510
Published to coincide with the 25th anniversary of the Americans with Disabilities Act (ADA), an acclaimed disability scholar tells the untold story of how a group of leftist Berkeley hippies managed to make an alliance with conservative Republicans to bring about a truly bipartisan bill.
"A lively and well-researched legal saga suited to general readers interested in current events and disability issues." —*Library Journal*
Includes bibliographical references and index.

Ford, Richard T.
Rights Gone Wrong: How Law Corrupts the Struggle for Equality. Richard Thompson Ford. Farrar, Straus and Giroux 2011. 288 p.
ISBN 9780374250355
Grades: Adult   342.7308
1. Racism 2. Social justice 3. Civil rights 4. United States 5. Society and culture — Race
LC 2011010705
New York Times Notable Book, 2011.
Argues that civil rights laws do very little to combat less-overt forms of discrimination and prejudice.
Includes bibliographical references and index.

Goldstone, Lawrence
On Account of Race: The Supreme Court, White Supremacy, and the Ravaging of African American Voting Rights. Lawrence Goldstone. Counterpoint Press 2020. xii, 283 pages
ISBN 9781640093928
Grades: Adult   342.7308
1. African Americans 2. Suffrage 3. African American history 4. 19th century 5. 20th century 6. History writing — Judicial branch — United States 7. History writing — African American — Civil rights — United States 8. Politics and global affairs — Civil and human rights
LC 2019037734
The award-winning Constitutional Law historian and author of Inherently Unequal examines case-based evidence to reveal the Supreme Court's long-standing support of white supremacy in the form of "state rights" and how bias has enabled imbalances in key judicial powers.
"This well-sourced and accessible account makes a convincing case that America's highest court played a key role in stalling Black progress for a century." —*Publishers Weekly*
Includes bibliographical references (pages 241-271) and index.

Greene, Jamal
How Rights Went Wrong: Why Our Obsession with Rights Is Tearing America Apart. Jamal Greene. Houghton Mifflin Harcourt 2021. 288 p.
ISBN 9781328518118
Grades: Adult   342.7308
1. Affirmative action 2. Discrimination 3. Civil rights 4. United States 5. Politics and global affairs — Social issues and policies
LC 2020034165
An eminent constitutional scholar reveals how the explosion of rights is dividing America, and shows how we can build a better system of justice.
"Greene delves deeply into the legal, cultural, and political matters behind rights conflicts, and laces his account with feisty legal opinions and colorful character sketches. This incisive account persuades." —*Publishers Weekly*
Includes bibliographical references and index.

PUBLIC LIBRARY CORE COLLECTION: NONFICTION
Twentieth Edition

Healy, Thomas
*The **Great** Dissent: How Oliver Wendell Holmes Changed His Mind and Changed the History of Free Speech in America.* Thomas Healy. Henry Holt and Company 2013. 320 p.
ISBN 9780805094565
Grades: Adult   **342.7308**
1. Abrams, J, 1886-1953 2. Holmes, Oliver Wendell, 1841-1935 3. Freedom of speech 4. Change (Psychology) 5. Trials 6. New York City 7. 20th century 8. History writing — Judicial branch — United States 9. History writing — Early 20th century — United States

LC 2012047539

Robert F. Kennedy Book Award, 2014.

Based on newly discovered letters and memos, this riveting scholarly history of the conservative justice who became a free-speech advocate and established the modern understanding of the First Amendment reconstructs his journey from free-speech skeptic to First Amendment hero.

Includes bibliographical references and index.

Hing, Bill Ong
★ *Humanizing Immigration: How to Transform Our Racist and Unjust System.* Bill ONG Hing. Beacon Press 2023. 248 p.
ISBN 9780807008027
Grades: Adult   **342.7308**
1. Immigration and emigration law 2. Human rights 3. Immigration and emigration 4. United States

LC 2023013085

First book to argue that immigrant and refugee rights are part of the fight for racial justice; offers a humanitarian approach to reform and abolition.

"Humanizing Immigration is a stirring call to action, urging readers to act from a place of empathy, not fear." —*Booklist*

Includes bibliographical references and index.

Luxenberg, Steve
★ *Separate: The Story of Plessy V. Ferguson, and America's Journey from Slavery to Segregation.* Steve Luxenberg. W. W. Norton & Company 2019. 560 p.
ISBN 9780393239379
Grades: Adult   **342.7308**
1. Plessy, Homer Adolph 2. Harlan, John Marshall, 1833-1911 3. Tourgée, Albion Winegar, 1838-1905 4. Brown, Henry Billings, 1836-1913 5. Martinet, Louis A, 1849-1917 6. Segregation 7. Segregation in transportation 8. Civil rights workers 9. Racism 10. African American history 11. Civil rights 12. Legislation 13. Race relations 14. United States history 15. 19th century 16. History writing — African American — Civil rights — United States 17. History writing — Judicial branch — United States

LC 2018043111

New York Times Notable Book, 2019.

The award-winning author of Annie's Ghosts documents the story of the infamous 19th-century Supreme Court ruling in favor of segregation, tracing the half-century of history that shaped the ruling and the reverberations that are still being felt today.

"This engrossing work builds to the courtroom drama in which Tourgée argues passionately but unsuccessfully on behalf of Homer Plessy to a Supreme Court, including, Brown, who wrote the majority opinion, and Harlan, the one-time slave owner, whose only dissenting vote revealed separate but equal hypocrisy." —*Library Journal*

Includes bibliographical references and index.

McCraw, David Edward
Truth in Our Times: Inside the Fight for Press Freedom in the Age of Alternative Facts. David E. McCraw. All Points Books 2019. 304 p.
ISBN 9781250184429
Grades: Adult   **342.7308**
1. McCraw, David Edward 2. Lawyers 3. Freedom of the press 4. Libel and slander 5. Press and politics 6. Journalism 7. Press law 8. Newspapers 9. Fake news 10. Censorship 11. Politics and government 12. United States 13. 21st century 14. Autobiographies and memoirs 15. Politics and global affairs — Mass media and politics 16. Arts and Entertainment — Writing and Publishing

LC 2018045141

A prominent New York Times newsroom lawyer whose scathing reply to Trump's demand for a retraction about his sexual abuses went viral in October 2016 shares insight into the conflicts and controversies impacting press freedom in today's America.

Includes index.

Prager, Joshua
*The **Family** Roe: An American Story.* Joshua Prager. W W Norton & Company 2021. 656 p.
ISBN 9780393247718
Grades: Adult   **342.7308**
1. McCorvey, Norma, 1947-2017 2. Wade, Henry 3. Trials (Abortion) 4. Abortion 5. Reproductive rights 6. Women's rights 7. Birth control 8. Pro-choice movement 9. Pro-life movement 10. Legislation 11. United States history 12. United States 13. 20th century 14. History writing — United States 15. Society and culture — Gender — Women — Reproductive rights 16. Politics and global affairs — Civil and human rights

National Book Critics Circle Award for Nonfiction finalist, 2021; Pulitzer Prize for General Nonfiction finalist, 2022.

Despite her famous pseudonym, no one knows the truth about "Jane Roe," Norma McCorvey (1947-2017), whose unwanted pregnancy in 1970 opened a great fracture in American life. Journalist Joshua Prager spent years with Norma, discovered her personal papers, a previously unseen trove, and witnessed her final moments. With an explosive revelation at the core of the case, he tells her full story for the first time.

"Journalist Prager (The Echoing Green) reveals in this trenchant account the identity of the child at the center of the Supreme Court's 1973 Roe v. Wade decision that legalized abortion. . . . Nuanced, fine-grained, and gripping, this is a masterful study of the human lives behind a landmark case." —*Publishers Weekly*

Purdum, Todd S.
*An **Idea** Whose Time Has Come: Two Presidents, Two Parties, and the Battle for the Civil Rights Act of 1964.* Todd S. Purdum. Henry Holt and Co. 2014. 400 pages
ISBN 9780805096729
Grades: Adult   **342.7308**
1. Civil Rights Movement 2. Civil rights 3. Political culture 4. Politics and government 5. United States 6. 20th century 7. History writing — African American — Civil rights — United States 8. History writing — 1960s — United States 9. Adult books for young adults

LC 2013038545

A top Washington journalist recounts the dramatic political battle to pass the Civil Rights Act of 1964.

"Those battling the neo-Confederates and nullificationists of today will want this book to see how it's done. Readers with an interest in American history and the American promise will find it a must-read as well." —*Kirkus*

Includes bibliographical references and index.

Richards, Leonard L.
Who Freed the Slaves?: The Fight Over the Thirteenth Amendment. Leonard L. Richards. The University of Chicago Press 2015. 322 p.
ISBN 9780226178202
Grades: Adult   **342.7308**
1. Ashley, James Mitchell, 1824-1896 2. Slavery 3. Legislation 4. Politicians 5. United States Civil War, 1861-1865 6. Freed people 7. United States history 8. United States 9. American Civil War era (1861-1865) 10. History writing — African American — Enslavement — United States 11. History writing — Politicians — United States

LC 2014023200

Provides the full story behind the 13th Amendment of the U.S. Constitution, highlighting the work of James Ashley, a firebrand congressman from Toledo, Ohio who fought hard for the law.

ESSENTIAL AND RECOMMENDED TITLES
343.73 Military, defense, public property, public finance, tax, commerce (trade), industrial law — United States

"It... provides a perceptive explanation as to how and why the promise of the 13th Amendment as an instrument for civil rights never came to fruition. In doing so, it reminds us that freedom is not a given; principled, pragmatic, and persistent advocates must work to realize and secure it." —*Library Journal*
Includes bibliographical references and index.

Risen, Clay
The Bill of the Century: The Epic Battle for the Civil Rights Act. Clay Risen. St Martins Press 2014. 320 p.
ISBN 9781608198245
Grades: Adult   **342.7308**
1. Segregation 2. Racism 3. African Americans 4. African American history 5. Civil rights 6. Legislation 7. Race relations 8. Politics and government 9. United States history 10. United States 11. 1960s 12. 20th century 13. History writing — African American — Civil rights — United States
LC 2014004662
Offers a full account of the complex battle to get the Civil Rights bill passed.
"A work of high academic quality written with a journalist's flair for telling a tale." —*Choice*

Strossen, Nadine
Hate: Why We Should Resist It with Free Speech, Not Censorship. Nadine Strossen. Oxford University Press 2018. 208 p.
ISBN 9780190859121
Grades: Adult   **342.7308**
1. Hate speech 2. Freedom of speech 3. Censorship 4. Constitutional law 5. Politics and global affairs — Civil and human rights
LC 2017054213
Dispelling rampant confusion about "hate speech," this book explains how U.S. law appropriately distinguishes between punishable and protected discriminatory speech. It shows that more speech-restrictive laws consistently have suppressed vital expression about public issues, targeting minority viewpoints and speakers; and that "counterspeech" has more effectively promoted equality and societal harmony.
"Strossen succeeds in lucidly explaining the relevant legal issues in a way that benefits both professional and lay readers." —*Library Journal*
Includes bibliographical references and index.

Weiner, Mark Stuart
Black Trials: Citizenship from the Beginnings of Slavery to the End of Caste. Mark S. Weiner. Alfred A. Knopf 2004. xvii, 421 p.
ISBN 9780375409813
Grades: 11 12 Adult   **342.7308**
1. Slavery 2. Race relations 3. African Americans 4. Legislation 5. African American history 6. History writing — African American — Enslavement — United States 7. Adult books for young adults
LC 2004040860
Examines how the role of Blacks in America has evolved from the colonial period to the present day as exemplified in American courts of laws, providing an insightful analysis of fourteen key legal cases that transformed American civic identity.
"This book is the best of its' kind—a serious, deeply felt reflection on the weight of history on contemporary affairs." —*Publishers Weekly*
Includes bibliographical references (p. [373]-403) and index.

Wexler, Jay
Holy Hullabaloos: A Road Trip to the Battlegrounds of the Church/State Wars. Jay Wexler. Beacon Press 2009. 272p.
ISBN 9780807000441
Grades: Adult   **342.7308**
1. Automobile travel 2. Freedom of religion 3. Church and state 4. Voyages and travels 5. United States 6. History writing — United States
LC 2008047405
A lighthearted account of a church-and-state law professor's cross-country visits to the places and people responsible for some of today's most hotly contested Supreme Court cases includes the author's encounters with a Cambridge bar whose liquor license was challenged by a nearby church and the Austin Capitol site where the Ten Commandments are controversially posted.
"This is a rare treat, a combination of thoughtful analysis and quirky humor that illuminates an issue that rarely elicits a laugh and that is central to the American body politic." —*Publishers Weekly*
Includes bibliographical references.

343.73 Military, defense, public property, public finance, tax, commerce (trade), industrial law — United States

Klobuchar, Amy
★ *Antitrust: Taking on Monopoly Power from the Gilded Age to the Digital Age.* Amy Klobuchar. Alfred A. Knopf 2021. 607 p.
ISBN 9780525654896
Grades: Adult   **343.73**
1. Roosevelt, Theodore, 1858-1919 2. Antitrust law 3. Business regulation 4. Monopolies 5. Government regulation 6. Antitrust law and competition 7. Politics and government 8. Legislation 9. United States 10. Business and economics — Economics — Contemporary U.S. economy 11. Politics and global affairs — General
LC 2020044843
An exploration of antitrust laws and their enforcement, and of the importance of antitrust for the American people.
"Even readers with only minimal knowledge of American business or the economy will be able to follow Klobuchar's analysis of anticompetitive business practices, and they may be surprised by how engaging the topic can be." —*Library Journal*
Includes index.

Witt, John Fabian
Lincoln's Code: The Laws of War in American History. John Fabian Witt. Free Press 2012. 240 p.
ISBN 9781416569831
Grades: Adult   **343.73**
1. Lincoln, Abraham, 1809-1865 2. Military law 3. War (International law) 4. United States Civil War, 1861-1865 5. United States history 6. American Civil War era (1861-1865) 7. History writing — Wars and conflicts — American Civil War
LC 2012006187
New York Times Notable Book, 2012; Pulitzer Prize for History finalist, 2013.
A Yale historian and author of the Accidental Republic presents the story of the pioneering American role in establishing modern laws of war, recounting decades of controversy and debate that resulted in a code of conduct adopted by the 16th President in the final years of the Civil War that influenced subsequent military conflicts.

343.7309 Public utilities — United States

Chertoff, Michael
Exploding Data: Reclaiming Our Cybersecurity in the Digital Age. Michael Chertoff. Atlantic Monthly Press 2018. 288 p.
ISBN 9780802127938
Grades: Adult   **343.7309**
1. Data protection 2. Internet 3. Privacy rights 4. Computer security 5. Information warfare 6. Legislation 7. Politics and government 8. United States 9. 21st century 10. Science Writing — Computing, the Internet, and Technology 11. Politics and global affairs — National security 12. Politics and global affairs — World politics — United States
LC 2018012763
The former Secretary of Homeland Security and author of Homeland Security: Assessing the First Five Years outlines powerful arguments for new laws and policies to protect society and individual autonomy from cyber-security threats.

PUBLIC LIBRARY CORE COLLECTION: NONFICTION
Twentieth Edition

"A tremendous resource for any reader about ever-shifting threats embedded in data collection and control." —*Library Journal*

Includes bibliographical references.

---

344 Labor, social service, education, cultural law

Maher, Kris

Desperate: An Epic Battle for Clean Water and Justice in Appalachia. Kris Maher. Scribner 2021. 352 p.

ISBN 9781501187346

Grades: Adult   344

1. Blankenship, Donald Leon 2. Water contamination 3. Coal mines and mining 4. Water-supply 5. Business corruption 6. Community organization 7. Mines and mineral resources 8. West Virginia 9. Appalachian region 10. Politics and global affairs — Environmental issues and policies 11. Nature Writing — Environmental Issues 12. Society and culture — Urban and regional studies

The story of one determined lawyer who waged a seven-year legal battle against Massey Energy—the most powerful coal company in West Virginia—over clean drinking water for the residents of Mingo County.

"It's both a case study in exploitation of the little guy and a playbook for confronting it. A rigorous accounting of a remarkably hard-fought battle for clean water." —*Kirkus*

344.04 Miscellaneous social problems and services

Bilott, Robert

Exposure: Poisoned Water, Corporate Greed, and One Lawyer's Twenty-year Battle Against Dupont. Robert Bilott, with Tom Shroder. Atria Books. 2019. xii, 386 p.

ISBN 9781501172816

Grades: Adult   344.04

1. Bilott, Robert, 1965- 2. Lawyers 3. Corporations 4. Corporate cover-ups 5. Hazardous waste 6. Illegal hazardous waste disposal 7. Chemical industry and trade 8. Water pollution 9. Pollution 10. West Virginia 11. Page to screen 12. Life stories — Law and order 13. Judges and lawyers 13. Business and economics — Corruption and scandal 14. Nature Writing — Environmental Issues 15. Adult books for young adults

LC Bl2019027138

Green Prize for Sustainable Literature: Adult Nonfiction, 2020.

In 1988, Rob Bilott began a legal battle against DuPont that would consume the next twenty years of his life, uncovering the worst case of environmental contamination in modern history and a corporate cover-up that put the health of hundreds of thousands of people at risk. Representing a single farmer who was convinced the creek on his property had been poisoned by runoff from a nearby DuPont landfill, Rob ultimately discovers the truth about PFAS—unregulated, toxic chemicals used in the manufacturing of Teflon and a host of other household goods.

Includes index; Inspiration for the movie Dark waters.

344.73 Labor, social service, education, cultural law — United States

Boschert, Sherry

37 Words: Title IX and Fifty Years of Fighting Sex Discrimination. Sherry Boschert. The New Press 2022. 352 p.

ISBN 9781620975831

Grades: Adult   344.73

1. Discrimination in education 2. Sex discrimination against women 3. Gender equity 4. Educational reform 5. Educational policy 6. Politics and global affairs — Civil and human rights

LC 2021046896

A sweeping history of the federal legislation that prohibits sex discrimination in education, published on the fiftieth anniversary of Title IX.

"Readers will finish this book with a clearer understanding of Title IX's impact, its shortcomings, and the continued threats faced by female students as they seek access to educational opportunities." —*Library Journal*

Includes bibliographical references and index.

Driver, Justin

The Schoolhouse Gate: Public Education, the Supreme Court, and the Battle for the American Mind. Justin Driver. Pantheon 2018. 576 p.

ISBN 9781101871652

Grades: Adult   344.73

1. Students 2. Public schools 3. Civil rights 4. Educational law and legislation 5. Judicial review 6. Judicial power 7. Constitutional law 8. Politics and government 9. United States 10. Society and culture — Education 11. Politics and global affairs — Judicial politics 12. History writing — Judicial branch — United States

LC 2017058167

An constitutional law scholar and clerk to such justices as Stephen Breyer and Sandra Day O'Connor presents a cautionary assessment of public schools to reveal how Supreme Court rulings in recent decades are undermining the constitutional rights of students.

"Readers with the ability to grapple with complex constitutional issues will find much to learn from Drivers independent thinking and unique insights." —*Publishers Weekly*

Includes index.

Okrent, Daniel

The Guarded Gate: Bigotry, Eugenics, and the Law That Kept Two Generations of Jews, Italians, and Other European Immigrants Out of America. Daniel Okrent. Scribner 2019. xvi, 478 pages : Illustration

ISBN 9781476798035

Grades: Adult   344.73

1. Eugenics 2. Immigration policy 3. Xenophobia 4. Prejudice 5. Immigration and emigration law 6. Nativism 7. Discrimination 8. Racism 9. Antisemitism 10. Scientists 11. Involuntary sterilization 12. Nazism 13. Race relations 14. United States history 15. 1890s 16. 1900s (Decade) 17. 1910s 18. 1920s 19. History writing — Immigration — United States 20. Society and culture — Immigration 21. Society and culture — Race

LC 2019006830

National Jewish Book Award, 2019; New York Times Notable Book, 2019.

The author of the Pulitzer finalist, Great Fortune, examines how eugenics and government-supported anti-immigration initiatives in the 1920s changed policies to ban discriminated-against groups from the U.S. for more than 40 years.

"A frighteningly timely book about a particularly ugly period in American history, a bigotry-riddled chapter many thought was closed but that shows recent signs of reopening. In his latest book, Okrent the former managing editor of Life magazine and editor at large at Time Inc, chronicles a time when white-supremacist policymakers joined forces with pseudo-scientists promoting eugenics, creating widespread anti-immigration sentiment throughout the country." —*Kirkus*

Includes bibliographical references and index; Includes bibliographical references (pages 403-451) and index.

344.7301 Labor law — United States

Sack, Steven Mitchell

The Employee Rights Handbook: Effective Legal Strategies to Protect Your Job from Interview to Pink Slip. Steven Mitchell Sack. Legal Strategies Publications 2010. xvii, 620 p. : Footnotes

ISBN 9780963630674

Grades: Adult   344.7301

1. Employee rights 2. Labor laws and legislation 3. Business and economics — General

LC 2010926886

"The author advises readers on topics from avoiding prehiring abuses and protecting on-the-job rights through postemployment litigation and finding and

ESSENTIAL AND RECOMMENDED TITLES
344.7304 Miscellaneous social problems and services — United States

hiring a lawyer. Readers looking for an all-in-one employee legal primer or layperson's quick reference should find this a useful tool." —*Library Journal*
Includes index.

Steingold, Fred S.
The Employer's Legal Handbook, 16th Ed. Attorney Fred S. Steingold. Nolo 2023. 484 pages
ISBN 9781413330915
Grades: Adult   344.7301
1. Labor laws and legislation 2. Business and economics — Business advice 3. Business and economics — General 4. Law — Corporate, business, and finance
LC Bl2017026668
Provides the information for employers on the most common and current employment law issues, including hiring, wage and hour laws, employee discipline and performance reviews, benefits, and family and medical leave, employee privacy, and layoffs.
Includes index.

Thomas, Gillian
Because of Sex: One Law, Ten Cases, and Fifty Years That Changed American Women's Lives at Work. Gillian Thomas. St. Martin's Press 2016. 272 p.
ISBN 9781137280053
Grades: Adult   344.7301
1. Sex discrimination in employment 2. Sexism in employment 3. Sex discrimination against women 4. Women's rights 5. Sex laws 6. History writing — Women's history
LC 2015033086
The 1964 Civil Rights Act is best known as a monumental achievement of the civil rights movement, but it also revolutionized the lives of American women. Title VII of the law made it illegal to discriminate "because of sex." but Congress did not specify how that would affect a "Mad Men" world where women played mainly supporting roles. The Supreme Court had to endow the phrase with meaning, and its decisions dramatically changed how the nation sees working women—women like Ida Phillips, denied an assembly line job because having small children deemed her unreliable; or Kim Rawlinson, who fought to be a prison guard because she believed that being 5'3" and 115 pounds didn't mean she couldn't do a "man's job"; or Ann Hopkins, refused a partnership at Price Waterhouse because the men in charge thought she needed "a course at charm school."
"The author merges the personal stories with the legal intricacies of the litigation, and crafts a moving and informative account of a struggle for equality that remains incomplete." —*Publishers Weekly*

344.7304 Miscellaneous social problems and services — United States

Cohen, Adam
★ *Imbeciles: The Supreme Court, American Eugenics, and the Sterilization of Carrie Buck.* Adam Cohen. Penguin Press 2016. 400 p.
ISBN 9781594204180
Grades: Adult   344.7304
1. Buck, Carrie, 1906-1983 2. Taft, William H. (William Howard), 1857-1930 3. Holmes, Oliver Wendell, 1841-1935 4. Brandeis, Louis Dembitz, 1856-1941 5. Involuntary sterilization 6. Eugenics 7. Discrimination 8. Prejudice 9. Trials 10. History writing — Judicial branch — United States
LC 2015044207
Describes a dark moment in American history, when the Supreme Court agreed, in 1927, to support eugenic sterilization for "undesirables," including epileptics and the "feebleminded," resulting in the sterilization of 70,000 Americans.
"A shocking tale about science and law gone horribly wrong, an almost forgotten case that deserves to be ranked with Dred Scott, Plessy, and Korematsu as among the Supreme Court's worst decisions." —*Kirkus*

Nourse, Victoria F.
In Reckless Hands: Skinner V. Oklahoma and the Near Triumph of American Eugenics. Victoria F. Nourse. W. W. Norton & Co. 2008. 256 p.
ISBN 9780393065299
Grades: Adult   344.7304
1. Skinner, Jack T, d.1977 2. Eugenics 3. Trials 4. United States history 5. United States 6. Oklahoma 7. 20th century 8. True Crime — Investigations and Trials 9. History writing — Judicial branch — United States 10. Adult books for young adults
LC 2008013140
Booklist Editors' Choice, 2008.
An account of the controversial early twentieth-century effort to sterilize criminals and the mentally ill profiles the activities at Oklahoma's McAlester prison, the trial of Jack Skinner, and the influence of Nazi Germany's eugenics practices on the outcome of an ensuing Supreme Court case.
"The author provides a legal history of the Supreme Court case that served to increase the recognition of individual rights, although it fell short of ending the practice and debate of eugenics in the US. This book deserves attention from those interested in the history and politics of the legal system." —*Choice*
Includes bibliographical references and index.

344.7305 Social law — United States — Public safety and morals

Anderson, Carol
★ *The Second: Race and Guns in a Fatally Unequal America.* Carol Anderson. Bloomsbury Publishing 2021. 304 p.
ISBN 9781635574258
Grades: Adult   344.7305
1. Gun ownership 2. Gun control 3. Violence against African Americans 4. Racism 5. Racial profiling 6. Right to bear arms 7. Constitutional amendments 8. Discrimination in law enforcement 9. Race relations 10. United States 11. Society and culture — Race 12. Society and culture — Violence and crime — Criminal justice system 13. Politics and global affairs — Civil and human rights
Historian and award-winning, bestselling author of White Rage Carol Anderson powerfully illuminates the history and impact of the Second Amendment, how it was designed, and how it has consistently been constructed to keep African Americans powerless and vulnerable. The Second is neither a "pro-gun" nor an "anti-gun" book; the lens is the citizenship rights and human rights of African Americans.
"An important but too-compact analysis that might leave readers wishing for more. Like Anderson's previous works, this is essential for everyone interested in U.S. history." —*Library Journal*

Chemerinsky, Erwin
Presumed Guilty: How the Supreme Court Empowered the Police and Subverted Civil Rights. Erwin Chemerinsky. Liveright Publishing 2021. 320 p.
ISBN 9781631496516
Grades: Adult   344.7305
1. Police misconduct 2. Police brutality 3. Racism in law enforcement 4. Racism in the criminal justice system 5. African American civil rights 6. Searches and seizures 7. Civil rights 8. United States 9. Society and culture — Violence and crime — Criminal justice system 10. History writing — Judicial branch — United States 11. Politics and global affairs — Judicial politics 12. Politics and global affairs — Civil and human rights
LC 2021012402
For the greater part of its existence, Chemerinsky shows, deference to and empowerment of the police have been the modi operandi of the Supreme Court. From its conception in the late eighteenth century until the Warren Court in 1953, the Supreme Court rarely ruled against the police, and then only when police conduct was truly shocking. Animating seminal cases and justices from the Court's history, Chemerinsky—who has himself litigated cases dealing with police misconduct for decades—shows how the Court has time and again refused to impose constitutional checks on police, all the while deliberately gutting remedies Americans might use to challenge police misconduct.

"A thoughtful, provocative, and instructive must-read for anyone concerned with justice and domestic tranquility." —*Library Journal*

Includes bibliographical references and index.

Friedman, Barry

★ *Unwarranted: Policing Without Permission.* Barry Friedman. Farrar, Straus and Giroux 2017. 416 p.

ISBN 9780374280451

Grades: Adult   344.7305

1. Electronic surveillance 2. Privacy rights 3. Searches and seizures 4. Intelligence service 5. Espionage 6. Civil rights 7. Law enforcement 8. Constitutional law 9. Political surveillance 10. Privacy 11. Legislation 12. Politics and government 13. United States 14. Politics and global affairs — Civil and human rights 15. Politics and global affairs — National security

LC 2016033246

As the debate about out-of-control policing heats up, an authority on constitutional law offers a provocative account of how our rights have been eroded.

Includes index.

Schwartz, Joanna C.

★ *Shielded: How the Police Became Untouchable.* Joanna Schwartz. Viking Press 2023. 320 p.

ISBN 9780593299364

Grades: Adult   344.7305

1. Police 2. Criminal justice system 3. Police misconduct 4. Corruption 5. Criminal justice reform 6. United States 7. Society and culture — Violence and crime — Criminal justice system

In the wake of high-profile murders that have brought much-needed attention to the pervasiveness of police misconduct, a UCLA law professor exposes the many ways in which our legal system protects police at all costs, shedding light on our failing criminal justice system.

"Rigorous research, in-depth analysis, and poignant case studies make this a must-read study of an urgent social issue." —*Publishers Weekly*

345 Criminal law

Kadri, Sadakat

The Trial: A History, from Socrates to O.J. Simpson. Sadakat Kadri. Random House 2005. xviii, 459 p. : Illustration

ISBN 9780375505508

Grades: Adult   345

1. Trials 2. Criminal justice system 3. True Crime — Investigations and Trials

LC 2005042925

Ranging from ancient Greece to the present day, a history of the criminal trial begins with the trial of Socrates and continues over the course of more than two thousand years, detailing the events, outcomes, and implications of the changing world of criminal justice.

"This history of the trial from ancient times to the present provides . [a] history of the various forms and purposes of trials throughout Western civilization. The result is a magnificent book suitable for all sorts of people, from inquisitive high school students to blue-chip lawyers." —*Choice*

Includes bibliographical references (p. [355]-435) and index.

Minow, Martha

When Should Law Forgive? Martha Minow. W.W. Norton & Company 2019. 252 p.

ISBN 9780393081763

Grades: Adult   345

1. Pardon 2. Forgiveness 3. Law 4. Clemency 5. Punishment 6. Fairness 7. Criminal justice system 8. Impartial writing 9. Society and culture — Violence and crime — Criminal justice system 10. Politics and global affairs — Political philosophy

LC 2019014868

The former Harvard Law School dean and Pro Bono Task Force chair of the Legal Services Corporation explores contradictions in how criminal acts and financial debts are forgiven and how offering pardon for justified grievances can render laws more just.

Includes bibliographical references and index.

Sands, Philippe

East West Street: On the Origins of Genocide and Crimes Against Humanity. Philippe Sands. Alfred A. Knopf 2016. 464 p.

ISBN 9780385350716

Grades: Adult   345

1. Lauterpacht, Hersch, 1897-1960 2. Lemkin, Raphael, 1900-1959 3. Genocide 4. Crimes against humanity 5. Nuremberg war crime trials, 1946-1949 6. Trials (Crimes against humanity) 7. Human rights (International law) 8. Holocaust victims 9. Trials (Genocide) 10. Family secrets 11. War crimes 12. Trials 13. 1940s 14. History writing — Wars and conflicts — Holocaust — World War II 15. True Crime — Investigations and Trials 16. Adult books for young adults

LC 2016933268

Baillie Gifford Prize for Non-Fiction, 2016; British Book Award for Narrative Nonfiction of the Year, 2017.

Pieces together how the lives of humanitarian-law professors Rafael Lemkin and Hersch Lauterpacht—as well as the life of Hitler's personal lawyer, who ordered the death of more than a million Jews and Poles, including the families of Lemkin and Lauterpacht—converged in October 1946 at the International Military Tribunals at Nuremberg.

"Readers interested in history, political science, and/Or religion shouldn't miss this compelling work with unforgettable characters." —*Library Journal*

Schiff, Stacy

The Witches: Salem, 1692. Stacy Schiff. Little, Brown 2015. xiv, 498 pages, 16 unnumbered pages of plates : Illustration; Color

ISBN 9780316200608

Grades: Adult   345

1. Witchcraft 2. Puritanism 3. Puritans 4. Hysteria (Social psychology) 5. Malicious accusation 6. Superstition 7. Witch hunting 8. Trials (Witchcraft) 9. United States history 10. Massachusetts 11. Salem, Massachusetts 12. 1690s 13. 17th century 14. Colonial America (1600-1775) 15. History writing — Women's history 16. History writing — Colonial America — United States

Booklist Editors' Choice, 2015.

The Pulitzer Prize-winning author of Cleopatra analyzes the Salem Witch Trials to offer key insights into the role of women in its events while explaining how its tragedies became possible.

"This fully documented narrative, if a bit exhausting and disorganized, will find a welcome audience among readers of witchcraft or colonial histories as well as Schiff's legion of fans." —*Library Journal*

Includes bibliographic references (pages 481-482) and index.

Schneps, Leila

Math on Trial: How Numbers Get Used and Abused in the Courtroom. Leila Schneps and Coralie Colmez. Basic Books 2013. 272 p.

ISBN 9780465032921

Grades: Adult   345

1. Statistics 2. Probabilities 3. Trials 4. Judicial error 5. Science Writing — Mathematics 6. True Crime — Investigations and Trials

LC 2012040624

Mother and daughter mathematicians describe the harm that can be done when mathematical arguments are improperly used and discuss ten trials where they were misused as evidence, including the Dreyfus Affair, the Amanda Knox Case and Charles Ponzi's original scheme.

Includes bibliographical references and index.

ESSENTIAL AND RECOMMENDED TITLES
345.43 Criminal law — Germany

345.43 Criminal law — Germany

King, David
The Trial of Adolf Hitler: The Beer Hall Putsch and the Rise of Nazi Germany. David King. W. W. Norton & Company 2017. 336 p.
ISBN 9780393241693
Grades: Adult   345.43
1. Hitler, Adolf, 1889-1945 2. Politicians 3. Trials (Treason) 4. Coups d'etat 5. Prisoners 6. Prison sentences 7. Fame 8. Propaganda 9. Nazi propaganda 10. Nationalism 11. German history 12. Between the Wars (1918-1939) 13. 1920s 14. 20th century 15. History writing — Europe — Germany 16. Life stories — Politics — Politicians
LC 2017008985
Documents the lesser-known story of the scandalous courtroom drama that paved the way for the rise of the Nazi Party, recounting the 1924 trial of Hitler and nine associates who successfully threw off charges of high treason and used the trial to gain international attention and launch an improbable path to power.
"King (Death in the City of Light) affirms his reputation as a first-rate narrative historian in this well-researched analysis of Adolf Hitler's trial for treason in the aftermath of the 1923 Beer Hall Putsch." —*Publishers Weekly*
Includes bibliographical references and index.

345.567 Criminal law — Iraq

Newton, Michael A.
Enemy of the State: The Trial and Execution of Saddam Hussein. Michael A. Newton & Michael P. Scharf. St. Martin's Press 2008. 320 p.
ISBN 9780312385569
Grades: 11 12 Adult   345.567
1. Hussein, Saddam, 1937-2006 2. Trials (Crimes against humanity) 3. Trials (Murder) 4. Crimes against humanity 5. Political leadership 6. Politics and government 7. Iraq 8. Baghdad, Iraq 9. History writing — Wars and conflicts — Iraq War
LC 2008021087
A behind-the-scenes account documents the events surrounding the executed Iraqi dictator's capture and the assemblage of the High Tribunal, describing how its team of judges and prosecutors was prepared to run a fair trial in the face of such obstacles as international upheavals and the disapprovals of the U.K. and the U.N.
Includes bibliographical references.

345.5694 Criminal law — Israel and Palestine

Lipstadt, Deborah E.
The Eichmann Trial. Deborah E. Lipstadt. Nextbook Schocken 2010. 256 p.
ISBN 9780805242607
Grades: Adult   345.5694
1. Eichmann, Adolf, 1906-1962 2. War crime trials 3. Holocaust (1933-1945) 4. War crimes 5. Jerusalem, Israel 6. History writing — Wars and conflicts — Holocaust — World War II 7. True Crime — Investigations and Trials
LC 2010028620
The National Jewish Book Award-winning author of History on Trial presents a reassessment of the groundbreaking 1960 trial of Nazi SS Lieutenant Colonel Adolf Eichmann by an Israeli court while exploring the controversial processes it introduced and its reflection of world views on genocide.
"Lipstadt has done a great service by untethering the trial from [Hannah] Arendt's polarizing presence, recovering the event as a gripping legal drama, as well as a hinge moment in Israel's history and in the world's delayed awakening to the magnitude of the Holocaust." —*New York Times Book Review*
Includes bibliographical references.

345.73 Criminal law — United States

Abrams, Dan
Theodore Roosevelt for the Defense: The Courtroom Battle to Save His Legacy. Dan Abrams and David Fisher. Hanover Square Press 2019. 400 p.
ISBN 9781335016447
Grades: Adult   345.73
1. Roosevelt, Theodore, 1858-1919 2. Former presidents 3. Trials (Libel) 4. Politicians 5. Political corruption 6. Actions and defenses 7. 20th century 8. History writing — Presidency — 20th century — United States 9. History writing — Early 20th century — United States 10. Life stories — Politics — Politicians
LC Bl2019008611
Chronicles the epic 1915 libel case in which Theodore Roosevelt, weighing a last presidential run, turned on former allies to challenge corruption in the political party that made him.
"Many of the questions the trial raised about the effects of money in politics, the dangers of blind allegiance to party politics, and oversize corporate political influence will resonate with contemporary readers. Legal eagles and history buffs will enjoy this one." —*Publishers Weekly*

Bazelon, Emily
★ *Charged: The New Movement to Transform American Prosecution and End Mass Incarceration.* Emily Bazelon. Random House 2019. xxxi, 409 pages : Illustration
ISBN 9780399590016
Grades: Adult   345.73
1. Criminal justice system 2. Injustice 3. Mass incarceration 4. Prosecution 5. Public prosecutors' misconduct 6. Public prosecutors 7. Sentences (Criminal procedure) 8. Imprisonment 9. Punishment 10. United States 11. Society and culture — Violence and crime — Criminal justice system
Library Journal Best Books, 2019; Los Angeles Times Book Prize for Current Interest, 2019.
An investigative journalist exposes the unchecked power of the prosecutor as a driving force in America's mass incarceration crisis, offering strategic recommendations for reversing discriminatory practices without changing the law.
"A vitally important new entry in the continued heated debates about criminal justice." —*Kirkus*
Includes bibliographical references (pages 337-391) and index.

Berman, Geoffrey
Holding the Line: Inside the Nation's Preeminent Us Attorney's Office and Its Battle with the Trump Justice Department. Geoffrey Berman, former US Attorney for the Southern District of New York. Penguin Press 2022. xv, 331 pages
ISBN 9780593300299
Grades: Adult   345.73
1. Berman, Geoffrey, 1959- 2. Trump, Donald, 1946- 3. District attorneys 4. Public prosecutors 5. Lawyers 6. Political corruption 7. Politics and government 8. United States 9. 2010s 10. 2020s 11. Autobiographies and memoirs 12. Politics and global affairs — Judicial politics 13. Life stories — Law and order — Judges and lawyers
LC 2022026842
The gripping and explosive memoir of serving as US Attorney for the Southern District of New York, in the face of the Justice Department's attempts to protect Trump's friends and punish his enemies.
"An instructive, highly readable account of the law, its protectors, and its enemies." —*Kirkus*
Includes index.

Bookman, Marc
A Descending Spiral: Exposing the Death Penalty in 12 Essays. Marc Bookman. The New Press 2021. 208 p.
ISBN 9781620976548
Grades: Adult   345.73

PUBLIC LIBRARY CORE COLLECTION: NONFICTION
Twentieth Edition

1. Capital punishment 2. Criminal justice system 3. Social advocacy 4. Society and culture — Violence and crime — Criminal justice system 5. Politics and global affairs — Civil and human rights

LC 2020053612

Powerful, wry essays offering modern takes on a primitive practice, from one of our most widely read death penalty abolitionists.

"Readers interested in the death penalty and injustice in the U.S. criminal justice system, as well as those who enjoyed Bryan Stevenson's Just Mercy, will appreciate this title." —*Library Journal*

Boyle, Kevin
Arc of Justice: A Saga of Race, Civil Rights, and Murder in the Jazz Age. Kevin Boyle. H. Holt 2004. 415 p, 8 p. of plates : Illustration
ISBN 9780805071450
Grades: Adult   345.73

1. Sweet, Ossian, 1895-1960 2. Darrow, Clarence, 1857-1938 3. Trials (Murder) 4. African Americans 5. Racism 6. African American history 7. Civil rights 8. Race relations 9. Detroit, Michigan 10. United States 11. 1920s 12. 20th century 13. History writing — Roaring 20s — United States 14. True Crime — Murder 15. History writing — African American — Civil rights — United States

LC 2004047352

National Book Award for Nonfiction, 2004; New York Times Notable Book, 2004; National Book Critics Circle Award for Nonfiction finalist, 2004; Pulitzer Prize for History finalist, 2005.

The grandson of a slave, Dr. Ossian Sweet moved his family to an all-white Detroit neighborhood in 1925. When his neighbors attempted to drive him out, Sweet defended himself—resulting in the death of a white man and a murder trial for Sweet. There followed one of the most important (and shockingly unknown) cases in Civil Rights history. Also caught up in the intense courtroom drama were legal giant Clarence Darrow and the newly formed National Association for the Advancement of Colored People (NAACP).

"Boyle has brilliantly rescued from obscurity a fascinating chapter in American history that had profound implications for the rise of the Civil Rights movement." —*Publishers Weekly*

Includes bibliographical references (p. [347]-395) and index.

Canon, Dan
★ *Pleading Out: How Plea Bargaining Creates a Permanent Criminal Class.* Dan Canon. Basic Books 2022. 336 p.
ISBN 9781541674677
Grades: Adult   345.73

1. Plea bargaining 2. Criminal law 3. Criminal justice system 4. Prison sentences 5. Innocence (Law) 6. Mass incarceration 7. Injustice 8. Society and culture — Violence and crime — Criminal justice system 9. Politics and global affairs — Civil and human rights

LC 2021050421

Most Americans believe that the jury trial is the backbone of our criminal justice system. But in fact, the vast majority of cases never make it to trial: almost all criminal convictions are the result of a plea bargain, a deal made entirely out of the public eye. Law professor and civil rights lawyer Dan Canon argues that plea bargaining may swiftly dispose of cases, but it also fuels an unjust system. This practice produces a massive underclass of people who are restricted from voting, working, and otherwise participating in society. And while innocent people plead guilty to crimes they did not commit in exchange for lesser sentences, the truly guilty can get away with murder.

"Full of persuasive evidence of how the courts are used by those in power to enforce the status quo, this is a cogent call for change." —*Publishers Weekly*

Includes bibliographical references and index.

Coates, Laura Gayle
Just Pursuit: A Black Prosecutor's Fight for Fairness in an Unfair System. Laura Coates. Simon & Schuster 2022. 272 p.
ISBN 9781982173760
Grades: Adult   345.73

1. Coates, Laura Gayle 2. Racism in the criminal justice system 3. Criminal justice system 4. Justice 5. Women public prosecutors 6. African Americans 7. Judicial system 8. Life stories — Law and order — Judges and lawyers 9. Society and culture — Violence and crime — Criminal justice system

LC 2021041619

A powerful true story and groundbreaking account of bias in the courtroom from CNN senior legal analyst Laura Coates, recounting her time as a Black female prosecutor for the US Department of Justice.

"In this eye-opening work, Coates (law, George Washington Univ.), a former federal prosecutor, confronts the many injustices in the American legal system, particularly for non-white people and women. . . . Readers will appreciate Coates's much-needed fresh perspective of the inner workings of the prosecutorial system, and the book's heartfelt storytelling." —*Library Journal*

Dybdahl, Thomas L.
When Innocence Is Not Enough: Hidden Evidence and the Failed Promise of the Brady Rule. Thomas L. Dybdahl. New Press 2023. 224 p.
ISBN 9781620977040
Grades: Adult   345.73

1. Criminal justice system 2. Innocence (Law) 3. Legal malpractice 4. Public prosecutors' misconduct 5. Corruption 6. Judicial system 7. Trials 8. United States 9. Society and culture — Violence and crime — Criminal justice system 10. True Crime — Investigations and Trials

A gripping work of narrative nonfiction, told across time, that exposes what's at stake when prosecutors conceal evidence—and what we can do about it.

"The devastating impact of a prosecutor's failure to disclose information favorable to the defense's case is mapped in this persuasive analysis by former public defender Dybdahl....This is an open-and-shut case." —*Publishers Weekly*

Goldberg, Carrie
Nobody's Victim: Fighting Psychos, Stalkers, Pervs and Trolls. Carrie Goldberg and Jeannine Amber. Plume 2019. 304 pages
ISBN 9780525533771
Grades: Adult   345.73

1. Goldberg, Carrie 2. Women lawyers 3. Victims of crimes 4. Computer crimes 5. Sex crimes 6. Sexual harassment 7. Stalkers 8. Extortion 9. Internet predators 10. Criminal law 11. Human rights 12. Civil rights 13. Autobiographies and memoirs 14. Society and culture — Violence and crime 15. Life stories — Law and order — Judges and lawyers 16. Life stories — Facing adversity — Victims of crime 17. True Crime — General

LC 2018060245

Riveting and an essential timely conversation-starter, Nobody's Victim invites readers to join Carrie on the front lines of the war against sexual violence and privacy violations as she fights for revenge porn and sextortion laws, uncovers major Title IX violations, and sues the hell out of tech companies, schools, and powerful sexual predators. Her battleground is the courtroom; her crusade is to transform clients from victims into warriors. In gripping detail, Carrie shares the diabolical ways her clients are attacked and how she, through her unique combination of advocacy, badass relentlessness, risk-taking, and client-empowerment, pursues justice for them all. There are stories about a woman whose ex-boyfriend made fake bomb threats in her name and caused a national panic; a fifteen-year-old girl who was sexually assaulted on school grounds and then suspended when she reported the attack; and a man whose ex-boyfriend used a dating app to send more than 1,200 men to ex's home and work for sex. With breathtaking honesty, Carrie also shares her own shattering story about why she began her work and the uphill battle of building a business. While her clients are a diverse group—from every gender, sexual orientation, age, class, race, religion, occupation, and background—the offenders are not. They are highly predictable. In this book, Carrie offers a taxonomy of the four types of offenders she encounters most often at her firm: Assholes, psychos, pervs, and trolls.

Includes bibliographical references and index.

Houppert, Karen
Chasing Gideon: The Elusive Quest for Poor People's Justice. Karen Houppert. The New Press 2013. 288 p.
ISBN 9781595588692
Grades: Adult   345.73

ESSENTIAL AND RECOMMENDED TITLES
345.73 Criminal law — United States

1. Legal assistance to poor people 2. Right to counsel 3. Poor people 4. Civil rights 5. Society and culture — Violence and crime — Criminal justice system 6. Society and culture — Wealth and class — Poverty

LC 2012047464

On the 50th anniversary of Gideon v. Wainwright, the landmark case that led to free legal counsel for those who needed it, a veteran journalist investigates the way justice is delivered to the poor—and discovers a crisis in our nation's courts.

Earlier and shorter versions of the chapters a Perfect Storm and Death in Georgia were first published in the Nation; Includes bibliographical references.

Lewis, Anthony
Gideon's Trumpet. Anthony Lewis. Vintage Books 1989. 277 p.
ISBN 9780679723127
Grades: 11 12 Adult   345.73
1. Gideon, Clarence Earl 2. Wainwright, Louie L. 3. Right to counsel 4. History writing — Judicial branch — United States

LC 88040504

Edgar Allan Poe Award for Best Fact Crime, 1965.

The story of a convict's defense of his contention that a person on trial should not be denied the assistance of counsel.

"His description of procedures, and his explication of the way new interpretations of law evolve, humanize the Supreme Court without lessening their majesty." —*Kirkus*

Includes bibliographical references (p. [265]-268) and index; Originally published: New York : Random House, 1964.

Lithwick, Dahlia
Lady Justice: Women, the Law, and the Battle to Save America. Dahlia Lithwick. Penguin 2022. 384 p.
ISBN 9780525561385
Grades: Adult   345.73
1. Trump, Donald, 1946- 2. Presidents 3. Women lawyers 4. Legal ethics 5. Law 6. Resistance to government 7. Opposition (Political science) 8. Injustice 9. Human rights 10. Social advocacy 11. Politics and government 12. United States 13. 21st century 14. Liberal writing 15. Politics and global affairs — Civil and human rights 16. Life stories — Identity — Gender 17. Life stories — Law and order — Judges and lawyers 18. History writing — Early 21st century — United States

Los Angeles Times Book Prize for Current Interest, 2022.

After the sudden shock of Donald Trump's victory over Hillary Clinton in 2016, many Americans felt lost and uncertain. It was clear he and his administration were going to pursue a series of retrograde, devastating policies. Immediately, women lawyers all around the country, independently of each other, sprang into action, and they had a common goal: They weren't going to stand by in the face of injustice, while Trump, Mitch McConnell, and the Republican party did everything in their power to remake the judiciary in their own conservative image. With unparalleled access to her subjects, she has written a luminous book, not about the villains of the Trump years, but about the heroes.

Mandery, Evan J.
A Wild Justice: The Death and Resurrection of Capital Punishment in America. Evan J. Mandery. W. W. Norton & Company 2013. 496 p.
ISBN 9780393239584
Grades: Adult   345.73
1. Capital punishment 2. Legislation 3. United States 4. 20th century 5. History writing — United States 6. Society and culture — Violence and crime — Criminal justice system

LC 2013010126

A professor and former capital defense attorney discusses the history of the two Supreme Court cases that were responsible for changing the laws regarding the death penalty in America and polarizing the nation.

Includes bibliographical references and index.

Rabinowitz, Dorothy
No Crueler Tyrannies: Accusation, False Witness, and Other Terrors of Our Times. Dorothy Rabinowitz. Free Press 2003. xi, 239 p.
ISBN 9780743228343
Grades: Adult   345.73
1. Child sexual abuse investigation 2. Trials (Child sexual abuse) 3. False testimony 4. Child witnesses 5. Essays 6. True Crime — Sex Crimes 7. True Crime — Investigations and Trials

LC 2002044670

The columnist collects and re-examines her stories of injustice, false accusations, and judicial perversions, revealing the measures she took to free victims who were wrongly accused of crimes they did not commit.

"This book reexamines high-profile cases of the 1980s and 1990s involving mass sexual abuse. Demonstrating that overzealous prosecutors and indifferent courts led to the prosecution of many innocents, Rabinowitz provides in-depth analyses of the major cases, especially those that involved child-care workers. This gripping, well-written book about social injustice and public hysteria is recommended for social science and law collections." —*Library Journal*

These articles were previously published individually in the Wall Street journal—T.P. verso; Includes index.

Rapping, Jonathan
Gideon's Promise: A Public Defender Movement to Transform Criminal Justice. Jonathan Rapping. Beacon Press 2020. 256 p.
ISBN 9780807064627
Grades: Adult   345.73
1. Rapping, Jonathan 2. Legal assistance to poor people 3. Public defenders 4. Criminal justice system 5. Judicial system 6. Imprisonment 7. Mass incarceration 8. Organizational behavior 9. Justice 10. Right to counsel 11. Constitutional law 12. United States 13. Autobiographies and memoirs 14. Society and culture — Violence and crime — Criminal justice system 15. Life stories — Law and order — Judges and lawyers

LC 2019059060

Drawing from his own experiences as well as cutting-edge research in the fields or organizational and cultural psychology, a public defender, revealing the pervasive issues inherent in our current system of public defense, lays the foundation for how model public defense programs should work to end mass incarceration.

"Rapping, a MacArthur 'Genius grant' recipient and former public defender, describes in this impressive debut the history and philosophy of Gideon's Promise, his criminal justice reform organization.... This optimistic, well-articulated account is a must-read for policy makers and criminal-justice advocates." —*Publishers Weekly*

Includes bibliographical references and index.

Rudolf, David S.
American Injustice: Inside Stories from the Underbelly of the Criminal Justice System. David S. Rudolf. Custom House 2022. 352 p.
ISBN 9780062997357
Grades: Adult   345.73
1. Rudolf, David S. 2. Lawyers 3. Criminal justice system 4. Judicial system 5. Law enforcement 6. Malicious accusation 7. Legal malpractice 8. Public prosecutors' misconduct 9. Suspects (Criminal investigation) 10. Prisoners 11. Innocence (Law) 12. Prejudice 13. Corruption 14. Incompetence 15. Injustice 16. Society and culture — Violence and crime — Criminal justice system 17. True Crime — Investigations and Trials 18. Life stories — Law and order — Prisoners and inmates

LC 2021036086

In the past thirty years alone, more than 2,800 innocent American prisoners—their combined sentences surpassing 25,000 years—have been exonerated and freed after being condemned for crimes they did not commit. Terrifyingly, this number represents only a fraction of the actual number of persons wrongfully accused and convicted over the same period. Renowned criminal defense and civil rights attorney David Rudolf has spent decades defending the wrongfully accused. In American Injustice, he draws from his years of experience in the American criminal legal system to shed light on the misconduct that exists at all levels of law enforcement and the tragic consequences that follow in its wake. In American Injustice, Rudolf gives a voice to those who have been the victim of wrongful accusations and shows in the starkest terms the human impact of legal wrongdoing.

"Defense attorney Rudolf debuts with a searing look at systemic failures in the U.S. justice system.... Enriched by Rudolf's firsthand experience and heartfelt compassion for his clients, this is a harrowing call for change." —*Publishers Weekly*

Includes index.

Trainum, James L.
How the Police Generate False Confessions: An Inside Look at the Interrogation Room. James L. Trainum. Rowman & Littlefield 2016. xix, 308 pages : Illustration
ISBN 9781442244641
Grades: Adult   345.73
1. Confession (Law) 2. Police questioning 3. Self-incrimination 4. Law — Criminal law
LC 2017478440

Despite the rising number of confirmed false confession cases, most people have a hard time grasping why someone would confess to a crime they did not commit, or even why a guilty person would admit to something that could put them in jail for life. How the Police Generate False Confessions takes you inside the interrogation room, exposing the tactics that law enforcement uses to make confessions happen. James L. Trainum reveals how innocent people can become suspects and then confessed criminals even when they have not committed a crime. Using real stories, he looks at the inherent coerciveness of the interrogation process and why so many false confessions contain so many of the details that only the true perpetrator would know. More disturbingly, the book examines how these same processes corrupt witness and victim statements, create lying informants and cooperators, and induce innocent people to plead guilty. Trainum also offers recommendations for change in the U.S. by looking at how other countriesare changing the process to prevent such miscarriages of justice. The reasons that people falsely confess can be complex and varied; throughout How the Police Generate False Confessions Trainum encourages readers to critically evaluate confessions on their own by gaining a better understanding of the interrogation process.

"Using numerous examples and backed by persuasive academic research, Trainum proposes a better way that is already at work in countries with similar criminal justice systems. His book will hit a nerve with a public newly concerned with abuses of police power, and hopefully will influence those tasked with law enforcement and public policy as well." —*Publishers Weekly*

Includes bibliographical references (pages 293-299) and index.

Turow, Scott
★ *Ultimate* Punishment: A Lawyer's Reflections on Dealing with the Death Penalty. Scott Turow. Farrar, Straus, and Giroux 2003. 164 p.
ISBN 9780374128739
Grades: Adult   345.73
1. Ryan, George H. 2. Criminal justice system 3. Innocence (Law) 4. Capital punishment 5. United States 6. Adult books for young adults 7. Society and culture — Violence and crime — Criminal justice system
LC 2003007873
Robert F. Kennedy Book Award, 2004.

Explores America's uneasy relationship with capital punishment from colonial days through Illinois Governor George Ryan's commutation of the sentences of 164 death row inmates before he left office in 2003.

Includes bibliographical references (p. [127]-164).

Watson, Bruce
Sacco and Vanzetti: The Judgment of Mankind. Bruce Watson. Viking 2007. 448 p.
ISBN 9780670063536
Grades: Adult   345.73
1. Sacco, Nicola, 1891-1927 2. Vanzetti, Bartolomeo, 1888-1927 3. Sacco-Vanzetti case 4. Trials (Murder) 5. Social life and customs 6. Massachusetts 7. True Crime — Investigations and Trials
LC 2006103092

Documents the infamous 1927 trial and execution of Nicola Sacco and Bartolomeo Vanzetti, from the anarchist bombings in Washington, D.C, for which they may have been wrongfully convicted to the fierce public debates that occurred as a result of the case.

"The author has written a well-researched page-turner. Highly recommended." —*Library Journal*

Includes bibliographical references and index.

345.7302 Organized crime — Law — United States

Stone, Geoffrey R.
★ *Sex* and the Constitution: Sex, Religion, and Law from America's Origins to the Twenty-First Century. Geoffrey R. Stone. Liveright Publishing Corporation 2017. 704 p.
ISBN 9780871404695
Grades: Adult   345.7302
1. Sexuality 2. Law 3. Constitutional law 4. Sex laws 5. Christianity and sexuality 6. Obscenity (Law) 7. Birth control 8. Abortion 9. Homosexuality 10. Criminal law 11. United States 12. Politics and global affairs — Judicial politics 13. History writing — United States 14. Society and culture — Sex and sexuality
LC 2016047264

A monumental work of scholarship, Sex and the Constitution illuminates how the clash between sex and religion has defined our nation's history.

"This title is a commanding synthesis of scholarship on over two centuries of American legal debate and practice regarding these issues, and would work well as the core text for a course of the subject." —*Publishers Weekly*

Includes bibliographical references and index.

345.744 Criminal law — Massachusetts

Robertson, Cara
The Trial of Lizzie Borden: A True Story. Cara Robertson. Simon & Schuster 2019. 288 p.
ISBN 9781501168376
Grades: Adult   345.744
1. Borden, Lizzie, 1860-1927 2. Trials (Murder) 3. Murder 4. Murder suspects 5. Massachusetts 6. 1890s 7. True Crime — Historical Crime 8. True Crime — Murder
LC 2018037560
Booklist Editors' Choice, 2019.

Drawing on 20 years of research and recently discovered evidence an account of the infamous Lizzie Borden trial explores professional and public opinions while considering how Gilded Age values and fears influenced the case.

"Robertson methodically rebuts the numerous theories advanced at the time and since, some of which pointed to other members of the household. The end result is a superior, page-turning true crime narrative that will leave most readers believing that the jury got it wrong." —*Publishers Weekly*

Includes bibliographical references and index.

345.747 Criminal law — New York

Davis, Kevin
The Brain Defense: Murder in Manhattan and the Dawn of Neuroscience in America's Courtrooms. Kevin Davis. Penguin Press 2017. 384 p.
ISBN 9781594206337
Grades: Adult   345.747
1. Weinstein, Herbert 2. Trials (Murder) 3. Insanity defense 4. Insanity (Law) 5. Brain 6. True crime — Murder 7. Science writing — General
LC 2016043485

In 1991, the police were called to East 72nd St. in Manhattan, where a woman's body had fallen from a twelfth-story window. The woman's husband, Herbert Weinstein, soon confessed to having hit and strangled his wife after an argument, then dropping her body out of their apartment window to make it look like a suicide. The 65-year-old Weinstein, a quiet, unassuming retired advertis-

ESSENTIAL AND RECOMMENDED TITLES
345.759 Criminal law — Florida

ing executive, had no criminal record, no history of violent behavior—not even a short temper. How, then, to explain this horrific act? Journalist Kevin Davis uses the perplexing story of the Weinstein murder to present a riveting, deeply researched exploration of the intersection of neuroscience and criminal justice.

"A thoroughly researched, clearly presented book that suggests that imprecise brain science will become increasingly more common as evidence in criminal cases." —*Kirkus*

345.759 Criminal law — Florida

Smith, Clive Stafford
The Injustice System: A Murder in Miami and a Trial Gone Wrong. Clive Stafford Smith. Viking 2012. 352 p.
ISBN 9780670023707
Grades: Adult   345.759
1. Maharaj, Kris 2. Judicial error 3. Trials (Murder) 4. Criminal justice system 5. Businesspeople 6. Business partners 7. Innocence (Law) 8. False imprisonment 9. Murder 10. True Crime — Investigations and Trials 11. True Crime — Murder
LC 2012019068

The award-winning criminal lawyer and author of Eight O'Clock Ferry to the Windward Side shares the story of the most discouraging case of his career, during which he defended an innocent Miami businessman whose murder conviction reflects disturbing and fundamental flaws in today's legal system.

Includes bibliographical references and index.

345.761 Criminal law — Alabama

Morrison, Melanie
Murder on Shades Mountain: The Legal Lynching of Willie Peterson and the Struggle for Justice in Jim Crow Birmingham. Melanie S. Morrison. Duke University Press 2018. 264 p.
ISBN 9780822371175
Grades: Adult   345.761
1. Peterson, Willie, 1896-1940 2. Trials (Rape) 3. Lynching 4. Hate crimes 5. Racism 6. Civil rights 7. Crimes against African Americans 8. African American civil rights 9. Race relations 10. United States history 11. Alabama 12. Southern States 13. Birmingham, Alabama 14. 1930s 15. 20th century 16. History writing — African American — Civil rights — United States 17. Society and culture — Race
LC 2017039036

Melanie S. Morrison tells the tragic story of the murder and attempted murder of three young women in 1930s Birmingham, Alabama, and the aftermath, which saw a reign of terror unleashed on the town's Black community, the wrongful conviction and death sentencing of Willie Peterson, and a Black-led effort to free Peterson.

Includes bibliographical references and index.

345.763 Criminal law — Louisiana

Van Meter, Matthew
Deep Delta Justice: A Black Teen, His Lawyer, and Their Groundbreaking Battle for Civil Rights in the South. Matthew Van Meter. Little, Brown & Company 2020. 290 pages
ISBN 9780316435031
Grades: Adult   345.763
1. Sobol, Richard B. 2. Duncan, Gary 3. Trials 4. Judicial system 5. African American defendants 6. Civil rights lawyers 7. Civil Rights Movement 8. Racism in the criminal justice system 9. Social justice 10. Racism 11. African American history 12. Civil rights 13. Louisiana 14. Southern States 15. 1960s 16. History writing — African American — Civil rights — United States 17. Life stories — Law and order 18. Politics and global affairs — Civil and human rights
LC Bl2020015425

In 1966 in a small town in Louisiana, a 19-year-old Black man named Gary Duncan pulled his car off the road to stop a fight between a group of four white kids and two of Gary's own cousins. After putting his hand on the arm of one of the white children, Duncan was arrested for assault. A member of the local branch of the NAACP, Duncan used his contacts to reach Richard Sobol, a 29-year-old born and bred New Yorker working that summer in a Black firm ("the most radical law firm") in New Orleans, to represent him. In this powerful work of character-driven history, Van Meter brings alive how one court case changed the course of justice in the South, and eventually the entire country.

"This deeply researched and vividly written chronicle is the definitive account of one of the civil rights movement's most unheralded victories." —*Publishers Weekly*

Includes bibliographical references and index.

345.773 Criminal law — Illinois

Bogira, Steve
Courtroom 302: A Year Behind the Scenes in an American Criminal Courthouse. Steve Bogira. Vintage Books 2006. 401 p.
ISBN 9780679752066
Grades: 11 12 Adult   345.773
1. Criminal courts 2. Criminal justice system 3. Criminal justice personnel 4. Criminals 5. True Crime — Investigations and Trials 6. Adult books for young adults
LC Bl2006004313

Follows a year in the events of a felony courthouse and the lives of men and women on both sides of the law, chronicling cases from the point-of-view of the prisoners' lockup, the jury room, the spectators' gallery, and the judge's chambers.

"Bogira provides a balanced view of the realities of the day-to-day, assembly-line grind that marks so much of the process from arrest to final disposition. The brilliance of Bogira's insights will lead many to hope that he will follow this debut with proposals to cure the many ills he has diagnosed." —*Publishers Weekly*

Includes bibliographical references (p. 359-383) and index; Originally published: New York : A. Knopf, 2005.

345.775 Criminal law — Wisconsin

Strang, Dean A.
Worse Than the Devil: Anarchists, Clarence Darrow, and Justice in a Time of Terror. Dean A. Strang. The University of Wisconsin Press 2013. 268 p.
ISBN 9780299293949
Grades: Adult   345.775
1. Darrow, Clarence, 1857-1938 2. Trials 3. Judicial corruption 4. Anarchists 5. Italian Americans 6. Conspiracies 7. United States history 8. Milwaukee, Wisconsin 9. 1910s 10. 20th century 11. History writing — Scandals 12. History writing — United States 13. True Crime — Investigations and Trials
LC 2012032689

"Strang, a criminal defense lawyer and professor of law, examines the dramatic case of the Bay View Eleven, a group of Italian immigrants arrested after a Milwaukee riot in 1917. In this in-depth study, he analyzes how their trial, coming on the heels of a police station bombing, was grossly mismanaged and sensationalized—essentially acting as proxy for the other tragedy." —*Publishers Weekly*

Includes bibliographical references and index.

346.04 Property

Lessig, Lawrence
The Future of Ideas: The Fate of the Commons in a Connected World. Lawrence Lessig. Random House 2001. xiii, 352 p.

ISBN 9780375505782

Grades: Adult 346.04

1. Intellectual property 2. Copyright and electronic data processing 3. Internet 4. Information society 5. Legislation 6. Science Writing — Computing, the Internet, and Technology

LC 2001031968

Explores the meaning of intellectual property in the new high-tech digital age, addressing the legal, social, and economic factors at work and provides a thought-provoking argument that those qualities that have made the Internet a dynamic force for creativity, freedom, and innovation could destroy the Intenet's potential.

Includes bibliographical references and index.

Norwick, Kenneth P.

The Legal Guide for Writers, Artists and Other Creative People: Protect Your Work and Understand the Law. Kenneth P. Norwick with Cooper Knowlton. Pate Street Publishing Co. 2017. 288 pages

ISBN 9781624144493

Grades: Adult 346.04

1. Artists 2. Authors 3. Copyright 4. Intellectual property 5. Legislation 6. Law — Trademark, patent, and intellectual property

LC Bl2017041447

Enables creators to understand their legal rights and safeguard their work from risks in both cyberspace and traditional media.

Includes index.

346.73 Private law — United States

Addison, Corban

Wastelands: The True Story of Farm Country on Trial. Corban Addison; foreword by John Grisham. Alfred A. Knopf 2022. 352 p.

ISBN 9780593320822

Grades: Adult 346.73

1. Pork industry and trade 2. Pig farming 3. Agribusiness 4. Corporations 5. Animal waste 6. Agricultural pollution 7. Neighbors 8. Trials 9. Lawyers 10. Environmentalists 11. North Carolina 12. Business and economics — Industries — Agriculture and food 13. True Crime — Investigations and Trials 14. Nature Writing — Environmental Issues 15. Life stories — Facing adversity — Victims of crime 16. Nonfiction that reads like fiction

LC 2021048239

Taking readers into the heart of a legal battle over the future of America's farmland, this riveting book stars a courageous group of locals in the coastal plain of North Carolina who, tired of polluting practices, brought suit against one of the world's most powerful companies—and won.

"A novelist and trial attorney tells the true story of North Carolina landowners who fought for justice from a multinational corporation over the deleterious practices of large-scale hog farming." —*Kirkus*

Includes index.

Bellos, David

Who Owns This Sentence?: A History of Copyrights and Wrongs. David Bellos and Alexandre Montagu. W.W. Norton & Company 2024. 384 p.

ISBN 9781324073710

Grades: Adult 346.73

1. Copyright 2. Fair use (Copyright) 3. Intellectual property 4. Trademarks 5. Corporate power 6. Capitalism 7. Creation (Literary, artistic, etc.) 8. History 9. Arts and Entertainment — General 10. Business and economics — General 11. History writing — Arts and culture

LibraryReads Favorites, 2024.

Copyright is everywhere. Your smartphone incorporates thousands of items of intellectual property. Not only books but wallpaper, computer programs, pop songs, cartoon characters, snapshots, and cuddly toys are now deemed to be intellectual properties—making copyright a labyrinthine construction of laws with colorful and often baffling rationales covering almost all products of human creativity. It wasn't always so. Principled arguments against copyright arose from the start and nearly abolished it in the nineteenth century. Nonetheless, countless revisions have made copyright ever stronger.

"A gimlet-eyed analysis of a system that protects a corporate status quo at the expense of independent invention." —*Kirkus*

Jacoby, Melissa B.

★ *Unjust Debts: How Our Bankruptcy System Makes America More Unequal.* Melissa B. Jacoby. The New Press 2024. 304 p.

ISBN 9781620977866

Grades: Adult 346.73

1. Bankruptcy 2. Public debt 3. Corporate power 4. Bailouts (Government policy) 5. Institutional racism 6. Income inequality 7. Civil rights 8. Injustice 9. Politics and global affairs — General 10. Society and culture — Wealth and class 11. Business and economics — Economics — Socioeconomics

LC 2023055115

Bankruptcy is the busiest federal court in America. In theory, bankruptcy in America exists to cancel or restructure debts for people and companies that have way too many—a safety valve designed to provide a mechanism for restarting lives and businesses when things go wrong financially. In this brilliant and paradigm-shifting book, legal scholar Melissa B. Jacoby shows how bankruptcy has also become an escape hatch for powerful individuals, corporations, and governments, contributing in unseen and poorly understood ways to race, gender, and class inequality in America.

"Jacoby's assured prose brings extraordinary clarity to an intentionally opaque and labyrinthine system. It's an eye-opening look at the laws that undergird American inequality." —*Publishers Weekly*

Includes bibliographical references.

Kaiser, Robert G.

Act of Congress: How America's Essential Institution Works, and How It Doesn't. Robert G. Kaiser. Alfred A. Knopf 2013. 304 p.

ISBN 9780307700162

Grades: Adult 346.73

1. Financial services industry and trade 2. Global Financial Crisis, 2008-2009 3. Politics and government 4. United States 5. Politics and global affairs — World politics — United States

LC 2012038245

Documents the journey of a financial reform bill in the wake of the 2008 economic collapse by focusing on two of the major players behind the legislation—Congressman Barney Frank and Senator Christopher Dodd.

Includes bibliographical references and index.

Oller, John

White Shoe: How a New Breed of Wall Street Lawyers Changed Big Business and the American Century. John Oller. E.P. Dutton 2019. 448 p.

ISBN 9781524743253

Grades: Adult 346.73

1. Corporate lawyers 2. Corporations 3. Big business 4. Wealth 5. Free enterprise 6. Law firms 7. Businesspeople 8. Lawyers 9. Wall Street, New York City 10. New York City 11. 20th century 12. Business and economics — Economics — History 13. Life stories — Law and order — Judges and lawyers 14. History writing — Early 20th century — United States

LC 2018029007

A former Manhattan lawyer presents a rollicking account of how an ambitious new class of attorneys in the 20th century devised and implemented the strategies that launched the era of American big business and international Wall Street prominence.

"Oller doesnt shy away from detailing early corporate lawyers role as tools of monopolistic robber barons, or the endemic prejudice against Jewish lawyers. That balance makes this a valuable addition to the literature on Americas transformation during the Gilded Age." —*Publishers Weekly*

Includes bibliographical references and index.

ESSENTIAL AND RECOMMENDED TITLES
346.7301 Private law — United States — Persons and domestic relations

Russell, Carrie
Complete Copyright for K-12 Librarians and Educators: For K-12 Librarians and Educators. Carrie Russell. American Library Association - ALA Editions 2023. 196 p.
ISBN 9780838939642
Grades: Professional   346.73
1. Copyright 2. Fair use (Copyright) 3. School libraries 4. Librarians 5. Law — Trademark, patent, and intellectual property 6. Professional materials — General
LC 2022057381
This resource offers clear guidance for providing materials to students while carefully observing copyright law.
Includes bibliographical references and index.

Winkler, Adam
We the Corporations: How American Businesses Won Their Civil Rights. Adam Winkler. Liveright Publishing Corporation 2018. xxiv, 471 pages : Illustration
ISBN 9780871407122
Grades: Adult   346.73
1. Lobbying 2. Business and politics 3. Business 4. Business and economics — Economics — Contemporary U.S. economy 5. Politics and global affairs — Civil and human rights 6. Book club best bets
LC 2017051893
New York Times Notable Book, 2018; National Book Critics Circle Award for Nonfiction finalist, 2018.
Traces the two-hundred-year history of corporate America's battle to achieve constitutional freedom from federal control, examining the civil rights debates and key events that shaped the controversial 2010 Supreme Court decision to extend constitutional protections to businesses.
"Winkler employs an evocative, fast-paced storytelling style, making for an entertaining and enlightening book that will likely complicate the views of partisans on both sides of the issue." —*Publishers Weekly*
Includes bibliographical references (pages 405-444) and index.

346.7301 Private law — United States — Persons and domestic relations

Cenziper, Debbie
★ *Love Wins: The Lovers and Lawyers Who Fought the Landmark Case for Marriage Equality.* Debbie Cenziper & Jim Obergefell. William Morrow 2016. 304 p.
ISBN 9780062456083
Grades: Adult   346.7301
1. Same-sex marriage 2. Civil rights 3. Gay men 4. Lesbians 5. Marriage law 6. Lawyers 7. Gay couples 8. Lesbian couples 9. LGBTQIA+ rights 10. Legislation 11. Human rights 12. Civil rights 13. United States history 14. United States 15. 21st century 16. Society and culture — LGBTQIA+ 17. Politics and global affairs — Civil and human rights 18. History writing — LGBTQIA+
LC 2016014548
Documents the inspirational story of the partners, lawyers, judges, and activists behind the groundbreaking Supreme Court case that legalized same-sex marriage in all fifty states.
"Uplifting, well-written story of personal courage and political empowerment." —*Kirkus*

Issenberg, Sasha
★ *The Engagement: A Quarter Century of Defending, Defining, and Expanding Marriage in America.* Sasha Issenberg. Pantheon Books 2021. 928 p.
ISBN 9781524748739
Grades: Adult   346.7301
1. Same-sex marriage 2. Social change 3. 21st century 4. History writing — LGBTQIA+ 5. History writing — Early 21st century — United States
LC 2019051707

On June 26, 2015, the United States Supreme Court ruled that state bans on gay marriage were unconstitutional, making same-sex unions legal throughout the United States. But the road to victory was much longer than many know. In this seminal work, Sasha Issenberg takes us back to Hawaii in the 1990s, when that state's supreme court first started grappling with the issue, and traces the fight for marriage equality from the enactment of the Defense of Marriage Act in 1996 to the Goodridge decision that made Massachusetts the first state to legalize same-sex marriage, and finally to the seminal Supreme Court decisions of Windsor and Obergefell. This meticulously reported work sheds new light on every aspect of this fraught history and brings to life the perspectives of those who fought courageously for the right to marry as well as those who fervently believed that same-sex marriage would destroy the nation. It is sure to become the definitive book on one of the most important civil rights fights of our time.
"Journalist Issenberg (Outpatients) depicts both sides of the debate over same-sex marriage in this comprehensive history. . . . The result is a definitive portrait of a key victory in the battle for LGBTQ rights." —*Publishers Weekly*
Includes bibliographical references and index.

Kaplan, Roberta A.
Then Comes Marriage: United States V. Windsor and the Defeat of DOMA. Roberta Kaplan with Lisa Dickey; Foreword by Edie Windsor. W. W. Norton & Company 2015. 320 p.
ISBN 9780393248678
Grades: Adult   346.7301
1. Windsor, Edie 2. Marriage law 3. Same-sex marriage 4. LGBTQIA+ rights 5. Lesbian couples 6. Gay couples 7. Gay marriage 8. Lesbians 9. Legislation 10. Human rights 11. Civil rights 12. Society and culture — LGBTQIA+ 13. Politics and global affairs — Civil and human rights
LC 2015023636
LibraryReads Favorites, 2015.
Roberta Kaplan's gripping story of her defeat of the Defense of Marriage Act (DOMA) before the Supreme Court.
"Readers with an interest in constitutional law and Supreme Court politics, as well as the road to marriage equality, will find this account deliciously gripping." —*Library Journal*
Includes index.

Lapidus, Lenora M.
★ *The Rights of Women: The Authoritative ACLU Guide to Women's Rights.* Lenora M. Lapidus, Emily J. Martin, Namita Luthra. New York University Press 2009. xvii, 412 p.
ISBN 9780814752296
Grades: Adult   346.7301
1. Women 2. Legislation 3. Law — General
LC 2008047033
The Rights of Women is a comprehensive guide that explains in detail the rights of women under present U.S. law, and how these laws can be used in the continuing struggle to achieve full gender equality at home, in the workplace, at school, and in society at large.
Rev. ed. of: The rights of women / Susan Deller Ross ... [et al.]. 3rd ed, completely rev. and up-to-date. c1993; Includes bibliographical references and index.

346.7302 Private law — United States — Juristic acts, contracts, agency

Leamer, Laurence
The Price of Justice: A True Story of Greed and Corruption. Laurence Leamer. Times Books 2013. 384 p.
ISBN 9780805094718
Grades: Adult   346.7302
1. Caperton, Hugh 2. Blankenship, Donald Leon 3. Coal mines and mining 4. Business corruption 5. Coal industry and trade 6. Judicial corruption 7. Political corruption 8. Exploitation 9. Manipulation by men 10. Conspiracies 11. Judges 12. Deception 13. Corporate greed 14. Corporate accountability 15. Fair

trial 16. Mines and mineral resources 17. Greed 18. Appalachian Region 19. True Crime — Investigations and Trials 20. Business and economics — Corruption and scandal

LC 2012041537

Describes how the tyrannical head of a large energy conglomerate bought judges, disregarded safety standards for mine workers, and polluted drinking water until challenged by two lawyers who brought him to justice.

Includes bibliographical references and index.

Lindner, Dan
★ *A Guide to Federal Contracting, 2nd Ed.: Principles and Practices.* Dan Lindner. Bernan Press 2022. x, 622 pages
ISBN 9781636710525
Grades: Adult   346.7302
1. Contracts 2. Government contracts 3. Business and economics — General

LC 2017046917

The second edition of a Guide to Federal Contracting, provides a succinct yet thorough treatment of federal contracting requirements and regulations—demystifying the volumes of regulations and policies of the federal government.

"There are other, less-expensive guides, but none are as complete or authoritative. This is an essential resource for large public and academic libraries where federal contracts play an important role." —*Booklist*

Includes bibliographical references (pages 577-582) and index.

346.7303 Torts — United States

McGinty, Brian
Lincoln's Greatest Case: The River, the Bridge, and the Making of America. Brian McGinty. Liveright Publishing Corporation, a Division of W.W. Norton & Company 2015. 320 p.
ISBN 9780871407849
Grades: Adult   346.7303
1. Lincoln, Abraham, 1809-1865 2. Trials 3. Lawyers 4. Steamboats 5. Railroads 6. Presidents 7. Transportation 8. United States 9. Biographies 10. Life stories — Politics — Politicians 11. History writing — Antebellum America — United States

LC 2014036938

It may seem unlikely that a single liability suit, the Effie Afton case, could help launch Abraham Lincoln's political career while determining the future of rail transportation in the U.S. However, in Lincoln's Greatest Case, legal historian Brian McGinty demonstrates how Lincoln's courtroom performance assured that trains would win over steamboats in the competition to dominate inland transportation. His intelligence, wit, and skill during the trial also helped convince political supporters that he could be a successful campaigner. This detailed and intriguing account illuminates a critical moment in transportation history and a pivotal event in Lincoln's ascent to the presidency.

"McGinty's book gives us the best accounting of Lincoln, the lawyer, to date. Highly recommended." —*Library Journal*

346.7304 Property law — United States

Butler, Rebecca P.
★ *Copyright for Teachers & Librarians in the 21st Century.* Rebecca P. Butler. Neal-Schuman Publishers 2011. xvii, 276 p. : Illustration
ISBN 9781555707385
Grades: Adult Professional   346.7304
1. Copyright 2. Fair use (Copyright) 3. Teachers 4. Law — Trademark, patent, and intellectual property 5. Professional materials — General 6. Educator resources — General

LC 2011012600

Here is a practical copyright handbook designed to help librarians, media specialists, technology coordinators and specialists, and teachers stay within copyright law while making copyrighted print, non-print, and Web sources available to students and others.

Includes bibliographical references and index.

Crews, Kenneth D.
★ *Copyright Law for Librarians and Educators: Creative Strategies and Practical Solutions.* Kenneth D. Crews. ALA Editions 2020. 308 p.
ISBN 9780838916292
Grades: Professional   346.7304
1. Copyright 2. Fair use (Copyright) 3. Librarians 4. Teachers 5. Law — Trademark, patent, and intellectual property 6. Professional materials — General

LC 2019051377

This newly revised and updated edition by respected copyright authority Crews offers timely insights and succinct guidance for LIS students, librarians, and educators alike.

Includes bibliographical references and index.

Decherney, Peter
Hollywood's Copyright Wars: From Edison to the Internet. Peter Decherney. Columbia University Press 2012. xii, 287 p. : Illustration
ISBN 9780231159463
Grades: Adult   346.7304
1. Copyright 2. Arts and Entertainment — Movies and Television

LC 2011041745

Beginning with Thomas Edison's aggressive copyright disputes and concluding with recent lawsuits against YouTube, Hollywood's Copyright Wars follows the struggle of the film, television, and digital media industries to influence and adapt to copyright law.

Includes bibliographical references (p. [243]-274) and index.

Elias, Stephen
The Foreclosure Survival Guide, 9th Ed.: Keep Your House or Walk Away with Money in Your Pocket. Attorneys Stephen Elias and Amy Loftsgordon; with bankruptcy updates by Attorney Leon Bayer. Nolo 2023. 339 p.
ISBN 9781413330991
Grades: Adult   346.7304
1. Foreclosure 2. Homeowners 3. Mortgage loans 4. House selling 5. Business and economics — General 6. Law — Real estate and housing

LC 2015009962

This book is for homeowners who can't make their mortgage payments. It provides a thorough, easy-to-understand, compassionate look at the foreclosure process and available options so that homeowners can determine if they should give up their home, file for bankruptcy, fight the foreclosure, or explore loss mitigation (foreclosure alternative) options.

Includes bibliographical references and index.

Fishman, Stephen
★ *The Copyright Handbook, 15th Ed.: What Every Writer Needs to Know.* Stephen Fishman, J.D... Nolo 2024. 386 pages
ISBN 9781413331134
Grades: Adult   346.7304
1. Copyright 2. Writing 3. Law — Trademark, patent, and intellectual property 4. Language arts and studies — Writing skills 5. Arts and Entertainment — Writing and publishing

LC Bl2014048732

Everything writers—and anyone working with words—need to know about producing and protecting content both in print and online. Includes a look at the exploding field of artificial intelligence (AI) and its impact on copyright.

Includes bibliographical references and index.

Gasaway, Laura N.
Copyright Questions and Answers for Information Professionals: From the Columns of Against the Grain. Laura N. Gasaway. Purdue University Press 2013. 298 p.
ISBN 9781557536396
Grades: Adult   346.7304

ESSENTIAL AND RECOMMENDED TITLES
346.7307 Commercial law — United States

1. Fair use (Copyright) 2. Copyright 3. Professional materials — General
LC Oc2013003292

"All in all, there are answers to well over 300 questions concerning copyright, fair use, and related issues. The appendix provides a chart to assist in knowing when a book passes into public domain." —*Library Journal*
Includes index.

Harris, Lesley Ellen
Licensing Digital Content: A Practical Guide for Librarians. Lesley Ellen Harris. ALA Editions 2018. xviii, 181 pages
ISBN 9780838916308
Grades: Professional   346.7304
1. Copyright 2. Libraries and electronic publishing 3. Librarians 4. United States 5. Professional materials — Library management
LC 2017044800

In its new edition, this resource remains a must-have for all information professionals who deal with licenses for electronic resources.

"The revised version of this book is well organized and updated to help professionals with the licensing process. The book includes detailed chapters, analysis, terminology, a thorough index, and examples of copyright law, all compiled by an expert in the field." —*Booklist*
Includes bibliographical references and index.

Lessig, Lawrence
Remix: Making Art and Commerce Thrive in the Hybrid Economy. Lawrence Lessig. Penguin Press 2008. 256 p.
ISBN 9781594201721
Grades: Adult   346.7304
1. Copyright and electronic data processing 2. Cultural industry and trade 3. Creativity 4. Copyright 5. Collaboration 6. Social life and customs 7. United States 8. 21st century 9. 20th century 10. Arts and Entertainment — General 11. Society and culture — Media and technology
LC 2008032392

Argues that future generations are being harmed by a restrictive copyright system that protects corporate interests, in a report that calls for an end of the practice of criminalizing artists who build on the creative works of others and for implementing a collaborative and profitable "hybrid economy" that protects both creative and ethical needs.

"As Lessig sees it, if intellectual-property law is left as it is an entire generation will be criminalized. He argues that the ways in which young people break copyright laws help them to become the sort of people we want them to be creative and collaborative. Kids today are simply not going to give up downloading music and using copyrighted material in YouTube videos: They belong to a culture for which remix is the essential art. Lessig's proposals for revising copyright are compelling, because they rethink intellectual-property rights without abandoning them." —*The New Yorker*
Includes bibliographical references and index.

Lobel, Orly
You Don't Own Me: How Mattel v. MGA Entertainment Exposed Barbie's Dark Side. Orly Lobel. W. W. Norton & Company 2018. 320 p.
ISBN 9780393254075
Grades: Adult   346.7304
1. Bryant, Carter 2. Trials 3. Intellectual property 4. Labor disputes 5. Intellectual property infringement 6. Toy industry and trade 7. Business competition 8. Barbie dolls 9. Business and economics — General
LC 2017027183

Argues that the battle between Mattel, the makers of the iconic Barbie doll, and MGA, the company that created the Bratz dolls, was not just a war over best-selling toys, but a war over intellectual property.

"The end result is a thoroughly researched book that explains the legalese of patent, property, and copyright law in laymans terms while providing an entertaining narrative." —*Publishers Weekly*
Includes bibliographical references and index.

346.7307 Commercial law — United States

O'Neill, Cara
Chapter 13 Bankruptcy, 17th Ed.: Keep Your Property & Repay Debts Over Time. Attorney Cara O'Neill. Nolo 2024. 394 p. : Illustration
ISBN 9781413331783
Grades: Adult   346.7307
1. Bankruptcy 2. Law — Corporate, business, and finance 3. Business and economics — Personal finance
LC Bl2018095009

This book simplifies the bankruptcy chapter often considered intimidating—Chapter 13. Debtors learn about the filing process, property issues, and the repayment plan, as well as about choosing a bankruptcy lawyer, the types of legal motions that could arise, and recovering financially after bankruptcy.
Includes index.

346.79401 Private law — California — Persons and domestic relations

Becker, Jo
★ *Forcing the Spring:* Inside the Fight for Marriage Equality. Jo Becker. Penguin Press 2014. 480 p.
ISBN 9781594204449
Grades: Adult   346.79401
1. Gay and Lesbian Movement 2. Gay marriage 3. Lesbian marriage 4. Gay men 5. Lesbians 6. Political activists 7. Civil rights 8. LGBTQIA+ rights 9. Human rights 10. Civil rights 11. United States 12. Politics and global affairs — Civil and human rights 13. Society and culture — LGBTQIA+
LC 2014005342

New York Times Notable Book, 2014.

Draws on interviews and in-depth reporting to present an insider's account of a national civil rights struggle to stop Proposition 8, which removed the right of gay men and women to marry, and the campaign to undermine the Defense of Marriage Act.

"Becker's chronicle of a legal battle reveals deeper changes in the cultural and political landscape of a nation grappling with old prejudices and changing public opinion that continue to resonate." —*Booklist*

Yoshino, Kenji
Speak Now: Marriage Equality on Trial. Kenji Yoshino. Crown 2015. 376 pages
ISBN 9780385348805
Grades: Adult   346.79401
1. Hollingsworth, Dennis, 1967- 2. Perry, Kristin 3. Gay marriage 4. Gay and Lesbian Movement 5. Political activists 6. Gay men 7. Lesbians 8. Civil rights 9. LGBTQIA+ rights 10. Human rights 11. Civil rights 12. United States 13. Politics and global affairs — Civil and human rights 14. Society and culture — LGBTQIA+
LC 2014042967

Stonewall Book Awards: Israel Fishman Non-fiction Award, 2016.

Drawing on interviews with lawyers and witnesses on both sides of the case, a prominent legal scholar—and newly married gay man—takes readers deep inside the groundbreaking federal suit against Proposition 8, which rescinded the right of same-sex couples to marry in the state of California.

"This is the well-told story of one of the most important civil trials in recent American history, Hollingsworth v. Perry, the 12-day trial challenging the constitutionality of California's Proposition 8. Because this case was tried in federal court, most of America was aware that it might end up being argued before the US Supreme Court. Yoshino takes the reader behind the scenes of both sides of this civil trial. Well beyond its outcome, however, this case is all about why trials can be crucial to the American system of justice." —*Choice*

347 Procedure and courts

Zerwick, Phoebe
Beyond Innocence: The Life Sentence of Darryl Hunt. Phoebe Zerwick. Atlantic Monthly Press 2022. 320 p.
ISBN 9780802159373
Grades: Adult   347
1. Innocence (Law) 2. Judicial error 3. Racism in the criminal justice system 4. Racism 5. African American prisoners 6. Criminal justice system 7. Coping 8. Post-traumatic stress disorder 9. Racism in law enforcement 10. North Carolina 11. Society and culture — Race 12. Society and culture — Violence and crime — Criminal justice system 13. True Crime — Investigations and Trials

A deeply reported, gripping narrative of injustice, exoneration, and the lifelong impact of incarceration, Beyond Innocence is the poignant saga of one remarkable life that sheds vitally important light on the failures of the American justice system at every level.

"Zerwick's portrait of Hunt is a reminder of the trauma caused by the American justice system and offers an essential narrative of the lasting impacts of incarceration." —*Library Journal*

347.73 Civil procedure and courts of the United States

Bharara, Preet
Doing Justice: A Prosecutor's Thoughts on Crime, Punishment, and the Rule of Law. Preet Bharara. Alfred A. Knopf 2019. 368 p.
ISBN 9780525521129
Grades: Adult   347.73
1. Criminal justice system 2. Social justice 3. Law 4. Fairness 5. Judgment 6. Crime 7. Punishment 8. Politics and government 9. United States 10. Politics and global affairs — Civil and human rights 11. Society and culture — Violence and crime — Criminal justice system

LC 2018053931
From a one-time federal prosecutor for the Southern District of New York comes an important overview of the way the American justice system works, and why the rule of law is essential to U.S. society, in a book that uses case histories, personal experiences and more.

"He former federal prosecutor for the Southern District of New York skillfully explains how he approached his job, offering a mixture of guiding principles and compelling anecdotes." —*Kirkus*

Biskupic, Joan
★ *Nine* Black Robes: Inside the Supreme Court's Drive to the Right and Its Historic Consequences. Joan Biskupic. HarperCollins 2023. 352 p.
ISBN 9780063052789
Grades: Adult   347.73
1. Trump, Donald, 1946- 2. Judges 3. Judicial system 4. Constitutional law 5. Trials 6. Law 7. Political questions and judicial power 8. Courts 9. Ideology 10. United States 11. Law — General 12. History writing — Judicial branch — United States

With unparalleled access to key players, a CNN senior legal analyst and Supreme Court expert provides an urgent and inside look at the history-making era in the Supreme Court during the Trump and post-Trump years, including its reversal of Roe v. Wade.

"Devoted Court-watchers will devour this behind-the-scenes expose." —*Booklist*

Breyer, Stephen G.
★ *The* Authority of the Court and the Peril of Politics. Stephen Breyer. Harvard University Press 2021. 101 p.
ISBN 9780674269361
Grades: Adult   347.73
1. Rule of law 2. Judicial review 3. Fairness 4. Public opinion 5. Political questions and judicial power 6. United States 7. Speeches, addresses, etc. 8. Politics and global affairs — Judicial politics

LC 2021017885

Americans increasingly believe the Supreme Court is a political body in disguise. But Justice Stephen Breyer disagrees. Arguing that judges are committed to their oath to do impartial justice, Breyer aims to restore trust in the Court. In the absence of that trust, he warns, the Court will lose its authority, imperiling our constitutional system.

"Based on his 2021 lecture at Harvard Law School, Supreme Court Justice Breyer offers a selected history of court cases, a defense of judicial impartiality, and recommendations for promoting the public's respect for and acceptance of the role of the judiciary in the future." —*Kirkus*

Includes bibliographical references.

Making Our Democracy Work: A Judge's View. by Stephen Breyer. Alfred A. Knopf 2010. 336 p.
ISBN 9780307269911
Grades: Adult   347.73
1. Judicial review 2. Separation of powers 3. Judicial power 4. Judicial system 5. Constitutional history 6. Political questions and judicial power 7. United States 8. History writing — Judicial branch — United States

LC 2010016839
A Supreme Court justice outlines an accessible profile of the legislative branch's duties that explains its responsibility to safeguard the public while ensuring the cooperation of other government branches, sharing the stories behind key historical decisions.

Includes bibliographical references.

Chemerinsky, Erwin
Closing the Courthouse Door: How Your Constitutional Rights Became Unenforceable. Erwin Chemerinsky. Yale University Press 2017. 256 p.
ISBN 9780300211580
Grades: Adult   347.73
1. Freedom 2. Political rights 3. Civil rights 4. State (Political science) 5. Constitutional law 6. Politics and global affairs — Judicial politics

LC 2016941955
A leading legal scholar, using many stories of people whose rights have been trampled yet had no legal recourse, explores how the constitutional right to seek justice has been restricted by the Supreme Court.

"A dramatic challenge to understand the shakiness of the foundations we take for granted and where energies committed to redress should be directed." —*Kirkus*

Cohen, Adam
★ *Supreme* Inequality: The Supreme Court's Fifty-year Battle for a More Unjust America. Adam Cohen. Penguin Group USA 2020. 448 p.
ISBN 9780735221505
Grades: Adult   347.73
1. Judicial power 2. Equality 3. Equality before the law 4. Political questions and judicial power 5. Discrimination 6. Election law 7. Politics and government 8. United States 9. Liberal writing 10. Politics and global affairs — Judicial politics 11. History writing — Judicial branch — United States

LC 2019031002
The Time senior writer and author of Imbeciles traces the increasingly conservative direction of the Supreme Court throughout the past half-century, exploring the appointments and rulings of Justices who have supported the reversals of egalitarian law. As the nation comes to grips with two new Trump-appointed justices, Cohen proves beyond doubt that the modern Court has been one of the leading forces behind the nation's soaring level of economic inequality, and that an institution revered as a source of fairness has been systematically making America less fair.

"Weaving legal, political, and social history, Cohen creates a richly detailed, but accessible, account for all interested in the personalities and politics that have shaped and are continuing to shape not only the U.S. criminal justice system but also the fabric of American life. A must-read." —*Library Journal*

Includes bibliographical references and index.

Coyle, Marcia
The Roberts Court: The Struggle for the Constitution. Marcia Coyle. Simon & Schuster 2013. 384 p.

ESSENTIAL AND RECOMMENDED TITLES
347.73 Civil procedure and courts of the United States

ISBN 9781451627510
Grades: Adult   347.73
1. Roberts, John G, 1955- 2. Judicial review 3. Judges 4. Law and politics 5. Political questions and judicial power 6. Gun control 7. Campaign funds 8. Immigration and emigration 9. Conservatism 10. Liberalism 11. Medical care 12. Social life and customs 13. United States 14. 21st century 15. Politics and global affairs — Judicial politics
LC 2012051637

A National Law Journal correspondent and forefront expert on the Supreme Court traces the first seven years of the Roberts Court to report on its direction and the resolutions of five landmark cases on race, guns, immigration, campaign finance and health care.

"In this insightful, important look at the Roberts court, Coyle also explores the broader implications for American politics and justice." —*Booklist*
Includes bibliographical references and index.

Finkelman, Paul
★ *Landmark Decisions of the United States Supreme Court*. Paul Finkelman, Melvin I. Urofsky. CQ Press 2008. xix, 791p.
ISBN 9780872894099
Grades: Adult   347.73
1. Constitutional law 2. Politics and global affairs — General 3. Law — General
LC 2007042588

An important reference that provides the historical context and constitutional perspective of more than 1,000 of the most important Supreme Court cases. Landmark Decisions of the United States Supreme Court offers an unparalleled history of the Supreme Court and its impact on American democracy and society.
Includes bibliographical references and indexes.

Friedman, Barry
The Will of the People: How Public Opinion Has Influenced the Supreme Court and Shaped the Meaning of the Constitution. Barry Friedman. Farrar, Straus and Giroux 2009. 688 p.
ISBN 9780374220341
Grades: Adult   347.73
1. Judicial process 2. Judicial system 3. Public opinion 4. Politics and government 5. United States 6. History writing — Judicial branch — United States
LC 2008054247

An account of the relationship between the public and the Supreme Court challenges complaints about the legitimacy of an appointed judicial authority, citing historical precedents that demonstrate how and why the rulings of justices have not overly strayed from public opinion.

"This book is a thought-provoking and authoritative history of the Supreme Court's relationship to popular opinion. Friedman's contribution to [the] discussion is the breadth and detail of his historical canvas, and it's a significant one." —*New York Times Book Review*
Includes bibliographical references and index.

Ginsburg, Ruth Bader
★ *My Own Words*. Ruth Bader Ginsburg with Mary Hartnett and Wendy W. Williams. Simon & Schuster 2016. 288 p.
ISBN 9781501145247
Grades: Adult   347.73
1. Ginsburg, Ruth Bader. 1933-2020 2. Judges 3. Civil rights 4. Women's rights 5. Feminists 6. Women judges 7. Autobiographies and memoirs 8. Essays 9. Life stories — Law and order — Judges and lawyers
LC 2016031635

Offers a collection of engaging, serious, and playful writings and speeches from the Supreme Court justice on topics ranging from gender equality and the workings of the Court to Judaism and the value of looking beyond U.S. shores when interpreting the Constitution.

"The variety of subjects is impressive, and Ginsburgs gift for concision enables her to discuss them in enough detail to engage interest while leaving the reader wanting more." —*Publishers Weekly*
Includes bibliographical references and index.

Graetz, Michael J.
The Burger Court and the Rise of the Judicial Right. Michael J. Graetz and Linda Greenhouse. Simon & Schuster 2016. 512 p.
ISBN 9781476732503
Grades: Adult   347.73
1. Burger, Warren Earl, 1907-1995 2. Judges 3. Constitutional law 4. Judicial system 5. Courts 6. Political questions and judicial power 7. United States 8. 20th century 9. History writing — Judicial branch — United States
LC 2015031713

Drawing on the personal papers of justices as well as other archives, a first-of-its-kind book provides a fresh perspective at the Warren Burger Supreme Court, digging down to the roots of its most significant decisions and shows how their legacy affects us today.

"Two powerhouse law historians/Journalists deliver a major contribution to the history of the Supreme Court." —*Kirkus*
Includes bibliographical references and index.

Hirshman, Linda R.
Sisters in Law: How Sandra Day O'Connor and Ruth Bader Ginsburg Went to the Supreme Court and Changed the World. Linda Hirshman. HarperCollins 2015. 320 p.
ISBN 9780062238467
Grades: Adult   347.73
1. O'Connor, Sandra Day, 1930-2023 2. Ginsburg, Ruth Bader. 1933-2020 3. Judges 4. Women's rights 5. Women judges 6. Civil rights 7. Politics and government 8. United States 9. 20th century 10. Biographies 11. History writing — Judicial branch — United States 12. Life stories — Law and order — Judges and lawyers 13. History writing — Women's history
LC 2015002577

Amelia Bloomer Lists, 2016; Library Journal Best Books, 2015.

An account of the intertwined lives of the first and second woman Supreme Court justices examines their respective religious and political beliefs while sharing insights into how they have influenced interpretations of the Constitution to promote equal rights for women.
Includes bibliographical references and index.

Kaplan, David A.
The Most Dangerous Branch: Inside the Supreme Court's Assault on the Constitution. David A. Kaplan. Crown Publishing 2018. 446 p.
ISBN 9781524759902
Grades: Adult   347.73
1. Judges 2. Judicial power 3. Constitutional law 4. Political parties 5. Separation of powers 6. Power 7. Liberal writing 8. History writing — Judicial branch — United States 9. Politics and global affairs — Judicial politics 10. Life stories — Law and order — Judges and lawyers
LC 2018004533

Kaplan presents a sweeping narrative of the justices' aggrandizement of power over the decades—from Roe v. Wade to Bush v. Gore to Citizens United, to rulings during the 2017-18 term. But the arrogance of the Court isn't partisan: Conservative and liberal justices alike are guilty of overreach. Challenging conventional wisdom about the Court's transcendent power, the Most Dangerous Branch is sure to rile both sides of the political aisle.

"In his penetrating if anxious analysis of Supreme Court jurisprudence, Kaplan laments recent decisions lacking judicial restraint and pleads for narrow exercise of the courts power despite public pressure and ample temptation to rule broadly on controversial matters." —*Booklist*
Includes bibliographical references and index.

O'Brien, David M
★ *Storm Center: The Supreme Court in American Politics*. David M. O'Brien, University of Virginia. W.W. Norton & Company 2017. xxi, 456 pages : Illustration
ISBN 9780393603538
Grades: Adult   347.73
1. Judicial process 2. Political questions and judicial power 3. United States 4. Politics and global affairs — General

PUBLIC LIBRARY CORE COLLECTION: NONFICTION
Twentieth Edition

An inside look at the workings of the Supreme Court.
Includes bibliographical references (pages 367-412) and index.

O'Connor, Sandra Day
★ *Out of Order: Stories from the History of the Supreme Court.* Sandra Day O'Connor. Random House 2013. 160 p.
ISBN 9780812993929
Grades: Adult   347.73
1. Trials 2. Courts 3. Judicial system 4. United States 5. Politics and global affairs — Judicial politics

LC 2012025708

The former Supreme Court Justice and author of Lazy B shares stories about the history and evolution of the Supreme Court that traces the roles of key contributors while sharing the events behind important transformations.
Includes bibliographical references and index.

Olsen, Lise
Code of Silence: Sexual Misconduct by Federal Judges, the Secret System That Protects Them, and the Women Who Blew the Whistle. Lise Olsen. Beacon Press 2021. 264 p.
ISBN 9780807008676
Grades: Adult   347.73
1. Judges 2. Federal judges 3. Judicial corruption 4. Sexual harassment of women 5. Sexual violence victims 6. Whistle blowers 7. Federal courts 8. Justice 9. Impeachments 10. United States 11. Politics and global affairs — Judicial politics 12. Society and culture — Violence and crime 13. Life stories — Facing adversity — Victims of crime

LC 2021012855

A book about lawbreaking federal judges, the secret disciplinary system that protects them, and brave women who blew the whistle.
"This captivating, eloquent book will resonate with anyone seeking justice and accountability; give to readers of Deborah Tuerkheimer's Credible: Why We Doubt Accusers and Protect Abusers." —*Library Journal*
Includes bibliographical references and index.

Robin, Corey
The Enigma of Clarence Thomas. Corey Robin. Metropolitan Books, Henry Holt and Company 2019. 208 p.
ISBN 9781627793834
Grades: Adult   347.73
1. Thomas, Clarence, 1948- 2. Racism 3. Conservatism 4. Judges 5. African American judges 6. Political questions and judicial power 7. Politics and government 8. United States 9. Biographies 10. History writing — Judicial branch — United States 11. Politics and global affairs — Judicial politics 12. Life stories — Law and order — Judges and lawyers

LC 2019012026

An analysis of the controversial Supreme Court justice examines Thomas' opinions against a backdrop of his autobiographical and political writings, revealing his pessimistic beliefs about the absolute racism of white people and the impossibility of progress.
Includes bibliographical references and index.

Shesol, Jeff
Supreme Power: Franklin Roosevelt vs. the Supreme Court. Jeff Shesol. W.W. Norton 2010. 512 p.
ISBN 9780393064742
Grades: Adult   347.73
1. Roosevelt, Franklin D. (Franklin Delano), 1882-1945 2. Judicial system 3. Political leadership 4. Presidents 5. Political questions and judicial power 6. Politics and government 7. United States 8. 20th century 9. History writing — Presidency — 20th century — United States 10. History writing — Judicial branch — United States

LC 2009046365

New York Times Notable Book, 2010.

Chronicles Franklin Roosevelt's battle with the Supreme Court, which culminated in him trying to suppress its conservative justices by expanding the size of the court, an attempt which failed and divided the Democratic party.
"This is an impressive and engaging book an excellent work of narrative history. It is deeply researched and beautifully written. Even readers who already know the outcome will find it hard not to feel the suspense that surrounded the battle, so successfully does Shesol recreate the atmosphere of this great controversy." —*New York Times Book Review*
Includes bibliographical references and index.

Simon, James F.
Eisenhower vs. Warren: The Battle for Civil Rights and Liberties. James F. Simon. Liveright Publishing Corporation 2018. 464 p.
ISBN 9780871407559
Grades: Adult   347.73
1. Warren, Earl, 1891-1974 2. Eisenhower, Dwight D. (Dwight David), 1890-1969 3. School integration 4. Civil Rights Movement 5. Social change 6. Civil rights 7. African Americans 8. Race relations 9. Politics and government 10. United States 11. 1950s 12. 1960s 13. Impartial writing 14. History writing — African American — Civil rights — United States

LC Bl2018003663

Traces the bitter 1950s rivalry between President Eisenhower and Chief Justice Earl Warren and how it framed the tumultuous future of the modern civil rights movement.
"This is a cogently written book, especially given the complexity of many of the issues. Simon does great justice to an important segment of a critical period in American history." —*Booklist*

Toobin, Jeffrey
The Nine: Inside the Secret World of the Supreme Court. Jeffrey Toobin. Doubleday 2007. VIII, 369 p. : Color illustration
ISBN 9780385516402
Grades: 11 12 Adult   347.73
1. Judicial review 2. Judges 3. Law and politics 4. Conservatism 5. Political questions and judicial power 6. Social life and customs 7. United States 8. 21st century 9. 20th century 10. Politics and global affairs — Judicial politics

LC 2007020287

J. Anthony Lukas Book Prize, 2008; New York Times Notable Book, 2007.

Drawing on interviews with the Supreme Court justices and other insiders, a look at the powerful, often secretive world of the Supreme Court offers profiles of each justice and how their individual styles affect the way in which they wield their power.
"Beautifully written, this is an essential purchase for all libraries interested in the contemporary Supreme Court." —*Library Journal*
Includes bibliographical references (p. [351]-353) and index.

Vladeck, Stephen I.
The Shadow Docket: How the Supreme Court Uses Stealth Rulings to Amass Power and Undermine the Republic. Stephen Vladeck. Basic Books 2023. 352 p.
ISBN 9781541602632
Grades: Adult   347.73
1. Judicial discretion 2. Conservatism 3. Secrecy 4. Law 5. Government accountability 6. Power 7. Separation of powers 8. Politics and government 9. United States 10. 21st century 11. Politics and global affairs — Judicial politics 12. Politics and global affairs — Political parties 13. Debut title

The Supreme Court has always had the authority to issue emergency rulings in exceptional circumstances. But since 2017, the Court has dramatically expanded its use of the behind-the-scenes "shadow docket," regularly making decisions that affect millions of Americans without public hearings and without explanation, through cryptic late-night rulings—green-lighting restrictive voting laws and bans on abortion, and curtailing immigration and COVID vaccine mandates. But Americans of all political stripes should be worried about what the shadow docket portends for the rule of law, argues Supreme Court expert Stephen Vladeck.
"This insightful and accessible account raises an important alarm." —*Publishers Weekly*
Includes bibliographical references and index.

ESSENTIAL AND RECOMMENDED TITLES
352.23 Chief executives

Waldman, Michael
*The **Supermajority**: How the Supreme Court Divided America.* Michael Waldman. Simon & Schuster 2023. 388 p.
ISBN 9781668006061
Grades: Adult   347.73
1. Judicial system 2. Judicial review 3. Civil rights 4. Privacy 5. Abortion 6. Gun control 7. Climate change 8. Conservatism 9. Polarization (Social sciences) 10. Democracy 11. Politics and government 12. United States 13. Politics and global affairs — Judicial politics 14. History writing — Judicial branch — United States

In The Supermajority, Michael Waldman explores the tumultuous 2021 2022 Supreme Court term. He draws deeply on history to examine other times the Court veered from the popular will, provoking controversy and backlash. And he analyzes the most important new rulings and their implications for the law and for American society. It was the most turbulent term in memory—with the leak of the opinion overturning Roe v. Wade, the first Black woman justice sworn in, and the justices turning on each other in public, Waldman previews the 2022-2023 term and how the brewing fights over the Supreme Court and its role that already have begun to reshape politics.

"Brisk yet detailed, this is a valuable overview of how America's highest court became such a lightning rod." —*Publishers Weekly*

Includes bibliographical references and index.

352.23 Chief executives

Emanuel, Rahm
*The **Nation** City: Why Mayors Are Now Running the World.* Rahm Emanuel. Random House Inc 2020. 240 p.
ISBN 9780525656388
Grades: Adult   352.23
1. Emanuel, Rahm, 1959- 2. Mayors 3. Municipal government 4. Cities and towns 5. Municipal services 6. Government accountability 7. Social responsibility 8. Political science 9. Political leadership 10. Politics and government 11. United States 12. 21st century 13. Life stories — Politics — Politicians 14. Society and culture — Urban and regional studies 15. Politics and global affairs — General

LC 2019024936

At a time of anxiety about the effectiveness of our national government, Rahm Emanuel provides a clear vision, for both progressives and centrists, of how to get things done in America today—a bracing, optimistic vision of America's future from one of our most experienced and original political minds.

"At its best, Emanuel's chronicle offers a revelatory view into how mayors run cities, and provokes readers to ponder whether cities really might save the world." —*Booklist*

Includes bibliographical references.

Lieven, Dominic
In the Shadow of the Gods: The Emperor in World History. Dominic Lieven. Viking Press 2022. 608 p.
ISBN 9780735222199
Grades: Adult   352.23
1. Rulers 2. Women rulers 3. Leadership 4. History 5. World leaders 6. Imperialism 7. History writing — General

This history of the men and women who led the world's great empires looks at figures such as Constantine, Suleyman, Louis XIX and Queen Victoria, and the shared characteristics that drove them.

"A sweeping survey of the evolution of the role of the emperor in terms of geopolitical leadership, empire building, and diplomacy....A consistently engaging comparison-contrast look at the mechanics of empire." —*Kirkus*

352.230973 Presidents — United States

Raphael, Ray
Mr. President: How and Why the Founders Created a Chief Executive. Ray Raphael. Alfred A. Knopf 2012. 324 p.
ISBN 9780307595270
Grades: 11 12 Adult   352.230973
1. Executive power 2. Political leadership 3. Reasoning 4. Constitutional law 5. Separation of powers 6. Debates and debating 7. Power 8. Politicians 9. Federal government 10. Presidents 11. Politics and government 12. United States 13. 18th century 14. Early America (1784-1819) 15. History writing — Presidency — United States

LC 2011033471

Offers the exciting story of how the American presidency was shaped during the Constitutional Convention, in a history that includes Gouverneur Morris, James Madison, Alexander Hamilton, Benjamin Franklin and George Washington, each jockeying for position and trying to see his vision for the office of the president realized.

"Raphael here delves into the Constitutional Convention of 1787 to elucidate compromises that created the presidency. Saving readers the tedium of digesting Madison's secret journal of the proceedings, Raphael converts it and supplementary sources into a dramatized narrative that emphasizes how differently the office could have been framed." —*Booklist*

Includes bibliographical references and index.

352.3 Executive management

Connelly, Matthew James
*The **Declassification** Engine: What History Reveals About America's Top Secrets.* Matthew Connelly. Pantheon Books 2023. 560 p.
ISBN 9781101871577
Grades: Adult   352.3
1. Government information 2. Secrecy in government 3. Political surveillance 4. Security classification (Government documents) 5. Archives 6. Public administration 7. Freedom of information 8. Government accountability 9. Politics and government 10. United States history 11. United States 12. Politics and global affairs — National security 13. History writing — United States

LC 2022019182

Before World War II, transparent government was a proud tradition in the United States. In all but the most serious of circumstances, classification, covert operations, and spying were considered deeply un-American. Since then, we have radically departed from that open tradition, allowing intelligence agencies, black sites, and classified laboratories to grow unchecked. Officials insist that only secrecy can keep us safe, but its true costs have gone unacknowledged for too long.

"The U.S. government is hopelessly awash in secret information, and this gripping history describes how we got that way and lays out the dismal consequences....Yet more evidence, brilliantly delivered, of the extent of the U.S. government's dysfunction." —*Kirkus*

Includes bibliographical references and index.

352.37 Means of obtaining objectives

Howley, Kerry
Bottoms up and the Devil Laughs: A Journey Through the Deep State. Kerry Howley. Alfred A. Knopf 2023. 256 p.
ISBN 9780525655497
Grades: Adult   352.37
1. Women veterans 2. Intelligence officers 3. Electronic surveillance 4. Electronic information resources 5. Internet security 6. Secrets 7. Presidential election, 2016 8. Secrecy in government 9. Security classification (Government documents) 10. Leaks (Disclosure of information) 11. Whistle blowers 12. Politics and global affairs — National security 13. Life stories — Law and order —

PUBLIC LIBRARY CORE COLLECTION: NONFICTION
Twentieth Edition

Criminals and law-breakers 14. Science Writing — Computing, the Internet, and Technology 15. Society and culture — Media and technology

National Book Critics Circle Award for Nonfiction finalist, 2023.

In this groundbreaking work of narrative nonfiction, Kerry Howley investigates the curious implications of living in the age of the indelible. Bottoms up and the Devil Laughs tells the true story of intelligence specialist Reality Winner, a lone young woman who stuffs a state secret under her skirt and trusts the wrong people to help. Following Winner's unlikely journey from rural Texas to a federal courtroom, Howley maps a hidden world, drawing in John Walker Lindh, Lady Gaga, Edward Snowden, a rescue dog named Outlaw Babyface Nelson, and a mother who will do whatever it takes to get her daughter out of jail.

"A literate, readable meditation on the surveillance state and its discontents." —*Kirkus*

355 Military science

Brooks, Rosa
How Everything Became War and the Military Became Everything: Tales from the Pentagon. Rosa Brooks. Simon & Schuster 2016. 448 p.
ISBN 9781476777863
Grades: Adult   355
1. National security 2. Military policy 3. War (International law) 4. Armed Forces 5. Terrorism 6. Just war doctrine 7. Militarism 8. Antiterrorist policy 9. Military strategy 10. Military history 11. United States 12. Politics and global affairs — National security
LC 2016005348

A former top Pentagon official, daughter of anti-war activists, wife of an Army Green Beret and human rights activist presents a scholarly examination of how a constant state of war is contrary to America's founding values, undermines international rules and compromises future security.

Includes bibliographical references and index.

Capozzola, Christopher
Bound by War: How the United States and the Philippines Built America's First Pacific Century. Christopher Capozzola. Perseus Books Group 2020. 496 p.
ISBN 9781541618275
Grades: Adult   355
1. International relations 2. Alliances 3. Colonialism 4. Geopolitics 5. American people in Asia 6. Military history 7. Military policy 8. United States 9. Pacific Area 10. Philippines 11. 20th century 12. History writing — Asia — Southeast Asia 13. History writing — United States 14. History writing — Military 15. History writing — Wars and conflicts
LC 2019057160

Ever since US troops occupied the Philippines in 1898, generations of Filipinos have served in and alongside the US armed forces. In Bound by War, historian Christopher Capozzola reveals this forgotten history, showing how war and military service forged an enduring, yet fraught, alliance between Americans and Filipinos. Telling the epic story of a century of conflict and migration, Bound by War is a fresh, definitive portrait of this uneven partnership and the two nations it transformed.

"Readers will savor this detailed study of an underexamined aspect of American foreign policy." —*Publishers Weekly*

Includes bibliographical references and index.

France, John
Perilous Glory: The Rise of Western Military Power. John France. Yale University Press 2011. 438 p.
ISBN 9780300120745
Grades: Adult   355
1. Military history 2. Military art and science 3. Military strategy 4. History writing — Military
LC 2011006437

Looks at the history of warfare from ancient Mesopotamia to the Gulf War.

Gans, John
White House Warriors: How the National Security Council Transformed the American Way of War. John Gans. Liveright Publishing Corporation 2019. 272 p.
ISBN 9781631494567
Grades: Adult   355
1. International relations 2. Defense planning 3. Military strategy 4. National security 5. Military policy 6. United States 7. Impartial writing 8. Politics and global affairs — World politics — United States
LC 2018054255

A revelatory history of the elusive National Security Council reveals how staffers operating in the shadows have driven foreign policy clandestinely for decades and is partially responsible for present-day escalations of hostility and polarization in American government.

"This book is essential reading for all interested in politics, government, and contemporary U.S. history." —*Booklist*

Includes bibliographical references and index.

Hanson, Victor Davis
The Soul of Battle: From Ancient Times to the Present Day, How Three Great Liberators Vanquished Tyranny. Victor Davis Hanson. Anchor Books 2001. 480 p.
ISBN 9780385720595
Grades: Adult   355
1. Epaminondas, b. ca. 420 B.C.E 2. Sherman, William Tecumseh, 1820-1891 3. Patton, George S, 1885-1945 4. Military history 5. Motivation 6. Military tactics 7. Command of troops 8. History writing — Military — Military leadership
LC 00063979

Argues that American generals Sherman and Patton, as well as Athenian general Epaminondas, were the greatest military leaders in history.

"Hanson narrates the success of three military campaigns-Epaminondas defeat of the Spartans in the fourth century B.C, Sherman's march through Georgia and the Carolinas during the Civil War, and Patton's race into Germany at the head of the Third Army in 1944-45. In Hanson's view, the individual traits of spontaneity and creativity that are nourished in a free society are assets, not hindrances, in warfare." —*Booklist*

Includes bibliographical references (p. 463-468) and index; Originally published: New York : Free Press, 1999.

Hastings, Max
Warriors: Portraits from the Battlefield. Max Hastings. Knopf 2005. xxiii, 354 p. : Illustration; Map
ISBN 9781400044412
Grades: Adult   355
1. Soldiers 2. War 3. Combat 4. History writing — Military 5. Adult books for young adults
LC 2005044302

Assessing the experiences of thirteen soldiers, airmen, and sailors, a military historian explores what it meant to be a warrior during the wars of the nineteenth and twentieth centuries, examining their triumphs, tragedies, and motivations.

Includes bibliographical references and index.

Kindsvatter, Peter S.
American Soldiers: Ground Combat in the World Wars, Korea, and Vietnam. Peter S. Kindsvatter; foreword by Russell F. Weigley. University Press of Kansas 2003. xxiii, 432 p, 16 p. of plates : Illustration
ISBN 9780700612291
Grades: Adult   355
1. Combat 2. Marines 3. Soldiers 4. 20th century 5. History writing — Military
LC 2002012957

By capturing the core 'Band of brothers' experience across several generations of warfare, Kindsvatter celebrates the American soldier while helping us to better understand war's lethal reality, and why soldiers persevere in the face of its horrors.

ESSENTIAL AND RECOMMENDED TITLES
355.001 Philosophy and theory

"Mining twentieth-century foot soldiers' memoirs and novels, Kindsvatter integrates this literature of personal experience into a generalized assessment of what combat was like and how men reacted to it. Kindsvatter's illuminating work is about coping with fear at the foxhole level, and it powerfully conveys the psychology and military sociology of combat in the draft-era armies." —*Booklist*
Includes bibliographical references (p. 405-420) and index.

Petraeus, David Howell
Conflict: The Evolution of Warfare from 1945 to Ukraine. David Petraeus, Andrew Roberts. HarperCollins 2023. 256 p.
ISBN 9780063293137
Grades: Adult   355
1. War 2. Military history 3. Command of troops 4. Guerrilla warfare 5. Cold War 6. Arab-Israeli conflict 7. Israel-Arab War, 1948-1949 8. Korean War, 1950-1953 9. Vietnam War, 1961-1975 10. Israel-Arab War, 1967 11. Israel-Arab War, 1973 12. Persian Gulf War, 1991 13. Iraq War, 2003-2011 14. Russo-Ukrainian War, 2014- 15. 20th century 16. History writing — Wars and conflicts 17. History writing — Military

Two leading authorities—an acclaimed historian and the outstanding battlefield commander and strategist of our time—collaborate on an examination of war since 1945.

"Petraeus, a retired army general who held command positions in Iraq and Afghanistan and formerly served as director of the CIA, joins forces with esteemed historian Roberts to present a thoroughly researched and remarkably informative survey and analysis of wars around the world since the end of WWII." —*Booklist*

Roach, Mary
★ *Grunt: The Curious Science of Humans at War.* by Mary Roach. W. W. Norton & Co. 2016. 256 p.
ISBN 9780393245448
Grades: 10 11 12 Adult   355
1. Military art and science 2. Military research 3. War and civilization 4. Technology and war 5. Technological innovations 6. United States 7. Science Writing — General 8. History writing — Military — Military Today 9. Adult books for young adults
LC 2016008754
LibraryReads Favorites, 2016; School Library Journal Best Books: Best Adult Books 4 Teens, 2016.

Explores the science of keeping humans healthy and focused in the extreme environments of war, drawing on interviews with doctors, uniform designers, trainers and weapons testers to illuminate how soldiers are conditioned to survive traumas ranging from heat and panic to exhaustion and noise.

"Roach's book is not for the squeamish or those who envision war as a glorious enterprise; it is a captivating look at the lengths scientists go to in order to reduce the horrors of war." —*Publishers Weekly*

Vickers, Michael G.
By All Means Available: Memoirs of a Life in Intelligence, Special Operations, and Strategy. Michael G. Vickers. Alfred A. Knopf 2023. 576 p.
ISBN 9781101947708
Grades: Adult   355
1. Vickers, Michael G. 2. Special forces 3. Intelligence service 4. War on Terrorism, 2001-2009 5. Terrorism prevention 6. Special operations (Military science) 7. National security 8. Strategy 9. Asian history 10. Afghanistan 11. 1970s 12. 1980s 13. Autobiographies and memoirs 14. History writing — Spies and spying 15. Life stories — Law and order — Spies and secret agents 16. Politics and global affairs — Terrorism
LC 2022037618

A veteran member of the intelligence community recounts his remarkable career, from his days leading the CIA's secret war against the Soviets in Afghanistan to his role in the global war on terror.

"A masterful, fully compelling assessment of key intelligence and special operations missions over recent decades." —*Kirkus*

355.001 Philosophy and theory

Tyson, Neil deGrasse
Accessory to War: The Unspoken Alliance Between Astrophysics and the Military. Neil deGrasse Tyson, Avis Lang. W W Norton 2018. 448 p.
ISBN 9780393064445
Grades: Adult   355.001
1. Astrophysics 2. Technological innovations 3. Military engineering 4. Military art and science 5. Science 6. Military-industrial complex 7. Defense industry and trade 8. Military planning 9. Policy sciences 10. Research 11. Science Writing — Space and Flight 12. History writing — Military — Weapons 13. Science Writing — Physics
LC 2018019206

From early celestial navigation to satellite-enabled warfare, a well-researched book provides a thought-provoking exploration of the centuries-old relationship between science and military power.

"Well paced and skillfully written, the narrative seamlessly integrates science lessons, military strategy, and world history—surely suiting military and science buffs alike." —*Publishers Weekly*

355.009 Military science — History, geographic treatment, biography

Chamberlin, Paul Thomas
The Cold War's Killing Fields: Rethinking the Long Peace. Paul Thomas Chamberlin. HarperCollins 2018. 592 p.
ISBN 9780062367204
Grades: Adult   355.009
1. Cold War 2. Military history 3. War casualties 4. World politics 5. Great powers 6. War 7. History writing — Cold War
LC Bl2018080039

Offers an international military history of the Cold War arguing that the decade-long superpower struggles were one of the three great conflicts of the 20th century alongside the two World Wars, and reveals how bloody the "Long Peace" actually was.

Matloff, Judith
No Friends but the Mountains: Dispatches from the World's Violent Highlands. Judith Matloff. Basic Books 2017. 272 pages
ISBN 9780465097883
Grades: Adult   355.009
1. Mountains 2. Violence 3. Social conflict 4. Mountain life 5. Effect of environment on humans 6. Social isolation 7. Civil war 8. Interethnic conflict 9. Sierra Madre Mountains, Mexico 10. Politics and global affairs — Terrorism 11. History writing — Wars and conflicts
LC 2016043569

A veteran war correspondent travels to different conflict zones around the world, from Albania to NEPAL and to Mexico, to investigate why a disproportionate amount of conflicts occur in remote mountain communities and how the drugs, terrorism and instability there affects us all.

"A tightly focused study of mountain societies that hints at future conflicts." —*Kirkus*
Includes bibliographical references and index.

355.0092 Military science — Biography

Toler, Pamela D.
Women Warriors: An Unexpected History. Pamela D. Toler. Beacon Press 2019. 240 pages
ISBN 9780807064320
Grades: Adult   355.0092
1. Women and war 2. Women soldiers 3. Women warriors 4. Courage 5. History writing — Women's history 6. History writing — Wars and conflicts 7. Adult books for young adults

LC 2018028811

From Vikings and African queens to cross-dressing military doctors and WWII Russian fighter pilots, Women Warrior reclaims lost stories of women for whom battle was not a metaphor, debunking the pervasive claim that women do not, and should not, fight.

"Toler blows past all expectations with this thoroughly delightful, personable, and crucially important history of women warriors…Her captivating writing style, which is marked by disarmingly cheeky footnotes, makes this trip through so much forgotten history an exceedingly pleasurable reading experience, and her subjects, from the famous (Joan of Arc) to the criminally overlooked (Buffalo Calf Road Woman, who likely killed Custer) are a treat to learn about. An absolute research gem, Women Warriors is a historians roar all libraries should welcome." —Booklist

Includes bibliographical references and index.

355.009437 Military history — Czech Republic and Slovakia

McNamara, Kevin J.
Dreams of a Great Small Nation: The Mutinous Army That Threatened a Revolution, Destroyed an Empire, Founded a Republic, and Remade the Map of Europe. Kevin J. McNamara. PublicAffairs 2016. 464 p.
ISBN 9781610394840
Grades: Adult   355.009437
1. Murder 2. International relations 3. Soviet Union history 4. European history 5. Czech Republic 6. Slovakia 7. Czechoslovakia 8. 1910s 9. Between the Wars (1918-1939) 10. Russian Revolution and Civil War (1917-1921) 11. History writing — Europe — Eastern Europe
LC 2016930908

Documents the history-shaping murder of an Austrian by a Czech soldier in 1918 Chelyabinsk during a railway brawl, detailing how the event sparked violent reactions, massive military engagements and a plan by fugitive philosophy professor Tomas Masaryk to reclaim and establish the Czechoslovakia homeland.

"McNamara's work presents a vital first entry that opens the doors on this integral part of World War I history and the shaping of the Soviet-influenced Eastern European political and social fabric." —Library Journal

355.00947 Military science—Russia

Rappaport, Helen
Caught in the Revolution: Petrograd, Russia, 1917—a World on the Edge. Helen Rappaport. St. Martin's Press 2017. 448 p.
ISBN 9781250056641
Grades: Adult   355.00947
1. War and society 2. Revolutions 3. Social change 4. Visitors 5. Russian history 6. Soviet Union history 7. St. Petersburg, Russia 8. Russian Revolution and Civil War (1917-1921) 9. Romanov Dynasty (1613-1917) 10. History writing — Wars and conflicts — Russian Revolution 11. History writing — Europe — Russia
LC 2016043110

The New York Times best-selling author of the Romanov Sisters presents a gripping portrait of Petrograd at the outbreak of the Russian Revolution, drawing on foreign-national eyewitness accounts to trace key events as recorded in letters and journals.

Includes bibliographical references and index.

355.00973 Military history — United States

Beschloss, Michael R.
★ *Presidents of War.* Michael Beschloss. Crown 2018. 752 p.
ISBN 9780307409607
Grades: Adult   355.00973
1. Military strategy 2. War 3. Unconventional warfare 4. Executive power 5. Political leadership 6. Presidents 7. Military history 8. United States 9. History writing — Wars and conflicts 10. History writing — Presidency — United States
LC 2018007697

The best-selling author of the Conquerors charts the controversial leadership, public reputations and evolving political powers of American wartime presidents from the War of 1812 through Vietnam, including Lincoln, Wilson and LBJ.

"With ample detail and enticing storytelling, this readable work will be enjoyed by students and American history buffs." —Publishers Weekly

Dower, John W.
Cultures of War: Pearl Harbor : Hiroshima : 9-11 : Iraq. John W. Dower. W.W. Norton : 2010. 576 p.
ISBN 9780393061505
Grades: Adult   355.00973
1. War and society 2. World War II 3. September 11 Terrorist Attacks, 2001 4. Iraq War, 2003-2011 5. Military strategy 6. Military history 7. Military policy 8. United States 9. 21st century 10. 20th century 11. History writing — Wars and conflicts
LC 2010020395

National Book Award for Nonfiction finalist, 2010.

Presents a comparative analysis of September 11 and the subsequent War on Terror with Pearl Harbor and World War II, addressing institutional failures of intelligence and imagination and the driving forces behind Pan-Asian and Pan-Islam movements.

"The author draws astute ironies between Pearl Harbor and 9/11 in terms of the overweening arrogance of military superpowers. The author moves back and forth between these two definitive eras in history, providing a brilliant examination of the willful self-delusion and selective reasoning involved in the highest levels of decision making—from Japan's spectacularly ill-advised bombing of Pearl Harbor to the Bush Administration's bundling of weapons of mass destruction and Osama bin Laden as justification for invasion of Iraq. An unrelenting, incisive, masterly comparative study." —Kirkus

Includes bibliographical references and index.

Glatthaar, Joseph T.
The American Military: A Concise History. Joseph T. Glatthaar. Oxford University Press 2018. x, 142 pages : Illustration
ISBN 9780190692810
Grades: Adult   355.00973
1. Military life 2. Military engineering 3. Military history 4. Armed Forces 5. United States history 6. United States 7. History writing — United States 8. History writing — Military
LC 2018000396

Explores the origins of the U.S. military, from the 13 colonies to today's ongoing conflicts in the Middle East, examining the challenges of unconventional warfare, including terrorism and cyberwar, and looking to the future of the U.S. military.

"Glatthaar (UNC Chapel Hill) delivers a masterpiece of compression, covering US arms from the colonial beginnings to yesterday in four chapters and 127 pages." —Choice

Includes bibliographical references (pages 131-135) and index.

Scahill, Jeremy
Dirty Wars: The World Is a Battlefield. Jeremy Scahill. Nation Books 2013. 384 p.
ISBN 9781568586717
Grades: Adult   355.00973
1. Special operations (Military science) 2. Terrorism 3. Assassination 4. Intelligence service 5. Antiterrorist policy 6. Military history 7. United States history 8. United States 9. 21st century 10. Page to screen 11. Politics and global affairs — Terrorism
LC 2012051769

A sobering expose of secret war programs currently being conducted behind the scenes of the War on Terror, drawing on interviews with CIA agents, merce-

ESSENTIAL AND RECOMMENDED TITLES
355.009747 Military history — New York

naries and other operators to reveal the human consequences of night raids, drone strikes and other unofficial "dirty-war" tactics.

355.009747 Military history — New York

Cohen, Eliot A.
Conquered into Liberty: Two Centuries of Battles Along the Great Warpath That Made the American Way of War. Eliot A. Cohen. Free Press 2011. 416 p.
ISBN 9780743249904
Grades: Adult   355.009747
1. War 2. Military strategy 3. Military history 4. New York (State) 5. Canada 6. 17th century 7. 18th century 8. History writing — Wars and conflicts
LC 2011023717
The author of Supreme Command documents the turbulent history of a contested corridor between Albany and Montreal, offering analyses of a series of pivotal battles to explain how they shaped American military culture for more than a century.
"This is an engaging account of the wars fought on the Great Warpath... a delightful-to-read piece of American history." —*Kirkus*
Includes bibliographical references and index.

355.02 War and warfare

Armitage, David
Civil Wars: A History in Ideas. David Armitage. Alfred A. Knopf 2017. 320 p.
ISBN 9780307271136
Grades: Adult   355.02
1. Civil war 2. Military history 3. War and civilization 4. History writing — Wars and conflicts — Civil Wars
LC 2016023404
A highly original history, tracing civil war, the least understood and most intractable form of organized human aggression, from Ancient Rome through the centuries to present day.
Includes bibliographical references and index.

Arnold, James R.
Jungle of Snakes: A Century of Counterinsurgency Warfare from the Philippines to Iraq. James R. Arnold. Bloomsbury Press 2009. 304 p.
ISBN 9781596915039
Grades: Adult   355.02
1. Unconventional warfare 2. World politics 3. War 4. Military history 5. United States 6. Great Britain 7. France 8. 20th century 9. History writing — Wars and conflicts
LC 2008054018
A former central intelligence agency director presents a history of modern warfare that evaluates how the post-cold war era has been fraught by such challenges as terrorism, insurgency, and guerilla tactics, in an account that also discusses America's struggles for civilian support and the nation's failure to learn from past mistakes throughout the occupation of Iraq.
Includes bibliographical references and index.

Boot, Max
Invisible Armies: An Epic History of Guerrilla Warfare from Ancient Times to the Present. Max Boot. Liveright Pub. Corporation 2012. 576 p.
ISBN 9780871404244
Grades: Adult   355.02
1. Guerrilla warfare 2. Unconventional warfare 3. Military strategy 4. Insurgency 5. Terrorism 6. History writing — Wars and conflicts 7. History writing — Microhistory
LC 2012028522
Describes the history of unconventional and nontraditional warfare from the nomads used by Alexander the Great to the shadowy modern battlefields of the post-9/11 era and featuring a diverse cast of historical tacticians and revolutionaries from Mao Zedong to Edward Lansdale.
Includes bibliographical references and index.

Gordin, Michael D.
Red Cloud at Dawn: Truman, Stalin, and the End of the Atomic Monopoly. Michael D. Gordin. Farrar, Straus and Giroux 2009. 416 p.
ISBN 9780374256821
Grades: Adult   355.02
1. Truman, Harry S, 1884-1972 2. Stalin, Joseph, 1879-1953 3. Nuclear weapons 4. Arms race 5. Cold War 6. World politics 7. Nuclear arms control 8. International relations 9. United States 10. Soviet Union 11. 20th century 12. 1950s 13. History writing — Cold War 14. History writing — Military — Weapons
LC 2009001424
The author of Five Days in August explores the covert process through which nations develop and hide their weapons programs and how other states detect nuclear proliferation, examining the role of intelligence in arms development and political decision-making.
Includes bibliographical references and index.

Hedges, Chris
War Is a Force That Gives Us Meaning. Chris Hedges. PublicAffairs 2002. 211 p.
ISBN 9781586480493
Grades: Adult   355.02
1. Hedges, Chris 2. War 3. Nationalism 4. Military history 5. 20th century 6. History writing — Wars and conflicts
LC 2002068136
New York Times Notable Book, 2002; National Book Critics Circle Award for Nonfiction finalist, 2002.
Looks at the appeal of war, arguing that the ideas of combat are noble and glorious, providing a purpose for living for some people.
"This moving book examines the continuing appeal of war to the human psyche... This should be required reading in this post-9/11 world as we debate the possibility of war with Iraq." —*Library Journal*
Includes bibliographical references (p. [192]-195) and index.

Langewiesche, William
The Atomic Bazaar: The Rise of the Nuclear Poor. William Langewiesche. Farrar, Straus and Giroux 2007. 179 p. : Map
ISBN 9780374106782
Grades: Adult   355.02
1. Nuclear weapons 2. Nuclear nonproliferation 3. World politics 4. Politics and government 5. Pakistan 6. 21st century 7. Politics and global affairs — World politics — Asia 8. History writing — Military — Weapons
LC 2006102539
In his shocking and revelatory new work, celebrated journalist William Langewiesche investigates the burgeoning threat of nuclear-weapons production and the inexorable drift of nuclear-weapons technology from the hands of the rich into the hands of the poor. As more unstazble and undeveloped nations acquire the ultimate arms, the stakes of state-sponsored nuclear activity have soared to frightening heights.
"Langewiesche's bracing expose of nuclear criminality blasts away the ubiquitous misinformation usually attendant on this alarming subject." —*Booklist*

355.0209 War and warfare — History, geographic treatment, biography

Boot, Max
★ *War Made New: Technology, Warfare, and the Course of History, 1500 to Today.* Max Boot. Gotham Books 2006. 624 p, 16 p. of plates : Illustration; Map
ISBN 9781592402229
Grades: Adult   355.0209

1. Military history 2. War 3. Military art and science 4. History writing — Military — Weapons 5. History writing — Technological innovations

LC 2006015518

An analysis of the pivotal role of technology in modern warfare focuses on four historical periods that shaped the rise and fall of empires, in a narrative account that covers such topics as gunpowder, the Industrial Revolution, and stealth aircraft.

A Council on Foreign Relations book—Jacket; Includes bibliographical references (p. [481]-516) and index.

Hanson, Victor Davis
The Father of Us All: War and History, Ancient and Modern. Victor Davis Hanson. Bloomsbury Press 2010. 259 p.
ISBN 9781608191659
Grades: Adult   355.0209
1. Military history 2. War and society 3. Ancient history 4. History 5. Ancient Greece (800 B.C.E.-640 C.E.) 6. Essays 7. History writing — Wars and conflicts

LC 2009041714

A sweeping survey on how war has shaped historical societies evaluates conflicts from Ancient Greece to the present while sharing essays that impart lessons on how to draw from past examples to address modern challenges. By the best-selling author of a War Like No Other.

"This anthology brings together 13 of Hanson's essays and reviews, revised and re-edited. They have appeared over the past decade in periodicals from the American Spectator to the New York Times. Hanson's introductory generalization that war is a human enterprise that seems inseparable from the human condition structures such subjects as an eloquent answer to the question Why Study War?, a defense of the historicity of the film 300, about the Persian Wars, in a masterpiece of envelope pushing, and a comprehensive and dazzling analysis of why America fights as she does. The pieces are well written, sometimes elegantly so, and closely reasoned." —*Publishers Weekly*

MacMillan, Margaret
War: How Conflict Shaped Us. Margaret MacMillan. Random House 2020. 336 p.
ISBN 9781984856135
Grades: Adult   355.0209
1. War and society 2. Military history 3. War 4. Cost of war 5. Technology and war 6. History writing — Wars and conflicts

LC 2020014498

New York Times Notable Book, 2020.

From the internationally renowned historian and bestselling author of Paris 1919 comes a provocative argument that war is an essential aspect of human nature, and that peace is an aberration in history.

"Like a great general, MacMillan marshals strands of culture, economics, technology, strategy, tactics, and even music, art, literature, and movies, clearing away the smoke of battle to reveal war's inner structure and impact. This is an erudite yet clearly written synthesis, sure to appeal to many readers." —*Booklist*

Includes bibliographical references and index.

355.20973 Military resources — United States

Klare, Michael T.
All Hell Breaking Loose: The Pentagon's Perspective on Climate Change. Michael T. Klare. Metropolitan Books 2019. 304 pages
ISBN 9781627792486
Grades: Adult   355.20973
1. Climate change 2. Global environmental change 3. Droughts 4. Food supply 5. Epidemics 6. Environmental policy 7. Refugees 8. National security 9. International cooperation 10. Politics and government 11. Armed Forces 12. Military policy 13. United States 14. Nature writing — Environmental issues 15. Politics and global affairs — Environmental issues and policies

LC Bl2019033834

The author of Resource Wars reveals how the American military regards climate change as a top threat to national security and is developing new strategies for responding to catastrophic weather, droughts and food shortages.

355.3 Organization and personnel of military forces

Newitz, Annalee
Stories Are Weapons: Psychological Warfare and the American Mind. Annalee Newitz. W W Norton & Co. Inc 2024. 240 p.
ISBN 9780393881516
Grades: Adult   355.3
1. Misinformation 2. Fake news 3. Propaganda 4. Psychological warfare 5. Military strategy 6. Political culture 7. Political psychology 8. International relations 9. Storytelling 10. United States history 11. United States 12. Politics and global affairs — World politics — United States

Annalee Newitz traces the way disinformation, propaganda, and violent threats—the essential tool kit for psychological warfare—have evolved from military weapons deployed against foreign adversaries into tools in domestic culture wars.

"Readers interested in politics and modern-day culture wars will find Newitz's work fascinating." —*Booklist*

Stengel, Richard
Information Wars: How We Lost the Global Battle Against Disinformation and What We Can Do About It. Richard Stengel. Atlantic Monthly Press 2019. 357 p.
ISBN 9780802147981
Grades: Adult   355.3
1. Fake news 2. Information warfare 3. Propaganda 4. Russo-Ukrainian War, 2014- 5. Social media 6. Political corruption 7. Mass media and world politics 8. Terrorism 9. International relations 10. Russia 11. United States 12. Politics and global affairs — Mass media and politics 13. Politics and global affairs — National security 14. Politics and global affairs — Terrorism

LC 2019033532

The former Under Secretary of State for Public Diplomacy and Public Affairs presents an insider's account of how the U.S. tried, and failed, to combat the disinformation that directly influenced the 2016 election and continues to impact global society.

Includes bibliographical references (pages [319]-339) and index.

355.4 Military operations

Gaddis, John Lewis
On Grand Strategy. John Lewis Gaddis. Penguin Group USA 2018. 304 p.
ISBN 9781594203510
Grades: Adult   355.4
1. Strategy 2. Leadership 3. Military art and science 4. Civilization, Western 5. History writing — General 6. Business and economics — Business advice — Leadership and management

LC 2018285468

Distilled from the Yale University seminar, "Studies in Grand Strategy," a master class in strategic thinking surveys statecraft from the ancient Greeks through FDR and beyond as vital historical lessons for future world leaders.

Marx, Karl
★ *The Communist Manifesto.* Karl Marx and Friedrich Engels. Penguin Books 2006. 119 p.
ISBN 9780143037514
Grades: 11 12 Adult   355.4
1. Communism 2. Political science 3. World politics 4. Social contract 5. Socialism 6. Politics and global affairs — Political philosophy

LC 2006043993

Examines the theory and goals expounded by Marx in the Communist Manifesto and the influence on Marx of Hegel, Feuerbach, and other philosophers.

ESSENTIAL AND RECOMMENDED TITLES
355.409 Military operations — History

Second presentation explores Rousseau's concept of social order and its implications for individual freedom and the good of society.

First published in 1848; Translation of: Manifest der Kommunistischen Partei.

355.409 Military operations — History

Nolan, Cathal J.
The Allure of Battle: A History of How Wars Have Been Won and Lost. Cathal J. Nolan. Oxford University Press 2017. VIII, 709 p.
ISBN 9780195383782
Grades: Adult   355.409
1. Battles 2. Military history 3. War 4. History writing — Military
LC 2016016391

Cathal Nolan's the Allure of Battle shows that while wars have shaped the history of the modern world, their outcomes are decided by many other factors. The book argues that major battles are not decisive to the outcome of wars; rather, wars depend on longer-term attrition in which the side that wins gradually and remorselessly overwhelms the other with larger arsenals and greater reserves of manpower.

"His focus on Europe may disappoint readers who would like more on American wars, and there is some repetition. Nonetheless, this is one of the most valuable military histories in years. A must-read for students of military history." —*Kirkus*

Includes bibliographical references and index.

355.5 Military training

Ambinder, Marc
The Brink: President Reagan and the Nuclear War Scare of 1983. Marc Ambinder. Simon & Schuster 2018. 320 p.
ISBN 9781476760377
Grades: Adult   355.5
1. Reagan, Ronald 2. Cold War 3. Nuclear warfare 4. Political leadership 5. World politics 6. International relations 7. United States 8. Soviet Union 9. 1980s 10. History writing — Cold War
LC Bl2018080040

Documents the story of the 1983 war game that intensified nuclear brinkmanship between the U.S. and the former Soviet Union, recounting a series of close calls that tested period leadership over the course of an anxious two-year nuclear stalemate. Illustrations.

Man, John
Ninja: 1,000 Years of the Shadow Warrior. John Man. William Morrow 2013. VI, 288 p. : Map
ISBN 9780062222022
Grades: Adult   355.5
1. Ninjutsu 2. Ninja 3. Martial artists 4. Assassination 5. Civil war 6. Feudalism 7. Japanese history 8. Japan 9. 15th century 10. True Crime — Historical Crime 11. History writing — Asia — Japan
LC 2012031912

Blends mythology and anthropology to trace the history of the warriors with extraordinary skills in combat, climbing, deception, disguise, and camouflage from their first appearance in feudal Japan to the present.

Includes bibliographical references and index.

355.6 Military administration

Cotton, Tom
Sacred Duty: A Soldier's Tour at Arlington National Cemetery. Tom Cotton. William Morrow & Co 2019. 352 pages
ISBN 9780062863157
Grades: Adult   355.6
1. Cotton, Tom 2. Cemeteries 3. Memorials 4. Funerals 5. Military cemeteries 6. National cemeteries 7. Memorialization 8. Military service 9. Nationalism 10. Military history 11. Arlington, Virginia 12. United States 13. History writing — Military — Military units 14. Life stories — Law and order — Armed forces personnel
LC 2019006676

The conservative Arkansas senator presents an intimate and uplifting portrait of Arlington National Cemetery's Old Guard, in a historical memoir that draws on his tradition-inspired service as a unit platoon leader in wartime.

"An Arkansas senator and Bronze Star recipient delivers a first book full of information, history, and remarkable facts about true heroes. A must-read for military members and their families that is sure to appeal to patriotic Americans of all stripes." —*Kirkus*

355.8 Military equipment and supplies

Kaplan, Fred M.
The Bomb: Presidents, Generals, and the Secret History of Nuclear War. Fred Kaplan. Simon & Schuster 2020. 384 p.
ISBN 9781982107291
Grades: Adult   355.8
1. Nuclear weapons 2. Weapons of mass destruction 3. Nuclear warfare 4. Military policy 5. Defense planning 6. National security 7. Atomic bomb 8. United States 9. Politics and global affairs — National security 10. History writing — Military — Weapons 11. History writing — Wars and conflicts — Atomic Bomb — World War II
LC Bl2020002407

The national-security columnist for Slate and Pulitzer Prize finalist, combining deep reporting with historical research, and discussing theories that have dominated nightmare scenarios, presents a history of American policy on nuclear war.

"A well-written, exhaustively researched history of American leaders' efforts to manage their nuclear arsenal." —*Kirkus*

Kean, Sam
The Bastard Brigade: The True Story of the Renegade Scientists and Spies Who Sabotaged the Nazi Atomic Bomb. Sam Kean. Little Brown & CO 2019. 416 p.
ISBN 9780316381680
Grades: Adult   355.8
1. Sabotage 2. Espionage 3. Atomic bomb 4. Nazis 5. Scientists 6. Assassination 7. Weapons research 8. World War II 9. Nuclear weapons 10. Research 11. Weapons 12. Germany 13. History writing — Wars and conflicts — World War II 14. History writing — Military — Weapons
LC 2019939370

The best-selling author of the Disappearing Spoon traces the remarkable story of how a renegade group of soldiers, scientists and spies prevented Hitler from obtaining a nuclear bomb.

"Vivid derring-do moves swiftly through a carefully constructed espionage thriller." —*Kirkus*

Kunetka, James W.
The General and the Genius: Groves and Oppenheimer : The Unlikely Partnership That Built the Atom Bomb. James Kunetka. Regnery Publishing 2015. 384 p.
ISBN 9781621573388
Grades: Adult   355.8
1. Groves, Leslie R, 1896-1970 2. Oppenheimer, J. Robert, 1904-1967 3. Atomic bomb 4. Physicists 5. Generals 6. Military engineering 7. Los Alamos, New Mexico 8. United States 9. Biographies 10. Collective biographies 11. History writing — Wars and conflicts — Atomic Bomb — World War II 12. Life stories — Science, technology, and medicine — Scientists and inventors 13. Life stories — Law and order — Armed forces personnel
LC 2015004467

Describes how Leslie Richard Groves of the Army Corps of Engineers enlisted the help of theoretical physicist J. Robert Oppenheimer on a three-year collaboration that resulted in the U.S. beating the Nazis to the invention of the atomic bomb. 20,000 first printing.

357 Mounted forces and warfare

Cotterell, Arthur
Chariot: The Astounding Rise and Fall of the World's First War Machine. Arthur Cotterell. Overlook Press 2005. 352 p.
ISBN 9781585676675
Grades: Adult 357
1. Military art and science 2. Ancient military history 3. Vehicles 4. History writing — Military — Weapons
LC 2004065980

Traces the rise and fall of chariot use in civilizations throughout the ancient world, recounting key military confrontations in which the chariot played a significant role in the outcome of battles and directly impacted the fates of nations, in an account that also reveals the chariot's role in sports, as a religious symbol, and as an element in literature and film.

"This work is a welcome addition to a collection specializing in military history or ancient history but will appeal to general readers as well because the writing is accessible despite the plethora of detail." —*Library Journal*

Includes bibliographical references and index.

358 Air and other specialized forces and warfare; engineering and related services

Baker, Nicholson
Baseless: My Search for Secrets in the Ruins of the Freedom of Information Act. Nicholson Baker. Penguin Press 2020. xiv, 450 p.
ISBN 9780735215757
Grades: Adult 358
1. Baker, Nicholson, 1957- 2. Biological weapons 3. Authors, American 4. Government information 5. Military secrets 6. Secrecy in government 7. Cold War 8. Intelligence service 9. United States 10. Politics and global affairs — National security 11. History writing — Cold War 12. History writing — Conspiracy theories
LC 2019043384

The National Book Critics Circle Award-winning author presents a deeply researched assessment of the Freedom of Information Act that reveals how deliberate obstructions, from extensive wait times to copious redactions, conceal government corruption and human-rights violations.

"This flowing account reveals the dark side of wartime strategies clouded by denials of FOIA requests. It will fascinate Cold War-era historians and readers concerned about access to government information." —*Library Journal*

Includes bibliographical references and index.

Emery, Theo
Hellfire Boys: The Birth of the U.S. Chemical Warfare Service and the Race for the World's Deadliest Weapons. Theo Emery. Little Brown & Co. 2017. 368 p.
ISBN 9780316264105
Grades: Adult 358
1. World War I 2. Chemical warfare 3. Chemical weapons 4. Military engineering 5. Military art and science 6. Weapons of mass destruction 7. First World War era (1914-1918) 8. History writing — Wars and conflicts — World War I 9. History writing — Military — Weapons 10. History writing — Military — Military units
LC Bl2017037105

Traces the actions of the "Hellfire Battalion," a group of American engineers who were trained in gas warfare and were sent to the front lines in France to launch multiple assaults against the Germans.

Guillemin, Jeanne
Biological Weapons: From the Invention of State-sponsored Programs to Contemporary Bioterrorism. Jeanne Guillemin. Columbia University Press 2005. xii, 258 p.
ISBN 9780231129428
Grades: Adult 358
1. Biological warfare 2. Biological terrorism 3. International security 4. Terrorism 5. War 6. World politics 7. History writing — Military — Weapons
LC 2004051911

A timely account of how resources for biological weapons programs were mobilized and why such weapons have never been deployed in major conflicts offers an understanding of the relevance of the historical restraints placed on the use of biological weapons and looks at what can to done to prevent their proliferation in the post-September 11th world.

"This is a history of biological weaponry, beginning with the British, American and Japanese programs that predate WWII. Admirably free of finger-pointing, shrillness and Luddite tendencies, the book ranks high as a historical introduction to the subject and a handbook on contemporary remedies." —*Publishers Weekly*

Includes bibliographical references (p. [207]-242) and index.

Tucker, Jonathan B.
War of Nerves: Chemical Warfare from World War I to Al-qaeda. Jonathan B. Tucker. Pantheon Books 2006. xi, 479 p. : Illustration
ISBN 9780375422294
Grades: Adult 358
1. Chemical warfare 2. Chemical weapons 3. Biological warfare 4. Biological weapons 5. History writing — Military — Weapons
LC 2005050053

Traces the military applications of toxic weaponry from World War I to the present day, the development of potent nerve agents during the Cold War, and the efforts of such terrorist groups as Al-Qaeda to acquire deadly nerve agents.

"This book makes a sobering case for a less poisonous world." —*New York Times Book Review*

Includes bibliographical references (p. 451-456) and index.

358.400941 Air forces — Great Britain

Hamilton-Paterson, James
Marked for Death: The First War in the Air. James Hamilton-Paterson. Pegasus 2016. 416 p.
ISBN 9781681771588
Grades: Adult 358.400941
1. Fighter planes 2. Military aviation 3. World War I 4. Aerial operations 5. Military aircraft 6. History writing — Wars and conflicts — World War I 7. History writing — Military — Aviation History
LC 2017304411

A dramatic and fascinating account of aerial combat during World War I, revealing the terrible risks taken by the men who fought and died in the world's first war in the air.

"Best of all, the authorwho has a solid body of fiction to his creditis a consummate storyteller; not only does the book tell a fascinating story, it is nearly impossible to put down." —*Kirkus*

359 Sea forces and warfare

Stavridis, James
Sea Power: The History and Geopolitics of the World's Oceans. James Stavridis. Penguin Group USA 2017. 368 p.
ISBN 9780735220591
Grades: Adult 359
1. Sea-power 2. Naval history 3. Geopolitics 4. International security 5. Navigation 6. Oceans 7. History writing — Wars and conflicts
LC 2016056758

ESSENTIAL AND RECOMMENDED TITLES
359.00973 Naval forces — United States

A general and former commander of NATO describes the history and geography of the world's oceans and the battles that have spanned them during the whole of human existence, from the Athenians to the nuclear submarines of the 20th century Cold War.

"A highly readable, instructive look at the role of the oceans in our civilization, past and present." —*Kirkus*

To Risk It All: Nine Conflicts and the Crucible of Decision. Admiral James Stavridis. Penguin Press 2022. 336 p.
ISBN 9780593297742
Grades: Adult   359
1. Military history 2. Military strategy 3. Leadership 4. Risk-taking 5. Risk analysis 6. Decision-making 7. Biographies 8. History writing — Military — Naval history

Told through the thrilling and heroic stories of nine famous acts of leadership in battle from the U.S. Navy's nearly 250-year history, one of the great naval leaders of our time draws from them a set of insights we can all put to use when confronted with fateful choices.

"Retired U.S. Navy admiral Stavridis (coauthor, 2034) unpacks nine instances of critical decision-making in this insightful mix of naval history and leadership guide." —*Publishers Weekly*

359.00973 Naval forces — United States

Hornfischer, James D.
Who Can Hold the Sea: The U.S. Navy in the Cold War, 1945-1960. James D. Hornfischer. Bantam Books 2022. 640 p.
ISBN 9780399178641
Grades: Adult   359.00973
1. Sea power 2. World politics 3. Cold War 4. Naval history 5. United States 6. 20th century 7. History writing — Military — Naval history 8. HIstory Writing — Wars and conflicts 9. History writing — Cold War
LC 2021043097

Combining narrative history with high-seas adventure, this thrilling book brings to life the dramatic rise of the Navy's crucial postwar role in a series of exciting episodes that include the controversial atomic bomb tests on warships at Bikini Atoll; the refinement of sonar and the developing science of undersea warfare. Maps.

Combining narrative history with high-seas adventure, this thrilling book brings to life the dramatic rise of the Navy's crucial postwar role in a series of exciting episodes that include the controversial atomic bomb tests on warships at Bikini Atoll; the refinement of sonar and the developing science of undersea warfare.

"This excellent naval history elucidates how the atomic bomb and nuclear power shaped the geopolitical rivalry between the U.S. and the Soviet Union." —*Publishers Weekly*

Includes index.

Toll, Ian W.
★ *Six Frigates: The Epic History of the Founding of the U.S. Navy.* Ian W. Toll. W.W. Norton & Co. 2006. xii, 560 p, 16 p. of plates : Illustration; Color; Map
ISBN 9780393058475
Grades: 11 12 Adult   359.00973
1. Sea-power 2. Military power 3. Frigates 4. Pirates 5. Founding fathers of the United States 6. Naval history 7. United States 8. History writing — Military — Naval history 9. Debut title
LC 2006020769

Describes the origins and early history of the American Navy, discussing the debates by the founding fathers over the need for a permanent military, the decision to construct six heavy frigates, the campaign against Tripoli, and the War of 1812.

"This is a must-read for fans of naval history and the early American Republic." —*Publishers Weekly*

Includes bibliographical references (p. [525]-540) and index.

359.9 Specialized combat forces engineering and related services

Couch, Dick
The Warrior Elite: The Forging of Seal Class 228. Dick Couch; photographs by Cliff Hollenbeck. Three Rivers Press 2003. x, 330 p. : Illustration
ISBN 9781400046959
Grades: 11 12 Adult   359.9
1. Commando troops 2. Special forces 3. Armed Forces 4. Navy SEALs 5. History writing — Military — Special Forces 6. Adult books for young adults
LC Bl2004107971

A former Navy SEAL and Vietnam War hero chronicles the grueling physical training and psychological conditioning that every SEAL must successfully endure in order to graduate.

"This book is unique. Couch, a Vietnam-era SEAL and retired naval reserve captain was given the most complete access possible. On view is much serious thought by serious thinkers on the making of warriors at the dawn of the twenty-first century." —*Booklist*

Sequel: The finishing school; Originally published: New York : Crown Publishers, 2001. With a new postscript.

Denver, Rorke
Worth Dying For: A Navy Seal's Call to a Nation. Rorke Denver and Ellis Henican. Howard Books 2016. 224 p.
ISBN 9781501124112
Grades: Adult   359.9
1. Denver, Rorke 2. War on Terrorism, 2001-2009 3. Terrorism prevention 4. Soldiers 5. Special forces 6. Special operations (Military science) 7. Navy SEALs 8. History writing — Military — Special Forces
LC 2015034024

A Navy SEAL commander explores the practical and philosophical questions of heroic service that have emerged about America's past decade at war, from the qualities of heroes and the reasons we fight to how war impacts families and whether or not soldiers can be held accountable for wartime actions.

Klay, Phil
Uncertain Ground: Citizenship in an Age of Endless, Invisible War. Phil Klay. Penguin Press 2022. 272 p.
ISBN 9780593299241
Grades: Adult   359.9
1. Klay, Phil 2. War and society 3. War 4. Citizenship 5. Soldiers 6. Politics and government 7. Armed Forces 8. Military policy 9. United States 10. 21st century 11. 2000s (Decade) 12. 2010s 13. 2020s 14. Essays 15. Life stories — Law and order — Armed forces personnel 16. History writing — Military — Military Today 17. History writing — Wars and conflicts
LC 2021027476

When Phil Klay left the Marines a decade ago, after serving as an officer in Iraq, he found himself part of the community of veterans who have no choice but to grapple with the meaning of their wartime experiences-for themselves and for the country. American identity has always been bound up in war-from the revolutionary war of our founding, to the civil war that ended slavery, to the two world wars that launched America as a superpower. What did the current wars say about who we are as a country, and how should we respond as citizens? Unlike previous eras of war, few other Americans have had to do any real grappling with the endless, invisible wars of the post-9/11 world at all; in fact, increasingly, few people are even aware they are still going on. It's as if there's a dark star with a strong gravitational force that draws a relatively small number of soldiers and their families into its orbit, while remaining inconspicuous to most other Americans. In the meantime, the consequences of American military action abroad may be out of sight and out of mind, but they are very real indeed.

"Klay, a former U.S. Marine and author of the acclaimed novel Redeployment, offers essays on war, violence, and literature in this new book." —*Library Journal*

Includes index.

PUBLIC LIBRARY CORE COLLECTION: NONFICTION
Twentieth Edition

Parrish, Thomas D.
The Submarine: A History. Thomas Parrish. Viking 2004. x, 576 p. : Illustration
ISBN 9780670033133
Grades: Adult
359.9
1. Submarines 2. Warships 3. History writing — Military — Naval history 4. Adult books for young adults
LC 2003070515

Chronicles the history and evolution of submarines and of the inventors and engineers who developed them, from eighteenth-century conception to twentieth-century reality, and discusses the military deployment, strategic implications, and future of the submarine.

"This brilliant, dramatic account of submarines and the men who sailed in them is a required acquisition for every military history collection." —*Choice*

Includes bibliographical references (p. 547-557) and index.

361.4 Group work

Berman, Sarah
Don't Call It a Cult: The Shocking Story of Keith Raniere and the Women of Nxivm. Sarah Michelle Berman. Steerforth Press 2021. 320 p.
ISBN 9781586422752
Grades: Adult
361.4
1. Raniere, Keith 2. Cults 3. Cult members 4. Sexual slavery 5. Control 6. Abusive men 7. Coercion 8. Extortion 9. Corruption 10. Secret societies 11. Dominance (Psychology) 12. Manipulation (Social sciences) 13. Forced labor 14. True Crime — General 15. Life stories — Law and order — Criminals and law-breakers

They draw you in with the promise of empowerment, self-discovery, women helping women. The more secretive those connections are, the more exclusive you feel. Little did you know, you just joined a cult.

"This deep dive behind the headlines isn't to be missed." —*Publishers Weekly*

361.7 Private action

Schwab, Tim
★ *The Bill Gates Problem: Reckoning with the Myth of the Good Billionaire.* Tim Schwab. Metropolitan Books, Henry Holt and Company 2023. 336 p.
ISBN 9781250850096
Grades: Adult
361.7
1. Gates, Bill, 1955- 2. Billionaires 3. Charitable contributions 4. Charities 5. Influence (Literary, artistic, etc.) 6. Philanthropists 7. Power 8. Control 9. United States 10. Society and culture — Social activism and philanthropy 11. Business and economics — Corruption and scandal 12. Politics and global affairs — General 13. Debut title
LC 2023024698

Investigates the Gates Foundation, interrogating how Bill Gates uses philanthropy as a political tool with no accountability.

"Schwab's deep reporting offers a convincing and informative alternative to the established image of the Gates Foundation." —*Booklist*

Includes bibliographical references and index.

362.1 People with physical illnesses

Coste, Joanne Koenig
Learning to Speak Alzheimer's: A Groundbreaking Approach for Everyone Dealing with the Disease. Joanne Koenig Coste. Houghton Mifflin 2004. xv, 240 p. : Illustration
ISBN 9780618485178
Grades: Adult
362.1
1. Alzheimer's disease 2. Caregivers 3. Medical care 4. People with Alzheimer's disease 5. Science writing — Medicine and health

LC Bl2009016680

A new approach to dealing with Alzheimer's disease offers a five step method for caring for people with progressive dementia, while offering hundreds of practical tips to ease life for patients and caregivers.

A pioneer in the care and treatment of Alzheimer's introduces her groundbreaking approach to dealing with the disease, offering a five step approach to caring for people with progressive dementia while offering hundreds of practical tips that can make life easier for patient and caregiver alike.

A Mariner book; Includes bibliographical references (p. 217-220), discography (p. 222-223), filmography (p. 220-222), and index; Reprint. Originally published: 2003.

Johnson, Steven
Extra Life : A Short History of Living Longer. Steven Johnson. Riverhead Books 2021. 304 p.
ISBN 9780525538851
Grades: Adult
362.1
1. Life expectancy 2. Medical care 3. Public health 4. Quality of life 5. Technological innovations 6. Science Writing — Biology 7. Society and culture — Illness and disease
LC 2020033229

As a species, humans have doubled their life expectancy in one hundred years. Medical breakthroughs, public health institutions, rising standards of living, and the other advances of modern life have given each person about 20,000 extra days on average. This book attempts to help the reader understand where that progress came from and what forces keep people alive longer. The author also considers how to avoid decreases in life expectancy as public health systems face unprecedented challenges, and what current technologies or interventions could reduce the impact of future crises. This work illuminates the power of common goals and public resources; the work of activists struggling for reform, and of scientists sharing their findings open-source-style; and of non-profit agencies spreading innovations around the world.

"With this latest work, best-selling author Johnson (Where Good Ideas Come From) attempts to explain the significant factors causing increased life spans and to broaden readers' understanding of those factors. . . . A smoothly written book of medical wonder that pays specific attention to racial disparities in health care." —*Library Journal*

Includes bibliographical references and index.

Kelly, Christopher R.
Am I Dying?!: A Complete Guide to Your Symptoms—and What to Do Next. Christopher Kelly, M.D, M.S; Marc Eisenberg, M.D, F.A.C.C… William Morrow 2019. xii, 337 p.
ISBN 9780062847607
Grades: Adult
362.1
1. Health risk assessment 2. Symptoms 3. Diagnosis 4. Self-care 5. Reference books 6. Science writing — Medicine and health — Illness and disease 7. Health
LC Bl2018197570

Presents the most common symptoms—from bloating and chest pain to fatigue, rashes, and weakness—and provides guidance on seeking medical care, including whether to make a doctor's appointment or go to the hospital.

Includes index.

Liverpool, Layal
Systemic: How Racism Is Making Us Sick. by Layal Liverpool. Astra House 2024. 320 p.
ISBN 9781662601675
Grades: Adult
362.1
1. Racism in medical care 2. Health services accessibility 3. Discrimination 4. Medical care services 5. Social medicine 6. Stereotypes 7. Microaggressions 8. Medical care 9. Racism 10. Society and culture — Race 11. Politics and global affairs — Public health
LC 2023053833

Sharing her journey to show how racism, woven into our societies as well as into medicine and science, is harmful to our health, a virologist, immunologist and science journalist reveals the fatal stereotypes that keep people of color undiagnosed, untreated and unsafe, and tells us what we can do about it.

ESSENTIAL AND RECOMMENDED TITLES
362.1089 Ethnic groups — Health services

"An urgent study of how ethnic minority patients are medically disadvantaged because they are economically and socially disadvantaged—and they are dying because of it." —*Kirkus*

Includes bibliographical references and index.

Malone, Sharon
Grown Woman Talk: Your Guide to Getting and Staying Healthy. Sharon Malone, M.D. Crown 2024. 256 p.
ISBN 9780593593868
Grades: Adult   362.1
1. Malone, Sharon, 1959- 2. Women 3. African American women 4. Health 5. Women's health services 6. African American women physicians 7. Medical care 8. Aging 9. Advice 10. Institutional racism 11. Intersectionality 12. Patient advocacy 13. Science Writing — Medicine and health 14. Society and culture — Gender — Women 15. Society and culture — Race
LC 2023048707

For all women who have often not been seen or heard, this practical guide, written by the chief medical officer of Alloy Women's Health, combines emerging practices with the latest research to empower us to become effective and efficient advocates in getting the care we deserve.

"A remarkable, accessible offering of feasible action steps that will help women feel more in control of medical issues related to heart health, hormones, cancer, and much more. Written from a social justice lens." —*Library Journal*

Includes bibliographical references and index.

Nuila, Ricardo
The People's Hospital: Hope and Peril in American Medicine. Ricardo Nuila. Scribner 2023. 368 p.
ISBN 9781501198045
Grades: Adult   362.1
1. Medical care 2. Health insurance 3. Medically uninsured people 4. Medical care services 5. Physicians 6. Patients 7. Debut title 8. Science Writing — Medicine and health 9. Life stories — Science, technology, and medicine 10. Politics and global affairs — Public health

Recounting the stories of five individuals denied access to health insurance, a physician, who emphasizes people over payments, interweaves their dramas into a singular narrative that contradicts the established idea that the only way to receive good healthcare is with good insurance.

"Physician Nuila debuts with a troubling yet inspirational look at the state of healthcare for America's 'Most medically and financially vulnerable.'…This is an urgent and essential call for a more humane healthcare system." —*Publishers Weekly*

Yurkiewicz, Ilana
Fragmented: A Doctor's Quest to Piece Together American Health Care. Yurkiewicz, Ilana, M.D. W W Norton & Company 2023. 288 p.
ISBN 9780393881196
Grades: Adult   362.1
1. Medical care 2. Medical care reform 3. Physicians 4. Physician and patient 5. Science writing — Medicine and health 6. Society and culture — Illness and disease

An award-winning physician-writer exposes how pervasive cracks in the health care system cost us time, energy, and lives—and how we can fix them.

"An engaging read that paints an honest picture of how a broken system impacts patients and providers." —*Kirkus*

Zaitchik, Alexander
Owning the Sun: A People's History of Monopoly Medicine from Aspirin to Covid-19 Vaccines. Alexander Zaitchik. Counterpoint 2022. 304 p.
ISBN 9781640095069
Grades: Adult   362.1
1. Medical care 2. Public health 3. Patent laws and legislation 4. Monopolies 5. Vaccines 6. Drug industry and trade 7. COVID-19 (Disease) 8. History of medicine 9. United States 10. Business and economics — Industries — Medical 11. Society and culture — Illness and disease
LC 2021044915

Telling the story of one of the most contentious fights in human history—the legal right to control the production of lifesaving medicines—this first-in-kind history traces the rise of medical monopoly in the U.S. and its subsequent globalization.

"Part history lesson on intellectual property and part damning critique of the private interests that blocked an attempt to subject COVID vaccines to IP restrictions, Zaitchik's book is highly informative and deeply troubling reading. It will appeal to readers concerned with equitable access to medicine and responsible corporate governance." —*Library Journal*

Includes bibliographical references and index.

362.1089 Ethnic groups — Health services

Fisher, Thomas
★ *The Emergency: A Year of Healing and Heartbreak in a Chicago Er.* by Thomas Fisher. One World 2022. 224 p.
ISBN 9780593230671
Grades: Adult   362.1089
1. Fisher, Thomas, (Board-certified emergency medicine physician) 2. African Americans 3. Marginalized people 4. Social medicine 5. Racism in medical care 6. Covid 19 disease 7. Social justice 8. Equality 9. Hospitals 10. Emergency medical services 11. Health 12. Medical care 13. Chicago, Illinois 14. Autobiographies and memoirs 15. Life stories — Science, technology, and medicine — Healthcare professionals 16. Society and culture — Race 17. Society and culture — Illness and disease 18. Science Writing — Medicine and health — Doctors and nurses
LC 2021039073

From a renowned emergency room doctor and healthcare policy expert comes the riveting story of a year in the life of an emergency room on the South Side of Chicago during a pandemic—and a powerful argument that American healthcare is designed to sacrifice the lives of the most vulnerable.

"Shedding light on the social justice implications on the health care system and an important snapshot of a grim moment in time, this account will appeal to a wide range of readers." —*Library Journal*

Includes index.

Geronimus, Arline T.
★ *Weathering: The Extraordinary Stress of Ordinary Life in an Unjust Society.* Arline T. Geronimus. Little, Brown Spark 2023. 352 p.
ISBN 9780316257978
Grades: Adult   362.1089
1. Institutional racism 2. Income inequality 3. Poverty 4. Marginalized people 5. Injustice 6. Stress 7. Health 8. Life expectancy 9. Quality of life 10. Social policy 11. Society and culture — Race 12. Society and culture — Illness and disease 13. Politics and global affairs — Public health

America has woken up to what many of its citizens have known for centuries and to what public health statistics have evidenced for decades: Systemic injustice takes a physical, too often deadly, toll on Black, brown, working class and poor communities, and any group who experiences systemic cultural oppression or economic exploitation. Until now, there has been little discussion about the insidious effects of social injustice on the body. Weathering shifts the paradigm, shining a light on the topic and offering a roadmap for hope.

"A persuasive hypothesis, an enlightening biopsychosocial study of health inequities fostered by racism and classism in America, and an urgent call for compassion and social justice." —*Booklist*

Villarosa, Linda
★ *Under the Skin: The Hidden Toll of Racism on American Lives and on the Health of Our Nation.* Linda Villarosa. Doubleday 2022. 304 p.
ISBN 9780385544887
Grades: Adult   362.1089
1. Racism 2. Inequality 3. African Americans 4. Marginalized people 5. Racism in medical care 6. Medical care 7. United States 8. Society and culture — Race 9. Science Writing — Medicine and health 10. Business and economics — Industries — Medical 11. Antiracist literature

PUBLIC LIBRARY CORE COLLECTION: NONFICTION
Twentieth Edition

J. Anthony Lukas Book Prize, 2023.

From an award-winning writer at the New York Times Magazine and a contributor to the 1619 Project comes a landmark book that tells the full story of racial health disparities in America, revealing the toll racism takes on individuals and the health of our nation.

"An eye-opening, heartbreaking study of the racism deeply embedded in U.S. medicine and society; critical for any reader interested in racism's effects on quality of life." —*Library Journal*

362.10973 Health services — United States

Alexander, Brian
★ *The* **Hospital**: *Life, Death, and Dollars in a Small American Town.* Brian Alexander. St. Martin's Press 2021. 320 p.
ISBN 9781250237354
Grades: Adult   362.10973
1. Hospitals 2. Small towns 3. Health policy 4. Public health 5. Physicians 6. Patients 7. Hospital administrators 8. Medical care 9. Ohio 10. United States 11. Politics and global affairs — Public health 12. Life stories — Science, technology, and medicine 13. Society and culture — Urban and regional studies
LC 2020040125

By following the struggle for survival of one small-town hospital, and the patients who walk, or are carried, through its doors, the Hospital takes readers into the world of the American medical industry in a way no book has done before. Author Brian Alexander argues that no plan will solve America's health crisis until the deeper causes of that crisis are addressed. Meanwhile, Bryan, a town of 8,500 people in Ohio's northwest corner, is still trying to recover from the Great Recession. As local leaders struggle to address the town's problems, and the hospital fights for its life amid a rapidly consolidating medical and hospital industry, a 39-year-old diabetic literally fights for his limbs, and a 55-year-old contractor lies dying in the emergency room. With these and other stories, Alexander strips away the wonkiness of policy to reveal Americans' struggle for health against a powerful system that's stacked against them, but yet so fragile it blows apart when the Covid-19 pandemic hits.

"The time Alexander spent embedded in the community gives continuity and depth to the stories of the individuals he connected with and puts a human face on broader issues of social inequality. This expertly reported account will resonate and find a wide audience." —*Library Journal*

Includes bibliographical references and index.

Rosenthal, Elisabeth
An **American** *Sickness: How Healthcare Became Big Business and How You Can Take It Back.* Elisabeth Rosenthal. Penguin Press 2017. 384 p.
ISBN 9781594206757
Grades: Adult   362.10973
1. Medical care 2. Medical care services 3. Health insurance 4. Health policy 5. Insurance companies 6. Medically uninsured people 7. Business corruption 8. Business and economics — Industries — Medical 9. Business and economics — Corruption and scandal 10. Politics and global affairs — Public health
LC 2016042934

Booklist Editors' Choice, 2017.

An award-winning New York Times reporter reveals expensive dysfunctions in America's healthcare system, outlining practical guidelines for recognizing misleading information and obtaining the care and pharmaceuticals needed to safeguard family health interests.

"After laying out the problem, Rosenthal presents solutions both personal and societal in this commanding and necessary call to arms." —*Booklist*

Snyder, Timothy
★ *Our* **Malady**: *Lessons in Liberty from a Hospital Diary.* Timothy Snyder. Crown 2020. 179 pages
ISBN 9780593238899
Grades: Adult   362.10973
1. Medical care reform 2. Medical care 3. United States 4. Politics and global affairs — Public health 5. Science Writing — Medicine and health

LC 2020024457

From the author of on Tyranny comes an urgent diagnosis of an American malady: Our heartless system of commercial medicine and our politics of pain. On December 29, 2019, historian Timothy Snyder fell gravely ill. Unable to stand, barely able to think, he waited for hours in an emergency room before being correctly diagnosed and rushed into surgery. Over the next few days, as he clung to life and the first light of a new year came through his window, he found himself reflecting on the fragility of health, not recognized in America as a human right, but without which all rights and freedoms have no meaning. And he had no idea how much worse things could get. Now, American hospitals, long understaffed and undersupplied, are buckling under waves of coronavirus patients. The federal government has responded with willful ignorance, misinformation, and profiteering. Even with public life at a standstill, thousands of Americans continue to die, needlessly, every single day. In this eye-opening cri de coeur, Snyder traces the societal forces that led us here and outlines the lessons we must learn to survive. In examining some of the darkest moments of recent history and of his own life, Snyder finds glimmers of hope, and principles that could lead us out of ourcurrent malaise. Only by enshrining healthcare as a human right, elevating the authority of doctors and medical knowledge, and planning for our children's future can we create an America where everyone is truly free.

"Snyder writes with passion and clarity, using personal observations, historical references, and case studies to raise the call for reforming the current health care system; stating that without changes, true freedom remains elusive for many." —*Library Journal*

Includes bibliographical references (pages 149-179).

362.1109747 Hospitals — New York

Manheimer, Eric
Twelve *Patients: Life and Death at Bellevue Hospital.* Eric Manheimer. Grand Central Pub. 2012. 272 p.
ISBN 9781455503889
Grades: Adult   362.1109747
1. Hospital patients 2. Hospital care 3. Public hospitals 4. Hospitals 5. Science Writing — Medicine and health
LC 2012005513

The medical director of Bellevue Hospital in New York, uses the lives and conditions of 12 different patients, from a Riker's Island prisoner to a suicidal private school student, to take a snapshot of modern society.

"Manheimer offers a window onto a unique hospital and the wisdom of a healer who tends with equal skill to patients and the world." —*Publishers Weekly*

Includes index.

Oshinsky, David M.
Bellevue: *Three Centuries of Medicine and Mayhem at America's Most Storied Hospital.* David Oshinsky. Doubleday 2016. 384 p.
ISBN 9780385523363
Grades: Adult   362.1109747
1. Hospital care 2. Hospitals 3. History of medicine 4. Hospital patients 5. Public hospitals 6. New York City 7. History writing — Science, technology, and medicine 8. History writing — United States 9. Science Writing — Medicine and health
LC 2016027568

Booklist Editors' Choice, 2016; ALA Notable Book, 2018.

A history of the iconic public hospital on New York City's East Side describes the changes in American medicine from 1730 to modern times as it traces building's origins as an almshouse and pesthouse to its current status as a revered place of first-class care.

Includes bibliographical references and index.

ESSENTIAL AND RECOMMENDED TITLES
362.1109763 Hospitals — Louisiana

362.1109763 Hospitals — Louisiana

Fink, Sheri
Five Days at Memorial: Life and Death in a Storm-ravaged Hospital. Sheri Fink. Crown Publishers 2013. 432 p.
ISBN 9780307718969
Grades: Adult   362.1109763
1. Hospitals 2. Medical malpractice 3. Survival (after hurricanes) 4. Death 5. Hurricanes 6. Euthanasia 7. Disaster relief 8. Hurricane Katrina, 2005 9. New Orleans, Louisiana 10. Page to screen 11. History writing — Natural disasters and tragedies 12. True Crime — Investigations and Trials
LC 2013019693

ALA Notable Book, 2014; Booklist Editors' Choice, 2013; J. Anthony Lukas Book Prize, 2014; Library Journal Best Books, 2013; LibraryReads Favorites, 2013; Los Angeles Times Book Prize for Current Interest, 2013; National Book Critics Circle Award for Non-Fiction, 2013; New York Times Notable Book, 2013; Andrew Carnegie Medal for Excellence in Non-Fiction finalist, 2014.

A Pulitzer Prize-winning doctor, reporter, and author reconstructs five days at Memorial Medical Center after Hurricane Katrina destroyed its generators to reveal how caregivers were forced to make life-and-death decisions without essential resources, an experience that raised key issues about practitioner responsibilities and end-of-life care.

"Fink draws those few days in the hospital's life with a fine, lively pen, providing stunningly framed vignettes of activities in the hospital and sharp pocket profiles of many of the characters. She gives measured consideration to such explosive issues as class and race discrimination in medicine, end-of-life care, medical rationing and euthanasia, and she presents the injection of some patients with a cocktail of drugs to reduce their breathing in such a manner that readers will be able to fully fashion their own opinions." —*Kirkus*

Also published in large print format; Adapted into a TV show on Apple TV, 2022; Includes bibliographical references and index.

362.17 Specific services

Gawande, Atul
★ *Being Mortal: Medicine and What Matters in the End.* Atul Gawande. Metropolitan Books : 2014. 304 p.
ISBN 9780805095159
Grades: Adult   362.17
1. Terminal Care 2. Quality of Life 3. Aging 4. Science Writing — Medicine and health 5. Family and relationships — Aging and death 6. Society and culture — Illness and disease
LC 2014017442

Booklist Editors' Choice, 2014; Indies' Choice Book Awards, Adult Nonfiction, 2015; New York Times Notable Book, 2014.

A prominent surgeon argues against modern medical practices that extend life at the expense of quality of life while isolating the dying, outlining suggestions for freer, more fulfilling approaches to death that enable more dignified and comfortable choices.

"A sensitive, intelligent and heartfelt examination of the processes of aging and dying." —*Kirkus*
Includes bibliographical references.

Lyons, Anna
We All Know How This Ends: Lessons About Life and Living from Working with Death and Dying. Anna Lyons & Louise Winter. Green Tree 2021. 256 pages
ISBN 9781472966810
Grades: Adult   362.17
1. Life 2. Death 3. Funerals 4. Grief 5. Family and Relationships — Aging and Death 6. Self-Help — Mental health — Grief and loss

This book explores lessons learned about life, death, love and loss. It is a practical guide to rethinking death. It discusses life and living, as much as death and dying. It's a reflection on the beauties, blessings and tragedies of life, the exquisite agony and ecstasy of being alive, and the fragility of everything we hold dear. It's as simple and as complicated as that.

"This should be required reading for all the living." —*Booklist*

McLaughlin, Kathleen
Blood Money: The Story of Life, Death, and Profit Inside America's Blood Industry. by Kathleen McLaughlin. One Signal Publishers/Atria 2023. 288 p.
ISBN 9781982171964
Grades: Adult   362.17
1. Blood banks 2. Corruption 3. Social classes 4. Inequality 5. United States 6. Society and culture — General
LC 2022034219

An award-winning journalist exposes how businesses have turned blood plasm into a precious commercial good which is marketed by private industry by feeding on the most vulnerable in our society through the practice of pay-for-plasma schemes.

"A disturbing, painful story that smoothly combines the personal and the universal." —*Kirkus*
Includes index.

362.18 Emergency services

Hazzard, Kevin M.
American Sirens: The Incredible Story of the Black Men Who Became America's First Paramedics. Kevin Hazzard. Hachette Books 2022. 336 p.
ISBN 9780306926075
Grades: Adult   362.18
1. First responders 2. Ambulance service 3. Paramedics 4. Medical care 5. African Americans 6. Race relations 7. Pittsburgh, Pennsylvania 8. United States 9. 1970s 10. 20th century 11. Society and culture — Race 12. History writing — African American — United States 13. Life stories — Science, Technology, and medicine — Healthcare professionals
LC 2022006917

The story of a group of Black men in Pittsburgh who became the first paramedics in America and forever changed how emergency medicine is administered, only to find their history and legacy erased.

"A mostly inspiring account of the early days of American emergency services and the Black men who advanced the level of care and attention....Good history and an admirable effort to document the achievements of a pioneering Black organization." —*Kirkus*
Includes bibliographical references.

362.196 Specific conditions

France, David
How to Survive a Plague: The Inside Story of How Citizens and Science Tamed AIDS. by David France. Alfred A. Knopf 2016. 640 p.
ISBN 9780307700636
Grades: Adult   362.196
1. AIDS activists 2. People with HIV 3. Gay and Lesbian Movement 4. AIDS (Disease) 5. People with AIDS 6. Gay men 7. LGBTQIA+ rights 8. New York (State) 9. United States 10. 1980s 11. 1990s 12. History writing — LGBTQIA+ 13. Society and culture — Illness and disease — Epidemics 14. Society and culture — LGBTQIA+
LC 2016010685

Baillie Gifford Prize for Non-Fiction, 2017; Lambda Literary Award for LGBT Nonfiction, 2017; New York Times Notable Book, 2016; Stonewall Book Awards: Israel Fishman Non-fiction Award, 2017.

A definitive history of the successful battle to halt the AIDS epidemic, written by the creator of and inspired by the seminal documentary of the same name, also shares the poignant stories of gay activists who resolved to make their life battles purposeful.

Includes bibliographical references and index.

PUBLIC LIBRARY CORE COLLECTION: NONFICTION
Twentieth Edition

Shilts, Randy
★ *And the Band Played On: Politics, People, and the AIDS Epidemic.* Randy Shilts. St. Martin's Griffin 2007. xxiii, 630 p.
ISBN 9780312009946
Grades: 11 12 Adult   362.196
1. AIDS (Disease) 2. Page to screen 3. Science Writing — Medicine and health — Illness and disease 4. Society and culture — Illness and disease — Epidemics

LC 87016528
National Book Critics Circle Award for Nonfiction finalist, 1987.
An examination of the AIDS crisis exposes the federal government for its inaction, health authorities for their greed, and scientists for their desire for prestige in the face of the AIDS pandemic.
"Shilts successfully weaves comprehensive investigative reporting and commercial page-turner pacing, political intrigue and personal tragedy into a landmark work." —*Publishers Weekly*
Includes bibliographical references and index.

362.1962 Services to patients with respiratory diseases

Brenner, Marie
★ *The Desperate Hours: One Hospital's Fight to Save a City on the Pandemic's Front Lines.* Marie Brenner. Flatiron Books 2022. 336 p.
ISBN 9781250805737
Grades: Adult   362.1962
1. COVID-19 (Disease) 2. COVID-19 Pandemic, 2020- 3. Communicable diseases 4. Viruses 5. Cities and towns 6. Epidemics 7. Hospitals 8. Hospital workers 9. Physicians 10. Nurses 11. Medical personnel 12. Hospital patients 13. Sick people 14. Death 15. Persistence 16. Courage 17. Duty 18. New York City history 19. 21st century 20. Society and culture — Illness and disease — Epidemics 21. Life stories — Science, technology, and medicine — Healthcare professionals 22. Science Writing — Medicine and health — Doctors and nurses 23. History writing — Early 21st century — United States

In the spring of 2020, COVID-19 arrived in New York City. Before long, America's largest metropolis was at war against a virus that mercilessly swept through its five boroughs. It became apparent that if Covid wasn't somehow halted, the death count in New York alone would be in the hundreds of thousands. And if New York's hospitals failed, what chance did the rest of the country have? In The Desperate Hours, journalist Marie Brenner, having been granted unprecedented 18-month access to the entire New York-Presbyterian hospital system, tells the story of the doctors, nurses, residents, researchers, and suppliers who tried to save lives across Manhattan, Queens, and Brooklyn.
"This is a powerful look at life on the front lines of a pandemic." —*Publishers Weekly*

Christakis, Nicholas A.
Apollo's Arrow: The Profound and Enduring Impact of Coronavirus on the Way We Live. Nicholas A. Christakis. Little, Brown Spark 2020. xvi, 368 p.
ISBN 9780316628211
Grades: Adult   362.1962
1. COVID-19 (Disease) 2. Epidemics 3. Plague 4. Epidemiology 5. Diseases 6. Public health 7. Immunity 8. Misinformation 9. Preparedness 10. Social isolation 11. Medical care 12. Social forecasting 13. Science Writing — Medicine and health — Illness and disease 14. Society and culture — Illness and disease — Epidemics 15. Politics and global affairs — Public health

Apollo's Arrow offers a riveting account of the impact of the coronavirus pandemic as it swept through American society in 2020, and of how the recovery will unfold in the coming years. Drawing on momentous (yet dimly remembered) historical epidemics, contemporary analyses, and cutting-edge research from a range of scientific disciplines, bestselling author, physician, sociologist, and public health expert Nicholas A. Christakis explores what it means to live in a time of plague—an experience that is paradoxically uncommon to the vast majority of humans who are alive, yet deeply fundamental to our species.
Includes bibliographical references and index.

Ferguson, Niall
Doom: The Politics of Catastrophe. Niall Ferguson. Penguin 2021. 496 p.
ISBN 9780593297377
Grades: Adult   362.1962
1. COVID-19 (Disease) 2. Disasters 3. Political leadership 4. Epidemics 5. Natural disasters 6. Emergency planning 7. Disaster relief 8. Denial (Psychology) 9. Failure 10. History writing — Natural disasters and tragedies 11. History writing — Plague and famine 12. Politics and global affairs — General 13. Society and culture — General

LC 2020043578
Setting the great crisis of 2020 in broad historical perspective, Niall Ferguson challenges the conventional wisdom that our failure to cope better with disaster was solely a crisis of political leadership, as opposed to a more profound systemic problem. Pandemics, like earthquakes, wildfires, financial crises and wars, are hard to predict; there is no cycle of history to help us anticipate the next catastrophe. But when disaster strikes, we ought to be better prepared than the Romans were when Vesuvius erupted, or medieval Italians when the Black Death struck. The facile answer is to blame poor leadership. While populist leaders have certainly performed poorly in the face of the pandemic, more profound problems have been exposed by COVID-19. Only when we understand the central challenge posed by disaster in history can we see that this was also a failure of an administrative state and economic elites that had grown myopic over much longer than just a few years.
"Historian Ferguson (Civilization) turns his analytical mind to catastrophes and disasters worldwide, in this latest work.... An exemplary and thought-provoking work from a renowned author that will not disappoint." —*Library Journal*
Includes bibliographical references and index.

Goldberg, Emma
Life on the Line: Young Doctors Come of Age in a Pandemic. Emma Goldberg. Harper 2021. 320 p.
ISBN 9780063073388
Grades: Adult   362.1962
1. COVID-19 (Disease) 2. Physicians 3. Residents (Medicine) 4. Young adults 5. Medical personnel 6. Hospitals 7. Epidemics 8. Communicable diseases 9. Medical care 10. Racism in medical care 11. Sick people 12. Death 13. Suffering 14. Fear 15. Self-sacrifice 16. New York City history 17. 21st century 18. Science Writing — Medicine and health — Doctors and nurses 19. Science Writing — Medicine and health — Illness and disease 20. Life stories — Science, technology, and medicine — Healthcare professionals 21. Society and culture — Illness and disease — Epidemics

In March 2020, soon-to-graduate medical students in New York City were nervously awaiting "match day" when they would learn where they would begin their residencies. Only a week later, these young physicians learned that they would be sent to the front lines of the desperate battle to save lives as the coronavirus plunged the city into crisis. Journalist Emma Goldberg offers an up-close portrait of six bright yet inexperienced health professionals, each of whom defies a stereotype about who gets to don a doctor's white coat. Goldberg illuminates how the pandemic redefines what it means for them to undergo this trial by fire as caregivers, colleagues, classmates, friends, romantic partners and concerned family members.
"New York Times reporter Goldberg debuts with a vivid and heart-wrenching portrayal of six doctors who graduated from medical school during the 'First-wave peak' of Covid-19 in New York City." —*Publishers Weekly*

McSwane, J. David
★ *Pandemic, Inc.: Chasing the Capitalists and Thieves Who Got Rich While We Got Sick.* J. David McSwane. Signal Press 2022. 288 p.
ISBN 9781982177744
Grades: Adult   362.1962
1. COVID-19 Pandemic, 2020- 2. Political corruption 3. Business corruption 4. Swindlers and swindling 5. United States 6. Business and economics — Corruption and scandal

In this brilliant—and shocking—nonfiction thriller, an award-winning ProPublica investigative reporter connects the dots between backdoor deals and

ESSENTIAL AND RECOMMENDED TITLES
362.19681 Cerebrovascular diseases

the spoils systems to provide the definitive account of how this pandemic was so catastrophically mishandled.

"McSwane...introduces the sketchy world of opportunists and their slippery network of connections, sparking fresh outrage over the time wasted and lives lost while greed and profit trumped public health and safety." —*Booklist*

Meyer, Robert
Every Minute Is a Day: A Doctor, an Emergency Room, and a City Under Siege. Robert Meyer, MD, and Dan Koeppel. Crown 2021. xix, 233 p.
ISBN 9780593238592
Grades: Adult   362.1962
1. Meyer, Robert (Robert H.) 2. COVID-19 Pandemic, 2020- 3. COVID-19 (Disease) 4. Emergency physicians 5. Cousins 6. Hospitals 7. Hospital patients 8. Diseases 9. Treatment 10. Emergency medical services 11. New York City 12. Life stories — Science, technology, and medicine — Healthcare professionals 13. Science Writing — Medicine and health — Doctors and nurses 14. Science Writing — Medicine and health — Illness and disease 15. Society and culture — Illness and disease — Epidemics
LC 2021012301

When Dan Koeppel texted his cousin Robert Meyer, a senior doctor in the emergency room at Montefiore Medical Center in the Bronx, at the beginning of the Covid-19 crisis in the United States, he expected to hear that things were hectic. On a scale of 1-10, ten being overwhelmed, where do you think you are? Koeppel asked. Meyer's grave reply—100—was merely the cusp of the crisis that has since touched every part of the globe. As fast-paced and high-tempo as the ER in which it takes place, Every Minute Is a Day is at its core an incomparable primary source and an account of unrelenting compassion. This fascinating, heartbreaking book will clarify this epoch-making moment for those who live through it and be consulted for generations to come.

"Meyer, an emergency room physician, teams up with his cousin, New York Times journalist Koeppel, to create a dramatic first-person account of the doctor's experience during the first six months of the pandemic at Montefiore, the largest hospital in one of America's poorest urban counties, the Bronx. . . . Touching evidence of compassion and sacrifice during the worst of the pandemic." —*Kirkus*

Nocera, Joseph
The Big Fail: What the Pandemic Revealed About Who America Protects, and Who It Leaves Behind. Joe Nocera and Bethany McLean. Portfolio/Penguin 2023. 432 p.
ISBN 9780593331026
Grades: Adult   362.1962
1. Epidemics 2. Public health 3. COVID-19 Pandemic, 2020- 4. Health policy 5. Health services accessibility 6. Capitalism 7. United States 8. Society and culture — Illness and disease — Epidemics 9. Business and economics — General 10. Politics and global affairs — Public health
LC 2023019683

In this page-turning economic, political and financial history, the collaborators behind the modern business classic All the Devils are Here offer a damning indictment of American capitalism, revealing what the pandemic did to the economy and the people who profited from it.

"A damning report card presenting a distressingly exhaustive array of pandemic fumbles." —*Kirkus*

Thrasher, Steven W.
★ *The Viral Underclass: The Human Toll When Inequality and Disease Collide.* Steven W. Thrasher. Celadon Books 2022. 352 p.
ISBN 9781250796639
Grades: Adult   362.1962
1. Social status 2. COVID-19 Pandemic, 2020- 3. Viruses 4. Equality 5. Inequality 6. Society and culture — Wealth and class 7. Society and culture — Illness and disease
LC 2021060451

Drawing from heart-rending stories of friends, activists and teachers navigating COVID, HIV and other viruses, a preeminent LGBTQ scholar and journalist presents, for the first time, his unified theory of one of the most pressing social justice issues of our time—how viruses expose the fault lines of society.

"Rigorous scholarship and intimate portraits of life and death on the margins make this a must-read." —*Publishers Weekly*

Includes bibliographical references and index.

362.19681 Cerebrovascular diseases

Taylor, Jill Bolte
My Stroke of Insight: A Brain Scientist's Personal Journey. Jill Bolte Taylor. Viking 2008. 183 p : Illustration
ISBN 9780670020744
Grades: Adult   362.19681
1. Neuroscientists 2. People who have had strokes 3. Strokes 4. Brain 5. Autobiographies and memoirs 6. Science Writing — Medicine and health — Disabilities and disorders 7. Science Writing — Biology 8. Life stories — Facing adversity — Medical issues

Traces the Harvard brain scientist author's massive left-hemisphere stroke at the age of thirty-seven, during which she observed the disparate functioning of her right and left brain and came into a realization that she could tap feelings of calm and well-being from her kinesthetic right hemisphere to promote her recovery and a positive outlook.

Self-published in 2006.

362.1969 Other diseases

Hotez, Peter J.
Preventing the Next Pandemic: Vaccine Diplomacy in a Time of Anti-science. Peter J. Hotez. Johns Hopkins University Press 2021. xiii, 192 pages : Illustration
ISBN 9781421440385
Grades: Adult   362.1969
1. Epidemics 2. Public health 3. Anti-vaccination movement 4. Communicable diseases 5. Vaccination 6. Vaccines 7. Preventive medicine 8. Science Writing — Medicine and health — Illness and disease 9. History writing — Science, technology, and medicine

Touching on a range of disease, from leishmaniasis, schistosomiasis, and Middle East Respiratory Syndrome (MERS) to COVID-19, Preventing the Next Pandemic has always been a timely goal, but it will be even more important in a COVID and post-COVID world.

"Hotez convincingly explains why science and public health are bigger than boundaries, more powerful than political differences." —*Booklist*

Includes bibliographical references and index.

362.19699 Patients with tumors and miscellaneous communicable diseases

Fessler, Pam
Carville's Cure: Leprosy, Stigma, and the Fight for Justice. Pam Fessler. Liveright Publishing Corporation 2020. 352 p.
ISBN 9781631495038
Grades: Adult   362.19699
1. People with leprosy 2. Leprosy 3. Stigma (Social psychology) 4. Skin diseases 5. Treatment 6. Ostracism 7. Patients' rights 8. Involuntary treatment 9. Imprisonment 10. Injustice 11. Social isolation 12. Louisiana 13. 20th century 14. Life stories — Facing adversity — Medical issues — Physical illness 15. Science Writing — Medicine and health — Illness and disease 16. History writing — Regional history — United States 17. Life stories — Science, technology, and medicine — Healthcare professionals
LC 2020008057

ALA Notable Book, 2021.

Explores the hidden history of Carville, the only leprosy colony in the continental United States which lasted from 1894 to 1999, and the shameful treatment of the thousands of Americans who were needlessly exiled there.

"NPR correspondent Fessler's polished and compassionate debut examines the history of Hansen's disease (the modern name for leprosy) in America through the story of the Louisiana Leper Home in Carville, LA.... Readers will be enlightened and encouraged."—*Publishers Weekly*

Includes bibliographical references.

Hutton, Andrea
Bald Is Better with Earrings: A Survivor's Guide to Getting Through Breast Cancer. Andrea Hutton. HarperWave 2015. xiv, 205 pages
ISBN 9780062375650

Grades: Adult   362.19699

1. Patients 2. Cancer 3. Breast cancer 4. Science writing — Medicine and health — Illness and disease 5. Science writing — Medicine and health — Women's health 6. Self-Help — Personal growth — Happiness

LC Bl2015026747

A guide for women with breast cancer shares step-by-step coverage of how to navigate the emotional and physical challenges of every stage of treatment.

Written in the style of a warm and practical-minded best friend, a guide for women with breast cancer shares step-by-step coverage of how to navigate the emotional and physical challenges of every stage of treatment.

"Readers will be equally overwhelmed and overjoyed by Hutton's prescriptions. This book could be a lifesaver for breast cancer club members."—*Library Journal*

362.1988 Obstetrical surgery and abortion

Andrews, Becca
★ *No Choice: The Destruction of Roe V. Wade and the Fight to Protect a Fundamental American Right.* Becca Andrews. PublicAffairs 2022. 256 p.
ISBN 9781541768390

Grades: Adult   362.1988

1. Human rights 2. Women's rights 3. Reproductive rights 4. Abortion 5. Pro-choice movement 6. Legislation 7. United States 8. 20th century 9. 21st century 10. Society and culture — Gender — Women — Reproductive rights 11. Politics and global affairs — Civil and human rights

Discusses the states and communities hardest hit by the reversal of Roe v. Wade, telling the stories of those most at risk, but also profiles the people who are doing groundbreaking, inspiring work to ensure safe, legal access to a fundamental part of health care.

"This is a valuable introduction to the current state of abortion rights in America."—*Publishers Weekly*

Blair, Gabrielle Stanley
★ *Ejaculate Responsibly: A Whole New Way to Think About Abortion.* Gabrielle Blair. Workman Publishing 2022. 137 pages
ISBN 9781523523184

Grades: Adult   362.1988

1. Human reproduction 2. Sexual ethics 3. Birth control 4. Sterilization (Birth control) 5. Men 6. Sexuality 7. Abortion 8. American people 9. North American people 10. United States 11. Society and culture — Sex and sexuality 12. Society and culture — Gender — Women — Reproductive rights

LC Bl2022033608

In a series of 28 brief arguments reframing the abortion issue, Gabrielle Blair deftly makes the case for moving the abortion debate away from controlling and legislating women's bodies and instead directs the focus on men's lack of accountability in preventing unwanted pregnancies.

"Flashes of acerbic humor and eye-opening statistics bolster Blair's common-sense case. This polemic has the power to change minds."—*Publishers Weekly*

Foster, Diana Greene
The Turnaway Study: Ten Years, a Thousand Women, and the Consequences of Having—or Being Denied—an Abortion. Diana Greene Foster. Scribner 2020. 360 p.
ISBN 9781982141561

Grades: Adult   362.1988

1. Reproductive rights 2. Abortion 3. Women's rights 4. Birth control 5. Pregnant women 6. Unplanned pregnancy 7. Impartial writing 8. Society and culture — Gender — Women — Reproductive rights 9. Politics and global affairs — Public health

LC 2020004923

The principal investigator of the Turnaway Study and internationally renowned expert on contraception presents an illuminating report on the long-term consequences of receiving versus being denied an abortion in accordance with the access of today's America.

"Policy makers and abortion rights activists should consider it a must-read." —*Publishers Weekly*

Kolbert, Kathryn
Controlling Women: What We Must Do Now to Save Reproductive Freedom. Kathryn Kolbert & Julie F. Kay. Hachette Books 2021. 288 p.
ISBN 9780306925634

Grades: Adult   362.1988

1. Abortion 2. Women's rights 3. Reproductive rights 4. United States 5. Society and culture — Gender — Women — Reproductive rights 6. Politics and global affairs — Civil and human rights 7. History writing — United States 8. History writing — Women's history

LC 2021005512

The definitive account of the battle for reproductive freedom and how advocates for those rights can fight back against the current assault on Roe v. Wade led by conservative state legislatures and anti-abortion judges.

"Kolbert and Kay, both attorneys who have spent their legal careers in service of reproductive justice, co-author a concise and pragmatic discourse on abortion rights.... An essential guide."—*Library Journal*

Includes bibliographical references and index.

Luthra, Shefali
★ *Undue Burden: Life and Death Decisions in Post-roe America.* Shefali Luthra. Doubleday 2024. 336 p.
ISBN 9780385550086

Grades: Adult   362.1988

1. Abortion policy 2. Abortion 3. Women's rights 4. Reproductive rights 5. Women's health services 6. Inequality 7. Science Writing — Medicine and health 8. Politics and global affairs — Social issues and policies 9. Society and culture — Gender — Women — Reproductive rights

The author presents this timely examination of human rights, healthcare, and economic and racial inequality in America through the perspectives of patients, providers, activists, and lawmakers, as the landscape of abortion rights continues to shift, forcing people to cross state lines to seek life-saving care.

"Luthra's well-researched, compelling book will appeal to anyone who is interested in the human cost of reproductive rights in America."—*Booklist*

Matthews, Hannah
You or Someone You Love: Reflections from an Abortion Doula. Hannah Matthews. Atria Books 2023. 256 p.
ISBN 9781668005255

Grades: Adult   362.1988

1. Abortion 2. Reproductive rights 3. Abortion policy 4. Abortion providers 5. Reproductive health 6. Public health 7. Health policy 8. Society and culture — Gender — Women — Reproductive rights

LC 2022054541

Rise: A Feminist Book Project List, 2024.

An eye-opening, transformative, and actionable journey through radical and compassionate community abortion care and support work: What it looks like, how each and every one of us can practice and incorporate it into our daily lives, and what we can imagine and build together in a post-Roe v. Wade United States.—.

"Abortion doula Matthews normalizes abortion experiences in her compassionate, affirming debut....Readers looking to support loved ones or offer themselves grace will find Matthews a wise guide."—*Publishers Weekly*

Includes bibliographical references and index.

ESSENTIAL AND RECOMMENDED TITLES
362.19892 Pediatric care

Peters, Rebecca Todd
Trust Women: A Progressive Christian Argument for Reproductive Justice. Rebecca Todd Peters. Beacon Press 2018. 240 p.
ISBN 9780807069981
Grades: Adult   362.1988
1. Abortion 2. Motherhood 3. Faith (Christianity) 4. Public opinion 5. Sexism 6. Misogyny 7. Social control 8. Christianity 9. Religions 10. Society and culture — Gender — Women — Reproductive rights 11. Politics and global affairs — Religion and politics 12. Spirituality and Religion — Christianity — Political Aspects
LC 2017042045

Rebecca Todd Peters, a Presbyterian minister and social ethicist, argues that the shaming and judging associated with abortion reflects deep, often unspoken patriarchal and racist assumptions about women and women's sexual activity. These assumptions are at the heart of what she calls the justification framework, which governs our public debate about abortion, and disrupts our ability to have authentic public discussions about the health and well-being of women and their families.

Includes bibliographical references and index.

Rankin, Lauren
Bodies on the Line: At the Front Lines of the Fight to Protect Abortion in America. Lauren Rankin. Counterpoint 2022. 256 p.
ISBN 9781640094741
Grades: Adult   362.1988
1. Abortion 2. Medical care 3. Abortion clinics and referral services 4. Pro-choice movement 5. Society and culture — Gender — Women — Reproductive rights
LC 2021037793

Collecting the stories of brave clinic escorts who have fought the "abortion wars" on the front lines, and drawing on research and input from abortion rights experts, this book makes a clear case for the right to an abortion as a fundamental part of human dignity.

"This history of abortion clinic escorts in the United States by writer and activist Rankin is timely, engaging, and full of compassion....It is both a celebration of devoted volunteer clinic escorts and a call to action to improve the circumstances under which people seek health care." —*Library Journal*

Includes bibliographical references.

Shah, Meera
You're the Only One I've Told: The Stories Behind Abortion. Dr. Meera Shah. Chicago Review Press 2020. 298 pages
ISBN 9781641603638
Grades: Adult   362.1988
1. Shah, Meera 2. Abortion 3. Abortion providers 4. Unplanned pregnancy 5. Pro-life movement 6. Family planning 7. Abortion clinics and referral services 8. Reproductive rights 9. Medical care 10. Women 11. Women's health services 12. Legislation 13. Society and culture — Gender — Women — Reproductive rights 14. Life stories — Facing adversity — Medical issues 15. Life stories — Science, technology, and medicine — Healthcare professionals
LC 2020939551

Chief medical officer of Planned Parenthood Hudson Peconic tells the myriad stories of diverse individuals whose abortion experiences bring vital and threatened reproductive rights to life.

"A strong contribution to discussions of reproductive rights." —*Kirkus*
Includes bibliographical references (pages 289-298).

362.19892 Pediatric care

Klass, Perri
A Good Time to Be Born: How Science and Public Health Gave Children a Future. Perri Klass. W. W. Norton & Company 2020. VIII, 376 p. : Illustration
ISBN 9780393609998
Grades: Adult   362.19892

1. Child health 2. Children 3. Women physicians 4. Medical research 5. Babies 6. Sanitation 7. Public health 8. Medical care 9. Vaccines 10. Science Writing — Medicine and health — medical breakthroughs 11. History writing — Science, technology, and medicine
LC 2020022472

A history of the world-transforming fight against child mortality interweaves the author's experiences as a medical student and doctor while paying tribute to the barrier-breaking women who introduced new approaches and scientific ideas about sanitation and vaccination.

"Klass masterfully introduces readers to the people coming up with solutions for many of the dangers of childhood and shows how the pediatric specialty over time has worked to improve children's lives. Essential reading for parents." —*Library Journal*

362.2 People with mental illness and disabilities

Bering, Jesse
Suicidal: Why We Kill Ourselves. Jesse Bering. The University of Chicago Press 2018. 272 p.
ISBN 9780226463322
Grades: Adult   362.2
1. Suicide 2. Social psychology 3. Depression 4. Mental illness 5. Society and culture — Psychology and human behavior
LC 2018021904

Uses scientific studies, personal stories, and cross-species comparisons to explore the science and psychology of suicide.

"Bering illuminates a murky, misunderstood human quandary with compassion, confessional honesty, and academic perception." —*Kirkus*
Includes bibliographical references and index.

Hylton, Antonia
Madness: Race and Insanity in a Jim Crow Asylum. Antonia Hylton. Legacy Lit 2024. 288 p.
ISBN 9781538723692
Grades: Adult   362.2
1. Psychiatric hospitals 2. Psychiatric hospital patients 3. Segregation 4. African Americans 5. Mental illness 6. Race (Social sciences) 7. Slavery 8. Racism in medical care 9. Mental health policy 10. Maryland 11. History writing — African American — United States 12. Science Writing — Medicine and health — Mental health 13. Society and culture — Race 14. Life stories — Facing adversity — Medical issues — Mental illness 15. Life stories — Identity — Race and ethnicity 16. Debut title

Tracing the legacy of slavery to the treatment of Black people's bodies and minds in our current healthcare system, a Peabody and Emmy award-winning journalist tells the 93-year-old history of Crownsville Hospital, one of the nation's last segregated asylums.

"This well-researched title is an important chronicle of the treatment of Black Americans and their mental health during the Jim Crow era." —*Library Journal*

Insel, Thomas R.
Healing: Our Path from Mental Illness to Mental Health. Thomas Insel, MD.. Penguin Press 2022. 384 p.
ISBN 9780593298046
Grades: Adult   362.2
1. Mental health 2. Mental health services 3. Mental health policy 4. Mental illness 5. Public health 6. Medical care reform 7. United States 8. Science Writing — Medicine and health — Mental health 9. Politics and global affairs — Public health
LC 2021033983

As director of the National Institute of Mental Health, Dr. Thomas Insel was giving a presentation when the father of a boy with schizophrenia yelled from the back of the room, "Our house is on fire and you're telling me about the chemistry of the paint! What are you doing to put out the fire?" Dr. Insel knew in his heart that the answer was not nearly enough. The gargantuan American mental health industry was not healing millions who were desperately in need. He left his position atop the mental health research world to investigate all that was broken-and what a better path to mental health might look like. In the United States, we have treatments that work, but our system fails at every stage to deliver care well. Mental illnesses are medical problems, but he discovers that the cures for the crisis are not just medical, but social. This path to healing, built upon what he calls the three Ps (people, place, and purpose), is more straightforward than we might imagine. Dr. Insel offers a comprehensive plan for our failing system and for families trying to discern the way forward.

"Insel offers a sense of hopeful solutions. . . . It's as compassionate as it is comprehensive." —*Publishers Weekly*

Includes bibliographical references and index.

Kissinger, Meg
While You Were Out: An Intimate Family Portrait of Mental Illness in an Era of Silence. Meg Kissinger. Celadon Books 2023. 320 p.
ISBN 9781250793775
Grades: Adult   362.2
1. Kissinger, Meg 2. Women journalists 3. Families 4. People with mental illnesses 5. Mental illness 6. Depression 7. Bipolar disorder 8. Family secrets 9. Suicide victims 10. Treatment 11. Mental health 12. Medical care 13. North American people 14. American people 15. Autobiographies and memoirs 16. Life stories — Facing adversity — Medical issues — Mental illness 17. Life stories — Arts and culture — Writing — Journalists 18. Family and Relationships — Illness and the Family 19. Science Writing — Medicine and health — Mental health 20. Debut title
LC 2023002648

Growing up in the 1960s in the suburbs of Chicago, Meg Kissinger's family seemed to live a charmed life. With eight kids and two loving parents, the Kissingers radiated a warm, boisterous energy. But behind closed doors, a harsher reality was unfolding—a heavily medicated mother hospitalized for anxiety and depression, a manic father prone to violence, and children in the throes of bipolar disorder and depression, two of whom would take their own lives. While You Were Out begins as the personal story of one family's struggles and then opens outward, as Kissinger details how childhood tragedy catalyzed a journalism career focused on exposing our country's flawed mental health care.

"An impassioned argument for reform in caring for the afflicted." —*Kirkus*

Includes bibliographical references.

Paperny, Anna Mehler
Hello I Want to Die Please Fix Me: Depression in the First Person. Anna Mehler Paperny. The Experiment 2020. 352 p.
ISBN 9781615194926
Grades: Adult   362.2
1. Paperny, Anna Mehler 2. Mental health 3. Depression 4. Mental illness 5. People with depression 6. Women 7. People with mental illnesses 8. Autobiographies and memoirs 9. Canadian literature 10. Life stories — Facing adversity — Medical issues — Mental illness 11. Science Writing — Medicine and health — Mental health
LC Bl2020009832

Loan Stars Favourites, 2019; Hilary Weston Writers' Trust Prize for Nonfiction finalist, 2019.

An investigative report on how depression is treated today shares stories from the author's personal journey with suicidal depression and draws on interviews with patients and experts to explore how current systems need to change.

"An eye-opening and humane book treatment of a difficult subject." —*Kirkus*

Originally published: Toronto : Random House Canada, 2019.

Tweedy, Damon
Facing the Unseen: The Struggle to Center Mental Health in Medicine. Damon Tweedy, M.D.. St. Martin's Press 2024. 304 p.
ISBN 9781250284891
Grades: Adult   362.2
1. Tweedy, Damon 2. Medicine 3. Mental health 4. Medical care 5. Mental health services 6. Physicians 7. People with mental illnesses 8. Psychology 9. Psychiatry 10. Crisis intervention 11. Medical care reform 12. Science Writing — Medicine and health — Mental health 13. Science Writing — Medicine and health — Doctors and nurses 14. Society and culture — Illness and disease
LC 2023051593

As much as we all might wish that mental health problems, with their elusive causes and unsettling behaviors, simply did not exist, millions of people suffer from them, sometimes to an extreme extent. Many others face addiction to alcohol and other drugs, as overdose and suicide deaths abound. Yet the vast majority of doctors receive minimal instruction in treating these conditions during their lengthy medical training. In powerful, compassionate prose, Tweedy argues for a more comprehensive and integrated approach where people with mental illness have a health care system that places their full well-being front and center.

"Tweedy offers a moving reminder that no individual is merely ordinary and calls for more available and comprehensive mental health care." —*Booklist*

Includes bibliographical references.

362.28 Suicide

Case, Anne
Deaths of Despair and the Future of Capitalism. Anne Case, Angus Deaton. Princeton University Press 2020. 312 pages : Illustration
ISBN 9780691190785
Grades: Adult   362.28
1. Capitalism and inequality 2. Depression 3. Suicide 4. Blue collar workers 5. Drug overdoses 6. Alcoholism 7. Unhappiness 8. Working class 9. Economics 10. United States 11. 20th century 12. Business and economics — Economics 13. Society and culture — Wealth and class
LC 2019040360

New York Times Notable Book, 2020.

This book documents the decline of white-working class lives over the last half-century and examines the social and economic forces that have slowly made these lives more difficult. Case and Deaton argue that market and political power in the United States have moved away from labor towards capital-as unions have weakened and politics have become more favorable to business, corporations have become more powerful. Consolidation in some American industries, healthcare especially, has brought an increase in monopoly power in some product markets so that it is possible for firms to raise prices above what they would be in a freely competitive market. This, the authors argue, is a major cause of wage stagnation among working-class Americans and has played a substantial role in the increase in deaths of despair. Case and Deaton offer a way forward, including ideas that, even in our current political situation, may be feasible and improve lives.

"Complementing their candid prose with enlightening charts and graphs, Case and Deaton make the scale and immediacy of the problem crystal clear. This is an essential portrait of America in crisis." —*Publishers Weekly*

Includes bibliographical references (pages 265-291) and index.

Martin, Clancy W.
How Not to Kill Yourself: A Portrait of the Suicidal Mind. Clancy Martin. Pantheon Books 2023. 400 p.
ISBN 9780593317051
Grades: Adult   362.28
1. Suicide 2. Suicidal behavior 3. Ethics 4. Self-destructive behavior 5. Philosophy 6. Autobiographies and memoirs 7. Life stories — Facing adversity
LC 2022036118

Based on his viral essay "I'm Still Here," the acclaimed writer and professor of philosophy chronicles his own multiple suicide attempts and discusses how the desire to kill oneself is almost always temporary and avoidable.

"This provocative dive into a difficult subject shouldn't be missed." —*Publishers Weekly*

Includes index.

ESSENTIAL AND RECOMMENDED TITLES
362.29 Substance abuse

362.29 Substance abuse

Berenson, Alex
★ *Tell Your Children: The Truth About Marijuana, Mental Illness, and Violence.* Alex Berenson. Simon & Schuster 2019. 256 p.
ISBN 9781982103668
Grades: Adult   362.29
1. Marijuana 2. Mental health 3. Marijuana abuse 4. Violence and drugs 5. Teenage drug abusers 6. Teenagers 7. Decriminalization of marijuana 8. Society and culture — Illness and disease — Addiction
LC Bl2018192602

A report from an award-winning author and former New York Times reporter reveals the link between teenage marijuana use and mental illness, and a hidden epidemic of violence caused by the drug—facts that the author believes have been ignored as the U.S. rushes to legalize cannabis.

"Those who favor legalization are likely to remain unmoved, but Berenson is certainly meticulous and coherent about making his case, and his well-written treatise never descends into Reefer Madnesslike hysteria." —*Publishers Weekly*

Dufton, Emily
Grass Roots: The Rise and Fall and Rise of Marijuana in America. Emiliy Dufton. Basic Books 2017. 336 p.
ISBN 9780465096169
Grades: Adult   362.29
1. Medical marijuana 2. Decriminalization of marijuana 3. Drug control 4. Marijuana in popular culture 5. Marijuana 6. Drug culture 7. Legislation 8. United States 9. Society and culture — Illness and disease
LC 2017956164

A chronicle of marijuana's journey toward and away from legalization examines how grassroots activists from the 1970s nearly secured its decriminalization before conservative parents and the Reagan administration transformed cannabis into a focus for the War on Drugs.

"Dufton's balanced and thoroughly researched book traces the long and still unwinding history of marijuana policy and activism in the U.S." —*Booklist*

Eyre, Eric
Death in Mud Lick: A Coal Country Fight Against the Drug Companies That Delivered the Opioid Epidemic. Eric Eyre. Scribner 2020. 320 p.
ISBN 9781982105310
Grades: Adult   362.29
1. Opioid epidemic 2. Addiction 3. Corruption 4. Drug industry and trade 5. Secrecy 6. Prescription drugs 7. Opioid abuse 8. Opioids 9. Prescription drug abuse 10. Small towns 11. West Virginia 12. United States 13. 21st century 14. Society and culture — Illness and disease — Addiction 15. Business and economics — Industries — Medical
LC Bl2020004776

Edgar Allan Poe Award for Best Fact Crime, 2021.

A Pulitzer Prize-winning reporter presents an urgent investigation into the role of corporate and government greed on the opioid epidemic as it devastatingly unfolded throughout small and vulnerable Appalachian communities.

"This is an infuriating story, compellingly told, and adds another layer to the reporting of the opioid crisis laid out in Beth Macy's Dopesick (2018). It is also a tale of compassionate people deeply wronged and a dogged journalist who won't stand for it." —*Booklist*

Fisher, Carl Erik
★ *The Urge: Our History of Addiction.* Carl Erik Fisher. Penguin 2022. 448 p.
ISBN 9780525561446
Grades: Adult   362.29
1. Fisher, Carl Erik 2. Psychiatrists 3. Alcoholics 4. Addicts 5. Drug abuse 6. Compulsive behavior 7. Addiction 8. Recovery movement 9. Temperance movements 10. Rehabilitation 11. Treatment 12. Science Writing — Medicine and health — Addiction 13. Life stories — Facing adversity — Medical issues — Addiction 14. Society and culture — Illness and disease — Addiction
LC 2021034504

A history of addiction and the treatments that have provided hope and relief for a number of people, including the author.

"Fisher makes a striking debut by skillfully combining a cultural history of addiction with his own story of recovery.... There's as much history here as there is heart." —*Publishers Weekly*

Includes bibliographical references and index.

Garcia, Angela
★ *The Way That Leads Among the Lost: Life, Death, and Hope in Mexico City's Anexos.* Angela Garcia. Farrar, Straus and Giroux 2024. 288 p.
ISBN 9780374605780
Grades: Adult   362.29
1. Garcia, Angela, 1971- 2. Drug abuse 3. Drug addicts 4. Drug abuse treatment centers and clinics 5. Drug addiction 6. Violence 7. Loss 8. Families 9. Family relationships 10. Drugs 11. Childhood 12. Mexico 13. Mexico city, Mexico 14. Autobiographies and memoirs 15. Life stories — Relationships — Family 16. Society and culture — Ethnic studies 17. Society and culture — Violence and crime 18. Society and culture — Wealth and class 19. History Writing — Latin America — Mexico
LC 2023045467

Journies into Mexico City's and California's anexos, the informal addiction treatment centers where mothers send their children to escape the violence of the drug war. Index.

"Garcia's outstanding book adds compassion and insight to this important social and political discussion." —*Booklist*

Includes bibliographical references and index.

Inglis, Lucy
Milk of Paradise: A History of Opium. Lucy Inglis. Pegasus Books 2019. 448 p.
ISBN 9781643130552
Grades: Adult   362.29
1. Opium industry and trade 2. Opium 3. Opioids 4. Narcotics 5. Social history 6. Opioid abuse 7. Opium addiction 8. Drug use 9. History writing — Science, technology, and medicine 10. History writing — Microhistory
LC Bl2018196003

The creator of the award-winning Georgian London blog presents an authoritative history of opium that explores its many uses and controversies, covering subjects ranging from the heroin underworld to the development of synthetic opiates.

"The narrative offers breadth rather than depth, but Inglis builds interest by emphasizing the places where intersections among historical strands yielded unexpected results and new trajectories in our relationship with opium; heroin, for example, was originally marketed as relief for tuberculosis symptoms, while the medical crisis of WWI encouraged Mexican opium production." —*Booklist*

Kennedy, Patrick J.
★ *Profiles in Mental Health Courage.* Patrick J. Kennedy & Stephen Fried. Dutton 2024. 320 p.
ISBN 9780593471760
Grades: Adult   362.29
1. People with mental illnesses 2. Recovering addicts 3. Psychotherapy patients 4. Mental illness 5. Addiction 6. Mental health 7. Life stories — Facing adversity — Medical issues — Mental illness 8. Life stories — Facing adversity — Medical issues — Addiction 9. Science Writing — Medicine and health — Mental health
LC 2023058101

Portrays those who have struggled with their mental health. This book offers deeply compelling stories about the bravery and resilience of those living with a variety of mental illnesses and addictions.

"Richly informative, harrowing, and moving, these courageously shared tales cast much-needed light on the many obstacles to mental health." —*Booklist*

Kuhn, Cynthia
Buzzed: The Straight Facts About the Most Used and Abused Drugs from Alcohol to Ecstasy. Cynthia Kuhn, PhD, Scott Swartzwelder, PhD, Wilkie Wilson,

PhD, Duke University and Duke University School of Medicine, with Leigh Heather Wilson and Jeremy Foster. W. W. Norton & Company 2019. 398 pages, 8 unnumbered pages of plates
ISBN 9780393356465
Grades: Adult   362.29
1. Drug abuse 2. Drugs 3. Reference books — Medicine
LC 2019015003
The essential source for understanding how drugs affect the body and behavior.
Includes bibliographical references and index.

Macy, Beth
★ *Dopesick: Dealers, Doctors, and the Drug Company That Addicted America*. Beth Macy. Little Brown & Co. 2018. 336 p.
ISBN 9780316551304
Grades: Adult   362.29
1. Opioid abuse 2. Drug addiction 3. Drug industry and trade 4. Heroin 5. Opioids 6. Prescription drugs 7. Prescription drug abuse 8. Drug addicts 9. Opioid epidemic 10. United States 11. Page to screen 12. Society and culture — Illness and disease — Addiction 13. Business and economics — Industries — Medical 14. Adult books for young adults
LC 2017961068
ALA Notable Book, 2019; Booklist Editors' Choice, 2018; Library Journal Best Books, 2018; Los Angeles Times Book Prize for Science and Technology, 2018; New York Times Notable Book, 2018; Andrew Carnegie Medal for Excellence in Non-Fiction Finalist, 2019; Kirkus Prize for Nonfiction finalist, 2018.

In a book that includes deeply human and unforgettable portraits of the families and first responders affected, the author takes readers into the epicenter of America's more than 20-year struggle with opioid addiction.

"Award-winning Virginia-based journalist Macy, author of best-sellers Factory Man (2014) and Truevine (2016), carefully constructs the through line from the midnineties introduction of the prescription painkiller OxyContin to the current U.S. opioid crisis: 300,000 deaths over the last 15 years, with that number predicted to double in the next 5." —*Booklist*

★ *Raising Lazarus: Hope, Justice, and the Future of America's Overdose Crisis*. Beth Macy. Little Brown & Company 2022. 352 p.
ISBN 9780316430227
Grades: Adult   362.29
1. Opioid epidemic 2. Opioid abuse 3. Drug industry and trade 4. Public health 5. Opioids 6. Heroin 7. Fentanyl 8. Drug addiction 9. Prescription drug abuse 10. Drug addicts 11. United States 12. Society and culture — Illness and disease — Addiction 13. Business and economics — Industries — Medical

In this complex story of public health, big pharma, dark money, politics, race and class, the New York Times best-selling author of Dopesick takes us to the forefront of the opioid crisis where we meet the everyday heroes fighting to stem the tide of drug overdose.

"A profoundly disconcerting book that, with luck, will inspire reform to aid the dopesick and punish their suppliers." —*Kirkus*

Marshall, McMillan
Among the Bros: A Fraternity Crime Story. Max Marshall. Harper 2023. 352 p.
ISBN 9780063099531
Grades: Adult   362.29
1. College students 2. Young men 3. Fraternities 4. Elite (Social sciences) 5. Privilege (Social psychology) 6. Drug abuse 7. Drug smuggling 8. Secrets 9. Greed 10. Murder 11. Investigative journalism 12. Life stories — Law or order — Criminals and law-breakers 13. Society and culture — Education — Higher education 14. True Crime — Drugs 15. Debut title
LC 2023013190
When Max Marshall arrived on the campus of the College of Charleston in 2018, he hoped to investigate a small-time fraternity Xanax trafficking ring. Instead, he found a homicide, several student deaths, and millions of dollars circulating around the Deep South. He also opened up an elite world hidden to outsiders. Behind the pop culture cliches of "Greek life" lies one of the major breeding grounds of American power: 80 percent of Fortune 500 executives, 85 percent of Supreme Court justices, and all but four presidents since 1825 have been fraternity members. With unprecedented immersion, this book takes readers inside that bubble.

"In this sobering debut, journalist Marshall digs into the deadly hubris underpinning an organized crime ring at the College of Charleston…The result is a fast-paced and frightening campus crime saga." —*Publishers Weekly*

McGreal, Chris
American Overdose: The Opioid Tragedy in Three Acts. Chris McGreal. PublicAffairs 2018. 320 p.
ISBN 9781610398619
Grades: Adult   362.29
1. Opioid abuse 2. Chronic pain 3. Prescription drugs 4. Prescription drug abuse 5. Pain control 6. Drug addiction 7. Drug industry and trade 8. Greed 9. Corruption 10. Heroin smuggling 11. Opioid epidemic 12. Drug abuse 13. Treatment 14. United States 15. Society and culture — Illness and disease — Addiction 16. Business and economics — Industries — Medical 17. Business and economics — Corruption and scandal 18. Science Writing — Medicine and health — Addiction
LC 2018025909
Describes how the current opioid crisis was driven by greed, incompetence and indifference and exposes Big Pharma's control of the healthcare system and the how the FDA was duped into pushing painkillers.

"This urgent, readable chronicle, which names names and pulls no punches, clearly and compassionately illuminates the evolution of Americas mass addiction problem." —*Publishers Weekly*

Includes bibliographical references and index.

Quinones, Sam
Dreamland: The True Tale of America's Opiate Epidemic. by Sam Quinones. Bloomsbury Press 2014. 320 p.
ISBN 9781620402504
Grades: Adult   362.29
1. Drug addiction 2. Heroin addiction 3. Narcotics 4. Oxycodone 5. Analgesics 6. Medical care 7. Drug traffic 8. United States 9. Mexico 10. True Crime — Drugs 11. Society and culture — Illness and disease — Addiction
LC 2014025398
National Book Critics Circle Award for Non-Fiction, 2015.

An explosive true account of addiction, marketing and the making of an epidemic weaves together the story of Purdue Pharma's campaign to market OxyContin, while, at the same time, a massive influx of black tar heroin took the county by storm through an almost unbreakable marking and distribution system.

"Journalist Quinones weaves an extraordinary story, including the personal journeys of the addicted, the drug traffickers, law enforcement, and scores of families affected by the scourge, as he details the social, economic, and political forces that eventually destroyed communities in the American heartland and continues to have a resounding impact." —*Booklist*

Featuring … (or with …) a Mexican town, a drug company, a letter to the editor, pain doctors & pill mills, a true tale of drug marketing & the search for happiness in an age of Excess; Includes bibliographical references and index.

★ *The Least of US: True Tales of America and Hope in the Time of Fentanyl and Meth*. Sam Quinones. Bloomsbury Publishing 2021. 288 p.
ISBN 9781635574357
Grades: Adult   362.29
1. Fentanyl 2. Opioid abuse 3. Drug industry and trade 4. Opioid epidemic 5. Drug abuse 6. Drug addiction 7. Methamphetamine 8. Drug addicts 9. Public health 10. United States 11. Society and culture — Illness and disease — Addiction

National Book Critics Circle Award for Nonfiction finalist, 2021.

From the best-selling author of Dreamland comes a searing follow-up that explores fentanyl and the quiet yet groundbreaking steps communities are taking to end the opioid crisis nationwide.

ESSENTIAL AND RECOMMENDED TITLES
362.292 Alcohol

Highly recommended for those interested in social justice and the strength of communities. Quinones argues that community can and must save 'The least of us.' —*School Library Journal*

Ramsey, Donovan X.
★ *When* Crack Was King: A People's History of a Misunderstood Era. Donovan X. Ramsey. One World 2023. 384 p.
ISBN 9780525511809
Grades: Adult   362.29
1. Crack (Drug) 2. Cocaine 3. Drug control 4. Epidemics 5. Resilience 6. Criminal justice system 7. African Americans 8. Marginalized people 9. Drugs 10. United States 11. 20th century 12. 1980s 13. 1990s 14. HIstory Writing — United States 15. Society and culture — Urban and regional studies 16. Society and culture — Race 17. Debut title

National Book Critics Circle Award: John Leonard Prize finalist, 2023.

A kaleidoscopic account of the crack cocaine era and a community's ultimate resilience—told through a cast of characters whose lives illuminate the dramatic rise and fall of the epidemic.

"Passionate, important reportage on a tragic era in American history from an author who lived through it." —*Kirkus*

Rieder, Travis
In Pain: A Bioethicist's Personal Struggle with Opioids. Travis Rieder. HarperCollins 2019. 320 pages
ISBN 9780062854643
Grades: Adult   362.29
1. Rieder, Travis 2. Opioids 3. Pain 4. Drug withdrawal symptoms 5. Accidents 6. Wounds and injuries 7. Pain control 8. Opium addiction 9. Opioid abuse 10. Drug addiction 11. Prescription drug abuse 12. Bioethics 13. Opioid epidemic 14. Treatment 15. Autobiographies and memoirs 16. Life stories — Facing adversity — Medical issues — Addiction 17. Society and culture — Illness and disease — Addiction 18. Science Writing — Medicine and health — Addiction

LC Bl2019015139

A bioethicist's eloquent and riveting memoir of opioid dependence and withdrawal is a harrowing personal reckoning and clarion call for change not only for government but medicine itself, revealing the lack of crucial resources and structures to handle this insidious nationwide epidemic.

"With this smart, riveting, real-life account, the author proves himself a convincing and effective advocate for opioid use reform. A harrowing cautionary narrative that speaks to patients and physicians alike on the ugly reality of the enduring opioid epidemic." —*Kirkus*

Weil, Andrew
Mind Over Meds: Know When Drugs Are Necessary, When Alternatives Are Better— and When to Let Your Body Heal on Its Own. Andrew Weil, MD… Little, Brown and Company 2017. xiv, 289 p.
ISBN 9780316269704
Grades: Adult   362.29
1. Alternative medicine 2. Science writing — Medicine and health — Alternative medicine 3. Science writing — Medicine and health

LC OC2018158460

The Harvard graduate, public health professor and best-selling author of Spontaneous Happiness explores the dangers of overmedication while outlining lifestyle changes and alternative treatments for common ailments.

"Weil's (Univ. of Arizona; Spontaneous Happiness, Healthy Aging) revolutionary book casts a critical eye on modern medicine, examining the very serious risks that medicine can carry." —*Library Journal*

Includes bibliographical references (pages 239-277) and index.

Westhoff, Ben
Fentanyl, Inc.: How Rogue Chemists Are Creating the Deadliest Wave of the Opioid Epidemic. Ben Westhoff. Atlantic Monthly Press 2019. 288 p.
ISBN 9780802127433
Grades: Adult   362.29
1. Opioid epidemic 2. Drug control 3. Drug industry and trade 4. Chemical industry and trade 5. Opioid abuse 6. Drug overdoses 7. Cartels 8. Drug dealers 9. Drug addicts 10. Law enforcement 11. Society and culture — Illness and disease — Addiction 12. Society and culture — Violence and crime 13. Politics and global affairs — Public health

LC 2019033267

An in-depth investigation into the dangerous world of synthetic drugs predicts a next wave in the opioid epidemic while examining the roles of black-market Chinese drug factories, European harm reduction activists and American dealers and users.

Includes bibliographical references and index.

362.292 Alcohol

Johnston, Ann Dowsett
Drink: The Intimate Relationship Between Women and Alcohol. Ann Dowsett Johnston. HarperWave 2013. 256 p.
ISBN 9780062241795
Grades: Adult   362.292
1. Johnston, Ann Dowsett 2. Women 3. Alcoholic women 4. Drinking 5. Addiction 6. Rehabilitation 7. Alcohol 8. Autobiographies and memoirs 9. Canadian literature 10. Science Writing — Medicine and health — Addiction 11. Life stories — Facing adversity — Medical issues — Addiction 12. Society and culture — Illness and disease — Addiction

LC 2013026103

An exploration of the rise in alcohol consumption and abuse among women in recent years. Drink covers health risks, marketing, current trends and sociological underpinnings of this new epidemic. The author beautifully weaves reportage with her personal recovery story into a compelling and informative narrative addressing one of the most pressing issues for women today.

362.4 People with physical disabilities

Blake, Melissa
Beautiful People: My Thirteen Truths About Disability. Melissa Blake. Hachette Go 2024. xiv, 256 pages : Illustration
ISBN 9780306830426
Grades: Adult   362.4
1. Blake, Melissa (Blogger) 2. Women journalists 3. People with disabilities 4. Marginalized people 5. Ableism 6. Bullies and bullying 7. Trolls (Online) 8. Human rights activists 9. Disability rights movement 10. Advocacy for people with disabilities 11. Empowerment 12. Social acceptance 13. Social justice 14. American people 15. Autobiographies and memoirs 16. Life stories — Facing adversity — Medical issues — Living with disabilities 17. Life stories — Identity 18. Science Writing — Medicine and health — Disabilities and disorders 19. Society and culture — General

LC Bl2024005150

The disability activist and social media influencer shares her story of living with a genetic bone and muscular disorder and the struggles that millions like her face in a society that makes them feel invisible.

"Throughout the book, the author is ebullient, humorous, and compassionate, balancing exuberant optimism and joie de vivre with crystal-clear convictions and a deeply critical eye." —*Kirkus*

Includes bibliographical references (pages 247-256).

Kisor, Henry
Traveling with Service Animals: By Air, Road, Rail, and Ship Across North America. Henry Kisor and Christine Goodier. University of Illinois Press 2019. xii, 249 pages : Illustration
ISBN 9780252084508
Grades: Adult   362.4
1. Working animals 2. Animals 3. People with disabilities 4. Travel writing — General 5. Society and culture — General

LC 2019014752

"Chicago Sun-Times columnist Kisor and freelance travel writer Goodier, both seasoned travelers with service dogs, offer a guide for those wishing to do the same. Only dogs and miniature horses are recognized by the U.S. government as service animals. Coverage is for North America only, and includes chapters on air travel (getting through TSA, negotiating airports), train travel (finding elusive potty stops), cruise ships (dining and onshore excursions), and on the road, including buses." —*Library Journal*

Includes index.

Sjunneson, Elsa

Being Seen: One Deafblind Woman's Fight to End Ableism. Elsa Sjunneson. Tiller Press 2021. 256 p.

ISBN 9781982152376

Grades: Adult   362.4

1. Sjunneson, Elsa, 1985- 2. People with disabilities 3. LGBTQIA+ people 4. Ableism 5. Social marginality 6. Social criticism 7. Social change 8. Women authors 9. People who are blind 10. Women 11. People who are blind and deaf 12. People who are deaf 13. Autobiographies and memoirs 14. Biographies 15. Life stories — Facing adversity — Medical issues — Living with disabilities 16. Life stories — Politics — Activists and reformers 17. Society and culture — General

LC 2021011846

In this blend of memoir, media criticism and cultural critique, the Deafblind writer and four-time Hugo Award finalist discusses how the media represents disability in books, movies and TV, as well as her efforts to fight ableism.

"In this sharp and thought-provoking memoir, Sjunneson, who describes herself as Deafblind and queer, shares anecdotes and insights about growing up in an ableist world." —*Booklist*

Includes bibliographical references.

362.4083 Children with disabilities — Social welfare

Solomon, Andrew

Far from the Tree: Parents, Children and the Search for Identity. Andrew Solomon. Scribner 2012. 672 p.

ISBN 9780743236713

Grades: Adult   362.4083

1. Children with disabilities 2. Identity 3. Parent and child 4. United States 5. Family and Relationships — Disabled Family Members

LC 2012020878

J. Anthony Lukas Book Prize, 2013; National Book Critics Circle Award for Non-Fiction, 2012; New York Times Notable Book, 2012.

The National Book Award-winning author explores the consequences of extreme personal differences between parents and children, describing his own experiences as a gay child of straight parents while evaluating the circumstances of people affected by physical, developmental or cultural factors that divide families.

Includes bibliographical references and index.

362.40973 Children with disabilities — United States

Nielsen, Kim E.

A Disability History of the United States. Kim E. Nielsen. Beacon Press 2012. 272 p.

ISBN 9780807022023

Grades: Adult   362.40973

1. People with disabilities 2. Disabilities 3. Sociology 4. Social history 5. Science Writing — Medicine and health — Disabilities and disorders

LC 2012014236

Covers the entirety of disability history, from pre-1492 to the present.

"American history examined sensitively and skillfully from the bottom up, grounded in the often shabby and sometimes exemplary treatment of disabled individuals.... A lively historical record that fills a gap in the literature." —*Kirkus*

Includes bibliographical references and index.

362.5 Poor people

Adler, Kevin F.

When We Walk By: Forgotten Humanity, Broken Systems, and the Role We Can Each Play in Ending Homelessness in America. Kevin F. Adler and Donald W. Burnes, with Amanda Banh and Andrijana Bilbija. North Atlantic Books 2023. xxiii, 299 p.

ISBN 9781623178840

Grades: Adult   362.5

1. Homelessness 2. Homeless people 3. Housing policy 4. Sociology 5. Marginalized people 6. Social isolation 7. Nonprofit organizations 8. Empathy 9. Social advocacy 10. United States 11. Society and culture — Wealth and class — Poverty 12. Society and culture — Social activism and philanthropy

LC 2023017244

When We Walk by takes an urgent look at homelessness in America, showing us what we lose—in ourselves and as a society—when we choose to walk past and ignore our neighbors in shelters, insecure housing, or on the streets. And it brilliantly shows what we stand to gain when we embrace our humanity and move toward evidence-based people-first, community-driven solutions, offering social analysis, economic and political histories, and the real stories of unhoused people. Authors Kevin F. Adler and Donald W. Burnes recast chronic homelessness in the U.S. as a byproduct of twin crises: Our social services systems are failing, and so is our humanity.

"This comprehensive overview of homelessness offers updates on current research, analysis, and solution-oriented practices, all presented through an especially empathetic lens." —*Booklist*

Includes bibliographical references (p. 242 -288) and index.

Coombes, Joshua

Do Something for Nothing: Seeing Beneath the Surface of Homelessness, Through the Simple Act of a Haircut. Joshua Coombes. Akashic Books 2021. 217 p. : Illustration

ISBN 9781617759352

Grades: Adult   362.5

1. Coombes, Joshua 2. Hairdressers 3. Homeless people 4. Haircutting 5. Love 6. Shame 7. Resilience 8. Homelessness 9. Stigma (Social psychology) 10. Toleration 11. Kindness 12. Autobiographies and memoirs 13. Life stories — General 14. Society and culture — Wealth and class — Poverty

In 2015, while working at a London hair salon, Joshua Coombes took to the streets with his scissors to build relationships with people sleeping rough in the capital. This inspired him to begin posting transformative images on social media to amplify their voices. These stories resonated and thousands of people got involved in their own way. #DoSomethingForNothing was born—a movement that encourages people to connect their skills and time to those who need it. Via the simple act of a haircut, readers are taken on a geographical and emotional journey into the lives of humans experiencing homelessness in different cities across the world.

"In this uplifting book, Coombes deftly illustrates how reaching out and listening can break down barriers in an often indifferent world." —*Booklist*

Desmond, Matthew

★ *Poverty, by America.* Matthew Desmond. Crown 2023. 288 p.

ISBN 9780593239919

Grades: Adult   362.5

1. Poverty 2. Wealth 3. Social marginality 4. Income inequality 5. Wages 6. Corporate power 7. Governmental reform 8. Social advocacy 9. Economics 10. United States 11. Society and culture — Wealth and class — Poverty 12. Society and culture — General 13. Book club best bets

The United States, the richest country on earth, has more poverty than any other advanced democracy. Why? In this landmark book, acclaimed sociologist Matthew Desmond draws on history, research, and original reporting to show how affluent Americans knowingly and unknowingly keep poor people poor. Elegantly written and fiercely argued, this compassionate book gives us new ways of thinking about a morally urgent problem.

ESSENTIAL AND RECOMMENDED TITLES
362.60973 Older people — Social welfare — United States

"This thoughtful investigation of a critically important subject, a piercing title by an astute writer who is both passionate and fearless, is valuable reading for all concerned with affecting positive change." —*Booklist*

Kidder, Tracy
★ *Rough Sleepers: Dr. Jim O'Connell's Urgent Mission to Bring Healing to Homeless People.* Tracy Kidder. Random House 2022. 320 p.
ISBN 9781984801432
Grades: Adult   362.5
1. Physicians 2. Homelessness 3. Homeless people 4. Physician and patient 5. Healing 6. Boston, Massachusetts 7. Massachusetts 8. Autobiographies and memoirs 9. Society and culture — Wealth and class — Poverty 10. Life stories — Science, technology, and medicine — Healthcare professionals

Tells the story of an inspiring doctor who made a difference by helping to create a program to care for Boston's homeless community.

"Keenly observed and fluidly written, this is a compassionate report from the front lines of one of America's most intractable social problems." —*Publishers Weekly*

Kozol, Jonathan
Rachel and Her Children: Homeless Families in America. Jonathan Kozol. Crown Publishers 1988. IX, 261 p.
ISBN 9780449903391
Grades: 11 12 Adult   362.5
1. Homeless people 2. Poor people 3. Poverty 4. Society and culture — Wealth and class — Poverty
LC 87022273
Robert F. Kennedy Book Award, 1989.

Argues that homelessness is caused by the lack of low-cost housing, describes the experiences of the homeless, and explains why the current welfare system is inadequate and misdirected.

"While the individual stories that Kozol tells so affectingly point out the vivid realities of urban poverty, the book also supplies statistics that detail the more abstract-and inhuman-attitudes that contemporary society assumes when attempting to deal with its victims." —*Booklist*

Includes bibliographical references (p. 249-252) and index.

Messenger, Tony
Profit and Punishment: How America Criminalizes the Poor in the Name of Justice. Tony Messenger. St. Martin's Press 2021. 320 p.
ISBN 9781250274649
Grades: Adult   362.5
1. Poor people 2. Criminal justice system 3. Criminal justice reform 4. Poverty 5. Inequality 6. United States 7. Society and culture — Violence and crime — Criminal justice system 8. Society and culture — Wealth and class — Poverty
LC 2021034260

Anchored by stories of three single mothers living in poverty, a Pulitzer Prize winner, in a feat of exceptional reporting, presents a comprehensive look at modern-day debtor's prisons and how they've destroyed the lives of poor Americans.

"Profit and Punishment is persuasive and enraging, a book that will stir readers from both sides of the aisle to support reform." —*Booklist*

Includes bibliographical references and index.

Sokolik, Vicki
★ *If You See Them: Young, Unhoused, and Alone in America.* Vicki Sokolik. Spiegel & Grau 2024. 336 p.
ISBN 9781954118492
Grades: Adult   362.5
1. Homelessness 2. Poverty 3. Homeless children 4. Homeless teenagers 5. Homeless people 6. Shelters for the homeless 7. Social advocates 8. Social advocacy 9. Social action 10. Community activism 11. American people 12. North American people 13. Florida 14. Autobiographies and memoirs 15. Society and culture — Wealth and class — Poverty 16. Society and culture — Urban and regional studies 17. Life stories — Facing adversity

A moving exploration of the crisis of homeless youth—told through the inspiring stories of a woman on the frontlines and the kids themselves.

"Brutally realistic and never preachy, Sokolik advocates strongly for these needy, overlooked children." —*Booklist*

362.60973 Older people — Social welfare — United States

Aronson, Louise
Elderhood: Redefining Aging, Transforming Medicine, Reimagining Life. Louise Aronson. Bloomsbury Publishing 2019. 446 p.
ISBN 9781620405468
Grades: Adult   362.60973
1. Seniors 2. Aging 3. Medical care 4. Geriatrics 5. Health 6. Family and Relationships — Aging and Death 7. Science Writing — Medicine and health
LC 2018040491
ALA Notable Book, 2020; Pulitzer Prize for General Nonfiction finalist, 2020.

Reminiscent of Oliver Sacks, noted Harvard-trained geriatrician Louise Aronson uses stories from her quarter century of caring for patients, and draws from history, science, literature, popular culture, and her own life to weave a vision of old age that's neither nightmare nor utopian fantasy—a vision full of joy, wonder, frustration, outrage, and hope about aging, medicine, and humanity itself.

"Aronson's deep empathy, hard-won knowledge, and vivid reportage makes for one of the best accounts around of the medical mistreatment of the old." —*Publishers Weekly*

Includes bibliographical references.

362.7 Young people

Benforado, Adam
A Minor Revolution: How Prioritizing Kids Benefits Us All. Adam Benforado. Crown 2023. 384 p.
ISBN 9781984823045
Grades: Adult   362.7
1. Children's rights 2. Child abuse 3. Child welfare 4. United States 5. Society and culture — Social activism and philanthropy
LC 2022026405

A revelatory investigation into how America is failing its children, and an urgent manifesto on why helping them is the best way to improve all of our lives—from the New York Times bestselling author of Unfair: The New Science of Criminal Injustice.

"Deeply researched and passionately argued, this is an irrefutable call for change." —*Publishers Weekly*

Includes bibliographical references and index.

Edelman, Marian Wright
Lanterns: A Memoir of Mentors. Marian Wright Edelman. Beacon Press 1999. xxi, 180 p. : Illustration
ISBN 9780807072141
Grades: Adult   362.7
1. Edelman, Marian Wright, 1939- 2. Mentoring 3. African American women social reformers 4. Personal conduct 5. Children 6. Autobiographies and memoirs 7. Life stories — Relationships 8. History writing — African American — United States
LC 99044228

The African American lawyer and president of the Children's Defense Fund describes the positive influences of family, church members, teachers, colleagues, and other social reformers in her life.

"Throughout this absorbing memoir, Edelman's voice resounds with spirituality, a reliance on her faith, and a belief in equality." —*Booklist*

Includes bibliographical references (p. 177-180).

Elliott, Andrea
★ *Invisible Child: Poverty, Survival, and Hope in an American City.* Andrea Elliott. Random House 2021. 448 p.

ISBN 9780812986945
Grades: Adult   362.7
1. Coates, Dasani, 2001- 2. Homeless children 3. African American children 4. Homelessness 5. Shelters for the homeless 6. Violence 7. Poverty 8. Addiction 9. Gentrification of cities 10. Education 11. Survival 12. Marginalized children 13. New York City 14. New York (State) 15. Biographies 16. Life stories — Facing adversity 17. Society and culture — Wealth and class — Poverty
LC 2021012357
J. Anthony Lukas Book Prize, 2022; Pulitzer Prize for General Nonfiction, 2022.

A Pulitzer Prize-winning reporter follows eight years in the life of a young girl in Brooklyn as her family navigates the world of homeless shelters, violence and addiction, as well as her eventual enrollment in a Pennsylvania boarding school.

"Expanding on her five-part series on child homelessness that appeared in the New York Times in 2013, this absorbing debut by Pulitzer Prize-winning investigative reporter Elliott follows Dasani, the oldest of eight siblings, between 2012 and 2020." —*Library Journal*

Includes index.

Hayasaki, Erika
Somewhere Sisters: A Story of Adoption, Identity, and the Meaning of Family. Erika Hayasaki. Algonquin Books of Chapel Hill 2022. 320 p.
ISBN 9781616209124
Grades: Adult   362.7
1. Vietnamese American children 2. Twin sisters 3. Adopted children 4. International adoption 5. Identity 6. Families 7. Family relationships 8. Sisters 9. Identical twins 10. Collective biographies 11. Life stories — Relationships — Family 12. Family and relationships — Parenting — Adoption 13. Society and culture — General
LC 2022018472

Identical twins Isabella and Hà were born in Vietnam and raised on opposite sides of the world, each knowing little about the other's existence, until they were reunited as teenagers, against all odds.

"Fascinating and moving on its own, the sisters' complex story of growing up, both together and apart, is complemented by Hayasaki's illumination of the personal, psychological, and sociocultural realities of adoption." —*Booklist*

Includes bibliographical references.

Lockhart, Chris
★ *Walking* the Bowl: A True Story of Murder and Survival Among the Street Children of Lusaka. Chris Lockhart and Daniel Mulilo Chama. Hanover Square Press 2022. 304 p.
ISBN 9781335425744
Grades: Adult   362.7
1. Murder investigation 2. Murder victims 3. Homeless children 4. Violence 5. Urban poor people 6. Inequality 7. Survival 8. Poverty 9. Poor people 10. Marginalized children 11. Zambia 12. Life stories — Facing adversity 13. True Crime — Murder 14. Society and culture — Wealth and class — Poverty

For readers of Behind the Beautiful Forevers and Nothing to Envy, this is a breathtaking real-life story of four street children in contemporary Zambia whose lives are drawn together and forever altered by the mysterious murder of a fellow street child. Based on years of investigative reporting and unprecedented fieldwork, Walking the Bowl immerses readers in the daily lives of four unforgettable characters: Lusabilo, a determined waste picker; Kapula, a burned-out brothel worker; Moonga, a former rock crusher turned beggar; and Timo, an ambitious gang leader. These children navigate the violent and poverty-stricken underworld of Lusaka, one of Africa's fastest growing cities. When the dead body of a ten-year-old boy is discovered under a heap of garbage in Lusaka's largest landfill, a murder investigation quickly heats up due to the influence of the victim's mother and her far-reaching political connections. The children's lives become more closely intertwined as each child engages in a desperate bid for survival against forces they could never have imagined. Gripping and fast-paced, the book exposes the perilous aspects of street life through the eyes of the children who survive, endure and dream there, and what emerges is an ultimately hopeful story about human kindness and how one small good deed, passed on to others, can make a difference in the face of seemingly insurmountable odds.

"Fans of Behind the Beautiful Forevers and Strength in What Remains will flock to this riveting and deeply reported portrait of life on the margins." —*Publishers Weekly*

Pryce, Jessica
★ *Broken:* Transforming Child Protective Services—notes of a Former Caseworker. Jessica Pryce. Amistad Press 2024. 256 p.
ISBN 9780063036192
Grades: Adult   362.7
1. Pryce, Jessica 2. Child welfare 3. Social workers 4. Child protective services 5. African American families 6. Poor people 7. Racism 8. Unconscious bias 9. Psychic trauma 10. Parent-separated children 11. Social advocacy 12. Welfare reform 13. Family and Relationships — Families 14. Life stories — Politics — Activists and reformers 15. Society and culture — General

Dr. Jessica Pryce knows the child welfare system firsthand and, in this long overdue book, breaks it down from the inside out, sharing her professional journey and offering the crucial perspectives of caseworkers and Black women impacted by the system. In the book, she walks alongside her close friends and even her family as they navigate the system, while sharing her own reckoning with the requirements of her job and her role in the systemic harm. With a renewed commitment to strengthening families in her role as activist, Pryce invites the child welfare workforce to embark on a journey of self-reflection and radical growth.

"Parents and child-welfare professionals will benefit from this excellent work that gives an insider's view of child protective services. Pair with We Were Once a Family by Roxanna Asgarian." —*Library Journal*

Roberts, Dorothy E.
Torn Apart: How the Child Welfare System Destroys Black Families—and How Abolition Can Build a Safer World. Dorothy Roberts. Basic Books 2022. 384 p.
ISBN 9781541675445
Grades: Adult   362.7
1. Child welfare 2. African American families 3. Social work 4. Racism 5. Legislation 6. United States 7. Society and culture — Race 8. Society and culture — Social activism and philanthropy
LC 2021036512

An award-winning scholar exposes the foundational racism of the child welfare system and calls for radical change Many believe the child welfare system protects children from abuse. But as Torn Apart uncovers, this system is designed to punish Black families. Drawing on decades of research, legal scholar and sociologist Dorothy Roberts reveals that the child welfare system is better understood as a "family policing system" that collaborates with law enforcement and prisons to oppress Black communities. Child protection investigations ensnare a majority of Black children, putting their families under intense state surveillance and regulation. Black children are disproportionately likely to be torn from their families and placed in foster care, driving many to juvenile detention and imprisonment. The only way to stop the destruction caused by family policing, Torn Apart argues, is to abolish the child welfare system and liberate Black communities.

"Readers at every level, especially policy-makers and -implementers, might well embrace this work as a primer for moving past a harmful system and creating a reimagined ideology and infrastructure to humanely care for families and keep children safe. Roberts's latest is necessary reading." —*Library Journal*

Includes bibliographical references and index.

Saldana, Stephanie
What We Remember Will Be Saved: A Story of Refugees and the Things They Carry. Stephanie Saldaña. Broadleaf Books 2023. xiv, 280 p.
ISBN 9781506484211
Grades: Adult   362.7
1. Refugees 2. Forced relocations 3. Personal belongings 4. Loss 5. Memory 6. Culture 7. Oral tradition 8. Immigration and emigration 9. Refugee camps 10. Home (Concept) 11. Resilience 12. Southwest Asian (Middle Eastern) people 13. Syrian people 14. Iraqi people 15. Syria 16. Iraq 17. Europe 18. Life sto-

ESSENTIAL AND RECOMMENDED TITLES
362.7086 Young people by miscellaneous social attributes

ries — Facing adversity — War and oppression — Refugees 19. Society and culture — Ethnic studies

LC 2022056982

Eggplant seeds, a lullaby in a vanishing language, an embroidered dress. When people flee their homes, the things they save speak of beauty and suffering and the indomitable human spirit. In an era of mass migration in which more than 100 million people are displaced comes this lyrical portrait of Syrian and Iraqi refugees and the belongings they carry. What We Remember Will Be Saved is a book of hope, home, and the stories we hold within us when everything else has been lost.

"Readers won't soon forget the compelling stories of these brave individuals, revealed so poignantly by Saldaña's beautiful writing." —*Booklist*

Includes bibliographical references.

362.7086 Young people by miscellaneous social attributes

Madrick, Jeffrey G
Invisible Americans: The Tragic Cost of Child Poverty. Jeff Madrick. Random House Inc 2020. 240 pages
ISBN 9780451494184
Grades: Adult   362.7086
1. Poor children 2. Child welfare 3. Poor people 4. Economic policy 5. Racism 6. Poverty 7. United States 8. Society and culture — Wealth and class — Poverty

LC 2019022606

Citing the alarming percentage of children who live in poverty in today's America, an urgent report examines contributing factors, including government indifference, a failing social welfare system and entrenched racism, while outlining a politically feasible option for next steps.

"With passionate advocacy, Madrick addresses a systemic problem with a simple solution. His argument will appeal to those who champion economic policy change that centers the child." —*Library Journal*

Includes index.

362.73 Institutional and related services

Kenneally, Christine
Ghosts of the Orphanage: A Story of Mysterious Deaths, a Conspiracy of Silence, and a Search for Justice. Christine Kenneally. PublicAffairs 2023. 304 p.
ISBN 9781541758513
Grades: Adult   362.73
1. Orphanages 2. Child abuse 3. Psychic trauma 4. Violence 5. Death 6. Justice 7. Orphans 8. United States history 9. 20th century 10. True Crime — Murder 11. Family and relationships — Abuse 12. History Writing — United States

LC 2022026574

NSW Premier's Literary Awards, Douglas Stewart Prize for Non Fiction, 2024.

An award-winning journalist and author exposes the horrible events that took place in twentieth-century orphanages using the stories of survivors who expose the violence, abuse, trauma and deaths that were commonplace and their quests for justice.

"An important look into the dark past of orphanages globally. It's also a deep dive into the ways these horrific stories were kept out of the public eye for so long." —*Library Journal*

Includes bibliographical references and index.

Leach, Samantha
★ *The Elissas: Three Girls, One Fate, and the Deadly Secrets of Suburbia.* Samantha Leach. Legacy Lit 2023. 256 p.
ISBN 9780306826917
Grades: Adult   362.73
1. Teenage girls 2. At-risk youth 3. Female friendship 4. Privilege (Social psychology) 5. Opioid abuse 6. Addiction 7. Self-destructive behavior 8. Institutional care 9. Death of women 10. Loss 11. Youth culture 12. Social pressure 13. Suburban life 14. Life stories — Relationships — Growing up 15. Life stories — Facing adversity — Medical issues — Addiction 16. Life stories — Facing adversity — Coping with death 17. Society and culture — General 18. Debut title

LC 2022057941

A writer seeking to understand the death of her childhood best friend Elissa, focuses on her last years at a therapeutic boarding school and discovers Elissa's closest friends who shared both her name and a penchant for partying also died, offering a chilling account of the secret lives of young suburban women.

"A poignant and heartfelt mix of sociology and memoir." —*Kirkus*

Moody, Anne
The Children Money Can Buy: Stories from the Frontlines of Foster Care and Adoption. Anne Moody. Rowman & Littlefield 2018. 266 p.
ISBN 9781538108024
Grades: Adult   362.73
1. Foster home care 2. Adoption 3. Foster children 4. Adoptive families 5. Child welfare 6. Family and Relationships — Parenting — Adoption 7. Society and culture — General

LC 2017034191

Foster care and adoption can be rewarding ways to become parents. But the system itself seems almost rigged for failure, confusion, fraud, and disappointment. This book takes readers on an insider's tour of the system, its successes and failures, and the joys adoption can bring through the real stories of those involved on all sides.

Includes index.

362.734 Adoption

Guida-Richards, Melissa
What White Parents Should Know About Transracial Adoption: An Adoptee's Perspective on Its History, Nuances, and Practices. Melissa Guida-Richards; forward by Paula Guida. North Atlantic Books 2021. 200 p.
ISBN 9781623175825
Grades: Adult   362.734
1. Interracial adoption 2. International adoption 3. Adoptive parents 4. Adopted children 5. Interracial families 6. Ethnic identity 7. Race awareness in children 8. Psychology 9. Family and Relationships — Parenting — Adoption 10. Society and culture — Race 11. Society and culture — Ethnic studies

LC 2021019827

A guide for white parents of transracially or transnationally adopted children.

"A much-needed volume from an adoptee's perspective; sure to be a must-read for parents who adopt. Recommend alongside Nicole Chung's memoir All You Can Ever Know." —*Library Journal*

Includes bibliographical references and index.

Sisson, Gretchen E.
★ *Relinquished: The Politics of Adoption and the Privilege of American Motherhood.* Gretchen Sisson. St. Martin's Press 2024. 320 p.
ISBN 9781250286772
Grades: Adult   362.734
1. Adoption 2. Motherhood 3. Parenting 4. Birthparents 5. Reproductive rights 6. Women's rights 7. Feminism 8. American people 9. North American people 10. United States 11. Interviews 12. Family and Relationships — Parenting — Adoption 13. Society and culture — Gender — Women — Reproductive rights

LC 2023036051

Rooted in long-term study, this powerful analysis of hundreds of heartrending interviews with American mothers who placed their children for domestic adoption reveals adoption to be a constrained choice for those for whom abortion is inaccessible, or for whom parenthood is untenable.

"The result is a devastating and urgent condemnation of America's adoption industry." —*Publishers Weekly*

Includes bibliographical references and index.

PUBLIC LIBRARY CORE COLLECTION: NONFICTION
Twentieth Edition

362.76092 Abused children — Social welfare — Biography

Glatt, John
The Family Next Door: The Heartbreaking Imprisonment of the 13 Turpin Siblings and Their Extraordinary Rescue. John Glatt. St. Martin's Press 2019. 320 p.
ISBN 9781250202130
Grades: Adult   362.76092
1. Turpin, David Allen, 1961- 2. Turpin, Louise Ann, 1968- 3. Child abuse 4. Child abuse victims 5. Captives 6. Family violence 7. Child abusers 8. Courage in children 9. Families 10. California 11. True Crime — Domestic Crime
LC 2019006614

An investigative journalist details the disturbing case of Louise and David Turpin who outwardly displayed the perfect picture of domestic bliss, but in reality perpetrated shocking abuse, including isolation, torture and near starvation on their thirteen children.

"This chilling portrayal of abuse and secrecy may leave readers looking differently at their neighbors." —*Publishers Weekly*

362.77 Social problems of and services to young people

Kozol, Jonathan
Fire in the Ashes: Twenty-five Years Among the Poorest Children in America. Jonathan Kozol. Random House 2012. 368 p.
ISBN 9781400052462
Grades: Adult   362.77
1. Inequality 2. Urban schools 3. Poor children 4. Poverty 5. Inner city 6. Poor families 7. Marginalized people 8. Urban education 9. Education 10. Race (Social sciences) 11. Child welfare 12. Children 13. United States 14. 21st century 15. Society and culture — Education 16. Society and culture — Race 17. Society and culture — Wealth and class — Poverty
LC 2012005183
Booklist Editors' Choice, 2012.

Continuing the stories of inner-city children he has known for many years, the author shares the personal journeys of youths who have struggled to work through formidable racial and economic inequalities while approaching adulthood.

362.82 Families

Fessler, Ann
The Girls Who Went Away: The Hidden History of Women Who Surrendered Children for Adoption in the Decades Before Roe V. Wade. Ann Fessler. Penguin Press 2006. 354 p.
ISBN 9781594200946
Grades: Adult   362.82
1. Birthmothers 2. Adoption 3. Unplanned pregnancy 4. Single mothers 5. 1950s 6. 1960s 7. Family and Relationships — Parenting — Adoption 8. Adult books for young adults
LC 2005058179
Booklist Editors' Choice, 2006; National Book Critics Circle Award for Nonfiction finalist, 2006.

This book brings to light the lives of 1.5 million single American women in the years following World War II who, under enormous social and family pressure, were coerced to give up their newborn children. It tells not of wild and carefree sexual liberation, but rather of a devastating double standard that has had punishing long-term effects on these women and on the children they gave up. Single pregnant women were shunned by family and friends, evicted from schools, sent away to maternity homes to have their children alone, and often treated with cold contempt by doctors, nurses, and clergy. The majority of the women interviewed by Fessler, herself an adoptee, have never spoken of their experiences, and most have been haunted by grief and shame their entire adult lives.

"These knowing oral histories are an emotional boon for birth mothers and adoptees struggling to make sense of troubled pasts." —*Publishers Weekly*
Includes bibliographical references and index.

Snyder, Rachel Louise
No Visible Bruises: What We Don't Know About Domestic Violence Can Kill Us. Rachel Louise Snyder. Bloomsbury Publishing 2019. VIII, 307 pages
ISBN 9781635570977
Grades: Adult   362.82
1. Family violence 2. Family violence victims 3. Violence against women 4. Abused women 5. Partner abuse 6. Public health 7. Family and Relationships — Abuse 8. Society and culture — Gender — Women

Library Journal Best Books, 2019; New York Times Notable Book, 2019; National Book Critics Circle Award for Nonfiction finalist, 2019; Kirkus Prize for Nonfiction finalist, 2019.

A journalist explores America's epidemic of domestic violence and how it has been misunderstood, sharing insights into what domestic violence portends about other types of violence and what countermeasures are needed today.

Although domestic violence is a difficult subject, this sympathetic look at victims, perpetrators, and intervention efforts by law enforcement and social agencies makes for compelling reading. Journalist Snyder takes readers beyond headlines and mind-numbing statistics, sharing specific cases brought to life through her thorough research.' —*Booklist*

Includes bibliographical references (pages 285-297) and index.

362.83 Social problems of and services to groups of people — Women

Freeman, Amanda
Getting Me Cheap: How Low-wage Work Traps Women and Girls in Poverty. Amanda Freeman and Lisa Dodson. The New Press 2022. 256 p.
ISBN 9781620977422
Grades: Adult   362.83
1. Poor women 2. Poor people 3. Minimum wage 4. Low-wage workers 5. Poverty 6. Economics 7. United States 8. Society and culture — Wealth and class — Poverty 9. Society and culture — Gender
LC 2022025494

Sociologists Lisa Dodson and Amanda Freeman follow women in the food, health care, home care, and other low-wage industries as they struggle to balance mothering with bad jobs and without public aid. While these women tend to the needs of well-off families, their own children frequently step into premature adult roles, providing care for siblings and aging family members. Based on years of in-depth field work and hundreds of eye-opening interviews, Getting Me Cheap explores how America traps millions of women and their children into lives of stunted opportunity and poverty in service of giving others of us the lives we seek.

"Readers will leave with a better understanding of the complexity of the lives of women working in low-wage jobs and what needs to change to provide them with the support they need." —*Library Journal*

Includes bibliographical references and index.

Goudeau, Jessica
★ *After the Last Border: Two Families and the Story of Refuge in America.* Jessica Goudeau. Viking 2020. 336 p.
ISBN 9780525559139
Grades: Adult   362.83
1. Women refugees 2. American Dream 3. Immigration policy 4. Refugee policy 5. Immigration and emigration law 6. Christian women 7. Muslim women 8. United States history 9. Austin, Texas 10. 21st century 11. Society and culture — Immigration 12. Politics and global affairs — Immigration
LC 2019033736

J. Anthony Lukas Book Prize, 2021.

Documents the intimate stories of two refugees in present-day Texas, describing how a Christian from Myanmar and a Muslim from Syria narrowly es-

ESSENTIAL AND RECOMMENDED TITLES
362.87 Displaced persons

caped their home countries only to be introduced to the worst and best of the American dream.

"An excellent choice for readers seeking to understand the human effects of government immigration and refugee policy. Goudeau's sometimes heartbreaking narratives personalize the refugee crisis in ways cold news accounts cannot." —*Library Journal*

Includes bibliographical references and index.

Isenberg, Sheila
Women Who Love Men Who Kill: 35 True Stories of Prison Passion. Sheila Isenberg. Diversion Books 2021. 256 p.

ISBN 9781635768091

Grades: Adult   **362.83**

1. Mate selection for women 2. Prisoners 3. Death row prisoners 4. Murderers 5. Romantic love 6. Letter writing 7. Dating 8. Online dating 9. Men-women relations 10. True Crime — Murder 11. Life stories — Law and order — Prisoners and inmates 12. Life stories — Relationships — Couples 13. Family and Relationships — Dating and Marriage

At once disturbing and fascinating, Women Who Love Men Who Kill is a compelling psychological study of prison passion in the new millennium. Through extensive research and interviews with women who seek relationships with convicted killers through snail and e-mail, and through conversations with psychiatrists, social workers, and prison officials, Isenberg sheds light on why these women are drawn into relationships with incarcerated outcasts.

"Isenberg updates her groundbreaking 1991 volume about women who seek out relationships with men incarcerated on murder charges. . . . Isenberg's is a compelling, research-driven book." —*Library Journal*

Originally published: New York : Simon & Schuster, 1991.

Kristof, Nicholas D.
Half the Sky: Turning Oppression into Opportunity for Women Worldwide. Nicholas D. Kristof and Sheryl WuDunn. Alfred A. Knopf 2009. xxii, 294 p. : Illustration

ISBN 9780307267146

Grades: Adult   **362.83**

1. Women's rights 2. Crimes against women 3. Women 4. Human rights 5. Oppression (Psychology) 6. Political persecution 7. Violence against marginalized women 8. Intersectionality 9. Developing countries 10. Page to screen 11. Society and culture — Gender — Women

Amelia Bloomer List, 2010.

Two Pulitzer Prize winners issue a call to action against our era's most pervasive human rights violation: the oppression of women in the developing world. They show that a little help can transform the lives of women and girls abroad and that the key to economic progress lies in unleashing women's potential.

Includes bibliographical references (p. 259-278) and index.

362.87 Displaced persons

Bittle, Jake
★ *The Great Displacement: Climate Change and the Next American Migration.* Jake Bittle. Simon & Schuster 2023. 320 p.

ISBN 9781982178253

Grades: Adult   **362.87**

1. Climate change 2. Natural disasters 3. Environmental disasters 4. Environmental forecasting 5. Droughts 6. Wildfires 7. Floods 8. Migration, Internal 9. Refugees 10. Displacement (Psychology) 11. Disaster relief 12. Environmental policy 13. Environmental degradation 14. United States 15. Nature Writing — Environmental Issues 16. Politics and global affairs — Environmental issues and policies 17. Life stories — Facing adversity — War and oppression — Refugees 18. Debut title

A human-centered narrative with national scope, this first book to report on climate migration in the U.S. tells the stories of those already experiencing life on the move, while detailing just how radically climate change with transform our lives.

"Presenting powerful and moving evidence, the author ends with a plea for comprehensive environmental policy change and urgent action." —*Booklist*

Nayeri, Dina
★ *The Ungrateful Refugee: What Immigrants Never Tell You.* Dina Nayeri. Catapult 2019. 336 p.

ISBN 9781948226424

Grades: Adult   **362.87**

1. Nayeri, Dina 2. Child refugees 3. Girls 4. Immigrant families 5. Assimilation (Sociology) 6. Identity 7. Immigration and emigration 8. Immigrants 9. Refugees 10. Refugee camps 11. Autobiographies and memoirs 12. Life stories — Facing adversity — War and oppression — Refugees 13. History writing — Immigration — United States 14. Life stories — Arts and culture — Writing — Authors

LC Bl2019020952

Kirkus Prize for Nonfiction finalist, 2019.

The author of Refuge draws on first-person testimonies in an urgent portrait of the refugee crisis that reveals how it happened and the harmful ways that Western governments respond to the inhumane conditions refugees endure.

"Nayeri is unflinching when it comes to the realities of refugee life. The larger notion of the refugee story is considered, and Nayeri deftly explores the balance between truth and storytelling when it comes to the expectations of both the telling and the hearing of these accounts." —*Library Journal*

Paxson, Margaret
The Plateau. Maggie Paxson. Riverhead Books 2019. 368 p.

ISBN 9781594634758

Grades: Adult   **362.87**

1. Paxson, Margaret 2. Refugees 3. Altruism 4. Asylum, Right of 5. World War II 6. Child Refugees 7. Resistance to government 8. Ethics 9. Anthropologists 10. Villages 11. Jewish people 12. French history 13. Le Chambon-sur-Lignon, France 14. France 15. 20th century 16. Autobiographies and memoirs 17. Society and culture — Social activism and philanthropy 18. Life stories — Politics — Activists and reformers 19. History writing — Europe — France

LC 2018050747

In a remote pocket of Nazi-held France, ordinary people risked their lives to rescue many hundreds of strangers, mostly Jewish children. Was this a fluke of history, or something more? Anthropologist Maggie Paxson, certainties shaken by years of studying strife, arrives on the Plateau to explore this phenomenon: what are the traits that make a group choose selflessness?

"Throughout, Paxson keeps asking questions and probing, never settling for assumptions. An elegant, intensive study that grapples with an enormous idea: How to be good." —*Kirkus*

Vince, Gaia
Nomad Century: How Climate Migration Will Reshape Our World. Gaia Vince. Flatiron Books 2022. 336 p.

ISBN 9781250821614

Grades: Adult   **362.87**

1. Climate change 2. Human geography 3. Migration, Internal 4. Global warming 5. Effect of environment on humans 6. Immigration and emigration 7. Nature Writing — Environmental issues 8. Society and culture — General

An urgent investigation of the most underreported, seismic consequence of climate change: How it will force us to change where—and how—we live.

"Journalist Vince (Transcendence) warns of a 'Great upheaval' in global migration resulting from climate change in this bracing clarion call." —*Publishers Weekly*

362.88 Victims of crimes

Belkin, Lisa
Genealogy of a Murder: Four Generations, Three Families, One Fateful Night. Lisa Belkin. W.W. Norton & Company 2023. 416 p.

ISBN 9780393285253

Grades: Adult **362.88**
1. Police 2. Prisoners 3. Parolees 4. Robbery 5. Murder victims 6. Violent crimes 7. Physicians 8. Punishment 9. Rehabilitation 10. Criminal justice system 11. Connecticut 12. 1960s 13. True Crime — Murder 14. Society and culture — Violence and crime — Criminal justice system 15. Life stories — Facing adversity — Victims of crime

The multigenerational tale of three families whose paths collide one summer night in 1960 with the murder of a police officer.

"Journalist Belkin offers a historical example of the 'Butterfly Effect'—the concept that the smallest of individual actions can impact an unknowable number of others—in analyzing a tragedy with intergenerational effects that occurred through a combination of personal responsibility, small decisions, and random circumstances." —*Booklist*

Franscell, Ron
Shadowman: An Elusive Psycho Killer and the Birth of FBI Profiling. Ron Franscell. Berkley 2022. 256 p.
ISBN 9780593199275
Grades: Adult **362.88**
1. Meirhofer, David, 1949-1974 2. Serial murderers 3. Criminal behavior 4. Criminal profiling 5. Criminal psychology 6. Criminal investigation 7. Serial murder investigation 8. United States 9. Montana 10. True Crime — Murder 11. Society and culture — Violence and crime 12. History writing — United States

LC 2021021990

This edge-of-your-seat, real-life thriller tells the true story of the first time in history the FBI created a psychological profile to catch a serial killer—a profile that fit the killer to a T when he was finally caught.

"In this riveting book, Franscell (Alice & Gerald: A Homicidal Love Story) details the crimes that led to the first psychological profile created by the FBI's Behavioral Science Unit.... A thrilling book about the lengths to which investigators went to catch an elusive killer and a pivotal moment in the history of criminal investigation." —*Library Journal*

Includes bibliographical references.

Mar, Alex
Seventy Times Seven: A True Story of Murder and Mercy. Alex Mar. Penguin Press 2023. 400 p.
ISBN 9780525522157
Grades: Adult **362.88**
1. Pelke, Bill 2. Cooper, Paula 3. Pelke, Ruth 4. Murder 5. Forgiveness 6. Murder victims 7. Faith 8. Death row 9. Death row prisoners 10. Justice 11. Criminal justice system 12. African American children 13. Girls 14. 1980s 15. True Crime — Murder 16. History Writing — United States 17. Society and culture — Violence and crime

Weaving an unforgettable narrative of an act of violence and its aftermath, this masterful work recounts the murder of Ruth Pelke, a beloved Bible teacher, at the hands of a 15-year-old Black girl, and the victim's grandson's ensuing campaign to spare her life in the ultimate act of forgiveness.

"Deeply reported and vividly written, this is a harrowing and thought-provoking portrait of crime and punishment." —*Publishers Weekly*

Rose, Jacqueline
On Violence and on Violence Against Women. Jacqueline Rose. Farrar, Straus & Giroux 2021. 368 p.
ISBN 9780374284213
Grades: Adult **362.88**
1. Violence against women 2. Sexual violence 3. Rape 4. Assault and battery 5. Murder 6. Violence against marginalized people 7. Violence against marginalized women 8. Feminism 9. Gender identity 10. Ethnic identity 11. Power 12. Violence 13. Essays 14. Society and culture — Violence and crime 15. Society and culture — Gender

LC 2020057030

Why has violence, and especially violence against women, become so much more prominent and visible across the world? To explore this question, Jacqueline Rose tracks the multiple forms of today's violence—historic and intimate, public and private—as they spread throughout our social fabric, offering a new, provocative account of violence in our time. From trans rights and #MeToo to the sexual harassment of migrant women, from the trial of Oscar Pistorius to domestic violence in lockdown, from the writing of Roxanne Gay to Hisham Mitar and Han Kang, she casts her net wide.

"This is an urgent book that deserves to be read in classes on feminist theory and gender studies. It's also meant for all readers who are interested in learning more about the ways in which power is literally mapped onto our bodies." —*Library Journal*

Rubenhold, Hallie
★ *The Five: The Untold Lives of the Women Killed by Jack the Ripper.* Hallie Rubenhold. Houghton Mifflin Harcourt 2019. VIII, 333 pages : Illustration
ISBN 9781328663818
Grades: Adult **362.88**
1. Jack, the Ripper 2. Women murder victims 3. Working class women 4. Whitechapel murders, 1888 5. Women 6. London, England history 7. Victorian era (1837-1901) 8. 19th century 9. Collective biographies 10. Society and culture — Violence and crime 11. Life stories — Facing adversity — Victims of crime 12. History writing — Women's history 13. True Crime — Historical Crime 14. History writing — Europe — United Kingdom

LC 2018038562

Baillie Gifford Prize for Non-Fiction, 2019.

Researched portraits of the five women murdered by Jack the Ripper in 1888 reveal each victim's historically relevant and diverse background while discussing the cultural and gender disadvantages that made them vulnerable.

"A lively if morbid exercise in Victorian social history essential to students of Ripperiana." —*Kirkus*

Includes bibliographical references (pages 312-323) and index.

362.88086 Victims of crimes — People by miscellaneous social attributes

Yeung, Bernice
In a Day's Work: The Fight to End Sexual Violence Against America's Most Vulnerable Workers. Bernice Yeung. New Press 2018. 272 p.
ISBN 9781620973158
Grades: Adult **362.88086**
1. Sexual harassment 2. Women immigrants 3. Sexual violence victims 4. Sex crimes 5. Workplace violence 6. Society and culture — Gender — Women 7. Society and culture — Violence and crime

LC 2017053297

Amelia Bloomer List, 2019; Pulitzer Prize for General Nonfiction finalist, 2019.

Yeung takes readers on a journey across the country, introducing us to women who came to America to escape grinding poverty only to encounter sexual violence in the United States. In a Day's Work exposes the underbelly of economies filled with employers who take advantage of immigrant women's need to earn a basic living. When these women find the courage to speak up, Yeung reveals, they are too often met by apathetic bosses and underresourced government agencies.

362.88092 Victims of crimes — Biography

Weinman, Sarah
The Real Lolita: The Kidnapping of Sally Horner and the Novel That Scandalized the World. Sarah Weinman. Ecco 2018. xii, 306 pages : Illustration
ISBN 9780062661920
Grades: Adult **362.88092**
1. Nabokov, Vladimir Vladimirovich, 1899-1977 2. Horner, Sally 3. Kidnapping victims 4. Authors 5. Writing 6. Inspiration 7. Kidnapping 8. Eleven-year-old girls 9. 1940s 10. True Crime — Historical Crime

Crime Writers of Canada Awards of Excellence Best Nonfiction Book, 2019; Macavity Award for Best Non-Fiction, 2019.

ESSENTIAL AND RECOMMENDED TITLES
362.883 Rape

A gripping true-crime investigation of the 1948 abduction of Sally Horner details the crime itself and how it inspired Vladimir Nabokov's classic novel, Lolita.

"This intricate balance of journalism and cultural critique is perfect for historical crime readers, feminist scholars, victims' rights advocates, and literature lovers. Recommended as a squirm-inducing read-along with Nabokov's novel." —*Library Journal*

Also published in large print format; Includes bibliographical references and index.

362.883 Rape

Herman, Judith Lewis
Truth and Repair: How Trauma Survivors Envision Justice. Judith L. Herman, MD.. Basic Books 2023. 288 p.
ISBN 9781541600546
Grades: Adult 362.883
1. Sexual violence victims 2. Family violence victims 3. Sex crimes 4. Justice 5. Patriarchy 6. Psychology 7. Violence 8. Psychic trauma 9. Society and culture — Violence and crime 10. Society and culture — Psychology and human behavior
LC 2022046067

From one of America's most influential psychiatrists comes a manifesto for reimagining justice, based on the testimony of trauma survivors.

"An intriguing exploration of alternative methods of justice for trauma survivors." —*Library Journal*

Includes bibliographical references and index.

Krakauer, Jon
Missoula: Rape and the Justice System in a College Town. Jon Krakauer. Doubleday 2015. 384 p.
ISBN 9780385538732
Grades: Adult 362.883
1. Rape 2. Universities and colleges 3. Rape victims 4. Victims of crimes 5. Acquaintance rape 6. Violence in universities and colleges 7. Rape case prosecution 8. Date rape 9. College football 10. Sexism in universities and colleges 11. College student rape victims 12. Injustice 13. Sexism 14. Human rights 15. Civil rights 16. Society and culture — Education — Higher education 17. Society and culture — Violence and crime 18. Adult books for young adults
LC 2015002686

School Library Journal Best Books: Best Adult Books 4 Teens, 2015.

In Missoula, Krakauer chronicles the searing experiences of several women in Missoula—the nights when they were raped; their fear and self-doubt in the aftermath; the way they were treated by the police, prosecutors, defense attorneys; the public vilification and private anguish; their bravery in pushing forward and what it cost them.

"Krakauer has done considerable research into acquaintance rape, and his recounting of trials, both legal and university proceedings, is riveting. His focus on quoting from testimony means that it is harder for readers to understand the motivations of someone like Kirsten Pabst, a former prosecutor who became a lawyer for an accused football player; an interview with her could have been useful. A raw and difficult but necessary read." —*Kirkus*

363 Other social problems and services

Chachra, Deb
How Infrastructure Works: Inside the Systems That Shape Our World. Deb Chachra. Riverhead Books 2023. 336 p.
ISBN 9780593086599
Grades: Adult 363
1. Public works 2. Municipal engineering 3. Infrastructure 4. Inequality 5. Climate change 6. Civil engineering 7. Society and culture — Urban and regional studies 8. Politics and global affairs — Environmental issues and policies 9. Debut title
LC 2023014882

A new way of seeing the essential systems hidden inside our walls, under our streets, and all around us.

"Materials scientist Chachra reminds readers of the ubiquity, endurance, and necessity of infrastructural networks while enthusiastically arguing for their public funding in her insightful debut." —*Publishers Weekly*

Includes bibliographical references and index.

363.1 Public safety programs

Boghosian, Heidi
"I Have Nothing to Hide": And 20 Other Myths About Surveillance and Privacy. Heidi Boghosian. Beacon Press 2021. 240 p.
ISBN 9780807061268
Grades: Adult 363.1
1. Electronic surveillance 2. Communication technology 3. Privacy rights 4. Data protection 5. Technology policy 6. Civil rights 7. National security 8. United States 9. Society and culture — Media and technology 10. Politics and global affairs — Civil and human rights 11. Politics and global affairs — National security
LC 2021006674

Dispels widespread myths about mass surveillance, privacy, and autonomy in the digital age.

"An accessible and informative introduction to the issues surrounding the rise in surveillance technology." —*Publishers Weekly*

Includes bibliographical references.

Singer, Jessie
There Are No Accidents: The Deadly Rise of Injury and Disaster—who Profits and Who Pays the Price. Jessie Singer. Simon & Schuster 2022. 320 p.
ISBN 9781982129668
Grades: Adult 363.1
1. Accidents 2. Inequality 3. Power 4. Wounds and injuries 5. Disasters 6. Accidental death 7. United States 8. History writing — United States 9. Politics and global affairs — General 10. Society and culture — Wealth and class

In this moving investigation of common tragedies, a journalist tracks accidental death in America from turn of the century to today, proving that what we call accidents are hardly random, rather who lives and dies by accident in America is defined by money and power.

"Journalist Singer's work analyzes the increasing incidence of 'Accidental' deaths and injuries in the United States, as exemplified by the 2006 death of her best friend, who was killed on his bike by a drunk driver.... Spanning the genres of business, political science, and public health, Singer's work will challenge readers personally and philosophically." —*Library Journal*

363.11 Occupational and industrial hazards

Hamby, Chris
Soul Full of Coal Dust: A Fight for Breath and Justice in Appalachia. Chris Hamby. Little Brown & Co. 2019. 384 p.
ISBN 9780316299473
Grades: Adult 363.11
1. Corporate cover-ups 2. Coal miners 3. Miners 4. Business corruption 5. Business and economics — Corruption and scandal
LC Bl2018192156

New York Times Notable Book, 2020.

An urgent report by a Pulitzer Prize-winning journalist uncovers the sobering resurgence of black lung disease in Appalachia, the cover-up activities of Big Coal and the awareness activities of regional mining communities.

"Pulitzer Prize-winning investigative reporter Hamby has compiled years of research into his story of coal miners in Appalachia who have endured black lung disease, and of their struggles to secure benefits from coal companies whose purposely hijacked safety procedures had led to their disability.... An engrossing read for those interested in social justice." —*Library Journal*

363.12 Transportation hazards

Gwynne, S. C.
His Majesty's Airship: The Life and Tragic Death of the World's Largest Flying Machine. S. C. Gwynne. Scribner 2023. 416 p.
ISBN 9781982168278
Grades: Adult   363.12
1. Thomson, Christopher Birdwood, Baron, 1875-1930 2. Airships 3. Accidents 4. Air travel 5. English history 6. 20th century 7. History Writing — Europe — United Kingdom 8. History writing — Military — Aviation History
LC 2022058230

The tragic story of the British airship R101—which went down in a spectacular hydrogen-fueled fireball in 1930, killing more people than died in the Hindenburg disaster seven years later—has been largely forgotten. In His Majesty's Airship, historian S.C. Gwynne resurrects it in vivid detail, telling the epic story of great ambition gone terribly wrong.

"Historian Gwynne (Empire of the Summer Moon) delivers a fascinating account of the bad decisions, distractions, naivete, and sheer incompetence behind the crash of the massive British airship R101 in a field outside Beauvais, France, in October 1930." —*Publishers Weekly*

Includes bibliographical references and index.

Leinbach, Michael D.
Bringing Columbia Home: The Final Mission of a Lost Space Shuttle and Her Crew. Michael D. Leinbach, and Jonathan H. Ward. Arcade Publishing 2018. 352 p.
ISBN 9781628728514
Grades: Adult   363.12
1. Space vehicle accidents 2. Space shuttles 3. Space shuttle accidents 4. Explosions 5. Space exploration 6. Astronauts 7. Aviation history 8. History writing — Natural disasters and tragedies 9. History writing — United States
LC 2017046190

Mike Leinbach was the launch director of the space shuttle program when Columbia disintegrated on reentry before a nation's eyes on February 1, 2003. And it would be Mike Leinbach who would be a key leader in the search and recovery effort as NASA, FEMA, the FBI, the US Forest Service, and dozens more federal, state, and local agencies combed an area of rural east Texas the size of Rhode Island for every piece of the shuttle and her crew they could find.

"A gripping account of a fatal tragedy and the impressive and deeply emotional human response that ensued." —*Kirkus*

Includes bibliographical references and index.

363.15 Hazards in health care facilities

Green, Elon
Last Call: A True Story of Love, Lust, and Murder in Queer New York. Elon Green. Celadon Books 2021. 272 p.
ISBN 9781250224354
Grades: Adult   363.15
1. Anderson, Peter Stickney 2. Serial murderers 3. Murder 4. Trials (Murder) 5. Crimes against gay men and lesbians 6. Homophobia 7. New York City 8. 1990s 9. True Crime — Murder
LC 2020040971

Edgar Allan Poe Award for Best Fact Crime, 2022.

This gripping true-crime narrative tells the story of the Last Call Killer and the decades-long chase to find him. And at the same time, it paints a portrait of his victims and a vibrant community navigating threat and resilience.

"The Last Call Killer brutally murdered several gay men in 1980s and '90s New York City. However, journalist Green's first book is more than just a standard true crime exploration of these killings." —*Booklist*

Includes bibliographical references.

363.17 Hazardous materials

Higginbotham, Adam
★ *Midnight in Chernobyl: The Untold Story of the World's Greatest Nuclear Disaster.* Adam Higginbotham. Simon & Schuster 2019. 320 p.
ISBN 9781501134616
Grades: Adult   363.17
1. Chernobyl Nuclear Accident, 1986 2. Nuclear accidents 3. Political corruption 4. Government cover-ups 5. Secrecy in government 6. Nuclear reactors 7. Nuclear power plants 8. Radioactive fallout 9. Radioactive pollution 10. Radiation injuries 11. Radioactivity 12. Nuclear power 13. Accidents 14. Health hazards 15. Soviet Union history 16. European history 17. Ukraine 18. 1980s 19. 1990s 20. History writing — Natural disasters and tragedies 21. Science Writing — General

ALA Notable Book, 2020; Andrew Carnegie Medal for Excellence in Non-Fiction, 2020; Booklist Editors' Choice, 2019; New York Times Notable Book, 2019.

Draws on 20 years of research, recently declassified files and interviews with first-person survivors in an account of the 1986 Chernobyl nuclear power plant disaster that also reveals how propaganda and secrets have created additional dangers.

"Written with authority, this superb book reads like a classic disaster story and reveals a Soviet empire on the brink." —*Kirkus*

Iversen, Kristen
Full Body Burden: Growing up in the Nuclear Shadow of Rocky Flats. Kristen Iversen. Crown Publishers 2012. 416 p.
ISBN 9780307955630
Grades: Adult   363.17
1. Iversen, Kristen 2. Nuclear warfare facilities 3. Secrecy in government 4. Growing up 5. Plutonium 6. Radioactive waste sites 7. Women authors, American 8. Radioactive pollution 9. Health hazards 10. Colorado 11. Autobiographies and memoirs 12. Life stories — Arts and culture — Writing — Authors 13. Nature Writing — Environmental Issues 14. Adult books for young adults
LC 2011045902

ALA Notable Book, 2013; School Library Journal Best Books: Best Adult Books 4 Teens, 2012.

A narrative report by a woman who grew up near the Rocky Flats nuclear weapons facility describes the secrets that dominated her childhood, the strange cancers that afflicted her neighbors, her brief employment at Rocky Flats, and the efforts of residents to achieve legal justice.

Includes bibliographical references and index.

Moore, Kate
The Radium Girls: The Dark Story of America's Shining Women. Kate Moore. Sourcebooks, Inc. 2017. 480 p.
ISBN 9781492649359
Grades: Adult   363.17
1. Radioactive pollution 2. Women's rights 3. Occupational health and safety 4. Employee rights 5. Radium 6. Radiation 7. World War I 8. Health hazards 9. Women's participation in wars 10. 20th century 11. History writing — Women's history 12. Business and economics — Corruption and scandal
LC 2016040681

Goodreads Choice Award, 2017; LibraryReads Favorites, 2017; Booklist Editors' Choice, 2017; ALA Notable Book, 2018.

Recounts the struggles of hundreds of women who were exposed to radium while working factory jobs during World War I, describing how they were mislead by their employers and became embroiled in a battle for workers' rights.

"Moore's well-researched narrative is written with clarity and a sympathetic voice that brings these figures and their struggles to life." —*Library Journal*

Includes bibliographical references and index; Originally published as: The Radium Girls : They paid with their lives, their final fight was for justice, in 2016 in the United Kingdom by Simon & Schuster UK.

ESSENTIAL AND RECOMMENDED TITLES
363.2 Police services

Schlosser, Eric
Command and Control: Nuclear Weapons, the Damascus Accident, and the Illusion of Safety. Eric Schlosser. The Penguin Press 2009. xxiii, 632 pages
ISBN 9781594202278
Grades: Adult — **363.17**
1. Cold War 2. Weapons of mass destruction 3. Nuclear weapons 4. Nuclear accidents 5. Hydrogen bomb 6. Missile silos 7. Laboratories 8. Disasters 9. Military history 10. United States 11. Science Writing — Physics 12. History writing — Military — Weapons 13. History writing — Natural disasters and tragedies
ALA Notable Book, 2014; New York Times Notable Book, 2013; Pulitzer Prize for History finalist, 2014.

Presents a minute-by-minute account of an H-bomb accident that nearly caused a nuclear disaster, examining other near misses and America's growing susceptibility to a catastrophic event.

Includes bibliographical references (pages 583-611) and index.

363.2 Police services

Butler, Paul
Chokehold: Policing Black Men. Paul Butler. New Press, the 2017. 256 p.
ISBN 9781595589057
Grades: Adult — **363.2**
1. Discrimination in law enforcement 2. African American men 3. Criminal justice system 4. Racism 5. Discrimination 6. Police 7. Public relations 8. Police brutality 9. Police misconduct 10. Racism in criminology 11. Race relations 12. Civil rights 13. United States 14. 21st century 15. Society and culture — Race 16. Society and culture — Violence and crime — Criminal justice system 17. Politics and global affairs — Civil and human rights
LC 2017000239

An African American former federal prosecutor and author of Let's Get Free uses new data to argue that white men commit the majority of violent crime in the United States and discusses the problem of Black-on-Black violence and how to keep communities safer without relying so much on the police.

"Smart, filled rightfully with righteous indignation, and demanding broad discussion and the widest audience." —*Kirkus*

Cox, Joseph
Dark Wire: The Incredible True Story of the Largest Sting Operation Ever. Joseph Cox. PublicAffairs 2024. 336 p.
ISBN 9781541702691
Grades: Adult — **363.2**
1. Undercover operations 2. Organized crime 3. Electronic surveillance 4. Computer networks 5. Cell phones 6. Computer security 7. Data encryption (Computer science) 8. Sting operations 9. Privacy rights 10. International cooperation 11. Criminal investigation 12. Organized crime investigation 13. True Crime — Investigations and Trials 14. True Crime — Organized Crime, Mafia, and Gangs 15. Science Writing — Computing, the Internet, and Technology
LC 2023044541

In 2018, a powerful app for secure communications called Anom took root among organized criminals. They believed Anom allowed them to conduct business in the shadows. Except for one thing: It was secretly run by the FBI. Backdoor access to Anom and a series of related investigations granted American, Australian, and European authorities a front-row seat to the underworld. Tens of thousands of criminals worldwide appeared in full view of the same agents they were trying to evade—a sprawling global economy as efficient and interconnected as the legal one. But as the FBI started to lose control of Anom, did the agency go too far?

"A fast-moving, exciting blend of white-hat technology and old-school gumshoe drudgery." —*Kirkus*

Includes bibliographical references.

Gross, Neil
Walk the Walk: How Three Police Chiefs Defied the Odds and Changed Cop Culture. Neil Gross. Metropolitan Books 2023. 240 p.
ISBN 9781250777522
Grades: Adult — **363.2**
1. Police 2. Criminal justice reform 3. Law enforcement 4. Culture 5. Criminal justice system 6. Society and culture — Violence and crime — Criminal justice system

Taking readers deep inside three unusual police departments in California, Colorado and Georgia, this book, informed by research, and by turns gripping, tragic and inspirational, follows the chiefs—and their officers and detectives—as they worked to replace aggressive culture with something better.

"Tightly focused and consistently persuasive, this is a crucial guide to solving a pressing social issue." —*Publishers Weekly*

Kaba, Mariame
No More Police: A Case for Abolition. Mariame Kaba and Andrea J. Ritchie; with a foreword by Kandace Montgomery and Miski Noor for Black Visions. The New Press 2022. 240 p.
ISBN 9781620976784
Grades: Adult — **363.2**
1. Police 2. Police ethics 3. Discrimination in law enforcement 4. Criminal justice system 5. Criminal justice reform 6. Social movements 7. Violence against marginalized people 8. Public safety 9. Discrimination 10. Social justice 11. Police brutality 12. United States 13. Society and culture — Violence and crime — Criminal justice system
LC 2022015112

A persuasive primer on police abolition from two veteran organizers.

"Two seasoned activists make a convincing case for defunding the police.…The book is deeply researched and flawlessly argued, and the plan they lay out is practical, compassionate, and circumspect." —*Kirkus*

Includes bibliographical references and index.

Lankford, Andrea
Trail of the Lost: The Relentless Search to Bring Home the Missing Hikers of the Pacific Crest Trail. Andrea Lankford. Hachette Books 2023. 336 p.
ISBN 9780306831959
Grades: Adult — **363.2**
1. Lankford, Andrea 2. Women authors 3. Park rangers 4. Hikers 5. Trails 6. Wilderness areas 7. Missing men 8. Cold cases (Criminal investigation) 9. Social media 10. Searching 11. Internet searching 12. Amateur detectives 13. Missing persons investigation 14. Pacific Crest Trail 15. California 16. Oregon 17. Washington (State) 18. Life stories — Nature and outdoors 19. Nature Writing — Natural Landscapes 20. True Crime — Cold Cases and Unsolved Mysteries

As a park ranger with the National Park Service's law enforcement team, Andrea Lankford led search and rescue missions in some of the most beautiful (and dangerous) landscapes across America, from Yosemite to the Grand Canyon, leaving the force after twelve years. Two decades later, however, she stumbles across a mystery that pulls her right back where she left off: Three young men have vanished from the Pacific Crest Trail, the 2,650-mile trek made famous by Cheryl Strayed's Wild, and no one has been able to find them.

"A gut-wrenching and compelling investigation of long-distance treks gone wrong." —*Kirkus*

Includes bibliographical references.

Raymond, Edwin
An Inconvenient Cop: My Fight to Change Policing in America. Lt. Edwin Raymond (Ret.), NYPD, with Jon Sternfeld. Viking 2023. 352 p.
ISBN 9780593653166
Grades: Adult — **363.2**
1. Raymond, Edwin, 1986- 2. Police 3. Whistle blowers 4. Police misconduct 5. Police corruption 6. Criminal justice reform 7. Institutional racism 8. Haitian people in the United States 9. American people 10. New York City 11. Autobiographies and memoirs 12. Life stories — Law and order — Police and law officers 13. Society and culture — Violence and crime — Criminal justice system
LC 2023022720

The highest-ranking whistleblower in NYPD history offers a rare, often shocking view of American policing that exposes institutional violence and corruption and presents a vision of radical hope and potential for change that could reform police departments across the country.

PUBLIC LIBRARY CORE COLLECTION: NONFICTION
Twentieth Edition

"Former NYPD lieutenant Raymond tracks his path from an impoverished childhood as the son of Haitian immigrants in Flatbush to a police officer, activist, and whistleblower." —*Booklist*

Includes bibliographical references.

Taibbi, Matt
I Can't Breathe: A Killing on Bay Street. Matt Taibbi. Spiegel & Grau 2017. 256 pages
ISBN 9780812988840
Grades: Adult   363.2
1. Garner, Eric, 1970-2014 2. African American men 3. Black Lives Matter movement 4. Police brutality 5. Injustice 6. Racism 7. African Americans 8. Criminal justice system 9. Police 10. Discrimination in law enforcement 11. Urban problems 12. Politics and government 13. New York City 14. 21st century 15. Society and culture — Violence and crime — Criminal justice system 16. Society and culture — Race 17. Politics and global affairs — Civil and human rights

LC Bl2017035731

Booklist Editors' Choice, 2017.

On July 17, 2014, a forty-three-year-old Black man named Eric Garner died on a Staten Island sidewalk after a police officer put him in what has been described as an illegal chokehold during an arrest for selling bootleg cigarettes. The final moments of Garner's life were captured on video and seen by millions. His agonized last words, "I can't breathe," became a rallying cry for the nascent Black Lives Matter protest movement.

"This is a necessary and riveting work." —*Booklist*

363.20973 Police services — United States

Purnell, Derecka
Becoming Abolitionists: Police, Protests, and the Pursuit of Freedom. Derecka Purnell. Astra House 2021. 311 p.
ISBN 9781662600517
Grades: Adult   363.20973
1. Purnell, Derecka 2. Social movements 3. Racism in law enforcement 4. Police brutality 5. Public safety 6. Antiracism 7. Peace movements 8. Social advocacy 9. Justice and politics 10. Social justice 11. Society and culture — Social activism and philanthropy 12. Society and culture — Violence and crime — Criminal justice system 13. Life stories — Politics — Activists and reformers

A human rights lawyer, writer, and organizer discusses alternatives to traditional policing and draws on the examples of worldwide movements rooted in rebellion, risk-taking and revolutionary love that have pushed a new generation of activists towards abolition of police.

"Purnell is able to deftly lead the reader through the ins and outs of the abolitionist mindset so that it is clear and comprehensible for all, including those who, like her, might be initially skeptical." —*Booklist*

Includes bibliographical references.

363.25 Detection of crime (Criminal investigation)

Bowden, Mark
The Last Stone: A Masterpiece of Criminal Interrogation. Mark Bowden. Atlantic Monthly Press 2019. 304 p.
ISBN 9780802147301
Grades: Adult   363.25
1. Journalists 2. Detectives 3. Cold cases (Criminal investigation) 4. Prisoners 5. Missing persons investigation 6. Questioning 7. Deception 8. Child sexual abusers 9. Missing children 10. Girls 11. True Crime — Sex Crimes

LC 2018058489

The author of Black Hawk Down documents the story of how five skilled detectives navigated the deceptions of a prisoner who hid his role in the 1975 disappearance of two young sisters.

"An intriguing firsthand look at the nebulous justice meted out by necessities of time and the desire for closure, as seen through the focused lens of a seasoned journalist." —*Library Journal*

Cooper, Sean Patrick
The Shooter at Midnight: Murder, Corruption, and a Farming Town Divided. Sean Patrick Cooper. Penguin Books 2024. 368 p.
ISBN 9780143135449
Grades: Adult   363.25
1. Murder investigation 2. Political corruption 3. Police corruption 4. American people 5. Missouri 6. True Crime — Murder

LC 2023034877

In 1990, when Cathy Robertson is murdered in a close-knit town still reeling from the aftereffects of the farming crisis, a neighbor is sentenced for the crime, some believe wrongly, in this gripping story about the fault-lines of a fracturing America that continue to cut across the farm belt today.

"Journalist Cooper debuts with an enthralling account of the murder that tore apart a hard-hit farming community in Missouri." —*Publishers Weekly*

Includes bibliographical references and index.

Cross, Kim
In Light of All Darkness: Inside the Polly Klaas Kidnapping and the Search for America's Child. Kim Cross. Grand Central Publishing 2023. 320 p.
ISBN 9781538725061
Grades: Adult   363.25
1. Klaas, Polly Hannah, 1981-1993 2. Kidnapping investigation 3. Murder 4. Kidnapping victims 5. Murder victims 6. Missing children 7. United States 8. California 9. Impartial writing 10. True Crime — Murder 11. True Crime — Investigations and Trials

LC 2023020949

A New York Times best-selling author, journalist and historian presents a comprehensive account of the kidnapping of Polly Klaas from her bedroom by a stranger in 1993 that triggered one of the largest manhunts in FBI history.

"Cross' coverage is polished and respectful, with a clear expression of ideas and heartfelt but dispassionate reporting. True crime and police procedural aficionados will find her treatment thoroughly informative and incredibly moving." —*Booklist*

Includes bibliographical references and index.

Dudley, Renee
The Ransomware Hunting Team: A Band of Misfits' Improbable Crusade to Save the World from Cybercrime. Renee Dudley and Daniel Golden. Farrar, Straus and Giroux 2022. 352 p.
ISBN 9780374603304
Grades: Adult   363.25
1. Computer crimes 2. Computer security 3. Computer networks 4. Computer technicians 5. Cyberterrorism 6. Crime prevention 7. True Crime — General 8. Science Writing — Computing, the Internet, and Technology

LC 2022022942

This real-life technological thriller follows a band of misfits who have used their extraordinary skills to save millions of ransomware victims from paying billions of dollars to criminals, tracking the ups and downs of their work as they take on the biggest cybersecurity threats of our time.

Journalists Dudley and Golden (author of Spy Schools, 2017) explore with verve and fascinating detail the assorted group of unpaid, self-taught experts in the U.S. and Europe who make it their duty to protect the innocent from ransomware, which the authors define as 'An unholy marriage of hacking and cryptography' and 'Kidnapping updated for the digital age.' —*Booklist*

Includes bibliographical references and index.

Fabricant, M. Chris
Junk Science and the American Criminal Justice System. M. Chris Fabricant. Akashic Books 2022. 368 p.
ISBN 9781636140308
Grades: Adult   363.25

ESSENTIAL AND RECOMMENDED TITLES
363.25 Detection of crime (Criminal investigation)

1. Fabricant, M. Chris 2. Defense attorneys 3. Expert evidence 4. Forensic pathology 5. Crime laboratories 6. Scientific errors 7. Criminal investigation 8. Malicious accusation 9. Judicial error 10. Racism in the criminal justice system 11. Prisoners 12. Death row prisoners 13. Injustice 14. True Crime — Investigations and Trials 15. Society and culture — Violence and crime — Criminal justice system 16. Life stories — Law and order — Prisoners and inmates 17. Science Writing — General

From CSI to Forensic Files to the celebrated reputation of the FBI crime lab, "forensic scientists" have long been mythologized in American popular culture as infallible crime solvers. Judges and juries put their faith in "expert witnesses" and innocent people have been executed as a result. In 2012, the Innocence Project began searching for prisoners convicted by junk science, and three men, each convicted of capital murder, became M. Chris Fabricant's clients. Junk Science and the American Criminal Justice System chronicles the fights to overturn their wrongful convictions and to end the use of the "science" that destroyed their lives. Weaving together courtroom battles from Mississippi to Texas to New York City, Fabricant takes the reader on a journey into the heart of a broken, racist system of justice and the role forensic science plays in maintaining the status quo.

"'Follow the science' turns out to be a mistake in the criminal justice system, as Fabricant, the Innocence Project's director of strategic litigation, forcefully demonstrates in his impressive debut….This j'accuse provides a broader look at a deeply disturbing aspect of a criminal justice system already considered racist and biased by many." —*Publishers Weekly*

Holes, Paul
***Unmasked:** My Life Solving America's Cold Cases.* Paul Holes with Robin Gaby Fisher. Celadon Books 2022. 336 p.
ISBN 9781250622792
Grades: Adult   363.25
1. Detectives 2. Cold cases (Criminal investigation) 3. Criminal investigation 4. Crime 5. Interpersonal relations 6. Autobiographies and memoirs 7. Life stories — Law and order 8. True Crime — Investigations and trials
LC 2021059410

An icon in the true crime world, the cold case investigator who finally caught the Golden State Killer provides an insider account of some of the most notorious cases in contemporary American history and opens up to the most intimate scenes of his life.

"In this candid, poignant memoir, Holes, with cowriter Fisher (After the Fire: A True Story of Friendship and Survival), reflects on a long career as a criminalist and detective….A captivating memoir of a life dedicated to cold cases." —*Library Journal*

Humes, Edward
*The **Forever** Witness: How DNA and Genealogy Solved a Cold Case Double Murder.* Edward Humes. Dutton 2022. 384 p.
ISBN 9781524746278
Grades: Adult   363.25
1. Criminal investigation 2. Genetic genealogy 3. Cold cases (Criminal investigation) 4. DNA 5. Murder 6. Murderers 7. Privacy 8. True Crime — Forensic Sciences 9. True Crime — Murder
LC 2021058094

After 30 years, Detective Jim Scharf and CeCe Moore solve the murder of a teenage couple with the help of genetic genealogy, which brings up questions of consent and privacy despite the fact we have the tools to catch the many killers responsible for approximately 250,000 murders in the U.S.

"Humes' writing is suspenseful yet also journalistic, providing fascinating details about the case, technological advances in police work, and genetic genealogy." —*Booklist*

Includes bibliographical references and index.

Krouse, Erika
★ ***Tell** Me Everything: The Story of a Private Investigation.* Erika Krouse. Flatiron Books 2022. 336 p.
ISBN 9781250240309
Grades: Adult   363.25

1. Krouse, Erika 2. Women private investigators 3. Sex crime investigation 4. Rape 5. Sexual harassment in universities and colleges 6. Adult child sexual abuse victims 7. Life change events 8. Social justice 9. Autobiographies and memoirs 10. Life stories — Facing adversity — Abuse survivors 11. Life stories — Law and order 12. True Crime — Sex Crimes
LC 2021047705

Edgar Allan Poe Award for Best Fact Crime, 2023.

In this part memoir, part literary true crime, the author becomes consumed by a sexual assault investigation that grows into a national scandal and a historic civil rights case, and, when everything around her implodes, she must figure out how to win the case without losing herself.

"In this memoir, Krouse, a creative writing teacher at the Lighthouse Writers Workshop in Denver, explores her role as a private investigator working on a complex and eventually high-profile sexual assault case along with its relevance to her own history of abuse….An exceptionally well-told, perceptive examination of a sexual abuse scandal and its personal and social relevance." —*Kirkus*

Monroe, Jana
***Hearts** of Darkness: Serial Killers, the Behavioral Science Unit, and My Life as a Woman in the FBI.* Jana Monroe; foreword by Joe Navarro. Abrams Press 2023. 320 p.
ISBN 9781419766114
Grades: Adult   363.25
1. Monroe, Jana 2. Women FBI agents 3. Psychology 4. Criminal profilers 5. Criminal behavior 6. Forensic psychology 7. Serial murderers 8. Sexism in employment 9. Psychic trauma 10. North American people 11. American people 12. Autobiographies and memoirs 13. Life stories — Law and order — Police and law officers 14. True Crime — Forensic Sciences 15. True Crime — Murder 16. Debut title

Jana Monroe was no ordinary cop. One of the first analysts—and, at the time, the only female agent—in the world-renowned FBI Behavioral Sciences Unit at Quantico, she consulted on more than 850 homicide cases, including infamous serial killers Ted Bundy, Jeffrey Dahmer, Edmund Kemper, and Aileen Wuornos. Monroe was also the model for Clarice Starling in the movie version of the Silence of the Lambs; she even helped train Jodie Foster for her Oscar-winning role. In Hearts of Darkness, Monroe steps out from the shadows to tell the story of her astonishing life in shaping law enforcement and intelligence analysis.

"Monroe, who helped train Jodie Foster for her role as Clarice Starling in the film the Silence of the Lambs, chronicles her prolific time in the FBI (she worked about 850 cases)…A gripping and readable memoir that's an essential read for audiences who want to understand the history of the FBI and the BSU." —*Library Journal*

Includes bibliographical references and index.

Norton, Laurah
*Lay **Them** to Rest: On the Road with the Cold Case Investigators Who Identify the Nameless.* Laurah Norton. Hachette Books 2023. xxi, 324 p.
ISBN 9780306828805
Grades: Adult   363.25
1. Norton, Laurah 2. Podcasters 3. Cold cases (Criminal investigation) 4. Murder victims 5. Dead 6. Identification 7. Forensic anthropology 8. Technological innovations 9. Genetic code 10. Marginalized people 11. Forensic scientists 12. Criminal investigation 13. True Crime — Forensic Sciences 14. Life stories — Facing adversity — Victims of crime 15. Life stories — Science, technology, and medicine — Scientists and inventors 16. Science Writing — General
LC 2023013020

Introducing readers to the history and evolution of forensic science, the author incorporates stories of real-life John & Jane Does from around the world and examines how rapidly evolving identification methods have helped solve the most iconic cold cases.

"A comprehensive study of the difficult task of figuring out the identities of faceless victims of violent crime…Norton's dive into forensic technology reveals a dark world that is being slowly illuminated by science and dedication." —*Kirkus*

Includes bibliographical references and index.

PUBLIC LIBRARY CORE COLLECTION: NONFICTION
Twentieth Edition

Tau, Byron
★ *Means* of Control: How the Hidden Alliance of Tech and Government Is Creating a New American Surveillance State. Byron Tau. Crown Publishers 2024. 336 p.
ISBN 9780593443224
Grades: Adult   363.25
1. Big data 2. Surveillance 3. Government contractors 4. Technology 5. Politics and government 6. High technology industry and trade 7. United States 8. Business and economics — Industries — Technology 9. Politics and global affairs — General

A journalist based in Washington, D.C, exposes the U.S. government's alliance with data brokers, tech companies and advertisers to reshape surveillance and privacy as we know it, in this sobering and eye-opening defining story of our era.

"Filled with shocking revelations and first-rate reporting, this will have readers thinking twice before they post." —*Publishers Weekly*

Tuerkheimer, Deborah
Credible: Why We Doubt Accusers and Protect Abusers. Deborah Tuerkheimer. HarperWave 2021. 320 p.
ISBN 9780063002746
Grades: Adult   363.25
1. Sexual violence 2. Rape culture 3. Sexual violence victims 4. Unconscious bias 5. Society and culture — Violence and crime 6. Society and culture — Gender

In this landmark book, a former prosecutor, legal expert, and leading authority on sexual violence examines why we are primed to disbelieve allegations of sexual abuse—and how we can transform a culture and a legal system structured to dismiss accusers.

"Harrowing survivor stories and the lack of easy solutions make Credible a difficult but necessary read urging individuals to start changing the way they think about allegations of abuse and the women who make them." —*Booklist*

363.28 Services of special kinds of security and law enforcement agencies

Molnar, Petra
The Walls Have Eyes: Surviving Migration in the Age of Artificial Intelligence. Petra Molnar; [foreword by E. Tendayi Achiume]. The New Press 2024. 320 p.
ISBN 9781620978368
Grades: Adult   363.28
1. Border security 2. Technological innovations 3. Immigration and emigration 4. Refugees 5. Forced relocations 6. Electronic surveillance 7. Political surveillance 8. Artificial intelligence 9. Corporations 10. High technology industry and trade 11. Political persecution 12. Social control 13. Politics and global affairs — Immigration 14. Politics and global affairs — Civil and human rights 15. Society and culture — Immigration 16. Society and culture — Media and technology 17. Debut title

LC 2023056025
As more people are displaced by war, economic instability, and a warming planet, more countries are turning to AI-driven technology to "manage" the influx. Based on years of researching borderlands across the world, lawyer and anthropologist Petra Molnar's the Walls Have Eyes is a truly global story—a dystopian vision turned reality, where your body is your passport and matters of life and death are determined by algorithm. Examining how technology is being deployed by governments on the world's most vulnerable with little regulation, Molnar also shows us how borders are now big business, with defense contractors and tech start-ups alike scrambling to capture this highly profitable market.

"In this unsettling debut study, Molnar…draws attention to a recent proliferation of digital technologies…This is a grave wake-up call." —*Publishers Weekly*

Includes bibliographical references.

Sohn, Amy
The Man Who Hated Women: Sex, Censorship, and Civil Liberties in the Gilded Age. Amy Sohn. Farrar, Straus and Giroux 2021. 304 p. : Illustration
ISBN 9781250174819
Grades: Adult   363.28
1. Comstock, Anthony, 1844-1915 2. Postal inspectors 3. Women's rights 4. Women social advocates 5. Reproductive rights 6. Women 7. Freedom of speech 8. Pornography 9. Sexuality 10. Legislation 11. Social life and customs 12. Moral conditions 13. United States 14. 19th century 15. 20th century 16. Biographies 17. History writing — Gilded Age — United States 18. History writing — Women's history 19. Life stories — People in history

LC 2021002669
A narrative history about Anthony Comstock, US Postal Inspector and vice hunter, and the remarkable women who opposed him.

"Novelist Sohn (The Actress) delivers an engrossing account of U.S. post office special agent Anthony Comstock's anti-vice crusade and the women who opposed it.... Blending colorful details of life at the turn of the 20th century with sharp insights into just how revolutionary these new ideas were, this fascinating history deserves a wide readership." —*Publishers Weekly*

Includes bibliographical references and index.

363.32 Social conflict

Barron, Justine
They Killed Freddie Gray: The Anatomy of a Police Brutality Cover-up. Justine Barron; foreword by Rabia Chaudry. Arcade Publishing 2023. 264 p.
ISBN 9781950994250
Grades: Adult   363.32
1. Gray, Freddie 1989-2015 2. African American men 3. Death 4. Suspects (Criminal investigation) 5. Police brutality 6. Trials (Murder) 7. Criminal evidence 8. Witnesses 9. Police cover-ups 10. Conspiracies 11. True Crime — Police and Lawyers 12. True Crime — Investigations and Trials 13. Society and culture — Violence and crime — Criminal justice system 14. Debut title

They Killed Freddie Gray exposes a conspiracy among Baltimore leaders to cover up what actually happened to Freddie Gray, who was fatally injured in police custody in April 2015. After Gray's death, Baltimore became ground zero for Black Lives Matter and racial justice protests that exploded across the country. Yet the cause of Gray's death has remained a mystery. This book revisits a pivotal moment in US criminal justice history, providing new insight into what happened, the historical structures of power that allowed it to happen, and the personalities and dynamics involved.

"Barron's writing is powered by outrage over Gray's death and the failure to hold anyone accountable. Readers will be troubled." —*Publishers Weekly*

Moore, Wes
★ *Five Days:* The Fiery Reckoning of an American City. Wes Moore with Erica L. Green. One World 2020. 256 p.
ISBN 9780525512363
Grades: Adult   363.32
1. Gray, Freddie, 1989-2015 2. Police brutality 3. Police misconduct 4. Civil rights 5. Police and African Americans 6. African American civil rights 7. Classism 8. Racism 9. Race relations 10. Baltimore, Maryland 11. 2010s 12. Oral histories 13. Society and culture — Race

LC 2019048820
An account of the 2015 police-brutality killing of Freddie Gray retraces key events from the perspectives of seven insiders, including a conflicted Baltimore Police Department captain, the victim's sister and the owner of the Baltimore Orioles.

"Moore provides important context in the history of Baltimore's racial and income inequality and the emergence of the Black Lives Matter movement. Readers will be enthralled by this propulsive account." —*Publishers Weekly*

Includes index.

ESSENTIAL AND RECOMMENDED TITLES
363.325 Terrorism

363.325 Terrorism

Bergen, Peter L.
Manhunt: The Ten-year Search for Bin Laden—from 9/11 to Abbottabad. Peter L. Bergen. Crown Publishers 2012. 288 p.
ISBN 9780307955579
Grades: Adult   363.325
1. Bin Laden, Osama, 1957-2011 2. Terrorists 3. Special operations (Military science) 4. War on Terrorism, 2001-2009 5. Terrorism prevention 6. United States 7. Politics and global affairs — Terrorism 8. History writing — Wars and conflicts — War in Afghanistan
LC 2012004258

The author of the best-selling Holy War, Inc. presents a definitive account of the decade-long search for Osama bin Laden, sharing coverage of such topics as the CIA analyst team that gathered critical intelligence and what bin Laden's demise means for al Qaeda.

Includes bibliographical references and index.

Carroll, Rory
There Will Be Fire: Margaret Thatcher, the Ira, and Two Minutes That Changed History. Rory Carroll. G. P. Putnam's Sons 2023. 400 p.
ISBN 9780593419496
Grades: Adult   363.325
1. Thatcher, Margaret 2. Magee, Patrick, 1951- 3. Terrorism 4. Attempted assassination 5. The Troubles, 1968-1998 6. Politics and government 7. Great Britain 8. Ireland 9. Northern Ireland 10. 20th century 11. History writing — Europe — United Kingdom — Northern Ireland
LC 2022052213

Drawing on interviews and original reporting, revealing new information and weaving together previously unconnected threads, a veteran journalist, in this book that reads like a thriller, recounts how the IRA came close to killing Margaret Thatcher and the epic manhunt that followed,.

"A lucid history of the Troubles in all its manifold complexities." —*Kirkus*

Includes bibliographical references.

Lehr, Dick
White Hot Hate: A True Story of Domestic Terrorism in America's Heartland. Dick Lehr. Mariner Books 2021. 304 p.
ISBN 9780358359906
Grades: Adult   363.325
1. Domestic terrorism 2. Small towns 3. Somali Americans 4. Immigrants 5. Racism 6. Islamophobia 7. White supremacy movements 8. Militia movement 9. Vigilantes 10. FBI agents 11. Undercover operations 12. Explosives 13. Conspiracies 14. Extremism 15. 21st century 16. Society and culture — Violence and crime 17. Politics and global affairs — Terrorism 18. True Crime — Organized Crime, Mafia, and Gangs 19. History writing — Early 21st century — United States
LC 2021014689

In the spring of 2016, as immigration debates rocked the United States, three men in a militia group known as the Crusaders grew aggravated over one Kansas town's growing Somali community. They decided that complaining about their new neighbors and threatening them directly wasn't enough. The men plotted to bomb a mosque, aiming to kill hundreds and inspire other attacks against Muslims in America. But they would wait until after the presidential election, so that their actions wouldn't hurt Donald Trump's chances of winning. An FBI informant befriended the three men, acting as law enforcement's eyes and ears for six months. His secretly taped conversations with the militia were pivotal in obstructing their plans and were a lynchpin in the resulting trial and convictions for conspiracy to use a weapon of mass destruction.

"A strong addition to true crime sections, this disturbing work will also appeal to readers interested in the development of modern hate groups." —*Library Journal*

Includes bibliographical references and index.

Soufan, Ali H.
The Black Banners Declassified: How Torture Derailed the War on Terror After 9/11. Ali Soufan, with Daniel Freedman. W. W. Norton & Co. 2020. xxx, 594 pages : Illustration
ISBN 9780393540727
Grades: Adult   363.325
1. Military intelligence 2. Antiterrorist policy 3. Terrorism 4. Terrorists 5. September 11 Terrorist Attacks, 2001 6. Politics and government 7. United States 8. 2000s (Decade) 9. History writing — September 11, 2001 — United States
LC 2020023446

The definitive account of an FBI special agent's al-Qaeda story, unredacted for the first time. In the fight against al-Qaeda, former FBI special agent Ali H. Soufan became a legend on the basis of his deft questioning of prisoners, which often short-circuited al-Qaeda plots in the pipeline. Physical or mental violence played no part in this success. He never laid a hand on the suspected terrorists. Other U.S. intelligence agencies took orders directly from the Oval Office, using other methods. The CIA's decision to employ "enhanced interrogation techniques" backfired, says Soufan. It made the job of defending the United States more difficult and dangerous.

"The best and most original book published in the West on al-Qaeda, this is highly recommended." —*Library Journal*

Includes bibliographical references (pages 569-572) and index.

Toobin, Jeffrey
★ *Homegrown: Timothy McVeigh and the Rise of Right-wing Extremism.* Jeffrey Toobin. Simon & Schuster 2023. 448 p.
ISBN 9781668013571
Grades: Adult   363.325
1. McVeigh, Timothy, 1968-2001 2. Oklahoma City Bombing, April 19, 1995 3. Right-wing extremists 4. White supremacists 5. Bombers (Airplanes) 6. Domestic terrorism 7. Extremism 8. Trials 9. Prisoners 10. Executions and executioners 11. Political violence 12. Political culture 13. North American people 14. American people 15. United States 16. Biographies 17. Life stories — Law and order — Criminals and law-breakers 18. Politics and global affairs — Terrorism 19. True Crime — Investigations and Trials

New York Times bestselling author Jeffrey Toobin traces the dramatic history and profound legacy of Timothy McVeigh, who once declared, "I believe there is an army out there, ready to rise up, even though I never found it." but that doesn't mean his army wasn't there. With news-breaking reportage, Toobin details how McVeigh's principles and tactics have flourished in the decades since his death in 2001, reaching an apotheosis on January 6 when hundreds of rioters stormed the Capitol. Homegrown reveals how the story of Timothy McVeigh and the Oklahoma City bombing is not only a powerful retelling of one of the great outrages of our time, but a warning for our future.

"A riveting account of the man behind the 1995 Oklahoma City bombing and the legacy of his actions, which reverberate today....An authoritative, disheartening, depressingly relevant page-turner." —*Kirkus*

Wood, Graeme
The Way of the Strangers: Encounters with the Islamic State. Graeme Wood. Random House Inc 2017. 224 p.
ISBN 9780812988758
Grades: Adult   363.325
1. Fundamentalism 2. Violence 3. World politics 4. International security 5. Terrorists 6. Islam 7. Terrorism 8. Southwest Asia and North Africa (Middle East) history 9. Southwest Asia and North Africa (Middle East) 10. 21st century 11. Politics and global affairs — Terrorism
LC 2017302379

Governor General's Literary Award for English-Language Nonfiction, 2017.

The writer of the Atlantic's cover story, "What ISIS Really Wants," presents an intimate and unsettling examination of the motivations that drive the men and women of the Islamic State, sharing the stories of individual followers against a backdrop of the violent events of today.

PUBLIC LIBRARY CORE COLLECTION: NONFICTION
Twentieth Edition

363.3250956 Terrorism — Middle East

Mekhennet, Souad
I Was Told to Come Alone: My Journey Behind the Lines of Jihad. Souad Mekhennet. Henry Holt and Co. 2017. 304 p.
ISBN 9781627798976
Grades: Adult   363.3250956
1. Emwazi, Mohammed, -2015 2. Mekhennet, Souad 3. Islam 4. Women journalists 5. Foreign correspondents 6. Jihad 7. Terrorism 8. Extremism 9. Investigative journalism 10. Autobiographies and memoirs 11. Impartial writing 12. Life stories — Arts and culture — Writing — Journalists 13. Politics and global affairs — Terrorism 14. Adult books for young adults
LC 2016054740
Booklist Editors' Choice, 2017.
Washington Post national security correspondent Souad Mekhennet is a Muslim who grew up in Germany. Viewed by Muslims as an interviewer they can trust, she often has access to significant newsmakers who won't meet with other Western journalists. In I Was Told to Come Alone, Mekhennet traces her life and career, offering insight into the experiences of Arabs and Muslims living in Europe. She also vividly portrays the people she's interviewed (including several jihadis) and the places of conflict she's visited as a reporter.
"A riveting memoir and a literary bombshell that effectively eviscerates every preconception, misconception, and prejudice readers have about the Arab world, I Was Told to Come Alone reinforces the singular significance of journalism, especially foreign journalism, at a time when it is facing its greatest challenges." —*Booklist*

363.33 Control of firearms

Auster, Paul
Bloodbath Nation. Paul Auster; photographs by Spencer Ostrander. Grove Press 2023. 160 p.
ISBN 9780802160454
Grades: Adult   363.33
1. Gun ownership 2. Gun accidents 3. Gunshot victims 4. Gunshot wounds 5. Death 6. Victims of violent crimes 7. Mass shootings 8. Law 9. Gun control 10. United States 11. Society and culture — Violence and crime 12. Politics and global affairs — General
LC 2022041759
Traces centuries of America's use and abuse of guns, exploring the bitter divide between our gun control and anti-gun control camps and how gun violence has become so prevalent and out of proportion to the rest of the world.
"In this brief but remarkably moving work, Auster blends personal and historical commentary, anecdotal and statistical evidence, sober analysis, and passionate appeals for reform, sketching the origins and present reality of American gun violence....A harrowing, haunting reflection on the routine slaughter wrought by guns." —*Kirkus*

Erdozain, Dominic
One Nation Under Guns: How Gun Culture Distorts Our History and Threatens Our Democracy. Dominic Erdozain. Crown 2024. 304 p.
ISBN 9780593594315
Grades: Adult   363.33
1. Guns 2. Gun ownership 3. Right to bear arms 4. Gun control 5. Freedom 6. Constitutional law 7. Racism 8. Nationalism 9. Violence and guns 10. United States history 11. History writing — United States 12. Politics and global affairs — Civil and human rights 13. Society and culture — Violence and crime
LC 2023034012
Taking us on a thought-provoking historical journey, the author shows how the nation's Founders did not intend the Second Amendment to guarantee the individual right to bear arms and argues that, to save our democracy, we must fight for the Founders' true idea of what it means to be free.
"A fast-paced, reader-friendly polemic that demolishes gun-culture myths. Will attract many readers." —*Library Journal*
Includes bibliographical references and index.

363.34 Disasters

Dolin, Eric Jay
A Furious Sky: The Five-hundred-year History of America's Hurricanes. Eric Jay Dolin. Liveright Publishing 2020. xxvii, 392 p.
ISBN 9781631495274
Grades: Adult   363.34
1. Hurricanes 2. Storms 3. Natural disasters 4. Effect of environment on humans 5. Meteorology 6. Weather forecasting 7. Global warming 8. Climate change 9. United States history 10. Atlantic Ocean 11. Gulf of Mexico 12. History writing — Natural disasters and tragedies 13. Science Writing — Weather 14. Nature Writing — Environmental Issues
LC 2019059367
Kirkus Prize for Nonfiction finalist, 2020.
Presents the five-hundred-year story of American hurricanes, from the nameless storms that threatened Columbus' New World voyages, to the devastation wrought by Hurricane Maria in Puerto Rico and the escalation of hurricane season as a result of global warming.
Includes bibliographical references and index.

Jensen, Robert A.
Personal Effects: What Recovering the Dead Teaches Me About Caring for the Living. Robert A. Jensen, with James Hider. St. Martin's Press 2021. 304 p.
ISBN 9781250267993
Grades: Adult   363.34
1. Jensen, Robert A. (Robert Andrew) 2. Executives 3. Disaster relief 4. Disasters 5. Emergencies 6. Disaster victims 7. Death 8. Dead 9. Tragedy 10. Identification 11. Life stories — Business — Working life 12. Life stories — Facing adversity — Coping with death 13. Life stories — Facing adversity — Disasters and tragedies
LC 2021016221
You have seen Robert A. Jensen—you just never knew it. As the owner of the world's largest disaster management company, he has spent most of his adult life responding to tragedy. From the Oklahoma City bombing, 9/11, and the Bali bombings, to the 2004 South Asian Tsunami, Hurricane Katrina, the 2010 Haitian Earthquake, and the Grenfell Tower Fire, Jensen has been at the practical level of international incidents, assisting with the recovery of bodies, identifying victims, and repatriating and returning their personal effects to the surviving family members. He is also, crucially, involved in the emotional recovery that comes after a disaster: Helping guide the families, governments, and companies involved, telling them what to expect and managing the unmanageable. Personal Effects is an unsparing, up-close look at the difficult work Jensen does behind the yellow tape and the lessons he learned there.
"Jensen's thoroughly engrossing personal account invites readers to witness an almost unseen arena of disaster management." —*Library Journal*
Includes index.

363.350973 Civil defense — United States

Graff, Garrett M.
Raven Rock: The Story of the U.S. Government's Secret Plan to Save Itself—While the Rest of Us Die. Garrett M. Graff. Simon & Schuster 2017. 560 pages
ISBN 9781476735405
Grades: Adult   363.350973
1. National security 2. Crisis management 3. Secrecy in government 4. Emergency planning 5. Military planning 6. Nuclear warfare 7. Cold War 8. Military secrets 9. Civil defense 10. Politics and government 11. Armed Forces 12. United States 13. Politics and global affairs — National security 14. Politics and global affairs — World politics — United States 15. History writing — Cold War 16. History writing — Military
LC 2017004895
Describes the secret Doomsday plans, developed for over 60 years, that would evacuate high-ranking government officials in the event of a massive terrorist or nuclear attack on Washington, DC, while leaving ordinary citizens to fend for themselves.

ESSENTIAL AND RECOMMENDED TITLES
363.37 Fire hazards

"A chilling portrait of how the government planned to continue to function during and after a nuclear holocaust is brilliantly told in this new valuable addition to Cold War literature that goes beyond policy and delves into logistical plans." —*Library Journal*

Includes bibliographical references and index.

363.37 Fire hazards

Gee, Alastair
Fire in Paradise: An American Tragedy. Alastair Gee and Dani Anguiano. Norton 2020. 272 p.
ISBN 9781324005148
Grades: Adult   363.37
1. Wildfires 2. Climate change 3. Business corruption 4. Disasters 5. California 6. Society and culture — Urban and regional studies 7. Nature Writing — Natural Disaster 8. Politics and global affairs — Environmental issues and policies
LC Bl2020011201

An account of the 2018 Camp Fire that razed the town of Paradise, California draws on hundreds of interviews with residents, firefighters, police and scientific experts to document its horrific impact, including the establishment of an unfolding refugee crisis.

"A vividly descriptive, compelling, well-researched, page-turning work of narrative nonfiction, both heartbreaking and uplifting." —*Library Journal*

Johnson, Lizzie
★ *Paradise: One Town's Struggle to Survive an American Wildfire.* Lizzie Johnson. Crown 2021. 304 p. : Illustration; Map
ISBN 9780593136386
Grades: Adult   363.37
1. Wildfires 2. Natural disasters 3. Fire fighters 4. Disaster victims 5. Survival 6. Business corruption 7. Disasters 8. Cities and towns 9. Fires 10. United States history 11. California 12. 21st century 13. History writing — Regional history — United States 14. History writing — Natural disasters and tragedies 15. Life stories — Facing adversity — Disasters and tragedies 16. Society and culture — Urban and regional studies 17. Nature Writing — Natural Disaster 18. Politics and global affairs — Environmental issues and policies 19. Debut title
LC 2021012297

A San Francisco Chronicle reporter, drawing on years of on-the-ground reporting and reams of public records, provides a first-hand account of California's Camp Fire—the nation's deadliest wildfire in a century, investigating root causes and how to avert future tragedies as the climate crisis unfolds.

"The definitive story of an American tragedy and a notable cautionary tale of climate change, corporate negligence, and insufficient planning. Highly recommended." —*Library Journal*

Includes bibliographical references and index.

Vaillant, John
★ *Fire Weather: A True Story from a Hotter World.* John Vaillant. Alfred A. Knopf 2023. 414 p.
ISBN 9781524732851
Grades: Adult   363.37
1. Forest fires 2. Wildfires 3. Climate change 4. Oil industry and trade 5. Environmental degradation 6. Environmental disasters 7. Tar sands 8. Mines and mineral resources 9. Greenhouse gases 10. Alberta 11. 2010s 12. History writing — Natural disasters and tragedies 13. Nature Writing — Environmental Issues 14. Nature Writing — Natural Disaster
LC 2022044338

Baillie Gifford Prize for Non-Fiction, 2023; Shaughnessy Cohen Prize for Political Writing (Canada), 2024; Pulitzer Prize for General Nonfiction finalist, 2024; National Book Award for Nonfiction finalist, 2023; Hilary Weston Writers' Trust Prize finalist, 2023.

In May 2016, the city of Fort McMurray in Alberta, Canada, burned to the ground, forcing 88,000 people to flee their homes. It was the largest evacuation ever of a city in the face of a forest fire, raising the curtain on a new age of increasingly destructive wildfires. This book is a suspenseful account of one of North America's most devastating forest fires—and a stark exploration of our dawning era of climate catastrophes.

"Journalist Vaillant (The Tiger) offers a gripping account of the May 2016 fire that engulfed the city of Fort McMurray in the Canadian province of Alberta, destroying thousands of homes and forcing the evacuation of 88,000 people." —*Publishers Weekly*

A Borzoi Book published by Alfred A. Knopf; Nominated for the Hilary Weston Writers' Trust Prize for Nonfiction, 2023; Includes bibliographical references and index.

363.3709745 Fire hazards — Rhode Island

James, Scott
Trial by Fire: A Devastating Tragedy, a Hundred Lives Lost, and a Fifteen-year Search for Truth. Scott James. Thomas Dunne Books 2020. 384 p.
ISBN 9781250131263
Grades: Adult   363.3709745
1. Nightclubs 2. Fires 3. Rock concerts 4. Fireworks 5. Rhode Island 6. History writing — Natural disasters and tragedies 7. True Crime — General
LC 2020019383

All it took for a hundred people to die during a show by the hair metal band Great White was a sudden burst from two giant sparklers that ignited the acoustical foam lining the Station nightclub. But who was at fault? Trial by Fire is the heart-wrenching story of the fire's aftermath because while the fire, one of America's deadliest, lasted fewer than two minutes, the search for the truth would take twenty years.

"This is not an easy book, but it is well worth reading for true crime fans who are tired of serial killers." —*Booklist*

Includes bibliographical references and index.

363.4 Controversies related to public morals and customs

Okrent, Daniel
Last Call: The Rise and Fall of Prohibition, 1920-1933. Daniel Okrent. Scribner 2010. 480 p.
ISBN 9780743277020
Grades: 11 12 Adult   363.4
1. Prohibition 2. Drinking 3. Alcohol 4. Bootleggers 5. United States history 6. 1920s 7. 20th century 8. History writing — Early 20th century — United States
LC 2009051127

ALA Notable Book, 2011; New York Times Notable Book, 2010.

Okrent explores the origins, implementation, and failure of that great American delusion known as Prohibition. "Last Call" explains how Prohibition happened, what life under it was like, and what it did to the country.

Includes bibliographical references and index.

363.4509861 Illegal drugs — Colombia

Muse, Toby
Kilo: Inside the Deadliest Cocaine Cartels—from the Jungles to the Streets. Toby Muse. William Morrow & Company 2020. 303 p.
ISBN 9780062905291
Grades: Adult   363.4509861
1. Muse, Toby 2. War correspondents 3. Cocaine traffic 4. Cocaine smuggling 5. Drug cartels 6. Gangsters 7. Farmers 8. Wealth 9. Poverty 10. Coca industry and trade 11. Colombia 12. Life stories — Law and order — Criminals and law-breakers 13. Society and culture — Violence and crime 14. Life stories — Arts and culture — Writing — Journalists
LC Bl2020004943

PUBLIC LIBRARY CORE COLLECTION: NONFICTION
Twentieth Edition

Seasoned war correspondent Toby Muse has witnessed each level of the cocaine business, fueled by the appetite for the drug in America and Europe. In this riveting chronicle, he takes the reader inside Colombia's notorious cartels to offer a never before look at the drug trade. Piercing this veiled world, Kilo is a gripping portrait of a country struggling to end this deadly trade even as the riches flow. A human portrait of criminals and the shocking details of their lives, Kilo is a chilling, unforgettable story that takes you deep into the belly of the beast.

"Cocaine darkens the souls of all it touches in a foreign correspondent's chilling eyewitness account of the barbarous world of Colombian drug trafficking. . . . An unrelentingly tragic yet indispensable expose." —*Kirkus*

363.5 Housing

Podemski, Max
A Paradise of Small Houses: The Evolution, Devolution, and Potential Rebirth of Urban Housing. Max Podemski. Beacon Press 2024. 272 p. : Illustration
ISBN 9780807007785
Grades: Adult   363.5
1. Houses 2. Small houses 3. Apartments 4. Architecture 5. Cities and towns 6. Regionalism 7. Urban economic development 8. Real estate 9. Gentrification of cities 10. Housing policy 11. Urban planning 12. United States 13. Arts and Entertainment — Architecture 14. Society and culture — Urban and regional studies 15. Debut title
LC 2023033566

The Philadelphia row house. The New York tenement. The Boston triple-decker. Every American city has its own iconic housing style, structures that have been home to generations of families and are symbols of identity and pride. Max Podemski, an urban planner for the city of Los Angeles and lifelong architecture buff, has spent his career in and around these buildings. Deftly combining his years of experience with extensive research, Podemski walks the reader through the history of our dwelling spaces—and offers a blueprint for how time-tested urban planning models can help us build the homes the United States so desperately needs.

"A thoughtful history of affordable housing that establishes the basis for reasoned discussion and well-informed policy." —*Kirkus*
Includes bibliographical references and index.

Ross, Andrew
Sunbelt Blues: The Failure of American Housing. Andrew Ross. Metropolitan Books 2021. 288 p.
ISBN 9781250804228
Grades: Adult   363.5
1. Social problems 2. Low-wage workers 3. Housing 4. Low-income housing 5. Real estate investment 6. Housing policy 7. Homelessness 8. Florida 9. Society and culture — Wealth and class 10. Society and culture — Urban and regional studies 11. Politics and global affairs — General
LC 2021021699

Once the main approach to Disney World, where vacationers found lodging on their way to the Magic Kingdom, the fifteen-mile Route 192 corridor in Osceola has become a site of shocking contrasts. At one end, absentee investors snatch up foreclosed properties to turn into extravagant vacation homes for affluent visitors, destroying affordable housing in the process. At the other, underpaid theme park workers, displaced families, and disabled and elderly people subsisting on government checks are technically homeless, living crammed into dilapidated, roach-infested motels or even in tent camps in the woods. Through visceral, frontline reporting from the motels and encampments dotting central Florida, renowned sociologist Andrew Ross exposes the overlooked housing crisis sweeping America's suburbs and rural areas.

"Ross calls to end market-driven housing and empower residents to make reform; for dwellers and policy-makers, reading this book may be a first step toward that empowerment." —*Library Journal*
Includes bibliographical references and index.

363.509794 Housing — California

Dougherty, Conor
Golden Gates: The Fight for Housing—and Democracy—in America's Most Prosperous City. Conor Dougherty. Penguin Press 2020. 384 p.
ISBN 9780525560210
Grades: Adult   363.509794
1. Housing 2. Working class 3. Urban planning 4. Home ownership 5. Discrimination in housing 6. San Francisco, California 7. California 8. Society and culture — Urban and regional studies 9. Business and economics — Economics — History 10. Business and economics — Economics — Socioeconomics
LC 2019039425

An economics reporter at the New York Times, through ground-level reporting, chronicles America's housing crisis from its West Coast epicenter, revealing the decades of history and economic forces that have brought us here.

"Readers who assume there's no solution to sky-high rents in America's big cities should consult this detailed and optimistic counter-narrative." —*Publishers Weekly*
Includes bibliographical references and index.

363.6 Public utilities and related services

Clark, Anna
The Poisoned City: Flint's Water and the American Urban Tragedy. Anna Clark. Henry Holt & Co. 2018. 336 p.
ISBN 9781250125149
Grades: Adult   363.6
1. Public health 2. Water-supply 3. Lead contamination 4. Government accountability 5. Municipal government 6. State governments 7. Social advocacy 8. Health policy 9. Public works 10. Health hazards 11. Flint, Michigan 12. Michigan 13. Society and culture — Urban and regional studies 14. Politics and global affairs — Public health
LC 2018021437

Documents the 2014 poisoning of the residents of Flint, Michigan, by contaminated water, and the ensuing 18-month activism case that only got the state to admit its complicity after 12 people died and many others suffered permanent injuries.

"A compelling must-read about issues of environmental activism, urban issues, systemic racism, and the accountability of the government to the people whom it serves." —*Library Journal*

Heacox, Kim
National Geographic the National Parks: An Illustrated History. Kim Heacox. National Geographic 2016. 367 pages : Color; Illustration
ISBN 9781426215599
Grades: Adult   363.6
1. National parks and reserves 2. United States 3. Arts and Entertainment — Photography 4. History writing — United States
LC 2015014107

A lavishly photographed celebration of the National Park Service's 100th anniversary combines top-selected National Geographic photography with expert historical coverage of topics ranging from the Grand Canyon to the Statue of Liberty.

A tribute to the National Park Service collects photographs of the country's parks, artifacts, and memorabilia, with stories about sites, rangers, and the history of the service.

"Gorgeous in every way, and essential for travel and history shelves." —*Library Journal*
Includes index.

ESSENTIAL AND RECOMMENDED TITLES
363.7 Environmental problems

363.7 Environmental problems

Campbell, Hayley
All the Living and the Dead: From Embalmers to Executioners, an Exploration of the People Who Have Made Death Their Life's Work. Hayley Campbell. St. Martin's Press 2022. 288 pages
ISBN 9781250281845
Grades: Adult   363.7
1. Culture 2. Grief 3. Death 4. Dead 5. Society and culture — General

We are surrounded by death. It is in our news, our nursery rhymes, our true-crime podcasts. Yet from a young age, we are told that death is something to be feared. How are we supposed to know what we're so afraid of, when we are never given the chance to look? Fuelled by a childhood fascination with death, journalist Hayley Campbell searches for answers from the people who choose to make a living by working with the dead. Along the way, Campbell encounters funeral directors, embalmers, a man who dissects cadavers for anatomy students, and a former executioner who is responsible for ending 62 lives. She sits in a van with gravediggers who have already dug their own graves, holds a brain at an autopsy, visits a cryonics facility in Michigan, and goes for late-night Chinese with a homicide detective. Through Campbell's probing, reverent interviews with these people who see death every day, Campbell pieces together the psychic jigsaw to ask- Why would someone choose a life of working with the dead? And what does dealing with death every day do to you as a person? A dazzling work of cultural criticism, All the Living and the Dead weaves together reportage with memoir, history, and philosophy, to offer readers a fascinating look into the psychology of Western death.

"Journalist Campbell (The Art of Neil Gaiman) delivers a gripping look at professionals who deal with the end of life and their efforts to give people 'Dignity in death.'…This is a vivid and open-minded look at a taboo topic." —*Publishers Weekly*

Eklof, Johan
The Darkness Manifesto: On Light Pollution, Night Ecology, and the Ancient Rhythms That Sustain Life. Johan Eklöf, translated from the Swedish by Elizabeth DeNoma. Scribner 2023. 256 p.
ISBN 9781668000892
Grades: Adult   363.7
1. Night 2. Light pollution 3. Light and darkness 4. Nature 5. Effect of humans on nature 6. Translations — Swedish to English 7. Nature Writing — Environmental issues
LC 2022037888

A Swedish conservationist and bat scientist, in this persuasive, meticulously researched book, urges us to appreciate natural darkness, its creatures and its unique benefits for the sake of the environment, our own wellbeing and all life on earth.

"A captivating, poetic call for greater awareness of the natural cycles of the world." —*Kirkus*

Tranlsation of: Mörkermanifestet. Sweden : Natur & Kultur, c2020; Copyright 2020 by Johan Eklöf and Natur & Kultur, English language translation copyright 2022 by Elizabeth DeNoma - t.P. verso; Includes bibliographical references and index.

Hendrickson, Debra
★ *The Air They Breathe: A Pediatrician on the Frontlines of Climate Change.* Debra Hendrickson. Simon & Schuster 2024. 240 p.
ISBN 9781501197130
Grades: Adult   363.7
1. Climate change 2. Children 3. Air pollution 4. Health 5. Public health 6. Health policy 7. Ethics 8. Air quality 9. Science Writing — Medicine and health 10. Society and culture — Illness and disease

"Pediatrician Hendrickson debuts with an affecting report on climate change's dire effects on young people…This visceral study is not easily forgotten." —*Publishers Weekly*

Lustgarten, Abrahm
★ *On the Move: The Overheating Earth and the Uprooting of America.* Abrahm Lustgarten. Farrar, Straus and Giroux 2024. 384 p.
ISBN 9780374171735
Grades: Adult   363.7
1. Climate change 2. Global warming 3. Environmental refugees 4. Migration, Internal 5. Environmental disasters 6. Forced relocations 7. United States 8. Science Writing — Weather 9. Nature Writing — Environmental Issues 10. Nature Writing — Natural Disaster 11. Politics and global affairs — Environmental issues and policies
LC 2023040981

Humanity is on the precipice of a great climate migration, and Americans will not be spared. Tens of millions of people are likely to be driven from the places they call home. Poorer communities will be left behind, while growth will surge in cities and regions most attractive to climate refugees. America will be changed utterly. On the Move is the definitive account of what this massive population shift might look like. The United States will be rendered unrecognizable by four unstoppable forces: Wildfires in the West; frequent flooding in coastal regions; extreme heat and humidity in the South; and droughts that will make farming all but impossible across much of the nation.

"ProPublica environmental reporter Lustgarten delivers an urgent examination of how the U.S. will be affected by migrations driven by global warming…Readers will be unnerved." —*Publishers Weekly*

Includes bibliographical references and index.

Prickett, Pamela J.
★ *The Unclaimed: Abandonment and Hope in the City of Angels.* Pamela Prickett and Stefan Timmermans. Crown 2024. 336 p.
ISBN 9780593239056
Grades: Adult   363.7
1. Death 2. Dead 3. Abandonment (Psychology) 4. Loneliness 5. Homelessness 6. Inequality 7. Social marginality 8. Local government 9. Social workers 10. Undertakers 11. Urban problems 12. Social isolation 13. Social problems 14. Los Angeles, California 15. Family and Relationships — Aging and Death 16. Society and culture — Urban and regional studies
LC 2023048688

In this extraordinary work of narrative nonfiction, two sociologists investigate the rising number of unclaimed dead in America today, following four individuals in Los Angeles at risk of going unclaimed, and introducing us to the scene investigators, notification officers and crematorium workers who care for them when no one else will.

"A poignant and disturbing book, researched and written with appropriate sensitivity, care, and dignity." —*Kirkus*

Includes bibliographical references and index.

363.72 Sanitation

Flowers, Catherine Coleman
Waste: One Woman's Fight Against America's Dirty Secret. Catherine Coleman Flowers; foreword by Bryan Stevenson. The New Press 2020. 210 p.
ISBN 9781620976081
Grades: Adult   363.72
1. Flowers, Catherine Coleman 2. Sewage disposal 3. Sanitation 4. Environmentalists 5. Racism in environmental policy 6. Environmental justice 7. Environmental policy 8. Public health 9. Climate change 10. Environmental degradation 11. United States 12. Politics and global affairs — Environmental issues and policies 13. Society and culture — Wealth and class — Poverty
LC 2020027724

The Equal Justice Initiative's "Erin Brockovich of Sewage" traces her evolution as an activist and the growing environmental justice movement on behalf of rural Americans whose are losing access to basic sanitation because of racism, poverty and climate change.

PUBLIC LIBRARY CORE COLLECTION: NONFICTION
Twentieth Edition

Franklin-Wallis, Oliver
★ *Wasteland: The Secret World of Waste and the Urgent Search for a Cleaner Future.* Oliver Franklin-Wallis. Hachette Books 2023. 336 p.
ISBN 9780306827112
Grades: Adult   363.72
1. Solid waste disposal 2. Solid waste 3. Environmental degradation 4. Sustainable living 5. Garbage collection 6. Solid waste management 7. Nature Writing — Environmental Issues 8. Business and economics — Industries

An award-winning investigative journalist takes us on a shocking journey inside the waste industry, the secretive multibillion dollar world underpinning the modern economy, to tell a new story of humanity based on what we leave behind, and, along the way, shares a blueprint for building a healthier, more sustainable world.

"Wasteland is an all-encompassing journey into what we throw away. The author's penetrating insight into how we both create and are threatened by this garbage shows the striking connection between humanity and our planet." —*Booklist*

Roy, Saumya
Castaway Mountain: Love and Loss Among the Wastepickers of Mumbai. Saumya Roy. Astra House 2021. 300 p.
ISBN 9781662600951
Grades: Adult   363.72
1. Landfills 2. Hazardous waste sites 3. Ragpickers 4. Solid waste 5. Poor families 6. Squatter families 7. Scavenging 8. Diseases 9. Gangs 10. Survival 11. Fathers and daughters 12. Consumerism 13. Mumbai, India 14. Society and culture — Wealth and class — Poverty 15. Society and culture — Urban and regional studies 16. Nature Writing — Environmental Issues 17. Life stories — Facing adversity

The story of a girl who becomes obsessed with picking through the enormous Deonar garbage mountains in Mumbai in an effort to exploit urban overconsumption to find treasure that could lift her family's fortunes.

"Readers of Behind the Beautiful Forevers will be drawn to this harrowing portrait." —*Publishers Weekly*

Published in the UK by Profile Books as Mountain tales: Love and loss in the municipality of castaway belongings, 2021.

363.7209749 Sanitation — New Jersey

Fagin, Dan
Toms River: A Small Town, a Cancer Cluster, and the Epic Quest to Expose Pollution's Hidden Consequences. Dan Fagin. Bantam Books 2013. xv, 538 p. : Map
ISBN 9780553806533
Grades: Adult   363.7209749
1. Corporate cover-ups 2. Pollution 3. Illegal hazardous waste disposal 4. Cancer 5. Water pollution 6. Dye industry and trade 7. Investigative journalism 8. Business corruption 9. Chemical industry and trade 10. Health hazards 11. New Jersey 12. Nature Writing — Environmental Issues 13. Business and economics — Corruption and scandal

National Academies Communication Award, 2014; Pulitzer Prize for General Nonfiction, 2014.

Recounts the decades-long saga of the New Jersey seaside town plagued by childhood cancers caused by air and water pollution due to the indiscriminate dumping of toxic chemicals.

Includes bibliographical references and index.

363.738 Pollutants

Bell, Alice R.
Our Biggest Experiment: An Epic History of the Climate Crisis. Alice Bell. Counterpoint 2021. 384 p.
ISBN 9781640094338
Grades: Adult   363.738
1. Environmental sciences 2. Environmentalists 3. Science 4. Global warming 5. Climate change 6. Fossil fuels 7. Climatology 8. Earth sciences 9. Research 10. Nature Writing — Environmental Issues 11. History writing — Science, technology, and medicine 12. Science Writing — General

LC 2020053206

Drawing from science, politics and technology, this illuminating book sheds new light on the little-known scientists throughout history who helped build our modern understanding of climate change.

"The discovery of climate change arrived not with a bang but slowly over many centuries of lesser-known findings, writes activist and journalist Bell (Can We Save the Planet?) in this thorough and sweeping history of the climate crisis. . . . Bell makes a convincing case that in order to effectively deal with climate change, people must understand how the world got to this point." —*Publishers Weekly*

Includes bibliographical references.

Berners-Lee, Mike
The Carbon Footprint of Everything. Mike Berners-Lee. Greystone Press 2022. 312 p.
ISBN 9781771645768
Grades: Adult   363.738
1. Climate change 2. Global warming 3. Environmental degradation 4. Environmental responsibility 5. Consumer economics 6. Politics and global affairs — Environmental issues and policies 7. Business and economics — Economics — Consumerism

The Carbon Footprint of Everything breaks items down by the amount of carbon they produce, creating a calorie guide for the carbon-conscious. With engaging writing, leading carbon expert Mike Berners-Lee shares new carbon calculations based on recent research. He considers the impact of the pandemic on the carbon battle—especially the embattled global supply chain—and adds items we didn't consider a decade ago, like bitcoin and other cryptocurrencies.

This new edition of How Bad Are Bananas? (2010) comes with a new title and updated numbers. The numbers are, as Berners-Lee states, 'The best estimate we can get of the full climate change impact of something.' —*Booklist*

Carson, Rachel
★ *Silent Spring.* Rachel Carson; introduction by Linda Lear; afterword by Edward O. Wilson; drawings by Lois and Louis Darling. Houghton Mifflin 2002. xix, 378 p. : Illustration
ISBN 9780618253050
Grades: 11 12 Adult   363.738
1. Insect pests 2. Poisons 3. Environmental degradation 4. Pesticides 5. Environmentalism 6. Nature Writing — Environmental Issues

LC BL2002012485

Discusses the reckless annihilation of fish and birds by the use of pesticides and warns of the possible genetic effects on humans.

"Understand, yes, and shudder, for she has drawn a living portrait of what is happening to this balance nature has decreed in the science of life—and what man is doing (and has done) to destroy it and create a science of death." —*Kirkus*

Includes bibliographical references (p. [301]-355) and index; Originally published in 1962.

Fox, Porter
The Last Winter: The Scientists, Adventurers, Journeymen, and Mavericks Trying to Save the World. Porter Fox. Little Brown & Company 2021. 384 p.
ISBN 9780316460927
Grades: Adult   363.738
1. Climate change 2. Global environmental change 3. Effect of humans on nature 4. Winter 5. Scientists 6. Adventurers 7. Journalists 8. Voyages and travels 9. Snow 10. Ice 11. Environmentalism 12. Nature Writing — Environmental issues 13. Science Writing — Weather 14. Travel Writing — General

As the planet warms due to greenhouse gas emissions, winter as we know it is disappearing. In the last fifty years, the Northern Hemisphere lost a million square miles of spring snowpack and in the US alone, snow cover has been reduced by 15-30%. On average, winter has shrunk by a month in most northern latitudes. In this deeply researched and adventure-filled book, journalist Porter Fox travels along the edge of the Northern Hemisphere's snow line to track the

ESSENTIAL AND RECOMMENDED TITLES
363.8 Food supply

scope of this drastic change, and ultimately, predict what the future of winter-or lack thereof-will look like. This original research will be animated by five harrowing and illuminating journeys- each grounded by interviews with idiosyncratic, charismatic experts in their respective fields and Fox's own narrative of growing up on a remote island in Northern Maine.

"Fox (Northland), editor of the literary journal Nowhere, spotlights a warming world in this moving travelogue about snowy places and the people who inhabit them. . . . Environmentalists will find much to savor in this exciting yet distressing tale." —*Publishers Weekly*

Goodell, Jeff
The **Heat** *Will Kill You First: Life and Death on a Scorched Planet*, Jeff Goodell. Little Brown & Company 2023. 352 p.
ISBN 9780316497572
Grades: Adult 363.738
1. Climate change 2. Temperature 3. Global warming 4. Climatic extremes 5. Heat 6. Nature Writing — Environmental issues

A New York Times best-selling journalist shares an explosive new understanding of heat in this searing examination of the impact that rising temperatures will have on our lives and on our planet.

"A sobering assessment of the risks of global warming." —*Publishers Weekly*

Holthaus, Eric
The **Future** *Earth: A Radical Vision for What's Possible in the Age of Warming*. Eric Holthaus. HarperOne 2020. 247 pages
ISBN 9780062883162
Grades: Adult 363.738
1. Climate change 2. Climatology 3. Global environmental change 4. Politics and global affairs — Environmental issues and policies 5. Nature Writing — Environmental Issues

A hopeful book about climate change shows readers how to reverse the short- and long-term effects of climate change over the next three decades.

"Climate journalist Holthaus imagines a different world in his cautionary but guardedly optimistic debut about how humanity might meet the climate change challenge. . . . Serious and substantial, this will give readers plenty to consider." —*Publishers Weekly*

Includes bibliographical references (pages 231-247).

Kolbert, Elizabeth
Field *Notes from a Catastrophe: Man, Nature, and Climate Change*. Elizabeth Kolbert. Bloomsbury Pub. 2006. 210 p. : Illustration; Map
ISBN 9781596911253
Grades: 11 12 Adult 363.738
1. Global warming 2. Climate change 3. Global temperature changes 4. Global environmental change 5. Nature Writing — Environmental Issues
ALA Notable Book, 2007; New York Times Notable Book, 2006.

A New Yorker writer tackles the controversial issue of global warming from every angle, incorporating interviews with researchers and environmentalists, explaining the science and the studies, unpacking the politics, drawing parallels to lost ancient civilizations, and presenting the personal tales of those who are being affected most.

"On the burgeoning shelf of cautionary but occasionally alarmist books warning about the consequences of dramatic climate change, Kolbert's calmly persuasive reporting stands out for its sobering clarity." —*Publishers Weekly*
Includes bibliographical references (p. 195-203) and index.

O'Brien, Keith
Paradise *Falls: The True Story of an Environmental Catastrophe*. Keith O'Brien. Pantheon Books 2022. 352 p.
ISBN 9780593318430
Grades: Adult 363.738
1. Chemical plants 2. Hazardous waste sites 3. Community activism 4. Women radicals 5. Industrial wastes 6. Environmentally induced diseases 7. Pollution 8. Communities 9. Health hazards 10. New York (State) 11. 1970s 12. 20th century 13. Collective biographies 14. Life stories — Politics — Activists and reformers 15. Nature writing — Environmental issues
LC 2021038250

From the New York Times best-selling journalist, the staggering, hidden story of an unlikely band of mothers who discovered the deadly secret of Love Canal, and exposed one of America's most devastating environmental disasters.

"O'Brien's (Fly Girls) meticulously researched and gripping history of the massive environmental disaster at Love Canal draws readers into the unrest, anxiety, and bewilderment of everyday people discovering their beloved neighborhood is poisoned and deadly." —*Library Journal*
Includes bibliographical references and index.

Rich, Nathaniel
Losing *Earth: A Recent History*. Nathaniel Rich. MCD/Farrar, Straus and Giroux 2019. x, 206 pages : Illustration
ISBN 9780374191337
Grades: Adult 363.738
1. Global warming 2. Global environmental change 3. Greenhouse effect, Atmospheric 4. Oil industry and trade 5. Environmentalism 6. Nature Writing — Environmental Issues 7. Science writing — Weather
LC 2018056269
Booklist Editors' Choice, 2019.

An account of the failures that prevented the world from committing to taking measures against climate change documents key negotiations against the backdrop of 1980s history while explaining what the choices of the past mean for today's world.
Includes bibliographical references (pages 205-206).

Thunberg, Greta
★ *The* **Climate** *Book: The Facts and the Solutions*. Greta Thunberg. The Penguin Press 2023. 352 p.
ISBN 9780593492307
Grades: Adult 363.738
1. Environmental protection 2. Climate change 3. Environmentalism 4. Environmentalists 5. Climate change mitigation 6. Social participation 7. Nature Writing — Environmental issues 8. Politics and global affairs — Environmental issues and policies
LC Bl2022038954

Gathering together the wisdom of over 100 experts, the world's leading climate activist arms us with the knowledge we need to combat climate disaster, showing there is hope, but only if we listen to the science before it's too late.

"The contributors to this multifaceted and vast source of climate knowledge offer irreproachable statistical analyses and impassioned altruistic assessments, making it a definitive book on climate change." —*Booklist*
Originally published in the UK by Allen Lane, London, in 2022.

363.8 Food supply

Puleo, Stephen
Voyage *of Mercy: The Uss Jamestown, the Irish Famine, and the Remarkable Story of America's First Humanitarian Mission*. Stephen Puleo. St. Martin's Press 2020. xviii, 313 pages : Illustration
ISBN 9781250200471
Grades: Adult 363.8
1. Forbes, R. B. (Robert Bennet), 1804-1889 2. Mathew, Theobald, 1790-1856 3. Famines 4. Food relief 5. Humanitarianism 6. Economic assistance, American 7. Warships 8. Ireland 9. United States 10. 1840s 11. Irish Potato Famine (1845-1852) 12. 19th century 13. History writing — Europe — Ireland 14. History writing — Antebellum America — United States
LC 2019043128

A historian tells the extraordinary story of Ireland's great potato famine in the late 1840s, the Jamestown voyage and the commitment of thousands of ordinary Americans to offer relief to Ireland, establishing the US as the leader in international aid.

PUBLIC LIBRARY CORE COLLECTION: NONFICTION
Twentieth Edition

"An uplifting historical account of humanitarianism with lessons in this increasingly isolationist time." —*Kirkus*

Includes bibliographical references (pages [283]-303) and index.

363.9 Population problems

Rutherford, Adam
Control: The Dark History and Troubling Present of Eugenics. Adam Rutherford. W.W. Norton & Company 2022. 288 p.
ISBN 9781324035602
Grades: Adult   **363.9**
1. Eugenics 2. Gene editing 3. Medical ethics 4. Social movements 5. Social control 6. Racism 7. Classism 8. Science Writing — Biology 9. History writing — Science, technology, and medicine

LC 2022027417

How did an obscure academic idea pave the way to the Holocaust within just fifty years? Inspired by Darwin's ideas about evolution, the concept of race purification through eugenics arose in Victorian England and quickly spread to America, where it was embraced by presidents, funded by Gilded Age monopolists, and enshrined into racist American laws that became the ideological cornerstone of the Third Reich. Adam Rutherford explains why eugenics remains so tempting to powerful people who wish to improve society through reproductive control, and the scientific impossibility of doing so.

"A century of efforts to breed, sterilize, or slaughter the way to grasp control over 'Who lives' is lambasted in this stinging study of the eugenics movement." —*Publishers Weekly*

Includes bibliographical references and index.

363.96 Birth control

Wade, Sabia
Birthing Liberation: How Reproductive Justice Can Set Us Free. Sabia Wade. Chicago Review Press 2023. 272 p.
ISBN 9781641607964
Grades: Adult   **363.96**
1. Reproductive rights 2. Justice 3. Racism 4. Childbirth 5. Medical care 6. Marginalized people 7. Racism in medical care 8. Science Writing — Medicine and health 9. Society and culture — Race 10. Debut title

"This deeply empathetic overview of medical racism will outrage and has the power to inspire change." —*Publishers Weekly*

364 Criminology

Crump, Benjamin
Open Season: Legalized Genocide of Colored People. Ben Crump. Amistad 2019. 272 pages
ISBN 9780062375094
Grades: Adult   **364**
1. Crump, Benjamin, 1969- 2. African American lawyers 3. Civil rights lawyers 4. Civil rights 5. Racism 6. Racism in the criminal justice system 7. Trials (Murder) 8. Genocide 9. Racial profiling 10. Police brutality 11. Crime and race 12. Judicial system 13. African Americans 14. Voter suppression 15. Voter fraud 16. Legislation 17. African American history 18. Race relations 19. United States 20. Autobiographies and memoirs 21. History writing — African American — Civil rights — United States 22. Life stories — Law and order — Judges and lawyers 23. Society and culture — Race

The president of the National Bar Association and a civil rights attorney chronicles his most memorable legal battles, including Trayvon Martin and Michael Brown, and describes the hidden and systemic injustices minorities face in the U.S. legal system.

364.1 Criminal offenses

Bernstein, Carl
★ *All the President's Men.* Carl Bernstein, Bob Woodward. Simon & Schuster 1999. 349 p. : Illustration
ISBN 9780684863559
Grades: 11 12 Adult   **364.1**
1. Bernstein, Carl, 1944- 2. Woodward, Bob, 1943- 3. Watergate Scandal 4. Political corruption 5. Politicians 6. Criminal investigation 7. Presidents 8. United States 9. 1970s 10. 20th century 11. Page to screen 12. History writing — Presidency — 20th century — United States 13. History writing — 1970s — United States 14. History writing — Scandals

LC 98054773

The two Washington Post reporters present the inside story of their inquiry into the persons involved in the Watergate scandal.

"Bernstein and Woodward, the two Washington Post journalists who broke the Big Story, tell how they did it by old fashioned seat-of-the-pants reporting—in other words, lots of intuition and a thick stack of phone numbers." —*Kirkus*

Includes index; Originally published: New York : Simon & Schuster, 1974.

Bugliosi, Vincent
★ *Helter Skelter: The True Story of the Manson Murders.* Vincent Bugliosi with Curt Gentry. W. W. Norton 1994. 687 p. : Illustration; Map
ISBN 9780393322231
Grades: 11 12 Adult   **364.1**
1. Manson, Charles, 1934-2017 2. Murderers 3. Trials (Murder) 4. Mind control 5. Murder 6. California 7. Page to screen 8. True Crime — Murder 9. Nonfiction that reads like fiction

LC Bl2005022570

Edgar Allan Poe Award for Best Fact Crime, 1975.

The prosecutor of the Tate-LaBianca trials presents the inside story behind the Manson killings, explaining how Charles Manson was able to make his "family" murder for him, chronicling the investigation, and describing the court trial that brought him and his accomplices to justice.

Includes index; Originally published: New York : Norton, 1974.

Bullough, Oliver
Moneyland: The Inside Story of the Crooks and Kleptocrats Who Rule the World. Oliver Bullough. St. Martin's Press 2019. 320 p.
ISBN 9781250208705
Grades: Adult   **364.1**
1. Money laundering 2. Organized crime 3. Political corruption 4. Business corruption 5. Crime prevention 6. Business and economics — Corruption and scandal

An investigative journalist's deep dive into the corrupt workings of the world's kleptocrats takes him from ruined towns on the edge of Siberia, to Bond-villain lairs in London and Manhattan.

"An indefatigable investigative journalist, Bullough has traveled the world, from Siberia to the Seychelles, to untangle this web of deceit, avarice, and amorality. The result is an eye-opening and stomach-churning expos of financial transgressions on a global scale that threatens democracy and the institutions charged with its protection." —*Booklist*

Includes bibliographical references and index.

Capote, Truman
★ *In Cold Blood: A True Account of a Multiple Murder and Its Consequences.* Truman Capote. Vintage Books 1994. 343 p.
ISBN 9780679745587
Grades: 11 12 Adult   **364.1**
1. Smith, Perry Edward, 1928-1965 2. Clutter family 3. Hickok, Richard Eugene, 1931-1965 4. Murder 5. Crime scenes 6. Murder victims 7. Murder investigation 8. Criminals 9. Sixteen-year-old girls 10. Small town life 11. Violence 12. United States history 13. Kansas 14. 1950s 15. 20th century 16. Page to screen 17. True Crime — Murder 18. Adult books for young adults 19. Nonfiction that reads like fiction

ESSENTIAL AND RECOMMENDED TITLES
364.1 Criminal offenses

LC 93006282

Edgar Allan Poe Award for Best Fact Crime, 1966.

Presents Capote's masterful account of the senseless 1959 murders of four members of a farm family in Holcomb, Kansas, and the search for the killers, Richard Eugene Hickock and Perry Edward Smith.

Appeared originally in the New Yorker in slightly different form; Originally published: New York : Random House, 1965.

De Leon, Jason

★ *Soldiers* and Kings: Survival and Hope in the World of Human Smuggling. Jason De Leon. Viking Press 2024. 400 p.

ISBN 9780593298589

Grades: Adult   364.1

1. Human smuggling 2. Immigration and emigration 3. Migrant workers 4. Smuggling 5. Smugglers 6. Undercover operations 7. Anthropologists 8. North American history 9. Latin America 10. Mexico 11. Biographies 12. Nonfiction that reads like fiction 13. Life stories — Facing adversity

LC 2023017436

An internationally recognized anthropologist, who embedded himself within a group of smugglers moving migrants across Mexico over the course of seven years, presents this first-ever, character-driven look at human smuggling that revolves around the life and death of one coyote who falls in love and tries to leave smuggling behind.

"An exemplary ethnography of central importance to any discussion of immigration policy or reform." —*Kirkus*

Includes bibliographical references and index.

Dray, Philip

At the Hands of Persons Unknown: The Lynching of Black America. Philip Dray. Random House 2002. xii, 528 p, 8 p. of plates : Illustration

ISBN 9780375754456

Grades: Adult   364.1

1. Crimes against African Americans 2. Lynching 3. Race relations 4. Southern States 5. United States 6. History writing — African American — Civil rights — United States

LC 2001040366

Robert F. Kennedy Book Award, 2003; Pulitzer Prize for History finalist, 2003.

A history of lynching in America describes its common use, especially in the southern United States, and discusses the crusade by a handful of Black and white citizens to eliminate the shameful practice.

"Dray balances moral indignation with a sound understanding of history and politics. The result is vital, hard-hitting cultural history." —*Publishers Weekly*

Includes bibliographical references (p. [467]-477) and index.

Eig, Jonathan

Get Capone: The Real Story of America's Legendary Gangster. Jonathan Eig. Simon & Schuster 2010. 480 p. cm.

ISBN 9781416580591

Grades: Adult   364.1

1. Capone, Al, 1899-1947 2. Criminals 3. Arrest 4. Gangsters 5. Organized crime 6. Prohibition 7. Tax evasion 8. Crime bosses 9. Chicago, Illinois 10. 1930s 11. Biographies 12. True Crime — Organized Crime, Mafia, and Gangs 13. History writing — Roaring 20s — United States 14. Life stories — Law and order — Criminals and law-breakers

LC 2009033949

Traces the criminal investigation of the notorious mobster, documenting his rise during the Prohibition era, the legal strategy that enabled his prosecution, and the possibility that he was innocent of the St. Valentine's Day massacre.

"The author rescues the narrative of AL Capone from the realm of pop melodrama, offering vibrant historical storytelling and a nuanced, enigmatic portrait of Capone and his Chicago milieu. An impressive, accessible history of a troubled time." —*Kirkus*

Includes bibliographical references and index.

Fenton, Justin

We Own This City: A True Story of Crime, Cops, and Corruption. Justin Fenton. Random House 2021. 352 p.

ISBN 9780593133668

Grades: Adult   364.1

1. Jenkins, Wayne, 1980- 2. Police corruption 3. Drug traffic 4. Organized crime 5. Police misconduct 6. Crime 7. 2010s 8. Page to screen 9. True Crime — Organized Crime, Mafia, and Gangs 10. True Crime — Police and Lawyers

LC 2020020879

Documents the corrupt activities of sergeant Wayne Jenkins and the Gun Trace Task Force of 2015-2017 Baltimore, revealing how they skimmed confiscated drugs and money while planting evidence to hide their crimes, triggering wrongful convictions and at least two deaths.

"Baltimore Sun reporter Fenton, whose coverage of the Baltimore riots that followed the death of Freddie Gray led to a Pulitzer Prize nomination, debuts with a searing look at that city's recent police corruption scandal." —*Publishers Weekly*

Made into a TV show on HBO starting in 2022; Includes bibliographical references and index.

Fox, Margalit

The Talented Mrs. Mandelbaum: The Rise and Fall of an American Organized-crime Boss. by Margalit Fox. Random House 2024. 384 p.

ISBN 9780593243855

Grades: Adult   364.1

1. Mandelbaum, Fredericka, 1825-1894 2. Thieves 3. Criminals 4. Receiving stolen goods 5. Organized crime 6. Ambition 7. Resilience 8. Corruption 9. New York (State) 10. United States 11. New York city 12. 19th century 13. Biographies 14. True Crime — Historical crime 15. Life stories — Law and order — Criminals and law-breakers 16. True Crime — Organized Crime, Mafia, and Gangs

LC 2023044598

Painting a vibrant portrait of Gilded Age New York—and of a once-famous, now-forgotten heroine, this unforgettable story of America's first lady of organized crime who, by the mid-1880s, amassed a huge fortune, recounts how she turned theft into a viable, scalable business.

"Fox's detailed descriptions of intricate heists make for a transfixing tale." —*Publishers Weekly*

Includes bibliographical references and index.

Gleeson, John

The Gotti Wars: Taking Down America's Most Notorious Mobster. John Gleeson. Simon & Scribner 2022. 336 p.

ISBN 9781982186920

Grades: Adult   364.1

1. Gleeson, John, 1953 July 14- 2. Gotti, John 3. Lawyers 4. Public prosecutors 5. Crime bosses 6. Organized crime 7. Betrayal 8. Trials (Murder) 9. Jury tampering 10. Wire-tapping 11. Electronic surveillance 12. Justice 13. New York City 14. True Crime — Organized Crime, Mafia, and Gangs 15. True Crime — Investigations and Trials 16. Life stories — Law and order — Judges and lawyers

This epic, page-turning courtroom drama is a brilliantly told crime story of a tenacious prosecutor who managed to end John Gotti's reign with a murder conviction that subsequently took down the Mafia altogether.

"In this exceptional debut, former federal prosecutor Gleeson chronicles his efforts to bring Gambino family crime boss John Gotti to justice." —*Publishers Weekly*

Honig, Elie

Untouchable: How Powerful People Get Away with It. Elie Honig. Harper 2023. 288 p.

ISBN 9780063241503

Grades: Adult   364.1

1. Crime 2. Elite (Social sciences) 3. Power 4. Rich people 5. Criminal justice system 6. Judicial corruption 7. Injustice 8. Society and culture — Violence and crime — Criminal justice system 9. Society and culture — Wealth and class

PUBLIC LIBRARY CORE COLLECTION: NONFICTION
Twentieth Edition

A CNN senior legal analyst and nationally best-selling author explores America's two-tier justice system, explaining how the rich, the famous, and the powerful—including, most notoriously, Donald Trump—manipulate the legal system to escape justice and get away with vast misdeeds.

"CNN legal analyst Honig (Hatchet Man) delivers a disturbing analysis of how the U.S. justice system makes it so difficult to hold the wealthy and well-connected to account for their crimes....His fluid prose and sharp analysis amount to a slam-dunk case that American justice is far from blind." —*Publishers Weekly*

Posner, Gerald L.
Case Closed: Lee Harvey Oswald and the Assassination of JFK. Gerald L. Posner. Random House 1993. xv, 607 p. : Illustration
ISBN 9780679418252
Grades: Adult   364.1
1. Kennedy, John F. (John Fitzgerald), 1917-1963 2. Oswald, Lee Harvey, 1939-1963 3. Assassination 4. Conspiracies 5. Presidents 6. United States history 7. United States 8. 1960s 9. 20th century 10. History writing — Presidency — 20th century — United States 11. True Crime — Murder 12. History writing — Conspiracy theories
LC 93012821
Pulitzer Prize for History finalist, 1994.
An intensive reexamination of the Kennedy assassination uses new interviews, recently disclosed documents, the latest film advances, and more to prove that Oswald acted alone.
Includes bibliographical references (p. [579]-585) and index.

Reilly, Ryan J.
★ *Sedition Hunters: How January 6th Broke the Justice System.* Ryan J. Reilly. Public Affairs 2023. 320 p.
ISBN 9781541701809
Grades: Adult   364.1
1. Capitol Riot, Washington, D.C, 2021 2. Riots 3. Political violence 4. Presidential election, 2020 5. Justice 6. Domestic terrorism 7. Politics and government 8. United States 9. 2020s 10. Politics and global affairs — General 11. History writing — Early 21st century — United States
Recounting the January 6th attack on the Capitol building, a Justice reporter for NBC News, in this work of incredible reportage, gets to know the would-be revolutionaries, obsessive online sleuths and FBI agents, shining a light on a justice system struggling to maintain order in our polarized country.
"Reilly debuts with a detailed and riveting report of the January 6, 2021, Capitol riot that illuminates the work of a little-known cottage industry involved in the subsequent federal investigation: the 'Sedition hunters.'...The result is a crucial new window onto a historic event." —*Publishers Weekly*

Shannon, Elaine
Hunting Leroux: The Inside Story of the Dea Takedown of a Criminal Genius and His Empire. Elaine Shannon. William Morrow 2019. xiv, 354 pages, [16] pages of plates : Illustration
ISBN 9780062859136
Grades: Adult   364.1
1. Le Roux, Paul Calder 2. Computer crimes 3. Organized crime 4. Undercover operations 5. Criminals 6. Drug traffic 7. Crime bosses 8. Cartels 9. Murder investigation 10. Drug enforcement agents 11. Crime 12. Biographies 13. Life stories — Law and order — Criminals and law-breakers 14. True Crime — Drugs
The story of Paul LeRoux, the twisted-genius entrepreneur and cold-blooded killer who brought revolutionary innovation to international crime, and the exclusive inside story of how the DEA's elite, secretive 960 Group brought him down.
Includes bibliographical references (pages 335-342) and index.

Tyson, Timothy B.
The Blood of Emmett Till. Timothy B. Tyson. Simon & Schuster 2017. 304 p.
ISBN 9781476714844
Grades: Adult   364.1
1. Till, Emmett, 1941-1955 2. Lynching 3. Crimes against African Americans 4. Racism 5. Trials (Murder) 6. Hate crimes 7. Civil Rights Movement 8. African Americans 9. Race relations 10. United States history 11. Southern States 12. Mississippi 13. 20th century 14. True Crime — Murder 15. True Crime — Historical Crime 16. History writing — African American — Civil rights — United States
LC 2016021595
ALA Notable Book, 2018; New York Times Notable Book, 2017; Robert F. Kennedy Book Award, 2018; Longlisted for the National Book Award for Nonfiction, 2017.
Though several books have covered the 60-year-old case of Emmett Till's lynching in Mississippi, historian Timothy Tyson's new history freshly illuminates the trial of Till's murderers. He analyzes the trial transcript, which had been missing since 1955, interviews the key witness (now 80 years old) to Till's allegedly inappropriate behavior, and provides details from a recent FBI investigation. This riveting account immerses readers in the case and offers the definitive summary of its impact on subsequent history.
"Cinematically engaging, harrowing, and poignant, Tyson's monumental work illuminates Emmett Till's murder and serves as a powerful reminder that certain stories in history merit frequent retelling." —*Publishers Weekly*
Includes bibliographical references and index.

Vorobyov, Niko
Dopeworld: Adventures in the Global Drug Trade. Niko Vorobyov. St. Martin's Press 2020. 432 p.
ISBN 9781250270016
Grades: Adult   364.1
1. Vorobyov, Niko 2. Drug traffic 3. Drug dealers 4. Drug abuse 5. Drug control 6. Drug culture 7. Drugs 8. Cartels 9. Organized crime 10. Journalists 11. Decriminalization of drugs 12. True Crime — Drugs 13. Life stories — Law and order — Criminals and law-breakers 14. Travel Writing — General 15. History writing — Microhistory
LC 2020010724
Just as Anthony Bourdain's No Reservations did for the world of food, Dopeworld is an intoxicating journey into the world of drugs. From the cocaine farms in South America to the streets of Manila, Dopeworld traces the emergence of psychoactive substances and our intimate relationship with them. As a former drug dealer turned subversive scholar, with unparalleled access to drug lords, cartel leaders, street dealers and government officials, journalist Niko Vorobyov attempts to shine a light on the dark underbelly of the drug world.
"Vorobyov makes a persuasive case for the legalization of drugs in what he aptly calls 'A true crime, gonzo, social, historical-memoir meets fucked-up travel book.' It could well become a classic." —*Publishers Weekly*
Includes bibliographical references; Originally published: London : Hodder & Stoughton, 2019.

Weinman, Sarah
★ *Unspeakable Acts: True Tales of Crime, Murder, Deceit, and Obsession.* Sarah Weinman; introduction by Patrick Radden Keefe. Ecco Press 2020. 288 pages
ISBN 9780062839886
Grades: Adult   364.1
1. True-crime television programs 2. Popular culture 3. Victims of crimes 4. Podcasts 5. Murder 6. Murderers 7. Criminal investigation 8. Essays 9. True Crime — Murder 10. Society and culture — Violence and crime
LC Bl2020016866
Anthony Award for Best Critical/Nonfiction, 2021.
An anthology of modern true-crime writing illustrating the appeal of this powerful and popular genre; as a collection, they, showcase writing about true crime across the broadest possible spectrum, while also reflecting what makes crime stories so transfixing and irresistible to the modern reader.
"This anthology is essential reading for all true crime fans." —*Booklist*

ESSENTIAL AND RECOMMENDED TITLES
364.106 Organized crime

364.106 Organized crime

Bowden, Mark
Life Sentence: The Brief and Tragic Career of Baltimore's Deadliest Gang Leader. Mark Bowden. Pgw 2023. 320 p.
ISBN 9780802162427
Grades: Adult 364.106
1. Gangs 2. Organized crime 3. Gang members 4. Criminal justice system 5. Street life 6. Drug traffic 7. Poverty 8. Baltimore, Maryland 9. United States 10. True Crime — Organized Crime, Mafia, and Gangs 11. Society and culture — Violence and crime

In this unprecedented deep dive into inner-city ganglife, Mark Bowden takes readers inside a Baltimore gang, offers an in-depth portrait of its notorious leader, and chronicles the 2016 FBI investigation that landed eight gang members in prison.

"A gripping and revealing glimpse into Baltimore gang life and the city's efforts to combat street violence….A powerful, nuanced depiction of gang violence in America that makes a strong case for meaningful reform beyond policing." —*Kirkus*

Croke, Ken
Riding with Evil: Taking Down the Notorious Pagan Motorcycle Gang. Ken Croke, with Dave Wedge. William Morrow & Company 2022. 304 p.
ISBN 9780063092402
Grades: Adult 364.106
1. Croke, Ken 2. Government investigators 3. Law enforcement 4. Motorcycle gangs 5. White supremacists 6. Organized crime 7. Drug smuggling 8. Violent crimes 9. Undercover operations 10. Autobiographies and memoirs 11. Life stories — Law and order — Police and law officers 12. True Crime — Organized Crime, Mafia, and Gangs 13. True Crime — Police and Lawyers 14. Nonfiction that reads like fiction

Longtime ATF agent Ken Croke had earned the right to coast to the end of a storied career, having routinely gone undercover to apprehend white supremacists, gun runners, and gang members. But after a chance encounter with an associate of the Pagan Motorcycle Gang created an opening, he transformed himself into "Slam," a monstrous, axe-handle wielding enforcer whose duty was to protect the leadership "mother club" at all costs. He befriended the club's most violent and criminally insane members and lived among them for two years, covertly building a case that would eventually take down the top members of the gang in a massive federal prosecution, even as he risked his marriage, his sanity, and his life.

"Croke, with the help of bestseller Wedge (The Last Days of John Lennon with James Patterson), debuts with a nail-biting account of how he became the first ATF agent to infiltrate the Pagans, a violent white supremacist motorcycle gang….This engrossing account about the realities of undercover work is must reading for true crime aficionados." —*Publishers Weekly*

Dudley, Steven S.
Ms-13: The Making of America's Most Notorious Gang. Steven Dudley. Hanover Square Press 2020. 352 p.
ISBN 9781335005540
Grades: Adult 364.106
1. Gangs 2. Organized crime 3. Gang members 4. Immigrants 5. Refugees 6. Salvadoran Americans 7. Hispanic American gangs 8. Prisons 9. Criminal justice system 10. Street life 11. Drug traffic 12. Violent crimes 13. Los Angeles, California 14. United States 15. El Salvador 16. True Crime — Organized Crime, Mafia, and Gangs 17. Society and culture — Violence and crime 18. Life stories — Law and order — Criminals and law-breakers

LC BI2020013289

Looks at the most dangerous street gang in America—the MS13—as seen through the lives of one family caught in its malicious web.

"An outstanding book for true crime readers." —*Library Journal*

Nadeau, Barbie Latza
The Godmother: Murder, Vengeance, and the Bloody Struggle of Mafia Women. Barbie Latza Nadeau. Penguin Books 2022. 240 p.
ISBN 9780143136118
Grades: Adult 364.106
1. Maresca, Pupetta, 1935-2021 2. Women 3. Mafia 4. Organized crime 5. Collective biographies 6. True Crime — Organized Crime, Mafia, and Gangs 7. Life stories — Identity — Gender 8. Life stories — Law and order — Criminals and law-breakers

LC 2022001193

In The Godmother, investigative journalist Barbie Latza Nadeau tells the stories of the women who have risen to prominence, and fallen out of favor, in the Italian mob, beginning with the most infamous of these women: Pupetta Maresca. A Mafia woman born and raised, Pupetta avenged her husband's murder, firing 29 shots at the man who killed him. Woven throughout Pupetta's story is Nadeau's diligent research, and her personal interviews with the Mafia women themselves. Nadeau takes readers inside the Mafia families to paint a complete and complex portrait of the real culture that has shaped the Mafia, and the women who are part of it.

"Fans of Mafia-related pop culture and history will enjoy Nadeau's book, even as it overturns everything we thought we knew about the Mafia." —*Library Journal*

Includes bibliographical references.

Rubinstein, Julian
★ *The Holly: Five Bullets, One Gun, and the Struggle to Save an American Neighborhood.* Julian Rubinstein. Farrar, Straus & Giroux 2021. 400 p.
ISBN 9780374168919
Grades: Adult 364.106
1. Violent crimes 2. Violence and guns 3. Violence in gangs 4. Former gang members 5. Community development 6. Gentrification of cities 7. Public safety 8. Local government 9. Police and African Americans 10. Racism in law enforcement 11. Gangs 12. Race relations 13. United States history 14. Denver, Colorado 15. Society and culture — Violence and crime — Criminal justice system 16. Society and culture — Race 17. History writing — Regional history — United States 18. Antiracist literature

LC 2020057989

On the last Friday evening of the summer of 2013, five shots rang out in the parking lot of a new Boys & Girls Club in a part of northeast Denver known as the Holly. Long a destination for African American families fleeing the Jim Crow South, the Holly had become an "invisible city" within a historically white metropolis. While shootings weren't uncommon, the identity of the shooter that night came as a shock. Much more than the story of a shooting, the Holly is a multigenerational crime story that explores the porous boundaries between a city's elites and its most disadvantaged citizens, as well as the fraught interactions of police, confidential informants, activists, gang members, and ex-gang members trying—or not—to put their pasts behind them.

"This is a gripping deep dive into media underreporting and too-quick judgment, and, most shockingly, into how the criminal-justice industrial complex may be invested in systemic corruption designed to keep drug wars going." —*Booklist*

Includes bibliographical references.

364.106089 Organized crime — Ethnic and national groups

English, T. J.
The Corporation: An Epic Story of the Cuban American Underworld. T.J. English. William Morrow 2018. 400 p.
ISBN 9780062568960
Grades: Adult 364.106089
1. Gangsters 2. Organized crime 3. Cuban people in the United States 4. Cuban Americans 5. Crime bosses 6. Criminals 7. Murder 8. True crime — Organized crime, Mafia, and gangs 9. History writing — United States

LC 2017039510

A multigenerational history of the Cuban mob in the U.S., written by the best-selling author of Havana Nocturne, examines the role of South Florida's exile community in building a criminal empire as part of a plot to reclaim Cuba from the Castro regime.

"English capably covers half a century of criminal enterprise, avoiding the clichs of the true-crime genre while stocking his narrative with familiar players: the capos and goons, the cops and informants, a mistress or two, and John F. Kennedy." —*Kirkus*

Includes bibliographical references and index.

364.1060973 Organized crime — United States

Maier, Thomas
Mafia Spies: The Inside Story of the Cia, Gangsters, JFK, and Castro. Thomas Maier. Simon & Schuster 2019. xii, 388 pages
ISBN 9781510741713
Grades: Adult   364.1060973
1. Giancana, Sam, 1908-1975 2. Rosselli, Johnny, 1905-1976 3. Kennedy, John F. (John Fitzgerald), 1917-1963 4. Castro, Fidel, 1926-2016 5. Espionage 6. Organized crime 7. Assassins 8. Mafia 9. Gangsters 10. Spies 11. Undercover operations 12. Murder 13. Political intrigue 14. International intrigue 15. Subversive activities 16. Attempted assassination 17. International relations 18. Cuba 19. United States 20. 1960s 21. 20th century 22. History writing — Spies and spying 23. True Crime — Organized Crime, Mafia, and Gangs 24. History writing — 1960s — United States

LC Bl2019010606

The definitive account of America's most remarkable espionage plots ever—with CIA agents, mob hitmen, and James Bond-like killing devices together in a top-secret mystery full of surprise twists and deadly intrigue. In the early 1960s, two top gangsters, Johnny Roselli and Sam Giancana, were hired by the CIA to kill Cuba's Communist leader, Fidel Castro, only to wind up murdered themselves amidst Congressional hearings and a national debate about the JFK assassination.

"As he has done before, Maier offers another deft translation of murky American history, focused on dynamic, improbable protagonists." —*Kirkus*

364.10973 Criminal offenses — United States

Bowden, Mark
The Case of the Vanishing Blonde: And Other True Crime Stories. Mark Bowden. Atlantic Monthly Press 2020. 232 p.
ISBN 9780802128447
Grades: Adult   364.10973
1. Crime 2. Criminal investigation 3. Murder 4. Murder investigation 5. Detectives 6. Private investigators 7. Cold cases (Criminal investigation) 8. Police corruption 9. Investigative journalism 10. Essays 11. True Crime — General 12. Life stories — Law and order

LC 2020025999

These captivating true-crime stories, spanning Mark Bowden's long and illustrious career, cover a variety of crimes complicated by extraordinary circumstances. The Case of the Vanishing Blonde collects six of his most riveting pieces—accounts spanning four decades of searing characters and unsettling tales to illustrate all manner of crimes and the ways technology has progressively altered criminal investigation.

"This true crime master expands the limits of the genre, digging to find answers and revealing that even the most horrific crimes are often linked to a larger story about America." —*Library Journal*

364.13 Political and related offenses

Hale, Grace Elizabeth
In the Pines: A Lynching, a Lie, a Reckoning. Grace Elizabeth Hale. Little, Brown & Company 2023. xxxviii, 215 p.
ISBN 9780316564748
Grades: Adult   364.13
1. Hale, Grace Elizabeth 2. Women historians 3. Families 4. Small towns 5. Sheriffs 6. African American prisoners 7. Rape suspects 8. Murder 9. Police cover-ups 10. Family secrets 11. Racism 12. Racism in the criminal justice system 13. Local history 14. Mississippi 15. History writing — Regional history — United States 16. History writing — African American — United States 17. Society and culture — Race 18. Life stories — Law and order 19. Life stories — Relationships — Family

Grace Hale was home from college when she first heard the family legend. In 1947, while her beloved grandfather had been serving as a sheriff in the Piney Woods of south-central Mississippi, he prevented a lynch mob from killing a Black man who was in his jail on suspicion of raping a white woman—only for the suspect to die the next day during an escape attempt. Years later, as a rising scholar of white supremacy, Hale revisited the story about her grandfather and Versie Johnson. What she discovered would upend everything she thought she knew about her family, the tragedy, and this haunted strip of the South.

"In 1947, Versie Johnson, a Black man, was lynched in the town of Prentiss, MS. In this deeply personal tale, Hale (history, Univ. of Virginia; Cool Town) uncovers the truth about the role Sheriff Oury Berry, her grandfather, played in Johnson's murder." —*Library Journal*

Includes bibliographical references and index.

364.15 Offenses against the person

Abdulali, Sohaila
What We Talk About When We Talk About Rape. Sohaila Abdulali. New Press 2018. 224 p.
ISBN 9781620974735
Grades: Adult   364.15
1. Rape 2. Rape victims 3. Violence against women 4. Violence against marginalized women 5. Sexual violence 6. Social justice 7. Society and culture — Gender — Women 8. Society and culture — Violence and crime

LC 2018034364

Amelia Bloomer List, 2019.

The acclaimed viral Mumbai journalist draws on personal experiences, inspiring survivor testimonies and meticulous research in an urgent call to action that illuminates the socio-economics and cultural realities of rape from the perspectives of survivors, counselors and activists.

"She writes in a conversational style and injects a levity that, rather than betraying the seriousness of her subject, makes it more possible to handle the necessary yet horrifying details of rape of all kinds." —*Booklist*

Includes bibliographical references and index.

Barr, John
Start by Believing: Larry Nassar's Crimes, the Institutions That Enabled Him, and the Brave Women Who Stopped a Monster. John Barr and Dan Murphy. Hachette Books 2020. 320 p.
ISBN 9780316532150
Grades: Adult   364.15
1. Nassar, Larry 2. Women athletes 3. Child sexual abuse 4. Physicians 5. Child sexual abusers 6. Child gymnasts 7. Sex crimes 8. Sexual violence victims 9. Sports corruption 10. Universities and colleges 11. Girls 12. Life stories — Facing adversity — Abuse survivors 13. Life stories — Law and order — Criminals and law-breakers 14. True crime — Sex crimes 15. Sports and Competition — Olympic Sports

LC 2019031505

For decades, osteopathic physician Larry Nassar built a sterling reputation as the go-to doctor for America's Olympians while treating countless others at his office on Michigan State University's campus. It was largely within the high-pressure world of competitive gymnastics that Nassar exploited young girls, who were otherwise motivated by fear and intimidation, sexually assaulting hundreds of them under the guise of medical treatment. Following the paths traveled by courageous women—featuring a once-shy Christian attorney and a brash, outspoken Olympic medalist—Barr and Murphy detail the stories of those who fought back against the dysfunction within their sport to claim a far-from-inevitable victory.

ESSENTIAL AND RECOMMENDED TITLES
364.15 Offenses against the person

"The authors' exhaustive research and relentless pursuit of the truth create an unsettling and stark record of the abuse scandal that sent shockwaves across America and which continues to resonate deeply." —*Library Journal*

Includes index.

Brodsky, Alexandra
Sexual Justice: Supporting Victims, Ensuring Due Process, and Resisting the Conservative Backlash. Alexandra Brodsky. Metropolitan Books 2021. x, 322 p.

ISBN 9781250262547

Grades: Adult   364.15

1. Sexual harassment 2. Crimes against women 3. Sex discrimination against women 4. Sexual violence victims 5. Due process of law 6. Criminal justice system 7. Social responsibility 8. Victims of crimes 9. Civil rights 10. Legislation 11. Human rights 12. Civil rights 13. Society and culture — Violence and crime 14. Society and culture — Sex and sexuality 15. Politics and global affairs — Civil and human rights

LC 2021002313

In the past few years, a remarkable number of sexual harassment victims have come forward with their stories, demanding consequences for their assailants and broad societal change. Each prominent allegation, however, has also set off a wave of questions—some posed in good faith, some distinctly not—about the rights of the accused. The national conversation has grown polarized, inflamed by a public narrative that wrongly presents feminism and fair process as warring interests. Sexual Justice is an intervention, pointing the way to common ground. Drawing on the core principles of civil rights law, and the personal experiences of victims and the accused, Alexandra Brodsky details how schools, workplaces, and other institutions can—indeed, must—address sexual harassment in ways fair to all.

"A level-headed, thoughtful, and necessary book." —*Booklist*

Includes bibliographical references and index.

Caruana Galizia, Paul
★ *A Death in Malta: An Assassination and a Family's Quest for Justice.* Paul Caruana Galizia. Riverhead Books 2023. 295 p.

ISBN 9780593543733

Grades: Adult   364.15

1. Caruana Galizia, Paul, 1988- 2. Galizia, Daphne Caruana, 1964-2017 3. Women journalists 4. Murder victims 5. Assassination 6. Children of murder victims 7. Mothers and sons 8. Families 9. Political corruption 10. Scandals 11. Justice 12. Politics and government 13. Western European people 14. Maltese people 15. Malta 16. Collective biographies 17. Life stories — Facing adversity — Victims of crime 18. Life stories — Facing adversity — Coping with death 19. True Crime — Murder 20. History writing — Europe

LC 2023010824

An archipelago off the southern coast of Italy, Malta is a picturesque gem eroded by a climate of corruption, polarization, inequality, and a virtual absence of civic spirit. In this unpromising soil, a fearless journalist took root. Daphne Caruana Galizia fashioned herself into the country's lonely voice of conscience, making her at once the island's best-known figure and its most reviled. In 2017, a campaign of intimidation against her culminated in a car bombing that took her life. A Death in Malta is at once a study in heroism and the powerful story of a family's crusade for accountability, with reverberations far beyond their homeland.

"Galizia combines memoir, true crime, and history as he details Malta's complicated past for a riveting and unnerving story that remains fully unresolved." —*Booklist*

Cutler, Max
Cults: Inside the World's Most Notorious Groups and Understanding the People Who Joined Them. Max Cutler with Kevin Conley. Gallery Books 2022. 416 p.

ISBN 9781982133542

Grades: Adult   364.15

1. Cults 2. Cult leaders 3. Cult members 4. Manipulation (Social sciences) 5. True Crime — General 6. Society and culture — General

Discusses what goes on inside the minds of cult leaders and the people who join them.

"A fascinating overview of famous cult leaders which serves as an introduction to the topic." —*Library Journal*

Gourevitch, Philip
We Wish to Inform You That Tomorrow We Will Be Killed with Our Families: Stories from Rwanda. Philip Gourevitch. Farrar, Straus, and Giroux 1998. 355 p. : Map

ISBN 9780374286972

Grades: 11 12 Adult   364.15

1. Tutsi (African people) 2. Genocide 3. Hutu (African people) 4. Interethnic relations 5. Politics and government 6. Rwanda 7. History writing — Wars and conflicts — Civil Wars 8. History writing — Civil wars and genocide — Africa

LC 98022132

Los Angeles Times Book Prize for Current Interest, 1998; National Book Critics Circle Award for Non-Fiction, 1998; Guardian First Book Award, 1999.

In 1994, when the Rwanda government called on everyone in the Hutu majority to kill everyone in the Tutsi minority, 800,000 Tutsis were murdered. This haunting work is an anatomy of the killings and a vivid history of the genocide's background and aftermath.

"In 1994, the world was informed of the inexplicable mass killings in Rwanda, in which over 800,000 were killed in 100 days. Gourevitch . . . spent over three years putting together an oral history of the mass killing that occurred in this small country." —*Library Journal*

Kantor, Jodi
She Said: Breaking the Sexual Harassment Story That Ignited a Movement. Jodi Kantor & Megan Twohey. Penguin Press 2019. 310 pages

ISBN 9780525560340

Grades: Adult   364.15

1. Me Too Movement 2. Sex crimes 3. Sexual harassment 4. Investigative journalism 5. Sexual harassment of women 6. Feminism 7. Women's rights 8. Investigative journalists 9. Empowerment 10. Women 11. United States 12. Page to screen 13. Society and culture — Gender — Women

LC 2019300465

New York Times Notable Book, 2019.

The Pulitzer Prize-winning reporters who broke the story of Harvey Weinstein's sexual abuses discuss the suspenseful untold story of their investigation, the way it changed their careers and whether or not the #MeToo movement changed things for the better.

"Both admirable and suspenseful, the narrative is a fitting testament to the power of persistence and dedication in exposing critical crimes. Keenly executed, exemplary spadework dedicated to justice for all women caught in the crosshairs of privileged power." —*Kirkus*

Made into a theatrical movie released in 2022; Includes bibliographical references (pages 267-297) and index.

King, David
Six Days in August: The Story of Stockholm Syndrome. David King. W.W. Norton & Company 2020. 282 p.

ISBN 9780393635089

Grades: Adult   364.15

1. Bank robberies 2. Stockholm syndrome 3. Hostages 4. Bank robbers 5. Hostage negotiations 6. Police 7. Stockholm, Sweden 8. Sweden 9. 1970s 10. True Crime — Heists and Robbery 11. Society and culture — Psychology and human behavior

LC 2019058100

The definitive account of the bizarre hostage drama that gave rise to the term "Stockholm syndrome."

"Engrossing, well researched, and tailor-made for true crime enthusiasts." —*Library Journal*

Includes bibliographical references and index.

PUBLIC LIBRARY CORE COLLECTION: NONFICTION
Twentieth Edition

Larson, Erik
★ The **Devil** in the White City: Murder, Magic, and Madness at the Fair That Changed America. Erik Larson. Crown Publishers 2003. xi, 447 p. : Illustration; Map
ISBN 9780609608449
Grades: 11 12 Adult   364.15
1. Mudgett, Herman W, 1861-1896 2. Burnham, Daniel Hudson, 1846-1912 3. Serial murderers 4. Serial murders 5. Architects 6. Murder 7. Deception 8. United States history 9. Chicago, Illinois 10. 1890s 11. 19th century 12. History writing — Gilded Age — United States 13. True Crime — Historical Crime 14. True Crime — Murder 15. Adult books for young adults 16. Nonfiction that reads like fiction 17. Book club best bets
LC 2002154046
Booklist Editors' Choice, 2003; Edgar Allan Poe Award for Best Fact Crime, 2004; Library Journal Best Books, 2003; International Horror Guild Award for Best Nonfiction, 2003; National Book Award for Nonfiction finalist, 2003.
An account of the Chicago World's Fair of 1893 relates the stories of two men who shaped the history of the event—architect Daniel H. Burnham, who coordinated its construction, and serial killer Herman Mudgett.
"Larson's breathtaking new history is a novelistic yet wholly factual account of the fair and the mass murderer who lurked within it." —*Publishers Weekly*
Includes bibliographical references (p. [423]-429) and index.

Miller, T. Christian
A **False** Report: A True Story of Rape in America. T. Christian Miller and Ken Armstrong. Crown Publishers 2018. 320 p.
ISBN 9781524759957
Grades: Adult   364.15
1. Rape 2. Rape victims 3. Police charges 4. Rape investigation 5. Serial rapists 6. Misogyny 7. Sexism 8. Page to screen 9. True Crime — Sex Crimes
LC 2017037935
Booklist Editors' Choice, 2018.
Two Pulitzer Prize-winning journalists present the true story of two detectives who teamed up to discern the truth about a case involving a teen who was charged with falsely reporting a rape, an investigation that revealed the work of a serial rapist in multiple states.
"This timely, well-researched, highly readable account will appeal to readers interested in true crime and social justice issues." —*Booklist*
Adapted into the television series Unbelievable, Fall 2019.

Moore, Michael Scott
The **Desert** and the Sea: 977 Days Captive on the Somali Pirate Coast. Michael Scott Moore. Harperwave 2018. 304 p.
ISBN 9780062449177
Grades: Adult   364.15
1. Moore, Michael Scott 2. Hostages 3. Pirates 4. Terrorism 5. Hostage taking 6. Journalists 7. Kidnapping 8. Kidnapping victims 9. Somalia 10. 21st century 11. Autobiographies and memoirs 12. Politics and global affairs — Terrorism 13. Life stories — Facing adversity — War and oppression — Hostages and POWs 14. True Crime — Organized Crime, Mafia, and Gangs
LC Bl2018072609
A journalist and the author of Sweetness and Blood chronicles his three years of captivity by Somali pirates, offering an exploration of foreign policy, religious extremism and the costs of survival in the process.

Murakami, Haruki
Underground. Haruki Murakami; translated from the Japanese by Alfred Birnbaum and Philip Gabriel. Vintage International 2001. x, 366 p; Map
ISBN 9780375725807
Grades: Adult   364.15
1. Religious terrorism 2. Terrorism 3. Violence 4. Survival 5. Japan 6. 1990s 7. Politics and global affairs — Terrorism 8. History writing — Asia — Japan
LC 00069310
Covers the 1995 Tokyo Gas Attack, during which agents of a Japanese cult released sarin gas into the subway system, as documented in interviews with its survivors, perpetrators, and victims's family members.

"All the debacle's surreal and horrific qualities rush to the fore, though Murakami keeps the tone under control. By keeping the atmosphere immediate, the author allows the irreducible humanity of each person to emerge." —*Kirkus*

Schwartzman, Nancy
Roll Red Roll: Rape, Power, and Football in the American Heartland. Nancy Schwartzman with Nora Zelevansky. Hachette Books 2022. 288 p.
ISBN 9780306924361
Grades: Adult   364.15
1. Rape of teenagers 2. Football 3. Sexual violence 4. High school football players 5. Rape culture 6. Rapists 7. Gang rape 8. Teenage girls 9. Rape 10. Social media 11. Violence against women 12. Power 13. Ohio 14. United States 15. True Crime — Sex Crimes
A thoughtfully reported narrative about a rape case at the center of a deeply polarized steel town in the American Midwest, exploring what creates a culture where sexual violence is tacitly understood and condoned, and how to make a difference.
"This compelling account offers heartbreaking evidence of the pervasive, systemic, and toxic misogyny that thrives in many American communities." —*Booklist*

Standiford, Les
Bringing **Adam** Home: The Abduction That Changed America. Les Standiford with Detective Sergeant Joe Matthews. Ecco 2011. 304 p.
ISBN 9780061983900
Grades: Adult   364.15
1. Walsh, Adam 2. Kidnapping 3. Kidnapping victims 4. Murder investigation 5. Crimes against children 6. United States history 7. Florida 8. 20th century 9. Biographies 10. True Crime — Murder
LC 2010043572
Relates the full, twenty-seven-year story behind the abduction and murder of Adam Walsh, the six-year-old son of "America's Most Wanted" host John Walsh, as well as the decades-long search for the boy's elusive killer.

Stout, David
The **Kidnap** Years: The Astonishing True History of the Forgotten Kidnapping Epidemic That Shook Depression-era America. David Stout. Sourcebooks 2020. xxix, 430 pages
ISBN 9781492694793
Grades: Adult   364.15
1. Kidnapping 2. Crime 3. Gangsters 4. Missing persons 5. Prohibition 6. Depressions, 1929-1941 7. United States history 8. United States 9. Depression era (1929-1941) 10. 1930s 11. 20th century 12. True Crime — Historical Crime 13. History writing — Great Depression — United States
LC 2019032997
Chronicles the less-remembered outbreak in kidnappings in Great Depression America, sharing insight into how the crime's low legal risks led to a sweep of abductions throughout the country.
"Stout presents a deeply researched, perfectly paced history of kidnappings that affected everyone from bank presidents and lumber barons to beer brewers and the children of wealthy families. Interspersed with the nail-biting tales of the kidnappings are details about the trials, the criminals, and the formation of the FBI and J. Edgar Hoover's rise to power." —*Library Journal*
Includes bibliographical references and index.

Swift, Earl
Hell Put to Shame: The 1921 Murder Farm Massacre and the Horror of America's Second Slavery. Earl Swift. Mariner Books 2024. 384 p.
ISBN 9780063265387
Grades: Adult   364.15
1. Johnson, James Weldon, 1871-1938 2. White, Walter, 1893-1955 3. African Americans 4. Mass murder 5. Peonage 6. Agricultural laborers 7. Indentured servants 8. Debt 9. Landowners 10. Trials (Murder) 11. Governors 12. Racism 13. African American civil rights workers 14. Justice 15. Georgia 16. 1920s 17. History writing — African American — United States 18. True Crime —

ESSENTIAL AND RECOMMENDED TITLES
364.152 Homicide

Historical Crime 19. Life stories — Politics — Activists and Reformers — Civil Rights Leaders

Tells the forgotten story of the mass killing of 11 Black farmhands on a Georgia plantation in the spring of 1921—a crime which exposed for the nation the existence of the "peonage system," a form of legal enslavement established after the Civil War across the American South.

"A gripping, memorable work that wholly confronts a hellish past that continues to bleed into the present." —*Kirkus*

Talty, Stephan
The Good Assassin: How a Mossad Agent and a Band of Survivors Hunted Down the Butcher of Latvia. Stephan Talty. Houghton Mifflin Harcourt 2020. xiv, 304 pages
ISBN 9781328613080
Grades: Adult   364.15
1. Cukurs, Herbert, 1900-1965 2. Medad, Jacob, 1919-2012 3. Fugitives 4. Holocaust (1933-1945) 5. War criminals 6. Jewish people 7. Mossad agents 8. Assassination 9. Undercover operations 10. Spies 11. Justice 12. Nazis 13. Intelligence service 14. Religious persecution 15. Brazil 16. Uruguay 17. Israel 18. 1960s 19. History writing — Spies and spying 20. History writing — Wars and conflicts — Holocaust — World War II 21. Society and culture — Violence and crime — Genocide
LC 2019027262

Provides the untold story of an Israeli spy's epic journey to bring the notorious Butcher of Latvia to justice—a case that altered the fates of all ex-Nazis.

"A fast-paced, recommended work that enthralls, edifies, and reveals the disturbing extent to which Latvians and others participated in genocide." —*Library Journal*

Includes bibliographical references and index.

364.152 Homicide

Ahmed, Azam
Fear Is Just a Word: A Missing Daughter, a Violent Cartel, and a Mother's Quest for Vengeance. Azam Ahmed. Random House 2023. 304 p.
ISBN 9780593448410
Grades: Adult   364.152
1. Mothers 2. Women vigilantes 3. Villages 4. Murder 5. Drug dealers 6. Violence 7. Drug traffic 8. Revenge 9. Women murder victims 10. Disappeared people 11. Mexico 12. True Crime — Organized Crime, Mafia, and Gangs 13. History Writing — Latin America — Mexico 14. Life stories — Facing adversity — Victims of crime
LC 2023010530

A global investigative correspondent for the New York Times describes the true story of how a mother living in the once-quiet Mexican village of San Fernando became a vigilante against the Zeta cartel that murdered her daughter.

"A dispiriting yet necessary study of how a criminal enterprise can swallow a nation whole." —*Kirkus*

Includes bibliographical references and index.

Appelman, J. Reuben
While Idaho Slept: The Hunt for Answers in the Murders of Four College Students. J. Reuben Appelman. HarperCollins 2023. 304 p.
ISBN 9780063346697
Grades: Adult   364.152
1. Murder 2. College students 3. Mass media 4. Mass murder investigation 5. Idaho 6. History Writing — Regional history — United States 7. True Crime — Murder

In this thought-provoking, literary chronicle of a small-town murder investigation, the author recounts the brutal killings of four University of Idaho students, exploring our societal fascination with true crime, the media's involvement and the future of homicide investigations as he humanizes the four victims, examining the richness of their lives.

"Journalist Appelman (The Kill Jar) painstakingly traces the fallout from the murders of four University of Idaho students in this well-researched account." —*Publishers Weekly*

Asgarian, Roxanna
We Were Once a Family: A Story of Love, Death, and Child Removal in America. Roxanna Asgarian. Farrar, Straus and Giroux 2023. 320 p.
ISBN 9780374602291
Grades: Adult   364.152
1. Adoption 2. Foster care 3. Lesbian couples 4. African American children 5. Foster children 6. Child abuse 7. Child neglect 8. African American families 9. Birthparents 10. Child custody 11. Traffic accidents 12. Suicide pacts 13. Child murder victims 14. Child welfare 15. Child protective services 16. Bureaucracy 17. Injustice 18. Debut title 19. Life stories — Facing adversity — Disasters and tragedies 20. Family and Relationships — Parenting — Adoption 21. True Crime — Domestic Crime 22. True Crime — Murder

Los Angeles Times Book Prize for Current Interest, 2023; Andrew Carnegie Medal for Excellence in Non-Fiction, 2024; National Book Critics Circle Award for Non-Fiction, 2023.

This shocking expose of the foster care and adoption systems that continue to fail America's most vulnerable children recounts the murder-suicide of a white married couple and their six Black children, revealing a pattern of abuse and neglect that went ignored with fateful consequences.

"Throughout, Asgarian makes clear that the endemic failures that led to this shocking tragedy continue to affect countless families caught up in the child welfare system. Sensitive, impassioned, and eye-opening, this is a must-read." —*Publishers Weekly*

Includes bibliographical references.

Bonner, Betsy
The Book of Atlantis Black: The Search for a Sister Gone Missing. Betsy Bonner. Tin House Books 2020. 280 p.
ISBN 9781947793774
Grades: Adult   364.152
1. Bonner, Betsy 2. Black, Atlantis, 1976-2008 3. Missing women 4. Murder investigation 5. Sisters 6. Adult child abuse victims 7. Women poets 8. Women musicians 9. Drug abuse 10. Mental illness 11. Searching 12. Clues 13. Memories 14. Interpersonal relations 15. Family relationships 16. Autobiographies and memoirs 17. Life stories — Facing adversity — Coping with death 18. Life stories — Relationships — Family 19. True Crime — Murder
LC 2020004078

A young woman is found dead on the floor of a Tijuana hotel room. An ID in a nearby purse reads "Atlantis Black." the police report states that the body does not seem to match the identification, yet the body is quickly cremated and the case is considered closed.So begins Betsy Bonner's search for her sister, Atlantis, and the unraveling of the mysterious final months before Atlantis's disappearance, alleged overdose, and death. Through a history only she and Atlantis shared—a childhood fraught with abuse and mental illness, Atlantis's precocious yet short rise in the music world, and through it all an unshakable bond of sisterhood—Bonner finds questions that lead only to more questions and possible clues that seem to point in no particular direction. In this haunting memoir and piercing true crime account, Bonner must decide how far she will go to understand a sister who, like the mythical island she renamed herself for, might prove impossible to find.

"A haunting, profound investigative memoir that will resonate with readers as both a compelling true crime story and an affecting literary work. Bonner creates a sense of closeness with readers that makes this book a challenge to put down or forget." —*Library Journal*

Brown, Vanessa
The Forest City Killer: A Serial Murderer, a Cold-case Sleuth, and a Search for Justice. Vanessa Brown. ECW Press 2019. 328 p.
ISBN 9781770415034
Grades: Adult   364.152
1. Serial murder investigation 2. Serial murders 3. Cold cases (Criminal investigation) 4. London, Ontario 5. Ontario 6. Canada 7. Canadian literature 8. True crime — Murder 9. True Crime — Cold Cases and Unsolved Mysteries

PUBLIC LIBRARY CORE COLLECTION: NONFICTION
Twentieth Edition

Loan Stars Favourites, 2019.

Investigates a cold-case serial killer case from London, Ontario in the 1960s.

Callahan, Maureen
American Predator: The Hunt for the Most Meticulous Serial Killer of the 21st Century. Maureen Callahan. Viking 2019. 304 pages

ISBN 9780525428640

Grades: Adult   364.152

1. Keyes, Israel 2. Serial murderers 3. Serial murder investigation 4. Murderers 5. Detectives 6. True Crime — Murder 7. True Crime — Investigations and Trials

LC 2018058203

An investigative journalist documents the story of enigmatic serial killer Israel Keyes and the efforts of the Anchorage PD and the FBI to capture him, discussing what his case reveals about twenty-first-century law enforcement.

Cameron, Silver Donald
Blood in the Water: A True Story of Revenge in the Maritimes. Silver Donald Cameron. Viking 2021. 244 p. : Illustration

ISBN 9781586422936

Grades: Adult   364.152

1. Boudreau, Phillip 2. Murder 3. Fishers 4. Revenge 5. Criminals 6. Stealing 7. Bullies and bullying 8. Power 9. Law 10. Self-esteem 11. Small towns 12. Coastal towns 13. Nova Scotia 14. Canadian literature 15. True Crime — Murder 16. Society and culture — Violence and crime

Writing for Change Award (Nova Scotia), 2021.

Recounts a brutal murder in a small Acadian fishing community in Nova Scotia that raises urgent questions of right and wrong.

"An often gripping, insightful examination of a well-known crime and the Acadian milieu in which it took place." —*Kirkus*

Cep, Casey N.
★ *Furious* Hours: Murder, Fraud, and the Last Trial of Harper Lee. Casey Cep. Knopf 2019. 304 p.

ISBN 9781101947869

Grades: Adult   364.152

1. Lee, Harper 2. Maxwell, Willie 3. Serial murderers 4. Women true crime writers 5. Rural life 6. Rural crimes 7. Race relations 8. Trials (Murder) 9. Creativity 10. United States history 11. Alabama 12. 20th century 13. Biographies 14. True crime — Murder 15. Life stories — Arts and culture — Writing — Authors 16. Life stories — Law and order — Criminals and law-breakers 17. Book club best bets

LC 2018043337

Gold Dagger Award for Best Nonfiction of the Year, 2020; New York Times Notable Book, 2019.

Documents the remarkable story of 1970s Alabama serial killer Willie Maxwell and the true-crime book on the Deep South's racial politics and justice system that consumed Harper Lee in the years after to Kill a Mockingbird.

"Cep has vividly and insightfully retrieved a grimly fascinating true-crime story and done Lee justice in a fresh and compelling portrait of this essential American writer." —*Booklist*

Includes bibliographical references.

Collins, Max Allan
Eliot Ness and the Mad Butcher: Hunting America's Deadliest Unidentified Serial Killer at the Dawn of Modern Criminology. Max Allan Collins, A. Brad Schwartz. William Morrow & Company 2020. 576 p.

ISBN 9780062881977

Grades: Adult   364.152

1. Ness, Eliot 2. Detectives 3. Public officials 4. Serial murderers 5. Serial murder investigation 6. Cities and towns 7. Depressions, 1929-1941 8. Public safety 9. Political corruption 10. Murder investigation 11. Cleveland, Ohio 12. Depression era (1929-1941) 13. Biographies 14. Life stories — Law and order — Police and law officers 15. True Crime — Police and Lawyers 16. True Crime — Murder 17. True Crime — Historical Crime 18. History writing — Great Depression — United States

LC 2020005488

In 1934, the nation's most legendary crime-fighter—fresh from taking on the greatest gangster in American history—arrived in Cleveland, a corrupt and dangerous town about to host a world's fair. It was to be his coronation, as well as the city's. Instead, terror descended, as headless bodies started turning up. The young detective, already battling the mob and crooked cops, found his drive to transform American policing subverted by a menace largely unknown to law enforcement: a serial murderer. As Ness zeroed in on a suspect powerful forces thwarted his quest for justice. In this battle between a flawed hero and a twisted monster—by turns horror story, political drama, and detective thriller—Collins and Schwartz find an American tragedy, classic in structure, epic in scope.

"A successful blend of history and suspense, this volume will appeal to readers interested in true crime and law enforcement. Readers intrigued by the Mad Butcher may also enjoy James Jessen Badal's in the Wake of the Butcher." —*Library Journal*

Includes bibliographical references and index.

Cooper, Becky
We Keep the Dead Close: A Murder at Harvard and a Half Century of Silence. Becky Cooper. Grand Central Publishing 2020. 464 p.

ISBN 9781538746837

Grades: Adult   364.152

1. Britton, Jane Sanders, 1945-1969 2. Murder investigation 3. Cold cases (Criminal investigation) 4. Murder victims 5. Women graduate students 6. Cambridge, Massachusetts 7. Debut title 8. True Crime — Cold Cases and Unsolved Mysteries 9. True Crime — Murder 10. Society and culture — Gender — Women 11. Society and culture — Education — Higher education

LC 2020022711

Documents the unsolved 1969 murder of Harvard student Jane Britton, sharing insights into how the case was clouded by false rumors and the realities of gender inequality and institutional silence in period academic circles.

"This book succeeds as both a true-crime story and a powerful portrait of a young woman's remarkable quest for justice." —*Kirkus*

Includes bibliographical references.

Corcoran, Katherine
In the Mouth of the Wolf: A Murder, a Coverup, and the True Cost of Silencing the Press. Katherine Corcoran. Bloomsbury Publishing 2022. 320 p.

ISBN 9781635575033

Grades: Adult   364.152

1. Martinez, Regina 2. Murder 3. Journalists 4. Murder victims 5. Corruption 6. Cold cases (Criminal investigation) 7. Mexican people 8. Violence 9. Women journalists 10. True Crime — Murder 11. True Crime — Organized Crime, Mafia, and Gangs 12. History writing — Latin America — Mexico 13. True Crime — Cold Cases and Unsolved Mysteries

A former Associated Press bureau chief describes the story of Mexican Gulf Coast journalist Regina Martinez who was murdered in cold blood for uncovering and publicizing the disappearance of thousands of Mexican people.

"Corcoran, former Associated Press bureau chief for Mexico and Central America, debuts with this captivating story of the murder of a Mexican journalist and her own mission to contest the official version of events." —*Booklist*

Cornwell, Patricia Daniels
Ripper: The Secret Life of Walter Sickert. Patricia Daniels Cornwell. Thomas & Mercer 2016. 304 p.

ISBN 9781503936874

Grades: Adult   364.152

1. Sickert, Walter Richard, 1860-1942 2. Jack, the Ripper 3. Whitechapel murders, 1888 4. Serial murderers 5. Murder 6. Serial murders 7. Murderers 8. London, England history 9. Whitechapel (London, England) 10. 1880s 11. 19th century 12. True Crime — Murder 13. True Crime — Historical Crime

LC Bl2017000501

From New York Times bestselling author Patricia Cornwell comes Ripper: The Secret Life of Walter Sickert, a comprehensive and intriguing expose of one of the world's most chilling cases of serial murder—and the police force that failed to solve it.

ESSENTIAL AND RECOMMENDED TITLES
364.152 Homicide

Denton, Sally
The Colony: Faith and Blood in a Promised Land. Sally Denton. Liveright Publishing Corporation 2022. 336 p.
ISBN 9781631498077
Grades: Adult   364.152
1. Mass murder 2. Mormons 3. Polygamy 4. Fundamentalism 5. Family secrets 6. Violence 7. Violence against women 8. Mexico 9. True Crime — Murder 10. History writing — Latin America — Mexico
LC 2021062619
A best-selling investigative journalist, revisiting the 2019 killings of women and children who were fundamentalist Mormons in Northern Mexico, picks up where the initial, incomplete reporting on the attacks ended, delving into the complex story of the LeBaron clan and their recent alliance with the NXIVM sex cult.
"Investigative journalist Denton (The Bluegrass Conspiracy) probes the 2019 massacre of nine women and children as part of a larger study of fundamentalist Mormon sects in Mexico." —*Library Journal*
Includes bibliographical references and index.

Douglas, John E.
When a Killer Calls: A Haunting Story of Murder, Criminal Profiling, and Justice in a Small Town. John Douglas and Mark Olshaker. Dey Street Books 2022. 240 p.
ISBN 9780063074477
Grades: Adult   364.152
1. Douglas, John E. 2. FBI agents 3. Criminal profilers 4. Small towns 5. Serial murderers 6. Child murder victims 7. Serial murder investigation 8. Girls 9. Child kidnapping victims 10. Missing children 11. South Carolina 12. 1980s 13. Media tie-ins 14. True Crime — Murder 15. True Crime — Investigations and Trials 16. Life stories — Law and order — Police and law officers 17. Life stories — Facing adversity — Victims of crime
From the legendary FBI criminal profiler, author, and inspiration for the Netflix show Mindhunter comes a chilling journey inside the mind and crimes of Larry Gene Bell, one of the most dangerous serial killers Douglas confronted, and the desperate effort to identify and catch him.
"FBI profiler Douglas and Olshaker (Mindhunter) tell the riveting story of how the FBI, working with local law enforcement officers, cracked the case of a particularly nasty killer.... Peppered with other FBI profiling cases, this is required reading for those interested in the early years of the FBI's Behavioral Science Unit." —*Publishers Weekly*

Eisenberg, Emma Copley
★ *The Third Rainbow Girl: The Long Life of a Double Murder in Appalachia.* Emma Copley Eisenberg. Hachette Books 2019. 336 p.
ISBN 9780316449236
Grades: Adult   364.152
1. Murder 2. Murder investigation 3. Suspicion 4. Communities 5. Rural life 6. Cold cases (Criminal investigation) 7. West Virginia 8. Appalachian Region 9. Autobiographies and memoirs 10. True Crime — Murder 11. Life stories — General
LC Bl2020004072
New York Times Notable Book, 2020.
A stunningly written investigation of the murder of two young women—showing how a violent crime casts a shadow over an entire community.
"The book is more than just another true crime memoir; Eisenberg has crafted a beautiful and complicated ode to West Virginia. Exquisitely written, this is a powerful commentary on society's notions of gender, violence, and rural America. Readers of literary nonfiction will devour this title in one sitting." —*Booklist*

Ervin, Kristine S.
Rabbit Heart: A Mother's Murder, a Daughter's Story. Kristine S. Ervin. Counterpoint 2024. 304 p.
ISBN 9781640096370
Grades: Adult   364.152
1. Ervin, Kristine S. 2. Murder 3. Families of murder victims 4. Children of murder victims 5. Violence against women 6. Identity 7. Grief 8. Death of mothers 9. Mothers 10. Families 11. Justice 12. Oklahoma 13. Autobiographies and memoirs 14. Life stories — Facing adversity — Coping with death 15. True Crime — Murder
LC 2023041428
Weaving together themes of power, gender and justice, the author, who was just eight years old when her mother was brutally murdered, recounts her drive to know her mother, and in the process, reckons with contradictions of what a woman is allowed to be and what a "true" victim looks like.
"Poet and essayist Ervin grapples in her moving debut memoir with the emotional damage caused by a parent's violent death." —*Publishers Weekly*
Includes bibliographical references.

Eustace, Nicole
★ *Covered with Night: A Story of Murder and Indigenous Justice in Early America.* Nicole Eustace. Liveright Publishing Corporation 2021. 464 p.
ISBN 9781631495878
Grades: Adult   364.152
1. Murder 2. Criminal justice system 3. Murder investigation 4. Violence against Indigenous people 5. Indigenous peoples of North America 6. United States 7. Colonial America (1600-1775) 8. 18th century 9. History writing — Colonial America — United States 10. True Crime — Murder 11. History writing — Indigenous peoples — United States
LC 2020050130
Pulitzer Prize for History, 2022; National Book Award for Nonfiction finalist, 2021.
An immersive tale of the killing of a Native American man and its far-reaching consequences for Colonial America. In the summer of 1722, on the eve of a conference between the Five Nations of the Iroquois and British-American colonists, two colonial furtraders brutally attacked an Indigenous hunter in colonial Pennsylvania. The crime set the entire mid-Atlantic on edge, with many believing that war was imminent. Frantic efforts to resolve the case created a contest between Native American forms of justice, centered on community, forgiveness, and reparations, and an ideology of harsh reprisal, based on British law, that called for the killers' execution.
"NYU history professor Eustace (1812: War and the Passions of Patriotism) delivers an immersive account of the fallout from the 1722 killing of a Seneca Indian hunter by two white fur traders in Pennsylvania.... Early American history buffs will be fascinated." —*Publishers Weekly*
Includes bibliographical references and index.

Faleiro, Sonia
The Good Girls: An Ordinary Killing. Sonia Faleiro. Grove Press 2021. 352 p.
ISBN 9780802158208
Grades: Adult   364.152
1. Shakya, Padma 2. Shakya, Lalli 3. Teenage girls 4. Cousins 5. Sexual violence victims 6. Gang rape 7. Honor killings 8. Caste 9. Gender role 10. Injustice 11. Criminal investigation 12. Small towns 13. Girls 14. Child murder victims 15. India 16. 2010s 17. True Crime — Sex Crimes 18. Society and culture — Gender — Women 19. Society and culture — Wealth and class — Poverty
An award-winning journalist investigates the mysterious 2014 deaths of two teenage girls in a tiny Indian village and how it led to a national conversation about sex, violence and codes of honor.
"In incisive prose, Faleiro, who offers no opinion on what actually happened, examines India's family honor system and the grueling lives of lower caste women." —*Publishers Weekly*

Fieseler, Robert W.
Tinderbox: The Untold Story of the up Stairs Lounge Fire and the Rise of Gay Liberation. Robert W. Fieseler. Liveright Publishing 2018. 320 p.
ISBN 9781631491641
Grades: Adult   364.152
1. Violence against gay men and lesbians 2. Mass murder 3. Arson 4. Gay bars and restaurants 5. Homophobia 6. Gay and Lesbian Movement 7. Homosexuality 8. Legislation 9. United States 10. New Orleans, Louisiana 11. 1970s

PUBLIC LIBRARY CORE COLLECTION: NONFICTION
Twentieth Edition

12. History writing — LGBTQIA+ 13. Society and culture — LGBTQIA+ 14. History writing — 1970s — United States 15. History writing — Regional history — United States

LC 2018004765

Edgar Allan Poe Award for Best Fact Crime, 2019; Library Journal Best Books, 2018.

A reconstruction of the 1973 fire that devastated New Orleans' subterranean gay community describes how the up Stairs Lounge and dozens of innocent patrons were targeted in what became a catalyzing event in the gay liberation movement.

"Though Fieseler's prose leans toward overreach—Humidity, so thick with vapor that breathing air could feel like crying tears, would almost routinely reach 100 percent—his attention to detail and intricate exploration of the material is spot-on. Fieseler shines a bright light on a dark and largely forgotten moment in the history of the gay rights movement." —*Publishers Weekly*

Includes bibliographical references and index.

Gerard, Sarah

Carrie Carolyn Coco: My Friend, Her Murder, and an Obsession with the Unthinkable. Sarah Gerard. Zando Books 2024. 368 p.

ISBN 9781638930464

Grades: Adult **364.152**

1. Gerard, Sarah 2. Women authors 3. Female friendship 4. Women murder victims 5. Stabbing victims 6. Roommates 7. Death of friends 8. Tragedy 9. Families of murder victims 10. Families of murderers 11. Questions and answers 12. Memorialization 13. True Crime — Murder 14. Life stories — Facing adversity — Victims of crime 15. Life stories — Relationships — Friendship

Author Sarah Gerard turns her keen observational eye and penetrating prose to the murder of her friend Carolyn Bush, examining the multi-faceted reasons for her death. On the night of September 28, 2016, twenty-five-year-old Carolyn was brutally stabbed to death in her New York City apartment by her roommate Render Stetson-Shanahan, leaving friends and family of both reeling. What emerged from Sarah's relentless instinct to follow the story and its characters to their darkest ends is a book that is at once a striking homage to Carolyn's life, a chilling excavation of a brutal crime, and a captivating whydunit with a shocking conclusion.

"In this wrenching blend of memoir and true crime, novelist Gerard (True Love) unpacks the murder of her friend, Carolyn Bush, through conversations with the friends and family of both the victim and her killer." —*Publishers Weekly*

Glatt, John

The *Doomsday* Mother: Lori Vallow, Chad Daybell, and the End of an American Family. John Glatt. St. Martin's Press 2022. 292 p.

ISBN 9781250276674

Grades: Adult **364.152**

1. Daybell, Chad, 1968- 2. Vallow, Lori, 1973- 3. Mormons 4. Husband and wife 5. Stepfathers 6. Stepchildren 7. Religious fanaticism 8. Delusions 9. Child murders 10. Filicide 11. Murder investigation 12. Idaho 13. Hawaii 14. True Crime — Murder 15. True Crime — Domestic Crime 16. Life stories — Law and order — Criminals and law-breakers

LC 2021044957

At first, the residents of Kauai Beach Resort took little notice of their new neighbors. The glamorous blonde and her tall husband fit the image of the ritzy gated community. The couple seemed to keep to themselves—until the police knocked on their door with a search warrant. Lori Vallow and Chad Daybell had fled to Hawaii in the midst of being investigated for the disappearance of Lori's children back in Idaho—Tylee and JJ—who hadn't been seen alive in five months. Author and journalist John Glatt takes readers deeper into the devastating crimes of Lori Vallow and Chad Daybell in an attempt to unravel the lethal relationship of this doomsday couple.

"This definitive look at a case Glatt considers the most 'Terrifying' of his decades of experience as a journalist is must reading for true crime fans." —*Publishers Weekly*

★ The *Perfect* Father: The True Story of Chris Watts, His All-american Family, and a Shocking Murder. John Glatt. St. Martin's Press 2020. x, 288 p.

ISBN 9781250231611

Grades: Adult **364.152**

1. Watts, Chris (Christopher Lee), 1985- 2. Murder 3. Family violence 4. Husband and wife 5. Pregnant women 6. Women murder victims 7. Child murder victims 8. Oil workers 9. Women executives 10. Secrets 11. Confession (Law) 12. Extramarital affairs 13. Murder investigation 14. Denver, Colorado 15. True Crime — Murder 16. True Crime — Domestic Crime

LC 2020009570

Documents the August 2018 murders of Shanann Watts and her young daughters, describing how viewers watched her husband's televised plea for help less than 24 hours before he confessed to killing his family.

"Fans of the Investigation Discovery show Nightmare Next Door are sure to appreciate this gripping read." —*Library Journal*

Tangled Vines: Power, Privilege, and the Murdaugh Family Murders. John Glatt. St. Martin's Press 2023. 304 p.

ISBN 9781250283481

Grades: Adult **364.152**

1. Murdaugh, Alex (Richard Alexander), 1968- 2. Murder 3. Families 4. Lawyers 5. Crime 6. Corruption 7. Power 8. South Carolina 9. Life stories — Law and order — Criminals and law-breakers 10. True Crime — Murder

LC 2023015052

A best-selling true crime author reconstructs the rise of the prestigious Murdaugh family and the shocking double murder that led to the downfall of its patriarch, Alex Murdaugh.

"This real-life Southern noir lingers." —*Publishers Weekly*

Includes index.

Hale, Kathleen

★ *Slenderman:* Online Obsession, Mental Illness, and the Violent Crime of Two Midwestern Girls. Kathleen Hale. Grove Press 2022. 368 p.

ISBN 9780802159809

Grades: Adult **364.152**

1. Juvenile delinquents 2. Twelve-year-old girls 3. Attempted murder 4. Mental illness 5. Schizophrenia 6. Internet 7. True Crime — Murder

LC 2022022692

Using court transcripts, police reports, individual reporting and exclusive interviews, this page-turning true crime story recounts the attempted murder of 12-year-old Bella Leutner at the hands of two girls who believed they needed a sacrifice to keep Slenderman—a figure born on the internet—at bay.

"As the first researcher into the case to draw extensively from transcripts of vital records, Hale has produced what stands as the most accurate account to date of this horrifying episode. This is a must for true crime fans." —*Publishers Weekly*

Includes bibliographical references.

Hannig, Anita

The **Day** I Die: The Untold Story of Assisted Dying in America. Anita Hannig. Sourcebooks 2022. 297 p.

ISBN 9781728244914

Grades: Adult **364.152**

1. Assisted suicide 2. Euthanasia 3. Right to die 4. Physician-assisted suicide 5. Life stories — Facing adversity — Coping with death 6. Family and relationships — Aging and death 7. Life stories — Science, technology, and medicine — Healthcare professionals 8. Science Writing — Medicine and health

LC 2021052668

The Day I Die is a major work of nonfiction that tackles the one issue we'll all eventually come to face-our final days, hours, and minutes. With clarity and empathy, award-winning anthropologist Anita Hannig uncovers the stigma against the practice of assisted dying, untangles the legalities and logistics of pursuing an assisted death in America today, and profiles the dedicated advocates and medical personnel involved. In intimate, lyrical detail, Hannig explains why someone might choose an assisted death and how that decision impacts their loved ones. In a time when nearly 80 percent of Americans die in hospitals and nursing homes, medical assistance in dying could transform the way we die for the better, allowing more people to define the terms of their own death.

ESSENTIAL AND RECOMMENDED TITLES
364.152 Homicide

"If all goes well, assisted death mimics the process of dying calmly during sleep. Haunting and deeply informative." —*Publishers Weekly*

Includes bibliographical references.

Harman, Claire
Murder by the Book: The Crime That Shocked Dickens's London. Claire Harman. Alfred A. Knopf 2019. 256 p.

ISBN 9780525520399

Grades: Adult   **364.152**

1. Courvoisier, Francois Benjamin, d. 1840 2. Russell, William, Lord, 1767-1840 3. Ainsworth, William Harrison, 1805-1882 4. Murder 5. Murder in literature 6. Books and reading 7. Trials (Murder) 8. Nobility 9. Murder victims 10. Murder suspects 11. Criminals 12. Confession (Law) 13. Guilt (Law) 14. Antiheroes and antiheroines 15. Publishers and publishing 16. London, England history 17. Victorian era (1837-1901) 18. 19th century 19. True Crime — Historical crime 20. True Crime — Murder

LC 2018029773

Traces the lesser-known story of a Victorian-era murder that rocked literary London, revealing how the killer organized his defense by blaming his behavior on a popular crime novel.

This is a Borzoi Book; Includes bibliographical references and index.

Hawes, Jennifer
Grace Will Lead Us Home: The Charleston Church Massacre and the Hard, Inspiring Journey to Forgiveness. Jennifer Berry Hawes. St. Martin's Press 2019. 352 p.

ISBN 9781250117762

Grades: Adult   **364.152**

1. Hate crimes 2. Mass shootings 3. Crimes against African Americans 4. Social psychology 5. Psychic trauma 6. Forgiveness 7. Massacres 8. Grief 9. Race relations 10. South Carolina 11. United States 12. Southern States 13. 21st century 14. History writing — Early 21st century — United States 15. Society and culture — Race 16. Adult books for young adults

LC Bl2018053071

New York Times Notable Book, 2019.

Follows the experiences of the survivors and victims' families following the 2015 shootings at Charleston's Mother Emanuel AME Church, chronicling the events and emotions that came in the aftermath of the shooting.

"A groundbreaking, accessible work of investigative reporting that spans a variety of topics, including gun violence and the historic role of the Emanuel AME Church. It will appeal to general readers interested in these topics, as well as historians and political scientists." —*Library Journal*

Herman, Eleanor
The Royal Art of Poison: Fatal Cosmetics, Deadly Medicine, Filthy Palaces, and Murder Most Foul. Eleanor Herman. St. Martin's Press 2018. 288 p.

ISBN 9781250140869

Grades: Adult   **364.152**

1. Courts and courtiers 2. Poisons 3. Poisoning 4. Power 5. Murder victims 6. Cosmetics 7. Dirtiness 8. Diseases 9. Rulers 10. Forensic anthropology 11. Adult books for young adults 12. True Crime — Historical Crime 13. History writing — Europe

LC 2017060759

This history of the role that poison has played in centuries of royal courts discusses both the intentional poisoning of royals by their underlings as well as the unintentional health effects of the makeup and medications they commonly used.

"Murder and scandal always sell, and Herman applies this philosophy to her examination—and frequent exhumation—of history's dubiously dispatched royalty." —*Booklist*

Includes bibliographical references and index.

Hortis, C. Alexander
The Witch of New York: The Trials of Polly Bodine and the Cursed Birth of Tabloid Justice. Alex Hortis. Pegasus Crime 2024. 368 p.

ISBN 9781639363919

Grades: Adult   **364.152**

1. Bodine, Polly 2. Trials (Murder) 3. Women murder suspects 4. Scandals 5. Tabloid newspapers 6. Publicity 7. Murder in mass media 8. Public opinion 9. Misogyny 10. Libel and slander 11. Judgment 12. New York City history 13. New York City 14. True Crime — Historical Crime 15. Life stories — Law and order 16. History writing — Regional history — United States

On Christmas night, 1843, in a serene village on Staten Island, shocked neighbors discovered the burnt remains of twenty-four-year-old mother Emeline Houseman and her infant daughter, Ann Eliza. When an ambitious district attorney charges Polly Bodine (Emeline's sister-in-law) with a double homicide, the new "penny press" explodes. Polly is a perfect media villain: She's a separated wife who drinks gin, commits adultery, and has had multiple abortions. The Witch of New York is the first narrative history about the dueling trial lawyers, ruthless newsmen, and shameless hucksters who turned the Polly Bodine case into America's formative tabloid trial.

"Hortis's fastidious historical detail makes the episode come to life, and he successfully evokes contemporary tabloid scandals like the Amanda Knox trial without stretching the point too far." —*Publishers Weekly*

Jimenez, Stephen
The Book of Matt: Hidden Truths About the Murder of Matthew Shepard. Stephen Jimenez. Steerforth Press 2013. 368 p.

ISBN 9781586422141

Grades: Adult   **364.152**

1. Shepard, Matthew, 1976-1998 2. Young gay men 3. Violence against gay men and lesbians 4. Drug use 5. Drug industry and trade 6. Methamphetamine 7. Hate crimes 8. Murder 9. True Crime — Murder 10. True Crime — Drugs 11. Society and culture — Violence and crime

LC 2013431178

A controversial account of the 1998 murder of Matthew Shepard describes the evening of the assault that ended his life and the ways in which the victim became a symbol of anti-hate crime activism, sharing additional details that suggest that Shepard was killed for more complicated and daunting reasons.

"In claiming that Shepard was killed because of drugs, and the 'Gay panic' story was offered as a cover and heavily pushed by media and politicians as part of a larger agenda, Jimenez completely changes the meaning and impact of Shepard's death." —*Publishers Weekly*

Jobb, Dean
The Case of the Murderous Dr. Cream: The Hunt for a Victorian Era Serial Killer. Dean Jobb. Algonquin Books of Chapel Hill 2021. 384 p.

ISBN 9781616206895

Grades: Adult   **364.152**

1. Cream, Thomas Neill, 1850-1892 2. Forensic sciences 3. Serial murderers 4. Physicians 5. Serial murders 6. London, England 7. United States 8. Victorian era (1837-1901) 9. Biographies 10. True Crime — Murder 11. True Crime — Historical Crime 12. History writing — General 13. Life stories — Law and order — Criminals and law-breakers

LC 2021002158

Framed around one salacious trial in 1891 London, a fascinating and vividly told true-crime narrative about the hunt for one of the first known serial killers, whose poisoning spree in the US, Canada, and England coincided with the birth of forensic science as well as the public's growing appetite for crime fiction such as Sir Arthur Conan Doyle's Sherlock Holmes novels.

"A lively account of an early international serial killer's crimes. In his latest, journalist and creative nonfiction professor Jobb richly embellishes his grim central tale with carefully researched setting, detail, and social mores of the late Victorian era." —*Kirkus*

Includes bibliographical references.

Keefe, Patrick Radden
★ *Say Nothing: A True Story of Murder and Memory in Northern Ireland*. Patrick Radden Keefe. Doubleday 2019. 304 p.

ISBN 9780385521314

Grades: Adult   **364.152**

1. McConville, Jean 2. The Troubles, 1968-1998 3. Murder 4. Kidnapping 5. Domestic terrorism 6. Political violence 7. British history 8. Belfast, Northern

Ireland 9. Northern Ireland 10. 1970s 11. 20th century 12. True Crime — Murder 13. History writing — Europe — United Kingdom — Northern Ireland

LC 2018031745

ALA Notable Book, 2020; Library Journal Best Books, 2019; New York Times Notable Book, 2019; Orwell Prize, 2019; National Book Critics Circle Award for Non-Fiction, 2019; Kirkus Prize for Nonfiction finalist, 2019; Longlisted for the National Book Award for Nonfiction, 2019.

Documents the notorious abduction and murder of I.R.A. Troubles victim Jean McConville in 1972 Belfast, exploring how the case reflected the brutal conflicts of Northern Ireland and their ongoing repercussions.

"Tinged with immense sadness, this work never loses sight of the humanity of even those who committed horrible acts in support of what they believed in." —*Publishers Weekly*

Kenda, Joe

Killer Triggers. Joe Kenda. Blackstone 2021. 200 p.

ISBN 9781982678357

Grades: Adult   364.152

1. Kenda, Joe 2. Detectives 3. Murderers 4. Murder 5. Crime 6. Criminal investigation 7. Colorado 8. 1980s 9. 1990s 10. Autobiographies and memoirs 11. Life stories — Law and order — Police and law officers 12. True Crime — Murder

The most common triggers for homicide are fear, rage, revenge, money, lust, and, more rarely, sheer madness. This isn't an exact science, of course. Any given murder can have multiple triggers. Sex and revenge seem to be common partners in crime. Rage, money, and revenge make for a dangerous trifecta of triggers, as well. This book offers my memories of homicide cases that I investigated or oversaw. In each case, I examine the trigger that led to death. I chose this theme for the book because even though the why of a murder case may not be critical in an investigation, it can sometimes lead us to the killer.

"In this exceptional memoir, Kenda chronicles the highlights of his twenty-one years as a Colorado Springs, Colo, homicide detective. . . . This is must reading for true crime fans." —*Publishers Weekly*

King, David

Death in the City of Light: The Serial Killer of Occupied Paris. David King. Crown 2011. 432 p.

ISBN 9780307452894

Grades: Adult   364.152

1. Petiot, Marcel 2. Serial murderers 3. Physicians 4. Serial murders 5. World War II 6. German occupation, World War II 7. French history 8. France 9. 1940s 10. True Crime — Investigations and Trials 11. True Crime — Murder 12. History writing — Wars and conflicts — World War II

LC 2011014412

Booklist Editors' Choice, 2011.

Documents the World War II effort to catch a physician serial killer in Paris, describing the covert information network that the chief French detective built with such groups as mobsters, nightclub owners, and Resistance fighters.

"This fascinating, often painful account combines a police procedural with a vivid historical portrait of culture and law enforcement in Nazi-occupied France." —*Publishers Weekly*

Includes bibliographical references and index.

King, Greg

Nothing but the Night: Leopold & Loeb and the Truth Behind the Murder That Rocked 1920s America. Greg King and Penny Wilson. St. Martin's Press 2022. 352 p.

ISBN 9781250272669

Grades: Adult   364.152

1. Leopold, Nathan Freudenthal, 1904-1971 2. Loeb, Richard A, 1905-1936 3. Young men 4. Murder 5. Ransom 6. Trials (Murder) 7. Lifers (Prisoners) 8. Chicago, Illinois 9. 1920s 10. True Crime — Historical Crime 11. True Crime — Murder

LC 2022014440

Nearly a hundred years ago, two wealthy and privileged teenagers—Nathan Leopold and Richard Loeb—were charged and convicted in a gruesome crime that would lead to the original "Trial of the Century": Well-to-do Jewish scions, full of promise, had killed fourteen-year-old Bobby Franks for the thrill of it. Using twenty-first century investigative tools, forensics, and a modern understanding of the psychology of these infamous killers, Nothing but the Night turns history on its head. Nothing but the Night pulls readers into the troubled world of Leopold and Loeb, revealing a more horrifying tale of passion, obsession, and betrayal than history ever imagined.

"King and Wilson, coauthors of the Last Voyage of the Andrea Doria, return with an intriguing deep dive into the horrific 1924 murder of 14-year-old Bobby Franks in Chicago….This is a disturbing and well-documented look at one of the 20th century's most infamous murders." —*Publishers Weekly*

Includes bibliographical references and index.

Kroll, Andy

A Death on W Street: The Murder of Seth Rich and the Age of Conspiracy. Andy Kroll. Public Affairs 2022. 368 p.

ISBN 9781541751149

Grades: Adult   364.152

1. Political consultants 2. Murder victims 3. Rumor 4. Conspiracy theories 5. Deception 6. Misinformation 7. Libel and slander 8. Propaganda 9. Murder in mass media 10. Press and politics 11. Life stories — Facing adversity — Victims of crime 12. Politics and global affairs — Mass media and politics 13. True Crime — Murder 14. History writing — Conspiracy theories 15. Debut title

Describes how the murder of a DNC political staffer launched conspiracy theories on social media and intensified the culture wars when Fox News broadcast unfounded theories that ultimately ensnared Hillary Clinton, a DC pizzeria and Alex Jones.

An unfortunate young man goes from murder victim to QAnon icon….An exemplary investigation, exactly as the author describes it: 'A true-crime story for the post-truth era.' —*Kirkus*

Includes bibliographical references and index.

Lake, Dianne

Member of the Family: My Story of Charles Manson, Life Inside His Cult, and the Darkness That Ended the Sixties. Dianne Lake, and Deborah Herman. William Morrow 2017. 336 p.

ISBN 9780062695574

Grades: Adult   364.152

1. Lake, Dianne 2. Manson, Charles, 1934-2017 3. Cults 4. Child abuse victims 5. Growing up 6. Brainwashing 7. Manipulation (Social sciences) 8. Autobiographies and memoirs 9. Life stories — Facing adversity — Abuse survivors

LC 2017277072

An inside account by the youngest member of Charles Manson's cult describes her involuntary indoctrination by her parents at age 14 and the manipulation, psychological control and physical abuse that she endured before she was rescued and adopted by the police officer who arrested her.

Lauren, Jillian

Behold the Monster: Confronting America's Most Prolific Serial Killer. Jillian Lauren; foreword by Michael Connelly. Sourcebooks 2023. 352 p.

ISBN 9781728267753

Grades: Adult   364.152

1. Little, Samuel, 1940-2020 2. Serial murderers 3. Serial murders 4. Serial rapists 5. Women murder victims 6. Confession (Law) 7. Prisoners 8. Lifers (Prisoners) 9. Serial murder investigation 10. California 11. True Crime — Murder

The best-selling author of Some Girls draws on correspondence and conversations with imprisoned serial killer Samuel Little and four of his surviving victims, recounting Little's confession to dozens of additional murders and what the interviews reveal about the criminal psyche.

"Bestseller Lauren (Some Girls) recounts the murders of Samuel Little, America's most prolific serial killer, in this wildly original blend of narrative nonfiction and true crime reporting…Lauren convincingly sketches Little, his victims, his relatives, and the lawmen and women who dedicated their lives to catching him." —*Publishers Weekly*

Originally published by E.P. Dutton, New York, in 2021; Includes bibliographical references.

ESSENTIAL AND RECOMMENDED TITLES
364.152 Homicide

Leovy, Jill
Ghettoside: A True Story of Murder in America. Jill Leovy. Spiegel & Grau 2014. 336 pages
ISBN 9780385529983
Grades: Adult   364.152
1. Murder 2. African American men 3. Inner city violence 4. Detectives 5. Ghettoes, African American 6. Murderers 7. Crime and race 8. African American communities 9. Los Angeles, California 10. True Crime — Murder 11. Society and culture — Race
LC 2013046367
New York Times Notable Book, 2015; National Book Critics Circle Award for Nonfiction finalist.
Discusses the hundreds of murders that occur in Los Angeles each year, and focuses on the story of the dedicated group of detectives who pursued justice at any cost in the killing of Bryant Tennelle.
"Readers may come for Leovy's detective story; they will stay for her lucid social critique." —*Publishers Weekly*

Lowry, Beverly
Deer Creek Drive: A Reckoning of Memory and Murder in the Mississippi Delta. Beverly Lowry. Alfred A. Knopf 2022. 304 p.
ISBN 9780525657231
Grades: Adult   364.152
1. Murder 2. White privilege 3. Mothers and daughters 4. Race relations 5. Mississippi 6. 1940s 7. Biographies 8. True Crime — Murder
LC 2021053204
Describes the 1948 murder of Southern society matron Idella Thompson, who was stabbed 150 times while home alone with her daughter, who was convicted of the murder and later freed in a tale of white privilege that still resonates today.
"Lowry elegantly details Southern daily life and the struggles for equality that eventually led to desegregation." —*Publishers Weekly*
Includes bibliographical references and index.

MacLean, Harry N.
Starkweather: The Untold Story of the Killing Spree That Changed America. Harry N. MacLean. Counterpoint 2023. 336 p.
ISBN 9781640095410
Grades: Adult   364.152
1. Starkweather, Charles Raymond, 1938-1959 2. Fugate, Caril Ann 3. Serial murderers 4. Serial murders 5. Murder 6. Teenage murderers 7. Nebraska 8. 1950s 9. True Crime — Murder
LC 2023019009
Drawing on new material, reporting and conclusions, this definitive story of 19-year-old Charles Starkweather, who, in 1958, murdered 10 people with his 14-year-old girlfriend, recounts this shocking event that served as the inspiration for the movie Natural Born Killers and Springsteen's iconic album Nebraska.
"Though the subject matter is bleak, this book is expertly written. Crime aficionados will enjoy." —*Library Journal*

Marzano-Lesnevich, Alexandria
The Fact of a Body: A Murder and a Memoir. Alexandria Marzano-lesnevich. St Martins Pr 2017. 320 p.
ISBN 9781250080547
Grades: Adult   364.152
1. Marzano-Lesnevich, Alexandria 2. Law students 3. Family secrets 4. Psychic trauma 5. Capital punishment 6. Adult child abuse victims 7. Autobiographies and memoirs 8. True Crime — Investigations and Trials 9. Life stories — Facing adversity — Abuse survivors 10. Nonfiction that reads like fiction
LC 2017003049
Lambda Literary Award for Lesbian Memoir/Biography, 2018.
A National Endowment for the Arts fellow documents the story of how a summer job at a Louisiana law firm and the case of a convicted murderer and child molester changed her views about the death penalty and forced her to confront traumatic secrets in her own family.

"She poses a greater philosophical and legal question of one's past and how that determines cause in an exquisite and thought-provoking comparison study." —*Library Journal*

Matney, Mandy
Blood on Their Hands: Murder, Corruption, and the Fall of the Murdaugh Dynasty. Mandy Matney. William Morrow & Company 2023. 288 p.
ISBN 9780063269217
Grades: Adult   364.152
1. Murdaugh, Alex (Richard Alexander), 1968- 2. Murder 3. Families 4. Lawyers 5. Crime 6. Corruption 7. Family violence 8. Power 9. South Carolina 10. Life stories — Law and order — Criminals and law-breakers 11. True Crime — Murder
"The result is both an engrossing true crime saga and a galvanizing ode to boots-on-the-ground journalism." —*Publishers Weekly*

McCracken, Patti
The Angel Makers: Arsenic, a Midwife, and Modern History's Most Astonishing Murder Ring. Patti McCracken. William Morrow & Company 2023. 320 p.
ISBN 9780063275034
Grades: Adult   364.152
1. Serial murderers 2. Women murderers 3. Serial murders 4. Midwives 5. Arsenic 6. 1920s 7. Life stories — Law and order — Criminals and law-breakers 8. True Crime — Murder 9. True Crime — Historical Crime
Tells the story of a 1920s midwife who may have been the century's most prolific killer leading a murder ring of women responsible for the deaths of at least 160 men.
"Journalist McCracken debuts with a compulsively readable account of a group of women who operated a murder ring for years during the early 20th century in the Hungarian village of Nagyrév....This is a must for true crime fans." —*Publishers Weekly*

McDiarmid, Jessica
Highway of Tears: A True Story of Racism, Indifference, and the Pursuit of Justice for Missing and Murdered Indigenous Women and Girls. Jessica McDiarmid. Atria Books 2019. 320 p.
ISBN 9781501160288
Grades: Adult   364.152
1. First Nations (Canada) 2. Indigenous women 3. Violence against women 4. Missing women 5. Women murder victims 6. Violence against marginalized women 7. Roads 8. Racism 9. Intersectionality 10. Social justice 11. Criminal justice system 12. Missing children 13. Girls 14. British Columbia 15. Canadian literature 16. Society and culture — Race 17. Society and culture — Gender — Women 18. Society and culture — Violence and crime — Criminal justice system 19. History writing — Indigenous peoples — Canada 20. Life stories — Facing adversity — Victims of crime 21. True Crime — Murder
LC Bl2019033987
Shortlisted for the Charles Taylor Prize for Literary Non-Fiction, 2020.
Along northern Canada's Highway 16, a yellow billboard reads GIRLS, DON'T HITCHHIKE. KILLER ON THE LOOSE. The highway is a 450-mile stretch of dirt and asphalt, surrounded by rugged wilderness and snowy mountain peaks. It is known as the Highway of Tears. It is here that countless women and girls—most of them Indigenous—have vanished since 1969. Highway of Tears explores the true story of what has happened along this troubled road. Journalist Jessica McDiarmid reassembles the lives of the victims—who they were, where they came from, who loved them, and what led them to the highway—and takes us into their families' determined fight for the truth.

McGarrahan, Ellen
Two Truths and a Lie: A Murder, a Private Investigator, and Her Search for Justice. Ellen McGarrahan. Random House 2021. 336 p.
ISBN 9780812998665
Grades: Adult   364.152
1. Tafero, Jesse, 1946-1990 2. McGarrahan, Ellen 3. Murder investigation 4. Crime and the press 5. Judicial error 6. Corruption 7. Women private investi-

gators 8. Justice 9. Grief 10. Florida 11. Autobiographies and memoirs 12. True Crime — Murder 13. Life stories — Law and order — Police and law officers
LC 2020009767

An investigative reporter-turned-private detective describes the brutal state execution of a possibly innocent man that haunted her career, her decision to reopen the case and the complex web of crime and corruption that her investigation exposed.

"Journalist and private investigator McGarrahan's debut is an engrossing, authoritative fusion of true crime and memoir." —*Kirkus*

McGough, Matthew
The Lazarus Files: A Cold Case Investigation. by Matthew McGough. Henry Holt 2019. 595 pages
ISBN 9780805095593
Grades: Adult   364.152
1. Rasmussen, Sherri 2. Lazarus, Stephanie 3. Women murder victims 4. Cold cases (Criminal investigation) 5. Police corruption 6. Murder 7. Women murder suspects 8. Police 9. Women detectives 10. Love triangles 11. Former girlfriends 12. Los Angeles, California 13. 1980s 14. True Crime — Murder 15. True Crime — Investigations and Trials
LC 2018037256

Traces the investigation surrounding a deeply reported cold case from 1986 Los Angeles that remained unsolved until DNA evidence shockingly implicated a woman LAPD detective.

McNamara, Michelle
I'll Be Gone in the Dark: One Woman's Obsessive Search for the Golden State Killer. Michelle McNamara, introduction by Gillian Flynn, afterword by Patton Oswalt. HarperCollins 2018. 368 p.
ISBN 9780062319784
Grades: Adult   364.152
1. McNamara, Michelle, 1970-2016 2. Cold cases (Criminal investigation) 3. Home invasions 4. Criminal investigation 5. Crimes against women 6. Violence against women 7. Serial rapists 8. Serial murders 9. Searching 10. Page to screen 11. True crime — Murder 12. True crime — Sex crimes 13. Adult books for young adults 14. Nonfiction that reads like fiction
LC 2017301180

Anthony Award for Best Critical/Nonfiction, 2019; Goodreads Choice Award, 2018; Library Journal Best Books, 2018.

An account of the unsolved Golden State Killer case, written by the late author of the TrueCrimeDiary.Com website traces the rapes and murders of dozens of victims and the author's determined efforts to help identify the killer and bring him to justice.

"McNamara's posthumously published book tells both the nightmarish story of the Golden State Killer (GSK) and the neighborhoods he terrorized and her own story of true-crime addiction." —*Booklist*

Metzl, Jonathan M.
★ *What We've Become: Living and Dying in a Country of Arms.* Jonathan M. Metzl. W W Norton & Company 2024. 320 p.
ISBN 9781324050254
Grades: Adult   364.152
1. Gun control 2. Violence 3. Violence and guns 4. Safety 5. Public health 6. Freedom 7. Civil rights 8. United States 9. Society and culture — Violence and crime 10. History Writing — United States 11. Politics and global affairs — Civil and human rights

"Metzl traces the shooter's path to that day while honoring the victims and their families in this essential study of how mass shootings in the U.S. have become commonplace." —*Booklist*

Miles, Kathryn
Trailed: One Woman's Quest to Solve the Shenandoah Murders. Kathryn Miles. Algonquin Books of Chapel Hill 2022. 336 p.
ISBN 9781616209094
Grades: Adult   364.152
1. Williams, Julie, -1996 2. Winans, Lollie, -1996 3. Murder 4. Murderers 5. Hikers 6. Women murder victims 7. Investigations 8. Virginia 9. True Crime — Murder 10. History writing — Regional History — United States
LC 2021057136

On the 20th anniversary of the murder, a journalist starts looking into the lives of Lollie Winans and Julie Williams, who were killed while backpacking in Virginia's Shenandoah National Park, revealing evidence of cover-ups and incompetence that possibly led to the apprehension of the wrong suspect.

"An award-winning science writer investigates the 1996 backcountry murders of two hikers….Gripping and thoughtful, this book will appeal to those with an interest in true-crime stories and unsettling truths about places deemed safe for all." —*Kirkus*

Includes bibliographical references.

Mitchell, Jerry
★ *Race Against Time: A Reporter Reopens the Unsolved Murder Cases of the Civil Rights Era.* Jerry Mitchell. Simon & Schuster 2020. 320 pages
ISBN 9781451645132
Grades: Adult   364.152
1. Mitchell, Jerry 2. Investigative journalists 3. Cold cases (Criminal investigation) 4. Trials (Murder) 5. Civil rights workers 6. Murder investigation 7. Civil Rights Movement 8. Murder 9. Journalists 10. Southern states 11. Mississippi 12. Alabama 13. United States 14. Autobiographies and memoirs 15. Biographies 16. Life stories — Arts and culture — Writing — Journalists 17. True Crime — Cold Cases and Unsolved Mysteries 18. Nonfiction that reads like fiction
LC 2019030562

An award-winning investigative journalist recounts the 1964 "Mississippi Burning" murders of three civil rights workers by the KKK, describing his role in reopening the case and bringing its mastermind and participating Klansmen to justice.

"A fine work of investigative journalism and an essential addition to the history of the civil rights movement." —*Kirkus*

Includes bibliographical references and index.

Montillo, Roseanne
Deliberate Cruelty: Truman Capote, the Millionaire's Wife, and the Murder of the Century. Roseanne Montillo. Atria Books 2022. 320 p.
ISBN 9781982153731
Grades: Adult   364.152
1. Capote, Truman, 1924-1984 2. Woodward, Ann, 1916-1975 3. Authors 4. Socialites 5. Murderers 6. Suicide 7. Murder victims 8. Upper class 9. Scandals 10. Long Island, New York 11. United States 12. 20th century 13. 1950s 14. True Crime — Murder 15. True Crime — Historical crime

Describes how author Truman Capote became obsessed with the true crime story of a Manhattan socialite who shot her banking heir husband in 1955 and discusses how publication of his book led to her suicide and his own scandalous downfall.

"In this engrossing account, research librarian Montillo (Atomic Women: The Untold Stories of the Scientists Who Helped Create the Nuclear Bomb) recreates a tragic cause célèbre….True crime fans particularly interested in bloodshed among the upper classes will enjoy this dark look at two intertwined and unhappy lives." —*Publishers Weekly*

Murdoch, Sierra Crane
★ *Yellow Bird: Oil, Murder, and a Woman's Search for Justice in Indian Country.* Sierra Crane Murdoch. Random House 2020. 400 p.
ISBN 9780399589157
Grades: Adult   364.152
1. Yellow Bird, Lissa 2. Clarke, Kristopher 3. Indigenous women 4. Oil workers 5. Missing persons investigation 6. Women former convicts 7. Missing men 8. Arikara (North American people) 9. Indigenous peoples of North America 10. Recession (Economics) 11. Oil industry and trade 12. Business corruption 13. Criminal investigation 14. Indigenous reservations 15. North Dakota 16. Biographies 17. Life stories — Law and order 18. True Crime — Murder 19. Life stories — Identity — Race and ethnicity
LC 2019022833

ESSENTIAL AND RECOMMENDED TITLES
364.152 Homicide

New York Times Notable Book, 2020; Oregon Book Awards, Sarah Winnemucca Award for Creative Nonfiction, 2021; Pulitzer Prize for General Nonfiction finalist, 2021.

Tells the true crime story of a murder on an Indian reservation, and the unforgettable Arikara woman who becomes obsessed with solving it.

"Required reading for all fans of true crime, particularly those interested in the intersections of poverty and environmental justice, along with Native studies." —*Library Journal*

Nelson, David B.
Boys Enter the House: The Victims of John Wayne Gacy and the Lives They Left Behind. David B. Nelson. Chicago Review Press 2021. 336 p.
ISBN 9781641604864
Grades: Adult   364.152
1. Gacy, John Wayne, 1942-1994 2. Murder victims 3. Families of murder victims 4. Serial murders 5. Murderers 6. Murder 7. Serial murderers 8. Boys 9. Child murder victims 10. Illinois 11. Chicago, Illinois 12. True Crime — Murder

Through the testimony of siblings, parents, friends, lovers, and other witnesses close to the case, Boys Enter the House retraces the footsteps of these victims as they make their way to the doorstep of the Gacy house itself.

"Journalist Nelson debuts with a moving and meticulously researched account of the lives of the victims of serial killer John Wayne Gacy, who brutalized and murdered 33 boys and young men between January 1972 and December 1978, burying most of them beneath his house on the outskirts of Chicago.... Nelson succeeds in giving Gacy's victims a voice. This is a must for true crime fans." —*Publishers Weekly*

O'Connell, Mark
A Thread of Violence: A Story of Truth, Invention, and Murder. Mark O'Connell. Doubleday 2023. 304 p.
ISBN 9780385547628
Grades: Adult   364.152
1. MacArthur, Malcolm 2. Socialites 3. Heirs and heiresses 4. Money 5. Debt 6. Bank robberies 7. Murder 8. Conspiracies 9. Trials 10. Prisoners 11. Crime in the news media 12. Dublin, Ireland 13. Ireland 14. Life stories — Law and order — Criminals and law-breakers 15. True Crime — Heists and Robbery 16. True Crime — Murder

An award-winning author tells the true crime tale of a Dublin socialite who squandered all his money and planned and executed a 1982 bank robbery that left two innocent people dead and whose conviction created an infamous political scandal.

"Swirling together dogged reporting with questions about the media's coverage of crime, O'Connell manages a gripping account that casts a skeptical eye on its own genre. Even readers put off by profiles of killers will be piqued." —*Publishers Weekly*

O'Neill, Tom
★ *Chaos: Charles Manson, the Cia, and the Secret History of the Sixties*. Tom O'Neill, with Dan Piepenbring. Little, Brown & Company 2019. 528 p.
ISBN 9780316477550
Grades: Adult   364.152
1. O'Neill, Tom 2. Manson, Charles, 1934-2017 3. Investigative journalists 4. Murder investigation 5. Murder suspects 6. Police misconduct 7. Police cover-ups 8. Public prosecutors 9. Intelligence service 10. Conspiracies 11. 1960s 12. True Crime — Historical Crime 13. True Crime — Murder
LC Bl2019011669

A journalist's 20-year obsession with the 1969 Manson murders brings shocking revelations about one of the most infamous crimes in American history: Carelessness from police, misconduct by prosecutors and even potential surveillance by intelligence agents.

Oppenheimer, Mark
Squirrel Hill: The Tree of Life Synagogue Shooting and the Soul of a Neighborhood. Mark Oppenheimer. Alfred A. Knopf 2021. 320 p.
ISBN 9780525657194
Grades: Adult   364.152
1. Neighborhoods 2. Jewish Americans 3. Synagogues 4. Mass shootings 5. Hate crimes 6. Antisemitism 7. Victims of violent crimes 8. Collective memory 9. Healing 10. Resilience 11. Pittsburgh, Pennsylvania 12. 21st century 13. History writing — Jewish history 14. History writing — Early 21st century — United States 15. Life stories — Facing adversity — Victims of crime 16. Society and culture — Violence and crime 17. Society and culture — Urban and regional studies

A portrait of the struggles and triumphs of one of America's renowned Jewish neighborhoods in the wake of unspeakable tragedy that highlights the hopes, fears, and tensions all Americans must confront on the road to healing.

"A devastating story of loss that becomes a story of societal resilience; essential reading for anyone seeking insight on gun violence." —*Library Journal*

Rae-Venter, Barbara
I Know Who You Are: How an Amateur DNA Sleuth Unmasked the Golden State Killer and Changed Crime Fighting Forever. Barbara Rae-Venter. Ballantine Books 2023. 256 p.
ISBN 9780593358894
Grades: Adult   364.152
1. Criminal investigation 2. Cold cases (Criminal investigation) 3. DNA 4. DNA research 5. Forensic scientists 6. Serial murderers 7. Rapists 8. California 9. True Crime — Forensic Sciences
LC 2022035338

A retiree researching her family history explains how she used her knowledge of DNA data to uncover the culprit of the Golden State Killer crime spree, a cold case that had baffled law enforcement for decades.

"Fascinating true-crime reportage infused with cinematic suspense." —*Kirkus*

Ralph, Laurence
Sito: An American Teenager and the City That Failed Him. Laurence Ralph. Grand Central Publishing 2024. 299 p.
ISBN 9781538740323
Grades: Adult   364.152
1. Teenage murder victims 2. Gangs 3. Street life 4. Violent crimes 5. Imprisonment 6. Mental health 7. Family relationships 8. Intergenerational trauma 9. Despair 10. Race relations 11. Racism in law enforcement 12. San Francisco, California 13. Life stories — Facing adversity — Victims of crime 14. Society and culture — Race 15. Society and culture — Violence and crime — Criminal justice system
LC 2023036571

Through the story of 19-year-old Luis Alberto Quiñonez, aka Sito, who was shot to death in the Mission District of San Francisco, the author, writing as both a person enmeshed in Sito's family and as an expert on the entanglement of class and violence, explores the systemic issues that perpetuate gang participation.

"Through a heart-wrenching study of a youth's murder, Ralph reveals a larger picture of social decay, despair, and violence." —*Kirkus*

Includes bibliographical references.

Rear, Rachel
Catch the Sparrow: A Search for a Sister and the Truth of Her Murder. Rachel Rear. Bloomsbury Publishing Place USA 2022. 256 p.
ISBN 9781635577235
Grades: Adult   364.152
1. Rear, Rachel 2. Kupchynsky, Stephanie 3. Women murder victims 4. Stepsisters 5. Violence against women 6. Investigations 7. Criminal justice system 8. Murder 9. Crime 10. Families 11. Autobiographies and memoirs 12. True Crime — Murder 13. Life stories — Facing adversity — Victims of crime

Growing up, Rachel Rear knew the story of Stephanie Kupchynsky's disappearance. The beautiful violinist and teacher had fled an abusive relationship on Martha's Vineyard and made a new start for herself near Rochester, NY. She was at the height of her life-in a relationship with a man she hoped to marry and close to her students and her family. And then, one morning, she was gone.

"A New York City public schoolteacher's account of her quest to discover the truth behind her stepsister's brutal murder.... A chillingly candid memoir and work of true crime." —*Kirkus*

PUBLIC LIBRARY CORE COLLECTION: NONFICTION
Twentieth Edition

Rubin, Kathy Kleiner
A Light in the Dark: Surviving More Than Ted Bundy. Kathy Kleiner Rubin and Emilie Le Beau Lucchesi. Chicago Review Press 2023. 287 p.
ISBN 9781641608688
Grades: Adult   364.152
1. Bundy, Ted, 1946-1989 2. Victims of violent crimes 3. Attempted murder 4. Serial murderers 5. Terminal illness 6. Serial murders 7. Lupus 8. Cancer survivors 9. Autobiographies and memoirs 10. True Crime — Murder 11. Debut title 12. Life stories — Facing adversity — Victims of crime 13. Life stories — Facing adversity — Medical issues — Physical illness 14. History Writing — United States

"In this beautifully told portrait of courage, Rubin tells her story of being a survivor…Rubin's story demonstrates the far-reaching ramifications of violent crime, showing how it destroys families and loved ones and leaves a wake of physical pain and emotional wreckage." —*Booklist*

Schechter, Harold
Murderabilia: A History of Crime in 100 Objects. Harold Schechter. Workman Publishing 2023. 282 pages : Illustration; Color
ISBN 9781523515295
Grades: Adult   364.152
1. Murder 2. Murderers 3. Serial murders 4. Serial murderers 5. True Crime — Murder

LC 2023012300

A veteran true crime writer presents 100 murder-related artifacts spanning from 1808-2014, including the false teeth of a female serial killer and the newly cracked cipher of the Zodiac killer, to better understand those who we typically label monsters in lieu of learning how they actually became one.

"A sound addition to true crime collections and collections in colleges, especially those with concentrations in criminology or criminal justice." —*Booklist*
Includes index.

Sides, Hampton
Hellhound on His Trail: The Stalking of Martin Luther King, Jr. And The International Hunt for His Assassin. Hampton Sides. Doubleday 2010. 320 p.
ISBN 9780385523929
Grades: Adult   364.152
1. King, Martin Luther, Jr, 1929-1968 2. Ray, James Earl, 1928-1998 3. African American civil rights workers 4. Murderers 5. Social history 6. Civil Rights Movement 7. Assassination 8. United States 9. 1960s 10. 20th century 11. True Crime — Historical Crime 12. True Crime — Murder 13. History writing — African American — Civil rights — United States

LC 2009043659

From the acclaimed bestselling author of "Ghost Soldiers" and "Blood and Thunder," a taut, intense narrative about the assassination of Martin Luther King, Jr, and the largest manhunt in American history—a sixty-five-day search that led investigators to Canada, Portugal, and England.

"Sides begins with Ray's escape from a maximum security prison in Missouri the prior April. In short, crisp chapters, Sides then cuts back and forth between Ray's movements during the ensuing year and King's increasing challenges during the same period, as a fraying civil rights movement struggled to transform hard-won legal equality into economic justice. Along the way, we're treated to vignettes featuring J. Edgar Hoover's vicious anti-King smear tactics; George Wallace's race-driven politics of hate during the 1968 presidential campaign; and an embittered Lyndon Johnson's estrangement from King over the ongoing war in Vietnam. None of this is new, but Sides ensures that it's still compulsively readable." —*Milwaukee Journal Sentinel*

Stashower, Daniel
American Demon: Eliot Ness and the Hunt for America's Jack the Ripper. Daniel Stashower. Minotaur Books 2022. 352 p.
ISBN 9781250041166
Grades: Adult   364.152
1. Ness, Eliot 2. Murder victims 3. Dismemberment 4. Serial murders 5. Cities and towns 6. Detectives 7. Humiliation 8. Murder investigation 9. Cleveland, Ohio 10. 1930s 11. True Crime — Murder 12. True Crime — Historical Crime 13. Life stories — Law and order — Police and law officers

LC 2022009070

On September 5th, 1934, a young beachcomber made a gruesome discovery on the shores of Cleveland's Lake Erie: the lower half of a female torso, neatly severed at the waist. Over the next four years, twelve more bodies would be scattered across the city. Some were beheaded while still alive. Amid the growing uproar, Cleveland's besieged mayor turned to his newly-appointed director of public safety: Eliot Ness. Ness had come to Cleveland fresh from his headline-grabbing exploits in Chicago, where he and his band of "Untouchables" led the frontline assault on AL Capone's bootlegging empire. Now he would confront a case that would redefine his storied career.

"A riveting and illuminating account of an iconic figure's involvement in a notorious murder investigation." —*Kirkus*
Includes bibliographical references and index.

Thompson, Jamie
Standoff: Race, Policing, and a Deadly Assault That Gripped a Nation. Jamie Thompson. Henry Holt & Company 2020. xix, 294 p.
ISBN 9781250204219
Grades: Adult   364.152
1. Police murders 2. Police 3. Mass shootings 4. Mass murder 5. Protests, demonstrations, vigils, etc. 6. Hostage negotiations 7. Public relations 8. Police brutality 9. Racism in law enforcement 10. Dallas, Texas 11. 21st century 12. Impartial writing 13. Society and culture — Violence and crime — Criminal justice system 14. Society and culture — Race 15. History writing — Early 21st century — United States

LC 2019055941

On the evening of July 7, 2016, protesters gathered in cities across the nation after police shot two Black men, Philando Castile and Alton Sterling. As officers patrolled a march in Dallas, a young man stepped out of an SUV wearing a bulletproof vest and carrying a high-powered rifle. He killed five officers and wounded eleven others. An award-winning journalist documents the shooting, offering character portraits of its first responders, negotiator, doctors and victims while examining how the tragedy reflects ongoing challenges in racial injustice and law enforcement.

"This standout account is both a riveting page-turner and a nuanced portrait of one of contemporary America's most divisive social issues." —*Publishers Weekly*
Includes bibliographical references and index.

Weinman, Sarah
Scoundrel: How a Convicted Murderer Persuaded the Women Who Loved Him, the Conservative Establishment, and the Courts to Set Him Free. Sarah Weinman. Ecco, an imprint of HarperCollins Publishers 2022. 320 p.
ISBN 9780062899767
Grades: Adult   364.152
1. Smith, Edgar, 1934-2017 2. Murderers 3. Swindlers and swindling 4. Fame 5. Crime 6. Murder 7. Manipulation (Social sciences) 8. New Jersey 9. Biographies 10. Life stories — Law and order — Criminals and law-breakers 11. True Crime — Murder

LC 2021044151

Tells the astonishing true story of a murderer who conned the people around him—including conservative thinker William F. Buckley—into helping set him free.

"With this enthralling book, Weinman (The Real Lolita) details the twisted, extraordinary story of a murderer who manipulated his way to freedom and fame.... The book is a must-read for true crime fans, but it will appeal to nonfiction readers across genres for its thrilling blend of crime, media, and politics in mid-century America." —*Library Journal*
Includes bibliographical references and index.

White, Richard
Who Killed Jane Stanford?: A Gilded Age Tale of Murder, Deceit, Spirits and the Birth of a University. Richard White. W.W. Norton & Company 2022. 384 p.
ISBN 9781324004332
Grades: Adult   364.152

ESSENTIAL AND RECOMMENDED TITLES
364.158092 Stalkers

1. Stanford, Jane Lathrop, 1828-1905 2. Murder 3. Cold cases (Criminal investigation) 4. Corruption 5. Deception 6. Conspiracies 7. Poisoning 8. Secrecy 9. Hawaii 10. 20th century 11. True Crime — Cold Cases and Unsolved Mysteries 12. History writing — Early 20th century — United States

LC 2022005007

A premier historian penetrates the fog of corruption and cover-up still surrounding the murder of a Stanford University founder to establish who did it, how, and why.

"Reading like a conversational history lecture in book form, Stanford professor emeritus White's (California Exposures, 2020) mostly captivating book chronicles the deception around the death of Jane Stanford, cofounder of Stanford University." —*Booklist*

Includes bibliographical references and index.

Wiehl, Lis W.
Hunting Charles Manson: The Quest for Justice in the Days of Helter Skelter. Lis Wiehl. Nelson Books 2018. 319 p.
ISBN 9780718092085
Grades: Adult   364.152

1. Manson, Charles, 1934-2017 2. Cults 3. Trials (Murder) 4. Murderers 5. Mass murder investigation 6. Murder 7. California 8. True Crime — Murder

LC 2017059418

Recounts the life of Charles Manson, describing his troubled past, his formation of a group of dedicated followers, the murder spree that resulted from his orders, intense investigation by law enforcement, final capture, homicide trial, and imprisonment.

"Mystery writer, lawyer, and legal analyst Wiehl presents an accessible reboot of prosecutor Vincent Bugliosi's classic Helter Skelter that for the most part doesn't add new information to the highly publicized case." —*Library Journal*

Hunting the Unabomber: The FBI, Ted Kaczynski, and the Capture of America's Most Notorious Domestic Terrorist. Lis Wiehl, with Lisa Pulitzer. Nelson Books 2020. xiv, 317 p.
ISBN 9780718092122
Grades: Adult   364.152

1. Kaczynski, Theodore John, 1942-2023 2. Terrorists 3. Domestic terrorism 4. Bombing investigation 5. Serial murder investigation 6. Former college teachers 7. Bombers (People) 8. FBI agents 9. Life stories — Law and order — Criminals and law-breakers 10. Life stories — Law and order — Police and law officers 11. True Crime — Investigations and Trials

LC 2019031034

On April 3, 1996, a team of FBI agents closed in on an isolated cabin in remote Montana, marking the end of the longest and most expensive investigation in FBI history. The cabin's lone inhabitant was a former mathematics prodigy and professor who had abandoned society decades earlier. Few people knew his name, Theodore Kaczynski, but everyone knew the mayhem and death associated with his nickname: the Unabomber.

"The action progresses with drama and nail-biting intensity, the conclusion foregone yet nonetheless compelling. A true-crime masterpiece." —*Booklist*

Includes bibliographical references and index.

Williamson, Elizabeth
★ *Sandy Hook: An American Tragedy and the Battle for Truth.* Elizabeth Williamson. E P Dutton 2022. 352 p.
ISBN 9781524746575
Grades: Adult   364.152

1. Sandy Hook Elementary School Shooting, Newtown, Conn, 2012 2. School shootings 3. Conspiracy theories 4. Mass shootings 5. Crimes against children 6. Violence in schools 7. Loss 8. Elementary schools 9. Mass murder 10. Connecticut 11. True Crime — Murder 12. History writing — United States 13. Life stories — Facing adversity — Victims of crime

Drawing on hours of interviews and exclusive sources and access, a New York Times journalist documents Sandy Hook and its aftermath, where a conspiracy theorists have forced the victims and survivors to defend that an event even occurred.

"New York Times reporter Williamson's searing debut demonstrates that the Jan. 6, 2021, attack on the Capitol had its roots in the deeply troubling efforts to claim that the 2012 massacre of 26 first-graders and staff members at Sandy Hook Elementary School in Newtown, Conn, was a hoax. . . . She has produced the definitive account of this dark chapter of American history." —*Publishers Weekly*

364.158092 Stalkers

Freitas, Donna
Consent: A Memoir of Unwanted Attention. Donna Freitas. Little, Brown & Company 2019. 352 p.
ISBN 9780316450522
Grades: Adult   364.158092

1. Freitas, Donna 2. Women graduate students 3. College teachers 4. Stalkers 5. Mentors 6. Teacher-student relationships 7. Sexual harassment 8. Sexual consent 9. Sexism in universities and colleges 10. Autobiographies and memoirs 11. Life stories — Facing adversity — Abuse survivors 12. Life stories — Relationships 13. Family and Relationships — Abuse

LC 2018956641

Donna Freitas delivers a forensic examination of the years she spent stalked by her professor, and uses her nightmarish experience to examine the ways in which we stigmatize, debate, and attempt to understand consent today.

"Any reader interested in current discussions on consent and its importance should pick up this heartfelt and harrowing book." —*Library Journal*

364.16 Offenses against property

Behar, Richard
Madoff: The Final Word. Richard Behar. Avid Reader Press 2024. 400 p.
ISBN 9781476726892
Grades: Adult   364.16

1. Madoff, Bernard L. 2. Swindlers and swindling 3. Investment advisers 4. Ponzi schemes 5. White collar crime 6. Victims of crimes 7. Fraud 8. Biographies 9. True Crime — General 10. Life stories — Law and order — Criminals and law-breakers

Fifteen years after Bernie Madoff's arrest, renowned investigative journalist Richard Behar delivers the definitive account of history's largest—and longest-running—financial fraud.

"A penetrating account of the web of lies that won the late con man Bernie Madoff his billions." —*Kirkus*

Betz-Hamilton, Axton
The Less People Know About US: a Mystery of Betrayal, Family Secrets, and Stolen Identity. Axton Betz-Hamilton. Grand Central Publishing 2019. 288 p.
ISBN 9781538730287
Grades: Adult   364.16

1. Betz-Hamilton, Axton 2. Deception 3. Identity theft 4. Families 5. Betrayal 6. Debt 7. Moving to a new home 8. Suspicion 9. Paranoia 10. Social isolation 11. Family secrets 12. Identity 13. Teenagers with eating disorders 14. Teenage girls 15. Autobiographies and memoirs 16. Life stories — Facing adversity — Victims of crime 17. True Crime — General 18. Family and Relationships — Families

LC 2019011217

Edgar Allan Poe Award for Best Fact Crime, 2020.

Describes the impact of identity theft on the author's family at a time when banks and authorities were unwilling to help, revealing how her parents and she endured nightmarish victimization at the hands of a loved one.

Bilefsky, Dan
The Last Job: The. Dan Bilefsky. W.W. Norton & Company 2019. 304 p.
ISBN 9780393609516
Grades: Adult   364.16

1. Burglary 2. Jewelry theft 3. Seniors 4. Thieves 5. Police 6. Bunglers and bungling 7. London, England 8. True Crime — Heists and Robbery

LC 2018046576

The definitive account of one of the most brazen jewel heists in history. Over Easter weekend 2015, a motley crew of six English thieves, several in their sixties and seventies, couldn't resist coming out of retirement for one last career-topping heist. Their target: the Hatton Garden Safe Deposit, in the heart of London's medieval diamond district.

"Former New York Times London correspondent Bilefsky makes good use of his access to the Scotland Yarders investigating the biggest burglary in English history to recreate a daring theft carried out by five thieves, who ended their retirement from a life of crime in 2015 by breaking into safety-deposit boxes." —*Publishers Weekly*

Includes bibliographical references and index.

Dolnick, Edward

The Rescue Artist: A True Story of Art, Thieves, and the Hunt for a Missing Masterpiece. Edward Dolnick. Harper Collins Publishers 2005. 270 p. : Illustration; Color

ISBN 9780060531171

Grades: 11 12 Adult 364.16

1. Munch, Edvard, 1863-1944 2. Art thefts 3. Robbery investigation 4. Museum thefts 5. Norway 6. True Crime — Heists and Robbery 7. Arts and Entertainment — Painting, Drawing, and Sculpture 8. Adult books for young adults

LC 2004062060

Edgar Allan Poe Award for Best Fact Crime, 2006.

Traces the theft of Edvard Munch's "The Scream" from Oslo's National Gallery in 1994, recounting the efforts of art detective Charley Hill to recover the painting in an investigation ranging from the estates of aristocrats to the art underworld.

"[A] tightly woven, fast-paced story." —*School Library Journal*

Includes bibliographical references (p. [245]-249) and index.

Greenberg, Andy

Sandworm: A New Era of Cyberwar and the Hunt for the Kremlin's Most Dangerous Hackers. Andy Greenberg. Doubleday 2019. 368 pages

ISBN 9780385544405

Grades: Adult 364.16

1. Cyberterrorism 2. Computer crimes 3. Spies 4. Hackers 5. Electronic intelligence 6. National security 7. Computer security 8. True Crime — General 9. Politics and global affairs — National security 10. Science Writing — Computing, the Internet, and Technology 11. Society and culture — Media and technology

LC 2019006755

The award-winning Wired senior writer and author of This Machine Kills Secrets documents the story of the hunt to identify and track an elite team of Russian agents behind the world's most dangerous digital attacks.

Includes bibliographical references.

Tracers in the Dark: The Global Hunt for the Crime Lords of Cryptocurrency. Andy Greenberg. Doubleday 2022. 368 p.

ISBN 9780385548090

Grades: Adult 364.16

1. Computer crimes 2. White collar crime 3. International crime 4. Cryptocurrencies 5. Bitcoin 6. Black market 7. High technology 8. Organized crime 9. Business corruption 10. Police corruption 11. True Crime — Organized Crime, Mafia, and Gangs 12. Science Writing — Computing, the Internet, and Technology 13. Life stories — Law and order — Criminals and law-breakers 14. Life stories — Law and order — Police and law officers 15. Nonfiction that reads like fiction

LC 2022005413

With unprecedented access to the major players in federal law enforcement and private industry who have cracked the Bitcoin blockchain, a veteran cybersecurity reporter presents this thrilling, globe-spanning story of dirty cops, drug bazaars, trafficking rings and the biggest takedown of an online narcotics market in the history of the internet.

"Greenberg follows up 2019's Sandworm, which focused on Russian computer hackers, with this spellbinding story of the efforts of law-enforcement agencies around the world to bring down the criminal elements who use cryptocurrency (Bitcoin, for example) to fund their illegal activities....Lively, highly relevant, and more than a little scary." —*Booklist*

Includes bibliographical references.

Hammer, Joshua

The Falcon Thief: A True Tale of Adventure, Treachery, and the Hunt for the Perfect Bird. Joshua Hammer. Simon & Schuster 2020. 288 pages

ISBN 9781501191886

Grades: Adult 364.16

1. Wildlife crimes 2. Falcons 3. Rare and endangered birds 4. Birds 5. Smugglers 6. Detectives 7. Obsession 8. Eggs 9. Nests 10. True Crime — General 11. Nature Writing — Animal Studies — Birds and Birding

LC 2019031607

Documents the true story of Irish national Jeffrey Lendrum and his globetrotting adventures as a smuggler of rare birds, detailing the efforts of British wildlife detective Andy McWilliam to protect the world's endangered birds of prey.

"A sleek, winning nonfiction thriller." —*Kirkus*

Includes bibliographical references and index.

Hvistendahl, Mara

★ *The Scientist and the Spy: A True Story of China, the FBI, and Industrial Espionage.* Mara Hvistendahl. Penguin Group USA 2020. 320 p.

ISBN 9780735214286

Grades: Adult 364.16

1. Business intelligence 2. Trade secrets 3. Spies 4. Governmental investigations 5. Big business 6. Chinese people in the United States 7. Agribusiness 8. Agricultural technology 9. International relations 10. Business corruption 11. Chinese people 12. United States 13. China 14. Life stories — Law and order — Spies and secret agents 15. True Crime — General 16. Business and economics — Industries — Agriculture and food 17. Nonfiction that reads like fiction

LC 2019037842

In September 2011, sheriff's deputies in Iowa encountered three ethnic Chinese men near a field where a farmer was growing corn seed under contract with Monsanto. What began as a simple trespassing inquiry mushroomed into a two-year FBI operation in which investigators bugged the men's rental cars, used a warrant intended for foreign terrorists and spies, and flew surveillance planes over corn country—all in the name of protecting trade secrets of corporate giants Monsanto and DuPont Pioneer. Hvistendahl gives a gripping account of this unusually far-reaching investigation, which pitted a veteran FBI special agent against Florida resident Robert Mo, who after his academic career foundered took a questionable job with the Chinese agricultural company DBG—and became a pawn in a global rivalry.

"This engaging book has something for everyone; it can be read as a spy thriller, an examination of U.S.-China relations, or a case study of agricultural espionage." —*Library Journal*

Includes bibliographical references and index.

Jobb, Dean

A Gentleman and a Thief: The Daring Jewel Heists of a Jazz Age Rogue. Dean Jobb. Algonquin Books 2024. 432 p.

ISBN 9781643752839

Grades: Adult 364.16

1. Gem theft 2. Jewel thieves 3. Jewelry theft 4. Swindlers and swindling 5. Thieves 6. Prisoners 7. Fugitives 8. Escapes 9. Romantic love 10. United States 11. 1920s 12. True Crime — Heists and Robbery 13. Life stories — Law and order — Criminals and law-breakers

LC 2024005157

Depicts the true story of Arthur Barry, one of the world's most successful burglars who stole jewels worth $60 million dollars from a Rockefeller, a Woolworth heiress and an oil magnate during the jazz age.

"Jobb follows up The Case of the Murderous Dr. Cream with a top-shelf work of true crime focused on lovestruck 'Gentleman thief' Arthur Barry (1896-1981)." —*Publishers Weekly*

Includes bibliographical references and index.

ESSENTIAL AND RECOMMENDED TITLES
364.16 Offenses against property

Johnson, Kirk W.
The Feather Thief: Beauty, Obsession, and the Natural History Heist of the Century. Kirk Wallace Johnson. Viking 2018. x, 308 p, 16 unnumbered pages of plates : Illustration; Color
   ISBN 9781101981610
Grades: Adult   **364.16**
   1. Johnson, Kirk W. 2. Rist, Edwin 3. Investigative journalism 4. Thieves 5. Natural history 6. Feathers 7. Birds 8. Stealing 9. Trials (Robbery) 10. Fly tying 11. Ornithologists 12. Natural history museums 13. Naturalists 14. Life stories — Law and order — Criminals and law-breakers 15. Nature Writing — Animal Studies — Birds and Birding 16. True Crime — Heists and Robbery
   ALA Notable Book, 2019.
   Documents the astonishing 2009 theft of an invaluable collection of ornithological displays from the British Museum of Natural History by a talented American musician, tracing the author's years-long investigation to track down the culprit and understand his motives, which were possibly linked to an obsession with the Victorian art of salmon fly-tying.
   "This is a remarkably compelling story of obsession and history and a man who so loved his art that he would break the law for it." —*Booklist*
   Also published in large print format.

Keefe, Patrick Radden
   ★ *Rogues: True Stories of Grifters, Killers, Rebels, and Crooks.* Patrick Radden Keefe. Doubleday 2022. 304 p.
   ISBN 9780385548519
Grades: Adult   **364.16**
   1. Swindlers and swindling 2. Crime 3. Criminals 4. Rebels 5. Corruption 6. Investigative journalism 7. Literary journalism 8. Essays 9. Life stories — Law and order — Criminals and law-breakers 10. True Crime — General
   LC 2021047117
   Patrick Radden Keefe has garnered prizes for his meticulously-reported, hypnotically engaging work on the many ways people behave badly. Rogues brings together a dozen of his most celebrated articles from the New Yorker. As Keefe says in his preface, "They reflect on some of my abiding preoccupations: Crime and corruption, secrets and lies, the permeable membrane separating licit and illicit worlds, the bonds of family, the power of denial." the appearance of his byline in the New Yorker is always an event, and collected here for the first time readers can see his work forms an always enthralling but deeply human portrait of criminals and rascals, as well as those who stand up against them.
   "A strong collection of essays of most interest to true crime readers, but also on display is a model of journalistic credibility." —*Library Journal*

Kolhatkar, Sheelah
   Black Edge: Inside Information, Dirty Money, and the Quest to Bring Down the Most Wanted Man on Wall Street. Sheelah Kolhatkar. Random House 2017. 368 pages
   ISBN 9780812995800
Grades: Adult   **364.16**
   1. Cohen, Steven A, 1956- 2. White collar crime 3. Hedge funds 4. Investments 5. Business corruption 6. Corporate crime 7. Insider trading in securities 8. Securities industry and trade 9. United States 10. Business and economics — Business leaders and entrepreneurs 11. Business and economics — Corruption and scandal
   LC 2016031776
   Longlisted for the Andrew Carnegie Medal for Excellence in Non-Fiction, 2018.
   Traces the rise and fall of stock trader Steven Cohen and his hedge fund, SAC Capital, to offer insight into personalities behind the largest insider-trading investigation in Wall Street history while revealing how Cohen continues to make billions as a free man.
   "Well-written, with pointed characterizations of the ambitious players and their motives, this book is highly recommended for readers interested in finance, crime, and politics." —*Library Journal*

Levin, Josh
   The Queen: The Forgotten Life Behind an American Myth. Josh Levin. Little, Brown & Company 2019. 412 p.
   ISBN 9780316513302
Grades: Adult   **364.16**
   1. African American women 2. Welfare recipients 3. Stereotypes 4. Swindlers and swindling 5. Fraud 6. Murder suspects 7. Racism 8. Prejudice 9. Public opinion 10. Chicago, Illinois 11. 1970s 12. Biographies 13. Life stories — Law and order — Criminals and law-breakers 14. True Crime — Cold Cases and Unsolved Mysteries 15. Society and culture — Race 16. History writing — 1970s — United States
   LC 2019934174
   National Book Critics Circle Award for Biography, 2019.
   On the South Side of Chicago in 1974, Linda Taylor reported a phony burglary, concocting a lie about stolen furs and jewelry. The detective who checked it out soon discovered she was a welfare cheat who drove a Cadillac to collect ill-gotten government checks. And that was just the beginning: Taylor, it turned out, was also a kidnapper, and possibly a murderer. But nobody—not the journalists who touted her story, not the police, and not presidential candidate Ronald Reagan—seemed to care about anything but her welfare thievery.
   "Levin does a terrific job of balancing his portrait of a criminal, of the racism of police who didnt bother to solve the three murders connected to Taylor, and of the widespread stereotyping of Blacks that grew out of her crimes and a president's distortions." —*Booklist*
   Includes bibliographical references and index.

Michel, Casey
   American Kleptocracy: How the U.S. Created the World's Greatest Money Laundering Scheme in History. Casey Michel. St. Martin's Press 2021. x, 349 p.
   ISBN 9781250274526
Grades: Adult   **364.16**
   1. Money laundering 2. International banking 3. Tax havens 4. Financial institutions 5. White collar crime 6. Business ethics 7. Business and politics 8. Corruption 9. United States 10. Business and economics — Corruption and scandal 11. Business and economics — Industries — Finance 12. Politics and global affairs — General
   LC 2021026596
   A remarkable debut by one of America's premier reporters on financial corruption, Casey Michel's American Kleptocracy offers an explosive investigation into how the United States of America built the largest illicit offshore finance system the world has ever known.
   "Michel's clear prose helps make a complicated subject comprehensible, and leaves readers with some hope that financial corruption may not be so inevitable after all." —*Booklist*
   Includes bibliographical references and index.

Mueller, Tom
   Crisis of Conscience: Whistleblowing in an Age of Fraud. Tom Mueller. Riverhead Books 2019. 596 pages
   ISBN 9781594634437
Grades: Adult   **364.16**
   1. Whistle blowing 2. Whistle blowers 3. Business corruption 4. Political corruption 5. Ethics 6. Informers 7. Fraud 8. Secrecy 9. Business and economics — Corruption and scandal 10. Life stories — Law and order 11. History writing — Scandals
   A riveting account of the heroes who are combating corporate, medical and government fraud traces the rise of whistleblowing through a series of important cases that reflect fundamental questions about the balance between free speech and state power.
   Includes bibliographical references and index.

Posner, Gerald L.
   God's Bankers: A History of Money and Power at the Vatican. by Gerald Posner. Simon & Schuster 2015. 496 p.
   ISBN 9781416576570
Grades: Adult   **364.16**

PUBLIC LIBRARY CORE COLLECTION: NONFICTION
Twentieth Edition

1. Corruption 2. Banks and banking 3. Religious corruption 4. 21st century 5. 20th century 6. Spirituality and religion — Christianity — Catholicism 7. True Crime — General 8. Nonfiction that reads like fiction

LC 2014021061

From a master chronicler of legal and financial misconduct, a magnificent investigation nine years in the making, this book traces the political intrigue and inner workings of the Catholic Church. Decidedly not about faith, belief in God, or religious doctrine, this book is about the church's accumulation of wealth and its byzantine entanglements with financial markets across the world. Told through 200 years of prelates, bishops, cardinals, and the Popes who oversee it all, Gerald Posner uncovers an eyebrow-raising account of money and power in perhaps the most influential organization in the history of the world.

"The destruction of documents, stonewalling by prelates, and closed Vatican archives made Posner's work harder, necessitating conjectures. This sad tale is known in its outlines, but Posner provides much more detail." —*Choice*

Renner, Rebecca

★ *Gator Country: Deception, Danger, and Alligators in the Everglades.* Rebecca Renner. Flatiron Books 2023. 256 p.

ISBN 9781250842572

Grades: Adult   364.16

1. Babauta, Jeff 2. Poaching 3. Alligators 4. Undercover wildlife agents 5. Environmental protection 6. Undercover operations 7. Wildlife conservation 8. Wildlife 9. Everglades, Florida 10. Florida 11. Life stories — Nature and outdoors 12. Nature Writing — Animal studies 13. Debut title 14. True Crime — General

LC 2023018604

Describes the true story of Officer Jeff Babauta who became a "Florida Man" and went undercover to establish the Sunshine Alligator Farm in Florida to infiltrate the shady world of illegal poachers throughout the Everglades.

"Beautifully evoking the 'Sawgrass plains and wild strands of jungle' of its author's home state, this tale of power, politics, and tradition is a triumph." —*Publishers Weekly*

Schneier, Bruce

A Hacker's Mind: How the Powerful Bend Society's Rules, and How to Bend Them Back. Bruce Schneier. W W Norton & Company 2023. 352 p.

ISBN 9780393866667

Grades: Adult   364.16

1. Hacking 2. Hackers 3. Culture 4. Exploitation 5. Power 6. Society and culture — Media and technology 7. Business and economics — General 8. Politics and global affairs — General

The legendary cybersecurity expert and New York Times best-selling author discusses ways that developing a hacker's mindset can help us better understand the systems and institutions that underpin our society.

"Schneier's deep dive into this cross-section of technology and humanity makes for investigative gold." —*Booklist*

Shapiro, Scott J.

★ *Fancy Bear Goes Phishing: The Dark History of the Information Age, in Five Extraordinary Hacks.* Scott J. Shapiro. Farrar Straus & Giroux 2023. 432 p.

ISBN 9780374601171

Grades: Adult   364.16

1. Philosophy 2. Technology 3. Hacking 4. Internet 5. Information management 6. Knowledge management 7. Hackers 8. Computer security 9. Espionage 10. Computer crimes 11. History Writing — Science, technology, and medicine 12. Science Writing — Computing, the Internet, and Technology

"Written for readers without deep technical backgrounds, this is an engaging and thought-provoking examination of the human elements of technology." —*Booklist*

Sisman, Adam

The Professor and the Parson: A Story of Desire, Deceit, and Defrocking. Adam Sisman. Counterpoint 2020. 288 pages

ISBN 9781640093287

Grades: Adult   364.16

1. Peters, Robert Parkins 2. Swindlers and swindling 3. Fraud 4. Impostors 5. Priest impersonators 6. Eccentric men 7. Narcissism 8. Bigamy 9. 20th century 10. Biographies 11. True Crime — General 12. Life stories — Law and order — Criminals and law-breakers 13. History writing — Europe — United Kingdom

LC 2019026530

The National Book Critics Circle Award-winning author of Boswell's Presumptuous Task describes his investigation into the true life of fraudulent priest Robert Parkin Peters and how he cheated his way through bigamous marriages, religious posts and academic positions.

"A captivating true tale that makes even the most intricate con-artist movies look cartoonish." —*Kirkus*

Originally published: London : Profile Books, 2019.

Taub, Jennifer

Big Dirty Money: The Shocking Injustice and Unseen Cost of White Collar Crime. Jennifer Taub. Viking 2020. xxxvi, 298 p.

ISBN 9781984879974

Grades: Adult   364.16

1. White collar crime 2. Corruption 3. Social classes 4. Income inequality 5. Rich people 6. Law reform 7. Injustice 8. Inequality 9. Social problems 10. Wealth 11. Economics 12. United States 13. 21st century 14. Business and economics — Economics — Socioeconomics 15. Business and economics — Corruption and scandal 16. Society and culture — Wealth and class 17. Society and culture — Violence and crime — Criminal justice system

LC 2020024366

A Harvard Law School visiting scholar and banking law advocate reveals how unchecked white-collar crimes, from fraud and embezzlement to obstruction of justice and bribery, continue to benefit the wealthy at the expense of everyday Americans.

"A significant manifesto for judicial reform that aims at cracking the cabal of big-money grifters at the top." —*Kirkus*

Includes bibliographical references and index.

Whitlock, Craig

★ *Fat Leonard: How One Man Bribed, Bilked, and Seduced the U.S. Navy.* Craig Whitlock. Simon & Schuster 2024. 464 p.

ISBN 9781982131630

Grades: Adult   364.16

1. Business corruption 2. Fraud 3. Defense contracts 4. Bribery 5. Extortion 6. Military secrets 7. National security 8. United States history 9. Naval history 10. Malaysian people 11. 21st century 12. Biographies 13. True Crime — General 14. Life stories — Law and order — Criminals and law-breakers 15. History writing — Military — Naval history

This story of one of the most significant public corruption scandals in American history chronicles how a Malaysian defense contractor defrauded the U.S. Navy of tens of millions of dollars and put our nation's security at risk.

"The result is an entertaining picaresque about a magnetic rogue that also spotlights troubling rot in the U.S. military." —*Publishers Weekly*

Yeebo, Yepoka

Anansi's Gold: The Man Who Looted the West, Outfoxed Washington, and Swindled the World. Yepoka Yeebo. Bloomsbury Publishing Place USA 2023. 384 p.

ISBN 9781635574739

Grades: Adult   364.16

1. Blay-Miezah, John Ackah 2. Swindlers and Swindling 3. Fraud 4. Ghanaian people 5. African people 6. African history 7. Ghana 8. 20th century 9. Biographies 10. Life stories — Law and order — Criminals and law-breakers 11. True Crime — Heists and Robbery 12. Nonfiction that reads like fiction

"British Ghanian journalist Yeebo tells the story of John Ackah Blay-Miezah, one of the world's most prolific con artists, who tricked many people worldwide into giving him their money." —*Library Journal*

ESSENTIAL AND RECOMMENDED TITLES
364.1628 Theft of specific items

364.1628 Theft of specific items

Finkel, Michael
The Art Thief: A True Story of Love, Crime, and a Dangerous Obsession. Michael Finkel. Alfred A. Knopf 2023. 240 p.
ISBN 9780525657323
Grades: Adult   364.1628
1. Breitwieser, Stéphane, 1971- 2. Thieves 3. Art thefts 4. Couples 5. Stealing 6. Desire 7. Aesthetics 8. Art museums 9. Criminal investigation 10. Trials (Robbery) 11. Western European people 12. French people 13. Europe 14. Biographies 15. Life stories — Law and order — Criminals and law-breakers 16. True Crime — Heists and Robbery 17. Arts and Entertainment — Painting, Drawing, and Sculpture 18. Nonfiction that reads like fiction
LC 2022049664

For centuries, works of art have been stolen in countless ways from all over the world, but no one has been quite as successful at it as the master thief Stéphane Breitwieser. Carrying out more than two hundred heists over nearly eight years—in museums and cathedrals all over Europe—Breitwieser, along with his girlfriend who worked as his lookout, stole more than three hundred objects, until it all fell apart in spectacular fashion. This is a riveting story of art, crime, love, and an insatiable hunger to possess beauty at any cost.

"Finkel will have art history and true crime lovers obsessively turning the pages of this suspenseful, smartly written work until its shocking conclusion." —*Library Journal*

This is a Borzoi book—Colophon.

364.2 Causes of crime and delinquency

Muhammad, Khalil Gibran
The Condemnation of Blackness: Race, Crime, and the Making of Modern Urban America. Khalil Gibran Muhammad. Harvard University Press 2010. 380 p.
ISBN 9780674035973
Grades: Adult   364.2
1. African Americans 2. Racism in the criminal justice system 3. Racism in the judicial system 4. Racism 5. Race relations 6. United States 7. 20th century 8. History writing — African American — Civil rights — United States 9. Society and culture — Violence and crime — Criminal justice system 10. Antiracist literature

Lynch mobs, chain gangs, and popular views of Black southern criminals that defined the Jim Crow South are well known. We know less about the role of the urban North in shaping views of race and crime in American society.

"A brilliant work that tells us how directly the past has formed us." —*New York Review of Books*

364.3 Offenders

Burgess, Ann Wolbert
A Killer by Design: Murderers, Mindhunters, and My Quest to Decipher the Criminal Mind. Ann Wolbert Burgess and Steven Matthew Constantine. Hachette Books 2021. 320 p.
ISBN 9780306924866
Grades: Adult   364.3
1. Burgess, Ann Wolbert 2. Psychiatric nurses 3. Forensic medicine 4. Criminal profiling 5. Crime forecasting 6. Serial murderers 7. Serial murder investigation 8. Psychology 9. United States 10. Autobiographies and memoirs 11. Life stories — Law and order 12. Life stories — Science, technology, and medicine — Healthcare professionals 13. True Crime — Murder 14. Society and culture — Violence and crime
LC 2021011086

In A Killer by Design, Ann Wolbert Burgess reveals how her pioneering research on sexual assault and trauma caught the attention of the FBI, and steered her right into the middle of a chilling serial murder investigation in Nebraska. Over the course of the next two decades, she helped the budding Behavioral Science Unit—better known as the "Mindhunters" unit—identify, interview, and track down dozens of notoriously violent offenders, including Ed Kemper ("The Co-Ed Killer"), Dennis Rader ("BTK"), Henry Wallace ("The Taco Bell Strangler"), Jon Barry Simonis ("The Ski-Mask Rapist"), and many others. As one of the first women trailblazers within the FBI's hallowed halls, Burgess knew many were expecting her to crack under pressure and recoil in horror—but she was determined to protect future victims at any cost. This book pulls us directly into the investigations as she experienced them, interweaving never-before-seen interview transcripts and crime scene drawings alongside her own vivid recollections to provide unprecedented insight into the minds of deranged criminals and the victims they left behind.

"An empathetic, insightful behind-the-scenes look at criminal profiling that will be appreciated by true crime fans and readers curious about forensic or criminal psychology." —*Library Journal*

Includes bibliographical references and index.

Hayes, Christopher
A Colony in a Nation. Chris Hayes. W W Norton & Co. Inc 2017. 256 p.
ISBN 9780393254228
Grades: Adult   364.3
1. Racism 2. Race relations 3. Racism in the criminal justice system 4. Criminal justice system 5. Law enforcement 6. Discrimination 7. Civil rights 8. Social life and customs 9. United States 10. 21st century 11. Politics and global affairs — Civil and human rights 12. Society and culture — Race 13. Society and culture — Violence and crime — Criminal justice system
LC 2016053392

New York Times Notable Book, 2017.

An Emmy Award-winning news anchor and New York Times best-selling author argues that there are really two Americas—a Colony and a Nation.

"A timely and impassioned argument for social justice." —*Kirkus*

364.36 Juvenile delinquents

Henning, Kristin
The Rage of Innocence: How America Criminalizes Black Youth. Kristin Henning. Pantheon Books 2021. 288 p.
ISBN 9781524748906
Grades: Adult   364.36
1. Racism in the criminal justice system 2. Racism in law enforcement 3. African American children 4. African American young men 5. Public relations 6. Racial profiling 7. Punishment 8. Marginalized children 9. Alienation 10. Injustice 11. Police 12. Society and culture — Race 13. Society and culture — Violence and crime — Criminal justice system 14. Family and Relationships — Growing Up
LC 2021002180

In the Margins Book Awards: Advocacy and Social Justice, 2022.

Drawing on 25 years of experience representing Black youth in Washington, DC's juvenile courts, the author, in this timely book, makes a powerfully compelling case that the crisis in racist American policing begins with its relationship to Black children.

"Copiously documented and passionately argued, this is a powerful and persuasive call for change." —*Publishers Weekly*

Includes bibliographical references and index.

Hobbs, Jeff
Children of the State: Stories of Survival and Hope in the Juvenile Justice System. Jeff Hobbs. Scribner 2023. 384 p.
ISBN 9781982116361
Grades: Adult   364.36
1. Juvenile delinquency 2. Juvenile delinquents 3. Teenagers 4. Violent crimes 5. Juvenile justice system 6. Juvenile corrections 7. Correctional personnel 8. Prison reform 9. Hope 10. Despair 11. North American people 12. American people 13. United States 14. Life stories — Law and order — Prisoners and inmates 15. Life stories — Relationships — Growing up 16. Society and culture — Violence and crime — Criminal justice system

LC 2022020137

There has been very little written about juvenile detention and the path to justice. For many kids, a mistake made at age thirteen or fourteen—often resulting from external factors coupled with a biologically immature brain—can resonate through the rest of their lives, making high school difficult, college nearly impossible, and a middle-class life a mere fantasy. Here, in Children of the State, Jeff Hobbs challenges any preconceived perceptions about how the juvenile justice system works—and demonstrates in brilliant, piercing prose: No one so young should ever be considered irredeemable.

"Bestseller Hobbs (Show Them You're Good) offers a gripping and harrowing study of the American juvenile justice system….Deeply researched and fluidly written, this is a searing portrait of an ongoing tragedy." —*Publishers Weekly*

364.4 Prevention of crime and delinquency

Evangelista, Patricia
★ *Some* People Need Killing: A Memoir of Murder in My Country. Patricia Evangelista. Random House 2023. xvi, 428 p.
ISBN 9780593133132
Grades: Adult   364.4
1. Duterte, Rodrigo Roa, 1945- 2. Evangelista, Patricia 3. Drug control 4. Presidents 5. Extrajudicial executions 6. Drug dealers 7. Drug addicts 8. Police brutality 9. Women journalists 10. Authoritarianism 11. Vigilantes 12. Political violence 13. Violence against marginalized people 14. Politics and government 15. Philippines 16. History writing — Asia — Southeast Asia 17. Politics and global affairs — World politics — Asia 18. Politics and global affairs — Political figures 19. Society and culture — Violence and crime 20. Nonfiction that reads like fiction 21. Debut title

LC 2023019108

In this thoroughly reported and deeply human chronicle of the Philippines' drug war and Rodrigo Duterte's assault on the country's struggling democracy, a trauma journalist immerses herself in the world of killers and survivors, capturing the atmosphere of fear created when an elected president decides some lives are worth less than others.

"Analytical, ambitious, and told with empathy, this will stand as a definitive historical account of the Philippines' drug war." —*Booklist*

364.6 Penology

Austen, Ben
Correction: Parole, Prison, and the Possibility of Change. Ben Austen. Flatiron Books 2023. 323 p.
ISBN 9781250758804
Grades: Adult   364.6
1. Corrections 2. Prisons 3. Parole 4. Prisoners 5. Parolees 6. Punishment 7. Mass incarceration 8. Ethics 9. Criminal justice policy 10. Criminal justice system 11. United States 12. Life stories — Law and order — Prisoners and inmates 13. Society and culture — Violence and crime — Criminal justice system 14. Politics and global affairs — General

LC 2023006824

The United States, alone, locks up a quarter of the world's incarcerated people. And yet apart from clichés—paying a debt to society; you do the crime, you do the time—there is little sense collectively in America what constitutes retribution or atonement. We don't actually know why we punish. Ben Austen's powerful exploration offers a behind-the-scenes look at the process of parole. Told through the portraits of two men imprisoned for murder, and the parole board that holds their freedom in the balance, Austen's unflinching storytelling forces us to reckon with some of the most profound questions underlying the country's values around crime and punishment.

"A cleareyed, compassionate, urgent appeal for prison reform." —*Kirkus*
Includes bibliographical references and index.

Davis, Angela Y.
Abolition: Politics, Practices, Promises. Angela Y. Davis. Haymarket Books 2024. 272 p.
ISBN 9798888900536
Grades: Adult   364.6
1. Abolitionists 2. Civil rights 3. Violence 4. Oppression (Psychology) 5. Freedom 6. Criminal justice system 7. Prison corruption 8. Prison industry and trade 9. Prisons 10. Alternatives to imprisonment 11. Feminism 12. Social problems 13. Political science 14. Essays 15. Society and culture — Violence and crime — Criminal justice system

For over fifty years, Angela Y. Davis has been at the forefront of collective movements for abolition and feminism and the fight against state violence and oppression. This essential collection of Davis's writing over the years, the first of two volumes, shows how her thinking has sharpened and evolved even as she has remained uncompromising in her commitment to collective liberation. In pieces that address the history of abolitionist practice and thought in the United States and globally, the unique contributions of women to abolitionist struggles, and stories and lessons of organizing inside and beyond the prison walls, Davis is always curious, always incisive, and always learning.

"The first volume of a collection of essays by former political prisoner and prison abolitionist Davis…A must-read essay collection for anyone invested in racial equity." —*Kirkus*

Hardy, Jason Matthew
★ *The Second* Chance Club: Hardship and Hope After Prison. Jason Hardy. Simon & Schuster 2020. 288 pages
ISBN 9781982128593
Grades: Adult   364.6
1. Hardy, Jason Matthew 2. Parolees 3. Parole officers 4. Former convicts 5. Criminals 6. Parole 7. Recidivism 8. Probation 9. Rehabilitation 10. Louisiana 11. Autobiographies and memoirs 12. Society and culture — Violence and crime — Criminal justice system 13. Life stories — Law and order — Police and law officers 14. Life stories — Law and order — Prisoners and inmates

LC 2019035155

A former parole officer shines a bright light on a huge yet hidden part of our justice system through the intertwining stories of seven parolees striving to survive the chaos that awaits them after prison in this illuminating and dramatic book.

"A powerful, necessary book with revelatory passages on nearly every page." —*Kirkus*
Includes bibliographical references and index.

Scott-Clark, Cathy
The Forever Prisoner: The Full and Searing Account of the Cia's Most Controversial Covert Program. Cathy Scott-Clark and Adrian Levy. Atlantic Monthly Press 2022. 464 p.
ISBN 9780802158925
Grades: Adult   364.6
1. Prisoners 2. Torture 3. Military interrogation 4. Intelligence service 5. Politics and government 6. United States 7. 21st century 8. History writing — Spies and spying

Based on four years of intensive reporting, on interviews with key protagonists who speak candidly for the first time, and on thousands of previously classified documents, the Forever Prisoner is a powerful chronicle of a shocking experiment that remains in the headlines twenty years after its inception, even as US government officials continue to thwart efforts to expose war crimes.

"British journalists Scott-Clark and Levy team up again to take a hard look at the CIA's program of rendition and torture after 9/11….A forceful book that demands greater oversight of the nation's intelligence services and justice for the wrongly imprisoned." —*Kirkus*

Sered, Danielle
Until We Reckon: Violence, Mass Incarceration, and a Road to Repair. Danielle Sered. New Press 2019. 336 p.
ISBN 9781620974797
Grades: Adult   364.6

ESSENTIAL AND RECOMMENDED TITLES
364.66 Capital punishment

1. Restorative justice 2. Imprisonment 3. Prison reform 4. Mass incarceration 5. Prisons 6. Violence 7. Crime 8. Criminal justice system 9. Responsibility 10. Punishment 11. Victims of crimes 12. Criminals 13. Society and culture — Violence and crime — Criminal justice system 14. True Crime — General

LC 2018047561

Asking us to reconsider the purposes of incarceration, an award-winning leader in the movement to end mass incarceration shows how her organization, which offers alternatives to people who commit serious violent crime, has produced immensely promising results.

Includes bibliographical references and index.

364.66 Capital punishment

Chammah, Maurice
★ *Let the Lord Sort Them: The Rise and Fall of the Death Penalty.* Maurice Chammah. Crown Publishing 2021. 368 p.
ISBN 9781524760267
Grades: Adult **364.66**
1. Capital punishment 2. Criminal justice system 3. Public prosecutors 4. Death row prisoners 5. Executions and executioners 6. Public opinion 7. Racism in the criminal justice system 8. Politics and government 9. Texas 10. United States 11. Impartial writing 12. Society and culture — Violence and crime — Criminal justice system 13. Life stories — Law and order — Prisoners and inmates 14. Life stories — Law and order — Judges and lawyers 15. Politics and global affairs — General

LC 2020025171

A history of the death penalty in Texas and its influence on the 1972 Supreme Court ruling examines the contributions of key prosecutors, judges and defendants while explaining how the state's example reflects critical vulnerabilities in the American criminal justice system.

"Chammah uses Texas as the focus of his history of the death penalty in the United States. . . . A readable, well-documented legal history that will appeal to a broad audience." —*Library Journal*

Includes index.

Prejean, Helen
The Death of Innocents: An Eyewitness Account of Wrongful Executions. Helen Prejean. Random House 2005. xvi, 310 p.
ISBN 9780679440567
Grades: Adult **364.66**
1. Capital punishment 2. Death row prisoners 3. Judicial system 4. Prisoners 5. Legislation 6. Politics and government 7. United States 8. True Crime — General 9. Society and culture — Violence and crime — Criminal justice system

LC 2004054154

Raises constitutional questions about the legality of the death penalty and reveals how race, poverty, publicity, and prosecutorial ambition can determine who lives and dies after a murder conviction.

"The author reexamines the cases of two men she fervently believes were executed for crimes they did not commit. In addition to providing a searing indictment of capital punishment, Prejean also exposes the fundamental inadequacies of the American court system. Expect demand for this extremely thought-provoking book." —*Booklist*

Includes bibliographical references and index.

364.8 Discharged offenders

Miller, Reuben Jonathan
Halfway Home: Race, Punishment, and the Afterlife of Mass Incarceration. Reuben Jonathan Miller. Little Brown & Company 2021. 352 p.
ISBN 9780316451512
Grades: Adult **364.8**
1. Racism in the criminal justice system 2. Criminal justice reform 3. Inequality 4. Mass incarceration 5. Punishment 6. Discrimination 7. Racism in the judicial system 8. Criminal justice system 9. Injustice 10. Judicial system 11. United States 12. Society and culture — Violence and crime — Criminal justice system 13. Society and culture — Race

A Chicago Cook County Jail chaplain and mass-incarceration sociologist examines the lifelong realities of a criminal record, demonstrating how America's justice system is less about rehabilitation and more about structured disenfranchisement.

"Striking a unique balance between memoir and sociological treatise, this bracing account makes clear just how high the deck is stacked against the formerly incarcerated." —*Publishers Weekly*

364.973 Crime — United States

Alexander, Michelle
The New Jim Crow: Mass Incarceration in the Age of Colorblindness. Michelle Alexander. New Press 2010. 352 p.
ISBN 9781595581037
Grades: Adult **364.973**
1. Criminal justice system 2. African American prisoners 3. Mass incarceration 4. Racism 5. Interethnic relations 6. Prejudice 7. African Americans 8. Suffrage 9. Intersectionality 10. Race relations 11. United States 12. Society and culture — Race 13. History writing — African American — Civil rights — United States 14. Antiracist literature 15. Book club best bets

LC 2009022519

Street Lit Book Award Medal: Adult Non-Fiction, 2013.

Argues that the War on Drugs and policies that deny convicted felons equal access to employment, housing, education, and public benefits create a permanent under caste based largely on race.

"Most provocatively, she reveals how both the move toward colorblindness and affirmative action may blur our vision of injustice: 'most Americans know and don't know the truth about mass incarceration'—but her carefully researched, deeply engaging, and thoroughly readable book should change that." —*Publishers Weekly*

The 10th anniversary edition published in 2020 contains a new preface that discusses the impact of the book; Includes bibliographical references and index.

Forman, James
Locking up Our Own: Crime and Punishment in Black America. James Forman, Jr. Farrar, Straus and Giroux 2017. 352 p.
ISBN 9780374189976
Grades: Adult **364.973**
1. Criminal justice system 2. African American police 3. African American judges 4. Racism in the criminal justice system 5. Racism in the judicial system 6. Racism in law enforcement 7. African American politicians 8. Criminal justice policy 9. Death control 10. Social justice 11. Race relations 12. United States 13. 1970s 14. Essays 15. Society and culture — Race 16. Society and culture — Violence and crime — Criminal justice system 17. History writing — African American — United States 18. Antiracist literature

LC 2016041345

New York Times Notable Book, 2017; Pulitzer Prize for General Nonfiction, 2018; Longlisted for the Andrew Carnegie Medal for Excellence in Non-Fiction, 2018; Longlisted for the National Book Award for Nonfiction, 2017.

In Locking up Our Own, author James Forman Jr. offers historical background to the U.S. War on Crime's aggressive policing and long criminal sentences. African American leaders welcomed these approaches, which began in the 1970s, but the measures now seem to be disproportionately targeting poor Black men. Forman, a Yale law professor and former public defender, offers a thought-provoking perspective on combating drugs and violent crime.

"Possibly controversial, undoubtedly argumentative, Forman's survey offers a refreshing breath of fresh air on the crisis in American policing." —*Publishers Weekly*

Includes index.

PUBLIC LIBRARY CORE COLLECTION: NONFICTION
Twentieth Edition

Pratt, Victoria
The Power of Dignity: How Transforming Justice Can Heal Our Communities. Judge Victoria Pratt; foreword by Senator Cory Booker. Seal Press 2022. 304 p.
ISBN 9781541674837
Grades: Adult   364.973
1. Pratt, Victoria 2. Criminal justice system 3. Respect 4. Fairness 5. Justice 6. Criminal justice reform 7. Dignity 8. United States 9. Society and culture — Violence and crime — Criminal justice system 10. Life stories — Law and order — Judges and lawyers

LC 2021056788

Newark Municipal Court's former chief judge discusses how her reforms transformed her courtroom into a place of problem-solving and a resource for healing, showing how we can transform courtrooms, neighborhoods and our nation to support the vulnerable and heal community rifts.

"A criminal justice professor and former judge discusses how courts can foster trust among the criminal offenders and victims the American legal system too often dehumanizes....Timely and hopeful, this book offers insight into how procedural justice can not only help to heal people and society, but also a judicial system in dire need of reform." —*Kirkus*

Includes bibliographical references.

365 Penal and related institutions

Applebaum, Anne
★ *Gulag: A History.* Anne Applebaum. Doubleday 2003. 677 p. : Illustration; Map; Portrait
ISBN 9780767900560
Grades: Adult   365
1. Forced labor 2. Prisons 3. Convict labor 4. Concentration camps 5. Politics and government 6. Soviet Union history 7. Soviet Union 8. 20th century 9. History writing — Communism — Europe — Russia

LC 2002041344

Booklist Editors' Choice, 2003; Library Journal Best Books, 2003; New York Times Notable Book, 2003; Pulitzer Prize for General Nonfiction, 2004; National Book Award for Nonfiction finalist, 2003; National Book Critics Circle Award for Nonfiction finalist, 2003.

Chronicles the history of the Soviet concentration camp system from its start after the Russian Revolution to its collapse, discussing its creation and the way of life for those who lived there.

"This describes how, largely under Stalin's watch, a regulated, centralized system of prison labor—unprecedented in scope—gradually arose out of the chaos of the Russian Revolution. Applebaum details camp life, including strategies for survival; the experiences of women and children in the camps; sexual relationships and marriages between prisoners; and rebellions, strikes and escapes. Applebaum's lucid prose and painstaking consideration of the competing theories about aspects of camp life and policy are always compelling." —*Publishers Weekly*

Includes bibliographical references and index.

Bauer, Shane
American Prison: A Reporter's Undercover Journey into the Business of Punishment. Shane Bauer. Penguin Press 2018. 368 p.
ISBN 9780735223585
Grades: Adult   365
1. Prison industry and trade 2. Criminal justice system 3. Corruption 4. Prison corruption 5. Prisoners 6. Prison guards 7. Correctional personnel 8. Prison industrial complex 9. Mass incarceration 10. Corrections 11. Investigative journalists 12. Privatization 13. Chain-gangs 14. Imprisonment 15. Prisons 16. Social life and customs 17. Louisiana 18. United States 19. 21st century 20. Society and culture — Violence and crime — Criminal justice system 21. Business and economics — Corruption and scandal 22. Adult books for young adults 23. Book club best bets

LC 2018018293

ALA Notable Book, 2019; J. Anthony Lukas Book Prize, 2019; Library Journal Best Books, 2018; New York Times Notable Book, 2018; Robert F. Kennedy Book Award, 2019; Kirkus Prize for Nonfiction finalist, 2018.

The investigative journalist draws on his experiences working in a Louisiana private prison to connect today's brutal for-profit prison system to the Civil War-era mass incarcerations of African-American workers.

"Bauer's amazing book examines one of slaverys toxic legacies, using convicted people to make profit, through a dual approach." —*Booklist*

Includes bibliographical references and index.

Campbell, Deborah
A Disappearance in Damascus: A Story of Friendship and Survival in the Shadow of War. Deborah Campbell. St Martin's Press 2016. 341 pages
ISBN 9781250147875
Grades: Adult   365
1. Mahmood, Ahlam A. 2. Campbell, Deborah, 1970- 3. Political prisoners 4. Iraq War, 2003-2011 5. Refugees 6. Journalists 7. Iraq 8. Syria 9. Autobiographies and memoirs 10. Canadian literature 11. Life stories — Relationships — Friendship 12. History writing — Wars and conflicts — Iraq War 13. Life stories — Arts and culture — Writing — Journalists 14. Adult books for young adults

BC Book Prizes, Hubert Evans Non-Fiction Prize, 2017; Hilary Weston Writers' Trust Prize, 2016.

The true story of an amazing friendship between 2 women—the award-winning Canadian journalist Deborah Campbell and Ahlam, an Iraqi woman who worked as a "fixer" for Western media in Syria as it plunged into war.

"Campbells captivating writing allows readers to see inside the life of a foreign correspondent and the bonds forged and broken through investigative reporting." —*Booklist*

Includes bibliographical references.

Fedderly, Eva
These Walls: The Battle for Rikers Island and the Future of America's Jails. Eva Fedderly. Avid Reader Press 2023. 224 p.
ISBN 9781982193911
Grades: Adult   365
1. Jails 2. Prisoners 3. Correctional institutions 4. Criminal justice reform 5. Criminal justice system 6. Rikers Island (N.Y.) 7. New York (State) 8. History Writing — United States 9. Society and culture — Violence and crime — Criminal justice system

This riveting blend of on-the-ground reporting and sweeping social and architectural history discusses the decision to close Rikers Island and what it will really mean for reformists, justice architects, abolitionists, city government officials, prison guards and the incarcerated themselves.

"A bracing look at how the nation's jails—and the nation itself—ought to be reformed." —*Kirkus*

Gessen, Masha
Never Remember: Searching for Stalin's Gulags in Putin's Russia. Masha Gessen, Michael Friedman. Columbia Global Reports 2018. 176 pages
ISBN 9780997722963
Grades: Adult   365
1. Stalin, Joseph, 1879-1953 2. Putin, Vladimir Vladimirovich, 1952- 3. Political prisoners 4. Political persecution 5. Totalitarianism 6. Despotism 7. Communism 8. Stalinism 9. Memories 10. Mass burials 11. Concentration camps 12. Politics and government 13. Soviet Union history 14. Russia 15. Soviet Union 16. 21st century 17. 20th century 18. History writing — Europe — Russia 19. Politics and global affairs — World politics — Europe 20. Politics and global affairs — Civil and human rights

LC 2018303220

A photographic history of the Soviet gulags goes in search of the memory of these labor camps, from Sandarmokh, a forested site of mass executions, to Kolyma, a deadly mining camp in the Far East.

"Friedman's moody, panoramic black-and-white photos of the memorial sites convey a narrative that's fragmented, blurry, and ultimately incomplete, perfectly underscoring Gessen's text. The combination is a powerful meditation on contemporary Russia as seen through its relationship to the past." —*Publishers Weekly*

ESSENTIAL AND RECOMMENDED TITLES
365 Penal and related institutions

Kimmerle, Erin H.
We Carry Their Bones: The Search for Justice at the Dozier School for Boys. Erin Kimmerle. William Morrow & Company 2022. 320 p.
ISBN 9780063030244
Grades: Adult   365
1. Kimmerle, Erin H. 2. Juvenile correctional institutions 3. Boys' schools 4. Forensic anthropologists 5. Child prisoners 6. Institutional child abuse 7. Forced labor 8. Murder victims 9. School closings 10. Cemeteries 11. Exhumation 12. Small towns 13. Secrets 14. Racism 15. DNA fingerprinting 16. Justice 17. True Crime — Historical Crime 18. True Crime — Forensic Sciences 19. Society and culture — Violence and crime — Criminal justice system 20. Society and culture — Race 21. History writing — Regional history — United States

The Arthur G. Dozier Boys School was a well-guarded secret in Florida for over a century, until reports of cruelty, abuse, and "mysterious" deaths shut the institution down in 2011. Established in 1900, the juvenile reform school accepted children as young as six years of age for crimes as harmless as truancy or trespassing. The boys sent there, many of whom were Black, were subject to brutal abuse, routinely hired out to local farmers by the school's management as indentured labor, and died either at the school or attempting to escape its brutal conditions. In the wake of the school's shutdown, Erin Kimmerle, a leading forensic anthropologist, stepped in to locate the school's graveyard to determine the number of graves and who was buried there, thus beginning the process of reuniting the boys with their families through forensic and DNA testing.

"Gripping investigation into a corrupt, dangerous Florida reform school, the institution featured in Colson Whitehead's the Nickel Boys....A horrific story of true crime, unjust punishment, and the quest for justice for the victims of a cruel state." —*Kirkus*

Minian, Ana Raquel
★ *In the Shadow of Liberty: The Invisible History of Immigrant Detention in the United States.* Ana Raquel Minian. Viking 2024. 384 p.
ISBN 9780593654255
Grades: Adult   365
1. Immigrants 2. History of immigrants 3. Immigration prisons 4. Immigration and emigration 5. Imprisonment 6. Due process of law 7. Immigration policy 8. Human rights policy 9. United States history 10. United States 11. History writing — Immigration — United States 12. Life stories — People in history 13. Society and culture — Immigration
LC 2023033975

Weaving together the stories of four migrants seeking to escape the turmoil of their homelands for the promise of America, a noted historian exposes immigrant detention in the U.S., showing how the changing political climate surrounding immigration has played out in individual lives, and at what cost.

"In this harrowing account of immigrants' experiences in American detention centers, Minian outlines the central role incarceration has played in the past century of U.S. immigration policy…It's a must-read for anyone invested in U.S. immigration policy." —*Publishers Weekly*

Includes bibliographical references.

Norton, Jack
The Jail Is Everywhere: Fighting the New Geography of Mass Incarceration. Jack Norton, Lyda Pelot-hobbs, Judah Schept; foreword by Ruth Wilson Gilmore. Verso Books 2024. 256 p.
ISBN 9781804291313
Grades: Adult   365
1. Mass incarceration 2. Imprisonment 3. Jails 4. Social justice 5. Prison reform 6. Criminal justice system 7. Essays 8. Society and culture — Violence and crime — Criminal justice system

"Activists involved on the ground will find this valuable, while others will receive a substantial education in the politics and economics of incarceration." —*Publishers Weekly*

Oshinsky, David M.
Worse Than Slavery: Parchman Farm and the Ordeal of Jim Crow Justice. David M. Oshinsky. Free Press 1996. xiv, 306 p, [16] p. of plates : Illustration
ISBN 9780684822983
Grades: Adult   365
1. Criminal justice system 2. Prisoners 3. Mississippi 4. True Crime — General 5. History writing — African American — Civil rights — United States
LC 95052880
Robert F. Kennedy Book Award, 1997.

Draws on police records, prison documents, and oral history to examine Mississippi's state penitentiary and Jim Crow justice, from the era of the cottonfield chain gangs to the 1960s.

Includes bibliographical references (p. 257-298) and index.

Rayman, Graham
★ *Rikers: An Oral History.* Graham Rayman and Reuven Blau. Random House 2023. 432 p.
ISBN 9780593134214
Grades: Adult   365
1. Correctional institutions 2. Prisoners 3. Rikers Island (N.Y.) 4. New York (State) 5. Oral histories 6. History Writing — United States 7. Society and culture — Violence and crime — Criminal justice system
LC 2022017211

Drawing on interviews with more than 130 people comprising a broad cross-section of lives Rikers has touched, with stories spanning from the 1970s to today, two prize-winning journalists offer a 360-degree view inside the country's largest detention complex for the first time.

"If there were ever an argument for prison reform, it's in these pages." —*Kirkus*

Includes index.

Solzhenitsyn, Aleksandr Isaevich
★ *The Gulag Archipelago 1918-1956: An Experiment in Literary Investigation.* Aleksandr I. Solzhenitsyn; translated from the Russian by Thomas P. Whitney and Harry Willetts; abridged by Edward E. Ericson. Perennial 2002. xxiv, 472 p. : Illustration; Map; Portrait
ISBN 9780060007768
Grades: Adult   365
1. Prisons 2. Political prisoners 3. Concentration camps 4. Soviet Union 5. History writing — Communism — Europe — Russia
LC 2001046504

An account of four decades of oppression describes individual escapes and attempted escapes from Stalin's camps, a disciplined, sustained resistance put down with tanks after forty days, and the forced removal and extermination of millions of peasants, in a special abridged edition of the classic by the Russian Nobel laureate.

Includes bibliographical references and index; Previously published: New York : Harper & Row, 1985.

★ *The Gulag Archipelago, 1918-1956: An Experiment in Literary Investigation.* Aleksandr I. Solzhenitsyn; translated from the Russian by Harry Willetts; foreword by Anne Applebaum. Harper Perennial Modern Classics 2007. xviii, 558, 24 pages : Illustration
ISBN 9780061253737
Grades: Adult   365
1. Political prisoners 2. Prisons 3. Concentration camps 4. Soviet Union 5. History writing — Communism — Europe — Russia
LC Bl2017038566

Describes individual escapes and attempted escapes from Stalin's camps.
Includes bibliographical references.

Thompson, Heather Ann
Blood in the Water: The Attica Prison Uprising of 1971 and Its Legacy. Heather Ann Thompson. Pantheon 2016. 720 p.
ISBN 9780375423222
Grades: Adult   365
1. Prison riots 2. Violence in prisons 3. Prisoner abuse 4. Police brutality 5. Criminal justice system 6. Police misconduct 7. Police corruption 8. Civil rights 9. Prisoners 10. Human rights 11. Civil rights 12. New York (State)

PUBLIC LIBRARY CORE COLLECTION: NONFICTION
Twentieth Edition

13. 1970s 14. True Crime — General 15. Society and culture — Violence and crime — Criminal justice system 16. History writing — 1970s — United States

LC 2016000477

New York Times Notable Book, 2016; Pulitzer Prize for History, 2017.

An account of the infamous 1971 Attica prison uprising, the state's violent response, and the victims' decades-long quest for justice draws on previously unreleased information while detailing how the event has influenced civil rights practices in the criminal justice system.

"Thompson's superb and thorough study serves as a powerful tale of the search for justice in the face of the abuses of institutional power." —*Publishers Weekly*

Includes index.

365.45092 Political prisoners

Jang, Lucia
Stars Between the Sun and Moon: One Woman's Life in North Korea and Escape to Freedom. Lucia Jang and Susan McClelland; with an afterword by Stephan Haggard. Douglas & McIntyre 2014. 287 pages

ISBN 9781771620352

Grades: Adult   365.45092

1. Jang, Lucia 2. Totalitarianism 3. Famines 4. Human trafficking 5. Political refugees 6. Forced labor 7. Abused women 8. Human trafficking victims 9. Dictatorship 10. North Korea 11. Autobiographies and memoirs 12. Canadian literature 13. Life stories — Facing adversity — War and oppression — Refugees 14. History writing — Asia — North and South Korea

The memoir of a determined young North Korean woman who endured famine, an unlawful marriage and harsh imprisonment, and who finally managed to escape to Canada.

"An emotional and engrossing work that sheds light on daily life in this opaque country. Highly recommended for readers interested in North Korea as well as those who enjoy inspirational stories. Fans of Barbara Demick's Nothing to Envy will especially appreciate this work." —*Library Journal*

368.38 Health insurance, accident insurance, disability income insurance

Cohn, Jonathan
The Ten Year War: Obamacare and the Unfinished Crusade for Universal Coverage. Jonathan Cohn. St Martins Press 2021. 416 p.

ISBN 9781250270931

Grades: Adult   368.38

1. Health insurance 2. Medical care 3. National health insurance 4. Public health 5. Medical care reform 6. Legislation 7. United States 8. Politics and global affairs — Public health

The Affordable Care Act, better known as "Obamacare," was the most sweeping and consequential piece of legislation of the last half century. It has touched nearly every American in one way or another, for better or worse, and become the defining political fight of our time. Veteran journalist Jonathan Cohn offers the compelling, authoritative history of how the law came to be, why it looks like it does, and what it's meant for average Americans. Drawn from hundreds of hours of interviews, plus private diaries, emails and memos, the Ten Year War takes readers to Capitol Hill and to town hall meetings, inside the West Wing and, eventually, into Trump Tower, as the nation's most powerful leaders try to reconcile pragmatism and idealism, self-interest and the public good, and ultimately two very different visions for what the country should look like.

"In a book that took 10 years to research and write, journalist Cohn offers a thorough history of the persistent controversy over health care insurance in the U.S." —*Kirkus*

369 Associations

Stewart, Nikita
Troop 6000: The Girl Scout Troop That Began in a Shelter and Inspired the World. Nikita Stewart. Ballantine Books 2020. 304 p.

ISBN 9781984820754

Grades: Adult   369

1. Homelessness 2. Shelters for the homeless 3. City life 4. Homeless children 5. Girls 6. New York City 7. Society and culture — Urban and regional studies

LC 2019038599

Describes how hardworking mother of five Giselle Burgess rose from poverty and homelessness to establish Girl Scout troops in 15 New York City shelters to bring pride, life-skill training and community to disadvantaged urban girls.

"A tale of how grassroots spirit and gritty determination can bloom into hope." —*Kirkus*

370 Education

Chu, Lenora
Little Soldiers: An American Boy, a Chinese School, and the Global Race to Achieve. Lenora Chu. HarperCollins 2017. 368 pages

ISBN 9780062367853

Grades: Adult   370

1. Chu, Lenora 2. Public education 3. Learning 4. Early childhood education 5. Education 6. Stress in children 7. Educational tests and measurements 8. Comparison 9. Shanghai, China 10. China 11. Autobiographies and memoirs 12. Impartial writing 13. Society and culture — Education

LC 2017276381

A hard-hitting exploration of China's widely acclaimed yet insular education system shares insights into how their examples are shaping the future of American parenting and education.

"Little Soldiers offers fascinating peeks inside the worlds largest educational system and at the future intellectual 'Soldiers' American kids will be facing." —*Booklist*

370.1 Philosophy and theory, education for specific objectives, educational psychology

Emdin, Christopher
Ratchetdemic: Reimagining Academic Success. Christopher Emdin. Beacon Press 2021. 224 p.

ISBN 9780807089507

Grades: Adult   370.1

1. Student achievement 2. Public education 3. Urban education 4. Study methods 5. Identity 6. Self-fulfillment 7. Marginalized children 8. Racism in education 9. Education 10. United States 11. Society and culture — Education 12. Society and culture — Race 13. Society and culture — Urban and regional studies

LC 2021012706

Bestselling author and educator Christopher Emdin advocates a new identity and sensibility for educators which bridges the seemingly disparate worlds of the ivory tower and urban classroom. Highlighting the major inequities in urban education, Emdin argues in favor of a simple solution: That being "ratchetdemic," or both ratchet and academic (like having rap battles about science) can empower students to embrace themselves, their background, and their education.

"A must-read for educators, students, parents, and anyone with a vested interest in an equal education system." —*Library Journal*

Includes bibliographical references and index.

ESSENTIAL AND RECOMMENDED TITLES
370.15 Educational psychology

370.15 Educational psychology

Berens, Kimberly Nix
Blind Spots: *Why Students Fail and the Science That Can Save Them.* Kimberly Nix Berens, Ph.D. Collective Book Studio 2020. 226 p.
ISBN 9781951412098
Grades: Adult   370.15
1. Educational reform 2. Education 3. United States 4. Society and culture — Education

"The writing is strong and the topic is intriguing, accessible to readers with little prior knowledge of education practices. A well-argued challenge to educational orthodoxy that calls for a systemic overhaul." —*Kirkus*

LaGarde, Jennifer
Fact vs. Fiction: *Teaching Critical Thinking Skills in the Age of Fake News.* Jennifer LaGarde and Darren Hudgins. International Society for Technology in Education 2018. xi, 147 p.
ISBN 9781564847041
Grades: Adult Professional   370.15
1. Critical thinking 2. Fake news 3. Information literacy 4. Mass media 5. Educator resources — General
LC 2018051063

"A thought-provoking resource for teachers and librarians seeking to foster their students' critical thinking." —*School Library Journal*
Includes bibliographical references (pages 133-140) and index.

Sarma, Sanjay E.
Grasp: The Science Transforming How We Learn. Sanjay Sarma, with Luke Yoquinto. Doubleday 2020. 304 p.
ISBN 9780385541824
Grades: Adult   370.15
1. Learning 2. Cognition 3. Research institutes 4. Brain 5. Intelligence 6. Teaching 7. Education 8. Cognitive neuroscience 9. Science Writing — Biology 10. Society and culture — Education
LC 2019054620

As the head of Open Learning at MIT, Sanjay Sarma has a daunting job description: to fling open the doors of the MIT experience for the benefit of the wider world. But if you're going to undertake such an ambitious project, it behooves you to ask: how exactly does learning work? What conditions are most conducive? Are our traditional classroom methods actually effective? Grasp takes readers across multiple frontiers, from fundamental neuroscience to cognitive psychology and beyond, as it explores the future of learning. Along the way, Sarma debunks long-held views, while equipping readers with a set of practical tools for absorbing and retaining information across a lifetime. He presents a vision for learning that's more inclusive and democratic—revealing a world bursting with powerful learners, just waiting for the chance they deserve.

"Compelling advice on how to improve education.... Delightful as well as convincing in its plea that educators place learning over winnowing and access over exclusivity." —*Kirkus*
Includes bibliographical references.

Ticktin, Allie
Play to Progress: Lead Your Child to Success Using the Power of Sensory Play. Allie Ticktin, MA, OTD, OTR/L, founder, Play 2 Progress. TarcherPerigee, an imprint of Penguin Random House LLC 2021. xxiii, 242 pages : Illustration
ISBN 9780593191927
Grades: Adult   370.15
1. Sensory stimulation 2. Play 3. Senses and sensation in children 4. Child development 5. Family and Relationships — Parenting
LC 2020055868

A game-changing book on child development—and the importance of physical play—for this digital and screen age.

"Full of fun, this guide is worth a look for parents of young children." —*Publishers Weekly*
Includes bibliographical references (pages 229-231) and index.

370.8 Groups of people

Fishman, Elly
Refugee High: *Coming of Age in America.* Elly Fishman. The New Press 2021. 288 p.
ISBN 9781620975084
Grades: Adult   370.8
1. High schools 2. Teenage refugees 3. Teenage immigrants 4. Marginalized teenagers 5. Marginalized children 6. Student achievement 7. Cultural differences 8. Racism 9. Xenophobia 10. Secondary education 11. Urban education 12. Education 13. Immigration and emigration 14. United States 15. Life stories — Facing adversity — War and oppression — Refugees 16. Society and culture — Education 17. Society and culture — Immigration 18. Life stories — Relationships — Growing up
LC 2021001818

For a century, Chicago's Roger C. Sullivan High School has been a home to immigrant and refugee students. In 2017, during the worst global refugee crisis in history, its immigrant population numbered close to three hundred—or nearly half the school—and many were refugees new to the country. These young people came from thirty-five different countries, speaking among themselves more than thirty-eight different languages. Refugee High is a riveting chronicle of the 2017-18 school year at Sullivan High, a time when anti-immigrant rhetoric was at its height in the White House. Equal parts heartbreaking and inspiring, it raises vital questions about the priorities and values of a public school and offers an eye-opening and captivating window into the present-day American immigration and education systems.

"Educators and general readers alike will find this vividly intimate work insightful." —*Library Journal*

370.89 Ethnic groups in education

Ewing, Eve L.
Ghosts in the Schoolyard: *Racism and School Closings on Chicago's South Side.* Eve L. Ewing. The University of Chicago Press 2018. xiii, 222 pages : Illustration; Map
ISBN 9780226526027
Grades: Adult   370.89
1. African Americans 2. Racism in education 3. Public schools 4. High schools 5. School closings 6. African American neighborhoods 7. Protests, demonstrations, vigils, etc. 8. Education 9. South Side, Chicago, Illinois 10. Chicago, Illinois 11. Society and culture — Education 12. Society and culture — Race 13. Society and culture — Urban and regional studies 14. Adult books for young adults
LC 2018010065

Booklist Editors' Choice, 2018.
"Failing schools. Underprivileged schools. Just plain bad schools." That's how Eve L. Ewing opens Ghosts in the Schoolyard: Describing Chicago Public Schools from the outside. But Ewing knows Chicago Public Schools from the inside: as a student, then a teacher, and now a scholar who studies them. And that perspective has shown her that public schools are not buildings full of failures—they're an integral part of their neighborhoods, at the heart of their communities, storehouses of history and memory that bring people together.
Includes bibliographical references and index.

Yacovone, Donald
★ *Teaching* White Supremacy: *America's Democratic Ordeal and the Forging of Our National Identity.* Donald Yacovone. Pantheon Books 2022. 496 p.
ISBN 9780593316634
Grades: Adult   370.89
1. Discrimination in education 2. White nationalism 3. Educational policy 4. Racism 5. Race relations 6. United States history 7. United States 8. History writing — United States 9. Society and culture — Education 10. Society and culture — Race
LC 2021058205

PUBLIC LIBRARY CORE COLLECTION: NONFICTION
Twentieth Edition

The lifetime Associate at Harvard University's Hutchins Center for African and African American Research and recipient of the NAACP Image Award reveals the systematic ways in which white supremacist ideology has infiltrated American culture and how it has been at the heart of our collective national identity.

"An outstanding contribution to the historical literature of American racism and racist ideologies." —*Kirkus*

Includes bibliographical references and index.

370.92 Educators — Biography

Walker, Vanessa Siddle
*The **Lost** Education of Horace Tate: Uncovering the Hidden Heroes Who Fought for Justice in Schools.* Vanessa Siddle Walker. Two Rivers Distribution 2018. 320 p.
ISBN 9781620971055
Grades: Adult   370.92
1. Tate, Horace, 1922-2002 2. Racism in education 3. Segregation in education 4. African American teachers 5. Social justice 6. Civil Rights Movement 7. African American civil rights 8. Race relations 9. Georgia 10. United States 11. History writing — African American — Civil rights — United States
LC 2018007468

The author of Behind Every Movement draws on hidden archives to reveal the achievements of a devoted network of African-American educators who battled Southern school segregation and inequality on either side of Brown v. Board of Education .

"Walker's extensively documented work is a much-needed corrective contextualizing the landscape of school desegregation; required reading for those interested in the past, present, and future of education of African American children." —*Library Journal*

370.973 Education — United States

Robinson, Ken
Creative Schools: The Grassroots Revolution That's Transforming Education. Ken Robinson, Lou Aronica. Viking Press 2015. 272 p.
ISBN 9780670016716
Grades: Adult   370.973
1. Educational reform 2. Education 3. Educational policy 4. Educational innovations 5. Educational tests and measurements 6. Learning by discovery 7. Schools 8. Society and culture — Education
LC 2015001098

In a book filled with anecdotes, observations and recommendations from professionals on the front line of transformative education, case histories and groundbreaking research, the author of the Element argues for an end to our outmoded industrial educational system and proposes a highly personalized, organic approach that draws on today's unprecedented technological and professional resources to engage all students, develop their love of learning and enable them to face the real challenges of the 21st century.

"For readers who are ardent about changing education for the better, believing that they can be part of the forces that will revolutionize the future." —*Library Journal*

371.01 Specific kinds of schools

Berkshire, Jennifer
*The **Education** Wars: A Citizen's Guide and Defense Manual.* Jennifer C. Berkshire, Jack Schneider. The New Press 2024. 192 p.
ISBN 9781620978542
Grades: Adult   371.01
1. Public schools 2. Educational policy 3. Culture conflict 4. Social values 5. Education 6. Religion and politics 7. Politics and education 8. Politics and culture 9. Right and left (Political science) 10. Banned books 11. Religious discrimination 12. United States 13. Society and culture — Education

Explaining the sudden obsession with race and gender in schools, as well as the ascendancy of book-banning efforts, this timely book outlines the core issues driving the education wars, laying out what's at stake for parents, teachers, and students and providing a roadmap for ensuring public education survives this present assault.

"By outlining the core issues, the authors show a path for protecting the fundamentals of what makes public schools so important. This is a good addition to a growing body of protest." —*Booklist*

371.010973 Public schools — United States

Brill, Steven
Class Warfare: Inside the Fight to Fix America's Schools. by Steven Brill. Simon & Schuster 2011. 352 p.
ISBN 9781451611991
Grades: Adult   371.010973
1. Public schools 2. School improvement programs 3. Educational policy 4. Educational reform 5. Education 6. Politics and government 7. United States 8. 21st century 9. Society and culture — Education
LC 2011016196

Booklist Editors' Choice, 2011.

Looks at why many of America's schools are failing and offers ways to improve grades K-12 and offer children a better future.

Ravitch, Diane
Slaying Goliath: The Passionate Resistance to Privatization and the Fight to Save America's Public Schools. Diane Ravitch. Alfred A. Knopf 2020. 352 p.
ISBN 9780525655374
Grades: Adult   371.010973
1. Education 2. Public schools 3. Educational policy 4. Public education 5. United States 6. Society and culture — Education
LC 2019022776

An in-depth look at the failed efforts to privatize public schools and the victories of those who have fought to save America's public school system.

"This extensive analysis is required reading for anyone concerned about American education." —*Library Journal*

Includes bibliographical references and index.

371.1 Schools and their activities

Kozol, Jonathan
Letters to a Young Teacher. Jonathan Kozol. Crown Publishers 2007. x, 288 p.
ISBN 9780307393715
Grades: 11 12 Adult Professional   371.1
1. Kozol, Jonathan 2. First-year teachers 3. Teachers 4. Teaching 5. Education 6. Social life and customs 7. United States 8. 20th century 9. Adult books for young adults 10. Society and culture — Education
LC 2007002689

The author shares a series of personal reflections, anecdotes, wisdom, and guidance in his letters to Francesca, a first-year teacher in a Boston elementary school, as he attempts to help her deal with the challenges she encounters.

"The book will delight and encourage first-year (or for that matter, 40th-year) teachers who need Kozol's reminders of the ways that their beautiful profession can bring joy and beauty, mystery and mischievous delight into the hearts of little people in their years of greatest curiosity." —*Publishers Weekly*

Includes bibliographical references.

Robbins, Alexandra
★ *The **Teachers**: A Year Inside America's Most Vulnerable, Important Profession.* Alexandra Robbins. Dutton 2023. 336 p.
ISBN 9781101986752

ESSENTIAL AND RECOMMENDED TITLES
371.1020973 Teaching — United States

Grades: Adult   **371.1**
1. Teachers 2. Teaching 3. Public schools 4. Public education 5. Job stress 6. Quality of work life 7. United States 8. Interviews 9. Society and culture — Education 10. Life stories — Education — Scholars and educators 11. Life stories — Business — Working life

LC 2022042500

Alexandra Robbins goes behind the scenes to tell the true, sometimes shocking, always inspirational stories of three teachers as they navigate a year in the classroom. She follows Penny, a southern middle school math teacher who grappled with a toxic staff clique at the big school in a small town; Miguel, a special ed teacher in the western United States who fought for his students both as an educator and as an activist; and Rebecca, an East Coast elementary school teacher who struggled to schedule and define a life outside of school. Robbins also interviewed hundreds of other teachers nationwide who share their secrets, dramas, and joys.

"The steady, measured prose doesn't diminish the drama of the situation, making this something that should be read by anyone interested in the state of education today." —*Booklist*

Includes bibliographical references.

371.1020973 Teaching — United States

Goldstein, Dana
The Teacher Wars: A History of America's Most Embattled Profession. Dana Goldstein. Doubleday 2014. 368 pages.
ISBN 9780385536950

Grades: Adult Professional   **371.1020973**
1. Teaching 2. Teachers 3. Education 4. Educational reform 5. Teachers' Unions 6. Public schools 7. Social classes 8. United States 9. History writing — United States 10. Society and culture — Education

LC 2014007024

Booklist Editors' Choice, 2014; New York Times Notable Book, 2014.

Traces 175 years of teaching in America to demonstrate how educators have characteristically endured shifting and often impossible expectations, comparing the practices and test scores of other nations while revealing the cultural and political factors compromising education today.

371.14 Organization of teaching force

Baker, Nicholson
Substitute: Going to School with a Thousand Kids. Nicholson Baker. Penguin Group USA 2016. 416 p.
ISBN 9780399160981

Grades: Adult   **371.14**
1. Baker, Nicholson, 1957- 2. Substitute teachers 3. Classroom management 4. Curriculum planning 5. Teaching 6. Autobiographies and memoirs 7. Life stories — Education — Scholars and educators 8. Society and culture — Education

LC Bl2016032188

Describes how the National Book Critics Circle Award-winning author became an on-call substitute teacher in pursuit of the realities of American public education, describing his complex difficulties with helping educate today's students in spite of flawed curriculums and interpersonal challenges.

"An affecting (long-exposure) snapshot revealing real-life concerns." —*Kirkus*

371.19 Community-school relations

Bauer, Susan Wise
Rethinking School: How to Take Charge of Your Child's Education. Susan Wise Bauer. W. W. Norton & Company 2018. xiv, 264 pages
ISBN 9780393285963

Grades: Adult   **371.19**
1. Student achievement 2. Education 3. Parenting 4. Educator resources — General

LC 2017051513

A best-selling expert on education shows how to make the school system work for your child. Our K-12 school system is an artificial product of market forces. It isn't a good fit for all—or even most—students. It prioritizes a single way of understanding the world over all others, pushes children into a rigid set of grades with little regard for individual maturity, and slaps "disability" labels over differences in learning style. Caught in this system, far too many young learners end up discouraged, disconnected, and unhappy. And when they struggle, school pressures parents, with overwhelming force, into "fixing" their children rather than questioning the system. With boldness, experience, and humor, Susan Wise Bauer turns conventional wisdom on its head: When a serious problem arises at school, the fault is more likely to lie with the school, or the educational system itself, than with the child. In five illuminating sections, Bauer teaches parents how to flex the K-12 system, rather than the child. She closely analyzes the traditional school structure, gives trenchant criticisms of its weaknesses, and offers a wealth of advice for parents of children whose difficulties may stem from struggling with learning differences, maturity differences, toxic classroom environments, and even from giftedness (not as much of a "gift" as you might think!). Rethinking School is a guide to one aspect of sane, humane parenting: Negotiating the twelve-grade school system in a way that nurtures and protects your child's mind, emotions, and spirit."

The author of the Well-trained Mind offers a critique of the U.S. public school system where she closely analyzes the traditional school structure, dissects its weaknesses, and offers a wealth of advice for parents of children whose difficulties may stem from struggling with learning differences, maturity differences, toxic classroom environments, and more.

"Bauer's guide to the various options available to struggling kids, inside and outside the educational system, will be both comforting and instructive to their parents." —*Publishers Weekly*

Includes bibliographical references and index.

371.260973 Educational tests — United States

Reese, William J.
Testing Wars in the Public Schools: A Forgotten History. William J. Reese. Harvard University Press 2013. 298 p.
ISBN 9780674073043

Grades: Adult   **371.260973**
1. Educational tests and measurements 2. Public schools 3. 19th century 4. Society and culture — Education 5. History writing — United States

LC 2012033665

Despite claims that written exams narrowed the curriculum, ruined children's health, and turned teachers into automatons, once tests took root in American schools their legitimacy was never seriously challenged. William Reese puts today's battles over standards and benchmarks into perspective by showcasing the history of the pencil-and-paper exam.

Includes bibliographical references and index.

371.30281 Techniques of study

Donaldson-Pressman, Stephanie
The Learning Habit: A Groundbreaking Approach to Homework and Parenting That Helps Our Children Succeed in School and Life. Stephanie Donaldson-Pressman, Rebecca Jackson, Dr. Robert M. Pressman. A Perigee Book 2014. xiii, 306 p. : Illustration
ISBN 9780399167119

Grades: Adult   **371.30281**
1. Homework 2. Study skills 3. Parenting 4. Families 5. Family and Relationships — Parenting

LC 2014011124

A groundbreaking approach to building learning habits for life, based on a major new study revealing what works—and what doesn't Life is different for kids today. Between standardized testing, the Common Core Curriculum, copi-

PUBLIC LIBRARY CORE COLLECTION: NONFICTION
Twentieth Edition

ous homework assignments, and seemingly endless amounts of "screen time," it's hard for kids—and parents—to know what's most essential. How can parents help their kids succeed—not just do well "on the test"—but develop the learning habits they'll need to thrive throughout their lives? This important and parent-friendly book presents new solutions based on the largest study of family routines ever conducted. The Learning Habit offers a blueprint for navigating the maze of homework, media use, and the everyday stress that families with school-age children face; turning those "stress times" into opportunities to develop the eight critical skills kids will need to succeed in college and in the highly competitive job market of tomorrow—skills including concentration and focus, time management, decision-making, goal-setting, and self-reliance. Along with hands-on advice and compelling real-life case studies, the book includes 21 fun family challenges for parents and kids, bringing together the latest research with simple everyday solutions to help kids thrive, academically and beyond.

Includes bibliographical references (pages 281-289) and index.

371.39 Other methods of instruction

Davies, Simone
The **Montessori** *Toddler: A Parent's Guide to Raising a Curious and Responsible Human Being.* Simone Davies; illustrated by Hiyoko Imai. Workman Publishing 2019. 248 p. : Color; Illustration

ISBN 9781523506897

Grades: Adult   371.39

1. Parenting 2. Montessori method of education 3. Reference books 4. Family and Relationships — Growing up 5. Family and Relationships — Parenting

LC 2019007032

Examines how to incorporate the Montessori education principles into daily routines at home, offering tips on setting up the home, discussing how to cultivate cooperation and set limits, and providing useful skills toddlers can learn.

371.7 Student welfare

Cox, John Woodrow
Children *Under Fire: An American Crisis.* John Woodrow Cox. Ecco 2021. 320 p.

ISBN 9780062883933

Grades: Adult   371.7

1. Gun control 2. School shootings 3. Mass shootings 4. United States 5. Society and culture — Violence and crime

Based on the Pulitzer-finalist series on the effects of gun violence on children, a urgent call to action investigates the effectiveness of gun safety reforms and the ongoing realities of traumatized survivors of community and campus shootings.

"Washington Post reporter Cox debuts with a hard-hitting report on the impact of gun violence on American children. . . . Balancing sound research with moving profiles of victims and activists, Cox makes an impeccable case for how to solve the problem and why it's essential to do so now." —*Booklist*

Cullen, David
Parkland: *Birth of a Movement.* Dave Cullen. HarperCollins 2019. 385 p.

ISBN 9780062882943

Grades: Adult   371.7

1. High school students 2. School shootings 3. Gun control 4. Mass shootings 5. Schools and guns 6. Violence in schools 7. Student movements 8. Teenage social advocates 9. Marjory Stoneman Douglas High School Shooting, Parkland, Florida, 2018 10. Florida 11. Society and culture — Social activism and philanthropy 12. Society and culture — Violence and crime 13. True Crime — Murder 14. Adult books for young adults

LC Bl2018196564

The author of Columbine offers a deeply moving account of the extraordinary teenage survivors of Parkland who became activists and pushed back against the NRA and Congressional leaders—inspiring millions of Americans to join their grassroots #neveragain movement.

"Cullen, the author of the groundbreaking Columbine (2009), brings his eloquence, expertise, combination of deep research and concision, and unbiased perspective to yet another mass school shooting, revealing its deepest layers and resonance." —*Booklist*

Grigoriadis, Vanessa
Blurred *Lines: Rethinking Sex, Power, and Consent on Campus.* Vanessa Grigoriadis. Houghton Mifflin Harcourt 2017. 320 p.

ISBN 9780544702554

Grades: Adult   371.7

1. Rape 2. Universities and colleges 3. Rape victims 4. Violence in universities and colleges 5. Victims of crimes 6. Acquaintance rape 7. Rape case prosecution 8. Date rape 9. Sexism in universities and colleges 10. College student rape victims 11. Human rights 12. Civil rights 13. Society and culture — Education — Higher education 14. Society and culture — Violence and crime

LC 2017297003

A National Magazine Award winner draws on extensive on-campus research to examine the sexual revolution of today's America, exploring such subjects as how young women are both protecting and expressing themselves, how young men are becoming more sensitive and aggressive and how schools can make college a safer experience.

"Grigoriadis adds context to the often-polarizing topics with numerous first-person accounts. Her view that 'We, as a society, are terrified to look at boys as boys rather than men and give them a break as such' seems to make excuses for criminal behavior. However, the breadth of her research, including her discussion of how university administrators deal with rape allegations and her exploration of toxic gender roles and stereotypes, are reason enough to pick up this book." —*Publishers Weekly*

Includes bibliographical references (pages 297-321) and index.

Hirsch, Jennifer S.
Sexual *Citizens: A Landmark Study of Sex, Power, and Assault on Campus.* Jennifer S. Hirsch and Shamus Khan. W.W. Norton & Company 2020. 384 p.

ISBN 9781324001706

Grades: Adult   371.7

1. Rape 2. Universities and colleges 3. College students 4. Power 5. Social responsibility 6. Higher education 7. Sexual violence 8. Causation 9. Rape culture 10. Sexuality 11. Society and culture — Education — Higher education 12. Society and culture — Sex and sexuality 13. Adult books for young adults

LC Bl2019037477

The fear of campus sexual assault has become an inextricable part of the college experience. Research has shown that by the time they graduate, as many as one in three women and almost one in six men will have been sexually assaulted. But why is sexual assault such a common feature of college life? And what can be done to prevent it? Drawing on the Sexual Health Initiative to Foster Transformation (SHIFT) at Columbia University, the most comprehensive study of sexual assault on a campus to date, Jennifer S. Hirsch and Shamus Khan present an entirely new framework that emphasizes sexual assault's social roots.

"Taking into account gender, sexuality, and race, Hirsch and Khan do an excellent job of exploring the complexities of sexual assault and how to make campuses safer for all students." —*Booklist*

Includes bibliographical references and index.

Lysiak, Matthew
Newtown: *An American Tragedy.* Matthew Lysiak. Gallery Books 2013. 352 p.

ISBN 9781476753744

Grades: Adult   371.7

1. Sandy Hook Elementary School Shooting, Newtown, Conn, 2012 2. School shootings 3. Mass shootings 4. Crimes against children 5. Violence in schools 6. Elementary schools 7. Mass murder 8. Connecticut 9. True Crime — Murder

LC 2013034956

Chronicling the horrific events of December 14, 2012, this first comprehensive account of the Sandy Hook shootings sheds new light on the unstable killer, Adam Lanza, and shows how this American tragedy became a lighting rod for political agendas, much like Columbine 10 years earlier.

ESSENTIAL AND RECOMMENDED TITLES
371.826 Students by miscellaneous social attributes

Quinones, John
★ *One Year in Uvalde: A Story of Hope and Resilience.* John Quinones and Maria Elena Salinas. Hyperion Books 2024. 240 p.
ISBN 9781368107013
Grades: Adult   371.7
1. Grief 2. Violence and guns 3. Mass shootings 4. School shootings 5. Hope 6. Social advocacy 7. Communities 8. Gunshot victims 9. School children 10. Loss 11. Elementary schools 12. American people 13. North American people 14. Texas 15. History writing — United States 16. Society and culture — Violence and crime 17. True Crime — Murder

A narrative that builds on year-long ABC News reporting from Uvalde, Texas, chronicles how the community is forging on through grief with hope and activism in the shadow of tragedy.

"Vivid testimony on how violence both tears a community apart and pulls it together." —*Kirkus*

Roig-Debellis, Kaitlin
Choosing Hope: Moving Forward from Life's Darkest Hours. Kaitlin Roig-Debellis with Robin Gaby Fisher. G.P. Putnams Sons 2015. 288 p.
ISBN 9780399174452
Grades: Adult   371.7
1. Roig-Debellis, Kaitlin 2. Sandy Hook Elementary School Shooting, Newtown, Conn, 2012 3. Mass shootings 4. School shootings 5. Loss 6. Crimes against children 7. Consolation 8. Grief 9. Autobiographies and memoirs 10. Life stories — Facing adversity — Victims of crime
LC 2015015834

A teacher who saved the lives of fifteen elementary school students during the Sandy Hook shooting shares her experience with others in the hopes that they too can overcome their own personal tragedies, regardless of their magnitude.

"Though it may strike some readers as Pollyannaish, the author's sunny optimism about the teaching profession is sincere. Her account of the shooting, her struggle to keep despair at bay in both herself and her students, and her ultimate triumph as a survivor seeking to make a difference help balance the book and redeem it from excessive sentimentality. A flawed but still courageous and inspiring book from a genuine hero." —*Kirkus*

371.826 Students by miscellaneous social attributes

Mufleh, Luma
★ *Learning America: One Woman's Fight for Educational Justice for Refugee Children.* Luma Mufleh. Mariner Books 2022. 256 p.
ISBN 9780358569725
Grades: Adult   371.826
1. Mufleh, Luma 2. Arab Americans 3. Women educators 4. Lesbians 5. Refugees 6. Child refugees 7. Soccer teams 8. Schools 9. Literacy 10. Marginalized children 11. Social advocacy 12. Education 13. Society and culture — Education 14. Society and culture — Immigration 15. Life stories — Facing adversity — War and oppression — Refugees 16. Life stories — Education — Scholars and educators

Luma Mufleh—a Muslim woman, a gay refugee from hyper-conservative Jordan—joins a pick-up game of soccer in Clarkston, Georgia. The players, 11- and 12-year-olds from Liberia and Afghanistan and Sudan, have attended local schools for years. Drawn in as coach of a ragtag but fiercely competitive team, Mufleh discovers that few of her players can read a word. Learning America traces the story of how Mufleh grew a group of kids into a soccer team and then into a nationally acclaimed network of schools for refugee children. The journey is inspiring and hard-won: Fugees schools accept only those most in need; no student passes a grade without earning it; the failure of any student is the responsibility of all. Mufleh delivers provocative, indelible portraits of student after student making leaps in learning that aren't supposed to be possible for children born into trauma.

"Founding director of the nonprofit Fugees Family, an organization devoted to educational justice for refugee and immigrant children, Mufleh makes her book debut with an absorbing account of her journey from a Jordanian immigrant to an influential educational leader and activist." —*Kirkus*

371.829 Ethnic and national groups

Givens, Jarvis R.
★ *School Clothes: A Collective Memoir of Black Student Witness.* Jarvis R. Givens. Beacon Press 2023. 256 p.
ISBN 9780807054819
Grades: Adult   371.829
1. African Americans 2. Education 3. Public schools 4. Racism 5. Discrimination in education 6. Learning and scholarship 7. Resistance (Psychology) 8. United States history 9. Society and culture — Education 10. History writing — African American — United States 11. Life stories — Education — Scholars and educators 12. Life stories — Identity — Race and ethnicity
LC 2022043505

Black students were forced to live and learn on the Black side of the color line for centuries, through the time of slavery, Emancipation, and the Jim Crow era. And for just as long—even through to today—Black students have been seen as a problem and a seemingly troubled population in America's public imagination. Through over one hundred firsthand accounts from the nineteenth and twentieth centuries, Professor Jarvis Givens offers a powerful counter-narrative in School Clothes to challenge such dated and prejudiced storylines.

"This book, which will appeal especially to educators and historians, triumphantly rewrites Black students into a history that has ignored them. An eloquently necessary study." —*Kirkus*

Includes bibliographical references and index.

Love, Bettina L.
Punished for Dreaming: How School Reform Harms Black Children and How We Heal. Bettina L. Love. St. Martin's Press 2023. 336 p.
ISBN 9781250280381
Grades: Adult   371.829
1. African American children 2. Discrimination in education 3. Racism in education 4. Educational reform 5. Public schools 6. Social justice 7. School choice 8. Educational policy 9. Prisons 10. Education 11. Inequality 12. United States 13. Society and culture — Education 14. Society and culture — Race
LC 2023019663

The cofounder of the Abolitionist Teaching Network, chronicling 40 years of educational reform, reveals the devastating effect on 25 Black Americans caught in the intersection of economic gain and racist ideology and offers a new way forward with all children at its core.

"Punished for Dreaming is an important—though enraging and heartbreaking—read." —*Booklist*

Includes bibliographical references and index.

Picower, Bree
Reading, Writing, and Racism: Disrupting Whiteness in Teacher Education and in the Classroom. Bree Picower; foreword by Bettina L. Love. Beacon Press 2021. 216 p.
ISBN 9780807033708
Grades: Adult   371.829
1. Racism in education 2. Discrimination in education 3. Teaching 4. Teacher training 5. Racism 6. Public schools 7. Social justice 8. Ideology 9. United States 10. Society and culture — Education 11. Society and culture — Race 12. Antiracist literature
LC 2020022060

When racist curriculum "goes viral" on social media, it is typically dismissed as an isolated incident from a "bad" teacher. Educator Bree Picower, however, holds that racist curriculum isn't an anomaly. It's a systemic problem that reflects how Whiteness is embedded and reproduced in education. In Reading, Writing, and Racism, Picower argues that White teachers must reframe their understanding about race in order to advance racial justice and that this must begin in teacher education programs.

"Picower's honest introspection about her own positionality builds an ethos of racial humility and dedication to dismantling racism in education." —*Booklist*
Includes bibliographical references and index.

371.85 Greek-letter societies

Hechinger, John
★ *True Gentlemen: The Broken Pledge of America's Fraternities.* John Hechinger. PublicAffairs 2017. 336 p.
ISBN 9781610396820
Grades: Adult   371.85
1. Fraternities 2. College students 3. Personal conduct 4. Universities and colleges 5. Campus life 6. Initiations (into trades, societies, etc.) 7. Hazing 8. Drug use 9. Racism 10. Education 11. Higher education 12. Social life and customs 13. United States 14. 20th century 15. Society and culture — Education — Higher education
LC 2017008179
A Pulitzer Prize-finalist journalist investigates modern fraternity culture, particularly the embattled Sigma Alpha Epsilon, who have been involved in hazing rituals that resulted in deaths, racism and sexual assaults on campus and discusses whether or not an institution so broken can be saved.

"A highly disquieting but important investigation of one of the most influential subcultures in American higher education." —*Kirkus*

371.9 Special education

Flink, David
Thinking Differently: An Inspiring Guide for Parents of Children with Learning Disabilities. David Flink. William Morrow 2014. x, 308 pages : Illustration
ISBN 9780062225931
Grades: Adult   371.9
1. Attention-deficit hyperactivity disorder 2. Learning disabilities 3. Children with learning disabilities 4. Educator resources — General 5. Family and Relationships — General 6. Family and Relationships — Parenting
LC 2015300888
When parents are told their child has a learning disability, they need more information. Thinking Differently is just the resource to meet that need. David Flink, leader of Eye to Eye, a national mentoring program for children with learning differences,explains each learning disability in layman's terms to prepare parents to speak knowledgeably with teachers about their child's specific challenges…".
Includes bibliographical references (pages 295-297) and index.

Hixenbaugh, Michael
★ *They Came for the Schools: One Town's Fight Over Race and Identity, and the New War for America's Classrooms.* Michael Hixenbaugh. Mariner Books 2024. 288 p.
ISBN 9780063307247
Grades: Adult   371.9
1. Education 2. Public education 3. Racism 4. Identity 5. Educational policy 6. Church and education 7. Texas 8. United States 9. Society and culture — Education
Explains how a school board win for the conservative right in one Texas suburb inspired a Christian nationalist campaign now threatening to undermine public education in America—from an NBC investigative reporter and co-creator of the Peabody Award—winning and Pulitzer Prize finalist Southlake podcast.

"What emerges is an extraordinarily detailed analysis of current conservative thought and political activity. It's a vital work of reportage." —*Publishers Weekly*

371.91 Students with physical disabilities

Marschark, Marc
★ *How Deaf Children Learn: What Parents and Teachers Need to Know.* Marc Marschark and Peter C. Hauser. Oxford University Press 2012. IX, 156 p. : Illustration
ISBN 9780195389753
Grades: Adult Professional   371.91
1. People who are deaf 2. Children who are deaf 3. Parent and child 4. Science writing — Medicine and health 5. Educator resources — General 6. Educator resources — Primary education
LC 2011012553
"The authors believe the best way to lead deaf children to academic success is by understanding who they are, what they know, and how they think. After reading this book, parents who may be feeling inadequate about their parenting skills or fearful about providing a good education for their deaf or hard-of-hearing child should be more at ease, and teachers will gain insight into the complexities involved in deaf education and be better equipped to teach these children." —*Library Journal*
Includes bibliographical references and index.

372 Primary education

Montessori, Maria
★ *The Montessori Method.* Maria Montessori; [translated from the Italian by Anne E. George]; introduction by J. McV. Hunt. Schocken Books 1964. xxxix, 376 p. : Illustration
ISBN 9780805209228
Grades: Adult   372
1. Montessori method of education 2. Educator resources — General
LC 64024014
This book is Montessori's own exposition of the theory behind her innovative educational techniques. She shows parents, teachers and administrators how to 'Free a child to learn through his own efforts'.
Translation of IL metodo della pedagogia scientifica; Reprint. Edition first published by Schocken Books in 1964; text unaltered from original edition; Includes bibliographical references (p. xxxv-xxxix).

372.21 Preschool education

Alvarez, Celine
The Natural Laws of Children: Why Children Thrive When We Understand How Their Brains Are Wired. Celine Alvarez; translated by Sherab Chodzin Kohn. Shambhala 2019. VIII, 354 p. : Illustration
ISBN 9781611806731
Grades: Adult   372.21
1. Education 2. Early childhood education 3. Montessori method of education 4. Activity programs in education 5. Educator resources — General 6. Family and Relationships — Growing Up
LC 2018050411
A powerful, neuroscience-based approach to revolutionize early childhood learning through natural creativity, strong human connections, spontaneous free play, and more.

"An indispensable resource for teachers and parents alike, this highly readable book offers strategies, anecdotes, and evidence without downplaying the complexity of the cognitive science that informs it." —*Library Journal*
Shambhala Publications is distributed worldwide by Penguin Random House, Inc, and its subsidiaries—T.P. verso; Includes bibliographical references and index; Originally published: Paris, France : Les Arnes, [2016], under title Les lois naturelles de l'enfant.

Christakis, Erika
The Importance of Being Little: What Preschoolers Really Need from Grownups. Erika Christakis. Viking Press 2015. 384 p.

ESSENTIAL AND RECOMMENDED TITLES
372.210973 Day care — Preschool education — United States

ISBN 9780525429074
Grades: Adult   372.21
1. Early childhood education 2. Preschool children 3. Learning 4. Children 5. Child psychology 6. Educational reform 7. Preschool education 8. Educational policy 9. Educational tests and measurements 10. Personal conduct 11. Society and culture — Education 12. Family and Relationships — Parenting
LC 2015044529

Drawing on her strong foundation in the study of child development and early education, as well as her classroom experience, the author challenges the conventional wisdom about early childhood, encouraging parents to rethink how and where young children learn best.

"A deep, provocative analysis of the current modes of teaching preschoolers and what should be changed to create a more effective learning environment for everyone." —*Kirkus*

372.210973 Day care — Preschool education — United States

Tough, Paul
★ *How Children Succeed: Grit, Curiosity, and the Hidden Power of Character.* Paul Tough. Houghton Mifflin Harcourt 2012. 256 p.
ISBN 9780547564654
Grades: Adult   372.210973
1. Early childhood education 2. Success (Concept) 3. Characters and characteristics 4. Intelligence 5. Persistence 6. Self-control 7. Optimism 8. Self-confidence 9. Society and culture — Education
LC 2012019000

Booklist Editors' Choice, 2012; New York Times Notable Book, 2012.

Challenges conventional views about standardized testing to argue that success is more determined by self-discipline, and describes the work of pioneering researchers and educators who have enabled effective new teaching methods.

"Well-written and bursting with ideas." —*Kirkus*
Includes bibliographical references and index.

372.4 Reading

Cleaver, Samantha
Raising an Active Reader: The Case for Reading Aloud to Engage Elementary School Youngsters. Samantha Cleaver. Rowman & Littlefield 2020. xviii, 181 p.
ISBN 9781475849288
Grades: Adult   372.4
1. Reading comprehension 2. Literacy 3. Active learning 4. Educator resources — English Language Arts
LC 2019051662

Raising an Active Reader explains research on reading aloud with children who are in early elementary school (grades K-3). Upon completion, adults will know how read aloud works for children who are learning to read, and how the ABCs of Active Reading (Ask questions, Build vocabulary, and make Connections) build important reading skills.

"This book will prove a valuable resource for parents, teachers, and librarians on the vital topic of reading aloud. With many titles geared toward reading aloud to babies, toddlers, and preschoolers, this helpful work will be ideal for school libraries." —*Library Journal*
Includes bibliographical references.

Gurdon, Meghan Cox
The Enchanted Hour: The Miraculous Power of Reading Aloud in the Age of Distraction. Meghan Cox Gurdon. HarperCollins 2019. 304 p.
ISBN 9780062562814
Grades: Adult   372.4
1. Books and reading 2. Reading aloud 3. Intellectual life 4. Cognitive neuroscience 5. Bonding (Interpersonal relations) 6. Household activities 7. Reading 8. Arts and Entertainment — Writing and Publishing 9. Society and culture — Psychology and human behavior

LC Bl2018192389

A Wall Street Journal writer looks at how reading aloud makes adults and children smarter, happier, healthier, more successful and more closely attached, even as technology pulls in the other direction.

"Gurdon combines a consciously old-fashioned, anti-technology perspective with modern, data-driven cognitive arguments to advocate for face-to-face reading with children early and often. Gurdon focuses especially on the value of the picture book to build connection, regulate attention and emotional awareness, transmit cultural values, and give children feelings of mastery through repetition." —*Publishers Weekly*

Smart, Maya Payne
Reading for Our Lives: A Literacy Action Plan from Birth to Six. Maya Payne Smart. Avery, an imprint of Penguin Random House 2022. VIII, 231 pages : Illustration
ISBN 9780593332177
Grades: Adult   372.4
1. Reading (Elementary) 2. Reading aloud 3. School readiness 4. Literacy 5. Education 6. Children 7. Parenting 8. Family and Relationships — Parenting 9. Society and culture — Education
LC 2022010712

Reading for Our Lives challenges the bath-book-bed mantra and the idea that reading aloud to our kids is enough to ensure school readiness. Instead, it gives parents easy, immediate, and accessible ways to nurture language and literacy development from the start. Through personal stories, historical accounts, scholarly research, and practical tips, this book presents the life-and-death urgency of literacy, investigates inequity in reading achievement, and illuminates a path to a true, transformative education for all."

"Parents will find Smart's solid advice well worth returning to." —*Publishers Weekly*
Includes bibliographical references (pages 201-223) and index.

Trelease, Jim
★ *Jim Trelease's Read-aloud Handbook.* [Jim Trelease]; edited and revised by Cyndi Giorgis. PENGUIN BOOKS 2019. 358 p. : Illustration
ISBN 9780143133797
Grades: Professional   372.4
1. Reading aloud 2. Language arts and studies — Reading skills 3. Educator resources — Primary education 4. Educator resources — English Language Arts 5. Professional materials — Programming
LC 2019014911

The classic million-copy bestselling handbook on reading aloud to children—revised and updated for a new generation of readers.

"Like its predecessors, this is an excellent choice to recommend to parents and also useful for beginning teachers and librarians." —*School Library Journal*

Portions of this book were originally published in pamphlet form—T.P. verso; Includes bibliographical references and index; the Read-Aloud Handbook first published in Penguin Books 1982. First revised edition published 1985. Second revised edition (with the title the New Read-Aloud Handbook) published 1989—T.P. verso.

372.41 Instructional materials, reading readiness, methods of instruction and study

Cox, Marge
Kids' Books and Maker Activities: 150 Perfect Pairings. Marge Cox; foreword by Tom Bober. Libraries Unlimited 2023. xiv, 359 pages
ISBN 9781440875670
Grades: Professional   372.41
1. Creative activities for children and students 2. Reading (Elementary) 3. Handicraft for children 4. Handicraft 5. Books 6. Children 7. Professional materials — Programming 8. Professional materials — School media centers
LC 2022037469

Providing connections to the new AASL standards and the ISTE Standards for Students with simple directions for using a variety of books to create maker activities, this book can help elementary teachers and librarians to enhance and deepen the reading experience. Featured books represent a variety of genres for kindergarten through sixth-grade students and highlights very current titles as well as classics.

Includes bibliographical references and index.

372.6 Language arts (Communication skills)

Farmer, Lesley S. J.
★ *Impactful Community-based Literacy Projects.* Lesley S. J. Farmer; foreword by Lois Bridges. ALA Editions 2021. 131 p.
ISBN 9780838948033
Grades: Professional   **372.6**
1. Libraries and community 2. Literacy 3. Reading programs 4. Communication 5. Social action 6. Professional materials — General
LC 2020025998
Complete with links to additional resources and support materials, this resource details the steps needed to create effective and sustainable projects in your own community.

Includes bibliographical references and index.

373 Secondary education

Cullen, David
Columbine. Dave Cullen. Twelve 2009. x, 417 p.
ISBN 9780446546935
Grades: 10 11 12 Adult   **373**
1. Columbine High School Shooting, Littleton, Colo, 1999 2. Teenage murderers 3. School shootings 4. News media 5. Mass murder 6. Mass shootings 7. Psychology 8. Colorado 9. True Crime — Murder
LC 2008031441
ALA Notable Book, 2010; Edgar Allan Poe Award for Best Fact Crime, 2010; Goodreads Choice Award, 2009; New York Times Notable Book, 2009.

Ten years in the making and a masterpiece of reportage, "Columbine" is an award-winning journalist's definitive account of one of the most shocking massacres in American history.

Hobbs, Jeff
Show Them You're Good: A Portrait of Boys in the City of Angels the Year Before College. Jeff Hobbs. Scribner 2020. 336 p.
ISBN 9781982116330
Grades: Adult   **373**
1. High school seniors 2. Student achievement 3. College applicants 4. Adolescence 5. Masculinity 6. Friendship 7. Family relationships 8. Asian American children 9. Undocumented immigrants 10. Race (Social sciences) 11. Social classes 12. Young men 13. High school students 14. Higher education 15. Boys 16. Ambition in children 17. Anxiety in children 18. Hispanic American children 19. Los Angeles, California 20. United States 21. Life stories — Relationships — Growing up 22. Society and culture — Gender — Men 23. Society and culture — Education 24. Society and culture — Wealth and class
LC Bl2020013211
Four teenage boys are high school seniors at two very different schools within the city of Los Angeles, the second largest school district in the nation with nearly 700,000 students. Author Jeff Hobbs, writing with heart, sensitivity, and insight, stunningly captures the challenges and triumphs of being a young person confronting the future—both their own and the cultures in which they live—in contemporary America.

"It's sure to cheer school librarians looking for true stories of male high school students known for something besides their athletic talents or troubles with the law. A unique slice of male high school life with strong crossover appeal for YA readers." —*Kirkus*

373.1102 High school teaching

Cushman, Kathleen
Fires in Our Lives: Advice for Teachers from Today's High School Students. Kathleen Cushman, Kristien Zenkov, Meagan Call-Cummings and the youth of what kids can do. The New Press 2021. xii, 194 pages : Illustration
ISBN 9781620975435
Grades: Adult   **373.1102**
1. Teaching 2. Education 3. High school students 4. Teacher-student relationships 5. Educator resources — General 6. Educator resources — Secondary education 7. Society and culture — Education
LC 2020049144
A sequel to the classic Fires in the Bathroom that illuminates what adolescents most need from teachers in today's upsetting times.

"For anyone interested in inspiring students and helping them develop their full potential as global citizens." —*Library Journal*

Includes bibliographical references (pages 177-185) and index.

Keizer, Garret
Getting Schooled: The Reeducation of an American Teacher. Garret Keizer. Metropolitan Books 2014. 320 pages
ISBN 9780805096439
Grades: Adult   **373.1102**
1. Keizer, Garret 2. High schools 3. High school teachers 4. Public schools 5. Education 6. Vermont 7. Autobiographies and memoirs 8. Life stories — Education — Scholars and educators 9. Society and culture — Education
LC 2013042594
Perhaps no profession is so constantly discussed, regulated, and maligned by non-practitioners as teaching. The voices of the teachers themselves are conspicuously missing. Defying this trend, teacher and writer Garret Keizer takes us to school—literally—in this arresting account of his return to the same rural Vermont high school where he taught fourteen years ago.

"[A]t once a sympathetic portrait of a school, a searing indictment of a culture that uses working-class children as cannon fodder, and, unexpectedly, a page-turner." —*Publishers Weekly*

373.18 Students — Secondary education

Thorpe, Helen
The Newcomers: Finding Refuge, Friendship, and Hope in an American Classroom. Helen Thorpe. Scribner 2017. 416 p.
ISBN 9781501159091
Grades: Adult   **373.18**
1. Teenage immigrants 2. Teenage refugees 3. Secondary education 4. High school students 5. English language 6. Americanization 7. Society and culture — Education 8. Adult books for young adults
LC Bl2017036773
Traces the lives of twenty-two immigrant teens throughout the course of a year at Denver's South High School who attended a specially created English Language Acquisition class and who were helped to adapt through strategic introductions to American culture.

373.236 Lower level

Fagell, Phyllis L.
★ *Middle School Matters: The 10 Key Skills Kids Need to Thrive in Middle School and Beyond—and How Parents Can Help.* Phyllis L. Fagell, LCPC.. Lifelong 2019. xix, 298 pages
ISBN 9780738235080
Grades: Adult   **373.236**
1. Adolescence 2. Home and school 3. Middle school education 4. Middle school students 5. Parenting 6. Educator resources — General 7. Family and Relationships — Growing up 8. Family and Relationships — Parenting
LC 2019022000

ESSENTIAL AND RECOMMENDED TITLES
374 Adult education

Middle school is its own important, distinct territory, and yet it's either written off as an uncomfortable rite of passage or lumped in with other developmental phases. Based on her many years working in schools, professional counselor Phyllis Fagell sees these years instead as a critical stage that parents can't afford to ignore (and though "middle school" includes different grades in various regions, Fagell maintains that the ages make more of a difference than the setting). Though the transition from childhood to adolescence can be tough for kids, this time of rapid physical, intellectual, moral, social, and emotional change is a unique opportunity to proactively build character and confidence. Fagell helps parents use the middle school years as a low-stakes training ground to teach kids the key skills they'll need to thrive now and in the future, including making good friend choices, negotiating conflict, regulating their own emotions, be their own advocates, and more. To answer parents' most common questions and struggles with middle school-aged children, Fagell combines her professional and personal expertise with stories and advice from prominent psychologists, doctors, parents, educators, school professionals, and middle schoolers themselves.

"Readers will appreciate Fagell's straightforward advice on the wide array of challenges that can appear during the influential years between elementary and high school. This is a must-read for all parents and educators of kids in this unique and often misunderstood age group." —*Booklist*

Includes bibliographical references (pages 257-280) and index.

374 Adult education

Rose, Mike
Back to School: Why Everyone Deserves a Second Chance at Education. Mike Rose. New Press, the 2012. 256 p.
ISBN 9781595587862
Grades: Adult **374**
1. Adult learners 2. Adult education 3. Higher education 4. Education 5. Universities and colleges 6. Society and culture — Education — Higher education
LC 2012021135

It's a statistic that's sure to surprise: Close to 45 percent of postsecondary students in the United States today do not enroll in college directly out of high school and many attend part-time. Following a tradition of self-improvement as old as the Republic, the "nontraditional" college student is becoming the norm. Back to School is the first book to look at the schools that serve a growing population of "second-chancers," exploring what higher education-in the fullest sense of the term-can offer ourrapidly changing society and why it is so critical to support the institutions that make it possible for millions of Americans to better their lot in life. In the anecdotal style of his bestselling Possible Lives, Rose crafts rich and moving vignettes of people in tough circumstances who find their way; who get a second. .. or third. .. or even fourth chance; and who, in a surprising number of cases, reinvent themselves as educated, engaged citizens. Rose reminds us that our nation's economic and civic future rests heavily on the health of the institutions that serve millions of everyday people-not simply the top twenty universities in U.S. News and World Report-and paints a vivid picture of the community colleges and adult education programs that give so many a shot at reaching their aspirations.

Includes bibliographical references.

378 Higher education (Tertiary education)

Perkins, Anne Gardiner
Yale Needs Women: How the First Group of Girls Rewrote the Rules of an Ivy League Giant. Anne Gardiner Perkins. Sourcebooks 2019. xv, 367 p.
ISBN 9781492687740
Grades: Adult **378**
1. Women college students 2. Sexism in education 3. Feminism 4. Sexism in universities and colleges 5. Universities and colleges 6. New Haven, Connecticut 7. Society and culture — Education — Higher education 8. History writing — Women's history 9. Society and culture — Gender — Women 10. Life stories — Education
LC 2019024227

Yale University, along with the rest of the Ivy League, kept its gates closed to women until the class of 1969. The reason for letting them in? As an incentive for men to attend. Yale Needs Women is the story of why the most elite schools in the nation refused women for so long, and what the first women to enter those halls faced when they stepped onto campus.

Includes bibliographical references and index.

Selingo, Jeffrey J.
College (un)bound: The Future of Higher Education and What It Means for Students. Jeffrey J. Selingo. Houghton Mifflin Harcourt 2013. 224 p.
ISBN 9780544027077
Grades: Adult **378**
1. Higher education 2. College students 3. Educational policy 4. Educational reform 5. Education 6. Campus life 7. College costs 8. Universities and colleges 9. United States 10. Society and culture — Education — Higher education
LC 2013001941

Discusses the problems facing four-year colleges in the wake of the 2008 recession that left graduates with enormous debts and slim job prospects in a tough economy and describes institutions that are innovating to better prepare students in the future.

Includes bibliographical references and index.

378.1 Organization and activities in higher education

Bain, Ken
What the Best College Students Do. Ken Bain. The Belknap Press of Harvard University Press 2012. 289 pages
ISBN 9780674066649
Grades: 11 12 Adult **378.1**
1. Student achievement 2. College students 3. Society and culture — Education — Higher education
LC 2012015548

"A soundly encouraging guide for college students to think deeply and for as long as it takes." —*Kirkus*

Includes bibliographical references (pages 263-280) and index.

Belasco, Andrew
The Enlightened College Applicant: A New Approach to the Search and Admissions Process. Andrew Belasco and Dave Bergman. Rowman & Littlefield 2023. xi, 248 pages
ISBN 9781475865219
Grades: Adult Professional **378.1**
1. College applications 2. College application essays 3. College choice 4. Universities and colleges 5. United States 6. Educator Resources — Secondary education 7. Family and Relationships — General 8. Self-Help — General
LC 2022046353

The Enlightened College Applicant presents a no-nonsense account of how students should approach the college search and admissions process.

"The authors address tangible costs of college, helping readers carve through recruitment language and dive into the realities and (dis)advantages of institutions, from Ivies to in-state schools. Families seeking enlightenment about how to rationally and reasonably advise their teens in the higher-education arms race would do well to seek out this title." —*Booklist*

Includes bibliographical references and index.

Brenner, Andrea
How to College: What to Know Before You Go (and When You're There). Andrea Malkin Brenner and Lara Hope Schwartz. St. Martin's Griffin 2019. VIII, 294 pages : Illustration
ISBN 9781250225184
Grades: 10 11 12 Adult **378.1**
1. College student orientation 2. College freshmen 3. College students 4. Student finance 5. Higher education 6. Personal conduct 7. United States
LC 2019000551

A practical guide to help first-year students and their families transition smoothly from high school to college prepares students to succeed and thrive as they adapt to college.

"Some of the best advice comes from other college students and professors. Anyone planning to attend college will find this practical guide useful." —Booklist

Includes bibliographical references (pages 283-284) and index.

Bruni, Frank
Where You Go Is Not Who You'll Be: An Antidote to the College Admissions Mania. Frank Bruni. Grand Central Pub. 2015. 176 p.

ISBN 9781455532704

Grades: Adult   378.1

1. Universities and colleges 2. College choice 3. Competition 4. Higher education 5. Social classes 6. Society and culture — Education — Higher education

LC 2014049043

Over the last few decades, Americans have turned college admissions into a terrifying and occasionally devastating process, preceded by test prep, tutors, all sorts of stratagems, all kinds of rankings, and a conviction among too many young people that their futures will be determined and their worth established by which schools say yes and which say no. That belief is wrong. It's cruel. And in WHERE YOU GO IS NOT WHO YOU'LL BE, Frank Bruni explains why, giving students and their parents a new perspective on this brutal, deeply flawed competition and a path out of the anxiety that it provokes. Bruni, a bestselling author and a columnist for the New York Times, shows that the Ivy League has no monopoly on corner offices, governors' mansions, or the most prestigious academic and scientific grants. Through statistics, surveys, and the stories of hugely successful people who didn't attend the most exclusive schools, he demonstrates that many kinds of colleges-large public universities, tiny hideaways in the hinterlands-serve as ideal springboards. And he illuminates how to make the most of them. What matters in the end are a student's efforts in and out of the classroom, not the gleam of his or her diploma. Where you go isn't who you'll be. Americans need to hear that-and this indispensable manifesto says it with eloquence and respect for the real promise of higher education.

"Written in a lively style but carrying a wallop, this is a book that family and educators cannot afford to overlook as they try to navigate the treacherous waters of college admissions." —Kirkus

Fiske, Edward B.
Fiske Guide to Getting into the Right College. Edward B. Fiske & Bruce G. Hammond. Sourcebooks 2016. 385 p.

ISBN 9781492633303

Grades: Adult   378.1

1. College choice 2. Universities and colleges 3. United States 4. Reference books — Study guides

LC BL2016029392

Provides information on each step of the college admissions process, including selecting a college, writing application essays, handling college interviews, and obtaining financial aid.

Includes index.

Hessler, Peter
Other Rivers: A Chinese Education. Peter Hessler. Penguin Press 2024. 480 p.

ISBN 9780593655337

Grades: Adult   378.1

1. Hessler, Peter, 1969- 2. Authors 3. English language teachers 4. Working abroad 5. Families 6. Universities and colleges 7. Public education 8. Teacher-student relationships 9. Generations 10. Economic development 11. Urbanization 12. Dictatorship 13. Social control 14. Attitude 15. Social change 16. China 17. Impartial writing 18. Travel Writing — Asia and the South Pacific 19. Travel Writing — Living Abroad 20. Society and culture — Education

More than two decades after teaching English during the early part of China's economic boom, chronicled in his book River Town, Peter Hessler returned to Sichuan Province to instruct students from the next generation. At the same time, Hessler and his wife enrolled their twin daughters in a local state-run elementary school, where they were the only Westerners. Over the years, Hessler had kept in close contact with many of the people he had taught in the 1990s. By reconnecting with these individuals—members of China's "Reform generation," now in their forties—while teaching current undergrads, Hessler gained a unique perspective on China's incredible transformation.

"Returning to Sichuan Province after a long absence, an American journalism teacher experiences heightened surveillance, pandemic lockdowns, and other challenges in a changing China." —Booklist

Parini, Jay
The Art of Teaching. Jay Parini. Oxford University Press 2005. xi, 160 p.

ISBN 9780195169690

Grades: Adult   378.1

1. Parini, Jay 2. College teachers 3. College teaching 4. Autobiographies and memoirs 5. Educator resources — General

LC 2004005443

In a deeply personal memoir filled with humor, encouragement, and hard-won wisdom about the teacher's craft, the distinguished critic and author furnishes valuable insights into the many challenges educators face, as well as a discussion of such topics as politics in the classroom, the importance of a disciplined approach to life, fostering relationships with students, and balancing one's teaching load with research and writing.

"The author offers musings about teaching's demands and what it takes to not lose one's other, creative self while meeting those demands in this memoir-cum-advice book for novice instructors. This warm guide should inform, entertain, and inspire young teachers as they seek to waken a student to his or her potential." —Publishers Weekly

Rosenfeld, Seth
Subversives: The FBI's War on Student Radicals, and Reagan's Rise to Power. Seth Rosenfeld. Farrar, Straus and Giroux 2012. 528 p.

ISBN 9780374257002

Grades: Adult   378.1

1. Reagan, Ronald 2. Hoover, J. Edgar, 1895-1972 3. Student movements 4. College students 5. Subversive activities 6. Political participation 7. Politics and government 8. California 9. 1960s 10. History writing — 1960s — United States

LC 2011041204

A narrative report on the FBI's covert involvement with future President Ronald Reagan, radical Mario Savio and liberal university president Clark Kerr to suppress the 1960s student movement at Berkeley reveals J. Edgar Hoover's campaign of planted news stories, illegal break-ins and other acts designed to undermine the Democratic party.

Includes bibliographical references.

Rudd, Mark
Underground: My Life with Sds and the Weathermen. Mark Rudd. William Morrow 2009. 352 p.

ISBN 9780061472756

Grades: 11 12 Adult   378.1

1. Rudd, Mark 2. Protest movements 3. Social advocates 4. Radicals 5. Revolutions 6. United States history 7. 20th century 8. Autobiographies and memoirs 9. History writing — 1960s — United States 10. Life stories — Politics — Activists and reformers

LC 2010292486

A leader of the Columbia University student uprising of 1968 and fugitive member of the notorious Weather Underground describes how he and his friends helped to organize the Days of Rage protests in 1969 and plotted to overthrow the government in a failed bombing attempt.

Selingo, Jeffrey J.
Who Gets in and Why: A Year Inside College Admissions. Jeffrey J. Selingo. Scribner 2020. xiv, 306 p.

ISBN 9781982116293

Grades: 10 11 12 Adult   378.1

1. Discrimination in universities and colleges 2. Educational reform 3. College applicants 4. Higher education Policy 5. Education 6. Inequality 7. Univer-

ESSENTIAL AND RECOMMENDED TITLES
378.3 Student aid and related topics

sities and colleges 8. United States 9. Society and culture — Education — Higher education

LC Bl2020018371

New York Times Notable Book, 2020.

A higher-education journalist draws on insider access to explain the nuts and bolts of college admissions today, outlining the unexpected agendas that reflect which and why prospective students receive admission into better schools.

"This well-researched work is an invaluable tool for college-bound students and their families, guidance counselors, and college admissions personnel." —*Library Journal*

Includes bibliographical references and index.

Tough, Paul
The Years That Matter Most: How College Makes or Breaks Us. Paul Tough. Houghton Mifflin Harcourt 2019. VIII, 390 pages
ISBN 9780544944480

Grades: Adult   378.1

1. Universities and colleges 2. Equal education policy 3. Social mobility 4. College student orientation 5. College students 6. White privilege 7. Inequality 8. United States 9. Society and culture — Education — Higher education 10. Society and culture — Wealth and class

LC 2019013123

Drawing on new research, the book reveals how the landscape of higher education has shifted in recent decades and exposes the hidden truths of how the system works and whom it works for. And it introduces us to the people who really make higher education go: Admissions directors trying to balance the class and balance the budget, College Board officials scrambling to defend the SAT in the face of mounting evidence that it favors the wealthy, researchers working to unlock the mysteries of the college-student brain, and educators trying to transform potential dropouts into successful graduates.

"Drawing on broad reading and visits to campuses across the country, Tough's work offers an indictment of American society and political structures and persuasively argues that universities must fulfill the American commitment to equality of opportunity." —*Library Journal*

Includes bibliographical references and index.

Ventrone, Jillian
From the Marine Corps to College: Transitioning from the Service to Higher Education. Jillian Ventrone. Rowan & Littlefield 2014. VII, 215 pages
ISBN 9781442237209

Grades: Adult   378.1

1. Marines 2. Veterans 3. Education 4. Educator resources — Secondary education 5. History writing — Wars and conflicts

LC 2014013314

"Despite its limitations, this title will appeal to marines and do well in libraries serving this population; otherwise, it is a supplemental purchase." —*Library Journal*

Includes bibliographical references (pages 207-209) and index.

378.3 Student aid and related topics

Goldrick-Rab, Sara
Paying the Price: College Costs, Financial Aid, and the Betrayal of the American Dream. Sara Goldrick-Rab. The University of Chicago Press 2016. 368 p.
ISBN 9780226404349

Grades: Adult   378.3

1. College costs 2. Student aid 3. Higher Education 4. Wisconsin 5. Society and culture — Education — Higher education

LC 2016007474

For the last decade, sociologist Sara Goldrick-Rab has been studying what happens when economically vulnerable people try to make their way through public higher education.

"This cogent and persuasive argument for a more humane and efficient program to make higher education accessible to all capable students draws upon thorough research and an array of personal portraits. Highly recommended for parents and taxpayers." —*Library Journal*

Includes bibliographical references and index.

Mitchell, Josh
The Debt Trap: How Student Loans Became a National Catastrophe. Josh Mitchell. Simon & Schuster 2021. 288 p.
ISBN 9781501199448

Grades: Adult   378.3

1. Student loans 2. Student aid 3. Student finance 4. Debt 5. College costs 6. Education 7. Higher education 8. Higher education policy 9. Finance 10. Economics 11. United States 12. Society and culture — Education — Higher education 13. Business and economics — Industries — Finance 14. Life stories — Education

Charting the 70-year history of student debt in America, a reporter in the Washington bureau of the Wall Street Journal tells the untold story of the scandals, scams, predatory actors and government malpractice that have created today's central economic issue.

"Parents, students, and educators will find it enthralling and possibly be moved to push for industry reforms." —*Booklist*

378.73 Colleges — United States

Bok, Derek Curtis
The Struggle to Reform Our Colleges. Derek Bok. Princeton University Press 2017. 228 p.
ISBN 9780691177472

Grades: Adult   378.73

1. Universities and colleges 2. Higher education 3. Student achievement 4. Educational reform 5. United States 6. Society and culture — Education — Higher education

LC 2017012202

Why efforts to improve American higher educational attainment haven't worked, and where to go from here.

Includes bibliographical references and index.

Cottom, Tressie McMillan
Lower Ed: How For-profit Colleges Deepen Inequality in America. Tressie McMillan Cottom. The New Press 2016. 256 p.
ISBN 9781620970607

Grades: Adult   378.73

1. Universities and colleges 2. Higher education 3. For-profit universities and colleges 4. Education 5. Social life and customs 6. United States 7. Society and culture — Education — Higher education

LC 2016048195

Drawing on her personal experience as a former counselor at two for-profit colleges and interviews with students, senior executives and activists, a renowned sociologist reveals how for-profit schools have become so successful and deciphers the benefits, credentials pitfalls and real costs of a for-profit education.

"The best book yet on the complex lives and choices of for-profit students." —*New York Times Book Review*

Mettler, Suzanne
Degrees of Inequality: How the Politics of Higher Education Sabotaged the American Dream. Suzanne Mettler. Basic Books, a member of the Perseus Books Group 2014. 320 p.
ISBN 9780465044962

Grades: Adult   378.73

1. Higher education 2. For-profit universities and colleges 3. Higher education policy 4. Universities and colleges 5. Income inequality 6. Poor people 7. Equal education policy 8. Educational innovations 9. Society and culture — Education — Higher education

LC 2013043678

PUBLIC LIBRARY CORE COLLECTION: NONFICTION
Twentieth Edition

An acclaimed political scientist describes how political partisanship, corporate interests and for-profit colleges have negatively impacted America's higher education system, which has been skewed to benefit only those in the highest income brackets.

"Though the book orbits the central theme of the for-profits and their outsized political influence, [Mettler] frames this with a history of higher education and its attendant laws, as well as an excellent introduction to political science that explains—in approachable language—the myriad impacts of law and the ways in which the intentions of legislators are often deformed." —*Publishers Weekly*

Williams, Juan
I'll Find a Way or Make One: A Tribute to Historically Black Colleges and Universities. Juan Williams and Dwayne Ashley with Shawn Rhea. Amistad 2004. xxiv, 453 p. : Illustration
ISBN 9780060094539
Grades: Adult   **378.73**
1. African American universities and colleges 2. African Americans 3. Education 4. African American history 5. Society and culture — Ethnic studies
LC 2004046450

A commemorative exploration of the history and cultural significance of 108 American Historically Black Colleges and Universities discusses how post-Civil War abolitionists worked to formally educate newly freed slaves; provides a wealth of historical narrative, personal memoir, and archival material; and identifies prominent African-Americans who have graduated to become societal leaders.

An exploration of the history of 107 historically Black American colleges and universities discusses how post-Civil War abolitionists worked to educate newly freed slaves and provides personal memoirs and archival material.

"The authors explore America's 107 historically Black colleges and universities, in existence for 172 years, showing how the schools were created and how Black and white abolitionists united to educate newly freed slaves." —*Library Journal*

Includes bibliographical references (p. [433]-435) and index.

379 Public policy issues in education

Duncan, Arne
How Schools Work: An Inside Account of Failure and Success from One of the Nation's Longest-serving Secretaries of Education. Arne Duncan. Simon & Schuster 2018. 352 p.
ISBN 9781501173059
Grades: Adult   **379**
1. Schools 2. Public schools 3. Educational policy 4. Discrimination in education 5. Politics and education 6. Education 7. Inequality 8. United States 9. Society and culture — Education
LC 2018016716

Examines some of the problems that plague the American public school system, identifies solutions that have worked in the past, and celebrates the hero teachers, staffers, and adminstrators the author met as the Obama Secretary of Education.

"Duncan's experienced perspective will interest anyone invested in American public education." —*Publishers Weekly*

379.1 Specific elements of support and control of public education

Ravitch, Diane
The Death and Life of the Great American School System: How Testing and Choice Are Undermining Education. Diane Ravitch. Basic Books 2009. 296 p.
ISBN 9780465014910
Grades: Adult   **379.1**
1. Public schools 2. Educational reform 3. School choice 4. Program evaluation in education 5. Educational tests and measurements 6. Educational policy 7. Society and culture — Education
LC 2009050406

Discusses how school choice, misapplied standards of accountability, the No Child Left Behind mandate, and the use of a corporate model have all led to a decline in public education and presents arguments for a return to strong neighborhood schools and quality teaching.

"The author provides an important and highly readable examination of the educational system, how it fails to prepare students for life after graduation, and how we can put it back on track. Anyone interested in education should definitely read this accessible, riveting book." —*Library Journal*

Includes bibliographical references and index.

379.2 Specific policy issues in public education

Green, Kristen
Something Must Be Done About Prince Edward County: A Family, a Virginia Town, a Civil Rights Battle. Kristen Green. Harpercollins 2015. 349 p.
ISBN 9780062268679
Grades: Adult   **379.2**
1. Green, Kristen 2. School integration 3. Family secrets 4. Race relations 5. Civil rights movement 6. School desegregation decision, 1954 7. Forgiveness 8. Virginia 9. Autobiographies and memoirs 10. Life stories — General 11. Society and culture — Race
LC 2015295454

Booklist Editors' Choice, 2015.

Combining hard-hitting investigative journalism and a sweeping family narrative, this provocative true story reveals a little-known chapter of American history: the period after the Brown v. Board of Education decision when one Virginia school system refused to integrate.

"Green's work brims with real-life detail from the journalist's eye and ear and joins the likes of Diane McWhorter's Carry Me Home in further developing the dimensions of the South's desegregation struggleparticularly from the perspective of white communitiesfor general readers and scholars of the late 20th-century civil rights movement." —*Library Journal*

Harris, Adam
★ *The State Must Provide: Why America's Colleges Have Always Been Unequal - and How to Set Them Right.* Adam Harris. Ecco Press 2021. 336 p.
ISBN 9780062976482
Grades: Adult   **379.2**
1. Universities and colleges 2. Racism in universities and colleges 3. African American universities and colleges 4. Racism 5. Higher education 6. Race relations 7. Discrimination in universities and colleges 8. Institutional racism 9. United States 10. Society and culture — Education — Higher education 11. Society and culture — Race 12. History writing — United States

The definitive chronicle of higher education's failed attempts at equality and the long road still in front of us to remedy centuries of racial discrimination—and poses a daring solution to help solve the underfunding of HBCUs. Told through a vivid cast of characters, the State Must Provide examines what happened before and after schools were supposedly integrated in the twentieth century, and why higher education remains broken to this day.

"Profound and thought-provoking, this work is recommended for anyone who wants to understand the structural inequities of the U.S. educational system." —*Library Journal*

Kozol, Jonathan
★ *An End to Inequality: Breaking Down the Walls of Apartheid Education in America.* Jonathan Kozol; [foreword by Theodore M. Shaw]. The New Press 2024. 192 p.
ISBN 9781620978726
Grades: Adult   **379.2**
1. Segregation in education 2. Marginalized students 3. Educational policy 4. School integration 5. Education 6. Racism in education 7. Children's rights

ESSENTIAL AND RECOMMENDED TITLES
379.73 Educational policy—United States

8. Equal education policy 9. Education and culture 10. Society and culture — Education 11. History Writing — United States 12. Society and culture — Race
LC 2023049416

The New York Times best-selling author of Death at an Early Age returns to urban schools to expose the deepening racial isolation and the harmful effects of punitive instruction and coercive uniformity on underprivileged students.

"An inspired and insightful analysis of race-based challenges in the American school system." —*Kirkus*

Includes bibliographical references and index.

Margolick, David

Elizabeth and Hazel: Two Women of Little Rock. David Margolick. Yale University Press 2011. 320 p.
ISBN 9780300141931
Grades: 11 12 Adult   **379.2**

1. Eckford, Elizabeth, 1941- 2. Massery, Hazel Bryan, 1942- 3. African American students 4. Racism 5. Interracial friendship 6. High school students 7. Female friendship 8. School integration 9. Little Rock, Arkansas 10. 1950s 11. History writing — African American — Civil rights — United States
LC 2011014101

Booklist Editors' Choice, 2011.

Looks at the lives of the two women at the center of a famous historic photograph taken during the Little Rock school desegregation crisis in 1957, in a book that discusses how each dealt with the fallout from that day.

"Margolick draws on interviews and press reports of the time to present a very nuanced analysis of how Elizabeth and Hazel were affected by the scene that made them famous. . . . A complex look at two women at the center of a historic moment." —*Booklist*

Includes bibliographical references and index.

Martin, Rachel Louise

A Most Tolerant Little Town: The Explosive Beginning of School Desegregation. Rachel Louise Martin. Simon & Schuster 2023. 384 p.
ISBN 9781665905145
Grades: Adult   **379.2**

1. Small towns 2. School integration 3. Racism in education 4. Equal education policy 5. Protests, demonstrations, vigils, etc. 6. African American students 7. Social conflict 8. Violence against African Americans 9. Bombings 10. Social change 11. Race relations 12. United States history 13. Tennessee 14. Southern States 15. 1950s 16. History writing — African American — Civil rights — United States 17. History writing — Regional history — United States 18. History writing — Post World War II - 1959 — United States 19. Life stories — People in history — Witness to history
LC 2022042647

This portrait of the first school to attempt to implement court-ordered desegregation in the wake of Brown v. Board of Education focuses on its impact on Clinton, Tennessee, a small town living through a tumultuous turning point for America.

"A timely contribution to the literature of the post-Brown v. Board Civil Rights Movement." —*Kirkus*

Includes bibliographical references and index.

Wilder, Craig Steven

Ebony and Ivy: Race, Slavery, and the Troubled History of America's Universities. by Craig Wilder. Bloomsbury 2013. 352 p.
ISBN 9781596916814
Grades: Adult   **379.2**

1. Universities and colleges 2. Race relations 3. Slavery 4. Higher education 5. African Americans 6. United States history 7. History writing — African American — Enslavement — United States 8. Society and culture — Education 9. Society and culture — Education — Higher education 10. Society and culture — Race
LC 2013011971

Booklist Editors' Choice, 2013; BCALA Literary Award for Nonfiction, 2014; Hurston/Wright Legacy Award: Nonfiction, 2014.

A leading African-American historian of race in America exposes the uncomfortable truths about race, slavery and the American academy, revealing that our leading universities, dependent on human bondage, became breeding grounds for the racist ideas that sustained it.

"A groundbreaking history that will no doubt contribute to a reappraisal of some deep-rooted founding myths." —*Kirkus*

379.73 Educational policy—United States

Fitzpatrick, Cara

The Death of Public School: How Conservatives Won the War Over Education in America. Cara Fitzpatrick. Basic Books 2023. 368 p.
ISBN 9781541646773
Grades: Adult   **379.73**

1. Public schools 2. Public education 3. Political culture 4. Conservatism 5. School choice 6. Private schools 7. Charter schools 8. Government accountability 9. Educational policy 10. Society and culture — Education 11. Politics and global affairs — General 12. History writing — United States 13. Debut title
LC 2022050482

America has relied on public schools for 150 years, but the system is increasingly under attack. With declining enrollment and diminished trust in public education, policies that steer tax dollars into private schools have grown rapidly. To understand how we got here, the Death of Public School argues, we must look back at the turbulent history of school choice. Cara Fitzpatrick uncovers the long evolution of school choice, a story full of fascinating people and changing political alliances, to show how education is now poised to become a private commodity rather than a universal good.

"Pulitzer winner Fitzpatrick's informative debut outlines the recent history of public education reform, detailing the intellectual underpinnings and political wrangling behind successive movements for school privatization." —*Publishers Weekly*

Includes bibliographical references and index.

381 Commerce (Trade)

Castleman, Michael

The Untold Story of Books: A Writer's History of Publishing. Michael Castleman. The Unnamed Press 2024. 270 pages
ISBN 9781961884083
Grades: Adult   **381**

1. Books 2. Books and reading 3. Literature and history 4. Publishers and publishing 5. Self-publishers and publishing 6. Booksellers 7. Bookstores 8. Bookselling 9. Printing presses 10. Copyright 11. Arts and Entertainment — Writing and Publishing 12. History writing — Microhistory 13. Society and culture — General

A deeply researched, fascinating history of the idiosyncratic book business—aimed at authors, aspiring authors, booksellers, industry professionals, and everyone who loves to read books.

"Castleman presents a sweeping 600-year chronicle of the book business…Bibliophiles will be enthralled." —*Publishers Weekly*

Del Rey, Jason

Winner Sells All: Amazon, Walmart, and the Battle for Our Wallets. Jason Del Rey. HarperBusiness 2023. 320 p.
ISBN 9780063076327
Grades: Adult   **381**

1. Consumerism 2. Commercialization 3. Shopping 4. Online shopping 5. Electronic commerce 6. Retail industry and trade 7. Business and economics — Industries — Retail products and services

This key to understanding how Amazon and Walmart are changing the way we shop, live and work chronicles the business clash of this generation—a war waged for our loyalty and money, with hundreds of billions of dollars at stake and millions of jobs on the line.

"An eye-opening look at a battle of corporate titans that shows few signs of slowing down." —*Kirkus*

PUBLIC LIBRARY CORE COLLECTION: NONFICTION
Twentieth Edition

Fili, Louise
*The **Cognoscenti's** Guide to Florence: Shop and Eat Like a Florentine.* Louise Fili & Lise Apatoff. Princeton Architectural Press 2017. 224 p.
ISBN 9781616896362
Grades: Adult   381
1. Shopping 2. Restaurants 3. Walking 4. Florence, Italy 5. Travel writing — Europe 6. Reference — Travel guides

Shop and eat like a Florentine with this pocket-sized guide to the best of the magnificent Tuscan city known for its art, culture, and cuisine. Celebrated graphic designer and self-described Italophile Louise Fili, with connoisseur of all things Lisa Apatoff, takes you on eight walks through Florence, discussing more than seventy of the city's most alluring shop—some run by the same families for generations, others offering young entrepreneurs' fresh interpretations of traditional techniques.

Jacobs, Ryan McMahon
*The **Truffle** Underground: A Tale of Mystery, Mayhem, and Manipulation in the Shadowy Market of the World's Most Expensive Fungus.* Ryan Jacobs. Clarkson Potter 2019. VI, 279 p.
ISBN 9780451495693
Grades: Adult   381
1. Truffles 2. Mushrooms 3. Black market 4. Cooks 5. Restaurateurs 6. Farmers 7. Smuggling 8. Counterfeits and counterfeiting 9. Food industry and trade 10. Cooking 11. France 12. Italy 13. Food writing — Investigations 14. Food Writing — Food and Culture 15. True Crime — Investigations and Trials
LC 2018053998

Documents the crimes at each level of a truffle's path from ground to plate, including planting poisoned meatballs to remove competitor's dogs, foragers robbed of their harvest at gunpoint, and crime syndicates stealing scientific secrets.

"This deeply researched and eye-opening account of the lengths people will go for wealth, gratification, and a taste of the prized fungus will captivate readers." —*Publishers Weekly*

Includes bibliographical references.

King, Ross
***Bookseller** of Florence: The Story of the Manuscripts That Illuminated the Renaissance.* Ross King. Atlantic Monthly Press 2021. 480 p.
ISBN 9780802158529
Grades: Adult   381
1. Vespasiano, da Bisticci, 1421-1498 2. Illumination of books and manuscripts 3. Manuscripts 4. Books and reading 5. Booksellers 6. Florence, Italy 7. Italy 8. Renaissance (1300-1600) 9. History writing — Renaissance — Europe 10. History writing — Europe — Italy

Loan Stars Favourites, 2021.

The Renaissance in Florence conjures images of beautiful frescoes and elegant buildings—the dazzling handiwork of the city's skilled artists and architects. But equally important for the centuries to follow were geniuses of a different sort: Florence's manuscript hunters, scribes, scholars, and booksellers, who blew the dust off a thousand years of history and, through the discovery and diffusion of ancient knowledge, imagined a new and enlightened world.

"Art historian King (Brunelleschi's Dome) delivers a richly detailed portrait of 15th-century Florence and the important role booksellers played in disseminating ancient Greek and Latin texts that were vital to the Renaissance. . . . This expert account shines a new light on the Renaissance." —*Publishers Weekly*

MacGillis, Alec
***Fulfillment**: Winning and Losing in One-click America.* Alec MacGillis. Farrar, Straus and Giroux 2021. 352 p.
ISBN 9780374159276
Grades: Adult   381
1. Bezos, Jeffrey 2. Corporate profits 3. Electronic commerce 4. Business and politics 5. Big business 6. Blue collar workers 7. COVID-19 (Disease) 8. Equality 9. Economics 10. United States 11. 20th century 12. Business and economics — Industries — Retail products and services
LC 2020046596

Examines how Amazon's trillion-dollar network of delivery hubs, data centers and corporate campuses reflects the company's increasing influence over local and federal governments.

"MacGillis' sprawling, fascinating account presses pause on the continuously unfurling effects of a monolithic company on not only our consumption, but also our livelihoods, communities, and government." —*Booklist*

Includes bibliographical references and index.

Minter, Adam
***Secondhand**: Travels in the New Global Garage Sale.* Adam Minter. Bloomsbury 2019. 304 p.
ISBN 9781635570106
Grades: Adult   381
1. Consumerism 2. Secondhand industry and trade 3. Consumer behavior 4. Used clothing 5. Society and culture — Urban and regional studies 6. Business and economics — Economics — Consumerism
LC Bl2019027524

From the author of Junkyard Planet comes a global exploration of the hidden market for used stuff and a travelogue that follows unwanted, obsolete objects' journeys into a reusable future.

Montero, David
★ *The **Stolen** Wealth of Slavery: A Case for Reparations.* David Montero. Legacy Lit 2024. 272 p.
ISBN 9780306827174
Grades: Adult   381
1. Slavery 2. Capitalism 3. Reparations for historical injustices 4. African Americans 5. Corporations 6. Slave trade 7. Banks and banking 8. Shipping industry and trade 9. Wealth 10. Misconceptions 11. Atrocities 12. Corporate accountability 13. Social movements 14. United States history 15. United States 16. History writing — African American — Enslavement — United States 17. Business and economics — Economics — History 18. Society and culture — Violence and crime — Genocide
LC 2023036573

It has long been maintained that the North wasn't complicit in the horrors of slavery. The truth, however, is that large Northern banks were critical to the financing of slavery; that they saw their fortunes rise dramatically from their involvement in the business of enslavement; and that white business leaders and their surrounding communities created enormous wealth from the enslavement and abuse of Black bodies. Journalist David Montero meticulously showcases exactly what was stolen, who stole it, and to whom it is owed, calling for corporate reparations as he details contemporary movements to hold companies accountable for past atrocities.

"Montero persuasively argues that profitable businesses owe reparations to people who continue to suffer from historic injustices." —*Library Journal*

Patterson, James
*The **Secret** Lives of Booksellers and Librarians: Their Stories Are Better Than the Bestsellers.* James Patterson and Matt Eversmann. Little Brown & Company 2024. 352 p.
ISBN 9780316567534
Grades: Adult   381
1. Booksellers 2. Librarians 3. Books 4. Books and reading 5. Collective biographies 6. Life stories — Arts and culture 7. History Writing — Arts and culture 8. Life stories — Education — Scholars and educators

Showcasing the smart and talented people who live between the pages, this inspiring collection of true stories, as told to one of the greatest novelists of our time, invites us into a world where we can feed our curiosities, discover new voices and find whatever we want or require.

"With its bite-sized chapters, this collection of profiles doesn't go into much depth, but it will appeal to readers looking for some quick, bookish inspiration." —*Booklist*

Wartzman, Rick
***Still** Broke: Walmart's Remarkable Transformation and the Limits of Socially Conscious Capitalism.* Rick Wartzman. PublicAffairs 2022. IX, 258 p.

ESSENTIAL AND RECOMMENDED TITLES
381.141 Department stores

ISBN 9781541757998
Grades: Adult — **381**
1. Chain stores 2. Corporate accountability 3. Business ethics 4. Capitalism 5. Labor-management relations 6. Retail industry and trade 7. United States 8. Business and economics — Industries — Retail products and services 9. Business and economics — Economics — Socioeconomics
LC 2022013116
With unparalleled access to key executives and change-makers, an award-winning author goes inside Walmart's transformation, showing in novelistic detail how the company has gotten to where it is, interrogating the role of business in American life and asking what the future of our economy and country can be.
"A well-written account of a corporate American juggernaut and its implications for society as a whole." —*Kirkus*
Includes bibliographical references and index.

381.141 Department stores

Satow, Julie
When Women Ran Fifth Avenue: Glamour and Power at the Dawn of American Fashion. Julie Satow. Doubleday 2024. 336 p.
ISBN 9780385548755
Grades: Adult — **381.141**
1. Department stores 2. Fashion 3. Women executives 4. American people 5. Consumerism 6. United States 7. New York city 8. 20th century 9. Arts and Entertainment — Fashion 10. History Writing — Women's history 11. Life stories — Business — Business leaders 12. Business and economics — Business leaders and entrepreneurs 13. Business and economics — Industries — Retail products and services
LC 2023039182
Rich with personal drama and trade secrets, an award-winning journalist takes us back to the golden age of American department stores and the three visionary women—Hortense Odium of Bonwit Teller; Dorothy Shaver of Lord & Taylor; and Geraldine Stutz of Henri Bendel—who led them.
"An investigation into three women who oversaw New York City department stores between the 1920s and 1970s…The illuminating stories of these unexpected tastemakers are both complementary and well contextualized." —*Kirkus*
Includes index.

381.142 E-commerce (Electronic commerce)

Mattioli, Dana
★ *The Everything War: Amazon's Ruthless Quest to Own the World and Remake Corporate Power.* Dana Mattioli. Little, Brown and Company 2024. 320 p.
ISBN 9780316269773
Grades: Adult — **381.142**
1. Corporate greed 2. Corporations 3. Business corruption 4. Monopolies 5. Power 6. Electronic commerce 7. Management 8. Business and economics — Industries — Technology 9. Business and economics — Industries — Retail products and services 10. Business and economics — Corruption and scandal
From veteran Amazon reporter for the Wall Street Journal comes an untold, devastating exposé of Amazon's endless strategic greed, from destroying Main Street to remaking corporate power, in pursuit of total domination, by any means necessary.
"This is investigative journalism at its finest." —*Publishers Weekly*

381.4 Commerce (Trade) — Specific products and services

Lorr, Benjamin
The Secret Life of Groceries: The Dark Miracle of the American Supermarket. Benjamin Lorr. Avery, an imprint of Penguin Random House 2020. 328 pages
ISBN 9780553459395
Grades: Adult — **381.4**
1. Supermarkets 2. Food industry and trade 3. Grocery industry and trade 4. Grocery industry and trade employees 5. Food 6. Commercial products 7. Grocery shopping 8. Food writing — Investigations 9. Business and economics — Industries — Agriculture and food
LC 2020004949
In the tradition of Fast Food Nation and The Omnivore's Dilemma, an extraordinary investigation into the human lives at the heart of the American grocery store. What does it take to run the American supermarket? How do products get to shelves? Who sets the price? and who suffers the consequences of increased convenience end efficiency? in this alarming exposae, author Benjamin Lorr pulls back the curtain on this highly secretive industry. Combining deep sourcing, immersive reporting, and compulsively readable prose, Lorr leads a wild investigation in which we learn: the secrets of Trader Joe's success from Trader Joe himself, Why truckers call their job "sharecropping on wheels," What it takes for a product to earn certification labels like "organic" and "fair trade."
"Lorr's exploration of the systems and individuals that create the modern grocery store will move readers to ask far more probing questions about what they're putting on the table. For fans of Michael Pollan's work and Michael Ruhlman's Grocery (2017)." —*Booklist*
Includes bibliographical references (pages 277-316) and index.

384 Communications

Basinger, Jeanine
The Star Machine. Jeanine Basinger. A. A. Knopf 2007. xiv, 586 p. : Illustration
ISBN 9781400041305
Grades: Adult — **384**
1. Film industry and trade 2. Films 3. Actors and actresses 4. Social life and customs 5. United States 6. 20th century 7. Biographies 8. Arts and Entertainment — Movies and Television
LC 2007005268
In an entertaining compilation of Hollywood lore, trivia, and analysis, a leading film historian provides a close-up look at the golden era of filmmaking and the creation of stars at the height of the studio system, from the 1930s to the 1950s, explaining how the star machine worked, the grooming of actors, and the careers of such actors as Tyrone Power, Errol Flynn, Lana Turner, and others.
Includes bibliographical references (p. [555]-557) and index.

Goldman, William
Adventures in the Screen Trade: A Personal View of Hollywood and Screenwriting. William Goldman. Warner Books 1984. xiii, 594 p.
ISBN 9780446391177
Grades: Adult — **384**
1. Goldman, William, 1931-2018 2. Screenplay writing 3. Film industry and trade 4. Screenwriters 5. Creativity 6. Arts and Entertainment — Movies and Television
LC BL 99758446
The Academy Award-winning screenwriter and bestselling author combines observations on Hollywood stars, studios, power plays, filming, directors, and producers with a point-by-point review of script writing.
Includes index.

384.55 Television

Hastings, Reed
No Rules Rules: Netflix and the Culture of Reinvention. Reed Hastings and Erin Meyer. Penguin Press 2020. 288 p.
ISBN 9781984877864
Grades: Adult — **384.55**
1. Hastings, Reed, 1960- 2. Chief executive officers 3. Corporate culture 4. Adaptability 5. Communication in organizations 6. Business innovations

7. Business and economics — Business advice — Leadership and management
8. Life stories — Business — Business leaders

LC 2019058039

Netflix cofounder Reed Hastings reveals for the first time the unorthodox culture behind one of the world's most innovative, imaginative, and successful companies. There has never before been a company like Netflix. It has led nothing short of a revolution in the entertainment industries, generating billions of dollars in annual revenue while capturing the imaginations of hundreds of millions of people in over 190 countries. But to reach these great heights, Netflix has had to reinvent itself over and over again. This type of unprecedented flexibility would have been impossible without the counterintuitive and radical management principles that cofounder Reed Hastings established from the very beginning. Hastings rejected the conventional wisdom under which other companies operate and defied tradition to instead build a culture focused on freedom and responsibility, one that has allowed Netflix to adapt and innovate as the needs of its members and the world have simultaneously transformed.

"Aspiring tech moguls should flock to Hastings and Meyer's energetic and fascinating account." —*Publishers Weekly*

Includes index.

Hayes, Dade

Binge *Times: Inside Hollywood's Furious Billion-dollar Battle to Take Down Netflix.* Dade Hayes & Dawn Chmielewski. William Morrow and Company 2022. 256 p.

ISBN 9780062980007

Grades: Adult   384.55

1. Internet 2. Entertainment industry and trade 3. Streaming technology (Telecommunications) 4. Technological innovations 5. Internet videos 6. Films 7. Film industry and trade 8. Business and economics — Industries — Entertainment and media 9. Arts and Entertainment — Movies and television

The first comprehensive account of the biggest wake-up call in the history of the entertainment business: the pivot to streaming.

"This will appeal to readers of business and media books as it reports on the difficult launches of several streaming services." —*Library Journal*

Napoli, Lisa

Up All Night: Ted Turner, Cnn, and the Birth of 24-hour News. Lisa Napoli. Harry N. Abrams 2020. 304 p.

ISBN 9781419743061

Grades: Adult   384.55

1. Turner, Ted 2. Current events 3. Broadcast journalism 4. Mass media 5. Politics and global affairs — Mass media and politics 6. Society and culture — Media and technology 7. Business and economics — Industries — Entertainment and media

LC Bl2020013378

Blends media and history in an account of the founding of CNN by Ted Turner and a motley assortment of cable-television visionaries, big-league rejects and non-union newcomers, whose collective successes exceeded their wildest ambitions.

"A page-turning hybrid of biography, media analysis, and business history." —*Kirkus*

385 Railroad transportation

Ambrose, Stephen E.

Nothing *Like It in the World: The Men Who Built the Transcontinental Railroad, 1863-1869.* Stephen E. Ambrose. Simon & Schuster 2000. 471 p. : Illustration

ISBN 9780684846095

Grades: 11 12 Adult   385

1. Transcontinental railroad (United States) 2. Railroad workers 3. Railroads 4. The West (United States) history 5. United States history 6. United States 7. 19th century 8. History writing — Technological innovations 9. History writing — Westward expansion — United States 10. Adult books for young adults

LC 00041005

New York Times Notable Book, 2000.

Chronicles the race to finish the transcontinental railroad in the 1860s and the exploits, sacrifices, triumphs, and tragedies of the individuals who made it happen.

"Ambrose's scholarship seems impeccable. . . . He writes a brisk, colloquial, straightforward prose that not only is easy to read but also bears the reader on shoulders of wonder and excitement." —*New York Times Book Review*

Includes bibliographical references and index.

Parks, Tim

Italian *Ways: On and off the Rails from Milan to Palermo.* Tim Parks. W.W. Norton & Company 2013. 320 p.

ISBN 9780393239324

Grades: Adult   385

1. Parks, Tim 2. Railroad travel 3. Transportation 4. Train passengers 5. Train rides 6. Social life and customs 7. Voyages and travels 8. Italy 9. Travel Writing — Europe 10. Travel Writing — Living Abroad 11. Travel Writing — Modes of Transportation — by Train

LC 2013011386

English ex-pat Tim Parks (a resident in Italy since 1981) explores the wonderful, awful experience of traveling Italy with wry, insightful humor. Riding the rails from Italy top to bottom presents an up-close experiences of Italian life, past and present. With memorable vignettes of those he meets along the way (many of whom hate the train system) interspersed with railway history (he boards cars from pre-World War II, to modern high-speed ones), this entertaining travelogue delivers a slice of Italian culture at large.

385.09 Railroad atlases — Specific areas

Zoellner, Tom

Train: *Riding the Rails That Created the Modern World - from the Trans-siberian to the Southwest Chief.* Tom Zoellner. Viking Adult 2014. 384 pages

ISBN 9780670025282

Grades: Adult   385.09

1. Trains 2. Railroad travel 3. Public transportation 4. Railroads 5. History writing — Microhistory 6. Travel Writing — Modes of Transportation — by Train

LC 2013036816

Do you love trains or wonder what the world would be like without them? Then climb on board the Train express! Combining fascinating social history and a sparkling travelogue, author (and train buff) Tom Zoellner engagingly chronicles the innovation and sociological impact of railway technologies that have changed and continue to change the world. Lucky him, he also travels to such far-flung locales as India, Britain, Russia, China, Peru, Spain, and the United States, soaking up local culture and riding an assortment of trains, from old stalwarts to modern bullet trains.

"An absorbing and lively reflection on an enduring marvel of modern industrial technology." —*Booklist*

Includes bibliographical references and index.

385.0973 Railroad transportation — United States

Hiltzik, Michael A.

Iron *Empires: Robber Barons, Railroads, and the Making of Modern America.* Michael Hiltzik. Houghton Mifflin Harcourt 2020. 416 p.

ISBN 9780544770317

Grades: Adult   385.0973

1. Big business 2. Capitalists and financiers 3. Industrialists 4. Railroads 5. Economics 6. United States history 7. United States 8. Gilded Age (1865-1898) 9. 19th century 10. 20th century 11. History writing — Gilded Age — United States 12. Business and economics — Industries — Transportation

LC 2019033911

From Pulitzer Prize-winner Michael Hiltzik, the epic tale of the clash for supremacy between America's railroad titans.

ESSENTIAL AND RECOMMENDED TITLES
387.2 Ships

"Pulitzer Prize-winning Los Angeles Times journalist Hiltzik chronicles the men who controlled the colossal railroad organizations that transformed the United States during the 19th century.... Lively storytelling and accessible writing makes Hiltzik's work suitable for all types of readers interested in railroad history." —*Library Journal*

Includes bibliographical references and index.

387.2 Ships

Graham, Ian
Fifty Ships That Changed the Course of History: A Nautical History of the World. Ian Graham. Firefly Books 2016. 224 pages : Illustration; Color
ISBN 9781770857193
Grades: Adult   387.2
1. Ships 2. Navigation 3. History writing — Exploration
LC Bl2018012054

Looks at fifty ships that have influenced human civilization and world history from ancient times to the present, covering such famous vessels as the Amistad, the Mayflower, the Bismarck, and the HMS Beagle.

"Well researched and illustrated, this 'Reference-y' title will be a good addition to any collection covering seafaring and transport." —*Booklist*

Includes bibliographical references (pages 218-219) and index.

387.243 Passenger ships — Power-driven

Henry, John
Great White Fleet: Celebrating Canada Steamship Lines Passenger Ships. by John Henry; foreword by Paul Martin. Dundurn Press 2013. 142 p. : Illustration; Color; Map
ISBN 9781459710467
Grades: Adult   387.243
1. Passenger ships 2. Steamboats 3. Voyages and travels 4. North Atlantic Region 5. North Atlantic Ocean 6. 20th century 7. Canadian literature 8. History writing — Canada

The history of the passenger steamers of Canada Steamship Lines. Known as the Great White Fleet, Canada Steamship Lines operated 51 passenger steamers from 1913-1965 that plied the waterways from the Great Lakes to the St. Lawrence Seaway.

Includes bibliographical references (p. [136]-138) and index.

387.5 Ocean transportation (Marine transportation)

Ujifusa, Steven
Barons of the Sea: And Their Race to Build the World's Fastest Clipper Ship. Steven Ujifusa. Simon & Schuster 2018. 448 p.
ISBN 9781476745978
Grades: Adult   387.5
1. Clipper-ships 2. Shipping industry and trade 3. Shipping 4. Ships 5. Ocean travel 6. Import export business 7. Trading companies 8. Business competition 9. International trade 10. Tea industry and trade 11. Opium industry and trade 12. Shipbuilders 13. Design and construction 14. United States 15. 19th century 16. Business and economics — Industries — Transportation 17. Nonfiction that reads like fiction
LC 2017037340

Describes the competition between merchants who imported luxury goods from China during the 1800s and their cutthroat race to build the best, fastest and most profitable clipper ships to promote their genteel, but sordid business.

"A vivid account of larger-than-life if not always attractive characters and a technological marvel that briefly captivated the Victorian world." —*Kirkus*

Includes bibliographical references and index.

387.7 Air transportation

Cooke, Julia
Come Fly the World: The Jet-age Story of the Women of Pan Am. Julia Cooke. Houghton Mifflin Harcourt 2021. 352 p.
ISBN 9780358251408
Grades: Adult   387.7
1. Flight attendants 2. Gender role in the work environment 3. Airlines 4. Commercial aviation 5. 1960s 6. 1970s 7. Collective biographies 8. Life stories — Identity — Gender 9. Business and economics — Industries — Transportation 10. Society and culture — Gender — Women
LC 2020034163

A lively, unexpected portrait of the jet-age stewardesses serving on iconic Pan Am airways between 1966 and 1975.

"A breezy account of Pan American World Airways in its glory days is smoothly interwoven with the engagingly complex stories of several longtime flight attendants." —*Kirkus*

Includes bibliographical references and index.

Holmes, Richard
Falling Upwards: How We Took to the Air. Richard Holmes. Pantheon Books 2013. 400 p.
ISBN 9780307379665
Grades: Adult   387.7
1. Balloonists 2. Ballooning 3. Balloons (Aeronautics) 4. Aviation history 5. Science Writing — Space and Flight
LC 2013011128

Documents the experiences of the enigmatic pioneers of human flight including Sophie Blanchard, John Wise and Felix Nadar to offer insight into the character qualities that inspired their ambitions and the ways in which their achievements have shaped culture, technology and meteorology. By the award-winning author of the Age of Wonder.

Includes bibliographical references and index.

388 Transportation

McPhee, John
Uncommon Carriers. John McPhee. Farrar, Straus, and Giroux 2006. 248 p.
ISBN 9780374280390
Grades: 11 12 Adult   388
1. Freight and freightage 2. Transportation 3. Trucking industry and trade 4. Trains 5. Tankers 6. Barges 7. Cargo handling 8. Freighters 9. Travel writing — Modes of transportation — Boating 10. Adult books for young adults 11. Business and economics — Industries — Transportation
LC 2006007953

New York Times Notable Book, 2006.

A staff writer for the New Yorker recounts his experiences with the freight transportation workers he has encountered during rides between Atlanta and Tacoma, from an eighteen-wheel hazmat tank operator to the skipper of a twenty-foot scale model of an ocean liner.

"The author sums up eight years of riding around with people who haul freight in vehicles ranging from 18-wheelers to towboats." —*Library Journal*

Also published in large print format.

Standage, Tom
A Brief History of Motion: From the Wheel, to the Car, to What Comes Next. Tom Standage. Bloomsbury Publishing 2021. 256 p.
ISBN 9781635573619
Grades: Adult   388
1. Transportation 2. Wheels 3. Automobiles 4. Railroads 5. Bicycles 6. Traffic congestion 7. Traffic accidents 8. Transportation, Automotive 9. Engineering 10. Transportation forecasting 11. Environmentalism 12. History writing — Technological innovations 13. History writing — Science, technology, and medicine 14. Science Writing — Great Engineering Feats

PUBLIC LIBRARY CORE COLLECTION: NONFICTION
Twentieth Edition

Beginning around 3,500 BCE with the wheel—a device that didn't catch on until a couple thousand years after its invention—Standage zips through the eras of horsepower, trains, and bicycles, revealing how each successive mode of transit embedded itself in the world we live in, from the geography of our cities to our experience of time to our notions of gender. Then, delving into the history of the automobile's development, Standage explores the social resistance to cars and the upheaval that their widespread adoption required. Today—after the explosive growth of ride-sharing and years of breathless predictions about autonomous vehicles—the social transformations spurred by coronavirus and overshadowed by climate change create a unique opportunity to critically reexamine our relationship to the car.

"Journalist Standage (Writing on the Wall) delivers a brisk and entertaining history of personal transportation.... Full of easy-to-understand history lessons and technical explanations, this is a well-informed look at how innovation, when properly guided, can pave the way to a brighter future." —*Publishers Weekly*

Includes bibliographical references and index.

388.09 Transportation — History, geographic treatment, biography

Humes, Edward

Door to Door: The Magnificent, Maddening, Mysterious World of Transportation. Edward Humes. Harper 2016. 384 p.

ISBN 9780062372079

Grades: Adult   388.09

1. Transportation 2. Infrastructure 3. Business and economics — Industries — Transportation

LC 2015037315

A Pulitzer Prize-winning journalist discusses the truths and challenges behind our modern world of transportation, describes the car culture that built modern America and predicts a coming revolution that stands to change every aspect of our lives.

"This timely book will inspire many readers to change their habits and their views of the future." —*Booklist*

Includes bibliographical references.

388.1 Roads

Kimble, Megan

★ *City Limits: Infrastructure, Inequality, and the Future of America's Highways.* Megan Kimble. Crown 2024. 352 p.

ISBN 9780593443781

Grades: Adult   388.1

1. Freeways 2. Urban planning 3. Cities and towns 4. City life 5. Pollution 6. Social history 7. Urban sprawl 8. Social advocacy 9. Urban transportation 10. Grassroots movement 11. Roads 12. Segregation 13. Society and culture — Urban and regional studies

LC 2023034296

Using ground-level reporting, an investigative reporter exposes how powerful groups are undermining urban communities in the quest to build more highways that take away homes and exacerbate existing patterns of segregation and sprawl.

"By seamlessly combining an expansive history of urban anti-highway organizing with an intriguing up-close look at present-day Texas politics, Kimble delivers an invigorating window onto American grassroots activism." —*Publishers Weekly*

Includes bibliographical references and index.

Mask, Deirdre

*The **Address** Book: What Street Addresses Reveal About Identity, Race, Wealth, and Power.* Deirdre Mask. St. Martin's Press 2020. 320 p.

ISBN 9781250134769

Grades: Adult   388.1

1. Urban planning 2. Street names 3. Social classes 4. Inequality 5. United States 6. Society and culture — Urban and regional studies

LC 2019048694

Finalist for the Hurston/Wright Legacy Awards for Nonfiction, 2021; Kirkus Prize for Nonfiction finalist, 2020.

Tells the story of how streets got their names and houses their numbers, and why something as seemingly mundane as an address can save lives or enforce power.

"An impressive book-length answer to a question few of us consider: 'Why do street addresses matter? . . . combines deep research with skillfully written, memorable anecdotes to illuminate the vast influence of street addresses as well as the negative consequences of not having a fixed address . . . A standout book of sociological history and current affairs." —*Kirkus*

Includes bibliographical references and index.

388.4 Local transportation

Lashinsky, Adam

Wild Ride: Inside Uber's Quest for World Domination. Adam Lashinsky. Portfolio 2017. 288 p.

ISBN 9780735211391

Grades: Adult   388.4

1. Ridesharing 2. Entrepreneurship 3. Computer industry and trade 4. High technology 5. Technological innovations 6. Business innovations 7. Business 8. Business and economics — Industries — Technology 9. Business and economics — Industries — Transportation

LC 2017006832

Describes the history of Uber and the startup's rapid growth, including its contributions to on-demand economy and the mobile revolution while also fighting politicians and tax companies all around the world and the company's expansion into vastly different industries.

388.474 Parking facilities

Grabar, Henry

Paved Paradise: How Parking Explains the World. Henry Grabar. Penguin Group USA 2023. 384 p.

ISBN 9781984881137

Grades: Adult   388.474

1. Automobile parking 2. Parking lots 3. Transportation, Automotive 4. Urban transportation 5. Infrastructure 6. Society and culture — Urban and regional studies 7. Politics and global affairs — Environmental issues and policies

We do ridiculous things for parking, contorting our professional, social, and financial lives to get a spot. Since the advent of the car, we have deformed—and in some cases demolished—our homes and our cities in a Sisyphean quest for cheap and convenient car storage. As a result, much of the nation's most valuable real estate is now devoted exclusively to empty and idle vehicles, even as many Americans struggle to find affordable housing. Can this really be the best use of our finite resources and space? Why have we done this to the places we love? Is parking really more important than anything else?

"Grabar, the urban affairs columnist at Slate, traveled to various cities and conducted interviews to investigate why parking spaces are so important to Americans....Grabar offers an intriguing, wide-ranging, readable perspective of the urban American parking scene, its issues, and possible future." —*Library Journal*

390 Customs, etiquette, folklore

Jenkins, Jessica Kerwin

All the Time in the World: A Book of Hours. Jessica Kerwin Jenkins. Nan A. Talese/Doubleday 2013. 303 p. : Illustration

ISBN 9780385535410

Grades: Adult   390

ESSENTIAL AND RECOMMENDED TITLES
390.09 Customs, etiquette & folklore — History, geographic treatment, biography

1. Social life and customs 2. Time 3. Literary curiosities 4. Life 5. Arts and Entertainment — General
LC 2013000795

A follow-up to Encyclopedia of the Exquisite presents a miscellany of engaging stories about intriguing customs, traditions and guilty pleasures pursued throughout history, from the day-long ceremony of laying a royal Elizabethan tablecloth to Nostradamus's beliefs about the aphrodisiac power of jam.

Includes bibliographical references (pages 267-303).

Narayan, Shoba
The Milk Lady of Bangalore: An Unexpected Adventure. by Shoba Narayan. Algonquin Books of Chapel Hill 2018. 224 p.
ISBN 9781616206154
Grades: Adult **390**

1. Narayan, Shoba 2. Community life 3. Cows 4. Milk 5. Women cookbook authors 6. Female friendship 7. Cooks 8. Social life and customs 9. India 10. Autobiographies and memoirs 11. Life stories — Identity 12. Food writing — Food and culture
LC 2017023398

A writer and cookbook author describes her return to Bangalore and how she bonded with the local milk lady, offered to buy her a new cow and gained a new perspective on the spiritual and historical role the animal plays in India.

"An absolute joy to read. Through her close encounters with the bovine kind, Narayan shows how Indian traditions are incorporated into contemporary ways of life." —*Library Journal*

390.09 Customs, etiquette & folklore — History, geographic treatment, biography

Sagan, Sasha
For Small Creatures Such as We: Rituals for Finding Meaning in Our Unlikely World. Sasha Sagan. G. P. Putnam's Sons 2019. 304 p.
ISBN 9780735218772
Grades: Adult **390.09**

1. Sagan, Sasha (Alexandra Rachel Druyan) 2. Rites and ceremonies 3. Spirituality 4. Nature 5. Secularism 6. Celebrations 7. Science 8. Family relationships 9. Children of celebrities 10. Science Writing — General 11. Spirituality and Religion — General 12. Life stories — Religion and spirituality — Personal faith
LC 2019021246

The daughter of astronomer Carl Sagan and writer Ann Druyan describes how motherhood inspired her investigations into the phenomena behind treasured human milestones to provide her daughter with a secular appreciation of the natural world.

391 Customs

Bari, Shahidha K.
Dressed: A Philosophy of Clothes. Shahidha Bari. Vintage Arrow 2022. 330 p.
ISBN 9781541645981
Grades: Adult **391**

1. Fashion 2. Costume 3. Philosophy 4. Clothing 5. Identity 6. Arts and Entertainment — Fashion 7. History writing — Arts and culture
LC 2019033789

We all get dressed. But how often do we pause to think about the place of our clothes in our world? What unconscious thoughts do we express when we dress every day? Dressed ranges freely from suits to suitcases, from Marx's coat to Madame X's gown. Through art and literature, film and philosophy, philosopher Shahidha Bari unveils the surprising personal implications of what we choose to wear. The impeccable cut of Cary Grant's suit projects masculine confidence, just as Madonna's oversized denim jacket and her armful of orange bangles loudly announces big ambition. How others dress tells us something fundamental about them—we can better understand how people live and what they think through their garments. Clothes tell our stories.

"Devoted fashion students will eagerly eat up every word of Bari's well-researched and passionate work." —*Publishers Weekly*

Includes bibliographical references and index; Originally published: London : Jonathan Cape, 2019.

DeJean, Joan E.
The Essence of Style: How the French Invented High Fashion, Fine Food, Chic Cafes, Style, Sophistication, and Glamour. Joan DeJean. Free Press 2005. 303 p. : Illustration
ISBN 9780743264136
Grades: 11 12 Adult **391**

1. Louis XIV, King of France, 1638-1715 2. Fashion 3. Cooking, French 4. Haute cuisine 5. Social life and customs 6. France 7. 17th century 8. History writing — Europe — France 9. Adult books for young adults
LC 2005040019

An exploration of how French culture during the reign of Louis XIV has had an enduring influence on modern traditions and style cites the French origins of haute cuisine, interior design, and the consumption of celebratory champagne.

"An unusual and delightfully educational perspective on snob appeal." —*Booklist*

Includes bibliographical references (p. 277-286) and index.

Edwards, Lydia
How to Read a Dress: A Guide to Changing Fashion from the 16th to the 20th Century. Lydia Edwards. Bloomsbury Academic 2017. 211 pages : Color; Illustration
ISBN 9781472533272
Grades: Adult **391**

1. Women's clothing 2. Fashion 3. Arts and Entertainment — Fashion 4. History writing — General
LC 2016029748

Fashion is ever-changing, and while some styles mark a dramatic departure from the past, many exhibit subtle differences from year to year that are not always easily identifiable. With overviews of each key period and detailed illustrations for each new style, How to Read a Dress is an authoritative visual guide to women's fashion across five centuries.

"Although the intended audience is fashion students, anyone interested in history or women's fashion will enjoy this volume." —*Booklist*

Includes bibliographical references and index.

Ford, Tanisha C.
Dressed in Dreams: A Black Girl's Love Letter to the Power of Fashion. Tanisha C. Ford. St. Martin's Press 2019. 304 p.
ISBN 9781250173539
Grades: Adult **391**

1. Ford, Tanisha C. 2. Clothing 3. Fashion 4. African American women 5. Growing up 6. Cultural appropriation 7. African-American history 8. African American college teachers 9. African Americans 10. Identity 11. Race relations 12. United States 13. Autobiographies and memoirs 14. Arts and Entertainment — Fashion 15. Adult books for young adults
LC 2019001794

The history of Black American fashion is discussed, including the author's own story of growing up in the Midwest while trying to find her own personal style, and how Black fashion has been appropriated by the mainstream America.

"A winning look at Black girl fashion and a solid addition for all collections." —*Library Journal*

Thanhauser, Sofi
Worn: A People's History of Clothing. Sofi Thanhauser. Pantheon Books 2022. 304 p.
ISBN 9781524748395
Grades: Adult **391**

1. Clothing 2. Fashion 3. Effect of humans on nature 4. Textile fabrics 5. History writing — Arts and culture 6. Arts and Entertainment — Fashion
LC 2021014453

Telling five stories—of linen, cotton, silk, synthetics and wool—this sweeping, engaging social history, drawn from years of intensive research and reporting from around the world, discusses the clothes we wear and where they come from, illuminating our world in unexpected ways.

"Thanhauser, an artist who teaches writing at the Pratt Institute, debuts with a captivating and deeply researched study of the five main fabrics from which clothing is made: Linen, cotton, silk, synthetics, and wool. . . . Thanhauser unearths the secret life of fabrics with skill and precision." —*Publishers Weekly*

Includes bibliographical references and index.

391.009 History, geographic treatment, biography

Cox, Caroline
The World Atlas of Street Fashion. Caroline Cox. Yale University Press 2017. 399 pages : Illustration; Color
ISBN 9780300224030
Grades: Adult   **391.009**
1. Fashion history 2. Street life 3. Subcultures 4. Fashion photography 5. Street photography 6. Clothing 7. 21st century 8. 20th century 9. Arts and Entertainment — Photography
LC Bl2018004000

A global tour of street fashion, organized by continent, shows the history of each look and how it has developed over time.
Includes index.

Leventon, Melissa
What People Wore When: A Complete Illustrated History of Costume from Ancient Times to the Nineteenth Century for Every Level of Society. Melissa Leventon. St. Martin's Griffin 2008. 352 p. : Illustration; Color
ISBN 9780312383213
Grades: 11 12 Adult   **391.009**
1. Clothing 2. Arts and Entertainment — Fashion
LC 2008012938

A history of costume and fashion spanning the civilizations of ancient Greece and Egypt through nineteenth-century Europe, including the clothing, footwear, accessories, and hairstyles of individuals from all levels of society.

"This attractive book will appeal to teens looking for quick answers for a last-minute assignment, and it will also be of interest to budding fashionistas and social historians. Leventon has combined current research on costume and dress through the ages with the detailed beauty of the work of two 19th-century illustrators, Auguste Racinet and Friedrich Hottenroth, to provide a historical and thematic examination of fashion and dress that is both comprehensive and readable." —*School Library Journal*

Includes bibliographical references (p. 346-347) and index.

391.4 Kinds of garments; accessories; buttons

Crowe, Lauren Goldstein
The Towering World of Jimmy Choo: A Glamorous Story of Power, Profits and the Pursuit of the Perfect Shoe. Lauren Goldstein Crowe and Sagra Maceira de Rosen. Bloomsbury USA 2009. 240 p.
ISBN 9781596913912
Grades: Adult   **391.4**
1. Choo, Jimmy, 1961- 2. Mellon, Tamara, 1967- 3. Women's shoes 4. Fashion design 5. Fashion 6. Luxury 7. Social life and customs 8. London, England 9. 1990s 10. 20th century 11. Biographies 12. Business and economics — Business leaders and entrepreneurs 13. Arts and Entertainment — Fashion 14. Life stories — Arts and culture — Fashion
LC 2008044378

Traces the rise of a London society girl to the head of one of the world's most famous shoe brands, describing how Tamara Yeardye convinced shoemaker Jimmy Choo to launch a factory-produced luxury footwear line and overcame daunting challenges at every stage.
Includes index.

391.5 Hairstyles

Dabiri, Emma
Twisted: The Tangled History of Black Hair Culture. Emma Dabiri. Harper Perennial 2020. 259 pages : Illustration
ISBN 9780062966728
Grades: Adult   **391.5**
1. Identity 2. Feminism 3. Racism 4. Discrimination 5. Women 6. Hairstyles 7. Personal space 8. Personal conduct 9. Social history 10. Society and culture — Race 11. Life stories — Identity — Race and ethnicity

Describes the stigmatism of Black hair and its encoded racism through history, from pre-colonial Africa through the Harlem Renaissance, to the modern Natural Hair Movement.

"Part memoir, part social history, and sure to become the definitive book on the politics, culture, and economics of Black hair." —*Kirkus*

Includes bibliographical references (pages 245-255); Originally published in Great Britain with the title Don't Touch My Hair : Penguin Books, 2019.

391.6 Personal appearance

Aitken-Smith, Trent
The Tattoo Dictionary: An A-z Guide to Choosing Your Tattoo. Trent Aitken-Smith; illustrated by Ashley Tyson. Mitchell Beazley 2016. 255 p. : Illustration
ISBN 9781784721770
Grades: Adult   **391.6**
1. Tattooing 2. Arts and Entertainment — General 3. History writing — Arts and culture
LC Bl2017046237

A book that includes over one hundred tattoo designs explains the true meanings behind them, from sailors' swallows and Mexican skulls to prisoners' barbed wire and intricate Maori patterns.
Includes index.

Hankir, Zahra
Eyeliner: A Cultural History. Zahra Hankir. Penguin Group USA 2023. 272 p.
ISBN 9780143137092
Grades: Adult   **391.6**
1. Cosmetics 2. Feminine beauty (Aesthetics) 3. Individuality 4. Social history 5. Cosmetics industry and trade 6. Beauty care 7. Beauty products 8. Society and culture — General

From the distant past to the present, with fingers and felt-tipped pens, metallic powders and gel pots, humans have been drawn to lining their eyes. The aesthetic trademark of figures ranging from Nefertiti to Amy Winehouse, eyeliner is one of our most enduring cosmetic tools; ancient royals and Gen Z beauty influencers alike would attest to its uniquely transformative power. It is undeniably fun—yet it is also far from frivolous.

"This captivating account reveals the complex significance of a seemingly simple adornment." —*Publishers Weekly*

392 Customs of life cycle and domestic life

Feiler, Bruce
Life Is in the Transitions: Mastering Transitions in a Nonlinear Age. Bruce Feiler. Penguin Press 2020. 352 p.
ISBN 9781594206825
Grades: Adult   **392**
1. Personal conduct 2. Life change events 3. Change (Psychology) 4. Human life cycle 5. Society and culture — Psychology and human behavior
LC 2019044488

The best-selling author of Council of Dads presents a pioneering study of the disruptions that are upending contemporary life, outlining bold recommenda-

ESSENTIAL AND RECOMMENDED TITLES
392.5 Wedding and marriage customs

tions for how to manage today's incremental transitions with more meaning, balance and satisfaction.

"All this advice is laid out in logical, sequential chapters, and occasional graphs and checklists bolster Feiler's reasoning. His relaxed, informal style is reassuring, and the numerous anecdotes gleaned from his wide variety of interview subjects keep the narrative fresh. His encouraging counsel will appeal to many." —*Booklist*

Includes bibliographical references and index.

392.5 Wedding and marriage customs

Monger, George
Marriage Customs of the World: An Encyclopedia of Dating Customs and Wedding Traditions. George P. Monger. ABC-CLIO 2013. 2 v. (xxxiii, 743 p.) : Illustration
ISBN 9781598846638
Grades: Adult   392.5
1. Marriage customs and rites 2. Dating 3. Mate selection 4. Encyclopedias 5. Reference — Encyclopedias 6. Society and culture — General 7. Reference — Weddings
                             LC 2012031375

This book presents a comprehensive overview of global courtship and marriage customs, from ancient history to contemporary society, demonstrating the vast differences as well as the similarities across all of human culture.

"As little is published on this subject, this set would be a good addition to public and academic libraries." —*Booklist*

Includes bibliographical references and index.

393 Death customs

Doughty, Caitlin
From Here to Eternity: Traveling the World to Find the Good Death. Caitlin Doughty. W. W. Norton & Company 2017. 224 p.
ISBN 9780393249897
Grades: Adult   393
1. Doughty, Caitlin 2. Death 3. Mourning customs 4. Burial 5. Funerals 6. Rites and ceremonies 7. Mortality 8. Death education 9. Society and culture — General 10. Travel Writing — General 11. Adult books for young adults
                             LC 2017025059

LibraryReads Favorites, 2017.

Describes death customs and rituals from around the world, exploring how they compare to the impersonal American system and how mourners respond best when they participate in caring for the deceased.

"These observances demonstrate how to diminish the stigma associated with death, burial, and eternal remembrance. Death gets the last word in this affably written, meticulously researched study of funerary customs." —*Kirkus*

Herring, Lucinda
Reimagining Death: Stories and Practical Wisdom for Home Funerals and Green Burials. Lucinda Herring; foreword by David Spangler. North Atlantic Books 2019. xix, 272 p.
ISBN 9781623172923
Grades: Adult   393
1. Burial 2. Environmental responsibility 3. United States 4. Self-Help — Mental health — Grief and loss 5. Self-Help — Personal growth 6. Family and Relationships — Aging and Death
                             LC 2018031617

For all those seeking to reclaim their innate and legal right to care for their own dead, create home funeral vigils, and choose greener after-death care options that are less toxic and more sustainable for the earth More natural after-death care options are transforming the paradigm of the existing funeral industry, helping families and communities recover their instinctive capacity to care for a loved one after death and do so in creative, nourishing, and healing ways. In reclaiming these practices and creating new, innovative options, we are greening the gateway of death and returning home to ourselves, our bodies, and the earth. Lucinda Herring reminds us of the sacredness of death itself; her compelling stories, poetry, and guidance come from years of experience as a home funeral/Green burial consultant and licensed funeral director dedicated to more natural and healing death practices. In Reimagining Death she shares with readers her experience caring for her own mother after death. Through storytelling and resources Herring also reveals to families the gifts of partnering with nature, home funeral vigils, sacred care at death, conscious dying (through the story of a Death with Dignity with accompanying photos of one man's planned death and after-death care), bringing laughter and a greater lightness of being to death, natural burials, and emerging eco-conscious dispositions. A valuable resource in planning for all deaths in all circumstances (with a chapter on what to do when a death occurs outside of the home), this book also guides readers on how to create an advance after-death care directive.

For all those seeking to reclaim their innate and legal right to care for their own dead, create home funeral vigils, and choose greener after-death care options that are less toxic and more sustainable for the earth.

Pringle, Heather Anne
The Mummy Congress: Science, Obsession, and the Everlasting Dead. Heather Pringle. Hyperion 2001. 368 p.
ISBN 9780786865512
Grades: 11 12 Adult   393
1. Mummies 2. Human remains (Archaeology) 3. Forensic anthropology 4. Physical anthropology 5. Human body 6. History writing — Archaeology 7. Adult books for young adults
                             LC 00054487

Booklist Editors' Choice, 2001.

A study of the mysteries of mummies explores the world of the scientists who devote their own lives to the study of them and examines how mummies have been used, venerated, worshiped, collected, and studied over the course of nearly seven thousand years of history.

"More astounding than all the fright flicks about shambling, gauze-wrapped menaces wound together." —*Booklist*

Includes bibliographical references (p. [343]-352) and index.

394 General customs

Schutt, Bill
Cannibalism: A Perfectly Natural History. by Bill Schutt. Algonquin Books 2017. 329 pages
ISBN 9781616204624
Grades: Adult   394
1. Cannibalism 2. Animal behavior 3. Human behavior 4. Taboo 5. Animal food habits 6. Sociocultural anthropology 7. Science Writing — Biology 8. Society and culture — Psychology and human behavior 9. Nature Writing — Animal Studies 10. History writing — Microhistory 11. Adult books for young adults
                             LC 2016023112

Eating one's own kind is completely natural behavior in thousands of species, including humans. Throughout history we have engaged in cannibalism for reasons of famine, burial rites, and medicinal remedies. With unexpected wit and a wealth of knowledge, biologist Bill Schutt takes us on a tour of the field, dissecting exciting new research on the topic.

"With plenty of examples of cannibalism in humans past and present, Schutt's well researched and suspenseful work is a must read for anyone who's interested in the topic—and can stomach the gore." —*Publishers Weekly*

Published simultaneously in Canada by Thomas Allen & Son Limited.

Visser, Margaret
The Gift of Thanks: The Roots, Persistence, and Paradoxical Meanings of a Social Ritual. Margaret Visser. Houghton Mifflin Harcourt 2009. 458 p.
ISBN 9780151013319
Grades: Adult   394
1. Gratitude 2. Thank-you notes 3. Generosity 4. Attitude 5. Society and culture — Psychology and human behavior

PUBLIC LIBRARY CORE COLLECTION: NONFICTION
Twentieth Edition

LC 2009014018

This inquiry into all aspects of gratitude ranges from the unusual determination with which parents teach their children to thank, to the difference between speaking the words and feeling them, to the ways different cultures handle the complex matters of giving, receiving, and returning favors and presents. It also illuminates the modern battle of social scientists to pin down the notion of thankfulness and discover its biological and evolutionary roots.

Includes bibliographical references and index; Originally published: Toronto : HarperCollins, 2008.

394.1 Eating, drinking; using drugs

Anthony, Jason C.
Hoosh: Roast Penguin, Scurvy Day, and Other Stories of Antarctic Cuisine. Jason C. Anthony. University of Nebraska Press 2012. 286 p.
ISBN 9780803226661
Grades: Adult 394.1
1. Food habits 2. Outdoor cooking 3. Antarctica history 4. Antarctica 5. Food Writing — Food and Culture

LC 2012011994

"A singular, engrossing take on a region that until now has been mostly documented from a scientific angle or romanticized by adventurers." —*Kirkus*
Includes bibliographical references.

Bittman, Mark
Animal, Vegetable, Junk: A History of Food, from Sustainable to Suicidal. Mark Bittman. Houghton Mifflin Harcourt 2021. 304 p.
ISBN 9781328974624
Grades: 9 10 11 12 Adult 394.1
1. Agricultural technology 2. Civilization 3. Agriculture 4. Agribusiness 5. Food habits 6. Environmentalism 7. United States 8. Business and economics — Industries — Agriculture and food 9. History writing — General

LC 2020034051

From hunting and gathering to GMOs and ultraprocessed foods, an expansive tour of human history rewrites the story of our species—and points the way to a better future.

"An expert's vigorous argument for systemic food reform." —*Kirkus*
Includes bibliographical references and index.

Cheever, Susan
Drinking in America: Our Secret History. Susan Cheever. Twelve 2015. 240 p.
ISBN 9781455513871
Grades: Adult 394.1
1. Drinking customs 2. National characteristics, American 3. Alcoholic beverages 4. Social drinking 5. United States history 6. United States 7. Food Writing — Food and Culture 8. History writing — United States

LC 2015025648

Presents an exploration of the history of drinking in the United States and its effects on the American character.

Includes bibliographical references and index.

Collingham, E. M.
Curry: A Tale of Cooks and Conquerors. Lizzie Collingham. Oxford University Press 2006. 352 p.
ISBN 9780195172416
Grades: Adult 394.1
1. Cooking, Indic 2. Cooking (Curry) 3. Food habits 4. Civilization 5. India 6. History writing — Arts and culture 7. Food writing — History and microhistory 8. Food Writing — Food and Culture 9. History writing — Asia — South Asia — India

LC 2005016641

An authoritative history of the foods of India, complete with delicious recipes, ranges from the imperial kitchen of the Mughal invader Babur to the smoky cookhouse of the British Raj and includes information on the influence of various food traditions on the evolution of Indian specialties.

Includes bibliographical references and index.

Cowen, Tyler
An Economist Gets Lunch: New Rules for Everyday Foodies. Tyler Cowen. Dutton 2012. 304 p.
ISBN 9780525952664
Grades: Adult 394.1
1. Food habits 2. Food industry and trade 3. Economics 4. Food writing — General

LC 2011035174

An influential economist challenges popular opinions about the superiority of locally grown and expensive foods, demonstrating how to eat responsibly without submitting to fashion-driven trends.

Includes bibliographical references and index.

Downie, David
A Taste of Paris: A History of the Parisian Love Affair with Food. David Downie. St. Martin's Press 2017. 320 p.
ISBN 9781250082930
Grades: Adult 394.1
1. Food 2. Gastronomy 3. Cooking, French 4. Food habits 5. Voyages and travels 6. Paris, France 7. France 8. Essays 9. Food writing — Food and culture 10. Travel Writing — Europe

LC 2017018869

A critically acclaimed author, using his trademark wit and informative style, embarks on a quest to discover "What is it about the history of Paris that has made it a food lover's paradise?" by following the contours of history and geography of the city.

"Downie relishes in debunking myths about French culinary exceptionalism ... while unabashedly proclaiming his adoration for French culture and history in and out of the kitchen. Readers don't have to be foodies to get the flavor of the French character in this delightful, thoroughly researched culinary history." —*Publishers Weekly*

Goulding, Matt
Grape, Olive, Pig: Deep Travels Through Spain's Food Culture. by Matt Goulding; edited by Nathan Thornburgh; designed by Doulgas Hughmanick. Harper Wave 2016. xiii, 347 pages : Illustration; Color
ISBN 9780062394132
Grades: Adult 394.1
1. Food habits 2. Social life and customs 3. Cooking 4. Food 5. Voyages and travels 6. Spain 7. Food writing — Food and culture 8. Travel Writing — Europe

LC 2016018185

IACP Cookbook Awards, Literary Food Writing, 2017.

A celebration of the culture and cuisine of Spain contextualizes meals with the stories behind them, offering a tour of everything from Barcelona's tapas bars to the coastal Cadiz bluefin tuna hunts to the small-plate flavors of Madrid.

An Anthony Bourdain book.

Rice, Noodle, Fish: Deep Travels Through Japan's Food Culture. Matt Goulding; edited by Nathan Thornburgh. HarperWave 2015. 352 p. : Color; Illustration
ISBN 9780062394033
Grades: Adult 394.1
1. Goulding, Matt 2. Food tourism 3. Cooking, Japanese 4. Ramen 5. Sushi 6. Food habits 7. Voyages and travels 8. Japan 9. Food writing — Food and culture 10. Travel writing — Asia and the south pacific

LC 2015005013

A gastronomic tour of Japan by the founders of the political and culinary "Roads & Kingdoms" website combines detailed narrative, insider advice and practical information with lavish full-color photography celebrating the traditions of seven key regions.

ESSENTIAL AND RECOMMENDED TITLES
394.1 Eating, drinking; using drugs

Henaut, Stephane
*A **Bite-sized** History of France: Gastronomic Tales of Revolution, War, and Enlightenment.* Stéphane Henaut and Jeni Mitchell. New Press 2018. 256 p.
ISBN 9781620972519
Grades: Adult   394.1
1. Gastronomy 2. Food 3. Food habits 4. Dinners and dining 5. Cooking, French 6. Social history 7. Cooking 8. Social life and customs 9. France 10. Food writing — Food and culture 11. Food writing — History and microhistory 12. History writing — Europe — France
LC 2018001242

Describes the history of France through a gastronomic lens, discussing the country's legendary cuisine and wine, from Roquefort cheese to cognac and croissants along with the social and political trends that influenced its innovations and traditions.

"Henault and Mitchell are often witty (perhaps most amusingly illustrated by a chapter called War and Peas) even as they present their exceptionally well-researched material. This culinary history is a treat for Francophiles." —*Publishers Weekly*

Includes bibliographical references and index.

Kauffman, Jonathan
***Hippie** Food: How Back-to-the-landers, Longhairs, and Revolutionaries Changed the Way We Eat.* Jonathan Kauffman. William Morrow & Company 2018. 352 p.
ISBN 9780062437303
Grades: Adult   394.1
1. Food habits 2. Counterculture 3. Diet 4. Natural foods 5. Sustainable agriculture 6. Food supply 7. Health food industry and trade 8. Cooking (Natural foods) 9. Cooking, American 10. Impartial writing 11. Food writing — History and microhistory
LC 2017278622

A narrative history of the alternative-foods movement of the past half century explores the diverse fringe trends, charismatic personalities and counterculture elements that have rendered quotidian wholefoods, from whole grain bread and tofu to yogurt and brown rice, part of the mainstream American diet.

"An astute, highly informative food expos that educates without bias, leaving the culinary decision-making to readers." —*Kirkus*

Pollan, Michael
*The **Omnivore's** Dilemma: A Natural History of Four Meals.* Michael Pollan. Penguin Press 2006. 450 p.
ISBN 9781594200823
Grades: Adult   394.1
1. Food habits 2. Corn 3. Natural foods 4. Food consumption 5. Omnivores 6. Food 7. Diet 8. Food writing — Investigations 9. Adult books for young adults
LC 2005056557

James Beard Foundation Book Awards, Writing and Literature, 2007; New York Times Notable Book, 2006; National Book Critics Circle Award for Nonfiction finalist, 2006.

Offers insight into food consumption in the twenty-first century, explaining how an abundance of unlimited food varieties reveals the responsibilities of consumers to protect their health and the environment.

"The author defines the Omnivore's Dilemma as the confusing maze of choices facing Americans trying to eat healthfully in a society that he calls notably unhealthy. He seeks answers to this dilemma by taking readers through the industrial, organic, and hunter-gatherer stages of the food chain. This folksy narrative provides a wealth of information about agriculture, the natural world, and human desires." —*Library Journal*

Includes bibliographical references (p. [417]-435) and index.

Standage, Tom
*An **Edible** History of Humanity.* Tom Standage. Walker & Company 2009. 288 p.
ISBN 9780802715883
Grades: Adult   394.1

1. Food habits 2. Food industry and trade 3. Agriculture 4. Food 5. Food Writing — Food and Culture 6. History writing — General 7. Adult books for young adults
LC 2009005610

A lighthearted chronicle of how foods have transformed human culture throughout the ages traces the barley- and wheat-driven early civilizations of the near East through the corn and potato industries in America, comparing the progress of farming cultures to those of hunter-gatherers while citing the pivotal contributions of global trade.

Includes bibliographical references and index.

*A **History** of the World in 6 Glasses.* Tom Standage. Walker & Co. 2005. 240 p.
ISBN 9780802714473
Grades: Adult   394.1
1. Beverages 2. Drinking 3. Tea 4. Coffee 5. Soft drinks 6. History writing — Microhistory 7. Food writing — History and microhistory 8. Food writing — Non-alcoholic beverages 9. Food writing — Beer, wine, and liquor
LC 2004061209

An offbeat history of the world traces the story of humankind from the Stone Age to the twenty-first century from the perspective of six different drinks—beer, wine, spirits, coffee, tea, and cola—describing their pervasive influence during pivotal eras of world history, from humankind's adoption of agriculture to the advent of globalization.

"Standage has the ability to connect the smallest detail to the big picture and a knack for summarizing vast concepts in a few sentences." —*Publishers Weekly*

Includes bibliographical references and index.

Terry, Bryant
***Black** Food: Stories, Art, and Essays.* Edited by Bryant Terry; photographs by Oriana Koren. Ten Speed Press 2021. 304 p.
ISBN 9781984859723
Grades: Adult   394.1
1. African Americans 2. Cooking, African American 3. Cooking 4. Food habits 5. United States 6. Food writing — Food and culture 7. History writing — African American — United States
LC 2021003655

A beautiful, rich, and groundbreaking book exploring Black foodways within America and around the world, curated by food activist and author of Vegetable Kingdom Bryant Terry.

A James Beard Award-winning chef, educator and author presents a joyful celebration of Black culture by interweaving food, experiences and community through poetry, essays and recipes including Crispy Cassava Skillet Cakes,, Meatballs with Egusi and Squash and Jerk Chicken Ramen.

"Whether read straight through or browsed section by section, this meaningful book brings Black foodways into focus and will leave a lasting impact." —*Library Journal*

Includes index.

Williams, Wyatt
***Springer** Mountain: Meditations on Killing and Eating.* Wyatt Williams. University of North Carolina Press 2021. 128 p.
ISBN 9781469665481
Grades: Adult   394.1
1. Meat 2. Vegetarianism 3. Animal welfare 4. Farm animal welfare 5. Animals 6. Violence 7. Hunting 8. Food writing — Food and culture 9. Society and culture — Violence and crime

Drawing on years of investigative reporting, Wyatt Williams offers a powerful look at why we kill and eat animals. In order to understand why we eat meat, the restaurant critic and journalist investigated factory farms, learned to hunt game, worked on a slaughterhouse kill floor, and partook in Indigenous traditions of whale eating in Alaska. In Springer Mountain, he tells about his experiences while charting the history of meat eating and vegetarianism.

"Similar to Michael Pollen's the Omnivore's Dilemma, this engaging narrative will catch readers' attention and lead them to take a deeper look at the where, how, and why behind the food they consume." —*Library Journal*

PUBLIC LIBRARY CORE COLLECTION: NONFICTION
Twentieth Edition

Wrangham, Richard W.
Catching Fire: How Cooking Made Us Human. Richard Wrangham. Basic Books 2009. 320 p.
ISBN 9780465013623
Grades: 11 12 Adult   394.1
1. Prehistoric humans 2. Cooking 3. Human evolution 4. Fire 5. Food habits 6. Social life and customs 7. Division of labor 8. Food values 9. Prehistoric era (Stone Age) 10. History writing — Ancient 11. Food writing — History and microhistory
LC 2009001742

Presents the theory that it was the introduction of cooking in the prehistoric past that led to physiological changes in the human brain and such advancements in human behavior as the development of social skills, bonding, and the division of labor in family groups.

"This is a plainspoken and thoroughly gripping scientific essay that presents nothing less than a new theory of human evolution.... [This book] contains serious science yet is related in direct, no-nonsense prose. It is toothsome, skillfully prepared brain food." —*New York Times*

Includes bibliographical references.

394.2646 Halloween

Morton, Lisa
Trick or Treat: A History of Halloween. Lisa Morton. Reaktion Books 2012. 229 p. : Illustration; Color
ISBN 9781780230474
Grades: Adult   394.2646
1. Halloween 2. Holidays 3. Trick or treat 4. Halloween candy 5. Halloween decorations 6. Halloween costumes 7. History writing — General
LC Bl2013007309

Bram Stoker Award for Best Nonfiction, 2012.

Every year, children and adults alike take to the streets dressed as witches, demons, animals, celebrities, and more. They carve pumpkins and play pranks, and the braver ones watch scary movies and go on ghost tours. There are parades, fireworks displays, cornfield mazes, and haunted houses and, most important, copious amounts of bite-sized candy. The popularity of Halloween has spread around the globe to places as diverse as Russia, China, and Japan, but its association with death and the supernatural and its inevitable commercialization has made it one of our most misunderstood holidays. How did it become what it is today?

394.2649 Thanksgiving

Baker, James W.
Thanksgiving: The Biography of an American Holiday. James W. Baker; foreword by Peter J. Gomes. University of New Hampshire Press; 2009. xii, 273 p. : Illustration
ISBN 9781584658016
Grades: 9 10 11 12 Adult   394.2649
1. Thanksgiving Day 2. Holidays 3. History writing — Microhistory
LC 2009012348

In this, the first in-depth study of the most American of holidays, James Baker sweeps away lingering myths and misconceptions to show how this celebration day was born and grew to be an essential part of our national spirit. Thanksgiving: The Biography of an American Holiday opens with an overview of the popular mythos of the holiday before discussing its possible religious and cultural precedents. This classic Yankee holiday is examined in historical and contemporary detail that embraces everything from proclamations, sermons, and local and regional traditions to family reunions, turkey dinners, and recipes. Thanksgiving's evolving face is illustrated with charming and often revealing period prints that chart our changing attitudes: the influence of Victorian sentiment in Thanksgiving's development, Progressive utilitarianism, intellectual "debunking," patriotic wartime reclamation, and 1960s-era protest. Thanksgiving remains controversial up to the present day, as Mayflower descendants, Native Americans, and commercial exploiters compete for the American public's opinion of the holiday's contemporary significance and its future status. This is an intelligent and illuminating introduction to a beloved holiday and a fascinating cultural history of America and Americana.

"This is destined to become the accepted text for research on the history and myth of this most American holiday, and it will be an enjoyable, fascinating read both for students and for anyone looking for a good story." —*Library Journal*

Includes bibliographical references and index.

Hillstrom, Laurie Collier
The **Thanksgiving** *Book: A Companion to the Holiday Covering Its History, Lore, Traditions, Foods, and Symbols, Including Primary Sources, Poems, Prayers, Songs, Hymns, and Recipes : Supplemented by a Chronology, Bibliography with Web Sites.* Laurie C. Hillstrom. Omnigraphics 2008. xi, 328 p. : Illustration
ISBN 9780780804036
Grades: Adult   394.2649
1. Thanksgiving Day 2. Society and culture — Sociology 3. Society and culture — General
LC 2007025708

Provides information about the history, lore, traditions, foods, and symbols of the Thanksgiving celebration. Features include narrative overviews and primary source documents, chronology, and resources for further information.

Includes bibliographical references (p. 309-316) and index.

394.2663 Christmas

Flanders, Judith
Christmas: A Biography. Judith Flanders. St Martin's Press 2017. 304 p.
ISBN 9781250118349
Grades: Adult   394.2663
1. Christmas 2. Holidays 3. Spirituality and Religion — Christianity 4. History writing — Microhistory 5. History writing — Arts and culture
LC 2017027330

The best-selling author of the Making of Home presents a tour of Christmas holiday traditions from the original festival through today, touching on subjects ranging from gift wrap and the holiday parade to the first gag holiday gift book and the first official appearance of Santa Claus.

"Christmas evokes both memories of the past and expectations for future celebrations, but Flanders posits that the holiday never was the quiet, thoughtful, religious observance we think it was. Separating fact from myth and traditional practice, Flanders provides a well-researched 'Biography' of how Christmas came to be observed through the ages and in various cultures." —*Booklist*

Forbes, Bruce David
Christmas: A Candid History. Bruce David Forbes. University of California Press 2007. xiv, 179 p. : Illustration; Color
ISBN 9780520251045
Grades: 9 10 11 12 Adult   394.2663
1. Christmas 2. Holidays 3. Spirituality and Religion — Christianity 4. History writing — Microhistory
LC 2007000366

Written for everyone who loves and is simultaneously driven crazy by the holiday season, Christmas: A Candid History provides an enlightening, entertaining perspective on how the annual Yuletide celebration got to be what it is today. In a fascinating, concise tour through history, the book tells the story of Christmas—from its pre-Christian roots, through the birth of Jesus, to the holiday's spread across Europe into the Americas and beyond, and to its mind-boggling transformation through modern consumerism. Packed with intriguing stories, based on research into myriad sources, full of insights, the book explores the historical origins of traditions including Santa, the reindeer, gift giving, the Christmas tree, Christmas songs and movies, and more. The book also offers some provocative ideas for reclaiming the joy and meaning of this beloved, yet often frustrating, season amid the pressures of our fast-paced consumer culture.

Includes bibliographical references (p. 163-170) and index.

ESSENTIAL AND RECOMMENDED TITLES
394.8 Dueling and suicide

Stibbe, Nina
An Almost Perfect Christmas. Nina Stibbe. Little, Brown and Co. 2018. 240 p.
ISBN 9780316415811
Grades: Adult 394.2663
1. Christmas cooking 2. Holidays 3. Family traditions 4. Family recipes 5. Christmas 6. Christmas presents 7. Food writing — Food and culture 8. Humor writing — Social humor
LC 2018944946

From perennially dry turkeys to Christmas pudding fires, from the round robin code of conduct to the risks and rewards of re-gifting, an Almost Perfect Christmas is an ode to the joy and insanity of the most wonderful time of the year.

"Funny, smart, sweet, and tender, this is greater than a gift book and readable any time of year." —*Booklist*

394.8 Dueling and suicide

Durkheim, Emile
★ *Suicide: A Study in Sociology:.* Translated by John A. Spaulding and George Simpson. Edited, with an introd, by George Simpson. Free Press 1951. 405 p. Map
ISBN 9780684836324
Grades: Adult 394.8
1. Suicide 2. Society and culture — Sociology
LC 51009585

Emile Durkheim's Suicide addresses the phenomenon of suicide and its social causes. Written by one of the world's most influential sociologists, this classic argues that suicide primarily results from a lack of integration of the individual into society. Suicide provides readers with an understanding of the impetus for suicide and its psychological impact on the victim, family, and society.

Bibliographical footnotes.

395 Etiquette (Manners)

Alkon, Amy
*Good Manners for Nice People: Who Sometimes Say F*ck.* Amy Alkon. St. Martin's Griffin 2014. x, 289 pages
ISBN 9781250030719
Grades: Adult 395
1. Courtesy 2. Etiquette 3. Social life and customs 4. United States 5. 21st century 6. Society and culture — General
LC 2014008115

Combining science with humor, this in-your-face modern guide to manners for regular people provides a new set of rules for our 21st century lives that show us how to avoid being rude and stand up to those who are.

Berman, Lea
Treating People Well: The Extraordinary Power of Civility at Work and in Life. Lea Berman and Jeremy Bernard. Simon & Schuster 2018. 256 p.
ISBN 9781501157981
Grades: Adult 395
1. Courtesy 2. Cooperation 3. Success in business 4. Social skills 5. Etiquette 6. Respect 7. Business etiquette 8. Business and economics — Business advice
LC 2017061756

Two former White House Social Secretaries draw on their experiences to convey the importance of treating everyone well regardless of differences, covering subjects ranging from how to make friends with strangers to overcoming the challenges of difficult colleagues.

"Berman and Bernard winningly call on their experiences as White House social secretaries under, respectively, George W. Bush and Barack Obama to make a case that manners and civility can be the basis for success in work and life." —*Publishers Weekly*

Dresser, Norine
Multicultural Manners: Essential Rules of Etiquette for the 21st Century. Norine Dresser. John Wiley & Sons 2005. xviii, 285 p. : Map
ISBN 9780471684282
Grades: Adult 395
1. Etiquette 2. Multiculturalism 3. United States 4. Language arts and studies — General 5. Reference — General
LC 2004027079

Reveals the dos and don'ts of international etiquette, covering body language, food, child rearing, clothing, colors, entertaining, weddings, funerals, and gift giving.

Includes bibliographical references (p. 259-269) and index.

Forni, Pier Massimo
The Civility Solution: What to Do When People Are Rude. P.M. Forni. St. Martin's Press 2008. xxi, 166 p.
ISBN 9780312368494
Grades: Adult 395
1. Courtesy 2. Etiquette 3. Reference — General
LC 2008009448

A founder of the Johns Hopkins Civility Project presents dozens of real-world examples and strategic advice on how to conduct oneself when confronted with the rude behavior of others, in a guide that makes recommendations for breaking rude cycles by being both polite and assertive.

Includes bibliographical references (p. [161]-166).

Post, Lizzie
Emily Post's Etiquette. Lizzie Post and Daniel Post Senning; illustrations by Eight Hour Day. 2022. 407 pages : Illustration
ISBN 9781984859396
Grades: Adult 395
1. Etiquette 2. Social life and customs 3. Personal conduct 4. Courtesy 5. Business etiquette 6. Online etiquette 7. Entertaining 8. Society and culture — General 9. Family and relationships — General 10. Reference — General
LC 2021042568

A completely revised and stylishly illustrated 20th edition-and centennial celebration-of the American classic, Emily Post's Etiquette, focused on the need-to-know etiquette of today.

For the past one hundred years, Emily Post has been America's definitive source for how to navigate—and enhance—every social interaction. This centennial edition has been updated for our increasingly diverse and intersectional world. Post and Senning—great-great grandchildren of Emily Post—continue the Post family legacy of upholding traditions while moving forward with the times. From table manners and gift-giving to video meetings, AI and home security, and tipping practices in the age of rideshares and payment screens, you'll move through your world with confidence and ease.

"Using common courtesy and concern for the well-being of others as basic tenets, this centenary offering from Emily Post's great-great grandchildren seeks to guid readers through digital age social minefields and conundrums." —*Booklist*

Includes index; Completely revised and updated — Spine.

Emily Post's Etiquette: Manners for Today. Lizzie Post, Daniel Post Senning; illustrations by Janice Richter. William Morrow & Company 2017. xi, 722 pages : Illustration
ISBN 9780062439253
Grades: Adult 395
1. Etiquette 2. Personal conduct 3. Social life and customs 4. Courtesy 5. Business etiquette 6. Online etiquette 7. Entertaining 8. Society and culture — General 9. Family and relationships — General

A revised and updated edition addresses such contemporary issues as social-media etiquette, email and texting and covering tattoos and piercings before interviews, as well as such classic conundrums as names and titles, official forms of address and dress codes.

PUBLIC LIBRARY CORE COLLECTION: NONFICTION
Twentieth Edition

395.2 Etiquette for stages in life cycle

Doty, Cate
Mergers and Acquisitions: Or, Everything I Know About Love I Learned on the Wedding Pages. Cate Doty. Putnam 2021. 400 p.
ISBN 9780593190449
Grades: Adult   **395.2**
1. Doty, Cate 2. Weddings 3. Women journalists 4. Marriage customs and rites 5. Marriage 6. Childhood 7. Journalists 8. Women 9. Men-women relations 10. United States 11. Autobiographies and memoirs 12. Life stories — Arts and culture — Writing — Journalists 13. Life stories — Relationships — Couples 14. Family and Relationships — Dating and Marriage 15. Arts and Entertainment — Writing and Publishing

A compulsively readable behind-the-scenes memoir that takes readers inside the weddings section of the New York Times—the good, bad, and just plain weird—through the eyes of a young reporter just as she's falling in love herself.

"Doty's love-filled memoir will delight readers hoping for an inside look at the wedding section, and fans of uplifting memoirs." —*Library Journal*

395.4 Social correspondence

Allert, Tilman
Heil Hitler: On the Meaning of a Gesture. Tilman Allert. Henry Holt and Company 2008. 128 p.
ISBN 9780312428303
Grades: 11 12 Adult   **395.4**
1. Salutations 2. Nazism 3. Rites and ceremonies 4. Third Reich, 1933-1945 5. History writing — Europe — Germany
LC 2007035667

Provides a critical look at the origins, history, and dissemination of the infamous Heil Hitler salute in Nazi Germany from its compulsory adoption in 1933, assessing its meaning in terms of a symbol of loyalty to the Nazi regime, as a means of vesting Hitler with a divine aura, and as a ritual of consent that paved the way for the erosion of social morality.

Translation of: Der deutsche Gruss; Published in paperback as The Hitler salute, 2009; Includes bibliographical references and index.

Scott, Andy
One Kiss or Two?: The Art and Science of Saying Hello. Andy Scott. Overlook Press 2018. 304 p.
ISBN 9781468316018
Grades: Adult   **395.4**
1. Social life and customs 2. Communication 3. Social psychology 4. Salutations 5. Multiculturalism 6. Body language 7. Human behavior 8. Social groups 9. Sociology 10. Anthropology 11. Society and culture — Psychology and human behavior
LC Bl2018037444

In an increasingly global and connected world, our ways of saying hello have become more confusing than ever. This book is essential reading for anyone traveling and working in the cross-cultural, modern age and global citizens determined to avoid social gaffes in important situations.

"Emphasizing the virtue of human connection throughout, Scotts buoyant study is reminiscent of the work of A.J. Jacobs in its breezy mix of pop sociology, personal anecdote, and self-help." —*Publishers Weekly*

395.5 Etiquette by situations

Blyth, Catherine
The Art of Conversation: A Guided Tour of a Neglected Pleasure. by Catherine Blyth. Gotham Books 2009. 289 p.
ISBN 9781592404193
Grades: Adult   **395.5**
1. Conversation 2. Oral communication 3. Interpersonal communication 4. Personal conduct 5. Interpersonal relations 6. Listening 7. Family and Relationships — General
LC 2008024276

Draws on examples from history, literature, and other disciplines to offer advice on how to rebuild conversational tools in order to make more qualitative connections with other people.

Schweitzer, Sharon
Access to Asia: Your Multicultural Guide to Building Trust, Inspiring Respect, and Creating Long-lasting Business Relationships. Sharon Schweitzer, J.D, Liz Alexander, Ph.D.. John Wiley & Sons, Inc. 2015. xxiv, 374 pages: Illustration
ISBN 9781118919019
Grades: Adult   **395.5**
1. Business etiquette 2. Corporate culture 3. Intercultural communication 4. Management 5. Asia 6. Business and economics — Business advice 7. Business and economics — Economics — World economy
LC 2014039933

"Beautifully constructed and expertly written in straightforward language; will make it far easier for anyone to navigate the cultural differences of doing business in Asia." —*Kirkus*

Includes bibliographical references (pages 343-350) and index.

Tower, Jeremiah
★ *Table Manners: How to Behave in the Modern World and Why Bother.* Jeremiah Tower; illustrations by Libby VanderPloeg. Farrar, Straus and Giroux 2016. 148 pages : Illustration
ISBN 9780374272340
Grades: Adult   **395.5**
1. Reference — General 2. Food writing — Cooking and cookbooks — Entertaining 3. Food writing — General
LC 2016007141

Funny and practical, a modern guide to table manners for all occasions by one of the world¡s most acclaimed chefs and restaurateurs tells readers how to behave, what to talk about, what to wear and how to eat, and serves up advice on everything from RSVPs, iPhones and running late to food allergies and what to do when you are served something disgusting.

Includes bibliographical references and index.

398.2 Folk literature

Bly, Robert
More Than True: The Wisdom of Fairy Tales. Robert Bly. Henry Holt and Company 2018. 192 p.
ISBN 9781250158192
Grades: Adult   **398.2**
1. Wisdom 2. Archetype (Psychology) 3. Personal conduct 4. Literary criticism 5. Fairy tale writing 6. Essays 7. Arts and Entertainment — Writing and Publishing 8. Arts and Entertainment — Writing and Publishing — Literary criticism
LC 2017024789

Bly looks at six tales that have stood the test of time and have captivated the poet for decades, from "The Six Swans" to "The Frog Prince." Drawing on his own creative genius, and the work of a range of thinkers from Kirkegaard and Yeats to Freud and Jung, Bly turns these stories over in his mind to bring new meaning and illumination to these timeless tales.

Includes bibliographical references and index.

Pullman, Philip
★ *Fairy Tales from the Brothers Grimm: A New English Version.* [edited by] Philip Pullman. Viking 2012. 400 p.
ISBN 9780670024971
Grades: Adult   **398.2**

ESSENTIAL AND RECOMMENDED TITLES
398.2093802 Persons (Individuals) — Folklore — Greece — Ancient

1. Parent and child 2. Stepmothers 3. Translations — German to English 4. Mythology, folklore, and legends 5. Adult books for young adults
LC 2012027181
Booklist Editors' Choice, 2012.

Presents mature and scholarly retellings of fifty favorite and lesser-known fairy tales on the two hundredth anniversary of the Grimm brothers' Children's and Household Tales, in a volume that includes such stories as Cinderella, Rapunzel, and Briar-Rose.

"Pullman's collection is noteworthy for the energetic pace of the stories and the subtle adaptations that make it accessible to modern readers. This is a collection for librarians and teachers to read aloud and to encourage listeners to imagine and retell in their own words." —*School Library Journal*

Includes bibliographical references.

Schonwerth, Franz Xaver von

The Turnip Princess: And Other Newly Discovered Fairy Tales. Franz Xaver von Schönwerth; compiled and edited with a foreword by Erika Eichenseer; translated with an introduction and commentary by Maria Tatar; illustrations by Engelbert Suss. Penguin Books 2015. 264 p.
ISBN 9780143107422
Grades: Adult   398.2
1. Anthologies 2. Mythology, folklore, and legends
LC Bl2015033117

Presents over seventy of the author's dark and violent fairy tales, thought lost until they were discovered in a German municipal archive.

"These eminently enjoyable tales offer a rich new take on the material of the Grimms and Andersen." —*Library Journal*

Seale, Yasmine

Aladdin: A New Translation. Translated by Yasmine Seale; edited by Paulo Lemos Horta. Liveright Publishing 2018. 144 p.
ISBN 9781631495168
Grades: Adult   398.2
1. Genies 2. Magic lamps 3. Aladdin (Legendary character) 4. Southwest Asia and North Africa (Middle East) 5. Arab countries 6. Translations — Arabic to English 7. Mythology, folklore, and legends
LC 2018036789

A new translation of the beloved folktale highlights the whimsy and also the darker themes often lost in previous English translations of the story of a rebellious 15-year old who is double-crossed by a sorcerer and saved by a princess.

"This exhilarating translation will thrill fans of darker, more complex fairy tales and upend readers preconceived image of Aladdin." —*Publishers Weekly*

Includes bibliographical references.

398.2093802 Persons (Individuals) — Folklore — Greece — Ancient

Wroe, Ann

Orpheus: The Song of Life. Ann Wroe. Overlook Press 2012. 262 p. : Illustration
ISBN 9781590207789
Grades: Adult   398.2093802
1. Orpheus (Greek mythology) 2. History writing — Ancient — Greece 3. History writing — Arts and culture

A history of the legend of Orpheus traces his mythical achievements and enduring influence, covering topics ranging from his passion for Eurydice to his role in inspiring Plato and Monteverdi and his treatment by the early Church.

Includes bibliographical references (p. 247-253) and index; Originally published: London : Jonathan Cape, 2011.

398.24 Tales and lore of plants and animals

Turvey, Samuel

★ *The Tomb of the Mili Mongga: Fossils, Folklore, and Adventures at the Edge of Reality.* Samuel Turvey. Bloomsbury Sigma 2024. 320 p.
ISBN 9781399409773
Grades: Adult   398.24
1. Islands 2. Exploration 3. Indigenous peoples 4. Animals 5. Anthropology 6. Biodiversity 7. Culture 8. Folklore, Indigenous 9. Evolution 10. Indonesia 11. History writing — Exploration 12. Travel Writing — Asia and the South Pacific 13. History Writing — Asia — Southeast Asia

"The prose is evocative…and Turvey weaves the natural history and folklore into an invigorating treatise on the nature of belief and knowledge. Vivid and transportive, this is a winner." —*Publishers Weekly*

398.45 Paranormal beings of human and semihuman form

Braudy, Leo

Haunted: On Ghosts, Witches, Vampires, Zombies, and Other Monsters of the Natural and Supernatural Worlds. Leo Braudy. Yale University Press 2016. 306 p.
ISBN 9780300203806
Grades: Adult   398.45
1. Monsters 2. Fear 3. Supernatural 4. Paranormal phenomena 5. Dracula, Count (Fictitious character) 6. Frankenstein's monster (Fictitious character) 7. Vampires 8. Zombies 9. Impartial writing 10. Society and culture — Pop culture 11. Science writing — Weird science 12. Arts and Entertainment — Writing and Publishing — Literary criticism
LC 2016937700

This book explores how fear has been shaped into images of monsters and monstrosity. From the Protestant Reformation to contemporary horror films and fiction, he explores four major types: the monster from nature (King Kong), the created monster (Frankenstein), the monster from within (Mr. Hyde), and the monster from the past (Dracula). Drawing upon deep historical and literary research, Braudy discusses the lasting presence of fearful imaginings in an age of scientific progress, viewing the detective genre as a rational riposte to the irrational world of the monstrous.

Includes index.

400 Language

Pinker, Steven

The Language Instinct. Steven Pinker. W. Morrow and Co. 1994. 494 p. : Illustration
ISBN 9780688121419
Grades: Adult   400
1. Language and languages 2. Speech 3. Science Writing — Biology
LC 93031842

The codirector of the MIT Center for Cognitive Science explains how language works, how it differs from thought, why adults have difficulty learning foreign languages, and why computers cannot learn human language.

"The author argues that an innate grammatical machinery of the brain exists, which allows children to reinvent language on their own. Basing his ideas on Noam Chomsky's Universal Grammar theory, Pinker describes language as a discrete combinatorial system that might easily have evolved via natural selection. Pinker steps on a few toes . but his work, while controversial, is well argued, challenging, often humorous, and always fascinating." —*Library Journal*

Includes bibliographical references (p. 447-472) and index.

PUBLIC LIBRARY CORE COLLECTION: NONFICTION
Twentieth Edition

401 Philosophy and theory

Everett, Daniel Leonard
How Language Began: The Story of Humanity's Greatest Invention. Daniel Everett. Liveright Publishing Corporation, a division of W. W. Norton & Company 2017. 384 p.
ISBN 9780871407955
Grades: Adult **401**
1. Oral communication 2. Semiotics 3. Psycholinguistics 4. Grammar 5. Language and languages 6. Speech 7. Society and culture — General 8. History writing — General
LC 2017025673

A pioneering linguist upends widely held beliefs about the acquisition and use of language by debunking theories on a wide range of disciplines and through citing examples from his four decades of field work with Amazonian hunter-gatherers.

"In this provocative and ambitious book, linguist Everett . demonstrates the complex and expansive nature of human language and its many communicative forms." —*Library Journal*

Includes bibliographical references and index.

Lieberman, David J.
Mindreader: Find Out What People Really Think, What They Really Want, and Who They Really Are. David J. Lieberman, PhD.. Rodale 2022. xiv, 220 pages
ISBN 9780593236185
Grades: Adult **401**
1. Psycholinguistics 2. Body language 3. Deception 4. Interpersonal communication 5. Self-Help — General 6. Science Writing — Medicine and health — Psychology
LC 2021047599

A New York Times best-selling author and longtime consultant to the FBI, CIA and NSA takes "people reading" to a whole new level, showing readers how to apply cutting-edge methods to countless everyday situations.

"This accessible pop psychology volume makes for a solid primer on getting into other people's heads." —*Publishers Weekly*

Includes bibliographical references (pages 191-218).

Pinker, Steven
The Stuff of Thought: Language as a Window into Human Nature. Steven Pinker. Viking 2007. IX, 499 p. : Illustration
ISBN 9780670063277
Grades: 11 12 Adult **401**
1. Language and languages 2. Thought and thinking 3. Language and culture 4. Language acquisition 5. Human nature 6. Human behavior 7. Speech 8. Philosophy 9. Science Writing — Biology
LC 2007026601

The Pulitzer Prize finalist author presents an accessible study of the relationship between language and human nature, explaining how everything from swearing and innuendo to prepositions and baby names reveal facts about key human concepts, emotions, and relationships.

"The author's vivid prose and down-to-earth attitude will once again attract an enthusiastic audience outside academia." —*Publishers Weekly*

Includes bibliographical references (p. [459]-481) and index.

Wolfe, Tom
The Kingdom of Speech. Tom Wolfe. Little Brown & Co. 2016. 160 p.
ISBN 9780316404624
Grades: Adult **401**
1. Speech 2. Human evolution 3. Language and culture 4. Oral communication 5. Social history 6. Society and culture — Psychology and human behavior
LC 2016942707

Taking readers on a rollicking ride through history, a master storyteller and reporter, whose legend began in journalism, presents a paradigm-shifting argument that speech, not evolution, is responsible for humanity's complex societies and achievements.

"Wolfe is at his best when portraying the lives of the scientists and their respective eras, and his vibrant study manages to be clever, funny, serious, satirical, and instructive." —*Publishers Weekly*

Yang, Charles D.
The Infinite Gift: How Children Learn and Unlearn the Languages of the World. Charles Yang. Scribner 2006. VII, 273 p. : Illustration
ISBN 9780743237567
Grades: Adult **401**
1. Language acquisition 2. Linguistics 3. Child development 4. Science Writing — General
LC 2006044307

Draws on cutting-edge scientific findings to address key issues about language development, demonstrating how human beings are born with an innate ability to speak any language but customize their communication abilities to accommodate the language that they hear.

"Anyone with the slightest interest in the English language should read his book." —*Library Journal*

Includes bibliographical references (p. 239-257) and index.

410 Linguistics

Crystal, David
★ *How Language Works: How Babies Babble, Words Change Meaning, and Languages Live or Die.* David Crystal. Overlook Press 2006. xii, 500 p. : Illustration; Map
ISBN 9781585678488
Grades: 11 12 Adult **410**
1. Linguistics 2. Language and languages 3. Words 4. Speech 5. Science Writing — Biology 6. Arts and Entertainment — Writing and Publishing
LC Bl2006030001

A lighthearted exploration of the origin, function and purpose of language addresses a wide range of topics to offer insight into what can be learned through verbal and body language, from the role of gestures and the evolution of grammar to the intricacies of different languages and the layout of the human throat.

"Crystal offers an impeccably organized guide to language and communication that brings clarity to a scholarly subject, and is sure to become a standard reference." —*Publishers Weekly*

Includes bibliographical references (p. 485-486) and index; Originally published: London : Penguin Books, 2005.

Deutscher, Guy
★ *Through the Language Glass: Why the World Looks Different in Other Languages.* Guy Deutscher. Metropolitan Books/Henry Holt and Co. 2010. 304 p, 8 p. of plates : Illustration; Color
ISBN 9780805081954
Grades: Adult **410**
1. Language and culture 2. Language and languages 3. Grammar 4. Sociolinguistics 5. Arts and Entertainment — Writing and Publishing 6. History writing — General
LC 2010001042

Library Journal Best Books, 2010.

A masterpiece of linguistics scholarship, at once erudite and entertaining, confronts the thorny question of how—and whether—culture shapes language and language, culture.

"Deutscher combines erudition, wry humor, and serious interpretation in this elegant and charmingly accessible study of the relation among language, culture, and thought and of how we have engaged in and reflected upon language over the years." —*Library Journal*

Includes bibliographical references (p. [274]-292) and index.

ESSENTIAL AND RECOMMENDED TITLES
410.92 Linguists

410.92 Linguists

Chomsky, Noam
Global Discontents: Conversations on the Rising Threats to Democracy. Noam Chomsky; interviews with David Barsamian. Metropolitan Books 2017. 240 pages
ISBN 9781250146182
Grades: Adult   410.92
1. Dissenters 2. Intellectuals 3. World politics 4. International security 5. Democracy 6. Capitalism 7. Terrorism 8. Climate change 9. Inequality 10. Discontent 11. Interviews 12. Liberal writing 13. Politics and global affairs — General 14. Society and culture — General
LC 2017276923

In a collection of wide-ranging interviews conducted by the award-winning director of Alternative Radio, the author of Who Rules the World? makes radical recommendations for addressing issues that threaten the world of the near future, including climate change, nuclear war, state surveillance, economic inequality and religion in American politics.

"Every page of this lively, probing, and sharp collection delivers a searing observation from linguist and political-thinker Chomsky." —*Publishers Weekly*

411 Writing systems of standard forms of languages

Ferrara, Silvia
The Greatest Invention: A History of the World in Nine Mysterious Scripts. Silvia Ferrara; translated from the Italian by Todd Portnowitz. Farrar, Straus and Giroux 2022. 288 p.
ISBN 9780374601621
Grades: Adult   411
1. Writing 2. Inscriptions 3. Extinct languages 4. Signs and symbols 5. Writing methods and systems 6. Communication 7. Civilization 8. Translations — Italian to English 9. History writing — Technological innovations 10. History writing — Microhistory 11. Arts and Entertainment — Writing and Publishing 12. History writing — Ancient
LC 2021044938

The L where a tabletop meets the legs, the T between double doors, the D of an armchair's oval backrest—all around us is an alphabet in things. But how did these shapes make it onto the page, never mind form such complex structures as this sentence? In The Greatest Invention, Silvia Ferrara takes a profound look at how—and how many times—human beings have managed to produce the miracle of written language, taking us back in time to Mesopotamia, Crete, China, Egypt, Central America, Easter Island, and beyond. As Ferrara demonstrates, in the shadows and swirls of these ancient inscriptions, not only are we able to decipher the stories these peoples sought to record, but we can also tease out the timeless truths of human nature, of our ceaseless drive to connect, create, and be remembered.

"Ferrara (Cypro-Minoan Inscriptions), professor of Aegean civilization at the University of Bologna, takes an entertaining and complex look at how written language has evolved." —*Publishers Weekly*

Originally published in Italian as La grande invenzioneby Giangiacomo Feltrinelli Editore, Milan, in 2019; Includes bibliographical references.

Hazrat, Florence
An Admirable Point: A Brief History of the Exclamation Mark. Florence Hazrat. Godine 2023. 176 p.
ISBN 9781567927870
Grades: Adult   411
1. Punctuation 2. History Writing — Microhistory 3. Arts and Entertainment — Writing and publishing 4. Debut title
LC 2022038098

Few punctuation marks elicit quite as much love or hate as the exclamation point. It's bubbly and exuberant, an emotional amplifier whose flamboyantly dramatic gesture lets the reader know: Here be feelings! an Admirable Point explores how ! came about in the first place some six hundred years ago, and uncovers the many ways in which ! has left its mark on art, literature, (pop) culture, and just about any sphere of human activity—from Beowulf to spam emails, ee cummings to neuroscience. Whether you think it's over-used, or enthusiastically sprinkle your writing with it, ! is inescapable.

A cross between a microhistory and the recent wave of witty grammar books, this slim book is so chock-full of interesting facts and ideas that it will leave most readers saying, Wow! —*Booklist*

Houston, Keith
Shady Characters: The Secret Life of Punctuation, Symbols, & Other Typographical Marks. Keith Houston. W.W. Norton & Company 2013. 320 p.
ISBN 9780393064421
Grades: Adult   411
1. Punctuation 2. Signs and symbols 3. Type and type-founding 4. Writing 5. History writing — Microhistory 6. Arts and Entertainment — Writing and Publishing
LC 2013017324

Revealing the secret history of punctuation, this delightful tour of 2,000 years of the written word, from ancient Greece to the Internet, explores the parallel histories of language and typography throughout the world and across time.
Includes bibliographical references and index.

413.028 Auxiliary techniques and procedures apparatus, equipment, materials

Stamper, Kory
Word by Word: The Secret Life of Dictionaries. Kory Stamper. Pantheon Books 2017. 320 pages
ISBN 9781101870945
Grades: Adult   413.028
1. English language 2. Words 3. Vocabulary 4. Lexicography 5. Language and languages 6. Lexicographers 7. Dictionaries 8. History writing — Arts and culture 9. Society and culture — General 10. History writing — Microhistory
LC 2016024253

While most of us might take dictionaries for granted, the process of writing them is in fact as lively and dynamic as language itself. Stamper cracks open the complex, obsessive world of lexicography, from the agonizing decisions about what and how to define, to the knotty questions of usage in an ever-changing language.

"Word by Word offers marvelous insight into the messy world behind the tidy definitions on the page." —*Booklist*
Includes bibliographical references and index.

415 Grammar of standard forms of languages

Pinker, Steven
Words and Rules: The Ingredients of Language. Steven Pinker. Basic Books 1999. xi, 348 p. : Illustration
ISBN 9780465072699
Grades: Adult   415
1. Language and languages 2. Grammar, Comparative and general 3. Verbs 4. Words 5. Terms and phrases 6. Science Writing — Biology
LC 99043013

An examination of the human ability to use language by an MIT professor traces the history and evolution of the English language, the theories of Noam Chomsky, the way children learn to use language, and much more.

"This book with its crisp prose and neat analogies, makes required reading for anyone interested in cognition and language." —*Publishers Weekly*
Includes bibliographical references (p. 313-333) and index.

418 Standard usage (Prescriptive linguistics)

Briggs, Kate
This Little Art. Kate Briggs. Fitzcarraldo Editions. 2018. 392 p.

PUBLIC LIBRARY CORE COLLECTION: NONFICTION
Twentieth Edition

ISBN 9781910695456
Grades: Adult — 418
1. Briggs, Kate 2. Translating and interpreting 3. Reading 4. Translators 5. Essays 6. Autobiographies and memoirs 7. Life stories — Arts and culture — Writing 8. Arts and Entertainment — Writing and Publishing 9. Arts and Entertainment — Writing and Publishing — Literary criticism
LC Bl2018125872

Part-essay, part-memoir, This Little Art is a manifesto and a song for the practice of literary translation.

"Lucid and engaging, Briggss book is essential, not just for translators, but anyone who has felt the magic of reading." —*Publishers Weekly*

Castillo, Elaine
★ *How to Read Now: Essays.* Elaine Castillo. Viking 2022. 304 p.
ISBN 9780593489635
Grades: Adult — 418
1. Storytelling 2. Racism in literature 3. Imperialism 4. Literature and society 5. Books and reading 6. Essays 7. Society and culture — Race 8. Antiracist literature 9. Book club best bets
LC 2022002699

An exploration and manifesto investigating the power of reading—and our potential to become radically better readers in the world.

"Castillo's knowledge, along with her firebrand style and generous humor, result in a dynamic and necessary look at the state of storytelling. This one packs a powerful punch." —*Publishers Weekly*

Includes bibliographical references.

Dehaene, Stanislas
Reading in the Brain: The Science and Evolution of a Cultural Invention. Stanislas Dehaene. Viking 2009. 400 p.
ISBN 9780670021109
Grades: Adult — 418
1. Reading 2. Books and reading 3. Brain 4. Comprehension 5. Science Writing — Biology
LC 2009009389

An accessible introduction to the process through which the brain reads considers a paradox through which the human brain adapted to create and recognize words, in an account that draws on pioneering research to offer insight into language, spelling logic, dyslexia, and more.

Includes bibliographical references and index.

Lahiri, Jhumpa
Translating Myself and Others. Jhumpa Lahiri. Princeton University Press 2022. 184 p.
ISBN 9780691231167
Grades: Adult — 418
1. Lahiri, Jhumpa 2. Translating and interpreting 3. Translators 4. Writing 5. Literature 6. United States 7. Autobiographies and memoirs 8. Essays 9. Arts and Entertainment — Writing and Publishing — Literary criticism 10. Life stories — Arts and culture — Writing 11. Arts and Entertainment — Writing and Publishing
LC 2021047885

Drawing on Ovid's myth of Echo and Narcissus to explore the distinction between writing and translating, a Pulitzer Prize-winning author talks broadly about writing, desire and freedom as she reflects on her emerging identity as a translator.

"Though the topic of translation studies might have a limited non-academic readership, Lahiri writes so beautifully that this collection will have broad appeal for anyone interested in literary essays." —*Library Journal*

Includes bibliographical references and index.

Wolf, Maryanne
Reader, Come Home: The Reading Brain in a Digital World. Maryanne Wolf. HarperCollins 2018. 160 p.
ISBN 9780062388780
Grades: Adult — 418
1. Books and reading 2. Thought and thinking 3. Technology and civilization 4. Brain 5. Child development 6. Electronic books 7. Critical thinking 8. Neuroscience 9. Digital media 10. Cognition 11. Physiology 12. Science Writing — Biology
LC Bl2018117004

Draws on the author's extensive research from Proust and the Squid to consider the future of the reading brain and its capacity for critical thinking, empathy and reflection in today's highly digitized world.

"Overall, a hopeful look at the future of reading that will resonate with those who worry that we are losing our ability to think in the digital age." —*Library Journal*

419 Sign languages

Tennant, Richard A.
The American Sign Language Handshape Dictionary. Richard A. Tennant, Marianne Gluszak Brown; illustrated by Valerie Nelson-Metlay. Clerc Books, Gallaudet University Press 1998. 407 p. : Illustration
ISBN 9781563680434
Grades: Adult — 419
1. American Sign Language 2. Dictionaries 3. Language arts and studies — Sign language 4. Educator resources — General
LC 97048389

The unique feature of this dictionary is that it is organized by handshape rather than by alphabetical order. An American Sign Language learner can look up an unfamiliar sign by looking for the handshape rather than by looking up the word in an alphabetical English glossary. At the same time, an English speaker can look up a sign for a specific word by looking at the Index of English Glossaries located at the end of the dictionary. The introduction includes a history of sign language in the United States. Detailed instructions explain the organization of the handshape sections and the ordering of signs. The illustrations are clear and are described in terms of configuration, location, movement, orientation, and nonmanual markers."

Includes index.

420 Specific languages

Bragg, Melvyn
★ *The Adventure of English: The Biography of a Language.* Melvyn Bragg. Arcade Pub. 2004. xii, 322 p. : Illustration; Color
ISBN 9781559707107
Grades: Adult — 420
1. English language 2. Etymology 3. Words 4. Arts and Entertainment — Writing and Publishing
LC 2003019583

Library Journal Best Books, 2004.

A history of the English language traces its evolution from a Germanic dialect around 500 A.D. to its modern form, noting the influence of such groups and individuals as early Anglo-Saxon tribes, Alfred the Great, and William Shakespeare.

"The author offers a biography of the English language, highlighting key individuals, places, and literature that advanced it, as well as the political and social trends that influenced it. Bragg discusses its evolution in the English colonies, devoting four chapters to the United States and one each to India, the West Indies, and Australia. Well researched yet more accessible to a wide audience than scholarly treatments by linguists or historians." —*Library Journal*

Includes bibliographical references (p. [303]-312) and index.

Cassell, Kay Ann
★ *Reference and Information Services: An Introduction.* Kay Ann Cassell & UMA Hiremath. ALA Neal-Schuman 2023. 522 p.
ISBN 9780838937334
Grades: Professional — 420

ESSENTIAL AND RECOMMENDED TITLES
420.141 Discourse analysis — linguistics — English language

1. Reference services (Libraries) 2. Information services 3. Reference sources 4. Professional materials — General

The fifth edition of Reference and Information Services: An Introduction is consciously aimed at arming the reference librarian with the skills, expertise, and mindset needed to keep up with changing resources and best practices.

"The sections on subject areas are especially helpful and include resources pertaining to law and business, geography, health information, and biographical information. Readers may be intrigued by the section on 'Reference as Programming,' which suggests different ways to help users navigate library resources." —*Library Journal*

Includes bibliographical references and indexes.

McCrum, Robert
★ *The Story of English*. Robert McCrum, William Cran, Robert MacNeil. Penguin Books 2003. xxi, 468 p. : Map
ISBN 9780142002315
Grades: 11 12 Adult   **420**
1. English language 2. Language and languages 3. Language arts 4. Grammar 5. Canadian literature 6. Arts and Entertainment — Writing and Publishing
LC 2002029818

Thoroughly revised and updated, the new edition of the international bestseller tells the anecdotal history of the English language from its obscure Anglo-Saxon origins to its present status as the world's most prominent, expressive, and fast-growing international language.

Sequel: Do you speak American?; Includes bibliographical references (p. [437]-438) and index.

420.141 Discourse analysis — linguistics — English language

Fridland, Valerie
★ *Like, Literally, Dude: Arguing for the Good in Bad English*. Valerie Fridland. Viking 2023. 352 p.
ISBN 9780593298329
Grades: Adult   **420.141**
1. English language 2. Oral communication 3. Slang 4. Language and languages 5. Linguistics 6. Society and culture — General
LC 2022030931

A lively linguistic exploration of the speech habits we love to hate—and why our "like"s and "literally"s actually make us better communicators.

"Scholarly yet accessible, and often very witty, this is a winning look at how language evolves." —*Publishers Weekly*

Includes biographical references and index.

420.9 English language — History

Hitchings, Henry
The Language Wars: A History of Proper English. Henry Hitchings. Farrar, Straus and Giroux 2011. 416 p.
ISBN 9780374183295
Grades: Adult   **420.9**
1. English language 2. Language and languages 3. Grammar, Comparative and general 4. Arts and Entertainment — Writing and Publishing 5. History writing — Microhistory
LC 2011010701

Examines modern debates about correct language use while exploring the roles of morality, politics and class on historical style arguments, evaluating the input of key contributors while covering topics ranging from regional accents and slang to political correctness and e-communications.

"As the author points out, there is probably not a person alive who does not have some bee in his bonnet about the way other people speak and write. Maybe it is the errant apostrophe, the splitting of the poor old infinitive, or the use of like as a comma. Or perhaps it is the exclamation mark, once known as the shriek mark. Mr Hitchings's book is a corrective to some of these linguistic prejudices. It is bracing to learn, for example, that the prohibition on splitting the infinitive is fairly recent. Pre-Victorians did not object. Chaucer was a splitter, and even Shakespeare had a go. Same story with the apostrophe: in the 18th-century authors were sprinkling apostrophes over everything. Mr Hitchings reviews such matters with cool erudition. He is resolutely relaxed about usage, understanding that correctitude and intelligibility are not the same." —*The Economist*

Includes bibliographical references and index.

421 Writing system, phonology, phonetics of standard English

Crystal, David
Spell It Out: The Curious, Enthralling and Extraordinary Story of English Spelling. David Crystal. St Martins Press 2013. 336 p.
ISBN 9781250003478
Grades: 11 12 Adult   **421**
1. Spelling 2. Language and languages 3. Words 4. English language 5. Arts and Entertainment — Writing and Publishing
LC 2013010521

A lesser-known history of English spelling by the award-winning author of the Story of English in 100 Words is presented through engaging, pithy chapters that cover such topics as the introduction of the Roman alphabet, each letter's origins and the development of long and short vowels.

Rosen, Michael
Alphabetical: How Every Letter Tells a Story. Michael Rosen. Counterpoint Press 2015. 448 p.
ISBN 9781619024830
Grades: Adult   **421**
1. Writing 2. Alphabet 3. Writing methods and systems 4. History writing — Microhistory
LC 2014035051

How on Earth did we fix upon our twenty-six letters, what do they really mean, and how did we come to write them down in the first place? Michael Rosen takes you on an unforgettable adventure through the history of the alphabet in twenty-six vivid chapters, fizzing with personal anecdotes and fascinating facts. Starting with the mysterious Phoenicians and how sounds first came to be written down, he races on to show how nonsense poems work, pins down the strange story of OK, traces our five lost letters and tackles the tyranny of spelling, among many many other things. His heroes of the alphabet range from Edward Lear to Phyllis Pearsall (the inventor of the A-Z), and from the two scribes of Beowulf to rappers. Each chapter takes on a different subject—whether it's codes, umlauts or the writing of dictionaries. Rosen's enthusiasm for letters positively leaps off the page, whether it's the story of his life told through the typewriters he's owned or a chapter on jokes written in a string of gags and word games. This is the book for anyone who's ever wondered why Hawaiian only has a thirteen-letter alphabet or how exactly to write down the sound of a wild raspberry.

"Rosen also is mellow about correctness in usage and punctuation (Our personal histories and feelings are wrapped up in what the letters and their means of transmission mean to each of us) and shows little sorrow for the disappearance of handwriting in schools; in fact, he thinks our current emphasis on it doesn't make much sense. A delightfully informative book about letters, their meanings, and the words and meanings we derive from them." —*Kirkus*

Includes bibliographical references and index.

422 Etymology of standard English

Crystal, David
The Story of English in 100 Words. David Crystal. St. Martin's Press 2012. xxi, 260 p. : Illustration
ISBN 9781250003461
Grades: Adult   **422**
1. Etymology 2. Language and languages 3. Words 4. Native language 5. English language 6. Arts and Entertainment — Writing and Publishing
LC 2012003038

Demonstrates how the history of English vernacular is reflected in one hundred words with sources in key influences and events, from "roe" and "loaf" to "fopdoodle" and "twittersphere."

Includes index; Originally published: Profile Books, LTD : Great Britain, 2011.

Nuttall, Jennifer Anne
★ *Mother Tongue: The Surprising History of Women's Words.* Jenni Nuttall. Viking Press 2023. 288 p.
ISBN 9780593299579
Grades: Adult   422
1. Language and languages 2. Women 3. Equality 4. Language and history 5. Feminism 6. Language and culture 7. Linguistics 8. History Writing — Arts and culture 9. History Writing — Women's history 10. Arts and Entertainment — Writing and publishing

An enlightening linguistic journey through a thousand years of feminist language—and what we can learn from the vivid vocabulary that English once had for women's bodies, experiences, and sexuality.

"A fresh, informative perspective on women's lives through the centuries." —*Kirkus*

Rosten, Leo
The New Joys of Yiddish. Leo Rosten; revisions and commentary by Lawrence Bush; illustrations by R.O. Blechman. Crown Publishers 2001. xxxii, 458 p. : Illustration
ISBN 9780609607855
Grades: Adult   422
1. Yiddish language 2. English language 3. Reference books — Language learning 4. Spirituality and Religion — Judaism
LC 2001028366

An updated version of the informal dictionary which offers the history and folklore behind Yiddish and Hebrew words as well as literal translations adds information on linguistic and cultural changes since Rosten's day.

Includes bibliographical references.

423 Dictionaries of standard English

Ammer, Christine
The American Heritage Dictionary of Idioms. Christine Ammer. Houghton Mifflin Harcourt 2013. V, 506 pages
ISBN 9780547676586
Grades: 11 12 Adult   423
1. Americanisms 2. English language 3. Idioms 4. United States 5. Reference — Dictionaries
LC 2012026443

Covering almost ten thousand phrases, including bite the bullet, take the cake, buy the farm, and says who, a unique reference on common American vocabulary and idiomatic expressions defines each entry and provides a contextual sentence.

Covering over ten thousand phrases, including "bite the bullet," "take the cake," and "buy the farm," a reference on common American vocabulary and idiomatic expressions defines each entry and provides a contextual sentence.

"This book makes for fun browsing and could be very helpful to foreign speakers." —*Choice*

Brewer, Ebenezer Cobham
★ *Brewer's Dictionary of Phrase & Fable.* Edited by Susie Dent. Brewer's 2012. xxii, 1480 p. : Illustration
ISBN 9780550107640
Grades: 6 7 8 9 10 11 12 Adult   423
1. Allusions 2. English language 3. Literature 4. Mythology 5. Dictionaries 6. Reference — Dictionaries
LC 2012464049

Provides definitions of typical phrases and words and explains their historical origins.

Corbeil, Jean-Claude
★ *Merriam-webster's Visual Dictionary.* Under the direction of Jean-Claude Corbeil. Merriam-Webster, Incorporated 2012. 1112 pages : Color; Illustration; Map
ISBN 9780877791515
Grades: 6 7 8 9 10 11 12 Adult   423
1. Picture dictionaries 2. Reference — Dictionaries
LC 2013498156

25,000 terms and their definitions with 8,000 full-color illustrations of a wide variety of objects from all aspects of life.

More than 20,000 words in the English language are grouped into similar categories—such as astronomy, house, human being, plants and society—and explained using detailed, labeled illustrations.

Includes index.

Espy, Willard R.
Words to Rhyme With: A Rhyming Dictionary.. Willard R. Espy. Facts on File 2006. xix, 683 p.
ISBN 9780816063031
Grades: Adult   423
1. English language 2. Dictionaries 3. Reference books 4. Language arts — General
LC 2005051122

Lists more than 80,000 rhyming words, including single, double, and triple rhymes, and offers information on rhyme schemes, meter, and poetic forms.

Includes index.

Garner, Bryan A.
Garner's Modern English Usage. Bryan A. Garner. Oxford University Press 2016. LVI, 1056 pages
ISBN 9780190491482
Grades: Adult   423
1. English language 2. Dictionaries 3. Reference — Writing 4. Reference — Dictionaries
LC 2016591307

Illustrates with actual examples, cited with chapter and verse, all the linguistic blunders that modern writers and speakers are pone to, whether in word choice, syntax phrasing, punctuation, or pronunciation.

This book is a successor to three editions (1998, 2003, 2009) of Garner's Modern American Usage—Title page verso; Revision of: Garner, Bryan A. Garner's modern American usage. Third edition. New York : Oxford University Press, 2009; Includes bibliographical references and index.

Ogilvie, Sarah
The Dictionary People: The Unsung Heroes Who Created the Oxford English Dictionary. Sarah Ogilvie. Alfred A. Knopf 2023. 336 p.
ISBN 9780593536407
Grades: Adult   423
1. Murray, James A. H, 1837-1915 2. Language and languages 3. English language 4. Lexicographers 5. Lexicography 6. 19th century 7. History writing — Arts and culture 8. History writing — Europe — United Kingdom 9. Arts and Entertainment — Writing and Publishing

For the first time ever, this thrilling literary detective story, doubling as a celebration of words, language, people and one of mankind's greatest achievements, unravels the mystery of the contributors from around the world who, for over 70 years, helped to codify the way we read, write and speak.

"The whimsical narrative is also educational, providing extensive insight into the process used to trace the origins of words. Readers will be enthralled." —*Publishers Weekly*

Winchester, Simon
The Professor and the Madman: A Tale of Murder, Insanity, and the Making of the Oxford English Dictionary. Simon Winchester. HarperCollins 1998. xi, 242 p. : Illustration
ISBN 9780060175962
Grades: Adult   423

ESSENTIAL AND RECOMMENDED TITLES
425.55 English language — Pronouns

1. Murray, James A. H, 1837-1915 2. Minor, William Chester, 1834-1920 3. Lexicography 4. Lexicographers 5. Psychiatric hospital patients 6. Language and languages 7. Etymology 8. Civil War veterans 9. 19th century 10. Biographies 11. History writing — General 12. Life stories — Education — Scholars and educators 13. Adult books for young adults 14. Nonfiction that reads like fiction

LC 98010204

New York Times Notable Book, 1998; National Book Critics Circle Award for Nonfiction finalist, 1998.

Describes how more than ten thousand definitions were submitted for the first Oxford English Dictionary from Dr. W.C. Minor, an American Civil War criminal who was considered both a genius and a lunatic.

"The author relates the story of the Oxford English Dictionary's first editor and the expatriate American murderer who contributed more than 10,000 quotations as examples. Best of all, among the entertaining tangents one learns a great deal about the making of that grandest of all reference works." —*Library Journal*

Includes bibliographical references (p. [239]-242).

425.55 English language — Pronouns

Baron, Dennis E.
What's Your Pronoun?: Beyond He and She. Dennis Baron. Liveright Publishing 2020. 272 p.
ISBN 9781631496042
Grades: Adult **425.55**
1. Grammar, Comparative and general 2. Pronouns 3. Gender identity 4. Gender equity 5. Etiquette 6. Identity 7. Fairness 8. English language 9. Grammar 10. Society and culture — Gender 11. Society and culture — General 12. Arts and Entertainment — Writing and Publishing

LC 2019021998

The University of Illinois linguistics professor and national commentator on language issues explores evolving debates regarding modern pronoun usage, tracing the history of pronouns, the creations of new gender pronouns and the role of pronouns in establishing identity and rights.

"Based on decades of research, Baron's masterly work documents the historical and continued importance of personal pronouns. Those interested in gender politics or English grammar, or who feel that 'He' and 'She' are inadequate, would benefit greatly from perusing this book." —*Library Journal*

Includes bibliographical references and index.

427 Historical and geographic variations, modern nongeographic variations of English

Bailey, Richard W.
Speaking American: A History of English in the United States. Richard W. Bailey. Oxford University Press 2011. 240 p.
ISBN 9780195179347
Grades: Adult **427**
1. English language 2. Americanisms 3. Language and languages 4. United States 5. Arts and Entertainment — Writing and Publishing

LC 2011011042

Investigates the history and continuing evolution of American English, from the 16th century to the present, to celebrate the endless variety and remarkable inventiveness that have always been at the heart of our language. By the author of Images of English: A Cultural History of the Language.

Includes bibliographical references and index.

Crystal, David
★ *English as a Global Language.* David Crystal. Cambridge University Press 2012. xv, 212 pages : Illustration; Map
ISBN 9781107611801
Grades: Adult **427**
1. English language 2. Language arts and studies — Linguistics

LC 2013498883

Written in a detailed and fascinating manner, this book is ideal for general readers interested in the English language.

Includes bibliographical references (pages 192-201) and index.

★ *The Stories of English.* David Crystal. Overlook Press 2004. [viii], 584 p. : Illustration; Map
ISBN 9781585676019
Grades: Adult **427**
1. Language and languages 2. Linguistics 3. English language 4. History writing — General 5. Arts and Entertainment — Writing and Publishing

LC 2004054727

A history of the English language draws on the diversity of dialects and regional accents around the world, as well as the dialects that appear in a variety of literary classics, to explain the significance of the language.

"The author traces the diverse and unpredictable influences that have shaped English into an unruly family of dialects, creoles, and patois. Crystal acknowledges the emergence during the fourteenth and fifteenth centuries of a prestigious standard version of English. Yet he shows in instance after instance that the tempests of linguistic change have often overwhelmed the custodians of the King's English, compelling them to accommodate forces they could not control. And though he never loses his focus on language, Crystal allows some of its more colorful users—including Chaucer, Shakespeare, Samuel Johnson, and Thomas Jefferson—to bring their personalities and voices into the chronicle." —*Booklist*

Includes bibliographical references (p. [551]-560) and indexes.

Holder, R. W.
How Not to Say What You Mean: A Dictionary of Euphemisms. R.W. Holder. Oxford University Press 2007. xvi, 410 p.
ISBN 9780199208395
Grades: 11 12 Adult **427**
1. English language 2. Vocabulary 3. Synonyms and antonyms 4. Humor writing — General 5. Reference — Dictionaries

LC 2007037558

This thoroughly updated new edition of How Not to Say What You Mean celebrates 20 years of R. W. Holder's popular and successful dictionary of euphemisms, offering a delightful collection of jocular and evasive expressions for sex, death, murder, crime, prison, and much more.

"Holder's collection, first published in 1987, has become the standard reference in the UK." —*Booklist*

Includes bibliographical references (p. [xi]-xvi).

McWhorter, John H.
Talking Back, Talking Black: Truths About America's Lingua Franca. John McWhorter. Bellevue Literary Press 2017. 192 p.
ISBN 9781942658207
Grades: Adult **427**
1. African Americans 2. English language 3. Language and languages 4. Language and culture 5. Racism 6. Sociolinguistics 7. Race awareness 8. United States 9. Essays 10. Society and culture — General 11. Society and culture — Race

LC BI2017005933

A linguistic expert explains the fundamentals and rich history of Black English while carefully examining the cultural, educational and political issues that have undermined recognition of the transformative, empowering dialect.

"This is an engaging look at the English language as spoken by many Black Americans as well as the long history of stereotyping that has prevented an objective analysis of a rich language tradition." —*Booklist*

428 Standard English usage (Prescriptive linguistics)

Brandreth, Gyles Daubeney
Have You Eaten Grandma?: Or, the Life-saving Importance of Correct Punctuation, Grammar, and Good English. Gyles Brandreth. Atria Books 2019. 320 p.

ISBN 9781982127404

Grades: Adult **428**

1. Writing 2. Grammar 3. Punctuation 4. Errors 5. English language 6. Arts and Entertainment — Writing and Publishing

In this brilliantly funny and accessible guide to proper punctuation and so much more, Gyles Brandreth explores the linguistic horrors of our times, tells us what we've been doing wrong and shows us how, in the future, we can get it right every time. Covering everything from dangling participles to transitive verbs, from age-old conundrums like "lay" vs. "lie," to the confounding influences of social media on our everyday language, Have You Eaten Grandma? is an endlessly useful and entertaining resource for all.

Curzan, Anne
★ *Says Who?: A Kinder, Funner Usage Guide for Everyone Who Cares About Words.* Anne Curzan. Crown 2024. 272 p.
ISBN 9780593444092

Grades: Adult **428**

1. English language 2. Grammar 3. Words 4. Speech 5. Writing 6. Lexicography 7. Social change 8. Society and culture — General 9. Arts and Entertainment — Writing and Publishing

LC 2023048686

Our use of language naturally evolves and is a living, breathing thing that reflects who we are. Says Who? offers clear, nuanced guidance that goes beyond "right" and "wrong" to empower us to make informed language choices. Never snooty or scoldy (yes, that's a "real" word!), this book explains where the grammar rules we learned in school actually come from and reveals the forces that drive dictionary editors to label certain words as slang or unacceptable. Linguist and veteran English professor Anne Curzan helps us use our new knowledge about the developing nature of language and grammar rules to become caretakers of language rather than gatekeepers of it.

"Highly recommended for all writers and speakers of English who want to understand why the language works the way it does." —*Library Journal*

Includes bibliographical references and index.

428.1 Vocabulary — English language — Usage (Applied linguistics)

Elster, Charles Harrington
How to Tell Fate from Destiny: And Other Skillful Word Distinctions. Charles Harrington Elster; [illustrations by Chi Birmingham]. Houghton Mifflin Harcourt 2018. VIII, 312 pages : Illustration
ISBN 9781328884077

Grades: Adult **428.1**

1. English language 2. Reference — Writing

LC 2018028262

If you have trouble distinguishing the verbs imitate and emulate, the relative pronouns that and which, or the adjectives pliant, pliable, and supple, never fear—How to Tell Fate from Destiny is here to help! with more than 500 headwords, the book is replete with advice on how to differentiate commonly confused words and steer clear of verbal trouble.

Includes bibliographical references (pages [299]-301) and index.

428.2 English language grammar

Garner, Bryan A
The Chicago Guide to Grammar, Usage, and Punctuation. Bryan A. Garner. The University of Chicago Press 2016. xxvii, 583 pages
ISBN 9780226188850

Grades: Adult **428.2**

1. English language 2. Grammar 3. Reference — Writing

LC 2015047425

Discusses standard literary English with sections about usage, grammar, punctuation, and word formation.

Includes bibliographical references (pages 497-505) and indexes.

Hult, Christine A
The Handy English Grammar Answer Book. Christine A. Hult, Ph.D… Visible Ink Press 2016. xii, 419 pages : Illustration
ISBN 9781578595204

Grades: Adult **428.2**

1. English language 2. Grammar 3. Language arts and studies — Writing skills

LC 2015015787

Explains the rules of English grammar, explores common mistakes, and offers situational examples of correct usage.

Includes index.

Norris, Mary
Between You and Me: Confessions of a Comma Queen. Mary Norris. W W Norton & Co. 2015. 240 p.
ISBN 9780393240184

Grades: Adult **428.2**

1. Norris, Mary (Editor) 2. Editors 3. Writing 4. Language and languages 5. Grammar 6. Autobiographies and memoirs 7. Life stories — Arts and culture — Writing 8. Arts and Entertainment — Writing and Publishing

LC 2014043252

Library Journal Best Books, 2015.

A New Yorker copy veteran presents laugh-out-loud descriptions of some of the most common and vexing errors in language and usage, drawing on examples from classic literature and pop culture while sharing anecdotes from her work with celebrated writers.

"In countless laugh-out-loud passages, Norris displays her admirable flexibility in bending rules when necessary. She even makes her serious quest to uncover the reason for the hyphen in the title of the classic novel Moby-Dick downright hilarious. A funny book for any serious reader." —*Kirkus*

Truss, Lynne
Eats, Shoots & Leaves: The Zero Tolerance Approach to Punctuation. Lynne Truss; Pat Byrnes, illustrator. Gotham Books 2009. 176 p. : Illustration
ISBN 9781592404889

Grades: 8 9 10 11 12 Adult **428.2**

1. Language and languages 2. English language 3. Language arts 4. Writing 5. Philosophy 6. Grammar 7. Humor writing — General

LC 2009291769

Looks at the history of punctuation and the rules governing the use of apostrophes, commas, dashes, hyphens, colons, and semicolons.

"The author dissects common errors that grammar mavens have long deplored (often, as she readily points out, in isolation) and makes . . . arguments for increased attention to punctuation correctness. . . . Truss serves up delightful, unabashedly strict and sometimes snobby little book, with cheery Britishisms (Lawks-a-mussy!) dotting pages that express a more international righteous indignation." —*Publishers Weekly*

Watson, Cecelia
Semicolon: The Past, Present, and Future of a Misunderstood Mark. Cecelia Watson. HarperCollins 2019. 160 p.
ISBN 9780062853059

Grades: Adult **428.2**

1. Punctuation 2. Grammar 3. Language and languages 4. Arts and Entertainment — Writing and Publishing

LC 2018045968

An engaging, existential chronicle of the polarizing punctuation mark traces its emergence in the wake of 19th-century grammar books and the ways it has been embraced or reviled by forefront authors.

"Sprightly and scholarly, this will appeal to grammar geeks who are patient with Watson's free-range sensibility." —*Kirkus*

Includes bibliographical references and index.

ESSENTIAL AND RECOMMENDED TITLES
440 French and related Romance languages

440 French and related Romance languages

Nadeau, Jean-Benoit
★ *The Story of French.* Jean-Benoit Nadeau and Julie Barlow. St. Martin's Press 2006. 483 p.
ISBN 9780312341831
Grades: 11 12 Adult **440**
1. French language 2. Linguistics 3. Language and languages 4. Canadian literature 5. French Canadian literature 6. History writing — Arts and culture 7. Arts and Entertainment — Writing and Publishing 8. Society and culture — General

Quebec Writers' Federation Literary Awards, Mavis Gallant Prize for Non-fiction, 2007.

Explores the origins and evolution of the French language, from the first extant document written in French in the mid-ninth century and the purging of Latin from the French courts to the obsession of French speakers to protect the purity of the language.

"This is a well-told, highly accessible history of the French language that leads to a spirited discussion of the prospects for French in an increasingly English-dominated world." —*New York Times*

460 Spanish, Portuguese, Galician

The Story of Spanish. Jean-Benoit Nadeau and Julie Barlow. St. Martin's Press 2013. 496 p.
ISBN 9780312656027
Grades: Adult **460**
1. Spanish language 2. Linguistics 3. Language and languages 4. Canadian literature 5. French Canadian literature 6. Arts and Entertainment — Writing and Publishing 7. History writing — Microhistory
LC 2013002633

Jean-Benoit Nadeau and Julie Barlow chronicle the history of the Spanish language.

Includes bibliographical references and index.

470 Latin and related Italic languages

Ostler, Nicholas
Ad Infinitum: A Biography of Latin. Nicholas Ostler. Walker & Co. 2007. 400 p.
ISBN 9780802715159
Grades: Adult **470**
1. Language and culture 2. Latin language 3. Language and languages 4. Speech 5. History writing — General
LC Bl2007012214

A study of the Latin language examines its role in the evolution of Western culture and civilization; its relationship with ancient Greek language, science, and philosophy; its place in the Catholic Church; and its function as an ancestor of modern-day languages.

"In four parts, Ostler covers the origins and development of Latin in the Roman world, Latin's taking over the church, its medieval continuation and fracturing into vernaculars, and a nuanced rebirth in the Renaissance and its legacy in the contemporary world. Incredibly well documented, with examples from antiquity to the modern era." —*Library Journal*

473 Dictionaries of classical Latin

Stone, Jon R.
★ *Latin for the Illiterati: A Modern Phrase Book for an Ancient Language.* Jon R. Stone. Routledge 2009. xxii, 338 p.
ISBN 9780415777674
Grades: Adult **473**

1. Latin language 2. Reference — Language learning 3. Reference — Dictionaries
LC 2010481624

This revised and updated edition includes a brand new foreword by Richard LaFleur and more than fifteen hundred new entries and abbreviations. Organized alphabetically within the categories of verba (common words and expressions), dicta (common phrases and familiar sayings), and abbreviations, this practical and helpful reference guide is a comprehensive compendium of more than 7,000 Latin words, expressions, phrases, and sayings taken from the world of art, music, law, philosophy, theology, medicine and the theatre, as well as witty remarks and sage advice from ancient writers such as Virgil, Ovid, Cicero, and more.

Previous ed.: 1996.

483 Dictionaries of classical Greek

Liddell, Henry George
A Greek-english Lexicon. Compiled by Henry George Liddell and Robert Scott. Clarendon Press; 1996. xlv, 2042, xxxi, 320 p.
ISBN 9780198642268
Grades: Adult **483**
1. Greek language 2. Reference — Language learning 3. Reference — Dictionaries
LC 95032369

Liddell & Scott's Greek-English Lexicon is the most comprehensive and up-to-date ancient Greek dictionary in the world. Used by every student of ancient Greek in the English-speaking world, the dictionary covers every surviving ancient Greek author and text discovered up to 1940, from the Pre-Classical Greek of Homer and Hesiod to Classical Greek to the Hellenistic Period, including the Greek Old and New Testaments. This monumental work is now available with a brand new Revised Supplement. Representing the culmination of thirteen years' work, the new Supplement is a complete replacement of the 1968 Supplement. Nearly twice the size of the 1968 edition, with over 20,000 entries, it adds to the dictionary words and forms from papyri and inscriptions discovered between 1940 and the 1990s as well as a host of other revisions, updatings, and corrections to the main dictionary. Linear B forms are shown within entries for the first time, and the Revised Supplement gives the dictionary a date-range from 1200 BC to 600 AD. It is fully cross-referenced to the main text, but additions have been designed to be easily used without constant reference to the main text.

With a revised supplement, 1996; Includes bibliographical references.

492.4 Hebrew

Glinert, Lewis
The Story of Hebrew. Lewis Glinert. Princeton University Press 2016. 296 pages
ISBN 9780691153292
Grades: Adult **492.4**
1. Linguistics 2. Hebrew language 3. Israel 4. Society and culture — Ethnic studies 5. History writing — Jewish history
LC 2016022084

An examination of the Hebrew language, and its transition from the language of the Judaic scriptures, through its decline and abandonment, and eventually to its re-adoption in the 20th century in a largely unchanged form.

"This is a must-read for students of language and Jewish history." —*Publishers Weekly*

Includes bibliographical references (p. 253-260) and index.

493 Non-Semitic Afro-Asiatic languages

Dolnick, Edward
The Writing of the Gods: The Race to Decode the Rosetta Stone. Edward Dolnick. Scribner 2021. 352 p.
ISBN 9781501198939

Grades: Adult **493**
1. Young, Thomas, 1773-1829 2. Champollion, Jean-Francois, 1790-1832 3. Egyptian hieroglyphics 4. Scholars and academics 5. Language and languages 6. Extinct languages 7. Translating and interpreting 8. International competition 9. Egyptology 10. Archaeology 11. History writing — Archaeology 12. History writing — Ancient — Egypt 13. History writing — Historical mysteries 14. Life stories — Education — Scholars and educators

LC 2021022972

In this riveting true story, two rival geniuses—one English, one French—embarked on a high-stakes intellectual race to decipher the Rosetta Stone, which, once solved, would open a door that had been locked for 2,000 years.

"When the Rosetta Stone was discovered by French soldiers in 1799, 'The first guesses were that it might take two weeks to decipher,' according to this stimulating history of a linguistic puzzle that took 20 years to solve.... The result is an immersive and knowledgeable introduction to one of archaeology's greatest breakthroughs." —*Publishers Weekly*

Includes bibliographical references and index.

495.111 Chinese language — writing systems

Tsu, Jing
Kingdom of Characters: The Language Revolution That Made China Modern. Jing Tsu. Riverhead 2022. 336 p.
ISBN 9780735214729
Grades: Adult **495.111**
1. Chinese characters 2. Intercultural communication 3. Chinese language 4. Calligraphy 5. Language and languages 6. Speech 7. Civilization 8. Chinese history 9. China 10. 20th century 11. History writing — Asia — China 12. Arts and Entertainment — Writing and Publishing

LC 2021017006

Pulitzer Prize for General Nonfiction finalist, 2023.

With unforgettable characters and an unexpected perspective on the major events of China's turbulent 20th century, this fascinating volume shows how 100 years of linguistic innovation turned China into one of the most powerful countries of the modern era.

"Tsu, a professor of East Asian language and literature at Yale, debuts with an immersive history of the effort to transform the written Chinese language's vast and complex set of characters into a modern communication technology.... Tsu sheds light on the intriguing interplay between Chinese language and politics." —*Publishers Weekly*

Includes bibliographical references and index.

499 Non-Austronesian languages of Oceania, Austronesian languages, miscellaneous languages

Pukui, Mary Kawena
Hawaiian Dictionary: Hawaiian-english, English-hawaiian. Mary Kawena Pukui, Samuel H. Elbert. University of Hawaii Press 1986. xxvi, 572 p.
ISBN 9780824807030
Grades: Adult **499**
1. English language 2. Dictionaries 3. Reference — Language learning

LC 85024583

Includes definitions, a grammar, and a pronunciation key.
Bibliography: P. [565]-572.

Schor, Esther H.
Bridge of Words: Esperanto and the Dream of a Universal Language. Esther Schor. Metropolitan Books 2016. 384 p.
ISBN 9780805090796
Grades: Adult **499**
1. Language and languages 2. History writing — General

LC 2015018907

In 1887, Ludwig Lazarus Zamenhof, a Polish Jew, had the idea of putting an end to tribalism by creating a universal language, one that would be equally accessible to everyone in the world. The result was Esperanto, a utopian scheme full of the brilliance, craziness, and grandiosity that characterize all such messianic visions. In this first full history of a constructed language, poet and scholar Esther Schor traces the life of Esperanto.

"Must reading for those fascinated by linguistics and utopian endeavors and an essential volume for every library's language collection." —*Booklist*

500 Natural sciences and mathematics

Brockman, John
This Idea Is Brilliant: Lost, Overlooked, and Underappreciated Scientific Concepts Everyone Should Know. John Brockman. HarperPerennial 2018. 864 p.
ISBN 9780062698216
Grades: Adult **500**
1. Science 2. Essays 3. Science writing — General

LC Bl2018001260

As science informs public policy, decision making, and so many aspects of our everyday lives, a scientifically literate society is crucial. In that spirit, Edge.Org publisher and author of Know This, John Brockman, asks 206 of the world's most brilliant minds the 2017 Edge Question: What scientific term or concept ought to be more widely known?

Bryson, Bill
★ *A Short* History of Nearly Everything. Bill Bryson. Broadway Books 2003. IX, 544 p.
ISBN 9780767908177
Grades: 9 10 11 12 Adult **500**
1. Science 2. History writing — Science, technology, and medicine 3. Science Writing — General 4. Adult books for young adults 5. Humor writing — Classic humorists

LC 2003046006

New York Times Notable Book, 2003; Royal Society General Prizes for Science Books, 2004.

The author traces the Big Bang through the rise of civilization, documenting his work with a host of the world's most advanced scientists and mathematicians to explain why things are the way they are.

"Neither oversimplified nor overstuffed, this exceptionally skillful tour of the physical world covers the basic principles and still has room for profiles of some of the more engaging scientists." —*New York Times Book Review*

Includes bibliographical references (p. 517-527) and index.

Dawkins, Richard
Science in the Soul: Selected Writings of a Passionate Rationalist. Richard Dawkins. Random House 2017. 320 p.
ISBN 9780399592249
Grades: Adult **500**
1. Evolution 2. Reason 3. Truth 4. Science 5. Nature 6. Rationalism 7. Essays 8. Science writing — General 9. Nature writing — General

LC 2017025118

An evolutionary biologist and provocateur, in a collection of 42 essays, focuses on what science is and how it is done, the inexhaustible wonders of nature, the importance of critical thinking and the great minds who have changed his life.

"These 41 short pieces suitably capture evolutionary biologist Dawkins's reputation as a fierce proponent of rationalism, who possesses an exacting and questioning scientific mind and an acerbic wit." —*Library Journal*

Du Sautoy, Marcus
The Great Unknown: Seven Journeys to the Frontiers of Science. Marcus du Sautoy. Viking 2017. 464 p.
ISBN 9780735221802
Grades: Adult **500**

ESSENTIAL AND RECOMMENDED TITLES
500 Natural sciences and mathematics

1. Scientific discoveries 2. Theory of knowledge 3. Science 4. History writing — Science, technology, and medicine 5. Science writing — General

LC 2016056835

The award-winning author of the Music of the Primes and popular presenter of Netflix's the Story of Math explores the once-ridiculed theories of history's greatest innovators and the outer reaches of human knowledge to consider what discoveries may lie beyond the predictive powers of science.

This brilliant, well-written exploration of our universe's biggest mysteries will captivate the curious and leave them pondering 'Natural phenomena that will never be tamed and known.' —*Publishers Weekly*

Includes bibliographical references and index.

Feynman, Richard P.
★ *The Meaning of It All: Thoughts of a Citizen Scientist*. Richard P. Feynman. Addison Wesley 1998. 133 p.
ISBN 9780201360806
Grades: 11 12 Adult **500**

1. Feynman, Richard P, (Richard Phillips), 1918-1988 2. Physicists 3. Religion and science 4. Science 5. United States history 6. 20th century 7. Science Writing — Physics

LC 97048250

In a series of previously unpublished lectures given at the University of Washington in 1963, one of the century's leading physicists reveals his thoughts on religion, life, politics, and science.

Includes index.

Goldacre, Ben
Bad Science: Quacks, Hacks, and Big Pharma Flacks. Ben Goldacre. Faber and Faber 2010. xii, 288 p. : Illustration
ISBN 9781452655895
Grades: Adult **500**

1. Pseudoscience 2. Scientific errors 3. Science in mass media 4. Experiments 5. Clinical trials 6. Misinformation 7. Medical research 8. Placebo (Medicine) 9. Experimental medicine 10. Science 11. Drug industry corruption 12. Science Writing — Medicine and health 13. Business and economics — Corruption and scandal

While exposing quack doctors and nutritionists, bogus credentialing programs, and biased scientific studies, the author takes the media to task for its willingness to throw facts and proof out the window in its quest to sell more copies. He also teaches you how to evaluate placebo effects, double-blind studies, and sample size, so that you can recognize bad science when you see it.

"The author has written a very funny and biting book critiquing what he calls Bad Science. Under this heading he includes homeopathy, cosmetics manufacturers whose claims about their products defy plausibility, proponents of miracle vitamins, and drug companies and physicians who design faulty studies and manipulate the results. While it is a very entertaining book, it also provides important insight into the horrifying outcomes that can result when willful anti-intellectualism is allowed equal footing with scientific methodology." —*Boston Globe*

Originally published, in different form: London : Fourth Estate, 2008; Includes bibliographical references (p. [259-273) and index.

Hawking, Stephen
★ *Brief Answers to the Big Questions*. Stephen W. Hawking. Bantam Dell Pub Group 2018. 144 p.
ISBN 9781984819192
Grades: Adult **500**

1. Questions and answers 2. Science 3. Cosmogony 4. Science Writing — General

LC Bl2018179891

The world-famous cosmologist and #1 best-selling author of a Brief History of Time leaves us with his final thoughts on the universe's biggest questions in a posthumous work.

Munroe, Randall
How To: Absurd Scientific Advice for Common Real-world Problems. Randall Munroe. Riverhead Books 2019. 307 pages : Illustration
ISBN 9780525537090
Grades: Adult **500**

1. Science 2. Essays 3. Humor writing — General 4. Science writing — General 5. Science writing — Physics

LC Bl2019023579

The creator of the web comic xkcd and best-selling author of What If? and Thing Explainer shares inadvisable advice for responding to today's problems, from using social-media for weather forecasts to powering a home by destroying the fabric of space-time. Illustrations.

"With illustrated formulas that humorously explain the science behind Munroe's conjectures, this book is sure to entertain and educate thinkers from high school on up." —*Library Journal*

Includes bibliographical references (pages 292-299) and index.

Thing Explainer: Complicated Stuff in Simple Words. Randall Munroe. Houghton Mifflin Harcourt 2015. 61 pages : Illustration
ISBN 9780544668256
Grades: Adult **500**

1. Science 2. Technology 3. Science writing — General

LC Bl2015042919

The creator of the popular webcomic "xkcd" uses line drawings and common words to provide simple explanations for how things work, including microwaves, bridges, tectonic plates, the solar system, the periodic table, helicopters, and other essential concepts.

The New York Times best-selling author of What If? and the creator of the webcomic xkcd uses line drawings and common words to provide simple explanations for how things work, including microwaves, bridges, tectonic plates, helicopters and much more.

What If? 2: Additional Serious Scientific Answers to Absurd Hypothetical Questions. Randall Munroe. Riverhead Books 2022. 320 p.
ISBN 9780525537113
Grades: Adult **500**

1. Science 2. Questions and answers 3. Hypothesis 4. Humorous writing 5. Science writing — General 6. Humor writing — General

The millions of people around the world who read and loved What If? still have questions, and those questions are getting stranger. Thank goodness Randall Munroe is here to help. Planning to ride a fire pole from the Moon back to Earth? The hardest part is sticking the landing. Hoping to cool the atmosphere by opening everyone's freezer door at the same time? Maybe it's time for a brief introduction to thermodynamics. Before you go on a cosmic road trip, feed the residents of New York City to a T. rex, or fill every church with bananas, be sure to consult this practical guide for impractical ideas.

"Former NASA roboticist Munroe continues his quest to answer the world's unlikeliest questions....A delight for science geeks with a penchant for oddball thought experiments." —*Kirkus*

★ *What If?: Serious Scientific Answers to Absurd Hypothetical Questions*. Randall Munroe. Houghton Mifflin Harcourt 2014. xii, 303 pages : Illustration
ISBN 9780544272996
Grades: Adult **500**

1. Science 2. Questions and answers 3. Science writing — General 4. Humor writing — General 5. Books for reluctant readers

LC 2014016311

YALSA Quick Picks for Reluctant Young Adult Readers, 2016.

The creator of the webcomic xkcd.Com provides hilarious and scientifically informative answers to questions that can never be physically solved, but are fun to think about.

Those who enjoyed the irreverent style of Allie Brosh's best-selling memoir, Hyperbole and a Half, will enjoy Munroe's serious and silly musings on everything from science to romance. One question submitted to his blog: 'If all digital data were stored on punch cards, how big would Google's data warehouse be?' was even answered by the search-engine behemoth. The response, 'No comment.' —*School Library Journal*

PUBLIC LIBRARY CORE COLLECTION: NONFICTION
Twentieth Edition

Novella, Steven
*The **Skeptics'** Guide to the Universe: How to Know What's Really Real in a World Increasingly Full of Fake.* Dr. Steven Novella with Bob Novella, Cara Santa Maria, Jay Novella, and Evan Bernstein. Grand Central Publishing 2018. xviii, 494 p.

ISBN 9781538760536

Grades: Adult   500

1. Science 2. Scientific errors 3. Pseudoscience 4. Conspiracy theories 5. Logic 6. Argumentation 7. Skepticism 8. Philosophy 9. Media tie-ins 10. Science Writing — General 11. Science Writing — Weird science

LC 2018013089

Based on the podcast known for battling sloppy reasoning, bad arguments and superstitions with logical thinking, the "Skeptical Rogues" help readers try to make sense of an increasingly crazy world using critical thinking skills, science and philosophy.

"This important addition to the literature of skepticism deserves shelf space beside the works of such notables as Michael Shermer, James Randi, Robert A. Baker, and Martin Gardner." —*Booklist*

Based on a podcast; Includes bibliographical references and index.

Ritchie, Stuart
Science Fictions: How Fraud, Bias, Negligence, and Hype Undermine the Search for Truth. Stuart Ritchie. Metropolitan Books 2020. 320 p.

ISBN 9781250222695

Grades: Adult   500

1. Science 2. Scientific errors 3. Research 4. Fraud 5. Unconscious bias 6. Negligence 7. Information 8. Scientists 9. Science Writing — General

LC 2020011654

Science is how we understand the world. Yet failures in peer review and mistakes in statistics have rendered a shocking number of scientific studies useless—or, worse, badly misleading. As Science Fictions makes clear, the current system of research funding and publication not only fails to safeguard us from blunders but actively encourages bad science. By illustrating the many ways that scientists go wrong, Ritchie gives us the knowledge we need to spot dubious research and points the way to reforms that could make science trustworthy once again.

"Thorough and detailed, this is a sobering and convincing treatise for anyone invested in the intellectual credibility of science." —*Publishers Weekly*

Rovelli, Carlo
There Are Places in the World Where Rules Are Less Important Than Kindness: And Other Thoughts on Physics, Philosophy and the World. Carlo Rovelli; Translated by Erica Segre and Simon Carnell. Riverhead Books 2022. 288 p.

ISBN 9780593192153

Grades: Adult   500

1. Physics 2. Political culture 3. Art 4. Philosophy 5. Metaphysics 6. Science 7. Essays 8. Translations — Italian to English 9. Science Writing — Physics 10. Society and culture — Philosophy

LC 2021038390

One of the world's most prominent physicists and fearless free spirit, Carlo Rovelli is also a masterful storyteller. In this collection of writings, the logbook of an intelligence always on the move, he follows his curiosity and invites us on a voyage through science, literature, philosophy and politics. Written with his usual clarity and wit, these pieces, most of which were first published in Italian newspapers, range widely across time and space—from Newton's alchemy to Einstein's mistakes, from Nabokov's butterflies to Dante's cosmology, from travels in Africa to the consciousness of an octopus, from mind-altering psychedelic substances to the meaning of atheism.

"Theoretical physicist Rovelli (The Order of Time) considers politics, art, philosophy, and science in this provocative collection of 46 previously published essays." —*Publishers Weekly*

Originally published in Italian asCi sono luoghi al mondo dove piu che le regole e importante la gentilezza by RCS Media Group, Milan, in 2018; English translation published in Great Britain by Allen Lane, an imprint of Penguin Random House UK.

Rutherford, Adam
*The **Complete** Guide to Absolutely Everything: Adventures in Math and Science.* Adam Rutherford and Hannah Fry. W.W. Norton & Company 2022. 288 p.

ISBN 9780393881578

Grades: Adult   500

1. Science 2. Mathematics 3. Life 4. Time 5. Cosmology 6. Technology 7. Questions and answers 8. Scientific discoveries 9. Science Writing — General

Geneticist Adam Rutherford and mathematician Hannah Fry guide readers through time and space, through our bodies and brains, showing how emotions shape our view of reality, how our minds tell us lies, and why a mostly bald and curious ape decided to begin poking at the fabric of the universe. Rutherford and Fry shine as science sleuths, wrestling with some truly head-scratching questions: Where did time come from? Do we have free will? Does my dog love me? Both rigorous and playful, The Complete Guide to Absolutely Everything (Abridged) is a celebration of the weirdness of the cosmos, the strangeness of humans, and the joys and follies of scientific discovery.

"The title suggests that the authors aren't just authoritative but witty and accessible, with their work adding to the groundswell of recent books on the basics of the universe for lay readers." —*Library Journal*

"Rutherford and Fry (cohosts of the podcast The Curious Cases of Rutherford and Fry) offer an informative and entertaining look into the science behind everyday phenomena and questions (e.g., do humans have free will? Do dogs feel love for their owners?)." —*Library Journal*

Includes bibliographical references.

Sagan, Carl
Billions and Billions: Thoughts on Life and Death at the Brink of the Millennium. Carl Sagan. Random House 1997. xii, 241 p. : Illustration

ISBN 9780679411604

Grades: Adult   500

1. Science 2. Essays 3. Science Writing — General

LC 96052730

The author draws on the most recent research into science, mathematics, and space in a study of the mysteries of life, addressing such topics as global warming, the abortion debate, life on Mars, and his own battle with myelodysplasia.

"This collection of essays covers such topics as: the invention of chess, life on Mars, global warming, abortion, international affairs, the nature of government, and the meaning of morality. Writing with clarity and an understanding of human nature, Sagan offers hope for humanity's future." —*Library Journal*

Includes bibliographical references (p. [231]-234) and index.

Smil, Vaclav
How the World Really Works: The Science Behind How We Got Here and Where We're Going. Vaclav Smil. Viking Press 2022. 384 p.

ISBN 9780593297063

Grades: Adult   500

1. Environmental responsibility 2. Sustainable development 3. Technological innovations 4. Technology and civilization 5. Science 6. Politics and global affairs — Environmental issues and policies 7. History writing — Technological innovations

LC 2022006318

We have never had so much information at our fingertips and yet most of us don't know how the world really works. This book explains seven of the most fundamental realities governing our survival and prosperity. From energy and food production, through our material world and its globalization, to risks, our environment and its future, How the World Really Works offers a much-needed reality check—because before we can tackle problems effectively, we must understand the facts.

"In seven chapters, Smil, the author of more than 40 books on science, nature, and current affairs, explores the science behind essential contemporary topics: Energy generation, food production, material dependence, globalization, large-scale risks, responses to environmental threats, and predictive uncer-

ESSENTIAL AND RECOMMENDED TITLES
500.201 Physical sciences — Philosophy

tainty....An exceptionally lucid, evenhanded study of the scientific basis of our current and future lives." —*Kirkus*

First published in hardcover in Great Britain by Viking, an imprint of Penguin Random House Ltd, London, in 2022; Includes bibliographical references and index.

Strevens, Michael
The *Knowledge* Machine: How Irrationality Created Modern Science. Michael Strevens. Liveright Publishing Corporation 2020. x, 350 p.
ISBN 9781631491375
Grades: Adult   **500**
1. Irrationalism (Philosophy) 2. Theory of knowledge 3. Science 4. Philosophy 5. Perception 6. History writing — Science, technology, and medicine 7. Science Writing — General
LC 2020018496

Citing historical events from Newton's alchemy to Hurricane Sandy's storm surge, a paradigm-shifting investigation into the origins and structure of science urges scientists to intentionally disregard religion, theoretical beauty and philosophy to channel focus into tangible experimentation and observation.

"A thought-provoking and likely-to-be-controversial explanation of how scientists finally got it right. One of the better examinations of the origins of the scientific revolution." —*Kirkus*

Includes bibliographical references and index.

Wilkinson, Karen
The *Art* of Tinkering: Meet 150+ Makers Working at the Intersection of Art, Science & Technology. Karen Wilkinson & Mike Petrich. Weldon Owen 2013. 223 pages : Color; Illustration
ISBN 9781616286095
Grades: Adult   **500**
1. Technology 2. Inventions 3. Arts and Entertainment — Crafts and hobbies
LC Bl2014003406

Displays the best exhibits, artwork, and projects in the Exploratorium museum, including a city built out of one hundred thousand toothpicks and a musical instrument that is powered by the ocean.

Exploratorium—Cover; Includes index.

Woodford, Chris
Atoms Under the Floorboards: The Surprising Science Hidden in Your Home. Chris Woodford. Bloomsbury Sigma 2015. 336 pages : Illustration
ISBN 9781472912220
Grades: 10 11 12 Adult   **500**
1. Home furnishings 2. Scientific discoveries 3. Science 4. Adult books for young adults 5. Science writing — General
LC Bl2015018531

Explains scientific concepts by using household examples, including what kitchen knives and golf clubs have in common, how much heat energy a typical home holds in the winter, and why sunlight makes clothes look brighter.

Includes bibliographical references (pages 295-328) and index.

500.201 Physical sciences — Philosophy

Ball, Philip
Patterns in Nature: Why the Natural World Looks the Way It Does. Philip Ball. The University of Chicago, Ill. :Press 2016. 288 pages : Illustration; Color
ISBN 9780226332420
Grades: 10 11 12 Adult   **500.201**
1. Geometry in nature 2. Nature 3. Nature writing — General 4. Science writing — General 5. Science writing — Geology
LC 2015034568

The natural world is replete with patterned order underpinned by scientific and mathematical principles. Take, for example, the veins of a leaf to the fingerprint-like blotches of the leopard and the labyrinthine structure of a termite's nest to the majestic profile of a mountain range. These patterns have inspired artists, writers, designers, and musicians for thousands of years. Patterns in Nature: Why the Natural World Looks the Way It Does explores the science behind the amazing diversity of patterns in the natural world and takes readers on a visual tour of some of the world's most incredible natural wonders. Featuring awe-inspiring galleries of nature's most ingenious designs, Patterns in Nature is a synergy of art and science that will fascinate artists and nature lovers alike.

"This is formidable eye candy for the I-love-science crowd, sure to spark a sense of impressed wonder at the beauty of our universe and our ability to photograph it." —*Publishers Weekly*

Includes bibliographical references.

501 Philosophy and theory

Greenfieldboyce, Nell
★ *Transient* and Strange: Notes on the Science of Life. Nell Greenfieldboyce. W.W. Norton & Company 2024. 240 p.
ISBN 9780393882346
Grades: Adult   **501**
1. Greenfieldboyce, Nell 2. Women scientists 3. Women radio journalists 4. Science journalism 5. Nature writing 6. Everyday life 7. Memories 8. Interpersonal relations 9. Essays 10. Science Writing — General 11. Nature Writing — Personal Responses 12. Life stories — Relationships 13. Life stories — Science, technology, and medicine 14. Debut title

In her career as a science reporter, Nell Greenfieldboyce has reported from inside a space shuttle, the bottom of a coal mine, and the control room of a particle collider. In this, her debut book, she delivers a wholly original collection of powerful, emotionally raw, and unforgettable personal essays that probe the places where science touches our lives most intimately. Expertly weaving her own experiences of motherhood and marriage with an almost devotional attention to the natural world, Greenfieldboyce grapples with the weighty dualities of life: Birth and death, constancy and impermanence, memory and doubt, love and aging.

"Greenfieldboyce dazzles with her auspicious first outing." —*Publishers Weekly*

502 Science — Miscellany

Balakrishnan, Chris
How to Win Friends and Influence Fungi: Collected Quirks of Science, Tech, Engineering, and Math from Nerd Nite. Dr. Chris Balakrishnan and Matt Wasowski. St. Martin's Press 2024. 320 p.
ISBN 9781250288349
Grades: Adult   **502**
1. Science 2. Medicine 3. Technology
LC 2023036005

The co-founders of the global science organization Nerd Nite bring readers a collection of fascinating STEM topics.

"Delightful and eminently readable. This book about the Nerd Nite empire will be an excellent addition to science collections." —*Library Journal*

507.1 Science education

Tesoriero, Heather Won
The Class: A Life-changing Teacher and His World-changing Kids. Heather Won Tesoriero. Ballantine Books 2018. 288 p.
ISBN 9780399181849
Grades: Adult   **507.1**
1. Bramante, Andy 2. Teacher-student relationships 3. High school students 4. Science projects 5. Science fairs 6. Science fair experiments 7. Science teachers 8. Science 9. Gifted teenagers 10. Greenwich, Connecticut 11. Science Writing — General 12. Society and culture — Education

Traces a year in the life of a visionary high school science teacher, describing how he left a successful corporate career to guide a diverse range of students through prestigious science competitions, personal challenges and college applications.

Includes bibliographical references and index.

508 Natural history

Attenborough, David
A Life on Our Planet: My Witness Statement and a Vision for the Future. David Attenborough. Grand Central Publishing 2020. 272 p.
ISBN 9781538719985
Grades: Adult **508**
1. Attenborough, David, 1926- 2. Environmental degradation 3. Pollution 4. Biodiversity 5. Extinction 6. Environmental disasters 7. Television personalities 8. Environmentalism 9. Effect of humans on nature 10. Natural history 11. Nature Writing — Environmental Issues 12. Nature Writing — Personal Responses

In this scientifically informed account of the environmental changes occurring in the world over the last century, award-winning broadcaster and natural historian shares a lifetime of wisdom and a hopeful vision for the future.

"In this companion to the 2020 documentary of the same name, filmmaker, natural historian and best-selling author Attenborough recounts a life spent exploring and documenting wild places.... Longtime devotees as well as newcomers will find much to learn about the man and his mission." —*Library Journal*

Includes bibliographical references and index.

Darwin, Charles
★ *The Voyage of the Beagle: Journal of Researches into the Natural History and Geology of the Countries Visited During the Voyage of H.M.S. Beagle Round the World.* Charles Darwin; introduction by Steve Jones. Modern Library 2001. xix, 468 p. : Illustration
ISBN 9780375756801
Grades: 11 12 Adult **508**
1. Geology 2. Natural history 3. Trips around the world 4. Exploration 5. South America 6. 19th century 7. Nature writing — Natural Landscapes 8. Travel writing — Historic Journeys

LC 00046294

A youthful Charles Darwin records his impressions of the flora, fauna, and geology of the South American coasts.

Originally published: New York : P.F. Collier & Son, 1909.

Dillard, Annie
Pilgrim at Tinker Creek. Annie Dillard. Harper Perennial 1998. 288 p.
ISBN 9780061233326
Grades: 9 10 11 12 Adult **508**
1. Nature 2. Women and nature 3. Seasons 4. Virginia 5. Blue Ridge Mountains 6. Essays 7. Nature Writing — Personal Responses

LC 98029765

Pulitzer Prize for General Nonfiction, 1975.

Presents a series of connected essays that chronicle a year at Tinker Creek in Virginia's Blue Ridge valley. Observant, deeply contemplative, and beautifully written, Pilgrim at Tinker Creek challenges listeners to study their surroundings beyond their familiar surfaces and uncover new and refreshing milieus.

Originally published: New York : Harper's Magazine Press, 1974.

Teaching a Stone to Talk: Expeditions and Encounters. Annie Dillard. Harper & Row 1982. 177 p.
ISBN 9780060150303
Grades: Adult **508**
1. Nature 2. Life 3. Spirituality 4. Spirituality and Religion — General

LC 82047520

The Pulitzer Prize-winning writer shares her sharply observed, keenly felt encounters with the natural world—in landscapes of Eastern woods and farmlands, the Pacific Northwest coast, and tropical islands and rivers.

"In the fourteen penses that make up this book {the author bears witness, reflects on her observations of the order and disorder, the splendor and horror of the natural world." —*The New Yorker*

Gould, Stephen Jay
The Richness of Life: The Essential Stephen Jay Gould. Stephen Jay Gould; edited by Paul McGarr and Steven Rose; with an introduction by Steven Rose; and a foreword by Oliver Sacks. Norton 2007. xiv, 654 p. : Illustration
ISBN 9780393064988
Grades: 11 12 Adult **508**
1. Gould, Stephen Jay 2. Natural history 3. Evolution 4. Science writing — Biology

LC 2006029208

Collects forty-four key segments from the late renowned paleontologist and evolutionary biologist's best-selling and award-winning books, papers, and essays, in a collection that includes an assortment of previously unpublished articles and speeches.

Includes bibliographical references and index.

Heinrich, Bernd
A Naturalist at Large: The Best Essays of Bernd Heinrich. Bernd Heinrich. Houghton Mifflin Harcourt 2018. 244 p.
ISBN 9780544986831
Grades: Adult **508**
1. Natural history 2. Science 3. Men and nature 4. Bird behavior 5. Wildlife 6. Trees 7. Insects 8. Animals 9. Biology 10. Autobiographies and memoirs 11. Essays 12. Life stories — Science, technology, and medicine — Scientists and inventors 13. Nature Writing — Personal Responses

LC 2017046210

National Outdoor Book Award for Natural History Literature, 2018.

From the acclaimed scientist and writer, essays collected for the first time in book form, on ravens and other birds, insects, trees, elephants, and more: Once again 'Passionate observations [that] superbly mix memoir and science.'(New York Times).

Includes bibliographical references and index.

Keffer, Ken
Earth Almanac: Nature's Calendar for Year-round Discovery. Ken Keffer; illustrations by Jeremy Collins. Skipstone 2020. 251 p.: Illustration; Color
ISBN 9781680512823
Grades: Adult **508**
1. Phenology 2. Natural history 3. Almanacs 4. North America 5. Nature writing — General

LC 2019036902

Earth Almanac presents the greatest hits of North American nature. Structured around phenology, the study of seasonal patterns in nature, these day-by-day descriptions offer insight into activities and connections throughout the natural world. Beginningwith the Winter Solstice in December, Earth Almanac highlights a wide range of natural history, including mammals, birds, fish, reptiles, insects, intertidal and marine life, trees, plants, fungi, environmental activists, and more, all the while revealing the ebb and flow of nature across the planet. Each season features more than 90 entries, and sidebars throughout provide calls to environmental action, citizen science opportunities, and details on special dates or holidays. It makes an excellent gift to celebrate the fiftieth anniversary of Earth Day (April 22, 2020).

Macdonald, Helen
★ *Vesper Flights.* Helen MacDonald. Grove Press 2020. 288 p.
ISBN 9780802128812
Grades: Adult **508**
1. Macdonald, Helen, 1970- 2. Effect of environment on humans 3. Memory 4. Wildlife 5. Nature and culture 6. Childhood 7. Climate change 8. Nostalgia 9. Nature 10. Essays 11. Nature Writing — Personal responses

LC Bl2020016185

The award-winning author of H Is for Hawk presents a collection of essays about humanity's relationship with nature, exploring subjects ranging from captivity and immigration to ostrich farming and the migrations of songbirds from the Empire State Building.

"English naturalist Macdonald (H Is for Hawk) offers meditations on the natural world and its inhabitants in an inviting collection of 41 new and previously

ESSENTIAL AND RECOMMENDED TITLES
508.092 Natural history — Biography

published essays that are infused with wonder, nostalgia, and melancholy. . . . The message throughout is clear: the world humans enjoy today may not be around tomorrow, so it should not be taken for granted." —*Publishers Weekly*

Peck, Robert McCracken
A Glorious Enterprise: The Academy of Natural Sciences of Philadelphia and the Making of American Science. Robert McCracken Peck and Patricia Tyson Stroud; photographs by Rosamond Purcell. University of Pennsylvania Press 2012. xvii, 437 p. : Illustration; Color
ISBN 9780812243802
Grades: Adult 508
1. Natural history 2. History writing — Science, technology, and medicine 3. Science Writing — Biology
LC 2011034991

A history of the renowned museum recounts key moments in its evolution as a research and education center, as well as the role of such individuals as Thomas Jefferson and John James Audubon in championing its purpose.

"Highly recommended for all academic libraries and larger public library systems. Readers of all levels will find this book useful." —*Library Journal*
Includes bibliographical references and index.

Preston, Diana
The Evolution of Charles Darwin: The Epic Voyage of the Beagle That Forever Changed Our View of Life on Earth. Diana Preston. Atlantic Monthly Press 2022. 448 p.
ISBN 9780802160188
Grades: Adult 508
1. Darwin, Charles, 1809-1882 2. Evolution 3. Natural history 4. Naturalists 5. Natural selection 6. History writing — Exploration 7. Science Writing — Biology
LC 2022024449

When twenty-two-year-old aspiring geologist Charles Darwin boarded the HMS Beagle in 1831 with his microscopes and specimen bottles-invited by ship's captain Robert FitzRoy who wanted a travel companion at least as much as a ship's naturalist-he hardly thought he was embarking on what would become perhaps the most important and epoch-changing voyage in scientific history. Diana Preston chronicles the epic voyage as it unfolded, tracing Darwin's growth from untested young man to accomplished adventurer and natural scientist in his own right.

"An exciting biography of the immortal naturalist's legendary journey....An irresistible scientific biography and adventure story with a happy ending." —*Kirkus*
Includes bibliographical references.

Pyle, Robert Michael
Nature Matrix: New and Selected Essays. Robert Michael Pyle. Counterpoint 2020. 288 pages
ISBN 9781640092761
Grades: Adult 508
1. Pyle, Robert Michael 2. Nabokov, Vladimir Vladimirovich, 1899-1977 3. Astor, John Jacob, 1763-1848 4. Natural history 5. Nature study 6. Wilderness areas 7. Naturalists 8. Essays 9. Nature Writing — Personal Responses
LC 2019017872

A selection of nature-themed essays by the biologist author of Magdalena Mountain explores such subjects as his early years as a national park ranger, the "wilderness" of modern times and the life of Vladimir Nabokov.

"Pyle proves yet again that he is one of the most nourishing nature writers at work today." —*Kirkus*

Steelquist, Robert
The Northwest Coastal Explorer: Your Guide to the Places, Plants, and Animals of the Pacific Coast. Robert Steelquist. Timber Press 2016. 283 pages : Illustration; Color
ISBN 9781604696318
Grades: Adult 508

1. Coastal ecology 2. Natural areas 3. Natural history 4. Pacific Coast (North America) 5. North Pacific Ocean 6. Reference — Travel guides 7. Nature writing — General 8. Travel Writing — United States
LC 2015047572

A fun, engaging, and full-color field guide to the marine life in Oregon, Washington, and British Columbia.
Includes bibliographical references (pages 271-273) and index.

Wohlleben, Peter
The Secret Wisdom of Nature: Trees, Animals, and the Extraordinary Balance of All Living Things - Stories from Science and Observation. Peter Wohlleben and translated by Jane Billinghurst. Greystone Books 2019. 272 p. (Mysteries of nature trilogy, 3)
ISBN 9781771643887
Grades: Adult 508
1. Biotic communities 2. Biodiversity 3. Habitats 4. Ecology 5. Adaptation 6. Competition (Biology) 7. Animals 8. Species 9. Translations — German to English 10. Science Writing — Biology 11. Nature Writing — General
LC Bl2019004698

In The Secret Wisdom of Nature, master storyteller and international sensation Peter Wohlleben takes readers on a thought-provoking exploration of the vast natural systems that make life on Earth possible. In this tour of an almost unfathomable world, Wohlleben describes the fascinating interplay between animals and plants and answers such questions as: how do they influence each other? Do lifeforms communicate across species boundaries? And what happens when this finely tuned system gets out of sync? By introducing us to the latest scientific discoveries and recounting his own insights from decades of observing nature, one of the world's most famous foresters shows us how to recapture our sense of awe so we can see the world around us with completely new eyes.

"This deep appreciation for ecology includes a passionate look at many animals, including wolves, salmon, and bears, and reflections on how their presence affects everything around them, from what they eat to plants and trees, bodies of water, rivers, and the very air they pass through." —*Booklist*

508.092 Natural history — Biography

McAnulty, Dara
Diary of a Young Naturalist. Dara McAnulty. Milkweed Editions 2021. 224 p.
ISBN 9781571311801
Grades: Adult 508.092
1. McAnulty, Dara 2. Naturalists 3. Environmentalists 4. Autistic teenagers 5. Nature 6. Friendship 7. Family relationships 8. Teenage social advocates 9. Natural history 10. Seasons 11. Autism spectrum disorders 12. Neurodivergent people 13. Northern Ireland 14. Autobiographies and memoirs 15. Life stories — Politics — Activists and reformers 16. Life stories — Facing adversity — Medical issues — Living with disabilities 17. Nature Writing — General
LC 2020041386

British Book Award for Narrative Nonfiction of the Year, 2021.

A world-renowned youth climate activist chronicles a year in the life of his Northern Ireland home, describing the beauty of his biosphere while juggling exams, friendships, campaigning and living with the complexities of autism.

"Not a nature guide as such, but should appeal to many, including fans of nature writing, those who'd like to read about a naturalist on the spectrum, and, of course, all who find inspiration in nature." —*Library Journal*
First published by Little Toller Books in 2020.

508.4 Natural history — Europe

Flannery, Tim F.
Europe: A Natural History. Tim Flannery with Luigi Boitani. Atlantic Monthly Press 2019. 288 p.
ISBN 9780802129161

PUBLIC LIBRARY CORE COLLECTION: NONFICTION
Twentieth Edition

Grades: Adult **508.4**
1. Natural history 2. Paleontology 3. Zoology 4. Geology 5. Prehistoric animals 6. Wildlife conservation 7. Prehistoric humans 8. Neanderthals 9. European history 10. Europe 11. Australian literature 12. History writing — Europe 13. Science Writing — Paleontology

LC 2018047048

An ecological account of Europe and the forces shaping life on it.

"Throughout, the author employs crisp, lively language suitable for readers without a background in natural history; the level of research and detail, however, means that it can also be used as an uncommonly approachable natural history textbook." —*Library Journal*

First published in Australia in 2018 by the Text Publishing Company.

509 Science—History, geographic treatment, biography

Al-Khalili, Jim
The **House** of Wisdom: How Arabic Science Saved Ancient Knowledge and Gave Us the Renaissance. Jim Al-Khalili. Penguin Press 2011. 352 p.
ISBN 9781594202797
Grades: 9 10 11 12 Adult **509**
1. Islam and science 2. Religion and science 3. European Renaissance 4. Ancient science 5. Science 6. Southwest Asia and North Africa (Middle East) history 7. History writing — Science, technology, and medicine 8. Science Writing — General 9. Spirituality and Religion — Islam 10. History writing — Southwest Asia and North Africa (Middle East)

LC 2010053136

Challenges popular misconceptions to reveal the unrecognized scientific accomplishments of medieval Islam, profiling innovations that played significant roles in bridging the ancient and modern worlds while promoting the European Renaissance.

Holmes, Richard
The **Age** of Wonder: How the Romantic Generation Discovered the Beauty and Terror of Science. Richard Holmes. Pantheon Books 2009. 576 p.
ISBN 9780375422225
Grades: Adult **509**
1. Herschel, William, 1738-1822 2. Herschel, Caroline Lucretia, 1750-1848 3. Davy, Humphry, Sir, 1778-1829 4. Science 5. Scientists 6. Romanticism 7. Scientific discoveries 8. Great Britain 9. 18th century 10. Science Writing — General 11. History writing — General

LC 2008049587

ALA Notable Book, 2010; Library Journal Best Books, 2009; National Book Critics Circle Award for Non-Fiction, 2009; National Academies Communication Award, 2010; New York Times Notable Book, 2009; Royal Society General Prizes for Science Books, 2009.

The Age of Wonder" explores the earliest ideas of deep time and space, and the explorers of "dynamic science": an infinite, mysterious Nature waiting to be discovered. Three lives dominate the book: William Herschel, his sister Caroline, and Humphry Davy.

Includes bibliographical references and index.

Kean, Sam
The **Icepick** Surgeon: Murder, Fraud, Sabotage, Piracy, and Other Dastardly Deeds Perpetrated in the Name of Science. Sam Kean. Little, Brown & Company 2021. 360 p.
ISBN 9780316496506
Grades: Adult **509**
1. Scientists 2. Science 3. Research 4. Experiments 5. Obsession 6. Corruption 7. Criminal behavior 8. History writing — Science, technology, and medicine 9. True Crime — Historical Crime 10. Science Writing — General

Science is usually a force for good in the world. But sometimes, when obsession gets the better of scientists, they twist a noble pursuit into something sinister. Bestselling author Sam Kean tells the true story of what happens when unfettered ambition pushes otherwise rational men and women to cross the line in the name of science, trampling ethical boundaries and often committing crimes in the process. The Icepick Surgeon fuses the drama of scientific discovery with the illicit thrill of a true-crime tale. Kean shows that, while science has done more good than harm in the world, rogue scientists do exist, and when we sacrifice morals for progress, we often end up with neither.

"In this witty, thought-provoking book, best-selling author Kean (The Bastard Brigade; the Disappearing Spoon) explores crimes committed in the name of scientific discovery. . . . A lively, compelling addition to the true crime and popular science genres." —*Library Journal*

Includes bibliographical references and index.

Lightman, Alan P.
The **Discoveries**. Alan Lightman. Pantheon Books 2005. xviii, 553 p. : Illustration
ISBN 9780375421686
Grades: 11 12 Adult **509**
1. Research 2. Technology 3. Scientists 4. Scientific discoveries 5. Science 6. Historiography 7. 20th century 8. Essays 9. Science Writing — General 10. Adult books for young adults

LC 2005040854

Booklist Editors' Choice, 2005.

Examines the impact of some of the most noteworthy scientific advances of the twentieth century, including the personalities and human drama involved, and draws on the original papers of Einstein, Bohr, Hubble, and other scientists.

"This book chronicles 25 landmark findings in astronomy, physics, chemistry, and biology in the 20th century. Beginning with Max Planck's quantum theory and ending with Paul Berg's recombinant DNA, these breakthroughs are academically and playfully explored via the nature of the unknown, the circumstances and influences of discovery, and, most originally, the actual words of the scientists." —*Library Journal*

Includes bibliographical references and index.

Weinberg, Steven
To Explain the World: The Discovery of Modern Science. Steven Weinberg. Harper 2015. 368 p.
ISBN 9780062346650
Grades: Adult **509**
1. Ancient science 2. Medieval science 3. Science 4. Greece 5. History writing — Science, technology, and medicine 6. Science Writing — General 7. History writing — General

LC 2014030253

A Nobel Prize-winning physicist presents a masterful commentary on the history of science that examines historic clashes and collaborations between science and the competing realms of religion, technology, poetry, mathematics and philosophy, from the Ancient Greece to the world of today,.

"The author provides an almost 100-page appendix of technical notes, mathematical explanations of many of the theories and ideas discussed in the book." —*Choice*

Includes bibliographical references.

509.2 Scientists

Reser, Anna
Forces of Nature: The Women Who Changed Science. Anna Reser, Leila McNeill. Frances Lincoln 2021. 272 p. : Illustration
ISBN 9780711248977
Grades: Adult **509.2**
1. Women scientists 2. Women's history 3. Scientific discoveries 4. Women inventors 5. Science 6. Illustrated books 7. Collective biographies 8. Life stories — Science, technology, and medicine — Scientists and inventors 9. History writing — Women's history 10. History writing — Science, technology and medicine 11. Science Writing — General

From the ancient world to the present women have been critical to the progress of science, yet their importance is overlooked, their stories lost, distorted, or actively suppressed. Forces of Nature sets the record straight and charts the fascinating history of women's discoveries in science.

ESSENTIAL AND RECOMMENDED TITLES
509.22 History of Science — general works

"This expansive history from Reser and McNeill, historians and coeditors of Lady Science magazine, sheds light on women's contributions to science throughout history.... Full of eye-opening information, this unique perspective on women's history will enthrall history buffs, science enthusiasts, and feminists." —*Publishers Weekly*

"The authors cover an impressive amount of ground, and the condensed profiles peppered throughout keep things moving. Full of eye-opening information, this unique perspective on women's history will enthrall history buffs, science enthusiasts, and feminists." —*Publishers Weekly*

Includes bibliographical references and index.

509.22 History of Science — general works

Black, Alexandra
Scientists Who Changed History. Contributors: Alexandra Black, Alethea Doran, Joanna Edwards, Richard Gilbert, Janet Mohun, Victoria Pyke, Penny Warren. DK Publishing 2019. 320 pages : Illustration; Color
ISBN 9781465482488
Grades: Adult   509.22
1. Scientists 2. Biographies 3. Life stories — Science, technology, and medicine 4. Science writing — General 5. History writing — Science, technology, and medicine
LC Bl2019026980

The second title in DK's new illustrated biography series, Scientists Who Changed History profiles trailblazing individuals from Greek mathematicians, such as Archimedes and Hipparchus, through physicists of the early 20th-century, such as Marie Curie and Albert Einstein, to modern greats such as Stephen Hawking and Tim Berners-Lee.

"This comprehensively researched and beautifully designed reference work contains profiles of over 80 scientists, mathematicians, engineers, and inventors whose work changed the world." —*Booklist*

Includes index.

510 Mathematics

Benjamin, Arthur
The Magic of Math: Solving for X and Figuring Out Why. Arthur Benjamin. Basic Books 2015. 321 pages : Illustration
ISBN 9780465054725
Grades: Adult   510
1. Mathematics 2. Mathematics fun 3. Science writing — Mathematics
LC Bl2015034757

An engaging introduction to the beauty, simplicity and fun of mathematical formulas explains its essentials and disciplines through everyday examples, mnemonics and brain-teasing tricks. By the author of the Secrets of Mental Math.

Includes index.

Cheng, Eugenia
How to Bake Pi: An Edible Exploration of the Mathematics of Mathematics. Eugenia Cheng. Basic Books 2015. 320 p.
ISBN 9780465051717
Grades: Adult   510
1. Mathematics 2. Food 3. Cooking 4. Mathematicians 5. Science Writing — Mathematics 6. Food Writing — General
LC Bl2015018104

Booklist Editors' Choice, 2015.

A math expert uses cooking to shed light on the heart of mathematics.

"Despite her zeal for mathematical logic, Cheng recognizes that such logic begins in faith—irrational faith—and ultimately requires poetry and art to complement its findings. A singular humanization of the mathematical project." —*Booklist*

Clegg, Brian
Are Numbers Real?: The Uncanny Relationship of Mathematics and the Physical World. Brian Clegg. St. Martin's Press 2016. 320 p.
ISBN 9781250081049
Grades: Adult   510
1. Mathematics 2. Number concept 3. Arithmetic 4. Number theory 5. Science Writing — Mathematics
LC 2016027287

The critically acclaimed author of Ten Billion Tomorrows and the Final Frontier presents an accessible, in-depth look at the history of numbers and their applications in life and science, from math's surreal presence in the virtual world to the debates about the role of math in science.

"Clegg is an outstanding science writer, and this book lives up to his usual standard. Highly recommended for those interested in math or science." —*Library Journal*

Includes bibliographical references.

Dunham, William
The Mathematical Universe: An Alphabetical Journey Through the Great Proofs, Problems, and Personalities. William Dunham. Wiley & Sons 1994. VI, 314 p. : Illustration
ISBN 9780471536567
Grades: Adult   510
1. Mathematics 2. Mathematicians 3. Science Writing — Mathematics
LC 93046702

Travels through mathematical concepts from arithmetic to zero to explore the wonders of the Fibonacci series, Russell's Paradox, and the theory of Pythagoras.

"In this history of mathematics, Dunham sheds light not only on the personalities—eccentric, vain, brilliant—of major mathematicians, but also on contemporary social issues, such as multiculturalism and gender equity. Readers who want to understand the cultural significance of mathematics would do well to begin with this book." —*Booklist*

Includes bibliographical references (p. 297-307) and index.

Ellenberg, Jordan
★ *How Not to Be Wrong: The Power of Mathematical Thinking*. Jordan Ellenberg. The Penguin Press 2014. 480 pages
ISBN 9781594205224
Grades: Adult   510
1. Mathematics 2. Mathematical analysis 3. Everyday life 4. Science writing — Mathematics
LC 2014005394

In How Not to Be Wrong, Jordan Ellenberg shows us that math isn't confined to abstract incidents that never occur in real life, but rather touches everything we do—the whole world is shot through with it. Math allows us to see the hidden structures underneath the messy and chaotic surface of our world. It's a science of not being wrong, hammered out by centuries of hard work and argument. Armed with the tools of mathematics, we can see through to the true meaning of information we take for granted: How early should you get to the airport? What does "public opinion" really represent? Why do tall parents have shorter children? Who really won Florida in 2000? And how likely are you, really, to develop cancer? How Not to Be Wrong presents the surprising revelations behind all of these questions and many more, using the mathematician's method of analyzing life and exposing the hard-won insights of the academic community to the layman—minus the jargon. Ellenberg pulls from history as well as from the latest theoretical developments to provide those not trained in math with the knowledge they need.

Ellenberg finds the common-sense math at work in the everyday world, and his vivid examples and clear descriptions show how 'Math is woven into the way we reason.' —*Publishers Weekly*

Includes bibliographical references and index.

Parker, Matt
Humble Pi: When Math Goes Wrong in the Real World. Matt Parker. Riverhead Books 2020. 336 pages

ISBN 9780593084687
Grades: Adult **510**
1. Mathematics 2. Errors 3. Science Writing — Mathematics
LC 2019029057

This tour of real-world mathematical disasters reveals the importance of math in everyday life. All sorts of seemingly innocuous mathematical mistakes can have significant consequences. Exploring and explaining a litany of glitches, near misses, and mathematical mishaps involving the internet, big data, elections, street signs, lotteries, the Roman Empire, and an Olympic team, Matt Parker uncovers the ways math trips us up.

"Nonsense, blunders, and delusions make for good reading, so Parker's relentless litany will have a wide appeal. Fun reading for nonmathematicians." —*Kirkus*

Includes index; Originally published: London : Allen Lane, 2019.

Seife, Charles

Proofiness: The Dark Arts of Mathematical Deception. Charles Seife. Viking 2010. 320 p.
ISBN 9780670022168
Grades: 9 10 11 12 Adult **510**
1. Mathematics 2. Pseudoscience 3. Statistics 4. Science Writing — Mathematics 5. Adult books for young adults
LC 2010012127

The bestselling author of "Zero" shows how mathematical misinformation pervades—and shapes—our daily lives.

"The author examines the many ways that people fudge with numbers, sometimes just to sell more moisturizer but also to ruin our economy, rig our elections, convict the innocent and undercount the needy.... [This book] reveals the truly corrosive effects on a society awash in numerical mendacity. This is more than a math book; it's an eye-opening civics lesson." —*New York Times Book Review*

Includes bibliographical references and index.

Stewart, Ian

Visions of Infinity: The Great Mathematical Problems. Ian Stewart. Basic Books 2013. 320 p.
ISBN 9780465022403
Grades: Adult **510**
1. Mathematics 2. Mathematicians 3. Science Writing — Mathematics
LC BI2013003267

A celebrated mathematician, explaining why mathematical problems exist, what drives mathematicians to solve them, and why their efforts matter in the context of science as a whole, presents a fascinating history of mathematics as told through 14 of its greatest problems.

Yates, Kit

The Math of Life and Death: 7 Mathematical Principles That Shape Our Lives. Kit Yates. Scribner 2020. 256 p.
ISBN 9781982111878
Grades: Adult **510**
1. Mathematics 2. Statistics 3. Misinformation 4. Errors 5. Science Writing — Mathematics 6. Society and culture — Psychology and human behavior
LC 2019024831

A first book by an Oxford-trained mathematician illuminates seven mathematical principles that shape our lives, from the controversies of DNA testing to the probabilities that shaped the Chernobyl disaster.

"A welcome addition to the math-for-people-who-hate-math genre." —*Kirkus*

Includes bibliographical references and index.

510.76 Mathematics — Examinations

Szpiro, George

Poincare's Prize: The Hundred-year Quest to Solve One of Math's Greatest Puzzles. George G. Szpiro. Dutton 2007. IX, 309 p.
ISBN 9780525950240

Grades: 11 12 Adult **510.76**
1. Perelman, Grigori, 1966- 2. Mathematics 3. Science Writing — Mathematics
LC 2007012792

Booklist Editors' Choice, 2007.

Traces the hundred-year effort to solve the Poincare Conjecture and its successful solution by Grigory Perelman, an impoverished Russian recluse who refused all prizes and academic appointments while solving an array of mathematical conundrums.

Never has mathematics provided more fascinating human drama! —*Booklist*

Includes bibliographical references and index.

510.9 Mathematics — History

Brooks, Michael

The Art of More: How Mathematics Created Civilization. Michael Brooks. Pantheon Books 2022. 256 p.
ISBN 9781524748999
Grades: Adult **510.9**
1. Mathematics 2. Civilization 3. History 4. Mathematicians 5. Applied mathematics 6. Equations 7. Technological innovations 8. History writing — Science, technology, and medicine 9. Science Writing — Mathematics 10. Life stories — Science, technology, and medicine 11. History writing — Technological innovations
LC 2021024094

In this captivating, sweeping history, Michael Brooks makes clear that mathematics was one of the foundational innovations that catapulted humanity from a nomadic existence to civilization, and that it has been instrumental in every subsequent great leap of humankind—from charting the movements of celestial bodies, to navigating the globe, to tracking the dissemination of viruses. And the trailblazing mathematicians who devoted their lives to taming numbers come to life in Brooks's telling. The Art of More brings mathematics back into the heart of what it means to be human.

"A more or less chronological history and compelling case that advances in mathematics provided the foundation for the advance of civilization.... Not a mathematics-is-fun romp but a serious, persuasive effort to describe how its discoveries paralleled human progress." —*Kirkus*

Originally published in the UK by Scribe, London, in 2021; Includes bibliographical references.

Kitagawa, Kate

The Secret Lives of Numbers: A Hidden History of Math's Unsung Trailblazers. Kate Kitagawa and Timothy Revell. William Morrow & Company 2024. 352 p.
ISBN 9780063206052
Grades: Adult **510.9**
1. Mathematics 2. Mathematicians 3. Women mathematicians 4. Marginalized people 5. Science Writing — Mathematics 6. History Writing — General 7. Life stories — Science, technology, and medicine

Spanning six continents and thousands of years of untold stories, as well as just about every mathematical discipline, a renowned math historian and a science journalist/Mathematician make the case that the history of math is infinitely deeper, broader and richer than the narrative we think we know.

"A fine history of mathematics that seeks to decouple it from its traditional Eurocentric focus and usually succeeds." —*Kirkus*

Merzbach, Uta C.

A History of Mathematics. Uta C. Merzbach and Carl B. Boyer. John Wiley 2011. xx, 668 p. : Illustration
ISBN 9780470525487
Grades: Adult **510.9**
1. Mathematics 2. Science writing — Mathematics
LC 2010003424

For more than forty years, a History of Mathematics has been the reference of choice for those looking to learn about the fascinating history of humankind's re-

ESSENTIAL AND RECOMMENDED TITLES
510.92 Mathematicians

lationship with numbers, shapes, and patterns. This revised edition features up-to-date coverage of topics such as Fermat's Last Theorem and the Poincare Conjecture, in addition to recent advances in areas such as finite group theory and computer-aided proofs.

Includes bibliographical references (p. 633-646) and index.

Pickover, Clifford A.
The Math Book: From Pythagoras to the 57th Dimension, 250 Milestones in the History of Mathematics. Clifford A. Pickover. Sterling Pub. 2009. 527, 1 p. : Color illustration
ISBN 9781402788291
Grades: 8 9 10 11 12 Adult   510.9
1. Mathematics 2. Science writing — Mathematics
LC 2008043214

"Pickover's love of mathematics shines through the text and images, and it is likely that the reader will catch at least some of his enthusiasm." —*Choice*

Includes bibliographical references (p. 518-525) and index.

510.92 Mathematicians

Shetterly, Margot Lee
★ *Hidden Figures: The American Dream and the Untold Story of the Black Women Mathematicians Who Helped Win the Space Race.* Margot Lee Shetterly. William Morrow 2016. xviii, 346 pages
ISBN 9780062363596
Grades: 10 11 12 Adult   510.92
1. Women mathematicians 2. African American women 3. Space programs 4. Racism in politics and government 5. Racism in employment 6. Race relations 7. International competition 8. 20th century 9. Page to screen 10. Science writing — Space and flight 11. Adult books for young adults 12. History writing — African American — United States

ALA Notable Book, 2017; Amelia Bloomer List, 2017; BCALA Literary Award for Nonfiction, 2017; Booklist Editors' Choice: Adult Books for Young Adults, 2016; National Academies Communication Award, 2017.

An account of the previously unheralded but pivotal contributions of NASA's African-American women mathematicians to America's space program describes how they were segregated from their white counterparts by Jim Crow laws in spite of their groundbreaking successes.

"Shetterly's highly recommended work offers up a crucial history that had previously and unforgivably been lost. We'd do well to put this book into the hands of young women who have long since been told that there's no room for them at the scientific table." —*Library Journal*

Adapted into a film by the same name in 2016.

511 General principles of mathematics

Alexander, Amir R.
Infinitesimal: How a Dangerous Mathematical Theory Shaped the Modern World. Amir Alexander. Scientific American/Farrar, Straus and Giroux 2014. 368 pages
ISBN 9780374176815
Grades: Adult   511
1. Calculus 2. Mathematics 3. Renaissance science 4. Religion and science 5. Theories 6. Science 7. Catholic theology 8. Religions 9. European history 10. 16th century 11. 17th century 12. Science Writing — Mathematics 13. History writing — Europe
LC 2013033923

The epic battle over a mathematical concept that shook the old order and shaped the world as we know it.

"The author navigates even the most abstract mathematical concepts as deftly as he does the layered social history, and the result is a book about math that is actually fun to read. A fast-paced history of the singular idea that shaped a multitude of modern achievements." —*Kirkus*

Includes bibliographical references and index.

Thompson, Erica
Escape from Model Land: How Mathematical Models Can Lead Us Astray and What We Can Do About It. Erica Thompson. Basic Books 2022. 304 p.
ISBN 9781541600980
Grades: Adult   511
1. Mathematics 2. Mathematical models 3. Models and model making 4. Science Writing — Mathematics

"A complex subject rendered in accessible terms, with good advice for using models without drowning in data." —*Kirkus*

511.3 Mathematical logic (Symbolic logic)

Fortnow, Lance
The Golden Ticket: P, Np, and the Search for the Impossible. Lance Fortnow. Princeton University Press 2013. 200 p.
ISBN 9780691156491
Grades: Adult   511.3
1. Mathematics 2. Computer science 3. Algorithms 4. Equations 5. Computational complexity 6. Computer algorithms 7. Science Writing — Mathematics 8. Science Writing — Computing, the Internet, and Technology
LC 2012039523

Provides a nontechnical introduction to the P-NP problem in computing—which asks whether every problem than can be verified quickly by a computer can also be solved quickly by a computer—its rich history, and its algorithmic implications for everything we do with computers and beyond.

Includes bibliographical references and index.

512 Algebra

Conway, John Horton
The Book of Numbers. John H. Conway, Richard K. Guy. Copernicus 1996. IX, 310 p. : Illustration; Color
ISBN 9780387979939
Grades: Adult   512
1. Number theory 2. Science writing — Mathematics
LC 95032588

Explores number theory and patterns that emerge in arithmetic, algebra, and geometry.

Includes bibliographical references and index.

Singh, Simon
Fermat's Enigma: The Epic Quest to Solve the World's Greatest Mathematical Problem. Simon Singh; foreword by John Lynch. Walker 1997. xviii, 315 p. : Illustration
ISBN 9780802713315
Grades: Adult   512
1. Wiles, Andrew, 1953- 2. Mathematicians 3. Mathematics 4. 1990s 5. Science Writing — Mathematics 6. Adult books for young adults
LC 97020748

New York Times Notable Book, 1997.

The story of Fermat's Last Theorem, devised by the seventeenth-century French mathematician Pierre de Fermat, recounts the struggles of three and a half centuries of scientists to devise a proof for it.

"This vivid account is fascinating reading for anyone interested in mathematics, its history, and the passionate quest for solutions to unsolved riddles." —*School Library Journal*

Also published as Fermat's last theorem; Includes bibliographical references (p. 301-305) and index.

PUBLIC LIBRARY CORE COLLECTION: NONFICTION
Twentieth Edition

519.2 Probabilities

Mazur, Joseph
Fluke: The Math and Myth of Coincidences. Joseph Mazur. Basic Books 2016. 272 p.
ISBN 9780465060955
Grades: 11 12 Adult   519.2
1. Coincidence 2. Chance 3. Mathematics 4. Mathematics in nature 5. Science Writing — Mathematics
LC 2015043288

Presents a mathematical guide to understanding why life can seem to be one big coincidence—and why the odds of just about everything are better than we think.

"The author draws examples and illustrations from a variety of fields—law enforcement, economics, the sciences—and, when he unavoidably gets into some fairly complicated mathematical discussions, he explains his terms and remembers that, for the most part, his readers aren't mathematicians. An ideal book, then, for the lay reader who is curious about the nature of coincidence." —*Booklist*

Includes bibliographical references and index.

519.5 Statistical mathematics

Wheelan, Charles J.
Naked Statistics: Stripping the Dread from the Data. Charles Wheelan. W. W. Norton & Co. 2013. xviii, 282 pages : Illustration
ISBN 9780393071955
Grades: 11 12 Adult   519.5
1. Statistics 2. Mathematics 3. Probabilities 4. Information services 5. Mathematical analysis 6. Science Writing — Mathematics
LC 2012034411

The author takes on the stuffy study of statistics to describe and demystify another essential discipline by explaining how Netflix knows which movies you'll like and how to catch schools that cheat on standardized tests.

"Wheelan has provided an intuitive presentation of statistical concepts without getting bogged down by extensive data lists or computation. The author begins by generally introducing each idea with an idealized situation to illustrate that statistical setting and its impact on effective interpretation, and then moves on to current real-world settings to legitimize his discussion. He also clearly discusses subtleties that can be encountered, showing how data users must be careful to avoid oversimplifying the implications of a given result. The presentation is nonthreatening, yet readers will find it a suitably thoughtful consideration of statistical ideas." —*Choice*

Includes bibliographical references (pages 261-267) and index.

520 Astronomy and allied sciences

Christian, Carol
A Question and Answer Guide to Astronomy. Carol Christian,Space Telscope Science Institute, Baltimore, USA, Jean-Rene Roy, Laval University, Quebec, Canada. Cambridge University Press 2017. xiv, 344 p. : Color; Illustration
ISBN 9781316615263
Grades: Adult   520
1. Astronomy 2. Science writing — Astronomy
LC 2016040127

Contains 250 questions and answers about astronomy, particular for the amateur astronomer.

English translation published 2010, revised 2016—T.P. verso; Includes bibliographical references (pages 325-332) and index; First published 2008 as 250 reponses ?vos questions sur l'astronomie—T.P. verso.

Levesque, Emily
The Last Stargazers: The Enduring Story of Astronomy's Vanishing Explorers. Emily Levesque. Sourcebooks 2020. xvi, 313 p.
ISBN 9781492681076
Grades: 11 12 Adult   520
1. Levesque, Emily 2. Astronomy 3. Women astronomers 4. Astronomical observatories 5. Telescopes 6. Astronomers 7. Research 8. Autobiographies and memoirs 9. Life stories — Science, technology, and medicine — Scientists and inventors 10. Science writing — Space and flight
LC 2020005285

Amidst the lonely quiet of stargazing to wild bears loose in the observatory, these love stories of astronomy show how scientists are going beyond the machines to infuse important creativity and intimate passion into the stars, inspiring future generations to peer skyward in pursuit of the universe's secrets.

Includes bibliographical references and index.

Lintott, Chris
Accidental Astronomy: How Random Discoveries Shape the Science of Space. Chris Lintott. Basic Books 2024. 336 p.
ISBN 9781541605411
Grades: Adult   520
1. Astronomy 2. Scientific discoveries 3. Good luck 4. Hypothesis 5. Astronomers 6. Cosmology 7. Astrophysics 8. Space sciences 9. Science writing — Astronomy
LC 2023049966

A professor of astrophysics discusses the ways in which luck defines his field of study and how both amateurs and scientific professionals must be looking at the right place and right time in the sky.

Lintott's awe-inspiring reflections on the universe's unknowable origin and development is fused with a distinctly human idea, that many of the most profound discoveries in astronomy were not made by 'Deliberate moves,' but rather by 'Stumbling accidents.' —*Booklist*

Originally published in 2024 by Torva in the United Kingdom; Includes bibliographical references and index.

Plait, Philip C.
Under Alien Skies: A Sightseer's Guide to the Universe. Philip Plait. W W Norton & Company 2023. 304 p. : Illustration
ISBN 9780393867305
Grades: Adult   520
1. Cosmology 2. Planets 3. Astronomy 4. Space 5. Science writing — Space and flight

Drawing on the latest scientific research and his prodigious imagination, a renowned astronomer and science communicator takes us on an immersive tour of the universe to view ten of the most spectacular sights outer space has to offer, including the strange, beautiful shadows cast by a hundred thousand stars.

"Diagrams and vivid color photos enhance the presentation. This will change how readers think about space." —*Publishers Weekly*

Ridpath, Ian
Stars & Planets: The Complete Guide to the Stars, Constellations, and the Solar System. Ian Ridpath & Wil Tirion. Princeton University Press 2017. 400 pages : Illustration; Color
ISBN 9780691177885
Grades: Adult   520
1. Astronomy 2. Planets 3. Stars 4. Observing things 5. Science writing — Astronomy
LC Bl2018003900

Offers information about all eighty-eight constellations of the Northern and Southern skies and provides simple star charts for easy identification.

Includes index.

Sagan, Carl
Cosmos. Carl Sagan. Random House 2002. xvi, 365 p. : Illustration; Color; Map
ISBN 9780375508325
Grades: Adult   520
1. Astronomy 2. Science 3. Science Writing — Space and Flight
LC 2002069744

ESSENTIAL AND RECOMMENDED TITLES
520.9 Astronomy — History

Hugo Award for Best Related Non-Fiction Book, 1981.
A complete guide for the layman to modern thinking in all areas of astronomy and cosmology.
"Based on the author's television series of the same name, this volume covers the 10- to 20-billion-year history of the universe, from the big bang and subsequent evolution of molecular material through the evolution of human culture."
—*Library Journal.* {review of 1980 edition
Originally published: New York : Random House, 1980; Includes bibliographical references (p. [350]-355) and index.

Sanders, Ella Frances
Eating the Sun: Small Musings on a Vast Universe. Ella Frances Sanders. Penguin Books, an imprint of Penguin Random House LLC 2019. 160 p.
ISBN 9780143133162
Grades: Adult   520
1. Astronomy 2. Astrophysics 3. Everyday life 4. Natural history 5. Physics 6. Evolution 7. Time 8. Relativity (Physics) 9. Photosynthesis 10. Cosmology 11. Solar system 12. Earth 13. Science Writing — Space and Flight 14. Science Writing — Biology
Explores the principles, laws, and wonders of the universe, the solar system, the world, and daily life alongside these phenomena.

Trefil, James
Space Atlas: Mapping the Universe and Beyond. James Trefil; with a foreword by Buzz Aldrin. National Geographic 2019. 351 pages : Illustration; Color; Map
ISBN 9781426219696
Grades: Adult   520
1. Astronomy 2. Planets 3. Solar system 4. Sun 5. Reference — Atlases 6. Science writing — Astronomy 7. Science writing — Space and Flight
LC 2018410255
In this guided tour of our planetary neighborhood, the Milky Way and other galaxies, and beyond, detailed maps and fascinating imagery from recent space missions partner with clear, authoritative scientific information. Starting with the sun and moving outward into space, acclaimed science writer and physicist James Trefil illuminates each planet, the most important moons, significant asteroids, and other objects in our solar system. Looking beyond, he explains what we know about the Milky Way and other galaxies—and how we know it, with clear explanations of the basics of astrophysics, including dark matter and gravitational waves. For this new edition, and to celebrate the 50th anniversary of his moonwalk, astronaut and American hero Buzz Aldrin offersa new special section on Earth's moon and its essential role in space exploration past and future.
Includes bibliographical references and indexes.

Tyson, Neil deGrasse
To Infinity and Beyond: A Journey of Cosmic Discovery. Neil deGrasse Tyson, Lindsey Nyx Walker. National Geographic Books 2023. 320 p.
ISBN 9781426223303
Grades: Adult   520
1. Astronomy 2. Cosmology 3. Astrophysics 4. Stars 5. Planets 6. Galaxies 7. Astronomical discoveries 8. Space exploration 9. Space 10. Science Writing — Space and Flight
LC 2023000808
No one can make the mysteries of the universe more comprehensible—and fun—than Neil deGrasse Tyson. With wit, charm, and everyday analogies, he brings planetary science down to earth and principles of astrophysics within reach. In this entertaining book, illustrated with vivid photographs and art, readers travel with him through space and time, starting with the big bang and voyaging to the far reaches of the universe and beyond.
"Buoyed by eye-popping photos of supernovas and distant galaxies, this is equal parts entertaining and informative." —*Publishers Weekly*
Includes bibliographical references and index.

520.9 Astronomy — History

Sobel, Dava
A More Perfect Heaven: How Copernicus Revolutionized the Cosmos. Dava Sobel. Walker Pub. 2011. 272 p.
ISBN 9780802717931
Grades: 11 12 Adult   520.9
1. Copernicus, Nicolaus, 1473-1543 2. Rhaticus, Georg Joachim, 1514-1576 3. Astronomy 4. Astronomers 5. Mathematicians 6. Solar system 7. Poland 8. 16th century 9. Biographies 10. Science Writing — Space and Flight 11. Science Writing — Physics 12. Life stories — Science, technology, and medicine — Scientists and inventors 13. Adult books for young adults 14. Book club best bets
LC 2011024772
The best-selling author of Galileo's Daughter traces the story of the reclusive 16th-century cleric who introduced the revolutionary idea that the Earth orbits the sun, in an account that describes the dangerous forces and complicated personalities that marked the publication of Copernicus's findings.
Includes bibliographical references and index.

520.92 Astronomers

Tyson, Neil deGrasse
Letters from an Astrophysicist. Neil deGrasse Tyson. W W Norton & Company 2019. 247 p.
ISBN 9781324003311
Grades: Adult   520.92
1. Tyson, Neil deGrasse 2. Cosmology 3. Astronomy 4. Astrophysics 5. Science 6. Space and time 7. Cosmogony 8. Astrophysicists 9. Life on other planets 10. Letters 11. Science writing — Physics 12. Adult books for young adults
LC 2019030198
Astrophysicist Neil deGrasse Tyson has attracted one of the world's largest online followings with his fascinating, widely accessible insights into science and our universe. Now, Tyson invites us to go behind the scenes of his public fame by revealing his correspondence with people across the globe who have sought him out in search of answers. In this hand-picked collection of 101 letters, Tyson draws upon cosmic perspectives to address a vast array of questions about science, faith, philosophy, life, and of course, Pluto. His succinct, opinionated, passionate, and often funny responses reflect his popularity and standing as a leading educator.

522 Astronomy — Techniques, procedures, apparatus, equipment, materials

Johnson, George
Miss Leavitt's Stars: The Untold Story of the Woman Who Discovered How to Measure the Universe. George Johnson. W.W. Norton 2005. xiv, 162 p. : Illustration (Great discoveries)
ISBN 9780393051285
Grades: Adult   522
1. Leavitt, Henrietta Swan, 1868-1921 2. Women astronomers 3. Astronomy 4. Social life and customs 5. United States 6. 20th century 7. Biographies 8. Science Writing — Space and Flight 9. Life stories — Science, technology, and medicine — Scientists and inventors
LC 2005002823
Recounts the story of Radcliffe-educated Henrietta Swan Leavitt, who in the face of ill health and progressing hearing loss discovered a new law that enabled astronomers to use variable stars in order to measure the universe.
"This book is a fine tribute to a remarkable woman of science." —*Publishers Weekly*
Includes bibliographical references (p. 149-150) and index.

PUBLIC LIBRARY CORE COLLECTION: NONFICTION
Twentieth Edition

523 Specific celestial bodies and phenomena

Shore, Linda
 The *Total Skywatcher's Manual: 275+ Skills and Tricks for Exploring Stars, Planets & Beyond*. Linda Shore, David Prosper & Vivian White of the astronomical society of the Pacific. Weldon Owen 2015. Color; Illustration
 ISBN 9781616288716
 Grades: Adult   523
 1. Stars 2. Constellations 3. Astronomy 4. Science writing — Astronomy
 LC Bl2015041893
 Shares useful information for beginning and advanced stargazers, including sky charts and diagrams, advice on choosing equipment, and suggestions for DIY projects.
 Includes index.

523.01 Astrophysics

Cliff, Harry
 How to Make an Apple Pie from Scratch: In Search of the Recipe for Our Universe, from the Origins of Atoms to the Big Bang. Harry Cliff. Doubleday 2021. 384 p.
 ISBN 9780385545655
 Grades: Adult   523.01
 1. Particles (Nuclear physics) 2. Matter 3. Higgs bosons 4. Cosmology 5. Physicists 6. Large Hadron Collider (France and Switzerland) 7. Big Bang Theory (Astronomy) 8. Physics 9. Chemistry 10. Astronomy 11. Science Writing — Physics
 LC 2020047429
 By an experimental physicist who works on the Large Hadron Collider, a mind-altering look at the foundational questions bedeviling modern physics, among them: Where does matter come from? Carl Sagan famously said, "If you wish to make an apple pie from scratch, you must first invent the universe." but what fundamental matter is the universe made of? What banged in the Big Bang? and how did that matter arise from nothing into the world we now know? Harry Cliff—a University of Cambridge particle physicist and acclaimed science presenter—sets out in pursuit of answers.
 "Physicist Cliff (The Sun) takes readers on an enthusiastic tour of the universe and modern physics in this enlightening survey. . . . Cliff describes complex ideas vividly and accessibly, and he's got a knack for making theory exciting. This enlightening and entertaining outing is worth savoring." —*Publishers Weekly*
 Includes bibliographical references and index.

Prescod-Weinstein, Chanda
 The Disordered Cosmos: A Journey into Dark Matter, Spacetime, and Dreams Deferred. Chanda Prescod-Weinstein. Bold Type Books 2021. 288 p.
 ISBN 9781541724709
 Grades: Adult   523.01
 1. Astrophysics 2. Cosmology 3. Particles (Nuclear physics) 4. Dark matter (Astronomy) 5. Astrophysicists 6. Sexism in science 7. Racism 8. Science Writing — Physics 9. Science Writing — Space and Flight
 LC 2020040651
 Los Angeles Times Book Prize for Science and Technology, 2021.
 From a star theoretical physicist, a journey into the world of particle physics and the cosmos—and a call for a more just practice of science.
 "Part introduction to quantum mechanics and cosmology, part memoir, and part sociological study, this work challenges readers to question the nature of how science is done in contemporary society, as well as what it means when everyone has a seat at the cosmological table." —*Library Journal*
 Includes bibliographical references and index.

Tyson, Neil deGrasse
 ★ *Astrophysics for People in a Hurry*. Neil deGrasse Tyson. 2017. 144 p.
 ISBN 9780393609394
 Grades: Adult   523.01
 1. Astrophysics 2. Cosmology 3. Space and time 4. Cosmogony 5. Science writing — Physics 6. Adult books for young adults
 LC 2017005442
 Goodreads Choice Award, 2017; LibraryReads Favorites, 2017.
 The notable host of StarTalk reveals just what people need to be fluent and ready for the next cosmic headlines: from the Big Bang to black holes, from quarks to quantum mechanics, and from the search for planets to the search for life in the universe.
 "Substituting down-to-earth wit for unnecessary jargon, Tyson presents ideas in clean, straightforward language and allows for the awesome nature of the universe to impress itself on readers unadorned." —*Kirkus*
 Includes index.

523.1 The universe, galaxies, quasars

Alexander, Stephon
 Fear of a Black Universe: An Outsider's Guide to the Future of Physics. Stephon Alexander. Basic Books 2021. 272 p.
 ISBN 9781541699632
 Grades: Adult   523.1
 1. Alexander, Stephon 2. Cosmology 3. Quantum theory 4. African American scientists 5. Physics 6. Discrimination 7. Marginalized people 8. Research 9. Science Writing — Physics
 LC 2021001977
 A leading cosmologist looks the three principles that shape all theories of the universe: the principle of invariance, the quantum principle and the principle of emergence and how they help solve some of physics' greatest mysteries.
 "Theoretical physicist Alexander (The Jazz of Physics) searches the far reaches of the cosmos while addressing the experiences of marginalized people in STEM fields in his refreshing survey. . . . The result is both an excellent work of advocacy and a welcoming introduction to physics." —*Publishers Weekly*
 Includes bibliographical references and index.

Berman, Bob
 Earth-shattering: Violent Supernovas, Galactic Explosions, Biological Mayhem, Nuclear Meltdowns, and Other Hazards to Life in Our Universe. Bob Berman. Little, Brown & Company 2019. 336 p.
 ISBN 9780316511353
 Grades: Adult   523.1
 1. Big Bang Theory (Astronomy) 2. Cosmology 3. Explosions 4. Catastrophism 5. Supernovae 6. Nuclear explosions 7. Science Writing — Space and Flight 8. Science Writing — Physics
 LC 2018026997
 A heart-pumping exploration of the biggest explosions in history, from the Big Bang to mysterious activity on Earth and everything in between. In Earth-Shattering, astronomy writer Bob Berman guides us through an epic, all-inclusive investigation into these instances of violence both mammoth and microscopic.
 "This lively menagerie of astrophysical oddities will entertain any reader whos ever wondered what the biggest, most dangerous bangs in the universe might be." —*Publishers Weekly*
 Includes index.

Cham, Jorge
 Frequently Asked Questions About the Universe. Jorge Cham and Daniel Whiteson. Riverhead Books 2021. 324 pages : Illustration
 ISBN 9780593189313
 Grades: Adult   523.1
 1. Cosmology 2. Science 3. Astrophysics 4. Science Writing — Space and Flight
 LC 2021001503
 A physics professor and a popular online cartoonist use their signature brand of humor honed on their podcast "Daniel and Jorge Explain the Universe" to provide short, accessible and lighthearted answers to questions about time, space, gravity, and wormholes.

ESSENTIAL AND RECOMMENDED TITLES
523.1 The universe, galaxies, quasars

"Physicist Whiteson and cartoonist Cham (We Have No Idea) bring their podcast Daniel and Jorge Explain the Universe to the page in this amusing intro to the mysteries of the cosmos.... Entertaining and satisfying, this is sure to please." —*Publishers Weekly*
Includes index.

Chown, Marcus
Infinity in the Palm of Your Hand: Fifty Wonders That Reveal an Extraordinary Universe. Marcus Chown. Diversion Books 2019. 214 p.
ISBN 9781635765946
Grades: Adult   523.1
1. Science 2. Theories 3. Information 4. Science Writing — General 5. Adult books for young adults

Explores some of the most profound and important science about us, our world, and beyond by examining some astonishing facts that reveal the vast complexities of the universe.

"A genial tour of the universe and its mysteries...Heavy stuff lightly spunjust the thing for the science buff in the house." —*Kirkus*
Originally published: London : Michael O'Mara Books, 2018.

Cox, Brian
Universal: A Guide to the Cosmos. Brian Cox and Jeff Forshaw. Da Capo Press 2017. 320 pages
ISBN 9780306822704
Grades: Adult   523.1
1. Astrophysics 2. Space sciences 3. Astronomy 4. Cosmology 5. General relativity (Physics) 6. Big Bang Theory (Astronomy) 7. Empiricism 8. Questioning 9. Science 10. Science Writing — Space and Flight 11. Science Writing — Physics
LC 2017930821

Providing explanations, diagrams and photos, two physicists reveal how we can all understand some of the most fundamental questions about our Earth, Sun, solar system and the galaxies beyond, presenting a world of simple questions with sublime answers.

Frank, Adam
Light of the Stars: Alien Worlds and the Fate of the Earth. Adam Frank. W.W. Norton & Company, Inc. 2018. 288 p.
ISBN 9780393609011
Grades: Adult   523.1
1. Cosmology 2. Human ecology 3. Exobiology 4. Civilization 5. Earth 6. Science writing — Physics 7. Science writing — Space and flight
LC 2017061640
Booklist Editors' Choice, 2018.

The astrophysicist traces beliefs about alien intelligence from the ancient Greeks to the theories of today's leading minds, drawing on the latest research to consider how other worlds may have addressed civilization-driven climate change.
Includes bibliographical references and index.

Greene, B.
The Fabric of the Cosmos: Space, Time, and the Texture of Reality. Brian Greene. A.A. Knopf 2004. xii, 569 p. : Illustration
ISBN 9780375412882
Grades: Adult   523.1
1. Cosmology 2. String theory (Nuclear physics) 3. Heisenberg uncertainty principle 4. Physics 5. Science Writing — Physics 6. Adult books for young adults
LC 2003058918
New York Times Notable Book, 2004.

A foremost string theorist discusses such topics as Newton's perspectives on space, Einstein's fusion of space and time, and recent breakthroughs on multidimensional universe theory.

"Frogs in bowls, falling eggs, loaves of bread, pennies on balloons, ping pong balls in molasses, and babushka dolls are just some of the analogies used to explain complex concepts cleverly. After reading this book, you will never look at a starry night sky the same way again." —*Library Journal*
Includes bibliographical references (p. [543]-544) and index.

Until the End of Time: Mind, Matter, and Our Search for Meaning in an Evolving Universe. Brian Greene. Random House Inc 2020. 320 pages
ISBN 9781524731670
Grades: Adult   523.1
1. Cosmology 2. Big Bang Theory (Astronomy) 3. Physics 4. Quantum theory 5. Black holes (Astronomy) 6. Consciousness 7. Purpose in life 8. Entropy 9. Philosophy 10. Science Writing — Physics 11. Society and culture — Psychology and human behavior
LC 2019022442
New York Times Notable Book, 2020.

The Columbia University theoretical physicist and best-selling author of the Elegant Universe explores subjects ranging from quantum mechanics to black holes, sharing insights into how human life and consciousness emerged from chaos.

"Curious readers interested in some of the most fundamental questions of existence, and willing to invest some time and thought, will be richly rewarded by his fascinating exploration." —*Publishers Weekly*
Includes bibliographical references and index.

Hawking, Stephen
A Brief History of Time. Stephen W. Hawking. Bantam Books 1998. IX, 212 p. : Illustration
ISBN 9780553380163
Grades: 11 12 Adult   523.1
1. Cosmology 2. Astronomy 3. Time 4. Big Bang Theory (Astronomy) 5. Black holes (Astronomy) 6. Physics 7. Space and time 8. Science Writing — Physics

Stephen W. Hawking, widely regarded as the most brilliant physicist since Einstein, discusses in a friendly and self-deprecating manner age-old questions about the origin and fate of the universe. Difficult concepts are made simple by Hawking's familiar, accessible prose.
Includes index.

★ *A Briefer History of Time.* Stephen Hawking and Leonard Mlodinow. Bantam Books 2005. 162 p. : Color illustration
ISBN 9780553804362
Grades: 11 12 Adult   523.1
1. Cosmology 2. Astronomy 3. Time 4. Grand unified theories (Nuclear physics) 5. Big Bang Theory (Astronomy) 6. Black holes (Astronomy) 7. Science Writing — Physics 8. Adult books for young adults
LC 2005042949

A shorter, more accessible edition of a now-classic survey of the origin and nature of the universe features new full-color illustrations and an expanded, easier to understand treatment of the volume's more important theoretical concepts.

"Hawking and Mlodinow provide one of the most lucid discussions of this complex topic ever written for a general audience. Readers will come away with an excellent understanding of the apparent contradictions and conundrums at the forefront of contemporary physics." —*Publishers Weekly*
Includes bibliographical references and index.

Kaku, Michio
The God Equation: The Quest for a Theory of Everything. Michio Kaku. Doubleday 2021. 256 p.
ISBN 9780385542746
Grades: Adult   523.1
1. Cosmology 2. Big bang theory (Astronomy) 3. Physics 4. Quantum theory 5. Science writing — Physics
LC 2020034243

A renowned theoretical physicist and New York Times best-selling author of Hyperspace and the Future of Humanity, tells the story of one of the greatest quests in all of science.

"Theoretical physicist and best-selling author Kaku (The Future of Humanity, 2018) eloquently reviews the structure of our universe, highlighting contributions from intellectual giants and those continuing the daunting, decades-long quest for the elusive theory of everything." —*Booklist*

Parallel Worlds: A Journey Through Creation, Higher Dimensions, and the Future of the Cosmos. Michio Kaku. Doubleday 2005. xvii, 428 p. : Illustration
ISBN 9780385509862
Grades: 11 12 Adult   523.1
1. Cosmology 2. Big Bang Theory (Astronomy) 3. Superstring theories 4. Parallel universes 5. Hyperspace 6. Fourth dimension 7. Science Writing — Physics
LC 2004056039
Booklist Editors' Choice, 2004.

A distinguished physicist sheds new light on the groundbreaking discoveries that have revolutionized the field of cosmology and transformed understanding of the universe, offering an incisive explanation of the multiverse M-theory and its implications in terms of the fate of our own universe.

"This is a riveting popular treatment of the string revolution in physics written by a pioneering theorist in the field. Kaku expounds comprehensibly on why astrophysicists love strings and branes and the way they resolve various vexatious cosmological paradoxes." —*Booklist*

Includes bibliographical references (p. [403]-405) and index.

Lightman, Alan P.
Searching for Stars on an Island in Maine. Alan Lightman. Pantheon Books 2018. 240 p.
ISBN 9781101871867
Grades: Adult   523.1
1. Cosmology 2. Philosophy 3. Religion and science 4. Science writing — General 5. Society and culture — Philosophy
LC 2017014750

The acclaimed author of Einstein's Dreams presents a lyrical meditation on religion and science as they relate to the human yearning for permanence and certainty in spite of discoveries that prove the world's impermanent and uncertain nature.

"Lightman's illuminating language and crisp imagery aim to ignite a sense of wonder in any reader whos ever pondered the universe, our world, and the nature of human consciousness." —*Publishers Weekly*

Mack, Katie
The ***End*** of Everything: (astrophysically Speaking). Katie Mack. Scribner 2020. 240 p.
ISBN 9781982103545
Grades: Adult   523.1
1. Quantum theory 2. Astrophysics 3. End of the universe 4. Cosmology 5. Physicists 6. String theory (Nuclear physics) 7. Dark matter (Astronomy) 8. Science Writing — Physics
LC Bl2020016348
New York Times Notable Book, 2020.

An eye-opening look at five ways the universe could end, and the mind-blowing lessons each scenario reveals about the most important concepts in cosmology.

"Readers with some background in physical sciences, philosophers of science, and anyone wondering what to read after Brian Greene's Until the End of Time will relish this blend of wit and deep thought." —*Library Journal*

Includes index.

Marchant, Jo
The ***Human*** Cosmos: A Secret History of the Stars. Jo Marchant. Dutton 2020. xii, 386 p.
ISBN 9780593183014
Grades: Adult   523.1
1. Cosmology 2. Civilization 3. Culture 4. Effect of environment on humans 5. Astronomy 6. Technology 7. Humans 8. Sense of wonder 9. History writing — Arts and culture 10. Science Writing — Space and flight
LC 2020004943

Revealing how early cultures celebrated the mysteries of a night sky now hidden by today's pollution and tech, the best-selling author of Cure invites readers to reconnect the human experience to the remarkable cosmic cycles that shaped it.

Includes bibliographical references and index.

McTier, Moiya
The ***Milky*** Way: An Autobiography of Our Galaxy. Via Moiya McTier. Grand Central Publishing 2022. 192 p.
ISBN 9781538754153
Grades: Adult   523.1
1. Cosmology 2. Astronomy 3. Physics 4. Galaxies 5. Milky Way 6. Science writing — Astronomy 7. Science Writing — Space and Flight
LC 2022004461

An astrophysicist and folklorist presents an out-of-this-world autobiography of the Milky Way that recounts the history and future of the universe in accessible but scientific detail, detailing what humans have discovered about everything, from its formation to its eventual death.

"McTier, writing as the Milky Way, cleverly covers the origins of the universe, how it might end, and key players in the history of space science, all in a droll, dignified voice gently scornful of human foible….The result is truly stellar." —*Publishers Weekly*

"Astrophysicist McTier delivers in her debut a delightful report on the Milky Way's inner workings, told from the galaxy's imagined point of view." —*Publishers Weekly*

Includes bibliographical references and index.

Pontzen, Andrew
The ***Universe*** in a Box: Simulations and the Quest to Code the Cosmos. Andrew Pontzen. Riverhead Books 2023. 288 p.
ISBN 9780593330487
Grades: Adult   523.1
1. Cosmology 2. Astrophysics 3. Computer simulation 4. Scientific forecasting 5. Mathematical models 6. Astronomy 7. Physics 8. Quantum theory 9. 20th century 10. 21st century 11. Science writing — Astronomy 12. Science writing — Physics

Cosmologist Andrew Pontzen explains how physicists model the universe's most exotic phenomena, from black holes and colliding galaxies to dark matter and quantum entanglement, enabling them to study the evolution of virtual worlds and to shed new light on our reality.

"An enthralling analysis of simulation, a formidable technology that may usher in a new era of cosmology." —*Kirkus*

Randall, Lisa
Dark Matter and the Dinosaurs: The Astounding Interconnectedness of the Universe. Lisa Randall. Ecco Press 2015. 256 p.
ISBN 9780062328472
Grades: Adult   523.1
1. Dark matter (Astronomy) 2. Astrophysics 3. Life 4. Life sciences 5. Evolution 6. Earth history 7. Science writing — Physics
LC Bl2015035307

The renowned particle physicist and New York Times best-selling author of Warped Passages draws on original research into dark matter to illuminate the surprising connections between deep space and life on Earth.

"Writing in a deceptively chatty narrative style, Randall provides a fascinating window into the ex c itement of discovery and the rigor required to test and elaborate new hypotheses. A top-notch science book from a leading researcher." —*Kirkus*

Tegmark, Max
Our Mathematical Universe: My Quest for the Ultimate Nature of Reality. Max Tegmark. Alfred A. Knopf 2013. 432 pages
ISBN 9780307599803
Grades: Adult   523.1
1. Tegmark, Max 2. Cosmology 3. Mathematical physics 4. Astronomy 5. Parallel universes 6. Autobiographies and memoirs 7. Science Writing — Mathematics 8. Life stories — Science, technology, and medicine — Scientists and inventors

ESSENTIAL AND RECOMMENDED TITLES
523.1 The universe, galaxies, quasars

LC 2013016020

Max Tegmark leads us on an astonishing journey through past, present, and future, and through the physics, astronomy and mathematics that are the foundation of his work, most particularly his hypothesis that our physical reality is a mathematical structure and his theory of the ultimate multiverse. In a dazzling combination of both popular and ground-breaking science, he not only helps us grasp his often mind-boggling theories (his website gives a flavor of how they might boggle the mind), but he also shares with us some of the often surprising triumphs and disappointments that have shaped his life as a scientist.

"Lively and lucid, the narrative invites general readers into debates over computer models for brain function, over scientific explanations of consciousness, and over prospects for finding advanced life in other galaxies." —*Booklist*

Tonelli, Guido
Genesis: *The Story of How Everything Began.* Guido Tonelli; translated from the Italian by Erica Segre and Simon Carnell. Farrar Straus & Giroux 2021. 240 p.
ISBN 9780374600488
Grades: Adult   **523.1**
1. Cosmology 2. Cosmogony 3. Life 4. Particles (Nuclear physics) 5. Astronomy 6. Scientific discoveries 7. Evolution 8. Translations — Italian to English 9. Science Writing — Physics 10. Science Writing — Space and Flight

LC 2020050642

Guido Tonelli, the acclaimed, award-winning particle physicist and a central figure in the discovery of the Higgs boson (the "God particle"), reveals the extraordinary story of our genesis—from the origins of the universe, to the emergence of life on Earth, to the birth of human language with its power to describe the world. Evoking the seven days of biblical creation, Tonelli takes us on a brisk, lively tour through the evolution of our cosmos and considers the incredible challenges scientists face in exploring its mysteries. Genesis both explains the fundamental physics of our universe and marvels at the profound wonder of our existence.

"Einstein meets Ovid in Tonelli's compelling account of how the universe was born and how it has since evolved. Grounded in theoretical science but sustained by artistic fervor, this account not only illuminates the precepts of modern cosmology for nonspecialists, but also endows those precepts with rare imaginative power." —*Booklist*

English translation originally published in 2021 by Profile Books Ltd, Great Britain; Originally published: Milan : Feltrinelli Editore, 2019; Translated from the Italian.

Tucker, Wallace H.
Chandra's *Cosmos: Dark Matter, Black Holes, and Other Wonders Revealed by Nasa's Premier X-ray Observatory.* Wallace H. Tucker. Smithsonian Books 2017. 304 p.
ISBN 9781588345875
Grades: Adult   **523.1**
1. Astronomy 2. Space telescopes 3. Extrasolar planets 4. Dark matter (Astronomy) 5. Black holes (Astronomy) 6. Astronomical observatories 7. Science Writing — Space and Flight 8. Science Writing — Physics

LC 2016016560

Presents the scientific discoveries achieved through the Chandra X-ray Observatory, including galaxy clusters, black holes, dark matter, and dark energy.

"Its one astonishment after another in this invaluable, imagination-stirring overview of cutting-edge astrophysics." —*Booklist*

Includes bibliographical references and index.

Tyson, Neil deGrasse
Cosmic *Queries: Startalk's Guide to Who We Are, How We Got Here, and Where We're Going.* Neil deGrasse Tyson with James Trefil; edited by Lindsey N. Walker. National Geographic 2021. 312 p.
ISBN 9781426221774
Grades: Adult   **523.1**
1. Astronomy 2. Cosmology 3. Astrophysics 4. Curiosities and wonders 5. Physics 6. Media tie-ins 7. Science Writing — Physics 8. Science Writing — Space and flight

LC 2020038953

A legendary astrophysicist offers a unique spin on the mysteries and curiosities of the cosmos, building on rich material from his beloved StarTalk podcast, while a renowned physicist takes on a big questions that humanity has been posing for millennia.

"As expected from National Geographic publications, the book is beautifully illustrated. . . . Casual readers and science buffs alike will appreciate Tyson's folksy approach to explaining difficult scientific concepts." —*Library Journal*

Includes bibliographical references and index.

Startalk: *Everything You Ever Need to Know About Space Travel, Sci-fi, the Human Race, the Universe, and Beyond.* with Neil deGrasse Tyson. National Geographic 2016. 302 pages : Color; Illustration
ISBN 9781426217272
Grades: Adult   **523.1**
1. Cosmology 2. Earth sciences 3. Humans 4. Space exploration 5. Science Writing — Space and Flight

LC 2016019357

A sumptuously photographed companion to the celebrated scientist's popular podcast and National Geographic Channel series combines the subjects of his most favorite Emmy-nominated talks with comprehensive fun facts, thought-provoking sidebars and vivid imagery.

Contributing editors, Charles Liu, astrophysics professor at the City University of New York's College of Staten Island, and Jeffrey Lee Simons, social media director of StarTalk Radio.

Welcome *to the Universe: An Astrophysical Tour.* Neil deGrasse Tyson, Michael A. Strauss, and J. Richard Gott. Princeton University Press 2016. 432 p.
ISBN 9780691157245
Grades: 11 12 Adult   **523.1**
1. Cosmology 2. Astronomy 3. Astrophysics 4. Relativity (Physics) 5. Space and time 6. Stars 7. Planets 8. Black holes (Astronomy) 9. Wormholes (Astrophysics) 10. Galaxies 11. Science Writing — Space and Flight 12. Science Writing — Physics 13. Adult books for young adults

LC 2016013487

Three of today's leading astrophysicists offer a guided tour of the cosmos, discussing the latest discoveries in the field, exploring why Pluto lost its planet status, and covering everything you need to know about planets, stars, galaxies, black holes, wormholes and time travel.

"An accessible and comprehensive overview of our universe by three eminent astrophysicists, based on an introductory course they have taught at Princeton University." —*Kirkus*

Includes bibliographical references and index.

Whitehouse, David
The Alien *Perspective: A New View of Humanity and the Cosmos.* David Whitehouse. Icon Books 2022. 255 p.
ISBN 9781785787492
Grades: Adult   **523.1**
1. Humans 2. Human evolution 3. Life on other planets 4. Consciousness 5. Cosmology 6. Scientific forecasting 7. Science Writing — Space and Flight 8. Science Writing — Biology

In David Whitehouse's most ambitious book to date he explores how human evolution has been intertwined with the workings of the cosmos from the very beginning, and what the far-distant future may hold, both for the universe and for ourselves. Given enough time, Whitehouse contends, we must communicate with intelligent aliens whose divergent perspective will transform our understanding of the universe. Drawing the thread of human consciousness from the cave to the cosmos, the author of Apollo 11: The Inside Story charts our future journey to the end of space and time, and considers whether something of humanity could remain at the end of it all.

"Whitehouse (Apollo 11: The Inside Story; Space 2069) uses his background as a former BBC correspondent and science editor to attempt to answer the eternal question: Is there life on other planets? The book looks at this question through the lens of many kinds of intelligent life (not just humankind), the history of Earth as it relates to other planets, and what's already known about the universe." —*Library Journal*

Includes index.

PUBLIC LIBRARY CORE COLLECTION: NONFICTION
Twentieth Edition

523.2 Planetary systems

Kaltenegger, Lisa
★ *Alien Earths: The New Science of Planet Hunting in the Cosmos.* Lisa Kaltenegger. St. Martin's Press 2024. 320 p.
ISBN 9781250283634
Grades: Adult 523.2
1. Extrasolar planets 2. Life on other planets 3. Extraterrestrial anthropology 4. Space exploration 5. Life (Biology) 6. Cosmology 7. Space sciences 8. Cartography 9. Science Writing — Space and Flight 10. Science writing — Astronomy
LC 2023056123

An astrophysicist unlocks the mysteries of alien worlds, from lava planets to multi-sun systems, using Earth as a key and humanity's curiosity as fuel, in a thrilling quest to answer whether we are alone in the universe.

"The breezy prose makes the sophisticated science accessible, and armchair astronomers will be entranced by the descriptions of remarkable exoplanets." —*Publishers Weekly*

Includes index.

Lang, Kenneth R.
The Cambridge Guide to the Solar System. Kenneth R. Lang. Cambridge University Press 2011. xxv, 475 p. : Illustration; Color
ISBN 9780521198578
Grades: Adult 523.2
1. Solar system 2. Science writing — Astronomy
LC 2011411432

"Anyone with a need for information on the solar system should find fulfillment in the pages of this handsome work, and it is a beautiful browsing book." —*Booklist*

Includes indexes.

Summers, Michael E.
Exoplanets: Diamonds Worlds, Super-earths, Pulsar Planets, and the New Search for Life Beyond Our Solar System. Michael Summers, and James Trefil. Smithsonian Books 2017. 240 p.
ISBN 9781588345943
Grades: Adult 523.2
1. Extrasolar planets 2. Space environment 3. Life on other planets 4. Habitable planets 5. Space exploration 6. Planets 7. Aliens 8. Science writing — Space and flight
LC 2016018596

Booklist Editors' Choice, 2017.

The past few years have seen an incredible explosion in our knowledge of the universe. Since its 2009 launch, the Kepler satellite has discovered more than two thousand exoplanets, or planets outside our solar system. More exoplanets are being discovered all the time, and even more remarkable than the sheer number of exoplanets is their variety. In Exoplanets, astronomer Michael Summers and physicist James Trefil explore these remarkable recent discoveries: Planets revolving around pulsars, planets made of diamond, planets that are mostly water, and numerous rogue planets wandering through the emptiness of space.

"These revelations, how they were made, imaginative voyages to five un-Earthly types of planets, and their implications for life and intelligence elsewhere than on Earth are concisely illuminated by astrophysicists Summers and Trefil in this marvelously fascinating and wonderfully accessible illustrated book." —*Booklist*

Includes index.

523.3 Moon

Boyle, Rebecca
Our Moon: How Earth's Celestial Companion Transformed the Planet, Guided Evolution, and Made Us Who We Are. Rebecca Boyle. Random House 2024. 304 p.
ISBN 9780593129722
Grades: Adult 523.3
1. Satellites 2. Orbits 3. History 4. Civilization 5. Culture 6. Influence (Psychology) 7. Gravity 8. Astronomy 9. Science 10. Calendars 11. Time measurements 12. Space exploration 13. Moon 14. Science Writing — Space and Flight 15. History writing — Microhistory 16. Debut title

An acclaimed journalist takes us on a incredible cultural and scientific tour throughout history to reveal the intimate role our 4.5-billion-year-old cosmic companion has played in our biological and cultural evolution, showing us that the Moon belongs to everybody and nobody at all.

"An appealing literary trip to the moon and an appreciation of the moon's immense importance." —*Booklist*

523.43 Mars

Aldrin, Buzz
Mission to Mars: My Vision for Space Exploration. Buzz Aldrin; with Leonard David. National Geographic 2013. 258 p.
ISBN 9781426210174
Grades: Adult 523.43
1. Space colonies 2. Space flight to Mars 3. Space exploration 4. Mars probes 5. Space tourism 6. Exploration 7. Mars (Planet) 8. Science Writing — Space and Flight
LC Bl2013020786

The history-making astronaut, aerospace engineer and respected advocate for space colonization outlines a plan for taking humans to Mars within the next quarter century, posing business-specific arguments while outlining practical strategies for travel and planetary homesteading.

"Aldrin makes a daring proposal for further space exploration in this exciting glimpse of the new new frontier." —*Publishers Weekly*

523.44 Asteroids (Planetoids)

Lauretta, D. S.
The Asteroid Hunter: A Scientist's Journey to the Dawn of Our Solar System. Dante S. Lauretta. Grand Central Publishing 2024. 336 p.
ISBN 9781538722947
Grades: Adult 523.44
1. Space exploration 2. Space probes 3. Soil science 4. Asteroids 5. Astronomers 6. Planetary theory 7. Planetology 8. Engineering design 9. American people 10. United States 11. Science writing — Astronomy
LC 2023040980

The Principal Investigator of NASA's historic OSIRIS-Rex Asteroid Sample Return Mission offers a behind-the-scenes account of his team's daring quest to retrieve an asteroid sample—one that held the potential to not only unlock the secrets of life's origins but also to avert an unprecedented disaster.

"The message is that the U.S. government can still complete remarkable projects, a resonant, hopeful conclusion that is much needed in these chaotic times. Lauretta's account of a historic mission is an impressive combination of fascinating science and human inspiration." —*Kirkus*

Includes bibliographical references and index.

523.7 Sun

Baron, David
American Eclipse: A Nation's Epic Race to Catch the Shadow of the Moon and Win the Glory of the World. David Baron. Liveright Publishing Corporation, a division of W.W. Norton & Company 2017. xiii, 330 p.
ISBN 9781631490163
Grades: Adult 523.7
1. Watson, James C. (James Craig), 1838-1880 2. Mitchell, Maria, 1818-1889 3. Edison, Thomas A. (Thomas Alva), 1847-1931 4. Science 5. Eclipses 6. Astronomy 7. Astronomers 8. Civilization 9. United States

ESSENTIAL AND RECOMMENDED TITLES
523.8 Stars

10. American Westward Expansion (1803-1899) 11. 19th century 12. History writing — Science, technology, and medicine

LC 2017009679

Booklist Editors' Choice, 2017.

Documents the efforts of three late-19th-century scientists to observe the rare total solar eclipse of 1878, citing how the respective ambitions of James Craig Watson, Maria Mitchell and Thomas Edison, juxtaposed against the challenges of the Wild West, helped America's early pursuits as a scientific superpower.

"With a wealth of choice details about their lives, Baron brilliantly presents these three pioneers, their ambitions, and their struggles." —*Booklist*

Includes bibliographical references and index.

Nordgren, Tyler E.

Sun, Moon, Earth: The History of Solar Eclipses, from Omens of Doom to Einstein and Exoplanets. Tyler Nordgren. Basic Books 2016. 256 p.

ISBN 9780465060924

Grades: 10 11 12 Adult   523.7

1. Eclipses 2. Astronomy 3. Archaeoastronomy 4. Lunar eclipses 5. Solar eclipses 6. Science 7. Solar system 8. Sun 9. Moon 10. History writing — Science, technology, and medicine 11. Science Writing — Space and Flight 12. Adult books for young adults

LC 2016013888

Ahead of the first total eclipse of the sun in 40 years, which will take place on August 21, 2017, an astronomer describes how solar eclipses were treated and interpreted by past civilizations, philosophers and Victorian scientists.

"A charming natural history of eclipses and a guide to witnessing the awe-inspiring event yourself." —*Kirkus*

Includes bibliographical references and index.

523.8 Stars

Fletcher, Seth

Einstein's Shadow: A Black Hole, a Band of Astronomers, and the Quest to See the Unseeable. Seth Fletcher. Ecco Press 2018. 288 p.

ISBN 9780062312020

Grades: Adult   523.8

1. Astrophysics 2. Astronomers 3. Black holes (Astronomy) 4. Relativity (Physics) 5. Space and time 6. Radio telescopes 7. Radio astronomy 8. Physics 9. Philosophy 10. Science Writing — Physics 11. Science Writing — Space and Flight 12. Life stories — Science, technology, and medicine — Scientists and inventors

LC 2018276358

Traces the efforts of an elite scientific team that put Einstein's theory to an ultimate test during a historic mission to photograph a black hole, addressing key questions about time, space and the nature of the universe.

Impey, Chris

Einstein's Monsters: The Life and Times of Black Holes. Chris Impey. W.W. Norton & Company 2019. 304 p.

ISBN 9781324000938

Grades: Adult   523.8

1. Black holes (Astronomy) 2. Gravity 3. Physics 4. String theory (Nuclear physics) 5. General relativity (Physics) 6. Science Writing — Physics 7. Science Writing — Space and Flight

LC 2018019192

An astronomer and critically-acclaimed author answers questions on the cutting edge of astrophysics to explores the fascinating science of black holes and their role in theoretical physics from Einstein's equations of general relativity to testing string theory.

Includes bibliographical references and index.

Tirion, Wil

The Cambridge Star Atlas. Wil Tirion. Cambridge University Press 2011. 1 atlas (vi, 90 p.) : Color illustration; Color; Map

ISBN 9780521173636

Grades: Adult   523.8

1. Astronomy 2. Stars 3. Atlases 4. Reference books — Science 5. Science Writing — Space and Flight

LC 2012589778

Provides information about the moon, star charts and monthly sky maps covering that which is visible each month in different hemispheres.

Includes bibliographical references (p. 90).

526 Mathematical geography

Sobel, Dava

Longitude: The True Story of a Lone Genius Who Solved the Greatest Scientific Problem of His Time. Dava Sobel. Walker 1995. VIII, 184 p.

ISBN 9780802713124

Grades: 11 12 Adult   526

1. Harrison, John, 1693-1776 2. Longitude 3. Clock and watch makers 4. Orientation 5. Directions (Geography) 6. Measurement 7. British history 8. 18th century 9. Page to screen 10. Science Writing — Great Engineering Feats 11. History writing — Technological innovations 12. History writing — Europe — United Kingdom 13. History writing — Enlightenment — Europe 14. Adult books for young adults

LC 95017402

ALA Notable Book, 1997; British Book Award for Book of the Year, 1997; School Library Journal Best Books: Best Adult Books 4 Teens, 1996.

Traces the forty-year endeavor of John Harrison to safeguard financial interests and the lives of countless sailors by building the first chronometer, a mechanical device that would enable effective timekeeping on the sea.

"Sobel tells his story (and the larger history of the search for longitude) clearly, entertainingly, and with a fine sense of the era in which it took place. Breezily written and full of fascinating characters and facts, here's a science book as enjoyable as any novel." —*Kirkus*

Includes bibliographical references (p. 177-180) and index.

526.09 Cartography — History

Garfield, Simon

On the Map: A Mind-expanding Exploration of the Way the World Looks. Simon Garfield. Gotham Books 2013. 368 p.

ISBN 9781592407798

Grades: Adult   526.09

1. Cartography 2. Maps 3. Surveying 4. History writing — Microhistory

LC 2013375048

ALA Notable Book, 2014.

Examines the pivotal relationship between mapping and civilization, demonstrating the unique ways that maps relate and realign history in an account that also shares engaging cartography stories and map lore.

529 Chronology

Burdick, Alan

Why Time Flies: A Mostly Scientific Investigation. by Alan Burdick. Simon & Schuster 2017. 352 p.

ISBN 9781416540274

Grades: Adult   529

1. Time measurements 2. Time 3. Science Writing — General

LC 2016025791

The award-winning author of Out of Eden presents an intimate exploration of how life is organized around time and its conflicting perceptions, drawing on international travels and research lab visits where he witnessed fascinating time-altering phenomena.

"A highly illuminating intellectual investigation." —*Kirkus*

Includes bibliographical references and index.

PUBLIC LIBRARY CORE COLLECTION: NONFICTION
Twentieth Edition

530 Physics

Czerski, Helen
Storm in a Teacup: The Physics of Everyday Life. Helen Czerski. 2017. 336 p.
ISBN 9780393248968
Grades: 11 12 Adult   530
1. Science 2. Physics 3. Science Writing — Physics 4. Adult books for young adults
LC 2016046555

Explanations of scientific principles as they can be observed in everyday examples, from the billowing cloud appearance of milk in hot drinks to how ducks keep their feet warm while walking on ice, reveal how they are linked to major challenges, including climate change and the energy crisis.
Includes bibliographical references and index.

Einstein, Albert
★ *The Evolution of Physics: The Growth of Ideas from Early Concepts to Relativity and Quanta.* Albert Einstein and Leopold Infeld. Simon and Schuster 1938. x, 319, 1 p. Illustration; Plate; Diagram
ISBN 9780671201562
Grades: Adult   530
1. Physics 2. Relativity (Physics) 3. Quantum theory 4. Science Writing — Physics
LC 38027272

Clear and concise explanations of the development of theories explaining physical phenomena.
"An exposition for the layman of the growth of ideas in physical science." —*Publishers Weekly*

Feynman, Richard P.
★ *Six Easy Pieces: Essentials of Physics, Explained by Its Most Brilliant Teacher.* Richard P. Feynman; originally prepared for publication by Robert B. Leighton and Matthew Sands; new introduction by Paul Davies. Addison Wesley 1995. xxix, 145 p. : Illustration
ISBN 9780201409550
Grades: 11 12 Adult   530
1. Physics 2. Atoms 3. Science 4. Science Writing — Physics
LC 94030894

The six easiest chapters from Feynman's celebrated lectures on physics, which the Nobel Prize-winning scientist delivered from 1961 to 1963 at the California Institute of Technology, have been reprinted in this volume.
Includes index.

Gray, Theodore W.
Reactions: An Illustrated Exploration of Elements, Molecules, and Change in the Universe. Theodore Gray; photographs by Nick Mann. Black Dog & Leventhal Publishers 2017. VII, 216 pages : Illustration; Color
ISBN 9780316391221
Grades: Adult   530
1. Chemical elements 2. Chemistry 3. Molecules 4. Science writing — Biology 5. Science writing — Chemistry 6. Science writing — General
LC 2017020093

In a follow-up to the Elements and Molecules, a internationally best-selling author and app creator demonstrates how the focus of his first two books combine to create chemical reactions including combustion, photosynthesis, respiration and oxidation.
Provides an illustrated exploration at how molecules come together in the reactions that shape the world.
Includes index.

Rovelli, Carlo
★ *Seven Brief Lessons on Physics.* Carlo Rovelli. Riverhead Books 2016. 96 p.
ISBN 9780399184413
Grades: 10 11 12 Adult   530
1. Physics 2. Science 3. Relativity (Physics) 4. Gravity 5. Science Writing — Physics
LC Bl2016001513

A introduction to modern physics by a founder of the loop quantum gravity theory shares seven succinct lessons on topics ranging from general relativity and quantum mechanics to elementary particles and black holes. An international best-seller.

Stanley, Matthew
Einstein's War: How Relativity Triumphed Amid the Vicious Nationalism of World War I. Matthew Stanley. Dutton 2019. 384 p.
ISBN 9781524745417
Grades: Adult   530
1. Einstein, Albert, 1879-1955 2. Eddington, Arthur Stanley, Sir, 1882-1944 3. Scientists 4. Relativity (Physics) 5. Science 6. World War I 7. Political persecution 8. Alliances 9. Cooperation 10. History writing — Science, technology, and medicine 11. History writing — Wars and conflicts — World War I 12. Life stories — Science, technology, and medicine — Scientists and inventors
LC 2019001286

The history of science podcaster behind What the If?!? reveals how the life of Einstein and the acceptance of his theory of relativity were challenged by the harsh realities of World War I and nationalist bigotry that criminalized his ideas.
"Fans of popular science, Einstein, physics, and World War I will find this to be entertaining and informative." —*Library Journal*
Includes bibliographical references and index.

530.01 Philosophy and theory

Krauss, Lawrence Maxwell
The Greatest Story Ever Told—so Far: Why Are We Here? Lawrence M. Krauss. Pocket Books 2017. 320 p.
ISBN 9781476777610
Grades: Adult   530.01
1. Physics 2. Cosmology 3. Gravity 4. Space and time 5. Quantum theory 6. Cosmogony 7. Solar system origin 8. Science Writing — Physics 9. Science Writing — Space and Flight
LC Bl2017004042

An award-winning theoretical physicist and best-selling author of a Universe from Nothing traces the dramatic discovery of the counterintuitive world of reality, explaining how readers can shift their perspectives to gain greater understandings of our individual roles in the universe.
"An admirable complement to the author's previous book and equally satisfying for those willing to read carefully." —*Kirkus*

Wilczek, Frank
Fundamentals: Ten Keys to Reality. Frank Wilczek. Penguin Press 2021. 272 p.
ISBN 9780735223790
Grades: Adult   530.01
1. Reality 2. Physics 3. Space and time 4. Matter 5. Energy 6. Cosmology 7. Science Writing — Physics
LC 2020020086

One of our great contemporary scientists reveals the 10 profound insights that illuminate what everyone should know about the physical world.
"In his fifth book on the nature of physical reality, MIT physics professor Wilczek delivers a breathtaking feat of popularization, especially in the 'Simplified' way he presents and dissects 10 fundamental principles in fields of study ranging from cosmology to quantum mechanics." —*Kirkus*
Includes index.

ESSENTIAL AND RECOMMENDED TITLES
530.092 Physicists

530.092 Physicists

Einstein, Albert
★ *A Stubbornly Persistent Illusion: The Essential Scientific Writings of Albert Einstein.* Edited, with commentary, by Stephen Hawking. Running Press 2007. xi, 468 p. : Illustration
ISBN 9780762430031
Grades: Adult   **530.092**
1. Einstein, Albert, 1879-1955 2. Physicists 3. Physics 4. Science 5. Experiments 6. Quantum theory 7. Relativity (Physics) 8. German history 9. 20th century 10. Essays 11. Science Writing — Physics
LC Bl2007020342

Brings together a compilation of the most important works by Albert Einstein, presenting his papers on the Theory of Relativity, quantum theory, statistical mechanics, the photoelectric effect, and other studies that transformed modern physics.

"Hawking adds a brief but effective introduction to each section, making this gem of a collection really shine." —*Publishers Weekly*

Includes bibliographical references and index.

*The **Ultimate** Quotable Einstein.* Collected and edited by Alice Calaprice; with a foreword by Freeman Dyson. Princeton University Press 2011. xxviii, 578 p. : Illustration
ISBN 9780691138176
Grades: Adult   **530.092**
1. Einstein, Albert, 1879-1955 2. Reference — Quotations
LC 2010002855

Here is the definitive new edition of the hugely popular collection of Einstein quotations that has sold tens of thousands of copies worldwide and been translated into twenty-five languages.

Includes bibliographical references and index.

530.1 Theories and mathematical physics

Hawking, Stephen
★ *Black Holes and Baby Universes and Other Essays.* Stephen Hawking. Bantam Books 1993. IX, 182 p.
ISBN 9780553095234
Grades: 11 12 Adult   **530.1**
1. Hawking, Stephen, 1942-2018 2. Cosmology 3. Physics 4. Astronomy 5. Unified field theories 6. Time 7. Black holes (Astronomy) 8. Science 9. Physicists 10. Philosophy 11. Essays 12. Biographies 13. Science Writing — Space and Flight
LC 93008269

A collection of essays from the noted scientist includes personal reminiscences, a call for better science education, and explorations of the origins of the universe.

"The author sprinkles his explanations with a wry sense of humor and a keen awareness that the sciences today delve not only into the far reaches of the cosmos, but into the inner philosophical world as well." —*New York Times Book Review*

Includes index.

*The **Nature** of Space and Time.* Stephen Hawking and Roger Penrose. Princeton University Press 1996. VIII, 141 p. : Illustration
ISBN 9780691037912
Grades: 11 12 Adult   **530.1**
1. Space and time 2. Theories 3. Quantum theory 4. Astrophysics 5. Cosmology 6. Speeches, addresses, etc. 7. Science Writing — Space and Flight
LC 95035582

"This volume takes the form of a debate between Hawking and Penrose at Cambridge in 1994. At the center of the discussion is a pair of powerful theories: the quantum theory of fields and the general theory of relativity. The issue is howif at allone can merge the two into a quantum theory of gravity. A substantial background in theoretical physics is needed for full comprehension." —*Library Journal*

Includes bibliographical references (p. [139]-141).

Kaku, Michio
★ *Hyperspace: A Scientific Odyssey Through Parallel Universes, Time Warps, and the Tenth Dimension.* Michio Kaku. Oxford University Press 1994. xvi, 359 p. : Illustration
ISBN 9780195085143
Grades: Adult   **530.1**
1. Superstring theories 2. Hyperspace 3. Physics 4. Research 5. Social life and customs 6. United States 7. 20th century 8. Science Writing — Space and Flight 9. Science Writing — Physics
LC 93007910

Offers insights into research on the tenth dimension, time warps, black holes, and multiple universes.

"This is an overview of the major scientists, discoveries, and ideas involved in an ongoing quest for synthesizing quantum mechanics and relativity physics into a superstring theory of our entire universe." —*Library Journal*

Includes bibliographical references (p. 353-354) and index.

530.11 Relativity theory

Carroll, Sean M.
*The **Biggest** Ideas in the Universe: Space, Time, and Motion.* Sean Carroll. E.P. Dutton 2022. 160 p.
ISBN 9780593186589
Grades: Adult   **530.11**
1. Physics 2. Science 3. General relativity (Physics) 4. Cosmology 5. Space 6. Science Writing — Physics 7. Science Writing — Space and flight

A theoretical physicist—and a genius for making complex notions entertaining—shows how physics offers deep insights into the workings of the universe, in this inspiring introduction to a way of seeing that will resonate across cultural and generation boundaries for many years to come.

"Fundamental physics for the nonphysicist....No-nonsense, not-dumbed-down explanations of basic laws of the universe that reward close attention." —*Kirkus*

*From **Eternity** to Here: The Quest for the Ultimate Theory of Time.* Sean Carroll. Dutton 2009. 448 p.
ISBN 9780525951339
Grades: Adult   **530.11**
1. Space and time 2. Physics 3. Time 4. Physical sciences 5. Science Writing — General
LC 2009023828

A cofounder of the blog Cosmic Variance outlines a comprehensive vision of the universe that attempts to explain why time moves forward, building on a premise that time owes its existence to conditions before the Big Bang and may be explained by theoretical space-time properties.

"Understanding time requires an acquaintance with entropy, relativity, cosmology, thermodynamics and statistical mechanics, which Carroll enthusiastically delivers at great length. Not for the scientifically disinclined, but determined readers will come away with a rewarding grasp of a complex subject." —*Kirkus*

Includes bibliographical references and index.

Einstein, Albert
*The **Meaning** of Relativity.* Albert Einstein. Princeton University Press 2005. xxiv, 166 p. : Illustration (The Stafford Little lectures, 1921)
ISBN 9780691120270
Grades: 11 12 Adult   **530.11**
1. Relativity (Physics) 2. Science writing — Physics
LC 2004111082

PUBLIC LIBRARY CORE COLLECTION: NONFICTION
Twentieth Edition

Simplified version of Einstein's theories that explain that the measurements of motion or rest are relative to the motion or rest of the observer.

Including the Relativistic theory of the non-symmetric field; Includes index.

Gleick, James
Time Travel: A History. James Gleick. Pantheon Books 2016. 256 p.
ISBN 9780307908797
Grades: Adult   530.11
1. Space and time 2. Time travel 3. Science writing — General
LC 2016002323
Booklist Editors' Choice, 2016.

Presents an exploration of time travel that details its subversive origins, evolution in literature and science, and enduring influence on the understanding of time itself.

Rovelli, Carlo
The Order of Time. Carlo Rovelli; translated by Erica Segre and Simon Carnell. Riverhead Books 2018. 224 p.
ISBN 9780735216105
Grades: Adult   530.11
1. Space and time 2. Time 3. Cosmology 4. Philosophy 5. Translations — Italian to English 6. Science writing — General
LC 2017060293

The best-selling author of Seven Brief Lessons on Physics presents an accessible exploration of the nature of time that illuminates the questions debated by physicists and philosophers, challenging assumptions that time is linear or even measurable while explaining the critical role of perception.

Originally published in Italian: L'ordine del tempo (Milan : Adelphi Edizioni, 2017); Includes bibliographical references and index.

530.12 Quantum mechanics (Quantum theory)

Ananthaswamy, Anil
Through Two Doors at Once: The Elegant Experiment That Captures the Enigma of Our Quantum Reality. Anil Ananthaswamy. Penguin Group USA 2018. 304 p.
ISBN 9781101986097
Grades: Adult   530.12
1. Quantum theory 2. Experiments 3. Light 4. Physics 5. Reality 6. Science Writing — Physics
LC 2018008272

The award-winning author of the Man Who Wasn't There traces the story of the "double-slit" experiment that demonstrated how a sunbeam split into two paths, which challenged 19th-century understandings about light and the nature of reality, triggering debates that continue today.

"An engaging and accessible history of a fascinating and baffling experiment that remains inconclusive to this day. Recommended for those interested in the subject or anyone wishing to delve further into the double-slit experiment." —*Library Journal*

Carroll, Sean M.
Something Deeply Hidden: Quantum Worlds and the Emergence of Spacetime. Sean Carroll. E.P. Dutton 2014. 345 p.
ISBN 9781524743017
Grades: Adult   530.12
1. Quantum theory 2. Reality 3. Space and time 4. Physics 5. Science Writing — Physics
LC Bl2019021305

A Caltech physicist and author of the Big Picture argues in favor of the Many Worlds theory of quantum behavior that argues that there are innumerable multiple worlds with copies of everything and everyone in them.

Includes bibliographical references and index.

Cox, Brian
The Quantum Universe: And Why Anything That Can Happen, Does. Brian Cox and Jeff Forshaw. Da Capo Press 2012. 256 p.
ISBN 9780306819643
Grades: Adult   530.12
1. Quantum theory 2. Physics 3. Mechanics 4. Science Writing — Physics
LC 2011942393

The authors of the best-selling Why Does E=MC2? render fundamental scientific principles in the areas of quantum mechanics comprehensive and engaging to lay readers, working through obscure and vague aspects to explain related natural world observations, how the quantum world was constructed and why it is important.

Crease, Robert P.
The Quantum Moment: How Planck, Bohr, Einstein, and Heisenberg Taught Us to Love Uncertainty. Robert P. Crease and Alfred Scharff Goldhaber. W.W. Norton & Company 2014. 352 p.
ISBN 9780393067927
Grades: Adult   530.12
1. Quantum theory 2. Popular culture 3. Physics 4. Creativity 5. Science writing — Physics
LC 2014011427
Booklist Editors' Choice, 2014.

Describes how the early-20th-century discoveries in quantum physics found their way into today's modern language and collective culture, appearing in everything from television shows and movies to coffee mugs and T-shirts to art forms like sculpture and prose.

Though the authors acknowledge that many of those appropriating the jargon of quantum physics have no clue as to its scientific meaning, readers will learn to appreciate the imaginative process that transforms quantum formulas into new metaphors for understanding the human condition. An exhilarating romp for the intellectually adventurous! —*Booklist*

Includes bibliographical references and index.

Greene, B.
★ *The Hidden Reality: Parallel Universes and the Deep Laws of the Cosmos.* Brian Greene. Alfred A. Knopf 2011. 384 p.
ISBN 9780307265630
Grades: Adult   530.12
1. Cosmology 2. Relativity (Physics) 3. Physics 4. String theory (Nuclear physics) 5. Quantum theory 6. Science Writing — Physics
LC 2010042710

Discusses recent discoveries in physics and cosmology to explore a range of multiverse proposals, and examines how the knowledge that some aspects of reality may lie beyond human comprehension might affect scientific progress.

"The author explores the possibility that there is not one big uncharted universe, but many. Those universes take the form of Swiss cheese, suds in a bubble bath, passageways right out of Star Trek, and realms right next to us. The danger of writing a mind-blower like the Hidden Reality is that, if the author isn't careful, it can become mind-numbing to read. A caution here upfront: There are points where Greene walks perilously close to that precipice. Black holes, parallel universes, the idea that we and our world may have doppelgngers in different dimensions are heady concepts. For some, such conjecture is religious heresy; for others, it aims to answer the ultimate questions as to how and why we are here, with science, not faith, forming a necessary and—so far—inadequate, bridge to explore the mystery. What Greene does exceedingly well is to lay out the prevailing theories, advanced by the brightest human minds, as to how the whole of everything may be ordered." —*Christian Science Monitor*

Hawking, Stephen
★ *The Universe in a Nutshell.* Stephen Hawking. Bantam Books 2001. VIII, 216 p; Illustration; Color
ISBN 9780553802023
Grades: 11 12 Adult   530.12

ESSENTIAL AND RECOMMENDED TITLES
530.14 Field and wave theories

1. Quantum theory 2. String theory (Nuclear physics) 3. Time 4. Space and time 5. Physics 6. Relativity (Physics) 7. Cosmology 8. Science Writing — Space and Flight 9. Science Writing — Physics 10. Adult books for young adults

LC 2001035757

Royal Society General Prizes for Science Books, 2002.

The author explores recent scientific breakthroughs in the fields of supergravity, supersymmetry, quantum theory, superstring theory, and p-branes as he searches for the Theory of Everything that lies at the heart of the cosmos.

"Admirers of Hawking's previous book will continue to appreciate his ability not only to air fresh, provocative ideas but also to say what he means clearly and without watering down his material or condescending to his audience—he even injects humor into his narrative. The profuse, beautifully rendered illustrations contribute greatly to the reader's understanding of his points." —*Booklist*

Includes index.

Kakalios, James

The Amazing Story of Quantum Mechanics: A Math-free Exploration of the Science That Made Our World. James Kakalios. Penguin Group USA 2010. 336 p. : Illustration

ISBN 9781592404797

Grades: 9 10 11 12 Adult   530.12

1. Quantum theory 2. Science in popular culture 3. Mechanics 4. Physics 5. Comic books, strips, etc. 6. Pulp periodicals 7. Science Writing — Physics

LC 2010029568

Explains how everyday products were made possible by quantum mechanics, covering the Schrödinger equation, the Heisenberg uncertainty principle, and nanoscience.

Though the book does not quite live up to the subtitle's promise of a math-free text, readers need no more than basic algebra to accompany comic-book heroes into well-illustrated explanations of quantum packets of light energy, of the wave functions of particles, and even of the angular spin inherent in both energy and matter. These basic principles illuminate the solid-state physics of semiconductors, the atomic magnetism of MRIs, and the nanotechnology of high-capacity storage batteries. And all of this conceptual heavy lifting comes with entertaining episodes from DC Comics and H. G. Wells' fiction. Physics has never been more fun! —*Booklist*

Lloyd, Seth

Programming the Universe: A Quantum Computer Scientist Takes on the Cosmos. Seth Lloyd. Knopf 2006. xii, 221 p. : Illustration

ISBN 9781400040926

Grades: Adult   530.12

1. Quantum theory 2. Mathematical models 3. Microcomputers 4. Quantum computers 5. Computer programming 6. Science Writing — Computing, the Internet, and Technology

LC 2005050408

New York Times Notable Book, 2006.

Is the universe actually a giant quantum computer? According to Seth Lloyd—professor of quantum-mechanical engineering at MIT and originator of the first technologically feasible design for a working quantum computer—the answer is yes. This book illuminates the professional and personal paths that led him to this remarkable conclusion. All interactions between particles in the universe, Lloyd explains, convey not only energy but also information—in other words, particles not only collide, they compute. And what is the entire universe computing, ultimately? "Its own dynamical evolution," he says. "As the computation proceeds, reality unfolds." to elucidate his theory, Lloyd examines the history of the cosmos, posing questions that in other hands might seem unfathomably complex: How much information is there in the universe? What information existed at the moment of the Big Bang and what happened to it? How do quantum mechanics and chaos theory interact to create our world? Could we attempt to re-create it on a giant quantum computer?

Includes bibliographical references (p. 219-221).

Rovelli, Carlo

Helgoland: Making Sense of the Quantum Revolution. Carlo Rovelli; translated from the Italian by Erica Segre and Simon Carnell. Riverhead Books 2021. 256 p.

ISBN 9780593328880

Grades: Adult   530.12

1. Quantum theory 2. Physics 3. Reality 4. Science Writing — Physics

LC 2020049573

The best-selling author of offers a startling new look at quantum theory.

"Physicist Rovelli (The Order of Time) dazzles with this look at the 'Almost psychedelic experience' of understanding quantum theory." —*Publishers Weekly*

Includes bibliographical references and index; Originally published in Italian under the title Helgoland by Adelphi Edizioni, Milan in 2020—Title page verso.

530.14 Field and wave theories

Hawking, Stephen

★ *The Grand Design.* Stephen Hawking and Leonard Mlodinow. Bantam Books 2010. 198 p. : Illustration; Color

ISBN 9780553805376

Grades: 11 12 Adult   530.14

1. Physics 2. Cosmology 3. Quantum theory 4. Evolution 5. Creation 6. Science Writing — Physics

LC 2010287390

Presents a new study of the cosmos that will blow peoples' minds, presented in clear, concise language this is easy to understand.

Includes index.

Rovelli, Carlo

Reality Is Not What It Seems: The Elementary Structure of Things. Carlo Rovelli; translated by Simon Carnell and Erica Segre. Riverhead Books, an imprint of Penguin Random House LLC 2017. 256 p.

ISBN 9780735213920

Grades: Adult   530.14

1. Physics 2. Gravity 3. Space-time 4. Quantum gravity 5. Science 6. Science Writing — Physics

LC 2016036293

The theoretical physicist author of the best-selling Seven Brief Lessons on Physics traces how the human image of the world has changed throughout history, demonstrating the evolution of the idea of reality while touching on subjects ranging from the Higgs boson to quantum gravity.

"Rovellis work is challenging, but his excitement is contagious and he delights in the possibilities of human understanding." —*Publishers Weekly*

Originally published in Italian under the title: La Realta non e come ci appare; English translation published in Great Britain by Allen Lane, an imprint of Penguin Random House UK; Includes bibliographical references and index.

530.4 States of matter

Miodownik, Mark

Liquid Rules: The Delightful and Dangerous Substances That Flow Through Our Lives. Mark Miodownik. Houghton Mifflin Harcourt 2019. 288 p.

ISBN 9780544850194

Grades: Adult   530.4

1. Liquids 2. Matter 3. Science 4. Materials science 5. Chemistry 6. Physics 7. Molecules 8. Sustainability 9. Transatlantic flights 10. Science Writing — Chemistry

LC 2018024866

Sometimes explosive, often delicious, occasionally poisonous, but always interesting: the New York Times-bestselling author of Stuff Matters shows us the secret lives of liquids: the shadow counterpart of our solid "stuff."

"In this informative, casual narrative, Miodownik (Stuff Matters), a science professor at University College London, gives a guided tour of the strange, wondrous liquids that flow through everyday life." —*Publishers Weekly*

Originally published in Great Britain by Penguin Books, 2018; Includes bibliographical references and index.

PUBLIC LIBRARY CORE COLLECTION: NONFICTION
Twentieth Edition

530.8 Measurement

Vincent, James
Beyond Measure: The Hidden History of Measurement from Cubits to Quantum Constants. James Vincent. W.W. Norton & Company 2022. VIII, 423 p.
ISBN 9781324035855
Grades: Adult **530.8**
1. Measurement 2. Observing things 3. Numbers 4. Mathematical analysis 5. Science 6. History 7. Science Writing — General 8. History writing — Science, technology, and medicine

A revelatory and vibrant story of measurement which will make you look at the world around you anew. We measure rainfall and radiation, the depths of space and the emptiness of atoms, calories and steps, happiness and fear. If we could not measure then we could not observe the world around us; we could not experiment, learn, and co-operate. But why did this urge to measure flourish? And when did measurement become ubiquitous? It is a tale that tracks humanity's search for dependable truths in a chaotic universe.

"A survey of the history of measurement and how it has shaped human progress." —*Kirkus*

531 Classical mechanics

Panek, Richard
The Trouble with Gravity: Solving the Mystery Beneath Our Feet. Richard Panek. 2019. 320 pages
ISBN 9780544526747
Grades: Adult **531**
1. Gravity 2. Mass (Physics) 3. Physics 4. Gravitational waves 5. Physicists 6. Science Writing — Physics 7. History writing — Science, technology, and medicine

LC 2018057178
An award-winning science writer traces our millennia-long effort to understand the phenomenon of gravity—the greatest mystery in physics, and a force that has shaped our universe and our minds in ways we have never fully understood until now.

"Teen and adult readers interested in better understanding the force of gravity and gaining insight into humanity's expanding knowledge of the universe will find this highly recommended book to be both accessible and enjoyable." —*Library Journal*

Includes bibliographical references and index.

537 Electricity and electronics

Bodanis, David
Electric Universe: The Shocking True Story of Electricity. David Bodanis. Crown Publishers 2005. 308 p.
ISBN 9781400045501
Grades: 11 12 Adult **537**
1. Electricity 2. Force 3. Energy 4. Electrons 5. Science Writing — Chemistry 6. Adult books for young adults

LC 2004011275
Booklist Editors' Choice: Adult Books for Young Adults, 2005; Royal Society General Prizes for Science Books, 2006.

A popular history of the science of electricity follows the work of the scientists and pioneers who investigated its unique properties and secrets and discusses the influence of their scientific breakthroughs on our ability to harness its power.

"As a storyteller, author David Bodanis is wonderful. This book is directed at a general audience, but it should be required reading for all scientific professionals." —*Science Books & Films*

Includes bibliographical references (p. 267-288) and index.

539.7 Atomic and nuclear physics

Greene, B.
★ *The Elegant Universe: Superstrings, Hidden Dimensions, and the Quest for the Ultimate Theory.* Brian Greene. W. W. Norton 1999. xiii, 448 p. : Illustration
ISBN 9780393046885
Grades: Adult **539.7**
1. Superstring theories 2. Cosmology 3. Relativity (Physics) 4. Quantum theory 5. Physics 6. Science Writing — Physics

LC 98025695
ALA Notable Book, 2000; Library Journal Best Books, 1999; New York Times Notable Book, 1999; Royal Society General Prizes for Science Books, 2000; Pulitzer Prize for General Nonfiction finalist.

[Greene] develops one fresh new insight after another … in the great tradition of physicists writing for the masses, the elegant universe sets a standard that will be hard to beat."

"The author makes the terribly complex theory of strings accessible to all. He possesses a remarkable gift for using the everyday to illustrate what may be going on in dimensions beyond our feeble human perception." —*Publishers Weekly*

Includes bibliographical references (p. 427-428) and index.

Levin, Janna
Black Hole Blues: And Other Songs from Outer Space. Janna Levin. Alfred A. Knopf 2016. 241 pages
ISBN 9780307958198
Grades: Adult **539.7**
1. Gravitational waves 2. Black holes (Astronomy) 3. Astronomy 4. Science Writing — Space and Flight 5. Science Writing — Physics

LC 2015046692
Recounts the fifty-year search for gravitational waves, explaining how the waves are created in the collision of black holes and why they can never be detected by telescope, and profiles four scientists currently engaged in the quest.

"A superb alignment of author and subject: Levin is among the best contemporary science writers, and LIGO is arguably the most compelling experiment on the planet." —*Kirkus*

Includes bibliographical references (pages 225-231) and index.

Levitt, Dan
What's Gotten into You: The Story of Your Body's Atoms, from the Big Bang Through Last Night's Dinner. Dan Levitt. HarperCollins 2023. 368 p.
ISBN 9780063251182
Grades: Adult **539.7**
1. Human body 2. Matter 3. Atoms 4. Chemical elements 5. Humans 6. Biology 7. Science 8. Science Writing — Biology

Tells the awe-inspiring story of the elements that make up the human body, and how these building blocks of life travelled billions of miles and across billions of years to make us who we are.

"What are we actually made of? And where did it come from? These two questions propel Levitt's exploration in an epic atomic odyssey….From stars to Homo sapiens, this book tackles sprawling subject matter—the birth and expansion of the universe, the origin of life, and how humans came to be what we are." —*Booklist*

Sheehy, Suzie
The Matter of Everything: How Curiosity, Physics, and Improbable Experiments Changed the World. Suzie Sheehy. Alfred A. Knopf 2023. 320 p.
ISBN 9780525658757
Grades: Adult **539.7**
1. Particles (Nuclear physics) 2. Physics 3. Particle accelerators 4. Scientific discoveries 5. Science Writing — Physics 6. History Writing — Science, technology, and medicine

LC 2022021649
Celebrating human ingenuity, creativity and curiosity, an accelerator physicist introduces us to the people who, through a combination of genius, persis-

ESSENTIAL AND RECOMMENDED TITLES
541 Physical chemistry

tence and luck, staged the experiments that changed the course of history, giving rise to the technology that ushered us into the modern world.

"Physicist Sheehy debuts with a terrific history of experiments that have changed the course of science....With punchy writing and vivid historical details, Sheehy brilliantly captures the curiosity that fuels science, the frustration of 'False starts and failures,' and the thrill of finding answers that are bound to raise more questions." —*Publishers Weekly*

Originally published in the UK as the matter of everything: Twelve experiments that changed our world by Bloomsbury, London, in 2022; Includes bibliographical references and index.

Still, Ben
Particle Physics Brick by Brick: Atomic and Subatomic Physics Explained... in Lego. Dr. Ben Still. Firefly Books 2018. 176 p.
ISBN 9780228100126
Grades: Adult **539.7**
1. Physics 2. Particles (Nuclear physics) 3. LEGO toys 4. Quantum theory 5. Cosmology 6. Building blocks (Toys) 7. Visual perception 8. Science — Physics and physical science
LC Bl2018197504

Particle Physics Brick by Brick is a succinct introduction for anyone that wants to gain a basic understanding of the atomic world, its elements and how they interact. By using tangible substitutes—bricks—it brings the unseen atomic world into the realm of the visual.
Includes index.

541 Physical chemistry

Gray, Theodore W.
Molecules: The Elements and the Architecture of Everything. Theodore Gray. Black Dog & Leventhal Publishers 2014. 240 p.
ISBN 9781579129712
Grades: Adult **541**
1. Molecules 2. Organic compounds 3. Science — Chemistry — Atoms and molecules
LC Bl2014050626

Provides an illustrated look at the chemical structures that compose every material in the world, from soaps and solvents to painkillers and sweeteners, featuring anecdotes about each item featured as well as diagrams of compounds.

"Readers who wish to learn more about chemistry would be better served with another work that isn't so strongly focused on photography. Those already familiar with the topic are sure to enjoy the images." —*Library Journal*

546 Inorganic chemistry

Challoner, Jack
The Elements: The New Guide to the Building Blocks of Our Universe. Jack Challoner. Carlton Books 2012. 160 p. : Illustration; Color
ISBN 9781780971254
Grades: Adult **546**
1. Chemical elements 2. Periodic law 3. Science writing — Chemistry
LC Bl2013000870

Presents photographic representations of the one hundred and eighteen elements in the period table, along with facts, figures and stories about each one.
Includes index.

Gray, Theodore W.
★ *The Elements: A Visual Exploration of Every Known Atom in the Universe.* Theodore Gray; photographs by Theodore Gray and Nick Mann. Black Dog & Leventhal Publishers 2009. 240 p.
ISBN 9781579128142
Grades: 11 12 Adult **546**
1. Chemical elements 2. Atoms 3. Periodic law 4. Chemistry 5. Science — Chemistry — Elements and compounds

LC 2009034931
YALSA Best Books for Young Adults, 2010.

The elements are what we—and everything around us—are made of. But how many elements have you seen in their pure, raw, uncombined form? This book presents photographic representations of the 118 elements in the period table, along with facts, figures and stories about each one.

"This gorgeously photographed guide to the elements can be used as a visual reference, but its brief entries are packed with intriguing tidbits that also make it a fascinating read." —*Library Journal*

Kean, Sam
The Disappearing Spoon: And Other True Tales of Madness, Love, and the History of the World from the Periodic Table of the Elements. Sam Kean. Little, Brown and Co. 2010. VI, 391 p. : Illustration
ISBN 9780316051644
Grades: 11 12 Adult **546**
1. Periodic law 2. Chemical elements 3. Chemistry 4. Carbon 5. Silicon 6. Gold 7. Chemicals 8. Scientists 9. Science Writing — Chemistry 10. Adult books for young adults
LC 2009040754

The periodic table of the elements is a crowning scientific achievement, but it's also a treasure trove of passion, adventure, obsession, and betrayal. These tales follow carbon, neon, silicon, gold, and all the elements in the table as they play out their parts in human history.

"With the anecdotal flourishes of Oliver Sacks and the populist accessibility of Malcolm Gladwell, but without the latter's occasional facileness, he makes even the most abstract concepts graspable for armchair scientists. His keen sense of humor is a particular pleasure." —*Entertainment Weekly*

549 Mineralogy

Pough, Frederick H.
★ *A Field Guide to Rocks and Minerals.* Frederick H. Pough, photographs by Jeffrey Scovil. Houghton Mifflin 1996. xv, 396 p. : Plate (The Peterson field guide series, 7)
ISBN 9780395910962
Grades: Adult **549**
1. Rocks 2. Science writing — Geology
LC 94049005

Describes hundreds of minerals and lists their geographic distribution, physical properties, chemical composition, and crystalline structure.

Sponsored by the National Audubon Society, the National Wildlife Federation, and the Roger Tory Peterson Institute; Includes bibliographical references (p. 377-181) and index.

550 Earth sciences

Alvarez, Walter
A Most Improbable Journey: A Big History of Our Planet and Ourselves. Walter Alvarez. W W Norton & Company 2016. 288 p.
ISBN 9780393292695
Grades: Adult **550**
1. Human evolution 2. Science 3. Science Writing — General
LC 2016022704

Famed geologist Walter Alvarez expands our view of human history by revealing the cosmic, geologic, and evolutionary forces that have shaped us.

Lambert, David
The Field Guide to Geology. David Lambert and the Diagram Group. Facts on File 2007. 304 p. : Illustration; Map
ISBN 9780816065103
Grades: 11 12 Adult **550**
1. Geology 2. Science writing — Weather
LC 2006048533

An updated title provides information on earth's origin, the shaping of the continents, the forming of rocks, erosion, earth's geological history, and the impact of the oceans and rivers.

Rev. ed. of: The field guide to geology. Updated ed. c1998; Includes bibliographical references and index.

551 Geology, hydrology, meteorology

Bjornerud, Marcia
Geopedia: A Brief Compendium of Geologic Curiosities. Marcia Bjornerud; illustrations by Haley Hagerman. Princeton University Press 2022. xv, 184 pages : Illustration
ISBN 9780691212579
Grades: Adult   551
1. Geology 2. Rocks 3. Minerals 4. Science Writing — Geology
LC 2021019929

Geoscientists are magpies for words, and with good reason. The sheer profusion of minerals, landforms, and geologic events produced by our creative planet demands an immense vocabulary to match. Marcia Bjornerud shows how this lexicon reflects not only the diversity of rocks and geologic processes but also the long history of human interactions with them. With wit and warmth, she invites all readers to celebrate the geologic glossary—a gallimaufry of allusions to mythology, imports from diverse languages, embarrassing anachronisms, and recent neologisms."

"Will fascinate and delight nearly all readers but particularly word lovers, rock lovers, and geology hobbyists." —*Library Journal*

Includes bibliographical references (pages 183-184).

551.2 Volcanoes, earthquakes, thermal waters and gases

Gates, Alexander E.
Encyclopedia of Earthquakes and Volcanoes. Alexander E. Gates and David Ritchie. Checkmark Books 2007. xvi, 346 p. : Illustration; Map
ISBN 9780816071203
Grades: 11 12 Adult   551.2
1. Earthquakes 2. Volcanoes 3. Encyclopedias 4. Reference books — Science 5. Science Writing — Geology
LC Bl2007011320

Provides information on earthquakes and volcanic eruptions in various regions of the world, major quakes and eruptions throughout history, and geologic and scientific terms.

Authors' names in reverse order on 2nd ed; Includes bibliographical references (p. 313-315) and index.

551.31 Glaciology

Pollack, H. N.
A World Without Ice. Henry Pollack. Avery 2009. xv, 287 p. : Illustration; Map
ISBN 9781583333570
Grades: 11 12 Adult   551.31
1. Glaciers 2. Ice 3. Global warming 4. Climate change 5. Nature Writing — Environmental Issues
LC 2009030326

A cowinner of the 2007 Nobel Peace Prize shares a comprehensive survey of ice as a force of nature while describing potential catastrophic consequences of ice shortages, in a reference that outlines recommended steps for avoiding environmental threats.

"Seldom has a scientist written so well and so clearly for the lay reader. Pollack's explanations of how researchers can tell that the climate is warming faster than normal are free of the usual scientific jargon and understandable. All readers concerned about global warming and students writing papers on the topic will want this excellent and important volume." —*Library Journal*

Includes bibliographical references and index.

551.41 Geomorphology

Proulx, Annie
★ *Fen,* Bog and Swamp: A Short History of Peatland Destruction and Its Role in the Climate Crisis. Annie Proulx. Scribner 2022. 208 p.
ISBN 9781982173357
Grades: Adult   551.41
1. Wetland conservation 2. Wetland ecology 3. Marshes 4. Swamps 5. Bog bodies 6. Greenhouse gases 7. Environmental degradation 8. Climate change 9. Nature conservation 10. Natural history 11. Nature Writing — Natural Landscapes 12. Nature Writing — Environmental Issues

National Book Critics Circle Award for Nonfiction finalist, 2022.

A lifelong environmentalist, Annie Proulx brings her wide-ranging research and scholarship to the subject of wetlands and the vitally important yet little understood role they play in preserving the environment—by storing the carbon emissions that greatly contribute to climate change. Fens, bogs, swamps, and marine estuaries are the earth's most desirable and dependable resources, and in four stunning parts, Proulx documents the long-misunderstood role of these wetlands in saving the planet.

"Fans of Proulx's fiction, even those with marginal interest in peatlands, will be intrigued by the snippets of memoir and the habits of a writer's mind that this collection reveals." —*Library Journal*

551.45 Plane and coastal regions

Goodell, Jeff
The Water Will Come: Rising Seas, Sinking Cities, and the Remaking of the Civilized World. Jeff Goodell. Little Brown & Co. 2017. 336 p.
ISBN 9780316260244
Grades: Adult   551.45
1. Sea level 2. Climate change 3. Coast changes 4. Floods 5. Global warming 6. Climatology 7. Nature Writing — Environmental Issues
LC Bl2017042941

An acclaimed journalist uses fact, science and on-the-ground reporting to provide an account of the coming new age of great flooding, due to rapidly rising sea levels that promise to inundate our coasts and transform existing landscapes.

"A frightening, scientifically grounded, and starkly relevant look at how climate change will affect coastal cities." —*Kirkus*

Rush, Elizabeth A.
Rising: Dispatches from the New American Shore. Elizabeth Rush. Milkweed Editions 2018. 256 p.
ISBN 9781571313676
Grades: Adult   551.45
1. Rush, Elizabeth A. 2. Climate change 3. Coasts 4. Sea level 5. Hurricanes 6. Coast changes 7. Coastal ecology 8. Natural disasters 9. Politics and global affairs — Environmental issues and policies
LC 2017059870

ALA Notable Book, 2019; Library Journal Best Books, 2018; Pulitzer Prize for General Nonfiction finalist, 2019.

A journalist, weaving firsthand accounts from the people and places imperiled by climate change in the United States today, takes readers to the places hardest hit by the rising seas, which are transforming the coastline of the U.S. in irrevocable ways.

Includes bibliographical references.

ESSENTIAL AND RECOMMENDED TITLES
551.46 Oceanography and submarine geology

551.46 Oceanography and submarine geology

Casey, Susan
The Underworld: Journeys to the Depths of the Ocean. Susan Casey. Doubleday 2023. 320 p.
ISBN 9780385545570
Grades: Adult   551.46
1. Oceans 2. Oceanography 3. Ocean bottom 4. Deep-sea sounding 5. Marine biology 6. Marine ecology 7. Climate change 8. Science Writing — Biology 9. Nature Writing — Natural Landscapes
LC 2023002536
Drawing on interviews with marine geologists, marine biologists and oceanographers, a premiere chronicler of the aquatic world and New York Times best-selling author provides a fascinating history of deep-sea exploration and shows how urgent it is that we understand the ocean in a time of increasing threats from climate change.
"Casey plunges deep into the saltwater Underworld to reveal the jagged mountain ranges, seemingly bottomless valleys, and bizarrely unfamiliar wildlife there." —*Library Journal*
Includes bibliographical references.

Czerski, Helen
The Blue Machine: How the Ocean Works. Helen Czerski. W W Norton & Co. Inc 2023. 416 p.
ISBN 9781324006718
Grades: Adult   551.46
1. Oceans 2. Oceanography 3. Biotic communities 4. Physics 5. Science Writing — Physics 6. Science Writing — Biology 7. Nature Writing — Natural Landscapes
A scientist's exploration of the "ocean engine"—the physics behind the ocean's systems—and why it matters.
"The book is packed with statistics…diligent environmentalists will be pleased with the author's rigor. A compelling read for science buffs and ocean enthusiasts." —*Kirkus*

Scales, Helen
The Brilliant Abyss: Exploring the Majestic Hidden Life of the Deep Ocean, and the Looming Threat That Imperils It. Helen Scales. Atlantic Monthly Press 2021. 288 p.
ISBN 9780802158222
Grades: Adult   551.46
1. Oceans 2. Oceanography 3. Marine ecology 4. Nature 5. Effect of environment on humans 6. Nature Writing — Natural Landscapes
A marine biologist brings to vibrant life the extraordinary ecosystem of the deep ocean, which has a huge effect on our daily life, in this fascinating book that is at once a revelation and a clarion call to preserve this vast unseen world.
"A fascinating international glimpse of Earth's last frontier that will draw in readers concerned for the health of our oceans." —*Library Journal*

Winchester, Simon
Atlantic: Great Sea Battles, Heroic Discoveries, Titanic Storms, and a Vast Ocean of a Million Stories. Simon Winchester. William Morrow 2010. 492 p.
ISBN 9780061702587
Grades: Adult   551.46
1. Oceans 2. Civilization 3. Atlantic Ocean 4. History writing — Microhistory
LC 2010015229
Blends history and anecdote, geography and reminiscence, and science and exposition, to relate the saga of the Atlantic Ocean, setting it against the backdrop of mankind's intellectual evolution.
"Writing the history of the Atlantic Ocean from tectonic labor pains to its lead role in modern European and American history might be one of the more difficult tasks Simon Winchester has set for himself. Luckily, the author comes armed with a knowledge almost as vast and deep as his subject, as well as a clever yet functional organizational scheme that divides his oceanic biography Atlantic into the seven ages of a man's life as proposed by Shakespeare. A formidable writer and storyteller, Winchester still gets distracted by the occasional unworthy anecdote or superfluous specificity, but for all the densely packed information in this work, the one thing it never becomes, quite appropriately, is dry." —*Entertainment Weekly*

551.46092 Oceanographers

Ballard, Robert D.
Into the Deep: An Explorer's Life. Robert D. Ballard and Christopher Drew. National Geographic 2021. 336 p.
ISBN 9781426220999
Grades: Adult   551.46092
1. Ballard, Robert D. 2. Oceanographers 3. Marine biologists 4. Underwater exploration 5. Adventurers 6. Adventure 7. Oceans 8. Oceanography 9. Dyslexia 10. Shipwrecks 11. Autobiographies and memoirs 12. Life stories — Facing adversity — Medical issues — Living with disabilities 13. Life stories — Science, technology, and medicine — Scientists and inventors 14. Adventure writing — Exploration
LC 2020044366
Oceanographer and marine biologist Robert D. Ballard looks back on a long and storied life that includes accomplishments ranging from discovering new life-forms to finding the wreck of the Titanic.
"This exciting memoir, recounted by a wonderful storyteller, will be relished by readers who enjoy adventure, oceanography, underwater archaeology, and scientific discovery." —*Library Journal*
Includes bibliographical references and index.

Widder, Edith
Below the Edge of Darkness: A Memoir of Exploring Light and Life in the Deep Sea. Edith Widder, Ph.D.. Random House 2021. 352 p.
ISBN 9780525509240
Grades: Adult   551.46092
1. Widder, Edith 2. Marine biologists 3. Women marine biologists 4. Bioluminescence 5. Underwater exploration 6. Marine biology 7. Marine organisms 8. Marine animals 9. United States 10. Autobiographies and memoirs 11. Life stories — Science, technology, and medicine — Scientists and inventors 12. Science Writing — Biology
LC 2020051565
An in-depth examination of oceanic bioluminescence, a little-explored scientific field that focuses on how marine life uses light to communicate in the darkness of the deep oceans, including a look at the legendary Giant Squid.
"In her first book, Widder, a veteran marine scientist and co-founder of the Ocean Research & Conservation Association, offers a captivating, watery-world personal memoir about exploring bioluminescence ('pure magic of living light') and an urgent plea to protect the world's largest ecosystem." —*Kirkus*
Includes bibliographical references and index.

551.5 Meteorology

Williams, Jack
★ *The Ams Weather Book: The Ultimate Guide to America's Weather.* Jack Williams. University of Chicago, Ill. :Press 2009. xi, 316 p. : Color illustration; Color; Map
ISBN 9780226898988
Grades: 9 10 11 12 Adult   551.5
1. Climatology 2. Meteorology 3. Weather 4. Science writing — Weather
LC 2008035916
Discusses the variety of weather patterns found in America, introduces the science behind meteorology, and answers common weather questions.
"This work, with its attractive, easy-to-understand graphics, offers a useful, engaging basic introduction to a wide variety of weather-related topics." —*Choice*
Copublished with the American Meteorological Society; Includes index.

PUBLIC LIBRARY CORE COLLECTION: NONFICTION
Twentieth Edition

551.51 Composition, regions, dynamics of atmosphere

Kean, Sam
Caesar's Last Breath: Decoding the Secrets of the Air Around Us. Sam Kean. Little, Brown & Co. 2017. 384 p.
ISBN 9780316381642
Grades: Adult   551.51
1. Air 2. Atmosphere 3. Chemistry 4. Chemical elements 5. Science Writing — Chemistry
LC BI2017021331
An engaging round-the-globe journey through the periodic table explains how the air we breathe reflects the world's history, tracing the origins and ingredients of the atmosphere to explain air's role in reshaping continents, steering human progress and powering revolutions.
"A witty book that turns the science of the stuff we breathe into a delightful romp through history." —*Kirkus*

Owens, Jay
Dust: The Modern World in a Trillion Particles. Jay Owens. Abrams Books 2023. 320 p.
ISBN 9781419764165
Grades: Adult   551.51
1. Dust 2. Pollution 3. Smoke 4. Smog 5. Climate change 6. Arid regions 7. Deserts 8. Radioactive fallout 9. Environmental degradation 10. Effect of humans on nature 11. Nature Writing — Environmental Issues 12. Science Writing — General 13. Debut title
A London-based researcher and writer describes how the progress of the 20th century has created a profound threat to life in the 21st century by examining the smallest substance on earth: Dust.
"Readers will be fascinated by what enormous insights Owens conveys by thoughtfully examining something as tiny as a dust particle." —*Booklist*

551.57 Hydrometeorology

Barnett, Cynthia
Rain: A Natural and Cultural History. by Cynthia Barnett. Crown Publishers 2014. 320 p.
ISBN 9780804137096
Grades: Adult   551.57
1. Rain and rainfall 2. Weather 3. Droughts 4. Physical geography 5. Climate change 6. Earth sciences 7. Nature writing — General 8. Science writing — Weather
LC 2014034180
A natural history of rain draws on myriad disciplines to trace the ocean-filling torrents from 4 billion years ago through the storms of the present world's climate change while sharing stories about humanity's efforts to control rain through science and magic.
"Barnett explores every facet of the substance. A seamless blending of personal narrative with scientific and cultural explanations makes the book both informative and entertaining." —*Library Journal*
Includes bibliographical references and index.

551.6 Climatology and weather

Fagan, Brian M.
The **Long** *Summer:* How Climate Changed Civilization. Brian Fagan. Basic Books 2004. xvii, 284 p. : Illustration
ISBN 9780465022816
Grades: 11 12 Adult   551.6
1. Climate change 2. History of civilization 3. Global warming 4. Prehistoric humans 5. Effect of humans on nature 6. Climatology 7. Environmentalism 8. Effect of environment on humans 9. Nature Writing — Environmental Issues
LC 2003013917
The anthropologist-author of "The Little Ice Age" analyzes the seminal impact of climatic change on the evolution of all of human history.
Includes bibliographical references (p. 253-269) and index.

Lynas, Mark
Six Degrees: Our Future on a Hotter Planet. by Mark Lynas. National Geographic 2008. 336 p.
ISBN 9781426202131
Grades: 11 12 Adult   551.6
1. Global warming 2. Climate change 3. Environmentalism 4. Effect of environment on humans 5. Nature Writing — Environmental Issues 6. Adult books for young adults
LC 2007030864
Royal Society General Prizes for Science Books, 2008.
Features a degree-by-degree account of how the effects of global climate change will impact people, the environment, and natural species in every region of the world, and offers recommendations on what can be done to manage the problem.
Originally published: London : Fourth Estate, 2007.

551.7 Historical geology

Childs, Craig
Atlas of a Lost World: Travels in Ice Age America. Craig Childs. Pantheon 2018. 288 p.
ISBN 9780307908650
Grades: Adult   551.7
1. Ice Age (Geology) 2. Paleo-Indigenous peoples of North America 3. Anthropology 4. Archaeology 5. Paleoecology 6. Fossil mammals 7. Natural history 8. Ancient geography 9. Prehistoric humans 10. Antiquities 11. North America 12. Prehistoric era (Stone Age) 13. History writing — Ancient 14. History writing — Archaeology 15. History writing — United States 16. History writing — Canada
LC 2017033037
In a blend of science and personal narrative that takes readers on a fascinating journey through prehistory, the author of Apocalyptic Planet, chronicling the last millennia of the Ice Age and tracing the First People in North America, shows how much has changed since the time of mammoth hunters, and also what hasn't changed.

Macdougall, J. D.
Frozen Earth: The Once and Future Story of Ice Ages. Doug Macdougall. University of California Press 2004. xi, 256 p. : Illustration
ISBN 9780520239227
Grades: 11 12 Adult   551.7
1. Ice age (Geology) 2. Paleoclimatology 3. Global environmental change 4. Nature Writing — Environmental Issues 5. Adult books for young adults
LC 2004008502
Explores the causes and effects of ice ages, explains how the Pleistocene Ice Age shaped the earth's landscape and influenced human evolution, and offers speculation and explanations of future climate changes.
"The author presents the scientific history behind ice ages, emphasizing the roles of four great scientists in the field.... Macdougall's account promotes a welcome reasoning attitude toward ice-age research and its relevance to global warming." —*Booklist*
Includes bibliographical references (p. 245-248) and index.

553.6 Other economic materials

Kurlansky, Mark
Salt: A World History. Mark Kurlansky. Walker and Co. 2001. xii, 484 p. : Illustration; Map
ISBN 9780142001615
Grades: 11 12 Adult   553.6

ESSENTIAL AND RECOMMENDED TITLES
553.7 Water

1. Salt 2. Commodity exchanges 3. Mines and mineral resources 4. Food writing — History and microhistory 5. History writing — Microhistory 6. Adult books for young adults

LC 2002391600

New York Times Notable Book, 2002.

Explores the role of salt in shaping history, discussing how one of the world's most sought-after commodities has influenced economics, science, politics, religion, and eating customs.

"Throughout his engaging, well-researched history, Kurlansky sprinkles witty asides and amusing anecdotes. A piquant blend of the historic, political, commercial, scientific and culinary, the book is sure to entertain as well as educate." —*Publishers Weekly*

Includes bibliographical references (p. 453-465) and index.

553.7 Water

Brady, Amy
Ice: From Mixed Drinks to Skating Rinks - a Cool History of a Hot Commodity. Amy Brady. Putnam Publishing Group 2023. 400 p.
ISBN 9780593422199
Grades: Adult   553.7

1. Ice 2. United States 3. History Writing — Microhistory 4. History Writing — United States 5. Society and culture — General

"Overflowing with intriguing arcana and colorful personalities, this is an eye-opener." —*Publishers Weekly*

Solomon, Steven
Water: The Epic Struggle for Wealth, Power, and Civilization. Steven Solomon. Harper 2010. 608 p.
ISBN 9780060548308
Grades: Adult   553.7

1. Water 2. Natural resources 3. Water-supply 4. Droughts 5. Scarcity 6. History writing — General 7. Nature Writing — Environmental Issues

LC 2009027500

Booklist Editors' Choice, 2010.

A narrative account of how water has shaped human society from the ancient past to the present.

"Solomon's unprecedented inquiry into the history, science, and politics of water use provides fascinating and ample testimony to the need to place a higher value on water and its preservation." —*Booklist*

553.8 Gems

Judah, Hettie
Lapidarium: The Secret Lives of Stones. Hettie Judah. Penguin Books 2023. 336 p.
ISBN 9780143137412
Grades: Adult   553.8

1. Precious stones 2. Mines and mineral resources 3. Stone 4. Gems 5. History 6. Science 7. Archaeology 8. Mythology in literature 9. Geology 10. Science Writing — Geology 11. History writing — Microhistory

LC 2022027524

Through the realms of art, myth, geology, philosophy and power, this brilliant history of the minerals and materials that have allowed humanity to evolve and create explores a treasure trove of 60 stones from around the world and the stories that accompany them.

"Readers can dip in and out, digesting tiny pearls of fascinating information that make for lively conversation starters. A fresh and enjoyable addition to materials history." —*Booklist*

Includes bibliographical references and index.

560 Paleontology

Halliday, Thomas
★ *Otherlands: A Journey Through Earth's Extinct Worlds.* Thomas Halliday. Random House 2022. 368 p.
ISBN 9780593132883
Grades: Adult   560

1. Paleobiology 2. Paleoecology 3. Extinct animals 4. Fossils 5. Geological time 6. Natural history 7. Science Writing — Paleontology 8. Science Writing — Biology

Mining the most recent paleontological advances, a paleobiologist recreates 16 extinct worlds, rendered here with a novelist's eye for detail and drama, bringing us up close to the intricate relationships of these ancient worlds, allowing us to discover the inner working—and the fragility—of our own.

"Halliday's brilliantly imaginative reconstructions, his deft marshalling of complex science, offers a thrilling experience of deep-time nature for pop-science buffs." —*Library Journal*

Includes bibliographical references and index.

Thompson, Ida
★ *The Audubon Society Field Guide to North American Fossils.* Ida Thompson; with photographs by Townsend P. Dickinson; visual key by Carol Nehring. Knopf : 1982. 846 p. : Illustration; Color (The Audubon Society field guide series)
ISBN 9780394524122
Grades: Adult   560

1. Fossils 2. Science writing — Paleontology

LC 81084772

AIDS in identifying eight hundred species of common North American fossils with color photographs and line drawings.

A Chanticleer Press edition; Includes index.

567.9 Reptiles

Brusatte, Stephen
★ *The Rise and Fall of the Dinosaurs: A New History of a Lost World.* Stephen Brusatte. HarperCollins 2018. 400 p.
ISBN 9780062490421
Grades: Adult   567.9

1. Dinosaurs 2. Evolution 3. Paleontology 4. Science Writing — Paleontology 5. Adult books for young adults

LC 2017038066

Booklist Editors' Choice: Adult Books for Young Adults, 2018; Goodreads Choice Award, 2018; Library Journal Best Books, 2018.

The "resident paleontologist" for BBC's Walking with Dinosaurs presents a narrative scientific history of the dinosaur eras that examines their origins, habitats, extinction and living legacy, chronicling nearly 200 million years of their evolution from small shadow dwellers through the emergences of prehistoric ancestors that became more than 10,000 modern bird species.

"His explanations of how sauropods became so large, the reasons for the dominance of Tyrannosaurus rex, the evolution of flying ability in some dinosaurs, and the factors leading to the demise of most of these creatures are carefully crafted and presented. Brusatte is not shy about saying what is not yet known, while making it clear that this is a truly exciting period, in which new fossils are being uncovered at a dizzying pace." —*Publishers Weekly*

Includes bibliographical references and index.

Lacovara, Kenneth
Why Dinosaurs Matter. Kenneth Lacovara. Simon & Schuster 2017. 120 p.
ISBN 9781501120107
Grades: Adult   567.9

1. Dinosaurs 2. Climate change 3. Extinction 4. Paleontology 5. Fossils 6. Consequences 7. Effect of humans on nature 8. Environmentalism 9. Nature Writing — Environmental Issues 10. Science Writing — Paleontology

LC Bl2017038106

A paleontologist examines the importance of the way dinosaurs lived and may have died, the meaning of fossils, the nature of deep time, and humans' place in the world as the earth moves into an uncertain environmental future.

"As paleontologist Lacovara has dug up the bones of some mighty dinosaurs, . . . he's just the man to tell us what dinosaurs can tell us about ourselves." —*Library Journal*

Paul, Gregory S.

The **Princeton** *Field Guide to Dinosaurs.* Gregory S. Paul. Princeton University Press 2016. 360 pages : Illustration; Color; Map
ISBN 9780691167664
Grades: Adult **567.9**
1. Dinosaurs 2. Nature writing — Animal Studies 3. Science writing — Paleontology 4. Reference — General

LC 2016933929

World-renowned dinosaur illustrator and researcher Gregory Paul provides comprehensive visual and textual coverage of the great Mesozoic animals that gave rise to the living dinosaurs, the birds. Paul presents thorough descriptions of more than 735 dinosaur species and features more than 600 color and black-and-white images, including unique skeletal drawings, "life" studies, and scenic views.

Includes bibliographical references (page 350) and index.

Pim, Keiron

Dinosaurs *the Grand Tour: Everything Worth Knowing About Dinosaurs from Aardonyx to Zuniceratops.* Keiron Pim with field notes by Jack Horner; illustrated by Fabio Pastori. The Experiment 2019. 352 pages : Illustration; Color
ISBN 9781615195190
Grades: 10 11 12 Adult **567.9**
1. Dinosaurs 2. Science writing — Paleontology

LC 2019039264

Collects information on paleontological expeditions, highlights from recent research, and profiles over three hundred dinosaurs, providing information on anatomy and evolution.

"Information is provided for each dinosaur on name pronunciation, the creature's diet and weight, where bones have been found, and when it lived. Dramatic illustrations and silhouettes of the dinosaur accompany each profile. Interspersed in the text are short explanations of various aspects of dinosaur lore, such as the Bone Wars." —*Booklist*

First published in Great Britain as the Bumper Book of Dinosaurs by Square Peg/Random House, 2013. First published in North America in revised form by the Experiment, LLC, in 2016; Includes bibliographical references and index.

569 Fossil mammals

Brusatte, Stephen

The **Rise** *and Reign of the Mammals: A New History, from the Shadow of the Dinosaurs to Us.* Steve Brusatte. Mariner Books 2022. 416 p.
ISBN 9780062951519
Grades: Adult **569**
1. Mammals 2. Evolution 3. Survival 4. Extinct mammals 5. Prehistoric animals 6. Natural history 7. Science Writing — Biology 8. Science Writing — Paleontology 9. Nature Writing — Animal Studies

In his acclaimed book the Rise and Fall of the Dinosaurs, American paleontologist Steve Brusatte enchanted readers with his definitive history of the dinosaurs. Now, picking up the narrative in the ashes of the extinction event that doomed T-rex and its kind, Brusatte explores the remarkable story of the family of animals that inherited the Earth—mammals—and brilliantly reveals that their story is every bit as fascinating and complex as that of their predecessors.

"Dinosaurs fascinate everyone, and Brusatte, professor of paleontology and adviser to the Jurassic World film franchise, has named more than 15 new species. However, mammals are his first love, and this delightful account will convert many readers….Throughout, the author employs lucid prose and generous illustrations to describe the explosion of mammal species that followed the disappearance of dinosaurs." —*Kirkus*

Johanson, Donald C.

Lucy: *The Beginnings of Humankind.* Donald C. Johanson and Maitland A. Edey. Simon and Schuster 1981. 409 p, [4] leaves of plates : Illustration
ISBN 9780671250362
Grades: 11 12 Adult **569**
1. Australopithecus afarensis 2. Prehistoric humans 3. Evolution 4. Ethiopia 5. Africa 6. Prehistoric era (Stone Age) 7. Science Writing — Biology 8. History writing — Ancient

LC 80021759

Johanson, the discoverer, in 1974, of "Lucy"—the oldest skelton of an erect-walking human yet found—reports the story of his internationally acclaimed find and speculates on its meaning for the understanding of our origin.

Includes bibliographical references (p. 385-389) and index.

569.9 Humans and related genera

Pattison, Kermit

Fossil *Men: The Quest for the Oldest Fossil Skeleton and the Battle to Define Human Origins.* Kermit Pattison. William Morrow 2018. 352 p.
ISBN 9780062410283
Grades: Adult **569.9**
1. Neanderthals 2. Prehistoric humans 3. Physical anthropology 4. Fossils 5. Human evolution 6. Archaeology 7. Excavations (Archaeology) 8. Forensic anthropology 9. Paleontology 10. Scientific discoveries 11. Prehistoric era (Stone Age) 12. Science Writing — Biology 13. Science Writing — Paleontology

Discusses the search for the fossilized remains of the earliest human ancestors in the hopes that the discoveries will offer new insights into the development, origins and evolution of the human species and reveals what is known about existing fossils.

Wragg Sykes, Rebecca

Kindred: *Neanderthal Life, Love, Death and Art.* Rebecca Wragg Sykes. Bloomsbury Sigma 2020. 400 pages, 8 unnumbered pages of plates : Illustration; Color
ISBN 9781635579895
Grades: Adult **569.9**
1. Prehistoric humans 2. Neanderthals 3. Evolution 4. Social life and customs 5. Human behavior 6. Culture 7. Scientific discoveries 8. Science Writing — General 9. History writing — Ancient 10. History writing — Archaeology

This book sheds new light on where Neanderthals lived, what they ate, and the increasingly complex Neanderthal culture that researchers have discovered.

"Accumulated from the approximately 200 known Neanderthal sites, the information that Sykes evocatively and enthusiastically presents enables readers to appreciate Neanderthals as sentient creatures, and possibly imagine themselves sharing, Jean Auel-like, a Pleistocene encounter with them." —*Booklist*

Includes bibliographical references and index.

570 Biology

Sinclair, David A.

Lifespan: *The Revolutionary Science of Why We Age - and Why We Don't Have to.* David A. Sinclair, Ph.D, A.O. with Matthew D. LaPlante; illustrations by Catherine L. Delphia. Atria Books 2019. 416 p.
ISBN 9781501191978
Grades: Adult **570**
1. Longevity 2. Cytology 3. Life expectancy 4. Aging 5. Science Writing — Biology

LC 2019007196

From an acclaimed Harvard professor and one of Time's most influential people, this paradigm-shifting book shows how almost everything we think we know about aging is wrong, offers a front-row seat to the amazing global effort to

ESSENTIAL AND RECOMMENDED TITLES
570.1 Biology — Philosophy and theory

slow, stop, and reverseaging, and calls readers to consider a future where aging can be treated.

Includes bibliographical references (pages 315-367) and index.

Zimmer, Carl
Life's Edge: Searching for What It Means to Be Alive. Carl Zimmer. Dutton 2021. 364 p.
ISBN 9780593182710
Grades: Adult **570**
1. Life sciences 2. Life (Biology) 3. Biodiversity 4. Science Writing — Biology
LC 2020039762

The New York Times "Matter" columnist investigates the science community's conflicting views on what it actually means to be alive as demonstrated by laboratory attempts to recreate life and the examples of particularly remarkable life forms.

"The question of what it means to be alive has flowed through four centuries of scientific history like an underground river,' writes journalist Zimmer (She Has Her Mother's Laugh) in this stimulating inquiry into biological fundamentals." —*Publishers Weekly*

Includes bibliographical references and index.

570.1 Biology — Philosophy and theory

Jabr, Ferris
★ *Becoming Earth: How Our Planet Came to Life.* Ferris Jabr. Random House 2024. 272 p.
ISBN 9780593133972
Grades: Adult **570.1**
1. Life 2. Evolution 3. Cosmogony 4. Nature 5. Organisms 6. Biodiversity 7. Interdependence in nature 8. Geodynamics 9. Effect of humans on nature 10. Environmental degradation 11. Fossil fuels 12. Climate change 13. Climate change mitigation 14. Biology 15. Geology 16. Earth 17. Nature Writing — Environmental Issues 18. Nature Writing — Natural Landscapes 19. Science Writing — Biology 20. Science Writing — Geology 21. Debut title
LC 2023038723

One of humanity's oldest beliefs is that our world is alive. Though once ridiculed by some scientists, the idea of Earth as a vast interconnected living system has gained acceptance in recent decades. We, and all living things, are more than inhabitants of Earth—we are Earth, an outgrowth of its structure and an engine of its evolution. Becoming Earth is an exhilarating journey through the hidden workings of our planetary symphony—its players, its instruments, and the music of life that emerges—and an invitation to reexamine our place in it. How well we play our part will determine what kind of Earth our descendants inherit for millennia to come.

"Jabr's survey of current Earth science is a masterwork of journalism—exhaustively researched, wide-ranging, simultaneously intricate in detail and accessible to general readers…Popular science writing at its very best." —*Kirkus*

Includes bibliographical references and index.

570.92 Biologists

Wilson, Edward O.
★ *Letters to a Young Scientist.* Edward O. Wilson. Liveright Publishing Corporation, a Division of W.W. Norton & Company 2013. 256 pages
ISBN 9780871403773
Grades: 9 10 11 12 Adult **570.92**
1. Wilson, Edward O. 2. Advice 3. Scientists 4. Science 5. Biologists 6. Naturalists 7. Science Writing — General 8. Nature Writing — General 9. Adult books for young adults
LC 2012051412

Green Prize for Sustainable Literature: Adult Nonfiction, 2014.

Weaves together more than twenty letters that illuminate the author's career and his motivations for becoming a biologist, explaining how success in the sciences depends on a passion for finding a problem and solving it.

"Critically aware of his—and his successors'—moments in time, and what kinds of problems the next generation of scientists will be dealing with (e.g., environmental issues), Wilson ultimately offers an encouraging call to arms: 'Time is growing short…you are needed.' —*Publishers Weekly*

Includes index.

571.0919 Space

Roach, Mary
Packing for Mars: The Curious Science of Life in the Void. Mary Roach. W. W. Norton 2010. 336 p. : Illustration
ISBN 9780393068474
Grades: 9 10 11 12 Adult **571.0919**
1. Space biology 2. Space exploration 3. Astronautics 4. Space sciences 5. Gravity 6. Science Writing — Space and Flight 7. Adult books for young adults
LC 2010017113

Library Journal Best Books, 2010.

Describes the weirdness of space travel, answers questions about the long-term effects of living in zero gravity on the human body, and explains how space simulations on Earth can provide a preview to life in space.

"The author explores the organic aspects of the space program, such as the dangerous bane of space motion sickness and the challenges of space hygiene…. She devotes one chapter to space food and another to zero-gravity elimination, which is a serious matter, even with a term like fecal popcorning. An impish and adventurous writer with a gleefully inquisitive mind and a standup comic's timing, Roach celebrates human ingenuity (the odder the better), and calls for us to marshal our resources, unchain our imaginations, and start packing for Mars." —*Booklist*

571.2 Plants and microorganisms

Schlanger, Zoe
★ *The Light Eaters: How the Unseen World of Plant Intelligence Offers a New Understanding of Life on Earth.* Zoë Schlanger. Harper 2024. 304 p.
ISBN 9780063073852
Grades: Adult **571.2**
1. Plants 2. Botany 3. Plant physiology 4. Plant growth 5. Life cycles 6. Biological discoveries 7. Intelligence 8. Communication 9. Survival 10. Science Writing — Biology 11. Nature Writing — Gardens
LC 2023037601

LibraryReads Favorites, 2024.

It takes tremendous biological creativity to be a plant. To survive and thrive while rooted in a single spot, plants have adapted ingenious methods of survival. What is intelligent life if not a vine that grows leaves to blend into the shrub on which it climbs, a flower that shapes its bloom to fit exactly the beak of its pollinator, a pea seedling that can hear water flowing and make its way toward it? Zoë Schlanger takes us across the globe, digging into her own memories and into the soil with the scientists who have spent their waking days studying these amazing entities up close.

"Schlanger, a staff writer at the Atlantic, debuts with an astounding exploration of the remarkable abilities of plants and fungi." —*Publishers Weekly*

Includes bibliographical references and index.

571.6 Cell biology

Martinez Arias, Alfonso
The Master Builder: How the New Science of the Cell Is Rewriting the Story of Life. Alfonso Martinez Arias. Basic Books 2023. 336 p.
ISBN 9781541603271

PUBLIC LIBRARY CORE COLLECTION: NONFICTION
Twentieth Edition

Grades: Adult   **571.6**

1. Cells 2. Organisms 3. Life (Biology) 4. Biological growth 5. Developmental biology 6. Biological research 7. Science Writing — Biology

LC 2022049294

What defines who we are? For decades, the answer has seemed obvious: our genes, the "blueprint of life." In The Master Builder, biologist Alfonso Martinez Arias argues we've been missing the bigger picture. It's not our genes that define who we are, but our cells. Drawing on new research from his own lab and others, Martinez Arias reveals that we are composed of a thrillingly intricate, constantly moving symphony of cells. Both their long lineage—stretching back to the very first cell—and their intricate interactions within our bodies today make us who we are.

"A rich, detailed exploration of the vitality of cells." —Kirkus

Includes bibliographical references and index.

Mukherjee, Siddhartha

★ *The Song of the Cell: An Exploration of Medicine and the New Human.* Siddhartha Mukherjee. Scribner 2022. 576 p.

ISBN 9781982117351

Grades: Adult   **571.6**

1. Cells 2. Health 3. Diseases 4. Medical care 5. Physicians 6. Medical research 7. Gene editing 8. Human physiology 9. Medical innovations 10. Science Writing — Biology 11. Science Writing — Medicine and health 12. Life stories — Science, technology, and medicine

Presenting revelatory and exhilarating stories of scientists, doctors and the patients whose lives may be saved by their work, Siddhartha Mukherjee, drawing on his own experience as a researcher, doctor and prolific reader, explores medicine and our radical new ability to manipulate cells.

"A better understanding of the cell holds immense power for medicine according to this eye-opening account from Pulitzer winner Mukherjee (The Emperor of All Maladies)." —Publishers Weekly

Stanger, Ben

From One Cell: A Journey into Life's Origins and the Future of Medicine. Ben Stanger. W W Norton & Company 2023. 320 p.

ISBN 9781324005421

Grades: Adult   **571.6**

1. Cells 2. Biology 3. Medical research 4. Genes 5. Human body 6. DNA 7. Science Writing — Biology

This exploration of the spectacular yet commonplace journey of the development of human life from a single cell to birth draws on the latest research into how life and the body take shape.

"Ultimately, the author delivers an informative package of how this field of medicine has developed and where it might be going." —Kirkus

---

572.8 Biochemical genetics

Cech, Thomas

The Catalyst: RNA and the Quest to Unlock Life's Deepest Secrets. Thomas R. Cech. W.W. Norton & Company 2024. 320 p.

ISBN 9781324050681

Grades: Adult   **572.8**

1. Cytology 2. Biochemistry 3. Cell physiology 4. Cell division 5. Molecular biology 6. Biological research 7. Scientific forecasting 8. Science Writing — Biology 9. Science Writing — Medicine and health 10. Debut title

Exploring the most transformative breakthroughs in biology since the discovery of the double helix, a Nobel Prize-winning scientist unveils the RNA age.

"Nobel Prize winner and National Medal of Science awardee Cech explains RNA, telomerase, CRISPR, mRNA vaccines, such as those created during the pandemic, and much more in this wide-ranging work that explores the science of RNA and profiles the scientists redefining the frontier of medicine." —Library Journal

Heine, Steven J.

Dna Is Not Destiny: The Remarkable, Completely Misunderstood Relationship Between You and Your Genes. Steven J. Heine. W W Norton & Co. Inc. 2017. 336 p.

ISBN 9780393244083

Grades: Adult   **572.8**

1. DNA 2. Social psychology 3. Genetics 4. Genes 5. Genomes 6. Epigenetics 7. Public opinion 8. Misconceptions 9. Science 10. Science Writing — Medicine and health

LC 2017000693

A leading cultural psychologist challenges current understandings about the role of DNA in health, drawing on his own genome sequencing results to explain what genes can actually tell us and why psychological biases can render people vulnerable to media hype.

"An accessible contribution to what the author calls 'Genetic literacy' and a satisfyingly hard-edged work of popular science." —Kirkus

Tabery, James

★ *Tyranny of the Gene: Personalized Medicine and Its Threat to Public Health.* James Tabery. Alfred A. Knopf 2023. 352 p.

ISBN 9780525658207

Grades: Adult   **572.8**

1. Genomes 2. Public health 3. Medical care 4. Human genome 5. Genetics 6. Society and culture — Illness and disease 7. Politics and global affairs — Public health 8. Science Writing — Medicine and health

Exposing the origin story of personalized medicine, one of power, politics and greed, and tracing its path from the Human Genome Project to the present, this thought-provoking book serves as a warning cry about the current trajectory of health care and charts a path to a more equitable alternative.

"This damning take on scientific bias is not to be missed." —Publishers Weekly

---

572.86 DNA

Markel, Howard

The Secret of Life: Rosalind Franklin, James Watson, Francis Crick, and the Discovery of Dna's Double Helix. Howard Markel. W.W. Norton & Company 2021. 608 p.

ISBN 9781324002239

Grades: Adult   **572.86**

1. Franklin, Rosalind, 1920-1958 2. Watson, James D, 1928- 3. Crick, Francis, 1916-2004 4. Wilkins, Maurice, 1916-2004 5. Pauling, Linus, 1901-1994 6. DNA 7. Genetic code 8. Genetics 9. Genomes 10. Jewish women 11. Women scientists 12. History of medicine 13. Scientists 14. Collective biographies 15. Biographies 16. Life stories — Science, technology, and medicine — Scientists and inventors 17. History writing — Science, technology, and medicine 18. Science Writing — Biology 19. History writing — Women's history

LC 2021013018

Drawing on archival research, including interviews with James Watson and Franklin's sister, this authoritative history of the race to unravel DNA's structure focuses on Rosalind Franklin, the lone Jewish woman among young male scientists, finally giving the woman at the center of this drama her due.

"One of the greatest scientific discoveries of the 20th century was also the scientific heist of the century, according to this action-packed history. Historian Markel (The Kelloggs) recreates the 1953 elucidation of DNA's structure by Cambridge University's James Watson and Francis Crick and their rivalry with the King's College team of Rosalind Franklin and Maurice Wilkins." —Publishers Weekly

Includes bibliographical references and index.

ESSENTIAL AND RECOMMENDED TITLES
573.8 Nervous and sensory systems

573.8 Nervous and sensory systems

Higgins, Jackie
Sentient: How Animals Illuminate the Wonder of Our Human Senses. Jackie Higgins. Atria Books 2022. 288 p.
ISBN 9781982156558
Grades: Adult   573.8
1. Animal physiology 2. Animal behavior 3. Perception 4. Senses and sensation 5. Evolution 6. Neuroscience 7. Science Writing — Biology 8. Nature Writing — Animal Studies

There is a scientific revolution stirring in the field of human perception. Research has shown that the extraordinary sensory powers of our animal friends can help us better understand the same powers that lie dormant within us. From the harlequin mantis shrimp with its ability to see a vast range of colors, to the bloodhound and its hundreds of millions of scent receptors; from the orb-weaving spider whose eyes recognize not only space but time, to the cheetah whose ears are responsible for its perfect agility, these astonishing animals hold the key to better understanding how we make sense of the world around us.

Higgins does a great job at describing scientific studies and their results, and at connecting them to humans, making for a moving and perspective-shifting examination of 'The everyday miracle of being sentient.' —*Publishers Weekly*

Originally published in the UK under the title Sentient: What animals reveal about our senses by Picador, London, in 2021.

575 Specific parts of and physiological systems in plants

Darwin, Charles
★ *The***Origin** *of Species by Means of NaturalSelection, Or, the Preservation of Favored RacesIn the Struggle for Life: By Means of NaturalSelection or the Preservation of Favored Races InThe Struggle for Life.* Charles Darwin. Modern Library 1993. xvi, 689 p.
ISBN 9780679600701
Grades: Adult   575
1. Natural selection 2. Evolution 3. Essays 4. Science writing — General
LC 93003598

States the evidence for a theory of evolution, explains how evolution takes place, and discusses instinct, hybrids, fossils, distribution, and classification.

Includes index.

576.5 Genetics

Isaacson, Walter
★ *The Code Breaker: Jennifer Doudna, Gene Editing, and the Future of the Human Race.* Walter Isaacson. Simon & Schuster 2021. 448 p.
ISBN 9781982115852
Grades: Adult   576.5
1. Doudna, Jennifer A. 2. Human genetics 3. Women scientists 4. CRISPR (Genetics) 5. Nobel PRize winners 6. Gene editing 7. Human genome 8. Genetics 9. Genetic research 10. Biographies 11. Life stories — Science, technology, and medicine — Scientists and inventors 12. Science — Biology — Genetics 13. Science Writing — Medicine and health
LC 2020043552

The bestselling author of Leonardo da Vinci and Steve Jobs returns with a gripping account of how the pioneering scientist Jennifer Doudna, along with her colleagues and rivals, launched a revolution that will allow us to cure diseases, fend off viruses, and enhance our children.

"Biographer Isaacson (Leonardo da Vinci) depicts science at its most exhilarating in this lively biography of Jennifer Doudna, the winner of the 2020 Nobel Prize in chemistry for her work on the CRISPR system of gene editing." —*Publishers Weekly*

Includes bibliographical references and index.

Raff, Jennifer
Origin: A Genetic History of the Americas. Jennifer Raff. Twelve, Hachette Book Group 2022. 352 p.
ISBN 9781538749715
Grades: Adult   576.5
1. Paleontology 2. Genetics 3. Anthropology 4. DNA 5. Indigenous peoples 6. North America 7. South America 8. Science Writing — Paleontology
LC 2021031909

In this study of both past and present, a celebrated anthropologist tells the story of who the first peoples in America were based on their complete genomes, providing a glimpse into how the tools of genetics reveal details about human history and evolution.

"When did humans first arrive in the Americas? Who were they? Where did they come from? Raff (anthropology, Univ. of Kansas) tackles these questions using anthropological genetics. . . . A thorough yet conversational outlining of the peopling of the Americas that will update any anthropology or world history collection." —*Library Journal*

Includes bibliographical references and index.

Zimmer, Carl
She Has Her Mother's Laugh: The Powers, Perversions, and Potential of Heredity. Carl Zimmer. Dutton, an imprint of Penguin Random House LLC 2018. 544 p.
ISBN 9781101984598
Grades: Adult   576.5
1. Heredity 2. Genetics 3. Genetic research 4. Human evolution 5. Science writing — Biology
LC 2017046101

National Academies Communication Award, 2019; New York Times Notable Book, 2018.

The award-winning columnist and author of Parasite Rex presents a history of our understanding of heredity and how it has shaped human society, chronicling the transitions brought about by genetic research and sharing anecdotal insights into his own family's experiences while making predictions about how evolving understandings are likely to impact the future.

Includes bibliographical references and index.

576.8 Evolution

Black, Riley
The Last Days of the Dinosaurs: An Asteroid, Extinction, and the Beginning of Our World. Riley Black. St. Martin's Press 2022. 304 p.
ISBN 9781250271044
Grades: Adult   576.8
1. Dinosaurs 2. Asteroids 3. Extinction 4. Mass extinctions 5. Evolution 6. Biotic communities 7. Excavations (Paleontology) 8. Natural history 9. Collisions (Astrophysics) 10. North America 11. Science Writing — Biology 12. Science Writing — Paleontology
LC 2021052246

Science Books and Films Prize for Excellence in Science Books, Young Adult Science Book, 2023.

The Last Days of the Dinosaurs by Riley Black tells the story of the extinction of these prehistoric creatures and the beginning of our world.

Walks readers through what happened in the days, years, centuries and million years after an asteroid led to the mass extinction of the dinosaurs and half of known species, and how this worst single day in the history of life on Earth allowed for evolutionary opportunities.

"Black (Written in Stone) combines science information with beautiful prose, providing snapshots of various dinosaurs just before, during, and after the asteroid impact." —*Library Journal*

Includes bibliographical references.

PUBLIC LIBRARY CORE COLLECTION: NONFICTION
Twentieth Edition

Brannen, Peter
The **Ends** *of the World: Volcanic Apocalypses, Lethal Oceans, and Our Quest to Understand Earth's Past Mass Extinctions.* Peter Brannen. Ecco Press 2017. 256 p.
ISBN 9780062364807
Grades: Adult 576.8
1. Mass extinctions 2. Extinction 3. Environmental disasters 4. Disaster forecasting 5. Environmental forecasting 6. Climate change 7. Nature writing — Natural disaster
LC Bl2017017905

A vivid tour of Earth's five mass extinctions profiles the vibrant worlds that were destroyed and rebuilt during each cycle, explaining what today's scientists are learning from ancient fossils about 21st-century climate change.

"If readers have time for only one book on the subject, this wonderfully written, well-balanced, and intricately researched (though not too dense) selection is the one to choose." —*Library Journal*

Catania, Kenneth
Great Adaptations: Star-nosed Moles, Electric Eels & Other Tales of Evolution's Mysteries Solved. Kenneth Catania. Princeton University Press 2020. 240 p.
ISBN 9780691195254
Grades: Adult 576.8
1. Adaptation 2. Animal adaptation 3. Animal anatomy 4. Animal behavior 5. Moles (Animals) 6. Electric Eel 7. Wasps 8. Snakes 9. Shrews 10. Evolution 11. Biology 12. Sense of wonder 13. Science 14. Nature Writing — Animal Studies 15. Science Writing — Biology
LC Bl2020052401

Science Books and Films Prize for Excellence in Science Books, Young Adult Science Book, 2022.

From star-nosed moles that have super-sensing snouts to electric eels that paralyze their prey, animals possess unique and extraordinary abilities. In Great Adaptations, Kenneth Catania presents an entertaining and engaging look at some of nature's most remarkable creatures. Telling the story of his biological detective work, Catania sheds light on the mysteries behind the behaviors of tentacled snakes, tiny shrews, zombie-making wasps, and more. He shows not only how studying these animals can provide deep insights into how life evolved, but also how scientific discovery can be filled with adventure and fun.

"The joy Catania takes in the process of exploring the natural world will delight readers." —*Publishers Weekly*

Includes bibliographical references and index.

Costa, James T.
Darwin's Backyard: How Small Experiments Led to a Big Theory. James T. Costa. W. W. Norton & Company 2017. 416 p.
ISBN 9780393239898
Grades: Adult 576.8
1. Darwin, Charles, 1809-1882 2. Naturalists 3. Natural selection 4. Experiments 5. Evolution 6. Science 7. Science Writing — Biology 8. Life stories — Science, technology, and medicine — Scientists and inventors
LC 2017017865

Goes beyond the portrait of Charles Darwin as a brilliant thinker to concentrate on him as a nimble experimenter delving into some of evolution's great mysteries.

"An instructive and entertaining look at Darwin's 'Experimentising' and how it can be readily duplicated using mostly simple household tools." —*Kirkus*

Darwin, Charles
Charles Darwin: The Beagle Letters. Edited by Frederick Burkhardt; introduction by Janet Browne. Cambridge University Press 2008. 500 p.
ISBN 9780521898386
Grades: Adult 576.8
1. Darwin, Charles, 1809-1882 2. Naturalists 3. Expeditions 4. Biological discoveries 5. Natural selection 6. Voyages and travels 7. Fossils 8. Collectors and collecting 9. Science Writing — Biology
LC Bl2009001752

A chronicle of the correspondences sent by and to Darwin while on the HMS Beagle in 1831, including details of the five-year journey, the observations that led to "The Origin of Species," and his feelings about the role he played.

"The complete correspondence both to and from Charles Darwin during his five years circumnavigating the globe on the HMS Beagle, beginning in 1831, documents his growth as a naturalist and offers a picture of life in the England he left behind. It is fascinating to watch Darwin attempt to come to grips with the huge amount of data he collected and make sense of the patterns he observed. We get an intimate look at an adventurous young Darwin, so unlike his more familiar, sedentary older self who would write on the Origin of Species." —*Publishers Weekly*

Dawkins, Richard
★ *The* **Ancestor's** *Tale: A Pilgrimage to the Dawn of Evolution.* Richard Dawkins. Houghton Mifflin 2004. xii, 673 p. : Illustration
ISBN 9780618005833
Grades: Adult 576.8
1. Humans 2. Life (Biology) 3. Evolution 4. Philosophy 5. Science Writing — Biology
LC 2004059864

New York Times Notable Book, 2004.

A renowned biologist provides a sweeping chronicle of more than four billion years of life on Earth, shedding new light on evolutionary theory and history, sexual selection, speciation, extinction, genetics, and geographical dispersal.

"The author sets out on a pilgrimage tracing the history of the human species back to the very origins of life, marking along the way 39 rendezvous points where the human genealogical path crosses that of other terrestrial species. Lively and daring, a book certain to draw even casual readers deep into the adventure and controversy of science." —*Booklist*

Includes bibliographical references (p. 624-645) and index.

The **Greatest** *Show on Earth: The Evidence for Evolution.* Richard Dawkins. Free Press 2009. 480 p.
ISBN 9781416594789
Grades: Adult 576.8
1. Evolution 2. Biology 3. Humans 4. Science 5. Genetics 6. Science Writing — Biology
LC 2009025330

The acclaimed author of the God Delusion and Selfish Gene lays out evidence in defense of the theory of evolution in a thrilling tour into our distant past and into the the interstices of life on Earth that will be released in time for the 150th anniversary of Charles Darwin's on the Origin of Species.

Includes bibliographical references and index.

Gee, Henry
A **(very)** *Short History of Life on Earth: 4.6 Billion Years in 12 Pithy Chapters.* Henry Gee. St. Martin's Press 2021. 208 p.
ISBN 9781250276650
Grades: Adult 576.8
1. Life 2. Human evolution 3. Evolution 4. Earth history 5. Science Writing — Biology 6. Science Writing — Geology
LC 2021029254

Royal Society General Prizes for Science Books, 2022.

Takes the reader through the last 4.6 billion years of history of Life on Earth with infectious enthusiasm and intellectual rigor.

"Gee (The Accidental Species), a paleontologist and senior editor at the science journal Nature, finds beauty in adversity in this eloquent account of how life evolved on Earth.... Action-packed and full of facts, this well-told tale will delight lay readers." —*Publishers Weekly*

Originally published in the United Kingdom by Picador; Includes bibliographical references and index.

Gould, Stephen Jay
The **Structure** *of Evolutionary Theory.* Stephen Jay Gould. Belknap Press of Harvard University Press 2002. xxii, 1433 p. : Illustration
ISBN 9780674006133
Grades: 11 12 Adult 576.8

ESSENTIAL AND RECOMMENDED TITLES
576.8 Evolution

1. Evolution 2. Human evolution 3. Science Writing — Biology

LC 2001043556

Presents a critique of classical Darwinism, covering its core elements, history, and origins, and offers a new structure of evolutionary thought.

"This is a history and analysis of classical and twentieth-century evolutionary theory." —*Booklist*

Includes bibliographical references (p. 1344-1387) and index.

Green, Jaime
The Possibility of Life: Science, Imagination, and Our Quest for Kinship in the Cosmos. Jaime Green. Hanover Square Press 2023. 288 p.

ISBN 9781335463548

Grades: Adult   576.8

1. Cosmology 2. Science 3. Life on other planets 4. Popular culture 5. Space 6. Essays 7. Science writing — Space and flight 8. Society and culture — Pop culture

"An insightful examination of life—not only on Earth, but also where it might exist on the myriad of newly discovered planets and distant stars….Ingenious writing about the cosmos and life itself." —*Kirkus*

Johnson, Sarah Stewart
The Sirens of Mars: Searching for Life on Another World. Sarah Stewart Johnson. Crown 2020. xiii, 266 p.

ISBN 9781101904817

Grades: Adult   576.8

1. Johnson, Sarah Stewart 2. Women scientists 3. Planets 4. Life on other planets 5. Extreme environments 6. Biology 7. Geology 8. Astronomy 9. Mars probes 10. Space exploration 11. Astronomical discoveries 12. Mars (Planet) 13. Science Writing — Space and Flight 14. Life stories — Science, technology, and medicine — Scientists and inventors 15. Nature Writing — Personal Responses

LC 2020007280

New York Times Notable Book, 2020.

Mars was once similar to Earth, but today there are no rivers, no lakes, no oceans. Coated in red dust, the terrain is bewilderingly empty. And yet multiple spacecraft are circling Mars, sweeping over Terra Sabaea, Syrtis Major, the dunes of Elysium, and Mare Sirenum—on the brink, perhaps, of a staggering find, one that would inspire humankind as much as any discovery in the history of modern science. In this beautifully observed, deeply personal book, Georgetown scientist Sarah Stewart Johnson tells the story of how she and other researchers have scoured Mars for signs of life, transforming the planet from a distant point of light into a world of its own.

"A vivid, poetic account that leaves readers eager to see what's next in the quest to find extraterrestrial life." —*Kirkus*

Includes bibliographical references and index.

Kershenbaum, Arik
The Zoologist's Guide to the Galaxy: What Animals on Earth Reveal About Aliens—and Ourselves. Arik Kershenbaum. Penguin Press 2021. 368 p.

ISBN 9781984881960

Grades: Adult   576.8

1. Life on other planets 2. Evolution 3. Aliens 4. Logic 5. Extraterrestrial anthropology 6. Cosmobiology 7. Space biology 8. Space 9. Science Writing — Space and Flight 10. Science Writing — Biology

LC 2020027476

Using universal laws that govern life on Earth, a noted Cambridge zoologist presents an engaging, scientifically sound exploration of what life may be like on other planets and in space, discussing such speculative topics as supersonic animals and alien emotion.

"In this enjoyable and informative book, Cambridge zoologist Kershenbaum argues that because the theory of natural selection and the laws of biology are universal, they can be applied to habitats other than Earth to understand how complex life may evolve in those places." —*Kirkus*

Includes bibliographical references and index.

Larson, Edward J.
Evolution: The Remarkable History of a Scientific Theory. Edward J. Larson. Modern Library 2004. xiv, 337 p. : Illustration

ISBN 9780679642886

Grades: 11 12 Adult   576.8

1. Evolution 2. Paleontology 3. Sociobiology 4. Genetics 5. Philosophy 6. Science Writing — Biology 7. Science Writing — Paleontology

LC 2003064888

Traces the history of evolutionary theory, from the eighteenth-century emergence of paleontology, through the breakthroughs of Darwin, to the backlash against evolutionism, to its resurrection through the science of genetics.

"This is an overview of evolutionary thought from ancient speculations to the emergence of a neo-Darwinian synthesis. It focuses on those essential facts, events, and ideas that have contributed to the successes of scientific evolutionism. Larson is to be commended for stressing the value of both scientific inquiry and the evolutionary framework. This outstanding book is highly recommended for all academic and public libraries." —*Library Journal*

Includes bibliographical references (p. [326]-331) and index.

Lister, Adrian
Darwin's Fossils: The Collection That Shaped the Theory of Evolution. Adrian Lister. Smithsonian Books 2018. 160 p.

ISBN 9781588346179

Grades: Adult   576.8

1. Darwin, Charles, 1809-1882 2. Evolution 3. Fossils 4. Science Writing — Biology 5. History writing — Exploration

LC 2017046415

Reveals how Darwin's study of fossils shaped his scientific thinking and led to his development of the theory of evolution.

"Richly illustrated with photos from the fossil collection and line drawings produced when Darwin was alive, Listers work is an essential acquisition for every library prizing quality books on evolution." —*Booklist*

Copyrighted by the Trustees of the Natural History Museum, London; Includes bibliographical references and index.

Loeb, Abraham
Extraterrestrial: The First Sign of Intelligent Life Beyond Earth. Avi Loeb. Houghton Mifflin Harcourt 2021. 240 p.

ISBN 9780358278146

Grades: Adult   576.8

1. Aliens 2. Life on other planets 3. Astrophysics 4. Astronomers 5. Theories 6. Astronomy 7. UFOs 8. Human-alien encounters 9. Science Writing — Space and flight

LC 2020023329

Harvard's top astronomer lays out his controversial theory that our solar system was recently visited by advanced alien technology from a distant star.

"Loeb's thought-provoking work of popular science will entertain those who wonder if humans are alone in the universe." —*Publishers Weekly*

Losos, Jonathan B.
Improbable Destinies: Fate, Chance, and the Future of Evolution. Jonathan B. Losos. Riverhead Books 2017. 384 p.

ISBN 9780399184925

Grades: Adult   576.8

1. Evolution 2. Adaptation 3. Natural selection 4. Science Writing — Biology

LC 2016054594

A Harvard museum curator draws on the latest breakthroughs in evolutionary biology to challenge popular assumptions about how evolution works, examining how tiny, random convergences, from mutations to butterfly sneezes, have triggered remarkable evolutionary changes.

"A cheerful, delightfully lucid primer on evolution and the predictive possibilities within the field." —*Kirkus*

Includes bibliographical references and index.

PUBLIC LIBRARY CORE COLLECTION: NONFICTION
Twentieth Edition

Margulis, Lynn
Symbiotic Planet: A New Look at Evolution. Lynn Margulis. Basic Books 1998. VI, 147 p. : Illustration
ISBN 9780465072712
Grades: 11 12 Adult   576.8
1. Symbiosis 2. Evolution 3. Science Writing — Biology
LC 98038921

A visionary scientist proposes her theory that cooperation in nature has been as influential as competition in the evolution of life, presenting a case for the importance of symbiosis in the development of sex, movements, minds, and life on land.

"From the origin of life to the classification and phylogeny of living organisms, from a discussion of Gaia—the belief that Earth operates like a living being—to a discussion of the underlying reasons for sex, iconoclastic biologist Margulis . . . takes on many of the big questions in biology. In a book that is part autobiography and part biological primer, Margulis . advances the idea that a large part of organic evolution can be explained by symbiosis." —*Publishers Weekly*

Includes bibliographical references (p. 131-136) and index.

Markel, Howard
Origin Story: The Trials of Charles Darwin. Howard Markel. W.W. Norton & Company 2024. 352 p.
ISBN 9781324036746
Grades: Adult   576.8
1. Darwin, Charles, 1809-1882 2. Biologists 3. Hypothesis 4. Evolution 5. Sick people 6. Grief 7. Death of children 8. Natural selection 9. Public opinion 10. Religion and science 11. Debates and debating 12. British people 13. English people 14. Biographies 15. Life stories — Science, technology, and medicine — Scientists and inventors 16. Science Writing — Biology 17. History writing — Science, technology, and medicine

By early morning of June 30, 1860, a large crowd began to congregate in front of Oxford University's brand-new Museum of Natural History. The occasion was the annual meeting of the British Association for the Advancement of Science, and the subject of discussion was Charles Darwin's new treatise: fact or fiction? Without fear of exaggeration, Darwin's thesis would forever change our understanding of the life sciences and the natural world. And yet the author himself was nowhere to be found in the debate hall—instead, he was miles away, seeking respite from a spate of illnesses that had plagued him for much of his adult life.

"Medical historian Markel (The Secret of Life) presents a gripping account of the period between 1858 and 1860 when Darwin wrote and published on the Origin of Species." —*Publishers Weekly*

McCalman, Iain
Darwin's Armada: Four Voyages and the Battle for the Theory of Evolution. Iain McCalman. Norton 2009. 432 p.
ISBN 9780393068146
Grades: Adult   576.8
1. Darwin, Charles, 1809-1882 2. Hooker, Joseph Dalton, Sir, 1817-1911 3. Huxley, Thomas Henry, 1825-1895 4. Wallace, Alfred Russel, 1823-1913 5. Naturalists 6. Evolution 7. Scientific discoveries 8. Voyages and travels 9. Biology 10. British history 11. 19th century 12. Australian literature 13. Science Writing — Biology
LC 2009016055

Western Australian Premier's Book Award for Non-Fiction, 2009.

Profiles three British voyagers who became fierce defenders of Darwin's theory of evolution, tracing the lives and scientific discoveries of Joseph Hooker, Thomas Huxley, and Alfred Wallace during respective voyages to the southern hemisphere.

Includes bibliographical references and index.

Moore, Kathleen Dean
Earth's Wild Music: Celebrating and Defending the Songs of the Natural World. Kathleen Dean Moore. Random House 2021. 256 pages
ISBN 9781640093676
Grades: Adult   576.8
1. Music 2. Nature 3. Climate change 4. Environmental protection 5. Philosophy 6. Extinction 7. Wildlife 8. Wilderness areas 9. Songs 10. Essays 11. Nature Writing — Environmental Issues 12. Nature Writing — Personal Responses 13. Politics and global affairs — Environmental issues and policies

A tireless advocate for environmental activism in the face of climate change gathers together new and selected essays about the music she finds in the natural world.

"Exceedingly knowledgeable, experienced, and expressive, this former philosophy professor shares tales of her adventures in the far north, prairies, woods, and beyond, all while emphasizing Earth's gloriously varied soundscape." —*Booklist*

Newitz, Annalee
Scatter, Adapt, and Remember: How Humans Will Survive a Mass Extinction. Annalee Newitz. Doubleday 2013. 320 p.
ISBN 9780385535915
Grades: Adult   576.8
1. Survival 2. Extinction 3. End of the world 4. Humans 5. Apocalyptic literature 6. Nature Writing — General 7. Science Writing — Biology
LC 2012042409

A speculative, optimistic work of popular science suggests practical ways to promote the human race's survival of a mass extinction induced by climate change, pandemics and catastrophic natural disasters, citing innovations ranging from the bacteria labs of St. Louis to the underground cities of central Turkey.

"Humans may be experts at destroying the planet, but we are no slouches at preserving it, either, and Newitz's shrewd speculations are heartening." —*Kirkus*

Nye, Bill
Undeniable: Evolution and the Science of Creation. Bill Nye with Corey Powell. St. Martin's Press 2014. 320 p.
ISBN 9781250007131
Grades: Adult   576.8
1. Natural history 2. Creationism 3. Religion and science 4. Evolution 5. Science Writing — Biology 6. Society and culture — Education
LC 2014027163

Revealing the mechanics of evolutionary theory, the scientist, engineer and inventor presents a compelling argument for the scientific unviability of creationism and insists that creationism's place in the science classroom is harmful not only to our children, but to the future of the greater world as well.

"The straightforward, accessible language and clear explanations make this ideal reading to understand lifes origins, especially for those new to the evidence of evolution." —*Library Journal*

Includes bibliographical references and index.

Stott, Rebecca
★ *Darwin's Ghosts:* The Secret History of Evolution. Rebecca Stott. Spiegel & Grau 2012. 320 p.
ISBN 9781400069378
Grades: Adult   576.8
1. Darwin, Charles, 1809-1882 2. Evolution 3. Science 4. Scientists 5. Naturalists 6. Science Writing — Biology 7. History writing — General
LC 2011041951

New York Times Notable Book, 2012.

Evolution was not discovered single-handedly, Rebecca Stott argues, contrary to what has become standard lore, but is an idea that emerged over many centuries, advanced by daring individuals across the globe who had the imagination to speculate on nature's extraordinary ways, and who had the courage to articulate such speculations at a time when to do so was often considered heresy.

Includes bibliographical references and index.

ESSENTIAL AND RECOMMENDED TITLES
576.801 Philosophy and theory

576.801 Philosophy and theory

Wilson, David Sloan
Evolution for Everyone: How Darwin's Theory Can Change the Way We Think About Our Lives. David Sloan Wilson. Delacorte Press 2007. VIII, 390 p.
ISBN 9780385340212
Grades: 11 12 Adult   **576.801**
1. Evolution 2. Life sciences 3. Science Writing — Biology
LC 2006023685

Wilson outlines the basic principles of evolution with stories that entertain as much as they inform, and shows how, properly understood, these principles can illuminate the length and breadth of creation, from the origin of life to the nature of religion. Now everyone can move beyond the sterile debates about creationism and intelligent design to share Darwin's panoramic view of animal and human life, seamlessly connected to each other. Evolution, as Wilson explains, is not just about dinosaurs and human origins, but about why all species behave as they do—from beetles that devour their own young, to bees that function as a collective brain, to dogs that are smarter in some respects than our closest ape relatives. And basic evolutionary principles are also the foundation for humanity's capacity for symbolic thought, culture, and morality.

"Rather than catalog its successes, denounce its detractors or in any way present evolutionary theory as the province of expert tacticians like himself, Wilson invites readers inside and shows them how Darwinism is done, and at lesson's end urges us to go ahead, feel free to try it at home. The result is a sprightly, absorbing and charmingly earnest book that manages a minor miracle, the near-complete emulsifying of science and the real world, ingredients too often kept stubbornly, senselessly apart." —*New York Times Book Review*

Includes bibliographical references (p. [351]-376) and index.

576.839 Extraterrestrial life

Ward, Peter Douglas
Life as We Do Not Know It: The Nasa Search for (and Synthesis Of) Alien Life. Peter Ward. Penguin 2007. xxi, 298 p. : Illustration
ISBN 9780143038498
Grades: 11 12 Adult   **576.839**
1. Life on other planets 2. Civilization 3. Astronomy 4. Space biology 5. Research 6. Aliens 7. Science Writing — Space and Flight 8. Adult books for young adults
LC Oc2007070096

Library Journal Best Books, 2005.

A revealing exploration of the latest NASA research into the possibility of extraterrestrial life also poses a hypothesis about the origins of life on Earth, examining the controversial idea of creating non-DNA life in a laboratory as well as the scientific possibilities of the range of life throughout the universe.

"The author believes researchers might be taking the wrong approach by looking only for earthly DNA-based life forms. Truly alien life, he argues, might have completely different origins. . . . The science is neatly laid out, and readers willing to follow his daring, scientifically based speculations will find their imaginations spurred." —*Publishers Weekly*

Includes bibliographical references (p. 263-284) and index; Originally published: New York: Viking, 2005.

577 Ecology

Carroll, Sean M.
The Big Picture: On the Origins of Life, Meaning, and the Universe Itself. Sean Carroll. Dutton est. 1852, an imprint of Penguin Random House LLC 2016. 352 p.
ISBN 9780525954828
Grades: Adult   **577**
1. Cosmology 2. Scientific discoveries 3. Life 4. Semantics 5. Naturalism 6. Evolution 7. Physical laws 8. Philosophy 9. Science writing — Physics 10. Society and culture — Philosophy
LC 2015050590

The award-winning Caltech physicist and author of the Particle at the End of the Universe shares sweeping perspectives into how human purpose and meaning naturally fit into a scientific worldview.

"Carroll is the perfect guide on this wondrous journey of discovery. A brilliantly lucid exposition of profound philosophical and scientific issues in a language accessible to lay readers." —*Kirkus*

Includes bibliographical references and index.

Roman, Joe
Eat, Poop, Die: How Animals Make Our World. Joe Roman. Little, Brown Spark 2023. VII, 277 p.
ISBN 9780316372923
Grades: Adult   **577**
1. Animals 2. Animal behavior 3. Digestion 4. Animal droppings 5. Biodegradation 6. Food chains (Ecology) 7. Biotic communities 8. Habitats 9. Ecology 10. Climate change mitigation 11. Nature Writing — Animal Studies 12. Nature Writing — Natural Landscapes 13. Nature Writing — Environmental Issues 14. Science Writing — Biology

If forests are the lungs of the planet, then animals migrating across oceans, streams, and mountains—eating, pooping, and dying along the way—are its heart and arteries, pumping nitrogen and phosphorus from deep-sea gorges up to mountain peaks, from the Arctic to the Caribbean. Without this conveyor belt of crucial, life-sustaining nutrients, the world would look very different. Eat, Poop, Die takes readers on an exhilarating global adventure, revealing the remarkable ways in which the most basic biological activities of animals make and remake the world—and how a deeper understanding of these cycles provides us with opportunities to undo the damage humanity has wrought on the planet.

"A book dealing with feces and carcasses may not sound like an appetizing read, but conservation biologist and marine ecologist Roman…delivers a thought-provoking, accessible text…With expert knowledge and wry humor, Roman returns animals to their rightful place at the center of the environment." —*Kirkus*

Includes bibliographical references.

Vigliotti, Jonathan
Before It's Gone: Stories from the Front Lines of Climate Change in Small Town America. Jonathan Vigliotti. Signal Press 2024. 288 p.
ISBN 9781668008171
Grades: Adult   **577**
1. Climate change 2. Global warming 3. Small towns 4. Rural life 5. Nature 6. Effect of environment on humans 7. Effect of humans on nature 8. United States 9. History Writing — Regional history — United States 10. Nature Writing — Environmental issues 11. Society and culture — Urban and regional studies 12. Debut title

A veteran journalist embarks on a poignant American odyssey, tracing the human toll of climate change that is no longer just a warming future, guiding readers across our current wildfire-ravaged landscapes, hurricane-battered coasts and vanishing ecosystems.

"Vigliotti debuts with an on-the-ground, journalistic, story-driven look at the impacts of climate change on individuals across the country, detailing the devastation already being experienced through wildfires, floods, coastline loss, and vast economic impact." —*Library Journal*

577.2 Specific factors affecting ecology

Hanson, Thor
Hurricane Lizards and Plastic Squid: The Fraught and Fascinating Biology of Climate Change. Thor Hanson. Basic Books 2021. 304 p.
ISBN 9781541672420
Grades: Adult   **577.2**
1. Hanson, Thor 2. Biologists 3. Climate change 4. Adaptation 5. Biotic communities 6. Animal migration 7. Global environmental change 8. Evolution 9. Nature Writing — Animal Studies 10. Nature Writing — Environmental Issues 11. Science Writing — Biology

PUBLIC LIBRARY CORE COLLECTION: NONFICTION
Twentieth Edition

LC 2021005928

Biologist Thor Hanson tells the remarkable story of how plants and animals are responding to climate change: Adjusting, evolving, and sometimes dying out. Anole lizards have grown larger toe pads, to grip more tightly in frequent hurricanes. Warm waters cause the development of Humboldt squid to alter so dramatically that fishermen mistake them for different species. Brown pelicans move north, and long-spined sea urchins south, to find cooler homes. And when coral reefs sicken, they leave no territory worth fighting for, so aggressive butterfly fish transform instantly into pacifists. A story of hope, resilience, and risk, Hurricane Lizards and Plastic Squid is a reminder of how unpredictable climate change is as it interacts with the messy lattice of life.

"Biologist Hanson (Buzz: The Nature and Necessity of Bees) explores ways in which plants and animals adjust to climate change, which fall into three categories: Move, adapt, or die.... This compelling read will spark the interest of everyone who cares about what is happening to the natural world." —*Library Journal*

Includes bibliographical references and index.

Welz, Adam
The End of Eden: Wild Nature in the Age of Climate Breakdown. Adam Welz. Bloomsbury Publishing Place USA 2023. 320 p.
ISBN 9781635575224
Grades: Adult   577.2
1. Climate change 2. Nature 3. Animals 4. Nature conservation 5. Wildlife conservation 6. Extinction 7. Environmental degradation 8. Nature Writing — Animal studies 9. Nature Writing — Environmental issues 10. Science Writing — Biology

Inviting us to meet wild species on our own terms in a range of ecosystems spanning the globe, this radical new kind of environmental journalism connects humans to nature in a more empathetic way than ever before and encourages us to defend the natural world before it's too late.

"Photographer and filmmaker Welz draws on decades of experience as an 'Old-school naturalist' in this overview of the devastating impact of global warming on several species around the world." —*Booklist*

577.3 Forest ecology

Pearce, Fred
A Trillion Trees: Restoring Our Forests by Trusting in Nature. Fred Pearce. Greystone Books 2022. 320 p.
ISBN 9781771649407
Grades: Adult   577.3
1. Trees 2. Forest conservation 3. Environmental degradation 4. Nature 5. Forests 6. Climate change 7. Nature Writing — Environmental Issues

A freelance author, journalist and environmental consultant takes readers on a spectacular tour of forests around the world from Ecuador and Nigeria to North America and illustrates the pace of their destruction and discusses why some are beginning to recover.

"Environmental journalist Pearce returns with an exploration of what trees and forests do, how humans have used them, and what must be done to maintain them....An exhilarating and informative look at the world's forests and how we can help them thrive." —*Kirkus*

Originally published in the UK under the title a trillion trees: How we can reforest our world by Granta, London, in 2021.

Rawlence, Ben
The Treeline: The Last Forest and the Future of Life on Earth. Ben Rawlence. St. Martin's Press 2022. 304 p.
ISBN 9781250270238
Grades: Adult   577.3
1. Climate change 2. Trees 3. Global warming 4. Biogeography 5. Forests 6. Environmentalism 7. Physiology 8. Nature Writing — Environmental issues
LC 2021039555

Combining reportage with the latest science, this journey is filled with the wonder and awe at the incredible creativity and resilience of trees and mysterious workings of the forest upon which we rely for the air we breathe.

"After becoming intrigued by the yew tree behind his home, Rawlence (City of Thorns, 2016) embarked on a grand investigation of the forest-tundra ecotone, aka the treeline, which serves as a transition zone between northerly ecosystems. . . . A title of the utmost importance at a time of tremendous peril, the Treeline is a game-changer." —*Booklist*

Includes bibliographical references and index.

577.5 Ecology of miscellaneous environments

Lawson, Nancy
The Humane Gardener: Nurturing a Backyard Habitat for Wildlife. Nancy Lawson. Princeton Architectural Press 2017. 223 p. : Color; Illustration
ISBN 9781616895549
Grades: Adult   577.5
1. Gardening to attract wildlife 2. Garden ecology 3. Reference books 4. Nature writing — Animal studies 5. Nature writing — Gardens
LC 2016029007

A philosophical and practical guide for the gardener who wants to create a backyard garden in harmony with nature.

"This gorgeously written, well-argued title will help backyard gardeners see all creatures, from insects to elk, as visitors to be welcomed rather than pests to be removed." —*Library Journal*

Includes bibliographical references.

Schilthuizen, Menno
Darwin Comes to Town: How the Urban Jungle Drives Evolution. Menno Schilthuizen. Picador USA 2018. 304 p.
ISBN 9781250127822
Grades: Adult   577.5
1. Cities and towns 2. Nature 3. Urban ecology 4. Urbanization 5. Evolution 6. Adaptation 7. Biotic communities 8. Natural selection 9. Science Writing — Biology 10. Nature Writing — Environmental Issues 11. Society and culture — Urban and regional studies
LC 2017059153

An evolutionary biologist explains how scientists are discovering that evolution can actually happen very quickly in the most unlikely of places—the heart of the city.

577.6 Aquatic ecology

Egan, Dan
★ *The Death and Life of the Great Lakes.* Dan Egan. W.W. Norton & Company 2017. 384 p.
ISBN 9780393246438
Grades: Adult   577.6
1. Lake ecology 2. Water quality 3. Lakes 4. Organism introduction 5. Great Lakes 6. Great Lakes region 7. Nature writing — Environmental issues 8. Science writing — General
LC 2016039546

Booklist Editors' Choice, 2017; Los Angeles Times Book Prize for History, 2017; National Academies Communication Award, 2018; New York Times Notable Book, 2017; Wisconsin Library Association Literary Award, 2018.

Traces the scientific, historical, and ecological factors endangering the Great Lakes, discussing late-nineteenth century efforts to connect the lakes to the Atlantic, which unexpectedly introduced invasive species from the natural world.

"Egan. effectively calls attention to the inherent fragility of the Great Lakes in this thought-provoking investigation, providing a modern history of the lakes . and the problems that have plagued them." —*Publishers Weekly*

Includes bibliographical references and index.

ESSENTIAL AND RECOMMENDED TITLES
577.68 Wetland ecology

577.68 Wetland ecology

Struzik, Edward
Swamplands: Tundra Beavers, Quaking Bogs, and the Improbable World of Peat. Edward Struzik. Island Press 2021. 297 p.
ISBN 9781642830804
Grades: Adult   577.68
1. Swamps 2. Bogs 3. Wetlands 4. Marshes 5. Bog bodies 6. Wildlife 7. Biodiversity 8. Endangered ecosystems 9. Biotic communities 10. Habitat conservation 11. Canadian literature 12. Nature Writing — Natural Landscapes 13. Nature Writing — Environmental Issues 14. Science Writing — Biology

In a world filled with breathtaking beauty, we have often overlooked the elusive magic of certain landscapes. A cloudy river flows into an Arctic wetland where sandhill cranes and muskoxen dwell. Further south, cypress branches hang low over dismal swamps. Places like these—collectively known as swamplands or peatlands—often go unnoticed for their ecological splendor. They are as globally significant as rainforests, yet, because of their reputation as wastelands, they are being systematically drained and degraded. Swamplands celebrates these wild places, as journalist Edward Struzik highlights the unappreciated struggle to save peatlands by scientists, conservationists, and landowners around the world.

"Struzik writes with immediacy and a sense of awe, bewitching readers with the unexpected beauty of peatlands." —*Booklist*

Includes bibliographical references and index.

577.69 Saltwater wetland and seashore ecology

Nicolson, Adam
Life Between the Tides. Adam Nicolson; animals and heroes by Kate Boxer; maps and figures by Rosie Nicolson. Farrar, Straus and Giroux 2022. 352 p.
ISBN 9780374251437
Grades: Adult   577.69
1. Tide pools 2. Tide pool ecology 3. Seashore ecology 4. Mollusks 5. Crustacea 6. Marine invertebrates 7. Seashore animals 8. Animal behavior 9. Beauty in nature 10. Human-animal relationships 11. Scotland 12. Great Britain 13. Nature Writing — Natural Landscapes 14. Nature Writing — Animal Studies
LC 2021044058

Inside each rockpool, tucked into one of the infinite crevices of the tidal coastline, lies a rippling, silent, unknowable universe. Below the stillness of the surface course different currents of endless motion—the ebb and flow of the tide, the steady forward propulsion of the passage of time, and the tiny lifetimes of its creatures, all of which coalesce into the grand narrative of evolution. In Life Between the Tides, Adam Nicolson investigates one of the most revelatory habitats on earth. For Nicolson, who writes "with scientific rigor and a poet's sense of wonder" (The American Scholar), the world of the rockpools is infinite and as intricate as our own.

"In the mode of Rachel Carson's the Edge of the Sea, distinguished British writer Nicolson (The Seabird's Cry, 2018) succeeds gloriously in conveying the marvels of a stretch of Scottish tidal coast, mixing history, science, and precise descriptions bright with inventive metaphors and profound revelations." —*Booklist*

Originally published in 2021 by William Collins, Great Britain, as the Sea Is Not Made of Water: Life Between the Tides; Includes bibliographical references and index.

577.7 Marine ecology

Ellis, Richard
★ *The Empty Ocean: Plundering the World's Marine Life.* Written and illustrated by Richard Ellis. Island Press; Shearwater Books 2003. xiv, 367 p. : Illustration
ISBN 9781559639743
Grades: 11 12 Adult   577.7
1. Marine animals 2. Rare and endangered animals 3. Rare and endangered plants 4. Marine biology 5. Marine ecology 6. Marine plants 7. Oceans 8. Nature Writing — Animal Studies — Endangered Species 9. Adult books for young adults
LC 2003002077
New York Times Notable Book, 2003.

Explains the detrimental affects that commercial fishing and other depletions of marine wildlife have on ocean ecology, and suggests remedies for the growing problem.

"Rather than writing the Silent Spring of the oceans, [Ellis] has produced a book that is likely to provide the inspiration and source materials for such a badly needed work . It is also a splendid example of history illuminating ecology, with well-chosen facts that enable us to picture a largely invisible catastrophe." —*New York Times Book Review*

Includes bibliographical references (p. 307-350).

Scales, Helen
What the Wild Sea Can Be: The Future of the World's Ocean. Helen Scales. Atlantic Monthly Press 2024. 352 p.
ISBN 9780802162991
Grades: Adult   577.7
1. Oceans 2. Marine pollution 3. Marine ecology 4. Effect of humans on nature 5. Environmentalism 6. Forecasting 7. Nature 8. Science Writing — Biology 9. Nature Writing — Animal studies 10. Nature Writing — Environmental issues
LC 2024010009

In this bracing yet hopeful exploration the ocean's future, an acclaimed marine biologist takes us into the realms of animals that epitomize today's increasingly challenging conditions, offering innovative ideas for protecting coastlines and cleaning the toxic seas to maintain a sense of awe and wonder at the majesty beneath the waves.

"Marine biologist Scales follows the Brilliant Abyss (2021), a look at deep-sea exploration, with this thorough overview of the current dismal state of the oceans and the diverse animals who depend on their vitality." —*Booklist*

Includes bibliographical references and index.

578 Natural history of organisms and related subjects

Roberts, Jason
★ *Every Living Thing: The Great and Deadly Race to Know All Life.* Jason Roberts. Random House 2024. 432 p.
ISBN 9781984855206
Grades: Adult   578
1. Linné, Carl von, 1707-1778 2. Buffon, Georges Louis Leclerc, comte de, 1707-1788 3. Biology 4. Nature 5. Classification 6. Scientists 7. Naturalists 8. 18th century 9. Collective biographies 10. Life stories — Science, technology, and medicine — Scientists and inventors 11. Science Writing — Biology 12. Nature Writing — Animal studies
LC 2023024942

The best-selling author of a Sense of the World tells the story of two scientific rivals and their mission to survey all life and the clash of ideas that had profound consequences for humanity.

"Roberts provides a thorough accounting of the divergent outlooks of his dual subjects and offers illuminating insight into how politics secured Linnaeus's legacy while consigning Buffon to relative obscurity." —*Publishers Weekly*

Includes bibliographical references and index.

578.4 Adaptation

Forbes, Peter
Dazzled and Deceived: Mimicry and Camouflage. Peter Forbes. Yale University Press 2009. xv, 283 p, 16 p. of plates : Illustration; Color; Map
ISBN 9780300125399
Grades: Adult   578.4

PUBLIC LIBRARY CORE COLLECTION: NONFICTION
Twentieth Edition

1. Mimicry (Biology) 2. Camouflage (Biology) 3. Science writing — Biology

LC 2009023577

Dazzled and Deceived tells the unique and fascinating story of mimicry and camouflage in science, art, warfare, and the natural world. Discovered in the 1850s by the young English naturalists Henry Walter Bates and Alfred Russel Wallace in the Amazonian rainforest, the phenomenon of mimicry was seized upon as the first independent validation of Darwin's theory of natural selection. But mimicry and camouflage also created a huge impact outside the laboratory walls. Peter Forbes's cultural history links mimicry and camouflage to art, literature, military tactics, and medical cures across the twentieth century, and charts its intricate involvement with the perennial dispute between evolution and creationism.

"Forbes has produced a colorful look at camouflage in nature and battle, with a focus on the two world wars. [The book] straddles the worlds of evolutionary biology, art, and military strategy with a world-class cast of characters..." —*Boston Globe*

Includes bibliographical references (p. [256]-276) and index.

Simon, Matt

The Wasp That Brainwashed the Caterpillar: Evolution's Most Unbelievable Solutions to Life's Biggest Problems. Matt Simon; illustrated by Vladimir Stankovic. Penguin Books 2016. xii, 260 pages : Illustration
ISBN 9780143128687
Grades: 11 12 Adult   578.4

1. Animal adaptation 2. Predation (Biology) 3. Parasitism 4. Natural selection 5. Essays 6. Nature writing — Animal studies 7. Adult books for young adults

LC 2016001823

Alex Award, 2017.

Profiles animals that have adapted to solve some of nature's more perplexing problems of everyday life, from the pangolin's keratinized armor and the anglerfish's mating habits to the axolotl's regenerative limbs.

Includes bibliographical references (pages 243-260).

578.6 Miscellaneous nontaxonomic kinds of organisms

Anthony, Leslie

The Aliens Among US: How Invasive Species Are Transforming the Planet - and Ourselves. Leslie Anthony. Yale University Press 2017. 367 pages
ISBN 9780300208900
Grades: Adult   578.6

1. Biotic communities 2. Biological invasions 3. Adaptation 4. Competition (Biology) 5. Effect of humans on nature 6. Habitat conservation 7. Animal habitations 8. Species 9. Science Writing — Biology 10. Nature Writing — General 11. Adult books for young adults

LC 2017937194

A thoughtful, accessible look at the rapidly growing issue of invasive plants, animals, and microbes around the globe with a focus on the scientific issues and ecological, health, and other challenges.

Includes bibliographical references and index.

578.769 Saltwater wetlands — Biology

Carson, Rachel

The Edge of the Sea. Rachel Carson; with illustrations by Bob Hines. Houghton Mifflin 1955. 276 p. : Illustration
ISBN 9780844670140
Grades: 7 8 9 10 11 12 Adult   578.769

1. Seashore biology 2. Seashore animals 3. Seashore 4. Seashore ecology 5. Biology 6. Coastal ecology 7. Nature 8. Nature Writing — Animal Studies 9. Science Writing — Biology

LC 54010759

Introduces a world of teeming life where the sea meets the land.

578.77 Oceans — Biology

Bradley, James

Deep Water: The World in the Ocean. James Bradley. Harperone 2024. 464 p.
ISBN 9780063390171
Grades: Adult   578.77

1. Oceans 2. Environmentalism 3. Oceanography 4. Marine biology 5. Marine ecology 6. Science Writing — General 7. Nature Writing — Environmental Issues

In this thrilling work—a blend of history, science, nature writing, and environmentalism—acclaimed writer James Bradley plunges into the unknown to explore the deepest recesses of the natural world.

"This expansive report from novelist Bradley (Ghost Species) studies ocean ecosystems as a means of exploring the interconnectedness of life on Earth." —*Publishers Weekly*

Carson, Rachel

Under the Sea Wind. Rachel Carson. Penguin Books 2007. 184 p.
ISBN 9780143104964
Grades: 11 12 Adult   578.77

1. Marine biology 2. Marine ecology 3. Sea birds 4. Marine animals 5. Atlantic Ocean 6. Nature Writing — Animal Studies

Uses the life and migrations of Scomber the mackerel and Anguilla the eel to depict marine ecology along the Atlantic shore.

Originally published: United States : Simon and Schuster, 1941.

Sardet, Christian

Plankton: Wonders of the Drifting World. Christian Sardet; edited by Rafael D. Rosengarten and Theodore Rosengarten; translated from the French by Christian Sardet and Dana Sardet; prologue by Mark Ohman. University of Chicago Press 2015. 222 pages : Illustration; Color
ISBN 9780226188713
Grades: Adult   578.77

1. Science writing — Biology

LC 2014034445

"A fascinating book that will cause readers to think deeply about plankton and its importance to human and animal life. A biology or general science background is not necessary to read this book; the reader needs only a desire to learn more about these intriguing organisms." —*Library Journal*

Includes bibliographical references (pages 215-216) and index; Originally published in France as Plancton, aux origines du vivant. (c) 2013 Les Editions Eugen Ulmer, Paris—Title page verso; Translated from the French.

579.2 Viruses and subviral organisms

Ireland, Tom

The Good Virus: The Amazing Story and Forgotten Promise of the Phage. Tom Ireland. W W Norton & Company 2023. 304 p.
ISBN 9781324050834
Grades: Adult   579.2

1. Viruses 2. Communicable diseases 3. Microbiology 4. Bacteria 5. Medical microbiology 6. Bacteriology 7. Science Writing — Biology

How a mysterious, super-powerful, yet long-neglected, microbe rules our world and can rescue our health in the age of antibiotic resistance.

"Tiny viruses that prey on bacteria could open a new front against infectious disease, according to this fascinating primer...The result is a captivating portrait of an overlooked remedy." —*Publishers Weekly*

579.5 Fungi

Sheldrake, Merlin

Entangled Life: How Fungi Make Our Worlds, Change Our Minds and Shape Our Futures. Merlin Sheldrake. Random House 2020. 352 p.
ISBN 9780525510314

ESSENTIAL AND RECOMMENDED TITLES
579.6 Mushrooms

Grades: Adult **579.5**
1. Fungi 2. Mycology 3. Botany 4. Biotic communities 5. Organisms 6. Life 7. Science Writing — Biology
LC 2019049709

Royal Society General Prizes for Science Books, 2021.

Citing the ubiquitous role of fungi in the environment, a scientific tour of examples ranging from yeast to psychedelics reveals the complex fungi networks that link plants together and make most biological life processes possible.

"From bread to booze to the very fiber of life, the world turns on fungi, and Sheldrake provides a top-notch portrait." —*Kirkus*

Includes bibliographical references and index.

579.6 Mushrooms

Borsato, Diane
Mushrooming: An Illustrated Guide to the Fantastic, Delicious, Deadly, and Strange World of Fungi. Diane Borsato; illustrations by Kelsey Oseid. The Experiment 2023. 231 pages : Color; Illustration
ISBN 9781615199587
Grades: Adult **579.6**
1. Mushrooms 2. Edible mushrooms 3. Wild foods 4. Poisonous plants 5. Plants in art 6. North America 7. Visual nonfiction 8. Nature Writing — Flowers and plants
LC 2022041056

A vibrant, illustrated guide to over 100 common and charismatic mushrooms, with storytelling that explores the connection between humans, fungi, and art."

"This guide merits an enthusiastic recommendation for both public and academic libraries. The illustrations alone, saturated with eye-pleasing, earthy colors, are worth the price." —*Booklist*

Includes index; Originally published in Canada by Douglas & McIntyre in 2022—Copyright page.

Lincoff, Gary
The Audubon Society Field Guide to North American Mushrooms. Gary H. Lincoff; visual key by Carol Nehring. Knopf : 1981. 926 p. : Illustration; Color
ISBN 9780394519920
Grades: Adult **579.6**
1. Mushrooms 2. Fungi 3. United States 4. Canada 5. Reference books 6. Nature Writing — Flowers and plants
LC 81080827

Covers 725 species, with full-color photographs, descriptions, identification keys, notes on folklore, and advice on edibility.

Includes index.

McKnight, Kent H.
A Field Guide to Mushrooms, North America. Kent H. McKnight and Vera B. McKnight; illustrations by Vera B. McKnight. Houghton Mifflin 1998. xii, 429 p. : Illustration; Color (The Peterson field guide series, 34)
ISBN 9780395910900
Grades: Adult **579.6**
1. Mushrooms 2. Identification 3. North America 4. Reference books 5. Nature writing — Flowers and plants
LC Bl2006021494

More than 1,000 species of mushrooms described in detail. Over 700 paintings and drawings reveal subtle field marks that cannot be captured into photographs.

Sponsored by the National Audubon Society and the National Wildlife Federation; Reprint. Originally published: 1987; Includes bibliographical references (p. 407) and index.

580 Plants (Botany)

Darcey, Cheralyn
Flowerpaedia: 1000 Flowers and Their Meanings. Cheralyn Darcey. Rockpool Publishing 2017. 258 p. : Illustration
ISBN 9781925429466
Grades: Adult **580**
1. Flowers 2. Dictionaries 3. Reference books 4. Nature writing — Flowers and plants
LC Bl2018193106

An A-Z reference guide of over one thousand flowers explains what each flower means emotionally, spiritually, and symbolically.

Includes bibliographical references (page 258) and index.

Mabey, Richard
The Cabaret of Plants: Forty Thousand Years of Plant Life and the Human Imagination. Richard Mabey. W. W. Norton & Company 2016. 400 p.
ISBN 9780393239973
Grades: Adult **580**
1. Botany 2. Plants 3. Nature 4. Natural history
LC 2015033568

Taking readers from the Himalayas to Madagascar to the Amazon to our backyards, a renowned naturalist presents a sweeping botanical history in which he explores dozens of plant species that have challenged our imaginations, awoken our wonder and upturned our ideas about history, science, beauty and belief.

"What Mabey does best is invite readers to think about plants in a radical new way, even posing the question as to whether a plant's sensory abilitieselectrostatic charges, chemical communication through pheromones and bio- a coustic sound wavesactually constitute intelligence. An unusual and vastly entertaining journey into the world of mysterious plant life as experienced by a gifted nature writer." —*Kirkus*

Includes bibliographical references and index; First published in Great Britain in 2015 under the title: The cabaret of plants: Botany and the imagination.

580.9 History, geographic treatment, biography

Sevigny, Melissa L.
★ *Brave the Wild River: The Untold Story of Two Women Who Mapped the Botany of the Grand Canyon.* Melissa L. Sevigny. W W Norton & Company 2023. 304 p.
ISBN 9780393868234
Grades: Adult **580.9**
1. Clover, Elzada 2. Jotter, Lois 3. Women botanists 4. Botany 5. Plants 6. Exploration 7. Grand Canyon 8. Colorado River 9. 20th century 10. 1930s 11. Collective biographies 12. Life stories — Nature and outdoors 13. Life stories — Science, technology, and medicine — Scientists and inventors 14. History Writing — Regional history — United States 15. History Writing — Women's history 16. Nonfiction that reads like fiction

National Outdoor Book Award for History/Biography, 2023.

The riveting tale of two pioneering botanists and their historic boat trip down the Colorado River and through the Grand Canyon.

"A breath-catching, enlightening, and significant work of scientific, environmental, and women's history." —*Booklist*

580.92 Botanists

Kassinger, Ruth
★ *A Garden of Marvels: How We Discovered That Flowers Have Sex, Leaves Eat Air, and Other Secrets of Plants.* Ruth Kassinger. William Morrow & Co. 2014. 256 p.
ISBN 9780062048998
Grades: Adult **580.92**

1. Botany 2. Plants 3. Horticulture 4. Gardeners 5. Gardens 6. Nature Writing — Gardens 7. Nature Writing — Personal Responses

LC 2014002824

In the tradition of the Botany of Desire and Wicked Plants, the author of Paradise Under Glass gives us a witty and engaging history of the first botanists interwoven with stories of today's extraordinary plants found in the garden and the lab.

"[A]n informal, entertaining account of how early researchers discovered how plants work and what scientists are still learning about plants today." —Kirkus

580.973 Botany — History — United States

Johnson, Victoria

★ *American* Eden: David Hosack, Botany, and Medicine in the Garden of the Early Republic. Victoria Johnson. Liveright Publishing Corporation 2018. 461 p.

ISBN 9781631494192

Grades: Adult   580.973

1. Hosack, David, 1769-1835 2. Botany 3. Botanical gardens 4. Physicians 5. Horticulture 6. Nature study 7. Botanists 8. United States history 9. Early America (1784-1819) 10. 19th century 11. Biographies 12. History writing — Antebellum America — United States 13. Life stories — People in history 14. Nature Writing — Gardens

New York Times Notable Book, 2018; National Book Award for Nonfiction finalist, 2018; Pulitzer Prize for History finalist, 2019.

The untold story of Hamilton's—and Burr's—personal physician, whose dream to build America's first botanical garden inspired the young Republic.

"A brilliant evocation of a man and his time. Plant lovers, history buffs, New Yorkaphiles, those interested in early medicine, even Hamiltonians—all will find this engrossing." —Library Journal

Includes bibliographical references and index.

581.4 Adaptation

Chace, Teri Dunn

Seeing Seeds: A Journey into the World of Seedheads, Pods, and Fruit. Photography by Robert Llewellyn; written by Teri Dunn Chace. Timber Press 2015. 284 pages : Color; Illustration

ISBN 9781604694925

Grades: Adult   581.4

1. Seeds 2. Arts and Entertainment — Photography 3. Nature writing — Flowers and plants 4. Science writing — Biology

LC 2015006910

Provides an overview of how seeds are formed and dispersed, and profiles common seeds from garden flowers, herbs, fruits and vegetables, and shrubs and trees.

Includes bibliographical references and index.

581.6 Miscellaneous nontaxonomic kinds of plants

Davis, Wade

One River: Explorations and Discoveries in the Amazon Rain Forest. Wade Davis. Simon & Schuster 1996. 537 p. : Illustration

ISBN 9780684808864

Grades: Adult   581.6

1. Schultes, Richard Evans, 1915-2001 2. Plowman, Timothy 3. Ethnobotanists 4. Botanists 5. Ethnobotany 6. Hallucinogenic plants 7. Medicinal plants 8. Amazon Valley 9. Nature Writing — Natural Landscapes

LC 96021516

Booklist Editors' Choice, 1996; Governor General's Literary Awards, English-language Non-fiction finalist.

An account of two generations of ethnobotanists who explored the Amazon, Richard Evans Schultes in the 1940s, and his students Timothy Plowman and Wade Davis in the 1970s, and their research into hallucinogenic and medicinal plants.

"Davis writes magnificently, with verve when describing his many adventurous field trips, accurately and efficiently when telling science or history, and with vivid fantasy when portraying hallucinogenic trances." —New York Times Book Review

Includes bibliographical references (p. 493-515) and index.

Pollan, Michael

★ *This* Is Your Mind on Plants. Michael Pollan. Penguin Press 2021. 352 p.

ISBN 9780593296905

Grades: Adult   581.6

1. Pollan, Michael 2. Drug use 3. Opium 4. Caffeine 5. Drugs 6. Plants 7. History writing — Microhistory 8. Science Writing — Biology 9. Society and culture — General 10. Science Writing — Medicine and health — Mental health

LC 2021003519

In this unique blend of history, science and memoir, a #1 New York Times best-selling author examines and experiences three plant drugs—opium, caffeine and mescaline—from several very different angles and contexts, exploring the powerful human attraction to psychoactive plants.

"A wide-ranging investigation that will interest anyone curious about consciousness-altering substances and their varying legality." —Library Journal

Includes bibliographical references and index.

Quave, Cassandra Leah

The Plant Hunter: A Scientist's Quest for Nature's Next Medicines. Cassandra Leah Quave. Viking 2021. 304 p.

ISBN 9781984879110

Grades: Adult   581.6

1. Quave, Cassandra Leah 2. People with disabilities 3. Medicinal plants 4. Ethnobotany 5. Herbal medicine 6. Ethnobotanists 7. Women scientists 8. Marriage 9. Gathering (of wild foods, seeds, medicinal plants, etc.) 10. Motherhood 11. Diseases 12. Nature 13. Autobiographies and memoirs 14. Science writing — Medicine and health 15. Life stories — Science, technology, and medicine — Scientists and inventors 16. Life stories — Facing adversity — Medical issues — Living with disabilities

LC 2021011104

Weaving together science, botany and an adventure-filled memoir to recount her own journey, a leading medical ethnobotanist, who studies plants to treat life-threatening illnesses, searches for natural compounds that could help save us from the antibiotic-resistant microbes that plague us all.

"Quave's inviting memoir demonstrates grit and determination and explains some of the fascinating and critical uses of plants for healing." —Library Journal

Includes bibliographical references and index.

Stewart, Amy

Wicked Plants: The Weed That Killed Lincoln's Mother & Other Botanical Atrocities. Amy Stewart; etchings by Briony Morrow-Cribbs; illustrations by Jonathon Rosen. Algonquin Books of Chapel Hill 2009. xvii, 235 p. : Illustration

ISBN 9781565126831

Grades: Adult   581.6

1. Poisonous plants 2. Dangerous plants 3. Plants 4. Botany 5. Nature Writing — General

LC 2009006192

Reveals the truth behind the harmful—even deadly—effects that many plants can have. From exploding shrubs to the weed that killed Abraham Lincoln's mother, not all plants are good for the garden.

"Stewart's book has two components: in-depth discussions of uniquely wicked plants like angel's trumpet, ergot and the water hyacinth and then guides to certain types of plants that share one common characteristic. These categories include common, garden-variety plants that have the potential to be killers (azalea, black locust, daphne, foxglove, lantana, etc.); blindness-inducing plants (poison sumac, tansy mustard, milky mangrove, etc.); and poison-producing plants that have been used to kill (curare, strychnine vine, kombe, upas tree, etc.).

ESSENTIAL AND RECOMMENDED TITLES
581.63 Beneficial plants

What makes Stewart's book even more fascinating is that it deftly blends botany, politics, and history into a very appealing format." —*PopMatters*
Includes bibliographical references (p. 233-[236]).

581.63 Beneficial plants

Drori, Jonathan
Around the World in 80 Plants. Jonathan Drori; illustrated by Lucille Clerc. Laurence King Publishing 2021. 216 pages : Illustration; Color
ISBN 9781786272300
Grades: Adult **581.63**
1. Humans and plants 2. Plants 3. Plant ecology 4. Botany 5. Nature Writing — General
LC Bl2021008834

Jonathan Drori takes another trip across the globe, bringing to life the science of plants by revealing how their worlds are intricately entwined with our own history, culture and folklore. From the seemingly familiar tomato and dandelion to the eerie mandrake and Spanish "moss" of Louisiana, each of these stories is full of surprises. Some have a troubling past, while others have ignited human creativity or enabled whole civilizations to flourish.

"Drori (Around the World in 80 Trees), a former trustee of the Royal Botanic Gardens, again masterfully blends science, history, and culture in this globe-spanning introduction to botany.... An accessible and colorful volume, this will charm even readers who know little about the plant-world." —*Publishers Weekly*
Includes index.

581.7 Plant ecology, plants characteristic of specific environments

Lowman, Margaret
The Arbornaut: A Life Discovering the Eighth Continent in the Trees Above Us. Meg Lowman. Farrar, Straus and Giroux 2021. 368 p.
ISBN 9780374162696
Grades: Adult **581.7**
1. Lowman, Margaret 2. Botanists 3. Women biologists 4. Rain forest ecology 5. Forest canopy ecology 6. Trees 7. Climate change 8. Environmentalists 9. Tree ecology 10. Research 11. Plants 12. Autobiographies and memoirs 13. Life stories — Science, technology, and medicine — Scientists and inventors 14. Science Writing — Biology 15. Nature Writing — General
LC 2021010520

Biologist, botanist, and conservationist Meg Lowman-aka "CanopyMeg"—takes us on an adventure into the "eighth continent" of the world's treetops, along her journey as a tree scientist, and into climate action.

"Lowman shines in her ability to combine accessible science with exciting personal anecdotes that effectively convey the 'Thrill of aerial exploration' and bolster her case that trees—and sustainable ecosystems—are worth studying, protecting, and preserving." —*Publishers Weekly*
Includes index.

582.16 Trees

Drori, Jonathan
Around the World in 80 Trees. Jonathan Drori; illustrations by Lucille Clerc. Laurence King Publishing 2018. 240 pages : Color; Illustration
ISBN 9781786271617
Grades: Adult **582.16**
1. Trees 2. Nature writing — Flowers and plants
LC Bl2018146060

"This exploration is both educational and visually exceptional." —*Publishers Weekly*
Includes bibliographical references (pages 230-234) and index.

Farmer, Jared
Elderflora: A Modern History of Ancient Trees. Jared Farmer. Basic Books 2022. 448 p.
ISBN 9780465097845
Grades: Adult **582.16**
1. Forests 2. Trees 3. Old growth forests 4. Old growth forest conservation 5. Forestry 6. Natural history 7. Industrial revolution 8. Climate change 9. Landscape assessment 10. Human ecology 11. Nature conservation 12. Nature Writing — Natural Landscapes 13. Science Writing — Biology 14. History writing — Microhistory
LC 2022014665

Examines the complex history of the world's oldest trees and the challenges they faced through imperial expansion and the industrial revolution, as well as the current threat of global climate change.

"An ingenious examination of old trees, mixing history, politics, and science." —*Kirkus*
Includes bibliographical references and indexes.

Hugo, Nancy R.
Seeing Trees: Discover the Extraordinary Secrets of Everyday Trees. by Nancy Ross Hugo; photography by Robert J. Llewellyn. Timber Press 2011. 242 p. : Color illustration
ISBN 9781604692198
Grades: Adult **582.16**
1. Trees 2. Identification 3. Nature writing — General
LC 2010052455

National Outdoor Book Award for Nature and the Environment, 2011.
Introduces trees, describing such topics as leaves, flowers, fruit, cones, and bark and profiling the uniques features of ten common North American trees.

"This fascinating celebration of trees will delight gardeners, botanists, students of natural history, and nature photographers." —*Library Journal*
Includes bibliographical references and index.

Lewis, Daniel
Twelve Trees: The Deep Roots of Our Future. Daniel Lewis. Avid Reader Press 2024. 336 p.
ISBN 9781982164058
Grades: Adult **582.16**
1. Trees 2. Forests 3. Environmental protection 4. Climate change 5. Nature 6. Plants 7. Nature Writing — General

A compelling global exploration of nature and survival as seen via a dozen species of trees that represent the challenges facing our planet, and the ways that scientists are working urgently to save our forests and our future.

"A well-informed, staunch defense of trees' capacity to multiply biodiversity and support life on Earth." —*Kirkus*

Logan, William Bryant
Sprout Lands: Tending the Endless Gift of Trees. William Bryant Logan. W.W. Norton & Company 2019. 384 p.
ISBN 9780393609417
Grades: Adult **582.16**
1. Trees 2. Sustainable living 3. Humans and plants 4. Sustainable societies 5. Humans and trees 6. Tree care 7. Forestry 8. Pruning 9. Nature Writing — Natural Landscapes 10. Nature Writing — Personal Responses
LC 2018055376

A practicing arborist discusses how people once used trees as an endless and self-renewing source of food and building materials, and presents practical knowledge about how we can again learn to tend to them in this way.

"Bryant knows trees, and much more. Tree loverseven those who consider pollarded trees ghastly and strangewill be drawn in by Bryant's vast cultural and scientific references, and charmed by passages that read like prose poems." —*Library Journal*
Includes bibliographical references and index.

PUBLIC LIBRARY CORE COLLECTION: NONFICTION
Twentieth Edition

Rodd, Tony
Trees: A Visual Guide. Tony Rodd and Jennifer Stackhouse. University of California Press 2008. 304 p. : Color illustration; Color; Map
ISBN 9780520256507
Grades: Adult   582.16
1. Trees 2. Nature writing — Flowers and plants
LC 2007043797

Beautifully illustrated and designed, this gorgeous reference book explores the world of trees from every perspective—-from the world's great forests to the lifespan of a single leaf. Arresting color photographs of a wide variety of trees and close-ups of many of their remarkable features provide an enormous amount of information in a highly accessible format. The volume illustrates how trees grow and function, looks at their astounding diversity and adaptations, documents the key role they play in ecosystems, and explores the multitude of uses to which we put trees—from timber and pharmaceuticals to shade and shelter. A highly absorbing read cover to cover or dipped into at random, Trees: A Visual Guide delves into many specific topics: the details of flowers, bark, and roots; profiles of favorite trees; how animals and insects interact with trees; trees in urban landscapes; the role trees play in our changing climate; deforestation and reforestation; and much more. With clear diagrams, illustrations, and intriguing sidebars on many featured topics, this unique volume is a complete visual guide to the magnificence of the arboreal world.

"This is a beautifully photographed visual guide to one of the most important resources of the natural world." —*Booklist*

Includes bibliographical references and index.

Simard, S.
★ *Finding the Mother Tree: Discovering the Wisdom of the Forest.* Suzanne Simard. Alfred A. Knopf 2021. 368 p.
ISBN 9780525656098
Grades: Adult   582.16
1. Simard, S. (Suzanne) 2. Women ecologists 3. Forest conservation 4. Tree conservation 5. Ecologists 6. Sexism 7. Trees 8. Environmentalists 9. Family history 10. People with cancer 11. Women 12. Autobiographies and memoirs 13. Nature Writing — Personal Responses 14. Life stories — Science, technology, and medicine — Scientists and inventors 15. Nature Writing — Gardens 16. Life stories — Nature and outdoors
LC 2020029993

National Outdoor Book Award for Natural History Literature, 2021; BC and Yukon Book Prizes, Bill Duthie Booksellers' Choice Award, 2022.

The world's leading forest ecologist, in her first book, draws us into the intimate world of trees, where she brilliantly illuminates the fascinating and vital truth that trees are a complex, interdependent circle of life.

"Simard's science fascinates, and so too does her life. This is an engaging memoir of scientific discovery." —*Library Journal*

Includes bibliographical references and index.

Wohlleben, Peter
Forest Walking: Discovering the Trees and Woodlands of North America. Peter Wohlleben, Jane Billinghurst. Greystone Books 2022. 240 pages
ISBN 9781771643313
Grades: Adult   582.16
1. Forests 2. Trees 3. Senses and sensation 4. Forest ecology 5. Forest animals 6. Beauty in nature 7. Biotic communities 8. Nature 9. Walking 10. United States 11. Canada 12. Translations — German to English 13. Nature writing — Natural landscapes 14. Science writing — Biology

Helps readers become a "forest detective" on their next outdoor adventure by decoding nature's signs by following tree roots, crossing streams and turning over rocks to awaken the ancient past and thrilling present of the ecosystem around them.

"Being in the woods can force one to slow down and offers an opportunity to hone senses, the authors write, and they offer a guide to navigating woodland areas….The survey is poetic and full of marvels, and readers will be encouraged by the authors' insistence that a simple walk is all one needs to find adventure."
—*Publishers Weekly*

The Heartbeat of Trees: Embracing Our Ancient Bond with Forests and Nature. Peter Wohlleben; translated by Jane Billinghurst. Greystone Books 2021. 240 p.
ISBN 9781771646895
Grades: Adult   582.16
1. Trees 2. Nature 3. Humans and trees 4. Effect of environment on humans 5. Plants 6. Nature and culture 7. Translations — German to English 8. Nature Writing — General 9. Science writing — Biology

Drawing on science and cutting-edge research, a renowned forester proves that, despite an era of cell phone addiction, climate change and urban life, the age-old ties linking humans to the forest remain alive and intact.

"Wohlleben sticks with the formula that made his earlier work so popular. This latest book will appeal to fans of popular science and anyone curious about natural history." —*Library Journal*

Originally published by Ludwig Verlag in German as DAS geheime Band zwischen Mensch und Natur: Erstaunliche Erkenntnisse uber die 7 Sinne des Menschen, den Herzschlad der Baume und die Frage, ob Pflanzen ein Bewusstsein haben, 2019; Translated from the German.

The Hidden Life of Trees: What They Feel, How They Communicate: Discoveries from a Secret World. Peter Wohlleben, foreword by Tim Flannery. Greystone Books 2016. 240 p. (Mysteries of nature trilogy, 1)
ISBN 9781771642484
Grades: Adult   582.16
1. Wohlleben, Peter, 1964- 2. Men and nature 3. Trees 4. Forests 5. Nature 6. Beauty in nature 7. Life cycles 8. Forest animals 9. Translations — German to English 10. Nature writing — Personal responses 11. Science writing — Biology
LC Bl2016036121

Indies' Choice Book Awards, Adult Nonfiction, 2017.

Draws on research and engaging forester stories to reveal how trees nurture each other and communicate, outlining the life cycles of "tree families" that support mutual growth, share nutrients, and contribute to a resilient ecosystem.

"In this spirited exploration, he guarantees that readers will never look at these life forms in quite the same way again." —*Library Journal*

Translated from the German DAS geheime Leben der Baume by Jane Billinghurst; Originally published by Ludwig Buchverlag, 2015.

582.16097 Trees — North America

Brockman, Christian Frank
Trees of North America: A Field Guide to the Major Native and Introduced Species North of Mexico. by C. Frank Brockman; illustrated by Rebecca Merrilees; revised by Jonathan P. Latimer and Karen Stray Nolting with David Challinor. St. Martin's Press 2001. 280 p. : Color illustration; Color; Map (A golden guide)
ISBN 9781582380926
Grades: 8 9 10 11 12 Adult   582.16097
1. Trees 2. Identification 3. United States 4. North America 5. Canada 6. Science — Plants — Trees
LC 2001272405

Presents a handbook for the identification of over five hundred species of trees by illustration and text.

Includes bibliographical references (p. 271).

Little, Elbert L.
The Audubon Society Field Guide to North American Trees: Eastern Region. Elbert L. Little; photos. by Sonja Bullaty and Angelo Lomeo, and others; visual key by Susan Rayfield and Olivia Buehl. Knopf : Distributed by Random House 1980. 1 volume : Illustration; Color
ISBN 9780394507606
Grades: Adult   582.16097
1. Trees 2. Identification 3. Canada 4. United States 5. Reference books 6. Nature writing — Flowers and plants
LC 79003474

ESSENTIAL AND RECOMMENDED TITLES
585 Pinophyta

Identifies and illustrates 360 species in the area ranging from the eastern seaboard to the Rocky Mountains.
Includes indexes.

Petrides, George A.
A Field Guide to Western Trees: Western United States and Canada. George A. Petrides; illustrated by Olivia Petrides. Houghton Mifflin 1998. xiv, 428 p. : Color illustration; Map; Color (The Peterson field guide series)
ISBN 9780395904541
Grades: 7 8 9 10 11 12 Adult   582.16097
1. Trees 2. Identification 3. Reference books 4. Nature writing — Flowers and plants
LC 98013624

This newly designed field guide features detailed descriptions of 387 species, arranged in six major groups by visual similarity. The 47 color plates and 5 text drawings show distinctive details needed for identification. Color photographs and 295 color range maps accompany the species descriptions.

Sponsored by the National Audubon Society, the National Wildlife Federation, and the Roger Tory Peterson Institute; Includes bibliographical references (p. 408-411) and index.

Sibley, David
★ *The Sibley Guide to Trees.* Written and illustrated by David Allen Sibley. Alfred A. Knopf 2009. xxxviii, 426 p. : Color illustration; Color; Map
ISBN 9780375415197
Grades: Adult   582.16097
1. Trees 2. Reference books 3. Nature writing — Flowers and plants
LC Bl2009026363

Featuring more than 4,100 detailed paintings and five hundred maps, highlights the similarities and distinctions between approximately six hundred North American tree species.

Includes bibliographical references (p. 398-399) and indexes.

585 Pinophyta

Preston, Richard
The Wild Trees: A Story of Passion and Daring. Richard Preston. Random House 2007. 294 p. : Illustration; Map
ISBN 9781400064892
Grades: 11 12 Adult   585
1. Forest conservation 2. Tree climbing 3. Forests 4. Trees 5. Redwood 6. Northern California 7. Nature Writing — Natural Landscapes 8. Adult books for young adults 9. Nonfiction that reads like fiction
LC 2006048646

Booklist Editors' Choice: Adult Books for Young Adults, 2007; Science Books and Films Prize for Excellence in Science Books, Science Book for High School Readers, 2008.

The best-selling author of the Hot Zone takes a close-up look at the world's tallest trees, the coast redwoods that grow only in the coastal regions of California, and at the previously unknown ecosystem that the trees form high in the air in the forest canopy, profiling the scientists and researchers that study this unique, labyrinthine ecological niche.

"There is something so elementally boyish in searching out the biggest and tallest, poring over maps and measurements, dubbing these trees with names lifted from J.R.R. Tolkein's Middle Earth. . . . Preston knows how to fold the science into the seams of his narrative, and his dry humor crops up, pleasurably, at the edges of his observations." —*Cleveland Plain Dealer*

590 Animals

Aryee, Patrick
30 Animals That Made Us Smarter: Stories of the Natural World That Inspired Human Ingenuity. Patrick Aryee. Island Press 2022. 377 p.
ISBN 9781642832679
Grades: Adult   590
1. Technological innovations 2. Animals 3. Engineering design 4. Biotechnology 5. Animal behavior 6. Inventions 7. Nature 8. Nature Writing — Animal studies 9. Science Writing — Biology 10. History writing — Science, technology, and medicine

Did you know that mosquitoes' mouthparts are helping to develop pain-free surgical needles? Who'd have thought that the humble mussel could inspire so many useful things, from plywood production to a "glue" that can cement the crowns on teeth? Or that the design of polar bear fur may one day help keep humans warm in space? In everything from fashion to architecture, medicine to transportation, it may surprise you how many extraordinary inventions have been inspired by the natural world. In 30 Animals That Made Us Smarter, join wildlife biologist, TV host, and BBC podcaster Patrick Aryee as he tells stories of biomimicry, or innovations inspired by the natural world, that enrich our lives every day—and in some cases, save them.

"This fascinating book explores numerous examples of biomimicry, the relatively new scientific field in which humans create innovative technology inspired by animals." —*Booklist*

Brookshire, Bethany
Pests: How Humans Create Animal Villains. Bethany Brookshire. Ecco Press 2022. 352 p.
ISBN 9780063097254
Grades: Adult   590
1. Animals 2. Pests 3. Animals and history 4. Animals and civilization 5. History Writing — General 6. Nature Writing — General

At the intersection of science, history and narrative journalism, this eye-opening study reveals why we deem certain animals "pests" and others not, and what this tells us about our own perceptions, beliefs and actions, as well as our place in the natural world.

"Page-turning stories of creatures most of us despise, mostly undeservedly....Chronicling her travels around the world to interview experts, the author delivers fascinating accounts of a score of widely deplored pests, from the no-brainers (rats, mice, pigeons) to the controversial (snakes, deer, raccoons) to a few shockers....Outstanding, possibly mind-changing natural history." —*Kirkus*

Montgomery, Sy
How to Be a Good Creature: A Memoir in Thirteen Animals. by Sy Montgomery; illustrated by Rebecca Green. Houghton Mifflin Harcourt 2018. 208 p.
ISBN 9780544938328
Grades: Adult   590
1. Animals 2. Empathy 3. Nature 4. Human-animal relationships 5. Autobiographies and memoirs 6. Life stories — Nature and outdoors 7. Nature Writing — Animal Studies
LC 2018022314

A naturalist and adventurer discusses the personalities and quirks of thirteen animals who have profoundly affected her, exploring themes of learning to become empathetic, creating families, coping with loss, and the otherness and sameness of people and animals.

Nezhukumatathil, Aimee
World of Wonders: In Praise of Fireflies, Whale Sharks, and Other Astonishments. Aimee Nezhukumatathil. Milkweed Editions 2020. 184 p. : Illustration
ISBN 9781571313652
Grades: Adult   590
1. Nezhukumatathil, Aimee 2. Animals 3. Nature 4. Philosophy of nature 5. Plants 6. Race (Social sciences) 7. Wildlife 8. Motherhood 9. Effect of environment on humans 10. Essays 11. Nature Writing — General
LC 2020010522

Kirkus Prize for Nonfiction finalist, 2020.

From beloved, award-winning poet Aimee Nezhukumatathil comes a debut work of nonfiction-a collection of essays about the natural world, and the way its inhabitants can teach, support, and inspire us.

"A lyrical exploration of a woman finding her true home in the world, interspersed with hauntingly beautiful descriptions of the lives of the animals and plants that illuminate it, this natural history will appeal to nature lovers and readers who relish thoughtful, introspective works. Also suggest to fans of Margaret Renkl's Late Migrations." —Library Journal

Orlean, Susan
On Animals. Susan Orlean. Avid Reader Press 2021. 288 p.
ISBN 9781982181536
Grades: Adult   590
1. Animals 2. Pet owners 3. Pets 4. Humans and pets 5. Farm animals 6. Wild animals as pets 7. Wildlife 8. Human-animal relationships 9. Essays 10. Life stories — Relationships — Pets and Owners 11. Family and Relationships — Pets and Owners 12. Nature Writing — Animal Studies

Examining animal-human relationships through captivating stories she has written over the course of her career, the author, in this book that is equal parts wonderful and profound, celebrates the cross-species connections that grace our collective existence.

"Fans of Orlean's prolific writing will be happy to have these favorites in one set." —Library Journal

Stewart, Tracey
Do Unto Animals: A Friendly Guide to How Animals Live, and How We Can Make Their Lives Better. Tracey Stewart; illustrations by Lisel Ashlock. Artisan 2015. 199 pages : Color; Illustration
ISBN 9781579656232
Grades: Adult   590
1. Animal habitations 2. Animal communication 3. Pets 4. Livestock 5. Human-animal relationships 6. Nature writing — Animal Studies
LC 2015010995

A former veterinary technician and animal advocate through hundreds of wonderful illustrations, homemade projects and expert advice provides insight into the secret lives of animals and the kindest ways to live with and alongside them.
Includes index.

590.2 Animals — Miscellany

Cooke, Lucy
The Truth About Animals: Stoned Sloths, Lovelorn Hippos, and Other Tales from the Wild Side of Wildlife. Lucy Cooke. Perseus Books Group 2018. 304 p.
ISBN 9780465094646
Grades: Adult   590.2
1. Animals 2. Misconceptions 3. Animal behavior 4. Sloths 5. Zoology 6. Nature Writing — Animal Studies
LC 2019301387

An uproarious tour of some of the basest instincts and vice-related mysteries of the animal world includes profiles of drunken moose, cheating penguins, lazy worker ants, castrating hippos and porn-peddling Chinese pandas.

Originally published under the title the unexpected truth about animals : a menagerie of the misunderstood by Doubleday, 2017.

590.73 Collections and exhibits of living mammals

Charman, Isobel
The Zoo: The Wild and Wonderful Tale of the Founding of London Zoo: 1826-1851. Isobel Charman. Pegasus Books 2017. 349 p.
ISBN 9781681773568
Grades: Adult   590.73
1. Zoo animals 2. Zoos 3. Captive wild animals 4. Georgian era (1714-1837) 5. History writing — Europe — United Kingdom 6. History writing — Arts and culture

Relates the creation of the London Zoo, the first zoo in history, describing the role of the diplomats, traders, scientists, and amateur naturalists who were charged with collecting animals from around the world, and the characters—both animal and human—who became part of it.

A deeply researched, terrifically entertaining exploration of the London Zoo 'Through the eyes of some of the people who made it happen.' —Kirkus

591.4 Physical adaptation

MacPhee, R. D. E.
End of the Megafauna: The Fate of the World's Hugest, Fiercest, and Strangest Animals. Ross D. E. MacPhee; with Illustrations by Peter Schouten. W.W. Norton & Company 2018. 144 p.
ISBN 9780393249293
Grades: Adult   591.4
1. Extinct animals 2. Body size 3. Extinction 4. Causation 5. Evolution 6. Animal morphology 7. Extinct mammals 8. Paleontology 9. Prehistoric era (Cenozoic, Pleistocene) 10. Science Writing — Paleontology 11. Science Writing — Biology 12. Nature Writing — Animal Studies
LC 2018029730

Investigates the yet-unsolved disappearances of the planet's giant prehistoric animals, exploring leading extinction theories to reveal the implausibility of human overhunting and catastrophic climate change and how new technologies may be able to reintroduce extinct species.

Includes bibliographical references and index.

591.47 Protective and locomotor adaptations, color

Barnett, Cynthia
★ *The Sound of the Sea: Seashells and the Fate of the Oceans.* Cynthia Barnett. W.W. Norton & Company 2021. 336 p.
ISBN 9780393651447
Grades: Adult   591.47
1. Shells 2. Mollusks 3. Shellfish 4. Effect of humans on nature 5. Marine ecology 6. Climate change 7. Wildlife habitat destruction 8. Overfishing 9. Natural history 10. Nature Writing — Animal Studies — Fish and Fishing 11. Nature Writing — Environmental Issues
LC 2021016248

Seashells have been the most coveted and collected of nature's creations since the dawn of humanity. They were money before coins, jewelry before gems, art before canvas. In The Sound of the Sea, acclaimed environmental author Cynthia Barnett blends cultural history and science to trace our long love affair with seashells and the hidden lives of the mollusks that make them. Spiraling out from the great cities of shell that once rose in North America to the warming waters of the Maldives and the slave castles of Ghana, Barnett has created an unforgettable account of the world's most iconic seashells. She begins with their childhood wonder, unwinds surprising histories like the origin of Shell Oil as a family business importing exotic shells, and charts what shells and the soft animals that build them are telling scientists about our warming, acidifying seas.

"A delightful, informative and momentous read for both enthusiasts and those who've never picked up a sea shell." —Library Journal

Includes bibliographical references and index.

Cheshire, James
Where the Animals Go: Tracking Wildlife with Technology in 50 Maps and Graphics. James Cheshire, Oliver Uberti. W. W. Norton & Company 2017. 174 pages : Illustration; Color; Map
ISBN 9780393634020
Grades: Adult   591.47
1. Animals 2. Animal behavior 3. Tracking and trailing 4. Maps 5. Wildlife 6. Digital mapping 7. Nature Writing — Animal Studies

Incorporating sophisticated infographics, a comprehensive, data-driven portrait of the behaviors of the planet's wildlife draws on pioneering research made possible by current advances in satellite, camera and other digital technologies to reveal nature's unique talents and survival skills.

Includes bibliographical references.

ESSENTIAL AND RECOMMENDED TITLES
591.5 Behavior

Emlen, Douglas John
Animal Weapons: The Evolution of Battle. by Douglas J. Emlen; illustrated by David J. Tuss. Henry Holt and Company 2014. 304 p.
ISBN 9780805094503
Grades: Adult 591.47
1. Animal weapons 2. Animal defenses 3. Defensive (Military science) 4. Animals 5. Biology 6. Weapons 7. Nature Writing — Animal Studies
LC 2014004772

An exploration of the extreme weapons seen in the animal world—teeth, horns, and claws—draws parallels to the way humans develop and employ their own weapons.

"Emlen's excellent writing will draw in readers intrigued by astonishingly powerful weapons, both in the wild and in the military, and how they have evolved owing to selective pressures. Though Philip Street's Animal Weapons describes a greater variety of animal defenses, Emlen's book is a more compelling read because it focuses on the parallels between animal and humans in this regard." —*Library Journal*

Includes bibliographical references and index.

591.5 Behavior

Braitman, Laurel
Animal Madness: How Anxious Dogs, Compulsive Parrots, and Elephants in Recovery Help Us Understand Ourselves. Laurel Braitman. Simon & Schuster 2014. 384 pages
ISBN 9781451627008
Grades: Adult 591.5
1. Animal behavior 2. Mental illness 3. Convalescence 4. Nature writing — Animal studies 5. Adult books for young adults
LC 2014000791

For the first time, a historian of science draws evidence from across the world to show how humans and other animals are astonishingly similar when it comes to their feelings and the ways in which they lose their minds.

"Braitman's gradual accretion of reasons to believe in animal emotional states that we can relate to, including the loopy ones, gives pause and sparks curiosity." —*Kirkus*

Durrani, Matin
Furry Logic: The Physics of Animal Life. Matin Durrani, Liz Kalaugher. Bloomsbury Sigma 2017. 304 p.
ISBN 9781472914095
Grades: Adult 591.5
1. Biomechanics 2. Animal behavior 3. Biophysics 4. Zoology 5. Physics 6. Adult books for young adults 7. Nature writing — Animal studies
LC 2016497302

The properties of physics are behind many of the ways animals go about their daily lives. Scientists researching the field of biomechanics have discovered that the way cats and dogs lap up milk can be explained by the laws of surface tension, the way ants navigate is due to magnetic fields, and why pistol shrimps are able to generate enough force to destroy aquarium glass using their claws!

"Another offbeat factoid in a book full of them is the way that elephants raise one foot from the ground in order to use their other three to triangulate vibrations. Light science reading that informs while it entertains good for dipping into and out of." —*Kirkus*

Grandin, Temple
★ *Animals in Translation: Using the Mysteries of Autism to Decode Animal Behavior.* Temple Grandin and Catherine Johnson. Scribner 2005. 356 p.
ISBN 9780743247696
Grades: 11 12 Adult 591.5
1. Animal behavior 2. Senses and sensation 3. Autistic people 4. Sensory stimulation 5. Animals 6. Autism spectrum disorders 7. Neurodivergent people 8. Nature Writing — Animal Studies 9. Science Writing — Medicine and health — Disabilities and disorders 10. Adult books for young adults
LC 2004058498

An animal scientist draws on her experience as an autistic to identify commonalities between animals and autistics, offering insight into how animals process sensory information and how they often possess unrecognized savant-level talents.

"This fascinating book will teach readers to see as animals see, to be a little more visual and a little less verbal, and, as a unique analysis of animal behavior, it belongs in all libraries." —*Booklist*

Includes bibliographical references (p. [337]-342) and index.

Keim, Brandon
Meet the Neighbors: Animal Minds and Life in a More-than-human World. Brandon Keim. W W Norton & Co. Inc 2024. 384 p.
ISBN 9781324007081
Grades: Adult 591.5
1. Human-animal relationships 2. Animal intelligence 3. Animal behavior 4. Animal communication 5. Animal rights 6. Wildlife conservation 7. Wildlife biologists 8. Wildlife researchers 9. Animal habitations 10. Nature Writing — Animal Studies

Inviting readers to discover an expanded sense of community and kinship beyond our own species, an acclaimed scientist, in this wide-ranging, wonder-filled exploration of animals' inner lives, shows the people—philosophers, ecologists, wildlife doctors—who are reimagining our relationships to the wild creatures populating our communities.

"Science journalist Keim…investigates what animals think and feel in this bracing inquiry." —*Publishers Weekly*

Roach, Mary
★ *Fuzz: When Nature Breaks the Law.* Mary Roach. W.W. Norton & Company 2021. 336 p.
ISBN 9781324001935
Grades: Adult 591.5
1. Animals and civilization 2. Animal behavior 3. Wildlife management 4. Humans and wild animals 5. Human-animal relationships 6. Nature Writing — Animal Studies 7. Society and culture — Urban and regional studies 8. Science Writing — General
LC 2021006594

LibraryReads Favorites, 2021.

Join "America's funniest science writer" (Peter Carlson, Washington Post) Mary Roach on an irresistible investigation into the unpredictable world where wildlife and humans meet. What's to be done about a jaywalking moose? A grizzly bear caught breaking and entering? A murderous tree? As New York Times best-selling author Mary Roach discovers, the answers are best found not in jurisprudence but in science: the curious science of human-wildlife conflict, a discipline at the crossroads of human behavior and wildlife biology.

"Intrepid, witty, and elucidating.... Roach's quirky angle on a timely topic will go down easy with readers of all ages." —*Booklist*

Includes bibliographical references and index.

Wilson, Edward O.
Genesis: The Deep Origin of Societies. Edward O. Wilson. Liveright Publishing Corporation 2019. 224 p.
ISBN 9781631495540
Grades: Adult 591.5
1. Animal behavior 2. Behavior evolution 3. Evolution 4. Behavior genetics 5. Science Writing — Biology
LC 2018050101

Forming a 21st-century statement on Darwinian evolution, one shorn of "religious and political dogma," the author offers a bold work of scientific thought and synthesis.

"A challenging read best suited for specialists in the fields of evolutionary biology and sociobiology." —*Library Journal*

Includes bibliographical references and index.

Yong, Ed
★ *An Immense World: How Animal Senses Reveal the Hidden Realms Around Us.* Ed Yong. Random House 2022. 480 p.

ISBN 9780593133231
Grades: Adult   591.5
1. Senses and sensation 2. Animal behavior 3. Physiology 4. Neuroscience 5. Science Writing — Biology 6. Nature Writing — Animal studies
LC 2021046048

Andrew Carnegie Medal for Excellence in Non-Fiction, 2023; Royal Society General Prizes for Science Books, 2023; National Book Critics Circle Award for Nonfiction finalist, 2022.

The Pulitzer Prize-winning New York Times best-selling author of I Contain Multitudes examines how the world of animal senses can help us understand and transform the way we perceive our world.

"Pulitzer-winning journalist Yong (I Contain Multitudes) reveals in this eye-opening survey animals' world through their own perceptions....This is science writing at its best." —Publishers Weekly

Includes bibliographical references and index.

591.56 Behavior relating to life cycle

Cooke, Lucy
Bitch: On the Female of the Species. Lucy Cooke. Basic Books 2022. 368 p.
ISBN 9781541674899
Grades: Adult   591.56
1. Animals 2. Gender role 3. Animal behavior 4. Women biologists 5. Sex differences 6. Evolution 7. Zoology 8. Sexism in science 9. Nature Writing — Animal Studies 10. Science Writing — Biology 11. Life stories — Science, technology, and medicine — Scientists and inventors

A fierce, funny, and revolutionary look at the queens of the animal kingdom.

Studying zoology made Lucy Cooke feel like a sad freak. Not because she loved spiders or would root around in animal feces: All her friends shared the same curious kinks. The problem was her sex. Being female meant she was, by nature, a loser. Since Charles Darwin, evolutionary biologists have been convinced that the males of the animal kingdom are the interesting ones—dominating and promiscuous, while females are dull, passive, and devoted. In Bitch, Cooke tells a new story. Whether investigating same-sex female albatross couples that raise chicks, murderous mother meerkats, or the titanic battle of the sexes waged by ducks, Cooke shows us a new evolutionary biology, one where females can be as dynamic as any male. This isn't your grandfather's evolutionary biology. It's more inclusive, truer to life, and, simply, more fun.

"Noted TED speaker and author Cooke dives into sex and gender across the animal kingdom, dispelling all the misogynist notions of females being the weaker sex....This book elevates not just the science itself but the scientists that have been marginalized for too long." —Booklist

Includes bibliographical references and index.

Safina, Carl
Beyond Words: What Animals Think and Feel. Carl Safina. Henry Holt and Company 2015. 320 p.
ISBN 9780805098884
Grades: Adult   591.56
1. Animal behavior 2. Elephants 3. Wolves 4. Whales 5. Animal intelligence 6. Comparative psychology 7. Nature writing — Animal studies 8. Adult books for young adults
LC 2014045385

Booklist Editors' Choice, 2015.

Weaving decades of field observations with exciting new discoveries about the brain, Carl Safina's landmark book offers an intimate view of animal behavior to challenge the fixed boundary between humans and nonhuman animals.

"With forays into neurology and diverse animal-behavior studies, Safina reveals that ours is just one of many powerful minds at work on Earth and that we share many profound traits with our fellow animals. By turns mesmerizing, thrilling, and tragic, Safinas enlightening inquiry into animal intelligence calls for a new, compassionate perspective before we unwittingly drive our precious animal kin into extinction." —Booklist

A John Macrae Book; Includes bibliographical references and index.

Toomey, David
Kingdom of Play: What Ball-bouncing Octopuses, Belly-flopping Monkeys, and Mud-sliding Elephants Reveal About Life Itself. David Toomey. Scribner 2024. 288 p.
ISBN 9781982154462
Grades: Adult   591.56
1. Animals 2. Animal behavior 3. Play 4. Play behavior in animals 5. Social behavior in animals 6. Experiments 7. Evolution 8. Biology 9. Nature Writing — Animal Studies 10. Science Writing — Biology
LC 2023029396

In Kingdom of Play, science writer David Toomey takes us on a fast-paced and entertaining tour of playful animals and the scientists who study them. From octopuses on Australia's Great Barrier Reef to meerkats in the Kalahari Desert to brown bears on Alaska's Aleutian Islands, we follow adventurous researchers as they conduct experiments seeking answers to new, intriguing questions: when did play first appear in animals? How does play develop the brain, and how did it evolve? And does play direct and possibly accelerate evolution? Through a close examination of both natural selection and play, Toomey argues that life itself is fundamentally playful.

"Toomey takes a wonderful...approach to chronicling just how playful diverse animals are and the benefits they accrue from this practice while explaining the science involved in watching animals play, making for a fun and absorbing read." —Booklist

Includes bibliographical references and index.

Zernicka-Goetz, Magdalena
The Dance of Life: The New Science of How a Single Cell Becomes a Human Being. Magdalena Zernicka-Goetz and Roger Highfield. Basic Books 2020. VII, 289 pages
ISBN 9781541699069
Grades: Adult   591.56
1. Pregnancy 2. Embryology 3. Fetus 4. Embryonic stem cells 5. Human fertility 6. Gene editing 7. Biological growth 8. Science Writing — Biology
LC 2019020177

Scientists have long struggled to make pregnancy easier, safer, and more successful. In The Dance of Life, developmental and stem-cell biologist Magdalena Zernicka-Goetz takes us to the front lines of efforts to understand the creation of a human life. She has spent two decades unraveling the mysteries of development, as a simple fertilized egg becomes a complex human being of forty trillion cells. Zernicka-Goetz's work is both incredibly practical and astonishingly vast: Her groundbreaking experiments with mouse, human, and artificial embryo models give hope to how more women can sustain viable pregnancies.

"Meaty and entertaining, with the effort extended well worth the energy." —Kirkus

Includes bibliographical references and index.

591.59 Communication

Mustill, Tom
How to Speak Whale: A Voyage into the Future of Animal Communication. Tom Mustill. Grand Central Publishing 2022. 272 p.
ISBN 9781538739112
Grades: Adult   591.59
1. Mustill, Tom 2. Animal communication 3. Biologists 4. Documentary filmmakers 5. Humans and whales 6. Whales 7. Whale sounds 8. Artificial intelligence 9. Language and languages 10. Animal behavior 11. Human-animal communication 12. Human-animal relationships 13. Nature Writing — Animal Studies 14. Science Writing — Computing, the Internet, and Technology
LC 2022019457

Drawing from his experience as a naturalist and wildlife filmmaker, the author, who survived a whale encounter, examines how scientists and start-ups around the world are decoding animal communications and what the consequences of such human interaction could be.

"Following a close encounter with a breaching humpback whale, biologist-turned filmmaker Mustill sets about answering the question of whether hu-

ESSENTIAL AND RECOMMENDED TITLES
591.6 Miscellaneous nontaxonomic kinds of animals

mans and whales will one day be able to communicate with each other." —*Library Journal*
  Includes bibliographical references.

591.6 Miscellaneous nontaxonomic kinds of animals

Simon, Matt
  Plight of the Living Dead: What the Animal Kingdom's Real-life Zombies Reveal About Nature — and Ourselves. Matt Simon. Penguin Group USA 2018. 272 p.
  ISBN 9780143131410
  Grades: Adult   591.6
  1. Parasites 2. Mind control 3. Predation (Biology) 4. Evolution 5. Brainwashing 6. Neuroscience 7. Nature Writing — Animal Studies
  LC 2018004526
  Chronicles the evolutionary history of mind control and real-life zombies, and what it reveals about nature and humanity.
  "Simons work is easily the most fun one could ever expect to have reading about the mind-controlling insects, insidious fungi, and parasites living alongside humanity." —*Publishers Weekly*
  Includes bibliographical references.

591.68 Rare and endangered animals

O'Connor, Maura R.
  Resurrection Science: Conservation, De-extinction and the Precarious Future of Wild Things. Maura R. O'Connor. St. Martin's Press 2015. 288 p.
  ISBN 9781137279293
  Grades: 10 11 12 Adult   591.68
  1. Evolution 2. Rare and endangered animals 3. Wildlife conservation 4. Nature writing — Animal studies — Endangered species 5. Science writing — Biology
  LC 2015004485
  A tour of current advances in biology and ethics demonstrates how humans are increasingly in control of evolution, exploring how as the scientific community endeavors to save near-extinct species, the creatures being saved become less wild and more dependent.

Preston, Christopher J.
  Tenacious Beasts: Wildlife Recoveries That Change How We Think About Animals. Christopher J. Preston. The MIT Press 2023. 312 p.
  ISBN 9780262047562
  Grades: Adult   591.68
  1. Wildlife reintroduction 2. Wildlife 3. Wildlife conservation 4. Climate change 5. Animal populations 6. Human-animal relationships 7. Nature Writing — Animal Studies — Endangered Species
  LC 2022011919
  Conventional wisdom is that wild animals are being wiped out. But conventional wisdom skips some important details. Wildlife is rebounding. Not everywhere. Not every species. But a handful of wildlife populations have reached numbers unimaginable in a century. This book tracks-and tries to understand-these dramatic rebounds. It shines a light on species returning to forests and farms, prairies and oceans, rivers and cities. It asks how these transformations can be happening and what they have to teach.
  "This makes for an excellent recommendation to readers searching for thoughtful but hopeful books on the future of nature." —*Library Journal*
  Includes bibliographical references and index.

591.7 Animal ecology, animals characteristic of specific environments

Safina, Carl
  ★ *Becoming Wild: How Animal Cultures Raise Families, Create Beauty, and Achieve Peace.* Carl Safina. Henry Holt and Company 2020. xiv, 368 pages : Illustration; Color
  ISBN 9781250173331
  Grades: Adult   591.7
  1. Animal societies 2. Social behavior in animals 3. Animals 4. Culture 5. Sperm whale 6. Macaws 7. Chimpanzees 8. Communities 9. Nature writing — Animal studies 10. Adult books for young adults
  LC 2019040495
  ALA Notable Book, 2021; New York Times Notable Book, 2020.
  The author brings readers close to three non-human cultures—what they do, why they do it, and how life is for them.
  "Safina writes with awe and wonder of what he observed and learned from the cultures of these remarkable animals, making us reconsider our sense of uniqueness.... An involving, even addictive chronicle." —*Booklist*
  Includes bibliographical references and index.

Ward, Ashley
  The Social Lives of Animals. Ashley Ward. Basic Books 2022. 384 p.
  ISBN 9781541600836
  Grades: Adult   591.7
  1. Animal groups 2. Animal communication 3. Animal behavior 4. Social behavior in animals 5. Zoology 6. Nature Writing — Animal Studies
  LC 2021024308
  A biologist, in this insightful, engaging and entertaining book, searches for a more accurate picture of how animals build societies, showing that the social impulses we've long thought separated humans from other animals might actually be our strongest connection to them.
  "Ward shares research and personal observations about the social behavior of animals from around the world, from Antarctic krill to the commonplace pigeon....Ward's lively and oftentimes surprising observations and quirky and wry writing will appeal to readers." —*Booklist*
  Includes bibliographical references and index.

591.77 Marine animals

Imbler, Sabrina
  How Far the Light Reaches: A Life in Ten Sea Creatures. Sabrina Imbler. Little Brown & Company 2022. 320 p.
  ISBN 9780316540537
  Grades: Adult   591.77
  1. Imbler, Sabrina 2. Marine biology 3. Survival 4. Marine animals 5. Sexuality 6. Families 7. Writing 8. Nature 9. Race (Social sciences) 10. Interpersonal relations 11. Essays 12. Science Writing — Biology 13. Life stories — Identity 14. Life stories — Science, technology and medicine
  Los Angeles Times Book Prize for Science and Technology, 2022.
  Exploring themes of adaptation, survival, sexuality, and care, and weaving the wonders of marine biology with stories of their own family, relationships, and coming of age, How Far the Light Reaches is a book that invites us to envision wilder, grander, and more abundant possibilities for the way we live.
  "In this captivating debut, science writer Imbler shines a light on the mysterious sea creatures that live in Earth's most inhospitable reaches, drawing parallels to their own experience of adaptation and survival....Imbler's ability to balance illuminating science journalism with candid personal revelation is impressive, and the mesmerizing glints of lyricism are a treat." —*Publishers Weekly*

Kingdon, Amorina
  ★ *Sing Like Fish: How Sound Rules Life Under Water.* Amorina Kingdon. Crown 2024. 288 p.
  ISBN 9780593442777
  Grades: Adult   591.77

PUBLIC LIBRARY CORE COLLECTION: NONFICTION
Twentieth Edition

1. Underwater exploration 2. Sounds 3. Noise 4. Water pollution 5. Marine animals 6. Marine biology 7. Nature sounds 8. Aquatic animals 9. Aquatic biology 10. Aquatic ecology 11. Nature Writing — Animal Studies — Fish and Fishing 12. Science Writing — Biology

LC 2023056614

Synthesizing historical discoveries with the latest scientific research, an award-winning science journalist takes us beneath the surface of the ocean to show the repercussions of human-made sound on the marine world's delicate acoustic ecosystems, issuing a clarion call for humans to address the ways we invade these critical soundscapes.

"With historical insight and contemporary science, award-winning writer Kingdon details how the sonic array of the sea sings in ways humans cannot hear." —*Library Journal*

Includes bibliographical references and index.

591.9709 Animals — North America — History

Flores, Dan L.
Wild New World: The Epic Story of Animals and People in America. Dan Flores. W.W. Norton & Company 2022. 384 p.

ISBN 9781324006169

Grades: Adult   591.9709

1. Wildlife 2. Human ecology 3. Effect of humans on nature 4. Indigenous peoples of North America 5. Colonialism 6. Extinction 7. Rare and endangered animals 8. Human-animal relationships 9. North America 10. Nature Writing — Animal Studies — Endangered Species 11. History writing — United States 12. History writing — Canada 13. History writing — Latin America — Mexico

LC 2022027350

National Outdoor Book Award for Natural History Literature, 2023.

A deep-time history of how humans engaged wildlife in North America, by the author of Coyote America. In 1908, a cowboy discovered bones from an extinct giant bison near Folsom, New Mexico. When archeologists found handmade weapons embedded in the fossils, the discovery vastly expanded our continent's known human history, but also revealed the long-standing danger Homo sapiens have presented to their fellow animals. Dan Flores celebrates the astonishing bestiary that arose on our continent and introduces the complex human characters who studied America's animals, hastened their eradication, and are working to recover them.

"A distinguished scholar of the U.S. West, Flores (Coyote America) surveys human-wildlife interactions across North America, from the emergence of its flora and fauna and the Pleistocene mass extinctions to the impact of white settlement and the decline (and sometimes rescue) of species in recent centuries." —*Library Journal*

Includes bibliographical references and index.

592 Invertebrates

Attenborough, David
Life in the Undergrowth. David Attenborough. Princeton University Press 2005. 288 p.

ISBN 9780691127033

Grades: 11 12 Adult   592

1. Invertebrates 2. Insects 3. Adaptation 4. Natural history 5. Media tie-ins 6. Nature Writing — Animal Studies 7. Adult books for young adults

LC 2005934727

National Outdoor Book Award for Nature and the Environment, 2006.

A richly illustrated companion to the Animal Planet television program offers a rare, close-up study of the secret life of invertebrates, focusing on a broad spectrum of tiny, diverse creatures that have had a profound impact on not only the evolutionary cycle but also the environmental health of the planet.

"This wonderful exploration of invertebrates exceeds the requirements for a great nature book through the strength of its photographs and the quality of its prose." —*Publishers Weekly*

Meinkoth, Norman August
The Audubon Society Field Guide to North American Seashore Creatures. Norman A. Meinkoth. A.A. Knopf 1981. 799 p. : Color illustration; Map (The Audubon Society field guide series)

ISBN 9780394519937

Grades: 7 8 9 10 11 12 Adult   592

1. Marine invertebrates 2. Reference books 3. Nature writing — Animal Studies

LC 81080828

Presents a comprehensive guide to more than six hundred species of sea creatures living along the coasts of North America, with full-color photographs, anecdotes, identification key, and other information.

Includes index.

594 Mollusks and molluscoids

Bailey, Elisabeth
The Sound of a Wild Snail Eating. Elisabeth Bailey. Algonquin Books 2010. 224 p.

ISBN 9781565126060

Grades: Adult   594

1. Bailey, Elisabeth 2. Companionship 3. Snails 4. People with terminal illnesses 5. Women 6. Bonding (Human-animal) 7. Human-animal relationships 8. Autobiographies and memoirs 9. Nature Writing — Personal responses 10. Life stories — Relationships — Pets and Owners 11. Family and Relationships — Pets and Owners 12. Adult books for young adults

LC 2010018603

Library Journal Best Books, 2010; National Outdoor Book Award for Natural History Literature, 2010; William Saroyan International Prize for Writing, Nonfiction category, 2012.

Bedridden and suffering from a neurological disorder, the author recounts the profound effect on her life caused by a gift of a snail in a potted plant and shares the lessons learned from her new companion about her the meaning of her life and the life of the small creature.

"A small, short book filled with an enormous amount of natural history and science about snails; also, an acknowledgment of an individual's determination to recover and regain life with humor and insight. Highly recommended." —*Library Journal*

Rehder, Harald Alfred
The Audubon Society Field Guide to North American Seashells. Harald A. Rehder, with photographs by James H. Carmichael, Jr; visual key by Carol Nehring and Mary Beth Brewer. Knopf 1981. 894 p. : Illustration; Color (The Audubon Society field guide series)

ISBN 9780394519135

Grades: 7 8 9 10 11 12 Adult   594

1. Shells 2. Identification 3. North America 4. Reference books 5. Nature writing — General

LC 80084239

Surveys the habitat, range, behavior, biology, and reproductive habits of marine mullusks.

"The more than 700 color plates are arranged according to shape and color rather than family or genus, making identification very simple for even the rankest amateur. . . . The text gives the common name, scientific name, description, habitat, range, and comments for each species. This is the most comprehensive field guide to North American seashells." —*Library Journal*

Includes index.

Scheel, David
Many Things Under a Rock: The Mysteries of Octopuses. David Scheel; illustrations by Laurel. W.W. Norton & Company 2023. 288 p.

ISBN 9781324020691

Grades: Adult   594

1. Octopuses 2. Marine biology 3. Animal behavior 4. Nature Writing — Animal studies 5. Science Writing — Biology

ESSENTIAL AND RECOMMENDED TITLES
595.7 Insects

LC 2023009900

A behavioral ecologist's chronicles his decades-long obsession with octopuses: His discoveries, adventures and new scientific understanding of their behaviors.

"The detailed descriptions of octopus behavior and stimulating research on their perceptive faculties makes for a complex portrait of a surprising animal."
—*Publishers Weekly*

Includes bibliographical references and index.

595.7 Insects

Brock, James P.
Kaufman Field Guide to Butterflies of North America. Jim P. Brock and Kenn Kaufman; with the collaboration of Rick and Nora Bowers and Lynn Hassler. Houghton Mifflin 2003. 391 p. : Color illustration; Color; Map
ISBN 9780618768264
Grades: Adult   595.7
1. Butterflies 2. North America 3. Reference books 4. Nature writing — Animal Studies
LC 2006287515

The most user-friendly butterfly guide ever published, still handy and compact.

Previously published as the Kaufman focus guide to Butterflies of North America—P. [6].

Holldobler, Bert
The Superorganism: The Beauty, Elegance, and Strangeness of Insect Societies. Bert Holldobler and Edward O. Wilson; line drawings by Margaret C. Nelson. W.W. Norton & Company 2008. 576 p.
ISBN 9780393067040
Grades: 11 12 Adult   595.7
1. Insect societies 2. Sociobiology 3. Social behavior in insects 4. Animal behavior 5. Animal societies 6. Insect behavior 7. Social behavior in animals 8. Nature Writing — Animal Studies

New York Times Notable Book, 2008.

The Pulitzer Prize-winning authors present a lavishly detailed account of the extraordinary lives of social insects that draws on more than two decades of research and offers insight into how bees, termites, and other insect societies thrive in systems of altruistic cooperation, complex communication, and labor division.

Includes bibliographical references and index.

MacNeal, David
Bugged: The Insects Who Rule the World and the People Obsessed with Them. David MacNeal; with illustrations by Michael Kennedy. St. Martin's Press 2017. 288 p.
ISBN 9781250095503
Grades: Adult   595.7
1. Insects 2. Entomology 3. Entomologists 4. Humans and insects 5. Adult books for young adults
LC 2017006880

Explores the relationship between humans and insects from a historical and cultural point of view.

"MacNeal delivers a joy-filled dose of science, reminding readers that the strange and alien creatures in our midst are not to be feared, but celebrated."
—*Publishers Weekly*

Includes bibliographical references and index.

Nicholls, Steve
Alien Worlds: How Insects Conquered the Earth and Why Their Fate Will Determine Our Future. Steve Nicholls. Princeton University Press 2023. 496 p.
ISBN 9780691253589
Grades: Adult   595.7
1. Insects 2. Entomology 3. Insect behavior 4. Evolution 5. Insect societies 6. Animal ecology 7. Biotic communities 8. Nature Writing — Animal Studies 9. Science Writing — Biology

Life on Earth depends on the busy activities of insects, but global populations of these teeming creatures are currently under threat, with grave consequences for us all. Alien Worlds presents insects and other arthropods as you have never seen them before, explaining how they conquered the planet and why there are so many of them, and shedding light on the evolutionary marvels that enabled them to thrive. Blending glorious imagery with entertaining and informative science writing, this book takes you inside the hidden realm of insects and reveals why their fate carries profound implications for our own.

"Among countless other interesting facts, readers will soak up vivid details of carnivorous plants and learn about insects' ability to jump great distances or walk on water. They will also enjoy the generous selection of beautiful, occasionally gruesome photographs spread throughout the text. Exemplary popular science." —*Kirkus*

Includes bibliographical references and index.

Paulson, Dennis
Dragonflies & Damselflies: A Natural History. Dennis Paulson. Princeton University Press 2019. 224 pages : Color; Illustration
ISBN 9780691180366
Grades: Adult   595.7
1. Damselflies 2. Dragonflies 3. Nature writing — Animal Studies 4. Science writing — Biology 5. Science writing — General
LC 2018961573

Dragonflies and damselflies are often called birdwatchers' insects. Large, brightly colored, active in the daytime, and displaying complex and interesting behaviors, they have existed since the days of the dinosaurs, and they continue to flourish. Their ancestors were the biggest insects ever, and they still impress us with their size, the largest bigger than a small hummingbird. There are more than 6,000 odonate species known at present, and you need only visit any wetland on a warm summer day to be enthralled by their stunning colors and fascinating behavior. In this lavishly illustrated natural history, leading dragonfly expert Dennis Paulson offers a comprehensive, accessible, and appealing introduction to the world's dragonflies and damselflies.

"The appreciation of this group will be enhanced for everyone reading this work." —*Choice*

First published in the UK in 2019 by Ivy Press; Includes bibliographical references (pages 218-219) and index.

Schmidt, Justin O.
The Sting of the Wild. Justin O. Schmidt. Johns Hopkins University Press 2016. 280 p.
ISBN 9781421419282
Grades: Adult   595.7
1. Poisonous insects 2. Insect pests 3. Insects 4. Nature writing — Animal studies
LC 2015026989

In The Sting of the Wild, the colorful Dr. Schmidt takes us on a journey inside the lives of stinging insects, seeing the world through their eyes as well as his own. He explains how and why they attack and reveals the powerful punch they can deliver with a small venom gland and a "sting," the name for the apparatus that delivers the venom. We learn which insects are the worst to encounter and why some are barely worth considering.

"Schmidts tales will prove infectiously engaging even to entomophobes."
—*Publishers Weekly*

Includes bibliographical references and index.

Sverdrup-Thygeson, Anne
Buzz, Sting, Bite: Why We Need Insects. by Anne Sverdrup-Thygeson; translated by Lucy Moffatt. Simon & Schuster 2019. 256 pages
ISBN 9781982112875
Grades: Adult   595.7
1. Insects 2. Humans and insects 3. Entomology 4. Translations — Norwegian to English 5. Science Writing — Biology 6. Nature Writing — General
LC 2018059668

An enthusiastic, witty and informative introduction to the world of insects explains why we—and the planet we inhabit—could not survive without them.

"A classy and brightly informative appreciation of insects all you could ask for in a popular natural history." —*Kirkus*

Originally published in 2018 in Norway by J.M. Stenersens Forlag as Insektenes Planet; Published in the UK by Mudlark as Extraordinary insects, 2019; Includes bibliographical references and index; Translated from the Norwegian.

595.7097 Insects — North America

Milne, Lorus Johnson
★ *The Audubon Society Field Guide to North American Insects and Spiders*. Lorus and Margery Milne; visual key by Susan Rayfield. Knopf 1980. 989 p. : Illustration; Color
ISBN 9780394507637
Grades: Adult 595.7097
1. Insects 2. Spiders 3. Identification 4. North America 5. Reference books 6. Nature writing — Animal Studies
LC 80007620

Identifies, discusses, and illustrates every important family and species in North America, providing information on the habits and characteristics of each insect and spider covered.

A Chanticleer Press edition; Includes index.

595.717 Ecology — Insects

Waldbauer, Gilbert
What Good Are Bugs?: Insects in the Web of Life. Gilbert Waldbauer. Harvard University Press 2003. 366 p; Illustration
ISBN 9780674010277
Grades: 11 12 Adult 595.717
1. Insects 2. Entomology 3. Animal behavior 4. Nature Writing — Animal Studies 5. Adult books for young adults
LC 2002027335

Looks at the behavior of insects and their importance to life on Earth. Includes bibliographical references (p. 317-342) and index.

595.76 Beetles

Lewis, Sara
Silent Sparks: The Wondrous World of Fireflies. Sara Lewis. Princeton University Press 2016. 240 p.
ISBN 9780691162683
Grades: 10 11 12 Adult 595.76
1. Fireflies 2. Insects 3. Nature writing — Animal studies
LC 2015037057

For centuries, the beauty of fireflies has evoked wonder and delight. Yet for most of us, fireflies remain shrouded in mystery: How do fireflies make their light? What are they saying with their flashing? And what do fireflies look for in a mate? In Silent Sparks, noted biologist and firefly expert Sara Lewis dives into the fascinating world of fireflies and reveals the most up-to-date discoveries about these beloved insects.

Includes bibliographical references and index.

595.77 Flies (Diptera) and fleas

Balcombe, Jonathan P.
Super Fly: The Unexpected Lives of the World's Most Successful Insects. Jonathan Balcombe. Penguin Group USA 2021. 352 p.
ISBN 9780143134275
Grades: Adult 595.77
1. Flies 2. Insects 3. Nature Writing — Animal studies 4. Science Writing — Biology
LC 2020019489

National Outdoor Book Award for Natural History Literature, 2021.

A biologist puts a spotlight on lowly, annoying flies and describes the vital roles they actually play in every ecosystem as pollinators, waste-disposers and food source, highlighting unique types including the Petroleum Fly and the Chocolate Midge.

"This is an excellent overview of what we know and what we're discovering about flies." —*Booklist*

Includes bibliographical references and index.

595.78 Moths and butterflies

Williams, Wendy
The Language of Butterflies: How Thieves, Hoarders, Scientists, and Other Obsessives Unlocked the Secrets of the World's Favorite Insect. Wendy Williams. Simon & Schuster 2020. 240 pages
ISBN 9781501178061
Grades: Adult 595.78
1. Butterflies 2. Insects 3. Lepidoptera 4. Nature writing — Animal studies
LC 2019025246

In this fascinating book from the New York Times bestselling author of the Horse, Wendy Williams explores the lives of one of the world's most resilient creatures—the butterfly—shedding light on the role that they play in our ecosystem and in our human lives.

"This fascinating book will be of interest to anyone who has ever admired a butterfly, and to everyone who cares about preserving these stunning creatures." —*Library Journal*

Includes bibliographical references and index.

595.79 Ants, bees, and wasps

Frey, Kate
The Bee-Friendly Garden: Design an Abundant, Flower-filled Yard That Nurtures Bees and Supports Biodiversity. Kate Frey and Gretchen LeBuhn. Ten Speed Press 2016. IX, 213 pages : Color; Illustration
ISBN 9781607747635
Grades: Adult 595.79
1. Bees 2. Gardening to attract wildlife 3. Arts and Entertainment — Crafts and hobbies — Garden and nature 4. Science writing — General
LC 2015025815

A guide to gardening shows readers how to create an organic, pesticide-free, and ecologically sustainable bee garden that can provide an impressive increase in yields and better-tasting produce.

Beautifully illustrated, a guide written by an award-winning garden designer and a bee expert shows readers how to create an organic, pesticide-free and ecologically sustainable bee garden that can provide an impressive increase in yields and better-tasting produce.

"Frey and LeBuhn's accessible and inspiring advice, if correctly followed by growers around the world, could profoundly help restore diminishing bee populations to thriving good health, which is essential to our crops and our well-being." —*Booklist*

Includes index.

Sumner, Seirian
Endless Forms: The Secret World of Wasps. Seirian Sumner. Harper 2022. 304 p.
ISBN 9780063029927
Grades: Adult 595.79
1. Wasps 2. Insect pollinators 3. Predatory animals 4. Insect behavior 5. Insects 6. Evolution 7. Social behavior in animals 8. Nature Writing — Animal Studies 9. Science Writing — Biology 10. Debut title

ESSENTIAL AND RECOMMENDED TITLES
597 Cold-blooded vertebrates

In this eye-opening and entertaining work of popular science in the spirit of the Mosquito, Entangled Life, and the Book of Eels, a leading behavioural ecologist transforms our understanding of wasps, exploring these much-maligned insects' secret world, their incredible diversity and complex social lives, and revealing how they hold our fragile ecosystem in balance. Wasps are diverse and beautiful by every measure, and they are invaluable to planetary health, Seirian Sumner reminds us; we'd do well to appreciate them as much as their cuter cousins, the bees.

"Entomologist Sumner debuts with a tour de force on the world of wasps, delving into their daily lives, economic value to society, and the important ecological niches they fill....Funny, informative, and zippy." —*Publishers Weekly*
Includes bibliographical references.

Wilson, Edward O.
Tales from the Ant World. Edward O. Wilson. Liveright Publishing 2020. 240 p.
ISBN 9781631495564
Grades: Adult   **595.79**
1. Wilson, Edward O. 2. Ants 3. Insects 4. Habitats 5. Humans and insects 6. Entomologists 7. Natural history 8. Insect behavior 9. Nature Writing — Animal Studies 10. Science Writing — Biology 11. Life stories — Science, technology, and medicine — Scientists and inventors
LC 2020017595

Edward O. Wilson recalls his lifetime with ants—from his first boyhood encounters in the woods of Alabama to perilous journeys into the Brazilian rainforest. "Ants are the most warlike of all animals, with colony pitted against colony... Their clashes dwarf Waterloo and Gettysburg," writes Edward O. Wilson in his most finely observed work in decades. In a myrmecological tour to such far-flung destinations as Mozambique and New Guinea, the Gulf of Mexico's Dauphin Island and even his parents' overgrown yard back in Alabama, Wilson thrillingly evokes his nine-decade-long scientific obsession with more than 15,000 ant species.

"Wilson's passion for his subject, for the scientific method, and for the natural world comes through clearly in this enjoyable survey." —*Publishers Weekly*
Includes bibliographical references and index.

Wilson, Joseph S.
The Bees in Your Backyard: A Guide to North America's Bees. Joseph S. Wilson & Olivia Messinger Carril. Princeton University Press 2016. 288 pages : Color; Illustration
ISBN 9780691160771
Grades: Adult   **595.79**
1. Bees 2. Honeybee 3. Bumblebees 4. Beekeeping 5. Nature writing — Animal Studies 6. Reference — General
LC 2015007075

The Bees in Your Backyard provides an engaging introduction to the roughly 4,000 different bee species found in the United States and Canada, dispelling common myths about bees while offering essential tips for telling them apart in the field.

"This is the best general guide to bees this reviewer has seen." —*Choice*
Includes index.

---
597 Cold-blooded vertebrates

Gilbert, Carter Rowell
★ *National Audubon Society Field Guide to Fishes.* Carter R. Gilbert, James D. Williams. Alfred A. Knopf 2002. 607 p. : Illustration; Color; Map
ISBN 9780375412240
Grades: 7 8 9 10 11 12 Adult   **597**
1. Fishes 2. Identification 3. Visual nonfiction 4. Nature Writing — Animal Studies — Fish and Fishing
LC 2002020773

Covering both freshwater and saltwater species of fish, this fully revised edition brings a new level of accuracy and usefulness to the National Audubon Society's acclaimed field guides.
Rev. ed. of: National Audubon Society field guide to fishes, whales & dolphins / by the National Audubon Society staff. 1983; a Chanticleer Press edition.

Svensson, Patrik
The Book of Eels: Our Enduring Fascination with the Most Mysterious Creature in the Natural World. Patrik Svensson. Ecco 2020. 320 p.
ISBN 9780062968814
Grades: Adult   **597**
1. Eels 2. Marine animals 3. Effect of humans on nature 4. Humans 5. Europe 6. Nature writing — Animal studies — Fish and fishing
LC 2019054460

National Outdoor Book Award for Natural History Literature, 2020; New York Times Notable Book, 2020.

A first book by the Sydsvenskan arts and culture journalist draws on research in literature, history and marine biology in a portrait of the enigmatic European eel that share insights into the species' complicated origins and nature.

"An account of the mysterious life of eels that also serves as a meditation on consciousness, faith, time, light and darkness, and life and death.... a highly readable place to begin learning. Unsentimental nature writing that sheds as much light on humans as on eels." —*Kirkus*
Includes bibliographical references and index.

597.15 Behavior — Fishes

Balcombe, Jonathan P.
What a Fish Knows: The Inner Lives of Our Underwater Cousins. Jonathan Balcombe. Scientific American/Farrar, Straus, and Giroux 2016. 224 p.
ISBN 9780374288211
Grades: Adult   **597.15**
1. Fishes 2. Animal communication 3. Animal intelligence 4. Animal behavior 5. Nature Writing — Animal Studies — Fish and Fishing
LC 2015048629

The author of Second Nature challenges popular misconceptions to explore the complex lives of the planet's diverse fish species, drawing on the latest understandings in animal behavior and biology to reveal their self-awareness, elaborate courtship rituals and cooperative intelligence.

"This is a lively and surprising work that makes a strong argument for sport and food fishing reform." —*Library Journal*
Includes bibliographical references and index.

597.176 Freshwater fishes

Page, Lawrence M.
★ *Peterson Field Guide to Freshwater Fishes of North America North of Mexico.* Lawrence M. Page, Brooks M. Burr; illustrations by Eugene C. Beckham III ... [et al.]; maps by Griffin E. Sheehy. Houghton Mifflin Harcourt 2011. xix, 663 p. : Illustration; Color; Map
ISBN 9780547242064
Grades: Adult   **597.176**
1. Freshwater fishes 2. Reference books 3. Nature writing — Animal Studies
LC 2010049219

This second edition incorporates almost 150 more freshwater fish species, plus all-new maps and a collection of new and revised plates.
Rev. ed. of: A field guide to freshwater fishes : North America north of Mexico. 1991; Includes bibliographical references (p. 635) and index.

PUBLIC LIBRARY CORE COLLECTION: NONFICTION
Twentieth Edition

597.3 Sharks

Graham, Jasmin
Sharks Don't Sink: Adventures of a Rogue Shark Scientist. Jasmin Graham. Pantheon Books 2024. 224 p.
ISBN 9780593685259
Grades: Adult   597.3
1. Graham, Jasmin 2. Women marine biologists 3. African American scientists 4. Sharks 5. Marine biology 6. Wildlife conservation 7. Marginalized people 8. Nature 9. Wildlife 10. Marine animals 11. Women scientists 12. Autobiographies and memoirs 13. Life stories — Science, technology, and medicine — Scientists and inventors 14. Nature Writing — Animal studies 15. Life stories — Nature and outdoors

LC 2023050534

A marine biologist and co-founder of Minorities in Shark Sciences shares how she flourished outside of academia by remembering the important lesson she learned from sharks: Keep moving forward, in this guidebook to respecting and protecting some of nature's most misunderstood and vulnerable creatures—and grant the same grace to ourselves.

"Vivid prose…and Graham's palpable enthusiasm for her work make this sing. It's an impassioned tale of ambition and advocacy." —*Publishers Weekly*

Skomal, Gregory
Chasing Shadows: My Life Tracking the Great White Shark. Greg Skomal with Ret Talbot. William Morrow, an Imprint of HarperCollins Publishers 2023. 368 p.
ISBN 9780063090835
Grades: Adult   597.3
1. Skomal, Gregory 2. Great white shark 3. Shark attacks 4. Animal behavior 5. New England 6. Nature Writing — Animal studies

LC 2023003938

As shark attacks continue to rise along the coast of New England, Dr. Greg Skomal, the leading great white shark expert in the country, takes readers on a gripping exploration of these apex predators and the factors in their resurgence.

"In this highly accessible work of narrative nonfiction, marine biologist and white shark expert Skomal, a regular on the Discovery Channel's megahit Shark Week, describes the lives of white sharks and chronicles his career tracking them over three decades." —*Kirkus*

Includes index.

597.9 Reptiles

McGinnis, Samuel M
★ *Peterson Field Guide to Western Reptiles and Amphibians.* Samuel M. McGinnis and Robert C. Stebbins; illustrations by Robert C. Stebbins; sponsored by the National Audubon Society, the National Wildlife Federation and the Roger Tory Peterson Institute. Houghton Mifflin Harcourt Company 2018. xi, 560 p. : Illustration; Color; Map
ISBN 9781328715500
Grades: Adult   597.9
1. Reptiles 2. Amphibians 3. Reference books 4. Nature writing — Animal Studies

LC 2017059616

This is the most comprehensive and trusted guide to reptiles and amphibians of western North America. The new edition retains the realistic and accurate paintings by Robert Stebbins and includes 160 color photographs for additional detail. All range maps are up to date and placed within their species accounts. Family, genus, species, and subspecies names have been updated to the currently accepted usage. Illustrations of eggs and larvae, which can aid in identifying salamanders and frogs, are a particularly helpful feature.

Revised edition of: A field guide to western reptiles and amphibians / text and illustrations by Robert C. Stebbins. 3rd ed. 2003; Includes bibliographical references and index.

597.92 Turtles

Montgomery, Sy
★ *Of Time and Turtles: Mending the World, Shell by Shattered Shell.* Sy Montgomery; with illustrations by Matt Patterson. Mariner Books 2023. 272 p.
ISBN 9780358458180
Grades: Adult   597.92
1. Turtles 2. Tortoises 3. Animal rescue 4. Injured animals 5. Sick animals 6. Reptiles 7. Wildlife 8. Animal shelters 9. Animal welfare 10. Human-animal relationships 11. Massachusetts 12. Nature Writing — Animal Studies 13. Life stories — Nature and outdoors

LibraryReads Favorites, 2023.

When acclaimed naturalist Sy Montgomery and wildlife artist Matt Patterson arrive at Turtle Rescue League, they are greeted by hundreds of turtles recovering from injury and illness. Endangered by cars and highways, pollution and poachers, these turtles—with wounds so severe that even veterinarians would have dismissed them as fatal—are given a second chance at life. The League's founders, Natasha and Alexxia, live by one motto: Never give up on a turtle. Montgomery turns to these little understood yet endlessly surprising creatures to probe the eternal question: How can we make peace with our time?

"This book expertly demonstrates the advantage that the slowed-down lives of turtles can have on humans. Fans of Montgomery's previous works will love this, and so will nature enthusiasts and environmentalists." —*Library Journal*

598 Birds

Barnes, Simon
The Meaning of Birds. Simon Barnes. W.W. Norton & Company 2018. 208 p.
ISBN 9781681776262
Grades: Adult   598
1. Birds 2. Humans and birds 3. Human-animal relationships 4. Nature writing — Animal studies — Birds and birding

LC Bl2017046417

An illustrated examination of the lives of birds looks at how they achieve the miracle of flight, why they sing, what they tell us about the seasons of the year, the uses of feathers, and what the migration of birds can tell us about climate change.

"This is an entertaining peek into the world of birds and birding that is sure to delight nature lovers." —*Booklist*

Includes index; Originally published: London : Head of Zeus, 2016.

Birkhead, T. R.
Bird Sense: What It's Like to Be a Bird. by Tim Birkhead. Walker & Company 2012. 288 p.
ISBN 9780802779663
Grades: Adult   598
1. Birds 2. Animal behavior 3. Senses and sensation 4. Nature Writing — Animal Studies — Birds and Birding

LC 2011043684

Describes the senses of birds that enable them to interpret their environments and interact with one another, drawing on cutting-edge science to explain how bird senses compare with those of humans and how they are able to detect distant and extraordinary elements from an upcoming storm to the Earth's magnetic field.

Includes bibliographical references and index.

Birkhead, Tim
Birds and Us: A 12,000-year History from Cave Art to Conservation. Tim Birkhead. Princeton University Press 2022. 496 p.
ISBN 9780691239927
Grades: Adult   598
1. Humans and birds 2. Birds 3. Bird protection 4. Nature 5. Human-animal relationships 6. Nature writing — Animal studies — Birds and birding 7. History writing — Arts and culture

ESSENTIAL AND RECOMMENDED TITLES
598 Birds

A sweeping and lyrical history of the relationship between birdlife and humankind over twelve millennia, exploring how birds have captured our imaginations & inspired our culture and our science. In Birds and Us award-winning writer and ornithologist Tim Birkhead takes us on an epic and dazzling journey through our mutual history with birds, from the ibises mummified and deified by Ancient Egyptians to Renaissance experiments on woodpecker anatomy, from Victorian obsessions with egg collecting to the present fight to save endangered species and restore their habitats. Weaving in stories from his own life as a scientist, including far-flung expeditions to Neolithic caves in Spain and the guillemot colonies of the Faroe Islands, this ambitious book is the culmination of a lifetime's research & unforgettably demonstrates how birds shaped us, and how we have shaped them.

"This beautifully produced volume is replete with drawings, photographs, maps, and vivid color plates. A fascinating, authoritative avian history." —*Kirkus*

Includes bibliographical references and index.

Burton, Robert
Audubon North American Birdfeeder Guide. Robert Burton and Stephen W. Kress. DK Pub. 2009. 224 p. : Color illustration; Color; Map
ISBN 9780756658830
Grades: Adult **598**
1. Bird attracting 2. Bird behavior 3. North America 4. Nature writing — Animal Studies — Birds and Birding

LC 2004059363

An illustrated handbook of bird identification provides tips on the art of birdwatching, closeup illustrations, locator maps, birding etiquette, essential equipment, and tips on the best ways to attract, feed, and observe various bird species in one's own backyard.

From the National Audubon Society comes a richly illustrated handbook of bird identification that provides helpful tips on the art of birdwatching, closeup illustrations, locator maps, birding etiquette, essential equipment, and tips on the best ways to attract, feed, and observe various bird species in one's own backyard.

Includes index.

Kaufman, Kenn
The Birds That Audubon Missed: Discovery and Desire in the American Wilderness. Kenn Kaufman. Avid Reader Press 2024. 384 p.
ISBN 9781668007594
Grades: Adult **598**
1. Audubon, John James, 1785-1851 2. Ornithology 3. Birds 4. Animals 5. Ornithologists 6. Naturalists 7. Scientific discoveries 8. Nature 9. United States 10. 19th century 11. Biographies 12. Nature Writing — Animal studies — Birds and birding 13. Life stories — Science, technology, and medicine — Scientists and inventors

LC 2023057178

From a new angle, a renowned bird expert and artist explores the scientific discoveries of John James Audubon and his fierce competition as they stumbled toward an understanding of the natural world by considering the birds these people discovered and, especially, the ones they missed.

"It's a high-flying study of Audubon's scientific contributions and major missteps." —*Publishers Weekly*

Includes bibliographical references and index.

Kumar, Priyanka
Conversations with Birds. Priyanka Kumar. Milkweed Editions 2022. 281 pages
ISBN 9781571313997
Grades: Adult **598**
1. Kumar, Priyanka, 1973- 2. Birds 3. Bird watching 4. Bird watchers 5. Animals 6. Conservation of natural resources 7. Ecology 8. Nature 9. Women authors, American 10. Biotic communities 11. Human-animal relationships 12. Environmental degradation 13. The West (United States) 14. Essays 15. Autobiographies and memoirs 16. Nature Writing — Animal Studies — Birds and Birding 17. Nature Writing — Environmental Issues 18. Life stories — Arts and culture — Writing

LC 2022010014

The acclaimed filmmaker and novelist presents a collection of essays that focus on her journey through the American west tracking the avian world while rediscovering her own place in the landscape.

"Novelist Kumar (Take Wing and Fly Here) wows in this sparkling exploration of her relationship with the birds that serve as her 'Almanac' and help her tune 'Into the seasons' and to herself....These outstanding reflections will inspire and enlighten, and are perfect for readers of Diane Ackerman." —*Publishers Weekly*

Lederer, Roger J.
Beaks, Bones, and Bird Songs: How the Struggle for Survival Has Shaped Birds and Their Behavior. Roger J. Lederer. Timber Press 2016. 288 p.
ISBN 9781604696486
Grades: Adult **598**
1. Birds 2. Bird behavior 3. Evolution 4. Nature Writing — Animal Studies — Birds and Birding 5. Science Writing — Biology

LC 2015045261

Describes the evolution of birds and the strategies they use to survive in the current world environment, with the need to find food, overcome hazardous weather, evade predators, successfully reproduce, and migrate.

"This is an exceptional overview of the life, adaptations, and impressive skill sets of wild birds." —*Library Journal*

Includes bibliographical references and index.

Robbins, Jim
The Wonder of Birds: What They Tell Us About Ourselves, the World, and a Better Future. by Jim Robbins. Spiegel & Grau 2017. 256 p.
ISBN 9780812993530
Grades: Adult **598**
1. Birds 2. Humans and birds 3. Human-animal relationships 4. Nature writing — Animal studies — Birds and birding

LC 2016049366

Montana Book Award, 2017.

From New York Times science writer Jim Robbins comes a powerful examination of the fascinating and surprising world of birds: How they enrich our lives, help sustain the planet, and have a lot to teach us about being human.

Includes bibliographical references and index.

Sibley, David
★ *Sibley's Birding Basics.* Written and illustrated by David Allen Sibley. Alfred A. Knopf 2002. 154 : Illustration; Color
ISBN 9780375709661
Grades: Adult **598**
1. Bird watching 2. Birds 3. Nature writing — Animal Studies — Birds and Birding 4. Reference — General

LC 2002020768

A noted bird painter and author of the Sibley Guide to Bird Life and Behavior offers an easy-to-follow introduction to birding, explaining how to identify various species of birds from their habitats, behaviors, characteristic feathers, and sounds and providing tips on where to look for birds.

Stokes, Donald W.
The New Stokes Field Guide to Birds. Donald & Lillian Stokes. Little, Brown 2013. xv, 574 p. : Color illustration; Color; Map
ISBN 9780316213929
Grades: Adult **598**
1. Birds 2. Bird watching 3. Identification 4. The West (United States) 5. The West (Canada) 6. North America 7. Reference books 8. Nature writing — Animal Studies — Birds and Birding

LC Bl2013010778

Presents a resource that covers all species of birds including all subspecies in the western regions of North America, with detailed information on range maps, migration routes, bird shape, significant plumages, habitat, and scientific and common names.

Includes indexes.

PUBLIC LIBRARY CORE COLLECTION: NONFICTION
Twentieth Edition

Tan, Amy
★ *The Backyard Bird Chronicles.* Written and illustrated by Amy Tan; foreword by David Allen Sibley. Alfred A. Knopf 2024. 320 p.
ISBN 9780593536131
Grades: Adult   598
1. Tan, Amy 2. Birds 3. Bird watching 4. Nature 5. Humans and nature 6. Bird behavior 7. Illustrated books 8. Nature Writing — Personal responses 9. Nature Writing — Animal studies — Birds and birding

Mapping the passage of time through daily entries, thoughtful questions and beautiful original sketches, the best-selling author of the Joy Luck Club shares her search for solace which turned into an opportunity to connect with nature in a meaningful way and imagine the intricate lives of the birds she admired.

"Bird lovers may not learn much, but Tan's enthusiasm and jaunty descriptions of her avian subjects enchant. This hits the mark." —*Publishers Weekly*

598.072 Bird watching

Alderfer, Jonathan K.
National Geographic Birding Essentials: All the Tools, Techniques, and Tips You Need to Begin and Become a Better Birder. Jonathan Alderfer and Jon L. Dunn. National Geographic 2007. 224 p. : Color illustration
ISBN 9781426201356
Grades: Adult   598.072
1. Bird watching 2. Birds 3. Reference books 4. Nature writing — Animal Studies — Birds and Birding
LC 2007030960

Offers tips and advice for how to improve bird watching skills, from choosing equipment and guides to where to watch and what features to look for when trying to identify a bird.
Includes bibliographical references and index.

Floyd, Ted
How to Know the Birds: The Art & Adventure of Birding. Ted Floyd; illustrations by N. John Schmitt. National Geographic 2019. 303 pages : Illustration
ISBN 9781426220036
Grades: Adult   598.072
1. Bird watching 2. Birds 3. United States 4. Nature writing — Animal studies — Birds and birding
LC 2018037630

Offers a holistic approach to bird-watching by noting how behaviors, settings, and seasonal cycles connect with shape, song, color, gender, and other characteristics traditionally used to identify species.

"Highly recommended for those interested in the natural world. This is a book to be read; there is nothing else quite like it." —*Library Journal*
Includes index.

Gentile, Olivia
Life List: A Woman's Quest for the World's Most Amazing Birds. Olivia Gentile. Bloomsbury 2009. 353 p.
ISBN 9781596911697
Grades: Adult   598.072
1. Snetsinger, Phoebe, 1931-1999 2. Women bird watchers 3. Bird watching 4. Cancer 5. Self-fulfillment 6. Women travelers 7. Diagnosis 8. Social life and customs 9. United States 10. 20th century 11. Nature Writing — Animal Studies — Birds and Birding
LC 2008027036

Features the saga of Phoebe Snetsinger, a wife, mother, and birdwatcher.
"Compassionate and comprehensive." —*Kirkus*

Jones, Darryl N.
The Birds at My Table: Why We Feed Wild Birds and Why It Matters. Darryl Jones. Comstock Publishing Associates, an imprint of Cornell University Press 2018. 352 pages
ISBN 9781501710780
Grades: Adult   598.072
1. Birds 2. Wildlife 3. Animal behavior 4. Human-animal relationships 5. Australian literature 6. Nature Writing — Animal Studies — Birds and Birding
LC 2017046553

Darryl Jones is fascinated by bird feeders. Not the containers supplying food to our winged friends, but the people who fill the containers. Why do people do this? Jones asks in The Birds at My Table. Does the food even benefit the birds? What are the unintended consequences of providing additional food to our winged friends? Jones takes us on a wild flight through the history of bird feeding.
Includes bibliographical references and index.

Strycker, Noah K.
The Thing with Feathers: The Surprising Lives of Birds and What They Reveal About Being Human. Noah Strycker. Riverhead Books, a member of Penguin Group (USA) 2014. 256 p.
ISBN 9781594486357
Grades: Adult   598.072
1. Bird behavior 2. Bird watching 3. Natural history 4. Human-animal relationships 5. Nature Writing — Animal Studies — Birds and Birding
LC 2013030320

The Thing with Feathers by Noah Strycker is a fun and profound look at the lives of birds, illuminating their surprising world—and deep connection with humanity.

"Strycker . here combines the latest in ornithological science with snippets of history and his own vast experience in the field to hatch a thoroughly entertaining examination of bird behavior." —*Booklist*
Includes bibliographical references and index.

Tougias, Robert
Birder on Berry Lane: Three Acres, Twelve Months, Thousands of Birds. by Robert Tougias; with illustrations by Mark Szantyr. Charlesbridge 2020. 256 p.
ISBN 9781623545413
Grades: Adult   598.072
1. Bird watching 2. Bird watchers 3. Bird migration 4. Backyards 5. Birdsongs 6. Bird sounds and calls 7. Seasons 8. Animal life cycles 9. Nature Writing — Animal Studies — Birds and Birding 10. Science Writing — Biology
LC 2019019734

A writer, birder and naturalist presents a month-by-month guide to the birds that flock to his New England backyard, revealing the miracles of the ordinary in the subtle changes, season to season and the ecosystem of the land surrounding him.

"Bird-loving readers will adore Tougias's celebratory account of how wild animals can become an intrinsic part of one's daily life." —*Publishers Weekly*
Includes bibliographical references and index.

598.097 Birds — North America

Bull, John L.
★ *The National Audubon Society Field Guide to North American Birds.* John Bull and John Farrand, Jr; revised by John Farrand; visual Key by Amanda Wilson and Lori Hogan. Knopf 1994. 796 p. : Illustration; Color
ISBN 9780679428527
Grades: 7 8 9 10 11 12 Adult   598.097
1. Birds 2. Identification 3. North America 4. Visual nonfiction 5. Nature Writing — Animal Studies — Birds and Birding
LC 94007768

A revised edition of the popular field guide includes hundreds of all new, full-color photographs, along with information on diverse species of eastern birds, their characteristics, habitats and ranges, identification tips, and more.
Rev. ed. of: The Audubon Society field guide to North American birds. 1977; Includes index.

ESSENTIAL AND RECOMMENDED TITLES
598.147 Feathers

Floyd, Ted
Smithsonian Field Guide to the Birds of North America. Ted Floyd; edited by Paul Hess and George Scott; designed by Charles Nix; maps by Paul Lehman; photographs by Brian E. Small ... [et al.]. Collins 2008. VII, 512 p. : Color illustration; Color; Map
ISBN 9780061120404
Grades: Adult   598.097
1. Birds 2. North America 3. Nature Writing — Animal Studies — Birds and Birding
LC 2008001395
A reference guide to North American wild birds features descriptive entries on 730 species, essays on bird behavior and identification, and maps based on the latest range information.
"Ideal for beginners, but also has formidable resources for experienced birders. Perfect for field use. Birders of any experience level will be happy with this volume on their bookshelf." —*Publishers Weekly*
Includes bibliographical references (p. 483) and indexes.

Peterson, Roger Tory
Peterson Field Guide to Birds of Western North America. Roger Tory Peterson; with contributions from Michael DiGiorgio ... [et al.]. Houghton Mifflin Harcourt 2020. xiv, 493 p. : Illustration; Color; Map
ISBN 9781328762221
Grades: 5 6 7 8 9 10 11 12 Adult   598.097
1. Birds 2. Nature writing — Animal Studies — Birds and Birding 3. Science writing — Biology
LC 2020009023
Each book in this series covers all the different species of a particular type of plant or animal, providing hundreds of color illustrations and range maps so that both nature enthusiasts and backyard observers can easily identify a particular type of flora or fauna.
Presents illustrations and detailed descriptions of the most common species of birds found in the western areas of North America, with advice on bird identification and maps indicating the range of each species.
Includes index; Rev. ed. of: A field guide to Western birds. 4th ed. 2010.

Peterson Field Guide to Birds of Eastern and Central North America. Roger Tory Peterson; with contributions from Michael DiGiorgio ... [et al.]. Houghton Mifflin Harcourt 2020. xiv, 445 p. : Illustration; Color; Map
ISBN 9781328771438
Grades: 5 6 7 8 9 10 11 12 Adult   598.097
1. Birds 2. North America 3. Nature writing — Animal Studies — Birds and Birding 4. Science writing — Biology
LC 2020004429
Presents illustrations and detailed descriptions of the most common species of birds found in the eastern and central areas of North America, with advice on bird identification and maps indicating the range of each species.
Includes index.

Sibley, David
Sibley Birds East: Field Guide to Birds of Eastern North America. Written and illustrated by David Allen Sibley. Alfred A. Knopf 2003. xxv, 438 pages : Color; Illustration
ISBN 9780307957917
Grades: 11 12 Adult   598.097
1. Birds 2. North America 3. Nature writing — Animal Studies — Birds and Birding
LC BL2003007994
A new edition of the eastern North American guide for bird enthusiasts profiles 550 species, and features new illustrations and maps, in a guide specifically designed for use in the field.
"All the qualities to be expected in a field guide are here. Image reproduction is crisp, colors are distinct, shading shows well, and despite the very small size, range map colors are clear. Sibley has accomplished the difficult task of condensing [The Sibley guide to birds] to practical field size." —*Library Journal*
Includes indexes.

★ *Sibley* Birds West: Field Guide to Birds of Western North America. Written and illustrated by David Allen Sibley. Alfred A. Knopf 2016. xxv, 471 pages : Color; Illustration
ISBN 9780307957924
Grades: Adult   598.097
1. Birds 2. Nature writing — Animal Studies — Birds and Birding 3. Reference — General
LC Bl2016012774
Features clear and detailed descriptions of 650 species of birds from the western regions of North America and several new maps and illustrations that feature depicted species from at least six different views.
A Scott & Nix edition; Includes indexes.

The Sibley Guide to Birds. Written and illustrated by David Sibley. Alfred A. Knopf 2000. 544 p. : Color illustration; Color; Map
ISBN 9780679451228
Grades: 11 12 Adult   598.097
1. Birds 2. Bird behavior 3. Identification 4. North America 5. Nature Writing — Animal Studies — Birds and Birding 6. Adult books for young adults
LC 00041239
Library Journal Best Books, 2000.
A new edition of the North American guide for bird enthusiasts profiles hundreds of species, and features new full-color illustrations and migration-range maps, in a guide specifically designed for use in the field.
"Published to universal acclaim in 2000, Sibley expands the first edition of his guide by over 50 pages, with more than 100 species added... More than 600 paintings are new, the range maps revised, and information on habitat, behavior, and food preferences—largely lacking previously—enhance this superb guide." —*Library Journal*

598.147 Feathers

Hanson, Thor
Feathers: The Evolution of a Natural Miracle. Thor Hanson. Basic Books 2011. 256 p.
ISBN 9780465020133
Grades: 11 12 Adult   598.147
1. Feathers 2. Body covering (Anatomy) 3. Science Writing — Biology 4. History writing — Microhistory
Science Books and Films Prize for Excellence in Science Books, Young Adult Science Book, 2012.
A biologist presents the natural history of feathers, applying the findings of paleontologists, ornithologists, biologists, engineers, and art historians to answer questions about the origin of feathers, their evolution, and their uses throughout the ages.
"Readers from science buffs to those interested in cultural history will find this a worthwhile afternoon's read." —*Publishers Weekly*

598.15 Behavior — Birds

Ackerman, Jennifer
The **Bird** *Way: A New Look at How Birds Talk, Work, Play, Parent, and Think*. Jennifer Ackerman. Penguin Press 2020. 352 p.
ISBN 9780735223011
Grades: Adult   598.15
1. Bird behavior 2. Animal intelligence 3. Birds 4. Animal behavior 5. Ornithology 6. Nature writing — Animal studies — Birds and birding
LC 2020002317
Draws on paradigm-changing scientific research into bird emotions and intelligence to explore advanced behaviors ranging from communicating and giving gifts to forming cooperative groups and dancing.
"A brightly original book sure to please any nature lover." —*Kirkus*
Includes bibliographical references and index.

PUBLIC LIBRARY CORE COLLECTION: NONFICTION
Twentieth Edition

Attenborough, David

The Life of Birds. David Attenborough. Princeton University Press 1998. 320 p. : Color illustration

ISBN 9780691016337

Grades: 11 12 Adult   598.15

1. Bird behavior 2. Ornithology 3. Bird watching 4. Bird ecology 5. Extinct birds 6. Flightless birds 7. Forest birds 8. Media tie-ins 9. Nature Writing — Animal Studies — Birds and Birding

LC 98030705

A survey of birds around the world explores their nesting, hunting, mating, and parenting behavior, and describes the threat to their existence presented by man.

"Well illustrated with color photographs, Attenborough's latest goes a long way to converting all readers into bird lovers." —*Booklist*

Includes bibliographical references and index.

Erickson, Laura

The Love Lives of Birds: Courting and Mating Rituals. Laura Erickson. Storey Publishing 2020. 152 p.

ISBN 9781635862751

Grades: Adult   598.15

1. Bird behavior 2. Birds 3. Courtship of animals 4. Parental behavior in animals 5. Ornithology 6. Bird watching 7. Nature Writing — Animal Studies — Birds and Birding

LC 2020029587

Ornithologist Laura Erickson combines her bird expertise with a touch of romance writing in this exploration of the courtship and mating rituals of 35 bird species. From the lifelong devotion of the American crow to the dalliances of the eastern bluebird, from the bald eagle's dazzling aerial display to the male ruby-throated hummingbird's reputation as a "deadbeat dad"—courtship, mating, and parenting differ dramatically among birds.

"Terrific color illustrations by Veronica Lilja add to the fun. Bird enthusiasts and nature lovers in general shouldn't miss this." —*Publishers Weekly*

598.156 Birds — Life cycle

Weidensaul, Scott

A World on the Wing: The Global Odyssey of Migratory Birds. Scott Weidensaul. W.W. Norton & Company 2021. 432 p. : Illustration

ISBN 9780393608908

Grades: Adult   598.156

1. Bird migration 2. Birds 3. Animal migration 4. Migratory animals 5. Nature Writing — Animal Studies — Birds and Birding

LC 2020028997

Offers exhilarating exploration of the science and wonder of global bird migration.

"Many mysteries of bird life and migration are revealed in this compelling and illuminating in-the-field narrative complete with maps and photographs." —*Booklist*

Includes bibliographical references and index.

598.177 Sea birds

Nicolson, Adam

The Seabird's Cry: The Lives and Loves of the Planet's Great Ocean Voyagers. Adam Nicolson. Henry Holt and Company 2018. 400 pages : Illustration; Map

ISBN 9781250134189

Grades: Adult   598.177

1. Sea birds 2. Marine ecology 3. Bird behavior 4. Puffins 5. Ornithology 6. Bird migration 7. Oceans 8. Rare and endangered animals 9. Extinction 10. Hebrides 11. Nature Writing — Animal Studies — Birds and Birding

LC 2017031320

Describes the plight of seabirds, whose numbers are on the decline, and relays the importance of their voyages on sustaining life on Earth.

"Marveling at lives lived in some of the harshest places on the planet, Nicolson writes lyrically of birds most of us only briefly notice when visiting a rocky shoreline, beings possessing extraordinary forms of understanding we have never shared." —*Booklist*

Includes bibliographical references and index; Originally published: London : William Collins, 2017.

598.7 Miscellaneous orders of land birds

Davies, N. B.

Cuckoo: Cheating by Nature. Nick Davies; with field drawings by James McCallum. Bloomsbury USA 2015. xx, 289 pages, 8 unnumbered pages of plates : Illustration; Color; Map

ISBN 9781620409527

Grades: Adult   598.7

1. Cuckoos 2. Birds 3. Ornithology 4. Deception 5. Nature writing — Animal studies — Birds and birding

LC Bl2015012933

A gifted biologist's careful and beguiling study of why cuckoos have got away with tricking other birds into hatching and raising their young for thousands of years.

"He describes experiments involving recorded bird calls, radio transmitters, and egg substitutions, and he reports findings that suggest how predators and prey continue to adapt. Readers may gain some respect, if not affection, for a hard-to-understand bird." —*Booklist*

Includes bibliographical references and index; First published in Great Britain 2015—Title page verso.

Dunn, Jon L.

The Glitter in the Green: In Search of Hummingbirds. Jon Dunn. Basic Books 2021. 320 p.

ISBN 9781541618190

Grades: Adult   598.7

1. Hummingbirds 2. Bird watching 3. Bird behavior 4. Habitats 5. Rare and endangered birds 6. Bird migration 7. Voyages and travels 8. Natural history 9. Western Hemisphere 10. Nature Writing — Animal Studies — Birds and Birding 11. Nature Writing — Animal Studies — Endangered Species

LC 2020038844

Hummingbirds are a glittering, sparkling collective of over three hundred wildly variable species. For centuries, they have been revered by indigenous Americans, coveted by European collectors, and admired worldwide for their unsurpassed metallic plumage and immense character. Yet they exist on a knife-edge, fighting for survival in boreal woodlands, dripping cloud forests, and subpolar islands. They are, perhaps, the ultimate embodiment of evolution's power to carve a niche for a delicate creature in even the harshest of places. Nature writer Jon Dunn encounters birders, scientists, and storytellers in his quest to find these beguiling creatures, immersing us in the world of one of Earth's most charismatic bird families.

"Natural history writer Dunn (Orchid Summer) takes readers on a wondrous globe-trotting pilgrimage to seek out hummingbirds as their populations are threatened. . . . Dunn's vivid prose, balanced with just the right amount of detail, will captivate birders and non-birders alike." —*Publishers Weekly*

Montgomery, Sy

The Hummingbirds' Gift: Wonder, Beauty, and Renewal on Wings. Sy Montgomery. Atria Books 2021. 96 p. : Illustration

ISBN 9781982176082

Grades: Adult   598.7

1. Hummingbirds 2. Birds 3. Wildlife rescue 4. Habitats 5. Nature Writing — Animal Studies — Birds and Birding

A naturalist and beloved New York Times best-selling author, who rescues abandoned hummingbirds, shows just how amazing these tiny creatures are and celebrates their very existence on our planet.

ESSENTIAL AND RECOMMENDED TITLES
598.8 Perching birds (Passeriformes)

"Montgomery's bright, richly illustrated chronicle stirs renewed appreciation for human empathy, skill, and wonder and for a miraculous winged species." —*Booklist*

Shunk, Stephen A.
Peterson Reference Guide to Woodpeckers of North America. Stephen A. Shunk. Houghton Mifflin Harcourt 2016. xi, 298 pages : Illustration; Color
ISBN 9780618739950
Grades: Adult   **598.7**
1. Woodpeckers 2. North America 3. Nature Writing — Animal Studies — Birds and Birding
LC Bl2016018082

Presents a comprehensive guide to twenty-three species of woodpeckers, describing their anatomy, physical features, distribution, habitat, behavior, diet, and conservation status.

Sponsored by the Roger Tory Peterson Institute and the National Wildlife Federation; Includes bibliographical references (pages 264-293) and index.

598.8 Perching birds (Passeriformes)

Heinrich, Bernd
White Feathers: The Nesting Lives of Tree Swallows. Bernd Heinrich. Houghton Mifflin Harcourt 2020. 352 p.
ISBN 9781328604415
Grades: Adult   **598.8**
1. Bird behavior 2. Swallows 3. Nature Writing — Animal Studies — Birds and Birding
LC 2019024927

An acclaimed scientist, naturalist and best-selling author offers an engaging, detailed look at the lives of wild birds, after becoming fascinated by a pair of swallows who have a preference for white feathers as nest lining.

"This inviting work will draw in naturalists and birders, along with anyone wishing to learn more about animal behavior from a trusted guide." —*Library Journal*

Includes bibliographical references and index.

598.9 Birds of prey

Ackerman, Jennifer
★ *What an Owl Knows: The New Science of the World's Most Enigmatic Birds.* Jennifer Ackerman. Penguin 2023. 368 p.
ISBN 9780593298886
Grades: Adult   **598.9**
1. Owls 2. Birds of prey 3. Nocturnal animals 4. Bird behavior 5. Animal communication 6. Bird sounds and calls 7. Social behavior in animals 8. Nature conservation 9. Nature Writing — Animal Studies — Birds and Birding 10. Science Writing — Biology
LC 2022053096

For millennia, owls have captivated and intrigued us. With their forward gaze and quiet flight, owls are often a symbol of wisdom, knowledge, and foresight. But what does an owl really know? And what do we really know about owls? Though our fascination goes back centuries, scientists have only recently begun to understand in deep detail the complex nature of these extraordinary birds. Jennifer Ackerman illuminates the rich biology and natural history of these birds and reveals remarkable new scientific discoveries about their brains and behavior.

"Ackerman's latest vivid and compelling narrative is enlivened by her own passion for owls and her excitement over discoveries in the wild that show that, for humans, owls continue to be full of surprises." —*Booklist*

Includes bibliographical references and index.

Davis, Jack E.
The Bald Eagle: The Improbable Journey of America's Bird. Jack E. Davis. Liveright Publishing Company 2022. 608 p.
ISBN 9781631495250
Grades: Adult   **598.9**
1. Bald eagle 2. Bald Eagle (Symbol) 3. Birds 4. United States 5. Nature Writing — Animal studies — Birds and birding 6. History writing — United States
LC 2021054960

The bald eagle is regal but fearless, a bird you're not inclined to argue with. For centuries, Americans have celebrated it as "majestic" and "noble," yet savaged the living bird behind their national symbol as a malicious predator of livestock and, falsely, a snatcher of babies. Taking us from before the nation's founding through inconceivable resurgences of this enduring all-American species, Jack E. Davis contrasts the age when native peoples lived beside it peacefully with that when others, whether through hunting bounties or DDT pesticides, twice pushed Haliaeetus leucocephalus to the brink of extinction. Filled with spectacular stories of Founding Fathers, rapacious hunters, heroic bird rescuers, and the lives of bald eagles themselves-monogamous creatures, considered among the animal world's finest parents—The Bald Eagle is a much-awaited cultural and natural history that demonstrates how this bird's wondrous journey may provide inspiration today, as we grapple with environmental peril on a larger scale.

"Pulitzer Prize winner Davis (The Gulf: The Making of an American Sea) presents the story of the United States' national bird. . . . This fascinating and readable work will appeal to fans of the majestic bald eagle and to those interested in the natural, cultural, and political history of the United States." —*Library Journal*

Includes bibliographical references and index.

Duncan, James R.
Owls of the World. James Duncan. Johns Hopkins University Press 2018. 192 pages : Color; Illustration
ISBN 9781421427188
Grades: Adult   **598.9**
1. Owls 2. Nature writing — Animal Studies — Birds and Birding
LC Bl2018191746

"There is no shortage of books devoted to the world's owls, and for good reason. Owls fascinate. This coffee tablesized book is most noteworthy for its splendid photos of owls, which make the book a visual treat." —*Choice*

Includes bibliographical references (pages 187-188) and index.

Meiburg, Jonathan
A Most Remarkable Creature: The Hidden Life and Epic Journey of the World's Smartest Birds of Prey. Jonathan Meiburg. Alfred A. Knopf 2021. 384 p.
ISBN 9781101875704
Grades: Adult   **598.9**
1. Birds of prey 2. Birds 3. Rare and endangered birds 4. Natural history 5. Voyages and travels 6. South America 7. Nature Writing — Animal studies — Birds and birding 8. Science Writing — Biology
LC 2020033130

A first book by an award-winning natural-science writer introduces readers to the remarkable world of the caracara, a social bird of prey, discussing how the species baffled Darwin and why it has remained confined to a small South American region.

"Meiburg elevates himself to the top ranks of science writers with this enthralling debut on the obscure caracara. . . . Fans of literary nature narratives will be thrilled by his lyrical account, and eager to see where Meiburg goes next." —*Publishers Weekly*

Includes bibliographical references and index.

Montgomery, Sy
The Hawk's Way: Encounters with Fierce Beauty. Sy Montgomery. Atria Books 2022. 96 p.
ISBN 9781668001967
Grades: Adult   **598.9**
1. Hawks 2. Birds of prey 3. Nature Writing — Animal Studies — Birds and Birding

PUBLIC LIBRARY CORE COLLECTION: NONFICTION
Twentieth Edition

Invites readers into the wonderous world of hawks where they will learn about the extraordinary abilities of these magnificent creatures and what they can teach us about nature, life and love.

"Naturalist Montgomery (The Soul of an Octopus) explores what can be learned from birds of prey in this impassioned introduction to falconry." —*Publishers Weekly*

Safina, Carl

★ *Alfie* and Me: What Owls Know, What Humans Believe. Carl Safina. W W Norton & Company 2023. 352 p.

ISBN 9781324065463

Grades: Adult   **598.9**

1. Safina, Carl, 1955- 2. Owls 3. Wildlife 4. Birds 5. Friendship 6. Nature 7. Ecologists 8. Human-animal relationships 9. Nature Writing — Animal studies — Birds and birding 10. Life stories — Nature and outdoors

A moving account of raising, then freeing, an orphaned screech owl, whose lasting friendship with the author illuminates humanity's relationship with the world.

"Interwoven with Safina's broad experience with other cultures' views on animals and the world and of how they related to Alfie's life, and richly illustrated with photographs, this a beautifully illuminating work of up-close natural history." —*Booklist*

Slaght, Jonathan C.

Owls of the Eastern Ice: A Quest to Find and Save the World's Largest Owl. Jonathan C. Slaght. Farrar, Straus and Giroux 2020. 256 p.

ISBN 9780374228484

Grades: Adult   **598.9**

1. Slaght, Jonathan C. 2. Owls 3. Birds of prey 4. Rare and endangered birds 5. Russia 6. Nature Writing — Animal Studies — Birds and Birding 7. Travel Writing — Asia and the South Pacific

LC 2020003420

Minnesota Book Award for General Nonfiction, 2021; New York Times Notable Book, 2020.

A field conservationist tracks his five-year study of the elusive Blakiston's fish owl of eastern Russia, where his small scientific monitoring team immersed themselves in local culture while learning about the species' survival behaviors and shrinking habitat.

"Slaght's extensive field research is rendered into clear, readable prose, making it a solid choice for bird lovers, but also for armchair travelers looking for eco-adventure on the fringes of civilization." —*Library Journal*

Includes bibliographical references.

599 Mammals

Drew, Liam

I, Mammal: The Story of What Makes Us Mammals. Liam Drew. Bloomsbury Sigma 2018. 288 pages

ISBN 9781472922892

Grades: Adult   **599**

1. Humans 2. Mammals 3. Human evolution 4. Human anatomy 5. Human physiology 6. Natural history 7. Science Writing — Biology

LC Bl2018000456

A freelance writer and former neurobiologist examines the biology, evolution and traits of humans and explores the anatomical and physiological attributes that make us mammals and that ultimately separate us from other members of the same scientific class designation.

"With wit and passion, Drew, a freelance writer and former neurobiologist, explores what it means to be a mammal by taking an evolutionary look at how and where mammals arose." —*Publishers Weekly*

Murie, Olaus J.

★ *A Field* Guide to Animal Tracks. Olaus J. Murie and Mark Elbroch; illustrated by Olaus J. Murie and Mark Elbroch. Houghton Mifflin Company 2005. xxvi, 391 p. : Illustration; Color (The Peterson field guide series)

ISBN 9780618517435

Grades: Adult   **599**

1. Animal tracks 2. Animals 3. North America 4. Reference books 5. Nature writing — Animal Studies

LC 2005013108

A new edition of the classic guide to animal tracking includes descriptions of habitats, habits, signs, and much more, providing thousands of line drawings of bird, reptiles, amphibians, and insects that leave tracks.

Includes bibliographical references (p. 371-378) and index.

Nowak, Ronald M.

Walker's Mammals of the World. Ronald M. Nowak. Johns Hopkins University Press 1999. 2 v. (li, 1936 p.) : Illustration

ISBN 9780801857898

Grades: 11 12 Adult   **599**

1. Mammals 2. Nature writing — Animal Studies 3. Science writing — Biology

LC 98023686

Gives an historical account of the world's mammals since 3,000 B.C, and then provides detailed information about every mammal on earth, divided by genus.

Includes bibliographical references (v. 2, p. 1747-1919) and index.

599.097 Mammals — North America

Whitaker, John O.

★ *National* Audubon Society Field Guide to North American Mammals. John O. Whitaker, Jr. Knopf 1996. 937 p. : Illustration; Color; Map

ISBN 9780679446316

Grades: 6 7 8 9 10 11 12 Adult   **599.097**

1. Mammals 2. Identification 3. North America 4. Visual nonfiction 5. Nature Writing — Animal Studies

LC 95081456

Presents information on 390 species of North American mammals, along with keys for identification, range maps, and information on tracks and anatomy.

A Chanticleer Press edition—P. opposite t.P; Includes index.

599.4 Bats

Taylor, Marianne

Bats: An Illustrated Guide to All Species. Marianne Taylor, Merlin D. Tuttle, science editor & photographer. Smithsonian Books 2018. 400 pages : Color; Illustration; Map

ISBN 9781588346476

Grades: Adult   **599.4**

1. Bats 2. Nature writing — Animal Studies 3. Science writing — Biology 4. Reference — General

LC 2018043061

Bats: An Illustrated Guide to All Species explores bats and their fundamental role in our ecosystems through lavish full-color photographs and lively narrative. From the Giant Golden Crowned Flying Fox, a megabat with a wingspan of more than five feet, to the aptly named Bumblebee Bat, the world's smallest mammal, the number and diversity of bat species have proven to be both rich and underestimated. Nocturnal, fast-flying, and secretive, bats are difficult to observe and catalog. This richly illustrated handbook presents bats' evolution, biology, behavior, and ecology. It offers in-depth profiles of four hundred megabats and microbats and detailed summaries of all the species identified to date. Complete with an introduction exploring bats' natural history and their unique adaptations to life on the wing, Bats includes close-up images of these animals' delicate and intricate forms and faces, each shaped by evolution to meet the demands of an extraordinarily specialized life.

"This comprehensive, clear, and concise guide is sure to appeal to any armchair enthusiast or researcher with an interest in the topic." —*Booklist*

Includes indexes.

ESSENTIAL AND RECOMMENDED TITLES
599.5 Cetaceans and sea cows

599.5 Cetaceans and sea cows

Hoare, Philip
The Whale: In Search of the Giants of the Sea. Philip Hoare. HarperCollins 2010. 448 p.
ISBN 9780061976216
Grades: 11 12 Adult 599.5
1. Whales 2. Whaling 3. Marine biology 4. Nature Writing — Animal Studies 5. Adult books for young adults
LC Bl2009036210
Samuel Johnson Prize for Nonfiction, 2009.
An extraordinary journey into the underwater world of the whale.
Originally published: London : Fourth Estate, 2008.

Hoyt, Erich
Encyclopedia of Whales, Dolphins and Porpoises. Erich Hoyt; principal photography by Brandon Cole; illustrations by Uko Gorter. Firefly Books 2017. 300 p. : Illustration; Color; Map
ISBN 9781770859418
Grades: Adult 599.5
1. Marine mammals 2. Cetacea 3. Whales 4. Dolphins 5. Encyclopedias 6. Reference books 7. Nature writing — Animal Studies 8. Science writing — Biology
LC 2017300268
In [this book], award-winning author and whale researcher Erich Hoyt takes readers into the field for an intimate encounter with some 90 species of cetaceans that make their homes in the world's oceans. Drawing on decades of firsthand experience and a comprehensive familiarity with the current revolution in cetacean studies, Hoyt provides unique insights into the life histories of these compelling marine mammals. Here are discoveries about cetacean biology and behavior, from the physical differences and adaptations among the baleen and toothed whales to their highly intelligent hunting and feeding methods. The courtship and mating practices, family relationships and the lifelong bonds among some family members are fascinating. The symphonic composer of the whale world is the humpback whale, whose complex 30-minute songs reverberate across the liquid universe of the ocean. Some cetaceans survive deep diving and negotiate lengthy migrations across oceans. This book is a fascinating compilation of the latest data on cetaceans and an impassioned argument for the ongoing need for international protection of at-risk populations and their increasingly damaged habitat."
Includes bibliographical references (page 297) and index.

Pyenson, Nick
Spying on Whales: The Past, Present, and Future of Earth's Most Awesome Creatures. Nick Pyenson. Viking 2018. xii, 322 pages : Illustration; Map
ISBN 9780735224568
Grades: Adult 599.5
1. Whales 2. Marine biology 3. Marine mammals 4. Evolution 5. Rare and endangered animals 6. Adult books for young adults 7. Nature Writing — Animal Studies — Endangered Species
Loan Stars Favourites, 2018; Library Journal Best Books, 2018.
Tracing the evolution of whales from small land-roamers to the intelligent, massive creatures of today, an award-winning Smithsonian researcher shares scientific and archaeological insights into their mysteries and survival challenges.
Includes bibliographical references and index.

599.53 Dolphins and porpoises

Neiwert, David A.
Of Orcas and Men: What Killer Whales Can Teach Us. David Neiwert. Overlook Pr. 2015. 368 p.
ISBN 9781468308655
Grades: Adult 599.53
1. Killer whale 2. Humans and whales 3. Natural history 4. Animal intelligence 5. Captive wild animals 6. Whales 7. Humans and wild animals 8. Effect of humans on nature 9. Wildlife conservation 10. Human-animal relationships 11. Puget Sound 12. Washington (State) 13. Nature Writing — Animal Studies — Endangered Species 14. Nature Writing — Environmental Issues
LC 2015010796
A revelatory history of orcas evaluates them as one of the planet's most intelligent animals, challenging beliefs about their "killer" natures while citing the threats to their populations. By the author of Strawberry Days .
"This narrative is perhaps a bit long but accessible and persuasive. The author authoritatively presents his facts and will likely inspire readers to share what they've learned from his call to action to ensure the orcas' survival. His tone isn't alarmist or strident, but his message is urgent. A wide-ranging, interesting book that should be required reading for school-aged environmentalists." —*Kirkus*

599.638 Giraffe and okapi

Peterson, Dale
Giraffe Reflections. Text by Dale Peterson; photographs by Karl Ammann. University of Calif. Press 2013. 221 pages : Color; Illustration
ISBN 9780520266858
Grades: Adult 599.638
1. Nature writing — Animal Studies 2. Science writing — Biology
LC 2012038611
Presents a cultural, historical, and pictorial history of giraffes, describing their biology and behavior and demonstrating their grace and elegance through over one hundred photographs.
This comprehensive look at the gentle giants who are the world's tallest and second-biggest land animals, offers gorgeous photographs of the endangered creatures in their natural habitat with information on their biology, behavior and history.
Includes bibliographical references (pages 216-218) and index.

599.64 Bovids

Castello, Jose R.
Bovids of the World: Antelopes, Gazelles, Cattle, Goats, Sheep, and Relatives. Jose R. Castello; foreword by Brent Huffman and Colin Groves. Princeton University Press 2016. 664 pages : Illustration; Color; Map
ISBN 9780691167176
Grades: Adult 599.64
1. Nature writing — Animal Studies
LC 2015035946
Bovids are a diverse group of ruminant mammals that have hooves and unbranched hollow horns. Bovids of the World is the first comprehensive field guide to cover all 279 bovid species, including antelopes, gazelles, cattle, buffaloes, sheep, and goats. From the hartebeest of Africa and the takin of Asia to the muskox of North America, bovids are among the world's most spectacular animals and this stunningly illustrated and easy-to-use field guide is an ideal way to learn more about them.
Includes bibliographical references and index.

Duncan, Dayton
Blood Memory: The Tragic Decline and Improbable Resurrection of the American Buffalo. Dayton Duncan and Ken Burns. Alfred A. Knopf 2023. 320 p.
ISBN 9780593537343
Grades: Adult 599.64
1. American bison 2. Human-animal relationships 3. Natural history 4. Hunting 5. Extinction 6. Indigenous peoples of North America — History 7. Wildlife recovery 8. Wildlife conservation 9. Effect of humans on nature 10. United States history 11. Great Plains (United States) 12. American Westward Expansion (1803-1899) 13. Nature Writing — Animal Studies 14. History writing — Westward expansion — United States
LC 2023008422

This work of natural history tells the epic saga of the American buffalo, from prehistoric times to today, capturing a young republic's heedless rush to conquer the continent and the dawn of the conservation era, which saved our nation's official mammal from extinction.

"Fortunately, this tale of conquest, bloodshed, and environmental disaster is also a story of resilience and resistance as Duncan profiles diverse men and women who rescued the buffalo from extinction and others involved in the ongoing pursuit of justice for crimes against Native Americans." —*Booklist*

Includes bibliographical references and index.

Rinella, Steven

American Buffalo: In Search of a Lost Icon. Steven Rinella. Spiegel & Grau 2008. 288 p.

ISBN 9780385521680

Grades: Adult   599.64

1. Rinella, Steven 2. Buffaloes 3. Hunting 4. American bison 5. Symbolism 6. Alaska 7. Nature Writing — Animal Studies — Endangered Species 8. Sports and Competition — Hunting

LC 2008013624

A correspondent for "Outside" magazine details his participation in a hunt for American bison in the Alaskan wilderness while reflecting on the history of the buffalo and the future of an animal that has haunted the American imagination.

"In 2005, [Rinella] won an Alaska state lottery permit making him one of 24 hunters allowed to kill one wild buffalo each to thin out the Copper River herd in the Wrangell-Saint Elias National Park. The book's core is Rinella's entertaining and often harrowing account of that hunting trip into Alaska's frozen south-central wilderness, where he bagged his first buffalo. But entwined throughout that story line is an engaging back story a stampede of facts and factoids, legends and lore, hard-core science and staggering history of North America's largest land animal. Everything you ever wanted to know about the buffalo or didn't going back to Pleistocene days." —*USA Today*

599.65 Deer

Delorme, Geoffroy

Deer Man: Seven Years of Living in the Wild. Geoffroy Delorme; translated by Shaun Whiteside. Greystone Books 2022. 224 p.

ISBN 9781771649797

Grades: Adult   599.65

1. Delorme, Geoffroy 2. Nature 3. Photographers 4. Authors 5. Deer 6. Wildlife 7. Wilderness survival 8. Effect of environment on humans 9. Autobiographies and memoirs 10. Nature Writing — Personal Responses 11. Life stories — Nature and outdoors

A nature photographer and writer describes how and why he left human society and lived among the deer in the forest for seven years and describes the beauty, pain, fear and joy of living life as a part of nature.

"Delorme, a young man more comfortable with animals than humans, moves into a forest in France and lives among a community of roe deer....Delorme presents an unusual tale of adaptability, survival, and animal behavior that calls for our understanding of and respect for nature." —*Booklist*

Howsare, Erika

The Age of Deer: Trouble and Kinship with Our Wild Neighbors. Erika Howsare. Catapult 2024. 256 p.

ISBN 9781646221349

Grades: Adult   599.65

1. Deer 2. Effect of humans on nature 3. Human-animal relationships 4. Anthropology 5. Wildlife 6. Hunting 7. Nature Writing — Personal Responses 8. Nature Writing — Animal Studies

In this masterful hybrid of nature writing and cultural studies, the author investigates our connection with deer, from mythology to biology, offering a unique and intimate perfective on a very human relationship while inviting us to contemplate the paradoxes of how we interact with and shape the natural world.

"A nature writer with a poet's eye and a scholar's acuity, Howsare catalogs the variety of ways the two species have interacted over time, balancing her personal observations with broad research that aims to move the needle from love-hate to understanding-acceptance." —*Booklist*

599.66 Odd-toed ungulates

Fowlds, Grant

Saving the Last Rhinos: The Life of a Frontline Conservationist. Grant Fowlds and Graham Spence. Pegasus Books 2020. 336 p.

ISBN 9781643135069

Grades: 9 10 11 12 Adult   599.66

1. Fowlds, Grant 2. Wildlife conservationists 3. Wildlife conservation 4. Rhinoceros 5. Wildlife refuges 6. Wildlife rescue 7. Poaching 8. Wildlife crimes 9. South Africa 10. Vietnam 11. Autobiographies and memoirs 12. Life stories — Politics — Activists and reformers 13. Life stories — Nature and outdoors 14. Nature Writing — Animal Studies — Endangered Species

What would drive a man to "smuggle" rhino horns back into Africa at great risk to himself? This is just one of the situations Grant Fowlds has put himself in as part of his ongoing fight against poaching, in order to prove a link between southern Africa and the illicit, lucrative trade in rhino horn in Vietnam. Growing up on a farm in the eastern Cape of South Africa, Fowlds developed a deep love of nature, turning his back on hunting to focus on saving wildlife of all kinds and the environment that sustains both them and us. He is a passionate conservationist who puts himself on the front line of protecting rhinos in the wild.

"An eye-opening account of the life of a famed conservationist that not only shows the pitfalls he faces on the job but also the hope he finds in others who are determinedly fighting to preserve wildlife." —*Library Journal*

Includes index; Originally published: Johannesburg, South Africa : Jonathan Ball Publishers, 2019.

599.67 Elephants

Wood, Levison

The Last Giants: The Rise and Fall of the African Elephant. Levison Wood. Black Cat 2020. 272 p.

ISBN 9780802158475

Grades: Adult   599.67

1. Wood, Levison, 1982- 2. African elephant 3. Rare and endangered animals 4. Social behavior in animals 5. Mammals 6. Animal behavior 7. Elephants 8. Effect of humans on nature 9. Voyages and travels 10. Botswana 11. Nature Writing — Animal Studies — Endangered species 12. Travel Writing — Africa

LC 2020038634

The Last Giants is a comprehensive exploration of the fascinating past, difficult present, and imperiled future of the African elephant.

"Comprehensively yet accessibly conveying Wood's lifelong fascination with African elephants, his discussion will appeal to anyone keen on learning more about them." —*Publishers Weekly*

599.75 Cat family

Pittman, Craig

Cat Tale: The Wild, Weird Battle to Save the Florida Panther. Craig Pittman. Hanover Square Press 2020. 352 pages

ISBN 9781335938800

Grades: Adult   599.75

1. Florida panther 2. Panthers 3. Wildlife conservation 4. Rare and endangered animals 5. Extinction 6. Wildlife conservationists 7. Wildlife biologists 8. Florida 9. Nature Writing — Animal Studies — Endangered Species 10. Adult books for young adults

LC Bl2020002934

ESSENTIAL AND RECOMMENDED TITLES
599.756 Tiger

The award-winning journalist traces the story of the unlikely rescue of the Florida panther from extinction while revealing the political factors and colorful personalities that are impacting the species today.

"A bright, intriguing story of people and panthers with strong appeal for readers interested in endangered species." —*Kirkus*

Williams, Jim
Path of the Puma: The Remarkable Resilience of the Mountain Lion. Jim Williams, with Joe Glickman and a foreword by Douglas Chadwick. Patagonia, Inc. 2018. 288 p.
ISBN 9781938340727
Grades: Adult   **599.75**
1. Puma 2. Wild cats 3. Wildlife 4. Wildlife conservation 5. Nature Writing — Animal Studies
LC Bl2019003695

During a time when most wild animals are experiencing decline in the face of development and climate change, the intrepid mountain lion—also known as a puma, a cougar, and by many other names— has experienced reinvigoration as well as expansion of territory. What makes this cat, the fourth carnivore in the food chain—just ahead of humans—so resilient and resourceful?

"The many spectacular landscape photographs are a treasure on their own and worth the cover price. A handsome book that is well-balanced, instructive, and authoritative." —*Kirkus*

599.756 Tiger

Vaillant, John
The Tiger: A True Story of Vengeance and Survival. by John Vaillant. Alfred A. Knopf 2010. 352 p.
ISBN 9780307268938
Grades: Adult   **599.756**
1. Tigers 2. Hunting 3. Poaching 4. Wildlife conservation 5. Tiger attacks 6. Siberian tigers 7. Wildlife habitat destruction 8. Russia 9. Canadian literature 10. Nature Writing — Animal Studies — Endangered Species 11. Nature Writing — Environmental Issues
LC 2010004068

ALA Notable Book, 2011; BC Book Prizes, Hubert Evans Non-Fiction Prize, 2011; British Columbia Award for Canadian Non-Fiction, 2011; CBA Libris Award for Non-Fiction Book of the Year, 2011; Library Journal Best Books, 2010.

Documents the efforts of a tiger conservation leader who was forced to hunt a man-eating tiger through the brutal Siberian winter, an effort that familiarized him with the creature's history, motives, and unique method of attack.

"What makes The Tiger a grand addition to the animal-pursuit subgenre is the sensitive way in which Vaillant . evokes his cat. Few writers have taken such pains to understand their monsters, and few depict them in such arresting prose." —*New York Times Book Review*

A Borzoi Book.

599.769 Otters

Darlington, Miriam
Otter Country: An Unexpected Adventure in the Natural World. Miriam Darlington. Tin House 2024. 368 p.
ISBN 9781959030348
Grades: Adult   **599.769**
1. Darlington, Miriam 2. Otters 3. Voyages and travels 4. Ecology 5. Wildlife 6. Stream ecology 7. Animal behavior 8. Great Britain 9. Autobiographies and memoirs 10. Nature Writing — Animal studies 11. Life stories — Nature and outdoors 12. Travel writing — Europe
LC 2023042708

Over the course of a single year, Darlington takes readers on a winding expedition in pursuit of these elusive creatures—from her home in Devon, England, and through the wilds of Scotland, Wales, the Lake District, and the countryside of Cornwall. As she's drawn deeper into wilder habitats, trekking through changing landscapes, seasons, and weather, Darlington meets biologists, conservationists, fishing and hunting enthusiasts, and poets—enriching her understanding, admiration, and awe of the wild otter. With each encounter, she reveals the scientific, environmental, and cultural importance of this creature and the places it calls home.

"An at times peculiar though wholly affectionate, informative, and bubbly work of nature writing." —*Booklist*

Includes bibliographical references.

599.773 Canis lupus and Canis rufus

Blakeslee, Nate
American Wolf: A True Story of Survival and Obsession in the West. Nate Blakeslee. Crown Publishers 2017. 336 p.
ISBN 9781101902783
Grades: Adult   **599.773**
1. Wolves 2. Rare and endangered animals 3. Wildlife management 4. Wildlife conservation 5. Effect of humans on nature 6. Yellowstone National Park 7. The West (United States) 8. Nature Writing — Animal Studies 9. Adult books for young adults
LC 2017008953

The story of O-Six, a female wolf in Yellowstone National Park who became something of a social media star, and the challenges she, her pups, and her pack faced from hunters, cattle ranchers, and other Yellowstone wolves. It is also a larger story of the clash in the American West between those who want to restore the wolf population of Yellowstone, and those who oppose it.

"The fight between federal and state control of Yellowstones wolves is embodied in O-Six's story, told with great immediacy and empathy in a tale that reads like fiction. This one will grab readers and impel them into the heart of the conflict." —*Booklist*

Busch, Robert
The Wolf Almanac: A Celebration of Wolves and Their World. Robert H. Busch; foreword by Rick Bass. The Lyons Press 2018. xiv, 303 pages : Color; Illustration; Map
ISBN 9781493033751
Grades: Adult   **599.773**
1. Wolves 2. Reference — General 3. Nature writing — Animal Studies
LC 2017057201

The Wolf Almanac is the most widely respected compendium on wolves. With hundreds of full-color photos, graphs, charts, maps, and more, The Wolf Almanac covers every aspect of the wolf kingdom, from the animal's evolution, to its anatomy, physiology, behavior, social dynamics, and interactions with other species. Important updates about wolf conservation and reintroductions are included, making The Wolf Almanac an indispensable addition to any naturalist's library.

Includes bibliographical references and index.

Lopez, Barry Holstun
★ *Of Wolves and Men.* Barry Lopez; with photographs by John Bauguess; including a new afterword by the author and expanded bibliography. Scribner Classics 2004. IX, 323 p. : Illustration
ISBN 9780743249362
Grades: 11 12 Adult   **599.773**
1. Wolves 2. Humans and wolves 3. Rare and endangered animals 4. Nature 5. Essays 6. Nature Writing — Animal Studies
LC 2004045429

A National Book Award finalist, originally published twenty-five years ago, examines the relationship between wolves and humans throughout history, drawing on a range of historical, mythological, and literary sources to discuss what wolves represent to people and present a case for their protection.

"The author infuses his natural history of the long relationship between wolves and humankind with both myth and science." —*Booklist*

Includes bibliographical references (p. 295-308) and index; Originally published: New York : Scribner, 1978.

McIntyre, Rick
The Reign of Wolf 21: The Saga of Yellowstone's Legendary Druid Pack. Rick McIntyre; foreword by Marc Bekoff. Greystone Books 2020. xvi, 256 p.
ISBN 9781771645249
Grades: Adult   599.773
1. Wolves 2. Wolf packs 3. Survival 4. Animal behavior 5. Courtship of animals 6. Competition 7. Cooperation 8. Natural selection 9. Predatory animals 10. Gray wolves 11. Wildlife 12. Rare and endangered mammals 13. National parks and reserves 14. Protectiveness 15. Yellowstone National Park 16. United States 17. Nature Writing — Animal Studies — Endangered Species 18. Science Writing — Biology

LC Bl2020069016

In the follow-up to The Rise of Wolf 8, Rick McIntyre profiles one of Yellowstone's most revered alpha males, Wolf 21. Leader of the Druid Peak Pack, Wolf 21 was known for his unwavering bravery, his unusual benevolence (unlike other alphas, he never killed defeated rival males), and his fierce commitment to his mate, the formidable Wolf 42. Wolf 21 and Wolf 42 were attracted to each other the moment they met, but Wolf 42's jealous sister interfered viciously in their relationship. After an explosive insurrection within the pack, the two wolves came together at last as leaders of the Druid Peak Pack, which dominated the park for more than 10 years. McIntyre recounts the pack's fascinating saga with compassion and a keen eye for detail, drawing on his many years of experience observing Yellowstone wolves in the wild.

"Like Thomas McNamee, David Mech, Barry Lopez, and other literary naturalists with an interest in wolf behavior, McIntyre writes with both elegance and flair, making complex biology and ethology a pleasure to read. Fans of wild wolves will eat this one up." —*Kirkus*

599.775 Vulpes

Brand, Adele
The Hidden World of the Fox. Adele Brand. William Morrow & Company 2019. 224 p.
ISBN 9780062966100
Grades: Adult   599.775
1. Foxes 2. Predatory animals 3. Animal adaptation 4. Effect of humans on nature 5. Human-animal relationships 6. Nature Writing — Animal Studies

LC Bl2019023587

A mammal ecologist's intimate portrait of the fox draws on scientific research in multiple countries to share insights into the species' evolution, its highly adaptable nature and the cultural history it has inspired. Adele Brand's observations have convinced her that the fox is arguably the most modern of all wildlife, uniquely suited to survival in the rapidly expanding urban/Wild interface.

599.78 Bears

Dickie, Gloria
Eight Bears: Mythic Past and Imperiled Future. Gloria Dickie. W W Norton & Company 2023. 336 p.
ISBN 9781324005087
Grades: Adult   599.78
1. Bears 2. Animals 3. Wildlife 4. Wildlife conservation 5. Nature 6. Climate change 7. Nature Writing — Animal Studies

"Journalist Dickie debuts with a superb study of the eight surviving species of bears...It's a winning combination of travel and environmental reporting." —*Publishers Weekly*

599.786 Polar bear

Williams, Kale
The Loneliest Polar Bear: A True Story of Survival and Peril on the Edge of a Warming World. Kale Williams. Crown 2021. 288 p.
ISBN 9781984826336
Grades: Adult   599.786
1. Polar bear 2. Polar bear cubs 3. Zoos 4. Rare and endangered animals 5. Climate change 6. Wildlife conservation 7. Human-animal relationships 8. Ohio 9. Nature Writing — Animal studies — Endangered species

LC 2020049765

The heartbreaking but hopeful story of abandoned polar bear cub, Nora, discussing the efforts of dedicated zookeepers, veterinarians and conservationists who are working to rescue the species from extinction.

"The story of a polar bear cub named Nora reveals the complex relationship among humans, animals, and the world we share." —*Kirkus*

Includes bibliographical references and index.

599.789 Giant panda

Croke, Vicki
The Lady and the Panda: The True Adventures of the First American Explorer to Bring Back China's Most Exotic Animal. Vicki Constantine Croke. Random House 2005. xix, 372 p. : Illustration
ISBN 9780375507830
Grades: 11 12 Adult   599.789
1. Harkness, Ruth 2. Women explorers 3. Women zoologists 4. Giant panda 5. Rare and endangered animals 6. China 7. 1930s 8. Biographies 9. Nature Writing — Animal Studies — Endangered Species 10. Life stories — People in history — Explorers 11. Adult books for young adults

LC 2004051356

Booklist Editors' Choice: Adult Books for Young Adults, 2005.

Recounts the adventures of Ruth Harkness, an American bohemian socialite, who, in 1936, ventured into one of the most dangerous, unexplored regions of the world on a quest to bring back the first live giant panda to reach the West.

"This well-written, exhaustively researched and documented book should be on every library's shelves." —*Library Journal*

Includes bibliographical references (p. [301]-361).

599.8 Primates

Goodall, Jane
★ *In the Shadow of Man.* Jane Goodall; photos. by Hugo van Lawick. Houghton Mifflin 1971. xx, 297 p. : Illustration
ISBN 9780395127261
Grades: 11 12 Adult   599.8
1. Chimpanzees 2. Social behavior in animals 3. Social behavior in chimpanzees 4. Primatologists 5. Animal behavior 6. Nature Writing — Animal Studies — Primates

LC 71162007

A personal account of the author's life among wild chimpanzees in Africa offers insight into animal behavior and draws parallels between chimpanzee and human relationships.

Includes bibliographical references (p. [287]-289).

599.88 Great apes and gibbons

Waal, F. B. M. de
Bonobo: The Forgotten Ape. Frans de Waal; photographs, Frans Lanting. University of California Press 1997. xv, 210 p. : Illustration; Color; Map
ISBN 9780520205352
Grades: 11 12 Adult   599.88

ESSENTIAL AND RECOMMENDED TITLES
599.884 Gorilla

1. Primatologists 2. Bonobos 3. Photographs 4. Animal behavior 5. Nature Writing — Animal Studies — Primates

LC 96041095

Booklist Editors' Choice, 1997.

Describes the habits and behavior of the bonobo, the ape believed to be biologically closest to humans, which has an egalitarian, female-dominant society based on broad sexual contact, and discusses the risks the animals face.

"The subject of this monograph is the bonobo, a species of ape. In six chapters, de Waal describes the history of the discovery of bonobos as a separate species; he compares them with common chimps; he describes their natural habitat and their . use of sex as social currency, particularly in moderating aggression; he examines bonobo social structure in relation to that of common chimps and humans; and he finishes with an exploration of bonobos' highly developed sense of empathy." —*The New Scientist*

Includes bibliographical references (p. 195-200) and index.

599.884 Gorilla

Fossey, Dian
★ *Gorillas* in the Mist. Dian Fossey. Houghton Mifflin 2000. xviii, 326 p; Illustration; Map
ISBN 9780618083602
Grades: 11 12 Adult   599.884
1. Fossey, Dian, 1932-1985 2. Gorillas 3. Animal behavior 4. Women and gorillas 5. Humans and gorillas 6. Wildlife conservation 7. Apes 8. Biology 9. Page to screen 10. Nature Writing — Animal Studies — Primates

LC 2001265471

Dian Fossey's classic account of four gorilla families—the basis for the major movie starring Sigourney Weaver.

"Whatever the mountain gorillas' future, their immediate past is here in Fossey's vibrant and invaluable study." —*Kirkus*

Includes bibliographical references (p. [287]-311).

599.885 Chimpanzees

Waal, F. B. M. de
★ *Mama's* Last Hug: Animal Emotions and What They Tell Us About Ourselves. Frans de Waal; with photographs and drawings by the author. W.W. Norton & Company 2019. 336 p.
ISBN 9780393635065
Grades: Adult   599.885
1. Emotions in animals 2. Empathy 3. Emotions 4. Animal behavior 5. Human behavior 6. Human nature 7. Compassion 8. Fairness 9. Human-animal relationships 10. Nature Writing — Animal Studies 11. Society and culture — Psychology and human behavior 12. Adult books for young adults

LC 2018047218

ALA Notable Book, 2020; Library Journal Best Books, 2019; New York Times Notable Book, 2019.

The influential primatologist draws on renowned primate studies in an exploration of animal emotions that touches on such subjects as expressions, animal sentience, and free will.

"Most of the author's observations involve the spontaneous behavior of chimpanzees, bonobos, and other primates, but readers will also be rewarded with tales of birds, dogs, horses, elephants, and rats. As he has shown in nearly all of his books, de Waal is a skilled storyteller, and his love for animals always shines through." —*Kirkus*

Includes bibliographical references and index.

599.9 Humans

Hagerty, Alexa
★ *Still* Life with Bones: Genocide, Forensics, and What Remains. Alexa Hagerty. Crown 2023. 288 p.
ISBN 9780593443132
Grades: Adult   599.9
1. Hagerty, Alexa 2. Anthropologists 3. Forensic anthropology 4. Dead 5. Mass burials 6. Identification 7. Bones 8. DNA 9. Genocide 10. War crimes 11. Political violence 12. Psychic trauma 13. Families of murder victims 14. Loss 15. Injustice 16. South American history 17. Guatemala 18. Argentina 19. Latin America 20. History writing — Regimes and political violence — Latin America 21. Society and culture — Violence and crime — Genocide 22. Life stories — Science, technology, and medicine — Scientists and inventors 23. True Crime — Forensic Sciences 24. Debut title

LC 2022039668

In the wake of genocidal violence in Latin American nations, families of the missing searched for the truth. Young scientists joined their fight against impunity. Gathering evidence in the face of intimidation and death threats, they pioneered the field of forensic exhumation for human rights. In Still Life with Bones, anthropologist Alexa Hagerty learns to see the dead body with a forensic eye. Working with forensic teams at mass grave sites and in labs, Hagerty discovers how bones bear witness to crimes against humanity and how exhumation can bring families meaning after unimaginable loss.

"Intense and emotional, this is a vital rumination on political violence." —*Publishers Weekly*

Includes bibliographical references.

Krause, Johannes
A Short History of Humanity: A New History of Old Europe. Johannes Krause with Thomas Trappe; translated from the German by Caroline Waight. Random House 2021. 288 p.
ISBN 9780593229422
Grades: Adult   599.9
1. Human population genetics 2. Human remains (Archaeology) 3. Human genetics 4. Prehistoric humans 5. Archaeology 6. Anthropology 7. Immigration and emigration 8. Antiquities 9. Europe 10. Translations — German to English 11. History writing — Archaeology 12. History writing — Arts and culture

LC 2020043748

A founding director of the Max Planck Institute and the editor-in-chief of Berlin's Tagesspiegel introduce the revolutionary science of archaeogenetics while explaining how new DNA sequencing technologies are revealing essential details about human evolution.

"Krause (archaeogenetics, Max Planck Inst.), who helped discover the ancient Denisova hominins in Russia, and journalist Trappe have written a splendid account of human origins, migrations, and pathogens from the perspective of recent DNA evidence.... Scientific yet accessible, this original book offers much insight to readers of European history." —*Library Journal*

Includes bibliographical references and index; Originally published in Germany by Propyläen Verlag in 2019; Translated from the German.

Meals, Roy A.
Bones: Inside and Out. Roy A. Meals, MD.. W. W. Norton & Company 2020. x, 294 p. Illustration
ISBN 9781324005322
Grades: Adult   599.9
1. Bones 2. Human anatomy 3. Culture 4. Skeleton 5. Human remains (Archaeology) 6. Civilization 7. Symbolism 8. Science Writing — Biology 9. History writing — Archaeology

LC 2020013491

A 500-million-year history of bone as a focus for understanding vertebrate life and human culture examines the biological makeup of bones, how medical innovations have enhanced human knowledge and what can be learned from bones even millions of years later.

"This appealing and kaleidoscopic narrative on bone topics, ranging from x-ray technology to the Paris catacombs, will appeal to readers interested in medicine and medical history, anthropology, archaeology, and material culture. Enjoyable and recommended." —*Library Journal*

Includes bibliographical references and index.

PUBLIC LIBRARY CORE COLLECTION: NONFICTION
Twentieth Edition

599.93 Genetics, sex and age characteristics, evolution

Bohme, Madelaine
Ancient Bones: Unearthing the Astonishing New Story of How We Became Human. Madelaine Bohme, Rudiger Braun, Florian Breier; foreword by David R. Begun; translated by Jane Billinghurst. Greystone books 2020. 337 p. : Illustration
ISBN 9781771647519
Grades: Adult 599.93
1. Human evolution 2. Evolution 3. Humans 4. Prehistoric humans 5. Scientific discoveries 6. Translations — German to English 7. Science Writing — Biology 8. History writing — Ancient

Ancient Bones takes readers behind the scenes of this incredible discovery, and invites readers to explore theories concerning early hominins to prehistoric humans, how climate and the environment were driving forces behind evolution, and how pivotal evolutionary steps'from our ability to communicate using complex speech to walking upright and using our hands to create'were necessary for humans to evolve and live on this planet.

"In this exciting investigation into the long and ancient path of humans, the authors explore the connections among evolution, climate, and environment.... An impressive introduction to the burgeoning recalibration of paleoanthropology." —*Kirkus*

Includes bibliographical references and index; Originally published in 2019 as Wie wir Menschen wurden by Wilhelm Heyne Verlag, Munich in the Random House GmbH publishing group; Translated from the German.

Desilva, Jeremy
First Steps: How Upright Walking Made Us Human. Jeremy Desilva. HarperCollins 2021. 320 p.
ISBN 9780062938497
Grades: Adult 599.93
1. Humans 2. Human evolution 3. Human physiology 4. Genetics 5. Civilization 6. History writing — General 7. Science writing — Biology

A Dartmouth anthropologist whose team discovered two ancient human species explores how our evolution toward bipedalism rendered us dominant, innovative, more compassionate and more susceptible to health problems.

"DeSilva provides a scholarly yet accessible conversation on the origins of human bipedalism. A great introduction to human origins, anthropology, and primatology for general audiences." —*Library Journal*

Finkel, Elizabeth
The Genome Generation. Elizabeth Finkel. Melbourne University Press 2012. xiv, 274 p. : Illustration
ISBN 9780522856477
Grades: Adult 599.93
1. Gene mapping 2. Human genetics 3. DNA research 4. Genetic engineering 5. Genetic code 6. Genetic research 7. Australian literature 8. Science Writing — Biology

"With consummate skill and a flair for storytelling, Finkel, an award-winning journalist and molecular biologist, uncoils the mystery of the genome and its ramifications." —*Choice*

Includes bibliographical references (p. 215-264) and index.

Leakey, Richard E.
The Origin of Humankind. Richard Leakey. BasicBooks 1994. xvi, 171 p. : Illustration; Map
ISBN 9780465031351
Grades: 11 12 Adult 599.93
1. Human evolution 2. Prehistoric humans 3. Evolution 4. Prehistoric era (Stone Age) 5. Science Writing — Biology 6. History writing — Ancient
LC 94003617

Discusses the evolution of the human species, relates the distinctions that set humans apart from apes, and explains how and why we developed social and cultural organizations.

"This is a worthwhile addition to many kinds of libraries: Public, general, science, biological, and psychological." —*Science Books & Films*

Includes bibliographical references (p. 159-164) and index.

Rutherford, Adam
Humanimal: How Homo Sapiens Became Nature's Most Paradoxical Creature—a New Evolutionary History. Adam Rutherford. The Experiment, LLC 2019. 256 pages
ISBN 9781615195312
Grades: Adult 599.93
1. Human evolution 2. Humans 3. Evolution 4. Animals 5. Science writing — Biology
LC Bl2019001361

The author of A Brief History of Everyone Who Ever Lived draws on current genetic research to explore the paradox of the human identity as a member of the animal kingdom that is distinct from all others.

"A smooth, expert, and often startling history that emphasizes that no behavior separates us from other animals, but we remain an utterly unique species." —*Kirkus*

Originally published in 2018 as the Book of Humans.

Tattersall, Ian
Masters of the Planet: Seeking the Origins of Human Singularity. Ian Tattersall. Palgrave Macmillan 2012. 272 p.
ISBN 9780230108752
Grades: 11 12 Adult 599.93
1. Prehistoric humans 2. Human evolution 3. Genetic psychology 4. Humans 5. Evolution 6. Homo erectus 7. Neanderthals 8. Science Writing — Biology
LC 2011034415

An award-winning Museum of Natural History curator and author traces the evolution of homo sapiens to demonstrate how they prevailed among other early humans because of their unique cognitive ability, in an account that also explains how their superior mental abilities were acquired.

Includes bibliographical references and index.

Vince, Gaia
Transcendence: How Humans Evolved Through Fire, Language, Beauty, and Time. Gaia Vince. Basic Books 2020. 320 p.
ISBN 9780465094905
Grades: Adult 599.93
1. Human evolution 2. Technology 3. Communication 4. Culture 5. Civilization 6. Sociocultural anthropology 7. Storytelling 8. Beauty 9. Effect of environment on humans 10. Technological innovations 11. Science writing — Biology
LC Bl2020004892

The author of Adventures in the Anthropocene traces the dramatic evolutionary changes that enabled intelligence in humans, explaining how our species established dominion through our growing understandings of four key elements.

Originally published: London : Allen Lane, 2019.

Wilson, Edward O.
★ *The Social Conquest of Earth.* Edward O. Wilson. Liveright Pub. Corporation 2012. 352 p.
ISBN 9780871404138
Grades: Adult 599.93
1. Social evolution 2. Human evolution 3. Evolution 4. Philosophy 5. Science Writing — Biology
LC 2011052680

Booklist Editors' Choice, 2012; New York Times Notable Book, 2012.

An acclaimed biologist and author of the Pulitzer Prize-winning the Ants discusses how morality, religion and the creative arts are biological in nature and defends his theory that the origin of the human condition is due to group, not family, selection. ".

"Wilson is a prolific and popular biological theorist, and this significant addition to his legacy of thought will be controversial, provocative, and influential." —*Library Journal*

Includes bibliographical references and index.

ESSENTIAL AND RECOMMENDED TITLES
600 Technology (Applied sciences)

Woolfson, Esther
Between Light and Storm: How We Live with Other Species. Esther Woolfson. Pegasus Books 2022. 368 p.
ISBN 9781639362769
Grades: Adult **599.93**
1. Nature 2. Animals 3. Animal rights 4. Effect of humans on nature 5. Climate change 6. Ethics 7. Human-animal relationships 8. Nature Writing — Animal studies 9. Nature Writing — Environmental issues

A landmark book about the fraught relationship between humans and animals that takes us from Genesis to climate change. Beginning with the very origins of life on Earth, Woolfson considers pre-historic human-animal interaction and traces the millennia-long evolution of conceptions of the soul and conscience in relation to the animal kingdom, and the consequences of our belief in human superiority. Woolfson examines some of the most complex ethical issues surrounding our treatment of animals and argues passionately and persuasively for a more humble, more humane, relationship with the creatures who share our world.

"This expansive book traces humanity's relationship with other species through scientific studies, philosophical, literary, religious, and historical writings, and personal anecdotes….It documents the history of our relationship with, in particular our mistreatment of, the animals around us as well as a philosophical argument towards a more humane world." —*Booklist*

Originally published in the UK by Granta, London, in 2020.

Yi, Sang-hui
Close Encounters with Humankind: A Paleoanthropologist Investigates Our Evolving Species. Sang-hee Lee with Shin-young Yoon. W. W. Norton & Company 2018. 304 p.
ISBN 9780393634822
Grades: Adult **599.93**
1. Forensic anthropology 2. Prehistoric humans 3. Human evolution 4. Paleontology 5. Science Writing — Biology 6. Science Writing — Paleontology

Explores how the field enables new insights into some of the world's leading evolutionary questions, drawing on cutting-edge findings to explore such topics as the life cycles of ancient people, the origins of social nature and the common traits between today's humans and Neanderthals.

"Lee, professor of anthropology at the University of California, Riverside, approaches an array of topics in the field of human evolution with candor, clarity, and brevity." —*Publishers Weekly*

Originally published in Korea by ScienceBooks Publishing Co, Ltd, Seoul, a division of Minumsa Publishing Group.

600 Technology (Applied sciences)

Doorley, Rachelle
Tinkerlab: A Hands-on Guide for Little Inventors. Rachelle Doorley. Roost Books 2014. xv, 219 pages : Color; Illustration
ISBN 9781611800654
Grades: Adult **600**
1. Creative activities and seat work 2. Inventions 3. Arts and Entertainment — Crafts and hobbies 4. Family and Relationships — General
LC 2013027910

Features creative experiments designed to encourage young children to use their natural curiosity to explore, test, play, and tinker.

"Young children will relish the projects provided here. From paper houses to marble runs to marker explosions, Doorley's designs have more of an engineering essence than those found in the standard arts and crafts book, and they will also take more preparation, but early educators, in particular, will delight in the volume's possibilities. For all budding inventors." —*Library Journal*

Includes bibliographical references (page 216).

Macaulay, David
The Way Things Work Now: From Levers to Lasers, Windmills to Wi-fi, a Visual Guide to the World of Machines. David Macaulay, with Neil Ardley. Houghton Mifflin Harcourt 2016. 400 p.
ISBN 9780544824386
Grades: 4 5 6 7 8 9 10 11 12 Adult **600**
1. Technology 2. Machinery 3. Mechanics 4. Science 5. Toy and movable books 6. Science — Technology
LC Bl2016040252

The sweeping new update to the worldwide bestseller, the New Way Things Work includes all new sections on the technology that most impacts our everyday lives.

"Macaulay's brilliantly designed, engagingly informal diagrams and cutaways bring within the grasp of even casual viewers a greater understanding of the technological wonders of both past and present." —*Kirkus*

Revised and updated — Cover; Originally published as the new way things work: Boston, MA : Houghton Mifflin, 1988.

604.82 Women — Technology

Marcal, Katrine
Mother of Invention: How Good Ideas Get Ignored in an Economy Built for Men. Katrine Marcal; translated by Alex Fleming. Abrams Press 2021. 304 p.
ISBN 9781419758041
Grades: Adult **604.82**
1. Technological innovations 2. Inventions 3. Sexism 4. Unconscious bias 5. Patriarchy 6. Male domination (Social structure) 7. Sexism in science 8. Sexism in business 9. Women inventors 10. Translations — Swedish to English 11. History writing — Women's history 12. Business and economics — Women and the workplace 13. Society and culture — Gender — Women 14. History writing — Technological innovations

Discusses how gender bias has affected innovation, technology, and history.

"Marcal draws on a range of primary and secondary sources for her interdisciplinary critique of literature, sociology, and anthropology, and calls on practitioners in those fields to work toward equality. A must-read." —*Library Journal*

Originally published: Stockholm : Mondial, 2020; Translated from the Swedish.

607 Education, research, related topics

Creighton, Margaret S.
The Electrifying Fall of Rainbow City: Spectacle and Assassination at the 1901 World's Fair. Margaret Creighton. W.W. Norton & Company 2016. 320 p.
ISBN 9780393247503
Grades: Adult **607**
1. McKinley, William, 1843-1901 2. Exhibitions 3. Scandals 4. Social values 5. Buffalo, New York 6. 1900s (Decade) 7. 20th century 8. History writing — Early 20th century — United States
LC 2016018256

Traces the events surrounding the 1901 Pan American Exposition in Buffalo, New York, describing how it was organized to bring millions into the region before the assassination of President William McKinley and a host of controversies reshaped the dawn of the century.

"An excellent and entertaining history for all readers." —*Library Journal*

Includes bibliographical references and index.

609 Technology — History, geographic treatment, biography

Agrawal, Roma
Nuts and Bolts: Seven Small Inventions That Changed the World in a Big Way. Roma Agrawal. W. W. Norton & Company, Inc. 2023. 336 p.
ISBN 9781324021520
Grades: Adult **609**
1. Engineering 2. Technology 3. Inventions 4. Technological innovations 5. Science Writing — General 6. History Writing — Technological Innovations

A structural engineer examines the seven most basic building blocks of engineering that have shaped the modern world.

"In this wide-ranging history, structural engineer Agrawal (Built) surveys how seven objects—the nail, wheel, spring, magnet, lens, string, and pump—transformed the world." —*Publishers Weekly*

Harford, Tim
50 Inventions That Shaped the Modern Economy. Tim Harford. Riverhead Books 2017. 321 pages
ISBN 9780735216136
Grades: Adult **609**
1. Inventions 2. Technological innovations 3. Economic history 4. Essays 5. History writing — Science, technology, and medicine 6. Business and economics — Economics — History

Describes the history of economic change through the 50 inventions that had the most impact and explores the hidden connections they share, from paper money and the horse collar, to bar codes and spreadsheets.

"And while the essays stand on their own, he has a broader point to make. 'Inventions shape our lives in unpredictable ways,' he writes, 'And while they're solving a problem for someone, they're often creating a problem for someone else.' Harford's contagious delight in his subject reminds readers not to take for granted the impact of objects and ideas so familiar they're easy to overlook." —*Kirkus*

Includes index.

610 Medicine and health

Hotz, Julia
★ *The Connection Cure: The Prescriptive Power of Movement, Nature, Art, Service, and Belonging.* Julia Hotz. Simon & Schuster 2024. 288 p.
ISBN 9781668030332
Grades: Adult **610**
1. Holistic medicine 2. Alternative medicine 3. Mind and body 4. Social interaction 5. Health 6. Environmental health 7. Society and culture — Illness and disease 8. Self-Help — Personal growth — Happiness 9. Science Writing — Medicine and health
LC 2024011197

Investigating "social prescriptions"—referrals to community activities and resources instead of solely pharmaceutical prescriptions, a solutions-focused journalist tours the world, meeting the doctors, nurses, therapists and social workers who have started to flip the script as well as the patients who have benefited from this life-changing and lasting "medicine."

"With interesting stories and a broad canvas, Hotz connects readers to a different way of thinking about health and wellness." —*Kirkus*

Luger, Chelsey
★ *The Seven Circles: Indigenous Teachings for Living Well.* Chelsey Luger and Thosh Collins. HarperOne, an imprint of HarperCollinsPublishers 2022. 248 pages : Color; Illustration
ISBN 9780063119208
Grades: Adult **610**
1. Indigenous peoples of North America 2. Philosophy, Indigenous 3. Health 4. Well-being 5. Self-care 6. North America 7. Self-Help — Personal growth — Happiness 8. Self-Help — Personal growth — Spirituality
LC 2022016120

Drawing from traditions spanning multiple tribes, the Native American founders of an Indigenous wellness initiative reclaim ancient wisdom for health and wellbeing, developing a holistic model called The Seven Circles, a holistic approach for modern living rooted in timeless teachings from their ancestors.

"Many self-help readers, especially fans of Eckhart Tolle's The Power of Now and James Clear's Atomic Habits, will likely want to implement Luger and Collins's guidance into their own lives." —*Library Journal*

Includes bibliographical references (pages 244-248).

Porter, Roy
The Greatest Benefit to Mankind: A Medical History of Humanity. Roy Porter. W. W. Norton 1998. xvi, 831 p. : Illustration
ISBN 9780393046342
Grades: Adult **610**
1. Medicine 2. Diseases 3. Social medicine 4. Treatment 5. Medical care 6. Science Writing — Medicine and health
LC 98010219

Los Angeles Times Book Prize for History, 1998; New York Times Notable Book, 1998; National Book Critics Circle Award for Nonfiction finalist, 1998.

Explores the development of medicine against the backdrop of the religious, scientific, philosophical, and political beliefs of each age, and unearths a treasure trove of medicinal oddities.

"Porter's study traces Western medical thought and practices from their origins in classical Greece to today's biomedical developments. Although scholarly, the text is elegantly written, accessible to the general reader, and filled with fascinating details." —*Library Journal*

British ed. published with subtitle: A medical history of humanity from antiquity to the present; Includes bibliographical references (p. 719-764) and index.

610.1 Medicine — Philosophy

Mukherjee, Siddhartha
The Laws of Medicine: Field Notes from an Uncertain Science. Siddhartha Mukherjee. Simon & Schuster 2015. 120 p.
ISBN 9781476784847
Grades: Adult **610.1**
1. Medical care 2. Physicians 3. Medicine 4. Science 5. Philosophy 6. Science Writing — Medicine and health
LC Bl2015034883

The Pulitzer Prize-winning author of the Emperor of All Maladies and one of the world's premiere cancer researchers reveals an urgent philosophy on the little-known principles that govern medicine and how understanding these principles can empower us all.

Rakel, David
The Compassionate Connection: The Healing Power of Empathy and Mindful Listening. David Rakel, MD, with Susan K. Golant, MA.. W.W. Norton & Company 2018. xiv, 280 p. : Illustration
ISBN 9780393247749
Grades: Adult **610.1**
1. Healing 2. Compassion 3. Interpersonal relations 4. Interpersonal communication 5. Mind and body 6. Self-Help — Relationships 7. Spirituality and Religion — Body, mind, and spirit 8. Family and Relationships — General
LC 2017056375

Draws on a range of disciplines to outline the concept of bio-psycho-spiritual authentic awareness and how to strengthen empathy bonds with others to promote healing and overall wellness.

Includes bibliographical references and index.

610.28 Auxiliary techniques and procedures; apparatus, equipment, materials

Allen, Marshall
★ *Never Pay the First Bill: And Other Ways to Fight the Health Care System and Win.* Marshall Allen. Portfolio 2021. 288 p.
ISBN 9780593190005
Grades: Adult **610.28**
1. Medical care 2. Medical errors 3. Patient advocacy 4. Personal finance 5. Health insurance 6. Politics and global affairs — Public health 7. Business and economics — Industries — Medical
LC 2021005233

Every year, millions of Americans are overcharged and underserved while the health care industry makes record profits. We know something is wrong, but the layers of bureaucracy designed to discourage complaints make pushing back seem impossible. At least, this is what the health care power players want you to

ESSENTIAL AND RECOMMENDED TITLES
610.69 Medical personnel and relationships

think. Never Pay the First Bill is the guerilla guide to health care the American people and employers need. Drawing on 15 years of investigating the health care industry, reporter Marshall Allen shows how companies and individuals have managed to force medical providers to play fair, and shows how you can, too. He reveals the industry's pressure points and how companies and individuals have fought overbilling, price gouging, insurance denials, and more to get the care they deserve.

Includes bibliographical references and index.

610.69 Medical personnel and relationships

Goldberg, Sana
How to Be a Patient: The Essential Guide to Navigating the World of Modern Medicine. Sana Goldberg, RN.. Harper Wave 2019. xxvi, 432 pages
ISBN 9780062797186
Grades: Adult   610.69
1. Communication in medicine 2. Physician and patient 3. Science writing — Medicine and health
LC 2018041369

A registered nurse and public health advocate provides a quick-reference guide for confronting the challenges of trying to navigate common medical situations, from making the most of routine appointments to understanding hospital culture.

From registered nurse and public health advocate Sana Goldberg, a timely, accessible, and comprehensive handbook to navigating common medical situations. From the routine to the unexpected, How to Be a Patient is your ultimate guide to better healthcare.Let's face it: Nobody likes going to the doctor. It can be uncomfortable, nerve wracking, expensive—and that's just for routine care! When it's an emergency—how do you choose between the ER, Urgent Care, or waiting-until-Monday? And for everything in between, how do you get an accurate diagnosis and timely treatment when something is off? In How to Be a Patient, registered nurse and outspoken public health advocate Sana Goldberg provides readers with an honest guide to the complicated and often-intimidating medical landscape. At once a quick-reference pocket guide and a lifelong framework for approaching your healthcare, this invaluable resource empowers readers to take charge of their wellbeing. It lifts the veil on a complicated, fractured system, giving patients the tools communicate with its players and sidestep its most vexing realities. Warm and trustworthy, Goldberg's advice is as expert as it is easy-to-understand, as she calls on years of first-hand nursing experience to help readers confront challenges, take advantage of opportunities, and maximize insurance resources while fending off hidden fees that slip by unnoticed. From setting yourself up when all is well and making the most of routine appointments, to understanding hospital culture for a more positive experience, How to Be a Patient is relevant for readers at any age.

"This essential resource, which can also double as ready reference, complements Karen A. Friedman and Sara L. Merwins the Informed Patient but can, and should, stand on its own." —*Library Journal*

Wilson, F. Perry
How Medicine Works and When It Doesn't: Learning Who to Trust to Get and Stay Healthy. F. Perry Wilson, MD MSCE.. Grand Central Publishing 2023. 320 p.
ISBN 9781538723609
Grades: Adult   610.69
1. Physician and patient 2. Medical care 3. Physicians 4. Medical research 5. Health 6. Patients 7. Trust 8. United States 9. Science Writing — Medicine and health — Doctors and nurses 10. Life stories — Science, technology, and medicine — Healthcare professionals
LC 2022037037

Blending personal anecdotes with hard science, an accomplished physician, researcher, and science communicator pulls back the curtain on medicine and medical research, revealing how progress is made—and how to rebuild trust between doctors and patients.

"The result is a trenchant, empowering look at how to fix doctor-patient relationships." —*Publishers Weekly*

Includes bibliographical references.

610.73 Nursing and services of allied health personnel

DiGregorio, Sarah
★ *Taking Care: The Story of Nursing and Its Power to Change Our World.* Sarah DiGregorio. Harper 2023. 368 p.
ISBN 9780063071285
Grades: Adult   610.73
1. Nursing 2. Nurses 3. History of medicine 4. Medical care 5. Sexism in medicine 6. Discrimination 7. Public health 8. Social values 9. Life stories — Science, technology, and medicine — Healthcare professionals 10. Science Writing — Medicine and health — Doctors and nurses 11. History writing — Science, technology, and medicine

Nurses have always been vital to human existence. A nurse was likely there when you were born and a nurse might well be there when you die. Yet despite being celebrated during the Covid-19 epidemic, nurses are often undermined and undervalued in ways that reflect misogyny and racism, and that extend to their working conditions—and affect the care available to everyone. In Taking Care, journalist Sarah DiGregorio chronicles the lives of nurses past and tells the stories of those today—caregivers at the vital intersection of health care and community who are actively changing the world, often invisibly.

"Striking an expert balance between the big picture and intimate portraits of individual caregivers, this is an enlightening study of a crucial yet often overlooked profession." —*Publishers Weekly*

Patterson, James
ER Nurses: True Stories from America's Greatest Unsung Heroes. James Patterson and Matt Eversmann, with Chris Mooney. Little, Brown & Company 2021. 304 p.
ISBN 9780759554269
Grades: Adult   610.73
1. Hospitals 2. Nurses 3. Nursing 4. Medical care 5. Medical emergencies 6. Medical personnel 7. Emergency medical services 8. Life stories — Science, technology, and medicine — Healthcare professionals 9. Life stories — Facing adversity — Medical issues 10. Science Writing — Medicine and health — Doctors and nurses

Around the clock, across the country, these highly skilled and compassionate men and women sacrifice and struggle for us and our families. You have never heard their true stories. Not like this. From big-city and small-town hospitals. From behind the scenes. From the heart. This book will make you laugh, make you cry, make you understand. When we're at our worst, E.R. nurses are at their best.

"Patterson and Eversmann present brief but meaningful first-person narratives that illustrate the true realities of nursing 'At the center of it all.'. . . These readable bite-sized snippets represent a significant caregiver demographic of women and men who exhibit the labor-intensive focus, compassion, dedication, and passion necessary to be an emergency nurse." —*Kirkus*

Smilios, Maria
★ *The Black Angels: The Untold Story of the Nurses Who Helped Cure Tuberculosis.* Maria Smilios. G. P. Putnam's Sons 2023. 448 p.
ISBN 9780593544921
Grades: Adult   610.73
1. African American nurses 2. Nurses 3. Hospitals 4. People with tuberculosis 5. African American women 6. Racism 7. Marginalized people 8. Racism in medical care 9. New York City 10. United States 11. 20th century 12. 1920s 13. Collective biographies 14. Life stories — Science, technology, and medicine — Healthcare professionals 15. Science Writing — Medicine and health — Doctors and nurses 16. History Writing — African American — United States 17. Nonfiction that reads like fiction
LC 2023028358

Tells true story of the Black nurses who helped cure a deadly tuberculosis plague in 1929 New York City.

"Informative, enthralling, and sometimes appalling, this is American history at its best." —*Booklist*

Includes bibliographical references and index.

PUBLIC LIBRARY CORE COLLECTION: NONFICTION
Twentieth Edition

610.92 Medicine — Biography

Blackstock, Uche
Legacy: A Black Physician Reckons with Racism in Medicine. Uche Blackstock. Viking Press 2023. 304 p.
ISBN 9780593491287
Grades: Adult   610.92
1. Blackstock, Uche 2. Racism in medical care 3. Physicians 4. Racism 5. Medical care 6. Autobiographies and memoirs 7. Life stories — Science, technology, and medicine — Healthcare professionals 8. Science Writing — Medicine and health — Doctors and nurses 9. Debut title

Part searing indictment of our healthcare system, part generational family memoir, part call to action, a physician and thought leader on bias and racism in healthcare recounts her journey to finally seizing her own power as a health equity advocate against the backdrop of the pandemic and the Black Lives Matter movement.

"A Black physician reflects on her career in medicine and the many inequities of American health care." —*Kirkus*

Brown, Jasmine
Twice as Hard: The Stories of Black Women Who Fought to Become Physicians, from the Civil War to the 21st Century. Jasmine Brown. Beacon Press 2023. 224 pages
ISBN 9780807025086
Grades: Adult   610.92
1. Crumpler, Rebecca Lee, 1835-1895 2. Chinn, May Edward, 1896-1980 3. Jones, Edith Irby, 1927-2019 4. Elders, Joycelyn, 1933- 5. African American women physicians 6. African American physicians 7. Women physicians 8. Persistence 9. Determination 10. United States history 11. 19th century 12. 20th century 13. Biographies 14. Life stories — Science, technology, and medicine — Healthcare professionals 15. Science Writing — Medicine and health — Doctors and nurses 16. Life stories — Facing adversity — Personal transformation 17. Debut title
LC 2022043511

Presents the long-erased stories of nine pioneering Black women physicians beginning in 1860, when a Black woman first entered medical school, including Dr. Rebecca Lee Crumpler, who provided medical care for newly freed slaves, to Dr. Joycelyn Elders, who became the first African American U.S. surgeon general. These women needed to work twice as hard and be twice as good, and their ultimate success serves as instruction and inspiration for new generations considering a career in medicine or science.

"In this well-researched reclamation of neglected yet invaluable history, Brown, a medical student at the University of Pennsylvania and a former Rhodes scholar, looks at nine trailblazing Black women who became physicians despite the odds." —*Booklist*

Includes bibliographical references and index.

Campbell, Olivia
Women in White Coats: How the First Women Doctors Changed the World of Medicine. Olivia Campbell. Park Row Books 2021. 352 p.
ISBN 9780778389392
Grades: Adult   610.92
1. Blackwell, Elizabeth, 1821-1910 2. Anderson, Elizabeth Garrett, 1836-1917 3. Jex-Blake, Sophia, 1840-1912 4. Women physicians 5. Medical care 6. Feminism 7. Women's rights 8. Women's movement 9. Women's health services 10. Patriarchy 11. Sexism in medicine 12. History of medicine 13. 19th century 14. Collective biographies 15. Life stories — Science, technology, and medicine — Healthcare professionals 16. History writing — Women's history 17. History writing — Science, technology, and medicine 18. Science Writing — Medicine and health — Doctors and nurses 19. Life stories — Identity — Gender

In the early 1800s, women were dying in large numbers from treatable diseases because they avoided receiving medical care. Motivated by personal loss and frustration over inadequate medical care, Elizabeth Blackwell, Elizabeth Garrett Anderson and Sophia Jex-Blake fought for a woman's place in the male-dominated medical field. For the first time ever, Women in White Coats tells the complete history of these three pioneering women who, despite countless obstacles, earned medical degrees and paved the way for other women to do the same. Though very different in personality and circumstance, together these women built women-run hospitals and teaching colleges—creating for the first time medical care for women by women.

"Journalist Campbell debuts with an inspirational group portrait of the first three women who became licensed doctors in the U.S. and the U.K. . . . This entertaining account adds a valuable chapter to the history of women and medicine." —*Publishers Weekly*

Deer, Brian
The Doctor Who Fooled the World: Science, Deception, and the War on Vaccines. Brian Deer. Johns Hopkins University Press 2020. 320 p.
ISBN 9781421438009
Grades: Adult   610.92
1. Wakefield, Andrew J. 2. Anti-vaccination movement 3. Deception 4. Propaganda 5. Former physicians 6. Communicable diseases 7. Health policy 8. Corruption 9. Conspiracies 10. Vaccination 11. Vaccines 12. Preventive medicine 13. Science Writing — Medicine and health — Medical breakthroughs 14. Science Writing — Medicine and health — Illness and disease
LC 2019033966

Andrew Wakefield, a former British doctor, has been a leading proponent of the discredited view that vaccines cause autism. The discrediting of Wakefield and the anti-vax position he propelled is due largely to the work of Brian Deer, an investigative reporter from the United Kingdom. In this book Deer tells the story of how Wakefield fabricated research results for his Lancet paper, failed to disclose financial conflicts of interest, manipulated researchers and parents, and lied to the public.

"This riveting history of Andrew Wakefield's career as an advocate for the discredited link between the measles vaccine and autism serves as a stirring demonstration of the process and power of investigative journalism. . . . Readers who love a good debunking will find Deer's narrative logical, exciting, and enraging." —*Publishers Weekly*

Includes index; Also published in Australia in 2020 by Scribe Publications.

Fauci, Anthony S.
Expect the Unexpected: Ten Lessons on Truth, Service, and the Way Forward. Anthony Fauci. National Geographic Society 2021. 80 p.
ISBN 9781426222450
Grades: Adult   610.92
1. Fauci, Anthony S, 1940- 2. Physicians 3. Public health 4. Diseases 5. Leadership 6. United States 7. Interviews 8. Autobiographies and memoirs 9. Life stories — Science, technology, and medicine — Healthcare professionals 10. Science Writing — Medicine and health — Doctors and nurses

The world-renowned infectious disease specialist looks back on his career helping to combat some of the most dangerous diseases to strike humankind such AIDS and Ebola, as well as his role as the face of White House Coronavirus Task Force.

"This glowing compilation of quotes and anecdotes drawn from published speeches and interviews with renowned infectious disease specialist Fauci (Harrison's Principles of Internal Medicine) offers bite-size morsels of wisdom and autobiographical tales from his decades-long career in public service. . . . Those craving more of Fauci's wisdom will love this charming work of self-help." —*Publishers Weekly*

Nimura, Janice P.
★ *The Doctors Blackwell: How Two Pioneering Sisters Brought Medicine to Women—and Women to Medicine.* Janice P. Nimura. W.W. Norton & Company 2021. 352 p.
ISBN 9780393635546
Grades: Adult   610.92
1. Blackwell, Elizabeth, 1821-1910 2. Blackwell, Emily, 1826-1910 3. Women physicians 4. Women 5. Sexism in medicine 6. Sisters 7. Women medical personnel 8. Women's health services 9. Medical care 10. United States 11. 19th century 12. Collective biographies 13. Life stories — Science, technology, and medicine — Healthcare professionals 14. History writing — Women's history 15. Science Writing — Medicine and health — Doctors and nurses

ESSENTIAL AND RECOMMENDED TITLES
611 Human anatomy, cytology, histology

16. History writing — Science, technology, and medicine 17. Nonfiction that reads like fiction

LC 2020023919

The vivid biography of two pioneering sisters who, together, became America's first female doctors and transformed New York's medical establishment by creating a hospital by and for women. Both sisters were tenacious and visionary; they were also judgmental, uncompromising, and occasionally misogynistic—their convictions as 19th-century women often contradicted their ambitions. From Bristol, England, to the new cities of antebellum America, this work of rich history follows the sister doctors as they transform the nineteenth century medical establishment and, in turn, our contemporary one.

"With the fiercely intelligent, prickly sisters at the center, Nimura's engrossing and enlightening group biography is highly recommended." —*Booklist*

Includes bibliographical references and index.

611 Human anatomy, cytology, histology

Newman, Magdalena
Normal: A Mother and Her Beautiful Son. Magdalena Newman; with Hilary Liftin. 2020. 256 pages
ISBN 9781328593122
Grades: Adult   611
1. Newman, Nathaniel 2. Newman, Magdalena 3. Mothers and sons 4. Medical genetics 5. Families 6. Family relationships 7. Washington (State) 8. Seattle, Washington 9. Autobiographies and memoirs 10. Life stories — Facing adversity — Medical issues 11. Life stories — Relationships — Parent and child

LC 2019023276

A moving memoir from the mother of a child with Treacher Collins Syndrome, with a foreword by R.J. Palacio, author of Wonder.

"Readers looking for an inspiring story about the power of the human spirit will find one here." —*Publishers Weekly*

Radke, Heather
Butts: A Backstory. Heather Radke. Avid Reader Press 2022. 224 p.
ISBN 9781982135485
Grades: Adult   611
1. Radke, Heather 2. Buttocks 3. Human body 4. Women 5. Science Writing — Biology 6. Society and culture — Pop culture 7. Society and culture — Gender — Women 8. History Writing — General

Whether we love them or hate them, think they're sexy, think they're strange, consider them too big, too small, or anywhere in between, humans have a complicated relationship with butts. It is a body part unique to humans, critical to our evolution and survival, and yet it has come to signify so much more: Sex, desire, comedy, shame. But why? In Butts: A Backstory, reporter, essayist, and RadioLab contributing editor Heather Radke is determined to find out.

"A fun, fascinating, and surprisingly empowering exploration of the history and cultural significance of the butt." —*Library Journal*

Roach, Mary
★ *Stiff: The Curious Lives of Human Cadavers.* Mary Roach. W.W. Norton & Co. 2003. 303 p. : Illustration
ISBN 9780393050936
Grades: 11 12 Adult   611
1. Human experimentation in medicine 2. Dead 3. Human dissection 4. Medical research 5. Forensic sciences 6. Forensic scientists 7. Forensic medicine 8. Cannibalism 9. Transplantation of organs, tissues, etc. 10. True Crime — Forensic Sciences 11. Science Writing — Biology 12. Adult books for young adults 13. Nonfiction that reads like fiction

LC 2002152908

Alex Award, 2004; Booklist Editors' Choice: Adult Books for Young Adults, 2003; Garden State Teen Book Award (New Jersey), Nonfiction, 2006; School Library Journal Best Books: Best Adult Books 4 Teens, 2003; YALSA Best Books for Young Adults, 2004.

A look inside the world of forensics examines the use of human cadavers in a wide range of endeavors, including research into new surgical procedures, space exploration, and a Tennessee human decay research facility.

"Roach writes in an insouciant style and displays her metier in tangents about bizarre incidents in pathological history. Death may have the last laugh, but, in the meantime, Roach finds merriment in the macabre." —*Booklist*

Includes bibliographical references (p.[295]-303).

Switek, Brian
Skeleton Keys: The Secret Life of Bone. Brian Switek. Riverhead Books 2019. 288 p.
ISBN 9780399184901
Grades: Adult   611
1. Skeleton 2. Human anatomy 3. Bones 4. Human remains (Archaeology) 5. Forensic anthropology 6. Evolution 7. Science Writing — Biology 8. Adult books for young adults

LC 2018037813

Presents a natural and cultural history of bone that explains how human skeletons evolved over 500 million years, what they do inside the body and how they record a person's history.

Includes bibliographical references and index.

612 Human physiology

Bryson, Bill
The Body: A Guide for Occupants. Bill Bryson. Doubleday 2019. 400 p.
ISBN 9780385539302
Grades: Adult   612
1. Human anatomy 2. Human physiology 3. Human body 4. Science Writing — Biology 5. Humor writing — Classic humorists

LC 2019012407

LibraryReads Favorites, 2019; Loan Stars Favourites, 2019.

The award-winning author presents an engaging head-to-toe tour of the human body that shares anecdotal insights into its functions, ability to heal and vulnerability to disease.

Includes bibliographical references and index.

Cassidy, Cody
And Then You're Dead: What Really Happens If You Get Swallowed by a Whale, Are Shot from a Cannon, or Go Barreling Over Niagara. Cody Cassidy and Paul Doherty, PhD.. Penguin Books 2017. xiii, 235 pages
ISBN 9780143108443
Grades: Adult   612
1. Human anatomy 2. Human physiology 3. Accidents 4. Science Writing — General 5. Science Writing — Medicine and health 6. Adult books for young adults

LC 2016040949

In a delightfully gruesome look at the actual science behind the most outlandish, cartoonish and impossible deaths imaginable, the senior staff scientist at the San Francisco Exploratorium Museum and a writer examine a vast array of fantastic scenarios, teaching readers about physics, astronomy, anatomy and more along the way.

"With bite-size morsels of astonishing science and the perfect combination of smart-alecky writing and black humor, this page-turner will surely debunk any misapprehension that science is dull." —*Booklist*

Includes bibliographical references.

612.044 Exercise and sports

Lieberman, Daniel
Exercised: Why Something We Never Evolved to Do Is Healthy and Rewarding. Daniel E. Lieberman. Pantheon Books 2021. xix, 440 p.
ISBN 9781524746988
Grades: Adult   612.044

1. Exercise 2. Physical fitness 3. Physical education and training 4. Health 5. Human evolution 6. Science Writing — Medicine and health 7. Society and culture — Illness and disease

LC 2020009066

A natural history of exercise by the Harvard University paleoanthropologist challenges popular myths about the evolution of physical activity while outlining anthropological approaches to exercising effectively in the modern world.

"His illuminating and frequently humorous work will delight fitness mavens and make those pesky workout sessions more rewarding for everyone else." —*Publishers Weekly*

Includes bibliographical references and index.

612.1 Specific functions, systems, organs

George, Rose
Nine Pints: A Journey Through the Money, Medicine, and Mysteries of Blood. Rose George. Metropolitan Books/ Henry Holt and Company 2018. 304 p.
ISBN 9781627796378
Grades: Adult   612.1
1. Blood 2. Phlebotomy 3. Blood donors 4. Science Writing — Biology

LC 2018013647

Library Journal Best Books, 2018.

A freelance journalist explores the science, traditions and myths surrounding blood, from ancient bloodletting practices to the development of mass blood donations during the Blitz and from researchers working on synthetic blood to the lucrative business of plasma transfusions.

"The author packs her book with the kinds of provocative, witty, and rigorously reported facts and stories sure to make readers view the integral fluid coursing through our veins in a whole new way. An intensive, humanistic examination of blood in all its dazzling forms and functions." —*Kirkus*

Includes bibliographical references and index.

Jauhar, Sandeep
Heart: A History. Sandeep Jauhar. Farrar Straus & Giroux 2018. 272 p.
ISBN 9780374168650
Grades: Adult   612.1
1. Jauhar, Sandeep, 1968- 2. Heart 3. Cardiology 4. History of medicine 5. Surgery 6. Autobiographies and memoirs 7. Life stories — Science, technology, and medicine — Healthcare professionals 8. History writing — Science, technology, and medicine 9. Adult books for young adults 10. Book club best bets

LC 2017055262

The leading cardiologist and author of Doctored and Intern examines the recent dismantling of historical taboos and the development of transformative heart procedures that have changed how we live and what we understand about illness.

Schutt, Bill
Pump: A Natural History of the Heart. Bill Schutt; illustrated by Patricia J. Wynne. Algonquin Books of Chapel Hill 2021. 240 p; Illustration
ISBN 9781616208936
Grades: Adult   612.1
1. Heart 2. Anatomy 3. Biology 4. Science Writing — Biology 5. History writing — Science, technology and medicine

LC 2021019011

Zoologist Bill Schutt delivers a look at hearts from across the animal kingdom, from insects to whales to humans.

"Zoologist Schutt (American Museum of Natural History; author of the best-selling Cannibalism: A Perfectly Natural History) turns his wry lens on the heart and circulatory system in this entertaining read. . . . An engaging, often droll look at the engine of life and the long history of efforts to understand it." —*Library Journal*

Includes bibliographical references.

612.3 Digestive system

Albright, Mary Beth
★ *Eat & Flourish: How Food Supports Emotional Well-being.* Mary Beth Albright. Countryman Press, a division of W. W. Norton & Company, Independent Publishers Since 1923 2023. 256 p.
ISBN 9781682686904
Grades: Adult   612.3
1. Nutrition 2. Food 3. Well-being 4. Mental health 5. Food habits 6. Food Writing — General 7. Science Writing — Medicine and health — Mental health

LC 2022028999

A lively and evidence-based argument that a whole food diet is essential for good mental health. Food has power to nourish your mind, supporting emotional wellness through both nutrients and pleasure. In this groundbreaking book, journalist Mary Beth Albright draws on cutting-edge research to explain the food/Mood connection. She redefines "emotional eating" based on the science, revealing how eating triggers biological responses that affect humans' emotional states both immediately and long-term.

"Albright, who writes about food for the Washington Post, debuts with a fun and illuminating look at how food affects mental health….The result is a first-rate program for eating better." —*Publishers Weekly*

Includes bibliographical references and index.

Collen, Alanna
10% Human: How Your Body's Microbes Hold the Key to Health and Happiness. Alanna Collen. HarperCollins 2015. 320 p.
ISBN 9780062345981
Grades: Adult   612.3
1. Health 2. Microorganisms 3. Bacteria 4. Microbiology 5. Human body 6. Science writing — Biology

LC 2015004721

An argument for the importance of gut bacteria in the human body and how this affects our health and well-being.

"Collen never claims that she has uncovered the answers to modern health woes, but she points out the markers that may one day lead to such answers. Everything you wanted to know about microbes but were afraid to ask." —*Kirkus*

Nelson, Bryn
Flush: The Remarkable Science of an Unlikely Treasure. Bryn Nelson, PhD.. Grand Central Publishing 2022. 352 p.
ISBN 9781538720028
Grades: Adult   612.3
1. Feces 2. Microbiology 3. Recycling (Waste, etc.) 4. Sustainability 5. Problem solving 6. Science Writing — Biology 7. Science Writing — Chemistry

LC 2022019468

An award-winning science writer examines the untapped potential of human feces as a source of potent medicine, sustainable power and natural fertilizer to restore the world's depleted lands.

"Nelson, an award-winning science writer with a background in microbiology, believes that human excrement is a valuable resource, and he examines the subject from many different perspectives….An authoritative, informative, and entertaining book that will change the thinking about what comes out of our bodies." —*Kirkus*

Includes bibliographical references and index.

Price, Catherine
Vitamania: Our Obsessive Quest for Nutritional Perfection. Catherine Price. Penguin Press 2015. xv, 318 pages
ISBN 9781594205040
Grades: Adult   612.3
1. Vitamins 2. Vitamins in human nutrition 3. Food supplements 4. Nutritionally induced diseases 5. Nutrition 6. Food 7. Science Writing — Medicine and health

LC 2014036657

ESSENTIAL AND RECOMMENDED TITLES
612.6 Reproduction, development, maturation

Delves into the big business of synthetic vitamins and dietary supplements and uncovers the truths about the long-held nutritional myths the industry has been championing for the past century.

"Prices sharp wit, skillful and vivid translation of science into story, and valiant inquisitiveness (she insists on tasting synthetic vitamins and gets buzzed on the militarys caffeinated meat sticks) make for an electrifying dissection of our vitamin habit in contrast to our irrevocable need for naturally nutrient-rich food." —*Booklist*

Includes bibliographical references and index.

Roach, Mary
Gulp: Adventures on the Alimentary Canal. Mary Roach. W.W. Norton & Company 2013. 336 p.
ISBN 9780393081572
Grades: 10 11 12 Adult 612.3
1. Digestion 2. Food habits 3. Gastrointestinal system 4. Digestive organs 5. Science Writing — Biology 6. Food writing — Investigations
LC 2012050391

Booklist Editors' Choice, 2013.

The humor scientist behind Stiff: The Curious Lives of Human Cadavers and Spook: Science Tackles the Afterlife takes a tour of the human digestive system, explaining why the stomach doesn't digest itself and whether constipation can kill you.

Includes bibliographical references.

612.6 Reproduction, development, maturation

Attia, Peter
★ *Outlive: The Science & Art of Longevity*. Peter Attia, MD, with Bill Gifford. Harmony 2023. 482 pages : Illustration
ISBN 9780593236598
Grades: Adult 612.6
1. Longevity 2. Aging 3. Nutrition 4. Exercise 5. Science Writing — Medicine and health — Aging and longevity 6. Self-Help — Personal growth — Aging
LC Bl2023011132

Drawing on the latest science and challenging mainstream medicine, a visionary physician and leading longevity expert presents a well-founded strategic and tactical approach to extending lifespan while also improving our physical, cognitive and emotional health.

"This stands a notch above other fare aimed at boosting health and longevity." —*Publishers Weekly*

Rethinking medicine to live better longer—Dust jacket; Includes bibliographical references (pages 431-470) and index.

Day, John D.
The Longevity Plan: Seven Life-Transforming Lessons from Ancient China. Dr. John D. Day and Jane Ann Day with Matthew LaPlante. Harper, an imprint of HarperCollinsPublishers 2017. 288 p.
ISBN 9780062319814
Grades: Adult 612.6
1. Day, John D, Dr 2. Longevity 3. Aging 4. Centenarians 5. Personal conduct 6. Social life and customs 7. China 8. Autobiographies and memoirs 9. Life stories — Personal growth 10. Family and relationships — Aging and death
LC Bl2017027411

A doctor shares his story and findings about the time he spent in Longevity Village, a mountainous region in China where most people live past 100 in very good health, and reveals the seven principles that work together to create health, happiness and longevity.

"Practical, applicable health guidance validated by a remarkable collective of revered Chinese elders." —*Kirkus*

Includes bibliographical references and index.

Diamant, Anita
★ *Period. End of Sentence: A New Chapter in the Fight for Menstrual Justice*. Anita Diamant; with a foreword by Melissa Berton, founder of the Pad Project. Scribner 2021. 208 p.
ISBN 9781982144289
Grades: Adult 612.6
1. Menstruation 2. Women 3. Girls 4. Social justice 5. Social advocates 6. Physiology 7. Essays 8. Society and culture — Gender — Women

Rise: A Feminist Book Project List, 2022.

Illuminates the many ways that menstrual injustice can limit opportunities, erode self-esteem, and even threaten lives. This powerful examination of the far-ranging and quickly evolving movement for menstrual justice introduces today's leaders and shows us how we can be part of the change.

"A life-improving title that should be made as widely available as possible." —*Booklist*

Includes bibliographical references and index.

Dolnick, Edward
Seeds of Life: From Aristotle to Da Vinci, from Shark's Teeth to Frog's Pants, the Long and Strange Quest to Discover Where Babies Come from. Edward Dolnick. Basic Books 2017. 272 pages
ISBN 9780465082957
Grades: Adult 612.6
1. Human reproduction 2. Conception 3. Scientific discoveries 4. Scientists 5. Experiments 6. Human anatomy 7. Religion and science 8. Science 9. 17th century 10. 18th century 11. 19th century 12. History writing — Science, technology, and medicine 13. Science Writing — Biology 14. Science Writing — Medicine and health
LC 2016054195

Kirkus Prize for Nonfiction finalist, 2017.

An upbeat history of the early scientists who engaged in genius or quack experiments in their effort to explain human conception profiles the remarkable theories that reflected period innovation, religious beliefs and personal biases.

"The best sort of science history, explaining not only how great men made great discoveries, but why equally great men, trapped by prejudices and what seemed to be plain common sense, missed what was in front of their noses." —*Kirkus*

Includes bibliographical references and index.

Eliot, Lise
Pink Brain, Blue Brain: How Small Differences Grow into Troublesome Gaps—and What We Can Do About It. Lise Eliot. Houghton Mifflin Harcourt 2009. 432 p.
ISBN 9780618393114
Grades: Adult 612.6
1. Gender gap 2. Developmental neurobiology 3. Sex differences 4. Stereotypes 5. Brain 6. Child development 7. Biological growth 8. Society and culture — Gender
LC 2009014746

A neuroscientist shatters the myths about gender differences, arguing that the brains of boys and girls are largely shaped by how they spend their time, in a book where she offers parents and teachers concrete ways to avoid reinforcing harmful stereotypes.

"This is an important book and highly recommended for parents, teachers, and anyone who works with children." —*Library Journal*

Includes bibliographical references and index.

Emera, Deena
A Brief History of the Female Body: An Evolutionary Look at How and Why the Female Form Came to Be. Deena Emera. Sourcebooks 2023. 320 p.
ISBN 9781728249407
Grades: Adult 612.6
1. Women 2. Human physiology 3. Human evolution 4. Sex differences 5. Debut title 6. Science Writing — Biology 7. Society and culture — Gender — Women 8. Science Writing — Medicine and health
LC 2022055161

PUBLIC LIBRARY CORE COLLECTION: NONFICTION
Twentieth Edition

Offers a deep dive into the complexities of the female body through its evolution over millions of years.

"Biologist Emera's enlightening debut traces the evolutionary history of women's bodies." —*Publishers Weekly*

Includes bibliographical references.

Enright, Lynn

Vagina: A Re-Education. Lynn Enright. Allen & Unwin 2019. 229 pages : Illustration

ISBN 9781911630012

Grades: Adult   612.6

1. Vagina 2. Women 3. Human anatomy 4. Human physiology 5. Identity 6. Physiology 7. Anatomy 8. Health 9. Society and culture — Gender — Women 10. History writing — Women's history

This indispensable book sifts through myths and misinformation with the aim of empowering women with vital knowledge about their own bodies.

"A necessary resource on an often-stigmatized subject, this book will appeal to anyone looking to learn more about the vagina and women's health." —*Library Journal*

Includes bibliographical references.

Esty, Katharaine C.

Eightysomethings: A Practical Guide to Letting Go, Aging Well, and Finding Unexpected Happiness. Katharine Esty, PhD.. Skyhorse Publishing 2019. VIII, 231 pages : Illustration

ISBN 9781510743120

Grades: Adult   612.6

1. Aging 2. Quality of life 3. Seniors 4. Octogenarians 5. Family and Relationships — Aging and Death 6. Society and culture — Psychology and human behavior

LC Bl2019027387

This invaluable guide will help the historical number of eightysomethings live fulfilled, happy lives long into their twilight years. Personal stories illustrate how real people in their eighties are living and how they make sense of their lives.

Includes bibliographical references.

Gunter, Jen

★ *Blood: The Science, Medicine, and Mythology of Menstruation.* Dr. Jen Gunter. Citadel Press 2024. 320 p.

ISBN 9780806540689

Grades: Adult   612.6

1. Menstruation 2. Female reproductive system 3. Women's health services 4. Human reproduction 5. Human physiology 6. Sexism in medicine 7. Science Writing — Medicine and health 8. Society and culture — Gender — Women 9. Society and culture — Sex and sexuality

Most people who menstruate can expect to have hundreds of periods in a lifetime. So why is real information so hard to find? Despite its significance, most education about menstruation focuses either on increasing the chances of pregnancy or preventing it. And while both are important for many people, those who menstruate deserve to know more about their bodies than just what happens in service to reproduction. At a time when charlatans, politicians, and social media are succeeding in propagating damaging misinformation with real and devastating consequences, Dr. Jen provides the antidote with science, myth busting, and no-nonsense facts.

"Requisite reading. A no-nonsense, educational, science-backed, in-depth title about menstruation and the impact it can have on one's body. This title will empower readers to better understand their bodies and to advocate for themselves in medical situations." —*Library Journal*

The Vagina Bible: The Vulva and the Vagina - Separating the Myth from the Medicine. Jen Gunter. Citadel Press 2019. 432 pages

ISBN 9780806539317

Grades: Adult   612.6

1. Vagina 2. Women 3. Female reproductive system 4. Gynecology 5. Sexual health 6. Anatomy 7. Science Writing — Medicine and health 8. Society and culture — Gender — Women

LC Bl2019026835

Dr. Jen Gunter now delivers the definitive book on vaginal health, answering the questions you've always had but were afraid to ask—or couldn't find the right answers to. She has been called Twitter's resident gynecologist, the Internet's OB/GYN, and one of the fiercest advocates for women's health—and she's here to give you the straight talk on the topics she knows best.

Includes bibliographical references.

Hazard, Leah

Womb: The Inside Story of Where We All Began. Leah Hazard. Ecco Press 2023. 304 p.

ISBN 9780063157620

Grades: Adult   612.6

1. Human body 2. Organs (Anatomy) 3. Female reproductive system 4. History Writing — Microhistory 5. Science writing — Biology

A groundbreaking, triumphant investigation of the uterus—from birth to death, in sickness and in health, throughout history and into our possible future—from a midwife and acclaimed writer.

"Hazard (Hard Pushed: A Midwife's Story), a practicing National Health Service (NHS) midwife, fearlessly tackles the myths, history, and science of the uterus in this new book....A revelatory, straightforward, and important work." —*Library Journal*

Mansberg, Ginni

The M Word: How to Thrive in Menopause. Ginni Mansberg. Murdoch Books 2020. 314 pages

ISBN 9781911632382

Grades: Adult   612.6

1. Menopause 2. Women 3. Health 4. Science Writing — Medicine and health — Women's health — Menopause 5. Science Writing — Medicine and health — Women's health

"Perimenopausal and menopausal women, as well as health-care professionals, will appreciate the wealth of evidence, advice, and topics covered in Mansberg's candid guide." —*Publishers Weekly*

Includes bibliographical references and index.

Mendelson, Zoe

Pussypedia: A Comprehensive Guide. Words by Zoe Mendelson; art by Maria Conejo. Hachette Go, an imprint of Hachette Books 2021. xxxviii, 387 pages : Illustration; Color

ISBN 9780306924286

Grades: Adult   612.6

1. Vagina 2. Sexual health 3. Female reproductive system 4. Women 5. Health 6. Reference — Health 7. Self-Help — Personal growth — Sex 8. Society and culture — Gender — Women

LC Bl2021018413

Through over 30 chapters, Pussypedia not only gives the reader information, but teaches them how to read science, how to consider information in its context, and how to accept what we don't know rather than search for conclusions. It also weaves in personal anecdotes from the authors and their friends—sometimes funny, sometimes sad, often cringe-worthy, and always extremely personal—to do away with shame and encourage curiosity, exploration, and agency."

"Women looking to ditch the shame will find this smart, inclusive, and practical guide the perfect resource." —*Publishers Weekly*

Includes bibliographical references (pages 329-367) and index.

Nilsson, Lennart

A Child Is Born. [photography], Lennart Nilsson; text, Lars Hamberger; translated from the Swedish by Linda Schenck. Delacorte Press 2020. 219 p. : Color illustration

ISBN 9780593157961

Grades: Adult   612.6

1. Pregnancy 2. Childbirth 3. Science writing — Medicine and health — Women's health — Pregnancy and childbirth

LC 2003043854

ESSENTIAL AND RECOMMENDED TITLES
612.7 Musculoskeletal system, integument

A new edition of the classic work on the miracle of human reproduction contains historic new photos of life before birth, accompanied by a detailed account of every stage of development and advice for expectant parents.

Merloyd Lawrence book; Includes index.

Roach, Mary
Bonk: The Curious Coupling of Science and Sex. Mary Roach. Norton 2008. 288 p.
ISBN 9780393064643
Grades: Adult   612.6
1. Sex (Biology) 2. Sexuality 3. Sex customs 4. Sexual excitement 5. Orgasm 6. Orgasm, Female 7. Science Writing — Biology
LC 2007051990
Booklist Editors' Choice, 2008.

Roach shows how and why sexual arousal and orgasm can be so hard to achieve and what science is doing to make the bedroom a more satisfying place.

"Tucked between the jokes and anecdotes, you will find lessons on impotence, orgasm, unusual and unusually brave scientists, and the sexual behaviour of other species, including a hilarious description of porcupine sex."—*The New Scientist*

Includes bibliographical references.

Walters, Jacqueline
The Queen V: Everything You Need to Know About Intimacy, Sex, and Down There Healthcare. Dr. Jackie Walters. Andy Cohen Books, Henry Holt and Company 2020. xxxiv, 265 pages : Illustration
ISBN 9781250209177
Grades: Adult   612.6
1. Sexual health 2. Vagina 3. Women 4. Human body 5. Science writing — Medicine and health — Women's health — Menopause 6. Science writing — Medicine and health — Women's health — Pregnancy and childbirth 7. Science writing — Medicine and health — Women's health
LC 2019038046

The celebrity OB-GYN and star of Married to Medicine outlines 12 principles for caring for the female reproductive system, sharing straightforward advice on taboo subjects ranging from libido and contraception to fertility and labiaplasty.

In The Queen V, the beloved OB-GYN, celebrity doctor, and star of Bravo's Married to Medicine reveals the twelve principles behind a happy and healthy vagina...and other lady parts. After twenty years of private obstetrics and gynecological practice, there's nothing Dr. Jackie Walters hasn't seen. And now, in her new book, the widely-adored OB-GYN invites you to put your feet in the stirrups and investigate. Whether she's covering libido, contraceptives, labiaplasty, or fertility, Dr. Jackie educates readers with her characteristic grace and pragmatism. Both funny and informative, she brings you on a quest through the female reproductive system—answering all the burning (and itching, and smelling...) questions you've always been afraid to ask. Dr. Jackie knows that every woman is different, and she's designed a reading experience that's tailor-made for each individual. After taking a fun quiz to uncover your own vaginal personality (V.P.), you'll embark upon an eye-opening journey of self-discovery. Are you a Mary Jane, a Sanctified Snatch, or a Notorious V.A.G.? What's the shape of your vaginal flower-rosebud, tulip, or carnation? Dr. Jackie reveals the answer and doles out advice so personal you'll feel like you're in the office talking to her. For every time you've been draped in a paper gown and too embarrassed to ask that question, Dr. Jackie has you covered. Her book is a woman's guide to self-awareness that will educate, entertain, and empower others to achieve vaginal liberation. It's a must-read for anyone who owns (or loves) a vagina.

Includes bibliographical references (pages 237-251) and index.

612.7 Musculoskeletal system, integument

Everts, Sarah
The Joy of Sweat: The Strange Science of Perspiration. Sarah Everts. W.W. Norton & Company 2021. 304 p.
ISBN 9780393635676
Grades: Adult   612.7
1. Sweat 2. Body fluids 3. Body odor 4. Human body 5. Human physiology 6. Science Writing — Biology
LC 2020053349

A taboo-busting romp through the shame, stink, and strange science of sweating. Sweating may be one of our weirdest biological functions, but it's also one of our most vital and least understood.

"Everts, a professor of journalism at Carleton University, argues in her fascinating debut that 'sweat may be sticky, stinky, and gross,' but it's one of humans' most crucial and least understood bodily functions. . . . Packed full of information and unexpected tidbits, this is hard to put down."—*Publishers Weekly*

Includes bibliographical references and index.

Lyman, Monty
The Remarkable Life of the Skin: An Intimate Journey Across Our Surface. Monty Lyman. Atlantic Monthly Press 2020. xvii, 283 pages : Illustration
ISBN 9780802129406
Grades: Adult   612.7
1. Skin 2. Human body 3. Body covering (Anatomy) 4. Human skin color 5. Skin care 6. Skin diseases 7. Physiology 8. Science Writing — Biology
LC 2020026004

An engaging exploration of the human body's skin and its multifaceted physical, psychological and social relevance explains how our skin provides a habitat to a complex world of microorganisms and physical functions that are vital to health and survival.

"At first blush dermatology may not seem the most enticing subject, but this brilliant synthesis will be an engrossing read for anyone interested in human health and biology."—*Library Journal*

Includes bibliographical references and index; Originally published: London : Bantam Press, 2019.

Meals, Roy A.
Muscle: The Gripping Story of Strength and Movement. Roy A. Meals, M.D.. W.W. Norton & Company 2023. 304 p.
ISBN 9781324021445
Grades: Adult   612.7
1. Muscles 2. Musculoskeletal system 3. Muscle strength 4. Exercise 5. Human anatomy 6. Human physiology 7. History of medicine 8. Science Writing — Biology 9. Science Writing — Medicine and health

Muscle tissue powers every heartbeat, blink, jog, jump, and goosebump. It is the force behind the most critical bodily functions, including digestion and childbirth, as well as extreme feats of athleticism. In this lively, lucid book, orthopedic surgeon Roy A. Meals takes us on a wide-ranging journey through anatomy, biology, history, and health to unlock the mysteries of our muscles. Brimming with fun facts and infectious enthusiasm, Muscle sheds light on the astonishing, essential tissue that moves us through life.

"Meals (Bones), a professor of orthopedic surgery at UCLA, delivers a thorough overview of muscles and how they operate....The result is a strong primer on an essential part of the human body."—*Publishers Weekly*

612.8 Nervous system

Benjamin, A. K.
Let Me Not Be Mad: My Story of Unravelling Minds. A. K. Benjamin. Dutton 2019. IX, 291 pages
ISBN 9781524744380
Grades: Adult   612.8
1. Benjamin, A. K. 2. Psychiatric hospitals 3. Psychiatric hospital patients 4. Psychologist and patient 5. Neuropsychology 6. Psychologists 7. Mental illness 8. Mental health 9. London, England 10. Autobiographies and memoirs 11. Science Writing — Medicine and health — Mental health 12. Life stories — Science, technology, and medicine — Healthcare professionals
LC 2018050850

Inspired by the author's years spent working as a clinical neuropsychologist at a London hospital, a multilayered personal account reveals the impact of his relationships with mentally disordered patients on his own perceptions of reality, sanity and healthcare.

"A well-conceived and -written exploration of the traps hidden in the art of mental healing." —Kirkus

Includes bibliographical references (page 289).

Burnett, Dean

Idiot Brain: What Your Head Is Really up To. Dean Burnett. W.W. Norton & Company 2016. 336 p.

ISBN 9780393253788

Grades: Adult   612.8

1. Consciousness 2. Brain 3. Neuroscience 4. Memory 5. Science Writing — Biology

LC 2016009451

A delightful tour of our mysterious, mischievous gray matter from neuroscientist and massively popular Guardian blogger Dean Burnett.

"Burnett manages to both entertain and inform in engaging ways that would benefit the performance of the most humorless pedant." —Kirkus

Includes bibliographical references and index.

Eagleman, David

The Brain: The Story of You. David Eagleman. Pantheon Books 2015. 256 p.

ISBN 9781101870532

Grades: Adult   612.8

1. Brain 2. Neuroscience 3. Medical research 4. Humans 5. Media tie-ins 6. Science Writing — Biology

LC 2015023281

The best-selling author of Incognito examines how the human brain creates the multisensory experiences that culminate in human reality, examining the brain's role in everything from developmental disorders to extreme sports while speculating on the provocative potential of scanning a brain into a computer, in a companion to the PBS series.

"This is a straightforward, stimulating companion book to the PBS series on the subject." —Publishers Weekly

Livewired: The Inside Story of the Ever-changing Brain. David Eagleman. Pantheon Books 2020. 320 p.

ISBN 9780307907493

Grades: Adult   612.8

1. Brain 2. Neuroplasticity 3. Adaptation 4. Learning 5. Biological growth 6. Neurobiology 7. Science Writing — Biology

LC 2020000081

The magic of the brain is not found in the parts it's made of but in the way those parts unceasingly reweave themselves in an electric living fabric. With his hallmark clarity and enthusiasm, David Eagleman reveals the myriad ways that the brain absorbs experience: Developing, redeploying, organizing, and arranging the data it receives from the body's own absorption of external stimuli, which enables us to gain the skills, the facilities, and the practices that make us who we are.

"Neuroscientist Eagleman (The Brain) delivers an intellectually exhilarating look at neuroplasticity. . . . Eagleman's skill as teacher, bold vision, and command of current research will make this superb work a curious reader's delight." —Publishers Weekly

Includes bibliographical references and index.

Holmes, Bob

Flavor: The Science of Our Most Neglected Sense. Bob Holmes. W.W. Norton & Company 2017. 320 p.

ISBN 9780393244427

Grades: Adult   612.8

1. Taste 2. Taste buds 3. Flavor 4. Senses and sensation 5. Science Writing — Biology

LC 2016046897

A journey into the surprising science of the sense of flavor by a veteran New Scientist correspondent outlines narrative principles in neurobiology and modern food production to reveal the broad range of factors that can affect one's appreciation of what we consume.

Independent Publishers Since 1923; Includes bibliographical references and index.

McGee, Harold

★ *Nose Dive: A Field Guide to the World's Smells.* Harold McGee. Penguin Press 2020. 654 p.

ISBN 9781594203954

Grades: Adult   612.8

1. Odors 2. Smell 3. Food writing — General 4. Science Writing — Biology

LC 2020003220

The James Beard Award-winning author presents a sensory tour of the universe's smells from the ambrosial to the malodorous that reveals the science behind scent and how humans perceive it in nature, products and food.

"Perfect for foodies, those interested in science, and the innately curious. Engagingly written, this would be a wonderful ready reference to have on hand." —Library Journal

Includes bibliographical references and index.

Nakazawa, Donna Jackson

The Angel and the Assassin: The Tiny Brain Cell That Changed the Course of Medicine. Donna Jackson Nakazawa. Random House Inc 2020. 320 pages

ISBN 9781524799175

Grades: Adult   612.8

1. Nakazawa, Donna Jackson 2. Cells 3. Healing 4. Brain 5. Brain diseases 6. Treatment 7. Medical innovations 8. Medical research 9. Autoimmune diseases 10. Mind and body 11. Preventive medicine 12. Autobiographies and memoirs 13. Science Writing — Biology 14. Life stories — Facing adversity — Medical issues 15. Science Writing — Medicine and health — Illness and disease 16. Science Writing — Medicine and health — Medical breakthroughs

LC 2019034927

The award-winning journalist, Guillain-Barre Syndrome patient and author of Childhood Disrupted reveals the role of microglia on brain health and disease, describing emerging treatments for brain diseases ranging from depression to Alzheimer's.

"Indispensable for psychology professionals and students and fans of Susannah Cahalan's Brain on Fire: My Month of Madness." —Library Journal

Includes bibliographical references and index.

Sapolsky, Robert M.

Behave: The Biology of Humans at Our Best and Worst. Robert M. Sapolsky. Penguin Press 2017. 496 p.

ISBN 9781594205071

Grades: Adult   612.8

1. Neurophysiology 2. Neurobiology 3. Human behavior 4. Human nature 5. Humans 6. Brain 7. Developmental neurobiology 8. Instinct 9. Physiology 10. Society and culture — Psychology and human behavior 11. Science writing — Biology

LC 2016056755

Los Angeles Times Book Prize for Science and Technology, 2017.

A professor of biology and neurology at Stanford reveals what makes humans do the things they do, delving into environmental stimuli, things that trigger the nervous system, hormonal responses and how they work in conjunction with evolutionary and cultural factors.

"An exemplary work of popular science, challenging but accessible." —Kirkus

Thomson, Helen

Unthinkable: An Extraordinary Journey Through the World's Strangest Brains. Helen Thomson. HarperCollins 2018. 256 p.

ISBN 9780062391162

Grades: Adult   612.8

1. Brain diseases 2. Thought and thinking 3. Consciousness 4. Neuroscience 5. Memory 6. Science Writing — Biology

LC 2018303642

ESSENTIAL AND RECOMMENDED TITLES
613 Personal health and safety

An award-winning science writer draws on years investigating some of the world's rarest brain disorders and the cases of nine extraordinary people to share insights into how the brain shapes life in unexpected, alarming and vibrant ways.

"Thomson has a gift for making the complex and strange understandable and relatable." —*Library Journal*

Ward, Ashley
Where We Meet the World: The Story of the Senses. Ashley Ward. Basic Books 2023. 304 p.
ISBN 9781541600850
Grades: Adult 612.8
1. Senses and sensation 2. Evolution 3. Biology 4. Perception 5. Neuroscience 6. Science writing — Biology

The thrilling story of how our senses evolved and how they shape our encounters with the world.

"In this fascinating exploration of the world of the senses, biologist Ward draws from a range of sciences to uncover how our perceptions intertwine with our emotions and behavior, as well as with the broader cultures around us." —*Booklist*

Willeumier, Kristen
★ *Biohack Your Brain: How to Boost Cognitive Health, Performance & Power.* Dr. Kristen Willeumier, with Sarah Toland. William Morrow, an imprint of HarperCollinsPublishers 2020. xi, 288 pages
ISBN 9780062994325
Grades: Adult 612.8
1. Brain 2. Brain diseases 3. Cognition 4. Science Writing — Medicine and health — Brain function and memory
LC Bl2020068694

The "Your Brain Health" neuroscience podcaster outlines recommendations for promoting brain health and resilience throughout life, outlining helpful techniques for preventing memory loss and other neurodegenerative disorders.

"A beneficial overview of the brain, what we know about it, and what we're still discovering." —*Library Journal*

Includes bibliographical references (pages 239-267) and index.

613 Personal health and safety

Ashton, Jennifer
The New Normal: A Roadmap to Resilience in the Pandemic Era. Jennifer Ashton. William Morrow and Company 2021. 288 p.
ISBN 9780063083233
Grades: Adult 613
1. Covid-19 (Disease) 2. Epidemics 3. Diseases 4. Public health 5. Health 6. Resilience 7. World health 8. Science Writing — Medicine and health — Illness and disease 9. Society and culture — Illness and disease — Epidemics

The Chief Medical Correspondent at ABC News presents a guide to resilience in the era of COVID, sharing insights into how to understand evolving medical updates, adapt to evolving norms and make responsible choices throughout the pandemic.

"Ashton gamely offers a roadmap for the COVID-era, with thoughtful chapters on how the pandemic is affecting our bodies, minds, diets, exercise routines, sleep habits, and more. . . . A brief medical how-to guide on navigating life and finding answers to common questions." —*Library Journal*

Beck, Amanda Martinez
More of You: The Fat Girl's Field Guide to the Modern World. Amanda Martinez Beck. Broadleaf Books 2022. 149 p.
ISBN 9781506474243
Grades: Adult 613
1. Body image 2. Fat women 3. Human body 4. Christian life 5. Self-esteem 6. Self-Help — Personal growth — Self-esteem 7. Spirituality and Religion — Christian living

Too often, fatness has been viewed as a moral failing. Fat Christian women in particular are shamed and marginalized by the message that they are failing God because they can't change their bodies. More of You will challenge that status quo, teaching readers to resist the shame and guilt that is pressed onto them by the world and instead to embrace their bodies, take up space, and learn to navigate the world in ways that allow them to flourish.

"This is an outstanding addition to fat positivity literature." —*Publishers Weekly*

Includes bibliographical references.

Block, Jennifer
Everything Below the Waist: Why Health Care Needs a Feminist Revolution. Jennifer Block. St. Martin's Press 2019. 304 pages
ISBN 9781250110053
Grades: Adult 613
1. Women 2. Feminism 3. Women's health services 4. Reproductive health 5. Sexuality 6. Public health 7. Gender equity 8. Sexism 9. Health 10. Medical care 11. United States 12. Politics and global affairs — Public health 13. Society and culture — Gender — Women 14. Science Writing — Medicine and health
LC 2019007959

The award-winning journalist and author of Pushed presents a critical assessment of women's healthcare in present-day America, citing declining life expectancies and common examples of how today's healthcare routinely compromises women's sexual lives.

"Thought-provoking, empowering information that all women should have; essential for public and consumer health libraries." —*Library Journal*

Includes bibliographical references and index.

Bohannon, Cat
★ *Eve: How the Female Body Drove 200 Million Years of Human Evolution.* Cat Bohannon. Alfred A. Knopf 2023. 612 p.
ISBN 9780385350549
Grades: Adult 613
1. Women 2. Anatomy 3. Physiology 4. Human evolution 5. Human behavior 6. Adaptation 7. Sex differences 8. Prehistoric humans 9. Anthropology 10. Society and culture — Gender — Women 11. Science Writing — Biology 12. Science Writing — Paleontology 13. Debut title
LC 2022060219

Eve is not only a sweeping revision of human history, it's an urgent and necessary corrective for a world that has focused primarily on the male body for far too long. Picking up where Sapiens left off, Eve will completely change what you think you know about evolution and why Homo sapiens has become such a successful and dominant species.

"From rising-star scientist Bohannon, Eve investigates the evolution of the female body to answer important questions that male-directed science has not been asking." —*Library Journal*

Includes bibliographical references and index.

Cleghorn, Elinor
Unwell Women: Misdiagnosis and Myth in a Man-Made World. Elinor Cleghorn. E.P. Dutton 2021. 304 p.
ISBN 9780593182956
Grades: Adult 613
1. Cleghorn, Elinor 2. Sick women 3. Diagnostic errors 4. Sexism in medicine 5. Patriarchy 6. Misogyny 7. Women 8. Medical care 9. Medical malpractice 10. History of medicine 11. Society and culture — Gender — Women 12. Science Writing — Medicine and health 13. History writing — Science, technology, and medicine 14. History writing — Women's history 15. Life stories — Facing adversity — Medical issues — Physical illness
LC 2020053644

In Unwell Women, Elinor Cleghorn explores this almost unbelievable history of how medicine has failed women, and shows how the legacy of disenfranchisement and discrimination is alive and well in the contemporary relationship between women and sickness. When Cleghorn was finally correctly diagnosed with an autoimmune disease after years of being told her symptoms were anything from psychosomatic to a possible pregnancy, she was inspired to unpack the roots of the perpetual misunderstanding, mystification, and misdiagnosis of women's bodies. Packed with character studies and case histories of women who have suffered, challenged, and rewritten medical orthodoxy—and the men who

PUBLIC LIBRARY CORE COLLECTION: NONFICTION
Twentieth Edition

controlled their fate—this is a revolutionary examination of the relationship between women, illness, and medicine.

"A feminist historian and cultural critic explores how age-old myths about gender roles and behaviors have shaped the history of medicine.... Powerful, provocative, necessary reading." —*Kirkus*

Includes bibliographical references.

Comen, Elizabeth

★ *All in Her Head: The Truth and Lies Early Medicine Taught Us About Women's Bodies and Why It Matters Today*. Elizabeth Comen. Harperwave 2024. 320 p.

ISBN 9780063293014

Grades: Adult   613

1. Medical care 2. Women 3. Women's health services 4. Medicine 5. Science writing — Medicine and health 6. History Writing — Science, technology, and medicine 7. Society and culture — Gender — Women

"Meticulously researched and conveyed in lucid prose, this fascinates and outrages in equal measure." —*Publishers Weekly*

Common

★ *And Then We Rise: A Guide to Loving and Taking Care of Self*. Common. HarperOne, an imprint of HarperCollinsPublishers 2024. 209 pages

ISBN 9780063215177

Grades: Adult   613

1. Self-care 2. Mind and body 3. Physical fitness 4. Nutrition 5. Mental health 6. Spirituality 7. Self-Help — Personal growth

LC Bl2024001703

A self-help book from the noted musical artist and actor.

"The rapper, actor, and advocate blends self-help with activist passion…Common asks readers to better themselves, empowering them with the grace and courage to do so." —*Kirkus*

Includes bibliographical references (page 205).

Crowley, Chris

Younger Next Year: Live Strong, Fit, Sexy, and Smart —Until You're 80 and Beyond. Chris Crowley and Henry S. Lodge, MD; with Allan J. Hamilton, MD.. Workman Publishing Company 2019. xiii, 321 p.

ISBN 9781523507924

Grades: Adult   613

1. Longevity 2. Science Writing — Medicine and health — Aging and longevity 3. Science writing — Medicine and health — Men's health

Draws on the research into the science of aging to explain how men over the age of fifty can turn back their biological clocks to live stronger, healthier, injury-free, and more alert lives.

Previously published as: Younger next year : a guide to living like 50 until you're 80 and beyond, 2004.

Falter, Suzanne

The Extremely Busy Woman's Guide to Self-Care: Do Less, Achieve More, and Live the Life You Want. Suzanne Falter. Sourcebooks Inc. 2019. 288 p.

ISBN 9781492698531

Grades: Adult   613

1. Self-care 2. Self-Help — General 3. Self-Help — Personal growth — Happiness 4. Self-Help — Personal growth — Motivation

LC Bl2019029090

A dedicated self-care guide for today's over-scheduled women draws on the author's experiences as a highly stressed workaholic who, in the face of a tragedy, discovered simple strategies for promoting wholeness and balance.

Hamblin, James

Clean: The New Science of Skin and the Beauty of Doing Less. James Hamblin. Riverhead Books 2020. 280 pages

ISBN 9780525538318

Grades: Adult   613

1. Hygiene 2. Beauty care 3. Skin care 4. Science Writing — Medicine and health — Hygiene and beauty

Clean reveals the harm that excessive soap, washing and skin-care products are doing to our health and environment—and introduces a new way to think about cleanliness.

"A quick, engaging read for everyone concerned with caring for their skin, and the science behind it." —*Library Journal*

If Our Bodies Could Talk: A Guide to Operating and Maintaining a Human Body. James Hamblin. Doubleday 2016. 352 p.

ISBN 9780385540971

Grades: Adult   613

1. Human body 2. Health 3. Medical care 4. Wellness lifestyle 5. Lifestyles and health 6. Science Writing — Medicine and health

LC 2016046694

Explores the stories behind persistent health questions that are subject to mischaracterization and oversimplification by marketing and the media, covering health topics ranging from sleep and aging to diet and the immune system.

"He does a stellar job with nutrition, covering supplements, multivitamins, energy drinks, and gluten. He calls out medical misinformation and marketing myths. He is troubled… by how money, politics, and industry distort scientific data and muddle health policy. Educational, entertaining, and a bit eccentric." —*Booklist*

Harrison, Christy

The Wellness Trap: Break Free from Diet Culture, Disinformation, and Dubious Diagnoses, and Find Your True Well-Being. Christy Harrison, MPH, RD.. Little, Brown Spark 2023. 311 pages

ISBN 9780316315609

Grades: Adult   613

1. Alternative medicine 2. Medical misconceptions 3. Misinformation 4. Well-being 5. Self-care 6. Diet 7. Self-Help — Personal growth — Diet and nutrition 8. Science Writing — Medicine and health — Diet and nutrition 9. Business and economics — Industries

LC Bl2023014661

Weaving together history, memoir, reporting, and practical advice, Harrison illuminates the harms of wellness culture while re-imagining our society's relationship with well-being.

"This title demonstrates that the wellness industry differs from true well-being as much as spa treatments differ from Audre Lorde's original idea of self-care for activists. A valuable addition to conversations about race, class, ableism, and diet culture." —*Library Journal*

Includes bibliographical references (pages 267-298) and index.

Hecht, M. E.

Two Old Broads: Stuff You Need to Know That You Didn't Know You Needed to Know. M.E. Hecht, MD and Whoopi Goldberg. Harper Horizon 2022. xvii, 222 pages

ISBN 9780785241645

Grades: Adult   613

1. Senior women 2. Health 3. Aging 4. Self-Help — Personal growth — Aging 5. Science Writing — Medicine and health — Aging and longevity 6. Science Writing — Medicine and health — Women's health

LC Bl2022034198

Both hilarious and helpful, this practical and unapologetic health and lifestyle guide tells it like it is for all of us who left middle age in the dust and want to be present, positive and as extraordinary as ever in our golden years.

"While this advice is not new, it is a fun, often sassy reminder that no one is just a number." —*Library Journal*

Includes index.

McGregor, Alyson J.

Sex Matters: How Male-Centric Medicine Endangers Women's Health and What We Can Do About It. Alyson J. McGregor. Hachette Go 2020. 254 p.

ISBN 9780738246765

Grades: Adult   613

1. Women 2. Medical care 3. Medical research 4. Patient advocacy 5. Sexism in medicine 6. Patriarchy 7. Discrimination 8. Women's health services

ESSENTIAL AND RECOMMENDED TITLES
613.2 Dietetics

9. Self-care 10. Health 11. Society and culture — Gender — Women 12. Science Writing — Medicine and health

LC Bl2020013069

Sex Matters tackles one of the most urgent, yet unspoken issues facing women's health care today: All models of medical research and practice are based on male-centric models that ignore the unique biological and emotional differences between men and women—an omission that can endanger women's lives. Sex Matters is an empowering roadmap for reinventing modern medicine—and for self-care.

"The author is to be commended for showing how medicine has long skewed male and harmed women. . . . Good ammunition for mandating sex- and gender-based differences in health professional education, research, and practice."
—*Kirkus*

Includes bibliographical references and index.

Raphael, Rina
The Gospel of Wellness: Gyms, Gurus, Goop, and the False Promise of Self-Care. Rina Raphael. Henry Holt and Company 2022. 304 p.
ISBN 9781250793003
Grades: Adult   613

1. Self-care 2. Wellness lifestyle 3. Women 4. Stress management 5. Well-being 6. Control 7. Marketing 8. Deception 9. Sexism 10. Exploitation 11. Pseudoscience 12. Consumerism 13. Obsession 14. Health 15. Society and culture — Gender — Women 16. Science writing — Medicine and health 17. Business and economics — Industries — Retail products and services

Women are pursuing their health like never before. Whether it's juicing, biohacking, clutching crystals, or sipping collagen, today there is something for everyone, as the wellness industry has grown from modest roots into a $4.4 trillion entity and a full-blown movement promising health and vitality in the most fashionable package. But why suddenly are we all feeling so unwell? The truth is that deep within the underbelly of self-care—hidden beneath layers of clever marketing—wellness beckons with a far stronger, more seductive message than health alone. It promises women the one thing they desperately desire: control. What happens when the cure becomes as bad as the disease?

"Raphael delivers an eye-opening, cautionary study of the contemporary, amorphous meaning of wellness." —*Booklist*

Wilson, Jessica
It's Always Been Ours: Rewriting the Story of Black Women's Bodies. Jessica Wilson. Hachette Go 2023. 320 p.
ISBN 9780306827693
Grades: Adult   613

1. Wilson, Jessica 2. Body image 3. Racism 4. African American women 5. Health 6. Food 7. Food habits 8. Culture 9. Eating disorders 10. Institutional racism 11. Life stories — Science, technology, and medicine — Healthcare professionals 12. History Writing — African American — United States 13. Science Writing — Medicine and health 14. Society and culture — General

A dietitian, storyteller and community organizer offers a cultural discussion of body image, food, health and wellness by focusing on the bodies of Black women and how our culture's obsession with thin, white women reinforces racist ideas and ideals.

"This fiery polemic and celebration stands out among contemporary books on the subject of Black women's bodies." —*Kirkus*

613.2 Dietetics

Barrett, Pearl
Trim Healthy Mama Trim Healthy Table: More Than 300 All-New Healthy and Delicious Recipes from Our Homes to Yours. Pearl Barrett & Serene Allison. Harmony Books 2017. 559 pages : Color; Illustration
ISBN 9780804189989
Grades: Adult   613.2

1. Dieting 2. Weight loss 3. Nutrition 4. Recipes 5. Cookbooks 6. Food writing — Cooking and cookbooks — Cooking for health

LC 2017030325

The best-selling authors share tips and more than 250 recipes for promoting health in entire families through better eating, offering time-saving advice and culinary options that focus on quick-and-easy one-pot meals that minimize sugar and processed foods.

Includes indexes; Gather the family, eat up, and trim down—Cover.

Campbell, T. Colin
The China Study: The Most Comprehensive Study of Nutrition Ever Conducted and the Startling Implications for Diet, Weight Loss and Long-Term Health. T. Colin Campbell, PhD, Thomas M. Campbell II, MD.. BenBella Books 2017. xxx, 451 p. : Illustration
ISBN 9781942952831
Grades: Adult   613.2

1. Nutrition 2. Nutritionally induced diseases 3. Science writing — Medicine and health — Diet and nutrition

LC Bl2017051571

The updated and expanded edition of a groundbreaking book describes the findings of a comprehensive nutritional study that shows the relationship between a diet high in animal protein and an increased risk of developing disease.

Includes bibliographical references (pages 389-438) and index.

Cruikshank, Tiffany
Meditate Your Weight: The 21-Day Retreat to Optimize Your Metabolism and Feel Great. Tiffany Cruikshank, LAc, MAOM; with Mariska Van Aalst. Harmony Books 2016. 321 pages
ISBN 9780804187961
Grades: Adult   613.2

1. Weight loss 2. Metabolism 3. Science writing — Medicine and health — Diet and nutrition 4. Self-Help — Personal growth — Meditation 5. Science writing — Medicine and health — Alternative medicine

LC 2015033619

An international yoga teacher and meditation, health and wellness expert presents a 21-day weight-loss plan that employs daily journaling and meditation practice to coach readers through the various mental blocks, thoughts, habits and behaviors and help them achieve and sustain a healthy weight and body image.

Includes bibliographical references (pages 305-311) and index.

Ehrenreich, Barbara
Natural Causes: An Epidemic of Wellness, the Certainty of Dying, and Killing Ourselves to Live Longer. Barbara Ehrenreich. Twelve 2018. 288 p.
ISBN 9781455535910
Grades: Adult   613.2

1. Death education 2. Aging 3. Life expectancy 4. Longevity 5. Health 6. Society and culture — Illness and disease

LC 2017041893

The respected cellular immunologist and author of the best-selling Nickel and Dimed shares cautionary insights into today's healthcare practices to identify the cellular sources of aging and illness while revealing how most treatments are aggressive and offer only the illusion of control and better survivability at the cost of life quality.

"In assessing our quest for a longer, healthier life, Ehrenreich provides a contemplative vision of an active, engaged health care that goes far beyond the physical restraints of the body and into the realm of metaphysical possibilities." —*Booklist*

Hari, Johann
★ *Magic Pill: The Extraordinary Benefits and Disturbing Risks of the New Weight-loss Drugs.* Johann Hari. Crown Publishing 2024. 272 p.
ISBN 9780593728635
Grades: Adult   613.2

1. Hari, Johann 2. Journalists 3. Prescription drugs 4. Weight loss 5. Health 6. Body image 7. Psychology 8. Mental health 9. Risk 10. Patients 11. Physicians 12. Drug industry and trade 13. Science Writing — Medicine and health 14. Business and economics — Industries — Medical 15. Life stories — Facing adversity — Medical issues

LC 2023059013

To answer questions about the new drugs transforming weight loss—and leading from his personal experience taking Ozempic—a journalist embarks on a journey from Iceland to Minneapolis to Tokyo to interview the leading experts in the world to answer those questions, in this essential guide to the revolution that's already begun.

"Hari explores obesity-related medical concerns...all the while peppering the book with anecdotes designed to remind readers that the choices they make about weight loss often have far less to do with the number on the scale than they do with the stories they have been told about their bodies." —*Library Journal*

Includes bibliographical references and index.

Ludwig, David

Always Hungry?: Conquer Cravings, Retrain Your Fat Cells, and Lose Weight Permanently. David Ludwig, MD, PhD.. Grand Central Life & Style 2016. xxiii, 357 pages : Illustration

ISBN 9781455533862

Grades: Adult 613.2

1. Metabolism 2. Recipes 3. Weight loss 4. Self-care 5. Dieting 6. Science writing — Medicine and health — Diet and nutrition

LC 2015032645

Inspired by the New York Times op-ed "Always Hungry," ALWAYS HUNGRY? will change everything readers ever thought about weight loss, diet, and health. Groundbreaking new research shows that calorie counting does not work for weight loss: one diet causes weight gain whereas another diet with the same calorie count doesn't. It's your fat cells that are to blame for causing excessive hunger and increased weight. By eating the wrong foods, our fat cells are triggered to take in too many calories for themselves, setting off a dangerous chain reaction of increased appetite and a slower metabolism. Now, Harvard Medical School's David Ludwig, MD, PhD, offers an impeccably researched diet that will turn dieting on its head, teaching readers to reprogram their fat cells, tame hunger, boost metabolism, and lose weight—for good.

A leading obesity researcher and top endocrinologist at Boston Children's Hospital and Harvard Medical School presents a groundbreaking diet program that debunks the myth that calorie balance is the key to weight loss and teaches readers how to reprogram their fat cells to lose weight without counting calories or feeling hungry.

"Ludwig's meal plans and recipes are excellent. This quality book on the basics of losing weight will appeal to all types of readers." —*Library Journal*

Includes bibliographical references (pages 325-347) and index.

Moss, Michael

★ *Hooked: Food, Free Will, and How the Food Giants Exploit Our Addictions.* Michael Moss. Random House 2021. xxviii, 274 p.

ISBN 9780812997293

Grades: Adult 613.2

1. Food habits 2. Diet 3. Nutrition 4. Obesity 5. Processed foods 6. Food additives 7. Food industry and trade 8. Manipulation (Social sciences) 9. Addiction 10. Compulsive eating 11. Food science 12. Food writing — Investigations 13. Science Writing — Medicine and health — Illness and disease 14. Society and culture — Illness and disease — Addiction

Everyone knows how hard it can be to maintain a healthy diet. But what if some of the decisions we make about what to eat are beyond our control? Is it possible that processed food is addictive, like drugs or alcohol? Motivated by these questions, investigative reporter Michael Moss began searching for answers, to find the true peril in our food. In Hooked, Moss explores the science of addiction and uncovers what the scientific and medical communities—as well as food manufacturers—already know, which is that food can, in some cases, be even more addictive than alcohol, cigarettes, or drugs. A gripping account of the legal battles, insidious marketing campaigns, and cutting-edge food science that have brought us to our current public health crisis, Hooked lays out all that the food industry is doing to exploit and deepen our addictions.

"Readers are sure to find much fascinating—and frightening—food for thought in this fast-paced survey." —*Publishers Weekly*

Salt, Sugar, Fat: How the Food Giants Hooked Us. Michael Moss. Random House 2013. 352 p.

ISBN 9781400069804

Grades: Adult 613.2

1. Nutrition 2. Food habits 3. Food industry and trade 4. Salt 5. Sugar 6. Food 7. Compulsive eating 8. Addiction 9. Food writing — Investigations

LC 2012033034

James Beard Foundation Book Awards, Writing and Literature, 2014.

Traces the rise of the processed food industry and how addictive salt, sugar, and fat have enabled its dominance in the past half century, revealing deliberate corporate practices behind current trends in obesity, diabetes, and other health challenges.

Published in Canada as Sugar, salt, fat: Toronto : Signal, 2013.

Oakes, John G. H.

★ *The Fast: The History, Science, Philosophy, and Promise of Doing Without.* John Oakes. Avid Reader Press 2024. 224 p.

ISBN 9781668017418

Grades: Adult 613.2

1. Fasting 2. Detoxification (Health) 3. Self-care 4. Self-control 5. Religious life 6. Rites and ceremonies 7. Spiritual life 8. Food habits 9. Food consumption 10. Culture 11. Health 12. Science Writing — Medicine and health 13. Spirituality and Religion — Body, mind, and spirit

LC 2023044307

We fast all the time, even when we're not conscious of doing so. A fast manifests the idea of holding back, resisting the animal impulse to charge ahead. Its flip side is similarly everywhere: Call it splurging, self-indulgence, or a variant of "self-care." Based on extensive historical, scientific, and cultural research and reporting, the Fast illuminates the numerous facets of this act of self-deprivation. John Oakes interviews doctors, spiritual leaders, activists, and others who guide him through this practice—and embarks on fasts of his own—to deliver a book that supplies readers curious about fasting with profound new understanding, appreciation, and inspiration.

"Broad in scope and rich in insight, this provides plenty to ponder." —*Publishers Weekly*

Includes bibliographical references and index.

Prescott, Matthew

Food Is the Solution: What to Eat to Save the World : 80+ Recipes for a Greener Planet and a Healthier You. Matthew Prescott; foreword by Academy Award-winning director James Cameron. Flatiron Books 2018. 272 pages : Color; Illustration

ISBN 9781250144454

Grades: Adult 613.2

1. Cooking (Vegetables) 2. Recipes 3. Vegan cooking 4. Veganism 5. Vegetarian cooking 6. Vegetarianism 7. Cookbooks 8. Food writing — Cooking and cookbooks — Ingredients 9. Science writing — General 10. Self-Help — Personal growth

LC Bl2018001272

A senior food policy director for the Humane Society presents a sumptuously designed cookbook of environmentally friendly, healthy, plant-based recipes that can be a major part of supporting key collective agendas in ecological responsibility and sustainability.

Includes bibliographical references (pages 258-263) and index.

Sanfilippo, Diane

Practical Paleo: A Customized Approach to Health and a Whole-Foods Life-Style. Diane Sanfilippo. Victory Belt Pub. 2016. 480 p. : Color illustration

ISBN 9781628600025

Grades: Adult 613.2

1. Cooking (Natural foods) 2. High-protein diet 3. Prehistoric humans 4. Nutrition 5. Food writing — Cooking and cookbooks — Cooking for health 6. Science writing — Medicine and health — Diet and nutrition 7. Science writing — Medicine and health — Diet and nutrition — Weight loss

LC Bl2012027906

Jam-packed with more than 100 easy recipes, all with notes about common food allergens, a collection of meal plans targets the right way to eat to improve blood sugar regulation and athletic performance, as well as brain, joint, skin, heart, digestive and immune system health.

ESSENTIAL AND RECOMMENDED TITLES
613.25 Weight-losing diet

Presents a collection of meal plans targeted toward alleviating specific medical conditions and improving joint, skin, heart, and digestive and immune system health, and discusses the benefits of adopting a paleo lifestyle.

Includes index.

Zimberoff, Larissa
Technically Food: Inside Silicon Valley's Mission to Change What We Eat. Larissa Zimberoff. Harry N Abrams 2021. 288 p.
ISBN 9781419747090
Grades: Adult   613.2
1. Food industry and trade 2. Ethics 3. Food substitutes 4. Food habits 5. Agricultural technology 6. Technology 7. Business and economics — Industries — Agriculture and food

Through news-breaking revelations, the author examines the trade-offs of replacing real food with technology-driven approximations.

"This fascinating overview of efforts to create a sustainable, cruelty-free meat substitute will take a well-deserved place on the shelf alongside works such as Michael Pollan's The Omnivore's Dilemma and Mary Roach's Gulp. . . . An engaging, thorough examination of the transformation of the food industry as it relates to sustainability and creating alternatives to the slaughterhouse." —*Library Journal*

613.25 Weight-losing diet

Meltzer, Marisa
This Is Big: How the Founder of Weight Watchers Changed the World — and Me. Marisa Meltzer. Little, Brown and Company 2020. xi, 290 pages
ISBN 9780316414005
Grades: Adult   613.25
1. Nidetch, Jean 2. Meltzer, Marisa, 1977- 3. Weight control 4. Diet 5. Dieting 6. Diet industry and trade 7. Body image 8. Self-perception 9. Self-esteem 10. Biographies 11. Autobiographies and memoirs 12. Life stories — Facing adversity 13. Life stories — Arts and culture — Writing — Journalists
LC 2019945559

Marisa Meltzer began her first diet at the age of five. Fast forward nearly four decades, Marisa comes across an obituary for Jean Nidetch, the Queens, New York housewife who founded Weight Watchers in 1963. Weaving Jean's incredible story as weight loss maven and pathbreaking entrepreneur with Marisa's own journey through Weight Watchers, she chronicles the deep parallels, and enduring frustrations, in each woman's decades-long efforts to lose weight and keep it off.

"A straightforward memoir of struggling with obesity and finding inspiration from the founder of Weight Watchers. Her story will resonate with readers who have struggled with weight and body image issues." —*Kirkus*

613.6 Personal safety and special topics of health

Canterbury, Dave
Bushcraft 101: A Field Guide to the Art of Wilderness Survival. Dave Canterbury. Adams Media 2014. 256 pages
ISBN 9781440579776
Grades: Adult   613.6
1. Camping 2. Outdoor life 3. Outdoor recreation 4. Wilderness survival 5. Reference books — Handbooks, manuals, etc. 6. Sports and Competition — General 7. Reference books — Sports
LC 2014012976

Offers survival skills on using the surrounding wilderness as a useful resource, including how to manufacture needed tools, how to collect and cook food, and how to guard against the elements.

Includes index.

Rawles, James Wesley
Tools for Survival: What You Need to Survive When You're on Your Own. James Wesley, Rawles. Plume 2015. xxxii, 315 pages
ISBN 9780452298125
Grades: Adult   613.6
1. Survival 2. Alternative lifestyles 3. Reference — Instructional materials
LC 2014032904

A preparedness expert describes how to survive any disaster event—from a minor disruption to the end of the world—including preserving food and cooking; welding and blacksmithing; the basics of timber, firewood and lumber; firefighting; and more. By the author of How to Survive the End of the World as We Know It.

Includes index.

Sprinkle, Timothy
Lost and Stranded: Expert Advice on How to Survive Being Alone in the Wilderness. Timothy Sprinkle. Skyhorse Publishing 2018. 275 p.
ISBN 9781510727700
Grades: Adult   613.6
1. Outdoor recreation 2. Outdoor life 3. Wilderness survival 4. Wilderness areas 5. Wilderness living 6. Dangerous animals 7. Emergencies 8. Safety 9. Nature Writing — General 10. Adventure writing — Survival

Breaking down the perils that can befall hikers, hunters, and other outdoor enthusiasts, information from expert sources fills in the details around exactly how each scenario plays out on the ground, followed by suggestions on how to avoid or survive each risk factor—making this book a vital resource for outdoor travelers.

Includes bibliographical references and index.

613.7 Physical fitness

Bercovici, Jeff
Play On: The New Science of Elite Performance at Any Age. Jeff Bercovici. Houghton Mifflin Harcourt 2018. 288 p.
ISBN 9780544809987
Grades: Adult   613.7
1. Aging 2. Sports sciences 3. Athletes 4. Training 5. Sports 6. Men 7. Sports and Competition — General 8. Science Writing — Biology
LC 2017050323

A lively, thoroughly researched tour of the latest in fitness science and technology, and the strategies of elite and amateur athletes who are performing at peak levels for decades longer than before.

"Bercovici smartly separates science from quackeryavoiding GMO foods wont help, he argues, but taking creatine willwhile offering colorful reportage on sports trainers, physiologists, and gurus, and using his own achy frame to road test their wares, from -286 F cryotherapy chamber to an exercise/torture device called the Versaclimber." —*Publishers Weekly*

Includes bibliographical references and index.

Bondy, Dianne
Yoga Where You Are: Customize Your Practice for Your Body + Your Life. Dianne Bondy and Kat Heagberg; foreword by Jes Baker; photos by Andrea Killam. Shambhala 2020. xv, 253 pages : Color; Illustration
ISBN 9781611807868
Grades: Adult   613.7
1. Hatha yoga 2. Yoga 3. Sports and recreation — Yoga
LC 2019053634

Everything you need to build a custom yoga practice that supports YOU, just where you are. This empowering guide celebrates readers of all backgrounds, body sizes, and abilities. It offers poses, variations, sequences, and tools to find freedom in your practice, make it truly your own, and deepen your self-compassion and love.

"This thoughtfully written and visually appealing book will be a welcome addition to any yogi's library." —*Publishers Weekly*

Includes index.

PUBLIC LIBRARY CORE COLLECTION: NONFICTION
Twentieth Edition

Brooks, Amanda
Run to the Finish: The Everyday Runner's Guide to Avoiding Injury, Ignoring the Clock, and Loving the Run. Amanda Brooks. Lifelong Books 2020. 288 p.
ISBN 9780738285993
Grades: Adult   613.7
1. Running 2. Marathons 3. Runners 4. Training 5. Sports and competition — Racing
LC 2019043017

In her first book, popular runner blogger Amanda Brooks lays out the path to finding greater fulfillment in running for those who consider themselves "middle of the pack runners"—they're not trying to win Boston (or even qualify for Boston); they just want to get strong and stay injury-free so they can continue to enjoy running.

"While there are plenty of books about running, few are as approachable and helpful as this one. Highly recommended for anyone looking to improve their running ability." —*Library Journal*

Includes bibliographical references and index.

Current, Austin
Science of Strength Training: Understand Anatomy and Physiology to Transform Your Body. Austin Current, CSCS, CISSN.. DK 2021. 224 pages : Illustration; Color
ISBN 9780744026955
Grades: Adult   613.7
1. Weight training 2. Muscles 3. Muscle strength 4. Exercise 5. Health 6. Science Writing — Medicine and Health — Exercise
LC Bl2021010148

Discusses the benefits and physiology of strength training, provides workout plans and more than one hundred individual exercises, and includes nutritional information and dietary advice.

Includes bibliographical references (pages 222-224) and index.

Esmonde-White, Miranda
Aging Backwards: Reverse the Aging Process and Look 10 Years Younger in 30 Minutes a Day. Miranda Esmonde-White. Harper Wave 2018. VI, 278 pages : Illustration
ISBN 9780062859327
Grades: Adult   613.7
1. Rejuvenation 2. Longevity 3. Aging 4. Physical fitness 5. Preventive medicine 6. Science writing — Medicine and health — Exercise 7. Science writing — Medicine and health — Aging and longevity
LC 2014028452

From PBS personality and injury prevention and recovery specialist Miranda Esmond-White comes an eye-opening guide to anti-aging, arming readers with tools they need to turn back the hands of time.

Includes bibliographical references (pages 269-271); Originally published: New York : Harper Wave, 2014.

Green, Louise
Big Fit Girl: Embrace the Body You Have. Louise Green. Greystone Books 2017. xi, 236 p. : Illustration
ISBN 9781771642125
Grades: Adult   613.7
1. Physical fitness for women 2. Fat women 3. Science writing — Medicine and health — Women's health 4. Science writing — Medicine and health — Exercise 5. Self-Help — Personal growth — Motivation
LC Bl2017009337

Offers a guide for plus-sized women to overcome cultural stereotypes and achieve high levels of fitness, from motivation, gear, and goals to appropriate nutrition for athletes and overcoming performance plateaus.

Includes bibliographical references (pages 225-226) and index.

Grossman, Gail Boorstein
Restorative Yoga for Life: A Relaxing Way to De-Stress, Re-Energize, and Find Balance. Gail Boorstein Grossman. Adams Media 2015. 254 pages : Color; Illustration
ISBN 9781440575204
Grades: Adult   613.7
1. Hatha yoga 2. Relaxation 3. Science writing — Medicine and health — Alternative medicine
LC 2014026432

A certified YogaKids trainer demonstrates how to practice a restorative form of yoga that focuses on prop-aided physical and mental relaxation while treating a range of ailments, from headaches and digestive imbalances to weight gain and back pain.

Includes index.

Hayes, Bill
Sweat: A History of Exercise. Bill Hayes. Bloomsbury publishing 2022. 336 p.
ISBN 9781620402283
Grades: Adult   613.7
1. Exercise 2. Physical fitness 3. Sports and Competition — General 4. History writing — General 5. Travel Writing — General

Exercise is our modern obsession, and we have the fancy workout gear and fads from HIIT to spin classes to hot yoga to prove it. Exercise-a form of physical activity distinct from sports, play, or athletics-was an ancient obsession, too, but as a chapter in human history, it's been largely overlooked. In Sweat, Bill Hayes runs, jogs, swims, spins, walks, bikes, boxes, lifts, sweats, and downward-dogs his way through the origins of different forms of exercise, chronicling how they have evolved over time, dissecting the dynamics of human movement.

"At once a book about exercise history, and a travelogue, a literary discovery tour, and another of Hayes's personal and exhilarating memoirs." —*Library Journal*

Lacerda, Daniel
2,100 Asanas: The Complete Yoga Poses. Daniel Lacerda, Founder of Mr. Yoga, Inc. Black Dog & Leventhal Publishers 2015. 736 p. : Color; Illustration
ISBN 9781631910104
Grades: Adult   613.7
1. Hatha yoga 2. Yoga 3. Exercise 4. Science writing — Medicine and health — Exercise
LC 2015026283

An extensive catalog of yoga asanas for practitioners of any experience level showcases the form's beauty and athleticism and is organized under eight major types, from standing and seated poses to inversion and quadruped poses.

Includes index.

Lasater, Judith
Yoga Myths: What You Need to Learn and Unlearn for a Safe and Healthy Yoga Practice. Judith Hanson Lasater. Shambhala 2020. xiv, 255 pages : Illustration
ISBN 9781611807967
Grades: Adult   613.7
1. Hatha yoga 2. Sports and recreation — Yoga
LC 2019042112

In Yoga Myths, Judith Hanson Lasater draws on almost fifty years of experience as a yoga instructor and physical therapist to address the most common mistakes in our yoga practice and provide clear instructions for correcting these errors. Focusing on the eleven "myths" most detrimental to our practice, Lasater provides a comprehensive discussion of what the myth is, why it can hurt us, and how we can avoid it through step-by-step instructions and guiding photos. This book will allow you to return to the inherent wisdom, natural goodness, and spiritual wholeness of yoga and avoid life altering injuries for as long as you practice."

ESSENTIAL AND RECOMMENDED TITLES
613.9 Birth control, reproductive technology, sex hygiene, sexual techniques

"This wise and detailed guidebook (accompanied by black-and-white photos) will help students and teachers alike to remember to listen to their bodies and practice yoga with awareness." —*Publishers Weekly*

Includes bibliographical references (page 243) and index.

Macedo, Diane
The Sleep Fix: Practical, Proven, and Surprising Solutions for Insomnia, Snoring, Shift Work, and More. Diane Macedo. William Morrow, an imprint of HarperCollinsPublishers 2021. VIII, 371 pages : Illustration

ISBN 9780063040021

Grades: Adult   613.7

1. Sleep 2. Insomnia 3. Sleep disorders 4. Science Writing — Medicine and health — Sleep 5. Self-Help — Personal growth — Motivation

LC Bl2021029847

A renowned ABC News anchor/correspondent and former insomniac presents cutting-edge research, expert advice, intimate stories and easy-to-implement solutions to help millions of people get the sleep they need.

"Macedo's guide is jam-packed with information—so much so that readers may experience a bit of overload and wish for chapter summaries to keep it all straight. Still, those struggling with sleep are sure to find this a valuable resource." —*Publishers Weekly*

Includes bibliographical references (pages 337-355) and index.

Pohlman, Dean
Yoga Fitness for Men: Build Strength, Improve Performance, Increase Flexibility. Dean Pohlman. DK Publishing 2018. 191 pages : Color; Illustration

ISBN 9781465473486

Grades: Adult   613.7

1. Hatha yoga 2. Science writing — Medicine and health — Men's health 3. Science writing — Medicine and health — Alternative medicine 4. Science writing — Medicine and health — Exercise

LC Bl2018085674

Perfect for beginners! with straightforward language and easy-to-follow steps, Yoga Fitness for Men will teach you how to execute the yoga postures you need for greater endurance, flexibility, balance, and strength. Prop the book in front of your mat and let the full-color, step-by-step photography guide you through everything you need to know for an effective yoga practice.

"A solid introduction or supplemental guide for men wishing to try yoga." —*Library Journal*

Includes index.

Stanley, Jessamyn
Every Body Yoga: Let Go of Fear, Get on the Mat, Love Your Body. Jessamyn Stanley. Workman Publishing 2017. IX, 222 pages : Color; Illustration

ISBN 9780761193111

Grades: Adult   613.7

1. Hatha yoga 2. Yoga 3. Exercise 4. Physical fitness 5. Science writing — Medicine and health — Alternative medicine

LC 2017009009

An internationally recognized, stereotype-shattering yogi welcomes people of all shapes and sizes to start practicing yoga with simple instructions for 50 basic yoga poses and 10 sequences and reinforces the idea that yoga is about how someone feels, not looks.

★ *Yoke: My Yoga of Self-Acceptance.* Jessamyn Stanley. Workman Publishing 2021. 198 pages : Color; Illustration

ISBN 9781523505210

Grades: Adult   613.7

1. Yoga 2. Hatha yoga 3. Exercise 4. Mind and body therapies 5. Sports and competition — General 6. Self-Help — Personal growth — Self-esteem

LC 2021003537

In a series of deeply honest, funny, gritty, thoughtful, and largely autobiographical essays, Yoke explores issues of self-love, body-positivity, race, sex and sexuality, cannabis, and more, all through the lens of an authentic yoga practice. Every reader is invited to find this authentic spirit of yoga in their own lives and practice.

"Abstract, funny, heartfelt, and inspiring, Yoke is a fundamental book for those learning to feel present in their emotions and to take up space for themselves, both on the yoga mat and off." —*Booklist*

Wayne, Peter
The Harvard Medical School Guide to Tai Chi: 12 Weeks to a Healthy Body, Strong Heart, and Sharp Mind. Peter M. Wayne, with Mark Fuerst. Shambhala 2013. xiii, 336 p. : Illustration

ISBN 9781590309421

Grades: Adult   613.7

1. Health 2. Tai chi 3. Exercise therapy 4. Science writing — Medicine and health — Alternative medicine

LC 2012025187

Presents the basic principles of tai chi and provides instructions for integrating tai chi into everyday activities to improve health and well-being.

Includes bibliographical references and index.

Zadra, Antonio
When Brains Dream: Exploring the Science and Mystery of Sleep. Antonio Zadra and Robert Stickgold. W. W.Norton & Company 2021. 304 p.

ISBN 9781324002833

Grades: Adult   613.7

1. Dreams 2. Sleep 3. Neuroscience 4. Memory 5. Sleep disorders 6. Research 7. Science Writing — Biology

LC 2020027749

Two world-renowned sleep and dream researchers present a comprehensive exploration of human dreaming that draws on up-to-date neuroscience research to illuminate what dreams are, where they come from, why we have them and what they mean.

"A deep exploration into the world of dreams that is highly recommended for anyone interested in delving more into this topic." —*Library Journal*

Includes bibliographical references and index.

613.9 Birth control, reproductive technology, sex hygiene, sexual techniques

Kerner, Ian
She Comes First: The Thinking Man's Guide to Pleasuring a Woman. Ian Kerner. ReganBooks 2004. xii, 228 p.

ISBN 9780060538255

Grades: Adult   613.9

1. Orgasm, Female 2. Oral sex 3. Sex education for adults 4. Family and Relationships — Dating and Marriage

LC 2004041787

A man's guide on how to enhance a woman's sexual experience through oral sex outlines a system of intimate techniques designed to maximize female gratification.

"Dispelling the widely held myth of genital penetration as the apogee of sexual pleasure, Kerner, who holds a doctorate in clinical sexology, offers this witty, well-researched manual for 'Consistently leading women to orgasm' through cunnilingus." —*Publishers Weekly*

Includes bibliographical references (p. [225]-226).

Schrock, Leslie
Fertility Rules: The Definitive Guide to Male and Female Reproductive Health. Leslie Schrock; medical editor: Jane van Dis, MD:obstetrics/gynecology; scientific editor:Christopher De Jonge, PhD, HCLD (ABB):urology/andrology; expert contributors: Michaela Burns, women's health physical trainer, Aliza Marogy, registered nurse. Simon Element 2023. xxvi, 322 pages : Illustration

ISBN 9781668000144

Grades: Adult   613.9

1. Conception 2. Human fertility 3. Reproductive health 4. Science Writing — Medicine and health — Fertility and sexual health 5. Science Writing —

Medicine and health — Women's health 6. Science Writing — Medicine and health — Men's health

LC B12023020530

Leslie Schrock is back with the first preconception guide for both male and female fertility. Based on cutting-edge science, Fertility Rules offers a holistic plan for every age and stage of the process, whether you're planning to conceive or in the throes. Unlike some other fertility books, it also includes practical content tailored to help the mental health of prospective parents."

"This is a definitive and highly useful guide to reproductive health." —Booklist

Includes bibliographical references (pages 273-307) and index.

613.9071 Birth control, reproductive technology, sex hygiene, sexual techniques — Sex education — Secondary level

Smiler, Andrew P.
Dating and Sex: A Guide for the 21st Century Teen Boy. by Andrew P. Smiler, PhD.. Magination Press, American Psychological Association 2016. 288 pages : Illustration
ISBN 9781433820458
Grades: Adult   613.9071
1. Sex education for teenagers 2. Dating 3. Sexuality 4. Interpersonal attraction 5. Teenage boys 6. Growing up — My body — Let's talk about sex 7. Growing up — Relationships — Dating

LC 2015019582

Presents information about dating and sex for teenage boys, including such topics as puberty, asking someone out on a date, and sexual orientation.

Includes bibliographical references (pages 261-276) and index.

Vernacchio, Al
For Goodness Sex: Changing the Way We Talk to Teens About Sexuality, Values, and Health. AL Vernacchio, with Brooke Lea Foster. Harper 2014. xiii, 254 pages
ISBN 9780062269515
Grades: Adult   613.9071
1. Sexual ethics 2. Teenagers 3. Parent and teenager 4. Sex education for adults 5. Science writing — Medicine and health 6. Educator resources — General

LC 2014019134

A high school sexuality educator presents a new approach to sex education for parents and teens that challenges traditional teaching models and instead embraces 21st-century realities by promoting healthy sexuality, values and body image in young people, in a book that includes real-life examples from the classroom, exercises and quizzes.

614 Forensic medicine; incidence of injuries, wounds, disease; public preventive medicine

Balko, Radley
★ *The Cadaver King and the Country Dentist: A True Story of Injustice in the American South.* Radley Balko and Tucker Carrington. PublicAffairs 2018. 336 p.
ISBN 9781610396912
Grades: Adult   614
1. Hayne, Steven (Forensic pathologist) 2. West, Michael (Dentist) 3. Brooks, Levon, 1959- 4. Brewer, Kennedy 5. Criminal justice system 6. Racism in the criminal justice system 7. Judicial error 8. Trials (Rape) 9. Trials (Murder) 10. Mississippi 11. Society and culture — Violence and crime — Criminal justice system 12. True crime — Investigations and trials

LC 2017009508

Relates the stories of two innocent men who were wrongly accused and convicted of crimes due largely to the legally condoned failures perpetrated by invalid forensic science and institutional racism.

"Through the intensive scrutiny of how the men were speedily tried, convicted, and then released after years in prison, the authors uncover an unholy alliance of racist cops and prosecutors with questionable death investigations and misapplied forensics. This work should spark both admiration and outrageand, one hopes, reform." —Booklist

Includes bibliographical references and index.

Bass, William M.
Death's Acre: Inside the Legendary Forensic Lab the Body Farm Where the Dead Do Tell Tales. Bill Bass and Jon Jefferson; foreword by Patricia Cornwell. G. P. Putnam's Sons 2003. xii, 304 p, 16 p. of plates : Illustration
ISBN 9780399151347
Grades: 9 10 11 12 Adult   614
1. Forensic anthropology 2. Crime laboratories 3. Dead 4. Skeleton 5. Human body 6. Identification 7. Tennessee 8. True Crime — Forensic Sciences 9. Adult books for young adults

LC 2003046908

Nowhere is there another lab like Dr. Bill Bass's: on a hillside in Tennessee, human bodies decompose in the open air, aided by insects, bacteria and birds, unhindered by coffins or mausoleums. At the "Body Farm," nature takes its course, with corpses buried in shallow graves, submerged in water, concealed beneath slabs of concrete, locked in trunks of cars. As stand-ins for murder victims, they serve the needs of science—and the cause of justice.

"The author explains the process of decomposition and how bones give clues to identify: Approximate age, sex, height, and race, all of which are needed to bring the forensic scientist one step closer to putting a name to a corpse. He describes some of the cases he has been involved with and laughs at himself when he shares stories of mistakes and assumptions. Young adults will gain insight into the forensic process and appreciate Bass's dedication to the truth and his work." —School Library Journal

Includes index.

Blum, Deborah
The Poisoner's Handbook: Murder and the Birth of Forensic Medicine in Jazz Age New York. Deborah Blum. Penguin Press 2010. 336 p.
ISBN 9781594202438
Grades: 11 12 Adult   614
1. Poisoning 2. Forensic sciences 3. Forensic medicine 4. Forensic toxicology 5. Toxicology 6. Poisoners 7. United States history 8. New York (State) 9. 1920s 10. 20th century 11. True Crime — Forensic Sciences 12. History writing — Roaring 20s — United States

LC 2009026461

Chronicles the story of New York City's first forensic scientists to describe Jazz Age poisoning cases, including a family's inexplicable balding, Barnum and Bailey's Blue Man, and the crumbling bones of factory workers.

"Blum effectively balances the fast-moving detective story with a clear view of the scientific advances that her protagonists brought to the field. Caviar for true-crime fans and science buffs alike." —Kirkus

Includes bibliographical references and index.

Butcher, Barbara
What the Dead Know: Learning About Life as a New York City Death Investigator. Barbara Butcher. Simon & Schuster 2023. 288 p.
ISBN 9781982179380
Grades: Adult   614
1. Butcher, Barbara 2. Women forensic scientists 3. Government investigators 4. Death 5. Dead 6. Murder victims 7. Accident victims 8. People with depression 9. Lesbians 10. Alcoholic women 11. Sobriety 12. North American people 13. American people 14. New York City 15. Autobiographies and memoirs 16. Life stories — Law and order 17. Life stories — Business — Working life 18. True Crime — Forensic Sciences

A deeply personal memoir of more than 20 years of death-scene investigations by New York City death investigator Barbara Butcher.

"Butcher's relaxed writing style allows her to show off her engaging personality, which often lends moments of humor despite the heavy topic, making this a recommended addition to any public-library collection." —Booklist

ESSENTIAL AND RECOMMENDED TITLES
614.4 Incidence of and public measures to prevent disease

Maples, William R.
Dead Men Do Tell Tales. William R. Maples and Michael Browning. Doubleday 1994. 292 p, [32] p. of plates : Illustration
ISBN 9780385474900
Grades: Adult   614
1. Maples, William R, died 1997 2. Physical anthropologists 3. Physical anthropology 4. Forensic anthropology 5. True Crime — Forensic Sciences 6. History writing — Historical mysteries
LC 94012290

While explaining the behavior of maggots and the biology of putrefaction a forensic anthropologist recounts his strangest and most horrifying criminal cases, from puzzles of dismemberment to the revelation of the identity of long-buried skeletons.

Includes index.

614.4 Incidence of and public measures to prevent disease

Honigsbaum, Mark
The Pandemic Century: One Hundred Years of Panic, Hysteria, and Hubris. Mark Honigsbaum. W. W. Norton & Company 2019. 448 p.
ISBN 9780393254754
Grades: Adult   614.4
1. Epidemics 2. Diseases 3. Epidemiology 4. Communicable diseases 5. Social medicine 6. Public health 7. History of medicine 8. SARS (Disease) 9. Ebola virus disease 10. Zika virus infection 11. Influenza Epidemic, 1918-1919 12. Science Writing — Medicine and health — Illness and disease 13. History writing — Plague and famine 14. History writing — Science, technology, and medicine
LC 2018048424

Chronicles the last century of scientific struggle against deadly contagious disease—from the 1918 Spanish influenza pandemic to the recent SARS, Ebola and Zika epidemics—examining related epidemiological mysteries and the role of disease in exacerbating world conflicts.

Includes bibliographical references and index.

Kang, Lydia
Patient Zero: A Curious History of the World's Worst Diseases. Lydia Kang, MD, and Nate Pedersen. Workman Publishing 2021. 352 p.
ISBN 9781523513291
Grades: Adult   614.4
1. Epidemics 2. Emerging infectious diseases 3. Diseases 4. Science 5. History writing — Science, technology and medicine 6. Society and culture — Illness and disease 7. Science Writing — Medicine and health — Illness and disease
LC 2021027209

A very timely history of disease outbreaks, from the authors of Quackery: Stories of outbreaks (and their patient zeros), plus chapters on the science, culture, and cures for different types of epidemics and pandemics. Popular reading on a timely topic.

"Kang and Pedersen (co-authors of Quackery: A Brief History of the Worst Ways to Cure Everything) return with a compendium of brief, informative chapters on significant disease outbreaks throughout the world, from the 1800s to the present day.... Kang and Pedersen's entertaining narrative style makes the informative content engaging." —*Library Journal*

Kennedy, Jonathan
Pathogenesis: A History of the World in Eight Plagues. Jonathan Kennedy. Crown 2023. 336 p.
ISBN 9780593240472
Grades: Adult   614.4
1. Epidemics 2. Plague 3. Biohistory 4. Diseases 5. Communicable diseases 6. History Writing — Plague and famine 7. Society and culture — Illness and disease — Epidemics 8. Debut title
LC 2022052387

Drawing on the latest research in fields ranging from genetics and anthropology to archaeology and economics, this revelatory book takes us through 60,000 years of history to show how the major transformations in history have been shaped by eight major outbreaks of infectious disease.

"Revisiting the theme of William H. McNeill's Plagues and Peoples (1976), sociologist and public health scholar Kennedy debuts with a virtuoso analysis of the fallout from encounters between deadly viral and bacterial pathogens and human populations that lacked immunity." —*Publishers Weekly*

Includes index.

Kenny, Charles
The Plague Cycle: The Unending War Between Humanity and Infectious Disease. Charles Kenny. Simon & Schuster 2021. 320 pages
ISBN 9781982165338
Grades: Adult   614.4
1. Civilization 2. Communicable diseases 3. Epidemics 4. Diseases 5. Public health 6. Plague 7. Globalization 8. Climate change 9. Prosperity 10. History writing — Science, technology, and medicine 11. Science Writing — Medicine and health — Illness and disease 12. Society and culture — Illness and disease — Epidemics

Reveals the relationship between civilization, globalization, prosperity, and infectious disease over the past five millennia. It harnesses history, economics, and public health, and charts humanity's remarkable progress, providing a fascinating and timely look at the cyclical nature of infectious disease.

"A timely, lucid look at the role of pandemics in history." —*Kirkus*

Kinch, Michael S.
Between Hope and Fear: A History of Vaccines and Human Immunity. Michael Kinch. Pegasus Books 2018. 360 p.
ISBN 9781681777511
Grades: Adult   614.4
1. Vaccines 2. Communicable diseases 3. Epidemics 4. Vaccination 5. Anti-vaccination movement 6. Immunity 7. Health policy 8. Microbiology 9. Immunology 10. History writing — Science, technology, and medicine 11. Science Writing — Medicine and health — Illness and disease 12. Science Writing — Medicine and health — Medical breakthroughs
LC BI2018080363

The author of A Prescription for Change presents an informed examination of the science of immunity, the public policy implications of vaccine denial and the real-world outcomes of failing to vaccinate.

"Kinch (radiation oncology, Washington Univ; director, Ctr. for Research Innovation in Business; Prescription for Change), ostensibly writing to refute the dangerous rise of antivaccinators, provides readers with an interdisciplinary cornucopia of meticulously researched information on the intersection of history, disease, and vaccine invention." —*Library Journal*

Manaugh, Geoff
Until Proven Safe: The History and Future of Quarantine. Geoff Manaugh and Nicola Twilley. MCD/Farrar, Straus and Giroux 2021. 320 p.
ISBN 9780374126582
Grades: Adult   614.4
1. Quarantine 2. Epidemics 3. COVID-19 (Disease) 4. Social isolation 5. Society and culture — Illness and disease — Epidemics 6. History writing — Plague and famine
LC 2021006853

Journalists Geoff Manaugh and Nicola Twilley explore the history and future of quarantine, from the Black Death to Big Data.

"A captivating survey of the uses and abuses of quarantines, from the days of the Black Death to the lockdowns of Covid-19. Journalists Manaugh and Twilley meld a global view of a timely subject with vividly detailed accounts of quarantines, whether of people or hazardous plants, animals, and chemicals such as nuclear waste." —*Kirkus*

Includes bibliographical references and index.

PUBLIC LIBRARY CORE COLLECTION: NONFICTION
Twentieth Edition

McNeil, Donald G.
★ *The Wisdom of Plagues: Lessons from 25 Years of Covering Pandemics.* Donald G. McNeil Jr. Simon & Schuster 2024. 384 p.

ISBN 9781668001394

Grades: Adult   614.4

1. Epidemiology 2. Epidemics 3. COVID-19 (Disease) 4. COVID-19 Pandemic, 2020- 5. Public health 6. Anti-vaccination movement 7. Vaccination 8. Health policy 9. Science policy 10. Mass media and culture 11. Mass media bias 12. Plague 13. United States 14. Society and culture — Illness and disease — Epidemics 15. Politics and global affairs — Public health

LC 2023018091

An award-winning New York Times reporter reflects on 25 years of covering pandemics—how governments react to them, how the media covers them, how they are exploited and what we can do to prepare for the next one.

"McNeil goes on to elucidate how skepticism, denialism, fatalism, rumors, false remedies, and cultural misunderstandings help fuel the spread of pandemics. Hard lessons that should never be forgotten." —*Booklist*

Includes bibliographical references and index.

Price, Polly J.
Plagues in the Nation: How Epidemics Shaped America. Polly J. Price. Beacon Press 2022. 272 p.

ISBN 9780807043493

Grades: Adult   614.4

1. Epidemics 2. Plague 3. Communicable diseases 4. COVID-19 (Disease) 5. Emergency planning 6. Social conflict 7. Public health 8. Politics and government 9. United States history 10. United States 11. Society and culture — Illness and disease — Epidemics 12. Politics and global affairs — Public health 13. History writing — United States

LC 2021056250

In this narrative history of the US through major outbreaks of contagious disease, from yellow fever to the Spanish flu, from HIV/AIDS to Ebola, Polly J. Price examines how law and government affected the outcome of epidemics—and how those outbreaks in turn shaped our government. Price presents a fascinating history that has never been fully explored and draws larger conclusions about the gaps in our governmental and legal response. Plagues in the Nation examines how our country learned—and failed to learn—how to address the panic, conflict, and chaos that are the companions of contagion, what policies failed America again and again, and what we must do better next time.

"A pointed study of how divisiveness and conflict undermine the nation's response to disease. Law professor and legal historian Price offers an authoritative history of America's flawed responses to epidemics." —*Kirkus*

Includes bibliographical references and index.

Quammen, David
★ *Spillover: Animal Infections and the Next Human Pandemic.* David Quammen. W.W. Norton & Co. 2012. 587 p.

ISBN 9780393066807

Grades: Adult   614.4

1. Epidemics 2. Communicable diseases 3. Public health 4. Ebola virus disease 5. AIDS (Disease) 6. Avian influenza 7. Science Writing — Medicine and health — Illness and disease 8. Society and culture — Illness and disease 9. Society and culture — Illness and disease — Epidemics

Booklist Editors' Choice, 2012; New York Times Notable Book, 2012; Andrew Carnegie Medal for Excellence in Non-Fiction finalist, 2013; National Book Critics Circle Award for Nonfiction finalist, 2012.

Examines the emergence and causes of new diseases all over the world, describing a process called "spillover" where illness originates in wild animals before being passed to humans and discusses the potential for the next huge pandemic.

"A wonderful, eye-opening account of humans versus disease that deserves to share the shelf with such classics as Microbe Hunters and Rats, Lice and History." —*Kirkus*

Includes bibliographical references (p. [523]-558) and index.

Schama, Simon
Foreign Bodies: Pandemics, Vaccines, and the Health of Nations. Simon Schama. Ecco Press 2023. 320 p.

ISBN 9781328974839

Grades: Adult   614.4

1. Vaccines 2. Viruses 3. Epidemics 4. Public health 5. Vaccination 6. Diseases 7. Medical research 8. Society and culture — Illness and disease 9. History Writing — Plague and famine

A best-selling author and historian presents a history of vaccines, including not only the scientific stories behind disease eradication but also the political, cultural, and personal factors that have impacted their development.

"Historian Schama (The Story of the Jews) examines in this insightful study the scientific battle against epidemic diseases over the past three centuries, as scientists contended with both the contagions and human intransigence." —*Publishers Weekly*

Senthilingam, Meera
Outbreaks and Epidemics: Battling Infection from Measles to Coronavirus. Meera Senthilingam. Icon Books 2020. 176 p.

ISBN 9781785785634

Grades: Adult   614.4

1. Epidemics 2. Plague 3. Diseases 4. Communicable diseases 5. Coronavirus infections 6. Public health 7. Medicine 8. Science Writing — Medicine and health — Illness and disease 9. History writing — Plague and famine 10. History writing — Science, technology, and medicine 11. Society and culture — Illness and disease — Epidemics

A journey through the history and science of epidemics and pandemics—from measles to coronavirus.

"Of considerable interest to anyone who wishes to learn about infections, how they spread, and how they are managed. Required reading for anyone new to learning about issues of public health." —*Library Journal*

614.5 Incidence of and public measures to prevent specific diseases and kinds of diseases

Allen, Arthur
★ *The Fantastic Laboratory of Dr. Weigl: How Two Brave Scientists Battled Typhus and Sabotaged the Nazis.* Arthur Allen. W.W. Norton & Company 2014. 352 p.

ISBN 9780393081015

Grades: Adult   614.5

1. Weigl, Rudolf, 1883-1957 2. Fleck, Ludwik, 1896-1961 3. World War II 4. Resistance to military occupation 5. Anti-Nazi movement 6. Scientists 7. Typhoid fever 8. Poland 9. History writing — Wars and conflicts — World War II 10. History writing — Wars and conflicts — Resistance — World War II

LC 2014003246

Describes the true story of how the eccentric Polish scientist tasked by the Nazis to create a typhus vaccine hid the intelligentsia from the Gestapo by hiring them to work in his laboratory.

"Allen is unflinching in his retelling of this monstrous era, but he manages to avoid writing a depressing narrative. Instead, Weigl, Fleck and their vaccines illuminate the inherent social complexities of science and truth and reinforce the overriding good of man." —*Kirkus*

Includes bibliographical references and index.

Barry, John M.
★ *The Great Influenza: The Epic Story of the Deadliest Plague in History.* John M. Barry. Viking 2004. 546 p. : Illustration

ISBN 9780670894734

Grades: 9 10 11 12 Adult   614.5

1. Influenza Epidemic, 1918-1919 2. Plague 3. Influenza 4. Vaccines 5. Communicable diseases 6. Epidemics 7. Medicine 8. Preventive medicine 9. United States 10. 1910s 11. 20th century 12. History writing — Plague and famine 13. Science Writing — Medicine and health — Illness and disease 14. Adult books for young adults

ESSENTIAL AND RECOMMENDED TITLES
614.5 Incidence of and public measures to prevent specific diseases and kinds of diseases

LC 2003057646

Booklist Editors' Choice, 2004; National Academies Communication Award, 2005.

An in-depth account of the deadly influenza epidemic of 1918, a plague that took the lives of millions of people around the world, examines the causes of the pandemic, its devastating impact on early twentieth-century society, the researchers who risked their lives to confront the disease, and the lasting implications of the crisis and the scientific discoveries that resulted.

Includes bibliographical references (p. [507]-527) and index.

Cantor, Norman F.
In the Wake of the Plague: The Black Death and the World It Made. Norman F. Cantor. Harper Collins Perennial 2002. 245 p. : Illustration; Map
ISBN 9780060014346
Grades: 11 12 Adult   614.5
1. Black Death 2. Plague 3. Civilization, Medieval 4. Medieval period (476-1492) 5. History writing — Plague and famine 6. History writing — Medieval — Europe

LC 2001051819

Through profiles of merchants, peasants, priests, and kings, argues that despite devastation, the Black Death resulted in a scientific revoltuion, a new wave of art, and the emergence of independent farmers.

"By animating history and demonstrating our times' connections to even as remote an event as the Black Death, Cantor's erudite excursion proves most engrossing." —*Booklist*

Includes bibliographical references (p. [221]-230) and index; Originally published: New York : Free Press, 2001.

Crosby, Molly Caldwell
The American Plague: The Untold Story of Yellow Fever, the Epidemic That Shaped Our History. Molly Caldwell Crosby. Berkley Books 2006. VIII, 308 p., 16 p. of plates : Illustration; Map
ISBN 9780425212028
Grades: 11 12 Adult   614.5
1. Yellow fever 2. Epidemics 3. Medicine 4. United States history 5. Memphis, Tennessee 6. United States 7. 19th century 8. 1870s 9. History writing — Science, technology, and medicine 10. History writing — Plague and famine 11. Science Writing — Medicine and health — Illness and disease 12. History writing — United States

LC 2006050497

Traces the impact on American history of yellow fever from the mid-seventeenth century onward, examining in particular the near-destruction of Memphis from the disease and the efforts of four men to combat the deadly scourge.

"The author offers a forceful narrative of a disease's ravages and the quest to find its cause and cure." —*Publishers Weekly*

Map on lining papers; Includes bibliographical references (p. [283]-296) and index.

Farmer, Paul
Fevers, Feuds, and Diamonds: Ebola and the Ravages of History. Paul Farmer. Farrar, Straus and Giroux 2020. 688 p.
ISBN 9780374234324
Grades: Adult   614.5
1. Ebola virus disease 2. Epidemics 3. Humanitarian assistance 4. Injustice 5. Public health 6. Exploitation 7. Communicable diseases 8. Africa 9. Society and culture — Illness and disease — Epidemics 10. Science Writing — Medicine and health — Illness and disease

LC 2020027255

The Harvard University global-health authority documents the 2014 Ebola crisis and the stories of victims and first responders while revealing the centuries of exploitation, injustice and state failures that rendered it history's worst outbreak.

Includes bibliographical references and index.

Gates, Bill
★ *How to Prevent the Next Pandemic.* Bill Gates. Alfred A. Knopf 2022. 272 p.
ISBN 9780593534489
Grades: Adult   614.5
1. Covid-19 (Disease) 2. COVID-19 Pandemic, 2020- 3. Communicable diseases 4. Epidemics 5. Preventive medicine 6. Emergency planning 7. International cooperation 8. Epidemiology 9. Science Writing — Medicine and health — Illness and disease 10. Society and culture — Illness and disease — Epidemics

LC 2021062526

Bill Gates...lays out clearly and convincingly what the world should have learned from COVID-19 and what all of us can do to ward off another disaster like it. Relying on the shared knowledge of the world's foremost experts and on his own experience of combating fatal diseases through the Gates Foundation, he first helps us understand the science of infectious diseases. Then he shows us how the nations of the world, working in conjunction with one another and with the private sector, can not only ward off another COVID-like catastrophe but also eliminate all respiratory diseases, including the flu.

"This book is a possible future blueprint for pandemic preparedness, which means that it's best audiences might be governments and NGOs, rather than individuals." —*Library Journal*

Includes bibliographical references and index.

Holt, Nathalia
Cured: How the Berlin Patients Defeated HIV and Forever Changed Medical Science. Nathalia Holt. Dutton, published by the Penguin Group 2014. 368 p.
ISBN 9780525953920
Grades: Adult   614.5
1. World health 2. People with HIV 3. Gene therapy 4. HIV (Viruses) 5. AIDS (Disease) 6. Treatment 7. Preventive medicine 8. Science Writing — Medicine and health — Illness and disease 9. History writing — Plague and famine 10. Society and culture — Illness and disease — Epidemics

LC 2013037181

An award-winning research scientist and HIV fellow at the Ragon Institute reveals the science behind the discovery of a potential cure for HIV, tracing the groundbreaking contributions of the two Berlin Patients and how their cases have influenced HIV researchers throughout the world.

"[I]n this accessible and fascinating account, Holt . juggles genetic mysteries, research perils, the agonies of these two reserved and sensitive men diagnosed with what was considered a death sentence, and the dogged doctors who successfully treated them during the later stages of AIDS epidemic." —*Publishers Weekly*

Includes bibliographical references.

Johnson, Steven
The Ghost Map: The Story of London's Deadliest Epidemic— and How It Changed the Way We Think About Disease, Cities, Science, and the Modern World. Steven Johnson. Riverhead Books 2006. 299 p. : Illustration; Map
ISBN 9781594489259
Grades: 11 12 Adult   614.5
1. Cholera 2. Epidemics 3. Communicable diseases 4. Diseases 5. Public health 6. London, England history 7. 19th century 8. History writing — Plague and famine 9. History writing — Europe — United Kingdom 10. Science Writing — Medicine and health — Illness and disease 11. History writing — Science, technology, and medicine

LC 2006023114

Library Journal Best Books, 2006; New York Times Notable Book, 2006.

A thrilling historical account of the worst cholera outbreak in Victorian London—and a brilliant exploration of how Dr. John Snow's solution revolutionized the way we think about disease, cities, science, and the modern world. The ghost map is an endlessly compelling and utterly gripping account of that London summer of 1854, from the microbial level to the macrourban-theory level—including, most important, the human level.

PUBLIC LIBRARY CORE COLLECTION: NONFICTION
Twentieth Edition

"From Snow's discovery of patient zero to Johnson's compelling argument for and celebration of cities, this makes for an illuminating and satisfying read." —*Publishers Weekly*

Includes bibliographical references (p. [285]-290) and index.

Kelly, John
The **Great Mortality:** *An Intimate History of the Black Death, the Most Devastating Plague of All Time.* John Kelly. HarperCollins Publishers 2005. xvii, 304 p. : Illustration

ISBN 9780060006921

Grades: 11 12 Adult 614.5

1. Black Death 2. Plague 3. Epidemics 4. Floods 5. Health 6. European history 7. Asian history 8. Europe 9. 14th century 10. Medieval period (476-1492) 11. History writing — Plague and famine 12. History writing — Medieval — Europe 13. Science Writing — Medicine and health — Illness and disease

LC 2004054213

Chronicles the Great Plague that devastated Asia and Europe in the fourteenth century, documenting the experiences of people who lived during its height while describing the decline of moral boundaries that also marked the period.

"Western Europe is the primary focus of Kelly's compact history, which is intimate in that it highlights many particular persons' passages through the crucible years, 1348-49. Kelly proceeds chronologically, beginning with the plague's prehistory in north central Asia and its spread through China before empire-building Mongols brought it west. This sweeping, viscerally exciting book contributes to a literature of perpetual fascination: the chronicles of pestilence." —*Booklist*

Includes bibliographical references and index.

Lewis, Michael
★ *The* **Premonition:** *A Pandemic Story.* Michael Lewis. W W Norton & Company 2021. 304 p.

ISBN 9780393881554

Grades: Adult 614.5

1. Public health 2. Medical care 3. Covid-19 (disease) 4. Epidemics 5. Physicians 6. Scientists 7. Technological innovations 8. Politics and government 9. United States 10. 21st century 11. Life stories — Science, technology, and medicine — Healthcare professionals 12. Politics and global affairs — Public health 13. Society and culture — Illness and disease — Epidemics 14. Science Writing — Medicine and health — Illness and disease

The #1 best-selling author's nonfiction narrative pits a band of medical visionaries against the wall of ignorance that was the official response of the Trump administration to the outbreak of COVID-19.

"Maverick doctors, scientists, and public health officials took charge of the fight against Covid-19 when the CDC and the Trump administration failed to act, according to this illuminating rehash of recent history." —*Publishers Weekly*

Oshinsky, David M.
★ *Polio:* **An American Story.** David M. Oshinsky. Oxford University Press 2005. 342, 16 p. of plates : Illustration

ISBN 9780195152944

Grades: 11 12 Adult 614.5

1. Salk, Jonas, 1914-1995 2. Vaccines 3. Viruses 4. Poliomyelitis 5. United States 6. 1940s 7. 1950s 8. Science Writing — Medicine and health — Illness and disease 9. History writing — Plague and famine 10. History writing — United States 11. Adult books for young adults

LC 2004025249

Pulitzer Prize for History, 2006.

This comprehensive and gripping narrative covers all the challenges, characters, and controversies in America's relentless struggle against polio. Funded by philanthropy and grassroots contributions, Salk's killed-virus vaccine (1954) and Sabin's live-virus vaccine (1961) began to eradicate this dreaded disease.

"This book is a rich and illuminating analysis that convincingly grounds the ways and means of modern American research in the response to polio." —*New York Times Book Review*

Includes bibliographical references and index.

Preston, Richard
Crisis **in the Red Zone:** *The Story of the Deadliest Ebola Outbreak in History, and of the Outbreaks to Come.* by Richard Preston. Random House 2019. 384 p.

ISBN 9780812998832

Grades: Adult 614.5

1. Ebola virus disease 2. Epidemics 3. Public health 4. Virus diseases 5. Diseases 6. Humanitarian assistance 7. International relations 8. Health policy 9. West Africa 10. Africa 11. 2010s 12. Science Writing — Medicine and health — Illness and disease 13. Society and culture — Illness and disease — Epidemics

LC 2019010492

Chronicles the 2013-2014 Ebola outbreak in West Africa and the global efforts of health professionals to contain the virus, and provides an urgent wake-up call about the future of emerging viruses.

"Medical thriller, cautionary tale, and a public health call-to-arms are all bundled together in this powerful read." —*Booklist*

The **Hot** *Zone.* Richard Preston. Random House 1994. xiii, 300 p. : Map (Dark biology, 1)

ISBN 9780606142304

Grades: 11 12 Adult 614.5

1. Ebola virus disease 2. Diseases 3. Epidemics 4. Viruses 5. History of medicine 6. Africa 7. Science Writing — Medicine and health — Illness and disease 8. Adult books for young adults 9. Nonfiction that reads like fiction

LC 94013415

Garden State Teen Book Award (New Jersey), Nonfiction, 1998; YALSA Best Books for Young Adults, 1996; School Library Journal Best Books: Best Adult Books 4 Teens, 1995.

A highly infectious, deadly virus from the central African rain forest suddenly appears in the suburbs of Washington, D.C. There is no cure. In a few days 90 percent of its victims are dead. A secret military SWAT team of soldiers and scientists is mobilized to stop the outbreak of this exotic "hot" virus. The Hot Zone tells this dramatic story, giving a hair-raising account of the appearance of rare and lethal viruses and their "crashes" into the human race.

"Ebola, a lethal virus that slumbers in an unknown host somewhere in the rain forest, sneaked into the United States in 1989 in a shipment of primates that ended up in a monkey house in Reston, Virginia. This virus jumps between species easily, and takes only weeks to kill its victim, with gory hemorrhaging from various orifices. Preston tells the suspenseful tale of its detection, and gives vivid life to the members of the SWAT team that, for eighteen bio-hazardous days, combatted the strain now known as Ebola Reston." —*The New Yorker*

Volumes 1 and 3 of this series are nonfiction titles, while volume 2 is a fictional novel.

Quammen, David
★ **Breathless:** *The Scientific Race to Defeat a Deadly Virus.* David Quammen. Simon & Schuster 2022. 352 p.

ISBN 9781982164362

Grades: Adult 614.5

1. COVID-19 (Disease) 2. COVID-19 Pandemic, 2020- 3. Coronaviruses 4. Epidemics 5. Viruses 6. Virology 7. Vaccines 8. Public health 9. Communicable diseases 10. Scientists 11. Science Writing — Medicine and health — Illness and disease 12. Science Writing — Medicine and health — Medical breakthroughs 13. Life stories — Science, technology, and medicine

National Book Award for Nonfiction finalist, 2022.

The story of the worldwide scientific quest to decipher the coronavirus SARS-CoV-2, trace its source and make possible the vaccines to fight the Covid-19 pandemic.

"An authoritative new history of Covid-19 and its predecessors....Unsettling global health news brilliantly delivered by an expert." —*Kirkus*

Smith, Michael
Cabin **Fever:** *The Harrowing Journey of a Cruise Ship at the Dawn of a Pandemic.* by Michael Smith and Jonathan Franklin. Doubleday, a division of Penguin Random House LLC 2022. 288 p.

ISBN 9780385547406

Grades: Adult 614.5

ESSENTIAL AND RECOMMENDED TITLES
614.5 Incidence of and public measures to prevent specific diseases and kinds of diseases

1. COVID-19 (Disease) 2. COVID-19 Pandemic, 2020- 3. Cruise ships 4. Ship passengers 5. Seniors 6. Ships 7. Voyages and travels 8. Society and culture — Illness and disease — Epidemics 9. Business and economics — Industries — Retail products and services
LC 2021049293

The story of the Holland America cruise ship Zaandam, which set sail with 1,200 passengers days before COVID-19 shut down the world in March 2020 and found itself denied safe harbor everywhere.

"A harrowing thriller that brings the wide-ranging impacts of the COVID pandemic into the microcosmic enclosed world of a cruise ship." —*Library Journal*

Spinney, Laura
★ *Pale Rider: The Spanish Flu of 1918 and How It Changed the World.* Laura Spinney. PublicAffairs 2017. VIII, 332 pages : Illustration; Map; Portrait
ISBN 9781610397674
Grades: Adult   614.5
1. Influenza Epidemic, 1918-1919 2. Influenza 3. Epidemics 4. Sick people 5. Viruses 6. Vaccines 7. Epidemiology 8. 1910s 9. 1920s 10. History writing — Science, technology, and medicine 11. History writing — Plague and famine 12. Science Writing — Medicine and health — Illness and disease
LC 2017933356

Describes the enormous-scale human disaster caused by the 1918 Spanish Flu and uses the latest findings in history, virology, epidemiology, psychology and economics to show how the pandemic permanently changed global politics, race relations, medicine, religion and the arts.

"A compelling, expert account of a half-forgotten historical catastrophe." —*Kirkus*

Wadman, Meredith
The Vaccine Race: Science, Politics, and the Human Costs of Defeating Disease. Meredith Wadman. Viking 2017. 400 p.
ISBN 9780525427537
Grades: Adult   614.5
1. Vaccination 2. Communicable diseases 3. Vaccines 4. Human experimentation in medicine 5. Health policy 6. Measles 7. United States 8. 1960s 9. History writing — Science, technology, and medicine 10. Science Writing — Medicine and health — Medical breakthroughs
LC 2016044189

Longlisted for the Andrew Carnegie Medal for Excellence in Non-Fiction, 2018.

Documents the controversial story of the development of the first widely used normal human cell line, paving the way for some of the world's most important vaccines, against a backdrop of the devastating rubella epidemic of the mid-1960s.

Includes bibliographical references and index.

Wasik, Bill
Rabid: A Cultural History of the World's Most Diabolical Virus. Bill Wasik and Monica Murphy. Viking 2012. 240 p.
ISBN 9780670023738
Grades: Adult   614.5
1. Diseases 2. Animals as carriers of disease 3. Rabies 4. Science Writing — Medicine and health — Illness and disease
LC 2011043903

Library Journal Best Books, 2012.

Charts the history, science and cultural mythology of rabies, documenting how before its vaccine the disease caused fatal brain infections and sparked the creations of famous monsters including werewolves, vampires and zombies.

Includes index.

Werb, Dan
The Invisible Siege: The Rise of Coronaviruses and the Search for a Cure. Dan Werb. Crown 2022. 304 p.
ISBN 9780593239230
Grades: Adult   614.5

1. COVID-19 (Disease) 2. Epidemics 3. Virus diseases 4. Coronaviruses 5. COVID-19 Pandemic, 2020- 6. Coronavirus infections 7. Society and culture — Illness and disease — Epidemics 8. Science Writing — Medicine and health — Illness and disease 9. History writing — Science, technology, and medicine
LC 2021052956

Science in Society Book Award (Canadian Science Writers' Association), for Adult Nonfiction, 2022; Hilary Weston Writers' Trust Prize, 2022.

Drawing on decades of scientific investigation, an epidemiologist, tracing the rise of the coronavirus family and society's desperate attempt to counter its threat, tells the story of a group of scientists who foresaw the danger and spent decades working to stop a looming pandemic.

"Great for those who want to understand the science of fighting pandemics while trying to avoid conspiracy theories and politicization." —*Library Journal*

Includes bibliographical references and index.

Wright, Lawrence
★ *The Plague Year: America in the Time of Covid.* Lawrence Wright. Alfred a Knopf 2021. 288 p.
ISBN 9780593320723
Grades: Adult   614.5
1. COVID-19 (Disease) 2. COVID-19 Pandemic, 2020- 3. Epidemics 4. Medical care 5. Physicians and nurses 6. Public health 7. Science Writing — Medicine and health — Illness and disease 8. Society and culture — Illness and disease — Epidemics 9. Politics and global affairs — Public health 10. History writing — Plague and famine

Honoring to the medical professionals around the country who've risked their lives to fight the virus, the Pulitzer Prize-winning author provides essential information—and fascinating historical parallels—examining the medical, economic, political, and social ramifications of the COVID-19 pandemic.

"While there are already several other books about COVID-19 and its sociological impact on the United States, this wide-ranging yet deeply personal account is a great starting point. At times infuriating, unbelievable, heartbreaking, and even witty, Wright's narrative is sorely needed." —*Library Journal*

Xuecun, Murong
Deadly Quiet City: True Stories from Wuhan. Murong Xuecun. The New Press 2023. VII, 309 pages
ISBN 9781620977927
Grades: Adult   614.5
1. Xuecun, Murong 2. Quarantine 3. COVID-19 (Disease) 4. COVID-19 Pandemic, 2020- 5. 21st century 6. Interviews 7. History writing — Asia — China 8. Science writing — Medicine and health 9. Society and culture — Illness and disease — Epidemics 10. Life stories — Facing adversity

"Fear—of a novel virus, an oppressive government, and death—is the common denominator in this tragic account constructed from interviews about the many hardships brought on by the COVID-19 outbreak and strictly enforced Chinese lockdowns at the start of the pandemic....These stories of suffering, propaganda, and abolition of personal freedoms will inform, sadden, and enrage readers." —*Booklist*

Originally published in Australia by Hardie Grant, Richmond, Victoria, in 2022.

Zuckerman, Gregory
A Shot to Save the World: The Inside Story of the Life-or-Death Race for a COVID-19 Vaccine. Gregory Zuckerman. Portfolio/Penguin 2021. xxiii, 355 pages
ISBN 9780593420393
Grades: Adult   614.5
1. COVID-19 (Disease) 2. Vaccines 3. COVID-19 Pandemic, 2020- 4. Vaccine industry and trade 5. Business and economics — Industries — Medical 6. Science Writing — Medicine and health
LC Bl2021027035

Chronicles the efforts to develop a vaccine for COVID-19, describing how a small, unlikely group of scientists and executives overcame corporate clashes and unexpected drama to create effective, lifesaving vaccines within a short amount of time.

"An intensely researched, rewarding account of an impressive medical triumph." —*Kirkus*

Includes bibliographical references (pages 345-355).

615 Pharmacology and therapeutics

Vanderbes, Jennifer

★ *Wonder* Drug: The Secret History of Thalidomide in America and Its Hidden Victims. by Jennifer Vanderbes. Random House 2023. 336 p.
ISBN 9780525512264

Grades: Adult   615

1. Drug industry and trade 2. Ethics 3. Drug industry corruption 4. Drugs 5. Corruption 6. Birth defects 7. United States history 8. Business and economics — Industries — Medical 9. History Writing — Science, technology, and medicine 10. Nonfiction that reads like fiction

LC 2022049196

This gripping, never-before-told story of thalidomide, the most notorious drug of the 20th century that harmed scores of Americans, and its origins were linked to the Nazis, gives voice to the unrecognized victims of this epic scandal and exposes the deceptive practices of Big Pharma that continue to endanger lives today.

"Vanderbes makes a complex and important story understandable...This is a medical must-read." —*Booklist*

Includes bibliographical references and index.

615.3 Organic drugs

Borrell, Brendan

The **First Shots**: The Epic Rivalries and Heroic Science Behind the Race to the Coronavirus Vaccine. Brendan Borrell. Mariner Books 2021. 320 p.
ISBN 9780358569848

Grades: Adult   615.3

1. COVID-19 (Disease) 2. Public health 3. Vaccines 4. Medical research 5. COVID-19 Pandemic, 2020- 6. Vaccine industry and trade 7. Page to screen 8. Politics and global affairs — Public health 9. Society and culture — Illness and disease — Epidemics 10. Science Writing — Medicine and health — Illness and disease

Heroic science. Chaotic politics. Billionaire entrepreneurs. Award-winning journalist Brendan Borrell brings the defining story of our times alive through compulsively readable, first-time reporting on the players leading the fight against a vicious virus. The First Shots, soon to be the subject of an HBO limited series with superstar director and producer Adam McKay (Succession, Vice, the Big Short), draws on exclusive, high-level access to weave together the intense vaccine-race conflicts among hard-driving, heroic scientists and the epic rivalries among Washington power players that shaped 18 months of fear, resolve, and triumph.

"Journalist Borrell debuts with a powerful behind-the-scenes look at Operation Warp Speed, the effort to develop a Covid-19 vaccine in record time.... The result is a page-turning introduction to a key part of the pandemic." —*Publishers Weekly*

Chevallier, Andrew

Encyclopedia of Herbal Medicine: 550 Herbs and Remedies for Common Ailments. Andrew Chevallier, FNIMH.. DK 2023. 351 pages : Illustration; Color
ISBN 9780744081794

Grades: Adult   615.3

1. Medicinal plants 2. Science writing — Medicine and health — Alternative medicine 3. Reference — Encyclopedias

LC BI2016021377

Provides an herb directory with photographic index, guidelines for growing medicinal plants and making home remedies, and historical and cultural perspectives for herbal medicine around the world.

With a focus on safety, a reference guide to natural remedies includes information on 550 key herbs—such as ginger, lavender, thyme and dandelion—and their uses as remedies in common ailments and how to grow, harvest and process home treatments.

"Though this selection should not be used as a medical reference on its own, it goes into enough depth for average readers looking for home remedies." —*Library Journal*

Includes bibliographical references (page 322) and indexes.

Davidson, Tish

The Vaccine Debate. Tish Davidson. Greenwood 2019. xii, 236 pages : Illustration
ISBN 9781440843532

Grades: Adult   615.3

1. Science writing — Medicine and health — Illness and disease — Vaccination

LC 2018030122

Providing accurate, accessible information on vaccines and the controversies that surround them, this book outlines the history of vaccine regulation and interactions between vaccines and the immune system, and thoughtfully considers each vaccine debate.

"This is an excellent resource for public, consumer-health, and school libraries." —*Booklist*

Includes bibliographical references and index.

615.5 Therapeutics

Offit, Paul A.

You Bet Your Life: From Blood Transfusions to Mass Vaccination, the Long and Risky History of Medical Innovations. Paul A. Offit, MD.. Basic Books 2021. 258 p.
ISBN 9781541620391

Grades: Adult   615.5

1. Medical innovations 2. Human experimentation in medicine 3. Clinical trials 4. Risk 5. Physician and patient 6. Medicine 7. History writing — Science, technology, and medicine 8. Science Writing — Medicine and health — Medical breakthroughs 9. Life stories — Science, technology, and medicine

Every medical decision—whether to have chemotherapy, an X-ray, or surgery—is a risk, no matter which way you choose. In You Bet Your Life, physician Paul A. Offit argues that, from the first blood transfusions four hundred years ago to the hunt for a COVID-19 vaccine, risk has been essential to the discovery of new treatments. More importantly, understanding the risks is crucial to whether, as a society or as individuals, we accept them. Told in Offit's vigorous and rigorous style, You Bet Your Life is an entertaining history of medicine. But it also lays bare the tortured relationships between intellectual breakthroughs, political realities, and human foibles. Our pandemic year has shown us, with its debates over lockdowns, masks, and vaccines, how easy it is to get everything wrong. You Bet Your Life is an essential read for getting the future a bit more right.

"A well-written and informative look at the reality of medical advancement, including poignant examples of its often-fatal repercussions." —*Library Journal*

Includes bibliographical references and index.

615.7 Pharmacokinetics

Blaser, Martin J.

Missing Microbes: How the Overuse of Antibiotics Is Fueling Our Modern Plagues. Dr. Martin Blaser. Henry Holt and Company 2014. 288 pages
ISBN 9780805098105

Grades: Adult   615.7

1. Antibiotics 2. Drug resistance in microorganisms 3. Diseases 4. Science Writing — Medicine and health — Illness and disease 5. Society and culture — Illness and disease

LC 2013042578

A critically important and startling look at the harmful effects of overusing antibiotics, from the field's leading expert Tracing one scientist's journey toward

ESSENTIAL AND RECOMMENDED TITLES
615.8 Specific therapies and kinds of therapies

understanding the crucial importance of the microbiome, this revolutionary book will take readers to the forefront of trail-blazing research while revealing the damage that overuse of antibiotics is doing to our health: Contributing to the rise of obesity, asthma, diabetes, and certain forms of cancer. In Missing Microbes, Dr. Martin Blaser invites us into the wilds of the human microbiome where for hundreds of thousands of years bacterial and human cells have existed in a peaceful symbiosis that is responsible for the health and equilibrium of our body. Now, this invisible eden is being irrevocably damaged by some of our most revered medical advances—antibiotics—threatening the extinction of our irreplaceable microbes with terrible health consequences.

"A masterful work of preventive health and superb science writing."—*Booklist*

Includes index.

English, Camper
Doctors and Distillers: The Remarkable Medicinal History of Beer, Wine, Spirits, and Cocktails. Camper English. Penguin Books 2022. 400 p.
ISBN 9780143134923
Grades: Adult   615.7
1. Alcoholic beverages 2. Drinking 3. Therapeutics 4. Medicine 5. Food writing — History and microhistory
LC 2021058521

In Doctors and Distillers, cocktail expert Camper English reveals how and why the contents of our medicine and liquor cabinets were, until surprisingly recently, one and the same.

"For the curious imbiber, or simply those looking for a few choice trivia tidbits to drop at cocktail parties, this is a winner." —*Publishers Weekly*

Includes bibliographical references and index.

Kempner, Joanna
Psychedelic Outlaws: The Movement Revolutionizing Modern Medicine. by Joanna Kempner, PhD.. Hachette Books 2024. 320 p.
ISBN 9780306828942
Grades: Adult   615.7
1. Medical care 2. Medicine 3. Mushrooms 4. Headache 5. Hallucinogenic mushrooms 6. Drug testing 7. Pain control 8. Medical research 9. 20th century 10. 21st century 11. Science Writing — Medicine and health
LC 2024001704

An award-winning sociologist unearths how a group of ordinary people debilitated by excruciating pain developed their own medicine from home-grown psilocybin mushrooms—crafting near-clinical grade dosing protocols—and fought for recognition in a broken medical system.

"Kempner tells a convoluted story with sympathy and respect, adding her personal experience to solid research." —*Kirkus*

Includes bibliographical references and index.

Kramer, Peter D.
★ *Ordinarily* Well: The Case for Antidepressants. Peter D. Kramer. Farrar, Straus and Giroux 2016. 336 p.
ISBN 9780374280673
Grades: Adult   615.7
1. Antidepressants 2. Psychotropic drugs 3. Depression 4. Mental health 5. Science Writing — Medicine and health — Mental health
LC 2015036472

An eminent psychologist and writer discusses the value of antidepressant drugs.

"Kramer (Listening to Prozac), a psychiatrist and professor at Brown Medical School, makes an energetic and personal case for the role of antidepressants in easing crippling depression. Starting with the history of psychotherapy, when infinite patience was the norm in treatment for depression, Kramer delves into the breakthrough use of imipramine for treatment in the mid-1950s that helped redefine the disorder and invigorate psychopharmacology. Kramer shows that the tools may be imperfect, but people battling severe depression are lucky to have them." —*Publishers Weekly*

Includes index.

Pollan, Michael
How to Change Your Mind: What the New Science of Psychedelics Teaches Us About Consciousness, Dying, Addiction, Depression, and Transcendence. Michael Pollan. Penguin 2018. 496 p.
ISBN 9781594204227
Grades: Adult   615.7
1. Drug use 2. Altered states of consciousness 3. Medical research 4. Psychedelic experience 5. Mental illness 6. Page to screen 7. Science Writing — Medicine and health — Mental health
LC 2018006190

New York Times Notable Book, 2018.

The best-selling author of the Omnivore's Dilemma presents a groundbreaking investigation into the medical and scientific revolution currently taking place in the field of psychedelic drugs, drawing on a range of experiences to trace the criminalization of such substances as LSD and psychedelic mushrooms and how they may offer treatment options for difficult health challenges.

"This nuanced and sophisticated exploration, which asks big questions about meaning-making and spiritual experience, is thought-provoking and eminently readable." —*Publishers Weekly*

Made into a TV show on Netflix, 2022.

Slater, Lauren
Blue Dreams: The Science and the Story of the Drugs That Changed Our Minds. Lauren Slater. Little Brown & Co. 2018. 368 p.
ISBN 9780316370646
Grades: Adult   615.7
1. Psychotropic drugs 2. Drug industry and trade 3. Pharmaceutical research 4. Science 5. Medicine 6. Research 7. Mental health 8. Neurochemistry 9. Prozac 10. History writing — Science, technology, and medicine 11. Science Writing — Medicine and health — Mental health
LC B12018004078

Explores the discovery, invention, science and people behind today's major psychotropic drugs, from the earliest, Thorazine and Lithium, to Prozac, Ecstasy, "magic mushrooms" and through today's most cutting-edge memory drugs and neural implants.

615.8 Specific therapies and kinds of therapies

Fleming, Renee
★ *Music and Mind: Harnessing the Arts for Health and Wellness.* Renee Fleming. Viking Press 2024. 320 p.
ISBN 9780593653197
Grades: Adult   615.8
1. Music therapy 2. Art therapy 3. Human evolution 4. Child development 5. Neuropsychology 6. Music and technology 7. Art and technology 8. Brain 9. Cognitive neuroscience 10. Mind and body 11. Mind and body therapies 12. Essays 13. Science Writing — Medicine and health — Brain function and memory

A growing body of research has shown music and arts therapies to be effective tools for addressing a widening array of conditions, from providing pain relief and alleviating anxiety and depression, to regaining speech after stroke or traumatic brain injury, and improving mobility for people with disorders that include Parkinson's disease and MS. In Music and Mind, Renee Fleming draws upon her own experience as an advocate to showcase the breadth of this booming field, inviting leading experts to share their discoveries. In addition to describing therapeutic benefits, the book explores evolution, brain function, childhood development, and technology as applied to arts and health.

"The result is an expansive and thought-provoking look at the dynamic intersection between art and science." —*Publishers Weekly*

Hongoltz-hetling, Matthew
If It Sounds Like a Quack: A Journey to the Fringes of American Medicine. Matthew Hongoltz-hetling. Public Affairs 2023. 320 p.
ISBN 9781541788879
Grades: Adult   615.8

PUBLIC LIBRARY CORE COLLECTION: NONFICTION
Twentieth Edition

1. Alternative medicine 2. Quacks and quackery 3. Medical care 4. Public health 5. Misinformation 6. United States 7. Science Writing — Medicine and health 8. History Writing — United States

"A wry, wide-ranging investigation into the 'alternative medicine' business and the dangers it poses….A walk on the weird side with an author who knows when to be funny and when to be serious." —*Kirkus*

Kelley, Margot Anne
A Gardener at the End of the World. Margot Anne Kelley. Godine 2024. 240 p.
ISBN 9781567927344
Grades: Adult   615.8
1. Kelley, Margot Anne 2. Gardening 3. COVID-19 Pandemic, 2020- 4. Human ecology 5. Nature 6. Seeds 7. Gardens 8. Viruses 9. Rural life 10. Epidemics 11. Maine 12. 2020s 13. Autobiographies and memoirs 14. Life stories — Nature and outdoors 15. Nature Writing — Personal responses 16. Nature Writing — Gardens
LC 2023039462

A gardener's pandemic journal that combines memoir with an exploration of the natural world both inside and outside the garden.

"A well-written chronicle of a gardening year, a pandemic, and their intertwined histories. Will appeal to a broad range of readers." —*Library Journal*

Louv, Richard
Our Wild Calling: How Connecting with Animals Can Transform Our Lives; and Save Theirs. by Richard Louv. Algonquin Books of Chapel Hill 2019. 288 p.
ISBN 9781616205607
Grades: Adult   615.8
1. Animals 2. Nature 3. Pet therapy 4. Human-animal communication 5. Human-animal relationships 6. Nature Writing — Animal Studies 7. Adult books for young adults
LC 2019019787

The bestselling author of the landmark work Last Child in the Woods now shows how cultivating the powerful, mysterious, and fragile bond between humans and other animals can improve our mental, physical, and spiritual health, protect our planet, and serve as an antidote to the loneliness of our species.

Includes bibliographical references and index.

Taylor, Madisyn
Unmedicated: The Four Pillars of Natural Wellness. Madisyn Taylor. Beyond Words 2018. xxxviii, 165 p.
ISBN 9781582706573
Grades: Adult   615.8
1. Mind and body therapies 2. Depression 3. Anxiety disorders 4. Alternative medicine 5. Self-Help — Mental health — Depression 6. Spirituality and Religion — Body, mind, and spirit 7. Science writing — Medicine and health — Alternative medicine
LC 2018170141

The cofounder of the holistic lifestyle website DailyOM presents a gentle and accessible step-by-step guide to moving from excessive reliance on medications to fundamentally healing yourself through four pillars of natural wellness. Madisyn Taylor was plagued by depression and anxiety, suffering from chronic physical problems that left her desperate for solutions. Spending decades searching for answers, she first turned to the medical community, which put her on a rollercoaster course of numerous doctors, tests, and an unhealthy reliance on medications that left her numb and lifeless. With her happiness and future on the line, she then made the decision to become unmedicated, reaching out to the natural, holistic health realm. And after years of practice and research, Madisyn developed an integrative wellness program that put her back in the driver's seat of her health, and ultimately, her life. Unmedicated is her thoughtful account of how she broke free from binding mental chains and physical ailments to be happy, healthy, and productive; it is also a guide for you to apply her practical techniques to your own healing journey. Madisyn offers a daily program of easy-to-follow actions based on four pillars that will build a lifelong foundation for health: clear your mind; strengthen your body; nurture your spirit; and find your tribe. Whether you want to be happy and stay happy, find relief from depression and anxiety, or heal and create a healthy change, Unmedicated is a gentle, compassionate, and achievable path that empowers you to take back your life and live fully.

"Taylor. . .shares her story of her own overreliance on medications that numbed her to her full potential in this instructive take on holistic medicine." —*Publishers Weekly*

Includes bibliographical references.

615.9 Toxicology

Bradbury, Neil
A Taste for Poison: Eleven Deadly Molecules and the Killers Who Used Them. Neil Bradbury. St. Martin's Press 2022. 288 p.
ISBN 9781250270757
Grades: Adult   615.9
1. Poisoners 2. Poisoning 3. Poisons 4. True Crime — General 5. History writing — Science, technology, and medicine 6. Science Writing — Biology 7. Debut title
LC 2021026597

Blending popular science, medical history and true crime, a Professor of Physiology and Biophysics explores, on a cellular level, the poisons used by spurned lovers, shady scientists, medical professionals and political assassins throughout history.

"Physiology and biophysics professor Bradbury debuts with an accessible and fascinating study of poisons, using real murder cases to explain how the chemicals affect the human body." —*Publishers Weekly*

Includes bibliographical references.

Hanna-Attisha, Mona
What the Eyes Don't See: A Story of Crisis, Resistance, and Hope in an American City. Mona Hanna-Attisha. Oneworld Publications 2018. 240 p.
ISBN 9780399590832
Grades: Adult   615.9
1. Hanna-Attisha, Mona 2. Women pediatricians 3. Water-supply 4. Cities and towns 5. Lead contamination 6. Alliances 7. Scandals 8. Public health 9. Public works 10. Women immigrants 11. Municipal government 12. State governments 13. Health hazards 14. Flint, Michigan 15. Michigan 16. Autobiographies and memoirs 17. Adult books for young adults 18. Life stories — Science, technology, and medicine — Healthcare professionals 19. Life stories — Politics — Activists and reformers 20. Society and culture — Social activism and philanthropy 21. Politics and global affairs — Public health
LC 2018002721

New York Times Notable Book, 2018.

A compelling firsthand account of the Flint water crisis traces how 100,000 Americans were poisoned by lead in their water supply with the government's awareness, tracing the pediatrician author's efforts to prove exposure in the face of brutal backlash.

"Essential for all readers who care about children, health, and the environment. This should be required reading for public servants as an incisive cautionary tale, and for pediatricians and youth advocates as a story of heroism in the ranks of people who have the capacity to make a difference." —*Library Journal*

616 Diseases

Brody, Jane E.
Jane Brody's Guide to the Great Beyond: A Practical Primer to Help You and Your Loved Ones Prepare Medically, Legally, and Emotionally for the End of Life. Jane Brody. Random House 2009. xxiv, 287 p. : Illustration
ISBN 9781400066544
Grades: Adult   616
1. Palliative treatment 2. Terminal care 3. Family and Relationships — Aging and Death 4. Self-Help — Mental health — Grief and loss
LC 2008016583

ESSENTIAL AND RECOMMENDED TITLES
616 Diseases

A guide to proactively prepare for the end of life covers topics ranging from financial planning and medical issues to emotional considerations, with advice on health care proxies, wills, funeral preparations, and palliative care.

Covering topics ranging from financial planning and medical issues to emotional considerations, the best-selling author of Jane Brody's Nutrition Book offers a thoughtful guide to help readers proactively prepare for the end of life, with advice on health care proxies, wills, funeral preparations, palliative care, and more.

"An instructive, inspiring and reassuring work full of compassion and humor (along with several cartoons from various New Yorker illustrators), this volume belongs on every family's bookshelf." —*Publishers Weekly*

Includes bibliographical references and index.

Kolata, Gina Bari
Mercies in Disguise: A Story of Hope, a Family's Genetic Destiny, and the Science That Rescued Them. Gina Kolata. St. Martin's Press 2017. 272 pages
ISBN 9781250064349
Grades: Adult   616
1. Baxley family 2. Baxley, Amanda 3. Medical genetics 4. Families 5. Medical ethics 6. Brain diseases 7. Medical research 8. Genetics 9. Genetic screening 10. Health 11. Heredity 12. Nervous system 13. Diseases 14. Science Writing — Medicine and health — Illness and disease 15. Family and Relationships — Illness and the Family 16. Science Writing — Medicine and health — Medical breakthroughs 17. Nonfiction that reads like fiction
LC 2016044044

A New York Times science reporter follows a family through genetic illness and one courageous daughter who decides her fate shall no longer be decided by a genetic flaw.

"Kolatas book reads like a medical thriller and readers will be caught up in the lives of the protagonists." —*Publishers Weekly*

Includes index.

Lalkhen, Abdul-Ghaaliq
An Anatomy of Pain: How the Body and the Mind Experience and Endure Physical Suffering. Dr. Abdul-Ghaaliq Lalkhen. Scribner 2021. 256 p.
ISBN 9781982160982
Grades: Adult   616
1. Pain 2. Pain control 3. Chronic pain 4. Nervous system 5. Senses and sensation 6. Suffering 7. Analgesics 8. Treatment 9. Science Writing — Medicine and health

An authoritative examination of the science of pain includes coverage of the current landscape of treatments, including opioids, while illuminating the complex body and brain interactions that trigger pain and its perception.

"This splendid book—informative, empathic, and wise—about a universal experience will surely promote healing." —*Booklist*

Lustig, Robert H.
Metabolical: The Lure and the Lies of Processed Food, Nutrition, and Modern Medicine. Robert H. Lustig, MD, MSL.. HarperWave, an imprint of HarperCollinsPublishers 2021. VIII, 407 pages : Illustration
ISBN 9780063027718
Grades: Adult   616
1. Chronic diseases 2. Treatment 3. Science Writing — Medicine and health — Diet and nutrition
LC 2021002178

The New York Times bestselling author of Fat Chance and pediatric neuroendocrinologist explains the eight pathologies that underlie all chronic disease, proposing an urgent manifesto and strategy to cure both us and the planet.

"This indictment of the food industry lands as a must-read guide to a healthier world." —*Publishers Weekly*

Includes index.

Mukherjee, Siddhartha
★ *The Gene: An Intimate History.* Siddhartha Mukherjee. Scribner 2016. 592 p.
ISBN 9781476733500
Grades: Adult   616
1. Genetics 2. Heredity 3. Genes 4. Science Writing — Biology
LC 2015039962

ALA Notable Book, 2017; Library Journal Best Books, 2016; New York Times Notable Book, 2016.

From the Pulitzer Prize-winning, best-selling author of the Emperor of All Maladies comes a magnificent history of the gene and a response to the defining question of the future: What becomes of being human when we learn to "read" and "write" our own genetic information?

"Sobering, humbling, and extraordinarily rich reading from a wise and gifted writer who sees how far we have comebut how much farther we have to go to understand our human nature and destiny." —*Kirkus*

Includes bibliographical references and index.

O'Rourke, Meghan
★ *The Invisible Kingdom: Reimagining Chronic Illness.* Meghan O'Rourke. Riverhead Books 2022. 288 p.
ISBN 9781594633799
Grades: Adult   616
1. O'Rourke, Meghan 2. Chronic diseases 3. Sick people 4. People with chronic illnesses 5. Autoimmune diseases 6. Medical care 7. Diagnosis 8. Uncertainty 9. Science Writing — Medicine and health — Illness and disease 10. Life stories — Facing adversity — Medical issues — Physical illness
LC 2021048490

National Book Award for Nonfiction finalist, 2022.

A silent epidemic of chronic illnesses afflicts tens of millions of Americans: These are diseases that are poorly understood, frequently marginalized, and can go undiagnosed and unrecognized altogether. Renowned writer Meghan O'Rourke delivers a revelatory investigation into this elusive category of "invisible" illness that encompasses autoimmune diseases, post-treatment Lyme disease syndrome, and now long COVID. Drawing on her own medical experiences as well as a decade of interviews with doctors, patients, researchers, and public health experts, O'Rourke traces the history of Western definitions of illness, and reveals how inherited ideas of cause, diagnosis, and treatment have led us to ignore a host of hard-to-understand medical conditions, ones that resist easy description or simple cures.

"This work may serve as an affirmation that people living with chronic illness are not alone. For those close to one with chronic illness or who would like to learn more, this firsthand account is both moving and educational." —*Library Journal*

Warraich, Haider
The Song of Our Scars: The Untold Story of Pain. Haider Warraich. Basic Books 2022. 320 p.
ISBN 9781541675308
Grades: Adult   616
1. Warraich, Haider 2. Pain 3. Chronic pain 4. Physicians 5. Medical care 6. Treatment 7. United States 8. Autobiographies and memoirs 9. Life stories — Facing adversity — Medical issues — Physical illness 10. Life stories — Science, technology, and medicine — Healthcare professionals 11. Science Writing — Medicine and health — Illness and disease
LC 2021038446

A physician at Brigham and Women's Hospital, Harvard Medical School and the VA Boston Healthcare System, himself a sufferer of chronic pain, shows that only by reckoning with both pain's complicated history and its biology can today's doctors adequately treat their patients' suffering.

"A must-read for anyone with chronic pain and those in the health professions." —*Library Journal*

Includes bibliographical references and index.

PUBLIC LIBRARY CORE COLLECTION: NONFICTION
Twentieth Edition

616.0072 Diseases—Humans—Medical research

Jena, Anupam B.
Random Acts of Medicine: The Hidden Forces That Sway Doctors, Impact Patients, and Shape Our Health. Anupam B. Jena, M.D, PH.D. and Christopher Worsham, M.D.. Doubleday 2023. 336 p.
ISBN 9780385548816
Grades: Adult   616.0072
1. Medical care 2. Hospitals 3. Economics 4. Physicians 5. Hospital patients 6. Treatment 7. Economic indicators 8. Statistics 9. Health policy 10. United States 11. Science Writing — Medicine and health 12. Business and economics — Industries — Medical 13. Business and economics — Economics — Socioeconomics

A book at the intersection of health and economics reveals the hidden side of medicine and how unexpected—but predictable—events can profoundly affect our health.

"An ingenious exploration of 'natural experiments' that influence medical care." —*Kirkus*

616.02 Special topics of diseases

Butler, Katy
The Art of Dying Well: A Practical Guide to a Good End of Life. Katy Butler. Scribner 2019. xi, 274 pages : Illustration
ISBN 9781501135316
Grades: Adult   616.02
1. Terminal care 2. Death 3. Human comfort 4. Decision-making 5. Self-Help — Mental health — Grief and loss 6. Family and Relationships — Aging and Death
LC 2018037020

Draws on patient insights to counsel readers on how to navigate the health-care system for best-possible life quality and how to achieve an optimal end-of-life experience.

"Journalist Butler offers a straightforward, well-organized, nondepressing guide to managing the run-up to one's inevitable demise." —*Publishers Weekly*

Includes bibliographical references (pages 231-256) and index.

Ely, Wes
Every Deep-Drawn Breath: A Critical Care Doctor on Healing, Recovery, and Transforming Medicine in the ICU. Wes Ely, MD.. Scribner 2021. 288 p.
ISBN 9781982171148
Grades: Adult   616.02
1. Ely, Wes 2. Critical Care 3. Intensive Care Units 4. Physician and patient 5. Hospital patients 6. People with critical Illnesses 7. Medicine 8. Medical care reform 9. Medical care 10. Treatment 11. Science Writing — Medicine and health — Doctors and nurses 12. Life stories — Science, technology, and medicine — Healthcare professionals
LC 2021020531

Over the next ten years, 40 to 60 million people in this country will be admitted to the ICU. Most of these hospitalizations will be sudden, unexpected, and harrowing, experiences that can alter patients and their families physically and emotionally, with effects that endure for years. Every Deep-Drawn Breath is a rich blend of science, medical history, profoundly humane patient stories, and personal reflection. Dr. Wes Ely's mission is to prevent patients from being inadvertently harmed by the technology that is keeping them alive. For decades, millions of ICU survivors left the hospital with disabling symptoms including newly acquired dementia, depression, PTSD, and nerve damage, all now recognized as Post Intensive Care Syndrome, or PICS (a severe subset of Long Covid symptoms). Dr. Ely's groundbreaking investigations advanced the understanding of PICS and introduced crucial changes that reshaped intensive care: Minimizing sedation, maximizing mobility, attending to the family, and providing supportive aftercare.

"Meaningful, thought-provoking insight into the world of critical care." —*Kirkus*

Includes bibliographical references and index.

Fersko-Weiss, Henry
Caring for the Dying: The Doula Approach to a Meaningful Death. Henry Fersko-Weiss. Conari Press, an imprint of Red Wheel/Weiser, LLC 2017. xiv, 222 pages
ISBN 9781573246965
Grades: Adult   616.02
1. Terminal care 2. Family and Relationships — Aging and Death 3. Self-Help — Mental health — Grief and loss
LC 2016041229

Provides a way to care for the dying based on the model of care birth doulas provide.

An Open Center Book—Title page.

Green, Stefanie
This Is Assisted Dying: A Doctor's Story of Empowering Patients at the End of Life. Stefanie Green. Scribner 2022. 288 p.
ISBN 9781982129460
Grades: Adult   616.02
1. Green, Stefanie 2. Terminal care 3. Death 4. Women physicians 5. Aging 6. Autobiographies and memoirs 7. Canadian literature 8. Life stories — Science, technology, and medicine — Healthcare professionals 9. Science Writing — Medicine and health 10. Family and relationships — Aging and death

In this candid and powerfully emotional book, a leading pioneer in medically assisted dying, shares the voices of her patients, her colleagues and her own narrative, changing the way people think about their choices at the end of life.

"A humane, cleareyed view of how and why one can leave the world by choice." —*Kirkus*

Lamas, Daniela J.
You Can Stop Humming Now: A Doctor's Stories of Life, Death, and in Between. Daniela J. Lamas. Little Brown & Co. 2018. 304 p.
ISBN 9780316393171
Grades: Adult   616.02
1. Critical care 2. Physicians 3. Medicine 4. Patients 5. Second chances 6. Life change events 7. Science Writing — Medicine and health
LC 2017947289

A critical care doctor examines the lives of people who were given a second chance through treatments and technologies including a man whose heart was replaced by a battery-operated pump and a man who found a kidney donor on social media.

"This thoughtful, reflective, and beautifully rendered book examines the costs of modern medicine. Readers who enjoy books by Oliver Sacks and Atul Gawande, or Paul Kalanithi's When Breath Becomes Air will find this volume moving and provocative." —*Library Journal*

Volandes, Angelo E.
The Conversation: A Revolutionary Plan for End-of-life Care. Angelo Volandes. Bloomsbury 2015. 256 p.
ISBN 9781620408544
Grades: Adult   616.02
1. Terminal care 2. Last days 3. Palliative treatment 4. Quality of life 5. Physician and patient 6. Death 7. Medical ethics 8. Science Writing — Medicine and health
LC 2014028386

Harvard Medical School physician Angelo Volandes offers a solution to traumatic end-of-life care: Talking, medicine's oldest and least technological tool in the proverbial black bag.

"Written with passion and clarity, this book moves beyond others on the topic by including empirical evidence of how to make such conversations about end-of-life care most effective." —*Library Journal*

Includes bibliographical references and index.

ESSENTIAL AND RECOMMENDED TITLES
616.07 Pathology

616.07 Pathology

Dettmer, Philipp
Immune: A Journey into the Mysterious System That Keeps You Alive. Philipp Dettmer. Random House 2021. 304 p.
ISBN 9780593241318
Grades: Adult   616.07
★ 1. Immune system 2. Immunology 3. Human physiology 4. Science Writing — Biology 5. Science Writing — Medicine and health
LC 2021010071

Although everyone who has ever had a cold is familiar with the human immune system and its importance, few understand just how complex and intricate the immune system is. In Immune, Internet creator and storyteller Philipp Dettmer takes readers on a journey through the fortress of the human body and its defenses. There is a constant battle raging just under our skin, full of stories of invasion, strategy, defeat, and noble self-sacrifice. In fact, in the time you've been reading this, your immune system has identified and eradicated multiple cancer cells that started to grow in your body. Enlivened by engaging full-color graphics and immersive descriptions, Immune turns one of the most intricate, interconnected, and pervasive subjects in biology—immunology—into a gripping adventure through an alien landscape.

"Pop science writer Dettmer (creator of the popular YouTube channel Kurzgesagt ['in a nutshell']) has written a volume explaining human immunity, which works on an extremely complex multi-systemic, even multi-cellular and micro-cellular level.... Bringing both insight and humor to an important and relevant topic, Dettmer's book is essential reading, especially in light of the COVID-19 pandemic." —*Library Journal*

Richtel, Matt
★ *An Elegant Defense: The Extraordinary New Science of the Immune System : A Tale in Four Lives.* Matt Richtel. William Morrow 2019. 416 p.
ISBN 9780062698537
Grades: Adult   616.07
1. Immune system 2. Immunology 3. Sick people 4. Autoimmune diseases 5. Immunologic diseases 6. People with cancer 7. History of medicine 8. Science Writing — Medicine and health — Illness and disease 9. History writing — Science, technology, and medicine
LC 2018038019

A terminal cancer patient rises from the grave. A medical marvel defies HIV. Two women with autoimmunity discover their own bodies have turned against them. An Elegant Defense uniquely entwines these intimate stories with science's centuries-long quest to unlock the mysteries of sickness and health, and illuminates the immune system as never before.

"Pulitzer Prize-winning reporter, nonfiction writer, and crime novelist Richtel adroitly mingles cellular biology, scientific history, medical research, and patients experiences as he explains how the immune system primarily protects our health but is also implicated in cancer, AIDS, and autoimmune disorders." —*Booklist*
Includes index.

616.1 Specific diseases

Case, Molly
How to Treat People: A Nurse's Notes. Molly Case. W.W. Norton & Company 2019. 272 p.
ISBN 9781324003465
Grades: Adult   616.1
1. Case, Molly 2. Nurses 3. Nursing 4. Father and adult daughter 5. Caregivers 6. Hospital patients 7. Autobiographies and memoirs 8. Life stories — Facing adversity — Medical issues — Physical illness

The nurse behind the popular "Nursing the Nation" video poem presents an engaging memoir of the human body and its care that describes the teen surgery that inspired her career and the intricate experiences of patients being tended by strangers.

616.2 Diseases of respiratory system

Mackenzie, Debora
Covid-19: The Pandemic That Never Should Have Happened and How to Stop the Next One. Debora Mackenzie. Hachette Books 2020. 279 p.
ISBN 9780306924248
Grades: Adult   616.2
1. COVID-19 (Disease) 2. Viruses 3. Epidemics 4. Diseases 5. Quarantine 6. Epidemiology 7. Public health 8. World health 9. Health policy 10. Health planning 11. Preventive medicine 12. Politics and global affairs — Public health 13. Society and culture — Illness and disease — Epidemics 14. Science Writing — Medicine and health — Illness and disease
LC Bl2020016355

Over the last 30 years of epidemics and pandemics, we learned nearly every lesson needed to stop this coronavirus outbreak in its tracks. We heeded almost none of them. The result is a pandemic on a scale never before seen in our lifetimes. In this captivating, authoritative, and eye-opening book, science journalist Debora MacKenzie lays out the full story of how and why it happened: the previous viruses that should have prepared us, the shocking public health failures that paved the way, the failure to contain the outbreak, and most importantly, what we must do to prevent future pandemics.

"MacKenzie delivers a wise and accurate account of the COVID-19 pandemic, supplying readers with an objective assessment of where we are, how we got here, and how to prepare for future emerging infections.... Surely one of the best books available about the virus that has altered how we live and work, worry and interact with others." —*Booklist*
Includes bibliographical references.

616.3 Diseases of digestive system

Gordon, Aubrey
"You Just Need to Lose Weight": And 19 Other Myths About Fat People. Aubrey Gordon. Beacon Press 2023. 224 p.
ISBN 9780807006474
Grades: Adult   616.3
1. Body size 2. Discrimination 3. Social justice 4. Stereotypes 5. Body awareness 6. Self-acceptance 7. Obesity 8. Fat people 9. United States 10. Life stories — Facing adversity 11. Society and culture — Psychology and human behavior
LC 2022043203

The co-host of The Maintenance Phase podcast and creator of Your Fat Friend equips you with the facts to debunk common anti-fat myths and with tools to take action for fat justice.

"Densely written, this thought-provoking treatise on fatness will give readers of all sizes plenty to think about." —*Booklist*
Includes bibliographical references.

Scarlata, Kate
Mind Your Gut: The Science-based, Whole-body Guide to Living Well with Ibs. Kate Scarlata, MPH, RDN, and Megan Riehl, PsyD; foreword by William D. Chey, MD.. Hachette Go 2024. xii, 370 pages : Illustration
ISBN 9780306832338
Grades: Adult   616.3
1. Inflammatory bowel disease 2. Nutritional therapy 3. Digestive organs 4. Diseases 5. Science Writing — Medicine and health — Diet and nutrition 6. Science Writing — Medicine and health — Illness and disease
LC 2023044405

A world-renowned digestive health specialist and registered dietitian and a prominent GI psychologist present a comprehensive, holistic approach to managing IBS that offers science-based interventions, targeted mind-gut behavioral strategies, delicious gut-soothing recipes and nutrition tips.

"This helpful resource from dietitian Scarlata (coauthor of the Low-FODMAP Diet) and health psychologist Riehl outlines strategies for managing irritable bowel syndrome...This gets the job done." —*Publishers Weekly*
Includes bibliographical references (pages 335-356) and index.

PUBLIC LIBRARY CORE COLLECTION: NONFICTION
Twentieth Edition

616.4 Diseases of endocrine, hematopoietic, lymphatic, glandular systems; diseases of male breast

Castro, M. Regina
★ *The Essential* Diabetes Book: A Complete Guide to Prevent, Manage and Live Well with Diabetes. M. Regina Castro. Mayo Foundation 2022. 320 p.
ISBN 9781893005792
Grades: Adult 616.4
1. Diabetes 2. Chronic diseases 3. Medical genetics 4. Self-care 5. Medical care 6. Health 7. Original Spanish-language materials 8. Science Writing — Medicine and health — Illness and disease

This newly revised third edition, while helping readers understand and manage their diabetes, outlines the most up-to-date information on new medications, advances in insulin delivery and the latest diabetes technology being used by medical experts.

616.462 Diabetes mellitus

Taubes, Gary
★ *Rethinking* Diabetes: What Science Reveals About Diet, Insulin, and Successful Treatments. Gary Taubes. Alfred A. Knopf 2024. 512 pages
ISBN 9780525520085
Grades: Adult 616.462
1. Diabetes 2. History of medicine 3. Research 4. Diet 5. Nutrition 6. Insulin 7. History Writing — Science, technology, and medicine 8. Science Writing — Medicine and health — Illness and disease

An eye-opening, comprehensive history of diabetes research and treatment, by award-winning journalist and the best-selling author of Why We Get Fat.

"Exhaustively researched and providing cautionary insight into the fallibilities of medical advice, this intrigues." —*Publishers Weekly*

Includes bibliographical references (pages [435]-470) and index.

616.7 Diseases of musculoskeletal system

Abril, Andy
Mayo Clinic Guide to Fibromyalgia. Andy Abril, M.D, and Barbara K. Bruce, Ph.D.. May Foundation for Medical 2019. 270 p.
ISBN 9781893005495
Grades: Adult 616.7
1. Fibromyalgia 2. Chronic diseases 3. Science writing — Medicine and health — Illness and disease

Dispels myths and provides research-based practical strategies and worksheets for managing the symptoms of those suffering with the often-misunderstood condition of fibromyalgia through personal stories of patients and their doctors.

"In clear, lucid language, Abril and Bruce offer the newest guidelines and advice for every step of a patient's journey, from the sometime elusive diagnosis to treatment and the daily management of pain and limitations." —*Publishers Weekly*

Fishman, Loren
Yoga for Arthritis: The Complete Guide. Loren M. Fishman, Ellen Saltonstall. W.W. Norton 2008. 335 p. : Illustration
ISBN 9780393330588
Grades: Adult 616.7
1. Arthritis 2. Yoga 3. Exercise therapy 4. Science writing — Medicine and health — Exercise 5. Science writing — Medicine and health — Illness and disease 6. Sports and recreation — Yoga
LC 2007044693

A comprehensive, user-friendly medical yoga program designed for management and prevention of arthritis.

"Modifications appear for various levels of ability, and photographs and illustrations clearly depict proper alignment." —*Library Journal*

Includes bibliographical references and index.

Hagberg, Eva
How to Be Loved: A Memoir of Lifesaving Friendship. Eva Hagberg Fisher. Houghton Mifflin Harcourt 2019. 240 p.
ISBN 9780544991156
Grades: Adult 616.7
1. Hagberg, Eva 2. People with chronic illnesses 3. People with cancer 4. Friendship 5. Immunologic diseases 6. Belonging 7. Life change events 8. Love 9. Lesbian authors 10. Diseases 11. Autobiographies and memoirs 12. Life stories — Facing adversity — Medical issues — Physical illness 13. Science Writing — Medicine and health — Illness and disease 14. Family and Relationships — Friendship 15. Life stories — Relationships — Friendship
LC 2018006363

A luminous memoir about how friendship saved one woman's life, for anyone who has loved a friend who was sick, grieving, or lost—and for anyone who has struggled to seek help or accept it."

"It is the revelation that love can be unconditional and profound that makes this memoir stand out from many similar ones." —*Kirkus*

616.8 Diseases of nervous system and mental disorders

Alterman, Sara Faith
Let's Never Talk About This Again: A Memoir. Sara Faith Alterman. Grand Central Publishing 2020. 288 p.
ISBN 9781538748671
Grades: Adult 616.8
1. Alterman, Ira 2. People with Alzheimer's disease 3. Alzheimer's disease 4. Authors 5. Podcasters 6. Erotic fiction writing 7. Loss 8. Eccentrics and eccentricities 9. Fathers and daughters 10. Family secrets 11. Family relationships 12. Autobiographies and memoirs 13. Media tie-ins 14. Family and relationships — Families 15. Life stories — Relationships — Family 16. Family and Relationships — Aging and Death 17. Science Writing — Medicine and health — Illness and disease
LC 2019058222

The producer of the Mortified series describes the innocence of her youth in suburban New England before her discovery that her father was a campy sex writer whose career she assumed when he developed early onset Alzheimer's.

"Entertaining, moving, and at times uncomfortable, this will especially resonate with those caring for an aging parent." —*Publishers Weekly*

Based on a podcast.

Bond, Melissa
Blood Orange Night: My Journey to the Edge of Madness. Melissa Bond. Gallery Books 2022. 288 p.
ISBN 9781982188276
Grades: Adult 616.8
1. Bond, Melissa 2. Women journalists 3. Mothers 4. Insomniacs 5. Prescription drug abuse 6. Insomnia 7. Physicians 8. Children with disabilities 9. Addicts 10. Family and addiction 11. Healing 12. Parent and child 13. Autobiographies and memoirs 14. Life stories — Facing adversity — Medical issues — Addiction 15. Family and Relationships — Illness and the Family 16. Society and culture — Illness and disease — Addiction
LC 2021045637

A memoir details a woman's accidental descent into prescription benzodiazepine dependence and the life-threatening impacts of the drugs' long-term use.

"Making her book debut, journalist and poet Bond, a blogger for Mad in America, recounts her unintended overuse of popularly prescribed benzodiazepine drugs, which led to addiction and a long, painful process of withdrawal." —*Kirkus*

Cacioppo, Stephanie
Wired for Love: A Neuroscientist's Journey Through Romance, Loss, and Essence of Human Connection. Stephanie Cacioppo. Flatiron Books 2022. 352 p.
ISBN 9781250790606
Grades: Adult 616.8

ESSENTIAL AND RECOMMENDED TITLES
616.8 Diseases of nervous system and mental disorders

1. Cacioppo, John T. 2. Cacioppo, Stephanie, 1974- 3. Romantic love 4. Neuroscience 5. Interpersonal relations 6. Death of married men 7. Courtship 8. People with cancer 9. Grief 10. Autobiographies and memoirs 11. Science Writing — Biology 12. Life stories — Relationships — Couples 13. Family and Relationships — Dating and Marriage

LC 2021047706

Sharing her moving personal story, from astonishment to unbreakable bond to grief and healing, the world's foremost neuroscientist of romantic love shares revelatory insights into how and why we fall in love, what makes love last and how we process love lost.

"A leading neuroscientist analyzes the 'power of love'—why it evolved, how it functions, how it can be harnessed to strengthen our bodies and open our minds…a beautiful testament to romantic love, scientific passion, and the endless possibility of connection."—*Kirkus*

Includes bibliographical references.

Cahalan, Susannah
Brain on Fire: My Month of Madness. by Susannah Cahalan. Free Press 2012. 288 p.
ISBN 9781451621372
Grades: Adult   616.8

1. Cahalan, Susannah 2. Diagnostic errors 3. Epidemic encephalitis 4. Memory 5. Identity 6. Determination 7. Autoimmune diseases 8. Self-discovery 9. United States 10. Autobiographies and memoirs 11. Science Writing — Medicine and health — Illness and disease 12. Life stories — Facing adversity — Medical issues 13. Adult books for young adults

LC 2012012670

An account of the author's struggle with a rare brain-attacking autoimmune disease traces how she woke up in a hospital room with no memory of baffling psychotic symptoms, describing the last-minute intervention by a doctor who identified the source of her illness.

"Cahalan expertly weaves together her own story and relevant scientific and medical information about autoimmune diseases, which are about two-thirds environmental and one-third genetic in origin. So, she writes, an external trigger, such as a sneeze or a toxic apartment, probably combined with a genetic predisposition toward developing aggressive antibodies to create her problem. A compelling health story."—*Booklist*

Davis, Patti
Floating in the Deep End: How Caregivers Can See Beyond Alzheimer's. Patti Davis. Liveright Publishing 2021. 320 p.
ISBN 9781631497988
Grades: Adult   616.8

1. Davis, Patti, 1952- 2. Reagan, Ronald 3. Alzheimer's disease 4. Caregivers 5. Fathers and daughters 6. People with Alzheimer's disease 7. People with dementia 8. Home health care 9. Family relationships 10. Family and Relationships — Illness and the Family 11. Life stories — Relationships — Parent and child 12. Life stories — Facing adversity — Medical issues

LC 2021025725

In a singular account of battling Alzheimer's, Patti Davis eloquently weaves personal anecdotes with practical advice tailored specifically for the overlooked caregiver. After losing her father, Ronald Reagan, Davis founded a support group for family members and friends of Alzheimer's patients; drawing on those years, Davis reveals the surprising struggles and gifts of this cruel disease. From the challenges of navigating disorientation to the moments when guilt and resentments creep in, readers are guided gently through slow-burning grief. Along the way, Davis shares how her own fractured family came together, and how her father revealed his true self—always kind, even when he couldn't recognize his own daughter.

"Davis is a wise, thoughtful, empathetic, skilled, graceful support for the many people facing AD in a loved one. A must-read."—*Library Journal*

Dearen, Jason
Kill Shot: A Shadow Industry, a Deadly Disease. by Jason Dearen. Avery 2020. 304 p.
ISBN 9780593085783
Grades: Adult   616.8

1. Meningitis 2. Epidemics 3. Drugs 4. Drug industry and trade 5. Science Writing — Medicine and health 6. Society and culture — Illness and disease 7. True Crime — Drugs

LC 2020013132

An award-winning investigative journalist's horrifying true crime story of America's deadliest drug contamination outbreak and the greed and deception that fueled it.

"A disturbing dive into a barely regulated area of the pharmaceutical industry. If you like fast-paced forensic thrillers a la Kathy Reichs, you'll love this tale of death and mayhem, from the opening exhumation to the final courtroom drama. . . . A harrowing, fast-paced tale of blind greed and sloppy science." —*Kirkus*

Includes index.

Fitzmaurice, Simon
It's Not Yet Dark: A Memoir. Simon Fitzmaurice. Houghton Mifflin Harcourt 2017. 176 p.
ISBN 9781328916716
Grades: Adult   616.8

1. Fitzmaurice, Simon 2. People with amyotrophic lateral sclerosis 3. Amyotrophic lateral sclerosis 4. Personal conduct 5. Determination 6. Autobiographies and memoirs 7. Life stories — Facing adversity — Medical issues

LC 2017016109

In 2008, Simon Fitzmaurice was diagnosed with ALS, or Lou Gehrig's disease. He was given four years to live. In 2010, in a state of lung-function collapse, Simon knew with crystal clarity that now was not his time to die. Against all prevailing medical opinion, he chose to ventilate in order to stay alive. In It's Not yet Dark, the young filmmaker, a husband and father of five small children, draws us deeply into his inner world.

"Fitzmaurice communicates well, making his own case and advocating for the right of the afflicted to make their own choices in how they will live and die. A fine and heartfelt memoir from an author hopeful in his determination to endure against the odds."—*Kirkus*

Frank, Lone
The Pleasure Shock: The Rise of Deep Brain Stimulation and Its Forgotten Inventor. Lone Frank. E.P. Dutton 2018. 336 p.
ISBN 9781101986530
Grades: Adult   616.8

1. Heath, Robert G. (Robert Galbraith), 1915-1999 2. Mental illness 3. Physicians 4. Brain 5. Science 6. Medical ethics 7. Research 8. Treatment 9. Biographies 10. Life stories — Science, technology, and medicine — Scientists and inventors 11. Science Writing — Medicine and health — Mental health 12. History writing — Science, technology, and medicine

LC 2017029957

An assessment of mid-20th-century Tulane psychiatrist Robert G. Heath's brain-pacemaker experiments shares insights into his controversial work with convicts, members of the gay community and the CIA's notorious "mind control" project and how much of his work has been suppressed or adapted as mainstream therapies for mental illness and addiction. By the award-winning author of My Beautiful Genome.

"Frank has written an excellent, balanced portrait of an inventive psychiatrist with a complicated legacy."—*Publishers Weekly*

Includes bibliographical references.

Karlawish, Jason
★ *The Problem of Alzheimer's: How Science, Culture, and Politics Turned a Rare Disease into a Crisis and What We Can Do About It.* Jason Karlawish. St. Martin's Press 2021. 336 p.
ISBN 9781250218735
Grades: Adult   616.8

1. Alzheimer's disease 2. People with Alzheimer's disease 3. Dementia 4. Brain diseases 5. Caregivers 6. Home health care 7. Patient advocacy 8. Medical research 9. Quality of life 10. Science Writing — Medicine and health — Illness and disease 11. Society and culture — Illness and disease

LC 2020026249

Part case studies, part meditation on the past, present and future of the disease, the Problem of Alzheimer's traces the disease from its beginnings to its recognition as a crisis. While it is an unambiguous account of decades of missed opportunities and our health care systems' failures to take action, it tells the story of the biomedical breakthroughs that may allow Alzheimer's to finally be prevented and treated by medicine and also presents an argument for how we can live with dementia: the ways patients can reclaim their autonomy and redefine their sense of self, how families can support their loved ones, and the innovative reforms we can make as a society that would give caregivers and patients better quality of life.

"As science and medicine continue to study Alzheimer's, Karlawish suggests, advances in technology, assisted living arrangements, and other lifestyle changes can be used to help people live well with the disease." —*Library Journal*

Includes bibliographical references and index.

Kiper, Dasha
★ *Travelers* to Unimaginable Lands: Dementia and the Hidden Workings of the Mind. Dasha Kiper; foreword by Norman Doidge. Random House 2023. 240 p.

ISBN 9780399590535

Grades: Adult   **616.8**

1. People with Alzheimer's disease 2. People with dementia 3. Alzheimer's disease 4. Caregivers 5. Dementia 6. Science Writing — Medicine and health — Illness and disease 7. Life stories — Facing adversity — Medical issues — Mental illness 8. Family and relationships — Illness and the family

In these poignant but unsentimental stories of parents and children, husbands and wives, the author dispels the myth of the perfect caregiver; and, relying on a wide breadth of cognitive and neurological research and borrowing from philosophy and literature, she explores the existential dilemmas created by Alzheimer's disease.

"The author's clear reasoning skillfully illuminates psychological concepts, and her poignant experiences bring them to life, sensitively broaching issues of free will, identity, and loss." —*Publishers Weekly*

Leschziner, Guy
The **Nocturnal** Brain: Nightmares, Neuroscience, and the Secret World of Sleep. Guy Leschziner. St. Martin's Press 2019. 288 pages

ISBN 9781250202703

Grades: Adult   **616.8**

1. Sleep disorders 2. Sleep deprivation 3. Sleep 4. Neuroscience 5. Nightmares 6. Insomnia 7. Sleepwalking 8. Sleep apnea 9. Narcolepsy 10. Science Writing — Medicine and health — Illness and disease 11. Science Writing — Biology 12. Life stories — Science, technology, and medicine — Healthcare professionals

LC 2019005309

A clinical neurologist and global authority on narcolepsy presents a tour of the sleeping human brain, sharing remarkable patient stories that demonstrate the neuroscience behind what happens in different mind states.

"Readers will find Leschziners stories fascinating, and might even pick up a few tips for getting a more restorative nights sleep in the process." —*Publishers Weekly*

Includes bibliographical references and index.

Mace, Nancy L.
★ The **36-Hour** Day: A Family Guide to Caring for People Who Have Alzheimer Disease, Other Dementias, and Memory Loss. Nancy L. Mace and Peter V. Rabins. Johns Hopkins University Press 2021. xx, 341 p. (Johns Hopkins Press Health Book)

ISBN 9781421441702

Grades: Adult   **616.8**

1. Alzheimer's disease 2. Dementia 3. Family and Relationships — Disabled Family Members 4. Science Writing — Medicine and health — Brain function and memory

LC 2016033545

Originally published in 1981, The 36-Hour Day was the first book of its kind. Forty years later, with dozens of other books on the market, it remains the definitive guide for people caring for someone with dementia. Now in a new and updated edition, this best-selling book features thoroughly revised chapters on the causes of dementia, managing the early stages of dementia, the prevention of dementia, and finding appropriate living arrangements for the person who has dementia when home care is no longer an option.

Includes index.

Navab, Pedram
Sleep Reimagined: The Fast Track to a Revitalized Life. Dr. Pedram Navab, FAASM.. Countryman Press, an imprint of W.W. Norton & Company 2023. xvi, 169 pages

ISBN 9781682687116

Grades: Adult   **616.8**

1. Sleep 2. Insomnia 3. Cognitive therapy 4. Science Writing — Medicine and health — Sleep 5. Self-Help — Mental health

LC 2022045895

A neurologist and sleep medicine specialist of 15 years presents a 6-step cognitive behavioral therapy program that guides readers to new and improved sleep in as little as four weeks.

"Navab's supportive and optimistic tone, combined with an approachable action plan, make this a useful addition to public and consumer health collections." —*Library Journal*

Includes bibliographical references and index.

Pelayo, Rafael
★ *How to Sleep*: The New Science-Based Rules for Sleeping Through the Night. Rafael Pelayo, MD.. Artisan 2020. 160 pages

ISBN 9781579659578

Grades: Adult   **616.8**

1. Sleep 2. Sleep disorders 3. Insomnia 4. Treatment 5. Science Writing — Medicine and health — Sleep

LC 2020020140

A Stanford University sleep-medicine clinician challenges conventional recommendations for overcoming more complicated cases of insomnia while outlining best practices and flexible approaches for managing jet lag, circadian rhythms and daylight exposure.

"Anyone struggling to get enough shut-eye should give these practical tips a look." —*Publishers Weekly*

Includes index.

Powell, Tia
Dementia Reimagined: Building a Life of Joy and Dignity from Beginning to End. Tia Powell, MD.. Avery 2019. 310 pages

ISBN 9780735210905

Grades: Adult   **616.8**

1. Alzheimer's disease 2. Dementia 3. Medical care 4. People with Alzheimer's disease 5. Science writing — Medicine and health — Illness and disease 6. Science writing — Medicine and health 7. Science writing — Medicine and health — Psychology

LC 2018049886

The cultural and medical history of dementia and Alzheimer's disease by a leading psychiatrist and bioethicist who urges us to turn our focus from cure to care.

A leading psychiatrist and bioethicist draws on historical research, family experiences and the latest focus on Alzheimer's in a cultural and medical history of dementia that urgently calls for a return to care-oriented approaches.

Includes bibliographical references (pages 279-298) and index.

Reiss, Benjamin
Wild Nights: How Taming Sleep Created Our Restless World. Benjamin Reiss. Basic Books 2017. 288 p.

ISBN 9780465061952

Grades: Adult   **616.8**

1. Sleep 2. Lifestyle change 3. Social change 4. Industrialization 5. Sleep disorders 6. Sleeping customs 7. Sleep-wake cycle 8. Science Writing — Medicine and health

ESSENTIAL AND RECOMMENDED TITLES
616.85 Miscellaneous diseases of nervous system and mental disorders

LC 2016043568

Based on centuries of literary, medical and scientific writings, an English professor explains how the modern rules of sleeping, which have been ingrained in our culture for two centuries, have had a detrimental impact on our overall well-being.

"This is a captivating examination and Reiss gives readers much to ponder long into the night." —*Publishers Weekly*

Includes bibliographical references and index.

Sacks, Oliver
The Man Who Mistook His Wife for a Hat and Other Clinical Tales. Oliver Sacks. Summit Books 1985. xvi, 233 p. : Illustration
ISBN 9780684853949

Grades: 11 12 Adult   616.8

1. Neurologists 2. Neurology 3. Physician and patient 4. Medical care 5. Science Writing — Medicine and health

LC 85017220

Presents a series of stories about men and women who, representing both medical and literary oddities, raise fundamental questions about the nature of reality.

"Sacks introduces the reader to real people who suffer from a variety of neurological syndromes which includes symptoms such as amnesia, uncontrolled movements, and musical hallucinations. Sacks recounts their stories in a riveting, compassionate, and thoughtful manner." —*Library Journal*

Spine title: The man who mistook his wife for a hat; Includes bibliographical references.

616.85 Miscellaneous diseases of nervous system and mental disorders

Adam, David
The Man Who Couldn't Stop: OCD and the True Story of a Life Lost in Thought. David Adam. Sarah Crichton Books 2014. 324 p.
ISBN 9780374223953

Grades: Adult   616.85

1. Adam, David, 1972- 2. Coping 3. Journalists 4. Compulsive behavior 5. OCD 6. Great Britain 7. Autobiographies and memoirs 8. Life stories — Facing adversity — Medical issues — Mental illness

LC 2014017387

An intimate look at the power of intrusive thoughts, how our brains can turn against us, and living with obsessive compulsive disorder.

"For all the impressive marshaling of information, it is Adam's own story of his struggles with the condition, which his infant daughter forced him to confront instead of uneasily accepting, that is the most captivating aspect of this impressive work." —*Booklist*

Originally published in UK.

Bass, Ellen
★ *The Courage to Heal: A Guide for Women Survivors of Child Sexual Abuse*. Ellen Bass & Laura Davis. Collins Living 2008. xxxiv, 606 p.
ISBN 9780061284335

Grades: Adult   616.85

1. Child sexual abuse 2. Women 3. Adult child abuse victims 4. Psychology 5. Self-Help — General 6. Science writing — Medicine and health — Psychology 7. Family and Relationships — Abuse

LC 2008011616

Offers inspiration and encouragement to women who have been sexually abused as children, providing self-help guidelines, a timely Resource Guide, healing tools, and new stories, insights, and wisdom.

Includes bibliographical references (p. 525-585) and index.

Boyes, Alice
The Anxiety Toolkit: Strategies for Fine-Tuning Your Mind and Moving Past Your Stuck Points. Alice Boyes, PhD.. Perigee 2015. 232 pages
ISBN 9780399169250

Grades: Adult   616.85

1. Anxiety 2. Treatment 3. Self-Help — Mental health — Anxiety and stress 4. Science Writing — Medicine and health — Psychology

LC 2014040065

Drawing on extensive social psychology research, and the author's training and clinical experience in Cognitive-Behavioral therapy, the Anxiety Toolkit offers actionable strategies that anyone can use to manage their anxiety—both personal and professional.

"Boyes's tone is friendly but never saccharine, and endlessly practical. Her tips and exercises, drawn from cognitive behavioral therapies that she herself has administered, should make a valuable reference for anxiety sufferers, and an ideal companion to readers undergoing psychotherapy themselves." —*Publishers Weekly*

Includes bibliographical references (pages 210-216) and index.

Brownstein, Gabriel
★ *The Secret Mind of Bertha Pappenheim: The Woman Who Invented Freud's Talking Cure*. Gabriel Brownstein. PublicAffairs 2024. 336 p.
ISBN 9781541774643

Grades: Adult   616.85

1. Pappenheim, Bertha, 1859-1936 2. Freud, Sigmund, 1856-1939 3. Psychiatrist and patient 4. Hysteria 5. Psychotherapy 6. Feminists 7. Social advocacy 8. Healing 9. Psychoanalysis 10. Sexism in medicine 11. History 12. Vienna, Austria 13. History writing — Science, technology, and medicine 14. Life stories — Facing adversity — Medical issues — Mental illness 15. Society and culture — Psychology and human behavior

LC 2023047264

This unusual work of science, history and psychology brings to life Bertha Pappenheim, a brilliant feminist thinker, a crusader against human trafficking and a pioneer in 19th-century Vienna who developed "the talking cure", while telling a parallel story of the neuroscience of a condition now called FND.

"Infused with emotion from Brownstein's own personal losses, the result is a riveting look at the boundaries between neurology and psychology and the gender dynamics of medicine. This captivates." —*Publishers Weekly*

Includes bibliographical references and index.

Bullmore, Edward T.
The Inflamed Mind: A Radical New Approach to Depression. Edward Bullmore. Picador 2019. xv, 240 pages : Illustration
ISBN 9781250318145

Grades: Adult   616.85

1. Neuroscience 2. Depression 3. Mental health 4. Psychiatry 5. Brain 6. Science Writing — Medicine and health — Mental health

Worldwide, depression will be the single biggest cause of disability in the next 20 years. But treatment for it has not changed much in the last three decades. In the world of psychiatry, time has apparently stood still... until now.

"Readers looking for current treatments for depression or self-help advice will not find it here, but those concerned with the science behind depression or autoimmune disorders will discover the current state of research very compelling." —*Library Journal*

Includes bibliographical references and index.

Buque, Mariel
Break the Cycle: A Guide to Healing Intergenerational Trauma. Dr. Mariel Buqué.. Dutton 2024. 288 pages
ISBN 9780593472491

Grades: Adult   616.85

1. Intergenerational trauma 2. Families 3. Mental health 4. Psychic trauma 5. Holistic medicine 6. Self-Help — Mental health — Post-traumatic stress disorder 7. Science Writing — Medicine and health — Psychology 8. Family and Relationships — Families

The definitive, paradigm-shifting guide to healing intergenerational trauma-weaving together scientific research with practical exercises and stories from the therapy room-from Dr. Mariel Buqué, PhD, a Columbia University-trained trauma-informed psychologist and practitioner of holistic healing.

PUBLIC LIBRARY CORE COLLECTION: NONFICTION
Twentieth Edition

"Readers seeking a practical and psychologically grounded approach to healing familial wounds will find value here." —*Publishers Weekly*

Includes bibliographical references and index.

Clein, Emmeline
★ *Dead Weight: Essays on Hunger and Harm.* Emmeline Clein. Alfred A. Knopf 2024. 304 p.

ISBN 9780593536902

Grades: Adult   616.85

1. Clein, Emmeline 2. Women 3. Girls 4. People with eating disorders 5. Anorexia nervosa 6. Bulimia 7. Dieting 8. Body image 9. Social acceptance 10. Feminine beauty (Aesthetics) 11. Popular culture 12. Life stories — Facing adversity — Medical issues 13. Science Writing — Medicine and health — Mental health 14. Society and culture — Gender — Women 15. Society and culture — Illness and disease — Addiction 16. Debut title

LC 2023022274

A writer recounts her own struggles with disordered eating in the context of historical figures and pop culture celebrities to reveal the economic, cultural and political history of an epidemic that has wreaked havoc on generations of women.

"Taking on the labyrinth of our current medical, social, and economic systems we can hardly see, let alone know how to escape from, Clein critiques with clarity and nuance. She can't look away, and her writing asks that we don't, either." —*Booklist*

Includes bibliographical references.

Crampton, Caroline
A Body Made of Glass: A Cultural History of Hypochondria. Caroline Crampton. Ecco Press 2024. 336 p.

ISBN 9780063273900

Grades: Adult   616.85

1. Crampton, Caroline 2. Anxiety disorders 3. Culture 4. Hypochondria 5. Mental illness 6. Mental health 7. Social life and customs 8. Neuroses 9. United States 10. Autobiographies and memoirs 11. Science Writing — Medicine and health — Mental health 12. Life stories — Facing adversity — Medical issues — Mental illness

LC 2023044384

A book that is part cultural history, part literary criticism and part memoir explores the world of hypochondria.

"In this riveting, genre-bending memoir, journalist Crampton…traces the cultural and historical lineage of hypochondria." —*Publishers Weekly*

Includes bibliographical references and index.

Cregan, Mary
The Scar: A Personal History of Depression and Recovery. Mary Cregan. W.W. Norton & Company 2019. 256 p.

ISBN 9781324001720

Grades: Adult   616.85

1. Cregan, Mary 2. Depression 3. Suicidal behavior 4. Death of babies 5. Psychiatric hospitals 6. Treatment 7. People with depression 8. Women 9. Autobiographies and memoirs 10. Life stories — Facing adversity — Medical issues — Mental illness 11. Science Writing — Medicine and health — Mental health

LC 2018050858

The author reflects on the death of her newborn daughter and the depression caused by the event while considering her experiences as part of the larger history of understanding depression.

"While there are quite a few memoirs on depression, Cregan's debut stands out for its personal and profound insights into a subject that can be difficult to grasp." —*Library Journal*

Includes bibliographical references.

Dakwar, Elias
The Captive Imagination: Addiction, Reality, and Our Search for Meaning. Elias Dakwar. HarperCollins 2024. 379 p.

ISBN 9780063340480

Grades: Adult   616.85

1. Addiction 2. Medical care 3. Purpose in life 4. Psychology 5. Reality 6. Neuroscience 7. Hallucinogenic drugs 8. Society and culture — Illness and disease — Addiction 9. Society and culture — Psychology and human behavior

Drawing on his research with hallucinogenic compounds and meditation-based treatments, fifteen years of clinical experience and recent findings from neuroscience, an addiction specialist examines how psychedelics can shed light on the broader systemic and cultural shifts needed to alleviate suffering, beginning with the most vulnerable among us.

"A potent, incisive reconsideration of a fundamental human behavior." —*Kirkus*

Dittrich, Luke
★ *Patient H.M.: A Story of Memory, Madness and Family Secrets.* Luke Dittrich. Random House 2016. 320 p.

ISBN 9780812992731

Grades: Adult   616.85

1. H, M, 1926-2008 2. Scoville, William Beecher, 1906-1984 3. Neurosurgeons 4. Neuroscience 5. Amnesia 6. Experimental medicine 7. Medical research 8. Epilepsy 9. Nervous system 10. Brain 11. Medical ethics 12. Memory 13. Surgery 14. Research 15. 1950s 16. Biographies 17. Science Writing — Medicine and health — Mental health 18. Life stories — Facing adversity — Medical issues — Living with disabilities

LC 2015048638

Los Angeles Times Book Prize for Science and Technology, 2016.

Explores the scientific, ethical, and human dimensions of the 1953 brain operation by William Beecher Scoville on an epileptic patient that transformed understandings of memory science and triggered profound legal and medical debates.

"Though long, there's not a wasted word in the book, which should make readers glad we live in the age of Prozac and not the scalpel. A mesmerizing, maddening story and a model of journalistic investigation." —*Kirkus*

Donvan, John
In a Different Key: The Story of Autism. John Donvan and Caren Zucker. Crown Publishers 2016. 448 p.

ISBN 9780307985675

Grades: Adult   616.85

1. People with disabilities 2. Autistic people 3. Autism spectrum disorders 4. Neurodivergent people 5. Science Writing — Medicine and health — Disabilities and disorders

LC 2015024706

Pulitzer Prize for General Nonfiction finalist, 2017.

The story of the discovery of autism and the first child diagnosed with the disorder draws on extensive research to trace how understandings about the condition have evolved through eight decades and how it has affected families in different historical periods.

"This book will not educate researchers with new information on autism. It will, however, introduce a human aspect to the chronology. Parents of autistic children will recognize themselves in many of these stories but also learn more about the truth behind them. Autistic individuals will take away lessons to forgive the past and to recognize the vast spectrum of differencenot just among those on the autism spectrum but among all people, who are always learning and growing." —*Library Journal*

Fleming, Jory
How to Be Human: An Autistic Man's Guide to Life. Jory Fleming with Lyric Winik. Simon & Schuster 2021. 192 p.

ISBN 9781501180507

Grades: Adult   616.85

1. Fleming, Jory 2. Autistic people 3. College students 4. Disabilities 5. Autism spectrum disorders 6. Neurodivergent people 7. United States 8. Autobiographies and memoirs 9. Life stories — Facing adversity — Medical issues — Living with disabilities

LC 2020029847

A remarkable and unforgettable memoir from the first man with autism to attend Oxford on a Rhodes scholarship, revealing what life is really like inside a

ESSENTIAL AND RECOMMENDED TITLES
616.85 Miscellaneous diseases of nervous system and mental disorders

world constructed for neurotypical minds while celebrating the many gifts of being different.

"A deeply moving memoir from the first autistic student to attend Oxford as a Rhodes Scholar. . . . Fleming's extraordinary journey will inspire any reader weighing what it means to be human in a troubled world." —*Kirkus*

Freeman, Hadley
Good Girls: A Story and Study of Anorexia. Hadley Freeman. Simon & Schuster 2023. 288 p.
ISBN 9781982189839
Grades: Adult   616.85
1. Freeman, Hadley 2. Anorexia nervosa 3. Eating disorders 4. Body image 5. OCD 6. Food habits 7. People with eating disorders 8. Shame 9. Compulsive eating 10. Treatment 11. Autism spectrum disorders 12. Autobiographies and memoirs 13. Life stories — Facing adversity — Medical issues

The bestselling author of House of Glass shares her twenty-year experience as an "functional anorexic," and her journey to recovery and examines recent discoveries have been made about the illness, including its connection to autism, OCD and metabolic rate.

"If you need to understand anorexia, look no further. This is the book for you." —*Kirkus*

Glass, Charles
Soldiers Don't Go Mad: A Story of Brotherhood, Poetry, and Mental Illness During the First World War. Charles Glass. Penguin Press 2023. 336 p.
ISBN 9781984877956
Grades: Adult   616.85
1. Sassoon, Siegfried, 1886-1967 2. Owen, Wilfred, 1893-1918 3. Mental health 4. Friendship 5. World War I 6. Poets 7. Post-traumatic stress disorder 8. War and society 9. Literature 10. War neuroses 11. Gay men 12. World War I veterans 13. Psychic trauma 14. Medical care 15. Soldiers 16. History Writing — Wars and conflicts — World War I 17. Life stories — Law and order — Armed forces personnel 18. Life stories — Facing adversity — Medical issues — Mental illness
LC 2023007303

Drawing on rich source materials as well as his own deep understanding of trauma and war, the author documents the friendship between two great WWI poets and patients at Craiglockhart War Hospital for treatment of shell shock to investigate the roots of what we now know as PTSD.

"Thoroughly researched and lucidly written, this is an immersive look at the healing power of art and a forceful indictment of the inhumanity of war." —*Publishers Weekly*

Includes bibliographical references and index.

Gutman, Matt
★ *No Time to Panic: The New Science of Panic Attacks and My Quest to Conquer Anxiety.* Matt Gutman. Doubleday 2023. 256 p.
ISBN 9780385549059
Grades: Adult   616.85
1. Gutman, Matt, 1977- 2. Mental health 3. Panic disorders 4. Panic attacks 5. California 6. Autobiographies and memoirs 7. Life stories — Facing adversity — Medical issues — Mental illness 8. Science Writing — Medicine and health — Mental health
LC 2023000750

Unflinching, perceptive and often funny, ABC News's chief national correspondent shares his personal journey into the science and treatment of panic attacks after his career was almost derailed by them, offering readers a roadmap to peace of mind.

"Both warm and candid, this book is sure to offer helpful doses of hope, humor, and wisdom to anyone suffering from panic disorder. Insightful reading." —*Kirkus*

Includes bibliographical references.

Guyenet, Stephan J.
The Hungry Brain: Outsmarting the Instincts That Make Us Overeat. Stephan J. Guyenet, Ph.D.. Flatiron Books 2017. 288 p.
ISBN 9781250081193
Grades: Adult   616.85
1. Overeating 2. Brain chemistry 3. Obesity 4. Diet 5. Neuroscience 6. Science Writing — Biology
LC 2016057553

Explores how the brain|s dual thinking processes regulate when, what and how much we eat.

"This fun, insightful, and important text will appeal to both science lovers and fitness fanatics." —*Publishers Weekly*

Kazdin, Cole
★ *What's Eating Us: Women, Food, and the Epidemic of Body Anxiety.* Cole Kazdin. St. Martin's Essentials 2023. 304 p.
ISBN 9781250282842
Grades: Adult   616.85
1. Kazdin, Cole 2. Women journalists 3. Eating disorders 4. Body dysmorphic disorder 5. Body image 6. Stigma (Social psychology) 7. Dieting 8. Weight loss 9. Diet industry and trade 10. Mental health 11. Self-acceptance 12. People with eating disorders 13. Women 14. Science Writing — Medicine and health — Mental health 15. Food writing — Investigations 16. Society and culture — Gender — Women 17. Society and culture — Illness and disease — Addiction 18. Life stories — Facing adversity — Medical issues — Mental illness
LC 2022038005

Women of all ages struggle with disordered eating, preoccupation with food, and body anxiety. Journalist Cole Kazdin was one such woman, and she set out to see if the impossibility of her own full recovery from an eating disorder was all in her head. Kazdin takes us to the doorstep of the diet industry and research community, exposing the flawed systems that claim to be helping us, and revealing disordered eating for the crisis that it is: a mental illness with the second highest mortality rate (after opioid-related deaths) that no one wants to talk about. What would it feel like to be free? Who can help us with this? We can.

"This work will appeal to readers who enjoy memoirs and general nonfiction, but Kadzin's conversational tone and writing style make this book accessible to all readers." —*Library Journal*

Includes bibliographical references.

Kluger, Jeffrey
The Narcissist Next Door: Understanding the Monster in Your Family, in Your Office, in Your Bed—in Your World. Jeffrey Kluger. Riverhead Books 2014. 277 pages
ISBN 9781594486364
Grades: Adult   616.85
1. Narcissism 2. Science writing — Medicine and health — Psychology
LC 2014006297

A lively and perceptive exploration of narcissism that examines its causes, the science and psychology at its core, and the opportunities and challenges it presents to those who suffer from it (and those who contend with it in others).

From an award-winning senior writer at Time, an eye-opening exploration of narcissism, how to recognize it, and how to handle it. The odds are good that you know a narcissist-probably a lot of them. The odds are also good that they are intelligent, confident, and articulate-the center of attention. They make you laugh and they make you think. The odds are also that this spell didn't last. Narcissists are everywhere. There are millions of them in the United States alone: entertainers, politicians, business people, your neighbors. Recognizing and understanding them is crucial to your not being overtaken by them, says Jeffrey Kluger, in his provocative new book about this insidious disorder. With insight and wit, Kluger frames the surprising new research on narcissism and explains the complex, exasperating personality disorder. He reveals how narcissism and narcissists affect our lives at work and at home, on the road, and in the halls of government; what to do when we encounter narcissism; and how to neutralize its effects before it's too late. As a Time writer and science editor, Kluger knows how to take science's new ideas and transform them into smart, accessible insights. Highly readable and deeply engaging, this book helps us understand narcissism and narcissists more fully.

An award-winning Time senior writer outlines provocative advice on how to recognize narcissistic personality disorder in other people while sharing counsel on how to protect oneself from the condition's destructive cycles.

"In addition to being informative and engaging, Kluger's account provides some effective tools for dealing with potential narcissists." —*Publishers Weekly*

Includes index.

Kriss, Alexander

Borderline: The Biography of a Personality Disorder. Alexander Kriss, PhD.. Beacon Press 2024. 288 p.

ISBN 9780807007815

Grades: Adult   616.85

1. Kriss, Alexander 2. Psychologists 3. Borderline Syndrome (Psychiatry) 4. People with mental illnesses 5. Treatment 6. Psychotherapy 7. Patients 8. Personality disorders 9. Biographies 10. Life stories — Facing adversity — Medical issues — Mental illness 11. Science Writing — Medicine and health — Mental health 12. Society and culture — Psychology and human behavior

LC 2023044313

An intimate, compassionate, and expansive portrait of Borderline Personality Disorder that rejects the conventional wisdom that the condition is untreatable and those diagnosed with it are "difficult," told by a psychologist who specializes in BPD.

"A revealing exploration of borderline personality disorder and the future of therapies addressing it." —*Kirkus*

Includes bibliographical references and index.

LeFavour, Cree

Lights On, Rats Out: A Memoir. Cree LeFavour. Grove Press 2017. 244 pages

ISBN 9780802125965

Grades: Adult   616.85

1. LeFavour, Cree 2. Young women 3. Self-harm 4. Psychiatrists 5. Self-injurious behavior 6. Scars 7. Dependency 8. Self-hate 9. Personal conduct 10. Healing 11. Psychiatric hospitals 12. Psychotherapists 13. Psychotherapy 14. Autobiographies and memoirs 15. Life stories — Facing adversity — Medical issues — Mental illness 16. Life stories — Facing adversity — Personal transformation

LC 2016048377

A young college graduate one year into her increasingly obsessive treatment with a psychiatrist begins to organize her days around a compulsion to harm herself with lit cigarettes. By the James Beard Award-nominated author of Fish.

A searing, brilliant memoir revealing the therapeutic process and its ability 'To turn our ghosts into ancestors.' —*Booklist*

McBride, Karyl

Will I Ever Be Good Enough?: Healing the Daughters of Narcissistic Mothers. Karyl McBride. Free Press 2008. xvi, 243 p.

ISBN 9781416551324

Grades: Adult   616.85

1. Mothers and daughters 2. Narcissism 3. Self-acceptance 4. Interpersonal relations 5. Psychological growth 6. Family and Relationships — Families

A resource for daughters of mothers with narcissistic personality disorder explains how to manage feelings of inadequacy and abandonment in the face of inappropriate maternal expectations and conditional love.

"In this book aimed at women whose mothers have narcissistic personality disorder, McBride presents specific steps toward recovery that daughters of any age can use as they grieve for the love and support they didn't receive, set healthy boundaries with their mothers and access an internal mother as a source of self-comforting. The author provides parenting tips as well as advice on maintaining healthy love relationships and friendshipsall of which tend to be weak points of the daughters of narcissistic mothers." —*Publishers Weekly*

Includes bibliographical references (p. 227-232).

Milliken, Kirsten

PLAYDHD: Permission to Play... A Prescription for Adults with ADHD. Kirsten Milliken, Ph.D, PCC, psychologist and ADHD coach; design and illustration by Morgan Pickard, Howler Monkey Design Studio. Bookbaby 2016. 144 pages : Illustration; Color

ISBN 9780997004502

Grades: Adult   616.85

1. Attention-deficit hyperactivity disorder 2. Science writing — Medicine and health — Psychology 3. Self-Help — Personal growth

LC Bl2017005825

"This book is a must for those with ADHD and their loved ones." —*Publishers Weekly*

Includes bibliographical references (pages 140-144).

Moe, John

The Hilarious World of Depression. John Moe. St. Martin's Press 2020. 256 p.

ISBN 9781250209283

Grades: Adult   616.85

1. Moe, John 2. People with depression 3. Mental health 4. Family and suicide 5. Self-destructive behavior 6. Grief 7. Loss 8. Autobiographies and memoirs 9. Media tie-ins 10. Life stories — Facing adversity — Medical issues — Mental illness

LC 2019058396

The host of the podcast The Hilarious World of Depression offers a moving portrait of what it means to be depressed.

"Moe's edifying, enjoyable take on the realities of living with depression will uplift any reader." —*Publishers Weekly*

Based on a podcast.

Morris, David J.

The Evil Hours: A Biography of Posttraumatic Stress Disorder. David J. Morris. Houghton Mifflin Harcourt 2015. 336 p.

ISBN 9780544086616

Grades: Adult   616.85

1. Morris, David J, 1971- 2. Post-traumatic stress disorder 3. War 4. Soldiers 5. Combat 6. Veterans 7. Psychology 8. Mental health 9. Autobiographies and memoirs 10. Life stories — Facing adversity — Medical issues — Mental illness 11. Science Writing — Medicine and health — Mental health

LC 2014034487

An examination of the role of PTSD in American life by an ex-Marine, war correspondent and PTSD patient shares discussions of its widespread impact on families and the taboos that challenge its treatments.

"Though its incidence among combat veterans has brought post-traumatic stress disorder to the fore, the National Institute of Mental Health estimates that one in every 30 American adults suffers from the condition. Seasoned war correspondent Morris, also a former marine infantry officer with PTSD, here draws on personal experience, interviews, and scientific studies to present the big picture." —*Library Journal*

An Eamon Dolan Book.

O'Sullivan, Suzanne

The Sleeping Beauties: And Other Stories of Mystery Illness. Suzanne O'Sullivan. Pantheon Books 2021. 320 p.

ISBN 9781524748371

Grades: Adult   616.85

1. Psychosomatic disorders 2. Hysteria (Social psychology) 3. Diseases 4. Mind and body 5. Neuropsychology 6. Science Writing — Medicine and health — Mental health 8. Society and culture — Psychology and human behavior 7. History writing — Science, technology, and medicine

LC 2021005258

A riveting exploration of the phenomenon of psychosomatic disorders, mass hysteria, and other culture-bound syndromes occurring around the world. In Sweden, hundreds of refugee children fall asleep for months and years at a time. In upstate New York, teenage girls develop involuntary twitches and seizures that spread like a contagion. She presents these curious and often distressing case studies of seeming mass hysteria with compassion and humanity, persuasively arguing that psychological suffering demands much greater respect and discussion than it's given at present. In attempting to understand the complexity of psy-

ESSENTIAL AND RECOMMENDED TITLES
616.85 Miscellaneous diseases of nervous system and mental disorders

chogenic illness, O'Sullivan has given us a book of both fascination and serious concern as these syndromes continue to proliferate around the globe.

"O'Sullivan has written a medical page-turner that makes a compelling argument for a holistic approach to health care." —*Library Journal*

Petersen, Andrea
On Edge: A Journey Through Anxiety. Andrea Petersen. Crown 2017. 336 p.
ISBN 9780553418576
Grades: Adult 616.85
1. Petersen, Andrea 2. Anxiety disorders 3. Mental health 4. Neuroscience 5. Determination 6. Anxiety 7. Autobiographies and memoirs 8. Life stories — Facing adversity — Medical issues — Mental illness
LC 2016050111

A compassionate account of living with anxiety, complemented by deep reportage on the science of anxiety disorders, traces the author's personal journey of trying to understand and manage her own case from neuroscientific, spiritual and genetic perspectives.

"Sensitive and frank personal views on anxiety backed by substantial research and analysis of the evolution of treatment methods and drugs to alleviate symptoms." —*Kirkus*

Includes bibliographical references and index.

Power, Thomas J.
If Your Adolescent Has ADHD: An Essential Resource for Parents. Thomas J. Power, PhD, Linda Wasmer Andrews. Oxford University Press 2018. xi, 218 p.
ISBN 9780190873103
Grades: Adult 616.85
1. Science writing — Medicine and health — Psychology 2. Science writing — Medicine and health — Children's health
LC 2017037994

Provides evidence-based treatments and behavioral strategies for parents of adolescents coping with attention-deficit hyperactivity disorder as they transition through high school into college, work, and moving away from home.

Includes bibliographical references and index.

Riley, Alex
★ *A Cure for Darkness: The Story of Depression and How We Treat It.* Alex Riley. Scribner 2021. 416 p.
ISBN 9781501198779
Grades: Adult 616.85
1. Riley, Alex 2. Depression 3. People with depression 4. Psychotherapy 5. Antidepressants 6. Mental health services 7. History of medicine 8. Treatment 9. Science Writing — Medicine and health — Mental health 10. Society and culture — Psychology and human behavior 11. Life stories — Facing adversity — Medical issues — Mental illness

What is depression? Is it a persistent low mood or a complex range of symptoms? Is it a single diagnosis or a diversity of mental disorders requiring different treatments? Since 2015, author Alex Riley has received both cognitive behavioral therapy and antidepressants for his own depression. Expanding from his own experience, he tracks treatments through history, from the "talking cure" to electroconvulsive therapy to magic mushrooms. Reporting on the field of global mental health from its colonial past to the present day, Riley highlights a range of scalable therapies, including how a group of grandmothers stands on the frontline of a mental health revolution.

"An essential book that brings much-needed awareness to depression and the lingering stigma and misinformation surrounding it." —*Library Journal*

Rodgers, Jodi
★ *How to Find a Four-Leaf Clover: What Autism Can Teach Us About Difference, Connection, and Belonging.* Jodi Rodgers. Little, Brown Spark 2024. 304 p.
ISBN 9780316471978
Grades: Adult 616.85
1. Autism spectrum disorders 2. Difference 3. Communities 4. Autistic people 5. Social advocates 6. Neurodivergent people 7. Belonging 8. Social integration 9. Life stories — Science, technology, and medicine — Healthcare professionals 10. Science writing — Medicine and health — Disabilities and disorders 11. Life stories — Facing adversity — Medical issues — Living with disabilities

The Love on the Spectrum star and disability rights advocate shares stories from her expansive career working within the autistic community and calls for a more inclusive and accepting society.

"Memorable, poignant, and heartwarming, Rodgers's stories provide welcome insight into the lives of autistic people." —*Library Journal*

Ronson, Jon
★ *The Psychopath Test: A Journey Through the Madness Industry.* Jon Ronson. Riverhead Books 2011. 288 p.
ISBN 9781594488016
Grades: Adult 616.85
1. Antisocial personality disorders 2. Mental illness 3. Psychopathology 4. Mental health 5. Personality disorders 6. Science Writing — Medicine and health — Mental health
LC 2011003133

In this madcap journey, a bestselling journalist investigates psychopaths and the industry of doctors, scientists, and journalists who study them.

Schreiber, Flora Rheta
Sybil. by Flora Rheta Schreiber. Warner Books 1974. 460 p. : Illustration
ISBN 9780808505174
Grades: Adult 616.85
1. Schreiber, Flora Rheta, 1918-1988 2. Dissociative identity disorder 3. People with mental illnesses 4. Autobiographies and memoirs 5. Page to screen 6. Science Writing — Medicine and health — Mental health 7. Life stories — Facing adversity — Medical issues — Mental illness 8. Family and Relationships — Abuse 9. True Crime — Domestic Crime
LC BL 99747888

Records the life of a young woman who assumed sixteen personalities, possibly due to abuse by her neurotic mother, and describes the events and outcome of her eleven years in psychoanalysis.

"This is the true story of Sybil I. Dorsett, a battered child possessed by 16 different personalities. The author skillfully evokes Sybil's patient work during 11 years of psychoanalysis and her eventual success in integrating these selves into a unified personality." —*Library Journal*

Includes index; Originally published: Chicago : Regnery, 1973.

Senator, Susan
Autism Adulthood: Strategies and Insights for a Fufilling Life. Susan Senator. Skyhorse Publishing 2016. 280 pages
ISBN 9781510704237
Grades: Adult 616.85
1. Parents of autistic children 2. Autistic people 3. Family relationships 4. People with developmental disabilities 5. Parent caregivers for people with disabilities 6. Autism spectrum disorders 7. Autobiographies and memoirs 8. Science Writing — Medicine and health — Disabilities and disorders 9. Family and Relationships — Parenting 10. Life stories — Facing adversity — Medical issues
LC Bl2016013890

Discusses the mysteries of autism adulthood, including ways to make it manageable and enjoyable, and shares stories from real families and their approaches.

"Straightforward and to the point, Senator's book addresses many parents' worst fears and inspires them to step up and create a situation and a community that can support their child in their absence. This is a must-read for any parent with a child on the autism spectrum as well as caregivers, siblings, and extended family. Suitable for any library with parenting and autism collections." —*Library Journal*

Included bibliographical resources.

Smith, R. Garth
ASD, the Complete Autism Spectrum Disorder Health & Diet Guide: The Complete Autism Spectrum Disorder Health & Diet Guide. R. Garth Smith,

PUBLIC LIBRARY CORE COLLECTION: NONFICTION
Twentieth Edition

MBBS, FRCPC, Susan Hannah, BA, BScH, and Elke Sengmueller, BASc, RD.. Robert Rose 2014. 408 pages
ISBN 9780778804734
Grades: Adult   616.85
1. Gluten-free diet 2. Recipes 3. Autism spectrum disorders 4. Cookbooks 5. Family and Relationships — General 6. Food writing — Cooking and cookbooks — Cooking for health

LC Oc2014020110

"With sections for all parts of the day, there are plenty of recipes to work through for even the pickiest/limited eater. This should be required reading for anyone wanting to best address healthy options for Autistic people."—*Publishers Weekly*

Includes index.

Specter, Emma
More, Please: On Food, Fat, Bingeing, Longing, and the Lust for Enough. Emma Specter. HarperCollins 2024. 320 p.
ISBN 9780063278370
Grades: Adult   616.85
1. Compulsive eating 2. Eating disorders 3. Culture 4. Food habits 5. Body image 6. Fat people 7. Desire 8. Identity 9. LGBTQIA+ people 10. Growing up 11. United States 12. Society and culture — General 13. Life stories — Facing adversity — Medical issues 14. Science Writing — Medicine and health

An unflinching and deeply reported look at the realities of binge-eating disorder from a rising culture commentator and writer for Vogue.

"In this 'Hybrid memoir-in-interviews,' Vogue culture writer Specter blends her own struggles with binge eating and body image with the voices of prominent body-positive writers, including Carmen Maria Machado and Roxane Gay, to show how representation can be a healing agent."—*Kirkus*

Stewart, Alison
Junk: Digging Through America's Love Affair with Stuff. Alison Stewart. Chicago Review Press 2016. 304 p.
ISBN 9781613730553
Grades: Adult   616.85
1. Consumer society 2. Compulsive hoarding 3. Housekeeping 4. Society and culture — Pop culture 5. Society and culture — Psychology and human behavior

LC 2015050224

When journalist and author Alison Stewart was confronted with emptying her late parents' overloaded basement, a job that dragged on for months, it got her thinking: how did it come to this? Why do smart, successful people hold on to old Christmas bows, chipped knick-knacks, and books they would likely never reread? Junk details Stewart's three-year investigation into America's stuff, lots and lots and lots of stuff.

"Absorbing and enjoyably compelling research on the packrat conundrum in our society." —*Kirkus*

Includes bibliographical references.

Summerscale, Kate
The Book of Phobias and Manias: A History of Obsession. Kate Summerscale. Penguin Group USA 2022. 240 p.
ISBN 9780593489758
Grades: Adult   616.85
1. Obsession 2. Fear 3. Mania 4. Phobias 5. Psychology 6. Compulsive behavior 7. History writing — General 8. Society and culture — Psychology and human behavior

Phobias and manias are deeply personal experiences, and among the most common anxiety disorders of our time, but they are also clues to our shared past. The award-winning author Kate Summerscale uses rich and riveting case studies to trace the origins of our obsessions, unearthing a history of human strangeness, from the middle ages to the present day, and a wealth of explanations for some of our most powerful aversions and desires.

"Exquisitely detailed and consistently insightful, this is an entertaining guide to humanity's compulsions." —*Publishers Weekly*

Turban, Jack L.
★ *Free to Be: Understanding Kids & Gender Identity.* by Jack Turban, MD.. Atria Books 2024. 320 p.
ISBN 9781668017043
Grades: Adult   616.85
1. Transgender children 2. Transgender teenagers 3. Gender dysphoria 4. Gender identity 5. Gender role and children 6. Parenting 7. Transgenderism 8. Medical care 9. Mental health 10. Gender role 11. LGBTQIA+ children 12. LGBTQIA+ teenagers 13. United States 14. Society and culture — Gender 15. Science Writing — Medicine and health

LC 2023053072

An authoritative guide to understanding and navigating gender identity from an acclaimed expert on the mental health of transgender and gender diverse youth.

"Thoroughly researched and buoyed by empathetic patient stories, this ranks among the best guides available for parents of trans children and teens." —*Publishers Weekly*

Includes bibliographical references and index.

Van der Kolk, Bessel A.
The Body Keeps the Score: Brain, Mind, and Body in the Healing of Trauma. Bessel A. van der Kolk, M.D.. Viking 2014. xvi, 443 pages : Illustration
ISBN 9780670785933
Grades: Adult   616.85
1. Post-traumatic stress disorder 2. Behavior therapy 3. Science writing — Medicine and health — Psychology 4. Science writing — Medicine and health — Alternative medicine

LC 2014021365

A forefront expert on traumatic stress outlines his own take on healing, explaining how traumatic stress affects brain processes and how to use innovative treatments to reactivate the mind's abilities to trust, engage others and experience pleasure.

Includes bibliographical references and index.

Wilson, Sarah
First, We Make the Beast Beautiful: A New Journey Through Anxiety. Sarah Wilson. Dey Street 2018. 312 pages
ISBN 9780062836786
Grades: Adult   616.85
1. Wilson, Sarah, 1974- 2. Anxiety 3. Mental health 4. Coping 5. Spirituality 6. Australian literature 7. Society and culture — Psychology and human behavior

Challenges cultural beliefs about anxiety from the perspectives of medical and spiritual leaders to explore how the condition needs to be viewed less as a burdensome affliction and more as a source of divine growth.

"Amusing, practical, and filled with delightful asides, this book will appeal to anxiety-prone readers, who will find much to calm them in these pages." —*Publishers Weekly*

Includes bibliographical references; Originally published in Australia in 2017 by Pan Macmillan Australia Pty Ltd.—Title page verso.

Winfrey, Oprah
What Happened to You?: Conversations on Trauma, Resilience, and Healing. Oprah Winfrey, Bruce D. Perry. Flatiron Books 2021. 304 p.
ISBN 9781250223180
Grades: Adult   616.85
1. Winfrey, Oprah, 1954- 2. Psychic trauma 3. Childhood 4. Health 5. Distress (Psychology) 6. Healing 7. Resilience 8. Growing up 9. Society and culture — Psychology and human behavior 10. Life stories — Personal growth

Oprah Winfrey and a renowned brain development and trauma expert discuss the impact of trauma and adversity and how healing must begin with a shift to asking, "What happened to you?" rather than "What's wrong with you?".

"Though many of these issues have been addressed before, Perry and Winfrey's partnership is notable, and their book is worthy of attention. A candid guidebook to exorcising mental trauma." —*Kirkus*

ESSENTIAL AND RECOMMENDED TITLES
616.8522 Anxiety disorders

Wood, David Bowne
★ *What* Have We Done: The Moral Injury of Our Longest Wars. David Wood. Little Brown & Co. 2016. 320 p.
ISBN 9780316264150
Grades: Adult   **616.85**
1. Political ethics 2. War 3. Killing (Ethics) 4. History writing — Wars and conflicts
LC 2016932416

Featuring portraits of combat veterans and leading mental health researchers, a Pulitzer Prize-winning journalist presents a meticulously researched and deeply personal look at war and those who volunteer for it, and, too often, receive the scars of moral injury.

616.8522 Anxiety disorders

Stern, Amanda
Little Panic: Dispatches from an Anxious Life. Amanda Stern. Grand Central Pub 2018. 416 p.
ISBN 9781538711927
Grades: Adult   **616.8522**
1. Stern, Amanda 2. Growing up 3. Fear 4. Panic disorders 5. Parent and child 6. Anxiety disorders 7. Self-destructive behavior 8. Anxiety 9. New York City 10. Autobiographies and memoirs 11. Life stories — Facing adversity — Medical issues — Mental illness 12. Life stories — Relationships — Growing up 13. Family and Relationships — Growing Up
LC 2017963706

The author of the Frankly Frannie series presents a relatable, darkly comic memoir about her lifelong struggles with anxiety, tracing her upbringing by a bohemian mother and sanitized, affluent father in a transforming New York City.

616.86 Substance abuse (Drug abuse)

Beattie, Melody
Codependent No More: Stop Controlling Others and Start Caring for Yourself. Melody Beattie. Hazelden 1987. 231 p.
ISBN 9780894864025
Grades: Adult   **616.86**
1. Codependency 2. Self-care 3. Self-Help — Mental health — Addiction 4. Self-Help — Relationships
LC 86082660

The healing touchstone of millions, this modern classic by one of America's best-loved and most inspirational authors holds the key to understanding codependency and to unlocking its stultifying hold on your life.
Bibliography: P. 217-222.

Whitaker, Holly
★ *Quit Like a Woman*: The Radical Choice to Not Drink in a Culture Obsessed with Alcohol. Holly Whitaker. The Dial Press 2019. 304 p.
ISBN 9781984825056
Grades: Adult   **616.86**
1. Whitaker, Holly 2. Sobriety 3. Alcoholism 4. Alcoholic women 5. Women drug abusers 6. Twelve-step programs 7. Male domination (Social structure) 8. Social control 9. Treatment 10. Autobiographies and memoirs 11. Society and culture — Illness and disease — Addiction 12. Science Writing — Medicine and health — Addiction 13. Life stories — Facing adversity — Medical issues — Addiction
LC 2019029710

Written in a relatable voice that is honest and witty, Quit Like a Woman is at once a groundbreaking look at drinking culture and a road map to cutting out alcohol in order to live our best lives without the crutch of intoxication. You will never look at drinking the same way again.

"Part self-help, part recovery memoir, this personal account provides useful and inspiring techniques for addiction recovery." —*Library Journal*

616.89 Mental disorders

Aviv, Rachel
★ *Strangers to Ourselves*: Unsettled Minds and the Stories That Make Us. Rachel Aviv. Farrar, Straus and Giroux 2022. 288 p.
ISBN 9780374600846
Grades: Adult   **616.89**
1. Aviv, Rachel 2. People with mental illnesses 3. Psychotherapy patients 4. Psychiatric hospital patients 5. Mental illness 6. Psychiatry 7. Identity 8. Life stories — Facing adversity — Medical issues — Mental illness 9. Science Writing — Medicine and health — Mental health
LC 2022021878

Raising fundamental questions about how we understand ourselves in periods of crisis and distress, the author draws on deep, original reporting as well as unpublished journals and memoirs to write about people who have come up against the limits of psychiatric explanations for who they are.

"This eye-opening examination makes for a valuable addition to modern discourse around mental illness." —*Publishers Weekly*
Includes bibliographical references.

Blumenthal, Brett
52 Small Changes for the Mind: Improve Memory - Minimize Stress - Increase Productivity - Boost Happiness. Brett Blumenthal. Chronicle Books 2015. 320 pages
ISBN 9781452131672
Grades: Adult   **616.89**
1. Mental health 2. Stress management 3. Well-being 4. Self-Help — Personal growth 5. Self-Help — General 6. Self-Help — Personal growth — Happiness
LC 2014039167

A wellness expert offers a plan for better memory, decreased stress, improved productivity and lasting happiness by making one small, attainable change every week, whether it be eating more brain-powering foods or developing music appreciation.

Encourages readers to make small daily changes that will promote wellness, overall health, and happiness.

Cahalan, Susannah
★ *The Great* Pretender: The Undercover Mission That Changed Our Understanding of Madness. Susannah Cahalan. Grand Central Publishing 2019. 336 p.
ISBN 9781538715284
Grades: Adult   **616.89**
1. Rosenhan, David L. 2. Mental illness 3. Mental Health Services 4. Human experimentation in psychology 5. Psychiatric hospitals 6. Psychiatric hospital patients 7. Psychopharmacology 8. Medical Personnel 9. Psychiatry 10. Diagnosis 11. United States 12. Science Writing — Medicine and health — Mental health 13. Life stories — Science, technology, and medicine — Healthcare professionals 14. History writing — Science, technology, and medicine
LC 2019017569

The award-winning, bestselling author investigates the 50-year-old mystery behind a dramatic experiment that broke open the field of psychology, closing down institutions and changing mental health diagnosis forever.
Includes bibliographical references and index.

Canfield, Jack
The 30 Day Sobriety Solution: How to Cut Back or Quit Drinking in the Privacy of Your Own Home. Jack Canfield and Dave Andrews. Atria Books 2016. xxii, 563 pages : Illustration
ISBN 9781476792958
Grades: Adult   **616.89**
1. Alcoholics 2. Alcoholism 3. Rehabilitation 4. Treatment 5. Self-Help — Personal growth 6. Self-Help — Mental health — Addiction 7. Self-Help — Personal growth — Motivation
LC 2015005948

A groundbreaking program to help you cut back or quit drinking entirely—in the privacy of your own home.

PUBLIC LIBRARY CORE COLLECTION: NONFICTION
Twentieth Edition

Jack Canfield, the #1 New York Times bestselling author of the Chicken Soup for the Soul; franchise and coauthor of The Success Principles, and Dave Andrews, a recovery expert, join forces to present a revolutionary program to help you cut back or quit drinking entirely—in the privacy of your own home. Alcohol kills one person every ten seconds worldwide, according to the World Health Organization. Thankfully, now, for anyone who feels that alcohol has become a problem—and for the 23.5 million Americans living in recovery and looking to be reinspired—this new program introduces a groundbreaking model for sobriety that you can achieve in your own home. The 30-Day Sobriety Solution grew out of Jack Canfield's decades-long work in self-esteem and success training. Its principles were carefully developed into a program by Dave Andrews and tested by thousands whose amazing stories of recovery are shared throughout the book. Organized into five phases that span 30-day periods, this book guides you through each day with practical exercises that, over time, allow you to more easily make positive choices again and again. "The Sobriety System" is an empowerment program that moves systematically from beliefs (including limiting ones) to feelings and emotions to concrete actions and behaviors that promote better outcomes. Integrating neuroscience, cognitive therapy, proven tools, and teachings, The 30-Day Sobriety Solution is a clear, practical daily program that will help you achieve your goals—whether that's getting sober or just cutting back—and create positive, permanent change in your life.

The best-selling co-creator of the Chicken Soup for the Soul franchise and a celebrity sobriety expert outline a groundbreaking model for recovery that incorporates self-esteem therapy exercises into five 30-day phases for making positive, incremental choices.

Includes bibliographical references and index.

Deisseroth, Karl
Projections: A Story of Human Emotions. Karl Deisseroth. Random House 2021. 272 p.
ISBN 9781984853691
Grades: Adult   616.89
1. Neuropsychiatry 2. People with mental illnesses 3. Mental illness 4. Psychiatrist and patient 5. Emotions 6. Suffering 7. Brain 8. Human evolution 9. Research 10. Physiology 11. Science Writing — Medicine and health — Mental health 12. Science Writing — Biology

Karl Deisseroth has spent his life pursuing truths about the human mind, both as a practicing clinical psychiatrist and as a researcher who created the revolutionary field of optogenetics, which allows us to decipher the brain's inner workings using light. In Projections, he combines his groundbreaking access to the brain's inner circuitry with a deep empathy for his patients to examine what mental illness reveals about the mind and the origin of human feelings.

"Deisseroth, professor of psychiatry at Stanford University, melds the personal with the clinical in his masterful debut on how the human mind works and what can be learned when it goes awry. . . . Writing with abundant empathy, Deisseroth brings his patients' struggles to life as he educates about both neuroscience and humanity." —Publishers Weekly

Foulkes, Lucy
★ *Losing Our Minds: The Challenge of Defining Mental Illness.* Lucy Foulkes. St. Martin's Press 2022. 240 p.
ISBN 9781250274175
Grades: Adult   616.89
1. Psychiatry 2. Teenagers 3. Mental illness 4. Mental health 5. Philosophy 6. Diagnosis 7. Science Writing — Medicine and health — Mental health
LC 2021037780

Public awareness of mental illness has been transformed in recent years, but our understanding of how to define it has yet to catch up. Too often, psychiatric disorders are confused with the inherent stresses and challenges of human experience. A narrative has taken hold that a mental health crisis has been building among young people. In this profoundly sensitive and constructive book, psychologist Lucy Foulkes argues that the crisis is one of ignorance as much as illness. Have we raised a 'snowflake' generation? Or are today's young people subjected to greater stress, exacerbated by social media, than ever before? Foulkes shows that both perspectives are useful but limited. The real question in need of answering is: how should we distinguish between 'normal' suffering and actual illness?

"Foulkes is a compassionate, rational guide through modern-day mental issues that are neither easily categorized nor treated." —Kirkus

Originally published in the UK by Jonathan Cape, 2021; Includes bibliographical references and index.

Gildiner, Catherine
Good Morning, Monster: Five Heroic Journeys to Recovery. Catherine Gildiner. St. Martin's Press 2020. 359 pages
ISBN 9781250271488
Grades: Adult   616.89
1. Gildiner, Catherine, 1948- 2. Women psychologists 3. Psychotherapy patients 4. Psychic trauma 5. Psychotherapy 6. Psychotherapist and patient 7. Psychological growth 8. Healing 9. Women psychotherapists 10. Psychologists 11. Autobiographies and memoirs 12. Life stories — Facing adversity — Medical issues — Mental illness 13. Life stories — Science, technology, and medicine — Healthcare professionals 14. Science Writing — Medicine and health — Doctors and nurses

A therapist creates moving portraits of five of her most memorable patients, men and women she considers psychological heroes.

"Clinical psychologist Gildiner (Too Close to the Falls) shares heart-wrenching stories of child abuse in this pull-no-punches narrative about five of her patients. . . . These painful accounts will break anyone's heart, and also inspire awe for the ways people who suffered horrific abuse were able to find a measure of recovery." —Publishers Weekly

Previously published: Toronto :.

Gottman, Julie Schwartz
Fight Right: How Successful Couples Turn Conflict into Connection. Julie Schwartz Gottman, PhD and John Gottman, PhD.. Harmony 2024. 344 pages : Illustration
ISBN 9780593579657
Grades: Adult   616.89
1. Psychotherapy 2. Couples 3. Psychology 4. Interpersonal communication 5. Interpersonal relations 6. Conflict resolution 7. Family and Relationships — Dating and Marriage 8. Self-Help — Relationships
LC 2023023993

Conflict is the top reason couples seek help—but it's also an opportunity for greater intimacy, deeper connection, and lasting love according to this essential guide from the world's leading relationship scientists and bestselling authors of the Seven Principles of Making Marriage Work.

Includes bibliographical references (pages 336-340) and index.

Grinker, Roy Richard
Nobody's Normal: How Culture Created the Stigma of Mental Illness. Roy Richard Grinker. W. W. Norton & Company 2021. 448 p.
ISBN 9780393531640
Grades: Adult   616.89
1. Grinker, Roy Richard, 1961- 2. People with mental illnesses 3. Stereotypes 4. Stigma (Social Psychology) 5. Psychiatry 6. Mental illness 7. Social psychology 8. Treatment 9. Science Writing — Medicine and health — Mental health 10. Society and culture — Illness and disease
LC 2020030381

The author of Unstrange Minds presents a compassionate history of evolving attitudes toward mental illness and the ongoing fight to end related stigmas, sharing the story of his own family's four-generation involvement in psychiatry.

With the eye of an anthropologist and a family legacy of psychiatry, Grinker explores how the contemporary United States came to its current understanding of mental illness and what is considered 'Normal.' —School Library Journal

Includes bibliographical references and index.

Haig, Matt
Notes on a Nervous Planet. Matt Haig. Penguin Books 2019. 272 p.
ISBN 9780143133421
Grades: Adult   616.89
1. Depression 2. Anxiety 3. Panic attacks 4. Coping 5. Technology 6. Mental illness 7. Stress management 8. Personal conduct 9. Autobiographies and mem-

ESSENTIAL AND RECOMMENDED TITLES
616.89 Mental disorders

oirs 10. Life stories — Facing adversity — Medical issues — Mental illness 11. Society and culture — Psychology and human behavior

LC 2018032891

A follow-up to the best-selling Reasons to Stay Alive shares a broad analysis of how modern life feeds anxiety, examining factors ranging from inequality and sleep disorders to social media and current events.

"By challenging readers to rethink their role in the modern world, Haigs book will embolden them to keep learning and pursuing their passions in order to ease anxiety." —*Publishers Weekly*

Harrington, Anne
Mind Fixers: Psychiatry's Troubled Search for the Biology of Mental Illness. Anne Harrington. W.W. Norton & Company 2019. 384 p.
ISBN 9780393071221
Grades: Adult   616.89
1. Mental illness 2. Psychotropic drugs 3. Neuropsychiatry 4. Psychiatry 5. Biology 6. Medicine 7. Biochemistry 8. Psychiatrist and patient 9. Neurochemistry 10. Public health 11. Impartial writing 12. Science Writing — Medicine and health — Mental health 13. History writing — Science, technology, and medicine

Documents the unfulfilled 1980s quest to identify the biological basis of mental illness, documenting the cultural upheavals, activism, public policy change, rivalries and profit-mongering that shaped efforts to address mental illness with biochemical treatments.

"In this erudite work, Harrington explores the history of psychiatry from the French neurologist Jean-Martin Charcot to the Swiss American neurologist Adolf Meyer to Sigmund Freud and up to the present day." —*Booklist*

Includes bibliographical references and index.

Jamison, Kay Redfield
Fires in the Dark: Healing the Unquiet Mind. Kay Redfield Jamison. Alfred A. Knopf 2023. 336 p.
ISBN 9780525657170
Grades: Adult   616.89
1. Rivers, W. H. R. (William Halse Rivers), 1864-1922 2. Osler, William, Sir, 1849-1919 3. Jamison, Kay Redfield 4. Physicians 5. Psychologists 6. Mental illness 7. Psychic trauma 8. Suffering 9. Psychotherapy 10. Treatment 11. Religions 12. Rites and ceremonies 13. Occultism 14. Empathy 15. Healing 16. Science Writing — Medicine and health — Mental health 17. History writing — Science, technology, and medicine 18. Life stories — Science, technology, and medicine — Healthcare professionals

LC 2022038323

A professor and acclaimed author of An Unquiet Mind discusses how the brain processes and reacts to trauma and explores the history of physical treatments for mental illness and the ancient and modern importance of religion in healing the mind.

"It's an eloquent, wide-ranging, and edifying look at healing relationships of all kinds." —*Publishers Weekly*

Includes bibliographical references and index.

Kandel, Eric R.
★ *The Disordered Mind: What Unusual Brains Tell Us About Ourselves.* Eric R. Kandel. Farrar, Straus and Giroux 2018. 352 p.
ISBN 9780374287863
Grades: Adult   616.89
1. Self 2. Neuroscience 3. Brain diseases 4. Mental health 5. Mind and body 6. Consciousness 7. Human anatomy 8. Decision-making 9. Identity 10. Science Writing — Biology

LC 2017049274

A Nobel Prize-winning neuroscientist draws on his extensive research to explore how the mind and one's individual sense of self arise from the physical matter of the brain, explaining what brain disorders can teach us about human nature.

"Emphasizing advances in the fields of genetics, brain imaging, and animal research, Kandel writes about decision-making, sense of self, emotion, mood, addiction, and gender identity." —*Booklist*

Includes bibliographical references and index.

Kohli, Sahaj Kaur
★ *But What Will People Say?: Navigating Mental Health, Identity, Love, and Family Between Cultures.* Sahaj Kaur Kohli, MA, LGPC.. Penguin Life 2024. 272 p.
ISBN 9780593491195
Grades: Adult   616.89
1. Psychiatry 2. Marginalized people 3. Culture 4. Acculturation 5. Mental health 6. Identity 7. Love 8. Families 9. Psychic trauma 10. Guilt 11. Personal conduct 12. Psychology 13. Science Writing — Medicine and health — Mental health 14. Society and culture — Psychology and human behavior 15. Family and relationships — General

LC 2023050100

A writer, therapist and founder of Brown Girl Therapy, a wellness organization for adult children of immigrants challenges the long-held, Eurocentric mental health models that were focused on individuality instead of collective healing and offers an alternative.

"It's the book she longed for in her youth; hopefully, it will be a guide for others facing similar challenges." —*Booklist*

Includes bibliographical references and index.

Lieberman, Jeffrey A.
Malady of the Mind: Schizophrenia and the Path to Prevention. Jeffrey A. Lieberman, MD.. Scribner 2023. 320 p.
ISBN 9781982136420
Grades: Adult   616.89
1. Schizophrenia 2. People with schizophrenia 3. Delusions 4. Mental illness 5. Psychiatry 6. Medical innovations 7. Preventive medicine 8. Diagnosis 9. Treatment 10. History of medicine 11. Science Writing — Medicine and health — Mental health 12. Science Writing — Medicine and health — Illness and disease 13. History writing — Science, technology, and medicine

LC 2021055774

This powerful portrait of schizophrenia, the most malignant and mysterious mental illness, by renowned psychiatrist Jeffrey Lieberman, interweaves cultural and scientific history with dramatic patient profiles and clinical experiences to impart a revolutionary message of hope. For the first time in history, we can effectively treat schizophrenia, limiting its disabling effects—and we're on the verge of being able to prevent the disease's onset entirely.

"The result is a brilliant examination of a long-misunderstood disorder." —*Publishers Weekly*

Includes bibliographical references.

Shrinks: The Untold Story of Psychiatry. Jeffrey A. Lieberman with Ogi Ogas. Little Brown & Co. 2015. 304 p.
ISBN 9780316278867
Grades: Adult   616.89
1. Psychiatry 2. Mental illness 3. People with mental illnesses 4. History writing — Microhistory 5. Science Writing — Medicine and health — Mental health

LC BI2015006112

A former president of the American Psychiatric Association presents the fascinating story of psychiatry's origins, downfall and redemption.

"A lively defense of psychiatry that extols brain science and pharmaceutical treatment. A contrasting approach is found in Philip Thomas's Psychiatry in Context; critical of routine overuse of pharmaceuticals, Thomas makes a case for understanding the unique experience of each patient, even in schizophrenia." —*Library Journal*

Marchant, Jo
Cure: A Journey into the Science of Mind Over Body. by Jo Marchant. Crown Publishers 2016. 288 p.
ISBN 9780385348157
Grades: Adult   616.89
1. Mind and body therapies 2. Mind and body 3. Alternative medicine 4. Healing 5. Placebo (Medicine) 6. Impartial writing 7. Science Writing — Medicine and health

LC 2015024707

Drawing on the latest research and traveling the world to interview physicians, patients and researchers on the cutting edge of a new world of medicine, an award-winning science writer presents a rigorous, skeptical, deeply reported examination into the science behind the vast potential of the mind's ability to heal the body.

Nerenberg, Jenara
Divergent Mind: Thriving in a World That Wasn't Designed for You. Jenara Nerenberg. HarperOne 2019. 256 p.
ISBN 9780062876799
Grades: Adult   616.89
1. Nerenberg, Jenara 2. Women 3. Neuropsychology 4. Autistic women 5. Brain 6. Diagnosis 7. Sexism in medicine 8. Sensitivity (Personal quality) 9. Mental health 10. Sex differences 11. Neurodivergent people 12. Life stories — Facing adversity — Medical issues — Living with disabilities 13. Science Writing — Medicine and health — Mental health 14. Society and culture — Gender — Women

LC 2019033534

A journalist who suffered into adulthood with autism and ADHD reveals why these conditions are often overlooked and misdiagnosed in women and shares real stories from fellow females to dispel widely-held misconceptions while offering a path forward.

"An extraordinary, jaw-dropping take on a topic with which many women will identify. Of special interest to those in the human resources, counseling, and education fields." —*Library Journal*

Includes bibliographical references.

Nesse, Randolph M.
Good Reasons for Bad Feelings: Insights from the Frontier of Evolutionary Psychiatry. Randolph M. Nesse, MD.. Dutton 2019. 384 p.
ISBN 9781101985663
Grades: Adult   616.89
1. Mental illness 2. Genetics 3. Human evolution 4. Psychiatry 5. Science Writing — Medicine and health — Mental health

LC 2018045094

A founder of the field of evolutionary medicine uses his decades of experience as a psychiatrist to provide a much-needed new framework for making sense of mental illness.

"Nesse fully meets his modest but laudable goal of providing a conversation-starter on why mental illness should be viewed from an evolutionary perspective." —*Publishers Weekly*

Pratt, Misty
All in Her Head: How Gender Bias Harms Women's Mental Health. Misty Pratt. Greystone Books 2024. 336 p.
ISBN 9781771649711
Grades: Adult   616.89
1. Women 2. Medical care 3. Mental illness 4. Gender role 5. Mental health 6. Sexism in medicine 7. History Writing — Women's history 8. Science Writing — Medicine and health — Mental health

Sharing her own history of mental illness, a science writer and medical researcher paints a picture of a system that's failing women on multiple levels, and explores stereotypes, debunks myth and challenges misconceptions to give women the hope and courage to reframe and reclaim their mental health.

"This title deftly brings awareness to biases and dismissive attitudes about women patients and the barriers they face when they seek treatment and relief." —*Library Journal*

Rosen, Jonathan
★ *The* Best Minds: A Story of Friendship, Madness, and the Tragedy of Good Intentions. Jonathan Rosen. Penguin Press 2023. 560 p.
ISBN 9781594206573
Grades: Adult   616.89
1. Laudor, Michael 2. Rosen, Jonathan, 1963- 3. People with schizophrenia 4. Male friendship 5. Mental illness 6. Schizophrenia 7. Murder 8. Friendship 9. Women murder victims 10. New York (State) 11. Autobiographies and memoirs 12. Life stories — Relationships — Friendship 13. Science writing — Medicine and health — Mental health 14. Life stories — Facing adversity — Medical issues — Mental illness 15. Family and relationships — Friendship 16. True Crime — Murder

LC 2022038816

Pulitzer Prize for Memoir or Autobiography finalist, 2024.

An acclaimed author investigates the forces that led his closest childhood friend, a paranoid schizophrenic with brilliant promise who defied the odds and graduated from Yale Law School, to kill the woman he loved, in this exploration of the ways in which we understand—and fail to understand—mental illness.

"An affecting, thoughtfully written portrait of a friendship broken by mental illness and its terrible sequelae." —*Kirkus*

Includes bibliographical references and index.

Sederer, Lloyd I.
The Family Guide to Mental Health Care. Lloyd I. Sederer, MD; foreword by Glenn Close. W.W. Norton & Company 2013. xxii, 312 pages
ISBN 9780393707946
Grades: Adult   616.89
1. Mental health services 2. Mental illness 3. Family and Relationships — General 4. Reference books — Psychology 5. Science writing — Medicine and health — Psychology

LC 2013007244

Counsels those dealing with a family member's mental illness on medications, medical privacy laws, depression, anxiety, bipolar illness, and eating disorders, and includes a checklist of questions to ask at a doctor's visit.

Includes bibliographical references (pages [269]-271) and index.

Stern, Adam
Committed: Dispatches from a Psychiatrist in Training. Adam Stern. Houghton Mifflin Harcourt 2021. 224 p.
ISBN 9780358434733
Grades: Adult   616.89
1. Stern, Adam (Psychiatrist) 2. Psychiatrists 3. Residents (Medicine) 4. Interpersonal relations 5. Psychiatry 6. Psychological growth 7. Love 8. Loss 9. Medical students 10. Interns (Medicine) 11. Autobiographies and memoirs 12. Life stories — Science, technology, and medicine — Healthcare professionals 13. Science Writing — Medicine and health — Doctors and nurses

LC 2020057716

In his memoir, Stern pulls back the curtain on the intense and emotionally challenging lessons he and his fellow doctors learned while studying the human condition, and ultimately, the value of connection. The narrative focuses on these residents, their growth as doctors, and the life choices they make as they try to survive their grueling four-year residency. Rich with drama, insight, and emotion, Stern shares engrossing stories of life on the psychiatric wards, as well as the group's experiences as they grapple with impostor syndrome and learn about love and loss.

"Stern debuts with a mesmerizing memoir of the four years he spent in a psychiatry residency program at Harvard.... Compassionate and candid, this is as human as it gets." —*Publishers Weekly*

Torrey, E. Fuller
Surviving Schizophrenia: A Family Manual. E. Fuller Torrey, M.D... Harper Perennial 2019. xxii, 496 pages : Illustration
ISBN 9780062880802
Grades: Adult   616.89
1. Schizophrenia 2. Science writing — Medicine and health — Psychology

LC Bl2013053517

Describes the symptoms, causes, and treatment of schizophrenia, tells those concerned how to take care of a schizophrenic, and discusses legal and ethical problems related to the mental illness.

Includes bibliographical references and index; First published 1983.

ESSENTIAL AND RECOMMENDED TITLES
616.8900835 Adolescent psychiatry

616.8900835 Adolescent psychiatry

Hibbs, B. Janet
The Stressed Years of Their Lives: Helping Your Kid Survive and Thrive During Their College Years. B. Janet Hibbs, Ph.D, M.F.T. & Anthony Rostain, M.D, M.A... St. Martin's Press 2019. xiii, 322 pages : Illustration
ISBN 9781250113139
Grades: Adult   616.8900835
  1. College students 2. Psychology 3. Mental health 4. Educator resources — General 5. Family and Relationships — Parenting 6. Science writing — Medicine and health — Psychology
LC 2018041166

A guide for parents of college-bound students cites the emergence of mood disorders and other mental-health challenges in mid to late adolescence, sharing counsel on typical versus atypical mental health and what behaviors necessitate intervention.

From two leading child and adolescent mental health experts comes a guide for the parents of every college and college-bound student who want to know what's normal mental health and behavior, what's not, and how to intervene before it's too late. "I canthink of no better guide than the Stressed Years of Their Lives for overwhelmed parents and stressed-out kids for navigating these turbulent times. This is required reading for the college set."—Brigid Schulte, author of the New York Times bestselling Overwhelmed All parenting is in preparation for letting go. However, the paradox of parenting is that the more we learn about late adolescent development and risk, the more frightened we become for our children, and the more we want to stay involved in their lives. This becomes particularly necessary, and also particularly challenging, in mid- to late adolescence, the years just before and after students head off to college. These years coincide with the emergence of many mood disorders and other mental health issues. When family psychologist Dr. B. Hibbs's own son came home from college mired in a dangerous depressive spiral, she turned to Dr. Anthony Rostain. Dr. Rostain has a secret superpower: He understands the arcane rules governing privacy and parental involvement in students' mental health care on college campuses, the same rules that sometimes hold parents back from getting good care for their kids. Now, these two doctors have combined their expertise to corral the crucial emotional skills and lessons that every parent and student can learn from a successful launch from home to college.

"Packing in just the right amount of statistics and real-world scenarios, two doctors offer sound advice on how parents can better prepare their children for the challenging college years that lie ahead of them."—*Kirkus*

Includes bibliographical references (pages 297-314) and index.

616.9 Other diseases

Finlay, B. Brett
Let Them Eat Dirt: Saving Your Child from an Oversanitized World. B. Brett Finlay, PhD, Marie-Claire Arrieta, PhD.. Algonquin Books of Chapel Hill 2016. xiii, 288 pages
ISBN 9781616206499
Grades: Adult   616.9
  1. Bacteria 2. Medical microbiology 3. Pathogenic microorganisms 4. Family and Relationships — Parenting 5. Science writing — Medicine and health — Children's health 6. Science writing — Biology
LC 2016018794

Drawing on recent scientific findings that suggest that exposure to infectious microbes can actually promote long-term health in children links microbe imbalances to a range of health problems while sharing insights into the pros and cons of such parenting choices as natural childbirth, breastfeeding, antibiotics and having pets.

Draws on scientific findings suggesting that exposure to infectious microbes can promote long-term health to link microbe imbalances to a range of health problems while sharing insights into the pros and cons of natural childbirth, breastfeeding, antibiotics, and having pets.

Includes bibliographical references.

Hernandez, Daisy
The Kissing Bug: A True Story of a Family, an Insect, and a Nation's Neglect of a Deadly Disease. Daisy Hernandez. Tin House 2021. 336 p.
ISBN 9781951142520
Grades: Adult   616.9
  1. Hernandez, Daisy 2. Communicable diseases 3. Medical care 4. Health 5. Discrimination 6. Inequality 7. Racism in medical care 8. Death of aunts 9. Grief 10. Families 11. Epidemics 12. Insects 13. Death of family members 14. United States 15. Family and Relationships — Illness and the family 16. Society and culture — Illness and disease
LC 2020057435

Growing up in a New Jersey factory town in the 1980s, Daisy Hernandez believed that her aunt had become deathly ill from eating an apple. No one in her family, in either the United States or Colombia, spoke of infectious diseases, and even into her thirties, she only knew that her aunt had died of a rare illness called Chagas. But as Hernandez dug deeper, she discovered that Chagas—or the kissing bug disease—is more prevalent in the United States than the Zika virus. Today, more than three hundred thousand Americans have Chagas. Why do some infectious diseases make headlines and others fall by the wayside? After her aunt's death, Hernandez begins searching for answers about who our nation chooses to take care of and who we ignore.

"Blending family and medical history, this account is especially relevant in an era of pandemics." —*Library Journal*

Includes bibliographical references and index.

Ingels, Darin
The Lyme Solution: A 5-part Plan to Fight the Inflammatory Auto-immune Response and Beat Lyme Disease. Darin Ingels, ND, FAAEM.. Avery 2018. xi, 372 p. : Illustration
ISBN 9780735216303
Grades: Adult   616.9
  1. Lyme disease 2. Naturopathy 3. Science writing — Medicine and health — Illness and disease 4. Science Writing — Medicine and health — Alternative medicine
LC Bl2018000933

Shares comprehensive, whole-body approaches to treating acute and chronic Lyme disease, outlining a five-step plan that involves prevention, early detection, bolstering the immune system, strategic uses of medication and overall lifestyle quality improvement.

Includes bibliographical references (pages 339-359) and index.

Monosson, Emily
★ *Blight: Fungi and the Coming Pandemic.* Emily Monosson. W.W. Norton & Company 2023. 288 p.
ISBN 9781324007012
Grades: Adult   616.9
  1. Fungi 2. Pathogenic microorganisms 3. Communicable diseases 4. Infection 5. Extinction 6. Mycology 7. Medicine 8. Environmentalism 9. Science Writing — Biology 10. Science Writing — Medicine and health — Illness and disease
LC 2023009948

Fungi are everywhere. Most are harmless; some are helpful. A few are killers. Collectively, infectious fungi are the mostdevastating agents of disease on earth, and a fungus that can persist in the environment without its host is here to stay. In Blight, Emily Monosson documents how trade, travel, and a changing climate are making us all more vulnerable to invasion.

"Monosson keeps the discussions of fungi biology accessible, and the battery of case studies of fungal outbreaks underscores the urgency of the threat. This wake-up call should not go unheeded." —*Publishers Weekly*

Includes bibliographical references and index.

Randall, David K.
Black Death at the Golden Gate: The Race to Save America from the Bubonic Plague. David K. Randall. W. W. Norton & Co. 2019. 273 pages
ISBN 9780393609455
Grades: Adult   616.9

1. Plague 2. Black Death 3. Quarantine 4. Immigrants 5. Racism 6. Hygiene 7. Sanitation 8. Diseases 9. Animal control (Public health) 10. History of medicine 11. Government cover-ups 12. Corruption 13. Preventive medicine 14. San Francisco, California 15. 20th century 16. History writing — Plague and famine 17. History writing — Science, technology, and medicine 18. History writing — Early 20th century — United States 19. Science Writing — Medicine and health

LC 2018055377

Traces the massive effort to contain an outbreak of bubonic plague in 1900 San Francisco, detailing how the process was complicated by virulent racism, pseudoscience, and political cover-ups.

Includes bibliographical references and index.

Zaman, Muhammad H.
Biography of Resistance: The Epic Battle Between People and Pathogens. Muhammad H. Zaman, Ph.D.. Harper Wave 2020. 304 pages
ISBN 9780062862976

Grades: Adult   616.9

1. Antibiotics 2. Drug resistance in microorganisms 3. Pathogenic microorganisms 4. Virus diseases 5. Public health 6. Science writing — Medicine and health

LC 2020002198

An award-winning Boston University educator and researcher provides a chilling look at the rise of antibiotic-resistant superbugs, explaining how we got here and what we must do to address this growing global health crisis.

"Recommended for readers interested in the history of science and medicine, and how human response to global issues informs and impacts pathogen research and antibacterial use." —*Library Journal*

Includes bibliographical references and index.

616.97 Diseases of immune system

MacPhail, Theresa
Allergic: Our Irritated Bodies in a Changing World. Theresa MacPhail. Random House 2023. 352 p.
ISBN 9780593229194

Grades: Adult   616.97

1. Allergy 2. Allergens 3. People with allergies 4. Allergic reaction 5. Food allergy 6. Air pollution 7. Immune system 8. Effect of environment on humans 9. Science Writing — Medicine and health — Illness and disease 10. Nature Writing — Environmental Issues 11. Society and culture — Illness and disease

LC 2022032275

Hay fever. Peanut allergies. Eczema. Either you have a frustrating allergy, or you know someone who does. Billions of people worldwide-an estimated 30 to 40 percent of the global population-have some form of allergy; millions have one severe enough to actively endanger their health. Even more concerningly, over the last decade, the number of people diagnosed with allergy has been steadily increasing. Medical anthropologist Theresa MacPhail, herself an allergy sufferer whose father died of a bee sting, set out to understand why.

"The author's examination of the science of immunology from a social and cultural perspective will give readers plenty of relevant, thought-provoking information." —*Kirkus*

Includes index.

Myers, Amy
★ The *Autoimmune* Solution: Prevent and Reverse the Full Spectrum of Inflammatory Symptoms and Diseases. Amy Myers, M.D.. HarperOne, an imprint of HarperCollinsPublsihers 2015. VIII, 390 pages : Illustration
ISBN 9780062347473

Grades: Adult   616.97

1. Autoimmune diseases 2. Science writing — Medicine and health — Alternative medicine 3. Science writing — Medicine and health — Diet and nutrition 4. Science writing — Medicine and health — Illness and disease

LC 2014017620

A leader in the paleo and functional medicine worlds introduces an accessible, easy-to-follow, and scientifically-proven plan for preventing and reversing the full spectrum of autoimmune diseases.

"Americans who suffer from psoriasis, type 1 diabetes, and other autoimmune diseases and want to treat them without conventional medicine will find many alternative ideas in this guide from medical doctor Myers." —*Booklist*

Includes bibliographical references (pages 358-380) and index.

616.99 Tumors and miscellaneous communicable diseases

Brem, Rachel
No Longer Radical: Understanding Mastectomies and Choosing the Breast Cancer Care That's Right for You. Rachel F. Brem, MD, Christy B. Teal, MD.. Simon Element 2023. VIII, 307 pages
ISBN 9781668001134

Grades: Adult   616.99

1. Breast cancer 2. Mastectomy 3. Preventive medicine 4. Women's health services 5. People with cancer 6. Advice 7. Treatment 8. Science Writing — Medicine and health — Illness and disease 9. Society and culture — Gender — Women

LC 2022057975

No Longer Radical is an essential read for everyone whose lives have been touched by breast cancer. Leaders in the field of breast cancer treatment at George Washington University—Dr. Rachel Brem is director of breast imaging and Dr. Christy Teal is the surgical director of the breast care center—have created a life-saving guide for detecting, preventing, and treating this devastating disease. No Longer Radical puts control of your healthcare into your own hands. The book covers essential topics that women must be prepared to think about when their medical history puts them at risk for breast cancer.

"An invaluable, forthright, upbeat resource." —*Booklist*

Includes bibliographical references (pages 257-278) and index.

Brown, Theresa
Healing: When a Nurse Becomes a Patient: A Memoir. Theresa Brown, RN.. Algonquin Books of Chapel Hill 2022. 256 p.
ISBN 9781643750699

Grades: Adult   616.99

1. Brown, Theresa 2. People with cancer 3. Cancer 4. Breast cancer 5. Nurses 6. Oncology nurses 7. Medical care 8. Compassion 9. Physician and patient 10. Patient advocacy 11. Advice 12. Autobiographies and memoirs 13. Biographies 14. Life stories — Science, technology, and medicine — Healthcare professionals 15. Life stories — Facing adversity — Medical issues — Physical illness 16. Science Writing — Medicine and health — Doctors and nurses 17. Business and economics — Industries — Medical

LC 2021052738

A registered nurse and author of The Shift tells the powerfully personal story of her own fight with breast cancer, including her surprise at the lack of compassion she encountered.

"With her aptly named and timed work, best-selling author and oncology nurse Brown (The Shift) weaves her multiple worlds together in this deeply personal memoir of her times as both registered nurse and cancer patient.... This moving and enlightening memoir is recommended for memoir readers and those interested in health care journeys and struggles." —*Library Journal*

Includes bibliographical references.

Fung, Jason
★ The *Cancer* Code: A Revolutionary New Understanding of a Medical Mystery. Dr. Jason Fung. Harper Wave, an imprint of HarperCollinsPublishers 2020. VIII, 360 pages : Illustration
ISBN 9780062894007

Grades: Adult   616.99

1. Cancer 2. Tumors 3. Treatment 4. Science Writing — Medicine and health — Illness and disease

LC 2020019321

ESSENTIAL AND RECOMMENDED TITLES
616.99 Tumors and miscellaneous communicable diseases

Author Dr. Jason Fung returns with a biography of cancer in which he offers a radical new paradigm for understanding cancer and issues a call to action for reducing risk moving forward.

Includes bibliographical references (pages 313-342) and index.

Funk, Kristi
Breasts: The Owner's Manual : Every Woman's Guide to Reducing Cancer Risk, Making Treatment Choices, and Optimizing Outcomes. Dr. Kristi Funk. Thomas Nelson 2018. xxiii, 392 pages : Illustration
ISBN 9780785218722
Grades: Adult 616.99
1. Breast cancer 2. Treatment 3. Preventive medicine 4. Science Writing — Medicine and health — Women's health 5. Science Writing — Medicine and health — Illness and disease
LC 2018000692

A holistic guide to total breast health arms women with the most up-to-date tools for prevention and includes compassionate and complete explanations of treatment options.

Includes bibliographical references (pages 309-380) and index.

Graeber, Charles
The Breakthrough: Immunotherapy and the Race to Cure Cancer. Charles Graeber. Grand Central Pub 2018. 352 p.
ISBN 9781455568505
Grades: Adult 616.99
1. Immunotherapy 2. Cancer research 3. Cancer 4. Treatment 5. Science Writing — Medicine and health — Medical breakthroughs
LC Bl2018183865

The New York Times best-selling author of The Good Nurse, details the astonishing scientific discovery of the code to unleashing the human immune system to fight—and possibly even cure—cancer.

"Graeber concisely reviews the science of cancer and the natural functioning of the immune system. He introduces researchers and oncologists in the field and provides stories of patients with melanoma, kidney cancer, sarcoma, and leukemia." —*Booklist*

Ingrassia, Lawrence
A Fatal Inheritance: How a Family Misfortune Revealed a Deadly Medical Mystery. Lawrence Ingrassia. Henry Holt and Company 2024. 304 p.
ISBN 9781250837226
Grades: Adult 616.99
1. Ingrassia, Lawrence 2. Families 3. Medical genetics 4. Patients 5. Genetics 6. Cancer research 7. Cancer 8. Medical research 9. Autobiographies and memoirs 10. Life stories — Facing adversity — Medical issues 11. Family and relationships — Illness and the family 12. Science writing — Medicine and health — Medical breakthroughs
LC 2023055907

Weaving his own moving family story with this sweeping history of cancer research, Lawrence Ingrassia delivers an intimate, gripping tale that sits at the intersection of memoir and medical thriller.

"This is an emotionally charged narrative about genetic proneness to cancer, the promise of scientific discovery, hope, loss, grief, and, especially, familial love." —*Booklist*

Includes bibliographical references and index.

Mukherjee, Siddhartha
★ *The Emperor of All Maladies: A Biography of Cancer.* Siddhartha Mukherjee. Scribner 2010. xiv, 571 p, 8 p. of plates : Illustration
ISBN 9781439107959
Grades: Adult 616.99
1. Cancer 2. Oncology 3. Chemotherapy 4. Leukemia 5. Diseases 6. People with cancer 7. Science Writing — Medicine and health — Illness and disease
LC 2010024114

ALA Notable Book, 2012; Booklist Editors' Choice, 2010; Guardian First Book Award, 2011; New York Times Notable Book, 2010; Pulitzer Prize for General Nonfiction, 2011; National Book Critics Circle Award for Nonfiction finalist, 2010.

A historical assessment of cancer addresses both the courageous battles against the complex disease and the misperceptions and hubris that have compromised modern understandings, covering such topics as ancient-world surgeries and the developments of present-day treatments.

"Mukherjee's formidable intelligence and compassion produce a stunning account of the effort to disrobe the emperor of maladies." —*Publishers Weekly*

Includes bibliographical references (p. 537-541) and index.

Raza, Azra
The First Cell: And the Human Costs of Pursuing Cancer to the Last. Azra Raza. Basic Books 2019. 336 p.
ISBN 9781541699526
Grades: Adult 616.99
1. Raza, Azra 2. Oncologists 3. People with cancer 4. Physician and patient 5. Cancer 6. Terminal illness 7. Compassion 8. Treatment 9. Preventive medicine 10. Science Writing — Medicine and health — Illness and disease 11. Life stories — Science, technology, and medicine — Healthcare professionals
LC 2019016257

A world-class oncologist and coeditor of the 3QuarksDaily website explores the medical, scientific, cultural and personal impact of cancer while outlining more beneficial alternatives to today's high-cost, largely ineffective treatments.

Includes bibliographical references and index.

Roth, Andrew J.
Managing Prostate Cancer: A Guide for Living Better. Andrew J. Roth, MD.. Oxford University Press 2015. xi, 354 pages : Illustration
ISBN 9780199336920
Grades: Adult 616.99
1. Men 2. Physician and patient 3. Prostate cancer 4. Science writing — Medicine and health — Illness and disease 5. Science writing — Medicine and health — Men's health 6. Science writing — Medicine and health
LC 2015016699

No one can forecast the outcome of prostate cancer. Diagnosis, treatment decisions, and treatment complications are fraught with uncertainty and distress. In Prostate Cancer without a Crystal Ball, Dr. Andrew Roth teaches patients with prostate-cancer and their loved ones strategies for how to live better with the questions and challenges that arise with this diagnosis. These tools will also help healthcare givers to provide improved support for their patients and families.

A psychiatrist who specializes in support for cancer patients provides the emotional skills and strategies needed to healthfully deal with the challenges that a prostate cancer diagnosis brings to daily life. These tools, which he terms "Emotional Judo," will also help healthcare givers to provide improved support for their patients and families.

"Roth offers a first-rate overview of how best to respond to a diagnosis of prostate cancer." —*Booklist*

Includes bibliographical references (pages 331-336) and index.

Servan-Schreiber, David
Anticancer: A New Way of Life. David Servan-Schreiber. Viking 2008. 304 p.
ISBN 9780670020348
Grades: Adult 616.99
1. Medicine 2. People with cancer 3. Research 4. Healing 5. Cancer 6. Alternative medicine 7. Treatment 8. Preventive medicine 9. Science Writing — Medicine and health — Illness and disease
LC 2008015721

The author describes his treatment for brain cancer, challenges beliefs about the body's ability to heal, identifies the environmental and lifestyle factors that promote cancer growth, and outlines conventional and alternative therapies.

"Servan-Schreiber underscores that his advice should be an adjunct to, not a replacement for, conventional treatments like surgery and chemotherapy, in this spirited mixture of good medical information, helpful suggestions and alternative medicine." —*Publishers Weekly*

Includes bibliographical references and index.

PUBLIC LIBRARY CORE COLLECTION: NONFICTION
Twentieth Edition

Walsh, Patrick C.
Dr. Patrick Walsh's Guide to Surviving Prostate Cancer. Patrick C. Walsh, M.D, and Janet Farrar Worthington. Grand Central Life & Style 2018. xvi, 524 pages : Illustration
ISBN 9781538727478
Grades: Adult 616.99
1. Prostate cancer 2. Science writing — Medicine and health — Men's health 3. Society and culture — Gender — Men
LC Bl2018072795
This guide covers every aspect of prostate cancer, from potential causes including diet to tests for diagnosis, curative treatment, and innovative means of controlling advanced stages of cancer.
Includes index.

617 Surgery, regional medicine, dentistry, ophthalmology, otology, audiology

Clements, Carol
Better Balance for Life: Banish the Fear of Falling with Simple Activities Added to Your Everyday Routine a 10-Week Plan. Carol Clements. The Experiment 2018. 182 p.
ISBN 9781615194155
Grades: Adult 617
1. Self-Help — Personal growth — Aging 2. Science writing — Medicine and health — Exercise
LC 2017026289
As you age, stumbling blocks are everywhere: the bottom step, the roadside curb, and even the living room carpet. But you don't have to live in fear of falling. With Better Balance for Life, you will learn all-new, simple activities to help you build strength and increase flexibility to improve your balance! in this ten-week program, personal trainer Carol Clements shows you effortless moves to slide into your everyday routine.
"These excellent illustrated instructions that can easily be performed will help seniors increase their strength and avoid injury." —*Library Journal*
Includes bibliographical references.

Laar, Arnold van de
Under the Knife: A History of Surgery in 28 Remarkable Operations. Arnold van de Laar. St. Martin's Press 2018. 320 p.
ISBN 9781250200105
Grades: Adult 617
1. Surgery 2. Medicine 3. Surgeons 4. Translations — Dutch to English 5. History writing — Science, technology, and medicine 6. Science Writing — Medicine and health — Medical breakthroughs 7. History writing — Microhistory
LC 2018019684
From the story of the desperate man from seventeenth-century Amsterdam who grimly cut a stone out of his own bladder to Bob Marley's deadly toe, Under the Knife offers a wealth of fascinating and unforgettable insights into medicine and history via the operating room.
"Beyond his interesting review of surgical history, van de Laar also offers insight into the thought process and philosophy of those who cut to heal." —*Booklist*
Translation of: Onder het mes : De beroemdste patiënten en operaties uit de geschiedenis van de chirurgie; Includes bibliographical references and index; Originally published: Amsterdam : Thomas Rap, 2014; Translated from the Dutch.

Otto, Mary
Teeth: The Story of Beauty, Inequality, and the Struggle for Oral Health in America. Mary Otto. The New Press 2016. 288 pages
ISBN 9781620971444
Grades: Adult 617
1. Dental care 2. Medical care 3. Inequality 4. Health policy 5. Dentistry 6. Tooth care 7. Poverty 8. Beauty 9. United States 10. Society and culture — Illness and disease 11. Business and economics — Industries — Medical 12. Society and culture — Wealth and class — Poverty
LC 2016041484
Takes readers on a disturbing journey into the role teeth play in our health and our social mobility. Muckraking and paradigm-shifting, Teeth exposes for the first time the extent and meaning of our oral health crisis.
"A focused, well-researched depiction of the dental industry's social and cultural relevance and its dire need for reform." —*Kirkus*
Includes bibliographical references and index.

Rutkow, Ira M.
Empire of the Scalpel: The History of Surgery. Ira Rutkow. Scribner 2022. 352 p.
ISBN 9781501163746
Grades: Adult 617
1. Surgery 2. Medicine 3. Medical care 4. Medical technology 5. Surgeons 6. History writing — Science, technology and medicine 7. Science Writing — Medicine and health 8. History writing — Microhistory
LC 2021048634
Looks at the history of surgery from the Stone Age to today and traces its incredible progress from fledgling science to the seemingly impossible modern feat of organ transplants.
"Surgeon and medical historian Rutkow (Surgery: An Illustrated History) writes a chronological history of surgery (primarily in Western societies) that begins with 'Stone Age surgeries.' . . . This is a well-documented and jargon-free work, aimed at helping laypeople better understand surgery and its practitioners." —*Library Journal*
Includes bibliographical references and index.

617.1 Injuries and wounds

Aschwanden, Christie
Good to Go: What the Athlete in All of Us Can Learn from the Strange Science of Recovery. Christie Aschwanden. W.W. Norton & Company 2019. 312 p.
ISBN 9780393254334
Grades: Adult 617.1
1. Sports 2. Physiology 3. Sports medicine 4. Sports injuries 5. Athletes 6. Stress 7. Physical education and training 8. Health 9. Sports and Competition — General 10. Science Writing — Medicine and health — Medical breakthroughs
LC 2018050104
Noting the recovery themes that have dominated fitness-industry recommendations in recent years, a popular science writer examines the latest athletic trends, rituals and training practices to determine if any help the body recover and achieve optimal performance.
Includes bibliographical references and index.

Fainaru-Wada, Mark
League of Denial: The NFL, Concussions, and the Battle for Truth. Mark Fainaru-Wada; and Steve Fainaru. Crown Archetype 2013. 399 p.
ISBN 9780770437541
Grades: 11 12 Adult 617.1
1. Football injuries 2. Brain concussions 3. Corporate cover-ups 4. Head 5. Sports injuries 6. Business corruption 7. Professional football 8. Sports medicine 9. Football 10. Violence in sports 11. Cognitive neuroscience 12. Wounds and injuries 13. Science Writing — Medicine and health — Illness and disease 14. Sports and Competition — Football
LC Bl2013043145
Award-winning ESPN investigative reporters Mark Fainaru-Wada and Steve Fainaru reveal how the NFL, over a period of nearly two decades, sought to cover up and deny mounting evidence of the connection between football and brain damage.

ESSENTIAL AND RECOMMENDED TITLES
617.4 Surgery by systems and regions

Rountree, Sage
The Athlete's Guide to Recovery: Rest, Relax, and Restore for Peak Performance. Sage Rountree. Rowman & Littlefield 2024. xiii, 234 pages : Illustration
ISBN 9781538181478
Grades: Adult   617.1
1. Sports injuries 2. Athletes 3. Physiology 4. Physical fitness 5. Sports medicine 6. Science Writing — Medicine and health — Exercise 7. Sports and Competition — General
LC 2023028112

Recovery—physical and mental—is a red-hot topic, and the worlds of sports, technology, and commerce have all taken note. This second edition of the Athlete's Guide to Recovery helps readers sort through the hype to focus on the practices and devices that really make a difference in recovery and lead to peak performance.

"Perfect for athletes in need of a reminder that being quick with their recovery efforts isn't a quick fix. This impressive book shows how slowing down speeds up results in the gym, on the road, and beyond." —*Library Journal*
Includes bibliographical references (pages 205-225) and index.

617.4 Surgery by systems and regions

Jones, Chip
The Organ Thieves: The Shocking Story of the First Heart Transplant in the Segregated South. Chip Jones. Jeter Publishing 2020. 399 p.
ISBN 9781982107529
Grades: Adult   617.4
1. Human experimentation in medicine 2. African Americans 3. Racism in medical care 4. Medical ethics 5. Racism 6. Medical malpractice 7. Heart 8. Transplantation of organs, tissues, etc. 9. Medical care 10. Southern States 11. 1960s 12. History writing — Science, technology, and medicine 13. Science Writing — Medicine and health 14. History writing — African American — United States 15. Society and culture — Race 16. True crime — General
LC Bl2020015982

An investigation into how racial inequality has shaped the heart transplant race describes how in 1968 an injured Black man checked into a hospital before his heart was removed and donated without his family's knowledge or consent.

"A dramatic and fine-grained expose of the mistreatment of Black Americans by the country's white medical establishment." —*Publishers Weekly*

Kean, Sam
The Tale of the Dueling Neurosurgeons: The History of the Human Brain as Revealed by True Stories of Trauma, Madness, and Recovery. Sam Kean. Little, Brown and Company 2014. 400 pages.
ISBN 9780316182348
Grades: Adult   617.4
1. Brain 2. Neuroscience 3. Brain diseases 4. Neurology 5. Physicians 6. Physiology 7. History writing — Science, technology, and medicine 8. Science Writing — Medicine and health — Medical breakthroughs
LC 2014004910

Offers fascinating tales of the brain and the history of neuroscience, explores the brain's secret passageways, and recounts the forgotten tales of the ordinary individuals whose struggles, resilience and deep humanity made neuroscience possible.

"Entertaining and quotable, Kean's writing is sharp, and each individual story brings the history of neuroscience to life. Compulsively readable, wicked scientific fun." —*Kirkus*
Includes bibliographical references and index.

Swartz, Mimi
Ticker: The Quest to Create an Artificial Heart. Mimi Swartz. Crown 2018. 304 p.
ISBN 9780804138000
Grades: Adult   617.4
1. Frazier, O. Howard 2. Cohn, Billy 3. Artificial heart 4. Surgeons 5. Heart 6. Cardiology 7. Heart surgeons 8. Implants, Artificial 9. Human experimentation in medicine 10. Houston, Texas 11. Science Writing — Medicine and health — Illness and disease
LC 2017058910

A two-time National Magazine Award winner traces the medical and technological quest to develop a successful artificial heart implant, chronicling the evolution of cardiac medicine while exploring the pioneering work of two Texas Heart Institute innovators.

"Told in an appropriately over-the-top style, this is a quintessentially Texas story: Sprawling, unpredictable, and teeming with risk and opportunity." —*Publishers Weekly*
Includes bibliographical references and index.

Wellons, Jay
All That Moves Us: Life Lessons from a Pediatric Neurosurgeon. Jay Wellons. Random House Inc 2022. 272 p.
ISBN 9780593243381
Grades: Adult   617.4
1. Neurosurgeons 2. Physicians 3. Physician and patient 4. Pediatric surgeons 5. Autobiographies and memoirs 6. Life stories — Science, technology, and medicine — Healthcare professionals 7. Science Writing — Medicine and health — Doctors and nurses

A pediatric neurosurgeon shares moments from his life and career that show what his young patients have taught him about courage while he literally held their lives in his hands.

Wellons, chief of the division of pediatric neurosurgery at Vanderbilt University Medical Center, shares in his powerful and intimate debut his stories of 'Remarkable children and our journeys together.' —*Publishers Weekly*

617.5 Regional medicine

Laskas, Jeanne Marie
Concussion. Jeanne Marie Laskas. Random House 2015. 269 pages, 8 unnumbered pages of plates : Illustration
ISBN 9780812989267
Grades: Adult   617.5
1. Omalu, Bennet I. (Bennet Ifeakandu) 2. Sports 3. Football injuries 4. Sports injuries 5. Sports medicine 6. Brain concussions 7. Corporate cover-ups 8. Head 9. Professional football 10. Football 11. Violence in sports 12. Cognitive neuroscience 13. Wounds and injuries 14. Page to screen 15. Science Writing — Medicine and health — Illness and disease 16. Sports and Competition — Football
Booklist Editors' Choice, 2015.

Tells the true story of how forensic neuropathologist Bennet Omalu discovered a dangerous secret that the National Football League desperately tried to keep silent.

"Effectively sobering. Suffice it to say that Pop Warner parents will want to armor their kids from head to toe upon reading it." —*Kirkus*

617.8 Otology and audiology

Owen, David
Volume Control: Hearing in a Deafening World. David Owen. Riverhead Books 2019. 292 pages
ISBN 9780525534228
Grades: Adult   617.8
1. Medical innovations 2. Deafness 3. Hearing 4. Cochlear implants 5. Medical care services 6. Science writing 7. Science Writing — Medicine and health
LC 2019000860

Citing the millions of Americans suffering from hearing loss and the stigmas and costs that challenge treatment, a New Yorker staff writer outlines the science of hearing while profiling the remarkable new technologies of today's medical community.

Includes bibliographical references and index.

PUBLIC LIBRARY CORE COLLECTION: NONFICTION
Twentieth Edition

617.9 Operative surgery and special fields of surgery

Mezrich, Joshua D.
When Death Becomes Life: Notes from a Transplant Surgeon. Joshua D. Mezrich. HarperCollins 2019. 368 p.
ISBN 9780062656209
Grades: Adult   617.9
1. Mezrich, Joshua D. 2. Transplantation of organs, tissues, etc. 3. Surgeons 4. Medicine 5. Organ donors 6. Transplant surgeons 7. Transplant recipients 8. Donation of organs, tissues, etc. 9. Autobiographies and memoirs 10. Life stories — Science, technology, and medicine — Healthcare professionals 11. History writing — Science, technology, and medicine
LC Bl2018192007

A portrait of the extraordinary field of organ transplantation draws on a century of advancement to discuss its pioneers, science and ethical challenges as well as the ways that organ transplants have revolutionized medical care.

"The author presents a history of a procedure, the invention of breakthrough treatments such as dialysis, and the development of medications to prevent rejection. Woven into this history are personal accounts of success, failure, perfect procedures, and frightening complications. Mezrich relieves the tension with humor, balancing clinical perspective with heart-rending stories, and through it all maintains enthusiasm and wonder at the process." —*Library Journal*

618.1 Gynecology

Allmen, Tara
Menopause Confidential: A Doctor Reveals the Secrets to Thriving Through Midlife. Tara Allmen, MD.. HarperOne 2016. 248 pages
ISBN 9780062447265
Grades: Adult   618.1
1. Menopause 2. Middle-aged women 3. Family and Relationships — Growing up 4. Science writing — Medicine and health 5. Science writing — Medicine and health — Women's health
LC 2016028325

An authoritative guide to understanding and navigating the hormonal changes and health issues women experience in midlife and beyond, from one of the leading medical experts in the field. The physical changes that occur after women turn forty are unavoidable—and can be unnerving. Menopause affects every aspect of life—from sex and sleep to mood and mental clarity to weight and body temperature. While there are a number of resources available, many are confusing and contradictory. Now, Manhattan gynecologist Dr. Tara Allmen, an experienced, nationally board-certified menopause practitioner and the recipient of the 2015 Doctor's Choice National Award for Obstetrics & Gynecology, shares her knowledge to help women be their happiest and healthiest, and turn this challenging time into an exciting one. Written in her effervescent yet assured voice, Menopause Confidential provides simple strategies and cutting-edge information on: hormonal changes and the symptoms of perimenopause and menopause; the health risks associated with midlife—from cutting through the conflicting opinions and advice about health screenings (Do I really need a colonoscopy? How often should I get a mammogram?) to common medical conditions, such as osteoporosis; various remedies, bothallopathic and natural, to combat symptoms and empower women to make the best choices for their individual needs; practical tips and resources for mitigating the effects of menopause. Fifty-one-year-old Dr. Allmen knows firsthand what women are going through, and shares stories of her own personal travails and solutions. Women can't turn back the clock, but they can take control of their health and flourish in midlife. Menopause Confidential encourages them to be informed, be proactive, and be their greatest selves.

An authoritative guide to understanding and navigating the hormonal changes and health challenges women experience at midlife and beyond sifts through contradictory recommendations to offer cutting-edge strategies on subjects ranging from mammograms and osteoporosis to natural and traditional therapies.

"Board-certified gynecologist and nationally certified menopause practitioner Allmen offers a comprehensive health guide for women over 40." —*Library Journal*
Includes bibliographical references and index.

Brighten, Jolene
Is This Normal?: Judgment-Free Straight Talk About Your Body. Dr. Jolene Brighten. Simon Element 2023. VIII, 468 pages : Illustration
ISBN 9781982196394
Grades: Adult   618.1
1. Gynecology 2. Women 3. Reproductive health 4. Sexuality 5. Sexual health 6. Menstruation 7. Science Writing — Medicine and health — Women's health 8. Science Writing — Medicine and health — Fertility and sexual health
LC Bl2023012017

A naturopathic endocrinologist and certified sex counselor answers women's questions about their reproductive anatomy, with topics including menstruation, postpartum health, libido, acne, orgasms, and discharges and offers charts, checklists and diagrams in an honest, easy-to-understand guide to the female body.

"A good addition to women's health and consumer health collections. Readers wanting more scientific information will want to pick up Vagina Obscura by Rachel E. Gross." —*Library Journal*
Includes bibliographical references (pages 389-450) and index.

Corinna, Heather
What Fresh Hell Is This?: Perimenopause, Menopause, Other Indignities, and You. Heather Corinna. Hachette Go 2021. VIII, 324 pages
ISBN 9780306874765
Grades: Adult   618.1
1. Menopause 2. Self-Help — Personal growth — Aging 3. Science Writing — Medicine and health — Women's health — Menopause
LC 2020058525

An informative, blisteringly funny, somewhat cranky and always spot-on guide to perimenopause and menopause by the award-winning sex ed/health educator and author of S.E.X.

"This newest work by Corinna is an excellent option for readers experiencing menopause or living alongside someone who is." —*Library Journal*
Includes bibliographical references and index.

Dunn, Jancee
Hot and Bothered: What No One Tells You About Menopause and How to Feel Like Yourself Again. Jancee Dunn. G.P. Putnam's Sons 2023. xii, 289 pages
ISBN 9780593542569
Grades: Adult   618.1
1. Menopause 2. Women 3. Health 4. Aging 5. Science Writing — Medicine and health — Women's health — Menopause
LC 2023004715

The New York Times best-selling author of How to Not Hate Your Husband After Kids recounts how she was completely surprised by the symptoms of menopause and researched a guide to help other women cope with the changes.

"Premenopausal and perimenopausal women will appreciate this witty and informative resource." —*Publishers Weekly*
Includes bibliographical references (pages 245-279) and index.

Eig, Jonathan
The Birth of the Pill: How Four Crusaders Reinvented Sex and Launched a Revolution. Jonathan Eig. W. W. Norton & Company 2014. 400 p.
ISBN 9780393073720
Grades: Adult   618.1
1. McCormick, Katherine Dexter, 1876-1967 2. Pincus, Gregory, 1903-1967 3. Rock, John, 1890-1984 4. Sanger, Margaret, 1879-1966 5. Oral contraceptives 6. Birth control 7. Feminism 8. Contraception 9. United States 10. Collective biographies 11. Life stories — Science, technology, and medicine — Scientists and inventors 12. Society and culture — Sex and sexuality
LC 2014019355
ALA Notable Book, 2015; Booklist Editors' Choice, 2014.

ESSENTIAL AND RECOMMENDED TITLES
618.1 Gynecology

We know it simply as "the pill," yet its genesis was anything but simple. Jonathan Eig's masterful narrative revolves around four principal characters: the fiery feminist Margaret Sanger, who was a champion of birth control in her campaign for the rights of women but neglected her own children in pursuit of free love; the beautiful Katharine McCormick, who owed her fortune to her wealthy husband, the son of the founder of International Harvester and a schizophrenic; the visionary scientist Gregory Pincus, who was dismissed by Harvard in the 1930s as a result of his experimentation with in vitro fertilization but who, after he was approached by Sanger and McCormick, grew obsessed with the idea of inventing a drug that could stop ovulation; and the telegenic John Rock, a Catholic doctor from Boston who battled his own church to become an enormously effective advocate in the effort to win public approval for the drug that would be marketed by Searle as Enovid.

Includes bibliographical references and index.

Gross, Rachel E.
Vagina Obscura: An Anatomical Voyage. Rachel E. Gross. W. W. Norton & Company 2022. 320 p.
ISBN 9781324006312
Grades: Adult   618.1
1. Vagina 2. Women 3. Female reproductive system 4. Anatomy 5. Women's rights 6. Marginalized people 7. Science Writing — Biology 8. Society and culture — Gender — Women — Reproductive rights 9. Science Writing — Medicine and health 10. Society and culture — Gender — Women 11. History writing — Science, technology, and medicine 12. History writing — Women's history
LC 2021049425

Full of wit and wonder, this scientific journey to the center of the new female body uses modern tools and fresh perspectives to see the organs traditionally bound up in reproduction within a new biology of change and resilience.

"Libraries catering to readers interested in history, anthropology, anatomy, and women's and gender studies will want to add this insightful and dynamic book to their collection." —*Library Journal*

Includes bibliographical references and index.

Gupta, Shalene
The Cycle: Confronting the Pain of Periods and Pmdd. Shalene Gupta. Flatiron Books 2024. 240 p.
ISBN 9781250882899
Grades: Adult   618.1
1. Gupta, Shalene 2. Women 3. Menstruation 4. Women's health services 5. Menstruation disorders 6. Premenstrual syndrome 7. Pain 8. Depression 9. Anger 10. Chronic diseases 11. Stigma (Social psychology) 12. Medical care 13. Sexism in medicine 14. Society and culture — Gender — Women 15. Society and culture — Illness and disease 16. Life stories — Facing adversity — Medical issues — Physical illness 17. Science Writing — Medicine and health

Uncovering the hidden epidemic of premenstrual dysphoric disorder (PMDD), the author, sharing her own experience with this widespread chronic illness, provides this deeply researched, movingly intimate and refreshingly hopeful book for those navigating a world ill-equipped to support their health.

"An informative melding of memoir and research." —*Kirkus*

Hallman, J. C.
Say Anarcha: A Young Woman, a Devious Surgeon, and the Harrowing Birth of Modern Women's Health. J. C. Hallman. Henry Holt and Company 2023. 448 p.
ISBN 9781250868466
Grades: Adult   618.1
1. Sims, J. Marion (James Marion), 1813-1883 2. Jackson, Anarcha, approximately 1821-1869 3. Human experimentation in medicine 4. Gynecologists 5. Surgeons 6. Gynecology 7. Vagina 8. Women's health services 9. Medical ethics 10. Enslaved women 11. Misogyny 12. Racism in medical care 13. North American people 14. American people 15. Ambition 16. United States history 17. 19th century 18. Collective biographies 19. Life stories — Science, technology, and medicine — Healthcare professionals 20. Life stories — Facing adversity — War and oppression — Enslaved people 21. History writing — African American — Enslavement — United States 22. History writing — Science, technology, and medicine 23. History writing — Women's history

LC 2023007478
A dual biography reckons with the birth of women's health and brings forth the forgotten Black woman who was at its center.

For more than a century, Dr. J. Marion Sims was hailed as the "father of modern gynecology." He founded a hospital in New York City and had a profitable career treating gentry and royalty in Europe, becoming one of the world's first celebrity surgeons, but he wasn't the hero he had made himself appear to be. Sims's greatest medical claim was the result of several years of experimental surgeries—without anesthesia—on a young enslaved woman known as Anarcha; his so-called cure for obstetric fistula forever altered the path of women's health. Little was known about the woman herself. The written record would have us believe Anarcha disappeared; she did not.

"A staggeringly researched book that serves as an indictment of Sims' hubris and an homage to Anarcha." —*Kirkus*

Haver, Mary Claire
★ *The New Menopause: Navigating Your Path Through Hormonal Change with Purpose, Power, and Facts.* Mary Claire Haver, MD.. Rodale 2024. xiv, 304 pages
ISBN 9780593796252
Grades: Adult   618.1
1. Menopause 2. Treatment 3. Health 4. Middle-aged women 5. Women 6. Science Writing — Medicine and health — Women's health — Menopause 7. Self-Help — General
LC 2023053299

A pioneering women's health advocate presents this comprehensive, authoritative, science-backed book in which she covers all aspects of menopause, including neurological, musculoskeletal, psychological and sexual issues, and provides tools for taking charge of your health at this pivotal life stage.

"It's an informative manual on an important yet underdiscussed health matter." —*Publishers Weekly*

Includes bibliographical references (pages 269-291) and index.

Love, Susan M.
★ *Dr. Susan Love's Breast Book.* Susan M. Love, M.D; with Elizabeth Love and Karen Lindsey; illustrations by Marcia Williams. Da Capo Lifelong 2015. xiii, 690 pages : Illustration
ISBN 9780738218212
Grades: Adult   618.1
1. Breast 2. Breast cancer 3. Cancer 4. Diagnosis 5. Diseases 6. Science Writing — Medicine and health — Illness and disease
LC 2015458675

Offers the most cutting-edge information for those at risk of getting breast cancer or those who already have it, including the latest in genetic research, advances in imaging, recognition of breast density as a risk factor, a section focused on personalized medicine and much more.

A Merloyd Lawrence Book; Includes bibliographical references (pages 579-639) and index.

Norman, Abby
Ask Me About My Uterus: A Quest to Make Doctors Believe in Women's Pain. Abby Norman. Nation Books 2018. 320 p.
ISBN 9781568585819
Grades: Adult   618.1
1. Norman, Abby 2. Endometriosis 3. Chronic pain 4. Women's health services 5. Sexism in medicine 6. Women 7. Human body 8. Autobiographies and memoirs 9. Life stories — Facing adversity — Medical issues — Physical illness 10. Society and culture — Gender — Women 11. Society and culture — Illness and disease
LC 2017043712

An empowering memoir, which advocates for recognition of women's health issues, follows the author's years-long journey to discover why she was in constant pain, which was dismissed by doctors, and puts her trials into a broader historical, sociocultural and political context to put an end to the belief that being a woman is a preexisting condition.

Includes bibliographical references and index.

PUBLIC LIBRARY CORE COLLECTION: NONFICTION
Twentieth Edition

Parker, Lara
Vagina Problems: Endometriosis, Painful Sex, and Other Taboo Topics. Lara Parker. St. Martin's Griffin 2020. 240 p.
ISBN 9781250240682
Grades: Adult   618.1
1. Parker, Lara (Writer and editor) 2. Women 3. Chronic pain 4. Sexism in medicine 5. Endometriosis 6. Women's health services 7. Treatment 8. Empowerment 9. Health 10. Autobiographies and memoirs 11. Life stories — Facing adversity — Medical issues — Physical illness 12. Society and culture — Gender — Women 13. Society and culture — Illness and disease
LC 2020024208

With unflinching honesty, Lara Parker, the Deputy Director for BuzzFeed, shares her day-to-day challenges of living, working, and loving with chronic pain caused by endometriosis in this raw, darkly humorous, and hopeful memoir.

"A solid purchase for public and consumer health libraries." —*Library Journal*

618.175 Menopause disorders

Gunter, Jen
The Menopause Manifesto: Own Your Health with Facts and Feminism. Dr. Jen Gunter. Citadel 2021. xiii, 370 p.
ISBN 9780806540665
Grades: Adult   618.175
1. Menopause 2. Women 3. Middle age 4. Health 5. Science Writing — Medicine and health — Women's health — Menopause 6. Society and culture — Gender — Women

The only thing predictable about menopause is its unpredictability. Factor in widespread misinformation, a lack of research, and the culture of shame around women's bodies, and it's no wonder women are unsure what to expect during the menopause transition and beyond. Menopause is not a disease—it's a planned change, like puberty. And just like puberty, we should be educated on what's to come years in advance, rather than the current practice of leaving people on their own with bothersome symptoms and too much conflicting information. Knowing what is happening, why, and what to do about it is both empowering and reassuring.

"Like her previous guide, Gunter's latest book will find a wide audience, with its clear writing and up-to-date research." —*Library Journal*

618.2 Obstetrics

Curtis, Glade B.
Your Pregnancy Week by Week. Glade B. Curtis, M.D, M.P.H, OB/GYN and Judith Schuler, M.S.. DaCapo Lifelong 2016. xii, 463 pages : Illustration
ISBN 9780738218939
Grades: Adult   618.2
1. Fetus 2. Pregnancy 3. Biological growth 4. Science writing — Medicine and health — Women's health — Pregnancy and childbirth 5. Family and Relationships — Parenting
LC 2016303069

A completely revised edition of the detailed pregnancy handbook that has been helping expectant parents for the last quarter century provides up-to-date information on the latest medical tests and procedures, safe exercises for moms and helpful hints for fathers.

Includes index.

Fisher, Susan J.
Taking Charge of Your Pregnancy: The New Science for a Safe Birth and a Healthy Baby. Susan J. Fisher with Becky Cabaza. Houghton Mifflin Harcourt 2021. 290 p. : Illustration
ISBN 9780358409076
Grades: Adult   618.2
1. Pregnancy 2. Childbirth 3. Prenatal care 4. Obstetrics 5. Science writing — Medicine and health — Women's health — Pregnancy and childbirth
LC 2020050867

Complete with helpful illustrations, practical tips, and the essential questions to ask healthcare providers, this groundbreaking guide, based on decades of research and the latest scientific advances, provides expert advice to empower expecting parents.

"This is worth a place on any expectant mother's bookshelf." —*Publishers Weekly*

Includes bibliographical references (pages 245-280) and index.

Harshe, January
Birth Without Fear: The Judgment-free Guide to Taking Charge of Your Pregnancy, Birth, and Postpartum. January Harshe. Hachette Books 2019. xix, 267 pages
ISBN 9780316515597
Grades: Adult   618.2
1. Childbirth 2. Pregnancy 3. Pregnant women 4. Hygiene 5. Science writing — Medicine and health — Women's health — Pregnancy and childbirth 6. Science writing — Medicine and health — Women's health
LC 2018020001

The founder of the global online community Birth Without Fear presents an all-encompassing, nonjudgmental and empowering guide to pregnancy, childbirth and postpartum life that puts mothers first.

An empowering, inclusive guide to pregnancy, childbirth, and postpartum life that puts mothers first—not a particular philosophy or agenda—and offers passionate and straightforward guidance on the issues that matter most to them, so that they can havethe kind of parenting experience they desire.

"Practical, positive, and empowering." —*Booklist*

Includes bibliographical references (pages 241-244) and index.

Murkoff, Heidi Eisenberg
★ *What* to Expect When You're Expecting. Heidi Murkoff and Sharon Mazel; foreword by Charles J. Lockwood, MD, Professor of obstetrics and gynecology and public health, Dean, Morsani College of Medicine, University of South Florida. Workman Publishing 2016. xii, 644 p. : Illustration
ISBN 9780761189244
Grades: Adult   618.2
1. Pregnancy 2. Childbirth 3. Postnatal care 4. Science writing — Medicine and health — Women's health — Pregnancy and childbirth 5. Family and Relationships — Growing up 6. Family and Relationships — Parenting
LC 2015044527

Offers advice, insight, and tips for moms and dads, discussing pregnancy and birthing practices, prenatal screenings, postpartum birth control, and nutrition.

Includes index.

Oster, Emily
★ *Cribsheet:* A Data-Driven Guide to Better, More Relaxed Parenting, from Birth to Preschool. Emily Oster. Penguin Press 2019. xxv, 322 pages : Illustration
ISBN 9780525559252
Grades: Adult   618.2
1. Pregnancy 2. Pregnant women 3. Parenthood 4. Parenting 5. Decision-making 6. Hygiene 7. Family and Relationships — Parenting 8. Reference — Instructional materials
LC 2018041564

From the author of EXPECTING BETTER, an economist's guide to the early years of parenting with Expecting Better, award-winning economist Emily Oster spotted a need in the pregnancy market for advice that gave women the information they needed to make the best decision for their own pregnancies. By digging into the data, Oster found that much of the conventional pregnancy wisdom was wrong. In Cribsheet, she now tackles an even great challenge: decision making in the early years of parenting. As any new parent knows, there is an abundance of often-conflicting advice hurled at you from doctors, family, friends, and the internet. From the earliest days, parents get the message that they must make certain choices around feeding, sleep, and schedule or all will be lost. There's a rule—or three—for everything. But the benefits of these choices can be overstated, and the tradeoffs can be profound. How do you make your own best decision? Armed with the data, Oster finds that the conventional wisdom doesn't

ESSENTIAL AND RECOMMENDED TITLES
618.3 Diseases, disorders, management of pregnancy, childbirth, puerperium

always hold up. She debunks myths around breastfeeding (not a panacea), sleep training (not so bad!), potty training (wait until they're ready or possibly bribe with M&Ms), language acquisition (early talkers aren't necessarily geniuses), and many other topics. She also shows parents how to think through freighted questions like if and how to go back to work, how to think about toddler discipline, and how to have a relationship and parent at the same time. Economics is the science of decision-making, and CRIBSHEET is a thinking parent's guide to the chaos and frequent misinformation of the early years. Emily Oster is a trained expert—and mom of two—who can empower us to make better, less fraught decisions—and stay sane in the years before preschool.

Includes bibliographical references (pages 297-311) and index.

★ *The Unexpected: Navigating Pregnancy During and After Complications.* Emily Oster and Nathan Fox, MD.. Penguin Press 2024. xxii, 247 pages
ISBN 9780593652770
Grades: Adult   618.2
1. Pregnancy complications 2. Pregnancy 3. Health 4. Pregnant women 5. Prenatal care 6. Science Writing — Medicine and health — Women's health — Pregnancy and childbirth 7. Family and Relationships — General
LC 2023038447

Laying out the data on recurrence and treatments shown to lower or mitigate risks for such conditions as preeclampsia, miscarriage and preterm birth, the New York Times best-selling author of Expecting Better, with insights from a lauded maternal fetal medicine specialist, makes the hardest parts of pregnancy a little bit less so.

"A vital reference that steers women toward healthy and successful pregnancies." —*Library Journal*

Includes bibliographical references (pages 229-237) and index.

Rope, Kate
Strong as a Mother: How to Stay Healthy, Happy, and (most Importantly) Sane from Pregnancy to Parenthood : The Only Guide to Taking Care of You! Kate Rope. St. Martin's Griffin 2018. xii, 388 pages
ISBN 9781250105585
Grades: Adult   618.2
1. Pregnancy 2. Pregnant women 3. Hygiene 4. Science Writing — Medicine and health — Women's health — Pregnancy and childbirth
LC 2017059644

Kate Rope's Strong as a Mother is a practical and compassionate guide to preparing for a smooth start to motherhood. Everyone knows the secret to having "the Happiest Baby on the Block." This is your guide to being the Sanest Mommy on the Block. It will prepare you with humor and grace for what lies ahead, give you the tools you need to take care of yourself, permission to struggle at times, and professional advice on how to move through it when you do. This book will become a dog-eared resource on your nightstand, offering you the same care and support that you are working so hard to provide to your child. It will help you prioritize your emotional health, set boundaries and ask for help, make choices about feeding and childcare that feel good to you, get good sleep, create a strong relationship with your partner, make self care an everyday priority, trust your instincts, and actually enjoy the hardest job you will ever love.

"Rope's book offers women commonsense guidance and vigorous reassurances on coping with the tumultuous changes of pregnancy and parenthood." —*Publishers Weekly*

Includes index.

Tang, Karen
★ *It's Not Hysteria: Everything You Need to Know About Your Reproductive Health (but Were Never Told).* Karen Tang, MD, MPH.. Flatiron Books 2024. VIII, 373 p. : Illustration
ISBN 9781250894151
Grades: Adult   618.2
1. Reproductive health 2. Women's health services 3. Gynecology 4. Sexual health 5. Sexism in medicine 6. Patient advocacy 7. Society and culture — Gender — Women 8. Science Writing — Medicine and health 9. Debut title
LC 2023048068

On a mission to transform how we engage with our bodies and our healthcare, a board-certified gynecologist and staunch advocate provides a comprehensive guide to common conditions and potential treatment options for reproductive health, educating and empowering women and those assigned female at birth.

"The result is a comprehensive resource for understanding gynecological health." —*Publishers Weekly*

Includes bibliographical references (pages 323-357) and index.

618.3 Diseases, disorders, management of pregnancy, childbirth, puerperium

White, Kate
Your Guide to Miscarriage & Pregnancy Loss: Hope and Healing When You're No Longer Expecting. Kate White, M.D, OB-GYN and miscarriage survivor. Mayo Clinic Press 2021. xi, 384 pages : Illustration; Color
ISBN 9781893005747
Grades: Adult   618.3
1. Miscarriage 2. Grief 3. Science Writing — Medicine and health — Women's health — Pregnancy and childbirth 4. Self-Help — Mental health — Grief and loss
LC Bl2021026094

A medical professional who has cared for women having miscarriages for more than twenty years and experienced two miscarriages herself answers questions about miscarriage diagnosis and treatment, and offers guidance for handling grief and the healing process.

"For readers who have experienced pregnancy loss, this is sure to be a welcome resource." —*Publishers Weekly*

Includes index.

618.6 Normal puerperium

Serrallach, Oscar
The Postnatal Depletion Cure: A Complete Guide to Rebuilding Your Health and Reclaiming Your Energy for Mothers of Newborns, Toddlers, and Young Children. Dr. Oscar Serrallach. Grand Central Life & Style 2018. xv, 287 pages
ISBN 9781478970293
Grades: Adult   618.6
1. Postnatal care 2. Family and Relationships — Parenting 3. Science writing — Medicine and health — Women's health — Pregnancy and childbirth 4. Science writing — Medicine and health — Women's health
LC 2017046606

A guide to navigating postpartum depression by treating the nutrient depletion, sleep loss and emotional shifts that affect women for years after childbirth also shares insights into how pregnancy affects the body and how to find support.

A revolutionary program of postnatal care, inspired by one of the most viewed GOOP articles ever, that teaches mothers to reclaim their health and energy up to 10 years after giving birth.

While postpartum depression has become a recognizable condition, THE POSTNATAL DEPLETION CURE is the first book to treat the nutrient depletion, sleep loss, and emotional shifts that afflict women up to a decade after giving birth. Most mothers have experienced exhaustion, pain, forgetfulness, indecision, low energy levels, moodiness, or some form of baby brain. And it's no wonder: The process of growing a baby depletes a mother's body in substantial ways—on average, a mother's brain shrinks 5% during pregnancy, and the placenta saps her of essential nutrients that she needs to be healthy and contented. But with postnatal care ending after 6 weeks, most women never learn how to rebuild their strength and care for their bodies after childbirth. As a result, they can suffer from the effects of depletion for many years, without knowing what's wrong as well as getting the support and treatments that they need. Any woman who has read What to Expect When You're Expecting needs a copy of THE POSTNATAL DEPLETION CURE. Filled with trustworthy advice, protocols for successful recovery, and written by a compassionate expert in women's health, THE POSTNATAL DEPLETION CURE will help every mother restore her energy, replenish her body, and reclaim her sense of self.

"A practical volume that will be of use to mothers everywhere." —*Library Journal*

Includes bibliographical references.

618.7 Puerperal diseases

Fox Starr, Rebecca
Beyond the Baby Blues: Anxiety and Depression During and After Pregnancy. Rebecca Fox Starr. Rowman & Littlefield 2018. xi, 141 pages
ISBN 9781442273900
Grades: Adult   618.7
1. Postpartum depression 2. Science writing — Medicine and health — Women's health — Pregnancy and childbirth 3. Science writing — Medicine and health — Women's health

LC 2017023086

"This work promises to be a valuable refuge for expectant mothers and their families confronting the specter of prenatal and postpartum depression." —*Publishers Weekly*

Includes bibliographical references and index.

618.8 Obstetrical surgery

Somerstein, Rachel
★ *Invisible* Labor: The Untold Story of the Cesarean Section. Rachel Somerstein. Ecco Press 2024. 256 p.
ISBN 9780063264410
Grades: Adult   618.8
1. Somerstein, Rachel 2. Surgery 3. Pregnancy 4. Medical care 5. Cesarean section 6. Childbirth 7. Maternal health services 8. United States 9. Essays 10. Collective autobiographies and memoirs 11. Society and culture — Gender — Women 12. Life stories — Identity — Gender 13. Life stories — Facing adversity — Medical issues

This incisive and personal look at the science of the cesarean section exposes the ways modern medical technology promotes its overuse and can sometimes lead to significant and life-changing consequences.

"This excellent debut investigation from Somerstein explores the history of and controversies surrounding the C-section." —*Publishers Weekly*

618.92 Pediatrics

Barkley, Russell A.
Taking Charge of ADHD: The Complete, Authoritative Guide for Parents. Russell A. Barkley, PhD.. The Guilford Press 2013. xvi, 363 pages
ISBN 9781462508518
Grades: Adult   618.92
1. Attention-deficit hyperactivity disorder 2. Child rearing 3. Family and Relationships — Parenting

LC 2012050510

Provides a step-by-step plan for ADHD diagnosis and treatment, behavior management, strategies for helping children succeed at school and in social situations, and information on advances in research.

"The author reports on his own theory, recent research, and strategies for parents in the challenge of raising children with attention problems. His view is that attention-deficit hyperactivity disorder (ADHD) is a 'Disorder of self-regulation' and that the problems of inattention, overactivity, and lack of inhibition become a developmental disability when extreme. ADHD is described as a neurologically based disorder with a probable genetic base." —*Science Books & Films*

Includes bibliographical references (pages 329-349) and index.

Bryson, Tina Payne
The Bottom Line for Baby: From Sleep Training to Screens, Thumb Sucking to Tummy Time—what the Science Says. Tina Payne Bryson, Ph.D... Ballantine Books 2020. xxvii, 297 pages
ISBN 9780593129968
Grades: Adult   618.92
1. Baby care 2. Parent and baby 3. Baby psychology 4. Family and Relationships — Parenting

LC 2019053246

What the Science Says About Your Biggest Questions and Concerns.

The co-author of the best-selling The Whole-Brain Child presents an A-to-Z guide for baby and toddler care, drawing on the most reliable and up-to-date research to separate fact from fiction on such topics as breastfeeding, circumcision and allergies.

"Psychotherapist Bryson (No-Drama Discipline) offers a splendid guide to help parents and caregivers 'wade through the cacophony' of sometimes conflicting information and opinions about baby care.... Parents, grandparents, and caretakers would do well to pick up this comprehensive work." —*Publishers Weekly*

Includes bibliographical references (pages 239-285) and index.

Burke Harris, Nadine
The Deepest Well: Healing the Long-Term Effects of Childhood Adversity. Nadine Burke Harris, M.D... Houghton Mifflin Harcourt 2018. xvi, 251 pages
ISBN 9780544828704
Grades: Adult   618.92
1. Psychic trauma in children 2. Adult child abuse victims 3. Society and culture — Children's studies 4. Science writing — Medicine and health — Psychology 5. Family and Relationships — Growing Up

LC Bl2017046716

Explores the relationship between childhood stress and adult health problems, drawing on scientific insights and personal stories to outline beneficial health interventions.

Includes bibliographical references (pages 235-242) and index.

DiGregorio, Sarah
Early: An Intimate History of Premature Birth and What It Teaches Us About Being Human. Sarah DiGregorio. HarperCollins 2020. 320 p.
ISBN 9780062820303
Grades: Adult   618.92
1. DiGregorio, Sarah 2. Premature babies 3. Neonatal intensive care 4. Premature labor 5. Mothers 6. Premature baby care 7. Medical ethics 8. Newborn baby care 9. Obstetrics 10. Medical innovations 11. Science Writing — Medicine and health — Medical breakthroughs 12. Life stories — Facing adversity — Medical issues 13. Family and Relationships — Illness and the Family 14. Family and Relationships — Parenting

LC Bl2020002787

Inspired by the author's harrowing experience giving birth to her premature daughter, a compelling and empathetic work that combines memoir with rigorous reporting to tell the story of neonatology—and to meditate on the questions raised by premature birth.

"A well-written, carefully researched book that should be of vital interest to potential parents and their friends and families." —*Library Journal*

Goh, Suzanne
Magnificent Minds: The New Whole-Child Approach to Autism. Suzanne Goh, MD.. TarcherPerigee, an imprint of Penguin Random House LLC 2024. xvii, 332 pages : Illustration
ISBN 9780593712719
Grades: Adult   618.92
1. Autistic children 2. Parents of autistic children 3. Autism spectrum disorders 4. Social skills in children 5. Treatment 6. Parenting 7. Science Writing — Medicine and health — Children's health 8. Science Writing — Medicine and health — Disabilities and disorders 9. Family and Relationships — Parenting

LC 2023043550

ESSENTIAL AND RECOMMENDED TITLES
618.92 Pediatrics

Pediatric neurologist Dr. Suzanne Goh has spent decades working with autistic children, and in this practical and research-based guide she shares her renowned and revolutionary model of care: an innovative, whole-child approach that combines optimal medical treatment with the most effective strategies for advancing cognition, communication, and behavior.

"Pediatric neurologist Goh provides a sensitive primer on how parents can take a holistic approach to raising autistic children." —*Publishers Weekly*

Includes bibliographical references (pages 297-321) and index.

Grandin, Temple
Navigating Autism: 9 Mindsets for Helping Kids on the Spectrum. Temple Grandin, Debra Moore. W.W. Norton & Company 2021. xiv, 362 pages : Illustration
ISBN 9780393714845
Grades: Adult   618.92
1. Autistic children 2. Parents of autistic children 3. Autism spectrum disorders 4. Science Writing — Medicine and health — Disabilities and disorders 5. Family and Relationships — Disabled Family Members 6. Educator resources — General
LC 2021014663

Empowering strategies for anyone who works with children and teens on the spectrum. International best-selling writer and autist Temple Grandin joins psychologist Debra Moore in presenting nine strengths-based mindsets necessary to successfully work with young people on the autism spectrum. Examples and stories bring the approaches to life, and detailed suggestions and checklists help readers put them to practical use."

"Those with a vested interest in helping children on the spectrum will find this a valuable resource worth returning to." —*Publishers Weekly*

A Norton Professional book; Includes bibliographical references (pages 319-338) and index.

Keene, Nancy
Childhood Leukemia: A Guide for Families, Friends & Caregivers. Nancy Keene. Childhood Cancer Guides 2018. xvi, 476 p. : Illustration
ISBN 9781941089040
Grades: Adult   618.92
1. Science writing — Medicine and health — Illness and disease 2. Science writing — Medicine and health — Children's health
LC 2017031837

The go-to guide for families of children with leukemia. Reviewed by renowned experts, it contains up-to-date medical information along with practical advice and poignant stories from more than 150 families of children with leukemia. Definitive, comprehensive and easy to read.

Includes bibliographical references and index.

Marcus, Amy Dockser
We the Scientists: How a Daring Team of Parents and Doctors Forged a New Path for Medicine. Amy Dockser Marcus. Riverhead Books 2023. xxx, 222 pages
ISBN 9780399576133
Grades: Adult   618.92
1. Growth disorders 2. Rare diseases 3. Medical genetics 4. Children with disabilities 5. Medical research 6. Treatment 7. Science Writing — Medicine and health — Disabilities and disorders
LC 2022023324

A Pulitzer Prize-winning reporter follows a group of parent advocates who collaborate with researchers and doctors in search of a cure for a rare and genetic condition, becoming citizen scientists in an extraordinary social experiment that reveals new pathways for treating disease and conducting research.

"The story of a painful but inspiring search for a cure for a fatal disease.... A moving argument for a more focused, humane, and efficient system for conducting medical research." —*Kirkus*

Includes bibliographical references (pages 203-213) and index.

Nigg, Joel T.
Getting Ahead of ADHD: What Next-Generation Science Says About Treatments That Work — and How You Can Make Them Work for Your Child. Joel T. Nigg. Guilford Press 2017. 272 p.
ISBN 9781462524938
Grades: Adult   618.92
1. Neuroscience 2. Children with ADHD 3. Genes 4. Nutrition 5. Exercise 6. Sleep 7. Alternative medicine 8. Attention-deficit hyperactivity disorder 9. Neurodivergent people 10. Science Writing — Medicine and health

Presents exciting treatment advances to maximize the positive effects of healthy nutrition, exercise, and sleep, and minimize the damage from stress and other known risk factors.

"Parents will find reassurance, hope, and step-by-step action plans in this coherent guide to the current and evolving science on ADHD." —*Publishers Weekly*

Porto, Anthony
The Pediatrician's Guide to Feeding Babies & Toddlers: Practical Answers to Your Questions on Nutrition, Starting Solids, Allergies, Picky Eating, and More. Anthony Porto, MD, MPH, Dina DiMaggio, MD.. Ten Speed Press 2016. VIII, 247 pages : Illustration
ISBN 9781607749011
Grades: Adult   618.92
1. Children 2. Food habits 3. Babies 4. Nutrition 5. Science writing — Medicine and health — Children's health 6. Science writing — Medicine and health — Diet and nutrition
LC 2015031409

An authoritative guide written by a team of medical and culinary experts—including a pediatrician, pediatric gastroenterologist, pediatric allergist and a personal chef—helps parents give their children the optimum nutrition they need to thrive during the crucial first years of life.

Includes bibliographical references and index.

Prizant, Barry M.
★ *Uniquely Human: A Different Way of Seeing Autism.* Barry M. Prizant, PhD; with Tom Fields-Meyer. Simon & Schuster 2022. x, 256 pages
ISBN 9781476776231
Grades: Adult   618.92
1. Autistic children 2. Autism spectrum disorders 3. Family and Relationships — Parenting 4. Science writing — Medicine and health — Psychology
LC 2014035241

In a book that aims to be essential reading for any parent, teacher, therapist or caregiver of a person with autism, one of the world's leading authorities on autism suggests a major shift in understanding autism and offers inspiring stories and practical advice drawn from his more than four-decade career.

"This positive volume should reassure parents and caregivers of kids with autism and any other disability that their kids are not broken, but, indeed, special." —*Booklist*

Originally published by Simon & Schuster in 2015. Expanded and revised version published in 2022; Simon & Schuster nonfiction original hardcover; Includes bibliographical references (pages 237-242) and index.

Saline, Sharon
What Your ADHD Child Wishes You Knew: Working Together to Empower Kids for Success in School and Life. Dr. Sharon Saline; foreword by Laura Markham. A TarcherPerigee Book 2018. xviii, 254 p.
ISBN 9780143132394
Grades: Adult   618.92
1. Attention-deficit hyperactivity disorder 2. Children with ADHD 3. Parent and child 4. Family and Relationships — General 5. Science writing — Medicine and health — Psychology
LC 2018017661

A veteran psychologist presents a proven roadmap to help ADHD kids succeed in school and life. You've read all the expert advice, but despite countless efforts to help your child cope better and stay on track, you're still struggling with everyday issues like homework, chores, getting to soccer practice on time, and simply getting along without pushback and power struggles. What if you could work with your child, motivating and engaging them in the process, to create positive change once and for all? In this insightful and practical book, veteran psychologist Sharon Saline shares the words and inner struggles of children and teens living with ADHD—and a blueprint for achieving lasting success by working together. Based on more than 25 years of experience counseling young people and their families, Dr. Saline's advice and real-world examples reveal how parents can shift the dynamic and truly help kids succeed. Topics include: * Setting mutual goals that foster cooperation * Easing academic struggles * Tackling everyday challenges, from tantrums and backtalk to staying organized, building friendships, and more. With useful exercises and easy-to-remember techniques, you'll discover a variety of practical strategies that really work, creating positive change that will last a lifetime.

Saul, Richard
ADHD Does Not Exist: The Truth About Attention Deficit and Hyperactivity Disorder. Richard Saul. HarperWave 2014. 336 pages
ISBN 9780062266736
Grades: Adult   618.92
1. Attention-deficit hyperactivity disorder 2. Diagnosis 3. Mental health 4. Science Writing — Medicine and health — Mental health
LC 2013030794
Over the course of half a century, physician Richard Saul has worked with thousands of patients demonstrating symptoms of ADHD. Based on his experience, he offers a shocking conclusion: ADHD is not a condition on its own, but rather a symptom complex caused by over twenty separate conditions—from poor eyesight and giftedness to bipolar disorder and depression—each requiring its own specific treatment.

Schwarz, Alan
ADHD Nation: Children, Doctors, Big Pharma, and the Making of an American Epidemic. Alan Schwarz. Scribner 2016. 352 p.
ISBN 9781501105913
Grades: Adult   618.92
1. Diagnostic errors 2. Drug industry and trade 3. Diseases 4. Attention-deficit hyperactivity disorder 5. Neurodivergent people 6. Science Writing — Medicine and health — Disabilities and disorders
LC 2016018493
A cautionary assessment of what the author believes to be widespread misdiagnoses of ADHD argues that doctors and pharmaceutical companies are improperly targeting adults and children for commercial gain, sharing the dramatic stories of two patients while denouncing the work of ADHD expert Keith Conners.
"In this powerful, necessary book, Schwarz exposes the dirty secrets of the growing ADHD epidemic." —*Kirkus*
Includes bibliographical references and index.

Sears, Robert W.
The Allergy Book: Solving Your Family's Nasal Allergies, Asthma, Food Sensitivities, and Related Health and Behavioral Problems. Robert W. Sears, MD, FAAP, and William Sears, MD, FRCP.. Little, Brown and Company 2015. xviii, 332 pages
ISBN 9780316324809
Grades: Adult   618.92
1. Science writing — Medicine and health — Allergies 2. Science writing — Medicine and health — Children's health
LC Bl2015014077
America's most trusted name in pediatrics presents an authoritative guide to treating and preventing nasal allergies, asthmas, food allergies and intolerances and more, which uses a proven science-based approach for both treatment and prevention.
Provides science-based information for parents on treating and preventing allergies in children to avoid chronic and long-term health complications, including nasal allergies, asthmas, and food allergies and intolerances.
"The authors warn readers about hidden sources of allergens (eggs can turn up in canned soups and in salad dressings), and discuss healthy eating, favoring fruits and vegetables over gluten-filled foods. Even allergy-free people will benefit from checking out the Searses easy-to-read, clearly laid-out guidebook." —*Booklist*
Includes index.

Trubo, Richard
Caring for Your Baby and Young Child: Birth to Age 5. Steven P. Shelov, MD, MS, FAAP, editor-in-chief,Associate Dean, Undergraduate Medical EducationWinthrop University Hospital, Mineola, New York,Professor of Pediatrics, Stony Brook School ofMedicine Stony Brook, New York; Tanya RemerAltmann, MD. Bantam Books 2014. xxxix, 917 pages : Illustration
ISBN 9780553393828
Grades: Adult   618.92
1. Child care 2. Child development 3. Baby care 4. Family and Relationships — Parenting
LC 2014013096
Provides a comprehensive guide to early child care from birth to preschool, covering topics ranging from food allergies, sleeping habits, autism and breastfeeding.
Includes index.

Vlock, Deborah
Parenting Children with Mental Health Challenges: A Guide to Life with Emotionally Complex Kids. Deborah Vlock. Rowman & Littlefield 2018. xx, 177 pages
ISBN 9781538105245
Grades: Adult   618.92
1. Parent and child 2. Family and Relationships — Parenting 3. Science writing — Medicine and health — Psychology
LC 2018009447
Written by a mother, expressly for other parents, this work supports parents as they help their kids manage life with mental illness. It offers insight into the various life "hurdles" every mom or dad must guide their children over—but which loom higher and more frightening when a child's emotional disorder is thrown into the mix.
"Readers who feel overwhelmed by the numerous and ever-present challenges of parenting a child with mental health issues will find opportunities to feel connected, supported, and hopeful in this book." —*Booklist*
Includes bibliographical references and index.

620 Engineering and allied operations

Hammack, William Scott
★ *Things We Make: The Unknown History of Invention from Cathedrals to Soda Cans.* Bill Hammack. Sourcebooks 2023. 272 p.
ISBN 9781728215754
Grades: Adult   620
1. Engineering 2. Products 3. Inventions 4. Buildings 5. Technological innovations 6. Failure 7. History Writing — Technological innovations 8. Society and culture — General 9. Science writing — General
LC 2022038493
From Stonehenge to microchips, discover the one simple method used to engineer the world as we know it.
"An informative book about how the impulse of engineers to solve real-world problems is the source of progress....Hammack writes with admirable clarity, authority, and wisdom." —*Kirkus*
Includes bibliographical references.

620.009 Engineering — History, geographic treatment, biography

Winchester, Simon
★ *The Perfectionists: How Precision Engineers Created the Modern World.* Simon Winchester. HarperCollins 2018. 384 p.
ISBN 9780062652553
Grades: Adult   620.009

ESSENTIAL AND RECOMMENDED TITLES
620.1 Engineering mechanics and materials

1. Inventions 2. Technology 3. Modern history 4. History writing — Science, technology, and medicine 5. Science writing — General

LC Bl2018052538

Booklist Editors' Choice, 2018.

Traces the development of technology from the Industrial Age to the Digital Age to explore the crucial role of precision in advancement, in a chronicle that stands as both an homage and cautionary assessment for the future.

"Winchester smoothly mixes history, science, and biographical sketches to pay homage to the work of precision engineers [A] rollicking work of pop science that entertains and informs." —*Publishers Weekly*

Published in Great Britain under the title: Exactly: How Precision Engineers Created the Modern World.

620.1 Engineering mechanics and materials

Miodownik, Mark
Stuff Matters: Exploring the Marvelous Materials That Shape Our Manmade World. Mark Miodownik. Houghton Mifflin Harcourt 2014. 256 p.
ISBN 9780544236042
Grades: Adult   620.1

1. Materials science 2. Manufacturing processes 3. Chemistry 4. Scientific discoveries 5. Science Writing — Chemistry

LC 2013047575

National Academies Communication Award, 2015; New York Times Notable Book, 2014; Royal Society General Prizes for Science Books, 2014.

A world-leading materials scientist presents an engrossing collection of stories that explain the science and history of materials, from the plastic in our appliances to the elastic in our underpants, revealing the miracles of engineering that seep into our everyday lives.

"At a time when science is maligned, first-rate storyteller Miodownik entertains and educates with pop-culture references, scholarly asides, and nods to everyone from the Six Million Dollar Man to the Luminre brothers. A delight for the curious reader."—*Booklist*

Reprint of: London : Penguin, 2013.

Ploszajski, Anna
Handmade: A Scientist's Search for Meaning Through Making. Anna Ploszajski. St Martins Press 2023. 320 p.
ISBN 9781472971081
Grades: Adult   620.1

1. Materials science 2. Engineering 3. Engineering design 4. Industrial design 5. Design and construction 6. Nature craft 7. Handicraft 8. Scientists 9. Science Writing — General 10. Science Writing — Chemistry 11. Science Writing — Physics

A fresh and entertaining perspective on materials science involving the craftspeople who have built their careers around working with certain materials. From atomic structures to theories about magnetic forces, scientific progress has given us a good grasp on the properties of many different materials. However, most scientists cannot measure the temperature of steel just by looking at it, or sculpt stone into all kinds of shapes, or know how it feels to blow up a balloon of glass. Handmade is the story of materials through making and doing.

"Further enlivened by Hana Ayoob's illustrations, Handmade is exactly the sort of hybrid memoir that invites discussion and will likely spark further research." —*Booklist*

Originally published in the UK by Bloomsbury Sigma, London, in 2021.

621 Applied physics

Twilley, Nicola
★ *Frostbite: How Refrigeration Changed Our Food, Our Planet, and Ourselves.* Nicola Twilley. Penguin Press 2024. 384 p.
ISBN 9780735223288
Grades: Adult   621

1. Refrigeration and refrigerating machinery 2. Refrigerators 3. Food habits 4. Food industry and trade 5. Biochemistry 6. Food science 7. Food supply 8. Cold 9. Food writing — History and microhistory 10. Food writing — Food and culture

LC 2023048094

An engaging and far-reaching exploration of refrigeration, tracing its evolution from scientific mystery to globe-spanning infrastructure, and an essential investigation into how it has remade our entire relationship with food—for better and for worse.

"This distinctive history tells us not to take our household fridge for granted; it has profoundly affected the composition of our meals and made handy leftovers possible." —*Booklist*

Includes bibliographical references and index.

621.3 Electrical, magnetic, optical, communications, computer engineering; electronics, lighting

McAlister, Michael
Taunton's Wiring Complete: Includes the Latest in Wi-fi, Smart-house Technology. Michael McAlister & Michael Litchfield. The Taunton Press 2017. 284 p. : Color; Illustration
ISBN 9781631868382
Grades: Adult   621.3

1. Electric wiring 2. Electric equipment 3. Houses 4. House and Home — DIY, maintenance, and repair 5. Reference books — Handbooks, manuals, etc.

LC 2017014083

Shares information and instructions with homeowners for different wiring projects, including installing recessed lighting, stripping cable, and running power to an outbuilding.

At head of title: Taunton's; Includes bibliographical references and index.

621.43 Internal-combustion engines

Vance, Ashlee
When the Heavens Went on Sale: The Misfits and Geniuses Racing to Put Space Within Reach. Ashlee Vance. Ecco Press 2023. 448 p.
ISBN 9780062998873
Grades: Adult   621.43

1. Rockets (Aviation) 2. Space flight 3. Space tourism 4. Artificial satellites 5. High technology industry and trade 6. Corporations 7. Venture capitalists 8. Privatization 9. Capitalism 10. Space exploration 11. Space 12. Science Writing — Space and Flight 13. Science Writing — Great Engineering Feats 14. Business and economics — Industries — Technology

LC 2022040831

With the launch of SpaceX's Falcon 1 rocket in 2008, Silicon Valley began to realize that the universe itself was open for business. Ashlee Vance tells the remarkable story of this frenzied intergalactic land grab by following four pioneering companies—Astra, Firefly, Planet Labs, and Rocket Lab—as they build new space systems and attempt to launch rockets and satellites into orbit by the thousands. With the public fixated on the space tourism being driven by the likes of Elon Musk, Jeff Bezos, and Richard Branson, these new, scrappy companies arrived with a different set of goals: to make rocket and satellite launches fast and cheap, thereby opening Earth's lower orbit for business.

"In this exciting account, Vance (Elon Musk), a journalist at Bloomberg Businessweek, shines light on some of the lesser known private sector efforts to capitalize on outer space, telling how aerospace companies Astra, Firefly, Planet Labs, and Rocket Lab have used scrappiness and innovation in their quest to turn a profit from rockets and satellites." —*Publishers Weekly*

Includes index.

PUBLIC LIBRARY CORE COLLECTION: NONFICTION
Twentieth Edition

623.4 Ordnance

Sheinkin, Steve
Bomb: The Race to Build—and Steal—the World's Most Dangerous Weapon. Steve Sheinkin. Henry Holt & Co. 2012. 192 p.
ISBN 9781596434875
Grades: 5 6 7 8 9 10 11 12 Adult   **623.4**
1. Atomic bomb 2. Nuclear power research 3. Spies 4. World War II 5. Military history 6. United States history 7. United States 8. 20th century 9. Second World War era (1939-1945) 10. Narrative nonfiction for kids and teens 11. History books — Wars — Atomic Bomb — World War II

ALA Notable Children's Book, 2013; Jefferson Cup Award for Older Readers, 2013; Robert F. Sibert Informational Book Medal, 2013; School Library Journal Best Nonfiction Books, 2012; YALSA Award for Excellence in Nonfiction, 2013; National Book Award for Young People's Literature finalist, 2012; Newbery Honor Book, 2013.

Recounts the scientific discoveries that enabled atom splitting, the military intelligence operations that occurred in rival countries, and the work of brilliant scientists hidden at Los Alamos.

624.1 Structural engineering and underground construction

Hunt, Will
Underground: A Human History of the Worlds Beneath Our Feet. by Will Hunt. Spiegel & Grau 2019. 288 p.
ISBN 9780812996746
Grades: Adult   **624.1**
1. Underground areas 2. Underground construction 3. Exploration 4. Subways 5. Tunnels 6. Caves 7. Natural history 8. Burial 9. Excavation 10. Mines and mineral resources 11. Adventure writing — Exploration 12. Travel Writing — General 13. Nature Writing — Natural Landscapes

LC 2018005540

The first book by an urban adventurer, spelunker and photographer explores the history, science, architecture and mythology of the subterranean landscape to evaluate humanity's relationship with the underground, from sacred caves and hidden catacombs to abandoned mines and subway systems.

"This unique book is a real-life Journey to the Center of the Earth, a maze of dark corners and subterranean denizens that encompass unknown or forgotten worlds." —*Library Journal*

625.2 Railroad rolling stock

Solomon, Brian
The Field Guide to Trains: Locomotives and Rolling Stock. Brian Solomon. Voyageur Press 2016. 208 pages : Illustration; Color
ISBN 9780760349977
Grades: Adult   **625.2**
1. Locomotives 2. Transportation — Trains and rail service

LC 2015047962

This book is an indispensable illustrated resource for railfans and families on road trips, filled with easy-to-find information on locomotives and rolling stock, such as railroad cars, coaches, and wagons.

Includes bibliographical references and index.

628 Sanitary engineering

Kostigen, Thomas
Hacking Planet Earth: How Geoengineering Can Help Us Reimagine the Future. Thomas Kostigen. TarcherPerigee 2020. 352 p.
ISBN 9780593187548
Grades: Adult   **628**
1. Climate change 2. Environmental engineering 3. Climatic extremes 4. Global warming 5. Effect of humans on nature 6. Technological innovations 7. Science Writing — Great Engineering Feats 8. Science Writing — Weather

LC 2019029958

Explores the cutting-edge technologies on the frontlines of geoengineering projects that have been developed in responses to climate change, from ultraviolet shields to laser-triggered rainstorms.

"A highly optimistic, sincere account of those leading the charge to solve a grave problem that some still choose to ignore." —*Kirkus*

Includes bibliographical references and index.

628.4 Waste technology, public toilets, street cleaning

Humes, Edward
★ *Total Garbage: How We Can Fix Our Waste and Heal Our World.* Edward Humes. Avery, an imprint of Penguin Random House 2024. 288 p.
ISBN 9780593543368
Grades: Adult   **628.4**
1. Solid waste disposal 2. Solid waste reduction 3. Waste products 4. Plastics 5. Food waste 6. Energy consumption 7. Environmental policy 8. Environmental engineering 9. Renewable energy sources 10. Electric vehicles 11. Energy technology 12. Nature Writing — Environmental Issues 13. Science Writing — General 14. Business and economics — Industries

LC 2023043542

A Pulitzer Prize-winning journalist explores the pervasive yet hard-to-see wastefulness that permeates our daily lives and shows how individuals and communities are making a real difference for health, prosperity, quality of life and the fight against climate change for a cleaner, greener world.

"Total Garbage is an engaging and uplifting book that offers compelling stories from experts and activists and strong recommendations to cut through the complacency or resignation that stymie efforts to create a greener, cleaner, more efficient world." —*Booklist*

Includes bibliographical references and index.

629.13 Aeronautics

Vanhoenacker, Mark
Imagine a City: A Pilot's Journey Home. Mark Vanhoenacker. Alfred A. Knopf 2022. 416 p.
ISBN 9780525657507
Grades: Adult   **629.13**
1. Vanhoenacker, Mark 2. Pilots 3. Commercial aviation 4. Cities and towns 5. Voyages and travels 6. Travel Writing — General

LC 2021040947

A pilot's world travels, from the author of Skyfaring.

"As he marvels at the locales he's visited, Vanhoenacker offers a taste of the high life that informs and awes in equal measure. Jet-setters will be enthralled." —*Publishers Weekly*

629.132 Mechanics of flight flying and related topics

Hampton, Dan
Chasing the Demon: A Secret History of the Quest for the Sound Barrier, and the Band of American Aces Who Conquered It. Dan Hampton. William Morrow & Company 2018. 400 p.
ISBN 9780062688729
Grades: Adult   **629.132**
1. Military aviation 2. Test pilots 3. Supersonic planes 4. High-speed aviation 5. Aeronautical engineers 6. Military aircraft 7. Cold war 8. Pilots 9. Aviation history 10. Speed 11. 1940s 12. History writing — Military — Aviation History 13. History writing — Technological innovations

LC 2018024770

ESSENTIAL AND RECOMMENDED TITLES
629.2 Motor land vehicles, cycles

The New York Times best-selling author of Viper Pilot and the Flight chronicles another thrilling chapter in American aviation history: the race to break the sound barrier.

"Author of the New York Times best-selling Viper Pilot and a decorated military pilot well acquainted with flying supersonic fighter jets, Hampton chronicles the U.S. effort to break the sound barrier, starting with the founding of the U.S. Air Force in 1947 and ending with Capt. Chuck Yeager's triumph on October 14, 1947." —*Library Journal*

629.2 Motor land vehicles, cycles

Schwartz, Samuel I.
No One at the Wheel: Driverless Cars and the Road of the Future. Samuel I. Schwartz with Karen Kelly. PublicAffairs/Hachette Book Group 2018. 256 p.
ISBN 9781610398657
Grades: Adult   629.2
1. Automobiles 2. Autonomous vehicles 3. Traffic safety 4. Technological innovations 5. Transportation 6. Forecasting 7. Science Writing — Computing, the Internet, and Technology
LC 2018021594

The country's leading transport expert describes how the driverless vehicle revolution will transform highways, cities, workplaces and laws not just here, but across the globe.
Includes bibliographical references and index.

629.222 Vehicles powered by fossil fuels and human-powered vehicles

Milchtein, Chaya M.
★ *Mechanic Shop Femme's Guide to Car Ownership: Uncomplicating Cars for All of Us.* Chaya M. Milchtein. Little, Brown Spark 2024. 293 p.
ISBN 9780316565516
Grades: Adult   629.222
1. Automobiles 2. Maintenance and repair 3. Automobile purchasing 4. Women automobile mechanics 5. Transportation — Automotive 6. House and Home — DIY, maintenance, and repair 7. Reference — Consumer guides

Automotive educator, journalist, and social media influencer Chaya M. Milchtein is a queer woman who has spent the last decade deeply entrenched in the automotive industry. She also understands that queer folks and women often find it daunting to buy a car and, subsequently, deal with the realities of getting it insured and repaired. Chaya speaks to readers of all identities and socio-economic backgrounds, arming them with the necessary knowledge to navigate the intimidating automotive industry.

"Affably written, Mechanic Shop Femme's Guide to Car Ownership should find a large audience in public libraries, especially among those traditionally left out of the car-buying and maintenance process." —*Booklist*
Includes bibliographical references (pages 275-278) and index.

Parissien, Steven
The Life of the Automobile: The Complete History of the Motor Car. Steven Parissien. Thomas Dunne Books 2014. 432 pages
ISBN 9781250040633
Grades: Adult   629.222
1. Automobiles 2. Transportation 3. Mass production 4. Automobile industry and trade 5. History writing — Technological innovations
LC 2013045750

This all-encompassing world history of the most important transport innovation of the modern age explores the impact, development and significance of the automobile through its tumultuous and colorful 130-year history.

"This elegant and authoritative work demonstrates the historical links among people, machines, and cultures on a global scale." —*Library Journal*
Includes bibliographical references and index.

629.227 Cycles

Rosen, Jody
Two Wheels Good: The History and Mystery of the Bicycle. Jody Rosen. Crown 2022. 320 p.
ISBN 9780804141499
Grades: Adult   629.227
1. Bicycles 2. Bicycling 3. Bicyclists 4. Choice of transportation 5. Transportation 6. Environmental engineering 7. History writing — Microhistory 8. Sports and Competition — Racing — Cycling 9. Travel Writing — Modes of Transportation — Cycling
LC 2021054101

The bicycle is a vestige of the Victorian era, seemingly at odds with our age of smartphones and ride-sharing apps and driverless cars. Yet we live on a bicycle planet. Across the world, more people travel by bicycle than any other form of transportation. Almost anyone can learn to ride a bike—and nearly everyone does. In Two Wheels Good, writer and critic Jody Rosen reshapes our understanding of this ubiquitous machine, an ever-present force in humanity's life and dream life—and a flash point in culture wars—for more than two hundred years.

"A lively social history of the bicycle....Fans of bicycling and how-the-world-works reportage alike will find this a great pleasure." —*Kirkus*
Includes bibliographical references and index.

629.4 Astronautics

Grush, Loren
★ *The Six: The Untold Story of America's First Women Astronauts.* Loren Grush. Scribner 2023. 416 p.
ISBN 9781982172800
Grades: Adult   629.4
1. Ride, Sally 2. Resnik, Judith, 1949-1986 3. Fisher, Anna Lee 4. Sullivan, Kathryn D. 5. Lucid, Shannon, 1943- 6. Seddon, Rhea 7. Women astronauts 8. Space flight 9. Space exploration 10. Space programs 11. Sexism 12. Sex discrimination against women 13. North American people 14. American people 15. United States history 16. Collective biographies 17. Life stories — Science, technology, and medicine — Astronauts and pilots 18. History writing — Women's history 19. Science Writing — Space and Flight 20. Debut title

When NASA sent astronauts to the moon in the 1960s and 70s the agency excluded women, arguing that only military test pilots—a group then made up exclusively of men—had the right stuff. It was an era in which women were steered away from jobs in science and deemed unqualified for space flight. Eventually, though, NASA recognized its blunder and opened the application process to a wider array of hopefuls, regardless of race or gender. In The Six, acclaimed journalist Loren Grush shows the first of these brilliant and courageous women—Sally Ride, Judy Resnik, Anna Fisher, Kathy Sullivan, Shannon Lucid, and Rhea Seddon—who helped build the tools that made the space program run.

"Based on archival material and interviews with the surviving pioneering female astronauts and the families of those who have passed, this is a well-rounded narrative of the lives of these trailblazing women." —*Booklist*

Holt, Nathalia
★ *Rise of the Rocket Girls: The Women Who Propelled Us, from Missiles to the Moon to Mars.* Nathalia Holt. Little Brown & Co. 2016. 304 p.
ISBN 9780316338929
Grades: Adult   629.4
1. Space exploration 2. Women scientists 3. Women engineers 4. Space flight 5. Gender role 6. Women 7. Adult books for young adults 8. History writing — Women's history 9. Science Writing — Space and Flight
LC 2015954384

School Library Journal Best Books: Best Adult Books 4 Teens, 2016.
Traces the pivotal achievements of the elite female science recruits at the Jet Propulsion Laboratory, where in the mid-20th century they transformed rocket design and enabled the creations of the first American satellites.

PUBLIC LIBRARY CORE COLLECTION: NONFICTION
Twentieth Edition

"This is an excellent contribution to American history, valuable not only for what it reveals about the space program and gender equality but even more as great reading. Book clubs will be lining up." —*Booklist*

Launius, Roger D.
The Smithsonian History of Space Exploration: From the Ancient World to the Extraterrestrial Future. Roger D. Launius. Smithsonian Books 2018. 400 p.
ISBN 9781588346377
Grades: Adult   629.4
1. Astronautics 2. Space flight 3. Space flight to Mars 4. Space exploration 5. Illustrated books 6. Science Writing — Space and Flight 7. Adult books for young adults
LC 2018017014

Offers an illustrated history of space exploration, from the pioneering work of ancient astronomers to the latest technological and mechanical marvels that allow extraterrestrial exploration, as well as what the future may hold.

Weinersmith, Kelly
★ *A City on Mars: Can We Settle Space, Should We Settle Space, and Have We Really Thought This Through?* Kelly Weinersmith, Zach Weinersmith. The Penguin Press 2023. 384 p.
ISBN 9781984881724
Grades: Adult   629.4
1. Space exploration 2. Space colonies 3. Forecasting 4. Technology 5. Space 6. Science writing — Space and flight
Hugo Award for Best Related Non-Fiction Book, 2024.

The authors of the best-selling popular science book Soonish discuss the future of space settlements, explore what would be needed to have space kids, build space farms and create nations, ultimately questioning whether or not it's actually a good idea.

"Forceful, engaging and funny, it is an essential reality check for anyone who has ever looked for home in the night sky." —*New York Times*

Wolfe, Tom
★ *The Right Stuff.* Tom Wolfe. Farrar, Straus, Giroux 1983. 436 p.
ISBN 9780312427566
Grades: 11 12 Adult   629.4
1. Astronauts 2. Space flight 3. Space accidents 4. Test pilots 5. Astronautics 6. Space programs 7. Courage 8. United States history 9. United States 10. 1960s 11. 20th century 12. Page to screen 13. Science Writing — Space and Flight 14. History writing — 1960s — United States 15. History writing — Technological innovations 16. Nonfiction that reads like fiction
LC 84162805

National Book Award for Nonfiction, 1980; National Book Critics Circle Award for Nonfiction finalist, 1979.

The moments of grandeur and weakness, the aspirations, and the problems of America's astronauts are revealed in an exploration of the dimensions of their inner lives in space, on the moon, and on the earth.

"This volume chronicles the handful of adrenaline-junkie military test pilots who became the Mercury astronauts. Their story is juxtaposed against that of Chuck Yeager, the ace of aces pilot who broke the sound barrier but couldn't apply to the space program because he lacked a college degree.... A terrific read from beginning to end." —*Library Journal*

629.40973 United States. National Aeronautics and Space Administration

Brinkley, Douglas
★ *American Moonshot: John F. Kennedy and the Great Space Race.* Douglas Brinkley. HarperCollins 2019. 448 p.
ISBN 9780062655066
Grades: Adult   629.40973
1. Kennedy, John F. (John Fitzgerald), 1917-1963 2. Space programs 3. Space exploration 4. Cold War 5. Astronauts 6. Presidents 7. International competition 8. Exploration 9. Moon 10. Space 11. United States 12. History writing — Cold War 13. History writing — 1960s — United States 14. Science Writing — Space and Flight 15. History writing — Science, technology, and medicine
LC 2019300429

The historian author of Cronkite draws on new primary source material and firsthand interviews in a reassessment of the space program that examines the political, cultural and scientific factors that launched NASA and the space race.

Tyson, Neil deGrasse
Space Chronicles: Facing the Ultimate Frontier. Neil deGrasse Tyson; edited by Avis Lang. W. W. Norton 2012. 240 p.
ISBN 9780393082104
Grades: 11 12 Adult   629.40973
1. Space flight 2. Space exploration 3. Space policy 4. Astronautics 5. Science Writing — Space and Flight
LC 2011032481

Presents the astrophysicist's views on the future of space travel and America's role in that future, giving his readers an eye-opening manifesto on the importance of space exploration for America's economy, security, and morale.
Includes index.

629.43 Unmanned space flight

Stern, Alan
Chasing New Horizons: Inside the Epic First Mission to Pluto. Alan Stern and David Grinspoon. Picador 2018. 320 p.
ISBN 9781250098962
Grades: Adult   629.43
1. Pluto (Dwarf planet) 2. Science writing — Space and flight
LC 2017060114

A New Horizons Principal Investigator and an award-winning NASA advisor share a behind-the-scenes account of the science, politics, egos and public expectations that shaped the New Horizons' mission to Pluto and beyond, citing the endeavor's boundary-breaking achievements and how they reflect the collective power of shared human goals.

"Armchair space explorers and budding scientists will relish this inspiring aerospace adventure." —*Library Journal*
Includes index.

629.44 Auxiliary spacecraft

Jones, Tom
Space Shuttle Stories: Firsthand Astronaut Accounts from All 135 Missions. Tom Jones. Smithsonian Books 2023. 319 pages : Illustration; Color
ISBN 9781588347541
Grades: Adult   629.44
1. Space shuttles 2. Astronauts 3. Space flight 4. Space vehicles 5. Space exploration 6. Space photography 7. United States 8. Oral histories 9. Visual nonfiction 10. Science Writing — Space and flight 11. Life stories — Science, technology, and medicine — Astronauts and pilots
LC 2023013350

With more than 600 photos from the NASA archives, this major contribution to the historical record of a momentous era of spaceflight invites readers to experience all 135 NASA space shuttle missions, from Columbia's maiden flight in 1981 to the final launch of Atlantis in 2011.

"The outstanding visuals and firsthand storytelling make this an attractive resource." —*Booklist*
Includes bibliographical references (pages 314-315) and index.

Kitmacher, Gary
Space Stations: The Art, Science, and Reality of Working in Space. Dr. Gary Kitmacher, Ron Miller, Robert Pearlman; foreword, Nicole Stott. Smithsonian Books 2018. 240 pages : Illustration; Color
ISBN 9781588346322

ESSENTIAL AND RECOMMENDED TITLES
629.45 Manned space flight

Grades: Adult   **629.44**

1. Space stations 2. Space exploration 3. Exploration 4. Space 5. Science writing — Space and Flight 6. History writing — Science, technology, and medicine

LC 2018004838

A rich visual history of real and fictional space stations, illustrating pop culture's influence on the development of actual space stations and vice versa.

"Covering technical breakthroughs as well as Star Trek and comic book references, their work will win high marks from space buffs and sf fans alike." —*Booklist*

Copyrighted by Elephant Book Company Limited; Includes bibliographical references (page 239) and index.

629.45 Manned space flight

Cook, Kevin
The *Burning* Blue: *The Untold Story of Christa McAuliffe and Nasa's Challenger Disaster*. Kevin Cook. Henry Holt and Company 2021. 320 p.
ISBN 9781250755551
Grades: Adult   **629.45**

1. McAuliffe, Christa, 1948-1986 2. Challenger (Space shuttle) 3. Challenger (Space shuttle) Accident, January 28, 1986 4. Women teachers 5. Astronauts 6. Space flight 7. Teachers 8. Biographies 9. Science Writing — Space and flight 10. History writing — United States 11. Life stories — Science, technology, and medicine — Astronauts and pilots 12. Life stories — Education — Scholars and educators

LC 2020052641

Infused with drama, immediacy and compelling characters, thirty-five years after NASA's revitalization program ended tragically with the Challenger explosion, this book uncovers the untold story of the disastrous order to launch that ill-fated, unforgettable morning.

"Journalist Cook (Ten Innings at Wrigley) delivers a crisp account of the January 1986 Challenger disaster focused on Christa McAuliffe, the first teacher selected to join a space mission. . . . This is an informative overview of a preventable tragedy that looms large in the history of the space program." —*Publishers Weekly*

Includes bibliographical references and index.

Donovan, Jim
★ *Shoot for the Moon: The Space Race and the Extraordinary Voyage of Apollo 11*. James Donovan. Little, Brown 2019. 448 p.
ISBN 9780316341783
Grades: Adult   **629.45**

1. Cold War 2. Apollo 11 (Spacecraft) 3. Space flight to the moon 4. Space exploration 5. Astronauts 6. Technology 7. Space programs 8. International competition 9. Exploration 10. Moon 11. 1960s 12. History writing — Cold War 13. Science Writing — Space and Flight 14. History writing — Science, technology, and medicine

LC 2018947611

Published to coincide with the mission's 50th anniversary, a meticulously researched account of the Apollo 11 program also examines its astronauts, flight controllers and engineers, as well as its role in shaping the Mercury and Gemini missions.

"Drawing on dozens of interviews with the era's engineers and scientists, Donovans history is a powerfully written and irresistible celebration of the Apollo missions." —*Booklist*

Fishman, Charles
★ *One Giant Leap: The Impossible Mission That Flew Us to the Moon*. Charles Fishman. Simon & Schuster 2019. 416 p.
ISBN 9781501106293
Grades: Adult   **629.45**

1. Technological innovations 2. Space flight to the moon 3. Scientists 4. Engineers 5. Space programs 6. Politics and government 7. Exploration 8. Moon 9. United States 10. 1960s 11. 20th century 12. History writing — Technological innovations 13. History writing — Science, technology, and medicine 14. History writing — 1960s — United States

LC Bl2019011666

The award-winning author of the Wal-Mart Effect shares the story of the remarkable NASA scientists and engineers who created America's space program and fulfilled President Kennedy's mandate to put a man on the Moon before 1970.

"With the upcoming 50th anniversary of the Apollo 11 landing, this compelling read is highly recommended for all public libraries." —*Library Journal*

Higginbotham, Adam
★ *Challenger: A True Story of Heroism and Disaster on the Edge of Space*. Adam Higginbotham. Avid Reader Press 2024. 496 p.
ISBN 9781982176617
Grades: Adult   **629.45**

1. Challenger (Space shuttle) 2. Challenger (Space shuttle) Accident, January 28, 1986 3. Astronauts 4. Space flight 5. United States 6. 20th century 7. Science Writing — Space and flight 8. History writing — United States

Based on fascinating new archival research and deep reporting, this gripping and riveting narrative provides the definitive story of the 1986 Challenger disaster and how it led to America changing its view of itself.

"A deeply researched, fluently written study in miscommunication, hubris, and technological overreach." —*Kirkus*

Simultaneously published in Great Britain by Viking press, 2024.

Kaku, Michio
★ *The Future of Humanity: Terraforming Mars, Interstellar Travel, Immortality, and Our Destiny Beyond Earth*. Michio Kaku. Doubleday 2018. 416 p.
ISBN 9780385542760
Grades: Adult   **629.45**

1. Scientific forecasting 2. Technological forecasting 3. Space colonies 4. Space flight 5. Astrophysics 6. High technology 7. Artificial intelligence 8. Science Writing — General

LC 2017046597

The co-founder of string field theory and best-selling author of the Future of the Mind traverses the frontiers of astrophysics, artificial intelligence and technology to outline a remarkable vision of humanity's future in space, from colonizing Mars to traveling to distant galaxies.

"Kakus writings have garnered a reputation for combining hard science with clever speculation, and his latest book continues that winning trend. A breathtaking voyage through what is almost certainly the next major period in the history of humanity." —*Booklist*

Kluger, Jeffrey
★ *Apollo 8: The Thrilling Story of the First Mission to the Moon*. Jeffrey Kluger. Henry Holt and Co. 2017. 336 p.
ISBN 9781627798327
Grades: Adult   **629.45**

1. Apollo 8 (Spacecraft) 2. Space flight to the moon 3. Astronauts 4. Cold War 5. 1960s 6. History writing — 1960s — United States 7. History writing — Cold War

LC 2016046157

In Apollo 8, acclaimed science writer Jeffrey Kluger provides a you-were-there reading experience as he recounts the preparations that culminated in the first manned flight to the moon. Drawing on his interviews with crew members Frank Borman, Jim Lovell, and Bill Anders, as well as the NASA Oral History Project and other records, Kluger enriches the personal and technical details of the mission with facets of the Cold War-era politics that spurred the race to the moon.

"Readers will relish Kluger's multisensory prose, and the whole gamut of space flight comes alive in the details. Moreover, extensive interviews lend authenticity to the dialogue and character sketches." —*Publishers Weekly*

Includes bibliographical references and index.

PUBLIC LIBRARY CORE COLLECTION: NONFICTION
Twentieth Edition

Kurson, Robert
★ *Rocket Men: The Daring Odyssey of Apollo 8 and the Astronauts Who Made Man's First Journey to the Moon.* Robert Kurson. Random House 2018. 352 p.
ISBN 9780812988703
Grades: Adult   629.45
1. Apollo 8 (Spacecraft) 2. Space flight to the moon 3. Astronauts 4. Space exploration 5. Space programs 6. Space vehicles 7. International competition 8. Science Writing — Space and Flight

LC 2017009386

Shares the lesser-known inside story of the dangerous Apollo 8 mission, focusing in particular on the lives and families of astronaut heroes Frank Borman, Jim Lovell and Bill Anders, while illuminating the political factors that prompted America to risk lives to save the Apollo program and define the space race.

An exuberant history of a major turning point in early American spaceflight, possibly 'The riskiest and most thrilling of all the Apollo missions.' —*Kirkus*

Includes bibliographical references and index.

Launius, Roger D.
Apollo's Legacy: Perspectives on the Moon Landings. Roger D. Launius. Smithsonian Books 2019. 264 p.
ISBN 9781588346490
Grades: Adult   629.45
1. Space flight to the moon 2. Space programs 3. Space exploration 4. Technological innovations 5. Public opinion 6. Aviation history 7. Impartial writing 8. History writing — Science, technology, and medicine 9. History writing — Technological innovations 10. Science Writing — Space and Flight 11. History writing — United States

LC 2018032602

A space historian explores the many-faceted stories told about the meaning of the Apollo program and how it forever altered American society, and weaves in stories from important moments in Apollo's history to draw readers into his analysis. (science).

Includes bibliographical references and index.

Nelson, Craig
Rocket Men: The Epic Story of the First Men on the Moon. Craig Nelson. Viking 2009. 416 p.
ISBN 9780670021031
Grades: Adult   629.45
1. Space flight to the moon 2. Astronauts 3. Space flight 4. Astronautics 5. Space programs 6. United States 7. 1960s 8. Science Writing — Space and Flight 9. Adult books for young adults

LC 2008051175

Recreates the story of the Apollo 11 moon mission through interviews, NASA oral histories, and declassified CIA documents.

"A thorough recounting as full in human terms as in scientific and technical detail of NASA's first manned Moon landing. The definitive account of a watershed in American history." —*Kirkus*

Includes bibliographical references and index.

Shesol, Jeff
Mercury Rising: John Glenn, John Kennedy, and the New Battleground of the Cold War. Jeff Shesol. W.W. Norton & Company 2021. 416 p.
ISBN 9781324022114
Grades: Adult   629.45
1. Glenn, John, 1921-2016 2. Kennedy, John F. (John Fitzgerald), 1917-1963 3. Project Mercury 4. Space flight 5. Space programs 6. Space policy 7. Astronautics 8. International competition 9. International relations 10. United States 11. Soviet Union 12. History writing — Science, technology, and medicine 13. History writing — United States 14. Science Writing — Space and flight

LC 2020051050

If the United States couldn't catch up to the Soviets in space, how could it compete with them on Earth? That was the question facing John F. Kennedy at the height of the Cold War—a perilous time when the Soviet Union built the wall in Berlin, tested nuclear bombs more destructive than any in history, and beat the United States to every major milestone in space. The race to the heavens seemed a race for survival—and America was losing.

"In this dramatic account, Shesol (Supreme Power: Franklin Roosevelt vs. the Supreme Court) tells the story of the first manned American spaceflight into orbit.... This well-researched and exciting read is recommended for those interested in the history of the space race or the Cold War." —*Library Journal*

Includes bibliographical references and index.

Stone, Robert
Chasing the Moon: The People, the Politics, and the Promise That Launched America into the Space Age. Robert Stone and Alan Andres. Ballantine Books 2019. 240 p.
ISBN 9781524798123
Grades: Adult   629.45
1. Space policy 2. Space exploration 3. Space programs 4. Space flight to the moon 5. Space flight 6. International competition 7. Aviation history 8. United States history 9. 20th century 10. Media tie-ins 11. Science writing — Space and flight 12. Adult books for young adults

LC 2018059390

A companion to PBS's American Experience draws on eyewitness accounts and newly discovered archival material to chronicle the stories of the visionaries who helped America win the space race with the first lunar landing.

"In an informative companion book to the PBS miniseries of the same name, documentary filmmaker Stone, the program's writer, producer, and director, and Andres, a consulting producer and researcher on the series, chronicle the quest for space travel that culminated in Neil Armstrong's first step on the lunar surface." —*Kirkus*

Includes bibliographical references and index.

Stuart, Colin
How to Live in Space: Everything You Need to Know for the Not-so-distant Future. Colin Stuart. Smithsonian Books 2018. 192 p.
ISBN 9781588346384
Grades: Adult   629.45
1. Space flight 2. Space stations 3. Life on other planets 4. Terraforming 5. Space colonies 6. Science Writing — Space and Flight 7. Adult books for young adults

LC 2018011524

An amusing and informative illustrated guide to life beyond our own planet that covers everything from training for and living in space to the future of space travel and tourism Now that suborbital space tourism is predicted to become a billion-dollar industry in the next ten years and NASA has announced its plans for landing humans on Mars in the 2030s, the dream of traveling and living in space is taking on new reality. But given that life on Earth can be complicated enough, how can we survive and thrive in the zero-gravity, absolute-zero far reaches of space? Look no further: How to Live in Space is chock-full of all the essential information you need to equip yourself for life beyond our blue planet. Grounded in space science, planetary biology, and rocket science, this accessible guide propels readers through takeoff, life in orbit, terraforming, and the long-term effects of space on the human body. Infographics and full-color illustrations help How to Live in Space to answer your burning questions, including: How do you sleep in microgravity? How do you grow food without water? Will your muscles waste away out there? How do you protect yourself from radiation? This is a light-hearted yet informative guide to a life far from terra firma.

"Suitable for space-happy tweens as well as nonscientist adults, Stuart's captivating handbook has something to amaze and entertain every reader." —*Publishers Weekly*

Includes index.

Swift, Earl
Across the Airless Wilds: The Lunar Rover and the Triumph of the Final Moon Landings. Earl Swift. Custom House 2021. 384 p. : Illustration
ISBN 9780062986535
Grades: Adult   629.45
1. Space flight to the moon 2. Space exploration 3. Space programs 4. Scientists 5. Astronauts 6. Engineers 7. United States history 8. 20th century 9. History

ESSENTIAL AND RECOMMENDED TITLES
629.47 Astronautical engineering

writing — Science, technology, and medicine 10. Science Writing — Space and flight 11. History writing — United States

LC 2021006863

Earl Swift rediscovers the final three Apollo Moon landings, arguing that these overlooked missions-distinguished by the use of the revolutionary Lunar Roving Vehicle-were the pinnacle of human exploration.

"Journalist Swift (Chesapeake Requiem) chronicles the work of the engineers, geologists, project managers, and astronauts who took lunar rovers to the moon in this detailed history." —*Publishers Weekly*

Includes bibliographical references and index.

Virts, Terry
How to Astronaut: An Insider's Guide to Leaving Planet Earth. Terry Virts. Workman Publishing Company 2020. IX, 310 p.

ISBN 9781523509614

Grades: Adult   629.45

1. Virts, Terry, 1967- 2. Astronauts 3. Astronautics 4. Space flight 5. Space exploration 6. Training 7. Essays 8. Science Writing — Space and flight 9. Life stories — Science, technology and medicine — Astronauts and pilots

LC Bl2020018719

A behind-the-scenes look at the training, basic rules, lessons and procedures of space travel by the former astronaut, space-shuttle pilot and International Space Station commander includes coverage of the realities of living long-term in space.

"This is an eye-opening insider's view on what it's really like to be an astronaut: the joys, the dangers, the fear, and the day-to-day reality of it. Virts' writing is humorous, playful, down to earth, and often wise." —*Booklist*

Includes index.

Walker, Stephen
Beyond: The Astonishing Story of the First Human Being to Leave Our Planet and Journey into Space. Stephen Walker. HarperCollins 2021. 400 p.

ISBN 9780062978158

Grades: Adult   629.45

1. Gagarin, Yuri Alekseyevich, 1934-1968 2. Astronauts 3. Men 4. Space programs 5. Space flight 6. Astronautics 7. Cold war 8. International competition 9. Space exploration 10. Aviation history 11. Soviet Union 12. 20th century 13. Biographies 14. Life stories — Science, technology, and medicine — Astronauts and pilots 15. Science Writing — Space and flight 16. History writing — Europe — Russia

A 60th-anniversary tribute to Russia's history-making first space mission documents the story of cosmonaut Yuri Gagarin, the program's repurposing of a nuclear ballistic missile and the Cold War challenges that shrouded the mission in secrecy.

"Walker provides a thrilling account of the first manned space flight, which began in total secrecy, concealed from the U.S. by the Iron Curtain." —*Library Journal*

Wohlforth, Charles P.
Beyond Earth: Our Path to a New Home in the Planets. Charles Wohlforth and Amanda R. Hendrix. Pantheon Books 2016. 288 p.

ISBN 9780804197977

Grades: Adult   629.45

1. Space flight 2. Astronautics 3. Space exploration 4. Space colonies 5. Science writing — Space and flight

LC 2016009498

A leading planetary scientist and an award-winning science writer present a chronicle of the developments and initiatives that have transformed the idea of space colonization into an achievable goal, sharing arguments in favor of targeting Saturn's moon, Titan.

"On the whole, the fictional chapters are entertaining, chilling, and put the science in a more human context. The two halves work together to create a striking, reality-based possible future thats seen through the lens of current knowledge." —*Publishers Weekly*

Includes index.

629.47 Astronautical engineering

Guthrie, Julian
How to Make a Spaceship: A Band of Renegades, an Epic Race, and the Birth of Private Spaceflight. Julian Guthrie, foreword by Richard Branson, afterword by Stephen Hawking. Penguin Group USA 2016. 400 p.

ISBN 9781594206726

Grades: Adult   629.47

1. Diamandis, Peter H. 2. Aeronautical engineers 3. Space flight 4. Science writing — Space and flight

LC Bl2016030308

Traces the efforts of science prodigy Peter Diamandis and other pioneering space hopefuls to create the private spaceflight industry, launching a historic race to win the $10 million XPrize and inspiring the triumphant 2004 launch of SpaceShipOne.

"Guthrie well captures the high-risk, buccaneering spirit of privately financed spaceflight." —*Booklist*

629.8 Automatic control engineering

Davis, Joshua
Spare Parts: Four Undocumented Teenagers, One Ugly Robot, and the Battle for the American Dream. Joshua Davis. Farrar, Straus, and Giroux 2014. 240 pages

ISBN 9780374183370

Grades: Adult   629.8

1. Robotics 2. Undocumented immigrants 3. Robots 4. Remotely operated submersibles 5. Mexican American teenagers 6. Boys 7. Phoenix, Arizona 8. Adult books for young adults 9. Society and culture — Education

LC 2014018569

Booklist Editors' Choice, 2014.

Tells the story of four Mexican American high school students who built a submersible robot and entered it in a national competition.

"Davis pulls no punches as he describes the grim sociopolitical atmosphere that allows the oppression of talented people for no morally acceptable reason. The four young inventors and their struggles helped spur the DREAMers movement, and their story will also be told in a forthcoming Hollywood movie. This is important reading." —*Booklist*

Waldman, Jonathan
Sam: One Robot, a Dozen Engineers, and the Race to Revolutionize the Way We Build. Jonathan Waldman. Avid Reader Press 2020. 288 pages

ISBN 9781501140594

Grades: Adult   629.8

1. Engineers 2. Construction industry and trade 3. Technological innovations 4. Robots 5. Change 6. Bricklayers 7. Science writing — Computing, the internet, and technology 8. Adult books for young adults

LC Bl2019037483

A true story of innovation centers on a scrappy team of engineers—far from the Silicon Valley limelight—and their quest to achieve a surprisingly difficult technological feat: Building a robot that can lay bricks.

"As one learns a great deal about geology from John McPhee and computers from Tracy Kidder, Waldman offers a lively, accessible overview of the bricklayer's art, which is much more complex than one might think." —*Kirkus*

630.89 Agriculture — Ethnic and national groups

Baszile, Natalie
We Are Each Other's Harvest: Celebrating African American Farmers, Land, and Legacy. Natalie Baszile. Amistad Press 2021. 224 p.

ISBN 9780062932563

Grades: Adult   630.89

1. Effect of environment on humans 2. Agriculture 3. Farmers 4. African American farmers 5. African Americans 6. Essays 7. Society and culture — Race 8. Nature Writing — Natural Landscapes

The author of the novel Queen Sugar gathers together essays, poems, photographs, quotes, conversations and first-person stories to examine Black people's connection to the American land from Emancipation to today.

"Novelist Baszile (Queen Sugar) explores the legacy of 'Black and brown farmers' in this winning anthology of essays, poems, photographs, and interviews." —Publishers Weekly

630.9 Agriculture — History

Connell, John
The Farmer's Son: Calving Season on a Family Farm. John Connell. Houghton Mifflin Harcourt 2019. 256 pages
ISBN 9781328577993
Grades: Adult   630.9

1. Connell, John, 1986- 2. Farm life 3. Family relationships 4. Cattle 5. Family farms 6. Calves 7. Sheep 8. Lambs 9. Faith (Christianity) 10. Communities 11. Animal life cycles 12. Ireland 13. Autobiographies and memoirs 14. Life stories — Nature and outdoors — Farmers and ranchers 15. Family and Relationships — Families 16. Life stories — Facing adversity — Medical issues — Mental illness 17. Nature Writing — Animal Studies

LC 2018042556

Traces a calving season on the author's family farm in Ireland, where, after a decade's absence, he found hope and healing in his family, routines, faith, and community.

First published, titled the cow book : a story of life on an Irish family farm, in Great Britain by Granta Books, 2018.

Genoways, Ted
This Blessed Earth: A Year in the Life of an American Family Farm. Ted Genoways. W.W. Norton & Company 2017. 288 p.
ISBN 9780393292572
Grades: Adult   630.9

1. Hammond family 2. Farm life 3. Family farms 4. Farmers 5. Ranchers 6. Ranch life 7. Inheritance and succession 8. Agriculture 9. Industrialization 10. Nebraska 11. Nature Writing — General 12. Family and Relationships — Families

LC 2017025062

A portrait of the American small farm examines one family's fight to preserve their legacy, following them from harvest to harvest as they are confronted by encroaching pipelines, climate change, and shifting trade policies.

"By following a single family through time, the book captures the complex reality of farmers in America today both in terms of the future of the industry and of their everyday lives. It is an unvarnished portrait striking for both its depth and humanity." —Publishers Weekly

Includes bibliographical references.

631.4 Soil science

Montgomery, David R.
What Your Food Ate: How to Heal Our Land and Reclaim Our Health. David R. Montgomery and Anne Bikle. W.W. Norton & Company, Inc. 2022. 496 p.
ISBN 9781324004530
Grades: Adult   631.4

1. Soils 2. Soil biology 3. Soil conservation 4. Food supply 5. Health 6. Sustainable agriculture 7. Nature Writing — Environmental Issues 8. Science Writing — Biology 9. Business and economics — Industries — Agriculture and food

LC 2022010303

Are you really what you eat? David R. Montgomery and Anne Bikle take us far beyond the well-worn adage to deliver a new truth: the roots of good health start on farms. What Your Food Ate marshals evidence from recent and forgotten science to illustrate how the health of the soil ripples through to that of crops, livestock, and ultimately us. Unfortunately, conventional agricultural practices unravel these vital partnerships and thereby undercut our well-being. Can farmers and ranchers produce enough nutrient-dense food to feed us all? Can we have quality and quantity? With their trademark thoroughness and knack for integrating information across numerous scientific fields, Montgomery and Bikle chart the way forward. Navigating discoveries and epiphanies about the world beneath our feet, they reveal why regenerative farming practices hold the key to healing sick soil and untapped potential for improving human health.

"This fascinating look at how soil health affects the health of plants, livestock, and people will appeal to those interested in regenerative agriculture, the welfare of livestock, soil science, and more." —Library Journal

Includes bibliographical references and index.

631.5 Cultivation and harvesting

Bradley, Steve
Pruning Simplified: A Visual Guide to 50 Trees and Shrubs. Steven Bradley. Timber Press 2019. 192 pages : Color; Illustration
ISBN 9781604698886
Grades: Adult   631.5

1. Pruning 2. Shrubs 3. Trees 4. Arts and Entertainment — Crafts and hobbies — Garden and nature

LC Bl2019012456

Filled with expert advice, a plant-by-plant guide profiles 50 of the most popular trees and shrubs and provides easy-to-follow instructions for pruning and shaping each one.

Explains how to prune fifty popular trees and shrubs, providing plant-by-plant instructions and illustrations.

"British horticulturist Bradley, known for his long career providing gardening advice, focuses his latest book on the evergreen subject of pruning. He outlines the many reasons for pruning, basic pruning techniques, and necessary equipment in brief, using general terms to start with, before moving on to the specific details for pruning 50 plants commonly grown in residential gardens." —Booklist

Includes index.

Gough, Robert E.
The Complete Guide to Saving Seeds: 322 Vegetables, Herbs, Flowers, Fruits, Trees, and Shrubs. Robert Gough and Cheryl Moore-Gough. Storey Pub. 2011. VIII, 311 p. : Color illustration
ISBN 9781603425742
Grades: Adult   631.5

1. Plant propagation 2. Seeds 3. Arts and Entertainment — Crafts and hobbies — Garden and nature

LC 2010051179

A full-color resource explains how to gather, clean, and store seeds for three hundred different kinds of vegetables, fruits, herbs, flowers, trees, and shrubs, as well as how to propagate and care for new seedlings.

Includes bibliographical references (p. 292-293) and index.

Halleck, Leslie F.
Plant Parenting: Easy Ways to Make More Houseplants, Vegetables, and Flowers. Leslie F. Halleck. Timber Press 2019. 255 p.
ISBN 9781604698725
Grades: Adult   631.5

1. Plant propagation 2. Arts and Entertainment — Crafts and hobbies — Garden and nature

LC 2018043092

A horticulture expert provides a starting point for beginners looking to dabble in plant propagation, providing simple instructions for the most practical techniques for cutting, layering, dividing, seed starting and saving and controlling pests.

Includes index.

ESSENTIAL AND RECOMMENDED TITLES
631.8 Fertilizers, soil conditioners, growth regulators

631.8 Fertilizers, soil conditioners, growth regulators

Pleasant, Barbara
The Complete Compost Gardening Guide: Banner Batches, Grow Heaps, Comforter Compost, and Other Amazing Techniques for Saving Time and Money, and Producing the Most Flavorful, Nutritious Vegetables Ever. Barbara Pleasant & Deborah L. Martin. Storey Pub. 2008. 319 p. : Color illustration; Color; Map
ISBN 9781580177030
Grades: Adult   631.8
1. Compost 2. Arts and Entertainment — Crafts and hobbies — Garden and nature
LC 2007049729
Explains how to transform one's garden into a nourishing, organic environment with the use of compost customized to the special needs and soil of each garden.
Includes bibliographical references (p. 293) and index.

632 Plant injuries, diseases, pests

Dickinson, Richard
Weeds of North America. Richard Dickinson and France Royer. The University of Chicago Press 2014. xxxii, 797 pages : Illustration; Color
ISBN 9780226076447
Grades: Adult   632
1. Weeds 2. Nature writing — Flowers and plants 3. Science writing — Biology 4. History writing — General
LC 2013038953
Organized by plant family and featuring more than 500 species, a visually stunning and informative guide to North American weeds at every stage of growth provides much-needed background on these intrusive organisms, arming readers with the knowledge they need to win the battle with weeds.
Includes bibliographical references (pages 761-764) and index.

633.8 Other crops grown for industrial processing

Zuckerman, Jocelyn C.
Planet Palm: How Palm Oil Ended up in Everything - and Endangered the World. Jocelyn C. Zuckerman. The New Press 2021. 272 p.
ISBN 9781620975237
Grades: Adult   633.8
1. Agricultural products 2. Plantations 3. Food industry and trade 4. Cosmetics industry and trade 5. Corporate power 6. Business corruption 7. Forced labor 8. Environmental degradation 9. Tropics 10. Business and economics — Industries — Agriculture and food 11. Nature Writing — Environmental Issues 12. Politics and global affairs — Civil and human rights 13. Food writing — Investigations
LC 2020057136
Over the past few decades, palm oil has seeped into every corner of our lives. Worldwide, palm oil production has nearly doubled in just the last decade: Oil-palm plantations now cover an area nearly the size of New Zealand, and some form of the commodity lurks in half the products on U.S. grocery shelves. But the palm oil revolution has been built on stolen land and slave labor; it's swept away cultures and so devastated the landscapes of Southeast Asia that iconic animals now teeter on the brink of extinction. Fires lit to clear the way for plantations spew carbon emissions to rival those of industrialized nations. Jocelyn Zuckerman's groundbreaking work of journalism compels us to examine the connections between the choices we make at the grocery store and a planet under siege.
"'Pay attention to palm oil,' Zuckerman nearly shouts in this crucial and exemplary work of investigative planetary journalism." —*Booklist*
Includes bibliographical references and index.

634 Orchards, fruits, forestry

Ralph, Ann
Grow a Little Fruit Tree: Simple Pruning Techniques for Small-Space, Easy-Harvest Fruit Trees. Ann Ralph. Storey Publishing 2015. 168 pages : Illustration; Color
ISBN 9781612120546
Grades: Adult   634
1. Fruit trees 2. Arts and Entertainment — Crafts and hobbies — Garden and nature
LC 2014025665
Outlines simple but effective techniques for growing apples, plums, cherries, peaches, and other fruits on small trees that take up less space and require minimal care in home gardens.
Includes index.

634.9 Forestry

Mathews, Daniel
Trees in Trouble: Wildfires, Infestations, and Climate Change. Daniel Mathews. Counterpoint Press 2020. 256 pages : Illustration
ISBN 9781640091351
Grades: Adult   634.9
1. Forest management 2. Trees 3. Climate change 4. Forests 5. Forestry 6. Forest ecology 7. Forest fires 8. The West (United States) 9. Nature writing — Environmental issues
LC 2019017930
The author of The Natural History of the Pacific Northwest Mountains examines the devastating effects of climate change in the Western and Rocky Mountain states, drawing on in-depth reportage to illuminate the essential work of today's activists.
"Eco-conscious readers, even those unversed in this seemingly niche subject, will be intrigued and enlightened by Matthews's thoughtful work." —*Publishers Weekly*
Includes bibliographical references and index.

Reid, John W.
Ever Green: Saving Big Forests to Save the Planet. John W. Reid and Thomas E. Lovejoy. W.W. Norton & Company 2022. 320 p.
ISBN 9781324006039
Grades: Adult   634.9
1. Forests 2. Conservation of natural resources 3. Global environmental change 4. Forestry 5. Nature Writing — Environmental Issues
LC 2021050573
Climage change.
"With stunning photographs, lively anecdotes, fresh perspectives, spirited prose, and realistic and just solutions, this is deeply informative and inspiring forest advocacy." —*Booklist*
Includes bibliographical references and index.

635 Garden crops (Horticulture)

Bellamy, Andrea
Small-Space Vegetable Gardens: Growing Great Edibles in Containers, Raised Beds, and Small Plots. Andrea Bellamy. Timber Press 2014. 213 pages : Color; Illustration
ISBN 9781604695472
Grades: Adult   635
1. Vegetable gardening 2. Arts and Entertainment — Crafts and hobbies — Garden and nature
LC 2014009485
Offers advice, tips, and techniques on choosing a space to garden, how to care for the plants, and preparing the soil.

"Recommended for readers interested in gardening on a smaller scale or growing food where lack of physical space is challenging." —*Library Journal*
Includes bibliographical references and index.

Belsinger, Susan
Grow Your Own Herbs: The 40 Best Culinary Varieties for Home Gardens. Susan Belsinger and Arthur O. Tucker; with photographs by Shawn Linehan. Timber Press 2019. 201 pages : Color; Illustration
   ISBN 9781604699296
Grades: Adult   635
   1. Cooking (Herbs) 2. Herb gardening 3. Herbs 4. Recipes 5. Arts and Entertainment — Crafts and hobbies — Garden and nature 6. Food writing — Cooking and cookbooks — Ingredients
                                                  LC Bl2019015117
Provides basic gardening information, including soil, watering and potting for growing over 40 herbs in your own backyard, including basil, bay laurel, lemon verbena and tarragon, along with instructions for preserving, storing and using them in recipes.
Includes bibliographical references (pages 190-191) and index.

Bohmig, Franz
   ★ *The Month-by-Month Gardening Guide: Daily Advice for Growing Flowers, Vegetables, Herbs & Houseplants.* Franz Böhmig; translated by Michael Ashdown. Timber Press 2022. 422 pages : Color; Illustration
   ISBN 9781643261416
Grades: Adult   635
   1. Gardening 2. Vegetable gardens 3. House plants 4. Herbs 5. Flowers 6. Arts and Entertainment — Crafts and hobbies — Garden and nature
                                                  LC 2021042436
Sharing thousands of tasks and chores broken down for every week of the year, this must-have primer on what to do and when covers vegetables, herbs, flowers and houseplants, and is for both new and experienced gardeners alike.
"This is the thirtieth German edition—and the first English-language edition—of a compendium originally published in Germany in 1964....Overall, a volume bursting with useful advice, especially for new gardeners." —*Booklist*
Includes index.

Coleman, Eliot
   ★ *The New Organic Grower: A Master's Manual of Tools and Techniques for the Home and Market Gardener.* Eliot Coleman; photographs by Barbara Damrosch. Chelsea Green Publishing 2018. xi, 288 p. : Color; Illustration
   ISBN 9781603588171
Grades: Adult   635
   1. Vegetable gardening 2. Organic gardening 3. Truck farming 4. Organic farming 5. Science writing — General
                                                  LC 2018015247
Shares information on soil, farm economics and labor, crop planning, equipment, green manures, tillage, organic fertilizers, pests, and livestock.
"This thirtieth-anniversary edition of a foundational book on small-scale organic growing has been revised and updated to reflect the changes that have happened in the intervening years." —*Booklist*
Includes bibliographical references (pages 261-275) and index.

Cranshaw, Whitney
Garden Insects of North America: The Ultimate Guide to Backyard Bugs. Whitney Cranshaw and David Shetlar. Princeton University Press 2017. 704 p.
   ISBN 9780691167442
Grades: Adult   635
   1. Garden pests 2. Nature writing — Animal Studies 3. Reference — General
                                                  LC 2017013286
This second edition of Garden Insects of North America solidifies its place as the most comprehensive guide to the common insects, mites, and other "bugs" found in the backyards and gardens of the United States and Canada. Featuring 3,300 full-color photos and concise, detailed text, this fully revised book covers the hundreds of species of insects and mites associated with fruits and vegetables, shade trees and shrubs, flowers and ornamental plants, and turfgrass—from aphids and bumble bees to leafhoppers and mealybugs to woollybears and yellowjacket wasps—and much more. This new edition also provides a greatly expanded treatment of common pollinators and flower visitors, the natural enemies of garden pests, and the earthworms, insects, and other arthropods that help with decomposing plant matter in the garden.
Includes bibliographical references and index.

Durber, Sarah
Make Your Own Indoor Garden. Sarah Durber. White Owl 2021. 112 pages : Illustration
   ISBN 9781526774583
Grades: Adult   635
   1. House plants 2. Indoor gardening 3. Arts and Entertainment — Crafts and hobbies — Garden and nature
This book aims to cover the most commonly asked questions by new plant owners and will help people who want to have more greenery in their lives but don't know where to start. It will advise on the best plant for a variety of home conditions so that everyone should be able to find plants that suit their space. Having and maintaining an indoor garden can be possible for anyone, the book will give you step by step guides to creating and designing your own terrariums, cacti & succulent gardens and even kokedamas (Japanese for Moss Ball).
"A useful resource for anyone who wants a photo-ready plant display, particularly if they need help with getting started or plant maintenance." —*Library Journal*

Erickson, Laura
   ★ *100 Plants to Feed the Birds: Turn Your Home Garden into a Healthy Bird Habitat.* Laura Erickson. Storey Publishing 2022. 256 pages : Color; Illustration
   ISBN 9781635864380
Grades: Adult   635
   1. Bird attracting 2. Gardening 3. Birds 4. Plants 5. Nature Writing — Flowers and plants 6. Nature Writing — Animal studies — Birds and birding
                                                  LC 2022030265
In-depth profiles offer planting and care guidance for 100 native plant species that provide food and shelter for birds throughout the year, from winter all the way through breeding and migrating periods."
"Deeply engaging photos of birds and plants and actionable suggestions make this a winner. It is the kind of book readers treasure once found, so put it on display and be ready for more requests for books on bird gardening." —*Library Journal*
Includes index.

Frey, Kate
Ground Rules: 100 Easy Lessons for Growing a More Glorious Garden. Kate Frey. Timber Press 2018. Color; Illustration
   ISBN 9781604698787
Grades: Adult   635
   1. Gardening 2. Essays 3. Arts and Entertainment — Crafts and hobbies — Garden and nature
                                                  LC 2018024164
An expert sustainable gardener and biodiversity farm consultant outlines 100 simple rules for a thriving home garden, touching on subjects ranging from healthy soil and strategic watering to attracting birds and when to re-pot a container.
Outlines one hundred rules for a thriving home garden, touching on subjects ranging from healthy soil and strategic watering to attracting birds and when to re-pot a container.
Includes bibliographical references and index.

Holmes, Kier
The Garden Refresh: How to Give Your Yard Big Impact on a Small Budget. Kier Holmes. Timber Press 2022. 255 pages : Color; Illustration
   ISBN 9781643260815
Grades: Adult   635
   1. Gardening 2. Arts and Entertainment — Crafts and hobbies — Garden and nature 3. House and Home — Outdoor areas

ESSENTIAL AND RECOMMENDED TITLES
635 Garden crops (Horticulture)

LC 2021049395

Overflowing with design tips, plant selection and how to address problematic situations, this accessible guide offers all of the essential information to creative a productive and lush garden that can be used and enjoyed.

"Holmes's easygoing style will get any gardener's creativity sparking." —*Publishers Weekly*

Includes index.

Iannotti, Marie
The Beginner's Guide to Growing Heirloom Vegetables: The 100 Easiest-to-grow, Tastiest Vegetables for Your Garden. by Marie Iannotti. Timber Press 2011. 250 p. : Color illustration
ISBN 9781604691887
Grades: Adult   635
1. Vegetable gardening 2. Vegetables 3. Arts and Entertainment — Crafts and hobbies — Garden and nature

LC 2011018441

Presents information on growing one hundred heirloom vegetables, providing advice on germination, exposure, spacing, soil, and harvesting for each variety.

Includes bibliographical references (p. 242-243) and index.

Jabbour, Niki
★ *Groundbreaking Food Gardens: 73 Plans That Will Change the Way You Grow Your Garden.* Niki Jabbour. Storey Pub. 2014. 263 p. : Color illustration
ISBN 9781612120614
Grades: Adult   635
1. Food crops 2. Fruit 3. Vegetable gardening 4. Vegetables 5. Arts and Entertainment — Crafts and hobbies — Garden and nature

LC 2013030517

Featuring contributions from such gardening superstars as Amy Stewart, Jessi Bloom and Joe Lampl, this must-have gardening resource presents 73 plans for unique and inspiring food gardens along with photographs, plant lists, the story behind the design and more.

Presents seventy-three plans for unique food gardens along with photographs, plant lists, and the story behind the design.

"Every plan is accompanied by full-color illustrations, growing tips, and tweakable lists of crop possibilities. The abundance of creative advice here will help perk up the gardens of both novice and professional growers." —*Booklist*

Includes bibliographical references and index.

Growing Under Cover: Techniques for a More Productive, Weather-Resistant, Pest-Free Vegetable Garden. Niki Jabbour. Storey Publishing 2020. 215 pages : Illustration; Color
ISBN 9781635861310
Grades: Adult   635
1. Vegetable gardening 2. Arts and Entertainment — Crafts and hobbies — Garden and nature

LC 2020028928

Niki Jabbour shows how to use row covers, shade cloth, low tunnels, cold frames, hoophouses, and other protective structures to create controlled growing spaces for vegetables to thrive.

"Her guidance will prove invaluable for vegetable gardeners determined to safeguard and prolong a robust harvest throughout the year." —*Publishers Weekly*

Includes index.

Niki Jabbour's Veggie Garden Remix: 224 New Plants to Shake up Your Garden and Add Variety, Flavor, and Fun. Niki Jabbour. Storey Publishing 2018. 231 pages : Color; Illustration
ISBN 9781612126708
Grades: Adult   635
1. Vegetables 2. Vegetable gardening 3. Arts and Entertainment — Crafts and hobbies — Garden and nature

LC 2017034219

Presents planting and growing advice for 224 varieties of unusual vegetable and herbs from around the world, including the Cape gooseberry, Middle Eastern molokhia, Asian celtuce, Japanese winter squash, and Thai basil.

"Loaded with lush photos throughout, this attractive book will appeal to gardeners and gourmands alike." —*Publishers Weekly*

Includes index.

Laing, Olivia
The Garden Against Time: In Search of a Common Paradise. Olivia Laing. W.W. Norton & Company 2024. 336 p.
ISBN 9780393882001
Grades: Adult   635
1. Laing, Olivia 2. Women authors 3. Gardens 4. Gardening 5. Effect of humans on nature 6. Colonialism 7. Social classes 8. Paradise 9. Utopias 10. Imagination 11. History 12. Social life and customs 13. Great Britain 14. Nature Writing — Gardens 15. History writing — Microhistory 16. Arts and Entertainment — Writing and Publishing

From the improbable queer utopia conjured by Derek Jarman on the beach at Dungeness to the fertile vision of a common Eden propagated by William Morris, new modes of living can and have been attempted amidst the flower beds, experiments that could prove vital in the coming era of climate change. Olivia Laing's The Garden Against Time is a humming, glowing tapestry, a beautiful and exacting account of the abundant pleasures and possibilities of gardens: not as a place to hide from the world but as a site of encounter and discovery, bee-loud and pollen-laden.

"Laing examines how historical British gardens reflect the periods in which they were designed and contemporaneous understandings of paradise on Earth? This is well worth seeking out." —*Publishers Weekly*

Lavelle, Christine
How to Create a Wildlife Garden: Encouraging Birds, Bees, Butterflies and Nature into Your Outside Space. Christine and Mick Lavelle. Lorenz Books 2021. 256 p.
ISBN 9780754835202
Grades: Adult   635
1. Gardening to attract wildlife 2. Gardening 3. Wildlife attracting 4. Arts and Entertainment — Crafts and hobbies — Garden and nature 5. Nature Writing — Gardens

"Gardeners of all stripes will appreciate the encouraging advice on how to foster a deep and mutually beneficial relationship with the natural world." —*Publishers Weekly*

Includes index; Originally published: London: Lorenz, 2007.

Lavoipierre, Frederique
Garden Allies: The Insects, Birds, and Other Animals That Keep Your Garden Beautiful and Thriving. Frederique Lavoipierre. Timber Press 2021. 304 p.
ISBN 9781643260082
Grades: Adult   635
1. Gardening 2. Horticulture 3. Life cycles 4. Insects 5. Insect pollinators 6. Agricultural pests 7. Nature writing — Gardens

An illustrated guide to the animals and insects that live in our yards and gardens and act as helpful friends by pollinating and keeping pests in check and includes information on welcoming and nurturing these creatures.

"All in all, an excellent resource for any gardener willing to press pause before turning to the pesticide." —*Booklist*

LeHoullier, Craig
Epic Tomatoes: How to Select & Grow the Best Varieties of All Time. Craig LeHoullier. Storey Publishing 2015. 255 p. : Color; Illustration
ISBN 9781612124643
Grades: Adult   635
1. Tomatoes 2. Arts and Entertainment — Crafts and hobbies — Garden and nature

LC 2014029010

PUBLIC LIBRARY CORE COLLECTION: NONFICTION
Twentieth Edition

Offers advice on growing and harvesting tomatoes and takes a look at the author's thirty-three favorite varieties, including the Green Giant, Red Zebra, and Yellow Oxheart.

Includes bibliographical references and index.

Loades, Greg
The Modern Cottage Garden: A Fresh Approach to a Classic Style. Greg Loades; with photography by Neil Hepworth. Timber Press 2020. 227 pages : Color; Illustration
ISBN 9781604699081
Grades: Adult   635
1. Gardening 2. Plants 3. Arts and Entertainment — Crafts and hobbies — Garden and nature
LC Bl2020052338

The editor of the Alpine Gardener presents a new style of planting, in this design-forward guide that teaches gardeners how to blend together big, colorful blooms and a striking mix of grasses and native plants into one space.

"Loades, editor of the Alpine Gardener, inspires with this delightful exploration of the process of creating a 'Modern cottage garden'. . . . Gorgeous, full-page color photos of gardens designed using Loades's approach will propel readers to the nearest plant nursery." —*Publishers Weekly*

Includes bibliographic references (page 214) and index.

McLaughlin, Chris
The Good Garden: How to Nurture Pollinators, Soil, Native Wildlife, and Healthy Food—All in Your Own Backyard. Chris McLaughlin. Island Press 2023. 300 pages : Color; Illustration
ISBN 9781642832150
Grades: Adult   635
1. Gardening 2. Sustainability 3. Organic gardening 4. Vegetable gardening 5. Gardening to attract wildlife 6. Nature Writing — Gardens
LC Bl2023003295

Drawing from established traditions, such as permaculture and French intensive gardening, and McLaughlin's hard-earned experience, The Good Garden is a joyful guide for newbies and experienced gardeners alike. It will teach you the fundamentals, including how to choose the right plant varieties for your microclimate, and proven methods to fight pests without chemicals. You will also discover the nuances of developing a green thumb, from picking species to attract specific types of pollinators to composting techniques based on time available. Lovely four-color photography will show you good gardening in action.

"Enhanced with numerous lovely color photographs, this inviting book is a wonderful overview on sustainable gardening." —*Library Journal*

Includes bibliographical references (pages 271-283) and index.

Murphy, Emily
Grow Now: How We Can Save Our Health, Communities, and Planet-one Garden at a Time. Emily Murphy. Timber Press 2022. 247 p.
ISBN 9781643260471
Grades: Adult   635
1. Gardening 2. Organic gardening 3. Arts and Entertainment — Crafts and hobbies — Garden and nature 4. Nature Writing — Gardens
LC 2021049339

A regenerative organic gardener, photographer, podcaster and designer shares her simple principles for regenerative gardening to foster biodiversity and improve soil health by choosing plants that cycle more carbon back into the earth and vegetables that improve soil fertility.

"With a list of related sources and a bibliography, Murphy offers a positive and doable approach to addressing our climate crisis." —*Booklist*

Includes index.

Pleasant, Barbara
Homegrown Pantry: A Gardener's Guide to Selecting the Best Varieties & Planting the Perfect Amounts for What You Want to Eat Year-Round. Barbara Pleasant. Storey Publishing 2017. 319 p. : Color; Illustration
ISBN 9781612125787
Grades: Adult   635
1. Food crops 2. Food 3. Vegetables 4. Herbs 5. Fruit 6. Canning and preserving 7. Arts and Entertainment — Crafts and hobbies — Garden and nature 8. Food writing — Cooking and cookbooks — Methods
LC 2016055527

Presents guidance on how to stock a pantry for year-round use, discussing fifty-five crops and how best to harvest and preserve them, including canning, pickling, and fermenting, and at what amounts.

Includes index.

★ *Starter Vegetable Gardens: 24 No-Fail Plans for Small Organic Gardens.* Barbara Pleasant; photography by John Gruen. Storey Pub. 2010. 179 p. : Illustration; Color; Map
ISBN 9781603425292
Grades: Adult   635
1. Vegetable gardening 2. Arts and Entertainment — Crafts and hobbies — Garden and nature 3. Nature Writing — Gardens
LC 2009049114

Presents a guide to cultivating an efficient and beautiful vegetable garden, from growing seedlings to preventing diseases, and provides twenty-four different plans for optimum crop yield.

"From simple bag gardens to bountiful food cornucopias, each garden plan is laid out with precise lists of materials and plants based on detailed landscape plans suitable for small city gardens as well as larger suburban backyards. Along with year-by-year overviews that allow gardeners to anticipate growth and adapt to changes, Pleasant provides essential cultivation and maintenance techniques." —*Booklist*

Includes index.

Roach, Margaret
★ *A Way to Garden: A Hands-on Primer for Every Season.* Margaret Roach. Timber Press 2019. 336 p.
ISBN 9781604698770
Grades: Adult   635
1. Roach, Margaret 2. Gardens 3. Gardening 4. Women gardeners 5. Periodical writers 6. Podcasters 7. Plant growth 8. Autobiographies and memoirs 9. Nature Writing — Gardens 10. Nature Writing — Personal Responses
LC 2018043086

Offers practical gardening advice as well as an exploration of the underlying connections between the yearly cycles of gardening and the stages of life.

"Readers will appreciate Roach's focus on gardening as a way anyone can help make the world a better place and her approach, combining horticultural how-to and woo-hoo (her term), which balances precise learned information with ones own intuition." —*Booklist*

Includes bibliographical references and index.

Schwartz, Bobbie
Garden Renovation: Transform Your Yard into the Garden of Your Dreams. Bobbie Schwartz. Timber Press 2017. 259 pages : Illustration; Color
ISBN 9781604696127
Grades: Adult   635
1. Gardens 2. Landscape gardening 3. Gardening 4. Design and construction 5. Arts and Entertainment — Crafts and hobbies — Garden and nature 6. House and Home — Outdoor areas
LC 2016055618

A guide to garden makeovers provides information on tackling problem areas, deciding where to start, and how to choose the right plants and design plans.

Includes bibliographical references and index.

Slatalla, Michelle
Gardenista: The Definitive Guide to Stylish Outdoor Spaces. Michelle Slatalla, with the editors of Gardenista; edited by Julie Carlson; photographs by Matthew Williams. Artisan 2016. IX, 397 pages : Color; Illustration
ISBN 9781579656522
Grades: Adult   635
1. Gardens 2. Outdoor living spaces 3. Design and construction 4. House and Home — Outdoor areas
LC 2016012874

ESSENTIAL AND RECOMMENDED TITLES
635.022 Gardening — Photographs

"The end result is a display of outdoor living space that integrates plants, color, balance, design, and also functionality." —*Publishers Weekly*
Includes index.

Smith, Edward C.
The Vegetable Gardener's Bible: Discover Ed's High-Yield W-O-R-D System for All North American Gardening Regions. Edward C. Smith. Storey Pub. 2009. 351 p. : Color illustration; Color; Map
ISBN 9781603424752
Grades: Adult　　　　　　　　　　　　　　　　　　　　635
1. Organic gardening 2. Vegetable gardening 3. Arts and Entertainment — Crafts and hobbies — Garden and nature
LC 2009023862

A fully updated 10th-anniversary edition covers more vegetables, fruits and herbs than the first edition and includes full-color photos, extended-season growing advice, sections on organic gardening and solutions for small-space gardening.
First ed. published in 2000; Includes bibliographical references (p. 338) and index.

The Vegetable Gardener's Container Bible: How to Grow a Bounty of Food in Pots, Tubs, and Other Containers. Edward C. Smith. Storey Pub. 2011. 263 p. : Color illustration
ISBN 9781603429757
Grades: Adult　　　　　　　　　　　　　　　　　　　　635
1. Container gardening 2. Vegetable gardening 3. Arts and Entertainment — Crafts and hobbies — Garden and nature
LC 2010051167

Presents information about growing vegetables in containers, covering such topics as selecting suitable pots, starting plants from seeds, and managing pests and diseases, with advice on individual vegetables and herbs.
Includes index; Previously published as: Incredible vegetables from self-watering containers. North Adams, MA : Storey Pub, c2006.

Walliser, Jessica
★ *Attracting Beneficial Bugs to Your Garden: A Natural Approach to Pest Control.* Jessica Walliser. Timber Press 2014. 240 p. : Color illustration
ISBN 9781604693881
Grades: Adult　　　　　　　　　　　　　　　　　　　　635
1. Beneficial insects 2. Garden pests 3. Arts and Entertainment — Crafts and hobbies — Garden and nature
LC 2013015303

Profiles nineteen bugs which are helpful to gardeners, with descriptions, illustrations, and a list of their benefits, along with planting and zone details about thirty-nine plants which can be used to attract them.
"While the subject matter and close-up photographs of insects eating insects may make some readers squirm, dedicated gardeners will discover enough solid information and genuine motivation to finally put down their bug spray." —*Booklist*
Includes bibliographical references (p. 222-224) index.

Plant Partners: Science-Based Companion Planting Strategies for the Vegetable Garden. Jessica Walliser. Storey Publishing 2020. 205 pages : Color; Illustration
ISBN 9781635861334
Grades: Adult　　　　　　　　　　　　　　　　　　　　635
1. Vegetable gardening 2. Plants 3. Arts and Entertainment — Crafts and hobbies — Garden and nature
LC 2020029583

Plant Partners delivers a research-based rationale for companion planting, offering gardeners dozens of ways they can use scientifically tested plant partnerships to benefit the garden as a whole.
"Walliser's lively guide will aid many a horticulturally minded reader." —*Publishers Weekly*
Includes bibliographical references (pages 190-199) and index.

Webb, Leah M.
The Seven-Step Homestead: A Guide for Creating the Backyard Microfarm of Your Dreams. Leah M. Webb. Storey Publishing 2023. 231 p.
ISBN 9781635864113
Grades: Adult　　　　　　　　　　　　　　　　　　　　635
1. Gardening 2. Organic gardening 3. Vegetable gardening 4. Kitchen gardens 5. Fruit growing 6. Fruit trees 7. Chickens 8. Nature Writing — Gardens
LC 2022049891

In this one-of-a-kind guide for those who want to grow more of their own food, a homesteader and garden consultant shares her strategy for implementing a homestead plan in seven stages by starting small and gradually adding more features each year.
"A superb guide for virtually all seasons, landscapes, and gardeners." —*Booklist*
Includes index.

Ziegler, Lisa Mason
Vegetables Love Flowers: Companion Planting for Beauty and Bounty. Lisa Mason Ziegler. Cool Springs Press 2018. 176 pages : Color; Illustration
ISBN 9780760357583
Grades: Adult　　　　　　　　　　　　　　　　　　　　635
1. Flowers 2. Vegetables 3. Plants 4. Arts and Entertainment — Crafts and hobbies — Garden and nature
LC 2017043293

A guide to pairing vegetables and flowers to create a bountiful garden includes tips, timetables, and planting schedules for companion planting.
In an introduction to one of the oldest, yet most radical, ways to improve and beautify a vegetable garden, the author walks readers through the ins and outs of planting flowers and vegetables together, from how it works to which plants go together.
Includes bibliographical references and index.

635.022 Gardening — Photographs

Woods, Christopher
Gardenlust: A Botanical Tour of the World's Best New Gardens. Christopher Woods. Timber Press 2018. 414 pages : Color; Illustration
ISBN 9781604697971
Grades: Adult　　　　　　　　　　　　　　　　　　　　635.022
1. Gardens 2. Arts and Entertainment — Crafts and hobbies — Garden and nature 3. Arts and Entertainment — Photography 4. Travel writing — General
LC 2018019654

A renowned gardening authority explores the world's most beautiful gardens in an illustrated guide to over 50 locations in the Americas, Europe, Africa, Australia and Asia including the Geelong Botanic Gardens, Sunnylands Center and Gardens and the Golden Rock Inn.
A pictorial tour of the world's most innovative new gardens includes the Tree Museum in Rapperswill, Switzerland; the Aloe Farm in Hartbeespoort, South Africa; Ichiyaga Forest in Tokyo, Japan; and Mordecai Children's Garden in Denver, Colorado.
"A recommended purchase for public libraries that have patrons interested in gardening as well as those who combine gardening and travel." —*Booklist*
Includes bibliographical references and index.

635.09 Gardening — History

Obama, Michelle
American Grown: The Story of the White House Kitchen Garden and Gardens Across America. Michelle Obama. Crown Publishers 2012. 256 p.
ISBN 9780307956026
Grades: Adult　　　　　　　　　　　　　　　　　　　　635.09
1. Kitchen gardens 2. Vegetable gardening 3. Nutrition 4. Gardens 5. Washington, D.C. 6. Essays 7. Nature Writing — Gardens
LC 2012015935

A sumptuously photographed guide by the First Lady describes how her daughters and she planted a vegetable garden on the White House's South Lawn as part of an initiative to raise awareness about childhood obesity, in a reference that shares gardening tips, recipes and advice for making healthier food choices.

635.0978 Gardening — Western States (U.S.)

Dungy, Camille T.
Soil: The Story of a Black Mother's Garden. Camille T. Dungy. Simon & Schuster 2023. 272 p.
ISBN 9781982195304
Grades: Adult   635.0978
1. Dungy, Camille T, 1972- 2. Gardens 3. African American women 4. Plants 5. Multiculturalism 6. Race (social sciences) 7. Landscape 8. Motherhood 9. Environmental justice 10. Freedom 11. Nature 12. African Americans 13. Women poets 14. Colorado 15. Autobiographies and memoirs 16. Life stories — Nature and outdoors 17. Life stories — Identity — Race and ethnicity 18. Nature Writing — Gardens

"In this meditative outing, poet Dungy (Guidebook to Relative Strangers) reflects on race and history while discussing the garden she maintains outside her Colorado home....Fans of Dungy's poetry will delight in her sparkling prose, and the wide-ranging meditations highlight the connections between land, freedom, and race." —*Publishers Weekly*

635.9 Flowers and ornamental plants

Bainbridge, David A
Gardening with Less Water: Low-Tech, Low-Cost Techniques : Use up to 90% Less Water in Your Garden. David A. Bainbridge. Storey Publishing 2015. 127 pages : Color; Illustration
ISBN 9781612125824
Grades: Adult   635.9
1. Xeriscaping 2. Gardening 3. Horticulture 4. Landscape gardening 5. Water conservation 6. Nature Writing — Gardens
LC 2015036487
Presents inexpensive methods of irrigating plants with efficient water systems, discussing such techniques as clay pots, wicks, porous hoses, vertical pipes, and grow tubes.

"Beyond soaker hoses, the title offers a varied range of scalable options for growers of all types committed to the exploration and use of optimal water-sparing techniques." —*Library Journal*
Includes index.

Baldwin, Debra Lee
Succulents Simplified: Growing, Designing, and Crafting with 100 Easy-Care Varieties. Debra Lee Baldwin. Timber Press 2013. 272 p. : Color illustration
ISBN 9781604693935
Grades: Adult   635.9
1. Drought-tolerant plants 2. Landscape gardening 3. Succulent plants 4. Arts and Entertainment — Crafts and hobbies — Garden and nature 5. Arts and Entertainment — Crafts and hobbies
LC 2012038829
A complete primer on choosing, growing and designing with succulents. Along with gorgeous photos packed with design ideas, Debra offers her top 100 plant picks and explains how to grow and care for succulents no matter where you live. Step-by-step projects, including a cake-stand centerpiece, special-occasion bouquets, a vertical garden, and a succulent topiary sphere, will inspire you to express your individual style—.

"This fresh and entertaining volume certainly deserves a green thumbs up." —*Library Journal*
Includes bibliographical references (p. 260) and index.

Benzakein, Erin
Floret Farm's Cut Flower Garden: Grow, Harvest & Arrange Stunning Seasonal Blooms. Erin Benzakein with Julie Chai; photographs by Michaele M. Waite. Chronicle Books 2017. 308 pages : Color; Illustration
ISBN 9781452145761
Grades: Adult   635.9
1. Flower arrangement 2. Arts and Entertainment — Crafts and hobbies — Garden and nature 3. Arts and Entertainment — Crafts and hobbies
LC 2016011482
A guide to arranging fresh cut flowers year-round features advice for planting, cultivating, and harvesting over one hundred and seventy-five flower varieties, along with step-by-step instructions for floral decor for every season.

Floret Farm's Discovering Dahlias: A Guide to Growing and Arranging Magnificent Blooms. Erin Benzakein with Jill Jorgensen and Julie Chai; photographs by Chris Benzakein. Chronicle Books 2021. 223 pages : Color; Illustration
ISBN 9781452181752
Grades: Adult   635.9
1. Flower gardening 2. Flower arrangement 3. Arts and Entertainment — Crafts and hobbies — Garden and nature
LC 2020024459
The renowned floral designer and best-selling author of Floret Farm's Cut Flower Garden shares professional secrets for growing, cultivating and arranging the versatile dahlia, providing a variety classification overview and step-by-step instructions for creating show-stopping bouquets.
Includes index.

Branhagen, Alan
Native Plants of the Midwest: A Comprehensive Guide to the Best 500 Species for the Garden. Alan Branhagen. Timber Press 2016. 440 p. : Color; Illustration; Map
ISBN 9781604695939
Grades: Adult   635.9
1. Native plants for cultivation 2. Arts and Entertainment — Crafts and hobbies — Garden and nature 3. House and Home — Sustainable living
LC Oc2018091642
"As more people are incorporating more natives in their landscapes for their own pleasure, pollinators, and birds, this book will be used by novice and experienced gardeners alike." —*Booklist*
Includes bibliographical references and index.

Brown, George E.
Essential Pruning Techniques: Trees, Shrubs, and Conifers. George E. Brown; revised and enlarged by Tony Kirkham; with photography from Andrea Jones and a new foreword by Hugh Johnson. Timber Press 2017. 404 p.
ISBN 9781604692884
Grades: Adult   635.9
1. Trees 2. Shrubs 3. Conifers 4. Pruning 5. Nature writing — Gardens 6. Nature writing — Flowers and plants
LC 2016017684
Pruning is an indispensable part of garden maintenance, but it is also one of the most difficult. Successful pruning requires a thorough knowledge of a plant's growth and flowering habits. In Essential Pruning Techniques, Tony Kirkham, the head of the arboretum and gardens at the Royal Botanic Gardens, Kew shares his decades of knowledge and expertise and expands on the groundbreaking work done by George E. Brown. Step-by-step photographs clearly show the general principles of pruning, and profiles of 379 woody plants include advice on habit, attributes, reasons for pruning, and the best time to prune. Essential Pruning Techniques is a must-have reference for home gardeners and professionals.

"All in all, an even more excellent text for shaping trees, shrubs, and conifers." —*Booklist*

This work incorporates portions of The Pruning of Trees, Shrubs and Conifers, first published in 1972 by Faber and Faber Limited ... by the estate of George E. Brown; Includes bibliographical references and index.

ESSENTIAL AND RECOMMENDED TITLES
635.9 Flowers and ornamental plants

Carey, Jenny Rose
The Ultimate Flower Gardener's Guide: How to Combine Shape, Color, and Texture to Create the Garden of Your Dreams. Jenny Rose Carey. Timber Press 2022. 363 pages : Color; Illustration
ISBN 9781643260389
Grades: Adult 635.9
1. Flower gardening 2. Gardens 3. Flowers 4. Arts and Entertainment — Crafts and hobbies — Garden and nature
LC 2021042434
Proposing a holistic approach to flower gardening with a refreshing twist, a renowned gardener brings flower shape and texture to the forefront, instead of concentrating on color, helping homeowners make plant choices that come together in an aesthetically pleasing way.
"A detailed and handy reference." —*Booklist*
Includes index.

Chapman, Baylor
★ *Decorating with Plants: What to Choose, Ways to Style, and How to Make Them Thrive.* Baylor Chapman; photographs by Aubrie Pick. Artisan 2019. 272 pages : Color; Illustration
ISBN 9781579657765
Grades: Adult 635.9
1. House plants 2. Plants 3. Arts and Entertainment — Crafts and hobbies — Textiles and needlework 4. House and Home — Interior Decorating and Furnishings
LC 2018030427
Focusing on houseplants, which are more popular than ever before, the founder of a San Francisco-based plant design studio presents this complete guide to |greening| any space along with ideas and inspiration for adding plants to every room in the home.
"Chapmans inviting tone mixed with the gorgeous photography makes for an ideal volume for the brown- and green-thumbed alike." —*Publishers Weekly*
Includes index.

Chezar, Ariella
★ *Seasonal Flower Arranging: Fill Your Home with Blooms, Branches, and Foraged Materials All Year Round.* Ariella Chezar with Julie Michaels; photography by Erin Kunkel. Ten Speed Press 2019. xvi, 204 pages : Color; Illustration
ISBN 9780399580765
Grades: Adult 635.9
1. Flower gardening 2. Flower arrangement 3. Arts and Entertainment — Crafts and hobbies
LC 2018023747
Provides step-by-step instructions for thirty-nine themed floral arrangements and projects that reflect the changing seasons and the wild beauty of nature.
"The combination of instructions, photographs, and elegant prose makes for a delightful companion for gardeners, florists, or armchair naturalists." —*Publishers Weekly*
Includes index.

Cowden, Meg McAndrews
★ *Plant Grow Harvest Repeat: Grow a Bounty of Vegetables, Fruits, and Flowers by Mastering the Art of Succession Planting.* Meg McAndrews Cowden. Timber Press 2022. 287 pages : Color; Illustration
ISBN 9781643260617
Grades: Adult 635.9
1. Organic gardening 2. Gardening 3. Arts and Entertainment — Crafts and hobbies — Garden and nature
LC 2021049337
An organic gardener teaches you how to implement succession into your home garden, inspiring you to create an even more productive, beautiful and enjoyable garden across the seasons.
"This master class will entice seasoned gardeners and newbies alike." —*Publishers Weekly*
Includes bibliographical references (page 277) and index.

Deardorff, David C
What's Wrong with My Houseplant?: Save Your Indoor Plants with 100% Organic Solutions. David Deardoff and Kathryn Wadsworth. Timber Press 2016. 292 p. : Color; Illustration
ISBN 9781604696332
Grades: Adult 635.9
1. House plants 2. Organic gardening 3. Arts and Entertainment — Crafts and hobbies — Garden and nature
LC 2015013389
Provides advice on caring for over one hundred thirty different houseplants, including watering, sunlight exposure, potting space, and organic solutions to common plant problems.
Includes bibliographical references and index.

Druse, Kenneth
The New Shade Garden. Ken Druse. Stewart, Tabori & Chang 2015. 255 pages : Color; Illustration
ISBN 9781617691041
Grades: Adult 635.9
1. Arts and Entertainment — Crafts and hobbies — Garden and nature 2. Science writing — General
LC Bl2015015164
Presents a comprehensive guide to creating a shade garden with emphasis on the adjustments necessary for a changing climate, offering advice on such subjects as sustainable watering, container gardening, and dealing with foraging animals.
"Even in cutlines, his delight in gardening percolates: for example, he notes attentively that prairie dropseed smells like popcorn. Druse sells shade masterfully." —*Publishers Weekly*
Includes index.

Edwards, Adrienne L.
Firescaping Your Home: A Manual for Readiness in Wildfire Country. Adrienne Edwards and Rachel Schleiger. Timber Press 2023. 263 pages : Illustration; Color
ISBN 9781643261355
Grades: Adult 635.9
1. Landscape gardening 2. Wildfires 3. Houses 4. Natural disasters 5. Native plants 6. Landscape plants 7. California 8. Oregon 9. Washington (State) 10. House and Home — Remodeling and renovation 11. House and Home — Outdoor areas 12. Reference — Instructional materials
LC 2022034284
There is currently no comprehensive guide to help homeowners minimize wildfire risks while optimizing the ecological integrity of wildland areas. Living in fire-prone landscapes should not mean that you must scrape all vegetation hundreds of feet away from structures. This book will empower readers to evaluate fire risks on their own property and take simple, actionable steps to mitigate them. The book will include specific recommendations, examples, and resources for planting and maintenance, making it an essential resource for western homeowners.
"Ecologists Edwards and Schleiger debut with a solid manual on how California, Oregon, and Washington State residents can make their homes fire resistant and landscape responsibly…West Coast denizens will want to study up." —*Publishers Weekly*
Includes bibliographical references (pages 236-247) and index.

Gidding, John
At Home with Nature: A Guide to Sustainable, Natural Landscaping. John Gidding. Countryman Press, an imprint of W.W. Norton & Company 2023. 192 pages : Illustration; Color
ISBN 9781682687093
Grades: Adult 635.9
1. Native plants 2. Gardening 3. Natural landscaping 4. Landscape architecture 5. Landscape gardening 6. United States 7. House and Home — Outdoor areas 8. Nature Writing — Gardens
LC Bl2023005605

Go from manicured lawn to eco-conscious garden with this step-by-step guide from HGTV star John Gidding.

"Readers looking to upgrade their yards while making them more sustainable will find this to be a great starting point." —*Publishers Weekly*

Includes index.

Hay Hinsdale, Emily L.

What Is My Plant Telling Me?: An Illustrated Guide to Houseplants and How to Keep Them Alive. Emily L. Hinsdale; illustrations by Loni Harris. Simon Element 2022. xvi, 191 pages : Color; Illustration

ISBN 9781982189815

Grades: Adult   **635.9**

1. House plants 2. Indoor gardening 3. Nature Writing — Flowers and plants 4. Arts and Entertainment — Crafts and hobbies — Garden and nature

LC 2021043099

Keep your house plants alive and thriving with this illustrated, accessible guide to popular house plants for new and experienced plant-parents alike.

"Budding green thumbs will find these handy tips worth returning to." —*Publishers Weekly*

Includes index.

Helm, Ben

The Water Gardener's Bible: A Step-by-Step Guide to Building, Planting, Stocking, and Maintaining a Backyard Water Garden. Ben Helm, Kelly Billing. Rodale 2008. 192 p. : Illustration; Color; Map

ISBN 9781594866586

Grades: Adult   **635.9**

1. Arts and Entertainment — Crafts and hobbies — Garden and nature

LC 2007045129

An accessible reference to water gardening provides guidelines for creating and managing gardens of any size, counseling readers on such details as water-garden kits, selecting aquatic plants and fish, and electrical and child safety.

Includes bibliographical references and index.

Isabel, Agatha

Houseplant Hookups: All the Dirt You Need to Find the Perfect Match. Agatha Isabel; illustrated by Mai Ly Degnan. Gibbs Smith 2023. 111 p.

ISBN 9781423663461

Grades: Adult   **635.9**

1. House plants 2. Indoor gardening 3. Nature craft 4. Nature Writing — Flowers and plants

Houseplant Hookups approaches plant care like modern dating. You'll find out how to choose the right plant partner, where to find them, and what happens when they come home with you. You'll learn how to start a loving relationship and watch it grow—literally…. These 35 plant profiles are far more helpful than your average Tinder bio, so you'll be able to decide if a relationship with a fiddle-leaf fig is more likely to be a fling or a forever kind of love.

"Isabel shares her expertise and knowledge of houseplants in this amusing, informative book, best for neophyte horticulturists who might not yet have a green thumb." —*Library Journal*

Includes index.

Johnsen, Jan

★ *Gardentopia: Design Basics for Creating Beautiful Outdoor Spaces*. Jan Johnsen. The Countryman Press, a division of W. W. Norton & Company 2019. 286 p.

ISBN 9781682683965

Grades: Adult   **635.9**

1. Landscape gardening 2. Arts and Entertainment — Crafts and hobbies — Garden and nature

LC 2018050566

Includes index.

Keville, Kathi

The Aromatherapy Garden: Growing Fragrant Plants for Happiness and Well-being. Kathi Keville. Timber Press 2016. 276 pages : Color; Illustration

ISBN 9781604695496

Grades: Adult   **635.9**

1. Aromatherapy 2. Arts and Entertainment — Crafts and hobbies — Garden and nature 3. Science writing — Medicine and health — Alternative medicine

LC 2015029697

Presents a guide to creating a garden of fragrant plants, with descriptions and therapeutic uses for each plant and advice for making herbal blends and vinegars, teas, scents, and body oils.

"With such rich descriptions, readers will long for the actual aroma." —*Publishers Weekly*

Includes index.

Martin, Tovah

★ *The Indestructible Houseplant: 200 Beautiful Plants That Everyone Can Grow*. Tovah Martin; photographs by Kindra Clineff. Timber Press 2015. 288 pages : Color; Illustration

ISBN 9781604695014

Grades: Adult   **635.9**

1. House plants 2. Arts and Entertainment — Crafts and hobbies — Garden and nature 3. House and Home — Interior Decorating and Furnishings

LC 2014042918

An expert gardener and best-selling author offers plant profiles with information on light, water care and blooming times for an array of hardy, pretty, resilient and easy-to-find indoor plants that even the most neglectful gardener can grow.

Profiles two hundred house plants that are low-maintenance and good for beginners, and includes tips on potting, watering, fertilization, and home decorating using house plants.

"The green-thumb-challenged will give Martin a standing ovation for this much-needed book created for windowsill-gardener wannabees desiring plants to survive tough love and transform lives. New England-based Martin appreciates interest in an indoor gardening approach requiring minimal time investment." —*Booklist*

Includes index.

The New Terrarium: Creating Beautiful Displays for Plants and Nature. Tovah Martin; photographs by Kindra Clineff. Clarkson Potter/Publishers 2009. 176 p. : Illustration; Color

ISBN 9780307407313

Grades: Adult   **635.9**

1. Terrariums 2. Arts and Entertainment — Crafts and hobbies — Garden and nature

LC 2008027713

One of America's favorite gardeners introduces the whimsical yet practical world of gardens under glass—the perfect way to spark creativity while incorporating favorite plants in a home.

Includes index.

The Unexpected Houseplant: 220 Extraordinary Choices for Every Spot in Your Home. Tovah Martin; photography by Kindra Clineff. Timber Press 2012. 328 p.

ISBN 9781604694260

Grades: Adult   **635.9**

1. House plants 2. Indoor gardening 3. Arts and Entertainment — Crafts and hobbies — Garden and nature 4. House and Home — Interior Decorating and Furnishings

LC Oc2012633870

The Unexpected Houseplant, by renowned plant authority Tovah Martin, offers a revolutionary approach to houseplants. Instead of the typical varieties, Martin suggests hundreds of creative choices—brilliant spring bulbs, lush perennials brought in from the garden, quirky succulents, and flowering vines and small trees. Along with loads of visual inspiration, you will learn how to make unusual selections, where to best position plants in the home, and valuable tips on watering, feeding, and pruning.

"All indoor plant hobbyists in every geographic area will enjoy and learn from this book. Its' fresh approach deserves a thumbs-up." —*Library Journal*

Includes bibliographical references and index.

ESSENTIAL AND RECOMMENDED TITLES
635.9 Flowers and ornamental plants

McIndoe, Andrew
*The **Creative** Shrub Garden: Eye-Catching Combinations for Year-Round Interest.* Andy McIndoe. Timber Press 2014. 247 p. : Color illustration
ISBN 9781604694345
Grades: Adult 635.9
1. Shrubs 2. Arts and Entertainment — Crafts and hobbies — Garden and nature
LC 2013040985
A professional garden designer describes the benefits of planting low-maintenance, hardy shrubs to beautify a home and garden and offers tips for choosing the best types based on climate, soil type and pruning requirements.
Describes the benefits of planting low-maintenance, hardy shrubs to beautify a home and garden and offers tips for choosing the best types based on climate, soil type, and pruning requirements.
"A plant directory; alphabetical guide for planting and maintaining various shrubs, including container planting; suggested readings; and an index round out this comprehensive text sure to please gardeners who love perennials." —*Booklist*
Includes bibliographical references (p. 235) and index.

Offolter, Enid
Welcome to the Jungle: Rare Tropical Houseplants to Collect, Grow, and Love. Enid Offolter; photographs by Sonya Revell. Ten Speed Press 2022. 217 pages : Color; Illustration
ISBN 9781984859945
Grades: Adult 635.9
1. House plants 2. Tropical plants 3. Plants 4. Arts and Entertainment — Crafts and hobbies — Garden and nature
LC 2021034250
Called "the Houseplant Queen" by the New York Times, the owner and founder of NSE Tropicals plant nursery, through tips, professional advice, behind-the-scenes stories from fellow plant collectors, and inspiration, shows you how to up your plant game with 50 highly sought-after botanicals.
"Offolter, owner of a tropical plant nursery, shares her love for collecting and looking after houseplants in this smart guide….Offolter's buoyant approach will inspire casual and serious collectors alike." —*Publishers Weekly*
Includes indexes and glossary.

Ondra, Nancy J
Container Theme Gardens: 42 Combinations, Each Using 5 Perfectly Matched Plants. Nancy J. Ondra, photography by Rob Cardillo. Storey Publishing 2016. 267 p. : Color; Illustration
ISBN 9781612123981
Grades: Adult 635.9
1. Container gardening 2. Arts and Entertainment — Crafts and hobbies — Garden and nature
LC 2015031345
Demonstrates how to create designer container gardens using groups of plants selected to be ideal growing companions, sharing recommendations for various preferences from a simple salad garden to a combination for attracting hummingbirds.
Includes bibliographical references and index.

Penick, Pam
*The **Water-Saving** Garden: How to Grow a Gorgeous Garden with a Lot Less Water.* Pam Penick. Ten Speed Press 2016. 233 pages : Color; Illustration
ISBN 9781607747932
Grades: Adult 635.9
1. Xeriscaping 2. Water conservation 3. Drought-tolerant plants
LC 2015025964
A guide to growing gardens in drought-prone areas teaches home gardeners how to use minimal water to achieve maximum results, from using permeable paving and irrigation to limiting grass and timing the planting season.
"With the growing popularity of permaculture and sustainable cultivation techniques, Penick's how-to offers gardeners at all levels of experience much timely advice on working with one of the Earth's most precious natural resources." —*Booklist*
Includes bibliographical references and index.

Pleasant, Barbara
*The **Complete** Houseplant Survival Manual: Essential Know-How for Keeping (Not Killing) More Than 160 Indoor Plants.* Barbara Pleasant; photography by Rosemary Kautzky. Storey Pub. 2005. xvii, 365 p. : Color illustration
ISBN 9781580175692
Grades: Adult 635.9
1. House plants 2. Arts and Entertainment — Crafts and hobbies — Garden and nature
LC 2005014205
A definitive home gardening handbook provides comprehensive, hands-on advice on how to care for 160 common houseplants, with helpful information on how to identify different plants, how to select the right container and soil mixture, lighting needs, feeding and watering, propagation, and how to identify causes, symptoms, and remedies for common problems on a plant by plant basis.
Provides hands-on advice on how to care for 160 common houseplants, with information on containers, soil mixtures, lighting needs, feeding and watering, and propagation.
"Following an enlightening introduction that discusses the history, uses, and benefits that houseplants bestow, the manual is divided into three main sections. The first two are plant directories offering in-depth plant profiles of first flowering, then foliage, houseplants. The third is an extensive compilation of houseplant-care topics, from acclimatization to watering. With vivid color photographs, precise illustrations, appendixes listing helpful resources, definitions, and a cross-reference chart of botanical and common names, this is a must-have manual for anyone who shares home or office space with potted plants." —*Booklist*
Includes index.

Silver, Johanna
★ *The **Bold** Dry Garden: Lessons from the Ruth Bancroft Garden.* Johanna Silver; photographs by Marion Brenner. Timber Press 2016. 235 pages : Color; Illustration
ISBN 9781604696707
Grades: Adult 635.9
1. Landscape gardening 2. Water conservation 3. Xeriscaping 4. California 5. Essays 6. Arts and Entertainment — Crafts and hobbies — Garden and nature 7. Life stories — Arts and culture
LC 2016001680
"Replete with brilliant color photography, this hopeful book will win over anyone who doubts that a desolate landscape can support thriving life." —*Publishers Weekly*
Includes bibliographical references and index.

Stearns, Jen
*The **Inspired** Houseplant: Transform Your Home with Indoor Plants from Kokedama to Terrariums and Water Gardens to Edibles.* Jen Stearns. Sasquatch Books 2019. xi, 192 p. : Color; Illustration
ISBN 9781632171771
Grades: Adult 635.9
1. House plants 2. Arts and Entertainment — Crafts and hobbies — Garden and nature
LC 2018014482
Presents the basic principles of potting, watering, and pruning house plants, a guide for favorite plants, and instructions for such plant projects as a hanging air globe, succulent bowl, and an underwater landscape.
Includes index.

Stewart, Martha
★ *Martha's Flowers: A Practical Guide to Growing, Gathering, and Enjoying.* Martha Stewart with Kevin Sharkey. Clarkson Potter Publishers 2018. 287 pages : Color; Illustration
ISBN 9781984822345

PUBLIC LIBRARY CORE COLLECTION: NONFICTION
Twentieth Edition

Grades: Adult   **635.9**
1. Flower arrangement 2. Flower gardening 3. Flowers 4. Arts and Entertainment — Crafts and hobbies — Garden and nature

LC Bl2019002404

The well-known author and decorator discusses her love of flowers from a young age, describes the different flower gardens she has had, and provides gardening advice on planting, growing, troubleshooting, and arranging specific flowers.
Includes index.

Stuckey, Maggie
*The **Container** Victory Garden: A Beginner's Guide to Growing Your Own Groceries.* Maggie Stuckey; art by Janice Minjin Yang and Lee Johnston. Harper Celebrate 2023. xiv, 255 pages : Illustration; Color
ISBN 9780785255765
Grades: Adult   **635.9**
1. Container gardening 2. Vegetable gardening 3. Kitchen gardens 4. Nature Writing — Gardens

LC Bl2023003680

In this must-have gardening book filled with inspiration, first-person stories and full-color photos, a bestselling author and expert gardener provides all the essential information on planning, planting, nurturing and harvesting a successful container garden.
"Urban gardeners will appreciate the recommendations on making the most out of limited space." —*Publishers Weekly*
Includes index.

Tallamy, Douglas W.
★ *Nature's Best Hope: A New Approach to Conservation That Starts in Your Yard.* Douglas W. Tallamy. Timber Press 2019. 254 pages : Color; Illustration
ISBN 9781604699005
Grades: Adult   **635.9**
1. Human ecology 2. Native plants for cultivation 3. Natural landscaping 4. Arts and Entertainment — Crafts and hobbies — Garden and nature 5. Nature writing — Environmental Issues

LC Bl2020005246

The best-selling author of Bringing Nature Home outlines practical next-step approaches to conservation, instructing homeowners on how to turn yards into supportive wildlife habitats that do not require government regulation. Illustrations.
"Recent reports of massive declines in bird populations across North America make this book both timely and apposite. An essential addition to most gardening collections." —*Library Journal*
Includes bibliographical references (pages 231-243) and index.

Tophill, Frances
★ *Container Gardener's Handbook: Pots, Techniques, and Projects to Transform Any Space.* Frances Tophill; photography by Rachel Warne. Fox Chapel Publishing 2019. 160 pages : Color; Illustration
ISBN 9781620083307
Grades: Adult   **635.9**
1. Container gardening 2. Arts and Entertainment — Crafts and hobbies — Garden and nature

LC 2018043589

Presents forty-one step-by-step projects for creative and sustainable container gardens which cover a range of different planting schemes and types of containers, along with advice on what to grow and how to grow it.
Includes index.

Tychonievich, Joseph
Rock Gardening: Reimagining a Classic Style. Joseph Tychonievich. Timber Press 2016. 295 p. : Color; Illustration
ISBN 9781604695878
Grades: Adult   **635.9**
1. Rock gardens 2. Arts and Entertainment — Architecture 3. Arts and Entertainment — Crafts and hobbies — Garden and nature

LC OC2018139553

"This useful work targets a wide range of garden enthusiasts and/or horticulturalists. While comparable to the North American Rock Garden Society's Rock Garden Design and Construction, this stands on its own merits." —*Library Journal*
Includes bibliographical references and index.

Whitman, John
Fresh from the Garden: An Organic Guide to Growing Vegetables, Berries, and Herbs in Cold Climates. John Whitman. University of Minnesota Press 2017. 514 p.
ISBN 9780816698394
Grades: Adult   **635.9**
1. Organic gardening 2. Vegetable gardening 3. Berries 4. Herb gardening 5. Canada 6. Arts and Entertainment — Crafts and hobbies — Garden and nature

LC 2016027971

Emphasizing organic gardening, Whitman, a professional gardener and author, offers a guide to growing vegetables, berries, and herbs in cold climates, in areas where temperatures can get to 20 degrees below zero during the winter. He explains where to plant, planting seed, starting vegetables from seed indoors, caring for plants, propagation, solving growing problems, harvesting and culinary uses, and tools, materials, and gardening aids, then offers a guide to about 150 plants and how they grow.
"An excellent handbook deserving a larger audience than it may receive." —*Booklist*
Includes index.

636 Animal husbandry

Foer, Jonathan Safran
★ *We Are the Weather: Saving the Planet Begins at Breakfast.* Jonathan Safran Foer. Farrar, Straus and Giroux 2019. 192 p.
ISBN 9780374280000
Grades: Adult   **636**
1. Climate change 2. Global warming 3. Livestock 4. Animal culture 5. Sustainable agriculture 6. Politics and global affairs — Environmental issues and policies

LC 2019020218

Green Prize for Sustainable Literature: Adult Nonfiction, 2020.
An urgent call to action on climate change by the author of Eating Animals shares insight into the climate denial mindset while identifying meat farms as a primary source of environmental pollutants.
"In his desire to convince others to take action, Foer raises the philosophical bar, which is, perhaps, the most effective way of fomenting sincere and long-lasting commitment to this life-threatening crisis." —*Booklist*
Includes bibliographical references.

Grandin, Temple
Temple Grandin's Guide to Working with Farm Animals: Safe, Humane, Livestock Handling Practices for the Small Farm. Temple Grandin. Storey Publishing 2017. 181 p. : Illustration; Color
ISBN 9781612127446
Grades: Adult   **636**
1. Domestic animals 2. Nature writing — Animal Studies

LC 2016055528

The animal behavior expert provides insight into the minds of livestock and presents practical advice on how to handle these animals humanely.
Includes bibliographical references (pages 170-173) and index.

636.08 Specific topics in animal husbandry

★ *Animals Make Us Human: Creating the Best Life for Animals.* Temple Grandin & Catherine Johnson. Houghton Mifflin Harcourt 2009. 352 p.
ISBN 9780151014897

ESSENTIAL AND RECOMMENDED TITLES
636.088 Animals for specific purposes

Grades: 9 10 11 12 Adult **636.08**
1. Emotions in animals 2. Animal welfare 3. Consciousness in animals 4. Animal behavior 5. Human-animal relationships 6. Nature Writing — Animal Studies

LC 2008034892

Drawing on the latest research and her own work, Grandin identifies the core emotional needs of animals and explains how to fulfill them for dogs and cats, horses, farm animals, and zoo animals.

"Packed with fascinating insights, unexpected observations and a wealth of how-to tips, Grandin's peppy work ably challenges assumptions about what makes animals happy." —*Publishers Weekly*

636.088 Animals for specific purposes

Masson, J. Moussaieff
Lost Companions: Reflections on the Death of Pets. Jeffrey Moussaieff Masson. St. Martin's Press 2020. 272 pages
ISBN 9781250202239
Grades: Adult **636.088**
1. Death of pets 2. Pet owners 3. Grief 4. Loss 5. Psychology 6. Family and Relationships — Pets and Owners

LC 2019058388

A heartfelt exploration of human grief after the loss of a pet by the New York Times bestselling author of Dogs Never Lie About Love.

"Highly recommended for all animal lovers who inevitably must deal with the death of their pets." —*Library Journal*

Novello, Carol
Mutual Rescue: How Adopting a Homeless Animal Can Save You, Too. by Carol Novello with Ginny Graves. Grand Central Life & Style 2019. VIII, 264 pages
ISBN 9781538713532
Grades: Adult **636.088**
1. Pet adoption 2. Humans and pets 3. Animal shelters 4. Animal rescue 5. Abandoned animals 6. Animal welfare 7. Healing 8. Redemption 9. Human-animal relationships 10. Family and Relationships — Pets and Owners

LC 2018044758

Explores the role that pets play in human lives and uses scientific research to show how pets can help transform people suffering from mental, physical or spiritual pain.

Includes bibliographical references.

Weitzman, Gary
National Geographic Complete Guide to Pet Health, Behavior, and Happiness: The Veterinarian's Approach to At-Home Animal Care. Gary Weitzman, DVM, MPH, CAWA.. National Geographic 2019. 399 pages : Color; Illustration
ISBN 9781426219658
Grades: Adult **636.088**
1. Pets 2. Psychology 3. Animal behavior 4. Health 5. Reference — General 6. Nature writing — Animal studies — Pet care 7. Nature writing — Animal Studies

LC 2018027275

Combining first aid, medical reference, and tips and tricks of the trade, here is your go-to-guide for at-home animal care, focusing on dogs, cats, rabbits, birds, and more! Building on more than two decades of veterinary experience, Dr. Gary Weitzman covers topics including upset stomachs, house training, physical ailments and behavior tips. The president and CEO of the San Diego Humane Society and former co-host of the weekly NPR show The Animal House, 'Dr. Gary' brings a wealth of experience to essential veterinary questions, revealing basic first-aid techniques, when a trip to the vet is necessary, dietary recommendations, simple training techniques, necessary supplies, essential behavior cues, and much more.

Includes bibliographical references (pages 387-390) and index.

636.1 Horses

McDougall, Christopher
Running with Sherman: The Donkey with the Heart of a Hero. Christopher McDougall. Alfred A. Knopf 2019. 352 p.
ISBN 9781524732363
Grades: Adult **636.1**
1. McDougall, Christopher, 1962- 2. Donkeys 3. Animal rescue 4. Running 5. Animal welfare 6. Running races 7. Healing 8. Cooperation 9. Training 10. Human-animal relationships 11. Pennsylvania 12. Autobiographies and memoirs 13. Life stories — Relationships — Pets and Owners 14. Nature Writing — Animal Studies 15. Sports and Competition — Racing 16. Adult books for young adults

LC 2019009852

When Chris McDougall agreed to take in a donkey from an animal hoarder, he thought it would be no harder than the rest of the adjustments he and his family had made after moving from Philadelphia to the heart of Pennsylvania Amish country. But when he arrived, Sherman was in such bad shape he could barely move, and his hair was coming out in clumps. Chris decided to undertake a radical rehabilitation program designed not only to heal Sherman's body but to heal his mind as well. It turns out the best way to soothe a donkey is to give it a job, and so Chris decided to teach Sherman how to run. He'd heard about burro racing—a unique type of race where humans and donkeys run together in a call-back to mining days—and decided he and Sherman would enter the World Championship in Colorado.

This is a Borzoi book.

636.4 Swine

Montgomery, Sy
The Good Good Pig: The Extraordinary Life of Christopher Hogwood. Sy Montgomery. Ballantine Books 2006. 228 p, 8 p. of plates : Color illustration
ISBN 9780345481375
Grades: 11 12 Adult **636.4**
1. Montgomery, Sy 2. Pigs 3. Pet owners 4. Pigs as pets 5. Pets 6. Human-animal relationships 7. Social life and customs 8. New Hampshire 9. Autobiographies and memoirs 10. Family and Relationships — Pets and Owners 11. Life stories — Relationships — Pets and Owners 12. Adult books for young adults

LC 2005057094

An ardent nature lover and author of Journey of the Pink Dolphins describes her unique friendship with a pig named Christopher Hogwood, a once sickly piglet who helped her develop a new relationship with neighbors in her small-town community that gave her an anchor to family and home.

"Anyone who has ever loved a pet can enjoy reading about the relationship between Montgomery and her Christopher." —*Science Books & Films*

636.7 Dogs

Achterberg, Cara Sue
Another Good Dog: One Family and Fifty Foster Dogs. Cara Sue Achterberg. W W Norton & Co. Inc 2018. 304 p.
ISBN 9781681777931
Grades: Adult **636.7**
1. Achterberg, Cara Sue 2. Women and dogs 3. Dog adoption 4. Empty nesters 5. Volunteers 6. Animal welfare 7. Abandoned dogs 8. Human-animal relationships 9. Autobiographies and memoirs 10. Life stories — Relationships — Pets and owners 11. Family and Relationships — Pets and Owners

LC Bl2018109824

The best-selling author of Girls' Weekend describes her decision to convert her Pennsylvania farm into a foster home for dogs, recounting her experiences with dozens of remarkable canines throughout her first two years.

"Witty and full of love, her memoir beautifully captures the personalities of the dogs shes helped save and recounts the concurrent struggles in her family life, particularly watching her teenagers fly the nest. This easy read is a must for animal lovers and those interested in volunteering with animals and a good choice for reluctant readers." —*Booklist*

Bradshaw, John
★ *Dog* Sense: How the New Science of Dog Behavior Can Make You a Better Friend to Your Pet. John Bradshaw. Basic Books 2011. 320 p.
ISBN 9780465019441
Grades: Adult 636.7
1. Animal intelligence 2. Dogs 3. Zoology 4. Psychology 5. Animal behavior 6. Human-animal relationships 7. Nature Writing — Animal Studies 8. Family and Relationships — Pets and Owners

LC 2010054337

A renowned anthrozoologist shows how humans can live in harmony with their canine friends, explaining why positive reinforcement is a more effective way to control behavior and how to weigh a dog's unique personality against stereotypes about its breed.

"Pet owners and those interested in the animal mind will learn from this balanced, well-referenced guide to the science of canine behavior." —*Library Journal*

Bragg, Rick
The *Speckled* Beauty: A Dog and His People. Rick Bragg. Alfred A. Knopf 2021. 256 p.
ISBN 9780525658818
Grades: Adult 636.7
1. Bragg, Rick 2. Authors 3. Cancer survivors 4. Adopted dogs 5. Convalescence 6. Families 7. Abandoned dogs 8. Injured animals 9. Misbehavior 10. Compassion 11. Dogs as pets 12. Bonding (Human-animal) 13. Alabama 14. Autobiographies and memoirs 15. Animal biographies 16. Life stories — Relationships — Pets and Owners 17. Family and Relationships — Pets and Owners

In this heartwarming and hilarious story, the author shares how his life was transformed by Speck, a badly behaved, half-blind stray dog who helped him through a moment of looming uncertainty.

"A celebrated Southern memoirist delivers a spirited book about a hell-raising dog and his effect on the author's life." —*Kirkus*

Charleson, Susannah
Where the Lost Dogs Go: A Story of Love, Search, and the Power of Reunion. Susannah Charleson. Houghton Mifflin Harcourt 2019. 320 pages
ISBN 9781328995056
Grades: Adult 636.7
1. Charleson, Susannah 2. Lost dogs 3. Search dogs 4. Search and rescue operations 5. Humans and dogs 6. Reunions 7. Human-animal relationships 8. Family and Relationships — Pets and Owners 9. Life stories — Relationships — Pets and Owners

LC 2018046441

Draws on expert studies in animal behavior, lost-pet search tactics, and the psychology of loss in an analysis of the world of lost dogs and the power of reunion.

"Charleston [sic] suffuses her tale with insight and well-earned sentiment, skillfully weaving in anecdotes of searches for lost dogs with those of her blossoming relationship with a new addition to her household, rescued Maltese-poodle mix Ace…This inspiring and informative work will resonate with pet lovers everywhere." —*Publishers Weekly*

Coile, D. Caroline
Encyclopedia of Dog Breeds. D. Caroline Coile, Ph.D; illustrations by Michele Earle-Bridges. Barron's 2015. VII, 392 pages : Illustration; Color
ISBN 9780764167294
Grades: Adult 636.7
1. Dog breeds 2. Nature writing — Animal studies — Pet care — Dogs 3. Reference — Encyclopedias 4. Reference — General

LC 2015935573

Profiles each AKC breed, covering breed history, physical traits, health, longevity, behavior, and exercise needs.
Includes index.

Conaboy, Kelly
The *Particulars* of Peter: Dance Lessons, DNA Tests, and Other Excuses to Hang Out with My Perfect Dog. Kelly Conaboy. Grand Central Publishing 2020. 240 p.
ISBN 9781538717868
Grades: Adult 636.7
1. Conaboy, Kelly 2. Dogs 3. Dogs as pets 4. Women dog owners 5. Women and dogs 6. Dog adoption 7. Obsession 8. Human-animal relationships 9. Autobiographies and memoirs 10. Life stories — Relationships — Pets and Owners 11. Family and Relationships — Pets and Owners 12. Humor writing — General

LC 2020030166

From one of the Internet's most original voices, a hilarious journey through the odd corners of obsessive dog ownership and the author's own infatuation with her perfect dog Peter.

"Dog enthusiasts will especially delight in this book, but anyone looking for a good laugh will have a ball." —*Publishers Weekly*

Golbeck, Jennifer
The *Purest* Bond: Understanding the Human-Canine Connection. by Jen Golbeck, Ph.D, and Stacey Colino, M.S.. Atria Books 2023. 256 p.
ISBN 9781668007846
Grades: Adult 636.7
1. Human-animal relationships 2. Dog owners 3. Dogs as pets 4. Bonding (Human-animal) 5. Human-animal communication 6. Well-being 7. Mental health 8. Happiness 9. Companionship 10. Psychological growth 11. Unconditional love 12. Cognition in animals 13. Healing 14. Dogs 15. Family and Relationships — Pets and Owners

LC 2023003065

Blending groundbreaking research with uplifting real-life tales, this feel-good book explores the benefits our canine companions can have on our physical, emotional, cognitive and social well-being, often without our realizing it.

"An excellent addition to the field of canine cognition and emotional connection that is inclusive and easily digested." —*Library Journal*
Includes bibliographical references.

Habib, Rodney
★ The *Forever* Dog: Surprising New Science to Help Your Canine Companion Live Younger, Healthier, and Longer. Rodney Habib and Karen Shaw Becker with Kristin Loberg. Harper Wave, an imprint of HarperCollins Publishers 2021. xxiii, 433 p. : Illustration
ISBN 9781443461689
Grades: Adult 636.7
1. Dogs 2. Humans and dogs 3. Pets 4. Health 5. Canadian literature 6. Family and Relationships — Pets and Owners 7. Nature Writing — Animal Studies

New science to help your dog live a healthier life.

"For readers looking to keep tails wagging for as long as possible, this is a no-brainer." —*Publishers Weekly*
Includes index.

Herriot, James
James Herriot's Dog Stories. James Herriot. St. Martin's Griffin 2006. xxxiii, 426 p. : Illustration
ISBN 9780312364526
Grades: 11 12 Adult 636.7
1. Herriot, James 1916-1995 2. Dogs 3. Veterinarians 4. Dog owners 5. Dogs as pets 6. Human-animal relationships 7. Social life and customs 8. Yorkshire, England 9. Autobiographies and memoirs 10. Family and Relationships — Pets and Owners 11. Life stories — Relationships — Pets and Owners 12. Life stories — Nature and outdoors

LC 2007274677

ESSENTIAL AND RECOMMENDED TITLES
636.7 Dogs

Here are the complete dog stories from his much-beloved memoirs: a handsome collection of tales, available for the first time in trade paperback, that will warm the hearts of dog lovers around the world. Featuring a special introduction by the author and his own accompanying notes to each specially illustrated story, this tribute from man to dog is a volume no Herriot fan will want to be without.

"A good choice for dog lovers." —*School Library Journal*
Originally published: New York : St. Martin's Press, 1986.

James Herriot's Favorite Dog Stories. James Herriot; illustrations by Lesley Holmes. St. Martin's Press 1996. 169 p. : Color illustration
ISBN 9780312146313
Grades: 11 12 Adult   636.7
1. Herriot, James 1916-1995 2. Dogs 3. Veterinarians 4. Dogs as pets 5. Dog owners 6. Human-animal relationships 7. Autobiographies and memoirs 8. Family and Relationships — Pets and Owners 9. Life stories — Nature and outdoors
LC 96018796

Watercolor illustrations accompany a collection of ten stories about dogs—from border collies and sheepdogs to the exploits of Tricki Woo, the unforgettable Pekinese.

"This is a collection of 10 previously published dog stories written in Herriot's heartwarming style. Each tale is accompanied by new attractive watercolor illustrations. A dog-lover's delight." —*School Library Journal*

Horowitz, Alexandra

★ *Being a Dog: Following the Dog into a World of Smell*. Alexandra Horowitz. Scribner 2016. 368 p.
ISBN 9781476795997
Grades: Adult   636.7
1. Dogs 2. Smell 3. Cognition in animals 4. Animal behavior 5. Human-animal relationships 6. Nature Writing — Animal Studies
LC 2016006968

The author of the New York Times best-selling Inside of a Dog explains how dogs perceive the world through their acute sense of smell and how humans can reconnect with their own underused senses to further human-canine bonds and gain insights into dog cognition.

"Both dog lovers and pop science readers will want to stick their noses in this book, and they may find themselves using their noses, like Horowitz and dogs everywhere, to experience the world more vividly." —*Publishers Weekly*

★ *Inside of a Dog: What Dogs See, Smell, and Know*. Alexandra Horowitz. Scribner 2009. x, 353 p.
ISBN 9781416583400
Grades: Adult   636.7
1. Dogs 2. Animal behavior 3. Dog owners 4. Zoology 5. Psychology 6. Nature Writing — Animal Studies

A psychologist offers insight into the canine mind, drawing on current cognitive research to illuminate a dog's perceptual abilities and the experiences that shape dog behavior, with stories about the author and her canine friend.

Includes bibliographical references (p. 303-332) and index.

Our Dogs, Ourselves: The Story of a Singular Bond. Alexandra Horowitz. Scribner 2019. 352 p.
ISBN 9781501175008
Grades: Adult   636.7
1. Dogs 2. Humans and dogs 3. Dog owners 4. Dogs as pets 5. Animal welfare 6. Human-animal relationships 7. Family and Relationships — Pets and Owners 8. Nature Writing — Animal Studies
LC 2019017043

We keep dogs and are kept by them. We love dogs and (we assume) we are loved by them. We buy them sweaters, toys, shoes; we are concerned with their social lives, their food, and their health. The story of humans and dogs is thousands of years old but is far from understood. In Our Dogs, Ourselves, Alexandra Horowitz explores all aspects of this unique and complex interspecies pairing.

Includes bibliographical references.

★ *The Year of the Puppy: How Dogs Become Themselves*. Alexandra Horowitz. Viking 2022. 304 p.
ISBN 9780593298008

Grades: Adult   636.7
1. Horowitz, Alexandra 2. Dogs 3. Puppies 4. Dog owners 5. Dog training 6. Biological growth 7. Identity 8. Personality 9. Psychology 10. Animal behavior 11. Nature Writing — Animal Studies 12. Family and Relationships — Pets and Owners 13. Life stories — Relationships — Pets and Owners

The author of the classic Inside of a Dog, by observing her puppy Quid from week to week, makes new sense of a dog's behavior, keeping a lens on the puppy's point of view as she researches the science of early dog development.

"A detailed, highly illuminating portrait of puppies and our relationships with them." —*Kirkus*

Hunger, Christina

How Stella Learned to Talk: The Groundbreaking Story of the World's First Talking Dog. Christina Hunger. William Morrow & Company 2021. 320 p.
ISBN 9780063046832
Grades: Adult   636.7
1. Hunger, Christina 2. Speech therapists 3. Dog training 4. Women and dogs 5. Communication 6. Dogs as pets 7. Humans and dogs 8. Human-animal communication 9. Life stories — Pets and Owners 10. Family and Relationships — Pets and Owners 11. Nature Writing — Animal Studies

An incredible, revolutionary true story and surprisingly simple guide to teaching your dog to talk from a speech-language pathologist who has taught her dog to communicate using simple paw-sized buttons associated with different words.

"Hunger, a speech-language pathologist, . . . realized that her methods for helping speech-inhibited children learn to communicate might also help her dog, Stella, learn to communicate her needs. . . . This fascinating study of the untapped potential in human-dog interaction includes end-of-chapter bullet-points for dog owners who are game to try on their own." —*Booklist*

Kavin, Kim

The Dog Merchants: Inside the Big Business of Breeders, Pet Stores, and Rescuers. Kim Kavin. Lyons Press 2016. 336 p.
ISBN 9781681771403
Grades: Adult   636.7
1. Pet industry and trade 2. Dogs as pets 3. Dog breeding 4. Dogs 5. Family and Relationships — Pets and Owners
LC 2015014827

Reveals the complex network behind the $11 billion-a-year business of selling dogs; discusses how all dogs are treated, from puppy mills to high-kill shelters; and shows how all dog lovers can come together, with one voice as consumers, on behalf of canines everywhere.

"A scathing indictment of an industry run amok; belongs on every pet lover's bookshelf." —*Kirkus*

Includes bibliographical references and index.

McConnell, Patricia B.

★ *The Other End of the Leash: Why We Do What We Do Around Dogs*. Patricia B. McConnell. Ballantine Books 2002. 246 p.
ISBN 9780345446794
Grades: Adult   636.7
1. Dog training 2. Dogs 3. Dog owners 4. Human-animal relationships 5. Family and Relationships — Pets and Owners

A fascinating glimpse into the world of dogs explores humans' relationships with their canine companions and the mysteries of human-canine communication, provides new insights into human and dog interaction, and explains how readers can retrain themselves to avoid sending conflicting messages to their pets.

"Good reading for dog lovers and an immensely useful manual for dog owners." —*Washington Post*

Melville, Wilma

★ *Hero Dogs: How a Pack of Rescues, Rejects, and Strays Became America's Greatest Disaster-search Partners*. Wilma Melville with Paul Lobo. St. Martin's Press 2019. 336 p.
ISBN 9781250179913

PUBLIC LIBRARY CORE COLLECTION: NONFICTION
Twentieth Edition

Grades: Adult   636.7

1. Melville, Wilma 2. Dog training 3. Search and rescue operations 4. Dog rescue 5. Search dogs 6. Rescue dogs 7. Natural disasters 8. Bombings 9. Dog trainers 10. Bonding (Human-animal) 11. Human-animal relationships 12. Autobiographies and memoirs 13. History writing — Natural disasters and tragedies 14. Life stories — Relationships — Pets and Owners 15. Life stories — Business — Working life

LC 2018039819

Recounts how the author turned a band of shelter dogs into one of America's foremost disaster-response teams during such catastrophes as the Oklahoma City bombing, the Septemner 11 terrorist attacks, and Hurricane Katrina.

"Melville, a canine search-and-rescue handler who was inspired to launch the National Disaster Search Dog Foundation (SDF) after volunteering to help look for Oklahoma City bombing survivors in 1995, shares the struggles of establishing and maintaining the organization." —*Publishers Weekly*

Miller, Pat
★ *The Power of Positive Dog Training*. Pat Miller. Wiley Pub. 2008. xvi, 272 p. : Illustration
ISBN 9780470241844
Grades: Adult   636.7

1. Dog training 2. Dogs 3. Animal behavior 4. Humans and dogs 5. Nature Writing — Animal studies — Pet care — Dogs

LC 2008001313

2nd edition; Includes bibliographical references (p. 257-260) and index.

Monks of New Skete
The Art of Raising a Puppy. the Monks of New Skete; [photographs by the Monks of New Skete]. Little, Brown and Co. 2011. x, 341 p. : Illustration
ISBN 9780316083270
Grades: Adult   636.7

1. Puppies 2. Dog training 3. Nature writing — Animal studies — Pet care — Dogs

LC 2011002744

For more than thirty years the Monks of New Skete have been among America's most trusted authorities on dog training, canine behavior, and the animal/Human bond. In their two now-classic bestsellers, How to be Your Dog's Best Friend and THE ART OF RAISING a PUPPY, the Monks draw on their experience as long-time breeders of German shepherds and as trainers of dogs of all breeds to provide—brilliantly distilled—the indispensable information and advice that every dog owner needs. This new edition of THE ART OF RAISING a PUPPY features new photographs throughout, along with updated chapters on play, crating, adopting dogs from shelters and rescue organizations, raising dogs in an urban environment, and the latest developments in canine health and canine behavioral theory.

This new edition of the classic best-seller from the long-time breeders of German shepherds and dog trainers features new photos and updated chapters on play, crating, adopting shelter dogs and the latest developments in canine health and behavioral theory.

Completely revised and updated; Includes bibliographical references (p. [329]-331) and index.

Nichols, Kerry
Puppy Brain: How Our Dogs Learn, Think, and Love. Kerry Nichols. Celadon Books 2024. VIII, 392 pages : Illustration
ISBN 9781250867919
Grades: Adult   636.7

1. Dogs 2. Puppies 3. Puppy care 4. Dog training 5. Animal behavior 6. Nature Writing — Animal Studies — Pet care — Dogs

LC 2023047170

Explains how to raise a happy, healthy, and emotionally resilient dog and forge a fulfilling bond with them.

"A must-read for any dog lover, whether you're adopting your first puppy or your last." —*Kirkus*

Includes index.

Sutherland, Amy
Rescuing Penny Jane: One Shelter Volunteer, Countless Dogs, and the Quest to Find Them All Homes. Amy Sutherland. HarperCollins 2017. 304 p.
ISBN 9780062377234
Grades: Adult   636.7

1. Sutherland, Amy 2. Animal rescue 3. Animal shelter workers 4. Animal shelters 5. Animal welfare 6. Autobiographies and memoirs 7. Life stories — Relationships — Pets and owners

LC Bl2017006986

A best-selling author and columnist for the Boston Globe describes what it was like working at an animal shelter helping to train scared, aggressive and previously-neglected dogs eventually find love and permanent homes.

"An inside look at the experiences of shelter dogs that is sure to appeal to dog and animal lovers." —*Kirkus*

Tomlinson, Tommy
Dogland: Passion, Glory, and Lots of Slobber at the Westminster Dog Show. Tommy Tomlinson. Avid Reader Press 2024. 288 p.
ISBN 9781982149321
Grades: Adult   636.7

1. Tomlinson, Tommy 2. Dog shows 3. Show dogs 4. Journalists 5. Competition 6. Humans and dogs 7. Dogs as pets 8. Dog breeding 9. Human-animal relationships 10. Nature Writing — Animal Studies 11. Life stories — Relationships — Pets and Owners 12. Family and Relationships — Pets and Owners

LC 2024000817

From a Pulitzer Prize finalist and the author of The Elephant in the Room comes the first inside account of the Westminster Dog Show—America's oldest and most beloved dog show—following one dog on his quest to become a champion.

"The result is an amusing, extremely readable look at the fancy (what insiders call the dog show world) that will appeal to dog lovers." —*Booklist*

Wynne, Clive D. L.
★ *Dog Is Love: Why and How Your Dog Loves You*. Clive Wynne. Houghton Mifflin Harcourt 2019. 272 pages
ISBN 9781328543967
Grades: Adult   636.7

1. Dogs 2. Humans and dogs 3. Emotions in animals 4. Animal behavior 6. Bonding (Human-animal) 7. Human-animal relationships 8. Family and Relationships — Pets and Owners 9. Nature Writing — Animal Studies

LC 2019002729

A pioneering canine behaviorist draws on cutting-edge research to show that a single, simple trait—the capacity to love—is what makes dogs such perfect companions for humans, and to explain how we can better reciprocate their affection.

Includes bibliographical references and index.

636.737 Herding dogs

Orlean, Susan
Rin Tin Tin: The Life and the Legend. Susan Orlean. Simon & Schuster 2011. 320 p.
ISBN 9781439190135
Grades: 11 12 Adult   636.737

1. Rin-Tin-Tin (Dog) 2. German shepherd dog 3. Working dogs 4. Dogs in films 5. Animal biographies 6. Arts and Entertainment — Movies and Television 7. Nature Writing — Animal Studies 8. Adult books for young adults

LC 2011024476

Booklist Editors' Choice 2011; New York Times Notable Book, 2011.

Chronicles the rise of the iconic German shepherd character while sharing the stories of the real WWI dog and the canine performer in the 1950s television show, and explores Rin Tin Tin's relevance in the military and popular culture.

Includes bibliographical references and index.

ESSENTIAL AND RECOMMENDED TITLES
636.752 Sporting dogs

636.752 Sporting dogs

Grogan, John
★ *Marley & Me: Life and Love with the World's Worst Dog.* John Grogan. Morrow 2005. xi, 291 p. : Illustration
ISBN 9780060817084
Grades: Adult   636.752
1. Grogan, John, 1957- 2. Labrador retrievers 3. Dogs as pets 4. Men and dogs 5. Dogs 6. Mischief 7. Human-animal relationships 8. Florida 9. Page to screen 10. Family and Relationships — Pets and Owners 11. Adult books for young adults
LC 2005040010

Follows the life story of an exuberant Labrador retriever who gets into perpetual trouble and experiences a range of inspiring adventures, from shutting down an entire beach to guarding a seventeen-year-old neighbor after a stabbing attack.

"Dog lovers will love this account of Grogan's much loved canine." —*Publishers Weekly*

636.755 Terriers

Dickey, Bronwen
Pit Bull: The Battle Over an American Icon. Bronwen Dickey. Alfred A. Knopf 2016. 288 p.
ISBN 9780307961761
Grades: Adult   636.755
1. Dogs as pets 2. Dog owners 3. Pit bull terriers 4. Family and Relationships — Pets and Owners 5. Nature writing — Animal studies
LC 2015033292

Describes how the loyal and affectionate dog breed that once earned presidential recognition for their roles on the battlefields of Gettysburg and the Marne and appeared in films and TV, became demonized and stigmatized through urban dog-fighting rings.

"This exceptional, thoroughly researched, and expertly written work is a must for all libraries." —*Library Journal*

636.8 Cats

Bradshaw, John
★ *Cat Sense: How the New Feline Science Can Make You a Better Friend to Your Pet.* John Bradshaw. Basic Books 2013. 320 p.
ISBN 9780465031016
Grades: 9 10 11 12 Adult   636.8
1. Animal intelligence 2. Cats 3. Animal behavior 4. Cat owners 5. Zoology 6. Cats as pets 7. Psychology 8. Human-animal relationships 9. Nature Writing — Animal Studies 10. Family and Relationships — Pets and Owners 11. Adult books for young adults
LC 2013020749

The best-selling anthrozoologist author draws on the latest scientific and behavioral research to explain the origins, evolution and modern-day needs of domestic cats, revealing how an understanding of a cat's ancient instincts is an essential part of a healthy cat-human relationship.

"Bradshaw teases out a better understanding of what our cats want (and need) from their owners.... This fascinating book will be a bible for cat owners." —*Booklist*

Includes bibliographical references and index.

Brown, Sarah L.
The Hidden Language of Cats: How They Have Us at Meow. Sarah Brown. Dutton 2023. 272 p.
ISBN 9780593186411
Grades: Adult   636.8
1. Cats 2. Humans and cats 3. Animal behavior 4. Cats as pets 5. Domestication 6. Adaptation 7. Human-animal communication 8. Family and Relationships — Pets and Owners 9. Nature Writing — Animal Studies
LC 2023009025

Drawing on 30 years of experience, a renowned cat behavior scientist references historical records and examines modern scientific studies of cat-human communication to reveal previously unexplored secrets of how cats all over the world have learned to talk to us.

"With her lighthearted yet authoritative approach, Brown helps us better understand our feline companions." —*Kirkus*

Includes bibliographical references and index.

Galaxy, Jackson
★ *Total Cat Mojo: The Ultimate Guide to Life with Your Cat.* Jackson Galaxy with Mikel Delgado and Bobby Rock. TarcherPerigee Book 2017. xviii, 365 pages : Illustration
ISBN 9780143131618
Grades: Adult   636.8
1. Cats 2. Health 3. Nature writing — Animal studies — Pet care — Cats 4. Reference — General
LC 2017026753

The star of Animal Planet's My Cat from Hell describes how to keep your feline pets happy and healthy by harnessing their |cat mojo| which allows them to safely stay in touch with their natural instincts in your home.

A TarcherPerigee book.

Herriot, James
James Herriot's Cat Stories. James Herriot; with illustrations by Lesley Holmes. St. Martin's Press 1994. xiii, 161 p. : Color illustration
ISBN 9780312113421
Grades: 11 12 Adult   636.8
1. Herriot, James 1916-1995 2. Veterinarians 3. Cats 4. Humans and cats 5. Cats as pets 6. Human-animal relationships 7. Yorkshire, England 8. Autobiographies and memoirs 9. Family and Relationships — Pets and Owners 10. Life stories — Nature and outdoors
LC 94020131

A renowned writer on animals offers a collection of stories about the cats he has known.

Losos, Jonathan B.
The Cat's Meow: How Cats Evolved from the Savanna to Your Sofa. Jonathan Losos. Viking Press 2023. 400 p.
ISBN 9781984878700
Grades: Adult   636.8
1. Cats 2. Cats as pets 3. Humans and cats 4. Domestication 5. Animal behavior 6. Wild cats 7. Animal habitations 8. Nature Writing — Animal Studies
LC 2022034185

The domestic cat has, from its evolutionary origins in Africa, been transformed in comparatively little time into one of the most successful and diverse species on the planet. Jonathan Losos, writing as both a scientist and a cat lover, explores how researchers today are unraveling the secrets of the cat, past and present, using all the tools of modern technology, from GPS tracking and genomics to forensic archaeology. In addition to solving the mysteries of your cat's past, it gives us a cat's-eye view of today's habitats, including meeting wild cousins around the world whose habits your sweet house cat sometimes eerily parallels.

"This head-to-paw guide to domestic cat behavior is the purr-fect addition for cat and science lovers who want to learn more about Felis catus and their large, wild cousins." —*Library Journal*

Includes bibliographical references and index.

Schotz, Susanne
The Secret Language of Cats: How to Understand Your Cat for a Better, Happier Relationship. Susanne Schotz; translated by Peter Kuras. Hanover Square Press 2018. 265 pages : Illustration
ISBN 9781335013897

PUBLIC LIBRARY CORE COLLECTION: NONFICTION
Twentieth Edition

Grades: Adult   636.8
1. Cats 2. Animal communication 3. Animal sounds 4. Animal behavior 5. Human-animal communication 6. Nature writing — Animal studies — Pet care — Cats

LC Bl2018184204

A Swedish professor of phonetics and leading authority on cat communication provides a crash course in speaking cat, describing what feline vocalizations mean in different situations and provides practical advice to help better understand your pets.
Includes bibliographical references.

Tucker, Abigail
The Lion in the Living Room: How House Cats Tamed Us and Took Over the World. Abigail Tucker. Simon & Schuster 2016. 256 pages
ISBN 9781476738239
Grades: 11 12 Adult   636.8
1. Cats as pets 2. Cats 3. Humans and cats 4. Human-animal relationships 5. History writing — Microhistory 6. Family and Relationships — Pets and Owners 7. Debut title

LC 2016000722

Discusses the natural history of domesticated felines, despite offering humans no practical benefits, through visiting researchers who discovered feline bones in the first human settlements and searching for house cats on the loose in Florida.

"Tucker's informative interviews with werewolf cat breeders, cat lobbyists, and Internet star Little Bub's owner round out a thoughtful look at the illogical human love of felines." —*Publishers Weekly*
Includes bibliographical references and index.

636.80092 Cats — Biography

Myron, Vicki
★ *Dewey: The Small-Town Library Cat Who Touched the World.* Vicki Myron, with Bret Witter. Grand Central Pub. 2008. 288 p.
ISBN 9780446407410
Grades: Adult   636.80092
1. Dewey (Marmalade cat) 2. Cats 3. Libraries 4. Mascots 5. Pets 6. Humans and cats 7. Abandoned cats 8. Bonding (Human-animal) 9. Human-animal relationships 10. Social life and customs 11. Iowa 12. Family and Relationships — Pets and Owners 13. Adult books for young adults 14. Nonfiction that reads like fiction

LC 2008004498

Traces the author's discovery of a half-frozen kitten in the drop-box of her small-community Iowa library and the feline's development into an affable library mascot whose intuitive nature prompted hundreds of abiding friendships.

"Myron's beguiling, poignant, and tender tale of survival, loyalty, and love is an unforgettable study in the mysterious and wondrous ways animals, and libraries, enrich humanity." —*Booklist*
Also published in large print format.

637 Processing dairy and related products

Kurlansky, Mark
Milk!: A 10,000-Year Food Fracas. Mark Kurlansky. Bloomsbury 2018. 352 p.
ISBN 9781632863829
Grades: Adult   637
1. Dairy products 2. Milk 3. Dairying 4. Beverages 5. Food habits 6. Animal rights 7. Genetically engineered organisms 8. Food writing — History and microhistory

LC 2017039795

Profoundly intertwined with human civilization, milk has a compelling and a surprisingly global story to tell. Tracing the liquid's diverse history from antiquity to the present, Mark Kurlansky details its curious and crucial role in cultural evolution, religion, nutrition, politics, and economics.

"A fascinating and comprehensive book that will keep readers engaged and entertained. The recipes, especially those on the historical side, are a unique and complimentary addition. Will appeal to both foodies and readers of world history. Highly recommended." —*Library Journal*
Includes bibliographical references and index.

638 Insect culture

Black, Scott Hoffman
Gardening for Butterflies: How You Can Attract and Protect Beautiful, Beneficial Insects. the Xerces Society (Scott Hoffman Black, Brianna Borders, Candace Fallon, Eric Lee-Mader, Matthew Shepherd); foreword by Robert Michael Pyle. Timber Press 2016. 287 pages : Color; Illustration
ISBN 9781604695984
Grades: Adult   638
1. Butterflies 2. Butterfly gardening 3. Arts and Entertainment — Crafts and hobbies — Garden and nature 4. Nature writing — Animal Studies

LC 2015029810

Discusses the life cycle of butterflies and the current threats to their existence and describes how to design and maintain a butterfly garden and select appropriate plants.

Explaining why butterflies are in danger, and why they matter, an optimistic call to arms by the experts at the Xerces Society provides home gardeners with everything they need to create a beautiful, beneficial, butterfly-filled garden no matter the size of their space.

"This book will help even those without green thumbs support the much-needed effort to assist and protect pollinators." —*Booklist*
Includes bibliographical references (pages 572-574) and index.

Flottum, Kim
The Backyard Beekeeper: An Absolute Beginner's Guide to Keeping Bees in Your Yard and Garden. Kim Flottum. Quarry Books 2018. 240 p. : Color; Illustration
ISBN 9781631593321
Grades: Adult   638
1. Honeybee 2. Beekeeping 3. Science writing — General 4. House and Home — Sustainable living 5. Nature writing — Animal Studies

LC 2019302955

Features information about bees, beeswax, and the modern rules of beekeeping with do-it-yourself tips for safe and fun beekeeping.
Includes index.

Nordhaus, Hannah
The Beekeeper's Lament: How One Man and Half a Billion Honey Bees Help Feed America. Hannah Nordhaus. Harpercollins 2011. 256 p.
ISBN 9780061873256
Grades: Adult   638
1. Bees 2. Beekeeping 3. Pollination 4. Bee products 5. Nature Writing — Animal Studies 6. Nature Writing — Environmental Issues 7. Adult books for young adults 8. Business and economics — Industries — Agriculture and food

LC 2011283445

An awarding-winning journalist tells the extraordinary story of John Miller, one of America's foremost migratory beekeepers, who, despite mysterious epidemics that threaten American honey populations—and the nation's agribusiness—forges on and moves ahead in a new natural world.

639 Hunting, fishing, conservation, related technologies

Swift, Earl
Chesapeake Requiem: A Year with the Watermen of Vanishing Tangier Island. Earl Swift. Dey Street 2018. 434 pages : Illustration; Map
ISBN 9780062661395

ESSENTIAL AND RECOMMENDED TITLES
639.2 Commercial fishing, whaling, sealing

Grades: Adult **639**

1. Crabs 2. Fishers 3. Island life 4. Islands 5. Sea level 6. Coastal towns 7. Community life 8. Climate change 9. Global warming 10. Crabbing 11. Chesapeake Bay 12. Virginia 13. Society and culture — Urban and regional studies 14. Nature Writing — Environmental Issues 15. History writing — Regional history — United States

LC 2018024659

Presents a 200-year history of Chesapeake Bay's Tangier Island crabbing community while explaining how rapidly rising sea levels will render the island uninhabitable within 20 years.

Includes bibliographical references (pages 383-417) and index.

639.2 Commercial fishing, whaling, sealing

Clark, Doug Bock
The Last Whalers: Three Years in the Far Pacific with a Courageous Tribe and a Vanishing Way of Life. Doug Bock Clark. Little Brown & Co. 2019. 384 p.
ISBN 9780316390620
Grades: Adult **639.2**

1. Whalers 2. Hunting and gathering societies 3. Indigenous peoples 4. Rites and ceremonies 5. Whaling 6. Islands 7. Indonesia 8. Islands of the Pacific 9. Society and culture — Ethnic studies 10. Adventure writing — Adventure travel

LC BI2018192737

New York Times Notable Book, 2019.

Deeply empathetic and richly reported, The Last Whalers is a riveting, powerful chronicle of the collision between one of the planet's dwindling indigenous peoples and the irresistible enticements and upheavals of a rapidly transforming world.

"Over several years, Clark lived among the Lamalerans in an attempt to tell their story and, in a larger context, the human story. The result is a wonderful ethnography that comes alive through a novelistic approach in which Clark explains whale hunting culture and keys in on a few individuals and their families in his effort to inform readers about their lives, ultimately exemplifying how the juggernaut nature of the modern world impacts all of its inhabitants." —*Library Journal*

Malarkey, Tucker
Stronghold: One Man's Quest to Save the World's Wild Salmon. Tucker Malarkey. Spiegel & Grau 2019. 352 pages
ISBN 9781984801692
Grades: Adult **639.2**

1. Rahr, Guido 2. Salmon 3. Wildlife conservation 4. Fishery conservation 5. Pacific salmon 6. Freshwater fishes 7. Fly fishing 8. Environmentalists 9. Sustainability 10. Oregon 11. Alaska 12. Russia 13. Biographies 14. Nature Writing — Animal Studies — Fish and Fishing 15. Nature Writing — Environmental Issues 16. Life stories — Nature and outdoors

LC 2018047731

A nonfiction debut by the author of the best-selling An Obvious Enchantment documents the story of fly fisherman and environmentalist Guido Rahr and his dangerous mission to protect the world's last major salmon habitat.

"This fascinating account of Rahr's crusade to get a multinational salmon conservation effort off the ground will be an enjoyable read for those interested in wilderness conservation and salmon ecology." —*Library Journal*

639.9 Conservation of biological resources

Owens, Delia
The Eye of the Elephant: An Epic Adventure in the African Wilderness. Delia and Mark Owens. Houghton Mifflin 1992. VIII, 305 p. : Color illustration
ISBN 9780395423813
Grades: 11 12 Adult **639.9**

1. Owens, Delia 2. Owens, Mark 3. Elephants 4. Wildlife conservationists 5. Wildlife conservation 6. Africa 7. Autobiographies and memoirs 8. Biographies 9. Nature Writing — Animal Studies 10. Life stories — Science, technology, and medicine — Scientists and inventors

LC 92017691

Two naturalists describe how a battle to save the elephants of Africa turned into a fight for their lives when commercial poachers heard of their work.

Includes bibliographical references (p. [290]-291) and index.

639.97 Specific kinds of animals

Gyllenhaal, Anders
A Wing and a Prayer: The Race to Save Our Vanishing Birds. Anders and Beverly Gyllenhaal. Simon & Schuster 2023. 320 p.
ISBN 9781982184551
Grades: Adult **639.97**

1. Birds 2. Rare and endangered birds 3. Climate change 4. Bird protection 5. Wildlife conservation 6. Habitat conservation 7. Extinction 8. Nature Writing — Animal Studies — Birds and Birding 9. Nature Writing — Environmental Issues

For the past year, veteran journalists Anders and Beverly Gyllenhaal traveled more than 25,000 miles across the Americas, chronicling costly experiments, contentious politics, and new technologies to save our beloved birds from the brink of extinction. Through this compelling drama, A Wing and a Prayer offers hope and an urgent call to action: birds are dying at an unprecedented pace. But there are encouraging breakthroughs across the hemisphere and still time to change course, if we act quickly.

"In this eye-opening account, married duo Anders and Beverly Gyllenhaal, retired journalists and avid birders, survey efforts to combat the decline in the North American bird population." —*Publishers Weekly*

640 Home and family management

Allen, Brigette
Living Without Plastic: More Than 100 Easy Swaps for Home, Travel, Dining, Holidays, and Beyond. Brigette Allen and Christine Wong. Workman Pub CO 2020. 255 pages : Color; Illustration
ISBN 9781579659400
Grades: Adult **640**

1. Plastic scrap 2. Plastics 3. Environmental protection 4. Pollution prevention 5. Solid waste reduction 6. Sustainable living 7. Plastic bag pollution 8. Plastic bottles 9. Plastic marine debris 10. Community activism 11. Environmentalism 12. Nature Writing — Environmental Issues

LC 2020015896

Every year, the world produces more than 300 million tons of plastic. These products will never break down and will endlessly pollute our oceans, air, land, and food chain. But the good news is that there are many steps, small and large, we can take to change our plastic-using habits. The introductory chapter walks readers through the different types of plastic and terminology. Then, starting with two of the most prevalent problems—the plastic water bottle and the plastic shopping bag—the book continues with the actions we can take each day to achieve a plastic-free life, organized into thematic lifestyle categories covering food, health and beauty, home, special occasions, and more.

"This is a clarion, convincing wake-up call to the scope of the global plastic problem and what readers can do about it." —*Publishers Weekly*

Includes index.

Bowers, Sharon
Home Ec for Everyone: Practical Life Skills in 118 Projects. Sharon and David Bowers; illustrated by Sophia Nicolay. Workman Publishing 2021. 228 pages : Illustration; Color
ISBN 9781523512379
Grades: Adult **640**

1. Homemaking 2. Houses 3. Life skills 4. Do-it-yourself work 5. Maintenance and repair 6. House and Home — General

LC 2020046563

Bried, Erin

How to Sew a Button: And Other Nifty Things Your Grandmother Knew. Erin Bried. Ballantine Books 2009. xxii, 278 p. : Illustration

ISBN 9780345518750

Grades: 11 12 Adult 640

1. Homemaking 2. Handicraft 3. Life skills 4. Arts and Entertainment — Crafts and hobbies

LC 2009036046

Offers clear, step-by-step instructions of the domestic arts that would've been taught once upon a time in a Home Economics course, such as cooking, hemming a pair of pants, folding a fitted sheet, writing a thank-you note and much more.

"This would be a good gift for folks on their own for the first time and will circulate widely in public and school libraries." —*Booklist*

Includes index.

Presents step-by-step instructions for more than one hundred basic domestic life skills from building a fire and hemming pants to rolling a pie crust and planting a vegetable garden, in a guide that includes tips for saving money.

"These anecdotes and tutorials gleaned from subject experts and grandmothers who were children during the Great Depression cover a broad swath of homemaking skills. Instead of systematic how-tos, Bried presents these lessons as a means to improve the quality of the reader's life." —*Library Journal*

Carroll, Ryder

★ *The Bullet Journal Method: Track the Past, Order the Present, Design the Future.* Ryder Carroll. Portfolio/Penguin 2018. 310 pages

ISBN 9780525533337

Grades: Adult 640

1. Personal diaries 2. Time management 3. Business and economics — General 4. Self-Help — Personal growth

LC 2018041565

A digital product designer and inventor of the Bullet Journal organizational system shows us how to track the past, order the present and design the future, providing the structure needed to go from passenger and pilot of your own life.

Includes bibliographical references (pages 298-302) and index.

Mendelson, Cheryl

★ *Home Comforts: The Art and Science of Keeping House.* Cheryl Mendelson; illustrations by Harry Bates. Scribner 1999. x, 884 p. : Illustration

ISBN 9780684814650

Grades: Adult 640

1. Homemaking 2. House and Home — Cleaning, caretaking, and organizing

LC 99037555

Ranging from suggestions on the care of musical instruments to tips on maintaining home safety, a celebration of and guide to the finer points of keeping house offers a contemporary, creative, and positive take on a traditional subject.

"Mendelson includes sections on food, clothing, cleanliness, daily life, and safety, with information on negligence, domestic employment laws, insurance, and even the impact of clothing label laws on our laundry. Preferred methods are explained in detail, and some alternatives are offered for those who need to compromise. This is a valuable tool." —*Library Journal*

Includes bibliographical references (p. [847]-855) and index.

Stewart, Martha

★ *The Martha Manual: How to Do (Almost) Everything.* Martha Stewart. Houghton Mifflin Harcourt 2019. 400 pages : Illustration; Color

ISBN 9781328927323

Grades: Adult 640

1. Entertaining 2. Gardening 3. Homemaking 4. Maintenance and repair 5. Houses 6. House and Home — Cleaning, caretaking, and organizing 7. House and Home — DIY, maintenance, and repair

LC 2018051333

An authoritative handbook by the domestic-lifestyle expert shares hundreds of ideas and instructions for homemaker skills, from transporting a decorated cake and folding an American flag to playing a classic lawn game and bathing a cat.

"This wide-ranging guide is designed as a household reference that sums up the breadth of Stewart's expertise." —*Booklist*

Includes index.

Sundeen, Mark

The Unsettlers: In Search of the Good Life in Today's America. Mark Sundeen. Riverhead Books 2017. 336 p.

ISBN 9781594631580

Grades: Adult 640

1. Sustainable living 2. Sustainable development 3. Sustainable communities 4. Simple life 5. Homesteading 6. Urban agriculture 7. Alternative lifestyles 8. Civilization 9. United States 10. 21st century 11. Society and culture — General

LC 2016026360

In a world of immersive journalism steeped in a distinctively American social history and sparked by a personal quest, the author chronicles the quest for the simple life through both the stories of three very different couples and the visionaries, ascetics and artists that inspired each of them to create a sustainable, ethical and authentic existence.

"An engaging read for those with an interest in sustainable living, urban farming, and homesteading." —*Library Journal*

Watkins, Julia

Simply Living Well: A Guide to Creating a Natural, Low-Waste Home. Julia Watkins. Houghton Mifflin Harcourt 2020. xiv, 271 p. : Color; Illustration

ISBN 9780358202189

Grades: Adult 640

1. House cleaning 2. Solid waste reduction 3. Kitchen gardens 4. Homemaking 5. House and Home — Sustainable living

LC 2019045719

Easy recipes, DIY projects, and other ideas for living a beautiful and low-waste life, from the expert behind

@simply.Living.Well on Instagram.

Includes bibliographical references (pages 262-263) and index.

---

641 Food and drink

Kingsolver, Barbara

★ *Animal, Vegetable, Miracle: A Year of Food Life.* Barbara Kingsolver, with Steven L. Hopp and Camille Kingsolver; original drawings by Richard A. Houser. Harper Collins 2007. 370 p. : Illustration

ISBN 9780060852559

Grades: 11 12 Adult 641

1. Kingsolver, Barbara 2. Hopp, Steven L, 1954- 3. Natural foods 4. Farm life 5. Rural life 6. Agriculture 7. Food habits 8. Diet 9. Social life and customs 10. Appalachian Region, Southern 11. Autobiographies and memoirs 12. Life stories — Nature and outdoors — Simple living 13. Food writing — Memoirs and biographies 14. Adult books for young adults

LC 2006053516

ALA Notable Book, 2008; Book Sense Book of the Year Nonfiction, 2008; Green Prize for Sustainable Literature, 2008; James Beard Foundation Book Awards, Writing and Literature, 2008.

Follows the author's family's efforts to live on locally- and home-grown foods, an endeavor through which they learned lighthearted truths about food production and the connection between health and diet.

"This is a serious book about important problems. Its concerns are real and urgent. It is clear, thoughtful, often amusing, passionate and appealing. It may give you a serious case of supermarket guilt, thinking of the energy footprint left by each out-of-season tomato, but you'll also find unexpected knowledge and

ESSENTIAL AND RECOMMENDED TITLES
641.01 Philosophy and theory

gain the ability to make informed choices about whatand howyou're willing to eat." —*Washington Post Book World.*
Includes bibliographical references.

Moskowitz, Isa Chandra
Veganomicon: The Ultimate Vegan Cookbook. Isa Chandra Moskowitz & Terry Hope Romero. DaCapo Life Long 2007. 432 : Illustration; Color
ISBN 9780738218991
Grades: Adult **641**
1. Gluten-free diet 2. Low-fat diet 3. Milk-free diet 4. Recipes 5. Vegan cooking 6. Vegetarian cooking 7. Cookbooks 8. Food writing — Cooking and cookbooks — Courses 9. Food writing — Cooking and cookbooks — Vegetarian and vegan
LC 2017394132

Contains a collection of vegan recipes, with advice on stocking the vegan pantry, equipment, and cooking techniques and options for appetizers, breakfast, salads, soups, casseroles, one-pot meals, pasta, breads, cookies, and desserts.

The 10th anniversary edition of this popular vegan cookbook features over 250 recipes for all occasions, including 25 new dishes added to the original ones and also now has options for soy-free, gluten-free and low-fat versions.\20170801\.
Includes indexes.

641.01 Philosophy and theory

Mohammadi, Kamin
Bella Figura: How to Live, Love, and Eat the Italian Way. Kamin Mohammadi. Alfred A. Knopf 2018. 284 pages
ISBN 9780385354011
Grades: Adult **641.01**
1. Mohammadi, Kamin 2. Cooking, Italian 3. Gastronomy 4. Travel writers 5. Voyages and travels 6. Italy 7. Self-Help — Personal growth — Fashion and style 8. Self-Help — Personal growth — Happiness 9. Travel Writing — Europe
LC 2017055692

An Iranian exile and British journalist describes how in spite of her successful career she began to experience stress-related health setbacks and accepted a friend's invitation to Florence, where she discovered the Italian approach to slowing down and enjoying everyday life.

Waters, Alice
★ *We Are What We Eat: A Slow Food Manifesto.* Alice Waters; with Bob Carrau and Cristina Mueller. Penguin Press 2021. 240 p.
ISBN 9780525561538
Grades: Adult **641.01**
1. Slow food movement 2. Gastronomy 3. Food habits 4. Food industry and trade 5. Convenience foods 6. Local foods 7. United States 8. Food writing — Investigations
LC 2021008353

From chef and food activist Alice Waters, an impassioned plea for a radical reconsideration of the way each and every one of us cooks and eats.

"Waters is a food-world legend, and this is an ideal title for discussion groups, sure to provoke passionate thoughts and feelings." —*Booklist*
Includes bibliographical references.

Wilson, Bee
The Way We Eat Now. Bee Wilson. Basic Books 2019. 384 p.
ISBN 9780465093977
Grades: Adult **641.01**
1. Food habits 2. Food supply 3. Food 4. Nutrition 5. Health 6. Food consumption 7. Diet 8. Food Writing — Food and Culture 9. Food writing — History and microhistory 10. Society and culture — General

An award-winning food writer takes us on a global tour of what the world eats—and shows us how we can change it for the better.

"This compelling overview of global eating habits by acclaimed food writer and Wall Street Journal columnist Wilson…seesaws back and forth between alarming paradoxes…Wilsons many fans and new converts alike will find her arguments convincing. This diet advice goes down easy." —*Booklist*
Includes bibliographical references and index.

641.2 Food and drink — Beverages (Drinks)

Bosker, Bianca
Cork Dork: A Wine-Fueled Adventure Among the Obsessive Sommeliers, Big Bottle Hunters, and Rogue Scientists Who Taught Me to Live for Taste. Bianca Bosker. Penguin Group 2017. 352 p.
ISBN 9780143128090
Grades: Adult **641.2**
1. Bosker, Bianca 2. Wine tasting 3. Lifestyle change 4. Wine and wine making 5. Senses and sensation 6. Autobiographies and memoirs 7. Life stories — Personal growth 8. Food writing — Memoirs and biographies
LC 2016029203

A tech reporter describes her introduction to the world of master sommeliers and her in-depth investigation into the source of their interests and skills, an effort marked by work with elite tasting groups, encounters at exclusive New York restaurants, visits to California winemakers and more.

"An interesting look at those with an unquenchable thirst for those unique bottles of vinicultural perfection." —*Booklist*

Neiman, Ophelie
Wine Isn't Rocket Science: A Quick and Easy Guide to Understanding, Buying, Tasting, and Pairing Every Type of Wine. Ophelie Neiman; illustrations by Yannis Varoutsikos; translated by Nysa Kline. Black Dog & Leventhal Publishers 2017. 272 p. : Illustration; Color
ISBN 9780316431309
Grades: Adult **641.2**
1. Recipes 2. Wine and wine making 3. Food writing — Beer, wine, and liquor 4. Food writing — Cooking and cookbooks — Entertaining
LC OC2018017219

"This book is a terrific introduction to an often intimidating subject." —*Publishers Weekly*
Includes index.

O'Meara, Mallory
Girly Drinks: A World History of Women and Alcohol. Mallory O'Meara. Hanover Square Press 2021. 352 p.
ISBN 9781335282408
Grades: Adult **641.2**
1. Drinking 2. Alcoholic beverages 3. Feminism 4. Sexism 5. Gender role 6. Social life and customs 7. Patriarchy 8. Women 9. Women bartenders 10. Distilling industry and trade 11. Brewing industry and trade 12. Wine and wine making 13. Alcohol 14. History writing — Women's history 15. Food writing — Beer, wine, and liquor 16. Food writing — History and microhistory 17. Society and culture — Gender — Women

A history of the female distillers, brewers, and drinkers who have a played a key role in the development and consumption of alcohol.

"Provoking both thought and laughter, this serves as bracing refreshment from a master textual mixologist." —*Publishers Weekly*

Risen, Clay
American Whiskey, Bourbon, & Rye: A Guide to the Nation's Favorite Spirit. Clay Risen. Sterling Epicure 2013. 297 pages : Color; Illustration
ISBN 9781402798405
Grades: Adult **641.2**
1. Recipes 2. Whiskey 3. Food writing — Beer, wine, and liquor
LC Bl2013049547

Offers brief histories, ratings, and tasting notes for two hundred and six types of American whiskey, including Eagle Rare, Jim Beam, and Whistlepig.

"Risen . deftly combines history and assessment in this informative volume that covers more than 200 of the titular spirits." —*Library Journal*
Includes bibliographical references and index.

PUBLIC LIBRARY CORE COLLECTION: NONFICTION
Twentieth Edition

Zraly, Kevin
Windows on the World Complete Wine Course. Kevin Zraly. Sterling Epicure 2014. xxi, 346 pages : Illustration; Color
ISBN 9781454913641
Grades: Adult   641.2
1. Vineyards 2. Wine and wine making 3. Food writing — Beer, wine, and liquor

LC Bl2014041180

Looks at how and where wine is made and how this affects its quality and pricing, including information on how the professionals taste and rate wine and a country-by-country tour of the latest vintages.

"The casual browser will find fascinating trivia and facts about wine in numerous sidebars, but may not be able to resist becoming involved in the main text, making this difficult to put down. Highly recommended for all wine connoisseurs." —*Library Journal*
Includes index.

641.3 Food

Adarme, Adrianna
The Year of Cozy: 125 Recipes, Crafts, and Other Homemade Adventures. Adrianna Adarme. Rodale 2015. x, 259 pages : Color; Illustration
ISBN 9781623365103
Grades: Adult   641.3
1. Comfort food 2. Handicraft 3. Do-it-yourself work 4. Recipes 5. Cookbooks 6. Arts and Entertainment — Crafts and hobbies 7. Self-Help — Personal growth — Creativity 8. Food writing — Cooking and cookbooks — Narrative cookbooks

LC 2015034972

From blogger, recipe developer, and photographer Adrianna Adarme comes a beautiful book of advice for simplifying, beautifying, and living a more thoughtful life. Organized by the months of the year, and by categories such as "Live," "Do," and "Make," Adarme shares ideas for activities, recipes, and projects that make the little moments in life just as exciting as the big. Like her blog, a Cozy Kitchen, the Year of Cozy features warm and comforting photos and cozy inspiration. Adarme gives us special (but totally doable) things we can do for others and ourselves. From recipes to DIY crafts, Adarme focuses on easy, inexpensive undertakings that have a big reward: Happiness. The best moments in life don't require stuff, they just require intention. Adarme's clear and easy-to-follow instructions and recipes will excite and motivate you to march into your kitchen and craft closet to make something you can be proud of.
Includes index.

Barber, Dan
The Third Plate: Field Notes on a New Cuisine. by Dan Barber. The Penguin Press 2014. 496 pages
ISBN 9781594204074
Grades: Adult   641.3
1. Cooking, American 2. Natural foods 3. Cooking (Natural foods) 4. Seasonal cooking 5. Agriculture 6. Sustainability 7. United States 8. Food writing — Investigations

LC 2013039966

Green Prize for Sustainable Literature: Adult Nonfiction, 2015; James Beard Foundation Book Awards, Writing and Literature, 2015.

Renowned chef Dan Barber introduces a new kind of cuisine that represents the future of American dining in THE THIRD PLATE. Barber explores the evolution of American food from the "first plate," or industrially-produced, meat-heavy dishes, to the "second plate" of grass-fed meat and organic greens, and says that both of these approaches are ultimately neither sustainable nor healthy. Instead, Barber proposes Americans should move to the "third plate," a cuisine rooted in seasonal productivity, natural livestock rhythms, whole-grains, and small portions of free-range meat. Barber's book charts a bright path for eaters and chefs alike towards a healthy and sustainable future for American cuisine.

"In this bold and impassioned analysis, Barber insists that chefs have the power to transform American cuisine to achieve a sustainable and nutritious future." —*Kirkus*
Includes bibliographical references and index.

Chaplin, Amy
Whole Food Cooking Every Day: Transform the Way You Eat with 250 Vegetarian Recipes Free of Gluten, Dairy, and Refined Sugar. Amy Chaplin; photographs by Anson Smart. Artisan 2019. 400 pages : Color; Illustration
ISBN 9781579658021
Grades: Adult   641.3
1. Cooking (Natural foods) 2. Natural foods 3. Recipes 4. Cookbooks 5. Food writing — Cooking and cookbooks — Chefs and restaurants 6. Food writing — Cooking and cookbooks — Ingredients 7. Food writing — Cooking and cookbooks — Cooking for health

LC 2018039183

The James Beard Award-winning author of a healthy eating cookbook shares her brilliant recipes incorporating whole foods that can transform a diet including Butternut Squash Soup with Toasted Hazelnut Milk and Sauteed Root Vegetables with Parsley, Poppy Seeds and Lemon. Illustrations.
Includes index.

David, Laurie
The Family Cooks: 100+ Recipes to Get Your Family Craving Food That's Simple, Tasty, and Incredibly Good for You. Laurie David; foreword by Katie Couric; photographs by Quentin Bacon. Rodale Books 2014. IX, 277 pages : Color; Illustration
ISBN 9781623362508
Grades: Adult   641.3
1. Cooking (Natural foods) 2. Families 3. Recipes 4. Cookbooks 5. Food writing — Cooking and cookbooks — Cooking for health 6. Food writing — Cooking and cookbooks — Cooking for the family 7. Self-Help — Personal growth — Diet and nutrition

LC 2014003505

Citing high-priced marketing campaigns designed to promote processed foods, a guide to promoting long-term healthy eating habits shares more than 100 recipes that emphasize minimal preparation times, healthy ingredients and low-stress cooking practices.

"Written primarily for busy families with children, David's attractive guide to reclaiming the family dinner will also appeal to young couples and professionals trying to shop smarter and eat less-processed meals at home." —*Library Journal*
Includes index.

Dinki, Nikki
Meat on the Side: Delicious Vegetable-Focused Recipes for Every Day. Nikki Dinki; photographs by Ellen Silverman. St. Martin's Griffin 2016. xviii, 270 pages : Color; Illustration
ISBN 9781250067166
Grades: Adult   641.3
1. Cooking (Vegetables) 2. Cookbooks 3. Food writing — Cooking and cookbooks — Ingredients

LC 2015043188

Shares plant-based recipes that feature some meat.

"For those who like flexible recipes that can be both meaty and meatless, this cookbook provides excellent choices." —*Library Journal*

DiSpirito, Rocco
Rocco's Healthy+Delicious: More Than 200 (Mostly) Plant-Based Recipes for Everyday Life. Rocco Dispirito. Harper Wave 2017. xiii, 383 pages : Color; Illustration
ISBN 9780062378125
Grades: Adult   641.3
1. Cooking (Natural foods) 2. Nutrition 3. Vegan cooking 4. Recipes 5. Cookbooks 6. Food writing — Cooking and cookbooks — Ingredients

ESSENTIAL AND RECOMMENDED TITLES
641.3 Food

7. Food writing — Cooking and cookbooks — Chefs and restaurants 8. Food writing — Cooking and cookbooks — Cooking for health

LC 2017012595

Presents the health benefits of eating a plant-based diet, with information about natural ingredients and a collection of recipes for snacks, smoothies, main dishes, sides, and desserts.

Includes index.

El-Waylly, Sohla
★ *Start Here: Instructions for Becoming a Better Cook*. Sohla El-Waylly. Knopf 2023. 656 pages :
ISBN 9780593320464
Grades: Adult   641.3

1. Cooking 2. Food preparation 3. Recipes 4. Food Writing — Cooking and cookbooks — Methods

A practical, information-packed, and transformative guide to becoming a better cook and conquering the kitchen, this is a must-have masterclass in leveling up your cooking. Across a dozen technique-themed chapters, from "Temperature Management 101" & "Break it Down & Get Saucy" to "Mix it Right," "Go to Brown Town," and "Getting to Know Dough," Sohla El-Waylly explains the hows and whys of cooking, introducing the fundamental skills that you need to become a more intuitive, inventive cook.

"This cookbook will be invaluable for readers who are getting started cooking. The recipes will motivate them to get in the kitchen, but experienced cooks and bakers will relish the abundance of information and interesting recipes too." —*Library Journal*

Foer, Jonathan Safran
Eating Animals. Jonathan Safran Foer. Little Brown & Co. 2009. 256 p.
ISBN 9780316069908
Grades: 11 12 Adult   641.3

1. Vegetarianism 2. Food 3. Animal welfare 4. Meat industry and trade 5. Food habits 6. Philosophy 7. Food consumption 8. Page to screen 9. Food writing — Investigations 10. Adult books for young adults

LC 2009034434

Booklist Editors' Choice, 2009.

Foer dissects our dietary choices in an intriguing look at why we eat the things we do.

Title adapted into a film by the same name in 2017.

Forte, Sara
The Sprouted Kitchen: A Tastier Take on Whole Foods. Sara Forte; photography by Hugh Forte. Ten Speed Press 2012. 241 p. : Color illustration
ISBN 9781607741145
Grades: Adult   641.3

1. Cooking (Cereals) 2. Cooking (Natural foods) 3. Recipes 4. Cooking 5. Cookbooks 6. Food writing — Cooking and cookbooks — Cooking for health

LC 2012008143

Sara Forte showcases her tasty take on whole foods with 100 easy, produce-rich recipes that take advantage of whole grains, unsaturated fats, natural sugar alternatives, and bright, seasonal flavors.

Includes index.

Ganeshram, Ramin
Future Chefs: Recipes by Tomorrow's Cooks Across the Nation and the World. Ramin Ganeshram; photography by Jean Paul Vellotti. Rodale 2014. xi, 276 pages : Color; Illustration
ISBN 9781623362065
Grades: Adult   641.3

1. Teenage cooks 2. Cooking 3. Recipes 4. Cookbooks 5. Food writing — Cooking and cookbooks — Courses

LC 2014025322

A curated collection of 150 recipes drawn from the experience and kitchens of young cooks all over America and the world, FutureChefs brings exciting and unique recipes to your kitchen for you or your kids to make at home! Here you'll find the real, cooking-obsessed tweens and teens from diverse social and cultural backgrounds—the face of America's culinary future. Veteran journalist and trained chef Ramin Ganeshram has crafted profiles of serious young chefs whose experience varies from culinary contest winners and prolific food bloggers to brand new cooks in the kitchen. Whether these kids have taken to cooking out of necessity, inspiration, or sheer passion, their stories all share common threads of creativity, hard work, and a look at what's ahead in America's culinary scene. This generation is more interested in hands-on cooking than ever, but they're lacking the platform to showcase their talents. FutureChefs is the perfect vehicle for these kids to share their passion, their stories, and, of course, their recipes.

Includes index.

Hamilton, Gabrielle
Prune. Gabrielle Hamilton. Random House 2014. 567 pages : Color; Illustration
ISBN 9780812994094
Grades: Adult   641.3

1. Cooking, French 2. Cooking, American 3. Recipes 4. Cookbooks 5. Food writing — Cooking and cookbooks — Regional 6. Food writing — Cooking and cookbooks — Chefs and restaurants 7. Food writing — Cooking and cookbooks — Methods

LC 2014003617

A full repertoire of the many recipes served at the beloved Lower East Side restaurant Prune over the last thirteen years from one of America's most recognized chefs and established literary talents. The recipes are written from the unique perspective of cook to cook, as if Gabrielle were addressing her own line cooks, some seasoned, some green, with all of the essential elements provided to getting a dish just right—all presented in a way that will make total sense to home cooks, too.

"Recipes range from a complex cold pork with tuna sauce to a simple butter-and-sugar sandwich. Despite the books address to fellow restaurateurs, skilled home chefs can find a number of ways to profit from a fair number of Hamilton's creations." —*Booklist*

Helwig, Jenna
Baby-Led Feeding: A Natural Way to Raise Happy, Independent Eaters. Jenna Helwig with Natalia Stasenko, MS, RD.. Houghton Mifflin Harcourt 2018. 205 pages : Color; Illustration
ISBN 9780544963405
Grades: Adult   641.3

1. Baby foods 2. Family and Relationships — Growing up 3. Food writing — Cooking and cookbooks — Cooking for the family

LC 2017051889

What if you could skip the tiny jars and pouches of bland baby food in favor of a more natural, flavor-filled, and family-friendly transition to solid foods? Baby-led feeding (also known as baby-led weaning) is just that. Feeding your baby a variety of healthy, wholesome solid foods, rather than relying solely on purees, is thought to promote motor skills and establish lifelong healthy eating habits. Here, author and food editor at Parents magazine Jenna Helwig gives an easy-to-follow introduction to this popular new method. With more than 100 ideas and recipes, this bright, photo-driven book includes chapters on the benefits of this approach, when and how to get started, essential safety and nutrition guidelines, frequently asked questions, basic fruit and vegetable prep, more complex finger foods, and family meals. All recipes have been reviewed by a registered dietitian and include nutrition information to ensure a healthy mealtime.

"The baby gets to choose (and have more variety) in this easy-to-use guide." —*Library Journal*

Includes index.

Hill, McKel
Nutrition Stripped: Whole-Food Recipes Made Deliciously Simple. McKel Hill, MS, RDN.. William Morrow 2016. 295 pages : Color; Illustration
ISBN 9780062419927
Grades: Adult   641.3

1. Cooking (Natural foods) 2. Natural foods 3. Recipes 4. Cookbooks 5. Food writing — Cooking and cookbooks — Ingredients 6. Food writing — Cooking and cookbooks — Cooking for health

PUBLIC LIBRARY CORE COLLECTION: NONFICTION
Twentieth Edition

LC Bl2016036178

Collects recipes from the Nutrition Stripped website, showing readers how to make simple, healthy meals, snacks, and beverages using whole foods.

"Best known for the anti-inflammatory turmeric milk recipe on her healthy living site, Nutrition Stripped, Hill offers elixirs and more in her first cookbook. But this is more than a cookbook; its a healthy living guide." —*Booklist*

Includes index.

Lakshmi, Padma

The Encyclopedia of Spices and Herbs: An Essential Guide to the Flavors of the World. Padma Lakshmi; with Judith Sutton and Kalustyan's Spice Shop; photographs by Evan Sung. Ecco 2016. xii, 335 pages : Color; Illustration

ISBN 9780062375230

Grades: Adult 641.3

1. Cooking (Herbs) 2. Cooking (Spices) 3. Herbs 4. Spices 5. Food writing — Cooking and cookbooks — Ingredients 6. Food writing — Cooking and cookbooks — Reference

LC Bl2016042330

The Emmy-nominated host of Top Chef presents an A-to-Z compendium of spices, herbs, salts, peppers and blends that combines sumptuous photography with culinary lore and advice.

"Cooks will appreciate Lakshmi's explanations of what goes into spice blends such as Chinese five spice powder, curries, dukkah, and garam masala. Full-color photographs appear every few pages, showing spices and herbs in various states, from just-harvested to finely ground." —*Library Journal*

Includes bibliographical references (pages 325-326) and index.

McFadden, Joshua

★ *Grains for Every Season: Rethinking Our Way with Grains.* Joshua McFadden with Martha Holmberg; photography by AJ Meeker, Ashley Marti, and David Alvarado. Artisan Books 2021. 349 pages : Color; Illustration

ISBN 9781579659561

Grades: Adult 641.3

1. Cooking (Cereals) 2. Cooking (Natural foods) 3. Grain 4. Cookbooks 5. Food Writing — Cooking and cookbooks — Chefs and restaurants 6. Food Writing — Cooking and cookbooks — Ingredients

LC 2021004797

The James Beard Award-winning author behind Six Seasons presents 200 recipes for salads, soups, pastas, pizzas and desserts all made from, and organized by, different grains including Meat Loaf with Barley and Mushrooms and Peanut Butter-Barley Cookies.

"McFadden's latest is destined to become a go-to cookbook." —*Library Journal*

Includes index.

McKoy, Bri

The Cook's Book: Recipes for Keeps & Essential Techniques to Master Everyday Cooking. Bri McKoy. Revell, a division of Baker Publishing Group 2023. 304 pages : Color; Illustration

ISBN 9780800742942

Grades: Adult 641.3

1. Cooking 2. Cookware 3. Kitchen utensils 4. Cookbooks 5. Food writing — Cooking and cookbooks — Reference 6. Food writing — Cooking and cookbooks — Methods

LC 2022044701

This foolproof, upbeat kitchen companion helps hesitant home cooks go beyond simple recipe reading, giving them the skills they need to master the art of confident cooking.

"The result is an excellent resource that budding home cooks will turn to time and again." —*Publishers Weekly*

Includes index.

Mitchell, Andie

Eating in the Middle: A Mostly Wholesome Cookbook. Andie Mitchell; photographs by Aran Goyoaga. Clarkson Potter 2016. 240 pages : Color; Illustration

ISBN 9780770433277

Grades: Adult 641.3

1. Cooking, American 2. Diet 3. Food 4. Health 5. Nutrition 6. Recipes 7. Cookbooks 8. Food writing — Cooking and cookbooks — Cooking for health 9. Food writing — Cooking and cookbooks — Regional

LC 2015034879

From the author of the New York times bestselling It was me all along, a cookbook for eating in balance, featuring mostly healthy recipes to help anyone stay fit, and a few "special occasion" sweets and entrees, with the author's moving story of weight loss and thoughts on managing cravings throughout.—.

In her first cookbook, the author—who struggled with obesity, lost weight and found balance in her eating habits—shares the recipes that helped her reach her goals and maintain her healthy size along with new anecdotes from her weight-loss journey and thoughts on managing cravings.

Includes index.

Murad, Noor

★ *Ottolenghi Test Kitchen: Extra Good Things : Bold, Vegetable-Forward Recipes Plus Homemade Sauces, Condiments, and More to Build a Flavor-packed Pantry.* Noor Murad & Yotam Ottolenghi; photography by Elena Heatherwick. Clarkson Potter/Publishers 2022. 253 pages : Color; Illustration

ISBN 9780593234389

Grades: Adult 641.3

1. Cooking 2. Cooking (Natural foods) 3. Vegetarian cooking 4. Sauces 5. Condiments 6. Cookbooks 7. Food writing — Cooking and cookbooks — Chefs and restaurants 8. Food writing — Cooking and cookbooks — Regional

LC 2022016182

These abundant, vegetable-forward recipes provide delicious, hearty meals, plus that extra takeaway—make-ahead condiments, sauces and a variety of toppings that will transform any dish into an Ottolenghi favorite.

"Long-standing Ottolenghi fans will find plenty of new favorites, while the title also serves as an accessible introduction for newcomers to his style and methods." —*Library Journal*

Includes fold-out pages; Includes index.

Nezhukumatathil, Aimee

Bite by Bite: Nourishments and Jamborees. Aimee Nezhukumatathil. Ecco Press 2024. 192 p.

ISBN 9780063282261

Grades: Adult 641.3

1. Nezhukumatathil, Aimee 2. Women authors 3. Filipino Americans 4. Indian Americans 5. Memories 6. Food 7. Culture 8. Family relationships 9. Taste 10. Flavor 11. Pleasure 12. Southeast Asian people 13. South Asian people 14. Filipino people 15. Indian people 16. American people 17. Essays 18. Autobiographies and memoirs 19. Book club best bets 20. Food writing — Memoirs and biographies 21. Food Writing — Food and Culture

A collection of short essays from the author of World of Wonders that investigate the relationship between humans and food, discussing how different dishes and traditions impact our identities and evoke associations and remembrances of joy, grief and desire.

"This whimsical and soothing work will appeal to fans of food writing, memoirs, intercultural stories, and poetry." —*Booklist*

Olmsted, Larry

Real Food/Fake Food: Why You Don't Know What You're Eating & What You Can Do About It. Larry Olmsted. Algonquin Books of Chapel Hill 2016. 320 p.

ISBN 9781616204211

Grades: Adult 641.3

1. Food 2. Fraud 3. Consumer education 4. Food substitutes 5. Food additives 6. Nutrition 7. Food writing — Investigations

LC 2016018797

You've seen the headlines: Parmesan cheese made from sawdust. Lobster rolls containing no lobster at all. Extra virgin olive oil that isn't. Fake foods are in our supermarkets, our restaurants, and our kitchen cabinets. Award-winning food journalist and travel writer Larry Olmsted exposes the pervasive and dangerous fraud perpetrated on unsuspecting Americans. Real Food/Fake Food

ESSENTIAL AND RECOMMENDED TITLES
641.3 Food

brings readers into the unregulated food industry, revealing the alarming truth: What we think we're eating is not what we're really eating.

"A provocative yet grounded look at the U.S. food industry. Though the prospect of finding quality food products may prove increasingly challenging for most consumers, Olmsted provides encouraging tips to help navigate the many obstacles." —*Kirkus*

Published simultaneously in Canada by Thomas Allen & Son Limited.

Robinson, Jo
Eating on the Wild Side: The Missing Link to Optimum Health. Jo Robinson; illustrations by Andie Styner. Little, Brown and Company 2013. VIII, 407 pages : Illustration
ISBN 9780316227940
Grades: Adult   641.3
1. Natural foods 2. Society and culture — General 3. Science writing — Medicine and health — Diet and nutrition
LC 2013934815

Describes how to replace modern fruits and vegetables, which are high in starch and sugar and lower in nutrients than earlier generations of the plants, with different varieties, easily located in grocery stores and farmers markets, that have better nutritional value.

Includes bibliographical references (pages 375-400) and index.

Rodale, Maria
Scratch: Home Cooking for Everyone Made Simple, Fun, and Totally Delicious. Maria Rodale, with Melanie Hansche; photographs by Con Poulos and Stacey Cramp. Rodale 2016. xxx, 352 pages : Color; Illustration
ISBN 9781623366438
Grades: Adult   641.3
1. Comfort food 2. Cooking 3. Seasonal cooking 4. Cookbooks 5. Food writing — Cooking and cookbooks — Cooking for health 6. Food writing — Cooking and cookbooks — Ingredients
LC 2016033950

Maria Rodale was raised on real food. She doesn't think of eating homemade, from scratch meals as part of a trend or movement; it has always been her life. Raised in a family of farmers, bakers, chefs, gardeners, and publishers, Maria is used to growing, cooking, reading and writing about, and eating organic, delicious food. And now, for the first time ever, she's sharing her tried-and-true family recipes. Scratch is full of comfort food recipes that aren't focused on any one healthy trend, but are instead innately healthy, because Maria inspires you to return to your kitchen and cook with real, organic food. Recipes like Pasta Fagiole, Maria's Fried Chicken, and Lamb & Barley Soup will be crowd pleasers for sure, but Maria throws in some unique-to-the-family recipes that are going to delight as well, such as her Pennsylvania Dutch Dandelion Salad with Bacon Dressing, Ardie's Pasties, and Homemade Hoppin' John (a black-eyed pea stew made with smoked turkey or ham). Besides sharing her family's favorite recipes, Maria's book also gives you a peek into her life as a Rodale, with personal family portraits and stories. With this cookbook, you can eat like the Rodale family every night of the week with delicious food to make at home, from scratch. Naturally healthy, bacon included.

The CEO and chairwoman of Rodale, Inc, inspires readers to return to their kitchens and cook with real, organic food by sharing her family¡s recipes as well as personal family stories and portraits.

"This down-to-earth, totally accessible cookbook will take any cook from breakfast to dessert." —*Publishers Weekly*

Includes index.

Saladino, Dan
Eating to Extinction: The World's Rarest Foods and Why We Need to Save Them. Dan Saladino. Farrar, Straus and Giroux 2022. 496 p.
ISBN 9780374605322
Grades: Adult   641.3
1. Food 2. Biodiversity 3. Globalization 4. Food security 5. Food supply 6. Rare and endangered plants 7. Rare and endangered animals 8. Food industry and trade 9. Food consumption 10. Food writing — Investigations
LC 2021041139

A global tour of some of the world's rarest and most endangered foods.

"Foodies and slow food enthusiasts will appreciate this deep dive into the history and diversity of global foods and the call to preserve them." —*Library Journal*

Originally published in 2021 by Jonathan Cape, Great Britain; Includes bibliographical references and index.

Schatzker, Mark
The Dorito Effect: The Surprising New Truth About Food and Flavor. Mark Schatzker. Simon & Schuster 2015. 288 p.
ISBN 9781476724218
Grades: Adult   641.3
1. Junk food 2. Nutrition 3. Taste 4. Dieting 5. Food portions 6. Canadian literature 7. Food writing — Investigations
LC 2014044543

The award-winning author of Steak argues that the key to reversing America's health crisis lies in the overlooked link between nutrition and flavor, explaining how technologically advanced but plentiful foods have been rendered less nutritious and taste-appealing.

"This is a provocative new take on American eating." —*Booklist*

Siegel, Matt
The Secret History of Food: Strange but True Stories About the Origins of Everything We Eat. Matt Siegel. Ecco Press 2021. 320 p.
ISBN 9780062973214
Grades: Adult   641.3
1. Food 2. Food habits 3. Cooking 4. Food writing — General 5. History writing — Arts and culture

Exploring cultural, scientific, sexual and culinary substructures, this essential read for all foodies, at turns both funny and fascinating, looks at the little-known history surrounding foods we know and love.

"A great addition to the celebrity cookbook shelf, as well as a go-to source for a variety of delicious recipes influenced by a range of cuisines." —*Library Journal*

Stark, Lizzie
★ *Egg: A Dozen Ovatures.* Lizzie Stark. 2023. 240 pages
ISBN 9780393531503
Grades: Adult   641.3
1. Eggs 2. Social history 3. Signs and symbols 4. Cooking (Eggs) 5. Faberge eggs 6. Egg decoration 7. Chickens 8. Natural history 9. History writing — Microhistory 10. Food writing — Food and culture 11. Food writing — History and microhistory
LC 2022048812

The egg is a paradox—both alive and not alive—and a symbol as old as culture itself. In this wide-ranging and delightful journey through its natural and cultural history, Lizzie Stark explores the egg's deep meanings, innumerable uses, and metabolic importance through a dozen dazzling specimens.

"This delightful paean to the egg is equal parts fun, philosophical, educational, and irreverent." —*Publishers Weekly*

Includes bibliographical references and index.

Tandoh, Ruby
★ *Eat Up: Food, Appetite and Eating What You Want.* Ruby Tandoh. Vintage Books 2022. 256 p.
ISBN 9780593466810
Grades: Adult   641.3
1. Food 2. Dieting 3. Food habits 4. Cooking 5. Appetite 6. Taste 7. Food writing — Food and culture

Filled with straight-talking, sympathetic advice on everything from mental health to recipe ideas and shopping tips, this is a book that clears away the fog, to help you fall back in love with food.

"A colorful, thoughtful collection that reads like memoir-meets-food science, perfect for foodies and anyone looking to examine their relationship with food and celebrate the joy of eating." —*Library Journal*

Originally published in the UK by Serpent's Tail, London, in 2018; Includes bibliography and index.

Thompson, Jennifer Trainer
Fresh Fish: A Fearless Guide to Grilling, Shucking, Searing, Poaching and Roasting Seafood. Jennifer Trainer Thompson; photographs by Keller + Keller. Storey Publishing 2016. 351 pages : Color; Illustration
ISBN 9781612128085
Grades: Adult   641.3
  1. Cooking (Fish) 2. Cookbooks 3. Food writing — Cooking and cookbooks — Ingredients 4. Food writing — Cooking and cookbooks — Regional
                              LC 2015041612
  Collects recipes that showcase the versatility of seafood, including such options as curried lobster roll and New-Haven style white clam pizza, and offers tips on everything from shucking oysters and roasting whole fish to organizing a clambake.
  Includes index.

Turshen, Julia
Simply Julia: 110 Easy Recipes for Healthy Comfort Food. Julia Turshen. Harper Wave, an imprint of HarperCollinsPublishers 2021. xxviii, 271 pages : Color; Illustration
ISBN 9780062993335
Grades: Adult   641.3
  1. Cooking 2. Comfort food 3. Food writing — Cooking and cookbooks — Cooking for health
                              LC 2020027738
  From cookbook author Julia Turshen comes a new collection of simple yet inspired recipes, in her most personal and visually arresting book to date.
  "Turshen writes from a home cook's perspective, and her fourth solo cookbook offers relaxed comfort food with a slew of creative, contemporary twists."
  —*Library Journal*
  Includes index.

Von Bremzen, Anya
National Dish: Around the World in Search of Food, History, and the Meaning of Home. Anya von Bremzen. Penguin Press 2023. 352 p.
ISBN 9780735223165
Grades: Adult   641.3
  1. Food habits 2. Food 3. Nationalism 4. Identity 5. Home (Concept) 6. Culture 7. Voyages and travels 8. France 9. Italy 10. Japan 11. Spain 12. Mexico 13. Turkey 14. Food Writing — Food and culture 15. Travel Writing — General
                              LC 2022049211
  National Dish peels back the layers of myth, commercialization, and fetishization around the great world cuisines. In so doing, it brings us to a deep appreciation of how the country makes the food, and the food the country.
  "Fans of food and travel writing will want to sink their teeth into this."
  —*Publishers Weekly*
  Includes bibliographical references and index.

Weil, Andrew
Fast Food, Good Food: More Than 150 Quick and Easy Ways to Put Healthy, Delicious Food on the Table. Andrew Weil, MD; photographs by Ditte Isager. Little, Brown and company 2015. 293 pages : Color; Illustration
ISBN 9780316329422
Grades: Adult   641.3
  1. Cooking (Natural foods) 2. Quick and easy cooking 3. Recipes 4. Cookbooks 5. Food writing — Cooking and cookbooks — Methods 6. Food writing — Cooking and cookbooks — Cooking for health
                              LC 2015931944
  These days, fewer people than ever are cooking meals at home. Convincing ourselves that we don't have time to cook, we've forgotten how fast, simple, and wonderfully satisfying it can be to prepare delicious meals in our own kitchens for the people we love. With guidance on following an anti-inflammatory diet and mouth-wateringly gorgeous photographs, FAST FOOD, GOOD FOOD will inspire the inner nutritionist and chef in every reader.

"Weil's accessible recipes will attract flexitarians, especially those with a penchant for seafood, vegetables, whole grains, and olive oil." —*Library Journal*
  Includes index.

Wong, Cecily
  ★ *Gastro Obscura: A Food Adventurer's Guide.* Cecily Wong, Dylan Thuras with additional writing by Rachel Rummel, Anne Ewbank, and Sam O'Brien. Workman Publishing 2021. 438 pages : Illustration; Color
ISBN 9781523502196
Grades: Adult   641.3
  1. Dinners and dining 2. Food 3. Curiosities and wonders 4. Voyages and travels 5. Trivia and miscellaneous facts 6. Food Writing — Food and culture 7. Travel Writing — General
                              LC 2021025589
  The team behind Atlas Obscura, a friendly tour-guide to the world's most amazing places, presents incredible ingredients, food adventures and edible wonders from around the world, including Chilean beer made from fog and 2,000-year-old egg ovens.
  "Armchair travelers and foodies will be left hungry, nostalgic, more knowledgeable about dishes from all over, and, most importantly, ready to try something different, whether it's found around the corner or across the world."
  —*Library Journal*
  An Atlas Obscura book—Cover; Includes index.

641.4 Food preservation and storage

West, Kevin
Saving the Season: A Cook's Guide to Home Canning, Pickling, and Preserving. Kevin West. Alfred A. Knopf 2013. 532 pages : Illustration; Color
ISBN 9780307599483
Grades: Adult   641.4
  1. Canning and preserving 2. Seasonal cooking 3. Recipes 4. Cookbooks 5. Food writing — Cooking and cookbooks — Methods
                              LC 2012037844
  A stylish, richly illustrated, practical guide for home cooks and preserving enthusiasts, the first cookbook from journalist Kevin West, author of the popular blog Savingtheseason.Com. Incorporating classic favorites and new flavors, West gives us more than one hundred recipes, organized by season, for sweet preserves and savory pickles; easy-to-can vegetables and fruits; condiments such as relishes, chutneys, and salsas; and cordials, candies, and cocktails. Interspersed with the recipes are chronicles of West's travels and the history of American preserving traditions from California to New Mexico to Long Island. A witty and erudite culinary companion, West makes a rich and entertaining story of the introductions to the recipes. Also included is a primer on preserving techniques that addresses issues of food safety and nutrition.
  Includes bibliographical references (pages 515-518) and index.

641.5 Cooking

Acheson, Hugh
The Chef and the Slow Cooker: A Cookbook. Hugh Acheson; photographs by Andy Lee. Clarkson Potter/Publishers 2017. 256 p.
ISBN 9780451498540
Grades: Adult   641.5
  1. Electric cooking 2. Quick and easy cooking 3. Cookbooks 4. Food writing — Cooking and cookbooks — Methods 5. Food writing — Cooking and cookbooks — Chefs and restaurants
                              LC 2017011173
  Presents a collection of recipes for the slow cooker, including options for broths, soups, beans, meats, fish, vegetables, butters, chutneys, and desserts.

ESSENTIAL AND RECOMMENDED TITLES
641.5 Cooking

Adler, Tamar
An Everlasting Meal: Cooking with Economy and Grace. Tamar Adler. Scribner 2011. xiii, 250 p.
ISBN 9781439181874
Grades: Adult　　　　　　　　　　　　　　　　641.5
1. Cooking 2. Gastronomy 3. Food preparation 4. Essays 5. Food writing — General
LC Bl2011028784

A practical guide to cooking and eating well regardless of financial circumstances explains how to shop and cook with an eye toward future meals while using scraps and leftovers to prepare nutritious, satisfying secondary foods.

"Improving upon M. F. K. Fisher's How to Cook a Wolf (1988) may seem impossible, yet riffing on it while injecting an up-to-date sensibility about cooking and food and the memories associated with kitchenry may, indeed, be Adler's contribution to food literature." —*Booklist*
Includes index.

Ali, Laila
Food for Life: Delicious & Healthy Comfort Food from My Table to Yours! Laila Ali; with Leida Scheintaub. St. Martin's Press 2017. 312 pages : Color; Illustration
ISBN 9781250131096
Grades: Adult　　　　　　　　　　　　　　　　641.5
1. Comfort food 2. Cooking 3. Cookbooks 4. Food writing — Cooking and cookbooks — Cooking for health
LC 2017045756

Collects one hundred hearty and flavor-focused recipes that can fit into any busy schedule, including oven "fried" chicken, cheesy cauliflower pizza, and heavenly lemon yogurt cake.
Includes bibliographical references and index.

Anderson, Pam
How to Cook Without a Book: Recipes and Techniques Every Cook Should Know by Heart. Pam Anderson. Broadway Books 2000. 290 p.
ISBN 9780767902793
Grades: 11 12 Adult　　　　　　　　　　　　　641.5
1. Quick and easy cooking 2. Recipes 3. Cookbooks 4. Food writing — Cooking and cookbooks — Methods
LC 99043776

Recalling an earlier era when cooks relied on sight, touch, and taste rather than cookbooks, the author encourages readers to rediscover the lost art of preparing food and use their imagination in the kitchen.

"Former executive editor of Cook's magazine and author of the Perfect Recipe, Anderson wants to teach Americans a new way to cook without relying on recipes. It's somewhat surprising, then, to discover that this book is full of recipes. However, readers may cotton to Anderson's method: Each chapter consists of a simple technique, basic recipe, variations, key points and a little mnemonic device used to recall the technique. The techniques are, for the most part, terrific time-savers." —*Publishers Weekly*

Andres, Jose
Vegetables Unleashed: A Cookbook. Jose Andres and Matt Goulding; photography by Peter Frank Edwards. Ecco 2019. 357 pages. : Color; Illustration
ISBN 9780062668387
Grades: Adult　　　　　　　　　　　　　　　　641.5
1. Cooking (Vegetables) 2. Vegetarian cooking 3. Recipes 4. Cookbooks 5. Food writing — Cooking and cookbooks — Vegetarian and vegan 6. Food writing — Cooking and cookbooks — Chefs and restaurants 7. Food writing — Cooking and cookbooks — Ingredients
LC Bl2019014702

A world-renowned Spanish chef and an award-winning food author present a collection of tricks and tips that focus on the vibrancy and diversity of vegetable-based dishes such as lentil stew, vegetable paella and the classic Spanish gazpacho.

"Recommendations for composting, in-season and farmer's-market shopping, and using seeds and scraps all underscore their waste-reducing ethos and their goal to get people excited about things that sprout from the ground." —*Booklist*
An Anthony Bourdain book; Includes index.

Apfelbaum, Chanie
★ *Totally Kosher: Tradition with a Twist! 150+ Recipes for the Holidays and Every Day.* Chanie Apfelbaum; photographs by Chanie Apfelbaum. Clarkson Potter/Publishers 2023. 319 pages : Color; Illustration
ISBN 9780593232613
Grades: Adult　　　　　　　　　　　　　　　　641.5
1. Cooking, Jewish 2. Cooking, Kosher 3. Kosher food 4. Cookbooks 5. Food writing — Cooking and cookbooks — Regional
LC 2022020787

The founder of the popular blog Busy in Brooklyn and author of the cookbook Millennial Kosher introduces home cooks to exciting ways to bring global flavors to a kosher kitchen through 150 modern recipes that keep kosher food exciting and delicious for the entire family.

"Fans of Apfelbaum's popular blog Busy in Brooklyn already know this is a must-have cookbook for kosher kitchens, but it's also a breath of fresh air for cooks looking for big flavors and a fun voice." —*Library Journal*
Includes index.

Aron, Jules
Vegan Cheese: Simple, Delicious, Plant-Based Recipes. Jules Aron. The Countryman Press 2017. 190 p. : Color; Illustration
ISBN 9781581574036
Grades: Adult　　　　　　　　　　　　　　　　641.5
1. Cheese 2. Recipes 3. Vegan cooking 4. Cookbooks 5. Food writing — Cooking and cookbooks — Vegetarian and vegan
LC Oc2018007570

"Aron's book is a useful, fun, and necessary addition to both the beginner and advanced vegan cooks repertoire." —*Publishers Weekly*
Includes index.

Baz, Molly
Cook This Book: Techniques That Teach & Recipes to Repeat. Molly Baz. Clarkson Potter/Publishers 2021. 303 pages : Illustration; Color
ISBN 9780593138274
Grades: Adult　　　　　　　　　　　　　　　　641.5
1. Cooking 2. Quick and easy cooking 3. Cookbooks 4. Food writing — Cooking and cookbooks
LC Bl2021008639

A new kind of foundational cookbook, this thoroughly modern guide to becoming a smarter, faster, more creative cook serves up clear and uncomplicated recipes that make cooking fun and will inspire a new generation to find joy in the kitchen.

"With its DIY approach to culinary expertise, this is a great starting point for home cooks wanting to develop flavor and technique." —*Library Journal*
Includes bibliographical references (page 295) and index.

Ben-Ishay, Melissa
Come Hungry: Salads, Meals, and Sweets for People Who Live to Eat. Melissa Ben-Ishay; photography by Ashley Sears. William Morrow, an imprint of HarperCollinsPublishers 2024. 279 pages : Color; Illustration
ISBN 9780063299276
Grades: Adult　　　　　　　　　　　　　　　　641.5
1. Cooking 2. Quick and easy cooking 3. Vegetarian cooking 4. Vegan cooking 5. Cookbooks 6. Food writing — Cooking and cookbooks — Vegetarian and vegan 7. Food writing — Cooking and cookbooks — Courses
LC Bl2024000247

In Come Hungry, Melissa shares her favorite everyday recipes and tips for creating nourishing, delicious meals the whole family will love. With flavorful ingredients and easy-to-follow instructions, Melissa encourages home cooks of all levels to cook outside of their comfort zones and reveals her go-to techniques for creating the perfect bite.

"This fresh, flavor-packed cookbook makes it easy to load up on vegetable-focused meals." —*Library Journal*
Includes index.

Berens, Abra
Ruffage: A Practical Guide to Vegetables. Abra Berens; photographs by E.E. Berger; illustrations by Lucy Engelman. Chronicle Books 2019. 464 p.
ISBN 9781452169323
Grades: Adult   **641.5**
1. Vegetarian cooking 2. Vegetables 3. Cooking (Vegetables) 4. Food writing — Cooking and cookbooks — Vegetarian and vegan
LC 2018022344

In this insightful and enchanting cookbook, new flavors, textures, techniques, and ways to enjoy all the vegetables you want to eat are revealed by chef and former farmer Abra Berens. Not only a terrific resource, with more than 300 recipes written in Berens' uniquely succinct style, the book also presents evocative storytelling to open each chapter, and photography that conveys the seasons and rugged beauty of Michigan farm country.

"Crammed with exciting ideas that encourage creativity, this lively book will quickly become an essential item in the home cook's library." —*Library Journal*
Contains photographs and illustrations.

Berry, Mary
Cooking with Mary Berry. Mary Berry. DK Publishing 2016. 256 pages : Color; Illustration
ISBN 9781465459510
Grades: Adult   **641.5**
1. Cooking 2. Recipes 3. Cookbooks 4. Food writing — Cooking and cookbooks — Regional 5. Food writing — Cooking and cookbooks — Chefs and restaurants
LC Bl2016040254

In her first cookbook for Americans, a British food writer and television host offers 150 of her favorite recipes, including Butternut Squash Soup, Chicken with Sage and Orange, Chelsea Buns and Lemon Cheesecake.

"This is a basic, go-to volume, with the flair that Berry's growing U.S. fan base will expect." —*Booklist*
Includes index.

Bhogal, Ravinder
Comfort and Joy: Irresistible Pleasures from a Vegetarian Kitchen. Ravinder Bhogal. Bloomsbury Publishing 2023. 272 pages
ISBN 9781526655370
Grades: Adult   **641.5**
1. Vegetarian cooking 2. Vegan cooking 3. Comfort food 4. Food writing — Cooking and cookbooks — Vegetarian and vegan

Comfort and Joy is a fresh take on vegetarian and vegan cooking; not geared towards health or denial but indulging all the senses with a decadent global larder. It is a cookbook of great bounty, promising fortifying curries and stews, the warm embrace of aromatic fried bhajis and rich, satisfying desserts. For Ravinder Bhogal, food should be made and shared with abundance in mind, and this sense of pleasure is conveyed on every page. From Miso Mushroom Carbonara to Crispy Aubergine with Caramel Sauce, this is food as pursuit of pleasure.

"Full of savory vegetarian recipes with an Indian flavor profile that are perfect for flavor-seeking foodies." —*Library Journal*

Bianco, Chris
Bianco: Pizza, Pasta, and Other Food I Like. Chris Bianco. Ecco 2016. xi, 212 p. : Illustration; Color
ISBN 9780062224378
Grades: Adult   **641.5**
1. Cooking, Italian 2. Cooking 3. Pizza 4. Recipes 5. Cookbooks 6. Food writing — Cooking and cookbooks — Courses 7. Food writing — Cooking and cookbooks — Regional
LC Bl2017039570

An award-winning chef presents the basic techniques of pizza making, with a discussion on dough, tomato sauce, and ingredients and options for pizza, sandwiches, pasta, and vegetable sides.

"Thanks to Bianco's focus on simple recipes and outstanding ingredients, home cooks get appealing, classic dishes great for any day of the week." —*Publishers Weekly*
Includes index.

Bittman, Mark
★ *Dinner for Everyone: 100 Iconic Dishes Made 3 Ways—easy, Vegan, or Perfect for Company.* Mark Bittman; photographs by Ava Brackett. Clarkson Potter/Publishers 2019. 432 pages : Color; Illustration
ISBN 9780385344760
Grades: Adult   **641.5**
1. Cooking 2. Quick and easy cooking 3. Recipes 4. Cookbooks 5. Food writing — Cooking and cookbooks — Methods
LC 2018003810

Provides instructions for one hundred dishes with three variations, easy, complex, and vegan.

"The all-out, or perfect-for-company recipes are for those who wish to take their time and cook for pleasure, not survival." —*Library Journal*
Includes index.

How to Cook Everything Fast: A Better Way to Cook Great Food. Mark Bittman; illustrations by Olivia de Salve Villedieu. Houghton Mifflin Harcourt 2014. 1056 pages : Illustration
ISBN 9780470936306
Grades: Adult   **641.5**
1. Quick and easy cooking 2. Cookbooks 3. Food writing — Cooking and cookbooks — Methods
LC Bl2014041639

Demonstrates how to minimize cooking times while becoming more intuitive in the kitchen, sharing hundreds of simple, flavorful dishes that can be prepared in fifteen to forty-five minutes.

"Bittman's latest is fantastic for busy, novice, and noncooks. It's also a practical tool for anyone who aspires but struggles to cook more often." —*Library Journal*
Includes index.

★ *How to Cook Everything Vegetarian: Simple Meatless Recipes for Great Food.* Mark Bittman; photography by Burcu Avsar & Zach DeSart; illustrations by Alan Witschonke. Houghton Mifflin Harcourt 2017. 830 pages : Color; Illustration
ISBN 9781118455647
Grades: 9 10 11 12 Adult   **641.5**
1. Cooking (Vegetables) 2. Recipes 3. Vegetarian cooking 4. Cookbooks 5. Food writing — Cooking and cookbooks — Ingredients 6. Food writing — Cooking and cookbooks — Vegetarian and vegan
LC 2017051874

Provides more than one thousand recipes and variations for simple meatless meals, including salads, soups, dairy, vegan, vegetables, fruit, pasta, grains, legumes, and meat substitutes.

"Bittman's evenhanded tone and his ability to cover a gamut of recipes . . . render this book as relevant today as it was when it first appeared, and confirm its status as an indispensable resource." —*Publishers Weekly*
Includes index.

★ *How to Cook Everything: Simple Recipes for Great Food.* Mark Bittman; illustrations by Alan Witschonke. J. Wiley 2019. VIII, 951 p.
ISBN 9781328545435
Grades: Adult   **641.5**
1. Cooking 2. Recipes 3. Quick and easy cooking 4. Cookbooks 5. Food writing — Cooking and cookbooks — Methods
LC 2008018984

A full-color 20th-anniversary edition includes hundreds of brand new features, recipes and variations plus old favorites from the previous editions, in many cases reimagined with new methods or flavors.

ESSENTIAL AND RECOMMENDED TITLES
641.5 Cooking

"The author presents more than 1000 basic recipes and simple and inventive variations. The enormous breadth of recipes along with Bittman's engaging, straightforward prose will appeal to cooks looking for reliable help with kitchen fundamentals." —*Publishers Weekly*
Includes bibliographical references and index.

How to Cook Everything: The Basics. Mark Bittman; photography by Romulo Yanes. Wiley 2012. IX, 486 p. : Color illustration
ISBN 9780470528068
Grades: Adult   641.5
1. Cooking 2. Recipes 3. Cookbooks 4. Food writing — Cooking and cookbooks — Methods
LC 2011048881
The New York Times columnist and author demonstrates fundamental cooking techniques while providing 171 recipes using basic staples and methods, covering everything from equipping a kitchen and stocking a pantry to making food selections and performing essential cooking tasks.
Includes index.

Mark Bittman's Kitchen Matrix: More Than 700 Simple Recipes and Techniques to Mix and Match for Endless Possibilities. Mark Bittman. Pam Krauss Books 2015. 304 p. : Illustration
ISBN 9780804188012
Grades: Adult   641.5
1. Cooking 2. Recipes 3. Cookbooks 4. Food writing — Cooking and cookbooks — Methods
LC 2015020733
An anthology of the best-selling food writer's popular Matrix writings is presented in the form of a boldly graphic cookbook that features single ingredients served up a dozen ways to demonstrate the versatility of recipe alterations.
"This unconventional cookbook can help proficient cooks develop ideas for creating their own recipe variations." —*Library Journal*

The VB6 Cookbook: More Than 350 Recipes for Healthy Vegan Meals All Day and Delicious Flexitarian Dinners at Night. Mark Bittman; photographs by Quentin Bacon. Clarkson Potter/Publishers 2014. 272 pages : Color; Illustration
ISBN 9780385344821
Grades: Adult   641.5
1. Recipes 2. Vegan cooking 3. Dieting 4. Cookbooks 5. Food writing — Cooking and cookbooks — Cooking for health 6. Food writing — Cooking and cookbooks — Vegetarian and vegan 7. Science writing — Medicine and health — Diet and nutrition
LC 2013050637
A companion to the Minimalist host's best-selling VB6 provides a broad selection of everyday vegan and vegetable-forward meals while outlining the potential health benefits of a diet that focuses on fruits and vegetables while minimizing meats and dairy.
Presents a meal plan which includes vegan recipes for breakfast and lunch and meat and fish based recipes for dinnertime, discussing the potential health benefits of a diet that focuses on fruits and vegetables while minimizing meats and dairy.
"Rather than overload readers with prescriptive rules, unfamiliar ingredients, and complicated preparations, Bittman gives them a memorable charge (eat more plants, less meat and processed foods) and tools to help them follow it." —*Library Journal*
Includes index.

Vb6: Eat Vegan Before 6:00 to Lose Weight and Restore Your Health... for Good : The Flexible Diet You Can Really Stick To, with More Than 60 Easy, Delicious Recipes. Mark Bittman; foreword by Dean Ornish, M.D.. Clarkson Potter/Publishers 2013. xi, 276 pages
ISBN 9780385344746
Grades: Adult   641.5
1. Vegan cooking 2. Dieting 3. Cookbooks 4. Food writing — Cooking and cookbooks — Vegetarian and vegan 5. Self-Help — Personal growth — Diet and nutrition 6. Food writing — Cooking and cookbooks — Cooking for health
LC 2012046866

The popular New York Times columnist builds on the theories of his hit book, Food Matters, to outline a menu plan that eliminates meat and animal products throughout the day to promote weight loss and overall better health.
Includes bibliographical references (pages 247-260) and index.

Blumenthal, Heston
Is This a Cookbook?: Adventures in the Kitchen. Heston Blumenthal. Bloomsbury Publishing 2022. 368 pages : Illustration
ISBN 9781526621504
Grades: Adult   641.5
1. Cooking 2. Cookbooks 3. Food writing — Cooking and cookbooks — Chefs and restaurants
Is this a cookbook? Well, it's full of Heston's typically brilliant, delicious & inventive recipes, including green gazpacho, beetroot and pea salad, quinoa with vegetables, Moroccan pasties, hemp panna cotta, banana and parsley smoothie, tomato and coffee muffins, parsnip granola, rice ice cream, sherry vinegar posset, cricket ketchup and thyme and orange kombucha, not forgetting popcorn chicken with real popcorn…. but there's so much more. Each of the 70 recipes is accompanied by Heston's thoughts, stories, insights and hacks, turning each cooking session into a journey that'll excite and inspire and reveal a whole world of culinary possibilities and fresh perspectives.
"Perfect as an introduction to gastronomy, Blumenthal's quirky and readable book will delight fans and create new ones." —*Library Journal*

Bourdain, Anthony
★ *Appetites: A Cookbook.* Anthony Bourdain, with Laurie Woolever. HarperCollins 2016. 320 p.
ISBN 9780062409959
Grades: Adult   641.5
1. Cooking 2. Dinners and dining 3. Cooking for families 4. Cooks 5. Recipes 6. Food habits 7. Food writing — Cooking and cookbooks — Narrative cookbooks 8. Food writing — Cooking and cookbooks — Chefs and restaurants
LC 2017394114
Draws on more than four decades of professional cooking and world traveling, as well as the author's more recent experiences as a father, to present a collection of personal home-cooking favorites that deconstructs the structural aspects of satisfying meals.
"In what might be his most accessible book yet, Bourdain reveals his 'Ina Gartenlike need to feed the people around me' with a terrific collection of recipes for family and friends." —*Publishers Weekly*

Bowen, Dana
Dynamite Kids Cooking School: Delicious Recipes That Teach All the Skills You Need. Dana Bowen & Sara Kate Gillingham. Clarkson Potter/Publishers 2022. 288 pages : Color; Illustration
ISBN 9780593138458
Grades: 4 5 6 7 8 9 10 11 12 Adult   641.5
1. Cooking 2. Dinners and dining 3. Cookbooks 4. Food books — Cookbooks
LC 2021058168
115 recipes from Brooklyn's The Dynamite Shop for young budding home chefs to cook for their families, themselves, or their communities, perfecting their kitchen skills along the way. When Sara Kate Gillingham and Dana Bowen founded The Dynamite Shop in Brooklyn, they wanted to create a space where kids could learn fundamental, practical kitchen skills that they could carry into their home kitchens and real life. But they also wanted to teach kids about food on a deeper level: how food connects us to the people we love, the communities we belong to, and the wider world.
A thorough volume from experienced instructors; a fine choice for juvenile cookbook collections. —*School Library Journal*
Includes index.

Bowien, Danny
Mission Vegan: Wildly Delicious Food for Everyone. Danny Bowien with JJ Goode. Ecco, an imprint of HarperCollinsPublishers 2022. xix, 251 pages : Color; Illustration

ISBN 9780063012981

Grades: Adult   641.5

1. Vegan cooking 2. Cooking, Asian 3. Cookbooks 4. Food writing — Cooking and cookbooks — Vegetarian and vegan 5. Food writing — Cooking and cookbooks — Regional

LC Bl2022025228

The cofounder and chef of the famous Mission Chinese Food restaurants in San Francisco and New York, making it his mission to find inspiration, joy and flavor in food, presents vegan recipes geared for the home cook, keeping the emphasis on experimenting in the kitchen and big flavor.

"Mixing bold ingredients and techniques, this enthralling collection will satisfy vegans and carnivores alike." —*Publishers Weekly*

Includes index.

Bracken, Peg

The I Hate to Cook Book. Peg Bracken; with a new foreword by Jo Bracken; drawings by Hilary Knight. Grand Central Pub. 2010. xiv, 207 p.

ISBN 9780446545921

Grades: Adult   641.5

1. Cooking 2. Recipes 3. Food writing — Cooking and cookbooks — Entertaining 4. Food writing — Cooking and cookbooks — Reference

LC 2009001249

A commemorative edition of a classic, humorous cookbook includes more than 180 easy recipes for those who fear the kitchen, from Philosopher's Chowder and Skinny Meatloaf to Fat Man's Shrimp and Immediate Fudge Cake.

Presents a commemorative edition of a classic, humorous cookbook that includes more than 180 easy recipes for those who fear the kitchen, covering such categories as entrees, side dishes, salads, vegetables, and desserts, along with household hints.

50th Anniversary Edition; Includes index.

Britton, Sarah

Naturally Nourished: Healthy, Delicious Meals Made with Everyday Ingredients. Sarah Britton. Clarkson Potter/Publishers 2017. 240 p. : Color; Illustration

ISBN 9780804185400

Grades: Adult   641.5

1. Vegetarian cooking 2. Cooking (Natural foods) 3. Nutrition 4. Cookbooks 5. Food writing — Cooking and cookbooks — Vegetarian and vegan 6. Food writing — Cooking and cookbooks — Cooking for health 7. Food writing — Cooking and cookbooks — Methods

LC 2018139474

An acclaimed holistic nutritionist and blogger simplifies whole food, vegetarian cooking for any budget and any night of the week with 100 recipes including Grilled Caesar Salad, Cauliflower Steaks, Baked Feta and Stone Fruit Ginger Salad.

Includes index.

Brown, Leanne

★ *Good and Cheap: Eat Well on $4/Day.* Leanne Brown. Workman Publishing 2015. xviii, 190 pages : Color; Illustration

ISBN 9780761184997

Grades: Adult   641.5

1. Recipes 2. Cookbooks 3. Food writing — Cooking and cookbooks — Courses 4. Food writing — Cooking and cookbooks — Methods

LC 2015011072

A call-to-arms guide to ending hunger shares 120 recipes for satisfying, healthful meals on a daily budget equivalent to the amount of government food-stamp allowances, offering complementary information about economical cooking methods.

Collects over one hundred recipes for daily meals that won't hurt the wallet, including such offerings as kale Caesar salad, Filipino chicken adobo, dark and spicy chili, and potato leek pizza.

"Brown estimates the cost per serving for all dishes, including potato leek pizzas, dark and spicy chili, and peanut chicken and broccoli with coconut rice." —*Library Journal*

A special edition of Good and Cheap; Includes index.

Carle-Sanders, Theresa

Outlander Kitchen : To the New World and Back Again: The Second Official Outlander Companion Cookbook. Theresa Carle-Sanders; [foreword by Diana Gabaldon; photography by Rebecca Wellman and Theresa Carle-Sanders]. Delacorte Press 2020. xviii, 331 pages : Color; Illustration

ISBN 9781984855152

Grades: Adult   641.5

1. Gabaldon, Diana 2. Cooking 3. Recipes 4. Cookbooks 5. Food writing — Cooking and cookbooks — Regional 6. Arts and Entertainment — Movies and Television

Includes more than 100 new easy-to-prepare recipes inspired by Diana Gabaldon's beloved Outlander and Lord John Grey series, as well as the hit Starz original show.

"Fans of Gabaldon's series will devour these accessible, well-conceived dishes." —*Publishers Weekly*

Cavallari, Kristin

True Roots: A Mindful Kitchen with More Than 100 Recipes Free of Gluten, Dairy, and Refined Sugar. Kristin Cavallari, with Mike Kubiesa. Rodale 2018. xviii, 252 pages : Color; Illustration

ISBN 9781623369163

Grades: Adult   641.5

1. Cooking (Natural foods) 2. Gluten-free diet 3. Milk-free diet 4. Recipes 5. Cookbooks 6. Food writing — Cooking and cookbooks — Cooking for health 7. Food writing — Cooking and cookbooks — Ingredients

LC Bl2018055271

A collection of healthy, clean-eating recipes from the actress and New York times bestselling author features such dishes as butternut squash pancakes, leek and zucchini quiche, raw honey planked salmon, and zesty quinoa salad.

Includes index.

Cayne, Alison

The Haven's Kitchen Cooking School: Recipes and Inspiration to Build a Lifetime of Confidence in the Kitchen. Alison Cayne. Artisan 2017. 374 pages : Illustration

ISBN 9781579656737

Grades: Adult   641.5

1. Cooking 2. Seasonal cooking 3. Recipes 4. Quick and easy cooking 5. Cookbooks 6. Food writing — Cooking and cookbooks — Methods 7. Food writing — Cooking and cookbooks — Chefs and restaurants

LC 2016038079

Presents cooking basics for beginners, discussing how to season vegetables and which knives to use for particular tasks, and includes such recipes as apple beignets, poached eggs, and beef bourguignon.

"This book will remain a staple in kitchens long after readers have mastered the basics of boiling an egg and searing a steak." —*Publishers Weekly*

Includes index.

Chang, David

★ *Eat a Peach: A Memoir.* David Chang with Gabe Ulla. Clarkson Potter/Publishers 2020. 448 pages

ISBN 9781524759216

Grades: Adult   641.5

1. Chang, David, 1977- 2. Restaurateurs 3. Cooking 4. Belonging 5. Self-acceptance 6. Reality television programs 7. Korean Americans 8. People with bipolar disorder 9. East Asian Americans 10. Autobiographies and memoirs 11. Food writing — Memoirs and biographies 12. Life stories — Arts and culture — Culinary arts 13. Life stories — Facing adversity — Medical issues — Mental illness

LC 2019052985

The star of Ugly Delicious traces his upbringing as a youngest son in a deeply religious Korean-American family, his search for identity, his struggles with manic depression and his unlikely rise as one of his generation's most influential chefs.

"Culinary-minded readers will find much instruction here (including a section on 33 rules for becoming a chef), as well as the intimate self-portrait of a

ESSENTIAL AND RECOMMENDED TITLES
641.5 Cooking

chef who works hard not to be at the top of his game, but instead always growing." —*Booklist*

Che, Hannah
★ *The Vegan Chinese Kitchen: Recipes and Modern Stories from a Thousand-year-old Tradition.* by Hannah Che. Clarkson Potter 2022. 304 p.
ISBN 9780593139707
Grades: Adult   641.5
1. Vegan cooking 2. Cooking, Chinese 3. Cookbooks 4. Food writing — Cooking and cookbooks — Regional 5. Food writing — Cooking and cookbooks — Vegetarian and vegan
LC 2021049177

Through stunning photography, stories and recipes, the creator of The Plant-Based Wok draws upon a fascinating subset of Chinese cookery that emphasizes umami-rich ingredients and can be traced back over centuries to Buddhist temple kitchens to introduce readers to a whole world of flavors and ingredients.

"Family photos interspersed with glamour shots of food feel right in a book whose style so perfectly aligns with its winning subject." —*Publishers Weekly*
Includes index.

Child, Julia
★ *The Way to Cook.* Julia Child; photographs by Brian Leatart and Jim Scherer. Knopf 1989. xi, 511 p. : Color illustration
ISBN 9780394532646
Grades: 11 12 Adult   641.5
1. Cooking 2. Food writing — Cooking and cookbooks — Reference
LC 88045838

Blending classic techniques with free-style American cooking and emphasizing freshness, lightness, and simpler preparations, this treasury of cooking from the "French Chef" features eight hundred master recipes and variations.
Includes index.

Christensen, Ashley
It's Always Freezer Season: How to Freeze Like a Chef with 100 Make-Ahead Recipes. Ashley Christensen and Kaitlyn Goalen; photography by Lauren Allen. Ten Speed Press 2021. 263 pages : Color; Illustration
ISBN 9781607746898
Grades: Adult   641.5
1. Make-ahead cooking 2. Frozen foods 3. Food writing — Cooking and cookbooks — Methods 4. Food writing — Cooking and cookbooks — Chefs and restaurants
LC 2020035243

A make-ahead freezer cookbook with 100 recipes from a James Beard Award-winning chef.

"This book will spur even experienced home cooks to see their freezers in a new light." —*Publishers Weekly*
Includes index.

Claiborne, Jenné
★ *Sweet Potato Soul: 100 Easy Vegan Recipes for the Southern Flavors of Smoke, Sugar, Spice, and Soul.* Jenné Claiborne. Harmony Books 2018. 223 pages : Illustration
ISBN 9780451498892
Grades: Adult   641.5
1. Vegan cooking 2. Cooking, African American 3. Cooking, American 4. Southern States 5. Cookbooks 6. Food writing — Cooking and cookbooks — Vegetarian and vegan
LC 2017013663

A vegan personal chef and popular blogger offers 100 soul food and Southern cooking plant-based recipes including Coconut Collard Salad, Peach-Date BBQ Jackfruit Sliders, Jalapeno Hush Puppies and Sweet Potato-Cinnamon Rolls.
Includes index.

Clark, Melissa
Comfort in an Instant: 75 Comfort Food Recipes for Your Pressure Cooker, Multicooker + Instant Pot. Melissa Clark. Clarkson Potter/Publishers 2018. 159 pages : Color; Illustration
ISBN 9780525576150
Grades: Adult   641.5
1. Comfort food 2. Pressure cooking 3. Recipes 4. Quick and easy cooking 5. Cookbooks 6. Food writing — Cooking and cookbooks — Methods
LC 2018019955

Collects classic comfort food recipes adapted for slow and pressure cookers, including such dishes as cheddar-spinach strata, matzo ball soup, chicken cacciatore, chili, and ginger-lemon cheesecake.

The New York Times columnist and author of Dinner in an Instant presents 75 classic comfort food recipes adapted for slow and pressure cookers, from Spicy Turkey Meatloaf and Weeknight Chicken Parm to Pork & Bean Chili and Shepherd's Pie.
Includes index.

★ *Dinner in an Instant: 75 Modern Recipes for Your Pressure Cooker, Slow Cooker, and Instant Pot.* Melissa Clark. Clarkson Potter/Publishers 2017. 159 pages : Color; Illustration
ISBN 9781524762964
Grades: Adult   641.5
1. Quick and easy cooking 2. Recipes 3. Cookbooks 4. Food writing — Cooking and cookbooks — Methods
LC 2017021737

With 75 all-new recipes, Melissa Clark, New York Times food columnist, web star, and our generation's authority on upping your cooking game without fuss, brings her signature flavor-forward dishes and dinner brand to everyone's favorite countertop appliance, the Instant Pot. With 75 recipes for slow cooker, pressure cooker, and other Instant Potregistered mark settings, Dinner in an Instant proves that home cooks do not have to sacrifice flavor and quality for the convenience of countertop appliance cooking. With Melissa's signature arsenal of flavors (garlic, ginger, preserved lemons, gochujang, harissa, and more!) and chock-full of tips—each of the recipes will be annotated with dietary information and notes on which setting is best for each dish. Recipes will also include instructions for cooking on multiple settings—busy home cooks can decide whether they want to have their dinner cook throughout the day while they tend to other tasks, or in a quick twenty minutes before the family sits down to eat. As in her previous book,Dinner,all of Melissa's recipes are never before published, fresh, approachable, and practical for weeknight cooking, without ever sacrificing quality and taste.

Trademark sign appears after Pot in title; Includes index.

Dinner: Changing the Game. Melissa Clark; photographs by Eric Wolfinger. Clarkson Potter 2017. 399 p. : Color; Illustration
ISBN 9780553448238
Grades: Adult   641.5
1. Cooking 2. Quick and easy cooking 3. Cookbooks 4. Food writing — Cooking and cookbooks — Methods 5. Food writing — Cooking and cookbooks — Courses 6. Food writing — Cooking and cookbooks — Regional
LC 2016013021

A collection of recipes for home cooks from the New York Times food columnist that are easy and quick enough to prepare on weeknights, includng such dishes as herb-marinated steak, maple-roasted tofu, and coconut curry chicken.
Includes index.

Kid in the Kitchen: 100 Recipes and Tips for Young Home Cooks. Melissa Clark with Daniel Gercke; photographs by David Malosh. Clarkson Potter 2020. 288 pages : Color; Illustration
ISBN 9780593232286
Grades: Adult   641.5
1. Cooking 2. Food writing — Cooking and cookbooks 3. Food writing — Cooking and cookbooks — Methods
LC 2020031610

The New York Times Food columnist and beloved home cooking authority, Melissa Clark, spins 100 all-new recipes for a robust new audience of home chefs: Kids ages 8-14! Melissa Clark, who has more range than any food writer today (and a young daughter to boot), marries the flavors beloved by adult fans of her bestselling cookbooks and her work in the New York Times with recipes that any kid age 8-14, whether cooking-curious or already kitchen-puttering, can make and build on.

"Clark has created a welcoming beginner's resource that will allow budding home cooks to find joy in the kitchen." —*Library Journal*

Includes index.

Cohen, Jake

Jew-Ish: Reinvented Recipes from a Modern Mensch. a cookbook by Jake Cohen; photography by Matt Taylor-Gross. Houghton Mifflin Harcourt 2021. xvii, 251 pages : Color; Illustration

ISBN 9780358353980

Grades: Adult   641.5

1. Cooking, Jewish 2. Food writing — Cooking and cookbooks — Regional

LC 2020036239

100 updated classic and all-new Jewish-style recipes from a bright new star in the food community.

"This fun collection will appeal to all home cooks looking for creative takes on modern cuisine with a Jew-ish flair, and anyone with a sense of humor." —*Library Journal*

Includes index.

Comerford, Hope

Fix-It and Forget-It Healthy 5-Ingredient Cookbook: 150 Easy and Nutritious Slow Cooker Recipes. Hope Comerford. Good Books 2019. 336 p. : Color; Illustration

ISBN 9781680994124

Grades: Adult   641.5

1. Quick and easy cooking 2. Cookbooks 3. Food writing — Cooking and cookbooks — Methods 4. Food writing — Cooking and cookbooks — Courses

LC Bl2019005951

A collection of recipes featuring five ingredients or less, including Southwestern chili, butternut squash soup, and spinach frittata, with tips on purchasing and using a slow cooker.

Includes index.

Coscarelli, Chloe

Chloe Flavor: Saucy, Spicy, Crunchy, Vegan. Chloe Coscarelli; photographs by Christina Holmes; foreword by Michael Symon. Clarkson Potter/Publishers 2018. 271 pages : Color; Illustration

ISBN 9780451499622

Grades: Adult   641.5

1. Vegan cooking 2. Quick and easy cooking 3. Recipes 4. Cookbooks 5. Food writing — Cooking and cookbooks — Vegetarian and vegan 6. Food writing — Cooking and cookbooks — Methods

LC 2017021732

Shares vegan recipes for over a hundred dishes that focus on simplicity and flavor, including fiesta taco bowl, oatmeal cake with coconut caramel glaze, and butternut bisque.

"For those who want to try vegan cooking, this is the perfect cookbook." —*Publishers Weekly*

Includes index.

Cristofano, Jana

Eat Well, Be Well: 100+ Healthy Re-Creations of the Food You Crave : Plant Based, Gluten-Free, Refined Sugar-Free. Jana Cristofano. Sterling Epicure 2020. 250 pages : Color; Illustration

ISBN 9781454933779

Grades: Adult   641.5

1. Cooking (Natural foods) 2. Gluten-free diet 3. Sugar-free diet 4. Vegan cooking 5. Food writing — Cooking and cookbooks — Cooking for health 6. Food writing — Cooking and cookbooks — Vegetarian and vegan

LC 2019019084

Satisfy your cravings and boost your vitality with good food that tastes great and is vegan."

"Not only fans of Cristofano's blog, but also everyday cooks looking to explore gluten-free and vegan recipes will find plenty to enjoy." —*Library Journal*

Includes bibliographical references (pages 242) and index.

Crocker, Betty

★ *Betty Crocker Cookbook: 1500 Recipes for the Way You Cook Today.* Betty Crocker. John Wiley & Sons 2011. 684 p. : Color illustration

ISBN 9780470906026

Grades: 11 12 Adult   641.5

1. Cooking 2. Recipes 3. Cookbooks 4. Food writing — Cooking and cookbooks

LC 2011009744

This 11th edition of The Betty Crocker Cookbook is the most thorough update in the book's 60-year history, with 1,100 all-new photos, 1,500 recipes, a fully contemporized design and features that highlight the heritage and expertise of this trusted classic. An exclusive bonus area on BettyCrocker.Com features 80 videos demonstrating recipes and techniques from the book, plus 400 additional recipes just for Big Red consumers.

In ringbinder; Includes index.

Curry, Kevin

Fit Men Cook: 100+ Meal Prep Recipes for Men and Women - Always #healthyaf, Never Boring. Kevin Curry. Touchstone 2018. 319 pages : Color; Illustration

ISBN 9781501178726

Grades: Adult   641.5

1. Cooking 2. Health 3. Nutrition 4. Recipes 5. Dieting 6. Cookbooks 7. Food writing — Cooking and cookbooks — Cooking for health 8. Science writing — Medicine and health — Diet and nutrition — Weight loss 9. Science writing — Medicine and health

LC 2018041649

The fitness influencer and creator of the best-selling Food & Drink app, FitMenCook, shares 100 satisfying, quick-prep recipes designed to support personal health goals on a budget.

Shares the importance of meal prep to create a healthier diet and offers over one hundred meal prep recipes, including savory quinoa cakes, orange miso salmon, roasted red pepper hummus, and mango cream ice pops.

Includes index.

Dada, Samah

Dada Eats Love to Cook It: 100 Plant-Based Recipes for Everyone at Your Table. Samah Dada; photography by Julia Gartland. Rodale Books 2021. 255 pages Color; Illustration

ISBN 9780593138236

Grades: Adult   641.5

1. Vegan cooking 2. Ketogenic diet 3. Low-carbohydrate diet 4. Gluten-free diet 5. Cookbooks 6. Food Writing — Cooking and cookbooks — Vegetarian and vegan 7. Food Writing — Cooking and cookbooks — Cooking for health

LC 2020030226

100+ indulgent meals and treats from the vegan- and keto-friendly rising star, all made with whole, unprocessed ingredients, including viral hits like brookie (brownie/cookie) pie and chocolate chip tahini cake.

"A winning debut that will delight home chefs looking to build cooking confidence or reinvent humble meals." —*Library Journal*

Includes index.

De Laurentiis, Giada

Happy Cooking: Make Every Meal Count— Without Stressing Out. Giada De Laurentiis. Pam Krauss Books 2015. 311 pages : Color; Illustration

ISBN 9780804187923

Grades: Adult   641.5

1. Cooking 2. Cookbooks 3. Food writing — Cooking and cookbooks — Chefs and restaurants

LC 2015022028

ESSENTIAL AND RECOMMENDED TITLES
641.5 Cooking

Outlines the author's year-round approach to enjoying a happy and healthy lifestyle based on strategic wellness practices, nutritious foods, and occasional indulgences.

DiGregorio, Sarah
Adventures in Slow Cooking: 120 Slow-Cooker Recipes for People Who Love Food. Sarah DiGregorio; photography by Andrew Purcell. William Morrow 2017. xxvii, 228 pages : Illustration; Color
ISBN 9780062661371
Grades: Adult   641.5
  1. Electric cooking 2. Recipes 3. Cooking 4. Cookbooks 5. Food writing — Cooking and cookbooks — Methods
LC Bl2017041532

Collects recipes for slow cooker meals, including such offerings as gingery cranberry chutney, farro puttanesca, and oxtail and short rib pho.

"Essential for most collections, this is an exciting and refreshingly unbiased guide to slow cooking." —*Library Journal*
  Includes index.

Disbrowe, Paula
Thank You for Smoking: Fun and Fearless Recipes Cooked with a Whiff of Wood Fire on Your Grill or Smoker. Paula Disbrowe; photographs by Johnny Autry. Ten Speed Press 2019. 233 pages : Color; Illustration
ISBN 9780399582134
Grades: Adult   641.5
  1. Recipes 2. Cooking 3. Cookbooks 4. Food writing — Cooking and cookbooks — Methods 5. Food writing — Cooking and cookbooks — Regional
LC 2018038937

Featuring an impressive array of smoke-infused recipes that extend well beyond the realm of rib joints, Thank You for Smoking shows home cooks how easy it is to rig a gas or charcoal grill or use a backyard smoker to infuse everything you love to eat—from veggies and greens to meat and fish—with a smoky nuance.

An award-winning author and grilling expert shows how to infuse everyday foods with smoky flavor with tips on how to create smoke-infused recipes such as Ginger Garlic Chicken and San Antonio-Style Flank Steak Tacos.

"Readers who enjoy trying new cooking techniques, and those looking for creative ways to incorporate smoky flavor into their foods will find this a treasure." —*Library Journal*
  Includes bibliographical references and indexes.

DiSpirito, Rocco
Now Eat This!: 150 of America's Favorite Comfort Foods, All Under 350 Calories. Rocco DiSpirito. Ballantine Books 2010. xxiii, 246 p. : Color illustration
ISBN 9780345520906
Grades: Adult   641.5
  1. Cooking, American 2. Low-calorie diet 3. Recipes 4. Cookbooks 5. Food writing — Cooking and cookbooks — Cooking for health
LC 2009052470

A popular chef takes 150 familiar recipes and puts a healthy spin on them, all without sacrificing the well-loved flavors of these classic American dishes.

"The author retools diet cookery in the hope of convincing even the most stubborn gourmand to cut calories without giving up delicious, satisfying foods." —*Booklist*

A Ballantine Books trade paperback original—Verso, t.P; Includes index.

Donofrio, Jeanine
★ *Love & Lemons: Simple Feel-Good Food: 125 Plant-Focused Meals to Enjoy Now or Make Ahead.* Jeanine Donofrio with Phoebe Moore; photography by Eva Kolenko. Avery, an imprint of Penguin Random House 2023. 271 pages : Color; Illustration
ISBN 9780593419106
Grades: Adult   641.5
  1. Vegetarian cooking 2. Quick and easy cooking 3. Make-ahead cooking 4. Cookbooks

LC 2022024974

Offering visual guides to reusing, mixing and matching ingredients for fresh, must-eat vegetarian meals, the creator of the hugely popular Love & Lemons blog provides both make-now recipes made with minimal prep and ingredients and make-ahead recipes for full meals destined for the freezer.

"Meatless Mondays will never be the same with this down-to-earth and delicious cookbook that provides oodles of stunning inspiration and encourages variation suited to individual style and taste." —*Library Journal*
  Includes index.

Drummond, Ree
★ *The Pioneer Woman Cooks: Come and Get It! : Simple, Scrumptious Recipes for Crazy Busy Lives.* Ree Drummond. William Morrow 2017. xvii, 381 pages : Illustration; Color
ISBN 9780062225269
Grades: Adult   641.5
  1. Quick and easy cooking 2. Recipes 3. Cookbooks 4. Food writing — Cooking and cookbooks — Chefs and restaurants 5. Food writing — Cooking and cookbooks — Methods
LC Bl2017037717

The Food Network star and best-selling author shares a collection of recipes that provide for the needs of today's busy families, outlining a wide range of quick-prepare, nutritious and satisfying options for every meal of the day.
  Includes index.

Esposito, Jennifer
Jennifer's Way Kitchen: Easy Allergen-Free, Anti-Inflammatory Recipes for a Delicious Life. Jennifer Esposito with Eve Adamson. Grand Central Life & Style 2017. 304 pages : Color; Illustration
ISBN 9781455596713
Grades: Adult   641.5
  1. Cooking (Natural foods) 2. Gluten-free diet 3. Sugar-free diet 4. Recipes 5. Cookbooks 6. Food writing — Cooking and cookbooks — Chefs and restaurants 7. Food writing — Cooking and cookbooks — Cooking for health
LC Bl2017038332

A collection of anti-inflammatory, allergen-free recipes from the actress and owner of New York City-based Jennifer's Way bakery features such offerings as spaghetti squash with garlic and oil, one-dish chicken with asparagus, and spring risotto.

"This solid foray into allergen-free cooking is packed with information that can help those with dietary problems." —*Publishers Weekly*

Gluten-free, grain-free, dairy-free, egg-free, soy-free, corn-free, refined sugar-free recipes from the owner of the beloved Jennifer's Way bakery; Includes index.

Fairchild, Barbara
The Bon Appetit Cookbook. Barbara Fairchild. Wiley 2006. xxiv, 792 p, 32 p. of plates : Illustration; Color
ISBN 9780764596865
Grades: 11 12 Adult   641.5
  1. Cooking 2. Food writing — Cooking and cookbooks — Courses
LC 2005005181

A comprehensive cooking compendium from America's leading food and entertaining magazine, Bon Appetit, selects more than 1,200 of the periodical's best-loved recipes for every meal, taste, budget, and occasion, including a variety of easy-to-make dishes that range from family favorites and classics to regional and international specialties.

"Mirroring the magazine on which it is based, this collection of 1,200 recipes is accessible, applicable to most home cooks' lives and a pleasure to cook from." —*Publishers Weekly*
  Includes index.

Fearnley-Whittingstall, Hugh
River Cottage Veg: 200 Inspired Vegetable Recipes. Hugh Fearnley-Whittingstall; photography by Simon Wheeler; illustrations by Mariko Jesse. Ten Speed Press 2013. 415 p. : Color illustration

PUBLIC LIBRARY CORE COLLECTION: NONFICTION
Twentieth Edition

ISBN 9781607744726
Grades: Adult 641.5
1. Vegetarian cooking 2. Recipes 3. Cookbooks 4. Food writing — Cooking and cookbooks — Vegetarian and vegan 5. Food writing — Cooking and cookbooks — Ingredients

LC Bl2013021941

Collects vegetarian recipes, including kale and mushroom lasagna, winter stir-fry with Chinese five-spice, and herby, peanutty, noodly salad.

Originally published in slightly different form in hardcover in Great Britain as River Cottage Veg Everyday by Bloomsbury Publishing Plc, London, in 2011—T.P. verso; Includes index.

Firth, Henry
Bosh!: Simple Recipes, Amazing Food, All Plants. Henry Firth & Ian Theasby. William Morrow 2018. 288 p. : Color; Illustration
ISBN 9780062820686
Grades: Adult 641.5
1. Vegetarian cooking 2. Cooking (Vegetables) 3. Cookbooks 4. Food writing — Cooking and cookbooks — Vegetarian and vegan 5. Food writing — Cooking and cookbooks — Ingredients

LC Bl2018071448

Shares over one hundred and forty plant-based recipes that span from daily meals to special-occasion fare, including sweet and sour crispy tofu, satay maki rolls, and creamy garlic mushroom toast.

Includes index.

Flanagan, Shalane
Run Fast, Cook Fast, Eat Slow: Quick-fix Recipes for Hangry Athletes. Shalane Flanagan & Elyse Kopecky; photography by Alan Weiner. Rodale 2018. 253 pages : Color; Illustration
ISBN 9781635651911
Grades: Adult 641.5
1. Cooking (Natural foods) 2. Natural foods 3. Recipes 4. Cookbooks 5. Food writing — Cooking and cookbooks — Cooking for health

LC Bl2018179666

A follow-up to the New York Times best-seller Run Fast. Eat Slow is aimed at busy young athletes looking for nutritious recipes to fuel their lives, in a book that includes recipes for such dishes as Superhero Muffins, Pizza Bolognese, Baked Avocado and more.

Collects energy-packed, whole food recipes to fuel athletes from a leading distance runner and a culinary nutritionist, for everything from snacks and meals to drinks and treats.

Includes index.

Flay, Bobby
Bobby at Home: Fearless Flavors from My Kitchen. Bobby Flay with Stephanie Banyas and Sally Jackson. Clarkson Potter/Publishers 2019. 255 pages : Color; Illustration
ISBN 9780385345910
Grades: Adult 641.5
1. Cooking 2. Recipes 3. Cookbooks 4. Food writing — Cooking and cookbooks — Chefs and restaurants 5. Food writing — Cooking and cookbooks — Entertaining

LC Bl2018052578

The James Beard Award-winning celebrity chef shares 165 advice-laden recipes, from pumpkin pancakes with apple-cider syrup to Korean BBQ chicken, that he prepares at home for friends and family members.

Includes index.

Sundays with Sophie: Flay Family Recipes for Any Day of the Week. Bobby Flay with Emily Timberlake and inspiration from Sophie Flay; photographs by Ed Anderson. Clarkson Potter/Publishers 2022. 255 pages : Color; Illustration
ISBN 9780593232408
Grades: Adult 641.5
1. Cooking 2. Cookbooks 3. Food writing — Cooking and cookbooks — Chefs and restaurants 4. Food writing — Cooking and cookbooks — Cooking for the family

LC 2021056954

One of the country's most celebrated chefs, along with his daughter, Sophie, invite you to pull up a chair at their family table to learn his secrets for delivering delicious, unbeatable meals for any night of the week, helping you to build a repertoire of classic, adaptable recipes that will make you a better cook.

"The Flays have slayed it with a casual family cookbook that covers the basics for beginners, but it is full of surprises for veteran home chefs." —*Library Journal*

Includes index.

Frank, Lois Ellen
Seed to Plate, Soil to Sky: Modern Plant-based Recipes Using Native American Ingredients. Lois Ellen Frank; Native American culinary advisor, Walter Whitewater; recipe testing & recipe development advisor, Marianne Sundquist. Hachette Go 2023. xvi, 302 pages : Color; Illustration
ISBN 9780306827297
Grades: Adult 641.5
1. Cooking, Indigenous 2. Vegan cooking 3. Cooking, American 4. Indigenous peoples of North America 5. Vegetables 6. Beans 7. Cacao beans 8. Chile peppers 9. Corn 10. Potatoes 11. Tomatoes 12. Vanilla 13. Southwest (United States) 14. Cookbooks 15. Food writing — Cooking and cookbooks — Regional 16. Food writing — Cooking and cookbooks — Vegetarian and vegan 17. Food writing — History and microhistory

LC 2022047494

Introducing the 'Magic 8' Native American plants—corn, beans, squash, chile, tomato, potato, vanilla and cacao, which forever changed the world's cuisines, this mouthwatering—and eye-opening—celebration of Indigenous foods and Southwestern flavors presents more than 100 plant-based recipes to transform your cooking.

"Thoughtful and informative, this is a strong addition to a long underpublished category." —*Publishers Weekly*

Includes bibliographical references (pages 279-287) and index.

Fuentes, Laura
The Best Homemade Kids' Snacks on the Planet: More Than 200 Healthy Homemade Snacks You and Your Kids Will Love. Laura Fuentes, founder of MOMables.Com. Fair Winds Press 2015. 240 pages : Color; Illustration
ISBN 9781592336616
Grades: Adult 641.5
1. Cooking (Natural foods) 2. Quick and easy cooking 3. Recipes 4. Snack foods 5. Cookbooks 6. Food writing — Cooking and cookbooks — Ingredients 7. Food writing — Cooking and cookbooks — Methods

LC 2014047820

Overflowing with quick and healthy ideas for the whole family, this cookbook features delicious recipes for more than 200 homemade snacks that solve the snack conundrum and can be made in minutes without fuss in the kitchen.

Provides recipes for over two hundred healthy homemade snacks that kids and adults will love, including caprese skewers, baked cheese twists, and Tex-Mex chicken salad bites.

Includes index.

Fuhrman, Joel
Eat to Live Quick & Easy Cookbook: 131 Delicious, Nutrient-Rich Recipes for Fast and Sustained Weight Loss, Reversing Disease, and Lifelong Health. Joel Fuhrman, M.D.. HarperOne 2017. VII, 294 pages : Color; Illustration
ISBN 9780062684950
Grades: Adult 641.5
1. Weight loss 2. Dieting 3. Nutrition 4. Recipes 5. Cookbooks 6. Food writing — Cooking and cookbooks — Cooking for health 7. Self-Help — Personal growth — Diet and nutrition

LC 2017013630

A full-color companion cookbook to the author's popular Eat to Live shares dozens of easy-to-prepare, plant-based recipes designed to promote health and weight loss.

"Most recipes take only minutes to assemble; vegans, nonvegans, and raw foodies also will find suitable options." —*Publishers Weekly*

Includes index.

ESSENTIAL AND RECOMMENDED TITLES
641.5 Cooking

Gardner, Lindsay
Why We Cook: 100+ Women on Food, Connection, and Identity. Lindsay Gardner. Workman Publishing 2021. 240 p.
ISBN 9781523509744
Grades: Adult   641.5
1. Food habits 2. Cooking 3. Women cooks 4. Food 5. Women restaurateurs 6. Food writing — Cooking and cookbooks — Narrative cookbooks 7. Food writing — Memoirs and biographies 8. Food writing — Food and culture

An inspirational and powerful book that celebrates women's stories and trailblazing achievements in today's culinary world, with personal essays, recipes, Q&As, illustrated quotes, and more from over 100 women in the world of food (restaurateurs, sommeliers, food producers, activists, writers, professional and home cooks).

"With Gardner's gorgeous watercolor illustrations, this book is a love letter to food and those who feed us." —*Booklist*

Garten, Ina
Barefoot Contessa at Home: Everyday Recipes You'll Make Over and Over Again. Ina Garten; photographs by Quentin Bacon. Clarkson Potter 2006. 256 p. : Color illustration
ISBN 9781400054343
Grades: Adult   641.5
1. Cooking 2. Menus 3. Recipes 4. Cookbooks 5. Food writing — Cooking and cookbooks — Chefs and restaurants 6. Food writing — Cooking and cookbooks — Entertaining
LC 2006014257

Collects recipes featuring elegant but easy-to-prepare dishes for breakfast, lunch, dinner, and dessert for both everyday meals or special occasions, accompanied by tips on the art of entertaining with style.
Includes indexes.

Barefoot Contessa Family Style: Easy Ideas and Recipes That Make Everyone Feel Like Family. Ina Garten; photographs by Maura McEvoy; food styling by Rori Trovato. Clarkson Potter 2002. 240 p. : Illustration
ISBN 9780609610664
Grades: Adult   641.5
1. Cooking 2. Recipes 3. Food writing — Cooking and cookbooks — Entertaining
LC 2002074979

Offers a collection of recipes for everday cooking, including clam chowder, penne with five cheeses, and linguine with shrimp scampi.

The Barefoot Contessa returns with a new assortment of family-style recipes, entertaining tips, and menu suggestions that include fresh, favorite dishes including Saffron Risotto with Butternut Squash, Goat Cheese Popovers, Steak with Balsamic Grilled Onions, and Linguine with Shrimp Scampi, among others.

"This is simple, elegant home cooking with good ingredients and a minimum of fuss. It takes a certain amount of chutzpah to include ordinary chicken noodle soup and mashed potatoes and gravy in a cookbook, but Garten pulls it off with heart and style." —*Publishers Weekly*
Includes index.

★ *Barefoot Contessa, How Easy Is That?: Fabulous Recipes & Easy Tips.* Ina Garten; photographs by Quentin Bacon. Clarkson Potter/Publishers 2010. 256 p. : Color illustration
ISBN 9780307238764
Grades: Adult   641.5
1. Cooking 2. Recipes 3. Cookbooks 4. Food writing — Cooking and cookbooks — Methods
LC 2010002025

Food Network guru Ina Garten offers simple yet appetizing dishes that save time and minimize stress in the kitchen. Featuring over 200 recipes, including everything from easy parmesan risotto and French toast bread pudding to spicy turkey meatballs.
Includes index.

★ *Cook Like a Pro: Recipes & Tips for Home Cooks.* Ina Garten; photographs by Quentin Bacon. Clarkson Potter/Publishers 2018. 272 pages : Color; Illustration
ISBN 9780804187046
Grades: Adult   641.5
1. Cooking 2. Recipes 3. Cookbooks 4. Food writing — Cooking and cookbooks — Chefs and restaurants 5. Food writing — Cooking and cookbooks — Methods
LC 2018006753

Presents simple, streamlined recipes with tips and techniques for cooking like a chef.
Includes index.

Cooking for Jeffrey: A Barefoot Contessa Cookbook. Ina Garten; photographs by Quentin Bacon; garden photographs by John M. Hall. Clarkson Potter/Publishers 2016. 256 pages : Color; Illustration
ISBN 9780307464897
Grades: Adult   641.5
1. Cooking 2. Cookbooks 3. Food writing — Cooking and cookbooks — Chefs and restaurants 4. Food writing — Cooking and cookbooks — Courses 5. Food writing — Cooking and cookbooks — Regional
LC 2016025974

Collects recipes for the author's most requested dishes, including brisket with onions and leeks, maple-roasted carrot salad, and vanilla rum panna cotta with salted caramel.

"True to form, this culinary love letter is as warm and comforting as Gartens dishes." —*Publishers Weekly*
Includes index.

★ *Go-To Dinners: Make Ahead, Freeze Ahead, Prep Ahead, Easy Assembled.* Ina Garten; photographs by Quentin Bacon. Clarkson Potter/Publishers 2022. 255 pages : Color; Illustration
ISBN 9781984822789
Grades: Adult   641.5
1. Cooking 2. Quick and easy cooking 3. Make-ahead cooking 4. Cookbooks 5. Food writing — Cooking and cookbooks — Methods 6. Food writing — Cooking and cookbooks — Chefs and restaurants
LC BL2022028178

The popular cooking show host and New York Times best-selling author shares her strategies for making delicious, satisfying and uncomplicated dinners including Overnight Mac & Cheese, Tuscan White Bean Soup, Chicken in a Pot with Orzo and Hasselback Kielbasa.

"Practical and practically faultless, this is a real treat." —*Publishers Weekly*
Includes indexes.

★ *Make It Ahead.* Ina Garten; photographs by Quentin Bacon; garden photographs by John M. Hall. Clarkson Potter/Publishers 2014. 272 pages : Color; Illustration
ISBN 9780307464880
Grades: Adult   641.5
1. Make-ahead cooking 2. Quick and easy cooking 3. Cookbooks 4. Food writing — Cooking and cookbooks — Methods
LC 2014004486

The Emmy Award-winning celebrity chef shares favorite make-ahead recipes and meal-planning tips for a variety of occasions, suggesting preparation options for low-stress dishes that improve if prepared in advance.

"A quieter, simpler, more accessible version of Martha Stewart in the kitchen. Make-ahead meals appended." —*Booklist*
Includes index.

★ *Modern Comfort Food: A Barefoot Contessa Cookbook.* Ina Garten; photographs by Quentin Bacon; party photographs by Jean-Pierre Uys. Clarkson Potter/Publishers 2020. 256 pages : Color; Illustration
ISBN 9780804187060
Grades: Adult   641.5
1. Comfort food 2. Food Writing — Cooking and cookbooks — Chefs and restaurants
LC BL2020046541

A collection of eighty-five all-new recipes by the James Beard Award-winning host of the Emmy Award-winning Food Network series features comforting twists on childhood favorites, including cheesy chicken enchiladas, tomato and goat cheese crostata, and banana rum trifle.

"Garten's cookbooks are perennial best sellers. Anyone in search of nostalgic American comfort food with a twist will enjoy her latest offering." —*Library Journal*

Includes indexes.

Gerard, Tieghan
★ *Half Baked Harvest Every Day: Recipes for Balanced, Flexible, Feel-good Meals.* Tieghan Gerard. Clarkson Potter/Publishers 2022. 288 pages : Color; Illustration
ISBN 9780593232552
Grades: Adult   641.5
1. Quick and easy cooking 2. Comfort food 3. Low-fat diet 4. Low-calorie diet 5. Cookbooks 6. Food Writing — Cooking and cookbooks
LC 2021028697

A food photographer, stylist and recipe developer offers 125 brand-new recipes that balance rich comfort with healthier and lighter ingredients and are fun to make including Pizza Pasta, Spicy Shrimp Tacos and Salty Chocolate Pretzel Rye Cookies.

"Gerard's best cookbook to date. Her farm-fresh interpretation of modern comfort food should appeal to a wide range of home cooks." —*Library Journal*

Includes index.

Gill, Sasha
East Meets Vegan: The Best of Asian Home Cooking, Plant-Based and Delicious. Sasha Gill. The Experiment 2019. 223 p. : Color; Illustration
ISBN 9781615195633
Grades: Adult   641.5
1. Vegetarian cooking 2. Cooking, Asian 3. Cookbooks 4. Food writing — Cooking and cookbooks — Vegetarian and vegan 5. Food writing — Cooking and cookbooks — Regional
LC 2018043596

Ninety affordable, delicious vegan recipes that capture the color, spice and flavor of dishes from six Asian countries: India, Thailand, Singapore, Malaysia, China, and Japan.

Includes bibliographical references and index; Published as Jackfruit and Blue Ginger in the UK, Australia, and New Zealand by Murdoch Books in 2019.

Good, Phyllis Pellman
Fix-It and Forget-It New Cookbook: 250 New Delicious Slow-Cooker Recipes! New York Times bestselling author Phyllis Good. Good Books 2013. 384 pages : Color; Illustration (Fix-it and Forget-it)
ISBN 9781561488001
Grades: Adult   641.5
1. Quick and easy cooking 2. Cooking 3. Recipes 4. Cookbooks 5. Food writing — Cooking and cookbooks — Methods
LC Bl2013041707

Presents over two hundred recipes designed for the slow cooker, from such easy-to-prepare dishes as wild rice with chicken and lentil soup to more advanced recipes including oatmeal tandy cake, beef carbonnade, and braised beef short ribs.

Includes index.

Gourdet, Gregory
Everyone's Table: Global Recipes for Modern Health. Gregory Gourdet and JJ Goode. Harper Wave, an imprint of HarperCollinsPublishers 2021. 393 pages : Color; Illustration
ISBN 9780062984517
Grades: Adult   641.5
1. Cooking 2. Gluten-free diet 3. Sugar-free diet 4. Cookbooks 5. Food writing — Cooking and cookbooks — Cooking for health 6. Food writing — Cooking and cookbooks — Chefs and restaurants
LC 2021002287

Beloved Top Chef star Gregory Gourdet's groundbreaking cookbook has the culinary sophistication and delight of Yottam Ottolenghi books and goes a step further, featuring only healthy recipes free of gluten, dairy, soy, refined sugar, and legumes.

"Gourdet, of Top Chef renown, gives clean eating a punchy makeover in this gratifying collection of 200 gluten-free and Paleo-friendly recipes." —*Publishers Weekly*

Includes index.

Gray, Jon
Ghetto Gastro Black Power Kitchen. Jon Gray, Pierre Serrao, and Lester Walker with Osayi Endolyn; foreword by Dr. Jessica B. Harris; photography by Nayquan Shuler and Joshua Woods. Artisan Books 2022. 304 p.
ISBN 9781648290169
Grades: Adult   641.5
1. Cooking, African American 2. African diaspora 3. Vegan cooking 4. Cookbooks 5. Essays 6. Food writing — Cooking and cookbooks — Chefs and restaurants 7. Food writing — Cooking and cookbooks — Narrative cookbooks

A Bronx-based creative and culinary collective that promotes Black excellence through recipes, art and words combine immersive and uplifting storytelling with 75 plant-based recipes including Strong Back Stew, Red Velvet Cake, Triboro Tres Leches and Chopped Stease.

"A wonderfully written and beautifully produced book. In keeping with Ghetto Gastro's multidisciplinary approach, this volume will offer readers an engaging excursion into food history and culture, with a myriad of appealing recipes." —*Library Journal*

Greenspan, Dorie
★ *Everyday Dorie: The Way I Cook.* Dorie Greenspan; photographs by Ellen Silverman. Houghton Mifflin Harcourt 2018. 357 pages : Color; Illustration
ISBN 9780544826984
Grades: Adult   641.5
1. Cooking 2. Cookbooks 3. Food writing — Cooking and cookbooks — Chefs and restaurants
LC 2017061484

The James Beard Award-winning and New York Times magazine columnist shares the irresistibly informal food she makes for her husband and friends—.

"Greenspan (Around My French Table), five-time James Beard Award winner, shares her favorite day-to-day recipes in this standout cookbook." —*Publishers Weekly*

A Rux Martin book; Includes index.

Greger, Michael
★ *The How Not to Diet Cookbook.* Michael Greger, M.D, FACLM; recipes by Robin Robertson. Flatiron Books 2020. xxi, 233 pages : Color; Illustration
ISBN 9781250199256
Grades: Adult   641.5
1. Dieting 2. Food habits 3. Food writing — Cooking and cookbooks — Cooking for health 4. Science Writing — Medicine and health — Diet and nutrition — Weight loss
LC 2020032573

The founder of Nutritionfacts.Org and best-selling author of How Not to Diet explains how to make mindful eating part of a healthy lifestyle, outlining satisfying, science-based options that promote weight loss without high expense or counting calories.

"In this well-rounded recipe collection, physician Greger argues persuasively that meals based on whole plant foods can lead to weight loss while still packing in flavor.... This is perfect for those looking to shed pounds and still eat well." —*Publishers Weekly*

100+ recipes for healthy, permanent weight loss—Cover; Includes bibliographical references (pages 222-226) and index.

Griffin, Brooke
Skinny Suppers: 125 Lightened Up, Healthier Meals for Your Family. Brooke Griffin. William Morrow, an Imprint of HarperCollins Publishers 2016. xi, 307 pages : Color; Illustration
ISBN 9780062419156

ESSENTIAL AND RECOMMENDED TITLES
641.5 Cooking

Grades: Adult   641.5
1. Low-calorie diet 2. Quick and easy cooking 3. Recipes 4. Cookbooks 5. Food writing — Cooking and cookbooks — Cooking for health 6. Science writing — Medicine and health — Diet and nutrition — Weight loss
LC 2015034595

Collects light recipes for quick-and-easy suppers from the Skinny Mom website founder, including such options as supreme pizza pasta casserole, loaded nacho soup, and un-sloppy Janes, with meal-planning techniques and time-saving grocery lists.

With most recipes taking less than half an hour to make, the founder of Skinny Mom, www.Skinnymom.Com, the fastest-growing healthy community of moms, combines her nutritional knowledge, cooking insights and great food, to help home cooks slim down their kitchen and provide their family with healthy, home-cooked meals.

"Having this cookbook on hand will be like having your own personal cheerleader in the kitchen." —*Booklist*

Includes index.

Guarnaschelli, Alex
★ *Cook It Up: Bold Moves for Family Foods.* Alex Guarnaschelli + Ava Clark; photographs by Suech and Beck. Clarkson Potter/Publishers 2023. 239 pages : Illustration; Color
ISBN 9780593577981
Grades: Adult   641.5
1. Cooking and teenagers 2. Cooking 3. Comfort food 4. Cookbooks 5. Food writing — Cooking and cookbooks — Cooking for the family
LC 2022055731

A Food Network host and judge on Chopped joins forces with her teenage daughter for a collection of modern family meal dishes including Nanny Ida's Crisp Potato Latkes, Baked Chicken Wings with Garlicky Ranch, Marinated Skirt Steak and Paprika Chicken.

"Family influences are clear throughout…and add a cozy, genuine feeling to the proceedings. Chefs of all ages will be inspired." —*Publishers Weekly*

Includes index.

Guetta, Benedetta Jasmine
Cooking Alla Giudia: A Celebration of the Jewish Food of Italy. Benedetta Jasmine Guetta. Artisan Books 2022. 351 pages : Color; Illustration
ISBN 9781579659806
Grades: Adult   641.5
1. Cooking, Jewish 2. Cooking, Italian 3. Kosher food 4. Cookbooks 5. Food Writing — Cooking and cookbooks — Regional
LC 2021045062

An Italian food writer and photographer pays tribute to the culinary heritage of Jews from Italy through a collection of kosher recipes including Goose Prosciutto and Salami, Deep-Fried Artichokes and Sweet and sour sardines.

"Guetta makes her U.S. debut with this fascinating deep dive into Jewish Italian food.…Two cultures, each steeped in culinary tradition, complement each other in this insightful guide." —*Publishers Weekly*

Includes bibliographical references (page 341) and indexes.

Hamshaw, Gena
Food 52 Vegan: 60 Vegetable-driven Recipes for Any Kitchen. Gena Hamshaw; photography by James Ransom. Ten Speed Press 2015. xii, 145 pages
ISBN 9781607747994
Grades: Adult   641.5
1. Vegan cooking 2. Veganism 3. Cooking (Vegetables) 4. Recipes 5. Cookbooks 6. Food writing — Cooking and cookbooks — Vegetarian and vegan 7. Food writing — Cooking and cookbooks — Ingredients
LC 2015002837

Presents a collection of hassle-free vegan recipes, including such offerings as baked kale chips, butternut squash mac and cheese, and blackberry coconut ice cream.

Includes index.

Hansen, Kim-Julie
Best of Vegan: 100 Recipes That Celebrate Comfort, Culture, and Community. Kim-Julie Hansen. Harper Design, an imprint of HarperCollinsPublishers 2022. 223 pages : Color; Illustration
ISBN 9780063230514
Grades: Adult   641.5
1. Vegan cooking 2. International cooking 3. Cookbooks 4. Food writing — Cooking and cookbooks — Vegetarian and vegan
LC Bl2022037725

From the founder of the popular Instagram account @bestofvegan, and author of Vegan Reset comes a versatile plant-based cookbook featuring over 100 recipes, including some of the most popular fare from the Best of Vegan community, exclusive dishes created with renowned international vegan authors and chefs, and a variety of staples for every occasion."

"The popular blog comes to life in this upbeat and fun cookbook that will be a hit with nouveau vegans looking for satisfying fare." —*Library Journal*

Includes index.

Hartnett, Angela
The Weekend Cook: Good Food for Real Life. Angela Hartnett. Bloomsbury Absolute 2022. 288 pages : Illustration
ISBN 9781472975010
Grades: Adult   641.5
1. Entertaining 2. Cooking 3. Cookbooks 4. Food writing — Cooking and cookbooks — Entertaining 5. Food writing — Cooking and cookbooks — Methods

Angela knows the secrets to throwing the most relaxed and enjoyable dinners for friends and family—sometimes mad, but always magical evenings that people talk about for months afterwards—and in this book she's going to share them. Great flavours and simple recipes abound in these pages, each one a joy to cook and eat, from satisfying one-pot dishes and comforting risottos to perfect party food and bakes to feed a hungry crowd. Collected in these pages are over 80 recipes from one of Britain's most-loved chefs, as well as time saving tips and cheats that will take the stress out of hosting and allow you to enjoy your dinner parties without breaking a sweat.

"Delivering elegance with ease, this is sure to become a go-to for all types of occasions." —*Publishers Weekly*

Hartwig, Melissa
The Whole30 Fast & Easy: 150 Simply Delicious Everday Recipes for Your Whole30. Melissa Hartwig, co-author of the New York Times best-selling the Whole30; photography by Ghazalle Badiozamani. Houghton Mifflin Harcourt 2017. xix, 300 pages : Color; Illustration
ISBN 9781328839206
Grades: Adult   641.5
1. Nutritional therapy 2. Nutrition 3. Food habits 4. Weight loss 5. Quick and easy cooking 6. Dieting 7. Recipes 8. Self-care 9. Cookbooks 10. Food writing — Cooking and cookbooks — Methods 11. Food writing — Cooking and cookbooks — Cooking for health
LC 2017302891

Presents Whole30 diet compliant meals in thirty minutes or less, including roasted salmon with tomatoes and fennel, shrimp stir-fry over cauliflower grits, and Moroccan chicken and sweet potatoes.

"Readers interested in preparing and serving healthier meals that come together quickly (even if theyre not participating in the Whole30 program) are sure to appreciate this thoughtful collection." —*Publishers Weekly*

Includes index.

The Whole30 Slow Cooker: 150 Totally Compliant Prep-and-go Recipes for Your Whole30. Melissa Hartwig; photography by Ghazalle Badiozamani. Houghton Mifflin Harcourt 2018. xxi, 313 pages : Color; Illustration
ISBN 9781328531049
Grades: Adult   641.5
1. Nutritional therapy 2. Nutrition 3. Food habits 4. Weight loss 5. Menu planning 6. Pressure cooking 7. Quick and easy cooking 8. Self-care 9. Cooking 10. Cookbooks 11. Food writing — Cooking and cookbooks — Methods 12. Food writing — Cooking and cookbooks — Cooking for health

PUBLIC LIBRARY CORE COLLECTION: NONFICTION
Twentieth Edition

LC 2018032711

Presents slow cooker recipes, including ribs, soups, and noodle bowls that comply with the Whole30 lifestyle.

"Each of the books' recipes includes modifications for the Instant Pot, as well as an additional chapter of more than 30 dishes best suited for the device, such as smoky beef and bacon chili, and Chinese sesame chicken."—*Publishers Weekly*

Includes index.

Hayden, Georgina

Nistisima. Georgina Hayden. Bloomsbury 2022. 304 pages :
ISBN 9781526630681
Grades: Adult   641.5

1. Cooking, Mediterranean 2. Cooking, Southwest Asian and North African 3. Vegan cooking 4. Food writing — Cooking and cookbooks — Vegetarian and vegan 5. Food writing — Cooking and cookbooks — Regional

In this book, Georgina draws on the history and culture around nistisimo cooking in the Mediterranean, Middle East and Eastern Europe to share the simple, nutritious and flavour-packed recipes at the heart of the practice. Whether you're vegan, vegetarian, or simply want to eat more plant-based food, Nistisima offers you tried and tested recipes that celebrate the very best of this tradition all bursting with flavour and all surprisingly vegan.

"While in a traditional sense the dishes presented here symbolize restraint, they will be a treat to the newcomers interested in preparing them."—*Booklist*

Headley, Brooks

Superiority Burger Cookbook: The Vegetarian Hamburger Is Now Delicious. Brooks Headley; with Julia Goldberg, Gabe Rosner, Matthew Silverstein, and Matt Sweeney; photographs by Sunny Shokrae. W. W. Norton & Company 2018. 223 pages : Color; Illustration
ISBN 9780393253986
Grades: Adult   641.5

1. Meat substitutes 2. Hamburger 3. Vegetarian cooking 4. Recipes 5. Cookbooks 6. Food writing — Cooking and cookbooks — Vegetarian and vegan 7. Food writing — Cooking and cookbooks — Chefs and restaurants

LC 2018015069

The chef-owner of America's most talked-about vegetarian restaurant located in New York City's East Village presents 90 delicious recipes, some of which are the restaurant's favorites, that are innovative, irresistible and incredibly simple to make.

Includes index.

Hesser, Amanda

★ *The Essential New York Times Cook Book: Classic Recipes for a New Century*. Amanda Hesser. W.W. Norton 2010. xxiv, 932 p. : Illustration
ISBN 9780393061031
Grades: Adult   641.5

1. Cooking 2. Recipes 3. Cookbooks 4. Food writing — Cooking and cookbooks — Reference

LC 2010033311

The newspaper|s food columnist presents a compendium of more than 1,000 of the best recipes from the past 150 years of food journalism, including classics like Plum Torte, David Eyre|s Pancake and Pamela Sherrid|s Summer Pasta to modern-day fava bean salad.

Presents a compendium of more than one thousand of the best recipes from the past 150 years of food journalism, covering categories that include appetizers, soups, salads, meat, fish, bread, vegetables, and desserts.

"The author spent six years combing the Times's vast recipe archive, cooking her way through more than 1000 recipes to assemble this indispensible tome culled from 150 years of the paper's food columns. This daunting compendium features both noteworthy classics (Osso Buco) and modern recipes (Smoked Mashed Potatoes) that have been tested and, in some cases, updated for the contemporary cook. Chapters begin with a time line and are arranged by type of food (e.g., soups, vegetables, cakes) then chronologically within the chapter, making for a fascinating historic overview of the interests of American cooks."—*Library Journal*

Text on lining papers; Includes bibliographical references and index.

Heuck, Lidey

★ *Cooking in Real Life: Delicious & Doable Recipes for Every Day*. Lidey Heuck; photography by Dane Tashima. Simon Element 2024. x, 276 pages : Color; Illustration
ISBN 9781668002155
Grades: Adult   641.5

1. Quick and easy cooking 2. Dinners and dining 3. Entertaining 4. Cookbooks 5. Food writing — Cooking and cookbooks — Methods 6. Food writing — Cooking and cookbooks — Entertaining

LC Bl2024005352

From the rising star who learned to cook when she worked for Ina Garten and inherited the Barefoot Contessa's intuition for what people want to cook comes a collection of 100 recipes that are cook-pleasing and crowd-pleasing and written with the shopper, chopper and dish-doer in mind.

"Every once in a while, a cookbook comes along that does it all, from simple to sophisticated, weeknight to showstopper and, with tons of kitchen inspiration too, this is that cookbook."—*Booklist*

Includes index.

Homolka, Gina

Skinnytaste Fast and Slow: Knockout Quick-fix and Slow Cooker Recipes. Gina Homolka with Heather K. Jones, R.D… Clarkson Potter/Publishers 2016. 304 p. : Color; Illustration
ISBN 9780553459609
Grades: Adult   641.5

1. Quick and easy cooking 2. Electric cooking 3. Low-calorie diet 4. Dieting 5. Recipes 6. Cookbooks 7. Food writing — Cooking and cookbooks — Methods

LC Bl2016054008

Shares over one hundred recipes for dishes that are easy to prep, whether for cooking in the oven, on the stovetop or in a slow cooker, including such options as Korean-style beef tacos, pizza-stuffed chicken roll-ups, and peach-strawberry crumble.

"With its attractive design and easy everyday dishes, Homolka's latest may strike advanced cooks as too basic, but these recipes are excellent for novices. Expect demand."—*Library Journal*

Includes index.

Skinnytaste One & Done: 140 No-Fuss Dinners for Your Instant Pot, Slow Cooker, Sheet Pan, Air Fryer, Dutch Oven, & More. Gina Homolka with Heather K. Jones, R.D.. Clarkson Potter/Publishers 2018. 303 pages : Illustration
ISBN 9781524762155
Grades: Adult   641.5

1. Quick and easy cooking 2. One-dish meals 3. Low-calorie diet 4. Dieting 5. Cookbooks 6. Food writing — Cooking and cookbooks — Methods 7. Food writing — Cooking and cookbooks — Cooking for health

LC 2018015876

Presents quick and easy, family-friendly recipes, with tips and nutritional information, for one-pot cooker convenience.

The award-winning blogger and best-selling author of The Skinnytaste Cookbook blends family-friendly, illustrated tips and nutritional information, in a collection that adapts her signature healthy, flavor-forward recipes for one-pot cooker convenience.

Includes index.

Hood, Ann

Kitchen Yarns: Notes on Life, Love, and Food. Ann Hood. W.W. Norton & Company, independent publishers since 1923 2018. 256 p.
ISBN 9780393249507
Grades: Adult   641.5

1. Hood, Ann, 1956- 2. Authors, American 3. Italian American families 4. Cooking 5. Cooking, Italian 6. Memories 7. Grief 8. Loss 9. Recipes 10. Providence, Rhode Island 11. Essays 12. Autobiographies and memoirs 13. Food writing — Memoirs and biographies 14. Life stories — Relationships — Family 15. Family and Relationships — Families

LC 2018027425

ESSENTIAL AND RECOMMENDED TITLES
641.5 Cooking

Howard, Vivian
This Will Make It Taste Good: A New Path to Simple Cooking. Vivian Howard; photographs by Baxter Miller. Voracious 2020. xvi, 331 pages : Color; Illustration
ISBN 9780316381123
Grades: Adult   641.5
1. Recipes 2. Flavor 3. Cooking for families 4. Quick and easy cooking 5. Food writing — Cooking and cookbooks — Chefs and restaurants 6. Food writing — Cooking and cookbooks — Ingredients
LC Bl2020068105

From caramelized onions to fruit preserves, make home cooking quick and easy with ten simple "kitchen heroes" in these 125 recipes from the New York Times bestselling and award-winning author of Deep Run Roots.

"Nothing overly composed nor requiring umpteen ingredients: This is home cooking, elevated." —*Booklist*
Includes index.

Hunt, Lindsay Maitland
Healthyish: A Cookbook with Seriously Satisfying, Truly Simple, Good-for-You (But Not Too Good-for-You) Recipes for Real Life. Lindsay Maitland Hunt; photography by Linda Pugliese. Abrams 2017. 255 pages : Color; Illustration
ISBN 9781419726569
Grades: Adult   641.5
1. Cooking 2. Recipes 3. Cookbooks 4. Food writing — Cooking and cookbooks — Courses 5. Food writing — Cooking and cookbooks — Methods
LC Bl2018000448

A collection of simple, healthy recipes features such dishes as toasted coconut muesli, hummus and veggie pita, summer corn soup, pork and mushroom stroganoff, and salmon and quinoa bowl.

"Whether you like to leave cooking till the last minute or enjoy whipping up a big batch of something to eat throughout the week, this book will serve you well." —*Library Journal*
Includes indexes.

Help Yourself: A Guide to Gut Health for People Who Love Delicious Food. Lindsay Maitland Hunt; photography by Linda Pugliese. Houghton Mifflin Harcourt 2020. 352 p.
ISBN 9780358008385
Grades: Adult   641.5
1. Cooking 2. Health 3. Low-calorie diet 4. Nutrition 5. Recipes 6. Cookbooks 7. Food writing — Cooking and cookbooks — Cooking for health 8. Self-Help — Diet and nutrition
LC 2019045851

Emphasizing plant-based and whole ingredients this cookbook offers more than 125 recipes, including Brussels Sprouts and Peanut Butter Curry Bowl and Seeded Almond Flour Waffles with Raspberry-Flax Smash, that will help restore microbial balance in the gut.

"This is a lightning bolt of lucidity in a crowded and jargon-laden field of often impractical and unsustainable dietary approaches." —*Publishers Weekly*
Includes bibliographical references and index.

Hussain, Nadiya
★ *Nadiya's Everyday Baking: From Weeknight Dinners to Celebration Cakes, Let Your Oven Do the Work.* Nadiya Hussain, Chris Terry. Clarkson Potter 2022. 272 pages
ISBN 9780593579053
Grades: Adult   641.5
1. Dinners and dining 2. Food habits 3. Cooking, British 4. Baking 5. Cooking 6. Recipes 7. Food writing — Cooking and cookbooks — Narrative cookbooks 8. Food Writing — Food and Culture
LC 2022938716

Loan Stars Favourites, 2022.

Presenting more than 90 sweet and savory recipes accompanied by gorgeous photos, the winner of the Great British Baking Show provides simple and achievable meals for any occasion or mood that are rewarding no matter what kind of day you're having. Alongside Nadiya's warm, inspirational voice, this is sure to become a new favorite for home cooks and bakers alike.

"Hussain puts her own spin on baking in this collection of appetizing recipes that showcases her infectious joy for food and penchant for playing with flavors." —*Library Journal*

Time to Eat: Delicious Meals for Busy Lives. Nadiya Hussain; photography by Chris Terry. Clarkson Potter Publishers 2020. 255 pages : Color; Illustration
ISBN 9780593233535
Grades: Adult   641.5
1. Quick and easy cooking 2. Make-ahead cooking 3. Food writing — Cooking and cookbooks — Cooking for the family
LC Bl2020071830

The Great British Baking Show winner and host of Time to Eat shares more than 100 recipes for family meals, complementing such series favorites as Instant Noodles and Peanut Butter & Jelly Traybake with time-saving and make-ahead tips.

"Great for home cooks who want to reduce waste and streamline effort. Plenty of family and budget-friendly options, British classics, and recipes that work for meal prep." —*Library Journal*

A Netflix original series—Cover; Includes index.

Jade, Holly
The Essential Book of Vegan Bakes: Irresistible Plant-Based Cakes and Treats. Holly Jade, creator of the little blog of vegan. Countryman Press, an imprint of W.W. Norton & Company 2022. 223 pages : Color; Illustration
ISBN 9781682687390
Grades: Adult   641.5
1. Vegan cooking 2. Baking 3. Cookbooks 4. Food writing — Cooking and cookbooks — Vegetarian and vegan 5. Food writing — Cooking and cookbooks — Methods
LC 2022017809

Creator of The Little Blog of Vegan, Holly Jade has made plant-based baking easier and better than ever for her growing audience. Her unabashedly decadent treats never sacrifice flavor and texture, from cakes and cookies to pastry and puddings. Now, with Holly's contemporary style and an arsenal of dynamic desserts, The Essential Book of Vegan Bakes has a recipe for every craving, whether readers are vegan veterans or newcomers to the plant-based scene."

"Vegans looking to sweeten up their repertoire should start here." —*Publishers Weekly*
Includes index.

Jaffrey, Madhur
Madhur Jaffrey's World Vegetarian. Madhur Jaffrey. Clarkson Potter 2002. IX, 758 p. : Color illustration
ISBN 9780609809235
Grades: Adult   641.5
1. Vegetarian cooking 2. Recipes 3. Cookbooks 4. Food writing — Cooking and cookbooks — Vegetarian and vegan
LC BL2002005317

An international assortment of more than 650 meatless recipes representing a host of ethnic culinary traditions includes soups and salads, vegetable dishes, beans and grains, and chutneys and sauces.

"A compendium of vegetarian recipes from all over the world. Grouped mostly into broad categories by main ingredient (beans, grain, vegetables, etc.), they are as likely to come from a Palestinian restaurant in Toronto, the nuns at the Ormylia Monastery in Macedonia, or a home cook in Mexico as from Jaffrey's own Indian background or her experience as a cooking teacher." —*Library Journal*

Reprint. Originally published: 1999; Includes index.

PUBLIC LIBRARY CORE COLLECTION: NONFICTION
Twentieth Edition

Jones, Anna
One: Pot, Pan, Planet: A Greener Way to Cook for You and Your Family. Anna Jones; photographs by Issy Croker. Alfred A. Knopf 2022. 329 pages : Color; Illustration
ISBN 9780593320327
Grades: Adult 641.5
1. Vegetarian cooking 2. Cooking (Vegetables) 3. One-dish meals 4. Cookbooks 5. Food Writing — Cooking and cookbooks — Vegetarian and vegan
LC 2021010010

With recipes for every occasion, these creative, delicious and satisfying vegetarian dishes are easy to prepare and keep sustainability at the center of every meal.

"Jones offers dozens of tempting vegetarian recipes that highlight creative ways to prepare a variety of seasonal, sustainable produce; perfect for anyone seeking unfussy plant-centered recipes and those new to vegetarian or vegan cooking." —*Library Journal*
Includes index.

Kane, Cyndi
Save-It-Forward Suppers: A Simple Strategy to Save Time, Money, and Sanity. Cyndi Kane; illustrations by Jeannine Bulleigh. William Morrow, an imprint of HarperCollinsPublishers 2022. xiii, 289 pages : Color; Illustration
ISBN 9780063042704
Grades: Adult 641.5
1. Quick and easy cooking 2. Make-ahead cooking 3. Cookbooks 4. Food Writing — Cooking and cookbooks — Methods
LC 2021041924

Providing 15 weekly menus and more than 100 recipes, this practical cookbook presents the author's 'Save-it-Forward' method to cut down on cooking time and food waste, transforming leftovers into something new every night.

"This will be a lifesaver for busy home cooks." —*Publishers Weekly*
Includes index.

Kanell, John
Preppy Kitchen: Recipes for Seasonal Dishes and Simple Pleasures. John Kanell with Rachel Holtzman; photographs by David Malosh with additional photographs by John Kanell and John Gruen. Simon Element 2022. 319 pages : Color; Illustration
ISBN 9781982178376
Grades: Adult 641.5
1. Seasonal cooking 2. Cookbooks 3. Food writing — Cooking and cookbooks — Methods
LC Bl2022029080

A cooking and baking expert, and founder of Preppy Kitchen, serves up his fan-favorite recipes and baked goods that can be made at home, along with inspirational crafts, from making flower arrangements and wreaths to pickling vegetables, and stunning photographs that bring these mouthwatering dishes to life.

"For home cooks looking to entertain with exciting meals, this is indispensable." —*Publishers Weekly*
Includes index.

Katzen, Mollie
The Heart of the Plate: Vegetarian Recipes for a New Generation. Recipes, photographs, and illustrations by Mollie Katzen. Houghton Mifflin Harcourt 2013. 456 pages : Color; Illustration
ISBN 9780547571591
Grades: Adult 641.5
1. Vegetarian cooking 2. International cooking 3. Cooking (Natural foods) 4. Recipes 5. Cookbooks 6. Food writing — Cooking and cookbooks — Vegetarian and vegan
LC 2013010180

Reinventing the traditional vegetarian repertoire, offers 250 recipes for simple and healthful dishes that celebrate vegetables in all their glory and juxtapose colors and textures to make weeknight dinners fresh and exciting.

A Rux Martin book; Includes index.

★ *The Moosewood Cookbook.* Mollie Katzen. Ten Speed Press 2014. xvi, 231 pages : Illustration
ISBN 9781607747390
Grades: Adult 641.5
1. Vegetarian cooking 2. Cooking (Natural foods) 3. Cookbooks 4. Food writing — Cooking and cookbooks — Vegetarian and vegan
LC 2014015685

Traditional cooking styles and eclectic cuisines are reflected in a collection of vegetarian recipes served at the Moosewood Restaurant.
Includes index.

Keller, Thomas
The French Laundry Cookbook. Thomas Keller with Susie Heller and Michael Ruhlman; photographs by Deborah Jones. Artisan 1999. IX, 325 p. : Illustration; Color
ISBN 9781579651268
Grades: Adult 641.5
1. Cooking, French 2. Haute cuisine 3. Restaurants 4. Cookbooks 5. Food writing — Cooking and cookbooks — Chefs and restaurants 6. Food writing — Cooking and cookbooks — Regional
LC 99032473

Offers one hundred and fifty recipes from The French Laundry kitchen, including "parmigiano-reggiano crisps with goat cheese mousse," "shrimp with avocado salsa," and "strawberry and champagne terrine."

"Epitomizing a love of ingredients (there is a resource guide to esoterica) and an almost magical approach to food, this is required for any real 'cookbook' collection." —*Library Journal*
Includes index.

Kieffer, Sarah
100 Morning Treats: With Muffins, Rolls, Biscuits, Sweet and Savory Breakfast Breads, and More. Sarah Kieffer. Chronicle Books 2023. 304 pages : Color; Illustration
ISBN 9781797216164
Grades: Adult 641.5
1. Breakfasts 2. Bread 3. Baking 4. Baked products 5. Cookbooks 6. Food writing — Cooking and cookbooks — Courses 7. Food writing — Cooking and cookbooks — Methods
LC 2022049798

The creator of Vanilla Bean Blog and best-selling author of 100 Cookies and Baking for the Holidays offers 100 breakfast recipes whether it's for a weekend, a morning at the office or sports practice from muffins to bread and coffeecakes.

"Although it isn't as accessible for beginners as those previous titles, experienced baking enthusiasts will find a lot to love." —*Library Journal*
Includes bibliographical references (page 297) and index.

★ *Baking for the Holidays: 50+ Treats for a Festive Season.* Sarah Kieffer. Chronicle Books 2021. 224 pages : Color; Illustration
ISBN 9781452180755
Grades: Adult 641.5
1. Holiday cooking 2. Christmas cooking 3. Baking 4. Food Writing — Cooking and cookbooks — Methods 5. Food Writing — Cooking and cookbooks — Courses
LC 2020058057

A festive baking book featuring more than 50 recipes to enjoy during the holiday season and all winter long.

"This approachable guide to baking for the holidays offers plenty of inspiration for bakers of all levels; it's a delightful seasonal complement to Kieffer's hit 100 Cookies." —*Library Journal*
Includes bibliographical references (page 217) and index.

Kimball, Christopher
Christopher Kimball's Milk Street: The New Home Cooking. with Matthew Card, J.M. Hirsch, Michelle Locke and Jennifer Baldino Cox. Little, Brown and Company 2017. xxv, 310 pages : Illustration; Color
ISBN 9780316437288
Grades: Adult 641.5

ESSENTIAL AND RECOMMENDED TITLES
641.5 Cooking

1. International cooking 2. Recipes 3. Cookbooks 4. Food writing — Cooking and cookbooks — Chefs and restaurants

LC Bl2017037212

A collection of recipes for the home cook, inspired by Christopher Kimball's Milk Street Television show and arranged by type of dish features such offerings as curry braised eggs, Vietnamese caramel fish, multigrain soda bread, and pumpkin tart.

"Overall, with its testing notes, short ingredient lists, and firm directions (each recipe has a don't section), this volume is a trustworthy and easy-to-use collection of international flavors from one of the nation's best cooking teachers." —*Booklist*

Includes index.

Christopher Kimball's Milk Street: Tuesday Nights. Christopher Kimball, J.M. Hirsch, Matthew Card, Michelle Locke, Jennifer Baldino Cox, and the editors and cooks of Milk Street; photography by Connie Miller. Little, Brown and Company 2018. IX, 405 pages : Illustration; Color

ISBN 9780316437318

Grades: Adult   641.5

1. Quick and easy cooking 2. Cookbooks 3. Food writing — Cooking and cookbooks — Methods 4. Food writing — Cooking and cookbooks — Chefs and restaurants

LC Bl2018186299

A collection of quick recipes for weeknight dining, inspired by Christopher Kimball's Milk Street Television show, include such dishes as yakiudon with pickled ginger, pork schnitzel, kale and white bean soup, Indonesian fried tofu salad, and three-cheese pizza.

"Milk Street's globally inspired approach to fast cooking is anything but bland. Turn to their latest for flavorful weeknight winners." —*Library Journal*

Includes index.

★ ***Milk Street 365: The All-Purpose Cookbook for Every Day of the Year***. Christopher Kimball; writing and editing, J.M. Hirsch, Michelle Locke and Dawn Yanagihara; recipes, Wes Martin, Courtney Hill, Diane Unger and the Milk Street kitchen cooks and recipe contributors; art direction, Jennifer Baldino Cox. Voracious 2024. 656 p.

ISBN 9780316538688

Grades: Adult   641.5

1. Cooking 2. Cookbooks 3. Food writing — Cooking and cookbooks — Reference 4. Food writing — Cooking and cookbooks — Courses

This is Milk Street's new and comprehensive guide to today's recipe repertoire, full of fresh flavors and simple yet game-changing techniques. This is everyday cooking you actually want to cook every day. Milk Street 365 is both inspiration and reference for the contemporary kitchen, with recipes that will change the way you cook at home—from soups, stews and salads to flatbreads, pizzas and noodles.

"Both newbie cooks and old hands in the kitchen will want a copy of this smartly written cookbook that delivers a year's worth of delicious dishes and invaluable culinary insight." —*Library Journal*

Includes index.

Milk Street: Cook What You Have ; Make a Meal Out of Almost Anything. Christopher Kimball; writing and editing by J.M.Hirsch, Michelle Locke and Dawn Yanagihara;recipes by Wes Martin, Diane Unger, Bianca Borges, Matthew Card, and the Cooks at Milk Street; art direction by Jennifer Baldino Cox and Ali Zeigler; pho. Voracious, Little, Brown and Company 2022. xxviii, 323 pages : Illustration; Color

ISBN 9780316387569

Grades: Adult   641.5

1. Cooking 2. Cookbooks 3. Food writing — Cooking and cookbooks — Methods 4. Food writing — Cooking and cookbooks — Chefs and restaurants

LC Bl2022030299

Encourages home cooks to make delicious meals with whatever they have on hand in the pantry through 225 recipes designed to teach an improvisational way to cook and include Portuguese-Style Tuna with Chickpeas and Hoisin-Ginger Noodles.

"This beautifully photographed and thoughtfully organized guide is a method of cooking, not just a cookbook." —*Booklist*

Includes index.

Milk Street: The New Rules : Recipes That Will Change the Way You Cook. Christopher Kimball; with writing and editing by J.M. Hirsch and Michelle Locke; recipes by Matthew Card, Diane Unger and the Cooks at Milk Street; art direction by Jennifer Baldino Cox and Brianna Coleman; photography by Connie Miller of CB Crea. Voracious, Little, Brown and Company 2019. xv, 302 pages : Illustration; Color

ISBN 9780316423052

Grades: Adult   641.5

1. Cooking 2. Recipes 3. Cookbooks 4. Food writing — Cooking and cookbooks — Chefs and restaurants 5. Food writing — Cooking and cookbooks — Regional

LC Bl2019032149

The Milk Street chef and his team offer such recipes as Vietnamese Chicken Salad and Malaysian-Style Noodles while demonstrating adaptable tips, tricks and ideas for dramatically improving preparation times and overall results.

"Highly recommended for fans of Kimball and Cook's Illustrated, with delicious recipes and sound techniques to improve and spice up everyday cooking routines." —*Library Journal*

Includes index.

Kingsley, Lisa

Smithsonian *American Table: The Foods, People, and Innovations That Feed Us*. Lisa Kingsley, in collaboration with Smithsonian Institution. Harvest, an imprint of HarperCollins Publishers 2023. 304 p.

ISBN 9780358008668

Grades: Adult   641.5

1. Cooking 2. Food 3. Food habits 4. Food preparation 5. Culture 6. History 7. Identity 8. Social life and customs 9. United States history 10. United States 11. Food Writing — Food and Culture 12. Food writing — History and microhistory

LC 2022049061

This historical exploration of the American table serves up an eye-opening look at what and how we've fed ourselves through the lens of location, immigration, ingenuity and culture, with an emphasis on the people, events and movements that have been left out of the dominant story.

"Suffused with facts, fun, and recipes, food and history enthusiasts will love this book." —*Library Journal*

Includes bibliographical references and index.

Klein, Dini

Prep *+ Rally: An Hour of Prep, a Week of Delicious Meals*. Dini Klein. Harvest, an imprint of William Morrow 2022. xi, 307 pages : Color; Illustration

ISBN 9780358645566

Grades: Adult   641.5

1. Quick and easy cooking 2. Make-ahead cooking 3. Cooking 4. Cookbooks 5. Food writing — Cooking and cookbooks — Methods 6. Food writing — Cooking and cookbooks — Cooking for the family

LC Bl2022028062

The rising Instagram star and founder of the popular meal-prep service Prep + Rally shows home cooks how just one hour of prep can result in four delicious, family-friendly weeknight meals, with one inexpensive weekly grocery bill.

"Look for this to become a perennial favorite for any cook looking to simplify meal planning and prep with delish results." —*Library Journal*

Includes index.

Kochilas, Diane

*The **Ikaria** Way: 100 Delicious Plant-based Recipes Inspired by My Homeland, the Greek Island of Longevity*. Diane Kochilas. St. Martin's Griffin 2024. 261 pages : Color; Illustration

ISBN 9781250880000

Grades: Adult   641.5

1. Local foods 2. Vegetarian cooking 3. Cooking, Mediterranean 4. Cooking, Greek 5. Greece 6. Cookbooks 7. Food writing — Cooking and cookbooks — Regional 8. Food writing — Cooking and cookbooks — Vegetarian and vegan

LC 2023036058

Brings the plant-based cuisine of Ikaria, Greece, to your dinner table, in a book that includes such recipes as Smoked Eggplant with Tahini and Walnuts, Mushroom-Red Petter Souvlaki, and many more.

"A thoroughly contemporary collection, elegantly presented." —*Booklist*

Includes index.

Koenig, Leah

Portico: Cooking and Feasting in Rome's Jewish Kitchen. Leah Koenig; photography by Kristin Teig. W.W. Norton & Company 2023. 333 pages : Color; Illustration

ISBN 9780393868012

Grades: Adult   641.5

1. Cooking, Jewish 2. Cooking, Italian 3. Restaurants 4. Jewish way of life 5. Rome, Italy 6. Italy 7. Cookbooks 8. Food Writing — Cooking and cookbooks — Regional

LC 2023009903

With more than 100 deeply flavorful recipes that maintain the integrity of tradition, this fascinating culinary tour of Rome's centuries-old Jewish community showcases the cuisine's elegantly understated vegetables, saucy braised meats and stews, rustic pastas, olive oil-fried foods and never-too-sweet desserts.

"Koenig's diligence with details will likely delight home cooks, especially those who keep kosher, armchair travelers, and history buffs looking to explore a lesser-known side of Jewish cuisine." —*Library Journal*

Includes bibliographical references (page 324) and index.

Krieger, Ellie

You Have It Made!: Delicious, Healthy Do-Ahead Meals. Ellie Krieger; with photography by Quentin Bacon. Houghton Mifflin Harcourt 2016. 352 pages : Color; Illustration

ISBN 9780544579309

Grades: Adult   641.5

1. Make-ahead cooking 2. Recipes 3. Cookbooks 4. Food writing — Cooking and cookbooks — Cooking for health 5. Food writing — Cooking and cookbooks — Methods

LC 2015028798

A longtime Food Network star and best-selling author offers make-ahead recipes for breakfast, salads, soups, entrees, vegetarian dishes and much more.

Shares over one hundred and forty recipes for dishes that can be made ahead of time, including blueberry-chia overnight oats in jars, herbed salmon salad, and pulled pork tacos with pineapple and pickled onions.

Lagasse, Emeril

Essential Emeril: Favorite Recipes and Hard-Won Wisdom from a Life in the Kitchen. Emeril Lagasse with Pam Hoenig. Oxmoor House 2015. 304 pages : Color; Illustration

ISBN 9780848744786

Grades: Adult   641.5

1. Cooking 2. Recipes 3. Cookbooks 4. Food writing — Cooking and cookbooks — Chefs and restaurants

LC Bl2015038121

The celebrity chef shares anecdotes, cooking instructions, and recipes for iconic dishes that have shaped his career from easy barbecue shrimp and duck confit with killer bacon waffles to lobster and saffron risotto and grilled calamari salad.

"More advanced than some of his other titles, Lagasse's latest showcases his skill. Emeril fans will savor these delicious and iconic dishes." —*Library Journal*

Includes indexes.

Lancaster, Bridget

Cooking at Home with Bridget & Julia: The TV Hosts of America's Test Kitchen Share Their Favorite Recipes for Feeding Family and Friends. Bridget Lancaster, Julia Collin Davison, and the editors at America's Test Kitchen. America's Test Kitchen 2017. xv, 304 pages : Color; Illustration

ISBN 9781945256165

Grades: Adult   641.5

1. Cooking 2. Recipes 3. Cookbooks 4. Food writing — Cooking and cookbooks — Cooking for the family 5. Food writing — Cooking and cookbooks — Chefs and restaurants

LC 2017018306

The television hosts share their favorite recipes, including muffin tin doughnuts, corned beef hash, hearty beef and vegetable stew, tomato and mozzarella tart, and florentine lace cookies.

Includes index.

Laperruque, Emma

Food52 Big Little Recipes: Good Food with Minimal Ingredients and Maximal Flavor. Emma Laperruque; photographs by James Ransom; illustrations by Hyesu Lee. Ten Speed Press 2021. IX, 165 pages : Color; Illustration

ISBN 9780399581588

Grades: Adult   641.5

1. Quick and easy cooking 2. Cookbooks 3. Food Writing — Cooking and cookbooks — Methods

LC 2020045750

Inspired by Food52's award-winning column, this cookbook features 60 new recipes that highlight minimalism and deliciousness to make every cooking step count, including Fried Toast with Sugared Tomatoes, Burrata & Chiles and Sesame Chicken with Artichokes & Arugula.

"This fundamental guide proves that cutting down the grocery list doesn't have to mean cutting down the flavor." —*Publishers Weekly*

Includes index.

Larsen, Jeffrey

★ *Gluten-Free Baking at Home: 102 Foolproof Recipes for Delicious Breads, Cakes, Cookies, and More.* Jeffrey Larsen; photographs by Kelly Puleio. Ten Speed Press 2019. 277 pages : Color; Illustration

ISBN 9780399582790

Grades: Adult   641.5

1. Baking 2. Gluten-free diet 3. Pies 4. Bread 5. Cookies 6. Recipes 7. Cookbooks 8. Food writing — Cooking and cookbooks — Methods 9. Food writing — Cooking and cookbooks — Cooking for health

LC 2018060697

A comprehensive, fully illustrated collection of more than 80 master recipes and variations for gluten- and allergen-free baked goods includes options ranging from chocolate chip cookies and banana bread to brioche and biscuits. Illustrations.

"A lovingly precise collection of gluten-free baking classics, stunning yet never showy. Highly recommended for bakers of all skill levels." —*Library Journal*

Includes bibliographical references and index.

Lawson, Nigella

★ *Cook, Eat, Repeat: Ingredients, Recipes, and Stories.* Nigella Lawson. Ecco Press 2021. 352 p. : Illustration

ISBN 9780063079540

Grades: Adult   641.5

1. Lawson, Nigella, 1960- 2. Cooking 3. Food 4. Food preparation 5. Comfort food 6. Holiday cooking 7. Food writing — Cooking and cookbooks — Narrative cookbooks 8. Life stories — Arts and culture — Culinary arts

A delicious and delightful combination of recipes intertwined with narrative essays about food, all written in Nigella Lawson's engaging and insightful prose….And in Cook, Eat, Repeat she reveals the rhythms and rituals of her kitchen through recipes that make the most of her favorite ingredients, with inspiration for family dinners, vegan feasts, and solo suppers, as well as new ideas for cooking during the holidays.

"This collection of family-friendly dishes that are on repeat in the Lawson household is sure to become a favorite for devotees and new readers alike." —*Library Journal*

ESSENTIAL AND RECOMMENDED TITLES
641.5 Cooking

★ *Simply* Nigella. Nigella Lawson; photographs by Keiko Oikawa. Flatiron Books 2015. xiii, 402 pages : Color; Illustration
ISBN 9781250073754
Grades: Adult 641.5
1. Cooking 2. Comfort food 3. Cookbooks 4. Food writing — Cooking and cookbooks — Chefs and restaurants
LC 2015036267

Whatever the occasion, food-in the making and the eating-should always be pleasurable. Simply Nigella taps into the rhythms of our cooking lives with recipes that are uncomplicated and relaxed yet always satisfying. From quick and calm workday dinners (Miso Salmon; Cauliflower & Cashew Nut Curry) to stress-free ideas when feeding a crowd (Chicken Traybake with Bitter Orange & Fennel) to the instant joy of bowlfood for cozy nights on the sofa (Thai Noodles with Cinnamon and Shrimp), here is food guaranteed to make everyone feel good. Whether you need to create some breathing space at the end of a long week (Asian-Flavored Short Ribs), indulge in a sweet treat (Lemon Pavlova; Chocolate Chip Cookie Dough Pots), or wake up to a strength-giving breakfast (Toasty Olive Oil Granola), Nigella's new cookbook is filled with recipes destined to become firm favorites. Simply Nigella is the perfect antidote to our busy lives: a calm and glad celebration of food to soothe and uplift.

"Home cooks who love planning relaxed meals by whim will be well served by Lawson's latest, which offers a winning selection of recipes for all occasions." —*Library Journal*

Includes index.

Leake, Lisa
100 Days of Real Food on a Budget: Simple Tips and Tasty Recipes to Help You Cut Out Processed Food Without Breaking the Bank. by Lisa Leake. William Morrow 2018. 295 pages : Color; Illustration
ISBN 9780062668554
Grades: Adult 641.5
1. Cooking (Natural foods) 2. Low-cost cooking 3. Recipes 4. Quick and easy cooking 5. Cookbooks 6. Food writing — Cooking and cookbooks — Methods
LC Bl2018156978

Shares shopping lists and meal plans designed to eliminate processed foods while on a tight budget.

Includes bibliographical references (page 278) and index.

★ *100 Days of Real Food: How We Did It, What We Learned, and 100 Easy, Wholesome Recipes Your Family Will Love*. Lisa Leake. William Morrow 2014. 360 pages : Color; Illustration
ISBN 9780062252555
Grades: Adult 641.5
1. Cooking (Natural foods) 2. Recipes 3. Cookbooks 4. Food writing — Cooking and cookbooks — Ingredients
LC Bl2014036664

Presents a hands-on cookbook and guide that provides family-friendly recipes and practical advice for eating wholesome natural food that is not highly processed or refined.

Includes bibliographical references and index.

Lee, Jennifer Tyler
Half the Sugar, All the Love: A Family Cookbook : 100 Easy, Low-sugar Recipes for Every Meal of the Day. Jennifer Tyler Lee and Anisha I. Patel, MD, MSPH.. Workman Publishing 2019. 216 pages : Color; Illustration
ISBN 9781523504237
Grades: Adult 641.5
1. Children 2. Detoxification (Health) 3. Nutrition 4. Cooking 5. Cookbooks 6. Food Writing — Cooking and cookbooks — Cooking for the family 7. Food Writing — Cooking and cookbooks — Cooking for health
LC 2019955696

Would you feed your child a candy bar for breakfast? Of course not. And yet today our children routinely consume three times the recommended daily allowance of added sugar, which puts them at an unprecedented risk for type 2 diabetes, high blood pressure, high cholesterol, excess weight, and even nonalcoholic fatty liver disease. Half the Sugar, All the Love is here to help, with 100 doctor-approved recipes that cut the sugar (by half or more!) without sacrificing the flavors our families love. The recipes rely on using fruits and vegetables to sweeten food naturally without adding sugar or sugar substitutes. It's an eye-opening education, a program of healthy eating, and a cookbook chock-full of easy, delicious recipes all in one. Pass the breakfast bars!

"This is a smart choice for families interested in improving their diet." —*Publishers Weekly*

Less sugar in every meal—back cover; Includes bibliographical references (pages 206-207) and index.

Lewis, John
*Badass Vegan: Fuel Your Body, Ph*ck the System, and Live Your Life Right*. John Lewis; created with Rachel Holtzman; recipes in collaboration with Chef Tara Punzone; food photography by Jackie Sobon; lifestyle photography by Cassie Fuertez, Adam Codeus, and Davy Greenberg. Avery, an imprint of Penguin Random House 2023. 319 pages : Illustration; Color
ISBN 9780593420737
Grades: Adult 641.5
1. Vegetarian cooking 2. Vegan cooking 3. Cooking (Vegetables) 4. Veganism 5. Health foods 6. Cookbooks 7. Food writing — Cooking and cookbooks — Vegetarian and vegan 8. Food writing — Cooking and cookbooks — Cooking for health
LC 2022012159

A health activist, wellness expert and "badass vegan" offers an irreverent and surprising four-part plan to help readers discover the huge health benefits of a plant-based lifestyle with over 75 recipes including Watermelon Gazpacho and Peanut Hoisin Seitan Wraps.

"Those curious about veganism will find this a powerful resource." —*Publishers Weekly*

Includes index.

Lightner, Jill
Cooking from Scratch: 120 Recipes for Colorful, Seasonal Food from PCc Community Markets. with Jill Lightner; photographs by Charity Burggraff. Sasquatch Books 2018. xxi, 279 pages : Color; Illustration
ISBN 9781632171887
Grades: Adult 641.5
1. Cooking (Natural foods) 2. Recipes 3. Seasonal cooking 4. Seattle, Washington 5. Cookbooks 6. Food writing — Cooking and cookbooks — Regional
LC 2018000128

120 simple and delicious recipes in a cookbook that's chock-full of nutritional information and expert advice from Seattle's popular grocer, PCC Community Markets.

"This diverse collection of easy-to-follow and flavorful recipes is a delicious, memorable addition to any home kitchen." —*Library Journal*

Includes index.

Lillien, Lisa
Hungry Girl 1-2-3: The Easiest, Most Delicious, Guilt-Free Recipes on the Planet. Lisa Lillien. St. Martin's Griffin 2010. xv, 333 p, [16] p. of plates : Color illustration
ISBN 9780312556181
Grades: Adult 641.5
1. Quick and easy cooking 2. Low-calorie diet 3. Low-fat diet 4. Recipes 5. Cookbooks 6. Food writing — Cooking and cookbooks — Cooking for health
LC 2009046743

With a focus on quick-to-prepare meals, offers recipes that require four ingredients or less and make use of the microwave, crockpot, and foil-pack baking, as well as some dishes that require no cooking.

Includes index.

Hungry Girl Simply 6: All-Natural Recipes with 6 Ingredients or Less. Lisa Lillien. St. Martin's Griffin 2019. 384 pages : Color; Illustration
ISBN 9781250154521
Grades: Adult 641.5
1. Quick and easy cooking 2. Low-calorie diet 3. Low-fat diet 4. Cookbooks 5. Food writing — Cooking and cookbooks — Cooking for health

PUBLIC LIBRARY CORE COLLECTION: NONFICTION
Twentieth Edition

LC 2018050709

A collection of recipes with six ingredients or less for meals, snacks, and desserts includes vegetarian and gluten-free recipes.

Includes index.

Madison, Deborah

In My Kitchen: A Collection of New and Favorite Vegetarian Recipes. Deborah Madison; photography by Erin Scott. Ten Speed Press 2017. 285 pages : Illustration

ISBN 9780399578885

Grades: Adult   641.5

1. Vegetarian cooking 2. Cooking 3. Recipes 4. Cookbooks 5. Food writing — Cooking and cookbooks — Vegetarian and vegan

LC 2016038957

Presents an updated collection of recipes from the country's leading authority on vegetarian cooking, including such dishes as cheese souffle, braised summer vegetables, and zucchini cake, with menu suggestions and tips for modifications.

"One glance will quickly show why the dishes here are Madison's go-to meals, and they will soon become readers favorites as well." —*Publishers Weekly*

Includes index.

Vegetarian Cooking for Everyone. Deborah Madison. Broadway Books 2007. x, 742 p, 24 p. of plates : Illustration; Color

ISBN 9780767927475

Grades: 11 12 Adult   641.5

1. Recipes 2. Vegetarian cooking 3. Food writing — Cooking and cookbooks — Vegetarian and vegan

LC 2007010075

The founding chef of San Francisco's Greens restaurant and award-winning author of The Greens Cookbook presents a lavishly illustrated cookbook of more than 1,400 innovative vegetarian and vegan recipes and comprehensive information on a myriad of vegetables dishes, in a tenth anniversary edition of the James Beard Award-winning cookbook.

"Following information on ingredients and techniques, the recipes focus mainly on vegetables and grains, aiming at flavor and variety, both often arrived at via assorted ethnic approaches." —*Publishers Weekly*

Includes index; Originally published: New York : Broadway Books, 1997.

Martin, Pat

Life of Fire: Mastering the Arts of Pit-Cooked Barbecue, the Grill, and the Smokehouse. Pat Martin and Nick Fauchald; photographs by Andrew Thomas Lee. Clarkson Potter/Publishers 2022. 317 pages : Illustration; Color

ISBN 9781984826121

Grades: Adult   641.5

1. Barbecuing 2. Cooking 3. Cookbooks 4. Food Writing — Cooking and cookbooks — Methods

LC 2021029082

One of the South's most acclaimed pitmasters reveals all he knows about the art of barbecue and open-flame cooking, in all the stages of a fire's life.

"The hours add up but the barbecuing never gets old in this satisfying outing." —*Publishers Weekly*

Includes index.

Mauro, Jeff

Come on Over: 111 Fantastic Recipes for the Family That Cooks, Eats, and Laughs Together. Jeff Mauro; photography by Ken Goodman. William Morrow 2021. IX, 294 pages : Color; Illustration

ISBN 9780062997081

Grades: Adult   641.5

1. Cooking 2. Cookbooks 3. Food writing — Cooking and cookbooks — Chefs and restaurants 4. Food writing — Cooking and cookbooks — Entertaining

LC 2020042432

A personality-filled cookbook for family and friendly gatherings from celebrity chef Jeff Mauro, co-host of the Kitchen on Food Network.

"Mauro's recipe introductions are personal, charming, friendly, and offer useful tips to enhance and instruct and are sure to engage. Put this at the center of your summertime cookbook display." —*Booklist*

Includes index.

McAlpine, Skye

A **Table** Full of Love: Recipes to Comfort, Seduce, Celebrate & Everything Else in Between. Skye McAlpine. Bloomsbury Publishing 2023. 319 pages : Color; Illustration

ISBN 9781639730490

Grades: Adult   641.5

1. Cooking 2. Entertaining 3. Cookbooks 4. Food writing — Cooking and cookbooks — Entertaining

LC Bl2023004734

The author of A Table for Friends shares recipes that will expand your culinary love language with sections entitled Comfort, Seduce, Nourish and Cocoon and with recipes including Spaghetti with Chiles and Hazelnut and Fusilli with Lardo, Almonds and Honey.

"Whether readers are looking for the perfect dish to woo or a way to comfort through food, McAlpine provides the tools and recipes to say it with love from a kitchen." —*Library Journal*

Includes index.

McFadden, Joshua

Six Seasons: A New Way with Vegetables. Joshua McFadden with Martha Holmberg; foreword by Barbara Damrosch and Eliot Coleman. Artisan 2017. 397 pages

ISBN 9781579656317

Grades: Adult   641.5

1. Cooking (Vegetables) 2. Recipes 3. Seasonal cooking 4. Cookbooks 5. Food writing — Cooking and cookbooks — Ingredients 6. Food writing — Cooking and cookbooks — Chefs and restaurants

LC OC2018135929

A chef and "vegetable whisperer" offers 225 vegetable-centric recipes that provide a new way to view and utilize their attributes throughout their growing seasons including Farro and Tomato Salad, Carrot and Beet Slaw and Fried Farro with Pickled Carrots and Runny Eggs.

"McFadden's debut cookbook is an invaluable resource for all things veggie." —*Booklist*

Includes index.

McGee, Harold

★ *On* Food and Cooking: The Science and Lore of the Kitchen. Harold McGee. Scribner 2004. x, 884 p. : Illustration

ISBN 9780684800011

Grades: Adult   641.5

1. Food 2. Cooking 3. Nutrition 4. Food science 5. Food in literature 6. Food habits 7. Health 8. Food writing — General

LC 2004058999

Looks at the history of milk, eggs, meat, fruits, vegetables, spices, grains, nuts, bread, sauces, sugars, alcohol, and food additives, and discusses nutrition and the principles of cooking.

"In this long-awaited revision of his classic on Food and Cooking (1984), McGee has incorporated current information and covers a greater range of ingredients and how they can be prepared to develop their diverse flavors." —*Library Journal*

Includes bibliographical references (p. 819-833) and index; Originally published: New York : Scribner, 1984.

McKinnon, Hetty

★ *Tenderheart:* A Cookbook About Vegetables and Unbreakable Family Bonds. Hetty Lui McKinnon. Knopf 2023. 528 pages : Illustration

ISBN 9780593534861

Grades: Adult   641.5

1. Vegetarian cooking 2. Cooking 3. Vegetables 4. Food writing — Cooking and cookbooks — Vegetarian and vegan

ESSENTIAL AND RECOMMENDED TITLES
641.5 Cooking

In this loving homage to her father, a Chinese immigrant in Australia, told in flavorful, vegetarian recipes, a James Beard Foundation finalist shares her love of vegetables which are the basis for over 180 recipes, including Miso Mushroom Ragu with Baked Polenta, Crispy Potato Tacos and Soy-Butter Boy Choy Pasta.

Home cooks will love the versatility and innovation she delivers, whether they are vegetarians or not, while readers will revel in the sweetness and beauty of her story. Library Journals.

Published in Australia by Plum in 2022.

Miglore, Kristen
★ *Food52* Genius Recipes: 100 Recipes That Will Change the Way You Cook. Kristen Miglore; photography by James Ransom. Ten Speed Press 2015. xvii, 251 pages : Color; Illustration
ISBN 9781607747970
Grades: Adult   641.5
1. Cooking 2. Recipes 3. Cookbooks 4. Food writing — Cooking and cookbooks 5. Food writing — Cooking and cookbooks — Chefs and restaurants
LC 2014034413

An essential collection of more than 100 foolproof recipes from food luminaries such as Julia Child, Alice Waters, and David Chang—curated, introduced, and photographed by the team behind the leading food website Food52. This debut title from Food52 Works, a new imprint from Ten Speed Press, draws from Food52's James Beard Award-nominated Genius Recipes column, which features inventive recipes that rethink cooking tropes and, simply put, are nothing short of genius. In this inspired book for the modern cook, Food52's executive editor Kristen Miglore combines new genius recipes, greatest hits from the column, and her own kitchen wisdom in a sleek, lushly illustrated package. Whether it's fail-safe Fried Chicken from Michael Ruhlman or the imaginative Black Pepper Tofu from Yotam Ottolenghi, once you try these recipes, you'll never need to go back to other versions. Plus with abundant how-to and finished dish photographs throughout, Genius Recipes is destined to become every home cook's go-to reference for smart, enjoyable cooking. .

"Miglore's addition to Food52's growing list of cookbooks is a treat for readers who enjoy casual gourmet food." —*Library Journal*
Includes index.

★ *Food52* Simply Genius: Recipes for Beginners, Busy Cooks & Curious People. Kristen Miglore; photography by James Ransom; illustrations by Eliana Rodgers. Ten Speed Press 2022. x, 275 pages : Illustration; Color
ISBN 9780399582943
Grades: Adult   641.5
1. Cooking 2. Quick and easy cooking 3. Cookbooks 4. Food writing — Cooking and cookbooks — Methods
LC 2021038258

Founding editor of Food52 and Genius Recipes shares brilliant cooking tips from popular cooks in simple, but rule-breaking recipes including Buttermilk-Marinated Roast Chicken, Mayonnaise d'Avocat, Roasted Butternut Squash & Red Onion with Tahini & Za'atar and Farro & Olive Salad.

"With a list for further reading, this book is a no-brainer for home cooks." —*Booklist*
Includes index.

Mullen, Seamus
Real Food Heals: Eat to Feel Younger + Stronger Every Day. Seamus Mullen with Genevieve Ko. Avery 2017. 319 pages : Illustration; Color
ISBN 9780735213852
Grades: Adult   641.5
1. Low-carbohydrate diet 2. Nutritional therapy 3. High-protein diet 4. Recipes 5. Self-Help — Personal growth — Diet and nutrition 6. Food writing — Cooking and cookbooks — Cooking for health
LC 2017012317

Healthy cooking reinvented by top chef Seamus Mullen, with over 125 Paleo-inspired recipes designed to revitalize your health every day.

Mullins, Brittany
Mostly Veggies: Easy Make-ahead Meals for Healthy Living. Brittany Mullins; photographs by Kristin Teig. Voracious, Little, Brown and Company 2023. 271 pages : Color; Illustration
ISBN 9780316427920
Grades: Adult   641.5
1. Vegetarian cooking 2. Cooking (Vegetables) 3. Make-ahead cooking 4. Quick and easy cooking 5. Menu planning 6. Health foods 7. Cookbooks 8. Food writing — Cooking and cookbooks — Vegetarian and vegan 9. Food writing — Cooking and cookbooks — Methods
LC Bl2023004799

Healthy doesn't have to be hard! Unlock the simplicity of veggie-forward cooking with bonus tips for planning and prepping your way to healthy, delicious eats for every meal.

"Busy home chefs looking to expand their vegetarian repertoire and streamline effort will find much to inspire them." —*Publishers Weekly*

Murad, Noor
Ottolenghi Test Kitchen: Shelf Love : Recipes to Unlock the Secrets of Your Pantry, Fridge, and Freezer. Noor Murad & Yotam Ottolenghi; photography by Elena Heatherwick. Clarkson Potter/Publisher 2021. 255 pages : Color; Illustration
ISBN 9780593234365
Grades: Adult   641.5
1. Cooking 2. Cooking (Natural foods) 3. Cooking, Southwest Asian and North African 4. Cookbooks 5. Food Writing — Cooking and cookbooks — Regional 6. Food Writing — Cooking and cookbooks — Chefs and restaurants
LC 2021024125

The revered team of chefs at the Ottolenghi Text Kitchen serve up simple yet unique Middle Eastern-inspired recipes that make use of every shelf in the pantry, fridge and freezer.

"An ideal introduction to Ottolenghi's culinary efforts; home cooks are guaranteed to discover several new go-to recipes for casual snacking, entertaining, and weeknight dinners." —*Library Journal*
Includes index.

Music, Carla Lalli
That Sounds so Good: 100 Real-Life Recipes for Every Day of the Week. Carla Lalli Music; photographs by Gentl and Hyers. Clarkson Potter/Publishers 2021. 287 pages : Color; Illustration
ISBN 9780593138250
Grades: Adult   641.5
1. Cooking 2. Quick and easy cooking 3. Cookbooks 4. Food Writing — Cooking and cookbooks — Methods 5. Food Writing — Cooking and cookbooks — Courses
LC 2020050815

The James Beard Award-winning author of Where Cooking Begins presents recipes for quick, easy-to-prepare meals that are filled with bold, unique flavors that use straightforward methods and swap-friendly ingredients.

"Thanks to its focus on casual gatherings and the connections we make by breaking bread together, Music's cookbook is sure to be a winner with many readers." —*Library Journal*
Includes index.

Where Cooking Begins: Uncomplicated Recipes to Make You a Great Cook. Carla Lalli Music. Clarkson Potter/Publishers 2019. 271 pages : Color; Illustration
ISBN 9780525573340
Grades: Adult   641.5
1. Cooking 2. Recipes 3. Cookbooks 4. Food writing — Cooking and cookbooks — Methods
LC 2018024658

PUBLIC LIBRARY CORE COLLECTION: NONFICTION
Twentieth Edition

"Home cooks looking to expand their repertoire with vibrant and easy meals need look no further than this remarkable, flavorsome new collection." —*Publishers Weekly*

Myers, Amy
*The **Autoimmune** Solution Cookbook: Over 150 Delicious Recipes to Prevent and Reverse the Full Spectrum of Inflammatory Symptoms and Diseases.* Amy Myers, MD.. HarperOne 2018. x, 325 pages : Color; Illustration
ISBN 9780062853547
Grades: Adult 641.5
1. Autoimmune diseases 2. Nutritional therapy 3. Recipes 4. Cookbooks 5. Self-Help — Personal growth — Diet and nutrition 6. Food writing — Cooking and cookbooks — Cooking for health
LC 2018010173

A companion cookbook to the best-selling the Autoimmune Solution provides dozens of recipes for foods that can help reduce inflammation and reverse other debilitating symptoms related to autoimmune disorders.

Includes bilbiographical references (pages 299-307) and index.

Nathan, Joan
King Solomon's Table: A Culinary Exploration of Jewish Cooking from Around the World. Joan Nathan; photographs by Gabriela Herman. Alfred A. Knopf 2017. xxviii, 382 p.
ISBN 9780385351140
Grades: Adult 641.5
1. Cooking, Jewish 2. Jewish way of life 3. Food habits 4. Food 5. Food writing — Cooking and cookbooks — Narrative cookbooks
LC 2016047294

Filled with historical details and personal histories, an around-the-world collection of recipes from a James Beard Award-winning cookbook author, with King Solomon's appetites and explorations in mind, showcases the diversity of Jewish cuisine.

Includes bibliographical references and index.

★ *My Life in Recipes: Food, Family, and Memories.* Joan Nathan. Alfred A. Knopf 2024. 496 p.
ISBN 9780525658986
Grades: Adult 641.5
1. Nathan, Joan 2. Women cooks 3. Women food writers 4. Jewish women 5. Cooking 6. Cooking, Jewish 7. Family history 8. Jewish families 9. Immigrant families 10. Voyages and travels 11. Marriage 12. Motherhood 13. Food preparation 14. Western European people 15. German people 16. American people 17. Autobiographies and memoirs 18. Life stories — Arts and culture — Culinary arts 19. Food writing — Memoirs and biographies 20. Food writing — Cooking and cookbooks — Narrative cookbooks

Before hummus was available in every grocery store—before shakshuka was a dish on every brunch menu—Joan Nathan taught home cooks how and why they should make these now-beloved staples themselves. Here, in her most personal book yet, the beloved authority on global Jewish cuisine uses recipes looks back at her own family's history—their arrival in America from Germany; her childhood in postwar New York and Rhode Island; her years in Paris, New York, Israel, and Washington, DC. Nathan shares her story—of marriage, motherhood, and a career as a food writer; of a life well-lived and centered around meals—and she punctuates it with all the foods she has come to love.

"For those seeking a healthy mix of typical yet well-executed European-Jewish dishes, paired with less familiar while still intriguing options, this will be a sure hit." —*Library Journal*

Nosrat, Samin
★ *Salt, Fat, Acid, Heat.* Samin Nosrat. Simon & Schuster 2017. 469 pages
ISBN 9781476753836
Grades: Adult 641.5
1. Cooking 2. Cooks 3. Food habits 4. Food science 5. Page to screen 6. Food writing — Cooking and cookbooks — Narrative cookbooks
LC 2016040649

A first book by the acclaimed chef from New York's Chez Panisse distills decades of professional experience into four simple elements that if properly applied can lead to better results in the kitchen, in a reference complemented by 100 essential remedies and dozens of variations.

"This exceptional debut is sure to inspire greater confidence in readers and enable them to create better meals on their own." —*Publishers Weekly*

Salt, Fat, Acid, Heat inspired the 2018 Netflix series of the same name; Includes bibliographical references and index.

Oliver, Jamie
Together: Memorable Meals Made Easy. Jamie Oliver; photography, David Loftus, Levon Biss & Paul Stuart; design James Verity. Flatiron Books 2021. 357 pages : Color; Illustration
ISBN 9781250821799
Grades: Adult 641.5
1. Quick and easy cooking 2. Entertaining 3. Cookbooks 4. Food Writing — Cooking and cookbooks — Chefs and restaurants
LC 2021038280

Taking the stress out of cooking by giving readers tips, tricks and hacks, this wonderful celebration of incredible food to share provides simple, achievable menus that can be mostly prepped ahead.

In tribute to health-care workers, internationally known chef Oliver . . . maximizes all the different ways a family or friends can enjoy time and food that say 'love.' —*Booklist*

Memorable meals made easy—Cover; Originally published in the United Kingdom in 2021 by Michael Joseph; Includes index.

Ottolenghi, Yotam
★ *Jerusalem: A Cookbook.* Yotam Ottolenghi, Sami Tamimi. Ten Speed Press 2012. 318 p. : Color illustration
ISBN 9781607743941
Grades: Adult 641.5
1. Cooking, Southwest Asian and North African 2. Recipes 3. Voyages and travels 4. Jerusalem, Israel 5. Cookbooks 6. Food writing — Cooking and cookbooks — Regional
LC 2012017560

The London restaurateur and best-selling author of Plenty offers a tribute to the vibrant cuisine of Jerusalem that explores its cross-cultural influences and includes such options as Charred Baby Okra with Tomato and Preserved Lemon, Clementine and Almond Cake and Braised Lamb Meatballs with Sour Cherries.

Includes index.

Oz, Daphne
*The **Happy** Cook: 125 Recipes for Eating Every Day Like It's the Weekend.* Daphne Oz; photographs by Amy Neunsinger. William Morrow 2016. 328 p. : Color; Illustration
ISBN 9780062426901
Grades: Adult 641.5
1. Cooking 2. Quick and easy cooking 3. Recipes 4. Cookbooks 5. Food writing — Cooking and cookbooks — Methods
LC 2016037715

"Tips, variations, and sidebars will guide inexperienced cooks to consider shortcuts and alternatives (try refrigerated piecrust, or include horseradish for its healing properties)." —*Booklist*

Includes index.

Page, Karen
The Flavor Bible: The Essential Guide to Culinary Creativity, Based on the Wisdom of America's Most Imaginative Chefs. Karen Page and Andrew Dornenburg; photographs by Barry Salzman. Little, Brown and Company 2008. xi, 380 p. : Color illustration
ISBN 9780316118408
Grades: Adult 641.5
1. Cooking 2. Flavor 3. Gastronomy 4. Food writing — Cooking and cookbooks — Reference
LC 2007033064

"The authors first discuss the four basic tastes and the roles played by weather, the season of the year, and other environmental factors in cooking. The

ESSENTIAL AND RECOMMENDED TITLES
641.5 Cooking

rest of the book is an extensive alphabetic guide to different culinary ingredients. Rather than just another collection of recipes, this is a unique resource that both beginning cooks and serious chefs will find wonderfully inspiring and immensely useful." —*Library Journal*

Paltrow, Gwyneth
It's All Easy: Delicious Weekday Recipes for the Super-Busy Home Cook. Gwyneth Paltrow with Thea Baumann; photographs by Ditte Isager. Goop press, Grand Central Life & Style 2016. xiv, 267 pages
ISBN 9781455584215
Grades: Adult 641.5
1. Quick and easy cooking 2. Recipes 3. Cookbooks 4. Food writing — Cooking and cookbooks — Methods
LC 2015044440

Collects more than one hundred healthy quick and easy recipes, including chopped salad with grilled shrimp, chocolate cinnamon overnight oats, and chicken enchiladas.
Includes index.

Pauline, Kathryn
A Dish for All Seasons: 125+ Recipe Variations for Delicious Meals All Year Round. Kathryn Pauline. Chronicle Books 2022. 287 pages : Color; Illustration
ISBN 9781797207711
Grades: Adult 641.5
1. Seasonal cooking 2. Cookbooks 3. Food writing — Cooking and cookbooks
LC 2021047869

A seasonal cookbook that features 26 base recipes that can be adapted for Spring, Summer, Fall and Winter for a total of over 100 creative weeknight dishes including Quesadillas, Veggie Burgers, Pesto, Panzanella, Focaccia and loaf cakes.
"Home cooks who like to color outside the lines will find plenty of inspiration." —*Publishers Weekly*
Includes index.

★ *Piecemeal: A Meal-Planning Repertoire with 120 Recipes to Make in 5+, 15+. Or 30+ Minutes.* Kathryn Pauline. Chronicle Books 2023. 288 pages : Color; Illustration
ISBN 9781797219868
Grades: Adult 641.5
1. Quick and easy cooking 2. Make-ahead cooking 3. Cookbooks 4. Food writing — Cooking and cookbooks — Methods
LC 2023005824

A new meals-in-minutes cookbook from recipe developer, photographer, and blogger Kathryn Pauline! Based on the idea that one go-to component can anchor several meals, Piecemeal is designed to help a busy home cook prepare delicious meals simply, in 15, 30, or 45 minutes. This strategy-based cookbook features recipes for 30 transformational components—such as grilled corn, turkey meatballs, tzatziki, roasted grapes—each used in three different ways, for a total of 120 delicious and adaptable recipes. The featured components were selected for maximum performance: Each is flavorful, storable, and versatile and can stand alone or be used in multiple ways.—.
"With its delicious, accurate, and reliable recipes, this title will fly off library shelves and become a staple for home cooks." —*Booklist*
30 bold ingredients + 90 variations; Includes index.

Pelosi, Dan
Let's Eat: 101 Recipes to Fill Your Heart & Home. Dan Pelosi; photographs by Andrew Bui. Union Square & Co. 2023. 291 pages : Color; Illustration
ISBN 9781454946397
Grades: Adult 641.5
1. Cooking, Italian 2. Cooking, American 3. Cooking for families 4. Food writing — Cooking and cookbooks — Regional 5. Debut title

In his debut cookbook, larger-than-life personality Dan Pelosi offers up a warm hug of home cooking, sharing both comfort food and connection with 101 of his nearest and dearest Italian American recipes. Some have been passed down through his family, and others have been cooked up from scratch—but all are made with love and accompanied by fun, meaningful stories to warm your heart while filling your belly.
"Just as practical as it is delectable, this cookbook successfully conveys the author's love of his family and cooking so that home cooks can bring his passion to their table." —*Library Journal*
Includes index.

Pepin, Jacques
★ *Jacques Pepin : New Complete Techniques.* Photographs by Léon Perer and Tom Hopkins. Black Dog & Leventhal Publishers : 2012. 736 p. : Illustration; Color
ISBN 9781579129118
Grades: Adult 641.5
1. Cooking 2. Cookbooks 3. Food writing — Cooking and cookbooks — Methods 4. Food writing — Cooking and cookbooks — Reference 5. Food writing — Cooking and cookbooks — Chefs and restaurants
LC Bl2012045422

Completely revised and updated with more than 1,000 color photographs and 30 percent new techniques, a classic seminal work by the culinary grand master provides instructions for every aspect of traditional cooking and is complemented by time-tested recipes that demonstrate how to put key techniques into practice.
Includes index.

★ *Jacques Pépin Cooking My Way: Recipes and Techniques for Economical Cooking.* Jacques Pépin. Harvest, an Imprint of William Morrow 2023. xvii, 269 pages : Color; Illustration
ISBN 9780358581802
Grades: Adult 641.5
1. Cooking 2. Low-cost cooking 3. Seasonal cooking 4. Painting, Modern 5. Cookbooks 6. Food writing — Cooking and cookbooks — Chefs and restaurants 7. Food writing — Cooking and cookbooks — Methods
LC 2023006863

Providing more than 150 recipes along with an illustrated menu for each season, the legendary master chef and cooking instructor offers practical techniques for saving money, time and cleanup effort without sacrificing taste.
"Complete with Pépin's own whimsical paintings, this handy resource demonstrates that efficiency doesn't have to mean sacrificing flavor." —*Publishers Weekly*
Includes index; Includes author's paintings with accompanying seasonal menus.

Perelman, Deb
★ *The Smitten Kitchen Cookbook.* Deb Perelman. Alfred A. Knopf 2012. xiv, 321 p. : Color illustration
ISBN 9780307595652
Grades: Adult 641.5
1. Cooking 2. Recipes 3. Cookbooks 4. Food writing — Cooking and cookbooks — Chefs and restaurants
LC 2012007711

The award-winning blogger for Smitten Kitchen presents a long-awaited first cookbook of 100 new and favorite recipes, from Mushroom Bourguignon and Pancetta to Buttered Popcorn Cookies and Chocolate Hazelnut Layer Cake, in a volume that features adapted options for busy home cooks.
Includes index.

★ *Smitten Kitchen Every Day: Triumphant and Unfussy New Favorites.* Deb Perelman. Alfred A. Knopf 2017. xvii, 330 pages
ISBN 9781101874813
Grades: Adult 641.5
1. Cooking, American 2. Recipes 3. Cookbooks 4. Food writing — Cooking and cookbooks — Regional 5. Food writing — Cooking and cookbooks — Ingredients 6. Food writing — Cooking and cookbooks — Chefs and restaurants
LC 2017010179

Shares unfussy, foolproof recipes that yield indulgent, flavorful dishes, including such options as sticky toffee waffles, bacony baked pintos, beefsteak skirt steak salad, and chocolate peanut butter icebox cake.

"Blogger and cookbook author Perelman (The Smitten Kitchen Cookbook) found she had to modify her approach to mealtime to accommodate a young, hungry family. This cookbook is her attempt to inspire herself and others to take a relaxed yet celebratory approach to feeding our families. The result is a joyous cookbook filled with delectable, creative possibilities for every meal." —*Publishers Weekly*

Includes index.

★ **Smitten** *Kitchen Keepers: New Classics for Your Forever Files*. Deb Perelman; photographs by Deb Perelman, styled by Barrett Washburne. Alfred A. Knopf 2022. xiii, 301 pages : Color; Illustration

ISBN 9780593318782

Grades: Adult   641.5

1. Cooking, American 2. Cookbooks 3. Food writing — Cooking and cookbooks

LC 2021060789

Here, in her third book, Perelman presents 100 new recipes (plus a few old favorites from her site) that aim to make shopping easier, preparation more practical and enjoyable, and food more reliably delicious for the home cook. What's a keeper? It's a brilliantly fuss-free lemon poppy seed cake. It's Perelman's favorite roasted winter squash. It's an epic quiche. It's a slow-roasted chicken on a bed of unapologetically schmaltzy croutons. It's the only apple crisp she will personally ever make. It's perfect spaghetti and meatballs. These are the fail-safe, satisfying recipes you'll rely on for years to come—from Perelman's forever files, to yours."

"Essential for all collections. The cookbook, like the recipes it shares, is a keeper." —*Library Journal*

Includes index.

Perry Lang, Adam

Serious *Barbecue: Smoke, Char, Baste, and Brush Your Way to Great Outdoor Cooking*. Adam Perry Lang, with J.J. Goode and Amy Vogler; photographs by David Loftus. Hyperion 2009. 390 p. : Color illustration

ISBN 9781401323066

Grades: Adult   641.5

1. Barbecuing 2. Recipes 3. Cookbooks 4. Food writing — Cooking and cookbooks — Methods

LC 2009001765

An introductory guide to barbecue cooking that covers everything from equipment fundamentals to preparing a diverse range of fare, including honey-glazed baby back ribs, quick cook Texas-style brisket, and rack of lamb crusted with grain mustard and chile powder.

Includes index.

Perry, Dawn

Ready, *Set, Cook: How to Make Good Food with What's on Hand (no Fancy Skills, Fancy Equipment, or Fancy Budget Required)*. Dawn Perry. Grand Central Publishing 2021. xiii, 322 pages : Color; Illustration

ISBN 9781982147266

Grades: Adult   641.5

1. Quick and easy cooking 2. Cookbooks 3. Food Writing — Cooking and cookbooks — Methods 4. Food Writing — Cooking and cookbooks — Reference

LC Bl2021027255

Former food director of Real Simple Dawn Perry used to wake up at the crack of dawn to hit the farmers market and scour specialty food stores for peak-season vegetables and lesser-known spices. But as she started to have a family, she became less interested in spending her mornings and weekends food shopping and meal prepping than building couch forts and making play-doh spaghetti. If you're time-crunched for any reason—early meeting at the office or late night on the town—this book will help. Dawn offers her very own playbook for getting good food on the table fast so you can spend more time doing what you love with your free time and energy."

"Perry's tutelage is a culinary windfall that will pay big dividends for busy home cooks." —*Publishers Weekly*

Includes index.

Peters, Meike

Noon: *Simple Recipes for Scrumptious Midday Meals and More*. Meike Peters. Chronicle Books 2023. 272 p.

ISBN 9781797222806

Grades: Adult   641.5

1. Lunches 2. Quick and easy cooking 3. Cookbooks 4. Food writing — Cooking and cookbooks — Courses 5. Food writing — Cooking and cookbooks — Methods

LC 2023007411

This bold new cookbook by James Beard Award-winning author and photographer Meike Peters invites us to indulge in simple, satisfying, and scrumptious meals to feed our midday cravings. With a few tricks and clever flavor combinations to keep your mind, body, and soul happy, Noon makes it easy to treat yourself throughout the day.

"Perfect for experienced cooks, who will relish Peters's imaginative takes on classic dishes as well as her inspired original culinary creations, and those new to the kitchen, who will feel empowered by the clear, easy-to-follow format and welcoming tone of the recipes." —*Library Journal*

Includes index.

Pierson, Joy

Vegan *Holiday Cooking from Candle Cafe: Celebratory Menus and Recipes from New York's Premier Plant-Based Restaurants*. Joy Pierson, Angel Ramos, & Jorge Pineda; photography by Jim Franco; forewords by Alicia Silverstone and Laura and Woody Harrelson. Ten Speed Press 2014. VIII, 168 pages : Color; Illustration

ISBN 9781607746478

Grades: Adult   641.5

1. Vegan cooking 2. Holiday cooking 3. Recipes 4. Cookbooks 5. Food writing — Cooking and cookbooks — Vegetarian and vegan 6. Food writing — Cooking and cookbooks — Chefs and restaurants

LC 2014005259

A first-of-its-kind vegan holiday cookbook from professional chefs takes plant-based fare to a fresh, inventive new level through special-occasion menus and recipes for main dishes and sides, along with wine and cocktail pairings, which will impress vegans and omnivores alike.

"You'll be proud to serve and eat these vegan foods, and party hosts won't be tempted to hide them at the end of their holiday buffet." —*Library Journal*

Pollan, Corky

The ***Pollan*** *Family Table: The Best Recipes and Kitchen Wisdom for Delicious, Healthy Family Meals*. Corky, Lori, Dana, and Tracy Pollan; foreword by Michael Pollan; photographs by John Kernick. Scribner 2014. xvii, 334 p. : Color; Illustration

ISBN 9781476746371

Grades: Adult   641.5

1. Cooking (Natural foods) 2. Cooking 3. Recipes 4. Cookbooks 5. Food writing — Cooking and cookbooks — Cooking for health

A family known for their commitment to fresh, local and healthy food presents a book of more than 100 of their best recipes.

Includes index.

Pollan, Michael

Cooked: *A Natural History of Transformation*. Michael Pollan. The Penguin Press 2013. 464 p.

ISBN 9781594204210

Grades: Adult   641.5

1. Cooking 2. Cooks 3. Four elements 4. Food habits 5. Food writing — Investigations

LC 2012039705

Library Journal Best Books, 2013.

A New York Times contributor and best-selling author of The Omnivore's Dilemma recounts the story of his culinary education and the roles of the four classical elements of fire, water, air and earth in transforming natural ingredients into delicious meals and drinks, in an account that traces his efforts to master classic recipes using one of the four elements.

ESSENTIAL AND RECOMMENDED TITLES
641.5 Cooking

"The author mixes journalistic encounters with tales of skilled, often relentlessly obsessive cooks who demonstrated the art of transforming the products of nature into tasty food and then tried, with spotty success, to teach him to do the same. Four sections describe this transformation with the four classical elements: Fire, water, air and earth." —*Kirkus*

Includes bibliographical references.

Porowski, Antoni
Antoni: Let's Do Dinner. Antoni Porowski with Mindy Fox; photographs by Paul Brissman. Houghton Mifflin Harcourt 2021. 271 pages : Color; Illustration
ISBN 9780358395324
Grades: Adult   641.5
1. Quick and easy cooking 2. Dinners and dining 3. Cookbooks 4. Food writing — Cooking and cookbooks — Chefs and restaurants
LC 2021010881

In the follow-up to his New York Times bestseller Antoni in the Kitchen, Queer Eye star Antoni Porowski shares exuberantly easy dinners for every night of the week."

"While there is no shortage of cookbooks on this subject, this resource has enough substance to be worthwhile for anyone seeking weeknight meal ideas and will be particularly appealing to Porowski's fans." —*Library Journal*

Includes index.

Powell, Julie
Julie and Julia: 365 Days, 524 Recipes, 1 Tiny Apartment Kitchen. Julie Powell. Little, Brown and Co. 2005. 309 p.
ISBN 9780316109697
Grades: Adult   641.5
1. Powell, Julie 2. Child, Julia 3. Women cooks 4. Cooking, French 5. Marriage 6. Bloggers 7. Recipes 8. Food habits 9. Men-women relations 10. United States 11. Autobiographies and memoirs 12. Page to screen 13. Life stories — Personal growth 14. Food writing — Memoirs and biographies
LC 2005007974

The author recounts how she escaped the doldrums of an unpromising career by mastering every recipe in Julia Child's 1961 classic, "Mastering the Art of French Cooking," a year-long endeavor that transformed her life.

"Both home cooks and devotees of Bridget Jones-style dishing will be caught up in Powell's funny, sharp-tongued but generous writing." —*Publishers Weekly*

Pulde, Alona
Forks Over Knives Family: Every Parent's Guide to Raising Healthy, Happy Kids on a Whole-Food, Plant-Based Diet. Alona Pulde, MD, and Matthew Lederman, MD, with Marah Stets, and Brian Wendel; recipes by Darshana Thacker. Touchstone 2016. xx, 300 pages : Color; Illustration
ISBN 9781476753324
Grades: Adult   641.5
1. Vegetarian cooking 2. Vegan cooking 3. Vegetarianism 4. Veganism 5. Baby foods 6. Cooking for families 7. Children 8. Babies 9. Nutrition 10. Cookbooks 11. Food writing — Cooking and cookbooks — Cooking for the family 12. Food writing — Cooking and cookbooks — Cooking for health
LC 2016011411

The best-selling authors of The Forks Over Knives Plan present a guide to a plant-based, whole-food lifestyle for entire families, sharing helpful tips, the latest scientific findings and more than 100 kid-friendly recipes.

"This is a manual, not a book that requires reading from front to back. Readers can pick morsels relevant to them and leave the rest. Over half of the book is a cookbook with delicious-sounding recipes from chef Darshana Thacker for both basic foods like muffins and baked ziti and more unusual fare such as Sunflower Seed Paté and Chickpeazella Sticks." —*Publishers Weekly*

Includes bibliographical references (pages 271-280) and index.

★ *The Forks Over Knives Plan: How to Transition to the Life-Saving, Whole-Food, Plant-Based Diet*. Alona Pulde, MD, and Matthew Lederman, MD; with Marah Stets and Brian Wendel, recipes by Darshana Thacker and Del Sroufe. Simon & Schuster 2014. x, 322 pages : Color; Illustration
ISBN 9781476753294
Grades: Adult   641.5
1. Cooking (Natural foods) 2. Menus 3. Natural foods 4. Recipes 5. Vegan cooking 6. Veganism 7. Cookbooks 8. Food writing — Cooking and cookbooks — Vegetarian and vegan 9. Science writing — Medicine and health — Diet and nutrition 10. Science writing — Medicine and health
LC 2014009582

The physician creators of the documentary by the same name present a four-week, celebrity-recommended plan for transitioning to a whole-food, plant-based diet to bolster the body's resistance to disease.

A Touchstone book; Includes bibliographical references (pages 291-293) and index.

Purviance, Jamie
Weber's Greatest Hits: 125 Classic Recipes for Every Grill. Jamie Purviance; photography by Ray Kachatorian. Houghton Mifflin Harcourt 2017. 318 pages : Color; Illustration
ISBN 9780544952379
Grades: Adult   641.5
1. Barbecuing 2. Outdoor cooking 3. Recipes 4. Cookbooks 5. Food writing — Cooking and cookbooks — Ingredients 6. Food writing — Cooking and cookbooks — Methods
LC Bl2017013608

Collects over one hundred barbecue recipes from the grilling company, including such offerings as grilled oysters, Korean beef barbecue, jerk-spiced ribs, and Greek seafood salad.

"Accompanied by all-new photographs and practical tips, these easy dishes will interest just about everyone." —*Library Journal*

Includes index.

Weber's Ultimate Grilling. Jamie Purviance; photography by Ray Kachatorian. Houghton Mifflin Harcourt 2019. 351 pages : Color; Illustration
ISBN 9781328589934
Grades: Adult   641.5
1. Barbecuing 2. Outdoor cooking 3. Recipes 4. Cookbooks 5. Food writing — Cooking and cookbooks — Entertaining 6. Food writing — Cooking and cookbooks — Methods
LC 2019010097

Shares advice and instruction on grilling, as well as over one hundred grilling recipes, including charred rib-eye steak with mushrooms, Tuscan rotisserie pork roast, spatchcocked chicken with chimichurri, and planked salon with gremolata.

"Purviance offers a banquet for visual learners in this easy-to-use guide for the grill." —*Publishers Weekly*

Includes index.

Ramsay, Gordon
★ *Quick and Delicious: 100 Recipes to Cook in 30 Minutes or Less*. Gordon Ramsay. Grand Central Publishing 2020. 250 pages : Color; Illustration
ISBN 9781538719336
Grades: Adult   641.5
1. Quick and easy cooking 2. Food Writing — Cooking and cookbooks — Chefs and restaurants 3. Food Writing — Cooking and cookbooks — Methods
LC Bl2020033663

The celebrity chef star of Kitchen Nightmares shares 100 tried-and-tested recipes for straightforward, expert-quality meals from his 3 Michelin-star restaurant and Las Vegas burger joint that can be made in 30 minutes or less.

"Chef, restaurateur, and TV personality Ramsay (Gordon Ramsay's Healthy, Lean & Fit) extends a guiding hand to those who need to quickly get dinner on the table in his excellent latest." —*Publishers Weekly*

Includes index.

Ray, Rachael
★ *This Must Be the Place: Dispatches & Food from the Home Front*. Rachael Ray; food photography by Kate Mathis. Ballantine Books 2021. xiii, 331 pages : Color; Illustration
ISBN 9780593357217
Grades: Adult   641.5

1. Ray, Rachael 2. Cooking 3. Cookbooks 4. Food Writing — Cooking and cookbooks — Chefs and restaurants 5. Food Writing — Cooking and cookbooks — Narrative cookbooks

LC Bl2021027361

The multi-Emmy Award-winning syndicated TV star offers more than 125 recipes straight from her home in upstate New York during the pandemic with personal stories on loss, gratitude and the special memories of what makes a house a home.

"Emmy Award-winning TV host Ray gets personal with enticing recipes and stories from her home." —*Publishers Weekly*

125+ recipes—Cover; Includes index.

Reichl, Ruth

My Kitchen Year: 136 Recipes That Saved My Life. Ruth Reichl. Random House 2015. 320 p.

ISBN 9781400069989

Grades: Adult　　　　　　　　　　　　　　　　　　　　641.5

1. Reichl, Ruth 2. Women food writers 3. Cooking 4. Women editors 5. Loss 6. Life change events 7. Recipes 8. Social life and customs 9. Self-discovery 10. Coping 11. United States 12. 2010s 13. 21st century 14. Essays 15. Autobiographies and memoirs 16. Life stories — Arts and culture — Culinary arts 17. Food writing — Cooking and cookbooks — Narrative cookbooks 18. Life stories — Personal growth

LC 2014029197

Recounts the author's emotional healing through cooking, with the recipes she used, after losing her job when Gourmet magazine was abruptly closed.

"Reichl has written some classics in food literature, including Tender at the Bone (1998); therefore, much attention will be accorded her latest book." —*Booklist*

Risbridger, Ella

The Year of Miracles: Recipes About Love + Grief + Growing Things. Ella Risbridger. Bloomsbury publishing place USA 2022. 288 p.

ISBN 9781526622631

Grades: Adult　　　　　　　　　　　　　　　　　　　　641.5

1. Love 2. Recipes 3. Grief 4. Loss 5. Healing 6. Psychological growth 7. Food Writing — Cooking and cookbooks — Narrative cookbooks

In Ella Risbridger's first book Midnight Chicken, she showed readers how food can serve as a light in our darkest days. Now, in The Year of Miracles, Ella shares her story of recovering from loss with the help of good food and good friends. The book celebrates making a fancy dinner even if you're just eating it with a spoon in front of the tv; having people over to dinner without overthinking it; finding late night snacks to ease you to sleep; and having seconds—of everything. Above all, it is a powerful testament to how cooking can help us get up and start again in the face of unimaginable hurt.

"This is a must for cookbook readers and Risbridger's fans, who will love curling up with this sequel and again enjoy how food, and the art of cooking it, have the power to heal." —*Booklist*

Roden, Claudia

★ *The Book of Jewish Food: An Odyssey from Samarkand to New York.* Claudia Roden. Knopf : 1996. xiv, 668 p. : Illustration

ISBN 9780394532585

Grades: Adult　　　　　　　　　　　　　　　　　　　　641.5

1. Cooking, Jewish 2. Kosher food 3. Recipes 4. Food writing — Cooking and cookbooks — Regional

LC 96028758

Eight hundred delicious recipes from around the world represent the finest in traditional and contemporary Jewish cookery, featuring dishes from such diverse places as Russia, Syria, India, North and South America, Africa, the Mediterranean, and Israel.

Eight hundred recipes from around the world represent the finest in traditional and contemporary Jewish cookery, featuring dishes from Russia, Syria, India, North and South America, Africa, the Mediterranean, and Israel.

Includes bibliographical references (p. [635]-636) and index.

Rodriguez, Ashley

Rooted Kitchen: Seasonal Recipes, Stories, and Ways to Connect with the Natural World. Ashley Rodriguez. Clarkson Potter/Publishers 2024. 271 pages : Color; Illustration

ISBN 9780593579329

Grades: Adult　　　　　　　　　　　　　　　　　　　　641.5

1. Seasonal cooking 2. Cooking (Wild foods) 3. Outdoor cooking 4. Cooking (Vegetables) 5. Gathering (of wild foods, seeds, medicinal plants, etc.) 6. Wild foods 7. Canning and preserving 8. Cookbooks 9. Food writing — Cooking and cookbooks — Methods 10. Food writing — Cooking and cookbooks — Ingredients

LC 2023016943

Deepen your relationship with the natural world through thoughtful essays and 75 delightfully inventive recipes that feature seasonal ingredients, plus techniques for foraging, preserving, and cooking over an open fire.

"Rodriguez encourages readers to commune with nature in this inspirational collection…Overall, this proves a thoughtful guide for those looking to forge a deeper connection to food." —*Publishers Weekly*

Includes index.

Roll, Rich

The Plantpower Way: Whole Food Plant-Based Recipes and Guidance for the Whole Family. Rich Roll and Julie Piatt. Avery 2015. xv, 319 pages : Illustration; Color

ISBN 9781583335871

Grades: Adult　　　　　　　　　　　　　　　　　　　　641.5

1. Vegetarian cooking 2. Vegan cooking 3. Cooking (Natural foods) 4. Recipes 5. Seasonal cooking 6. Cookbooks 7. Food writing — Cooking and cookbooks — Vegetarian and vegan 8. Food writing — Cooking and cookbooks — Ingredients

LC Bl2015017042

Presents more than one hundred and twenty whole food recipes for every meal of the day, plus recipes for smoothies, juices, and desserts, along with advice on maintaining a plant-based lifestyle.

Includes bibliographical references (pages 318-319), filmography (page 319), and index.

Roman, Alison

Dining In: Highly Cookable Recipes. Alison Roman; photographs by Michael Graydon and Nikole Herriott. Clarkson Potter/Publishers 2017. 303 pages : Color; Illustration

ISBN 9780451496997

Grades: Adult　　　　　　　　　　　　　　　　　　　　641.5

1. Cooking 2. Cookbooks 3. Food writing — Cooking and cookbooks — Courses

LC 2017026507

Collects trendsetting, quality recipes for home cooks, including such dishes as crispy kimchi and cheddar omelette, clam pasta with chorizo and walnuts, and cumin lamb chops with charred scallions and peanuts.

"These varied recipes are relaxed, doable, and anything but pedestrian. Striking color photographs and punchy writing further heighten the book's appeal." —*Library Journal*

Includes index.

Rondinelli-Hamilton, Lara

The Diabetes Cookbook: 300 Recipes for Healthy Living Powered by the Diabetes Food Hub. Lara Rondinelli-Hamilton, RD, LDN, CDE & Chef Jennifer Bucko Lamplough. American Diabetes Association 2019. x, 398 pages : Color; Illustration

ISBN 9781580406802

Grades: Adult　　　　　　　　　　　　　　　　　　　　641.5

1. Diabetes 2. Recipes 3. Cookbooks 4. Food writing — Cooking and cookbooks — Cooking for health

LC 2018009603

Backed by decades of evidence-based research, a cookbook from the American Diabetes Association shares low-carb, diabetes-friendly adaptations of clas-

ESSENTIAL AND RECOMMENDED TITLES
641.5 Cooking

sic favorites, including Slow Cooker Pulled Pork, Jalapeno Mac and Cheese and Paleo 10-Minute Taco Salad.

"The authors include standards like roasted turkey and vegetables, and salmon burgers (both are categorized as budget-friendly), but also surprise with mole pork tenderloin with zucchini and refried beans (in the chapter on low-glycemic index recipes); reduced-carb sangria; and, to satisfy snack cravings, sweet and spicy nuts. Directions are clear and succinct, and virtually all the ingredients can be sourced at the local grocery store." —*Publishers Weekly*

Includes bibliographical references and index.

Rosenstrach, Jenny
How to Celebrate Everything: Recipes and Rituals for Birthdays, Holidays, Family Dinners, and Every Day in Between. Jenny Rosenstrach; photography by Chelsea Cavanaugh. Ballantine Books 2016. xxix, 288 pages : Color; Illustration
ISBN 9780804176309
Grades: Adult   641.5
1. Dinners and dining 2. Entertaining 3. Families 4. Holiday cooking 5. Recipes 6. Cookbooks 7. Arts and Entertainment — Crafts and hobbies — Seasonal 8. Food writing — Cooking and cookbooks — Entertaining
LC 2016001416

From the creator of the popular blog and book Dinner: A Love Story and author of the New York Times bestseller Dinner: The Playbook comes a warm and inviting guide with more than one hundred time-tested recipes and a host of inspiring ideas for turning birthdays, holidays, and everyday occasions into cherished traditions. "Families crave rituals," says Jenny Rosenstrach, and by rituals she means not just the big celebrations—Valentine's Day dinners, Mother's Day brunches, Thanksgiving feasts—but the little ones we may not even realize are rituals: a platter of deluxe nachos on Super Bowl Sunday or a bowl of creamy mashed potatoes after every braces-tightening session. Whether simple or elaborate, daily or annually, these rituals all serve the same purpose for Rosenstrach: to bring comfort, connection, and meaning to everyday family life. Recipes here are organized into groupings unique to Rosenstrach but familiar to everyone: Our Family Rituals (think tomato sandwiches for lunch after a family walk to the market, or homemade popovers on sleepover mornings); Holidays We Didn't Invent, including Friday Challah and Easter Ham (yes, both, more on that inside); a Halloween Launch Party for trick-or-treaters, featuring a self-serve simmering pot of Chicken Chorizo Chili. A section on Birthdays includes Rosenstrach's legendary chocolate frosted "mud" cake as well as a one-size-fits-all party planner with menus that do not rely on pizza. Lastly, in Family Dinners you'll find celebratory Sunday meals (Soy-Glazed Grilled Pork Chops, Harissa Roasted Chicken, Summer Cobbler) alongside Rosenstrach's signature easy weeknight fare (Crispy Chickpeas and Yogurt, Shrimp Tacos with Avocado "Butter," and vegetable-packed Burrito Bowls)—all of which translate to prime quality time with the family. In this digital, overscheduled age, How to Celebrate Everything helps families slow down, capture the moments that matter—and eat well while doing it.

A best-selling author and the popular blogger behind dinneralovestory.com offers her own personal recipes, traditions, rituals and personal stories to help inspire readers to make lasting memories of family celebrations including birthdays, Sunday dinner, vacations, holidays and smaller occasions.

Includes index.

★ *The Weekday Vegetarians: 100 Recipes and a Real-Life Plan for Eating Less Meat.* Jenny Rosenstrach; photographs by Christine Han. Clarkson Potter Publishers 2021. 256 pages : Illustration; Color
ISBN 9780593138748
Grades: Adult   641.5
1. Vegetarian cooking 2. Vegan cooking 3. Cookbooks 4. Food Writing — Cooking and cookbooks — Vegetarian and vegan
LC 2021004529

You don't need to be a vegetarian to eat like one! with over 100 recipes, the New York Times bestselling author of Dinner: A Love Story and her family adopt a "weekday vegetarian" mentality. In her newest cookbook, creator of the beloved website Dinner:A Love Story and Cup of Jo columnist Jenny Rosenstrach writes about being a "weekday vegetarian," i.e. eating a vegetable-based diet during the week and saving meaty splurges for the weekend. One day, it hit Rosenstrach like a lightning bolt: she and her family needed to eat less meat—for their health and for the greater good of the environment. The Weekday Vegetarians shows readers how she got her family on board with meat-free meals. She uses "Hooks" that make any vegetarian dish irresistible—like spiced Crispy Chickpeas, Pizza Dough Croutons, and Sweet Chili Glaze; "Next-Level Sauces" like Vegan Caesar, Shakedown Pesto, and Yogurt-Harissa; and "Side Dishes That Make Everything Special" like Yogurt Flatbread. Organized by meal type, the Weekday Vegetarians offers one hundred recipes like Pizza Salad with White Beans in the Bowls & Salads chapter, Cauliflower Cutlets with Ranch Dressing in the chapter Skillet Mains, and Squash and Black Bean Tacos in the Tacos & Tortillas chapter, with excellent and practical tips, and food for thought written in her engaging, witty, and relatable voice. And who knows—maybe like Jenny's family, the more you practice being "weekday vegetarians," the more you will notice plant-based eating creeping into your weekends!

"This mightily proves that vegetarian cooking is not only approachable, but fun." —*Publishers Weekly*

From the New York Times bestselling author of Dinner: a love story; Includes index.

Rosso, Julee
The New Basics Cookbook. by Julee Rosso & Sheila Lukins; illustrated by Sheila Lukins. Workman Pub. 1989. xiii, 849 p. : Illustration; Color
ISBN 9780894803413
Grades: Adult   641.5
1. Cooking, American 2. Cookbooks 3. Food writing — Cooking and cookbooks — Methods 4. Food writing — Cooking and cookbooks — Reference
LC 88051581

Designed to reflect changing tastes and preferences, as well as new kitchen and culinary styles, this 950-recipe cookbook covers all sorts of dishes, with tips on setting up shop, buying and storing food, and more.

"It's a huge cookbook/reference work, filled with information on new ingredients and styles of cooking, practical advice on such subjects as entertaining and choosing wine, and more than 900 recipes. There are all sorts of dishes here, family favorites as well as company food, recipes that seem fresh and new but not, in general, overly trendy." —*Library Journal*

Includes bibliographical references (p. 801-803).

The Silver Palate Cookbook. Julee Rosso & Sheila Lukins with Michael McLaughlin; photographs by Patrick Tregenza and Susan Goldman; illustrations by Sheila Lukins. Workman 2007. xi, 452 p. : Color illustration
ISBN 9780761145974
Grades: Adult   641.5
1. Cooking 2. Gourmet cooking 3. Recipes 4. Cookbooks 5. Food writing — Cooking and cookbooks — Methods 6. Food writing — Cooking and cookbooks — Courses
LC 2007276244

Provides recipes for appetizers, soups, pasta, main dishes, vegetables, salads, breads, and desserts, and includes tips on planning menus and entertaining.

Includes index.

Ruhlman, Michael
Ratio: The Simple Codes Behind the Craft of Everyday Cooking. Michael Ruhlman. Scribner 2009. xxv, 224 p. : Illustration
ISBN 9781416566113
Grades: Adult   641.5
1. Cooking 2. Ratio and proportion 3. Recipes 4. Cookbooks 5. Food writing — Cooking and cookbooks — Methods
LC 2008032679

Demonstrates how to master western cooking fundamentals through an understanding of ingredient ratios, in a guide that introduces twenty-six basic recipes broken down into ratio-style measurements as well as a variety of accessible variations that enable more flavorful or creative taste combinations.

"While Ruhlman was attending the Culinary Institute of America for a book project, a chef showed him a copy of the golden rules, which boiled down the elements of (French) cooking into ratios. [In this volume] Ruhlman guides readers through the ratios for a variety of doughs, batters, stocks, sauces, custards and sausages, explaining their chemical and culinary basis in clear, earnest prose and providing tasteful recipes that lay out the technique for each formula." —*New York Times Book Review*

Saltz, Joanna
Delish: Eat Like Every Day's the Weekend. Joanna Saltz & the editors of Delish. Houghton Mifflin Harcourt 2018. 415 pages : Color; Illustration
ISBN 9781328498861
Grades: Adult 641.5
1. Cooking 2. Entertaining 3. Recipes 4. Quick and easy cooking 5. Cookbooks 6. Food writing — Cooking and cookbooks — Methods 7. Food writing — Cooking and cookbooks — Entertaining
LC 2018012229

Shares recipes for the home cook from the popular Internet food site, including such options as Boston cream pancakes, chicken fried steak fingers, pizza pinwheels, quesadilla burgers, avocado pesto linguine, and snickerdoodle blondies.

The popular internet food site collects 300 of its best recipes'including Unicorn Bark, Chicken Fried Cauliflower, Bacon Pickle Pizza, Sheet Pan Shrimp Boil and more'and pairs them with step-by-step full-color photos to make things easy for the home cook.

Includes index; Amazingly delicious recipes from the team behind Hearst's wildly popular Delish.Com website.

Samuelsson, Marcus
Marcus off Duty: The Recipes I Cook at Home. Marcus Samuelsson with Roy Finamore; photographs by Paul Brissman. Houghton Mifflin Harcourt 2014. 352 pages : Color; Illustration
ISBN 9780470940587
Grades: Adult 641.5
1. Samuelsson, Marcus 2. Cooking 3. Recipes 4. Cookbooks 5. Food writing — Cooking and cookbooks — Regional 6. Food writing — Cooking and cookbooks — Chefs and restaurants
LC 2014018169

The award-winning chef presents over one hundred twenty recipes he likes to prepare at home, incorporating Ethiopian, Swedish, Caribbean, Italian, and Southern soul food cuisines.

"Highly recommended for adventurous and well-traveled home cooks, as well as fans of Susan Feniger's Street Food." —*Library Journal*

A Rux Martin Book; Includes index.

Sarna, Shannon
Modern Jewish Comfort Food: 100 Fresh Recipes for Classic Dishes from Kugel to Kreplach. Shannon Sarna; photography by Doug Schneider; styling by Sheri Silver. Countryman Press, an imprint of W.W. Norton & Company 2022. 215 pages : Color; Illustration
ISBN 9781682686980
Grades: Adult 641.5
1. Cooking, Jewish 2. Comfort food 3. Cookbooks 4. Food writing — Cooking and cookbooks — Regional
LC 2022013057

Modern Jewish Comfort Food showcases recipes and variations that have shaped Jewish cuisine from around the world—including immigration waves from Europe, the Middle East, North Africa, New York City, and beyond. Sarna shares many traditional dishes, and then provides exciting variations that will bring heartwarming comfort to the home kitchen."

"This invigorating work takes Jewish cooking to a whole new level." —*Publishers Weekly*

Includes index.

Schinner, Miyoko Nishimoto
The Vegan Meat Cookbook: Meatless Favorites. Made with Plants. Miyoko Schinner; photographs by Eva Kolenko. Ten Speed Press 2021. 247 pages : Color; Illustration
ISBN 9781984858887
Grades: Adult 641.5
1. Meat substitutes 2. Vegan cooking 3. Cookbooks 4. Food writing — Cooking and cookbooks — Ingredients 5. Food writing — Cooking and cookbooks — Vegetarian and vegan
LC 2020035536

More than 100 recipes for meals featuring vegan meat, and recipes for making your own DIY vegan meats and cheese, from bestselling vegan author and entrepreneur Miyoko Schinner.

"Appetizing and accessible, these recipes could just as easily enhance a meat lover's diet as change minds about the place of plants in one's diet." —*Publishers Weekly*

Includes index.

Scott, Chris
Homage: Recipes and Stories from an Amish Soul Food Kitchen. Chris Scott with Sarah Zorn; photographs by Brittany Cornerly. Chronicle Books 2022. 271 pages : Illustration; Color
ISBN 9781797207742
Grades: Adult 641.5
1. Amish 2. Cooking, American 3. Cooking, African American 4. Cookbooks 5. Food writing — Cooking and cookbooks — Regional
LC 2021058073

A New York-based chef celebrates his African heritage and Amish country childhood with 100 unique dishes that blend the two including Chicken Fried Steak with Sassafras Country Gravy and Charred Radicchio Salad with Roasted Grapes and Shaved Amish Cheddar.

"Two cultures steeped in farming find rich common ground in this captivating tribute from chef Scott....This hits the spot." —*Publishers Weekly*

Includes index.

Scott, Ryan
The No-Fuss Family Cookbook: Simple Recipes for Everyday Life. Ryan Scott; photography by Chris Andre. Houghton Mifflin Harcourt 2021. xv, 272 pages : Color; Illustration
ISBN 9780358439141
Grades: Adult 641.5
1. Quick and easy cooking 2. Cooking and children 3. Cookbooks 4. Food writing — Cooking and cookbooks — Cooking for the family
LC 2020045799

An Emmy Award-winning chef—and dad—presents a heartfelt collection of kid-friendly recipes that are packed with clever hacks and pro tips for getting meals on the table (and cleaning up quickly).

"Home cooks looking to expand their repertoire of crowd-pleasing options will find these recipes irresistible." —*Publishers Weekly*

Includes index.

Segnit, Niki
★ *The Flavor Thesaurus: More Flavors : Plant-led Pairings, Recipes, and Ideas for Cooks*. Niki Segnit. Bloomsbury Publishing 2023. VI, 352 pages : Illustration; Color
ISBN 9781639731138
Grades: Adult 641.5
1. Flavor 2. Food 3. Taste 4. Cooking (Vegetables) 5. Vegetables 6. Cookbooks 7. Food Writing — Cooking and cookbooks — Reference 8. Food Writing — Cooking and cookbooks — Vegetarian and vegan
LC Bl2023018868

Explores the character and tasting notes of chickpea, fennel, pomegranate, kale, lentil, miso, mustard, rye, pine nut, pistachio, poppy seed, sesame, turmeric, and wild rice—as well as favorites like almond, avocado, garlic, lemon, and parsley—then expertly teaches readers how to pair them with ingredients that complement. With her celebrated blend of science, history, expertise, anecdotes, and signature sense of humor, Niki Segnit's More Flavors is a modern classic of food writing, and a brilliantly useful, engaging reference book for every cook's kitchen."

"Food lovers will enjoy Segnit's meander through food memories, recipes, and advice, along with all the practical uses for this flavor reference guide." —*Library Journal*

Includes bibliographical references (pages 307-315) and indexes.

ESSENTIAL AND RECOMMENDED TITLES
641.5 Cooking

Setareh, Saghar
Pomegranates & Artichokes: A Food Journey from Iran to Italy. Saghar Setareh. Interlink Books, an imprint of Interlink Publishing Group, Inc. 2023. 287 pages : Color; Illustration
ISBN 9781623717407
Grades: Adult   641.5
1. Cooking, Jewish 2. Cooking, Iranian 3. Cooking, Italian 4. Immigration and emigration 5. Iran 6. Italy 7. Mediterranean Region 8. Cookbooks 9. Food Writing — Cooking and cookbooks — Regional
LC 2023011637

This is the story of photographer and food writer Saghar Setareh's culinary journey from Iran to Italy, in which she describes the many parallels that link Middle Eastern and Mediterranean food cultures, and shows how ingredients and recipes—unconstrained by borders—are shared and transformed through the immigrant experience.

"Rich in images and stories, at once accessible to cooks, and crafted for readers, this is a work to cook from and reflect on." —*Library Journal*

Includes bibliographical references (pages 280-281) and index.

Shumski, Daniel
How to Instant Pot: Mastering All the Functions of the One Pot That Will Change the Way You Cook. Daniel Shumski. Workman Publishing 2017. VIII, 279 p. : Color; Illustration
ISBN 9781523502066
Grades: Adult   641.5
1. One-dish meals 2. Pressure cooking 3. Quick and easy cooking 4. Recipes 5. Cookbooks 6. Food writing — Cooking and cookbooks — Methods
LC Bl2017051578

Presents over one hundred recipes specifically designed for use in the Instant Pot, including such dishes as beef barbacoa tacos, gorzonzola polenta, beet and blue cheese salad, chipotle tomato soup, and saffron rice pudding.

Includes index.

Sifton, Sam
★ *The New York Times Cooking No-Recipe Recipes.* Sam Sifton; photographs by David Malosh and food styling by Simon Andrews. Ten Speed Press 2021. 242 pages : Color; Illustration
ISBN 9781984858474
Grades: Adult   641.5
1. Quick and easy cooking 2. Food writing — Cooking and cookbooks — Methods

A debut cookbook from the popular New York Times website and NYT Cooking mobile app provides one hundren vibrantly photographed "No Recipe Recipes" for weeknight meals, from smothered pork chops to fettucine with minted ricotta.

"Innovative, fun, and freeing, this outstanding offering will reenergize the creative spirits of novice and experienced home cooks alike." —*Publishers Weekly*

★ *See You on Sunday: A Cookbook for Family and Friends.* by Sam Sifton; photographs by David Malosh; food stylist: Simon Andrews. Random House 2019. 368 pages : Color; Illustration
ISBN 9781400069927
Grades: Adult   641.5
1. Cooking 2. Entertaining 3. Recipes 4. Cookbooks 5. Food writing — Cooking and cookbooks — Entertaining
LC 2018032051

The award-winning New York Times food editor celebrates the art of Sunday suppers and the joys of gathering with friends and family, complementing simple, traditional recipes for small and larger groups with tips about rendering classics distinctive.

"[D]elivers a lush and fun guide to creating memorable Sunday dinners for large groups of friends and family . . . This is an excellent resource for family meals that readers will turn to time and again." —*Publishers Weekly*

Includes index.

Thanksgiving: How to Cook It Well. Sam Sifton. Random House 2012. 133 p. : Illustration
ISBN 9781400069910
Grades: Adult   641.5
1. Holiday cooking 2. Thanksgiving Day 3. Cooking, American 4. Recipes 5. Cookbooks 6. Food writing — Cooking and cookbooks — Regional
LC 2012013919

A former New York Times restaurant critic and Thanksgiving Help Line contact presents an accessible and authoritative guide to cooking and surviving a stylish Thanksgiving dinner, drawing on his extensive experiences to counsel home cooks on everything from different ways to prepare a turkey and selecting accompanying wines to managing difficult relatives and timing side dishes.

Includes index.

Siva, Micah
Nosh: Plant-Forward Recipes Celebrating Modern Jewish Cuisine. Micah Siva. The Collective Book Studio 2024. 255 pages : Color; Illustration
ISBN 9781685553272
Grades: Adult   641.5
1. Vegetarian cooking 2. Vegan cooking 3. Cooking, Jewish 4. Jewish holiday cooking 5. Cookbooks 6. Food writing — Cooking and cookbooks — Vegetarian and vegan 7. Food writing — Cooking and cookbooks — Regional
LC Bl2024005278

Food is a central part of Jewish culture, and those who don't connect with the foods of yesterday may feel as though a part of their heritage is missing. Nosh is the vegetarian cookbook for the modern Jewish kitchen, drawing inspiration from history through a 21st century lens.

"In all, the bright photos and fresh take on Jewish cuisine elevate holiday menu making to new heights." —*Booklist*

Includes index.

Smith, Michelle
The Whole Smiths Good Food Cookbook: Delicious Real Food Recipes to Cook All Year Long. Michelle Smith. Houghton Mifflin Harcourt 2018. xxi, 261 pages : Color; Illustration
ISBN 9781328915092
Grades: Adult   641.5
1. Nutritional therapy 2. Cooking (Natural foods) 3. Nutrition 4. Recipes 5. Self-care 6. Cookbooks 7. Food writing — Cooking and cookbooks — Cooking for health 8. Self-Help — Personal growth — Diet and nutrition
LC 2017051915

Fully endorsed by Whole30, a collection of 150 recipes for the other 335 days of the year includes both gluten-free and low-grain options as well as meals that can be customized for dietary restraints.

Includes index.

Snodgrass, Alex
★ *The Defined Dish: Healthy and Wholesome Weeknight Recipes.* Alex Snodgrass; photography by Kristen Kilpatrick; foreword by Melissa Urban, co-creator of the Whole30.. Houghton Mifflin Harcourt 2020. xi, 291 pages : Color; Illustration
ISBN 9780358004417
Grades: Adult   641.5
1. Cooking (Natural foods) 2. Gluten-free diet 3. Wheat-free diet 4. Low-carbohydrate diet 5. Recipes 6. Quick and easy cooking 7. Cookbooks 8. Food writing — Cooking and cookbooks — Methods 9. Food writing — Cooking and cookbooks — Courses 10. Food writing — Cooking and cookbooks — Cooking for health
LC 2019032812

With gluten-free, dairy-free and grain-free recipes that sound and look way too delicious to be healthy, this is a cookbook people can turn to after completing a Whole30, when they're looking to reintroduce healthful ingredients like tortillas, yogurt, beans and legumes.

Whole30 endorsed—Cover; Includes index.

PUBLIC LIBRARY CORE COLLECTION: NONFICTION
Twentieth Edition

Dinner Tonight: 100 Simple, Healthy Recipes for Every Night of the Week. Alex Snodgrass; photography by Kristen Kilpatrick. William Morrow, an imprint of HarperCollinsPublishers 2023. 247 pages : Color; Illustration
ISBN 9780063278479
Grades: Adult   641.5
1. Dinners and dining 2. Quick and easy cooking 3. Food writing — Cooking and cookbooks — Methods 4. Food writing — Cooking and cookbooks — Cooking for health

LC 2023013425

The New York Times best-selling author of The Defined Dish offers flexible, simple and healthy weeknight dinner recipes including Seared Tuna with White Bean and Arugula Salad, Chicken Pot Pie Chowder, and 2AM Kimchi Noodles.

"An excellent choice for home cooks looking for deliciously uncomplicated weeknight meals that can also be impressive enough for company." —*Library Journal*

Includes index.

Snyder, Sabrina
Dinner Then Dessert: Satisfying Meals Using Only 3, 5, or 7 Ingredients. Sabrina Snyder with Jenny Wapner; photographs by Colin Price. Harper Design, an imprint of HarperCollinsPublishers 2021. 224 pages : Color; Illustration
ISBN 9780062995414
Grades: Adult   641.5
1. Quick and easy cooking 2. Desserts 3. Cookbooks 4. Food Writing — Cooking and cookbooks — Methods 5. Food Writing — Cooking and cookbooks — Courses

LC 2021005554

Learn how to make easy, practical, mouth-watering meals in this first-ever cookbook featuring over 100 full-color photos from the genius chef behind the very successful, no-nonsense food website Dinner Then Dessert.

"The easy-going style and kid-friendly meals will make this cookbook attractive to busy households looking to go beyond an uninspired dinner routine." —*Booklist*

Includes index.

Stewart, Martha
Martha Stewart's Cooking School: Lessons and Recipes for the Home Cook. Martha Stewart with Sarah Carey. Clarkson Potter/Publishers 2008. VII, 504 p. : Color illustration
ISBN 9780307396440
Grades: Adult   641.5
1. Cooking 2. Recipes 3. Cookbooks 4. Food writing — Cooking and cookbooks — Methods

LC Bl2008027017

Introduces common cooking methods, including techniques for making stocks and soups, eggs, pasta, vegetables, beans, and desserts, and broiling, braising, and sauteing meats and fish, along with recipes and descriptions of basic kitchen equipment, seasonings, and herbs.

Includes index.

Sussman, Adeena
Sababa: Fresh, Sunny Flavors from My Israeli Kitchen. Adeena Sussman. Avery, an imprint of Penguin Random House 2019. 368 pages : Color; Illustration
ISBN 9780525533450
Grades: Adult   641.5
1. Seasonal cooking 2. Cookbooks 3. Food writing — Cooking and cookbooks — Regional

LC 2019004726

An American food writer and expatriate living in Tel Aviv presents 125 recipes from Israel, including Freekeh and Roasted Grape Salad, Crudo with Cherries and Squeezed Tomatoes, Schug Marinated Lamb Chops and Tahini Caramel Tart. Illustrations.

"Sababa, which translates as everything is awesome, makes for an appropriate title for this outstanding collection of fresh variations on an old-world cuisine." —*Publishers Weekly*

Includes index.

★ *Shabbat:* Recipes and Rituals from My Table to Yours. Adeena Sussman; photography by Dan Perez; styling by Nurit Kariv. Avery, an imprint of Penguin Random House 2023. 383 pages : Color; Illustration
ISBN 9780593327777
Grades: Adult   641.5
1. Cooking, Jewish 2. Sabbath (Judaism) 3. Cookbooks 4. Food writing — Cooking and cookbooks — Regional

LC 2023005722

The author of Sababa returns with a collection of good-for-the-soul recipes that embody the spirit and pleasures of Shabbat.

"[Sussman] offers recipes that are modern and have a little something for everyone with plenty of vegan offerings, cocktails, and even breakfast. Readers will also find traditional Jewish dishes like matzo ball soup and kugel." —*Library Journal*

Includes index.

Symon, Michael
★ *Fix* It with Food: More Than 125 Recipes to Address Autoimmune Issues and Inflammation. Michael Symon and Douglas Trattner; [photographs by Ed Anderson]. Clarkson Potter/Publishers 2019. 255 pages : Color; Illustration
ISBN 9781984825537
Grades: Adult   641.5
1. Cooking 2. Health 3. Recipes 4. Cookbooks 5. Food writing — Cooking and cookbooks — Cooking for health

LC 2019008836

A health-focused cookbook by the celebrity cohost of Iron Chef America draws on his experiences with chronic illness and food-triggering pain to offer satisfying recipes that do not include red meat, white flour, sugar, dairy or alcohol.

Includes index.

Tam, Michelle
Ready or Not!: 150+ Make-Ahead, Make-Over, and Make-Now Recipes by Nom Nom Paleo. Michelle Tam + Henry Fong. Andrews McMeel Publishing 2017. 344 pages : Color; Illustration
ISBN 9781449478292
Grades: Adult   641.5
1. Cooking (Natural foods) 2. Quick and easy cooking 3. High-protein diet 4. Recipes 5. Cookbooks 6. Food writing — Cooking and cookbooks — Ingredients 7. Food writing — Cooking and cookbooks — Methods

LC Bl2017030627

Presents paleo diet recipes that are intended to be prepared quickly and with simple ingredients, including rustic chocolate cake, hangry soup, flank steak super salad, and sunnyside salad.

No gluten, grains, dairy, refined sugar, or excuses!—Cover; Includes indexes.

Taylor, Kathryne
Love Real Food: More Than 100 Feel-Good Vegetarian Favorites to Delight the Senses and Nourish the Body. Kathryne Taylor. Rodale 2017. xxvii, 243 pages : Color; Illustration
ISBN 9781623367411
Grades: Adult   641.5
1. Vegetarian cooking 2. Recipes 3. Cookbooks 4. Food writing — Cooking and cookbooks — Vegetarian and vegan

LC 2017007675

The author presents vegetarian recipes that are popular on her blog, including heirloom tomato pesto pizza, peanut butter chocolate chip cookies, and olive oil and black pepper popcorn.

ESSENTIAL AND RECOMMENDED TITLES
641.5 Cooking

Taylor, Nicole A.
★ *Watermelon* & *Red Birds: A Cookbook for Juneteenth and Black Celebrations*. Nicole A. Taylor. Simon & Schuster 2022. xiv, 270 pages : Color; Illustration
ISBN 9781982176211
Grades: Adult 641.5
1. Cooking, African American 2. Juneteenth 3. Cookbooks 4. Food Writing — Cooking and cookbooks — Regional 5. Food Writing — Cooking and cookbooks — Entertaining
LC Bl2022015689

In this collection of recipes and essays that both celebrate and investigate Juneteenth, a critically acclaimed food writer presents 75 delicious dishes that are simple, victory-garden-driven and approachable.

"Taylor delivers a comprehensive, celebratory, and informative Juneteenth cookbook that will make readers dream of summer." —*Library Journal*

Includes bibliographical references (pages 262-263) and index.

Teigen, Chrissy
Cravings: Hungry for More. Chrissy Teigen. Clarkson Potter 2018. 240 p.
ISBN 9781524759728
Grades: Adult 641.5
1. Teigen, Chrissy 2. Cooking 3. Cooks 4. Recipes 5. Quick and easy cooking 6. Autobiographies and memoirs 7. Food writing — Memoirs and biographies 8. Food writing — Cooking and cookbooks — Narrative cookbooks 9. Food writing — Cooking and cookbooks — Methods
LC 2017061197

Goodreads Choice Award, 2018.

A follow-up to Cravings is presented in the form of a culinary diary about the Sports Illustrated model's family life and features healthier, flavor-forward adaptations of recipes for such fare as pancakes, onion dip and banana bread.

Terry, Bryant
Vegan Soul Kitchen: Fresh, Healthy, and Creative African American Cuisine. Bryant Terry. Da Capo Press 2009. xxviii, 223 p, 8 p. of plates : Illustration; Color
ISBN 9780738212289
Grades: Adult 641.5
1. Vegan cooking 2. Cooking, African American 3. Local foods 4. Seasonal cooking 5. Cooking, American 6. Cooking 7. Cookbooks 8. Food writing — Cooking and cookbooks — Cooking for health 9. Food writing — Cooking and cookbooks — Vegetarian and vegan
LC 2008046945

Offers recipes for low-fat African American dishes made with fresh ingredients and minimal amounts of salt and refined sugar, along with tips on using healthy cooking techniques and buying local, seasonal products.

Includes bibliographical references (p. 201-202) and index.

★ *Vegetable Kingdom: The Abundant World of Vegan Recipes*. Bryant Terry; photographs by Ed Anderson. Ten Speed Press 2020. 249 p.: Color; Illustration
ISBN 9780399581045
Grades: Adult 641.5
1. Vegan cooking 2. Cooking (Natural foods) 3. Recipes 4. Cookbooks 5. Food writing — Cooking and cookbooks — Vegetarian and vegan
LC 2019038413

A guide to the fundamentals of plant-based cooking features over 100 recipes for such dishes as Dirty Cauliflower, Barbecued Carrots with Slow-Cooked White Beans and Millet Roux Mushroom Gumbo, as well as tips on vegan cooking.

"Terry's approach to food and its preparation is complex, even when recipes are simple. His previous book, Afro-Vegan, explored dishes of the African diaspora. This newest work broadens the global reach with international influences that blend traditional methods with the culinary techniques and training of the James Beard Award-winning chef and writer." —*Library Journal*

Includes index.

Thiessen, Tiffani
Pull up a Chair: Recipes from My Family to Yours. Tiffani Thiessen with Rachel Holtzman; photography by Rebecca Sanabria. Houghton Mifflin Harcourt 2018. xi, 323 pages : Color; Illustration
ISBN 9781328710307
Grades: Adult 641.5
1. Cooking 2. Recipes 3. Cookbooks 4. Food writing — Cooking and cookbooks — Cooking for the family 5. Food writing — Cooking and cookbooks — Entertaining
LC 2017059617

Presents a collection of family recipes from the television star with her take on classic American dishes, including roasted chicken potpie, whole grilled trout, arugula, grape, & ricotta pizza, and vanilla bean bread pudding with bourbon-caramel sauce.

"Thiessen's simple recipes and presentation truly inspire meals to reconnect and celebrate with friends and family." —*Publishers Weekly*

Includes index.

Thomas, Anna
Vegan Vegetarian Omnivore: Dinner for Everyone at the Table. Anna Thomas; photography by Victoria Pearson. W.W. Norton & Company 2016. 414 pages : Color; Illustration
ISBN 9780393083019
Grades: Adult 641.5
1. Cooking 2. Recipes 3. Cookbooks 4. Food writing — Cooking and cookbooks — Vegetarian and vegan 5. Food writing — Cooking and cookbooks — Ingredients
LC 2015043951

Presents a collection of 150 recipes to accommodate every type of eater, including vegans, vegetarians, and meat eaters, with options for appetizers, dips, sauces, salads, soups, pasta, sides, main courses, and desserts.

"Armed with nearly 200 of Thomas's versatile recipes, hosts can feel confident cooking one menu for all their guests." —*Library Journal*

Includes index.

Thomas, Haile
Living Lively: 80 Plant-Based Recipes to Activate Your Power and Feed Your Potential. Haile Thomas. William Morrow 2020. 256 p.: Illustration
ISBN 9780062943415
Grades: Adult 641.5
1. Vegetarian cooking 2. Cooking (Natural foods) 3. Recipes 4. Cookbooks 5. Food writing — Cooking and cookbooks — Vegetarian and vegan 6. Food writing — Cooking and cookbooks — Cooking for health
LC 2019054725

By a superstar eighteen-year-old activist and motivational speaker, and the youngest Certified Integrative Health Coach in America, an inspiring plant-based cookbook featuring 80 delicious, wholesome recipes to boost confidence, happiness, energy, and positivity along with "7 points of power" to motivate the next generation of leaders.

"Plant-based foodstuffs are the backbone of her 80 recipes, including comfort foods in new guises and variations, like chickpea flour pancakes, overnight oats, cauliflower steaks, and spicy Southwestern falafel." —*Booklist*

Turshen, Julia
Feed the Resistance: Recipes + Ideas for Getting Involved. Julia Turshen with contributions from Maya-CamilleBroussard, Anthony Thosh Collins and ChelseaLuger, Erika Council, Devita Davison, Cheryl Day,Jocelyn Delk Adams, Von Diaz, Yana Gilbuena, MikkiHalpin, Hawa Hassan, Jocelyn Jackson, CallieJayne, J. Chronicle Books 2017. 143 pages
ISBN 9781452168388
Grades: Adult 641.5

583

PUBLIC LIBRARY CORE COLLECTION: NONFICTION
Twentieth Edition

1. Cooking 2. Recipes 3. Cookbooks 4. Food writing — Cooking and cookbooks — Narrative cookbooks 5. Food writing — Cooking and cookbooks — Regional

LC 2017024414

A popular cookbook author offers a collection of recipes aimed at fostering community and providing sustenance for those actively fighting to |resist| social injustice and express support for civil rights along with political activism resources, lists and essays from other activists. Proceeds will be donated to the ACLU.

Includes index.

Now & Again: Go-to Recipes, Inspired Menus + Endless Ideas for Reinventing Leftovers. Julia Turshen; photographs by David Loftus. Chronicle Books 2018. 303 pages : Color; Illustration

ISBN 9781452164922

Grades: Adult   641.5

1. Cooking 2. Cookbooks 3. Food writing — Cooking and cookbooks

LC 2017040842

Offers over one hundred recipes and menu ideas for reinventing leftovers, including such dishes as kale salad with pepita dressing, baked saffron rice, chicken and black-eyed pea chili, and black forest cake.

Includes Index.

Small Victories: Recipes, Advice + Hundreds of Ideas for Home-cooking Triumphs. Julia Turshen; foreword by Ina Garten; photographs by Gentl + Hyers. Chronicle Books 2016. 303 pages

ISBN 9781452143095

Grades: Adult   641.5

1. Cooking 2. Recipes 3. Cookbooks 4. Food writing — Cooking and cookbooks — Methods

LC OC2018153478

Overflowing with instruction and inspiration, a writer and go-to recipe developer shares a lifetime of lessons learned through cooking thousands of meals along with more than 400 bold, flavorful recipes, that are simple and achievable, for breakfast, lunch, dinner and dessert.

"Home cooks aiming to produce delicious, unpretentious fare or those who enjoyed such cookbooks as Deb Perelman's the Smitten Kitchen Cookbook or Kristen Miglore's Food52 Genius Recipes would do well to add this to their shelves." —*Library Journal*

Includes index.

Twitty, Michael

★ *Koshersoul: The Faith and Food Journey of an African American Jew.* Michael W. Twitty. Amistad, an imprint of HarperCollins Publishers 2022. 320 p.

ISBN 9780062891754

Grades: Adult   641.5

1. Twitty, Michael, 1977- 2. Cooking, Jewish 3. Cooking, African American 4. Jewish history 5. African American history 6. Recipes 7. Food Writing — Cooking and cookbooks — Narrative cookbooks 8. Food Writing — Food and Culture

LC 2021059767

In Koshersoul, Michael W. Twitty considers the marriage of two of the most distinctive culinary cultures in the world today: the foods and traditions of the African Atlantic and the global Jewish diaspora. To Twitty, the creation of African-Jewish cooking is a conversation of migrations and a dialogue of diasporas offering a rich background for inventive recipes and the people who create them. The question that most intrigues him is not just who makes the food, but how the food makes the people. Jews of Color are not outliers, Twitty contends, but significant and meaningful cultural creators in both Black and Jewish civilizations. Koshersoul also explores how food has shaped the journeys of numerous cooks, including Twitty's own passage to and within Judaism.

"Twitty stuffs his follow-up to James Beard Award winner the Cooking Gene with wide-ranging ideas....Serving up a hefty helping of heart and wit, Twitty's narrative is thrilling in its originality." —*Publishers Weekly*

Includes bibliographical references.

Urban, Melissa

The Whole30 Friends & Family: 150 Recipes for Every Social Occasion. Melissa Hartwig Urban; photography by Ghazalle Badiozaman. Houghton Mifflin Harcourt 2019. xxi, 265 pages : Color; Illustration

ISBN 9780358112136

Grades: Adult   641.5

1. Cooking (Natural foods) 2. Dieting 3. Low-carbohydrate diet 4. Recipes 5. Diet and disease 6. Cookbooks 7. Food writing — Cooking and cookbooks — Cooking for health 8. Food writing — Cooking and cookbooks — Entertaining

LC 2019024061

Whole30 menus and recipes for everyday social occasions from birthday parties and baby showers, to movie night, date night, and more.

Includes index.

Villanova, Thibaud

Disney Enchanted Recipes. Thibaud Villanova; photography: Nicolas Lobbestaël; styling: Soizic Chomel de Varagnes; translation: Lisa MoHe Troyer. Insight Editions 2022. 143 pages : Illustration; Color

ISBN 9781647221546

Grades: Adult   641.5

1. Cooking 2. Disney characters 3. Cookbooks 4. Translations — French to English 5. Food writing — Cooking and cookbooks

LC Bl2022015825

Collects easy-to-prepare recipes inspired by Disney films, from main courses to desserts, with cooking tips and recipes for all skill levels, including such dishes as Princess Tiana's gumbo, Kronk's spinach puffs, Remy's soup, and Jack-Jack's cookies.

This cookbook and its stunning design will appeal to Disney lovers of all ages. While it suffers from some organizational choices, Disney fans will be inspired to cook. School.

Includes index.

Walch, Aubry

The Herbivorous Butcher Cookbook: 75+ Recipes for Plant-based Meats and All the Dishes You Can Make with Them. by Aubry and Kale Walch with Sandra Soria and Danny Seo; photographs by Rikki Snyder. Chronicle Books 2022. 240 pages : Illustration; Color

ISBN 9781797211954

Grades: Adult   641.5

1. Vegan cooking 2. Quick and easy cooking 3. Cookbooks 4. Food writing — Cooking and cookbooks — Vegetarian and vegan 5. Food writing — Cooking and cookbooks — Chefs and restaurants

LC 2021060637

75 innovative recipes for plant-based meats and standout vegan dishes from the Herbivorous Butcher Shop."

"There's nothing fake about the flavor or enthusiasm behind this marvelous endeavor." —*Publishers Weekly*

Includes index.

Walker, Danielle

Danielle Walker's Against All Grain: Meals Made Simple : Gluten-Free, Dairy-Free, and Paleo Recipes to Make Anytime. Written and photographed by Danielle Walker; cover photography by Jennifer Skog. Victory Belt Publishing 2014. 319 pages : Color; Illustration

ISBN 9781628600421

Grades: Adult   641.5

1. Cooking (Natural foods) 2. Gluten-free diet 3. High-protein diet 4. Milk-free diet 5. Recipes 6. Cookbooks 7. Food writing — Cooking and cookbooks — Cooking for health 8. Food writing — Cooking and cookbooks — Ingredients

LC Bl2014037018

In a follow-up to her New York Times best-selling Against All Grain the popular blogger offers 100 new, enjoyable, gluten-free, dairy-free and Paleo-friendly recipes, including a month of dinner ideas and complete shopping lists.

ESSENTIAL AND RECOMMENDED TITLES
641.5 Cooking

Offers one hundred gluten-free, dairy-free, and Paleo-friendly recipes, including a month of dinner ideas and complete shopping lists.
Includes index.

***Danielle** Walker's Healthy in a Hurry: Real Life, Real Food, Real Fast.* Danielle Walker. Ten Speed Press 2022. 329 p.
ISBN 9781984857668
Grades: Adult   641.5
1. Quick and easy cooking 2. Health 3. Cooking 4. Cookbooks 5. Food writing — Cooking and cookbooks — Cooking for health
LC 2021025482

The New York Times best-selling author of the Against All Grain series presents over 150 paleo, gluten-free and dairy-free recipes including lunches, freezer-friendly meals and sheet pan dinners like Curry Noodles with Shrimp and Pork Ragu over Creamy Polenta. Index.
"Whether home cooks have dietary restrictions or just want to eat healthy, this is a book that they will turn to time and again." —*Publishers Weekly*
Includes index.

Waters, Alice
The Art of Simple Food. Alice Waters; with Patricia Curtan, Kelsie Kerr & Fritz Streiff; illustrations by Patricia Curtan. Clarkson Potter 2007. IX, 405 p. : Illustration
ISBN 9780307336798
Grades: Adult   641.5
1. Cooking 2. Seasonal cooking 3. Food writing — Cooking and cookbooks — Ingredients
LC Bl2007022117

Reveals how to select seasonal, local, fresh, and sustainable foods; provides a series of lessons on everyday principles and practices of good eating; and presents more than two hundred recipes that range from appetizers to desserts.
"After a useful discussion of ingredients and equipment come chapters on techniques, such as making broth and soup. Each of these includes three or four recipes that rely on the technique described. The final third of the book divides many more recipes traditionally into salads, pasta and so forth. Waters taps an almost endless supply of ideas for appealing and fresh yet low-stress dishes." —*Publishers Weekly*
Includes index.

Weinstein, Bruce
*The **Great** Big Pressure Cooker Book: 500 Easy Recipes for Every Machine, Both Stovetop and Electric.* Bruce Weinstein and Mark Scarbrough; photographs by Tina Rupp. Clarkson Potter/Publishers 2015. 512 pages : Color; Illustration
ISBN 9780804185325
Grades: Adult   641.5
1. Pressure cooking 2. Quick and easy cooking 3. Cookbooks 4. Food writing — Cooking and cookbooks — Methods
LC 2014022862

Provides over five hundred recipes for stovetop and electric pressure cookers, including French toast bread pudding, osso bucco, tamarind beef stew, chicken fricassee, spicy steamed clams, and chocolate pudding.
Includes index.

Wells, Patricia
My Master Recipes: 165 Recipes to Inspire Confidence in the Kitchen, with Dozens of Variations. Patricia Wells; in collaboration with Emily Buchanan. William Morrow 2017. xxix, 466 pages : Color; Illustration
ISBN 9780062424822
Grades: Adult   641.5
1. Cooking 2. Gourmet cooking 3. Recipes 4. Cookbooks 5. Food writing — Cooking and cookbooks — Chefs and restaurants 6. Food writing — Cooking and cookbooks — Methods
LC Bl2017009407

A best-selling cookbook author, drawing on the lessons taught at her cooking schools in France, presents an instructional cookbook that provides a vast array of recipes that teach particular techniques—including blanching, searching, braising and steaming—and gives home cooks the knowledge and assurance to expand their cooking even further.
"Simple, seasonal dishes will send gourmands to the kitchen for leisurely cooking. Wells's recipes are fiercely precise and personal." —*Library Journal*
Includes index.

Winfrey, Oprah
Food, Health, and Happiness: 115 On-Point Recipes for Great Meals and a Better Life. Oprah Winfrey; with Lisa Kogan. Flatiron Books 2017. 231 pages : Color; Illustration
ISBN 9781250126535
Grades: Adult   641.5
1. Winfrey, Oprah, 1954- 2. Cooking (Natural foods) 3. Cooking 4. Cookbooks 5. Food writing — Cooking and cookbooks — Cooking for health
LC 2016963619

A four-color cookbook collecting 100 top-selected recipes by the iconic host of the Oprah Winfrey Show draws on the expertise of such fan-favorite chefs as Rosie Daley and Taryn Huebner and shares insights into how Winfrey learned to enjoy favorite meals while controlling her weight.
An Oprah book; Includes index.

Wolf, Robb
Wired to Eat: Turn off Cravings, Rewire Your Appetite for Weight Loss, and Determine the Foods That Work for You. Robb Wolf. Harmony Books 2017. xii, 388 p. : Illustration
ISBN 9780451498564
Grades: Adult   641.5
1. Low-carbohydrate diet 2. Recipes 3. Dieting 4. Food writing — Cooking and cookbooks — Cooking for health 5. Science writing — Medicine and health — Diet and nutrition 6. Science writing — Medicine and health — Diet and nutrition — Weight loss
LC BL2017031726

A recipe-complemented guide by the best-selling author of the Paleo Solution outlines a 30-day program based on the latest research to help readers rewire their appetites, regulate blood sugar, and lose weight more easily by consuming paleo-based, whole foods.
Includes bibliographical references (pages 354-373) and index.

Workman, Katie
Dinner Solved!: 100 Ingenious Recipes That Make the Whole Family Happy, Including You. Katie Workman; photographs by Todd Coleman. Workman Publishing 2015. xii, 372 pages
ISBN 9780761181873
Grades: Adult   641.5
1. Cooking, American 2. Cooking 3. Recipes 4. Cookbooks 5. Family and Relationships — Parenting 6. Food writing — Cooking and cookbooks — Regional 7. Food writing — Cooking and cookbooks — Vegetarian and vegan
LC 2015011304

Collects family-friendly recipes with "Fork-in-the-Road" variations that make it easy to adapt dishes to appeal to both adults and children, including appetizers, burgers, one-dish meals, vegetarian meals, and desserts.
Filled with a vast array of recipes and full-color photos, the author of the Mom 100 Cookbook, expanding on one of the most popular features of the first cookbook—her ingenious "Fork in the Road" recipe solution, shows home cooks how to turn one dish into two or more.

*The **Mom** 100 Cookbook: 100 Recipes Every Mom Needs in Her Back Pocket.* Katie Workman; photographs by Todd Coleman. Workman Pub. 2012. xxix, 366 p. : Color illustration
ISBN 9780761166030
Grades: Adult   641.5
1. Cooking 2. Recipes 3. Quick and easy cooking 4. Cookbooks 5. Food writing — Cooking and cookbooks — Methods 6. Food writing — Cooking and cookbooks — Cooking for the family
LC 2012001330

Contains several recipes designed to make life easier for mothers and choosy children.

"Families can use this practical, mix-and-match recipe collection to lessen the stress of meal planning." —*Library Journal*
Includes index.

Yearwood, Trisha
Trisha's Kitchen: Easy Comfort Food for Friends & Family. Trisha Yearwood; with Beth Yearwood Bernard; foreword by Garth Brooks. Houghton Mifflin Harcourt 2021. 287 pages : Illustration; Color
ISBN 9780358567370

Grades: Adult 641.5
1. Cooking 2. Comfort food 3. Cooking for families 4. Quick and easy cooking 5. Food writing — Cooking and cookbooks
LC 2021014683

The country music star, Food Network star and #1 bestselling author offers 125 comfort food recipes and family favorites that are easy to make, along with fun family stories and photos.

"A variety of comfort food ideas that will please Yearwood's fans and attract new foodies. These dishes will find an eager audience in home cooks of all levels." —*Library Journal*
Includes index.

Yeh, Molly
Home Is Where the Eggs Are: Farmhouse Food for the People You Love. Molly Yeh. William Morrow, an imprint of HarperCollinsPublishers 2022. xxx, 337 pages : Color; Illustration
ISBN 9780063052413

Grades: Adult 641.5
1. Cooking 2. Cooking, Jewish 3. Cooking, Chinese 4. Farm life 5. Cookbooks 6. Food writing — Cooking and cookbooks — Regional
LC 2022002983

The host of Food Network's Girl Meets Farm offers a collection of cozy, low-maintenance recipes that draw on her Chinese and Jewish heritage including Babka Cereal, Mozzarella Stick Salad, Doughnut Matzo Brei and Ham and Potato Pizza.

"If patrons are not already a fan of Yeh's cheerful culinary brand of pun-enriched and sprinkle-championing cooking, this charming paean to joys of farmhouse food and the bucolic life will win them over." —*Library Journal*
Includes index.

641.509 Cooking — History, geographic treatment, biography

Miller, Max
★ *Tasting History: Explore the Past Through 4,000 Years of Recipes.* Max Miller with Ann Volkwein; photography by Andrew Bui. Simon Element 2023. 255 pages
ISBN 9781982186180

Grades: Adult 641.509
1. Cooking 2. Food habits 3. History 4. Recipes 5. Food writing — Cooking and cookbooks 6. Food writing — History and microhistory
LC Bl2023013437

What began as a passion project when Max Miller was furloughed during Covid-19 has become a viral YouTube sensation. The Tasting History with Max Miller channel has thrilled food enthusiasts and history buffs alike as Miller recreates a dish from the past, often using historical recipes from vintage texts, but updated for modern kitchens as he tells stories behind the cuisine and culture. Now, with beautiful photographs portraying the dishes and historical artwork throughout, Tasting History compiles over sixty dishes.

"A wonderful contribution to the teaching of social history through the culinary pleasures of the day. Great for anyone who enjoys cooking or history." —*Library Journal*

Includes bibliographical references (pages 243-245) and index.

641.5092 Cooks

Bourdain, Anthony
The Nasty Bits: Collected Varietal Cuts, Usable Trim, Scraps, and Bones. Anthony Bourdain. Bloomsbury Pub. 2006. xii, 288 p.
ISBN 9781582344515

Grades: Adult 641.5092
1. Cooking 2. Food 3. Restaurants 4. Food industry and trade 5. Television programs 6. Voyages and travels 7. Food writing — General
LC 2005033245

Presents a candid collection of culinary misadventures, from scrounging for eel in backstreet Hanoi, to quarreling with raw-food activist Woody Harrelson and revealing the less than glamorous aspects of making television.

"The author is a vivid and witty writer, but his greatest gift is his ability to convey his passion for professional cooking." —*New York Times Book Review*
Includes bibliographical references.

Sanchez, Aaron
Where I Come From: Life Lessons from a Latino Chef. Aaron Sanchez. Harry N Abrams Inc 2019. 304 p.
ISBN 9781419738029

Grades: Adult 641.5092
1. Sanchez, Aaron 2. Mexican Americans 3. Celebrity chefs 4. Cooking 5. Cooks 6. Cooking, Latin American 7. Growing up 8. Mothers and sons 9. El Paso, Texas 10. New York City 11. New Orleans, Louisiana 12. Autobiographies and memoirs 13. Life stories — Arts and culture — Culinary arts 14. Food writing — Memoirs and biographies 15. Adult books for young adults
LC 2018958855

The award-winning co-star of MasterChef shares stories from his family life and culinary journey, detailing his upbringing by a fiercely talented restaurateur mother and his work beside some of New York's most distinguished chefs.

Sen, Mayukh
Taste Makers: Seven Immigrant Women Who Revolutionized Food in America. Mayukh Sen. W. W. Norton & Company, independent publishers since 1923 2022. 304 p.
ISBN 9781324004516

Grades: Adult 641.5092
1. Chao, Buwei Yang, 1889-1981 2. Zelayeta, Elena 3. Child, Julia 4. Kamman, Madeleine 5. Hazan, Marcella 6. Sahni, Julie 7. Batmanglij, Najmieh, 1947- 8. Women cooks 9. Women immigrants 10. Gender role 11. Immigration and emigration 12. Food 13. Cooking 14. United States 15. Collective biographies 16. Food writing — Memoirs and biographies 17. Food writing — Food and culture
LC 2021029600

America's modern culinary history told through the lives of seven pathbreaking chefs and food writers. Who's really behind America's appetite for foods from around the globe? This group biography from an electric new voice in food writing honors seven extraordinary women, all immigrants, who left an indelible mark on the way Americans eat today. Taste Makers stretches from World War II to the present, with absorbing and deeply researched portraits of figures including Mexican-born Elena Zelayeta, a blind chef; Marcella Hazan, the deity of Italian cuisine; and Norma Shirley, a champion of Jamaican dishes. In imaginative, lively prose, Mayukh Sen—a queer, brown child of immigrants—reconstructs the lives of these women in vivid and empathetic detail, daring to ask why some were famous in their own time, but not in ours, and why others shine brightly even today. Weaving together histories of food, immigration, and gender, Taste Makers will challenge the way readers look at what's on their plate—and the women whose labor, overlooked for so long, makes those meals possible.

"In this dazzling debut, James Beard Award-winning food writer Sen looks at the lives of seven remarkable immigrant women whose passion for their homeland's food transformed how Americans cook and eat. . . . What results is a vibrant, empathetic, and dynamic exploration of culture, identity, race, and gender." —*Publishers Weekly*

Includes bibliographical references and index.

ESSENTIAL AND RECOMMENDED TITLES
641.555 Timesaving cooking

641.555 Timesaving cooking

Weinstein, Bruce
The Kitchen Shortcut Bible: More Than 200 Recipes to Make Real Food Real Fast. Bruce Weinstein and Mark Scarbrough; photographs by Eric medsker. Little, Brown and Company 2018. 352 pages : Color; Illustration
ISBN 9780316509718
Grades: Adult   641.555
1. Quick and easy cooking 2. Recipes 3. Cookbooks 4. Food writing — Cooking and cookbooks — Methods
LC 2017964191
A collection of quick and easy recipes features such dishes as blender salsa verde, microwave pasta carbonara, one-skillet loaded mac and cheese, and no-churn butter pecan ice cream.
"Basic directions and easy-to-find ingredients guarantee this book will be embraced by everyday cooks, who will welcome a respite from complicated, time-consuming, and multi-ingredient recipes." —*Library Journal*
Includes index.

641.59 Cooking characteristic of specific geographic environments, ethnic cooking

Bishara, Rawia
Olives, Lemons & Za'atar: The Best Middle Eastern Home Cooking. Rawia Bishara; photography by Peter Cassidy. Kyle Books 2014. 224 pages : Illustration; Color
ISBN 9781906868840
Grades: Adult   641.59
1. Cooking, Southwest Asian and North African 2. Cookbooks 3. Food writing — Cooking and cookbooks — Regional
LC Bl2014006120
Draws on the author's Palestinian-Arab family life and her experiences as the owner of Brooklyn's Tanoreen restaurant to present a collection of Middle-Eastern recipes, including red snapper in grape leaves and cheese knafeh.
"Themes of food, family, and personal growth flow throughout this gorgeous cookbook, which balances both simple and challenging recipes." —*Library Journal*
Includes index.

Bitsoie, Freddie
New Native Kitchen: Celebrating Modern Recipes of the American Indian. Chef Freddie Bitsoie and James O. Fraioli; photography by Quentin Bacon; illustrations by Gabriella Trujillo. Abrams Press 2021. 287 p. : Color; Illustration
ISBN 9781419753558
Grades: Adult   641.59
1. Cooking, Indigenous 2. Cooking, American 3. Indigenous peoples of North America 4. Indigenous peoples of North America — Social life and customs 5. Food Preparation 6. Food Writing — Food and Culture 7. Food writing — Cooking and cookbooks — Narrative cookbooks 8. Society and culture — Ethnic studies
LC Bl2021029109
From Freddie Bitsoie, the former executive chef at Mitsitam Native Foods Cafe at the Smithsonian's National Museum of the American Indian, and James Beard Award-winning author James O. Fraioli, New Native Kitchen is a celebration of Indigenous cuisine. Accompanied by original artwork by Gabriella Trujillo and offering delicious dishes like Cherrystone Clam Soup from the Northeastern Wampanoag and Spice-Rubbed Pork Tenderloin from the Pueblo peoples, Bitsoie showcases the variety of flavor and culinary history on offer from coast to coast, providing modern interpretations of 100 recipes that have long fed this country.
"A diverse and flavorful cultural history comes alive in this riveting celebration of the country's past and present." —*Publishers Weekly*
Includes bibliographical references (pages 278-279) and index.

Bourdain, Anthony
★ *World Travel: An Irreverent Guide.* Anthony Bourdain and Laurie Woolever; illustrations by Wesley Allsbrook. Ecco 2020. 471 p. : Illustration
ISBN 9780062802798
Grades: Adult   641.59
1. Bourdain, Anthony 1956-2018 2. Celebrity chefs 3. International cooking 4. Voyages and travels 5. Food habits 6. Food industry and trade 7. Food 8. Food Writing — Food and Culture 9. Travel Writing — General
LC 2020013949
A guide to some of the world's most interesting places, as seen and experienced by writer, television host and relentlessly curious traveler Anthony Bourdain.
"An exhilarating and worthwhile choice for those planning an actual trip and for stay-at-home travelers." —*Library Journal*

Deetz, Kelley Fanto
Bound to the Fire: How Virginia's Enslaved Cooks Helped Invent American Cuisine. Kelley Fanto Deetz. The University Press of Kentucky 2017. 162 p.
ISBN 9780813174730
Grades: Adult   641.59
1. Enslaved people 2. Cooking, African American 3. Cooking, American 4. African Americans 5. African American cooks 6. Plantation life 7. Race relations 8. United States history 9. Virginia 10. History writing — African American — Enslavement — United States 11. Food writing — History and microhistory
LC 2017029779
In grocery store aisles and kitchens across the country, smiling images of 'Aunt Jemima' and other historical and fictional Black cooks can be found on various food products and in advertising. Although these images are sanitized and romanticized in American popular culture, they represent the untold stories of enslaved men and women who had a significant impact on the nation's culinary and hospitality traditions even as they were forced to prepare food for their oppressors.
"Scholarly yet readable, Deetz's book honors these American ancestors by reclaiming their rightful places and stories." —*Booklist*
Includes bibliographical references and index.

Diaz, Von
★ *Islas: A Celebration of Tropical Cooking : 125 Recipes from the Indian, Atlantic, and Pacific Ocean Islands.* Von Diaz; photography by Cybelle Codish, Lauren Vied Allen. Chronicle Books LLC 2023. 303 pages : Color; Illustration
ISBN 9781797215242
Grades: Adult   641.59
1. Cooking, Indic 2. Cooking 3. Islands 4. Tropics 5. Atlantic Ocean 6. Islands of the Pacific 7. Islands of the Indian Ocean 8. Cookbooks 9. Food writing — Cooking and cookbooks — Narrative cookbooks 10. Food writing — Cooking and cookbooks — Regional 11. Food writing — Cooking and cookbooks — Reference
LC 2023012952
A writer, documentary producer and author takes us on a culinary adventure through the islands spanning the Indian, Atlantic and Pacific Oceans, sharing 125 recipes, along with ancestral cooking techniques, stories from islanders and step-by-step guides for recreating them at home.
"Diaz explores the connecting threads that define the culture of islands around the world. Home chefs will delight in the rich history and mouthwatering dishes she has uncovered." —*Booklist*
Includes index.

Guy, Jerrelle
Black Girl Baking: Wholesome Recipes Inspired by a Soulful Upbringing. Jerrelle Guy, founder of Chocolate for Basil. Page Street Publishing Co. 2018. 207 pages : Color; Illustration
ISBN 9781624145124
Grades: Adult   641.59

PUBLIC LIBRARY CORE COLLECTION: NONFICTION
Twentieth Edition

1. Guy, Jerrelle, 1990- 2. Baking 3. Cooking, African American 4. Cooking (Natural foods) 5. Recipes 6. Cookbooks 7. Food writing — Cooking and cookbooks — Methods

LC 2017943529

Growing up sensitive and slightly awkward in a race-conscious space, Guy decided early on that good food is the most powerful way to connect, understand, and heal. She leads readers on a sensual baking journey, using the fives senses, as she retells foodmemories with ingredients that involve whole flours, less refined sugar, and vegan alternatives.

Includes index.

Hall, Carla
Carla's Comfort Foods: Favorite Dishes from Around the World. Carla Hall with Genevieve Ko; photography by Frances Janisch; design by Jennifer Barry. Atria Books 2014. xvii, 221 pages : Color; Illustration
ISBN 9781451662221
Grades: Adult   641.59

1. International cooking 2. Comfort food 3. Recipes 4. Cookbooks 5. Food writing — Cooking and cookbooks — Regional 6. Food writing — Cooking and cookbooks — Ingredients

LC 2013035094

The executive chef and co-host of the Chew presents 130 recipes that offer new variations on international and American South favorites, from Southern Chicken with Milk Gravy and West African Spicy-Sweet Stew to Irish Shepherd's Pie and Mexican Enchiladas.

Includes index.

Harris, Jessica B.
High on the Hog: A Culinary Journey from Africa to America. Jessica B. Harris. Bloomsbury USA 2011. 288 p.
ISBN 9781596913950
Grades: Adult   641.59

1. Cooking, African American 2. Food habits 3. African diaspora 4. Identity 5. Page to screen 6. Food writing — General 7. History writing — African American — United States

LC 2010024899

Cookbook author Jessica B. Harris has spent much of her life researching the food and foodways of the African Diaspora. High on the Hog is the culmination of years of her work, and the result is an engaging history of African American cuisine. Harris takes the reader on a harrowing journey from Africa across the Atlantic to America, tracking the trials that the people and the food have undergone along the way. From chitlins and ham hocks to fried chicken and vegan soul, Harris celebrates the delicious and restorative foods of the African American experience and details how each came to form such an important part of African American culture, history, and identity. Although the story of African cuisine in America begins with slavery, High on the Hog ultimately chronicles a history of triumph and survival.

"A narrative history—and travel memoir—of African American cuisine by the author of numerous popular cookbooks. Harris explains the rich provenance of African America's foodways and meals." —*Library Journal*

Includes index; Made into a TV series on Netflix.

Holland, Tanya
★ *Tanya Holland's California Soul: Recipes from a Culinary Journey West.* Tanya Holland with Maria C. Hunt and Dr. Kelley Fanto Deetz; foreword by Alice Walker; photographs by Aubrie Pick. Ten Speed Press 2022. 253 pages : Color; Illustration
ISBN 9781984860729
Grades: Adult   641.59

1. Cooking, African American 2. Seasonal cooking 3. Comfort food 4. Cooking, American 5. California 6. Southern states 7. Cookbooks

LC 2022005493

80+ comfort-filled recipes that trace the roots of modern California soul food to the Great Migration that brought African American culture to the West Coast—from the acclaimed chef and author of Brown Sugar Kitchen.

"There's something about the sun-soaked coloration of each page, and the tint of each photograph, that gives readers the sense of enjoying a comfy, home-cooked meal in the warm sunshine." —*Booklist*

Includes index.

Jenkins, Nancy Harmon
The New Mediterranean Diet Cookbook: A Delicious Alternative for Lifelong Health. Nancy Harmon Jenkins; with a foreword by Marion Nestle. Bantam Books 2009. xiii, 496 p.
ISBN 9780553385090
Grades: Adult   641.59

1. Cooking, Mediterranean 2. Low-fat diet 3. Recipes 4. Cookbooks 5. Food writing — Cooking and cookbooks — Cooking for health

LC 2008040982

Discusses the nutritional and health benefits of Mediterranean culinary practices and presents two hundred recipes adapted for the modern American kitchen.

"Jenkins' knowledge of these cuisines is both personal and informed. An essential purchase." —*Library Journal*

Prev. ed. published under title: The Mediterranean diet cookbook; Includes bibliographical references (p. 479-481) and index.

Johnson, J. J.
Between Harlem and Heaven: Afro-Asian-American Cooking for Big Nights, Weeknights, & Every Day. JJ Johnson and Alexander Smalls; with Veronica Chambers; photography by Beatriz da Costa; food styling by Roscoe Betsill. Flatiron Books 2018. 269 pages : Illustration; Color
ISBN 9781250108715
Grades: Adult   641.59

1. Cooking, African American 2. Cookbooks 3. Food writing — Cooking and cookbooks — Chefs and restaurants 4. Food writing — Cooking and cookbooks — Regional

LC 2018000426

Describes how the authors created the Afro-Asian-American flavor profile in their Harlem restaurant, and provides recipes for such dishes as pineapple black fried rice, grilled octopus salad, tamarind glazed oxtails, and West African peanut punch.

Includes index.

Karadsheh, Suzy
★ *The Mediterranean Dish: 120 Bold and Healthy Recipes You'll Make on Repeat.* Suzy Karadsheh with Susan Puckett; photographs by Caitlin Bensel. Clarkson Potter/Publishers 2022. 303 pages : Color; Illustration
ISBN 9780593234273
Grades: Adult   641.59

1. Cooking, Mediterranean 2. Cookbooks 3. Food writing — Cooking and cookbooks — Regional

LC 2021051906

Filled with easy-to-follow recipes, gorgeous photos, charming authentic stories and simple assemblies, the creator of The Mediterranean Dish website, in this long-awaited first cookbook, brings cross-culturally inspired dishes from throughout the Mediterranean into American home kitchens.

"This is as full of flavor as it is hospitality." —*Publishers Weekly*

Includes index.

Kattan, Fadi
★ *Bethlehem: A Celebration of Palestinian Food.* Fadi Kattan. Hardie Grant North America 2024. 240 p.
ISBN 9781958417287
Grades: Adult   641.59

1. Palestinian people 2. Food 3. Culture 4. Families 5. Cities and towns 6. Food habits 7. Recipes 8. Cooking, Southwest Asian and North African 9. Memories 10. Social life and customs 11. Bethlehem 12. Palestine 13. Southwest Asia and North Africa (Middle East) 14. Food writing — Cooking and cookbooks — Narrative cookbooks 15. Food Writing — Food and culture

ESSENTIAL AND RECOMMENDED TITLES
641.59 Cooking characteristic of specific geographic environments, ethnic cooking

Bethlehem is a celebration of Palestinian food and culture from one of the area's most dynamic chefs and a portrait of one of the most storied cities in the world.

"Augmented with beautiful photos, this ode to Palestinian culinary culture stuns." —*Publishers Weekly*

Kimball, Christopher
Tuesday Nights Mediterranean. Christopher Kimball; writing and editing by J.M. Hirsch and Michelle Locke; recipes by Matthew Card, Bianca Borges, Diane Unger and the cooks at Milk Street; art direction by Jennifer Baldino Cox and Brianna Coleman; photography by Connie Miller. Voracious 2021. xv, 283 pages : Illustration; Color
ISBN 9780316705998
Grades: Adult   641.59
1. Cooking, Mediterranean 2. Quick and easy cooking 3. Cookbooks 4. Food writing — Cooking and cookbooks — Regional
LC Bl2021008195

Each of these 125 Mediterranean dinners is ready in under 45 minutes, and many take just 20 minutes start to finish.

"Milk Street's winning formula for creating maximum flavor, balanced with weeknight convenience, shines here, and fans of Tuesday Nights will eagerly embrace this new collection. Highly recommended for all libraries." —*Library Journal*

Includes index.

Lawson, Nigella
At My Table: A Celebration of Home Cooking. Nigella Lawson. Flatiron Books 2017. 288 pages : Color; Illustration
ISBN 9781250154286
Grades: Adult   641.59
1. Cooking 2. Quick and easy cooking 3. Cooking, Mediterranean 4. Cooking, English 5. Recipes 6. Cookbooks 7. Food writing — Cooking and cookbooks — Methods 8. Food writing — Cooking and cookbooks — Chefs and restaurants
LC 2018000297

A recipe collection that celebrates home cooking offers recipes that are simple to prepare and feature new ingredients to enrich classic flavors and tastes, including such dishes as parmesan French toast, meatballs with orzo, and apple pork chops.

Includes index.

Lee, Edward
Buttermilk Graffiti: A Chef's Journey to Discover America's New Melting-Pot Cuisine. Edward Lee. Artisan, a Division of Workman Publishing Co, Inc. 2018. 272 p.
ISBN 9781579657383
Grades: Adult   641.59
1. Lee, Edward, 1972- 2. Restaurateurs 3. Automobile travel 4. Cooks 5. International cooking 6. Cooking 7. Voyages and travels 8. United States 9. Travel Writing — United States 10. Travel Writing — Modes of Transportation — Road Trips 11. Food writing — Food and culture 12. Food writing — Cooking and cookbooks — Chefs and restaurants
LC 2017051428

James Beard Foundation Book Awards, Writing and Literature, 2019.

A chef, restaurateur and author describes the two years he spent traveling the United States learning about the different cultures, traditions, memories and innovations that keep adding to, reshaping and helping to evolve what makes up American cuisine.

Lukas, Albert
★ *Sweet Home Cafe Cookbook: A Celebration of African American Cooking.* Albert Lukas and Jessica B. Harris, with contributions by Jerome Grant; foreword by Lonnie G. Bunch III; introduction by Jacquelyn Serwer; in association with the National Museum of African American History and Culture and Restaurant Associates. Smithsonian Books 2018. 216 pages : Illustration; Color
ISBN 9781588346407
Grades: Adult   641.59
1. Cooking, African American 2. Recipes 3. Cooking, American 4. Cookbooks 5. Food writing — Cooking and cookbooks — Regional 6. Food writing — Cooking and cookbooks — Chefs and restaurants
LC 2018016725

A celebration of African-American cooking focuses on locally sourced ingredients and includes modern adaptations of such traditional recipes as fried green tomatoes, grits, hush puppies, fried chicken, and gumbo.

A celebration of African-American cooking by the NMAAHC's Sweet Home Cafe focuses on locally sourced ingredients and includes modern adaptations of such traditional recipes as Fried Green Tomatoes, Maryland Crab Cakes and Jamaican Grilled Jerk Chicken.

"Named for the cafe at the National Museum of African American History and Culture in Washington, DC, this cookbook collects classic and contemporary dishes inspired by historically African American foods." —*Library Journal*

Includes bibliographical references (page 210) and index.

Miller, Klancy
★ *For the Culture: Phenomenal Black Women and Femmes in Food : Interviews, Inspiration, and Recipes.* Klancy Miller. HarperCollins Publishers 2023. xii, 305 pages
ISBN 9780358581277
Grades: Adult   641.59
1. African American businesspeople 2. Cooking, African American 3. Cooking, American 4. Recipes 5. African American farmers 6. African American-owned businesses 7. Restaurants 8. Success (Concept) 9. Cookbooks 10. Interviews 11. Food writing — Food and culture 12. Life stories — Arts and culture — Culinary arts 13. Food writing — Memoirs and biographies 14. Food writing — Cooking and cookbooks
LC 2023020180

A pastry chef, recipe developer and founder of for the Culture highlights and profiles the extraordinary Black women who influenced and shaped today's food and hospitality, including Toni Tipton-Martin, Mashama Bailey and Carla Hall along with their personal recipes.

"Honoring Black creators past and present from all over the food world, this book is a treasure and a love letter to Black women everywhere." —*Booklist*

Includes index.

Onwuachi, Kwame
★ *Notes from a Young Black Chef: A Memoir.* Kwame Onwuachi with Joshua David Stein. Alfred A. Knopf 2019. 288 p.
ISBN 9781524732622
Grades: Adult   641.59
1. Onwuachi, Kwame 2. African American cooks 3. Restaurateurs 4. Cooking, African American 5. Cooking 6. Cooks 7. Former gang members 8. Life change events 9. Cooking, American 10. Determination 11. Bronx, New York City 12. Nigeria 13. Autobiographies and memoirs 14. Life stories — Arts and culture — Culinary arts 15. Life stories — Facing adversity — Personal transformation 16. Food writing — Memoirs and biographies 17. Adult books for young adults 18. Antiracist literature
LC 2018036747

The Top Chef star traces his culinary coming-of-age in both the Bronx and Nigeria, discussing his eclectic training in acclaimed restaurants while sharing insights into the racial barriers that have challenged his career.

"A solid choice for fans of celebrity chef and pop culture memoirs." —*Library Journal*

Ottolenghi, Yotam
Ottolenghi Simple: A Cookbook. Yotam Ottolenghi, with Tara Wigley and Esme Howarth; photographs by Jonathan Lovekin. Ten Speed Press 2018. xiii, 307 pages : Color; Illustration
ISBN 9781607749165
Grades: Adult   641.59
1. Cooking, Southwest Asian and North African 2. Quick and easy cooking 3. Make-ahead cooking 4. Cookbooks 5. Food writing — Cooking and cookbooks — Regional 6. Food writing — Cooking and cookbooks — Chefs and restaurants 7. Food writing — Cooking and cookbooks — Methods

LC 2018020229

An author, chef, and restaurateur presents 130 Middle Eastern recipes that can be made easily in one or more ways: in 30 minutes or less, with 10 or fewer ingredients, in a single pot, using pantry staples, or prepared ahead of time for easy weeknight meals.

"Ottolenghi's many fans will want this book, but it will also appeal to home cooks looking for exciting, approachable recipes." —*Library Journal*

Includes bibliographical references and index.

Ottolenghi: The Cookbook. Yotam Ottolenghi and Sami Tamimi; photography by Richard Learoyd. Ten Speed Press 2013. xv, 287 pages : Color; Illustration

ISBN 9781607744184

Grades: Adult   641.59

1. Cooking, Mediterranean 2. Cooking, Southwest Asian and North African 3. Cookbooks 4. Food writing — Cooking and cookbooks — Regional

LC Bl2013037719

Shares 140 recipes from the Mediterranean-inspired chain restaurant, including options for such dishes as stuffed grape leaves, harissa-marinated chicken with red grapefruit salad, and sour cherry amaretti.

"Although Ottolenghi's latest will challenge readers in ways its predecessors did not, it reliably delivers unique recipes with flavor combinations unmatched in their inventiveness." —*Library Journal*

Includes index.

Parla, Katie

Tasting Rome: Fresh Flavors & Forgotten Recipes from an Ancient City. Katie Parla and Kristina Gill; foreword by Mario Batali. Clarkson Potter/Publishers 2016. 255 pages : Color; Illustration

ISBN 9780804187183

Grades: Adult   641.59

1. Cooking, Italian 2. Recipes 3. Cookbooks 4. Food writing — Cooking and cookbooks — Regional

LC 2015023715

Presents recipes for modern dishes influenced by Roman regional traditions and culture, demonstrating how classic favorites, street-food innovations, and forgotten recipes reveal Italy's unique culinary evolution.

Includes bibliographical references and index.

Pittman, Ann Taylor

The Global Pantry Cookbook: Transform Your Everyday Cooking with Tahini, Gochujang, Miso, and Other Irresistible Ingredients. Ann Taylor Pittman, Scott Mowbray; photography by Kevin Miyazaki. Workman Publishing 2023. 307 pages : Color; Illustration

ISBN 9781523516858

Grades: Adult   641.59

1. International cooking 2. Food 3. Cookbooks 4. Food writing — Cooking and cookbooks — Regional 5. Food writing — Cooking and cookbooks — Ingredients

LC 2023019343

This definitive cookbook from two James Beard Cookbook Award-winning authors teaches readers how to combine dozens of super-powered pantry items from around the globe—from aji amarillo to gochujang, Banyuls vinegar to za'atar—with proven test-kitchen techniques to build maximum flavor with minimal effort.

Includes index.

Raiford, Matthew

Bress 'N' Nyam: Gullah Geechee Recipes from a Sixth-Generation Farmer. Matthew Raiford, with Amy Paige Condon; photography by Siobhan Egan. The Countryman Press 2021. 240 pages : Color; Illustration

ISBN 9781682686041

Grades: Adult   641.59

1. Raiford, Matthew 2. Cooking, African American 3. African American farmers 4. African American families 5. African American cooks 6. Freed people 7. Cooking, American 8. Southern States 9. Food writing — Cooking and cookbooks — Narrative cookbooks 10. Food Writing — Food and Culture 11. History writing — African American — United States

LC 2020047976

Matthew Raiford pays homage to this cuisine that nurtured his family for seven generations. In 2010, Raiford's Nana handed over the deed to the Georgia family farm to him and his sister, and Raiford rose to the occasion, nurturing the farm that his great-great-great grandfather, a freed slave, purchased in 1874. In this collection of heritage and updated recipes, he traces a history of community and family brought together by food.

"With tips on recipe pairings and meal planning, Raiford's debut will have home cooks coming back for more." —*Library Journal*

Includes bibliographical references (pages 228-229) and index.

Roden, Claudia

Arabesque: A Taste of Morocco, Turkey, and Lebanon. Claudia Roden. Knopf 2006. 341 p. : Color illustration

ISBN 9780307264985

Grades: Adult   641.59

1. Cooking, Arabic 2. Cooking, Moroccan 3. Cooking, Turkish 4. Cooking, Lebanese 5. Food writing — Cooking and cookbooks — Narrative cookbooks

LC 2006045258

An authority on Middle Eastern and North African cuisine explores the culinary heritage of Morocco, Turkey, and Lebanon in a colorful cookbook that features more than 150 tempting recipes that transform the unique flavors, foods, cooking techniques, and traditions for the modern home cook.

Includes index; Originally published in Great Britain by Michael Joseph, Penguin Books, Ltd, London, in 2005—T.P. verso.

Rodriguez, Jessamyn Waldman

The Hot Bread Kitchen Cookbook: Artisanal Baking from Around the World. Jessamyn Waldman Rodriguez and the Bakers of Hot Bread Kitchen with Julia Turshen. Clarkson Potter/Publishers 2015. 301 pages

ISBN 9780804186179

Grades: Adult   641.59

1. Bread 2. International cooking 3. Recipes 4. Cookbooks 5. Food writing — Cooking and cookbooks — Courses 6. Food writing — Cooking and cookbooks — Methods 7. Food writing — Cooking and cookbooks — Regional

LC 2014048697

A cookbook from the New York-based bakery that supplies ethnic breads to dozens of retail outlets while employing and empowering immigrant women shares the baker's regional breads from the international locales these women called home.

This first cookbook from the nonprofit New York City-based bakery that supplies ethnic breads to dozens of retail outlets while employing and empowering immigrant women shares the baker's regional breads from the international locales these women called home.

"Hot Bread Kitchen's first cookbook foray is essential reading for serious foodies, bakers and anyone inspired by the bakery's philanthropic mission." —*Library Journal*

Includes bibliographical references and index.

Rosenthal, Phil

★ *Somebody Feed Phil the Book: Untold Stories, Behind-the-Scenes Photos and Favorite Recipes.* Phil Rosenthal and Jenn Garbee; location photography by Richard Rosenthal; food photography by Ed Anderson. Simon Element 2022. IX, 341 pages : Illustration; Color

ISBN 9781982170998

Grades: Adult   641.59

1. Rosenthal, Phil, 1960- 2. International cooking 3. Voyages and travels 4. Cookbooks 5. Media tie-ins 6. Food writing — Cooking and cookbooks — Regional

LC Bl2022030624

The host of the entertaining Netflix series Somebody Feed Phil presents never-before-heard stories from every episode of the first four seasons, along with more than 60 of viewers' most requested recipes from acclaimed international chefs and local legends alike.

ESSENTIAL AND RECOMMENDED TITLES
641.59 Cooking characteristic of specific geographic environments, ethnic cooking

"An irresistible hybrid cookbook/Travel book, ideal for readers planning a trip or a meal." —*Library Journal*
Includes index.

Samuelsson, Marcus
★ *The Rise: Black Cooks and the Soul of American Food.* Marcus Samuelsson, with Osayi Endolyn; recipes with Yewande Komolafe and Tamie Cook; photographs by Angie Mosier. Voracious 2020. xx, 326 pages; Color; Illustration
ISBN 9780316480680
Grades: Adult   641.59
1. Cooking, African American 2. African American cooks 3. Cooking, African 4. Multiculturalism 5. African diaspora 6. Recipes 7. Food preparation 8. Cooking, American 9. Food writing — Cooking and cookbooks — Narrative cookbooks 10. Food Writing — Food and Culture 11. Life stories — Identity — Race and ethnicity 12. Life stories — Arts and culture — Culinary arts

It is long past time to recognize Black excellence in the culinary world the same way it has been celebrated in the worlds of music, sports, literature, film, and the arts. Now, in the Rise, chef, author, and television star Marcus Samuelsson gathers together an unforgettable feast of food, culture, and history to highlight the diverse deliciousness of Black cooking today. Driven by a desire to fight against bias, reclaim Black culinary traditions, and energize a new generation of cooks, Marcus shares his own journey alongside 150 recipes in honor of dozens of top chefs, writers, and activists—with stories exploring their creativity and influence.

"Reminding us that Black food is not monolithic and is more than soul food, award-winning chef Samuelsson (The Red Rooster Cookbook) creates a groundbreaking resource devoted to Black foodways and the ongoing history of food as a part of racial justice." —*Library Journal*
Includes index.

Shepherd, Chris
Cook Like a Local: Flavors That Can Change How You Cook and See the World. Chris Shepherd; with Kaitlyn Goalen; photographs by Julie Goalen. Clarkson Potter/Publishers 2019. 288 pages : Illustration
ISBN 9781524761264
Grades: Adult   641.59
1. International cooking 2. Cooking 3. Recipes 4. Cookbooks 5. Food writing — Cooking and cookbooks — Chefs and restaurants 6. Food writing — Cooking and cookbooks — Regional
LC 2019013832

The James Beard Award-winning chef of Underbelly Hospitality in Houston champions, not appropriates, the city's diverse immigrant communities and their cuisines in this collection of recipes including Fried Chicken Tamales and Korean Braised Goat and Dumplings.

"Flavors from around the world redefine the concept of home cooking in this rich and satisfying collection." —*Publishers Weekly*
Includes index.

Sherman, Sean
★ *The Sioux Chef's Indigenous Kitchen.* Sean Sherman; with Beth Dooley. University of Minnesota Press 2017. 225 pages : Color; Illustration
ISBN 9780816699797
Grades: Adult   641.59
1. Indigenous peoples of North America 2. Recipes 3. Cookbooks 4. Food writing — Cooking and cookbooks — Regional 5. Food writing — Cooking and cookbooks — Chefs and restaurants
LC 2017020954

Here is real food—our indigenous American fruits and vegetables, the wild and foraged ingredients, game and fish. Locally sourced, seasonal, "clean" ingredients and nose-to-tail cooking are nothing new to Sean Sherman, the Oglala Lakota chef and founder of the Sioux Chef. In his breakout book, The Sioux Chef's Indigenous Kitchen, Sherman shares his approach to creating boldly seasoned foods that are vibrant, healthful, at once elegant and easy. Sherman dispels outdated notions of Native American fare—no fry bread or Indian tacos here—and no European staples such as wheat flour, dairy products, sugar, and domestic pork and beef. The Sioux Chef's healthful plates embrace venison and rabbit, river and lake trout, duck and quail, wild turkey, blueberries, sage, sumac, timpsula or wild turnip, plums, purslane, and abundant wildflowers. Contemporary and authentic, his dishes feature cedar braised bison, griddled wild rice cakes, amaranth crackers with smoked white bean paste, three sisters salad, deviled duck eggs, smoked turkey soup, dried meats, roasted corn sorbet, and hazelnut-maple bites. The Sioux Chef's Indigenous Kitchen is a rich education and a delectable introduction to modern indigenous cuisine of the Dakota and Minnesota territories, with a vision and approach to food that travels well beyond those borders.

"Oglala Lakota chef Sherman has set out to educate the U.S. about its indigenous fruits and vegetables. Starting from his base in the northern Midwest and Great Plains and extending into Navajo lands, he ably demonstrates just how tasty and sophisticated the produce of the nation's heartland can be." —*Booklist*
Includes bibliographical references (pages 209-210) and index.

Smalls, Alexander
Meals, Music, and Muses: Recipes from My African American Kitchen. Alexander Smalls with Veronica Chambers; food and author photography by Beatriz da Costa; food styling by Roscoe Betsill. Flatiron Books 2020. xiii, 224 p.: Illustration; Color
ISBN 9781250098092
Grades: Adult   641.59
1. Cooking, African American 2. Recipes 3. Cooking, American 4. Cookbooks 5. Food writing — Cooking and cookbooks — Regional 6. Food writing — Cooking and cookbooks — Chefs and restaurants
LC 2019054745

The acclaimed James Beard award-winning restaurateur, while sharing anecdotes from his childhood in the Low Country, and examinations of Southern musical tradition, presents classic African American dishes that originated in the South,.

"Home cooks are sure to give this excellent recipe collection a standing ovation." —*Publishers Weekly*
Includes index.

Snoop Dogg
Goon with the Spoon. by Snoop Dog and Earl. Chronicle Books 2023. 190 pages : Color; Illustration
ISBN 9781797213712
Grades: Adult   641.59
1. International cooking 2. Cooking, American 3. Comfort food 4. Cookbooks 5. Food writing — Cooking and cookbooks — Chefs and restaurants 6. Food writing — Cooking and cookbooks — Entertaining
LC 2023025183

Drawing inspiration from both rappers' musical catalogs, their favorite meals to cook and eat together and E-40's Filipino food business, this next-level soulful cookbook contains more than 65 crowd-pleasing dishes along with epic stories and behind-the-scenes photos that bring these masterpieces to life.

"Fans and newcomers alike will want to get cooking." —*Publishers Weekly*
Includes index.

Tandoh, Ruby
★ *Cook as You Are: Recipes for Real Life, Hungry Cooks, and Messy Kitchens.* Ruby Tandoh; illustrations by Sinae Park. Alfred A. Knopf 2022. 344 pages : Color; Illustration
ISBN 9780593321546
Grades: Adult   641.59
1. International cooking 2. Quick and easy cooking 3. Comfort food 4. Cookbooks 5. Food writing — Cooking and cookbooks — Methods 6. Food writing — Cooking and cookbooks — Chefs and restaurants
LC 2022001815

Presents over 100 affordable, accessible and delicious recipes for feeding one person or a whole family including Carrot, Lemon and Tahini Soup, Smoky Chicken, Okra and Chorizo Casserole and Tofu and Greens with Hot and Sour Chili Sauce.

"Perfect for those looking to rekindle their relationship with cooking via simple, low-pressure, and taste-focused recipes." —*Library Journal*
Includes index; Great Britain : Serpent's Tail, 2021.

PUBLIC LIBRARY CORE COLLECTION: NONFICTION
Twentieth Edition

Terry, Bryant
Afro-Vegan: *Farm-Fresh African, Caribbean & Southern Flavors Remixed.* Bryant Terry; photography by Paige Green. Ten Speed Press 2014. VIII, 215 pages color illustrations
ISBN 9781607745310
Grades: Adult **641.59**
1. Cooking, African American 2. Cooking, African 3. Cooking, Caribbean 4. Vegan cooking 5. Recipes 6. Cooking, American 7. Cookbooks 8. Food writing — Cooking and cookbooks — Regional 9. Food writing — Cooking and cookbooks — Vegetarian and vegan
LC 2013048560

The rising star chef, food activist and author of the Inspired Vegan remixes foods of the African diaspora to outline creative but comprehensive vegan recipes.

"Chef-author Terry . . . introduces the concept of food justice, a philosophy that he defines as good food being an everyday right, and not just a privilege. His book is also an introduction to the various ways (more than 100, in short) that African cuisine can go mainstream." —*Booklist*

Includes index.

Tipton-Martin, Toni
*The **Jemima** Code: Two Centuries of African American Cookbooks.* Toni Tipton-Martin; forewords by John Egerton and Barbara Haber. University of Texas Press 2015. xv, 246 pages : Illustration
ISBN 9780292745483
Grades: Adult **641.59**
1. Cooking, African American 2. Cookbook writing 3. African American women cooks 4. Recipes 5. Social history 6. African American cooks 7. Stereotypes 8. Cooks 9. Food habits 10. United States 11. Food writing — History and microhistory 12. Food writing — Cooking and cookbooks — Narrative cookbooks 13. History writing — African American — United States
LC 2014033779

Women of African descent have contributed to America's food culture for centuries, but their rich and varied involvement is still overshadowed by the demeaning stereotype of an illiterate "Aunt Jemima" who cooked mostly by natural instinct. To discover the true roles of Black women in the creation of American, and especially southern, cuisine, Toni Tipton-Martin has spent years amassing one of the world's largest private collections of cookbooks published by African American authors, looking for evidence of their impact on American food, families, and communities and for ways we might use that knowledge to inspire community wellness of every kind.

"In this collection of two centuries worth of Black cookbooks, from an 1827 manual to contemporary titles, Tipton-Martin . . . uncovers the central role of Black women in American food." —*Library Journal*

Includes index.

★ ***Jubilee:*** *Recipes from Two Centuries of African-American Cooking.* Toni Tipton-Martin. Clarkson Potter 2019. 319 pages : Illustration
ISBN 9781524761738
Grades: Adult **641.59**
1. Cooking, African American 2. African American cooks 3. Enslaved people 4. African Americans 5. Food 6. Recipes 7. Food habits 8. United States 9. Food writing — Cooking and cookbooks — Narrative cookbooks 10. Food writing — History and microhistory 11. Food Writing — Food and Culture 12. History writing — African American — United States
LC 2019006495

Booklist Editors' Choice, 2019.

Drawing from historical texts and rare African-American cookbooks, a collection of 125 recipes takes readers into the world of African-American cuisine made by enslaved master chefs, free caterers and Black entrepreneurs and culinary stars that goes far beyond soul food.

"More than a cookbook, this collections of recipes offers an excellent starting point for anyone interested in African American culinary history." —*Library Journal*

Includes bibliographical references and indexes.

Twitty, Michael
★ *The **Cooking** Gene: A Journey Through African-American Culinary History in the Old South.* Michael W. Twitty. HarperCollins Publishers 2017. 336 p.
ISBN 9780062379290
Grades: Adult **641.59**
1. Cooking, African American 2. Food habits 3. Cooking, American 4. Social life and customs 5. Southern States 6. 20th century 7. History writing — African American — United States 8. Food Writing — Food and Culture 9. Food writing — History and microhistory
LC 2017003374

James Beard Foundation Book Awards, Writing and Literature, 2018; Finalist for the Hurston/Wright Legacy Awards for Nonfiction, 2018; Kirkus Prize for Nonfiction finalist, 2017.

Food blogger (Afroculinaria), Judaic studies scholar, and Southerner Michael Twitty connects family history with food and culture in this wide-ranging—and often mouth-watering—study. Primarily a narrative cultural history that examines slavery, race relations, soul food, and even kosher cooking, the Cooking Gene includes recipes that Twitty extensively researched and personally tested.

641.5926872073 Mexican American cooking

Casares, Sylvia
*The **Enchilada** Queen Cookbook: Enchiladas, Fajitas, Tamales, and More Classic Recipes from Texas-Mexico Border Kitchens.* Sylvia Casares with Dotty Griffith. St. Martin's Griffin 2016. xii, 224 pages : Illustration; Color; Map
ISBN 9781250082916
Grades: Adult **641.5926872073**
1. Cooking, Mexican American 2. Cookbooks 3. Food writing — Cooking and cookbooks — Regional
LC 2016033309

Presents a recipe collection representing the best in Texas-Mexico border town cooking from the founder and chef of Texas' Sylvia's Enchilada Kitchen, including such dishes as salsa verde, corn and crab soup, Gulf coast fish tacos, and braised pork.

"A satisfying combination of autobiography and popular Mexican foods." —*Library Journal*

Includes index.

641.59296073 African American cooking

Richards, Todd
Soul: *A Chef's Culinary Evolution in 150 Recipes.* Todd Richards; foreword by Sean Brock. Oxmoor House 2018. 366 pages : Illustration; Color
ISBN 9780848754419
Grades: Adult **641.59296073**
1. Cooking, African American 2. Recipes 3. Cooking, American 4. Cookbooks 5. Food writing — Cooking and cookbooks — Regional

"Lovers of Southern cuisine will find grits, corn, shrimp, and peaches showcased, but in unexpected, delightful ways (grilled peach toast with pimiento cheese; and peach salsa, chicken liver pate on zucchini bread)." —*Publishers Weekly*

Includes index.

641.594 Cooking — Europe

Allibhoy, Omar
Spanish *Made Simple: Foolproof Spanish Recipes for Every Day.* Omar Allibhoy; photography by Martin Poole. Quadrille 2016. 207 pages : Color; Illustration
ISBN 9781849497602
Grades: Adult **641.594**

ESSENTIAL AND RECOMMENDED TITLES
641.594 Cooking — Europe

1. Cooking, Spanish 2. Recipes 3. Cookbooks 4. Food writing — Cooking and cookbooks — Regional

LC Bl2017032188

Presents recipes for one hundred classic Spanish dishes, including tuna-stuffed eggs, squid in black ink sauce, pea soup with Serrano ham, seafood paella, and roasted almond nougat.
Includes index.

Andrews, Colman
The Country Cooking of Ireland. by Colman Andrews; photographs by Christopher Hirsheimer; foreword by Darina Allen. Chronicle Books 2009. 383 p. : Illustration; Color
ISBN 9780811866705
Grades: Adult   641.594
1. Cooking, Irish 2. Food writing — Cooking and cookbooks — Regional

LC Bl2009032505

Portraits of the Irish countryside and its people accompany recipes and cooking instructions for traditional Irish fare.
"The author provides new perspectives on the often maligned Irish cuisine. The breathtakingly beautiful photographs are alone enough to convince, but Andrews, calling Irish cuisine one of the most exciting food stories in the world today, lets the dishes make his case. ... Andrews has done the near impossible in elevating a cuisine thought to be humble and drab into tantalizing fare that will have worldwide appeal." —*Publishers Weekly*
Includes bibliographical references (p. 365-369) and index.

Bastianich, Lidia
Felidia: Recipes from My Flagship Restaurant. Lidia Matticchio Bastianich with Chef Fortunato Nicotra and Tanya Bastianich Manuali; photographs by Jennifer May. Alfred A. Knopf 2019. xxxiii, 240 pages : Illustration; Color
ISBN 9781524733087
Grades: Adult   641.594
1. Cooking, Italian 2. Recipes 3. Cookbooks 4. Food writing — Cooking and cookbooks — Chefs and restaurants 5. Food writing — Cooking and cookbooks — Regional

LC 2018060923

The best-selling author and award-winning chef and her culinary partners share 115 recipes from their popular New York restaurant including Pasta Primavera; Linguine with Mussels, Clams and Broccoli; Pear and Pecorino Ravioli; Chicken Piazzaiola; Chocolate Hazelnut Flan and Open Cannoli.

Lidia Cooks from the Heart of Italy. Lidia Matticchio Bastianich and Tanya Bastianich Manuali, with David Nussbaum; photographs by Hirsheimer & Hamilton and Lidia Matticchio Bastianich. Alfred A. Knopf 2009. xv, 411 p. : Color illustration; Color; Map
ISBN 9780307267511
Grades: Adult   641.594
1. Cooking, Italian 2. Cooking 3. Recipes 4. Cookbooks 5. Food writing — Cooking and cookbooks — Regional

LC 2009022021

Shares recipes from lesser-known regions of Italy and secret dishes from famous areas, in a treasury that includes such options as risotto milan-style with marrow and saffron and roast lobster with bread crumb topping.
"Bastianich and daughter Tanya take readers on a culinary tour of Italy's 12 regions. Grouped by those areas, the recipes are simple enough for novice cooks. Included are appetizers, soups, salads and side dishes, condiments, pastas and risottos/Rice, vegetarian main courses (aside from pasta), fish and seafood, meat and poultry, and desserts. In addition, there are stories about the history of the dishes." —*Library Journal*
A feast of 175 regional recipes—jacket; Includes index.

Lidia's Commonsense Italian Cooking: 150 Delicious and Simple Recipes Anyone Can Master. Lidia Matticchio Bastianich and Tanya Bastianich Manuali; photographs by Marcus Nilsson. Alfred A. Knopf 2013. xxi, 277 pages : Color; Illustration
ISBN 9780385349444
Grades: Adult   641.594

1. Cooking, Italian 2. Recipes 3. Cookbooks 4. Food writing — Cooking and cookbooks — Regional 5. Food writing — Cooking and cookbooks — Chefs and restaurants

LC 2013005067

Collects recipes outlining accessible culinary tips that channel instructive elements from the author's television show while sharing preparation guidelines for such fare as citrus roasted veal, rustic ricotta tart, and raw garden salad.
This is a Borzoi book—Title page verso; Includes index.

Lidia's Family Table. Lidia Matticchio Bastianich, with David Nussbaum; photographs by Christopher Hirsheimer. Alfred A. Knopf 2004. xxiv, 419 p. : Color illustration
ISBN 9781400040353
Grades: Adult   641.594
1. Cooking, Italian 2. Recipes 3. Cookbooks 4. Food writing — Cooking and cookbooks — Cooking for the family 5. Food writing — Cooking and cookbooks — Regional

LC 2004022411

A guide to family cookery features more than two hundred master recipes for everyday dining and special family occasions, along with imaginative ideas for variations and improvisations, including seasonal salads, vegetables, soups, pastas, sauces, main courses, and desserts.
"Step-by-step photographs illustrate kitchen techniques, and charming photos of the author's grandchildren and other family scenes add to the appeal of this engaging, immensely practical book." —*Library Journal*
Includes index.

Lidia's Favorite Recipes: 100 Foolproof Italian Dishes, from Basic Sauces to Irresistible Entrées. Lidia Matticchio Bastianich and Tanya Bastianich Manuali; photographs by Marcus Nilsson. Alfred A. Knopf 2012. xv, 220 pages : Illustration
ISBN 9780307595669
Grades: Adult   641.594
1. Cooking, Italian 2. Recipes 3. Cookbooks 4. Food writing — Cooking and cookbooks — Regional 5. Food writing — Cooking and cookbooks — Chefs and restaurants

LC 2012023455

The proprietor of New York City's Felidia restaurant and her daughter present a collection of favorite Italian recipes, with nutritional information for ingredients and suggestions for recipe variations.
"More compact than Bastianichs other titles, this practical collection is perfect for families as well as readers who enjoyed Viana La Place and Evan Kleimans Cucina Rustica." —*Library Journal*
Includes index.

★ *Lidia's from Our Family Table to Yours: More Than 100 Recipes Made with Love for All Occasions.* Lidia Matticchio Bastianich and Tanya Bastianich Manuali; photographs by Armando Rafael. Alfred A. Knopf 2023. xvi, 213 pages : Color; Illustration
ISBN 9780525657422
Grades: Adult   641.594
1. Cooking, Italian 2. Quick and easy cooking 3. Cookbooks 4. Food writing — Cooking and cookbooks — Regional 5. Food writing — Cooking and cookbooks — Chefs and restaurants

LC 2022043358

In this deeply personal new cookbook, which doubles as a tribute to her mother, the Emmy Award-winning host of PBS's Lidia's Kitchen shares the dishes she cooks for those she loves most, presenting more than 100 delicious, flavorful and easy-to-make Italian recipes.
"While Bastianich has always been appreciated for her relaxed approach to food, this latest collection brings her sincerity, accessibility, and culinary talent to a new level. Home cooks won't be able to resist." —*Publishers Weekly*
Includes index.

Lidia's Mastering the Art of Italian Cuisine: Everything You Need to Know to Be a Great Italian Cook. Lidia Matticchio Bastianich, with Tanya Bastianich Manuali. Alfred A. Knopf 2015. xiii, 461 pages
ISBN 9780385349468

PUBLIC LIBRARY CORE COLLECTION: NONFICTION
Twentieth Edition

Grades: Adult   641.594

1. Cooking, Italian 2. Recipes 3. Cookbooks 4. Food writing — Cooking and cookbooks — Reference 5. Food writing — Cooking and cookbooks — Regional 6. Food writing — Cooking and cookbooks — Chefs and restaurants

LC 2015001871

The Emmy-winning host of "Lidia's Kitchen," along with her daughter, provides an authoritative guide to Italian cooking that features 400 recipes along with the techniques needed to master Italian cuisine and a comprehensive guide to the tools every kitchen should have to produce the best results.

"The book completes its course with a charming chapter on Italian culture and language, as well as an extensive glossary of food terms. With this passionate treatise on Italian food and culture, readers dreaming of la dolce vita may find armchair travels enough to satisfy their hunger." —*Publishers Weekly*

Lidia's: Celebrate Like an Italian. Lidia Matticchio Bastianich and Tanya Bastianich Manuali; photographs by Steve Giralt. Alfred A. Knopf 2017. xxvii, 383 pages

ISBN 9780385349482

Grades: Adult   641.594

1. Cooking, Italian 2. Recipes 3. Cookbooks 4. Food writing — Cooking and cookbooks — Chefs and restaurants 5. Food writing — Cooking and cookbooks — Entertaining 6. Food writing — Cooking and cookbooks — Regional

LC 2017010180

In a guide for entertaining with that distinctly Bastianich flare, the beloved TV chef and her daughter present 220 easy-to-follow recipes with a welcoming Italian flavor that are perfect for any occasion, including Fragoli Daiquiri, Mussels with Zucchini Salsaverde, Peach Almond Cake, Roasted Olives with Orange and Rosemary, Campanelle with Fennel and much more.

Includes index.

Behan, Ren

★ *The Sweet Polish Kitchen: A Celebration of Home Baking & Nostalgic Treats.* Ren Behan. Interlink Books, an imprint of Interlink Publishing Group, Inc. 2023. 192 pages : Illustration; Color

ISBN 9781623717179

Grades: Adult   641.594

1. Cooking 2. Baking 3. Desserts 4. Pastry 5. Poland 6. Cookbooks 7. Food writing — Cooking and cookbooks — Regional 8. Food writing — Cooking and cookbooks — Courses 9. Food writing — Cooking and cookbooks — Methods

LC Bl2023176648

A collection of traditional and modern Polish baking and dessert recipes including babkas, cheesecakes, tarts, pastries, and all things sweet and celebratory.

"Home cooks and bakers into all things cottage-core and soft living will love cozying up to this beautiful and functional book filled with lovely, simply elegant bakes." —*Booklist*

Includes index.

Bjork, Katrin

From the North: A Simple and Modern Approach to Authentic Nordic Cooking. Katrin Bjork founder of Modern Wifestyle. Page Street Publishing Co. 2018. 192 pages : Color; Illustration

ISBN 9781624145308

Grades: Adult   641.594

1. Cooking, Scandinavian 2. Entertaining 3. Recipes 4. Cookbooks 5. Food writing — Cooking and cookbooks — Regional

LC 2017952212

In From the North, Katrin Bjork celebrates the flavors of her childhood with fresh ingredients and unique twists. Her modern techniques make traditional Nordic cooking simple and approachable, no matter how far south your kitchen.

"This cookbook—with its solid, simple recipes—serves as an excellent introduction to Nordic cuisine." —*Publishers Weekly*

Includes index.

Child, Julia

Julia and Jacques Cooking at Home. Julia Child and Jacques Pepin, with David Nussbaum. Alfred Knopf 1999. xii, 430 p. : Color illustration

ISBN 9780375404313

Grades: Adult   641.594

1. Child, Julia 2. Pepin, Jacques, 1935- 3. Cooking, French 4. Recipes 5. Cookbooks 6. Food writing — Cooking and cookbooks — Regional

LC 98032418

Two culinary masters join their talents in a cookbook that demonstrates the best in traditional French home cooking, with an assortment of recipes that ranges from soups to desserts.

"A companion volume to the PBS series. For each show, the two chefs started out with ideas and ingredients but no set recipes, so they improvised as they went along, cooking a lot of their favorite traditional dishes and coming up with new ones as well. Dozens of boxes throughout the text provide information on a wide variety of topics." —*Library Journal*

★ *Mastering the Art of French Cooking.* Julia Child, Louisette Bertholle, Simone Beck; illustrations by Sidonie Coryn. Alfred A. Knopf 2018. xxxi, 684, xxxii pages : Illustration

ISBN 9780375413407

Grades: 11 12 Adult   641.594

1. Cooking, French 2. Recipes 3. Cookbooks 4. Food writing — Cooking and cookbooks — Regional

LC 2009288212

Explains for the novice American cook the special ingredients and cooking techniques involved in preparing the wide variety of French dishes featured.

This is a Borzoi Book—Title page verso; Includes index; Revised edition of: Mastering the art of French cooking / by Simone Beck, Louisette Bertholle, Julia Child. [1st ed]. 1961-1970.

Clark, Melissa

Dinner in French: My Recipes by Way of France. Melissa Clark. Clarkson Potter/Publishers 2020. 335 pages : Illustration; Color

ISBN 9780553448252

Grades: Adult   641.594

1. Cooking, French 2. Recipes 3. Seasonal cooking 4. Cookbooks 5. Food writing — Cooking and cookbooks — Methods 6. Food writing — Cooking and cookbooks — Regional

LC 2019013485

An authoritative but comprehensive French cookbook by the James Beard Award-winning New York Times food writer and author of Dinner shares 150 wide-ranging recipes and modern updates of classic favorites, from Ratatouille Sheet-pan Chicken to Scalloped Potato Gratin.

"This remarkable volume will entice avid home cooks to return to it time and again." —*Publishers Weekly*

Includes index.

Danford, Natalie

How to Eataly: A Guide to Buying, Cooking, and Eating Italian Food. Written by Natalie Danford; photographs by Francesco Sapienza; introduction by Oscar Farinetti, founder; forewords by Joe Bastianich, Lidia Bastianich, Mario Batali, and Adam & Alex Saper. Rizzoli 2014. 304 pages : Illustration; Color

ISBN 9780847843350

Grades: Adult   641.594

1. Cooking, Italian 2. Recipes 3. Cookbooks 4. Food writing — Cooking and cookbooks — Chefs and restaurants 5. Food writing — Cooking and cookbooks — Regional

LC Bl2014044028

Collects recipes from the Eataly food emporium experts for contemporary Italian classics, with information about Italian food and cooking, including how to source the best-quality ingredients, drink coffee Italian style, and cook pasta al dente.

Includes index.

De Laurentiis, Giada

★ *Giada's Italy: My Recipes for La Dolce Vita.* Giada De Laurentiis. Clarkson Potter 2018. 288 pages : Color; Illustration

ISBN 9780307987228

Grades: Adult   641.594

ESSENTIAL AND RECOMMENDED TITLES
641.594 Cooking — Europe

1. Cooking, Italian 2. Recipes 3. Cookbooks 4. Food writing — Cooking and cookbooks — Ingredients 5. Food writing — Cooking and cookbooks — Regional

LC 2017049489

A lavish exploration of the author's food heritage in her native Rome also celebrates the lifestyle traditions that define la bella vita, sharing authentic Italian recipes enhanced with a contemporary California twist, including Grilled Swordfish with Candied Lemon Salad, Spaghetti with Chianti and Fava Beans and Fennel Upside Down Cake.

Includes index.

Giada's Kitchen: New Italian Favorites. Giada De Laurentiis; photographs by Tina Rupp. Clarkson Potter/Publishers 2008. 240 p. : Color illustration
ISBN 9780307346599
Grades: Adult   641.594
1. Cooking, Italian 2. Cooking, Italian-American 3. Recipes 4. Cookbooks 5. Food writing — Cooking and cookbooks — Regional 6. Food writing — Cooking and cookbooks — Chefs and restaurants

LC 2008005004

The host of Food Network's Everyday Italian presents a new collection of nearly one hundred tempting recipes for classic Italian dishes with a California-inspired twist, including lighter versions of such traditional dishes as Osso Bucco, as well as regional specialties, pasta, salads, meats, desserts, and special meals for kids.

Includes index.

Dusoulier, Clotilde
Tasting Paris: 100 Recipes to Eat Like a Local. Clotilde Dusoulier. Clarkson Potter/Publishers 2018. 256 p.
ISBN 9780451499141
Grades: Adult   641.594
1. Cooking, French 2. Cultural fusion 3. Food habits 4. City life 5. Eating out 6. Multiculturalism 7. Recipes 8. Paris, France 9. Food writing — Cooking and cookbooks — Narrative cookbooks 10. Food writing — Food and culture

LC 2017025780

A culinary tour of the French capital and food destination includes iconic bistro and brasserie fare, as well as such newer dishes as carrot chickpea crepes and ratatouille tahini sandwiches.

"Chapters are organized by time of day, so that one for afternoon treats, for instance, proffers light sweets, which are differentiated from dinner desserts. The setup can be a bit confusing at first, but it does ultimately lend reading this volume the same feel as of discovering something new while strolling down a city street." —*Publishers Weekly*

Feinberg, Andrew
Franny's: Simple Seasonal Italian. Andrew Feinberg, Francine Stephens, Melissa Clark. Artisan 2013. IX, 366 pages : Illustration; Color
ISBN 9781579654641
Grades: Adult   641.594
1. Cooking, Italian 2. Cooking 3. Seasonal cooking 4. Cookbooks 5. Food writing — Cooking and cookbooks — Regional

LC 2012028954

Offers modern Southern Italian recipes including roasted romano beans with calabrese olives, linguine with meyer lemon, marinated artichokes, baked sausage and polenta, and bucatini alla puttanesca.

Includes index.

Garten, Ina
Barefoot in Paris: Easy French Food You Can Make at Home. Ina Garten; photographs by Quentin Bacon; food styling by Rori Trovato; styling by Miguel Flores-Vianna. Clarkson Potter/Publishers 2004. 238 p. : Color illustration
ISBN 9781400049356
Grades: Adult   641.594
1. Cooking, French 2. Cookbooks 3. Food writing — Cooking and cookbooks — Regional

LC 2004003280

Provides recipes for simple dishes from France, using fresh, quality ingredients to concoct new twists on traditional French favorites, including steak au poivre, and creme brulée.

Includes indexes.

Greenspan, Dorie
Around My French Table: More Than 300 Recipes from My Home to Yours. Dorie Greenspan; photographs by Alan Richardson. Houghton Mifflin Harcourt 2010. xiii, 530 p. : Color illustration
ISBN 9780618875535
Grades: Adult   641.594
1. Cooking, French 2. Recipes 3. Food writing — Cooking and cookbooks — Regional

LC 2010014232

A James Beard Award winner offers personable recipes for French home cooking, presenting more than three hundred recipes for hors d'oeuvres, salads, soups, meat dishes, fish, vegetables, and desserts, with a separate section on making dough, vinaigrettes, and sauces.

"A part-time Paris resident for more than a decade, Greenspan focuses on what French people really eat at home: Easy-to-prepare yet flavorful dishes that are suitable for just about any time of day. From Bacon and Eggs and Asparagus Salad to Chicken in a Pot to Veal Chops with Rosemary Butter, her offerings are hardy, mostly uncomplicated, and superbly appetizing. She also provides sidebars on a wide range of topics, including whether or not to wash raw chicken, several ways of cooking beets, mussels, and more." —*Publishers Weekly*

Includes product source list and index.

Hayden, Georgina
Greekish: Everyday Recipes with Greek Roots. Georgina Hayden. Bloomsbury Publishing (UBD) 2024. 288 pages : Illustration
ISBN 9781526630667
Grades: Adult   641.594
1. Cooking, Greek 2. Cooking, Mediterranean 3. Quick and easy cooking 4. Food writing — Cooking and cookbooks — Regional 5. Food writing — Cooking and cookbooks — Methods

Inspired by her Greek-Cypriot roots and Greek travels, Georgina has collected recipes that are easy, bursting with flavour and sure to be cooked on repeat. With fewer ingredients and less stress, the recipes include familiar Mediterranean classics, as well as plenty of Greek-influenced dishes with Georgina's twists.

"This inviting collection will appeal to anyone interested in expanding their Mediterranean repertoire." —*Publishers Weekly*

Hazan, Marcella
★ *Essentials of Classic Italian Cooking.* by Marcella Hazan; illustrated by Karin Kretschmann. A. A. Knopf 1992. xi, 688 p. : Illustration
ISBN 9780394584041
Grades: Adult   641.594
1. Cooking, Italian 2. Recipes 3. Cookbooks 4. Food writing — Cooking and cookbooks — Regional

LC 92052954

"This could readily assume the mantle of the definitive resource for Italian cuisine." —*Booklist*

Includes index.

Kahan, Paul
Cheers to the Publican, Repast and Present: Recipes and Ramblings from an American Beer Hall. Paul Kahan and Cosmo Goss with Rachel Holtzman; photographs, Peden + Munk; poems, Jason Pickleman. Lorena Jones Books, an imprint of Ten Speed Press 2017. xi, 324 pages : Color; Illustration
ISBN 9780399578564
Grades: Adult   641.594
1. Cooking, European 2. Recipes 3. Cookbooks 4. Food writing — Cooking and cookbooks — Chefs and restaurants

LC 2017013468

PUBLIC LIBRARY CORE COLLECTION: NONFICTION
Twentieth Edition

The chef behind an incredibly popular restaurant in Chicago, known for its beer-friendly cooking and massive communal tables, offers 125 recipes for meat, seafood and vegetable dishes along with entertaining stories from the kitchen and dining room.

Includes bibliographical references and index.

Keller, Thomas
Bouchon Bakery. Thomas Keller and Sebastien Rouxel with Susie Heller, Matthew McDonald, Michael Ruhlman, and Amy Vogler; photographs by Deborah Jones. Artisan 2012. 399 p. : Color illustration
ISBN 9781579654351
Grades: Adult   641.594
1. Baking 2. Cookbooks 3. Food writing — Cooking and cookbooks — Methods 4. Food writing — Cooking and cookbooks — Chefs and restaurants
LC 2012000695

Collects recipes from the famed Bouchon Bakery, including chocolate eclairs, cherry-whipped cream doughnuts, poached pears, and sourdough boule.

"[T]his lovely volume is a must-have for cooks who want to take baking to the next level." —*Publishers Weekly*

Includes index.

Klopotenko, Yevhen
★ *The Authentic Ukrainian Kitchen: Recipes from a Native Chef.* Yevhen Klopotenko; photographs by Dima Bahta and Vladyslav Nahornyi. Voracious/Little, Brown and Company 2024. 269 p.
ISBN 9780316559393
Grades: Adult   641.594
1. Cooking 2. Eastern European people 3. Ukrainian people 4. Ukraine 5. Cookbooks 6. Food writing — Cooking and cookbooks — Regional 7. Food writing — Cooking and cookbooks — Chefs and restaurants

Now, more than ever, Ukrainian cuisine and culture deserve to be known around the world. Here, Yevhen Klopotenko shares modern recipes for the dishes that best express Ukraine's unique culinary heritage and define the independent spirit of its people. Inside you'll find fresh ideas about how to use common vegetables, new approaches to fermentation and pickling, the delight of dumplings and simple baked goods, hearty long-simmered braises, and the pleasure of babka, torte, candied fruit, and so much more. Klopotenko is Ukraine's most internationally celebrated chef, and these recipes are the result of years of research into regional Ukrainian cooking.

"Klopotenko's passion for and pride in Ukrainian cuisine shine brightly in this insightful, illuminating cookbook, making it an outstanding introduction to the food and culture of this brave country." —*Library Journal*

Includes index.

Korkosz, Michal
Fresh from Poland: New Vegetarian Cooking from the Old Country. Michal Korkosz. The Experiment 2020. 245 pages : Color; Illustration
ISBN 9781615196555
Grades: Adult   641.594
1. Vegetarian cooking 2. Recipes 3. Cooking 4. Cookbooks 5. Food writing — Cooking and cookbooks — Regional 6. Food writing — Cooking and cookbooks — Ingredients 7. Food writing — Cooking and cookbooks — Vegetarian and vegan
LC 2019054739

The first Polish vegetarian cookbook, with new Polish recipes and meat-free versions of traditional dishes.

"This charming collection offers both traditional vegetable dishes of Poland, such as creamy cucumber salad and chilled beet soup, and vegetarian versions of the Polish canon. . . . A light and delicious take on a cuisine often underrepresented in cooking collections. Vegetarian or not, most cooks will find something to savor." —*Library Journal*

Includes index.

Ladner, Mark
The Del Posto Cookbook. Mark Ladner with Michael R. Wilson; forewords by Mario Batali and Joe Bastianich; food photography by Paulette Tavormina. Grand Central Life & Style 2016. xxxi, 239 pages : Color; Illustration
ISBN 9781455561544
Grades: Adult   641.594
1. Cooking, Italian 2. Restaurants 3. Cookbooks 4. Food writing — Cooking and cookbooks — Chefs and restaurants 5. Food writing — Cooking and cookbooks — Regional
LC OC2018159199

The celebrated chef at Mario Batali's and Lidia Bastianich's award-winning destination restaurant in New York City redefines excellence in Italian cooking in America, focusing on regional Italian ingredients and traditions to present a collection of sophisticated old-country recipes.

"In addition to a thorough index, Ladner provides a welcome rarity: an allergen guide, three pages of charts listing all the recipes and the common allergens they include." —*Publishers Weekly*

Includes index.

Lanza, Fabrizia
The Food of Sicily: Recipes from a Sun-Drenched Culinary Crossroads. Fabrizia Lanza with Kate Winslow; photographs by Guy Ambrosino. Artisan Books 2023. 319 p.
ISBN 9781579659868
Grades: Adult   641.594
1. Cooking, Italian 2. Appetizers 3. Soups 4. Pasta 5. Fish as food 6. Pizza 7. Sicily, Italy 8. Cookbooks

Celebrating Sicily's food culture while honoring everything that makes it special, this singular cookbook is both a collection of recipes and techniques and a vibrant, beautifully photographed profile of the land, the people, the history and so much more.

"The result is a valuable guide to an abundant region that will be a welcome companion in the kitchen—or on a trip to Sicily." —*Publishers Weekly*

Lebovitz, David
My Paris Kitchen: Recipes and Stories. David Lebovitz. Ten Speed Press 2014. 352 pages
ISBN 9781607742678
Grades: Adult   641.594
1. Lebovitz, David 2. Cooking, French 3. Cooking 4. Bloggers 5. Recipes 6. Food habits 7. Social life and customs 8. Paris, France 9. France 10. Food writing — Cooking and cookbooks — Narrative cookbooks 11. Food writing — Food and Culture
LC 2013032561

A collection of stories and 100 sweet and savory French-inspired recipes from Chez Panisse pastry chef turned popular food blogger David Lebovitz, reflecting the way modern Parisians eat today and featuring lush photography taken around Paris and in David's Parisian kitchen. French cooking has come a long way since the days of Escoffier. The culinary culture of France has changed and the current generation of French cooks, most notably in Paris, are incorporating ingredients and techniques from around the world. In My Paris Kitchen, David Lebovitz remasters the French classics, introduces lesser known French fare, and presents 100 recipes using ingredients foraged in the ethnic neighborhoods of Paris. Stories told in David's trademark style describe thequirks, trials, and joys of cooking, shopping, and eating in France, while food and location photographs reveal modern life in Paris.

"French food personalized and demystified for the home cook in the best way." —*Publishers Weekly*

Includes bibliographical references and index.

Morales, Bonnie Frumkin
Kachka: A Return to Russian Cooking. Bonnie Frumkin Morales; with Deena Prichep; photography by Leela Cyd. Flatiron Books 2017. 389 pages
ISBN 9781250087607
Grades: Adult   641.594

ESSENTIAL AND RECOMMENDED TITLES
641.594 Cooking — Europe

1. Cooking, Russian 2. Recipes 3. Cookbooks 4. Food writing — Cooking and cookbooks — Chefs and restaurants

LC 2017022390

"This fantastic cookbook from the chef at Kachka in Portland, Ore, is by turns funny, moving, informative, and appetite-whetting." —*Publishers Weekly*

Includes index.

Nolen, Jeremy
New German Cooking: Recipes for Classics Revisited. Jeremy and Jessica Nolen with Drew Lazor; photographs by Jason Varney. Chronicle Books 2014. 235 pages : Color; Illustration

ISBN 9781452128061

Grades: Adult   641.594

1. Cooking, German 2. Recipes 3. Cookbooks 4. Food writing — Cooking and cookbooks — Regional

LC 2014000717

Shares recipes for familiar German classics that have been updated to reflect contemporary dining preferences, including such options as smoked pork and bacon sausage, mushroom and sauerkraut goulash, and apple strudel.

Includes bibliographical references (page 228) index.

Pepin, Jacques
Essential Pepin: More Than 700 All-Time Favorites from My Life in Food. Jacques Pepin. Houghton Mifflin Harcourt 2011. xv, 685 p. : Illustration

ISBN 9780547232799

Grades: Adult   641.594

1. Cooking, French 2. Cooking 3. Recipes 4. Cookbooks 5. Food writing — Cooking and cookbooks — Regional 6. Food writing — Cooking and cookbooks — Methods

LC 2011016057

Collects updated versions of the James Beard Award-winning celebrity chef's favorite recipes from his six-decade career, discussing the international flavors that inspired his cuisine while providing on an accompanying DVD demonstrations of a complete range of cooking techniques. First serial, Food & Wine. TV tie-in.

"Pepin offers more than 700 of his best French and French-accented dishes from decades of cooking and teaching. They're simple without being dumbed down; approachable yet still adventurous. Whether he's explaining how to make Escoffier quenelles with mushroom sauce; black sea bass gravlax; chicken livers sauted with vinegar; duck cassoulet; artichoke hearts with tarragon and mushrooms; or tarte tatin, he makes it seem doable and shares tidbits of wisdom to boost confidence and kitchen knowledge. His head notes are brief but informative, warm but not cloying. Pepin's own line drawings accompany the recipes, and they are, appropriately, at once homey and sophisticated. A DVD teaching a variety of cooking techniques accompanies the book, promising to make even the more challenging recipes less intimidating. For serious cooks and beginners alike, this is an instant classic." —*Publishers Weekly*

Includes index.

★ *Jacques Pepin: Heart & Soul in the Kitchen.* Photography by Tom Hopkins Studio. Houghton Mifflin Harcourt 2015. IX, 435 pages : Illustration; Color

ISBN 9780544301986

Grades: Adult   641.594

1. Cooking 2. Recipes 3. Cookbooks 4. Food writing — Cooking and cookbooks — Chefs and restaurants 5. Food writing — Cooking and cookbooks — Narrative cookbooks 6. Food writing — Cooking and cookbooks — Entertaining

LC Bl2015038122

Shares two hundred recipes from the chef's final PBS series that emphasize his close relationship to the land and sea, including herbed omelet with shrimp, baked rabbit with mustard crust, and caramelized pear custard.

"Readers can expect effortless, entertaining-worthy fare...along with humorous and informative anecdotes from Pepin's storied career...Highly recommended for fans of the chef and most public libraries." —*Library Journal*

A Rux Martin Book; Includes index.

Peppler, Rebekah
Le Sud: Recipes from Provence-Alpes-Côte D'Azur. Rebekah Peppler; photographs by Joann Pai. Chronicle Books 2024. 278 pages : Color; Illustration

ISBN 9781797219530

Grades: Adult   641.594

1. Cooking, French 2. Cooking 3. Provence, France 4. French Alps 5. French Riviera 6. Southern France 7. Cookbooks 8. Food writing — Cooking and cookbooks — Regional

LC 2023046483

For centuries, artists, vacationers, and food writers have fallen hard for the charms of the south of France. And like many regions where landscapes and people happily crash into each other, the food is dynamic and exciting. In Le Sud, Rebekah Peppler distillsthe flavors, techniques, and spirit of Provence, the Alps, and Côte d'Azur into a never-before-seen collection of recipes, photographs, and stories that give us a fresh new look at the region.

"This sparkling collection will delight foodies and armchair travelers alike." —*Publishers Weekly*

Includes index; Text in english.

Ray, Rachael
Everyone Is Italian on Sunday. Rachael Ray. Atria Books 2015. IX, 396 pages : Color; Illustration

ISBN 9781476766072

Grades: Adult   641.594

1. Cooking, Italian 2. Recipes 3. Cookbooks 4. Food writing — Cooking and cookbooks — Regional 5. Food writing — Cooking and cookbooks — Chefs and restaurants

LC 2014043645

Presents a comprehensive collection of Italian recipes from the celebrated television chef, with traditional and original versions of options for appetizers, soups, risotto, pasta, meats, vegetables, cocktails, and desserts.

"For those who are looking for a new angle, this cookbook satisfies in spades." —*Publishers Weekly*

Includes index.

Roberts, Julius
The Farm Table. Julius Roberts. Ten Speed Press 2024. 318 pages : Color; Illustration

ISBN 9781984862662

Grades: Adult   641.594

1. Cooking, English 2. Farm life 3. Seasonal cooking 4. Sustainable agriculture 5. Sustainable living 6. England 7. Food writing — Cooking and cookbooks — Regional 8. Food writing — Cooking and cookbooks — Methods

LC 2023024415

Motivated to leave restaurant life in London behind, chef Julius Roberts decided to live sustainably on a small English farm. The books takes readers through a year on the author's farm season by season, with tales of country living and unfussy recipes using simple ingredients.

"Readers will relish these unpretentious but flavorful offerings." —*Publishers Weekly*

Includes index.

Scarpaleggia, Giulia
★ *Cucina Povera: The Italian Way of Transforming Humble Ingredients into Unforgettable Meals.* Giulia Scarpaleggia; photographs by Tommaso Galli. Artisan 2023. 319 pages : Color; Illustration

ISBN 9781648290565

Grades: Adult   641.594

1. Cooking, Italian 2. Italy 3. Cookbooks 4. Food writing — Cooking and cookbooks — Regional

LC 2022027919

A writer, podcaster and cooking school instructor reveals the soul of Italian food and "making do with what you've got," in a collection of peasant recipes including Polenta with Butter and Cheese and Chicken Cacciatore.

PUBLIC LIBRARY CORE COLLECTION: NONFICTION
Twentieth Edition

"This book is an invaluable cultural guide and history lesson in the foundations of Italian cooking that enthusiasts will not want to miss." —*Booklist*

Includes index.

Thorisson, Mimi
A Kitchen in France: A Year of Cooking in My Farmhouse. Mimi Thorisson; photographs by Oddur Thorisson. Clarkson Potter/Publishers 2014. 304 pages : Color; Illustration
ISBN 9780804185592
Grades: Adult 641.594
1. Thorisson, Mimi 2. Cooking, French 3. Cooking 4. Seasonal cooking 5. Recipes 6. Seasons 7. Cookbooks 8. Food writing — Cooking and cookbooks — Regional
LC 2013049107

A French-cooking blogger describes and photographs her family's meals—made using local ingredients—at their farmhouse in Medoc, including almond gazpacho, quail grilled over grapevines, and apple tart with orange flower water.

"Francophiles and armchair travelers who loved Dorie Greenspan's Around My French Table and David Lebovitz's My Paris Kitchen will gladly add this classic title to their collections." —*Library Journal*

Includes index.

Weiss, Luisa
Classic German Baking: The Very Best Recipes for Traditional Favorites, from Pfeffernusse to Streuselkuchen. Luisa Weiss; photographs by Aubrie Pick. Ten Speed Press 2016. xi, 275 pages
ISBN 9781607748250
Grades: Adult 641.594
1. Cooking, German 2. Baking 3. Recipes 4. Cookbooks 5. Food writing — Cooking and cookbooks — Methods 6. Food writing — Cooking and cookbooks — Courses 7. Food writing — Cooking and cookbooks — Regional
LC 2016015734

Presents a collection of recipes for classic German desserts, including glazed apple cake, chocolate-hazelnut cookie bars, lemon cream roll, braided almond-cream wreath and carrot-nut torte.

"Collected from various places and people—whether it's a cookbook or from her German assistant—this cookbook presents a beautiful piece of German tradition." —*Publishers Weekly*

Includes index.

White, Marco Pierre
White Heat. Marco Pierre White; photographs by Bob Carlos Clarke; food photography by Michael Boys. Mitchell Beazley 2015. 191 pages : Illustration; Color
ISBN 9781784720001
Grades: Adult 641.594
1. White, Marco Pierre 2. Cooks 3. Restaurants 4. Cooking, English 5. Photographs 6. Cookbooks 7. Visual nonfiction 8. Food writing — Cooking and cookbooks — Chefs and restaurants 9. Food writing — Cooking and cookbooks — Regional
LC Bl2015035889

A twenty-fifth-anniversary edition of the influential cookbook includes classic recipes and behind-the-scenes photographs of the award-winning chef in his kitchen.

"When first published in 1990, White Heat gave ordinary cooks a glimpse inside the astonishingly creative mind of superstar London chef Marco Pierre White. One of the first British chefs to win worldwide recognition, White became famous as much for his intense focus and incendiary temperament as for the brilliance of his simple and novel pairings of foods in ways that both built on classic technique and were wildly revolutionary." —*Booklist*

Includes index; 25th anniversary edition.

641.59458 Cooking — Sicily (Italy)

Vicenzino, Cettina
The Sicily Cookbook: Authentic Recipes from a Mediterranean Island. Cettina Vicenzino. DK Publishing 2020. 239 p.
ISBN 9781465491107
Grades: Adult 641.59458
1. Cooking, Italian 2. Cooking, Mediterranean 3. Recipes 4. Cookbooks 5. Food writing — Cooking and cookbooks — Regional

"This volume easily succeeds as an inspiring introduction to the flavors of Sicily. . . . beautifully captures Sicily's traditions and quirks with stunning images and insightful text." —*Publishers Weekly*

641.595 Cooking — Asia

Admony, Einat
Shuk: From Market to Table, the Heart of Israeli Home Cooking. Einat Admony & Janna Gur; photographs by Quentin Bacon. Artisan 2019. 367 pages : Color; Illustration
ISBN 9781579656720
Grades: Adult 641.595
1. Cooking, Israeli 2. Cookbooks 3. Food writing — Cooking and cookbooks — Regional 4. Food writing — Cooking and cookbooks — Chefs and restaurants
LC 2019018638

Taking readers on a culinary journey through Israel where they are introduced to the fragrances and flavors of the mishmash of foods represented in its shuks or markets, this book presents 140 home-cook-friendly recipes for creating a multicultural table.

Includes index.

Alikhani, Nasim
Sofreh: A Contemporary Approach to Classic Persian Cuisine. Nasim Alikhani; with Theresa Gambacorta; photographs by Quentin Bacon. Alfred A. Knopf 2023. xli, 355 pages : Color; Illustration
ISBN 9780593320747
Grades: Adult 641.595
1. Cooking, Iranian 2. Iran 3. Cookbooks 4. Food writing — Cooking and cookbooks — Regional 5. Food writing — Cooking and cookbooks — Chefs and restaurants
LC 2022014632

In her first cookbook, the owner of Sofreh, one of Brooklyn's most acclaimed restaurants, offers readers the true tastes of Iran, presenting the timeless, soul-satisfying food of Persia through more than 120 flavorful recipes.

"Fans of the restaurant will enjoy learning about Alikhani's personal journey from home cook in Iran to restauranteur in New York City and will delight in bringing her philosophy home with her authentic recipes." —*Library Journal*

Includes index.

Assil, Reem
Arabiyya: Recipes from the Life of an Arab in Diaspora. Reem Assil with Emily Katz; foreword by Alicia Garza; photographs by Alanna Hale; illustrations by Cece Carpio. Ten Speed Press 2022. VII, 295 pages : Color; Illustration
ISBN 9781984859075
Grades: Adult 641.595
1. Cookbooks 2. Food Writing — Cooking and cookbooks — Regional 3. Food Writing — Cooking and cookbooks — Chefs and restaurants
LC Bl2022011766

A James Beard Award semifinalist and California bakery owner highlights the origins and evolution of her native Arabic food with inspired recipes for flatbreads, dips, snacks and platters including Hazelnut-Praline Baklava Rolls with Milk and Honey and Chile-Onion-Stuffed Falafel.

"Part memoir, part cultural primer, but mostly cookbook, Assil's work is a delicious take on cuisines and cultures of the Arab diaspora." —*Library Journal*

Includes index.

ESSENTIAL AND RECOMMENDED TITLES
641.595 Cooking — Asia

Ayubi, Durkhanai
Parwana: Recipes and Stories from an Afghan Kitchen. Durkhanai Ayubi; recipes by Farida Ayubi; with assistance from Fatema Ayubi. Interlink Books, an imprint of Interlink Publishing Group, Inc. 2021. 255 pages : Color; Illustration
ISBN 9781623718756
Grades: Adult   641.595
1. Cooking 2. Food Writing — Cooking and cookbooks — Regional 3. Food Writing — Cooking and cookbooks — Narrative cookbooks
LC 2020039574

Authentic Afghan recipes with family narratives and stunning photography. Parwana tells one family's story of a region long afflicted by war, but with much more at its heart. Author Durkhanai Ayubi's parents, Zelmai and Farida Ayubi, fled Afghanistan with their young family in 1987, at the height of the Cold War. When their family-run restaurant Parwana opened its doors in Adelaide, Australia in 2009, their vision was to share an authentic piece of the Afghanistan the family had left behind-a country rich in culture, family memories infused with Afghanistan's traditions of generosity and hospitality. These recipes have been in the family for generations and include rice dishes, curries, meats, dumplings, Afghan pastas, sweets, drinks, chutneys and pickles, soups and breads. Some are celebratory special dishes while most are day to day dishes. Each has a story to tell. With beautiful food and location photography, this compilation offers valuable insights into the origins and heritage of Afghan cuisine and a fresh perspective to one of the oldest civilizations.

"This is an homage to the strength and spirit of refugees, as well as a delicious reminder of what adventurous U.S. cooks can create." —*Booklist*
Includes index.

Berg, Meliz
Dinner Tonight: Simple Meals Full of Mediterranean Flavor. Meliz Berg. Interlink Books, an imprint of Interlink Publishing Group, Inc, 2024. 223 p.
ISBN 9781623716899
Grades: Adult   641.595
1. Cooking, Mediterranean 2. Quick and easy cooking 3. Food writing — Cooking and cookbooks — Regional 4. Food writing — Cooking and cookbooks — Methods

Meliz Berg shares her go-to home cooking—quick and nourishing meals, instant dinners that come together with pantry essentials, clever shortcuts, one-pot and sheet-pan winners, easy Friday "fake-out" ideas, and lazy weekend inspiration for beautiful food that takes care of itself in the oven—perfect for stress-free gatherings with family and friends.

Inspired by her Turkish-Cypriot heritage, a self-taught cook and recipe developer follows up her best-selling cookbook with a second collection of quick and nourishing meals including One-Pot Orzo, Leftover Hummus Soup, Cheater's Lahmacun Pide Pockets and Tavuk Kebab Curry.

"While it may be necessary to stock up on a few Turkish spices to see these recipes through, once they acquire them, readers will delight in turning quick and easy meal inspiration into dinner for friends and family." —*Booklist*
Includes index.

Cailan, Alvin
Amboy: Recipes from the Filipino-american Dream. Alivin Cailan with Alexandra Cuerdo and Susan Choung; photography by Wyatt Conlon. Houghton Mifflin Harcourt 2020. 352 p.
ISBN 9781328931733
Grades: Adult   641.595
1. Cailan, Alvin 2. Cooks 3. Filipino Americans 4. Cooking, Philippine 5. Food preparation 6. Recipes 7. Restaurants 8. Children of immigrants 9. Entrepreneurs 10. Southeast Asian Americans 11. Southeast Asian people 12. Food writing — Cooking and cookbooks — Narrative cookbooks 13. Food Writing — Food and Culture 14. Life stories — Arts and culture — Culinary arts
LC 2019045713

Alvin Cailan has risen to become arguably the most high-profile chef in America's Filipino food movement. He took the food scene by storm when he opened the now-legendary Eggslut in Los Angeles, as well as hosting the popular the Burger Show on First We Feast's YouTube channel. Alvin's story of success, however, is an unlikely one. He emerged from his youth spent as part of an immigrant family in East LA feeling like he wasn't Filipino enough to be Filipino and not American enough to be an American, thus amboy, the term for a Filipino raised in America. He had to first overcome cultural traditions and family expectations to find his own path to success, and this unique cookbook tells that story through his recipes.

"It's impossible not to engage with Cailan's energy and commentary: His persona virtually leaps off the page. Readers who enjoy personality-driven memoirs will discover something inimitable and poignant here, in both Cailan's story and his delicious food." —*Library Journal*
Includes index.

Cho, Kristina
Mooncakes + Milk Bread: Sweet & Savory Recipes Inspired by Chinese Bakeries. Kristina Cho. Harper Horizon 2021. xxix, 274 pages : Color; Illustration
ISBN 9780785238997
Grades: Adult   641.595
1. Cooking, Chinese 2. Baking 3. Desserts 4. Cookies 5. Food Writing — Cooking and cookbooks — Regional 6. Food Writing — Cooking and cookbooks — Methods
LC Bl2021025527

A popular food blogger, focusing exclusively on Chinese bakeries and cafes, presents simple, easy-to-make interpretations of classic recipes for the modern baker, including sweet and savory baked buns, steamed buns, Chinese breads, unique cookies, juicy dumplings and more.

"In this delightful debut, Cho presents dozens of sweet and savory treats inspired by Chinese-American bakeshops. . . . This is a terrific introduction to a seldom explored baking niche." —*Publishers Weekly*
Includes index.

Chou, Hsiao-Ching
Chinese Soul Food: A Friendly Guide for Homemade Dumplings, Stir-Fries, Soups, and More. Hsiao-Ching Chou; photography by Clare Barboza. Sasquatch Books 2018. 256 pages : Color; Illustration
ISBN 9781632171238
Grades: Adult   641.595
1. Cooking, Chinese 2. Cookbooks 3. Food writing — Cooking and cookbooks — Regional
LC 2017041434

Presents eighty recipes for Chinese soul food that any home cook can make, including such dishes as pork and Chinese cabbage dumplings, vegetable fried rice with curry, wonton soup, red-braised beef shank, and pork spare ribs.

Showing that any kitchen can be a Chinese kitchen, an award-winning food journalist and cooking instructor presents 80 recipes for Chinese soul food that any home cook can make—including Dry-fried Green Beans, Lion's Head Meatballs, and Fragrant Crispy Duck Breast—in a book that includes a list of essential kitchen utensils and discusses the intricacies of soy sauce.

"This is a fun guide to creating favorite restaurant recipes at home." —*Publishers Weekly*
Includes bibliographical references and index.

Dunlop, Fuchsia
The Food of Sichuan. Fuchsia Dunlop; photography by Yuki Sugiura with additional location photography by Ian Cumming. W. W. Norton & Company 2019. 495 p.
ISBN 9781324004837
Grades: Adult   641.595
1. Cooking, Chinese 2. Cookbooks 3. Food writing — Cooking and cookbooks — Regional
LC 2019020111

Twenty years after the publication of her groundbreaking cookbook, Land of Plenty, the author returns to Sichuan and adds over 70 new, regional recipes for home cooks, including Mapo Tofu, Twice- Cooked Pork and Gong Bao Chicken.

This revised and updated edition first published in 2019 by Bloomsbury Publishing; Includes bibliographical references and index; First published in the UK in 2001 by Michael Joseph as Sichuan Cookery and in the US in 2003 by W. W. Norton & Company as Land of Plenty.

PUBLIC LIBRARY CORE COLLECTION: NONFICTION
Twentieth Edition

Eckhardt, Robyn
Istanbul & *Beyond: Exploring the Diverse Cuisines of Turkey*. Robyn Eckhardt; photographs by David Hagerman. Houghton Mifflin Harcourt 2017. 352 pages : Color; Illustration
ISBN 9780544444317
Grades: Adult   641.595
1. Cooking, Turkish 2. Cookbooks 3. Food writing — Cooking and cookbooks — Regional

LC 2017016108

The most extensive and lushly photographed Turkish cookbook to date, by two internationally acclaimed experts standing at the crossroads between the Mediterranean, the Middle East, and Asia, Turkey boasts astonishingly rich and diverse culinary traditions. Journalist Robyn Eckhardt and her husband, photographer David Hagerman, have spent almost twenty years discovering the country's very best dishes. Now they take readers on an unforgettable epicurean adventure, beginning in Istanbul, home to one of the world's great fusion cuisines. From there, they journey to the lesser-known provinces, opening a vivid world of flavors influenced by neighboring Syria, Iran, Iraq, Armenia, and Georgia.From village home cooks, community bakers, cafe chefs, farmers, and fishermen, they have assembled a broad, one-of-a-kind collection of authentic, easy-to-follow recipes: "The Imam Fainted" Stuffed Eggplant; Pillowy Fingerprint Flatbread; Pot-Roasted Chicken with Caramelized Onions; Stovetop Lamb Meatballs with Spice Butter; Artichoke Ragout with Peas and Favas; Green Olive Salad with Pomegranate Molasses; Apple and Raisin Hand Pies. Many of these have never before been published in English.

"This collection will delight and inspire home cooks who are unfamiliar with the regions food but are looking to broaden their culinary horizons." —*Publishers Weekly*

A Rux Martin book; Includes bibliographical references (page 343).

Gaw, Frankie
First Generation: Recipes from My Taiwanese-American Home. Frankie Gaw. Ten Speed Press 2022. 211 pages : Color; Illustration
ISBN 9781984860767
Grades: Adult   641.595
1. Cooking, Chinese 2. Taiwanese Americans 3. Taiwan 4. Cookbooks 5. Food writing — Cooking and cookbooks — Regional

LC 2022015031

The debut cookbook from the blogger behind Little Fat Boy offers 80 recipes reminiscent of his first-generation Taiwanese American childhood in the Midwest including LAP Cheong Corn Dogs, Honey-Mustard Glazed Taiwanese Popcorn Chicken and Stir-Fried Rice Cakes with Bolognese.

"Easy-to-follow recipes and the nostalgic stories behind them are sure to please enthusiastic cooks." —*Library Journal*
Includes index.

Hage, Salma
★ *The* **Levantine** *Vegetarian: Recipes from the Middle East*. Salma Hage. Phaidon (ADS) 2024. 272 pages : Illustration
ISBN 9781838667641
Grades: Adult   641.595
1. Cooking, Southwest Asian and North African 2. Vegetarian cooking 3. Cookbooks 4. Food writing — Cooking and cookbooks — Vegetarian and vegan 5. Food writing — Cooking and cookbooks — Regional

This glorious celebration of a bold vegetarian cuisine features 140 easy-to-make, bright, uplifting plant-based recipes, including classics such as falafels, hummus, and tabbouleh, as well as unique dishes reflective of region, religion, and culture across the Levantine. The food is fresh and delicious, whether its garlic-laced mezze dishes, pittas stuffed with pickles, tahini, and grilled vegetables, or sweet and spicy desserts. Covering a vast area straddling Africa, Asia, and the gateway to Europe, the book embraces the culinary traditions of all corners of the Cradle of Civilization.

"Hage extols the vegetarian bounty of the Levant in this appealing collection…Home cooks will treasure this." —*Publishers Weekly*

Helou, Anissa
Feast: Food of the Islamic World. Anissa Helou. ECCO 2018. 529 pages : Color; Illustration
ISBN 9780062363039
Grades: Adult   641.595
1. Cooking 2. Cooking, Southwest Asian and North African 3. Cooking, North African 4. Cooking, Indic 5. Recipes 6. Cookbooks 7. Food writing — Cooking and cookbooks — Regional

LC Bl2018190099

A collection of recipes from North Africa, the Mediterranean, and the Middle East.

"Renowned chef Helou takes readers on a culinary tour of the Muslim world, showcasing more than 300 recipes from the Middle East, Africa, and Indonesia, while exploring the history and tradition of Islamic cuisine." —*Library Journal*
Includes index.

Hong, Deuki
Koreatown: A Cookbook. Deuki Hong & Matt Rodbard; photographs by Sam Horine. Clarkson Potter/Publishers 2016. 272 pages : Color; Illustration
ISBN 9780804186131
Grades: Adult   641.595
1. Cooking, Korean 2. Recipes 3. Cookbooks 4. Food writing — Cooking and cookbooks — Regional

LC 2015009587

Collects recipes, stories, interviews, and photographs from Korean American neighborhoods across the country, to create a portrait of a culture and community through dishes that range from mixed rice bowls, spicy seafood noodle soup, and sweet soy-braised chicken.

Iyer, Raghavan
Indian Cooking Unfolded: A Master Class in Indian Cooking, with 100 Easy Recipes Using 10 Ingredients or Less. Raghavan Iyer; photography by TK.. Workman Publishing 2013. 330 pages : Color; Illustration
ISBN 9780761165217
Grades: Adult   641.595
1. Cooking, Indic 2. Recipes 3. Cookbooks 4. Food writing — Cooking and cookbooks — Regional 5. Food writing — Cooking and cookbooks — Methods 6. Food writing — Cooking and cookbooks — Courses

LC 2013004247

Reveals how to create one hundred of Indian cuisine's most popular dishes and is complemented by step-by-step photo gatefolds.

Jaffrey, Madhur
★ *Madhur Jaffrey's Instantly Indian Cookbook*. Madhur Jaffrey; photographs by Dana Gallagher. Alfred A. Knopf 2019. xiii, 170 pages : Color; Illustration
ISBN 9780525655794
Grades: Adult   641.595
1. Cooking, Indic 2. Pressure cooking 3. Recipes 4. Cookbooks 5. Food writing — Cooking and cookbooks — Methods 6. Food writing — Cooking and cookbooks — Regional

LC 2018040124

The James Beard Award-winning cookbook author presents new and classic Indian recipes that can be made using an Instant Pot, including South Indian mixed-vegetable korma, simple mung dal, butter chicken, Kerala lamb stew, and pork kabobs.

This is a Borzoi Book published by Alfred A. Knopf; Includes index.

Vegetarian India: A Journey Through the Best of Indian Home Cooking. Madhur Jaffrey. Alfred A. Knopf 2015. xxii, 416 pages : Illustration
ISBN 9781101874868
Grades: Adult   641.595
1. Cooking, Indic 2. Vegetarian cooking 3. Recipes 4. Cookbooks 5. Food writing — Cooking and cookbooks — Regional 6. Food writing — Cooking and cookbooks — Vegetarian and vegan

LC 2014048953

ESSENTIAL AND RECOMMENDED TITLES
641.595 Cooking — Asia

Presents a collection of Indian vegetarian recipes from the award-winning chef, with options for soups, dals, grains, eggs and dairy, chutneys, and desserts, and a separate section on ingredients.

"Jaffrey's fresh compilation features extraordinary variety and achieves approachability without oversimplification. Highly recommended for vegetarians and Indian food enthusiasts." —*Library Journal*

Includes index.

Joo, Judy
Korean Food Made Simple. Judy Joo; with Vivian Jao; Photography by Jean Cazals. Houghton Mifflin Harcourt 2016. 286 pages
ISBN 9780544663305
Grades: Adult   641.595
1. Cooking, Korean 2. Cookbooks 3. Food writing — Cooking and cookbooks — Regional
LC 2015049784

125 simple Korean recipes from the host of the Cooking Channel television show of the same name in Korean Food Made Simple, Judy Joo, host of the Cooking Channel's show of the same name and Food Network regular, brings Korean food to the masses, proving that it's fun and easy to prepare at home. As a Korean-American, Judy understands how to make dishes that may seem exotic and difficult accessible to the everyday cook. The book has over 100 recipes including well-loved dishes like kimchi, sweet potatonoodles (japchae), beef and vegetable rice bowl (bibimbap), and Korean fried chicken, along with creative, less-traditional recipes like Spicy Pork Belly Cheese Steak, Krazy Korean Burgers, and Fried Fish with Kimchi Mayo and Sesame Mushy Peas. In addition, there are chapters devoted to sauces, desserts, and drinks as well as a detailed list for stocking a Korean pantry, making this book a comprehensive guide on Korean food and flavors. Enjoying the spotlight as the hot Asian cuisine, Korean food is on the rise, and Judy's bold and exciting recipes are go-tos for making it at home.

"Cooks looking to make a first foray into Korean cooking or those wishing to enhance their knowledge will delight in Joos uncommon approach and her tasty creations." —*Publishers Weekly*

Kahate, Ruta
6 Spices 60 Dishes: Indian Recipes That Are Simple, Fresh, and Big on Taste. Ruta Kahate; photographs by Ghazalle Badiozamani. Chronicle Books 2023. 160 pages : Color; Illustration
ISBN 9781797216201
Grades: Adult   641.595
1. Cooking, Indic 2. Vegetarian cooking 3. Spices 4. Food writing — Cooking and cookbooks — Regional 5. Food writing — Cooking and cookbooks — Ingredients
LC 2022019426

60 delicious Indian recipes that use just 6 common spices."

"This largely vegetarian collection (with the exception of a few fish curries and meat-based stews) will find approval from the plant-based to the carnivorous." —*Booklist*

Includes index.

Kang, Mingoo
Jang: The Soul of Korean Cooking. Mingoo Kang with Joshua David Stein and Nadia Cho. Artisan, a division of Workman Publishing Co, Inc. 2024. 215 p.
ISBN 9781648291869
Grades: Adult   641.595
1. Cooking, Korean 2. Sauces 3. Chile peppers 4. Peppers 5. Fermented foods 6. Korea 7. Cookbooks 8. Food writing — Cooking and cookbooks — Regional 9. Food writing — Cooking and cookbooks — Chefs and restaurants
LC 2023033565

Showing readers how to cook with Jangs—umami sauces found in every meal—and one of the culinary world's best-hidden secrets, South Korea's best chef, in his first cookbook, weaves Jangs' history and methods into 60 accessible recipes to bring the sauces to life.

"Thanks to the ready availability of gochujang and such in grocery stores and on the internet, U.S. cooks can recreate this astonishing and delightful cuisine in their home kitchens. Color photographs make Kang's innovative cooking vividly attractive." —*Booklist*

Includes index; More than 60 recipes features gochujang, doenjang, and ganjang—cover.

Khan, Asma
Ammu: Indian Home-Cooking to Nourish Your Soul. Asma Khan of Darjeeling express. Interlink Books, an imprint of Interlink Publishing Group, Inc. 2022. 287 pages : Illustration; Color
ISBN 9781623718411
Grades: Adult   641.595
1. Cooking, Indic 2. Cookbooks 3. Food Writing — Cooking and cookbooks — Regional
LC 2021062644

Ammu is a collection of recipes from Asma Khan's childhood, from her Indian family kitchen. It is a celebration of where she comes from, of home cooking, and the inextricable link between food and love. It is also a chance for Asma to honor her ammu—mother—and to share with us the recipes that made her and rooted her to home. This book is a joyful celebration of memories of food, and its power to heal, restore, and comfort. It includes her ammu's comfort food from childhood, the recipes with which she was taught to cook, celebratory food for special occasions, and slow-cooked recipes passed through the generations of her family.

"Showing readers the connection between food and love, this book is highly recommended for families that cook together and beginner chefs seeking to recreate their own joys of enjoying food with family." —*Booklist*

Includes index.

Khan, Yasmin
Ripe Figs: Recipes and Stories from Turkey, Greece, and Cyprus. Yasmin Khan. W. W. Norton & Company 2021. 304 p.
ISBN 9781324006657
Grades: Adult   641.595
1. Cooking, Southwest Asian and North African 2. Immigration and emigration 3. Boundaries 4. Identity 5. Refugees 6. Cookbooks 7. Essays 8. Food Writing — Cooking and cookbooks — Narrative cookbooks 9. Food Writing — Food and culture 10. Travel Writing — Southwest Asia and North Africa (Middle East)
LC 2021004696

For thousands of years, the eastern Mediterranean has stood as a meeting point between East and West, bringing cultures and cuisines through trade, commerce, and migration. Traveling by boat and land, Yasmin Khan traces the ingredients that have spread through the region from the time of Ottoman rule to the influence of recent refugee communities.At the kitchen table, she explores what borders, identity, and migration mean in an interconnected world, and her recipes unite around thickets of dill and bunches of oregano, zesty citrus and sweet dates, thick tahini and soothing cardamom.

"Another must-have collection from Khan that will transport home cooks to the region and warmly guide them along as they recreate her comforting meals." —*Library Journal*

Includes index.

★ Zaitoun: Recipes from the Palestinian Kitchen.
Yasmin Khan; recipe photography by Matt Russell; travel photography by Raya Manaa'and Hosam Salem. W. W. Norton & Co. 2019. 256 p. : Illustration
ISBN 9781324002628
Grades: Adult   641.595
1. Cooking, Southwest Asian and North African 2. Recipes 3. Culture 4. Food habits 5. Social life and customs 6. Southwest Asia and North Africa (Middle East) 7. Palestine 8. Cookbooks 9. Food writing — Food and culture 10. Food writing — Cooking and cookbooks
LC 2018050132

A dazzling celebration of Palestinian cuisine, featuring more than 80 modern recipes, captivating stories, and stunning travel photography.

Includes index.

PUBLIC LIBRARY CORE COLLECTION: NONFICTION
Twentieth Edition

Kim, Bill
Korean BBQ: *Master Your Grill in Seven Sauces.* Bill Kim with Chandra Ram; photograps by Johnny Autry. Ten Speed Press 2018. 232 pages : Color; Illustration
ISBN 9780399580789
Grades: Adult   641.595
 1. Cooking, Korean 2. Barbecuing 3. Outdoor cooking 4. Cookbooks 5. Food writing — Cooking and cookbooks — Methods 6. Food writing — Cooking and cookbooks — Ingredients 7. Food writing — Cooking and cookbooks — Regional
LC 2017040334

Offers recipes from the chef that combine flavors and sauces from Korea and grilling, along with suitable substitutions for hard-to-find ingredients, including such dishes as spicy grilled crabs, lemongrass chicken, and kimchi potato salad.

"Although some of the recipes may seem daunting, Kim provides even the most basic cook with a guide to understanding their way around a grill." —*Library Journal*
 Includes index.

Kim, Eric
★ *Korean American: Food That Tastes Like Home.* Eric Kim; photographs by Jenny Huang. Clarkson Potter/Publishers 2022. 286 pages : Color; Illustration
ISBN 9780593233498
Grades: Adult   641.595
 1. Cooking, Korean 2. Cookbooks 3. Food Writing — Cooking and cookbooks — Regional
LC 2021031286

Showing how new culinary traditions can be forged to honor both your past and present, a New York Times staff writer, in his debut cookbook, shares his favorite recipes, along with personal essays and the history of Korean cooking in America.

"Drawing heavily from his Atlanta family's culinary heritage, New York Times food writer Kim maps out the intersection of Korean and American fare in this bold and delicious debut…Old traditions lead to delicious new flavor combinations in this heartfelt collection." —*Publishers Weekly*
 Includes index.

Kim, Hooni
My Korea: Traditional Flavors, Modern Recipes. Hooni Kim with Aki Kamozawa, photography by Kristin Teig. W. W. Norton & Company 2020. 272 p.
ISBN 9780393239720
Grades: Adult   641.595
 1. Cooking, Korean 2. Cooking, American 3. Recipes 4. Cookbooks 5. Food writing — Cooking and cookbooks — Regional 6. Food writing — Cooking and cookbooks — Chefs and restaurants
LC 2019057930

The long-awaited debut cookbook from the Michelin-star chef known for defining Korean food in America. Hooni Kim is a chef who cooks with jung sung, heart and devotion. My Korea embraces his gastronomic heritage. From simple rice cakes drenched in a spicy sauce to a 12-Hour Korean Ramyeon (ramen), Hooni uses his background in world-class French and Japanese kitch-ens to fine-tune techniques in classic Korean cuisine, which often originated in home kitchens. Readers will discover the Korean culinary trinity: gochujang, doenjang, and ganjang (Korean chili pepper paste, fermented soybean paste, and soy sauce). These key ingredients add a savory depth and flavor to the entire spectrum of Korean cuisine, from banchan to robust stews. Enhanced with gorgeous photography that highlights food creation and enjoyment across Korea today, My Korea brings a powerful culinary legacy into your kitchen.

"This thoughtful, comprehensive, and inventive volume sets a high bar for Korean cookbooks." —*Publishers Weekly*
 Includes index.

King, Niloufer Ichaporia
My Bombay Kitchen: Traditional and Modern Parsi Home Cooking. Niloufer Ichaporia King; foreword by Alice Waters. University of California Press 2007. xvi, 338 p. : Illustration; Map
ISBN 9780520249608
Grades: Adult   641.595
 1. Cooking, Indic 2. Cooking 3. Food writing — Cooking and cookbooks — Narrative cookbooks

A detailed guide to the culinary traditions of the Parsi population of India features 165 tempting recipes that capture one of India's most colorful regional cuisines and offers a personal overview of the ideas, tastes, ingredients, and cooking techniques of Parsi cuisine.

"She begins with a brief history of the Parsis and an introduction to her grandmother's and mother's kitchens and then presents more than 150 recipes, both sophisticated and homey, many of which will be unfamiliar even to most Indian-food lovers. The headnotes are informative and entertaining, and the book concludes with a selection of menus, a detailed glossary, a source guide, and a bibliography." —*Library Journal*
 Includes bibliographical references (p. 317-322) and index.

Krishna, Priya
★ *Indian-ish: Recipes and Antics from a Modern American Family.* Priya Krishna with Ritu Krishna; photography by Mackenzie Kelly; illustrations by Maria Qamar; foreword by Padma Lakshmi. Houghton Mifflin Harcourt 2019. IX, 241 pages : Illustration; Color
ISBN 9781328482471
Grades: Adult   641.595
 1. Cooking, Indic 2. Cooking, American 3. Recipes 4. Cookbooks 5. Food writing — Cooking and cookbooks — Regional
LC 2018043605

Collects recipes for the home cook that merge Indian and American cuisine, including such dishes as tomato-cheese masala toast, roti noodle stir-fry, herby avocado sandwich, and garlic-ginger chicken with cilantro and mint.

"Krishna's newest offering will delight cooks seeking to expand their palate and knowledge of Indian cuisine. With easy-to-follow recipes, the "Indian-ish" additions to many American homestyle favorites will appeal to even the pickiest eaters." —*Library Journal*
 Includes index.

Lee Molinaro, Joanne
★ *The Korean Vegan Cookbook: Reflections and Recipes from Omma's Kitchen.* Joanne Lee Molinaro. Avery, an imprint of Penguin Random House 2021. 335 pages : Color; Illustration
ISBN 9780593084274
Grades: Adult   641.595
 1. Cooking, Korean 2. Vegan cooking 3. Cookbooks 4. Food Writing — Cooking and cookbooks — Regional 5. Food Writing — Cooking and cookbooks — Vegetarian and vegan
LC 2020057487

The home cook and storyteller behind @thekoreanvegan on TikTok, in her debut cookbook, shares recipes and narrative snapshots of the food that shaped her family history.

"This tasty tribute is full of heart and flavor." —*Publishers Weekly*
 Includes index.

Lee, Lara
A Splash of Soy: Everyday Food from Asia. Lara Lee; photography by Louise Hagger. Bloomsbury Publishing 2023. 254 pages : Color; Illustration
ISBN 9781639730438
Grades: Adult   641.595
 1. Cooking, Asian 2. Quick and easy cooking 3. Cookbooks 4. Food writing — Cooking and cookbooks — Regional 5. Food writing — Cooking and cookbooks — Methods
LC Bl2023020905

Named after the simplicity and usefulness of soy, Lara Lee's new cookbook introduces 80 game-changing recipes that close the gap between classic Asian

ESSENTIAL AND RECOMMENDED TITLES
641.595 Cooking — Asia

dishes and quick-to-table family meals. There are recipes that only require a little chopping and a boiled kettle, as well as 15, 30, and 45 minute meals fit for weeknight dinners or no-fuss dinner parties."

"A fun, colorful option for those who love experimenting with bold flavors." —*Booklist*

Includes indexes; Orginally published : Great Britain : Bloomsbury Publishing, 2023.

Lopez-Alt, J. Kenji
★ *The Wok: Recipes and Techniques*. J. Kenji López-Alt. W.W. Norton & Company 2022. 658 pages : Color; Illustration
ISBN 9780393541212
Grades: Adult   641.595
1. Cooking, Chinese 2. Cooking 3. Cookbooks 4. Food Writing — Cooking and cookbooks — Methods
LC 2021052502

Presenting over 200 recipes, along with more than 1,000 color photos, the author of The Food Lab focuses on the wok, the most versatile pan in the kitchen, showing home cooks how to master the mechanics of a stir-fry and providing endless inspiration for brightening up dinner.

"Lopez-Alt's latest is an essential addition to any cookbook collection, providing both insights and inspiration for cooking." —*Library Journal*

Includes bibliographical references (pages 625-627) and index.

Maangchi
Maangchi's Real Korean Cooking: Authentic Dishes for the Home Cook. Maangchi with Lauren Chattman; photographs by Maangchi. Houghton Mifflin Harcourt 2015. 310 pages; Illustration; Color
ISBN 9780544129894
Grades: Adult   641.595
1. Cooking, Korean 2. Cookbooks 3. Food writing — Cooking and cookbooks — Regional
LC 2015004571

Offers a complete Korean cuisine cooking course for home chefs, with step-by-step, illustrated recipes for a variety of the country's best dishes, including bulgogi, Korean fried chicken, spicy beef and vegetable soup, and seafood-scallion pancake.

"Like Robert Danhi's Easy Thai Cooking and Bee Yin Low's Easy Chinese Recipes, this encouraging and instructional cookbook demystifies Asian home cooking. First-timers to Korean restaurants and grocery stores will be grateful for Maangchi's introductory chapters." —*Library Journal*

Includes bibiliographical references (page 301) and index.

Massih, Edy
★ *Keep It Zesty: A Celebration of Lebanese Flavors & Culture from Edy's Grocer*. Edy Massih. Harper, an imprint of HarperCollinsPublishers 2024. 244 pages : Color; Illustration
ISBN 9780063280908
Grades: Adult   641.595
1. Cooking, Lebanese 2. Grocers 3. Cookbooks 4. Food writing — Cooking and cookbooks — Regional 5. Food writing — Cooking and cookbooks — Chefs and restaurants
LC Bl2024009850

With personal anecdotes, stunning photos of food and lovingly preserved family pictures, the beloved chef and owner of Edy's Grocer shares 115+ recipes for traditional Lebanese fare with a modern twist—and that are dedicated to the women in his life who shaped Edy along the way.

"Written with a wonderful sense of humor and a great deal of heart, this cookbook debut is a first-rate introduction to the vibrant and appetizing world of Lebanese cuisine." —*Library Journal*

Includes index.

Meehan, Peter
Lucky Peach Presents 101 Easy Asian Recipes. Peter Meehan and the editors of Lucky Peach; photographs by Gabriele Stabile. Clarkson Potter/Publishers 2015. 271 pages : Color; Illustration

ISBN 9780804187794
Grades: Adult   641.595
1. Cooking, Asian 2. Quick and easy cooking 3. Recipes 4. Cookbooks 5. Food writing — Cooking and cookbooks — Regional 6. Food writing — Cooking and cookbooks — Methods
LC 2015015729

A collection of simple recipes for favorite Asian dishes from the popular indie food magazine, including dumplings, rice, soups, noodles, meat dishes, sauces, and desserts.

"Readers will also appreciate the surprising lack of prep for many dishes; few require chopping and dicing multitudes of vegetables or sourcing ingredients that are difficult to find in the U.S. This is an outstanding, practical guide sure to inspire even the most discouraged home cook." —*Publishers Weekly*

Includes index.

Morimoto, Masaharu
Mastering the Art of Japanese Home Cooking. Masaharu Morimoto. Ecco 2016. VII, 275 pages : Color; Illustration
ISBN 9780062344380
Grades: Adult   641.595
1. Cooking, Japanese 2. Cookbooks 3. Food writing — Cooking and cookbooks — Regional 4. Food writing — Cooking and cookbooks — Methods
LC Bl2016048973

A collection of traditional Japanese recipes for the home cook from the legendary chef and restaurateur features such dishes as miso soup, pork and cabbage dumplings, salt-grilled salmon, and chicken teriyaki.

"Soups, stir-fry, and noodles each have their own chapter and a section on the underappreciated art of simmering features fish simmered with sake, soy sauce, and sugar, as well as slow-cooked pork belly with beer-teriyaki glaze. The 177 color photos range from utilitarian instruction on flipping a Japanese omelet to an artistic interpretation of rice grains clustered in the hand of the chef." —*Publishers Weekly*

Includes index.

Nguyen, Andrea Quynhgiao
Ever-Green Vietnamese: Super-Fresh Recipes, Starring Plants from Land and Sea. Andrea Quynhgiao Nguyen; photographs by Aubrie Pick. Ten Speed Press 2023. 293 pages : Color; Illustration
ISBN 9781984859853
Grades: Adult   641.595
1. Cooking, Vietnamese 2. Vegetarian cooking 3. Cooking (Vegetables) 4. Natural foods 5. Cookbooks 6. Food writing — Cooking and cookbooks — Regional 7. Food writing — Cooking and cookbooks — Vegetarian and vegan
LC 2022015150

The award-winning author of six acclaimed books showcases how cooks in her home country of Vietnam use natural resourcefulness and Buddhist traditions to make Smoky Tofu-Nori Wontons, Steamed Veggie Bao, Fast Vegetarian Pho and Banh MI with Mayonnaise and Bologna.

"Detailed instructions and tantalizing recipes make this an excellent book for those wanting to incorporate plant-based options in Vietnamese cooking." —*Library Journal*

Includes index.

The Pho Cookbook: Easy to Adventurous Recipes for Vietnam's Favorite Soup and Noodles. Andrea Quynhgiao Nguyen. Ten Speed Press 2017. 160 pages : Color; Illustration
ISBN 9781607749585
Grades: Adult   641.595
1. Cooking, Vietnamese 2. Cookbooks 3. Food writing — Cooking and cookbooks — Courses 4. Food writing — Cooking and cookbooks — Regional
LC 2016022687

Looks at the Vietnamese dish's roots with information on ingredients and techniques and offers instructions for making different versions of the noodle soup and recipes for snacks, salads, companion dishes, and vegetarian and gluten-free options.

Includes bibliographical references and index.

PUBLIC LIBRARY CORE COLLECTION: NONFICTION
Twentieth Edition

★ ***Vietnamese*** *Food Any Day: Simple Recipes for True, Fresh Flavors.* Andrea Nguyen; photographs by Aubrie Pick. Ten Speed Press 2019. 233 pages : Illustration; Color

ISBN 9780399580352

Grades: Adult   **641.595**

1. Cooking, Vietnamese 2. Recipes 3. Quick and easy cooking 4. Cookbooks 5. Food writing — Cooking and cookbooks — Regional 6. Food writing — Cooking and cookbooks — Methods

LC 2018017922

Collects accessible, easy recipes for Vietnamese food, including such options as honey-glazed pork riblets, curry-scented grilled beef lettuce wraps, turmeric coconut rice, crispy lemongrass salmon, and orange-rum flan.

A collection of 80 accessible, easy recipes for fresh Vietnamese food includes such options as Honey-Glazed Pork Riblets, Chile Garlic Chicken Wings and No-churn Vietnamese Coffee Ice Cream. By the author of the Pho Cookbook.

"The first chapter is extremely useful in its offering of several sauces essential to Vietnamese dishes, such as Caramel sauce and Nuoc Cham. In many of the recipes, Nguyen gives notes on substitutions to make them vegetarian friendly. Beautiful photographs are a bonus." —*Library Journal*

Includes index.

Orkin, Ivan

*The **Gaijin** Cookbook: Japanese Recipes from a Chef, Father, Eater, and Lifelong Outsider.* Ivan Orkin and Chris Ying; photographs by Aubrie Pick. Houghton Mifflin Harcourt 2019. 256 pages : Color; Illustration

ISBN 9781328954350

Grades: Adult   **641.595**

1. Cooking, Japanese 2. Recipes 3. Cookbooks 4. Food writing — Cooking and cookbooks — Regional 5. Food writing — Cooking and cookbooks — Chefs and restaurants

LC 2019002730

"This passionate, welcoming volume serves as an excellent guide to Japanese home cooking." —*Publishers Weekly*

Includes index.

Pang, Kevin

*A **Very** Chinese Cookbook: 100 Recipes from China & Not China (but Still Really Chinese).* with Kevin Pang & Jeffrey Pang. America's Test Kitchen 2023. xi, 372 pages : Illustration; Color

ISBN 9781954210479

Grades: Adult   **641.595**

1. Cooking, Chinese 2. Cookbooks

LC Bl2023173229

The father and son behind America's Test Kitchen's Hunger Pangs present 100 fully-tested, foolproof recipes that celebrate Chinese cooking including Scallion Oil Noodles, Clay Pot Chicken Rice, Stir-Fried Beef with Gai Lan and Red-Braised Pork Belly.

Includes index.

Patel, Palak

Food *Is Love: Plant-Based Indian-Inspired Recipes to Feel Joy and Connection.* Palak Patel. Harvest, an imprint of William Morrow 2024. xxx, 245 pages : Color; Illustration

ISBN 9780063320642

Grades: Adult   **641.595**

1. Cooking, Indic 2. Vegetarian cooking 3. Vegan cooking 4. Cookbooks 5. Food writing — Cooking and cookbooks — Vegetarian and vegan 6. Food writing — Cooking and cookbooks — Regional

LC Bl2024012389

A Food Network veteran and acclaimed Indian vegan chef presents recipes designed to evoke specific feelings, from joy and comfort to nostalgia and love, reminding us that food is more than just sustenance, it's also a way to connect with our loved ones, express love for ourselves and others and celebrate life.

"Recipes are fairly simple to prepare and prepped for family-sized portions, giving plant-based eaters a great collection to peruse for weeknight meals." —*Booklist*

Includes index.

Ponseca, Nicole

***I** Am a Filipino and This Is How We Cook.* Nicole Ponseca & Miguel Trinidad with Rachel Wharton; foreword by Jose Antonio Vargas; photographs by Justin Walker. Artisan 2018. 352 p. : Color; Illustration

ISBN 9781579657673

Grades: Adult   **641.595**

1. Cooking, Philippine 2. Recipes 3. Cookbooks 4. Food writing — Cooking and cookbooks — Regional 5. Food writing — Cooking and cookbooks — Chefs and restaurants

LC 2018014210

Two trailblazing restaurateurs present a modern cookbook filled with a vast array of Filipino recipes that capture the unexpected and addictive flavors of this vibrant and diverse cuisine.

Includes index.

Raines, Abigail Sotto

Rice. *Noodles. Yum.: Everyone's Favorite Southeast Asian Dishes.* Abigail Sotto Raines. Page Street Publishing Co. 2019. 191 pages : Color; Illustration

ISBN 9781624147715

Grades: Adult   **641.595**

1. Cooking, Asian 2. Cooking, Southeast Asian 3. Recipes 4. Cookbooks 5. Food writing — Cooking and cookbooks — Regional

LC 2018957262

"This is an outstanding assembly of dishes, and a book sure to get plenty of use." —*Publishers Weekly*

Includes index.

Sahadi Whelan, Christine

Flavors *of the Sun: The Sahadi's Guide to Understanding, Buying, and Using Middle Eastern Ingredients.* Christine Sahadi Whelan; photographs by Kristin Teig. Chronicle Books 2021. 350 pages : Illustration; Color

ISBN 9781452182452

Grades: Adult   **641.595**

1. Cooking, Southwest Asian and North African 2. Food Writing — Cooking and cookbooks — Regional 3. Food Writing — Cooking and cookbooks — Ingredients

LC 2021011463

Flavors of the Sun is both a deep dive into the diverse array of ingredients from the Middle East as well as the story of a beloved Brooklyn institution, Sahadi's. For the first time, the people behind Sahadi's are sharing their expert knowledge of these sought-after ingredients in the form of over 120 recipes, plus buying guides, and side bar "10 More Ways to Use..." sections.

"Blending essential guidance with winning recipes, this debut will satisfy a variety of tastes; it pairs well with Eden Grinshpan's Eating Out Loud." —*Library Journal*

Includes index.

Sakai, Sonoko

Japanese *Home Cooking: Simple Meals, Authentic Flavors.* Sonoko Sakai; photographs by Rick Poon; illustrations by Juliette Bellocq. Roost Books 2019. 304 p.

ISBN 9781611806168

Grades: Adult   **641.595**

1. Cooking, Japanese 2. Quick and easy cooking 3. Cookbooks 4. Food writing — Cooking and cookbooks — Regional

LC 2018041562

The essential guide to Japanese home cooking—the ingredients, techniques and over 100 recipes—for seasoned cooks and beginners who are craving authentic Japanese flavors. Using high-quality, seasonal ingredients in simple preparations, Sakai offers recipes with a gentle voice and a passion for authentic Japanese cooking. Beginning with the pantry, the flavors of this cuisine are ex-

ESSENTIAL AND RECOMMENDED TITLES
641.595 Cooking — Asia

plored alongside fundamental recipes, such as dashi and pickles, and traditional techniques, like making noodles and properly cooking rice.
Includes index.

Serpico, Peter
Learning Korean: Recipes for Home Cooking. Peter Serpico with Drew Lazor; photography by Neal Santos. W.W. Norton & Company 2022. xix, 209 pages : Color; Illustration
ISBN 9781324003229
Grades: Adult   641.595
1. Cooking, Korean 2. Quick and easy cooking 3. Cookbooks 4. Food Writing — Cooking and cookbooks — Regional
LC 2022006957

Drawing from his decades of professional cooking experience to elevate the greatest hits of at-home Korean dishes, a James Beard Award-winning chef reveals new flavors, techniques and ways to enjoy one of the world's greatest cuisines.
"A great choice for dedicated home chefs looking for Korean cuisine, or cookbook readers looking for a new favorite chef." —*Library Journal*
Includes index.

Sodha, Meera
East: 120 Vegan and Vegetarian Recipes from Bangalore to Beijing. Meera Sodha; photography by David Loftus; art direction by John Hamilton; illustrations by Monika Forsberg. Flatiron Books 2020. 303 pages : Color; Illustration
ISBN 9781250750730
Grades: Adult   641.595
1. Cooking, Asian 2. Vegetarian cooking 3. Cookbooks 4. Food writing — Cooking and cookbooks — Regional 5. Food writing — Cooking and cookbooks — Vegetarian and vegan
LC 2020032572

Modern, vibrant, fuss-free food made from easy-to-find ingredients, East is a must-have whether you're vegan, vegetarian, or simply want to eat more delicious meat-free food. Meera Sodha's stunning new collection features brand-new recipes from a wide range of Asian cuisines. This cookbook is a collaboration between Sodha and the East Asian and South East Asian home cooks and gourmet chefs who inspired her along the way. There are noodles, curries, rice dishes, tofu, salads, sides, and sweets, all easy to make and bursting with exciting flavors.
"Sodha writes in a thoughtful and caring way with a sincerity that home cooks will find encouraging. Readers might also be inspired by Sodha's journey into veganism. This book is recommended for readers of all cooking levels. It is also recommended for libraries that do cooking programs for teens or adults." —*Booklist*
Originally published in the U.K. by Fig Tree, 2019; Includes bibliographical references (page 295) and index.

Made in India: Recipes from an Indian Family Kitchen. Meera Sodha; photography by David Loftus. Flatiron Books 2015. 319 pages : Color; Illustration
ISBN 9781250071019
Grades: Adult   641.595
1. Cooking, Indic 2. Cooking (Spices) 3. Recipes 4. Cookbooks 5. Food writing — Cooking and cookbooks — Regional
LC 2015950828

Presents a collection of over 130 family recipes for Indian dishes, with advice on ingredients, equipment, weights, and measurement and options for starters, meat entrees, vegetables, sides, breads, chutneys, and desserts.
"Sodha offers helpful sections explaining how each Indian ingredient tastes and the best ways to use it, and how to fix a dish thats too spicy or salty. The power of this book lies in its simplicityboth in terms of ingredients and technique." —*Publishers Weekly*
Includes index.

Solomonov, Michael
Israeli Soul: Easy, Essential, Delicious. Michael Solomonov and Steven Cook. Houghton Mifflin Harcourt 2018. 384 p.
ISBN 9780544970373
Grades: Adult   641.595
1. Cooking, Israeli 2. Kosher food 3. Recipes 4. Cooking, Southwest Asian and North African 5. Social life and customs 6. Israel 7. Philadelphia, Pennsylvania 8. Food writing — Cooking and cookbooks — Narrative cookbooks 9. Food Writing — Food and Culture 10. Food writing — Cooking and cookbooks — Chefs and restaurants
LC 2018017712

Presents a collection of recipes that focus on the great dishes which are the soul of Israeli cuisine, including such options as sabich, shawarma, hummus, falafel, mountain bread, and schnitzel.
"Whether they're seeking an entertaining travelogue, an engrossing gourmet history, or an amazing collection of admirably imitable Israeli cuisine, readers won't be disappointed by Philadelphia chef Solomonov and his business partner Cook's (Federal Donuts, 2017; Zahav, 2015) third collection." —*Booklist*
A Rux Martin book.

Zahav: A World of Israeli Cooking. Michael Solomonov and Steven Cook; produced by Dorothy Kalins; photography by Mike Persico; design by Don Morris Design. Houghton Mifflin Harcourt 2015. 368 pages : Color; Illustration
ISBN 9780544373280
Grades: Adult   641.595
1. Solomonov, Michael 2. Recipes 3. Cooking, Israeli 4. Cooks 5. Cooking, Southwest Asian and North African 6. Restaurateurs 7. Social life and customs 8. Israel 9. Philadelphia, Pennsylvania 10. Autobiographies and memoirs 11. Food writing — Cooking and cookbooks — Narrative cookbooks 12. Food writing — Memoirs and biographies 13. Life stories — Arts and culture — Culinary arts
LC 2015004346

A collection of recipes from a Philadelphia restaurant known for its modern take on Israeli cooking presents such offerings as hummus tehina, potato and kale borekas, and pomegranate-glazed salmon.
"Readers with an adventurous palate and an open mind will be richly rewarded by this terrific debut." —*Publishers Weekly*
A Rux Martin book; Includes index.

Tamimi, Sami
Falastin: A Cookbook. Sami Tamimi, Tara Wigley; foreword by Yotam Ottolenghi; photographs by Jenny Zarins. Ten Speed Press 2020. 352 p.
ISBN 9780399581731
Grades: Adult   641.595
1. Food 2. Recipes 3. Palestine 4. Cookbooks 5. Food writing — Cooking and cookbooks — Chefs and restaurants 6. Food writing — Cooking and cookbooks — Regional
LC 2019050435

A soulful tour of Palestinian cooking today from the Ottolenghi restaurants' executive chef and partner- 120 recipes shaped by his personal story as well as the history of Palestine.
"Ottolenghi alums Tamimi (coauthor, Jerusalem and Ottolenghi) and Wigley (coauthor, Ottolenghi Simple) set out on their own with this expert dive into the food of Palestine. The dishes overflow with bold flavors . . . Like the best cookbooks, this one opens a window to expand both palates and minds." —*Publishers Weekly*
Includes bibliographical references and index.

Teigen, Pepper (Vilailuck)
The Pepper Thai Cookbook: Family Recipes from Everyone's Favorite Thai Mom. Pepper Teigen; with Garrett Snyder. Clarkson Potter/Publishers 2021. 255 p. : Color; Illustration
ISBN 9780593137666
Grades: Adult   641.595
1. Cooking, Thai 2. Cooking for families 3. Cookbooks 4. Food writing — Cooking and cookbooks — Narrative cookbooks 5. Food writing — Cooking and cookbooks — Regional
LC Bl2021007858

In her debut cookbook, the author shares more that 80 fun and flavorful recipes, along with stories about her early days in the U.S. learning how to cook Thai

PUBLIC LIBRARY CORE COLLECTION: NONFICTION
Twentieth Edition

dishes with American ingredients and substitutes and what it's like to raise and live with a famous daughter.

"This is a great guide for readers ready to take the plunge into Thai cooking." —*Publishers Weekly*

Includes index.

Tila, Jet
101 Asian Dishes You Need to Cook Before You Die: Discover a New World of Flavors in Authentic Recipes. Jet Tila, award-winning chef and TV personality. Page Street Publishing Co. 2017. 192 pages : Color; Illustration
ISBN 9781624143823
Grades: Adult   641.595
1. Cooking, Asian 2. Recipes 3. Cookbooks 4. Food writing — Cooking and cookbooks — Regional 5. Food writing — Cooking and cookbooks — Chefs and restaurants

LC Bl2017025759

A collection of authentic Asian recipes for the home cook from the celebrity chef and television personality features such dishes as kung pao shrimp, Korean spicy grilled chicken, spicy tuna roll, and Vietnamese crispy imperial rolls.

"Readers of all skill levels and heat tolerances will appreciate Tila's instructions, which emphasize flavor without calling for hours of prep or multiple trips to specialty stores." —*Publishers Weekly*

Includes index.

Wang, Jason
Xi'an Famous Foods: The Cuisine of Western China, from New York's Favorite Noodle Shop. Jason Wang with Jessica K. Chou; photography by Jenny Huang. Abrams 2020. 303 pages : Color; Illustration
ISBN 9781419747526
Grades: Adult   641.595
1. Cooking, Chinese 2. Cooking (Noodles) 3. Recipes 4. Restaurateurs 5. Cookbooks 6. Food writing — Cooking and cookbooks — Chefs and restaurants 7. Food writing — Cooking and cookbooks — Regional 8. Food writing — Cooking and cookbooks — Narrative cookbooks

LC Oc2020002265

The CEO of Xi'an Famous Foods describes how he grew his successful restaurant to fourteen locations throughout New York and offers his never-before-published recipes, including Fried Chicken Wings with XFF Spices and Hot Oil-Seared Biang-Biang Noodles.

"While challenging for beginning cooks, this enjoyable offering features clear instructions and inspiring recipes that are well within the reach of the home kitchen." —*Library Journal*

Includes index.

Witte, Christina De
★ *Noodles, Rice, and Everything Spice: A Thai Comic Book Cookbook.* Christina De Witte and Mallika Kauppinen. Ten Speed Press 2023. 208 p.
ISBN 9781984861603
Grades: Adult   641.595
1. Cooking, Thai 2. Recipes 3. Social life and customs 4. Thailand 5. Cookbooks 6. Comics and Graphic novels 7. How-to books 8. Food books — History and culture 9. Food writing — Cooking and cookbooks — Regional

LC 2022042556

Showcasing real Thai food from the country's distinct culinary regions, an all-female, all-Thai team presents easy-to-follow comic book panes for 50 recipes and stories that share the secrets to making these dynamic, flavorful Thai dishes at home.

"De Witte and Kauppinen will easily convince them to get in the kitchen and make these mouthwatering favorites." —*Booklist*

Includes index.

Woo, Ronnie
Did You Eat Yet?: Craveable Recipes from an All-American Asian Chef. Ronnie Woo. Harvest, an imprint of William Morrow 2023. 288 pages : Color; Illustration
ISBN 9780358581697
Grades: Adult   641.595
1. Cooking, Asian 2. Cooking, American 3. Asian Americans 4. Cookbooks 5. Food writing — Cooking and cookbooks — Chefs and restaurants 6. Food writing — Cooking and cookbooks — Regional

LC 2022043526

Whether it's a health carb conscious recipe, an overly indulgent cheat meal, or stunning happy-hour fare, plus mouth-watering photographs throughout, Ronnie's over-the-top book delivers on flavor with memorable humor and offers a serious array to easily elevate your home cookingand make sure you and your loved ones are well fed."

"This first cookbook from chef and food TV personality Woo is a fun and wonderful introduction to his cooking, appropriate for all skill levels." —*Library Journal*

Includes index.

641.596 Cooking — Africa

Hassan, Hawa
In Bibi's Kitchen: The Recipes and Stories of Grandmothers from the Eight African Countries That Touch the Indian Ocean. Hawa Hassan with Julia Turshen; photographs by Khadija M. Farah & Jennifer May; illustrations by Araki Koman. Ten Speed Press 2020. 281 pages : Illustration; Color
ISBN 9781984856739
Grades: Adult   641.596
1. Cooking, African 2. Cooking 3. Recipes 4. Voyages and travels 5. East Africa 6. Cookbooks 7. Food writing — Cooking and cookbooks — Regional 8. Food writing — Cooking and cookbooks — Narrative cookbooks 9. Food writing — Food and culture

LC 2020003798

The best-selling cookbook author of Feed the Resistance teams up with the founder and CEO of a company that makes condiments inspired by Somalia to present seventy-five recipes and stories gathered from grandmothers of eight African nations.

Timothy, Duval
Food from Across Africa. Duval Timothy, Jacob Fodio Todd, Folayemi Brown; photography by Toby Glanville & Sophie Davidson; illustration by Duval Timothy. Ecco, an imprint of HarperCollinsPublishers 2016. 335 pages : Illustration; Color
ISBN 9780062467409
Grades: Adult   641.596
1. Cooking, African 2. Cookbooks

LC Bl2016024844

The founders of the bi-monthly London supper club, the Groundnut, present a treasury of classical and modern African recipes to celebrate the cuisine's diversity and heritage, sharing brief historical information for each entry while providing a host of complementary beverages, sides and desserts.

Includes indexes; Originally published: London : Michael Joseph, 2015.

Umah-Shaylor, Lerato
Africana: More Than 100 Recipes and Flavors Inspired by a Rich Continent. Lerato Umah-Shaylor. Amistad, an imprint of HarperCollinsPublishers 2023. 288 pages : Color; Illustration
ISBN 9780063277496
Grades: Adult   641.596
1. Cooking, African 2. Cookbooks 3. Food writing — Cooking and cookbooks — Regional

LC 2022044386

AFRICANA travels across the continent showcasing its vibrant and varied cuisines that are rich in flavor, diverse in culture and steeped in tradition. Combining recipes passed down the generations but with her own modern and inventive style, food writer and cook Lerato shares her own stories of Africa with a delectable sense of adventure. Discover how to cook some of the most iconic dishes from Nigeria to Madagascar, Morocco to South Africa."

ESSENTIAL AND RECOMMENDED TITLES
641.5972 Cooking — Mexico

"Home cooks with an appetite for food heritage and kitchen adventure will appreciate this passionate and welcoming exploration of tastes from across Africa." —*Publishers Weekly*
Includes index.

641.5972 Cooking — Mexico

Bayless, Rick
Authentic Mexican: Regional Cooking from the Heart of Mexico. Rick Bayless with Deann Groen Bayless; illustrations by John Sandford; photographs by Christopher Hirsheimer. William Morrow 2007. 384 pages, 16 unnumbered pages of plates : Illustration; Color; Map
ISBN 9780061373268
Grades: Adult   641.5972
1. Cooking, Mexican 2. Recipes 3. Cookbooks 4. Food writing — Cooking and cookbooks — Regional
LC
Collects recipes that show readers how to recreate the textures and flavors of Mexico's regional specialties in North American kitchens.
Includes bibliographical references (pages 357-361) and index.

★ *Fiesta at Rick's: Fabulous Food for Great Times with Friends*. Rick Bayless with Deann Groen Bayless; photographs by Paul Elledge. W. W. Norton 2010. 348 p. : Color illustration
ISBN 9780393058994
Grades: Adult   641.5972
1. Cooking, Mexican 2. Entertaining 3. Menus 4. Recipes 5. Cookbooks 6. Food writing — Cooking and cookbooks — Regional
LC 2010013128
"The book loosely packages recipes around fiestas, from a luxury guacamole and cocktail party for 12 to classic mole for 24, complete with game-plan checklists. The hardest thing about using this book isn't finding the ingredients (today, practically every small town has a great Mexican grocery), it's keeping yourself from eating everything before the guests arrive." —*New York Times Book Review*
Includes indexes.

Mexican Everyday. Rick Bayless, with Deann Groen Bayless; color photographs by Christopher Hirsheimer. Norton 2005. 336 p. : Color illustration
ISBN 9780393061543
Grades: Adult   641.5972
1. Cooking, Mexican 2. Recipes 3. Cookbooks 4. Food writing — Cooking and cookbooks — Regional
LC 2005023129
Presents easy-to-prepare recipes for nutritious Mexican dishes including salads, soups, soft tacos, enchiladas, tostadas, tortas, entrees, grilled fare, marinades, salsas, and desserts.
"Befitting the Mexican origins of these dishes, Bayless uses a wide variety of chiles, especially the deeply flavorful poblano. With virtually every recipe in the book, Bayless adds riffs that offer imaginative variations on the main recipe's techniques." —*Booklist*
Includes index.

★ *More Mexican Everyday: Simple, Seasonal, Celebratory*. Rick Bayless, with Deann Groen Bayless and David Tamarkin; photographs by Hirsheimer and Hamilton. W.W. Norton & Company 2015. 384 pages : Color; Illustration
ISBN 9780393081145
Grades: Adult   641.5972
1. Cooking, Mexican 2. Recipes 3. Seasonal cooking 4. Cookbooks 5. Food writing — Cooking and cookbooks — Methods 6. Food writing — Cooking and cookbooks — Regional
LC 2015005985
Presents easy-to-prepare recipes for Mexican dishes using seasonal ingredients, including salads, soups, tacos, enchiladas, tostadas, tortas, entrees, salsas, and desserts.

"Recipes conclude with quick summaries of ingredients to ease shopping. An effective starting point for the would-be home Mexican cook." —*Booklist*
Includes index.

Rick Bayless Mexico One Plate at a Time. Rick Bayless, with Jeanmarie Brownson and Deann Groen Bayless; color photographs by Gentl & Hayers; Mexican location photographs by James Baigrie; glossary photographs by James Isberner. Scribner 2000. x, 374 p. : Illustration; Color
ISBN 9780684841861
Grades: Adult   641.5972
1. Cooking, Mexican 2. Recipes 3. Cookbooks 4. Food writing — Cooking and cookbooks — Regional
LC 00058327
An authority on Mexican cuisine shares his wisdom and experience on cooking south of the border in this collection of 120 recipes that includes classics as well as some of his own creations.
"There are helpful questions and answers at the end of each section, based on questions generated by recipe testers, an addition that may be unique to the cookbook genre. There is much here for both neophytes and experienced cooks. Highly recommended for all public libraries." —*Library Journal*
Includes bibliographical references and index.

Camara, Gabriela
My Mexico City Kitchen: Recipes and Convictions. Gabriela Camara with Malena Watrous; photographs by Marcus Nilsson. Lorena Jones Books 2019. 367 pages : Illustration; Color
ISBN 9780399580574
Grades: Adult   641.5972
1. Cooking, Mexican 2. Recipes 3. Food habits 4. Mexico City, Mexico 5. Cookbooks 6. Food writing — Cooking and cookbooks — Regional 7. Food writing — Cooking and cookbooks — Chefs and restaurants
LC 2018042689
Inspired by the flavors, ingredients, and flair of culinary and cultural hotspot Mexico City, Gabriela Camara's style of fresh-first, vegetable-forward, legume-loving, and seafood-centric Mexican cooking is a siren call to home cooks who crave authentic, on-trend recipes they can make with confidence and regularity. With 150 recipes for Basicos (basics), Desayunos (breakfasts), Primeros (starters), Platos Fuertos (mains), and Postres (sweets), Mexican food-lovers will find all the dishes they want to cook—from Chilaquiles Verdes to Chiles Rellenos and Flan de Cajeta—and will discover many sure-to-be favorites, such as her signature tuna tostadas.
"This simple yet authentic and extensive collection could easily replace every other Mexican cookbook in your library's collection." —*Library Journal*
Includes index.

Gerson, Fany
My Sweet Mexico: Recipes for Authentic Pastries, Breads, Candies, Beverages, and Frozen Treats. Fany Gerson; photography by Ed Anderson. Ten Speed Press 2010. VII, 215 p. : Color illustration
ISBN 9781580089944
Grades: Adult   641.5972
1. Cooking, Mexican 2. Desserts 3. Recipes 4. Mexico 5. Cookbooks 6. Food writing — Cooking and cookbooks — Courses 7. Food writing — Cooking and cookbooks — Regional
LC 2010014469
The first cookbook to present authentic versions of beloved Mexican sweets plus a creative selection of new recipes rooted in traditional flavors and ingredients.
A volume of authentic Mexican sweet recipes is complemented by creative alternatives rooted in traditional flavors and ingredients, in a collection that shares culinary historical information and insights into the proper accompaniments for national celebrations.
"The author has dutifully catalogued the confections of her native Mexico. American readers who have only encountered the occasional tres leches cake in a Mexican restaurant will be stunned by the breadth and depth of recipes here, ranging from coffee-flavored corn cookies to guava caramel pecan rolls and hibiscus ice pops, all culled from Gerson's family, friends, and generous strangers."

Gerson's vivid descriptions, exacting instruction, and obvious passion for her subject matter make this volume a substantial read about the most tempting indulgences." —*Publishers Weekly*

Includes bibliographical references (p. 207-209) and index.

Hernandez, Eddie
Turnip Greens & Tortillas: A Mexican Chef Spices up the Southern Kitchen. Eddie Hernandez and Susan Puckett; photographs by Angie Mosier. Houghton Mifflin Harcourt 2018. VII, 310 pages : Color; Illustration
ISBN 9780544618824
Grades: Adult   641.5972
1. Cooking, Mexican 2. Cookbooks 3. Food writing — Cooking and cookbooks — Regional
LC 2017051352

A collection of recipes for Southern fare with a Mexican flair from the chef and restaurateur features such dishes as Cajun hash, cheeseburger tacos, chicken enchilada casserole, and Creole red beans and rice burritos.

"A stellar debut imbued with Hernandez's infectious excitement for cooking." —*Library Journal*

Includes index; a Rux Martin Book.

Jinich, Pati
Mexican Today: New and Rediscovered Recipes for Contemporary Kitchens. Pati Jinich; photography by Ellen Silverman. Houghton Mifflin Harcourt 2016. 320 pages : Color; Illustration
ISBN 9780544557246
Grades: Adult   641.5972
1. Cooking, Mexican 2. Recipes 3. Cookbooks 4. Food writing — Cooking and cookbooks — Regional
LC 2015042717

A collection of recipes from the host of PBS series Pati's Mexican Table for traditional Mexican dishes and modified recipes that show the evolution of Mexican food, including such options as guacamoles, salsa, tacos, enchiladas, and guisados.

"Many of her recipes can be made in advance or in less than 30 minutes and rely on easy-to-find ingredients. A highlight of this cookbook is its playful variations such as baked huevos rancheros casserole." —*Library Journal*

A Rux Martin Book.

★ *Treasures* of the Mexican Table: Classic Recipes, Local Secrets. Pati Jinich; photographs by Angie Mosier. Houghton Mifflin Harcourt 2021. VII, 406 pages : Color; Illustration
ISBN 9780358086765
Grades: Adult   641.5972
1. Cooking, Mexican 2. Cookbooks 3. Food Writing — Cooking and cookbooks — Regional 4. Food Writing — Cooking and cookbooks — Chefs and restaurants
LC 2021018574

The star of the three-time James Beard Award-winning PBS series Pati's Mexican Table presents more than 150 classic recipes, which are heirlooms passed down from generations, that paint a vivid picture of the richness of Mexico.

"For home cooks looking for recipes that go beyond Tex-Mex, Jinich's cookbook offers delicious insights about the rich and varied culinary culture of Mexico. Longtime viewers of her PBS cooking show will be drawn in, as will new fans." —*Library Journal*

Includes index.

Martinez, Rick
★ *Mi Cocina*: Recipes and Rapture from My Kitchen in México. Rick Martínez; photographs by Ren Fuller. Clarkson Potter/Publishers 2022. 303 pages : Color; Illustration
ISBN 9780593138700
Grades: Adult   641.5972
1. Cooking, Mexican 2. Cooks 3. Immigration and emigration 4. Cookbooks 5. Food Writing — Cooking and cookbooks — Regional 6. Food writing — Food and culture 7. Life stories — Arts and culture — Culinary arts
LC 2021034744

In his first cookbook, a beloved food writer introduces the diverse culinary treasures of Mexico, taking readers on a journey through each of the seven regions to explore 100 unique dishes, which are accompanied by essays on various topics, such as migration and culinary influence from other countries.

"Martínez manages to marry pragmatic, genuine, and delicious recipes with a beautiful narrative about his journey of self-discovery; will quickly become a favorite on cookbook shelves." —*Library Journal*

Includes index.

Presilla, Maricel E.
Gran Cocina Latina: The Food of Latin America. Maricel E. Presilla; photographs by Gentl & Hyers/Edge; drawings by Julio Figueroa. Norton & Company 2012. VII, 901 p, 32 p. of plates : Illustration; Color
ISBN 9780393050691
Grades: Adult   641.5972
1. Cooking, Latin American 2. Cooking, Caribbean 3. Cooking, Mexican 4. Recipes 5. Cookbooks 6. Food writing — Cooking and cookbooks — Regional
LC 2012017701

Presents five hundred recipes from the Latin world ranging from Mexico to Argentina and all the Spanish-speaking countries of the Caribbean including adobos, sofritos, empanadas, tamales, ceviches, moles, and flan.

Includes index.

Villasuso, Susana
Sobremesa: Tasty Mexican Recipes for Every Day. Susana Villasuso. Interlink Books, an imprint of Interlink Publishing Group, Inc. 2024. 239 pages : Illustration; Color
ISBN 9781623716882
Grades: Adult   641.5972
1. Cooking, Mexican 2. Dinners and dining 3. Cookbooks 4. Food writing — Cooking and cookbooks — Regional 5. Food writing — Cooking and cookbooks — Methods
LC Bl2024009696

Sobremesa means "relaxing at the table after a heavy meal," usually after getting together with family and friends. Mexican-born chef and recipe developer Susana Villasuso is on a mission to bring the flavors of Mexico to your table, and share her culture with the world. Inspired by the dishes she learned to cook from her mother and grandmother, this debut cookbook brings together authentic, modern, simple, and tasty recipes for feeding the whole family and for all occasions, made with everyday supermarket ingredients.

"Crisp and colorful photos showcase the vivid beauty of these meals and encourage cooks to make healthy and hearty Mexican platos a part of their weeknight repertoire." —*Booklist*

Includes bibliographical references (page 229) and index.

641.597291 Cooking — Cuba

Pelaez, Ana Sofia
The Cuban Table: A Celebration of Food, Flavors, and History. Ana Sofia Pelaez; photographs by Ellen Silverman. St. Martin's Press 2014. xi, 323 pages : Color; Illustration
ISBN 9781250036087
Grades: Adult   641.597291
1. Cooking, Cuban 2. Recipes 3. Cookbooks 4. Food writing — Cooking and cookbooks — Regional
LC 2014026974

A Cuban-American food writer and blogger offers an illustrated, comprehensive overview of Cuban cuisine, providing historical context for dishes that include Spanish and African ingredients as well as 110 delicious, authentic recipes.

"Let's hope Pelaez and Silverman undertake more collaborations. Their thorough and respectful treatment of their subject results in a compelling cookbook that conveys a strong sense of place." —*Library Journal*

Includes bibliographical references (page 313) and index.

ESSENTIAL AND RECOMMENDED TITLES
641.597295 Cooking — Puerto Rico

641.597295 Cooking — Puerto Rico

Maisonet, Illyanna
★ *Diasporican:* A Puerto Rican Cookbook. Illyanna Maisonet; foreword by Michael W. Twitty; Puerto Rico photographs by Erika P. Rodriguez; California and food photographs by Dan Liberti. Ten Speed Press 2022. 241 pages : Color; Illustration
ISBN 9781984859761
Grades: Adult   **641.597295**
1. Cooking, Caribbean 2. Cooking 3. Cookbooks 4. Food writing — Cooking and cookbooks — Regional
LC 2021060872

America's first Puerto Rican food columnist shares the results of documenting her family's food traditions through over 90 recipes, some passed down from her grandmother, for classic dishes including Tostones, Pernil, Arroz con Gandules and Flan de Queso.
"This one-of-a-kind cookbook is highly recommended for its combination of island flare, important history, and tons of personality." —*Booklist*
Includes index.

641.5973 Cooking — United States

Angelou, Maya
Great Food, All Day Long: Cook Splendidly, Eat Smart. Maya Angelou. Random House 2010. 176 p. : Illustration
ISBN 9781400068449
Grades: Adult   **641.5973**
1. Cooking, American 2. Memories 3. Weight loss 4. Health foods 5. Food habits 6. Food writing — Cooking and cookbooks — Narrative cookbooks
LC 2010017519

Beloved author Maya Angelou returns to the kitchen—both hers and ours—with her second cookbook, filled with time-tested recipes and the intimate, autobiographical sketches of how they came to be. Inspired by Angelou's own dramatic weight loss, the focus here is on good food, well-made and eaten in moderation. All the delicious dishes here can be eaten in small portions, and many times a day. More important, they can be converted into other mouth-watering incarnations. So Crown Roast of Pork becomes Pork Tacos and Pork Fried Rice, while Roasted Chicken becomes Chicken Tetrazzini and Chicken Curry. And throughout, Maya Angelou's rich and wise voice carries the food from written word to body-and-soul-enriching experience.

Hallelujah! the Welcome Table. Maya Angelou. Random House 2004. xiii, 218 p. : Color illustration
ISBN 9781400062898
Grades: Adult   **641.5973**
1. Angelou, Maya 2. Cooking, American 3. Cooking 4. Food writing — Cooking and cookbooks — Narrative cookbooks
LC 2004044902

Combining reminiscences with more than sixty of her personal recipes, the acclaimed author reflects on important moments of her life that centered around the dinner table.
"The author couples brief anecdotes from her life with more than 60 recipes for food enjoyed at that time. Readers will be torn between losing themselves in the evocative text and rushing to the kitchen to whip up such delights as her grandmother's caramel cake or the white bean cassoulet that Angelou prepared for food writer M.F.K. Fisher." —*Library Journal*

Batali, Mario
Mario Batali Big American Cookbook: 250 Favorite Recipes from Across the Usa. Mario Batali; with Jim Webster; art direction by Douglas Riccardi; photography by Quentin Bacon. Grand Central Life & Style 2016. xv, 495 pages
ISBN 9781455584710
Grades: Adult   **641.5973**
1. Cooking, American 2. Local foods 3. Recipes 4. Cookbooks 5. Food writing — Cooking and cookbooks — Regional 6. Food writing — Cooking and cookbooks — Chefs and restaurants
LC 2016022712

Presents two hundred fifty recipes using regional ingredients from around the United States, sharing such dishes as lobster pot pie, oyster fritters, shrimp and grits, key lime pie, stuffed cabbages, fried pickles, huevos rancheros, and Kahlua pork.
"Boosting recipes with color photographs, Batali makes every dish look like great fun, and its impossible not to share his enthusiasm." —*Booklist*
Includes index.

Brennan, Kathy
Keepers: Two Home Cooks Share Their Tried-and-True Weeknight Recipes and the Secrets to Happiness in the Kitchen. Kathy Brennan and Caroline Campion. Rodale 2013. xiv, 240 pages : Color; Illustration
ISBN 9781609613549
Grades: Adult   **641.5973**
1. Cooking 2. Cooking, American 3. Kitchens 4. Menus 5. Quick and easy cooking 6. Recipes 7. Cookbooks 8. Food writing — Cooking and cookbooks — Methods
LC 2013005481

A collection of 120 accessible, affordable recipes for families, written by two award-winning food journalists, draws on the expertise of professional chefs and the authors' own home-kitchen experiences to provide adaptations of classic dishes, old favorites and one-pot convenience meals that can be readily prepared on busy weeknights.
Includes index.

Falk, Daina
The Hungry Fan's Game Day Cookbook: 165 Recipes for Eating, Drinking & Watching Sports. Daina Falk. Oxmoor House 2016. 256 pages : Color; Illustration
ISBN 9780848745837
Grades: Adult   **641.5973**
1. Cooking, American 2. Recipes 3. Cookbooks 4. Food writing — Cooking and cookbooks — Methods
LC Bl2016032888

Offers game-day recipes from a nationally recognized sports expert and fan, including such options as Cajun shrimp skewers, empanadas, buffalo chicken salad, and Italian hero sandwich, along with signature recipes from professional athletes.
"Regardless of culinary preferences or skill level, every hungry sports fan can find something appealing in this go-to guide for game days all year long." —*Publishers Weekly*
Includes index.

Ferguson, Jesse Tyler
★ *Food* Between Friends. Jesse Tyler Ferguson, Julie Tanous; photographs by Eva Kolenko. Clarkson Potter 2021. 272 pages : Color; Illustration
ISBN 9780593136539
Grades: Adult   **641.5973**
1. Cooking, American 2. Food writing — Cooking and cookbooks — Regional
LC Bl2021005865

The Modern Family star and his "Julie & Jesse" co-blogger present a debut cookbook inspired by the traditional foods of their Southwestern and Southern hometowns, offering adaptations for such classic favorites as hatch green chile mac and cheese and grilled chicken with Alabama white BBQ sauce.
"An effervescent, accessible cookbook bolstered by a joyful friendship. Fans of comedy-infused cookbooks and festive, lighthearted cooking will enjoy these creative meals." —*Library Journal*
Includes index.

PUBLIC LIBRARY CORE COLLECTION: NONFICTION
Twentieth Edition

Guarnaschelli, Alex
The **Home** *Cook: Recipes to Know by Heart.* Alex Guarnaschelli. Clarkson Potter/Publishers 2017. 368 pages
   ISBN 9780307956583
Grades: Adult   641.5973
   1. Cooking, American 2. Recipes 3. Cookbooks 4. Food writing — Cooking and cookbooks — Courses 5. Food writing — Cooking and cookbooks — Reference
                                              LC 2016045628
   A collection of modern recipes from the accomplished chef that features vibrant international flavors, including such dishes as whole pork loin roast with Cajun rub, lamb tagine, and roasted eggplant dip with garlic butter naan.
   An accomplished chef and mom offers a cookbook that reflects the way modern people eat and presents 300 recipes that use vibrant international flavors including Glazed Five-spice Ribs, Roasted Eggplant Dip with Garlic Butter Naan and Dark Chocolate Rum Pie.
   Includes index.

Kinch, David
At Home in the Kitchen: Simple Recipes from a Chef's Night off. David Kinch with Devin Fuller. Ten Speed Press 2021. 288 p.
   ISBN 9781984858504
Grades: Adult   641.5973
   1. Cooking, American 2. Quick and easy cooking 3. California 4. Food writing — Cooking and cookbooks — Chefs and restaurants 5. Food writing — Cooking and cookbooks — Regional
   The James Beard Award-winning, three-Michelin-starred chef and co-owner of Manresa presents recipes for the dishes he cooks most often, including Brussels Sprouts with Cider and Goat Cheese, Mozzarella Crostini with Lemon and Tomato and Penne with a Walnut Sauce.
   "This is a solid choice for readers craving quick, adventurous dishes." —*Publishers Weekly*

Langholtz, Gabrielle
America: The Cookbook. Gabrielle Langholtz. Phaidon Press 2017. 767 pages : Color; Illustration; Map
   ISBN 9780714873961
Grades: Adult   641.5973
   1. Cooking, American 2. Recipes 3. Cookbooks 4. Food writing — Cooking and cookbooks — Regional
                                              LC 2017446984
   With 800 home-cooking recipes, America: The Cookbook is a celebration of the remarkable diversity of American food and food culture state by state. Features 50 essays and menus from a 'Who's who' of 100 foremost food experts and chefs.
   "Rather than simply offering a rote recitation of well-worn classics, Langholtz artfully includes recipes that show America's kaleidoscopic culinary landscape." —*Publishers Weekly*
   Includes index.

Lohman, Sarah
   ★ *Endangered Eating: America's Vanishing Foods.* Sarah Lohman. Norton 2023. 320 p.
   ISBN 9781324004660
Grades: Adult   641.5973
   1. Food habits 2. Food 3. Social life and customs 4. National characteristics, American 5. United States 6. Food writing — Food and culture
   A leading culinary historian looks at the ways American food traditions are in danger of being lost and discusses how we can reverse this trend by supporting community food organizations and producers.
   "A tasty sojourn through the landscape of America's endangered foods, served with a scoop of energy and a dash of hope." —*Kirkus*

McBride, Martina
Martina's Kitchen Mix: My Recipe Playlist for Real Life. Martina McBride. Oxmoor House 2018. 271 pages : Color; Illustration
   ISBN 9780848757632
Grades: Adult   641.5973
   1. Cooking, American 2. Seasonal cooking 3. Recipes 4. Cookbooks 5. Food writing — Cooking and cookbooks — Regional
                                              LC Bl2018190482
   The country music star shares recipes from her kitchen for meals, beverages, appetizers, and desserts, that feature fresh seasonal ingredients.
   Includes index.

Moulton, Sara
Sara Moulton's Home Cooking 101: How to Make Everything Taste Better. Sara Moulton. Oxmoor House 2016. 367 pages : Color; Illustration
   ISBN 9780848744410
Grades: Adult   641.5973
   1. Cooking, American 2. Recipes 3. Cookbooks 4. Food writing — Cooking and cookbooks — Methods 5. Food writing — Cooking and cookbooks — Chefs and restaurants
                                              LC Bl2016007835
   Collects more than one hundred fifty recipes that exhibit the essentials of flavor and taste, including such offerings as tomato paella soup, grilled jerk pork, and spicy greens ravioli.
   "Busy home cooks will find much to savor in this approachable, elegant collection of recipes." —*Publishers Weekly*
   Includes indexes.

Noyes, Brian
The Red Truck Bakery Farmhouse Cookbook: Sweet and Savory Comfort Food from America's Favorite Rural Bakery. Brian Noyes; photographs by Angie Mosier; foreword by Ronni Lundy. Clarkson Potter/Publishers 2022. 223 pages : Illustration; Color
   ISBN 9780593234815
Grades: Adult   641.5973
   1. Cooking, American 2. Comfort food 3. Virginia 4. Southern States 5. Cookbooks 6. Food writing — Cooking and cookbooks — Regional 7. Food writing — Cooking and cookbooks — Chefs and restaurants
                                              LC 2021056986
   The founder of the award-winning Red Truck Bakery offers more than 95 all-new recipes celebrating ingredients and traditions from the bakery's home on the edge of the Shenandoah Valley and the Blue Ridge mountains, bringing the comfort and charm of the farmhouse where the bakery started into your kitchen.
   "This is a must-have for lovers of Southern cooking." —*Publishers Weekly*
   Includes index.

Nunn, Emily
The **Comfort** *Food Diaries: My Quest for the Perfect Dish to Mend a Broken Heart.* Emily Nunn. Atria Books 2017. 320 p.
   ISBN 9781451674200
Grades: Adult   641.5973
   1. Nunn, Emily 2. Comfort food 3. Cooking, American 4. Voyages and travels 5. Food writers 6. Grief 7. Autobiographies and memoirs 8. Life stories — Arts and culture — Culinary arts 9. Food writing — Cooking and cookbooks — Narrative cookbooks 10. Life stories — Personal growth
                                              LC 2016055910
   A former New Yorker editor chronicles her quest to overcome the convergence of the sudden loss of her brother, being dumped by her fiancé, and being evicted from her apartment by cooking her way across the country while staying with friends and family.
   "Nourishing, truthful reflections on family, friends, and love all wrapped up in the idea of food as sustenance for both the body and the soul." —*Kirkus*
   Includes recipes.

Rombauer, Irma S.
   ★ *Joy of Cooking.* Irma S. Rombauer, Marion Rombauer Becker, Ethan Becker, John Becker, Megan Scott; illustrations by John Norton; papercuts by Anna Brones. Scribner 2019. xliv, 1156 pages : Illustration
   ISBN 9781501169717

ESSENTIAL AND RECOMMENDED TITLES
641.5974 Cooking — United States — New England

Grades: Adult   641.5973
1. Cooking, American 2. Cookbooks 3. Food writing — Cooking and cookbooks

LC Bl2019032676

Revised and updated with more than 600 new recipes, a new edition of the classic cookbook, which has become a kitchen bible, combines classic recipes, new dishes and indispensable reference information for today|s home cooks.

"In an era when thousands of recipes are at our fingertips online, this classic collection proves its worth as a source of dependable culinary guidance and reliable recipes; a first purchase." —Library Journal

Includes bibliographical references (pages 1077-1080) and indexes.

★ *Joy of Cooking*. Irma S. Rombauer, Marion Rombauer Becker, Ethan Becker; illustrated by John Norton. Scribner 2006. xiii, 1132 p. : Illustration
ISBN 9780743246262

Grades: Adult   641.5973
1. Cooking, American 2. Cookbooks 3. Food writing — Cooking and cookbooks — Regional

LC 2006051231

A classic guide to American cooking features thousands of traditional recipes and five hundred new dishes, in a volume that includes an array of favorite casserole, dessert, and soup options.

75th anniversary ed; Includes index.

Rosen, Ali

Bring It!: Tried and True Recipes for Potlucks and Casual Entertaining. Ali Rosen; photography by Noah Fecks. Running Press 2018. 239 pages
ISBN 9780762462728

Grades: Adult   641.5973
1. Cooking, American 2. Quick and easy cooking 3. Seasonal cooking 4. Recipes 5. Cookbooks 6. Food writing — Cooking and cookbooks — Entertaining

LC 2017955766

Presents advice about preparing foods for entertainment, discussing ingredients and serving sizes and providing a collection of recipes for appetizers, dips, salads, casseroles, main dishes, and desserts.

Wilson, Melba

★ *Melba's American Comfort: 100 Recipes from My Heart to Your Kitchen*. Melba Wilson; photography by Melissa Hom. 2016. 235 p.
ISBN 9781476795300

Grades: Adult   641.5973
1. Cooking, American 2. Cooking, African American 3. Comfort food 4. Cooking (Chicken) 5. Southern States 6. Harlem, New York City 7. Cookbooks 8. Food writing — Cooking and cookbooks — Regional 9. Food writing — Cooking and cookbooks — Chefs and restaurants

Wilson invites you to experience the delicious foods of her heritage. She melds the down-home country cooking of her Southern roots with the urban cultural influences of New York City. Also included is a treasure trove of delightful stories and wisdom from the heart of her bustling kitchen.

"Doyenne of contemporary cooking Wilson packs her Harlem restaurant nightly with fans eager for her fried chicken and other comfort foods from the noble culinary tradition of southern America." —Booklist

Includes index.

641.5974 Cooking — United States — New England

Samuelsson, Marcus

The Red Rooster Cookbook: The Story of Food and Hustle in Harlem. Marcus Samuelsson; photographs by Bobby Fisher; foreword by Hilton Als; text with April Reynolds; recipes and text with Roy Finamore; illustrations by Rebekah Maysles and Leon Johnson. Houghton Mifflin Harcourt 2016. 384 pages
ISBN 9780544639775

Grades: Adult   641.5974
1. International cooking 2. Cooking 3. Food 4. New York (State) 5. Cookbooks 6. Food writing — Cooking and cookbooks — Regional

LC 2016037226

A cookbook by the chef and owner of Red Rooster Harlem offers Southern comfort food and other multicultural recipes, including brown butter biscuits, killer collards, donuts with sweet potato cream, and Chinese steamed bass.

"Fisher's food and street photography colorfully captures the character of Samuelsson's dishes as well as the characters that inhabit his neighborhood." —Publishers Weekly

A Rux Martin Book; Includes index.

641.5975 Cooking — United States — Southern

Adams, Jocelyn Delk

Everyday Grand: Soulful Recipes for Celebrating Life's Big and Small Moments. Jocelyn Delk Adams with Olga Massov; photographs by Brittany Conerly. Clarkson Potter/Publishers 2023. 255 pages : Color; Illustration
ISBN 9780593236215

Grades: Adult   641.5975
1. Cooking, American 2. Comfort food 3. Southern States 4. Cookbooks 5. Food writing — Cooking and cookbooks — Regional

LC Bl2023007095

The founder and author behind Grandbaby Cakes presents her approachable take on comfort food to celebrate every day with over 80 Southern-inspired recipes including Georgia Peach Salad with Candied Pecans and Cornbread Croutons and Mojito-Marinated Skirt Steak with Chimichurri.

"For home cooks looking to whip up soul food fare with a bit of flare, this is a quality guide." —Publishers Weekly

Includes index.

Bragg, Rick

★ *The Best Cook in the World: Tales from My Momma's Table*. by Rick Bragg. Alfred A. Knopf 2018. 512 p.
ISBN 9781400040414

Grades: Adult   641.5975
1. Bragg, Rick 2. Families 3. Mothers and sons 4. Cooking, American 5. Autobiographies and memoirs 6. Life stories — Relationships — Parent and child 7. Food writing — Memoirs and biographies

LC 2017024979

Presents a food memoir, cookbook, and tribute to the author's mother, sharing classic family recipes—many of them pre-dating the Civil War—and preparation secrets for such traditional fare as short ribs, biscuits, and perfect mashed potatoes.

"For readers who crave soul with their recipes (some 75 here), this is a fitting tribute to foodways that are fast slipping away." —Library Journal

Includes recipes.

Brock, Sean

South: Essential Recipes and New Explorations. Sean Brock, with Lucas Weir and Marion Sullivan; photographs by Peter Frank Edwards. Artisan 2019. 374 pages : Color; Illustration
ISBN 9781579657161

Grades: Adult   641.5975
1. Seasonal cooking 2. Recipes 3. Cooking, American 4. Cookbooks 5. Food writing — Cooking and cookbooks — Regional 6. Food writing — Cooking and cookbooks — Chefs and restaurants

LC 2019016960

An award-winning chef, cookbook author, Nashville restauranteur and Southern cuisine promoter shares his mix-and-match component recipes for grits, fried chicken, collard greens, corn bread, tomato okra stew and buttermilk biscuits.

"Brimming with exquisite interpretations of Southern cooking, this is a great collection for intermediate to advanced cooks looking to broaden their culinary repertoire." —Library Journal

Includes index.

PUBLIC LIBRARY CORE COLLECTION: NONFICTION
Twentieth Edition

Brown, Kardea
The Way Home: A Celebration of Sea Islands Food and Family with Over 100 Recipes. Kardea Brown. Amistad, an imprint of HarperCollinsPublishers 2022. IX, 291 pages : Color; Illustration
ISBN 9780063085602
Grades: Adult　　　　　　　　　　　　　　　　　　641.5975
1. Cooking, American 2. Cooking, African American 3. Gullahs 4. Southern States 5. Cookbooks 6. Food writing — Cooking and cookbooks — Regional 7. Food writing — Cooking and cookbooks — Chefs and restaurants
LC Bl2022033407

Celebrating the Gullah/Geechee culinary traditions of her family and sharing family anecdotes, memories and helpful tips, the breakout star of Food Network's top-rated show Delicious Miss Brown presents dishes combining West African herbs, spices and grains with traditional Southern cooking to nourish you, body and soul.

"Just like a comfy homecooked meal, The Way Home is bound to leave readers craving more." —*Booklist*

Includes index.

Dissen, William Stark
Thoughtful Cooking: Recipes Rooted in the New South. William Stark Dissen; photography by Johnny and Charlotte Autry. Countryman Press, an imprint of W.W. Norton & Company 2024. 288 pages : Color; Illustration
ISBN 9781682688083
Grades: Adult　　　　　　　　　　　　　　　　　　641.5975
1. Cooking, American 2. Seasonal cooking 3. Sustainability 4. Cooking 5. Asheville, North Carolina 6. Southern States 7. Appalachian Region, Southern 8. Cookbooks 9. Food writing — Cooking and cookbooks — Regional 10. Food writing — Cooking and cookbooks — Chefs and restaurants
LC Bl2024006958

A long-anticipated cookbook from the chef and owner of The Market Place, Asheville's renowned farm-to-table restaurant.

"Written with the same love and care as Bill Smith's Seasoned in the South and Vivian Howard's Deep Run Roots, Dissen's irresistible tome of culinary love will be food for thought for readers seeking a grounded guide to cooking." —*Library Journal*

Includes index.

Gaines, Joanna
★ *Magnolia Table: A Collection of Recipes for Gathering.* Joanna Gaines with Marah Stets; photography by Amy Neunsinger. William Morrow 2018. 328 pages : Illustration; Color
ISBN 9780062820150
Grades: Adult　　　　　　　　　　　　　　　　　　641.5975
1. Recipes 2. Seasonal cooking 3. Cooking, American 4. Cookbooks 5. Food writing — Cooking and cookbooks — Entertaining 6. Food writing — Cooking and cookbooks — Regional
LC 2018438643

Jo Gaines believes there's no better way to celebrate family and friendship than through the art of togetherness, celebrating tradition, and sharing a great meal. She provides 125 classic recipes—from breakfast, lunch, and dinner to small plates, snacks, and desserts—presenting a modern selection of American classics, personal family favorites, and comfort food from the couple's new restaurant, Magnolia Table. Complemented by her love for her garden, these dishes also incorporate homegrown, seasonal produce at the peak of its flavor. Dishes include fried chicken with sticky poppy seed jam, white Cheddar bisque, peach caprese, and lemon pie.

Includes index.

Hall, Carla
Carla Hall's Soul Food: Everyday and Celebration. Carla Hall with Genevieve Ko. Harper Wave 2018. x, 322 pages : Color; Illustration
ISBN 9780062669834
Grades: Adult　　　　　　　　　　　　　　　　　　641.5975
1. Cooking, African American 2. Recipes 3. Cooking, American 4. Cookbooks 5. Food writing — Cooking and cookbooks — Regional 6. Food writing — Cooking and cookbooks — Chefs and restaurants
LC 2018020071

Presents a collection of recipes inspired by traditional African American cooking, including flaky buttermilk biscuits, grilled okra with spiced sprinkle, black-eyed pea salad with hot sauce vinaigrette, and oxtail stew with brown sauce.

Includes index.

Howard, Vivian
Deep Run Roots: Stories and Recipes from My Corner of the South. Vivian Howard. Little, Brown 2016. 576 p.
ISBN 9780316381109
Grades: Adult　　　　　　　　　　　　　　　　　　641.5975
1. Howard, Vivian (Vivian S.), 1978- 2. Cooking 3. Local foods 4. Cooking, American 5. Recipes 6. Social life and customs 7. North Carolina 8. Southern States 9. Food writing — Cooking and cookbooks — Narrative cookbooks 10. Food Writing — Food and culture 11. Food writing — Cooking and cookbooks — Chefs and restaurants
LC 2016931447

As much a storybook as it is a cookbook, Deep Run roots imparts the true tale of Southern food: Rooted in family and tradition, yet calling out to the rest of the world.

Lewis, Edna
In Pursuit of Flavor. by Edna Lewis, with Mary Goodbody; foreword by Mashama Bailey; illustrated by Louisa Jones Waller. Alfred A. Knopf 2019. 354 p.
ISBN 9780525655510
Grades: Adult　　　　　　　　　　　　　　　　　　641.5975
1. Food habits 2. Food preparation 3. Cooking, American 4. Food writing — Cooking and cookbooks — Narrative cookbooks 5. Food writing — Cooking and cookbooks — Chefs and restaurants
LC 2018035278

Decades before cornbread, shrimp and grits, and peach cobbler were mainstays on menus everywhere, Edna Lewis was pioneering the celebration of seasonal food as a distinctly American cuisine. In this James Beard Foundation Cookbook Hall of Fame-inducted cookbook, Miss Lewis (as she was almost universally known) shares the recipes of her childhood, spent in a Virginia farming community founded by her grandfather and his friends after emancipation, as well as those that made her one of the most revered American chefs of all time.

Includes index; Originally published: New York : Knopf, 1988.

Stone, Robyn
Add a Pinch Cookbook: Easier, Faster, Fresher Southern Classics. Robyn Stone; foreword by Ree Drummond. Clarkson Potter/Publishers 2017. 240 pages : Color; Illustration
ISBN 9780553496413
Grades: Adult　　　　　　　　　　　　　　　　　　641.5975
1. Quick and easy cooking 2. Cooking, American 3. Cookbooks 4. Food writing — Cooking and cookbooks — Regional
LC 2016044983

A blogger who was featured in Southern Living magazine offers 100 traditional Southern recipes that have been reworked to be faster and healthier including Southern Buttermilk Fried Chicken, Pepper Jelly Pork Medallions, Weeknight Chicken Pot Pie and Buttermilk Praline Cheesecake.

Includes index.

Wilkinson, Crystal
Praisesong for the Kitchen Ghosts: Stories and Recipes from Five Generations of Black Country Cooks. Crystal Wilkinson. Clarkson Potter 2024. 288 p.
ISBN 9780593236512
Grades: Adult　　　　　　　　　　　　　　　　　　641.5975
1. Wilkinson, Crystal 2. Cooking, African American 3. Cooking, American 4. Families 5. Recipes 6. African American women authors 7. African American

ESSENTIAL AND RECOMMENDED TITLES
641.5976 Cooking — United States — South Central

women 8. Appalachians (People) 9. Rural life 10. Food habits 11. Southern states 12. Kentucky 13. Appalachian Region 14. Autobiographies and memoirs 15. Cookbooks 16. Food Writing — Cooking and cookbooks — Narrative cookbooks 17. Life stories — Relationships — Family

LC 2023005847

As the keeper of her family's stories and treasured dishes, an O. Henry Prize-winning writer, in this part memoir, part cookbook, weaves those stories together with recipes, family photos and the untold heritage of Black Appalachia.

"Cookbook readers will delight in the beautiful exploration of ancestry, homeland, and food that Wilkinson weaves and relish bringing these foodways of Black Appalachians into their own homes." —*Library Journal*

Includes index.

641.5976 Cooking — United States — South Central

Hereford, Mason
Turkey and the Wolf: Flavor Trippin' in New Orleans. Mason Hereford with JJ Goode; photographs by William Hereford; illustrations by Leo Gonzales; lettering by Ashlee Arceneaux Jones. Ten Speed Press 2022. 243 pages : Illustration; Color
 ISBN 9781984858993
 Grades: Adult 641.5976
 1. Cooking, American 2. New Orleans, Louisiana 3. Southern States 4. Food writing — Cooking and cookbooks — Chefs and restaurants 5. Food writing — Cooking and cookbooks — Regional

LC 2021017837

Drawing inspiration from his childhood, the James Beard Award-nominated owner of Turkey and the Wolf in New Orleans puts a bold, fresh twist on some of the most beloved Southern dishes.

"This wild and laid-back cookbook will be a joy for those who are looking for a break from more serious cookbooks and want to dig in with junk food cravings." —*Library Journal*

Includes index.

Lambert, Miranda
*Y'all Eat Yet?: Welcome to the Pretty B*tchin' Kitchen*. Miranda Lambert with Holly Gleason. Dey St, an imprint of William Morrow 2023. 278 pages : Color; Illustration
 ISBN 9780063087781
 Grades: Adult 641.5976
 1. Cooking, American 2. Country musicians 3. Southern states 4. Texas 5. Louisiana 6. Cookbooks 7. Food writing — Cooking and cookbooks — Regional 8. Life stories — Arts and culture — Performing arts — Musicians and composers 9. Arts and Entertainment — Music — Country

LC Bl2023012846

With recipes collected from all the women in her life, including her mom, grandma and a colorful bunch of best friends, this book delivers food you want to make alongside charming stories that show why Miranda Lambert is one of the most beloved artists in country music today.

"The simple, straightforward recipes will appeal to beginning cooks, and fans of Lambert will love the pictures and background narrative. A celebrity cookbook definitely worth adding to library collections." —*Library Journal*

Includes index.

641.5977 Cooking — United States — Midwest

King, Maren Ellingboe
Fresh Midwest: Modern Recipes from the Heartland. Maren Ellingboe King; photographs by Maren Ellingboe King & Eliesa Johnson. Countryman Press, an imprint of W. W. Norton & Company 2022. xiii, 234 pages : Color; Illustration
 ISBN 9781682686966
 Grades: Adult 641.5977
 1. Cooking, American 2. Cooking 3. Cooking, Scandinavian 4. Middle West 5. Minnesota 6. Food writing — Cooking and cookbooks — Regional

LC 2022021411

In this debut cookbook, recipe developer and Minnesota native Maren Ellingboe King perfectly combines the nostalgia of traditional midwestern dishes and influences of her Scandinavian heritage with an emphasis on local, unprocessed ingredients. Ellingboe King celebrates the growing diversity of her home state with a modern take on traditional recipes by using fresh produce, more spice, and more heat, all while retaining the simplicity and approachability of her family's recipes."

"The result is a wonderful introduction to Midwestern cooking and its rich traditions." —*Publishers Weekly*

Includes index.

Rettke, Amanda
Homestead Recipes: Midwestern Inspirations, Family Favorites, and Pearls of Wisdom from a Sassy Home Cook. Amanda Rettke. William Morrow, an imprint of HarperCollinsPublishers 2022. xv, 283 pages : Illustration; Color
 ISBN 9780063008205
 Grades: Adult 641.5977
 1. Cooking, American 2. Cookbooks 3. Food Writing — Cooking and cookbooks — Regional

LC Bl2022011567

A food blogger, cake cookbook author and Minnesota homesteader provides 110 home-cooked recipes with chapters on breakfast, casseroles, soups, appetizers, meats, vegetables and desserts along with her trademark sassy commentary and beautiful photos.

"A spoonful of sugar, then several more, help the treats go down in this waistline-be-damned parade of comfort foods." —*Publishers Weekly*

Includes index.

Sever, Shauna
 ★ *Midwest Made: Big, Bold Baking from the Heartland*. Shauna Sever; photographs by Paul Strabbing. Running Press 2019. 318 pages : Color; Illustration
 ISBN 9780762464500
 Grades: Adult 641.5977
 1. Baking 2. Cooking, American 3. Recipes 4. Cookbooks 5. Food writing — Cooking and cookbooks — Methods 6. Food writing — Cooking and cookbooks — Regional

LC Bl2019034670

When it comes to defining what we know as all-American baking, everything from Bundt cakes to brownies have roots that can be traced to the great Midwest. German, Scandinavian, Polish, French, and Italian immigrant families baked their way to the American Midwest, instilling in it pies, breads, cookies, and pastries that manage to feel distinctly home-grown.

Includes index.

641.5979 Cooking — United States — Pacific Slope

Centeno, Josef
Ama: A Modern Tex-Mex Kitchen. Josef Centeno & Betty Hallock; photographs by Ren Fuller. Chronicle Books 2019. 272 pages : Color; Illustration
 ISBN 9781452155869
 Grades: Adult 641.5979
 1. Cooking, Mexican American 2. Cooking, American 3. Recipes 4. Cookbooks 5. Food writing — Cooking and cookbooks — Regional 6. Food writing — Cooking and cookbooks — Chefs and restaurants

LC 2018052019

A San Antonio native and Los Angeles chef and restauranteur introduces Tex-Mex, a cuisine that combines the deep traditions of Texan and Mexican cooking, in this collection of more than 100 recipes that celebrate down-home cooking and grilling at its most inspiring. Illustrations.

Includes index.

PUBLIC LIBRARY CORE COLLECTION: NONFICTION
Twentieth Edition

Trejo, Danny
Trejo's Tacos: Recipes and Stories from L.A. Danny Trejo with Hugh Garvey; photography by Ed Anderson. Clarkson Potter 2020. 223 p.
ISBN 9781984826855
Grades: Adult   **641.5979**
1. Cooking, Mexican American 2. Tacos 3. Recipes 4. Cookbooks 5. Food writing — Cooking and cookbooks — Regional 6. Food writing — Cooking and cookbooks — Chefs and restaurants
LC Bl2020046500

The legendary actor and L.A. restauranteur shares his favorite—and badass—recipes for bold, fun and versatile Mexican dishes along with stories about his lifelong love of food, in this cookbook that is symbolic of L.A.'s vibrant Latino culture.

"This fiendishly creative collection is a must-have for taco lovers." —*Publishers Weekly*

Wangler, Justin
Season: A Year of Wine Country Food, Farming, Family & Friends. Justin Wangler & Tracey Shepos Cenami; with culinary gardener Tucker Taylor, Jackson Family Wines; photographer, Alan Campbell; writer, Steve Siegelman; designers, Iain R. Morris & Suzi Hutsell. Cameron + Company 2018. 302 pages : Color; Illustration; Portrait
ISBN 9781944903374
Grades: Adult   **641.5979**
1. Cooking, American 2. Food and wine pairing 3. Recipes 4. Seasonal cooking 5. Cookbooks 6. Food writing — Cooking and cookbooks — Regional
LC 2018042526

A cookbook put together by the chefs and gardeners at Jackson Family Wines, offering season-specific recipes for every occasion.

"This high-end farmers almanac pairs seasonal food with Jackson Family wines... the entire package is an appealing advertisement for not just wines and food, but for the California wine country lifestyle." —*Publishers Weekly*

Includes bibliographical references and index.

641.598 Cooking — South America

Gutierrez, Sandra A.
Latinísimo: Home Recipes from the Twenty-One Countries of Latin America. Sandra A. Gutierrez; photographs by Kevin J. Miyazaki. Alfred A. Knopf 2023. xxvii, 557 pages : Color; Illustration
ISBN 9780525659259
Grades: Adult   **641.598**
1. Cooking, Latin American 2. Latin America 3. Cookbooks 4. Food writing — Cooking and cookbooks — Regional
LC 2022039482

A cookbook celebrating the cuisines and cultures of all twenty-one Latin American countries.

"The breadth of this cookbook, combined with its practical charm, makes this a perfect choice for libraries looking to get a great, all-in-one Latin American cookbook." —*Booklist*

Includes bibliographical references (page 543) and index.

Vasquez, Karla Tatiana
★ *The Salvisoul* Cookbook: Salvadoran Recipes & The Women Who Preserve Them. Karla Tatiana Vasquez; photography by Ren Fuller and Monica Torrento. Ten Speed Press 2024. 279 p. : Illustration; Color
ISBN 9781984861429
Grades: Adult   **641.598**
1. Cooking 2. Women 3. Salvadoran Americans 4. Immigrants 5. Communities 6. Survival 7. Recipes 8. Sharing 9. Food preparation 10. El Salvador 11. United States 12. Food writing — Cooking and cookbooks — Narrative cookbooks 13. Food writing — Food and culture 14. Life stories — Facing adversity 15. Debut title
LC 2023013449

A food historian and Salvadoran, through this collection of 80 recipes, shares the stories of the women in her life who reveal shared experiences of what it was like in El Salvador before the war, and what life was like as Salvadoran women surviving in their new home in the U.S.

"The bright photos sometimes seem at odds with the darker tales Vasquez's subjects share but serve as a reminder that in spite of hardship, food is always part of the journey. An essential for any cookbook collection." —*Booklist*

Includes index.

641.59861 Cooking — Colombia

Velasquez, Mariana
Colombiana: A Rediscovery of Recipes and Rituals from the Soul of Colombia. Mariana Velasquez. Harper Wave 2021. 288 p.
ISBN 9780063019430
Grades: Adult   **641.59861**
1. Cooking 2. Cookbooks 3. Food writing — Cooking and cookbooks — Regional
LC 2020047875

A cookbook featuring 100 recipes that offer a contemporary take on traditional Colombian cooking.

The James Beard-award-winning recipe developer and food stylist draws on the rich culinary traditions of her native Bogota, Columbia in a collection of 100 recipes including Tamarind Pork Tenderloin with Mint and Spicy Papaya and Charred Shrimp Gazpacho.

"For home cooks in search of a primer on Colombian food and culinary tradition, Velasquez is the ideal tutor." —*Publishers Weekly*

Includes bibliographical references and index.

641.59969 Cooking — Hawaii

Kysar, Alana
Aloha Kitchen: Recipes from Hawai'i. Alana Kysar; photography by Alana Kysar and Brooklyn Dombroski. Ten Speed Press 2019. 230 pages : Color; Illustration
ISBN 9780399581366
Grades: Adult   **641.59969**
1. Recipes 2. Cooking 3. Cookbooks 4. Food writing — Cooking and cookbooks — Regional
LC 2018034179

A native Hawaiian food blogger explores the multicultural influences behind the cuisine of the islands with recipes for such staples as saimin, loco moco, shave ice, and shoyu chicken, tracing their geographic origin and history on the islands.

"Kysar, a food blogger (Fix Feast Flair) born in Maui, presents an eye-opening portrait of the cultural diversity behind Hawaiis cuisine in 85 recipes celebrating the aloha spirit at the core of Hawaiian food." —*Publishers Weekly*

Includes index.

Simeon, Sheldon
Cook Real Hawaii. Sheldon Simeon with Garrett Snyder. Clarkson Potter/Publishers 2021. 302 pages : Color; Illustration
ISBN 9781984825834
Grades: Adult   **641.59969**
1. Cooking 2. Food writing — Cooking and cookbooks — Regional 3. Food writing — Cooking and cookbooks — Chefs and restaurants
LC 2020031835

The story of Hawaiian cooking, by a two-time Top Chef finalist and Fan Favorite, through 100 recipes that embody the beautiful cross-cultural exchange of the islands. On two seasons of Top Chef, Sheldon Simeon established himself as a leading young, creative chef (he was both a finalist and Fan Favorite on both seasons). The role he is even more proud to fill, though, is as the storyteller of Hawaiian cuisine and the many cultures that have come together there to create

ESSENTIAL AND RECOMMENDED TITLES
641.6 Cooking specific materials

it: the native Hawaiian traditions, Japanese influences, Portuguese cooking techniques, and dynamic flavors that are closest to Sheldon's heart.

"Great for home cooks wanting to explore Hawaiian cuisine at home, or those wanting to try new flavors and enhance their repertoire of fusion-inspired dishes." —*Library Journal*

Includes index.

641.6 Cooking specific materials

Anthony, Michael
V Is for Vegetables: Inspired Recipes and Techniques for Home Cooks from Artichokes to Zucchini. Michael Anthony with Dorothy Kalins; photographs by Maura McEvoy; design by Don Morris Design. Little, Brown and Company 2015. IX, 374 pages : Color; Illustration
ISBN 9780316373357
Grades: Adult   641.6
1. Cooking (Vegetables) 2. Recipes 3. Cookbooks 4. Food writing — Cooking and cookbooks — Vegetarian and vegan 5. Food writing — Cooking and cookbooks — Ingredients
LC Bl2015042210

Collects simple recipes and techniques for cooking imaginative vegetable-based dishes, including salads, herb sauces, gratins, and stews.

"With its distinctive recipes, this title can augment and supplement collections that already include classics such as James Peterson's Vegetables, Revised and Deborah Madison's Vegetable Literacy." —*Library Journal*

Includes index.

Berens, Abra
Grist: A Practical Guide to Cooking Grains, Beans, Seeds, and Legumes : 140+ Recipes and 160+ Variations. by Abra Berens; photographs by EE Berger; illustrations by Lucy Engelman, foreword by Adrian Lipscombe. Chronicle Books 2021. 448 pages : Illustration; Color
ISBN 9781797207131
Grades: Adult   641.6
1. Cooking (Cereals) 2. Cooking (Vegetables) 3. Vegetarian cooking 4. Cookbooks 5. Food Writing — Cooking and cookbooks — Ingredients 6. Food Writing — Cooking and cookbooks — Vegetarian and vegan
LC 2021018825

A practical guide to cooking grains, beans, seeds, and legumes, with 140+ recipes and 160+ variations."

"Berens demystifies grains, seeds, and legumes with her suggestions. An essential guide for home chefs looking to cook more than white rice and canned beans." —*Library Journal*

Includes index.

Pulp: A Practical Guide to Cooking with Fruit : 215+ Sweet and Savory Recipes and Variations, Including a Baker's Toolkit. by Abra Berens; photographs by EE Berger; illustrations by Lucy Engelman, foreword by Tim Mazurek. Chronicle Books 2023. 432 pages : Illustration; Color
ISBN 9781797207148
Grades: Adult   641.6
1. Cooking (Fruit) 2. Cooking (Vegetables) 3. Fruit 4. Vegetables 5. Desserts 6. Cookbooks 7. Food writing — Cooking and cookbooks — Ingredients
LC 2022045922

Providing more than 215 recipes that are alternately sweet and savory, this gorgeous follow-up to Ruffage and Grist shows home cooks and bakers alike how to incorporate fruit that grows in the Midwestern U.S. in main dishes to add variety and seasonality.

"Berens is a cookbook superstar, and her innovative way of creating books, and talking about and sharing food, is a pleasure to read." —*Library Journal*

Includes index.

Conner, Polly
★ *From Freezer to Cooker: Delicious Whole-Foods Meals for the Slow Cooker, Pressure Cooker, and Instant Pot.* Polly Conner & Rachel Tiemeyer; photography by Helene Dujardin. Rodale 2020. 256 p.
ISBN 9781635653120
Grades: Adult   641.6
1. Quick and easy cooking 2. Pressure cooking 3. Recipes 4. Cookbooks 5. Food writing — Cooking and cookbooks — Methods 6. Food writing — Cooking and cookbooks — Ingredients

The authors of from Freezer to Table share dozens of nutritious slow cooker, pressure cooker and Instant Pot meals that are designed for busy households and complemented by advice for preparing ahead by using frozen ingredients.

"[A] useful collection for home cooks pressed for time." —*Publishers Weekly*

Dragonwagon, Crescent
Bean by Bean: More Than 175 Recipes for Fresh Beans, Dried Beans, Cool Beans, Hot Beans, Savory Beans, Even Sweet Beans! Crescent Dragonwagon. Workman Pub. 2011. xiv, 370 p. : Color illustration
ISBN 9780761132417
Grades: Adult   641.6
1. Cooking 2. Beans 3. Cookbooks 4. Food writing — Cooking and cookbooks — Ingredients
LC Bl2012025556

Presents over one hundred recipes for appetizers, soups, salads, entrées, and desserts that feature beans as the main ingredient.

"Health food-focused readers will appreciate icons that identify vegan, vegetarian, gluten-free, and 'meatest' recipes, as well as the abundant variety of flavors and cultural influences in this exhaustive and inexpensive cookbook." —*Library Journal*

Includes index.

Fox, Jeremy
On Vegetables: Modern Recipes for the Home Kitchen. Jeremy Fox with Noah Galuten; foreword by David Chang; photographs by Rick Poon. 2017. 319 pages : Illustration; Color
ISBN 9780714873909
Grades: Adult   641.6
1. Cooking (Vegetables) 2. Cooking, American 3. California 4. Cookbooks 5. Food writing — Cooking and cookbooks — Ingredients 6. Food writing — Cooking and cookbooks — Regional 7. Food writing — Cooking and cookbooks — Chefs and restaurants
LC Bl2017015826

Includes index.

Franklin, Aaron
Franklin Steak: Dry-Aged, Live-Fired, Pure Beef. Aaron Franklin and Jordan Mackay; photography by Wyatt McSpadden; illustrations by Bryan B. Butler. Ten Speed Press 2019. VII, 215 pages : Color; Illustration
ISBN 9780399580963
Grades: Adult   641.6
1. Cooking (Beef) 2. Cookbooks 3. Food writing — Cooking and cookbooks — Ingredients 4. Food writing — Cooking and cookbooks — Methods 5. Food writing — Cooking and cookbooks — Regional
LC 2018045052

The be-all, end-all guide to cooking the perfect steak—from buying top-notch beef, seasoning to perfection, and finding or building the ideal cooking vessel—from the team behind the acclaimed and best-selling book Franklin Barbecue. Aaron Franklin may be the reigning king of brisket, but in his off-time, what he really loves to cook and eat at home is steak. So, in this follow-up to his New York Times best-selling book Franklin Barbecue, the pitmaster extraordinaire teaches readers how to cook his favorite food to absolute perfection. With their trademark rigor and expertise, Franklin and coauthor Jordan Mackay go deeper into the art and science of cooking steak than anyone has gone before. They travel the world—beyond Franklin's native Texas to Spain, Scotland, California, and Japan—to uncover global steak preparations and traditions. They demystify cattle breeds, explore the technique of dry-aging, and even teach readers how to build custom, backyard grill setups inspired by the best steak chefs in the world. For any meat-lover, backyard grill-master, or fan of Franklin's fun yet authoritative approach, this book is a must-have.

Includes bibliographical references and index.

PUBLIC LIBRARY CORE COLLECTION: NONFICTION
Twentieth Edition

Greenspan, Eric
The **Great** *Grilled Cheese Book: Grown-Up Recipes for a Childhood Classic.* Eric Greenspan; photography by Colin Price. Ten Speed Press 2018. 143 pages : Color; Illustration
ISBN 9780399580741
Grades: Adult 641.6
1. Sandwiches 2. Cooking (Cheese) 3. Recipes 4. Quick and easy cooking 5. Cookbooks 6. Food writing — Cooking and cookbooks — Methods 7. Food writing — Cooking and cookbooks — Ingredients
LC 2017049573

Offers fifty recipes for grilled cheese sandwiches, from the simple to the sophisticated, and includes tips on the best cheeses and breads and notes on the best cooking techniques.
Includes index.

Holmberg, Martha
★ **Simply** *Tomato: 100 Recipes for Enjoying Your Favorite Ingredient All Year Long.* Martha Holmberg; photographs by Ellen Silverman. Artisan 2023. 247 pages : Color; Illustration
ISBN 9781648290374
Grades: Adult 641.6
1. Cooking 2. Tomato sauces 3. Tomatoes 4. Cookbooks 5. Food writing — Cooking and cookbooks — Ingredients
LC 2022037519

Americans eat more tomatoes than any vegetable except for the potato. But what do we do with all those tomatoes? Acclaimed chef, cooking teacher, and author Martha Holmberg shares 75 recipes to turn the tomato into glorious dishes. Whether it's a fresh-off-the-vine tomato or a just-picked-from-the-supermarket-shelf tomato, Holmberg has ideas to make the best of our favorite summer fruit.

"Longtime food guru Holmberg chops up tomato myths into digestible pieces, along the way educating readers on every part of the fruit…For tomato lovers, this is destined to be an all-season favorite." —*Booklist*
Includes index.

Madison, Deborah
Vegetable *Literacy: Cooking and Gardening with Twelve Families from the Edible Plant Kingdom, with Over 300 Deliciously Simple Recipes.* Deborah Madison; photography by Christopher Hirsheimer and Melissa Hamilton. Ten Speed Press 2013. 405 pages : Color; Illustration
ISBN 9781607741916
Grades: Adult 641.6
1. Cooking (Vegetables) 2. Food crops 3. Recipes 4. Cookbooks 5. Food writing — Cooking and cookbooks — Ingredients 6. Food writing — Cooking and cookbooks — Vegetarian and vegan
LC 2012030968

Shows how vegetables from the same family can be interchanged to complement other flavors and includes over one hundred recipes, including grilled asparagus with tarragon butter, potato cakes with red chile molido, and chive and saffron crepes.
Includes bibliographical references (page 395) and index.

Mangini, Cara
The **Vegetable** *Butcher: How to Select, Prep, Slice, Dice, and Masterfully Cook Vegetables from Artichokes to Zucchini.* Cara Mangini. Workman Publishing 2016. Iv, 346 pages
ISBN 9780761180524
Grades: Adult 641.6
1. Cooking (Vegetables) 2. Vegetables 3. Recipes 4. Cookbooks 5. Food writing — Cooking and cookbooks — Ingredients 6. Food writing — Cooking and cookbooks — Vegetarian and vegan
LC 2016004215

Marrying the art of butchery with the joy of seasonal produce, an essential guide demystifies the world of vegetables, providing a complete vegetable education through 100 vegetarian recipes that celebrate the soul-satisfying flavor of each vegetable.
Includes index.

★ *The* **Vegetable** *Eater: The New Playbook for Cooking Vegetarian.* Cara Mangini. Workman Publishing 2024. 330 pages : Color; Illustration
ISBN 9781523514946
Grades: Adult 641.6
1. Cooking (Vegetables) 2. Seasonal cooking 3. Vegetarian cooking 4. Cookbooks 5. Food writing — Cooking and cookbooks — Ingredients 6. Food writing — Cooking and cookbooks — Vegetarian and vegan
LC 2023028661

The IACP Award winner and James Beard Award finalist, aka the Vegetable Butcher, presents a foundational education in vegetable cooking, making it approachable through uncomplicated lessons, with 100 nourishing, vegetable-forward recipes with season variations.

"With crisp photos and a clean layout, Mangini's low-hassle and lighter recipes will inspire both habitual vegetarians and carnivores looking to take on lunches and suppers in more cruciferous style." —*Booklist*
Includes index.

Mullen, Marissa
That **Cheese** *Plate Wants to Party: Festive Boards, Spreads, and Recipes with the Cheese by Numbers Method.* Marissa Mullen; illustrated by Sara Gilanchi. The Dial Press 2023. xii, 271 pages : Color; Illustration
ISBN 9780593446683
Grades: Adult 641.6
1. Cheese 2. Appetizers 3. Cooking (Cheese) 4. Cocktails 5. Entertaining 6. Parties 7. Cookbooks 8. Food writing — Cooking and cookbooks — Entertaining 9. Food writing — Cooking and cookbooks — Ingredients
LC 2022039276

Featuring 40 new cheese boards for parties of all kinds, along with drink pairings, color themes, floral arrangement tips, tablescape ideas, playlists and cheesy party games, this how-to guide shows how these communal meals celebrate the way we connect with each other.

"A gorgeous and helpful resource for anyone just starting out with cheese boards that takes readers from basic prep to boards or grazing tables, with all of the necessary steps in between." —*Library Journal*
Includes index.

Ottolenghi, Yotam
★ **Plenty** *More: Vibrant Vegetable Cooking from London's Ottolenghi.* Yotam Ottolenghi. Ten Speed Press 2014. x, 339 pages : Color; Illustration
ISBN 9781607746218
Grades: Adult 641.6
1. Cooking (Vegetables) 2. Vegetarian cooking 3. Recipes 4. Cookbooks 5. Food writing — Cooking and cookbooks — Chefs and restaurants 6. Food writing — Cooking and cookbooks — Vegetarian and vegan
LC 2014017924

"While the recipes require time and finesse . they are often revelatory, introducing textures and flavor combinations that readers won't find elsewhere." —*Library Journal*
Includes index.

Plenty: *Vibrant Vegetable Recipes from London's Ottolenghi.* Yotam Ottolenghi. Chronicle Books 2011. 287 p. : Color illustration
ISBN 9781452101248
Grades: Adult 641.6
1. Cooking (Vegetables) 2. Recipes 3. Cookbooks 4. Food writing — Cooking and cookbooks — Chefs and restaurants 5. Food writing — Cooking and cookbooks — Vegetarian and vegan
LC 2011036741

A collection of vegetarian recipes based on freshness and seasonality, and drawn from the diverse food cultures represented in London.
Includes bibliographical references and index.

ESSENTIAL AND RECOMMENDED TITLES
641.665 Poultry

Raichlen, Steven
The Brisket Chronicles: How to Barbecue, Braise, Smoke, and Cure the World's Most Epic Cut of Meat. Steven Raichlen; food photography by Matthew Benson. Workman Publishing 2019. IX, 278 pages : Illustration; Color
ISBN 9781523505487
Grades: Adult **641.6**
1. Cooking (Beef) 2. Cookbooks 3. Food writing — Cooking and cookbooks — Methods 4. Food writing — Cooking and cookbooks — Ingredients
LC Bl2019012911

Collects more than sixty recipes that incorporate America's favorite cut of meat, including such offerings as bacon-smoked brisket flat, Korean grilled brisket, old school pastrami, brisket ramen, and smoky brisket cheese pockets.

"Barbecue guru Raichlen (Project Smoke) turns his expert attention to that collagen-laced chest cut of beef known, in 1450 England, as bru-kette, revealing it as the modern-day centerpiece for an international menu of delicacies. Over 60 recipes and numerous cooking techniques are interwoven with a look at the foods history, along with brief profiles of a few of who Raichlen considers America's best pit masters." —*Publishers Weekly*
Includes index.

How to Grill Vegetables: The New Bible for Barbecuing Vegetables Over Live Fire. Steven Raichlen. Workman Publishing 2021. 325 p. : Color; Illustration
ISBN 9781523509843
Grades: Adult **641.6**
1. Vegetables 2. Cooking (Vegetables) 3. Barbecuing 4. Cookbooks 5. Food writing — Cooking and cookbooks — Ingredients
LC 2021010004

A New York Times best-selling cookbook author and grilling guru describes the basics of how to grill vegetables, whether they be the main dish or sides in recipes including Wood-Grilled Bruschetta and Spicy Smoked Chickpeas. 75,000 first printing.

"As always in his cookbooks, Raichlen provides a wealth of conveniently presented and highly useful information about equipment, ingredients, and techniques to guide both novice and experienced grill-tenders." —*Booklist*
Includes index.

Ripert, Eric
Seafood Simple. Eric Ripert; photographs by Nigel Parry. Random House 2023. 286 pages : Color; Illustration
ISBN 9780593449523
Grades: Adult **641.6**
1. Cooking (Seafood) 2. Cooking (Fish) 3. Seafood 4. Fish as food 5. Cookbooks 6. Food writing — Cooking and cookbooks — Ingredients 7. Food writing — Cooking and cookbooks — Chefs and restaurants
LC 2022054245

The three-Michelin-starred chef of Le Bernardin in New York City teaches readers how to master fish cookery at home through 85 straightforward, mouthwatering recipes, including Tuna Carpaccio, Crispy Fish Tacos, Shrimp Tempura and Miso Cod, for bringing out the vibrant flavor and incredible versatility of seafood.

"Such simple preparations demand the freshest catch, so access to good seafood markets is a necessity." —*Booklist*
Includes index.

Selengut, Becky
★ *Misunderstood Vegetables: How to Fall in Love with Sunchokes, Rutabaga, Eggplant, and More.* Becky Selengut; photography by Clare Barboza. Countryman Press, an imprint of W.W. Norton & Company 2024. 271 pages : Color; Illustration
ISBN 9781682688038
Grades: Adult **641.6**
1. Cooking (Vegetables) 2. Vegetables 3. Cookbooks 4. Food writing — Cooking and cookbooks — Ingredients 5. Food writing — Cooking and cookbooks — Vegetarian and vegan
LC Bl2024003843

Go from "What the heck is this" to "How does it taste so good" in this celebration of misfit vegetables.

"Even with the bounty of excellent vegetable-focused cookbooks that are available, this effortlessly entertaining and endlessly empowering book deserves its own spot in every kitchen." —*Library Journal*
Includes indexes.

Sharma, Nik
Veg-Table: Recipes, Techniques + Plant Science for Big-Flavored, Vegetable-Focused Meals. Recipes and photographs by Nik Sharma. Chronicle Books 2023. 351 pages : Color; Illustration
ISBN 9781797216317
Grades: Adult **641.6**
1. Cooking (Vegetables) 2. Vegetarian cooking 3. Cookbooks 4. Food writing — Cooking and cookbooks — Ingredients
LC 2023020292

Showcasing more than 50 vegetables, revealing their origins, biology and unique characteristics, this beautiful vegetable-focused recipe collection of big flavors and techniques has been perfected by rigorous testing and a deep scientific lens.

"Some contain meat, but the focus is 100 percent on the vegetables. Recipes are written in a conversational style, listing ingredients in both metric and U.S. measurements in bold within the text itself. Cook's notes follow each recipe, providing tips and possible substitution ideas, along with gorgeous photos and veggie glamour shots." —*Library Journal*
Includes bibliographical references (page 343) and index.

Steele, Lisa
★ *The Fresh Eggs Daily Cookbook: Over 100 Fabulous Recipes to Use Eggs in Unexpected Ways.* Lisa Steele. Harper Horizon 2022. xv, 299 pages : Illustration; Color
ISBN 9780785245261
Grades: Adult **641.6**
1. Cooking (Eggs) 2. Cookbooks 3. Food Writing — Cooking and cookbooks — Ingredients
LC Bl2022006467

Lisa Steele, founder of the popular blog Fresh Eggs Daily, shares the delightful and delicious recipes she uses each day to take advantage of the bounty provided by the feathered friends on her Maine farm."

"Steele lays down as many tips and recipes as her chickens do eggs in this innovative and plucky collection. . . . This will be hard to beat." —*Publishers Weekly*
Includes indexes.

641.665 Poultry

Pepin, Jacques
Art of the Chicken: A Master Chef's Paintings, Stories, and Recipes of the Humble Bird. Jacques Pépin. Harvest 2022. xxv, 228 pages : Illustration; Color
ISBN 9780358654513
Grades: Adult **641.665**
1. Pepin, Jacques, 1935- 2. Cooks 3. Chickens 4. Cooking (Chicken) 5. Cooking, French 6. Cooking, American 7. Recipes 8. Western European people 9. French people 10. North American people 11. American people 12. Life stories — Arts and culture — Culinary arts 13. Food writing — Cooking and cookbooks — Narrative cookbooks 14. Food writing — Memoirs and biographies
LC 2022935618

From legendary chef Jacques Pepin, a book celebrating his lifelong love of chickens, featuring dozens of his celebrated paintings and more than 50 recipes, along with a treasure trove of poignant and often humorous stories.

"It's a lovely book on its own, and also a winning companion volume to Pépin's memoir, the Apprentice." —*Publishers Weekly*
Includes index.

PUBLIC LIBRARY CORE COLLECTION: NONFICTION
Twentieth Edition

641.7 Specific cooking processes and techniques

Bittman, Mark
★ *How to Grill Everything: Simple Recipes for Great Flame-Cooked Food.* Mark Bittman; photography by Christina Holmes. Houghton Mifflin Harcourt 2018. VII, 568 pages : Color; Illustration
ISBN 9780544790308
Grades: Adult   641.7
1. Barbecuing 2. Barbecue cooking 3. Recipes 4. Cookbooks 5. Food writing — Cooking and cookbooks — Methods
LC 2017051933
"Regardless of ones grilling experience, fans of outdoor cooking will find this volume to be essential." —*Publishers Weekly*
Includes index.

Byrn, Anne
Skillet Love: From Steak to Cake : More Than 150 Recipes in One Cast-Iron Pan. Anne Byrn; photographs by Danielle Atkins. Grand Central Publishing 2019. xxv, 277 p. : Color; Illustration
ISBN 9781538763186
Grades: Adult   641.7
1. Comfort food 2. One-dish meals 3. Recipes 4. Cookbooks 5. Food writing — Cooking and cookbooks — Methods
LC 2019014326
A celebration of the cast-iron pan.
Includes index.

Franklin, Aaron
Franklin Barbecue: A Meat-Smoking Manifesto. Aaron Franklin and Jordan Mackay; photography by Wyatt McSpadden. Ten Speed Press 2015. IX, 213 pages : Color; Illustration
ISBN 9781607747208
Grades: Adult   641.7
1. Barbecuing 2. Recipes 3. Cooking 4. Cookbooks 5. Food writing — Cooking and cookbooks — Methods 6. Food writing — Cooking and cookbooks — Regional
LC 2014036177
A resource for home cooks from an award-winning pitmaster unlocks the secrets behind great barbecue, including building a smoker, curing the right wood, and tending fires, with recipes for brisket, spare ribs, beef ribs, and turkey breast.
Includes index.

Goldwyn, Meathead
★ *Meathead: The Science of Great Barbecue and Grilling.* Text and photos by Meathead Goldwyn; with Greg Blonder, Ph.D.. A Rux Martin Book, Houghton Mifflin Harcourt 2016. xv, 384 pages
ISBN 9780544018464
Grades: Adult   641.7
1. Barbecuing 2. Cookbooks 3. Food writing — Cooking and cookbooks — Methods
LC 2015049143
The founder and editor behind AmazingRibs.Com provides a definitive guide to understanding the science behind barbecuing and grilling, explaining how marinades work, the importance of digital thermometers, how to calibrate a grill or smoker, along with 118 delicious recipes.
"This highly recommended food-science focused guide to grilling and barbecue will satisfy amateurs and professionals alike." —*Library Journal*
Includes index.

Kimball, Christopher
Milk Street: The World in a Skillet. Christopher Kimball; writing and editing by J.M.Hirsch, Michelle Locke and Dawn Yanagihara;recipes by Wes Martin, Diane Unger, Matthew Card,and the cooks at Milk Street; art direction byJennifer Baldino Cox and Brianna Coleman;photography by. Voracious, Little, Brown and Company 2022. xv, 282 pages : Illustration; Color
ISBN 9780316387361
Grades: Adult   641.7
1. International cooking 2. Cookbooks 3. Food Writing — Cooking and cookbooks — Methods
LC Bl2022012204
Liberating the skillet from commonplace fare, the author shares what he's learned from his travels and from cooks in more than 35 countries through 125 recipes that will transform and expand the way you use this versatile piece of cookware.
"In this latest from the team at Kimball's Milk Street, a single pan takes on global cuisines to offer a delicious range of accessible dishes….Kitchen adventures beckon in this expansive and appetizing collection." —*Publishers Weekly*
At head of title: Milk Street; Includes index.

Leung, Bill
★ *The Woks of Life: Recipes to Know and Love from a Chinese American Family.* Bill, Judy, Sarah & Kaitlin Leung; food photographs by Sarah Leung & Kaitlin Leung; lifestyle photographs by Christine Han. Clarkson Potter/Publishers 2022. 319 pages : Illustration; Color
ISBN 9780593233894
Grades: Adult   641.7
1. Cooking, Chinese 2. Cookbooks 3. Food writing — Cooking and cookbooks — Regional
LC 2022016399
The funny and poignant family behind the hugely popular multigenerational blog The Woks of Life share 100 of their favorite home-cooked and restaurant-style Chinese recipes, along with game-changing Chinese cooking secrets, that will become a part of your family story, too.
"Covering a huge range of dishes and then some, this cookbook will thrill fans of the blog and appeal to cooks of all skill levels, including those looking for a challenge." —*Library Journal*
Includes index.

Moore, Matt
Serial Griller: Grillmaster Secrets for Flame-Cooked Perfection. Matt Moore; photographs by Andrea Behrends and Helene Dujardin. Houghton Mifflin Harcourt 2020. 309 pages : Illustration; Color
ISBN 9780358182696
Grades: Adult   641.7
1. Barbecuing 2. Cooking, American 3. Outdoor cooking 4. Recipes 5. Cookbooks 6. Food writing — Cooking and cookbooks — Methods
LC 2019042991
Taking us on a tour across America to round up authentic stories, covered recipes and practical tips from grill masters of the South and beyond, a self-proclaimed serial griller offers his own tried-and-true recipes for every part of the meal.
"Dedicated backyard grillers will find a lot to challenge them here." —*Booklist*
Includes index.

Rapoport, Adam
The Grilling Book: The Definitive Guide from Bon Appetit. Edited by Adam Rapoport; photography by Peden + Munk. Andrews McMeel Publishing, LLC 2013. 432 pages
ISBN 9781449427528
Grades: Adult   641.7
1. Barbecuing 2. Cookbooks 3. Food writing — Cooking and cookbooks — Methods
LC 2012952341
Features over three hundred fifty recipes for the grill, including rosemary-basted chicken, Yucatan-style pork chops, and corn with hoisin-orange butter.

Scott, Rodney
★ *Rodney Scott's World of BBQ: Every Day Is a Good Day.* Rodney Scott and Lolis Eric Elie. Clarkson Potter/Publishers 2021. 223 pages : Illustration; Color

ESSENTIAL AND RECOMMENDED TITLES
641.8 Cooking specific kinds of dishes and preparing beverages

ISBN 9781984826930
Grades: Adult **641.7**
1. Barbecuing 2. Cooking, American 3. Food writing — Cooking and cookbooks — Methods 4. Food writing — Cooking and cookbooks — Chefs and restaurants 5. Food writing — Cooking and cookbooks — Regional
LC Bl2021005596

The chef and co-owner of Rodney Scott's BBQ in Charleston, South Carolina, shares home-state traditions, tips on building a barbeque pit, and recipes for such dishes as pit-smoked turkey, barbecued spare ribs, smoked chicken wings, and hush puppies.

"With humor and candor, Scott brings readers into his home and invites them to stay a while. A standout collection for fans of BBQ." —*Library Journal*
Includes index.

Sheehan, Jessie
★ *Snackable Bakes: 100 Easy-Peasy Recipes for Exceptionally Scrumptious Sweets and Treats*. Jessie Sheehan. Countryman Press, an imprint of W.W. Norton & Company 2022. 240 pages : Color; Illustration
ISBN 9781682687376
Grades: Adult **641.7**
1. Baking 2. Desserts 3. Quick and easy cooking 4. Cookbooks 5. Food Writing — Cooking and cookbooks — Methods 6. Food Writing — Cooking and cookbooks — Courses
LC 2022003102

From Peppermint Stick No-Churn Ice Cream to Deeply Chocolaty Baked Donuts with Buttermilk Glaze and Sprinkles, this guide to snackable sweets shows readers how to create decadent delights in 20 minutes or less.

"Sheehan brings the irrepressible enthusiasm of her viral TikTok videos to a sumptuous collection of sweet treats designed to be made in under an hour. This excellent guide would satisfy just about any sugar craving." —*Publishers Weekly*
Includes index.

Symon, Michael
Michael Symon's Playing with Fire: BBQ and More from the Grill, Smoker, and Fireplace. Michael Symon and Douglas Trattner; photographs by Ed Anderson. Clarkson Potter/Publishers 2018. 239 pages : Color; Illustration
ISBN 9780804186582
Grades: Adult **641.7**
1. Barbecuing 2. Cooking (Meat) 3. Recipes 4. Cookbooks 5. Food writing — Cooking and cookbooks — Methods
LC 2017034644

"With just 42 main-dish recipes spread across the first 167 pages, the gaps are filled with an overabundance of 'pitmaster profiles,' in which barbecue chefs from across the country are briefly interviewed and their own eateries promoted. Meanwhile, Ed Anderson's color photography of savory cuts encrusted with dry rub or slathered with sauce is nearly enough to make Cleveland synonymous with mouthwatering. This is an excellent guide to live-fire cooking." —*Publishers Weekly*

641.8 Cooking specific kinds of dishes and preparing beverages

Beranbaum, Rose Levy
★ *The Cake Bible*. Rose Levy Beranbaum; edited by Maria D. Guarnaschelli; photographs by Vincent Lee; foreword by Maida Heatter. W. Morrow 1988. 555 p, 30 p. of plates : Illustration; Color
ISBN 9780688044022
Grades: Adult **641.8**
1. Cake 2. Food writing — Cooking and cookbooks — Courses
LC 88001369

Providing countless solutions and tips for commonly encountered baking problems, this comprehensive cake cookbook provides precise instructions for baking and decorating spectacular special-occasion cakes of any size up to eighteen inches in diameter.
Includes index; Bibliography: P. 538-539.

Greenspan, Dorie
Baking with Julia: Based on the PBS Series Hosted by Julia Child. Written by Dorie Greenspan; photographs by Gentl & Hyers. Morrow 1996. xvii, 480 p. : Illustration; Color
ISBN 9780688146573
Grades: Adult **641.8**
1. Baking 2. Recipes 3. Cookbooks 4. Food writing — Cooking and cookbooks — Methods
LC 96023061

A companion volume to the PBS series hosted by Julia Child presents more than 250 recipes for baked goods including simple white breads, muffins, pastry, chocolate creations, and a wedding cake.

"The 200 recipes are organized as a course in baking, with an early, energetic section on the basic batters and doughs for cakes and pastries. The book moves on to recipes of varying degrees of complexity. But the book's success is due to more than organization: the text never misses a chance to explain, expand and entertain." —*New York Times Book Review*
Includes index.

Baking: From My Home to Yours. Dorie Greenspan; photographs by Alan Richardson. Houghton Mifflin 2006. xiii, 514 p. : Illustration
ISBN 9780618443369
Grades: Adult **641.8**
1. Baking 2. Recipes 3. Cookbooks 4. Food writing — Cooking and cookbooks — Methods
LC 2006003101

Offers more than three hundred of the author's favorite recipes, including split-level pudding, gingered carrot cookies, and fold-over pear torte, and provides baking tips and a glossary.

"This collection of recipes covers all the baking bases, from muffins, cookies and brownies to spoon desserts, pies and cobblers. Instructions are clear and easy to follow, and Greenspan uses everyday ingredients readily available to the home chef. This is baking at its best." —*Publishers Weekly*
Includes index.

Stewart, Martha
★ *Martha Stewart's Baking Handbook*. Martha Stewart. Clarkson Potter/Publishers 2005. 415 p. : Color illustration
ISBN 9780307236722
Grades: Adult **641.8**
1. Baking 2. Recipes 3. Cookbooks 4. Food writing — Cooking and cookbooks — Methods
LC 2005053532

Combines instructions for a variety of baking techniques, a visual glossary of equipment, tips on storage and make-ahead preparation, and more than 250 recipes for cakes, pies, biscuits, muffins, scones, breads, and pastries.

"This volume may add to global warming as cooks all over the country start up their ovens to produce the extraordinary baked goods that Stewart proposes." —*Booklist*
Includes index.

641.81 Side dishes, sauces, garnishes

Barrow, Cathy
Bagels, Schmears, and a Nice Piece of Fish: A Whole Brunch of Recipes to Make at Home. Cathy Barrow; photographs by Linda XIao. Chronicle Books 2022. 207 p.
ISBN 9781797210551
Grades: Adult **641.81**
1. Bagels 2. Sandwiches 3. Food Writing — Cooking and cookbooks — Courses 4. Food Writing — Cooking and cookbooks — Methods
LC 2021035053

An award-winning author and cook provides home bakers with step-by-step, illustrated recipes and proper techniques for making classic New York bagels as well as information on slicing and storing as well as suggestions for what to "schmear" on them.

Beranbaum, Rose Levy

★ *The Baking Bible.* Rose Levy Beranbaum; photography by Ben Fink. Houghton Mifflin Harcourt 2014. xv, 560 pages : Illustration
ISBN 9781118338612
Grades: Adult   641.81
1. Baking 2. Cookbooks 3. Food writing — Cooking and cookbooks
LC 2014016319

Offers baking tips and techniques, with recipes for cakes, tarts, pies, cookies, and breads.

"Berenbaum successfully bridges the gap between popular home baking collections and professional texts." —*Library Journal*

★ *Rose's Baking Basics: 100 Essential Recipes, with More Than 600 Step-by-Step Photos.* Rose Levy Beranbaum; photography by Matthew Septimus. Houghton Mifflin Harcourt 2018. xxvi, 372 pages : Color; Illustration
ISBN 9780544816220
Grades: Adult   641.81
1. Baking 2. Cookies 3. Pies 4. Pastry 5. Bread 6. Recipes 7. Cookbooks 8. Food writing — Cooking and cookbooks — Methods
LC 2017058732

Provides illustrated no-fuss recipes for cookies, pies, pastries, cakes, and breads, including such options as marzipan cookies, chocolate butterscotch toffee, blueberry muffins, lemon meringue pie, cream puffs, and whole wheat sandwich bread.

"Instructions for creating related toppings and fillings such as classic ganache, along with solutions for problems during the baking process, will help guide new bakers to create treats such as basic chocolate cupcakes, apple cinnamon coffee cake, and butter biscuits. Lavish step-by-step photographs and storing information accompany each recipe." —*Library Journal*

Includes index.

Bittman, Mark

★ *Bittman Bread: No-Knead Whole-Grain Baking for Every Day.* Mark Bittman and Kerri Conan; photography by Jim Henkens. Houghton Mifflin Harcourt 2021. 241 pages : Color; Illustration
ISBN 9780358539339
Grades: Adult   641.81
1. Cooking (Bread) 2. Bread 3. Cookbooks 4. Food Writing — Cooking and cookbooks — Methods 5. Food Writing — Cooking and cookbooks — Courses
LC 2021018572

A former food columnist and author of more than 30 books presents simple, no-knead bread recipes for every taste and grain—including baguettes, hearty seeded loaves, sandwich bread, soft pretzels, cinnamon rolls, focaccia, pizza, waffles, and much more.

"After reading through the straightforward instructions and salivating at the recipes for crusty breads, pizzas, desserts, and more, readers will be excited to get started." —*Booklist*

Includes index.

★ *How to Bake Everything: Simple Recipes for Best Baking.* Mark Bittman; illustrated by Alan Witschinke. Houghton Mifflin Harcourt 2016. 703 pages : Illustration
ISBN 9780470526880
Grades: Adult   641.81
1. Baking 2. Recipes 3. Cookbooks 4. Food writing — Cooking and cookbooks — Methods
LC Bl2016040259

A comprehensive baker's resource collects more than two thousand recipes for a wide variety of baked products, sharing illustrated how-to instructions as well as advice for adapting recipes for vegan and other customizable needs.

Includes index.

Black, Sarah

One Dough, Ten Breads: Making Great Bread by Hand. Sarah Black; photography by Lauren Volo. Houghton Mifflin Harcourt 2016. xiv, 209 pages : Color; Illustration
ISBN 9780470260951
Grades: Adult   641.81
1. Bread 2. Recipes 3. Cookbooks 4. Food writing — Cooking and cookbooks — Courses 5. Food writing — Cooking and cookbooks — Methods
LC 2015004574

Teaches how to make artisan-style breads by hand, starting with simple, white dough, and then making small changes to ingredients, proportions, and shapes to craft ten foundation breads, and includes additional recipes that build on these basics.

"Black, who believes getting your hands in the dough is the best way to learn about bread, provides easy-to-follow directions for 10 types of bread, each created from one dough and with less than 30 minutes of active time." —*Publishers Weekly*

Conners, Rachel

Bakerita: 100+ No-Fuss Gluten-Free, Dairy-Free, and Refined Sugar-Free Recipes for the Modern Baker. Rachel Conners with Mary Goodbody. Houghton Mifflin Harcourt 2020. 288 pages : Color; Illustration
ISBN 9780358116677
Grades: Adult   641.81
1. Baking 2. Desserts 3. Gluten-free diet 4. Recipes 5. Cookbooks 6. Food writing — Cooking and cookbooks — Cooking for health 7. Food writing — Cooking and cookbooks — Methods
LC 2019033897

Amazingly delicious and beautiful gluten-free, grain-free, dairy-free, and refined sugar-free desserts from the popular Bakerita blog.

"A great choice for health-conscious bakers interested in exploring flavors beyond the nut-and-chocolate staples prevalent in gluten-free and vegan baking." —*Library Journal*

Includes index.

Day, Cheryl

Back in the Day Bakery, Made with Love: More Than 100 Recipes and Make-it-yourself Projects to Create and Share. Cheryl Day & Griffith Day. Artisan 2015. 302 pages
ISBN 9781579655563
Grades: Adult   641.81
1. Baking 2. Cake 3. Pies 4. Recipes 5. Cookbooks 6. Food writing — Cooking and cookbooks — Methods 7. Food writing — Cooking and cookbooks — Regional
LC 2014035874

Offers more than one hundred recipes for treats, breakfast pastries, breads, pizza, and condiments, including jam muffins, breakfast bread pudding, rustic plum pie, tomato pie, spoon bread, salted caramel popcorn, and rosemary focaccia.

The authors of the best-selling Back in the Day Bakery Cookbook share more than 100 new recipes for some of their Georgia bakery's most-requested treats, including Star Brownies, Cakette Party Cake and Chive Parmigiano-Reggiano Popovers.

"Though the Days are wordy at times, the narrative is instructive and warming. The inclusion of crafts like a marshmallow chandelier and a keepsake cake topper seems jarring rather than jovial, the only off note. This is a terrific sequel, and fans of Southern baking (not to mention baking in general) will want to add it to their collection." —*Publishers Weekly*

Includes bibliographical references and index.

Cheryl Day's Treasury of Southern Baking. Cheryl Day; photographs by Angie Mosier. ArtisanBooks 2021. 400 pages : Color; Illustration
ISBN 9781579658410
Grades: Adult   641.81
1. Baking 2. Cooking, American 3. Cookbooks 4. Food Writing — Cooking and cookbooks — Methods 5. Food Writing — Cooking and cookbooks — Chefs and restaurants

ESSENTIAL AND RECOMMENDED TITLES
641.81 Side dishes, sauces, garnishes

LC 2021004795

Combining her deep experience, the conversations she's had with family and her passion for collecting local cookbooks and handwritten recipes, one of the South's most respected bakers presents more than 200 tried-and-true recipes that celebrate the craft of from-scratch Southern baking.

"Day breaks down seemingly complex recipes and makes them accessible and easy to accomplish—her collection of recipes is an essential library addition for at-home and professional bakers alike."—*Booklist*

Includes index.

Emberling, Amy
Zingerman's Bakehouse. Amy Emberling & Frank Carollo; photographs by Antonis Achilleos. Chronicle Books 2017. 255 pages : Color; Illustration
ISBN 9781452156583
Grades: Adult   641.81
1. Baking 2. Recipes 3. Cookbooks 4. Food writing — Cooking and cookbooks — Methods 5. Food writing — Cooking and cookbooks — Chefs and restaurants

LC 2016057669

A collection of recipes from Michigan's renowned artisanal bakery in celebration of its twenty-fifth anniversary features such options as sour cream coffee cake, Jewish rye, challah, Boston cream pie, French crullers, and pecan sandies with bacon.

"All home bakers will recognize its merit, made visible in precise recipes, stunning photographs, and deeply reflective storytelling." —*Library Journal*

Includes indexes.

Forkish, Ken
Flour Water Salt Yeast: The Fundamentals of Artisan Bread and Pizza. Ken Forkish; photographs by alan Weiner. Ten Speed Press 2012. 265 p. : Color illustration
ISBN 9781607742739
Grades: Adult   641.81
1. Bread 2. Pizza 3. Recipes 4. Cookbooks 5. Food writing — Cooking and cookbooks — Courses 6. Food writing — Cooking and cookbooks — Methods

LC 2012012080

A treasury of recipes for world-class breads and pizzas is complemented by schedules that can be adapted for busy home bakers, sharing instructions for preparing high-quality artisan recipes using basic straight dough, pre-ferment dough and complex levain.

"Committed bakers will find plenty here to keep ovens hot and families plates filled with honest versions of one of the nations most beloved foods." —*Booklist*

Includes index.

Francois, Zoe
Holiday and Celebration Bread in Five Minutes a Day: Sweet and Decadent Baking for Every Occasion. Zoe Francois and Jeff Hertzberg, M.D; photographs by Sarah Kieffer and Zoe Francois. St. Martin's Press 2018. xix, 378 pages : Color; Illustration
ISBN 9781250077561
Grades: Adult   641.81
1. Bread 2. Holiday cooking 3. Recipes 4. Cookbooks 5. Food writing — Cooking and cookbooks — Courses 6. Food writing — Cooking and cookbooks — Methods

LC 2018017182

This new cookbook from the authors of the Artisan Bread in Five Minutes a Day series contains 100 recipes for every occasion, using stored doughs that can be used as the basis for celebration breads from all over the globe.

Offers one hundred recipes for holiday breads that use homemade, high-moisture yeast dough, including such breads as lavash, braided challah, monkey bread, sufganiyot, and panettone.

Includes index.

Goldman, Duff
Duff Bakes: Think and Bake Like a Pro at Home. Duff Goldman and Sara Gonzales; photography by Caren Alpert. William Morrow 2015. 343 pages : Color; Illustration
ISBN 9780062349804
Grades: Adult   641.81
1. Baking 2. Desserts 3. Recipes 4. Cookbooks 5. Food writing — Cooking and cookbooks — Chefs and restaurants 6. Food writing — Cooking and cookbooks — Methods

LC Bl2015046059

The graffiti artist-turned-Ace of Cakes star presents a collection of down-to-earth baking recipes that outlines the essentials that home cooks need to create satisfying favorites, from cookies and brownies to muffins and pizza dough.

"Rounded out with plenty of salient tips on everything from selecting the right blowtorch (hit the hardware store) to getting cheesecake out of a cake pan (briefly warm the bottom over the stove top), Goldman and Gonzalez's thoughtful instructions are sure to inspire and embolden readers." —*Publishers Weekly*

Greenspan, Dorie
★ *Baking with Dorie: Sweet, Salty & Simple.* Dorie Greenspan; photographs by Mark Weinberg. Houghton Mifflin Harcourt 2021. x, 389 pages : Color; Illustration
ISBN 9780358223580
Grades: Adult   641.81
1. Baking 2. Cookbooks 3. Food Writing — Cooking and cookbooks — Methods 4. Food Writing — Cooking and cookbooks — Courses

LC 2021013014

A James Beard Award-winning and New York Times best-selling cookbook author offers more than 150 new recipes with ingenious twists including Meringue Little Marvels, Double-Decker Caramel Cake, Coconut Milk Chocolate Marble Cake and Curd and Cream Shortcake.

"This thoroughly explained and understated-yet-elegant collection will keep bakers joyously busy."—*Booklist*

Includes index.

Hazan, Jack
Mind Over Batter: 75 Recipes for Baking as Therapy. Jack Hazan, MA, LMHC with Michael Harari; photography by Lauren Volo. Chronicle Books 2022. 272 pages : Color; Illustration
ISBN 9781797212302
Grades: Adult   641.81
1. Baking 2. Baked products 3. Mental health 4. Self-care 5. Cookbooks 6. Food writing — Cooking and cookbooks — Methods 7. Self-Help — Mental health

LC Bl2023010870

A self-care cookbook for using baking as therapy from licensed psychotherapist and master baker Jack Hazan, with 75 simple, therapeutic recipes."

"Hazan's point of view is simple, comforting, and helpful for those in need of some talk therapy, with the added bonus of baked goods." —*Library Journal*

Includes index.

Hoffman, Brian Hart
★ *Bake from Scratch; Volume Two.* Brian Hart Hoffman. 83 Press 2018. 400 pages : Color; Illustration
ISBN 9781940772486
Grades: Adult   641.81
1. Baking 2. Bread 3. Desserts 4. Cookbooks 5. Food writing — Cooking and cookbooks — Methods 6. Food writing — Cooking and cookbooks — Courses

LC Bl2018052577

Collects recipes for artisan breads, cakes, cookies, and confections for the home cook, including such dishes as spiced persimmon coconut cake, carrot coffee cake, honey pear swirl bread, apricot-almond hand pies, salted chocolate chip cookies, and pecan-toffee bites.

Includes index.

PUBLIC LIBRARY CORE COLLECTION: NONFICTION
Twentieth Edition

Hollis, B. Dylan
  ★ *Baking* Yesteryear: The Best Recipes from the 1900s to the 1980s. B. Dylan Hollis. DK 2023. 255 pages : Color; Illustration
  ISBN 9780744080049
  Grades: Adult   641.81
  1. Baking 2. History 3. 20th century 4. Cookbooks 5. Food writing — Cooking and cookbooks — Courses 6. Food writing — Cooking and cookbooks — Methods
  LC Bl2023023303
  A popular social media baker who shares treats made from antique cookbooks helps readers create baking recipes from the last century in a delicious decade-by-decade tour from Chocolate Potato Cake from the 1910s to Avocado Pie from the 1960s.
  Includes index.

Hollywood, Paul
  ★ *Bake:* My Best Ever Recipes for the Classics. Paul Hollywood; photographs by Haarala Hamilton. Bloomsbury Publishing 2022. 302 pages : Color; Illustration
  ISBN 9781635579291
  Grades: Adult   641.81
  1. Baking 2. Desserts 3. Bread 4. Cooking, British 5. Cookbooks 6. Food writing — Cooking and cookbooks — Methods 7. Food writing — Cooking and cookbooks — Courses
  LC Bl2022022409
  A professional chef and judge on The Great British Baking Show shares his favorite recipes for baking cakes, cookies and breads, each fully tested and tasted for at-home chefs who enjoy discovering new techniques, ingredients and influences.
  "Break out the Hollywood handshake because this book is filled with bakes that will become part of readers' regular rotations." —*Library Journal*
  Includes index.

Hussain, Nadiya
  ★ *Nadiya Bakes.* Nadiya Hussain; photography by Chris Terry. Clarkson Potter/Publishers 2021. 255 pages : Color; Illustration
  ISBN 9780593233733
  Grades: Adult   641.81
  1. Bread 2. Cookies 3. Pies 4. Baking 5. Cookbooks 6. Food Writing — Cooking and cookbooks — Methods 7. Food Writing — Cooking and cookbooks — Courses 8. Food Writing — Cooking and cookbooks — Chefs and restaurants
  LC 2021004506
  The host of the beloved Netflix series Time to Eat and Nadiya Bakes and winner of the Great British Baking Show returns to her true love, baking, with more than 100 delicious, Americanized recipes for sweet treats.
  "Like in her previous cookbooks, Hussain's recipes are filled with flavor and creativity while also being effortlessly attainable by home bakers." —*Library Journal*
  Over 100 must-try recipes for breads, cakes, biscuits, pies, and more—Cover; Includes index.

Kulaga, Agatha
  Ovenly: Sweet & Salty Recipes from New York's Most Creative Bakery. Agatha Kulaga & Erin Patinkin; photography by Winona Barton-Ballentine. Harlequin 2014. xxi, 217 pages : Color; Illustration
  ISBN 9780373892952
  Grades: Adult   641.81
  1. Bread 2. Baked products 3. Recipes 4. Cookbooks 5. Food writing — Cooking and cookbooks — Methods
  LC 2014005173
  Presents a collection of recipes from the award-winning Brooklyn bakery, with a discussion on baking tools and ingredients and options for breads, muffins, cookies, pies, brownies, and cakes.

"Complemented by an attractive design and step-by-step photographs of important techniques, this is a satisfying everyday baking collection perfect for readers who like substantial baked goods with a salty streak." —*Library Journal*
  Includes index.

Lahey, Jim
  The Sullivan Street Bakery Cookbook. Jim Lahey with Maya Joseph; photography by Squire Fox. W. W. Norton & Company 2017. 240 pages : Color; Illustration
  ISBN 9780393247282
  Grades: Adult   641.81
  1. Baking 2. Recipes 3. Cookbooks 4. Food writing — Cooking and cookbooks — Chefs and restaurants 5. Food writing — Cooking and cookbooks — Courses
  LC 2017029427
  Collects recipes for the Italian-inspired cafe dishes and breads from the popular Manhattan bakery, including such options as asparagus pizza, ciabatta, bran and blackberry muffins, oven-baked pasta, and brisket braised in black tea.
  "A terrific addition to the bread-making canon." —*Publishers Weekly*
  Includes bibliographical references and index.

Lomas, Vallery
  ★ *Life* Is What You Bake It: Recipes, Stories & Inspiration to Bake Your Way to the Top. Vallery Lomas. Clarkson Potter/Publishers 2021. 287 pages : Color; Illustration
  ISBN 9780593137680
  Grades: Adult   641.81
  1. Baking 2. Desserts 3. Cookbooks 4. Food writing — Cooking and cookbooks
  LC 2021004910
  A former lawyer who won The Great American Baking Show during the season that was unaired due to a judge's misconduct allegations debuts her first cookbook featuring Apple Cider Fritters, Lemon-Honey Madeleines, Crawfish Hand Pies and Grandma's Million Dollar Cake.
  "Lomas debuts with an inspiring collection that combines life lessons, family lore, and behind-the-scenes peeks at the reality show world with more than 100 indulgent recipes.... Aspiring baking champs need look no further." —*Publishers Weekly*
  Includes index.

Manning, Ivy
  Easy Soups from Scratch with Quick Breads to Match: 70 Recipes to Pair and Share. Ivy Manning; photographs by Dina Avila. Chronicle Books 2017. 175 pages : Color; Illustration
  ISBN 9781452155029
  Grades: Adult   641.81
  1. Bread 2. Recipes 3. Soups 4. Cookbooks 5. Food writing — Cooking and cookbooks — Courses
  LC 2016032627
  Presents a collection of seventy soup recipes, including Korean kimchi and tofu soup, roasted cauliflower and paprika soup, black bean soup with roasted red pepper cream, and coconut chicken soup.
  Includes index.

McDowell, Erin Jeanne
  The Fearless Baker: Simple Secrets for Baking Like a Pro. Erin Jeanne McDowell; photographs by Jennifer May. Houghton Mifflin Harcourt 2017. 383 pages : Color; Illustration
  ISBN 9780544791435
  Grades: Adult   641.81
  1. Baking 2. Cookbooks 3. Food writing — Cooking and cookbooks — Methods
  LC Bl2017043684
  Shares tips and techniques for baking to make professional-quality cakes, pies, and other desserts, and provides recipes for such confections as flourless cocoa cookies, apple cider pie, and strawberry popovers.

ESSENTIAL AND RECOMMENDED TITLES
641.81 Side dishes, sauces, garnishes

"Comprehensive tips on baking and decorating cakes and pies accompany tempting recipes, including for pound cupcakes made with honey-caramel glaze, mocha cake with a coffee and white chocolate ganache, and a simple cider caramel apple pie. Her clearly written recipes and tips, explained in a friendly, encouraging voice, will inspire confidence in experienced and novice bakers alike." —*Publishers Weekly*

A Rux Martin book; Includes index.

Nelson, Candace
The Sprinkles Baking Book: 100 Secret Recipes from Candace's Kitchen. Candace Nelson with Adeena Sussman; photographs by Amy Neunsinger. Grand Central Life & Style 2016. xiii, 321 pages : Color; Illustration

ISBN 9781455592579

Grades: Adult **641.81**

1. Desserts 2. Cake 3. Cupcakes 4. Baking 5. Recipes 6. Cookbooks 7. Food writing — Cooking and cookbooks — Methods 8. Food writing — Cooking and cookbooks — Chefs and restaurants

LC OC2018140580

The founder and pastry chef of Sprinkles Bakery and judge of Cupcake Wars shares the stories and recipes that have been a part of her life and her customers' lives, including 50 Sprinkles cupcake recipes in all their variations along with 50 of her favorite dessert recipes for cakes, pies, cookies, bars and more.

Includes bibliographical references and index.

Peterson, James
Sauces: Classical and Contemporary Sauce Making. James Peterson. Houghton Mifflin Harcourt 2017. xxi, 666 pages : Color; Illustration

ISBN 9780544819825

Grades: Adult **641.81**

1. Recipes 2. Sauces 3. Cookbooks 4. Food writing — Cooking and cookbooks — Courses

LC BI2017051518

Offers practical tips for making sauces, as well as hundreds of recipes for stocks, glaces, and purees using easy-to-follow charts, healthier ingredients, and standardized terminology.

Includes bibliographical references (pages 645-648) and index.

Poliafito, Renato
★ *Dolci!: American Baking with an Italian Accent.* Renato Poliafito; with Casey Elsass; photographs by Kevin Miyazaki. Alfred A. Knopf 2024. xi, 298 pages : Illustration; Color

ISBN 9780593537183

Grades: Adult **641.81**

1. Baking 2. Desserts 3. Cooking, Italian 4. Cooking, American 5. Cookbooks 6. Food writing — Cooking and cookbooks — Methods 7. Food writing — Cooking and cookbooks — Regional

LC 2023013872

A James Beard Award nominee and owner of a Brooklyn bakery and cafe celebrates the tastes and traditions of Italy combined with American innovations in a collection of recipes including Aperol Spritz Cake, Italian Krispie Treats and Sourdough Focaccias.

"Sophisticated photography takes readers to piazzas, Mediterranean rooftops, and Sicilian seascapes, making this another fine recommendation to armchair travelers as well as inspired bakers." —*Booklist*

Includes index.

Saltz, Joanna
★ *Delish Insane Sweets: Bake Yourself a Little Crazy.* Joanna Saltz & the Editors of Delish. Houghton Mifflin Harcourt 2019. 238 pages : Illustration; Color

ISBN 9780358193340

Grades: Adult **641.81**

1. Baking 2. Cookies 3. Cake 4. Cupcakes 5. Desserts 6. Cookbooks 7. Food writing — Cooking and cookbooks — Courses

LC 2019025607

The first dessert recipe collection from the editors of the wildly popular site and magazine, Delish.

100+ cookies bars & bites inside!; Includes index.

Seneviratne, Samantha
Bake Smart: Sweets and Secrets from My Oven to Yours. Samantha Seneviratne. Harper, an imprint of William Morrow 2023. 222 pages : Color; Illustration

ISBN 9780358715146

Grades: Adult **641.81**

1. Baking 2. Desserts 3. Cookbooks 4. Food writing — Cooking and cookbooks — Methods 5. Food writing — Cooking and cookbooks — Courses

LC 2023020173

A baker, food editor and recipe developer dispels myths and fussy procedures and provides home cooks with industry baking secrets to effortlessly make delicious sweets including Stuffed S'more Cookies, Lemony Hibiscus Doodles and Burnt Caramel Basque Cheesecake.

"Although Seneviratne admits that baking should be 'smart,' she comforts readers by advising that it's okay to bake imperfectly—the results will still be delicious." —*Booklist*

Includes index.

Silverton, Nancy
★ *The Cookie That Changed My Life: And More Than 100 Other Classic Cakes, Cookies, Muffins, and Pies That Will Change Yours.* Nancy Silverton with Carolynn Carreño; photographs by Anne Fishbein. Alfred A. Knopf 2023. VII, 497 pages : Color; Illustration

ISBN 9780593321669

Grades: Adult **641.81**

1. Baking 2. Desserts 3. Cookies 4. Cookbooks 5. Food writing — Cooking and cookbooks — Methods 6. Food writing — Cooking and cookbooks — Courses 7. Food writing — Cooking and cookbooks — Chefs and restaurants

LC 2022034670

In this veritable encyclopedia of what to bake, the James Beard award-winning chef and founder of the La Brea Bakery offers 100+ recipes for cookies, cakes, breads, breakfast pastries and much more, including her life-changing Peanut Butter Cookie.

"There's no shortage of excellent baking books available…but home bakers trying to up their dessert game will find that Silverton's superbly written guide hits the sweet spot." —*Library Journal*

Includes index.

Volger, Lukas
Bowl: Vegetarian Recipes for Ramen, Pho, Bibimbap, Dumplings, and Other One-dish Meals. Lukas Volger; photography by Michael Harlan Turkell. Houghton Mifflin Harcourt 2016. 255 pages : Color; Illustration

ISBN 9780544325289

Grades: Adult **641.81**

1. Soups 2. Stews 3. One-dish meals 4. Vegetarian cooking 5. Cooking, Asian 6. Recipes 7. Cookbooks 8. Food writing — Cooking and cookbooks — Vegetarian and vegan

LC 2015037777

Putting a vegetarian twist on ramen, pho, bibimbap, dumplings and burrito bowls, this unique cookbook, capturing the full flavor of the popular one-bowl meals, shows readers how to make improvisational meals full of seasonal produce and herbs that can be made quickly and inexpensively.

"A go-to cookbook for Asian-inspired vegetarian soups, noodle bowls, and dumplings." —*Library Journal*

Includes bibliographical references (pages 249-250) and index.

Westerhausen, Shelly
Every Season Is Soup Season: 85+ Souper-Adaptable Recipes to Batch, Share, Reinvent, and Enjoy. Shelly Westerhausen Worcel wth Wyatt Worcel. Chronicle Books 2023. 255 pages : Color; Illustration

ISBN 9781797220307

Grades: Adult

PUBLIC LIBRARY CORE COLLECTION: NONFICTION
Twentieth Edition

1. Soups 2. Cooking (Vegetables) 3. Quick and easy cooking 4. Cookbooks 5. Food writing — Cooking and cookbooks — Courses

LC 2023004575

85+ recipes for soups, soup fixings, and more. Includes index.

641.82 Main dishes

Bastianich, Lidia

★ *Lidia's* a Pot, a Pan, and a Bowl: Simple Recipes for Perfect Meals. Lidia Matticchio Bastianich and Tanya Bastianich Manuali; photographs by Armando Rafael. Alfred A. Knopf 2021. xxi, 193 pages : Color; Illustration

ISBN 9780525657408

Grades: Adult 641.82

1. Cooking, Italian 2. One-dish meals 3. Quick and easy cooking 4. Cookbooks 5. Food Writing — Cooking and cookbooks — Regional 6. Food Writing — Cooking and cookbooks — Methods

LC 2020050353

More than 100 recipes that use just one (or two) pots, pans, or bowls; from Lidia Bastianich."

"Readers who are familiar with homestyle Italian cooking will be reminded of its simple joys, while those looking to make something attainable in their kitchen will enjoy the simplicity offered here." —*Library Journal*

Includes index.

Clark, Melissa

★ *Dinner* in One: Exceptional & Easy One-Pan Meals. Melissa Clark; photographs by Linda XIao. Clarkson Potter/Publishers 2022. 255 pages : Color; Illustration

ISBN 9780593233252

Grades: Adult 641.82

1. One-dish meals 2. Quick and easy cooking 3. Cookbooks 4. Food writing — Cooking and cookbooks — Methods

LC Bl2022026746

A collection of 100 new, simple and delicious one-pan, one-pot, or one-sheet recipes that minimize clean-up times and include Miso-Glazed Salmon with Roasted Sugar Snap Peas, Cheesy Meatball Parm with Spinach and Gingery Coconut Noodles with Shrimp and Greens.

"As always, Clark has home cooks in mind with this collection of streamlined, crowd-pleasing recipes; perfect for beginning cooks and readers looking to build a repertoire of sure-fire dinner options." —*Library Journal*

Includes index.

Henry, Diana

From the Oven to the Table: Simple Dishes That Look After Themselves. Diana Henry. Mitchell Beazley 2019. 240 pages : Color; Illustration

ISBN 9781784726096

Grades: Adult 641.82

1. Cooking 2. Quick and easy cooking 3. One-dish meals 4. Cookbooks 5. Food writing — Cooking and cookbooks — Methods 6. Food writing — Cooking and cookbooks — Chefs and restaurants

LC Bl2019029485

"An appealing resource for home cooks, curious dabblers, serious chefs." —*Library Journal*

Includes index.

Le, Mike

That Noodle Life: Soulful, Savory, Spicy, Slurpy. Mike Le and Stephanie Le, creators of Iamafoodblog; photography by Mike Le. Workman Publishing 2021. 256 p.

ISBN 9781523505326

Grades: Adult 641.82

1. Cooking (Pasta) 2. Cooking (Noodles) 3. Cookbooks 4. Food Writing — Cooking and cookbooks — Ingredients 5. Food Writing — Cooking and cookbooks — Regional

LC 2021007904

Oh, noodles! You're so much fun. You're so beloved! All your magical shapes, flavors, and textures. But no one obsesses over you quite like Mike Le and Stephanie Le, the-husband-and-wife team who are superstars in the food blog world. Their humbly namediamafoodblog boasts 186,000 followers on Instagram and receives 500,000 page views each month-and in it they profess their undying love for noodles in the most delicious, clever, and visually striking ways. That Noodle Life is their 75-recipe celebration of the myriad pleasures of noodles. And let's just say it goes way beyond spaghetti and ramen. Inspired by the noodle- and macaroni-crazed cuisines of Asia, Italy, and the global melting pot, they dish up high-impact, soulful, slurpable flavor with minimal fuss. Gorgeous full-color photographs of every dish enhance the lively and sophisticated spreads. Dig into comfort noodles: Really Savory Sunday Sauce with Tagliatelle and French Onion Mac and Cheese. Quick weeknight noodles: Flash-Fried Ribeye with Crispy Chow Mein and Stay in Tonight Sesame Chili Oil Noodles-faster than takeout and far better. Sexy Date Night Noodles: Double Lobster Chitarra, Miso Clam Linguine, Bone Marrow and Beef Brisket Pho. And how to upgrade instant noodles to make them shine, recipes for making noodles from scratch, notes on essential ingredients, and noodle etiquette, including how to use a ramen vending machine in Japan. Plus, who wouldn't want to participate in the Lasagna Bracket Competition?

"The Les, popular bloggers, express their passion for the noodle in all its global guises…Photographs further set readers salivating and rushing to the kitchen to start pasta water boiling." —*Booklist*

Massov, Olga

★ *Hot Sheet: Sweet and Savory Sheet Pan Recipes for Every Day and Celebrations*. Olga Massov and Sanaë Lemoine; photographs by Johnny Miller. Harvest, an imprint of William Morrow 2024. 294 pages : Color; Illustration

ISBN 9780063243873

Grades: Adult 641.82

1. One-dish meals 2. Cooking 3. Cookbooks 4. Food writing — Cooking and cookbooks — Methods

LC 2023037595

Collects more than 100 recipes harnessing the power of the sheet pan, including breakfasts, starters, dinners and desserts.

"Home cooks interested in exploring and expanding their sheet pan repertoire will find this invaluable." —*Publishers Weekly*

Includes index.

Merchant, Jessica

Everyday Dinners: Real Life Recipes to Set Your Family up for a Week of Success. Jessica Merchant. Rodale 2021. 271 p. : Color; Illustration

ISBN 9780593137499

Grades: Adult 641.82

1. Cooking for families 2. Recipes 3. Menu planning 4. Dinners and dining 5. Quick and easy cooking 6. Cookbooks 7. Food writing — Cooking and cookbooks — Cooking for the family

LC 2020026690

The blogger behind the wildly popular site How Sweet Eats turns her attention to meal prepping to create quick weeknight dinners, which take 30 minutes or less, without sacrificing flavor.

"Merchant's method of meal prepping in short bursts will appeal to beginner home cooks looking for a structured dinnertime strategy, but anyone responsible for serving family dinners will find inspiration here." —*Library Journal*

Includes index.

Munno, Nadia Caterina

The Pasta Queen: A Just Gorgeous Cookbook : 100+ Recipes and Stories. Nadia Caterina Munno with Katie Parla. Gallery Books 2022. xlii, 244 pages : Illustration; Color

ISBN 9781982195151

Grades: Adult 641.82

1. Cooking (Pasta) 2. Cooking, Italian 3. Italy 4. Cookbooks 5. Food writing — Cooking and cookbooks — Ingredients 6. Food writing — Cooking and cookbooks — Regional

LC 2022014448

ESSENTIAL AND RECOMMENDED TITLES
641.822 Noodle and pasta dishes

Through more than 100 recipes, the TikTok star and social media sensation shares the dishes that have made her pasta royalty, as well as provides a visually stunning tour of Italy, revealing the country's rich heritage, along with stories about her own life and family.

"This 'just gorgeous' cookbook is truly that, and its assortment of recipes will please a variety of readers looking for bona fide Italian food for all occasions." —*Library Journal*

Includes index.

Pashman, Dan
Anything's Pastable: 81 Inventive Pasta Recipes for Saucy People. Dan Pashman. William Morrow, an imprint of HarperCollinsPublishers 2024. xi, 275 pages : Color; Illustration

ISBN 9780063291126

Grades: Adult   641.82

1. Cooking (Pasta) 2. Pasta 3. Cooking, Italian 4. Cookbooks 5. Food writing — Cooking and cookbooks — Ingredients 6. Food writing — Cooking and cookbooks — Regional

LC 2023023709

The innovative James Beard Award-winning podcaster who changed the way you think about pasta shapes with his invention of the viral sensation cascatelli now does the same for pasta sauces in this fun and charmingly obsessive cookbook.

"With just a handful of ingredients and some creativity, Pashman proves that anything truly is pastable." —*Booklist*

Includes index.

Reinhart, Peter
Perfect Pan Pizza: Square Pies to Make at Home, from Roman, Sicilian, and Detroit, to Grandma Pies and Focaccia. Peter Reinhart. Ten Speed Press 2019. 185 p. : Color illustration

ISBN 9780399581953

Grades: Adult   641.82

1. Pizza 2. Cooking, Italian 3. Cookbooks 4. Food writing — Cooking and cookbooks — Courses 5. Food writing — Cooking and cookbooks — Regional

LC 2018054093

A guide to pan pizza illustrates how to make several styles in a home oven, including Detroit-style deep-pan, focaccia, Sicilian, and Roman, and features recipes for such options as pepperoni deluxe, kundalini cauliflower, and bacon and egg.

Includes bibliographical references and index.

Roddy, Rachel
★ *An A-Z of Pasta: Recipes for Shapes and Sauces, from Alfabeto to Ziti, and Everything in Between*. Rachel Roddy; photography by Jonathan Lovekin. Alfred A. Knopf 2023. 352 pages : Illustration; Color

ISBN 9780593535394

Grades: Adult   641.82

1. Cooking (Pasta) 2. Cooking, Italian 3. Pasta 4. Cookbooks 5. Food writing — Cooking and cookbooks — Regional 6. Food writing — Cooking and cookbooks — Ingredients

LC 2022014616

An award-winning food writer presents the story of pasta and offers tips to bring your pasta dishes to the next level through recipes like Cavatelli with Sausage, Mint, and Tomato, Fregula with Clams and Bucatini with Cauliflower, Saffron and Anchovies.

"Readers will eagerly head to the kitchen to roll out a batch of fresh dough or rush to book a flight to il bel paese in search of these dishes. Possibly both." —*Booklist*

This is a Borzoi book published by Alfred A. Knopf—Title page verso; Includes index; Originally published : Great Britain : Penguin Books, 2020.

Vetri, Marc
Mastering Pizza: The Art and Practice of Handmade Pizza, Focaccia and Calzone. Marc Vetri and David Joachim; photography by Ed Anderson. Ten Speed Press 2018. 261 pages : Color; Illustration

ISBN 9780399579226

Grades: Adult   641.82

1. Pizza 2. Cooking, Italian 3. Cookbooks 4. Food writing — Cooking and cookbooks — Chefs and restaurants 5. Food writing — Cooking and cookbooks — Regional

LC 2017049095

A noted, award-winning chef and restauranteur offers a step-by-step guide for making the perfect pizza by selecting from a variety of base doughs with different hydration levels that can work perfectly in a regular home kitchen oven.

Includes bibliographical references and index.

641.822 Noodle and pasta dishes

Williams, Odette
★ *Simple Pasta: Pasta Made Easy. Life Made Better*. Odette Williams; photographs by Graydon Herriott. Ten Speed Press 2022. 243 pages : Illustration; Color

ISBN 9781984859921

Grades: Adult   641.822

1. Cooking (Pasta) 2. Pasta 3. Cooking, Italian 4. Cookbooks 5. Food writing — Cooking and cookbooks — Ingredients 6. Food writing — Cooking and cookbooks — Regional

LC Bl2022026260

Making homemade pasta simple, enjoyable and delicious, this cookbook, using three base doughs, showcases the endless possibilities for creating pasta dishes that are singular and memorable.

"Recommended for its versatility, humor and general deliciousness, this title won't disappoint pasta lovers looking to learn the craft of Italian cooking or just perk up weeknight meals." —*Library Journal*

Includes index.

Zanini De Vita, Oretta
Encyclopedia of Pasta. Oretta Zanini De Vita; translated by Maureen B. Fant; with a foreword by Carol Field. University of Calif. Press 2009. xxi, 374 p. : Illustration; Map

ISBN 9780520255227

Grades: Adult   641.822

1. Cooking (Pasta) 2. Recipes 3. Food writing — Cooking and cookbooks — Ingredients 4. Reference — Encyclopedias

LC 2009010522

Provides a complete history of pasta in Italian cooking, including the origins of each pasta shape, preparation techniques, and common pasta myths and misconceptions.

"This book provides a complete history of pasta in Italy, showcasing more than 300 types of pastafrom bucatini and gnocchetti to tortellini and ziti. Each entry is nicely displayed in a box and includes an overview of each pasta type: the primary ingredients, preparation techniques, the different names for each kind of pasta, how it is served, the region where it is found, and the author's remarks. This wonderful resource is destined to become the definitive book on pasta. It succeeds both as a scholarly achievement and as an entertaining and authentic overview of Italian history and geography." —*Library Journal*

Translated from the Italian; Includes bibliographical references and index.

641.83 Salads

Damuck, Jess
Salad Freak: Recipes to Feed a Healthy Obsession. Jess Damuck; foreword by Martha Stewart; photography by Linda Pugliese. Abrams 2022. 271 pages : Color; Illustration

ISBN 9781419758393

Grades: Adult   641.83

1. Salads 2. Cookbooks 3. Food Writing — Cooking and cookbooks — Courses 4. Food Writing — Cooking and cookbooks — Ingredients

LC Bl2022010196

Offering more than 100 inspired recipes, recipe developer and food stylist Jess Damuck shares her passion for making truly delicious salads. 'Salad Freak' encourages readers to discover and embrace their own salad obsessions. With the right recipes, you will want to eat salad for every meal and never get bored."

Putting the focus on a balance of flavors, textures, and colors, Damuck presents 100 punchy salads that are 'Anything but boring.' —*Publishers Weekly*

Includes index.

Rosen, Ilene
Saladish: A Crunchier, Grainier, Herbier, Heartier, Tastier Way with Vegetables. Ilene Rosen with Donna Gelb; photographs by Joseph De Leo; illustrations by Emma Dibben. Artisan 2018. 207 pages : Color; Illustration
ISBN 9781579656959
Grades: Adult 641.83
1. Salads 2. Cookbooks 3. Food writing — Cooking and cookbooks — Chefs and restaurants 4. Food writing — Cooking and cookbooks — Vegetarian and vegan
LC 2017036051

A collection of seasonally organized recipes for creative salads and vegetable dishes that blend a wide range of ingredients, flavors, and textures, features such options as Vietnamese-style tofu salad, roasted grapes, and Bosc pear and fennel slaw.

"Highly recommended for fans of grain bowls, meal-sized salads, and meatless meals." —*Library Journal*

Includes bibliographical references and index.

Schrijver, Darlene
The Salad Lab: Whisk, Toss, Enjoy! : Recipes for Making Fabulous Salads Every Day. Darlene Schrijver. Simon Element 2024. 272 pages : Color; Illustration
ISBN 9781668025246
Grades: Adult 641.83
1. Salads 2. Cookbooks 3. Food writing — Cooking and cookbooks — Courses
LC Bl2024012650

With both favorite and all-new recipes, TikTok's beloved salad recipe creator, The Salad Lab, shows readers how to make creative, unique and delicious salads through careful instructions and smart salad-making tips that are guaranteed to make anyone crave a healthy salad.

"Those looking to expand their salad options will find both a useful methodology and plenty of inspiration." —*Publishers Weekly*

Includes index.

641.85 Preserves and candy

Curl, Jami
Candy Is Magic: Real Ingredients, Modern Recipes. Jami Curl; photography by Maggie Kirkland; illustrations by Michelle Ott. Ten Speed Press 2017. VII, 303 pages
ISBN 9780399578397
Grades: Adult 641.85
1. Candy 2. Confectionery 3. Recipes 4. Cookbooks 5. Food writing — Cooking and cookbooks — Ingredients
LC 2016047716

Shares recipes for two hundred confectionaries made from real, natural ingredients, including donut magic dust, vanilla bean and roasted fruit caramels, and toasted coconut marshmallows.

Using only real, natural ingredients, a candy-maker extraordinaire and owner of the candy company Quin shares 200 achievable recipes for such delectable|and original|delights as Whole Roasted Strawberry Lollipops, Bergamot Caramels and Pinot Noir cotton candy.

"Curls enthusiasm for her craft makes this cookbook a pleasure to read; she is the ideal coach for would-be candy makers." —*Publishers Weekly. Annex*

Includes bibliographical references (pages 291-295) and index.

Goldstein, Joyce Esersky, author
Jam Session: A Fruit-preserving Handbook. Joyce Goldstein; photographs by Ed Anderson. Lorena Jones Books, an imprint of the Crown Publishing Group 2018. 263 p. : Color; Illustration
ISBN 9780399579615
Grades: Adult 641.85
1. Seasonal cooking 2. Jams and jellies 3. Cookbooks 4. Food writing — Cooking and cookbooks — Methods 5. Food writing — Cooking and cookbooks — Reference 6. Food writing — Cooking and cookbooks — Ingredients
LC 2018001021

Offers instructions for all-natural fruit preserving and includes ideas on how to use fruit preserves to elevate common foods.

Includes index.

641.86 Desserts

Adams, Jocelyn Delk
Grandbaby Cakes: Modern Recipes, Vintage Charm, Soulful Memories. Jocelyn Delk Adams. Surrey Books, an Agate Imprint 2015. 224 pages
ISBN 9781572841734
Grades: Adult 641.86
1. Cake 2. Baking 3. Recipes 4. Cookbooks 5. Food writing — Cooking and cookbooks — Courses 6. Food writing — Cooking and cookbooks — Methods 7. Food writing — Cooking and cookbooks — Regional
LC 2015013216

Cookbook featuring 50 vintage cakes with modern twists and memoir tracing the roots of the author's family recipes.

"Adams's cake recipes are familiar yet unlike any you'll find in similar cookbooks. An instant classic, this title belongs in most baking collections." —*Library Journal*

Includes index.

Arefi, Yossy
Snacking Cakes: Simple Treats for Anytime Cravings. Yossy Arefi; photo styling by Ali Slagle. Clarkson Potter/Publishers 2020. 191 pages : Color; Illustration
ISBN 9780593139660
Grades: Adult 641.86
1. Cake 2. Desserts 3. Baking 4. Cookbooks 5. Food writing — Cooking and cookbooks — Courses 6. Food writing — Cooking and cookbooks — Methods
LC Bl2020069440

The recipe developer, photographer, food stylist and cookbook author behind the award-winning blog Apt. 2B Baking Co. offers 50 effortless, one-bowl cake recipes including Cornmeal Peach Upside-Down Cake, Sweet Potato Cinnamon Sugar Cake and Salted Caramel Peanut Butter Cake.

"With 50 streamlined cake recipes, this little gem of a cookbook will quickly become a prized resource in many kitchens." —*Library Journal*

Includes index.

Barrow, Cathy
★ *Pie Squared: Irresistibly Easy Sweet & Savory Slab Pies.* Cathy Barrow; Photographs by Christopher Hirsheimer. Grand Central Life & Style 2018. xiv, 321 pages : Color; Illustration
ISBN 9781538729144
Grades: Adult 641.86
1. Desserts 2. Pastry 3. Pies 4. Recipes 5. Cookbooks 6. Food writing — Cooking and cookbooks — Courses 7. Food writing — Cooking and cookbooks — Methods
LC 2018003656

Shares recipes for the new food trend of slab pies, including such options as blueberry streusel, lemon cream, mushroom and kale, and Hawaiian pizza, along with such crust recipes as cracker, cornbread, cookie, and cheddar cheese crusts.

Includes bibliographical references and index.

ESSENTIAL AND RECOMMENDED TITLES
641.86 Desserts

Beranbaum, Rose Levy
★ *The Cookie Bible.* Rose Levy Beranbaum; photography by Matthew Septimus. Houghton Mifflin Harcourt 2021. xxix, 418 pages : Color; Illustration
ISBN 9780358353997
Grades: Adult   641.86
1. Cookies 2. Baking 3. Desserts 4. Cookbooks 5. Food writing — Cooking and cookbooks — Methods 6. Food writing — Cooking and cookbooks — Courses
LC 2021010883

An award-winning author and legendary baker presents this ultimate cookie book, in which she offers foolproof recipes with detail-oriented instructions that eliminate guesswork for whipping up irresistible, crowd-pleasing cookies for any occasion.

"Precision is Berenbaum's modus operandi, as she not only instructs readers on how to make perfect cookies, but explains why specific ingredients and techniques result in perfection. Indispensable for holiday (and year-round) cookie baking." —*Booklist*
Includes index.

Rose's Ice Cream Bliss. Rose Levy Beranbaum; photography by Matthew Septimus. Houghton Mifflin Harcourt 2020. 336 p.
ISBN 9781328506627
Grades: Adult   641.86
1. Ice cream, ices, etc. 2. Recipes 3. Cookbooks 4. Food writing — Cooking and cookbooks — Courses 5. Food writing — Cooking and cookbooks — Methods
LC 2019033902

An award-winning cookbook author offers foolproof recipes for making ice cream at home including classic flavors like Peanut Butter and Chocolate Fudge as well as the more exotic like Brown Sugar and Black Pepper, Roasted Corn and Red Wine.

"Serious ice cream makers will want to add this to the shelf." —*Publishers Weekly*
Includes index.

Byrn, Anne
★ *American Cake: From Colonial Gingerbread to Classic Layer, the Stories and Recipes Behind More Than 125 of Our Best-loved Cakes from Past to Present.* Anne Byrn. Rodale Inc. 2016. 344 pages : Color; Illustration
ISBN 9781623365431
Grades: Adult   641.86
1. Cake 2. Recipes 3. Cookbooks 4. Food writing — Cooking and cookbooks — Courses 5. Food writing — Cooking and cookbooks — Regional 6. Food writing — History and microhistory
LC 2016029092

Describes the rich history of American cake baking, from colonial times to the present, and includes such cake recipes as New Orleans king, chocolate stout, angel food, red velvet, and pineapple upside-down.

"These well researched and written pages go far beyond the average baking guide." —*Publishers Weekly*
Includes bibliographical references (pages 325-329) and index.

★ *American Cookie: The Snaps, Drops, Jumbles, Tea Cakes, Bars & Brownies That We Have Loved for Generations.* Anne Byrn; photography by Tina Rupp. Rodale 2018. 312 pages : Color; Illustration
ISBN 9781623365455
Grades: Adult   641.86
1. Cookies 2. Recipes 3. Cookbooks 4. Food writing — Cooking and cookbooks — Courses 5. Food writing — Cooking and cookbooks — Methods 6. Food writing — History and microhistory
LC Bl2018180646

Describes the rich history of American cookie baking, from colonial times to the present, and includes such cookie recipes as macaroons, snickerdoodles, American gingersnaps, lavender tea cookies, and black and white cookies.

"The introduction sets the stage, outlining the basic ingredients and supplies required for the recipes. Sidebars offer baking suggestions and historical notes,

and each recipe is introduced with a brief anecdote about its origins." —*Library Journal*
Includes bibliographical references (pages 295-299) and index.

A New Take on Cake: 175 Beautiful, Doable Cake Mix Recipes for Bundts, Layers, Slabs, Loaves, Cookies, and More! Anne Byrn; photographs by Danielle Atkins. Clarkson Potter/Publishers 2021. 383 pages : Color; Illustration
ISBN 9780593233597
Grades: Adult   641.86
1. Cake 2. Baking 3. Cookbooks 4. Food Writing — Cooking and cookbooks — Courses 5. Food Writing — Cooking and cookbooks — Methods
LC 2021013785

Home bakers can learn how to make 200 brand new and modernized classic cake recipes including Pumpkin Skillet Crumble, Strawberry Smash Cake and Double Chocolate Drop Cookies, in a new collection from the best-selling author of the Cake Mix Doctor.

"This inviting resource offers plenty of easy ideas for cake makers with the help of a mix." —*Library Journal*
Includes index.

Chang, Joanne
Pastry Love: A Baker's Journal of Favorite Recipes. Joanne Chang; photography by Kristin Teig. Houghton Mifflin Harcourt 2019. 463 pages : Color; Illustration
ISBN 9780544836488
Grades: Adult   641.86
1. Baking 2. Desserts 3. Pastry 4. Recipes 5. Cookbooks 6. Food writing — Cooking and cookbooks — Methods 7. Food writing — Cooking and cookbooks — Courses
LC 2019004919

An award-winning baker presents 125 of her favorite recipes—such as Strawberry Slab Pie, Mocha Chip Cookies and Malted Chocolate Cake—as well as lessons and techniques for both experienced bakers and beginners. Illustrations.

"An excellent volume of recipes that will work for bakers at any level." —*Library Journal*
Includes index.

Dodge, Abigail Johnson
Sheet Cake: Easy One-Pan Recipes for Every Day & Every Occasion. Abigail Johnson Dodge. Clarkson Potter/Publishers 2021. 175 pages : Color; Illustration
ISBN 9780593136102
Grades: Adult   641.86
1. Cake 2. Cookbooks 3. Food Writing — Cooking and cookbooks — Methods 4. Food Writing — Cooking and cookbooks — Courses
LC 2020052972

A totally new take on fuss-free baking with 50 easy-to-master recipes that put an inventive spin on beloved classic cakes, using one sheet pan and minimal supplies.

"Instruction comes by way of Dodge's fuss-free best practices and providing foolproof tips. . . . This is an all-around treat." —*Publishers Weekly*
Includes index.

Francois, Zoe
Zoe Bakes Cakes: Everything You Need to Know to Make Your Favorite Layers, Bundts, Loaves, and More. Zoe Francois; how-to and author photos by Sarah Keiffer. Ten Speed Press 2021. 261 pages : Color; Illustration
ISBN 9781984857361
Grades: Adult   641.86
1. Cake 2. Baking 3. Food writing — Cooking and cookbooks — Methods 4. Food writing — Cooking and cookbooks — Courses
LC Oc2021000933

An expert baker and the best-selling author of Artisan Bread in Five Minutes a Day offers 100 easy-to-follow cake recipes including Apple Cake with Honey-Bourbon Glaze, Lemon-Curd Pound Cake, Coconut-Candy Bar Cake, and Chocolate Devil's Food Cake.

"The recipes themselves are clearly written, though home bakers may find they need to flip through the book more than they'd like to locate subrecipes. Still, this is an excellent guide, and the tutorial alone is worth the price of admission." —*Publishers Weekly*

Includes index.

Gerson, Fany
Mexican Ice Cream: Beloved Recipes and Stories. Fany Gerson; photography by Justin Walker and Fernando Gomez Carbajal. Ten Speed Press 2017. 173 pages : Color; Illustration

ISBN 9781607747772

Grades: Adult   641.86

1. Cooking, Mexican 2. Desserts 3. Frozen desserts 4. Ice cream, ices, etc. 5. Recipes 6. Mexico 7. Cookbooks 8. Essays 9. Food writing — Cooking and cookbooks — Courses 10. Food writing — Cooking and cookbooks — Narrative cookbooks 11. Food writing — Cooking and cookbooks — Regional

LC 2016051341

Presents recipes for Mexican ice cream that showcase its diverse flavors, including such options as goat's milk caramel, avocado, rice pudding, and chocolate-chile, while exploring the cultural aspects of preparing and consuming ice cream in Mexico.

The chef behind Brooklyn's La Newyorkina and Dough brings the diverse flavors of Mexican ice cream to the home kitchen, providing recipes for making exotic, fresh and surprising flavors like Oaxacan-style Lime Sorbet, Avocado-Chocolate Ice Cream, and Rice-Almond Ice Cream with Cinnamon.

"[Gerson's] extensive expertise underpins this inspiring cookbook, which collects classic and modern recipes for sorbets, ice creams, and accompaniments." —*Library Journal*

Includes bibliographical references and index.

Greenspan, Dorie
Baking Chez Moi: Recipes from My Paris Home to Your Home Anywhere. Dorie Greenspan; photographs by Alan Richardson. Houghton Mifflin Harcourt 2014. IX, 477 pages : Color; Illustration

ISBN 9780547724249

Grades: Adult   641.86

1. Desserts 2. Cooking, French 3. Baking 4. Pastry 5. Macarons 6. Recipes 7. Cookbooks 8. Food writing — Cooking and cookbooks — Methods 9. Food writing — Cooking and cookbooks — Regional

LC 2014016312

The author of the award-winning Around My French Table presents a collection of 180 radically simple desserts from French home cooks and pastry chefs.

"Combining everyday desserts with doable versions of extremely popular treats (think macarons, eclairs, and crackle-top cream puffs), Greenspan's new collection is an instant classic." —*Library Journal*

A Rux Martin book; Includes index.

★ *Dorie's* Cookies. Dorie Greenspan. Houghton Mifflin Harcourt 2016. 517 pages : Color; Illustration

ISBN 9780547614847

Grades: Adult   641.86

1. Cookies 2. Baking 3. Recipes 4. Cookbooks 5. Food writing — Cooking and cookbooks — Methods

LC 2015042719

A James Beard Foundation Who's Who inductee presents an all-occasions collection of top-selected cookie recipes, including Blueberry Buttermilk Pie Bars, Snowy-Topped Brownie Drops and Pink-Peppercorn Thumbprints.

Gunst, Kathy
Rage Baking: The Transformative Power of Flour, Fury, and Women's Voices (a Cookbook with More Than 50 Recipes). Kathy Gunst and Katherine Alford; photography by Jerelle Guy. Tiller Press 2020. 181 p.

ISBN 9781982132675

Grades: Adult   641.86

1. Women political activists 2. Women and politics 3. Women 4. Baking 5. Presidential election, 2016 6. Recipes 7. Political participation 8. Anger 9. Essays 10. Food writing — Cooking and cookbooks — Narrative cookbooks

LC 2019046205

Combining food and the activism unleashed by the 2016 election, a collection of over 50 cookie, cake, tart and pie recipes also features essays, reflections and interviews with both well-known bakers and women activists.

"This resource will satisfy those looking for an outlet to quell their angst and bake some fantastic treats. An engaging choice for teens and up." —*Library Journal*

Includes index.

Heatter, Maida
★ *Happiness* Is Baking: Cakes, Pies, Tarts, Muffins, Brownies, Cookies : Favorite Desserts from the Queen of Cake. Maida Heatter; foreword by Dorie Greenspan; illustrations by Alice Oehr. Little, Brown and Company 2019. 287 pages : Color; Illustration

ISBN 9780316420570

Grades: Adult   641.86

1. Desserts 2. Baking 3. Cookbooks 4. Food writing — Cooking and cookbooks — Chefs and restaurants 5. Food writing — Cooking and cookbooks — Courses

LC Bl2019009880

A collection of the cookbook author's classic, foolproof recipes features such options as blueberry crumb cake, chocolate cupcakes, oatmeal molasses cookies, chocolate chip and almond biscotti, devil's food cake, and apricot tart.

"This is an excellent one-stop shop for Heatter's greatest hits, and a perfect introduction for any rising baker unfamiliar with her work." —*Booklist*

Includes index.

Kartes, Danielle
Butter, Flour, Sugar, Joy: Simple, Sweet Desserts for Everyone. Danielle Kartes; photography by Michael Kartes. Sourcebooks 2023. 215 p.

ISBN 9781728278018

Grades: Adult   641.86

1. Desserts 2. Baking 3. Cookbooks 4. Food writing — Cooking and cookbooks — Courses 5. Food writing — Cooking and cookbooks — Methods

LC 2023019165

An author and recipe developer with a boutique food photography business provides almost 80 delectable dessert recipes from cakes to no-churn ice cream including Cream Cheese Blondies, Brioche Cinnamon Rolls, Nutella Banana Cake and Blueberry Buckle.

"Kartes offers a refreshing and relaxed approach that is especially suitable for medium-level bakers. Both the decadent recipes and heartfelt stories about their origins will entice fans of Paula Deen and Taste of Home magazine." —*Library Journal*

Includes index.

Lane, Christina
Dessert for Two: Small Batch Cookies, Brownies, Pies, and Cakes. Christina Lane. The Countryman Press 2015. 231 pages : Color; Illustration

ISBN 9781581572841

Grades: Adult   641.86

1. Desserts 2. Recipes 3. Cookbooks 4. Food writing — Cooking and cookbooks — Courses 5. Food writing — Cooking and cookbooks — Methods

LC Bl2015010260

A collection of small-batch dessert recipes takes favorite sweet treats and scales down the recipes to make only two servings using small pans, ramekins and muffin cups, including Brûléed Lemon Bars, Banana Puddin', brownies, blondies and assorted cookies.

Includes index.

Lloyd, Bobbie
The Magnolia Bakery Handbook: A Complete Guide for the Home Baker : Baking Made Easy with 150 Foolproof Recipes & Techniques. Bobbie Lloyd, Chief Baking Officer. Harper Design, an imprint of HarperCollinsPublishers 2020. 300 pages : Color; Illustration

ISBN 9780062887214

Grades: Adult   641.86

ESSENTIAL AND RECOMMENDED TITLES
641.86 Desserts

1. Baking 2. Pastry 3. Desserts 4. Food writing — Cooking and cookbooks — Methods 5. Food writing — Cooking and cookbooks — Chefs and restaurants 6. Food writing — Cooking and cookbooks — Reference
LC BI2020069295

Published to coincide with the 25th anniversary of the bakery, which quickly became a landmark and destination in New York City, this gorgeous book offers close to 150 recipes, along with tips, tools and techniques for the home baker.
"A good selection for home bakers of all levels looking for something sweet." —*Library Journal*
Includes index.

Ludwinski, Lisa
Sister Pie: The Recipes & Stories of a Big-Hearted Bakery in Detroit. Lisa Ludwinski; photographs by E.E. Berger. Lorena Jones Books, an imprint of Ten Speed Press 2018. IX, 245 p. : Color; Illustration
ISBN 9780399579769
Grades: Adult   641.86
1. Pies 2. Pastry 3. Cookbooks 4. Food writing — Cooking and cookbooks — Courses 5. Food writing — Cooking and cookbooks — Methods
LC 2018003428

A collection of favorite recipes for sweet and savory pies from the owner of Detroit's Sister Pie bakery features such options as ginger peach biscuit, toasted marshmallow butterscotch, and sour cherry bourbon pie.
Includes index.

McDermott, Kate
★ *Art of the Pie: A Practical Guide to Homemade Crusts, Fillings, and Life*. Kate McDermott; photographs by Andrew Scrivani. The Countryman Press, a division of W. W. Norton & Company 2016. 352 pages : Color; Illustration
ISBN 9781581573275
Grades: Adult   641.86
1. Baking 2. Desserts 3. Pies 4. Recipes 5. Cookbooks 6. Food writing — Cooking and cookbooks — Methods 7. Food writing — Cooking and cookbooks — Courses
LC 2016017593

An award-winning, self-taught home baker who hosts instructional Pie Camps around the country provides detailed recipes and instructions for making, rolling and baking perfect pie crusts and fillings every time, including Blackberry, Peach and Rhubarb.
Provides detailed recipes and instructions for making, rolling, and baking perfect pie crusts and fillings every time, including such options as blackberry, peach, pumpkin, rhubarb, and savory supper pies.
"It's really all about the standards... McDermott excels, giving readers an informative guide they'll be referring to for years to come." —*Publishers Weekly*
Includes bibliographical references and index.

McDowell, Erin Jeanne
★ *The Book on Pie: Everything You Need to Know to Bake Perfect Pies*. Erin Jeanne McDowell; photographs by Mark Weinberg. Houghton Mifflin Harcourt 2020. 351 pages : Color; Illustration
ISBN 9780358229285
Grades: Adult   641.86
1. Baking 2. Baked products 3. Pies 4. Desserts 5. Food writing — Cooking and cookbooks
LC 2020023318

100 recipes for perfect pies by Food52 baking consultant, New York Times contributor, and top food stylist Erin Jeanne McDowell.
"McDowell writes with a welcoming voice; newbies will be heartened and old hands will be impressed. Get out the rolling pin, this book has a pie for everyone." —*Library Journal*
Includes index.

McKenney, Sally
★ *Sally's Cookie Addiction: Irresistible Cookies, Bars, Shortbread, and More from the Creator of Sally's Baking Addiction*. Sally McKenney. Race Point Publishing 2017. 199 pages : Color; Illustration

ISBN 9781631063077
Grades: Adult   641.86
1. Cookies 2. Recipes 3. Cookbooks 4. Food writing — Cooking and cookbooks — Courses
LC 2017018781

A collection of recipes for cookies, cookie bars, cookie dough dips, slice-and-bakes, and no-bakes includes such options as brown butter snickerdoodles, pinwheel cookies, fairy meringues, jam shortbread bars, and chocolate hazelnut thumbprints.
Includes index.

Miglore, Kristen
Food52 Genius Desserts: 100 Recipes That Will Change the Way You Bake. Kristen Miglore; photography by James Ransom. Ten Speed Press 2018. xi, 273 pages : Color; Illustration (Food52 Works)
ISBN 9781524758981
Grades: Adult   641.86
1. Desserts 2. Recipes 3. Cookbooks 4. Food writing — Cooking and cookbooks — Methods
LC 2017053167

A collection of game-changing dessert recipes includes the unconventional ingredients and methods used to make East 62nd Street Lemon Cake, Flourless Chocolate-Walnut Cookies, Butterscotch Budino, Peach Cobbler with Hot Sugar Crust, and Parsnip Cake with Blood Orange Buttercream.
Offers one hundred dessert recipes from the author's "Genius Recipes" column and the Food52 community, including peanut butter sandies, olive oil cake, French lemon cream tart, and baked caramel pears.
Includes index.

Mubarak, Heather
Stuffed: The Sandwich Cookie Book : 65 Mix & Match Recipes. Heather Mubarak. Chronicle Books 2023. 271 pages : Color; Illustration
ISBN 9781797214535
Grades: Adult   641.86
1. Cookies 2. Baking 3. Desserts 4. Cookbooks 5. Food writing — Cooking and cookbooks — Courses
LC 2022040564

A baking book with 65 mix-and-match recipes for cookie sandwiches."
"Mubarak's tempting array of sandwich cookies will prove to be the stuff of sweet dreams for home bakers." —*Library Journal*
Whoopie pies, macarons, ice cream sandwiches, and more!; Includes index.

Nederlanden, Elisabet der
★ *Holiday Cookies: Showstopping Recipes to Sweeten the Season*. Elisabet der Nederlanden; photography by Erin Scott. Ten Speed Press 2017. 161 pages : Color; Illustration
ISBN 9780399580253
Grades: Adult   641.86
1. Baking 2. Confectionery 3. Cookies 4. Holiday cooking 5. Recipes 6. Cookbooks 7. Food writing — Cooking and cookbooks — Methods 8. Food writing — Cooking and cookbooks — Courses
LC 2017015950

A collection of holiday cookie recipes from a veteran baker and recipe developer features such sweets as gingerbread cookies, black and whites, molasses spice cookies, fig and cardamom rugelach, and candy cane cookies.
Perfect for cookie exchanges, gift-giving and just enjoying throughout the season, a festive, full-color cookbook offers new inspiration for the best holiday baking through 50 tested recipes, including Gingerbread Houses, Peppermint Bark, Hazelnut Sandwich Cookies, Dark Chocolate-Hazelnut Fudge and many more.
Includes bibliographical references and index.

Nelson, Kim
Daisy Cakes Bakes: Keepsake Recipes for Southern Layer Cakes, Pies, Cookies, and More. Kim Nelson. Clarkson Potter/Publishers 2017. 222 pages : Color; Illustration

PUBLIC LIBRARY CORE COLLECTION: NONFICTION
Twentieth Edition

ISBN 9780451499417

Grades: Adult   641.86

1. Cake 2. Desserts 3. Quick and easy cooking 4. Recipes 5. Cookbooks 6. Food writing — Cooking and cookbooks — Methods

LC 2017044208

A collection of recipes from the founder of the Daisy Cakes mail-order bakery features such options as pumpkin whoopee pies, chocolate peanut butter bark, pecan pie, apple fritters, Mississippi mud cake, and buttermilk ice cream.

Includes index.

Ottolenghi, Yotam

Sweet: Desserts from London's Ottolenghi. Yotam Ottolenghi, Helen Goh with Tara Wigley. Ten Speed Press 2017. 363 pages : Illustration; Color

ISBN 9781607749141

Grades: Adult   641.86

1. Confectionery 2. Pastry 3. Desserts 4. Cookbooks 5. Food writing — Cooking and cookbooks — Methods 6. Food writing — Cooking and cookbooks — Chefs and restaurants

LC Bl2017045258

A collection of recipes for sweets, baked goods, and confections from the superstar chef, including such dishes as banana cakes with rum caramel, pineapple and star anise chiffon cake, pecan snowballs, and lemon and poppy seed cake.

"Modern, creative, appealing, and, most importantly, fun—this is Ottolenghi at the top of his game." —*Publishers Weekly*

Includes index.

Pansino, Rosanna

Baking All Year Round. Rosanna Pansino. Atria Books 2018. 255 pages : Color; Illustration

ISBN 9781501179822

Grades: Adult   641.86

1. Baking 2. Desserts 3. Holiday cooking 4. Recipes 5. Cookbooks 6. Food writing — Cooking and cookbooks — Methods

LC 2018015942

Offers eighty-five holiday recipes from the YouTube star, with a discussion on tools and baking terminology and options for cookies, cupcakes, brownies, cakes, and toppings for every holiday occasion.

Includes index.

Parks, Stella

★ *Bravetart: Iconic American Desserts.* Stella Parks; foreword by J. Kenji Lopez-Alt; photography by Penny De Los Santos. W.W. Norton & Company 2017. 395 pages : Illustration; Color

ISBN 9780393239867

Grades: Adult   641.86

1. Baking 2. Cooking, American 3. Desserts 4. Recipes 5. Cookbooks 6. Food writing — Cooking and cookbooks — Courses 7. Food writing — Cooking and cookbooks — Regional

LC 2017007009

"Parks, a senior editor at Serious Eats and the creator of the Bravetart blog, has written a cookbook that is as interesting to read as it is to cook from." —*Publishers Weekly*

Includes bibliographical references and index.

Pfeiffer, Jacquy

The Art of French Pastry. Jacquy Pfeiffer; with Martha Rose Shulman; photographs by Paul Strabbing. Alfred A. Knopf 2013. xxxi, 395 pages : Color; Illustration

ISBN 9780307959355

Grades: Adult   641.86

1. Pastry 2. Cooking, French 3. Cookbooks 4. Food writing — Cooking and cookbooks — Courses 5. Food writing — Cooking and cookbooks — Regional

LC 2013017643

"Anyone studying to be a professional baker will profit from Pfeiffer's guidance, and the amateur cook can vastly improve family desserts." —*Booklist*

A Borzoi book.

Roman, Alison

Sweet Enough. Alison Roman; photographs by Chris Bernabeo. Clarkson Potter/Publishers 2023. 303 pages : Color; Illustration

ISBN 9781984826398

Grades: Adult   641.86

1. Desserts 2. Baking 3. Pies 4. Cookbooks 5. Food writing — Cooking and cookbooks — Courses 6. Food writing — Cooking and cookbooks — Methods

LC 2022029048

Presenting dessert recipes that feel special and approachable, impressive and doable, a New York-based cook and New York Times bestselling author shows how to make simple yet sublime sweets that are a perfect finish to any dinner.

"Those who like a more casual, carefree approach to baking will appreciate this, where the aim is for a delicious, not perfect, result." —*Library Journal*

Includes index.

Saffitz, Claire

★ *What's for Dessert: Simple Recipes for Dessert People.* Claire Saffitz; photographs by Jenny Huang. Clarkson Potter/Publishers 2022. 367 pages : Color; Illustration

ISBN 9781984826985

Grades: Adult   641.86

1. Desserts 2. Quick and easy cooking 3. Cookbooks 4. Food writing — Cooking and cookbooks — Courses 5. Food writing — Cooking and cookbooks — Methods

LC Bl2022034174

Filled with decadent delights to satisfy any sweet tooth, this all-new collection of straightforward and simple recipes for dessert people is filled with loads of troubleshooting advice that readers have come to count on.

"Saffitz continues to convert cooks to bakers and wow the experienced with her charm, fun recipes, and excellent instruction in a book that is sure to become a classic." —*Library Journal*

Includes index.

Stewart, Martha

Martha Stewart's Cake Perfection: 100+ Recipes for the Sweet Classic, from Simple to Stunning. from the Kitchens of Martha Stewart; photographs by Lennart Weibull and others. Clarkson Potter 2020. 256 pages : Color; Illustration

ISBN 9780593138656

Grades: Adult   641.86

1. Cake 2. Baking 3. Cake decorating 4. Icings, Cake 5. Cooking 6. Cookbooks 7. Food writing — Cooking and cookbooks

LC Bl2020068160

An authoritative baking guide to 125 cakes provides basic though sophisticated options for a variety of occasions, offering expert tips for such mouthwatering and eye-appealing creations as Strawberry Ombre Cake, Coconut Chiffon Cake and Flourless Chocolate Gluten-Free Sheet Cake.

"The editors of Martha Stewart Living inspire in this sophisticated guide to cake making. Recipes run the gamut from simple pound cakes to more involved multilayer cakes, and each are accompanied by detailed instructions." —*Publishers Weekly*

Includes index.

Tosi, Christina

All About Cake. Christina Tosi with Courtney McBroom; photographs by Gabriele Stabile and Mark Ibold. Clarkson Potter/Publishers 2018. 287 pages : Illustration; Color

ISBN 9780451499523

Grades: Adult   641.86

1. Cake 2. Desserts 3. Quick and easy cooking 4. Recipes 5. Cookbooks 6. Food writing — Cooking and cookbooks — Courses 7. Food writing — Cooking and cookbooks — Methods 8. Food writing — Cooking and cookbooks — Chefs and restaurants

LC 2017050431

In this sugar-fueled cookbook, the chef, owner and founder of Milk Bar helps bakers of all levels to indulge in both classic flavors and true originals, revealing

ESSENTIAL AND RECOMMENDED TITLES
641.87 Preparing beverages

the method behind her team|s creativity to help invent any cake flavor imaginable.

All About Cookies. Christina Tosi with Shannon Salzano; photographs by Henry Hargreaves. Clarkson Potter/Publishers 2022. 271 pages : Color; Illustration

ISBN 9780593231975

Grades: Adult   **641.86**

1. Cookies 2. Baking 3. Cookbooks 4. Food writing — Cooking and cookbooks — Methods 5. Food writing — Cooking and cookbooks — Courses

LC 2021061789

The James Beard Award-winning chef, owner of Milk Bar and host of Bake Squad presents a collection of 100 new cookie recipes including sandies, sammies, chewies, bars and no-bakes including Golden Oaties, Pie Bars and Jelly Donut Sandwich cookies.

"A good addition to any comprehensive baking collection (as both a guide and an enjoyable read)." —*Library Journal*

At head of title: Milk Bar; Includes index.

Weller, Melissa

*A **Good** Bake: The Art and Science of Making Perfect Pastries, Cakes, Cookies, Pies, and Breads at Home.* Melissa Weller with Carrolynn Carreño; photographs by Johnny Miller. Alfred A. Knopf 2020. xl, 448 pages : Color; Illustration

ISBN 9781524733438

Grades: Adult   **641.86**

1. Baking 2. Baked products 3. Pastry 4. Bread 5. Cake 6. Cookies 7. Pies 8. Food writing — Cooking and cookbooks

LC 2019048763

A comprehensive baking bible for the twenty-first century from the James Beard nominee who has redefined American baking. With 120 scientifically grounded recipes for sweet and savory baked goods anyone can master.

"One of the most impressively thorough and extensive books on baking, this new book is chock-full of recipes that span from sourdough breads and pizzas." —*Library Journal*

Includes index.

Williams, Odette

Simple Cake: *All You Need to Keep Your Friends and Family in Cake : 10 Cakes, 15 Toppings, 30 Cake-Worthy Moments.* Odette Williams; photography by Nicole Franzen. Ten Speed Press 2019. 191 pages : Color; Illustration

ISBN 9780399581427

Grades: Adult   **641.86**

1. Cake 2. Recipes 3. Cookbooks 4. Food writing — Cooking and cookbooks — Courses 5. Food writing — Cooking and cookbooks — Methods

LC 2018025094

A nostalgic ode to the joy of homemade cake, beautifully photographed and with easy mix-and-match recipes for a sweet lift any day of the week—.

Includes index.

Wright, Caroline

Cake Magic!: *Mix & Match Your Way to 100 Amazing Combinations.* Caroline Wright. Workman Publishing 2016. 186 pages

ISBN 9780761182030

Grades: Adult   **641.86**

1. Baking 2. Cake 3. Desserts 4. Recipes 5. Cookbooks 6. Food writing — Cooking and cookbooks — Methods

LC 2016000666

It's a simple formula for dessert bliss: batter + syrup + frosting = 100 different cakes! An innovative and remarkable easy way to bake luscious, flavorful cakes, Cake Magic! is a full-color visual cookbook—photos in the front, recipes in the back—for every cake lover, for fans of The Genius of the Cake Mix Doctor series, and for home bakers who obsess over colorful cakes on Pinterest and Instagram (where cakes are consistently in the "most popular" feed). The key to the cakes' ease is the homemade Mix + Match Baking Mix—the foundation of every cake in the book. From there it's just a matter of mixing and matching batters, flavoring syrups (the secret step that makes these cake recipes so versatile), frostings, and, sometimes, topping to create uniquecakes. Want something decadent and fudgy? Darkest Chocolate Cake + Milky Caramel Syrup + Malted Milk Chocolate Frosting + crushed candy bars = Candy Bar Cake. Swap in Bourbon Syrup + Cream Cheese Frosting, and you have the grown-up Drunken Tuxedo Cake. There's nothing vanilla about these vanilla cakes (Cookies + Cream Cake, Caramel-Pineapple Upside-Down Layer Cake); ethereal coconut cakes; and nutty cakes like Elvis-Peanut Butter Cake + Bacon Syrup + Nutella Frosting, topped with candied bacon. Fit for the King, indeed. Includes valuable baking tips, vegan and gluten-free variations, plus how to tweak the recipes to make sheet cakes, Bundt cakes, and cupcakes.

In an innovative and easy full-color visual cookbook—which is filled with essential baking tips, vegan and gluten-free variations and ways to tweak the recipes to make sheet cakes, Bundt cakes and cupcakes—the simple formula for dessert bliss is revealed: batter + syrup + frosting = 100 different cakes.

Includes index.

641.87 Preparing beverages

Hoffman, Maggie

Batch *Cocktails: Make-Ahead Pitcher Drinks for Every Occasion.* Maggie Hoffman; photographs by Kelly Puleio. Ten Speed Press 2019. 153 pages : Color; Illustration

ISBN 9780399582530

Grades: Adult   **641.87**

1. Cocktails 2. Reference books 3. Food writing — Beer, wine, and liquor

LC 2018046944

Provides recipes for sixty-five pitcher cocktails for advance preparation to serve eight to twelve guests.

Includes index.

Ramirez, Elva

Zero Proof: *90 Non-Alcoholic Recipes for Mindful Drinking.* Elva Ramirez; photography by Robert Bredvad. Houghton Mifflin Harcourt 2021. 255 p.

ISBN 9780358211914

Grades: Adult   **641.87**

1. Recipes 2. Beverages 3. Nonalcoholic drinks 4. Cookbooks 5. Food writing — Non-alcoholic beverages

LC 2020039131

90 no-alcohol cocktail recipes from top bartenders across the country.

"For serious home bartenders, more involved projects will impress and satisfy. This makes going dry anything but a dry affair." —*Publishers Weekly*

Includes bibliographical references and index.

Rollich, Christiaan

Bar Chef: *Handcrafted Cocktails.* Christiaan Rollich and Carolynn Carreno. W. W. Norton & Company. 2019. 304 p.

ISBN 9780393651560

Grades: Adult   **641.87**

1. Bartending 2. Cocktails 3. Food writing — Beer, wine, and liquor

LC 2018053634

Celebrated Los Angeles bartender Christiaan Roellich approaches a drink the way a master chef approaches a dish: he draws on high-quality seasonal ingredients to create cocktails for every occasion. In Bar Chef, Rollich shares 100 original recipes for drinks that that are as beautiful as they are delicious, including the Quixote (gin with grapefruit); a Kentucky Sour (bourbon with homemade cola syrup); Eggnog for the holidays, and Rollich's signature drink, the Green Goddess (green tea vodka with cucumber, arugula, jalapeno, and absinthe), which has become a part of the language of LA. Including easy-to-follow recipes for syrups, tinctures, liqueurs, and bitters with herbs, spices, and seasonal fruit, Rollich guides you through his creative process, demystifying the craft of cocktail-making. With stunning color photography and the suave storytelling of your favorite bartender, Bar Chef will become a go-to bar book for home cooks and cocktail enthusiasts, inspiring and pleasing readers with every drink.

PUBLIC LIBRARY CORE COLLECTION: NONFICTION
Twentieth Edition

"This refreshing collection is a must-have for those seeking a no-nonsense approach to making high-end drinks." —*Publishers Weekly*

Tipton-Martin, Toni
Juke Joints, Jazz Clubs & Juice: Cocktails from Two Centuries of African American Cookbooks. Toni Tipton-Martin; photographs by Brittany Conerly. Clarkson Potter/Publishers 2023. 254 pages : Color; Illustration
ISBN 9780593233825
Grades: Adult   641.87
1. Cocktails 2. Alcoholic beverages 3. United States history 4. African Americans 5. Social life and customs 6. Drinking customs 7. United States 8. Food writing — Beer, wine, and liquor 9. Food writing — History and microhistory
LC 2023005867

Discover the fascinating, unexplored history of Black mixology and its enduring influence on cocktail and drinking culture through rediscovered recipes, from the James Beard Award-winning author of Jubilee. Toni Tipton-Martin's volume on Black culinary history celebrates the lore and people behind our favorite drinks. With cocktail recipes such as the Jerk-Spiced Bloody Mary, the Absinthe Frappe, and the Clover Leaf Cocktail, Juke Joints, Jazz Clubs, and Juice illustrates the essential influence that Black Americans have had on modern mixology.

"The new title from Tipton-Martin (Jubilee), James Beard Award winner and editor in chief of Cook's Country, is a stunning blend of recipes and history from behind the bar. Her inspiration was the lack of historical representation of African American mixologists and their contribution to the modern craft. Her detailed research is evident throughout, including chapter and recipe introductions that take readers back in time and make for fascinating reading." —*Library Journal*

Includes bibliographical references (pages 234-243) and indexes.

642 Meals and table service

Hudson, Kate
Pretty Fun: Creating and Celebrating a Lifetime of Tradition. Kate Hudson with Rachel Holtzman; photographs by Amy Neunsinger. Dey St, an imprint of William Morrow 2017. 258 pages : Color; Illustration
ISBN 9780062685766
Grades: Adult   642
1. Cooking 2. Entertaining 3. Parties 4. Recipes 5. Cookbooks 6. Food writing — Beer, wine, and liquor 7. Food writing — Cooking and cookbooks — Entertaining 8. House and Home — Interior Decorating and Furnishings
LC Bl2017044234

Outlines tips for celebrating special events, offers advice on organizing more meaningful gatherings, and provides recipes for healthy snacks and beverages.

The popular actress and author of the best-selling Pretty Happy outlines illustrated tips for celebrating special events, sharing advice on organizing meaningful gatherings while offering a range of recipes for healthy, indulgent and memorable snacks and beverages.

Includes bibliographical references (pages 257-258).

Roman, Alison
★ *Nothing Fancy: Unfussy Food for Having People Over.* Alison Roman; photographs by Michael Graydon and Nikole Herriott. Clarkson Potter/Publishers 2019. 319 pages : Illustration; Color
ISBN 9780451497017
Grades: Adult   642
1. Cooking 2. Entertaining 3. Quick and easy cooking 4. Seasonal cooking 5. Cookbooks 6. Food writing — Cooking and cookbooks — Methods 7. Food writing — Cooking and cookbooks — Entertaining 8. Food writing — Cooking and cookbooks — Courses
LC 2019001089

Bringing her signature laid-back, approachable style to the table, a social media superstar and newly minted New York Times columnist presents 150 recipes that are high on 'wow' factors and low on effort. Illustrations.

Includes index.

Zizka, Maria
The Hostess Handbook: A Modern Guide to Entertaining. Maria Zizka; photographs by Erin Scott. Artisan Books 2024. 304 p.
ISBN 9781648291807
Grades: Adult   642
1. Cooking 2. Entertaining 3. Parties 4. Dinners and dining 5. Cookbooks 6. Food writing — Cooking and cookbooks — Entertaining 7. Food writing — Cooking and cookbooks — Courses
LC 2023042591

Offering 100 easy entertaining recipes, party planning advice and curated menus, this go-to guide shows how to create warm, joyful and special celebrations that we never want to end, from an epic holiday bash to a casual get-together, or an inspired dinner party.

"Zizka's handbook and perky, can-do attitude will convince almost anyone to home-entertain." —*Booklist*

Includes bibliographical references and index.

643 Housing and household equipment

Branson, Gary D.
Home, Water & Moisture Problems: Prevention and Solutions. Gary Branson. Firefly Books 2003. 143 p. : Illustration; Map
ISBN 9781552978368
Grades: Adult   643
1. Maintenance and repair 2. Houses 3. House and Home — DIY, maintenance, and repair 4. House and Home — Remodeling and renovation
LC 2003533299

Includes index.

Bryson, Bill
★ *At Home: An Informal History of Private Life.* Bill Bryson. Doubleday 2010. 497 p. : Illustration
ISBN 9780767919388
Grades: Adult   643
1. Houses 2. Architecture, Domestic 3. Home (Social sciences) 4. Rooms 5. Furniture 6. Household activities 7. Bathrooms 8. Households 9. Home (Concept) 10. History writing — Microhistory 11. Humor writing — Classic humorists
LC 2010004008

Bryson, author of A Short History of Nearly Everything, takes readers on a tour of his house, a rural English parsonage, showing how each room has figured in the evolution of private life.

"It takes a very particular kind of thoughtfulness, as well as a bold temperament, to stuff all this research into a mattress that's supportive enough to loll about on while pondering the real subject of this bookthe development of the modern world. Bryson is fascinated by everything, and his curiosity is infectious." —*New York Times Book Review*

Includes bibliographical references (p. [455]-475) and index.

Byers, Charles T.
Ultimate Guide Home Repair and Improvement: Proven Money-Saving Projects: 3,400 Photos & Illustrations. Technical editor for updated edition: Charles T. Byers, assistant professor, residential remodeling technology, B.Sc, Thaddeus Stevens College of Technology. Creative Homeowner 2017. 599 pages : Color; Illustration
ISBN 9781580117838
Grades: Adult   643
1. Maintenance and repair 2. Houses 3. Design and construction 4. House and Home — DIY, maintenance, and repair 5. Reference books — Handbooks, manuals, etc.
LC Bl2016042011

Presents information on home maintenance and remodeling with more than three hundred step-by-step projects that cover such topics as masonry, plumbing, insulation, flooring, trimwork, siding, roofing, and windows.

Includes index.

ESSENTIAL AND RECOMMENDED TITLES
645 Household furnishings

Finkelstein, Elizabeth
Cheap Old Houses: An Unconventional Guide to Loving and Restoring a Forgotten Home. Elizabeth and Ethan Finkelstein; with Christina Poletto; photographs by Kelly Marshall. Clarkson Potter/Publishers 2023. 287 pages : Color; Illustration
ISBN 9780593578766
Grades: Adult   643
1. Houses 2. Renovation (Architecture) 3. Historic preservation 4. Historic buildings 5. Homeowners 6. Architecture 7. Photography 8. United States 9. Visual nonfiction 10. House and Home — Remodeling and renovation 11. House and Home — Interior decorating and furnishings 12. Arts and Entertainment — Architecture
LC 2022045258
With hundreds of beautiful photographs, the founders of the HGTV show and Instagram Cheap Old Houses features the stories of how fixer-upper homes were acquired and lovingly restored as well as inspiration for buying and preserving an historic house.
"The beautiful houses make it easy to overlook the shortage of practical advice." —*Publishers Weekly*
Includes index.

Scott, Jonathan
★ *Dream* Home: The Property Brothers' Ultimate Guide to Finding & Fixing Your Perfect House. Jonathan Scott & Drew Scott; photography by David Tsay. Houghton Mifflin Harcourt 2016. 304 pages : Color; Illustration
ISBN 9780544715677
Grades: Adult   643
1. Houses 2. Design and construction 3. House buying 4. House and Home — General 5. House and Home — DIY, maintenance, and repair 6. House and Home — Remodeling and renovation
LC 2015037674
The celebrity designers from "Property Brothers" and other hit HGTV series share comprehensive guidelines to buying, selling, and renovating a house in a reference that includes strategic tips on hidden costs and finding good deals on home products.
"Dream Home is full of ideas and is a good source for anyone looking to buy, sell, or renovate a property." —*Booklist*
Includes index.

Wing, Charles
How Your House Works: A Visual Guide to Understanding and Maintaining Your Home. Charlie Wing. Wiley 2018. xvi, 216 pages : Color; Illustration
ISBN 9781119467618
Grades: Adult   643
1. Buildings 2. Maintenance and repair 3. Houses 4. House and Home — DIY, maintenance, and repair
LC 2018008701
An illustrated guide to understanding how everything in a house works, including appliances, electrical, plumbing, heating, and air conditioning.
Includes index.

645 Household furnishings

McClain, John
The Designer Within: A Professional Guide to a Well-styled Home. John McClain; principal photographer Zeke Ruelas. Gibbs Smith 2022. 223 p.
ISBN 9781423660224
Grades: Adult   645
1. Interior decoration 2. House and Home — Interior decorating and furnishings
McClain's candid and humorous look into the entire design process, from conception to completion, will allow anyone to find the designer within themselves, and ultimately create the home of their dreams. This isn't a book about how to create a look for less, but rather a book with a detailed breakdown of professionally designed rooms. From kitchens to powder rooms, McClain dissects each space with actionable items for the reader to implement in their own home. The reader can apply one or all of his tips to start their own design process."
"Armchair designers looking for inspiration will find it on full display here." —*Publishers Weekly*

Parrella-Van Den Berg, Janet
White & Faded: Restoring Beauty in Your Home and Life. Janet Parrella-Van Den Berg; foreword by Liz Marie Galvan. Thomas Nelson 2023. 193 p.
ISBN 9781400243396
Grades: Adult   645
1. Interior decoration 2. Home furnishings 3. White (color) 4. Restoration 5. House and Home — Interior decorating and furnishings
Taking readers on a stunning photographic tour of her restored English homes, the founder of the U.K. brand White & Faded provides insights into both the literal and metaphorical aspects of white and faded, along with restoration tips, decorative ideas, inspiration and the author's own remarkable story of trauma, love and rediscovered identity.
"The author cleverly explores the restoration of the home and the spirit…Antique lovers, photographers, and those who repurpose home goods will want to check this out." —*Library Journal*

Petersik, Sherry
Lovable Livable Home: How to Add Beauty, Get Organized, and Make Your House Work for You. Sherry & John Petersik of Young House Love. Artisan 2015. 336 pages
ISBN 9781579656225
Grades: Adult   645
1. Interior decoration 2. Houses 3. Design and construction 4. House and Home — Interior Decorating and Furnishings 5. House and Home — Remodeling and renovation
LC 2015010991
Offers illustrated guidance for creating beautiful, functional, and practical living spaces, including advice, DIY projects, and inspirational examples of interior decoration from real homes.
The authors of Young House Love return with a new set of makeovers, completely doable DIY projects, and inspirational design ideas perfect for sprucing up everyday living with pets and kids.
Includes bibliographical references (pages 327-331) and index.

646 Sewing, clothing, management of personal and family life

Cline, Elizabeth L.
The Conscious Closet: The Revolutionary Guide to Looking Good While Doing Good. Elizabeth L. Cline. Plume 2019. xi, 348 pages : Illustration
ISBN 9781524744304
Grades: Adult   646
1. Clothing industry and trade 2. Environmental responsibility 3. Fashion 4. Clothing 5. Shopping 6. Green consumerism 7. Green products 8. Environmental ethics 9. Consumer economics 10. Sustainable living 11. Environmentalism 12. Social issues — Environment — Conservation 13. Arts and Entertainment — Fashion 14. Business and economics — Economics — Consumerism
An expert on fashion and the environment discusses ways to create an ethical and sustainable wardrobe, including tips on how to pare down your closet and find affordable clothes which minimize environmental and social impacts.
Includes bibliographical references.

Edwards, Zoe
Mend It, Wear It, Love It!: Stitch Your Way to a Sustainable Wardrobe. Zoe Edwards. DK Publishing 2021. 143 pages : Color; Illustration
ISBN 9780744026801
Grades: Adult   646
1. Clothing 2. Sewing 3. Arts and Entertainment — Crafts and hobbies — Textiles and needlework 4. House and Home — Sustainable living
LC Oc2021000548

PUBLIC LIBRARY CORE COLLECTION: NONFICTION
Twentieth Edition

Have you ever thrown good clothes away simply because you didn't know how to mend them? Have you got clothes that you can't bear to part with, but need a fresher look? Then this book is for you. With fast fixes and complete makeovers, Mend It, Wear It, Love It! has everything you need to mend and care for your clothes, and stitch your way to a more sustainable wardrobe.

"Throughout, color photographs of personalized garments show Edwards's projects in action. This primer on reworking old clothing is a must-read for stylish thrifters." —*Publishers Weekly*

Includes bibliographical references (page 142) and index.

Ishida, Sanae
***Sewing** Love: Handmade Clothes for Any Body.* Sanae Ishida; photography by Manuela Insixiengmay and Amy Johnson; styling by Rachel Grunig. Sasquatch Books 2022. xiv, 271 pages : Illustration; Color
ISBN 9781632172815
Grades: Adult 646
1. Sewing 2. Clothing 3. Arts and Entertainment — Crafts and hobbies — Textiles and needlework

LC 2021024200

Empowering you to solve the fit issues that come with buying commercial clothing designed to fit one "ideal" body type, the author, sharing her own inspiring personal story, provides gentle instruction in the simple art of pattern-making and garment sewing for loving the body you have.

"This guide to garment sewing is a must-read for crafters of all levels." —*Publishers Weekly*

Includes bibliographical references (pages 262-263) and index.

Karen, Dawnn
***Dress** Your Best Life: How to Use Fashion Psychology to Take Your Look — and Your Life — to the Next Level.* Dawnn Karen. Little, Brown Spark 2020. 280 p.
ISBN 9780316530996
Grades: Adult 646
1. Women's clothing 2. Fashion 3. Clothing 4. Arts and Entertainment — Fashion 5. Science writing — Medicine and health — Psychology 6. Self-Help — Personal growth — Fashion and style

LC Bl2020009829

Packed with practical tips and cutting-edge advice, Dress Your Best Life will teach you to harness the power of fashion for the life you want to live.

"This is a thoughtful and fashion-forward approach to figuring out what to wear—and understanding how clothes reflect lives well lived… Karen's very apt conclusion: don't be eye candy. Be soul food. Engaging, well-written, and (gulp) rather piercing commentary on getting dressed." —*Booklist*

Includes bibliographical references (pages 255-272) and index.

Montenegro, Sonya
***Mending** Life: A Handbook for Repairing Clothes and Hearts.* Sonya and Nina Montenegro. Sasquatch Books 2020. 191 pages : Color; Illustration
ISBN 9781632172525
Grades: Adult 646
1. Clothing 2. Needlework 3. Arts and Entertainment — Crafts and hobbies — Textiles and needlework

LC 2019015016

Teaching basic techniques along with more advanced stitches, this visually stunning, practical tool kit for repairing the clothes and belongings reveals how mending can strengthen not only the object we are repairing, but ourselves as well.

"With a guiding mantra that There's nothing broken that can't be fixed, this very accessible guide will encourage readers to look with hopeful possibility at their well-worn, well-loved clothes." —*Booklist*

Includes bibliographical references (page 182) and index.

646.2 Sewing and related operations

Conahan, Gillian
*The **Hero's** Closet: Sewing for Cosplay and Costuming.* Gillian Conahan; photographs by Karen Pearson. Abrams 2017. 207 pages : Color; Illustration
ISBN 9781419723964
Grades: Adult 646.2
1. Sewing 2. Costume 3. Cosplay 4. Arts and Entertainment — Crafts and hobbies — Textiles and needlework

LC Bl2017015805

Offers step-by-step instructions and patterns that covers the basics of sewing costumes.

Includes index.

Ishida, Sanae
***Sewing** Happiness: A Year of Simple Projects for Living Well.* Sanae Ishida. Sasquatch Books 2016. 225 : Illustration
ISBN 9781570619953
Grades: Adult 646.2
1. Ishida, Sanae 2. Machine sewing 3. Arts and Entertainment — Crafts and hobbies — Textiles and needlework

LC 2015040697

"The instructions are thorough, the tips and advice are generous, and the overall presentation is thoughtful." —*Library Journal*

Includes bibliographical references (pages 215).

Yaker, Rebecca
***Little** One-Yard Wonders: Irresistible Clothes, Toys, and Accessories You Can Make for Babies and Kids.* Rebecca Yaker & Patricia Hoskins. Storey Publishing 2014. 359 pages : Color; Illustration
ISBN 9781612121246
Grades: Adult 646.2
1. Machine sewing 2. Children's clothing 3. Arts and Entertainment — Crafts and hobbies — Textiles and needlework

LC 2013045043

Shares one hundred one projects for accessories, toys, and wearables for babies and children, focusing on single yards of fabric and minimal completion times.

"This title is a treasure trove of handmade kid's stuff, and sewists of all skill levels will find ideas and inspiration in this lighthearted collection." —*Library Journal*

Six sheets of pattern pieces in pocket; Includes index.

Yang, April
***Diy** Thrift Flip: Sewing Techniques for Transforming Old Clothes into Fun, Wearable Fashions.* April Yang, Coolirpa. Quarry 2024. 152 p.
ISBN 9780760383216
Grades: Adult 646.2
1. Machine sewing 2. Clothing 3. Recycling (Waste, etc.) 4. Sustainable living 5. Thrift shops 6. Tailoring 7. Used clothing 8. Fashion 9. Arts and Entertainment — Crafts and hobbies — Textiles and needlework

LC 2023050654

DIY Thrift Flip teaches how to shop and sew sustainably by providing how-tos for finding, upcycling, and customizing secondhand clothing with basic sewing instructions.

"Yang's handy and inventive guidance is an excellent source of inspiration for eco-conscious sewers." —*Publishers Weekly*

Includes index.

646.4 Clothing and accessories construction

Alicia, Anna
***Bags:** Sew 18 Stylish Bags for Every Occasion.* Anna Alicia; photography by Anna Batchelor. Hardie Grant, Quadrille 2019. 141 pages : Color; Illustration
ISBN 9781787133761

ESSENTIAL AND RECOMMENDED TITLES
646.6 Care of clothing and accessories

Grades: Adult   **646.4**
1. Handbags 2. Sewing 3. Arts and Entertainment — Crafts and hobbies — Textiles and needlework 4. Arts and Entertainment — Fashion

LC B12019038743

"Each project has a skill-level rating, keeping fledgling crafters from getting in over their heads. Laden with gorgeous color photography and easy-to-follow templates, Alicia's book will tempt many crafters into replicating her designs—and adding their own twists." —*Publishers Weekly*

Includes index.

Herbertson, Angie
Sewing Face Masks, Scrub Caps, Arm Slings, and More: Practical Projects for Comfort and Care. Angie Herbertson. Landauer Publishing 2021. 120 p.
    ISBN 9781947163669

Grades: Adult   **646.4**
1. Sewing 2. Protective clothing 3. Arts and Entertainment — Crafts and hobbies — Textiles and needlework

LC 2020914686

Presents 14 projects with instructions and patterns for health care and comfort, such as face masks, scrub caps, wheelchair caddies, arm slings, fidget mats, and more.

"Complete with an index of patterns, these straightforward and easy-to-follow projects are a great place for would-be crafters to begin." —*Publishers Weekly*

Hewett, Jen
Print, Pattern, Sew: Block-printing Basics + Simple Sewing Projects for an Inspired Wardrobe. Jen Hewett; photographs by Jen Siska. Roost Books 2018. 162 pages : Illustration
    ISBN 9781611804621

Grades: Adult   **646.4**
1. Textile printing 2. Dressmaking 3. Dress accessories 4. Arts and Entertainment — Crafts and hobbies — Textiles and needlework

LC 2017016294

Create bold block prints for a completely custom wardrobe—print fabrics, customize patterns, and sew garments that truly express your own style.

"This alluring how-to guide combines block printing with garment sewing to yield dreamy bohemian scarves, preppy printed aprons, elegant summer dresses, and more." —*Publishers Weekly*

Includes bibliographical references (page 162).

Quindt, Svetlana
The Costume Making Guide: Creating Armor & Props for Cosplay. Svetlana Quindt, aka Kamui Cosplay. Impact 2016. 128 pages : Color; Illustration
    ISBN 9781440345166

Grades: Adult   **646.4**
1. Cosplay 2. Costume design 3. Arts and Entertainment — Crafts and hobbies — Textiles and needlework 4. Arts and Entertainment — Fashion 5. Arts and Entertainment — Theater

LC B12017027597

Introduces costume making, offering tips and techniques on making bracers, armor, and weapons.

"Cosplay armor and props are the focus of Quindt's guide, which takes crafters through the steps of designing, fitting, and creating custom pieces." —*Library Journal*

Includes index.

646.6 Care of clothing and accessories

Misumi, Noriko
Mending with Love: Creative Repairs for Your Favorite Things. Noriko Misumi. Tuttle Publishing 2021. 88 p.
    ISBN 9780804854030

Grades: Adult   **646.6**

1. Sewing 2. Clothing 3. Arts and Entertainment — Crafts and hobbies — Textiles and needlework

Mending with Love shows you how to apply embroidery, patching, darning, felting, stamping and a little crochet to worn pieces of clothing or household items. Instead of stowing or throwing away damaged pieces that hold happy memories, you can employ these beautiful and sustainable ideas to give them a new life.

"The appended stitch instructions may be less useful than YouTube videos, but the book on the whole is a must-have for those looking to shrink their ecological footprint with beauty and warmth." —*Booklist*

646.7 Management of personal and family life

Allen, David
★ *Getting Things Done: The Art of Stress-Free Productivity.* David Allen. Penguin Books 2015. xxx, 317 pages
    ISBN 9780143126560

Grades: Adult   **646.7**
1. Time management 2. Self-management 3. Self-Help — Personal growth — Motivation

LC 2015002886

Based on the premise that productivity is directly proportional to one's ability to handle tasks in a relaxed manner, the author offers strategies for self-management that minimize stress and enhance one's focus and efficiency.

"This classic text will help those with their calendars loaded with responsibilities to juggle their engagements, pare down their to-do lists, and manage the stress of too many commitments." —*Library Journal*

Includes index.

Bowe, Whitney
The Beauty of Dirty Skin: The Surprising Science to Looking and Feeling Radiant from the Inside Out. Whitney Bowe, MD with Kristin Loberg. Little, Brown and Company 2018. VIII, 278 pages
    ISBN 9780316509824

Grades: Adult   **646.7**
1. Skin 2. Science writing — Medicine and health — Hygiene and beauty

LC B12018003629

A leading dermatologist and research scientist identifies a connection between a healthy gut and radiant, clear skin, outlining a twenty-one-day program for maximizing skin health and beauty through a strategic diet, appropriate sleep habits, and do-it-yourself practical skin-care strategies.

Includes bibliographical references (pages 253-265) and index.

Conley, Chip
★ *Learning to Love Midlife: 12 Reasons Why Life Gets Better with Age.* Chip Conley. Little, Brown Spark 2024. x, 223 pages : Illustration
    ISBN 9780316567022

Grades: Adult   **646.7**
1. Middle-aged people 2. Personal conduct 3. Change (Psychology) 4. Aging 5. Self-Help — Personal growth — Aging 6. Self-Help — Personal growth — Happiness

LC B12024000923

The midlife crisis is the butt of so many jokes, but this long-derided life stage has an upside. What if we could reframe our thinking about the natural transition of midlife not as a crisis, but as a chrysalis—a time when something profound awakens in us, as we shed our skin, spread our wings, and pollinate our wisdom to the world?

"Conley's enthusiasm for grasping the full potential of the midlife years is contagious and inspiring." —*Kirkus*

Includes bibliographical references (pages 211-213) and index.

Dunn, Jancee
★ *How Not to Hate Your Husband After Kids.* Jancee Dunn. Little, Brown and Company 2017. VIII, 269 pages
    ISBN 9780316267106

PUBLIC LIBRARY CORE COLLECTION: NONFICTION
Twentieth Edition

Grades: Adult   646.7

1. Dunn, Jancee 2. Communication in marriage 3. Marriage 4. Parenting 5. Family and Relationships — Dating and Marriage 6. Humor writing — Family and relationship humor

LC 2016946111

A candid account of the author's struggles to revitalize her post-baby marriage describes how she resented societal roles that made her the only caregiver to her new daughter and the counseling and research that were part of her effort to resolve unbalanced family dynamics.

Godas, Maru

Organic Beauty: An Illustrated Manual of Natural Cosmetics. Maru Godas. Smith Street Books (ADS) 2023. 128 pages : Color; Illustration

ISBN 9781922754783

Grades: Adult   646.7

1. Beauty care 2. Beauty products 3. Cosmetics 4. Skin care 5. Organic lifestyle 6. Plants 7. Arts and Entertainment — Crafts and hobbies 8. Reference — Instructional materials

Love for the senses unites Maru Godas' triple devotion to flowers, body care, and art in Organic Beauty. A beautifully illustrated guide to self-care, this book will teach how you to create your own cosmetics using only natural products. Learn what plants to use, how to collect and prepare them, and create your own masks, scrubs, balms, butter, hair lotions and much more with detailed step-by-step instructions.

"It's a wonderful guide to going natural with one's beauty care routine." —*Publishers Weekly*

Hakkakiyan, Ruya

A Beginner's Guide to America: For the Immigrant and the Curious. Roya Hakakian. Alfred A. Knopf 2021. 240 p.

ISBN 9780525656067

Grades: Adult   646.7

1. Hakkakiyan, Ruya 2. Immigrants 3. Social life and customs 4. National characteristics, American 5. Moving to a new country 6. Advice 7. Immigration and emigration 8. United States 9. Society and culture — Immigration 10. Life stories — Identity — Immigrants

LC 2020016857

Into the maelstrom of unprecedented contemporary debates about immigrants in the United States, this perfectly timed book gives us a portrait of what the new immigrant experience in America is really like. Written as a "guide" for the newly arrived, and providing "practical information and advice," Roya Hakakian, an immigrant herself, reveals what those who settle here love about the country, what they miss about their homes, the cruelty of some Americans, and the unceasing generosity of others. She captures the texture of life in a new place in all its complexity, laying bare both its beauty and its darkness as she discusses race, sex, love, death, consumerism, and what it is like to be from a country that is in America's crosshairs.

"Although narrated as advice for incoming immigrants, this personal, yet practical account is intended to challenge misconceptions and biases that native-born U.S. citizens have toward documented and undocumented immigrants. It is highly recommended for all." —*Library Journal*

Hu, Elise

Flawless: Lessons in Looks and Culture from the K-Beauty Capital. Elise Hu. Dutton 2023. 372 p.

ISBN 9780593184189

Grades: Adult   646.7

1. Hu, Elise 2. Women journalists 3. Korean Americans 4. Feminine beauty (Aesthetics) 5. Beauty care 6. Cosmetics industry and trade 7. Corporations 8. Marketing 9. Self-improvement 10. Image 11. Perfectionism 12. Sex discrimination 13. Consumerism 14. Seoul, Korea 15. Society and culture — Pop culture 16. Business and economics — Industries — Retail products and services 17. Debut title

K-Beauty has captured imaginations worldwide by promising a kind of mesmerizing perfection. Its skincare and makeup products work together to fascinate us, champion consumerism, and invite us to indulge. In the four years Elise Hu spent in Seoul as NPR's bureau chief, the global K-Beauty industry quadrupled. And fun as self-care consumerism may be, Elise turns her eye to the darker questions lurking beneath the surface of this story. What are the real financial, physical, and emotional costs of beauty work in a culture that valorizes endless self-improvement and codes it as empowerment?

"A well-researched, accessible, and fascinating look at Korean culture and the beauty industry." —*Booklist*

Johansen, Signe

★ *How to Hygge: The Nordic Secrets to a Happy Life.* Signe Johansen. St. Martin's Griffin 2017. 206 pages

ISBN 9781250122032

Grades: Adult   646.7

1. Life 2. Happiness 3. Well-being 4. Civilization 5. Scandinavia 6. Self-Help — Personal growth

LC 2016059131

A chef and writer who grew up in Norway—using the concept of 'hygge,' which values the idea of cherishing yourself, celebrating experiences over possessions and being kind to yourself and others—presents a how-to guide that combines recipes, helpful tips and more for cozy living at home the Danish way.

"Readers interested in simplifying their homes and lives are sure to find plenty of practical recipes and suggestions here that they can implement immediately." —*Publishers Weekly*

Includes bibliographical references (pages 202-204) and index.

Raskin, Allison

Overthinking About You: Navigating Romantic Relationships When You Have Anxiety, OCD, and/or Depression. Allison Raskin. Workman Publishing 2022. 208 p.

ISBN 9781523513222

Grades: Adult   646.7

1. Dating 2. Interpersonal relations 3. Mental illness 4. Mental health 5. Anxiety 6. Depression 7. OCD 8. Men-women relations 9. Autobiographies and memoirs 10. Interviews 11. Society and culture — Psychology and human behavior 12. Society and culture — Sex and sexuality 13. Life stories — Facing adversity — Medical issues — Mental illness

LC 2021030972

Interweaving interviews with clinical psychologists, a psychiatrist, a sexologist, relationship experts and real-life couples throughout, this memoir-driven self-help book explores the complex connection between brain and heart, helping readers feel better prepared to tackle dating and relationships with more confidence and less worry.

"This invaluable and empowering primer delivers on its promise to help readers date while struggling with mental illness." —*Publishers Weekly*

Real, Terrence

Us: Getting Past You and Me to Build a More Loving Relationship. Terrence Real; foreword by Bruce Springsteen. Goop Press/Rodale 2022. 320 p.

ISBN 9780593233672

Grades: Adult   646.7

1. Married people 2. Couples 3. Individualism 4. Intimacy 5. Interpersonal conflict 6. Interpersonal relations 7. Psychology 8. Family and Relationships — Dating and Marriage 9. Society and culture — Psychology and human behavior

LC 2021040825

At a time when toxic individualism is rending our society at every level, best-selling author and renowned marriage counselor Terrence Real sees how it poisons our most intimate relationships in his therapy practice where he works with couples on the brink of disaster. The good news: Warmer, closer, more passionate relationships are possible if you have the right tools. Us is a groundbreaking guide to a new science-backed skillset—one that will allow you to get past your kneejerk reactions and tap into your wiser, more collaborative self. With a novelist's flair, Real shares the stories of real couples whose relationships have been saved by these skills and pans out to the cultural landscape that reinforce our dysfunction.

"In this accessible outing, family therapist Real offers advice to help romantic partners feel more connected. This approachable take on healing relationships will enlighten." —*Publishers Weekly*

Includes bibliographical references and index.

ESSENTIAL AND RECOMMENDED TITLES
646.7 Management of personal and family life

Slice, Jessica
Dateable: Swiping Right, Hooking Up, and Settling Down While Chronically Ill and Disabled. Jessica Slice and Caroline Cupp. Hachette Go 2024. 272 p.
ISBN 9780306832734
Grades: Adult   646.7
1. People with disabilities 2. People with chronic illnesses 3. Dating 4. Sexuality 5. Social life and customs 6. Interpersonal relations 7. Self-Help — Relationships 8. Family and Relationships — Dating and Marriage
LC 2024001689

A disabled essayist and a bioethicist combine on this guide for disabled and chronically ill people on navigating the world of modern dating, including how to use apps and to develop satisfying sexual and romantic relationships.

"With plenty of useful tips, stories, and encouragement for readers to fashion their own approaches, this is a valuable resource." —*Publishers Weekly*

Includes bibliographical references and index.

Taillac, Victoire de
An Atlas of Natural Beauty: Botanical Ingredients for Retaining and Enhancing Beauty. Victoire de Taillac and Ramdane Touhami from Officine Universelle Buly. Simon & Schuster 2018. 256 pages : Color; Illustration
ISBN 9781501197352
Grades: Adult   646.7
1. Science writing — Medicine and health — Hygiene and beauty 2. Science writing — Medicine and health — Alternative medicine 3. Self-Help — Personal growth — Fashion and style
LC 2018033089

The aesthetic and heritage of a French apothecary are on display in this encyclopedic illustrated guide to home beauty recipes that use seeds, flowers, oils, fruits and herbs to smooth skin, brighten hair and make readers feel beautiful.

From Apricots with witch haze by way of chamomile, lavender and olives, AN ATLAS OF NATURAL BEAUTY explains the origins, history and uses past and present of over 80 versatile botanicals for retaining and enhancing one's beauty.

Includes indexes; Originally published in Great Britain in 2017 by Ebury Press—Title page verso.

Thomas, Mathilde
The French Beauty Solution: Time-Tested Secrets to Look and Feel Beautiful Inside and Out. Mathilde Thomas. Avery 2015. VIII, 263 pages : Illustration
ISBN 9781592409518
Grades: Adult   646.7
1. Skin 2. Women 3. Self-care 4. Human body 5. Science writing — Medicine and health — Hygiene and beauty
LC 2015003934

Cofounder of the international beauty company Caudalie shares the simple, natural, time-tested beauty secrets she learned growing up in France that any woman can use to look younger, healthier, and more radiant without harsh products or drastic procedures. When Mathilde Thomas moved from her native France to the United States to expand her skin-care company, Caudalie, she wanted to find out what American women wanted from their beauty routines. She interviewed thousands of women and was struck by how different the French and American approaches to beauty were. American women are all about the quick fix—the elusive product or procedure that will instantly solve a nagging beauty problem, even if it hurts, is wildly expensive, or is damaging in the longterm. The French, by contrast, approach beauty as an essential and pleasurable part of the day, a lifelong and active investment that makes you look and feel good. Mathilde used these insights to turn Caudalie into one of America's top beauty brands. Drawing on her company's twenty years of scientific skin-care expertise backed by the research of doctors and dermatologists—as well as the beauty secrets she learned growing up on a vineyard in Bordeaux—The French Beauty Solution covers everything from how to use natural ingredients such as oil and honey to wash your face; what foods to eat for healthier hair, skin, and nails; and the amazing properties of grapes and grapeseed oil. She also introduces an easy three-day grape cleanse that European aristocrats have been using to detox for hundreds of years. Blending stories, science, DIY recipes, and tons of savoir faire, The French Beauty Solution is the last beauty regimen you'll ever need.

The co-founder of the Caudalie skin-care line outlines natural French beauty secrets for promoting a younger and healthier appearance, including strategies ranging from tapping the detoxing properties of grapes to using honey as a face wash.

Includes index.

Tourles, Stephanie L.
Pure Skin Care: Nourishing Recipes for Vibrant Skin & Natural Beauty. Stephanie L. Tourles. Storey Publishing 2018. 247 p. : Color; Illustration
ISBN 9781635860504
Grades: Adult   646.7
1. Skin 2. Science writing — Medicine and health — Hygiene and beauty 3. Science writing — Medicine and health — Alternative medicine 4. Science writing — General
LC 2018012689

Shares recipes for facial cleansers and scrubs, masks, moisturizers, and steams, along with creams, balms, and exfoliants for the entire body, all formulated to meet the most up-to-date green beauty standards.

Includes bibliographical references (pages 238-239) and index.

Vanderbilt, Tom
★ *Beginners:* The Joy and Transformative Power of Lifelong Learning. Tom Vanderbilt. Alfred A. Knopf 2021. 320 p.
ISBN 9781524732165
Grades: Adult   646.7
1. Vanderbilt, Tom 2. Self-fulfillment 3. Learning 4. Skills 5. Fathers and daughters 6. Society and culture — Psychology and human behavior 7. Life stories — Personal growth
LC 2019057320

Inspired by his young daughter's insatiable need to know how to do almost everything, and stymied by his own rut of mid-career competence, Tom Vanderbilt begins a year of learning purely for the sake of learning. He tackles five main skills (and picks up a few more along the way), choosing them for their difficulty to master and their distinct lack of career marketability—chess, singing, surfing, drawing, and juggling. What he doesn't expect is that the circuitous paths he takes while learning these skills will prove even more satisfying than any knowledge he gains. Ultimately, he shares how his refreshed sense of curiosity opened him up to a profound happiness and a deeper connection to the people around him. It's about how small acts of reinvention, at any age, can make life seem magical.

"This enjoyable reminder to embrace the small acts of reinvention, at any age, that can make life seem magical will appeal to those who enjoyed Robert Pirsig's Zen and the Art of Motorcycle Maintenance." —*Publishers Weekly*

Includes bibliographical references.

Wiking, Meik
The Little Book of Lykke: Secrets of the World's Happiest People. Meik Wiking. William Morrow 2017. 285 pages : Color; Illustration
ISBN 9780062820334
Grades: Adult   646.7
1. Contentment 2. Happiness 3. Quality of life 4. Science writing — Medicine and health 5. Self-Help — General 6. Self-Help — Personal growth — Happiness
LC BI2017042108

Shares inspirational writings and suggestions for achieving happiness by practicing the art of seeking out the good that exists in the world, and discusses how small adjustments in behavior can deepen contentment and increase happiness.

The author of the New York Times best-selling the Little Book of Hygge shares a new collection of inspirational writings and suggestions for achieving happiness by practicing the art of seeking out the good that exists in today's world.

"Wiking provides common-sense, real-life applications for his advice in a light-hearted, easy-to-read presentation laced with statistics and personal anecdotes in support of his findings. Whether its used as a how-to or as inspirational reading, this little book is sure to bring a dose of happiness to all its readers." —*Booklist*

PUBLIC LIBRARY CORE COLLECTION: NONFICTION
Twentieth Edition

Yong, Sable
Die Hot with a Vengeance: Essays on Vanity. Sable Yong. Dey Street Books 2024. 304 p.
ISBN 9780063236486
Grades: Adult   646.7
1. Beauty 2. Self-discovery 3. Pride and vanity 4. Culture 5. Identity 6. Popular culture 7. Body image 8. Fashion 9. Beauty care 10. Interpersonal relations 11. Clothing industry and trade 12. Essays 13. Society and culture — Pop culture 14. Business and economics — Industries 15. Life stories — Identity

Journalist and former Allure editor Sable Yong debuts with a sharp-toothed and hilarious essay collection about beauty and vanity, examining their stigmatization in the cultural zeitgeist, and how to shift the focus to use both for powerful tools for self-exploration, interpersonal connection, and cultural change.

"Yong's take on beauty and fashion is revealing, playful, and heartfelt." —*Kirkus*

Ziegler, Sheryl
★ *Mommy Burnout: How to Reclaim Your Life and Raise Healthier Children in the Process.* Dr. Sheryl Ziegler. Dey St, an imprint of William Morrow 2018. xiii, 311 pages
ISBN 9780062683687
Grades: Adult   646.7
1. Motherhood 2. Mothers 3. Psychology 4. Family and Relationships — Parenting 5. Self-Help — General 6. Self-Help — Personal growth — Happiness
LC BI2017051387

A practical handbook for modern moms outlines positive, liberating recommendations for avoiding debilitating social messages that impose impossible standards of perfection, sharing relatable anecdotes and real-world suggestions for breaking burnout cycles and protecting children from the damage of overwhelmed-parenting dynamics.

"Although this book is well researched and broad in scope of topics, it's written for a singular audience—the heterosexual, middle-class mother. Beyond this limitation, the harrowing descriptions of how women are suffering are anxiety-inducing in their own right and may make the reader opt to put down the book and call her therapist." —*Booklist*

Includes bibliographical references (pages 287-302) and index.

646.7009 History, geographic treatment, biography of management of personal and family life

Weir, Laura
Cosy: The British Art of Comfort. Laura Weir; illustrations by Rose Electra Harris. HarperOne 2019. 162 p.
ISBN 9780062948168
Grades: Adult   646.7009
1. Contentment 2. Human comfort 3. Quality of life 4. Home (Concept) 5. Everyday life 6. Kindness 7. Well-being 8. Social life and customs 9. Great Britain 10. Society and culture — Psychology and human behavior
LC 2019013019

A lifestyle journalist introduces American readers to "coziness"—an unfussy way of creating comfort and joy.

Includes bibliographical references; Originally published as Cosy in Great Britain in 2018 by Yellow Kite—T.P. verso.

647.95 Eating and drinking places

Ahdoot, Dan
Undercooked: How I Let Food Become My Life Navigator and How Maybe That's a Dumb Way to Live. Dan Ahdoot. Crown 2023. 256 p.
ISBN 9780593240793
Grades: Adult   647.95
1. Ahdoot, Dan 2. Actors and actresses 3. Gastronomy 4. Food 5. Obsession 6. Food habits 7. Family relationships 8. North American people 9. American people 10. Jewish people 11. Southwest Asian (Middle Eastern) people 12. Iranian people 13. Essays 14. Autobiographies and memoirs 15. Food writing — Memoirs and biographies 16. Humor writing — Social humor 17. Life stories — Arts and culture — Performing arts — Actors and actresses
LC 2022036804

This collection of entertaining essays from the Cobra Kai actor, stand-up comic and host of Food Network's Raid the Fridge shows how food became his obsession and central in all his relationships, sharing his unconventional adventures—the result of letting his stomach be his guide.

"Whether he is skewering food restrictions or lamenting relationship regrets, Ahdoot's rib-tickling collection will satiate culinary adventurers." —*Publishers Weekly*

Cecchi-Azzolina, Michael
Your Table Is Ready: Tales of a New York City Maître D'. Michael Cecchi-Azzolina. St. Martin's Press 2022. 320 p.
ISBN 9781250281982
Grades: Adult   647.95
1. Cecchi-Azzolina, Michael 2. Restaurateurs 3. Restaurants 4. Food service 5. Restaurant workers 6. Consumers 7. Dinners and dining 8. Celebrities 9. North American people 10. American people 11. New York City 12. Autobiographies and memoirs 13. Life stories — Arts and culture — Culinary arts 14. Food writing — Memoirs and biographies
LC 2022035063

A front-of-the-house Kitchen Confidential from a career maître d'hotel who manned the front of the room in New York City's hottest and most in-demand restaurants. From the glamorous to the entitled, from royalty to the financially ruined, everyone who wanted to be seen—or just to gawk—at the hottest restaurants in New York City came to places Michael Cecchi-Azzolina helped run. His phone number was passed around among those who wanted to curry favor, during the decades when restaurants replaced clubs and theater as, well, theater in the most visible, vibrant city in the world.

"'A well-run dining room is an art, a ballet,' according to this riveting debut from Cecchi-Azzolina, a veteran of New York City's restaurant industry….Readers will gobble up the juicy gossip and decadent stories from a man who has seen it all." —*Publishers Weekly*

Chandler, Adam
Drive-Thru Dreams: A Journey Through the Heart of America's Fast-Food Kingdom. Adam Chandler. Flatiron Books 2019. 272 p.
ISBN 9781250090720
Grades: Adult   647.95
1. Fast food restaurants, chains, etc. 2. Fast foods 3. Multinational corporations 4. Fast food Restaurateurs 5. Fast food workers 6. Food habits 7. Social life and customs 8. United States 9. Food writing — History and microhistory 10. Food Writing — Food and Culture 11. Adult books for young adults
LC 2019002978

Most any honest person can own up to harboring at least one fast-food guilty pleasure. In Drive-Thru Dreams, Adam Chandler explores the inseparable link between fast food and American life for the past century. The dark underbelly of the industry's largest players has long been scrutinized and gutted, characterized as impersonal, greedy, corporate, and worse. But, in unexpected ways, fast food is also deeply personal and emblematic of a larger than life image of America.

"This fun, argumentative, and frequently surprising pop history of American fast food will thrill and educate food lovers of all speeds." —*Publishers Weekly*

Includes bibliographical references and index.

Friedman, Andrew
The Dish: The Lives and Labor Behind One Plate of Food. Andrew Friedman. Mariner Books 2023. 336 p.
ISBN 9780063135970
Grades: Adult   647.95
1. Restaurants 2. Food industry and trade 3. Agriculture 4. United States 5. Food Writing — General

Following one restaurant dish's production via real-time reportage in the kitchen, a food writer and podcaster, as various components are readied, finished, fired and plated, introduces all the players responsible for producing it,

ESSENTIAL AND RECOMMENDED TITLES
648 Housekeeping

providing a fascinating lens into the farm-to-table movement and the collaborative nature of restaurant work.

"Readers intrigued by the fine-dining industry will not only enjoy this work, but will be reminded to think more deeply about those serving them and working behind the kitchen door the next time they go out to eat." —*Booklist*

Levy, Shawn
★ *The Castle on Sunset: Life, Death, Love, Art, and Scandal at Hollywood's Chateau Marmont.* Shawn Levy. Doubleday 2019. 384 p.
ISBN 9780385543163
Grades: Adult   647.95
1. Hotels 2. Celebrities 3. Entertainment industry and trade 4. Hotel owners 5. Scandals 6. Film industry and trade 7. Films 8. Actors and actresses 9. Hollywood, California 10. History writing — Arts and culture 11. History writing — Regional history — United States 12. Arts and Entertainment — General
LC 2018023441

For ninety years, Hollywood's brightest stars have favored the Chateau Marmont as a home away from home. An apartment house-turned-hotel, it has been the backdrop for generations of gossip and folklore. The author of Rat Pack Confidential presents a deeply researched history of the iconic Hollywood hotel that explores its storied role in wild celebrity revelries, scandalous liaisons and creative breakthroughs.

"Levy focuses on Chateau Marmont as a living entity, bringing it to life through its guests and the changes on the Sunset Strip. This will appeal most to Hollywood history buffs, but may also pique the interest of general readers with its yarns of various stars." —*Library Journal*

Includes bibliographical references.

648 Housekeeping

Boyd, Nikki
★ *Beautifully Organized: A Guide to Function and Style in Your Home.* Nikki Boyd, creator of Athomewithnikki.Com. Paige Tate & Co. 2019. 224 pages : Color; Illustration
ISBN 9781944515683
Grades: Adult   648
1. Storage in the home 2. Interior decoration 3. House and Home — Cleaning, caretaking, and organizing
LC Bl2019009998

In a full-color guide, the creator of the firm At Home with Nikki shares her best advice for how to create an organized, beautiful and welcoming home, including the five steps every homeowner should go through: Assess, Declutter, Clean, Organize and Beautify.

Includes index.

Carlson, Julie
Remodelista: The Organized Home : Simple, Stylish Storage Ideas for All Over the House. Julie Carlson and Margot Guralnick; with the editors of Remodelista; photographs by Matthew Williams; creative direction by Alexa Hotz. Artisan 2017. 224 p.
ISBN 9781579656935
Grades: Adult   648
1. Interior decoration 2. Orderliness 3. Storage in the home 4. House and Home — Cleaning, caretaking, and organizing
LC 2017013398

The team behind Remodelista.Com shares over one hundred tips for creating an organized home using common everyday items, along with guidance on tackling problem zones and turning clutter into stylish design.

Includes index.

Casazza, Allie
Declutter Like a Mother: A Guilt-Free, No-Stress Way to Transform Your Home and Your Life. Allie Casazza. Nelson Books, an imprint of Thomas Nelson 2021. xxii, 201 pages
ISBN 9781400225637

Grades: Adult   648
1. Storage in the home 2. House cleaning 3. Orderliness 4. House and Home — Cleaning, caretaking, and organizing 5. Self-Help — Personal growth — Motivation
LC 2020053640

Successful business entrepreneur Allie Casazza shares her powerful and proven method for clearing the clutter in our minds by first clearing the clutter in our homes, the place where transformation begins."

"Readers looking for straightforward advice on streamlining one's possessions will get much from this reassuring, sensible road map." —*Publishers Weekly*

Includes bibliographical references (pages 199-200).

Cilley, Marla
The Chaos Cure: Clean Your House and Calm Your Soul in 15 Minutes.* Marla Cilley aka the Fly Lady. Seal Press 2018. 191 pages : Illustration
ISBN 9781580058025
Grades: Adult   648
1. House cleaning 2. Housekeeping 3. House and Home — General 4. House and Home — Cleaning, caretaking, and organizing 5. Self-Help — General
LC 2018959608

The "FlyLady" author of the best-selling Sink Reflections shares practical advice, quick fixes and helpful tricks for transforming a perpetually messy home by embracing housekeeping as an act of self-care.

Are you suffering from CHAOS, otherwise known as can't have anyone over syndrome? If your house is a jumble of dirty dishes, piles of paper, and never-ending laundry, you are probably afflicted. But don't give up hope, because now there's an antidote: the chaos cure.

Davis, KC
★ *How to Keep House While Drowning: A Gentle Approach to Cleaning and Organizing.* KC Davis. Simon Element 2022. 151 pages : Illustration; Color
ISBN 9781668002841
Grades: Adult   648
1. Housekeeping 2. House cleaning 3. Orderliness 4. Attention-deficit hyperactivity disorder 5. Anxiety 6. Depression 7. Fatigue 8. House and Home — Cleaning, caretaking, and organizing 9. Self-Help — Mental health
LC 2021059468

A professional therapist offers support and tips for those struggling to maintain a clean house while struggling with issues such anxiety, fatigue, depression, ADHD or a lack of support.

Ewer, Cynthia Townley
Cut the Clutter: A Simple Organization Plan for a Clean and Tidy Home. Cynthia Townley Ewer of OrganizedHome.Com. DK Publishing 2016. 240 pages : Color; Illustration
ISBN 9781465453051
Grades: Adult   648
1. House cleaning 2. Orderliness 3. Storage in the home 4. House and Home — Cleaning, caretaking, and organizing
LC Bl2016039921

Explains how to declutter, organize, and clean the home, with easy-to-remember tips for every job, from keeping the bathroom clean and doing the laundry to sorting out paperwork and organizing the family photo album.

"The book delves into the nitty-gritty of list-making, menu planning, and the cycles of cleaning. Its best used as a reference guide for specific chores... rather than as a method to follow strictly. This practical guide will be a solid resource for young adults and new parents." —*Publishers Weekly*

Includes index.

Kondo, Marie
★ *The Life-Changing Magic of Tidying Up: The Japanese Art of Decluttering and Organizing.* Marie Kondo; translated from Japanese by Cathy Hirano. Ten Speed Press 2014. 213 pages
ISBN 9781607747307
Grades: Adult   648

PUBLIC LIBRARY CORE COLLECTION: NONFICTION
Twentieth Edition

1. Homemaking 2. Housekeeping 3. Orderliness 4. Clutter 5. Storage in the home 6. Translations — Japanese to English 7. House and Home — Cleaning, caretaking, and organizing 8. Spirituality and Religion — General 9. Self-Help — Personal growth — Motivation

LC 2014017930

Presents a guide to cleaning and organizing a living space, discussing best methods for decluttering and the impact that an organized home can have on mood and physical and mental health.

Includes index; This English translation by Cathy Hirano first published in Great Britain by Ebury Publishing, an imprint of Random House UK, London—Copyright page.

★ *Marie Kondo's Kurashi at Home: How to Organize Your Space and Achieve Your Ideal Life.* Marie Kondo; photographs by Nastassia Brückin and Tess Comrie; translated from the Japanese by Cathy Hirano. Ten Speed Press 2022. 223 pages : Color; Illustration
 ISBN 9781984860781
Grades: Adult   648
1. Homemaking 2. Self-fulfillment 3. Happiness 4. House and Home — Cleaning, caretaking, and organizing 5. Self-Help — Personal growth — Motivation 6. Self-Help — Personal growth — Happiness

LC 2022005220

Inspired by the Japanese concept of kurashi, or 'way of life,' the #1 best-selling sensation and Netflix star, in this beautiful guide, empowers you to embrace what you love about your life and then reflect it in your home, activities and relationships.

"This book moves beyond the home to include everyday activities and lifestyle. It's likely to be in high demand due to Kondo's popularity." —*Library Journal*

Parts previously published in Mainichi ga tokimeku katazuke no mah; Includes index.

★ *Spark Joy: An Illustrated Master Class on the Art of Organizing and Tidying up.* Marie Kondo; translated from the Japanese by Cathy Hirano. Ten Speed Press 2016. xii, 291 pages
 ISBN 9781607749721
Grades: Adult   648
1. Storage in the home 2. Housekeeping 3. Homemaking 4. Orderliness 5. House and Home — Cleaning, caretaking, and organizing 6. Self-Help — Personal growth — Motivation

LC 2015035727

A follow-up to the best-selling The Life-Changing Magic of Tidying Up shares the highly sought Japanese cleaning consultant's detailed methods for organizing closets, folding clothes and minimizing clutter.

"Kondo presents not a decluttering manual but a way to look at the relationships and things that are meaningful in life." —*Library Journal*

Published in Japan as The Life-Changing Magic of Tidying Up 2 and The Illustrated Life-Changing Magic of Tidying Up by Sunmark Publishing, Inc, Tokyo, in 2012 and 2015, and is a combination of the two Japanese titles: Jinsei ga Tokimeko Katazuke no Maho2 and Irasuto de Tokimeku Katazuke no Maho; Includes index.

McCubbin, Tracy

Making Space, Clutter Free: The Last Book on Decluttering You'll Ever Need. Tracy McCubbin. Sourcebooks, Inc. 2019. 282 p.
 ISBN 9781492675198
Grades: Adult   648
1. House cleaning 2. Orderliness 3. Storage in the home 4. House and Home — Cleaning, caretaking, and organizing 5. Self-Help — Personal growth — Happiness 6. Self-Help — Personal growth — Motivation

LC 2019006715

A Los Angeles clutter guru shares her unique approach to conquering clutter and discovering emotional cleansing, providing empowering advice, tips and tricks for creating a beautiful home devoid of emotional baggage and clutter—one that sparks a newfound feeling of freedom.

"While many books concentrate on either the emotional aspects of clutter or tips for getting rid of it, McCubbin interweaves both, resulting in highly practical guidance." —*Library Journal*

Includes bibliographical references.

Richardson, Patric

Laundry Love: Finding Joy in a Common Chore. Patric Richardson with Karin B. Miller. Flatiron Books 2021. xx, 185 pages : Illustration
 ISBN 9781250235190
Grades: Adult   648
1. Laundry 2. House and Home — Cleaning, caretaking, and organizing 3. Self-Help — General

LC 2020031678

Patric Richardson, aka the "Laundry Evangelist," reveals his revolutionary methods for cleaning clothes—and making laundry loads more fun. Doing laundry is rarely anyone's favorite task. But to Patric Richardson, laundry isn't just fun—it's a way of life. After years of running Laundry Camp at the Mall of America for thousands of eager learners, he's ready to share his tips, tricks, and hacks—bringing surprise and delight to this commonly dreaded chore. Sorting your laundry? It's not all about whites and darks. Pondering the wash cycles? Every load, even your delicates, should be washed using express or quick-wash on warm. Facing expensive dry cleaning bills? You'll learn how to wash everything—yes everything—at home. And those basically clean but smelly clothes? Richardson has a secret for freshening those too (hint: It involves vodka, not soap). Changing your relationship with laundry can also change your life. Richardson's handy advice shows us how to save time and money (and the planet!) with our laundry—and he intersperses it all with a healthy dose of humor, real-life laundry stories, and lessons from his Appalachian upbringing and career in fashion. Laundry Love will make you wonder why you ever stressed about ironing, dry cleaning, or (god forbid) red wine spills on your new couch. No matter the issue, Richardson is here to help you make laundry miracles happen—wrinkles and stains be damned.

"Richardson's love for doing laundry is so infectious that readers just might find themselves dreading this mundane chore a bit less." —*Publishers Weekly*

Shearer, Clea

★ *The Home Edit Life: The No-Guilt Guide to Owning What You Want and Organizing Everything.* Clea Shearer & Joanna Teplin; photographs by Clea Shearer. Clarkson Potter/Publishers 2020. 255 pages : Color; Illustration
 ISBN 9780593138304
Grades: Adult   648
1. Storage in the home 2. Orderliness 3. House and Home — Cleaning, caretaking, and organizing

LC 2019056167

The stars of Home Edit outline holistic, tech-friendly approaches to rendering everyday work more productive and fulfilling through organization, offering customizable, guilt-free recommendations for everything from office spaces and holiday storage to luggage and pet supplies.

"Big photos of gorgeously organized spaces provide plenty of eye candy. This irresistible primer will delight and inspire the neat and messy alike." —*Publishers Weekly*

Includes index.

Wenzke, Ali

★ *The Art of Happy Moving: How to Declutter, Pack, and Start Over While Maintaining Your Sanity and Finding Happiness.* Ali Wenzke. William Morrow 2019. xiv, 271 pages : Color; Illustration
 ISBN 9780062869739
Grades: Adult   648
1. Moving to a new home 2. Family and Relationships — Friendship 3. House and Home — General 4. Self-Help — Personal growth — Happiness

LC Bl2019012822

A blogger who moved ten times in eleven years shares tips on managing the moving process, including how to successfully list your home, declutter and pack and transition to a new community.

ESSENTIAL AND RECOMMENDED TITLES
649 Child rearing; home care of people with disabilities and illnesses

Offers a comprehensive, step-by-step guide for every phase of the moving process, including how to choose the next neighborhood, how to say goodbye to friends, and how to build a new community.

"A less-onerous-than-Marie Kondo method guide to decluttering. Appended with a moving checklist, moving resolutions, questions to ask before hiring a mover or realtor, moving-day survival kit, donation value guide, and dream-home wish list." —*Booklist*

Includes index.

White, Dana
How to Manage Your Home Without Losing Your Mind: Dealing with Your House's Dirty Little Secrets. Dana K. White. W Publishing Group, an imprint of Thomas Nelson 2016. xv, 223 pages : Illustration

ISBN 9780718079956

Grades: Adult   648

1. Housekeeping 2. House cleaning 3. Orderliness 4. Clutter 5. Cleaning 6. House and Home — Cleaning, caretaking, and organizing

LC 2016008307

A decluttering expert who blogs at A Slob Comes Clean presents the strategies she has developed, tested and proved in her own home combined with her reality-based cleaning and organizing techniques that will help readers get rid of enormous amounts of stuff quickly and without drama.

---

649 Child rearing; home care of people with disabilities and illnesses

Adichie, Chimamanda Ngozi
Dear Ijeawele: Or a Feminist Manifesto in Fifteen Suggestions. Chimamanda Ngozi Adichie. Random House Inc 2017. 63 p.

ISBN 9781524733131

Grades: 11 12 Adult   649

1. Feminist theory 2. Feminism 3. Feminists 4. Advice 5. Child rearing 6. Letter writing 7. Gender wars 8. Women's role 9. Female friendship 10. Empowerment 11. Society and culture — Gender — Women 12. Family and Relationships — Parenting

LC Bl2017007979

Amelia Bloomer List, 2018.

Offers the author's advice to a childhood friend on raising a baby girl to be a feminist, in the form of fifteen suggestions for bringing up a girl to become a strong, independent woman.

"This excellent series of essays is award-winning author Adichie's (Americanah) response to a friend's question on how to raise her daughter as a feminist." —*Library Journal*

Altmann, Tanya Remer
What to Feed Your Baby: A Pediatrician's Guide to the Eleven Essential Foods to Guarantee Veggie-Loving, No-Fuss, Healthy-Eating Kids. Tanya Altmann, M.D, F.A.A.P. with Beth Saltz M.P.H, R.D.. HarperOne 2016. VII, 326 pages

ISBN 9780062404930

Grades: Adult   649

1. Food habits 2. Babies 3. Nutrition 4. Family and Relationships — Parenting 5. Science writing — Medicine and health — Children's health 6. Science writing — Medicine and health — Diet and nutrition

LC 2015033614

An American Academy of Pediatrics spokesperson and best-selling author of Mommy Calls shares strategies for raising children to love healthy foods, clarifying the contradictory information that challenges parenting choices while identifying 11 foundation foods critical to brain development and growth.

"This clear, thorough guide will take the angst and confusion out of feeding time for parents and youngsters alike." —*Publishers Weekly*

Includes bibliographical references and index.

Amer, Lindz
Rainbow Parenting: Your Guide to Raising Queer Kids and Their Allies. Lindz Amer. St. Martin's Griffin 2023. x, 242 pages : Illustration

ISBN 9781250836489

Grades: Adult   649

1. LGBTQIA+ children 2. Children 3. Parenting 4. Gender identity 5. Family and Relationships — Parenting 6. Family and Relationships — LGBTQIA+

LC 2022058225

Rainbow Parenting is an indispensable stepping stone for adults who want to raise and teach kids in a queer and gender-affirming way, but might not know how. Lindz Amer, the creator of Queer Kid Stuff, an award-winning LGBTQ+ educational webseries for children and families, is an expert guide, leading readers through practical applications, important LGBTQ+ history, key lessons in intersectionality, pronouns, social justice, and more. Divided by sections that address kids' individual ages—from infancy to kindergarten—this joyful and approachable book shares a bit of hope and starts with the understanding that anyone can spread queer joy.

"Filled with practical guidance and thoughtful commentary, this is a valuable resource for raising children beyond the gender binary." —*Publishers Weekly*

Includes bibliographical references (pages 219-228) and index.

Arment, Ainsley
The Wild + Free Family: Forging Your Own Path to a Life Full of Wonder, Adventure, and Connection. Ainsley Arment. HarperOne, an imprint of HarperCollinsPublishers 2022. x, 227 pages : Illustration

ISBN 9780062998231

Grades: Adult   649

1. Parenting 2. Parent and child 3. Children 4. Families 5. Family and Relationships — Parenting

LC Bl2022026673

Drawn from her family's stories and those shared by the Wild + Free community, the Wild + Free Family explores how to create a family culture that breaks the mold by seeking to connect with our children, unleash their gifts, pursue a shared vision together, and redeem generational brokenness, among so much more. Inside these pages are Ainsley's words of encouragement, honesty, and wisdom, guiding all parents to create a home where families can forge their own path to love stronger, live more fully, and grow closer to each other."

"For parents looking to 'Cast aside convention,' this is just right." —*Publishers Weekly*

Includes bibliographical references (pages 219-226).

Baxley, Traci
Social Justice Parenting: How to Raise Compassionate, Anti-racist, Justice-minded Kids in an Unjust World. Traci Baxley. Harper Wave 2021. 256 p.

ISBN 9780063082366

Grades: Adult   649

1. Parenting 2. Race awareness in children 3. Antiracism 4. Prejudice 5. Unconscious bias 6. Child rearing 7. Social justice 8. United States 9. Antiracist literature 10. Family and Relationships — Parenting 11. Society and culture — Race

LC 2021010020

A professor of education who has spent 30 years teaching diversity and inclusion presents this timely guide that encourages parents to acknowledge their influence in developing compassionate, socially conscious children.

"Baxley's meaty book is sure to provoke thought and positive dialogue; a must-read." —*Library Journal*

Boyce, W. Thomas
The Orchid and the Dandelion: Why Some Children Struggle and How All Can Thrive. W. Thomas Boyce MD.. Knopf 2019. 304 p.

ISBN 9781101946565

Grades: Adult   649

1. Developmental psychology 2. Child development 3. Heredity and environment (Psychology) 4. Parenting 5. Society and culture — Education 6. Family and relationships — Parenting

LC 2017060895

PUBLIC LIBRARY CORE COLLECTION: NONFICTION
Twentieth Edition

Based on groundbreaking research, a book on the idea that there are children who have the capacity to survive and thrive under any circumstances and those who are highly sensitive to their environment but, if properly nurtured, can survive and flourish.

"This fascinating study of nurture vs. nature and how parents can play a positive role in a childs life comes highly recommended." —*Library Journal*

Includes bibliographical references and index.

Brown, Emma

To Raise a Boy: Classrooms, Locker Rooms, Bedrooms, and the Hidden Struggles of American Boyhood. Emma Brown. One Signal Publishers 2021. 320 p.

ISBN 9781982128081

Grades: Adult   649

1. Masculinity 2. Gender identity 3. Growing up 4. Adolescence 5. Sexuality 6. Sexual violence 7. Child rearing 8. Trust 9. Respect 10. Parents 11. Journalists 12. Educators 13. Social change 14. Psychology 15. Boys 16. United States 17. Society and culture — Gender — Men 18. Family and Relationships — Parenting 19. Family and Relationships — Growing up 20. Life stories — Identity — Gender

LC 2020044541

How will I raise my son to be different? This question gripped Washington Post investigative reporter Emma Brown, who was at home nursing her six-week-old son when the #MeToo movement erupted. In search of an answer, Brown traveled around the country for two years, through towns urban and rural, affluent and distressed. In the course of her reporting, she interviewed hundreds of people—educators, parents, coaches, researchers, men, and boys—to understand the challenges boys face and how to address them. What Brown uncovered was shocking. From the reporter who brought Dr. Christine Blasey Ford's story to light, To Raise a Boy combines assiduous reporting, cutting-edge scientific research, and boys' powerful testimonials to expose the crisis in young men's emotional and physical health.

"In this empathetic account, Washington Post reporter Brown exposes the pressures society exerts on boys.... This authoritative and accessible consideration offers insights, solutions, and hope." —*Booklist*

Includes bibliographical references and index.

Ezzo, Gary

On Becoming Baby Wise: Giving Your Infant the Gift of Nighttime Sleep. Gary Ezzo, M.A. and Robert Bucknam, M.D... Parent-Wise Solutions, Inc. 2012. 279 pages : Illustration

ISBN 9781932740134

Grades: Adult   649

1. Child rearing 2. Babies 3. Parent and baby 4. Sleep 5. Family and Relationships — Parenting

LC Bl2014007776

Teaches parents about synchronized feedings so their baby will establish cycles for wake time and nighttime, giving both parent and child the rest they need.

Includes bibliographical references (ppages 267-269) and index.

Faber, Adele

★ *How to Talk so Kids Will Listen & Listen so Kids Will Talk*. Adele Faber & Elaine Mazlish; illustrations by Kimberly Ann Coe. Scribner Classics 2012. xiv, 345 p. : Illustration

ISBN 9781451663877

Grades: Adult   649

1. Parenting 2. Interpersonal communication 3. Family and Relationships — Parenting

LC Bl2012004319

Details a program for improving communication between parents and children, providing sample dialogues and role-playing exercises.

"This title has developed a cult following over the years, and this revised edition is a welcome arrival. An essential purchase." —*Library Journal*

With a new afterword, 'The Next Generation' by Joanna Faber; Includes bibliographical references (p. 333-334) and index.

Fradin, Kelly

Advanced Parenting: Advice for Helping Kids Through Diagnoses, Differences, and Mental Health Challenges. Kelly Fradin, MD.. Balance 2023. xviii, 317 pages

ISBN 9781538722466

Grades: Adult   649

1. Parenting 2. Children with learning disabilities 3. Children with developmental disabilities 4. Children with emotional illnesses 5. Children with disabilities 6. Family and Relationships — Parenting 7. Science Writing — Medicine and health — Children's health

LC 2022053112

A pediatrician provides empathy, support and evidence-based guidance to help parents manage the emotional stress and navigation of care when their child has medical issues, from ADHD and food allergies to anxiety and developmental delays.

"The advice manages the difficult feat of providing specific guidance while applying broadly to the myriad conditions a child might face. Thoughtful and practical, this delivers." —*Publishers Weekly*

Includes bibliographical references (pages 297-311) and index.

Galinsky, Ellen

★ *The Breakthrough Years: A New Scientific Framework for Raising Thriving Teens*. Ellen Galinsky. Flatiron Books 2024. VIII, 548 pages : Illustration

ISBN 9781250062048

Grades: Adult   649

1. Parenting 2. Adolescent psychology 3. Child development 4. Teenagers 5. Parent and teenager 6. Family and Relationships — Parenting

LC 2023037230

Blending cutting-edge research with engaging storytelling, the author offers readers a paradigm-shifting comprehensive understanding of adolescence.

"Overflowing with insight backed by scientific rigor, this is an essential companion for parents of adolescents." —*Publishers Weekly*

Includes bibliographical references and index.

Greene, Benjamin

★ *My Child Is Trans, Now What?: A Joy-Centered Approach to Support*. Ben V. Greene. Rowman & Littlefield 2024. 208 p.

ISBN 9781538186459

Grades: Adult   649

1. Parents of transgender children 2. Transgender children 3. Parenting 4. Coming out (Sexual or gender identity) 5. Gender identity 6. Gender nonconformity 7. Transitioning (Gender identity) 8. Family relationships 9. Family and Relationships — LGBTQIA+ 10. Family and Relationships — Parenting

LC 2023040342

With personal stories and experiences, key resources and emotional support, a full-time public speaker specializing in spreading awareness and understanding of the transgender community offers a judgment-free guide for parents and loved ones to help trans youth thrive.

"This warm and generous book will help a wide range of readers to support and celebrate children who are trans, nonbinary, and questioning." —*Booklist*

Includes bibliographical references and index.

Haelle, Tara

The Informed Parent: A Science-based Resource for Your Child's First Four Years. Tara Haelle and Emily Willingham, Ph.D.. A TarcherPerigee Book 2016. xii, 321 pages

ISBN 9780399171062

Grades: Adult   649

1. Child development 2. Child rearing 3. Families 4. Parenthood 5. Pregnancy 6. Baby care 7. Family and Relationships — Growing up 8. Family and Relationships — Parenting 9. Science writing — Medicine and health — Women's health — Pregnancy and childbirth

LC 2015046759

Science writers and parents themselves, the authors, sifting through research studies on dozens of essential topics, present the latest scientific research on

ESSENTIAL AND RECOMMENDED TITLES
649 Child rearing; home care of people with disabilities and illnesses

hone birth, breastfeeding, sleep training, vaccines and other important topics so that parents-to-be can make their own best-information decisions.

"For anyone headed into parenthood, this is a must-read, as it answers so many questions new parents are bound to ask. Easy-to-read, up-to-date information on the latest research into pregnancy, childbirth, and early childhood."
—*Kirkus*

Includes index.

Harrison, Valerie I.
Do Right by Me: Learning to Raise Black Children in White Spaces. Valerie I. Harrison and Kathryn Peach D'Angelo. Temple University Press 2020. 194 p.
ISBN 9781439919958
Grades: Adult 649
1. Interracial adoption 2. African American children 3. Race awareness in children 4. Adoption 5. Adoptive parents 6. Adopted children 7. Interracial families 8. Racism 9. White privilege 10. Race relations 11. United States 12. Family and Relationships — Parenting — Adoption 13. Society and culture — Race
LC 2020013140

Engaging in friendly dialogues, the two authors, through lively and intimate back-and-forth exchanges, share information on transracial adoption, understanding racism, developing a child's positive racial identity, racial disparities in healthcare and education and the violence of racism.

"This timely examination of discrimination and privilege is packed with insight and should be a great resource for white parents raising children of color." —*Publishers Weekly*

Includes bibliographical references and index.

Hawthorne, Britt
★ *Raising Antiracist Children: A Practical Parenting Guide*. Britt Hawthorne with Natasha Yglesias. Simon Element 2022. xiii, 303 pages : Illustration; Color
ISBN 9781982185428
Grades: Adult 649
1. Parenting 2. Child rearing 3. Antiracism 4. Moral development 5. Antiracist literature 6. Family and Relationships — Parenting
LC Bl2022016144

A nationally recognized teacher and advocate presents this interactive guide in which she shows parents/Caregivers how to strategically incorporate the tools of inclusivity into everyday life and parenting.

"This is a must-read that covers an essential topic well and is jam-packed with ideas to implement." —*Library Journal*

Includes bibliographical references (pages 279-290) and index.

Hibbs, B. Janet
You're Not Done Yet: Parenting Young Adults in an Age of Uncertainty. B. Janet Hibbs, M.F.T, Ph.D. and Anthony Rostain, M.D, M.A… St. Martin's Press 2024. 289 pages : Illustration
ISBN 9781250283238
Grades: Adult 649
1. Parent and adult child 2. Parenting 3. Adult children 4. Young adults 5. Family and Relationships — Parenting
LC 2023038136

An optimistic guide for parents with adult children who need help navigating the challenges to launching an independent life.

"Deeply researched, with extensive appendices, this valuable resource offers compassionate, actionable advice for families going through a transition increasingly beset with unprecedented challenges." —*Booklist*

Includes bibliographical references (pages 265-279) and index.

Huggins, Kathleen
★ *The Nursing Mother's Companion: The Breastfeeding Book Mothers Trust, from Pregnancy Through Weaning*. Kathleen Huggins, R.N, M.S, I.B.C.L.C; foreword by Jessica Martin-Weber; preface by Kelly Bonyata; appendix on drug safety by Philip O. Anderson. Harvard Common Press 2017. xii, 436 pages : Illustration
ISBN 9781558328822

Grades: Adult 649
1. Breast feeding 2. Family and Relationships — Growing up 3. Science writing — Medicine and health — Women's health — Pregnancy and childbirth
LC Bl2018125682

Breastfeeding is natural, but it is not always instinctive for either mothers or babies. The Nursing Mother's Companion has been among the best-selling books on breastfeeding for more than 30 years, with more than 1 million copies sold. It is respected and recommended by professionals, including the International Lactation Consultant Association, T. Berry Brazelton and the American Academy of Pediatrics, and is well loved by new parents for its encouraging and accessible style.

Includes bibliographical references (pages 407-414) and indexes.

Jaffe, Sarah W.
Wanting What's Best: Parenting, Privilege, and Building a Just World. Sarah W. Jaffe. Parenting Press 2022. 242 p.
ISBN 9781641607674
Grades: Adult 649
1. Parenting 2. Parenthood 3. Child welfare 4. Elitism 5. Privilege (Social psychology) 6. Social responsibility 7. Social advocacy 8. Family and Relationships — Parenting 9. Society and culture — Wealth and class 10. Society and culture — Social activism and philanthropy

When privileged parents say that they "want what's best" for their child, they don't consciously add "and not for other children." yet the practical effect of parents with privilege relentlessly pursuing their own child's interests is that other children are left behind. Author Sarah W. Jaffe interviewed dozens of parents who are resisting the cultural pressures to seek "the best" for only their kids while navigating some of the major decisions that parents make—about childcare, schools, how they use their time and money, and the legacy they hope to leave their kids. These may not feel like political decisions, but each either contributes to a system where only a few can thrive or takes a small step toward dismantling it.

"While acknowledging the challenges and fears of being a parent today, Jafffe talks with fellow parents who believe there doesn't have to be a choice between being a good parent and being a good citizen." —*Booklist*

Kendi, Ibram X.
★ *How to Raise an Antiracist*. Ibram X. Kendi. One World 2022. 224 p.
ISBN 9780593242537
Grades: Adult 649
1. Kendi, Ibram X. 2. Authors 3. Fatherhood 4. African American families 5. African American parent and child 6. Parenting 7. Race (Social sciences) 8. Race awareness 9. Racism in education 10. Racism 11. Race relations 12. United States 13. Society and culture — Race 14. Family and Relationships — Parenting 15. Life stories — Identity — Race and ethnicity 16. Life stories — Relationships — Parent and child 17. Antiracist literature

Massachusetts Book Awards, Nonfiction Award, 2022.

The tragedies and reckonings around racism that are rocking the country have created a specific crisis for parents, educators, and other caregivers: How do we talk to our children about racism? How do we teach children to be antiracist? How are kids at different ages experiencing race? How are racist structures impacting children? How can we inspire our children to avoid our mistakes, to be better, to make the world better? These are the questions Ibram X. Kendi found himself avoiding as he anticipated the birth of his first child. Like most parents or parents-to-be, he felt the reflex to not talk to his child about racism, which he feared would stain her innocence and steal away her joy. But research and experience changed his mind. He realized that teaching children about the reality of racism and the myth of race provides a protective education in our diverse and unequal world.

"Best-selling Kendi is an antiracism trailblazer and parents, educators, and everyone else who cares for children will seek his guidance." —*Booklist*

Kowal-Connelly, Suanne
Parenting Through Puberty: Mood Swings, Acne, and Growing Pains. Suanne Kowal-Connelly, MD, FAAP.. American Academy of Pediatrics 2019. xvii, 246 pages : Illustration
ISBN 9781610022125

Grades: Adult 649
1. Parent and teenager 2. Puberty 3. Family and Relationships — Parenting
LC Bl2018186502

Details the physical and emotional changes parents can expect to see in their child during puberty and explains how to help teenagers navigate through this tough time in their lives.

Includes bibliographical references and index.

Lahey, Jessica

The Addiction Inoculation: Raising Healthy Kids in a Culture of Dependence. Jessica Lahey. Harper, an imprint of HarperCollinsPublishers 2021. VIII, 323 pages
ISBN 9780062883780

Grades: Adult 649
1. Parenting 2. Child rearing 3. Drug abuse 4. Teenagers 5. Children 6. Drug use 7. Family and relationships — Parenting 8. Society and culture — Illness and disease — Addiction 9. Self-help — Mental health — Addiction

A comprehensive reference for parents and educators explains the origins of substance abuse while offering advice for how to identify risk factors and take steps to prevent vulnerable teens from developing an addiction disorder.

"This book combines expertise with humble personal experience to show how modeling, believing in our children, and valuing learning instead of accolades will go a long way toward preventing addiction." —*Library Journal*

Includes bibliographical references (pages [281]-309) and index.

The Gift of Failure: How the Best Parents Learn to Let Go so Their Children Can Succeed. Jessica Lahey. Harper 2015. 304 p.
ISBN 9780062299239

Grades: Adult 649
1. Self-reliance in children 2. Overprotectiveness in parents 3. Early childhood education 4. Child rearing 5. Parenting 6. United States 7. Family and relationships — Parenting 8. Debut title
LC 2014039146

A full-length guide based on the author's provocative essay on the website of the Atlantic counsels parents of school-aged children on how to overcome tendencies toward over-protectiveness to allow children to develop independence.

"Lahey's conversational tone, combined with research and narratives from both children and parents, delivers in-depth insight into the value of mistakes. With chapters on specific age groups (middle schoolers and high schoolers) and hot-button issues, such as household chores, homework, and friendships, any parent who needs assistance reining in the supermom tendencies will find sound advice here." —*Library Journal*

Lev, Arlene Istar

The Complete Lesbian & Gay Parenting Guide. Arlene Istar Lev. Berkley Books 2004. xvi, 379 p.
ISBN 9780425191972

Grades: Adult 649
1. Families 2. Gay parents 3. Parenting 4. United States 5. Family and Relationships — General 6. Family and Relationships — Parenting
LC 2004057080

A comprehensive and practical handbook for gay, lesbian, and alternative lifestyle parents shares sensible advice and personal real-life stories about the challenges of twenty-first-century family life, covering such topics as solo parenting, blended families, surrogacy, adoption and foster parenting, legal rights, bias, domestic partnership agreements, custody, and more.

Includes bibliographical references (p. [346]-349) and index.

Levine, Madeline

★ *Ready or Not: Preparing Our Kids to Thrive in an Uncertain and Rapidly Changing World.* Madeline Levine. Harper360 2020. 352 pages
ISBN 9780062657756

Grades: Adult 649
1. Parenting 2. Child rearing 3. Skills 4. Success (Concept) 5. Critical thinking 6. Curiosity 7. Adaptability 8. Collaboration 9. Persistence 10. Family and Relationships — Parenting
LC Bl2020000501

The New York Times best-selling author of The Price of Privilege and Teach Your Children Well explores how today's parenting techniques and our myopic educational system are failing to prepare children for their certain-to-be-uncertain future—and how we can reverse course to ensure their lasting adaptability, resilience, health and happiness.

"With thorough research backing her up, Levine delivers advice with intelligence and compassion, but also with realistic expectations of what it's like to parent as well as grow up in today's world. Best of all, she masterfully balances this realism with positivity. Another invaluable resource from Levine." —*Booklist*

Includes bibliographical references and index.

Lickona, Thomas

How to Raise Kind Kids: And Get Respect, Gratitude, and a Happier Family in the Bargain. Thomas Lickona. Penguin Books 2018. xxvii, 308 p.
ISBN 9780143131946

Grades: Adult 649
1. Parenting 2. Kindness 3. Education 4. Family and Relationships — Parenting 5. Science writing — Medicine and health — Psychology
LC 2017058211

Can you teach a child to be kind? This vital question is taking on a new urgency as our culture grows ever more abrasive and divided. We all want our kids to be kind. But that is not the same as knowing what to do when you catch your son being unkind. A world-renowned developmental psychologist, Dr. Thomas Lickona has led the character education movement in schools for forty years. Now he shares with parents the vital tools they need to bring peace and foster cooperation at home. Kindness doesn't stand on its own. It needs a supporting cast of other essential virtues—like courage, self-control, respect, and gratitude. With concrete examples drawn from the many families Dr. Lickona has worked with over the years and clear tips you can act on tonight, How to Raise Kind Kids will help you give and get respect, hold family meetings to tackle persistent problems, discipline in a way that builds character, and improve the dynamic of your relationship with your children while putting them on the path to ahappier and more fulfilling life.

With concrete examples drawn from the many families Dr. Lickona has worked with over the years and clear tips you can act on tonight, How to Raise Kind Kids will help you give and get respect, hold family meetings to tackle persistent problems, discipline in a way that builds character, and improve the dynamic of your relationship with your children while putting them on the path to a happier and more fulfilling life.

Includes bibliographical references (pages 283-295) and index.

Linn, Susan

Who's Raising the Kids?: Big Tech, Big Business, and the Lives of Children. Susan Linn. The New Press 2022. 320 p.
ISBN 9781620972274

Grades: Adult 649
1. Computers and children 2. Child psychology 3. Parenting 4. Smartphones 5. Internet addiction 6. High technology industry and trade 7. Advertising 8. Capitalism 9. Child mental health 10. Child welfare 11. Society and culture — Media and technology 12. Family and Relationships — Parenting

Even before the COVID-19 pandemic, digital technologies had become deeply embedded in children's lives, despite a growing body of research detailing the harms of excessive immersion in the unregulated, powerfully seductive, profit-driven world of the "kid-tech" industry. In Who's Raising the Kids? Susan Linn—one of the world's leading experts on the impact of Big Tech and big business on children—explores the roots and consequences of this monumental shift toward a digitized, commercialized childhood, focusing on kids' values, relationships, and learning.

"Linn's examination of how screens have taken over childhood is a must-read for any parent." —*Kirkus*

McCarthy, Catherine

Raising a Kid Who Can: Simple Strategies to Build a Lifetime of Adaptability and Emotional Strength. Catherine McCarthy, MD, Heather Tedesco, PhD, Jennifer Weaver, LCSW.. Workman Publishing 2023. 280 p.
ISBN 9781523518593

ESSENTIAL AND RECOMMENDED TITLES
649 Child rearing; home care of people with disabilities and illnesses

Grades: Adult **649**
1. Resilience in children 2. Emotions in children 3. Adaptability 4. Children 5. Parenting 6. Parent and child 7. Family and Relationships — Parenting

Providing scientifically based and actionable advice and strategies, three mental health professionals who work with families team up in this new approach to a parenting guide that helps parents focus only on what's truly essential for raising healthier, happier humans.

"It's a valuable guide for helping kids help themselves." —*Publishers Weekly*

Includes bibliographical references and index.

Mogel, Wendy
Voice Lessons for Parents: What to Say, How to Say It, and When to Listen. Wendy Mogel, PhD.. Scribner 2018. xvi, 302 pages
ISBN 9781501142390
Grades: Adult **649**
1. Interpersonal communication 2. Parent and child 3. Parenting 4. Family and Relationships — Growing up 5. Family and Relationships — Parenting 6. Self-Help — Relationships

LC BI2018004483

Presents an essential guide to the art of talking with children that demonstrates how a change of voice can transform conversations and ease parent-child relationships, sharing strategies for communicating with kids at different age levels.

The best-selling author of The Blessing of a Skinned Knee presents an essential guide to the new art of talking with children that demonstrates how a change of voice can transform conversations and ease parent-child relationships, sharing strategies for communicating with kids at different age levels as well as talking with family members, teachers, coaches and other caregivers about one's children.

Includes bibliographical references and index.

Morgenstern, Julie
Time to Parent: Organizing Your Life to Bring Out the Best in Your Child and You. Julie Morgenstern. Henry Holt and Company 2018. xvi, 335 p. : Illustration
ISBN 9781627797436
Grades: Adult **649**
1. Parenting 2. Time management 3. Self-Help — General 4. House and Home — Cleaning, caretaking, and organizing 5. Family and Relationships — Parenting

LC 2018001408

Intends to help parents and caregivers craft a life schedule that builds in quality time with children.

Morin, Amy
13 Things Mentally Strong Parents Don't Do: Raising Self-Assured Children and Training Their Brains for a Life of Happiness, Meaning, and Success. Amy Morin. William Morrow 2017. 342 pages
ISBN 9780062565730
Grades: Adult **649**
1. Parenting 2. Child rearing 3. Self-confidence in children 4. Family and Relationships — Parenting

LC 2017470363

In today's world, many parents over-react to events by trying to shield their children from pain and reality. But children need to learn skills that will help them become mentally strong adults. Morin offers advice for providing appropriate support, guidance, and encouragement to help children deal with challenges and flourish in their everyday lives.

"Her combination of common sense backed by research—amply cited—will help parents make a midcourse correction. While the title focuses on the negative, the book itself accentuates the positive." —*Publishers Weekly*

Includes bibliographical references (pages 333-342).

Murkoff, Heidi Eisenberg
★ *What to Expect the Second Year: From 12 to 24 Months.* Heidi Murkoff and Sharon Mazel; foreword by Mark D. Widome. Workman Pub. 2011. xvi, 512 p. : Illustration

ISBN 9780761163640
Grades: Adult **649**
1. Child rearing 2. Toddlers 3. Family and Relationships — Parenting

LC 2011281832

From the first birthday to the second, everything you need to know about caring for, nurturing, understanding, and keeping up with your incredible 1 year old.

Includes index.

Natterson, Cara Familian
★ *Decoding Boys: New Science Behind the Subtle Art of Raising Sons.* Cara Natterson, MD.. Random House Inc 2020. 288 pages
ISBN 9781984819031
Grades: Adult **649**
1. Teenage boys 2. Child rearing 3. Puberty 4. Parent and child 5. Sons 6. Parenting 7. Psychology 8. Boys 9. Family and Relationships — Parenting 10. Family and Relationships — Growing Up

LC 2019037589

Citing the less-recognized behavioral tendencies of male adolescence that complicate communications between parents and children, a guide to raising teen boys shares strategic guidelines on effective parenting, managing screen time and understanding the sources of negative behavior.

"An essential and approachable resource for parents of preteen and teenage boys." —*Library Journal*

Includes bibliographical references and index.

Naumburg, Carla
★ *You Are Not a Sh*tty Parent: How to Practice Self-Compassion and Give Yourself a Break.* Carla Naumburg, PhD.. Workman Publishing 2022. 219 pages
ISBN 9781523517114
Grades: Adult **649**
1. Parenting 2. Self-acceptance 3. Compassion 4. Stress 5. Family and Relationships — Parenting 6. Self-Help — Personal growth — Self-esteem

LC BI2022030036

The bestselling author of How to Stop Losing Your Sh*t with Your Kids has an important message for stressed-out parents who want to do better: the secret to being a more effective, more empathetic parent and raising happy, resilient kids starts with practicing compassion for yourself."

"The rare parenting book that readers will want to pick up again and again." —*Booklist*

Includes bibliographical references (pages 217-218).

Neifert, Marianne R.
The Essential Guide to Breastfeeding. Marianne Neifert. Sterling 2009. 312 p. : Illustration
ISBN 9781402758171
Grades: Adult **649**
1. Breast feeding 2. Science writing — Medicine and health — Women's health — Pregnancy and childbirth

LC 2009005248

Describes how to prepare for breastfeeding a newborn, from preparations before birth to breastfeeding with a busy schedule, proper storage, maintaining a healthy diet, and breastfeeding high-risk infants.

"The author combines detailed, readable medical explanations with practical tips for success and addresses potential challenges honestly rather than glossing over them with bland reassurances. Each chapter seems designed to stand alone, making it easy for time-pressed mothers to find the information they need without reading the entire book." —*Library Journal*

Includes index.

Nowicki, Stephen
Raising a Socially Successful Child: Teaching Kids the Nonverbal Language They Need to Communicate, Connect, and Thrive. Stephen Nowicki. Little, Brown Spark 2024. 265 p.
ISBN 9780316516471
Grades: Adult **649**

PUBLIC LIBRARY CORE COLLECTION: NONFICTION
Twentieth Edition

1. Child rearing 2. Nonverbal communication 3. Interpersonal communication 4. Social interaction in children 5. Body language 6. Children 7. Family and Relationships — Parenting

Reveals how to identify the nonverbal areas where a child might be struggling, and equips readers with a set of simple exercises for helping any child learn how to: Follow the rhythm of conversations, respect others' personal space and much more.

"Sound advice for teaching children about building enjoyable, positive, and meaningful relationships." —*Kirkus*

Includes bibliographical references (pages 244-256) and index.

Ockwell-Smith, Sarah
Ready, Set, Go!: A Gentle Parenting Guide to Calmer, Quicker Potty Training. Sarah Ockwell-Smith. A TarcherPerigee Book 2017. xiii, 191 pages

ISBN 9780143131908

Grades: Adult   649

1. Toilet training 2. Family and Relationships — Growing up 3. Family and Relationships — Parenting

LC 2018011129

A popular parenting expert presents this authoritative guide to potty-training that helps parents understand when to start the process, and provides step-by-step information on the most effective, gentle and compassionate approach, as well as how to handle setbacks.

Presents an authoritative guide to potty-training that helps parents understand when to start the process, and provides step-by-step information on the most effective, gentle, and compassionate approach, as well as how to handle setbacks.

"There is little new here, but potty training is of perennial interest to parents, and newbies may find this a solid starter manual." —*Library Journal*

Paul, Pamela
★ *How to Raise a Reader.* Pamela Paul, Maria Russo; illustrated by Dan Yaccarino. Workman Publishing 2019. 208 p.

ISBN 9781523505302

Grades: Adult   649

1. Books and reading 2. Children 3. Reading aloud 4. Families 5. Family and Relationships — Parenting 6. Arts and Entertainment — Writing and Publishing

LC Bl2019021047

A parent's guide to raising a lifelong reader, packed with practical ideas for engaging children of all ages in books, plus wonderful lists of books, arranged by age and subject matter, will keep the shelves stocked and young readers' interests high from birth through teens.

"With the bottom line that "If you want to raise a reader, be a reader," their primer is recommended for all worried parents and anyone looking for suggestions of what books to read or give to children." —*Publishers Weekly*

Includes index.

Perry, Philippa
★ *The Book You Wish Your Parents Had Read: (and Your Children Will Be Glad That You Did).* Philippa Perry. Pamela Dorman Books Life/Viking 2019. xv, 304 p.

ISBN 9781984879554

Grades: Adult   649

1. Parenting 2. Parent and child 3. Science writing — Medicine and health — Psychology 4. Self-Help — Personal growth 5. Family and Relationships — Parenting

LC 2019025255

In this absorbing, clever, and warm book, renowned psychotherapist Philippa Perry tells us what really matters and what behavior it is important to avoid—the vital dos and don'ts of parenting.

Includes bibliographical references and index.

Phelan, Thomas W.
1-2-3 Magic: Effective Discipline for Children 2-12. Thomas W. Phelan, PhD.. Sourcebooks 2016. xx, 265 p. : Illustration

ISBN 9781492631828

Grades: Adult   649

1. Child rearing 2. Parenting 3. Family and Relationships — Parenting

LC 2015021612

Outlines a three step parenting guide, offering readers tools to use in a variety of situations and advice for common problems.

Includes bibliographical references (pages 248-251) and index.

Ramesh, Jaya
Parenting at the Intersections: Raising Neurodivergent Children of Color. Jaya Ramesh, Priya Saaral. Parenting Press, an imprint of Chicago Review Press Incorporated 2024. xxv, 318 pages : Illustration

ISBN 9781641608893

Grades: Adult   649

1. Parenting 2. Marginalized children 3. Neurodivergent people 4. Children with developmental disabilities 5. Race awareness in children 6. Child rearing 7. Child development 8. Children with ADHD 9. Autistic people 10. Intersectionality 11. Social justice 12. Family and Relationships — Parenting 13. Society and culture — General 14. Antiracist literature

LC Bl2024001880

What if parenting were an act of social justice? In this part story-telling, part self-inquiry book, authors and therapists Jaya Ramesh and Priya Saaral situate parenting children of color with neurodivergence within the context of various interlocking systems of oppression including settler colonialism, White supremacy, ableism, and capitalism. These intersections engender isolation and loneliness. Using the voices of parents on the front lines and other experts, Parenting at the Intersections offer aninvitation to parents to slow down and reflect on their own parenting journeys.

"Therapists Ramesh and Saaral debut with an insightful guide on parenting kids of color with ADHD, autism, dyslexia, OCD, or other neurological conditions…It's an empathetic look at how to meet kids where they're at." —*Publishers Weekly*

Includes bibliographical references (pages 307-318).

Rinella, Steven
★ *Outdoor Kids in an Inside World: Getting Your Family Out of the House and Radically Engaged with Nature.* Steven Rinella. Random House 2022. xxviii, 171 pages : Illustration

ISBN 9780593129661

Grades: Adult   649

1. Natural history 2. Nature 3. Environmentalism 4. Family and Relationships — Parenting 5. Nature Writing — General

LC 2021048803

Helping families connect with nature—and each other, this timely guide shares parenting wisdom, practical advice and hands-on activities to help kids see their own place within the natural world.

"As useful as it is charming, this should go a long way toward convincing readers to get up, gather the family, and enjoy what nature has in store." —*Publishers Weekly*

Host of the show Meateater as seen on Netflix—Jacket; Includes index.

Rippon, Kelly
Parent Up: Inspire Your Child to Be Their Best Self. Kelly Rippon. Sourcebooks 2021. xxv, 197 pages

ISBN 9781728222356

Grades: Adult   649

1. Rippon, Kelly 2. Rippon, Adam 1989- 3. Single-parent families 4. Parenting 5. Parent and child 6. Maternal love 7. High achievement 8. Familial love 9. Self-confidence 10. Empathy 11. Loyalty 12. Child rearing 13. Family and Relationships — Parenting 14. Life stories — Relationships — Parent and child

LC 2020020041

From Kelly Rippon, single mother of six super achievers, including an Olympic medalist, comes a breakthrough parenting philosophy. Parent Up is a call to action for all parents to realize the power of being the most important, positive shaping force in your children's lives. Broken down into ten chapters that each present a key influence (from the influence of optimism to loyalty), Kelly shares her philosophy as well as relatable anecdotes from her own life to offer

ESSENTIAL AND RECOMMENDED TITLES
649.1 Child rearing

not only accessible parenting advice but to invite parents into their own journey of self-discovery. To her, becoming the ultimate influencer for your kids is the highest self-development experience a person can have.

The mother of Olympic medalist Adam Rippon draws on her experiences as a single parent of six high achievers to outline anecdotal philosophies about how to be a positive influencer in the development of a young person's best self.

"What sets this apart from other parenting books are Rippon's core ideals in action.... Rippon shares thoughtful insights, extensive experiences, and sound tips for everyone who interacts with children." —*Booklist*

Seldin, Tim
How to Raise an Amazing Child the Montessori Way. Tim Seldin. DK Pub. 2017. 208 pages : Color; Illustration
ISBN 9781465462305
Grades: Adult   649
1. Child rearing 2. Child development 3. Learning 4. Early childhood education 5. Cognition 6. Cognitive styles 7. Montessori method of education 8. Family and Relationships — Parenting
LC 2017302243

The president of the Montessori Foundation offers an inspirational handbook designed to help parents enhance a child's physical and intellectual growth from birth to six years of age, furnishing insights into each development stage; proven strategies for helping youngsters develop discipline, respect, and kindness; and tips on coping with problem behavior.

Child psychiatrist Seldin, president of the Montessori Foundation, here adapts key Montessori principles for the home environment, maintaining the core tenets of 'Kindness, partnership, and respect.' —*School Library Journal*

Includes bibliographical references (page 208) and index.

Siegel, Daniel J.
Parenting from the Inside Out: How a Deeper Self-Understanding Can Help You Raise Children Who Thrive. Daniel J. Siegel, M.D, and Mary Hartzell, M.Ed; with a new preface by the authors. Jeremy P. Tarcher/Penguin 2014. xxiv, 311 pages : Illustration
ISBN 9780399165108
Grades: Adult   649
1. Parent and child 2. Parenting 3. Self-perception 4. Family and Relationships — Parenting
LC 2013037883

Explores the extent to which our childhood experiences shape the way we parent, drawing on new findings in neurobiology and attachment research and explaining how interpersonal relationships directly impact the development of the brain. Offers parents a step-by-step approach to forming a deeper understanding of their own life stories.

Includes bibliographical references and index.

The Power of Showing Up: How Parental Presence Shapes Who Our Kids Become and How Their Brains Get Wired. Daniel J. Siegel, M.D, Tina Payne Bryson, Ph.D; illustrations by Tuesday Mourning. Ballantine Books 2020. xiv, 238 pages : Illustration
ISBN 9781524797713
Grades: Adult   649
1. Parent and child 2. Parenting 3. Family and Relationships — Parenting
LC 2019034765

Draws on the latest understandings in attachment research to explain the importance of a parent's involved presence in helping children feel safe, secure and loved.

Way, Niobe
Rebels with a Cause: Reimagining Boys, Ourselves, and Our Culture. Niobe Way. Dutton 2024. 322 p.
ISBN 9780593184264
Grades: Adult   649
1. Boys 2. Young men 3. Developmental psychology 4. Mental health 5. Depression 6. Addiction 7. Alienation 8. Suicide 9. Masculinity 10. Male friendship 11. Culture 12. Social psychology 13. Patriarchy 14. Bonding (Interpersonal relations) 15. Society and culture — Gender — Men 16. Society and culture — Psychology and human behavior
LC 2024012610

Dr. Niobe Way has spent her career researching social and emotional development and finds that boys and young men desperately want and need the same thing as everyone else: close friendships. Yet they and we grow up in a stereotyped "boy" culture, one that devalues and mocks those relationships, rather than recognizing that they're necessary for human survival. Way provides us not only with data-driven insight into the roots and consequences of this crisis of connection, but also offers us concrete and empirically tested strategies for creating a culture that better aligns with our human nature and our human needs.

"A thoughtful, well-informed look at contemporary boy culture and its many inherent problems." —*Kirkus*

Includes bibliographical references and index.

Wojcicki, Esther
How to Raise Successful People: Simple Lessons for Radical Results. Esther Wojcicki. Houghton Mifflin Harcourt 2019. 304 p.
ISBN 9781328974860
Grades: Adult   649
1. Parenting 2. Education 3. Child psychology 4. Child development 5. Success (Concept) 6. Motivation 7. Success in business 8. Trust 9. Family and Relationships — Parenting
LC 2018046436

The Godmother of Silicon Valley, legendary teacher, and mother of a Super Family shares her tried-and-tested methods for raising happy, healthy, successful children using Trust, Respect, Independence, Collaboration, and Kindness: TRICK.

"Written with honesty, heart, and a great deal of experience, How to Raise Successful People is a must-read for all parents." —*Booklist*

649.1 Child rearing

Bhattacharya, Shaoni
The Baby Book: Pregnancy, Birth, Baby & Childcare from 0 to 3. Writers Shaoni Bhattacharya, Claire Cross, Carol Dyce, Kate Ling, Susannah Marriott, Karen Sullivan, and Jo Wiltshire. DK Publishing 2016. 320 pages : Color; Illustration
ISBN 9781465444783
Grades: Adult   649.1
1. Child care 2. Childbirth 3. Pregnancy 4. Baby care 5. Family and Relationships — Parenting 6. Science writing — Medicine and health — Children's health
LC Bl2015056898

A comprehensive guide for modern parents covers pregnancy through the first three years with recommendations on everything from prenatal superfoods and labor tips to first checkups and breastfeeding practices.

"While books on this subject are abundant, readers will be naturally drawn to the warm style and sheer beauty of the DK titles. Libraries can't go wrong with this acquisition." —*Library Journal*

Includes index.

Hillsberg, Christina
License to Parent: How My Career as a Spy Helped Me Raise Resourceful, Self-Sufficient Kids. Christina Hillsberg, with Ryan Hillsberg. Putnam 2021. 288 p.
ISBN 9780593191118
Grades: Adult   649.1
1. Hillsberg, Christina 2. CIA agents 3. Women CIA agents 4. Spies 5. Husband and wife 6. Stepchildren 7. Children 8. Child rearing 9. Parenting 10. Life skills 11. Self-reliance 12. Independence in children 13. Intelligence service 14. Training 15. United States 16. Family and Relationships — Parenting 17. Life stories — Law and order — Spies and secret agents 18. Life stories — Relationships — Parent and child

Christina was a single, successful CIA analyst with a burgeoning career in espionage when she met fellow spy, Ryan, a hotshot field operative who turned her world upside down. They fell in love, married, and soon they were raising three children from his first marriage, and later, two more of their own. Told through honest and relatable parenting anecdotes, Christina shares their distinctive approach to raising confident, security-conscious, resilient children, giving practical takeaways rooted in CIA tradecraft along the way.

"With tips for staying safe online, living by one's principles, and finding a healthy balance with risk, this is a fascinating and useful take on parenting." —*Library Journal*

Pressman, Aliza

The 5 Principles of Parenting: Your Essential Guide to Raising Good Humans. Dr. Aliza Pressman. Simon Element 2024. xx, 346 pages

ISBN 9781668014530

Grades: Adult   649.1

1. Parenting 2. Parent and child 3. Child rearing 4. Family and Relationships — Parenting

LC Bl2024001548

Drawing on nearly twenty years' experience, a developmental psychologist, providing expert advice and strategies, helps parents chart a manageable course for raising good humans that's aligned to their own values and their children's unique temperaments.

"In this uplifting, practical parenting guide, developmental psychologist Pressman shares big-picture principles and advice on how to apply them." —*Booklist*

Includes bibliographical references (pages 317-323) and index.

Sole-Smith, Virginia

★ *Fat Talk: Parenting in the Age of Diet Culture*. Virginia Sole-Smith. Henry Holt & Co. 2023. 320 p.

ISBN 9781250831217

Grades: Adult   649.1

1. Fat children 2. Body image 3. Self-esteem in children 4. Parenting 5. Child development 6. Family relationships 7. Obesity 8. Eating disorders 9. Weight loss 10. Dieting 11. Body dysmorphic disorder 12. Social justice 13. American people 14. North American people 15. United States 16. Family and Relationships — Parenting 17. Society and culture — Psychology and human behavior

Reveals the impact of our weight-centric society on children and explores how America's focus on "solving the childhood obesity epidemic" has perpetuated disordered eating and bodying hatred and offers empowering advice to navigate these challenges.

"With its message of trusting our kids' bodies (and everyone else's) as they are as both a social justice issue and an act of love, this is a great place to begin." —*Booklist*

649.8 Home care of people with disabilities and illnesses

Applebaum, Allison

Stand by Me: A Guide to Navigating Modern, Meaningful Caregiving. Allison J. Applebaum, PhD.. Simon Element 2024. x, 333 pages : Illustration

ISBN 9781668005804

Grades: Adult   649.8

1. Caregivers 2. Mental health 3. Family relationships 4. Self-care 5. Patients 6. Family and Relationships — Illness and the Family 7. Self-Help — General 8. Science Writing — Medicine and health

LC 2023045095

The founder of the Caregivers Clinic at Memorial Sloan Kettering Cancer Center, a clinical psychologist, sharing her own personal journey, gives caregivers the practical tools and support they need to provide their loved ones with the best quality of life and care possible, while promoting their own wellbeing.

Includes bibliographical references (pages 271-309) and index.

Washington, Kate

★ *Already Toast: Caregiving and Burnout in America*. Kate Washington. Beacon Press 2021. 224

ISBN 9780807011508

Grades: Adult   649.8

1. Washington, Kate, 1972- 2. Caregivers 3. Women 4. Burn out (Psychology) 5. Home health care 6. Married people 7. Medical care 8. Women caregivers 9. Psychology 10. Family relationships 11. People with cancer 12. Men 13. United States 14. Autobiographies and memoirs 15. Life stories — Facing adversity — Medical issues 16. Family and Relationships — Illness and the family 17. Science Writing — Medicine and health — Illness and disease

LC 2020030912

Despite feeling profoundly alone while providing care to her sick husband, a writer discusses how she discovered she was one of millions of exhausted and stressed unpaid caregivers in America and argues that more should be done to support them.

"This moving, relatable story is sure to resonate with patrons who, if not already serving as a caregiver, may find themselves taking on that role soon enough." —*Library Journal*

Includes bibliographical references and index.

650.1 Personal success in business

Braswell, Porter

★ *Let Them See You: The Guide for Leveraging Your Diversity at Work*. Porter Braswell. Lorena Jones Books 2019. 213 p.

ISBN 9780399581403

Grades: Adult   650.1

1. Career development 2. Vocational guidance 3. Personnel management 4. Multiculturalism 5. Race relations 6. Self-Help — Career and financial success

LC 2018042897

In Let Them See You, Braswell outlines all the lessons he has learned from advising people of color on the front lines of the fast-changing workplace, such as how to scale not-so-invisible obstacles, create perceived value, get recognized, be true to yourself, build a personal brand, harness fear of failure, and embrace uncomfortable conversations.

A former Wall Street analyst and current technology entrepreneur offers a practical guide for entry- to mid-level professionals of color on how to exceed in the workplace when faced with obstacles and uncomfortable conversations based on his own experiences.

"This frank, inspiring book belongs in every library that supports job seekers, and leaders at all levels and of all ethnicities will learn from it." —*Booklist*

Includes bibliographical references and index.

Burkus, David

Friend of a Friend…: Understanding the Hidden Networks That Can Transform Your Life and Your Career. David Burkus. Houghton Mifflin Harcourt 2018. 256 p.

ISBN 9780544971264

Grades: Adult   650.1

1. Business networks 2. Networking 3. Career development 4. Networks 5. Interpersonal relations 6. Social networks 7. Business communication 8. Business and economics — Business Advice 9. Business and economics — Popular psychology

LC 2017045593

Burkus shows that most of your best connections do not come from close friends but rather from distant, even long-forgotten contacts; that it's the colleagues and influential acquaintances of your best friends who will play a major role in developing your connections; and that your most valuable network in business has much more to do with how you develop these secondary sources in order to springboard your career.

ESSENTIAL AND RECOMMENDED TITLES
650.1 Personal success in business

"This work offers thought-provoking case studies and practical guidelines on a popular but generally misunderstood topic. Of interest to social scientists, business professionals, and job seekers alike." —*Library Journal*

Includes bibliographical references and index.

Burnett, William
Designing Your Life: How to Build a Well-lived, Joyful Life. Bill Burnett and Dave Evans. Alfred A. Knopf 2016. xxxi, 238 pages : Illustration; Color
ISBN 9781101875322
Grades: Adult   650.1
1. Decision making 2. Design 3. Self-fulfillment 4. Vocational guidance 5. Business and economics — Careers 6. Self-Help — Personal growth
LC 2016008862

Outlines strategies for enabling a thriving life by incorporating "design thinking" habits that promote fulfillment and meaning by emulating the examples of the engineers of today's most popular technologies.

The executive director of the Design Program at Stanford and the co-founder of Electronic Arts outline strategies for enabling a thriving life by incorporating "design thinking" habits that promote fulfillment and meaning by emulating the examples of the engineers of today's most popular technologies.

Includes bibliographical references (pages 235-238).

Cast, Carter
The Right—and Wrong—Stuff: How Brilliant Careers Are Made and Unmade. Carter Cast. PublicAffairs 2017. 288 p.
ISBN 9781610397094
Grades: Adult   650.1
1. Success in business 2. Career development 3. Executive ability 4. Skills 5. Business and economics — Business advice 6. Business and economics — Popular psychology
LC 2017042061

Drawing on his own experiences, as well as meticulous research, the author, a former rising star at a Fortune 100 company whose career was derailed by his attitude, shows readers how, through five defining archetypes, they can recognize blind spots that can lead to downfall and provides new ways for readers to take charge of their careers.

"This relatable career manual should inspire plenty of white-collar professionals to work on serious self-accounting, take responsibility for their own mistakes, and form support teams of friends, managers, and mentors." —*Publishers Weekly*

Includes bibliographical references and index.

Dufu, Tiffany
Drop the Ball: Achieving More by Doing Less. Tiffany Dufu, foreword by Gloria Steinem. Flatiron Books 2017. 288 p.
ISBN 9781250071736
Grades: Adult   650.1
1. Dufu, Tiffany 2. Women executives 3. Businesspeople 4. Leadership 5. Autobiographies and memoirs 6. Business and economics — Women and the workplace 7. Life stories — Business — Business leaders
LC 2016037631

An inspiring memoir by a leading figure in the women's leadership movement counsels women on how to cultivate the essential skills of reevaluating expectations, setting realistic goals and meaningfully engaging with others in order to thrive in personal and professional arenas.

Includes index.

Economy, Peter
Wait, I'm Working with Who?!?: The Essential Guide to Dealing with Difficult Coworkers, Annoying Managers, and Other Toxic Personalities. Peter Economy. Career Press 2021. 206 p.
ISBN 9781632651853
Grades: Adult   650.1
1. Conflict resolution 2. Interpersonal relations 3. Interpersonal conflict 4. Industrial psychology 5. Business and economics — Business advice 6. Self-Help — Career and financial success

LC 2020051387

Who hasn't had to deal with a jerk at work? Whether it's a toxic team member who loves nothing better than to suck the life and excitement out of her colleagues or a bad boss who causes his employees to constantly dream of telling him to "Take this job and shove it!" or the difficult co-worker who isn't happy unless the office is filled with mayhem and drama, we've all had to deal with people on the job we would rather not. Based on proven approaches and the latest research and advice of workplace experts, this book will provide readers with detailed and unambiguous advice on how to deal with and neutralize the negative people in their work lives.

"This readable, practical book will have wide appeal. Anyone who has held a job, is entering the workforce, or has challenges with friends or family members will find this book informative, helpful, and easy to read and use." —*Booklist*

Includes bibliographical references.

Eikenberry, Kevin
The Long-Distance Teammate: Stay Engaged and Connected While Working Anywhere. Kevin Eikenberry and Wayne Turmel. Berrett-Koehler Publishers, Inc. 2021. VIII, 197 pages : Illustration
ISBN 9781523090303
Grades: Adult   650.1
1. Telecommuting 2. Career development 3. Self-Help — Career and financial success
LC 2020037957

What does it mean to "go to work" when you don't actually leave the house? This is the ultimate guide for remote workers who want to stay engaged as team members, maintain robust work relationships, and keep an eye on their long-term career goals.

"Full of concrete, real-world examples, this guide is written with both understanding and encouragement." —*Publishers Weekly*

Includes bibliographical references (pages 181-182) and index.

Fineman, Meredith
Brag Better: Master the Art of Fearless Self-Promotion. Meredith Fineman. Portfolio 2020. 288 p.
ISBN 9780593086810
Grades: Adult   650.1
1. Business communication 2. Success in business 3. Interpersonal communication 4. Communication 5. Business 6. Trademarks 7. Marketing 8. Business and economics — Business advice
LC 2020004061

An entrepreneur, writer and podcast host advocates for the power of talking about your accomplishments and offers tools and tips for bragging, including eliminating words that undermine your work and focusing on your personal brand and voice.

"Though the focus is on self-promotion, Fineman's upbeat ideas have crossover potential for finding confidence in other aspects of life. Women entrepreneurs will love these shrewd promotion strategies." —*Publishers Weekly*

Friedman, Ron
Decoding Greatness: How the Best in the World Reverse Engineer Success. Ron Friedman. Simon & Schuster 2021. 288 p.
ISBN 9781982135799
Grades: Adult   650.1
1. Knowledge 2. Ideas (Philosophy) 3. Success (Concept) 4. Creativity 5. Performance 6. Society and culture — Psychology and human behavior 7. Business and economics — Popular psychology

Drawing on the examples of top performers such as Agatha Christie, Andy Warhol, Barack Obama and Serena Williams, an award-winning psychologist discusses ways to examine their examples and develop the knowledge to develop new ideas.

"A practical and sophisticated handbook, useful for readers who wish to learn from the successful experiences of others and effectively apply the lessons to their own work and careers." —*Library Journal*

PUBLIC LIBRARY CORE COLLECTION: NONFICTION
Twentieth Edition

Green, Alison

Ask a Manager: How to Navigate Clueless Colleagues, Lunch-Stealing Bosses, and the Rest of Your Life at Work. Alison Green. Ballantine Books 2018. 287 p.

ISBN 9780399181818

Grades: Adult   650.1

1. Industrial psychology 2. Work 3. Work environment 4. Conflict resolution 5. Interpersonal relations 6. Business and economics — Careers 7. Business and economics — Business advice 8. Business and economics — Popular psychology

LC 2018288338

From the creator of the popular website Ask a Manager and New York magazine's work-advice columnist comes a witty, practical guide to navigating 200 difficult professional conversations—featuring all-new advice! There's a reason Alison Green has been called "the Dear Abby of the work world." Ten years as a workplace-advice columnist have taught her that people avoid awkward conversations in the office because they simply don't know what to say. Thankfully, Green does—and in this incredibly helpful book, she tackles the tough discussions you may need to have during your career.

Hansen, Morten T.

Great at Work: How Top Performers Do Less, Work Better, and Achieve More. Morten T. Hansen. Simon & Schuster 2018. VIII, 310 pages

ISBN 9781476765624

Grades: Adult   650.1

1. Ability 2. Motivation 3. Performance 4. Success in business 5. Self-management 6. Business and economics — Business advice — Leadership and management 7. Business and economics — General

LC Bl2017045786

Shares authoritative, practical advice on how to bolster individual performance, drawing on a study involving thousands of managers and employees to outline seven work practices for improving focus, scheduling, and organization.

The best-selling author of Great by Choice shares authoritative, practical advice on how to bolster individual performance, drawing on an in-depth study involving thousands of managers and employees to outline seven work practices for improving focus, scheduling and organization in accordance with the examples of inspiring high-achievers.

"Based on this work, Hansen identifies the seven key factors that make people work smarter, not harder: do less, then obsess; redesign your work; don't just learn, loop; have passion and purpose; be a forceful champion; fight over ideas but unite on decisions; and use disciplined collaboration." —*Booklist*

Includes bibliographical references (pages 263-289) and index.

Henry, Alan

Seen, Heard, and Paid: The New Work Rules for the Marginalized. Alan Henry. Rodale Press 2022. 288 p.

ISBN 9780593233351

Grades: Adult   650.1

1. Marginalized people 2. Discrimination in employment 3. Multiculturalism 4. Work 5. Success (Concept) 6. Business and economics — Business advice

For over twenty years, Alan Henry has written about using technology and productivity techniques to work and live better for publications such as Lifehacker, the New York Times, and Wired. But he found that as a Black man he didn't have access to some of the more powerful ways to hack your job—like only checking email once a day or blocking out time on your calendar to do deep work. In fact, he found that even when he landed a prestigious title at the Times, there were moments when he was still overlooked and excluded from the most interesting and career-boosting work. This led him to first explore these struggles in a Times piece titled "Productivity Without Privilege." Now he goes even deeper, interviewing experts across multiple fields to come up with powerful tools to overcome the forces of marginalization. In Seen, Heard, and Paid, Henry shares the new work rules that may finally allow people of color, women, and LGBTQ+ folks to have the same access to career advancement and rewarding work as those with more privilege.

"Readers who feel unseen at work, no matter their background or situation, will find powerful takeaways. This book is also great for teens and college students." —*Booklist*

Hill, Napoleon

Think and Grow Rich: The Landmark Bestseller—now Revised and Updated for the 21st Century. Napoleon Hill; rev. and expanded by Arthur R. Pell. Jeremy P. Tarcher/Penguin 2005. xv, 302 p.

ISBN 9781585424337

Grades: Adult   650.1

1. Carnegie, Andrew, 1835-1919 2. Success in business 3. Self-Help — Personal growth 4. Business and economics — General

LC 2005044133

An updated edition of the best-selling guide features anecdotes about such modern figures as Bill Gates, Dave Thomas, and Sir John Templeton, explaining how their examples can enable modern readers to pursue wealth and overcome personal stumbling blocks.

Orginally published: Meriden, Conn. : Ralston Society, 1937; Includes index.

Kramer, Andrea S.

Breaking Through Bias: Communication Techniques for Women to Succeed at Work. Andrea S. Kramer, Alton B. Harris. Bibliomotion, Inc. 2016. xxx, 226 p.

ISBN 9781629561042

Grades: Adult   650.1

1. Communication in management 2. Communication in organizations 3. Women 4. Sex discrimination 5. Stereotypes 6. Vocational guidance 7. Interpersonal communication 8. Business and economics — Women and the workplace

LC 2015040059

Argues that stereotypes about men, women, work, leadership, and family are to blame for the gender gap in employment and includes communication techniques that women can use to avoid the discriminatory consequences of these stereotypes.

Includes bibliographical references and index.

Mattel, Trixie

Working Girls: Trixie and Katya's Guide to Professional Womanhood. Trixie Mattel, Katya. Plume 2022. 240 p.

ISBN 9780593186114

Grades: Adult   650.1

1. Women office workers 2. Personal conduct 3. Career development 4. Advice 5. Female impersonators 6. Drag queens 7. Television personalities 8. Humorous writing 9. Humor writing — Social humor 10. Society and culture — LGBTQIA+ 11. Arts and Entertainment — Movies and Television

The immensely popular drag queens return with probably very misguided advice for women in the workplace, in this satirical guide to professional womanhood. In Working Girls, Trixie and Katya dole out both savvy and satirical advice for every stage of working life, from choosing a career path to sailing into a blissful retirement, in step-by-step guides, quizzes, the world's most bizarre aptitude test, and more. Searching for the perfect interview outfit? Agonizing over how to get that raise? Suspicious that your colleague doesn't really hope their email "finds you well"? Trixie and Katya have got you covered.

"For librarians serious about building up both their modern humor sections and their selections of books written by drag queens, this sequel is a must." —*Library Journal*

Mazzucato, Mariana

★ *The Big Con: How the Consulting Industry Weakens Our Businesses, Infantilizes Our Governments, and Warps Our Economies.* Mariana Mazzucato and Rosie Collington. Penguin Press 2023. 368 p.

ISBN 9780593492673

Grades: Adult   650.1

ESSENTIAL AND RECOMMENDED TITLES
650.1 Personal success in business

1. Business consultants 2. Consultants 3. Consulting firms 4. Business 5. Business and economics — Industries 6. Business and economics — Economics — History

Pulling back the curtain on the consulting industry, which weakens our businesses, infantilizes our governments and warps our economies, this important book argues brilliantly for building a new system in which public and private sectors work innovatively for the common good.

"Doggedly researched and elegantly written, this is a fascinating entry point into a critical yet underreported issue." —*Publishers Weekly*

Medini, Shari
***Parenting** While Working from Home: A Monthly Guide to Help Parents Balance Their Careers, Connect with Their Kids, Establish Their Inner Strength.* Shari Medini and Karissa Tunis, owners of AdoreThemParenting.Com. Skyhorse Publishing 2021. xiv, 185 pages
ISBN 9781510764828
Grades: Adult   650.1
1. Family and work 2. Work-life balance 3. Parenting 4. Telecommuting 5. Family and Relationships — Parenting 6. Self-Help — Relationships 7. Self-Help — Career and financial success
LC Bl2021001024

Parenting experts Karissa Tunis and Shari Medini share actionable tips, heartfelt insight, and planning strategies to help you enjoy your own parenting journey while working from home. Building on the authors' own experiences and the most common challenges they hear parents voicing today, Parenting While Working from Home encourages parents to make intentional changes that will result in happier families and thriving careers.

"Whether working from home while parenting as a temporary solution or a more long-term plan, readers will get advice for finding a rhythm, maintaining positivity, and balancing everything, while still having fun." —*Booklist*

Mulcahy, Diane
*The **Gig** Economy: The Complete Guide to Getting Better Work, Taking More Time Off, and Financing the Life You Want.* Diane Mulcahy. AMACOM, American Management Assoication 2016. 227 pages
ISBN 9780814437339
Grades: Adult   650.1
1. Career development 2. Part-time employment 3. Quality of work life 4. Flex time 5. Business and economics — General 6. Business and economics — Business leaders and entrepreneurs 7. Business and economics — Careers
LC 2016023117

Presents advice for managing employment in an economy characterized by contract work and freelance assignments, describing strategies for creating multiple sources of income, developing new skills, financing time off, and retaining a personal safety net.

"The book is filled with helpful step-by-step instructions, sound examples of good and bad approaches, and financial reality checks." —*Booklist*

Includes bibliographical references.

Norton, Michael
★ *The **Ritual** Effect: From Habit to Ritual, Harness the Surprising Power of Everyday Actions.* Michael Norton. Scribner 2024. x, 272 pages
ISBN 9781982153021
Grades: Adult   650.1
1. Time management 2. Change (Psychology) 3. Self-actualization 4. Behavior modification 5. Habit 6. Human behavior 7. Self-Help — Personal growth
LC Bl2024007130

Drawing on a decade of original research, a renowned social psychologist shows how we can shift from a 'habitual' mindset to a 'ritual' mindset, reminding us of the intention-filled acts that drive human behavior and create surprising satisfaction and enjoyment.

"A good-humored, gentle exhortation to transform the ordinary into the extraordinary and add a little magic to our lives." —*Kirkus*

Includes bibliographical references (pages 223-261) and index.

Pollak, Lindsey
***Recalculating:** Navigate Your Career Through the Changing World of Work.* Lindsey Pollak. Harper Business, an imprint of HarperCollinsPublishers 2021. 304 pages
ISBN 9780063067707
Grades: Adult   650.1
1. Career development 2. Job hunting 3. Employment interviewing 4. Career changes 5. Introverts 6. Success in business 7. Self-help — Career and financial success
LC 2020044792

A leading workplace expert provides an inspirational, practical, and forward-looking career playbook for recent grads, career changers, and transitioning professionals looking to thrive in today's rapidly evolving workplace.

Includes bibliographical references (pages 287-293) and index.

Porath, Christine Lynne
***Mastering** Civility: A Manifesto for the Workplace.* Christine Porath. Grand Central Publishing 2016. VIII, 230 pages
ISBN 9781455568987
Grades: Adult   650.1
1. Employee morale 2. Interpersonal relations 3. Organizational behavior 4. Work environment 5. Business and economics — Business advice
LC 2016028809

A full-length guide based on the author's New York Times article, "No Time to Be Nice at Work," demonstrates how to enhance workplace effectiveness by mastering the skills of professional civility.

"This book will arm readers with the tools they need to move from defeat to empowerment and prompt change in the workplace." —*Publishers Weekly*

Includes bibliographical references and index.

Steib, Mike
*The **Career** Manifesto: Discover Your Calling and Create an Extraordinary Life.* Mike Steib. TarcherPerigee 2018. xi, 274 p. : Illustration
ISBN 9780143129349
Grades: Adult   650.1
1. Career development 2. Vocational guidance 3. Business and economics — General 4. Self-Help — Personal growth
LC OC2018170784

An award-winning business leader uses his own experiences in his career as well as those of other successful business leaders to offer advice and exercises aimed at helping young professionals, entrepreneurs and creative people to bring purpose to their work and lives.

"His book lays out a sound and logical approach, with easily applicable and customizable advice aplenty." —*Publishers Weekly*

Includes bibliographical references and index.

Sutton, Robert I.
*The **Asshole** Survival Guide: How to Deal with People Who Treat You Like Dirt.* Robert I. Sutton. Houghton Mifflin Harcourt 2017. 224 p.
ISBN 9781328695918
Grades: Adult   650.1
1. Organizational behavior 2. Interpersonal conflict 3. Bullying in the workplace 4. Emotional abuse 5. Interpersonal relations 6. Business and economics — Business advice
LC 2017012053

The author of The No Asshole Rule provides field-tested, evidence-based and sometimes surprising strategies for dealing with toxic people|avoiding them, outwitting them, disarming them, sending them packing and developing protective psychological armor|as well as advice for not becoming toxic yourself.

Includes bibliographical references and index.

Vanek Smith, Stacey
***Machiavelli** for Women: Defend Your Worth, Grow Your Ambition, and Win the Workplace.* Stacey Vanek Smith. Gallery Books 2021. IX, 273 p.
ISBN 9781982121754

PUBLIC LIBRARY CORE COLLECTION: NONFICTION
Twentieth Edition

Grades: Adult   650.1

1. Machiavelli, Niccolo, 1469-1527 2. Women 3. Women professional employees 4. Women's rights 5. Sexism in employment 6. Philosophers 7. Philosophy 8. Power 9. Empowerment 10. Advice 11. Assertiveness 12. Negotiation 13. Work 14. Business and economics — Women and the workplace 15. Society and culture — Gender — Women 16. Society and culture — Philosophy

LC 2020049503

Women have been making strides towards equality for decades, or so we're often told. They've been increasingly entering male-dominated areas of the workforce and consistently surpassing their male peers in grades, university attendance, and degrees. They've recently stormed the political arena with a vengeance. But despite all of this, the payoff is—quite literally—not there: the gender pay gap has held steady at about 20% since 2000. And the number of female CEOs for Fortune 500 companies has actually been declining. So why, in the age of #MeToo and #TimesUp, is the glass ceiling still holding strong? And how can we shatter it for once and for all? Stacy Vanek Smith's advice: ask Machiavelli. Using the Prince as a guide and with charm and wit, Smith applies Renaissance politics to the 21st century, and demonstrates how women can take and maintain power in careers where they have long been cast as second-best.

"Though geared toward women, this playbook from NPR host Smith could work for any sex. . . . Guidance to relate to and follow." —*Booklist*

Includes bibliographical references and index.

Varol, Ozan O.

Think Like a Rocket Scientist: Simple Strategies You Can Use to Make Giant Leaps in Work and Life. Ozan Varol. PublicAffairs 2020. VII, 353 p.

ISBN 9781541762596

Grades: Adult   650.1

1. Creativity 2. Creativity in business 3. Business and economics — Business advice — Leadership and management

LC 2019041750

We're experiencing a second age of spaceflight, and the renaissance of rocket science is captivating the world. Movies and television shows set in this sphere consistently top the charts, and millions tune in to watch SpaceX launches. Although we glamorize rocket science, we assume that it's beyond comprehension by mere mortals who don't have a special kind of genius baked into their DNA (hence the common saying, "It's not rocket science"). Yet while the complex math and scientific details of building rockets may be out of our reach, the principles that guide the discipline don't have to be. In this mind-expanding book, Ozan Varol, an actual rocket scientist, shows how the strategies that built the Apollo 11 can help you achieve your own moon shot. Think Like a Rocket Scientist teaches you how to attack previously unsolved problems, how to overcome everyday obstacles to grand ambitions, and much more. A deeply knowledgeable scholar with a breezy, contrarian voice, Varol inspires us not only to dream big—but to achieve those dreams too.

Includes bibliographical references (pages 289-336) and index.

Vaynerchuk, Gary

Crushing It!: How Great Entrepreneurs Build Business and Influence— and How You Can, Too. Gary Vaynerchuk. HarperBusiness 2018. 272 p.

ISBN 9780062674678

Grades: Adult   650.1

1. Entrepreneurship 2. Internet marketing 3. Social media 4. Success in business 5. Trademarks 6. Marketing 7. Business and economics — Business leaders and entrepreneurs 8. Self-Help — Personal growth — Motivation

LC Bl2017045699

Shares new lessons and inspiration drawn from dozens of entrepreneurs who rejected traditional corporate careers in favor of pursuing their dreams.

Includes bibliographical references (pages 267-272).

Wasserman, Claire

Ladies Get Paid: The Ultimate Guide to Breaking Barriers, Owning Your Worth, and Taking Command of Your Career. Claire Wasserman. Gallery Books 2021. xx, 300 pages : Illustration

ISBN 9781982126902

Grades: Adult   650.1

1. Career development 2. Sex discrimination in employment 3. Equal pay for equal work 4. Success in business 5. Vocational guidance 6. Business and economics — Women and the workplace 7. Self-Help — Career and financial success

LC 2020029832

If you're looking to navigate a promotion or break the glass ceiling, Ladies Get Paid is your essential toolkit for achieving success. Filled with straightforward advice and inspiring stories, Ladies Get Paid encourages self-advocacy and activism as a way to advance your career and make more money. Covering topics as crucial and varied as how to find the perfect mentor, how to negotiate a raise, and how to become a leader, Ladies Get Paid is a reminder that you are valuable-both as an individual woman and as part of the female community.

"Personal stories like that of Beth Comstock, former vice chair of GE, plus a few mind-bending statistics . . . make this a 'Gottaread' playbook." —*Booklist*

Includes bibliographical references (pages 273-289) and index.

Webb, Caroline

How to Have a Good Day: Harness the Power of Behavioral Science to Transform Your Working Life. Caroline Webb. Crown Business 2016. 360 pages : Illustration

ISBN 9780553419634

Grades: Adult   650.1

1. Job satisfaction 2. Neuropsychology 3. Performance 4. Industrial psychology 5. Business and economics — General 6. Business and economics — Careers 7. Science writing — Medicine and health — Psychology

LC 2015026815

An economist and executive coach offers seven different practices to use to ensure you have a good day at work, including setting the right priorities, making productive use of time, having effective conversations, doing your very best work and sustaining energy. 7 charts.

Includes bibliographical references (pages 332-354) and index.

Williams, Joan

What Works for Women at Work: Four Patterns Working Women Need to Know. Joan C. Williams and Rachel Dempsey; foreword by Anne-Marie Slaughter. New York University Press 2018. xxxvii, 365 pages

ISBN 9781479814312

Grades: Adult   650.1

1. Office politics 2. Women 3. Gender role in the work environment 4. Glass ceiling 5. Human behavior 6. Stereotypes 7. Work 8. Business and economics — Women and the workplace 9. Business and economics — Popular psychology

LC Bl2018001611

Provides a guide for mastering office politics as a woman, describing four patterns that affect working women and presenting strategies for overcoming them.

"[F]illed with street-smart advice and plain old savvy about the way life works in corporate America." —*Booklist*

Includes bibliographical references (pages 307-347) and index.

Young, Scott H.

Get Better at Anything: 12 Maxims for Mastery. Scott H. Young. Harper Business, an imprint of HarperCollinsPublishers 2024. VIII, 291 pages : Illustration

ISBN 9780063256675

Grades: Adult   650.1

1. Career development 2. Ability 3. Success (Concept) 4. Learning 5. Business and economics — Popular psychology 6. Self-Help — Career and financial success

LC 2023049684

The author of the Wall Street Journal best-seller Ultralearning presents three key factors and twelve maxims that can help overcome the difficulties of learning new skills and help readers make advancement possible.

"This competent manual from Young presents advice on how readers can better pick up new skills…The result is a worthy complement to Adam Grant's Hidden Potential." —*Publishers Weekly*

Includes bibliographical references (pages 241-275) and index.

ESSENTIAL AND RECOMMENDED TITLES
650.14 Success in obtaining jobs and promotions

650.14 Success in obtaining jobs and promotions

Finkle, Jane
The Introvert's Complete Career Guide: From Landing a Job, to Surviving, Thriving, and Moving on Up. Jane Finkle. Career Press 2019. 232 pages
ISBN 9781632651310
Grades: Adult   650.14
1. Career development 2. Job hunting 3. Employment interviewing 4. Career changes 5. Introverts 6. Success in business 7. Self-help — Career and financial success
LC 2018038604

This handbook demonstrates how to use your introverted qualities to their best advantage, then add a few extroverted skills to round out a forceful combination for ultimate career success. Includes keys to navigating each stage of professional development—from self-assessment and job search to survival in a new position and career advancement.

"The book is a good tool for working introverts, and the tips and advice found here could also apply to young adults or older adults returning to the workforce." —*Booklist*

Includes bibliographical references.

Germer, Fawn
Coming Back: How to Win the Job You Want When You've Lost the Job You Need. Fawn Germer. St. Martin's Press 2021. 291 pages : Illustration
ISBN 9781250271655
Grades: Adult   650.14
1. Career development 2. Career changes 3. Job hunting 4. Baby boom generation 5. Generation X 6. Self-Help — Career and financial success
LC 2020040181

One of the nation's most popular leadership experts and global motivational speakers offers clear and candid advice for renewing or resuming your career.

"Aimed mainly at Gen Xers and baby boomers, Germer's book takes a markedly different approach than that of the average job-hunting guide. Her advice is intended to apply to a wide swath of those forty-, fifty-, and sixtysomethings who are unemployed, underemployed, or frustrated by their current job." —*Booklist*

Includes index.

Keller, Julia
Quitting: A Life Strategy : The Myth of Perseverance—and How the New Science of Giving up Can Set You Free. Julia Keller, PhD.. 2023. xxxi, 222 pages
ISBN 9781538722343
Grades: Adult   650.14
1. Persistence 2. Career changes 3. Self-preservation 4. Self-reliance 5. Self-Help — Personal growth — Happiness 6. Self-Help — Personal growth — Motivation
LC 2022037036

In Quitting: A Life Strategy, Pulitzer prize-winning journalist Julia Keller dives into "the neuroscience of nope," and the cultural messaging that drives our reluctance to throw in the towel, to dismantle the myth of perseverance once and for all. Combining reportage from the front lines of scientific research, pop culture, with conversations with people who have made profound change in their own lives and "Permission Slips" to guide readers in their own embrace of quitting, Keller gives readers the rationale and confidence they need to pull the plug and shape their own lives without fear-at work, at home, in our relationships, and beyond.

"Keller includes exercises, called permission slips, to help readers with their own strategic quitting, making this book practical and enlightening." —*Booklist*

Includes bibliographical references (pages 207-222).

Louis, Matthew J.
Mission Transition: Navigating the Opportunities and Obstacles to Your Post-military Career. Matthew J. Louis. HarperCollins Leadership 2019. xvii, 318 pages : Illustration
ISBN 9781400214754
Grades: Adult   650.14
1. Veterans 2. Career changes 3. Job hunting 4. Work 5. Self-Help — Career and financial success
LC 2019007471

A practical career-change guide to help transitioning veterans avoid false starts and make optimal career choices following active duty."

Includes bibliographical references (pages 293-310) and index.

651.56 Cooking for special situations, reasons, ages

Moskowitz, Isa Chandra
The Superfun Times Vegan Holiday Cookbook: Entertaining for Absolutely Every Occasion. Isa Chandra Moskowitz; photographs by Vanessa Rees and Joshua Foo. Little, Brown and Company 2016. 439 pages : Color illustrations
ISBN 9780316221894
Grades: Adult   651.56
1. Holiday cooking 2. Recipes 3. Vegan cooking 4. Cookbooks 5. Food writing — Cooking and cookbooks — Entertaining 6. Food writing — Cooking and cookbooks — Vegetarian and vegan
LC 2016941207

A best-selling vegan cookbook author presents her first book on entertaining, in a guide the includes menus and tips for every Holiday and every big celebration in between, as well as recipes for vegan versions of such dishes as Cinnamon Apple Crepes, Cheeseburger Pizza, Churro Biscotti, Biscuits and Gravy and many more.

Includes index.

Perlmutter, David
The Grain Brain Cookbook: More Than 150 Life-Changing, Gluten-Free Recipes to Transform Your Health. David Perlmutter, MD.. Little Brown and Company 2014. 337 pages : Color; Illustration
ISBN 9780316334259
Grades: Adult   651.56
1. Brain 2. Carbohydrates 3. Gluten-free diet 4. Recipes 5. Cookbooks 6. Food writing — Cooking and cookbooks — Cooking for health
LC 2014940575

Provides more than 150 delicious, gluten-free recipes, including Eggs Benedict with Zucchini Pancakes and Cauliflower "Couscous," to help maintain a healthy body and mind and reduce the risk of chronic diseases, in a follow-up to the best-selling Grain Brain.

"Recommended only for libraries where Perlmutter's books are in high demand." —*Library Journal*

Includes index.

Sarno, Chad
The Wicked Healthy Cookbook: Free. From. Animals. Chad Sarno, Derek Sarno, and David Joachim; foreword by Woody Harrelson; photographs by Eva Kosmas Flores. Grand Central Life & Style 2018. xii, 306 pages : Color; Illustration
ISBN 9781455570287
Grades: Adult   651.56
1. Cooking (Natural foods) 2. Cooking (Vegetables) 3. Recipes 4. Vegan cooking 5. Cookbooks 6. Food writing — Cooking and cookbooks — Courses 7. Food writing — Cooking and cookbooks — Ingredients 8. Food writing — Cooking and cookbooks — Vegetarian and vegan
LC 2018288838

Two former Whole Foods Market culinary experts combine innovative cooking techniques with attitude in a collection of vegan recipes that includes options for everyday meals and special occasions as well as tips for gluten-free cooking.

[This book] takes ... plant-based cooking to a whole new level. The chefs have pioneered innovative cooking techniques such as pressing and searing mushrooms until they reach a rich and delicious meat-like consistency. Inside, you'll find informative sidebars and must-have tips on everything from oil-free and gluten-free cooking (if you're into that) to organizing an efficient kitchen.

PUBLIC LIBRARY CORE COLLECTION: NONFICTION
Twentieth Edition

"This varied assortment will appeal mostly to herbivores wishing to comfort their inner carnivore." —*Publishers Weekly*

Includes index.

657 Accounting

Siegel, Joel G.
Accounting Handbook. Jae K, Ph.D. Shim, Joel G, Ph.D. Siegel, Nick Dauber, Anique A, Ph.D. Qureshi. Barrons Educational Series 2015. 1062 pages
ISBN 9780764166570
Grades: Adult 657
1. Accounting 2. Business and economics — General 3. Reference — Business 4. Reference books — Handbooks, manuals, etc.
LC 2014009657

Presents an overview of financial accounting, with a focus on financial statements, reporting requirements, and taxation, and features a dictionary of accounting terms.

Revised edition of: Accounting handbook / Joel G. Siegel, Jae K. Shim. 5th ed; Includes bibliographical references and index.

658 General management

Economy, Peter
Wait, I'm the Boss?!?: The Essential Guide for New Managers to Succeed from Day One. 2020. 190 p.
ISBN 9781632651648
Grades: Adult 658
1. Management 2. Leadership 3. Personnel management 4. Organizational change 5. Teams in the workplace 6. Self-Help — Career and Financial Success 7. Business and Economics — Business Advice — Leadership and Management

This guide explores the fundamental skills that every manager needs to understand, practice, and master, such as building teams and teamwork, setting goals, creating a fun and effective organizational culture, rewarding and motivating employees, leading organizational change, learning how to hire great employees, correcting poor performance, coaching and mentoring, delegation, communicating effectively, and dealing with layoffs and terminations.

"This book is for those who aspire to be managers, who are new managers, or who want a refresher. The conversational tone makes the book easy to read, and it is great as a reference guide to keep on the shelf." —*Booklist*

Peter, Laurence J.
The Peter Principle: Why Things Always Go Wrong. Laurence J. Peter and Raymond Hull. Collins Business 2009. 192 p.
ISBN 9780061699061
Grades: Adult 658
1. Executive ability 2. Work 3. Management 4. Humor writing — General 5. Business and economics — Business advice — Leadership and management
LC 2008044122

A re-release of the popular treatise on the rise and fall of civilizations as reflected by their professional organizations is based on a premise that every employee in a hierarchy tends to rise to his or her level of incompetence, an unfortunate fact that is shaping education, government, and business.

Webb, Maynard
Dear Founder: Letters of Advice for Anyone Who Leads, Manages, or Wants to Start a Business. Maynard Webb, with Carlye Adler. St. Martin's Press 2018. 272 p.
ISBN 9781250195647
Grades: Adult 658
1. New businesses 2. Leadership in business 3. Corporate culture 4. Entrepreneurs 5. Entrepreneurship 6. Supervisors 7. Organizational change 8. Letter writing 9. Business and economics — Business advice — Leadership and management 10. Business and economics — Popular psychology
LC 2018013472

Offers practical, profit-minded advice to entrepreneurs on subjects ranging from hiring and culture-building to raising money and pursuing goals.

"This recommended book provides honest guidance about the work that goes into a new company, delivered in digestible chunks for the entrepreneur on the go." —*Library Journal*

Includes index.

Wooldridge, Adrian
Masters of Management: How the Business Gurus and Their Ideas Have Changed the World—for Better and for Worse. Adrian Wooldridge; with a foreword by John Micklethwait. HarperBusiness 2011. xviii, 446 p.
ISBN 9780061771132
Grades: Adult 658
1. Industrial management 2. Corporate accountability 3. Reengineering (Management) 4. Business and economics — Business advice — Leadership and management
LC 2011015690

A complete update of the 1996 bestselling the witch doctors, a penetrating and engaging history of management theory that sorts the wisdom from the dross, and the wise men from the charlatans.

Rev. ed. of: Witch doctors / John Micklethwait. 1996.

658.1 Organization and financial management

Kawasaki, Guy
The Art of the Start 2.0: The Time-Tested, Battle-Hardened Guide for Anyone Starting Anything. Guy Kawasaki. Portfolio/Penguin 2015. x, 326 pages : Illustration
ISBN 9781591847847
Grades: Adult 658.1
1. Entrepreneurship 2. New businesses 3. Business and economics — Business leaders and entrepreneurs 4. Business and economics — General
LC 2015295069

Newly revised and updated, a 10th-anniversary edition of an iconic, best-selling guide for start-ups provides expert advice on a wealth of topics—including writing a business plan, recruiting, raising capital and branding.

Provides a guide to starting a business and becoming an entrepreneur in the twenty-first century, describing how to effectively use social media and crowdfunding and take advantage of easier, cheaper, more democratic establishment basics.

"An excellent guide packed with valuable information for students, would-be entrepreneurs, and practicing entrepreneurs." —*Library Journal*

Includes bibliographical references and index.

Stewart, James B.
Unscripted: The Epic Battle for a Media Empire and the Redstone Family Legacy. James B. Stewart, Rachel Abrams. Penguin Press 2023. xvi, 398 p.
ISBN 9781984879424
Grades: Adult 658.1
1. Redstone, Sumner 2. Redstone, Shari 3. Moonves, Leslie 4. Corporations 5. Rich families 6. Mass media executives 7. Fathers and daughters 8. Inheritance and succession 9. Scandals 10. Conflict in families 11. Power 12. Business and economics — Corruption and scandal 13. Life stories — Relationships — Family 14. Life stories — Business — Business leaders
LC 2022030865

In 2016, the fate of Paramount Global—the multibillion-dollar entertainment empire that includes Paramount, CBS, MTV, Nickelodeon, Showtime, and Simon & Schuster—hung precariously in the balance. Unscripted is an explosive and unvarnished look at the usually secret inner workings of two public companies, their boards of directors, and a wealthy, dysfunctional family in the throes of seismic changes, from journalists James B. Stewart and Rachel Abrams.

"An ugly yarn full of money-grubbing villains, irresistible in all its inglorious nastiness." —*Kirkus*

Includes bibliographical references and index.

ESSENTIAL AND RECOMMENDED TITLES
658.15 Financial management

658.15 Financial management

McKeever, Mike P
How to Write a Business Plan. Mike P. McKeever. Nolo 2017. 331 pages
ISBN 9781413323191
Grades: Adult   658.15
1. Small business 2. Finance 3. Planning 4. New businesses 5. Business and economics — General 6. Law — Corporate, business, and finance
LC 2016026296

Explains how to create the loan package necessary to finance a business and make it work, covering such topics as assessing the potential of a business idea, estimating operating expenses, and finding sources of financing.

Explains how to create the loan package necessary to finance a business and make it work, including how to assess the potential of a business idea, estimate operating expenses, find sources of financing, present the plan to lenders and investors and more, in a book that includes access to downloadable forms. Charts. Tables. Graphs. Forms.

Includes bibliographical references and index.

Rice, Condoleezza
Political Risk: How Businesses and Organizations Can Anticipate Global Insecurity. Condoleezza Rice and Amy Zegart. Twelve 2018. 336 p.
ISBN 9781455542352
Grades: Adult   658.15
1. World politics 2. Risk analysis 3. Business and politics 4. Management 5. Risk management 6. Success in business 7. Politics and global affairs — World politics 8. Business and economics — Business advice
LC 2017054476

Examines the topic of political risk, the authors look at the essential lessons, corrective measures and counterintuitive insights for executives, entrepreneurs and investors to navigate an uncertain, volatile world.

Includes bibliographical references and index.

658.3 Personnel management (Human resource management)

Coggan, Philip
Surviving the Daily Grind: Bartleby's Guide to Work. Philip Coggan. Economists Books 2024. 208 p.
ISBN 9781639364350
Grades: Adult   658.3
1. Employee morale 2. Employee motivation 3. Employees 4. Work 5. Work-life balance 6. Work ethic 7. Quality of work life 8. Psychological growth 9. Career development 10. Success in business 11. Self-Help — Personal growth 12. Business and economics — Popular psychology

We spend a lot of our time at work and would be depressed with nothing to do. But when it gets to Monday, many of us are already longing for the weekend and the prospect of escape. How did work become so tedious and stressful? And is there anything we can do to make it better? Based on his popular Economist Bartleby column, Philip Coggan rewrites the rules of work to help us survive the daily grind. Ranging widely, he encourages us to cut through mindless jargon, pointless bureaucracy and endless meetings to find a new, more creative—and less frustrating—way to get by and get things done at work.

"Coggan…provides an irreverent accounting of how overlong meetings, noisy office plans, incompetent managers, and other exasperating eccentricities of the modern workplace burden employees. The result is a pleasantly peppy lampooning of the plight of the modern professional." —*Publishers Weekly*

Cox, Gena
Leading Inclusion: Drive Change Your Employees Can See and Feel. Gena Cox, PhD.. Page Two 2022. 296 p.
ISBN 9781774581797
Grades: Adult   658.3
1. Work 2. Management 3. Corporate culture 4. Toleration 5. Multiculturalism 6. Marginalized people 7. Racism in employment 8. Sexism in employment 9. Organizational change 10. Business and economics — Business advice —

Leadership and management 11. Society and culture — Gender 12. Society and culture — Race

Drawing on her own experience in corporate America, an organizational psychologist and executive coach presents this revolutionary new book in which she shows you how to lead an inclusive organization, from the top down, and to seek solutions to the racially based discontent that pervades many employees' experiences.

"An outstanding source of information and advice for leaders who want to build inclusive work environments." —*Library Journal*

Includes bibliographical references and index.

Fuller, Pamela
★ *The Leader's Guide to Unconscious Bias: How to Reframe Bias, Cultivate Connection, and Create High-Performance Teams.* Pamela Fuller & Mark Murphy with Anne Chow. Simon & Schuster 2020. xi, 278 pages : Illustration
ISBN 9781982144319
Grades: Adult   658.3
1. Unconscious bias 2. Prejudice 3. Discrimination 4. Racism in employment 5. Sexism in employment 6. Stereotypes 7. Multiculturalism 8. Leadership 9. Personnel management 10. Business and economics — Business leaders and entrepreneurs
LC BI2020072000

The experts at FranklinCovey provide more than thirty unique tools to teach leaders how to overcome unconscious bias in the workplace to unlock the potential of every person they encounter.

"This timely book is full of opportunities for leaders and employees to rethink how to address and mitigate bias mistreatments in the workplace." —*Booklist*

Includes index.

Hamilton, Denise
★ *Indivisible: How to Forge Our Differences into a Stronger Future.* Denise Hamilton. Countryman Press, an imprint of W.W. Norton & Company 2024. 210 p. : Illustration
ISBN 9781682688380
Grades: Adult   658.3
1. Multiculturalism 2. Marginalized people 3. Corporate culture 4. Office environment 5. Cooperation 6. Attitude change 7. Social change 8. Social advocacy 9. Society and culture — Social activism and philanthropy 10. Business and economics — Business Advice
LC BI2024003049

In her groundbreaking debut, she challenges readers to move beyond current notions of diversity and inclusion to build communities, workplaces, and relationships that live up to that word. She urges us to reexamine long-held beliefs and habits and to dismantle hierarchies that shape our current society. If we want to repair the fraying stitches that bind us together, if we want to build a truly close-knit collective, we cannot settle for our present approach. It's time to recalibrate and identify a goal higher than inclusivity—the goal of indivisibility.

"Inclusion strategist Hamilton delivers guidance that has value beyond corporate offices; it is guidance for the business of living." —*Booklist*

Includes bibliographical references (pages 195-199) and index.

Harts, Minda
Right Within: How to Heal from Racial Trauma in the Workplace. Minda Harts. Seal Press 2021. IX, 277 pages
ISBN 9781541619623
Grades: Adult   658.3
1. Multiculturalism 2. Marginalized women 3. Microaggressions 4. Work 5. Business and economics — Women and the workplace 6. Self-Help — Career and financial success 7. Society and culture — Race
LC 2021022124

Through action points, exercises and clear-eyed coaching, as well as advice from therapists and faith leaders of color, this essential self-help book offers strategies for women of color to heal and thrive in the workplace, and strengthen their resolve across corporate America.

"Harts argues that we need to understand that racism kills both people and careers, and that workplace injustices do incredible harm.... A necessary addition to business collections." —*Booklist*

Includes index.

Hewlett, Sylvia Ann
#metoo in the Corporate World: Power, Privilege, and the Path Forward. Sylvia Ann Hewlett. Harper Business 2020. xviii, 232 pages : Illustration

ISBN 9780062899194

Grades: Adult 658.3

1. Sexual harassment 2. Me Too movement 3. Business corruption 4. Sexual violence victims 5. United States 6. Life stories — Facing adversity — Victims of crime 7. Society and culture — Violence and crime 8. Society and culture — Gender

LC Bl2020003094

Economist and award-winning author Sylvia Ann Hewlett blends vivid stories with powerful new data in assessing the impact of the #MeToo movement in corporate America and provides concrete action to help executives and companies create more inclusive and safe work environments for women, people of color, and LGBTQ employees.

"Hewlett admits that we are in the early stages of understanding #MeToo in business, but her clear and practical book should be required reading for corporate leaders." —*Booklist*

Includes bibliographical references (pages [197]-219) and index.

McAfee, Andrew
The Geek Way: The Radical Mindset That Drives Extraordinary Results. Andrew McAfee; foreword by Reid Hoffman. Little, Brown & Company 2023. 336 p.

ISBN 9780316436700

Grades: Adult 658.3

1. Corporate culture 2. Curiosity 3. Experiments 4. Cooperation 5. Collaboration 6. Honesty 7. Science 8. Business innovations 9. High technology industry and trade 10. Business and economics — Business Advice 11. Business and economics — Industries — Technology

What is "being geeky?" It's being a perennially curious person, one who's not afraid to tackle hard problems and embrace unconventional solutions. McAfee shows how the geeks have created a new culture based around four norms: science, ownership, speed, and openness. It's not deferential to experts, fond of planning and process, afraid of mistakes, or obsessed with "winning." but it explains everything from why Montessori babies turn out to be creative tinkerers to how newcomers are disrupting industry after industry. McAfee offers a new way to see the world and empowering tools for seizing the big opportunities of today and tomorrow.

"This volume in McAfee's stable of books will be a welcome addition to business collections in academic and public libraries." —*Booklist*

Includes bibliographical references and index.

Morris, Jim
★ *The Cancer Factory: Industrial Chemicals, Corporate Deception, and the Hidden Deaths of American Workers.* Jim Morris. Beacon Press 2024. 272 p.

ISBN 9780807059142

Grades: Adult 658.3

1. Occupational health and safety 2. Hazardous occupations 3. Environmental policy 4. Hazardous materials 5. United States 6. Business and economics — Industries 7. Politics and global affairs — Environmental issues and policies 8. Society and culture — Illness and disease 9. Debut title

LC 2023028973

Based on four decades of reporting and delving into scientific literature about toxic substances and health risks, this gripping story of one of the nation's worst, and best-documented, outbreaks of work-related cancer at the Goodyear Tire and Rubber Company chemical plant exposes the sometimes-deadly risks too many workers face.

"Well documented, lucidly written, and disturbing to read, this is an urgent wake-up call." —*Publishers Weekly*

Includes bibliographical references and index.

Newkirk, Pamela
Diversity, Inc.: The Failed Promise of a Billion-Dollar Business. Pamela Newkirk. Bold Type Books 2019. 261 p.

ISBN 9781568588223

Grades: Adult 658.3

1. Multiculturalism 2. Strategic planning 3. Marginalized people 4. Leadership 5. Employee selection 6. Business innovations 7. Business and economics — Popular psychology 8. Society and culture — Race

LC 2019941714

An award-winning journalist describes how well-intentioned and often costly workplace diversity initiatives have given way to a misguided industry and reveals the large gap between the rhetoric of inclusivity and actual accomplishments.

"A must-read.... A well-sourced and succinctly written report that addresses the overall lack of progress in three key sectors: academia, corporate America, and the Hollywood entertainment establishment.... The book is valuable for many reasons, not the least of which is the context Newkirk provides." —*Fortune*

Includes bibliographical references and index.

Richards, Shola
Making Work Work: The Positivity Solution for Any Work Environment. Shola Richards. Sterling Ethos 2016. xiv, 239 pages

ISBN 9781454918721

Grades: Adult 658.3

1. Self-actualization 2. Work environment 3. Business and economics — Business advice — Leadership and management 4. Business and economics — General 5. Self-Help — Personal growth

LC 2016016626

"Most books about creating a better work climate center on the role of management... Richard's focus on leading change from across title ranks will be appreciated by people at any stage of their careers who are seeking a more spirit-enriching workplace." —*Library Journal*

Includes bibliographical references (pages 219-220) and index.

Smith, Clint
How to Hire: The Essential Guide to Recruit & Retain the Right People. Clint Smith, founder & CEO, CareerPlug. Amplify, an imprint of Mascot Books 2023. 232 p.

ISBN 9781645433248

Grades: Adult 658.3

1. Personnel management 2. Employee selection 3. Employment interviewing 4. Business and economics — Business advice — Leadership and management

Hiring has never been more challenging. There are fewer qualified applicants with more employers competing for them. And most business owners are stuck trying to figure this out on their own. Most books on hiring are written for HR professionals. The strategies and processes described in this book are proven. Clint Smith has worked closely with hundreds of business owners to develop them. This playbook is the foundation for his company's hiring software, which is used by over 17,000 companies to hire over 100,000 people per year.

"Business leaders, entrepreneurs, and hiring managers will find a wealth of practical wisdom here, and just the right blend of general principles and actionable practices." —*Booklist*

Includes bibliographical references.

Tracy, Brian
Full Engagement!: Inspire, Motivate, and Bring Out the Best in Your People. Brian Tracy. American Management Association 2011. VIII, 226 p.

ISBN 9780814416891

Grades: Adult 658.3

1. Employee motivation 2. Organizational behavior 3. Organizational effectiveness 4. Performance 5. Business and economics — Business advice — Leadership and management

LC 2010048293

ESSENTIAL AND RECOMMENDED TITLES
658.4 Executive management

Tracy (president, Brian Tracy International and Business Growth Strategy) presents this guide to motivating team members which focuses on high-trust work environment creation, identifying and eliminating the fears that hinder productivity, goals and objectives, unlocking potential, the "X Factor," and recognizing and rewarding efforts.

Includes index.

Warzel, Charlie
Out of Office: The Big Problem and Bigger Promise of Working from Home. Charlie Warzel and Anne Helen Petersen. Alfred A. Knopf 2021. 256 p.
ISBN 9780593320099
Grades: Adult   658.3
1. Telecommuting 2. Corporate culture 3. Social change 4. Labor productivity 5. Work-life balance 6. Job satisfaction 7. Flex time 8. Business and economics — Business advice 9. Society and culture — General
LC 2021019080

A future-looking, game-changing book about the radical transformational potential of working from home.

Combining groundbreaking reporting and the couple's own experiences, two leading culture reporters describe how workers and employers are finding new ways of working that make people happier and more productive, and make companies more profitable—ultimately improving our lives and strengthening our communities.

"Never sacrificing meaningful analysis for easy answers, this is a remarkable examination of the rapidly-changing workplace." —*Publishers Weekly*

Includes bibliographical references.

Washington, Ella F.
The Necessary Journey: Making Real Progress on Equity and Inclusion. Ella F. Washington. Harvard Business School Press 2022. 256 p.
ISBN 9781647821289
Grades: Adult   658.3
1. Management 2. Multiculturalism 3. Social justice 4. Equality 5. Industrial management 6. Business and economics — Business advice — Leadership and management
LC 2022021837

Washington, an organizational psychologist, consultant, and professor of management, provides case studies of specific companies' journeys towards progress on diversity, equity, and inclusion.

"Highly useful for diversity officers, HR workers, CEOs, and activists in the business community." —*Kirkus*

Includes index.

658.4 Executive management

Abrams, Stacey
Level Up: Rise Above the Hidden Forces Holding Your Business Back. Stacey Abrams and Lara Hodgson, with Heather Cabot. Portfolio/Penguin 2022. 208 p.
ISBN 9780593539828
Grades: Adult   658.4
1. Small business 2. Success in business 3. Entrepreneurship 4. Business and economics — Business advice
LC 2021055166

A must-read guide for small business owners navigating a critical turning point: When you either level up or give up.

"This brilliantly written, deeply insightful look at small-business ownership is a must-have for public and academic libraries." —*Booklist*

Includes bibliographical references.

Bahcall, Safi
Loonshots: How to Nurture the Crazy Ideas That Win Wars, Cure Diseases, and Transform Industries. Safi Bahcall. St. Martin's Press 2019. 352 p.
ISBN 9781250185969
Grades: Adult   658.4
1. Creativity in business 2. Entrepreneurship 3. Success in business 4. Ideas (Philosophy) 5. Diffusion of innovations 6. Social groups 7. Business and economics — Business advice — Leadership and management 8. Business and economics — Popular psychology
LC 2018041158

What do James Bond and Lipitor have in common? What can we learn about human nature and world history from a glass of water? In Loonshots, physicist and entrepreneur Safi Bahcall reveals a surprising new way of thinking about the mysteries of group behavior that challenges everything we thought we knew about nurturing radical breakthroughs.

"This thorough, fascinating study will appeal to a broader audience than just business wonks." —*Booklist*

Includes bibliographical references and index.

Barsh, Joanna
Grow Wherever You Work: Straight Talk to Help with Your Toughest Challenges. Joanna Barsh. McGraw-Hill Education 2018. xiv, 254 pages
ISBN 9781260026467
Grades: Adult   658.4
1. Leadership in business 2. Leadership 3. Quality of work life 4. Work environment 5. Business and economics — Business advice — Leadership and management
LC 2017039530

"The essential coach's handbook for anyone in a position of leadership: engaging, wise, and extremely practical. A must-read for students of business, organizational communication, and psychology." —*Library Journal*

Includes bibliographical references and index.

Boden, Anne
Female Founders' Playbook: Insights from the Superwomen Who Have Made It. Anne Boden. Kagan Page 2024. 256 p.
ISBN 9781398616370
Grades: Adult   658.4
1. Women executives 2. Leadership in business 3. Role models 4. Success in business 5. Creativity in business 6. Finance 7. Business and economics — Business advice — Leadership and management 8. Business and economics — Business leaders and entrepreneurs 9. Business and economics — Industries — Finance 10. Life stories — Business — Business leaders
LC 2023054576

High-growth enterprises on a rocket ship growth trajectory and tech unicorns with a value of more than one billion pounds have the potential to transform the economy. But building a unicorn is not an easy task. And it's even more difficult for female-led enterprises than it is for male-led start-ups. Female Founders' Playbook brings together the experiences of the leading women entrepreneurs and VC investors. These successful businesswomen share their thoughts on every aspect of launching a high-growth business, from coming up with a unicorn-worthy idea, through to building a multi-talented team to winning investment. T—.

"Drawing on decades of experience, renowned fintech entrepreneur Boden delivers an accessible game plan for aspiring female founders…This is a welcome addition to any business collection." —*Booklist*

Includes bibliographical references and index.

Botelho, Elena L.
The CEO Next Door: What It Takes to Get to the Top, and Succeed. by Elena L. Botelho and Kim R. Powell with Tahl Raz. Currency 2017. 304 p.
ISBN 9781101906491
Grades: Adult   658.4
1. Chief executive officers 2. Executive ability 3. Career development 4. Success in business 5. Business and economics — Business advice — Leadership and management
LC 2017035471

Drawing on a database of more than 17,000 leaders, as well as interviews with CEO candidates, two business consultants, dispelling myths about what it takes to get to the top, reveal the common attributes and hidden insights to success that have helped more than 6 million CEOs land their jobs and how these can be applied to our own careers. Includes six charts.

PUBLIC LIBRARY CORE COLLECTION: NONFICTION
Twentieth Edition

"Botelho and Powell have created a thought-provoking look at successful leadership without the typical bluster." —*Publishers Weekly*

Includes bibliographical references and index.

Brown, Brene
★ *Dare to Lead: Brave Work, Tough Conversations, Whole Hearts*. Brene Brown. Random House 2018. xix, 298 pages

ISBN 9780399592522

Grades: Adult   658.4

1. Leadership 2. Management 3. Psychological growth 4. Courage 5. Business and economics — Popular psychology 6. Business and economics — Business advice — Leadership and management 7. Society and culture — Psychology and human behavior

Explores how to cultivate daring leaders by recognizing and developing the potential in people, sharing power, aligning authority with accountability, and not avoiding difficult conversations or situations.

"It's an absorbingly actionable handbook on creating a space for better work and more fulfilled people." —*Washington Post*

Includes bibliographical references (pages 277-286) and index.

Cerulo, Erica
Work Wife: The Power of Female Friendship to Drive Successful Businesses. Erica Cerulo and Claire Mazur. Ballantine Books 2019. 288 p.

ISBN 9781524796778

Grades: Adult   658.4

1. Women executives 2. Women-owned businesses 3. Female friendship 4. Business partnership 5. Collaboration 6. Success in business 7. Business and economics — Women and the workplace 8. Business and economics — Business advice — Leadership and management

LC 2018051136

When Erica Cerulo and Claire Mazur met in college in 2002, they bonded instantly. Fast-forward to 2010, when they founded the popular fashion and design website of a Kind. Now, in their first book, Cerulo and Mazur bring to light the unique power of female friendship to fuel successful businesses. Drawing on their own experiences, as well as the stories of other thriving "work wives," they highlight the ways in which vulnerability, openness, and compassion—qualities central to so many women's relationships—lend themselves to professional accomplishment and innovation.

"This insightful, engaging work is an essential guidebook for friends considering a business collaboration." —*Library Journal*

Davidds, Yasmin
Your Own Terms: A Woman's Guide to Taking Charge of Any Negotiation. Yasmin Davidds, PsyD with Ann Bidou. AMACOM, American Management Association 2015. xii, 260 pages

ISBN 9780814436028

Grades: Adult   658.4

1. Negotiation in business 2. Negotiation 3. Businesspeople 4. Women 5. Business and economics — General 6. Business and economics — Women and the workplace

LC 2015009457

A negotiating guide for women provides information about such topics as creating a strong presence, leveraging natural style, and handling difficult people.

Includes bibliographical references (pages 247-254) and index.

Duke, Annie
Thinking in Bets: Making Smarter Decisions When You Don't Have All the Facts. Annie Duke. Portfolio/Penguin 2018. 276 pages : Illustration

ISBN 9780735216358

Grades: Adult   658.4

1. Decision making 2. Business and economics — Business advice 3. Business and economics — General 4. Science writing — Medicine and health — Psychology

LC 2017042666

Poker champion turned business consultant Annie Duke teaches you how to get comfortable with uncertainty and make better decisions as a result. In Super Bowl XLIX, Seahawks coach Pete Carroll made one of the most controversial calls in football history: With 26 seconds remaining, and trailing by four at the Patriots' one-yard line, he called for a pass instead of a hand off to his star running back. The pass was intercepted and the Seahawks lost. Critics called it the dumbest play in history. But was the call really that bad? Or did Carroll actually make a great move that was ruined by bad luck? Even the best decision doesn't yield the best outcome every time. There's always an element of luck that you can't control, and there is always information that is hidden from view. So the key to long-term success (and avoiding worrying yourself to death) is to think in bets: How sure am I? What are the possible ways things could turn out? What decision has the highest odds of success? Did I land in the unlucky 10% on the strategy that works 90% of the time? Or is my success attributable to dumb luck rather than great decision making? Annie Duke, a former World Series of Poker champion turned business consultant, draws on examples from business, sports, politics, and (of course) poker to share tools anyone can use to embrace uncertainty and make better decisions. For most people, it's difficult to say "I'm not sure" in a world that values and, even, rewards the appearance of certainty. But professional pokerplayers are comfortable with the fact that great decisions don't always lead to great outcomes and bad decisions don't always lead to bad outcomes. By shifting your thinking from a need for certainty to a goal of accurately assessing what you know and what you don't, you'll be less vulnerable to reactive emotions, knee-jerk biases, and destructive habits in your decision making. You'll become more confident, calm, compassionate and successful in the long run.

Includes bibliographical references (pages 241-266) and index.

Ferrazzi, Keith
Never Eat Alone: And Other Secrets to Success, One Relationship at a Time. Keith Ferrazzi and Tahl Raz. Crown Business 2014. xvii, 379 p.

ISBN 9780385346658

Grades: Adult   658.4

1. Success in business 2. Business networks 3. Online social networks 4. Generosity 5. Interpersonal relations 6. Public relations 7. Business and economics — Careers

LC 2014381541

Explaining how to turn one-time contacts into a lifelong circle of mentors, colleagues, and friends, a guide to the art of networking reveals the fundamental principles of what it takes to build lasting, mutually beneficial relationships.

Gallo, Amy
Getting Along: How to Work with Anyone (Even Difficult People). Amy Gallo. Harvard Business Review Press 2022. 256 p.

ISBN 9781647821067

Grades: Adult   658.4

1. Conflict resolution 2. Interpersonal conflict 3. Personnel management 4. Work environment 5. Business and economics — Popular psychology

LC 2022020652

Workplace expert and Harvard Business Review podcast host Amy Gallo identifies eight familiar types of difficult coworkers—the insecure boss, the passive-aggressive peer, the know-it-all, the biased coworker, and others—and provides strategies tailored to dealing constructively with each one. She also shares principles that will help you turn things around, no matter who you're at odds with. Taking the high road isn't easy, but Gallo offers a crucial perspective on how work relationships really matter, as well as the compassion, encouragement, and tools you need to prevail—on your terms.

"This practical and empathetic guide to taking the high road is worth a look for workers lost in conflict." —*Publishers Weekly*

Includes index.

Gallo, Carmine
The Bezos Blueprint: Communication Secrets of the World's Greatest Salesman. Carmine Gallo. St. Martin's Press 2022. x, 258 pages : Illustration

ISBN 9781250278333

Grades: Adult   658.4

ESSENTIAL AND RECOMMENDED TITLES
658.4 Executive management

1. Bezos, Jeffrey 2. Business communication 3. Communication in management 4. Leadership 5. Business and economics — Business advice

LC 2022028658

Reveals the communication and leadership secrets of the Amazon founder, showing readers how to sharpen their writing, storytelling and communication skills to build the company or career of their dreams.

"Intended for professionals in a business setting, the book draws lessons from real excerpts of speeches and shareholder memos that Bezos has delivered over the past 20-plus years...An insightful guide to improving communication skills." —*Library Journal*

Includes bibliographical references (pages 235-245) and index.

***Talk** Like Ted: The 9 Public-Speaking Secrets of the World's Top Minds.* Carmine Gallo. St. Martin's Press 2014. x, 278 pages : Illustration

ISBN 9781250041128

Grades: Adult   658.4

1. Business presentations 2. Public speaking 3. Self-Help — Career and financial success 4. Language arts and studies — Public speaking 5. Reference — Business

LC 2013031049

Reveals the nine strategies of the gold-standard presentation method, drawing on interviews with TED conference speakers to outline methods for overcoming public speaking fears, motivating teams, and making a presentation dynamic.

"The author ... includes successful outlines and guides to using both audio-visual aides and effective body language. Dramatic composition and vigorous presentation make this a powerful tool to improve mastery of speaking skills." —*Kirkus*

Includes bibliographical references (pages 249-261) and index.

Gilkey, Charlie

***Start** Finishing: How to Go from Idea to Done.* Charlie Gilkey. Sounds True 2019. IX, 257 p. : Illustration

ISBN 9781683642633

Grades: Adult   658.4

1. Time management 2. Procrastination 3. Business and economics — General 4. Self-Help — Personal growth 5. Business and economics — Business advice — Leadership and management

LC 2018059665

Presents a 9-step method for success—including identifying your genius, building a success pack of supporters, navigating multiple projects, and overcoming the challenges that come with doing work that matters.

"For those interested in project management and entrepreneurship, this book offers creative solutions for developing habits and routines that will set them on a path to starting and finishing projects successfully." —*Booklist*

Includes bibliographical references (pages 253-257).

Goleman, Daniel

***Primal** Leadership: Unleashing the Power of Emotional Intelligence.* Daniel Goleman, Richard Boyatzis, Annie McKee. Harvard Business Review Press 2013. xxi, 306 p.

ISBN 9781422168035

Grades: Adult   658.4

1. Leadership 2. Management 3. Executive ability 4. Emotional intelligence 5. Business and economics — Business advice — Leadership and management

LC 2013018294

This refreshed edition of Primal Leadership illustrates why the book is all the more timely today as leaders face ever-increasing pressures—from globalization and the economic roller coaster to the hyper-speed of evolving information technologies and the ratcheting up of competitive forces.

Includes bibliographical references (pages 257-290) and index.

Goodall, Amanda

***Credible:** The Power of Expert Leaders.* Amanda Goodall. Public Affairs 2023. 304 p.

ISBN 9781541702509

Grades: Adult   658.4

1. Leadership 2. Success in business 3. Management 4. Success (Concept) 5. Business and economics — Business advice — Leadership and management

"A convincing argument that a company's success requires leaders to have specific industry expertise." —*Library Journal*

Horstman, Mark

*The **Effective** Manager.* Mark Horstman, cofounder, manager tools. Wiley 2016. xiv, 194 pages

ISBN 9781119244608

Grades: Adult   658.4

1. Executive ability 2. Management 3. Supervision of employees 4. Teams in the workplace 5. Business and economics — Business advice — Leadership and management

LC 2016018227

The Effective Manager is written for every manager, at every level. It focuses on what you can do now, today, with your team members, to improve their performance and get better results and retention. It even tells you how fast to roll out each of the 4tools—One on Ones, Feedback, Coaching and Delegation, week by week.

The how-to guide for exceptional management from the bottom up the Effective Manager is a hands-on practical guide to great management at every level. Written by the man behind Manager Tools, the world's number-one business podcast, this book distills the author's 25 years of management training expertise into clear, actionable steps to start taking today. First, you'll identify what "effective management" actually looks like: Can you get the job done at a high level? Do you attract and retain top talent without burning them out? Then you'll dig into the four critical behaviors that make a manager great, and learn how to adjust your own behavior to be the leader your team needs. You'll learn the four major tools that should be a part of every manager'srepertoire, how to use them, and even how to introduce them to the team in a productive, non-disruptive way. Most management books are written for CEOs and geared toward improving corporate management, but this book is expressly aimed at managers of anylevel-with a behavioral framework designed to be tailored to your team's specific needs. Understand your team's strengths, weaknesses, and goals in a meaningful way Stop limiting feedback to when something goes wrong Motivate your people to continuous improvement Spread the work around and let people stretch their skills Effective managers are good at the job and "good at people." the key is combining those skills to foster your team's development, get better and better results, and maintain a culture of positive productivity. The Effective Manager shows you how to turn good into great with clear, actionable, expert guidance.

Includes index.

Kethledge, Raymond Michael

***Lead** Yourself First: Inspiring Leadership Through Solitude.* Raymond M. Kethledge and Michael S. Erwin; foreword by Jim Collins. Bloomsbury Publishing USA 2017. 288 pages

ISBN 9781632866318

Grades: Adult   658.4

1. Leadership 2. Solitude 3. Self-improvement 4. Politicians 5. Leadership in business 6. Decision making 7. Perspective, Personal 8. Critical thinking 9. Distractions 10. Business and economics — Business advice — Leadership and management 11. Business and economics — Popular psychology

LC 2016044432

Citing examples from great leaders in politics, business, sports and the military, makes the case for leaders to unplug from daily life and spend time alone to improve clarity and creativity, balance their emotions and sustain certainty.

"This book is a rare gem, offering an optimistic message that there remain powerful leaders intent on being courageous and moral, and on finding 'Transcendent meaning' in their vocation." —*Publishers Weekly*

Includes bibliographical references and index.

Maroney, Tyler

*The **Modern** Detective: How Corporate Intelligence Is Reshaping the World.* Tyler Maroney. Riverhead Books 2020. 262 p.

ISBN 9781594632594

Grades: Adult   658.4

1. Maroney, Tyler 2. Business intelligence 3. Private investigators 4. Intelligence service 5. Ethics 6. Corruption investigation 7. White collar crime 8. Business security 9. Life stories — Law and order 10. Business and economics — Corruption and scandal 11. True Crime — General

LC 2020018425

An insider's tour of the world of 21st-century private investigators examines how today's detectives use unique creativity and resources to help catch corrupt politicians, international embezzlers and corporate purveyors of human-rights abuses.

"Readers do not need a background in private investigative work to appreciate this fascinating read. Hand this to readers interested in the work and life of a private investigator, the role of technology in investigative work, and political and white-collar crime." —Booklist

Includes index.

Mueller, Jennifer

Creative Change: Why We Resist It... How We Can Embrace It. Jennifer Mueller. Houghton Mifflin Harcourt 2017. 288 p.

ISBN 9780544703094

Grades: Adult   658.4

1. Creativity 2. Change 3. Success in business 4. Business innovations 5. Performance 6. Motivation 7. Decision making 8. Industrial productivity 9. Success (Concept) 10. Inspiration 11. Business and economics — Popular psychology

LC 2016036403

A forefront psychologist analyzes the paradox of how today's corporate leaders both desire and reject creative solutions, offering insight into the biases that compromise innovation while suggesting options for recognizing creative opportunities and overcoming unproductive beliefs.

"This enlightening book not only shows why people reject creativity but provides solutions on how to switch ones thinking and truly welcome it." —Publishers Weekly

Phillips, Collette A. M.

The Includers: The 7 Traits of Culturally Savvy, Anti-Racist Leaders. Collette A.M. Phillips. BenBella Books Inc. 2024. xvii, 231 pages

ISBN 9781637741382

Grades: Adult   658.4

1. Leadership 2. Ethics 3. Antiracism 4. Multiculturalism 5. Organizational change 6. Social change 7. Antiracist literature 8. Business and economics — Business advice — Leadership and management 9. Society and culture — Race

LC 2023025934

In The Includers, Colette Phillips shares data and real-life stories, focusing on the steps to take, qualities to hone, and people to emulate to become an "includer." by highlighting the experiences of real includers who have utilized their positions asleaders to fight for change, Phillips shows that this form of allyship isn't just possible, it's easy, sustainable, and necessary.

"The Includers will be a valuable addition to business collections in both public and academic libraries. Its message will benefit professionals in the business community and beyond." —Booklist

Includes bibliographical references (pages 213-218) and index.

Riel, Jennifer

Creating Great Choices: A Leader's Guide to Integrative Thinking. Jennifer Riel, Roger L. Martin. Harvard Business Review Press 2017. xvii, 242 p. : Illustration

ISBN 9781633692961

Grades: Adult   658.4

1. Problem solving 2. Thought and thinking 3. Decision making 4. Leadership 5. Business and economics — Business advice — Leadership and management

LC 2017012026

Conventional wisdom—and business school curricula—teaches us that making trade-offs is inevitable when it comes to hard choices. But sometimes, accepting the obvious trade-off just isn't good enough: the choices in front of us don't get us what we need. In those cases, rather than choosing the least worst option, we can use the models in front of us to create a new and better answer. This is integrative thinking. First introduced by Roger Martin in The Opposable Mind, integrative thinking is an approach to problem solving that uses opposing ideas as the basis for innovation. Now, in Creating Great Choices, Martin and fellow Rotman expert Jennifer Riel vividly show how they have refined and enhanced the understanding and practice of integrative thinking through their work teaching the concept and its principles to business and nonprofit executives, MBA students, even kids. Integrative thinking has been embraced by organizations such as Procter & Gamble, Deloitte, Verizon, and the Toronto District School Board—all seeking a replicable, thoughtful approach to creating a "third and better way" to make important choices in the face of unacceptable trade-offs. The book includes new stories of successful integrative thinkers that will demystify the process of creative problem solving. It lays out the authors' practical four-step methodology, which can be applied in virtually any context: Articulating opposing models Examining the models Generating possibilities Assessing prototypes Stimulating and practical, Creating Great Choices blends storytelling, theory, and hands-on advice to help any leader or manager facing a tough choice.

Includes bibliographical references.

Rubin, Robert Edward

The Yellow Pad: Making Better Decision in an Uncertain World. Robert E. Rubin. Penguin Press 2023. 336 p.

ISBN 9780593491393

Grades: Adult   658.4

1. Rubin, Robert Edward, 1938- 2. Decision-making 3. Crisis management 4. Social problems 5. Life stories — Business — Business leaders 6. Life stories — Politics 7. Politics and global affairs — General 8. Business and economics — General

LC 2022035034

The former U.S. Treasury Secretary and co-chairman of Goldman Sachs, armed with his most trusted tool—a simple yellow legal pad—offers this essential guide for anyone looking to make better decisions in life, work and public policy against the backdrop of a fundamentally uncertain world.

"With intellectual heft and plenty of actionable items, this is a smart prescription for better thinking." —Kirkus

Includes index.

Sally, David

One Step Ahead: Mastering the Art and Science of Negotiation. David Sally. St. Martin's Press 2020. x, 372 pages : Illustration

ISBN 9781250166395

Grades: Adult   658.4

1. Negotiation in business 2. Negotiation 3. Business and economics — Business advice

LC 2019054416

An innovative strategist and behavioral economist, drawing on 20 years of experience—and the stories of often misunderstood historical characters, introduces a revolutionary way of approaching negotiation that applies in any situation.

"Entertaining and conversational, this is an important tool for getting to yes, as well as understanding exactly what will prompt an opponent to say it." —Publishers Weekly

Includes bibliographical references (pages 327-361) and index.

Sandberg, Sheryl

Lean In: For Graduates. Sheryl Sandberg. Alfred A. Knopf 2014. 432 p.

ISBN 9780385353670

Grades: Adult   658.4

1. Women college graduates 2. Job hunting 3. Job applications 4. Women executives 5. Leadership 6. Business and economics — Business Advice 7. Business and economics — Women and the workplace

LC 2014002390

Expanded and updated for graduates just entering the workforce, a guide to finding and getting the most out of a first job shares professional advice for râesumâe writing, recommended interviewing practices, and salary negotiation.

"An expanded version of Facebook COO Sandberg's 2013 best-seller, this time with additional material aimed specifically at women just entering the

ESSENTIAL AND RECOMMENDED TITLES
658.7 Management of materials

workforce. Sandberg recruits a considerable number of women, and a couple of men, to add their voices to hers." —*Kirkus*

***Lean** In: Women, Work, and the Will to Lead.* Sheryl Sandberg. Alfred A. Knopf 2013. 208 p.
ISBN 9780385349949
Grades: Adult   658.4
1. Sandberg, Sheryl 2. Women executives 3. Leadership 4. Business and economics — Business Advice 5. Business and economics — Women and the workplace
LC 2012043371
New York Times Notable Book, 2013.

The Facebook chief operating officer and Fortune top-ranked businesswoman shares provocative, anecdotal advice for women that urges them to take risks and seek new challenges in order to find work that they can love and engage in passionately.

Scott, Kim Malone
***Radical** Candor: Be a Kick-Ass Boss Without Losing Your Humanity.* Kim Scott. St. Martin's Press 2017. 272 pages
ISBN 9781250103505
Grades: Adult   658.4
1. Management 2. Executives 3. Leadership 4. Decision-making 5. Honesty 6. Employee motivation 7. Personnel management 8. Business and economics — Business advice — Leadership and management 9. Business and economics — Business leaders and entrepreneurs
LC 2016044291

A high-profile business manager describes her development of an optimal management course designed to help business leaders become balanced and effective without resorting to insensitive aggression or overt permissiveness.

"Informational and clear, this is necessary reading for anyone who's having trouble coming to terms with an underperforming workforce." —*Publishers Weekly*

Snow, Shane
***Dream** Teams: Working Together Without Falling Apart.* Shane Snow. Portfolio/Penguin 2018. xiii, 286 pages : Illustration
ISBN 9780735217799
Grades: Adult   658.4
1. Cooperation 2. Success in business 3. Teams in the workplace 4. Work environment 5. Work 6. Business and economics — Business advice
LC 2018014633

Uses research from history, neuroscience, psychology, and business to explore and determine how and why some partnerships break down and others thrive.

"Entrepreneur, journalist, and author Snow (Smartcuts, 2014) explains how the composition of teams can make or break ideas, progress, and even the outcomes of battles. Using a combination of historical events (like the Battle of New Orleans, against the British, with General Andrew Jackson at the helm) and psychological research, Snow's narrative and perspective are clear: to become stronger, work must be collective in certain ways." —*Booklist*

Includes index.

Solovic, Susan Wilson
*The **One-Percent** Edge: Small Changes That Guarantee Relevance and Build Sustainable Success.* Susan Solovic with Ray Manley. AMACOM Books 2018. xxi, 256 p.
ISBN 9780814438800
Grades: Adult   658.4
1. Organizational change 2. Corporate culture 3. Organizational behavior 4. Success in business 5. Success (Concept) 6. Business and economics — Business Advice
LC 2017027592

When business is good, most leaders focus on maintaining the status quo. After all, why fix what's not broken? But doing the same thing leaves you vulnerable to new competitors and technologies. (Consider what happened to Polaroid when digital cameras hit the market, or to Firestone when Michelin introduced its superior radial tires.) to gain an advantage over old rivals and upstarts alike, The One-Percent Edge offers a simple but powerful formula: Make small, incremental improvements in seven areas of your business.

Includes index.

Spetzler, Carl S.
***Decision** Quality: Value Creation from Better Business Decisions.* Carl Spetzler, Hannah Winter, Jennifer Meyer. WILEY 2016. xviii, 237 pages : Illustration
ISBN 9781119144670
Grades: Adult   658.4
1. Decision making 2. Business and economics — Business advice
LC 2015043777

Add value with every decision using a simple yet powerful framework Few things are as valuable in business, and in life, as the ability to make good decisions. Can you imagine how much more rewarding your life and your business would be if every decision you made were the best it could be? Decision Quality empowers you to make the best possible choice and get more of what you truly want from every decision. Dr. Carl Spetzler is a leader in the field of decision science and has worked with organizations across industries to improve their decision-making capabilities. He and his co-authors, all experienced consultants and educators in this field, show you how to frame a problem or opportunity, create a set of attractive alternatives, identify relevant uncertain information, clarify the values that are important in the decision, apply tools of analysis, and develop buy-in among stakeholders. Their straightforward approach is elegantly simple, yet practical and powerful. It can be applied to all types of decisions. Our business and our personal lives are marked by a stream of decisions. Some are small. Some are large. Some are life-altering or strategic. How well we make those decisions truly matters. This book gives you a framework and thinking tools that will help you to improve the odds of getting more of what you value from every choice. You will learn: The six element of decisions quality, and how to apply them the difference between a good decision and a good outcome Why a decision can only be as good as the best of the available alternative Methods for making both 'significant' and strategic decisions the mental traps that undermine decision quality and how to avoid them How to deal with uncertainty—a factor in every important choice How to judge the quality of a decision at the time you're making it How organizations have benefited from building quality into their decisions. Many people are satisfied with 'good enough' when making important decisions.

Aimed at executive and management-level decision makers in every industry, Decision Quality: Value Creation from Better Business Decisions provides a proven and real-world-tested framework for improving business decision quality.

Includes bibliographical references and index.

658.7 Management of materials

Goodman, Peter S.
★ *How the World Ran Out of Everything: Inside the Global Supply Chain.* Peter S. Goodman. Mariner Books 2024. 480 p.
ISBN 9780063257924
Grades: Adult   658.7
1. International trade 2. International finance 3. Scarcity 4. Supply and demand 5. Supply-side economics 6. Deregulation 7. Freight and freightage 8. Transportation 9. Trucking industry and trade 10. COVID-19 Pandemic, 2020- 11. Business and economics — Economics — World economy 12. Business and economics — Industries — Transportation 13. Business and economics — Industries — Retail products and services

The New York Times's Global Economics Correspondent looks at the fascinating innerworkings of our global supply chain, how the COVID-19 pandemic exposed its dangerous vulnerabilities and offers solutions to make it more reliable and resilient.

"Readers will be drawn into supply-chain history, how it works today, and Goodman's ideas on how to change it to avoid another dysfunction." —*Booklist*

PUBLIC LIBRARY CORE COLLECTION: NONFICTION
Twentieth Edition

658.8 Management of marketing

Kerpen, Dave
Likeable Social Media: How to Delight Your Customers, Create an Irresistible Brand, and Be Generally Amazing on All Social Networks That Matter. by Dave Kerpen with Michelle Greenbaum, Robert Berk, and Carrie Kerpen. McGraw-Hill 2019. 296 p.
ISBN 9781260453287
Grades: Adult   658.8
1. Marketing 2. Social networks 3. Online social networks 4. Product management 5. Business and economics — General 6. Science writing — Computing, the internet, and technology — Internet
This updated edition of the bestselling classic is packed with expert advice and new case studies that demonstrate the latest best practices.

Kim, W. Chan
Blue Ocean Shift: Beyond Competing : Proven Steps to Inspire Confidence and Seize New Growth. W. Chan Kim, Renee Mauborgne. Hachette Books 2017. xi, 322 p. : Illustration
ISBN 9780316314046
Grades: Adult   658.8
1. New products 2. Market segmentation 3. Business and economics — Business advice — Leadership and management
LC Bl2017030275
Drawing on more than a decade of new work, the authors demonstrate how to move beyond competing, inspire confidence, and seize new growth, discussing how to take an organization into an uncontested market space.
Includes bibliographical references and index.

Marie, Jane
★ *Selling* the Dream: The Billion-Dollar Industry Bankrupting Americans. Jane Marie. Atria Books 2024. 320 p.
ISBN 9781982155773
Grades: Adult   658.8
1. Corporations 2. Sales 3. Marketing 4. Consumerism 5. Swindlers and swindling 6. Blue collar workers 7. Poor people 8. Self-employment 9. Sales personnel 10. Debt 11. Exploitation 12. Propaganda 13. Society and culture — Wealth and class 14. Business and economics — Economics — Consumerism 15. Business and economics — Industries — Retail products and services
LC 2023035155
We've all heard of Amway, Mary Kay, Tupperware, and LuLaRoe, but few know the nefarious way they and countless other multilevel marketing (MLM) companies prey on desperate Americans struggling to make ends meet. Featuring in-depth reporting and intimate research, Selling the Dream reveals how these companies—often owned by political and corporate elites, such as the Devos and the Van Andels families—have made a windfall in profit off of the desperation of the American working class.
"The result is an urgent and riveting exposé of the fraudulent tactics behind direct sales organizations." —*Publishers Weekly*
Includes bibliographical references and index.

Watkins, Alexandra
Hello, My Name Is Awesome: How to Create Brand Names That Stick. Alexandra Watkins. Berrett-Koehler Publishers 2014. x, 98 pages : Illustration
ISBN 9781626561861
Grades: Adult   658.8
1. Trademarks 2. Marketing 3. Business and economics — General
LC 2014018994
Naming a business or product has always been challenging—and sometimes costly—for entrepreneurs and inventors, but it's one of the most important decisions they have to make. Alexandra Watkins presents a foolproof model that anyone can use to create and evaluate brand names like a pro.
"Useful for readers who are naming anything more important than a household pet." —*Library Journal*
Includes index.

659.1 Advertising

Auletta, Ken
Frenemies: The Epic Disruption of the Ad Business (and Everything Else). Ken Auletta. Penguin Press 2018. 400 p.
ISBN 9780735220867
Grades: Adult   659.1
1. Advertising agencies 2. Marketing 3. Consumer behavior 4. Corporate accountability 5. Advertising 6. Mass media and culture 7. Telecommunication 8. Mass media 9. Technology 10. Business and economics — Economics — Consumerism 11. Business and economics — Industries — Technology
LC 2018006195
The "Annals of Communication" columnist and author of Googled presents an intimate and awareness-raising assessment of the changes buffeting the $2 trillion global advertising and marketing business as viewed by the industry's most powerful players.
Includes bibliographical references and index.

Wu, Tim
The Attention Merchants: The Epic Scramble to Get Inside Our Heads. Tim Wu. Knopf 2016. 304 p.
ISBN 9780385352017
Grades: Adult   659.1
1. Manipulation (Social sciences) 2. Advertising 3. Mass media 4. Technology 5. Marketing 6. Consumerism 7. Mass media and culture 8. Telecommunication 9. Information technology 10. Consumer behavior 11. United States 12. Business and economics — Economics — Consumerism 13. Business and economics — Industries — Entertainment and media
LC 2016010140
The award-winning author of The Master Switch, who coined the term "net neutrality," discusses the companies that want to attract and harvest human attention and their relentless attempts to influence our consumption and purchases.

659.2 Public relations

Elwood, Phil
All the Worst Humans: How I Made News for Dictators, Tycoons, and Politicians. Phil Elwood. Henry Holt and Company 2024. 272 p.
ISBN 9781250321572
Grades: Adult   659.2
1. Elwood, Phil (Philip) 2. Public relations 3. Political consultants 4. Public relations and politics 5. Press and politics 6. Communication in politics 7. Professional-client relations 8. Politicians 9. Dictators 10. Billionaires 11. Wealth 12. Power 13. Addiction 14. Depression 15. Ethics 16. Conscience 17. Life change events 18. Career changes 19. American people 20. Autobiographies and memoirs 21. Life stories — Business — Working life 22. Politics and global affairs — Political figures 23. Politics and global affairs — Mass media and politics
LC 2023055958
After nearly two decades in the Washington PR business, Phil Elwood wants to come clean, by exposing the dark underbelly of the very industry that's made him so successful. Elwood has worked for a murderer's row of questionable clients, including Gaddafi, Assad, and the government of Qatar. In All the Worst Humans, Elwood unveils how the PR business works, and how the truth gets made, spun, and sold to the public. But as he moved up the ranks, he felt worse and worse about the sleaziness of it all—until Elwood receives a shocking wake-up call from the FBI. This risky game nearly cost Elwood his life and his freedom.
"A breakneck-pace memoir of a career drumming up publicity for some of the worst human beings in the public eye." —*Kirkus*
Includes bibliographical references.

Gramm, Jeff
Dear Chairman: Boardroom Battles and the Rise of Shareholder Activism. Jeff Gramm. Harper Business 2016. 304 p.

ESSENTIAL AND RECOMMENDED TITLES
660.6 Biotechnology

ISBN 9780062369833
Grades: Adult **659.2**
1. Corporate governance 2. Corporations 3. Stockholders 4. Investors 5. Business and economics — Economics — History
LC 2015038177

Drawing on lively case studies and original letters from some of our most legendary and controversial investors and activists, a hedge-fund manager and an adjunct professor at Columbia Business School traces the rise in shareholder activism from the 1920s to today, providing a first-of-its-kind perspective on what it means to be a public company.

"Entertaining as well as intriguing, Gramm's work is a great read for both students of business and interested general readers." —*Library Journal*

Includes bibliographical references and index.

660.6 Biotechnology

Piore, Adam
The *Body Builders: Inside the Science of the Engineered Human*. Adam Piore. Ecco Press 2017. 400 pages
ISBN 9780062347145
Grades: Adult **660.6**
1. Biotechnology 2. Medical genetics 3. Human engineering 4. Genetic engineering 5. Science writing — Biology
LC BI2017004021

A tour of the current revolution in human augmentation explores how the world's most innovative engineers are helping people repair traumatic injuries while transcending physical and mental limitations.

"Piore writes gracefully, and with deep insight, about complex scientific endeavors that could ease human suffering but are fraught with myriad ethical perils." —*Publishers Weekly*

663 Beverage technology

Bryson, Lew
Tasting Whiskey: An Insiders Guide to the Unique Pleasures of the World's Finest Spirits. Lew Bryson. Storey Publishing 2014. 255 pages
ISBN 9781612123011
Grades: Adult **663**
1. Whiskey 2. Food writing — Beer, wine, and liquor
LC 2014023260

This full-color book on all things whiskey offers whiskey aficionados and fans detailed information on the history, flavors, and more of this celebrated spirit.

Includes index.

Cioletti, Jeff
Sakepedia: A Non-Traditional Guide to Japan's Traditional Beverage. Jeff Cioletti. Turner Publishing 2019. 201 p.
ISBN 9781683367741
Grades: Adult **663**
1. Food writing — Beer, wine, and liquor
LC 2018008896

Booze journalist, expert and International Kikisake-shi—that's a fancy term for "sake sommelier"—Jeff Cioletti is passionate about Japan's classic national beverage, but he's tired of it being so misunderstood. Sake been called "exotic," "mysterious," and even, at times, "intimidating." but Jeff's here to tell you that it's actually none of those things and he wants you to join him on his flavorful, unpretentious and de-mystifying journey across thousands of miles, centuries of tradition and hundreds of glasses of sake. Anyone who's enjoyed a good beer, wine or spirit from time to time and is looking for a new adventure is invited to come along.

Includes bibliographical references.

Easto, Jessica
How to Taste Coffee: Develop Your Sensory Skills and Get the Most Out of Every Cup. Jessica Easto. Agate 2023. 191 pages : Color; Illustration
ISBN 9781572843295
Grades: Adult **663**
1. Coffee 2. Senses and sensation 3. Taste 4. Smell 5. Touch 6. Flavor 7. Food writing — Non-alcoholic beverages
LC 2023007844

Featuring nineteen exercises designed to give you a more developed palate, an improved ability to choose the perfect coffee and an understanding of the power contained within these tiny beans, this interactive guide shows you how coffee stimulates the senses—and how to get the most out of drinking it.

"Illustrations, a resource sheet, and impeccably documented sources further elevate this savvy guide to tasting coffee in all its complexity." —*Booklist*

A Surrey book; Includes bibliographical references (pages 175-185) and index.

Hoalst-Pullen, Nancy
National Geographic Atlas of Beer: A Globe-Trotting Journey Through the World of Beer. Nancy Hoalst-Pullen & Mark W. Patterson; foreword & tasting tips by Garrett Oliver. National Geographic 2017. 303 pages : Color; Illustration; Map
ISBN 9781426218330
Grades: Adult **663**
1. Beer 2. Breweries 3. Food writing — Beer, wine, and liquor
LC 2017011583

Featuring 200 photos, 100 maps, interesting beer destinations and fascinating historical perspectives, an ultimate beer lover|s guide to the world explores beer history, geography, trends and tasting on six continents.

Presents a guide to beer and breweries in fifteen countries around the world, describing the history of beer, favorite destinations in each country, beer festivals, and unusual breweries,.

Includes bibliographical references and index.

Rogers, Adam
Proof: The Science of Booze. Adam Rogers. Houghton Mifflin Harcourt 2014. 256 p.
ISBN 9780547897967
Grades: Adult **663**
1. Liquors 2. Alcoholic beverages 3. Distillation 4. Beverage industry and trade 5. Science Writing — General 6. Food writing — General
LC 2013045770

Presents a look at the science of alcohol production and consumption, from the principles behind the fermentation, distillation, and aging of alcoholic beverages, to the psychology and neurobiology of what happens after it is consumed.

"The science here can be intimidating to process, but when enjoyed in leisurely sips, Rogers's cheeky and accessible writing style goes down smoothly, capturing the essence of this enigmatic, ancient social lubricant." —*Publishers Weekly*

Includes bibliographical references and index.

White, April
Apples to Cider: How to Make Sweet and Hard Cider at Home. April White with Stephen M. Wood of Farnum Hill Ciders. Quarry Books 2015. 151 p.
ISBN 9781592539185
Grades: Adult **663**
1. Cider 2. Food writing — Non-alcoholic beverages 3. Food writing — Beer, wine, and liquor
LC 2015000551

With these easy-to-follow instructions for first-time cidermakers and advanced techniques for the more experienced, you'll be on your way to making your own delicious cider at home.

"This book is a fine introduction to the basics of hard cider and will surely pique the interest of home brewers looking to stretch beyond beer and wine." —*Library Journal*

Includes bibliographical references and index.

PUBLIC LIBRARY CORE COLLECTION: NONFICTION
Twentieth Edition

664 Food technology

Danforth, Adam
Butchering Poultry, Rabbit, Lamb, Goat, and Pork: The Comprehensive Photographic Guide to Humane Slaughtering and Butchering. Adam Danforth, Photography by Keller + Keller. Storey Pub. 2014. IX, 446 pages : Color; Illustration
ISBN 9781612121826
Grades: Adult — 664
1. Animal welfare 2. Cooking (Meat) 3. Meat cutting 4. Meat 5. Recipes 6. Slaughter-houses and slaughtering 7. Canning and preserving 8. Food writing — Cooking and cookbooks — Ingredients 9. Science writing — General
LC 2013030702

Depicts the entire process of slaughtering and butchering small livestock, including chickens, rabbits, sheep, pigs and goats through detailed, explicit step-by-step photographs and also features information on food safety, freezing, packaging and equipment.
Includes bibliographical references (p. 436-437) and index.

Forkish, Ken
Evolutions in Bread: Artisan Pan Breads and Dutch-Oven Loaves at Home. Ken Forkish, James Beard Award-winning author of Flour water salt yeast; photographs by Alan Weiner. Ten Speed Press 2022. 249 pages : Color; Illustration
ISBN 9781984860378
Grades: Adult — 664
1. Bread 2. Baking 3. Cookbooks 4. Food writing — Cooking and cookbooks — Courses 5. Food writing — Cooking and cookbooks — Methods
LC BL2022028053

The New York Times best-selling author of Four Water Salt Yeast helps home bakers elevate their bread-making game with all-new recipes for same-day loaves, overnight cold-proof doughs and classic levains along with equipment lists, and important methods and techniques. Index.
"Chef Forkish turns his attention to developing doughs and techniques specifically for pans and Dutch ovens in his magnificent latest....This will be a sure-fire boon for home bread bakers." —*Publishers Weekly*
Includes index.

Lopez-Alt, J. Kenji
The Food Lab. J. Kenji Lopez-Alt. W W Norton & Co. 2015. 958 pages
ISBN 9780393081084
Grades: Adult — 664
1. Food science 2. Cooking, American 3. Cooking 4. Cooks 5. Food writing — Cooking and cookbooks — Narrative cookbooks
LC 2015016358

Collects easy-to-prepare, illustrated recipes for practicing simple, fool-proof techniques, based on the science of cooking, for creating great food, including blanching, defatting stock, emulsions, and knife skills.
"This indispensable kitchen manual, which suggests visualizing heat capacity as a coop full of Red Bull-energized chickens, makes food science accessible." —*Library Journal*

Redzepi, Rene
The Noma Guide to Fermentation: Foundations of Flavor. Renae Redzepi & David Zilber; photographs by Evan Sung; illustrations by Paula Troxler. Artisan 2018. 455 pages : Illustration; Color
ISBN 9781579657185
Grades: Adult — 664
1. Fermentation 2. Flavor 3. Fermented foods 4. Recipes 5. Food writing — Cooking and cookbooks — Chefs and restaurants 6. Food writing — Cooking and cookbooks — Methods
LC 2018003633

Describes how the chefs at the Copenhagen restaurant Noma make the fermented flavorings, based on fermentation traditions from throughout the world, that are basic to the foods they serve, and suggests possible uses for fermented foods.

"Practical applications abound, such as DIY lemon verbena kombucha, whiskey vinegar, and shoyu-buttermilk fried chicken (add shoyu to buttermilk for the marinade). Recipes are clearly written and accompanied by more than 500 photos." —*Publishers Weekly*
Includes index.

Tulleken, Chris van
Ultra-Processed People: The Science Behind the Food That Isn't Food. Chris Van Tulleken. W W Norton & Company 2023. 336 p.
ISBN 9781324036722
Grades: Adult — 664
1. Food 2. Food habits 3. Processed foods 4. Fast foods 5. Obesity 6. Health 7. Food industry and trade 8. Society and culture — General 9. Science Writing — Medicine and health 10. Food Writing — Investigations

Van Tulleken delves into the science and economics of UPF, reframing obesity as a "commerciogenic disease" driven by an unregulated industry and caused by the consumption of knowingly harmful, addictive substances. The book will use evidence to propose real solutions to the current obesity epidemic, both for policy makers and for readers. Threaded throughout is a highly engaging personal account of the author's own confused relationship with UPF as a doctor, parent and sibling.
"This impassioned polemic will make readers think twice about what they eat." —*Publishers Weekly*

Wade, Greg
★ *Bread* Head: Baking for the Road Less Traveled. Greg Wade with Rachel Holtzman; photography by E.E. Berger. W.W. Norton & Company 2022. 335 pages : Color; Illustration
ISBN 9780393866742
Grades: Adult — 664
1. Bread 2. Baking 3. Baked products 4. Cookbooks 5. Food writing — Cooking and cookbooks — Methods
LC 2022010762

At Publican Quality Breads in Chicago, Greg Wade bakes rich, flavorful, naturally leavened breads with local organic flours.[...]Wade, who is largely self-taught, presents a laid-back master class that any home cook can engage with: He explains what happens to your bread on a cellular level as it ferments and bakes, and walks readers through the different grains and the various forms they can take (i.e, cracked, sprouted, whole-grain, coarse-milled), describes their flavors, and sheds light on how they behave and what could be substituted with success."
"In this exceptional guide, Wade calls on his knowledge and good humor to show home bakers how to 'Increase the tools in your toolbox one by one'....This is sure to banish any remnants of sourdough fatigue." —*Publishers Weekly*
Includes index.

Winter, Ruth
A Consumer's Dictionary of Food Additives: Descriptions in Plain English of More Than 12,000 Ingredients Both Harmful and Desirable Found in Foods. Ruth Winter. Three Rivers Press 2009. 595 p.
ISBN 9780307408921
Grades: 11 12 Adult — 664
1. Food additives 2. Science writing — Medicine and health — Diet and nutrition 3. Reference — Dictionaries
LC 2008040601

Supplies consumers with vital information needed to judge the safety of a wide variety of food additives, updating the reference to encompass the more than twelve thousand ingredients in new food products, and offers detailed explanations of food production technologies, safe storage procedures, and the new label regulations.
Includes bibliographical references (p. 593-595).

ESSENTIAL AND RECOMMENDED TITLES
676 Pulp and paper technology

676 Pulp and paper technology

Basbanes, Nicholas A.
On Paper: The Everything of Its Two-Thousand-Year History. Nicholas A. Basbanes. Alfred A. Knopf 2013. 448 p.
ISBN 9780307266422
Grades: Adult **676**
1. Papermaking 2. Paper 3. Paper products 4. Paper industry and trade 5. Paper work 6. History writing — Microhistory
LC 2012050267

ALA Notable Book, 2014; Andrew Carnegie Medal for Excellence in Non-Fiction finalist, 2014.

An award-winning investigative journalist presents a sweeping history of paper that traces its invention in China 1,800 years ago through its myriad applications in business, trade and culture to illuminate paper's crucial role in the unfolding of political scandals, the making of laws and more.

"An unhurried book that will be enjoyed not only by bibliophiles, librarians, and archivists but by many readers engaged by the study of the past and present."
—*Library Journal*

Includes bibliographical references.

Kurlansky, Mark
Paper: Paging Through History. Mark Kurlansky. W W Norton & Co. 2016. 416 p.
ISBN 9780393239614
Grades: Adult **676**
1. Papermaking 2. Paper industry and trade 3. Paper 4. Printing 5. Books and reading 6. Civilization 7. History writing — Microhistory
LC 2016007084

The best-selling author of Cod and Salt presents a history of paper and the unexpected ways it shaped a modern world transitioning toward digital technologies, tracing the role of paper and paper-making in education, media, religion, commerce and art.

"Kurlansky profiles key individuals, from inventors to master printers, writers, artists, and revolutionaries, while incisively parsing technological breakthroughs and social conundrums." —*Booklist*

677 Textiles

Goldsmith, Becky
The Ultimate *Thread Guide: Everything You Need to Know to Choose the Perfect Thread for Every Project*. Becky Goldsmith. C&T Publishing 2019. 64 p. : Illustration; Color
ISBN 9781617458705
Grades: Adult **677**
1. Sewing 2. Arts and Entertainment — Crafts and hobbies — Textiles and needlework

"In addition to explanations about weight and thickness, Goldsmith provides practical guidance on which needles to use with which thread, whether for sewing by hand or with a machine. Her section dedicated to introducing various manufacturers and their particular offerings, meanwhile, will make for a handy shopping tool." —*Publishers Weekly*

Parkes, Clara
The Knitter's *Book of Yarn: The Ultimate Guide to Choosing, Using, and Enjoying Yarn*. by Clara Parkes. Potter Craft 2007. 255 p. : Illustration; Color
ISBN 9780307352163
Grades: Adult **677**
1. Knitting 2. Yarn 3. Arts and Entertainment — Crafts and hobbies — Textiles and needlework
LC 2007009363

A definitive guide to yarn explains how to pair a knitting project with the right type of available yarn, discussing the special characteristics and qualities of each category of yarn, the unique effects it creates, and available substitutions, and includes dozens of creative projects by experienced knitting designers.

Includes bibliographical references (p. 242) and index.

Prasad, Aarathi
Silk: A World History. Aarathi Prasad. William Morrow 2024. 320 p.
ISBN 9780063160255
Grades: Adult **677**
1. Silk 2. History 3. Silkworms 4. Moths 5. Spiders 6. Mollusks 7. Silk industry and trade 8. Textile fabrics 9. Materials science 10. Technological innovations 11. Nature Writing — Animal Studies 12. Science Writing — General 13. History writing — Microhistory
LC 2023046769

In a gorgeous history that spans continents and millennia, Aarathi Prasad weaves together the complex story of the queen of fabrics. Through the scientists who have studied silk, and the biology of the animals from which it has been drawn, Prasad explores the global, natural, and cultural history (and future) of a unique material that has fascinated the world for thousands of years.

"Prasad...offers a microhistory of one of the world's most luxurious fabrics, rooted in worms, crossing cultures and epochs, and dependent on science and secrets." —*Library Journal*

Includes bibliographical references and index.

Robson, Deborah
The Field *Guide to Fleece: 100 Sheep Breeds and How to Use Their Fibers*. Deborah Robson & Carol Ekarius. Storey Publishing 2013. 231 pages : Color; Illustration
ISBN 9781612121789
Grades: Adult **677**
1. Wool 2. Arts and Entertainment — Crafts and hobbies — Textiles and needlework
LC 2013003107

Provides different breeds of sheep and explains the best way to prepare their fleece for spinning, the natural colors of the fleece and how well it dyes, the best use for the wool, and fleece weights, staple lengths, and fiber diameters.

Includes bibliographical references (page 232) and index.

683.4 Small firearms

McWhirter, Cameron
American Gun: The True Story of the AR-15. Cameron McWhirter and Zusha Elinson. Farrar, Straus and Giroux 2023. 496 p.
ISBN 9780374103859
Grades: Adult **683.4**
1. Rifles 2. Assault weapons 3. Gunsmiths 4. Engineers 5. Right to bear arms 6. Violence and guns 7. Mass shootings 8. Gun control 9. Polarization (Social sciences) 10. Gun industry and trade 11. United States 12. Impartial writing 13. History writing — Technological innovations 14. History writing — Military — Weapons 15. Society and culture — Violence and crime 16. Life stories — Science, technology, and medicine — Scientists and inventors
LC 2023008699

In the 1950s, an obsessive firearms designer named Eugene Stoner invented the AR-15 rifle in a California garage. High-minded and patriotic, Stoner sought to devise a lightweight, easy-to-use weapon that could replace the M1s touted by soldiers in World War II. What he did create was a lethal handheld icon of the American century. In American Gun, the veteran Wall Street Journal reporters Cameron McWhirter and Zusha Elinson track the AR-15 from inception to ubiquity. In the 2000s, it would become the weapon of choice for mass shooters, prompting widespread calls for proscription even as the gun industry embraced it as a financial savior.

"Such a highly charged subject deserves a well-written analysis, grounded in facts and presented with journalistic detachment, and McWhirter and Elinson deliver on all counts." —*Booklist*

Includes bibliographical references and index.

PUBLIC LIBRARY CORE COLLECTION: NONFICTION
Twentieth Edition

684 Furnishings and home workshops

Barn the Spoon
Woodcraft: Master the Art of Green Woodworking with Key Techniques and Inspiring Projects. Barn the Spoon. DK Publishing 2019. 256 pages : Illustration; Color
ISBN 9781465479785
Grades: Adult   **684**
1. Wood-carving 2. Woodworking 3. Arts and Entertainment — Crafts and hobbies — Woodworking
LC 2019285189
Explores the craft of green woodworking and offers instructions on different green woodworking projects, including a bangle, frame stool, and shaving horse.
"Barn the Spoon—aka Barnaby Carder, a London-based woodworker known for his spoon-carving workshops—uses incredible mastery and a touch of humor to instruct readers in the art of green woodcraft, with smart, calculated lessons that lead up to the from-scratch creation of a captains chair." —*Booklist*
Includes index.

Christiana, Asa
Build Stuff with Wood: Make Awesome Projects with Basic Tools. Asa Christiana; foreword by Nick Offerman. Taunton Press, Inc. 2017. 202 pages : Color; Illustration
ISBN 9781631867118
Grades: Adult   **684**
1. Woodworking 2. Arts and Entertainment — Crafts and hobbies — Woodworking
LC 2017007163
Provides instructions for creating useful items from wood using only a few portable power tools, including an outdoor bench, postmodern coffee table, floating shelves, and hanging lamp.
"This solid, basic primer wonderfully reflects straightforward instruction with some very desirable projects." —*Library Journal*

Horwood, Roger
Woodworker's Handbook: The Beginner's Reference to Tools, Materials, and Skills, Plus Essential Projects to Make. Roger Horwood. Fox Chapel Publishing 2019. 168 pages : Color; Illustration
ISBN 9781497100657
Grades: Adult   **684**
1. Woodworking 2. Handicraft 3. Do-it-yourself work 4. Reference books — Handbooks, manuals, etc. 5. Arts and Entertainment — Crafts and hobbies — Woodworking
The complete reference handbook for DIY home woodworking, this is an absolute must-have guide for beginners and even experienced craftsmen. Every tool you'll need is laid out with guidance on safety measures, care instructions, and how and when to use it, from gauges and shaping tools to clamps, drills, and more. Every technique you'll use is described and detailed, from constructing to finishing. You'll know what type of woods to use for certain projects, how they cut, and their durability. After learning the crucial fundamentals of woodworking, you'll complete 5 step-by-step projects that are beautiful and useful items for everyday use, ranging from a dining room table to a bedside cabinet. Concise and practical, and useful even for experienced woodworkers, Woodworker's Handbook will help you practice and improve your skills—and learn new ones!
Includes index.

684.1 Furniture

Blair, Barb
Furniture Makeovers: Simple Techniques for Transforming Furniture with Paint, Stains, Paper, Stencils, and More. Barb Blair; photographs by J. Aaron Greene; foreword by Holly Becker. Chronicle Books 2013. 190 p. : Color illustration
ISBN 9781452104157
Grades: Adult   **684.1**
1. Furniture finishing 2. Painting 3. House and Home — Interior Decorating and Furnishings
LC Bl2013015035
Offers simple techniques to transforming drab furniture into showpieces, including easy-to-follow instructions for spray painting, applying gold leaf, wall papering, stenciling, and dip dyeing.
Includes index.

Hingley, Brian D.
Furniture Repair & Restoration. Brian D. Hingley. Creative Homeowner 2010. 175 p. : Color illustration
ISBN 9781580114783
Grades: Adult   **684.1**
1. Furniture 2. Furniture finishing 3. Arts and Entertainment — Crafts and hobbies
LC Bl2010012453
Presents a guide to repairing antique wooden furniture, and information on the tools, supplies, and equipment needed for each situation.
"With special sections on evaluation and repair of structural issues, this volume features an array of valuable information on furniture repair and refinishing. Geared toward beginners in wood restoration, the book highlights the author's professional experience, which shows through in the advice and thorough directions." —*Library Journal*
Green ed; Includes index.

Pourny, Christophe
★ *The Furniture* Bible. Christophe Pourny with Jen Renzi; foreword by Martha Stewart; photographs by James Wade; illustrations by Christophe Pourny. Artisan 2014. 304 pages : Illustration; Color
ISBN 9781579655358
Grades: Adult   **684.1**
1. Furniture finishing 2. Restoration 3. Furniture 4. Furniture industry and trade 5. Arts and Entertainment — Antiques and collectibles 6. Arts and Entertainment — Crafts and hobbies — Woodworking 7. House and Home — DIY, maintenance, and repair
LC 2014004628
A comprehensive guide to restoring, preserving and refinishing furniture draws on the author's experience as the son of a French atelier to outline such step-by-step techniques as ceruse, vernis anglais and water gilding.
A comprehensive guide to restoring, preserving, and refinishing furniture draws on the author's experience as the son of a French atelier to outline such step-by-step techniques as ceruse, vernis anglais, and water gilding.
"Pourny explains how to assess damage, make repairs, and complete a final finish. A strong section on furniture care and cleaning argues that using the right methods will prolong the life of furniture. This guide will find a wide audience among those who simply want to learn about and appreciate good furniture, as well as those who are more hands-on." —*Publishers Weekly*
Includes bibliographical references (pages 298-299) and index.

686 Printing and related activities

Lee, Marshall
Bookmaking: Editing, Design, Production. Marshall Lee; technical consultant Joseph Gannon. Norton 2004. 494 p. : Illustration
ISBN 9780393730180
Grades: Adult   **686**
1. Books 2. Book design 3. Editing 4. Arts and Entertainment — Writing and publishing
LC 2003059672
Updated to reflect changes in the bookmaking process and in publishing practices, covers all processes from preparation of a manuscript to both print and electronic distribution.
A Balance House book; Includes bibliographical references and index.

ESSENTIAL AND RECOMMENDED TITLES
686.2 Printing

Rivers, Charlotte
Little Book of Book Making: Timeless Techniques and Fresh Ideas for Beautiful Handmade Books. Charlotte Rivers. Potter Craft 2014. 192 pages : Illustration
ISBN 9780770435141
Grades: Adult   **686**
1. Book design 2. Bookbinding 3. Artists' books 4. Arts and Entertainment — Crafts and hobbies
LC 2013044724

Making books by hand has never been cooler, with this inspiring guide to 30 top bookmakers working today, plus 21 tutorials for essential techniques to make your own books. Crafters, artists, writers, and book lovers can't resist a beautifully handbound book. Packed with wonderfully eclectic examples, this book explores the intriguing creative possibilities of bookmaking as a modern art form, including a wide range of bindings, materials, and embellishments. Featured techniques include everything from Coptic to concertina binding, as well as experimental page treatments such as sumi-e ink marbling and wheat paste. In addition to page after page of inspiration from leading contemporary binderies, Little Book of Bookmaking includes a practical section of 21 easy-to-follow illustrated tutorials.

686.2 Printing

Smyth, Adam
The ***Book-makers:*** A History of the Book in Eighteen Lives. Adam Smyth. Basic Books 2024. 400 p.
ISBN 9781541605640
Grades: Adult   **686.2**
1. Books 2. Bookbinding 3. Bookbinders 4. Book industry and trade 5. Printing industry and trade 6. Culture 7. Europe 8. Arts and Entertainment — Writing and publishing 9. History Writing — Europe 10. Life stories — Arts and culture

Through profiles of 18 individuals who defined Western culture's most important object, this 500-year-old history of printed books celebrates those who first experimented in the art of printing, design and binding, changing the course of history.

"This lively and enlightening history of books and the people who made them is packed with fascinating people and facts and buttressed by a flood of informative illustrations scattered across the text and in folio." —*Library Journal*

688.7 Recreational equipment

Whitelaw, Ian
The ***History*** of Fly-Fishing in Fifty Flies. Ian Whitelaw; illustrations by Julie Spyropoulos. Stewart, Tabori & Chang 2015. 223 p. : Illustration; Color
ISBN 9781617691461
Grades: Adult   **688.7**
1. Flies, Artificial 2. Fly fishing 3. Sports and Competition — Fishing
LC Bl2015015009

Focuses on fifty flies chosen to represent the evolution of fly fishing, including the green drake, prince nymph, and bionic bug.
Includes bibliographical references (pages 218-219) and index.

690 Construction of buildings

Cory, Steve
Ultimate Guide: Porches : Building Techniques for Adding a New Porch to Your Home. Steve Cory. Creative Homeowner 2011. 191 p. : Illustration; Color (Creative Homeowner Ultimate Guide to…)
ISBN 9781580114912
Grades: Adult   **690**
1. Porches 2. House and Home — Outdoor areas
LC Bl2011035873

Describes the process of building a porch, covering such topics as design features, tools, materials, roofs, and elaborate porch styles.

"In this manual, the author shares numerous, clear illustrations and detailed construction information and techniques. His confident, expert instruction . Is apparent in the projects presented here. A solid addition to any home improvement collection." —*Library Journal*

At head of title: Creative homeowner; Includes index.

Thorstensen, Ole
Making Things Right: The Simple Philosophy of a Working Life. Ole Thorstensen; translated from the Norwegian by Seán Kinsella. Penguinbooks, an imprint of Penguin Random House 2018. 240 p.
ISBN 9780143130949
Grades: Adult   **690**
1. Thorstensen, Ole 2. Houses 3. Carpenters 4. Building 5. Work ethic 6. Small business 7. Work 8. Design and construction 9. Philosophy 10. Translations — Norwegian to English 11. Arts and Entertainment — Architecture
LC 2017058279

A carpenter and contractor, in this ode to manual labor, reflects on the philosophical aspects of life and work while renovating a loft, writing passionately about his profession and of the joy of seeing a vision for a space take shape.

Originally published in 2015 as En snekkers dagbok by Pelikanen Forlag.

Toht, David
★ ***Stanley*** Decks: A Homeowner's Guide. David Toht. The Taunton Press, Inc. 2017. 234 p.
ISBN 9781631864506
Grades: Adult   **690**
1. House and Home — DIY, maintenance, and repair 2. House and Home — General 3. House and Home — Outdoor areas
LC 2016037011

Offers step-by-step guidance on how to build a deck, including choosing materials, installing footings and ledgers, framing, and building stairs and railings.
Includes index.

700 The arts

Cumming, Robert
Art: A Visual History. Robert Cumming. DK Publishing 2015. 416 pages : Color; Illustration
ISBN 9781465436610
Grades: Adult   **700**
1. Art 2. History writing — Arts and culture 3. Reference books — Handbooks, manuals, etc.
LC 2015473824

A chronological book features information on the history of more than 650 artists, as well as details on the major schools and movements of the art world, from Ancient Greece to Pop Art, as well as an extended, detailed focus on 22 masterpieces.

Presents a visual guide to the history of art from ancient times to the modern day, discussing major artists, their key works, and significant themes and styles.

"With its solid, accessible information and hundreds of excellent, full-color reproductions, this is ideal for high school or college students as well as any art lover or museumgoer." —*Library Journal*

Includes index.

Fox, Dan
Pretentiousness: Why It Matters. Dan Fox. Coffee House Press 2016. 140 p.
ISBN 9781566894289
Grades: Adult   **700**
1. Performance 2. Authenticity (Philosophy) 3. Creation (Literary, artistic, etc.) 4. Creativity 5. Society and culture — Pop culture
LC 2015033491

New York Times Notable Book, 2016.

PUBLIC LIBRARY CORE COLLECTION: NONFICTION
Twentieth Edition

Pretentiousness is for anyone who has braved being different, whether that's making a stand against artistic consensus or running the gauntlet of the last bus home dressed differently from everyone else. It's an essential ingredient in pop music and high art. Why do we choose accusations of elitism over open-mindedness? What do our anxieties about "pretending" say about us? Co-editor of Frieze, Europe's foremost magazine of contemporary art and culture, Dan Fox has authored over two hundred essays, interviews, and reviews, contributed to numerous catalogues and publications produced by major international art galleries and institutions.

"His book stands as a convincing philosophical investigation into a wide-ranging concept that governs much of the way people behave."—*Publishers Weekly*

Updike, John
Always Looking: Essays on Art. by John Updike; edited by Christopher Carduff. Alfred A. Knopf 2012. xiii, 204 pages : Illustration
ISBN 9780307957306
Grades: Adult   700
1. Art, American 2. Art criticism 3. Art appreciation 4. Artists 5. Visual perception 6. Communication in art 7. Psychology 8. Social life and customs 9. United States 10. 20th century 11. Essays 12. Arts and Entertainment — Painting, Drawing, and Sculpture
LC 2012005986

A posthumous anthology of the author's art writings includes his 2008 lecture "The Clarity of Things" as well as fourteen essays on Western art and the characterization of American art.
Includes index.

700.1 Philosophy and theory of the arts

Dederer, Claire
★ *Monsters: A Fan's Dilemma.* Claire Dederer. Alfred A. Knopf 2023. 256 p.
ISBN 9780525655114
Grades: Adult   700.1
1. Arts 2. Personal conduct 3. Art 4. Ethics 5. Artists 6. Genius 7. Social ethics 8. Character 9. Celebrities 10. Arts and Entertainment — General 11. Society and culture — General
LC 2022032926

Los Angeles Times Book Prizes, Christopher Isherwood Prize for Autobiographical Prose, 2023.

Exploring the audience's relationship with artists from Woody Allen to Michael Jackson, a New York Times bestselling author, book critic, essayist and reporter, in this candid, deeply personal book, discusses whether and how we can separate artists from their art.

"By turns emotional and measured, this is a valuable meditation on some of the era's most urgent cultural questions." —*Library Journal*

A Borzoi book; Includes bibliographical references.

James, Jamie
The Glamour of Strangeness: Artists and the Last Age of the Exotic. Jamie James. Farrar, Straus & Giroux 2016. xii, 364 p.
ISBN 9780374163358
Grades: Adult   700.1
1. Artists 2. Expatriates 3. Immigrants 4. Art history 5. Voyages and travels 6. Arts and Entertainment — Painting, Drawing, and Sculpture

Exploration of a "rare, emotionally intense way of life" in which artists like Raden Saleh and Walter Spies abandon the cultures that created them and adopt an exotic alternative.

"Abundant primary sources inform James' sharply drawn, sympathetic portraits." —*Kirkus*

Includes bibliographical references (pages 325-341) and index.

Laing, Olivia
★ *The Lonely City: Adventures in the Art of Being Alone.* Olivia Laing. Picador 2016. 352 p.
ISBN 9781250039576
Grades: Adult   700.1
1. Laing, Olivia 2. Loneliness 3. Artists 4. City life 5. Loners 6. City dwellers 7. Social isolation 8. Art and society 9. Psychology 10. Autobiographies and memoirs 11. Life stories — Arts and culture 12. Arts and entertainment — General
LC 2015037147

What does it mean to be lonely? How do we live, if we're not intimately involved with another human being? How do we connect with other people, particularly if our sexuality or physical body is considered deviant or damaged? Does technology draw us closer together or trap us behind screens? Olivia Laing explores these questions by travelling deep into the work and lives of some of the century's most original artists, among them Andy Warhol, David Wojnarowicz, Edward Hopper, Henry Darger and Klaus Nomi. Part memoir, part biography, part dazzling work of cultural criticism, the Lonely City is not just a map, but a celebration of the state of loneliness.

"Laing's writing becomes expansive, exploring their biographies, sharing art analysis, and weaving in observations from periods of desolation that was at times "cold as ice and clear as glass."" —*Publishers Weekly*

Larson, Kay
Where the Heart Beats: John Cage, Zen Buddhism, and the Inner Life of Artists. Kay Larson. Penguin Press 2012. 384 p.
ISBN 9781594203404
Grades: Adult   700.1
1. Cage, John, 1912-1992 2. Postmodernism 3. Zen Buddhism 4. Composers 5. United States 6. Biographies 7. Arts and Entertainment — Music 8. Life stories — Arts and culture — Performing arts — Musicians and composers 9. Spirituality and Religion — Buddhism
LC 2011044714

A first book by a Zen Buddhist practitioner and leading art critic assesses the influence of Zen Buddhism on the work of composer John Cage, exploring the ways in which Zen transformed Cage's troubled psyche, his relationship with partner Merce Cunningham and his often indefinable music.
Includes bibliographical references and index.

Wu, Simon
Dancing on My Own: Essays on Art, Collectivity, and Joy. Simon Wu. Harper 2024. 256 p.
ISBN 9780063316201
Grades: Adult   700.1
1. Wu, Simon (Curator) 2. Identity 3. Art and society 4. Self-discovery 5. Fashion 6. Art 7. Social classes 8. Self 9. Happiness 10. Families 11. Essays 12. History writing — Arts and culture 13. Life stories — Identity 14. Arts and Entertainment — General 15. Life stories — Relationships — Growing up
LC 2023044132

An art critic, curator and writer presents a series of personal essays that explores class aspiration, the complexities of creating fashion and art and adopting a joyful approach to identity and the journey of self-discovery.

"This dynamic first outing heralds the arrival of a promising new talent." —*Publishers Weekly*

Includes bibliographical references.

700.89 Arts — Ethnic and national groups

Otfinoski, Steven
Latinos in the Arts. Steven Otfinoski. Facts on File 2007. x, 277 p. : Illustration
ISBN 9780816063949
Grades: Adult   700.89

ESSENTIAL AND RECOMMENDED TITLES
700.9 Arts — History, geographic treatment, biography

1. Hispanic Americans 2. 21st century 3. History writing — Latin America 4. Life stories — Arts and culture 5. Life stories — Arts and culture — Performing arts

LC 2006016900

Each volume in this invaluable resource contains more than 150 biographical profiles of Latinos who have influenced and continue to impact the Latino community, the United States, and the world in a variety of fields and professions.

Presents biographical profiles of Latino artists who have influenced and continue to impact the Latino community, the United States, and the world.

Includes bibliographical references (p. 247-248) and index.

700.9 Arts — History, geographic treatment, biography

Schloss, Edith
The Loft Generation: From the De Koonings to Twombly: Portraits and Sketches, 1942-2011. Edith Schloss; edited by Mary Venturini. Farrar, Straus & Giroux 2021. 320 p.

ISBN 9780374190088

Grades: Adult   **700.9**

1. Schloss, Edith, 1919-2011 2. Art and society 3. Women artists 4. Artists 5. Art critics 6. Intellectuals 7. Friendship 8. Abstract expressionism 9. Postwar life 10. 20th century 11. Life stories — Arts and culture — Artists 12. History writing — Arts and culture

LC 2021025297

The Loft Generation: From the de Koonings to Twombly is a firsthand account by an artist at the center of a landmark era in American art. Edith Schloss writes about the artists, poets, and musicians who were part of the postwar art movements in America and about her life as an artist in America and later in Italy, where she continued to paint and write until her death in 2011. Schloss was born in Germany and moved to New York City during World War II. She became part of a thriving community of artists and intellectuals, from Elaine and Willem de Kooning and Larry Rivers to John Cage and Frank O'Hara. She was both a working artist and an incisive art critic, and was a candid and gimlet-eyed observer of the close-knit community that was redefining American art.

"Rich in granular detail and rendered in eloquent and captivating prose, this is an intimate look at a pivotal era in its formative stages and offers an invaluable source for the study of one of the great art movements." —*Publishers Weekly*

700.92 Arts — Biography

Smee, Sebastian
The Art of Rivalry: Four Friendships, Betrayals, and Breakthroughs in Modern Art. Sebastian Smee. Random House 2016. 256 p.

ISBN 9780812994803

Grades: Adult   **700.92**

1. Picasso, Pablo, 1881-1973 2. Matisse, Henri, 1869-1954 3. Manet, Edouard, 1832-1883 4. Degas, Edgar, 1834-1917 5. Pollock, Jackson, 1912-1956 6. De Kooning, Willem, 1904-1997 7. Freud, Lucian 8. Bacon, Francis, 1909-1992 9. Artists 10. Modern art 11. Friendship 12. Creation (Literary, artistic, etc.) 13. Psychology 14. Australian literature 15. Biographies 16. Arts and Entertainment — Painting, Drawing, and Sculpture 17. Life stories — Arts and culture — Artists 18. Life stories — Relationships — Friendship 19. Family and Relationships — Friendship

LC 2015050361

Traces the stories of four pairs of artists whose relationships shaped and spurred their achievements and the cultural world, profiling the psychologically tense relationships of Picasso and Matisse, Manet and Degas, Pollack and de Kooning, and Lucian Freud and Francis Bacon.

"This ambitious and impressive work is an utterly absorbing read about four important relationships in modern art." —*Publishers Weekly*

Includes index; Includes bibliographical references.

701 Philosophy and theory of fine and decorative arts

Bosker, Bianca
Get the Picture: A Mind-Bending Journey Among the Inspired Artists and Obsessive Art Fiends Who Taught Me How to See. Bianca Bosker. Viking 2024. 384 p.

ISBN 9780525562207

Grades: Adult   **701**

1. Bosker, Bianca 2. Art 3. Obsession 4. Women journalists 5. Artists 6. Art collectors and collecting 7. Elite (Social sciences) 8. Art museums 9. Art galleries, Commercial 10. Creation (Literary, artistic, etc.) 11. Art and society 12. Art appreciation 13. Arts and Entertainment — Painting, Drawing, and Sculpture 14. Arts and Entertainment — General 15. Life stories — Arts and culture

LC 2023049037

Bianca Bosker's existence was upended when she wandered into the art world—and couldn't look away. Intrigued by artists who hyperventilate around their favorite colors and art fiends who max out credit cards to show hunks of metal they think can change the world, Bosker grew fixated on understanding why art matters and how she—or any of us—could engage with it more deeply. In Get the Picture, Bosker throws herself into the nerve center of art and the people who live for it: gallerists, collectors, curators, and, of course, artists themselves—to discover the inner workings of the art-canonization machine.

"Connoisseurs and neophytes alike will be charmed and captivated by Bosker's boundless curiosity and astute powers of observation." —*Publishers Weekly*

Includes bibliographical references and index.

Moss, Adam
★ *The Work of Art: How Something Comes from Nothing.* Adam Moss. Penguin 2024. 432 p.

ISBN 9780593297582

Grades: Adult   **701**

1. Art 2. Artists 3. Authors 4. Musicians 5. Poets 6. Creation (Literary, artistic, etc.) 7. Creativity 8. Inspiration 9. Psychology 10. Work 11. Patience 12. Arts and entertainment — General 13. Life stories — Arts and culture

LC 2023038445

From former editor-in-chief of New York magazine Adam Moss, a collection of illuminating conversations examining the very personal, rigorous, complex, and elusive work of making art. What is the work of art? In this guided tour inside the artist's head, Adam Moss traces the evolution of transcendent novels, paintings, jokes, movies, songs, and more. Weaving conversations with some of the most accomplished artists of our time together with the journal entries, napkin doodles, and sketches that were their tools, Moss breaks down the work—the tortuous paths and artistic decisions—that led to great art.

"A panoply of artists offer a rare peek into the mysteries and mundanities of the creative process in this captivating compendium…It's a must-read for creatives of all stripes." —*Publishers Weekly*

Shnayerson, Michael
Boom: Mad Money, Mega Dealers, and the Rise of Contemporary Art. Michael Shnayerson. PublicAffairs 2019. 272 p.

ISBN 9781610398404

Grades: Adult   **701**

1. Art collectors and collecting 2. Modern art 3. Art 4. Art and society 5. Art galleries, Commercial 6. Art dealers 7. Art as an investment 8. Marketing 9. Arts and Entertainment — Painting, Drawing, and Sculpture

LC 2018044679

A Vanity Fair editor discusses the explosive growth of the market for modern art and how it has created the largest unregulated financial market in the world through interviews with renowned art dealers such as Larry Gagosian and David Zwirner.

"Focusing on personalities as much as business development, Shnayersons writing is conversational and accessible, even for those without deep art knowledge. Fast-paced and eye-opening, this is a wildly entertaining business history." —*Publishers Weekly*

Includes bibliographical references and index.

702 Miscellany of fine and decorative arts

Congdon, Lisa

Art Inc.: The Essential Guide for Building Your Career as an Artist. Lisa Congdon; edited by Meg Mateo Ilasco; foreword by Jonathan Fields. Chronicle Books 2014. 184 pages : Color; Illustration

ISBN 9781452128269

Grades: Adult   702

1. Artists 2. Art 3. Vocational guidance 4. Reference — Vocational guidance

LC Bl2014034127

Presents advice for aspiring artists on the best ways to manage their career, discussing the use of social media for promotion, signing with a gallery, preparing for exhibitions, and pricing and selling artwork.

"A useful resource for young adults, emerging artists, and creative people of all ages who seek a career change." —*Library Journal*

Includes index.

702.8 Auxiliary techniques and procedures; apparatus, equipment, materials

Amore, Anthony M.

The Art of the Con: The Most Notorious Fakes, Frauds, and Forgeries in the Art World. Anthony M. Amore. Palgrave Macmillan Trade 2015. 272 p.

ISBN 9781137279873

Grades: Adult   702.8

1. Art forgeries 2. Art thefts 3. Swindlers and swindling 4. True Crime — Heists and Robbery 5. Arts and Entertainment — Painting, Drawing, and Sculpture

LC 2014046676

Art scams are today so numerous that the specter of a lawsuit arising from a mistaken attribution has scared a number of experts away from the business of authentication, and with good reason. Art scams are increasingly convincing and involve incredible sums of money. The cons perpetrated by unscrupulous art dealers and their accomplices are proportionately elaborate. The Art of the Con tells the stories of some of history's most notorious yet untold cons. They involve stolen art hidden for decades; elaborate ruses that involve the Nazis and allegedly plundered art; the theft of a conceptual prototype from a well-known artist by his assistant to be used later to create copies; the use of online and television auction sites to scam buyers out of millions; and other confidence scams incredible not only for their boldness but more so because they actually worked. Using interviews and newly released court documents, The Art of the Con will also take the reader into the investigations that led to the capture of the con men, who oftentimes return back to the world of crime.

"Of significant interest to art world aficionados, brokers, collectors, dealers, lawyers, professionals, and general readers, this ambitious, well-presented and well-documented survey belongs in public as well as academic and special libraries." —*Library Journal*

704 Special topics in fine and decorative arts

Farrington, Lisa E.

Creating Their Own Image: The History of African-American Women Artists. Lisa E. Farrington. Oxford University Press 2005. 354 p. : Illustration; Color

ISBN 9780195167214

Grades: 11 12 Adult   704

1. African American art 2. African American women artists 3. Arts and Entertainment — General 4. History writing — African American — United States

LC 2003066171

An expansive collection of artists, styles, and periods are woven together into a survey that demonstrates how African-American women artists have created an alternative vision of how women of color can, are, and might be presented in American culture.

"A richly detailed yet fluent work of trailblazing research, fresh interpretations, and cogent argument, Farrington's treatise discusses vital aesthetic as well as social and cultural issues and creates a vibrant context for such seminal artists as Augusta Savage, Faith Ringgold, Barbara Chase-Riboud, Kara Walker, and many more." —*Booklist*

Holladay, Wilhelmina Cole

A Museum of Their Own: National Museum of Women in the Arts. Wilhelmina Cole Holladay; text contributions by Philip Kopper. Abbeville Press 2008. 240 p. : Illustration; Color

ISBN 9780789210036

Grades: Adult   704

1. Holladay, Wilhelmina Cole, 1922-2021 2. Women artists 3. Museums 4. Art history 5. Washington (D.C.) 6. Arts and Entertainment — Museums and Collections

LC 2008021646

Until quite recently, the work of great women artists was ignored, forgotten, or denied; they were largely left out of museums and histories of art. Along came Wilhelmina Cole Holladay, who boldly rectified this oversight in 1981, by founding a museum that was initially housed in her residence, where docent-led tours of the collection were offered." "This thrilling account of the birth and early years of NMWA provides a lively, anecdotal, behind-the-scenes glimpse of the efforts of the countless dedicated individuals who have shared Mrs. Holladay's vision and, under her leadership, helped to expand the permanent collection, renovate the Museum, and fund a robust endowment. Today, NMWA boasts a sizable membership—among the ten largest museum memberships in the world—including twenty-nine active committees in states across the nation and in eight countries. Among the major exhibitions presented at the Museum have been retrospectives of important women artists—Lavinia Fontana, Berthe Morisot, CamilleClaudel, Lilla Cabot Perry, and Carrie Mae Weems." "Illustrating this captivating memoir are nearly 200 pictures, most in full color, including artworks, archival photographs, and candid images of the landmark events that led to the Museum's impressive growth. An additional feature is a color portfolio of "Selected Gifts and Promised Gifts of Wallace and Wilhelmina Holladay to the Museum." the remarkable story of NMWA, told through the eyes of its founder, is a priceless legacy for women today and for future generations." "Wilhelmina Cole Holladay, the founder and chair of the board of the National Museum of Women in the Arts.

"The National Museum of Women in the Arts . opened in 1987. It changed the status of women artists and the life of its founder, who now tells the museum's fascinating success story in an entertainingly anecdotal, inspiring, and beautifully illustrated [book]. This invaluable work of art history is enlivened by Holladay's encounters with artists . and gorgeous reproductions, many of works that will be new to even the most art-expert readers." —*Booklist*

Includes index.

704.03 Ethnic and national groups

Berlo, Janet Catherine

★ *Native North American Art.* Janet Catherine Berlo, University of Rochester, Ruth B. Phillips, Carleton University. Oxford University Press 2015. xxix, 410 p. : Illustration; Map

ISBN 9780199947546

Grades: Adult   704.03

1. Art, Indigenous 2. Antiquities 3. North America 4. Arts and Entertainment — Painting, Drawing, and Sculpture 5. History writing — Arts and culture

LC 2014004553

This lively introductory survey of indigenous North American arts from ancient times to the present explores both the shared themes and imagery found across the continent and the distinctive traditions of each region. Focusing on the richness of artwork created in the US and Canada, Native North American Art, Second Edition, discusses 3,000 years of architecture, wood and rock carvings, basketry, dance masks, clothing and more.

Includes bibliographical references (pages 353-392) and index.

ESSENTIAL AND RECOMMENDED TITLES
704.9 Iconography

Patton, Sharon F.
African-American Art. Sharon F. Patton. Oxford University Press 1998. 319 p. : Illustration; Color
ISBN 9780192842138
Grades: Adult   704.03
1. African American art 2. History writing — Arts and culture
LC 98190459

Discusses African American folk art, decorative art, photography, and fine arts.
Includes bibliographical references (p. 274-299) and index.

Stanislaus, Grace C.
Instill & Inspire: The John & Vivian Hewitt Collection of African-American Art. Text by Grace C. Stanislaus. University of Pittsburgh Press 2017. xiv, 152 pages : Illustration
ISBN 9780822945048
Grades: Adult   704.03
1. Hewitt, John H, 1924-2000 2. Hewitt, Vivian D. 3. African American art 4. Art 5. Arts and Entertainment — Painting, Drawing, and Sculpture 6. Arts and Entertainment — Museums and Collections
LC 2017014500

The John and Vivian Hewitt Collection of African-American Art represents works that celebrate the expression and passion of twenty artists, including Romare Bearden, Margaret Burroughs, Jonathan Green, Jacob Lawrence, Elizabeth Catlett, Ann Tanksley, and Henry Ossawa Tanner. This book contains all fifty-eight works from the collection, exquisitely reproduced in full color. Grace C. Stanislaus provides a text on the significance of the collection that is supplemented by interviews with Vivian Hewitt, David Taylor of the Gantt Center, art collectors Harmon and Harriett Kelley, and Nancy Washington.

704.9 Iconography

Beard, Mary
★ *How Do We Look: The Body, the Divine, and the Question of Civilization.* Mary Beard. W. W. Norton 2018. 240 pages : Illustration
ISBN 9781631494406
Grades: Adult   704.9
1. Art and religion 2. Civilization, Ancient 3. Religious art and symbolism 4. Sculpture 5. Architecture 6. Calligraphy 7. Islam and art 8. Christianity and art 9. Olmecs (Mexican people) 10. Ancient art 11. Art 12. Antiquities 13. Central America 14. Ancient Egypt 15. Ancient Greece 16. Arts and Entertainment — Painting, Drawing, and Sculpture 17. Spirituality and Religion — General 18. History writing — Ancient
LC 2018027575

From prehistoric Mexico to modern Istanbul, Mary Beard looks beyond the familiar canon of Western imagery to explore the history of art, religion, and humanity.
"Recommended for fans of this popular author, the Civilizations program, and those looking for brief foray into an alternative form of art appreciation." —*Library Journal*

Betts, Reginald Dwayne
★ *Redaction.* Titus Kaphar, Reginald Dwayne Betts. W.W. Norton & Company 2023. 160 p.
ISBN 9781324006824
Grades: Adult   704.9
1. Prisoners 2. Imprisonment 3. Legal documents 4. Criminal justice system 5. Mass incarceration 6. African Americans 7. Injustice 8. United States history 9. Poetry 10. Society and culture — Violence and crime — Criminal justice system
LC 2022019927

MacArthur fellows Reginald Dwayne Betts and Titus Kaphar present a stunning literary and artistic collaboration that confronts the abuses of the criminal justice system. In Redaction, they unite their different mediums to expose the ways the legal system exploitsand erases the poor and incarcerated from public consciousness. First exhibited at MoMA PS1, the fifty "Redaction" prints layer Kaphar's etched portraits of incarcerated individuals with Betts's poetry, which uses the legal strategy of redaction to craft verse out of legal documents. This volume also includes additional artwork, poetry, and an introduction by MoMA associate director Sarah Suzuki.
"The result is a brilliant and original condemnation of racial injustice." —*Publishers Weekly*

Hall, James
The Self-Portrait: A Cultural History : 120 Illustrations, 109 in Color. James Hall. Thames & Hudson 2014. 288 pages : Illustration; Color
ISBN 9780500239100
Grades: Adult   704.9
1. Art appreciation 2. Artists 3. Self-portraits 4. Arts and Entertainment — Painting, Drawing, and Sculpture
LC Bl2014017378

From the earliest myths of Narcissus to the prolific self-image-making of today, this all-encompassing cultural history of self-portraiture, filled with beautiful illustrations, offers insights into artists' personal, psychological and creative worlds.
From the earliest myths of Narcissus to the prolific self-image-making of today, this cultural history of self-portraiture, filled with illustrations, offers insights into artists' personal, psychological, and creative worlds.
Includes bibliographical references and index.

707.5 Art — Collecting

Obrist, Hans-Ulrich
Ways of Curating. Hans Ulrich Obrist with Asad Reza. Faber & Faber 2014. 176 p.
ISBN 9780865478190
Grades: Adult   707.5
1. Obrist, Hans-Ulrich 2. Art museums 3. Art curators 4. Museum curators 5. Museums 6. Autobiographies and memoirs 7. Arts and Entertainment — Painting, Drawing, and Sculpture 8. Arts and Entertainment — Museums and Collections 9. Life stories — Arts and culture
LC 2014016970

The world's most influential contemporary-art curator explores the history and practice of his craft.
"An essential title for museum professionals, curators, and students aspiring to these professions." —*Library Journal*

709 Arts — History, geographic treatment, biography

Boardman, John
★ *Greek Art.* John Boardman. Thames & Hudson 2016. 320 pages : Illustration; Color
ISBN 9780500204337
Grades: Adult   709
1. Art, Greek 2. History writing — Arts and culture
LC 2016933412

"This is a classic in the field made even more readable and useful than before. Highly recommended for all collections." —*Library Journal*
Includes bibliographical references (pages 314-316) and index.

Dasal, Jennifer
Artcurious: Stories of the Unexpected, Slightly Odd, and Strangely Wonderful in Art History. Jennifer Dasal. Penguin Books 2020. 256 p.
ISBN 9780143134596
Grades: Adult   709
1. Art history 2. Art 3. Art and society 4. Artists 5. Curiosities and wonders 6. Media tie-ins 7. Arts and Entertainment — Painting, Drawing, and Sculpture 8. History writing — Arts and culture
LC 2020013857

From the host of the ArtCurious podcast, this book looks at the world of art history, revealing some of the strangest, funniest, and most fascinating stories behind the world's great artists and masterpieces. It demonstrates why art history is, and continues to be, a riveting and relevant world to explore.

"Both art aficionados and novices will find something to appreciate in this offbeat and informative outing." —*Publishers Weekly*

Based on a podcast; Includes bibliographical references and index.

Dickerman, Leah
Dada: Zurich, Berlin, Hannover, Cologne, New York, Paris. Leah Dickerman; with essays by Brigid Doherty ... [et al.]. National Gallery of Art in association with D.A.P. 2005. xv, 519 p. : Illustration; Color
ISBN 9781933045207
Grades: Adult   709
1. Dadaism 2. 20th century 3. History writing — Arts and culture 4. Arts and Entertainment — Museums and Collections
LC 2005017984

"Seven scholars and curators contribute essays that examine each of the various Dada centers in turn. Each essay examines key locations (e.g., the Cabaret Voltaire), individuals, publications (including Merz magazine), and inventions (such as ready-mades and photomontage.) . Its comprehensive scholarship and color illustrations of many rarely seen works make this book essential for all art collections." —*Choice*

Catalog of an exhibition held at the Musee national d'art moderne, Centre Pompidou, Paris, Oct. 5, 2005-Jan. 9, 2006; at the National Gallery of Art, Washington, Feb. 19-May 14, 2006; and at the Museum of Modern Art, New York, June 18-Sept. 11, 2006; Includes bibliographical references (p. 490-503) and index.

Gombrich, E. H.
★ *The Story of Art.* E.H. Gombrich. Prentice-Hall 1995. 688 p. : Illustration; Color; Map
ISBN 9780134401997
Grades: Adult   709
1. Art history 2. Arts and Entertainment — General 3. History writing — Arts and culture
LC 96140698

An illustrated introduction to art appreciation with a survey of the major art periods and styles and descriptions of the work and world of the masters.
Includes bibliographical references (p. 646-654) and index.

Gompertz, Will
What Are You Looking At?: The Surprising, Shocking, and Sometimes Strange Story of One Hundred Years of Modern Art. Will Gompertz. E. P. Dutton 2012. 416 p.
ISBN 9780525952671
Grades: Adult   709
1. Art history 2. Modern art 3. 19th century 4. 20th century 5. History writing — Arts and culture 6. Arts and Entertainment — Painting, Drawing, and Sculpture
LC 2012027995

A BBC arts editor and former director of London's Tate Gallery presents an irreverent narrative tour of Modern Art that explains its cultural relevance and why it is so compelling, tracing a century's worth of movements, achievements and masterpieces that have reshaped the art world.

Hoving, Thomas
Art for Dummies. Thomas Hoving; foreword by Andrew Wyeth. IDG Books Worldwide, Inc. 1999. xxiv, 382 p, 32 p. of col. plates : Illustration; Color
ISBN 9780764551048
Grades: Adult   709
1. Art appreciation 2. History writing — Arts and culture
LC 99065838

Explains to the average person how to understand, appreciate, and evaluate art, and discusses starting an art collection and where to go to see art.

"In this delightful book, Hoving . leads readers gently through thousands of years of art history. His breathless enthusiasm is avuncular, scholarly, and quite infectiousan attitude that happily precludes condescension. A terrific book for students, travelers, tyros, and old hands alike." —*Library Journal*

Includes bibliographical references (p.367-368) and index.

Hughes, Robert
American Visions: The Epic History of Art in America. by Robert Hughes. Alfred A. Knopf 1997. IX, 635 p. : Illustration; Color
ISBN 9780679426271
Grades: Adult   709
1. Art 2. Art, American 3. Arts and Entertainment — General
LC 96045111
New York Times Notable Book, 1997.

Traces the history of art in America, from the early works of Native Americans to the present day, and includes critical commentaries, anecdotes, profiles, and hundreds of illustrations.

"Hughes has orchestrated a spectacular integration of facts, observations, and insights in this ambitious, lively, and gloriously illustrated volume." —*Booklist*

Includes bibliographical references and index.

Janson, H. W.
★ *Janson's History of Art: The Western Tradition.* Penelope J.E. Davies ... [et al.]. Prentice Hall 2011. xxxi, 1152 p. : Illustration; Color; Map
ISBN 9780205685172
Grades: Adult   709
1. Art history 2. History writing — Arts and culture
LC 2009022617

Rewritten and reorganized, this new edition weaves together the most recent scholarship, the most current thinking in art history, and the most innovative online supplements, including digital art library.

Includes bibliographical references and index.

Johnson, Paul
★ *Art: A New History.* Paul Johnson. Harper Collins 2003. x, 777 p. : Color illustration
ISBN 9780060530754
Grades: 11 12 Adult   709
1. Art history 2. Artists 3. Arts and Entertainment — Painting, Drawing, and Sculpture 4. Adult books for young adults
LC BL2003015116

A personal view of the history of art follows every period from prehistoric times to today, examining both major movements and lesser-known contributors.

"While [Johnson's] narrative is for the most part a conventional journey through the canon, his headlong pace, quirky views and pungent prose make it anything but dull." —*Publishers Weekly*

Includes index.

Kampen-O'Riley, Michael
Art Beyond the West: The Arts of the Islamic World, India and Southeast Asia, China, Japan and Korea, the Pacific, Africa, and the Americas. Michael Kampen O'Riley. Pearson 2013. 367 pages : Illustration; Map
ISBN 9780205887897
Grades: 11 12 Adult   709
1. Art history 2. Reference books 3. Arts and Entertainment — Painting, Drawing, and Sculpture
LC 2012026414

A major survey of the visual arts that lie outside the Western tradition—Art Beyond the West (3rd edition) presents the vast range of arts that lie outside of the Western tradition.

Includes bibliographical references (pages 357-361) and index.

ESSENTIAL AND RECOMMENDED TITLES
709.04 Arts — 20th century, 1900-1999

McPhee, John
The Ransom of Russian Art. John McPhee. Farrar, Straus and Giroux 1994. 181 p. : Color illustration
ISBN 9780374246822
Grades: Adult   709
1. Dodge, Norton Townshend, 1927-2011 2. American people in foreign countries 3. Dissenters, Artistic 4. American people 5. Soviet Union 6. Arts and Entertainment — Painting, Drawing, and Sculpture
LC 94014723
Reveals the clandestine activities of an American professor who retrieved eight thousand works of Soviet art by visiting dissident artists in the Soviet Union.
"McPhee's engaging narrative sheds light on this suppressed creative milieu." —*Publishers Weekly*

Petropoulos, Jonathan
The Faustian Bargain: The Art World in Nazi Germany. Jonathan Petropoulos. Oxford University Press 2000. xvii, 395 p. : Illustration
ISBN 9780195129649
Grades: Adult   709
1. Art treasures in war 2. Art 3. Nazis 4. German history 5. 20th century 6. Biographies 7. History writing — Arts and culture
LC 99033372
Profiles five key figures in the art world of Nazi Germany who plundered art masterpieces from museums and private collections across Europe at the behest of Adolf Hitler's Third Reich—museum director Ernst Buchner, art critic Robert Scholz, dealer Karl Haberstock, art historian Kajetan Muhlman, and sculptor Arno Breker.
"Spotlighting five groups—art museum directors, art dealers, art journalists, art historians, and artists—Petropoulos . details how each of these groups either directly or indirectly facilitated the theft of countless works of art and legitimized the Nazi regime." —*Library Journal*
Includes bibliographical references (p. 281-376) and index.

Robins, Gay
The Art of Ancient Egypt: Revised Edition. Gay Robins. Harvard University Press 2008. 271 p. : Illustration; Color; Map
ISBN 9780674030657
Grades: Adult   709
1. Ancient art 2. Art, Egyptian 3. History writing — Arts and culture 4. History writing — Ancient — Egypt
LC 2008004264
"The first chapter orients the reader in the cultural, technical, and iconographic contexts needed to explore the evolution of the Egyptian artistic tradition in subsequent chapters. Beginning with the predynastic origins (5000 BCE) and concluding in the Ptolemaic Period (304-30 BCE), Robins traces the development of sculpture, painting, funerary and religious art, and architecture with over 300 illustrations, many in color." —*Library Journal.* [review of 1997 edition]
Includes bibliographical references (p. 256-266) and index.

Schama, Simon
The Power of Art. Simon Schama. Ecco Press 2006. 448 p.
ISBN 9780061176104
Grades: Adult   709
1. Art history 2. Artists 3. Creativity 4. Arts and Entertainment — Painting, Drawing, and Sculpture
A companion to the author's PBS series documents the creation processes of eight master artists including Rembrandt, Van Gogh, and Picasso, in an account that discusses how each featured masterpiece was created under tremendous pressure in response to the artist's troubled time.
"The author presents eight remarkable artists who created their masterworks against a backdrop of personal and professional distress. From politically charged commentaries (David, Picasso, Turner and Rembrandt) to intensely personal visions of the world (van Gogh and Rothko) and the reinvention of the divine (Bernini and Caravaggio), Schama takes these masters' hallowed works off the museum wall and drags them through the mud and muck that went into their creation." —*Publishers Weekly*

Strickland, Carol
The Annotated Mona Lisa: A Crash Course in Art History from Prehistoric to Post-modern. Carol Strickland and John Boswell. Andrews and McMeel 2018. 222 p. : Illustration; Color
ISBN 9781449482138
Grades: 11 12 Adult   709
1. Art history 2. Art appreciation 3. Art 4. Arts and Entertainment — General 5. Adult books for young adults
LC 2017931253
Presents the history of art from prehistoric times to the present day, describing major artists and movements and detailing the influence of art on society through the ages.
Includes index.

Ward, Gerald W. R.
Chihuly: Through the Looking Glass. Gerald W.R. Ward. MFA Publications 2011. 149 p. : Color illustration
ISBN 9780878467648
Grades: Adult   709
1. Chihuly, Dale, 1941- 2. Glass sculpture 3. 21st century 4. 20th century 5. Arts and Entertainment — Painting, Drawing, and Sculpture
LC 2010941797
"The book covers a rich set of vibrant work inspired predominantly by natural forms and makes the most of its large format. The documentation is superb, the scope is expansive, and the text is expertly presented." —*Library Journal*
Catalog of an exhibition held at the Museum of Fine Arts, Boston, Apr. 10-Aug. 7, 2011; Includes bibliographical references.

709.04 Arts — 20th century, 1900-1999

Arnason, H. Harvard
★ *History of Modern Art: Painting, Sculpture, Architecture, Photography.* H.H. Arnason, Elizabeth C. Mansfield, National Humanities Centre. Pearson 2013. xvi, 816 p. : Illustration
ISBN 9780205259472
Grades: Adult   709.04
1. Modern art 2. Arts and Entertainment — Painting, Drawing, and Sculpture
LC 2012029474
A visual comprehensive overview of the modern art field.
Includes bibliographical references (pages 763-789) and index.

Barnes, Julian
Keeping an Eye Open: Essays on Art. Julian Barnes. Alfred A. Knopf 2015. 288 p.
ISBN 9781101874783
Grades: Adult   709.04
1. Modern art 2. Art criticism 3. Art technique 4. Romanticism in art 5. Realism in art 6. Art appreciation 7. Painting technique 8. 19th century 9. 20th century 10. Essays 11. Arts and Entertainment — Painting, Drawing, and Sculpture
LC 2015014317
A collection of essays traces the artistic evolution from Romanticism to Realism and Modernism to share insights into the opposing dynamics between experiencing art silently and the need to verbalize art's impact.
"Barnes knows that one of the immeasurable pleasures of art is its capacity to approach us from unexpected angles and excite our senses of wonder. The same may be said of his scholarly and astute yet accessible and exciting essays." —*Kirkus*
Originally published in Great Britain by Jonathan Cape.

English, Charlie
The Gallery of Miracles and Madness: Insanity, Modernism, and Hitler's War on Art. Charlie English. Random House 2021. 352 p.

ISBN 9780525512059

Grades: Adult 709.04

1. Prinzhorn, Hans, 1886-1933 2. Psychiatrists 3. People with mental illnesses 4. Artists 5. Art and mental illness 6. Modernism (Art) 7. Modernism (Aesthetics) 8. Censorship 9. Art and politics 10. Art and society 11. Murder 12. Art 13. Nazism 14. Third Reich, 1933-1945 15. Politics and government 16. German history 17. Germany 18. 20th century 19. History writing — Europe — Germany 20. History writing — Arts and culture 21. Life stories — Arts and culture 22. Arts and Entertainment — Painting, Drawing, and Sculpture

LC 2020044464

In the early 1920s, Hans Prinzhorn, a psychiatrist and aesthete, sought insight from the art of mental patients such as Franz Buhler. Buhler was a brilliant, well-known ironworker until his schizophrenia diagnosis, and his work was compared to that of Munch and Duhrer. Prinzhorn collected and published their work, inspiring the Modernist movement that was coming into fashion just as a young Adolf Hitler arrived in Vienna to begin his brief, failed career as a painter. The cultural cleansing was a precursor to the racial cleansing and Prinzhorns's patient artists would be caught up in both. Hitler developed the first gas chambers as a way to dispose of 70,273 patients, including Franz Buhler. In The Gallery of Miracles and Madness, the Nazis' cultural destruction, which would rightly be considered among the lesser sins of the Reich, puts the horror of the Holocaust into relief.

"In this fascinating account, journalist English (Book Smugglers of Timbuktu) unpacks Hitler's mad campaign against mentally ill artists.... In musing on the definition of art, limitations of clinical psychology, and the rise of fascism, English's story feels strikingly relevant." —*Publishers Weekly*

Includes bibliographical references and index.

Salle, David

How to See: Looking, Talking, and Thinking About Art. David Salle. W.W. Norton & Company 2016. VIII, 271 pages : Illustration

ISBN 9780393248135

Grades: Adult 709.04

1. Modern art 2. Art appreciation 3. 21st century 4. 20th century 5. Essays 6. Arts and Entertainment — Painting, Drawing, and Sculpture

LC 2016025215

The renowned artist whose work is among the permanent collections at the Whitney Museum and the National Gallery describes contemporary art in simple language and explores how an artist gives form to an idea and the difference between inventing and perfecting ideas.

"As he states in his introduction, Salle wants to avoid what he describes as the generalizing language of professional art writing (with its frequent recourse to broad art historical styles and obscure critical theory) and instead analyze art in direct and intimate fashion as befits a practicing artist. Although many may take issue with Salle's dismissal of art history and theory, his writing is refreshingly engaging and original: Conversational in tone, replete with personal anecdotes, and grounded in keen observational analysis." —*Library Journal*

Includes index.

709.1 Arts — Areas, regions, places in general

Khalili, Nasser D.

Islamic Art and Culture: A Visual History. Nasser D. Khalili. Overlook Press 2006. 186 p. : Color illustration; Color; Map

ISBN 9781585678396

Grades: 11 12 Adult 709.1

1. Art, Islamic 2. Islamic Empire 3. History writing — Arts and culture 4. Spirituality and Religion — Islam — History

LC Bl2006029795

An oversized visual history of Islamic civilization as reflected in its fine art spans 1,200 years and surveys a range of media, from architecture and painting to silk textiles and calligraphy, in a volume that also demonstrates the relationship between Islamic artists and their western peers.

An oversized visual history of Islamic civilization as reflected in its fine art spans 1,200 years and surveys a range of media, from architecture and painting to silk textiles and calligraphy, in a volume that also demonstrates the relationship between Islamic artists and their western peers.

Includes bibliographical references (p. 180-182) and index.

O'Kane, Bernard

Treasures of Islam: Artistic Glories of the Muslim World. [Bernard O'Kane]. Duncan Baird 2007. 224 p. : Illustration; Color; Map

ISBN 9781844834839

Grades: Adult 709.1

1. Art, Islamic 2. Architecture, Islamic 3. Southwest Asia and North Africa (Middle East) history 4. Islamic Empire 5. Arts and Entertainment — General 6. Spirituality and Religion — Islam 7. Adult books for young adults

LC Bl2007021891

Booklist Editors' Choice, 2007.

Presents a portrait of the cultural heritage of Islam looking at its artistic influences and offering examples of paintings, jewelry, sculpture, metalwork, and architecture.

"The wealth of glorious full-color illustrations make this beautifully designed book an excellent introduction to the art of Islam." —*Publishers Weekly*

Includes bibliographical references (p. 213-214) and index.

709.2 Arts — Biography

Ai, Weiwei

1000 Years of Joys and Sorrows. Ai Weiwei; translated by Allan H. Barr. Crown 2021. 352 p.

ISBN 9780553419467

Grades: Adult 709.2

1. Ai, Weiwei 2. Expatriate artists 3. Artists 4. Dissenters, Artistic 5. Social advocates 6. Families 7. Creativity 8. Chinese history 9. Autobiographies and memoirs 10. Life stories — Arts and culture 11. History writing — Asia — China

LC 2021028838

One of the world's most famous artists and activists presents a personal memoir and a history of the last 100 years of China, while shedding light on his own artistic process.

"Artist Ai Weiwei has penned an engrossing memoir that takes readers back and forth through time as he examines the life and legacy of his father, the renowned poet Ai Qing, as well as the evolution of his own political and artistic sensibilities, all in the shadow of the tremendous upheaval in China over the past century.... Highly recommended for those interested in art, memoir, politics, and history." —*Library Journal*

Aquino, Lucia

Leonardo Da Vinci. Preface by Mario Pomilio; [editor (English edition), Julie DI Filippo; translation, Miriam Hurley]. Rizzoli 2005. 173 p. : Illustration; Color

ISBN 9780847826773

Grades: Adult 709.2

1. Leonardo, da Vinci, 1452-1519 2. Arts and Entertainment — Painting, Drawing, and Sculpture

LC Bl2007009384

A discussion of the work of the Italian master includes commentary by famous art historians, a critical essay on the artist's life and art, a timeline, and a list of museums where the featured paintings can be found.

Includes bibliographical references (p. 173).

Hook, Philip

Rogues' Gallery: The Rise (and Occasional Fall) of Art Dealers, the Hidden Players in the History of Art. Philip Hook. Experiment 2017. 298 pages : Illustration; Color

ISBN 9781615194162

Grades: Adult 709.2

1. Art dealers 2. Collectors and collecting 3. Arts and entertainment — General 4. History writing — Arts and culture

ESSENTIAL AND RECOMMENDED TITLES
709.45 Fine arts — Italy, San Marino, Vatican City, Malta

LC 2017025490

Philip Hook takes the lid off the world of art dealing to reveal the brilliance, cunning, greed, and daring of its practitioners. In a richly anecdotal chronological narrative he describes the rise and occasional fall of the extraordinary men and women who over the centuries have made it their business to sell art to kings, merchants, nobles, entrepreneurs, and museums.

Originally published in the UK as Rogues' Gallery: A History of Art and Its Dealers by Profile Books Ltd in 2017; Includes bibliographical references and index.

Matisse, Henri
Henri Matisse: The Cut-Outs. Edited by Karl Buchberg, Nicholas Cullinan, Jodi Hauptman, and Nicholas Serota; with essays by Karl Buchberg, Nicholas Cullinan, Samantha Friedman, Flavia Frigeri, Markus Gross, Jodi Hauptman, Stephan Lohrengel, and Nicholas Serota. The Museum of Modern Art 2014. 298 pages : Illustration; Color
ISBN 9780870709159
Grades: Adult **709.2**
1. Matisse, Henri, 1869-1954 2. Collage 3. 20th century 4. Arts and Entertainment — Painting, Drawing, and Sculpture 5. Arts and Entertainment — Museums and Collections

LC Bl2015013492

Showcases the gouache-painted cut-outs created during the period of Matisse's life when he suffered from restricted physical mobility, while sharing new research on such topics as his methods and environmental ambitions for the works.

"The beautifully produced catalog of this exhibition includes essays that explore Matisses innovative process, brought to life by photographs of the artist with his assistants at work in his studio as well as a generous and representative selection of high-quality color reproductions of significant milestones from a decade of cut-out projects. Essential for art studio, history, and conservation collections." —*Choice*

Published in conjunction with the exhibition Henri Matisse: The Cut-Outs, at the Museum of Modern Art, New York. The exhibition is organized by the Museum of Modern Art, New York, in collaboration with Tate Modern, London—Title page verso; Includes bibliographical references (pages 279-283) and index.

Pham, Larissa
Pop Song: Adventures in Art & Intimacy. Larissa Pham. Catapult 2021. 276 p.
ISBN 9781646220267
Grades: Adult **709.2**
1. Pham, Larissa 2. Purpose in life 3. Identity 4. Feminism 5. Art 6. Desire 7. Love 8. Voyages and travels 9. Obsession 10. Interpersonal relations 11. Psychic trauma 12. Autobiographies and memoirs 13. Life stories — Identity 14. Life stories — Arts and culture — Artists

National Book Critics Circle Award: John Leonard Prize finalist, 2021.

A Brooklyn-based artist and writer shares her youthful attempts to find meaning in travel, sex, drugs and art, before sensing that she might need to turn her gaze upon herself.

"Pham seamlessly blends the personal and the cultural, the confessional and the critical, the cerebral and the sentimental, to create an exciting and imaginative memoir. A vital playlist that hits all the right notes." —*Kirkus*

Shaw, Jennifer Laurie
Exist Otherwise: The Life and Works of Claude Cahun. Jennifer L. Shaw. Reaktion Books 2017. 326 pages : Illustration; Color
ISBN 9781780237282
Grades: Adult **709.2**
1. Cahun, Claude, 1894-1954 2. Artists 3. Surrealism 4. Avant-garde (Aesthetics) 5. Art 6. France 7. Biographies 8. Life stories — Arts and culture — Artists 9. Arts and Entertainment — Painting, Drawing, and Sculpture

In the turmoil of the 1920s and '30s, Claude Cahun challenged gender stereotypes with her powerful photographs, montages, and writings, works that appear to our twenty-first-century eyes as utterly contemporary, or even from the future. She wrote poetry and prose for major French literary magazines, worked in avant-garde theater, and was both comrade of and critical outsider to the Surrealists. Exist Otherwise is the first work in English to the tell the full story of Claude Cahun's art and life, one that celebrates and makes accessible Cahun's remarkable vision.

Includes bibliographical references and index.

709.45 Fine arts — Italy, San Marino, Vatican City, Malta

Adams, Laurie
★ *Italian Renaissance Art.* Laurie Schneider Adams. Westview Press 2013. 436 pages : Illustration; Color
ISBN 9780813349022
Grades: Adult **709.45**
1. Art, Italian 2. Art, Renaissance (Europe) 3. Arts and Entertainment — Painting, Drawing, and Sculpture

LC Bl2014000066

Presents a survey of Italian Renaissance art, focusing on the principal works of the most important and innovative artists, along with information on women artists, Mannerism, and the late Renaissance period.

Includes bibliographical references and index.

709.51 Fine arts — China

Ai, Weiwei
Ai Weiwei: According to What? [editor, Deborah E. Horowitz]. DelMonico Books-Prestel 2012. 144 pages : Illustration; Color
ISBN 9783791352404
Grades: Adult **709.51**
1. Ai, Weiwei 2. Installations (Art) 3. Arts and Entertainment — Painting, Drawing, and Sculpture 4. Arts and Entertainment — Museums and Collections

LC Bl2013035266

Offers an introduction to Weiwei's work—from photographs and sculpture to documentation of several of his most well-known projects, including his collaboration on the "bird's nest" stadium for the 2008 Beijing Olympics.

This catalogue is published in conjunction with the exhibition Ai Weiwei: According to What?, organized by the Mori Art Museum, Tokyo, in association with the Hirshhorn Museum and Sculpture Garden, Smithsonian Institution, Washington, D.C.—T.P. verso; Exhibition held at the Hirshhorn Museum and Sculpture Garden, Washington, D.C, October 7, 2012-February 24, 2013; Indianapolis Museum of Art, Indianapolis, Indiana, April 5-July 28, 2013; Art Gallery of Ontario, Toronto, Ontario, August 31-October 27, 2013; Perez Art Museum Miami, Miami, Florida, November 28, 2013-March 16, 2014; Brooklyn Museum, Brooklyn, New York, April 18-August 10, 2014; Includes bibliographical references (pages 142-144).

Tregear, Mary
Chinese Art. Mary Tregear. Thames and Hudson 1997. 216 p. : Illustration; Color; Map
ISBN 9780500202999
Grades: 11 12 Adult **709.51**
1. Art, Chinese 2. History writing — Arts and culture

LC 96061015

Traces the history of Chinese painting and sculpture, and describes important movements and themes.

Includes bibliographical references (p. 201) and index.

709.73 Fine arts — United States

FitzGerald, Michael C.
★ *Picasso and American Art.* Michael FitzGerald; with a chronology by Julia May Boddewyn. Whitney Museum of American Art 2006. 400 p. : Illustration; Color
ISBN 9780300114522

Grades: Adult   709.73

1. Picasso, Pablo, 1881-1973 2. Art, American 3. Avant-garde (Aesthetics) 4. United States 5. 20th century 6. Arts and Entertainment — Painting, Drawing, and Sculpture 7. Arts and Entertainment — Museums and Collections

LC 2006001402

"A study of Picasso's influence on some of the most significant American artists of the 20th century. Fitzgerald moves chronologically, from the earliest Americans who engaged cubism in the teens (Max Weber, Marsden Hartley, Man Ray, Stuart Davis), through the modernist investigations of Arshile Gorky, Willem De Kooning and Jackson Pollack, and winds up with Roy Lichtenstien's pop-art and Jasper Johns' postmodern responses to Picasso. Fitzgerald takes great pains to triangulate exhibition specifics with the work and words of each artist to document the precise nature and extent of the influence in each case. There is a generous supply of images presented with the text, and they are as successful as Fitzgerald's prose in illuminating the complexities of Picasso's influence on these artists." —*Publishers Weekly*

The exhibition was organized by Michael FitzGerald, guest curator, in association with Dana Miller, associate curator, Whitney Museum of American Art; Published on the occasion of an exhibition organized by the Whitney Museum of American Art, New York and held also at the San Francisco Museum of Modern Art and Walker Art Center, Minneapolis; Includes bibliographical references and index.

Peiffer, Prudence

The Slip: The New York City Street That Changed American Art Forever. Prudence Peiffer. HarperCollins Publishers 2023. 384 p.

ISBN 9780063097209

Grades: Adult   709.73

1. Artists 2. Artists' studios 3. Influence (Literary, artistic, etc.) 4. Art 5. Film 6. Social life and customs 7. New York city 8. United States 9. 20th century 10. 1950s 11. 1960s 12. Collective biographies 13. Life stories — Arts and culture — Artists 14. Arts and Entertainment — Painting, Drawing, and Sculpture 15. Arts and Entertainment — Movies and Television 16. History Writing — Arts and culture

LC 2023013718

A group portrait of artists Robert Indiana, Ellsworth Kelly, Agnes Martin, James Rosenquist, Delphine Seyrig, Lenore Tawney, Jack Youngerman, and the street they all called home, Coenties Slip in the 1950s and 1960s.

"It's a gratifying deep dive into New York City art history." —*Publishers Weekly*

Includes bibliographical references and index.

709.8 Fine arts — South America

Barnitz, Jacqueline

Twentieth-Century Art of Latin America. Jacqueline Barnitz. University of Texas Press 2001. 415 p. : Illustration; Color; Map

ISBN 9781477308042

Grades: Adult   709.8

1. Art, Latin American 2. 20th century 3. Arts and Entertainment — Painting, Drawing, and Sculpture

LC 99050871

Booklist Editors' Choice, 2001.

This new edition has been refreshed throughout to include new scholarship on several modern movements, such as abstraction in the River Plate region and the Cuban avant-garde. A new chapter covers art since 1990. In all, 30 percent of the images in this edition are new, and thirty-four additional artists are discussed and illustrated.

"Latin American art, the fruit of violent collisions among diverse indigenous, European, and African cultures, is revealed as provocative and vibrant in Barnitz's well-illustrated and groundbreaking overview of its dazzling twentieth-century flowering." —*Booklist*

Includes bibliographical references and index.

711 Area planning (Civic art)

McGregor, James H.

Rome from the Ground up. James H.S. McGregor. Belknap Press of Harvard University Press 2005. 344 p. : Illustration; Color; Map

ISBN 9780674019119

Grades: Adult   711

1. Urban planning 2. Architecture 3. Voyages and travels 4. Italian history 5. Ancient Rome 6. Rome, Italy 7. History writing — Europe — Italy

LC 2005048213

In this multifaceted historical portrait of Rome, the practical world of each period is explored to reveal the complex urban forms and shifting realities of the many cities that constitute Rome.

"The author chronologically traces the successive periods of intense architecture and planning that helped Rome achieve strategic greatness, from the Etruscan management of the Tiber Island ford 3,000 years ago, to the city's unparalleled artistic stamp by Bramante and Michelangelo during the Renaissance, to Mussolini's monumental Fascist vision, to the precarious repairs heralding the Jubilee Year of 2000. Here is a walking tour in stately, inviting prose that renders wonderfully manageable a massive history lesson for the intellectually curious and adept." —*Publishers Weekly*

Includes bibliographical references and index.

712 Landscape architecture (Landscape design)

Alexander, Rosemary

★ *The Essential Garden Design Workbook: 3rd Edition.* Rosemary Alexander. Timber Press 2009. 391 p. : Illustration; Color; Plan

ISBN 9781604696615

Grades: Adult   712

1. Gardens 2. Design and construction 3. Arts and Entertainment — Crafts and hobbies — Garden and nature

LC 2009008564

Guides you through every stage of designing a garden. Hundreds of explanatory drawings and quick-reference diagrams make this workbook a vital addition to your garden-planning library.

"Now in its third edition. . . expand[s] on the distinguished and experienced authors' goal of providing guidance for a professional garden designer's career [and] . . .maintains the earlier editions' well-written, straightforward text, instructive line drawings, and beautiful, informative color photographs." —*Choice*

Includes bibliographical references and index.

Bohl, Loree

Fearless Gardening: Be Bold, Break the Rules, Grow What You Love. Loree Bohl. Timber Press, 2021. 259 p.

ISBN 9781604699623

Grades: Adult   712

1. Gardening 2. North America 3. Arts and Entertainment — Crafts and hobbies — Garden and nature

"Gardeners aspiring and experienced may feel emboldened and inspired by both permission to break the rules and gorgeous photos of Bohl's home garden." —*Booklist*

Brody, Mark

Mosaic Garden Projects: Add Color to Your Garden with Tables, Fountains, Birdbaths, and More. by Mark Brody; with Sheila Ashdown; with photographs by Justin Myers. Timber Press 2015. 304 pages : Illustration; Color

ISBN 9781604694871

Grades: Adult   712

1. Gardens 2. Mosaics 3. Color in design 4. Garden ornaments and furniture 5. Design and construction 6. Arts and Entertainment — Crafts and hobbies — Garden and nature 7. Arts and Entertainment — Crafts and hobbies — Ceramics

LC 2014020734

ESSENTIAL AND RECOMMENDED TITLES
712 Landscape architecture (Landscape design)

Presents detailed, step-by-step instructions for making mosaic garden structures and ornaments, including planters, stepping stones, tabletops, and a pagoda.

25 colorful step-by-step projects—Cover; Includes index.

Buchanan, Rita
Taylor's Master Guide to Landscaping. Rita Buchanan. Houghton Mifflin Co. 2000. 372 p. : Color illustration
ISBN 9780618055906
Grades: Adult **712**
1. Landscape gardening 2. Arts and Entertainment — Crafts and hobbies — Garden and nature
LC 99054110

Reveals the vital components of landscape design, offering advice on choosing a site, selecting plants, creating garden accessories, and maintaining a landscape.

The companion volume to Taylor's Master Guide to Gardening reveals the vital components of landscape design, urging readers to approach landscaping with function as well as form in mind and offering advice on choosing a site, selecting plants, creating garden accessories, and maintaining a landscape.

"Buchanan offers a comprehensive treatment of landscape design, emphasizing designing with plants and including extensive information about choosing and caring for plants, trees, shrubs, vines, and ground covers. A landmark work destined to become a classic."—*Library Journal*

A Frances Tenenbaum book; Includes index.

Chesshire, Charles
Japanese Gardening: A Practical Guide to Creating a Japanese-Style Garden with 700 Step-by-Step Photographs. Charles Chesshire. Lorenz Books, an imprint of Anness Publishing Ltd 2020. 256 p.
ISBN 9780754834953
Grades: Adult **712**
1. Japanese gardens 2. Gardens 3. Design and construction 4. Arts and Entertainment — Crafts and hobbies — Garden and nature

This inspiring book offers expert information on how to create the perfect Japanese-style garden in any location, large or small. It presents the history of Japanese gardens and the principles underlying them. Sections on the five classic Japanese garden styles (pond gardens, dry gardens, tea gardens, stroll gardens, and courtyard gardens) explain their key characteristics with practical tips on how to achieve them.

"This fascinating guide from garden designer Chesshire (Clematis: Inspiration, Selection and Practical Advice) lays out the spiritual and practical aspects of Japanese gardening.... For the gardener desiring a spiritually fulfilling and calming pursuit as well as a robust garden, this stimulating volume will show the way."—*Publishers Weekly*

Includes index.

Darke, Rick
The Living Landscape: Designing for Beauty and Biodiversity in the Home Garden. Rick Darke & Doug Tallamy; principal photography by Rick Darke. Timber Press 2014. 392 p. : Color illustration
ISBN 9781604694086
Grades: Adult **712**
1. Natural landscaping 2. Arts and Entertainment — Crafts and hobbies — Garden and nature
LC 2013040141

Describes how gardeners can support sustainability and biodiversity by including in their garden plants that provide food for birds and bugs and serve as a pollination source for bees, suggesting plants for every climate and region.

Describes how home gardeners can help support sustainability and biodiversity through including in their garden plants that provide food for birds and bugs and serve as a pollination source for bees, including suggested plants for every climate and region.

Includes bibliographical references (p. 367-368) and index.

Greayer, Rochelle
Cultivating Garden Style: Inspired Ideas and Practical Advice to Unleash Your Garden Personality. Rochelle Greayer. Timber Press, Inc. 2014. 323 pages : Color; Illustration
ISBN 9781604694772
Grades: Adult **712**
1. Gardening 2. Gardens 3. Design and construction 4. Arts and Entertainment — Crafts and hobbies — Garden and nature 5. House and Home — Interior Decorating and Furnishings 6. House and Home — Outdoor areas
LC 2014009479

Features examples of twenty-three different garden styles, with advice on selecting plants, trees, containers, and garden accessories to make a garden inviting and a reflection of individual taste.

"The extravagant use of color photos on each page brings visual clarity to otherwise improbable schemes. Whether depicting retro rockery, topiary, trellising, Danish or Zen features, the book offers needed guidance for designing outdoor space in a way that helps gardeners bring unique personality to their living, growing outdoor decor."—*Publishers Weekly*

Includes index.

Holmes, Roger
Midwest Home Landscaping: Including South-Central Canada. Roger Holmes & Rita Buchanan. Creative Homeowner Press 2006. 223 p. : Color illustration; Color; Map
ISBN 9781580112567
Grades: Adult **712**
1. Gardens 2. Landscape gardening 3. Design and construction 4. Ontario 5. Middle West 6. Arts and Entertainment — Crafts and hobbies — Garden and nature 7. House and Home — DIY, maintenance, and repair
LC Bl2007010605

Provides information and guidance on designing plantings for the home yard and includes do-it-yourself outdoor building projects.

"The authors offer 46 designs for 23 common landscaping situations. Illustrated installation instructions are followed by solid plant choices for zone 4. Zone 3 gardeners are advised on plant substitutions."—*Library Journal*

Includes index; Previous ed. published under title: Home landscaping : Midwest Region, including southern Canada. 1999.

Howcroft, Heidi
Garden Design: A Book of Ideas. Heidi Howcroft & Marianne Majerus. Firefly Books 2015. 320 p. : Color; Illustration
ISBN 9781770855243
Grades: Adult **712**
1. Gardens 2. Design and construction 3. Reference books 4. Arts and Entertainment — Crafts and hobbies — Garden and nature
LC Oc2016048116

More than 600 inspirational photographs, 24 case studies, [and] a must-have sourcebook for garden owners, architects and designers.

The possibilities in designing a garden are astonishing, and the choices you face can be overwhelming. The secret to creating a garden that reflects your desires is part common sense and part instinct. Howcroft and Majerus provide inspirational photographs, case studies, and a must-have sourcebook for garden owners, architects and designers.

Includes index.

Mansfield, Stephen
Japanese Stone Gardens: Origins, Meaning, Form. Stephen Mansfield; foreword by Donald Richie. Tuttle Pub. 2009. 160 p. : Illustration; Color; Map
ISBN 9784805310564
Grades: Adult **712**
1. Arts and Entertainment — Crafts and hobbies — Garden and nature
LC Bl2009035758

Japanese Stone Gardens provides a comprehensive introduction to the powerful mystique and dynamism of the Japanese stone garden—from their earliest use as props in animistic rituals, to their appropriation by Zen monks and priests to create settings conducive to contemplation and finally to their contemporary uses and meaning.

"An in-depth tour of 15 masterpiece stone gardens ancient and contemporary throughout Japan further deepens our appreciation for these landscapes of aesthetic precision and meditative repose in a book as lovely and restorative as its subject." —*Booklist*

Includes bibliographical references (p. 157) and index.

Pember, Mat
DIY Garden Projects: Step -by-Step Activities for Edible Gardening and Backyard Fun. Mat Pember and Dillon Seitchik-Reardon. Hardie Grant Books 2016. 383 pages : Color; Illustration
ISBN 9781743790991
Grades: Adult   712
1. Garden structures 2. Gardens 3. Design and construction 4. Arts and Entertainment — Crafts and hobbies — Garden and nature
LC Bl2016029905

Provides step-by-step instructions for thirty-eight activities in the garden, including garden basics, using recycled materials, and vertical gardening.

"Charming and hip projects emphasize recycled materials and small space gardens that will be attractive in urban settings. Highly recommended, especially where variety is desired." —*Library Journal*

Includes index.

Williams, Bunny
On Garden Style. Bunny Williams; written with Nancy Drew; book design by Doug Turshen with David Huang. Stewart, Tabori & Change 2015. 287 p. : Color; Illustration
ISBN 9781617691539
Grades: Adult   712
1. Gardening 2. Ornamental plants 3. Gardens 4. Design and construction 5. Garden structures 6. Arts and Entertainment — Crafts and hobbies — Garden and nature
LC Bl2015012051

A leading interior designer and a gardening journalist combine their expertise to provide an authoritative volume on how to design gardens of all kinds, as well as how to appreciate their aesthetic appeal.

Includes bibliographical references (pages 284-287).

712.09 Landscape architecture — History

Brown, Kendall H.
Quiet Beauty: The Japanese Gardens of North America. Kendall H. Brown; photographs by David M. Cobb. Tuttle Pub. 2013. 176 p. : Color illustration
ISBN 9784805311950
Grades: Adult   712.09
1. Arts and Entertainment — Crafts and hobbies — Garden and nature
LC 2012036548

Japanese gardens have been part of North American culture for almost 150 years. Quiet Beauty is a thought-provoking look at the history of their introduction to the world of North American gardening and how this aspect of Japanese culture has taken root and flourished.

"Yet, the 150-year history of Japanese gardens in American culture raises complicated questions about authenticity, design, style, and meaning. In this lavishly illustrated book, art historian Brown and photographer Cobb act as tour guides to 26 such gardens." —*Publishers Weekly*

Includes bibliographical references (p. 175).

712.092 Landscape architects

Howard, Hugh
Architects of an American Landscape: Henry Hobson Richardson, Frederick Law Olmsted, and the Reimagining of America's Public and Private Spaces. Hugh Howard. Atlantic Monthly Press 2022. 416 p.
ISBN 9780802159236
Grades: Adult   712.092
1. Olmsted, Frederick Law, 1822-1903 2. Richardson, Henry Hobson, 1838-1886 3. Architects 4. Landscape architects, American 5. Friendship 6. Public spaces 7. Parks 8. Buildings 9. Houses 10. Architecture, domestic 11. Design 12. Collective biographies 13. Biographies 14. Life stories — Arts and culture — Architects 15. Arts and Entertainment — Architecture 16. History writing — Gilded Age — United States 17. History writing — Arts and culture

As the nation recovered from a cataclysmic war, two titans of design profoundly influenced how Americans came to interact with the built and natural world around them through their pioneering work in architecture and landscape design. Frederick Law Olmsted is widely revered as America's first and finest parkmaker and environmentalist, the force behind Manhattan's Central Park, Brooklyn's Prospect Park, and the preservation of Yosemite and Niagara Falls. Yet his close friend and sometime collaborator, Henry Hobson Richardson, has been almost entirely forgotten today, despite his outsized influence on American architecture—from Boston's iconic Trinity Church to Chicago's Marshall Field Wholesale Store to the wildly popular "open plan" he conceived for family homes. Individually they created much-beloved buildings and public spaces. Together they married natural landscapes with built structures in train stations and public libraries that helped drive the shift in American life from congested cities to developing suburbs across the country.

"A well-researched dual biography, rich in historical context, presenting two gifted architects who as robust allies utterly transformed the look of American buildings and landscapes." —*Booklist*

715 Woody plants in landscape architecture

Foley, Caroline
Topiary, Knots and Parterres. Caroline Foley. Pimpernel Press Ltd, in association with the European Boxwood and Topiary Society 2017. 288 pages : Illustration; Color
ISBN 9781910258187
Grades: Adult   715
1. Hedges 2. Topiary work 3. Arts and Entertainment — Crafts and hobbies — Garden and nature
LC 2017431398

Topiary, knots, and parterres come in many guises, from the grand and imposing to the humble and folksy. In this book Caroline Foley—with the aid of diarists, writers, wits, designers, gardeners, and garden owners—traces their story through the centuries and across the world.

Includes bibliographical references (page 284) and index.

717 Structures in landscape architecture

Hayward, Gordon
Stone in the Garden: Inspiring Designs and Practical Projects. Gordon Hayward; illustrations by Gordon Morrison. W.W. Norton 2001. 224 p. : Illustration; Color
ISBN 9780393047790
Grades: Adult   717
1. Arts and Entertainment — Crafts and hobbies — Garden and nature
LC 00069945

A guide to using stones in the garden, walls, walkways, and terraces features more than one hundred drawings and photographs that give instructions on how to complete a wide range of projects.

A lavishly illustrated guide to using stone in your garden, walls, walkways, terraces, and more features more than one hundred detailed drawings and photographs that give readers intructions on how to complete a wide range of projects with confidence and finesse.

"The book's first half focuses on the philosophical and design considerations of stone forms as varied as walls, paths, terraces, and even benches. The second half is more practical, covering topics such as estimating the amount of stone

ESSENTIAL AND RECOMMENDED TITLES
720 Architecture

needed for a wall, the methods of cutting and laying stone, and building pools and fountains." —*Library Journal*

Includes bibliograhical references (p.) and index.

720 Architecture

Cornille, Didier
Who Built That?: Skyscrapers : An Introduction to Skyscrapers and Their Architects. Didier Cornille. Princeton Architectural Press 2014. 83 p. : Illustration; Color (Who built that?)
ISBN 9781616892708
Grades: Adult   720
1. Skyscrapers 2. Architecture 3. Architects 4. Buildings 5. Art and music — Visual arts — Architecture
LC 2014004388

An introduction to skyscrapers spotlights eight built between 1889 and 2010 in Europe, the United States, and Asia, with information about the architects, the circumstances when they were designed, and the elements that make them distinctive.

"Though the information is a little slight, the spare illustrations easily make up for itall of Cornilles drawings unmistakably reveal architectural components not visible in photographs, such as interior structures or foundations, and although theyre very minimalistic, its impossible not to see the structures grandeur in each illustration. Though this resembles a picture book, the sometimes elevated language makes this better suited to middle- or even high-school students who already have an interest in architecture or graphic design." —*Booklist*

Originally published as: Tous les gratte-ciel sont dans la nature, France, 2012; Illustrated by the author.

Glancey, Jonathan
The Story of Architecture. Jonathan Glancey. Dorling Kindersley 2000. 240 p. : Color illustration
ISBN 9780789459657
Grades: 11 12 Adult   720
1. Architecture 2. Architectural criticism 3. Architectural photography 4. Arts and Entertainment — Architecture
LC 00030434

An illustrated study of architecture spans some five thousand years as it captures the finest achievements of human construction; discusses a variety of architectural styles and movements; and profiles some of the world's great architects, past and present.

"Devoting nearly half the text to the modern period, Glancey condenses history's panorama into a series of colorful vignettes, each described as having some contemporary relevance. Driven by a contagious enthusiasm, the narrative is enlivened by chatty, sometimes offbeat commentary." —*Library Journal*

Includes index.

Mars, Roman
★ *The 99% Invisible City: A Field Guide to the Hidden World of Everyday Design.* Roman Mars and Kurt Kohlstedt. Houghton Mifflin Harcourt 2020. 384 p.
ISBN 9780358126607
Grades: Adult   720
1. Urban planning 2. Cities and towns 3. Design 4. Public works 5. Media tie-ins 6. Society and culture — Urban and regional studies
LC 2020023323

The creators of the record-setting 99% Invisible podcast celebrate the achievements of modern urban design and architecture, sharing the origin stories behind fundamental innovations, from power grids and fire escapes to drinking fountains and street signs.

"A user-friendly guide to all the overlooked things that make urban civilization tick. If you're an infrastructure nerd, a reader of David Macauley, Kate Ascher, or Brian Hayes, then you know that under the sidewalks of your town or city lies an endlessly complex world of pipes, cables, wires, and tunnels. If you want to understand the language spoken in that world, then this book is for you." —*Kirkus*

Based on a podcast; Includes bibliographical references and index.

Rybczynski, Witold
Mysteries of the Mall: And Other Essays. Witold Rybczynski. Farrar, Straus and Giroux 2015. 320 p.
ISBN 9780374269937
Grades: Adult   720
1. Cities and towns 2. Urban planning 3. Architecture and society 4. United States 5. Essays 6. Society and culture — Urban and regional studies 7. Arts and entertainment — Architecture
LC 2014046633

A collection of essays about modern life in our cities.

"A superb book for those interested in architectural history, written in an easygoing style by a man with encyclopedic knowledge and an obvious great love for building." —*Kirkus*

Includes index.

Watkin, David
A History of Western Architecture. David Watkin. Laurence King Publishing 2015. 736 pages : Illustration; Color
ISBN 9781780675978
Grades: Adult   720
1. Architecture 2. Architecture and society 3. Arts and Entertainment — Architecture

Traces the history of western architecture from the earliest times in Mesopotamia and Egypt to the eclectic styles of the twenty-first century. The author emphasizes that "traditional architecture has re-established itself as a solution to the many problems presented by new needs and new materials … This new edition covers. [structures] in [other areas of the world] as products of globalization, the attention paid to sustainability, energy; recycling elements of buildings; the passion for astonishing height but also architecture on a human scale, and urban planning [issues].

Includes bibliographical references (pages 720-724) and index; Previous edition: 2011. First edition published in 1986.

720.1 Architecture — Philosophy and theory

Goldhagen, Sarah Williams
Welcome to Your World: How the Built Environment Shapes Our Lives. Sarah Williams Goldhagen. Harper 2017. xxxiv, 347 pages : Illustration; Color
ISBN 9780061957802
Grades: Adult   720.1
1. Architecture 2. Architectural design 3. Urban beautification 4. Urban planning 5. Arts and Entertainment — Architecture 6. Society and culture — Urban and regional studies

One of the nation's chief architecture critics, drawing on new discoveries in cognitive psychology and neuroscience, takes readers on an eye-opening journey through some of the world's best and worst landscapes, buildings and cityscapes, revealing how the environments we build profoundly shape our feelings and memories.

"An eye-opening look at the ways in which carefully planned and executed design and architecture can expand cognitive faculties and improve daily life." —*Kirkus*

Includes bibliographical references (pages 309-335) and index.

720.9 History, geographic treatment, biography

Ching, Francis D. K.
★ *A Global History of Architecture.* Francis D.K. Ching, Mark Jarzombek, Vikramaditya Prakash. Wiley 2017. xiii, 850 p. : Illustration; Map
ISBN 9781118981337
Grades: Adult   720.9

PUBLIC LIBRARY CORE COLLECTION: NONFICTION
Twentieth Edition

1. Architecture 2. Arts and Entertainment — Architecture

LC 2017004046

A Global History of Architecture, Third Edition has been updated and revised throughout to reflect current scholarship, including an expanded section on contemporary global architecture. Spanning from 3,500 b.C.E. to the present, this unique guide is written by an all-star team of architectural experts in their fields who emphasize the connections, contrasts, and influences of architectural movements throughout history.

Includes bibliographical references (pages 811-820) and index.

Hollis, Edward
The Secret Lives of Buildings: From the Ruins of the Parthenon to the Vegas Strip in Thirteen Stories. Edward Hollis. Metropolitan Books, Henry Holt and Co. 2009. 352 p.
ISBN 9780805087857
Grades: Adult 720.9
1. Architecture and history 2. Architecture and society 3. Buildings 4. Architecture 5. Essays 6. Arts and Entertainment — Architecture

LC 2009018715

A narrative history of western architecture offers insight into its reflection of cultural influences and transformations, documenting some of the most dramatic examples of dynamic western architecture from Notre Dame's cathedral to the Berlin Wall.

Includes bibliographical references.

720.92 Architects

Storrer, William Allin
The Frank Lloyd Wright Companion. William Allin Storrer. University of Chicago, Ill. :Press 2006. xvi, 492 p. : Illustration
ISBN 9780226776217
Grades: Adult 720.92
1. Wright, Frank Lloyd, 1867-1959 2. Arts and Entertainment — Architecture

LC 2006044502

The comprehensive source for as-built plans of Wright's work.

"With this volume, Storrer surpasses his previous catalog of Wright's work, the Architecture of Frank Lloyd Wright (MIT Pr, 1978), by compiling detailed plans, photographs, and brief histories of every structure built by America's most widely known architect." —*Library Journal*

Includes index.

721 Architectural materials

Rybczynski, Witold
The Look of Architecture. Witold Rybczynski. Oxford University Press 2001. xiv, 130 p. : Illustration
ISBN 9780195156331
Grades: Adult 721
1. Architecture 2. Architectural design 3. Arts and Entertainment — Architecture 4. Adult books for young adults

LC 00053077

One of the nation's foremost experts on architecture discusses the role of style in the "language" of the discipline, and shows how Frank Gehry, Mies van der Rohe, Allan Greenberg, and others are influenced by it.

"The author's deeply informed enthusiasm is infectious, and his removal of architectural writing from an airily theoretical discourse to the realm of practical experience is empowering for the lay reader." —*Publishers Weekly*

Includes bibliographical references (p. 121-124) and index.

Smith, Nathan
Color Concrete Garden Projects: Make Your Own Planters, Furniture, and Fire Pits Using Creative Techniques and Vibrant Finishes. Nathan Smith & Michael Snyder; photographs by Charles Coleman. Timber Press 2015. 206 pages : Color; Illustration
ISBN 9781604695397
Grades: Adult 721
1. Garden ornaments and furniture 2. Concrete construction 3. Design and construction 4. Arts and Entertainment — Crafts and hobbies — Garden and nature

LC 2014048495

Presents step-by-step instructions for twenty garden projects that use concrete as a medium, from a tabletop candleholder and a doorstop to a large oval planter and a modern birdhouse.

"This book has taken concrete projects to a new high; there's nothing else quite as focused on the subject. For a general concrete container book, see Malin Nilsson and Camilla Arvidsson's Concrete Garden Projects. A true standout. . . superior instructions and innovative design and use of pigment. A must for any DIY collection." —*Library Journal*

Includes index.

724 Architecture from 1400

Curtis, William J. R.
Modern Architecture Since 1900. William J.R. Curtis. Phaidon 1996. 736 p. : Illustration; Color
ISBN 9780714835242
Grades: Adult 724
1. Architecture, Modern 2. 20th century 3. Arts and Entertainment — Architecture

LC 97112837

"The volume's well-detailed text is buttressed with 650 color and black-and-white illustrations. This should be a standard volume in all architecture collections." —*Library Journal*

Includes bibliographical references (p. 693-719) and index.

Huxtable, Ada Louise
On Architecture: Collected Reflections on a Century of Change. Ada Louise Huxtable. Walker & Co. 2008. 288 p.
ISBN 9780802717078
Grades: Adult 724
1. Architecture 2. Architectural criticism 3. Architecture and society 4. 20th century 5. Essays 6. Arts and Entertainment — Architecture

LC Bl2009005866

A forefront and passionate critic evaluates architecture as a pivotal and controversial component of twentieth-century culture, in a collection of articles that covers such topics as Le Corbusier's Carpenter Center at Harvard, the mid-century shifts in style, and her selections for best and worst architectural examples.

"The author presents her penetrating and tough-minded criticism spanning half a century. Centering largely on modernism, its masters and its discontents, the volume opens with an overview of the past four decades, including startlingly powerful pieces on the late '60s urban decay and the '90s reinvention of architecture." —*Publishers Weekly*

725 Architecture — Public structures

Blockley, David
Bridges: The Science and Art of the World's Most Inspiring Structures. David Blockley. Oxford University Press 2010. 288 p.
ISBN 9780199543595
Grades: 11 12 Adult 725
1. Bridges 2. Architecture 3. Structural engineering 4. Suspension bridges 5. Arches 6. Science Writing — Great Engineering Feats 7. Arts and Entertainment — Architecture

LC Bl2010016758

Explains the importance of bridges, the process of constructing the four main types, and the reasons behind bridge disasters around the world.

ESSENTIAL AND RECOMMENDED TITLES
726.5 Buildings associated with Christianity

Thompson, Erin L.
Smashing Statues: The Rise and Fall of America's Public Monuments. Erin L. Thompson. W. W. Norton & Company 2022. 224 p.
ISBN 9780393867671
Grades: Adult   **725**
1. Memorialization 2. Collective memory 3. Monuments 4. Public opinion 5. United States 6. History writing — United States
LC 2021041567

An urgent and fractious national debate over public monuments has erupted in America. Some people risk imprisonment to tear down long-ignored hunks of marble; others form armed patrols to defend them. Why do we care so much about statues? And who gets to decide which ones should stay up and which should come down?

"Thompson (Possession), a professor of art crime at the John Jay College of Criminal Justice, examines in this trenchant account 'The ideologies, hatreds, and ambitions' behind America's public monuments, and the debate over 'What we can and should do with them now.'... Full of intriguing historical tidbits and incisive cultural analysis, this is a worthy study of a complex and controversial issue." —*Publishers Weekly*

Includes bibliographical references and index.

726.5 Buildings associated with Christianity

Van Hensbergen, Gijs
The Sagrada Familia: Gaudi's Heaven on Earth. Gijs van Hensbergen. Bloomsbury 2017. 204 p.
ISBN 9781408854778
Grades: Adult   **726.5**
1. Gaudi, Antoni, 1852-1926 2. Churches 3. Architects 4. Architecture 5. Barcelona, Spain 6. spain 7. History writing — Europe — Spain 8. Arts and Entertainment — Architecture

Explores the history of the Sagrada Famâilia, the unfinished minor basilica designed by Antoni Gaudi.

"Van Hensbergen serves as an enthusiastic guide in this more than thorough account of one of the worlds most eccentric and stunning buildings." —*Publishers Weekly*

Includes index; Originally published : Barcelona : Rosa dels Vents, 2016.

726.6 Cathedrals

King, Ross
Brunelleschi's Dome: How a Renaissance Genius Reinvented Architecture. Ross King. Walker & Co. 2000. 194 p. : Illustration
ISBN 9780802713667
Grades: 11 12 Adult   **726.6**
1. Brunelleschi, Filippo, 1377-1446 2. Ghiberti, Lorenzo, 1378-1455 3. Architects 4. Domes 5. Architecture, Renaissance (Europe) 6. Architecture and religion 7. Cathedrals 8. European Renaissance 9. Design and construction 10. Buildings 11. Italian history 12. Florence, Italy 13. Italy 14. 15th century 15. Renaissance (1300-1600) 16. History writing — Renaissance — Europe 17. History writing — Europe — Italy 18. History writing — Technological innovations 19. Arts and Entertainment — Architecture
LC 00043524

Book Sense Book of the Year Nonfiction, 2001; Booklist Editors' Choice, 2000.

Describes how a fifteenth-century goldsmith and clockmaker, Filippo Brunelleschi, came up with a unique design for the dome to crown Florence's magnificent new cathedral, Santa Maria del Fiore.

"King illuminates the mysterious sources of inspiration and the secretive methods of architectural genius Filippo Brunelleschi in a fascinating chronicle of the building of his masterwork, the dome of Santa Maria del Fiore in Florence. A remarkable saga of how one incandescent mind performed the one matchless feat that would forever transform architecture from a mechanical craft into a creative art." —*Booklist*

Includes bibliographical references (p. [177]) and index; Simultaneously published: London : Chatto & Windus, 2000.

727 Buildings for educational and research purposes

Holway, Tatiana M.
The Flower of Empire: The Amazon's Largest Water Lily, the Quest to Make It Bloom, and the World It Helped Create. Tatiana Holway. Oxford University Press 2013. 336 p.
ISBN 9780195373899
Grades: Adult   **727**
1. Lindley, John, 1799-1865 2. Schomburgk, Robert H. (Robert Hermann), Sir, 1804-1865 3. Fads and crazes 4. Botany 5. Botanists 6. Exploration 7. Scientific discoveries 8. Flowers 9. Popular culture 10. Botanical gardens 11. British history 12. 19th century 13. History writing — Europe — United Kingdom 14. Nature Writing — Gardens
LC 2012034518

Narrates the story of the discovery of an Amazon water lily and its impact on Victorian life and culture, as prominent botanists of the day became obsessessed in their quest to make the flower bloom in England.

Meier, Richard
Building the Getty. Richard Meier. Alfred A. Knopf 1997. xii, 204 p. : Illustration
ISBN 9780375400438
Grades: Adult   **727**
1. Art centers 2. Los Angeles, California 3. Arts and Entertainment — Architecture
LC 97029326

"Charting his involvement in the Getty's construction, Meier recounts in an intriguingly candid, eminently personal style the formidable bureaucratic process entailed upon undertaking to realize this grandiose endeavor. Beginning with the competition itself, Meier's detailed reminiscences offer fascinating insights into the design process and the extraordinarily intricate procedures and systems, as well as endless setbacks, associated with executing a modern-day megalithic structure." —*Booklist*

728 Residential and related buildings

Barker, Margaret A.
Audubon Birdhouse Book: Building, Placing, and Maintaining Great Homes for Great Birds. Margaret A. Barker and Elissa Wolfson; foreword by Stephen W. Kress; carpentry by Chris Willett. Voyageur Press 2013. 160 p. : Illustration; Map
ISBN 9780760342206
Grades: Adult   **728**
1. Bird attracting 2. United States 3. Nature writing — Animal Studies — Birds and Birding 4. Arts and Entertainment — Crafts and hobbies — Woodworking
LC 2013018947

Produced in association with the National Audubon Society, Audubon Birdhouse Book explains how to build and place functional DIY bird homes that are safe and appropriate for more than 20 classic North American species, from wrens to raptors.

"Like Birdhouses You Can Build in a Day, this informative volume tailors designs to specific species. However, what sets this work apart is the inclusion of research and scientific study results on what makes a home suitable for a particular type of bird." —*Library Journal*

Includes bibliographical references (page 156) and index.

PUBLIC LIBRARY CORE COLLECTION: NONFICTION
Twentieth Edition

Bradbury, Dominic
Mountain Modern: Contemporary Homes in High Places. Dominic Bradbury; photographs by Richard Powers. Thames & Hudson 2014. 255 pages : Illustration; Color
ISBN 9780500517468
Grades: Adult   **728**
1. Architecture, Domestic 2. Interior decoration 3. Arts and Entertainment — Architecture
LC Bl2015006420

Showcases contemporary houses designed specifically for mountain settings and high-altitude locations, looking at how architects incorporate natural settings into their plans while highlighting interior design features.

Hirsch, William J.
Designing Your Perfect House: Lessons from an Architect. William J. Hirsch Jr. Dalsimer Press 2008. 239 p. : Color illustration
ISBN 9780979882005
Grades: Adult   **728**
1. Architecture, Domestic 2. Houses 3. Design and construction 4. Arts and Entertainment — Architecture 5. House and Home — General
LC 2007936951

This second edition of Designing Your Perfect House includes a bonus lesson, Building Green, Naturally.

"Drawing many examples from his own practice, he explains the process and philosophy of residential design as seen from a professional's view and discusses what to consider when creating one's dream home." —*Library Journal*

Includes bibliographical references and index.

Jordan, Wendy Adler
Universal Design for the Home: Great Looking, Great Living Design for All Ages, Abilities, and Circumstances. Wendy A. Jordan. Quarry Books 2008. 207 p. : Color illustration; Plan
ISBN 9781592533817
Grades: Adult   **728**
1. Barrier-free design 2. Houses 3. Design and construction 4. Arts and Entertainment — Architecture
LC 2007032663

Showcases newly built or renovated homes that are accommodating to all and discusses the inhabitants' lifestyles and physical challenges.

"This book shows how a home that is accommodating to all can also have a stylish decor. Color photographs and some before-and-after floor plans show how accessibility standards have been incorporated. A list of resources is provided." —*Library Journal*

Includes index.

Koones, Sheri
Prefabulous Small Houses. Sheri Koones; foreword by Robert Redford. The Taunton Press, Inc. 2016. 233 p.
ISBN 9781631864049
Grades: Adult   **728**
1. Ecological houses 2. Small houses 3. Houses 4. Design and construction 5. Architecture, Domestic 6. United States 7. House and Home — General 8. Arts and Entertainment — Architecture
LC 2016021033

In Prefabulous Small Houses, best-selling author Sheri Koones presents 32 stunning prefabricated homes from around North America. 250 beautiful photographs and floorplans show the amazing breadth of styles available to today's homeowners.

"Lack of an index might hamper the use of this volume, but a multitude of cost-effective, energy-efficient ideas can be found here." —*Library Journal*

Kotite, Erika
She Sheds: A Room of Your Own. Erika Kotite. Cool Springs Press 2017. 176 pages : Color; Illustration
ISBN 9781591866770
Grades: Adult   **728**
1. Interior decoration 2. Outdoor living spaces 3. Sheds 4. Women 5. House and Home — General 6. House and Home — Interior Decorating and Furnishings 7. House and Home — Outdoor areas
LC 2016033753

She Sheds provides inspiration, tips, and tricks to help create the hideaway of your dreams.

McAlester, Virginia
A Field Guide to American Houses: The Definitive Guide to Identifying and Understanding America's Domestic Architecture. Virginia Savage McAlester; with drawings bySuzanne Patton Matty and photographs by Steve Clicque; revised and expanded from the original edition written by Virginia and Lee McAlester; with drawings by Lauren Jarrett and model house drawings by Ju. Alfred A. Knopf 2013. xxv, 848 pages : Illustration
ISBN 9781400043590
Grades: Adult   **728**
1. Architecture, Domestic 2. United States 3. Arts and Entertainment — Architecture 4. Reference — Travel guides
LC 2013018432

A guide for architecture aficionados explains how to identify the various styles and periods of American domestic architecture, focusing on typical dwellings in everyday neighborhoods to place distinct styles and characteristics within historical frames.

Provides in-depth descriptions and illustrations of architectural styles and features of everyday domestic dwellings across the United States.

First edition published June 12, 1984.—Title page verso; Includes bibliographical references (pages 773-814) and index.

Pierce, D.
The Accessible Home: Designing for All Ages and Abilities. Deborah Pierce. The Taunton Press 2012. 234 pages : Color; Illustration
ISBN 9781600854910
Grades: Adult   **728**
1. Houses 2. Design and construction 3. Barrier-free design 4. House and Home — General 5. House and Home — DIY, maintenance, and repair 6. House and Home — Remodeling and renovation
LC 2012029176

Millions of baby boomers are approaching the golden years. While it's a marker worth celebrating, it can also be a reminder of uncertain times ahead. How will I manage? Can I stay in my home? The Accessible Home goes beyond ramps and grab-bars to help aging boomers, or those faced with disabilities, accomplish home accessibility on a deeper level. With a focus on closing the gap between home and homeowner, architect Deborah Pierce leads readers through the steps of universal design—from hiring the right architect to creating a pleasing space with the final details. Plus, an insider's look at 25 case studies shows that the best design is built in, not tacked on, and that "accessible" can be both beautiful and functional. The Accessible Home empowers people of all ages and challenges them to create homes that restore independence and the grace of daily living.

The idea of the accessible home has evolved beyond grab-bars and ramps to one where accessibility is built into the design, making living in the house easier both for people with disabilities and those without disabilities, young and old.

Includes index.

Susanka, Sarah
Creating the Not so Big House: Insights and Ideas for the New American Home. Sarah Susanka; photographs by Grey Crawford. Taunton Press; 2000. 258 p. : Color illustration
ISBN 9781561583775
Grades: Adult   **728**
1. Architecture 2. Interior architecture 3. Space (Architecture) 4. Architecture, Domestic 5. United States 6. 20th century 7. House and Home — General 8. House and Home — DIY, maintenance, and repair
LC 00044323

Offers a look at twenty-five examples of small house designs to show readers what they need to know to plan the home that best fits their goals and lifestyles.

ESSENTIAL AND RECOMMENDED TITLES
728.37 Separate houses

The sequel to the best-selling The Not so Big House offers a close-up, richly illustrated look at twenty-five outstanding examples of the best small-house designs to show readers what they need to know to create the home that best fits their goals and lifestyles.

"Architect Susanka has big ideas about small design. This book promotes well-designed, efficient, interesting modest-size homes. She includes 25 delightful examples of houses designed by architects from around the country." —*Booklist*

Includes index.

Not So Big Solutions for Your Home. Sarah Susanka. Taunton Press; 2002. 155 p. : Color illustration
ISBN 9781561586134
Grades: Adult   728
1. Architecture, Domestic 2. House construction 3. Interior architecture 4. House and Home — General
LC 2002007101

Offers ideas to increase usable space in a home and add warmth and character, including tips on designing a window seat, planning a recyling area, and using tile to personalize a kitchen or bathroom.

"The author presents a compilation of 31 essays from her Drawing Board column in Fine Homebuilding magazine that offer a number of solutions to household design problems both big and small. Susanka offers an eclectic mix: Tips on site selection, mud room design, planning to fit specific furniture, creating a family room that works, personalizing with tile, and planning window seats, pantries, TV placement, and floor plan changes." —*Library Journal*

From the pages of Fine homebuilding magazine; Contains articles originally written for Fine homebuilding magazine's Drawing board column.

Van Doren, Adam
The House Tells the Story: Homes of the American Presidents. Adam Van Doren; foreword by David McCullough. David R. Godine, Publisher 2015. 189 pages : Color; Illustration
ISBN 9781567925425
Grades: Adult   728
1. Van Doren, Adam, 1962- 2. Presidents 3. Arts and Entertainment — Architecture 4. History writing — United States
LC 2015000579

The author shares the illustrated letters he sent his friend, historian David McCullough, over the course of three years that depict the homes of former presidents, focusing on the small details of everyday life to provide a more intimate look at the presidents' lives.

"Warm, accessible, and harmonious, this book marries history with art for a uniquely American vision." —*Publishers Weekly*

Includes index.

Versaci, Russell
Creating a New Old House: Yesterday's Character for Today's Home. Russell Versaci; photographs by Erik Kvalsvik. Taunton Press 2003. 218 p. : Color illustration
ISBN 9781561586158
Grades: Adult   728
1. Architecture, Domestic 2. United States 3. Arts and Entertainment — Architecture
LC 2003004993

Featuring 18 homes, this guidebook by a Virginia-based architect offers ideas and techniques for instilling "core pillars of tradition" in new homes.

Wilhide, Elizabeth
Scandinavian Home: A Comprehensive Guide to Mid-Century Modern Scandinavian Designers. Elizabeth Wilhide. Quadrille Publishing 2016. 192 p. : Illustration; Color
ISBN 9781849497497
Grades: Adult   728
1. Architecture, Domestic 2. Architecture, Modern 3. Interior decoration 4. Scandinavia 5. House and Home — Interior Decorating and Furnishings
LC Bl2016032221

Explores the Scandinavian design movement, an approach characterized by the use of natural materials and organic forms with clean lines and comfort.

Includes index.

728.37 Separate houses

Mitchell, Ryan
Tiny House Living: Ideas for Building and Living Well in Less Than 400 Square Feet. Ryan Mitchell. Betterway Home 2014. 175 pages : Color; Illustration
ISBN 9781440333163
Grades: Adult   728.37
1. Small houses 2. House and Home — DIY, maintenance, and repair 3. House and Home — Sustainable living
LC Bl2014029615

Explores the philosophies behind the tiny house lifestyle, and provides guidance for the transition to a smaller space, including practical strategies for paring down possessions and design tricks to maximize function in available space.

Includes bibliographical references (pages 166-168) and index.

728.81 Castles

Morris, Marc
Castles: Their History and Evolution in Medieval Britain. Marc Morris. Pegasus 2017. 288 p.
ISBN 9781681773599
Grades: Adult   728.81
1. Castles 2. Medieval architecture 3. Architecture, British 4. Buildings 5. Great Britain 6. England 7. Ireland 8. Wales 9. Medieval period (476-1492) 10. History writing — Medieval — Europe 11. Arts and Entertainment — Architecture
LC 2017446173

From the author of the Norman Conquest and a Great and Terrible King comes a sweeping and stunning history of the most magnificent castles in Britain.

731.4 Sculpture — Techniques and procedures

Heaser, Sue
The Polymer Clay Techniques Book. Sue Heaser. North Light Books 1999. 128 p. : Illustration; Color
ISBN 9781581800081
Grades: Adult   731.4
1. Polymer clay sculpture 2. Arts and Entertainment — Crafts and hobbies — Ceramics
LC BL 00001414

A step-by-step guide to creating different crafts, such as buttons, beads, and mosaics, using polymer clay.

"The Polymer Clay Technique Book, in particular, has detailed step-by-step instructions for many techniques such as marbling, cutting, and making millefiori canes." —*Library Journal*

Includes bibliographical references (p. 126) and index.

736 Carving and carvings

Brown, Nancy Marie
Ivory Vikings: The Mystery of the Most Famous Chessmen in the World and the Woman Who Made Them. Nancy Marie Brown. Palgrave Macmillan Trade 2015. 256 p.
ISBN 9781137279378
Grades: Adult   736

PUBLIC LIBRARY CORE COLLECTION: NONFICTION
Twentieth Edition

1. Vikings 2. Civilization, Medieval 3. Chess sets 4. Chess 5. Antiquities 6. Scotland 7. Medieval period (476-1492) 8. History writing — Arts and culture 9. History writing — Medieval — Europe 10. Sports and Competition — Games

LC 2015002532

Draws on medieval Icelandic sagas, modern archaeology, art history, forensics, and the history of board games to discuss the Lewis chessman.

"This book is a delight for chess players, of course, but also for gamers of all sorts as well as anyone interested in the intricacies of the provenance of art and in endlessly fascinating minutiae the strength and uses of walrus skin, how to carve walrus ivory, and so much more." —*Booklist*

Includes bibliographical references.

Jones, Andrew

Stickmaking Handbook. Andrew Jones & Clive George. Guild of Master Craftsman Publications 2016. 143 pages : Illustration; Color
ISBN 9781784940980
Grades: Adult   **736**

1. Wood-carving 2. Staffs (Sticks, canes, etc.) 3. Arts and Entertainment — Crafts and hobbies — Woodworking

LC Bl2017008659

Explains how to carve a variety of traditional walking sticks using wood and alternative materials.

"There are few books on this traditional craft, making this title unique. Recommended as a different focus for woodworkers." —*Library Journal*

Includes index.

736.98 Paper cutting and folding

Hayakawa, Hiroshi

Kirigami Menagerie: 38 Paper Animals to Copy, Cut & Fold. Hiroshi Hayakawa. Sterling Pub. CO 2009. 128 p. : Color illustration
ISBN 9781600593185
Grades: 8 9 10 11 12 Adult   **736.98**

1. Origami 2. Animals in art 3. Arts and Entertainment — Crafts and hobbies — Papercrafts

LC 2008050622

In origami, a flat piece of paper is folded to create a dimensional object. Similarly, in traditional Japanese kirigami, paper is folded, cut, and unfolded to reveal complex patterns—like a paper snowflake. Here, author Hiroshi Hayakawa has ingeniously combined these two techniques to create a charming menagerie of 38 animals, from flocks of sheep and swirling dragons to stampeding ostriches and pandas in a bamboo grove.

"Hayakawa's delightful animals start out with cutout shapes that are folded and joined together with slits and tabs." —*Library Journal*

Includes index.

736.982 Origami

Baard, Nellianna van den

Better Living Through Origami: 20 Creative Paper Projects for a Beautiful Home. Nellianna van den Baard and Kenneth Veenenbos. Sew and so 2018. 127 pages : Illustration; Color
ISBN 9781446307120
Grades: Adult   **736.982**

1. Origami 2. Arts and Entertainment — Crafts and hobbies — Papercrafts

LC Bl2019001192

"Patterns for finished objects that are both contemporary and versatile feature instructions that can be readily executed, covering all of the elements more specifically and including graphics, patterns, and metric measurements." —*Booklist*

Includes index.

Morin, John

Inspired Origami: Projects to Calm the Mind and Soothe the Soul. John Morin and Camilla Sanderson. Running Press 2016. 120 pages : Color; Illustration
ISBN 9780762461752
Grades: Adult   **736.982**

1. Origami 2. Mindfulness 3. Arts and Entertainment — Crafts and hobbies — Papercrafts

LC Bl2018002539

Presents fifteen origami projects and explains how the practice of paper folding can calm people through mindfulness.

Includes index.

738 Ceramic arts

Nelson, Glenn C.

Ceramics: A Potter's Handbook. Glenn C. Nelson, Richard Burkett. Wadsworth/Thomson Learning 2002. 439 p. : Illustration; Color
ISBN 9780030289378
Grades: Adult   **738**

1. Ceramics 2. Arts and Entertainment — Crafts and hobbies — Ceramics

LC 2001096329

This text introduces students to the fundamentals of the ceramic arts, beginning with a history of ceramic materials and techniques up to the present day and then moving on to a detailed presentation of basic and complex ceramic techniques. Techniques and results are illustrated with b&w and color photos, with a portfolio of contemporary work of the last 50 years. This sixth edition incorporates new resources and materials available as well as current technical and safety information. Burkett is affiliated with San Diego State University.

Includes bibliographical references (p. 420-424) and index.

738.1 Techniques, procedures, apparatus, equipment, materials

Burnett, Jason Bige

Graphic Clay: Ceramic Surfaces & Printed Image Transfer Techniques. Jason Bige Burnett. Lark Crafts 2014. 160 pages : Illustration
ISBN 9781454707752
Grades: Adult   **738.1**

1. Pottery 2. Arts and Entertainment — Crafts and hobbies — Ceramics

LC 2014016141

Presents information about decorative imagery for ceramics, describing techniques for applying slip, prepping bisqueware, firing decals, creating silk-screen stencils, and transferring screen-print images.

"Intermediate and experienced artists with some existing ceramics skills can find much inspiration here." —*Library Journal*

Includes bibliographical references (pages 148-149) and index.

Muller, Kristin

The Potter's Studio Handbook: A Start-to-Finish Guide to Hand-Built and Wheel-Thrown Ceramics. Kristin Muller. Quarry Books 2007. 192 p. : Color illustration (Backyard Series)
ISBN 9781592533732
Grades: 9 10 11 12 Adult   **738.1**

1. Pottery 2. Artists' studios 3. Arts and Entertainment — Crafts and hobbies — Ceramics

LC 2007016693

"The author guides beginners through advanced students in equipping a ceramic studio, handling the design, preparing the clay, constructing slab projects, throwing on a wheel, glazing, and firing. The 16 clay projects featured here include teapots, vases, and dinner plates. Readers can draw inspiration from the creative painting and underglazing examples, as well as the unusual firing techniques for color and texture." —*Library Journal*

ESSENTIAL AND RECOMMENDED TITLES
739.27 Jewelry

Pavelka, Lisa
*The **Complete** Book of Polymer Clay: Step-by-Step Instructions, Original Projects, Inspirational Gallery.* Lisa Pavelka. Taunton Press 2010. 221 p. : Color illustration
ISBN 9781600851285
Grades: Adult   738.1
  1. Polymer clay sculpture 2. Arts and Entertainment — Crafts and hobbies — Jewelry and beadwork
                                                LC 2009042430
  The Complete Book of Polymer Clay is an encyclopedic book by renowned expert Lisa Pavelka includes the latest techniques, handy tips, and trade secrets.
  Includes bibliographical references (p. 216-217) and index.

Stone, Francesca
***Easy** Homemade Pottery: Make Your Own Stylish Decor Using Polymer and Air-Dry Clay.* Francesca Stone. Page Street Publishing 2021. 175 p.
ISBN 9781645671503
Grades: Adult   738.1
  1. Pottery 2. Polymer clay sculpture 3. Arts and Entertainment — Crafts and hobbies — Ceramics
  You'll be amazed by what you can create with polymer and air-dry clay. These affordable, easy-to-find clays present endless possibilities for artisan-quality home decor and gifts. Francesca Stone, creator of the decor blog Fall for DIY, presents simple step-by-step techniques for shaping and decorating clay with just a few household tools.
  "Stone gives good coverage of a fun new medium to explore. This book will appeal to a wide audience of clay artists, both beginning and more experienced." —*Library Journal*

Taylor, Brian J.
***Glaze:** The Ultimate Ceramic Artist's Guide to Glaze and Color.* Brian Taylor and Kate Doody. Barron's 2014. 320 pages : Color; Illustration
ISBN 9780764166426
Grades: Adult   738.1
  1. Arts and Entertainment — Crafts and hobbies — Ceramics
                                                LC Oc2014087346
  Anyone who loves creating ceramics knows that glazing can be a labor of great love or the bane of the entire ceramic process. In the instructional and inspirational Glaze, potters will find a wealth of guidance on the glazing process as several of today's leading ceramicists share the recipes and techniques behind their most stunning works of art—each selected specifically for its unique glaze.
  "Pottery was never so alluring. Appended are a glossary, a bibliography, an Orton cone chart, a directory of ceramic materials, and teachers and artists." —*Booklist*
  A Quarto book—Title page verso; Includes bibliographical references (page 305) and index.

739.27 Jewelry

Codina, Carles
*The **Complete** Book of Jewelry Making: A Full-Color Introduction to the Jeweler's Art.* [Carles Codina; translation from the Spanish, Laurie C. Jones]. Lark Books 2006. 160 p. : Color illustration
ISBN 9781579903046
Grades: 11 12 Adult   739.27
  1. Jewelry making 2. Arts and Entertainment — Crafts and hobbies — Jewelry and beadwork
                                                LC Oc2007055494
  "This book covers the basics, from the ABCs of metallurgy to such complicated techniques as enameling and lacquering. Most of the examples are contemporary, taken from European designers, and all blessed with great color photographs." —*Booklist*
  Includes bibliographical references (p. 160) and index.

DeCoster, Marcia
  ★ *Marcia Decoster's Beaded Opulence: Elegant Jewelry Projects with Right Angle Weave.* Marcia DeCoster. Lark Books 2009. 128 p. : Color illustration
ISBN 9781600592928
Grades: Adult   739.27
  1. Beadwork 2. Jewelry making 3. Arts and Entertainment — Crafts and hobbies — Jewelry and beadwork
                                                LC 2008050857
  "Uniformly good design characterizes both books." —*Library Journal*
  Includes index.

Haab, Sherri
*The **Art** of Metal Clay: Techniques for Creating Jewelry and Decorative Objects.* Sherri Haab. Watson-Guptill Publications 2010. 160 p. : Illustration; Color
ISBN 9780823099320
Grades: Adult   739.27
  1. Metal-work 2. Jewelry making 3. Arts and Entertainment — Crafts and hobbies — Jewelry and beadwork 4. Arts and Entertainment — Crafts and hobbies — Ceramics
                                                LC 2009043781
  Developed in Japan in the 1990s, metal clay consists of microscopic particles of silver or gold suspended in a pliable organic binder that can be worked with the hands and simple household tools. This book offers a comprehensive introduction to the medium designed specifically for crafters and jewelrymakers.
  "An essential project book for anyone interested in learning to work with metal clay. [The projects included involve] bronze and copper metal clays, etching, and enameling. An included DVD has additional projects." —*Library Journal*
  Includes index.

Michaels, Chris Franchetti
Teach Yourself Visually Jewelry Making & Beading. by Chris Franchetti Michaels. Wiley Pub. 2007. 290 p. : Illustration; Color (Teach Yourself Visually)
ISBN 9780470101506
Grades: Adult   739.27
  1. Jewelry making 2. Beadwork 3. Arts and Entertainment — Crafts and hobbies — Jewelry and beadwork
                                                LC Bl2007029159
  Presents illustrated step-by-step instructions for jewelry making and beading, with advice on techniques, supplies, and design, and diagrams for easy and intermediate projects.
  Includes bibliographical references (p. 284-285), videography (p. 284), and index.

Young, Anastasia
*The **Workbench** Guide to Jewelry Techniques.* Anastasia Young. Interweave Press LLC 2009. 320 p. : Color illustration
ISBN 9781596681699
Grades: Adult   739.27
  1. Jewelry making 2. Arts and Entertainment — Crafts and hobbies — Jewelry and beadwork
                                                LC 2009041385
  Presents a comprehensive workshop reference for jewelry making and includes tips on tool shapes, an introduction to the history of jewelry, and suggestions for photographing and promoting finished pieces.
  "This is a reference guide for all jewelers, amateur or professional. Includes extensive photographic illustrations of virtually all techniques needed to create quality jewelry. Also has an excellent chapter on design, and additional sections on photographing, exhibiting, marketing, and selling work." —*Library Journal*
  A Quarto Book — T.P. verso; Includes bibliographical references (p. 315) and index.

PUBLIC LIBRARY CORE COLLECTION: NONFICTION
Twentieth Edition

739.27028 Jewelry — Auxiliary techniques and procedures

McGrath, Jinks
The Complete Jewelry Making Course. Jinks McGrath. Barron's 2007. 144 p. : Color illustration
ISBN 9780764136603
Grades: Adult   739.27028
1. Jewelry making 2. Arts and Entertainment — Crafts and hobbies — Jewelry and beadwork
LC Bl2007026247
This comprehensive and heavily illustrated manual teaches the craft of jewelry making to students looking to create professional quality items.
Includes bibliographical references (p. 144) and index.

740 Graphic arts

Ogura, Yoshiko
The Complete Guide to Drawing for Beginners: 21 Step-by-Step Lessons: Over 450 Illustrations! Yoshiko Ogura. Tuttle Publishing 2020. 127 p.
ISBN 9784805315767
Grades: Adult   740
1. Drawing 2. Arts and Entertainment — Painting, Drawing, and Sculpture
"It's difficult to see how an in-person class could teach much more."—*Booklist*

740.9 History, geographic treatment, biography of graphic arts and of decorative arts

Harvey, Eleanor Jones
The Civil War and American Art. Eleanor Jones Harvey. Smithsonian American Art Museum; 2012. xvii, 316 pages : Illustration
ISBN 9780300187335
Grades: Adult   740.9
1. Art and society 2. Art, American 3. Art criticism 4. Art exhibitions 5. United States history 6. 19th century 7. American Civil War era (1861-1865) 8. Arts and Entertainment — Painting, Drawing, and Sculpture 9. History writing — Arts and culture 10. History writing — Antebellum America — United States
LC 2012029342
The American Civil War was arguably the first modern war. Its grim reality, captured through the new medium of photography, was laid bare. American artists could not approach the conflict with the conventions of European history painting, which glamorized the hero on the battlefield. Instead, many artists found ways to weave the war into works of art that considered the human narrative—the daily experiences of soldiers, slaves, and families left behind. Artists and writers wrestled with the ambiguity and anxiety of the Civil War and used landscape imagery to give voice to their misgivings as well as their hopes for themselves and the nation. This important book looks at the range of artwork created before, during, and following the war, in the years between 1859 and 1876. Author Eleanor Jones Harvey examines the implications of the war on landscape and genre painting, history painting, and photography, as represented in some of the greatest masterpieces of 19th-century American art. The book features extensive quotations from men and women alive during the war years, alongside text by literary figures including Emily Dickinson, Mark Twain, and Walt Whitman, among many others.
Collects the best artwork created before, during and following the Civil War, in the years between 1859 and 1876, along with extensive quotations from men and women alive during the war years and text by literary figures, including Emily Dickinson, Mark Twain and Walt Whitman.
Published in conjunction with the exhibition of the same name, on view at the Smithsonian American Art Museum in Washington, D.C, from November 16, 2012 through April 28, 2013, and at the Metropolitan Museum of Art, New York City, from May 21-September 2, 2013; Includes bibliographical references (pages 274-293) and index.

741.09 Drawing and drawings — History, geographic treatment, biography

Kline, Fred R.
Leonardo's Holy Child: The Discovery of a Leonardo Da Vinci Masterpiece: A Connoiseur's Search for Lost Art in America. Fred R. Kline. Pegasus Books 2016. 384 p.
ISBN 9781605989792
Grades: Adult   741.09
1. Leonardo, da Vinci, 1452-1519 2. Drawing 3. Art collectors and collecting 4. Art 5. Arts and entertainment — Painting, drawing, and sculpture
LC Bl2016018832
Fred Kline is a well-known art historian, dealer, connoisseur, and explorer who has made a career of scouring antique stores, estate sales, and auctions looking for unusual—and often misidentified—works of art. Many of the gems he has found are now in major museum collections like the Frick, the Getty, and the Metropolitan Museum of Art. But this book is about the discovery of one piece in particular: About ten years ago, when Kline was routinely combing through a Christie's catalog, a beautiful little drawing caught his eye. Attributed to Carracci, it came with a very low estimate, but Kline's every instinct told him that the attribution was wrong. He placed a bid at the low asking price and bought the drawing outright. And that was the beginning of how Kline discovered Leonardo da Vinci's model drawing for the Infant Jesus and the Infant St. John. It is the first work by da Vinci to have surfaced in over a century.
"Even the most casual museum goer will find something to appreciate in this fascinating account."—*Booklist*

Whistler, Catherine
Venice and Drawing, 1500-1800: Theory, Practice and Collecting. Catherine Whistler. Yale University Press 2016. xxxv, 344 pages : Illustration
ISBN 9780300187731
Grades: Adult   741.09
1. History writing — Arts and culture 2. Arts and Entertainment — Painting, Drawing, and Sculpture
LC 2015045305
"With its wealth of new information and its highlighting of superb examples of the craft, this book will be the gold standard for the study of Venetian drawings for years to come."—*Choice*
Includes bibliographical references (pages 290-325).

741.2 Techniques, procedures, apparatus, equipment, materials

Birch, Helen
Freehand: Sketching Tips and Tricks Drawn from Art. Helen Birch. Chronicle Books 2013. 224 pages : Color; Illustration
ISBN 9781452119779
Grades: Adult   741.2
1. Creation (Literary, artistic, etc.) 2. Drawing technique 3. Arts and Entertainment — Painting, Drawing, and Sculpture
LC 2013036430
Provides commentary on a selection of different freehand drawings, identifying tips, techniques, and different tools to inspire readers.
"Employing the formula of examples + explanations = inspiration, journalist and artist Birch presents the work of dozens of practicing contemporary artists, highlighting prominent techniques so that the reader can emulate and build upon them. Illustrations can be found on nearly every page, including many close-up views that break down for the reader what is happening in the more elaborate drawings."—*Library Journal*
Includes bibliographical references and index.

De Reyna, Rudy
How to Draw What You See. Rudy de Reyna. Watson-Guptill Publications 1996. 175 p. : Illustration
ISBN 9780823023752
Grades: Adult   741.2

ESSENTIAL AND RECOMMENDED TITLES
741.5 Cartoons, graphic novels, caricatures, comics

1. Drawing 2. Arts and Entertainment — Painting, Drawing, and Sculpture
LC BL 99786913

Provides lessons in dimensions, proportions, the recognition of basic structure, lighting, shading, and the selection and use of various drawing materials.

"This compact 35th anniversary edition touches on still life, landscapes, and figure drawing in pencil, charcoal, watercolor wash, acrylic, and ink. De Reyna's dedication and enthusiasm are evident on every page." —*Library Journal*

Includes index; Reprint. Originally published: C1970.

Eagle, Ellen
Pastel Painting Atelier: Essential Lessons in Techniques, Practices, and Materials. Ellen Eagle; foreword by Maxine Hong Kingston. Watson-Guptill Publications 2013. 192 pages : Illustration

ISBN 9780823008414

Grades: Adult   741.2

1. Arts and Entertainment — Painting, Drawing, and Sculpture
LC 2012018761

A complete primer for serious beginners through advanced artists traces the history, materials and techniques of pastel artwork, featuring the pieces of old masters as well as a selection of notable contemporaries to cover each stage, discussing formal techniques as well as steps for pursuing personal aesthetics.

Explores the history, materials, and techniques of pastel drawing, and highlights the works of old masters and contemporaries alike.

Edwards, Betty
Drawing on the Right Side of the Brain. Betty Edwards. Tarcher/Penguin 2012. xxxiii, 284 p. : Illustration

ISBN 9781585429202

Grades: 9 10 11 12 Adult   741.2

1. Cerebral dominance 2. Drawing technique 3. Visual perception 4. Arts and Entertainment — Painting, Drawing, and Sculpture 5. Reference — Instructional materials
LC 2012001232

Helps the reader gain access to right-brain functions, which affect artistic and creative abilities, by teaching drawing through unusual exercises designed to increase visual skills.

"This new edition of the hugely popular and influential drawing manual first published over 30 years ago incorporates new findings from neuroscience, like the discovery of brain plasticity, together with the tried-and-true exercises included in past editions." —*Library Journal*

Rev. and expanded ed. of: New drawing on the right side of the brain. 1999; Includes bibliographical references (p. 270-274) and index.

McKinley, Richard
Pastel Pointers: Top Secrets for Beautiful Pastel Paintings. Richard McKinley. North Light Books 2010. 127 p. : Illustration; Color

ISBN 9781440308390

Grades: Adult   741.2

1. Arts and Entertainment — Painting, Drawing, and Sculpture
LC 2010028709

This book covers everything from the fundamentals to get you going (how to lay out your palette, create an underpainting, evoke luminous effects) to inspirations that will keep you growing (plein air painting, working in a series, keeping a painting journal). Whether you're a beginner or an experienced painter anxious to explore the expressive possibilities of pastel, this is your guide to making the most of the medium.

Includes bibliographical references and index.

Micklewright, Keith
Drawing: Mastering the Language of Visual Expression. Keith Mickelwright. Harry N. Abrams 2005. 168 p. : Illustration; Color

ISBN 9780810992382

Grades: 11 12 Adult   741.2

1. Communication in art 2. Drawing technique 3. Arts and Entertainment — Painting, Drawing, and Sculpture
LC 2005005862

Gives a history of drawing and includes chapters on such subjects as proportion, light, dimension, visual relationships, materials, and movement, and discusses how drawing is like language because it brings thoughts to life.

Includes bibliographical references (p. 164) and index.

Price, Maggie
Painting with Pastels: Easy Techniques to Master the Medium. Maggie Price. North Light Books 2007. 128 p. : Illustration; Color

ISBN 9781581808193

Grades: Adult   741.2

1. Arts and Entertainment — Painting, Drawing, and Sculpture
LC 2006029048

From selecting the right materials to learning the fundamentals of composition, Maggie starts with the basics and progresses to 21 complete pastel demonstrations that detail specific painting techniques and effects.

Includes index.

Scheinberger, Felix
Dare to Sketch: A Guide to Drawing on the Go. Felix Scheinberger. Watson-Guptill 2017. 159 pages

ISBN 9780399579554

Grades: Adult   741.2

1. Drawing technique 2. Arts and Entertainment — Painting, Drawing, and Sculpture 3. Self-Help — Personal growth — Creativity
LC 2017020347

An inspirational, instructional, and visually stimulating guide to sketching and drawing. Dare to Sketch is filled with practical tips about which materials to use, a variety of subject matter ranging from easy to more challenging, and wisdom about overcoming creative blocks and fear of making mistakes.

The author of Urban Watercolor Sketching, covering all of the important basics, presents an inspirational, instructional and visually stimulating guide to sketching and drawing that showcases his unique and contemporary art style.

"Lots of practical advice helps with everything from how to confront a blank sketchbook to the best way to catch a subject that won't sit still." —*Library Journal*

Willenbrink, Mark
Drawing for the Absolute Beginner: A Clear & Easy Guide to Successful Drawing. Mark and Mary Willenbrink. North Light Books 2006. 128 p. : Illustration

ISBN 9781581807899

Grades: Adult   741.2

1. Drawing technique 2. Arts and Entertainment — Painting, Drawing, and Sculpture
LC 2006008900

A series of confidence-building exercises take the reader from the basic fundamentals of drawing to the complexities of creating landscapes, still lifes, people, and much more in this helpful guide for artists of all skill levels.

Includes index.

741.5 Cartoons, graphic novels, caricatures, comics

Abel, Jessica
Drawing Words, Writing Pictures: Making Comics from Manga to Graphic Novels. Jessica Abel, Matt Madden. First Second Books 2008. 206 p. : Illustration

ISBN 9781596431317

Grades: 9 10 11 12 Adult   741.5

1. Comics and graphic novel writing 2. Cartooning technique 3. Comic books, strips, etc. 4. Comic book illustration 5. Comics and Graphic novels 6. Art and music — Visual arts — Cartooning and animation 7. Art and music — Arts and crafts — Drawing and painting 8. How-to books

A course on comic creation—for college classes or for independent study—that centers on storytelling and concludes with making a finished comic. With chapters on lettering, story structure, and panel layout, the fifteen lessons offered—each complete with homework, extra-credit activities and supplementary reading suggestions—provide a solid introduction for people interested in making their own comics. Additional resources, lessons, and after-class help are available on the accompanying website, http://Www.Dw-wp.Com.

"This book offers step-by-step entry into a complicated series of skills in a nonscary and approachable way." —*Library Journal*

Mastering Comics: Drawing Words & Writing Pictures Continued. Jessica Abel and Matt Madden. First Second Books 2012. 336 p. : Illustration; Color
ISBN 9781596436176
Grades: 9 10 11 12 Adult   741.5
1. Comics and graphic novel writing 2. Cartooning technique 3. Comic books, strips, etc. 4. Comic book illustration 5. Comics and Graphic novels 6. Art and music — Visual arts — Cartooning and animation 7. Art and music — Arts and crafts — Drawing and painting 8. How-to books

Presents instructions for mastering the creation of comic books and graphic novels, providing guidelines for the intermediate cartoonist on technique, story generation, narrative tools, and business and industry insights.

Ai, Weiwei

Zodiac: A Graphic Memoir. Ai Weiwei, with Elettra Stamboulis; illustrated by Gianluca Costantini. Ten Speed Press 2024. 171 p.
ISBN 9781984862990
Grades: Adult   741.5
1. Ai, Weiwei 2. Artists 3. Dissenters 4. Political activists 5. Exiles 6. Growing up 7. Revolutions 8. Censorship 9. Totalitarianism 10. Freedom and art 11. Creation (Literary, artistic, etc.) 12. Chinese zodiac 13. Art and politics 14. East Asian people 15. Chinese people 16. China 17. Autobiographical comics 18. Comics and graphic novels 19. Life stories — Arts and culture — Artists 20. Life stories — Politics — Activists and reformers 21. Life stories — Facing adversity — War and oppression 22. Arts and Entertainment — Painting, Drawing, and Sculpture

LC 2023941102

Inspired by the twelve signs of the Chinese zodiac and their associated human characteristics, Ai Weiwei masterfully interweaves ancient Chinese folklore with stories of his life, family, and career. The narrative shifts back and forth through the years—at once in the past, present, and future—mirroring memory and our relationship to time. As readers delve deeper into the beautifully illustrated pages of Zodiac, they will find not only a personal history of Ai Weiwei and an examination of the sociopolitical climate in which he makes his art, but a philosophical exploration of what it means to find oneself through art and freedom of expression.

"This is a sage and inventive embroidery of philosophy, family memoir, and cultural history." —*Publishers Weekly*

Amano, Hugh

Let's Make Dumplings!: A Comic Book Cookbook. Hugh Amano, Sarah Becan. Ten Speed Press 2021. 208 p. (Let's make (Graphic novel cookbooks))
ISBN 9781984858757
Grades: Adult   741.5
1. Dumplings 2. Cooking, Asian 3. Comics and Graphic novels 4. Food writing — Food and culture 5. Food writing — Cooking and cookbooks — Narrative cookbooks

Including dumpling history and lore, this comic book cookbook invites readers to explore the big little world of Asian dumplings and proves that intricate folding styles and flavorful fillings are achievable in the home kitchen.

"Solid recipes (calling for either handmade and store-bought wrappers) and entertaining stories—including one about a forgetful cook who accidentally invented pot stickers—showcase the authors' detailed yet playful approach to their craft." —*Publishers Weekly*

B., David

Epileptic. David B.. Pantheon Books 2005. 368 p.
ISBN 9780375423185
Grades: 11 12 Adult   741.5
1. Brothers 2. Growing up 3. Artists 4. Escapism 5. Families 6. Epilepsy 7. Children with epilepsy 8. People with epilepsy 9. Alternative medicine 10. Family problems 11. Coping in children 12. Childhood 13. Treatment 14. Family relationships 15. Child artists 16. France 17. 1960s 18. 1970s 19. Autobiographical comics 20. Comics and Graphic novels 21. Autobiographies and memoirs 22. Translations — French to English 23. Family and Relationships — Illness and the Family 24. Science Writing — Medicine and health — Illness and disease 25. Life stories — Facing adversity — Medical issues 26. Adult books for young adults

LC 2004053419

A personal memoir told in the form of a graphic novel chronicles the author's experiences growing up with an older brother suddenly afflicted with epilepsy and the effects of the disease on the family, and the roots of his career as a cartoonist.

"The author's artwork is magnificent—gorgeously bold, impressionistic representations of the world not as it is but as he's taught himself to perceive it. . . . B.'s illustrations constantly underscore his writing's wrenching psychological depth; readers can literally see how the chaos of his childhood shaped his vision and mind." —*Publishers Weekly*

Originally published: Paris : L'Association, 2002.

Beaton, Kate

★ *Ducks: Two Years in the Oil Sands.* Kate Beaton. Drawn & Quarterly 2022. 448 p.
ISBN 9781770462892
Grades: Adult   741.5
1. Families 2. Oil 3. Oil industry and trade 4. Student loans 5. Women artists 6. Sexism in employment 7. Sexual harassment 8. Psychic trauma 9. Exploitation 10. Tar sands 11. Mines and mineral resources 12. Canada 13. Comics and graphic novels 14. Autobiographical comics 15. Life stories — Arts and culture — Artists

Rise: A Feminist Book Project List, 2023; Mike Wieringo Comic Book Industry Awards, Best Non-Fiction Graphic Work, 2023; OLA Best Bets, 2022; Doug Wright Awards: Best Book, 2023; Ignatz Awards, Outstanding Graphic Novel, 2023; Evergreen Award (Ontario), 2023.

Before there was Kate Beaton, there was Katie Beaton of the Cape Breton Beatons, specifically Mabou, a tight-knit seaside community where the lobster is as abundant as beaches, fiddles, and Gaelic folk songs. With the singular goal of paying off her student loans, Katie heads out west to take advantage of Alberta's oil rush—part of the long tradition of East Coasters who seek gainful employment elsewhere when they can't find it in the homeland they love so much. Katie encounters the harsh reality of life in the oil sands, where trauma is an everyday occurrence yet is never discussed.

"Beaton captures numerous poignant, sometimes heartbreaking moments throughout the book, but the cumulative effect of her many stories is even more impressive. She creates an indelible portrait of environmental degradation, fraught interpersonal relationships among a workforce largely disconnected from home, and greedy corporations that seem only vaguely aware of the difficult work's effect on their employees." —*Kirkus*

Bechdel, Alison

★ *Fun Home: A Family Tragicomic.* Alison Bechdel. Houghton Mifflin 2006. 240 p.
ISBN 9780618477944
Grades: 11 12 Adult   741.5
1. Bechdel, Alison, 1960- 2. Fathers and daughters 3. Closeted gay men 4. Lesbian teenagers 5. Brothers 6. Teachers 7. Gay men 8. Undertakers 9. Parent and child 10. Children of divorced parents 11. Funeral homes 12. Teacher-student relationships 13. Divorce 14. Death 15. Historic preservation 16. Cartoonists 17. Coming out (Sexual or gender identity) 18. Autobiographical comics 19. LGBTQIA+ comics 20. Autobiographies and memoirs 21. Comics and Graphic novels 22. Family and Relationships — Families 23. Life stories — Relationships — Growing up 24. Life stories — Arts and culture — Writing — Authors 25. Adult books for young adults

LC 2005030304

ALA Notable Book, 2007; Eisner Awards, Best Reality-Based Work, 2007; Lambda Literary Award for Biography/Autobiography, 2006; New York Times Notable Book, 2006; Rainbow List, 2008; National Book Critics Circle Award for Autobiography/Memoir finalist.

ESSENTIAL AND RECOMMENDED TITLES
741.5 Cartoons, graphic novels, caricatures, comics

An unusual memoir done in the form of a graphic novel by a cult favorite comic artist offers a darkly funny family portrait that details her relationship with her father, a historic preservation expert dedicated to restoring the family's Victorian home, funeral home director, high-school English teacher, and closeted homosexual.

"The recursively told story, which revisits the sites of tragic desperation again and again, hits notes that resemble Jeanette Winterson at her best. Bechdel presents her childhood as a 'still life with children' that her father created, and meditates on how prolonged untruth can become its own reality. She's made a story that's quiet, dignified and not easy to put down." —*Publishers Weekly*

★ *The Secret to Superhuman Strength*. Alison Bechdel. Houghton Mifflin Harcourt 2021. 256 p.
ISBN 9780544387652
Grades: Adult   741.5
1. Bechdel, Alison, 1960- 2. Physical fitness 3. Fads and crazes 4. Health 5. Growing up 6. Self-fulfillment 7. Cartoonists 8. Lesbians 9. Self-discovery 10. Comics and graphic novels 11. Autobiographical comics 12. Life stories — Identity — LGBTQIA+ 13. Science writing — Medicine and health 14. Society and culture — Pop culture 15. Spirituality and religion — Body, mind, and spirit
LC 2021002174

A comics and cultural superstar delivers a deeply layered story of her fascination, from childhood to adulthood, with every fitness craze throughout the years, from Jack LaLanne in the 60s to the existential oddness of present-day spin classes.

"Bechdel's ever-elegant drawings, with nuanced coloring provided by her partner Holly Rae Taylor, perfectly match the tonal shifts of her kaleidoscopic narrative, alternating between soul-searching angst and dry self-satire." —*Publishers Weekly*

Bell, Darrin
★ *The Talk*. Darrin Bell. Henry Holt & Company 2023. 352 p.
ISBN 9781250805140
Grades: Adult   741.5
1. Bell, Darrin 2. Cartoonists 3. Growing up 4. Multiracial children 5. African American children 6. African American men 7. Racism 8. Race awareness 9. Identity 10. Violence against African Americans 11. Police brutality 12. Social justice 13. Fatherhood 14. Protectiveness 15. North American people 16. American people 17. Autobiographical comics 18. Comics and graphic novels 19. Life stories — Identity — Race and ethnicity 20. Life stories — Relationships — Growing up 21. Society and culture — Race 22. Debut title 23. Adult books for young adults 24. Antiracist literature
Alex Awards, 2024.

Darrin Bell was six years old when his mother told him he couldn't have a realistic water gun. She said she feared for his safety, that police tend to think of little Black boys as older and less innocent than they really are. Through evocative illustrations and sharp humor, Bell examines how the Talk shaped intimate and public moments from childhood to adulthood. Drawing attention to the brutal murders of African Americans along the way, he brings us up to the moment of reckoning when people took to the streets protesting the murders of George Floyd and Breonna Taylor. And now Bell must decide whether he and his own son are ready to have the Talk.

"Part memoir and part intellectual awakening, Bell's memoir is a triumph. A beautifully drawn book, rich with insight, humor, and hard-won knowledge." —*Kirkus*
Illustrated by the author.

Bongiovanni, Archie
A Quick & Easy Guide to They/Them Pronouns. Archie Bongiovanni and Tristan Jimerson. Limerence Press 2018. 60 p.
ISBN 9781620104996
Grades: 7 8 9 10 11 12 Adult   741.5
1. Gender expression 2. Gender identity 3. Gender nonconformity 4. Nonbinary people 5. Comics and Graphic novels 6. Growing up — LGBTQIA+ 7. Social issues — Human rights — LGBTQIA+
Rainbow List, 2019; YALSA Great Graphic Novels for Teens, 2019.

A quick, easy and important educational comic guide to using gender-neutral pronouns.

"In addition to supplying best practices for allies, situational examples illustrate what its like to be misgendered and how that feels to someone who identifies as nonbinary." —*Library Journal*

Brosh, Allie
★ *Hyperbole and a Half: Unfortunate Situations, Flawed Coping Mechanisms, Mayhem, and Other Things That Happened*. Allie Brosh. Simon & Schuster 2013. 288 p.
ISBN 9781451666175
Grades: Adult   741.5
1. Brosh, Allie 2. Personal conduct 3. Growing up 4. Blogs 5. Comedians 6. People with depression 7. Women 8. United States 9. Comics and Graphic novels 10. Webcomics 11. Autobiographical comics 12. Autobiographies and memoirs 13. Biographies 14. Life stories — Arts and culture — Performing arts — Entertainers and celebrities 15. Life stories — Relationships 16. Life stories — Facing adversity — Medical issues — Mental illness 17. Humor writing — General
LC 2013025527
Library Journal Best Books, 2013; Goodreads Choice Award, 2013.

In a four-color, illustrated collection of stories and essays, Allie Brosh's debut chronicles the many "learning experiences" Brosh has endured as a result of her own character flaws, and the horrible experiences that other people have had to endure because she was such a terrible child. Possibly the worst child. For example, one time she ate an entire cake just to spite her mother.

★ *Solutions and Other Problems*. Allie Brosh. Simon & Schuster 2020. 496 p.
ISBN 9781982156947
Grades: 9 10 11 12 Adult   741.5
1. Brosh, Allie 2. Comedians 3. Personal conduct 4. Growing up 5. Blogs 6. People with depression 7. Women 8. Comics and Graphic novels 9. Webcomics 10. Autobiographical comics 11. Autobiographies and memoirs 12. Life stories — Arts and culture — Performing arts — Entertainers and celebrities 13. Life stories — Relationships 14. Life stories — Facing adversity — Medical issues — Mental illness 15. Humor writing — General 16. Adult books for young adults
Alex Award, 2021.

The creator of the award-winning Hyperbole and a Half presents a new collection of comedic, autobiographical and deceptively illustrated essays on topics ranging from childhood and very bad pets to grief, loneliness and powerlessness in modern life.

"This achingly accurate and consistently hilarious comic memoir finds Brosh moving forward and becoming a stronger, braver storyteller page by page." —*Publishers Weekly*

Brunetti, Ivan
Cartooning: Philosophy and Practice. Ivan Brunetti. Yale University Press 2011. 77 p. : Illustration; Color
ISBN 9780300170993
Grades: 11 12 Adult   741.5
1. Cartooning 2. Cartooning technique 3. Arts and Entertainment — Comics, Cartoons, and Animation
LC 2010940419

Provides lessons on the art of cartooning along with information on terminology, tools, techniques, and theory.
Includes bibliographical references (p. 77).

Bui, Thi
★ *The Best We Could Do: An Illustrated Memoir*. Thi Bui. Harry N Abrams Inc. 2017. 336 p. : Illustration
ISBN 9781419718779
Grades: 11 12 Adult   741.5
1. Bui, Thi 2. Child immigrants 3. Immigrant families 4. Immigrants, Vietnamese 5. Immigration and emigration 6. Vietnam War, 1961-1975 7. Identity 8. Family relationships 9. Acculturation 10. Coping 11. Asian history 12. Vietnam

PUBLIC LIBRARY CORE COLLECTION: NONFICTION
Twentieth Edition

13. 1970s 14. 20th century 15. Autobiographical comics 16. Comics and Graphic novels 17. Life stories — Identity — Immigrants 18. Family and Relationships — Families 19. Adult books for young adults

LC Bl2017000643

ALA Notable Book, 2018; Booklist Editors' Choice: Adult Books for Young Adults, 2017; Library Journal Best Books, 2017; Mike Wieringo Comic Book Industry Awards, Best Non-Fiction Graphic Work, 2018; YALSA Great Graphic Novels for Teens, 2018; National Book Critics Circle Award for Autobiography/Memoir finalist, 2017.

The debut graphic novel memoir from Thi Bui is an intimate look at one family's journey from their war-torn home in Vietnam to their new lives in America. Exploring the anguish of immigration and the lasting effects that displacement has on a child and her family, Bui documents the story of her family's daring escape after the fall of South Vietnam in the 1970s, and the difficulties they faced building new lives for themselves.

"In creatively telling a complicated story with the kind of feeling words alone rarely relay, The Best We Could Do does the very best that comics can do." —*Booklist*

Byrne, Eugene
Darwin: A Graphic Biography. Eugene Byrne and illustrated by Simon Gurr. Smithsonian Institute Press 2013. 104 p.

ISBN 9781588343529

Grades: 5 6 7 8 9 10 11 12 Adult   741.5

1. Darwin, Charles, 1809-1882 2. Naturalists 3. Evolution 4. Natural history 5. English history 6. 19th century 7. Comics and Graphic novels 8. Biographies 9. Life stories — Science, technology, and medicine — Scientists and inventors 10. Science Writing — Biology 11. Adult books for young adults

LC Bl2013046169

Depicts the life and adventures of a young Charles Darwin in graphic novel form, following the intrepid scientist on an expedition to discover new specimens of beetles and describing the world of the 1800s.

Chast, Roz
★ *Can't We Talk About Something More Pleasant?: A Memoir.* Roz Chast. St Martins Pr. 2014. 224 p. : Illustration

ISBN 9781608198061

Grades: Adult   741.5

1. Chast, Roz 2. Parent and adult child 3. Aging parents 4. Children of aging parents 5. Life change events 6. Cartoonists 7. Aging 8. Seniors 9. Autobiographical comics 10. Comics and Graphic novels 11. Autobiographies and memoirs 12. Family and Relationships — Aging and Death 13. Life stories — Facing adversity — Coping with death

LC Bl2014017757

Kirkus Prize for Nonfiction, 2014; Library Journal Best Books 2014; National Book Critics Circle Award for Autobiography, 2014; New York Times Notable Book, 2014; National Book Award for Nonfiction finalist, 2014.

Celebrates the final years of the author's aging parents' lives through cartoons, family photos, and documents that reflect the author's struggles with caregiver challenges.

"Chast brings her parents and herself to life in the form of her characteristic scratchy-lined, emotionally expressive characters, making the story both more personal and universal." —*Publishers Weekly*

Chelsea, David
Perspective in Action: Creative Exercises for Depicting Spatial Representation from the Renaissance to the Digital Age. David Chelsea. Watson-Guptill Publications 2017. 171 pages : Illustration; Color

ISBN 9781607749462

Grades: Adult   741.5

1. Perspective 2. Comics and graphic novel writing 3. Comics and Graphic novels 4. Arts and Entertainment — Painting, Drawing, and Sculpture

LC 2016045493

Using the graphic novel format, Perspective in Action features 33 easy-to-follow demonstrations to teach the major discoveries in perspective.

"Cleverly packaged in a graphic novel format, artist Chelsea's (Perspective! for Comic Book Artists) book covers all aspects of simple perspective drawing and depicts its more complex applications." —*Library Journal*

Chiefly illustrations; Includes index.

Delisle, Guy
Hostage. Guy Delisle. Drawn & Quarterly 2017. 432 pages : Color; Illustration

ISBN 9781770462793

Grades: Adult   741.5

1. Andre, Christophe 2. Hostages 3. Kidnapping 4. Kidnapping victims 5. Biographical comics 6. Comics and Graphic novels 7. Translations — French to English 8. Life stories — Facing adversity — War and oppression — Hostages and POWs

LC Bl2017016554

Recounts, in graphic novel format, the harrowing story of Christophe Andre, an administer with Doctors without Borders who was kidnapped and held by armed men while working in the Caucasus region.

"Delisle brings the reader so fully into Andre's world that a simple change in his routine becomes either harrowing or hopeful, and the mundane details of his daily existence, saving a piece of bread from his morning meal for a snack, enjoying some music drifting through the wall into his cell, become heroic acts of defiance." —*Library Journal*

Chiefly illustrations; Originally published in 2016 as S'enfuir by Dargaud; Translated from the French by Helge Dascher.

Pyongyang: A Journey in North Korea. Guy Delisle; [translated by Helge Dascher]. Drawn & Quarterly 2005. 176 p. : Illustration

ISBN 9781896597898

Grades: 11 12 Adult   741.5

1. Delisle, Guy 2. Communism 3. Cartoonists 4. Animators 5. Tour guides 6. Cartoons (Animated films) 7. Totalitarianism 8. Hotels 9. Canadian people in foreign countries 10. North Korea 11. 21st century 12. Autobiographies and memoirs 13. Comics and Graphic novels 14. Canadian literature 15. Translations — French to English 16. Travel Writing — Asia and the South Pacific 17. Life stories — Arts and culture — Artists 18. Adult books for young adults

YALSA Best Books for Young Adults, 2006; YALSA Great Graphic Novels for Teens, 2007.

One of the few Westerners granted access to North Korea documents his observations of the secretive society in this graphic travelogue that depicts the cultural alienation, boredom, and desires of ordinary North Koreans.

"Pyongyang will appeal to multiple audiences: Current events buffs, Persepolis fans and those who just love a good yarn." —*Publishers Weekly*

Translated from the French.

Derf
Kent State: Four Dead in Ohio. Derf Backderf. Abrams ComicArts 2020. 288 p.

ISBN 9781419734847

Grades: 10 11 12 Adult   741.5

1. Kent State shootings, May 4, 1970 2. College students 3. Vietnam War, 1961-1975 4. Student movements 5. Protest movements 6. Political participation 7. United States history 8. United States 9. Ohio 10. 1970s 11. 20th century 12. Comics and Graphic novels 13. History writing — 1970s — United States 14. Politics and global affairs — Civil and human rights 15. Adult books for young adults

LC Bl2020033759

Alex Award, 2021; Eisner Awards, Best Reality-Based Work, 2021; Mike Wieringo Comic Book Industry Awards, Best Non-Fiction Graphic Work, 2021; YALSA Great Graphic Novels for Teens, 2021.

A commemorative 50th anniversary graphic-novel account of the May 4, 1970 shootings of Vietnam War college student protesters by the Ohio National Guard draws on in-depth interviews to profile the tragedy's four victims.

"Backderf's tightly drawn, muscular figures and busy layouts anchored by choice period details are consistent with his established style, with flourishes (from hairstyles to smirks) that individualize the ensemble cast. His expertly

ESSENTIAL AND RECOMMENDED TITLES
741.5 Cartoons, graphic novels, caricatures, comics

crafted chronicle of this defining moment in U.S. history serves as a deeply moving elegy for the victims." —*Publishers Weekly*
Illustrated by the author.

Eisner, Will
★ *Comics* and Sequential Art: Principles and Practices from the Legendary Cartoonist. Will Eisner. W. W. Norton 2008. xii, 175 p. : Illustration
ISBN 9780393331264
Grades: 9 10 11 12 Adult　741.5
1. Drawing technique 2. Cartooning technique 3. Arts and Entertainment — Comics, Cartoons, and Animation 4. Adult books for young adults
LC 2008020042
"This guide by one of the veterans of the industry provides a solid framework in the principles of drawing comic art." —*Library Journal*
Rev. ed. of: Comics & sequential art. 1985; Includes index.

Findakly, Brigitte
Poppies of Iraq. Brigitte Findakly; co-written and illustrated by Lewis Trondheim. Farrar Straus & Giroux 2017. 120 p.
ISBN 9781770462939
Grades: 9 10 11 12 Adult　741.5
1. Culture 2. Childhood 3. Christian families 4. Growing up 5. Dictators 6. Iraq 7. Mosul, Iraq 8. Autobiographies and memoirs 9. Autobiographical comics 10. Comics and Graphic novels 11. Life stories — Relationships — Growing up 12. Family and Relationships — Growing Up
LC Bl2017036604
The author shares memories of her middle class childhood to create a family portrait that explores loss, tragedy, love, and the loneliness of exile.

Fingeroth, Danny
A Marvelous Life: The Amazing Story of Stan Lee. Danny Fingeroth. St. Martin's Press 2019. 320 p.
ISBN 9781250133908
Grades: Adult　741.5
1. Lee, Stan, 1922-2018 2. Comics and graphic novel writers 3. Comic book illustrators 4. Comic books, strips, etc. 5. Publishers and publishing 6. Biographies 7. Life stories — Arts and culture — Writing — Authors 8. Arts and Entertainment — Comics, Cartoons, and Animation
LC 2019031647
The definitive biography of the beloved—often controversial—co-creator of many legendary superheroes, a Marvelous Life: The Amazing Story of Stan Lee presents the origin of "Stan the Man," who spun a storytelling web of comic book heroic adventures into a pop culture phenomenon: the Marvel Universe.
"Lee remains a pivotal figure in the superhero genre that's come to dominate popular culture, and Fingeroth, a comics veteran who worked closely with Lee, gives evenhanded treatment to his accomplishments and foibles." —*Booklist*
Includes bibliographical references.

Forkish, Ken
★ *Let's Make Bread!: A Comic Book Cookbook.* Ken Forkish, Sarah Becan. Ten Speed Press 2024. 160 p. (Let's make (Graphic novel cookbooks))
ISBN 9781984860873
Grades: Adult　741.5
1. Cooking (Bread) 2. Bread 3. Comics and Graphic novels 4. Food writing — Food and culture 5. Food writing — Cooking and cookbooks — Narrative cookbooks
LC 2023027969
In this beginner-friendly comic book cookbook, the New York Times best-selling and award-winning author adapts his expert baking tips and recipes for making bread with a new twist, along with foolproof techniques for making your perfect loaf at home.
"The quick pace, methodical guidance, and visual style highly recommend this to teens eager to do more in the kitchen." —*Booklist*
Includes index.

Ghez, Didier
The Hidden Art of Disney's Golden Age: The 1930s. Didier Ghez; foreword by Pete Docter. Chronicle Books 2015. 207 pages : Illustration; Color
ISBN 9781452137438
Grades: Adult　741.5
1. Horvath, Ferdinand, 1891-1973 2. Hurter, Albert 3. Majolie, Bianca 4. Tenggren, Gustaf, 1896-1970 5. Animated films 6. Animation (Cinematography) 7. Animators 8. Cartoon characters 9. Disney characters 10. 20th century 11. Biographies 12. History writing — Arts and culture 13. Arts and Entertainment — Comics, Cartoons, and Animation
LC 2016439270
Introducing new biographical material about the artists and including largely unpublished artwork from the depths of the Walt Disney Archives and the Disney Animation Research Library, this volume offers a window into the most inspiring work created by the best Disney artists during the studio's early golden age.
Includes bibliographical references (pages 204-205) and index.

Gitlin, Marty
A Celebration of Animation: The 100 Greatest Cartoon Characters in Television History. Marty Gitlin and Joe Wos. Lyons Press 2017. 256 pages
ISBN 9781630762780
Grades: Adult　741.5
1. Cartoon characters 2. Television cartoon shows 3. Popular culture 4. Cartoons (Animated films) 5. Film history and criticism 6. Arts and Entertainment — Comics, Cartoons, and Animation
LC 2017025749
Explores the greatest cartoon characters in television history, providing such information about each character as its creator, debut, voice artist, and antagonists.

Gladstone, Brooke
The Influencing Machine: Brooke Gladstone on the Media. Brooke Gladstone; illustrated by Josh Neufeld; with additional penciling by Randy Jones and Susann Ferris-Jones. W. W. Norton 2011. xxii, 170 p. : Illustration; Color
ISBN 9780393077797
Grades: Adult　741.5
1. Mass media 2. Newspapers 3. Broadcast journalism 4. Television 5. Comics and Graphic novels 6. Arts and Entertainment — General
LC 2011009820
Library Journal Best Books, 2011; YALSA Great Graphic Novels for Teens, 2012.
The cohost of NPR's "On the Media" narrates, in cartoon form, two millennia of history of the influence of the media on the populace, from newspapers in Caesar's Rome to the penny press of the American Revolution to today.
Includes bibliographical references (p. 163-170).

Goldman, Seth
Mission in a Bottle: The Honest Guide to Doing Business Differently—and Succeeding. Seth Goldman and Barry Nalebuff; illustrated by Sungyoon Choi. Crown Business 2013. 278 p. : Color; Illustration
ISBN 9780770437497
Grades: Adult　741.5
1. Tea industry and trade 2. Soft drink industry and trade 3. Tea 4. Comics and Graphic novels 5. Business and economics — Business Advice
LC 2013004799
In graphic novel format, the cofounders of Honest Tea present the history of the company and provide practical advice on launching a successful business, perseverance, and creative problem-solving.
Chiefly illustrations.

Guibert, Emmanuel
Alan's War: The Memories of G.I. Alan Cope. Emmanuel Guibert; translation, Kathryn Pulver; lettering, Celine Merrien. First Second 2008. 304 p. : Illustration
ISBN 9781596430969

PUBLIC LIBRARY CORE COLLECTION: NONFICTION
Twentieth Edition

Grades: 10 11 12 Adult   741.5

1. Cope, Alan Ingram, 1925-1999 2. World War II 3. Military campaigns 4. Soldiers 5. Social life and customs 6. Europe 7. France 8. United States 9. Comics and Graphic novels 10. Biographical comics 11. Translations — French to English 12. Biographies 13. History writing — Wars and conflicts — World War II 14. Life stories — Law and order — Armed forces personnel 15. Adult books for young adults

LC 2007046190

A graphic-novel biography presents the life of Alan Cope, an American World War II veteran, from being drafted at eighteen, through his war-time experiences, to his decision to return to France after the war was over.

"This is a poignant and frank graphic memoir of young soldier who was told to serve his country in WWII and how it changed him forever. . . . Cope and Guibert forge a story that resonates with humanity." —*Publishers Weekly*

Translated from the French: Guerre d'Alan.

The **Photographer:** *Into War-Torn Afghanistan with Doctors Without Borders.* Illustrated by Emmanuel Guibert; written by Didier Lefevre and Frederic Lemercier; translated from the French by Alexis Siegel. First Second 2009. xi, 267 p. : Illustration; Color

ISBN 9781596433755

Grades: 11 12 Adult   741.5

1. Lefevre, Didier, 1957-2007 2. Photojournalists 3. Medical care 4. Humanitarian assistance 5. Asian history 6. Afghanistan 7. Autobiographical comics 8. Comics and Graphic novels 9. Autobiographies and memoirs 10. Translations — French to English 11. History writing — Asia — South Asia — Afghanistan 12. Life stories — Science, technology, and medicine — Healthcare professionals 13. Adult books for young adults

LC 2012288469

ALA Notable Book, 2010; School Library Journal Best Books: Best Adult Books 4 Teens, 2009; YALSA Great Graphic Novels for Teens, 2010.

In 1986, Afghanistan was torn apart by a war with the Soviet Union. This graphic novel/photo-journal is a record of one reporter's arduous and dangerous journey through Afghanistan, accompanying the Doctors Without Borders.

"The graphic novel combines traditional comic art with some of the four thousand photographs Lefevre shot while in Afghanistan. . . . Many images will stay with readers as both horrifying and glorious. The Afghan children being treated for burns, bullet wounds, and shrapnel are page by page next to the beauty of the Afghan mountainous landscapes. . . . [This book] has a powerful message and images of a part of the world that should be discussed more often." —*Voice of Youth Advocates*

Hall, Rebecca

★ **Wake:** *The Hidden History of Women-Led Slave Revolts.* Rebecca Hall; illustrated by Hugo Martinez; lettered by Sarula Bao. Simon & Schuster 2021. 208 p.

ISBN 9781982115180

Grades: Adult   741.5

1. Hall, Rebecca, 1963- 2. Women historians 3. African American women 4. Enslaved women 5. Enslaved people's resistance and revolts 6. Children of enslaved people 7. Historical research 8. Slavery 9. United States history 10. 18th century 11. Historical comics 12. Autobiographical comics 13. Comics and Graphic novels 14. History writing — African American — Enslavement — United States 15. History writing — Women's history 16. Life stories — Education — Scholars and educators 17. Antiracist literature

LC 2021001239

Rise: A Feminist Book Project List, 2022.

Wake tells the story of Dr. Rebecca Hall, a historian, granddaughter of slaves, and a woman haunted by the legacy of slavery. The accepted history of slave revolts has always told her that enslaved women took a back seat. But Rebecca decides to look deeper, and her journey takes her through old court records, slave ship captain's logs, crumbling correspondence, and even the forensic evidence from the bones of enslaved women from the "negro burying ground" uncovered in Manhattan. She finds women warriors everywhere. Using in-depth archival research and a measured use of historical imagination, Rebecca constructs the likely pasts of Adono and Alele, women rebels who fought for freedom during the Middle Passage, as well as the stories of women who led slave revolts in Colonial New York. We also follow Rebecca's own story as the legacy of slavery shapes life, both during her time as a successful attorney and later as a historian seeking the past that haunts her.

"An urgent, brilliant work of historical excavation." —*Kirkus*

Hart, Christopher

Cartooning for the Beginner. Christopher Hart. Watson-Guptill 2000. 144 p. : Illustration; Color

ISBN 9780823005864

Grades: 11 12 Adult   741.5

1. Cartooning technique 2. Arts and Entertainment — Painting, Drawing, and Sculpture

LC BL 00014882

"This guide to cartooning techniques covers the world of cartoon animals, animation, and edgy 'Toons." —*Library Journal*

Includes index.

Hedges, Chris

Days of Destruction, Days of Revolt. Chris Hedges and Joe Sacco. Nation Books 2012. 304 p. : Illustration

ISBN 9781568586434

Grades: Adult   741.5

1. Poor people 2. Crime 3. Social classes 4. United States 5. 20th century 6. Comics and Graphic novels 7. Society and culture — Wealth and class — Poverty

LC 2012004701

An award-winning cartoonist presents a scathing graphic report on the crises facing America's poor as reflected in the city of Camden, New Jersey, trace its descent from an industrial giant to a region torn by unemployment, open-air drug markets and budget cuts.

Includes bibliographical references and index.

Hennessey, Jonathan

The **United** *States Constitution: A Graphic Adaptation.* Written by Jonathan Hennessey; art by Aaron McConnell. Hill and Wang 2008. 149 p. : Color illustration

ISBN 9780809094875

Grades: 9 10 11 12 Adult   741.5

1. Constitutional history 2. Politics and government 3. United States history 4. United States 5. Comics and Graphic novels 6. Politics and global affairs — Political philosophy 7. Adult books for young adults

LC 2008017927

YALSA Great Graphic Novels for Teens, 2009.

An illustrated account of the American Constitution covers each article and amendment in a graphic format designed to render its meanings more relevant and accessible to modern readers, in a volume that addresses such topics as the separation of church and state, the break from the monarchy, and the limits imposed on presidential power.

Includes bibliographical references (p. 145).

Howe, Sean

Marvel Comics: The Untold Story. by Sean Howe. Harper 2012. 320 p.

ISBN 9780061992100

Grades: Adult   741.5

1. Comic books, strips, etc. 2. Comic book characters 3. Comic book illustrators 4. Comics and graphic novel writers 5. Copyright 6. Publishers and publishing 7. Popular culture 8. United States history 9. 20th century 10. Arts and Entertainment — Writing and Publishing 11. Business and economics — Industries — Entertainment and media

LC 2012015058

Pulp magazine publisher Marvin Goodman reluctantly expanded into the new field of comic books in 1939, but Marvel Comics didn't really make the scene until 1961. Author Sean Howe delivers the scoop on the notoriously contentious relationships among Marvel's artists, writers, and editors throughout its publishing history. Stan Lee and Jack Kirby take center stage, as do their famous creations—like the golden-boy Captain America, and lovable (if nerdy)

ESSENTIAL AND RECOMMENDED TITLES
741.5 Cartoons, graphic novels, caricatures, comics

Spiderman, four-color comic book heroes who are now among Hollywood's hottest stars.

Hulls, Tessa
★ *Feeding* Ghosts: A Graphic Memoir. Tessa Hulls. MCD / Farrar, Straus and Giroux 2024. 400 p.
ISBN 9780374601652
Grades: Adult   **741.5**
1. Hulls, Tessa, 1984- 2. Chinese American families 3. Women 4. Journalists 5. Mothers and daughters 6. Wanderers and wandering 7. Intergenerational relations 8. Intergenerational trauma 9. People with mental illnesses 10. Immigration and emigration 11. Political persecution 12. Familial love 13. Chinese history 14. East Asian people 15. Chinese people 16. American people 17. China 18. Hong Kong 19. United States 20. Comics and graphic novels 21. Autobiographical comics 22. Life stories — Relationships — Family 23. Life stories — Identity — Race and ethnicity 24. Life stories — Facing adversity — War and oppression — Refugees 25. Life stories — Facing adversity — Medical issues — Mental illness 26. History writing — Communist China — Asia — China 27. Debut title
LC 2023040893

In her evocative, genre-defying graphic memoir, Tessa Hulls tells the story of three generations of women in her family: Her Chinese grandmother, Sun Yi; her mother, Rose; and herself. Extensively researched and gorgeously rendered, Feeding Ghosts is Hulls's homecoming, a vivid journey into the beating heart of one family, set against the dark backdrop of Chinese history.

"A work that glimmers with insight, acumen, and an unwillingness to settle for simple answers." —*Kirkus*

Illustrated by the author; Includes bibliographical references.

Igort
The **Ukrainian** *and Russian Notebooks: Life and Death Under Soviet Rule.* Igort. Simon & Schuster 2016. 352 p.
ISBN 9781451678871
Grades: Adult   **741.5**
1. Politkovskaya, Anna 2. Totalitarianism 3. Crimes against humanity 4. State-sponsored terrorism 5. Women journalists 6. Human rights activists 7. Assassination 8. Atrocities 9. Genocide 10. Famines 11. Communism 12. Soviet Union history 13. Russian history 14. European history 15. Ukraine 16. Chechnya, Russia 17. Soviet Union 18. Historical comics 19. Comics and Graphic novels 20. Translations — Italian to English 21. History writing — Communism — Europe — Russia 22. History writing — Europe — Eastern Europe

Shares the stories of the survivors and witnesses of Soviet Rule that the graphic novelist collected over two years, covering events that include the Ukraine famine and the assassination of Russian journalists.

Originally published separately in Italian as Quaderni ucraini (2010) and Quaderni russi (2011) by Mondadori, strade Blu; Translated from the Italian by Jamie Richards.

Inman, Matthew
The **Terrible** *and Wonderful Reasons Why I Run Long Distances.* Oatmeal, Matthew Inman. Andrews McMeel 2014. 148 p.
ISBN 9781449459956
Grades: Adult   **741.5**
1. Long-distance running 2. Runners 3. Running 4. Alternative comics 5. Satirical comics 6. Comics and Graphic novels 7. Webcomics 8. Humor writing — Social humor 9. Sports and Competition — Racing — Track and Field
LC 2014937161

This is not just a book about running. It's a book about cupcakes. It's a book about suffering. It's a book about gluttony, vanity, bliss, electrical storms, ranch dressing, and Godzilla. It's a book about all the terrible and wonderful reasons we wake up each day and propel our bodies through rain, shine, heaven, and hell.

Jacob, Mira
Good Talk: A Memoir in Conversations. Mira Jacob. Random House 2018. 400 p.
ISBN 9780399589041
Grades: 11 12 Adult   **741.5**
1. Jacob, Mira, 1973- 2. Women authors 3. Interracial families 4. Indian Americans 5. Identity 6. Multiracial children 7. Mothers and sons 8. Families 9. Racism 10. Presidential election, 2016 11. United States 12. Autobiographies and memoirs 13. Autobiographical comics 14. Comics and Graphic novels 15. Life stories — Identity — Race and ethnicity 16. Society and culture — Race 17. Family and Relationships — Dating and Marriage 18. Adult books for young adults
LC 2017021147

Library Journal Best Books, 2019; New York Times Notable Book, 2019; National Book Critics Circle Award for Autobiography/Memoir finalist, 2019.

An intimate graphic memoir about American identity as it has shaped the author's interracial family in the aftermath of the 2016 elections.

"The narrative spans generations, drawing parallels between Jacob and her son but also highlighting the lack of social progress. Aided by the skillful story structure, Jacob's no-holds-barred vulnerability compels reflection and empathy. The unique art style combines photographic backgrounds with illustrations of characters framed in white, like paper cutouts." —*School Library Journal*

Jacobson, Sidney
The 9-11 Report: A Graphic Adaptation. Sid Jacobson; illustrated by Ernie Colon; with a foreword by Thomas H. Kean and Lee H. Hamilton. Hill and Wang 2006. x, 117 p. : Color illustration
ISBN 9780809057382
Grades: 9 10 11 12 Adult   **741.5**
1. September 11 Terrorist Attacks, 2001 2. War on Terrorism, 2001-2009 3. Terrorism 4. Terrorists 5. Hijacking of aircraft 6. Intelligence service 7. National security 8. United States 9. 21st century 10. Comics and Graphic novels 11. History writing — September 11, 2001 — United States 12. Adult books for young adults
LC 2006924343

YALSA Great Graphic Novels for Teens, 2007; YALSA Best Books for Young Adults, 2007; School Library Journal Best Books: Best Adult Books 4 Teens, 2006.

A graphic novel of the report of the 9/11 Commission reveals the Commission's findings regarding the terrorist attacks on the United States and its recommendations concerning what the United States government needs to do in its wake.

"The book aims to make . . . [The 9/11 Commission Report] more accessible to all readers and draw in young adults. . . . This graphic adaptation is an important and necessary part of any collection." —*School Library Journal*

Based on the final report of the National Commission on Terrorist Attacks upon the United States—Cover.

Anne **Frank**: *The Anne Frank House Authorized Graphic Biography.* Sid Jacobson and Ernie Colon. Hill and Wang 2010. 152 p. : Illustration; Color; Map
ISBN 9780809026852
Grades: 9 10 11 12 Adult   **741.5**
1. Frank, Anne, 1929-1945 2. Jewish children 3. Jewish people 4. Girls 5. Holocaust (1933-1945) 6. Amsterdam, Netherlands 7. Netherlands 8. Biographies 9. Comics and Graphic novels 10. History books — Wars — Holocaust — World War II 11. Biographies — Identity — Jewish 12. Biographies — Identity — Children and teenagers 13. Biographies — People in history — Holocaust

Drawing on the archives and expertise of the Anne Frank House, the best-selling authors of 9/11 Report: A Graphic Adaptation cover the short-but-inspiring life of the famed Jewish teen memoirist, from the lives of her parents to Anne's years keeping her private diary while hidden from the Nazis to her untimely death in a concentration camp.

Jones, Gerard
Men of Tomorrow: Geeks, Gangsters, and the Birth of the Comic Book. Gerard Jones. Basic Books 2004. xv, 384 p. : Illustration
ISBN 9780465036561
Grades: 11 12 Adult   **741.5**
1. Cartoonists 2. Comic books, strips, etc. 3. Literary criticism 4. Social life and customs 5. United States history 6. United States 7. 21st century 8. 20th cen-

PUBLIC LIBRARY CORE COLLECTION: NONFICTION
Twentieth Edition

tury 9. Biographies 10. Arts and Entertainment — Comics, Cartoons, and Animation

LC 2004009031

Springing from the depths of the Depression, the birth of the comic book superhero spawned a new genre that still resonates seventy years later, a journey chronicled in an in-depth look at the people and personalities behind the creations.

Katin, Miriam
We Are on Our Own: A Memoir. by Miriam Katin. Drawn & Quarterly, 2006. 122 p. : Illustration; Color
ISBN 9781896597201
Grades: 9 10 11 12 Adult   741.5
1. Toddlers 2. Jewish people 3. Household employees 4. Refugees, Jewish 5. Children and war 6. World War II 7. Nazis 8. Deception 9. Disguises 10. Survival 11. Loss 12. Staged deaths 13. Housekeepers 14. Eastern European people 15. Hungarian people 16. Budapest, Hungary 17. Autobiographical comics 18. Comics and Graphic novels 19. Autobiographies and memoirs 20. History writing — Wars and conflicts — Holocaust — World War II 21. Life stories — Facing adversity — War and oppression — War survivors 22. Adult books for young adults

LC 2006389448

A full-length illustrated graphic memoir about the author and her mother's escape on foot from the Nazi invasion of Budapest vividly recounts how they faked their deaths, abandoned their belongings and loved ones, and fled in disguise with German troops close behind, a journey after which the author struggled with her faith.

"This impressive book belongs in all serious graphic novel collections and is also a natural for Jewish studies." —*Booklist*

Sequel: Letting It Go.

Kawa, Abraham
Democracy. Abraham Kawa, illustrated by Alekos Papadatos. Bloomsbury 2015. 352 p.
ISBN 9781608197194
Grades: 11 12 Adult   741.5
1. Democracy 2. Political science 3. Philosophy 4. Ancient Greece 5. Comics and Graphic novels 6. Politics and global affairs — Political philosophy 7. History writing — Ancient — Greece

LC 2020289649

From a team including the artists of the *New York Times* bestseller Logicomix, another entertaining and educational graphic delight focusing on the origins and rise of democracy.

Kitchen, Denis
The Art of Harvey Kurtzman: The Mad Genius of Comics. by Denis Kitchen and Paul Buhle; introduction by Harry Shearer. Abrams ComicArts 2009. xiii, 241 p. : Illustration; Color
ISBN 9780810972964
Grades: Adult   741.5
1. Kurtzman, Harvey 2. Cartoonists 3. Arts and Entertainment — Comics, Cartoons, and Animation

LC 2008004809

Shares hundreds of illustrations, paintings, pencil sketches, illustrated correspondence, and vintage photos from this master of American comics.

Essential Harvey Kurtzman bibliography: P. 241; Includes bibliographical references (p. 238) and index.

Kneece, Mark
The Art of Comic Book Writing: The Definitive Guide to Outlining, Scripting, and Pitching Your Sequential Art Stories. Mark Kneece. Watson-Guptill Publications 2015. 184 pages : Illustration
ISBN 9780770436971
Grades: Adult   741.5
1. Comic books, strips, etc. 2. Arts and Entertainment — Crafts and hobbies 3. Language arts and studies — Writing skills

LC 2015007716

A successful writer and instructor offers practical advice, essential tools and simple examples for aspiring comic book writers at any level to use to better navigate the mysteries and pitfalls of getting published in the industry.

Includes index.

Kobabe, Maia
Gender Queer: A Memoir. by Maia Kobabe; colors by Phoebe Kobabe. Lion Forge, LLC 2019. 239 p.
ISBN 9781637150726
Grades: Adult   741.5
1. Kobabe, Maia 2. Nonbinary people 3. Genderqueer people 4. Gender identity 5. Gender nonconformity 6. LGBTQIA+ people 7. Asexuality 8. LGBTQIA+ comics 9. Autobiographical comics 10. Autobiographies and memoirs 11. Comics and Graphic novels 12. Biographies — Identity — LGBTQIA+ 13. Growing up — LGBTQIA+ 14. Adult books for young adults

Rainbow List, 2020; School Library Journal Best Books, 2019; Alex Award, 2020; YALSA Great Graphic Novels for Teens, 2020.

In 2014, Maia Kobabe, who uses e/em/eir pronouns, thought that a comic of reading statistics would be the last autobiographical comic e would ever write. At the time, it was the only thing e felt comfortable with strangers knowing about em. Now, Gender Queer is here. Maia's intensely cathartic autobiography charts eir journey of self-identity, which includes the mortification and confusion of adolescent crushes, grappling with how to come out to family and society, bonding with friends over erotic gay fanfiction, and facing the trauma and fundamental violation of pap smears. Started as a way to explain to eir family what it means to be nonbinary and asexual, Gender Queer is more than a personal story: It is a useful and touching guide on gender identity—what it means and how to think about it—for advocates, friends, and humans everywhere.

Krimstein, Ken
When I Grow Up: The Lost Autobiographies of Six Yiddish Teenagers. Ken Krimstein. Bloomsbury Publishing 2021. 256 p.
ISBN 9781635573701
Grades: Adult   741.5
1. Jewish teenagers 2. Growing up 3. Adolescence 4. Holocaust (1933-1945) 5. Teenagers 6. Ambition 7. Desire 8. Social life and customs 9. Eastern Europe 10. 1930s 11. Comics and Graphic novels 12. Biographical comics 13. Collective biographies 14. Life stories — Relationships — Growing up 15. History writing — Jewish history 16. Life stories — Facing adversity — War and oppression — Holocaust 17. History writing — Europe — Eastern Europe

Based on newly discovered, never-before-published autobiographies of Eastern European Jewish teens on the brink of WWII, this graphic nonfiction book presents the stories of six young men and women in riveting, almost cinematic narratives, full of humor, yearning, ambition and angst.

"By depicting the personalities of youth lost—with easy beauty and a lack of preciosity—rather than how they died, Krimstein conveys the depth of human and cultural loss that much more profoundly." —*Publishers Weekly*

Krug, Nora
★ *Belonging: A German Reckons with History and Home.* Nora Krug. Scribner 2018. 288 p.
ISBN 9781476796628
Grades: Adult   741.5
1. Krug, Nora 2. German Americans 3. Guilt 4. German people 5. Family secrets 6. Place (Philosophy) 7. Identity 8. Immigrants 9. Holocaust (1933-1945) 10. German American families 11. World War II 12. Family history 13. German history 14. Germany 15. 20th century 16. Autobiographies and memoirs 17. Autobiographical comics 18. Comics and Graphic novels 19. Life stories — Identity 20. Life stories — Arts and culture — Artists

LC Bl2018187724

Library Journal Best Books, 2018; National Book Critics Circle Award for Autobiography, 2018; YALSA Great Graphic Novels for Teens, 2019.

A graphic memoir by an award-winning artist tells the story of her attempt to confront the hidden truths of her family's wartime past in Nazi Germany and to comprehend the forces that have shaped her life, her generation and history.

ESSENTIAL AND RECOMMENDED TITLES
741.5 Cartoons, graphic novels, caricatures, comics

"The narrative is a deeply personal—and deeply moving—dive into national legacy and family history, with more text than most graphic novels and a graphic presentation that mixes documentary photographs, illustrations, and memories that predate the author's birth." —*Kirkus*

Kupperman, Michael
All the Answers. Michael Kupperman. Simon & Schuster 2018. 224 p.
ISBN 9781501166433
Grades: Adult   741.5
1. Kupperman, Joel 2. Child prodigies 3. Child celebrities 4. Fathers and sons 5. Fame 6. Propaganda 7. World War II 8. Jewish Americans 9. Alzheimer's disease 10. 20th century 11. Biographical comics 12. Biographies 13. Comics and Graphic novels 14. Life stories — Relationships — Parent and child 15. History writing — Wars and conflicts — Homefront — World War II
LC Bl2018080304
Library Journal Best Books, 2018.

Traces the life of the author's reclusive father, Joel Kupperman, Quiz Kid, who went from being a national sensation to removing himself from the world and living a secluded life in the woods of Connecticut.

"Kupperman's solid, line-heavy drawings, which impart credibility to the preposterous concepts of his humorous strips, are equally effective at conveying this real-life drama. His clear-eyed yet touching portrait of his father serves as a a powerful indictment of celebrity culture." —*Booklist*

Lee, Stan
Stan Lee's How to Draw Comics: From the Legendary Co-Creator of Spider-Man, the Incredible Hulk, Fantastic Four, X-Men, and Iron Man. Watson-Guptill Publications 2010. 224 p. : Illustration; Color
ISBN 9780823000838
Grades: 9 10 11 12 Adult   741.5
1. Drawing technique 2. Art and music — Visual arts — Cartooning and animation 3. Art and music — Arts and crafts — Drawing and painting 4. How-to books
LC 2010005781

The comic book icon explains drawing and creating comic book characters—from producing concepts and character sketches to laying out the final page of art.

"The author includes chapters on creating comics with computer programs and online resources and how to get work in the 21st century. The book begins with a brief history of comics, then focuses on action-adventure style, romance, humor, horror, and Japanese manga. This is the one book anyone interested in drawing comics should own." —*Library Journal*

Includes bibliographical references (p. 222) and index.

Leong, Sonia
101 Top Tips from Professional Manga Artists. Sonia Leong. Barron's 2013. 176 pages : Illustration; Color
ISBN 9781438002064
Grades: Adult   741.5
1. Cartooning technique 2. Comic strip characters 3. Japan 4. How-to books 5. Arts and Entertainment — Comics, Cartoons, and Animation
LC 2012948428

"Freelance comic artist and illustrator Leong and several contributing artists provide over 100 tips grouped and organized around basic topics, highlighting key aspects of manga such as character design, backgrounds, props, software and media, and even practices of successful professionals." —*Library Journal*

Includes index.

Lepore, Jill
★ *The Secret History of Wonder Woman.* by Jill Lepore. Alfred A. Knopf 2014. 432 p.
ISBN 9780385354042
Grades: Adult   741.5
1. Marston, William Moulton, 1893-1947 2. Wonder Woman (Fictitious character) 3. Comics and graphic novel writers 4. Comic books, strips, etc. 5. Nontraditional families 6. Comic book characters 7. History of women's rights 8. Literary criticism 9. Popular culture 10. Feminism 11. United States 12. 20th century 13. Arts and Entertainment — Comics, Cartoons, and Animation
LC 2014011064
ALA Notable Book, 2015; American History Book Prize, 2014; Booklist Editors' Choice 2014.

A cultural history of Wonder Woman traces the character's creation and enduring popularity, drawing on interviews and archival research to reveal the pivotal role of feminism in shaping her seven-decade story.

Includes bibliographical references and index.

Lewis, John
★ *March; Book One.* John Lewis, Andrew Aydin, and Nate Powell. Top Shelf Productions 2013. 121 pages : Illustration (March, 1)
ISBN 9781603093002
Grades: 8 9 10 11 12 Adult   741.5
1. Lewis, John, 1940-2020 2. King, Martin Luther, Jr, 1929-1968 3. Civil Rights Movement 4. Racism 5. Protests, demonstrations, vigils, etc. 6. African American civil rights 7. Student movements 8. Nonviolence 9. Segregation 10. Civil rights 11. Politicians 12. Rural children 13. Race relations 14. Alabama 15. United States 16. 20th century 17. Autobiographical comics 18. Comics and Graphic novels 19. Autobiographies and memoirs 20. Biographies 21. History writing — African American — Civil rights — United States 22. Life stories — Politics — Activists and reformers 23. Adult books for young adults 24. Society and culture — Race 25. Antiracist literature

ALA Notable Children's Book, 2014; Booklist Editors' Choice: Adult Books for Young Adults, 2013; Carter G. Woodson Book Awards: Secondary Level, 2017; Library Journal Best Books, 2013; School Library Journal Best Books, 2013; YALSA Great Graphic Novels for Teens, 2014; Coretta Scott King Honor Book for Authors, 2014.

A first-hand account of the author's lifelong struggle for civil and human rights spans his youth in rural Alabama, his life-changing meeting with Martin Luther King, Jr, and the birth of the Nashville Student Movement.

"This is superb visual storytelling that establishes a convincing, definitive record of a key eyewitness to significant social change." —*School Library Journal*

★ *March; Book Three.* John Lewis with Andrew Aydin; art by Nate Powell. Top Shelf Productions 2016. 246 p. : Illustration (March, 3)
ISBN 9781603094023
Grades: 8 9 10 11 12 Adult   741.5
1. Lewis, John, 1940-2020 2. Civil Rights Movement 3. Protests, demonstrations, vigils, etc. 4. Racism 5. Race relations 6. African American civil rights 7. Student movements 8. Nonviolence 9. Segregation 10. Civil rights 11. Politicians 12. United States 13. 1960s 14. 20th century 15. Autobiographical comics 16. Comics and Graphic novels 17. Autobiographies and memoirs 18. Biographies 19. History writing — African American — Civil rights — United States 20. Life stories — Politics — Activists and reformers 21. Adult books for young adults 22. Society and culture — Race 23. Antiracist literature

ALA Notable Children's Book, 2017; Booklist Editors' Choice: Books for Youth, 2016; Carter G. Woodson Book Awards: Secondary Level, 2017; Coretta Scott King Award, Author Category, 2017; Eisner Awards, Best Reality-Based Work, 2017; Flora Stieglitz Straus Award, 2017; Glyph Comics Awards, Best Writer, 2017; Glyph Comics Awards, Story of the Year, 2017; Library Journal Best Books, 2016; Michael L. Printz Award, 2017; Mike Wieringo Comic Book Industry Awards, Best Original Graphic Novel, 2017; Mike Wieringo Comic Book Industry Awards, Best Non-Fiction Graphic Work, 2017; National Book Award for Young People's Literature, 2016; Robert F. Sibert Informational Book Medal, 2017; School Library Journal Best Books, 2016; Walter Award, 2017; YALSA Award for Excellence in Nonfiction, 2017; YALSA Great Graphic Novels for Teens, 2017; SEE-IT Award finalist, 2017.

Congressman John Lewis, one of the key figures of the civil rights movement, joins co-writer Andrew Aydin and artist Nate Powell to bring the lessons of history to vivid life for a new generation, urgently relevant for today's world.

"Though Lewis and Aydin throw a lot at readers in this volume, their message, helped along seamlessly and splendidly by Powell's fantastic, cinematic artwork, is abundantly clear: the victories of the civil rights movement, symbol-

ized in particular by Barack Obama's inauguration, are hard-won and only succeeded through the dogged dedication of a wide variety of people." —*Booklist*
Series complete in 3 volumes.

★ *March; Book Two.* John Lewis, Andrew Aydin, and Nate Powell. Top Shelf Productions 2015. 160 p. : Illustration (March, 2)
ISBN 9781603094009
Grades: 8 9 10 11 12 Adult   741.5
1. Lewis, John, 1940-2020 2. Civil Rights Movement 3. Protests, demonstrations, vigils, etc. 4. Racism 5. Race relations 6. African American civil rights 7. Student movements 8. Nonviolence 9. Segregation 10. Civil rights 11. Politicians 12. United States 13. 1960s 14. 20th century 15. Autobiographical comics 16. Comics and Graphic novels 17. Autobiographies and memoirs 18. Biographies 19. History writing — African American — Civil rights — United States 20. Life stories — Politics — Activists and reformers 21. Adult books for young adults 22. Society and culture — Race 23. Antiracist literature

Carter G. Woodson Book Awards: Secondary Level, 2017; Eisner Awards, Best Reality-Based Work, 2016; Street Lit Book Award Medal: Graphic Novel, 2016; YALSA Great Graphic Novels for Teens, 2016; Harvey Awards, Best Graphic Album - Original, 2016.

The award-winning, best-selling series returns, as John Lewis' story continues through Freedom Rides and the legendary 1963 March on Washington.

"Heroism and steadiness of purpose continue to light up Lewis' frank, harrowing account of the civil rights movement's climactic days. . . . The contrast between the dignified marchers and the vicious, hate-filled actions and expressions of their tormentors will leave a deep impression on readers." —*Kirkus*

★ *Run; Book One.* Written by John Lewis and Andrew Aydin; art by L. Fury with Nate Powell. Abrams ComicArts 2018. 128 p. (Run (John Lewis), 1)
ISBN 9781419730696
Grades: 7 8 9 10 11 12 Adult   741.5
1. Lewis, John, 1940-2020 2. African American legislators 3. African American civil rights 4. Political campaigns 5. Legislators 6. Politicians 7. Politics and government 8. Georgia 9. United States 10. 20th century 11. Autobiographical comics 12. Comics and Graphic novels 13. Autobiographies and memoirs 14. Biographies 15. History writing — Politicians — United States 16. Life stories — Politics — Politicians 17. Adult books for young adults 18. Antiracist literature

LC 2018024127

In the Margins Book Awards: Nonfiction, 2022.

Tells the true story of John Lewis and his colleagues in the movement following the historic success of the Selma campaign and the Voting Rights Act.

"This living history gives faces and voices to the legends of the civil rights era and connects their struggles to the present." —*Publishers Weekly*

Mankoff, Robert
How About Never—Is Never Good for You?: My Life in Cartoons. Bob Mankoff. Henry Holt & Company 2014. 304 pages
ISBN 9780805095906
Grades: Adult   741.5
1. Mankoff, Robert 2. Cartoonists 3. Cartoons 4. Periodical editors 5. Growing up 6. Child artists 7. United States 8. Comics and Graphic novels 9. Autobiographies and memoirs 10. Biographies 11. Life stories — Arts and culture — Writing 12. Arts and Entertainment — Comics, Cartoons, and Animation 13. Life stories — Arts and culture — Artists 14. Adult books for young adults

LC 2013021129

Memoir in cartoons by the longtime cartoon editor of the New Yorker. People tell Bob Mankoff that as the cartoon editor of the New Yorker he has the best job in the world. Never one to beat around the bush, he explains to us, in the opening of this singular, delightfully eccentric book, that because he is also a cartoonist at the magazine he actually has two of the best jobs in the world. With the help of myriad images and his funniest, most beloved cartoons, he traces his love of the craft all the way back to his childhood, when he started doing funny drawings at the age of eight. Throughout, we see his commitment to the motto "Anything worth saying is worth saying funny."

Mauldin, Bill
Willie & Joe: The WWII Years. by Bill Mauldin; edited by Todd DePastino. Fantagraphics 2008. 650 p.
ISBN 9781560978381
Grades: Adult   741.5
1. World War II 2. Soldiers 3. Comics and Graphic novels

Presents a complete collection of the Willie & Joe creator's World War II cartoons, in a volume that offers insight into how Mauldin's works reflected his military service, sparked the ire of military leaders, and commemorated his war losses.

McCloud, Scott
Making Comics: Storytelling Secrets of Comics, Manga and Graphic Novels. Scott McCloud. Harper 2006. 264 p. : Illustration
ISBN 9780060780944
Grades: 11 12 Adult   741.5
1. Comics and graphic novel writing 2. Cartooning 3. Drawing 4. Storytelling 5. Comics and Graphic novels 6. Arts and Entertainment — Comics, Cartoons, and Animation 7. Adult books for young adults

LC 2006287667

Booklist Editors' Choice: Adult Books for Young Adults, 2006; YALSA Great Graphic Novels for Teens, 2007.

The author of Understanding Comics and Reinventing Comics instructs aspiring cartoonists on the art form's key techniques, sharing concise and accessible guidelines on such principles as capturing the human condition through words and images in a minimalist style.

"The author explores practical matters, including comics devices such as panels, word balloons, and sound effects; facial expressions and body language; the creation of convincing and evocative settings; and the different tools artists can use for the job, from pencils to computers. He also delves into the framing of images in panels, the flow of panels on a page, and the relationships between words and pictures in comics. . . . This is thoughtful, fascinating, stimulating, potentially controversial, and inspiring." —*Library Journal*

Includes bibliographical references (p. 256-257) and index.

Reinventing Comics. Harper Collins 2000. 237 p.
ISBN 9780060953508
Grades: 11 12 Adult   741.5
1. Cartoons 2. Comics and graphic novel writing 3. Comic book illustration 4. Comics and Graphic novels 5. Arts and Entertainment — Comics, Cartoons, and Animation

Explains how digital revolutions are affecting the comic strip business, from the artist's creation of the comic strips to the distribution of the finished product to the consumers.

"The author maps out 12 revolutions, which, he believes, need to take place for comics to survive and finally be recognized as a legitimate art form. The topics progress from the oldest of comic-related arguments (seeking respect) to the use of computer technology to renew and expand its audience. These brilliantly presented discussions concern comics as literature, comics as art, creators' rights, industry innovation, and public perception, among other topics." —*Library Journal*

★ *Understanding Comics: The Invisible Art.* Scott McCloud. Tundra Pub. 1993. 215 p. : Illustration; Color
ISBN 9780060976255
Grades: 9 10 11 12 Adult   741.5
1. Cartooning technique 2. Comic books, strips, etc. 3. Literary criticism 4. Comics and Graphic novels 5. Arts and Entertainment — Comics, Cartoons, and Animation 6. Adult books for young adults

LC 93184802

Harvey Awards, Best Graphic Album - Original, 1994.

Traces the 3,000 year history of storytelling through pictures, discussing the language and images used.

"The author traces the 3,000-year history (from Egyptian paintings on) of telling stories through pictures; describes the language of comicsits grammar and vocabulary; explains the use of different types of images ranging from ironic to realistic; depicts how artists convey movement and the passage of time and use

ESSENTIAL AND RECOMMENDED TITLES
741.5 Cartoons, graphic novels, caricatures, comics

various symbols as shorthand; and [seeks to demonstrate] the expressive emotional qualities of different drawing styles."—*Booklist. [review of 1993 edition]*
Includes bibliographical references.

Mizuki, Shigeru
Showa 1926-1939: A History of Japan. Shigeru Mizuki; translation by Zack Davisson. Drawn & Quarterly 2022. 533 pages : Illustration (Showa: a history of Japan, 1)
ISBN 9781770466258
Grades: Adult   741.5
1. Nanking Massacre, Nanjing, Jiangsu Sheng, China, 1937 2. World War II 3. Japanese history 4. Japan 5. Showa period (1926-1989) 6. Manga 7. Historical comics 8. Autobiographical comics 9. Comics and Graphic novels 10. Translations — Japanese to English 11. Autobiographies and memoirs 12. Adult books for young adults 13. Life stories — Law and order — Armed forces personnel 14. History writing — Asia — Japan

A look at the Showa period in Japanese history with events leading towads World War II.

Originally published: Montreal : Dran & Quarterly, 2013; Translated from the Japanese Komikku Showa-shi.

Neufeld, Josh
A.D.: New Orleans After the Deluge. Josh Neufeld. Pantheon Books 2009. 193 p. : Color illustration
ISBN 9780307378149
Grades: Adult   741.5
1. Natural disasters 2. Hurricane Katrina, 2005 3. Disaster victims 4. Storm damage 5. Survival (after hurricanes) 6. Hurricanes 7. United States history 8. New Orleans, Louisiana 9. 21st century 10. Comics and Graphic novels 11. Nature Writing — Natural Disaster 12. History writing — Natural disasters and tragedies
                                                                        LC 2008055687
YALSA Great Graphic Novels for Teens, 2010.

Uses graphic novel format to depict the events of Hurricane Katrina through six true stories of New Orleanians who survived the storm, including Denise, who experienced the chaos of the Superdome, and a doctor whose French Quarter home was unscathed.

"Graphic artist Neufeld paints an emotive portrait of New Orleans during and after Hurricane Katrina, as seen through the eyes of seven of the city's citizens. The opening panels coalesce into a long cinematic pan, a thrumming setup for the disaster. The half-page and quarter-page panels—satellite views of weather patterns and close inspections of neighborhoods—are crisp, and the two-page spreads are softly focused. Neufeld's words and images are commensurable and rhythmic, and the vernacular is sharp. Bristling with attitude and pungent with social awareness."—*Kirkus*

Ottaviani, Jim
Hawking. Written by Jim Ottaviani; art by Leland Myrick. First Second 2019. 304 p.
ISBN 9781626720251
Grades: 10 11 12 Adult   741.5
1. Hawking, Stephen, 1942-2018 2. Physicists 3. Scientists 4. People with amyotrophic lateral sclerosis 5. Physics 6. Biographies 7. Biographical comics 8. Comics and Graphic novels 9. Science Writing — Physics 10. Life stories — Science, technology, and medicine — Scientists and inventors 11. Adult books for young adults

YALSA Great Graphic Novels for Teens, 2020.

From his early days at the St Albans School and Oxford, Stephen Hawking's brilliance and good humor were obvious to everyone he met. A lively and popular young man, it's no surprise that he would later rise to celebrity status. At twenty-one he was diagnosed with ALS, a degenerative neuromuscular disease. Though the disease weakened his muscles and limited his ability to move and speak, it did nothing to limit his mind. He went on to do groundbreaking work in cosmology and theoretical physics for decades after being told he had only a few years to live.

"Hawking's divorces and emotional distance from his family are poignantly represented, but the story remains about science, which is delivered in an accessible form yet hardly watered down. This smart and wondrously exploratory scientific biography reveals as much about black holes as the man who explored them."—*Publishers Weekly*

Parker, Meghan
Teaching Artfully. Meghan Parker; [foreword, Nick Sousanis]. Clover Press 2021. 224 pages : Color; Illustration
ISBN 9781951038205
Grades: Professional   741.5
1. Parker, Meghan 2. Art teachers 3. Teaching 4. Art 5. Philosophy 6. Comics and Graphic novels 7. Educator resources — Arts & Humanities

First created as a Masters thesis in the Faculty of Education at Simon Fraser University, Teaching Artfully playfully and earnestly encourages us to see the arts as a way to connect with one another and find our common humanity. Creative people, educators and the general public are sure to connect with the call for meaningful engagement with the arts. Graphic novel lovers of all sorts will find an awakening in Parker's approach to the creation of space and opportunities for students to imagine and create new possibilities."

"A manual and call to arms for creative perspectives; librarians should loan this one to every art teacher and budding artist in sight."—*School Library Journal*

Created as a Master of Arts thesis in the Faculty of Education at Simon Fraser University; Includes bibliographical references.

Powell, Nate
★ *Lies My Teacher Told Me: Everything Your American History Textbooks Got Wrong.* James W. Loewen; adapted & illustrated by Nate Powell. The New Press 2024. 272 p.
ISBN 9781620977033
Grades: Adult   741.5
1. High schools 2. Secondary education 3. Indigenous peoples of North America in textbooks 4. Historical revisionism 5. Thanksgiving Day 6. Racism 7. Historiography 8. United States history 9. United States 10. Comics and Graphic novels 11. Social issues — Human rights — Race and ethnicity 12. Social issues — Education 13. History books — United States
                                                                        LC 2023017951
At last! the long-awaited graphic version of the multi-million copy bestselling corrective to American history myths—adapted by the famed National Book Award-winning artist behind John Lewis's March trilogy.

"The new format helps visualize some of the more concrete data Loewen cites in graphs and charts, but it also neatly emphasizes the importance of an emotional connection to history, a key argument Loewen makes about the pitfalls of traditional history classes."—*Booklist*

Radtke, Kristen
Seek You: Essays on American Loneliness. Kristen Radtke. Pantheon Books 2021. 352 p.
ISBN 9781524748067
Grades: Adult   741.5
1. Loneliness 2. Sociology 3. Human behavior 4. Personal conduct 5. Social isolation 6. Comics and Graphic novels 7. Autobiographical comics 8. Autobiographies and memoirs 9. Life stories — Relationships 10. Society and culture — Psychology and human behavior

Andrew Carnegie Medal for Excellence in Non-Fiction Finalist, 2022; Kirkus Prize for Nonfiction finalist, 2021.

When Kristen Radtke was in her twenties, she learned that, as her father was growing up, he would crawl onto his roof in rural Wisconsin and send signals out on his ham radio. Those CQ calls were his attempt to reach somebody—anybody—who would respond. In Seek You, Radtke uses this image as her jumping off point into a piercing exploration of loneliness and the ways in which we attempt to feel closer to one another. She looks at the very real current crisis of loneliness through the lenses of gender, violence, technology, and art. Ranging from the invention of the laugh-track to Instagram to Harry Harlow's experiments in which infant monkeys were given inanimate surrogate mothers, Radtke uncovers all she can about how we engage with friends, family, and strangers alike, and what happens—to us and to them—when we disengage. With her distinctive, emotionally charged drawings and unflinchingly sharp prose, Kristen Radtke masterfully reframes some of our most vulnerable and sublime moments.

"In often poetic prose accompanied by stunning illustration, Radtke weaves together personal anecdotes and examples drawn from physical and mental health studies to create a meditation on the causes and cost of isolation." —Library Journal

Illustrated by the author.

Redniss, Lauren
Thunder & Lightning: Weather Past, Present, Future. Lauren Redniss. Random House Inc. 2015. 272 p. : Illustration
ISBN 9780812993172
Grades: Adult   741.5
1. Weather 2. Meteorology 3. Climatology 4. Fog 5. Snow 6. Winds 7. Clouds 8. Rain and rainfall 9. Comics and Graphic novels 10. Science Writing — Weather

LC Bl2015042809

Focusing on the intricate nature of the world around us, as well as the personal relationship we all have to the weather, a National Book Award finalist—combining personal stories with history, interviews, scientific research and full-color photos—explores the transformative power of weather.

Riesman, Abraham
True Believer: The Rise and Fall of Stan Lee. Abraham Riesman. Crown 2020. 416 p.
ISBN 9780593135716
Grades: Adult   741.5
1. Lee, Stan, 1922-2018 2. Cartoonists 3. Comics and graphic novel writers 4. Popular culture 5. Jewish American men 6. Comic book illustrators 7. Comic books, strips, etc. 8. Publishers and publishing 9. Biographies 10. Life stories — Arts and culture — Artists 11. Arts and Entertainment — Comics, Cartoons, and Animation

LC 2020016622

The definitive, revelatory biography of Marvel Comics creator Stan Lee, an artist and entrepreneur who reshaped global pop culture at a steep personal cost. Stan Lee—born Stanley Martin Lieber in 1922—is one of the most beloved and influential entertainers to emerge from the twentieth century. True Believer chronicles every triumph and every misstep of an extraordinary life, and leaves it to readers to decide whether Lee lived up to the responsibilities of his own talent.

"This detailed, clear-eyed examination pulls back the curtain on one of America's great storytellers and is sure to reignite debates over Lee's legacy." —*Publishers Weekly*

Includes index.

Sacco, Joe
Footnotes in Gaza. Joe Sacco. Metropolitan Books 2009. 432 p.
ISBN 9780805073478
Grades: Adult   741.5
1. Arab-Israeli conflict 2. Arab-Israeli relations 3. Violence 4. Massacres 5. Historiography 6. Palestinian people 7. Southwest Asia and North Africa (Middle East) history 8. Gaza Strip 9. Egypt 10. 20th century 11. 1950s 12. Comics and Graphic novels 13. History writing — Arab-Israeli relations — Southwest Asia and North Africa (Middle East)

LC 2009028433

Oregon Book Awards, Pacific Northwest College of Art Graphic Literature Award, 2012.

From the great cartoonist-reporter, a sweeping, original investigation of a forgotten crime in the most vexed of places. Rafah, a town at the bottommost tip of the Gaza Strip, is a squalid place. Raw concrete buildings front trash-strewn alleys. The narrow streets are crowded with young children and unemployed men. On the border with Egypt, swaths of Rafah have been bulldozed to rubble. Rafah is today and has always been a notorious flashpoint in this bitterest of conflicts. Buried deep in the archives is one bloody incident, in 1956, that left 111 Palestinians dead, shot by Israeli soldiers. Seemingly a footnote to a long history of killing, that day in Rafah—cold-blooded massacre or dreadful mistake—reveals the competing truths that have come to define an intractable war. In a quest to get to the heart of what happened, Joe Sacco immerses himself in daily life of Rafah and the neighboring town of Khan Younis, uncovering Gaza past and present. Spanning fifty years, moving fluidly between one war and the next, alive with the voices of fugitives and schoolchildren, widows and sheikhs, Footnotes in Gaza captures the essence of a tragedy.

★ *Paying the Land.* Joe Sacco. Metropolitan Books 2020. 256 p.
ISBN 9781627799034
Grades: Adult   741.5
1. Denesuline (North American people) 2. Indigenous peoples of North America, Treatment of 3. First Nations (Canada) 4. Racism 5. Government relations with indigenous peoples 6. Mines and mineral resources 7. Comics and Graphic novels 8. Historical comics 9. History writing — Indigenous peoples — Canada 10. Politics and global affairs — Civil and human rights

LC 2019053376

Joe Sacco travels the frozen North to reveal a people in conflict over the costs and benefits of development. The mining boom is only the latest assault on indigenous culture: Sacco recounts the shattering impact of a residential school system that aimed to "remove the Indian from the child"; the destructive process that drove the Dene from the bush into settlements and turned them into wage laborers; the government land claims stacked against the Dene Nation; and their uphill efforts to revive a wounded culture.

"Harrowing and enlightening, Sacco presents another solemn, resonating dispatch." —*Booklist*

Chiefly illustrated.

Santiago, Wilfred
"21": The Story of Roberto Clemente : A Graphic Novel. by Wilfred Santiago. Fantagraphics 2011. 148 p. : Illustration
ISBN 9781560978923
Grades: 11 12 Adult   741.5
1. Clemente, Roberto, 1934-1972 2. Professional baseball players 3. Athletes 4. Baseball players 5. Puerto Rican people in the United States 6. Right fielders (Baseball) 7. Biographies 8. Comics and Graphic novels 9. Biographical comics 10. Biographies — Identity — Hispanics and Hispanic Americans 11. Sports and recreation — Baseball 12. Biographies — Athletes 13. Sports and recreation — Athletes

LC 2012289663

Booklist Editors' Choice: Adult Books for Young Adults, 2011; Library Journal Best Books, 2011; YALSA Great Graphic Novels for Teens, 2012.

A graphic tale inspired by the life of baseball star Roberto Clemente includes coverage of a wide range of topics from the ways in which prejudice challenged his career and his personal responsibilities to his achievements with the Pittsburgh Pirates and his triumphant 3,000th hit before his tragic fatal plane crash.

"Santiago skitters around formative scenes from Clemente's childhood—striking a complex chord of family, homeland, and a driving passion for baseball—before tracing significant moments from his professional career: Staring down racism with the same resolute demeanor with which he faced a high heater, snagging batting championships and fans' hearts many times over, and always looking for ways to honor his heritage." —*Booklist*

Includes bibliographical references.

Satrapi, Marjane
Chicken with Plums. Marjane Satrapi. Pantheon Books 2006. 96 p.
ISBN 9780375424151
Grades: 11 12 Adult   741.5
1. Khan, Nasser Ali 2. Musicians 3. Lost articles 4. Death 5. Quests 6. Married men 7. Husband and wife 8. Father and child 9. Men 10. Suicidal behavior 11. Decision-making 12. People with depression 13. Social life and customs 14. Iran 15. Tehran, Iran 16. 1950s 17. 20th century 18. Comics and Graphic novels 19. Page to screen 20. Family and Relationships — Families 21. Science Writing — Medicine and health — Mental health

LC 2006043156

The author relates the story of her great-uncle, Nasser Ali Khan, one of Iran's most acclaimed musicians, who discovers that his beloved instrument has been irrevocably damaged and renounces the world, its pleasures, and life itself.

"In graphic novel format, the author chronicles the life of her great-uncle Nasser Ali Khan. A revered musician, he takes to his bed and refuses sustenance

ESSENTIAL AND RECOMMENDED TITLES
741.5 Cartoons, graphic novels, caricatures, comics

after his frustrated wife breaks his taran Iranian luteover her knee. It takes him eight days to die, and in that time Satrapi reveals the futures of his children and unearths his past.... Satrapi's deceptively simple, remarkably powerful drawings match the precise but flexible prose she employs in adapting to her multiple roles as educator, folklorist, and grand-niece." —*The New Yorker*

★ *The Complete Persepolis*. Marjane Satrapi. Pantheon Books 2007. 341 p. : Illustration
ISBN 9780375714832
Grades: 11 12 Adult   741.5
1. Satrapi, Marjane, 1969- 2. Children and war 3. Teenage girls 4. Women's rights 5. Women's role 6. Iran-Iraq War, 1980-1988 7. Muslims 8. Young women 9. Misfits (People) 10. Alienation 11. Parent and adult child 12. Iranian revolution, 1979-1997 13. Social life and customs 14. Independence 15. Southwest Asia and North Africa (Middle East) history 16. Tehran, Iran 17. Iran 18. 1980s 19. 20th century 20. Autobiographies and memoirs 21. Autobiographical comics 22. Comics and Graphic novels 23. Family and Relationships — Growing up 24. Life stories — Relationships — Growing up 25. Adult books for young adults 26. History writing — Nationalism — Southwest Asia and North Africa (Middle East)
LC 2007060106

The great-granddaughter of Iran's last emperor and the daughter of ardent Marxists describes growing up in Tehran in a country plagued by political upheaval and vast contradictions between public and private life.

Contains the author's Persepolis (2003) and Persepolis 2 (2004).

Embroideries. Marjane Satrapi. Pantheon Books 2005. 144 p. : Illustration
ISBN 9780375423055
Grades: 11 12 Adult   741.5
1. Satrapi, Marjane, 1969- 2. Sexuality 3. Women's role 4. Female friendship 5. Regret 6. Virginity 7. Arranged marriage 8. Plastic surgery 9. Marriage 10. Family relationships 11. Social life and customs 12. Iran 13. 20th century 14. Comics and Graphic novels 15. History writing — Women's history 16. History writing — Southwest Asia and North Africa (Middle East)
LC 2004058660

A collection of stories and anecdotes, told in the form of a graphic novel, reveals the love and sex lives of a group of women as revealed during an afternoon of conversation and tea-drinking.

"Discussions of sex are frank and explicit and laced with high humor.... Satrapi's simple black-and-white cartooning style is tremendously effective, expertly portraying emotional nuances with just a few lines." —*School Library Journal*

Sattouf, Riad

The Arab of the Future 2: A Graphic Memoir : A Childhood in the Middle East (1984-1985). Riad Sattouf. Henry Holt & Co. 2016. 176 p.
ISBN 9781627793513
Grades: Adult   741.5
1. Sattouf, Riad 2. Assad, Hafez, 1930-2000 3. Antisemitism 4. Growing up 5. Dictatorship 6. Families 7. Cartoonists 8. Childhood innocence (Concept) 9. Totalitarianism 10. Fathers and sons 11. Oppression (Psychology) 12. Nationalism 13. Boys 14. Syria 15. Southwest Asia and North Africa (Middle East) 16. 1980s 17. Comics and Graphic novels 18. Autobiographical comics 19. Translations — French to English 20. Life stories — Relationships — Growing up 21. Life stories — Facing adversity — War and oppression 22. Life stories — Identity — Race and ethnicity
LC Bl2016039900

In a graphic account of his childhood, the author, now settled in his father's hometown of Homs, gets to go to school, where he dedicates himself to becoming a true Syrian in the country of the dictator Hafez Al-Assad, and the rest of his family also strains to fit in, until a single brutal act forces the family to make a dramatic change.

"Rather than being incongruous with the oppressive society and grim events he depicts, Sattouf's broadly cartoonish drawing style imparts a level of attachment that makes his story bearable." —*Booklist*

Sequel to: The Arab of the future.

The Arab of the Future: Growing up in the Middle East (1978-1984) : A Graphic Memoir. Riad Sattouf. Metropolitan Books 2015. 160 p. : Illustration
ISBN 9781627793445
Grades: Adult   741.5
1. Sattouf, Riad 2. Qaddafi, Muammar 3. Assad, Hafez, 1930-2000 4. Growing up 5. Dictatorship 6. Cartoonists 7. Families 8. Childhood 9. Totalitarianism 10. Fathers and sons 11. Oppression (Psychology) 12. Nationalism 13. Boys 14. Libya 15. Southwest Asia and North Africa (Middle East) 16. 20th century 17. Autobiographical comics 18. Comics and Graphic novels 19. Translations — French to English 20. Life stories — Relationships — Growing up 21. Life stories — Facing adversity — War and oppression 22. Life stories — Identity — Race and ethnicity
LC 2014041152

Los Angeles Times Book Prize for Graphic Novel, 2015.

The author recounts his nomadic childhood growing up in rural France, Gaddafi's Libya, and Assad's Syria, under the roof of his father, a Syrian Pan-Arabist, who drags his family along in his pursuit of grandiose dreams for the Arab nation.

"Caught between his parents, Sattouf makes the best of his situation by becoming a master observer and interpreter, his clean, cartoonish art making a social and personal document of wit and understanding." —*Publishers Weekly*

Sequel: The Arab of the future 2; Translated from the French Arabe du futur by Sam Taylor.

Schumacher, Michael

Will Eisner: A Dreamer's Life in Comics. Michael Schumacher. Bloomsbury 2010. 368 p.
ISBN 9781608190133
Grades: 11 12 Adult   741.5
1. Eisner, Will 2. Cartoonists 3. Cartoons 4. Illustrators 5. Literary criticism 6. Social life and customs 7. United States 8. 20th century 9. 21st century 10. Biographies 11. Arts and Entertainment — Comics, Cartoons, and Animation 12. Life stories — Arts and culture — Artists 13. Adult books for young adults
LC 2010011283

Depicts the artist's career over eight decades, from the dawn of comics' Golden Age in the late 1930s to the early 21st century when Pulitzers began being awarded to graphic novels, and features interviews with his family, friends and colleagues.

"Propelled by Eisner's geyserlike energy and output, Schumacher keenly chronicles Eisner's brilliant career within a lively history of American comics and creates an inspiring portrait of a perpetually diligent and innovative artist whose belief in comics as fine art fueled a new and fertile creative universe." —*Booklist*

Includes bibliographical references and index.

Spiegelman, Art

Co-Mix: A Retrospective of Comics, Graphics, and Scraps. Art Spiegelman. Drawn & Quarterly 2013. 192 p. : Illustration
ISBN 9781770461147
Grades: Adult   741.5
1. Spiegelman, Art 2. Comic books, strips, etc. 3. Comic book illustrators 4. Comics and graphic novel writers 5. Comic book illustration 6. Comics and graphic novel writing 7. Literary criticism 8. 20th century 9. Biographical comics 10. Comics and Graphic novels 11. Anthologies 12. Biographies 13. Arts and Entertainment — Comics, Cartoons, and Animation 14. Life stories — Arts and culture — Writing — Authors
LC Bl2013040412

A comprehensive retrospective of the career of the Pulitzer Prize-winning cartoonist includes full-page reproductions of his artwork as well as essays from curators and other artists who discuss his genre-defining work.

"Maus did much to 'Legitimize' comics to the wider world, but this thoughtfully curated, elegantly presented volume is an even more convincing testament to the potential of the medium." —*Booklist*

In the Shadow of No Towers. Art Spiegelman. Pantheon Books 2004. 42 p. : Color illustration
ISBN 9780375423079

PUBLIC LIBRARY CORE COLLECTION: NONFICTION
Twentieth Edition

Grades: 10 11 12 Adult   **741.5**
1. Spiegelman, Art 2. September 11 Terrorist Attacks, 2001 3. Grief 4. Anger 5. New York City 6. Comics and Graphic novels 7. Biographical comics 8. History writing — September 11, 2001 — United States

LC 2004043870

New York Times Notable Book, 2004.

The creator of Maus conveys experience of the September 11th tragedy in a series of drawings and text that capture the horror of the event, its impact on his own life, and the dangerous erosion of American democracy that has occured in the aftermath of the attack.

"The author provides a hair-raising and wry account of his family's frantic efforts to locate one another on September 11 as well as a morbidly funny survey of his trademark sense of existential doom. . . . This is a powerful and quirky work of visual storytelling by a master comics artist." —*Publishers Weekly*

★ *Maus: A Survivor's Tale.* Art Spiegelman. Pantheon Books 1997. 295 p. : Illustration

ISBN 9780679406419

Grades: 7 8 9 10 11 12 Adult   **741.5**
1. Spiegelman, Art 2. Spiegelman, Vladek, 1906-1982 3. Children of Holocaust survivors 4. Fathers and sons 5. Holocaust survivors 6. Jewish American men 7. Jewish Americans 8. Survival (in concentration camps, prisons, etc.) 9. Comics and graphic novel writers 10. Comic book illustrators 11. Holocaust (1933-1945) 12. Poland 13. Autobiographies and memoirs 14. Comics and Graphic novels 15. Biographies 16. History writing — Wars and conflicts — Holocaust — World War II 17. Life stories — Facing adversity — War and oppression — War survivors

LC 96032796

A son struggles to come to terms with the horrific story of his parents and their experiences during the Holocaust and in postwar America, in an omnibus edition of Spiegelman's two-part, Pulitzer Prize-winning best-seller.

"An undisputed classic and award-winning title (including a Pulitzer Prize in 1992) in which renowned cartoonist Spiegelman depicts his father's experiences as a World War II Nazi concentration camp survivor." —*Library Journal*

Spiegelman, Nadja

★ *I'm Supposed to Protect You from All This: A Memoir.* Nadja Spiegelman. Riverhead Books 2016. 288 p.

ISBN 9781594631924

Grades: Adult   **741.5**
1. Spiegelman, Nadja 2. Mouly, Francoise 3. Mothers and daughters 4. Autobiographies and memoirs 5. Life stories — Relationships — Parent and child 6. Adult books for young adults

LC 2016010834

Booklist Editors' Choice, 2016.

The daughter of Maus creator Art Spiegelman and New Yorker art director Francoise Mouly describes her coming-of-age discovery of her mother's complicated childhood, her investigation into four generations of family women and her own efforts to reinvent herself in New York.

Tisserand, Michael

Krazy: George Herriman, a Life in Black and White. Michael Tisserand. HarperCollins 2016. 560 pages

ISBN 9780061732997

Grades: Adult   **741.5**
1. Herriman, George, 1880-1944 2. Krazy Kat (Comic strip) 3. Comics and graphic novel writers 4. Passing (Identity) 5. Race (Social sciences) 6. Comic strip illustrators 7. Comic books, strips, etc. 8. Comics and graphic novel writing 9. Literary criticism 10. New Orleans, Louisiana 11. Biographies 12. Life stories — Arts and culture — Artists 13. Life stories — Identity — Race and ethnicity

LC Bl2016052808

New York Times Notable Book, 2017; National Book Critics Circle Award for Biography finalist, 2016.

A biography of the creator of the wildly popular Krazy Kat comic describes how the 19th-century New Orleans native hid his African-American racial identity in order to advance his art and career.

"Essential reading for comics fans and history buffs, Krazy is a roaring success, providing an indispensable new perspective on turn-of-the-century America." —*Kirkus*

Tomine, Adrian

The Loneliness of the Long-Distance Cartoonist. Adrian Tomine. Drawn and Quarterly 2020. 168 p.

ISBN 9781770463950

Grades: Adult   **741.5**
1. Tomine, Adrian, 1974- 2. Cartoonists 3. Self-consciousness 4. Fame 5. Men 6. Autobiographical comics 7. Comics and Graphic novels 8. Autobiographies and memoirs 9. Life stories — Arts and culture — Artists 10. Arts and Entertainment — Comics, Cartoons, and Animation

LC Bl2020017911

New York Times Notable Book, 2020.

A comedic memoir about fandom, fame, and other embarrassments from the life of a New York Times bestseller.

"Subtle, provocative, and sharply drawn—a portrait of the perpetually dissatisfied artist." —*Kirkus*

Illustrated by the author.

Voloj, Julian

Ghetto Brother: Warrior to Peacemaker. Julian Voloj; illustrated by Claudia Ahlering. NBM Comics Lit 2015. 127 p. : Illustration

ISBN 9781561639489

Grades: 11 12 Adult   **741.5**
1. Melendez, Benjy 2. Gang leaders 3. Nonviolence 4. Mediation 5. Gangs 6. Street life 7. Leadership 8. Immigrants, Puerto-Rican 9. Bronx, New York City 10. New York City 11. 1960s 12. 1970s 13. Biographical comics 14. Comics and Graphic novels 15. Adult books for young adults

LC 2015931382

Tells the true story of Benjy Melendez, a Bronx legend, son of Puerto-Rican immigrants, who founded, at the end of the 1960s, the notorious Ghetto Brothers gang.

"A fine documentary graphic novel of cultural and personal change for the better." —*Booklist*

Weldon, Glen

★ *The Caped Crusade: Batman and the Rise of Nerd Culture.* Glen Weldon. Simon & Schuster 2016. VIII, 324 p.

ISBN 9781476756691

Grades: Adult   **741.5**
1. Batman (Fictitious character) 2. Social history 3. Fans (People) 4. Comic book characters 5. Comic books, strips, etc. 6. Superheroes 7. Literary criticism 8. Popular culture 9. 20th century 10. Society and culture — Pop culture 11. Adult books for young adults 12. Arts and Entertainment — Writing and Publishing — Literary criticism

Explains Batman's rises and falls throughout the ages—and what his story tells us about ourselves.

"Ostensibly written with non-nerds in mind, this will, nevertheless, have huge appeal for members of the very group it attempts to dissect. Includes a truly spectacular, comprehensive bibliography." —*Booklist*

Includes bibliographical references (pages 289-305) and index.

Wolk, Douglas

★ *All of the Marvels: A Journey to the Ends of the Biggest Story Ever Told.* Douglas Wolk. Penguin Press 2021. 320 p.

ISBN 9780735222168

Grades: Adult   **741.5**
1. Comic books, strips, etc. 2. Literature and society 3. Popular culture 4. Superheroes 5. Literary criticism 6. United States 7. History writing — Arts and culture 8. Society and culture — Pop culture 9. Arts and Entertainment — Comics, Cartoons, and Animation

LC 2021013414

The first-ever full reckoning with Marvel Comics' interconnected, half-million-page story, a revelatory guide to the past 60 years of American cul-

ESSENTIAL AND RECOMMENDED TITLES
741.6 Graphic design, illustration, commercial art

ture—from an authority on the subject who read all 27,000+ Marvel superhero comics and lived to tell the tale.

"Wolk's light and humorous style appeals, and this work would be a marvelous addition to any library's collection. It will likely become a bible for serious comics fans and a useful introduction and reference guide for all others." —*Library Journal*

Includes bibliographical references and index.

Wood, Lawrence
Your Caption Has Been Selected: More Than Anyone Could Possibly Want to Know About the New Yorker Cartoon Caption Contest. Lawrence Wood; foreword by Bob Mankoff. St. Martin's Press 2024. 288 p.

ISBN 9781250333407

Grades: Adult   741.5

1. Cartoons 2. Contests 3. Humorous writing 4. Creativity 5. Newspaper comic strips 6. Arts and Entertainment — Comics, Cartoons, and Animation 7. Arts and Entertainment — Writing and publishing

LC 2024005563

A behind-the-scenes look at the New Yorker cartoon caption contest, its history, how it's judged, and the secrets to writing a winning caption.

"Wood has a great time here, mixing the bizarre, the jocular, and the wise into a clever package." —*Kirkus*

Includes bibliographical references.

741.6 Graphic design, illustration, commercial art

Bang, Molly
★ *Picture This: How Pictures Work.* Molly Bang. SeaStar Books 2000. 96 p. : Illustration; Color

ISBN 9781587170294

Grades: Adult   741.6

1. Illustration of books 2. Visual perception 3. Illustrated children's books 4. Art and music — Visual arts

LC 00024402

The illustrator of a retelling of "Little Red Riding Hood" provides a step-by-step account of her work to reveal the principles of illustration and the role of shape and color in expressing ideas and emotions.

"A must-have book for anyone wanting to learn or teach about art elements and principles and their connections to (picture book) art and visual perception." —*Kirkus*

Republished in 2016 by Chronicle Books.

Crumb, R.
R. Crumb: The Complete Record Cover Collection. R. Crumb. W.W. Norton 2011. Chiefly ill. (some col.)

ISBN 9780393082784

Grades: Adult   741.6

1. Crumb, R. 2. Sound recordings 3. Arts and Entertainment — General

LC Bl2011026934

A collection of album cover artwork from a founder of the underground comix movement includes the cover art for Janice Joplin's 1968 album "Cheap Thrills" and classic old-time music collections "Truckin' My Blues Away" and "Harmonica Blues."

"This volume is filled with the artist's designs for such ephemera as 'Unknown Detroit Bluesmen' or Cliff Edwards's 'I'm a Bear in a Ladies' Boudoir.' Starting in the 1970s, Mr. Crumb produced covers for reissues from labels like Yazoo, Blue Goose and Barrelhouse Records, and his love for the music is evident—a stippled Robert Johnson stares out in stark black and white, Bessie Smith sings 'Put a Little Sugar in My Bowl' and Charlie Patton gets his own mini-graphic novel. (The biggest act here is Big Brother and the Holding Company, with Janis Joplin done over to fit Crumb's zaftig ideal.) in this journeyman work, however, the discipline of playing second fiddle to his favorite musicians keeps the artist's self-loathing in check without taming the ribald humor that is also a hallmark of the blues. Few Crumb projects seem like so much fun to read about, to look at or to listen along to." —*Wall Street Journal*

In slipcase.

Marcus, Leonard S.
★ *Pictured Worlds: Masterpieces of Children's Book Art by 101 Essential Illustrators from Around the World.* Leonard S. Marcus. Abrams 2023. 431 pages ; Illustration; Color

ISBN 9781419738982

Grades: Adult   741.6

1. Illustrated children's books 2. Illustration of books 3. Children's book illustrators 4. Illustration 5. Art 6. Arts and Entertainment — Painting, Drawing, and Sculpture 7. Arts and Entertainment — Writing and Publishing

LC Bl2023012311

Highlights an international roster of 101 artists of the last 250 years whose touchstone achievements collectively chart the major trends and turning points in the history of children's book illustration."

"A work of art in itself, this volume about the picture book art form is a must-have for shelves celebrating children's books." —*School Library Journal*

Includes bibliographical references (pages 423-426).

Meder, Danielle
Draw Fashion Now: Techniques, Inspiration, and Ideas for Illustrating and Imagining Your Designs. Danielle Meder. Rockport 2016. 143 pages : Illustration; Color

ISBN 9781631591204

Grades: Adult   741.6

1. Fashion drawing 2. Arts and Entertainment — Fashion 3. Arts and Entertainment — Painting, Drawing, and Sculpture

LC Bl2016030336

Provides step-by-step instructions for drawing fashion designs from basic forms to finished products in environments such as red carpet events and live fashion runway shows.

"Fashion buffs and aspiring designers of any skill level will enjoy this fun guide." —*Library Journal*

With fashion paper dolls and a customizable, designer-inspired wardrobe—Cover; Includes bibliographical references (page 143).

Rees, Darrel
How to Be an Illustrator. Darrel Rees. Laurence King Publishing Ltd 2014. 167 pages : Illustration; Color

ISBN 9781780673288

Grades: Adult   741.6

1. Illustrators 2. Arts and Entertainment — General

LC Bl2014008473

Offers practical guidance to aspiring illustrators, including effective ways to approach would-be clients, how to negotiate contracts, and how to set up a studio.

"This guide . shares the author's insights on everything except the artistic aspects of the occupation, i.e, business concerns such as education, job hunting, project management, billing, and promoting yourself." —*Library Journal*

Rendgen, Sandra
Understanding the World: The Atlas of Infographics. Sandra Rendgen; ed. Julius Wiedemann. Taschen 2014. 456 pages : Illustration; Color

ISBN 9783836548830

Grades: Adult   741.6

1. Graphic arts 2. Graphic methods 3. Arts and Entertainment — General

LC Bl2014055105

Collects over 280 information graphics that render data on the environment, technology, economics, society, and culture into visual formats.

The atlas of infographics—Cover; Includes index.

742 Perspective in drawing

Brehm, Matthew T.
Drawing Perspective: How to See It, How to Apply It. Matthew Brehm. Barrons Educational Series, Inc. 2016. 144 pages : Illustration; Color
ISBN 9781438006598
Grades: Adult   742
1. Drawing technique 2. Perspective 3. Arts and Entertainment — Painting, Drawing, and Sculpture
LC 2014945484

A hands-on guide to perspective provides exercises designed to make drawing perspective effortless and easy.

"Dynamic layouts and simple structure make this guide fun to read and easy to comprehend." —*Library Journal*

Put your skills to the test! Includes a 32-page workbook with grids to fill in and artwork to complete—Cover; Includes bibliographical references (page 144) and index.

743 Drawing and drawings by subject

Vanderpoel, John Henry
The Human Figure. John H. Vanderpoel. Dover Publications 1958. 143 p. : Illustration
ISBN 9780486204321
Grades: Adult   743
1. Figure drawing 2. Arts and Entertainment — Crafts and hobbies
LC BL 99965426

The classic text on drawing human anatomy offers instructions on depicting such difficult areas as the lips, knee, ear, and nose.

Originally published: New York : Sterling Pub. Co, 1935.

743.4 Drawing human figures

Bradley, Barbara
Drawing People: How to Portray the Clothed Figure. Barbara Bradley. North Light Books 2003. 175 p. : Illustration; Color
ISBN 9781581803594
Grades: Adult   743.4
1. Drawing technique 2. Human figure in art 3. Arts and Entertainment — Painting, Drawing, and Sculpture
LC 2003042043

Teaches the fundamentals of any drawing, then illustrates how to draw clothed human figures that are active or at rest.

"The first part discusses proportion, perspective, and value, while the second part considers drawing folds and drapery. The final section offers tips on completing figures, including how to draw faces and hands and special instructions for drawing children. The result is a competent manual by a 25-year veteran of teaching at the Academy of Art College in San Francisco." —*Library Journal*

Includes index.

Hale, Robert Beverly
Anatomy Lessons from the Great Masters. Robert Beverly Hale and Terence Coyle. Watson-Guptill Publications 2000. 271 p. : Illustration
ISBN 9780823002818
Grades: Adult   743.4
1. Anatomy 2. Figure drawing 3. Arts and Entertainment — Painting, Drawing, and Sculpture
LC 2003265337

"Advanced students will find Hale and Coyle's Anatomy Lessons from the Great Masters a rich source of inspiration." —*Library Journal*

Includes bibliographical references (p. 263) and index.

Hart, Christopher
Human Anatomy Made Amazingly Easy. Christopher Hart. Watson-Guptill Publications 2000. 144 p. : Illustration
ISBN 9780823024971
Grades: 11 12 Adult   743.4
1. Drawing technique 2. Human figure in art 3. Arts and Entertainment — Painting, Drawing, and Sculpture
LC 00043514

Offers instructions for drawing seated, reclining, and standing figures, and features twelve projects from simple charcoal drawings to complex watercolors.

Includes index.

Huston, Steve
Figure Drawing for Artists: Making Every Mark Count. Steve Huston. Rockport Publishers 2016. 192 p. : Color; Illustration
ISBN 9781631590658
Grades: Adult   743.4
1. Figure drawing 2. Drawing technique 3. Human figure in art 4. Arts and Entertainment — Painting, Drawing, and Sculpture
LC 2018277532

Teaches human figure drawing techniques for both beginner and advanced students, offering specific instructions for areas such as the head, torso, arms, and feet.

Loomis, Andrew
Figure Drawing for All It's Worth: For All It's Worth. Andrew Loomis. Titan Books 2011. 204 p. : Illustration
ISBN 9780857680983
Grades: Adult   743.4
1. Anatomy 2. Figure drawing 3. Drawing technique 4. Arts and Entertainment — Painting, Drawing, and Sculpture
LC 2011381456

The illustrator Andrew Loomis (1892-1959) is revered among artists—including comics superstar Alex Ross—for his mastery of figure drawing and clean, Realist style. His hugely influential series of art instruction books have never been bettered, and Figure Drawing is the first in Titan's programme of facsimile editions, returning these classic titles to print for the first time in decades.

A book of fundamentals for an artistic career—Jkt; Originally published: New York : Viking Press, 1943.

Parks, Carrie
Secrets to Drawing Realistic Faces. Carrie Stuart Parks. North Light Books 2003. 140 p. : Illustration
ISBN 9781581802160
Grades: Adult   743.4
1. Drawing technique 2. Face in art 3. Arts and Entertainment — Painting, Drawing, and Sculpture
LC 2002023509

Provides examples and exercises to teach readers how to draw faces, covering shapes, shading, eyes, noses, lips, teeth, the head, and hair.

"Her useful and far-ranging discussion of materials includes an evaluation of pencils' graphite grades, kneaded and electric erasers, blending tools, and papers." —*Booklist*

Includes index.

Ryder, Anthony
The Artist's Complete Guide to Figure Drawing: A Contemporary Perspective on the Classical Tradition. Anthony Ryder. Watson-Guptill Publications 2000. 160 p. : Illustration
ISBN 9780823003037
Grades: Adult   743.4
1. Figure drawing 2. Drawing technique 3. Arts and Entertainment — Painting, Drawing, and Sculpture
LC 99022843

ESSENTIAL AND RECOMMENDED TITLES
743.6 Drawing animals

Demonstrates a three-step drawing method exploring outline, contour, and the capture of light, volume, and mass.
Includes index.

Winslow, Valerie L.
Classic *Human Anatomy: The Artist's Guide to Form, Function, and Movement.* Valerie L. Winslow. Watson-Guptill 2009. 303 p. : Illustration; Color
ISBN 9780823024155
Grades: Adult 743.4
1. Anatomy 2. Figure drawing 3. Drawing technique 4. Arts and Entertainment — Painting, Drawing, and Sculpture
LC 2009280099

The study of anatomy has long been essential training for painters and sculptures who want to accurately portray the human form. With hundreds of drawings and meticulously researched text, this book includes: an overview of the history of artistic anatomy; an introduction to the "language of anatomy" that makes the meaning of anatomical terms transparent, accessible, and memorable; entries on all major muscles and muscle groups, depicting each muscle's form, its interactions with the skeletal system, and its role in creating movement; instruction on capturing the human figure through quick "gesture" drawings as well as highly detailed renderings; a selection of finished life studies—some of the whole figure, others focusing on discrete regions of the body—that translate anatomical knowledge into expressive art; and quick-reference study aids, including a guide to anatomical terminology and a glossary.
"A significant contribution to the literature of art reference." —*Library Journal*
Includes bibliographical references (p. 295-296) and index.

743.6 Drawing animals

Hand, Diana
Draw Horses in 15 Minutes: Capture the Beauty of the Equine Form. Diana Hand. ILEX 2015. 112 p. : Illustration
ISBN 9781781572498
Grades: Adult 743.6
1. Horses in art 2. Drawing technique 3. Arts and Entertainment — Painting, Drawing, and Sculpture
LC Bl2016054519

Teaches essential skills and techniques for sketching horses, with guidance specific to each element of the horse's anatomy.
Includes bibliographical references (pages 111).

745 Decorative arts

Larson, Elsie
*A **Beautiful** Mess Happy Handmade Home: A Room-by-Room Guide to Painting, Crafting, and Decorating a Cheerful, More Inspiring Space.* Elsie Larson and Emma Chapman. Potter Style 2014. 240 pages : Color; Illustration
ISBN 9780770434052
Grades: Adult 745
1. Handicraft 2. Home furnishings 3. Interior decoration 4. Arts and Entertainment — Crafts and hobbies 5. House and Home — Interior Decorating and Furnishings
LC 2014008902

Give your home a "happiness makeover" with the more than 90 DIY projects, decorating tips, and inspiring ideas in this first-ever home decor book from the creators of the mega-popular style blog A Beautiful Mess.
"In the introduction, the authors instruct readers to identify what features stand out in favorite spaces of all kinds, to make lists of how rooms might be used unconventionally (playing cards in a dining room), and to do some soul searching (Make a list of 100 things about YOU.) the idea is to make home an expression of one's personality, a skill that the authors have clearly mastered." —*Publishers Weekly*
Includes bibliographical references (page 237) and index.

745.4 Pure and applied design and decoration

Black, Alexandra
Design: *The Definitive Visual History.* Writers, Alexandra Black, R.G. Grant, Ann Kay, Philip Wilkinson, Iain Zaczek. DK 2015. 480 pages : Illustration; Color
ISBN 9781465438010
Grades: Adult 745.4
1. Design 2. Arts and Entertainment — General
LC Bl2015040100

Traces the history of design from early cultures to contemporary design, profiling major movements, designers, and manufacturers.
DK Smithsonian—Cover; Includes index.

745.409034 Decoration — 19th century

Miller, Judith
Miller's Arts & Crafts: Living with the Arts & Crafts Style. Judith Miller. Millers, a division of Mitchell Beazley 2014. 239 pages : Illustration; Color
ISBN 9781845339432
Grades: Adult 745.409034
1. Arts and crafts movement 2. Arts and Entertainment — Painting, Drawing, and Sculpture
LC Oc2014163957

"Noteworthy for its breadth and its superb color images, this is an up-to-date resource for any art collection." —*Library Journal*
Includes index.

745.5 Handicrafts

Akiyama, Lance
Duct Tape Engineer: The Book of Big, Bigger, and Epic Duct Tape Projects. Lance Akiyama. Rockport Publishers 2017. 160 p. : Illustration
ISBN 9781631591303
Grades: Adult 745.5
1. Duct tape 2. Arts and Entertainment — Crafts and hobbies 3. House and Home — DIY, maintenance, and repair
LC 2016032103

"This volume will have great appeal to young adults and teens. And while the durability of cardboard and duct tape furniture may be questionable, it certainly is unique." —*Library Journal*

Chapin, Kari
★ *The Handmade Marketplace: Featuring New Online Strategies and Crafter Profiles.* Kari Chapin. Storey Publishing 2014. 247 pages
ISBN 9781612123356
Grades: Adult 745.5
1. Selling 2. Handicraft 3. Marketing 4. Business and economics — General 5. Arts and Entertainment — Crafts and hobbies
LC 2014004540

Presents advice on turning a creative interest into a profitable craft business, covering basic business start-up practices, marketing, networking, advertising and publicity, blogging, participating in craft fairs, and online selling.
Includes bibliographical references (pages 239-242) and index.

Corwin, Lena
Printing by Hand: A Modern Guide to Printing with Handmade Stamps, Stencils, and Silk Screens. by Lena Corwin; photography by Thayer Allyson Gowdy. Stewart, Tabori & Chang 2008. 144 p. : Color illustration
ISBN 9781584796725
Grades: Adult 745.5
1. Handicraft 2. Rubber stamping 3. Stenciling 4. Arts and Entertainment — Crafts and hobbies
LC 2007044503

A talented designer explains how to create a wide variety of unusual and innovative hand-printed fabrics, furnishings, accessories, and paper crafts by using stencils, master stamps, and screen printing, using step-by-step instructions to teach crafters the fundamentals of hand printing and offering an array of ingenious projects, from screen-printed bed linens to stationery.

Includes bibliographical references.

Falick, Melanie
Making a Life: Working by Hand and Discovering the Life You Are Meant to Live. Melanie Falick; photographs by Rinne Allen. Artisan 2019. 319 p.
  ISBN 9781579657444
Grades: Adult   745.5
  1. Artisans 2. Handicraft 3. Creation (Literary, artistic, etc.) 4. Semantics 5. Arts and Entertainment — Crafts and hobbies
                                                           LC 2019016973

A writer, crafter and maker describes her travels around the world to meet with 30 potters, weavers, painters, metalsmiths, woodworkers, and more to explore the personal, inspiring and resonating reasons that they create with their hands.

Gorges, Eric
A Craftsman's Legacy: Why Working with Our Hands Gives Us Meaning. Eric Gorges, with Jon Sternfeld. Algonquin Books 2019. 244 p.
  ISBN 9781616208363
Grades: Adult   745.5
  1. Gorges, Eric 2. Handicraft 3. Happiness 4. Purpose in life 5. Work-life balance 6. Artisanship 7. Creation (Literary, artistic, etc.) 8. Metal-work 9. Arts and Entertainment — Crafts and hobbies 10. Life stories — Arts and culture
                                                           LC 2018042246

The host of PBS's A Craftsman's Legacy makes the case that the craftsman's way—the philosophy, the skills, and the mindset—can provide a blueprint for all of us in our increasingly hurried, disposable world. In this book he tells the stories and shares the collective wisdom of these modern-day makers while also celebrating the culture of all craftsmen.

"Metalworker Gorges, who has profiled artisans of all stripes as host of the PBS series A Craftsman's Legacy, revisits some of his favorite interviews in this invigorating survey." —*Publishers Weekly*

Includes bibliographical references.

Minter, Laura
Mini Makers: Crafty Makes to Create with Your Kids. Laura Minter & Tia Williams. Guild of Master Craftsman Publications Ltd 2016. 159 pages : Illustration; Color
  ISBN 9781784941017
Grades: Adult   745.5
  1. Handicraft 2. Handicraft for children 3. Arts and Entertainment — Crafts and hobbies
                                                           LC Bl2017003624

Presents ideas for crafts designed for parents and children to complete together, including rainy-day games, musical instruments, dress up costumes, and a cardboard vessel.

"Parents and caregivers will find plenty of ideas for creative play in this imaginative collection." —*Library Journal*

Includes index.

Nicholas, Kristin
Crafting a Patterned Home: Painting, Printing, and Stitching Projects to Enliven Every Room. Kristin Nicholas; photographs by Rikki Snyder. Roost Books 2018. x, 191 pages Color; Illustration
  ISBN 9781611803495
Grades: Adult   745.5
  1. Handicraft 2. Home furnishings 3. Arts and Entertainment — Crafts and hobbies — Textiles and needlework 4. House and Home — Interior Decorating and Furnishings
                                                           LC 2017008660

Presents design ideas for adding patterns to home decor, giving advice on paints, materials, tools, the use of color, and the mixing and layering of different patterns, with projects for creating such items as pillows, murals, curtains, napkins, and upholstered chairs.

Pester, Sophie
Supercraft: Easy Projects for Every Weekend. Sophie Pester, Catharina Bruns. DK 2016. 175 pages : Illustration; Color
  ISBN 9781465449207
Grades: Adult   745.5
  1. Handicraft 2. Arts and Entertainment — Crafts and hobbies
                                                           LC Bl2016008207

Shares instructions for a year of crafts broken down by season, from knitting hats and cutomizing stationary to painting hangers and creating concrete letters.

"The aesthetic is fresh and contemporary, with lots of bright colors and modern art-inspired style. Numerous techniques are covered, including paper craft, painting, crochet, embroidery, weaving, origami, and sewing, making this a veritable buffet of ideas." —*Library Journal*

Pigza, Jessica
Bibliocraft: A Modern Crafter's Guide to Using Library Resources to Jumpstart Creative Projects. Jessica Pigza; photographs by Johnny Miller; photostyling by Shana Faust; illustrations by Sun Young Park. STC Craft 2014. 207 pages : Illustration; Color
  ISBN 9781617690969
Grades: Adult   745.5
  1. Arts and Entertainment — Crafts and hobbies
                                                           LC Bl2014014668

Encourages using the library as a source of both creative inspiration and materials for handicraft projects, showcasing the projects from celebrated designers, including watermark pillows, cyanotype throws, and cartouche embroidery.

"Though bibliophiles and fans of libraries will be drawn in by the theme of the book, crafters who haven't visited a library since childhood will be thrilled with the wealth of talented artists whose projects are featured. (Bibliophiles will also be pleased that no books are harmed in the making of these crafts." —*Library Journal*

A Melanie Falick book; Includes index.

Rodabaugh, Katrina
The Paper Playhouse: Awesome Art Projects for Kids : Using Paper, Boxes, and Books. Katrina Rodabaugh. Quarry Books 2015. 144 pages : Color; Illustration
  ISBN 9781592539802
Grades: Adult   745.5
  1. Handicraft 2. Arts and Entertainment — Crafts and hobbies
                                                           LC Bl2014053710

Offers different arts and crafts projects parents and their children can create together, including sculpture, printmaking, bookbinding, and collage.

"Craft projects using recycled or upcycled materials are perennially popular, and the kid-friendly angle adds a fun dimension." —*Library Journal*

Samuell, Kristine
A Year of Gingerbread Houses: Making & Decorating Gingerbread Houses for All Seasons. Kristine Samuell. Lark, an imprint of Sterling Publishing 2015. VII, 135 pages : Illustration; Color
  ISBN 9781454708919
Grades: Adult   745.5
  1. Gingerbread houses 2. Gingerbread 3. Arts and Entertainment — Crafts and hobbies — Seasonal
                                                           LC Bl2015032357

Provides step-by-step instructions for six gingerbread house projects, including a haunted hideaway, a winter wonderland, and a birthday picnic, with project templates; advice on planning, baking, and assembling houses; and decorating tips.

ESSENTIAL AND RECOMMENDED TITLES
745.5083 Handicrafts — Arts — Children

"One of the best gingerbread books available, Samuell's debut is essential for serious gingerbread architects and decorators." —*Library Journal*
Includes bibliographical references (page 131) and index.

745.5083 Handicrafts — Arts — Children

Neuburger, Emily K.
Show Me a Story: 40 Craft Projects and Activities to Spark Children's Storytelling. Emily K. Neuburger. Storey Pub. 2012. 144 p. : Color illustration
ISBN 9781603429887
Grades: Adult Professional   **745.5083**
1. Handicraft for children 2. Storytelling 3. Arts and Entertainment — Crafts and hobbies
LC 2012004610

Features instructions for creating and leading forty activities that encourage children to tell stories by using their imaginations, drawing, developing characters, and learning vocabulary.
Includes bibliographical references and index.

Van't Hul, Jean
The Artful Parent: Simple Ways to Fill Your Family's Life with Art and Creativity. Jean Van't Hul. Roost Books 2013. xxi, 320 p. : Color illustration
ISBN 9781590309643
Grades: Adult   **745.5083**
1. Child artists 2. Creative activities and seat work 3. Handicraft for children 4. Parent and child 5. Family and Relationships — General
LC 2012021168

Provides over sixty art projects for children designed to inspire creativity and imagination, including creating artful envelopes, tracing shadow shapes, and making collage frames.
"Parents, teachers, and child-care providers will all find useful ideas and inspiration here." —*Library Journal*
Includes bibliographical references (p. 298-309) and index.

745.53 Handicrafts — Leathers and furs

Gethin, Rosanna Clare
Sew Luxe Leather: Over 20 Stylish Leather Craft Accessories. Rosanna Clare Gethin. SewandSo 2018. 127 pages : Illustration; Color
ISBN 9781446306765
Grades: Adult   **745.53**
1. Leatherwork 2. Handicraft 3. Arts and Entertainment — Crafts and hobbies — Textiles and needlework
LC BL2018072028

"All are ordered by level of difficulty, easiest to most complex, and include tools, materials, and numbered directions, with accompanying color photographs." —*Booklist*
Includes index.

745.54 Papers

Descamps, Ghylenn
Beginner's Guide to Kirigami: 24 Skill-Building Projects Using Origami & Papercrafting Skills. Ghylenn Descamps. Fox Chapel Publishing 2019. 94 p.
ISBN 9781497100169
Grades: Adult   **745.54**
1. Paper work 2. Arts and Entertainment — Crafts and hobbies — Papercrafts
LC 2019024143

Gives instructions for making 24 kirigami projects. Also offers tips on using papercrafting tools, paper selection, and folding techniques.

Martin, Ann
The Art of Quilling Paper Jewelry: Techniques & Projects for Metallic Earrings & Pendants. Ann Martin. Interweave 2017. 144 pages : Color; Illustration
ISBN 9781632505774
Grades: Adult   **745.54**
1. Jewelry making 2. Arts and Entertainment — Crafts and hobbies — Jewelry and beadwork 3. Arts and Entertainment — Crafts and hobbies — Papercrafts
LC Bl2017035569

"This beautiful collection opens up numerous options for quilling beyond the standard surface decoration and may inspire crafters to give this ages-old craft a try." —*Library Journal*
Includes index.

Thuss, Rebecca
Paper to Petal: 75 Whimsical Paper Flower Ideas to Craft by Hand. Rebecca Thuss and Patrick Farrell; Foreword by Martha Stewart. Potter Craft 2013. 256 pages : Color; Illustration
ISBN 9780385345057
Grades: Adult   **745.54**
1. Paper flowers 2. Arts and Entertainment — Crafts and hobbies — Papercrafts
LC 2012048675

Shares step-by-step instructions for making dozens of sophisticated paper flowers, outlining creative projects ranging from wristlets and bookmarks to wreaths and a Mary Poppins-inspired flower.
Includes index.

745.57 Rubber and plastics

Akiyama, Lance
Rubber Band Engineer: Build Slingshot-Powered Rockets, Rubber Band Rifles, Unconventional Catapults, and More Guerilla Gadgets from Household Hardware. Lance Akiyama. Rockport 2016. 144 pages : Color; Illustration
ISBN 9781631591044
Grades: Adult   **745.57**
1. Toy making 2. Handicraft 3. Arts and Entertainment — Crafts and hobbies
LC Bl2016018730

Offers instructions for twenty-five different gadgets, including a crossbow, pneumatic magic box, and slingshot rocket.
Includes index.

745.592 Toys, models, miniatures, related objects

Frisoni, Christine-Lea
The Big Book of a Miniature House: Create and Decorate a House Room by Room. Christine-Lea Frisoni; translated by Stephen Haynes; photographs by Bertrand Runtz. Guild of Master Craftsman Publications Ltd 2014. 191 pages : Illustration; Color
ISBN 9781861089540
Grades: Adult   **745.592**
1. Dollhouses 2. Miniature craft 3. Interior decoration 4. Arts and Entertainment — Crafts and hobbies 5. House and Home — Interior Decorating and Furnishings
LC Bl2016021468

Provides instructions for building and decorating a miniature French country house and adding furniture, plants, and other adornments.

Smith, Sally J.
Fairy Houses: How to Create Whimsical Homes for Fairy Folk. Sally J. Smith. Cool Springs Press 2017. 192 pages
ISBN 9781591866725
Grades: Adult   **745.592**

1. Dollhouses 2. Fairies in art 3. Fairies 4. Miniature objects 5. Nature craft 6. Arts and Entertainment — Crafts and hobbies — Garden and nature 7. Arts and Entertainment — Crafts and hobbies

LC 2016033755

"While charming and sweet, the fairy houses here are not hardy enough to hold up to inclement weather and temperature. Nevertheless, this recommended title is fun and unique." —*Library Journal*

745.5928 Models and miniatures

Garfield, Simon
In Miniature: How Small Things Illuminate the World. Simon Garfield. Atria Books 2019. 323 pages
ISBN 9781501199585
Grades: Adult   745.5928
1. Collectibles 2. Collectors and collecting 3. Toys 4. Control 5. Models and model making 6. Miniature craft 7. Miniature objects 8. Dollhouses 9. Art 10. History 11. Arts and Entertainment — General 12. History writing — Arts and culture 13. History writing — Microhistory

LC 2020302037

Encouraging us to find greatness in the smallest of things, the author, focusing on miniatures—and bringing together history, psychology, art and obsession--explores what fuels the strong appeal of miniature objects among collectors, modelers and fans.

Includes bibliographical references and index; Originally published: Edingburgh : Canongate Books, 2018.

745.593 Useful objects

Oppenheimer, Betty
The Candlemaker's Companion: A Complete Guide to Rolling, Pouring, Dipping, and Decorating Your Own Candles. Betty Oppenheimer. Storey Books 2001. VII, 199 p. : Illustration
ISBN 9781580173667
Grades: Adult   745.593
1. Candlemaking 2. Arts and Entertainment — Crafts and hobbies

LC 00053802

From wax to wick to wrapping, the Candlemaker's Companion is a definitive guide to modern candle making. Learn how to create rolled, poured, molded, and dipped candles; play with your favorite scents and colors; and use specialty techniques to design glowing luminaria, candle holders, and other gorgeous accessories.

Includes bibliographical references and index.

745.594 Decorative objects

Bluhm, Lisa
Creative Soldered Jewelry & Accessories: 20+ Earrings, Necklaces, Bracelets & More. Lisa Bluhm. Lark 2015. 126 pages : Color; Illustration
ISBN 9781454708162
Grades: Adult   745.594
1. Jewelry making 2. Arts and Entertainment — Crafts and hobbies — Jewelry and beadwork

LC 2013044513

Presents step-by-step instructions for twenty-eight projects using todays most popular soldering torch and iron techniques, from fashionable cuffs and necklaces to unique frames and decorative bottle toppers.

"This is a practical introduction and overview of both hard and soft soldering for hobbyists. Creating fun pieces as part of the learning process is an added bonus." —*Library Journal*

Includes index.

Cetti, Livia
The Exquisite Book of Paper Flowers: A Guide to Making Unbelievably Realistic Paper Blooms. Livia Cetti; photographs by Addie Juell. STC Craft 2014. 192 pages : Illustration; Color
ISBN 9781617691003
Grades: Adult   745.594
1. Paper flowers 2. Arts and Entertainment — Crafts and hobbies — Papercrafts

LC Bl2014040851

Provides step-by-step instructions for creating twenty-five paper flowers from tissue and crepe paper, and explains how to combine the flowers to arrange garlands, wreaths, table decorations, and corsages.

A Melanie Falick book.

Combs, Rebecca Ann
Kumihimo: Basics & Beyond : 24 Braided and Beaded Jewelry Projects on the Kumihimo Disk. Rebecca Ann Combs. Kalmbach Books 2014. 95 p. : Color illustration
ISBN 9781627000437
Grades: Adult   745.594
1. Beadwork 2. Jewelry making 3. Arts and Entertainment — Crafts and hobbies — Jewelry and beadwork

LC Oc2013124525

Kumihimo Basics and Beyond presents techniques for creating all-cord braids and beaded braids, then teaches beaders how to transform them into finished jewelry.

Crowther, Janet
Make a Statement: 25 Handcrafted Jewelry & Accessory Projects. Janet Crowther & Katie Covington. Chronicle Books 2015. 143 pages : Illustration; Color
ISBN 9781452133201
Grades: Adult   745.594
1. Jewelry making 2. Costume jewelry 3. Fashion 4. Arts and Entertainment — Crafts and hobbies — Jewelry and beadwork

LC 2014004103

Presents twenty-five projects for handcrafting jewelry and other accessories, including earrings, bracelets, necklaces, hair combs, and shoe clips.

Includes bibliographical references (pages 138-140) and index.

Geary, Theresa Flores
The Illustrated Bead Bible: Terms, Tips & Techniques. Theresa Flores Geary; photographs by Debra Whalen. Sterling Pub. 2008. VIII, 406 p. : Color illustration
ISBN 9781402723537
Grades: Adult   745.594
1. Beadwork 2. Arts and Entertainment — Crafts and hobbies — Jewelry and beadwork

LC 2007026120

Offers information on bead types, styles, materials, and tools with tips and techniques for purchasing beads and materials.

"This may be the ultimate bead reference book. The majority of the text is made up of an illustrated alphabetical encyclopedia of beads, broadly defined, and beading terms. Additional chapters include tips and techniques, charts illustrating bead characteristics, and stitch diagrams." —*Library Journal*

Includes bibliographical references (p. 385-392) and index.

Gedeon, Jade
Beautiful Bracelets by Hand: Seventy-Five One-of-a-Kind Baubles, Bangles, and Other Wrist Adornments You Can Make at Home. Jade Gedeon. Page Street Publishing Co. 2014. 1 online resource (223 pages) : Color; Illustration
ISBN 9781624140907
Grades: Adult   745.594
1. Bracelets 2. Jewelry making 3. Arts and Entertainment — Crafts and hobbies — Jewelry and beadwork

LC BL2015009513

ESSENTIAL AND RECOMMENDED TITLES
745.594 Decorative objects

Offers instructions on creating different types of bracelets from different types of materials, including leather, metal, and wood.

"The majority of the bracelets in this book are so simple and easy to make that absolute beginners can duplicate them successfully. Much of the writing reads like corny catalog copy, but there's enough Gedeon to make this a worthwhile purchase, especially where beginners' jewelry-making titles are popular." —*Library Journal*

Includes index.

Karon, Karen
Advanced Chain Maille Jewelry Workshop: Weaving with Rings & Scales. Karen Karon. Interweave 2014. 159 pages
ISBN 9781620336595
Grades: Adult   745.594
1. Jewelry making 2. Chains (Jewelry) 3. Metal-work 4. Arts and Entertainment — Crafts and hobbies — Jewelry and beadwork
LC 2014011104

"For experienced jewelry makers, since basic chain maille techniques such as opening and closing jump rings properly are not covered. Those looking to go beyond the techniques addressed in most related books will find a wealth of information within these pages." —*Library Journal*

Includes index.

Katz, Amy
Seed Bead Chic: 25 Elegant Projects Inspired by Fine Jewelry. Amy Katz. Lark Jewelry & Beading 2014. 128 pages : Color; Illustration (Lark Jewelry & Beading Bead Inspirations)
ISBN 9781454708179
Grades: Adult   745.594
1. Beadwork 2. Jewelry making 3. Arts and Entertainment — Crafts and hobbies — Jewelry and beadwork
LC 2013047476

Upscale, elegant, chic: These 25 handcrafted projects look like the fine jewelry you'd find in high-end boutiques. But why splurge when all it takes to make them are some seed beads and intermediate-to-advanced skills? Featuring a variety of stitches—including the author's newly created right-angle ladder stitch—these stunning pieces cover everything from earrings to brooches. Gorgeous photographs, diagrams, and helpful tips make the beading process simple and pleasurable!

Amy Katz teaches how to make seed bead jewelry projects resembling beautiful fine jewelry. Along with the stunning photography, step-by-step instructions, and beading diagrams, this book will introduce Amy's newly invented beading stitch: the right angle ladder stitch. This book will position primarily toward the dedicated intermediate to advanced audience.

"Katz's projects are sophisticated in both style and technique. Jewelry makers looking for a challenge will find one here." —*Library Journal*

Includes index.

Legenhausen, Courtney
Fashion Jewelry: A Beginner's Guide to Jewelry Making. Courtney Legenhausen of Lotus Jewelry Studio. Lark 2017. 175 pages : Color; Illustration
ISBN 9781454710325
Grades: Adult   745.594
1. Jewelry making 2. Arts and Entertainment — Crafts and hobbies — Jewelry and beadwork
LC Bl2017029491

Provides instructions for creating sixteen stylish jewelry pieces using such techniques as bead stringing, wire wrapping, knotting, and hammering.

Includes index.

Pester, Sophie
Homemade Holiday: Craft Your Way Through More Than 40 Festive Projects. Sophie Pester, Catharina Bruns. DK Publishing 2017. 143 p. : Illustration; Color
ISBN 9781465463265
Grades: Adult   745.594
1. Christmas decorations 2. Handicraft 3. Arts and Entertainment — Crafts and hobbies — Seasonal
LC Bl2017037715

Presents step-by-step, illustrated instructions for festive craft projects for gifts, decorations, and homemade wrapping paper.

Van't Hul, Jean
The Artful Year: Celebrating the Seasons and Holidays with Family Arts and Crafts. Jean Van't Hul. Roost Books 2015. xv, 351 pages : Color; Illustration
ISBN 9781611801491
Grades: Adult   745.594
1. Family recreation 2. Handicraft 3. Holiday decorations 4. Recipes 5. Seasonal cooking 6. Cookbooks 7. Arts and Entertainment — Crafts and hobbies 8. Family and Relationships — General
LC 2013048889

Shares a collection of child-friendly holiday crafts and seasonal recipes to inspire and enrich family traditions.

Includes bibliographical references (pages 346-351).

Watanabe, Judi
The Complete Photo Guide to Cardmaking. Judi Watanabe. Creative Publishing International 2016. 256 pages : Illustration; Color (Complete Photo Guide)
ISBN 9781589238824
Grades: Adult   745.594
1. Greeting cards 2. Paper work 3. Arts and Entertainment — Crafts and hobbies — Papercrafts
LC Bl2016002838

Shows readers a range of paper crafting techniques, from washi tape, origami, and quilling to cut-outs, stamping, and die cutting, for designing cards for all occasions.

"Although this is a cardmaking book, scrapbookers, art journalers, and mixed-media artists will also appreciate the image-based tutorials and the abundance of inspiring photos." —*Library Journal*

Includes index.

Wiseman, Jill
Jill Wiseman's Beautiful Beaded Ropes: 24 Wearable Jewelry Projects in Multiple Stitches. Jill Wiseman. Lark Crafts 2012. 119 pages : Color; Illustration
ISBN 9781454703563
Grades: Adult   745.594
1. Beadwork 2. Jewelry making 3. Arts and Entertainment — Crafts and hobbies — Jewelry and beadwork
LC 2012002269

Join popular teacher and designer Jill Wiseman as she presents 24 beaded rope designs in this wonderful entry in Lark Jewelry & Beading's popular Beadweaving Master Class series. From dainty to heavy, and from simple to outrageously textured, these beautiful and wearable necklace, lariat, bangle, and bracelet projects (plus a few earrings!) utilize such popular stitch techniques as spiral rope, peyote, netting, herringbone, right angle weave, chevron, polygon weave, and oglala. Beginning and experienced beaders alike will love these high-quality projects from one of the most fun and innovative beaders on the scene today!—.

"Wiseman's designs have a lot of appeal and are easily customizable to suit individual tastes, and the variety of stitches used in the projects will pique beaders' interest." —*Library Journal*

Includes indexes.

Yamazaki, Hiromi
Japanese Paper Flowers: Elegant Kirigami Blossoms, Bouquets, Wreaths and More. Hiromi Yamazaki. Tuttle Publishing 2019. 96 pages : Color; Illustration
ISBN 9784805314982
Grades: Adult   745.594
1. Paper flowers 2. Handicraft 3. Arts and Entertainment — Crafts and hobbies — Papercrafts

LC Bl2019012564

Provides instructions on how to create thirty-one paper flower designs and includes projects that incorporate them, including wreaths, garlands, and jewelry.

"Whether or not they're already familiar with the Japanese art of origami, crafters can follow Yamazaki's instructions for fashioning exquisite and realistic-looking flowers from paper." —*Booklist*

745.5941646 Halloween — Handicrafts

Cupp, Lundy
Realistic Pumpkin Carving: 24 Scary, Spooky, and Spine-Chilling Designs. Lundy Cupp. Fox Chapel Publishing 2016. 96 pages : Illustration; Color
ISBN 9781565238947
Grades: Adult   745.5941646
1. Halloween decorations 2. Jack-o-lanterns 3. Vegetable carving 4. Pumpkin 5. Arts and Entertainment — Crafts and hobbies — Seasonal
LC 2017279887

Showcases realistic faces carved on pumpkins, discussing how to choose a pumpkin, describing the tools and equipment, and offering step-by-step instructions and twenty ready-to-use patterns.

"Create the perfect pumpkin for Halloween with this stunning book. Artist Cupp presents a collection of pumpkin carving patterns. The galleries of brilliantly carved pumpkins, squashes, and sweet potatoes are tantalizing, and the author's level of expertise is clearly on display." —*Library Journal*

Portions of this book were originally published in Woodcarving Illustrated magazine—Title page verso; Includes index.

745.6 Calligraphy, heraldic design, illumination

Doh, Jenny
Creative Lettering: Techniques & Tips from Top Artists. Jenny Doh. Lark 2013. 143 pages : Illustration; Color
ISBN 9781454704003
Grades: Adult   745.6
1. Lettering 2. Art technique 3. Arts and Entertainment — Crafts and hobbies
LC 2012021130

Provides step-by-step instructions for lettering from top artists, including advice on the best tools, techniques and tips, and font samples.

"Artists of all skill levels can enjoy this title." —*Library Journal*
Includes index.

Flor, Martina
The Golden Secrets of Lettering: Letter Design from First Sketch to Final Artwork. Martina Flor. Princeton Architectural Press 2017. 167 p. : Illustration
ISBN 9781616895730
Grades: Adult   745.6
1. Lettering 2. Art technique 3. Arts and Entertainment — Painting, Drawing, and Sculpture
LC 2016037057

"Readers with at least some prior drawing experience are best poised to benefit from this highly educational art instruction book." —*Library Journal*

Glynn, Kathy
Hand Lettering Step by Step: Techniques and Projects to Express Yourself Creatively. Kathy Glynn. Get Creative 6 2018. 143 p. : Illustration; Color
ISBN 9781942021858
Grades: Adult   745.6
1. Lettering 2. Handicraft 3. Art technique 4. Arts and Entertainment — Painting, Drawing, and Sculpture
LC 2017028519

"Each chapter contains step-by-step projects with lots of practical applications, including designs for love letters, monogrammed jewelry, business cards, fabric patterns, all sorts of signs, gift wrap, rubber stamps, and temporary tattoos.

Detailed, close-up photographs of various pen types, nibs from all angles, a great variety of inks, paints, and other supplies are featured throughout." —*Library Journal*

Includes bibliographical references (page 133) and index.

Owen, Imogen
Modern Calligraphy Workshop: The Creative Art of Pen, Brush and Chalk Lettering. Imogen Owen; photography by Kim Lightbody. Quadrille 2017. 143 p. : Illustration; Color
ISBN 9781849499071
Grades: Adult   745.6
1. Calligraphy 2. Arts and Entertainment — Painting, Drawing, and Sculpture
LC Bl2017044850

Instructs readers on how to write calligraphy to create hand-lettered stationery, art, and other decorations through the use of interactive sample alphabets, exercises, and step-by-step projects.

Includes index.

Rodriguez, Dina
The Big Awesome Book of Hand & Chalk Lettering. Dina Rodriguez. DK Publishing 2017. 206 pages : Illustration; Color
ISBN 9781465462725
Grades: Adult   745.6
1. Alphabets 2. Decorative arts 3. Lettering 4. Art technique 5. Arts and Entertainment — Painting, Drawing, and Sculpture 6. Arts and Entertainment — Crafts and hobbies 7. Arts and Entertainment — General
LC Bl2017027950

Uses step-by-step instructions and photographs to teach beginners how the master the art of hand lettering, how to compose phrases on the page, and how to make letters look dimensional.

Includes index.

Shepherd, Margaret
Learn Calligraphy: The Complete Book of Lettering and Design. Margaret Shepherd. Broadway Books 2001. 167 p. : Illustration
ISBN 9780767907323
Grades: Adult   745.6
1. Calligraphy 2. Art technique 3. Arts and Entertainment — Painting, Drawing, and Sculpture
LC 00053016

Offers step-by-step lessons on the techniques of calligraphy, providing historical information while suggesting advice for choosing alphabets for different messages and selecting the best materials.

Offers step-by-step lessons on the techniques of lettering Roman, Gothic, Celtic, Italic, and Bookhand calligraphy, providing historical information while suggesting advice for choosing alphabets for different messages and selecting the best materials.

Thorpe, Molly Suber
Modern Calligraphy: Everything You Need to Know to Get Started in Script Calligraphy. Molly Suber Thorpe; photography by Molly Suber Thorpe. St. Martin's Griffin 2013. VI, 184 pages : Illustration; Color
ISBN 9781250016324
Grades: Adult   745.6
1. Calligraphy 2. Writing materials and instruments 3. Arts and Entertainment — Painting, Drawing, and Sculpture
LC 2013013847

Calligraphy is about creating something uniquely beautiful, whether to celebrate a special occasion like marriage or to use every day in the form of stationery. Author Molly Suber Thorpe, an award-winning designer and calligrapher based in Los Angeles, works closely with her international clients to give them the distinctive products they're looking for. Now you can learn from this experienced expert how to master this fresh modern lettering style. The first book to teach this bold new style breaks the calligraphy process down into simple steps so anyone can learn to create their own stunning wedding invitations, thank you

ESSENTIAL AND RECOMMENDED TITLES
745.7 Decorative coloring

cards, gift tags, and more. Starting with an overview of the supplies—from paper to ink to pens—you will learn how to form letters, words, and then phrases by following Molly's clear step-by-step instructions, and by practicing with the provided templates. After mastering letter forms using a pointed pen and ink you can take it to the next level by learning how to use watercolor and gouache, or how to digitize your calligraphy. The twenty projects in the book provide lots of inspiration for making your own and are grouped into three sections: weddings, entertainment, and personal stationery. With loads of ideas, practice exercises, and helpful tips, soon you will be turning out gorgeous script calligraphy pieces like the ones featured in wedding magazines and popular websites like Pinterest!
Includes index.

745.7 Decorative coloring

Joyce, Anna
Stamp Stencil Paint: Making Extraordinary Patterned Projects by Hand. Anna Joyce; photography by Lisa Waringer; photostyling by Chelsea Fuss. STC Craft 2015. 144 pages : Illustration; Color
ISBN 9781617691775
Grades: Adult   745.7
1. Stenciling 2. Painting 3. Handicraft 4. Arts and Entertainment — Crafts and hobbies
LC Bl2015032839
Shares instructions for creating projects by stamping, stenciling, and painting, including beach towels, table linens, storage baskets, and plates.
A Melanie Falick book.

Sloan, Annie
Color Recipes for Painted Furniture and More: 40 Step-by-Step Projects to Transform Your Home. Annie Sloan. Cico Books 2013. 160 p. : Color illustration
ISBN 9781908862778
Grades: Adult   745.7
1. Painting 2. Arts and Entertainment — Crafts and hobbies
LC Bl2013013989
Presents instructions for using a variety of decorative and color mixing techniques to transform furniture, floors, lighting fixtures, and walls, describing such methods as painting, gilding, waxing, stenciling, marbling, and decoupage.
Includes index.

745.92 Floral arts

Crary, Calvert
The Encyclopedia of Cut Flowers: What Flowers to Buy, When to Buy Them, and How to Keep Them Alive for Longer. Calvert Crary with Bruce Littlefield. Black Dog & Leventhal Publishers/Hachette Book Group 2023. 368 p.
ISBN 9780762483280
Grades: Adult   745.92
1. Flowers 2. Flower arrangement 3. Arts and Entertainment — Crafts and hobbies — Garden and nature 4. Nature Writing — Flowers and plants 5. Reference — Encyclopedias
From Calvert Crary, author of Flower School and executive director of FlowerSchool NY and FlowerSchool LA, the Encyclopedia of Cut Flowers is a first-of-its-kind, beautiful yet practical guide to buying and caring for 146 different varieties of cut flowers, including information on how to get the most for your money by prolonging the life of your flowers.
"Authoritative, accessible, and visually enticing, this is a worthy offering from an expert who wants to let every blossom live out its life cycle with dignity." —*Booklist*

Cylinder, Carly
The Flower Chef: A Modern Guide to Do-It-Yourself Floral Arrangements. Carly Cylinder; edited by Amara Holstein. Grand Central Life & Style 2016. 223 pages : Color; Illustration
ISBN 9781455555499

Grades: Adult   745.92
1. Flower arrangement 2. Arts and Entertainment — Crafts and hobbies
LC 2015039431
Provides instructions for creating fresh and original floral designs, from buying and caring for flowers to using foam, vases, and other decorative elements to create arrangements.
"This book creates a needed foundation for aspiring designers." —*Library Journal*
Includes index.

Harampolis, Alethea
The Flower Recipe Book. Alethea Harampolis and Jill Rizzo of Studio Choo, photographs by Paige Green. Artisan 2013. 268 pages : Color; Illustration
ISBN 9781579655303
Grades: Adult   745.92
1. Flower arrangement 2. Arts and Entertainment — Crafts and hobbies
LC 2012046704
Offers step-by-step instructions with accompanying photographs to make over one hundred different floral arrangements in a variety of styles, from single blooms to overflowing and layered blossoms, using easily located flowers.

McLeary, Susan
Flowers for All: Modern Floral Arrangements for Beauty, Joy, and Mindfulness Every Day. Susan McLeary; photographs by EE Berger. Chronicle Books 2023. 172 pages : Color; Illustration
ISBN 9781797215662
Grades: Adult   745.92
1. Flower arrangement 2. Flowers 3. Arts and Entertainment — Crafts and hobbies — Garden and nature
LC 2022037938
A guide to creating gorgeous flower arrangements that enhance everyday life with natural beauty.
"This should be a no-brainer for novice florists." —*Publishers Weekly*

Turner, Tiffanie
The Fine Art of Paper Flowers: A Guide to Making Beautiful and Lifelike Botanicals. Tiffanie Turner; photographs by Tiffanie Turner and Aya Brackett. Watson-Guptill 2017. 1 online resource (vii, 254 pages) : Illustration
ISBN 9780399578373
Grades: Adult   745.92
1. Paper flowers 2. Flower arrangement 3. Arts and Entertainment — Crafts and hobbies — Papercrafts
LC Oc2018143426
Features step-by-step instructions for crafting over thirty of the author's lifelike paper flowers and their foliage, from bougainvillea to zinnias, along with instructions for using paper flowers in garlands, bouquets, and fashion accessories.

Underwood, Kiana
Color Me Floral: Stunning Monochromatic Arrangements for Every Season. Kiana Underwood; photographs by Nathan Underwood. Chronicle Books 2018. 240 pages : Color; Illustration
ISBN 9781452161174
Grades: Adult   745.92
1. Flower arrangement 2. Arts and Entertainment — Crafts and hobbies — Garden and nature
LC 2017020489
Organized by season, the book includes how-to's for 40 arrangements, including a lush green display for spring, an astonishing black bouquet for summer, a striking magenta design for fall, and an unexpected, oh-so-pretty pink arrangement for winter.
"She builds each arrangement in steps and includes photos—taken by her husband—at each stage. Using a pin frog (and eschewing floral foam), she indicates which specimen is inserted at what point, considering height, breadth, and mass." —*Publishers Weekly*
Includes index.

PUBLIC LIBRARY CORE COLLECTION: NONFICTION
Twentieth Edition

746 Textile arts

Adams, Liza
Needle Felting: From Basics to Bears with Step-by-Step Photos and Instructions for Creating Cute Little Bears and Bunnies from Natural Wools. Liza Adams. Stackpole Books 2016. 128 pages : Color; Illustration
ISBN 9780811716628
Grades: Adult **746**
1. Felt work 2. Textile crafts 3. Arts and Entertainment — Crafts and hobbies — Textiles and needlework
LC 2015045254

Make the cutest little creatures from wool! Needle felting is all the rage, and this book shows you how to create tiny bears, rabbits, dogs, cats, fairies, dolls, cupcakes, and more.

Lindsay, Virginia Keleher
Sewing to Sell: The Beginner's Guide to Starting a Craft Business : Bonus, 16 Starter Projects : How to Sell Locally & Online. Virginia Lindsay. StashBooks, C&T Publishing 2014. 151 pages : Color; Illustration
ISBN 9781607059035
Grades: Adult **746**
1. Small business 2. Selling 3. Management 4. Arts and Entertainment — Crafts and hobbies — Textiles and needlework
LC 2014013070

Provides tips for setting up a craft business along with instructions for sixteen sewing projects.

"Most appropriate for crafters who need a very basic guide to selling their handmade goods. Those looking to take their business to the next level will benefit from Kari Chapin's Grow Your Handmade Business and the Handmade Marketplace, which provide a more comprehensive view of operating a craft-based enterprise." —*Library Journal*

Includes bibliographical references (pages 149-150).

Susa, Sachiko
Sweet & Simple Needle Felted Animals: A Step-by-Step Visual Guide. Sachiko Susa. Tuttle Publishing 2017. 96 pages : Color; Illustration
ISBN 9784805314548
Grades: Adult **746**
1. Felt work 2. Handicraft 3. Arts and Entertainment — Crafts and hobbies — Textiles and needlework
LC Bl2017041724

Offers step-by-step illustrated instructions to create felt animals, including kittens, a dachshund puppy, and rabbits.

"Novices and experienced needle felters alike will enjoy making these irresistible miniatures." —*Booklist*

Wicker, Alden
★ *To* Dye For: How Toxic Fashion Is Making Us Sick - and How We Can Fight Back. Alden Wicker. Putnam Publishing Group 2023. 288 p.
ISBN 9780593422618
Grades: Adult **746**
1. Dye industry and trade 2. Dyes and dyeing 3. Toxins 4. Clothing industry and trade 5. Clothing 6. Arts and Entertainment — Fashion 7. Business and economics — Corruption and scandal

In To Dye For, Wicker reveals how clothing manufacturers have successfully swept consumers' concerns under the rug for more than 150 years, and why synthetic fashion and dyes made from fossil fuels are so deeply intertwined with the rise of autoimmune disease, infertility, asthma, eczema, and more. In fact, there's little to no regulation of the clothes and textiles we wear each day—from uniforms to fast fashion, outdoor gear, and even the face masks that have become ubiquitous in recent years. Wicker explains how we got here, what the stakes are, and what all of us can do in the fight for a safe and healthy wardrobe for all."

"A thought-provoking read for anyone who buys or wears clothes." —*Library Journal*

746.0463 Felt — Textiles — Arts

Lapierre, Corinne
Folk Embroidered Felt Birds: 20 Modern Folk Art Designs to Make & Embellish. Corinne Lapierre. Search Press Limited 2019. 96 pages : Color; Illustration
ISBN 9781782216988
Grades: Adult **746.0463**
1. Felt work 2. Embroidery 3. Birds in art 4. Arts and Entertainment — Crafts and hobbies — Textiles and needlework 5. Arts and Entertainment — Crafts and hobbies — Folkcrafts
LC 2018289826

"Lapierre provides clear introductory instructions on suggested materials and basic embroidery stitches, but the small size of the finished projects (based on the provided templates, most are a little over six inches long) and the detailed stitching work required to finish them make this an ideal challenge for more-experienced crafters." —*Booklist*

20 modern folk art designs to make & embellish— cover.

746.092 Textile handicrafters

Gilchrist, Abby
Modern Fabric: Twenty-Five Designers on Their Inspiration and Craft. Abby Gilchrist and Amelia Poole. Princeton Architectural Press 2021. 256 pages : Color; Illustration
ISBN 9781616898373
Grades: Adult **746.092**
1. Textile designers 2. Textile fabrics 3. Textile design 4. Arts and Entertainment — Crafts and hobbies — Textiles and needlework
LC 2020005884

The first collection of modern fabric designers and their work-a colorful and inspiring selection featuring fresh, bold patterns from an international group of today's up-and-coming and established textile stars.

"Not a 'How-to' or technical presentation but an exploration into the creative lives of contemporary fabric designers. This should appeal to quilters, sewers, and designers, both hobbyists and professionals." —*Library Journal*

746.1 Products and processes

Anderson, Sarah
The Spinner's Book of Yarn Designs: Techniques for Creating 80 Yarns. Sarah Anderson; foreword by Judith MacKenzie. Storey Publishing 2012. 255 pages : Color; Illustration
ISBN 9781603427388
Grades: Adult **746.1**
1. Arts and Entertainment — Crafts and hobbies — Textiles and needlework
LC 2012039869

Offers step-by-step instructions for spinning yarn, explaining the process of working with fleece and how to manipulate and combine the fibers for creating eighty different types of yarn, from mohair boucle to supercoils.

"Inventive, accessible, and fun, this book is an invitation to spinners of all skill levels to venture into uncharted territory and try out something new. This beautiful reference is an essential addition to any spinner's library." —*Publishers Weekly*

Includes bibliographical references (pages 248-249) and index.

Boggs, Jacey
Spin Art: Mastering the Craft of Spinning Textured Yarn. Jacey Boggs. Interweave Press 2011. 143 p. : Illustration; Color
ISBN 9781596683624
Grades: Adult **746.1**
1. Arts and Entertainment — Crafts and hobbies — Textiles and needlework
LC Bl2013019898

ESSENTIAL AND RECOMMENDED TITLES
746.4 Needlework and handwork

Presents step-by-step coverage of thirty yarn spinning techniques, including autowrap, halos, and spiral plying.
Includes index.

Daly, Fiona
Weaving on a Little Loom: Techniques, Patterns, and Projects for Beginners. Fiona Daly. Princeton Architectural Press 2018. 144 pages : Color; Illustration
ISBN 9781616897123
Grades: Adult   746.1
1. Weaving 2. Looms 3. Arts and Entertainment — Crafts and hobbies — Textiles and needlework
LC 2018006741

"Weaving, Daly explains, is not a weekend project but a commitment; her alluring book convinces readers its worth the time and effort." —*Publishers Weekly*

Includes index; Previously published: Little loom weaving. Berkeley, CA : Ulysses Press, 2017.

Dixon, Anne
The Handweaver's Pattern Directory: Over 600 Weaves for Four-Shaft Looms. Anne Dixon. Interweave Press 2007. 256 p. : Color illustration
ISBN 9781596680401
Grades: Adult   746.1
1. Hand weaving 2. Weaving 3. Arts and Entertainment — Crafts and hobbies — Textiles and needlework
LC 2007026351

Provides instructions on the basics of weaving and finishing techniques along with six hundred different weaving patterns for four-shaft looms.

"This guide to more than 600 different weaving patterns for four-shaft looms divides weaves into basic groups by structure (e.g., basic threadings, block drafts). Each weave is accompanied by warp threading and weaving drafts (the latter, explained in a handy extended flap), a tieup grid, closeup photos of the weave, and color photos of the actual woven fabric. Beginning weavers will appreciate the sections on weaving basics and finishing techniques as well as the glossary of common weaving terms." —*Library Journal*
Includes index.

The Weaver's Inkle Pattern Directory. Anne Dixon. Interweave Press 2012. 175 pages : Illustration; Color
ISBN 9781596686472
Grades: Adult   746.1
1. Arts and Entertainment — Crafts and hobbies — Textiles and needlework
LC 2012002086

Over 400 patterns for inkle weaving.
Includes bibliographical references and index.

Jarchow, Deborah
The Weaving Explorer: Ingenious Techniques, Accessible Tools & Creative Projects with Yarn, Paper, Wire & More. Deborah Jarchow & Gwen W. Steege. Storey Publishing 2019. 310 pages : Color; Illustration
ISBN 9781635860283
Grades: Adult   746.1
1. Hand weaving 2. Arts and Entertainment — Crafts and hobbies — Textiles and needlework
LC 2019033543

The Weaving Explorer takes inspiration from the world of folk weaving traditions, adding a contemporary spin by introducing an unexpected range of materials and home dec projects.
Includes index.

Mitchell, Syne
Inventive Weaving on a Little Loom: Discover the Full Potential of the Rigid-Heddle Loom, for Beginners and Beyond. Syne Mitchell. Storey Publishing 2015. 295 pages : Color; Illustration
ISBN 9781603429726
Grades: Adult   746.1

1. Hand weaving 2. Looms 3. Arts and Entertainment — Crafts and hobbies — Textiles and needlework
LC 2015019702

A handbook to the tabletop loom provides step-by-step photographs to outline techniques that can be applied to a range of contemporary projects, from pillows and curtains to bags and jewelry.
Includes bibliographical references and index.

Murphy, Marilyn
Woven to Wear: 17 Thoughtful Designs with Simple Shapes. Marilyn Murphy. Interweave Press 2013. 143 pages : Color; Illustration
ISBN 9781596686519
Grades: Adult   746.1
1. Hand weaving 2. Clothing 3. Arts and Entertainment — Crafts and hobbies — Textiles and needlework
LC 2012048056

A collection of woven wraps, shawls, and outwear that will appeal to beginner and advanced weavers alike.

"Beginners (or experienced weavers who could use a refresher) will appreciate the thorough introduction to weaving tools and technique." —*Library Journal*

Includes bibliographical references (page 142) and index.

Patrick, Jane
The Weaver's Idea Book: Creative Cloth on a Rigid-Heddle Loom. Jane Patrick. Interweave Press 2010. 239 p. : Color illustration
ISBN 9781596681750
Grades: Adult   746.1
1. Hand weaving 2. Arts and Entertainment — Crafts and hobbies — Textiles and needlework
LC 2009039518

Presents a wide variety of weave-structure patterns along with swatches illustrating the techniques, accompanied by step-by-step photos, as well as project ideas ranging from wearables to home decor.

"Patrick's collection of patterns and projects explores the possibilities of weaving on a rigid heddle loom. From basic plain weaves to finger-controlled and pick-up techniques, Patrick guides weavers of all skill levels. This is an excellent addition to any weaving collection." —*Library Journal*

Includes bibliographical references and index.

746.4 Needlework and handwork

Zimmermann, Elizabeth
★ *Knitting Without Tears: Basic Techniques and Easy-to-Follow Directions for Garments to Fit All Sizes.* Elizabeth Zimmermann. Scribner 1971. 120 p. Illustration
ISBN 9780684135052
Grades: Adult   746.4
1. Knitting 2. Arts and Entertainment — Crafts and hobbies — Textiles and needlework
LC 70140776

The author guides the novice and the experienced knitters in short-cuts and construction tricks and offers twenty original designs.
Bibliography: P. 118.

746.412 Basketry

Irish, Lora S.
Basket Essentials: Rib Basket Weaving; Techniques and Projects for DIY Woven Reed Baskets. Lora S. Irish. Fox Chapel Publishing 2020. 200 pages : Illustration
ISBN 9781497100145
Grades: Adult   746.412
1. Baskets 2. Basket making 3. Arts and Entertainment — Crafts and hobbies

Go beyond just following the steps and learn the methods to traditional basket weaving. With step-by-step instructions and photography for 3 rib basket projects, followed by 12 additional designs to accomplish independently, you'll acquire all the proper techniques you need to become a successful basket-weaver, from measuring and adding spokes to learning various weaving patterns.

"Her attractive illustrations and skillful instructions should inspire many newcomers to try out this laid-back craft." —*Publishers Weekly*

Includes index.

746.42 Nonloom weaving and related techniques

Katz, Emily
Modern Macrame: 33 Stylish Projects for Your Handmade Home. Emily Katz with Johanna Kunin; photographs by Nicole Franzen and Shannon Wolf. Ten Speed Press 2018. 247 pages : Color; Illustration
ISBN 9780399579578
Grades: Adult   746.42
1. Macrame 2. Handicraft 3. Interior decoration 4. Arts and Entertainment — Crafts and hobbies 5. Reference — Instructional materials
LC Bl2018157085

A guide to the traditional art of decorative knotting includes thirty-three projects for the home, including wall hangings, bohemian light fixtures, macrame baskets, rugs, and chairs.

"The step-by-step guidance for plant hangers, rugs, wall hangings, and general knotted miscellany will help even novice crafters achieve results that are both lovely and useful. Readers looking for an updated take on macrame will want to pick up this stylish and practical book." —*Publishers Weekly*

Includes index.

Zedenius, Fanny
Macrame: The Craft of Creative Knotting for Your Home. Fanny Zedenius; photography by Kim Lightbody. Quadrille 2017. 143 pages : Illustration; Color
ISBN 9781849499408
Grades: Adult   746.42
1. Macrame 2. Handicraft 3. Home furnishings 4. Arts and Entertainment — Crafts and hobbies 5. Reference — Instructional materials
LC Bl2017028164

Shares information on starting macrame, the most popular knots, and tips on how to create different patterns through various knot combinations, as well as over twenty projects to make for the home.

Includes index.

746.43 Knitting, crocheting, tatting

Abbondio, Sarah
Mini Amigurumi Animals: 26 Tiny Creatures to Crochet. Sarah Abbondio. Search Press 2020. 47 p.
ISBN 9781782219163
Grades: Adult   746.43
1. Crocheting 2. Amigurumi 3. Arts and Entertainment — Crafts and hobbies — Textiles and needlework

"Experienced amigurumi makers will enjoy the cuteness as they quickly whip up these small and delightful creatures. A must-have for all library craft collections." —*Booklist*

Atherley, Kate
The *Knitter's* Dictionary: Knitting Know-how from A to Z. Kate Atherley. Interweave 2018. 126 pages : Illustration
ISBN 9781632506382
Grades: Adult   746.43
1. Knitting 2. Dictionaries 3. Arts and Entertainment — Crafts and hobbies — Textiles and needlework
LC Bl2018191533

Provides an A-to-Z guide to knitting, offering entries on knitting language and abbreviations, extended information on such challenging topics as understanding gauge, and tips on making knitting patterns.

"Unlike many knitting books, the diagrams and drawings included here are clearly drawn and easy to decipher. The book is small but filled with enough useful information to make it a go-to reference in any knitting library." —*Publishers Weekly*

Includes bibliographical references (page 125).

Baca, Salena
Oversize Fashion Crochet: 6 Cozy Cardigans, Pullovers & Wraps Designed with Maximum Style and Ease. Salena Baca. Stackpole Books 2023. 32 pages : Color; Illustration
ISBN 9780811770477
Grades: Adult   746.43
1. Crocheting 2. Women's clothing 3. Clothing 4. Sweaters 5. Arts and Entertainment — Crafts and hobbies — Textiles and needlework
LC 2023012798

Get ready for cool weather, fast! You'll be ready to cozy up in no time with these 6 crochet designs made with bulky yarn and big hooks. Designs include pullovers, cardigans, ponchos, and wraps in easy-to-wear, popular oversized fit.

"A must for collections that serve crochet enthusiasts." —*Booklist*

Bassetti, Amanda
Arm Knitting. Amanda Bassetti. Barron's 2015. 144 pages : Color; Illustration
ISBN 9781438007304
Grades: Adult   746.43
1. Knitting 2. Hand weaving 3. Arts and Entertainment — Crafts and hobbies — Textiles and needlework
LC Bl2015036233

Offers step-by-step instructions to learn a range of arm knitting stitches and thirty projects they can be used to create.

"Hands down (or arms up), one of the best-ever beginner craft books." —*Booklist*

30 home and fashion projects for all your no-needle needs—Cover; Includes index.

Bergstrom, Lauren
Cute & Cuddly Crochet: Learn to Make Huggable Amigurumi Animals. Lauren Bergstrom. Walter Foster 2023. 128 p.
ISBN 9780760382905
Grades: Adult   746.43
1. Amigurumi 2. Crocheting 3. Soft toy making 4. Stuffed animals (Toys) 5. Arts and Entertainment — Crafts and hobbies — Textiles and needlework
LC Bl2023025850

While amigurumi animals are often very small, this book features instructions and tips for crocheting larger plushie animals that are perfect for baby gifts, birthday gifts for kids, home decor, and more. While crocheting a larger animal may sound intimidating or like more work, it isn't! Included in the book are helpful hints for working with bulky yarn, as well as how to stuff the animals. Cute & Cuddly Crochet also offers a guide for crochet basics, such as crochet techniques, stitches, how to do color changes, materials and where to source them, and much more. Accompanying the book are helpful videos from the author.

"The instructions are thorough and the projects are irresistible." —*Publishers Weekly*

Mini Crochet Creatures: 30 Amigurumi Animals to Make. Lauren Bergstrom. The Guild of Master Craftsman Publications 2018. 159 pages : Illustration; Color
ISBN 9781784943899
Grades: Adult   746.43
1. Amigurumi 2. Crocheting 3. Soft toy making 4. Stuffed animals (Toys) 5. Arts and Entertainment — Crafts and hobbies — Textiles and needlework
LC Bl2018183427

ESSENTIAL AND RECOMMENDED TITLES
746.43 Knitting, crocheting, tatting

Presents thirty designs for amigurumi animals, including a bunny, otter, butterfly, and elephant, providing detailed instructions and explanations of all the techniques used.

"Photos of the finished products in cleverly crafted settings (the sea creatures surf in ocean blue-green yarn) add whimsy to the books general appeal. While the projects are designed for novice crocheters, experts may want to craft this menagerie as well."—*Publishers Weekly*

Includes index.

Bernard, Wendy
Up, Down, All-Around Stitch Dictionary: More Than 150 Stitch Patterns to Knit Top Down, Bottom Up, Back and Forth, and in the Round. Wendy Bernard; photography by Thayer Allyson Gowdy; prop and wardrobe styling by Karen Schaupeter. Stewart, Tabori & Chang 2014. 288 pages : Illustration; Color
ISBN 9781617690990
Grades: Adult   746.43
1. Knitting 2. Arts and Entertainment — Crafts and hobbies — Textiles and needlework
LC Bl2014021762

Provides instructions for more than one hundred-fifty stitch patterns, ranging from lace and cables to colorwork and fancy edgings.

"As with any solid stitch dictionary, the swatches show multiple repeats of the pattern, and the color photos are clear and large enough to display detail. Charts are present as needed."—*Library Journal*

A Melanie Falick Book; Includes index.

Bliss, Debbie
★ *The Knitter's Book of Knowledge: A Complete Guide to Essential Knitting Techniques*. Debbie Bliss; illustrations by Cathy Brear; photography by Kim Lightbody. Lark 2015. 318 pages : Color; Illustration
ISBN 9781454709268
Grades: Adult   746.43
1. Knitting 2. Arts and Entertainment — Crafts and hobbies — Textiles and needlework
LC Bl2016032794

A guide to knitting techniques discusses equipment and materials, shows readers basic, embellishing, and finishing techniques, and provides time-saving tips.

"Years in the knitwear industry have made Bliss a leading expert, but her ability to share her knowledge in a cohesive manner is special indeed."—*Library Journal*

Includes index.

Budd, Ann
The Knitter's Handy Book of Top-Down Sweaters: Basic Designs in Multiple Sizes and Gauges. Ann Budd. Interweave Press LLC 2012. 263 pages : Illustration; Color
ISBN 9781596684836
Grades: Adult   746.43
1. Knitting 2. Sweaters 3. Arts and Entertainment — Crafts and hobbies — Textiles and needlework
LC 2012001366

Fiber and yarn enthusiasts nationwide will celebrate Ann Budd's latest addition to the Knitter's Handy Book series. Answering to a growing interest in knitting sweaters from the top down and knitting seamless sweaters that require little finishing, this handy book offers instructions for knitting five basic sweater types: Circular yoke, raglan, modified-drop shoulder, set-in sleeve, and saddle shoulder. Patterns are offered in multiple sizes and yarn gauges and for a broad age group. Following the basics for each of the five sweater types are three diverse patterns from top designers that illustrate some of the many ways that instructions can be used as springboards for creative expression, including color, texture, and shaping variations. Also included for intermediate to advanced knitters are personal design touches, detailed charts, clear instruction, and quick tips to expand knitting possibilities and maintain creative originality.

"Knitters who want to design their own sweaters but don't want to figure out all the math will appreciate Budd's straightforward approach to sweater design, while knitters who are just looking for patterns will enjoy the variety of ready-to-knit patterns in this collection."—*Library Journal*

Includes bibliographical references (page 262) and index.

New Directions in Sock Knitting: 18 Innovative Designs Knitted from Every Which Way. Ann Budd. Interweave 2015. 167 pages : Illustration; Color
ISBN 9781620339435
Grades: Adult   746.43
1. Knitting 2. Socks 3. Arts and Entertainment — Crafts and hobbies — Textiles and needlework
LC Bl2016001628

Presents a collection of sock patterns categorized by type of knitting construction, including top-down, toe-up, zigzag, boomerang, and u-turn.

Includes index.

Sock Knitting Master Class: Innovative Techniques + Patterns from Top Designers. Ann Budd. Interweave 2011. 183 p. : Color illustration
ISBN 9781596683129
Grades: Adult   746.43
1. Knitting 2. Socks 3. Arts and Entertainment — Crafts and hobbies — Textiles and needlework
LC 2010049008

Learn sock design from the masters while knitting 15+ spectacular, brand-new patterns featuring the widest variety of techniques.

Includes bibliographical references (p. 182) and index.

Chachula, Robyn
Unexpected Afghans: Innovative Crochet Designs with Traditional Techniques. Robyn Chachula. Interweave Press 2012. 159 pages : Illustration
ISBN 9781596682993
Grades: Adult   746.43
1. Crocheting 2. Arts and Entertainment — Crafts and hobbies — Textiles and needlework
LC 2012001563

Unexpected Afghans presents 29 innovative interpretations of a favorite at-home essential. From best-selling author Robyn Chachula comes an in-depth look into crocheting traditional afghans using contemporary techniques, colors and patterns. Expert designers including Kristin Omdahl, Kathy Merrick, Kimberly McAlindin, and many more, provide an abundance of fresh patterns and projects that are perfect for new and advanced crocheters as they start out beginner-friendly and become more complex, allowing a crocheter to build skills and confidence.

"With almost 30 different projects encompassing a variety of styles and techniques, this is an excellent value."—*Library Journal*

Includes bibliographical references and index.

Corkhill, Betsan
Crochet Therapy: The Soothing Art of Savoring Each Stitch. Betsan Corkhill. Abrams 2016. 144 pages : Color; Illustration
ISBN 9781419721113
Grades: Adult   746.43
1. Crocheting 2. Arts and Entertainment — Crafts and hobbies — Textiles and needlework
LC 2015955482

Crochet Therapy will inspire you to pick up a hook and take some time out of your hectic day to dive into colorful whorls of yarn. Focus, relax, and become more mindful by making more than 20 simple and colorful projects comprised of crocheted mandalas, soothing circles, and other beautiful motifs. Each repetitive pattern helps you engage with your materials, increase your well-being, and unlock your creativity. Mindfulness exercises accompany the patterns and complement the therapeutic effect of crocheting for achieving calm, stress relief, and becoming "effortlessly present" in your craft. Clear instructions and a host of finishing techniques round out the pretty projects and crocheted bounty.

"Corkhill's meditative projects, combined with the exercises throughout, will help crocheters reap the health and wellness benefits of mindful crafting." —*Library Journal*

20+ projects for finding your zen—Cover; Includes index.

PUBLIC LIBRARY CORE COLLECTION: NONFICTION
Twentieth Edition

Crowfoot, Jane
Ultimate Crochet Bible: A Complete Reference with Step-by-step Techniques. Jane Crowfoot. Collins & Brown 2010. 304 p. : Illustration; Color (C&B Crafts)
ISBN 9781843405634
Grades: Adult　746.43
1. Crocheting 2. Arts and Entertainment — Crafts and hobbies — Textiles and needlework
LC Bl2011026453
Provides step-by-step instructions for all aspects of crocheting, with information on such topics as choosing a hook; texture and lace stitches; Tunisian and entrelac crochet; working with color, beads and sequins; embellishments; and finishing techniques.
"This guide begins with an overview of the craft's origins and its requirements and necessities (for instance, hooks, needles, and knowledge of how to read a chart). Each chapter truly exposes the how-to details, not only in words but also, most important, in oversize illustrations. Included are a well-explained section of basics (for instance, how to differentiate between front and reverse sides and how to work crochet for left-handed crafters) and specific stitch categories: Texture and lace, thread, Tunisian entrelac, color, beads and sequins, edgings, and professional finishing techniques." —*Booklist*
Includes index.

Dassau, Jennifer
Knitting Short Rows: Techniques for Great Shapes & Angles. Jennifer Dassau. Interweave 2016. 143 pages : Illustration; Color
ISBN 9781632502582
Grades: Adult　746.43
1. Knitting 2. Arts and Entertainment — Crafts and hobbies — Textiles and needlework
LC Bl2017029398
Provides instructions for essential techniques to create seamless curves, soft angles, and finishing touches.
Includes index.

Durant, Judith
Cable Left, Cable Right: 94 Knitted Cables. Judith Durant; photography by Mars Vilaubi. Storey Publishing 2016. 216 pages : Color; Illustration
ISBN 9781612125169
Grades: Adult　746.43
1. Knitting 2. Arts and Entertainment — Crafts and hobbies — Textiles and needlework
LC 2015044820
"Each of the cables includes a full-color, close-up swatch illustrating clearly how the cables are formed as well as charted instructions. Helpful tips for troubleshooting including a clever approach to remedying loose stitches before and after cablesare supplied throughout." —*Library Journal*
Includes index.

Increase, Decrease: 99 Step-by-Step Methods. Judith Durant; photography by John Polak. Storey Publishing 2015. 256 pages : Color; Illustration
ISBN 9781612123318
Grades: Adult　746.43
1. Knitting 2. Arts and Entertainment — Crafts and hobbies — Textiles and needlework
LC 2014042919
Presents detailed instructions for making increases and decreases in knitting patterns, with a variety of techniques for bringing shape and structure to the finished garment.
Includes index.

Eckman, Edie
Around the Corner Crochet Borders: 150 Colorful, Creative Crocheted Edgings with Charts & Instructions for Turning the Corner Perfectly Every Time. Edie Eckman. Storey Pub. 2010. 316 p. : Illustration; Color
ISBN 9781603425384
Grades: Adult　746.43
1. Crocheting 2. Arts and Entertainment — Crafts and hobbies — Textiles and needlework
LC 2010001461
A crochet border is the perfect finishing touch on the edges of any fiber project, but creating one often means shaping the edging around an unforgiving 90-degree angle. It's no easy task, but Edie Eckman guides you through it with style and poise.
Includes index.

Beyond the Square Crochet Motifs: 144 Circles, Hexagons, Triangles, Squares, and Other Unexpected Shapes. Edie Eckman. Storey Pub. 2008. VI, 201 p. : Illustration; Color
ISBN 9781603428149
Grades: Adult　746.43
1. Crocheting 2. Arts and Entertainment — Crafts and hobbies — Textiles and needlework
LC Oc2012548281
Move beyond granny squares and get ready for crocheted circles, triangles, hexagons, and stars. Edie Eckman opens up the door to crocheting creativity with more than 140 motifs of every shape and size.
Includes index.

Connect the Shapes Crochet Motifs: Creative Techniques for Joining Motifs of All Shapes. Edie Eckman. Storey Publishing 2012. 271 pages : Illustration; Color
ISBN 9781603429733
Grades: Adult　746.43
1. Crocheting 2. Arts and Entertainment — Crafts and hobbies — Textiles and needlework
LC 2012013934
Presents 101 crochet motifs along with techniques for arranging and joining them together in a variety of patterns.
"Eckman's eye for color and design make this an excellent addition to any crafter's crochet collection." —*Library Journal*
Includes index.

The **Crochet** Answer Book: Solutions to Every Problem You'll Ever Face; Answers to Every Question You'll Ever Ask. Edie Eckman. Storey Publishing 2015. 408 pages : Color; Illustration
ISBN 9781612124063
Grades: 11 12 Adult　746.43
1. Crocheting 2. Arts and Entertainment — Crafts and hobbies — Textiles and needlework
LC 2014033696
Discusses a range of topics about crocheting, from foundation chains and yarn types to charts, gauges, granny squares, borders, and tunisian crochet, in a question-and-answer format.
"Eckman presents a definitively revised guide that reflects the latest trends. In her inimitable question-and-answer style, she features the most recently unearthed techniques (do remember: What's old is new again in this and other needlework books), like Tunisian crochet and Bruges and Clones laces. There are brief illustrations, now, for both left- and right-handed stitchers. And new yarns and new tools (or adaptive ones) are explored with helpful tips and caveats." —*Booklist*
Includes index.

Epstein, Nicky
Nicky Epstein, the Essential Edgings Collection: 500 of Her Favorite Original Borders. Nicky Epstein. Nicky Epstein Books, an imprint of Sixth&Spring Books 2012. 256 pages : Illustration; Color
ISBN 9781936096473
Grades: Adult　746.43
1. Knitting 2. Arts and Entertainment — Crafts and hobbies — Textiles and needlework
LC Bl2013039645

ESSENTIAL AND RECOMMENDED TITLES
746.43 Knitting, crocheting, tatting

Gaughan, Norah
Norah Gaughan's Knitted Cable Sourcebook: A Breakthrough Guide to Knitting with Cables and Designing Your Own. Photographs by Jared Flood. Abrams 2016. 275 pages : Illustration; Color
ISBN 9781419722394
Grades: Adult **746.43**
1. Knitting 2. Arts and Entertainment — Crafts and hobbies — Textiles and needlework
LC Bl2016042339

Presents more than one hundred and fifty cable stitch patterns, ranging from basic to complex, and information on how to mix and match cables in projects, along with instructions for fifteen garment patterns for wraps, sweaters, and accessories.

Green-Hite, Vincent
Knot Bad Amigurumi: Learn Crochet Stitches & Techniques to Create Cute Creatures with 25 Easy Patterns. Vincent Green-Hite. Quarry Books 2023. 128 pages : Color; Illustration
ISBN 9780760376775
Grades: Adult **746.43**
1. Amigurumi 2. Crocheting 3. Soft toy making 4. Arts and Entertainment — Crafts and hobbies — Textiles and needlework
LC 2022025861

Knot Bad Amigurumi features easy and fun techniques for creating unique and adorable crochet characters—including a turtle, bee, rocket ship, and boba tea, along with ideas for personalizing creations."

"This fun guide is a must-read for crocheters of all levels." —*Publishers Weekly*

Yarn Punk; Includes index.

Gullberg, Maria
Tapestry Crochet and More: A Handbook of Crochet Techniques and Patterns : Tapestry Crochet, Granny Squares, Lacy Stars, and 3d Patterns. Maria Gullberg; translator, Carol Huebscher Rhoades. Trafalgar Square 2016. 82 pages : Color; Illustration
ISBN 9781570767678
Grades: Adult **746.43**
1. Crocheting 2. Arts and Entertainment — Crafts and hobbies — Textiles and needlework
LC Bl2016047675

Presents tapestry crocheting techniques with practical tips and patterns for totes, hats, wrist warmers, and lace.

"This concealed ring-bound book focuses on tapestry crochet but also offers several other types of projects, including granny squares and three-dimensional flowers. The look of tapestry crochet is very distinctive and is rarely represented in craft books published in the U.S." —*Booklist*

Hatchard, Gurinder Kaur
Hooked on Shakespeare: Crochet Projects Inspired by the Bard. Gurinder Kaur Hatchard. Herbert Press Ltd 2023. 128 p.
ISBN 9781789941289
Grades: Adult **746.43**
1. Shakespeare, William, 1564-1616 2. Crocheting 3. Soft toy making 4. Arts and Entertainment — Crafts and hobbies — Textiles and needlework

From the iconic Romeo and Juliet to the three witches from Macbeth, Hatchard shares easy-to-make designs for crochet characters inspired by the works of William Shakespeare. Each project features an introduction to the play and the characters, and are perfect for beginning crocheters as well as advanced crochet enthusiasts.—adapted from back cover.

"A perfect addition to the crafty reader's shelf. Will have Shakespeare readers and English teachers crocheting characters in no time." —*Library Journal*

Herzog, Amy
Knit Wear Love: Foolproof Instructions for Knitting Your Best-Fitting Sweaters Ever in the Styles You Love to Wear. Amy Herzog; photography by Karen Pearson; photography creative direction and styling by Karen Schaupeter. Stewart, Tabori & Chang 2015. 192 pages : Illustration; Color
ISBN 9781617691393
Grades: Adult **746.43**
1. Knitting 2. Sweaters 3. Arts and Entertainment — Crafts and hobbies — Textiles and needlework
LC Bl2015012057

A guide to knitting sweaters explains how to customize such basic sweater patterns as cardigans, wraps, and pullovers to suit different shapes and personal styles, with a variety of customization details and twelve sizes.

"This classic-in-the-making will inspire knitters to make sweaters that fit well and suit their personal style." —*Library Journal*

STC Craft/A Melanie Falick Book; 24 sweaters for all shapes and sizes!—Cover; Mix-and-match patterns in 12 sizes and 3 gauges!—Page 4 of cover.

Hiatt, June
The Principles of Knitting: Methods and Techniques of Hand Knitting. June Hemmons Hiatt; illustrations by Jesse Hiatt. Simon & Schuster 2012. xx, 712 pages : Illustration
ISBN 9781416535171
Grades: Adult **746.43**
1. Knitting 2. Arts and Entertainment — Crafts and hobbies — Textiles and needlework
LC 2012418278

A revised and updated edition of a popular classic primer shares comprehensive guidelines for beginning and experienced knitters that demonstrate how to approach a full range of techniques.

A Touchstone Book; the comprehensive & timeless guide—Cover; Includes bibliographical references (pages 665-672) and index.

Hubert, Margaret
10 Granny Squares, 30 Blankets: Color Schemes, Layouts, and Edge Finishes for 30 Unique Looks. Margaret Hubert. Creative Publishing International 2016. 128 pages : Color; Illustration
ISBN 9781589238930
Grades: Adult **746.43**
1. Crocheting 2. Blankets 3. Arts and Entertainment — Crafts and hobbies — Textiles and needlework
LC Bl2016047704

Provides instructions for crocheting thirty blankets, including baby blankets and full-size throws, using combinations of ten different granny squares.

"Hubert is one of the crocheters responsible for rescuing granny squares from the 1970s nostalgia heap, and here she continues her quest to modernize this tried-and-true favorite." —*Library Journal*

The Complete Photo Guide to Crochet: 1200 Photos: Basics, Stitch Patterns, and Projects. Margaret Hubert. Creative Pub. International 2010. 272 p. : Color illustration
ISBN 9781589234727
Grades: 11 12 Adult **746.43**
1. Crocheting 2. Arts and Entertainment — Crafts and hobbies — Textiles and needlework
LC 2009031798

Reference for crocheters; includes instructions and diagrams for 200 stitch patterns, basic information about how to crochet, plus 20 patterns.

The Granny Square Book: Timeless Techniques & Fresh Ideas for Crocheting Square by Square. Margaret Hubert. Creative Pub. International 2011. 176 p. : Illustration; Color
ISBN 9781589236387
Grades: Adult **746.43**
1. Crocheting 2. Arts and Entertainment — Crafts and hobbies — Textiles and needlework

PUBLIC LIBRARY CORE COLLECTION: NONFICTION
Twentieth Edition

LC 2011013365

Granny squares are to crochet what pieced squares are to quilting. They originated with pioneer women using up precious scraps of yarn to make blankets for their families, and over the years, many recognized, named patterns have been handed down from one generation to the next. Beyond this treasury of 75 different granny square motifs, Margaret Hubert shows the evolution of the granny square, how it can be used and interpreted in different ways with different yarns, and how today's crocheter can design her own projects using the granny squares of her choice with the yarn choices of today. Just as Margaret learned from her grandmother and mother and then passed the skill down to her daughter and granddaughter, each generation finds new uses and artisticways to interpret granny squares.

Techniques for crocheting granny squares with basic instructions, 75 stitch patterns, and a variety of projects.

"Crocheters looking to move beyond basic granny squares, as well as new crocheters drawn to these traditional motifs, will enjoy this collection." —*Library Journal*

Huff, Mary Scott

The Mitten Handbook: Knitting Recipes to Make Your Own. Mary Scott Huff; photographs by Lesley Unruh. Abrams 2017. 158 pages : Illustration; Color

ISBN 9781419726620

Grades: Adult　　　　　　　　　　　　　　　　746.43

1. Mittens 2. Knitting 3. Recipes 4. Arts and Entertainment — Crafts and hobbies — Textiles and needlework

LC 2016961383

Shares twenty patterns for knitting mittens.

Impelen, Helgrid van

Big Knits Big Needles. Helgrid van Impelen; photography: Katja Schubert. DK Publishing 2015. 143 pages : Illustration; Color

ISBN 9781465453983

Grades: Adult　　　　　　　　　　　　　　　　746.43

1. Knitting 2. Sweaters 3. Arts and Entertainment — Crafts and hobbies — Textiles and needlework

LC 2016591051

20+ stylish patterns on giant needles for super-fast results.

"Sophisticated and more rustic styles are featured and should please a variety of tastes." —*Booklist*

Kartus, Lisa

Knit Fix: Problem Solving for Knitters. Lisa Kartus, author. Interweave Press 2006. 111 p. : Illustration; Color

ISBN 9781596680111

Grades: 11 12 Adult　　　　　　　　　　　　746.43

1. Knitting 2. Arts and Entertainment — Crafts and hobbies — Textiles and needlework

LC 2006002416

"Knitting teacher Kartus believes that there isn't any knitting faux pas that can't be fixed, and in this illustrated problem-solving manual, she proves her point." —*Library Journal*

Includes index.

Knight, Erika

500 Crochet Stitches: The Ultimate Crochet Stitch Bible. Pavilion. St. Martin's Griffin 2015. 287 pages : Illustration; Color

ISBN 9781250067302

Grades: Adult　　　　　　　　　　　　　　　　746.43

1. Crocheting 2. Stitches (Sewing) 3. Arts and Entertainment — Crafts and hobbies — Textiles and needlework

LC 2015016931

Presents an introduction to crocheting, discussing tools, equipment, basic and advanced stitches, edgings, and trims, with illustrations and detailed instructions for five hundred stitches.

"There are a number of crochet stitch dictionaries on the market, but most are focused on a specific type of stitch (e.g., edgings) or on motifs. This comprehensive work makes an excellent reference for crocheters of all skill levels." —*Library Journal*

Includes index.

750 Knitting Stitches: The Ultimate Knit Stitch Bible. [Erika Knight]. St. Martin's Griffin 2015. 287 pages : Color; Illustration

ISBN 9781250067180

Grades: Adult　　　　　　　　　　　　　　　　746.43

1. Knitting 2. Stitches (Sewing) 3. Arts and Entertainment — Crafts and hobbies — Textiles and needlework

LC 2015017155

Presents an introduction to knitting, discussing tools, equipment, techniques for basic and advanced stitches, colorwork, edgings, and trims, with illustrations and detailed instructions for 750 stitches.

"A close-up, full-color swatch is also included for each design, giving the knitter an idea of what multiple pattern repeats look like in a knitted sample. A directory of basic knitting abbreviations and a guide to knitting elementals appear in the introduction." —*Library Journal*

Includes index.

Leapman, Melissa

Mastering Color Knitting: Simple Instructions for Stranded, Intarsia, and Double Knitting. Melissa Leapman. Potter Craft 2010. 175 p. : Illustration; Color

ISBN 9780307586506

Grades: Adult　　　　　　　　　　　　　　　　746.43

1. Knitting 2. Arts and Entertainment — Crafts and hobbies — Textiles and needlework

LC 2010006097

Reveals how to create advanced results through stranded knitting, intarsia, and two-color double knitting techniques, with twelve projects and more than fifty stitch patterns that use multiple yarn colors or include reversible knitting options.

"Knitters who like to design their own projects will appreciate the variety of motifs in all three techniques, which can be used to create a one-of-a-kind garment or accessory." —*Library Journal*

Includes index.

Ludwig, Frauke

Essential Knit Sweaters: Patterns for Every Sweater You Ever Wanted to Wear Every Day. Frauke Ludwig. Stackpole Books 2024. 188 pages : Illustration; Color

ISBN 9780811772761

Grades: Adult　　　　　　　　　　　　　　　　746.43

1. Knitting 2. Sweaters 3. Arts and Entertainment — Crafts and hobbies — Textiles and needlework

LC 2023023579

Each of the designs is a classic, essential type of sweater everyone should own-jacket cardigan, turtleneck, oversize tunic, slouchy cardigan, hoodie, raglan pullover-and all knit in easy stitches but with added details to make them unique. Knitting tutorials and detailed instructions make the sweater designs accessible for beginner to advanced knitters.

"Knitwear designer Ludwig debuts with an inspired collection of women's sweater patterns…This has much to recommend it." —*Publishers Weekly*

Melville, Sally

Knitting Pattern Essentials: Adapting and Drafting Knitting Patterns for Great Knitwear. Sally Melville. Potter Craft 2013. 224 pages : Color; Illustration

ISBN 9780307965578

Grades: Adult　　　　　　　　　　　　　　　　746.43

1. Knitting 2. Arts and Entertainment — Crafts and hobbies — Textiles and needlework

LC 2012015715

An acclaimed instructor and author of the best-selling Knitting Experience series presents a comprehensive guide to sweater construction that reveals how

ESSENTIAL AND RECOMMENDED TITLES
746.43 Knitting, crocheting, tatting

to modify garment patterns so that finished products look and fit as desired, in a volume complemented by 10 customizable patterns.

Guides knitters on how to properly modify or create a pattern, including calculating personal measurements; creating a pattern from an existing garment; and shaping a variety of necklines, sides, sleeves, and hemlines.

Includes index.

Mullett-Bowlsby, Shannon
★ *Complete Crochet Course: The Ultimate Reference Guide.* Shannon & Jason Mullett-Bowlsby. Lark 2018. 335 pages : Illustration; Color
ISBN 9781454710523
Grades: Adult 746.43
1. Crocheting 2. Arts and Entertainment — Crafts and hobbies — Textiles and needlework
LC Bl2018029092

Presents a guide to every aspect of crocheting, describing tools, yarn, chart reading, basic and advanced stitches, colorwork and finishing techniques, with detailed instructions for five crochet projects.

"It's a well-organized reference, up-to-date with the different cable, ribbing, and pattern stitches that are now popular." —*Booklist*

Featuring more than 190 stitches, 125 tutorials, 98 techniques—Cover; Includes index.

Newton, Deborah
Finishing School: A Master Class for Knitters. Deborah Newton. Sixth&Spring Books 2011. 164 p. : Color illustration
ISBN 9781936096190
Grades: Adult 746.43
1. Knitting 2. Arts and Entertainment — Crafts and hobbies — Textiles and needlework
LC 2011013424

The word "finishing" fills many knitters, beginners and more experienced alike, with dread. Some even abandon projects at this stage, rather than complete the necessary steps to achieve beautiful, wearable garments. In Finishing School, master knitter and designer Deborah Newton, shares her expertise and love of (yes, love of) finishing with knitters of all skill levels. She takes them step by step through the ins and outs of blocking, seaming, edging and embellishments, giving knitters the confidence and skills needed to create professional-looking knitwear. In addition to in-depth instruction, the book includes patterns for 12 sweaters, jackets and scarves, many with variations.

Nico, Brooke
More Lovely Knitted Lace: Contemporary Patterns in Geometric Shapes. Brooke Nico. Lark 2016. 127 pages : Illustration; Color
ISBN 9781454709183
Grades: Adult 746.43
1. Knitting 2. Shapes 3. Arts and Entertainment — Crafts and hobbies — Textiles and needlework
LC Bl2017016125

Presents sixteen new lace knitting projects that use four basic shapes as the base for shawls, gauntlets, vests, and other wearables.

4 basic shapes, 16 stunning projects—Cover; Includes index.

Noldeke, Marisa
50 Knitted Wraps and Shawls. Marisa Noldeke. Stackpole Books 2020. 167 p.
ISBN 9780811738613
Grades: Adult 746.43
1. Knitting 2. Shawls 3. Arts and Entertainment — Crafts and hobbies — Textiles and needlework
LC Bl2020045589

With 50 patterns for knitted shawls and wraps to choose from, in so many styles and textures, choosing your first project will be a welcome challenge. From simple knit-purl designs to more complex colorwork, cables, and lace, there are designs to interest every level of knitter.

"This will be an excellent addition to the knitting library for crafters who enjoy experimenting with design choices to fashion stylish, one-size-fits-all creations." —*Publishers Weekly*

Ohrenstein, Dora
The Crocheter's Skill-Building Workshop. Dora Ohrenstein. Storey Publishing 2014. 255 pages : Color; Illustration
ISBN 9781612122465
Grades: Adult 746.43
1. Crocheting 2. Arts and Entertainment — Crafts and hobbies — Textiles and needlework
LC 2014028045

Covers basic crochet techniques and beyond, providing dozens of stitch-along swatches that teach specific skills that can be applied to five projects for a hat, shawl, neck warmer, bag and scarf.

Presents an introduction to crocheting, discussing basic and advanced stitches, yarns, shaping, texture, counting, and finishing, with patterns for seventy-five practice swatches demonstrating the various techniques.

Includes index.

Phelps, Isela
Loom Knitting Primer: A Beginner's Guide to Knitting on a Loom with Over 35 Fun Projects. Isela Phelps. St. Martin's Griffin 2016. 160 pages
ISBN 9781250084194
Grades: Adult 746.43
1. Knitting 2. Looms 3. Arts and Entertainment — Crafts and hobbies — Textiles and needlework
LC 2015041185

Presents an introduction to loom knitting, with detailed instructions on techniques for round and rectangular looms and thirty-five patterns for making hats, scarves, socks, cowls, and an afghan.

Fully revised and updated edition of the bestselling book; Cover title; Includes bibliographical references and index.

Radcliffe, Margaret
Circular Knitting Workshop: Essential Techniques to Master Knitting in the Round. by Margaret Radcliffe; photography by John Polak. Storey Pub, LLC 2012. 319 p. : Color illustration
ISBN 9781603429993
Grades: Adult 746.43
1. Knitting 2. Arts and Entertainment — Crafts and hobbies — Textiles and needlework
LC 2011025033

Provides step-by-step instructions for stitching items using the circular knitting method, a technique used to create socks, bags, gloves and mittens, sweaters, and vests.

"All knitters, from novice to expert, will find something new and useful in this comprehensive guide. Essential for knitting collections."—*Library Journal*

Includes index.

The Knitting Answer Book: Solutions to Every Problem You'll Ever Face; Answers to Every Question You'll Ever Ask. by Margaret Radcliffe. Storey Publishing 2015. 439 pages : Illustration; Color
ISBN 9781612124049
Grades: 9 10 11 12 Adult 746.43
1. Knitting 2. Arts and Entertainment — Crafts and hobbies — Textiles and needlework
LC 2014033661

Discusses a range of topics about knitting, from needle sizes and yarn weights to curling edges, chart reading, tight ribbing, and dropped stitches, in a question-and-answer format.

Includes bibliographical references (pages 415-428) and index.

*The **Knowledgeable** Knitter: Understand the Inner Workings of Knitting and Make Every Project a Success.* Margaret Radcliffe. Storey Publishing 2014. 295 pages : Illustration; Color
ISBN 9781612124148

Grades: Adult   746.43
1. Knitting 2. Arts and Entertainment — Crafts and hobbies — Textiles and needlework

LC 2014016057

Helps knitters with the challenges they face while undertaking a new project by demystifying and explaining every knitting technique, including how to read a pattern chart, select the right yarn, modify a pattern, fix a mistake, and create edges and seams.

Includes bibliographical references (pages 283-284) and index.

Righetti, Maggie

Crocheting in Plain English. Maggie Righetti. Thomas Dunne Books 2008. xviii, 268 p. : Illustration

ISBN 9780312353544

Grades: Adult   746.43
1. Crocheting 2. Arts and Entertainment — Crafts and hobbies — Textiles and needlework

LC 2008043913

Comprehensive, common-sense advice on all aspects of crocheting ranges from the basics for beginners to perfecting techniques for the advanced crocheter, and from selecting threads and yarns to blocking, cleaning, and storing crocheted articles, in a revised and updated edition of the best-selling crochet reference.

Includes bibliographical references (p. 261-263) and index.

Shida, Hitomi

Japanese Knitting Stitch Bible: 260 Exquisite Patterns. Hitomi Shida; translated from the Japanese with an introduction by Gayle Roehm. Tuttle Publishing 2017. 160 p. : Illustration; Color

ISBN 9781462919406

Grades: Adult   746.43
1. Knitting 2. Arts and Entertainment — Crafts and hobbies — Textiles and needlework 3. Arts and Entertainment — Fashion

LC Bl2017043744

Offers 260 original knitting patterns for experienced knitters, including variations on classic stitches, as well as unique new creations, with diagrams showing how to execute the basic stitches and instructions and diagrams for a sampling of projects.

"For intrepid knitters looking for a challenge, the pages of stunning stitches will prove well worth the effort." —*Publishers Weekly*

Spainhower, Courtney

Elemental Knits: A Perennial Knitwear Collection. Courtney Spainhower. Interweave 2020. 159 p.

ISBN 9781632506535

Grades: Adult   746.43
1. Knitting 2. Arts and Entertainment — Crafts and hobbies — Textiles and needlework

LC Bl2020000199

A collection of 20 customizable knitting patterns counsels do-it-yourself crafters on how to select practical patterns and fibers while creating wardrobe-enhancing fashions for different times of the year.

Stanfield, Lesley

100 Flowers to Knit & Crochet: A Collection of Beautiful Blooms for Embellishing Clothes, Accessories, Cushions and Throws. Lesley Stanfield. Search Press 2021. 128 p.

ISBN 9781800920286

Grades: Adult   746.43
1. Knitting 2. Crocheting 3. Arts and Entertainment — Crafts and hobbies — Textiles and needlework

This 15th anniversary edition of the best-selling book 100 Flowers to Knit and Crochet, with over 130,000 copies sold! an utterly delightful collection of designs for any knitting or crochet enthusiast, it not only includes the most beautiful flowers and leaves, but also a wonderful, whimsical collection of fruit and vegetables as well as butterflies. As most of the projects use only small amounts of yarn, it is the perfect way to use up scraps, or practise using novelty yarns. You can use them to decorate clothing, hats, bags and belts, embellish home accessories, or make a beautiful bouquet as an unusual display piece. There are so many flowers to choose from that there is sure to be something you will love, from simple spiral roses and two-tone fuchsias, to elaborate layered blooms and fabulous felted flowers.

"A standard for libraries that don't already own this classic reference." —*Booklist*

Includes index.

Stoller, Debbie

Stitch 'N Bitch Superstar Knitting: Go Beyond the Basics. Debbie Stoller; with photography by Gabrielle Revere. Workman Pub 2010. xii, 356 p. : Color illustration

ISBN 9780761135975

Grades: Adult   746.43
1. Knitting 2. Arts and Entertainment — Crafts and hobbies — Textiles and needlework

LC 2010051402

Presents instructions for a full array of advanced knitting techniques and skills, such as double-knitting, knitting lace, complicated color work, and beading, along with forty-one patterns for such items as sweaters, hats, socks, and scarves.

"Essential for the well-rounded knitting collection owing to the sections on techniques and designing; a few of the patterns are destined to be popular. The Frilly Filly Scarf (see pattern, above) is simple and sophisticated." —*Library Journal*

Includes index.

★ *Stitch* 'N Bitch: The Knitter's Handbook. Debbie Stoller; illustrations by Adrienne Yan; fashion photography by John Dolan. Workman 2003. 248 p. : Illustration; Color

ISBN 9780761128182

Grades: Adult   746.43
1. Knitting 2. Arts and Entertainment — Crafts and hobbies — Textiles and needlework

LC 2003053543

A guide to knitting offers instructions for a variety of techniques and stitches, as well as information on the different types of needles and yarns, tips on shopping for yarns, finishing techniques, and forty patterns.

"An introduction chronicles the history of knitting from the female perspective, while subsequent chapters cover topics such as yarn type, instruments, stitches, and patterns. Perhaps the most exciting bit is Stoller's knit as you learn technique: with every new stitch, she presents a new pattern, thereby allowing knitters to build on their knowledge. Essential for all crafts collections and perfect for a display." —*Library Journal*

Includes index.

Storey, Martin

Easy Fair Isle Knitting: 27 Projects with a Modern Twist. Martin Storey; photography by Steven Wooster. Trafalgar Square 2016. 128 pages : Illustration; Color

ISBN 9781570767852

Grades: Adult   746.43
1. Knitting 2. Arts and Entertainment — Crafts and hobbies — Textiles and needlework

LC Bl2016037437

Presents instructions for Fair Isle knitting projects for the novice that feature patterns with only two colors in each row of knitting, including scarves, cowls, hats, and pillows.

"Knitters who are drawn to Fair Isle colorwork but aren't taken with traditional geometric motifs will appreciate Storey's modern take on the technique." —*Library Journal*

ESSENTIAL AND RECOMMENDED TITLES
746.432 Knitting

Talley, Safiyyah
Knit 2 Socks in 1: Discover the Easy Magic of Turning One Long Sock into a Pair! Safiyyah Talley. Storey Publishing 2022. IX, 141 pages : Color; Illustration
ISBN 9781635864076
Grades: Adult   746.43
1. Knitting 2. Socks 3. Arts and Entertainment — Crafts and hobbies — Textiles and needlework
LC 2021051927

To stop knitters from losing interest in the second sock after the first one is done, this tried-and-true knitting technique is the most accessible way yet developed to knit two socks at a time, providing 21 different sock styles ranging in level of difficulty.

"Perfect for beginning knitters who find a traditional sock too intimidating or more experienced knitters who want to experiment with a new technique."—*Library Journal*
Includes index.

Todhunter, Tracey
Crochet, Learn It. Love It.: Techniques and Projects to Build a Lifelong Passion for Beginners up. Tracey Todhunter. Barron's Educational Series, Inc. 2016. 160 pages : Color; Illustration
ISBN 9781438007595
Grades: Adult   746.43
1. Crocheting 2. Arts and Entertainment — Crafts and hobbies — Textiles and needlework
LC 2015951472

"The tone is straightforward but friendly, and the written and photographed instructions are thorough, making this appropriate for crafters who learn best either visually or by following written instructions." —*Library Journal*
A Quarto book—Title page verso; Includes index.

Turner, Sharon
Teach Yourself Visually Knitting. Sharon Turner. Wiley Pub. 2010. 339 p. : Illustration; Color (Teach Yourself Visually)
ISBN 9780470528327
Grades: Adult   746.43
1. Knitting 2. Arts and Entertainment — Crafts and hobbies — Textiles and needlework
LC Bl2010003831

Uses color photographs and step-by-step instructions to provide a visual guide for creating a knitted scarf, hat, or sweater, covering such topics as casting, purling, correcting mistakes, and deciphering cryptic knitting patterns.
Includes index.

Weil, Anne
Knitting Without Needles: A Stylish Introduction to Finger and Arm Knitting. Anne Weil. Potter Craft 2015. 191 pages : Color; Illustration
ISBN 9780804186520
Grades: Adult   746.43
1. Knitting 2. Arts and Entertainment — Crafts and hobbies — Textiles and needlework
LC 2014036650

A guide to finger weaving explains how to create such projects as headbands, hats, scarves, and blankets.
Includes index.

Werker, Kim P.
Teach Yourself Visually Crochet. by Kim P. Werker and Cecily Keim. Wiley 2011. 280 p. : Color illustration (Teach Yourself Visually)
ISBN 9780470879979
Grades: Adult   746.43
1. Crocheting 2. Arts and Entertainment — Crafts and hobbies — Textiles and needlework
LC Bl2011003712

Uses color photographs and step-by-step instructions to provide a visual guide to crocheting, covering such topics as basic crochet stiches, advanced variations, blocks, edgings, patterns, and finishing.
Includes index.

Wood, Jennifer
Refined Knits: Sophisticated Lace, Cable, and Aran Lace Knitting. Jennifer Wood. Interweave 2016. 156 pages : Illustration; Color
ISBN 9781632500687
Grades: Adult   746.43
1. Lace and lace making 2. Knitting 3. Arts and Entertainment — Crafts and hobbies — Textiles and needlework
LC Bl2016011985

Knitwear designer Jennifer Wood combines lace, cable, and Aran lace knitting techniques into patterns for pullover sweaters, cardigans, cowls, and shrugs.

"The patterns are comprehensive, including written and charted instructions, schematics, and notes on construction as needed." —*Library Journal*
Includes bibliographical references (page 155) and index.

746.432 Knitting

Bestor, Leslie Ann
Cast On, Bind Off: 54 Step-by-Step Methods. Leslie Ann Bestor; photography by John Polak. Storey Publishing 2012. 215 pages : Color; Illustration
ISBN 9781603427241
Grades: Adult   746.432
1. Knitting 2. Arts and Entertainment — Crafts and hobbies — Textiles and needlework
LC 2012002769

Collects contemporary and creative cast-on and bind-off knitting methods, including the invisible circular cast on, the mobius cast on, and the Icelandic bind off.
Includes bibliographical references (page 209) and indexes.

Eaton, Jan
350+ Crochet Tips, Techniques, and Trade Secrets. Jan Eaton. St. Martins Griffin 2017. 160 pages; Illustration; Color
ISBN 9781250125101
Grades: Adult   746.432
1. Crocheting 2. Arts and Entertainment — Crafts and hobbies — Textiles and needlework
LC 2017938523

A treasury of tips, techniques, and trade secrets for crocheters provides step-by-step, illustrated instructions that cover everything from choosing the right hook and yarn to setting up a dye studio and managing yard ends.
Includes index.

Herzog, Amy
You Can Knit That: Foolproof Instructions for Fabulous Sweaters. Amy Herzog; photography by Karen Pearson. Abrams 2016. 175 pages : Illustration; Color
ISBN 9781419722479
Grades: Adult   746.432
1. Knitting 2. Sweaters 3. Arts and Entertainment — Crafts and hobbies — Textiles and needlework
LC 2015955480

Intends to provide knitters of all skill levels with the sweater-making confidence they need through instructions for six sweater styles—vests, all-in-one construction, drop shoulders, raglans, yokes, and set-in sleeves.

"Herzog's expertise, combined with her ability to explain clearly the hows and whys of sweater knitting, will build confidence even in the most reluctant knitters." —*Library Journal*
Includes bibliographical references (page 173).

PUBLIC LIBRARY CORE COLLECTION: NONFICTION
Twentieth Edition

Righetti, Maggie
Knitting in Plain English. Maggie Righetti. St. Martin's Press 1986. xiii, 241 p. : Illustration
ISBN 9780312458539
Grades: Adult   746.432
1. Knitting 2. Arts and Entertainment — Crafts and hobbies — Textiles and needlework
                               LC 86001800

An introduction to knitting covers patterns, gauges, yarns, needles, types of construction, casting on and off, increases, decreases, buttonholes, hems, color, pattern stitching, blocking, and alterations.

"This is one of the most comprehensive and accessible guides to crochet available. This isn't a quick-start guide: Righetti provides an overview of the necessary supplies, a brief history of crochet, and information about gauge before guiding beginners through their first stitch, an ideal approach for readers who wish to understand crochet in-depth." —*Library Journal*
Includes index.

Square, Vicki
The *Knitter's* Companion: Expanded and Updated! Vicki Square. Interweave 2010. 138 p. : Color illustration
ISBN 9781596683143
Grades: Adult   746.432
1. Knitting 2. Sweaters 3. Arts and Entertainment — Crafts and hobbies — Textiles and needlework
                               LC Oc2010090182

Now with an instructional DVD, an ideal knitting reference guide includes plenty of techniques, illustrations and definitions, covering everything from stitches, gauges, seams, borders and buttonholes to tassels, fringe, knitting with beads and more. By the author of Knit Kimono.

"This is an excellent ready reference for a variety of knitting techniques, including cast-ons, bind-offs, finishing, and other basics. The demonstrations on the DVDs show knitters exactly what they should be doing. Every knitting collection needs a reference; this one is affordable and accessible." —*Library Journal*
Includes index.

746.44 Embroidery

Brasfield, Hope
Satisfying Stitches: Learn Simple Embroidery Techniques and Embrace the Joys of Stitching by Hand. Hope Brasfield of Hopebroidery. Quarry 2023. 127 pages : Illustration; Color
ISBN 9780760377703
Grades: Adult   746.44
1. Embroidery 2. Needlework 3. Arts and Entertainment — Crafts and hobbies — Textiles and needlework
                               LC 2022027738

With Satisfying Stitches, you'll learn to create beautiful embroidery designs and discover how creative stitching can relieve stress and provide a sense of accomplishment."

"Highly recommended, especially for libraries looking to expand their beginner-embroidery offerings." —*Library Journal*
Includes index.

Chanin, Natalie
★ The *Geometry* of Hand-Sewing: A Romance in Stitches and Embroidery from Alabama Chanin and the School of Making. Natalie Chanin; photographs by Abraham Rowe and Rinne Allen; illustrations by Sun Young Park. Abrams 2017. 143 pages : Illustration; Color
ISBN 9781419726637
Grades: Adult   746.44
1. Stitches (Sewing) 2. Sewing 3. Arts and Entertainment — Crafts and hobbies — Textiles and needlework
                               LC Bl2017051001

Explains that all stitches are based on gridlines and provides instructions for more than one hundred stitches, from straight to herringbone, in a book that includes two plastic stitch cards that can be used for practice.

"Her tone throughout is as measured as her grids and as serene as the gray backgrounds appearing in the photos of each stitch." —*Publishers Weekly*
Includes indexes.

Christensen, Jo Ippolito
★ *The Needlepoint* Book. Jo Ippolito Christensen. Simon & Schuster 2015. xix, 537 p. : Illustration; Color
ISBN 9781476754086
Grades: Adult   746.44
1. Embroidery 2. Arts and Entertainment — Crafts and hobbies — Textiles and needlework
                               LC Oc2014027833

A revision of the profusely illustrated, so-called "Black Bible" of needlepoint, first published in 1976, includes new information on the latest stitches, materials, and techniques and hundreds of new photographs and informational charts.

"Even though the book is a reference, the text is enjoyable to read. Sage advice from Christensen and a variety of other needle artists can be found throughout." —*Library Journal*
Includes bibliographical references and indexes.

Eaton, Jan
Mary Thomas's Dictionary of Embroidery Stitches. Trafalgar Square Pub. 1998. 208 p. : Color illustration
ISBN 9781570761188
Grades: Adult   746.44
1. Embroidery 2. Arts and Entertainment — Crafts and hobbies — Textiles and needlework
                               LC 97081406

"A comprehensive dictionary offering more than 400 stitches, this edition includes 100 new stitches, all described and pictured in full-color diagrams. Essential for public libraries and embroidery collections." —*Library Journal*
Revised, full-color edition of this classic book, wtih over 100 new stitches; Includes index.

Frazer, Amy L.
Empowered Embroidery. Amy L. Frazer. Walter Foster Publishing 2021. 128 p. (Art Makers)
ISBN 9781633228849
Grades: Adult   746.44
1. Embroidery 2. Arts and Entertainment — Crafts and hobbies — Textiles and needlework

Featuring sketching and illustration instructions, basic stitches, embroidery techniques, and 6 projects with portraits of famous women, this book is a must-have tool for hands-on artists and crafters.

"Embroiderers looking to push their creativity will be rewarded by these projects." —*Publishers Weekly*

Galbraith, Melissa
How to Embroider Texture and Pattern: 20 Designs That Celebrate Pattern, Color, and Pop-up Stitching. Melissa Galbraith. Landauer Publishing 2023. 160 p.
ISBN 9781639810215
Grades: Adult   746.44
1. Embroidery 2. Needlework 3. Stitches (Sewing) 4. Arts and Entertainment — Crafts and hobbies — Textiles and needlework

Featuring 20 step-by-step embroidery projects of beautiful landscapes, desert canyons, unique flora, and more, How to Embroider Texture and Pattern is filled with vibrant embroidery patterns inspired by wanderlust that will challenge and grow your skills as you bring these beautiful outdoor scenes to life. Also included are easy-to-follow tutorials for over 20 need-to-know embroidery stitches, plus guidance for incorporating fabric prints into your projects to enhance the design, textural and 3D embroidery instruction, how to transfer a pat-

ESSENTIAL AND RECOMMENDED TITLES
746.44 Embroidery

tern, and other fundamental techniques. Have fun with color, create rich textures, and feel confident as you stitch your love for nature.

"Gorgeous projects and thorough instructions make this a superior embroidery guide." —*Publishers Weekly*

Ganderton, Lucinda
★ *Embroidery*. Lucinda Ganderton. DK 2015. 160 pages : Color; Illustration
ISBN 9781465436030
Grades: Adult 746.44
1. Embroidery 2. Needlework 3. Arts and Entertainment — Crafts and hobbies — Textiles and needlework
LC 2015431417

Demonstrates over two hundred stitches for embroidery, needlepoint, and dressmaking and offers advice on thread, needles, and fabrics.

"It's straightforward, simple, and easy to access, thanks not only to an appended index but also to an upfront visual table of contents. The quintessentially perfect reference." —*Booklist*

Previously published as: Stitch Sampler. 1999; Includes index.

Glass, Alison
Alison Glass Applique.: The Essential Guide to Modern Applique. Alison Glass. Lucky Spool Media 2014. 143 pages : Illustration; Color
ISBN 9781940655031
Grades: Adult 746.44
1. Applique 2. Quilting 3. Arts and Entertainment — Crafts and hobbies — Textiles and needlework
LC Bl2020045642

Former interior designer turned award-winning pattern and textile designer, Alison Glass, brings you fresh, creative projects guaranteed to add warmth and style to your home. You'll love making eye-catching quilts and home decor that rival boutique-style accessories but made by hand. Alison introduces readers to a variety of fabric types, threads and techniques suitable for creating wonderful textures in applique. She also includes a series of embroidery stitch instructions to get you started with hand-stitched embellishments. Who says applique has to be from a single fabric? Learn how to piece interesting improv components to cut large-scale applique shapes to add more layers to your quilts. From heirloom-quality needle-turn applique to modern jersey and big-stitch accents, this book includes step-by-step photographs covering each technique in detail (from raw-edge, to needle-turn to reverse applique). With two large pull-out pages packed with mix-and-match shapes to use, Alison gets you drawing, cutting, snipping, turning and stitching to express your own style through each fabulous layer. 14 unique projects for those new to applique and Alison Glass enthusiasts alike.

Higuchi, Yumiko
Embroidered Animals: Wild and Woolly Creatures to Stitch and Sew. Yumiko Higuchi. Roost Books 2021. 96 p.
ISBN 9781611808865
Grades: Adult 746.44
1. Embroidery 2. Animals in art 3. Arts and Entertainment — Crafts and hobbies — Textiles and needlework

A lively and accessible book featuring embroidery motifs and sewing projects that highlight the wonder and beauty of the animal kingdom with designs for foxes, cats, owls, zebras, and pandas. From elegant birds to adorable rabbits and wonderfully simple sheep, the 25 motifs and patterns in this book offer both a modern flair and an organic true-to-nature style. The whimsical animal designs—ranging from wild wolves, cheetahs, and giraffes to cuddly and cute bears, cats, dogs, monkeys, and pigs—can be incorporated into any of the sewing projects included, such as bags, pillows, bookmarks, and sachets, so that beginner and experienced embroiderers can mix and match patterns according to their own interest and skill.

"With technical instructions, templates, project directions, and the inspiration of Higuchi's beautiful samples, readers will have everything but the materials to make their own versions of these works of thread art." —*Booklist*

Lowry, Melissa
Vibrant Punch Needle Decor: Adorn Your Home with Colorful Florals & Geometric Patterns. Melissa Lowry. Page Street Publishing Co. 2020. 141 p.
ISBN 9781645670117
Grades: Adult 746.44
1. Embroidery 2. Arts and Entertainment — Crafts and hobbies — Textiles and needlework
LC Bl2020046010

Inspired by Melissa's Mexican heritage, these patterns reflect the vibrant colors and geometric patterns of traditional textiles, with a modern touch. The book includes full-size templates, so readers can replicate Melissa's signature designs. Beginners can get that amazing handmade look in a just an hour or two, creating beautiful pillows, hoop art, napkins and placements from scratch. Readers who want to dive deeper into the craft can tackle large-scale rugs and wall-hangings along with more detailed designs."

"Crafters will enjoy this imaginative design compilation that doubles as an educational sampling of traditional Mexican motifs and designs." —*Publishers Weekly*

Includes index.

Mornu, Nathalie
Embroider Your Life: Techniques + Motifs + Inspiration : Simple Techniques & 150 Stylish Motifs to Embellish Your World. Nathalie Mornu. Alpha 2017. 124 pages : Illustration; Color
ISBN 9781465464859
Grades: Adult 746.44
1. Embroidery 2. Needlework 3. Arts and Entertainment — Crafts and hobbies — Textiles and needlework
LC Bl2017037586

"Embroidery is on the upswing among crafters, and Mornu's nicely organized collection is full of helpful tutorials and clever ideas." —*Library Journal*

Ringquist, Rebecca
★ *Rebecca Ringquist's Embroidery Workshops: A Bend-the-Rules Primer*. Photography by Johnny Miller; photostyling by Shana Faust. STC Craft 2015. 156 pages : Illustration; Color
ISBN 9781617691416
Grades: Adult 746.44
1. Embroidery 2. Arts and Entertainment — Crafts and hobbies — Textiles and needlework
LC Bl2015014297

Teaches a variety of embroidery techniques, including stitching, tracing, drawing, layering, and mixing machine- and hand-sewing, and features projects that test each skill.

"Ringquist is a skilled instructor with a great deal of experience. Crafters who are intimidated by embroidery will find her free-spirited approach refreshing." —*Library Journal*

A Melanie Falick book.

Shimoda, Naoko
Artfully Embroidered: Motifs and Patterns for Bags and More. Naoko Shimoda. Interweave 2014. 119 pages : Illustration; Color
ISBN 9781620337288
Grades: Adult 746.44
1. Embroidery 2. Arts and Entertainment — Crafts and hobbies — Textiles and needlework
LC 2014036871

Artfully Embroidered reinvents vintage embroidery through a modern aesthetic. Traditional Japanese and western motifs are made new with color and embellishment, and 25 embroidered patterns demonstrate the beauty of the traditional designs while keeping the projects fresh and modern-looking for today's sewists.

"Sewists interested in exploring the world of embroidery will find a wealth of inspiration here, though beginners may need to consult a reference or an online tutorial to get themselves up to speed on the basics." —*Library Journal*

Includes two folded sheets of patterns inside pocket on page 3 of cover.

Watson, Sarah
***Pen to Thread:** 750+ Hand-Drawn Embroidery Designs to Inspire Your Stitches*. Sarah Watson. Interweave 2015. 159 pages : Illustration; Color
ISBN 9781620339527
Grades: Adult 746.44
1. Embroidery 2. Arts and Entertainment — Crafts and hobbies — Textiles and needlework
LC Bl2015054045

Shares over seven hundred and fifty motifs to embroider inspired by everyday items, nature, and food, along with tips for choosing fabric and stitching basics.

"Illustrator and fabric designer Watson brings her whimsical, hand-drawn designs to embroiderers in this collection of small and medium motifs." —*Library Journal*

Includes index.

746.46 Patchwork and quilting

Alexander, Lissa
***Oh, Scrap!:** Fabulous Quilts That Make the Most of Your Stash*. Lissa Alexander. Martingale 2018. 96 pages : Color; Illustration
ISBN 9781604688948
Grades: Adult 746.46
1. Patchwork 2. Quilting 3. Arts and Entertainment — Crafts and hobbies — Textiles and needlework
LC 2017044124

Best of all, with a dozen patterns to choose from you'll discover how to (finally!) use your unique stash to make scrap quilts that sing. Includes a preface by renowned quilt historian Barbara Brackman.

Belyea, Patricia
***East-Meets-West** Quilts: Explore Improv with Japanese-Inspired Designs*. Patricia Belyea; photography by Kate Baldwin. Abrams 2017. 191 pages : Color; Illustration
ISBN 9781419726590
Grades: Adult 746.46
1. Quilting 2. Patchwork 3. Arts and Entertainment — Crafts and hobbies — Textiles and needlework
LC Bl2017052290

The author presents her Quilt Manifesto of five rules for improvising while creating quilts and offers detailed instructions for fourteen quilt patterns using yukata cottons and inspired by Japanese design.

"The quilts' backs prove as interesting as the fronts, and Belyea's stitching designs are innovative, too. With fresh designs and useful directions, Belyea's book is both practical and aspirational." —*Publishers Weekly*

Beyer, Jinny
*A **Quilter's** Album of Patchwork Patterns: 4050 Pieced Blocks for Quilters*. Jinny Beyer. Breckling Press 2009. VII, 488 p. : Color illustration
ISBN 9781933308081
Grades: Adult 746.46
1. Patchwork 2. Quilting 3. Arts and Entertainment — Crafts and hobbies — Textiles and needlework
LC 2009021009

A visual encyclopedia of quilt block designs that provides quilters, designers, researchers, and patchwork enthusiasts with a comprehensive tool for finding, identifying and drafting more than 4050 unique patterns.

"The author pored through newspapers, catalogs, patterns, and magazines of the 1800s and 1900s to prepare illustrations—along with grids, dates, and multiple names—of more than 4,000 quilting blocks, the foundation of this genre of stitching. Yet providing that resource wasn't enough; Beyer enhances her encyclopedic reference by featuring mini catalogs of like-minded design styles, like bow ties, airplanes, the Red Cross, and kaleidoscope blocks. She also details her sources with commentary and explains how she categorized the blocks. Worthy of any quilting (and quilter's) library." —*Booklist*

Includes bibliographical references (p. 441-446) and index.

Brandvig, Jera
***Quilt** As-You-Go Made Vintage: 51 Blocks, 9 Projects, 3 Joining Methods*. Jera Brandvig. StashBooks 2017. 143 pages : Color; Illustration
ISBN 9781617454721
Grades: Adult 746.46
1. Patchwork quilts 2. Patchwork 3. Machine sewing 4. Arts and Entertainment — Crafts and hobbies — Textiles and needlework
LC 2017003179

Presents an innovative quilt-as-you-go technique for reversible quilts that encourages improvisation, providing patterns for nine quilting projects.

Doughty, Kathy
***Adding** Layers: Color, Design & Imagination : 15 Original Quilt Projects from Kathy Doughty of Material Obsession*. Kathy Doughty. C&T Publishing 2014. 127 pages : Color; Illustration
ISBN 9781607058472
Grades: Adult 746.46
1. Patchwork 2. Quilting 3. Arts and Entertainment — Crafts and hobbies — Textiles and needlework
LC 2013024143

"Techniques range from both simple to curved piecing to Y-seams and are best suited to intermediate quilters, although an ambitious beginner could easily follow Doughty's instructions and attempt any of the projects. Handy tips for everything from efficient cutting to design and layout are included." —*Library Journal*

1 folded sheet; Includes bibliographical references (page 127).

Gering, Jacquie
***Quilting** Modern: Techniques and Projects for Improvisational Quilts*. Jacquie Gering, Katie Pedersen. Interweave Press 2012. 175 p. : Illustration
ISBN 9781596683877
Grades: Adult 746.46
1. Patchwork 2. Machine quilting 3. Quilting 4. Arts and Entertainment — Crafts and hobbies — Textiles and needlework
LC 2011039245

Quilting Modern teaches quilters to use improvisational techniques to make graphic, contemporary quilts and quilted projects.

Includes bibliographical references and index.

***Walk:** Master Machine Quilting with Your Walking Foot*. Jacquie Gering. Lucky Spool Media, LLC 2016. 160 pages : Illustration; Color
ISBN 9781940655215
Grades: Adult 746.46
1. Machine quilting 2. Arts and Entertainment — Crafts and hobbies — Textiles and needlework
LC Bl2017037006

Covers the basics of quilting with a walking foot, featuring over forty traditional and advanced designs as well as tips for quilting with decorative stitches and reverse quilting.

Includes bibliographical references (page 159).

Gilleland, Diane
***All** Points Patchwork: English Paper Piecing Beyond the Hexagon, for Quilts & Small Projects*. Diane Gilleland. Storey Publishing 2015. 222 pages
ISBN 9781612124209
Grades: Adult 746.46
1. Quilting 2. Patchwork 3. Paper work 4. Arts and Entertainment — Crafts and hobbies — Textiles and needlework
LC 2014048235

A patchwork guide instructs quilters on how to use the traditional English paper piecing technique to achieve well-matched points, with step-by-step illustrations showing how to connect a variety of shapes, including diamonds, jewels, and curves.

ESSENTIAL AND RECOMMENDED TITLES
746.46 Patchwork and quilting

"An essential reference for quilters interested in EPP." —*Library Journal*
Includes bibliographical references (pages 204-205) and index.

Goertzen, Vanessa
★ *Charm* School: 18 Quilts from 5. Vanessa Goertzen of Lella Boutique. StashBooks 2017. 127 pages : Color; Illustration
ISBN 9781617452710
Grades: Adult   746.46
1. Patchwork quilts 2. Patchwork 3. Quilting 4. Arts and Entertainment — Crafts and hobbies — Textiles and needlework
LC 2016025934

"These cheery quilts demonstrate the versatility of charm squares and will inspire quilters to make use of these popular precuts." —*Library Journal*

Goldsworthy, Lynne
Quick & Easy Quilts: 20 Machine Quilting Projects. Lynne Goldsworthy; photography by Jan Baldwin. The Taunton Press 2017. 128 pages : Color; Illustration
ISBN 9781631869143
Grades: Adult   746.46
1. Patchwork 2. Quilting 3. Machine quilting 4. Patchwork quilts 5. Arts and Entertainment — Crafts and hobbies — Textiles and needlework
LC 2017026662

"These projects will appeal to quilters looking for attractive, modern projects featuring bold interpretations of traditional blocks." —*Library Journal*

First published in Great Britain in 2016 by Kyle Books, an imprint of Kyle Cathie Ltd; First published in the United States in 2017 by the Tauton Press.

Grisham, Candyce Copp
Dresden Quilt Blocks Reimagined: Sew Your Own Playful Plates : 25 Elements to Mix & Match. Candyce Copp Grisham. C&T Publishing, Inc. 2019. 79 p.
ISBN 9781617457937
Grades: Adult   746.46
1. Quilting 2. Patchwork quilts 3. Arts and Entertainment — Crafts and hobbies — Textiles and needlework
LC 2018054532

Mix and match the 4 edge treatments, 16 sizes, and endless fabric combinations to make Dresden Plate quilts.

Hartman, Elizabeth
Modern Patchwork: 12 Quilts to Take You Beyond the Basics. Elizabeth Hartman. StashBooks 2012. 143 p. : Color illustration
ISBN 9781607055488
Grades: Adult   746.46
1. Patchwork quilts 2. Quilting 3. Arts and Entertainment — Crafts and hobbies — Textiles and needlework
LC 2011040928

Presents detailed instructions for twelve quilts which demonstrate modern color design and utilize such intermediate techniques as curved seams and hexagon blocks, with a section on construction basics.

Hunter, Bonnie K.
String Frenzy: 12 More String Quilt Projects : Strips, Strings & Scrappy Things! Bonnie K. Hunter. C&T Publishing 2018. 95 pages
ISBN 9781617457326
Grades: Adult   746.46
1. Patchwork 2. Quilting 3. Arts and Entertainment — Crafts and hobbies — Textiles and needlework
LC 2018009853

A latest collection of playful string-quilt projects demonstrates the author's foundation piecing basics and instructs crafters on how to transform leftover fabric scraps into one-of-a-kind quilts.

"Short on fluff and long on useful information, this slim volume offers abundant, well-stated advice for creating unique heirloom quilts." —*Publishers Weekly*

Maxwell, Sarah
Fearless with Fabric: Fresh Quilts from Traditional Blocks : An Inspiring Guide to Making 14 Quilt Projects. Sarah J. Maxwell. Landauer Publishing 2020. 150 pages : Illustration; Color
ISBN 9781947163232
Grades: Adult   746.46
1. Quilting 2. Arts and Entertainment — Crafts and hobbies — Textiles and needlework

Inspiring readers to quilt outside of their comfort zone, a project book designed to build confidence shows how, through step-by-step instructions, to mix and match fabrics and colors.

"Maxwell's instruction stands out in its encouragements." —*Booklist*

Nyberg, Amanda Jean
No Scrap Left Behind: 16 Quilt Projects That Celebrate Scraps of All Sizes. Amanda Jean Nyberg. ShashBooks, an imprint of C&T Publishing 2017. 127 p.
ISBN 9781617453366
Grades: Adult   746.46
1. Patchwork 2. Quilting 3. Arts and Entertainment — Crafts and hobbies — Textiles and needlework
LC 2016030821

Presents sixteen quilt projects which are categorized by the use of fabric scraps to form squares, triangles, snippets, strips, and strings.

Redford, Catherine
Modern Machine Quilting: Make a Perfectly Finished Quilt on Your Home Machine. Catherine Redford. Fons & Porter 2017. 127 pages : Illustration; Color
ISBN 9781440246319
Grades: Adult   746.46
1. Machine quilting 2. Quilting 3. Patchwork 4. Arts and Entertainment — Crafts and hobbies — Textiles and needlework
LC Bl2018052901

A guide to creating quilts on a home sewing machine includes step-by-step instructions for planning, constructing, and finishing a quilt; presents a multitude of designs; and provides projects for quilting practice.
Includes index.

Rosenthal, Maxine
One-Block Wonders of the World: New Ideas, Design Advice, a Stunning Collection of Quilts. Maxine Rosenthal and Linda Bardes. C&T Publishing, Inc. 2017. 79 pages : Color; Illustration
ISBN 9781617455186
Grades: Adult   746.46
1. Patchwork 2. Quilting 3. Arts and Entertainment — Crafts and hobbies — Textiles and needlework
LC 2017013882

"Quilters familiar with making kaleidoscopic quilts will find plenty of inspiration; those new to this style will want to consult Rosenthal's earlier book One-Block Wonders for instructions." —*Library Journal*

Shaw, Robert
American Quilts: The Democratic Art. Robert Shaw. Sterling 2014. 375 pages : Illustration; Color
ISBN 9781454913979
Grades: Adult   746.46
1. Quilts 2. United States 3. Arts and Entertainment — Crafts and hobbies — Textiles and needlework
LC Bl2014042061

Presents a history of American quilt making over a four-hundred-year period, covering the evolution of the art and describing the cultural and social conditions under which the quilts were made, with 350 examples of works created by a diverse group of artists.

"The story of American quilting is eloquently told here, set within a broad geographic scope, putting Shaw's expansive curatorial background to full advantage." —*Library Journal*

Includes bibliographical references (pages 361-366) and index.

PUBLIC LIBRARY CORE COLLECTION: NONFICTION
Twentieth Edition

Stocker, Blair
Wise Craft Quilts: A Guide to Turning Beloved Fabrics into Meaningful Patchwork. Blair Stocker; foreword by Denyse Schmidt; photographs by Stephanie Congdon Barnes. Roost Books 2017. xv, 173 pages : Color; Illustration
ISBN 9781611803488
Grades: Adult   746.46
1. Patchwork quilts 2. Patchwork 3. Textile fabrics 4. Arts and Entertainment — Crafts and hobbies — Textiles and needlework
LC 2016012230
"There are so many innovative projects in this impressive collection that it's difficult to pick a standout. Quilters interested in nontraditional textiles will be inspired." —*Library Journal*
Includes bibliographical references.

Tomasson, Dara
Walk, Jog, Run: A Free-Motion Quilting Workout : Muscle-Memory-Building Exercises, Projects & Tips. Dara Tomasson. Stash Books 2020. 143 pages : Illustration; Color
ISBN 9781617459153
Grades: Adult   746.46
1. Machine quilting 2. Arts and Entertainment — Crafts and hobbies — Textiles and needlework
LC 2019049047
Free-motion quilting book how to get started and 10 projects.
"Tomasson, who blogs about and teaches free-motion quilting, fills this auspicious debut with instructions on the craft of using sewing machines to stitch something other than straight lines onto a quilt." —*Publishers Weekly*

Walters, Angela
Free-Motion Meandering: A Beginner's Guide to Machine Quilting. Angela Walters. StashBooks 2017. 79 pages : Color; Illustration
ISBN 9781617455209
Grades: Adult   746.46
1. Machine quilting 2. Arts and Entertainment — Crafts and hobbies — Textiles and needlework
LC 2017006148
Presents step-by-step, illustrated instructions for eight meandering stitches for beginners to practice, along with unique modifications for each, to improve free-motion quilting, disguise mistakes, and transition between designs with ease.

Wolfe, Victoria Findlay
Modern Quilt Magic; 5 Parlor Tricks to Expand Your Piecing Skills - 17 Captivating Projects. Victoria Findlay Wolfe. Stash Books, an imprint of C & T Publishing, Inc. 2017. 128 pages : Illustration; Color
ISBN 9781617455087
Grades: Adult   746.46
1. Patchwork 2. Quilting 3. Arts and Entertainment — Crafts and hobbies — Textiles and needlework
LC 2016059348
Presents detailed instructions for such quilting skills as partial-seams, y-seams, and free-form curves and offers seventeen projects which incorporate these techniques into quilts and pillows.

Wood, Sherri
The Improv Handbook for Modern Quilters: A Guide to Creating, Quilting & Living Courageously. Sherri Lynn Wood; photography by Sara Remington. STC Craft 2015. 174 pages : Illustration; Color
ISBN 9781617691386
Grades: Adult   746.46
1. Quilting 2. Arts and Entertainment — Crafts and hobbies — Textiles and needlework
LC Bl2015014300
Shares a flexible approach to quilting that features improvisational sewing and patchwork techniques, and includes ten patterns with loose parameters as well as mind exercises for experimenting with color.

"Improv quilting may not be to everyone's taste—it can be visually jarring at times—but many who love this style are downright passionate about it, and Wood provides a comprehensive overview of improvisational techniques." —*Library Journal*
A Melanie Falick book; Includes bibliographical references (pages 170-171).

746.5 Bead embroidery

Cox, Shelley
Bead Embroidery. Shelley Cox. Search Press 2013. 95 pages : Color; Illustration
ISBN 9781844489237
Grades: Adult   746.5
1. Arts and Entertainment — Crafts and hobbies — Textiles and needlework
LC Bl2014038270
Focuses on bead embroidery, presenting a brief history and discussing basic techniques, counted thread embroidery, bead embroidery, surface embroidery, and fringes.
RSN, Royal School of Needlework—Cover; Includes index.

746.6 Printing, painting, dyeing

Callahan, Gail
Hand Dyeing Yarn and Fleece: Dip-Dyeing, Hand-Painting, Tie-Dyeing, and Other Creative Techniques. Gail Callahan; photography by John Polak. Storey Pub. 2010. 168 p. : Illustration; Color
ISBN 9781603424684
Grades: Adult   746.6
1. Dyes and dyeing 2. Textile fibers 3. Yarn 4. Wool 5. Arts and Entertainment — Crafts and hobbies — Textiles and needlework
LC 2009028676
Provides instructions for dyeing yarn and fleece using various techniques, designs, and dyes, along with information on supplies and finding the right colors.
Includes bibliographical references (p. 164) and index.

Corwin, Lena
Lena Corwin's Made by Hand. Lena Corwin; photography by Maria Alexandra Vettese and Stephanie Congdon Barnes. STC Craft/A Melanie Falick Book, Stewart, Tabori & Chang 2013. 176 pages
ISBN 9781617690594
Grades: Adult   746.6
1. Dyes and dyeing 2. Handicraft 3. Knitting 4. Sewing 5. Textile crafts 6. Textile printing 7. Weaving 8. Arts and Entertainment — Crafts and hobbies — Textiles and needlework 9. Arts and Entertainment — General
LC 2013010186
Curates a collection of twenty-six studio classes hosted at the author's Brooklyn studio, offering step-by-step instructions for projects that use classic craft techniques showcased in modern styles.
STC Craft/A Melanie Falick book; Includes bibliographical references (page 175).

Duerr, Sasha
Natural Color: Vibrant Plant Dye Projects for Your Home and Wardrobe. Sasha Duerr; photography by Aya Brackett. Watson-Guptill Publications 2016. VI, 263 p.
ISBN 9781607749363
Grades: Adult   746.6
1. Dyes and dyeing 2. Textile fibers 3. Arts and Entertainment — Crafts and hobbies — Textiles and needlework
LC 2016002216

ESSENTIAL AND RECOMMENDED TITLES
746.7 Rugs

An illustrated guide to making natural plant dyes for clothing and home decor features more than two dozen projects, organized by season, including using mint to dye table runners and using sourgrass to color children's clothing.

"Duerr is knowledgeable and thorough, and fiber artists with an interest in incorporating natural dyeing into their work will find the information they need to get started, as well as insight into the dyeing process." —*Library Journal*

Includes bibliographical references (pages 254-255) and indexes.

Joyce, Anna
Hand Dyed: A Modern Guide to Dyeing in Brilliant Color for You and Your Home. Anna Joyce; photography by Dane Tashima. Abrams 2019. 159 pages : Color; Illustration
ISBN 9781419734281
Grades: Adult   746.6
1. Dyes and dyeing 2. Arts and Entertainment — Crafts and hobbies — Textiles and needlework
LC 2018936227

A guide to dyeing explains the classic techniques and materials needed to create colored and patterned pieces, including swaddling blankets, a tie-dye swimsuit, and festive cotton buntings.

"A wide range of crafters and textile artists should find this to be a useful resource." —*Library Journal*

Includes bibliographical references (page 158).

Swearington, Jen
Printing on Fabric: Techniques with Screens, Stencils, Inks, and Dyes. Jen Swearington. Lark Crafts 2013. 160 pages : Illustration; Color
ISBN 9781454703945
Grades: Adult   746.6
1. Textile printing 2. Arts and Entertainment — Crafts and hobbies
LC 2012006729

Provides an accessible guide to hand-printing fabric, and includes tips on translating design ideas into prints, the different modes of transfer, and how to use effective color combinations.

Includes bibliographical references (page 158) and index.

746.7 Rugs

Mezoff, Rebecca
★ *The Art of Tapestry Weaving: A Complete Guide to Mastering the Techniques for Making Images with Yarn*. Rebecca Mezoff; foreword by Sarah C. Swett. Workman Pub CO 2020. xi, 306 pages : Color; Illustration
ISBN 9781635861358
Grades: Adult   746.7
1. Tapestry 2. Hand weaving 3. Arts and Entertainment — Crafts and hobbies — Textiles and needlework
LC 2020024105

Rebecca Mezoff shares her techniques in this in-depth guide to every aspect of the process, from developing a color palette to selecting yarn, warping the loom, and weaving the image."

"The high level of detail in the explanations of everything from equipment to materials to techniques makes this book a must-have for the aspiring tapestry weaver." —*Booklist*

Includes index.

Rott, Ira
Crochet Animal Rugs: Over 20 Crochet Patterns for Fun Floor Mats and Matching Accessories. Ira Rott. SewandSo 2018. 143 pages : Color; Illustration
ISBN 9781446307007
Grades: Adult   746.7
1. Rugs 2. Home furnishings 3. Animals in art 4. Crocheting 5. Arts and Entertainment — Crafts and hobbies — Textiles and needlework
LC Bl2018168472

"Following the online success of her elephant-rug pattern, Rott, in her first book, expands her animal-themed designs beyond rugs to over 20 patterns that include matching pillows, bags, blankets, and other accessories and the original elephant rug." —*Booklist*

Includes index.

746.9 Other textile products

Bowles, Hamish
Vogue & The Metropolitan Museum of Art Costume Institute: Parties, Exhibitions, People. Hamish Bowles; foreword by Thomas P. Campbell; introduction by Anna Wintour; edited by Chloe Malle. Abrams 2014. 271 pages : Illustration; Color
ISBN 9781419714245
Grades: Adult   746.9
1. Balls (Parties) 2. Costume 3. Fashion photography 4. Arts and Entertainment — Fashion 5. Arts and Entertainment — Photography
LC Bl2014047080

Offers pictorial highlights of the Metropolitan Museum of Art's spring Costume Institute exhibitions of the twenty-first century, curated by Harold Koda and Andrew Bolton, as well as the Vogue fashion shoots they inspired and galas that opened them.

Carter, Ruth E.
★ *The Art of Ruth E. Carter: Costuming Black History and the Afro-Future, from Do the Right Thing to Black Panther*. Ruth E. Carter, foreword by Danai Gurira. Chronicle Books 2022. 152 p; Illustration
ISBN 9781797203065
Grades: Adult   746.9
1. Carter, Ruth E. 2. African American women 3. Costume design 4. Fashion designers 5. African Americans 6. Clothing 7. Costume 8. Fashion design 9. African Americans in films 10. Film 11. United States 12. Afrofuturism 13. Autobiographies and memoirs 14. Life stories — Arts and culture — Fashion 15. Arts and Entertainment — Fashion 16. Arts and Entertainment — Movies and television
LC 2021053651

In this definitive book, Carter shares her origins—recalling a trip to the sporting goods store with Spike Lee to outfit the School Daze cast and a transformative moment stepping inside history on the set of Steven Spielberg's Amistad. Carter's wisdom and stories are paired with deluxe visuals, including sketches, mood boards, and film stills. Danai Gurira, beloved for her portrayal of Okoye in Black Panther, has contributed a foreword. Fans will even get a glimpse behind the scenes of Black Panther: Wakanda Forever. This book is sure to inspire the next generation of artists and storytellers.

"An appealing read for anyone interested in moviemaking, and an essential for aspiring costumers. Carter's contributions to Black cinema make this a worthy inclusion in any library collection." —*Library Journal*

Faerm, Steven
Fashion Design Course: Principles, Practice, and Techniques: The Practical Guide for Aspiring Fashion Designers. Steven Faerm. Barron's 2017. 160 pages : Illustration; Color
ISBN 9781438011073
Grades: 11 12 Adult   746.9
1. Clothing 2. Fashion design 3. Vocational guidance 4. Arts and Entertainment — Crafts and hobbies — Textiles and needlework 5. Arts and Entertainment — Fashion
LC Bl2018004126

An introduction to fashion design offers practical exercises and interviews with industry professionals to help readers create their own collections and discover their unique design vision.

"The author takes readers through a thorough exploration of the fashion industry, from history to inspiration to the design process to landing a job. There are also 14 practical assignments to help budding designers learn more about the industry. Teens exploring careers in fashion will enjoy the practical advice from industry insiders, and fashion-mad readers of all ages will appreciate the information about how fashion design works." —*Library Journal*

Principles, practice, and techniques: the practical guide for aspiring fashion designers—Cover; Includes index.

Givhan, Robin
*The **Battle** of Versailles: The Night American Fashion Stumbled into the Spotlight and Made History.* Robin Givhan. Flatiron Books 2015. 320 pages
ISBN 9781250052902
Grades: Adult   746.9

1. Fashion shows 2. Fashion design 3. Fashion designers 4. Fashion merchandising 5. Social change 6. Fund raising 7. Textile industry and trade 8. African American fashion models 9. Versailles, France 10. 1970s 11. 20th century 12. Arts and Entertainment — Fashion

LC 2014040369

Conceived as a fundraiser for the restoration of King Louis XIV's palace, the world's elite gathered in Versailles' grand theater to view a fashion extravaganza of the best that French and American designers had to offer, while being entertained by LizaMinnelli and Josephine Baker. What they saw would forever alter the history of fashion. At the Battle of Versailles five Americans—Oscar de la Renta, Bill Blass, Anne Klein, Halston, and Stephen Burrows—faced off against the five French designers considered the best in the world—Yves Saint Laurent, Hubert de Givenchy, Pierre Cardin, Emanuel Ungaro, and Marc Bohan of Christian Dior. Against all odds, the American energy and the domination by their fearless models (ten of whom, in a ground-breaking move, were African-American) sent the audience reeling. By the end of the evening, the Americans had transformed their place on the world stage and sowed the seeds for changing the way race, gender, sexuality, and economics would be treated in fashion for decades to come. The in-fighting between ego-inflated designers, the unforeseen obstacles in staging the show on a shoestring, the triumphant win, the vastly different fates of the designers post-show—Robin Givhan's meticulous research brings the event alive and places it firmly in the history of fashion, offering an intimate examination of a single moment that teaches us how the culture of fashion as we now know it came to be.

"Readers need not be fashion mavens to enjoy this entertaining episode of history, enhanced by Givhan's effortless ability to illustrate the models and designers (particularly Lambert) who changed how we dress." —*Kirkus*

Grumbach, Didier
History of International Fashion. Didier Grumbach; photo editor Isabelle d'Hauteville. Interlink Books 2014. 462 pages : Illustration; Color
ISBN 9781566569767
Grades: Adult   746.9

1. Fashion design 2. Fashion 3. 20th century 4. Arts and Entertainment — Fashion

LC 2014004755

"Industry veteran Grumbach takes you through the history of fashion in this lavishly illustrated book, from its humble beginnings to today's superstar designers." —*Publishers Weekly*

Includes bibliographical references (pages 436-437) and index; Originally published in French as Histoires de la mode—Page facing title page.

Linett, Andrea
*The **Cool** Factor: A Guide to Achieving Effortless Style, with Secrets from the Women Who Have It.* Andrea Linett. Artisan 2016. 223 pages
ISBN 9781579656485
Grades: Adult   746.9

1. Fashion 2. Women's clothing 3. Science writing — Medicine and health — Hygiene and beauty 4. Self-Help — Personal growth — Fashion and style 5. Self-Help — Personal growth — Motivation

LC 2015034242

"Theres at least one tip or rule-busting—potentially game-changing—suggestion for any woman looking to cultivate a coherent wardrobe and unique style by using her eyes, judgment, and Linett's six principles." —*Publishers Weekly*

Includes index.

Lowit, Roxanne
Yves Saint Laurent. Roxanne Lowit, photographs; foreword by Pierre Bergé.. Thames & Hudson 2014. 1 volume (unpaged) : Illustration; Color
ISBN 9780500517604
Grades: Adult   746.9

1. Saint Laurent, Yves, 1936-2008 2. Fashion designers 3. Fashion design 4. 20th century 5. Arts and Entertainment — Fashion

LC 2014930896

A dazzling portrait of Yves Saint Laurent and his world of fashion over the last twenty-five years of his career, by legendary pioneer of backstage fashion photography, Roxanne Lowit. Yves Saint Laurent is a name synonymous with style, elegance, and high fashion. When he came on the scene at Dior and then started his own line, he quickly changed the way people regarded haute couture and the world of fashion itself. He revolutionized women's eveningwear when he introduced le smoking, a woman's tuxedo, and made couture accessible to a younger generation. Yves Saint Laurent is Roxanne Lowit's personal photographic history of Saint Laurent, the man and the fashion, from 1978, the year she first met him, to the last show he gave in 2002. With contributions from YSL's muses and admirers, including Catherine Deneuve, Betty Catroux, Lucie de la Falaise, Pat Cleveland, and Valerie Steele, this book represents the backstage experience at YSL's shows as Lowit experienced them herself. Whether surrounded by beautiful models or peeking at the catwalk from the wings, every moment was a magnificent photo opportunity. Lowit shares magical moments of YSL with the world; intimate, social, absorbed in fashion; and creates a unique portrait of this towering figure of postwar couture.

Secrest, Meryle
Elsa Schiaparelli: A Biography. Meryle Secrest. Alfred A. Knopf 2014. 352 p.
ISBN 9780307701596
Grades: Adult   746.9

1. Schiaparelli, Elsa, 1890-1973 2. Clothing industry and trade 3. Fashion designers 4. Women fashion designers 5. Fashion design 6. Biographies 7. Life stories — Arts and culture — Fashion

LC 2014025820

The first biography of the grand couturier, surrealist, and embattled figure (her medium was apparel), whose extraordinary work has stood the test of time.

"Richly illustrated and endlessly intriguing, Secrests biography illuminates the 'Daredevil swagger' of Schiaparellis clothes and the oft-besieged couturiers inexhaustible tenacity and dazzling creativity." —*Booklist*

Tonti, Lucianne
Sundressed: Natural Fabrics and the Future of Clothing. Lucianne Tonti. Island Press 2023. 240 p.
ISBN 9781642832716
Grades: Adult   746.9

1. Clothing industry and trade 2. Clothing 3. Recycling (Waste, etc.) 4. Environmental ethics 5. Environmentalism 6. Green consumerism 7. Environmental design 8. Consumer economics 9. Sustainable living 10. Environmental responsibility 11. Fashion 12. Business and economics — Industries — Manufacturing 13. Business and economics — Economics — Consumerism 14. Arts and Entertainment — Fashion 15. Business and economics — Industries — Retail products and services

From Mongolian goatherders, to Mulberry groves in China, and American hemp farms, a sustainable fashion consultant travels the world to showcase producers who are reforming the industry with clothes made from natural fabrics that can stand the test of time.

"Tonti's insightful book shines light into the darker corners of the fashion business and points to new ways forward." —*Kirkus*

Originally published in Australia by Black Inc, Collingwood, Victoria, in 2022.

ESSENTIAL AND RECOMMENDED TITLES
746.92 Costume

746.92 Costume

Dirix, Emmanuelle
Dressing the Decades: Twentieth-Century Vintage Style. Emmanuelle Dirix. Yale University Press 2016. 224 p.
ISBN 9780300215526
Grades: Adult 746.92
1. Fashion 2. Clothing 3. Fashion design 4. Arts and Entertainment — Fashion 5. History writing — United States
LC 2015953579

A visually dazzling tour of 20th-century fashion, spotlighting the leading designers and dominant styles of the past 100 years.

"Her well-informed narrative is often laced with socioeconomic observations, including discussion of Hollywood's impact on designers and vice versa, the class divisions of haute couture vs. ready-to-wear, and how various social and political movements transformed how we dress and consume fashion. The accompanying photos and illustrations ... are stunning and often drool-worthy." —*Library Journal*

Trubert-Tollu, Chantal
★ *The House of Worth 1858-1954: The Birth of Haute Couture.* Chantal Trubert-Tollu, Francoise Tetart-Vittu, Jean-Marie Martin-Hattemberg, Fabrice Olivieri; foreword by Christian Lacroix. Thames & Hudson 2017. 335 pages : Illustration; Color
ISBN 9780500519431
Grades: Adult 746.92
1. Worth, Charles Frederic, 1825-1895 2. Couture clothing 3. Fashion design 4. Fashion designers 5. 19th century 6. 20th century 7. Arts and Entertainment — Fashion
LC 2017944380

A history of the House of Worth, the worlds pioneering haute couture label, covers its founder, Charles Frederick Worth, the company's successes and failures, and its lasting legacy and influence in the realm of fashion.

"With gorgeous color images of Worth designs, paintings, and archival fashion drawings and photographs, this sumptuous book is recommended for readers interested in the history of haute couture and French fashion." —*Library Journal*

Includes bibliographical references (pages 324-325) and index; Translated from the French.

746.92092 Fashion design — Biography

Barker, Nigel
Models of Influence: 50 Women Who Reset the Course of Fashion. Nigel Barker. Harper Design 2015. 255 p. : Illustration; Color
ISBN 9780062345844
Grades: Adult 746.92092
1. Fashion models 2. Fashion history 3. 20th century 4. Arts and Entertainment — Fashion 5. Life stories — Identity — Gender 6. Arts and Entertainment — Photography
LC 2014930210

Interweaving .., photographs and ... anecdotes, [this book] profiles 50 women who have made an unforgettable impression on fashion, the modeling industry, and our notions of beauty. Eight chronological chapters, each of which spotlight an era, feature the stories and images of women who made their mark.

Includes bibliographical references (pages 252-255).

747 Interior decoration

Adams, Michael Henry
Style and Grace: African Americans at Home. Michael Henry Adams; photographs by Mick Hales. Bulfinch Press 2003. 160 p. : Color illustration
ISBN 9780821228470
Grades: Adult 747
1. African Americans 2. Interior decoration 3. Architecture, Domestic 4. New York City 5. 20th century 6. House and Home — Interior Decorating and Furnishings
LC 2003103036

Celebrating the African-American tradition of style and creativity in home design and decoration, this richly illustrated study looks at the unique homes of hip-hop entrepreneur Russell Simmons, photographer Gordon Parks, Congressman Charles Rangel, and other African-American artists and professionals.

Includes index.

Becker, Holly
Decorate: 1,000 Professional Design Ideas for Every Room in Your Home. Holly Becker & Joanna Copestick; photographs by Debi Treloar. Chronicle Books 2011. 288 p. : Color illustration
ISBN 9780811877893
Grades: Adult 747
1. Interior decoration 2. House and Home — Interior Decorating and Furnishings
LC 2010048053

Collects tips from such professional interior designers as Kelly Wearstler, Amy Butler, and Jonathan Adler for every room and every budget, along with photographs, line illustrations, checklists, shortcuts, and floor plans.

Blakeney, Justina
Jungalow: Decorate Wild : The Life and Style Guide. Justina Blakeney. Abrams 2021. 271 p. : Illustration
ISBN 9781419747052
Grades: Adult 747
1. Interior decoration 2. Women interior decorators 3. House and Home — Interior Decorating and Furnishings

In each chapter, Justina shares her distinctive point of view on everything design fans want to know—how to make bold choices with color and pattern, how to take cues from nature, how to authentically glean inspiration from their heritage and travels, how to break rules, and all the other paths to truly begin to decorate wild. Along the way, Justina also shares personal narratives, practical advice, and nuanced insight into how she lives in her own space—how she reconnects with nature, how she plays and stays inspired, how she gives herself permission to feel free and wild, and how readers can do the same.

"Blakeney's bold tips are sure to leave readers eager to find inspiration in the world, and to bring bright color into their homes." —*Publishers Weekly*

Includes bibliographical references.

The New Bohemians Handbook: Come Home to Good Vibes. Justina Blakeney; photography by Dabito. Abrams 2017. 287 p.: Color; Illustration
ISBN 9781419724824
Grades: Adult 747
1. Interior decoration 2. Bohemianism 3. House and Home — Interior Decorating and Furnishings 4. House and Home — DIY, maintenance, and repair
LC Bl2017045393

A guide to affordable bohemian interior design presents ways to enhance the environment of the room with plants, colors, and do-it-yourself projects.

A New York Times best-selling author, designer and artist guides readers through affordable DIY projects that use color and scent to add positive energy into their homes and enhance mood, productivity and relaxation.

Bradbury, Dominic
The Iconic Interior: Private Spaces of Leading Artists, Architects, and Designers. Dominic Bradbury; with photography by Richard Powers. Abrams 2012. 351 pages : Color; Illustration
ISBN 9781617690051
Grades: Adult 747
1. Interior decoration 2. 21st century 3. 20th century 4. Arts and Entertainment — Architecture
LC 2012007221

"With such a detailed description of the best of the best in 20th-century interior design and the range of styles represented, this book is an outstanding reference and fulfills Bradbury's intention of encouraging both amateurs and professionals to take a bold approach to design." —*Library Journal*

Includes bibliographical references and index.

Bridges, Sheila
Furnishing Forward: A Practical Guide to Furnishing for a Lifetime. Sheila Bridges; with photographs by Anna Williams. Bulfinch Press 2005. 184 p. : Color illustration

ISBN 9780821261804

Grades: Adult   747

1. Interior decoration 2. United States 3. House and Home — Interior Decorating and Furnishings

LC 2001016480

A distinguished designer shares professional and personal anecdotes in this full-color guide on how to make the transition to eclectic and classic furniture that will endure for years to achieve an individual and elegant home.

Brits, Louisa Thomsen
The Book of Hygge: The Danish Art of Comfort, Coziness, and Connection. Louisa Thomsen Brits. Plume 2017. 192 p.

ISBN 9780735214101

Grades: Adult   747

1. Human comfort 2. Interior decoration 3. House and Home — Interior Decorating and Furnishings 4. Self-Help — Personal growth — Happiness 5. Self-Help — Personal growth — Motivation

LC 2016033937

A full-color lifestyle guide to the centuries-old Danish art of togetherness and contentment shares advice for incorporating hygge practices into everyday life, from making coffee together at breakfast and sharing meals to sitting beside a fire or snuggling into bed with a good book.

"In increasingly fast-paced and competitive America, hygge has considerable appeal; readers may very well find reading Brits's compact and enjoyable book the literary version of the practice." —*Publishers Weekly*

Brown, Amanda
★ *Spruce:* A Step-by-Step Guide to Upholstery and Design. Amanda Brown; photography by Ryann Ford. Storey Publishing 2013. 392 pages

ISBN 9781612121376

Grades: Adult   747

1. Do-it-yourself work 2. House and Home — Interior Decorating and Furnishings 3. Reference — Instructional materials

LC 2013012590

Accompanied by photographs and step-by-step instructions, an introduction to the craft of upholstery provides all of the techniques and skills needed to reupholster any piece of furniture and become a master upholsterer.

"[P]erfectly matches complete, precisely written directions with correspondingly crisp, helpful photographs." —*Booklist*

Includes index.

Carter, Darryl
The Collected Home: Rooms with Style, Grace, and History. Darryl Carter with Trish Donnally; photographs by Gordon Beall. Clarkson Potter/Publishers 2012. 208 p. : Color illustration

ISBN 9780307953940

Grades: Adult   747

1. Interior decoration 2. House and Home — Interior Decorating and Furnishings

LC 2011043291

Explores the role of textures, multi-purpose furniture, and unexpected objects in rendering spaces both comfortable and eye-catching, outlining a range of short- and long-term steps for overall home design.

A follow-up to the New Traditional builds on the popular designer's aesthetic principles to explore the role of textures, multi-purpose furniture and unexpected objects in rendering spaces both comfortable and eye-catching, outlining a range of short- and long-term steps for overall home design.

Includes index.

The New Traditional: Reinvent, Balance, Define Your Home. Darryl Carter. Clarkson Potter 2008. 208 p. : Color illustration

ISBN 9780307408655

Grades: Adult   747

1. Interior decoration 2. House and Home — Interior Decorating and Furnishings

LC 2007045663

Presents an accessible guide to creating a stylish, inviting, and comfortable design that is responsive to the individual requirements of the people who live in it, explaining how to integrate modern elements with the classical using furnishings accessories, textiles, lighting, and color to make one's home a place to be enjoyed.

Includes index.

Gates, Erin T
★ *Elements* of Family Style: Elegant Spaces for Everyday Life. Erin Gates. Atria Books 2019. xi, 355 pages : Color; Illustration

ISBN 9781501137303

Grades: Adult   747

1. Interior decoration 2. House and Home — General 3. House and Home — Interior Decorating and Furnishings

LC Bl2019008480

Organized by room, this decorating guide offers advice, inspiration, and ideas for designing a home with children, pets, and all the messes of life, but still reflects the owner's personality and style.

Gill, Shira
Organized Living: Solutions and Inspiration for Your Home. Shira Gill; photography by Vivian Johnson. Ten Speed Press 2023. 280 pages : Color; Illustration

ISBN 9781984861184

Grades: Adult   747

1. Interior decoration 2. Interior decorators 3. Orderliness 4. House and Home — Cleaning, caretaking, and organizing 5. Self-Help — Personal growth — Motivation

LC 2022055487

A globally recognized home organizing expert and author of Minimalista showcases the homes of 25 international home organizers, introducing you to the aspirational spaces of the most organized people in the world and the passion that fuels their work, providing you with visual inspiration, expert tips and resources and clever organizing hacks.

"A fresh take on home organization that will likely serve as catnip for readers wanting peeks of the experts' homes and instructions on how to achieve it themselves." —*Library Journal*

Grove, Kirsten
Simply Styling: Fresh & Easy Ways to Personalize Your Home. Kirsten Grove of Simply Grove. Sterling 2016. xxii, 199 pages : Color; Illustration

ISBN 9781454918226

Grades: Adult   747

1. Interior decoration 2. Arts and Entertainment — General 3. House and Home — DIY, maintenance, and repair

LC Bl2016042188

Presents interior decorating advice on how to personalize a home, offering instructions for styling such items as a couch, coffee table, and bathtub, and such areas as the walls, foyer, and bedroom.

The stylist, editor and creator of the hugely popular blog Simply Grove helps readers get the stylish and comfortable home they¡ve longed for by guiding them every step of the way, going room by room and item by item, and providing them with easy-to-implement tips that they will find invaluable.

"With her blog, Simply Grove, self-taught interior stylist Grove's ideas have become quite influential, which has led to her contributing to numerous interior design publications and websites. Here, Grove explains how to achieve this popular look that she espouses of neutral-colored interiors bathed in light." —*Library Journal*

Includes index.

ESSENTIAL AND RECOMMENDED TITLES
747 Interior decoration

Gura, Judith
*The **Guide** to Period Styles for Interiors: From the 17th Century to the Present*. Judith Gura. Bloomsbury, Fairchild Books, an imprint of Bloomsbury Publishing Inc. 2016. xvi, 479 p.
ISBN 9781628924718
Grades: Adult   747
1. Interior decoration 2. Arts and Entertainment — Architecture
LC 2015005290

"This updated pictorial guide to interior design features fully revised sections and a new chapter on twenty-first-century styles. There are 350 photographs, a bibliography, a glossary, and a chronology. Every era is covered in a brief narrative, along with photos of prime examples (mostly individual furniture pieces) of the style." —*Booklist*
Includes bibliographical references and index.

Guralnick, Margot
Remodelista: The Low-Impact Home : A Sourcebook for Stylish, Eco-Conscious Living. Margot Guralnick & Fan Winston; with the editors of Remodelista; principal photography by Matthew Williams. Artisan 2022. 350 pages : Color; Illustration
ISBN 9781648290145
Grades: Adult   747
1. Interior decoration 2. Sustainable living 3. House and Home — Sustainable living
LC 2022010980

The experts behind Remodelista.com, in this highly visual guide, reveal a personalized, future-minded approach to creating a sustainable—and stylish—home by emphasizing conscientious consumerism and climate-aware choices.

"This lovely, practical collection will be just right for green-minded designers." —*Publishers Weekly*
Includes index.

Hays, Jeanine
Remix: Decorating with Culture, Objects, and Soul. Jeanine Hays and Bryan Mason; photographs by Patrick Cline, foreword by Danielle Colding. Clarkson Potter/Publishers 2013. 256 p.: Color; Illustration
ISBN 9780770433024
Grades: Adult   747
1. Interior decoration 2. African Americans 3. United States 4. House and Home — Interior Decorating and Furnishings
LC 2012038317

Profiling homes throughout Brooklyn, Manhattan, Philadelphia, Los Angeles and Washington, D.C, this excellent design resource, influenced by African-American culture, showcases authentically designed homes that celebrate diversity in design.

Includes index; Chapters include: Aphro-who? — Elements. The culture of color — Telling your story through pattern — Original art — Going global at home — Modern soulful homes. Maiysha Simpson: Brooklyn lullaby — Angela and Leon Belt: Artists in residence — Tara Bethea and BOA: a soulful abode — Malene Barnett: Island in the city — Jeanine Hays and Bryan Mason: Our homecoming.

Khemsurov, Monica
How to Live with Objects: A Modern Guide to More Meaningful Interiors. Monica Khemsurov & Jill Singer; photographs by Charlie Schuck. Clarkson Potter/Publisher 2022. 318 pages : Illustration; Color
ISBN 9780593235041
Grades: Adult   747
1. Interior decoration 2. House and Home — Interior decorating and furnishings
LC 2022003132

A stylish guide to artful objects, both new and vintage, and how to use them to design a remarkable home, from the founders of the trendsetting magazine Sight Unseen. With a collection of anecdotes, tours of remarkable homes, and modern and meaningful design advice, Monica Khemsurov and Jill Singer take you on a fun, educational, and highly visual journey through two questions at the core of their design philosophy: What are objects, and how do we live with them?

"Creative and fun, this will be invaluable to readers looking to foster a more meaningful connection with the objects they bring home." —*Publishers Weekly*
Includes index.

Lamb, Kelli
Home with Rue: Style for Everyone. Kelli Lamb; foreword by Nate Berkus. Ten Speed Press 2022. IX, 261 pages : Color; Illustration
ISBN 9781984860682
Grades: Adult   747
1. Interior decoration 2. House and Home — Interior decorating and furnishings
LC 2021039909

The editorial director of a bi-monthly digital home design magazine showcases images of real homes to explore a variety of complementary aesthetics along with expert insights and tips and tricks to help readers design the rooms of their dreams.

"Design aficionados looking to shake up their decor need look no further." —*Publishers Weekly*

Linsley, Leslie
Salvage Style: Decorate with Vintage Finds. Leslie Linsley. Hearst Books 2017. 160 pages : Color; Illustration
ISBN 9781588169280
Grades: Adult   747
1. Home furnishings 2. Interior decoration 3. House and Home — Interior Decorating and Furnishings
LC 2017287731

Decorate with repurposed, refurbished, and vintage items to stunning effect. Try wire cubbies for pretty bathroom storage; a tree trunk as a rustic nightstand; a bedspring as an inventive memo board; a breadbox to hold silverware and so much more!

"Crafts and design author Linsley (Nantucket: Island Living) turns her attention to using junkyard finds in home decor." —*Library Journal*
Includes index.

Merhi, Farah
★ *Inspire Your Home: Easy, Affordable Ideas to Make Every Room Glamorous*. Farah Merhi. Tiller Press 2019. 289 p.: Color; Illustration
ISBN 9781982131241
Grades: Adult   747
1. Interior decoration 2. House and Home — Interior Decorating and Furnishings
LC Bl2019032425

The Instagram star and founder of Inspire Me! Home Decor offers strategic interior design secrets for creating glamorous but cozy living spaces on a budget, sharing related advice for home cleaning, organizing and customizing.

Moss, Charlotte
Garden Inspirations. Charlotte Moss. Rizzoli 2015. 287 pages : Illustration; Color
ISBN 9780847844777
Grades: Adult   747
1. Gardens 2. Interior decoration 3. Arts and Entertainment — Crafts and hobbies — Garden and nature
LC Bl2016015787

Shares ideas for bringing the garden into the home, including decorating with flower arrangements and setting up garden seating, and showcases a selection of notable gardens.
Includes bibliographical references (pages 282-284).

Napier, Erin
Heirloom Rooms: Soulful Stories of Home. Erin Napier. Gallery Books 2023. 320 pages : Color; Illustration

PUBLIC LIBRARY CORE COLLECTION: NONFICTION
Twentieth Edition

ISBN 9781982190439
Grades: Adult   747
1. Interior decoration 2. Home furnishings 3. Houses 4. Home (Concept) 5. Essays 6. Visual nonfiction 7. House and Home — General
LC Bl2023112704

In this visual celebration of the homes we live in and love, the host of HGTV's Home Town shares a collection of personal essays as she walks us through every room in her home, telling the story of a family's life and encourage us to document our own homemade memories.

"Fans of Home Town will relish this insightful look at the cohosts' dream home and memories. This title will also likely appeal to readers who enjoy interior design and personalizing their own living spaces to create a homey feel."
—*Library Journal*

Needleman, Deborah

*The **Perfectly** Imperfect Home: How to Decorate & Live Well.* Deborah Needleman. Clarkson Potter/Publishers 2011. 255 p. : Illustration; Color
ISBN 9780307720139
Grades: Adult   747
1. Interior decoration 2. House and Home — Interior Decorating and Furnishings
LC 2011020194

Describes eighty items that are what the author identifies as all one needs to live comfortably, practically, and stylishly, from essential furnishings to aesthetic accents.

The editor-in-chief of the late cult magazine domino presents a follow-up to the best-selling domino: the book of decorating that describes 80 items that are what the author identifies as all one needs to live comfortably, practically and stylishly, from essential furnishings to aesthetic accents.

Includes index.

Spencer, Lara

Flea Market Fabulous: Designing Gorgeous Rooms with Vintage Treasures. Lara Spencer with Amy Feezor; foreword by Jonathan Adler; photographys by ChiChi Ubiña. Stewart, Tabori & Chang 2014. 182 pages : Color; Illustration
ISBN 9781617690952
Grades: Adult   747
1. Flea markets 2. Interior decoration 3. House and Home — General 4. House and Home — Interior Decorating and Furnishings
LC Bl2014036775

Presents information on how to find flea market treasures and incorporate them into home interiors, with tips on making a decorating plan, overcoming the limitations of each room, and the best ways to restore and reinvent flea market items.

The host of the HGTV show Flea Market Flip tackles nine common design dilemmas in nine different homes and solves them by finding and restoring flea-market finds to show that readers can achieve a gorgeous space at bargain prices.

Tanov, Erica

Design by Nature: Creating Layered, Lived-In Spaces Inspired by the Natural World. Erica Tanov; photographs by Ngoc Minh Ngo. Ten Speed Press 2018. 229 pages
ISBN 9780399579073
Grades: Adult   747
1. Interior decoration 2. House and Home — Interior Decorating and Furnishings 3. Arts and Entertainment — Fashion
LC 2017036480

The first design book that translates elements of nature—flora, water, and wood—into elements of decor for beautiful, lived-in, bohemian interiors, from acclaimed designer and tastemaker Erica Tanov.

Includes bibliographical references (pages 226-227) and index.

Taylor, Claude

How to Zoom Your Room: Room Rater's Ultimate Style Guide. Claude Taylor & Jessie Bahrey; illustrations by Chris Morris. Voracious/Little, Brown and Company 2022. IX, 245 pages : Color; Illustration
ISBN 9780316428125
Grades: Adult   747
1. Interior decoration 2. Internet 3. Meetings 4. Videoconferencing 5. Internet videos 6. House and home — Interior decorating and furnishings 7. Science Writing — Computing, the Internet, and Technology
LC Bl2022017430

The ultimate users' guide to curating your Zoom background from Room Raters, Twitter's foremost experts in on-screen décor."

"Loosely organized and branching out from the various rooms readers may want to stage (attic, kitchen, den), this is the easiest way yet to absorb design advice." —*Booklist*

747.7 Decoration of specific rooms of residential buildings

Gold, Jamie

Taunton's New Bathroom Idea Book. Jamie Gold. The Taunton Press, Inc. 2017. 217 pages
ISBN 9781631864056
Grades: Adult   747.7
1. Bathrooms 2. Interior decoration 3. House and Home — Remodeling and renovation 4. House and Home — Interior Decorating and Furnishings
LC 2016056526

Shares design ideas for different types of bathrooms, including half-baths, standard his-and-hers bathrooms, and luxury home spas.

Lee, Vinny

Kitchenalia: Furnishing and Equipping Your Kitchen with Flea Market Finds and Period Pieces. Vinny Lee. Jacqui Small 2014. 224 pages : Color; Illustration
ISBN 9781909342491
Grades: Adult   747.7
1. Interior decoration 2. Kitchens 3. Furniture 4. Design 5. Arts and Entertainment — Antiques and collectibles
LC Bl2015009104

Shows how to use vintage finds and accessories to furnish the kitchen, describing the themes that characterize seven distinct design styles as well as how to enhance each by focusing on furniture, surfaces, and other elements of the room.

"The variety of styles makes this book an inspiring choice for those looking for ideas on decorating kitchens." —*Library Journal*

Includes index.

747.98 Decorating with houseplants

Carter, Hilton

Wild Interiors: Beautiful Plants in Beautiful Spaces. Hilton Carter. CICO Books 2020. 224 p. : Illustration
ISBN 9781782498759
Grades: Adult   747.98
1. Interior decoration 2. House plants 3. House and Home — Interior decorating and furnishings

… Hilton Carter takes you on a magical plant journey that highlights 12 unique, green-filled, interiors. Full of plant care advice, including a room by room guide profiling the plants that are best suited to each one, Hilton brings his unique eye and love of plants to inspire you to create your own Wild Interiors.

ESSENTIAL AND RECOMMENDED TITLES
748.5 Stained, painted, leaded, mosaic glass

748.5 Stained, painted, leaded, mosaic glass

Rich, Chris
Stained Glass Basics: Techniques & Projects. by Chris Rich with Martha Mitchell and Rachel Ward. Sterling Pub. 1996. 144 p. : Illustration; Color
ISBN 9780806948768
Grades: Adult   748.5
1. Glass craft 2. Glass painting 3. Arts and Entertainment — Crafts and hobbies
LC 95054102

Introduces tools, materials, and techniques for working with stained glass, offers tips on safety, and suggests projects.

"This book presents the fundamental techniques of working with stained glass and is intended for those getting started in the craft. Excellent color photographs and diagrams show materials and tools, as well as the cutting, assembling, and soldering of glass items. The projects include hanging glass panels, boxes, and lamps." —*Library Journal*

A Sterling/Lark book; Includes index.

748.50282 Glass painting and staining

Stevenson, Christine Kellmann
Creative Stained Glass: Modern Designs & Simple Techniques. Christine Kellman Stevenson. Lark 2007. 128 p. : Illustration; Color
ISBN 9781600591327
Grades: Adult   748.50282
1. Arts and Entertainment — Crafts and hobbies
LC Oc2007073614

From in-a-weekend pieces to intricate designs that take more time, these 27 stained-glass projects shine with light, color, and texture, thanks to the great new glasses on the market today. More than 70 color photos present the techniques, all worked with easy-to-acquire, modern, and efficient tools.

Includes index; Originally published: 2004.

749 Furniture and accessories

Aronson, Joseph
The Encyclopedia of Furniture. Joseph Aronson. Crown Publishers 1965. IX, 484 p. Illustration
ISBN 9780517037355
Grades: Adult   749
1. Furniture 2. Furniture industry and trade 3. Furniture makers 4. Design 5. Encyclopedias 6. Reference books 7. Arts and Entertainment — Antiques and collectibles
LC 65024334

An illustrated up-to-date reference work which describes every period and development in furniture styling and construction.

Bibliography: P. [476]-479.

Kistler, Vivian Carli
The Complete Photo Guide to Framing and Displaying Artwork: 500 Full-Color How-To Photos. Vivian Carli Kistler. Creative Pub. International 2009. 192 p. : Illustration (Complete Photo Guide)
ISBN 9781589234222
Grades: Adult   749
1. Picture frames and framing 2. Arts and Entertainment — Crafts and hobbies
LC 2008046612

"In this guide, the author teaches the do-it-yourselfer to frame like a pro. Hundreds of photos illustrate conservation matting, working with premade elements or frame-building from scratch, glazing, and hanging." —*Library Journal*

Includes index.

Logan, M. David
Mat, Mount, and Frame It Yourself. M. David Logan. Watson-Guptill Publications 2002. 160 p. : Color illustration
ISBN 9780823030385
Grades: Adult   749
1. Picture frames and framing 2. Decorative arts 3. Arts and Entertainment — Crafts and hobbies
LC 2001093246

Explains how to use frames and mats to skillfully and economically present artwork.

"Logan does a great job of explaining everything and supplements the text with attractive photos. There is something here for framers of all skill levels." —*Library Journal*

Includes index.

Miller, Judith
Furniture. Judith Miller. DK Pub. 2005. 560 p. : Illustration; Color
ISBN 9780756613402
Grades: Adult   749
1. Furniture 2. Furniture industry and trade 3. Furniture makers 4. Design 5. Arts and Entertainment — Antiques and collectibles 6. Reference — Encyclopedias
LC Bl2006009577

A comprehensive reference spanning some three thousand years of design provides more than 3,500 full-color photographs and descriptions of furniture representing every style and form, along with an overview of decorative motifs from key periods, profiles of important designers and craftsmen, a study of important movements in furniture design, and more.

A comprehensive reference spanning some three thousand years of design provides more than 3,500 full-color photographs and descriptions of furniture representing every style and form, along with an overview of decorative motifs from key periods, profilesof important designers and craftsmen, and a study of important movements in furniture design.

Includes bibliographical references (p. 538-539) and index.

750.1 Painting — Philosophy and theory

Ward, Ossian
Look Again: How to Experience the Old Masters. Ossian Ward. Thames & Hudson 2019. 175 pages : Color; Illustration
ISBN 9780500239674
Grades: Adult   750.1
1. Painting 2. Visual perception 3. Arts and Entertainment — Painting, Drawing, and Sculpture 4. History writing — Arts and culture
LC Bl2019027947

"This book is a primer, preparing readers to stop reading and start looking." —*Booklist*

With over 100 illustrations; Includes bibliographical references (page 172) and index.

751.4 Painting — Techniques and procedures

Crilley, Mark
The Realism Challenge: Drawing and Painting Secrets from a Modern Master of Hyperrealism. Mark Crilley. Watson-Guptill Publications 2015. 152 pages : Color; Illustration
ISBN 9780385346290
Grades: Adult   751.4
1. Drawing technique 2. Painting technique 3. Arts and Entertainment — Painting, Drawing, and Sculpture
LC 2014024085

Discusses methods, tips, and techniques for creating realistic drawings and paintings with step-by-step process photos for over twenty works.

"Those with modest artistic skills can greatly improve their ability to draw and paint realistic objects by following the tips and tricks detailed here." —*Library Journal*

Includes index.

Jung, Kwan
Chinese Brush Painting: Step by Step. Kwan Jung. North Light Books 2003. 128 p. : Illustration; Color
ISBN 9781581802078
Grades: Adult   751.4
1. Painting technique 2. Watercolor painting 3. Painting 4. Arts and Entertainment — Painting, Drawing, and Sculpture

LC 2002071858

A guide to Chinese brush painting provides twelve projects that use a range of Chinese inks, brushes, and papers.

A stunning guide to Sumi-E, or Chinese brush painting, shows painters of all skill levels how to achieve the flowing, natural style of this uniqe art form by providing twelve easy-to-follow projects that use a range of Chinese inks, brushes, and papers.

Includes index.

Marine, Carol
Daily Painting: Paint Small and Often to Become a More Creative, Productive, and Successful Artist. Carol Marine. Watson-Guptill Publications 2014. x, 182 p. : Color; Illustration
ISBN 9780770435332
Grades: Adult   751.4
1. Painting technique 2. Arts and Entertainment — Painting, Drawing, and Sculpture 3. Self-Help — Personal growth — Creativity

LC BL2014050373

A blogger, teacher and painter describes how the practice of painting small projects daily can help artists at all levels grow, improve their technique and skill level and keep the creative ideas flowing.

Includes index.

Self, Caroline
Chinese Brush Painting: A Hands-on Introduction to the Traditional Art. by Caroline Self and Susan Self. Tuttle Pub. 2007. 64 p. : Illustration; Color
ISBN 9780804838771
Grades: 9 10 11 12 Adult   751.4
1. Painting technique 2. Art 3. Painting 4. Art and music — Arts and crafts — Drawing and painting 5. Culture and customs — Asia and the South Pacific — China 6. How-to books

LC 2006037838

Introduces the art of Chinese brush painting, discussing the principles of painting; materials; holding the brush; and how to paint calligraphy characters, an orchid, and landscapes.

"This introduces readers to the art of Chinese calligraphy and brush painting. The text is fluid and graceful . . . and the authors wrap succinct accounts of Chinese history and lore around their clear, step-by-step, illustrated instructions." —*Booklist*

Includes bibliographical references (p. 64).

751.42 Use of water-soluble mediums

Kersey, Geoff
Painting Successful Watercolours from Photographs. Geoff Kersey. Search Press 2015. 128 pages : Illustration; Color
ISBN 9781844489985
Grades: Adult   751.42
1. Landscape painting 2. Painting technique 3. Watercolor painting 4. Painting 5. Arts and Entertainment — Painting, Drawing, and Sculpture

LC Bl2014050761

A master watercolorist counsels developing artists on how to adapt and improve photographic source material to create successful paintings, displaying reference images, color charts and preparatory sketches beside finished works. Includes illustrated glossary.

Explores the author's artistic process for interpreting photographs to produce watercolors by detailing how twenty-seven of his own paintings evolved from photographs, with diagrams, color charts, and explanations of relevant painting techniques.

"This guide has solid crossover potential among avid travelers, hobbyist watercolor painters, and amateur photographers." —*Library Journal*

Includes index.

Kloosterboer, Lorena
Painting in Acrylics: The Indispensable Guide. Lorena Kloosterboer. Firefly Books 2014. 320 pages : Color; Illustration
ISBN 9781770854086
Grades: Adult   751.42
1. Acrylic painting 2. Painting technique 3. Arts and Entertainment — Painting, Drawing, and Sculpture

LC Bl2014055914

Provides an introduction to acrylic painting, with information on different paints, brushes, tools, surfaces, color theories, and painting techniques and advice on competitions and exhibits.

Includes index.

O'Connor, Birgit
Watercolor Essentials: Hands-on Techniques for Exploring Watercolor in Motion. Birgit O'Connor. North Light Books 2009. 127 p. : Color illustration
ISBN 9781600610943
Grades: Adult   751.42
1. Watercolor painting 2. Painting technique 3. Arts and Entertainment — Painting, Drawing, and Sculpture

LC 2008036576

"This is an exciting, comprehensive package for the beginning watercolor artist. O'Connor . keys her lessons to a 70-minute DVD. Her wet and loose technique and the personal touch of the DVD make this a great choice at a good price." —*Library Journal*

Includes index.

Robinson, Mario Andres
Lessons in Realistic Watercolor: A Contemporary Approach to Painting People and Places in the Classical Tradition. Mario Andres Robinson. Monacelli Studio 2016. 176 pages : Illustration; Color
ISBN 9781580934459
Grades: Adult   751.42
1. Realism in art 2. Watercolor painting 3. Painting technique 4. Arts and Entertainment — Painting, Drawing, and Sculpture

LC 2015038871

"Artists of intermediate skill level are best poised to benefit from these lessons." —*Library Journal*

Includes index.

Zickefoose, Julie
Baby Birds: An Artist Looks into the Nest. Julie Zickefoose. Houghton Mifflin Harcourt 2016. xxi, 333 pages : Illustration; Color
ISBN 9780544206700
Grades: Adult   751.42
1. Birds in art 2. Arts and Entertainment — Painting, Drawing, and Sculpture 3. Nature writing — Animal Studies — Birds and Birding

LC Bl2016011031

An artist and a wildlife rehabilitator presents a visually stunning book, combining art and natural history, that is filled with more than 400 watercolor paintings that capture the breathtakingly swift development of 17 different species of wild birds.

Collects over four hundred watercolor paintings depicting the rapid development of seventeen bird species that live at the author's wildlife sanctuary.

Includes bibliographical references (pages 326-327) and index.

ESSENTIAL AND RECOMMENDED TITLES
751.45 Oil painting

751.45 Oil painting

Griffel, Lois
Painting the Impressionist Landscape: Lessons in Interpreting Light and Color. Lois Griffel. Watson-Guptill Publications 2008. 144 p. : Color illustration
ISBN 9780823095193
Grades: Adult   751.45
1. Hawthorne, Charles Webster, 1872-1930 2. Color in art 3. Impressionism (Art) 4. Landscape painting 5. Painting technique 6. Art 7. Arts and Entertainment — Painting, Drawing, and Sculpture
LC BI2011004762
Offers a study of Hawthorne's theories about the use of color and light in impressionism, features examples with classic and local reproductions, and provides exercises for creating simple pieces using the theories.
Includes index; Reprint. Originally published: 1994.

751.7 Specific forms

Felisbret, Eric
Graffiti New York. Eric Felisbret DEAL CIA; contributions by Luke Felisbret SPAR ONE; foreword by James Prigoff. Abrams 2009. 339 p. : Illustration; Color
ISBN 9780810951464
Grades: 9 10 11 12 Adult   751.7
1. Street art 2. Graffiti 3. Popular culture 4. Visual nonfiction 5. Society and culture — Pop culture 6. Arts and Entertainment — Painting, Drawing, and Sculpture 7. Adult books for young adults 8. Books for reluctant readers
LC 2009011736
YALSA Quick Picks for Reluctant Young Adult Readers, 2011.
Presents the history of graffiti art in New York City, detailing the concepts, aesthetics, ideals, and social structures that have served as a cultural blueprint for graffiti movements across the world.

Ganz, Nicholas
★ *Graffiti World: Street Art from Five Continents.* Nicholas Ganz; edited by Tristan Manco. Abrams 2009. 391 p. (some folded) : Color illustration
ISBN 9780810980495
Grades: 11 12 Adult   751.7
1. Street art 2. Graffiti 3. Murals 4. Public art 5. Radical art 6. Mural painting and decoration 7. Art appreciation 8. 20th century 9. Art and music — Visual arts 10. Adult books for young adults 11. Books for reluctant readers
LC 2004004248
YALSA Quick Picks for Reluctant Young Adult Readers, 2006.
A history of graffiti art traces its evolution from the late 1960s to today, citing its reflection of hip-hop culture as well as its symbolism of youth art.
"Ganz's survey of graffiti art includes upward of 2,000 full-color photographs.... An ephemeral, often despised, yet irrefutably powerful mode of expression, graffiti has always been political, and although many of the street artists Ganz succinctly profiles have moved away from illegal spray painting, they have not compromised the inherent subversiveness of their work.... Ganz's global array captures the power and synergy of this vibrant alternative art world in which artists form crews and collectiveness to ensure that their art is seen."
—*Booklist*
Includes 8 folded pages; Includes bibliographical references (p. 390).

752 Color

Edwards, Betty
Color: A Course in Mastering the Art of Mixing Colors. Betty Edwards. Jeremy P. Tarcher/Penguin 2004. xvii, 206 p. : Illustration; Color
ISBN 9781585421992
Grades: Adult   752
1. Color in art 2. Arts and Entertainment — Painting, Drawing, and Sculpture
LC 2003067215

The author of The New Drawing on the Right Side of the Brain distills the complex principles of color theory into a practical, easy-to-follow method of working with color to produce harmonious and pleasing combinations, explaining how to see and use color and how to mix and combine hues.
Includes bibliographical references (p. 197-198) and index.

759.13 Painting — United States

Cohen-Solal, Annie
Mark Rothko: Toward the Light in the Chapel. Annie Cohen-Solal. Yale University Press 2015. 224 p.
ISBN 9780300182040
Grades: Adult   759.13
1. Rothko, Mark, 1903-1970 2. Painters 3. Jewish men 4. Immigrants 5. Art 6. Artists 7. Spirituality 8. United States 9. Biographies 10. Translations — French to English 11. Life stories — Arts and culture — Artists 12. Arts and Entertainment — Painting, Drawing, and Sculpture
LC 2014037767
Mark Rothko was not only one of the most influential American painters of the twentieth century; he was a scholar, an educator, and a deeply spiritual human being. Born Marcus Yakovlevich Rotkovitch, he emigrated from the Russian Empire to the United States at age ten, already well educated in the Talmud and carrying with him bitter memories of the pogroms and persecutions visited upon the Jews of Latvia. Few artists have achieved success as quickly, and by the mid-twentieth century, Rothko's artwork was being displayed in major museums throughout the world. In May 2012 his painting Orange, Red, Yellow was auctioned for nearly $87 million, setting a new Christie's record. Author Annie Cohen-Solal gained access to archival materials no previous biographer had seen. As a result, her book is an extraordinarily detailed portrait of Rothko the man and the artist, an uncommonly successful painter who was never comfortable with the idea of his art as a commodity.
"A defining and affecting tribute to a modern master." —*Booklist*
First published in French as Mark Rothko by Actes Sud (Arles, France, 2013); Includes bibliographical references and index.

Cross, William R.
Winslow Homer: American Passage. William R. Cross. Farrar, Straus and Giroux 2022. 320 p.
ISBN 9780374603793
Grades: Adult   759.13
1. Homer, Winslow, 1836-1910 2. Artists 3. Painters 4. Illustrators 5. Art 6. Social life and customs 7. United States 8. 19th century 9. Biographies 10. Life stories — Arts and culture — Artists 11. Arts and Entertainment — Painting, Drawing, and Sculpture
LC 2021057038
A deeply insightful scholar chronicles the life of the great painter and illustrator, revealing the man behind the images he created that depicted a rapidly changing America with an artist's eye and captured pivotal monuments of American culture.
"Drawing on abundant scholarship and archival sources, Cross chronicles in vibrant detail the career, travels, friendships, and prolific output of Winslow Homer (1836-1910)." —*Kirkus*
Includes bibliographical references and index.

Gerdts, William H.
American Impressionism. William H. Gerdts. Abbeville Press 2001. 368 p. : Illustration; Color
ISBN 9780789207371
Grades: Adult   759.13
1. Impressionism (Art) 2. Painting, American 3. United States 4. 19th century 5. Arts and Entertainment — Painting, Drawing, and Sculpture
LC 2001022419
More than four hundred illustrations along with photographs of the artists and excerpts from their letters and journals illustrate a new expanded edition of

the definitive study of American Impressionism by the preeminent scholar in the field.

"The best general source available on American Impressionism. [The] book covers the major artists in the movement, including expatriates working in Europe and regional schools throughout the United States during the late 19th and early 20th centuries. .The well-chosen illustrations include many full-page color reproductions as well as photographs of many of the artists." —*Library Journal*

Includes bibliographical references (p. 348-363) and index.

Herdrich, Stephanie L
★ *Sargent: The Masterworks.* Stephanie L. Herdrich. Rizzoli Electa 2018. 221 pages : Illustration; Color
ISBN 9780847862399
Grades: Adult   759.13
1. Sargent, John Singer, 1856-1925 2. Painters 3. Painting 4. Biographies 5. Arts and Entertainment — Painting, Drawing, and Sculpture
LC Bl2018053091

"This visual feast of Sargent's most acclaimed creations is time well spent for art students and curious general readers." —*Library Journal*

Includes bibliographical references.

Kamensky, Jane
A Revolution in Color: The World of John Singleton Copley. Jane Kamensky. W.W. Norton & Company 2016. 352 p.
ISBN 9780393240016
Grades: Adult   759.13
1. Copley, John Singleton, 1738-1815 2. Painters 3. Artists 4. Loyalists (United States history) 5. Intellectual life 6. United States history 7. United States 8. Revolutionary America (1775-1783) 9. Biographies 10. Life stories — Arts and culture — Artists 11. History writing — Early America — United States
LC 2016019022

American History Book Prize, 2016; Massachusetts Book Awards, Nonfiction Award, 2017.

Looks at the American Revolution as seen through the eyes of Boston-born painter John Singleton Copley.

"There may never be a better biography of Copley than this sumptuous, exquisitely told story of a man and his time." —*Kirkus*

Includes bibliographical references and index.

Levin, Gail
Edward Hopper: The Art and the Artist. Gail Levin. Norton : 1980. xv, 299 p. : Illustration; Color
ISBN 9780393315776
Grades: Adult   759.13
1. Hopper, Edward, 1882-1967 2. Artists 3. Realism in art 4. Realism 5. United States 6. Biographies 7. Arts and Entertainment — Painting, Drawing, and Sculpture 8. Arts and Entertainment — Museums and Collections
LC 79027958

Covers all phases of the prominent realist's work and reveals aspects of Hopper's personality and life that help explain his artistic development.

Accompanies the exhibition organized by the Whitney Museum and sponsored by Philip Morris Incorporated and the National Endowment for the Arts; to be held at Hayward Gallery, London, Feb. 11-Mar. 29, 1981, and four other museums, Apr. 22, 1981-Feb. 10, 1982; Includes bibliographical references (p. [72]-[74]) and index.

Livingston, Jane
The Paintings of Joan Mitchell. Jane Livingston; with essays by Linda Nochelin, Yvette Lee, and Jane Livingston. Whitney Museum; 2002. 237 p. : Color illustration
ISBN 9780520235687
Grades: Adult   759.13
1. Mitchell, Joan, 1926-1992 2. Abstract expressionism 3. Arts and Entertainment — Painting, Drawing, and Sculpture 4. Arts and Entertainment — Museums and Collections
LC 2001058514

Library Journal Best Books, 2002.

"This is a vivid portrait of the artist. Mitchell's compositions {are gorgeously reproduced here in vibrant color." —*Booklist*

Catalog of an exhibition held at the Whitney Museum of American Art, New York, June-Oct. 2002; Includes bibliographical references (p. 217-219) and index.

Lynes, Barbara Buhler
Georgia O'Keeffe Museum Collections. Barbara Buhler Lynes. Abrams 2007. 352 p. : Illustration; Color
ISBN 9780810909571
Grades: Adult   759.13
1. O'Keeffe, Georgia, 1887-1986 2. Art 3. Arts and Entertainment — Painting, Drawing, and Sculpture 4. Arts and Entertainment — Museums and Collections
LC 2006019894

Provides a comprehensive view of O'Keeffe's paintings, drawings, and sculptures, and documents the growth of the collection at the Georgia O'Keeffe Museum from its inception to its ten-year anniversary.

In association with Georgia O'Keeffe Museum; Includes bibliographical references (p. 348-349) and index.

Rothko, Mark
Rothko: The Color Field Paintings. Foreword by Christopher Rothko; essay by Janet Bishop; picture editor, Jenny Moussa Spring. Chronicle Books 2017. 120 p. : Color; Illustration
ISBN 9781452156606
Grades: Adult   759.13
1. Rothko, Mark, 1903-1970 2. History writing — Arts and culture 3. Arts and Entertainment — Painting, Drawing, and Sculpture
LC Oc2018144648

This collection presents fifty large-scale artworks from the American master's color field period (1949-1970) alongside essays by Rothko's son, Christopher Rothko, and San Francisco Museum of Modern Art curator of painting and sculpture Janet Bishop.

Includes bibliographical references.

Sewell, Darrel
Thomas Eakins. Organized by Darrel Sewell with essays by Kathleen A. Foster ... [et al.]; chronology by Kathleen Brown. Philadelphia Museum of Art 2001. xli, 446 p. : Illustration; Color
ISBN 9780300091113
Grades: Adult   759.13
1. Eakins, Thomas, 1844-1916 2. Arts and Entertainment — Painting, Drawing, and Sculpture
LC 2001053142

"This is clearly the definitive monograph on one of the most significant artists America has produced." —*Library Journal*

Exhibition held at Philadelphia Museum of Art, Oct. 4, 2001 to Jan. 6, 2002, Musee d'Orsay, Paris, Feb. 5 to May 12, 2002, the Metropolitan Museum of Art, New York, June 18 to Sept. 15, 2002; Includes bibliographical references and index.

759.4 French painting

Cogeval, Guy
Edouard Vuillard. Guy Cogeval with Kimberly Jones, Laurence des Cars, MaryAnne Stevens; contributions by Dario Gamboni, Elizabeth Easton, Mathias Chivot. National Gallery of Art 2003. xviii, 501 p. : Illustration; Color
ISBN 9780300097375
Grades: Adult   759.4
1. Vuillard, Edouard, 1868-1940 2. Arts and Entertainment — Museums and Collections
LC 2002151120

ESSENTIAL AND RECOMMENDED TITLES
759.5 Italian painting

"This authoritative study on an artist whose career spanned two centuries is recommended for all libraries that collect art books." —*Library Journal*

National Gallery of Art, Washington, 19 January-20 April 2003, Montreal Museum of Fine Arts, 15 May-24 August 2003, Galeries nationales du Grand Palais, Paris, 23 September 2003-4 January 2004, Royal Academy of Arts, London, 27 January-27 April 2004; Includes bibliographical references and index.

Kelder, Diane
The Great Book of French Impressionism. Diane Kelder. Abbeville Press 2001. 400 p. : Illustration; Color
ISBN 9780789206886
Grades: Adult   **759.4**
1. Painting, French 2. Impressionism (Art) 3. France 4. Arts and Entertainment — Painting, Drawing, and Sculpture

LC 2001266313

Traces the development of impressionism and draws on anecdotes and excerpts from contemporary essays and letters to explore the lives of the major Impressionists.

Includes bibliographical references (p. 394-395) and index.

King, Ross
The Judgment of Paris: The Revolutionary Decade That Gave the World Impressionism. Ross King. Walker & Co. 2006. xiii, 448 p, 8 p. of plates : Illustration; Color
ISBN 9780802714664
Grades: Adult   **759.4**
1. Manet, Edouard, 1832-1883 2. Meissonier, Jean Louis Ernest, 1815-1891 3. Painters 4. Visual art and society 5. Painting, French 6. Impressionism (Art) 7. Paris, France history 8. France 9. 19th century 10. Arts and Entertainment — Painting, Drawing, and Sculpture

LC 2005031089

Governor General's Literary Award for English-Language Nonfiction, 2006; ALA Notable Book, 2007.

Discusses the development of Impressionism in Paris during the 19th century.

"The book serves as an entertaining if broad account of a revolutionary transformation in visionnot least of all through art." —*Library Journal*

Includes bibliographical references (p. [423]-435) and index.

★ *Mad Enchantment: Claude Monet and the Painting of the Water Lilies.* Ross King. Bloomsbury USA 2016. 384 p.
ISBN 9781632860125
Grades: Adult   **759.4**
1. Monet, Claude, 1840-1926 2. Painters 3. Impressionism (Art) 4. Artists 5. Painting, French 6. Art history 7. Friendship 8. 1910s 9. Biographies 10. Arts and Entertainment — Painting, Drawing, and Sculpture 11. Life stories — Arts and culture — Artists

LC 2015049404

Booklist Editors' Choice, 2016; Charles Taylor Prize for Literary Non-Fiction (Canada), 2017; Hilary Weston Writers' Trust Prize for Nonfiction finalist, 2016.

Examines the life of the artist Claude Monet with a focus on the paintings of the water lilies in his garden at Giverny.

"Never before has the full drama and significance of Monets magnificent Water Lilies been conveyed with such knowledge and perception, empathy and wonder." —*Booklist*

Includes bibliographical references.

Shackelford, George T. M.
Monet: The Early Years. George T.M. Shackelford; with essays by Anthea Callen, Mary Dailey Desmarais, Richard Shiff, Richard Thomson. Kimbell Art Museum 2016. 206 pages : Illustration; Color
ISBN 9780300221855
Grades: Adult   **759.4**
1. Monet, Claude, 1840-1926 2. Exhibition catalogs 3. History writing — Arts and culture 4. Arts and Entertainment — Painting, Drawing, and Sculpture 5. Arts and Entertainment — Museums and Collections

LC 2016951792

This elegant volume is the first to be devoted to the young genius of Claude Monet (1840-1926). Bringing together the greatest paintings from his early career it features essays by distinguished scholars, focusing on the evolution of Monet's own distinctive mode of painting. Through the 1860s, the young painter absorbed and transformed a variety of influences, from the lessons of the Barbizon school and his mentor Boudin to the challenges posed by his friends Manet, Pissarro, Renoir, and Sisley. Artistic innovation and personal ambition shaped the work of the celebrated impressionist painter from the very start of his long and illustrious career.

"It offers a fresh, coherent reassessment of Monet's early career (185872) before he participated in impressionistic exhibitions." —*Choice*

Catalog of the exhibition at Kimbell Art Museum, Fort Worth, October 16, 2016 - January 29, 2017; Fine Arts Museums of San Francisco, February 25 - May 29, 2017; Errata sheet tipped in; Includes bibliographical references (pages 198-201).

Unger, Miles
Picasso and the Painting That Shocked the World. Miles J. Unger. Simon & Schuster 2018. 336 p.
ISBN 9781476794211
Grades: Adult   **759.4**
1. Picasso, Pablo, 1881-1973 2. Artists 3. Painters 4. Modern art 5. Creation (Literary, artistic, etc.) 6. Cubism 7. Painting 8. Biographies 9. Life stories — Arts and culture — Artists 10. Arts and Entertainment — Painting, Drawing, and Sculpture

LC 2017022812

Traces the story of Picasso's rise from an obscure young painter in Barcelona to one of the most influential artists of the 20th century, documenting the events of his first visit to Paris, his emergence as a leader of a group of bohemian artists, his gradual recognition by collectors and the 1906 creation of the disturbing masterpiece, Les Demoiselles d'Avignon.

"This engrossing book chronicles with precision and enthusiasm a painting with lasting impact in todays art world." —*Publishers Weekly*

Includes bibliographical references and index.

759.5 Italian painting

Brewer, John
The American Leonardo: A Tale of Obsession, Art and Money. John Brewer. Oxford University Press 2009. IX, 310 p, 8 p. of plates : Illustration
ISBN 9780195396904
Grades: Adult   **759.5**
1. Leonardo, da Vinci, 1452-1519 2. Hahn, Harry (Harry J.), b. 1897 3. Painting, Renaissance (Europe) 4. Art forgeries 5. United States history 6. 20th century 7. Arts and Entertainment — Painting, Drawing, and Sculpture 8. Nonfiction that reads like fiction

LC 2009008681

Charts the history of 20th century obsession with art, taste and money.

"In 1919, a Midwestern auto salesman named Harry Hahn and his French war bride got in touch with Joseph Duveen, the famous New York art dealer, with an offer to sell what they claimed was an original painting by Leonardo da Vinci. Duveen publicly dismissed the work as a fake, and the Hahns, taking him to court for slander, began a decades-long struggle for authentication that scrutinized not only the art world's elitism but the validity of connoisseurship itself. Brewer skillfully outlines the conditions that made America ripe for such an incident and explores how Old Master art became the currency with which the country's new millionaires established their cultural credibility." —*The New Yorker*

Includes bibliographical references and index.

King, Ross
Florence: The Paintings & Frescoes, 1250-1743. Introductions and essays by Ross King; painting descriptions by Anja Grebe. Black Dog & Leventhal 2015. x, 697 pages : Color; Illustration
ISBN 9781631910012

Grades: Adult   759.5
1. Painting, Italian 2. Art history 3. Art, European 4. Painting, Renaissance (Europe) 5. Florence, Italy 6. Arts and Entertainment — Painting, Drawing, and Sculpture

LC 2015026785

A comprehensive book on the paintings and frescoes of Florence, with more than 2,000 artworks from the city's great museums and churches.

"Written in an easy-to-read style, this surprisingly affordable tome, given its size and lavish illustrations, will interest general readers through art historians." —*Library Journal*

Includes bibliographical references.

★ *Leonardo and the Last Supper.* Ross King. Walker & Company 2012. 352 p.
ISBN 9780802717054
Grades: Adult   759.5
1. Leonardo, da Vinci, 1452-1519 2. Mural painting and decoration, Italian 3. Painting, Italian 4. Artists 5. Art and society 6. Art 7. 15th century 8. Canadian literature 9. Arts and Entertainment — Painting, Drawing, and Sculpture 10. Book club best bets

LC 2012005358

Governor General's Literary Award for English-Language Nonfiction, 2012; Booklist Editors' Choice 2012; ALA Notable Book, 2013; Shortlisted for the Charles Taylor Prize for Literary Non-Fiction.

Chronicles how Leonardo da Vinci created the mural painting, the Last Supper.

Michelangelo & The Pope's Ceiling. Ross King. Walker & Company 2003. 373 p, 8 p. of plates : Illustration; Color
ISBN 9780802713957
Grades: 11 12 Adult   759.5
1. Michelangelo Buonarroti, 1475-1564 2. Julius II, Pope, 1443-1513 3. Artists 4. Mural painting and decoration, Italian 5. Frescoes 6. Artistic rivalry 7. Mural painting and decoration, Renaissance (Europe) 8. Italian history 9. Vatican City 10. Italy 11. 16th century 12. Renaissance (1300-1600) 13. Age of exploration (1419-1610) 14. History writing — Renaissance — Europe 15. Arts and Entertainment — Painting, Drawing, and Sculpture

LC 2002038074

ALA Notable Book, 2004; Governor General's Literary Awards, English-language Non-fiction finalist.

An account of Michelangelo's creation of his masterpiece, the ceiling of the Sistine Chapel, from his original commission from Pope Julius II, through the artist's four years of work, to the final acclaim at the paintings' 1512 unveiling.

"This engaging narrative sets the record straight on a few points and is highly recommended for most public library collections." —*Library Journal*

Includes bibliographical references (p. [347]-356) and index.

Prose, Francine
Caravaggio: Painter of Miracles. Francine Prose. Atlas Books Harper Collins 2005. 149 p. : Color illustration (Eminent lives)
ISBN 9780060575601
Grades: 11 12 Adult   759.5
1. Caravaggio, Michelangelo Merisi da, 1573-1610 2. Painters 3. Social life and customs 4. Italy 5. Biographies 6. Arts and Entertainment — Painting, Drawing, and Sculpture 7. Life stories — Arts and culture — Artists

LC 2005040203

A National Book Award finalist presents the story of the tumultuous life of the Baroque Italian artist, offering insight into how he defined the aesthetic conventions of his time to create realistic portraits of everyday people and natural subjects.

"A contemporary of Shakespeare, Caravaggio was belligerent, contemptuous, and competitive, a revered artist and a notorious street fighter wanted for murder who died at 39 under tragic circumstances. Much has been written about Caravaggio and his dramatic paintings, especially his daringly earthy depictions of biblical scenes, but somehow Prose's concentrated interpretation has a stronger impact. Not only does she cover all the biographical essentials but she also more clearly and descriptively explicates the pioneering painter's unique perception of the miraculous in everyday life. Prose also reveals, with both subtlety and flourish, how Caravaggio's frank interpretations of violence and pain, fear and grief, dignity and transcendence are matched with a brilliant subversion of our sense of reality." —*Booklist*

Includes bibliographical references (p. 147-148).

Scotti, R. A.
Vanished Smile: The Mysterious Theft of Mona Lisa. R.A. Scotti. Knopf Books 2009. 256 p.
ISBN 9780307265807
Grades: Adult   759.5
1. Leonardo, da Vinci, 1452-1519 2. Art thefts 3. Painting 4. Art 5. Paris, France 6. 1910s 7. Arts and Entertainment — Painting, Drawing, and Sculpture 8. True Crime — Heists and Robbery

LC 2008047851

Reopens the case of one of the most perplexing art thefts ever committed—the still unsolved mystery of the disappearance of Leonardo da Vinci's "Mona Lisa" from the Louvre on August 21, 1911.

"The author reports on the 1911 theft of Mona Lisa. The lovely woman with the enigmatic smile was simply lifted off the wall and spirited away. The scandal was immense, the investigation feverish, the headlines screaming, and Scotti revels in every turn. Her lively, expert coverage encompasses the fascinating, many-chaptered story of Mona Lisa and ironic revelations about the frenzy among America's robber barons for old masters and the corresponding renaissance in art fraud. Scotti's avid, exciting true-life mystery yields intriguing disclosures and reaffirms Mona Lisa's unique powers." —*Booklist*

759.6 Spanish painting

Cumming, Laura
★ *The Vanishing Velazquez: A 19th Century Bookseller's Obsession with a Lost Masterpiece.* by Laura Cumming. Scribner 2016. 320 p.
ISBN 9781476762159
Grades: Adult   759.6
1. Snare, John 2. Velazquez, Diego, 1599-1660 3. Booksellers 4. Portrait painting 5. Biographies 6. Life stories — People in history — Witness to history 7. Arts and entertainment — Painting, drawing, and sculpture 8. Nonfiction that reads like fiction

LC 2015040220

James Tait Black Memorial Prize for Biography, 2016.

Describes the true story of a provincial bookseller who discovered an incredible portrait of King Charles I at a liquidation auction and his lifelong quest to prove it was painted by Diego Velazquez.

"Snare's story is noteworthy, but it is Cumming's spirited and clever narration that makes this enigma utterly engrossing." —*Publishers Weekly*

Originally published: London : Chatto & Windus, 2016 as The Vanishing Man: In Pursuit of Velazques.

759.81 Norwegian painting

Knausgaard, Karl Ove
So Much Longing in so Little Space: The Art of Edvard Munch. Karl Ove Knausgaard; translated from the Norwegian by Ingvild Burkey. Penguin Books 2019. 233 pages : Color; Illustration
ISBN 9780143133131
Grades: Adult   759.81
1. Munch, Edvard, 1863-1944 2. Artists 3. Art 4. Creation (Literary, artistic, etc.) 5. Authors 6. Painters 7. Art history 8. Art criticism 9. Expressionism (Art) 10. Abstract expressionism 11. Modern art 12. Literary criticism 13. Translations — Norwegian to English 14. Arts and Entertainment — Painting, Drawing, and Sculpture

LC 2018057501

The award-winning Norwegian novelist tackles nonfiction with his personal assessment of the work of the famous expressionist painter and fellow country-

ESSENTIAL AND RECOMMENDED TITLES
759.9493 Belgian painting

man, providing artistic insight with historical, biographical and autobiographical discussions surrounding works including My Struggle and Four Seasons.

"Fans of the author's acclaimed autobiographical novels will find this book to be of Rosetta Stone-like importance as he delves into Munch's exploration of memory and how the artist rendered the past in a way that still feels both intimate and universally relatable." —*Kirkus*

Includes bibliographical references; Originally published by Forlaget Oktober, 2017.

Ustvedt, Oystein
Edvard Munch: An Inner Life. Oystein Ustvedt; translated from the Norwegian by Alison McCullough. Thames & Hudson 2020. 223 pages : Illustration; Color
   ISBN 9780500295762

Grades: Adult   759.81

1. Munch, Edvard, 1863-1944 2. Modernism (Art) 3. Artists 4. Painters 5. Painting 6. Art 7. Biographies 8. Life stories — Arts and culture — Artists 9. Arts and Entertainment — Painting, Drawing, and Sculpture

   LC 2019949015

A renowned expert on Edvard Munch delivers this wonderfully illustrated volume on the life and work of the great artist.

"A beautifully produced introduction to a celebrated artist." —*Kirkus*

Includes bibliographical references (pages 208-213) and index; Translated from the Norwegian.

759.9493 Belgian painting

Gohr, Siegfried
★ *Magritte: Attempting the Impossible.* Siegfried Gohr. D.A.P./Distributed Art Publishers 2009. 323 p. : Illustration; Color
   ISBN 9781933045931

Grades: Adult   759.9493

1. Magritte, Rene, 1898-1967 2. Surrealism 3. Arts and Entertainment — Painting, Drawing, and Sculpture

   LC 2009022403

"This extremely well-illustrated tour de force combines new research with unique organization. Obligatory chapters introduce Magritte's early development (during which his work revealed the heavy influence of De Chirico, Leger, and Le Corbusier) and his use of other media (graphic design, illustration, drawings, collages) in addition to oil paintings. This structure will engage the novice's imagination and will intrigue the Magritte connoisseur. Gohr's book reminds readers that excellent art never ceases to provide new avenues for investigation, through both research and careful visual examination of the art as primary document." —*Choice Reviews*

Includes bibliographical references (p. 318-319) and indexes.

759.972 Mexican painting

Lozano, Luis-Martin
Frida Kahlo. [Luis-Martin Lozano; translated from the Spanish by Mark Eaton and Luisa Panichi]. Bulfinch Press 2000. 245 p. : Illustration; Color
   ISBN 9780821227664

Grades: Adult   759.972

1. Kahlo, Frida 2. Artists 3. Women artists 4. Picture books for adults 5. Biographies 6. Translations — Spanish to English 7. Arts and Entertainment — Painting, Drawing, and Sculpture 8. Life stories — Arts and culture — Artists

   LC 2001089093

Library Journal Best Books, 2001.

Presents an overview of the Mexican painter's life and work and features two hundred reproductions of her art, as well as details about her childhood, political beliefs, and marriage to Diego Rivera.

"In this illustrated survey of Frida Kahlo's work Lozano . explores her life and paintings in a series of essays that range from a poetic study by noted Mexican cultural critic Carlos Monsivis to a short, prosaic piece written in 1943 by her husband, Diego Rivera, to an academic essay by Lozano himself. Lozano uses Kahlo's own stunning images, offering high-quality reproductions of some of Kahlo's most famous works as well as some of her lesser-known pieces. Previously unseen photos of Kahlo at work in her studio are also included. The detail and clarity of the images is incredible." —*Library Journal*

760 Printmaking and prints

Harmon, Katharine A.
The Map as Art: Contemporary Artists Explore Cartography. Katharine Harmon; with essays by Gayle Clemans. Princeton Architectural Press 2009. 255 p. : Color illustration
   ISBN 9781568989723

Grades: Adult   760

1. Arts and Entertainment — Painting, Drawing, and Sculpture

   LC 2008030929

Arranged by themes including personal terrain, inner visions, and global reckoning, a catalog collects 350 works by an international range of artists creating map-related works of art.

Includes bibliographical references.

769.569 Postage stamps and related devices — History, geographic treatment, biography

Barron, James
The One-Cent Magenta: Inside the Quest to Own the Most Valuable Stamp in the World. James Barron. Algonquin Books of Chapel Hill 2017. 224 p.
   ISBN 9781616205188

Grades: Adult   769.569

1. Stamp collecting 2. Collectors and collecting 3. Postage stamps 4. Guyana 5. History writing — Arts and culture

   LC 2016038074

When it was issued in 1856, it cost a penny. In 2014, this tiny square of faded red paper sold at Sotheby's for nearly $9.5 million, the largest amount ever paid for a postage stamp at auction. Through the stories of the eccentric characters who have bought, owned, and sold the one-cent magenta in the years in between, James Barron delivers a fascinating tale of global history and immense wealth, and of the human desire to collect.

"Readers of history, microhistory, and narrative nonfiction, and those with an interest in stamps, will appreciate this absorbing tale of the rarefied world of high-stakes philately." —*Library Journal*

Published simultaneously in Canada by Thomas Allen & Son Limited.

769.92 Prints — Biography

Katsushika, Hokusai
Hokusai: Beyond the Great Wave. Edited by Timothy Clark. Thames & Hudson 2017. 352 pages : Color; Illustration
   ISBN 9780500094068

Grades: Adult   769.92

1. Katsushika, Hokusai, 1760-1849 2. Painting 3. Japanese history 4. Arts and Entertainment — Painting, Drawing, and Sculpture 5. Arts and Entertainment — Museums and Collections

   LC Bl2018029569

Examines the brush paintings, drawings, woodblock prints, and illustrated books of Hokusai and arranges them thematically into groups that are related to the major spiritual and artistic quests of his life.

This publication accompanies the exhibition 'Hokusai : Beyond the great wave' at the British Museum from 25 May to 13 August 2017 and the exhibition 'Hokusai - Fuji o koete' at Abeno Harukas Art Museum, Osaka, from 6 October to 19 November 2017—Title page verso; Includes bibliographical references (pages 334-339) and index.

PUBLIC LIBRARY CORE COLLECTION: NONFICTION
Twentieth Edition

770 Photography, computer art, cinematography, videography

Ang, Tom
Digital Photography Masterclass. Tom Ang. DK 2013. 360 pages : Color; Illustration
ISBN 9781465408563
Grades: Adult   770
1. Image processing 2. Photography 3. Digital photography 4. Arts and Entertainment — Photography
LC Bl2013033728
Explains how to see the world with a photographer's eyes through tutorials, image analyses, assignments, and step-by-step image manipulation exercises.
This must-have digital photography resource explains how to see the world with a photographer's eyes through tutorials, image analyses, assignments and step-by-step image manipulation exercises.
Includes index.

Campany, David
The Open Road: Photography & The American Road Trip. David Campany. Aperture Foundation 2014. 334 p; Illustration; Color; Map
ISBN 9781597112406
Grades: Adult   770
1. Artistic photography 2. Social life and customs 3. Voyages and travels 4. United States 5. Arts and Entertainment — Photography
LC 2014020321
The Open Road considers the photographic road trip as a genre in and of itself, and presents the story of photographers for whom the American road is muse. The book features David Campany's introduction to the genre and 18 chapters presented chronologically, each exploring one American road trip in depth through a portfolio of images and informative texts.

Cole, Teju
Blind Spot. Teju Cole. Random House 2017. 352 pages
ISBN 9780399591075
Grades: Adult   770
1. Cole, Teju 2. Voyages and travels 3. Photography 4. Authors 5. Perception 6. African American authors 7. Travel writing 8. Arts and Entertainment — Photography
LC 2016032505
The New York Times photography critic and award-winning author pairs more than 150 images with lyrical text to explore his complex relationship to the visual world through his great passions—writing and photography—in a testament to the art of seeing.

Fagans, Michael
iPhone Photography for Everybody. Michael Fagans. Amherst Media, Inc. 2017. 127 p. : Illustration; Color
ISBN 9781682032909
Grades: Adult   770
1. Photography 2. iPhone (Smartphone) 3. Digital photography 4. Artistic photography 5. Arts and Entertainment — Photography 6. Science writing — Computing, the Internet, and Technology
LC Bl2017050802
Offers advice on how to shoot exceptional images with an iPhone camera, covering such topics as context and composition, lighting, and portraits and selfies.
Includes index.

Freeman, Michael
The Photographer's Mind: Creative Thinking for Better Digital Photos. Michael Freeman. Focal Press 2011. 192 p. : Illustration; Color
ISBN 9780240815176
Grades: Adult   770
1. Digital cameras 2. Image processing 3. Photography 4. Digital photography 5. Arts and Entertainment — Photography
LC Bl2011023168

Describes the components of a good photograph—purpose, style, and technique—and offers illustrative examples of the concepts within each section that were created using digital technology.
"The author shares experience he has gained as a professional photographer to improve the quality of the digital pictures nearly everyone is now creating. The content is streamlined into three chapters, on intent, style, and process, that tackle both the practical and the intangible aspects of photography more thoughtfully than many similar books. Freeman is as adept at explaining composition as he is at discussing the problem of clich or the philosophy of the sublime." —*Library Journal*
Includes bibliographical references (p. 192) and index.

Gatcum, Chris
★ *The Beginner's Photography Guide.* Written by Chris Gatcum. DK Publishing 2016. 192 pages : Illustration; Color
ISBN 9781465449665
Grades: Adult   770
1. Photography 2. Digital photography 3. Arts and Entertainment — Photography
LC Bl2016009693
Provides practical advice on the techniques of digital photography, with information on such topics as equipment, exposure, focusing, lenses, light, flash, and image enhancement.
"Though perfect for novices, this manual will also be helpful to readers with prior knowledge of analog photography wishing to translate their skills to the digital realm." —*Library Journal*
Includes index.

Horenstein, Henry
Digital Photography: A Basic Manual. Henry Horenstein with Allison Carroll. Little, Brown and Co. 2011. 240 p. : Illustration; Color
ISBN 9780316020749
Grades: Adult   770
1. Photography 2. Digital photography 3. Arts and Entertainment — Photography
LC 2011018758
A professional photographer and author presents a step-by-step course for beginning digital photography enthusiasts, covering topics such as exposure controls, shutter speed and information on image editing, printing methods and file storage.
Includes index.

Lee, Corky
★ *Corky Lee's Asian America: Fifty Years of Photographic Justice.* Photographs by Corky Lee; edited by Chee Wang Ng & Mae Ngai. Clarkson Potter/Publishers 2024. 319 pages : Illustration; Color
ISBN 9780593580127
Grades: Adult   770
1. Lee, Corky, 1947-2021 2. Asian Americans 3. Politics and government 4. Social history 5. Social movements 6. Portrait photography 7. United States history 8. United States 9. Arts and Entertainment — Photography 10. Society and culture — Race 11. History writing — Early 21st century — United States 12. History writing — United States
LC 2023001435
A posthumous collection of over 200 breathtaking photographs that document the history and cultural impact of the Asian American social justice movement, through the lens of beloved photographer Corky Lee—the man who sought to change the world one photograph at a time.
"For this dynamic collection, Ng and Ngai gather images from the half century that the late photographer Corky Lee (1947-2021) spent documenting Asian American communities…This is a potent record of Asian Americans' continued struggle for equality." —*Publishers Weekly*
Includes bibliographical references(pages 303-305 and index.

ESSENTIAL AND RECOMMENDED TITLES
770.23 Photography as a profession, occupation, hobby

Peterson, Bryan
Learning to See Creatively: Design, Color, and Composition in Photography. Bryan Peterson. Amphoto Books 2015. 144 pages : Color; Illustration
ISBN 9781607748274
Grades: Adult   770
1. Artistic photography 2. Photography 3. Arts and Entertainment — Photography
LC 2014049147

Completely revised and updated throughout, Bryan Peterson's classic guide to creativity helps photographers visualize their work, and the world, in a whole new light by developing their photographic vision. Fully revised with 100 percent new photography, this best-selling guide takes a radical approach to creativity by explaining how it is not just an inherent ability but a skill that can be learned and applied. Using inventive photos from his own stunning portfolio, author and veteran photographer Bryan Peterson deconstructs creativity for photographers. He details the basic techniques that go into not only taking a particular photo, but also provides insights on how to improve upon it—helping readers avoid the visual pitfalls and technical dead endsthat can lead to dull, uninventive photographs. This revised edition features a complete section on color as a design element and all new photographs to illustrate Peterson's points. Learning to See Creatively is the definitive reference for any photographer looking for a fresh perspective on their work.
Includes index.

Taylor, David
Digital Photography Complete Course. Written by David Taylor, Tracy Hallett, Paul Lowe, Paul Sanders. DK 2015. 360 pages : Illustration; Color
ISBN 9781465436078
Grades: Adult   770
1. Photography 2. Digital photography 3. Arts and Entertainment — Photography
LC Bl2015031893

Using a combination of tutorials, step-by-step demonstrations, practical assignments and Q&As, a guide to digital photography explores a wide range of genres to help aspiring photographers build their skills.
"An affordable, uncomplicated way to learn about digital photography." —*Library Journal*
Includes index.

Willis, Deborah
Reflections in Black: A History of Black Photographers, 1840 to the Present. Deborah Willis. W. W. Norton 2000. xviii, 348 p. : Illustration; Color
ISBN 9780393048803
Grades: 11 12 Adult   770
1. African American photographers 2. African Americans in art 3. Photography 4. United States 5. 19th century 6. 20th century 7. Arts and Entertainment — Photography 8. Arts and Entertainment — Museums and Collections
LC 99055185

Library Journal Best Books, 2000.
The companion volume to a major exhibition at the Smithsonian Institution contains a photographic celebration of the power of family, endurance, spirituality, and the diverse range of the African-American experience over the last two centuries.
"Willis sketches important figures and traces both developments in photographic techniques and the practice of photography by African Americans.... A beautiful and informative album." —*Booklist*
Includes bibliographical references (p. 338-343) and index.

770.23 Photography as a profession, occupation, hobby

Fordham, Demetrius
★ *If You're Bored with Your Camera Read This Book.* Demetrius Fordham. Ilex 2017. 128 pages : Illustration; Color
ISBN 9781781574317
Grades: Adult   770.23
1. Photography 2. Digital photography 3. Arts and Entertainment — Photography
LC Bl2017044359

Shares tricks, tips, hacks, and exercises to help readers find new ideas for images and different techniques, covering such topics as creating an inspiration board, playing with shadows and highlights, and experimenting with double exposure.
Includes index.

770.9 History, geographical treatment, biography

Ang, Tom
Photography: The Definitive Visual History. Tom Ang. DK Publishing 2014. 480 pages : Illustration; Color
ISBN 9781465422880
Grades: Adult   770.9
1. Photography 2. Arts and Entertainment — Photography
LC Bl2014039324

Traces the history of photography from its origins in the 1820s to the digital photography of the twenty-first century, profiling key photographers, highlighting important techniques, and showcasing iconic photographic images.
"While too basic for a professional or serious student, this volume will appeal to photo enthusiasts and general readers. Those wanting an extensive single-volume overview should stick with Michael R. Peres's the Focal Encyclopedia of Photography." —*Library Journal*
Includes index.

Morris, Errol
Believing Is Seeing: Observations on the Mysteries of Photography. Errol Morris. Penguin Press 2011. 336 p.
ISBN 9781594203015
Grades: Adult   770.9
1. Documentary photography 2. Photojournalism 3. Truth 4. Reliability 5. Photography 6. Documentary films 7. Arts and Entertainment — Photography
LC 2011013101

New York Times Notable Book, 2011.
Presents an investigation into the truth behind a variety of documentary photographs throughout history, discussing the relationship between the photograph and the world they supposedly represent.
Includes bibliographical references and index.

770.92 Biography

Alinder, Mary Street
Group F.64: Edward Weston, Ansel Adams, Imogen Cunningham, and the Community of Artists Who Revolutionized American Photography. Mary Street Alinder. Bloomsbury USA 2014. 320 p.
ISBN 9781620405550
Grades: Adult   770.92
1. Photographers 2. Photography 3. Artists 4. California 5. 1930s 6. Arts and Entertainment — Photography
LC 2014011040

Chronicles the lives and careers of the members of the West Coast photography movement, including such famous names as Ansel Adams, Imogen Cunningham, Dorothea Lange, Willard Van Dyke, and Edward Weston.
As she chronicles the photographers friendships, tempestuous love lives, epic parties, scrambles to survive, passionate manifestos, heated public debates, social and environmental concerns, and hard-won exhibitions, Alinder achieves an f.64 degree of crisp and commanding detail in this landmark group portrait of the visionary photographers who succeeded in 'Forever changing our way of seeing.' —*Booklist*
Includes bibliographical references and index.

PUBLIC LIBRARY CORE COLLECTION: NONFICTION
Twentieth Edition

Brandow, Todd
Edward Steichen: Lives in Photography. Todd Brandow and William A. Ewing; with contributions by A.D. Coleman ... [et al.]. Foundation for the Exhibition of Photography; 2008. 335 p. : Illustration; Color
ISBN 9780393066265
Grades: Adult **770.92**
1. Steichen, Edward, 1879-1973 2. Artistic photography 3. Arts and Entertainment — Photography
LC 2007020128

A visual portrait of the influential and prolific fine-art photographer also includes an analysis of his commercial achievements and the continuing legacy of his exhibition, The Family of Man, in an account that features scholarly essays that evaluate such topics as his work with Conde Nast and his Museum of Modern Art directorship.

Published on the occasion of the exhibition organized by the Foundation for the Exhibition of Photography and Musee de l'Elysee, Lausanne; Exhibition itinerary, Jeu de Paume, Paris, October 9-December 30, 2007; Musee de l'Elysee, Lausanne, January 17-March 23, 2008; Palazzo Magnani, Reggio Emilia, April 12-June 8, 2008; Museo Nacional Centro de Arte Reina Sofia, June 24-September 22, 2008; Includes bibliographical references (p. 309-316) and index.

Curtis, Edward S.
Edward S. Curtis: One Hundred Masterworks. Christopher Cardozo; with contributions by A. D. Coleman, Louise Erdrich, Eric J. Jolly, and Michael Charles Tobias. Foundation for the Exhibition of Photography 2015. 183 p. : Illustration; Color
ISBN 9783791354217
Grades: Adult **770.92**
1. Curtis, Edward S, 1868-1952 2. Indigenous peoples of North America— History 3. Indigenous peoples of North America 4. Portraits 5. Photographers 6. Photography 7. Biographies 8. Arts and Entertainment — Photography
LC 2014049053

Showcasing Edward Curtis's most compelling and important works, this beautiful publication highlights both iconic and rarely seen images, demonstrating his artistry and mastery of photographic mediums, and his commitment to documenting and preserving for posterity the Native Americans' traditions and ways of life.

"This title succeeds at bringing the reader close to what it's like to view the artist's master prints in person. Excellent essays by Curtis expert Cardozo and historian, critic, and curator of photography A.D. Coleman discuss both Curtis's work and his printmaking technique." —Library Journal

Egan, Timothy
★ *Short* Nights of the Shadow Catcher: The Epic Life and Immortal Photographs of Edward Curtis. Timothy Egan. Houghton Mifflin Harcourt 2012. 352 p.
ISBN 9780618969029
Grades: Adult **770.92**
1. Curtis, Edward S, 1868-1952 2. Photographers 3. Indigenous peoples of North America 4. Portraits 5. United States history 6. 19th century 7. 20th century 8. Biographies 9. History writing — Indigenous peoples — United States 10. Life stories — Arts and culture — Artists 11. Life stories — People in history — Explorers 12. Life stories — People in history — Indigenous peoples
LC 2012022390

ALA Notable Book, 2013; Booklist Editors' Choice, 2012; New York Times Notable Book, 2012; Andrew Carnegie Medal for Excellence in Non-Fiction, 2013.

Recounts the pioneering photographer's life-risking effort to document the disappearing North American Indian nation, offering insight into the danger and resolve behind his venture, his elevation to an impassioned advocate, and the posthumous discovery of his achievements.

Galassi, Peter
Ansel Adams in Yosemite Valley: Celebrating the Park at 150. Peter Galassi. Little, Brown and Company 2014. 203 pages : Illustration; Color; Map
ISBN 9780316323406
Grades: Adult **770.92**
1. Adams, Ansel, 1902-1984 2. Landscape photography 3. Photographers 4. National parks and reserves 5. United States 6. Yosemite National Park 7. Yosemite Valley 8. Visual nonfiction 9. Arts and Entertainment — Photography
LC 2014940622

A luminous collection of photographs that Ansel Adams made in Yosemite National Park during his long and remarkably productive life, published to celebrate the 150th anniversary of President Abraham Lincoln's signing of the Yosemite Land Grant.

Includes bibliographic references (pages 32-33) and indexes.

771 Techniques, procedures, apparatus, equipment, materials

Ang, Tom
Digital Photographer's Handbook. Tom Ang. DK 2012. 408 p. : Color illustration
ISBN 9780756692421
Grades: Adult **771**
1. Digital cameras 2. Photography 3. Digital photography 4. Arts and Entertainment — Photography
LC 2012418315

A latest edition provides revised and updated coverage of expert techniques related to current trends and developments in digital photography to counsel novice through professional photographers on how to capture the best possible shots and enhance existing pictures.

Presents an introduction to digital photography, describing the latest equipment, software, and accessories and providing detailed information about techniques, design, lighting, digital image manipulation, and composition.

Includes bibliographical references (p. 398-399) and index.

Peterson, Bryan
Understanding Exposure: How to Shoot Great Photographs with Any Camera. Bryan Peterson. AmPhoto Books 2016. 168 pages
ISBN 9781607748502
Grades: Adult **771**
1. Photography 2. Arts and Entertainment — Photography
LC 2015025905

Provides detailed lessons on the elements of exposure and how each relates to depth of field, freezing and blurring action, and shooting in low light, demonstrating a diversity of creative choices in exposing a picture.

Includes bibliographical references and index.

777 Cinematography and videography

Pincus, Edward
The Filmmaker's Handbook: A Comprehensive Guide for the Digital Age. Steven Ascher & Edward Pincus; drawings by Carol Keller and Robert Brun; original photographs by Ted Spagna and Stephen McCarthy completely revised and updated by Steven Ascher with contributions by David Leitner. Plume 2012. 832 p.
ISBN 9780452297289
Grades: Adult **777**
1. Cinematography 2. Digital cinematography 3. Digital video 4. Filmmaking 5. Arts and Entertainment — Movies and Television 6. Reference books — Performing arts 7. Reference books — Handbooks, manuals, etc.
LC OC2012621105

A fully revised, comprehensive guide offers an in-depth exploration of today's recent technological advances, such as digital age filmmaking, while reviewing a collection of new methods and techniques in relation to various film formats and offering suggestions on the business aspects of financing and producing films.

Includes bibliographical references and index; Originally published as: The filmmaker's handbook / Edward Pincus and Steven Ascher. 1984.

ESSENTIAL AND RECOMMENDED TITLES
778 Specific fields and special kinds of photography

778 Specific fields and special kinds of photography

Harryhausen, Ray
The Art of Ray Harryhausen. Ray Harryhausen & Tony Dalton; with a foreword by Peter Jackson. Billboard Books 2006. xi, 230 p. : Illustration; Color; Portrait
ISBN 9780823084005
Grades: Adult — 778
1. Harryhausen, Ray 2. Animators 3. Film producers and directors 4. United States 5. Autobiographies and memoirs 6. Biographies 7. Arts and Entertainment — Movies and Television 8. Life stories — Arts and culture — Artists 9. Adult books for young adults
LC 2005930364

Library Journal Best Books, 2006.

In a follow-up to Ray Harryhausen: An Animated Life, the award-winning practitioner of stop-motion animation provides an illustrated guide to his life and work, furnishing a collection of essays and illustrations that chronicles the development of his film work and examines his innovative creations—including aliens, prehistoric creatures, mythological monsters, and more.

"The text is fun and informative, but the main feast here is the art, and the reproductions of the concept drawings and photos of the models are superb." —*Library Journal*

Companion vol. to Ray Harryhausen, an animated life, 2004; Includes index; First published in Great Britain 2005 by Aurum Press Ltd, London—T.P. verso.

Williams, Richard
The Animator's Survival Kit: A Manual of Methods, Principles and Formulas for Classical, Computer, Games, Stop Motion and Internet Animators. Richard Williams. Faber and Faber 2009. x, 382 p. : Illustration; Color; Portrait
ISBN 9780571238330
Grades: Adult — 778
1. Animation (Cinematography) 2. Drawing technique 3. Science writing — Computing, the Internet, and Technology 4. Arts and Entertainment — Comics, Cartoons, and Animation
LC 2010294449

The Academy Award-winning artist draws on his master instruction classes to demonstrate essential techniques required of animators of any skill level or method, in an updated edition that provides expanded coverage of such topics as animal gaits and liveaction.

Previous ed.: 2001; Title on accompanying DVD: The animator's survival kit animated.

778.7 Photography under specific conditions

Rotman, Jeffrey L.
The Last Fisherman: Witness to the Endangered Oceans. Jeffrey L. Rotman with Yair Harel; introduction by Les Kaufman. Abbeville Press 2014. 276 pages : Color; Illustration
ISBN 9780789211910
Grades: Adult — 778.7
1. Rotman, Jeffrey L. 2. Overfishing 3. Underwater photography 4. Nature writing — Natural Landscapes
LC 2014016848

"An excellent cautionary tale, this work offers much to celebrate, too. Highly recommended to all interested in nature, the oceans, and fishing." —*Library Journal*

Includes bibliographical references (page 270) and index.

778.9 Photography of specific subjects

Marks, Ann
Vivian Maier Developed: The Untold Story of the Photographer Nanny. Ann Marks. Atria Books 2021. 336 p. : Illustration
ISBN 9781982166724
Grades: Adult — 778.9
1. Maier, Vivian, 1926-2009 2. Street photography 3. Photographers 4. Women photographers 5. Nannies 6. Women artists 7. United States 8. Biographies 9. Life stories — Arts and culture — Artists 10. Arts and Entertainment — Photography
LC 2021018972

Vivian Maier, the photographer nanny whose work was famously discovered in a Chicago storage locker, captured the imagination of the world with her masterful images and mysterious life. Before posthumously skyrocketing to global fame, she had so deeply buried her past that even the families she lived with knew little about her. No one could relay where she was born or raised, if she had parents or siblings, if she enjoyed personal relationships, why she took photographs and why she didn't share them with others. Now, in this definitive biography, Ann Marks uses her complete access to Vivian's personal records and archive of 140,000 photographs to reveal the full story of her extraordinary life.

"With the keen eye of a detective and persistence of a genealogist, researcher Marks unravels the complicated story of 'nanny wonder' Vivian Maier (1926-2009), one of the 20th century's most enigmatic street photographers.... This definitive account will leave readers in awe." —*Publishers Weekly*

Includes bibliographical references and index.

Watkins, Carleton E.
Carleton Watkins: The Complete Mammoth Photographs. Weston Naef and Christine Hult-Lewis; with contributions by Michael Hargraves, Jack von Euw, and Jennifer A. Watts. J. Paul Getty Museum 2011. xxv, 572 p. : Illustration; Map
ISBN 9781606060056
Grades: Adult — 778.9
1. Watkins, Carleton E, 1829-1916 2. Landscape photography 3. California 4. Arts and Entertainment — Photography
LC 2011005241

Discusses the life and work of the nineteenth century landscape photographer, presenting a selection of photographs of the American West taken between 1858 and 1891.

Includes bibliographical references and index.

779 Photographic images

Addario, Lynsey
Of Love & War. Lynsey Addario. Penguin Press 2018. 272 p.
ISBN 9780525560029
Grades: Adult — 779
1. Addario, Lynsey 2. War and society 3. Photojournalists 4. Human rights 5. Women photojournalists 6. Essay writing 7. Injustice 8. Resilience 9. Refugees 10. Childbirth 11. Education 12. Courage 13. Afghanistan 14. Congo (Democratic Republic) 15. Sudan 16. Southwest Asia and North Africa (Middle East) 17. Africa 18. Autobiographies and memoirs 19. Politics and global affairs — Civil and human rights 20. Life stories — Arts and culture — Writing — Journalists 21. History writing — Wars and conflicts
LC 2018006212

The photojournalist presents a curated selection of images from her work in the Middle East, South Asia, and Africa, in a collection that features essays by such contributors as Dexter Filkins, Suzy Hansen, and Christy Turlington.

Buckland, Gail
Who Shot Rock & Roll: A Photographic History, 1955 to the Present. Gail Buckland. Knopf 2009. 304 p.
ISBN 9780307270160
Grades: Adult — 779
1. Rock music 2. Rock musicians 3. Music history and criticism 4. Social life and customs 5. United States 6. 20th century 7. 21st century 8. Arts and Entertainment — Music — Rock
LC 2009019122

A former curator of the Royal Photographic Society of Great Britain presents a chronicle of rare and previously unseen images marking more than half a century of rock-and-roll history, in a tribute to star performers and leading photographers that also includes album covers and live concert shots.

"Here are nearly 300 iconic photographs by those photographers who understood the power of the image in the formation and sustenance of rock-and-roll culture from 1955 onward. The care with which Buckland selects representative photographers and their most significant images is matched by her interpretive prowess. [She] carefully but deliberately argues that the art of rock photography has been sacrificed to the paparazzi and corporate art departments. In light of this inclusive, heady and visceral collection of the genre's best, it would be hard to argue otherwise." —*Publishers Weekly*

Includes bibliographical references and index.

Who Shot Sports: A Photographic History, 1843 to the Present. Gail Buckland. Alfred A. Knopf 2016. xii, 329 pages : Illustration; Color
ISBN 9780385352239
Grades: Adult   779
1. Arts and Entertainment — Photography 2. Sports and Competition — Sports History

LC 2015038089

Presents more than 280 amazing action photographs of athletes, including Willie Mays, Carl Lewis, Ian Botham, Kobe Bryant and Magic Johnson by such photographers as Robert Capa, Danny Lyon, Annie Leibovitz, Neil Leifer, Walter Iooss Jr. and Bob Martin.

Shows the range, cultural importance, and aesthetics of sports photography.

"Buckland writes with such authority that her thoughts on photography, as an art form, and her analysis of individual images in and out of the sports context make this a must-read for pop culture enthusiasts and anyone interested in photography." —*Publishers Weekly*

Includes bibliographical references (pages 305-309) and index.

Evans, Walker

American Photographs. Walker Evans; with an essay by Lincoln Kirstein. Museum of Modern Art 2012. 208 p. : Illustration
ISBN 9780870708350
Grades: Adult   779
1. Evans, Walker, 1903-1975 2. Artistic photography 3. United States 4. Between the Wars (1918-1939) 5. Arts and Entertainment — Photography

LC 2012940325

This seventy-fifth anniversary edition of American Photographs, made with new reproductions, recreates the original 1938 edition as closely as possible to make the landmark publication available for a new generation.

Friedman, Elias Weiss

The Dogist: Photographic Encounters with 1,000 Dogs. Elias Weiss Friedman. Artisan 2015. 303 pages : Color; Illustration
ISBN 9781579656713
Grades: Adult   779
1. Photography of dogs 2. Arts and Entertainment — Photography 3. Nature writing — Animal studies — Pet care — Dogs

LC 2015036708

A treasury of expressive and heartwarming canine portraits is complemented by subject stories and characteristics and is thematically organized under sections ranging from Puppies and Cones of Shame to Working Dogs and Dogs in Fancy Outfits.

A treasury of expressive canine portraits is complemented by subject stories and characteristics and is thematically organized under sections ranging from "Puppies" and "Cones of Shame" to "Working Dogs" and "Dogs in Fancy Outfits."

"This delightful collection of photographs is likely to catch the eye of readers who follow Friedman's blog, Facebook page, tweets, and/or Instagram account. Animal portraiture enthusiasts may be especially interested in this title as an exemplar of the genre." —*Library Journal*

Includes index.

Leibovitz, Annie

A Photographer's Life, 1990-2005. Annie Leibovitz. Random House 2006. 480 p; Illustration; Color
ISBN 9780375505096
Grades: Adult   779
1. Leibovitz, Annie, 1949- 2. Portrait photography 3. Arts and Entertainment — Museums and Collections

LC 2006045765

A visual narrative of the past fifteen years brings together more than three hundred photographs, including both personal images and professional work, that document her relationship with her late companion Susan Sontag, the birth of her daughters, the death of her father, and the world of such public figures as Demi Moore, Nelson Mandela, Bill Clinton, and others.

Women. [photographs by] Annie Leibovitz; [essay by] Susan Sontag. Random House 1999. 239 p. : Illustration; Color
ISBN 9780375500206
Grades: Adult   779
1. Leibovitz, Annie, 1949- 2. Photography 3. Arts and Entertainment — Photography

LC 99024968

The photographer turns her lens to a favorite topic, women, sharing her portraits of Hillary Rodham Clinton, Eudora Welty, Martina Navratilova, and Jodie Foster, as well as women from other walks of life, including a Navajo weaver, an astronaut, and a rancher.

Cover title.

Light, Michael

100 Suns: 1945-1962. Michael Light. Alfred A. Knopf 2003. 208 p. : Illustration; Color
ISBN 9781400041138
Grades: Adult   779
1. Nuclear weapons 2. United States 3. Science Writing — Physics 4. Adult books for young adults

LC 2003106275

Booklist Editors' Choice, 2003.

A collection of one hundred previously classified photographs depict the United States' above-ground nuclear tests set off between 1945 and 1962 in Nevada, New Mexico, and over the Pacific.

"The suns Light presents to readers in this . photography collection are manmade: Aboveground atomic detonations captured on film both in the Nevada desert and at sea, terrifyingly beautiful images that remind readers of the apocalyptic might of nuclear weapons." —*Booklist*

Images in this book were made by photographers in the U.S. Army Signal Corps ... [and] the 1352nd Photographic Group of the U.S. Air Force—Note on the photographs; Contains 100 photographs of nuclear tests; Includes bibliographical references.

Sartore, Joel

★ *The Photo Ark: One Man's Quest to Document the World's Animals*. Joel Sartore; foreword by Harrison Ford; introduction by Douglas H. Chadwick. National Geographic 2017. 399 pages : Color; Illustration
ISBN 9781426217777
Grades: Adult   779
1. Rare and endangered animals 2. Photography of animals 3. Wildlife photography 4. Arts and Entertainment — Photography 5. Nature writing — Animal Studies — Endangered Species

LC 2016038616

Representing National Geographic's Photo Ark—a major cross-platform initiative and lifelong project by a veteran photographer to make portraits of the world's animals, especially those that are endangered—this showcase of 600 photos presents a thought-provoking argument for saving all the species of our planet.

"Satore more than succeeds in his goal to provide people with an opportunity to become aware of these animals, many endangered, before they disappear." —*Publishers Weekly*

Includes index.

ESSENTIAL AND RECOMMENDED TITLES
779.092 Photographers

Shaughnessy, Jim
The Call of Trains: Railroad Photographs by Jim Shaughnessy. Text by Jeff Brouws. W.W. Norton & Co. 2008. 224 p. : Illustration
ISBN 9780393065923
Grades: Adult   779
1. Railroads 2. United States 3. Transportation — Trains and rail service
LC 2008001295

A celebration of the life and work of the renowned railroad photographer includes photographs taken between 1946 and 1988, and emphasizes the railroad culture of the fifties and sixties.

Celebrates the life and work of an eminent railroad photographer, in a volume of 170 duotone works taken between 1946 and 1988 that is complemented by a biographical essay and places an emphasis on railroad culture in the 1950s and 1960s.

"Shaughnessy began shooting trains in downtown Troy, New York (his hometown), in the middle 1940s. He eventually took lengthy trips, first in New England and Canada, later across the Midwest to the Southwest, to photograph trains. He initially focused on the big engines but quickly extended his purview to include railway workers, railway buildings, and the countrysides through which the trains rolled. A civil engineer rather than a professional photographer, he became as skilled as any pro. Appearing on full pages of this oversize volume, his pictures are engrossing, stunning masterpieces of photodocumentation." —*Booklist*

Includes bibliographical references (p. 222-223).

Smith, Joel
Edward Steichen: The Early Years. Joel Smith. Princeton University Press in association with the Metropolitan Museum of Art 1999. 167 p, 61 leaves of col. plates : Color illustration
ISBN 9780691048734
Grades: Adult   779
1. Steichen, Edward, 1879-1973 2. Artistic photography 3. Arts and Entertainment — Photography
LC 99026617

"Smith examines the photography of Edward Steichen. Alfred Stieglitz was a patron of Steichen's, and Smith discusses the interrelationship between Steichen's work and Stieglitz's shifting aesthetic interests, as well as the influence of Paris on Steichen's development." —*New York Times Book Review*

Includes bibliographical references (p. 40-46).

Smith, Patti
★ *A Book of Days.* Patti Smith. Bloomsbury Publishing 2022. 432 pages :
ISBN 9781526650986
Grades: Adult   779
1. Photographers 2. Musicians 3. Singers 4. Popular culture 5. Communication and technology 6. Photography 7. Social media 8. Virtual community 9. Visual nonfiction 10. Arts and entertainment — Writing and publishing 11. Society and culture — Pop culture

Showcases a year of the life of the acclaimed singer, songwriter, poet, painter and National Book Award-winning author through personal images of 365 days.

"A powerful melding of image and text inspired by Instagram yet original in its execution." —*Kirkus*

Stanton, Brandon
Humans. Brandon Stanton. St. Martin's Press 2020. 437 p.
ISBN 9781250114297
Grades: 9 10 11 12 Adult   779
1. Humans 2. Everyday life 3. Photography 4. Human behavior 5. Street photography 6. Artistic photography 7. Portrait photography 8. Collective autobiographies and memoirs 9. Interviews 10. Life stories — General 11. Society and culture — General
LC 2020030024

Brandon Stanton's new book, Humans ... shows us the world. Brandon Stanton created Humans of New York in 2010. What began as a photographic census of life in New York City, soon evolved into a storytelling phenomenon. A global audience of millions began following HONY daily. Over the next several years, Stanton broadened his lens to include people from across the world. Traveling to more than forty countries, he conducted interviews across continents, borders, and language barriers. Humans is the definitive catalogue of these travels. The faces and locations will vary from page to page, but the stories will feel deeply familiar. Told with candor and intimacy, Humans will resonate with readers across the globe-providing a portrait of our shared experience.

"Millions follow Stanton, and the empathy and love his work engenders will be a balm to many more." —*Booklist*

"A lovely, sometimes challenging testament to the universality of human nature." —*Kirkus*

779.092 Photographers

McCurry, Steve
The Iconic Photographs: The Iconic Photographs. Steve McCurry. Phaidon 2012. 270 p. : Color illustration
ISBN 9780714865133
Grades: Adult   779.092
1. Portrait photography 2. Artistic photography 3. Arts and Entertainment — Photography
LC Bl2012046509

Presents a retrospective collection of the photographer's work over the past thirty years.

779.2 Portraits — Photographs

Bethencourt, Kahran
Glory: Magical Visions of Black Beauty. Kahran and Regis Bethencourt. St. Martin's Press 2020. 256 p.
ISBN 9781250204561
Grades: Adult   779.2
1. African American children 2. African Americans 3. African people 4. Photography of children 5. Artistic photography 6. Beauty 7. Aesthetics 8. Visual nonfiction 9. Society and culture — Ethnic studies
LC 2020021905

The husband-and-wife team behind CreativeSoul Photography and the acclaimed AfroArt series combine striking photography of natural Black hairstyles with visual storytelling in a celebration of Black culture, heritage and self-acceptance.

"An exquisite pictorial love letter to Black children around the world." —*Kirkus*

780 Music

Bullock, Darryl W.
David Bowie Made Me Gay: 100 Years of LGBT Music. Darryl W. Bullock. Overlook Press 2017. 320 p.
ISBN 9781468315592
Grades: 11 12 Adult   780
1. Gay culture 2. Musicians 3. Music history and criticism 4. Popular culture 5. Arts and Entertainment — Music 6. History writing — LGBTQIA+ 7. History writing — Arts and culture 8. Adult books for young adults
LC Bl2017049523

The most comprehensive history of LGBT music ever compiled, encompassing a century of music by and for the LGBT community.

"Well-researched and brimming with intrigue, Bullock's comprehensive study not only makes the work of scores of musicians sing anew; it also demonstrates how the pendulum of acceptance can swing from era to era." —*Kirkus*

Crawford, Richard
America's Musical Life: A History. Richard Crawford. Norton 2001. xv, 976 p. : Illustration
ISBN 9780393048100

Grades: Adult **780**
1. Music, American 2. Music 3. Music history and criticism 4. United States 5. Arts and Entertainment — Music

LC 99047565

Library Journal Best Books, 2001.

An illustrated history of America's musical heritage ranges from the earliest examples of Native American traditional song to the innovative sound of contemporary rock and jazz.

"This survey of music in America covers blues, jazz, swing, pop, rock, hip hop . with economics and history as cultural backdrops. Well researched and sensitively constructed, this is highly recommended." —*Library Journal*

Includes bibliographical references (p. 897-923) and index.

Day, Timothy

★ *A Century of Recorded Music: Listening to Musical History.* Timothy Day. Yale University Press 2000. x, 306 p. : Illustration
ISBN 9780300084429

Grades: Adult **780**
1. Music history and criticism 2. Sound recordings 3. Sound 4. 20th century 5. Arts and Entertainment — Music

LC 00043490

"This work provides a narrative of the evolution of recording from cylinders (1887), shellac discs, and acoustic rerecording through the reproducing piano, electrical amplifications (1925), and magnetic tape to the long-playing record (1948) and compact disc of the 1980s. Day also discusses studio practices and the emergence of influential record producers, the role of radio and recordings in creating a mass audience, the expansion of recorded repertoire, and new ways to experience music. Recommended for all music collections." —*Choice*

Includes bibliographical references (p. [257]-259) and index.

Schonberg, Harold C.

★ *The Lives of the Great Composers.* Harold C. Schonberg. W. W. Norton 1997. 653 p. : Illustration
ISBN 9780393038576

Grades: Adult **780**
1. Composers 2. Life stories — Arts and culture — Performing arts — Musicians and composers 3. Reference books — Performing arts

LC 96013308

Profiles of the world's most outstanding composers from Bach to Schoenberg examines the lives, times, and music of each.

Includes bibliographical references (p. [621]-635) and index.

Tolan, Sandy

Children of the Stone: The Power of Music in a Hard Land. Sandy Tolan. Bloomsbury USA 2015. 356 p.
ISBN 9781608198139

Grades: Adult **780**
1. Aburedwan, Ramzi 2. Music and society 3. Refugees, Palestinian 4. Conservatories of music 5. Israeli West Bank Barrier 6. Boundaries 7. Israel 8. Biographies 9. Life stories — Facing adversity — War and oppression — Refugees 10. Society and culture — Education

LC 2014032528

Booklist Editors' Choice, 2015; Library Journal Best Books, 2015; Middle East Book Award, Honorable Mention, 2015.

Children of the Stone is the unlikely story of Ramzi Hussein Aburedwan, a kid from a Palestinian refugee camp who confronts an occupying army, gets an education, masters an instrument, dreams of something much bigger than himself, and then, through his charisma and persistence, inspires scores of others to work with him to make that dream real. That dream: a music school in the midst of a refugee camp, a school to transform the lives of thousands of children-as Ramzi's life was transformed-through music.

"This is an engrossing and powerful story, moving skillfully amid the failure of the never-ending battles and 'Peace' talks between Israel and Palestine and the determination of one brave young man to change his world." —*Booklist*

Includes bibliographical references and index.

Walker-Hill, Helen

From Spirituals to Symphonies: African-American Women Composers and Their Music. Helen Walker-Hill. Greenwood Press 2002. xvi, 401 p. : Illustration
ISBN 9780313299476

Grades: Adult **780**
1. Composers 2. African Americans 3. United States 4. Biographies 5. Arts and Entertainment — Music

LC 2001040600

"This excellent and beautifully produced publication will immediately interest those working in music history and women's studies." —*Choice*

Includes bibliographical references (p. [375]-377), discography (p. 378-379), and index.

780.26 Texts; treatises on music scores and recordings

Austerlitz, Saul

Money for Nothing: A History of the Music Video, from the Beatles to the White Stripes. Saul Austerlitz. Continuum 2006. IX, 250 pages
ISBN 9780826418180

Grades: Adult **780.26**
1. Music videos 2. Music 3. Popular music 4. Sound recording industry and trade 5. Arts and Entertainment — Movies and Television 6. Arts and Entertainment — Music

LC 2006029185

Money for Nothing begins with the earliest days of the music video, when Hollywood musicals, experimental animated films, Soundies, and Scopitones fused music and image in ways that would presage the eventual form of the MTV clip. As MTV and VH1 have morphed into lifestyle channels, the video no longer has the cultural impact it once had, but our era of YouTube and bloggers has revitalized the form, sparking a video resurgence among bands, directors, and fans.

"In this look back on the music video genre, film and music critic Austerlitz does an admirable job explaining how early pioneers like the Beatles and Bob Dylan paved the way for the Madonnas and Michael Jacksons of the 1980s, the decade in which the music video thrived." —*Publishers Weekly*

Includes videography (page 250).

Calamar, Gary

Record Store Days: From Vinyl to Digital and Back Again. Gary Calamar, Phil Gallo; edited by Scott Calamar; foreword by Peter Buck. Sterling Pub CO Inc 2010. 238 p.
ISBN 9781402772320

Grades: 11 12 Adult **780.26**
1. Music stores 2. Music industry and trade 3. Records, Phonograph 4. Vintage record stores 5. Digital music 6. Arts and Entertainment — Music

LC Bl2010016536

Uses interviews, photographs, anecdotes, and memorabilia to provide a nostalgic history of the record store in the United States and includes profiles of major shops and quotations from musicians, shop owners, and fans.

780.3 Music dictionaries

Hoffman, Miles

The NPR Classical Music Companion: An Essential Guide for Enlightened Listening. Miles Hoffman. Houghton Mifflin 2005. x, 306 p.
ISBN 9780618619450

Grades: Adult **780.3**
1. Music 2. Arts and Entertainment — Music — Classical 3. Reference books — Performing arts 4. Reference — Dictionaries

LC 2006273343

Recently revised for the latest wave of classical music fans, this popular introduction to the genre by NPR commentator Miles Hoffman teaches readers how to distinguish between good and bad performances, explains why opera was

ESSENTIAL AND RECOMMENDED TITLES
780.71 Music — Education

invented, and shares fascinating facts designed to heighten appreciation for the form.

Includes index; Originally published: The NPR classical music companion : Terms and concepts from A to Z, c1997.

780.71 Music — Education

Koenig, Joan
 The Musical Child: Using the Power of Music to Raise Children Who Are Happy, Healthy, and Whole. Joan Koenig. Houghton Mifflin Harcourt 2021. 288 p.
 ISBN 9781328612960
 Grades: Adult 780.71
 1. Koenig, Joan 2. Children and music 3. Child development 4. Music teachers 5. Music 6. Early childhood education 7. Neuroscience 8. Family and Relationships — Parenting 9. Arts and Entertainment — Music 10. Society and culture — Education
 LC 2020050865

Since opening her famed Parisian conservatory over three decades ago, Joan Koenig has led a global movement to improve children's lives and minds with the transformative power of music. In The Musical Child, Koenig shares stories from her classrooms, along with tips about how to use the latest research during the critical years when children are most sensitive to musical exposure—and most receptive to its benefits.

"Educators ready to approach music as a core skill will find these ideas easy to implement and worth exploring." —*Publishers Weekly*

Includes bibliographical references and index.

Tunstall, Tricia
 Changing Lives: Gustavo Dudamel, El Sistema, and the Transformative Power of Music. Tricia Tunstall. W.W. Norton 2012. 320 p.
 ISBN 9780393078961
 Grades: Adult 780.71
 1. Dudamel, Gustavo 2. Music 3. Children and music 4. Poor children 5. Teaching 6. Arts and Entertainment — Music — Classical 7. Society and culture — Social activism and philanthropy
 LC 2011026504

Reveals the effect that education can have on positive social change by examining the life of a conductor of the Los Angeles Philharmonic and the unique program that nurtured his talent back home in Venezuela and its current availability in the U.S.

Includes index.

780.9 History, geographic treatment, biography

Broyles, Michael
 ★ *Revolutions in American Music: Three Decades That Changed a Country and Its Sounds.* Michael Broyles. W.W. Norton & Company 2024. 416 p.
 ISBN 9780393634204
 Grades: Adult 780.9
 1. Music 2. Popular music 3. Race relations 4. Technology 5. Music industry and trade 6. Social change 7. United States history 8. Music history and criticism 9. United States 10. 1840s 11. 1920s 12. 1950s 13. Arts and Entertainment — Music 14. History writing — United States 15. History writing — Arts and culture 16. Life stories — Arts and culture — Performing arts — Musicians and composers

How did a European social dance craze become part of an American presidential election? Why did the recording industry become racially divided? Where did rock 'n' roll really come from? And how do all these things continue to reverberate in today's world? Michael Broyles combines broad historical perspective with an eye for the telling detail to tell the story of how unexpected connections between music, technology, and race across three tumultuous decades changed American culture.

"A well-researched and astute look at the evolution of American culture through popular music." —*Library Journal*

Burton-Hill, Clemency
 ★ *Year of Wonder: Classical Music to Enjoy Day by Day.* Clemency Burton-Hill. Harper 2018. 442 pages
 ISBN 9780062856203
 Grades: Adult 780.9
 1. Music 2. Music appreciation 3. Arts and Entertainment — Music 4. Arts and Entertainment — Music — Classical
 LC 2019564819

The award-winning violinist and BBC Radio personality shares a year's worth of expertly curated, savor-worthy classical music pieces reflecting a diverse range of historical periods, genres, cultures and composers.

"Burton-Hill's delightful and informative guide provides a daily dose of the beauty of classical music and also an enticing introduction to it." —*Publishers Weekly*

First published in Great Britain in 2017 by Headline Home—Title page verso; Includes bibliographical references (pages 411-428) and index.

Gioia, Ted
 Music: A Subversive History. Ted Gioia. Basic Books 2019. 528 p.
 ISBN 9781541644366
 Grades: Adult 780.9
 1. Popular culture 2. Music 3. Arts and Entertainment — Music 4. History writing — Arts and culture
 LC 2019001627

A music historian recounts four-thousand-years of music history focusing on the social outcasts, riffraff, insurgents and provocateurs who became trailblazers of this artistic expression and have repeatedly reinvented it, from Sappho to the Sex Pistols.

Includes bibliographical references and index.

Isacoff, Stuart
 Musical Revolutions: How the Sounds of the World Changed. Stuart Isacoff. Alfred A. Knopf 2022. 288 p.
 ISBN 9780525658634
 Grades: Adult 780.9
 1. Music history and criticism 2. Music and society 3. Musicians 4. Biographies 5. Arts and Entertainment — Music 6. Life stories — Arts and culture — Performing arts — Musicians and composers
 LC 2021045361

From the critically acclaimed author of Temperament, a narrative account of the most defining moments in musical history-classical, jazz, rock-all of which forever altered Western culture.

"Whether readers are dedicated musicologists or casual fans, they'll enjoy this thought-provoking dive into the history of Western music." —*Library Journal*

Includes bibliographical references and index.

Rosen, Charles
 The Classical Style: Haydn, Mozart, Beethoven. Charles Rosen. W. W. Norton 1997. xxx, 533 p.
 ISBN 9780393317121
 Grades: Adult 780.9
 1. Haydn, Franz Joseph, 1732-1809 2. Mozart, Wolfgang Amadeus, 1756-1791 3. Beethoven, Ludwig van, 1770-1827 4. Music history and criticism 5. 18th century 6. Arts and Entertainment — Music — Classical
 LC BL 98000020

Presents a detailed analysis of the musical styles and forms developed by Mozart, Haydn, and Beethoven.

"This remains simply the most important book on the classical style in music." —*Choice*

Includes bibliographical references and index.

PUBLIC LIBRARY CORE COLLECTION: NONFICTION
Twentieth Edition

Sachs, Harvey
Ten Masterpieces of Music. Harvey Sachs. Liveright Publishing Corporation 2021. 336 p.
ISBN 9781631495182
Grades: Adult   780.9
1. Music history and criticism 2. Essays 3. Arts and Entertainment — Music
LC 2021033585

Some pieces of music survive; most fall into oblivion. What gives the ten masterpieces selected for this book their extraordinary vitality? In this magisterial volume, Harvey Sachs takes readers into the heart of ten great works of classical music-works that have endured because they were created by composers who had a genius for drawing music out of their deepest wellsprings. These masters-Mozart and Beethoven; Schubert, Schumann, Berlioz, Verdi, and Brahms; Sibelius, Prokofiev, and Stravinsky-communicated their life experiences through music, and through music they universalized the intimate. By expanding our perceptions of these ten pieces-composed in the years between 1784 and 1966-Sachs, in lush,exquisite prose, invites us to consider why music stimulates, disturbs, exalts, and consoles us.

"Sachs's lively prose will draw readers in; were it not for his considerable technical discussion of the masterpieces, this book would be a first-rate choice for general readers. Heartily recommended to every serious lover of classical music." —*Library Journal*

Includes bibliographical references and index.

Spitzer, Michael
The Musical Human: A History of Life on Earth. Michael Spitzer. Bloomsbury 2021. 473 p.
ISBN 9781635576245
Grades: Adult   780.9
1. Music history and criticism 2. Civilization 3. Human evolution 4. Cognition 5. Musical ability 6. Creation (Literary, artistic, etc.) 7. Composition (Music) 8. History writing — Microhistory 9. Arts and Entertainment — Music 10. History writing — Arts and culture

Today music fills our lives. How we have created, performed and listened to this music throughout history has defined what our species is and how we understand who we are. Yet music is an overlooked part of our origin story. With insights from a wealth of disciplines, world-leading musicologist Michael Spitzer renders a global history of music on the widest possible canvas, looking at music in our everyday lives; music in world history; and music in evolution, from insects to apes, humans to AI. Through this journey we begin to understand how music is central to the distinctly human experiences of cognition, feeling and even biology, both widening and closing the evolutionary gaps between ourselves and animals in surprising ways.

"Touching on culture, history, science, anthropology, and philosophy, Spitzer discusses music from ancient times to the courts of medieval and Renaissance Europe to the modern era and everything in between, employing voluminous examples.... An exhaustive but not exhausting study, sublimely readable." —*Booklist*

Includes bibliographical references (395-451) and index.

780.92 Biography

Boilen, Bob
Your Song Changed My Life: From Jimmy Page to St. Vincent, Smokey Robinson to Hozier, Thirty-Five Beloved Artists on Their Journey and the Music That Inspired It. Bob Boilen. William Morrow 2016. 288 pages
ISBN 9780062344441
Grades: Adult   780.92
1. Musicians 2. Popular music 3. Music history and criticism 4. Media tie-ins 5. Arts and entertainment — Music
LC 2015046110

The host and creator of NPR's All Songs Considered asks well-known musicians to reflect on the auditory moments that inspired them and changed their lives, including Trey Anastasio, Carrie Brownstein, Colin Meloy, Jimmy Page and Dave Grohl.

Based on a podcast.

Geck, Martin
★ *Johann Sebastian Bach: Life and Work.* Martin Geck; translated from the German by John Hargraves; [foreword by Kurt Masur]. Harcourt 2006. 738 p. : Illustration
ISBN 9780151006489
Grades: Adult   780.92
1. Bach, Johann Sebastian, 1685-1750 2. Composers 3. Music, German 4. Music history and criticism 5. German history 6. 17th century 7. 18th century 8. Biographies 9. Translations — German to English 10. Arts and Entertainment — Music — Classical 11. Life stories — Arts and culture — Performing arts — Musicians and composers
LC 2006012390

Discusses Bach's musical accomplishments through the stages of his life, from his humble origins as a self-taught court musician to his role as kapellmeister and cantor of St. Thomas's Church.

"This book adds original scholarship to an exhaustive study of other studies of Bach. And although it is often dense with information, it is just as often entertaining: Rich in anecdotes and scintillating in its conjectures." —*New York Times*

Includes bibliographical references (p. 697-719) and index.

Moynahan, Brian
Leningrad: Siege and Symphony: The Story of the Great City Terrorized by Stalin, Starved by Hitler, Immortalized by Shostakovich. Brian Moynahan. Atlantic Monthly Press 2014. 496 p.
ISBN 9780802123169
Grades: Adult   780.92
1. Shostakovich, Dmitrii Dmitrievich, 1906-1975 2. World War II 3. Starvation 4. Musicians 5. Sieges 6. St. Petersburg, Russia 7. 1940s 8. History writing — Wars and conflicts — World War II
LC Bl2014044322

Describes the concert played in August 1942 by a cobbled-together group of starving survivors—who were cold, sick and weak from Stalin's purges and the Nazi invasion of Russia—which offered a glimmer of hope during the darkest days of World War II.

"Moynahan's rapturous commentary on the music at times amounts to puffery. theless an admirable tribute to the human spirit and artistic integrity. Highly recommended for all readers interested in the era and the wellsprings of artistic creation." —*Library Journal*

781.1 Basic principles of music

Gasser, Nolan
Why You Like It: The Science and Culture of Musical Taste. Nolan Gasser. Flatiron Books 2019. 576 p.
ISBN 9781250057198
Grades: Adult   781.1
1. Music appreciation 2. Popular music 3. Musicology 4. Musical style 5. Music 6. Arts and Entertainment — Music
LC 2018037896

The chief architect of the Pandora Radio song recommendation engine presents a groundbreaking examination of how the body and mind affect music tastes, discussing how the brain processes music and what qualities trigger such human responses as humming and dancing.

"The book is a sprawl, but serious music lovers will find much fascinating science and lore to browse." —*Publishers Weekly*

Includes bibliographical references and index.

Mauceri, John
For the Love of Music: A Conductor's Guide to the Art of Listening. John Mauceri. Alfred A. Knopf 2019. 224 pages
ISBN 9780525520658

ESSENTIAL AND RECOMMENDED TITLES
781.45 Conducting

Grades: Adult   **781.1**

1. Music appreciation 2. Classical music 3. Music history and criticism 4. Music 5. Listening 6. Performance art 7. Musical performance 8. Arts and Entertainment — Music — Classical

LC 2018051290

In this beautifully written guide, a protege of Leonard Bernstein, his colleague for 18 years, draws on his profound knowledge to answer the questions: Why should I listen to classical music? How can a get the most from the listening experience?

"Even those who know classical music well will learn something from this lively and enthusiastic primer." —*Kirkus*

Includes index.

Rogers, Susan E.

★ ***This Is What It Sounds Like: What the Music You Love Says About You.*** Susan Rogers and Ogi Ogas. W.W. Norton & Company 2022. 288 p.

ISBN 9780393541250

Grades: Adult   **781.1**

1. Rogers, Susan E. 2. Music 3. Listening 4. Music appreciation 5. Brain 6. Neuroscience 7. Personality 8. Identity 9. Arts and Entertainment — Music 10. Society and culture — Psychology and human behavior

One of the most successful female record producers of all time and an award-winning professor of cognitive neuroscience leads readers to musical self-awareness, explaining that we each possess a unique "listener profile" based on our brain's natural response to seven key dimensions of any song.

"As long as readers are up for a record pull, they won't be disappointed. Sure to appeal to many popular music lovers, particularly young adults." —*Library Journal*

Warsaw-Fan Rauch, Arianna

★ ***Declassified:*** *A Low-Key Guide to the High-Strung World of Classical Music.* Arianna Warsaw-Fan Rauch. G. P. Putnam's Sons 2022. 304 p.

ISBN 9780593331460

Grades: Adult   **781.1**

1. Music appreciation 2. Classical music 3. Music industry and trade 4. Classical musicians 5. Elitism 6. Autobiographies and memoirs 7. Arts and Entertainment — Music — Classical 8. Life stories — Arts and culture — Performing arts — Musicians and composers

LC 2022019089

Warsaw-Fan Rauch blows through the cobwebs of elitism and exclusion and invites everyone to love and hate this music as much as she does. She offers a backstage tour of the industry and equips you for every listening scenario, covering :the 7 main compositional periods (even the soul-crushingly depressing Medieval period), a breakdown of the instruments and their associated personality types (apologies to violists and conductors), what it's like to be a musician at the highest level (it's hard), how to steal a Stradivarius (and make no money in the process), and when to clap during a live performance (also: When not to).

"Cue vigorous applause and a standing ovation because Declassified is an enchanting and exhilarating tour de force." —*Booklist*

Includes bibliographical references and index.

781.45 Conducting

Mauceri, John

Maestros and Their Music: The Art and Alchemy of Conducting. by John Mauceri. Alfred A. Knopf 2017. 272 p.

ISBN 9780451494023

Grades: Adult   **781.45**

1. Conductors (Music) 2. Musical performance 3. Orchestras 4. Conducting 5. Orchestral music 6. Arts and Entertainment — Music — Classical

LC 2016055932

An accessible tour of the enigmatic craft of conducting by the celebrated international conductor explores how the art of his profession is itself a composition of legacy, tradition, and techniques that involve intricate communicative gestures.

"Symphony-lovers will be thrilled with the behind-the-scenes details, and aspiring conductors will enjoy the rich industry insight. Those simply curious about how classical music happens will feel drawn in by Mauceris palpable passion." —*Booklist*

Includes index.

781.49 Recording of music

Milner, Greg

Perfecting *Sound Forever: An Aural History of Recorded Music.* Greg Milner. Faber and Faber 2009. x, 416 p. : Illustration

ISBN 9780571211654

Grades: Adult   **781.49**

1. Music 2. Popular music 3. Sound 4. Music history and criticism 5. Sound recordings 6. Arts and Entertainment — Music

LC 2008055444

A history of recorded music reveals the behind-the-scenes processes through which recorded sound is captured and produced, in a chronicle that also covers major recording achievements, the innovators who influence the way music is experienced, and the current debate about faithful versus transcendent recording practices.

"The author begins in the late 19th century, tracing the evolution from Edison's invention of the phonograph to the contemporary use of digital music files. Broad in scope and steeped in detail, the book strikes a mostly well-maintained balance between the history of the technological development of recordings and the more approachable accounts of the people and events surrounding it." —*Kirkus*

Includes index.

781.6 Traditions of music

Almond, Steve

Rock *and Roll Will Save Your Life: A Book by and for the Fanatics Among Us (with Bitchin' Soundtrack).* Steve Almond. Random House Inc 2010. 222 p.

ISBN 9781400066209

Grades: Adult   **781.6**

1. Rock music 2. Rock musicians 3. Fans (People) 4. Autobiographies and memoirs 5. Arts and Entertainment — Music — Rock 6. Life stories — Arts and culture — Performing arts

LC 2010281026

The author of Candyfreak celebrates his love for rock and roll, in a humorous memoir about his life as an obsessed fan augmented by entertaining rock lists, surprising debates and discussions and homages to some of rock's most beloved bad songs.

"As a young writer plagued by self-doubt, Almond reveled in the emotional escape of music; the joy of his fanaticism is conveyed poignantlyand so completelythat we're infected with his touted salvation too. With well-placed interludes or reluctant exegeses, Almond peppers his pages with biting insights and funny vignettes; dismissing, for instance, Toto's Africa as … the lovechild of Muzak and Imperialism. Though the language feels a bit highbrow, Almond ultimately crafts a playful and intelligent read." —*Paste*

Horowitz, Joseph

★ ***Classical*** *Music in America: A History of Its Rise and Fall.* Joseph Horowitz. W.W. Norton 2005. xix, 606 p. : Illustration

ISBN 9780393057171

Grades: Adult   **781.6**

1. Classical music 2. Music history and criticism 3. United States 4. Arts and Entertainment — Music — Classical

LC 2004027754

A social history of classical music in America looks at top performers, explains how classical music failed to sustain its early popularity, and offers suggestions for broadening its appeal.

PUBLIC LIBRARY CORE COLLECTION: NONFICTION
Twentieth Edition

"Whether or not his conclusions are accepted in their totality, this fascinating book is an important social history and is highly recommended for all libraries." —*Library Journal*

781.62 Folk music

Strom, Yale
The Book of Klezmer: The History, the Music, the Folklore. Yale Strom. Chicago Review Press 2011. 381 p.
ISBN 9781613740637
Grades: Adult   **781.62**
1. Klezmer music 2. Music, Jewish 3. Folk music 4. Arts and Entertainment — Music — Folk

This remarkable book contains interviews and accounts of klezmer musicians and the music's history in Eastern Europe and the New World. Strom, who is a klezmer musician as well as historian and writer, interviewed survivors of the Holocaust when klezmer music came in danger of being annihilated along with the Jews during travels in Eastern Europe, along with present day klezmer musicians who have fueled its revival.

"This history of Klezmer music is divided into four chapters: 'From King David to Duvid the Klezmer,' 'From the Enlightenment to the Holocaust,' 'Klezmer in the New World, 1880-1960,' and 'From Zev to Zorn: The Masters of the Culture.' the first appendix, 'Klezmer Memories in the Memorial Books,' is one of the most moving sections, featuring a collection of commentaries on klezmer music and musicians from hundreds of memorial books written by Holocaust survivors." —*Library Journal*

Includes bibliographical references, discography, and index.

Young, Rob
Electric Eden: Unearthing Britain's Visionary Music. Rob Young. Faber and Faber 2011. 672 p.
ISBN 9780865478565
Grades: Adult   **781.62**
1. Music history and criticism 2. Folk music 3. 1960s 4. 1970s 5. 20th century 6. Arts and Entertainment — Music — Folk
LC 2011001987

Traces the 1960s effort to revive music in England that underscored the achievements of such period artists as Pink Floyd, Nick Drake and Led Zeppelin, providing insight into how their work reflected historical precedents while establishing models for present-day musicians.

"Young's narrative slips fluidly forward, backward, and through the cracks of canonical music history. And he doesn't just stick to music; like Greil Marcus with a thirst for ancient paganism and postmodern urban theory, Young weaves a poetic, philosophical tapestry as rich and heady as the songs he champions." —*AV Club*

Includes bibliographical references and index.

781.63 Popular music

Piston, Walter
Orchestration. Walter Piston. Norton 1955. 477 p. : Illustration
ISBN 9780393097405
Grades: Adult   **781.63**
1. Music 2. Orchestral music 3. Arts and Entertainment — Music
LC 55014230

A college-level music text that develops the student's knowledge of musical instruments, and their function in the orchestra.

781.64 Western popular music

Doggett, Peter
Electric Shock: From the Gramophone to the iPhone - 125 Years of Pop Music. Peter Doggett. Random House UK 2017. 728 pages
ISBN 9780099575191
Grades: Adult   **781.64**
1. Popular music 2. Music 3. Popular culture 4. Sound recording industry and trade 5. 20th century 6. 21st century 7. Arts and Entertainment — Music 8. History writing — Arts and culture 9. Society and culture — Pop culture
LC Bl2018020209

Tells the story of popular music, from the birth of recording in the 1890s to the digital age, from the first pop superstars of the twentieth century to the omnipresence of music in our lives, in hit singles, ringtones and on Spotify. The author takes us on a rollercoaster ride through the history of music.

"This exhaustive work will be indispensable and go well alongside such books as Ed Wards the History of Rock & Roll: Volume 1, 1920-1963 (2016) and Ann Powers Good Booty (2017)." —*Booklist*

Includes bibliographical references and index.

Hermes, Will
Love Goes to Buildings on Fire: Five Years in New York That Changed Music Forever. Will Hermes. Faber and Faber 2011. xi, 368 p. : Illustration
ISBN 9780865479807
Grades: Adult   **781.64**
1. Popular music 2. Popular culture 3. Music 4. Music history and criticism 5. Social life and customs 6. New York City 7. United States 8. 1970s 9. 20th century 10. Arts and Entertainment — Music
LC 2011008445

This is the first book to tell the full story of the New York City punk rock, hip-hop, disco, salsa, loft jazz scene, the downtown composers known in the mid-1970s as Minimalists, and the phenomenal and surprising ways they intersected. From New Year's Day 1973 to New Year's Eve 1977, the book moves panoramically from post-Dylan Greenwich Village, to the arson-scarred South Bronx barrios where salsa and hip-hop were created, to the Lower Manhattan lofts where jazz and classical music were reimagined, to ramshackle clubs like CBGB and the Gallery, where rock and dance music were hot-wired for a new generation.

Includes bibliographical references and index.

Houghton, Mick
Becoming Elektra: The True Story of Jac Holzman's Visionary Record Label. Mick Houghton. Jawbone 2010. 304 p. : Illustration; Color
ISBN 9781906002299
Grades: Adult   **781.64**
1. Holzman, Jac 2. Music 3. Sound recording industry and trade 4. Popular music 5. Sound recordings 6. Music history and criticism 7. Arts and Entertainment — Music
LC 2011477408

"Includes full-color reproductions of virtually every title in Elektra's catalog, themselves a revealing portrait of changing tastes and evolving consumer sophistication. Houghton's research is meticulous but he avoids the minutia that clogs many music books." —*Seattle Post-Intelligencer*

Includes bibliographical references, discography and index.

Lehman, David
A Fine Romance: Jewish Songwriters, American Songs. David Lehman. Nextbook/Schocken 2009. 249 p.
ISBN 9780805242508
Grades: Adult   **781.64**
1. Popular music 2. Music history and criticism 3. Arts and Entertainment — Music 4. History writing — Jewish history 5. Life stories — Arts and culture — Performing arts — Musicians and composers
LC 2009005942

This guidebook through the golden age of song examines the stories behind these classic songs and the Jewish musicians, composers, and lyricists who wrote them, including "Embraceable You," "White Christmas," and "Easter Parade."

"Lehman investigates the lasting impact of 20th-century Jewish popular songwriters in America, ranging from Irving Berlin's and Jerome Kern's early efforts in the 1910s through George Gershwin, Harold Arlen, Richard Rodgers, Lorenz Hart, and Oscar Hammerstein II to Leonard Bernstein and the early

ESSENTIAL AND RECOMMENDED TITLES
781.64 Western popular music

1960s. In fluid prose and expert foreshadowing and summations, the author conveys the personality of each musician or writer and recommends selected versions of his favorite songs." —*Library Journal*

Includes bibliographical references (p. [235]-249).

McNally, Dennis

On Highway 61: Music, Race, and the Evolution of Cultural Freedom. Dennis McNally. Counterpoint 2014. 384 p.

ISBN 9781619024496

Grades: Adult   781.64

1. African Americans 2. Popular music 3. Music 4. Race relations 5. African American music 6. Music history and criticism 7. United States history 8. Arts and Entertainment — Music 9. History writing — African American — United States

LC 2014014417

Traces the progression of music created by post-Civil War Black Americans "from ragtime to blues and jazz" and the white followers who adopted and embraced diversity and the sound to create bop, swing and rock and roll.

"A concise, Dylan-heavy history of the American relationship between race and music." —*Kirkus*

Powers, Ann

Good Booty: Love and Sex, Black and White, Body and Soul in American Music. Ann Powers. Dey Street Books 2017. 256 pages

ISBN 9780062463692

Grades: Adult   781.64

1. Popular music 2. Sound recording industry and trade 3. Sexuality 4. Race (Social sciences) 5. Singers 6. Musicians 7. Dancing 8. Metaphor 9. African American music 10. Music, American 11. Arts and Entertainment — Music 12. Society and culture — Sex and sexuality 13. Society and culture — Race 14. History writing — Arts and culture

LC Bl2017032952

The critic and correspondent for NPR Music explores the history of American popular music as an erotic art form, from 19th-century New Orleans and the Jazz Age in New York, to the screaming teens that welcomed the Beatles and modern day performers.

"Powers reveals an extraordinary breadth of knowledge and insight and has produced an absolutely essential addition to any pop-culture collection." —*Booklist*

Remnick, David

Holding the Note: Profiles in Popular Music. David Remnick. Alfred a Knopf Inc 2023. 256 p.

ISBN 9781400043613

Grades: Adult   781.64

1. Musicians 2. Music history and criticism 3. Popular music composers 4. Creativity 5. Seniors 6. Essays 7. Interviews 8. Collective biographies 9. Life stories — Arts and culture — Performing arts — Musicians and composers 10. Arts and Entertainment — Music

The greatest popular songs, whether it's Aretha Franklin singing "Respect" or Bob Dylan performing "Blind Willie McTell," have a way of embedding themselves in our memories. You remember a time and a place and a feeling when you hear that song again. In Holding the Note, David Remnick writes about the lives and work of some of the greatest musicians, songwriters, and performers of the past fifty years.

"There is acuity here, bemusement, tenderness, and gratitude." —*Booklist*

Sanneh, Kelefa

★ *Major Labels: A History of Popular Music in Seven Genres.* Kelefa Sanneh. Penguin 2021. 400 p.

ISBN 9780525559597

Grades: Adult   781.64

1. Popular music 2. Music history and criticism 3. Music industry and trade 4. Popular culture 5. Public opinion 6. 21st century 7. 20th century 8. Arts and Entertainment — Music 9. Society and culture — Pop culture

LC 2021008355

The entire history of popular music over the past fifty years refracted through the big genres that have defined and dominated it—including rock, country, punk, R&B, dance and hip-hop—woven together into a cosmic reckoning with music's evolution as a popular art form, as a huge cultural and economic force, and as an essential component to our identities, from Black Sabbath to Black Flag to Beyonce, and beyond.

"A thoroughly enjoyable and perceptive book that champions the art of popular music." —*Library Journal*

Includes index.

Sloan, Nate

Switched on Pop: How Popular Music Works, and Why It Matters. Nate Sloan and Charlie Harding. Oxford University Press 2020. 224 pages

ISBN 9780190056650

Grades: Adult   781.64

1. Popular music 2. Music history and criticism 3. Songwriting 4. Composition (Music) 5. Musicology 6. Media tie-ins 7. Arts and Entertainment — Music — Pop 8. Society and culture — Pop culture

Switched on Pop is the book based on the eponymous podcast that has been hailed by NPR, Rolling Stone, the Guardian, and Entertainment Weekly for its witty and accessible analysis of Top 40 hits. Through close studies of sixteen modern classics, musicologist Nate Sloan and songwriter Charlie Harding shift pop from the background to the foreground, illuminating the essential musical concepts behind two decades of chart-topping songs.

"In much the same way that Wendy Carlos's 1968 album Switched-on Bach introduced synthesizers to popular music, Sloan and Harding's ode to popular music reintroduces the Billboard Top 100 to the field of musicology and the snobbiest of vinyl collectors. A necessary addition to any music collection." —*Library Journal*

Based on a podcast.

Stanley, Bob

Let's Do It: The Birth of Pop Music: A History. Bob Stanley. Pegasus Books 2022. 624 p.

ISBN 9781639362509

Grades: Adult   781.64

1. Popular music 2. Music and society 3. Music industry and trade 4. Arts and Entertainment — Music 5. Arts and Entertainment — Music — Pop

The must-read music book of the year brings together all genres to tell the definitive story of the birth of Pop, from 1900 to the mid-fifties.

"Stanley's engaging narrative music study invites general readers as well as music mavens into a memorable world that provided the necessary antecedents for rock and roll." —*Library Journal*

Wald, Elijah

American Epic: When Music Gave America Her Voice. Elijah Wald, and Bernard McMahon. Touchstone Books 2016. 288 p.

ISBN 9781501135606

Grades: Adult   781.64

1. Music 2. Blues (Music) 3. Gospel music 4. Folk music 5. Media tie-ins 6. History writing — Arts and culture 7. Arts and entertainment — Music 8. History writing — United States

LC 2016001493

A companion book to the groundbreaking PBS and BBC documentary series celebrates the pioneers and artists of American roots music—blues, gospel, folk, Cajun, Appalachian, Hawaiian, Native American—without which there would be no jazz, rock, country R&B, or hip hop today.

How the Beatles Destroyed Rock 'n' Roll: An Alternative History of American Popular Music. Elijah Wald. Oxford University Press 2009. 336 p.

ISBN 9780195341546

Grades: 11 12 Adult   781.64

1. Rock groups 2. Popular music 3. Rock music 4. Music 5. Historiography 6. Social life and customs 7. United States 8. 21st century 9. Arts and Entertainment — Music — Pop 10. Arts and Entertainment — Music — Rock

LC 2008042265

Surveys the history of American popular music in terms of the changes in technology and their effect on ordinary listeners as they changed music from something to be listened to and danced to live to something to be bought in recorded form.

Includes bibliographical references and index.

781.642 Country music

Duncan, Dayton

★ *Country Music: An Illustrated History.* Dayton Duncan and Ken Burns. Alfred A. Knopf 2019. 464 pages

ISBN 9780525520542

Grades: Adult   781.642

1. Country music 2. Country musicians 3. Music history and criticism 4. Social life and customs 5. United States 6. Media tie-ins 7. Arts and Entertainment — Music — Country 8. History writing — United States 9. Life stories — Arts and culture — Performing arts — Musicians and composers

LC 2018047629

Spur Award for Contemporary Nonfiction, 2020.

The rich and colorful story of America's most popular music and the singers and songwriters who captivated, entertained, and consoled listeners throughout the twentieth century—based on the eight-part film series which aired on PBS in September 2019.

"Country music is America's music—which is to say, music from every culture and ethnicity. An essential guide." —*Kirkus*

Moss, Marissa R.

Her Country: How the Women of Country Music Became the Success They Were Never Supposed to Be. Marissa R. Moss. Henry Holt and Company 2022. 304 p.

ISBN 9781250793591

Grades: Adult   781.642

1. Women country musicians 2. Women singers 3. Country music 4. Gender role 5. Music industry and trade 6. Music history and criticism 7. Persistence 8. Nashville, Tennessee 9. Society and culture — Gender — Women 10. Arts and Entertainment — Music — Country 11. Life stories — Arts and culture — Performing arts — Musicians and composers 12. Life stories — Identity — Gender

LC 2021060818

It was only two decades ago, but, for the women of country music, 1999 seems like an entirely different universe. With Shania Twain, country's biggest award winner and star, and the Chicks topping every chart, country music was a woman's world: specifically, country radio and Nashville's Music Row. Cut to 2021, when women are only played on country radio 16% of the time, on a good day, and when only men have won Entertainer of the Year at the CMA Awards for a decade. Her Country is veteran Nashville journalist Marissa R. Moss's story of how in the past two decades, country's women fought back against systems designed to keep them down, armed with their art and never willing to just shut up and sing—and about how women can and do belong in the mainstream of country music, even if their voices aren't being heard as loudly.

Music journalist Moss debuts with an exuberant deep-dive into the careers of three country music stars who 'opened up a window to a musical world where women are in charge.' —*Publishers Weekly*

Includes bibliographical references.

781.643 Blues

Ferris, William R.

Give My Poor Heart Ease: Voices of the Mississippi Blues. [interviews by] William Ferris. University of North Carolina Press 2009. xiv, 302 p. : Illustration; Map

ISBN 9780807833254

Grades: Adult   781.643

1. African Americans 2. Blues (Music) 3. Blues musicians 4. Music history and criticism 5. African American music 6. Interviews 7. Arts and Entertainment — Music — Jazz and the Blues 8. Society and culture — Ethnic studies

LC 2009016647

Collects interviews and commentary on blues and gospel music from the Mississippi Delta area, and discusses how race relations, connections to the sacred, and Southern life helped mold this style of music.

"Ferris presents transcriptions of stories he captured via films and recording devices from the 1960s and 1970s of Mississippi blues practitioners, preachers, and Parchman Prison inmates. The enclosed CD and DVD bring the package together with stories, blues songs, and gospel recordings. B.B. King and Willie Dixon are the most famous artists included, but the stories of desperately poor sharecroppers and ex-inmates are just as engrossing. The comprehensive bibliography is a great resource." —*Library Journal*

This book was published with the assistance of the H. Eugene and Lillian Youngs Lehman Fund of the University of North Carolina Press—T.P. verso; Includes bibliographical references (p. [259]-269), discography (p. 269-284), filmography (p. 284-289) and index.

Lomax, Alan

★ *The Land Where the Blues Began.* Alan Lomax. Pantheon Books 1993. xv, 539 p. : Illustration

ISBN 9780385312851

Grades: Adult   781.643

1. Blues (Music) 2. Music, American 3. African American history 4. African Americans 5. Music history and criticism 6. Delta Region, Mississippi 7. Arts and Entertainment — Music — Jazz and the Blues

LC 91052627

National Book Critics Circle Award for Non-Fiction, 1993.

A journey of discovery through the Mississippi Delta explores the rich African-American musical heritage of the region, as recorded in the words and music of Muddy Waters, Fred Macdowell, Sid Hemphill, and other great masters of the blues.

"If it were a novel, Alan Lomax's long-awaited account of his adventures in the Mississippi Delta would be called sprawling and a must read. It is as delightful and hard to put down as any fictional epic." —*Booklist*

Includes bibliographical references (p. 509-514), discography, filmography, and index.

781.644 Soul

White, Adam

★ *Motown: The Sound of Young America.* Adam White with Barney Ales; foreword by Andrew Loog Oldham. Thames & Hudson Australia Pty, Limited. 2016. 400 p.

ISBN 9780500518298

Grades: Adult   781.644

1. Soul music 2. Popular music 3. African American music 4. Music history and criticism 5. 1960s 6. Visual nonfiction 7. Arts and Entertainment — Music

The music of 'Motown' needs no introduction. Berry Gordy's record label became a style unto itself, producing hit after suave, sassy and sophisticated hit, and shaped the careers of so many of the greatest musicians of all time. The label produced more US number-one hits than the Beatles, Elvis Presley, the Rolling Stones and the Beach Boys combined. Now, and with fresh new insights and an incredible visual narrative, the official, visual history of this momentous contribution to music and American culture is told in full.

"Working with Motown founder Berry Gordy's right-hand man Ales, he delivers a lavishly illustrated, wonderfully written history of Motown. Although the music and personalities involved in the Motown story have been richly mined (readers looking for salaciousness can refer to books such as Gerald Posner's Motown and the biographies by J. Randy Taraborrelli, alternatives to Gordy's self-serving autobiography To Be Loved), this is balanced insider knowledge that greatly exceeds the others visually, packed as it is with fabulous photographs and album art that celebrates the record label that provided the soundtrack to exciting and changing times, and readers will treasure the deep

ESSENTIAL AND RECOMMENDED TITLES
781.646 Reggae

dive into the era and the vast, firsthand information on Motown artists." —*Library Journal*

781.646 Reggae

Garnice, Michael
The Ultimate Guide to Great Reggae: The Complete Story of Reggae Told Through Its Greatest Songs, Famous and Forgotten. Michael Garnice. Equinox Publishing Ltd. 2016. 604 p.
ISBN 9781781790953
Grades: Adult   781.646
1. Reggae music 2. Reggae musicians 3. Music 4. Popular music 5. Arts and Entertainment — Music

The Ultimate Guide to Great Reggae" celebrates (and helps you find) the greatest songs of reggae. It focuses on every style of reggae, from mento to Jamaican R&B, ska, rock steady, dub, DJ, roots, dancehall and more. It opens with an exceptionally comprehensive brief history of reggae. This is followed by 52 chapters, each devoted to in-depth descriptions of the greatest songs for a particular artist or style.

781.648 Electronica

Matos, Michaelangelo
The Underground Is Massive: How Electronic Dance Music Conquered America. Michaelangelo Matos. Dey Street Books 2015. 368 p.
ISBN 9780062271785
Grades: Adult   781.648
1. Music and society 2. Technopop music 3. Electronic music 4. Dance music 5. Raves 6. Ecstasy (Drug) 7. Arts and Entertainment — Music
LC Bl2015006082

A music journalist chronicles the birth and escalating popularity of electronic dance music, describing how the Millennial generation's use of technology and social media helped fuel the rise and expansion of the musical subculture.

781.65 Jazz

DeVeaux, Scott Knowles
Jazz. Scott DeVeaux, University of Virginia, Gary Giddins, the Graduate Center, City University of New York. W. W. Norton & Company 2015. xix, 475 p, 66 variously numbered p, 16 unnumbered p. of plates : Illustration
ISBN 9780393937060
Grades: Adult   781.65
1. Music history and criticism 2. Jazz music 3. Arts and Entertainment — Music — Jazz and the Blues
LC 2014038121

This streamlined second edition exposes students to the expressive power of jazz and brings its greatest players to life.

"There are numerous histories of jazz on the market, but renowned critic Giddins and scholar DeVeaux's offering jumps immediately to the top of the list." —*Booklist*

Includes bibliographical references and index.

Marsalis, Wynton
Moving to Higher Ground: How Jazz Can Change Your Life. Wynton Marsalis with Geoffrey C. Ward. Random House 2008. 208 p.
ISBN 9781400060788
Grades: 10 11 12 Adult   781.65
1. Jazz music 2. Music and society 3. Music appreciation 4. Music, American 5. Music 6. United States 7. Arts and Entertainment — Music — Jazz and the Blues 8. Adult books for young adults
LC 2008016560

The Pulitzer Prize-winning musician offers his own take on jazz music as he discusses the secrets of listening to jazz, the different styles of various jazz musicians, its improvisational principles, and its influence on modern life and on one's view of the world around.

Morgenstern, Dan
Living with Jazz: A Reader. Dan Morgenstern; a reader edited by Sheldon Meyer. Pantheon Books 2004. xvii, 712 p.
ISBN 9780375420726
Grades: Adult   781.65
1. Music history and criticism 2. Jazz music 3. Arts and Entertainment — Music — Jazz and the Blues
LC 2004043432

A collection of essays, biographical profiles, and critical analyses by one of the twentieth century's leading jazz writers includes commentary on the work of jazz entertainers, including Duke Ellington, Ella Fitzgerald, John Coltrane, Dizzy Gillespie, and Louis Armstrong, as well as assessment of the role of jazz in contemporary culture and its influence on modern music.

"This is a compilation of nearly half a century of Morgenstern's profiles, liner notes, record and show reviews and other musings. Morgenstern reminisces about his introduction to jazz in a brief opening memoir, then segues into lengthy sections on his greatest heroes, Louis Armstrong and Duke Ellington. His exuberant characterizations make this monumental volume a stimulating guide to jazz in the second half of the 20th century." —*Publishers Weekly*

Includes index.

Myers, Marc
Why Jazz Happened. Marc Myers. University of California Press 2013. 248 p.
ISBN 9780520268784
Grades: Adult   781.65
1. Jazz music 2. Music industry and trade 3. Jazz musicians 4. Music history and criticism 5. Arts and Entertainment — Music — Jazz and the Blues
LC 2012022218

A comprehensive social history looks at the many forces that shaped this most American of art forms and the many influences that gave rise to jazz's post-war styles.

Includes bibliographical references and index.

Torgoff, Martin
Bop Apocalypse: Jazz, Race, the Beats, and Drugs. Martin Torgoff. Da Capo Press 2017. 320 p.
ISBN 9780306824753
Grades: Adult   781.65
1. Beat culture 2. Music and race (Social sciences) 3. Drugs 4. Jazz musicians 5. Music and society 6. Music history and criticism 7. Jazz music 8. History writing — Arts and culture 9. History writing — United States 10. Arts and entertainment — Music — Jazz and the Blues
LC 2016015902

Describes the history of drug culture in America, interweaving tales of the birth of jazz in New Orleans, the rise of swing and bebop and the start of the Beat Generation with the first drug laws and the development of the Federal Bureau of Narcotics.

"A textured story of human hope and hopelessness, of artistry that blossomed in the most daunting and, in some cases, demeaning circumstances." —*Kirkus*

Includes bibliographical references and index.

781.6509 Jazz — History

Chinen, Nate
Playing Changes: Jazz for the New Century. Nate Chinen. Pantheon Books 2018. 256 p.
ISBN 9781101870341
Grades: Adult   781.6509

1. Jazz music 2. Jazz musicians 3. Music history and criticism 4. African American jazz musicians 5. 21st century 6. Arts and Entertainment — Music — Jazz and the Blues

LC 2017058677

A leading jazz critic charts the origins of jazz history and the influence of commercialized jazz education on the true spirit of the genre and discusses the synergy between jazz and postmillennial hip-hop and R&B music.

"Chinens virtuoso jazz history will drive readers to listen to the music anew, or for the first time." —*Publishers Weekly*

Includes bibliographical references and index.

Cooke, Mervyn
The **Chronicle** *of Jazz*. Oxford University Press 2013. 256 p.
ISBN 9780199341009
Grades: Adult 781.6509
1. Jazz musicians 2. Jazz music composers 3. Jazz music 4. Music history and criticism 5. Arts and Entertainment — Music — Jazz and the Blues 6. Adult books for young adults

LC 2013019617

A year-by-year history of people and events, this lively multi-layered account tells the whole story of jazz music and its personalities.

"This handsome and attractive volume by music professor and writer Cooke covers the entire history of the jazz medium in one accessible and colorful resource." —*Booklist*

Originally published in 1998 (New York :Abbeville Press,1998).

Giddins, Gary
Weather Bird: *Jazz at the Dawn of Its Second Century*. Gary Giddins. Oxford University Press 2004. xxiv, 632 p.
ISBN 9780195156072
Grades: Adult 781.6509
1. Jazz music 2. Performing arts 3. Music history and criticism 4. Arts and Entertainment — Music — Jazz and the Blues

LC 2004000654

A companion volume to the landmark Visions of Jazz collects more than 140 writings celebrating jazz, with commentary on everything from modern jazz events and the current top musicians, to studies on the leading jazz figures of the past.

"This book collects more than 140 essays, articles, and reviews that Giddins wrote from 1990 to November 2003. The breadth and depth of his knowledge is extremely impressive, his ear is astounding, and his masterly style routinely achieves the near impossible in writing engagingly about something that inherently eludes description." —*Library Journal*

Includes index.

Gioia, Ted
The **History** *of Jazz*. Ted Gioia. Oxford University Press 2021. 444 p. : Illustration
ISBN 9780190087210
Grades: 11 12 Adult 781.6509
1. Jazz music 2. Music history and criticism 3. Arts and Entertainment — Music — Jazz and the Blues 4. Adult books for young adults

LC 2010023182

A panoramic history of the genre brings to life the diverse places in which jazz evolved, traces the origins of its various styles, and offers commentary on the music itself.

"The author relates the story of African American music from its roots in Africa to the international respect it enjoys today. This well-researched, extensively annotated volume covers the major trends and personalities that have shaped jazz. The excellent bibliography and list of recommended listening make this a valuable purchase for libraries building a jazz collection." —*Library Journal*

Includes bibliographical references (p. 399]-402), discography (p. 403-418), and index.

Kahn, Ashley
The **House** *That Trane Built: The Story of Impulse Records*. Ashley Kahn. W.W. Norton & Co. 2006. VIII, 338 p. : Illustration
ISBN 9780393058796
Grades: Adult 781.6509
1. Coltrane, John, 1926-1967 2. Sound recording industry and trade 3. Jazz music 4. Music history and criticism 5. Social life and customs 6. United States 7. 20th century 8. Arts and Entertainment — Music — Jazz and the Blues

LC 2005037218

Traces the story of Impulse Records and the pivotal contributions of avant-garde jazz musician John Coltrane in the 1960s and 1970s, explaining how the label was shaped by thirty-eight of his politically charged recordings.

"The author offers a fascinating insider's view of the sessions that produced not only Coltrane's classics but also top-grade albums by both fiery radicals and such timeless stars as Duke Ellington, Coleman Hawkins and Benny Carter." —*The Economist*

Includes bibliographical references (p. 321-324), discography (p. 299-320), and index.

Sandke, Randy
Where *the Dark and the Light Folks Meet: Race and the Mythology, Politics, and Business of Jazz*. Randall Sandke. Scarecrow Press 2010. x, 277 p.
ISBN 9780810866522
Grades: Adult 781.6509
1. Music 2. Music history and criticism 3. Jazz music 4. Arts and Entertainment — Music — Jazz and the Blues

LC 2009037977

Looks at the history and nature of jazz, challenging the theory that the music was solely created and driven by African Americans.

"This book is thoroughly researched and documented. This is an important addition to the literature of jazz." —*Choice*

Includes bibliographical references (p. 249-258) and index.

Tye, Larry
★ *The* **Jazzmen:** *How Duke Ellington, Louis Armstrong, and Count Basie Transformed America*. Larry Tye. Mariner Books 2024. 384 p.
ISBN 9780358380436
Grades: Adult 781.6509
1. Ellington, Duke, 1899-1974 2. Basie, Count, 1904-1984 3. Armstrong, Louis, 1901-1971 4. African American jazz musicians 5. Jazz music 6. Music history and criticism 7. Social change 8. African American history 9. Civil Rights Movement 10. Popular culture 11. African Americans 12. 20th century 13. Collective biographies 14. Interviews 15. Life stories — Arts and culture — Performing arts — Musicians and composers 16. Arts and Entertainment — Music — Jazz and the Blues 17. Society and culture — Pop culture

Based on more than 250 interviews, this meticulously researched history of Black America in the early-to-mid 1900s through three longtime kings of jazz—Duke Ellington, Louis Armstrong and Count Basie—who opened America's eyes and souls to their magnificent music, writing the soundtrack for the civil rights movement.

"The author's vivid style brings readers front and center into the myriad of clubs and studios where Armstrong, Basie, and Ellington played, as well as the social vibe of the cities and towns where their music left an indelible mark." —*Kirkus*

Ward, Geoffrey C.
Jazz: *A History of America's Music*. by Geoffrey C. Ward; based on a documentary film by Ken Burns written by Geoffrey C. Ward; with a preface by Ken Burns. Alfred A. Knopf 2000. x, 489 p. : Illustration; Color
ISBN 9780679445517
Grades: 11 12 Adult 781.6509
1. Music history and criticism 2. African American jazz musicians 3. Jazz music 4. Jazz musicians 5. Biographies 6. Arts and Entertainment — Music — Jazz and the Blues 7. Adult books for young adults

LC 00022604

ESSENTIAL AND RECOMMENDED TITLES
781.65092 Jazz — Biography

Library Journal Best Books, 2000; New York Times Notable Book, 2000.

A companion book to the PBS series furnishes a lavish photographic essay that celebrates the contributions of such artists as Louis Armstrong, Duke Ellington, Ella Fitzgerald, and John Coltrane.

"The illustrations are copious, including about 500 pieces and running from cover to cover; the text, picture captions, and sidebars reflect the research that went into the six-year project. A very competent and lovingly rendered history."
—*Booklist*

Includes bibliographical references (p. 465-470) and index.

781.65092 Jazz — Biography

Ratliff, Ben
The Jazz Ear: Conversations Over Music. Ben Ratliff. Times Books 2008. 256 p.
ISBN 9780805081466
Grades: Adult   781.65092
1. Jazz musicians 2. Jazz music 3. Music 4. Musicians 5. Social life and customs 6. United States 7. Interviews 8. Arts and Entertainment — Music — Jazz and the Blues 9. Adult books for young adults
LC 2008010122

An intimate exploration into the musical achievements of fifteen living jazz artists profiles jazz as one of the most ephemeral and improvisational performing art forms, in an account that offers insight into the conceptual nature of jazz while drawing on interviews with such figures as Sonny Rollins, Ornette Coleman, and Branford Marsalis.

"Originally published as a series in the New York Times, the 15 conversations presented here consist of Ratliff sitting down with such diverse and talented luminaries as Sonny Rollins, Pat Metheny, Paul Motian, and Dianne Reeves. The treasure of these conversations is not just their fluid and intimate manner but their focus on the recordings that had the greatest influence on the artists and their musical paths. An added bonus is the recommended-listening section, in which Ratliff shares his list of his subjects' seminal recordings. Highly recommended." —*Library Journal*

Includes bibliographical references and index.

781.66 Rock (Rock 'n' roll)

Hopper, Jessica
The First Collection of Criticism by a Living Female Rock Critic. Jessica Hopper. MCD x FSG Originals 2021. 428 p.
ISBN 9780374538996
Grades: Adult   781.66
1. Rock music 2. Rock musicians 3. Women musicians 4. Music critics 5. Essays 6. Arts and entertainment — Music — Rock 7. Life stories — Arts and culture — Performing arts — Musicians and composers 8. Life stories — Identity — Gender
LC Bl2015023805

Throughout her career, spanning more than two decades, Jessica Hopper, a revered and pioneering music critic, has examined women recording and producing music, in all genres, through an intersectional feminist lens. The First Collection of Criticism by a Living Female Rock Critic features oral histories of bands like Hole and Sleater Kinney, interviews with the women editors of 1970s-era Rolling Stone, and intimate conversations with iconic musicians such as Björk, Robyn, and Lido Pimienta. The collection also includes profiles and reviews of some of the most-loved, and most-loathed, women artists making music today: Fiona Apple, Kacey Musgraves, M.I.A, Miley Cyrus, Lana Del Rey.

"Rock music fans of all genders and stripes will find a lot to chew on in these pages." —*Library Journal*

Originally published: Chicago : Featherproof Books, 2015.

Kaye, Lenny
★ *Lightning Striking: Ten Transformative Moments in Rock and Roll*. Lenny Kaye. Ecco Press 2022. 400 p.
ISBN 9780062449207
Grades: Adult   781.66
1. Kaye, Lenny 2. Rock music 3. Rock musicians 4. Bands (Music) 5. Influence (Literary, artistic, etc.) 6. Popular music 7. Music history and criticism 8. Arts and Entertainment — Music — Rock 9. Life stories — Arts and culture — Performing arts — Musicians and composers 10. History writing — Arts and culture

Rock and roll was birthed in basements and garages, radio stations and dance halls, in cities where unexpected gatherings of artists and audience changed and charged the way music is heard and celebrated, capturing lightning in a bottle. Musician and writer Lenny Kaye explores ten crossroads of time and place that define rock and roll, its unforgettable flashpoints, characters and visionaries, how each generation came to be, how it was discovered by the world. Whether describing Elvis Presley's Memphis, the Beatles' Liverpool, Patti Smith's New York or Kurt Cobain's Seattle, Lightning Striking reveals the communal energy that creates a scene, a guided tour inside style and performance, to see who's on stage, along with the movers and shakers, the hustlers and hangers-on, and why everybody is listening.

"Touching on a dizzying array of famous and obscure musicians, bars, and clubs, Kaye brilliantly captures the ecstasy of what it was like to be there? This memorable history is electrifying." —*Publishers Weekly*

"Part history, part memoir, Lightning Striking is a fat, fun homage to the glory days of rock and roll and is full of vivid and revealing memories and anecdotes." —*Booklist*

Includes bibliographical references and discography.

Lang, Michael
The Road to Woodstock. Michael Lang. Ecco 2009. 304 p.
ISBN 9780061576553
Grades: 11 12 Adult   781.66
1. Lang, Michael, 1944-2022 2. Sound recording executives and producers 3. Woodstock Festival, 1969 4. Peace movements 5. Counterculture 6. Rock concerts 7. Music festivals 8. Promotion of special events 9. Music history and criticism 10. Performing arts festivals 11. United States history 12. United States 13. 1960s 14. 20th century 15. Autobiographies and memoirs 16. Life stories — General 17. Arts and Entertainment — Music — Folk 18. Arts and Entertainment — Music — Rock 19. Adult books for young adults
LC 2011477461

A fortieth anniversary tribute to the first Woodstock event, written by its co-creator, describes the events of the historical three-day performance, in an account that features rare photographs and recollections by such artists as the Grateful Dead, Crosby Stills & Nash, and the Who.

Waksman, Steve
This Ain't the Summer of Love: Conflict and Crossover in Heavy Metal and Punk. Steve Waksman. University of Calif. Press 2009. xi, 391 p. : Illustration
ISBN 9780520257177
Grades: Adult   781.66
1. Heavy metal music 2. Punk rock music 3. Music history and criticism 4. Arts and Entertainment — Music
LC 2008025957

"The number of fanzines and interviews cited is evidence that this is a comprehensively and enthusiastically researched book. As a critical study it provides an original critique of both the genres involved, and of genre itself; the only flipside is that this ends up playing second fiddle to a damn good story." —*PopMatters*

Roth Family Foundation music in America imprint—Prelim. p; Includes bibliographical references (p. 349-367), discography (p. 369-375), and index.

Womack, Kenneth
All Things Must Pass Away: Harrison, Clapton, and Other Assorted Love Songs. Kenneth Womack and Jason Kruppa. Chicago Review Press 2021. 288 p. : Illustration
ISBN 9781641603256
Grades: Adult   781.66
1. Harrison, George, 1943-2001 2. Clapton, Eric 3. Musicians 4. Rock musicians 5. Artistic rivalry 6. Competition 7. Male friendship 8. Rock music 9. Inter-

personal relations 10. Music history and criticism 11. 20th century 12. Collective biographies 13. Arts and Entertainment — Music 14. Life stories — Arts and culture — Performing arts — Musicians and composers

Reveals the foundations of Harrison and Clapton's friendship, focusing on the ways their encouragement and support of each other drove them to produce works that would cast long shadows over the evolving world of rock music.

"In a crowded field of Beatles-related books, one might wonder if there is need for another. With this entertaining and informative work, Womack and Kruppa offer an emphatic yes." —*Library Journal*

Includes bibliographical references and index.

781.66078 Rock music —Festivals

Austerlitz, Saul
Just a Shot Away: Peace, Love, and Tragedy with the Rolling Stones at Altamont. Saul Austerlitz. Thomas Dunne Books 2018. 304 p.
ISBN 9781250083197
Grades: Adult   781.66078
1. Rock concerts 2. Murder 3. Racism 4. Rock music 5. Counterculture 6. United States history 7. California 8. 1960s 9. 20th century 10. History writing — 1960s — United States

LC 2018001404

Explores how the 1969 Altamont Festival and the murder of 18-year-old Meredith Hunter during a performance by the Rolling Stones came to symbolize the end of an era and persistent racial tensions.

"Austerlitz (Money for Nothing) offers a blistering exploration of the deadly confluence of racism, stoned naivete, biker belligerence, and rockstar obliviousness that resulted in the murder of 18-year-old Berkeley arts student Meredith Hunter at the Rolling Stones' infamously disastrous concert in Altamont, Calif." —*Publishers Weekly*

Includes index.

781.6609 Rock music — History

Heller, Jason
Strange Stars: David Bowie, Pop Music, and the Decade Sci-Fi Exploded. Jason Heller. Melville House Publishing; London : Blackstock Mews 2018. 272 p.
ISBN 9781612196978
Grades: Adult   781.6609
1. Popular music 2. Popular culture 3. Music history and criticism 4. 1970s 5. 20th century 6. Arts and Entertainment — Music — Rock 7. Arts and Entertainment — Writing and Publishing 8. Arts and Entertainment — Writing and Publishing — Literary criticism

LC 2018013060

A Hugo Award-winning author and music journalist revisits a time of unparalleled creativity as the sci-fi world collides with the rock 'n' roll world of the 1970s, presenting a whole generation of revered musicians as the sci-fi obsessed conjurers they really were.

"The accessible title will have readers scouring local bookstores for old sf classics and used record bins for long-forgotten LPs such as Colonel Elliott & The Lunatics' Interstellar Reggae Drive (1973) and Zed's Visions of Dune (1979)." —*Library Journal*

Includes bibliographical references and index.

Hyden, Steven
Twilight of the Gods: A Journey to the End of Classic Rock. Steven Hyden. Dey Street Books 2018. 320 p.
ISBN 9780062657121
Grades: Adult   781.6609
1. Rock music 2. Rock musicians 3. Popular music 4. Musicians 5. Popular culture 6. Music history and criticism 7. Essays 8. Arts and Entertainment — Music — Rock 9. Society and culture — Pop culture

LC Bl2018072576

The author of the critically acclaimed Your Favorite Band Is Killing Me presents a frank and revelatory assessment of the current state of classic rock, assessing its past and future, its enduring impact and what its loss could mean in economic and cultural arenas.

McKeen, William
Everybody Had an Ocean: Music and Mayhem in 1960s Los Angeles. William McKeen. Chicago Review Press 2017. 422 p.
ISBN 9781613734919
Grades: Adult   781.6609
1. Popular culture 2. Popular music 3. Rock music 4. Musicians 5. Rock musicians 6. Social history 7. Music history and criticism 8. Los Angeles, California 9. Southern California 10. California 11. 1960s 12. 20th century 13. History writing — 1960s — United States 14. History writing — Arts and culture 15. Arts and Entertainment — Music — Rock

LC 2016029172

Los Angeles in the 1960s gave the world some of the greatest music in rock 'n' roll history: "California Dreamin'" by the Mamas and the Papas, "Mr. Tambourine Man" by the Byrds, and "Good Vibrations" by the Beach Boys, a song that magnificently summarized the joy and beauty of the era in three and a half minutes. But there was a dark flip side to the fun fun fun of the music, a nexus between naive young musicians and the hangers-on who exploited the decade's peace, love, and flowers ethos, all fueled by sex, drugs, and overnight success. One surf music superstar unwittingly subsidized the kidnapping of Frank Sinatra Jr. The transplanted Texas singer Bobby Fuller might have been murdered by the Mob in what is still an unsolved case. And after hearing Charlie Manson sing, Neil Young recommended him to the president of Warner Bros. Records. Manson's ultimate rejection by the music industry likely led to the infamous murders that shocked a nation. Everybody Had an Ocean chronicles the migration of the rock 'n' roll business to Southern California and how the artists flourished there. The cast of characters is astonishing—Brian and Dennis Wilson of the Beach Boys, Jan and Dean, eccentric producer Phil Spector, Cass Elliot, Sam Cooke, Ike and Tina Turner, Joni Mitchell, and scores of others—and their stories form a modern epic of the battles between innocence and cynicism, joy and terror. You'll never hear that beautiful music in quite the same way.

"Using a synthesis of memoirs and biographies, McKeen creates a sprawling, entertaining, and sometime lurid, narrative about artists who, bursting with creative energy, converged in L.A." —*Booklist*

Includes bibliographical references and index.

Reynolds, Simon
Shock and Awe: Glam Rock and Its Legacy, from the Seventies to the Twenty-First Century. Simon Reynolds. Dey Street Books 2016. 304 p.
ISBN 9780062279804
Grades: Adult   781.6609
1. Bowie, David, 1947-2016 2. Progressive rock music 3. Fame 4. Excess (Philosophy) 5. Rock music 6. Rock musicians 7. Music history and criticism 8. England 9. 1970s 10. 20th century 11. Biographies 12. Arts and Entertainment — Music — Rock

LC Bl2016045701

A definitive history of glam and glitter rock, celebrating its outlandish fashion and outrageous stars, shows how the original glam artists' obsession with fame, extreme fashion and theatrical excess are still prevalent today.

"For neo-glamsters, a blueprint for how to get things done; for oldsters, a nostalgic look into a shining, glittery era." —*Kirkus*

Robb, John
Punk Rock: An Oral History. John Robb; edited by Oliver Craske. PM Press 2012. xv, 562 p. : Illustration
ISBN 9781604860054
Grades: Adult   781.6609
1. Punk rock music 2. Rock music 3. Punk rock musicians 4. Rock musicians 5. Music history and criticism 6. Popular culture 7. British history 8. 20th century 9. Oral histories 10. Interviews 11. Arts and Entertainment — Music — Rock 12. History writing — Europe — United Kingdom

LC 2011939680

ESSENTIAL AND RECOMMENDED TITLES
782 Vocal music

Through more than 150 interviews with key players in the punk-rock scene, the author gives a thorough account of the rise of his important new genre, from its roots in the 1960s to the the influence of such acts as the Clash, the Sex Pistols, Henry Rollins and Black Flag, the Buzzcocks and many more.
Originally published: London : Ebury Press, 2006.

Savage, Jon
★ *1966: The Year the Decade Exploded*. Jon Savage. Faber & Faber 2016. 620 p.
ISBN 9780571277629
Grades: Adult   781.6609
1. Social history 2. Popular culture 3. Popular music 4. Counterculture 5. Social change 6. Culture 7. 1960s 8. History writing — General
LC Bl2016036637

Paying tribute to the year that shaped the pop future of the century, an exploration into the social and cultural heart of the decade, drawing on archival primary sources, reveals a unique chemistry of ideas, substances, freedom of expression and dialogue that exploded in unparalleled creativity.

Wiederhorn, Jon
Louder Than Hell: The Definitive Oral History of Metal. Jon Wiederhorn & Katherine Turman; introduction by Scott Ian of Anthrax; afterword by Rob Halford of Judas Priest. It Books 2013. xiii, 718 pages, 48 unnumbered pages of plates : Illustration; Color
ISBN 9780061958281
Grades: Adult   781.6609
1. Heavy metal music 2. Heavy metal groups 3. Counterculture 4. Industrial music 5. Death metal music 6. Music history and criticism 7. Popular culture 8. British history 9. United States history 10. 20th century 11. Oral histories 12. Interviews 13. Arts and Entertainment — Music — Rock
LC Bl2013023546

Offers a chronological look at the history of heavy metal music through the words of the artists themselves culled from over four hundred interviews conducted over twenty-five years.

Introduction and afterword responsibility statements from dust jacket.

782 Vocal music

Smith, Patti
Collected Lyrics: 1970-2015. Patti Smith. Ecco 2015. 308 p. : Illustration
ISBN 9780062345011
Grades: Adult   782
1. Rock music 2. Arts and Entertainment — Music
LC Bl2015043209

Collects the complete lyrics of the songs of Patti Smith, supplemented with images of the original manuscripts.

782.1 Operas and related dramatic vocal forms

Berger, William
Puccini Without Excuses: A Refreshing Reassessment of the World's Most Popular Composer. William Berger. Vintage Books 2005. 471 p.
ISBN 9781400077786
Grades: Adult   782.1
1. Puccini, Giacomo, 1858-1924 2. Classical music 3. Composers 4. Operas 5. Social life and customs 6. Italy 7. 19th century 8. Biographies 9. Arts and Entertainment — Music — Opera 10. Life stories — Arts and culture — Performing arts — Musicians and composers
LC 2005046157

A critical analysis of the life and work of the popular operatic composer reassesses Puccini's role in the history of music and his enduring legacy, in a study that encompasses a biographical profile, detailed discussions of each of his operatic works, recommended recordings and videos, trivia and anecdotes, and a helpful glossary.

"The author sets Puccini within his times before discussing the circumstances of each opera's premiere and famous interpreters of the roles, providing character lists and synopses and fleshing all this out with musical commentary. Chapters on opera production and the genre's relation to film are useful. Berger's lucid yet hardly dispassionate views are designed to elicit strong reactions, so this is not the first place one should go for an unbiased introduction to the composer's oeuvre. But the author's grounding information is helpful for the novice, and he refers to some of the current authoritative sources." —*Library Journal*
Includes bibliographical references (p. 411-423) and index.

Gay, John
The Beggar's Opera. Edited by Edgar V. Roberts; music edited by Edward Smith. University of Nebraska Press 1969. xxix, 238 p.
ISBN 9780803253612
Grades: Adult   782.1
1. Drama 2. Arts and Entertainment — Music — Opera
LC 68021878

The Beggar's Opera introduced to theater the ballad-opera and an immortal cast of characters.
Appendices (p. 84-238): A. The music of the beggar's opera, with keyboard accompaniments realized from the basses of John Christopher Pepusch by Edward Smith.—B. Chronology; Includes bibliographical references.

Hischak, Thomas S.
The Oxford Companion to the American Musical: Theatre, Film, and Television. Thomas Hischak. Oxford University Press 2008. xxxiv, 923 p. : Illustration
ISBN 9780195335330
Grades: 9 10 11 12 Adult   782.1
1. Musicals 2. Arts and Entertainment — Theater 3. Reference books — Performing arts 4. Reference — Dictionaries
LC 2007052436

A reference that covers American stage, film, and television musicals from 1860 to 2007 offers information on the musical productions and the historical evolution of the musical, as well as on performers, composers, and producers.

An engaging and authoritative reference that covers stage, film, and television musicals from 1860 to 2007 offers a wealth of information on the musical productions, the historical evolution of the musical, performers, composers, lyricists, producers, choreographers, and more, all enhanced by a listing of recommended recordings, cross-references, and a chronological listing of the musicals.

"This is an overview of the American musical theater on the stage, silver screen, and small screen. The 2000-plus entries are brief but detailed accounts of plots; production histories; careers of actors, dancers, musicians, lyricists, composers, choreographers, and directors; organizations; and genres (animated musicals, frontier musicals). . . . This thorough work provides enjoyable reading for anyone interested in American theatrical history in general and musicals in particular." —*School Library Journal*
Includes bibliographical references (p. 855-897), discography (p. 899-902), and index.

Maslon, Laurence
★ *Broadway: The American Musical*. Laurence Maslon; based on the documentary film by Michael Kantor. Applause Theatre & Cinema Books 2020. 505 p. : Illustration; Color; Map
ISBN 9781493047673
Grades: 11 12 Adult   782.1
1. Musicals 2. Broadway, New York City 3. New York City 4. Arts and Entertainment — Theater
LC Bl2010016394

Presents a history of the Broadway musical theater, including summaries of the shows, photographs of the stars, posters, sheet music, production stills, and essays by theater luminaries.
Includes bibliographical references and index.

Max, D. T.
Finale: Late Conversations with Stephen Sondheim. D. T. Max. HarperCollins 2022. 176 p.

ISBN 9780063279810
Grades: Adult   782.1
1. Sondheim, Stephen, 1930-2021 2. Creativity 3. Composers 4. Composition (Music) 5. Musicals 6. Aging 7. Gay men 8. American people 9. North American people 10. Interviews 11. Biographies 12. Arts and Entertainment — Music 13. Life stories — Arts and culture — Performing arts — Musicians and composers

Conducted during the last years of the iconic composer's life, a deeply personal collection of interviews highlights the legend's work and his opinions and thoughts on music, movies, family, New York, aging and the creative process.

"A loose latter-day chronicle of one of theater's irreplaceable voices; will be cherished by scholars and enthusiasts as a testament to Sondheim's creative process and to the man himself." —*Library Journal*

Miranda, Lin-Manuel

Hamilton: The Revolution. Lin-Manuel Miranda, with Jeremy McCarter. Grand Central Pub. 2016. 288 p.
ISBN 9781455539741
Grades: Adult   782.1
1. Miranda, Lin-Manuel, 1980- 2. Hamilton, Alexander, 1757-1804 3. Theater 4. Founding Fathers of the United States 5. Drama 6. Hip-hop culture 7. Popular culture 8. Musicals 9. Broadway, New York City 10. 21st century 11. Adult books for young adults 12. Arts and Entertainment — Theater
LC 2015957946

Goodreads Choice Award, 2016; School Library Journal Best Books: Best Adult Books 4 Teens, 2016.

The Tony Award-winning composer-lyricist-star takes readers behind the scenes of his groundbreaking hit musical, which is filled with romance, drama, violence, patriotism and adventure and details the many dramatic episodes in Alexander Hamilton's life.

"A treasure trove of information, they highlight his writing process, musical influences (ranging from show tunes to pop to hip-hop), amusing anecdotes, and so much more." —*Library Journal*

Mordden, Ethan

Anything Goes: A History of American Musical Theatre. Ethan Mordden. Oxford University Press 2013. 360 p.
ISBN 9780199892839
Grades: Adult   782.1
1. Musicals 2. Theater 3. Dancing 4. Composition (Music) 5. Choreography 6. Broadway, New York City 7. History writing — Arts and culture 8. Arts and Entertainment — Theater 9. History writing — United States
LC 2013000208

Anything Goes stages a grand revue of the musical from the 1920s through the 1970s, narrated in Mordden's famously witty, scholarly, and conversational style.

"Mordden brightly differentiates those forms, citing hundreds and analyzing dozens of examples of them in a sweeping narrative that, with plenty of sass and tang, wit and even a little snark, not to mention scholarly precision, is obviously the best-ever history of the musical and likely to remain so for a very long time." —*Booklist*

Discography; Includes bibliographical references and index.

Rose, Michael

The Birth of an Opera: Fifteen Masterpieces from Poppea to Wozzeck. Michael Rose. W.W. Norton & Company 2013. 480 p.
ISBN 9780393060430
Grades: Adult   782.1
1. Creation (literary, artistic, etc.) 2. Composition (Music) 3. Composers 4. Music history and criticism 5. Operas 6. Arts and Entertainment — Music — Opera 7. History writing — General
LC 2012039470

Including Monteverdi, Mozart, Puccini, Wagner and Berg, this guide describes the stories behind the writing and creation of fifteen different operas, detailing the circumstances of each composer's life and times and the impact their environment had on their art.

Includes bibliographical references and index.

Sondheim, Stephen

Look, I Made a Hat: Collected Lyrics (1981-2011) with Attendant Comments, Amplifications, Dogmas, Harangues, Digressions, Anecdotes and Miscellany. Stephen Sondheim. Alfred A. Knopf 2011. 480 p.
ISBN 9780307593412
Grades: Adult   782.1
1. Musicals 2. Librettos 3. Composition (Music) 4. Lyric writing 5. Songwriting 6. Arts and Entertainment — Music
LC 2011014604

A second volume of collected lyrics by the iconic music artist features accompanying discussions of his experiences in the theater, memories about some of his important collaborations and dissections of what he believes to be his most significant successes and failures, providing additional coverage of his creative process and non-sequitur pieces.

"With this chronological continuation of Finishing the Hat, musical theater lyricist and composer Sondheim has produced another delightful book that melds lyrics, anecdotes, opinions, and whimsy…As in the previous volume, Sondheim includes descriptions about each show, as well as running commentary. Sondheim's general essays (the harangues and dogmas of the subtitle) show him at his opinionated and literate best….Certainly all libraries owning the first volume will want the second." —*Library Journal*

782.1092 Operas — Biography

Suchet, John

Verdi: The Man Revealed. John Suchet. Pegasus Books 2018. 288 p.
ISBN 9781681777689
Grades: Adult   782.1092
1. Verdi, Giuseppe, 1813-1901 2. Composers 3. Classical music 4. Italy 5. Biographies 6. Arts and Entertainment — Music — Classical 7. Life stories — Arts and culture — Performing arts — Musicians and composers
LC 2019565070

Describes the life and career of Italy's greatest operatic composer, whose obsession with perfection drove his collaborators to incredible frustration and was also a landowner, farmer, politician and was outspoken in promoting Italian independence and criticizing the church.

"Obviously, music lovers will want this volume, but the subject is so lively and the presentation so attractive that it will appeal to all who value a solid biography." —*Library Journal*

782.25 Small-scale vocal forms

Marovich, Robert M.

A City Called Heaven: Chicago and the Birth of Gospel Music. Robert M. Marovich. University of Illinois Press 2015. x, 441 p.
ISBN 9780252039102
Grades: Adult   782.25
1. Gospel music 2. African American music 3. Popular music 4. African American musicians 5. African Americans in popular culture 6. African Americans 7. Music history and criticism 8. Chicago, Illinois 9. Arts and entertainment — Music — Christian and gospel

In A City Called Heaven, gospel announcer and music historian Robert Marovich shines a light on the humble origins of a majestic genre and its indispensable bond to the city where it found its voice: Chicago.

"Marovich's excellent book should appeal to both academic historians and Chicago-area music fans. It opens a window on an important part of 20th-century Americana that has been little explored heretofore." —*Library Journal*

Perry, Imani

May We Forever Stand: A History of the Black National Anthem. Imani Perry. The University of North Carolina Press 2018. xiv, 280 pages; Illustration
ISBN 9781469638607
Grades: Adult   782.25

ESSENTIAL AND RECOMMENDED TITLES
782.4 Secular forms

1. Johnson, James Weldon, 1871-1938 2. Johnson, John Rosamond 1873-1954 3. Civil rights 4. Social change 5. Intellectual life 6. African Americans 7. Faith (Christianity) 8. Race relations 9. United States 10. 20th century 11. Society and culture — Race 12. History writing — African American — United States

Hurston/Wright Legacy Award: Nonfiction, 2019.

In this rich, poignant, and readable work, Imani Perry tells the story of the Black National Anthem as it traveled from South to North, from civil rights to Black power, and from countless family reunions to Carnegie Hall and the Oval Office. Drawing on a wide array of sources, Perry uses "Lift Every Voice and Sing" as a window on the powerful ways African Americans have used music and culture to organize, mourn, challenge, and celebrate for more than a century.

782.4 Secular forms

Bostridge, Ian
Schubert's Winter Journey: Anatomy of an Obsession. Ian Bostridge. Alfred A. Knopf 2015. 336 p.
ISBN 9780307961631
Grades: Adult 782.4
1. Bostridge, Ian 2. Schubert, Franz, 1797-1828 3. Songwriting 4. Composition (Music) 5. Composers 6. Music history and criticism 7. Arts and Entertainment — Music — Classical
LC 2014020088

Library Journal Best Books 2014.

Drawing on his first-hand experience with Schubert's Winterreise, considered by many to be the single greatest piece of music ever written for the male solo voice; his musical knowledge; and his training as a scholar, the author explores the enigmas and subtle meanings of each of the 24 songs comprising this legendary masterpiece.

Includes bibliographical references and index.

782.42 Songs

Clague, Mark
O Say Can You Hear?: A Cultural Biography Of. Mark Clague. W.W. Norton & Company, Inc. 2022. 320 p.
ISBN 9780393651386
Grades: Adult 782.42
1. Patriotic music, American 2. National songs 3. Anthems 4. War of 1812 5. United States history 6. History writing — United States 7. Arts and Entertainment — Music
LC 2022008993

Weaving together the stories of America's national anthem and the country it represents, this book examines the origins of both text and music, alternate lyrics and translations and the song's use in sports, at times of war and for political protesting.

"A music historian and professor of musicology, Clague finds in America's national anthem 'A surprisingly rich archive offering insight into the conflicts and complexities that forged the United States.'...An engaging cultural history." —*Kirkus*

Includes bibliographical references and index.

Dylan, Bob
★ *The Philosophy of Modern Song.* Bob Dylan. Simon & Schuster 2022. 339 pages
ISBN 9781451648706
Grades: Adult 782.42
1. Popular music 2. Popular music (Vocal) 3. Music history and criticism 4. Storytelling 5. Popular music industry and trade 6. Music industry and trade 7. 20th century 8. Essays 9. Society and culture — Pop culture 10. Arts and Entertainment — Music

Dylan offers his extraordinary insight into the nature of popular music in essays focusing on songs by other artists, spanning from Stephen Foster to Elvis Costello, from Hank Williams to Nina Simone. Written in Dylan's unique prose—mysterious and mercurial, poignant and profound, and often laugh-out-loud funny—these essays are ostensibly about music, but are really meditations and reflections on the human condition.

"This is a fascinating and personalized journey through 20th-century popular music that's guided by one of its luminaries." —*Library Journal*

Gioia, Ted
Work Songs. Ted Gioia. Duke University Press 2006. xiii, 352 p.
ISBN 9780822337263
Grades: Adult 782.42
1. Working class 2. Arts and Entertainment — Music — Christian and Gospel 3. Arts and Entertainment — Music — Folk 4. Arts and Entertainment — Music — Jazz and the Blues
LC 2005026241

"Gioia poignantly tells the story of work songs sung by everyone from prehistoric hunters to today's consumers. His task involved drawing on multilayered and diverse resources that include travel literature, slave narratives, historical accounts and personal journals, myths and legends, biographies, and labor union writings; the focus is on the rhythms, melodies, and lyrics of music that has accompanied such tasks as raising and lowering sails, felling trees, and weaving and sewing garments. This book provides an opportunity to re-experience the history and dignity of our human toils. Highly recommended for public and academic libraries." —*Library Journal*

Includes bibliographical references (p. [313]-335) and index.

Lynskey, Dorian
33 Revolutions per Minute: A History of Protest Songs, from Billie Holiday to Green Day. Dorian Lynskey. Ecco 2011. 320 p.
ISBN 9780061670152
Grades: 11 12 Adult 782.42
1. Music 2. Popular music 3. Music history and criticism 4. Protest songs 5. Popular culture 6. United States history 7. British history 8. 21st century 9. 20th century 10. Arts and Entertainment — Music
LC 2010024247

Booklist Editors' Choice 2011.

A history of protest music embodied in 33 songs since the 1930s.

"The author delves into the protest song movement from 1939 to the present. Dividing the time into discrete sections, he focuses on particular examples but also provides information on related songs. The author traces the historical context, using valuable contemporary sources and quotations from the artists. Lynskey's flowing prose and well-turned phrases bring the times to life. He is especially adept at integrating the songs into the wider social milieu, which extends the appeal to cultural historians as well as music lovers." —*Library Journal*

Meacham, Jon
Songs of America: Patriotism, Protest, and the Music That Made a Nation. Jon Meacham and Tim McGraw. Random House 2019. 320 p.
ISBN 9780593132951
Grades: Adult 782.42
1. Music 2. Protest songs 3. Patriotic music 4. Music history and criticism 5. Arts and Entertainment — Music 6. History writing — Arts and culture 7. History writing — United States
LC 2019014364

A Pulitzer Prize-winning author and Grammy-winning music artist celebrate America and the music that inspired people and illuminated eras, from the Revolutionary War to the present.

"Not in the musicological class of Alan Lomax or at the historical heights of David Hackett Fischer's Liberty and Freedom, but worthy reading for the anthemically minded." —*Kirkus*

Includes bibliographical references and index.

Tweedy, Jeff
How to Write One Song. Jeff Tweedy. Dutton, Penguin Random House LLC 2020. 176 p.
ISBN 9780593183526

Grades: Adult   782.42

1. Songwriting 2. Music appreciation 3. Creativity 4. Writing 5. Inspiration 6. Arts and Entertainment — Music 7. Arts and Entertainment — Writing and Publishing

LC 2020030553

Perfect for gifting during the holidays and beyond, a thoughtful, counterintuitive book about creativity from the celebrated songwriter, leader of the band Wilco, and New York Times bestselling author of Let's Go (So We Can Get Back), inspiring others by taking the reader through the process of writing one song.

"Observing [musician] Tweedy's glowingly creative mind at work throughout this seriously fun book is truly illuminating." —*Booklist*

782.421 General principles of songs

Fernando, S. H, Jr.
From the Streets of Shaolin: The Wu-Tang Saga. S. H. Fernando, Jr. Hachette Books 2021. 528 p.
ISBN 9780306874468
Grades: Adult   782.421

1. Rap musicians 2. Hip-hop culture 3. Rap music 4. Music industry and trade 5. Popular culture 6. United States history 7. United States 8. 1990s 9. 20th century 10. Biographies 11. Arts and Entertainment — Music — Rap and R&B 12. Life stories — Arts and culture — Performing arts — Musicians and composers

This definitive history of the rap supergroup examines their genesis and evolution from their start in the housing projects of Staten Island to the hip-hop renaissance they helped usher in during the 1990s.

"Fernando brilliantly reconstructs the Wu-Tang story and, in the process, sketches a concise history of hip-hop and illuminates the challenges the group members encountered growing up." —*Library Journal*

Includes bibliographical references and index.

Mahon, Maureen
★ *Black Diamond Queens: African American Women and Rock and Roll.* Maureen Mahon. Duke University Press 2020. 408 p.
ISBN 9781478010197
Grades: Adult   782.421

1. African-American rock musicians 2. Rock music 3. Music and race (Social sciences) 4. African American women 5. Rock musicians 6. Music history and criticism 7. 20th century 8. Arts and Entertainment — Music — Rock 9. History writing — Arts and culture 10. History writing — Women's history 11. History writing — African American — United States 12. Life stories — Arts and culture — Performing arts — Musicians and composers

LC 2020014043

African American women have played a pivotal part in rock and roll-from laying its foundations and singing chart-topping hits to influencing some of the genre's most iconic acts. Despite this, Black women's importance to the music's history has been diminished by narratives of rock as a mostly white male enterprise. In Black Diamond Queens, Maureen Mahon draws on recordings, press coverage, archival materials, and interviews to document the history of African American women in rock and roll between the 1950s and the 1980s.

"With depth and breadth, Mahon's work centers the many African American women who heavily influence rock and roll, from LaVern Baker to Tina Turner." —*Booklist*

Includes bibliographical references and index.

782.42162 Folk songs

Polenberg, Richard
Hear My Sad Story: The True Tales That Inspired Stagolee, John Henry, and Other Traditional American Folk Songs. Richard Polenberg. Cornell University Press 2015. 280 p.
ISBN 9781501700026

Grades: Adult   782.42162

1. Folk music 2. Music history and criticism 3. Songs 4. Arts and Entertainment — Music — Folk

LC 2015016652

In Hear My Sad Story, Richard Polenberg describes the historical events that led to the writing of many famous American folk songs that served as touchstones for generations of American musicians, lyricists, and folklorists.

"A well-written primer of American folk culture that should be in any serious popular music collection." —*Library Journal*

Sandburg, Carl
The American Songbag. Carl Sandburg. Harcourt Brace Jovanovich 1990. xxix, 495 p. : Illustration
ISBN 9780156056502
Grades: Adult   782.42162

1. Folk music 2. Songwriting 3. Music history and criticism 4. Songs 5. Arts and Entertainment — Music 6. Arts and Entertainment — Music — Folk

LC BL 99712752

Two hundred and eighty songs and ballads trace the growth of America.

A Harvest/HBJ book; Includes bibliographical references (p. xvii-xviii) and index; Originally published: New York : Harcourt, Brace & Co, 1927.

782.42164 Western popular songs

Barlow, John Perry
Mother American Night: My Life and Crazy Times. John Perry Barlow with Robert Greenfield. Crown Archetype 2018. 304 p.
ISBN 9781524760182
Grades: Adult   782.42164

1. Barlow, John Perry, 1947-2018 2. Songwriters 3. Cattle ranchers 4. Political activists 5. Musicians 6. Libertarians 7. Campaigning 8. Autobiographies and memoirs 9. Life stories — Arts and culture — Performing arts — Musicians and composers

LC 2017050430

Traces the remarkable life story of the lyricist and political campaign manager, describing his upbringing among elite Wyoming ranchers, his vigorous advocacy of internet freedoms and his relationships with figures ranging from Jerry Garcia to Steve Jobs.

Belafonte, Harry
★ *My Song: A Memoir.* Harry Belafonte with Michael Shnayerson. Alfred A. Knopf, Inc. 2011. 448 p.
ISBN 9780307272263
Grades: Adult   782.42164

1. Belafonte, Harry, 1927-2023 2. African American singers 3. Singers 4. United States 5. Autobiographies and memoirs 6. Biographies 7. Arts and Entertainment — Music 8. Life stories — Arts and culture — Performing arts — Musicians and composers

LC 2011014602

New York Times Notable Book, 2011.

The National Medal of Arts recipient and former UNICEF Goodwill Ambassador shares the story of his life and career, from his impoverished childhood in Harlem and Jamaica and his racial barrier-breaking career to his commitment to numerous civil causes and his relationships with such figures as Eleanor Roosevelt, Martin Luther King, Jr. and Fidel Castro.

"The author covers his public career as an American entertainment icon (which solidified with his 1956 album, Calypso) and his interactions with many politicians and celebrities, e.g., Paul Robeson, Poitier, Marlon Brando, and Robert Kennedy, among many others. How these different strands interweavethe anger generated by the poverty and racial discrimination of his early years, the socially conscious reformer, and the well-respected entertainermake for a potent memoir of our times." —*Library Journal*

ESSENTIAL AND RECOMMENDED TITLES
782.42164 Western popular songs

Bogle, Donald
Heat Wave: The Life and Career of Ethel Waters. Donald Bogle. HarperCollins 2011. 352 p.
ISBN 9780061241734
Grades: Adult   782.42164
1. Waters, Ethel, 1900-1977 2. African American singers 3. Singers 4. African American women 5. United States 6. Biographies 7. Arts and Entertainment — Music 8. Life stories — Arts and culture — Performing arts — Musicians and composers
LC 2010029230

The best-selling author of Dorothy Dandridge examines the life and legacy of theatrical star Ethel Waters.
Includes bibliographical references.

Breihan, Tom
★ *The Number Ones: Twenty Chart-Topping Hits That Reveal the History of Pop Music.* Tom Breihan. Hachette Books 2022. 304 p.
ISBN 9780306826535
Grades: Adult   782.42164
1. Music history and criticism 2. Popular music 3. Popular music industry and trade 4. Pop musicians 5. United States 6. 20th century 7. 21st century 8. Arts and Entertainment — Music — Pop 9. Society and culture — Pop culture

Featuring the greatest pop artists of all times, this fascinating narrative of the history of popular music through the lens of the Billboard Hot 100, which began in 1958, revels a remarkably fluid and connected story of music that is as entertaining as it is enlightening. 22,500 first printing.
"An entertaining and informative survey of some milestones of popular music. This book should delight anyone who has felt the magic only pop music can provide." —*Library Journal*

Cohodas, Nadine
Princess Noire: The Tumultuous Reign of Nina Simone. Nadine Cohodas. Pantheon Books 2010. 464 p.
ISBN 9780375424014
Grades: Adult   782.42164
1. Simone, Nina, 1933-2003 2. Singers 3. African American singers 4. Civil rights 5. Cabarets 6. Music 7. Biographies 8. Arts and Entertainment — Music 9. Life stories — Arts and culture — Performing arts — Musicians and composers
LC 2009022252

A portrait of the mid-20th-century singer traces the challenges she faced acquiring her education, her 1959 debut at New York City's Town Hall and her relationships with such contemporaries as Lorraine Hansberry and James Baldwin.
"Looking at every aspect of Simone's work, from stage decorum to audience interaction, the author offers many rich insights into her subject's conflicted emotional world. Throughout, she nurtures the reader's empathy for the artist but takes care to avoid unfounded speculation on racism or gender bias. In fact, this is a 360-degree profile of Simone, offering solid critical insights at every turn." —*Choice*
Includes discography, bibliographical references, and index.

DiFranco, Ani
No Walls and the Recurring Dream: A Memoir. Ani DiFranco. Viking 2019. 320 pages
ISBN 9780735225176
Grades: Adult   782.42164
1. DiFranco, Ani 2. Women social reformers 3. Social reformers 4. Singers 5. Women singers 6. United States 7. Autobiographies and memoirs 8. Biographies 9. Liberal writing 10. Life stories — Arts and culture — Performing arts — Musicians and composers 11. Life stories — Politics — Activists and reformers 12. Arts and entertainment — Music
LC 2019003676

In her new memoir, No Walls and the Recurring Dream, Ani DiFranco recounts her early life from a place of hard-won wisdom, combining personal expression, the power of music, feminism, political activism, storytelling, philanthropy, entrepreneurship, and much more into an inspiring whole.

"DiFranco has defied convention yet remained true to herself. A must for her fans, this riveting, thought-provoking work will also appeal to anyone who enjoys a well-written autobiography." —*Library Journal*

Feinstein, Michael
The Gershwins and Me: A Personal History in Twelve Songs. Michael Feinstein, with Ian Jackman. Simon & Schuster 2012. 320 p.
ISBN 9781451645309
Grades: 10 11 12 Adult   782.42164
1. Gershwin, George, 1898-1937 2. Gershwin, Ira, 1896-1983 3. Feinstein, Michael 4. Songwriters 5. Songwriting 6. Composition (Music) 7. Music 8. Popular music 9. Musicians 10. Music history and criticism 11. Popular culture 12. United States history 13. 1970s 14. 20th century 15. Autobiographies and memoirs 16. Biographies 17. Life stories — Relationships — Friendship 18. Arts and Entertainment — Music
LC 2012006833

A five-time Grammy nominee presents an illustrated tribute to the lives and legacies of the Gershwins that is presented through the stories of 12 of their most enduring songs including "Strike up the Band" and "Love Is Here to Stay," in a volume that is complemented by a CD of original recordings.
Includes bibliographical references and index.

Friedwald, Will
★ *Sinatra! the Song Is You: A Singer's Art.* Will Friedwald. Chicago Review Press 2018. 632 p. : Illustration
ISBN 9781613737705
Grades: Adult   782.42164
1. Sinatra, Frank, 1915-1998 2. Singers 3. Social life and customs 4. United States 5. 20th century 6. Biographies 7. Arts and Entertainment — Music — Jazz and the Blues 8. Life stories — Arts and culture — Performing arts — Musicians and composers
LC 96043855

Drawing upon interviews with hundreds of his collaborators as well as with 'The Voice' himself, this book chronicles, critiques, and celebrates Frank Sinatra's five-decade career.
"Friedwald's commentary is alert and perceptive, and even more valuable is the wealth of pointed reminiscence drawn from interviews he has done with musicians who worked closely with Mr. Sinatra." —*New York Times Book Review*
Originally published: New York : Scribner, 1995; Includes bibliographical references, discography, and index.

Straighten up and Fly Right: The Life and Music of Nat King Cole. Will Friedwald. Oxford University Press 2020. 560 p.
ISBN 9780190882044
Grades: Adult   782.42164
1. Cole, Nat King, 1919-1965 2. Jazz musicians 3. Pianists 4. Jazz music 5. African American musicians 6. Biographies 7. Life stories — Arts and culture — Performing arts — Musicians and composers 8. Arts and Entertainment — Music — Jazz and the Blues
LC 2019049935

One of the most popular and memorable American musicians of the 20th century, Nat King Cole (1919-65) is remembered today as both a pianist and a singer, a feat rarely accomplished in the world of popular music. Now, in this complete life and times biography, author Will Friedwald offers a new take on this fascinating musician, framing him first as a bandleader and then as a star.
"Though needlessly exaggerating its subject's considerable accomplishments and sometimes mired in details, this well-researched, comprehensive work should became a standard biography along with Daniel Mark Epstein's Nat King Cole." —*Library Journal*
Includes bibliographical references and index.

Garfunkel, Art
What Is It All but Luminous: Notes from an Underground Man. Art Garfunkel. Alfred A. Knopf 2017. 256 p.
ISBN 9780385352475
Grades: Adult   782.42164

PUBLIC LIBRARY CORE COLLECTION: NONFICTION
Twentieth Edition

1. Garfunkel, Art, 1941- 2. Folk musicians 3. Folk music 4. Poetry writing 5. Growing up 6. Men-women relations 7. Autobiographies and memoirs 8. Arts and Entertainment — Music — Rock 9. Life stories — Arts and culture — Performing arts — Musicians and composers

LC 2016037296

Art Garfunkel writes about his life before, during, and after Simon & Garfunkel...about their folk-rock music in the roiling age that embraced and was defined by their pathbreaking sound. He writes about growing up in the 1940s and '50s (son of a traveling salesman), a middle class Jewish boy, living in a red brick semi-attached house in Kew Gardens, Queens, a kid who was different—from the age of five feeling his vocal cords "vibrating with the love of sound"...meeting Paul Simon in school, the funny guy who made Art laugh; their going on to junior high school together, of being twelve at the birth of rock'n'roll, both of them "captured" by it.

"Sensitive, soulful, sharp-tongued, and serious, Garfunkel vies for a place in the pantheon of singers." —*Booklist*

Gavin, James
★ *Stormy Weather: The Life of Lena Horne*. James Gavin. Atria 2009. 608 p.
ISBN 9780743271431
Grades: Adult   **782.42164**

1. Horne, Lena 2. African American women singers 3. Singers 4. African American women 5. Actors and actresses 6. Social life and customs 7. United States 8. 20th century 9. Biographies 10. Arts and Entertainment — Music 11. Life stories — Arts and culture — Performing arts — Musicians and composers

LC 2009008170

Profiles the Hollywood actress and singer, evaluating her painful childhood, the challenges she faced as a barrier-breaking African-American performer, and the ways in which she inspired other performers.

"Horne has had a life so rich in ups and downs as to make page after page eventful and suspenseful. This all the more so since the book is also two books in one: a thorough and fluent biography and a history of the slow social rise of Black people despite crippling discrimination and stinging humiliationsa history in which Horne's story is embedded." —*New York Times Book Review*

Harvilla, Rob
60 Songs That Explain the '90s. Rob Harvilla. Twelve 2023. xvii, 269 p.
ISBN 9781538759462
Grades: Adult   **782.42164**

1. Popular music 2. Memories 3. Rock music 4. Rap music 5. Rhythm and blues music 6. Popular culture 7. Music industry and trade 8. Music history and criticism 9. United States 10. 1990s 11. History writing — 1990s — United States 12. Arts and Entertainment — Music 13. Debut title

LC 2023026358

The 1990s were a chaotic and gritty and utterly magical time for music, a confounding barrage of genres and lifestyles and superstars, from grunge to hip-hop, from sumptuous R&B to rambunctious ska-punk, from Axl to Kurt to Missy to Santana to Tupac to Britney. Ringer music critic Rob Harvilla reimagines all the earwormy, iconic hits Gen Xers pine for with vivid historical storytelling, sharp critical analysis, rampant loopiness, and wryly personal ruminations on the most bizarre, joyous, and inescapable songs from a decade we both regret entirely and miss desperately.

"Overall, this is a solid introduction to the music of the 1990s that will be useful both to readers unfamiliar with the era's pop culture and to those seeking to immerse themselves in old favorites." —*Booklist*

Hilburn, Robert
★ *Paul Simon: The Life*. Robert Hilburn. Simon & Schuster 2018. 439 pages, 16 unnumbered pages of plates : Illustration; Color
ISBN 9781501112126
Grades: Adult   **782.42164**

1. Simon, Paul, 1941- 2. Rock musicians 3. Biographies 4. Life stories — Arts and culture — Performing arts — Musicians and composers

LC 2018015535

An intimate, candid portrait of the two-time Rock and Roll Hall of Fame member and first songwriter recipient of the Gershwin Prize, written with rare input by Simon himself, discusses his creative process, his marriages, his decision to leave Simon and Garfunkel and the challenges and sacrifices of living life at an ultimate level of music artistry.

Includes bibliographical references (pages 397-417) and index.

Jewel
Never Broken: Songs Are Only Half the Story. Jewel. Blue Rider Press 2015. 336 p.
ISBN 9780399174339
Grades: Adult   **782.42164**

1. Jewel, 1974- 2. Child abuse victims 3. Singers 4. Alaska 5. United States 6. Autobiographies and memoirs 7. Biographies 8. Life stories — Arts and culture — Performing arts — Musicians and composers 9. Life stories — Facing adversity — Abuse survivors 10. Adult books for young adults

LC 2015024911

The best-selling poet and multi-platinum singer and songwriter explores her struggles with abuse at the hands of unconventional and highly creative family members in Alaska before rising to unexpected fame and becoming a parent.

Kapilow, Robert
★ *Listening for America: Inside the Great American Songbook from Gershwin to Sondheim*. Rob Kapilow. W W Norton & Co. Inc 2019. 448 p.
ISBN 9781631490293
Grades: Adult   **782.42164**

1. Popular music 2. Musicals 3. Music history and criticism 4. Popular culture 5. United States 6. 20th century 7. Arts and Entertainment — Music 8. Arts and Entertainment — Theater 9. History writing — Arts and culture

LC 2019026121

A composer, conductor, and the host of the NPR's What Makes It Great? explores the songs and stories of eight of the twentieth century's most beloved American composers, including Porter, Gershwin and Sondheim and celebrates what makes their work unforgettable.

"A treat for music fans and a great addition to any performing arts or popular culture collection." —*Booklist*

Includes bibliographical references and index.

Kaplan, James
Sinatra: The Chairman. by James Kaplan. Doubleday 2015. 928 p. (Frank Sinatra (James Kaplan), 2)
ISBN 9780385535397
Grades: Adult   **782.42164**

1. Sinatra, Frank, 1915-1998 2. Jazz music 3. Jazz singers 4. Singers 5. United States 6. Biographies 7. Arts and Entertainment — Music — Jazz and the Blues 8. Life stories — Arts and culture — Performing arts — Musicians and composers

LC 2015008973

Booklist Editors' Choice, 2015.

Presents a behind-the-scenes examination of the life and career of the legendary performer that offers insight into his prolific accomplishments, multidimensional character, and complex relationships.

"An appropriately big book for an oversized artistic presence." —*Kirkus*

Mike D.
Beastie Boys Book. Mike D. and Adam Horovitz. Spiegel & Grau 2018. 576 p.
ISBN 9780812995541
Grades: Adult   **782.42164**

1. Mike D, 1965- 2. Horovitz, Adam 3. Yauch, Adam, 1964-2012 4. Rap music 5. Rap musicians 6. Music industry and trade 7. Popular culture 8. Mixtapes 9. 1980s 10. Society and culture — Pop culture 11. Arts and Entertainment — Music — Rap and R&B 12. Adult books for young adults

LC 2018004935

With a style as distinctive and eclectic as a Beastie Boys album, Beastie Boys Book upends the typical music memoir. Alongside the band narrative you will find rare photos, original illustrations, a cookbook by chef Roy Choi, a graphic

ESSENTIAL AND RECOMMENDED TITLES
782.42164 Western popular songs

novel, a map of Beastie Boys' New York, mixtape playlists, pieces by guest contributors, and many more surprises.

Moorer, Allison
I Dream He Talks to Me: A Memoir of Learning How to Listen. Allison Moorer. Hachette Books 2021. 288 p.
ISBN 9780306923074
Grades: Adult   782.42164
1. Moorer, Allison 2. Singers 3. Parents of autistic children 4. Love 5. Parenting 6. Resilience 7. Autistic children 8. Family relationships 9. Autism spectrum disorders 10. Neurodivergent people 11. Autobiographies and memoirs 12. Life stories — Relationships — Parent and child 13. Family and Relationships — Parenting 14. Family and Relationships — Disabled family members
LC 2021012467

The Grammy-nominated music discusses her journey parenting her son John Henry who has nonverbal autism and how she has sought understanding through heartbreak, adventure, confusion, and unending love.

"Grammy-nominated singer-songwriter Moorer follows her debut, Blood, with an equally vulnerable and uplifting account of raising a child on the autism spectrum.... Moorer's candor and self-doubt are achingly honest and oftentimes funny, making this not a story of heartbreak but a celebration of life's struggles and rewards." —*Publishers Weekly*

Palmer, Amanda
★ *The Art of Asking: Or How I Learned to Stop Worrying and Let People Help.* Amanda Palmer. Grand Central Pub. 2014. 224 p.
ISBN 9781455581085
Grades: Adult   782.42164
1. Palmer, Amanda, 1976- 2. Self-discovery 3. Caring 4. Communities 5. Musicians 6. Authors 7. Autobiographies and memoirs 8. Biographies 9. Life stories — Arts and culture — Performing arts 10. Life stories — Relationships

The lead singer of the Dresden Dolls reveals how she has used the power of social networking to meet basic survival needs, make friends, and strengthen communities by raising awareness and funds.

Questlove
Mo' Meta Blues: The World According to Questlove. Ahmir. Grand Central Publishing 2013. 282 pages, 16 unnumbered pages of plates : Illustration; Color
ISBN 9781455501359
Grades: Adult   782.42164
1. Questlove (Musician) 2. Hip-hop culture 3. Music appreciation 4. Race (Social sciences) 5. Drummers 6. Musicians 7. Autobiographies and memoirs 8. Biographies 9. Life stories — Arts and culture — Performing arts — Musicians and composers 10. Arts and Entertainment — Music — Rap and R&B
LC 2013932326

Questlove (aka Ahmir Thompson) is the drummer for the Grammy Award-winning group the Roots, which also serves as the house band on Late Night with Jimmy Fallon. He's also a producer, DJ, and cultural critic. Here Questlove discusses hip-hop, his life and career, his interactions with other musicians and artists like Jay Z and Common, and more. Part personal history, part history of the Roots, and part music critique, Mo' Meta Blues will appeal widely to pop culture fans as well as fans of the author.

Music Is History. Questlove. Abrams Image 2021. 320 p.
ISBN 9781419751431
Grades: Adult   782.42164
1. Music, American 2. Identity 3. Music and society 4. Music history and criticism 5. Essays 6. Society and culture — Pop culture 7. History writing — Arts and culture 8. History writing — United States 9. Arts and Entertainment — Music

Focusing on the years 1971 to the present, a Sundance award-winning director and bestselling author chooses one essential track from each year, revealing the pivotal role that American music plays around issues of race, gender, politics and identity.

"This inspired volume continues Questlove's thoughtful and thought-provoking work and is an enduring analysis of the effects of music on personal, political, and cultural histories." —*Library Journal*

Simmons, Nadirah
★ *First Things First: Hip-Hop Ladies Who Changed the Game.* Nadirah Simmons. Twelve 2024. 256 p.
ISBN 9781538740743
Grades: Adult   782.42164
1. Women rap musicians 2. Rap musicians 3. Rap music industry and trade 4. Rap music 5. Hip hop culture 6. Collective biographies 7. Life stories — Arts and culture — Performing arts — Musicians and composers 8. History Writing — Women's history 9. Arts and Entertainment — Music — Rap and R&B

This reframing of the history of hip-hop focuses on the notable firsts of women such as Lauryn Hill making history as the first rapper to an Album of the Year Grammy.

"Simmons happily rips up decades of hip-hop mythology to show the indispensable work of women in the game." —*Kirkus*

Simon, Carly
★ *Boys in the Trees: A Memoir.* Carly Simon. Flatiron Books 2015. 304 p.
ISBN 9781250095893
Grades: Adult   782.42164
1. Simon, Carly 2. Women singers 3. Singers 4. Popular music 5. Autobiographies and memoirs 6. Life stories — Arts and culture — Performing arts — Musicians and composers
LC 2015038193

The successful singer-songwriter describes her life growing up amidst the glamour of literary New York with her father who co-founded Simon & Schuster, her path to art and music, her marriage to James Taylor and her famously cryptic song lyrics.

"Memoirs by rock icons of the 1960s and '70s are flying fast and furious these days. This is one of the best, lively and memorable. Check the new album that accompanies the book, too." —*Kirkus*

Smarsh, Sarah
She Come by It Natural: Dolly Parton and the Women Who Lived Her Songs. Sarah Smarsh. Scribner 2020. 208 p.
ISBN 9781982157289
Grades: Adult   782.42164
1. Parton, Dolly, 1946- 2. Smarsh, Sarah 3. Women country musicians 4. Blue collar women 5. Poor women 6. Women's role 7. Feminism 8. Sexism 9. Social classes 10. Inequality 11. Women songwriters 12. Role models 13. Life stories — Arts and culture — Performing arts — Musicians and composers 14. Society and culture — Gender — Women 15. Society and culture — Wealth and class — Poverty 16. Life stories — Facing adversity

National Book Critics Circle Award for Nonfiction finalist, 2020.

Growing up amid Kansas wheat fields and airplane factories, Sarah Smarsh witnessed firsthand the particular vulnerabilities—and strengths—of women in working poverty. Meanwhile, country songs by female artists played in the background, telling powerful stories about life, men, hard times, and surviving. In her family, she writes, "country music was foremost a language among women. It's how we talked to each other in a place where feelings aren't discussed." and no one provided that language better than Dolly Parton. In She Come by It Natural, Smarsh explores the overlooked contributions to social progress by such women—including those averse to the term "feminism"—as exemplified by Dolly Parton's life and art.

"Smarsh's luminescent prose and briskly tempered storytelling make for an illuminating take on a one-of-a-kind artist." —*Publishers Weekly*

Smith, Danyel
Shine Bright: A Very Personal History of Black Women in Pop. Danyel Smith. Roc Lit 101 2021. 288 p.
ISBN 9780593132715
Grades: Adult   782.42164

1. African American women musicians 2. Popular music 3. African American singers 4. Women singers 5. Music history and criticism 6. Autobiographies and memoirs 7. Life stories — Arts and culture — Performing arts 8. Society and culture — Pop culture 9. Society and culture — Race 10. Arts and Entertainment — Music 11. History writing — Women's history

LC 2020057494

From a noted cultural critic comes a combination of memoir, criticism, and biography that tells the story of Black women in music—from the Dixie Cups to Gladys Knight to Janet Jackson, Whitney Houston, and Mariah Carey—as the foundational story of American pop.

"Smith (Bliss), host of the music podcast Black Girl Songbook, combines memoir, cultural history, and criticism in this masterful examination of the Black women artists who've indelibly shaped American popular music." —*Publishers Weekly*

Includes index.

Stanley, Bob

★ *The Story of the Bee Gees: Children of the World.* Bob Stanley. Pegasus Books 2024. 352 p.

ISBN 9781639365531

Grades: Adult   **782.42164**

1. Gibb, Barry, 1947- 2. Gibb, Maurice, 1949-2003 3. Gibb, Robin, 1949-2012 4. Popular music 5. Disco music 6. Rock groups 7. Musicians 8. 1970s 9. Biographies 10. Life stories — Arts and culture — Performing arts — Musicians and composers 11. Arts and entertainment — Music — Disco

"Music journalist Stanley (Let's Do It!) aims to restore the 'Misfit' Bee Gees to 'Their rightful place at the very top of pop's table' in this rewarding deep dive." —*Publishers Weekly*

Thomas, Richard F.

★ *Why Bob Dylan Matters.* Richard F. Thomas. Dey Street Books 2017. 256 p.

ISBN 9780062685735

Grades: Adult   **782.42164**

1. Dylan, Bob, 1941- 2. Folk music, American 3. Popular music 4. Rock music 5. Rock musicians 6. Creativity in music 7. Popular culture 8. Music and society 9. Music history and criticism 10. United States 11. Arts and Entertainment — Music — Rock 12. Arts and Entertainment — Music — Folk

LC 2017041732

A Harvard classics professor and expert on Bob Dylan expands on his popular seminar in a full-length, meditative examination of the Nobel Prize-winning lyricist's enduring influence, sharing insights into Dylan's formative experiences against a backdrop of western and classical literature.

"This new work doesn't simply examine Dylan's appeal or the deep meaning of his lyrics but tracks his cultural importance and ongoing relevance in today's tumbled-around world." —*Library Journal*

Tinsley, Omise'eke Natasha

Beyonce in Formation: Remixing Black Feminism. Omise'eke Natasha Tinsley. University of Texas 2018. 208 p.

ISBN 9781477318393

Grades: Adult   **782.42164**

1. Beyonce, 1981- 2. African American women singers 3. Feminists 4. Feminism 5. African American feminism 6. African American women 7. Sexuality 8. Music 9. Social life and customs 10. United States 11. 21st century 12. Society and culture — Gender — Women 13. Society and culture — Race

LC 2018014320

In the tradition of Roxanne Gay's Bad Feminist and Jill Lepore's best-selling cultural histories, Beyonce in Formation is the work of a daring intellectual who is poised to spark a new conversation about freedom and identity in America.

Includes bibliographical references and index.

Wald, Elijah

Dylan Goes Electric!: Newport, Seeger, Dylan, and the Night That Split the Sixties. Elijah Wald. Dey Street Books 2015. 256 p.

ISBN 9780062366689

Grades: Adult   **782.42164**

1. Dylan, Bob, 1941- 2. Folk-rock music 3. Popular music 4. Music 5. Folk music, American 6. Music history and criticism 7. Social life and customs 8. United States 9. 1960s 10. 20th century 11. Arts and Entertainment — Music — Rock

LC 2017561065

On the evening of July 25, 1965, Bob Dylan took the stage at Newport Folk Festival, backed by an electric band, and roared into his new rock hit, Like a Rolling Stone. The audience of committed folk purists and political activists who had hailed him as their acoustic prophet reacted with a mix of shock, booing, and scattered cheers. It was the shot heard round the world—Dylan's declaration of musical independence, the end of the folk revival, and the birth of rock as the voice of a generation—and one of the defining moments in twentieth-century music.

"Some of this material has been covered before, but rarely has it been done so knowingly, lovingly, and felicitously. All the players, too, are here (Joan Baez, Dave Van Ronk, Johnny Cash, et al.), and, though nostalgic, the book makes a major contribution to modern musical history." —*Booklist*

Weisman, Eliot

The Way It Was: My Life with Frank Sinatra. Eliot Weisman. Hachette Books 2017. 320 p.

ISBN 9780316470087

Grades: Adult   **782.42164**

1. Weisman, Eliot 2. Sinatra, Frank, 1915-1998 3. Road managers 4. Autobiographies and memoirs 5. Life stories — Arts and culture — Performing arts — Musicians and composers

LC Bl2017044202

Frank Sinatra's long-time manager and friend, who was one of the singer's most trust confidantes and advisors, tells the story of the final years of the iconic entertainer from the perspective from within his inner circle.

White, Ryan

Jimmy Buffett: A Good Life All the Way. by Ryan White. Touchstone 2017. 336 p.

ISBN 9781501132551

Grades: Adult   **782.42164**

1. Buffett, Jimmy 1946-2023 2. Rock music 3. Singers 4. Rock musicians 5. United States 6. Biographies 7. Life stories — Arts and culture — Performing arts — Musicians and composers 8. Arts and Entertainment — Music — Rock

LC 2016052808

The acclaimed music critic and author of Springsteen: Album by Album explores the life, achievements and legacy of the iconic music artist and writer, tracing the experiences that shaped Buffett's career while celebrating the enduring culture he inspired.

"A thorough, well-researched, and fully dimensional portrait of a multitalented and wildly popular and influential music and entrepreneurial star." —*Booklist*

Winder, Elizabeth

Parachute Women: Marianne Faithfull, Marsha Hunt, Bianca Jagger, Anita Pallenberg, and the Women Behind the Rolling Stones. Elizabeth Winder. Hachette Books 2023. 320 p.

ISBN 9781580059589

Grades: Adult   **782.42164**

1. Faithfull, Marianne 2. Hunt, Marsha 3. Jagger, Bianca 4. Pallenberg, Anita 5. Women rock musicians 6. Actors and actresses 7. Women 8. Fashion models 9. Artists 10. Music industry and trade 11. Sexism 12. Rock music 13. 1960s 14. 1970s 15. Collective biographies 16. Life stories — Arts and culture — Performing arts 17. Arts and Entertainment — Music — Rock 18. Life stories — Identity — Gender 19. History Writing — Women's history

Introduces the four women who inspired, styled, wrote for, remixed and ultimately helped create the legend of the Rolling Stones and transformed them into international stars, but who were themselves marginalized by the male-dominated rock world of the late '60s and early '70s.

"Poet Winder (Marilyn in Manhattan) paints a fascinating portrait of Marianne Faithfull, Marsha Hunt, Bianca Jagger, and Anita Pallenberg

ESSENTIAL AND RECOMMENDED TITLES
782.421643 Blues — Songs

(1942-2017), four women who styled, wrote lyrics for, and in equal measure enraptured and enraged the Rolling Stones." —*Publishers Weekly*

Wood, Damon
Working for the Man, Playing in the Band: My Years with James Brown. Damon Wood, with Phil Carson. Pgw 2018. 279 p.
ISBN 9781770413856
Grades: Adult   **782.42164**
1. Brown, James, 1933-2006 2. Wood, Damon 3. Soul music 4. Guitarists 5. Musicians 6. Soul musicians 7. African American musicians 8. Autobiographies and memoirs 9. Arts and Entertainment — Music — Jazz and the Blues 10. Life stories — Arts and culture — Performing arts — Musicians and composers
LC 2019393707

Guitarist Damon Wood spent six-and-a-half years playing for James Brown and the Soul Generals. Damon's narrative of this dramatic period in James Brown's illustrious career will fascinate his millions of fans.

"An insider's account that will delight both Brown fans and those interested in what it's like working for such a dedicated showman. Kudos to Wood for delivering the inside scoop on a demanding performer with exacting standards who brought it, every night." —*Library Journal*

Yaffe, David
Reckless Daughter: A Portrait of Joni Mitchell. David Yaffe. Sarah Crichton Books, Farrar, Straus and Giroux 2017. 544 p.
ISBN 9780374248130
Grades: Adult   **782.42164**
1. Mitchell, Joni, 1943- 2. Folk music 3. Women musicians 4. Folk musicians 5. Biographies 6. Life stories — Arts and culture — Performing arts — Musicians and composers 7. Arts and Entertainment — Music — Folk
LC 2017024370

A portrait of the music-culture icon shares insight into her use of experimental lyrics while revealing the inspirations behind her most famous songs, from her youth on the Canadian prairie to her early marriage and the child she gave up for adoption.

"A shimmering portrait of one artists life, illusions and all." —*Booklist*
Includes bibliographical references and index.

Zanes, Warren
Deliver Me from Nowhere: The Making of Bruce Springsteen's Nebraska. Warren Zanes. Crown 2023. 288 p.
ISBN 9780593237410
Grades: Adult   **782.42164**
1. Springsteen, Bruce 2. Musicians 3. Songwriters 4. Sound recordings 5. Influence (Psychology) 6. Rock music 7. Popular music 8. Arts and Entertainment — Music — Rock 9. Life stories — Arts and culture — Performing arts — Musicians and composers
LC 2022052300

The natural follow-up to Springsteen's hugely successful The River should have been the hit-packed album Born in the U.S.A, but instead, in 1982, he came out with Nebraska, an album consisting of a series of dark songs he had recorded exclusively by himself, for himself. But almost forty years later, Nebraska is arguably Springsteen's most important record—the lasting clue if you're looking to understand not just the artist's career and the vision behind it but the man himself.

"Even those who aren't convinced that Nebraska is Springsteen at his best will hear it with fresh ears." —*Kirkus*

782.421643 Blues — Songs

McCormick, Mack
Biography of a Phantom: A Robert Johnson Blues Odyssey. Robert. Smithsonian Books 2023. 272 p.
ISBN 9781588347343
Grades: Adult   **782.421643**
1. Johnson, Robert, 1911-1938 2. McCormick, Mack 3. Blues musicians 4. African American musicians 5. Death 6. Musicologists 7. Historical research 8. Blues (Music) 9. Folk music 10. Music history and criticism 11. North American people 12. American people 13. Mississippi 14. Southern States 15. 20th century 16. Biographies 17. Life stories — Arts and culture — Performing arts — Musicians and composers 18. Arts and Entertainment — Music — Jazz and the Blues 19. History writing — Early 20th century — United States
LC 2022047107

When blues master Robert Johnson's little-known recordings were rereleased to great fanfare in the 1960s, little was known about his life, giving rise to legends that he gained success by selling his soul to the devil. Biography of a Phantom is musicologist Mack McCormick's all-consuming search, from the late 1960s until McCormick's death in 2015, to uncover Johnson's life story. While Johnson died before achieving widespread recognition, his music took on a life of its own and inspired future generations. Filled with lush descriptive fieldwork and photographs, this book is an important historical object that deepens the understanding of a stellar musician.

"McCormick conveys a wild enthusiasm for his research and the music of Robert Johnson that readers will find contagious." —*Library Journal*
Includes bibliographical references and index.

782.421644 Soul music — Songs

Jackson family
The Jacksons: Legacy. Jackie, Tito, Jermaine, Marlon, Michael, and Randy Jackson; with Fred Bronson. Black Dog & Leventhal 2017. 320 pages
ISBN 9780316473736
Grades: Adult   **782.421644**
1. Jackson family 2. Bands (Music) 3. African American families 4. African American brothers 5. Soul musicians 6. Child celebrities 7. Soul music 8. Popular music 9. Fame 10. Growing up 11. Collective autobiographies and memoirs 12. Life stories — Arts and culture — Performing arts — Musicians and composers 13. Arts and Entertainment — Music — Rap and R&B 14. Life stories — Relationships — Family
LC 2017943146

Written by Jackie, Tito, Jermaine, Marlon and Michael, a first-person visual history of the Jacksons combines exclusive interviews, anecdotes, quotes and previously unseen family archive photos tracing their meteoric rise and history-making tours.

782.421649 Rap songs

Abdurraqib, Hanif
Go Ahead in the Rain: Notes to A Tribe Called Quest. Hanif Abdurraqib. University of Texas Press 2019. 200 p.
ISBN 9781477316481
Grades: Adult   **782.421649**
1. Abdurraqib, Hanif, 1983- 2. Rap music 3. Rap musicians 4. Hip-hop culture 5. Bands (Music) 6. Arts and Entertainment — Music — Rap and R&B 7. Life stories — Arts and culture — Performing arts — Musicians and composers 8. Society and culture — Pop culture
LC 2018031799

Kirkus Prize for Nonfiction finalist, 2019; Longlisted for the National Book Award for Nonfiction, 2019.

How does one pay homage to A Tribe Called Quest? The seminal rap group brought jazz into the genre, resurrecting timeless rhythms to create masterpieces such as The Low End Theory and Midnight Marauders. Poet and essayist Hanif Abdurraqib digs into the group's history and draws from his own experience to reflect on how its distinctive sound resonated among fans like himself. The result is as ambitious and genre-bending as the rap group itself.

"Abdurraqib frames himself as a participant in the story. His journey is integral as the music weaves into his existence, and he conveys the passion felt when art gives voice to our lives. This is his homage, written at times directly to readers and at others to the members of the group." —*Library Journal*

PUBLIC LIBRARY CORE COLLECTION: NONFICTION
Twentieth Edition

Abrams, Jonathan P. D.
★ *The Come* Up: An Oral History of the Rise of Hip-Hop. Jonathan Abrams. Crown 2022. 576 p.
ISBN 9781984825131
Grades: Adult 782.421649
1. Rap music 2. Rap musicians 3. Hip hop culture 4. Music and society 5. Music history and criticism 6. Popular culture 7. Bronx, New York City 8. New York City 9. United States 10. Oral histories 11. Arts and Entertainment — Music — Rap and R&B 12. History writing — Arts and culture
LC 2022016189

Drawing on more than 300 interviews conducted over three years with DJs, executives, producers and artists, a New York Times best-selling author offers the most comprehensive account to date of hip-hop's rise, conveying the drive, the stakes and the relentless creativity that ignited one of the greatest revolutions in modern music.

"Recommended for music historians, hip-hop fans, and casual listeners who want to add to their playlists." —*Library Journal*

Includes bibliographical references and index.

Ashon, Will
Chamber Music: Wu-Tang and America, in 36 Pieces. Will Ashon. Faber & Faber 2019. 374 pages
ISBN 9780571350001
Grades: Adult 782.421649
1. Rap music 2. Rap musicians 3. Music and society 4. African American musicians 5. Hip-hop culture 6. Social life and customs 7. New York City 8. 20th century 9. Arts and Entertainment — Music — Rap and R&B
LC Bl2019021748

Explores the iconic rap album and examines how it changed the world and continues to inspire new ways of looking, listening, and learning.

"This is nothing less than a literary tour de force through hundreds of years of American history as seen through one hip-hop band and one landmark album." —*Booklist*

Chuck D.
Chuck D Presents This Day in Rap and Hip-Hop History. with Duke Eatmon, Ron Maskell, Lorrie Boula, and Jonathan Bernstein; foreword by Shepard Fairey. Black Dog & Leventhal 2017. IX, 342 pages : Illustration; Color
ISBN 9780316430975
Grades: Adult 782.421649
1. Hip-hop culture 2. Rap music industry and trade 3. Rap music 4. Music history and criticism 5. Popular culture 6. 20th century 7. Arts and Entertainment — Music — Rap and R&B 8. History writing — Arts and culture
LC 2017568883

A comprehensive, chronological survey of rap and hip-hop from 1973 to the present, written by one of the industry's most influential lyricists, is based on his long-running show on Rapstation.Com and details the most iconic moments and relevant songs from the genre's recorded history.

Includes index.

Edwards, Paul
The Concise Guide to Hip-Hop Music: A Fresh Look at the Art of Hip-Hop, from Old-School Beats to Freestyle Rap. Paul Edwards. St. Martin's Griffin 2015. 232 pages
ISBN 9781250034816
Grades: Adult 782.421649
1. Rap music 2. Rap musicians 3. Music history and criticism 4. Arts and Entertainment — Music — Rap and R&B
LC 2014034012

In 1973, the music scene was forever changed by the emergence of hip-hop. Masterfully blending the rhythmic grooves of funk and soul with layered beats and chanted rhymes, artists such as DJ Kool Herc and Grandmaster Flash paved the way for an entire new genre and generation of musicians. In this comprehensive, accessible guide, Paul Edwards breaks down the difference between old school and new school, recaps the biggest influencers of the genre, and sets straight the myths and misconceptions of the artists and their music. Fans old and new alike will all learn something new about the history and development of hip-hop, from its inception up through the current day.

Includes bibliographical references and index.

Greenburg, Zack O'Malley
3 Kings: Diddy, Dr. Dre, Jay-Z, and Hip-Hop's Multibillion-Dollar Rise. Zack O'Malley Greenburg. Little, Brown 2018. 320 p.
ISBN 9780316316538
Grades: Adult 782.421649
1. Jay-Z, 1969- 2. Dr. Dre, 1965- 3. Diddy, 1969- 4. Rap musicians 5. Rap music 6. Hip-hop culture 7. African American businesspeople 8. African American entrepreneurs 9. African Americans 10. Social life and customs 11. United States 12. Biographies 13. Arts and Entertainment — Music — Rap and R&B 14. Business and economics — Business leaders and entrepreneurs 15. Adult books for young adults
LC 2017021046

Library Journal Best Books, 2018.

Tracing the careers of hip-hop's three most dynamic stars, this deeply reported history brilliantly examines the entrepreneurial genius of the first musician tycoons: Diddy, Dr. Dre, and Jay-Z.

"Greenburg details the thinking of these three tastemakers throughout their musical careers and into their corporate identities as they focus on shaping the way people enjoy their lives. Each approached rap music through a different outlet. Each carved out a different lasting mark. And all slowly but intentionally made decisions that impacted the business world on a grand scale. Greenburg offers a refreshing perspective on three immensely talented and popular personalities." —*Booklist*

Iandoli, Kathy
God Save the Queens: The Essential History of Women in Hip-Hop. Kathy Iandoli. Dey Street Books 2019. 320 pages
ISBN 9780062878502
Grades: Adult 782.421649
1. Women rap musicians 2. Hip-hop culture 3. Rap music 4. Women musicians 5. Sexism 6. Gender role 7. Sexuality 8. Music history and criticism 9. Arts and Entertainment — Music — Rap and R&B 10. History writing — Women's history 11. Society and culture — Gender — Women 12. Life stories — Arts and culture — Performing arts — Musicians and composers 13. Adult books for young adults
LC Bl2019035953

Paying tribute to the women of hip-hop, and exploring issues of gender, money, sexuality, violence, objectification and more, this important and monumental work of music journalism finally gives these influential artists the respect they have long deserved.

Includes bibliographical references and index.

Questlove
★ *Hip-Hop* Is History. Questlove with Ben Greenman. AUWA / MCD / Farrar, Straus and Giroux 2024. 352 p.
ISBN 9780374614072
Grades: Adult 782.421649
1. Rap music 2. Music history and criticism 3. Hip-hop culture 4. 20th century 5. 21st century 6. Arts and Entertainment — Music — Rap and R&B 7. History Writing — Arts and culture
LC 2023057423

The musician behind the band the Roots chronicles the 50-year history of hip-hop.

"Drawing on remarkably detailed information and a keen critical sensibility and working seamlessly with his coauthor, Greenman, Questlove traces the genre from its roots in the Bronx during the 1970s to its flourishing across the country in its many variations to its global impact in the present, highlighting landmark achievements and acknowledging the challenges artists and producers faced…Questlove's illuminating and insightful survey is as personal as it is expert." —*Booklist*

Includes index.

CLASSIFIED LIST OF WORKS
782.42166 Rock (Rock 'n' roll) songs

Westhoff, Ben
Dirty South: Outkast, Lil Wayne, Soulja Boy, and the Southern Rappers Who Reinvented Hip-Hop. Ben Westhoff. Chicago Review Press 2011. 288 p.
ISBN 9781569766064
Grades: Adult   782.421649
1. Rap music 2. Rap musicians 3. Popular music 4. Hip-hop culture 5. Music 6. Music history and criticism 7. Social life and customs 8. Southern States 9. 21st century 10. Arts and Entertainment — Music — Rap and R&B
LC 2010053907

"An exploration of the musical and personal terrain of what has come to be known as the Southern sound of rap by such artists as Lil Wayne, Young Jeezy, and Ludacris. Westhoff convincingly details how Southern rap music—party music, full of hypnotic hooks and sing-along choruses—took over from dominant East Coast and West Coast rap styles by replacing normal rap structures and metaphor-heavy rhymes in favor of chants, grunts and shouts. In fact, the beauty of Westhoff's descriptions of the genre as a whole and various songs in particular will make old fans as well as newbies want to search out and play classic CDs such as OutKast's Aquemini and Kings of Crunk by Lil Jon. And Westhoff's personal trips to the home bases of each artist he presents show how the personalities of the artists reinforce their music." —*Publishers Weekly*
Includes bibliographical references and index.

Original Gangstas: The Untold Story of Dr. Dre, Eazy-E, Ice Cube, Tupac Shakur, and the Birth of West Coast Rap. Ben Westhoff. Hachette Books 2016. VIII, 422 pages
ISBN 9780316383899
Grades: Adult   782.421649
1. Dr. Dre, 1965- 2. Wright, Eric, 1964-1995 3. Ice Cube 4. Shakur, Tupac, 1971-1996 5. Notorious B.I.G, 1972-1997 6. Rap musicians 7. Hip-hop culture 8. Inner city 9. Gangsta rap 10. Drugs 11. Cocaine traffic 12. Violence in gangs 13. Rap music industry and trade 14. Music industry and trade 15. Popular culture 16. South Central Los Angeles, California 17. Los Angeles, California 18. Oral histories 19. Arts and Entertainment — Music — Rap and R&B 20. Society and culture — Pop culture 21. History writing — African American — United States 22. Adult books for young adults
LC 2016941451

This wide-ranging history of West Coast rap offers in-depth biographies of its leading artists—including Eazy-E, Dr. Dre, Ice Cube, Tupac Shakur, and others—as well as accounts of the rivalries between them. It also offers insightful examinations of the glamorizing of thug life and the popularity of hip hop, the consequences of fame, and the still-unsolved murders of Tupac and Biggie Smalls.

"Westhoff's impressive research makes this an invaluable overview of the musical influences and legal nightmares of West Coast rap's main players." —*Publishers Weekly*
Includes index.

782.42166 Rock (Rock 'n' roll) songs

Cohen, Rich
The Sun and the Moon and the Rolling Stones. Rich Cohen. Spiegel & Grau 2016. 381 p.
ISBN 9780804179232
Grades: Adult   782.42166
1. Journalists 2. Rock musicians 3. Rock groups 4. Arts and Entertainment — Music — Rock 5. Life stories — Arts and culture — Performing arts — Musicians and composers
LC 2015035782

Describes the history of the English rock group, documenting the formation of the band in the 1960s, their rise to world fame, skills as innovative songwriters, and continuing endurance into the present day.

"A compact and conversant history that makes the story new again, capturing the Rolling Stones in all their Faustian glory." —*Kirkus*
Includes bibliographical references and index.

Cross, Charles R.
Here We Are Now: The Lasting Impact of Kurt Cobain. Charles R. Cross. It Books 2014. 192 pages
ISBN 9780062308214
Grades: Adult   782.42166
1. Cobain, Kurt, 1967-1994 2. Rock music 3. Music 4. Rock musicians 5. Addiction 6. Fashion 7. Alternative rock music 8. Alternative rock musicians 9. Rock groups 10. Depression 11. Grunge groups 12. Grunge music 13. Music history and criticism 14. Arts and Entertainment — Music — Rock
LC 2013045769

The author of the Kurt Cobain biography "Heavier Than Heaven" examines the legacy of the Nirvana frontman and discusses why he still matters twenty years after his death.

"This short but intriguing book explores the troubled musician as a kind of muse for seemingly unrelated fields (modern hip-hop, medical studies, high-end fashion) as well as a champion for gay and women's rights and racial equality." —*Library Journal*

Guesdon, Jean-Michel
All the Songs: The Story Behind Every Beatles Release. Preface by Patti Smith; Jean-Michel Guesdon & Philippe Margotin; Scott Freiman, consulting editor. Black Dog & Leventhal Publishers 2013. 671 pages : Illustration; Color
ISBN 9781579129521
Grades: Adult   782.42166
1. Songwriting 2. Lyric writing 3. Composition (Music) 4. Popular music 5. Rock music 6. Music history and criticism 7. Great Britain 8. Arts and Entertainment — Music — Rock
LC BI2013048728

Presents the stories behind the writing and recording of all 213 songs released by the Beatles, in a work arranged chronologically and illustrated with hundreds of photographs.

"Arranged chronologically by album, the book includes for each song basic information (songwriter, track length, number of takes, etc.), a brief discussion of how it was written and recorded, and an overall assessment. [N]umerous anecdotes and quotations from the group keep the book entertaining and accessible even to more casual music fans." —*Library Journal*
Includes bibliographical references (page 671) and index.

Hyden, Steven
Long Road: Pearl Jam and the Sound of a Generation. Steven Hyden. Hachette Books 2022. 256 p.
ISBN 9780306826429
Grades: Adult   782.42166
1. Rock groups 2. Rock musicians 3. Alternative rock music 4. Generation X 5. Popular culture 6. Rock music 7. Music history and criticism 8. Arts and Entertainment — Music — Rock 9. Life stories — Arts and culture — Performing arts — Musicians and composers
LC 2022019040

Ever since Pearl Jam first blasted onto the Seattle grunge scene three decades ago with their debut album, Ten, they have sold 85M+ albums, performed for hundreds of thousands of fans around the world, and have even been inducted into the Rock and Roll Hall of Fame. In Long Road, music critic and journalist Steven Hyden celebrates the life, career, and music of this legendary group, widely considered to be one of the greatest American rock bands of all time. Long Road is structured like a mix tape, using 18 different Pearl Jam classics as starting points for telling a mix of personal and universal stories.

"A music biography well suited to fans of both the band and 1990s pop culture." —*Kirkus*
Includes index.

Margotin, Philippe
The Rolling Stones: All the Songs : The Story Behind Every Track. Philippe Margotin and Jean-Michel Guesdon; translation by Richard George Elliott. Black Dog & Leventhal Publishers 2016. 703 p. : Illustration; Color
ISBN 9780316317740
Grades: Adult   782.42166

1. Rock music 2. England 3. Arts and Entertainment — Music — Rock
LC 2016564656

A visual, song-by-song history of the Rolling Stones covers their studio albums, compilation albums, and more than one hundred singles, providing photographs, musician lists, and recording and song development information.

Includes bibliographical references (pages 702-703), discography, and index; Translated from the French.

McCartney, Paul

★ *1964: Eyes of the Storm.* Photographs and reflections by Paul McCartney; introduction by Jill Lepore. Liveright Publishing Corporation, a division of W.W. Norton & Company 2023. 336 pages : Illustration
ISBN 9781324093060
Grades: Adult   782.42166

1. Bands (Music) 2. Concert tours 3. Photographs 4. Great Britain 5. United States 6. 1960s 7. Visual nonfiction 8. Arts and Entertainment — Music — Pop 9. Life stories — Arts and culture — Performing arts — Musicians and composers
LC Bl2023021282

McCartney recalls the pandemonium of British concert halls, followed by the hysteria that greeted the band on its first American visit. Candid recollections preceding each city portfolio that form an autobiographical account of the period McCartney remembers as the "Eyes of the Storm," plus a coda with subsequent events in 1964.

"This beautiful art book serves as a most welcome companion to Beatles scholarship and 1960s culture in general." —*Library Journal*

The Lyrics: 1956 to the Present. Paul McCartney; edited with an introduction by Paul Muldoon. Liveright Publishing 2021. 880 p. : Illustration
ISBN 9781631492563
Grades: Adult   782.42166

1. McCartney, Paul 2. Rock musicians 3. Songwriters 4. Songwriting 5. Singers 6. Memories 7. Interpersonal relations 8. Popular music 9. Music history and criticism 10. Arts and Entertainment — Music — Rock 11. Life stories — Arts and culture — Performing arts — Musicians and composers
LC 2021012488

From his early Liverpool days, through the historic decade of the Beatles, to Wings and his long solo career, The Lyrics pairs the definitive texts of 154 Paul McCartney songs with first-person commentaries on his life and music. Spanning two alphabetically arranged volumes, these commentaries reveal how the songs came to be and the people who inspired them: his devoted parents, Mary and Jim; his songwriting partner, John Lennon; his "Golden Earth Girl," Linda Eastman; his wife, Nancy McCartney; and even Queen Elizabeth, among many others. With images from McCartney's personal archives—handwritten texts, paintings, and photographs, hundreds previously unseen—The Lyrics, spanning sixty-four years, becomes the definitive literary and visual record of one of the greatest songwriters of all time.

"McCartney's contributions to culture are foundational, extending well beyond enthusiasts and devotees. This set serves as his testament of a career and a life dedicated to music." —*Library Journal*

2 volumes presented in a slipcase; Includes index.

Povey, Glenn

Echoes: The Complete History of Pink Floyd. Glenn Povey. Chicago Review Press 2010. 368 p. : Illustration; Color
ISBN 9781569763131
Grades: 11 12 Adult   782.42166

1. Progressive rock music 2. Psychedelic rock music 3. Rock music 4. Rock musicians 5. Music history and criticism 6. English history 7. England 8. 21st century 9. 20th century 10. Biographies 11. Life stories — Arts and culture — Performing arts — Musicians and composers 12. Arts and Entertainment — Music — Rock
LC 2011420528

Presents an account of the collective and individual careers of the members of Pink Floyd, dating from before the band's formation to the present day, that includes a comprehensive list of their stage, television, and radio performances.

"Long time fans will find Echoes a pleasure to read as well as to look at. For the most part, the book has the knowing and reverential feeling of liner notes. But occasionally some mordant humor comes through. A congenital defect of tribute volumes is that they tend to recite band lore that you already know about. For the most part, Povey avoids this tendency and digs up some of the strange bypaths of the band's long history." —*PopMatters*

Spitz, Bob

Led Zeppelin: The Biography. Bob Spitz. Penguin Books 2021. 688 p.
ISBN 9780399562426
Grades: Adult   782.42166

1. Rock groups 2. Heavy metal groups 3. Rock music 4. Rock musicians 5. Collective biographies 6. Life stories — Arts and culture — Performing arts — Musicians and composers 7. Arts and Entertainment — Music — Rock

Separating fact from fiction, which is sometimes astonishing and sometimes disturbing, the award-winning biographer brings the band's artistic journey to full and vivid life, showing how the 60s became the 70s, and how innocence became decadence as they took things to an entirely new level.

"Music biographer Spitz (The Beatles) calls on his supreme research and analytical skills to deliver the definitive story of one of the greatest rock groups of the 1970s. While this isn't the first (or second) telling of the Zeppelin saga, it reigns superior to its predecessors with an exhaustive history that never flags in momentum or spirit." —*Publishers Weekly*

Includes bibliographical references.

Tolokonnikova, Nadezhda

Rules for Rulebreakers: A Pussy Riot Guide to Revolution. Nadya Tolokonnikova. HarperOne 2018. 256 p.
ISBN 9780062741585
Grades: Adult   782.42166

1. Tolokonnikova, Nadezhda, 1989- 2. Art and politics 3. Punk rock music 4. Punk rock musicians 5. Feminism 6. Counterculture 7. Social advocacy 8. Political participation 9. Women 10. Rock musicians 11. Autobiographies and memoirs 12. Life stories — Politics — Activists and reformers 13. Society and culture — Social activism and philanthropy 14. Adult books for young adults
LC 2017059217

From a life of inspired action and creative rebellion, a feminist artist, activist and Pussy Riot founder shares her core principles and formative experiences, offering inspiration for opposing authoritarian leaders and governments that threaten to suppress individual rights and freedoms.

782.5 Vocal executants

Rapkin, Mickey

Pitch Perfect: The Quest for Collegiate a Cappella Glory. Mickey Rapkin. Gotham Books 2008. 288 p.
ISBN 9781592403769
Grades: Adult   782.5

1. Music 2. Page to screen 3. Arts and Entertainment — Music
LC 2007048222

Chronicles the competition between three contending groups for the Collegiate a Cappella championship, evaluating how their achievements reflect a rising surge in the music form's popularity, as well as the diversity that has shaped its expression.

784.18 Musical forms

Hamilton-Paterson, James

★ *Beethoven's Eroica: The First Great Romantic Symphony.* James Hamilton-Paterson. Basic Books 2017. 176 p.
ISBN 9781541697362
Grades: Adult   784.18

1. Beethoven, Ludwig van, 1770-1827 2. Classical music 3. Symphonies 4. Arts and entertainment — Music — Classical

ESSENTIAL AND RECOMMENDED TITLES
784.2 Full orchestra (Symphony orchestra)

LC Bl2017049925

A tribute to Beethoven's revolutionary Third Symphony explores how it was originally inscribed to Napoleon, broke the mold of the Viennese Classical style and revealed powerful new forms of musical expressiveness. By the award-winning author of Empire of the Clouds.

"Casual concertgoers and serious music aficionados alike will find much to savor in this elegant and insightful book." —Booklist

784.2 Full orchestra (Symphony orchestra)

Murakami, Haruki
★ *Absolutely* on Music: Conversations. Haruki Murakami with Seiji Ozawa; translated from the Japanese by Jay Rubin. Alfred A. Knopf 2016. 288 p.
ISBN 9780385354349
Grades: Adult   784.2
1. Ozawa, Seiji, 1935-2024 2. Music history and criticism 3. Writing 4. Male friendship 5. Authors 6. Classical music 7. Jazz music 8. Autobiographies and memoirs 9. Translations — Japanese to English 10. Life stories — Arts and culture — Performing arts — Musicians and composers 11. Arts and Entertainment — Music

LC 2016008866

Loan Stars Favourites, 2016.

A deeply personal, intimate conversation about music and writing illuminates the perspectives and shared interests of the internationally acclaimed, best-selling author of Colorless Tsukuru Tazaki and His Years of Pilgrimage and his close friend, the former conductor of the Boston Symphony Orchestra.

"A work that general readers will enjoy and the musical cognoscenti will devour." —Kirkus

Originally published as Ozawa Seiji-san to, ongaku ni tsuite hanashi o suru: Tokyo : Shinchosha, 2011; Translated from the Japanese.

Philip, Robert
The Classical Music Lover's Companion to Orchestral Music. Robert Philip. Yale University Press 2018. xviii, 949 pages
ISBN 9780300120691
Grades: Adult   784.2
1. Music history and criticism 2. Orchestral music 3. Arts and Entertainment — Music — Classical 4. Arts and Entertainment — Music

LC 2018954130

Robert Philip, scholar, broadcaster, and musician, has compiled an essential handbook for lovers of classical music, designed to enhance their listening experience to the full. Covering four hundred works by sixty-eight composers from Corelli to Shostakovich, from 1700 to 1950, this engaging companion explores and unpacks the most frequently performed works, including symphonies, concertos, overtures, suites, and ballet scores. It offers intriguing details about each piece while avoiding technical terminology that might frustrate the non-specialist reader. Philip identifies key features in each work, as well as subtleties and surprises that await the attentive listener, and he includes enough background and biographical information to illuminate the composer's intentions. Organized alphabetically from Bach to Webern, this compendium will be indispensable for classical music enthusiasts, whether in the concert hall or enjoying recordings at home.

Includes bibliographical references (pages 902-919) and index.

Sachs, Harvey
The Ninth: Beethoven and the Year 1824. Harvey Sachs. Random House 2010. 224 p.
ISBN 9781400060771
Grades: Adult   784.2
1. Beethoven, Ludwig van, 1770-1827 2. Music and society 3. Music 4. Music history and criticism 5. Composers 6. European history 7. 19th century 8. Arts and Entertainment — Music — Classical 9. History writing — Enlightenment — Europe

LC 2009019716

An analysis of Beethoven's seminal Ninth Symphony identifies it as a key cultural event that reflected major social upheavals, from the emergence of a dynamic Western world and changes in philosophical perspectives on individuality.

"This discussion of the cornerstone of Romantic music, whose influence extended deep into the twentieth century, is concise, thorough, and written from the heart of a great biographer, musicologist, and lover of fine music." —Booklist

Steinberg, Michael
The Symphony: A Listener's Guide. Michael Steinberg. Oxford University Press 1998. xvii, 678 p.
ISBN 9780195126655
Grades: 11 12 Adult   784.2
1. Symphonies 2. Arts and Entertainment — Music — Classical

LC BL 98013621

Presents an exhaustive listener's guide to the symphony, replete with musical examples, biographical details, historical background, and commentaries on more than one hundred major works.

"Steinberg describes 36 composers and, movement by movement, 118 symphonies, including all the standard repertory . as well as a few by less well known composers such as Gorecki, Harbison, Martinu, and Sessions. The writing varies from formal and factual to chatty, with candid asides and stories relevant to the composer, the composition, or an important performance." —Library Journal

Includes bibliographical references; Reprint. Originally published: 1995.

786.2092 Pianists

Hafner, Katie
A Romance on Three Legs: Glenn Gould's Obsessive Quest for the Perfect Piano. Katie Hafner. Bloomsburg USA 2008. 272 p.
ISBN 9781596915244
Grades: Adult   786.2092
1. Gould, Glenn 2. Steinway & Sons 3. Pianists 4. Piano 5. Design and construction 6. Autism spectrum disorders 7. United States history 8. 20th century 9. Arts and Entertainment — Music — Instruments 10. Adult books for young adults

LC 2007048808

Traces the complex and eccentric musician's psychologically charged relationship with a Steinway concert grand, from his discovery of the instrument and the seemingly endless coddling that went into its maintenance to his acquaintance with a long-suffering piano tuner.

"When Gould was paired with the right composer, Bach especially, he could make you wonder if he was altogether human. And reading Hafner on Gould is sometimes as much fun as listening to him play. And that's saying a lot." —Newsweek

Hough, Stephen
Rough Ideas: Reflections on Music and More. Stephen Hough. Farrar Straus & Giroux 2020. 304 p.
ISBN 9780374252540
Grades: Adult   786.2092
1. Hough, Stephen, 1961- 2. Classical music 3. Classical musicians 4. Pianists 5. Art 6. Culture 7. Musical performance 8. Composers 9. Essays 10. Arts and Entertainment — Music — Classical 11. Life stories — Arts and culture — Performing arts — Musicians and composers 12. Society and culture — General

LC Bl2020005922

A world-renowned classical pianist, composer and polymath candidly and engagingly discusses music and the life of a musician as well as people, places, books, paintings, the existence of God and the challenges of being a gay Catholic.

"Hough writes with wit, grace, and a singular point of view. His book offers rare insight into the mind of one of the leading performers of classical music." —Library Journal

Originally published: London : Faber & Faber, 2019.

786.5 Organs

Whitney, Craig R.
All the Stops: The Glorious Pipe Organ and Its American Masters. Craig R. Whitney. Public Affairs 2003. xxv, 321 p. : Illustration
ISBN 9781586481735
Grades: Adult   **786.5**
1. Organ music 2. Organists 3. Musical instruments 4. Design and construction 5. Music history and criticism 6. Music 7. Arts and Entertainment — Music — Instruments

LC 2002037025

New York Times Notable Book, 2003.

Presents a history of the pipe organ in the United States from the nineteenth-century until the present day.

"Whitney extolls the organ's eclectic heritage at a time when the instrument seems poised for a return to the mainstream, and his glossary of its colorful terminology will help novices tell a windchest from a bombarde." —*The New Yorker*

Includes discography (p. 273-274), bibliographical references (p. 301-303), and index.

786.7 Electronic instruments (Electrophones)

Warner, Daniel
Live Wires: A History of Electronic Music. Daniel Warner. Reaktion Books, Limited. 2017. 205 p. : Illustration
ISBN 9781780238241
Grades: Adult   **786.7**
1. Music 2. Electronic music 3. Technological innovations 4. Music history and criticism 5. Arts and Entertainment — Music

We live in an electronic world. Electronic sounds and electronic music have long permeated our sonic landscape. What began as the otherworldly sounds of the film score for the 1956 film Forbidden Planet and the rarefied, new timbres of Stockhausen's Kontakte a few years later, is now a common soundscape in technology, media and an array of musical genres and subgenres. Featuring the work of major figures from Schaeffer, Varese, Xenakis, Babbitt and Oliveros to Eno, Keith Emerson, Grandmaster Flash, Juan Atkins and Holly Herndon, Live Wires presents many of the powerful musical ideas that are being recycled, rethought and remixed by some of the most electrifying composers and musicians today.

"Though Warner's book would have benefited from more careful editing (for example, John Oswald of plunderphonics fame is mistakenly referred to as John Corbett), it is both informative and engaging, and it serves as a good overview of some of the most important electronic music repertoire and technology of the last century." —*Choice*

787 Stringed instruments (Chordophones)

Gaddy, K. R.
★ *Well of Souls: Uncovering the Banjo's Hidden History.* Kristina R. Gaddy; [foreword by Rhiannon Giddens]. W.W. Norton & Company 2022. 284 p.
ISBN 9780393866803
Grades: Adult   **787**
1. Banjo 2. Musical instruments 3. African Americans 4. Enslaved people 5. Slave trade 6. Rites and ceremonies 7. Cultural appropriation 8. Music, American 9. Social life and customs 10. United States history 11. United States 12. Arts and Entertainment — Music — Instruments 13. History writing — African American — United States

LC 2022027189

In an extraordinary story unfolding across two hundred years, Kristina Gaddy uncovers the banjo's key role in Black spirituality, ritual, and rebellion. Through meticulous research in diaries, letters, archives, and art, she traces the banjo's beginnings from the seventeenth century, when enslaved people of African descent created it from gourds or calabashes and wood. Gaddy shows how the enslaved carried this unique instrument as they were transported and sold by slaveowners throughout the Americas, to Suriname, the Caribbean, and the colonies that became U.S. states, including Louisiana, South Carolina, Maryland, and New York.

"This is a glorious and invaluable chronicle for music lovers and everyone interested in American culture." —*Booklist*

Includes bibliographical references and index.

Seeger, Pete
How to Play the 5-String Banjo: A Manual for Beginners. Pete Seeger. Hal Leonard Corporation 2002. 72 pages : Illustration
ISBN 9781597731645
Grades: Adult   **787**
1. Banjo 2. Arts and Entertainment — Music

LC Bl2014050878

Presents a history of the banjo, introduces strumming and fingering techniques, and offers advice on choosing and buying an instrument.

Includes bibliographical references (pages 70-71) and discography (page 72).

787.87 Guitars

Chappell, Jon
★ *Guitar All-in-One for Dummies.* Jon Chappell, Mark Phillips, and Desi Serna. John Wiley & Sons, Inc. 2020. xvi, 628 pages : Illustration
ISBN 9781119731412
Grades: Adult   **787.87**
1. Guitar 2. Arts and Entertainment — Music

LC Bl2014036815

Presents an easy-to-follow guide to the guitar, from the basics of the instrument to different guitar music styles, including guidance on purchasing and stringing guitars, chord and rhythm techniques, guitar theory, and chord exercises.

6 books in 1—Cover; Includes index.

Port, Ian S
The Birth of Loud: Leo Fender, Les Paul, and the Guitar-Pioneering Rivalry That Shaped Rock 'n' Roll. Ian S. Port. Scribner 2019. 320 p.
ISBN 9781501141652
Grades: Adult   **787.87**
1. Fender, Leo, 1909-1991 2. Paul, Les, 1915-2009 3. Business competition 4. Electric guitar 5. Guitar 6. Popular music 7. Rock music 8. Fender guitar 9. Competition 10. Arts and Entertainment — Music — Instruments

LC 2018024537

Chronicles the rivalry between the two men who innovated the electric guitar's sound—Leo Fender and Les Paul—and their competition to convince rock stars like the Beatles, Jimi Hendrix, and Eric Clapton to play the instruments they built.

"This smartly written and genuinely exciting book walks us through the bitter rivalry between Fender and Gibson and, since there is no way to tell this story without telling the story of rock n roll itself, also provides a jaunty if necessarily abbreviated history of rock." —*Booklist*

Includes bibliographical references.

790 Recreational and performing arts

Capelle, Philip B.
★ *Play Your Best Straight Pool.* Philip B. Capelle. Billiards Pr 2000. 416 p.
ISBN 9780964920422
Grades: Adult   **790**
1. Pool (Game) 2. Strategy 3. Sports and Competition — Games

ESSENTIAL AND RECOMMENDED TITLES
790.1 General kinds of recreational activities

Fletcher, Susan A.
Exploring the History of Childhood and Play Through 50 Historic Treasures. Susan A. Fletcher. Rowman & Littlefield 2020. xxvi, 299 p. : Illustration; Color
ISBN 9781538118740
Grades: Adult 790
1. Toys 2. Games 3. Play 4. Children 5. Social life and customs 6. United States 7. History writing — Arts and culture
LC 2019049614

Exploring the History of Childhood and Play in American History Through 50 Historic Treasures is a compilation of fifty iconic toys and games from American history. As the amount of leisure time available to children has increased in the United States, the number of toys available to them has also dramatically increased.

Includes bibliographical references (pages 249-284) and index.

790.1 General kinds of recreational activities

Ahuvia, Aaron
★ *The Things We Love: How Our Passions Connect Us and Make Us Who We Are.* Aaron Ahuvia. Little Brown & Co. 2022. 304 p.
ISBN 9780316498227
Grades: Adult 790.1
1. Consumer behavior 2. Cognitive neuroscience 3. Identity 4. Belonging 5. Marketing 6. Economics 7. Society and culture — Psychology and human behavior

Books, baseball cards, ceramic figurines, art, iPhones, clothing, cars, music, dolls, furniture, and even nature itself. If you're like most people, at some point in your life you've found yourself indulging in a love affair with some thing that brings you immense joy, comfort, or fulfillment. Why is it that we so often feel intense passion for objects? What does this tendency tell us about ourselves and our society?

"This stimulating volume is easy to love." —*Publishers Weekly*

Du Sautoy, Marcus
★ *Around the World in Eighty Games: From Tarot to Tic-Tac-Toe, Catan to Chutes and Ladders, a Mathematician Unlocks the Secrets of the World's Greatest Games.* Marcus du Sautoy. Basic Books 2023. 400 p.
ISBN 9781541601284
Grades: Adult 790.1
1. Games 2. Mathematics 3. Mathematical analysis 4. Mathematical models 5. Game theory 6. Problem solving 7. Science Writing — Mathematics
LC 2023006341

An award-winning mathematician explores the deep connections between math and the games we love, such as Monopoly and Connect 4, and explains how playing such games are an essential part of human psychology and culture.

"This meticulous and deeply researched survey will appeal to math-lovers and history buffs alike." —*Publishers Weekly*

Includes bibliographical references and index.

Johnson, Steven
Wonderland: How Play Made the Modern World. Steven Johnson. Riverhead Books 2016. 304 p.
ISBN 9780399184482
Grades: Adult 790.1
1. Technological innovations 2. Inventions 3. Technology 4. Amusements 5. Entertainment industry and trade 6. History 7. History writing — General 8. Science writing — General 9. Arts and Entertainment — General
LC 2016035344
Booklist Editors' Choice, 2016.

A history of popular entertainment explores the world-changing innovations humans have made while keeping themselves entertained and introduces the explorers, proprietors, showmen, and artists who became the innovators of leisure.

"This is a great book for all curious readers, especially the history-averse, who will enjoy the fast pace, topical diversity, and abundant trivia." —*Booklist*

Raab, Nathan
The Hunt for History: On the Trail of the World's Lost Treasures - from the Letters of Lincoln, Churchill, and Einstein to the Secret Recordings Onboard JFK's Air Force One. Nathan Raab, with Luke Barr. Scribner 2020. 288 p.
ISBN 9781501198908
Grades: Adult 790.1
1. Raab, Nathan, 1978- 2. Antique dealers 3. Collectors and collecting 4. Manuscripts 5. Historic documents 6. Lost articles 7. History 8. Life stories — Arts and culture — Writing 9. History writing — General
LC 2019024822

A preeminent rare documents dealer recounts his years spent finding, authenticating and protecting important historical artifacts, from letters written by Alexander Hamilton to an American flag carried by Neil Armstrong to the moon and back.

"With several chill-inducing moments combined with engaging writing, this book will hold readers' interest until the last page. May be of particular interest to fans of Antiques Roadshow or American Pickers." —*Library Journal*

Includes index.

791 Public performances

Hendrix, Grady
These Fists Break Bricks: How Kung Fu Movies Swept America and Changed the World. Grady Hendrix and Chris Poggiali. Mondo Books 2022. 333 p.
ISBN 9781736891605
Grades: Adult 791
1. Martial arts films 2. Films 3. Kung fu 4. Martial arts 5. Adventure films 6. Cult films 7. Film history and criticism 8. Visual nonfiction 9. Arts and Entertainment — Movies and Television

Moore, Rachel
The Artist's Compass: The Complete Guide to Building a Life and a Living in the Performing Arts. Rachel S. Moore, President and CEO of the Los Angeles Music Center. Touchstone 2016. xviii, 204 pages
ISBN 9781501126642
Grades: 11 12 Adult 791
1. Performing arts 2. Vocational guidance 3. Business and economics — Careers 4. Arts and Entertainment — General 5. Self-Help — Personal growth
LC 2015037025

Describes how to build and nurture a secure and successful career in the performing arts by approaching it like an entrepreneur.

"Moore is qualified to become a mentor to a whole new generation of artists, and they will benefit greatly from her advice." —*Publishers Weekly*

Includes bibliographical references (pages 181-186) and index.

791.06 Organizations and management; amusement parks

Snow, Richard
Disney's Land: Walt Disney and the Invention of the Amusement Park That Changed the World. Richard Snow. Scribner 2019. 432 pages
ISBN 9781501190803
Grades: Adult 791.06
1. Disney, Walt, 1901-1966 2. Amusement parks 3. Entrepreneurs 4. Architecture and society 5. Architecture, American 6. Design and construction 7. California 8. Business and economics — Industries — Entertainment and media 9. Arts and Entertainment — Architecture 10. Business and economics — Business leaders and entrepreneurs
LC 2019024840

A history of the conception and development of the iconic California theme park chronicles how Walt and Roy Disney and a small group of artists endured innumerable setbacks to create one of the world's most popular destinations.

Includes bibliographical references and index.

PUBLIC LIBRARY CORE COLLECTION: NONFICTION
Twentieth Edition

791.089 African American entertainers

Abdurraqib, Hanif
★ *A Little Devil in America: Notes in Praise of Black Performance.* Hanif Abdurraqib. Random House 2021. 272 p.
ISBN 9781984801197
Grades: Adult   791.089
1. African Americans in the performing arts 2. African American authors 3. Intellectual life 4. Performing arts 5. Race relations 6. United States 7. Autobiographies and memoirs 8. Arts and Entertainment — General 9. Society and culture — Race 10. Life stories — Arts and culture — Performing arts
LC 2020023086

Andrew Carnegie Medal for Excellence in Non-Fiction, 2022; National Book Critics Circle Award for Autobiography/Memoir finalist, 2021; National Book Award for Nonfiction finalist, 2021.

A poet, essayist and cultural critic presents a profound and lasting reflection on how Black performance is inextricably woven into the fabric of American culture.

"Told with humor and grace, Abdurraqib's stories will inspire and provoke thoughtful meditations on how Black lives matter in all areas of life and art." —*Library Journal*

Includes bibliographical references and index.

791.3 Circuses

Standiford, Les
★ *Battle for the Big Top: P.T. Barnum, James Bailey, John Ringling, and the Death-Defying Saga of the American Circus.* Les Standiford. Public Affairs 2021. 272 p.
ISBN 9781541762282
Grades: Adult   791.3
1. Barnum, P. T. (Phineas Taylor), 1810-1891 2. Ringling, John, 1866-1936 3. Ringling family 4. Bailey, James, 1847-1906 5. Circus 6. Circus owners 7. Businesspeople 8. Circus performers 9. Circus animals 10. History writing — Arts and culture 11. Arts and Entertainment — General 12. History writing — United States 13. Nonfiction that reads like fiction
LC 2020056749

Les Standiford brings to life a remarkable era when three circus kings, James Bailey, P.T. Barnum, and John Ringling, all vied for control of the vastly profitable and influential American Circus. Ultimately, the rivalry of these three men resulted in the creation of an institution that would surpass all intentions and, for 147 years, hold a nation spellbound.

"[Standiford] delivers a zippy history of Ringling Bros. Barnum & Bailey Circus.... Readers will relish this entertaining portrait of a bygone American institution." —*Publishers Weekly*

791.4 Motion pictures, radio, television

Hickey, Walt
★ *You Are What You Watch: How Movies and TV Affect Everything.* Walt Hickey; data visuals by Heather Jones. Workman Publishing 2023. 240 p.
ISBN 9781523515899
Grades: Adult   791.4
1. Mass media 2. Popular culture 3. Psychology 4. Physiology 5. Society and culture — Pop culture 6. Debut title
LC 2023020360

Pulitzer Prize-winning author and data expert Walt Hickey explains the power of entertainment to change our biology, our beliefs, how we see ourselves, and how nations gain power.

"Hickey presents a refreshing analysis of media consumption by explaining the human body's physiological responses to it...A worthy, fun dissection of pop culture that's full of infographics and data." —*Library Journal*

Includes bibliographical references and index.

791.43 Motion pictures

Arnold, Jeremy
Turner Classic Movies: The Essentials : 52 Must-See Movies and Why They Matter. Jeremy Arnold; foreword by Robert Osborne. Running Press 2016. 288 pages : Illustration; Color
ISBN 9780762459469
Grades: Adult   791.43
1. Films 2. Arts and Entertainment — General 3. Arts and Entertainment — Movies and Television 4. Arts and Entertainment — Photography
LC Bl2016018038

Presents fifty-two films that everyone should see and explains why each film is such a classic, including such notable films as "Duck Soup," "Sunset Boulevard," and "The Graduate."

Includes bibliographical references (pages 272-279) and index.

Auletta, Ken
★ *Hollywood Ending: Harvey Weinstein and the Culture of Silence.* Ken Auletta. Penguin Press 2022. 448 p.
ISBN 9781984878373
Grades: Adult   791.43
1. Weinstein, Harvey, 1952- 2. Coercion 3. Sex crimes 4. Sexual harassment of women 5. Sex discrimination in employment 6. Film producers and directors 7. Power 8. Hollywood, California 9. True Crime — Sex Crimes 10. Society and culture — Violence and crime 11. Life stories — Arts and culture — Performing arts

This biography of the disgraced Hollywood mogul looks at both his meteoric rise and how he used his position to indulge his sexual appetites for decades before facing a swift and dramatic downfall.

"Having revealed Harvey Weinstein's violent behavior two decades ago in a New Yorker profile, Auletta asks in Hollywood Ending whether Weinstein's sexual predation can be attributed to himself alone or to the Hollywood power game—and why it took so long to challenge it." —*Library Journal*

Ausaja, S. M. M.
Bollywood: The Films! the Songs! the Stars! S.M.M Ausajoa, Karan Bali, Aseem Chabbra, Rjesh Devraj; foreword by Amitabh Backchan. DK Publishing 2017. 360 p.
ISBN 9781465463296
Grades: Adult   791.43
1. Films 2. Film industry and trade 3. Film history and criticism 4. India 5. Arts and Entertainment — Movies and Television

"Public libraries should offer works on this topic, and academic libraries will want this as part of their cinema history collections. A fun book to browse, filled with ideas to entertain lovers of film and Indian culture." —*Library Journal*

Austerlitz, Saul
Kind of a Big Deal: How Anchorman Stayed Classy and Became the Most Iconic Comedy of the Twenty-First Century. Saul Austerlitz. Dutton 2023. IX, 308 p.
ISBN 9780593186848
Grades: Adult   791.43
1. Films 2. Comedy films 3. Influence (Psychology) 4. Actors and actresses 5. Screenwriters 6. Characters and characteristics in films 7. Sexism 8. Feminism 9. Masculinity 10. Mass media 11. Broadcast journalism 12. Arts and Entertainment — Movies and Television
LC 2022057221

Comedy historian Saul Austerlitz tells the history of how Anchorman was developed, written, and cast, and how it launched the careers of future superstars like Will Ferrell, Steve Carell, and Paul Rudd, also setting the stage for a whole decade of comedy to come and influencing films like The 40-Year-Old Virgin, Talladega Nights, Knocked Up, Superbad, and so many more. But Kind of a Big Deal isn't only a celebration of Anchorman—it's also a cultural analysis of the film's significance as a sly commentary on feminism, the media, fragile masculinity, 1970s nostalgia, and more.

ESSENTIAL AND RECOMMENDED TITLES
791.43 Motion pictures

"Anchorman fans will thoroughly enjoy this appraisal, and students of film criticism will learn from Austerlitz's readings. Sterling work." —*Booklist*

Barr, Patricia
Ultimate Star Wars. Written by Patricia Barr, Adam Bray, Daniel Wallace, Ryder Windham. DK Publishing 2015. 319 pages : Color; Illustration
ISBN 9781465436016
Grades: Adult   791.43
1. Star Wars films 2. Reference books — Performing arts
LC 2015297170

An in-depth, sumptuously illustrated survey of the characters and storylines from the Star Wars universe is chronologically organized and includes coverage of the films, and The Clone Wars and Rebels TV series. Movie tie-in.

Become an expert on the Star Wars galaxy! This book is an in-depth visual feast exploring the characters and storylines from the Star Wars galaxy. This is a beautifully illustrated guide that is structured chronologically and packed full of information about key characters and storylines from the Star Wars movie saga, The Clone Wars, and Rebels. Ultimate Star Wars will get new and old fans caught up and knowledgeable on all things Star Wars.

"Some pages contain several photos of the same structure so that all angles can be seen. The book also contains a contributers page where each artist is given credit. Middle and high school librarians should definitely consider adding this volume to their collections. Creative teens will appreciate the addition." —*Voice of Youth Advocates*

Characters, creatures, locations, technology, vehicles—Cover; Foreword by Anthony Daniels, C-3PO—Cover; Includes index.

Basinger, Jeanine
Hollywood: The Oral History. Jeanine Basinger and Sam Wasson. HarperCollins 2022. 832 p.
ISBN 9780063056947
Grades: Adult   791.43
1. Film industry and trade 2. Actors and actresses 3. Entertainment industry and trade 4. Hollywood, California 5. Oral histories 6. History writing — Arts and culture 7. Arts and Entertainment — Movies and television 8. Life stories — Arts and culture — Performing arts

A legendary film scholar and a New York Times best-selling author present the oral history of Hollywood through candid remarks from stars both in front and behind the camera including Bette Davis, Meryl Streep and Frank Capra.

"For fans of film history, this is an event: Film historians Basinger and Wasson teaming up to take us through the history of Hollywood (and, by extension, the American motion picture industry)....As close to a comprehensive Who's Who of American film as we're likely to see, and as close to a definitive history of American cinema as we've seen so far." —*Booklist*

Benson, Michael
Space Odyssey: Stanley Kubrick, Arthur C. Clarke, and the Making of a Masterpiece. Michael Benson. Simon & Schuster 2018. xii, 497 pages, 16 unnumbered pages of plates : Illustration; Color
ISBN 9781501163937
Grades: Adult   791.43
1. Kubrick, Stanley 2. Clarke, Arthur C. (Arthur Charles), 1917-2008 3. Filmmaking 4. Film producers and directors 5. Films 6. Science fiction films 7. Arts and Entertainment — Movies and Television
LC 2017051254

Published to coincide with the 50th anniversary of the film's release, this is the definitive story of the making of "2001: A Space Odyssey," acclaimed today as one of the greatest films ever made, and of director Stanley Kubrick and writer Arthur C. Clarke, who created this influential cinematic masterpiece.

Includes bibliographical references and index.

Bogle, Donald
Bright Boulevards, Bold Dreams: The Story of Black Hollywood. Donald Bogle. One World Ballantine Books 2005. xiv, 411 p. : Illustration
ISBN 9780345454188
Grades: Adult   791.43
1. African Americans in films 2. Films 3. African Americans 4. Actors and actresses 5. Biographies 6. Arts and Entertainment — Movies and Television
LC 2004054781

Celebrates Hollywood's glamorous African-American community, from the early twentieth century to the early 1970s, and profiles the accomplishments of such stars as the Nicholas brothers, Lena Horne, and Hattie McDaniel.

"Starting with Madame Sul-Te-Wan's work in D.W. Griffith's 1915 the Birth of a Nation and ending with the 1960s deaths of Louise Beavers, Nat King Cole and Dorothy Dandridge, Bogle tells the stories of the stars of Black Hollywood: Their outfits, their love affairs and their struggles for better roles. Bogle's lively style . and his many anecdotes will entertain and inform film students and Black history buffs alike." —*Publishers Weekly*

Includes bibliographical references (p. [383]-386) and index.

Carlson, Erin
I'll Have What She's Having: How Nora Ephron's Three Iconic Films Saved the Romantic Comedy. Erin Carlson. Hachette Books 2017. 304 p.
ISBN 9780316353885
Grades: Adult   791.43
1. Ephron, Nora 2. Films 3. Comedy films 4. Love in films 5. Film history and criticism 6. Arts and entertainment — Movies and television 7. Life stories — Arts and culture — Writing
LC 2017014826

A backstage assessment of the making of Nora Ephron's revered trilogy, When Harry Met Sally, You've Got Mail and Sleepless in Seattle, shares an intimate portrait of the writer's life and her enduring influence on a generation of Hollywood women.

Cavalier, Stephen
The World History of Animation. Stephen Cavalier. University of California Press 2011. 416 p. : Illustration; Color
ISBN 9780520261129
Grades: Adult   791.43
1. Animated films 2. Animation (Cinematography) 3. Animators 4. Television cartoon shows 5. Film history and criticism 6. Arts and Entertainment — Comics, Cartoons, and Animation
LC 2010931052

A lavishly illustrated volume with 250 color images traces the full history of animation from its very inception, looking at examples of the most groundbreaking work from around the globe and describing how animation technique has improved over the years.

Includes bibliographical references (p. 404-405) and index.

Clements, Jonathan
The Anime Encyclopedia: A Century of Japanese Animation. Jonathan Clements, Helen McCarthy. Stone Bridge Press 2015. xxiv, 1136 pages
ISBN 9781611720181
Grades: Adult   791.43
1. Animated films 2. Japan 3. Arts and Entertainment — Painting, Drawing, and Sculpture 4. Arts and Entertainment — Comics, Cartoons, and Animation 5. Arts and Entertainment — Movies and Television 6. Reference — Encyclopedias
LC 2014047174

Over 1,000 new entries, over 4,000 updates and corrections, countless old arguments ended (and new ones begun). The 3rd edition of the Anime Encyclopedia brings the landmark reference work up to date with six additional years of information on Japanese anime.

Includes bibliographical references (pages 961-968) and indexes.

Davis, Michael
Street Gang: The Complete History of Sesame Street. by Michael Davis. Viking 2009. 379 p.
ISBN 9780670019960
Grades: Adult   791.43
1. Television programs for children 2. Popular culture 3. Television and education 4. Television programs 5. Television 6. Film history and criticism 7. So-

PUBLIC LIBRARY CORE COLLECTION: NONFICTION
Twentieth Edition

cial life and customs 8. United States 9. 20th century 10. 21st century 11. Page to screen 12. Arts and Entertainment — Movies and Television 13. Adult books for young adults

LC 2008035498

A former family television editor for TV Guide traces the story of the landmark children's television show, from its origins at a dinner party by co-founder Joan Ganz Cooney and the creative achievements of Jim Henson to the Nixon administration's efforts to stop its funding and the advent of Elmo.

"Any grown-up fan will relish this account, gaining an even greater appreciation for the cultural contributions of Kermit, Big Bird, Oscar the Grouch and all their neighbors." —*Publishers Weekly*

Includes bibliographical references and index.

De Vise, Daniel

★ *The Blues Brothers: An Epic Friendship, the Rise of Improv, and the Making of an American Film Classic.* Daniel de Vise. Atlantic Monthly Press 2024. 480 p.

ISBN 9780802160980

Grades: Adult   791.43

1. Belushi, John, 1949-1982 2. Aykroyd, Dan, 1952- 3. Comedians 4. Friendship 5. Comedy films 6. Films and history 7. Film history and criticism 8. Film industry and trade 9. Improvisation (Acting) 10. Rhythm and blues music 11. Rhythm and blues musicians 12. Blues (Music) 13. United States 14. 1980s 15. 1970s 16. Life stories — Arts and culture — Performing arts — Actors and actresses 17. Arts and Entertainment — Movies and Television

LC 2023049667

Forty-four years since one of the most significant films of the 20th century hit theaters, this story of the epic friendship between John Belushi and Dan Aykroyd, the creative geniuses behind modern comedy, doubles as a behind-the-scenes narrative of how the film was made, scene by memorable scene.

"Will be popular with fans of pop culture and aficionados of film and TV history, as it not only covers the creation of the Blues Brothers abut also serves as a dual biography of Aykroyd and Belushi." —*Library Journal*

Includes bibliographical references and index.

Dixon, Wheeler W.

A Short History of Film. Wheeler Winston Dixon and Gwendolyn Audrey Foster. Rutgers University Press 2018. xxxviii, 465 pages, 16 unnumbered pages of plates : Illustration; Color; Portrait

ISBN 9780813595122

Grades: Adult   791.43

1. History 2. Film industry and trade 3. Films 4. Arts and Entertainment — Movies and Television 5. Society and culture — Media and technology

LC 2019296561

With more than 250 images, new information on international cinema (especially Polish, Chinese, Russian, Canadian, and Iranian filmmakers), an expanded section on African-American filmmakers, updated discussions of new works by major American directors, and a new section on the rise of comic book movies and computer generated special effects.

Includes glossary of film terms; Includes bibliographical references (pages 411-431) and index.

Elwes, Cary

As You Wish: Inconceivable Tales from the Making of The Princess Bride. Cary Elwes with Joe Layden. Touchstone 2014. 272 p.

ISBN 9781476764023

Grades: Adult   791.43

1. Elwes, Cary, 1962- 2. Actors and actresses 3. Filmmaking 4. Autobiographies and memoirs 5. Life stories — Arts and culture — Performing arts — Actors and actresses 6. Arts and entertainment — Movies and television

LC 2014014652

LibraryReads Favorites, 2014.

In a 25th anniversary, behind-the-scenes account of the making of the cult classic film, the lead actor shares never-before-told stories and exclusive photographs as well as interviews with Robin Wright, Billy Crystal and more.

Includes index.

Fischer, Paul

A **Kim** *Jong-Il Production: The Extraordinary True Story of a Kidnapped Filmmaker, His Star Actress, and a Young Dictator's Rise to Power.* Paul Fischer. Flatiron Books 2015. 368 p.

ISBN 9781250054265

Grades: Adult   791.43

1. Kim, Chong-Il, 1942-2011 2. Sin, Sang-ok, 1926-2006 3. Ch'oe, Un-hui, 1930-2018 4. Propaganda 5. Captives 6. Actors and actresses 7. Film producers and directors 8. Films 9. North Korea 10. Biographies 11. Life stories — Arts and culture — Performing arts 12. Life stories — Politics — Politicians 13. History writing — Asia — North and South Korea

LC 2014040366

Library Journal Best Books, 2015.

Before becoming the world's most notorious dictator, Kim Jong-Il ran North Korea's Ministry for Propaganda and its film studios. Conceiving every movie made, he acted as producer and screenwriter. Despite this control, he was underwhelmed by the available talent and took drastic steps, ordering the kidnapping of Choi Eun-Hee (Madam Choi)—South Korea's most famous actress—and her ex-husband Shin Sang-Ok, the country's most famous filmmaker.

"The most compelling facets of this book of astonishments are Fischers insights into the relationships between Choi, Shin, and their diabolical captor and Fischers canny perception of how Kim Jong-Il turned his oppressed, corrupt, and starving country into one vast theatrical production of fantasy, deceit, and terror, scripting lives of fear, ignorance, obedience, and deprivation." —*Booklist*

The **Man** *Who Invented Motion Pictures: A True Tale of Obsession, Murder, and the Movies.* Paul Fischer. Simon & Schuster 2022. 384 p.

ISBN 9781982114824

Grades: Adult   791.43

1. Le Prince, Louis Aime Augustin, 1842-1890 2. Artists 3. Inventors 4. Photography 5. Cinematography 6. Patents 7. Competition 8. Missing persons 9. Absence and presumption of death 10. Biographies 11. Life stories — Science, technology, and medicine — Scientists and inventors 12. Arts and Entertainment — Movies and Television 13. Arts and Entertainment — Photography 14. History writing — Technological innovations

An unputdownable story of the man who, before he could unveil his invention of the motion picture to the world, mysteriously vanished and was never seen or heard again, lost to history until now, in this never-before-told history of the motion picture.

"Was the man who invented cinematography kidnapped and murdered on the orders of Thomas Edison? Film producer Fischer (A Kim Jong-Il Production) raises that possibility in this fascinating portrait of 19th-century polymath Louis Le Prince." —*Publishers Weekly*

Fournier-Lanzoni, Remi

French Cinema, 2nd Ed.: From Its Beginnings to the Present. Rémi Fournier Lanzoni. Bloomsbury USA Academic 2015. 612 p.

ISBN 9781501303074

Grades: Adult   791.43

1. Films 2. Film history and criticism 3. Film industry and trade 4. French history 5. France 6. Arts and Entertainment — Movies and Television

An all-encompassing history of French motion pictures and cinematographic trends chronologically from 1895 to the present.

"Fournier Lanzoni (Wake Forest) updates the first edition of this model history of French cinema (CH, Sep'03, 41-0198) with an 84-page chapter titled 'The New Millennium.'…. Updated appendixes include France's Cannes award winners, the César Awards, box office toppers, and the country's successes at the Oscars. This second edition replaces the first." —*Choice*

Frankel, Glenn

High Noon: The Hollywood Blacklist and the Making of an American Classic. Glenn Frankel. Bloomsbury 2017. 304 p.

ISBN 9781620409480

Grades: Adult   791.43

1. Foreman, Carl 2. Film industry and trade 3. Screenplay writing 4. Hollywood Blacklist 5. Screenwriters 6. Blacklisting of authors 7. Communism 8. United States 9. 1950s 10. Arts and Entertainment — Movies and Television

ESSENTIAL AND RECOMMENDED TITLES
791.43 Motion pictures

LC 2017000380

Beginning in 1947, Hollywood came under intense scrutiny by the House Committee on Un-American Activities (HUAC), which was looking into alleged communist influences in Hollywood; ultimately hundreds of directors, actors, and screenwriters were blacklisted or boycotted by risk-averse studios. In High Noon, author Glenn Frankel explores the era through the production of the film by the same name. During the shoot, screenwriter Carl Foreman came under fire from HUAC, but he wasn't the only one affected by the political climate. Check it out if you're interested in the link between film and politics.

"A comprehensive guide to both a classic film and the era that created it." —*Kirkus*

Shooting Midnight Cowboy: Art, Sex, Loneliness, Liberation, and the Making of a Dark Classic. Glenn Frankel. Farrar, Straus and Giroux 2021. 416 p.
ISBN 9780374209018
Grades: Adult   791.43
1. Films 2. Filmmaking 3. Actors and actresses 4. New York City 5. Hollywood, California 6. 1960s 7. Arts and Entertainment — Movies and Television

LC 2020034903

A history of the making of the film Midnight Cowboy and the novel that inspired it.

"Midnight Cowboy is an acknowledged classic of American cinema, and Frankel provides us with the context we need to fully appreciate the film as a vivid snapshot of a specific time and place in American history." —*Booklist*

Includes bibliographical references and index.

Goetz, Kevin
Audienceology: How Moviegoers Shape the Films We Love. Kevin Goetz with Darlene Hayman. Tiller Press 2021. 224 p.
ISBN 9781982186678
Grades: Adult   791.43
1. Film industry and trade 2. Film audiences 3. Media fandom 4. Films 5. Film history and criticism 6. Arts and Entertainment — Movies and television

Audience-ology takes you to one of the most unknown places in Hollywood—a place where famous directors are reduced to tears and multi-millionaire actors to fits of rage. A place where dreams are made and fortunes are lost. This book is the chronicle of how real people have written and rewritten America's cinematic masterpieces by showing up, watching a rough cut of a new film, and giving their unfettered opinions so that directors and studios can salvage their blunders, or better yet, turn their movies into all-time classics.

"Goetz's goal is to give us a deeper appreciation of the role early audiences play in influencing what a movie ultimately looks like. . . . Absorbing reading for film fans." —*Booklist*

Includes bibliographical references and index.

Harris, Mark
Pictures at a Revolution: Five Movies and the Birth of the New Hollywood. Mark Harris. Penguin Press 2008. 496 p.
ISBN 9781594201523
Grades: Adult   791.43
1. Films, American 2. Filmmaking 3. Culture 4. Film history and criticism 5. Social life and customs 6. United States 7. 1960s 8. 20th century 9. Arts and Entertainment — Movies and Television

LC 2007032633

ALA Notable Book, 2009; Booklist Editors' Choice, 2008; New York Times Notable Book, 2008.

[Explores] the epic human drama behind the making of the five movies nominated for Best Picture in 1967—Guess Who's Coming to Dinner, The Graduate, In the Heat of the Night, Doctor Doolittle, and Bonnie and Clyde—and through them, the larger story of the cultural revolution that transformed Hollywood, and America, forever.

Includes bibliographical references and index.

Haygood, Wil
★ *Colorization:* One Hundred Years of Black Films in a White World. Wil Haygood. Alfred A. Knopf 2021. 432 p.
ISBN 9780525656876

Grades: Adult   791.43
1. African Americans in films 2. Race (Social sciences) 3. Racism 4. Films 5. Race relations 6. United States 7. Arts and Entertainment — Movies and Television 8. History writing — African American — United States

LC 2020056224

Explores the history of Black cinema and how it has served as a reflection of social realities and events, from the early racist films of D.W. Griffith to today's groundbreaking work of Black moviemakers and stars.

"Haygood's defining history is as moving as it is enlightening." —*Booklist*

This is a Borzoi Book published by Alfred A. Knopf; Includes bibliographical references and index.

Hirsch, Foster
★ *Hollywood* and the Movies of the Fifties: The Collapse of the Studio System, the Thrill of Cinerama, and the Invasion of the Ultimate Body Snatcher—television. Foster Hirsch. Alfred A. Knopf 2023. 736 p.
ISBN 9780307958921
Grades: Adult   791.43
1. Film industry and trade 2. Films 3. Postwar life 4. Film history and criticism 5. Los Angeles, California 6. Hollywood, California 7. United States 8. 1950s 9. 20th century 10. History Writing — United States 11. Arts and Entertainment — Movies and television 12. History Writing — Arts and culture

LC 2022055318

A comprehensive study of the changing attitudes of America in the 1950s as reflected by the films of that decade.

"A rich, expansive, and penetrating work of film and social history." —*Kirkus*

This is a Borzoi Book published by Alfred A. Knopf; Includes bibliographical references.

Jameson, A. D.
I Find Your Lack of Faith Disturbing: Star Wars and the Triumph of Geek Culture. A. D. Jameson. Farrar, Straus and Giroux 2018. 272 p.
ISBN 9780374537364
Grades: Adult   791.43
1. Star Wars films 2. Science fiction fandom 3. Fans (People) 4. Popular culture 5. Arts and Entertainment — Movies and Television 6. Society and culture — Pop culture 7. Adult books for young adults 8. Arts and Entertainment — Writing and Publishing — Literary criticism

LC 2017038357

A lifelong geek invites readers on an irreverent journey through modern geek culture as he shines new light on well-loved movie classics in the science fiction, fantasy and superhero genres, and discusses why he thinks these films should be taken seriously.

Includes bibliographical references and index.

Kael, Pauline
★ *The Age of Movies:* Selected Writings of Pauline Kael. Pauline Kael; edited by Sanford Schwartz. Library of America 2012. 750 p.
ISBN 9781598531091
Grades: Adult   791.43
1. Film reviews 2. Film evaluation 3. Film history and criticism 4. Arts and Entertainment — Movies and Television

LC 2011923053

A compendium of top-selected, signature writings by the influential former critic of the New Yorker offers insight into her capacity for capturing cinematic details and includes her appraisals of such works as Bonnie and Clyde, the Godfather and Last Tango in Paris.

Karp, Josh
Orson Welles's Last Movie: The Making of the Other Side of the Wind. Josh Karp. St Martin's Press 2015. 352 p.
ISBN 9781250007087
Grades: Adult   791.43
1. Welles, Orson, 1915-1985 2. Film producers and directors 3. Filmmaking 4. Arts and entertainment — Movies and television

PUBLIC LIBRARY CORE COLLECTION: NONFICTION
Twentieth Edition

LC 2015002464

In the summer of 1970 legendary but self-destructive director Orson Welles returned to Hollywood from years of self-imposed exile in Europe and decided it was time to make a comeback movie. Coincidentally it was the story of a legendary self-destructive director who returns to Hollywood from years of self-imposed exile in Europe. Welles swore it wasn't autobiographical.

"A fascinating story, much more than your typical making-of book." —*Booklist*

Kenny, Glenn

Made Men: The Story of Goodfellas. Glenn Kenny. Hanover Square Press 2020. 352 p.

ISBN 9781335016508

Grades: Adult   791.43

1. Film noir 2. Gangster films 3. Film producers and directors 4. Actors and actresses 5. Popular culture 6. Filmmaking 7. Film history and criticism 8. Arts and Entertainment — Movies and Television

LC Bl2020046755

When Goodfellas first hit the theatres in 1990, a classic was born. Few could anticipate the unparalleled influence it would have on pop culture, one that would inspire future filmmakers and redefine the gangster picture as we know it today. In the first ever behind-the-scenes story of Goodfellas, film critic Glenn Kenny chronicles the making and afterlife of the film that introduced America to the real modern gangster—brutal, ruthless, yet darkly appealing, the villain we can't get enough of. Featuring interviews with the film's major players, including Martin Scorsese and Robert De Niro, Made Men shines a light on the lives and stories wrapped up in the Goodfellas universe, and why its enduring legacy is still essential to charting the trajectory of American culture thirty years later.

"A must for any fan of Goodfellas, Scorsese, or movies in general." —*Library Journal*

The World Is Yours: The Story of Scarface. Glenn Kenny. Hanover Square Press 2024. 320 p.

ISBN 9781335449627

Grades: Adult   791.43

1. Gangster films 2. Actors and actresses 3. Film producers and directors 4. Influence (Psychology) 5. Filmmaking 6. Popular culture 7. Film history and criticism 8. Arts and Entertainment — Movies and Television 9. Life stories — Arts and culture — Performing arts

An unflinching confrontation of humanity's dark side, Brian De Palma's crime drama film Scarface gave rise to a cultural revolution upon its release in 1983. Its impact was unprecedented, making globe-spanning waves as a defining portrait of the gritty Miami street life. From Al Pacino's masterful characterization of Tony Montana to the iconic "Say hello to my little friend," Scarface maintains its reputation as an unwavering game changer in cult classic cinema. With brand-new interviews and untold stories of the film's production, longtime film critic Glenn Kenny takes us on an unparalleled journey through the making of American depictions of crime.

"Scarface fans should be sure to read this absolutely necessary book, and so should readers who enjoy a good book about moviemaking, even if they haven't seen this particular film." —*Booklist*

Klastorin, Michael

Close Encounters of the Third Kind: The Ultimate Visual History. Michael Klastorin; foreword by Steven Spielberg. Harper Design, an imprint of HarperColinsPublishers 2017. 188 pages : Illustration; Color

ISBN 9780062692993

Grades: Adult   791.43

1. Science fiction films 2. Arts and Entertainment — Painting, Drawing, and Sculpture 3. Arts and Entertainment — Movies and Television

LC Bl2017043939

Explores the creation, production, and legacy of the science fiction film and offers never-before-seen imagery from the archives.

Published to coincide with the sci-fi classic's 40th anniversary, and created in conjunction with Sony Pictures and Amblin Entertainment, a fully authorized behind-the-scenes book explores the creation, production and legacy of this iconic film, bringing together a gorgeous collection of on-set photography, concept art, storyboards and more.

Leamer, Laurence

Hitchcock's Blondes: The Unforgettable Women Behind the Legendary Director's Dark Obsession. Laurence Leamer. Putnam Publishing Group 2023. 368 p.

ISBN 9780593542972

Grades: Adult   791.43

1. Hitchcock, Alfred, 1899-1980 2. Blonde women 3. Actors and actresses 4. Manipulation (Social sciences) 5. Obsession 6. Desire 7. Film 8. Collective biographies 9. Life stories — Arts and culture — Performing arts — Actors and actresses 10. Life stories — Arts and culture — Performing arts — Directors and producers 11. Arts and Entertainment — Movies and television

Offering an intimate journey into the lives of eight legendary actresses whose stories help chart the course of the enigmatic director's career, this mesmerizing account takes a modern look at both the enduring art created by a man obsessed—and the private toll that fixation took on the women in his orbit.

"The author of Capote's Women digs into Hitchcock territory…Leamer excels at dissecting Hitchcock's filmic genius and odd proclivities." —*Kirkus*

Lebo, Harlan

★ *Citizen Kane: A Filmmaker's Journey.* Harlan Lebo. Thomas Dunne Books 2016. 368 p.

ISBN 9781250077530

Grades: Adult   791.43

1. Welles, Orson, 1915-1985 2. Film producers and directors 3. Biographies 4. Life stories — Arts and culture — Performing arts — Directors and producers 5. Arts and Entertainment — Movies and Television

LC 2015045237

In commemoration of the film's 75th anniversary, describes how newcomer Orson Welles won an unprecedented contract that gave him total creative control over his masterpiece, the dispute over who wrote the script and the plot by William Randolph Hearst to destroy the project.

"Lebo's book is highly readable; it's dense, lucid, and page-turning. Fans of Welles and classic Hollywood will be delighted by this comprehensive, intelligent work." —*Publishers Weekly*

Lenburg, Jeff

The Encyclopedia of Animated Cartoons. Jeff Lenburg; foreword by Chris Bailey. Facts on File/Checkmark Books 2009. xiv, 738 p, 32 p. of plates : Illustration; Color

ISBN 9780816065998

Grades: Adult   791.43

1. Animated films 2. Film history and criticism 3. Encyclopedias 4. Reference books 5. Arts and Entertainment — Comics, Cartoons, and Animation

LC 2007025676

Showcases silent cartoons, theatrical sound cartoon series, full-length animated features, animated television specials, and television cartoon series dating from 1911 to the present.

Includes bibliographical references (p. 697) filmographies, and index.

Lumet, Sidney

Making Movies. Sidney Lumet. Vintage Books 1996. x, 220 p.

ISBN 9780679756606

Grades: Adult   791.43

1. Films 2. Filmmaking 3. Film producers and directors 4. Cinematography 5. Filmmakers 6. Arts and Entertainment — Movies and Television

LC BL 99771663

The award-winning director journeys inside the world of film to illuminate the arduous process of creating movies, discussing the art and craft of directing, writers and actors, the camera, art direction, editing, sound tracks, and more.

"This is a book about the job of being a movie director. From the creation of the screeenplay to the final previews, Mr. Lumet explains every step in the process, drawing examples from his own career." —*New York Times Book Review*

Originally published: New York : Knopf, 1995.

ESSENTIAL AND RECOMMENDED TITLES
791.43 Motion pictures

Meslow, Scott
From Hollywood with Love: The Rise and Fall and Rise Again of the Romantic Comedy. Scott Meslow. Dey Street Books 2022. 416 p.
ISBN 9780063026292
Grades: Adult   791.43
1. Films 2. Comedy films 3. Popular culture 4. Filmmaking 5. Actors and actresses 6. Film producers and directors 7. Film history and criticism 8. Social life and customs 9. Hollywood, California 10. United States 11. Arts and Entertainment — Movies and Television 12. Arts and Entertainment — Comedy

An in-depth celebration of the romantic comedy's modern golden era and its role in our culture—tracking the genre from its heyday in the '80s and the '90s, through its unfortunate decline in the 2000s and up to its explosive reemergence in the age of streaming—features exclusive interviews with the directors, writers, and stars of the iconic films that defined the genre.

"Entertainment writer Meslow's first book is a delightful and humorous love letter to the romantic comedy flick.... Fans of the popular but often under-appreciated genre of romantic comedy will appreciate Meslow's book, which offers insight on the development of landmark films and how some of Hollywood's biggest names launched their careers." —*Library Journal*

Muir, John Kenneth
The Encyclopedia of Superheroes on Film and Television. John Kenneth Muir. McFarland & Co. 2008. VIII, 696 p. : Illustration
ISBN 9780786437559
Grades: 11 12 Adult   791.43
1. Television 2. Reference books — Performing arts 3. Reference — Encyclopedias
LC 2008019724

This updated edition of 2004's award-winning encyclopedia traces developments in the popular genre; new shows; latest films; and covers more superheroes. Each entry includes a detailed history, cast and credits, episode and film descriptions, critical commentaries, and data on arch-villains, comic-book origins and super powers, while placing each production into its historical context.

"Entries start with description and background of the hero. Live-action films are presented with reviewer comments and cast and crew. TV series also present reviewer comments and a description of the series. Episode guides include title, writer and director credits, and air dates as well as episode descriptions and guest casts. A good addition to the pop-culture collection." —*Booklist*

Includes bibliographical references (p. 681-684) and index.

Nashawaty, Chris
Caddyshack: The Making of a Hollywood Cinderella Story and the Remaking of American Comedy. Chris Nashawaty. Flatiron Books 2018. 288 p.
ISBN 9781250105950
Grades: Adult   791.43
1. Films 2. Comedy films 3. Media tie-ins 4. Arts and entertainment — Movies and television
LC 2017051033

An anecdotal account of the making of Caddyshack shares profiles of the comedy pioneers behind it, citing the influence of Harvard's National Lampoon and the film, Animal House before stories from the country-club summer jobs of Bill and Brian Doyle Murray inspired the film's wacky production throughout a memorable Florida summer.

"Nashawatys prose is lively, and his exhaustive research is bolstered by interviews with many of the films principle players, including the famously elusive Murray. A wonderful celebration of a passionately loved film." —*Booklist*

Includes bibliographical references.

Parke, Henry C.
The Greatest Westerns Ever Made and the People Who Made Them. Henry C. Parke and True West Magazine. Twodot 2024. 224 p.
ISBN 9781493074396
Grades: Adult   791.43
1. Western films 2. Films 3. Television programs 4. Cowboys 5. Indigenous peoples of North America in popular culture 6. Film producers and directors 7. Filmmakers 8. Actors and actresses 9. Film industry and trade 10. The West (United States) in art 11. Essays 12. Arts and Entertainment — Movies and Television 13. Life stories — Arts and culture — Performing arts

The Greatest Westerns Ever Made and the People Who Made Them provides an eclectic review of the Western film and television genre, from John Ford's classic black and white films to Deadwood and indie darlings. Screenwriter Henry C. Parke presents a nuanced look at Hollywood's dramatization of historic events, the common themes and archetypes of Western movies, and the characters we love (and sometimes love to hate). This book also features essays and interviews with influential Western filmmakers, character actors, the women of Western films, and the Native American perspective on Western films.

"The book's sections are devoted to (among other topics) classic western films and TV shows, actors, filmmakers, writers, the Native American perspective, the role of women in front of and behind the camera, and a profile of legendary stuntman Yakima Canutt." —*Booklist*

Robinson, Joanna
★ *MCU: The Reign of Marvel Studios.* Joanna Robinson, Dave Gonzales, Gavin Edwards. W W Norton & Co. Inc 2023. 512 p.
ISBN 9781631497513
Grades: Adult   791.43
1. Superheroes 2. Filmmaking 3. Popular culture 4. Success in business 5. Arts and Entertainment — Movies and television 6. Society and culture — Pop culture

Drawing on more than 100 interviews with actors, producers, directors and writers, this first book to tell the Marvel Studios story in full charts the stunning rise—and suddenly uncertain reign—of the Marvel Cinematic Universe—a studio forged by near-constant conflict despite its outward success.

"Marvel fans and film aficionados alike will appreciate this highly recommended, smashing insider look at one of entertainment's greatest success stories." —*Library Journal*

Rosenbaum, Jonathan
★ *Essential Cinema: On the Necessity of Film Canons.* Jonathan Rosenbaum. Johns Hopkins University Press 2004. 445 p.
ISBN 9780801878404
Grades: Adult   791.43
1. Films 2. Film history and criticism 3. Arts and Entertainment — Movies and Television

Although informed by Harold Bloom's The Western Canon, Rosenbaum (film critic for the Chicago Reader) differs from Bloom in a number of ways in his proposal for a canon of film. His canon is not exclusively Western, goes beyond purely aesthetic considerations, is a process of selection rather than reportage, and sees cultural criticism as valid. Individual films and directors are explored in 60 chapters that present the arguments for and against canonization, collectively illustrating Rosenbaum's idea of canonization.

"Every essay demonstrates Rosenbaum's fervent dedication to the cinema and, more important, that he has the knowledge and insight to support his impassioned opinions." —*Booklist*

Rosenzweig, Laura B.
Hollywood's Spies: The Undercover Surveillance of Nazis in Los Angeles. Laura B. Rosenzweig. New York University Press 2017. 320 p.
ISBN 9781479855179
Grades: Adult   791.43
1. Anti-Nazi movement 2. Film industry and trade 3. Jewish Americans 4. Undercover operations 5. Political participation 6. Political activists 7. United States history 8. Los Angeles, California 9. California 10. 1930s 11. 20th century 12. History writing — Wars and conflicts — Homefront — World War II 13. History writing — Jewish history

Tells the remarkable story of the Jewish moguls in Hollywood who established the first anti-Nazi Jewish resistance organization in the country in the 1930s. In April 1939, Warner Brothers studios released the first Hollywood film to confront the Nazi threat in the United States. Confessions of a Nazi Spy, starring Edward G. Robinson, told the story of German agents in New York City working to overthrow the U.S. government. The film alerted Americans to the dangers of Nazism at home and encouraged them to defend against it. Confessions of a Nazi Spy may have been the first cinematic shot fired by Hollywood against Nazis in America, but it by no means marked the political awakening of the film industry's Jewish executives to the problem. Hollywood's Spies tells the remarkable story of the Jewish moguls in Hollywood who paid private investigators to infiltrate Nazi groups operating in Los Angeles, establishing the first anti-Nazi Jewish resistance organization in the country—the Los Angeles Jewish Community Committee (LAJCC). Drawing on more than 15,000 pages of archival documents, Laura B. Rosenzweig offers a compelling narrative illuminating the role that Jewish Americans played in combating insurgent Nazism in the United States in the 1930s. Forced undercover by the anti-Semitic climate of the decade, the LAJCC partnered with organizations whose Americanism was unimpeachable, such as the American Legion, to channel information regarding seditious Nazi plots to Congress, the Justice Department, the FBI and the Los Angeles Police Department. Hollywood's Spies corrects the decades-long belief that American Jews lacked the political organization and leadership to assert their political interests during this period in our history and reveals that the LAJCC was one of many covert 'fact finding' operations funded by Jewish Americans designed to root out Nazism in the United States.

"Independent scholar Rosenzweig carefully examines the little-known surveillance of Nazis in Depression era Los Angeles." —*Choice*

Ryan, Maureen

Burn It Down: Power, Complicity, and a Call for Change in Hollywood. Maureen Ryan. Mariner Books 2023. 320 p.

ISBN 9780063269279

Grades: Adult   791.43

1. Prejudice 2. Harassment 3. Entertainment industry and trade 4. Scandals 5. Social change 6. Grassroots movement 7. Power 8. Responsibility 9. Social advocacy 10. Hollywood, California 11. Arts and Entertainment — Movies and Television 12. Society and culture — Pop culture

An expose of patterns of harassment and bias in Hollywood looks at the grassroots reforms under way and the labor and activist revolutions that recent scandals have ignited.

"Vanity Fair contributing editor Ryan exposes the ugly truths about the entertainment business and the harmful behaviors that have been accepted and normalized in Hollywood for more than a century." —*Library Journal*

Santopietro, Tom

The **Sound** *of Music Story: How One Young Nun, One Handsome Austrian Captain, and Seven Singing Von Trapp Children Inspired the Most Beloved Film of All Time*. Tom Santopietro. St. Martin's Press 2015. 288 p.

ISBN 9781250064462

Grades: Adult   791.43

1. Andrews, Julie 2. Plummer, Christopher. 1929-2021 3. Musical films 4. Singers 5. Musicals 6. Blended families 7. Immigrants 8. Folk music 9. 1960s 10. Arts and Entertainment — Movies and Television 11. Arts and Entertainment — Music — Folk

LC 2014033795

Published to coincide with the film's 50th anniversary, an ultimate fan book shares behind-the-scenes facts about The Sound of Music's filming in Austria and Hollywood and incorporates new interviews with production insiders, including Johannes von Trapp.

"A fun-to-read book, perfect for musical-lovers, aspiring moviemakers, and film buffs." —*Booklist*

Schechter, Harold

★ *Ripped from the Headlines!: The Shocking True Stories Behind the Movies Most Memorable Crimes*. Harold Schechter. Little a 2020. 374 p.

ISBN 9781542041805

Grades: Adult   791.43

1. Films 2. Cult Films 3. Crime 4. Film producers and directors 5. Screenwriters 6. Popular culture 7. Murderers 8. Psychopaths 9. Horror films 10. Film history and criticism 11. Essays 12. Arts and Entertainment — Movies and Television 13. True Crime — General 14. True Crime — Historical Crime

LC Bl2020016941

In this collection of revelatory essays, true-crime historian Harold Schechter takes a fascinating trip down the crossroads of fact and fiction to reveal the sensational real-life stories that are more shocking, taboo, and fantastic than even the most imaginative screenwriter can dream up.

"This fascinating look at the intersection of true crime and pop culture is a must." —*Library Journal*

Includes bibliographical references and index.

Schulman, Michael

★ *Oscar* Wars: A History of Hollywood in Gold, Sweat, and Tears. Michael Schulman. HarperCollins 2023. 400 p.

ISBN 9780062859013

Grades: Adult   791.43

1. Academy Awards (Films) 2. Films 3. Film industry and trade 4. Entertainment industry and trade 5. Celebrities 6. Culture 7. Hollywood, California 8. History writing — General 9. Arts and Entertainment — Movies and television 10. Life stories — Arts and culture — Performing arts

Chronicling the remarkable, sprawling history of the Academy Awards and the personal dramas that have played out on the stage and off camera, this entertaining exploration of the Oscars features a star-studded cast of some of the most powerful Hollywood players of today and yesterday.

"This Oscars history mixes all the expected glitz and glamour with enough industry intrigue to power an award-winning drama." —*Kirkus*

Schwartzel, Erich

Red Carpet: Hollywood, China, and the Global Battle for Cultural Supremacy. Erich Schwartzel. Penguin Press 2022. 400 p.

ISBN 9781984878991

Grades: Adult   791.43

1. Film 2. Film industry and trade 3. Finance 4. International relations 5. Asia 6. United States 7. China 8. Arts and Entertainment — Movies and television 9. History writing — Arts and culture 10. Business and economics — Industries — Entertainment and media

LC 2021027952

An eye-opening and deeply reported narrative that details the surprising role of the movie business in the high-stakes contest between the U.S. and China.

"Schwartzel makes an eye-opening debut with this accomplished account of how soft power helped China become one of the most influential players on the global stage.... It's a fascinating take on the crossroads of film and global politics." —*Publishers Weekly*

Includes bibliographical references and index.

Seal, Mark

★ *Leave* the Gun, Take the Cannoli: The Epic Story of the Making of the Godfather. Mark Seal. Gallery Books 2021. 352 p.

ISBN 9781982158590

Grades: Adult   791.43

1. Coppola, Francis Ford, 1939- 2. Puzo, Mario, 1920-1999 3. Creativity 4. Filmmaking 5. Film industry and trade 6. Film producers and directors 7. Interviews 8. Arts and Entertainment — Movies and Television

LC 2021023281

The incredible true story of the making of the Godfather-one of America's most popular cinematic masterpieces-featuring interviews with the director, producer, cast, and crew, just in time for the film's fiftieth anniversary.

"Seal, the author of the splendid the Man in the Rockefeller Suit (2011), makes us an offer we can't refuse with this detailed, fascinating, and frequently surprising look at the origins and filming of the Godfather.... For fans of books about moviemaking, this is a definite must-read." —*Booklist*

Includes bibliographical references.

Sestero, Greg

The **Disaster** *Artist: My Life Inside The Room, the Greatest Bad Movie Ever Made*. Greg Sestero, Tom Bissell. Simon & Schuster 2013. 288 p.

ISBN 9781451661194

Grades: Adult   791.43

1. Sestero, Greg, 1978- 2. Wiseau, Tommy 3. Filmmakers 4. Filmmaking 5. Films 6. Fame 7. Misfits (People) 8. Male friendship 9. Actors and actresses

ESSENTIAL AND RECOMMENDED TITLES
791.43 Motion pictures

10. Autobiographies and memoirs 11. Page to screen 12. Life stories — Relationships — Friendship 13. Arts and Entertainment — Movies and Television
LC 2013008798

This side-splittingly funny ode to cinematic hubris tells the story of the mysteriously wealthy misfit and producer, director and star of The Room, an international phenomenon to rival The Rocky Horror Picture Show.

"An improbably resonant tale of warped creativity and friendship."—*Kirkus*

Title adapted into a film in 2017; Includes bibliographical references and index.

Shelton, Ron
The Church of Baseball: The Making of Bull Durham : Home Runs, Bad Calls, Crazy Fights, Big Swings, and a Hit. Ron Shelton. Alfred A. Knopf 2022. 240 p.

ISBN 9780593319772

Grades: Adult   791.43

1. Shelton, Ron, 1945- 2. Film producers and directors 3. Screenwriters 4. Former baseball players 5. Sports films 6. Actors and actresses 7. Baseball 8. Minor league baseball 9. Filmmaking 10. Film history and criticism 11. Arts and Entertainment — Movies and Television 12. Life stories — Arts and culture — Performing arts — Directors and producers 13. Sports and Competition — Baseball 14. Debut title
LC 2021049945

Bull Durham, the breakthrough 1988 film about a minor league baseball team, is widely revered as the best sports movie of all time. But back in 1987, Ron Shelton was a first-time director and no one was willing to finance a movie about baseball—especially a story set in the minors. The jury was still out on Kevin Costner's leading-man potential, while Susan Sarandon was already seen as a has-been. There were doubts. But something miraculous happened, and The Church of Baseball attempts to capture why. Shelton brings to life the making of this beloved American movie.

"Shelton combines two biographies in this jaunty memoir, one detailing the making of the movie Bull Durham, which he wrote and directed, and the other tracking his own coming-of-age as a ballplayer and a filmmaker….A marvelous book about a classic movie."—*Booklist*

This is a Borzoi book published by Alfred A. Knopf.

Shepard, Jim
The Tunnel at the End of the Light: Essays on Movies and Politics. Jim Shepard. Tin House Books 2017. xxii, 261 p.

ISBN 9781941040720

Grades: Adult   791.43

1. Films 2. Philosophy 3. Essays 4. Arts and Entertainment — Movies and Television
LC 2017010540

Argues that the movies shape some of America's most destructive political assumptions and culturally critiques certain films, including "Chinatown," "The Third Man," and "Badlands."

Silver, Alain
★ *From the Moment They Met It Was Murder: Double Indemnity and the Rise of Film Noir*. Alain Silver and James Ursini. Running Press 2024. 336 p.

ISBN 9780762484935

Grades: Adult   791.43

1. Films 2. Film noir 3. Influence (Psychology) 4. Film producers and directors 5. Screenwriters 6. Actors and actresses 7. Film history and criticism 8. Arts and Entertainment — Movies and Television 9. Life stories — Arts and culture — Performing arts

A behind-the-scenes story of the quintessential film noir and cult classic, Billy Wilder's Double Indemnity—its true crime origins and crucial impact on film history—is told for the first time in this riveting narrative published for the film's 80th anniversary. Double Indemnity's impact on filmmakers and audiences is still felt eight decades after its release.

"Film lovers will eat up this book about Double Indemnity's true-crime origins."—*Library Journal*

Includes bibliographical references and index.

Singer, Matt
Opposable Thumbs: How Siskel & Ebert Changed Movies Forever. Matt Singer. Putnam 2023. 320 p.

ISBN 9780593540152

Grades: Adult   791.43

1. Siskel, Gene 2. Ebert, Roger 3. Film critics 4. Journalists 5. Television programs 6. Influence (Psychology) 7. Films 8. Debates and debating 9. Friendship 10. North American people 11. American people 12. Collective biographies 13. Life stories — Arts and culture — Writing — Journalists 14. Arts and Entertainment — Movies and Television

An award-winning editor and film critic raises the curtain on the often-antagonistic partnership, which later transformed into genuine friendship, between Robert Ebert and Gene Siskel, whose signature "Two thumbs up!" would become the most trusted critical brand in Hollywood—one that still lives on today.

"Anecdotes illuminate the pair's at times contentious behind-the-scenes dynamic…, and interviews with colleagues and loved ones offer insight into the critics' psychologies."—*Publishers Weekly*

Stratton, W. K.
The Wild Bunch: Sam Peckinpah, a Revolution in Hollywood, and the Making of a Legendary Film. W.K. Stratton. Bloomsbury Publishing Inc. 2019. 352 pages

ISBN 9781632862129

Grades: Adult   791.43

1. Peckinpah, Sam, 1925-1984 2. Western films 3. Film industry and trade 4. Film producers and directors 5. Filmmaking 6. Film history and criticism 7. Arts and Entertainment — Movies and Television
LC 2018024992

Chronicles the making of "The Wild Bunch," documenting the contributions of Mexican and Mexican-American actors and crew members and discussing how the film's dark, violent take on Western movies reflected the turbulent times in which it was created.

"Stratton's thorough research yields a fascinating perspective on how Peckinpah created a western of unparalleled realism and intensity."—*Publishers Weekly*

Tarantino, Quentin
Cinema Speculation. Quentin Tarantino. Harper 2022. 304 p.

ISBN 9780063112582

Grades: Adult   791.43

1. Tarantino, Quentin 2. Films 3. Fans (People) 4. Film industry and trade 5. Popular culture 6. Film history and criticism 7. 1970s 8. Arts and Entertainment — Movies and Television 9. Life stories — Arts and culture — Performing arts — Directors and producers

In addition to being among the most celebrated of contemporary filmmakers, Quentin Tarantino is possibly the most joyously infectious movie lover alive. For years he has touted in interviews his eventual turn to writing books about films. Now, with Cinema Speculation, the time has come, and the results are everything his passionate fans—and all movie lovers—could have hoped for. Organized around key American films from the 1970s, all of which he first saw as a young moviegoer at the time, this book is as intellectually rigorous and insightful as it is rollicking and entertaining.

"In his first nonfiction book, following his first novel, Once Upon a Time in Hollywood (2021), Tarantino brings the heat and exuberance of his movie expertise, storytelling artistry, and sharp humor to a dynamic mix of eyebrow-raising personal stories, zesty film history, and kickass film criticism."—*Booklist*

Thomson, David
The Fatal Alliance: A Century of War on Film. David Thomson. Harper 2023. xii, 435 p.

ISBN 9780063041417

Grades: Adult   791.43

1. War films 2. War in mass media 3. War and civilization 4. Violence in films 5. War propaganda 6. Art and war 7. Popular culture 8. Film industry and trade 9. Film history and criticism 10. Arts and Entertainment — Movies and Television 11. History writing — Wars and conflicts 12. History writing — Arts and culture

PUBLIC LIBRARY CORE COLLECTION: NONFICTION
Twentieth Edition

In The Fatal Alliance the acclaimed film critic David Thomson offers us one of his most provocative books yet—a rich, arresting, and troubling study of that most beloved genre: the war movie. Movies had only begun to exist by the beginning of World War I, yet in less than a century, had transformed civilian experience of war—and history itself—for millions around the globe.

"In this interesting and thought-provoking new book, Thomson takes on the war-movie genre...An insightful and important book." —*Booklist*

Includes bibliographical references and index.

★ *How to Watch a Movie.* David Thomson. Alfred A. Knopf 2015. 342 p.

ISBN 9781101875391

Grades: Adult   791.43

1. Film evaluation 2. Films 3. Film industry and trade 4. Popular culture 5. Cinematography 6. Arts and entertainment — Movies and television

LC 2014046757

A critic shares professional insights into how to derive more from a film experience, analyzing a range of iconic films to reveal metaphorical artistry techniques in the acting, filming, dialogue, and music.

"An enjoyably deep dive into the interaction between cinema and psyche." —*Kirkus*

Tietjen, Jill S

Hollywood, Her Story: An Illustrated History of Women and the Movies. Jill Tietjen and Barbara Bridges. Lyons Press 2019. 400 p.

ISBN 9781493037056

Grades: Adult   791.43

1. Women in films 2. Filmmaking 3. Women in the film industry and trade 4. Film industry and trade 5. Social history 6. Films 7. Actors and actresses 8. Arts and Entertainment — Movies and Television 9. Society and culture — Gender — Women 10. History writing — Women's history 11. Adult books for young adults

LC 2018050076

Building on the legacy of the author's previous work: HER STORY: A Timeline of the Women Who Changed America, this book will be an inclusive volume across all facets of the film industry from acting to directing, from producing to editing, from casting to wardrobe, from stunts to the technical advances in the industry. Women's contributions will be acknowledged from the late 1890s through 2017. Seeing them all in one book shows the impressive impact women have had on the movies.

Includes bibliographical references and index.

Turan, Kenneth

Not to Be Missed: 54 Favorites from a Lifetime of Film. Kenneth Turan. PublicAffairs 2014. xix, 345 p.

ISBN 9781586483968

Grades: Adult   791.43

1. Films 2. Film industry and trade 3. Film reviews 4. Actors and actresses 5. Arts and Entertainment — Movies and Television

LC 2014007773

A film critic for the Los Angeles Times presents a list of his favorite films of all-time, from All About Eve to Spirited Away, and offers anecdotes on the cultural impact, controversies, and history surrounding each.

"Turan's illuminating reflections do what the best essays on film always do: Send us to watch the movie, whether for the first time or the 20th." —*Publishers Weekly*

Includes index.

Vick, Tom

Asian Cinema: A Field Guide. Tom Vick. Collins 2007. xiv, 274 p. : Illustration

ISBN 9780061145858

Grades: Adult   791.43

1. Film industry and trade 2. Asia 3. Arts and Entertainment — Movies and Television

LC 2007026648

Looks at the past, present, and future of Asian film, offering historical background for each of four regions, context for the films, and portraits of selected films.

Includes bibliographical references (p. 258-264) and index.

Wasson, Sam

The Big Goodbye: Chinatown and the Last Years of Hollywood. Sam Wasson. Flatiron Books 2020. 336 pages

ISBN 9781250301826

Grades: Adult   791.43

1. Nicholson, Jack, 1937- 2. Polanski, Roman 3. Tate, Sharon, 1943-1969 4. Dunaway, Faye, 1941- 5. Evans, Robert, 1930-2019 6. Towne, Robert 7. Films 8. Film industry and trade 9. Film producers and directors 10. Actors and actresses 11. Screenplay writing 12. Characters and characteristics in films 13. Film history and criticism 14. Arts and Entertainment — Movies and Television 15. Life stories — Arts and culture — Performing arts — Actors and actresses 16. Life stories — Arts and culture — Performing arts — Directors and producers

LC 2019045207

A revealing account of the making of the classic film Chinatown describes Jack Nicholson at the height of his career, his doomed love affair with Anjelica Huston and Roman Polanski, still reeling from the savage death of his wife.

"Inimitable Wasson (Fifth Avenue, 5 A.M.) examines the development of the iconic film Chinatown (1974), beginning with the months leading up to the murder of director Roman Polanski's wife, Sharon Tate, in 1969 ... on par with Wasson's exceptional Fosse, this portrait of a neonoir classic will weave a spell over cinephiles." —*Library Journal*

Includes bibliographical references and index.

Fifth Avenue, 5 A.M.: Breakfast at Tiffany's and the Making of the Modern American Woman. Sam Wasson. Harpercollins 2010. 304 p.

ISBN 9780061774157

Grades: Adult   791.43

1. Hepburn, Audrey, 1929-1993 2. Women 3. Women's role 4. Transformations, Personal 5. United States 6. 20th century 7. History writing — Women's history 8. Society and culture — Gender — Women 9. Nonfiction that reads like fiction

LC 2009052439

Depicts the making of the iconic film "Breakfast at Tiffany's" in the late 1950s, drawing on interviews with those involved in the film's production, including the actors, producer Richard Shepherd, and Truman Capote's biographer.

"The author presents an irresistibly gossipy account of the production of Breakfast at Tiffany's (1961), charting the transformation of actress Audrey Hepburn into an icon of emerging sexual liberation: the good/bad girl, the lovable kook, independent and sexually experienced but sufficiently charming to bring home to mother. Rich in incident and set among the glitterati of America's most glamorous era, the book reads like a novel." —*Kirkus*

Weismann, Brad

Lost in the Dark: A World History of Horror Film. Brad Weismann. University Press of Massachussetts 2021. 264 p.

ISBN 9781496833211

Grades: Adult   791.43

1. Films 2. Horror films 3. Monster films 4. Film industry and trade 5. Film history and criticism 6. Arts and Entertainment — Movies and Television

A comprehensive and fun overview of moviegoers' favorite genre.

"Joining many recent books recounting the long and rich history of the horror film, this volume aims for inclusiveness and accessibility." —*Choice*

Williams, Marlena

Night Mother: A Personal and Cultural History of the Exorcist. Marlena Williams. Mad Creek Books 2023. 240 p.

ISBN 9780814258767

Grades: Adult   791.43

1. Film history and criticism 2. Family relationships 3. Death of mothers 4. Mothers and daughters 5. Feminism 6. Horror films 7. American people

ESSENTIAL AND RECOMMENDED TITLES
791.4302 Stock footage — Motion pictures

8. North American people 9. Grief 10. Guilt 11. Essays 12. Autobiographies and memoirs 13. Society and culture — Gender — Women 14. Life stories — Relationships — Family

LC 2023007266

Blends personal narrative with cultural criticism to explore the ways The Exorcist has influenced the author's life and American culture, tracing stories of the film's stars and analyzing infamous scenes while excavating the deeper stories the film tells about faith, family, illness, anger, guilt, desire, and death.—.

"An incredible work of film analysis, examining cultural context and interspersing personal history, that makes a great read for movie, horror, and pop-culture fans." —*Library Journal*

Includes bibliographical references.

Yang, Jeff
The Golden Screen: The Movies That Made Asian America. Jeff Yang. Black Dog & Leventhal 2023. IX, 294 p.
ISBN 9780762482221
Grades: Adult   791.43
1. Asian Americans 2. Films 3. Actors and actresses 4. Filmmakers 5. Popular culture 6. Film industry and trade 7. Film history and criticism 8. Society and culture — Ethnic studies 9. Arts and Entertainment — Movies and Television 10. Life stories — Arts and culture — Performing arts

In 2018, the critical and financial success of Crazy Rich Asians ignited new fires in Hollywood to create and back Asian-centric stories. Since then, the number of movies featuring Asian Americans, either in front or behind the camera, has boomed and ushered in a new era of filmmaking. But many films, like The Joy Luck Club in 1993, paved the way for Asian American-led films before Crazy Rich Asians and to today. The Golden Screen is an in-depth look at those films, and the factors that played into their success.

"A comprehensive, incisive, and gorgeous celebration of a century's worth of Asian actors, characters, and contributors who have helped shaped American perspectives and Asian American representation." —*Library Journal*

Includes index.

Yomota, Inuhiko
What Is Japanese Cinema?: A History. Yomota Inuhiko; translated by Philip Kaffen. Columbia University Press 2019. 248 p.
ISBN 9780231191630
Grades: Adult   791.43
1. Film 2. Film history and criticism 3. Japanese history 4. Japan 5. Translations — Japanese to English 6. Arts and Entertainment — Movies and Television

In this book, Yomota Inuhiko provides a concise history of Japanese film that shows how cinema tells the story of Japan's modern age. Discussing popular works alongside auteurist masterpieces, Inuhiko considers films in light of both Japanese cultural particularities and cinema as a worldwide art form.

Zucker, David
Surely You Can't Be Serious: The True Story of Airplane! David Zucker, Jim Abrahams, Jerry Zucker; interviews by Will Harris. St. Martin's Press 2023. 352 p.
ISBN 9781250289315
Grades: Adult   791.43
1. Zucker, David, 1947- 2. Abrahams, Jim, 1944- 3. Zucker, Jerry 4. Comedy films 5. Film producers and directors 6. Screenwriters 7. Comedy writing 8. Actors and actresses 9. Oral histories 10. Arts and Entertainment — Movies and Television 11. Arts and Entertainment — Comedy 12. Life stories — Arts and culture — Performing arts

Airplane! premiered on July 2nd, 1980. With a budget of $3.5 million it went on to make nearly $200 million in sales and has influenced a multitude of comedians on both sides of the camera. Surely You Can't Be Serious is the first-ever oral history of the making of Airplane! by the creators, and of the beginnings of the ZAZ trio (David Zucker, Jim Abrahams, and Jerry Zucker)—charting the rise of their comedy troupe Kentucky Fried Theater in Madison, Wisconsin all the way to premiere night.

"This is a wonderful book, full of laughs, surprises, high drama, low comedy, and that delightful feeling of excitement when the underdog scores big. For fans of the movie, a must-read. Ditto for fans of making-of books." —*Booklist*

791.4302 Stock footage — Motion pictures

Coppola, Francis Ford
Live Cinema and Its Techniques. Francis Ford Coppola. Liveright Publishing 2017. xiii, 210 pages : Illustration
ISBN 9781631493669
Grades: Adult   791.4302
1. Filmmaking 2. Films 3. Filmmakers 4. Mass media 5. Film industry and trade 6. Arts and Entertainment — Movies and Television

One of the masters of 20th-century cinema presents an indispensable and entertaining guide to a visionary new form of moviemaking that can be appreciated by the avid film buff and general movie lover alike.

"As in his films, Coppola knows how to tell a compelling story. Live cinema, in its new incarnation, and everyone it attracts, will benefit from his insights." —*Booklist*

Includes index.

D'Alessandro, Emilio
Stanley Kubrick and Me: Thirty Years at His Side. Emilio D'Alessandro with Filippo Ulivieri; translated by Simon Marsh. Arcade Publishing 2016. 352 p.
ISBN 9781628726695
Grades: Adult   791.4302
1. Kubrick, Stanley, 1928-1999 2. D'Alessandro, Emilio 3. Film producers and directors 4. Filmmaking 5. Filmmakers 6. Film industry and trade 7. Biographies 8. Life stories — Arts and culture — Performing arts — Directors and producers

LC 2015050645

This intimate portrait by his former personal assistant and confidante reveals the man behind the legendary filmmaker—for the first time.

"Hard-core Kubrick devotees won't learn much, but this easygoing and likable memoir humanizes an eccentric titan of cinema." —*Library Journal*

Harris, Mark
★ *Five Came Back: A Story of Hollywood and the Second World War*. Mark Harris. The Penguin Press 2014. 480 p.
ISBN 9781594204302
Grades: Adult   791.4302
1. Ford, John, 1894-1973 2. Wyler, William, 1902-1981 3. Huston, John, 1906-1987 4. Capra, Frank, 1897-1991 5. Stevens, George, 1904-1975 6. World War II 7. Films 8. Film industry and trade 9. World War II films 10. Films, American 11. War films 12. 1940s 13. Arts and Entertainment — Movies and Television 14. History writing — Wars and conflicts — World War II

LC 2013039983

Library Journal Best Books 2014.

Traces the World War II experiences of five legendary directors including John Ford, William Wyler, John Huston, Frank Capra and George Stevens to assess the transformative impact of the war and period beliefs on Hollywood.

"Narrative nonfiction that is as gloriously readable as it is unfailingly informative." —*Booklist*

Merritt, Tyler
I Take My Coffee Black: Reflections on Tupac, Musical Theater, Faith, and Being Black in America. Tyler Merritt with David Tieche; with a foreword by Jimmy Kimmel. Worthy 2021. 256 p.
ISBN 9781546029410
Grades: Adult   791.4302
1. Musicals 2. Faith (Christianity) 3. Racism 4. African American men 5. Growing up 6. Identity 7. Masculinity 8. Actors and actresses 9. African Americans 10. Race relations 11. United States 12. Autobiographies and memoirs 13. Life stories — Arts and culture — Performing arts — Actors and actresses 14. Life stories — Identity — Race and Ethnicity 15. Arts and Entertainment — Theater

LC 2021019943

By turns witty, insightful, touching, and laugh-out-loud funny, I Take My Coffee Black paints a portrait of Black manhood in America and enlightens, illuminates, and entertains—ultimately building the kind of empathy that might just be the antidote against the racial injustice in our society.

"Actor and comedian Merritt combines comedy, social commentary, autobiography, and religious musings to stunning effect in this kaleidoscopic take on race and religion in America.... Readers will be awed by Merritt's brutal honesty and inspiring grassroots approach to countering racial injustice and deep-seated prejudice." —*Publishers Weekly*

Includes bibliographical references.

Movsesian, Sona
The World's Worst Assistant. Sona Movsesian. Plume 2022. 288 p.
ISBN 9780593185513
Grades: Adult   791.4302
1. Movsesian, Sona 2. O'Brien, Conan 3. Television industry and trade 4. Personal assistants 5. Autobiographies and memoirs 6. Humor Writing — Social humor
LC 2022017150

Part satire based on her and Conan O'Brien's beloved alter egos, part memoir that evidences their sincere mutual trust and respect built over 12 years, this hilarious how-to-guide shows readers how to get away with being a terrible, yet unfireable employee.

Movsesian and her boss share a droll rapport and their anecdotes are a gas to read, a testament to the success of the 'world's worst assistant.' —*Booklist*

Shone, Tom
The Nolan Variations: The Movies, Mysteries, and Marvels Od Christopher Nolan. Tom Shone. Alfred A. Knopf 2020. 368 p.
ISBN 9780525655329
Grades: Adult   791.4302
1. Nolan, Christopher, 1970- 2. Film producers and directors 3. Filmmaking 4. Filmmakers 5. Screenwriters 6. Creation (literary, artistic, etc.) 7. Biographies 8. Life stories — Arts and culture — Performing arts — Directors and producers 9. Arts and Entertainment — Movies and Television 10. Society and culture — Pop culture

The Nolan Variations is a rare, intimate portrait of Christopher Nolan, one of the most profound and commercially successful directors at work today. In this in-depth exploration of his work—including The Dark Knight (2008), Inception (2010) and Dunkirk (2017)—Nolan discusses the evolution of his pictures; his thoughts on time, identity, perception, chaos, and daydreams. The book has been done with the full cooperation of Nolan, who has opened himself up more fully than ever before in his talks with Tom Shone.

"This is an erudite book, written primarily for serious film fans, but Shone's prose is easygoing and mostly nontechnical, and the text has plenty to say to readers of all levels of interest. A first-class book about an intriguing filmmaker." —*Booklist*

Stevens, Dana
Camera Man: Buster Keaton, the Dawn of Cinema, and the Invention of the Twentieth Century. Dana Stevens. Atria Books 2022. 288 p.
ISBN 9781501134197
Grades: Adult   791.4302
1. Keaton, Buster, 1895-1966 2. Film producers and directors 3. Vaudeville 4. Comedians 5. Film industry and trade 6. Actors and actresses 7. Films 8. Silent films 9. United States 10. 20th century 11. Biographies 12. Arts and Entertainment — Movies and Television 13. Life stories — Arts and culture — Performing arts — Actors and actresses

The chief film critic for Slate magazine presents a biography of the comedy legend and acclaimed filmmaker, from his vaudeville beginnings to his rise to Hollywood stardom as an actor and director during the silent film era.

"Slate film critic Stevens debuts with a masterful mix of cultural history, biography, and film criticism to consider of the work and legacy of silent film star Buster Keaton (1895-1966).... Combining the same ingredients that made Keaton's movies indelible—an elegant narrative, humor, and pathos—Stevens's account isn't one to miss." —*Publishers Weekly*

Stevens, George, Jr
Conversations at the American Film Institute with the Great Moviemakers: The Next Generation. [edited and with an introduction by] George Stevens, Jr. Alfred A. Knopf 2012. xxiii, 737 p. : Illustration
ISBN 9780307273475
Grades: Adult   791.4302
1. Film producers and directors 2. Filmmaking 3. Interviews 4. Arts and Entertainment — Movies and Television
LC 2011043741

A companion to the Emmy and Peabody Award-winning author's well-received collection of American Film Institute seminars with film pioneers draws on AFI conversations with moviemakers from the 1950s to today, including Steven Spielberg, Nora Ephron and George Lucas.

Collects American Film Institute conversations with filmmakers from the 1950s to today, including Steven Spielberg, Nora Ephron, and George Lucas.

Includes bibliographical references (p. 705) and index; Includes filmographies.

Thomson, David
The New Biographical Dictionary of Film. David Thomson. Alfred A. Knopf 2014. 1076 p.
ISBN 9780375711848
Grades: Adult   791.4302
1. Films 2. Actors and actresses 3. Life stories — Arts and culture — Performing arts 4. Reference books — Performing arts 5. Reference — Biographical dictionaries
LC 2010016450

Featuring three hundred new additions, an updated edition of the classic film reference provides more than 1,300 entries on leading international actors and actresses, directors, and producers, along with frequently provocative critical essays, profiles, and film analyses.

"This book—with its at times very opinionated perspective—is suitable for most medium-sized and large public libraries, for both reference and circulating collections. Libraries owning older editions will want to replace with this version." —*Booklist*

Waxman, Sharon
Rebels on the Backlot: Six Maverick Directors and How They Conquered the Hollywood Studio System. Sharon Waxman. HarperEntertainment 2005. xxi, 386 p. : Illustration
ISBN 9780060540173
Grades: Adult   791.4302
1. Film producers and directors 2. Film industry and trade 3. Hollywood, California 4. Arts and Entertainment — Movies and Television
LC 2004059269

Draws on more than one hundred interviews and a decade's worth of reportage to chronicle the rise of six influential directors from the 1990s, including Quentin Tarantino, David Fincher, and Spike Jonze, in a portrait of contemporary Hollywood that focuses on the development, shooting, and release of each director's major film.

Includes bibliographical references (p. [343]-373) and index.

791.43079 Motion pictures — Awards

Osborne, Robert
85 Years of the Oscar: The Official History of the Academy Awards. Robert Osborne. Abbeville Press Publishers 2013. 472 p. : Illustration
ISBN 9780789211422
Grades: Adult   791.43079
1. Films 2. Reference books — Performing arts 3. Arts and Entertainment — Movies and Television
LC 2013033021

ESSENTIAL AND RECOMMENDED TITLES
791.43092 Motion pictures — Biography

Reaccounts the last eighty-five years of the Oscars, including over 750 pictures, information on the ceremonies, trends, developments, and events that occured in the film industry and within the academy.
Includes bibliographical references and index.

791.43092 Motion pictures — Biography

Finch, Christopher
The Art of Walt Disney: From Mickey Mouse to the Magic Kingdoms. Christopher Finch. Abrams 2011. 503 p. : Illustration; Color; Map
ISBN 9780810998148
Grades: 7 8 9 10 11 12 Adult   791.43092
1. Disney, Walt, 1901-1966 2. Animators 3. Animation (Cinematography) 4. Film industry and trade 5. Cartoonists 6. Arts and Entertainment — Comics, Cartoons, and Animation 7. Adult books for young adults
LC 2004010016
Traces the career of the beloved cartoonist while exploring the diverse artistic and cinematographic techniques used to make his animated and live action films.
Includes index.

791.430973 Motion pictures — United States

Schickel, Richard
Keepers: The Greatest Films and Personal Favorites of a Moviegoing Lifetime. Richard Schickel. Alfred A. Knopf 2015. 320 p.
ISBN 9780375424595
Grades: Adult   791.430973
1. Film evaluation 2. Films 3. Film industry and trade 4. Popular culture 5. Arts and entertainment — Movies and television
LC 2014034997
A film critic and movie historian who has been watching cinema for 70 years and has seen almost 19,000 films brings viewers on a tour of his favorite movies, highlighting forgotten treasures and explaining what makes a film a hit or a flop.
"Schickel, who posits in his introduction that movies are about both nothing and everything, wholly succeeds in making readers care about every film hes seen." —*Publishers Weekly*

Thomson, David
The Big Screen: The Story of the Movies. David Thomson. Farrar, Straus and Giroux 2012. 528 p.
ISBN 9780374191894
Grades: Adult   791.430973
1. Films 2. Film producers and directors 3. Filmmaking 4. Actors and actresses 5. Arts and Entertainment — Movies and Television 6. History writing — Microhistory
LC 2012009140
Booklist Editors' Choice 2012.
Traces the rise, decline and influence of the film industry on the modern world, assessing its expressions in multiple media, its capacity for imitating and idealizing life and its role in the existences of everyday viewers. By the author of The New Biographical Dictionary of Film.
Includes bibliographical references and index.

Urwand, Ben
The Collaboration: Hollywood's Pact with Hitler. Ben Urwand. The Belknap Press of Harvard University Press 2013. 320 p.
ISBN 9780674724747
Grades: Adult   791.430973
1. Films, American 2. Nazism 3. World War II 4. Antisemitism 5. Greed 6. Film industry and trade 7. Art 8. Films 9. Germany 10. 20th century 11. Arts and Entertainment — Movies and Television 12. History writing — Wars and conflicts — World War II
LC 2013013576

Argues that Hollywood studios collaborated with Hitler during the 1930s by agree to not make movies that disparaged Germany, investing in German newsreels and even financing the production of German armaments.
Includes bibliographical references and index.

791.4372 Single films

Bingen, Steven
Easy Rider: 50 Years Looking for America. Steven Bingen; with Alan Dunn. Lyons Press 2020. xiv, 170 pages : Illustration
ISBN 9781493046430
Grades: Adult   791.4372
1. Arts and Entertainment — Movies and Television 2. History writing — United States
LC Bl2020000254
Includes bibliographical references (pages 149-161) and index.

Rinzler, J. W.
The Making of Aliens. J. W Rinzler. Titan Publishing Group 2020. 256 pages : Illustration
ISBN 9781789093100
Grades: Adult   791.4372
1. Filmmaking 2. Science fiction films 3. Films 4. Media tie-ins 5. Interviews 6. Arts and Entertainment — Movies and Television
A comprehensive and definitive volume telling the complete story of how Aliens was made, featuring new interviews with some of the cast and production crew, and including many rarely seen photos and illustrations from the Fox archives. As one of the most highly regarded movie sequels of all time, Aliens quickly embedded itself in the minds of cinema-goers around the world when it was released in 1986. Driven by the singular vision of director James Cameron and guided by producer Gale Ann Hurd, its relentless action and unforgettable characters helped cement its place as an undisputed classic of 1980s cinema. The Making of Aliens tells the complete story of how Cameron and Hurd, together with their immensely talented cast and crew, brought heroine Ellen Ripley back to the big screen and upped the stakes by introducing a whole army of aliens for her to face. Interviews with the cast and crew, alongside revealing photography and fascinating concept art, illustrate the film's eventful journey from its beginnings as a sequel that nobody wanted to make through to its transformation into one of the highest-grossing blockbusters of the decade.

791.44 Radio

Dunning, John
On the Air: The Encyclopedia of Old-Time Radio. John Dunning. Oxford University Press 1998. xvi, 822 p.
ISBN 9780195076783
Grades: Adult   791.44
1. Radio programs 2. Arts and Entertainment — Radio
LC 96041959
A comprehensive reference of the radio shows of the 1930s, 1940s, and 1950s has entries arranged in alphabetical order and includes each show's history, timeslot, network, advertisers, cast members, and much more.
"Dunning has compiled and organized a massive amount of research data on hundreds of radio shows aired from the 1920s through the 1960s. The entries, listed alphabetically by show title, each contain a treasure trove of information: Broadcast dates, casts and personnel, anecdotes, special analyses, and a detailed overview of each show's background, format, and content." —*Library Journal*
Rev. ed. of: Tune in yesterday. c1976; Includes bibliographical references (p. 747-757) and index.

Schwartz, A. Brad
★ *Broadcast Hysteria: Orson Welles's War of the Worlds and the Art of Fake News.* A. Brad Schwartz. Hill and Wang 2015. 304 p.
ISBN 9780809031610

PUBLIC LIBRARY CORE COLLECTION: NONFICTION
Twentieth Edition

Grades: Adult   791.44
1. Welles, Orson, 1915-1985 2. Radio broadcasting 3. Deception 4. Hoaxes 5. Mass media 6. 1930s 7. 20th century 8. Arts and Entertainment — Radio 9. History writing — Great Depression — United States 10. Society and culture — Media and technology

LC 2014040510

Retells the story of the famed radio play and its impact, examining how the broadcast became a major scandal and caused a debate over the power of radio broadcasting and the country's vulnerability in times of crisis.

"An entertaining assessment of a watershed moment in American life and its lasting effect on popular culture." —*Kirkus*

Includes bibliographical references and index.

791.45 Television

Armstrong, Jennifer Keishin
Seinfeldia: How a Show About Nothing Changed Everything. Jennifer Keishin Armstrong. Simon & Schuster 2015. 320 p.

ISBN 9781476756103

Grades: Adult   791.45
1. Seinfeld, Jerry 2. Television programs 3. Popular culture 4. Television 5. Television writing 6. Comedy writing 7. Screenwriters 8. Social life and customs 9. United States 10. 20th century 11. Arts and Entertainment — Movies and Television 12. Society and culture — Pop culture

LC 2015023755

An uproarious behind-the-scenes account of the creation of the hit television series describes how comedians Larry David and Jerry Seinfeld dreamed up the idea for an unconventional sitcom over coffee and how, despite network skepticism and minimal plotlines, achieved mainstream success.

"Armstrong offers a masterly look at one of the greatest shows. The research involved makes this a boon to television scholars, but Seinfeld enthusiasts will also enjoy this funny, highly readable book." —*Library Journal*

Includes bibliographical references and index.

Sex and the City and Us: How Four Single Women Changed the Way We Think, Live, and Love. Jennifer Keishin Armstrong. Simon & Schuster 2018. 288 p.

ISBN 9781501164828

Grades: Adult   791.45
1. Television programs 2. Popular culture 3. Television writing 4. Television 5. Comedy writing 6. Screenwriters 7. Social life and customs 8. United States 9. 20th century 10. Arts and Entertainment — Movies and Television 11. Society and culture — Pop culture

LC 2018000333

A retrospective of the award-winning series features interviews from the cast and writers that further explore how the show changes the way women everywhere see themselves.

Includes bibliographical references and index.

When Women Invented Television: The Untold Story of the Female Powerhouses Who Pioneered the Way We Watch Today. Jennifer Armstrong. HarperCollins 2021. 368 p.

ISBN 9780062973306

Grades: Adult   791.45
1. Phillips, Irna, 1901-1973 2. Berg, Gertrude, 1899-1966 3. Scott, Hazel 4. White, Betty, 1922-2021 5. Women in television 6. Women's history 7. Television industry and trade 8. Television programs 9. Popular culture 10. Actors and actresses 11. African Americans 12. 20th century 13. Collective biographies 14. History writing — Women's history 15. Life stories — Arts and culture — Performing arts — Actors and actresses 16. Life stories — Arts and culture — Performing arts — Entertainers and celebrities 17. Arts and Entertainment — Movies and Television 18. History writing — United States

Documents the lesser-known story of how four trailblazing women from the radio era, including Irna Phillips, Gertrude Berg, Hazel Scott and Betty White, helped establish the foundation of the modern television industry.

"In this compelling, well-researched work, Armstrong (Seinfeldia) uncovers the role women played in developing television, fighting for airtime as they launched sitcoms, soap operas, variety shows, and more." —*Library Journal*

Biskind, Peter
Pandora's Box: How Guts, Guile, and Greed Upended TV. Peter Biskind. William Morrow 2023. xiv, 383 p.

ISBN 9780062991669

Grades: Adult   791.45
1. Television programs 2. Cable television 3. Streaming technology (Telecommunications) 4. Business competition 5. Mass media executives 6. Television producers and directors 7. Television industry and trade 8. Popular culture 9. Arts and Entertainment — Movies and Television 10. Business and economics — Industries — Entertainment and media

LC 2023030841

Author of Easy Riders, Raging Bulls and Down and Dirty Pictures, cultural critic Peter Biskind turns his eye toward the new golden age of television, sparked by the fall of play-it-safe network TV and the rise of boundary-busting cable followed by streaming, that overturned both—based on exclusive, candid, and colorful interviews with executives, writers, showrunners, directors, and actors.

"Film historian and cultural critic Biskind takes a look at television's 'Second golden age,' which was ushered in by the cable networks (HBO, FX, AMC) and the streaming services (Netflix and its many competitors)…For readers interested in what goes on behind the scenes in the world of television, a must-read." —*Booklist*

Includes index.

Britt, Ryan
Phasers on Stun!: How the Making and Remaking of Star Trek Changed the World. Ryan Britt. Plume 2022. 432 p.

ISBN 9780593185698

Grades: Adult   791.45
1. Star Trek films 2. Popular culture 3. Television programs 4. Society and culture — Pop culture 5. Arts and Entertainment — Movies and Television

Including extensive interviews with current Star Trek showrunner Michael Chabon, and actors William Shatner and Jonathan Frakes, this book charts an out-of-this-world course through Star Trek's history, reveling bold choices that have allowed it to help shape the world that watched it.

"While Britt's insightful and entertaining history may not take fans where no one has gone before…he still offers a fun ride that few fans will be able to resist." —*Library Journal*

Includes bibliographical references.

Burnett, Carol
In Such Good Company: Eleven Years of Laughter, Mayhem, and Fun in the Sandbox. Carol Burnett. Crown Archetype 2016. 288 p.

ISBN 9781101904657

Grades: Adult   791.45
1. Burnett, Carol 2. Women comedians 3. Television comedies 4. Autobiographies and memoirs 5. Life stories — Arts and culture — Performing arts — Entertainers and celebrities 6. Arts and entertainment — Movies and television

LC 2016008433

Comedy legend Carol Burnett tells the hilarious behind-the-scenes story of her iconic weekly variety series, The Carol Burnett Show. Who but Carol Burnett herself has the timing, talent, and wit to pull back the curtain on the Emmy-Award winning show that made television history for eleven glorious seasons? In Such Good Company delves into little-known stories of the guests, sketches and antics that made the show legendary, as well as some favorite tales too good not to relive again.

"Burnett watched every episode afresh to research this book, and that attention to detail shows in her exhaustive accounts of major sketches. However, even nonfans will enjoy the nuggets of intrigue Burnett scatters throughout, in which she shines a light on the sexism she faced during her tenure as a leading lady of the small screen." —*Publishers Weekly*

ESSENTIAL AND RECOMMENDED TITLES
791.45 Television

Fischer, Jenna
The Office BFFs: Tales of the Office from Two Best Friends Who Were There. Jenna Fischer and Angela Kinsey. Dey Street Books 2022. 240 p.
ISBN 9780063007598
Grades: Adult   791.45
1. Fischer, Jenna, 1974- 2. Kinsey, Angela, 1971- 3. Actors and actresses 4. Television programs 5. Fame 6. Friendship 7. Collective autobiographies and memoirs 8. Life stories — Arts and culture — Performing arts — Actors and actresses 9. Life stories — Relationships — Friendship 10. Arts and Entertainment — Movies and Television
LC 2022007102

Receptionist Pam Beesly and accountant Angela Martin had very little in common when they toiled together at Scranton's Dunder Mifflin Paper Company. But, in reality, the two bonded in their very first days on set and, over the nine seasons of the series' run, built a friendship that transcended the show and continues to this day. Sharing everything from what it was like in the early days as the show struggled to gain traction, to walking their first red carpet—plus exclusive stories on the making of milestone episodes and how their lives changed when they became moms—The Office BFFs is full of the same warm and friendly tone Jenna and Angela have brought to their Office Ladies podcast.

"A smart, sweet look from inside The Office about how the show spawned enduring friendships and unexpected careers." —*Kirkus*

Greene, Andy
The Office: The Untold Story of the Greatest Sitcom of the 2000s : An Oral History. Andy Greene. Dutton 2020. 336 p.
ISBN 9781524744977
Grades: Adult   791.45
1. Television programs 2. Popular culture 3. Television 4. Television writing 5. Comedy writing 6. Television industry and trade 7. Actors and actresses 8. Social life and customs 9. United States 10. 21st century 11. Oral histories 12. Arts and Entertainment — Movies and Television 13. Society and culture — Pop culture
LC 2019037591

The untold stories behind The Office, one of the most iconic television shows of the twenty-first century, told by its creators, writers, and actors.

"A fond, funny, informative trip down Memory Lane for series buffs and newcomers alike." —*Kirkus*

Includes bibliographical references and index.

Gross, Edward
The Fifty Year Mission: The First 25 Years: The Complete, Uncensored, Unauthorized Oral History of Star Trek. Edward Gross and Mark A. Altman. Thomas Dunne Books 2016. 544 p.
ISBN 9781250065841
Grades: Adult   791.45
1. Star Trek films 2. Arts and entertainment — Movies and television 3. Society and culture — Pop culture 4. Adult books for young adults
LC 2015051257

This 1st volume of an extensive oral history of Star Trek includes the uncensored and never-before-told stories of more than 200 people involved in creating the Star Trek franchise. Providing solid context for a bevy of quotes, the authors focus on the original series and the six movies that the show inspired—and much of the entertainment comes from the different perspectives on the sometimes contentious relationships between contributors.

"Breathtaking in scope and depth, this is a must-read for Star Trek lovers as well as anyone who wants a better understanding of how television and film production works." —*Booklist*

Includes index.

Imperioli, Michael
Woke Up This Morning: The Definitive Oral History of The Sopranos. Michael Imperioli and Steve Schirripa, with Philip Lerman. William Morrow & Company 2021. 509 p.
ISBN 9780063090026
Grades: Adult   791.45
1. Television programs 2. Podcasts 3. Actors and Actresses 4. Television producers and directors 5. Memories 6. Conversation 7. Television production and direction 8. Oral histories 9. Arts and Entertainment — Movies and Television 10. Life stories — Arts and culture — Performing arts

Inspired by the incredibly successful Talking Sopranos podcast, The Sopranos stars Michael Imperioli (Christopher Moltisanti) and Steve Schirripa (Bobby Baccalieri) finally reveal all the Soprano family secrets in a surprising, funny, and honest new book. Woke up This Morning is the definitive behind-the-scenes history of the groundbreaking HBO series that became a worldwide cultural phenomenon, ushered in a new Golden Age of Television, and to this day continues to be one of the most binged shows of all time. Expanding on the podcast with exclusive interviews with the cast, crew, producers, writers, directors, and, of course, the series creator David Chase, Michael and Steve will tell all the incredible stories that The Sopranos fans have been waiting to hear for over twenty years.

"This is the ultimate book on The Sopranos, made by the people who lived it." —*Publishers Weekly*

Katz, Evan Ross
Into Every Generation a Slayer Is Born: How Buffy Staked Our Hearts. Evan Ross Katz. Hachette Books 2022. 384 p.
ISBN 9780306826689
Grades: Adult   791.45
1. Television programs 2. Influence (Psychology) 3. Television production and direction 4. Television writers 5. Television producers and directors 6. Fans (People) 7. Actors and actresses 8. Oral histories 9. Arts and Entertainment — Movies and Television 10. Life stories — Arts and culture — Performing arts
LC 2021036939

Over the course of its seven-year run, Buffy the Vampire Slayer cultivated a loyal fandom and featured a strong, complex female lead, at a time when such a character was a rarity. Evan Ross Katz explores the show's cultural relevance through a book that is part oral history, part celebration, and part memoir of a personal fandom that has universal resonance still, decades later. Katz—with the help of the show's cast, creators, and crew—reveals that although Buffy contributed to important conversations about gender, sexuality, and feminism, it was not free of internal strife, controversy, and shortcomings. Men—both on screen and off—would taint the show's reputation as a feminist masterpiece, and changing networks, amongst other factors, would drastically alter the show's tone.

"In this entertaining debut, pop culture critic Katz makes a convincing case for why 25 years on, Buffy the Vampire Slayer 'remains one of the best television series of all time.'…Mixing keen cultural analysis, wit, and an obsessive's zeal, this will have fans riveted." —*Publishers Weekly*

Includes bibliographical references and index.

Kaufman, Amy
Bachelor Nation: Inside the World of America's Favorite Guilty Pleasure. Amy Kaufman. E.P. Dutton 2018. 304 p.
ISBN 9781101985908
Grades: Adult   791.45
1. Television programs 2. Popular culture 3. Television history and criticism 4. Arts and entertainment — Movies and television
LC 2017486601

Presents an unauthorized, behind-the-scenes cultural history of The Bachelor franchise.

"Essential for fans of pop culture, this book could play an important role in courses on feminism and gender studies. It's also a fascinating and fun read for anyone who wants to think about how and why viewers continue to tune into shows like the Bachelor." —*Library Journal*

Nussbaum, Emily
Cue the Sun!: The Invention of Reality TV. Emily Nussbaum. Random House 2024. 416 p.
ISBN 9780525508991
Grades: Adult   791.45
1. Reality television programs 2. Television producers and directors 3. Television personalities 4. Documentary television programs 5. Deception 6. Television industry and trade 7. Television history and criticism 8. Arts and

Entertainment — Movies and Television 9. Life stories — Arts and culture — Performing arts

LC 2023045197

Who invented reality television, the world's most dangerous pop-culture genre—and why can't we look away? In this revelatory, deeply reported account of the rise of "dirty documentary"—from its contentious roots in radio to the ascent of Donald Trump—Emily Nussbaum unearths the origin story of the genre that ate the world, as told through the lively voices of the people who built it. At once gimlet-eyed and empathetic, Cue the Sun! explores the morally charged, funny, and sometimes tragic consequences of the hunt for something real inside something fake.

"Nussbaum charts unscripted television's evolution from Candid Camera's 1948 premier through the first season of The Apprentice in 2003…It's a rowdy and unsettling look at how reality conquered television." —*Publishers Weekly*

Includes index.

I Like to Watch: Arguing My Way Through the TV Revolution. Emily Nussbaum. Random House 2019. 365 p.

ISBN 9780525508960

Grades: Adult   791.45

1. Nussbaum, Emily, 1966- 2. Television programs 3. Television history and criticism 4. Popular culture 5. Media fandom 6. Critics 7. Arts and Entertainment — Movies and Television 8. Society and culture — Pop culture 9. Life stories — Arts and culture — Writing — Journalists

LC 2018055067

Nussbaum writes about her passion for television, beginning with Buffy the Vampire Slayer, the show that set her on a fresh intellectual path. She explores the rise of the female screw-up, how fans warp the shows they love, the messy power of sexual violence on TV, and the year that jokes helped elect a reality-television president.

Includes index.

Peisner, David

Homey Don't Play That!: The Story of In Living Color and the Black Comedy Revolution. David Peisner. Simon & Schuster 2018. 288 p.

ISBN 9781501143328

Grades: Adult   791.45

1. African American comedians 2. African Americans in television 3. Television comedies 4. African Americans 5. Actors and actresses 6. Society and culture — Race 7. Society and culture — Media and technology 8. Arts and Entertainment — Movies and Television

LC Bl2017051446

Library Journal Best Books, 2018.

Engaging behind-the-scenes stories about the boundary-breaking sketch comedy show draw on interviews with cast members, writers, producers and network executives to celebrate its enduring influence on comedy, race relations and the careers of some of today's biggest stars.

Press, Joy

Stealing the Show: How Women Are Revolutionizing Television. Joy Press. Atria Books 2018. 272 p.

ISBN 9781501137716

Grades: Adult   791.45

1. Women entertainers 2. Women in television 3. Women television producers and directors 4. Television programs 5. Television industry and trade 6. Television 7. Arts and entertainment — Movies and television 8. Society and culture — Gender — Women 9. Adult books for young adults

LC 2017032332

A leading cultural journalist traces the rise of the female showrunner and how women have become an integral part of today's television, sharing the stories of such boundary-breaking performers as Roseanne Barr, Diane English and Tina Fey.

Reiss, Mike

Springfield Confidential: Jokes, Secrets, and Outright Lies from a Lifetime Writing for the Simpsons. Mike Reiss, Mathew Klickstein; foreword by Judd Apatow. HarperCollins 2018. 320 p.

ISBN 9780062748034

Grades: Adult   791.45

1. Television writing 2. Television writers 3. Television programs 4. Cartoons 5. Arts and Entertainment — Movies and Television

LC 2017279142

The Simpsons' longest-serving writer and producer offers a humorous look at the writing and making of the legendary Fox series that has become one of the most revered artistic achievements in television history.

"Always honest, playful, and engaging, the book will provide fans with deep insight into the show's history but also into its daily production and future." —*Kirkus*

Seitz, Matt Zoller

The Sopranos Sessions. Matt Zoller Seitz & Alan Sepinwall. Abrams Press 2019. 471 pages

ISBN 9781419734946

Grades: Adult   791.45

1. Chase, David, 1945 August 22- 2. Essays 3. Arts and Entertainment — Movies and Television

LC Bl2019000366

Celebrating the 20th anniversary of one of the greatest TV series of all time, a collection of recaps, conversations and critical essays covers every episode and explores the show's artistry, themes and legacy.

Sepinwall, Alan

★ *TV (the Book): Two Experts Pick the Greatest American Shows of All Time.* Alan Sepinwall & Matt Zoller Seitz. Grand Central Publishing 2016. 352 p.

ISBN 9781455588190

Grades: Adult   791.45

1. Television history and criticism 2. Television programs 3. Mass media 4. Popular culture 5. Essays 6. Arts and Entertainment — Movies and Television 7. Adult books for young adults

LC 2016015540

While working at the Newark Star-Ledger, Matt Zoller Seitz and Alan Sepinwall created a popular column debating the merits of then-current television. Eventually they went on to successful careers as critics elsewhere, but the debate raged on and now comes to an epic conclusion in TV (the Book).

"The great debate: How do you pick the best show of all time?—The inner circle—No-doubt-about-it classics—Groundbreakers and workhorses—Outlier classics—Works in progress—A certain regard—Miniseries—TV-movies—Live plays made for television." —*Kirkus*

Includes index.

Shales, Tom

Live from New York: An Uncensored History of Saturday Night Live. Tom Shales and James Andrew Miller. Little, Brown 2014. 594 p, 16 p. of plates : Illustration

ISBN 9780316295048

Grades: Adult   791.45

1. Television 2. Television programs 3. Literary criticism 4. Stand-up comedy 5. Comedians 6. Arts and Entertainment — Movies and Television 7. Arts and Entertainment — Comedy 8. Adult books for young adults

LC 2002072958

A history of the long-running television series draws on backstage anecdotes and uncensored reminiscences to create an oral history of "Saturday Night Live."

Includes index.

Smith, Chris

The Daily Show (the Book): An Oral History as Told by Jon Stewart, the Correspondents, Staff and Guests. Chris Smith, foreword by Jon Stewart. Grand Central Publishing 2016. 304 p.

ISBN 9781455565382

Grades: Adult   791.45

1. Television writers 2. Television 3. Television programs 4. Comedians 5. Literary criticism 6. Stand-up comedy 7. United States 8. Oral histories 9. Bi-

ESSENTIAL AND RECOMMENDED TITLES
791.4502 Stock footage — Television

ographies 10. Arts and Entertainment — Movies and Television 11. Arts and Entertainment — Comedy

LC 2016952042

An uncensored history of the Emmy and Peabody Award-winning The Daily Show with Jon Stewart as told by its correspondents, writers and host shares behind-the-scenes stories as well as observations about its blend of news reportage and comedy and its enduring cultural and professional influence.

791.4502 Stock footage — Television

Burrows, James
★ *Directed by James Burrows: Five Decades of Stories from the Legendary Director of Taxi, Cheers, Frasier, Friends, Will & Grace, and More.* James Burrows, with Eddy Friedfeld; foreword by Glen and Les Charles. Ballantine Books 2022. 368 p.
ISBN 9780593358245
Grades: Adult 791.4502
1. Burrows, James, 1940- 2. Television producers and directors 3. Television comedies 4. Television production and direction 5. Television industry and trade 6. Actors and actresses 7. Autobiographies and memoirs 8. Life stories — Arts and culture — Performing arts — Directors and producers 9. Arts and Entertainment — Movies and Television

LC 2021047965

Legendary sitcom director James Burrows has spent five decades making America laugh. Here readers will find never-revealed stories behind the casting of the dozens of great sitcoms he directed, as well as details as to how these memorable shows were created, how they got on the air, and how the cast and crew continued to develop and grow. Burrows also examines his own challenges, career victories, and defeats, and provides advice for aspiring directors, writers, and actors. All this from the man who helped launch the careers of Ted Danson, Kelsey Grammer, Woody Harrelson, Jennifer Aniston, Debra Messing, and Melissa McCarthy, to name a few.

"A wonderful book about the world of television, easily as valuable as Levinson and Link's Stay Tuned (1981) and Bill Carter's Desperate Networks (2006)." —*Booklist*

Kamp, David
Sunny Days: The Children's Television Revolution That Changed America. David Kamp; foreword by Questlove. Simon & Schuster 2020. 320 p.
ISBN 9781501137808
Grades: Adult 791.4502
1. Television programs for children 2. Television programs 3. Television and education 4. Inner city children 5. Children 6. Race relations 7. Education 8. Social life and customs 9. United States 10. 1960s 11. 20th century 12. Arts and Entertainment — Movies and Television 13. Society and culture — Pop culture

LC 2019059612

Tells the behind-the-scenes story of the creation of the children's TV programs Sesame Street, the Electric Company, Mister Rogers' Neighborhood and more—which transformed the American childhood for the better, teaching kids about diversity, the ABCs and feminism.

"This passionate, highly engaging media history will thrill pop culture buffs and those who remember these shows from their childhood." —*Publishers Weekly*

Includes bibliographical references.

Lakshmi, Padma
Love, Loss, and What We Ate. Padma Lakshmi. Ecco Press 2016. 325 pages
ISBN 9780062202611
Grades: Adult 791.4502
1. Lakshmi, Padma 2. Cooks 3. Immigrants 4. Television personalities 5. Immigrant families 6. Growing up 7. Indian Americans 8. Cooking 9. Autobiographies and memoirs 10. Life stories — Arts and culture — Culinary arts 11. Life stories — Relationships — Growing up 12. Life stories — Identity — Immigrants

The host of the Emmy Award-winning Top Chef presents a memoir about her immigrant childhood and complicated life in front of the camera, tracing her formative experiences in her grandmother's South India kitchen and her relationships with people who influenced her culinary skills and career.

Trebek, Alex
The Answer Is ...: Reflections on My Life. Alex Trebek. Simon & Schuster 2020. 290 pages : Illustration; Color
ISBN 9781982157999
Grades: Adult 791.4502
1. Trebek, Alex, 1940-2020 2. Television personalities 3. Television game shows 4. Television game show hosts 5. Quiz shows 6. Fame 7. Growing up 8. Family relationships 9. Popular culture 10. Autobiographies and memoirs 11. Canadian literature 12. Biographies 13. Life stories — Arts and culture — Performing arts — Entertainers and celebrities 14. Arts and Entertainment — Movies and Television

LC 2020938903

Longtime Jeopardy! host and television icon Alex Trebek reflects on his life and career.

"Readers will likely come away from the memoir feeling even more comfortable with the author than they already did. An amiable, enjoyable series of glimpses into the life of an avuncular figure." —*Kirkus*

Van Ness, Jonathan
Love That Story: Observations from a Gorgeously Queer Life. Jonathan Van Ness. HarperOne 2022. 272 p.
ISBN 9780063082267
Grades: Adult 791.4502
1. Van Ness, Jonathan 2. Identity 3. Grief 4. Body image 5. White privilege 6. Compassion 7. Empathy 8. Optimism 9. Self-fulfillment 10. Essays 11. Society and culture — General 12. Life stories — Personal growth 13. Life stories — Identity — LGBTQIA+

In a candid and curious essay collection, a Queer Eye star takes a thoughtful, in-depth look at timely topics through the lens of his own personal experience—instances that have required him to learn, grow, and find a better understanding of the world around him.

791.45028 Acting — Television

Mulgrew, Kate
Born with Teeth: A Memoir. Kate Mulgrew. Little Brown & Co. 2015. 320 p.
ISBN 9780316334310
Grades: Adult 791.45028
1. Mulgrew, Kate, 1955- 2. Growing up 3. Actors and actresses 4. Adoption 5. unplanned pregnancy 6. Rape victims 7. Mothers and daughters 8. People with Alzheimer's disease 9. Determination 10. Autobiographies and memoirs 11. Life stories — Arts and culture — Performing arts — Actors and actresses 12. Arts and Entertainment — Movies and Television 13. Family and Relationships — Parenting — Adoption

LC 2015930445

A star known for her strong female roles in Star Trek: Voyager and Orange Is the New Black offers a deeply moving account of the price and rewards of a passionate life.

"Mulgrew's enjoyable narrative is compelling as she portrays her decades of acting work, personal triumphs and heartbreaks, and her mesmerizing life." —*Library Journal*

Nawaz, Zarqa
Laughing All the Way to the Mosque. Zarqa Nawaz. Little Brown & Co. 2016. 241 p.
ISBN 9781443416931
Grades: Adult 791.45028
1. Nawaz, Zarqa 2. Women television producers and directors 3. Muslim women 4. Muslims 5. Identity 6. Culture conflict 7. Ethnic identity 8. Autobiographies and memoirs 9. Canadian literature 10. Life stories — Relationships —

Growing up 11. Life stories — Arts and culture — Performing arts — Directors and Producers 12. Spirituality and Religion — Islam 13. Arts and Entertainment — Movies and Television 14. Humor writing — Social humor

A humorous account of growing up in a traditionally Muslim household in Canada.

"Nawaz's self-deprecating wit is endearing, and her simple, factual tone provides education without ever being boring. This memoir provides an important glimpse into the everyday life of a Western Muslim family, but, even better, it is a laugh-out-loud story that everyone can enjoy." —*Publishers Weekly*

Originally published in Canada (Toronto : HarperCollins Canada, [2014]).

791.4509 Television — History, geographic treatment, biography

Martin, Brett
Difficult Men: Behind the Scenes of a Creative Revolution: From The Sopranos and The Wire to Mad Men and Breaking Bad. Brett Martin. Penguin 2013. 288 p.
ISBN 9781594204197
Grades: Adult   791.4509
1. Television programs 2. Television industry and trade 3. Cable television 4. Television 5. Popular culture 6. Antiheroes and antiheroines 7. Social norms 8. Actors and actresses 9. 2000s (Decade) 10. 2010s 11. Arts and Entertainment — Movies and Television

LC 2012047001

Since when have morally ambiguous "good" guys become so hot in TV? In a fascinating assessment of programs that have helped TV emerge as a legitimate creative art form over the last 15 years, author Brett Martin explores the unique writing and production choices that have place shows like The Wire, Deadwood, The Sopranos, and Mad Men a cut above. Full of both serious commentary and behind-the-scenes info, this is a great read for anyone interested in today's more challenging shows.

791.456 Special aspects of television programs

Stelter, Brian
Top of the Morning: Inside the Cutthroat World of Morning TV. Brian Stelter. Grand Central Publishing 2013. 352 p.
ISBN 9781455512874
Grades: Adult   791.456
1. Couric, Katie, 1957- 2. Sawyer, Diane, 1945- 3. Lauer, Matt, 1957- 4. Gibson, Charles, 1943- 5. Television talk shows 6. Television talk show hosts and guests 7. Competition 8. Television personalities 9. Television industry and trade 10. Television newscasters and commentators 11. United States 12. Page to screen 13. Arts and Entertainment — Movies and Television

LC 2013932327

A staff writer at the New York Times uncovers the behind-the-scenes dirt on America's favorite morning television shows, featuring well-sourced gossip about Ann Curry, Katie Couric, Diane Sawyer, Charlie Gibson and Matt Lauer.

Adapted into the television series The Morning Show, Fall 2019.

791.457 Programs

McCormick, Brad
Extreme Sports: The World's Most Thrilling Activities. Brad McCormick. Tabby Entertainment 2023. 52 p.
ISBN 9781961408296
Grades: Adult   791.457
1. Extreme sports 2. Risk-taking 3. Sports 4. Sports and Competition — Extreme Sports

Extreme Sports: The World's Most Thrilling Activities is your ultimate guide to the heart-pounding, boundary-pushing activities that have captured the imagination of adventurers and athletes alike.

791.5 Puppetry and toy theaters

Blumenthal, Eileen
Puppetry: A World History. Eileen Blumenthal. Harry N. Abrams 2005. 271 p. : Illustration
ISBN 9780810955875
Grades: 11 12 Adult   791.5
1. Puppet theaters 2. Puppetry 3. Puppets 4. Puppeteers 5. Shadow theaters 6. Arts and Entertainment — Theater 7. Arts and Entertainment — Crafts and hobbies 8. Adult books for young adults

LC 2004029349

Booklist Editors' Choice, 2005.

An illustrated exploration of the cultural diversity and personalities of puppets throughout history examines the characterizations of numerous puppeteers, as well as the often sophisticated technology that has gone into their creations.

"This is a history of the puppet world, from prehistoric times to Tony-winning Broadway hit Avenue Q. This would be a welcome addition to the libraries of performing arts buffs who want to learn more about a lesser known form." —*Publishers Weekly*

Includes bibliographical references (p. 256-262) and index.

791.6 Pageantry

Mifflin, Margot
Looking for Miss America: A Pageant's 100-Year Quest to Define Womanhood. Margot Mifflin. Counterpoint 2020. 320 p.
ISBN 9781640092235
Grades: Adult   791.6
1. Beauty contests 2. Beauty contest industry and trade 3. Feminism 4. Racism in popular culture 5. Sexism 6. Beauty contestants 7. Feminine beauty (Aesthetics) 8. Femininity 9. United States 10. Society and culture — Gender — Women 11. Arts and Entertainment — General

LC 2019053730

Approaching its 100th anniversary, the pageant has survived scandal, protests, mockery, and the mutiny of a queen who got cold feet and skipped town the night she won. Looking for Miss America breaks down the blend of capitalism, patriotism, class anxiety and cultural mythology that has fueled the pageant, the racial biases it has perpetuated, and the social mobility it has enabled.

"This work offers a thought-provoking, balanced, and highly informative look at an institution that has perplexed and enticed Americans since its founding." —*Library Journal*

Includes bibliographical references.

792 Stage presentations

Adler, Stella
Stella Adler: The Art of Acting. Compiled and edited by Howard Kissel. Applause Books 2000. 271 p. : Illustration
ISBN 9781557833730
Grades: Adult   792
1. Acting 2. Arts and Entertainment — General

LC 00108803

Drawing on an archive of notebooks, transcriptions, and audiotapes, the lessons and insights Stella Adler brought to the craft of acting are presented.

"In this collection of Adler's papers Kissel has taken tapes, transcriptions, notebooks, and other sources to reconstruct an acting course in 22 lessons. The lessons are graduated from very basic matters to quite complex issues of textual analysis and decorum. Though mostly monologues, they include enough exercises and student responses to get the flavor of Adler's work. This is required reading for anyone interested in theater practice." —*Library Journal*

Brockett, Oscar G.
History of the Theatre. Oscar G. Brockett, Franklin J. Hildy. Pearson 2008. xii, 688 p. : Illustration; Map

ESSENTIAL AND RECOMMENDED TITLES
792.02 Miscellany

ISBN 9780205511860
Grades: Adult — 792
1. Theater 2. Drama 3. Film history and criticism 4. Arts and Entertainment — Theater
LC 2009291794

This 40th anniversary edition retains all of the traditional features that have made History of the Theatre the most successful text of its kind, including worldwide coverage, more than 530 photos and illustrations, useful maps, and the expertise of Oscar G. Brockett and Franklin J. Hildy, two of the most widely respected theatre historians in the field. As with every edition, the text reflects the current state of knowledge and brings the history of theatre up to the present. This tenth edition continues to provide the most thorough and accurate assessment of theatre history available.

"This edition, with its extensive bibliography and instructive images, ensures that this title will continue to be among the best resources on the market. This said, libraries that own the ninth edition may wish to pass on this one, since the information expanded in (and new to) the present volume is readily available elsewhere." —*Choice*

40th anniversary edition—Cover; Includes bibliographical references (p. 642-653) and index.

Dench, Judi
Shakespeare: The Man Who Pays the Rent. Judi Dench, with Brendan O'Hea; illustrations by Judi Dench. St. Martin's Press 2024. 288 p.
ISBN 9781250325778
Grades: Adult — 792
1. Dench, Judi, 1934- 2. Shakespeare, William, 1564-1616 3. Actors and actresses 4. Women celebrities 5. Acting 6. Interviews 7. Autobiographies and memoirs 8. Biographies 9. Life stories — Arts and culture — Performing arts — Actors and actresses 10. Arts and Entertainment — General
LC 2023056205

For the very first time, a noted actor opens up about every Shakespearean role she has played throughout her seven-decade career, from Lady Macbeth and Titania to Ophelia and Cleopatra.

"A compendium of great wit and wisdom with universal appeal. Both Shakespeare fans and novices, especially students who might find his language difficult to understand, will be delighted." —*Library Journal*

Originally published in the United Kingdom by Penguin Random House, London, in 2023.

Gillette, J. Michael
Designing with Light: An Introduction to Stage Lighting. J. Michael Gillette, Michael J. McNamara. McGraw-Hill Companies 2013. 379 p.
ISBN 9780073514239
Grades: Adult — 792
1. Stage lighting 2. Arts and Entertainment — Theater
LC 2012034637

The authors approach stage lighting design as an art that integrates the vision of director, actor, and playwright, and as a craft that provides practical solutions for the manipulation of stage space. The sixth edition offers a wealth of new information on new trends in lighting design.

Mamet, David
True and False: Heresy and Common Sense for the Actor. David Mamet. Pantheon Books 1997. x, 127 p.
ISBN 9780679442493
Grades: Adult — 792
1. Acting 2. Actors and actresses 3. Films 4. Popular culture 5. United States history 6. 20th century 7. Essays 8. Arts and Entertainment — Movies and Television
LC 97019336

Argues that the techniques taught in acting school, in particular the famous Stansilavsky Method, mislead aspiring actors and suggests ways for performers to remain true to the chararacters they represent.

"Mamet exhorts actors to show up early, have their lines down cold, and have a single objective for each scene. He contends that overthinking and too much emotional interpretation is not the actor's role. Essential reading for theater collections." —*Library Journal*

Moore, Sonia
The Stanislavski System: The Professional Training of an Actor : Digested from the Teachings of Konstantin S. Stanislavski. Sonia Moore. Penguin Books 1984. xvi, 96 p.
ISBN 9780140466607
Grades: Adult — 792
1. Method acting 2. Arts and Entertainment — General
LC 84002855

Provides an explanation of the art and practice of acting as taught by Stanislavski and briefly describes the style and achievements of his disciple, Eugene Vakhtangov.

Includes index; Bibliography: P. 91-92.

Riedel, Michael
Singular Sensation: The Triumph of Broadway. Michael Riedel. Avid Reader Press 2020. 336 p.
ISBN 9781501166631
Grades: Adult — 792
1. Drama 2. Theatrical producers and directors 3. Actors and actresses 4. Musicals 5. Theater 6. Film history and criticism 7. Broadway, New York City 8. New York City 9. 1990s 10. 2000s (Decade) 11. 20th century 12. Arts and Entertainment — Theater 13. History writing — Arts and culture 14. Life stories — Arts and culture — Performing arts

The 1990s was a decade of profound change on Broadway. A different breed of producers rose up to challenge the grip theater owners had long held on Broadway, and corporations began to see how much money could be made from live theater. And just as Broadway had clawed its way back into the mainstream of American popular culture, the September 11 attacks struck fear into the heart of Americans who thought Times Square might be the next target. But Broadway was back in business just two days later, buoyed by talented theater people intent on bringing New Yorkers together and supporting the economics of an injured city. Michael Riedel presents the drama behind every mega-hit or shocking flop, bringing readers into high-stakes premieres, fraught rehearsals, tough contract negotiations, intense Tony Award battles, and more. Broadway has triumphs and disasters, but the show always goes on.

"New York theater critic and author Riedel . . . considers the 1990s 'a decade of profound change on Broadway' and here pulls back the curtain on some of its most popular shows." —*Booklist*

Shapiro, James
★ *The Playbook: A Story of Theater, Democracy, and the Making of a Culture War*. James Shapiro. Penguin Press 2024. 384 p.
ISBN 9780593490204
Grades: Adult — 792
1. Drama 2. Theater and society 3. Politics and literature 4. Democracy 5. Anti-Communism 6. Culture conflict 7. United States history 8. United States 9. 20th century 10. Arts and Entertainment — Theater 11. History writing — Arts and culture 12. History writing — United States
LC 2023048102

This masterful history of the Federal Theatre Project, which entertained the public from 1935-1939, takes us through its most remarkable productions, from Shakespeare to modern plays that confronted the pressing issues of the day until it was shut down on the grounds it promoted "un-American" activity.

"Shapiro's exquisite backstage history also cannily reflects on present-day political implications. It's a bravura performance." —*Publishers Weekly*

Includes bibliographical references and index.

792.02 Miscellany

Butler, Isaac
The Method: How the Twentieth Century Learned to Act. Isaac Butler. Bloomsbury Publishing 2022. 416 p.

PUBLIC LIBRARY CORE COLLECTION: NONFICTION
Twentieth Edition

ISBN 9781635574777
Grades: Adult 792.02
1. Method acting 2. Acting 3. Performing arts 4. 20th century 5. Arts and Entertainment — Movies and Television 6. Arts and Entertainment — Theater 7. History writing — Arts and culture
LC 2021044374
National Book Critics Circle Award for Non-Fiction, 2022.

This must read for any fan of Broadway or American film, a critic and theater director chronicles the history of Method acting—an enthusiastic and engaging story of creative discovery and the birth of classic Hollywood.

"Butler (coauthor of The World Only Spins Forward: The Ascent of 'Angels in America') provides an excellent, thorough history of the preeminent school of American acting.... Butler has produced an essential study of this hugely influential theory and practice of American acting." —*Library Journal*

Includes bibliographic references.

Cohen, Robert
Acting Power: The 21st Century Edition. Robert Cohen. Routledge, Taylor & Francis Group 2013. xvi, 245 pages
ISBN 9780415658461
Grades: Adult 792.02
1. Acting 2. Arts and Entertainment — General
LC 2012037409
Includes bibliographical references (pages 230-235) and index.

Essin, Christin
Stage Designers in Early Twentieth-Century America: Artists, Activists, Cultural Critics. Christin Essin. Palgrave Macmillan 2012. xiii, 264 pages : Illustration
ISBN 9780230115071
Grades: Adult 792.02
1. Set designers 2. Theaters 3. 20th century 4. Arts and Entertainment — Theater 5. History writing — United States
LC 2012043581

By casting designers as authors, cultural critics, activists, entrepreneurs, and global cartographers, Essin tells a story about scenic images on the page, stage, and beyond that helped American audiences see the everyday landscapes and exotic destinations from a modern perspective.

"All these treatments are enlivened with case studies of specific productions. Essin's research is thorough, her writing is engaging, and her insights are rewarding." —*Choice*

Includes bibliographical references (pages 239-253) and index.

Fischer, Jenna
The Actor's Life: A Survival Guide. Jenna Fischer. BenBella Books 2017. 252 p.
ISBN 9781944648220
Grades: Adult 792.02
1. Acting 2. Vocational guidance 3. Reference books 4. Arts and Entertainment — General 5. Reference books — Performing arts
LC 2017048157

An established actor and one of the stars of The Office, with amusing candor and wit and drawing on her own memorable and hilarious experiences, presents this handy guide for getting established as a professional actor, providing invaluable advice personally acquired from her many years of struggle.

Includes bibliographical references and index.

Gillette, J. Michael
Theatrical Design and Production: An Introduction to Scene Design and Construction, Lighting, Sound, Costume, and Makeup. J. Michael Gillette. McGraw-Hill 2013. xvi, 624 p. : Illustration; Color
ISBN 9780073382227
Grades: Adult 792.02
1. Stage management 2. Theater 3. Theaters 4. Stage craft 5. Arts and Entertainment — Theater
LC 2012020022

"The author divides his standard text for undergraduate lighting design students into the two constituent elements of his craft—technology and design. He clearly and completely presents both technical and aesthetic design aspects." —*Library Journal*

Includes bibliographical references (p. 602-603) and index.

Hagen, Uta
★ *Respect for Acting*. Uta Hagen; with Haskel Frankel. John Wiley & Sons 2008. xiii, 226 p.
ISBN 9780470228487
Grades: Adult 792.02
1. Acting 2. Arts and Entertainment — General
LC 2008016843

"This classic treatise on the process and craft of acting has significantly benefited actors for three decades. Juxtaposed with Hagen's aesthetic is a wealth of practical information, creative ideas, and her uniquely useful object exercises." —*Library Journal*

Includes index; Originally published: New York : Macmillan, 1973.

Powell, Michael
The Acting Bible: The Complete Resource for Aspiring Actors. Michael Powell. Barron's 2010. 256 p. : Illustration; Color
ISBN 9780764163586
Grades: 10 11 12 Adult 792.02
1. Acting 2. Vocational guidance 3. Reference books — Handbooks, manuals, etc. 4. Arts and Entertainment — General
LC 2009941266

Presents a guide to acting, covering such topics as technique, vocal training, movement, observation, screen acting, auditions, and career options.

A Quintet book.—T.P. verso; Includes index.

Rannells, Andrew
Too Much Is Not Enough: A Memoir of Fumbling Toward Adulthood. Andrew Rannells. Crown Publishing 2019. xii, 251 pages
ISBN 9780525574859
Grades: Adult 792.02
1. Rannells, Andrew 2. Actors and actresses 3. Young men 4. Ambition 5. Acting 6. Auditions 7. Broadway, New York City 8. New York City 9. Autobiographies and memoirs 10. Life stories — Arts and culture — Performing arts — Actors and actresses 11. Arts and Entertainment — Movies and Television 12. Arts and Entertainment — Theater

The star of Broadway's The Book of Mormon and HBO's Girls presents a heartfelt coming-of-age memoir that recounts how, as a fiercely ambitious but sexually confused Midwestern teen, he haphazardly pursued his theatrical dreams in 1997 New York City.

"In a spirited debut saturated with personality and frank humor, Rannells tells the stories of his youth growing up as the fourth of five siblings in Omaha, Nebraska." —*Kirkus*

Seligman, Craig
Who Does That Bitch Think She Is?: Doris Fish and the Rise of Drag. Craig Seligman. PublicAffairs 2023. 352 p.
ISBN 9781541702165
Grades: Adult 792.02
1. Fish, Doris, 1952-1991 2. Drag queens 3. Drag shows 4. LGBTQIA+ people 5. Gay communities 6. History writing — LGBTQIA+ 7. Society and culture — LGBTQIA+ 8. Life stories — Identity — LGBTQIA+
LC 2022036158

In the 1970s, queer people were openly despised and drag queens scared the public; this was also the era when Doris Fish (born Philip Mills in 1952 in Australia) rose to drag queen stardom. He was a leader of the generation that prepared the world not just for drag queens on TV but for a society that is more tolerant and accepting of LGBTQ+ people. How did we get from there to here? Craig Seligman looks at Doris's life as a way to provide some answers while recounting this vivid era in LGBTQ+ history, giving needed insight to how drag has become the performance phenomenon we know today.

ESSENTIAL AND RECOMMENDED TITLES
792.089 Ethnic groups — Theater

"This honest and compassionate depiction of someone who was true to their passions will inspire readers, especially those interested in LGBTQIA+ history." —*Library Journal*

Includes bibliographical references and index.

Stanislavsky, Konstantin
An Actor's Work: A Student's Diary. Konstantin Stanislavski; translated and edited by Jean Benedetti. Routledge 2008. xxviii, 693 p.
ISBN 9780415422239
Grades: Adult   **792.02**
1. Method acting 2. Arts and Entertainment — Theater 3. Arts and Entertainment — General
LC 2007045357

Presents a new translation of the author's incomplete works "An Actor Prepares" and "Building a Character" which provides a system for acting and developing a character.

"This translation by Benedetti of Stanislavski's famous works will be greeted with excitement by actors everywhere." —*Library Journal*

Translated from the Russian.

Wasson, Sam
★ *Improv Nation: How We Made a Great American Art.* Sam Wasson. Houghton Mifflin Harcourt 2017. 464 p.
ISBN 9780544557208
Grades: Adult   **792.02**
1. Popular culture 2. Women comedians 3. Comedians 4. Theater 5. Stand-up comedy 6. Social life and customs 7. United States 8. 20th century 9. Arts and Entertainment — Comedy 10. Arts and Entertainment — Theater 11. Arts and Entertainment — Movies and Television
LC Bl2017041789

A sweeping history of the uniquely American art form of improv, which has never been more popular—from its beginnings during the McCarthy Era through the rise of such institutions as Second City, the Groundlings and the Upright Citizens Brigade and such performers as Tina Fey, Steve Carell and Bill Murray.

"While comedians today take up a large space in public life, Wasson reminds us that a lot of hard work has been done for them to get there. An entertaining book, recommended for aspiring comedians who want to historicize their practice." —*Kirkus*

792.089 Ethnic groups — Theater

Lane, Stewart F.
Black Broadway: African Americans on the Great White Way. Stewart F. Lane. Square One Publishers 2015. 288 p.
ISBN 9780757003882
Grades: Adult   **792.089**
1. Theater 2. African Americans 3. African American entertainers 4. African Americans in the performing arts 5. Drama 6. Theatrical producers and directors 7. Actors and actresses 8. Minstrel shows 9. Vaudeville 10. Musicals 11. New York City 12. Arts and Entertainment — Theater 13. History writing — African American — United States
LC 2014006513

An entertaining, poignant history of a Broadway of which few are aware.

"In this wonderfully illustrated and researched book, Tony Award-winning producer Lane chronicles the evolution of Black theater from the 1700s to today." —*Booklist*

Includes bibliographical references.

792.09 History, geographic treatment, biography

Levy, Reynold
They Told Me Not to Take That Job: Tumult, Betrayal, Heroics, and the Transformation of Lincoln Center. Reynold Levy. PublicAffairs 2015. xvii, 349 p. : Illustration; Color
ISBN 9781610393614
Grades: Adult   **792.09**
1. Levy, Reynold 2. Performing arts 3. Leadership 4. Success (Concept) 5. Businesspeople 6. Autobiographies and memoirs 7. Biographies 8. Life stories — Business — Business leaders 9. Arts and entertainment — General 10. Business and economics — Business leaders and entrepreneurs
LC 2014049065

The president of the Lincoln Center for the Performing Arts reveals the real story behind the $1.2 billion reinvention of Lincoln Center, and the trials and triumphs along with way, providing unique lessons for leaders in all kinds of organizations.

Includes bibliographical references (pages 324-335) and index.

Riedel, Michael
Razzle Dazzle: The Battle for Broadway. Michael Riedel. Simon & Schuster 2015. 352 p.
ISBN 9781451672169
Grades: Adult   **792.09**
1. Theater 2. Musicals 3. Cities and towns 4. Broadway, New York City 5. 1970s 6. 1980s 7. Arts and entertainment — Theater 8. Nonfiction that reads like fiction
LC 2015506947

A revered and provocative theater observer presents a grand history of the producers, directors, actors, and critics battling for creative and financial control of Broadway.

"While not functioning as an introduction or a detailed history of the American commercial theater, this book articulates a neglected but historically essential point of view." —*Library Journal*

792.2 Comedy and melodrama

Key, Keegan-Michael
★ *The History of Sketch Comedy: A Journey Through the Art and Craft of Humor.* by Keegan-Michael Key and Elle Key. Chronicle Books 2023. 256 p.
ISBN 9781797216836
Grades: Adult   **792.2**
1. Comedy writing 2. Television comedies 3. Television comedy writers 4. Humorous writing 5. Characters and characteristics in television 6. Comedians 7. Television history and criticism 8. Autobiographies and memoirs 9. Humor writing — General 10. Arts and Entertainment — Comedy 11. Arts and Entertainment — Movies and Television
LC 2022048189

Building on the popularity of their 2022 Webby Award-winning podcast, the authors, in this entertaining part memoir, part masterclass, take us on a rollicking ride through the history of comedy with the help of essays from such comedy greats as Jordan Peele, Mike Myers, Ken Jeong, Christopher Guest and Jim Carrey.

"A great addition to popular reading collections. Recommended for sketch comedy and improv enthusiasts and fans of Key & Peele skits." —*Library Journal*

Includes index.

792.6 Musical plays

Bloom, Ken
Broadway Musicals: The 101 Greatest Shows of All Time. Ken Bloom & Frank Vlastnik; new preface by Broadway's leading ladies; foreword by Jerry Orbach. Black Dog & Leventhal Publishers 2010. 344 pages : Illustration; Color

PUBLIC LIBRARY CORE COLLECTION: NONFICTION
Twentieth Edition

ISBN 9781579128494

Grades: 11 12 Adult   792.6

1. Musicals 2. Broadway, New York City 3. Arts and Entertainment — Theater

LC 2012398655

Offers an alphabetical survey of the most popular Broadway musicals in history, with commentaries, synopses, behind-the-scenes information, and lists of songs and cast members for each musical.

Includes index.

792.609 Musical plays — History, geographic treatment, biography

Stempel, Larry

★ *Showtime: A History of the Broadway Musical Theater.* Larry Stempel. W.W. Norton & Co. 2010. xx, 826 p, 16 p. of plates : Illustration; Color

ISBN 9780393067156

Grades: Adult   792.609

1. Musicals 2. Music history and criticism 3. Arts and Entertainment — Music 4. History writing — Regional history — United States

LC 2010019704

Presents the history of Broadway musicals over the past 150 years, examining their cultural context and historical significance, from the Astor Place Opera House riot of 1849 through the golden age of Show Boat and Oklahoma! and modern-day Rent.

Showtime brings the history of Broadway musicals to life in a narrative as engaging as the subject itself—beginning with the scandalous Astor Place Opera House riot of 1849 to such groundbreaking works as Company and Rent.

"Theater buffs will be delighted to find that this scholarly, definitive work is also a hugely entertaining read." —*Publishers Weekly*

Includes bibliographical references (p. 687-782), discography (p. 783-785), and index.

Viertel, Jack

The Secret Life of the American Musical: How Classic Broadway Shows Are Built. Jack Viertel. Sarah Crichton Books 2016. 336 p.

ISBN 9780374256920

Grades: Adult   792.609

1. Theater 2. Musicals 3. Music history and criticism 4. Broadway, New York City 5. Arts and entertainment — Theater 6. Arts and Entertainment — Writing and Publishing — Literary criticism

LC 2015023713

How do musicals make it to Broadway? In this entertaining and informative book, Broadway veteran (producer, critic, professor, executive, etc.) Jack Viertel draws on a range of examples—from The Music Man to Wicked to Hamilton—and personal experiences to paint a picture of how the process works. Taking readers step-by-step through all the phases of a typical musical-theater story, from opening numbers to finales, Viertel offers a colorful exploration of Broadway. And for those who want to know what to listen to post-reading, Viertel provides a list of soundtracks.

Includes index.

792.7 Variety shows and theatrical dancing

Feast, Fancy

Naked: On Sex, Work, and Other Burlesques. Essays by Fancy Feast. Algonquin Books of Chapel Hill 2023. 304 p.

ISBN 9781643752372

Grades: Adult   792.7

1. Feast, Fancy, 1988- 2. Stripteasers 3. Sex industry and trade 4. Sexuality 5. Desire 6. Love 7. Body image 8. Culture 9. United States 10. Essays 11. Society and culture — Sex and sexuality — Sex industry 12. Life stories — Arts and culture — Performing arts — Entertainers and celebrities

LC 2023021019

Burlesque performer, sex educator, and social worker Fancy Feast gives readers a backstage pass to the nightlife and sex industries, examining our culture's hang-ups and obsessions with bodies, desire, and even love.

"Honest, explicit, and sometimes vulnerable, this revealing debut offers much for readers to enjoy." —*Booklist*

Fox, Jesse David

Comedy Book: How Comedy Conquered Culture—and the Magic That Makes It Work. Jesse David Fox. Farrar, Straus and Giroux 2023. 336 p.

ISBN 9780374604714

Grades: Adult   792.7

1. Comedy writing 2. Comedians 3. Popular culture 4. United States 5. History writing — Arts and culture 6. Arts and Entertainment — Comedy 7. Society and culture — Pop culture

LC 2023018729

From a beloved comedy critic, a wisecracking, heartfelt, and overdue chronicle of comedy's boom-and its magic.

"This electric debut from Vulture editor Fox serves up trenchant observations on the roles context, laughter, timing, and other factors play in comedic movies, television shows, and standup sets from 1990 through the early 2020s." —*Publishers Weekly*

Includes bibliographical references and index.

Gold, Judy

Yes I Can Say That: When They Come for the Comedians We're All in Trouble. Judy Gold. Dey Street 2020. 224 p.

ISBN 9780062953759

Grades: Adult   792.7

1. Comedians 2. Censorship 3. Freedom of speech 4. Political correctness (Concept) 5. Arts and Entertainment — Comedy 6. Politics and global affairs — Mass media and politics 7. Humor writing — Social humor

LC 2019054781

A comedy veteran, in 10 impassioned polemics, frames comedy as a tool of empowerment—a way to reclaim hateful rhetoric and battle the democracy-crushing plight of censorship.

"A powerful, and powerfully funny, argument in support of how vital free speech is to comedy and comedy is to us." —*Booklist*

Includes bibliographical references.

Goodman, Elyssa

Glitter and Concrete: A Cultural History of Drag in New York City. Elyssa Maxx Goodman. Hanover Square Press 2023. 320 p.

ISBN 9781335449368

Grades: Adult   792.7

1. Drag shows 2. Drag queens 3. Drag kings 4. LGBTQIA+ people 5. Gender identity 6. Social marginality 7. Art and politics 8. Subcultures 9. Freedom of expression 10. New York City history 11. History writing — LGBTQIA+ 12. Society and culture — LGBTQIA+ 13. Life stories — Arts and culture — Performing arts — Entertainers and celebrities 14. Debut title

From the lush feather boas that adorned early female impersonators to the sequined lip syncs of barroom queens to the drag kings that have us laughing in stitches, drag has played a vital role in the creative life of New York City. But the evolution of drag in the city—as an art form, a community and a mode of liberation—has never before been fully chronicled. Informed by meticulous research and archival work, as well as original interviews with high-profile performers, Elyssa Maxx Goodman's history is a significant contribution to queer history and an essential read for anyone curious about the story that echoes beneath the heels.

"Goodman, a writer and columnist focused on the arts and LGBTQ+ culture, parlays her ardor for drag into a uniquely comprehensive, vibrant, and eye-opening history of the art form in New York City." —*Booklist*

Levy, Shawn

★ *In on the Joke: The Original Queens of Standup Comedy.* Shawn Levy. Doubleday 2022. 400 p.

ISBN 9780385545785

ESSENTIAL AND RECOMMENDED TITLES
792.7 Variety shows and theatrical dancing

Grades: Adult   792.7

1. Women stand-up comedians 2. Comic routines 3. Women comedians 4. Women's role 5. Stand-up comedians 6. Comedians 7. Social life and customs 8. Resilience 9. United States 10. 20th century 11. 1970s 12. Biographies 13. Arts and Entertainment — Comedy 14. Life stories — Arts and culture — Performing arts — Entertainers and celebrities 15. History writing — Women's history

Today, women are ascendant in stand-up comedy, even preeminent. They make headlines, fill arenas, spawn blockbuster movies. But just a few decades ago, the very idea of a female comedian seemed, to most of America, like a punch line. And it took a special sort of woman—indeed, a parade of them—to break and remake the mold. In on the Joke is the story of a group of unforgettable women who knocked down the doors of stand-up comedy so other women could get a shot.

"The book is insightful, moving, and well researched, with humorous anecdotes and fond memories of a group of women Levy clearly admires." —*Library Journal*

Mooney, Paul
Black Is the New White. by Paul Mooney. Simon Spotlight Entertainment 2009. 272 p.
ISBN 9781416587958
Grades: Adult   792.7

1. Mooney, Paul, 1941-2021 2. Television comedy writers 3. African American comedians 4. African-American celebrities 5. Social life and customs 6. United States 7. 21st century 8. Autobiographies and memoirs 9. Biographies 10. Arts and Entertainment — Comedy 11. Life stories — Arts and culture — Performing arts — Entertainers and celebrities

LC 2009019572

A contributor to Chappelle's Show, The Richard Pryor Show, Saturday Night Live, and may other programs recounts his many experiences with Pryor and describes his life as a TV writer, in a memoir that combines personal narrative with sharp, witty social insights.

Nesteroff, Kliph
The Comedians: Drunks, Thieves, Scoundrels, and the History of American Comedy. Kliph Nesteroff. Grove Press 2015. 512 p.
ISBN 9780802123985
Grades: Adult   792.7

1. Stand-up comedy 2. Stand-up comedians 3. Literary criticism 4. Comedians 5. Arts and Entertainment — Comedy

LC 2016479007

Explores and describes the history of stand-up comedy in America—beginning with vaudeville and moving through radio, late-night television, the counter-culture comedy icons of the 1960s, the first stand-up clubs in the 1970s and the cocaine-fueled boom of the 1980s.

"Both pop culture enthusiasts and entertainment scholars will relish this important history of American comedy." —*Library Journal*

Robinson, Phoebe
You Can't Touch My Hair and Other Things I Still Have to Explain. Phoebe Robinson. Penguin Group USA 2016. xxxii, 285 p.
ISBN 9780143129202
Grades: Adult   792.7

1. Robinson, Phoebe 2. Women comedians 3. African American women 4. Racism 5. Television comedy writers 6. Autobiographies and memoirs 7. Life stories — Arts and culture — Performing arts — Entertainers and celebrities 8. Life stories — Identity — Race and ethnicity 9. Antiracist literature 10. Book club best bets

LC 2016018322

Amelia Bloomer List, 2018.

The stand-up comedian and WNYC podcaster offers humorous, poignant essays describing her experience as a Black woman in modern America on topics such as how she's been questioned on her love of Billy Joel and U2 and why you can't touch her hair.

"A thought-provoking collection of essays that will find a welcome home among Black women and general readers who appreciate the humor in everyday situations." —*Library Journal*

Rosenfield, Stephen
Mastering Stand-Up: The Complete Guide to Becoming a Successful Comedian. Stephen Rosenfield. Chicago Review Press 2018. xiv, 256 p.
ISBN 9781613736920
Grades: Adult   792.7

1. Stand-up comedy 2. Arts and Entertainment — Comedy 3. Arts and Entertainment — General

LC Bl2017042209

An entertaining and sharply written guidefor both beginners breaking into comedy and professionals seeking to improve their sets and advance their careersexamines the work of great comedians such as Jerry Seinfeld, Eddie Izzard, Moms Mabley, Hannibal Buress, Sarah Silverman, Richard Pryor and more as a means of illustrating the most important techniques of performing and writing stand-up. Includes index.

Velour, Sasha
★ *The Big Reveal: An Illustrated Manifesto of Drag.* Sasha Velour. Harper 2023. 240 p.
ISBN 9780358508083
Grades: Adult   792.7

1. Velour, Sasha 2. Drag queens 3. Drag shows 4. Female impersonators 5. Gender identity 6. LGBTQIA+ people 7. LGBTQIA+ rights 8. Gay culture 9. Communities 10. Gender expression 11. North American people 12. American people 13. Society and culture — LGBTQIA+ 14. Life stories — Arts and culture — Performing arts 15. Life stories — Identity — LGBTQIA+ 16. Arts and entertainment — General

This book is a quilt, piecing together memoir, history, and theory into a living portrait of an artist and an art. Within these pages, illustrated throughout with photos and original artwork, Sasha Velour illuminates drag as a unique form of expression with a rich history and a revolutionary spirit. Each chapter strips off a new layer to reveal all the twists and turns in the life of a queen. As Sasha recalls her own journey, from the women who raised her, to learning the craft of an artist, to success, disaster, and more, she also uncovers the history of queer life around the world that made it all possible.

"Sasha Velour's memoir is a must-read for fans of drag, advocates of the LGBTQ community, and anyone looking for a path to revealing their truest self." —*Booklist*

Worley, Jennifer
Neon Girls: A Stripper's Education in Protest and Power. Jennifer Worley. HarperPerennial 2020. 261 pages : Illustration
ISBN 9780062971326
Grades: Adult   792.7

1. Worley, Jennifer 2. Stripteasers 3. Women labor unionists 4. Feminism 5. Sexism in employment 6. Women 7. Gender identity 8. Labor unions 9. Labor organizers 10. Nightclubs 11. Political participation 12. Social life and customs 13. San Francisco, California 14. 1990s 15. Autobiographies and memoirs 16. Life stories — Politics — Activists and reformers 17. Society and culture — Sex and sexuality — Sex industry

A former San Francisco stripper gives an account of how she led her fellow dancers to create the first strippers' union in the world and take control of the operation of their club.

"A fast-paced, engaging book that readers with an interest in feminist thought, memoirs, and labor activism will enjoy." —*Library Journal*

Zemeckis, Leslie Harter
Behind the Burly Q: The Story of Burlesque in America. Leslie Zemeckis. Skyhorse Publishing 2013. xxiv, 360 pages : Illustration
ISBN 9781620876916
Grades: Adult   792.7

1. Burlesque 2. Stripteasers 3. Traveling theater 4. Dancers 5. Biographies 6. Arts and Entertainment — Theater

LC 2015302007

Featuring interviews by performers and other notables of the industry, presents the history of American burlesque theater from its golden age through its decline and its current renaissance.

Includes bibliographical references (page 342-344) and index.

792.8 Ballet and modern dance

Alford, Henry
And Then We Danced: A Voyage into the Groove. Henry Alford. Simon & Schuster 2018. 224 p.

ISBN 9781501122255

Grades: Adult   **792.8**

1. Alford, Henry, 1962- 2. Dancers 3. Social life and customs 4. Misadventures 5. Dancing 6. Essays 7. Autobiographies and memoirs 8. Biographies 9. Arts and Entertainment — Dance 10. Humor writing — Social humor

LC 2017044367

A journalist and humorist's story about Zumba leads him to a journey through many forms of dance, including ballet, hip-hop, jazz and ballroom, and how this new passion changed his life.

Angyal, Chloe
Turning Pointe: *How a New Generation of Dancers Is Saving Ballet from Itself.* Chloe Angyal. Bold Type Books 2021. 288 p.

ISBN 9781645036708

Grades: Adult   **792.8**

1. Ballet 2. Dancing 3. Racism 4. Sexism

LC 2020046028

A reckoning with one of our most beloved art forms, whose past and present are shaped by gender, racial, and class inequities—and a look inside the fight for its future.

"Required reading for anyone who loves ballet and cares about its future." —*Library Journal*

Includes bibliographical references and index.

Copeland, Misty
★ *Ballerina* Body: *Dancing and Eating Your Way to a Leaner, Stronger, and More Graceful You.* Misty Copeland, with Charisse Jones; movement and dance photography by Henry Leutwyler, food photography by Amy Roth. Grand Central Life & Style 2017. xii, 226 p. : Color; Illustration

ISBN 9781455569878

Grades: Adult   **792.8**

1. Ballet dancers 2. Arts and Entertainment — Dance 3. Science writing — Medicine and health — Diet and nutrition 4. Science writing — Medicine and health — Exercise

LC OC2018136608

The celebrated ballerina and role model, Misty Copeland, shares the secrets of how to reshape your body and achieve a lean, strong physique and glowing health.

Includes index.

Craine, Debra
The Oxford Dictionary of Dance. Debra Craine, Judith Mackrell. Oxford University Press 2010. VI, 502 p. : Illustration

ISBN 9780199563449

Grades: Adult   **792.8**

1. Ballet 2. Dancing 3. Reference books — Performing arts 4. Arts and Entertainment — Music

LC 2010930321

"Very affordable, it is well worth adding to a dance collection in any library and provides a compact, handy way to access dance facts quickly." —*Booklist*

Previous ed.: 2000; Includes bibliographical references (p. [499]-502).

Hall, Jake
The Art of Drag. Jake Hall; Illustrated by Sofie Birkin, Helen LI, Jasjyot Singh Hans. Nobrow press 2020. 133 pages : Color; Illustration

ISBN 9781910620717

Grades: Adult   **792.8**

1. Drag shows 2. Theater 3. Drag kings 4. Drag queens 5. Gender identity 6. Sexuality 7. Illustrated books 8. History writing — LGBTQIA+ 9. Arts and Entertainment — Theater 10. History writing — Arts and culture 11. Society and culture — LGBTQIA+

LC 2019394940

The history of drag has been formed by many intersections: fashion, theatre, sexuality and politics—all coming together to create the show stopping entertainment millions witness today. In this extensive work, Jake Hall delves deep into the ancient beginnings of drag, to present day and beyond.

"This stylish coffee-table/conversation piece illuminates the history of drag from its ancient roots in mime and traditional theater to the present day." —*Publishers Weekly*

Includes bibliographical references and index.

Homans, Jennifer
★ *Apollo's* Angels: *A History of Ballet.* Jennifer Homans. Random House 2010. 464 p.

ISBN 9781400060603

Grades: Adult   **792.8**

1. Ballet 2. Ballet dancers 3. Dancing 4. Dancers 5. Arts and Entertainment — Dance

LC 2010006945

ALA Notable Book, 2012; New York Times Notable Book, 2010; National Book Critics Circle Award for Nonfiction finalist, 2010.

Unique among the arts, ballet has no written texts or standardized notation. It is a storytelling art passed on from teacher to student. A ballerina dancing today is a link in a long chain of dancers stretching back to sixteenth-century Italy and France: her graceful movements recall a lost world of courts, kings, and aristocracy, but her steps are also marked by the dramatic changes in dance and culture that followed. From ballet's origins in the Renaissance and the codification of its basic steps and positions under France's Louis XIV (himself an avid dancer), the art form wound its way through the courts of Europe, from Paris and Milan to Vienna and St. Petersburg. Jennifer Homans, a historian and critic who was also a professional dancer, traces the evolution of technique, choreography, and performance in clear prose, drawing readers into the intricacies of the art with vivid descriptions of dances and the artists who made them.

"A book of this breadth is going to have its own biorhythms—chapters that engage the author's mind and heart wholly, where everything clicks and the thinking is virtually kinetic, and chapters that don't come as easily. Ms. Homans is at her best when the ideological agenda at hand aspires to discipline, precision and refinement. Her French section is masterful, as are the chapters on the rise of the ballerina, the Danish style, Imperial Russian classicism, and British ballet." —*Wall Street Journal*

Includes bibliographical references.

Jacobs, Laura
★ *Celestial* Bodies: *How to Look at Ballet.* Laura Jacobs. Basic Books 2018. 272 p.

ISBN 9780465098477

Grades: Adult   **792.8**

1. Ballet 2. Choreography 3. Dancing 4. Arts and Entertainment — Dance 5. History writing — Arts and culture

LC 2017051470

In Celestial Bodies, dance critic Laura Jacobs makes the foreign familiar, providing a lively, poetic, and uniquely accessible introduction to the world of classical dance. Combining history, interviews with dancers, technical definitions, descriptions of performances, and personal stories, Jacobs offers an intimate and passionate guide to watching ballet and understanding the central elements of choreography.

"Ballet history, explanations of technique, interviews with dancers, first-person accounts of performances, and personal reflections on a variety of other re-

ESSENTIAL AND RECOMMENDED TITLES
792.809 Ballet and modern dance — History, geographic treatment, biography

lated topics are presented in engaging prose, enhanced by Jessica Roux's delicate illustrations." —*Booklist*

Includes bibliographical references and index.

Kessler, Lauren
Raising the Barre: Big Dreams, False Starts, and My Midlife Quest to Dance the Nutcracker. by Lauren Kessler. Da Capo Press a Member of the Perseus Books Group 2015. 256 p.

ISBN 9780738218311

Grades: Adult   792.8

1. Kessler, Lauren 2. Authors, American 3. Ballet dancers 4. Performance 5. Autobiographies and memoirs 6. Life stories — Personal growth 7. Arts and Entertainment — Dance

LC 2015026258

An award-winning author's journey to turn off the comfortable cruise-control of midlife and reclaim the daring of her girlhood by dancing in the world's most popular ballet, The Nutcracker, with a professional company.

"An amusingly shrewd memoir of following a lifelong dream." —*Kirkus*

Includes bibliographical references and index.

Minden, Eliza Gaynor
The Ballet Companion: A Dancer's Guide to the Technique, Traditions, and Joys of Ballet. Eliza Gaynor Minden. Fireside Book/Simon & Schuster 2005. xv, 331 p. : Illustration; Color

ISBN 9780743264075

Grades: 6 7 8 9 10 11 12 Adult   792.8

1. Arts and Entertainment — Dance 2. Reference books — Handbooks, manuals, etc.

LC 2005044102

An illustrated reference for dancers at all levels shares advice about how to train safely, observe appropriate etiquette, and learn the techniques of accomplished dancers, in a volume complemented by historical information.

A Fireside book; a Lark production; Includes bibliographical references (p. [316]-317) and index.

Morrison, Simon Alexander
Bolshoi Confidential: Secrets of the Russian Ballet from the Rule of the Tsars to Today. Simon Morrison. Liveright Publishing Corporation 2016. 512 p.

ISBN 9780871402967

Grades: Adult   792.8

1. Dance companies 2. Ballet dancers 3. Ballets 4. Russia 5. Arts and Entertainment — Dance

LC 2016031665

Booklist Editors' Choice, 2016.

A history of the Bolshoi Ballet from its beginnings in 1776 to today, describing the careers of those onstage and off, tracing its political ties to the varying Russian regimes, and detailing some of the best-loved ballets in its repertoire.

"A must for ballet buffs. Not the last word on the Bolshoi, but a look backstage that is both lively and learned." —*Kirkus*

Robb, Alice
★ *Don't Think, Dear: On Loving & Leaving Ballet.* Alice Robb. Mariner Books 2023. 320 p.

ISBN 9780358653332

Grades: Adult   792.8

1. Robb, Alice 2. Women ballet dancers 3. Ballet 4. Femininity 5. Dancers 6. Dancing 7. Self perception 8. Body image 9. Child ballet dancers 10. Girls 11. United States 12. Autobiographies and memoirs 13. Life stories — Arts and culture — Performing arts — Dancers and choreographers 14. Arts and Entertainment — Dance

LC 2022040833

A former student at the elite School of American Ballet describes how the strict codes of that world, which included thinness, stoicism and submission, forced her to grapple with the contradictions and challenges of modern womanhood.

"This engaging book will appeal to dance lovers and anyone interested in the entangled nature of patriarchy, race, and ballet. An elegantly incisive, meditative work." —*Kirkus*

Includes bibliographical references and index.

Valby, Karen
The Swans of Harlem: Five Black Ballerinas, Fifty Years of Sisterhood, and Their Reclamation of a Groundbreaking History. Karen Valby. Pantheon Books 2024. 288 p.

ISBN 9780593317525

Grades: Adult   792.8

1. Abarca, Lydia 2. McKinney, Gayle 3. Rohan, Sheila 4. Sells, Marcia Lynn 5. Shelton, Karlya 6. African American ballet dancers 7. African American women 8. Ballet 9. Women ballet dancers 10. Dance teachers 11. Racism 12. Inequality 13. Sisterhood 14. Fame 15. American people 16. Harlem, New York City 17. Collective biographies 18. Life stories — Arts and culture — Performing arts — Dancers and choreographers 19. Life stories — Identity — Race and ethnicity 20. History writing — African American — United States 21. Arts and Entertainment — Dance

LC 2023028575

Steeped in the glamour and grit of professional ballet, this captivating account of five extraordinarily accomplished Black ballerinas, The Swans of Harlem, celebrates both their historic careers and their 50-year sisterhood, offering a window into the history of Black ballet, hidden for too long.

"Valby gives each dancer space for their stories to naturally flow, writing them as fully realized individuals with their own hopes and dreams. A heartwarming addition to performing arts biographies." —*Library Journal*

Includes bibliographical references and index.

792.809 Ballet and modern dance — History, geographic treatment, biography

Fuhrer, Margaret
★ *American Dance: The Complete Illustrated History.* Margaret Fuhrer; foreword by Alicia Graf Mack. Voyageur Press 2014. 288 pages : Illustration; Color

ISBN 9780760345993

Grades: Adult   792.809

1. Modern dance 2. Arts and Entertainment — Dance 3. History writing — United States

LC 2014022261

A lavishly illustrated history of American dance; covers more than four centuries, from Native American ceremonial dances to the early 21st century; written by journalist and dancer Margaret Fuhrer.

A dance sampler that should prompt readers to further explore the multifaceted history of dance and maybe take a class! —*School Library Journal*

Includes bibliographical references (pages 277-279) and index.

792.9 Stage productions

Dromgoole, Dominic
Hamlet Globe to Globe. Dominic Dromgoole. Grove Press 2017. 320 p.

ISBN 9780802125620

Grades: Adult   792.9

1. Shakespeare, William, 1564-1616 2. Acting 3. Theater 4. Drama 5. Arts and Entertainment — Theater

LC 2017001313

New York Times Notable Book, 2017.

From the artistic director of Shakespeare's Globe Theatre in London comes an account of the theater's extraordinary two-year tour bringing Hamlet to every country on Earth, and an exploration of the play's history, meaning and impact.

"Sly, witty, and delightful a glorious Shakespearean romp." —*Kirkus*

PUBLIC LIBRARY CORE COLLECTION: NONFICTION
Twentieth Edition

793.2 Parties and entertainments

Watson, Ted Kennedy
Ted Kennedy Watson's Guide to Stylish Entertaining. Written, styled & photographed by Ted Kennedy Watson; foreword by Lisa Birnbach. Gibbs Smith 2022. 197 p.
ISBN 9781423657293
Grades: Adult   793.2
1. Entertaining 2. Table setting and decoration 3. Beverages 4. Cooking 5. House and Home — Interior decorating and furnishings 6. Food writing — Cooking and cookbooks — Entertaining

Stylish entertaining doesn't require perfection. It's not about flawlessly polished tableware or professionally arranged florals—it's about the small, creative touches that make each event unique. This uniquely informative entertaining/Hosting guide combines stylishly practical advice along with gorgeous photos as well as personal essays & ideas from tastemaker, award-winning retailer, best-selling author and daily blogger Ted Kennedy Watson. Like a trusted friend, he invites you into his homes and shares his secrets honed over the years that are sure to bring you much success and as he would stress, happiness, as you host your next gatherings."

"This will have readers ready to host in no time." —*Publishers Weekly*

793.3 Social, folk, national dancing

Flaherty, Meghan
Tango Lessons: A Memoir. Meghan Flaherty. Houghton Mifflin Harcourt 2018. 320 p.
ISBN 9780544980709
Grades: Adult   793.3
1. Flaherty, Meghan 2. Tango (Dance) 3. Intimacy 4. Dancing 5. Self-discovery 6. Psychic trauma 7. Women dancers 8. New York City 9. Autobiographies and memoirs 10. Life stories — Facing adversity — Personal transformation 11. Arts and Entertainment — Dance

LC 2017046214

Traces the author's decision to overcome trauma-related intimacy issues by taking dance lessons in New York's vibrant tango underground, where she learned unexpected lessons in strength, balance and love. A first book.

793.73 Puzzles and puzzle games

Jacobs, A. J.
The Puzzler: One Man's Quest to Solve the Most Baffling Puzzles Ever, from Crosswords to Jigsaws to the Meaning of Life. AJ Jacobs. Crown 2022. 256 p.
ISBN 9780593136713
Grades: Adult   793.73
1. Jacobs, A. J, 1968- 2. Journalists 3. Puzzles 4. Cognition 5. Thought and thinking 6. Autobiographies and memoirs 7. Life stories — Personal growth 8. Sports and Competition — Games

LC 2021053376

The New York Times bestselling author of The Year of Living Biblically goes on a journey to understand the enduring power of puzzles: Why we love them, what they do to our brains, and how they can improve our world.

A master of immersion journalism unpacks the history of the most popular puzzles, and aims to solve the most impossible head-scratchers, from a mutant Rubik's Cube, to the hardest corn maze in America, to the most sadistic jigsaw.

"This multifaceted memoir explores Jacobs's (Thanks a Thousand) personal relationship with puzzles but also discusses the broader history (and controversies) of puzzles….A fun, interactive exploration of the history and hidden world of puzzles." —*Library Journal*

793.74 Mathematical games and recreations

Stewart, Ian
Professor Stewart's Casebook of Mathematical Mysteries. Ian Stewart. Basic Books, a member of the Perseus Books Group 2014. x, 307 pages : Illustration
ISBN 9780465054978
Grades: Adult   793.74
1. Mathematics 2. Mathematics fun 3. Essays 4. Science writing — Mathematics

LC Bl2014045135

Offers mathematical games, puzzles, facts, and stories that tackle subjects ranging from prime numbers to Pi Day and other mathematical dates.

"Add a few jokes, a few serious applications, and plenty of references for further online exploration, and the result is another fine book from Stewart. Summing Up: Highly recommended. All levels/libraries." —*Choice*

793.8 Magic and related activities

Diaconis, Persi
Magical Mathematics: The Mathematical Ideas That Animate Great Magic Tricks. Persi Diaconis and Ron Graham; with a foreword by Martin Gardner. Princeton University Press 2012. xii, 244 p. : Color illustration
ISBN 9780691151649
Grades: Adult   793.8
1. Card tricks 2. Science writing — Mathematics 3. Arts and Entertainment — General

LC 2011014755

Magical Mathematics reveals the secrets of amazing, fun-to-perform card tricks—and the profound mathematical ideas behind them—that will astound even the most accomplished magician. Persi Diaconis and Ron Graham provide easy, step-by-step instructionsfor each trick, explaining how to set up the effect and offering tips on what to say and do while performing it. Each card trick introduces a new mathematical idea, and varying the tricks in turn takes readers to the very threshold of today's mathematical knowledge. For example, the Gilbreath principle—a fantastic effect where the cards remain in control despite being shuffled—is found to share an intimate connection with the Mandelbrot set. Other card tricks link to the mathematical secrets of combinatorics, graph theory, number theory, topology, the Riemann hypothesis, and even Fermat's last theorem. Diaconis and Graham are mathematicians as well as skilled performers with decades of professional experience between them. In this book they share a wealth of conjuring lore, including some closely guarded secrets of legendary magicians. Magical Mathematics covers the mathematics of juggling and shows how the I Ching connects to the history of probability and magic tricks both old and new. It tells the stories—and reveals the best tricks—of the eccentric and brilliant inventors of mathematical magic. Magical Mathematics exposes old gambling secrets through the mathematics of shuffling cards, explains the classic street-gambling scam of three-card monte, traces the history of mathematical magic back to the thirteenth century and the oldest mathematical trick—and much more.

Includes bibliographical references and index.

Miles, Bryan
101 Magic Tricks: Any Time, Any Place. Bryan Miles. Quarry 2016. 208 p. : Illustration
ISBN 9781631590726
Grades: Adult   793.8
1. Magic tricks 2. Arts and Entertainment — General

LC 2015025881

Presents step-by-step instructions for over one hundred magic tricks. Includes index.

Owen, Oscar
Mind-Blowing Magic Tricks for Everyone. Oscar Owen. Skyhorse Publishing 2021. 156 pages : Illustration
ISBN 9781510763302

ESSENTIAL AND RECOMMENDED TITLES
793.93 Adventure games

Grades: Adult **793.8**
1. Magic tricks 2. Coin tricks 3. Card tricks 4. Magic shows 5. Entertainments 6. Amusements 7. Arts and Entertainment — General

Learn to perform 50 unbelievable magic tricks that will impress and astonish any audience! No special equipment required! This book reveals some of magic's best-kept secrets, showing you step-by-step exactly how the tricks are done from multiple angles.

Posnanski, Joe
★ The *Life and Afterlife of Harry Houdini*. Joe Posnanski. Avid Reader Press 2019. xv, 316 pages : Illustration
ISBN 9781501137235
Grades: Adult **793.8**
1. Houdini, Harry, 1874-1926 2. Magicians 3. Escape artists 4. Legacies 5. Entertainers 6. Magic tricks 7. Performing arts 8. Fans (People) 9. Social life and customs 10. United States 11. 20th century 12. Biographies 13. Life stories — Arts and culture — Performing arts — Entertainers and celebrities 14. Arts and Entertainment — Theater

Award-winning journalist Joe Posnanski enters the world of Harry Houdini and his legions of devoted fans in an immersive, entertaining, and magical work on the illusionist's impact on American culture—and why his legacy endures to this day.

Includes bibliographical references (pages 313-316).

793.93 Adventure games

Barbarisi, Daniel
Dueling with Kings: High Stakes, Killer Sharks, and the Get-Rich Promise of Daily Fantasy Sports. Daniel Barbarisi. Touchstone 2017. 304 p.
ISBN 9781501146176
Grades: Adult **793.93**
1. Barbarisi, Daniel 2. Winning and losing 3. Fantasy sports 4. Fantasy football (Game) 5. Gambling 6. Autobiographies and memoirs 7. Sports and competition — Gambling and betting 8. Life stories — Sports
LC 2016052642

An assessment of the influential world of Daily Fantasy Sports describes the author's decision to quit his reporter job and embark on a quest to join the top percent of DFS shark players, describing the fierce billion-dollar industry of FanDuel, DraftKings and online juggernauts who wager millions every day.

794 Indoor games of skill

Roeder, Oliver
Seven Games: A Human History. Oliver Roeder. W.W. Norton & Company 2022. 272 p.
ISBN 9781324003779
Grades: Adult **794**
1. Board games 2. Card games 3. Games 4. Computer science 5. Technology 6. Machine learning 7. History writing — General 8. Sports and competition — Games
LC 2021038188

A group biography of seven enduring and beloved games, and the story of why—and how—we play them. Checkers, Backgammon, Chess, and Go. Poker, Scrabble, and Bridge. These seven games, ancient and modern, fascinate millions of people worldwide. In Seven Games, Oliver Roeder charts their origins and historical importance, the delightful arcana of their rules, and the behavioral design that make them pleasurable. Roeder introduces thrilling competitors, such as evangelical minister Marion Tinsley, who across forty years lost only three games of checkers; Shusai the Master, the last Go champion of Imperial Japan, defending tradition against "modern rationalism"; and an IBM engineer who created a backgammon program so capable at self-learning that NASA used it on the Space Shuttle. Throughout, Roeder tells the compelling story of how humans, pursuing scientific glory and competitive advantage, have invented AI programs better than any human player, and what that means for the games-and

for us. Funny, fascinating and profound, Seven Games is a story of obsession, psychology, history, and how play makes us human.

"With entertaining cultural profiles of the games of checkers, chess, go, Scrabble, backgammon, poker, and bridge, journalist Roeder (The Riddler) delivers a splashy narrative that successfully argues that games, more than just being forms of entertainment, help individuals develop strategies for navigating daily life. . . . This humanistic look at some of the most popular games in history will have readers hooked." —*Publishers Weekly*

Includes bibliographical references and index.

794.1 Chess

Fischer, Bobby
★ *Bobby* Fischer Teaches Chess. Bobby Fischer, Stuart Margulies, Donn Mosenfelder. Bantam Books 1972. 179 p. : Illustration
ISBN 9780553263152
Grades: Adult **794.1**
1. Chess 2. Arts and Entertainment — General
LC BL 99788921

Programmed text offers experienced as well as beginning players the opportunity to develop chess skills.

Originally published: New York : Xerox Learning Systems, 1966.

794.1092 Chess players

Chapin, Sasha
All the Wrong Moves: A Memoir About Chess, Love, and Ruining Everything. Sasha Chapin. Doubleday 2019. 224 p.
ISBN 9780385545174
Grades: Adult **794.1092**
1. Chapin, Sasha 2. Chess 3. Chess players 4. Journalists 5. Addiction 6. Competition 7. Tournaments 8. Obsession 9. Autobiographies and memoirs 10. Canadian literature 11. Sports and Competition — Games 12. Life stories — Personal growth
LC 2019000510

An award-winning journalist explores the consequences of obsessive addiction through his experiences as an amateur chess enthusiast, revealing how the game consumed his life, compelling two years of international travels in search of grandmaster challenges.

794.6 Bowling

Mullen, Michelle
Bowling Fundamentals. Michelle Mullen. Human Kinetics 2014. xiv, 127 p. : Illustration
ISBN 9781450465809
Grades: 9 10 11 12 Adult **794.6**
1. Bowling 2. Sports and Competition — General
LC 2003013368

Discusses essential skills, tactics and fundamentals-grip, stance, footwork, arm swing, timing, and release—and provides a base for solid technique.

794.8 Electronic games

Bissell, Tom
Extra Lives: Why Video Games Matter. Tom Bissell. Pantheon Books 2010. 240 p.
ISBN 9780307378705
Grades: Adult **794.8**
1. Video Games 2. Popular culture 3. Electronic games 4. Science Writing — Computing, the Internet, and Technology
LC 2009039602

PUBLIC LIBRARY CORE COLLECTION: NONFICTION
Twentieth Edition

Millions of adults spend hours every week playing video games, and the industry itself now reliably out earns Hollywood. But the wider culture seems to regard video games as, at best, well designed if mindless entertainment. Extra Lives is an impassioned defense of this assailed and misunderstood art form. Bissell argues that we are in a golden age of gaming-but he also believes games could be even better. He offers a fascinating and often hilarious critique of the ways video games dazzle and, just as often, frustrate. Along the way, we get firsthand portraits of some of the best minds (Jonathan Blow, Clint Hocking, Cliff Bleszinski, Peter Molyneux) at work in video game design today, as well as a shattering and deeply moving final chapter that describes, in searing detail, Bissell's descent into the world of Grand Theft Auto IV, a game whose themes mirror his own increasingly self-destructive compulsions.

Includes index.

Burak, Asi
Power Play: How Video Games Can Save the World. Asi Burak and Laura Parker. St. Martin's Press 2016. 256 pages

ISBN 9781250089335

Grades: Adult   794.8

1. Video games 2. Social change 3. Education 4. Nonprofit organizations 5. Social movements 6. Social forecasting 7. Learning 8. Open source (Software) 9. Video games industry and trade 10. Business and economics — Industries — Technology 11. Society and culture — Social activism and philanthropy 12. Science Writing — Computing, the Internet, and Technology 13. Business and economics — Industries — Entertainment and media

LC 2016036716

Explores how the Games for Change movement, which uses games as a platform to engage players in current social issues, is spearheading humanitarian and educational efforts around the globe in collaboration with the White House, NASA, the World Bank and the United Nations.

"These compelling examples of games for change are sure to engage gaming enthusiasts, activists, and game studies scholars." —*Library Journal*

McGonigal, Jane
Super Better: A Revolutionary Approach to Getting Stronger, Happier, Braver, and More Resilient*. Jane McGonigal. Penguin Press 2015. xii, 466 pages

ISBN 9781594206368

Grades: Adult   794.8

1. Internet games 2. Resilience 3. Arts and Entertainment — General 4. Science writing — Medicine and health — Psychology 5. Self-Help — Personal growth — Happiness

LC Bl2015032053

A renowned game designer and author of the best-selling Reality Is Broken describes how she recovered from a debilitating concussion by turning her therapeutic process into a digital game that became the subject of a major NIH research study.

*Powered by the science of games; Includes bibliographical references (pages 431-453) and index.

Miller, Megan
★ *The Ultimate* Unofficial Encyclopedia for Minecrafters: An A-Z Book of Tips and Tricks the Official Guides Don't Teach You. Megan Miller. Sky Pony Press 2015. 176 pages : Color; Illustration

ISBN 9781634506984

Grades: 4 5 6 7 8 9 10 11 12 Adult   794.8

1. Minecraft (Game) 2. Strategy 3. Games 4. Video games 5. Computer games 6. Arts and Entertainment — General 7. Sports and Competition — Games 8. Reference — General

LC 2015009136

A guidebook to the popular computer game covers all the best hacks for mining, farming, building, villagers, and the Nether.

Parkin, Simon
An Illustrated History of 151 Video Games: A Detailed Guide to the Most Important Games. Simon Parkin. Lorenz Books 2013. 255 pages : Color; Illustration

ISBN 9780754823902

Grades: Adult   794.8

1. Video games 2. Arts and Entertainment — Painting, Drawing, and Sculpture 3. Arts and Entertainment — General

LC Bl2015000018

Examines the evolution of video games, chronicles the history of gaming, and profiles key titles across all platforms.

Includes index.

Quinn, Zoe
Crash Override: How Gamergate Nearly Destroyed My Life, and How We Can Win the Fight Against Online Hate. Zoe Quinn. Public Affairs 2017. 256 p.

ISBN 9781610398084

Grades: Adult   794.8

1. Cyberbullying 2. Sexism 3. Internet 4. Misogyny 5. Bullies and bullying 6. Harassment 7. Society and culture — Media and technology 8. Adult books for young adults

LC 2017017273

Informed by the game-designer author's highly publicized experience with online harassment, an exploration of the problems of Internet abuse offers solutions for lawmakers, police, parents, corporations and individuals.

"She elevates diverse voices in her engaging, often-humorous writing. Whether readers are Internet devotees or not, Quinns writing provides important context for our increasingly online lives." —*Booklist*

Ruberg, Bonnie
★ *The Queer* Games Avant-Garde: How LBGTQ Game Makers Are Reimagining the Medium of Video Games. Bonnie Ruberg. 2020. 276 pages

ISBN 9781478005919

Grades: Adult   794.8

1. Video games 2. Gay culture 3. Gender identity 4. Queer theory 5. Video games industry and trade 6. Interviews 7. Society and culture — LGBTQIA+ 8. Society and culture — Gender

LC 2019041791

Stonewall Book Awards: Israel Fishman Non-fiction Award, 2021.

Through a series of interview-based profiles of influential and innovative contemporary LGBTQ game-makers and activists, The Queer Games Avant-Garde explores the queer gaming world as an artistic and social movement.

Includes bibliographical references and index.

795.4 Card games

Ho, Oliver
The Ultimate Book of Family Card Games. Oliver Ho. Sterling Children's Books 2012. x, 118 p. : Color illustration

ISBN 9781402750410

Grades: Adult   795.4

1. Card games 2. Games 3. Amusements 4. Playing cards 5. Children 6. Recreation 7. Sports and recreation — Games, puzzles, and play

LC 2010026522

Presents a collection of fifty card games, organized by type and difficulty, and complete with instructions, rules, and strategies.

Includes index.

795.41 Games in which skill is a major element

Hellmuth, Phil
Play Poker Like the Pros. Phil Hellmuth, Jr. Quill 2003. xviii, 394 p. : Illustration (A HarperResource book)

ESSENTIAL AND RECOMMENDED TITLES
795.412 Poker

ISBN 9780060005726
Grades: Adult   **795.41**
1. Poker 2. Arts and Entertainment — General
LC 2002032703

Describes the rules and basic and advanced strategies for a variety of poker games and includes tips on reading other players and beating online poker games.
Includes index.

McManus, James
★ *Positively Fifth Street: Murderers, Cheetahs, and Binion's World Series of Poker.* James McManus. Farrar, Straus, Giroux 2003. 422 p. : Illustration
ISBN 9780374236489
Grades: Adult   **795.41**
1. Binion, Ted, died 1998 2. Poker players 3. Trials (Murder) 4. Gamblers 5. Card games 6. Poker 7. Tournaments 8. Las Vegas, Nevada 9. Sports and Competition — Gambling and Betting 10. Sports and Competition — Games
LC 2002033882

New York Times Notable Book, 2003.

A chronicle of life in Las Vegas investigates the murder of poker player Ted Binion, revealing a secret world of kinky sex, black magic, and science lurking at the heart of gambling's World Series of Poker.

"McManus went to Las Vegas in May 2000 on assignment for Harper's to cover the World Series of Poker. He was to throw in coverage of the trial of Sandy Murphy, an ex-stripper, and her boyfriend, Rick Tabish, accused of murdering Ted Binion, the tournament's host. To satisfy his own gambling urge, McManus enter the poker competition and spends 10 days immersed in the culture of Vegas and gambling, rendering a fast-paced, riveting account of his progress through the tournament. A delicious inside look." —*Booklist*

Includes bibliographical references (p. [399]-403) and index.

795.412 Poker

Konnikova, Maria
The Biggest Bluff: How I Learned to Pay Attention, Master the Odds, and Win. Maria Konnikova. Penguin Press 2020. 400 p.
ISBN 9780525522621
Grades: Adult   **795.412**
1. Konnikova, Maria 2. Seidel, Erik, 1959- 3. Poker players 4. Human behavior 5. Mentors 6. Psychologists 7. Poker 8. Psychology 9. Gambling 10. United States 11. Autobiographies and memoirs 12. Society and culture — Psychology and human behavior 13. Sports and Competition — Gambling and Betting 14. Life stories — Sports 15. Business and economics — Popular psychology
LC 2020002627

New York Times Notable Book, 2020.

How a New York Times bestselling author and New Yorker contributor parlayed a strong grasp of the science of human decision-making and a woeful ignorance of cards into a life-changing run as a professional poker player, under the wing of a legend of the game.

"A smart and subtle delight—highly recommended for fans of cards and brain-hacking alike." —*Kirkus*

Includes index.

796 Athletic and outdoor sports and games

Cox, Michael
Zonal Marking: From Ajax to Zidane, the Making of Modern Soccer. Michael Cox. Bold Type Books 2019. 440 p.
ISBN 9781568589336
Grades: Adult   **796**
1. Soccer 2. Professional soccer 3. Soccer teams 4. Soccer players 5. Sports organizations 6. Strategy 7. Sports history 8. Europe 9. Sports and Competition — Soccer 10. Sports and Competition — Sports History

A respected soccer journalist presents this exciting tour of the game's most innovative teams and their unique contributions and tactics, tracing the development of soccer in the modern era.
Includes bibliographical references and index.

Crouse, Karen
Norwich: One Tiny Vermont Town's Secret to Happiness and Excellence. Karen Crouse. Simon & Schuster 2018. 272 p.
ISBN 9781501119897
Grades: Adult   **796**
1. Sports 2. Olympic athletes 3. Athletes 4. Growing up 5. Self-fulfillment in children 6. Vermont 7. Society and culture — Psychology and human behavior 8. History writing — Regional history — United States
LC 2017012269

Traces the history and achievements of the small Vermont community that has likely produced more Olympians per capita than any other place in the country, assessing its model for achieving excellence and a well-rounded life based on the counterintuitive practices of moderate competition, inclusion regardless of talent, and emphasis on childhood fun.

"Short and sweet, this important book highlights what's wrong with youth sports by focusing on a community that gets it right." —*Publishers Weekly*

Includes bibliographical references and index.

Litman, Laken
Strong Like a Woman: 100 Game-Changing Female Athletes. Laken Litman; foreword by Billie Jean King; introduction by Stephen Cannella. Universe 2022. 256 pages : Illustration; Color
ISBN 9780789341198
Grades: Adult   **796**
1. Women athletes 2. Sports and Competition — General
LC 2021946570

Marking the 50th anniversary of Title IX, this is an inspiring celebration of 100 women who are still paving the way for future generations of female athletes. This important and groundbreaking volume chronicles both the breadth and rich diversity of sports and the athletes who compete in them: from the global stage of the Olympics and the Paralympics and the Women's World Cup, to collegiate athletics, to Gen-X sports. From Janet Guthrie to Megan Rapinoe, and Billie Jean King to Aly Raisman, this is the ideal gift book for anyone involved with girls in athletics, whether as an athlete or coach, parent, daughter, sister, niece, or granddaughter.

Includes bibliographical references (pages 252-256).

Pesca, Mike
Upon Further Review: The Greatest What-ifs in Sports History. Mike Pesca. Twelve 2018. 320 p.
ISBN 9781455540365
Grades: Adult   **796**
1. Sports 2. Options, alternatives, choices 3. Athletes 4. Fans (People) 5. Essays 6. Media tie-ins 7. Sports and Competition — General
LC 2017041897

The host of The Gist podcast shares perspectives by some of history's greatest sports minds on how the world might have changed if iconic plays, trades, injuries or referee's calls had gone the other way.

Based on a podcast.

Rhoden, William C.
$40 Million Slaves: The Rise, Fall, and Redemption of the Black Athlete. William C. Rhoden. Crown Publishers 2006. xiii, 286 p. : Illustration
ISBN 9780609601204
Grades: Adult   **796**
1. Sports 2. Racism in sports 3. African American athletes 4. Social life and customs 5. United States 6. 19th century 7. 20th century 8. Sports and Competition — General 9. Adult books for young adults 10. History writing — African American — Civil rights — United States
LC 2005034952

A critical analysis of race, politics, and the history of American sports traces the origins and evolution of the Black athlete, arguing that every advance by Black athletes has been countered by a definite setback and that Black youngsters who are brought into big-time programs are cut off from their heritage and exploited by the media, team owners, and others.

Includes bibliographical references (p. 277-278) and index.

796.01 Sports — Philosophy

Afremow, James A.
The Champion's Mind: How Great Athletes Think, Train, and Thrive. Jim Afremow, PhD; foreword by Jim Craig, goalie for the 1980 U.S.. Rodale 2013. xvi, 269 pages
ISBN 9781623361488
Grades: Adult 796.01
1. Physical education and training 2. Sports 3. Sports and Competition — General

LC 2013032605

A sports psychologist offers tips and techniques for athletes looking to get into the "zone" while working with their team and offers fully customizable pre-performance routines to help athletes be ready to go at full-throttle when the game starts.

Includes bibliographical references (pages 249-251) and index.

Parry, John Weston
The Burden of Sports: How and Why Athletes Struggle with Mental Health. John Weston Parry. Rowman & Littlefield 2024. 296 p.
ISBN 9781538175538
Grades: Adult 796.01
1. Sports 2. Athletes 3. Mental health 4. Mass media and sports 5. Sports spectators 6. Social life and customs 7. Sports and competition — General 8. Science Writing — Medicine and health — Mental health

LC 2023027672

This book looks at how sports negatively impact the mental health and emotional well-being of athletes as well as the reactions of spectators and media to these athletes' struggles.

"It would be hard to find a current work in this area more thorough and complete than Parry's. Timely and important, this title has the potential to change the sports industry worldwide." —*Library Journal*

Includes bibliographical references and index.

Rotella, Robert J.
How Champions Think: In Sports and in Life. Dr. Bob Rotella, with Bob Cullen. Simon & Schuster 2015. 290 pages : Illustration
ISBN 9781476788623
Grades: Adult 796.01
1. Athletes 2. Sports 3. Success (Concept) 4. Psychology 5. Self-Help — Personal growth 6. Self-Help — Personal growth — Motivation 7. Sports and Competition — General

LC 2014044600

A preeminent sports psychologist shares his years of in-depth research and practical experience in a guide that aims to help readers achieve success in all aspects of their lives.

The preeminent sports psychologist and best-selling author, who has advised everyone from professional golfers to NBA superstars to business executives, shares his years of in-depth research and practical experience in a revolutionary guide that will help readers achieve success in all aspects of their lives.

"Rotella's liberal use of sports anecdotes and an effective piece on a coach's perspective (Kentucky basketball coach John Calipari) further underscore the importance of the core set of philosophies and behaviors he promotes, although his frequent and distractive allusions to faith and religion as one of the linchpins to an athlete's or a team's success may not appeal to more secular readers. A solid motivational text for the sports-minded and those interested in the bridging of athletics and exceptionalism." —*Kirkus*

Wertheim, L. Jon
This Is Your Brain on Sports. L. Jon Wertheim and Sam Sommers. Crown Archetype 2016. 272 p.
ISBN 9780553447408
Grades: Adult 796.01
1. Sports 2. Professional sports 3. Athletes 4. Winning and losing 5. Human behavior 6. Cognition and culture 7. Professional athletes 8. Competition 9. Neurology 10. Nationalism 11. Sports and Competition — General 12. Society and culture — Psychology and human behavior

LC 2015021731

The executive editor of Sports Illustrated and a psychologist join forces to examine the behavior of those involved in professional sports, explaining how athletes can successfully put aside personal trauma on game day and why people love to root for a loser.

"If sport s bring out the kooky, spooky, and creepy in us, Wertheim and Sommers give us a chance to understand ourselves and perhaps get a grip before we totally lose it." —*Kirkus*

Includes bibliographical references.

796.04 General kinds of sports and games

Nocera, Joseph
Indentured: The Inside Story of the Rebellion Against the NCAA. Joe Nocera and Ben Strauss. Portfolio 2016. IX, 369 p.
ISBN 9781591846321
Grades: Adult 796.04
1. College sports 2. College athletes

LC 2015044500

Asserts that the NCAA is a cartel that has acted to prevent college athletes from receiving any money for their labors, discussing the legal push to bring down this morally corrupt and hypocritical organization.

"Championship-level reporting on the boundaries of sport and business." —*Kirkus*

Includes index.

Schoenfeld, Bruce
★ *Game of Edges: The Analytics Revolution and the Future of Professional Sports.* Bruce Schoenfeld. W.W. Norton & Company, Inc. 2023. 288 p.
ISBN 9780393531688
Grades: Adult 796.04
1. Professional sports 2. Data processing 3. Technological innovations 4. Sports 5. Business and economics — Industries 6. Sports and competition — General

LC 2023009924

The story of how a new generation of tech-savvy franchise owners is reshaping every aspect of professional sports.

"A worthy spiritual sequel to Moneyball, this makes for a bracing look at a fundamental shift in professional sports." —*Publishers Weekly*

Includes index.

796.043 College sports

McIntire, Mike
Champions Way: Football, Florida, and the Lost Soul of College Sports. Mike McIntire. Norton 2017. 256 p.
ISBN 9780393292619
Grades: Adult 796.043
1. College sports 2. Universities and colleges 3. College athletes 4. Corruption 5. Whistle blowers 6. College football 7. Rape in universities and colleges 8. Florida 9. Society and culture — Education — Higher education 10. Sports and Competition — Football

LC 2017017863

A searing expose of how the multibillion dollar college sports empire fails universities, students, and athletes.

ESSENTIAL AND RECOMMENDED TITLES
796.06 Organizations, facilities, management

"McIntire summarizes the history of college sports and the social and economic culture of football in American universities, particularly in the South, convincingly arguing that these transgressions are widespread." —*Publishers Weekly*

796.06 Organizations, facilities, management

Kohan, Rafi
The Arena: Inside the Tailgating, Ticket-Scalping, Mascot-Racing, Dubiously Funded, and Possibly Haunted Monuments of American Sport. Rafi Kohan. Liveright Publishing Corporation 2017. 416 p.
ISBN 9781631491276
Grades: Adult 796.06
1. Stadiums 2. Sports 3. Sports facilities 4. Sports and competition — General 5. History writing — Arts and culture
LC 2017015161

Rafi Kohan's The Arena is a vivid exploration of what it's like behind the scenes at a modern American sports stadium, from tailgating and ticket scalpers to halftime shows and local traditions. It also includes a look at the role that big-ticket sports plays in both U.S. culture and local economies. Mixing humor, hands-on research, and sociological analysis, this is an entertaining and edifying look at sports as entertainment—and business.

"Kohan's curiosity and empathy are infectious as he demonstrates how human this corporate aspect of sports can be. He has created an immersive, informative work that will delight and enlighten a wide range of readers." —*Publishers Weekly*

796.07 Education, research, related topics

Davis, Seth
Getting to Us: How Great Coaches Make Great Teams. Seth Davis. Penguin Group USA 2018. 320 pages : Illustration
ISBN 9780735222724
Grades: Adult 796.07
1. Athletic coaches 2. Coaching (Athletics) 3. Sports 4. Sports and competition — Coaches
LC 2018285542

The acclaimed sports commentator and author of the best-selling When March Went Mad presents a guide for coaching leadership that identifies the characteristics of exemplary coaches and how to implement the examples of such forefront individuals as Urban Meyer, Dabot Swinney and Brad Stevens.

"Each chapter includes interviews with the selected coach, along with relatives, mentors, assistants, and former players as Davis relates the subject's life, career, and method. Although the coaches' styles vary from Harbaugh's in-your-face intensity to Boeheim's aloof practicality to Swinney's loquacious empathy, the nine essays fit together with what Davis views as the common keys to successful coaching." —*Library Journal*

Walker, Sam
The Captain Class: The Hidden Force That Creates the World's Greatest Teams. Sam Walker. Random House Inc 2017. 304 p.
ISBN 9780812997194
Grades: Adult 796.07
1. Sports teams 2. Athletes 3. Sportsmanship 4. Success (Concept) 5. Sports and competition — General 6. Society and culture — Psychology and human behavior 7. Business and economics — Business advice
LC 2016054597

A former Wall Street Journal global sports editor reveals the essential contributions of unconventional players behind the world's highest-performing sports teams, explaining how their unofficial leadership examples and counterintuitive strategies helped enable remarkable, long-term successes.

"Written for serious sports fans in lively language that also speaks to aspiring athletes and business professionals, this book offers a compelling argument for the value of inspired leadership." —*Publishers Weekly*

796.08 Groups of people

Thomas, Etan
We Matter: Athletes and Activism. Etan Thomas. Akashic 2018. 250 p.
ISBN 9781617755910
Grades: Adult 796.08
1. Athletes 2. Social advocacy 3. African Americans 4. Political activists 5. Social participation 6. Political participation 7. Sports 8. African American athletes 9. Former basketball players 10. Race relations 11. United States 12. Essays 13. Society and culture — Race 14. Sports and Competition — General 15. Adult books for young adults
LC 2017936007

Library Journal Best Books, 2018.

In interviews and essays, high-profile activist athletes explore the intersection of sports and politics.

"Recommended for not only high school and college students but all readers concerned with social activism and awareness. An excellent resource to spark discussions and motivate positive community expression and involvement." —*Library Journal*

796.082 Outdoor recreation — Women

Allred, Alexandra Powe
When Women Stood: The Untold History of Females Who Changed Sports and the World. Alexandra Allred. Rowman & Littlefield Publishing Group 2023. 320 p.
ISBN 9781538171349
Grades: Adult 796.082
1. Women athletes 2. Women's sports 3. Sex discrimination in sports 4. United States 5. Sports and Competition — General 6. Society and culture — Gender — Women
LC 2022025379

When Women Stood is an unapologetically new sport and social history that unveils the often-overlooked chronicle of women and their fight for equality. From early Amazons and suffragists to modern-day athletes and social influencers, this is an eye-opening history of women told through the always-influential world of sports.

"Allred's prose is direct, and she lucidly explains how these pioneers have challenged gender and racial stereotypes. The result is an enlightening account of women trailblazers." —*Publishers Weekly*

Includes bibliographical references and index.

Barnes, Katie
★ *Fair Play: How Sports Shape the Gender Debates.* Katie Barnes. St. Martin's Press 2023. 288 p.
ISBN 9781250276629
Grades: Adult 796.082
1. Women and sports 2. Sports 3. Sex discrimination in sports 4. Sex discrimination against women 5. Stereotypes 6. Sports journalism 7. Women athletes 8. Gender identity 9. Transgender people 10. Athletes 11. Intersex people 12. LGBTQIA+ people 13. Sports and competition — Sports history 14. Society and culture — LGBTQIA+
LC 2023022817

An award-winning LGBTQ+ journalist traces the evolution of women's sports as a pastime and a political arena, where equality and fairness have been fought over for generations, and discusses the controversy surrounding trans athletes and the much-needed solution that seeks to preserve opportunities for all going forward.

"Through interviews, deep research, and thoughtful observations, Barnes provides much-needed clarification on a topic that too often leads to confusion and discomfort. An important study on the policing of gender." —*Booklist*

Includes bibliographical references and index.

PUBLIC LIBRARY CORE COLLECTION: NONFICTION
Twentieth Edition

796.083 Outdoor recreation — Young people

Striniste, Nancy
Nature Play at Home: Creating Outdoor Spaces That Connect Children with the Natural World. Nancy Striniste; illustrations by Jen Ren. Timber Press 2019. 288 p.
ISBN 9781604698251
Grades: Adult   796.083
1. Outdoor recreation for children 2. Nature study 3. Play 4. House and Home — Outdoor areas
LC 2018038898

Access to technology has created a generation of children who are more plugged in than ever before—often with negative consequences. But there is a solution. Unrestricted outdoor play helps reduce stress, improve health, and enhance creativity, learning, and attention span. In Nature Play at Home, Nancy Striniste gives you the tools you need to make outdoor adventures possible in your own backyard. With hundreds of inspiring ideas and illustrated, step-by-step projects, this hardworking book details how to create playspaces that use natural materials—like logs, boulders, sand, water, and plants of all kinds. Projects include hillside slides, seating circles, sand pits, and more.

"Adults and children will delight in working together to build creations like hillside slides, mosaic streams, insect hotels, a living willow tunnel, and even a bamboo bower. Nature Play at Home is sure to inspire readers to take action in their backyards and encourage creative play in nature for years to come." —*Booklist*

Includes bibliographical references and index.

796.087 People with disabilities and illnesses, gifted people

Shriver, Timothy P.
Fully Alive: Discovering What Matters Most. Timothy P. Shriver. Sarah Crichton Books 2014. 304 p.
ISBN 9780374280918
Grades: Adult   796.087
1. Shriver, Timothy P. 2. Shriver family 3. Special Olympics 4. Athletes with disabilities 5. People with disabilities 6. People with developmental disabilities 7. Growing up 8. Sports 9. Autobiographies and memoirs 10. Life stories — People in history — Famous families 11. Sports and competition — Olympic sports
LC 2014020245

The chairman of Special Olympics shares inspiring stories about athletes with intellectual disabilities who have become champions in the face of seeming powerlessness and vulnerability, sharing additional insight into the Shriver family and their dedication to advocacy.

"Sincere, profound and deeply satisfying." —*Kirkus*

796.09 Sports — History

Wertheim, L. Jon
Glory Days: The Summer of 1984 and the 90 Days That Changed Sports and Culture Forever. L. Jon Wertheim. Houghton Mifflin Harcourt 2021. 288 p.
ISBN 9781328637246
Grades: Adult   796.09
1. Sports 2. Sports history 3. Professional sports 4. United States 5. 1980s 6. 20th century 7. Sports and Competition — Sports History
LC 2020033845

Looks at the sports stories that converged in the summer of 1984—the rise of Michel Jordan, ESPN's increasing media dominance, the Los Angeles Olympics and more—that shaped sports into the multimillion dollar industry of today.

"In the middle of the over-the-top 1980s, a span of 90 days in the summer of 1984 changed the course of American history, writes journalist Wertheim (Sports Illustrated). . . . Historians, sports fans, and any readers interested in American culture will find this a fascinating look at three months with lasting implications." —*Library Journal*

Includes bibliographical references and index.

796.092 Athletes

Walters, Billy
Gambler: Secrets from a Life at Risk. Billy Walters. Avid Reader 2023. 384 p.
ISBN 9781668032855
Grades: Adult   796.092
1. Walters, Billy 2. Sports betting 3. Gambling 4. Bets 5. Gamblers 6. Autobiographies and memoirs 7. Life stories — General 8. Sports and competition — Gambling and betting

The man described as "the Michael Jordan of sports betting" passes along everything he's learned about sports betting and show bettors how to use the information we all have at our fingertips to develop a sophisticated betting strategy.

"Warranted or not, the sour grapes will be less interesting for most readers than Walters' tips on how to gamble, which amount to warnings that almost any approach will lead to losses unless a person is willing to make a full-time job of doing legwork and research, learning how to handicap and acquiring other skills." —*Kirkus*

796.1 Miscellaneous games

Barbarisi, Daniel
Chasing the Thrill: Obsession, Death, and Glory in America's Most Extraordinary Treasure Hunt. Daniel Barbarisi. Alfred A. Knopf 2021. 368 p.
ISBN 9780525656173
Grades: Adult   796.1
1. Fenn, Forrest 2. Barbarisi, Daniel 3. Art dealers 4. Treasure troves 5. Codes (Communication) 6. Treasure hunters 7. Journalists 8. Searching 9. Competition 10. Obsession 11. Rocky Mountains 12. United States 13. Life stories — General 14. Travel Writing — United States 15. Adventure writing — General 16. Nonfiction that reads like fiction
LC 2020039356

When Forrest Fenn was told he was going to die, he came up with a plan to hide a chest full of jewels and gold in the wilderness, and publish a poem that would serve as a map leading to the treasure's secret location. Daniel Barbarisi first learned of Fenn's hunt in 2017 when a friend began decoding the poem and convinced Barbarisi to catalogue his search. What began as a great story documenting the history of Fenn's treasure hunt—the rumors, characters, and pitfalls—quickly turned into a personal quest, as Barbarisi found himself on a sometimes reckless and potentially dangerous path, despite having a family at home. Over the course of the next three years, several searchers would die, endless controversies would erupt, and one anonymous unknown would find the ultimate prize.

"Reminiscent of Douglas Preston's adventures, this modern-day treasure hunt is an entertaining thrill ride." —*Library Journal*

796.2 Activities and games requiring equipment

Gessner, David
Ultimate Glory: Frisbee, Obsession, and My Wild Youth. David Gessner. Riverhead Books 2017. 304 p.
ISBN 9780735210561
Grades: Adult   796.2
1. Gessner, David, 1961- 2. Competition 3. Athletes 4. Outdoor games 5. Sports 6. Frisbee (Game) 7. Training 8. Autobiographies and memoirs 9. Sports and Competition — General 10. Life stories — Sports
LC 2016048991

An acclaimed essayist and nature writer describes how he spent his youth playing Ultimate Frisbee and the fierce competition, camaraderie and epic par-

ESSENTIAL AND RECOMMENDED TITLES
796.323 Basketball

ties he survived while trying to win the national competition in a largely misunderstood sport.

"An anecdotal tour of a sport that has only been around for a few decades but that claims legions of adherents." —*Kirkus*

796.323 Basketball

Abdurraqib, Hanif
★ *There's Always This Year: On Basketball and Ascension.* Hanif Abdurraqib. Random House 2024. 336 p.
ISBN 9780593448793
Grades: Adult   **796.323**
1. Abdurraqib, Hanif, 1983- 2. African American authors 3. Basketball 4. Growing up 5. Basketball fans 6. Basketball players 7. Family relationships 8. Marginalized people 9. Social life and customs 10. Identity 11. Love 12. Loyalty 13. Home (Concept) 14. Ohio 15. 1990s 16. Family and Relationships — Growing up 17. Sports and Competition — Basketball 18. History writing — Regional history — United States
LC 2023025674

LibraryReads Favorites, 2024.

While Hanif Abdurraqib is an acclaimed author, a gifted poet, and one of our culture's most insightful music critics, he is most of all, at heart, an Ohioan. Growing up in Columbus in the '90s, Abdurraqib witnessed a golden era of basketball, one in which legends like LeBron were forged, and countless others weren't. His lifelong love of the game leads Abdurraqib into a lyrical, historical, and emotionally rich exploration of what it means to make it, who we think deserves success, the tensions between excellence and expectation, and the very notion of role-models, all of which he expertly weaves together with memoir.

"The acclaimed poet and cultural critic uses his lifelong relationship with basketball to muse on the ways in which we grow attached to our hometowns, even when they fail us…An innovative memoir encompassing sports, mortality, belonging, and home." —*Kirkus*

Includes index.

Abrams, Jonathan P. D.
Boys Among Men: How the Prep-to-Pro Generation Redefined the NBA and Sparked a Basketball Revolution. Jonathan Abrams. Crown Archetype 2016. 336 p.
ISBN 9780804139250
Grades: Adult   **796.323**
1. Basketball players 2. College basketball players 3. Sports and Competition — Basketball
LC 2015027590

Explores the trend of teenage basketball stars skipping college and going right into playing professionally, resulting in the 2005 age limit requirement instituted by the NBA, mandating that all players must attend college or another developmental program for at least a year.

"[T]his essential, well-researched book will appeal to readers interested in basketball's business side as well as the factors that have helped shape the modern NBA." —*Library Journal*

Blais, Madeleine
In These Girls, Hope Is a Muscle. Madeleine Blais. Warner Books 1996. VI, 266 p.
ISBN 9780446672108
Grades: 11 12 Adult   **796.323**
1. High school basketball 2. Basketball for children 3. Girls 4. Sports and Competition — Basketball 5. Sports and Competition — Teams
LC 95034477

YALSA Best Books for Young Adults, 1996; National Book Critics Circle Award for Nonfiction finalist, 1995.

A look at the trials and triumphs of high school girls' basketball chronicles one season of the Lady Hurricanes of Amherst, Massachusetts, as they learn loyalty and self-confidence on their way to a championship game.

"Alternately funny, exciting and moving, the book should be enjoyed not only by girls and women who have played sports but also those who wanted to but let themselves be discouraged." —*Publishers Weekly*

Originally published: New York : Atlantic Monthly Press, c1995.

Bradburd, Rus
All the Dreams We've Dreamed: A Story of Hoops and Handguns on Chicago's West Side. Rus Bradburd. Lawrence Hill Books 2018. 265 p.
ISBN 9781613739310
Grades: Adult   **796.323**
1. Harrington, Shawn 2. Urban violence 3. African American basketball players 4. Basketball coaches 5. Basketball 6. Guns 7. Race relations 8. Inner city violence 9. Society and culture — Violence and crime 10. True Crime — Organized Crime, Mafia, and Gangs 11. Society and culture — Race 12. Adult books for young adults
LC 2017054197

Booklist Editors' Choice, 2018.

A tale of courage, endurance, and friendship in one of America's most violent neighborhoods follows the experiences of coach Shawn Harrington and his John Marshall High School team over a series of three years marked by murder, racism, and corruption.

Chansky, Art
Blue Blood II: Duke-Carolina: The Latest on the Never-Ending and Greatest Rivalry in College Hoops. Art Chansky. St Martins Press 2018. 320 p.
ISBN 9781250193278
Grades: Adult   **796.323**
1. College basketball 2. Sports rivalry 3. College sports 4. North Carolina 5. Sports and Competition — Basketball 6. Sports and Competition — Rivalry
LC 2018410335

This follow-up to Blue Blood, published 13 years after the first book, tells the recent history of the Duke-Carolina college basketball rivalry and is a must-have for Duke and UNC fans, as well as college basketball fans in general.

Colton, Larry
Counting Coup: A True Story of Basketball and Honor on the Little Big Horn. Larry Colton. Warner Books 2000. 420 p.
ISBN 9780446526838
Grades: 11 12 Adult   **796.323**
1. Basketball for women 2. Indigenous athletes 3. Teenage girls 4. Indigenous women 5. High school students 6. Crow (Apsáalooke) (North American people) 7. Basketball 8. Indigenous peoples of North America — Social conditions 9. Indigenous peoples of North America 10. Montana 11. Biographies 12. Sports and Competition — Basketball 13. Sports and Competition — Teams 14. Adult books for young adults
LC 00024987

Alex Award, 2001; Booklist Editors' Choice: Adult Books for Young Adults, 2000; YALSA Best Books for Young Adults, 2002.

Profiles a Montana high-school girls' basketball team—made up of Crow Indian and white girls from a rural town—that carries on its shoulders the dreams and hopes of a Native American tribe during their winning season.

Includes index.

Dohrmann, George
★ *Play Their Hearts Out: A Coach, His Star Recruit, and the Youth Basketball Machine.* George Dohrmann. Balantine Books 2010. 416 p.
ISBN 9780345508607
Grades: 10 11 12 Adult   **796.323**
1. Keller, Joe 2. Walker, Demetrius 3. Basketball coaches 4. Basketball 5. Basketball players 6. Sports and Competition — Basketball
LC 2010015470

Pulitzer Prize-winning journalist George Dohrmann's remarkable debut offers an up-close and unforgettable narrative that reveals the gritty reality hiding behind the romanticized hoop dreams of America's basketball prodigies.

PUBLIC LIBRARY CORE COLLECTION: NONFICTION
Twentieth Edition

Feinstein, John
★ *The* **Back** *Roads to March: The Unsung, Unheralded, and Unknown Heroes of a College Basketball Season.* by John Feinstein. Doubleday 2020. 304 p.
ISBN 9780385544481
Grades: Adult   **796.323**
1. Basketball teams 2. College basketball players 3. College basketball 4. College basketball coaches 5. College sports 6. Competition 7. Sports and competition — Basketball
LC 2019047926

Sports journalist John Feinstein returns to his first love—college basketball—with a fascinating and compelling journey through a landscape of unsung, unpublicized and often unknown heroes of Division-1 college hoops.
"Feinstein writes with warmth and enthusiasm of a beloved sport in a book that will grab any fan." —*Kirkus*
Includes index.

★ *Last Dance: Behind the Scenes at the Final Four.* John Feinstein. Little, Brown 2006. 375 p.
ISBN 9780316160308
Grades: Adult   **796.323**
1. College basketball players 2. College basketball 3. Basketball tournaments 4. Basketball teams 5. College athletes 6. College basketball coaches 7. Basketball history 8. United States 9. Sports and Competition — Basketball 10. Adult books for young adults
LC 2005028478

A portrait of the NCAA Final Four competition is presented from the perspectives of schools, coaches, and players who have made it to college basketball's final weekend, in a collection that also includes accounts by officials, referees, and scouts.
"The author employs the 2005 [Final Four] weekend as the catalyst to discuss the history of the event, the key people, and, most significantly, the effect that involvement in the Final Four has had on participants' lives. The anecdotes are entertaining, and the insights into the tournament's logistics fascinating, but what will linger most are the remembrances of players, especially those who ended up on the losing side." —*Booklist*
Includes index.

A **March** *to Madness: The View from the Floor in the Atlantic Coast Conference.* John Feinstein. Little, Brown and Co. 1998. xvii, 464 p. : Illustration
ISBN 9780316277402
Grades: 11 12 Adult   **796.323**
1. Basketball 2. College basketball 3. College sports 4. Basketball teams 5. Basketball coaches 6. College basketball coaches 7. Sports and Competition — Basketball 8. Sports and Competition — Sports History
LC 97031060

Follows the eventful 1996-1997 season in college basketball's most competitive league, the Atlantic Coast Conference, offering behind-the-scenes portraits of the nine top teams and coaches in action.
"Feinstein covers one year with all of the teams in the perennially powerful Atlantic Coast Conference. After introducing each of the schools, their teams, their coaches, and their expectations for the 1996/97 basketball season, the book describes their progress week by week, culminating with Dean Smith's run to the NCAA Final Four. Such a detailed accounting of a sports season could seem interminable to readers, but Feinstein has again produced a narrative that is not only interesting but often exciting." —*Library Journal*
Includes index.

Fury, Shawn
Rise and *Fire: The Origins, Science, and Evolution of the Jump Shot — and How It Transformed Basketball Forever.* Shawn Fury. Flatiron Books 2016. 288 p.
ISBN 9781250062161
Grades: Adult   **796.323**
1. Basketball 2. Basketball players 3. Basketball history 4. Sports and Competition — Basketball
LC 2015040454

An analysis of the play that revolutionized baseball and has been a component in most of the game's top moments draws on in-depth research to cover the roles of equipment, the contributions of team rivalries and the achievements of legendary athletes.

Glockner, Andy
Chasing Perfection: *A Behind-the-Scenes Look at the High-Stakes Game of Creating an NBA Champion.* Andy Glockner. Da Capo Press 2016. 288 p.
ISBN 9780306824029
Grades: Adult   **796.323**
1. Basketball 2. Professional basketball 3. Professional basketball players 4. Basketball teams 5. Impartial writing 6. Sports and Competition — Basketball
LC Bl2016008751

A tour of the multi-million-dollar world of analytics, player identification, talent development and other methods employed by NBA teams to make champions demonstrates how the 2014-2015 NBA season reflected key practices shaping the game today.
"Highly recommended for NBA junkies who scour box scores." —*Library Journal*

Goodman, Matthew
The **City** *Game: Triumph, Scandal, and a Legendary Basketball Team.* Matthew Goodman. Ballantine Books 2019. IX, 350 p. : Illustration
ISBN 9781101882832
Grades: Adult   **796.323**
1. College sports 2. Basketball 3. Basketball teams 4. Scandals 5. Corruption 6. Gambling 7. Sports betting 8. Organized crime 9. Race relations 10. Social classes 11. New York City history 12. 20th century 13. 1950s 14. Sports and Competition — Basketball 15. Sports and Competition — Gambling and Betting 16. History writing — Post World War II - 1959 — United States 17. History writing — Scandals
LC Bl2019027021

The powerful story of a college basketball team who carried an era's brightest hopes—racial harmony, social mobility, and the triumph of the underdog—but whose success was soon followed by a shocking downfall.
"Recommended for anyone interested in the history of post-World War II basketball; relevant to issues within amateur athletics today." —*Library Journal*
Includes bibliographical references (p. 327-334) and index.

Lunardi, Joe
★ *Bracketology:* *March Madness, College Basketball, and the Creation of a National Obsession.* by Joe Lunardi with David Smale. Triumph Books 2021. 256 p.
ISBN 9781629378817
Grades: Adult   **796.323**
1. Basketball 2. Tournaments 3. College basketball 4. Basketball tournaments 5. Basketball teams 6. Sports 7. Basketball history 8. United States 9. Sports and Competition — Basketball
LC 2020048220

This books is about the process and history of selecting teams into the NCAA Tournament.
"A treat for any fan of March Madness—and college basketball in general." —*Kirkus*

MacMullan, Jackie
★ *Basketball:* *A Love Story.* by Jackie MacMullan and Rafe Bartholomew. Crown Archetype 2018. 448 p.
ISBN 9781524761783
Grades: Adult   **796.323**
1. Basketball 2. Basketball players 3. Basketball coaches 4. Professional basketball 5. Oral histories 6. Sports and Competition — Basketball 7. Adult books for young adults
LC 2018023541

Library Journal Best Books, 2018.
A revelatory history of basketball, published to coincide with a major ESPN and ABC series, draws on hundreds of interviews with leading athletes, coaches,

ESSENTIAL AND RECOMMENDED TITLES
796.323 Basketball

executives and journalists from the NBA, WNBA, NCAA and international leagues.

"Professional basketball fans will go to the net for this exciting history." —*Publishers Weekly*

Malinowski, Erik
Betaball: How Silicon Valley and Science Built One of the Greatest Basketball Teams in History. Erik Malinowski. Atria Books 2017. 320 p.

ISBN 9781501158193

Grades: Adult   796.323

1. Professional basketball 2. Basketball teams 3. Professional sports teams 4. Basketball 5. Sports and Competition — Basketball 6. Adult books for young adults

LC Bl2017039746

Describes how a venture capitalist and a Hollywood producer turned a declining franchise into one of the greatest teams in basketball, becoming a model organization for other professional sports teams for instilling workplace principles modeled after successful corporations.

"Much the way David Kaplan chronicled the creation of the 2016 champion Chicago Cubs in the Plan (2017), so free-lance sportswriter Malinowski has laid out the construction, piece by piece, of the powerhouse Golden State Warriors, who won NBA titles in 2015 and 2017, and in the 2016 regular season won a record-breaking 79 games... an insightful portrait of, yes, one of the all-time great NBA teams." —*Booklist*

McCallum, Jack
Dream Team: How Michael, Magic, Larry, Charles, and the Greatest Team of All Time Conquered the World and Changed the Game of Basketball Forever. Jack McCallum. Ballantine Books 2012. 352 p.

ISBN 9780345520487

Grades: 9 10 11 12 Adult   796.323

1. Basketball teams 2. Basketball players 3. Basketball history 4. United States 5. Biographies 6. Life stories — Sports — Athletes 7. Sports and Competition — Basketball 8. Sports and Competition — Olympic Sports

LC 2012006253

Documents the story of the Olympic squad that won the gold at the 1992 Barcelona Games, assessing the achievements and legacy of some of the NBA's greatest players, including Magic Johnson, Michael Jordan, and Charles Barkley.

"...[McCallum] effectively evokes the remarkable team while placing it within the larger historical context. Basketball and Olympics fans will welcome this nostalgic trip through the recent past." —*Kirkus*

Includes index.

Golden Days: West's Lakers, Steph's Warriors, and the California Dreamers Who Reinvented Basketball. Jack McCallum. Random House Inc 2017. 240 p.

ISBN 9780399179075

Grades: Adult   796.323

1. West, Jerry, 1938-2024 2. Curry, Stephen, 1988- 3. Basketball 4. Professional basketball 5. Professional basketball players 6. Basketball teams 7. 1970s 8. Sports and Competition — Basketball

LC 2017038872

Tells the interconnected stories of today's Golden State Warriors and the early-1970s Los Angeles Lakers, two extraordinary teams playing in extraordinary times and linked by one extraordinary man: Jerry West. By the New York Times best-selling author of Dream Team.

Montville, Leigh
Tall Men, Short Shorts: The 1969 NBA Finals: Wilt, Russ, Lakers, Celtics, and a Very Young Sports Reporter. Leigh Montville. Doubleday 2021. 336 p.

ISBN 9780385545198

Grades: Adult   796.323

1. Chamberlain, Wilt, 1936-1999 2. Russell, Bill, 1934-2022 3. Montville, Leigh 4. Basketball history 5. Sportswriters 6. Basketball teams 7. Autobiographies and memoirs 8. Life stories — Sports 9. Sports and Competition — Basketball 10. Sports and Competition — Sports History

LC 2021000519

A lively and colorful account of the 1969 NBA Finals—one of the greatest upsets in basketball history—through the eyes of future sports writing legend Leigh Montville, who was covering the coast-to-coast event as a brand-new twenty-four-year-old reporter for the Boston Globe.

"Sportswriter Montville (Sting Like a Bee) masterfully combines memoir and sports history in this thrilling deep dive into a legendary NBA championship battle." —*Publishers Weekly*

Includes bibliographical references and index.

Pearlman, Jeff
★ *Three-Ring Circus: Kobe, Shaq, Phil, and the Crazy Years of the Lakers Dynasty.* Jeff Pearlman. Houghton Mifflin Harcourt 2020. xix, 426 p.

ISBN 9781328530004

Grades: Adult   796.323

1. Bryant, Kobe, 1978-2020 2. O'Neal, Shaquille, 1972- 3. Jackson, Phil 4. Basketball teams 5. Basketball players 6. Interpersonal relations 7. Quarreling 8. Winning and losing 9. Basketball coaches 10. Professional basketball players 11. Professional basketball 12. Los Angeles, California 13. 1990s 14. 2000s (Decade) 15. Sports and Competition — Basketball 16. Sports and Competition — Sports History

LC 2019057830

Tells the story of the Lakers dynasty from 1996 through 2004, when Kobe Bryant and Shaquille O'Neal combined—and collided—to help bring the Lakers three straight championships and restore the franchise as a powerhouse.

"A must-read for all basketball fans." —*Library Journal*

Includes bibliographical references and index.

Powell, Michael
★ *Canyon Dreams: A Basketball Season on the Navajo Nation.* Michael Powell. Blue Rider Press 2019. 272 p.

ISBN 9780525534662

Grades: Adult   796.323

1. Indigenous peoples of North America 2. Navajo (Diné) (North American people) 3. High school students 4. Basketball 5. School sports 6. Indigenous reservations 7. Race relations 8. Arizona 9. Sports and Competition — Basketball 10. Society and culture — Race 11. Adult books for young adults

LC 2019034479

The moving story of a Navajo high school basketball team, its members struggling with the everyday challenges of high school, adolescence, and family, and the great and unique obstacles facing Native Americans living on reservations.

Ravin, Idan
The Hoops Whisperer: On the Court and Inside the Heads of Basketball's Best Players. Idan Ravin. Gotham Books 2014. VIII, 246 pages

ISBN 9781592408917

Grades: Adult   796.323

1. Ravin, Idan 2. Athletes 3. Basketball 4. Training 5. Autobiographies and memoirs 6. Life stories — Sports — Athletes 7. Sports and Competition — Basketball

Sharing his unorthodox drills and improvisational techniques in action, professional basketball's hottest trainer, recounting his own inspirational journey, reveals how faith, effort, dedication and passion can transform any player into a superstar—and anyone into a success.

Runstedtler, Theresa
Black Ball: Kareem Abdul-Jabbar, Spencer Haywood, and the Generation That Saved the Soul of the NBA. Theresa Runstedtler. Bold Type Books 2023. 368 p.

ISBN 9781645036951

Grades: Adult   796.323

1. African American basketball players 2. Basketball history 3. Discrimination in sports 4. Race relations 5. Basketball 6. Sports history 7. United States 8. 20th century 9. History Writing — African American — United States 10. Sports and competition — Basketball 11. Sports and competition — Sports history

A vital narrative history of 1970s pro basketball, and the Black players who shaped the NBA.

"Runstedtler's superior storytelling, buoyed by expert research, casts a new light on the league's complex history." —*Publishers Weekly*

Includes bibliographical references and index.

Serrano, Shea
Basketball (and Other Things): A Collection of Questions Asked, Answered, Illustrated. Shea Serrano; with illustrations by Arturo Torres. Abrams Image 2017. 239 pages : Color; Illustration
ISBN 9781419726477
Grades: Adult 796.323
1. Basketball 2. Questions and answers 3. Sports 4. Basketball fans 5. Sports and Competition — Basketball 6. Humor writing — General 7. Sports and Competition — Fans
LC 2017930301

Shares lighthearted coverage of a wide range of fan debates about basketball history, from Kobe Bryant's actual league dominance to what rules are not permitted in pickup games.

"An original work that captures the spirit of basketball. Highly recommended for die-hard NBA fans." —*Library Journal*

Simmons, Bill
The Book of Basketball: The NBA According to the Sports Guy. Bill Simmons. Ballantine/ESPN Books 2009. xi, 715 p. : Illustration
ISBN 9780345511768
Grades: 11 12 Adult 796.323
1. Basketball 2. Professional sports 3. Professional basketball 4. Professional basketball teams 5. Sports organizations 6. Sports and Competition — Basketball 7. Adult books for young adults
LC 2009036006

A lively and opinionated tour of the past, present, and future of pro basketball, written by ESPN's "Sports Guy" columnist, shares provocative insights on everything from major NBA events and underrated players to how the author believes Hall of Famers should be selected.

"The true NBA fan will dive into this hefty volume and won't resurface for about a week, emerging from the man cave unshaven, smelling of beer and pizza, grinning, and armed with NBA history, insight, anecdotes, statistics, and a dozen new examples of Simmons' Unintentional Comedy Scale. This is just plain fun. Expect significant demand from hoops junkies." —*Booklist*

Includes bibliographical references (p. [701]-702) and index.

Skelton, Marc
Pounding the Rock: Basketball Dreams and Real Life in a Bronx High School. Marc Skelton. Doubleday 2019. 256 p.
ISBN 9780385542654
Grades: Adult 796.323
1. Skelton, Marc, 1974- 2. High school basketball 3. Basketball coaches 4. Inner city schools 5. Basketball 6. High school students 7. Public education 8. High school teachers 9. High school basketball coaches 10. Bronx, New York City 11. New York City 12. Autobiographies and memoirs 13. Sports and Competition — Basketball 14. Life stories — Sports — Coaches, managers, and owners 15. Society and culture — Education
LC 2018027159

An account of the Bronx Fannie Lou Hamer Panthers 2016-2017 season shares insights into how a small, working-class high school has become a symbol of regeneration and how its coach inspires the team to balance their championships with academics.

"Skelton's game accounts are exciting and reveal details about his players, their lives, and off-court challenges." —*Kirkus*

Smith, Sam
Hard Labor: The Battle That Birthed the Billion-Dollar NBA. Sam Smith. Triumph Books 2017. 256 pages
ISBN 9781629372785
Grades: Adult 796.323
1. Professional basketball players 2. Labor unions 3. Negotiation 4. Basketball 5. Professional athletes 6. Basketball team owners 7. Wages 8. Sports and Competition — Basketball 9. Sports and Competition — Sports History 10. Business and economics — Industries — Entertainment and media
LC 2017026712

In Hard Labor, Sam Smith unearths this incredible and untold fight for players' rights and examines the massive repercussions for the NBA and sports in the United States in the 40 years since.

Sullivan, Matt
Can't Knock the Hustle: Inside the Season of Protest, Pandemic, and Progress with the Brooklyn Nets' Superstars of Tomorrow. Matt Sullivan. Dey Street 2021. 320 p.
ISBN 9780063036802
Grades: Adult 796.323
1. Durant, Kevin, 1988- 2. Irving, Kyrie, 1992- 3. Basketball players 4. Social justice 5. Covid-19 (Disease) 6. COVID-19 Pandemic, 2020- 7. Sports 8. Basketball 9. Fame 10. Social influence 11. Race relations 12. United States 13. Life stories — Sports 14. Sports and Competition — Basketball
LC 2021012801

An award-winning journalist's behind-the-scenes account from the epicenter of sports, social justice, and coronavirus, Can't Knock the Hustle is a lasting chronicle of the historic 2019-2020 NBA season, by way of the notorious Brooklyn Nets and basketball's renaissance as a cultural force beyond the game.

"More than a basketball book, this helps explain race relations, celebrity power, and personal choice in a changed world." —*Kirkus*

Includes bibliographical references.

Weitzman, Yaron
Tanking to the Top: The Philadelphia 76ers and the Most Audacious Process in the History of Professional Sports. Yaron Weitzman. Grand Central Publishing 2020. 288 pages
ISBN 9781538749722
Grades: Adult 796.323
1. Organizational change 2. Trading and swapping 3. Professional basketball players 4. Professional basketball 5. Basketball players 6. United States 7. Sports and competition — Basketball
LC 2019041816

The story of how the Philadelphia 76ers employed a rebuilding strategy of trading short-term winning for long-term success through minimal spending and accumulating low-level talent that could be traded away for future draft picks.

"Readers interested in the business of basketball, and how it affects teams and players above all, will find this a must-read." —*Library Journal*

Includes index.

796.332 American football

Anderson, Lars
Carlisle vs. Army: Jim Thorpe, Dwight Eisenhower, Pop Warner, and the Forgotten Story of Football's Greatest Battle. Lars Anderson. Random House 2007. 349 p. : Illustration
ISBN 9781400066001
Grades: Adult 796.332
1. Football history 2. Social life and customs 3. United States 4. 20th century 5. Sports and Competition — Football 6. Adult books for young adults
LC 2007008410

Booklist Editors' Choice, 2007.

Describes the November 1912 football matchup between college football powerhouse Army—which included cadet Dwight Eisenhower—and the Native American team from Carlisle, a team that was coached by the inventive Pop Warner and included Jim Thorpe.

"A forgotten football game in 1912, between Carlisle, led by Jim Thorpe and coached by the legendary Pop Warner, and Army, led by Dwight Eisenhower, be-

ESSENTIAL AND RECOMMENDED TITLES
796.332 American football

comes the launching point for a fascinating look at multiple levels of American popular culture." —*Booklist*

Includes bibliographical references (p. [323]-336) and index.

Benedict, Jeff
The Dynasty. Jeff Benedict. Avid Reader Press 2020. xii, 578 pages
ISBN 9781982134105
Grades: Adult 796.332
1. Belichick, Bill 2. Brady, Tom, 1977- 3. Kraft, Robert 4. Football teams 5. Football 6. Success (Concept) 7. Football coaches 8. Quarterbacks (Football) 9. Sports and Competition — Football 10. Sports and Competition — Teams
LC Bl2020019651

How was the Patriots dynasty built? And how did it last for two decades? In The Dynasty, acclaimed journalist Jeff Benedict provides richly reported answers in a sweeping account based on exclusive interviews with more than two hundred insiders, including team executives, coaches, players, players' wives, team doctors, lawyers, and more, as well as never-before-seen recordings, documents, and electronic communications.

"Smart, engaging sportswriting.... Good reading for organization builders as well as Pats fans." —*Kirkus*

Includes bibliographical references (pages 529-557) and index.

The System: The Glory and Scandal of Big-Time College Football. Jeff Benedict, Armen Keteyian. Doubleday 2013. 336 p.
ISBN 9780385536615
Grades: Adult 796.332
1. College sports 2. College football 3. Football 4. Universities and colleges 5. Sports corruption 6. Sports and Competition — Football
LC 2013362311

A revelatory account based on the authors' unprecedented access to the NCAA's highest-level programs throughout the 2012 season describes its high-powered system of billion-dollar television deals, high-priced coaches, football "hostessing," castoff athlete-students and paid test takers.

"An overwhelming recommendation for all readers who love or hate college sports." —*Library Journal*

Bissinger, H. G.
★ *Friday Night Lights: A Town, a Team, and a Dream*. H.G. Bissinger. Da Capo Press 2003. xiv, 367 p. : Illustration
ISBN 9780306812828
Grades: 11 12 Adult 796.332
1. Football 2. High school football 3. Football teams 4. Small town life 5. Social life and customs 6. Texas 7. Page to screen 8. Sports and Competition — Football 9. Sports and Competition — Teams
LC Bl2006017196

Chronicles a football season in Odessa, Texas, a depressed All-American town that lives and dies with the fortunes of its high school football team.

"It is a tricky balancing act, but Mr. Bissinger carries it off: Friday Night Lights offers a biting indictment of the sports craziness that grips not only Odessa but most of American society, while at the same time providing a moving evocation of its powerful allure." —*New York Times Book Review*

Originally published: Reading, MA : Addison-Wesley Pub. Co, 1990.

★ *The Mosquito Bowl: A Game of Life and Death in World War II*. Buzz Bissinger. HarperCollins 2022. 368 p.
ISBN 9780062879929
Grades: Adult 796.332
1. World War II 2. Marines 3. Football 4. Football players 5. War 6. College football players 7. Military history 8. Okinawa 9. Second world war era (1939-1945) 10. Life stories — Law and order — Armed forces personnel 11. History writing — Wars and conflicts — World War II 12. Life stories — Sports 13. Sports and competition — Football

This extraordinary, never-before-told story of WWII follows two U.S. Marine Corps regiments, comprised of some of the greatest football talent, as they played each other in a football game in the dirt and coral of Guadalcanal known as "The Mosquito Bowl" before they faced the darkest and deadliest days at Okinawa.

"Bissinger (Friday Night Lights) effortlessly combines sports and military history in this gritty account of a football game played by U.S. Marines on Guadalcanal in December 1944." —*Publishers Weekly*

Burke, Monte
Saban: The Making of a Coach. Monte Burke. Simon & Schuster 2015. 320 p.
ISBN 9781476789934
Grades: Adult 796.332
1. Saban, Nick 2. Football coaches 3. College football 4. Leadership 5. Biographies 6. Sports and Competition — Football 7. Sports and Competition — Coaches 8. Life stories — Sports — Coaches, managers, and owners
LC 2015018182

A portrait of the influential and controversial University of Alabama football coach shares insights into his winning "process," his early coaching years at the college and professional levels, and the defining events that shaped his career.

"With Saban's wins and losses over the years having been covered extensively in the media, Burke wisely focuses on the man rather than the play-by-play, and the result is a genuinely insightful look at a fierce competitor who nevertheless seems to care for his players both on and off the field." —*Booklist*

Includes bibliographical references.

Colt, George Howe
The Game: Harvard, Yale, and America in 1968. George Howe Colt. Scribner 2018. 352 p.
ISBN 9781501104787
Grades: Adult 796.332
1. College sports 2. College football 3. Young men 4. College students 5. United States history 6. 1960s 7. 20th century 8. Sports and Competition — Games 9. History writing — 1960s — United States 10. Sports and Competition — Football
LC 2018410267

From the author of the bestselling National Book Award finalist The Big House comes a story in the tradition of the Boys in the Boat about an unforgettable group of young athletes who battled in the legendary Harvard-Yale football game of 1968 amidst the sweeping currents of one of the most transformative years in American history.

"First-rate reporting and writing that will appeal to gridiron fans and general readers as well." —*Kirkus*

Dawidoff, Nicholas
Collision Low Crossers: A Year Inside the Turbulent World of NFL Football. Nicholas Dawidoff. Little Brown & Co. 2013. 496 pages
ISBN 9780316196796
Grades: Adult 796.332
1. Professional football 2. Football 3. United States 4. Sports and Competition — Football
LC 2013030013

An award-winning author and scholar describes what it was like to experience a year in the scouting department of the New York Jets and the time he spent with coach Rex Ryan, defensive player Darrelle Revis and quarterback Mark Sanchez.

Includes bibliographical references and index.

Easterbrook, Gregg
★ *The King of Sports: Football's Impact on America*. Gregg Easterbrook. Thomas Dunne Books 2013. 368 p.
ISBN 9781250011718
Grades: Adult 796.332
1. Football players 2. College football 3. Professional football 4. Sports 5. Football 6. Safety 7. United States 8. History writing — Arts and culture 9. Sports and Competition — Football 10. History writing — United States 11. Society and culture — Education
LC 2013023495

Using his year-long insider access to the Virginia Tech football program and extensive interviews with current and former college and pro-football players and coaches, the author of the ESPN.com blog "Tuesday Morning Quarterback" tackles football's place in American society.

"Easterbrook presents much to consider and discuss in his diagnosis and treatment plan, which should be of interest to a broad audience." —*Library Journal*

Includes bibliographical references and index.

Eatman, Nicholas

Friday, Saturday, Sunday in Texas: A Year in the Life of Lone Star Football, from High School to College to the Cowboys. Nicholas Eatman. Dey Street Books 2016. 304 p.

ISBN 9780062433312

Grades: Adult 796.332

1. High school football 2. College football 3. Professional football 4. High school football players 5. College football players 6. Professional football players 7. Football 8. Football players 9. Football teams 10. Texas 11. Sports and competition — Football 12. Sports and Competition — Teams

LC Bl2016041583

A veteran Texas sports writer follows three teams in three leagues—Plano Senior High School, Baylor University and the Dallas Cowboys—throughout the 2015 season, blending their stories into a revealing chronicle of Lone Star Football and highlighting the ups and downs, and even the parallels, that these teams experienced over the course of a year.

"A realistic look at football as its played in Texas." —*Booklist*

Eisenberg, John

The League: How Five Rivals Created the NFL and Launched a Sports Empire. John Eisenberg. Basic Books, an imprint of Perseus Books, LLC, a subsidiary of Hachette Book Group, Inc. 2018. 336 p.

ISBN 9780465048700

Grades: Adult 796.332

1. Bell, Bert, 1894-1959 2. Mara, Tim 3. Marshall, George Preston, 1896-1969 4. Rooney, Art, 1901-1988 5. Halas, George Stanley, 1895-1983 6. Professional football 7. Sports team owners 8. Football 9. United States 10. Sports and competition — Football 11. Sports and competition — Sports history

LC 2018012386

Part history of football, part extraordinary story of business ingenuity, a riveting story follows the five individuals who took an immense risk by investing in the professional game, shepherding the league through its rough early decades and building the most popular sport in America.

Includes bibliographical references and index.

Gaul, Gilbert M.

Billion-Dollar Ball: A Journey Through the Out-of-Control Money Culture of College Football. Gilbert Gaul. Viking Press 2015. 288 p.

ISBN 9780143108634

Grades: Adult 796.332

1. College football 2. Football 3. Higher education 4. Hypocrisy 5. Greed 6. College sports 7. Sports corruption 8. Society and culture — Education — Higher education 9. Sports and Competition — Football

LC 2015473475

A two-time Pulitzer Prize-winning journalist explores how college football has come to dominate some of the most prestigious universities, transforming athletic departments into wildly rich entertainment factories that put sports before education.

"Gaul's reporting is unassailable, but watch as his conclusions stir up a furor in the sports press. You don't even have to hate football to find this book valuableand certainly worth reading." —*Kirkus*

Horrigan, Joe

NFL Century: The One-Hundred-Year Rise of America's Greatest Sports League. Joe Horrigan. Crown Archetype 2019. 364 p.

ISBN 9781635653595

Grades: Adult 796.332

1. Professional football 2. Sports organizations 3. Football 4. United States 5. Sports and Competition — Football 6. Sports and Competition — Sports History

LC 2018057907

The NFL Hall of Fame executive director and host of the popular radio show, Pro Football Hall of Fame Radio, chronicles the history of the NFL through its founding in 1920 Ohio through its 100th anniversary season.

"This engagingly written chronicle of the most powerful and influential sports league in American history should be of wide interest." —*Library Journal*

Includes index.

Jaworksi, Ron

The Games That Changed the Game: The Evolution of the NFL in Seven Sundays. Ron Jaworksi, with Greg Cosell and David Plaut. ESPN Books 2010. 224 p.

ISBN 9780345517951

Grades: Adult 796.332

1. Professional football 2. Football players 3. Football 4. United States 5. Sports and Competition — Football 6. Sports and Competition — Sports History

LC 2010031008

A leading professional football analyst best known for his game tape breakdowns on Monday Night Football isolates seven historically significant games in which famous coaches demonstrated ideal executions of innovative strategies.

"Filled with anecdotes, player recollections, and other wonderful details, this should be the most popular football book of the season. Terrific reading." —*Booklist*

Includes index.

Myers, Gary

The Catch: One Play, Two Dynasties, and the Game That Changed the NFL. Gary Myers. Crown Publishers 2009. xiii, 252 p.

ISBN 9780307409089

Grades: Adult 796.332

1. Professional football 2. Football 3. Football players 4. Sports and Competition — Football

LC 2009014961

A behind-the-scenes retelling of the 1982 showdown between the Dallas Cowboys and the San Francisco 49ers explains its relevance to NFL history, drawing on interviews with leading figures to offer insight into the role of similar events on the rise and fall of franchises.

Oriard, Michael

Brand NFL: Making and Selling America's Favorite Sport. Michael Oriard. University of North Carolina Press 2007. 326 p.

ISBN 9780807831427

Grades: Adult 796.332

1. Football 2. Corporate sponsorship 3. Marketing 4. Professional football 5. Professional football players 6. Sports and Competition — Football

LC 2007008867

The evolution of how the NFL is marketed as entertainment rather than sport is detailed in a study that looks closely at the development of the sport and its unique place in American life.

Includes bibliographical references (p. [259]-307) and index.

Pearlman, Jeff

Boys Will Be Boys: The Glory Days and Party Nights of the Dallas Cowboys Dynasty. Jeff Pearlman. HarperCollins 2008. IX, 406 p. : Illustration; Color

ISBN 9780061256806

Grades: Adult 796.332

1. Professional football 2. Professional football players 3. Professional football coaches 4. Professional football teams 5. Football teams 6. Football 7. Scandals 8. Personal conduct 9. Social life and customs 10. Dallas, Texas 11. Sports and Competition — Football 12. Sports and Competition — Teams

ESSENTIAL AND RECOMMENDED TITLES
796.332 American football

Chronicles the rise and fall of the Dallas Cowboys during the 1990s, citing the contributions of owner Jerry Jones and coach Jimmy Johnson as well as the achievements of such players as Troy Aikman, Emmitt Smith, and Deion Sanders.

Includes bibliographical references (p. [389]-392) and index.

Football for a Buck: The Crazy Rise and Crazier Demise of the USFL. Jeff Pearlman. Houghton Mifflin Harcourt 2018. 320 p.
ISBN 9780544454385
Grades: Adult   796.332
1. Trump, Donald, 1946- 2. Football team owners 3. Professional football 4. Professional football players 5. Football 6. United States 7. 1980s 8. Sports and Competition — Football

LC 2018006360

Traces the three seasons of existence of the United States Football League, revealing its early success, how it launched the careers of many football superstars, and how it ultimately crashed and failed due to the influence of Donald Trump and other teamowners.

Includes bibliographical references and index.

Price, S. L.
Playing Through the Whistle: Steel, Football, and an American Town. S.L. Price. Atlantic Monthly Press 2016. 400 pages
ISBN 9780802125644
Grades: Adult   796.332
1. High school football 2. Working class 3. Steel towns 4. Steel industry and trade 5. Social problems 6. Deindustrialization 7. Race relations 8. Pennsylvania 9. Sports and Competition — Football 10. History writing — Regional history — United States 11. Society and culture — Wealth and class 12. Sports and Competition — Teams

LC 2018420187

A Sports Illustrated senior writer presents a moving epic of football in industrial America, tracing the story of Aliquippa, Pennsylvania's now-shuttered steel mill, and its legendary high school football team.

"From the rigidly stratified life in the 1920s and '30s during J&Ls 'despotic prime,' to the brief, postwar golden age, 'a moment of civic equipoise,' to today's 'company town without a company,' where the combination of unemployment, drugs, and crime crushes hope, Price's football story is really that of America's Rust Belt in poignant miniature." —*Kirkus*

Ribowsky, Mark
The Last Cowboy: A Life of Tom Landry. Mark Ribowsky. Liveright Pub. Corp. 2013. 720 p.
ISBN 9780871403339
Grades: Adult   796.332
1. Landry, Tom 2. Professional football 3. Professional football coaches 4. Christian men 5. Biographies 6. Sports and Competition — Coaches 7. Sports and Competition — Football 8. Life stories — Sports — Coaches, managers, and owners

LC 2013034731

A biography of the legendary professional football coach and strategist. After playing with the AAFC Yankees and NFL Giants, then as defensive coach of the Giants, Landry spent thirty years as head coach of the Dallas Cowboys, including twenty consecutive winning seasons. Discusses his relations to players, including those not sharing his temperament and background.

Rice, Jerry
America's Game: The NFL at 100. Jerry Rice and Randy O. Williams. Dey Street Books 2019. 544 p.
ISBN 9780062692900
Grades: Adult   796.332
1. Football teams 2. Football players 3. Football coaches 4. Sports organizations 5. Professional football 6. Football 7. United States 8. Sports and Competition — Football 9. Sports and Competition — Sports History

The authors of 50 Years, 50 Moments celebrate the first 100 years of the National Football League, interweaving history, personal stories, and observations of some of its greatest players, coaches, and advocates by leading contributors to chronicle the NFL's rise to a multi-billion-dollar brand.

Sando, Mike
The Football 100. Mike Sando, Dan Pompei, and the Athletic NFL Staff. William Morrow, an imprint of HarperCollinsPublishers 2023. xiii, 656 pages : Illustration
ISBN 9780063329096
Grades: Adult   796.332
1. Professional football players 2. Professional football 3. Football players 4. Football 5. Football history 6. United States 7. Essays 8. Collective biographies 9. Sports and Competition — Football

LC Bl2023173427

The sports media powerhouse, over the course of 100 essays, spanning more than 600 pages, reveals the greatest football players of all time—and uncovers the history of the NFL in the process, bringing to life the extraordinary athletic talents who changed the way the game is played.

"An engaging book that NFL fans will love and argue over endlessly." —*Kirkus*

The story of the greatest players in NFL history—Jacket; Includes index.

Savage, Phil
4th and Goal Every Day: Alabama's Relentless Pursuit of Perfection. Phil Savage with Ray Glier; preface by Nick Saban; foreword by Rece Davis. St Martin's Press 2017. 320 p.
ISBN 9781250130808
Grades: Adult   796.332
1. Football players 2. College football 3. College sports 4. Alabama 5. Sports and Competition — Football

LC 2017016459

The former general manager of the Cleveland Browns and current game commentator for the Alabama Crimson Tide Sports Network discusses how the college football team rebuilt itself to win four national titles in eight seasons through commitment to recruiting, practice and fundamentals.

"A football lifer gives insight into how the Alabama Crimson Tide continue to be the most dominant force in college football." —*Kirkus*

Weinreb, Michael
Season of Saturdays: A History of College Football in 14 Games. Michael Weinreb. Scribner 2014. 288 p.
ISBN 9781451627817
Grades: Adult   796.332
1. Football 2. College football 3. College sports 4. Sports and competition — Football

An award-winning sportswriter presents an engaging cultural history that highlights the key moments, games, personalities and scandals of American college football, tracing how it grew from a rugby offshoot to a complicated and ubiquitous part of the country's national identity.

Wickersham, Seth
★ *It's Better to Be Feared: The New England Patriots Dynasty and the Pursuit of Greatness.* Seth Wickersham. Liveright Publishing Corporation 2021. 506 p.
ISBN 9781631498237
Grades: Adult   796.332
1. Football teams 2. Professional football 3. Professional football players 4. 21st century 5. Sports and Competition — Football 6. Sports and Competition — Teams 7. Sports and Competition — Sports History

The explosive, long-awaited account of the making of the greatest dynasty in football history—from the acclaimed ESPN reporter who has been there from the very beginning. Over two unbelievable decades, the New England Patriots were not only the NFL's most dominant team, but also—and by far—the most secretive. How did they achieve and sustain greatness—and what were the costs?

"This enthralling behind-the-scenes tale of the New England Patriots is a piece of journalistic excellence from ESPN's Wickersham, who performed countless hours of interviews and observations with Patriots' and outside management, coaches, and players, especially quarterback Tom Brady and head coach Bill Belichick. . . . Patriots' fans will revel in all the little-known backstories, while all football fans and readers seeking astonishing success stories will relish this, too." —*Booklist*

Includes bibliographical references and index.

Yousse, Bower
Freddie Steinmark: Faith, Family, Football. Bower Yousse and Thomas J. Cryan. University of Texas Press 2015. xi, 253 pages
ISBN 9781477308219
Grades: Adult   **796.332**
1. Steinmark, Freddie 2. College football players 3. Football 4. Cancer 5. Texas 6. 1960s 7. Biographies 8. Sports and Competition — Football 9. Sports and Competition — Sports History 10. Life stories — Facing adversity — Medical issues — Physical illness 11. Life stories — Sports — Athletes
LC 2015004079

Freddie Steinmark tells the story of a legendary University of Texas football player whose courage on the field and in battling cancer still inspires the Longhorn nation.

Includes bibliographical references and index.

796.334 Soccer (Association football)

Abbot, Sebastian
The Away Game: The Epic Search for Soccer's Next Superstars. Sebastian Abbot. W W Norton & Company 2018. 336 p.
ISBN 9780393292206
Grades: Adult   **796.334**
1. Professional soccer 2. Soccer 3. Sports and competition — Soccer
LC 2017052648

Traces the audacious scouting program known as Football Dreams that for the past decade has strategically recruited young African boys to become the sport's future elites, describing the experiences of a group of talented hopefuls who train, compete and pursue their fortunes at Europe's top clubs.

"Abbots narrative features vivid profiles, engrossing play-by-play, and a sobering lesson: Bad breaks and cold business calculations sometimes trump ability in the making of champions." —*Publishers Weekly*

Anderson, Christopher
The Numbers Game: Why Everything You Know About Soccer Is Wrong. Chris Anderson and David Sally. Penguin Books 2013. 384 p.
ISBN 9780143124566
Grades: Adult   **796.334**
1. Soccer 2. Statistics 3. Sports 4. Sports and Competition — Soccer 5. Science Writing — Mathematics
LC 2013011448

A former professional goalkeeper turned soccer statistics guru, along with a behavioral analyst, presents this first book on soccer stats that reveals the numbers that truly count, exposing the sport's hidden rules.

Includes bibliographical references and index.

Bass, Amy
One Goal: A Coach, a Team, and the Game That Brought a Divided Town Together. Amy Bass. Hachette Books 2018. 288 p.
ISBN 9780316396547
Grades: Adult   **796.334**
1. Soccer 2. Immigrants 3. Race relations 4. Small town life 5. Small towns 6. Somali people 7. Maine 8. Sports and competition — Soccer 9. Society and culture — Immigration 10. Adult books for young adults
LC 2017034578

Library Journal Best Books, 2018.

In the tradition of Friday Night Lights and Outcasts United, ONE GOAL tells the inspiring story of the soccer team in a town bristling with racial tension that united Somali refugees and multi-generation Mainers in their quest for state—and ultimately national—glory. When thousands of Somali refugees resettled in Lewiston, Maine, a struggling, overwhelmingly white town, longtime residents grew uneasy. Then the mayor wrote a letter asking Somalis to stop coming, which became a national story. While scandal threatened to subsume the town, its high school's soccer coach integrated Somali kids onto his team, and their passion began to heal old wounds.

"Basss effective portrayal of Lewiston as a microcosm of Americas changing culture should be required reading for coaches, teachers, and those working with diverse populations." —*Publishers Weekly*

Also published in large print format.

Bennett, Roger
Men in Blazers Present Encyclopedia Blazertannica: A Suboptimal Guide to Soccer, America's. by Roger Bennett, Michael Davies. Random House Inc 2018. 240 p.
ISBN 9781101875988
Grades: Adult   **796.334**
1. Soccer 2. Soccer players 3. Media tie-ins 4. Sports and competition — Soccer
LC 2017028596

Two popular British soccer experts who host a podcast and a television show fill in the gaps for newly minted fans of the sport with great moments in the sport's history.

Based on a podcast.

Bensinger, Ken
★ *Red* Card: How the U.S. Blew the Whistle on the World's Biggest Sports Scandal. Ken Bensinger. Simon & Schuster 2018. 352 p.
ISBN 9781501133909
Grades: Adult   **796.334**
1. Sports corruption 2. Scandals 3. Soccer 4. Corruption investigation 5. White collar crime 6. Money laundering 7. Embezzlement 8. Bribery 9. Fraud 10. Business and economics — Corruption and scandal 11. Sports and Competition — Soccer
LC Bl2018063563

An award-winning journalist presents an account of the FIFA corruption scandal that implicated nearly every aspect of international soccer, sharing insights into the roles of key personalities while tracing the efforts of law officials to expose the truth.

"With the flair of a novelist, Bensinger meticulously chronicles the magnitude of corruption that permeates the worlds most popular sport." —*Publishers Weekly*

Clarke, Gemma
Soccerwomen: The Icons, Rebels, Stars, and Trailblazers Who Transformed the Beautiful Game. Gemma Clarke. Nation Books 2019. 304 p.
ISBN 9781568589213
Grades: Adult   **796.334**
1. Women soccer players 2. Women and sports 3. Women athletes 4. Soccer players 5. Professional soccer 6. Soccer for women 7. Professional athletes 8. Sports and Competition — Soccer 9. Adult books for young adults
LC 2018050633

Based on more than 50 interviews with current and former players and coaches, a British sports journalist celebrates the elite athletes of women's professional soccer, including profiles on Mia Hamm, Abby Wambach, Marta and Sun Wen.

"Similar to Gwendolyn Oxenham's recent Under the Lights and in the Dark, while offering more of a historical perspective on the women's game. Soccer fans will enjoy learning more about these athletes." —*Library Journal*

Includes bibliographical references.

Conn, David
The Fall of the House of FIFA: The Multimillion-Dollar Corruption at the Heart of Global Soccer. David Conn. Nation Books 2017. 328 p.
ISBN 9781568585963
Grades: Adult   **796.334**

ESSENTIAL AND RECOMMENDED TITLES
796.334 Soccer (Association football)

1. Soccer 2. Professional soccer 3. Soccer tournaments 4. Corruption 5. Scandals 6. Embezzlement 7. Money laundering 8. Bribery 9. Sports and Competition — Soccer 10. Business and economics — Corruption and scandal

LC 2017905020

Chronicles the history and staggering scale of corruption at the center of FIFA and paints revealing portraits of the power brokers at the center of the scandal.

"Conn's meticulous research and smooth writing style bring this unseemly chapter in FIFA history to a close, with realistic hope for the future of the most popular sport on earth." —*Library Journal*

Dohrmann, George
Switching Fields: Inside the Fight to Remake Men's Soccer in the United States. George Dohrmann. Ballantine Books 2022. 288 p.
ISBN 9781524798864
Grades: Adult   796.334
1. Soccer 2. Professional soccer 3. Professional sports 4. Soccer for children 5. Soccer coaching 6. Equality 7. Multiculturalism 8. United States 9. Sports and Competition — Soccer 10. Life stories — Sports

LC 2022010428

In Switching Fields, Pulitzer Prize-winning journalist George Dohrmann turns his investigative focus on the system that develops male soccer players in the United States, examining why the country has struggled for decades to produce first-class talent. But rather than just focus on the past, he looks forward, connecting with coaches and players who are changing the way talented prospects are unearthed and developed. Following these innovators' inspiring journeys, Dohrmann gives ever-hopeful U.S. soccer fans a reason to believe that a movement is underway to smash the developmental status quo—one that has put the United States on the verge of greatness.

"Juxtaposed against numerous accounts detailing the success of U.S. women's soccer, this call to action provides hope that there could be a way forward for men's soccer in this country." —*Booklist*

Galeano, Eduardo
Soccer in Sun and Shadow. by Eduardo Galeano; translated by Mark Fried. Verso 1998. VIII, 228 p.
ISBN 9781568584942
Grades: Adult   796.334
1. Soccer players 2. Soccer 3. Social life and customs 4. South America 5. 20th century 6. Sports and Competition — Soccer

LC 98006769

Presents observations and reflections on soccer showing both the tragedy and the triumph of the game throughout the years.

Includes bibliographical references (p. [211]-218) and index.

Goldblatt, David
★ *The Age of Football: Soccer and the 21st Century.* David Goldblatt. W.W. Norton & Co. 2020. 624 pages
ISBN 9780393635119
Grades: Adult   796.334
1. Soccer 2. Sports 3. Geopolitics 4. 21st century 5. Sports and Competition — Soccer

LC 2019052146

The "Game of Our Lives" podcaster and author of the best-selling the Ball Is Round presents a wide-reaching exploration of soccer and society that charts the sport's global cultural ascent, economic transformation and deep politicization.

"Superb: Essential reading not just for fans of the sport, but also for students of geopolitics." —*Kirkus*

Includes bibliographical references and index; First published in the UK by Macmillan Publishers International Limited under the title the age of football : the global game in the twenty-first century.

Honigstein, Raphael
Das Reboot: How German Soccer Reinvented Itself and Conquered the World. Raphael Honigstein. Nation Books,c2015 2015. 276 p.
ISBN 9781568585307

Grades: Adult   796.334
1. Soccer 2. Germany 3. Sports and Competition — Soccer

LC 2015947738

Guardian journalist and television pundit Raphael Honigstein charts the return of German soccer from the international wilderness of the late nineteen-nineties to Götze's moment of genius and asks, how did this come about? How did German soccer reinvent itself away from its efficient but unappealing and defensively-minded past to the free-flowing, attack-minded soccer that was on display in 2014? The answer takes him from California to Stuttgart, from Munich to the Maracaná, via Dortmund and Amsterdam. Packed with exclusive interviews with the key protagonists, Honigstein's book lifts the lid on the secrets of German soccer's success.

"Championship teams always have their books, but few are as thoughtful and edifying as this one." —*Booklist*

Hopcraft, Arthur
The Football Man: People and Passions in Soccer. Arthur Hopcraft; with a new foreword by Michael Parkinson. Aurum 2013. 253 p.
ISBN 9781781311516
Grades: Adult   796.334
1. Soccer 2. Sports and Competition — Soccer 3. Sports and Competition — Sports History

LC Oc2014001408

Written just two years after England's '66 triumph when the national game was at its zenith, Arthur Hopcraft's The Football Man is repeatedly quoted as the best book every written about the sport.

Includes index; Originally published: Harmondsworth: Penguin, 1971.

Kuper, Simon
Soccernomics: Why England Loses, Why Germany and Brazil Win, and Why the U.S, Japan, Australia, Turkey and Even Iraq Are Destined to Become the Kings of the World's Most Popular Sport. Simon Kuper and Stefan Szymanski. Nation Books 2009. 336 p.
ISBN 9781568584256
Grades: Adult   796.334
1. Soccer 2. Economics 3. Sports 4. Sports and Competition — Soccer

LC 2009023502

A pair of award-winning journalists draw on analogies from a range of disciplines to consider why forefront soccer teams win or lose World Cup competitions, offering insight into the playing styles of leading national teams as well as overall factors that influence how the game is played.

"Whether analyzing the relationship of spending to winning or applying game theory to the penalty kick, the authors' delight in discovery proves both persuasive and contagious. It's a fascinating book with the potential to effect genuine change in the sport." —*Booklist*

Includes bibliographical references and index.

Oxenham, Gwendolyn
Under the Lights and in the Dark: Untold Stories of Women's Soccer. Gwendolyn Oxenham. Icon Books 2017. 272 p.
ISBN 9781785781537
Grades: Adult   796.334
1. Women soccer players 2. Professional athletes 3. Soccer 4. Women's sports 5. Sports and Competition — Soccer

LC Bl2017040525

California-based writer Gwendolyn Oxenham presents an insider's look at women's soccer, following players across the world from Portland Thorns' Allie Long to FC Kansas City's Amy Rodriguez.

Vecsey, George
Eight World Cups: My Journey Through the Beauty and Dark Side of Soccer. George Vecsey. Times Books 2014. 288 p.
ISBN 9780805098488
Grades: Adult   796.334
1. Soccer 2. Soccer players 3. Tournaments 4. Sports and Competition — Soccer

809

PUBLIC LIBRARY CORE COLLECTION: NONFICTION
Twentieth Edition

LC 2013042574

A New York Times sports columnist presents this action-packed travelogue of the last eight World Cups during which he immersed himself in the great national leagues, historic clubs and devoted fans and met such stars as Socrates, Maradona, Baggio and Zidane.

"Vecsey's insights offer a unique look at the grace of the game as well as the underside of world soccer." —*Library Journal*

Includes bibliographical references and index.

Villoro, Juan

God Is Round. Juan Villoro; translated by Thomas Bunstead. Restless Books 2016. 240 p.

ISBN 9781632060587

Grades: Adult   796.334

1. Soccer 2. Soccer players 3. Sports 4. Essays 5. Translations — Spanish to English 6. Sports and Competition — Soccer

LC Bl2016016137

A brilliant and kaleidoscopic exploration of the world's favorite sport and the passion, hopes, rivalries, superstitions, and global solidarity soccer inspires from award-winning author and Mexico's leading sports journalist, Juan Villoro.

"For millions around the world, soccer is not just a game, but rather life itself and, as Villoro ably reveals, very much worth pursuing to the final whistle." —*Kirkus*

Wahl, Grant

★ *Masters of Modern Soccer: How the World's Best Play the Twenty-First-Century Game.* Grant Wahl. Crown Archetype 2018. 304 p.

ISBN 9780307408600

Grades: Adult   796.334

1. Soccer 2. Soccer players 3. Sports and competition — Soccer

LC 2017053620

The forefront Sports Illustrated soccer journalist and best-selling author of The Beckham Experiment profiles master players in every key position to reveal how elite athletes and coaches strategize on and off the field and perform in high-pressure game situations.

"One of the best books on the sport, alongside Raphael Honigstein's Das Reboot and Simon Kuper and Stefan Szymanski's Soccernomics, this gem of a work will appeal to longtime soccer fans and budding enthusiasts." —*Library Journal*

Includes index.

796.34 Racket games

Gingrich, Dayne

Pickleball Mindset: The Blueprint for Peak Performance. Dayne Gingrich and Jill Martin. Mindset Productions 2024. II, 251 pages : Illustration

ISBN 9798218369828

Grades: Adult   796.34

1. Racket games 2. Ball games 3. Sports 4. Sports and competition — General

Not just another book about how to play pickleball, Pickleball Mindset dives deep into how to think on the court.

Hinkson, Jim

Lacrosse for Dummies. Jim Hinkson and Joe Lombardi. John Wiley & Sons Canada, Ltd. 2010. xxvi, 330 p. : Illustration

ISBN 9780470738559

Grades: Adult   796.34

1. Lacrosse 2. Sports and Competition — General

LC 2010282483

The book offers everything the beginning player needs to know, from the necessary equipment to the basic rules of the game, with explanations of the women's game and the indoor game, too.

Previous ed.: 2003; Includes bibliographical references (p. 307-309) and index.

McAfee, Richard

Table Tennis: Steps to Success. Richard McAfee. Human Kinetics 2009. xx, 203 p. : Illustration

ISBN 9780736077316

Grades: 9 10 11 12 Adult   796.34

1. Table tennis 2. Sports and Competition — General

LC 2009004824

Combines the knowledge and experience of master instructor Richard McAfee with essential table tennis techniques and strategies for today's player.

McPhee, John

Levels of the Game. by John McPhee. Farrar, Straus & Giroux 1989. 149 p.

ISBN 9780374515263

Grades: Adult   796.34

1. Ashe, Arthur 2. Graebner, Clark, 1943- 3. Sports journalism 4. Tennis 5. Tennis players 6. Tennis tournaments 7. Competition 8. Professional tennis players 9. African American tennis players 10. African American men 11. Sports and Competition — Tennis

Narrates the events surrounding the 1968 championship tennis match at Forest Hills, focusing on the psychological game played by each of the opposing players, Arthur Ashe and Clark Graebner.

Levels of the game is a narrative of a tennis match played by Arthur Ashe and Clark Graebner at Forest Hills.—back cover; the contents of this book originally appeared in the New Yorker.

Parker, Vergil R.

Pickleball 101: A Complete and Comprehensive Guide Detailing the History, Rules, Techniques, and Strategies of This Fun and Fast-Growing Sport. Vergil R. Parker. 2023. 172 p.

ISBN 9798870543901

Grades: Adult   796.34

1. Racket games 2. Ball games 3. Sports 4. Rules 5. Strategy 6. Sports and competition — General

Lucky for you, this guidebook contains the most up-to-date game rules as well as helpful strategies and techniques to help you learn the sport, elevate your game, and ultimately experience the joy it can bring.

Simon, Rachel

Pickleball for All: Everything but The Kitchen Sink. Rachel Simon. Dey St, an imprint of William Morrow 2022. 196 pages : Color; Illustration

ISBN 9780063273047

Grades: Adult   796.34

1. Racket games 2. Sports 3. Sports history 4. Sports and competition — General 5. Sports and competition — Sports History

LC Bl2022026045

Weaving inspiring stories from the world's top players during their most exciting pickleball moments, and painting a portrait of a new American pastime, this fun-filled book shows how this sport was born, which has become a nationally growing phenomenon as a way to stay active, safe and entertained.

"Pickleball...may have been the 'perfect pandemic pastime,' but with an ever-growing number of enthusiasts, it has long outgrown its origin story. A timely resource on the racquet sport of the moment." —*Booklist*

Setup, stories, strategies—Cover; Includes bibliographical references (pages 189-194).

796.342 Tennis (Lawn tennis)

Fisher, Marshall Jon

A Terrible Splendor: Three Extraordinary Men, a World Poised for War, and the Greatest Tennis Match Ever Played. Marshall Jon Fisher. Crown 2009. 336 p.

ISBN 9780307393944

Grades: Adult   796.342

1. Professional tennis 2. Tennis 3. Tennis players 4. Tennis tournaments 5. Professional tennis players 6. Tournaments 7. Third Reich, 1933-1945

ESSENTIAL AND RECOMMENDED TITLES
796.352 Golf

8. 1930s 9. Sports and Competition — Tennis 10. Sports and Competition — Rivalry

LC 2008050527

Looks at the prominent figures and events surrounding the 1937 Davis Cup Tournament, specifically the match between Don Budge of the United States and Gottfried von Cramm of Germany.

"Richly detailed . the story moves from one nail-biting set to the next against a backdrop of improbably high personal and political stakes." —*Boston Globe*

Gallwey, W. Timothy
★ *The Inner Game of Tennis*. W. Timothy Gallwey. Random House 1997. xx, 122 p. : Illustration
ISBN 9780679778318
Grades: Adult   796.342
1. Tennis 2. Sports and Competition — Tennis

LC 97000895

Concentrates upon overcoming mental attitudes that adversely affect tennis performance, including learning to relax, effectively concentrating, and discarding bad habits.

Focuses on overcoming the mental attitudes that adversely affect tennis performance, including learning how to relax, effectively concentrating on one's game, and discarding bad habits.

Phillips, Rowan Ricardo
The Circuit: A Tennis Odyssey. Rowan Ricardo Phillips. Farrar, Straus and Giroux 2018. xvii, 256 p.
ISBN 9780374123772
Grades: Adult   796.342
1. Tennis tournaments 2. Tennis players 3. Professional tennis 4. Seasons 5. Competition 6. Winning and losing 7. Sports and Competition — Tennis 8. Life stories — Sports — Athletes

LC 2018017728

An award-winning poet describes the historic 2017 tennis season, from the Australian Open, which pitted Roger Federer against rival Rafael Nadal to the U.S. Open which saw the shocking return of Maria Sharapova.

796.352 Golf

Carter, Iain
Golf Wars: Liv and Golf's Bitter Battle for Power and Identity. Iain Carter. Bloomsbury Sport 2024. 288 p.
ISBN 9781399410168
Grades: Adult   796.352
1. Professional golf 2. Professional golfers 3. Golf 4. Sports tournaments 5. International competition 6. Corporate power 7. Ethics 8. Business ethics 9. Saudi Arabia 10. Sports and Competition — Golf

The battle for the future of professional golf has been blazing. The Saudi-backed organisation Liv Golf has struck at the very heart of the golfing establishment, setting up rival tournaments with enormous prize pots and pitting the game's most famous players against each other. Its tagline: golf but louder. With Liv now in its season and little sign of the struggle abating, BBC Golf Correspondent Iain Carter delivers the fascinating—and ongoing—account of a sporting upheaval. Carter covers every twist and turn, exploring how the PGA Tour and other traditional organisations are fighting back.

"A tale of 'arch disruptors,' big money, and murky ethics, this is Accidental Billionaires for the golf world." —*Publishers Weekly*

Coyne, Tom
A Course Called Scotland: Searching the Home of Golf for the Secret to Its Game. Tom Coyne. Simon & Schuster 2018. 336 p.
ISBN 9781476754284
Grades: Adult   796.352
1. Coyne, Tom 2. Authors 3. Golfers 4. Golf 5. Voyages and travels 6. Golf courses 7. Travel writing 8. Scotland 9. Sports and Competition — Golf 10. Travel Writing — Europe 11. Life stories — Sports

LC 2018015536

Describes the author's visit to Scotland, the birthplace of golf, playing on over 100 of the oldest and most-revered courses in the world, including St. Andrews, Turnberry, Dornoch and Troon.

"In this witty and charming follow-up to A Course Called Ireland, Coyne continues living a golfers dream by playing every links course in Scotland, golfs birthplace." —*Publishers Weekly*

Feinstein, John
The First Major: The Inside Story of the 2016 Ryder Cup. John Feinstein. Doubleday 2017. 304 p.
ISBN 9780385541091
Grades: Adult   796.352
1. Ryder Cup (Golf) 2. Golf 3. Tournaments 4. Sports and competition — Golf

LC 2017021758

A dramatic chronicle of the bitterly fought 2016 Ryder Cup discusses the multiple losses and recent death of Arnold Palmer that spurred a vengeful match between the American and European teams, citing the particular contributions of such figures as Phil Mickelson, Rory McIlroy and Patrick Reed.

"Golf fans will know what happened, of course, but Feinstein compellingly re-creates the excitement, sometimes shot by shot, especially in the classic McIlroy-Reed singles match, which has come to be a symbol of golf at its best, both for shotmaking and sportsmanship. A great moment in golf history, vividly captured." —*Booklist*

Frost, Mark
The Match: The Day the Game of Golf Changed Forever. Mark Frost. Hyperion 2007. 272 p.
ISBN 9781401302788
Grades: Adult   796.352
1. Lowery, Eddie 2. Golf 3. Golfers 4. Sports betting 5. 1950s 6. 20th century 7. Sports and Competition — Golf

LC 2007023325

In 1956, a casual bet between two millionaires eventually pitted two of the greatest golfers of the era—Byron Nelson and Ben Hogan—against top amateurs Harvie Ward and Ken Venturi. Frost recounts this dramatic tale from start to finish, detailing the match that vaulted golf out of the shadows and into the national spotlight.

"What makes this account so fresh and so exciting for golf fans is that—unlike any other re-creation of a great moment in sports history—Frost tells a story that, being virtually unknown, carries with it genuine suspense as to the outcome. Going well beyond the simple question of who will win, however, Frost makes us see this spur-of-the-moment match for what it was: the last hurrah of amateur golf. And, best of all, he captures one of those fleeting moments in sports when competing athletes reach a kind of transcendent perfection simultaneously. Superb narrative nonfiction." —*Booklist*

Includes bibliographical references.

Harig, Bob
Drive: The Lasting Legacy of Tiger Woods. Bob Harig. St. Martin's Press 2024. 336 p.
ISBN 9781250288752
Grades: Adult   796.352
1. Woods, Tiger 2. Golfers 3. African Americans 4. Biographies 5. Sports and Competition — Golf 6. Sports and Competition — Individual Athlete 7. Life stories — Sports — Athletes

LC 2023045825

A deep-dive into Tiger Woods' thrilling career, as seen through his iconic 2019 Masters comeback and win.

"A solid portrait of an athlete's lonely progress in battling pain, the yips, aging, and other obstacles." —*Kirkus*

Includes index.

PUBLIC LIBRARY CORE COLLECTION: NONFICTION
Twentieth Edition

Hogan, Ben
★ *Five Lessons: The Modern Fundamentals of Golf.* Ben Hogan with Herbert Warren Wind; drawings by Anthony Ravielli. Simon & Schuster 1985. 127 p. : Illustration
ISBN 9780671612979
Grades: Adult   796.352
1. Golf 2. Sports and Competition — Golf
LC 85014558
The professional golfer provides tips on the grip, stance, and swing of successful golf shots.
"The basics of hitting a ball with a club haven't changed much since this debuted, so this still offers valuable advice from one of the greats." —*Library Journal*
A Fireside book; Previously published in 1957.

Norton, Hughes
★ *Rainmaker: Superagent Hughes Norton and the Money-Grab Explosion of Golf from Tiger Woods to Liv And Beyond.* Hughes Norton and George Peper. Atria Books 2024. 243 p.
ISBN 9781668045268
Grades: Adult   796.352
1. Norton, Hughes 2. Sports agents 3. Athletes 4. Golf 5. Professional golfers 6. Contracts 7. Corporate sponsorship 8. Wealth 9. Success (Concept) 10. Scandals 11. Employee termination 12. American people 13. Autobiographies and memoirs 14. Life stories — Sports 15. Life stories — Business 16. Sports and Competition — Golf
Best known as golf's super-agent who represented Tiger Woods and Greg Norman, the author provides a glimpse into his meteoric rise and fall, with never-before-told stories and exclusive insights, revealing how, to protect his players and his career, he made ethical and moral choices he would later regret.
"Norton's engaging memoir provides a revealing glimpse into the cutthroat world of a sports agent, an insider's perspective on the evolution of professional golf, and colorful anecdotes about the personalities he met throughout his storied career." —*Booklist*
Includes bibliographical references and index.

Rotella, Robert J.
Golf Is Not a Game of Perfect. Bob Rotella with Bob Cullen. Simon & Schuster 1995. 224 p.
ISBN 9780684803647
Grades: Adult   796.352
1. Golf 2. Golfers 3. Sports and Competition — Golf 4. Sports and Competition — Coaches
LC 95001120
A coach and sports psychologist presents anecdotes about the golfers he has worked with while offering advice on how to handle the mental aspects of golfing and accept personal potentials and limits.

796.357 Baseball

Barry, Dan
Bottom of the 33rd: Hope and Redemption in Baseball's Longest Game. by Dan Barry. Harper 2011. 272 p.
ISBN 9780062014481
Grades: Adult   796.357
1. Minor league baseball 2. Baseball 3. Ball games 4. Baseball history 5. Statistics 6. United States 7. Sports and Competition — Baseball 8. Sports and Competition — Sports History
LC 2010051656
Details the longest game in baseball history, a grueling minor-league matchup between the Pawtucket Red Sox and the Rochester Red Wings that lasted more than eight hours, with the last of the 33 innings being postponed until two months later.
"Barry exploits the power of memory and nostalgia with literary grace and journalistic exactitude. He blends a vivid, moment-by-moment recreation of the game with what happens to its participants in the next 30 years." —*New York Times Book Review*

Brown, Tim
★ *The Tao of the Backup Catcher: Playing Baseball for the Love of the Game.* Tim Brown, with Erik Kratz. Twelve 2023. 304 p.
ISBN 9781538726556
Grades: Adult   796.357
1. Kratz, Erik 2. Baseball 3. Baseball players 4. Sports 5. Professional baseball 6. Catchers (Baseball) 7. Sports and competition — Baseball
"Baseball and sports lovers will likely forever revere and quote this book. It belongs in all general and many academic libraries." —*Library Journal*

Cohen, Rich
The Chicago Cubs: Story of a Curse. Rich Cohen. Farrar, Straus and Giroux 2017. 272 p.
ISBN 9780374120924
Grades: Adult   796.357
1. Professional baseball teams 2. Baseball teams 3. Baseball fans 4. Chicago, Illinois 5. Sports and Competition — Baseball 6. Sports and Competition — Teams
LC 2017025511
Combining reportage with memoir, the author chronicles the history of the Chicago Cubs and—drawing on interviews and travels with recent Cubs players, owners and coaching staff—tracks the famous curse that was placed on the team in 1945 by the owner of the Billy Goat Tavern.
"This is but one in what is already a succession of books on the Chicago Cubs' historic 2016 World Series championship—books that include Scott Simon's My Cubs and David Kaplans The Plan—but it might be the best, since it's both a deeply satisfying historical account of that colorful franchise and a compelling, all-too-painful personal narrative of one longtime, besotted Cubs fan." —*Booklist*
Includes bibliographical references.

Cook, Kevin
Ten Innings at Wrigley: The Wildest Ballgame Ever, with Baseball on the Brink. Kevin Cook. Henry Holt and Company 2019. 320 p.
ISBN 9781250182036
Grades: Adult   796.357
1. Baseball teams 2. Professional baseball 3. Baseball players 4. Professional baseball players 5. Baseball history 6. United States 7. 1970s 8. 20th century 9. Sports and Competition — Baseball 10. Sports and Competition — Sports History
LC 2018047864
A recap of a wild 1979 baseball game at Wrigley Field between the Chicago Cubs and Philadelphia Phillies that featured 45 runs and 11 homers from legendary players such as Mike Schmidt, Bruce Sutter and Tug McGraw.
Includes bibliographical references and index.

Creamer, Robert W.
Stengel: His Life and Times. Robert W. Creamer. University of Nebraska Press 1996. 349 p. : Illustration
ISBN 9780803263673
Grades: Adult   796.357
1. Stengel, Casey, 1890-1975 2. Professional baseball managers 3. Baseball history 4. Baseball players 5. Social life and customs 6. United States 7. 20th century 8. Biographies 9. Sports and Competition — Baseball 10. Sports and Competition — Coaches 11. Life stories — Sports — Athletes 12. Life stories — Sports — Coaches, managers, and owners
LC 95040143
A portrait of the colorful Casey Stengel examines the complex man behind the numerous stories and wild tales, detailing the patterns of extravagant success, failure, and comeback that characterized his life.
"Casey Stengel is remembered as either the shrewd, innovative New York Yankee manager who won 10 pennants and seven World Series from 1949 to 1960 or as the seemingly senile, aged master of malaprop who (mis)-managed

ESSENTIAL AND RECOMMENDED TITLES
796.357 Baseball

the legendarily inept New York Mets in the early 1960s. Creamer . dissolves the apparently disparate images and melds them into an inclusive vision of an unexpectedly complex man." —*Booklist*

Originally published: New York : Simon and Schuster, c1984. With new introd; Bison books—P. preceding t.P; Includes index.

Diamond, Jared M.
Swing Kings: The Inside Story of Baseball's Home Run Revolution. Jared Diamond. William Morrow & Co 2020. 352 p.

ISBN 9780062872104

Grades: Adult   796.357

1. Baseball 2. Home runs (Baseball) 3. Baseball players 4. Baseball bats 5. Professional baseball 6. Professional baseball players 7. 21st century 8. Sports and competition — Baseball

LC Bl2020004928

The Wall Street Journal national baseball writer presents a narrative account of the "home run boom" that describes the pivotal contributions of such figures as J. D. Martinez, Aaron Judge and Justin Turner.

"This breezy and engaging history will be a hit with baseball aficionados and casual fans alike." —*Publishers Weekly*

Eisenberg, John
The Streak: Lou Gehrig, Cal Ripken, and Baseball's Most Historic Record. John Eisenberg. Houghton Mifflin Harcourt 2017. 320 p.

ISBN 9780544107670

Grades: Adult   796.357

1. Ripken, Cal, Jr, 1960- 2. Gehrig, Lou, 1903-1941 3. Baseball Hall of Fame members 4. Professional baseball players 5. Baseball players 6. Baseball 7. Professional baseball 8. Shortstops (Baseball players) 9. First base players (Baseball) 10. Record setting 11. Statistics 12. Sports and Competition — Baseball 13. Sports and Competition — Sports History 14. Sports and Competition — Individual Athlete

LC 2017000811

Discusses the historic, game-playing records by both Lou Gehrig and Cal Ripken Jr. and dissects who had the more difficult achievement through probing research, meticulous analysis and colorful parallel storytelling.

"Eisenberg examines one of baseball's most venerated records while exploring what it all means, providing a compelling, thought-provoking history for fans of America's grand game." —*Kirkus*

Epplin, Luke
Our Team: The Epic Story of Four Men and the World Series That Changed Baseball. Luke Epplin. Flatiron Books 2021. 416 p.

ISBN 9781250313799

Grades: Adult   796.357

1. Doby, Larry 2. Veeck, Bill, 1914-1986 3. Feller, Bob, 1918-2010 4. Paige, Satchel, 1906-1982 5. Baseball history 6. African American baseball players 7. Baseball players 8. Baseball teams 9. Racism in baseball 10. Sports history 11. Race relations 12. United States 13. 1940s 14. Collective Biographies 15. Life stories — Sports — Athletes 16. Sports and Competition — Baseball 17. Sports and Competition — Sports history 18. History writing — United States

LC 2020047458

Tells the story of four men—Larry Doby, Bill Veeck, Bob Feller, and Satchel Paige—whose improbable union on the Cleveland Indians in the late 1940s would shape the immediate postwar era of Major League Baseball and beyond.

"Epplin has given us an entertaining account of this ball club, and we find ourselves rooting for them in the end. An enjoyable read for all sports fans." —*Library Journal*

Includes bibliographical references and index.

Feinstein, John
Where Nobody Knows Your Name: Life in the Minor Leagues of Baseball. John Feinstein. Doubleday 2014. 304 p.

ISBN 9780385535939

Grades: Adult   796.357

1. Minor league baseball 2. Baseball 3. Minor league baseball players 4. Baseball players 5. Sports and Competition — Baseball

LC 2013030645

During the 2012 season, sportswriter John Feinstein dug into minor league baseball, spending his time with players, managers, and other members of the Triple-A International League. It's a very different world than the majors, which becomes clear as Feinstein focuses on eight men in particular, among a larger cast. Some of them have worked in the majors while others haven't—but they all want to get there for good. From the Durham Bulls to the Lehigh Valley Iron Pigs, Where Nobody Knows Your Name offers a colorfully broad view of life in the minor leagues.

Formosa, Dan
Baseball Field Guide: An In-Depth Illustrated Guide to the Complete Rules of Baseball. Dan Formosa & Paul Hamburger. The Experiment 2023. 264 pages : Illustration

ISBN 9781615199549

Grades: Adult   796.357

1. Baseball 2. Rules 3. Sports and Competition — Baseball 4. Reference — General

LC 2022052459

For new and seasoned fans alike, this visual guide demystifies baseball's every rule.

"This book belongs on the shelves of most public libraries, especially those with sports fans." —*Booklist*

Includes index.

Geist, William
Little League Confidential: One Coach's Completely Unauthorized Tale of Survival. Bill Geist. Dell 1999. 217 p.

ISBN 9780440508779

Grades: Adult   796.357

1. Little League baseball 2. Humor writing — Social humor 3. Reference books — Sports 4. Sports and Competition — Baseball

LC BL 99003224

A journalist tells of his experiences coaching his son's Little League team, with anecdotes about a ballerina batter, an unfair umpire uncle, and other stories that provide a fresh perspective on an American institution.

"The author relates his decade of service as a little-league baseball coach. He admittedly distills his experiencesand those of othersinto a season-long docudrama journal. He tells of pompous coaches lecturing their miniplayers on the subtleties of the infield fly rule; he addresses the question of positioning a player with a personal-injury lawyer for a dad. The book is a wonderful effort filled with empathy for kids, impatience for pushy parents, and a good sense of humor." —*Booklist*

A Dell trade paperback; Originally published: New York : Macmillan, 1992.

Goldberger, Paul
Ballpark: Baseball in the American City. Paul Goldberger. Alfred A. Knopf 2019. 352 p.

ISBN 9780307701541

Grades: Adult   796.357

1. Baseball fields 2. Stadiums 3. Historic buildings 4. Baseball history 5. United States 6. Arts and Entertainment — Architecture 7. Sports and Competition — Baseball

LC 2018046223

This lavishly-illustrated look at the history of baseball through the lens of its ever-changing ballparks discusses the bond between American cities and the national pastime and how changes in the urban landscape have been reflected in stadium design.

Includes bibliographical references.

Halberstam, David
Summer of '49. David Halberstam. Harper Perennial 2006. 354 p. : Illustration

ISBN 9780060884260

PUBLIC LIBRARY CORE COLLECTION: NONFICTION
Twentieth Edition

Grades: 11 12 Adult   796.357

1. Baseball 2. Baseball teams 3. Professional baseball 4. Professional baseball teams 5. Social life and customs 6. United States 7. 1940s 8. Sports and Competition — Baseball 9. Sports and Competition — Teams

LC 89002886

Chronicles the 1949 pennant race between the Boston Red Sox and the New York Yankees, profiling the players, owners, and fans as major league baseball was poised on the brink of major changes.

"This book is ostensibly about the pennant race between the Yankees and Red Sox in 1949 and the 'rivalry' between Joe DiMaggio and Ted Williams. It is a study of all the elements and personalities that influenced baseball that year and beyond. Halberstam brings them together in such an enjoyable, interesting, and informative manner that a reader needn't be a baseball fan to appreciate the book." —Library Journal

Includes bibliographical references (p. [337]-339) and index; Originally published: New York : W. Morrow, 1989.

Hample, Zack

The **Baseball:** *Stunts, Scandals, and Secrets Beneath the Stitches.* Zack Hample. Anchor Books 2011. IX, 356 p. : Illustration

ISBN 9780307475459

Grades: 11 12 Adult   796.357

1. Baseball fans 2. Baseballs 3. Professional baseball 4. Professional baseball players 5. Baseball 6. Baseball history 7. United States 8. Sports and Competition — Baseball 9. History writing — Microhistory 10. Adult books for young adults

LC 2010043551

The best-selling author of Watching Baseball Smarter shares historical and modern stories about the ball at the center of America's favorite pastime while tracing the baseball's evolution from a string-wrapped walnut to today's invisible ink-stamped ball.

"The author covers basics such as what to watch for in pitchers, catchers, hitters, fielders and base runners; he also provides answers to such nagging questions as why spectators stretch in the seventh inning and why most ballplayers grab their crotches. Hample hits the equivalent of a reference book home run with his witty and loose styletaking a friendly for-a-fan-by-a-fan approach that doesn't hide his enormous depth of knowledge." —Publishers Weekly

Anchor sports; Includes index.

Jamieson, David

Mint Condition: How Baseball Cards Became an American Obsession. David Jamieson. Atlantic Monthly Press 2010. 320 p.

ISBN 9780802119391

Grades: Adult   796.357

1. Baseball cards 2. Collectors and collecting 3. Collectibles 4. Sports cards 5. Baseball 6. Popular culture 7. Sports and Competition — Baseball

LC 2010282449

Explores the fascinating world of baseball-card collecting from its roots in the tobacco industry to its rise in popularity to its bubble bursting in the 90s, in a book that looks at mad-genius designers, professional "graders" who rate the cards and the "doctors" who secretly alter them.

"For much of his book, Jamieson seems to be saying that greed and grown-ups have spoiled card collecting forever. But there's comfort in knowing that the cards have always appealed to baseball lovers and bottom-line business types for their own reasons. Even Jamieson holds out hope that they will find their proper place again in American kids' lives even if it's only in their closets." —Minneapolis Star Tribune

Kenny, Brian

Ahead of the Curve: Inside the Baseball Revolution. Brian Kenny. Simon & Schuster 2016. 512 p.

ISBN 9781501106330

Grades: Adult   796.357

1. Baseball 2. Statistics 3. Sports and competition — Baseball

LC 2015039474

The outspoken MLB Network commentator draws on stories from baseball's present and past to reveal the important role of analytical thinking in today's game, examining why baseball leaders have compromised teams by favoring traditional rather than logical strategies.

"When Miguel Cabrera captured Major League Baseball's elusive Triple Crown in 2012, Kenny refused to join the adulatory journalists lauding his selection as the American League's Most Valuable Player. Convinced that two-thirds of the Crown's jewels (namely, batting average and runs batted in) poorly measure a player's performance, Kenny argues that more-sophisticated metrics established Angels outfielder Mike Trout as a more deserving MVP. Recognizing Oaklands Moneyball transformation as a harbinger of things to come, Kenny predicts that as managers grow increasingly data-savvy, they will throw off the restraints of tradition when shifting infielders, setting a batting order, and using the bullpen. Perhaps unwelcome among fans who love the myth and nostalgia of the diamond, this bolt of analytical lightning will make sports talk shows crackle." —Booklist

Includes bibliographical references and index.

Kepner, Tyler

K: A History of Baseball in Ten Pitches. Tyler Kepner. Doubleday 2019. 320 p.

ISBN 9780385541015

Grades: Adult   796.357

1. Pitching (Baseball) 2. Pitchers (Baseball) 3. Batters (Baseball) 4. Baseballs 5. Baseball players 6. Professional baseball players 7. Baseball Hall of Fame members 8. Baseball history 9. United States 10. Sports and Competition — Baseball

LC 2018016158

A history of the national pastime as told through the craft of pitching draws on years of archival research and interviews with more than three hundred star athletes to reveal the colorful stories and folklore behind ten major pitches.

"From triumph to tragedy, readers trace the astonishingly diverse trajectories of the baseballs pitchers throw. Appreciative fans will keep this book zipping off library shelves." —Booklist

Includes bibliographical references and index.

Knight, Molly

The Best Team Money Can Buy: The Los Angeles Dodgers' Wild Struggle to Build a Baseball Powerhouse. Molly Knight. Simon & Schuster 2015. 324 p.

ISBN 9781476776293

Grades: Adult   796.357

1. Professional baseball teams 2. Professional baseball players 3. Baseball teams 4. Baseball 5. Sports 6. Management 7. Sports and Competition — Soccer 8. Business and economics — Industries — Entertainment and media

LC 2015017287

Documents the lucrative 2012 purchase of a bankrupt Los Angeles Dodgers team and the ensuing high-conflict deals involving new owners, managers and players, including controversy-marked rookie Yasiel Puig.

"A must-read for fans of the Dodgers and all Los Angeles sports teams. Knight's undercover work is like none other. Dodger fanatics, this book is for you." —Library Journal

Kornhauser, Jacob

The Cup of Coffee Club: 11 Players and Their Brush with Baseball History. Jacob Kornhauser. Rowman & Littlefield 2020. 208 pages

ISBN 9781538130810

Grades: Adult   796.357

1. Minor league baseball 2. Baseball players 3. United States 4. Biographies 5. Sports and Competition — Baseball 6. Sports and Competition — Individual Athlete 7. Life stories — Sports — Athletes

LC 2019038836

Most baseball players will never reach the major leagues. While many that do stay there for a long time, there are a select few that played in just one major league game. Cup of Coffee Club tells the stories of eleven of these players and their struggles to reach the major leagues, as well as their struggles to get back.

"This is one of the very best baseball books in years. Readers will put faces and names to what they knew on a subliminal level: Major-league baseball is really, really hard, and a lot of fine young players get left behind." —Booklist

Includes bibliographical references and index.

ESSENTIAL AND RECOMMENDED TITLES
796.357 Baseball

Kurkjian, Tim
I'm Fascinated by Sacrifice Flies: Inside the Game We All Love. Tim Kurkjian. St. Martin's Press 2016. 256 p.
ISBN 9781250077936
Grades: Adult   796.357
1. Sportscasters 2. Baseball 3. Sports and Competition — Baseball
LC 2015048747

An ESPN baseball analyst offers hilarious and insightful tales from the world of Major League Baseball.

"Kurkjian's celebrity and the joyous contents within the covers merit the investment." —*Booklist*

Kurlansky, Mark
The Eastern Stars: How Baseball Changed the Dominican Town of San Pedro De Macoris. Mark Kurlansky. Riverhead Books 2010. 288 p.
ISBN 9781594487507
Grades: Adult   796.357
1. Baseball 2. Baseball players 3. Sugar industry and trade 4. Migrant workers 5. Dominican Republic 6. Sports and Competition — Baseball 7. Adult books for young adults
LC 2009041036

A history of San Pedro in the Dominican Republic traces its rise from a small and impoverished region to an area that has produced some of Major League Baseball's greatest talents, citing the influence of sugar industry migrant workers and the role of race in transforming the sport. By the best-selling author of Cod.
Includes bibliographical references and index.

Law, Keith
Smart Baseball: The Story Behind the Old Stats That Are Ruining the Game, the New Ones That Are Running It, and the Right Way to Think About Baseball. Keith Law. William Morrow & Company 2017. 304 pages
ISBN 9780062490223
Grades: Adult   796.357
1. Baseball history 2. Statistics 3. Forecasting 4. Big data 5. Winning and losing 6. Baseball players 7. Baseball teams 8. Decision-making 9. Sports and Competition — Baseball 10. Science Writing — Mathematics
LC Bl2017016359

An ESPN senior baseball writer and statistical analyst looks at the numbers game of baseball, proving why some of the most trusted stats are surprisingly wrong, explaining what numbers actually work and exploring what the rise of Big Data means for the future of the sport.

"This book by ESPN sportswriter and analyst Law is both a primer on how sabermetrics are changing the way fans and professionals view baseball, as well as a thorough explanation of why traditional statistics are misleading or obsolete." —*Library Journal*

Lewis, Michael
★ *Moneyball: The Art of Winning an Unfair Game.* Michael Lewis. W. W. Norton 2003. xv, 288 p.
ISBN 9780393057652
Grades: 11 12 Adult   796.357
1. Baseball 2. Professional baseball scouting 3. Baseball players 4. Professional sports teams 5. Page to screen 6. Sports and Competition — Baseball 7. Adult books for young adults
LC 2003005089

New York Times Notable Book, 2003.

Examines the fallacy behind the major league baseball refrain that the team with the biggest wallet is supposed to win. Over the past four years the Oakland Athletics, a major league team with a minor league payroll, have had one of the best records in the country.

"With so many baseball books to choose from, it is difficult to single out a few as must-haves, but this one comes pretty close." —*Booklist*

Lindbergh, Ben
The Only Rule Is That It Has to Work: Our Wild Experiment Building a New Kind of Baseball Team. Ben Lindbergh, Sam Miller. Henry Holt & Co. 2016. 304 p.
ISBN 9781627795647
Grades: Adult   796.357
1. Baseball 2. Professional baseball scouting 3. Statistics 4. Minor league baseball 5. Minor league baseball teams 6. Sports and Competition — Baseball
LC 2016005561

Two statisticians describe what happened when they were given the chance to run the Sonoma Stompers, an independent minor-league team in California, according to the most advanced statistics.

"With honest and captivating prose, the authors compel readers to care about players that don't make a lot of money yet still have big league dreams and aspirations." —*Library Journal*

Megdal, Howard
The Baseball Talmud: The Definitive Position-by-Position Ranking of Baseball's Chosen Players. Howard Megdal. HarperCollins 2022. 320 p.
ISBN 9781637270011
Grades: Adult   796.357
1. Baseball players 2. Baseball 3. Jewish Americans 4. Professional baseball 5. Statistics 6. Biographies 7. Sports and Competition — Baseball 8. Sports and Competition — Sports History 9. History writing — Jewish history
LC 2008040534

This new, expanded edition of The Baseball Talmud rewrites the history of Jewish baseball and is a book that every baseball fan should own.

Montgomery, Patrick
Baseball's Great Expectations: Candid Stories of Ballplayers Who Didn't Live up to the Hype. Patrick Montgomery. Rowman & Littlefield 2024. 191 p.
ISBN 9781538181805
Grades: Adult   796.357
1. Baseball 2. Baseball players 3. Professional baseball players 4. Athletic ability 5. Expectation 6. Bad luck 7. Sports injuries 8. Failure 9. Winning and losing 10. Baseball history 11. Sports and Competition — Baseball 12. Life stories — Sports — Athletes

Stories of baseball idols and heroes are oft-repeated, but what about those players who everyone thought would be the next "great one" and have since disappeared from the sport? What happened after they failed to meet the weighty expectations placed on them? Baseball's Great Expectations reveals an often-overlooked side of professional baseball, of the struggles with injury, mental exhaustion, pressure, temptations, and sometimes just being in the wrong place at the wrong time. The path to baseball stardom is not as glamorous as it is sometimes made out to be, and this book reveals just how difficult the journey truly is.

"A fascinating exploration of the unfulfilled dreams of pro baseball players. Will appeal to fans of the sport." —*Library Journal*
Includes index.

Neyer, Rob
Power Ball: Anatomy of a Modern Baseball Game. Rob Neyer. Harper 2018. xii, 300 p.
ISBN 9780062853615
Grades: Adult   796.357
1. Baseball 2. Professional baseball 3. Strategy 4. Winning and losing 5. Sports 6. Baseball teams 7. Sports and Competition — Baseball
LC 2018027809

To show the many ways in which Major League Baseball has changed over the past 20 years, a former ESPN columnist and analytics pioneer dramatically recreates an action-packed 2017 game between the Oakland A's and eventual World Series Champion Houston Astros.
Includes index.

Nusbaum, Eric
Stealing Home: Los Angeles, the Dodgers, and the Lives Caught in Between. Eric Nusbaum. PublicAffairs 2020. xiii, 331 p.

ISBN 9781541742215

Grades: Adult 796.357

1. Mexican-Americans 2. Neighborhoods 3. Baseball fields 4. Municipal government 5. Urban planning 6. Injustice 7. Racism 8. Classism 9. Baseball history 10. United States history 11. California 12. Los Angeles, California 13. 20th century 14. History writing — Regional history — United States 15. Sports and Competition — Baseball 16. Sports and Competition — Sports History

LC 2019041742

Dodger Stadium is an American icon. The oldest ballpark west of the Mississippi—and the third oldest overall—it is a shrine to baseball and an essential feature of the Los Angeles cityscape. Yet the story of how it was built has a dark side. To clear space for the stadium, the city tore down low-income, Hispanic-friendly housing, resulting in a dramatic confrontation between the County Sheriff and the one family—the Arechigas—who refused to yield their home. In Stealing Home, Eric Nusbaum—a fluent Spanish-speaker, Dodgers fan, and lifelong Angeleno—tells the stories of the people whose homes were destroyed, their conflict with the bureaucrats and money men of Los Angeles, and shows how their lives were overrun by the wheel of history.

"Provocative, essential reading for students of California history." —*Kirkus*

Includes bibliographical references and index.

O'Brien, Keith

Charlie Hustle: The Rise and Fall of Pete Rose, and the Last Glory Days of Baseball. Keith O'Brien. Pantheon Books 2024. 512 p.

ISBN 9780593317372

Grades: Adult 796.357

1. Rose, Pete, 1941- 2. Baseball players 3. Baseball managers 4. Celebrities 5. Sports betting 6. Baseball betting 7. Compulsive gamblers 8. Womanizers 9. Deception 10. Corruption 11. Pariahs 12. American people 13. Cincinnati, Ohio 14. Biographies 15. Impartial writing 16. Life stories — Sports 17. Sports and Competition — Baseball 18. Sports and Competition — Gambling and Betting 19. Sports and Competition — Individual Athlete

LC 2023020621

Pete Rose is a legend. A baseball god. He compiled more hits than anyone in the history of baseball, a record he set decades ago that still stands today. He was a working-class white guy from Cincinnati who made it; less talented than tough, and rough around the edges. He was everything that America wanted and needed him to be, the American dream personified, until he wasn't. In the 1980s, Pete Rose came to be at the center of one of the biggest scandals in baseball history. He kept secrets, ran with bookies, took on massive gambling debts, and he was magnificently, publicly cast out for betting on baseball and lying about it.

"Sports biographies don't get much better than this enthralling and tragic account of the career of Pete Rose, Major League Baseball's all-time hits leader." —*Publishers Weekly*

Includes bibliographical references and index.

Perron, Cam

★ *Comeback* Season: My Unlikely Story of Friendship with the Greatest Living Negro League Baseball Players. Cam Perron with Nick Chiles; foreword by Hank Aaron. Gallery Books 2021. 288 p.

ISBN 9781982153601

Grades: Adult 796.357

1. Perron, Cam, 1994- 2. Baseball fans 3. African American baseball players 4. Negro Leagues players 5. Baseball 6. Friendship 7. Racism in sports 8. Interracial friendship 9. Professional baseball 10. Racism in baseball 11. Sports 12. Baseball history 13. United States 14. Autobiographies and memoirs 15. Sports and Competition — Baseball 16. Life stories — Sports 17. History writing — African American — United States

LC 2020038081

The uplifting, unlikely, and inspirational true story of the friendships formed between Cam Perron—a white, baseball-obsessed teenager from Boston—and hundreds of former professional Negro League players, who were still awaiting the recognition and compensation that they deserved from Major League Baseball more than fifty years after their playing days were over. Featuring the players' fascinating stories and original photographs.

"This heartfelt book, with a foreword by Hank Aaron, is a must-read, and Perron's personable writing succeeds in giving often overlooked players a voice." —*Library Journal*

Pessah, Jon

The Game: Inside the Secret World of Major League Baseball's Power Brokers. Jon Pessah. Little, Brown and Company 2015. 512 p.

ISBN 9780316185882

Grades: Adult 796.357

1. Baseball 2. Professional baseball 3. Baseball players 4. Baseball team owners 5. Contracts 6. Negotiation in business 7. Professional sports teams 8. Sports and competition — Baseball

LC 2015901927

The founding editor of ESPN the Magazine and Pulitzer Prize nominee presents the extraordinary inside story of baseball's last 20 years, during which the genius and struggle for power of three men saved the game from self-destruction.

"Labor strife and controversies over performance-enhancing drugs absolutely are essential to baseball's recent history, but the author presents them as virtually the only parts that matter. An important but incomplete picture of baseball's Bud Selig era." —*Kirkus*

Peta, Joe

Trading Bases: A Story About Wall Street, Gambling, and Baseball (Not Necessarily in That Order):. Joe Peta. Dutton 2013. 368 p.

ISBN 9780525953647

Grades: Adult 796.357

1. Baseball 2. Statistics 3. Gambling 4. Finance 5. Wall Street, New York City 6. Sports and Competition — Baseball 7. Business and economics — Economics — Contemporary U.S. economy

LC 2012043509

An ex-Wall Street trader improved on "Moneyball's" famed sabermetrics to place bets that would beat the Vegas odds on Major League Baseball games—with a 41 percent return in his first year. "Trading Bases" explains how he did it.

Includes index.

Posnanski, Joe

The Baseball 100. Joe Posnanski. Avid Reader Press 2021. 869 pages : Illustration

ISBN 9781982180584

Grades: Adult 796.357

1. Baseball players 2. Baseball history 3. Professional baseball players 4. Collective biographies 5. Sports and Competition — Baseball 6. Life stories — Sports — Athletes

LC Oc2021002865

An award-winning sportswriter presents this ultimate baseball resource that tells the story of the game through the extraordinary lives of its 100 greatest players by retracing their origins, illuminating their characters and placing their accomplishments in the context of baseball's past and present.

"Sportswriter Posnanski (The Soul of Baseball) knocks it out of the park with this fascinating deep dive into the careers of those he considers baseball's 100 greatest players. . . . Sure to inspire heated debate, this is a remarkable achievement." —*Publishers Weekly*

The Athletic; Includes index.

The Soul of Baseball: A Road Trip Through Buck O'Neil's America. Joe Posnanski. W. Morrow 2007. 276 p.

ISBN 9780060854034

Grades: 11 12 Adult 796.357

1. O'Neil, Buck, 1911-2006 2. Posnanski, Joe 3. African American baseball players 4. First base players (Baseball) 5. Professional baseball scouts 6. Travelers 7. Negro Leagues 8. Baseball history 9. Social life and customs 10. Voyages and travels 11. United States 12. 20th century 13. Biographies 14. Sports and Competition — Baseball 15. Sports and Competition — Individual Athlete 16. Life stories — Sports — Athletes 17. Adult books for young adults 18. Life stories — Sports — Coaches, managers, and owners

ESSENTIAL AND RECOMMENDED TITLES
796.357 Baseball

LC 2007296667

Documents the author's cross-country travels at the side of Negro Leagues champion Buck O'Neil, a journey during which the pair sought to recapture their love of the game, remembered O'Neil's history-making career, and explored the numerous challenges that the sport has overcome.

★ *Why We Love Baseball: A History in 50 Moments*. Joe Posnanski. Dutton 2023. 336 p.
ISBN 9780593472675
Grades: Adult   796.357
1. Baseball 2. Baseball players 3. Baseball teams 4. Memories 5. Winning and losing 6. Sports history 7. Sports and Competition — Baseball 8. Sports and Competition — Sports History

Joe Posnanski writes of major moments that created legends, and of forgotten moments almost lost to time. From nineteenth-century pitchers' duels to breaking the sport's color line in the '40s, all the way to the greatest trick play of the last decade and the slide home that became a meme, Posnanski's illuminating take allows us to rediscover the sport we love—and thought we knew.

"This work will likely enlighten even the most knowledgeable and die-hard baseball fans." —*Library Journal*

Rapp, David
Tinker to Evers to Chance: The Chicago Cubs and the Dawn of Modern America. David Rapp. 2018. 325 p.
ISBN 9780226415048
Grades: Adult   796.357
1. Evers, Johnny 2. Tinker, Joe, 1880-1948 3. Chance, Frank L. (Frank Leroy), 1877-1924 4. Baseball history 5. Professional baseball players 6. Professional baseball 7. Baseball players 8. 1900s (Decade) 9. Sports and Competition — Baseball 10. Sports and Competition — Sports History

LC 2017041630

Tinker to Evers to Chance examines this pivotal moment in American history, when baseball became the game we know today. Each man came from a different corner of the country and brought a distinctive local culture with him: Evers from the Irish-American hothouse of Troy, New York; Tinker from the urban parklands of Kansas City, Missouri; Chance from the verdant fields of California's Central Valley. The stories of these early baseball stars shed unexpected light not only on the evolution of baseball and on the enthusiasm of its players and fans all across America, but also on the broader convulsions transforming the US into a confident new industrial society. With them emerged a truly national culture.

"The compelling narrative not only details the feats these three achieved in helping establish a Cubs dynasty but also chronicles the metamorphosis of the new twentieth-century nation that embraced baseball as a game that reflected the urban strength developed in modern industry while also offering green-field comfort to city dwellers nostalgic for a rural past." —*Booklist*

Includes bibliographical references and index.

Reiter, Ben
Astroball: The New Way to Win It All. Ben Reiter. Crown Archetype 2018. 272 p.
ISBN 9780525576648
Grades: Adult   796.357
1. Baseball 2. Baseball teams 3. Professional baseball 4. Sports 5. Sports and Competition — Baseball 6. Sports and Competition — Teams

LC 2018019954

The Sports Illustrated writer who predicted the Houston Astros' unexpected rise to win the World Series three years before it happened offers an account of the team's breathtaking 2017 season.

Ripken, Bill
State of Play: The Old School Guide to New School Baseball. Bill Ripken. Diversion Books 2020. xxix, 209 pages : Illustration
ISBN 9781635766592
Grades: Adult   796.357
1. Baseball 2. Sports 3. Sports and Competition — Baseball

"A well-written account by one of baseball's most influential players. Fans of America's pastime and die-hard sabermetrics devotees will savor this informed perspective." —*Library Journal*

Ruck, Rob
Raceball: How the Major Leagues Colonized the Black and Latin Game. Rob Ruck. Beacon Press 2010. 288 p.
ISBN 9780807048054
Grades: 11-12 Adult   796.357
1. Baseball 2. Racism in sports 3. African American baseball players 4. Hispanic American baseball players 5. Baseball history 6. Latin America 7. Caribbean Area 8. United States 9. Sports and Competition — Baseball 10. Society and culture — Race

LC 2010037079

Discusses the intricate relationship between race and baseball, from the integration of the Major Leagues to the resulting decline of the Negro League and contemporary prominence of baseball players from the Caribbean.

Includes bibliographical references and index.

Rushin, Steve
The 34-Ton Bat: The Story of Baseball as Told Through Bobbleheads, Cracker Jacks, Jockstraps, Eye Black, and 375 Other Strange and Unforgettable Objects. Steve Rushin. Little, Brown and Company 2013. 288 p.
ISBN 9780316200936
Grades: Adult   796.357
1. Baseball history 2. Baseball players 3. Material culture 4. Sports and Competition — Baseball

LC 2013017752

Provides a history of America's pastime told through memorabilia and other tokens of the sport and its fans, including giant bats and balls, cards, team pennants, cracker jacks, eyeblack, pipe organs, and clogged stadium toilets.

Includes bibliographical references and index.

Sabathia, CC
Till the End. Cc Sabathia, with Chris Smith. One World 2021. 256 p.
ISBN 9780593133750
Grades: Adult   796.357
1. Sabathia, CC (Carsten Charles) 2. Baseball players 3. Resilience 4. Baseball 5. Families 6. Fame 7. Addiction 8. Alcoholism 9. Loss 10. Sports 11. Autobiographies and memoirs 12. Life stories — Sports — Athletes 13. Life stories — Facing adversity — Medical issues — Addiction 14. Sports and Competition — Baseball

LC 2020057521

The memoir of the life of one of the most beloved baseball players of his generation presents a raw, compelling story of baseball, family, fame, addiction, loss, and a champion's resilience.

"One of the best pitchers of his generation—and often the only Black man on his team—shares an extraordinary life in baseball. . . . Everything about Sabathia is larger than life, yet he tells his story with honesty and humility." —*Kirkus*

Sawchik, Travis
Big Data Baseball: Math, Miracles, and the End of a 20-Year Losing Streak. Travis Sawchik. Flatiron Books 2015. 288 p.
ISBN 9781250063502
Grades: Adult   796.357
1. Baseball 2. Baseball players 3. Baseball teams 4. Statistics 5. Sports and Competition — Baseball 6. Science Writing — Mathematics 7. Adult books for young adults

LC 2015011231

A sports writer for the Pittsburgh Tribune-Review describes how the General Manager of the Pirates, tired of a 20-year losing streak, adopted the strategies of big data, similar to those depicted in Moneyball, to help improve their game.

"Casual and hard-core baseball fans alike who enjoyed Moneyball are sure to be entertained and informed by this sort-of sequel." —*Library Journal*

PUBLIC LIBRARY CORE COLLECTION: NONFICTION
Twentieth Edition

Simon, Scott
My Cubs: A Love Story. Scott Simon. Blue Rider Press 2017. 160 p.
ISBN 9780735218031
Grades: Adult   796.357
1. Simon, Scott 2. Baseball fans 3. Professional baseball teams 4. Professional baseball 5. Baseball teams 6. Winning and losing 7. Chicago, Illinois 8. Sports and Competition — Baseball 9. Sports and Competition — Teams
LC 2017004698

The host of National Public Radio's Weekend Edition offers personal, heartfelt reflections on his beloved Chicago Cubs, replete with club lore, memorable anecdotes, frenetic fandom and wise and adoring intimacy that have made the world champion Cubbies baseball's most tortured—and now triumphant—franchise.

"There will be many books about the Cubs 2016 World Series win, but its doubtful any will surpass Simons for humor, poignancy, and, well, love." —*Booklist*

Stout, Glenn
Fenway 1912: The Birth of a Ballpark, a Championship Season, and Fenway's Remarkable First Year. Glenn Stout. Houghton Mifflin Harcourt 2011. 256 p.
ISBN 9780547195629
Grades: Adult   796.357
1. Baseball fields 2. Professional baseball 3. Professional baseball teams 4. Boston, Massachusetts 5. Sports and Competition — Baseball
LC 2011016068

A centennial tribute to the beloved ballpark shares the behind-the-scenes story of its tumultuous origins and first year, sharing coverage of such topics as the unorthodox blueprint that belies the park's notorious quirks, the construction contributions of local citizens and the history-making World Series battle between the Red Sox and the Giants.

"While some sports histories are bone-dry and distant, Stout imbues his account with a unique vibrancy and a razor-sharp intelligence. A wonderful sports book." —*Booklist*

Svrluga, Barry
The Grind: Inside Baseball's Endless Season. Barry Svrluga. Blue Rider Press 2015. 192 p.
ISBN 9780399176289
Grades: Adult   796.357
1. Professional baseball 2. Baseball players 3. Baseball 4. United States 5. Sports and Competition — Baseball
LC 2015016056

What's it like to live through sports' longest season, the 162-game Major League Baseball schedule? THE GRIND captures the frustration, impermanence, and glory felt by the players, the staff, and their families from the start of spring training to the final game of the year; classy baseball writing in the Roger Angell or Tom Boswell tradition.

"A quick and enjoyable read for any baseball lover, not just Nationals fans." —*Library Journal*
Includes bibliographical references and index.

Turbow, Jason
The Baseball Codes: Beanballs, Sign Stealing, and Bench-Clearing Brawls : The Unwritten Rules of America's Pastime. Jason Turbow with Michael Duca. Pantheon Books 2010. 304 p.
ISBN 9780375424694
Grades: Adult   796.357
1. Baseball 2. Baseball players 3. Rules 4. Baseball teams 5. Behavior 6. Sports and Competition — Baseball
LC 2009022253

A behind-the-scenes analysis of professional baseball's hidden rules reveals the impact of unwritten codes of conduct, retaliatory behaviors and cheating, providing dramatic examples as committed by such figures as Mickey Mantle, Willie Mays and Don Drysdale.

"The premise [of this book] is that ballplayers, managers, coaches and various other participants in the culture of baseball are all clued in to a value system, a mode of behavior that defines a gauzy ideal: the right way to play the game. [The authors] have collected dozens of stories from baseball history about situations that are not governed by the rule book but that pertain to the fuzzy notions of rightness and respect and that describe the contours of the so-called baseball codes. The stories the authors have unearthed to illustrate ballpark justice and morality are often delicious." —*New York Times Book Review*
Includes bibliographical references and index.

They Bled Blue: Fernandomania, Strike-Season Mayhem, and the Weirdest Championship Baseball Had Ever Seen: The 1981 Los Angeles Dodgers. Jason Turbow. Houghton Mifflin Harcourt 2019. 320 p.
ISBN 9781328715531
Grades: Adult   796.357
1. Valenzuela, Fernando, 1960- 2. Lasorda, Tommy 3. Pitchers (Baseball) 4. Baseball managers 5. Professional baseball teams 6. Cy Young Award winners 7. Baseball players 8. Professional baseball players 9. Los Angeles, California 10. 20th century 11. Sports and Competition — Baseball
LC 2018043599

Recounts the 1981 season of the Los Angeles Dodgers, including the break out pitcher Fernando Venezuela, Tommy Lasorda's monologues about bleeding Dodger blue, and their unexpected World Series win.

"Fluidly written and expertly paced, this exciting look at a turbulent team will thrill baseball enthusiasts of all stripes." —*Publishers Weekly*
Includes bibliographical references and index.

Wong, Stephen
Game Worn: Baseball Treasures from the Game's Greatest Heroes and Moments. Stephen Wong and Dave Grob; foreword by John Thorn; photography by Francesco Sapienza. Smithsonian Books 2016. 320 pages : Illustration; Color
ISBN 9781588345714
Grades: Adult   796.357
1. Sports uniforms 2. Baseball 3. Arts and Entertainment — Antiques and collectibles 4. Sports and Competition — Baseball
LC 2016015599

Photography, essays, and research on rare game-worn uniforms that bear witness to baseball history.

"This rare look at the importance of baseball garments is a visually striking compilation that reads like a Ken Burns documentary. A book for all baseball lovers." —*Library Journal*
Includes bibliographical references (pages 313-316) and index.

Smithsonian Baseball: Inside the World's Finest Private Collections. Stephen Wong; photographs by Susan Einstein. Smithsonian Books 2005. x, 286 p. Illustration; Color
ISBN 9780060838515
Grades: Adult   796.357
1. Baseball 2. Collectibles 3. Collectors and collecting 4. United States 5. Arts and Entertainment — Antiques and collectibles 6. Arts and Entertainment — Photography 7. Sports and Competition — Baseball
LC 2006297206

An oversized volume showcases 350 full-color photographs of twenty-one of the best private collections of baseball memorabilia, featuring numerous historical and previously unseen artifacts and providing eight expert essays on how to build a personal collection.
Includes bibliographical references (p. 286) and index.

Zminda, Don
Double Plays and Double Crosses: The Black Sox and Baseball in 1920. Don Zminda. Rowman & Littlefield 2021. 344 p.
ISBN 9781538142325
Grades: Adult   796.357
1. Sports betting 2. Baseball 3. Scandals 4. Baseball betting 5. Black Sox Scandal, 1919 6. Sports cover-ups 7. Sports corruption 8. Chicago, Illinois 9. 1920s 10. 20th century 11. Sports and Competition — Baseball 12. Sports and

ESSENTIAL AND RECOMMENDED TITLES
796.3576 Specific types of baseball

Competition — Gambling and Betting 13. History writing — Scandals 14. Sports and Competition — Sports History
LC 2020036349

This book is the exciting story of how one of the most infamous scandals in American history—the Black Sox scandal—continued for over a year following the "fixed" World Series of 1919 until the truth began to emerge. It is a story of gamblers and crooks; a story of teammates betraying one another; a story of investigations and cover-ups.

"One hundred years after the notorious Black Sox scandal, baseball scholars and historians will find this an essential study of a previously unexplored chapter of the game's history." —*Library Journal*

Includes bibliographical references and index.

796.3576 Specific types of baseball

Passan, Jeff
The *Arm*: Inside the Billion-Dollar Mystery of the Most Valuable Commodity in Sports. Jeff Passan. HarperCollins 2016. 368 p.
ISBN 9780062400369
Grades: Adult   796.3576
1. Baseball 2. Pitchers (Baseball) 3. Pitching (Baseball) 4. Baseball players 5. Arm 6. Sports injuries 7. Sports and Competition — Baseball
LC 2016303971

The Yahoo Sports lead columnist and author of Death to the BCS examines the franchise lifeblood role of pitchers in Major League Baseball and the considerable vulnerability of pitching arms, drawing on rare interviews with Daniel Hudson, Todd Coffey and Sandy Koufax to share insights into the impact of injuries on careers and teams.

"As Passan interviews professionals dealing with the problem—physicians, managers, trainers, pitchers, and even epidemiologists—he reports no magical breakthroughs. But he does give readers an insiders perspective on the threat hanging over every player who takes the mound." —*Booklist*

796.35764 Professional and semiprofessional baseball

Law, Keith
The *Inside* Game: Bad Calls, Strange Moves, and What Baseball Behavior Teaches Us About Ourselves. Keith Law. William Morrow 2020. VIII, 263 pages
ISBN 9780062942722
Grades: Adult   796.35764
1. Baseball 2. Professional baseball 3. Professional sports 4. Baseball players 5. Baseball teams 6. Decision-making 7. Social life and customs 8. United States 9. Sports and Competition — Baseball

Offers an era-spanning dissection of some of the best and worst decisions in modern baseball, explaining what motivated them, what can be learned from them, and how their legacy has shaped the game.

"Highly recommended for serious followers of baseball and readers interested in how statistical analysis and trends can be applied in any sport." —*Library Journal*

Includes bibliographical references and index.

796.42 Track and field

Alvarez, Noe
Spirit Run: A 6,000-Mile Marathon Through North America's Stolen Land. Noe Alvarez. Catapult 2020. xvii, 218 p.
ISBN 9781948226462
Grades: Adult   796.42
1. Alvarez, Noe 2. Children of immigrants 3. Distance running 4. Immigrants, Mexican 5. Long distance runners 6. Indigenous peoples of North America 7. First Nations (Canada) 8. Indigenous peoples 9. Indigenous activists 10. Endurance sports 11. Running 12. Self-discovery 13. United States 14. Canada 15. Mexico 16. Guatemala 17. North America 18. Central America 19. Autobiographies and memoirs 20. Life stories — Identity — Race and ethnicity 21. Society and culture — Ethnic studies 22. Society and culture — Social activism and philanthropy 23. Sports and Competition — Racing — Track and Field 24. Adult books for young adults

A debut memoir by the son of working-class Mexican immigrants describes his upbringing in Washington State, membership in the Peace and Dignity Journeys movement and competition in the Native American cultural marathon from Canada to Guatemala.

"This is a powerful American coming-of-age story about a Mexican American who seeks to embrace his heritage while forging his own path forward. Certain to make a lasting impression on readers across generations and backgrounds, all of whom will be inspired by the young Álvarez." —*Booklist*

Dixon, Matt
The *Well-Built* Triathlete: Turning Potential into Performance. Matt Dixon. VeloPress 2014. xii, 356 pages : Illustration
ISBN 9781937715113
Grades: Adult   796.42
1. Triathletes 2. Triathlon 3. Training 4. Sports and Competition — Racing
LC BL2014025090

A comprehensive, whole-body approach to training for triathletes identifies four pillars of performance—training, recovery, nutrition, and strength—and provides guidelines and advice for making improvements in each area.

Includes index.

Finn, Adharanand
The *Way* of the Runner: A Journey into the Fabled World of Japanese Running. Adharanand Finn. Pegasus Books 2016. 326 p.
ISBN 9781681771212
Grades: Adult   796.42
1. Running 2. Runners 3. Long-distance running 4. National characteristics, Japanese 5. Sports 6. Japan 7. Sports and Competition — Racing — Track and Field
LC 2017304780

The award-winning author of Running with the Kenyans turns his attention to Japan, the most running-obsessed country on earth, revealing a running culture that will fascinate and surprise anyone eager to explore why we run and how we might do it better.

"An elegant, well-written pleasure even for readers with no particular interest in foot racing." —*Kirkus*

Fitzgerald, Matt
Iron War: Dave Scott, Mark Allen & The Greatest Race Ever Run. Matt Fitzgerald with Bob Babbitt. VeloPress 2011. 324 p, 24 p. of plates : Illustration; Color; Map
ISBN 9781934030776
Grades: Adult   796.42
1. Scott, Dave 2. Allen, Mark, 1958- 3. Triathletes 4. Ironman triathlons 5. Endurance sports 6. Biographies 7. Sports and Competition — Extreme Sports 8. Life stories — Sports — Athletes
LC 2011027408

Weaving an examination of mental resolve into a gripping tale of athletic adventure, Iron War is a soaring narrative of two champions and the paths that led to their stunning final showdown.

"A true page-turner about a too-little-known great moment in sports." —*Booklist*

Friel, Joe
The *Triathlete's* Training Bible: The World's Most Comprehensive Training Guide. Joe Friel. VeloPress 2016. xv, 331 p. : Illustration
ISBN 9781937715441
Grades: Adult   796.42
1. Triathlon 2. Training 3. Sports and Competition — Racing
LC 2016034831

PUBLIC LIBRARY CORE COLLECTION: NONFICTION
Twentieth Edition

A comprehensive guide to triathlon training includes both power- and pace-based training, custom recovery plans, and techniques to build up speed and strength skills.

Includes bibliographical references and index.

Higdon, Hal
★ *Marathon: The Ultimate Training Guide : Advice, Plans, and Programs for Half and Full Marathons.* Hal Higdon. Rodale 2020. x, 294 p.
ISBN 9780593137734
Grades: Adult   796.42
1. Running 2. Long-distance running 3. Marathons 4. Training 5. Sports and Competition — General
LC 2011028075

A training guide for beginners, first-time marathoners, and women runners counsels readers on how to build speed and distance while maximizing one's performance and building on defensive running skills, in an updated edition by a senior writer for Runner's World magazine.

Includes index.

Karnazes, Dean
The Legend of Marathon: Retracing the Ancient Battle and Epic Run That Inspired the World's Greatest Foot Race. Dean Karnazes. Rodale Press 2014. 304 pages
ISBN 9781609614744
Grades: Adult   796.42
1. Pheidippides, fl. 490 B.C.E 2. Marathon, Battle of, Greece, 490 B.C.E 3. Marathon running 4. Marathon runners 5. Marathons 6. Endurance sports 7. Greece 8. Travel Writing — Retracing Historic Journeys 9. Sports and Competition — Sports History 10. Travel Writing — Europe
LC 2018300054

Ultramarathoner Dean Karnazes explores his Greek ancestry and, with the help of scholars, learns about the world's first marathon. He decides to follow the 153-mile run from Athens to Sparta to honor an ancient Greek runner as well as his own Greek heritage.

"This is a remarkable and inspiring memoir that will have casual and serious runners cheering." —*Publishers Weekly*

Magill, Pete
Build Your Running Body: A Total-Body Fitness Plan for All Distance Runners, from Milers to Ultramarathoners' Run Farther, Faster, and Injury-Free. Pete Magill, Thomas Schwartz, and Melissa Breyer; photographs by Diana Hernandez. The experiment 2014. xi, 434 pages : Illustration
ISBN 9781615191024
Grades: Adult   796.42
1. Long-distance running 2. Running 3. Training 4. Reference books — Handbooks, manuals, etc. 5. Reference books — Sports 6. Sports and Competition — General
LC 2014010816

Draws on the latest research in running physiology to provide training programs and strategies for improving running mileage while preventing injuries, and includes nutrition guidance and beginner's guidelines.

Includes index.

McDougall, Christopher
★ *Born to Run: A Hidden Tribe, Superathletes, and the Greatest Race the World Has Never Seen.* Christopher McDougall. Alfred A. Knopf 2009. 287 p.
ISBN 9780307266309
Grades: Adult   796.42
1. Indigenous peoples of Mexico 2. Ultramarathon running 3. Runners 4. Running 5. Tarahumara (Mexican people) 6. Marathon running 7. Marathon runners 8. Athletes 9. Endurance sports 10. Mexico 11. Sports and Competition — Racing — Track and Field
LC 2009922861

ALA Notable Book, 2010.

McDougall reveals the secrets of the world's greatest distance runners—the Tarahumara Indians of Copper Canyon, Mexico—and how he trained for the challenge of a fifty-mile race through the heart of Tarahumara country pitting the tribe against an odd band of super-athletic Americans.

"Implausibly difficult marathons, hundreds of miles long, and the ultra-elite competitive runners who tackle them for fun. A hidden, almost mythical, tribe in Mexico untouched by modern disease. Shoe manufacturers driven by corporate greed to sustain an industry that has created modern running injuries. An anthropological study of homo sapiens physiology and the course we took to survive while Neanderthals died out. It may seem farfetched, but Born to Run entwines all those strands and even pop-culture references into an engaging and inspirational read." —*PopMatters*

Mertens, Maggie
Better Faster Farther: How Running Changed Everything We Know About Women. Maggie Mertens. Algonquin Books 2024. 272 p.
ISBN 9781643753355
Grades: Adult   796.42
1. Women runners 2. Social history 3. Running 4. Gender role 5. Runners 6. Women and sports 7. Sports history 8. History Writing — Women's history 9. Sports and competition — Racing — Track and field

Introducing us to the women who have redefined society's image of strength and power, an award-winning journalist, recounting the story of how women broke into competitive running, transports us from that first boundary-breaking marathon in Greece, 1896, to today's most intense ultramarathons, whose current record holder is a woman—by a lot.

"Award-winning journalist Mertens takes readers on a fascinating deep dive into the myth of gender roles that set limitations on women's participation in athletics." —*Booklist*

Nolan, Ali
Master the Marathon: The Ultimate Training Guide for Women. Ali Nolan. Penguin Books 2021. xi, 226 pages : Illustration
ISBN 9780143135487
Grades: Adult   796.42
1. Women marathon runners 2. Marathon running 3. Marathons 4. Training 5. Sports and Competition — Racing — Track and Field 6. Science Writing — Medicine and health — Women's health
LC 2021012072

A no-nonsense, interactive guide that empowers all women at all levels to run their strongest, best marathon ever. As recently as 1966, women were forbidden to run in the marathon. Professionals—including doctors—believed it was physically impossible and dangerous for women to run more than a mile and a half. But as with many other barriers women have faced over time, we fought our way in. Today, women make up almost half of the marathoning population. Yet most marathon training manuals are written by men. And while these men are experts when it comes to how men can and should train, women need training programs tailored to our bodies to our unique strengths and weaknesses-so that we can avoid injuries and run at our peak. The programming in this book was created by a woman, specifically for women. Master the Marathon is a comprehensive guide to marathon training for women at all levels of running-beginner, intermediate, and advanced. The book takes you through everything you need to know to be preparedfor the 26.2 miles of the marathon, including detailed training plans, strength training programs, building your mental awareness of your physical body, nutrition, guidance on finding the best marathon for you, identifying and avoiding potential injuries, inspirational advice, and other unexpected pieces of wisdom. Both incredibly practical and deeply motivating, Master the Marathon will help you unlock the strength and determination inside you to embark on the spectacular journey that is the marathon."

"This worthy addition to running collections is sure to be popular with newbies as well as middle-of-the-pack and competitive runners embarking on their transformative marathon journey or in need of motivation to resume training after time away from the sport." —*Booklist*

Romanov, Nicholas S.
The Running Revolution: How to Run Faster, Farther, and Injury-Free—For Life. Dr. Nicholas Romanov with Kurt Brungardt. Penguin Books 2014. xv, 220 pages : Illustration
ISBN 9780143123194

ESSENTIAL AND RECOMMENDED TITLES
796.42071 Track and field — Education

Grades: Adult   796.42
1. Running 2. Training 3. Sports and Competition — General
LC 2014012161

Explains how to run more efficiently and with better biomechanics in order to minimize strain and injury, describing the best type of shoes, highlighting the safest type of foot strike, and outlining a four-week training program.

Provides both beginner and experienced runners with all the information they need to run more efficiently and with better biomechanics and to minimize strain and potential injury by describing the best type of shoes and the safest type of foot strike, in a book that includes more than 100 instructional photos and a four-week training program.

Includes index.

Shorter, Frank
My Marathon: Reflections on a Gold Medal Life. Frank Shorter with John Brant. Rodale 2016. xviii, 254 pages : Illustration
ISBN 9781623367244
Grades: Adult   796.42
1. Shorter, Frank, 1947- 2. Runners 3. Marathon running 4. Child abuse 5. Doping in sports 6. Dysfunctional families 7. Adult child abuse victims 8. Olympic medal winners 9. Endurance sports 10. Autobiographies and memoirs 11. Sports and Competition — Racing — Track and Field 12. Life stories — Sports — Athletes 13. Life stories — Facing adversity — Abuse survivors 14. Family and relationships — Abuse
LC Bl2016027627

The Olympian and founder of the United States Anti-Doping Agency discusses his life, including his athletic triumphs and the abuse he and his siblings suffered at the hands of his father.

Includes index.

Wade, Becky
Run the World: My 3,500-Mile Journey Through Running Cultures Around the Globe. Becky Wade. William Morrow 2016. 288 pages
ISBN 9780062416438
Grades: Adult   796.42
1. Wade, Becky 2. Runners 3. Marathon running 4. Cross-country runners 5. Marathon runners 6. Marathons 7. Running 8. Running races 9. Cross-country running 10. Endurance sports 11. Autobiographies and memoirs 12. Sports and Competition — Racing — Track and Field 13. Life stories — Sports — Athletes
LC 2017304785

An elite marathoner describes the year she spent running over 3,500 miles in nine different countries, living with host families and exploring diverse running communities and cultures all over the globe.

"Every so often a book comes along that becomes a cult classic for competitive runners but also has appeal to a broader audience... and this terrific debut is sure to join their ranks." —*Booklist*

796.42071 Track and field — Education

Futterman, Matthew
Running to the Edge: A Band of Misfits and the Guru Who Unlocked the Secrets of Speed. Matthew Futterman. Doubleday 2019. 288 p.
ISBN 9780385543743
Grades: Adult   796.42071
1. Larsen, Bob 2. Track and field coaches 3. Running 4. Speed 5. Physical fitness 6. Runners 7. Running races 8. Track and field athletes 9. Training 10. Biographies 11. Life stories — Sports — Coaches, managers, and owners 12. Sports and Competition — Racing — Track and Field
LC 2018049020

In the dusty hills above San Diego, Bob Larsen became America's greatest running coach. Starting with a ragtag group of high school cross country and track runners, Larsen set out on a decades-long quest to find the secret of running impossibly fast, for longer distances than anyone thought possible. Running to the Edge is a riveting account of Larsen's journey, and his quest to discover the unorthodox training secrets that would lead American runners (elite and recreational) to breakthroughs never imagined.

"A fascinating look at the history of U.S. distance running with plenty of grit, innovative approaches, near disasters, and fun." —*Library Journal*

796.4252 Marathon

Keflezighi, Meb
Meb for Mortals: How to Run, Think and Eat Like a Champion Marathoner. Meb Keflezighi with Scott Douglas. Rodale 2015. xi, 196 pages : Illustration
ISBN 9781623365479
Grades: Adult   796.4252
1. Long-distance running 2. Marathon running 3. Training 4. Sports and Competition — General
LC 2016301845

Describes in unprecedented detail how three-time Olympian Keflezighi prepares to take on the best runners in the world. More important, the book shows everyday runners how to implement the training, nutritional, and mental principles that have guided him throughout his long career, which in addition to the 2014 Boston win includes an Olympic silver medal and the 2009 New York City Marathon title.

"The format is clean and the writing is simple and strong, all making this book a valuable tool for anyone with their sights set on running a marathon." —*Publishers Weekly*

Includes index.

796.4809 Olympic Games — History

Goldblatt, David
The Games: A Global History of the Olympics. David Goldblatt. W. W. Norton & Company 2016. 464 p.
ISBN 9780393292770
Grades: Adult   796.4809
1. Olympic games 2. Sports history 3. Social history 4. Sports and state 5. 20th century 6. Impartial writing 7. History writing — Arts and culture 8. Sports and competition — Olympic sports
LC 2016022203

The definitive sports and social history of the modern Olympic Games—by one of the most celebrated sportswriters of our time.

Includes bibliographic references and index.

796.5 Outdoor life

Citro, Asia
150+ Screen-Free Activities for Kids: The Very Best and Easiest Playtime Activities from Funathomewithkids.Com. Asia Citro, MEd, creator of Fun at Home with Kids. Adams Media 2014. 255 pages : Color; Illustration
ISBN 9781440576157
Grades: Adult   796.5
1. Creative activities and seat work 2. Outdoor recreation for children 3. Family and Relationships — General 4. Family and Relationships — Parenting
LC 2014021922

Provides over one hundred fun and creative activities for children that take them away from screens and gadgets, including making "slime," crafting paints, and designing toys.

Includes bibliographical references and index.

Coburn, Broughton
Everest: Mountain Without Mercy. Broughton Coburn; introduction by Tim Cahill; afterword by David Breashears. National Geographic Society 2015. 256 p. : Color illustration; Color; Map
ISBN 9781426215858

PUBLIC LIBRARY CORE COLLECTION: NONFICTION
Twentieth Edition

Grades: 11 12 Adult   796.5

1. Mountaineering accidents 2. Extreme sports 3. Mount Everest 4. Sports and Competition — Extreme Sports 5. Sports and Competition — Mountaineering

LC 97010765

Photographs and firsthand accounts chronicle the 1996 Everest expedition that claimed eight lives.

"Review of previous edition: bringing an understated yet powerful Buddhist/Sherpa ethical perspective to the tragedy on Everest chronicled in Jon Krakauer's Into Thin Air, Coburn reports on the IMAX film crew who participated in the rescue effort when the May 1996 expeditions led by guides Rob Hall and Scott Fischer ended in death and crippling injury." —*Publishers Weekly*

Includes index.

796.51 Walking

Davis, Jennifer Pharr

The Pursuit of Endurance: Harnessing the Record-Breaking Power of Strength and Resilience. Jennifer Pharr Davis. Penguin Group USA 2018. 320 p.

ISBN 9780735221895

Grades: Adult   796.51

1. Davis, Jennifer Pharr 2. Long distance runners 3. World records 4. Endurance sports 5. Running 6. Distance running 7. Running races 8. Autobiographies and memoirs 9. Life stories — Sports — Athletes

LC 2018013087

Jennifer Pharr Davis, a record holder of the FKT (fastest known time) on the Appalachian Trail, reveals the secrets and habits behind endurance as she chronicles her incredible accomplishments in the world of endurance hiking, backpacking, and trail running.

"A captivating narrative guidebook that will inspire readers to test their own limits, on the trail and off." —*Kirkus*

Michaud-Skog, Summer

Fat Girls Hiking: An Inclusive Guide to Getting Outdoors at Any Size or Ability. Summer Michaud-Skog. Timber Press 2022. 224 p.

ISBN 9781643260396

Grades: Adult   796.51

1. Hiking 2. Outdoor recreation 3. Fat women 4. Outdoor life 5. Body image 6. Body movement 7. Adventure writing — Adventure travel

LC 2021049340

Rise: A Feminist Book Project List, 2023.

Provides practical advice for aspiring hikers with a body-positive bent and offers personal and heartfelt stories and reviews of trails to welcome and encourage people of all body types, sizes and backgrounds to enjoy outdoor recreation.

"Kudos to the author for changing the narrative on inclusiveness, breaking down stereotypes, and building body positivity with a clarion call to the outdoor industry: Increase diverse representation and offer plus-sized apparel and gear." —*Booklist*

Includes index.

Solnit, Rebecca

Wanderlust: A History of Walking. Rebecca Solnit. Viking 2000. VIII, 326 p. : Illustration

ISBN 9780670882090

Grades: Adult   796.51

1. Walking 2. Hiking 3. Voyages and travels 4. History writing — Microhistory 5. Nature Writing — Personal Responses

LC 99041153

A cultural history of walking explores the ancient practice, from ancient Greece to the present, delving into Wordsworth, Gary Snyder, Rousseau, Jane Austen, and other cultural and literary icons to show how this basic activity has been imagined througout history.

"The author presents a look at how the act of walking has influenced our history, our science, our literature, and the very way that we see ourselves as human beings. Drawing on a multitude of diverse disciplines, Solnit illustrates that walking has led to some of the best, and worst, incidents in all of history." —*Booklist*

Includes bibliographical references (p. [293]-318) and index.

Streets, Annabel

52 Ways to Walk: The Surprising Science of Walking for Wellness and Joy, One Week at a Time. Annabel Streets. G.P. Putnam's Sons 2022. xix, 267 pages : Illustration

ISBN 9780593419953

Grades: Adult   796.51

1. Walking 2. Exercise 3. Health 4. Happiness 5. Self-Help — Personal growth — Motivation 6. Science Writing — Medicine and health — Exercise

LC 2021053561

Encourages and inspires readers to improve how they walk, where they walk and who they walk with to attain the full range of mental and physical benefits of walking and get more out of life one step at a time.

"Streets carefully breaks down the psychological and physical benefits of each type of walk, and makes a solid case that getting some movement in outside can help one 'appreciate the exquisitely complicated and beautiful world we inhabit.' Readers ready to hit the pavement will find plenty of inspiration and information here." —*Publishers Weekly*

Includes bibliographical references (pages 225-258) and index.

Townsend, Chris

The Backpacker's Handbook. Chris Townsend. McGraw-Hill 2012. x, 468 p. : Illustration

ISBN 9780071754897

Grades: Adult   796.51

1. Backpacking 2. Reference books — Handbooks, manuals, etc. 3. Sports and Competition — General

LC 2011028816

Offers a handbook for all skill levels of hiking that covers a wide range of backbacking issues, including how to use a map and compass, survival skills, and tracking.

Includes index.

796.510973 Hiking — United States

Berger, Karen

America's Great Hiking Trails. Karen Berger; photography by Bart Smith; foreword by Bill McKibben. Rizzoli 2014. 335 pages : Color; Illustration

ISBN 9780789327413

Grades: Adult   796.510973

1. Hiking 2. United States 3. Sports and Competition — General 4. Travel writing — General 5. Reference — General

LC Oc2014124897

This lavishly illustrated celebration of more than 50,000 miles of America's most iconic trails celebrates the forty most important trails in America in forty-nine states and eight national parks.

Chamberlin, Silas

On the Trail: A History of American Hiking. Silas Chamberlin. Yale University Press 2016. 243 p.

ISBN 9780300219111

Grades: Adult   796.510973

1. Hiking 2. Voyages and travels 3. Travelers 4. Trails 5. History writing — Microhistory 6. Nature Writing — Natural Landscapes

LC 2016936121

The first history of the American hiking community and its contributions to the nation's vast network of trails.

"This winning, thought-provoking book offers insight into a relatively unknown aspect of environmental history." —*Library Journal*

ESSENTIAL AND RECOMMENDED TITLES
796.5109756 Hiking — North Carolina

796.5109756 Hiking — North Carolina

Spira, Timothy P.
Waterfalls and Wildflowers in the Southern Appalachians: Thirty Great Hikes. Timothy P. Spira. University of North Carolina Press 2015. 279 pages : Color; Illustration; Map
ISBN 9781469622644
Grades: Adult   796.5109756
1. Hiking 2. Natural history 3. Trails 4. Waterfalls 5. Wild flowers 6. Appalachian Region, Southern 7. Travel Writing — United States 8. Reference — Travel guides 9. Reference — General
LC 2014044782

If you love waterfalls, here are some of the best hikes in the Southern Appalachians. And if you love plants—or simply would like to learn more about them—you will be in hiking heaven.

"Biologist's will savor this handy hiking guide to a particularly beautiful region." —*Library Journal*
Includes index.

796.52 Walking and exploring by kind of terrain

Bukreev, Anatolii Nikolaevich
The Climb: Tragic Ambitions on Everest. Anatoli Boukreev and G. Weston DeWalt. St. Martin's Press 1997. xi, 255 p. : Illustration; Color; Map
ISBN 9780312168148
Grades: Adult   796.52
1. Bukreev, Anatolii Nikolaevich, 1958-1997 2. Mountaineering accidents 3. Search and rescue operations 4. Mount Everest Expedition, 1996 5. Blizzards 6. Adventure 7. Extreme sports 8. Mountaineering 9. Mount Everest 10. 1990s 11. Sports and Competition — Mountaineering 12. Sports and Competition — Extreme Sports 13. Adventure writing — Natural disaster 14. Nature Writing — Natural Disaster
LC 97023194

New York Times Notable Book, 1998.

Relates the true story of what happened when a climbing expedition to Mount Everest was overcome by snow, wind, and lack of oxygen.

"This is a first-person account of the tragic climbing experience in May 1996 on Mount Everest that left eight hikers dead and several others struggling to stay alive. Fast-paced and easy to read, Boukreev's story of adventure and survival will remain in the reader's memory long after the book is finished." —*Library Journal*

Gutman, Matt
The Boys in the Cave: Deep Inside the Impossible Rescue in Thailand. Matt Gutman. Modern Library 2018. 256 p.
ISBN 9780062909916
Grades: Adult   796.52
1. Caves 2. Search and rescue operations 3. Survival 4. Soccer teams 5. Cave diving 6. Lifesaving 7. Caving 8. Thailand 9. Adventure writing — Survival
LC 2018054756

From award-winning ABC News Chief National Correspondent Matt Gutman, and written using exclusive interviews and information comes the definitive account of the dramatic story that gripped the world: the miracle rescue of twelve boys and their soccer coach trapped in a flooded cave miles underground for nearly three weeks—a pulse-pounding page-turner by a reporter who was there every step of their journey out.

Isserman, Maurice
Continental Divide: A History of American Mountaineering. Maurice Isserman. W.W. Norton & Co. 2016. 416 p.
ISBN 9780393068504
Grades: Adult   796.52
1. Mountaineering 2. History writing — Arts and culture 3. Sports and competition — Mountaineering 4. Sports and competition — Sports history
LC 2016000548

A history of the role of mountains and mountaineering in America is told through four centuries of landmark climbs and environmental activism, citing the contributions of notables ranging from Lewis and Clark to John Muir and Teddy Roosevelt.

"This broad sweep of American mountaineering history will satisfy general history readers and outdoor adventurers alike." —*Library Journal*
Includes bibliographical references and index.

Krakauer, Jon
★ *Into Thin Air: A Personal Account of the Mount Everest Disaster.* Jon Krakauer. Villard 1997. 293 p. : Illustration
ISBN 9780679457527
Grades: 11 12 Adult   796.52
1. Krakauer, Jon 2. Mount Everest Expedition, 1996 3. Mountaineering accidents 4. Mountaineers 5. Expeditions 6. Adventure 7. Extreme sports 8. Mountaineering 9. Mount Everest 10. China 11. NEPAL 12. Himalaya Mountains 13. Adventure writing — Survival 14. Sports and Competition — Mountaineering 15. Sports and Competition — Extreme Sports 16. Travel Writing — Asia and the South Pacific 17. Adult books for young adults 18. Nonfiction that reads like fiction
LC 96030031

ALA Notable Book, 1998; Alex Award, 1998; Garden State Teen Book Award (New Jersey), Nonfiction, 2000; School Library Journal Best Books: Best Adult Books 4 Teens, 1997; YALSA Best Books for Young Adults, 1998; National Book Critics Circle Award for Nonfiction finalist, 1997; Pulitzer Prize for General Nonfiction finalist, 1998.

The author describes his spring 1996 trek to Mt. Everest, a disastrous expedition that claimed the lives of eight climbers, and explains why he survived.

"This tense, harrowing story is as mesmerizing and hard to put down as any well-written adventure novel." —*School Library Journal*
Map on lining papers; Includes bibliographical references (p. 293).

Tabor, James M.
Blind Descent: The Quest to Discover the Deepest Place on Earth. James M. Tabor. Random House 2010. xv, 286 p. : Color illustration
ISBN 9781400067671
Grades: Adult   796.52
1. Stone, W. C. (William C.) 2. Klimchuk, A. B. (Aleksandr Borisovich) 3. Caving 4. Caves 5. Underground areas 6. Sports and Competition — Extreme Sports 7. Adventure writing — Exploration

This is the story of the men and women who risked everything to find the deepest cave on Earth, earning their place in history beside the likes of Peary, Amundsen, Hillary, and Armstrong. Tabor focuses particularly on the heroic efforts of Bill Stone in the vast Cheve Cave of southern Mexico and Alexander Klimchouk in the supercave Krubera of the Republic of Georgia.

"The author examines the two polar opposites at the head of each of two major cave-diving expeditions: the win-at-all-costs, classic alpha-male, American Bill Stone, who led Mexican cave dives in Cheve and Huatula; and mild-mannered organization man, Ukrainian Alexander Klimchouk, who spearheaded the exploration of his country's notorious Krubera cave. Only one of these men came away with the distinction of having descended deeper into the earth's core than anyone else. Tabor expertly fashions a fly-on-the-wall narrative from the firsthand accounts of Stone, Klimchouk and their supporting casts of death-defying followers. A fascinating and informative introduction to the sport of cave diving, as well as a dramatic portrayal of a significant man-vs.-nature conflict." —*Kirkus*
Includes bibliographical references and index.

Taylor, Joseph E.
Pilgrims of the Vertical: Yosemite Rock Climbers and Nature at Risk. Joseph E. Taylor III.. Harvard University Press 2010. 384 p.
ISBN 9780674052871
Grades: Adult   796.52
1. Rock climbing 2. Mountaineering 3. Environmentalism 4. Mountaineers 5. Rock climbers 6. Environmentalists 7. Yosemite Valley 8. Sports and Competition — Mountaineering 9. Sports and Competition — Extreme Sports 10. Nature Writing — General

LC 2010021578
National Outdoor Book Award for History/Biography, 2010.

Using the history of Yosemite Valley as his focus, Taylor (history and geography, Simon Fraser University) charts the development of rock climbing over the 20th century. Tracing the sport from its beginnings with European mountain climbers and climbing clubs in the US West, the author shows how climbing has evolved into an individual activity that often puts a premium on risk-taking. Taylor also focuses on the contradictions inherent in a sport where enthusiasts pride themselves on their environmentalism, yet participate in an activity that leads to the degradation of their most favored locales. While directed mainly at an academic audience, this book will also interest rock climbers who are patient with academic jargon.

"Yosemite has been a climber magnet for decades, and it was here that many of rock climbing's highly ritualized set of norms and mores evolved. [This book] is at once a chronicle of how the sport evolved in Yosemite and a fascinating social history that considers climbing in the larger context of American life. For the general reader, the book makes a fine introduction to the history of climbing and Yosemite's special place in its development. For climbers, Pilgrims of the Vertical offers a somewhat idiosyncratic view of their sport." —*Wall Street Journal*

Includes bibliographical references and index.

796.522 Walking and exploring by kind of terrain — Mountains, hills, rocks

Burgman, John
High Drama: The Rise, Fall, and Rebirth of American Competition Climbing. John Burgman; foreword by Kynan Waggoner. Triumph Books 2020. 381 p.
ISBN 9781629377759
Grades: Adult   796.522
1. Rock climbing 2. Rock climbers 3. Competition 4. Free climbing 5. Indoor climbing 6. Extreme sports 7. Outdoor recreation 8. Sports and Competition — Mountaineering 9. Life stories — Sports — Athletes
LC 2020040381

High Drama explores rock climbing's transformation from a pursuit of select anti-establishment vagabonds to a sport embraced by competitors of all ages, social classes, and backgrounds. Climbing magazine's John Burgman weaves a multi-layered story of traditionalists and opportunists, grassroots organizers and business-minded developers, free-spirited rebels and rigorously coached athletes.

"Leaving no stone unturned, this exhaustive history will find an audience with climbing enthusiasts." —*Library Journal*

Includes bibliographical references.

Conefrey, Mick
The Ghosts of K2: The Epic Saga of the First Ascent. Mick Conefrey. Oneworld 2015. 336 p.
ISBN 9781780745954
Grades: Adult   796.522
1. Mountaineering 2. Mountains 3. Expeditions 4. K2 (Mountain), Pakistan 5. Adventure writing — Exploration
LC Bl2015052047
National Outdoor Book Award for History/Biography, 2016.

Mick Conefrey tells the story of three extraordinary expeditions filled with riveting drama and unimaginable tragedy: Fritz Wiessener's controversial attempt of 1939, the disastrous American expedition of 1953, and the huge Italian expedition of 1954 on which K2 was first climbed.

"An absorbing chronicle of K2's early history that all fans of mountaineering will enjoy." —*Library Journal*

Cordes, Kelly
The Tower: Mountain of Legends, Spire of Storms—Cerro Torre. Kelly Cordes. Patagonia Inc. 2014. 256 p.
ISBN 9781938340338
Grades: Adult   796.522
1. Mountains 2. Mountaineers 3. Mountaineering 4. Extreme sports 5. Extreme environments 6. South American history 7. Argentina 8. Sports and Competition — Mountaineering 9. Adventure writing — Adventure travel
LC 2014947861
National Outdoor Book Award for Outdoor Literature, 2015.

Patagonia's Cerro Torre, considered by many the most beautiful peak in the world, draws the finest and most devoted technical alpinists to its climbing challenges. But controversy has swirled around this ice-capped peak since Cesare Maestri claimed firstascent in 1959. Since then a debate has raged, with world-class climbers attempting to retrace his route but finding only contradictions. This chronicle of hubris, heroism, controversies and epic journeys offers a glimpse into the human condition, and why some pursue extreme endeavors that at face value have no worth.

Ellsworth, Scott
The World Beneath Their Feet: Mountaineering, Madness, and the Deadly Race to Summit the Himalayas. Scott Ellsworth. Little Brown & Company 2020. xix, 393 pages
ISBN 9780316434867
Grades: Adult   796.522
1. Mountaineers 2. International competition 3. Adventure 4. Expeditions 5. Mountaineering 6. Mount Everest 7. K2 (Mountain), Pakistan 8. Himalaya Mountains 9. 1930s 10. Adventure Writing — Exploration 11. Life stories — People in history — Explorers 12. Sports and Competition — Mountaineering 13. History writing — Exploration 14. Nonfiction that reads like fiction
LC Bl2020004653
National Outdoor Book Award for History/Biography, 2020.

As tension steadily rose between European powers in the 1930s, a different kind of battle was already raging across the Himalayas. Teams of mountaineers from Great Britain, Nazi Germany, and the United States were all competing to be the first to climb the world's highest peaks, including Mount Everest and K2. Unlike climbers today, they had few photographs or maps, no properly working oxygen systems, and they wore leather boots and cotton parkas. Amazingly, and against all odds, they soon went farther and higher than anyone could have imagined.

"An excellent overview of mountaineering and exploration in the Himalayas and Karakoram, set against the backdrop of 20th-century history, that will appeal to mountaineers and armchair adventurers." —*Library Journal*

Includes bibliographical references and index.

Hall, Andy
Denali's Howl: The Deadliest Climbing Disaster on America's Wildest Peak. Andy Hall. Dutton Adult 2014. 368 pages
ISBN 9780525954064
Grades: Adult   796.522
1. Mountaineering accidents 2. Mountaineering 3. Search and rescue operations 4. Mount Denali (Alaska) 5. Denali National Park and Preserve (Alaska) 6. Alaska 7. Sports and competition — Mountaineering 8. Adventure writing — Survival
LC 2013047600

Denali's Howl is the white-knuckle account of one of the most deadly climbing disasters of all time. In 1967, twelve young men attempted to climb Alaska's Mount McKinley—known to the locals as Denali—one of the most popular and deadly mountaineering destinations in the world. Only five survived. Journalist Andy Hall, son of the park superintendent at the time, investigates the tragedy. He spent years tracking down survivors, lost documents, and recordings of radio communications. In Denali's Howl, Hall reveals the full story of an expedition facing conditions conclusively established here for the first time: At an elevation of nearly 20,000 feet, these young men endured an "arctic super blizzard," with howling winds of up to 300 miles an hour and windchill that freezes flesh solid in minutes. All this without the high-tech gear and equipment climbers use today. As well as the story of the men caught inside the storm, Denali's Howl is the story of those caught outside it trying to save them—Hall's father among them. The book gives readers a detailed look at the culture of climbing then and now and raises uncomfortable questions about each player in this tragedy.

ESSENTIAL AND RECOMMENDED TITLES
796.54 Camping

Lowe, George
Letters from Everest: A New Zealander's Account of the Epic First Ascent. George Lowe. HarperCollins 2013. 176 p.
ISBN 9781775540335
Grades: 9 10 11 12 **796.522**
1. Lowe, George, 1924-2013 2. Mount Everest Expedition, 1953 3. Mountaineers 4. Mountaineering 5. Male friendship 6. Expeditions 7. Exploration 8. Mount Everest 9. New Zealand 10. 1950s 11. Letters 12. Autobiographies and memoirs 13. New Zealand literature 14. Life stories — People in history — Explorers 15. Adventure writing — Exploration 16. History writing — Exploration 17. Sports and Competition — Mountaineering

In this touching book, unpublished letters from the George Lowe collection are brought together for the first time to describe the day-to-day moments of the historic 1953 Everest expedition. Lowe met Hillary while working in New Zealand's Southern Alps just after the war and struck up a friendship. Little did he know it would be the beginning of a journey to the highest altitudes and latitudes of the planet.

Ralston, Aron
Between a Rock and a Hard Place. Aron Ralston. Atria Books 2004. xiii, 354 p. : Color illustration; Map
ISBN 9780743492812
Grades: 11 12 Adult **796.522**
1. Ralston, Aron 2. Rock climbing accidents 3. Rock climbing 4. Desert survival 5. Extreme sports 6. Utah 7. Page to screen 8. Adventure writing — Survival 9. Sports and Competition — Extreme Sports 10. Adult books for young adults
LC 2004303427

A mountaineer who survived a near-fatal accident by amputating his arm when it became trapped behind a boulder in Utah describes how he endured five days of hypothermia, dehydration, and hallucinations before managing his own rescue.

"With precious little water or food, his right arm pinned for nearly five days by a boulder in a narrow canyon shaft in central-eastern Utah, Ralston amputated the arm with his pocketknife, then rappelled and hiked his way to his own rescue. What makes his account of his ordeal extraordinary, too, is the detail and precision Ralston, a former mechanical engineer, brings to the telling, from the almost minute-by-minute chronology of his ordeal to topographical descriptions of the ground he's covered in his life as an outdoor adventurer." —*Booklist*

Book was adapted into a movie called 127 hours; Later published: 127 hours. New York : Atria Books, 2010; Also published in large print format; Includes bibliographical references (p. 353).

Synnott, Mark
The Third Pole: Mystery, Obsession, and Death on Mount Everest. Mark Synnott. Dutton 2021. 416 p.
ISBN 9781524745578
Grades: Adult **796.522**
1. Irvine, Andrew, 1902-1924 2. Synnott, Mark 3. Mount Everest Expedition, 1924 4. Mountaineering 5. Mountaineers 6. Explorers 7. Voyages and travels 8. Mount Everest 9. Sports and Competition — Mountaineering 10. Travel Writing — Asia and the South Pacific 11. Adventure Writing — Adventure travel 12. Travel Writing — Retracing Historic Journeys 13. Life stories — People in history — Explorers
LC 2020048322

The veteran Pararescuemen trainer and author of the Impossible Climb recounts how the unknown achievements of George Mallory and Sandy Irvine's ill-fated 1924 ascent inspired his own unlikely summit up Mount Everest.

"Professional climber and journalist Synnott chronicles his climb of Mount Everest in hopes of finding the remains, and an all-important camera, of George Mallory's climbing partner, Andrew Irvine. . . . A fine tale of adventure and exploration sure to please any fan of climbing and Everest lore." —*Kirkus*
Includes index.

Zuckerman, Peter
★ *Buried in the Sky: The Extraordinary Story of the Sherpa Climbers on K2's Deadliest Day.* Peter Zuckerman and Amanda Padoan. W.W. Norton & Co. 2012. 320 p.
ISBN 9780393079883
Grades: Adult **796.522**
1. Sherpa (NEPAlese people) 2. Mountaineers 3. Mountaineering accidents 4. Mountaineering 5. K2 (Mountain), Pakistan 6. Sports and Competition — Mountaineering
LC 2012008490

National Outdoor Book Award for History/Biography, 2012.

Presents the stories of the sharps who have acted as expert consultants to Westerners climbing the Himalayas, focusing in particular on Chhiring Dorje Sherpa and Pasang Lama, who survived when 11 other climbers died on K2 in August 2008.

Includes bibliographical references and index.

796.54 Camping

White, Dan
Under the Stars: How America Fell in Love with Camping. Dan White. Henry Holt and Co. 2016. 368 p.
ISBN 9781627791953
Grades: Adult **796.54**
1. Camping 2. Outdoor life 3. History writing — Arts and culture 4. History writing — Microhistory
LC 2015042691

From the Sierras to the Adirondacks and the Everglades, from remote wildernesses to public campgrounds and RV meccas, Dan White travels across America, searching through its history and landscapes to tell the story of how camping took hold of the national imagination and evolved alongside a changing country.

"An adventurous, informative, and irreverent look at outdoor recreation." —*Booklist*

Includes bibliographical references and index.

796.6 Cycling and related activities

Bambrick, Yvonne
The Urban Cycling Survival Guide: Need-to-Know Skills & Strategies for Biking in the City. Yvonne Bambrick; illustrated by Marc Ngui. ECW Press 2015. xx, 203 p. : Illustration; Color
ISBN 9781770412187
Grades: Adult **796.6**
1. Sports and Competition — Racing — Cycling
LC Bl2015010874

Presents a guide to cycling safely and understanding the rules of the road in urban areas, covering such topics as signals and communication, road-sharing, navigating obstacles, etiquette, and all-weather riding.

Includes bibliographical references (pages 194-199).

Leonard, Max
Lanterne Rouge: The Last Man in the Tour De France. Max Leonard. Pegasus 2015. 272 p.
ISBN 9781605987866
Grades: Adult **796.6**
1. Bicycle racing 2. Bicyclists 3. Losers 4. Bicycling 5. Sports and Competition — Racing — Cycling
LC Bl2015021574

Shares the lesser-known stories of last-place finishers in the Tour de France, recounting the inspirational and occasionally absurd events that shaped their efforts.

"Writer and amateur cyclist Leonard challenges what it means to achieve greatness through the mythos of the sport's underdogs. The author provides little information about the competitors we recognize as champions of the sport, instead populating the narrative with a strange sort of idol worship." —*Kirkus*

Moore, Tim
The Cyclist Who Went Out in the Cold: Adventures Riding the Iron Curtain. Tim Moore. Pegasus Books 2017. 368 p.
ISBN 9781681772998
Grades: Adult   **796.6**
1. Moore, Tim, 1964- 2. Bicycle touring 3. Travelers 4. Iron Curtain 5. Voyages and travels 6. Eastern Europe 7. Travel Writing — Europe
LC 2017302278

The author describes his bicycle tour through the old Iron Curtain territory, traveling 6,000 miles from the northern border between Russia and Norway to the Black Sea in Bulgaria while reflecting on what became of the Cold War Communist dream.

"An enjoyable account of an amazing human accomplishment." —*Kirkus*

Petersen, Grant
Just Ride: A Radically Practical Guide to Riding Your Bike. Grant Petersen; illustrations by Retsu Takahashi. Workman Pub. 2012. xi, 212 p. : Illustration
ISBN 9780761155584
Grades: Adult   **796.6**
1. Bicycles 2. Reference books — Handbooks, manuals, etc. 3. Sports and Competition — Racing — Cycling
LC 2012001429

Questions and debunks over eighty myths to highlight bicycling's inherently enjoyable nature, addressing everything from clothing and accessories to health, fitness, and safety.

"This piece of awesomeness should become a populist manifesto for bicyclists everywhere." —*Library Journal*
Includes index.

Weiss, Eben
★ *The Ultimate Bicycle Owner's Manual: The Universal Guide to Bikes, Riding, and Everything for Beginner and Seasoned Cyclists.* Eben Weiss, aka Bike Snob NYC.. Black Dog & Leventhal Publishers 2016. 240 p. : Illustration
ISBN 9780316352680
Grades: Adult   **796.6**
1. Bicycles 2. Maintenance and repair 3. Reference books 4. Sports and Competition — Racing — Cycling 5. Science writing — Medicine and health — Exercise 6. Sports
LC 2015041449

Everything you need to know to purchase, maintain, and ride a bike for recreation, commuting, competition, travel, and beyond! from the bike world's most beloved and trusted advocate.
Includes index.

796.62 Bicycle racing

Hamilton, Tyler
The Secret Race: Inside the Hidden World of the Tour De France: Doping, Cover-ups, and Winning at All Costs. Tyler Hamilton and Daniel Coyle. Bantam Dell 2012. 304 p.
ISBN 9780345530417
Grades: Adult   **796.62**
1. Hamilton, Tyler, 1971- 2. Armstrong, Lance 3. Bicycle racing 4. Doping in sports 5. Athletes 6. Drug use 7. People with depression 8. Men 9. Autobiographies and memoirs 10. Sports and Competition — Racing — Cycling 11. Sports and Competition — Individual Athlete 12. True Crime — Drugs 13. Life stories — Sports — Athletes
LC 2012288990

Hamilton pulls back the curtain on the Tour de France and takes us into the secret world of professional cycling like never before: the doping, the lying, and his years as Lance Armstrong's teammate on U.S. Postal.

796.72 Automobile racing

Hawley, Sam
Speed Duel: The Inside Story of the Land Speed Record in the Sixties. Sam Hawley. Firefly Books Ltd 2010. 360 p.
ISBN 9781554076338
Grades: Adult   **796.72**
1. Speed 2. Record setting 3. Dragsters 4. Automobiles, Racing 5. 1960s 6. Sports and Competition — Racing
LC 2012405437

Looks at the rivalry between Craig Breedlove and Art Arfons as they aspired to set new land speed records during the 1960s.

"Even readers who don't know a spark plug from a gear shift will be transfixed by Hawley's white-knuckled account of the ever-escalating competition to hold the Land Speed Record in the '60s and early '70s. Drawing from countless articles, profiles, documentaries, and interviews with the men and women who were there, Hawley traces the sport's evolution from its first four-wheeled record of 39mph in 1898, to today's jet-propelled 700mph-plus, recounting the creation, testing, and repair of legendary cars like the humble Green Monster and the charismatic Spirit of America." —*Publishers Weekly*

796.7209 Automobile racing — History

Baime, A. J.
★ *Go Like Hell: Ford, Ferrari, and Their Battle for Speed and Glory at Le Mans.* A. J. Baime. Houghton Mifflin Harcourt 2009. xv, 304 p. : Illustration; Color; Map
ISBN 9780618822195
Grades: Adult   **796.7209**
1. Ford, Henry, 1863-1947 2. Iacocca, Lee A, 1924-2019 3. Shelby, Carroll, 1923-2012 4. Grand Prix racing 5. Industrialists 6. Automobile designers 7. Automobiles 8. Sports cars 9. Ferrari automobile 10. Design and construction 11. Sports and Competition — Racing — Cars
LC 2008052948

Traces the story of how Henry Ford II competed against Enzo Ferrari for dominance in the speed- and style-driven 1960s automobile industry, revealing the contributions of visionary Lee Iacocca and former racing champion-turned-engineer Carroll Shelby.

"Baime tells an exciting story at a pace that manages to keep up with the drivers." —*Library Journal*
Includes bibliographical references (p. [260]-283) and index.

Bascomb, Neal
Faster: How a Jewish Driver, an American Heiress, and a Legendary Car Beat Hitler's Best. Neal Bascomb. Houghton Mifflin Harcourt 2020. 304 p.
ISBN 9781328489876
Grades: Adult   **796.7209**
1. Dreyfus, Rene 2. Schell, Lucy 3. Automobile racing 4. Automobile racing drivers 5. Discrimination in sports 6. Grand Prix racing 7. Nazism 8. Socialites 9. Jewish men 10. Persecution by Nazis 11. World War II 12. Between the Wars (1918-1939) 13. Sports and competition — Racing — Cars 14. History writing — Europe
LC 2019033972

For fans of Boys in the Boat and In the Garden of Beasts, the pulse-pounding story of how a Jewish race car driver and an American speed queen triumphed over Hitler's fearsome Silver Arrows on the eve of World War II.

"This rousing popular history fires on all cylinders." —*Publishers Weekly*
Includes bibliographical references and index.

796.8 Combat sports

Lee, Shannon
Be Water, My Friend: The Teachings of Bruce Lee. Shannon Lee. Flatiron Books 2020. 240 p.

ESSENTIAL AND RECOMMENDED TITLES
796.812 Wrestling

ISBN 9781250206688
Grades: Adult   **796.8**
1. Lee, Bruce, 1940-1973 2. Martial arts 3. Personal conduct 4. Psychological growth 5. Mind and body 6. Spiritual life 7. Philosophy 8. Society and culture — Philosophy 9. Sports and Competition — Martial Arts 10. Spirituality and Religion — General

LC 2020031675

The daughter of the legendary martial artist and president of the Bruce Lee Foundation shares insights into her father's life-shaping philosophies while demonstrating how the martial arts can be both a metaphor and tool of personal growth.

"This inspired guide will remind any reader that, while one cannot control external circumstance, how one responds is always a choice." —*Publishers Weekly*

796.812 Wrestling

Levi, Heather
The World of Lucha Libre: Secrets, Revelations, and Mexican National Identity. Heather Levi. Duke University Press 2008. xxii, 265 p.
ISBN 9780822342328
Grades: Adult   **796.812**
1. Lucha libre 2. Wrestling 3. Wrestlers 4. Social life and customs 5. Mexico 6. Sports and Competition — Wrestling

LC 2008023166

Ethnography of Mexican professional wrestling by a female wrestler and scholar, showing how the sport is linked to national affirmations and counter-narratives.

"A small but fascinating part of Levi's book is the fieldwork she did while preparing the text. While living in Mexico, Levi trained as a luchadora with a former professional wrestler. The experience of training is not the focus of the work, however, but rather a tool the author used to further illuminate her research." —*PopMatters*

Includes bibliographical references and index.

796.815 Oriental martial arts forms

Wertheim, L. Jon
Blood in the Cage: Mixed Martial Arts, Pat Miletich, and the Furious Rise of the Ufc. L. Jon Wertheim. Houghton Mifflin Harcourt 2009. 288 p.
ISBN 9780618982615
Grades: 10 11 12 Adult   **796.815**
1. Miletich, Patrick Jay, 1968- 2. Martial artists 3. Mixed martial arts 4. Self-defense 5. Martial arts 6. Social life and customs 7. United States 8. 21st century 9. Autobiographies and memoirs 10. Sports and Competition — Martial Arts 11. Life stories — Sports — Athletes

LC 2008036764

An inside look at the growing sport of mixed martial arts chronicles the life and career of Pat Miletich, a pioneer of mixed martial arts and six-time UFC champion, against the backdrop of the rise of the Ultimate Fighting Championship.

796.83 Boxing

Butler, Brin-Jonathan
The Domino Diaries: My Decade Boxing with Olympic Champions and Chasing Hemingway's Ghost in the Last Days of Castro's Cuba. Brin-Jonathan Butler. Picador 2015. 320 p.
ISBN 9781250043702
Grades: Adult   **796.83**
1. Butler, Brin-Jonathan 2. Boxing 3. Athletes 4. Journalists 5. Cuba 6. Autobiographies and memoirs 7. Life stories — Arts and culture — Writing — Journalists 8. Life stories — Sports

LC 2015012698

Brin-Jonathan Butler's story of his time chasing the American dream through Cuba Whether he's hustling his way into Mike Tyson's mansion for an interview, betting his life savings on a boxing match, becoming romantically entangled with one of Fidel Castro's granddaughters, or simply manufacturing press credentials to go where he wants-Brin-Jonathan Butler has always been the "act first, ask permission later" kind of journalist. This book is the culmination of Butler's decade spent in the trenches of Havana, trying to understand a culture perplexing to Westerners: one whose elite athletes regularly forgo multimillion-dollar opportunities to stay in Cuba and box for their country, while living in penury. Butler's fascination with this distinctly Cuban idealism sets him off on a remarkable journey, training with, befriending, and interviewing the champion boxers that Cuba seems to produce more than any other country. In the process, though, Butler gets to know the landscape of the exhilaratingly warm Cuban culture-and starts to question where he feels most at home.

"Focusing on Dickensian characters as well as boxing, Butler's gonzo journalism should have broad appeal." —*Library Journal*

Liebling, A. J.
★ *The Sweet Science.* A.J. Liebling; foreword by Robert Anasi. North Point Press 2004. xv, 267 p.
ISBN 9780374272272
Grades: Adult   **796.83**
1. Boxers (Sports) 2. Boxing 3. United States 4. Essays 5. Sports and Competition — Boxing

LC 2004049509

Here are the great events of boxing's American heyday: Sugar Ray Robinson's dramatic comeback, Rocky Marciano's rise to prominence, Joe Louis's unfortunate decline, brought so vividly to life that Sports Illustrated named the Sweet Science the best American sports book of all time.

Originally published: New York : Viking, 1956.

796.86 Fencing

Bennett, Alexander
Kendo: Culture of the Sword. Alexander C. Bennett. University of California Press 2015. 356 p.
ISBN 9780520284371
Grades: Adult   **796.86**
1. Kendo 2. Martial arts 3. Military art and science 4. Swordplay 5. Japan 6. Sports and competition — Martial arts 7. History writing — Asia — Japan

LC 2015004621

Kendo is the first book in English to provide an in-depth historical, cultural, and political account of the Japanese martial art of swordsmanship, from its beginnings in military training and arcane medieval schools to its widespread practice today as a global sport. Alexander Bennett shows how kendo evolved through a recurring process of 'Inventing tradition', which served the changing ideologies and needs of Japanese warriors and governments over the course of history. Kendo follows the development of Japanese swordsmanship from the aristocratic pretensions of medieval warriors in the Muromachi period, to the samurai elitism of the Edo regime, and to the patriotism of the Meiji state.

"A highly recommended, useful resource for all readers interested in this popular sport." —*Library Journal*

Includes bibliographical references and index.

796.93 Skiing and snowboarding

Vinton, Nathaniel
The Fall Line: How American Ski Racers Conquered a Sport on the Edge. Nathaniel Vinton. W. W. Norton & Company 2015. 384 p.
ISBN 9780393244779
Grades: Adult   **796.93**

PUBLIC LIBRARY CORE COLLECTION: NONFICTION
Twentieth Edition

1. Vonn, Lindsey 2. Miller, Bode, 1977- 3. Skiing 4. Skiers 5. Skis 6. United States 7. Sports and Competition — Olympic Sports 8. Sports and Competition — Sports History

LC 2014033594

A journey into the world's original extreme sport: Downhill ski racing.

"As the season progresses, Vinton adds rich historical context to each race venue, documenting course changes and rule revisions, while profiling past skiing greats, including Austrians Franz Klammer and Hermann Maier. The subtitle is a bit of a misnomer as this is not simply a story of American skiers but, instead, a primer on the history and current state of Alpine skiing." —*Booklist*

Includes index.

796.962 Ice hockey

Coffey, Wayne R.
★ *The Boys of Winter: The Untold Story of a Coach, a Dream, and the 1980 U.S. Olympic Hockey Team.* Wayne Coffey; foreword by Jim Craig. Crown Publishers 2005. xiii, 272 p. : Illustration
ISBN 9781400047659
Grades: 9 10 11 12 Adult   796.962

1. Hockey 2. Hockey teams 3. Hockey players 4. Olympic athletes 5. 1980s 6. Sports and Competition — Hockey 7. Sports and Competition — Teams 8. Sports and Competition — Olympic Sports 9. Adult books for young adults

LC 2004014163

Looks back at one of the greatest moments of twentieth-century sports history, the victory of the U.S. hockey team over the Soviet Union, assessing the meaning of the triumph and the paths of the players and coaches on both sides since 1980.

"The author offers a nuanced portrait of the 1980 Olympics miracle on ice and the gold medal-winning U.S. hockey team." —*School Library Journal*

Also published in large print format.

797.1 Aquatic sports

Krauzer, Steven M.
Kayaking: Whitewater and Touring Basics. by Steven Krauzer; introduction by John Viehman; illustrations by Ron Hildebrand. W.W. Norton 1995. 192 p. : Color illustration; Color; Map
ISBN 9780393313369
Grades: Adult   797.1

1. Kayaking 2. Kayaks 3. Sports and Competition — General

LC 95005527

A companion book to the Trailside PBS-TV series guides beginners from still waters to paddling downriver, exploring local waterways, or touring offshore islands, with a survey of the latest boat designs and equipment. TV tie-in.

A companion volume to the television series, Trailside; Includes bibliographical references and index.

Sleight, Steve
The Complete Sailing Manual. Steve Sleight. DK/Penguin Random House Publishing 2021. 448 pages : Color; Illustration
ISBN 9780744027495
Grades: Adult   797.1

1. Sailing 2. Reference books — Handbooks, manuals, etc. 3. Reference books — Sports 4. Sports and Competition — Boating and sailing

LC 2017448422

An illustrated, step-by-step guide to sailing, reviewing the parts of the boat, equipment, controls, and other basics; and discussing dinghy sailing, cruiser sailing, navigation, weather, practical boat care, and safety.

Foreword by Sir Ben Ainslie—Front cover; First American Edition: 2012; Includes index.

797.12 Types of vessels

Brown, Daniel James
★ *The Boys in the Boat: Nine Americans and Their Epic Quest for Gold at the 1936 Olympics.* Daniel James Brown. Viking 2013. 432 p.
ISBN 9780593512302
Grades: 11 12 Adult   797.12

1. Rowing 2. Working class men 3. Friendship 4. Rowers 5. Olympic athletes 6. Olympic games 7. Determination 8. Sports history 9. Athletes 10. Sports teams 11. American people 12. United States 13. 1930s 14. 20th century 15. Biographies 16. Page to screen 17. Sports and Competition — Olympic Sports 18. Sports and Competition — Racing — Boats 19. Sports and competition — Sports history 20. Nonfiction that reads like fiction 21. Book club best bets

LC 2013001560

ALA Notable Book, 2014; Indies' Choice Book Awards, Adult Nonfiction, 2014; Shortlisted for the James Tait Black Memorial Prize for Biography, 2013.

The Boys in the Boat describes how a group of working class youths from the University of Washington rowing team emerged from obscurity to defeat a field of elite international rivals at the 1936 Berlin Olympics. Sports fans who love a good "Cinderella story" will cheer this fast-paced, emotionally charged account of the players' and coaches' struggles set against stark Depression-era realities.

Also published in large print format; Includes bibliographical references and index.

Gilder, Ginny
Course Correction: A Story of Rowing and Resilience in the Wake of Title IX. Ginny Gilder. Beacon Press 2015. 272 p.
ISBN 9780807074770
Grades: Adult   797.12

1. Gilder, Ginny 2. Rowers 3. Rowing 4. Women Olympic athletes 5. Women athletes 6. United States 7. Autobiographies and memoirs 8. Biographies 9. Life stories — Sports — Athletes 10. Life stories — Identity — Gender 11. Sports and competition — Racing — Boats

LC 2014037358

Course Correction recounts the physical and psychological barriers Gilder overcame as she transformed into an elite athlete who reached the highest echelon of her sport. Set against the backdrop of unprecedented cultural change, Gilder's story personalizes the impact of Title IX, illustrating the life-changing lessons learned in sports but felt far beyond the athletic arena.

797.122 Canoeing

McGrath, Ben
Riverman: An American Odyssey. Ben McGrath. Alfred A. Knopf 2022. 304 p.
ISBN 9780451494009
Grades: Adult   797.122

1. Conant, Richard Perry 2. Outdoor life 3. Canoes 4. Canoeing 5. Rivers 6. Wilderness survival 7. Wanderers and wandering 8. Alternative lifestyles 9. Eccentrics and eccentricities 10. Journalists 11. Missing men 12. People with mental illnesses 13. Men 14. Biographies 15. Life stories — Nature and outdoors 16. Travel Writing — Modes of Transportation — Boating 17. Travel Writing — United States

Drawing on his own encounter with Dick Conant, this riveting true story follows the American folk hero who, living a remarkable life far outside the staid confines of modern existence, paddled the rivers of America until his disappearance in 2014 while on the way to Florida. Map(s).

"The captivating story of an inveterate river wanderer who left a mark on many he met along his journeys before suddenly vanishing….In this debut book, longtime New Yorker staff writer McGrath…delivers a worthy combination of character study, travelogue, and missing-person's story." —*Kirkus*

ESSENTIAL AND RECOMMENDED TITLES
797.2 Swimming and diving

797.2 Swimming and diving

Checkoway, Julie
The **Three-Year** *Swim Club: The Untold Story of Maui's Sugar Ditch Kids and Their Quest for Olympic Glory.* Julie Checkoway. Grand Central Pub. 2015. 448 p.
ISBN 9781455523443
Grades: Adult 797.2
1. Swimming 2. Poor children 3. Olympic games 4. Sugar plantations 5. Teachers 6. Japanese Americans 7. Swimmers 8. Coaching (Athletics) 9. East Asian Americans 10. Hawaii 11. 1930s 12. Sports and Competition — Swimming and Diving 13. Sports and Competition — Olympic Sports 14. Adult books for young adults
LC 2015947608
Offers an inspiring story of how a group of poor Japanese-American kids from Hawaii were transformed into Olympic-level swimming champions.
"Details about training, swim times, and the team's travels occasionally overwhelm Checkoway's tense, vivid, an d inspiring narrative. Not without its flaws, but a good choice for fans of David Halberstam's The Amateurs (1985), Daniel Boyne's The Red Rose Crew (2000), and similar books." —*Kirkus*

Graver, Dennis
Scuba Diving. Dennis K. Graver, EMT, SEI.. Human Kinetics 2017. IX, 245 pages : Color; Illustration
ISBN 9781492525769
Grades: 11 12 Adult 797.2
1. Scuba diving 2. Sports and Competition — General
LC 2016018110
Packed with full-color photographs and illustrations, Scuba Diving offers step-by-step instruction on preparing for and managing a dive safely with information on the latest equipment, gear selection, recommended dive locations, technologies and techniques. Dennis Graver explains the basics of diving, including managing underwater emergencies, avoiding underwater hazards and equalizing pressure in the ears, sinuses and mask. The comprehensive content and world class photography of Scuba Diving make it the finest scuba title on the market!
Includes bibliographical references (page 239) and index.

Means, Howard B.
★ *Splash!: 10,000 Years of Swimming.* Howard Means. Hachette Books 2020. 336 p.
ISBN 9780306845666
Grades: Adult 797.2
1. Swimming 2. Olympic games (Ancient) 3. Olympic games 4. History writing — Microhistory 5. Sports and Competition — Swimming and Diving 6. Sports and Competition — Olympic Sports
LC 2019056316
This history of 10,000 years of swimming from Ancient Egypt, Greece and Rome to today|s Olympic games and backyard pools also looks its influence on religion, segregation and sex.
"For a sport generally underrepresented in library collections, this is a superb account of swimming's long and remarkable history." —*Library Journal*
Includes bibliographical references and index.

Nestor, James
Deep: Freediving, Renegade Science, and What the Ocean Tells Us About Ourselves. James Nestor. Houghton Mifflin Harcourt 2014. 272 p.
ISBN 9780547985527
Grades: Adult 797.2
1. Skin diving 2. Marine biology 3. Marine animals 4. Sports and competition — Extreme sports 5. Science writing — Biology 6. Adult books for young adults
LC 2014002593
Booklist Editors' Choice: Adult Books for Young Adults, 2014.
Surveys the achievements of adventurous scientists, athletes and explorers to reveal how new understandings about deep-sea life, from telepathic coral to shark navigation, are expanding what is known about the natural world and the human mind.
"[B]rimming with vivid portraits, lucid scientific explanations, gripping (and funny) first-person accounts, and urgent facts about the ocean's endangerment, Nestor's Deep is galvanizing, enlightening, and invaluable." —*Booklist*

Tsui, Bonnie
Why We Swim. Bonnie Tsui. Algonquin Books 2020. 277 p.
ISBN 9781616207861
Grades: Adult 797.2
1. Swimming 2. Social history 3. Well-being 4. Swimmers 5. Water 6. Health 7. Survival 8. Sports and Competition — Swimming and Diving 9. Nature Writing — General 10. Sports and Competition — Sports History
LC 2019042645
We swim in freezing Arctic waters and piranha-infested rivers to test our limits. We swim for pleasure, for exercise, for healing. But humans, unlike other animals that are drawn to water, are not natural-born swimmers. We must be taught. Sharing stories of Olympic champions, a Baghdad swim club, and modern-day Japanese samurai swimmers, a New York Times contributor investigates what about water—despite its dangers—draws us to it time and time again.
"A study of swimming as sport, survival method, basis for community, and route to physical and mental well-being... an absorbing, wide-ranging story of humans' relationship with the water." —*Kirkus*
Includes bibliographical references.

797.32 Surfing (Surf riding)

Mackinnon, Al
Epic Surf Breaks of the World: Explore the Planet's Most Thrilling Waves. [authors, Al Mackinnon and others]. Lonely Planet 2020. 328 p. (Lonely Planet Epic Surf Breaks of the World)
ISBN 9781788686501
Grades: Adult 797.32
1. Surfing 2. Sports and Competition — General 3. Travel Writing — General
"The editors of this vibrant illustrated volume share tales of epic rides, advice on getting to the wave, and, most importantly, where to find the best breaks.... Surfers will immerse themselves in this bucket-list guidebook." —*Publishers Weekly*

798.4 Horse racing

Hillenbrand, Laura
★ *Seabiscuit: An American Legend.* Laura Hillenbrand. Random House 2001. xiii, 399 p. : Illustration
ISBN 9780375502910
Grades: 11 12 Adult 798.4
1. Self-acceptance 2. Seabiscuit (Race horse) 3. Thoroughbred horses 4. Horse trainers 5. Jockeys 6. Men and horses 7. Horse racing 8. Race horses 9. United States 10. 1930s 11. Animal biographies 12. Page to screen 13. Sports and Competition — Racing — Horses 14. Family and Relationships — Pets and Owners 15. Adult books for young adults 16. Nonfiction that reads like fiction
LC 2002090323
ALA Notable Book, 2002; Book Sense Book of the Year Nonfiction, 2002; Library Journal Best Books, 2001; New York Times Notable Book, 2001; School Library Journal Best Books: Best Adult Books 4 Teens, 2001; National Book Critics Circle Award for Nonfiction finalist, 2001.
To look at Seabiscuit one would never know that he had the potential to become the most popular racehorse of the 20th century. But, thanks to the efforts of his owner, his dedicated trainer, and his jockeys, Seabiscuit made racing history despite his stunted legs and knobby knees. The team's road to unimaginable fame and success (even President Roosevelt halted work to listen to the race between Seabiscuit and his foe, War Admiral) is the subject of this wildly popular and hugely compelling bestseller.

"This is a remarkable tale well told by a writer who deftly blends history and sport." —*The Economist*

Includes bibliographical references and index.

Prior-Palmer, Lara
Rough Magic: Riding the World's Loneliest Horse Race. Lara Prior-Palmer. Catapult 2019. 224 pages
ISBN 9781948226196

Grades: Adult   798.4

1. Prior-Palmer, Lara 2. Horse racing 3. Women and horses 4. Competition 5. Young women 6. Wild horses 7. Mongolia 8. Autobiographies and memoirs 9. Life stories — Sports — Athletes 10. Sports and competition — Racing — Horses 11. Adult books for young adults

LC 2018950159

For fans of Helen Macdonald's H Is for Hawk, this is the extraordinary debut memoir of a young woman who traveled to Mongolia to compete in the world's longest, toughest horse race, and emerged as its youngest and first-ever female winner.

"First-time author Prior-Palmer transforms from hopeless 19-year-old underdog into surprising champion of the grueling 2013 Mongol Derby in this exhilarating, visceral account of her attempt to win a 1,000-kilometer horse race across the Mongolian countryside." —*Publishers Weekly*

798.40092 Horse racing — Biography

Drape, Joe
American Pharoah: The Untold Story of the Triple Crown Winner's Legendary Rise. Joe Drape. Hachette Books 2016. x, 292 pages : Color; Illustration
ISBN 9780316268844

Grades: Adult   798.40092

1. American Pharoah (Horse) 2. Race horses 3. Horse racing 4. Triple Crown, American (Horse racing) 5. Sports and competition — Racing — Horses

LC Bl2016014449

Profiles the life and accomplishments of the Thoroughbred race horse American Pharoah, chronicling key events en route to him becoming the twelfth Triple Crown winner.

"A captivating story woven with an affectionate yet honest portrayal of the sometimes seedy sport of kings, this work will appeal to horse-racing fans and anyone who enjoys athlete biographies." —*Library Journal*

Includes bibliographical references (pages 275-278) and index.

798.400929 Racehorses — Sports — Biography

Ours, Dorothy
Man O' War: A Legend Like Lightning. Dorothy Ours. St. Martin's Press 2006. VIII, 342 p, 16 p. of plates : Illustration
ISBN 9780312340995

Grades: 11 12 Adult   798.400929

1. Horse racing 2. Race horses 3. Sports corruption 4. Social life and customs 5. United States 6. 20th century 7. Sports and Competition — Racing — Horses

LC 2006041631

The story of a legendary early twentieth-century racehorse offers insight into the sport during his career, describing the horse's rebellious early years, the rumors about race fixing that haunted his one defeat, and the role of arch-rival and Triple Crown winner Sir Barton.

"This book is clearly a labor of love, and it certifies Big Red's claim to immortality." —*New York Times Book Review*

Includes bibliographical references (p. 285-325) and index.

798.4010973 Gambling — Horse racing — United States

Lang, Arne K.
Sports Betting and Bookmaking: An American History. Arne K. Lang. Rowman & Littlefield 2016. xi, 293 p.
ISBN 9781442265530

Grades: Adult   798.4010973

1. Horse race betting 2. Sports betting 3. Bookmaking (Betting) 4. Gambling 5. Horse racing 6. Sports and competition — Gambling and betting

LC 2015047132

This book is a sweeping overview of bookmaking in the United States, from the first thoroughbred meet at Saratoga in 1863 through the modern day. The cultural war between bookmakers and their adversaries is a recurrent thread, and the decline of horse racing—and concurrent rise of team sports—is examined at length.

Includes bibliographical references and index.

799.1 Fishing

Cermele, Joe
★ *The Total Fishing Manual: 317 Essential Fishing Skills.* Joe Cermele and the editors of Field & Stream. Welden Owen 2013. 314 p; Color illustration
ISBN 9781616286293

Grades: Adult   799.1

1. Fishing 2. Sports and Competition — Fishing

LC Bl2013025585

A comprehensive guide to fishing, including information on the best lures for particular fish, picking the right rod, and how to troubleshoot a boat's motor.

Gathers comprehensive advice from top fishermen to counsel enthusiasts of any level on the methods used by professionals, providing coverage of such skills as properly baiting a hook, nabbing a good spot on a party fishing boat and landing a prime catch.

Includes index.

Messineo, Janet
Casting into the Light: Tales of a Fishing Life. Janet Messineo. Pantheon Books 2019. 320 pages
ISBN 9781524747640

Grades: Adult   799.1

1. Messineo, Janet 2. Fishing 3. Women fishers 4. Salt-water fishing 5. Atlantic Coast (United States) 6. Autobiographies and memoirs 7. Life stories — Nature and outdoors 8. Sports and Competition — Fishing 9. Life stories — Identity — Gender

LC 2018052725

The champion surfcaster and Martha's Vineyard Times columnist traces her efforts to break barriers in a strictly male sport, describing its unspoken ethics while sharing insider strategies on surf-fishing techniques, lures, baits and locations.

"An inspirational memoir of one woman's self-discovery while pursuing the elusive catch." —*Booklist*

Includes bibliographical references and index.

Schultz, Ken
Ken Schultz's Essentials of Fishing: The Only Guide You Need to Catch Freshwater and Saltwater Fish. Ken Schultz; fish illustrations by David Kiphuth. John Wiley & Sons 2009. 480 p.
ISBN 9781684425839

Grades: Adult   799.1

1. Fishing 2. Fishes 3. Fishing tackle 4. Fishing rods 5. Sports and Competition — Fishing 6. Reference — Instructional materials

Ken Schultz's Essentials of Fishing combines authoritative coverage of every aspect of fishing with a stunning visual presentation that is as thrilling and dramatic as the sport you love. Organized by topic, this information-packed reference offers fast and easy access to all of the fishing facts, instructions, and tips

ESSENTIAL AND RECOMMENDED TITLES
799.12 Angling

you need to get more bites, land more big ones, and have a lot more fun every time you dip a line in the water."

Essentials is a condensation of Ken Schultz's Fishing encyclopedia : Worldwide angling guide with new material added; Includes index.

799.12 Angling

Gierach, John
All Fishermen Are Liars. John Gierach. Simon & Schuster 2014. 256 p.
ISBN 9781451618310
Grades: Adult   799.12
1. Fly fishing 2. Fishing 3. Fishers 4. Humans and fish 5. Essays 6. Sports and Competition — Fishing 7. Nature Writing — Animal Studies — Fish and Fishing
LC 2013012784

From the Pacific Northwest to the Upper Midwest to the Canadian Maritimes, "America's best fishing writer" shares insights, musings and countless stories he has collected over a lifetime of fishing, proving that life's most valuable lessons are found while fly-fishing.

"An engaging autobiographical introduction opens the book, which includes 22 perceptive and witty essays, recalling numerous fishing trips and offering insights on fly rods and fly patterns. These lyrical essays explode with descriptions of beautiful places, big fish, and beautiful fish." —*Booklist*

A Fly Rod of Your Own. John Gierach; art by Glenn Wolff. Simon & Schuster 2017. 256 p.
ISBN 9781451618341
Grades: Adult   799.12
1. Fly fishing 2. Fishing 3. Essays 4. Sports and Competition — Fishing 5. Nature Writing — Animal Studies — Fish and Fishing
LC 2016019507

National Outdoor Book Award for Outdoor Literature, 2017.

Called "the voice of the common angler" by the Wall Street Journal, and a member of the Fly Fishing Hall of Fame, the author travels to remote fishing locations, from Alaska to the Canadian Maritimes, where he, with his sharp sense of humor and keen eye for observation of the fishing life, scrutinizes the art of fly-fishing.

"A must for fisherman and outdoor enthusiasts, this book may also have wider appeal, as it is as much about travel, friendships, and navigating today's world as it is about fly-fishing." —*Library Journal*

Meyers, Charlie
The Little Red Book of Fly Fishing: 250 Tips to Make You a Better Fisherman. Charlie Meyers and Kirk Deeter. Skyhorse Pub. 2010. xv, 201 p. : Color illustration
ISBN 9781602399815
Grades: Adult   799.12
1. Fly fishing 2. Sports and Competition — Fishing
LC 2009046448

Kirk Deeter of Field & Stream and Charlie Meyers of the Denver Post, crack open their notebooks and share expert advice on flies, casting, reading the water, and much more.

Includes bibliographical references and index.

Rosenbauer, Tom
The Orvis Fly-Fishing Guide. Tom Rosenbauer. Lyons Press 2017. VII, 400 pages : Color; Illustration
ISBN 9781493025794
Grades: Adult   799.12
1. Fly fishing 2. Sports and Competition — Fishing
LC 2016048926

Presents a comprehensive guide to fly fishing, with information on rods, lines, reels, and leaders, advice for casting and fly selection, and tactics for stream, freshwater, and salt water fishing.

Includes bibliographical references and index.

799.124 Fly fishing

Burke, Monte
Lords of the Fly: Madness, Obsession, and the Hunt for the World Record Tarpon. Monte Burke. Pegasus Books 2020. xvii, 278 pages : Illustration
ISBN 9781643135588
Grades: Adult   799.124
1. Fishers 2. Fishing 3. Environmental degradation 4. Fly fishing 5. Competition 6. Florida 7. 1970s 8. 1980s 9. Sports and Competition — Fishing 10. Nature Writing — Animal Studies — Fish and Fishing

In the late 1970s and early 1980s, something unique happened in the quiet little town on the west coast of Florida known as Homosassa. The best fly anglers in the world gathered together to chase the same Holy Grail: The world record for the world's most glamorous and sought-after fly rod species, the tarpon.

"A fascinating look at the narrow but wild world of tarpon fishing. Burke constructs the rise and fall of this unique fishing tale with impressive narrative control and an obvious reverence for its vivid characters. Ably captures the swagger, attitudes, and angling derring-do of a golden age of fishing history." —*Kirkus*

Includes bibliographical references.

Gierach, John
Dumb Luck and the Kindness of Strangers. John Gierach. Simon & Schuster 2020. 225 pages : Illustration
ISBN 9781501168581
Grades: Adult   799.124
1. Fly fishing 2. Fishing 3. Essays 4. Sports and Competition — Fishing 5. Nature Writing — Animal Studies — Fish and Fishing
LC 2020930580

In Dumb Luck and the Kindness of Strangers, Gierach looks back to the long-ago day when he bought his first resident fishing license in Colorado, where the fishing season never ends, and just knew he was in the right place. And he succinctly sums up part of the appeal of his sport when he writes that it is 'An acquired taste that reintroduces the chaos of uncertainty back into our well-regulated lives'.

"Gierach's inviting, down-to-earth, and humorous work shares a deep love of fly-fishing and the ways that it can be a metaphor for life." —*Publishers Weekly*

799.2 Hunting

Rinella, Steven
The Complete Guide to Hunting, Butchering, and Cooking Wild Game: Big Game. Steven Rinella. Spiegel & Grau 2015. 400 p; Illustration; Color; Map
ISBN 9780812994063
Grades: Adult   799.2
1. Big game animals 2. Hunting 3. Cooking (Game) 4. Hunting equipment 5. United States 6. Food writing — Cooking and cookbooks — Ingredients 7. Sports and Competition — Hunting
LC 2014013333

This comprehensive guide to big game hunting, organized by animal, provides novices and experts alike with step-by-step instructions and photographs to help readers prep, track, hunt and prepare their kills.

"Rinella doesnt offer too many tips beyond the obvious grilled steaks and jerky, though wild pig hunters will appreciate his simple but flavorful recipe for smoked ham. Its a minor flaw in a book thats terrifically informative and is sure to inspire hunters to start poring over maps and readying themselves for their next hunt." —*Publishers Weekly*

A Spiegel & Grau trade paperback original; Includes index.

The Complete Guide to Hunting, Butchering, and Cooking Wild Game; Volume 2. Steven Rinella. Spiegel & Grau 2015. xiii, 364 pages : Color; Illustration
ISBN 9780812987058
Grades: Adult   799.2

PUBLIC LIBRARY CORE COLLECTION: NONFICTION
Twentieth Edition

1. Cooking (Game) 2. Fowling 3. Game and game birds 4. Hunting 5. Hunting equipment 6. Recipes 7. Food writing — Cooking and cookbooks — Ingredients 8. Sports and Competition — Hunting

LC Bl2015052507

Provides information on hunting, butchering, and cooking small game and fowl, discussing the equipment needed, basic and advanced hunting strategies, how to field dress animals, and recipes for indoor and outdoor cooking.

Includes index.

801 Literature — Philosophy and theory

Chabon, Michael
Maps and Legends. Michael Chabon. McSweeney's Books 2008. 200 p.
ISBN 9781932416893
Grades: Adult   801
1. Books and reading 2. Authors 3. Readers 4. Authors and readers 5. Writing 6. Essays 7. Arts and Entertainment — Writing and Publishing

LC Bl2008009268

A series of linked essays about the enriching prospects of reading and writing argues for the importance of enjoying a diverse range of options rather than limiting oneself to studious or serious literature, in an anthology that also explores the Pulitzer Prize-winning author's own writings from a perspective of personal history.

Kundera, Milan
★ *The Curtain: An Essay in Seven Parts.* Milan Kundera; translated from the French by Linda Asher. HarperCollins Publishers 2006. VIII, 168 p.
ISBN 9780060841867
Grades: Adult   801
1. Literature 2. Philosophy 3. Arts and Entertainment — Writing and Publishing — Literary criticism

LC 2006043420

Traces the author's personal view of the history and significance of the novel in western civilization, arguing that a novel's development crosses international and language boundaries while serving to reveal previously unknown aspects of a reader's existence.

"The immediacy of Kundera's evocative prose and the rich tapestry he weaves compel us to pick up and read, or reread, the bountiful literary treasures of Western literature. This could be a book from which to draw a summer reading list." —*Library Journal*

Moore, Lorrie
See What Can Be Done: Essays, Criticism, & Commentary. Lorrie Moore. Alfred A. Knopf 2018. 416 p.
ISBN 9781524732486
Grades: Adult   801
1. Criticism 2. Modern literature 3. Authors 4. Political culture 5. Social change 6. Literary criticism 7. United States 8. Essays 9. Arts and Entertainment — Writing and Publishing 10. Arts and Entertainment — Writing and Publishing — Literary criticism

LC 2017006247

A treasury of more than 50 prose pieces by the cultural commentator and author of Bark reviews the literary achievements of her contemporaries, sharing perspectives on subjects ranging from the art of writing fiction and the historical imagination to terrorism and the continuing unequal state of race in America.

"Deft, graceful essays from a sharply incisive writer." —*Kirkus*
This is a Borzoi book.

Ozick, Cynthia
Critics, Monsters, Fanatics, and Other Literary Essays. Cynthia Ozick. Houghton Mifflin Harcourt 2016. 224 p.
ISBN 9780544703711
Grades: Adult   801
1. Criticism 2. Literary criticism 3. Essays 4. Arts and Entertainment — Writing and Publishing

LC 2015037560

An essay collection by the National Book Critics Circle Award-winning critic includes a selection of new pieces as well as the author's gauntlet-throwing views on the essential role of critics in establishing a vibrant literary community.

"This essay collection from novelist (Foreign Bodies) and literary critic Ozick takes a fresh look at renowned writers of the past and present." —*Publishers Weekly*

Schultz, Philip
Comforts of the Abyss: The Art of Persona Writing. Philip Schultz. W. W. Norton & Company 2022. 240 p.
ISBN 9780393531848
Grades: Adult   801
1. Schultz, Philip 2. Writing 3. Creation (Literary, artistic, etc.) 4. Authors, American 5. Poets, American 6. Arts and entertainment — Writing and publishing 7. Life stories — Arts and culture — Writing — Authors

LC 2021061122

Persona writing, a method of borrowing the voice and temperament of accomplished writers, offers aspiring writers imaginative distance and perspective needed to tell their stories. Through a candid and generous account of his own story, acclaimed poet Philip Schultz reveals how his early struggle to find inspiration in his negative inclinations led to the idea of persona writing, the philosophy on which he founded the Writers Studio in 1987.

"Poet Schultz delves into the written expression of real emotion in this eloquent guide to 'persona writing,' or developing a narrative voice and viewpoint different from one's own....This intimate account is sure to satisfy writers in the making." —*Publishers Weekly*

803 Literature — Dictionaries, encyclopedias, concordances

Baldick, Chris
★ *The Oxford Dictionary of Literary Terms.* Chris Baldick. 2015. x, 392 p.
ISBN 9780198715443
Grades: Adult   803
1. Literature 2. Criticism 3. English language 4. Literary form 5. Dictionaries 6. Reference books — Literature

LC 2014960115

The bestselling Oxford Dictionary of Literary Terms provides clear and concise definitions of the most troublesome literary terms, from abjection to zeugma.

Includes bibliographical references (pages [391]-392).

807 Education, research, related topics

Appleman, Deborah
Literature and the New Culture Wars. Deborah Appleman. W.W. Norton & Company 2022. 168 p.
ISBN 9781324019183
Grades: Adult   807
1. Secondary education 2. Public education 3. Teaching 4. Censorship 5. Banned books 6. Challenged books 7. Political culture 8. Books and reading 9. Literature 10. Society and culture — Education 11. Arts and Entertainment — Writing and Publishing

Our current "culture wars" have reshaped the politics of secondary literature instruction. Due to a variety of challenges from both the left and the right—to language or subject matter, to potentially triggering content, or to authors who have been canceled—school reading lists are rapidly shrinking. For many teachers, choosing which books to include in their curriculum has become an agonizing task with political, professional, and ethical dimensions. Can educators continue to teach troubling but worthwhile texts?

This is an invigorating call for educators 'to continue to teach challenging texts.' —*Publishers Weekly*

ESSENTIAL AND RECOMMENDED TITLES
808 Rhetoric and collections of literary texts from more than two literatures

808 Rhetoric and collections of literary texts from more than two literatures

Evans, Bec
Written: How to Keep Writing and Build a Habit That Lasts. Bec Evans & Chris Smith; foreword by Oliver Burkeman. Icon 2023. 272 pages : Illustration
ISBN 9781785789038
Grades: Adult **808**
1. Writing 2. Habit 3. Language arts and studies — Writing skills 4. Self-Help — Personal growth
LC Bl2023013800

Applying research from neuroscience and psychology, and based on the authors' own practice and findings, Written will show you how to manage your time effectively, how to visualize and set successful goals, how to recover from setbacks, and ultimately how to create writing habits that work for you. Along the way, you'll hear inspiring and relatable stories from other writers who have overcome their struggles to find success."

"Highly recommended for libraries serving strong writing communities." —*Booklist*

Includes bibliographical references.

Fish, Stanley Eugene
Winning Arguments: What Works and Doesn't Work in Politics, the Bedroom, the Courtroom, and the Classroom. Stanley Fish. Harper 2016. 212 pages
ISBN 9780062226679
Grades: Adult **808**
1. Persuasion (Rhetoric) 2. Debates and debating 3. Rhetoric 4. Language arts and studies — Public speaking
LC 2015046681

Stanley Fish, the notoriously brash and brilliant English and Law professor, has authored dozens of academic books on subjects ranging from Milton to freedom of speech. In 2011, Fish turned his eye to a more popular subject, the art of writing great sentences. His short, wise book How to Write a Sentence became an instant New York Times Bestseller and continues to be read by students and aspiring writers. Adam Haslet called the book, "deeper and more democratic than the Elements of Style." If great sentences are, in effect, performances at the highest level, Fish acts as a lively sportscaster giving the reader a blow-by-blow. In Winning Arguments, Fish employs this same wit and observational prowess as he guides readers through the "greatest hits" of rhetoric including landmark legal cases, arguments drawn from popular film and TV, and even Fish's own career. The success of books like Jay Heinrich's Thank You for Arguing demonstrate a clear audience for fun, intellectually nourishing books that make youfeel just a little bit smarter for having read them. Like How to Write a Sentence, Winning Arguments will become a modern classic.

hooks, bell
Remembered Rapture: The Writer at Work. Bell hooks. Henry Holt 1999. xvi, 237 p.
ISBN 9780805059090
Grades: Adult **808**
1. hooks, bell, 1952-2021 2. Writing 3. Critics 4. Women and literature 5. African Americans in literature 6. Feminism 7. Intellectual life 8. African American women 9. Literary criticism 10. African Americans 11. United States 12. Essays 13. Arts and Entertainment — Writing and Publishing
LC 98007998

With grace and insight, celebrated writer bell hooks untangles the complex personae of women writers. Born and raised in the rural South, hooks learned early the power of the written word and the importance of speaking her mind. Her passion for words is the heartbeat of this collection of essays. Remembered Rapture celebrates literacy, the joys of reading and writing, and the lasting power of the book. Once again, these essays reveal bell hooks's wide-ranging intellectual scope; she is a universal writer addressing readers and writers everywhere.

Lamott, Anne
Bird by Bird: Some Instructions on Writing and Life. Anne Lamott. Anchor Books 1995. xxxi, 239 p.
ISBN 9780385480017
Grades: Adult **808**
1. Writing 2. Authors 3. Arts and Entertainment — Writing and Publishing
LC 95010225

A step-by-step guide to writing and managing the writer's life covers each portion of a written project, addresses such concerns as writer's block and getting published, and offers awareness and survival tips.

Originally published: New York : Pantheon Books, 1994.

Larimer, Kevin
The Poets & Writers Complete Guide to Being a Writer: Everything You Need to Know About Craft, Inspiration, Agents, Editors, Publishing, and the Business of Building a Sustainable Writing Career. Kevin Larimer and Mary Gannon. Avid Reader Press 2020. 416 pages
ISBN 9781982123079
Grades: Adult **808**
1. Writing 2. Authors 3. Poets 4. Creation (Literary, artistic, etc.) 5. Fiction writing 6. Poetry writing 7. Storytelling 8. Creative writing 9. Book industry and trade 10. Publishers and publishing 11. Literary agents 12. Vocational guidance 13. Arts and Entertainment — Writing and Publishing
LC Bl2020010946

A Poets & Writers guide draws on the insights of published authors, literary agents and editors in an authoritative reference that includes coverage of pursuing an MFA, preparing submissions and marketing in today's digital world.

"A book of benefit to well-practiced as well as novice writers, full of useful advice, pointers, and prompts." —*Kirkus*

Includes bibliographical references and index.

O'Neil, Dennis
The DC Comics Guide to Writing Comics. by Dennis O'Neil; introduction by Stan Lee. Watson-Guptill 2001. 128 p. : Illustration
ISBN 9780823010271
Grades: 11 12 Adult **808**
1. Comics and graphic novel writing 2. Comic book illustration 3. Writing 4. Art and music — Arts and crafts — Drawing and painting 5. Art and music — Visual arts — Cartooning and animation 6. Adult books for young adults 7. How-to books
LC 2001026101

Discusses the basic elements of comic book writing including script writing, story development, subplots, and character development.

Includes index.

Strunk, William
★ *The Elements of Style.* William Strunk, Jr; with revisions, an introduction, and a chapter on writing by E.B. White; [foreword by Roger Angell]. Allyn and Bacon 1999. xviii, 105 p.
ISBN 9780205313426
Grades: Adult **808**
1. English language 2. Report writing 3. Language arts — Writing skills
LC 99016419

Offers advice on improving writing skills and promoting a style marked by simplicity, orderliness, and sincerity.

Includes index.

Woods, Geraldine
25 Great Sentences and How They Got That Way. Geraldine Woods. W.W. Norton & Company 2020. 336 p.
ISBN 9781324004851
Grades: Adult **808**
1. English language 2. Sentences (Grammar) 3. Writing 4. Rhetoric 5. Communication 6. Arts and Entertainment — Writing and Publishing
LC 2019047655

We all know the basic structure of a sentence: a subject/verb pair expressing a complete thought and ending with proper punctuation. But that classroom definition doesn't begin to describe the ways in which these elements can combine to resonate with us as we read, to make us stop and think, laugh or cry. Culled from fiction, nonfiction, drama, poetry, song lyrics, speeches, and even ads, these exemplary sentences are celebrated for the distinctive features—whether of structure, diction, connection/comparison, sound, or extremes—that underlie their beauty, resonance, and creativity. With dry humor and an infectious enjoyment that makes her own sentences a pleasure to read, Woods shows us the craft that goes into the construction of a memorable sentence.

"A practical, nonboring companion for writers aiming to hone their style." —*Kirkus*

Includes bibliographical references and index.

Zinsser, William Knowlton
Writing to Learn. William Zinsser. Perennial Library 1989. x, 256 p.
ISBN 9780062720405
Grades: 11 12 Adult   808
1. English language 2. Interdisciplinary approach in education 3. Reference books
LC BL 99995954

The author demonstrates the importance of clear writing in every subject, discussing writing as a means to access knowledge, and surveys the growing emphasis on writing in American education.

"Eschewing theory and philosophical breast-beating, Zinsser uses his own experience to reinforce the fact that clear, eloquent writing can be taught for every subject across the curriculum. A practical manual for teachers and a powerful reminder for everyone that good writing makes possible good thinking." —*American Libraries*

Includes index; Bibliography: P. [237]-247; Originally published: New York : Harper & Row, 1988.

808.02 Authorship techniques, plagiarism, editorial techniques

Anders, Charlie Jane
★ *Never Say You Can't Survive: How to Get Through Hard Times by Making up Stories.* Charlie Jane Anders. Tor.Com 2021. 288 p.
ISBN 9781250800015
Grades: Adult   808.02
1. Anders, Charlie Jane 2. Women authors 3. Writing 4. Creativity 5. Creation (Literary, artistic, etc.) 6. Fiction writing 7. Essays 8. Life stories — Arts and culture — Writing — Authors 9. Arts and Entertainment — Writing and Publishing

Hugo Award for Best Related Non-Fiction Book, 2022.

An internationally best-selling and critically acclaimed writer presents a nonfiction book that is part memoir, part personal anecdote and insight on how to foster creativity in unprecedented times.

"Anders gives both new and experienced writers questions, exercises, and encouragement that will spark ideas and keep them motivated to continue their work." —*Booklist*

Attenberg, Jami
1000 Words: A Writer's Guide to Staying Creative, Focused, and Productive All Year Round. [edited by] Jami Attenberg. Simon Element 2024. 261 pages
ISBN 9781668023600
Grades: Adult   808.02
1. Writing 2. Vocational guidance 3. Essays 4. Language arts and studies — Writing skills 5. Arts and Entertainment — Writing and Publishing 6. Self-Help — Personal growth — Creativity
LC Oc2024002004

The book extension of the growing writer's movement and challenge to write 1,000 words a day helps readers and writers discover how to uncover their creative desires and stay motivated and offers advice from over 50 well-known writers.

"Readers will want to refer to this book more than once, so it's an ideal purchase for public libraries." —*Booklist*

Dreyer, Benjamin
Dreyer's English: An Utterly Correct Guide to Clarity and Style. Benjamin Dreyer. Random House 2019. xviii, 291 pages : Illustration
ISBN 9780812995701
Grades: Adult   808.02
1. Writing 2. Grammar 3. Punctuation 4. English language 5. Language and languages 6. Editing 7. Arts and Entertainment — Writing and Publishing
LC 2018027979

As Random House's copy chief, Dreyer has upheld the standards of the legendary publisher for more than two decades. Now he distills everything he has learned from the myriad books he has copyedited and overseen into a useful guide not just for writers but for everyone who wants to put their best prose foot forward.

"In this user-friendly guide, Random House copy chief Dreyer invites readers into his life's work, explaining how to navigate written communication through examples from years spent buried in unpublished manuscripts." —*Booklist*

Includes bibliographical references and index.

Griffin, Susan
Out of Silence, Sound. Out of Nothing, Something: A Writer's Guide. Susan Griffin. Counterpoint 2023. xviii, 230 p.
ISBN 9781640094109
Grades: Adult   808.02
1. Griffin, Susan 2. Women authors 3. Writing 4. Creativity 5. Imagination 6. Self-awareness 7. Fiction writing 8. Creative writing 9. Advice 10. Arts and Entertainment — Writing and Publishing 11. Life stories — Arts and culture — Writing — Authors
LC 2022023050

The distinguished author of more than twenty-two books, Susan Griffin distills daily wisdom garnered from more than five decades teaching creative writing and editing manuscripts, as well as from her own writing. Organized according to a practical timeline, Out of Silence, Sound. Out of Nothing, Something. elucidates the process of writing from beginning to end, presenting an approach that is similar to the practice of meditation as it encourages and enlarges the mind's intrinsic capacity for creativity. An autobiographical account, a sometimes humorous, at times moving essay called "How I Learned to Write" is threaded throughout the book.

"Budding writers will find a bottomless well of wisdom, and seasoned ones will see the great lessons of their lives re-spun in beautiful, glowing prose." —*Booklist*

Kempton, Beth
The Way of the Fearless Writer: Mindful Wisdom for a Flourishing Writing Life. Beth Kempton. St. Martin's Essentials 2023. 257 pages
ISBN 9781250892133
Grades: Adult   808.02
1. Writing 2. Mindfulness 3. Mind and body 4. Philosophy, Buddhist 5. Language arts and studies — Writing skills 6. Self-Help — Personal growth — Creativity
LC Bl2023022866

Based on Buddhist thought, this book takes you on a sacred writing journey on which you'll learn how to free your mind so your body can create, transform your relationship to fear, write anytime, anywhere and share your words with confidence.

"Like Natalie Goldberg's 1986 classic, Writing Down the Bones, this book will inspire any writer who seeks a fresh way of working and living." —*Booklist*

Includes bibliographical references and index.

Kidder, Tracy
Good Prose: The Art of Nonfiction. Tracy Kidder and Richard Todd. Random House 2013. 224 p.
ISBN 9781400069750
Grades: Adult   808.02
1. Kidder, Tracy 2. Todd, Richard, 1949- 3. Writing 4. Nonfiction writing 5. Creative writing 6. Arts and Entertainment — Writing and Publishing

ESSENTIAL AND RECOMMENDED TITLES
808.06 Rhetoric of specific kinds of writing

LC 2012021165

The Pulitzer Prize and National Book Award-winning author and the editor of Atlantic Monthly share stories from their literary friendship and respective careers, offering insight into writing principles and mechanics that they have identified as elementary to quality prose.
Includes bibliographical references and index.

McCann, Colum
Letters to a Young Writer: Some Practical and Philosophical Advice. Colum McCann. Random House Inc 2017. 176 p.
ISBN 9780399590801
Grades: Adult   808.02
1. Creative writing 2. Writing 3. Authors 4. Books and reading 5. Literature 6. Essays 7. Arts and Entertainment — Writing and Publishing
LC 2016055256

A best-selling author and lecturer of creative writing at Hunter College in New York City presents a collection of essays featuring advice to writers just beginning to practice their craft.
"Pithy, wise, and gently encouraging advice from an acclaimed fiction writer." —*Kirkus*

Rubin, Daniel Joshua
27 Essential Principles of Story: Master the Secrets of Great Storytelling, from Shakespeare to South Park. Daniel Joshua Rubin. Workman Publishing Co. 2020. xi, 372 pages
ISBN 9781523507160
Grades: Adult   808.02
1. Storytelling 2. Arts and Entertainment — Writing and Publishing
LC 2020938343

A modern and actionable guide to the fundamentals of writing compelling, well-crafted, authentic stories in any medium, with lessons illustrated by novels, plays, films, music, video games, and TV, and writers from Shakespeare and Dostoevsky to Quentin Tarantino and Eminem.
"This is a no-brainer for both pro and would-be novelists." —*Publishers Weekly*

Scalzi, John
Don't Live for Your Obituary: Advice, Commentary, and Personal Observations on Writing. John Scalzi. Subterranean Press 2017. 469 pages
ISBN 9781596068582
Grades: Adult   808.02
1. Science fiction writing 2. Authors 3. Writing 4. Books and reading 5. Science fiction authors 6. Essays 7. Arts and Entertainment — Writing and publishing
LC 2017277896

A curated selection of that decade of advice, commentary and observations on the writing life, from one of the best-known science fiction authors working today. But more than that, it's a portrait of an era—ten years of drama, controversy and change in writing, speculative fiction and the world in general—from someone who was there when it happened— and who had opinions about it all.
"Above all [Scalzi] writes accessibly and so commonsensically that this book should appeal to writers in all disciplines, and even to SF readers who have no ambitions to write themselves." —*Publishers Weekly*

Sepetys, Ruta
★ *You: The Story: A Writer's Guide to Craft Through Memory.* Ruta Sepetys. Viking 2023. 217 pages
ISBN 9780593524381
Grades: Adult   808.02
1. Writing 2. Fiction writing 3. Memory 4. Language arts and studies — Writing skills 5. Arts and Entertainment — Writing and Publishing
LC 2022035024

A #1 New York Times best-selling author explains how life experiences help shape a writer.
"Part writing guide, part memoir, Sepetys' fresh, fun handbook is all inspiration." —*Booklist*

808.06 Rhetoric of specific kinds of writing

Febos, Melissa
★ *Body Work: The Radical Power of Personal Narrative.* Melissa Febos. Catapult 2022. 192 p.
ISBN 9781646220854
Grades: Adult   808.06
1. Febos, Melissa 2. Women authors, American 3. Writing 4. Autobiography 5. Storytelling 6. Freedom of expression 7. Psychic trauma 8. Healing 9. Advice 10. Essays 11. Life stories — Arts and culture — Writing — Authors 12. Arts and Entertainment — Writing and Publishing

In this mix of memoir and master class, Melissa Febos tackles the emotional, psychological, and physical work of writing intimately while offering an utterly fresh examination of the storyteller's life and the questions which run through it. How might we go about capturing on the page the relationships that have formed us? How do we write about our bodies, their desires and traumas? What does it mean for an author's way of writing, or living, to be dismissed as "navel-gazing"—or else hailed as "so brave, so raw"? And to whom, in the end, do our most intimate stories belong?
"Wide-ranging in its theoretical and historical breadth yet intimate in all ways, Febos's book offers the tools readers need to identify, access, process, and articulate hard-won stories of trauma and of love that their flesh holds." —*Library Journal*

Klein, Cheryl B.
The Magic Words: Writing Great Books for Children and Young Adults. Cheryl B. Klein. W. W. Norton & Company 2016. 368 p.
ISBN 9780393292244
Grades: Adult   808.06
1. Children's literature writing 2. Teenage literature writing 3. Reference books 4. Language arts — Writing and research
LC 2016014423

Guides writers through the major elements of fiction for middle grade and young adult readers and provides exercises, questions, and rules of thumb to help jump-start the creative process.
Includes bibliographical references and index.

Turabian, Kate L
Student's Guide to Writing College Papers. Kate L. Turabian; revised by Gregory G Colomb, Joseph M. Williams, Joseph Bizup, William T. Fitzgerald, and the University of Chicago Press editorial staff. University of Chicago Press 2019. xvii, 321 pages : Illustration
ISBN 9780226430263
Grades: Adult   808.06
1. Report writing 2. Language arts and studies — Writing skills 3. Reference — Writing
LC 2018060157

Friendly and authoritative, the fifth edition of Student's Guide to Writing College Papers combines decades of expert advice with new revisions based on feedback from students and teachers. Time-tested and teacher-approved, this book will prepare students to be better critical thinkers and help them develop a sense of inquiry that will serve them well beyond the classroom.

808.1 Rhetoric in specific literary forms

Deutsch, Babette
Poetry Handbook: A Dictionary of Terms. Babette Deutsch. Barnes & Noble Books 1981. xix, 203 p.
ISBN 9780064635486
Grades: 11 12 Adult   808.1
1. Literature 2. Poetry writing 3. Arts and Entertainment — Writing and Publishing
LC BL 99922903

Terms relating to poetry written in the English language are defined and illustrated by means of complete poems and verse excerpts.

Previously published: New York : Funk & Wagnalls, 1974.

Foster, Thomas C

How to Read Poetry Like a Professor: A Quippy and Sonorous Guide to Verse. Thomas C. Foster. Harper Perennial 2018. 212 p.

ISBN 9780062113788

Grades: Adult   808.1

1. Poetry writing 2. Literary criticism 3. Arts and Entertainment — Writing and Publishing — Literary criticism 4. Poetry

LC 2018295084

No literary form is as admired and feared as poetry. Admired for its lengthy pedigree—a line of poets extending back to a time before recorded history—and a ubiquitous presence in virtually all cultures, poetry is also revered for its great beauty and the powerful emotions it evokes. But the form has also instilled trepidation in its many admirers mainly because of a lack of familiarity and knowledge. Poetry demands more from readers—intellectually, emotionally, and spiritually—than other literary forms. Most of us started out loving poetry because it filled our beloved children's books from Dr. Seuss to Robert Louis Stevenson. Eventually, our reading shifted to prose, and later when we encountered poetry again, we had no recent experience to make it feel familiar. But reading poetry doesn't need to be so overwhelming. In an entertaining and engaging voice, Thomas C. Foster shows readers how to overcome their fear of poetry and learn to enjoy it once more.

Includes bibliographical references (pages 191-193) and index.

Hecht, Jennifer Michael

★ *The Wonder Paradox: Embracing the Weirdness of Existence and the Poetry of Our Lives.* Jennifer Michael Hecht. Farrar, Straus and Giroux 2023. 368 p.

ISBN 9780374292744

Grades: Adult   808.1

1. Art appreciation 2. Poetry and society 3. Poets 4. Literary criticism 5. Books and reading 6. Inspiration 7. Purpose in life 8. Sense of wonder 9. Spirituality 10. Arts and Entertainment — Writing and Publishing — Literary criticism 11. Spirituality and Religion — General

LC 2022049726

Religion once formed the rhythms and structures of society: marking time with calendars, carving out space for contemplation, creating connection, reinforcing legacy and morality. Now, for many, religion no longer runs the show. So where shall we find our magic? How do we celebrate milestones? Which texts can focus our attention but still offer space for inquiry, communion, and the chance to dwell for a dazzling instant in what can't be said? The answer, Jennifer Michael Hecht—the historian, poet, and bestselling author of Doubt—tells us, is poetry.

"Warmth and enthusiasm suffuse Hecht's enchanting prose, which make this book a moving, hopeful read." —*Library Journal*

Includes bibliographical references and index.

Higginson, William J.

The Haiku Handbook: How to Write, Teach, and Appreciate Haiku. William J. Higginson and Penny Harter; foreword by Jane Reichhold. Kodansha International 2013. xix, 331 p.

ISBN 9781568365404

Grades: Adult   808.1

1. Poetry writing 2. Poetry

LC 2009036628

In this groundbreaking and now-classic volume, the authors present haiku poets writing in English, Spanish, French, German, and five other languages on an equal footing with Japanese poets.

Includes bibliographical references and index; Originally published: New York : McGraw-Hill, c1985.

Hirsch, Edward

How to Read a Poem: And Fall in Love with Poetry. Edward Hirsch. Harcourt Brace & Co. 1999. xvi, 352 p.

ISBN 9780151004195

Grades: 11 12 Adult   808.1

1. Poetry writing 2. Literary criticism 3. Arts and Entertainment — Writing and Publishing

LC 98050065

ALA Notable Book, 2000; Booklist Editors' Choice, 1999.

An examination from an award-winning poet and critic of the reasons for and meanings of poetry offers an analysis of poems by Wordsworth, Plath, Neruda, and others to precisely delineate their unique power and their ineffable message.

"The author has gathered an eclectic group of poems from many times and places, with selections as varied as postwar Polish poetry, works by Keats and Christopher Smart, and lyrics from African American work songs. A prolific, award-winning poet in his own right, Hirsch suggests helpful strategies for understanding and appreciating each poem. The book is scholarly but very readable and incorporates interesting anecdotes from the lives of the poets." —*Library Journal*

Published by the Center for Documentary Studies in association with—; Includes bibliographical references (p. [323]-346) and index.

A Poet's Glossary. Edward Hirsch. Houghton Mifflin Harcourt 2014. VI, 730 pages

ISBN 9780151011957

Grades: Adult   808.1

1. Poetry writing 2. Arts and Entertainment — Writing and Publishing — Literary criticism 3. Reference — Dictionaries

LC 2014011675

The poet and author of How to Read a Poem (And Fall in Love with Poetry) explores the traditions of poets throughout time and around the world and provides definitions of the art form's devices, movements, "isms" and aesthetics.

"Offering definitions, a discussion of poetic techniques, and an unalloyed spiritual quality to his work, Hirsch's . alphabetically arranged glossary includes historical explanations, quotes, interpretative material, usage in various languages, and references to additional terms for even more clarification." —*Library Journal*

Includes index.

Leithauser, Brad

Rhyme's Rooms: The Architecture of Poetry. Brad Leithauser. Alfred A. Knopf 2022. 272 p.

ISBN 9780525655053

Grades: Adult   808.1

1. Poetry writing 2. Literary criticism 3. Language arts 4. Arts and Entertainment — Writing and publishing — Literary criticism 5. Arts and Entertainment — Writing and publishing

LC 2021025741

From the widely acclaimed poet, novelist, critic, and scholar, a lucid and edifying exploration of the building blocks of poetry and how they've been used over the centuries to assemble the most imperishable poems. We treasure our greatest poetry, Brad Leithauser reminds us in these pages, "not for its what but its how." in chapters on everything from iambic pentameter to how stanzas are put together to "rhyme and the way we really talk," Leithauser takes a deep dive into that how-the very architecture of poetry.

"A warm, well-considered celebration of a rich literary form." —*Kirkus*

This is a Borzoi book.

Oliver, Mary

A Poetry Handbook. Mary Oliver. Harcourt Brace & Co. 1994. VIII, 130 p.

ISBN 9780156724005

Grades: Adult   808.1

1. English language 2. American poetry 3. Poetry writing 4. Arts and Entertainment — Writing and Publishing — Literary criticism 5. Language arts and studies — Writing skills 6. Reference — Writing

LC 93049676

Offers advice on reading and writing poetry, and discusses imitation, sound, the line, poem forms, free verse, diction, imagery, revision, and workshops.

A Harvest original; Includes index.

ESSENTIAL AND RECOMMENDED TITLES
808.2 Rhetoric of drama

Orr, David
You, Too, Could Write a Poem: Selected Reviews and Essays, 2000-2015. David Orr. Penguin Books 2017. IX, 384 pages
ISBN 9780143128199
Grades: Adult   808.1
1. Poetry writing 2. Poetry 3. Arts and Entertainment — Writing and Publishing — Literary criticism 4. Language arts and studies — Writing skills
LC 2016040779

A collection of reviews and essays by David Orr, the New York Times poetry columnist and one of the most respected critics in America today, his best work of the past fifteen years in one place Poetry is never more vital, meaningful, or accessible than in the hands of David Orr. In the pieces collected here, most of them written originally for the New York Times, Orr is at his rigorous, conversational, and edifying best. Whether he is considering the careers of contemporary masters, such as Louise Gluck or Frederick Seidel, sizing up younger American poets, like Matthea Harvey and Matthew Zapruder, or even turning his attention to celebrities and public figures, namely Oprah Winfrey and Stephen Fry, when they choose to wade into the hotly contested waters of the poetry world, Orr is never any less than fully persuasive in arguing what makes a poem or poet great—or not.

The poetry columnist for the New York Times Book Review uses a collection of poems from contemporary masters and up-and-coming poets to provide examples of what he thinks makes a poem or a poet great or not.

Orr, Gregory
A Primer for Poets & Readers of Poetry. Gregory Orr. W. W. Norton & Company 2018. 325 pages
ISBN 9780393253924
Grades: Adult   808.1
1. Poetry writing 2. Language arts 3. Arts and Entertainment — Writing and Publishing — Literary criticism
LC 2017052637

An award-winning poet and beloved professor, using such poems as Theodore Roethke's "My Papa's Waltz" and Robert Hayden's "Those Winter Sundays," guides young poets toward a deeper understanding of how poetry can function in their lives, while also introducing the art in an exciting new way.
Includes bibliographical references (pages 321-325) and index.

Pinsky, Robert
Singing School: Learning to Write (and Read) Poetry by Studying with the Masters. Robert Pinsky. W. W. Norton & Company 2013. xv, 221 pages
ISBN 9780393050684
Grades: Adult   808.1
1. Poetry writing 2. Poetry — Collections
LC 2013022146

A former poet laureate provides informative introductions and sidebar notes for more than 80 poems by greats including William Butler Yeats, Emily Dickinson and George Herbert, in an effort to spark pleasure in reading and writing poems.

A former poet laureate provides introductions and sidebar notes for more than eighty poems by greats including William Butler Yeats, Emily Dickinson, and George Herbert, in an effort to spark pleasure in reading and writing poems.
Includes bibliographical references and index.

Sol, Adam
How a Poem Moves: A Field Guide for Readers Afraid of Poetry. Adam Sol. MisFit 2019. 200 p.
ISBN 9781770414563
Grades: Adult   808.1
1. Poetry writing 2. Literary criticism 3. Essays 4. Arts and Entertainment — Writing and Publishing 5. Arts and Entertainment — Writing and Publishing — Literary criticism
LC Bl2019005578

Developed from Adam Sol's popular blog, How a Poem Moves is a collection of 35 short essays that walks readers through an array of contemporary poems. Sol is a dynamic teacher, and in these essays, he has captured the humor and engaging intelligence for which he is known in the classroom. With a breezy style, Sol delivers essays that are perfect for a quick read or to be grouped together as a curriculum.

"His selections, largely derived from his time as a juror for the 2015 Griffin Poetry Prize, tend toward the relatively lesser-known, making this survey equally worthwhile for beginners who can learn from Sol's instruction and for more seasoned readers who will delight in the new discoveries contained within." —*Publishers Weekly*

Teicher, Craig Morgan
We Begin in Gladness: How Poets Progress : Essays. Craig Morgan Teicher. Graywolf Press 2018. 164 pages
ISBN 9781555978211
Grades: Adult   808.1
1. Essays 2. Arts and Entertainment — Writing and Publishing — Literary criticism 3. Language arts and studies — Writing skills
LC 2018934489

An acclaimed poet and critic, through luminous essays, considers how poets start out, how they learn to hear themselves and how they create lasting work, tracing the poetic development of the works of Sylvia Plath, John Ashbery and Louise Gluck, among others.

Tuama, Padraig O.
★ *Poetry Unbound: 50 Poems to Open Your World.* Pádraig Ó. Tuama. W W Norton & Company 2022. 304 p.
ISBN 9781324035473
Grades: Adult   808.1
1. Self-acceptance 2. History 3. Parenthood 4. Identity 5. Happiness 6. Resilience 7. Independence 8. Anthologies 9. Poetry

An immersive collection of poetry to open your world, curated by the host of Poetry Unbound. This inspiring collection, edited by Padraig O Tuama, presents fifty poems each with their own commentary and personal anecdotes alongside insights into the content of the poem. The poems gathered in this selection are from many walks of life, many experiences, many points of view. Engaging, accessible, diverse and inviting, Poetry Unbound is the perfect companion for everyone who wants to go deeper into poetry. Contains expanded reflections on poems as heard on the podcast, as well as exclusive new selections.

"The book is ideal for novices, while poetry devotees will surely find a handful (or two!) of new poets to relish." —*Booklist*

808.2 Rhetoric of drama

Vogler, Christopher
★ *The Writer's Journey: Mythic Structure for Writers.* Christopher Vogler; illustrated by Michele Montez. Michael Wiese Productions 2020. xxii, 492 pages : Illustration
ISBN 9781615933150
Grades: Adult   808.2
1. Screenplay writing 2. Narration (Rhetoric) 3. Mythology in literature 4. Creative writing 5. Writing 6. Arts and Entertainment — Movies and Television 7. Language arts and studies — Writing skills
LC 2019047080

Originally an influential memo Vogler wrote for Walt Disney Animation executives regarding the Lion King, the Writer's Journey details a twelve-stage, myth-inspired method that has galvanized Hollywood's treatment of cinematic storytelling. A format that once seldom deviated beyond a traditional three-act blueprint, Vogler's comprehensive theory of story structure and character development has met with universal acclaim, and is detailed herein using examples from myths, fairy tales, and classic movies.
Includes bibliographical references (page 471), filmography (pages 468-471) and index.

PUBLIC LIBRARY CORE COLLECTION: NONFICTION
Twentieth Edition

808.3 Rhetoric of fiction

Dufresne, John
Storyville!: An Illustrated Guide to Writing Fiction. John Dufresne; illustrated by Evan Wondolowski. W.W. Norton & Company 2020. x, 273 pages : Illustration
ISBN 9780393608403
Grades: Adult 808.3
1. Fiction writing 2. Creative writing 3. Writing 4. Language arts and studies — Writing skills 5. Reference — Writing
LC 2020000310

A smart and funny guide to writing fiction, with engaging infographics that bring storytelling techniques to life.

"An excellent addition for most library collections, laying out the basics for newbies and providing inspiration for seasoned writers." —*Booklist*

Koch, Stephen
The Modern Library Writer's Workshop: A Guide to the Craft of Fiction. Stephen Koch. Modern Library 2003. 246 p.
ISBN 9780375755583
Grades: Professional 808.3
1. Fiction writing 2. Reference — General
LC 2002032593

Compiling wisdom and advice from such masters of the craft as Henry James, E. M. Forster, Eudora Welty, and Toni Morrison, this readerly guide to fiction writing provides helpful observations and techniques for would-be fiction writers, covering such topics as cultivating one's creative imagination, the mechanics of plot and character development, and narrative thinking.

Includes bibliographical references (p. [215]-230) and index.

Mosley, Walter
Elements of Fiction. Walter Mosley. Grove Press 2019. xii, 115 pages
ISBN 9780802147639
Grades: Adult 808.3
1. Creative writing 2. Fiction writing 3. Language arts and studies — Writing skills 4. Reference — Writing
LC 2019033265

The award-winning author of the Easy Rawlins series presents a follow-up to This Year You Write Your Novel that offers conversational, instructive chapters demonstrating the essential elements of fiction, from character and plot development to context and description.

Percy, Benjamin
Thrill Me: Essays on Fiction. Benjamin Percy. Graywolf 2016. 160 p.
ISBN 9781555977597
Grades: Adult 808.3
1. Books and reading 2. Fiction writing 3. Writing 4. Books 5. Authors 6. Essays 7. Arts and Entertainment — Writing and Publishing
LC Bl2016044911

In his first nonfiction book, the best-selling author of The Dead Lands challenges the notion that literary and genre fiction are somehow mutually exclusive through 15 essays on the craft of fiction that look to disparate sources such as Jaws, Blood Meridian and The Girl with the Dragon Tattoo.

"Percys essays skillfully dissect the structure, mechanics, and concrete details of what makes good writing sparkle." —*Publishers Weekly*

Piercy, Marge
So You Want to Write: How to Master the Craft of Writing Fiction and Memoir. Marge Piercy and Ira Wood. Leapfrog Press; 2005. 324 p.
ISBN 9780972898454
Grades: Adult 808.3
1. Autobiography 2. Fiction writing 3. Reference books 4. Self-Help — General
LC Bl2006016096

Describes the elements that are necessary to write novels, short stories, and memoirs.
Includes index.

Salesses, Matthew
★ *Craft in the Real World: Rethinking Fiction Writing and Workshopping.* Matthew Salesses. Catapult 2021. 256 p.
ISBN 9781948226806
Grades: Adult 808.3
1. Writing 2. Creation (Literary, artistic, etc.) 3. White privilege 4. Fiction writing 5. Marginalized people 6. Creative writing 7. Writers conferences 8. Arts and Entertainment — Writing and Publishing

The traditional writing workshop was established with white male writers in mind; what we call craft is informed by their cultural values. In this bold and original examination of elements of writing—including plot, character, conflict, structure, and believability—and aspects of workshop—including the silenced writer and the imagined reader—Matthew Salesses asks questions to invigorate these familiar concepts. He upends Western notions of how a story must progress. How can we rethink craft, and the teaching of it, to better reach writers with diverse backgrounds? How can we invite diverse storytelling traditions into literary spaces?

"An insightful guide for readers, writers, and instructors from all walks of life." —*Kirkus*

Wood, James
How Fiction Works. James Wood. Farrar, Straus and Giroux 2008. 208 p.
ISBN 9780374173401
Grades: Adult 808.3
1. Books and reading 2. Literature 3. Literary criticism 4. English language 5. 20th century 6. Arts and Entertainment — Writing and Publishing
LC 2008010290

Library Journal Best Books, 2008; New York Times Notable Book, 2008.

What makes a story a story? What is style? What's the connection between realism and real life? These are some of the questions James Wood answers in How Fiction Works, the first book-length essay by the preeminent critic of his generation. Ranging widely—from Homer to David Foster Wallace, from What Maisie Knew to Make Way for Ducklings—Wood takes the reader through the basic elements of the art, step by step.

Includes bibliographical references and index.

808.5 Rhetoric of speech

Linklater, Kristin
Freeing the Natural Voice. Kristin Linklater; drawings by Douglas Florian. Drama Book Specialists 1976. 210 p. : Illustration
ISBN 9780896760714
Grades: Adult 808.5
1. Voice training 2. Arts and Entertainment — General
LC 75028172

Describes the mechanics of the voice and obstacles of spontaneous, effective vocal expression and details exercises for developing and strengthening the voice as a human and actor's instrument.

"Predicated on the basic assumptions that everyone has a voice capable of expressing a full range of emotions within a normal two- to four-octave scale and that daily stress compromises the voice's natural abilities and power {the author presents a simple and clear narrative, as well as a full set of exercises to cultivate and strengthen the voice." —*Library Journal*

Pinsky, Robert
The Sounds of Poetry: A Brief Guide. Robert Pinsky. Farrar, Straus and Giroux 1999. 129 p.
ISBN 9780374526177
Grades: 11 12 Adult 808.5
1. Oral interpretation of poetry 2. Arts and Entertainment — Writing and Publishing — Literary criticism

ESSENTIAL AND RECOMMENDED TITLES
808.53 Debating

LC BL 99009766

America's Poet Laureate offers a journey inside the world of poetry to explore the fundamental workings of this literary art, explaining how different sounds can be used to express meaning and images.

"By bringing his passion for the sound of language—so evident in his own poems—to his expert interpretations of the work of others, Pinsky cracks open the glass case that seems to separate poetry from everyday language, allowing the song of each poem to ring bright and clear." —*Booklist*

Includes bibliographical references (p. [119]-121) and index; Reprint. Originally published: C1998.

Rueckert, Veronica
Outspoken: Why Women's Voices Get Silenced and How to Set Them Free. Veronica Rueckert. HarperCollins 2019. 304 pages
ISBN 9780062879349
Grades: Adult   808.5
1. Communication 2. Interpersonal communication 3. Career development 4. Men-women communication 5. Society and culture — Gender — Women 6. Business and economics — Women and the workplace 7. History writing — Women's history

LC 2019016792

A Peabody Award-winning communications specialist and former host at Wisconsin Public Radio offers women practical tools, encouragement and advice for speaking with confidence and authority so that they will finally be heard.

"A practical and fascinating guide to liberating the female voice as a key to liberating the self." —*Kirkus*

Wellman, Victoria
Before You Say Anything: The Untold Stories and Failproof Strategies of a Very Discreet Speechwriter. Victoria Wellman. St. Martin's Press 2022. 288 p.
ISBN 9781250274021
Grades: Adult   808.5
1. Wellman, Victoria, (Speechwriter) 2. Speech writing 3. Speechwriters 4. Public speaking 5. Autobiographies and memoirs 6. Life stories — Arts and culture — Writing 7. Arts and Entertainment — Writing and publishing

LC 2021051087

Based on her own experiences and expertise, the founder and president of Manhattan-based speechwriting company The Oratory Laboratory shares her secrets for researching, crafting and delivering a professional-quality speech.

"The book is both a guide for aspiring orators and a poignant memoir about a writer with a gift for poignancy. Wellman's free spirit, penchant for romance, and enduring optimism appear in every lesson." —*Booklist*

808.53 Debating

Seo, Bo
Good Arguments: How Debate Teaches Us to Listen and Be Heard. Bo Seo. Penguin Press 2022. 342 pages
ISBN 9780593299517
Grades: Adult   808.53
1. Seo, Bo 2. Debates and debating 3. Scholars and academics 4. Argumentation 5. Persuasion (Psychology) 6. Interpersonal communication 7. Conflict resolution 8. Australian literature 9. Life stories — Education 10. Society and culture — Education

LC 2021058137

When Bo Seo was 8 years old, his family migrated from Korea to Australia. At the time, he did not speak English and struggled at school. But, then, something happened to change his life: He was introduced to debating. It turned out that debating was the perfect activity for someone shy. He went on to win world titles with the Australian schools and Harvard University teams. But debating isn't just about winning or losing: It's about information gathering, truth finding, lucidity, and persuasion. It's about being able to engage with views you disagree with, without the argument turning toxic.

"Delving into topics of communication, rhetoric, debate, and critical thinking, this illuminating book examines the fascinating world of competitive debate and offers much food for thought." —*Booklist*

Includes bibliographical references and index.

808.81 Collections in specific forms

Hirsch, Edward
Poet's Choice. Edward Hirsch. Harcourt 2006. xv, 432 p.
ISBN 9780151013562
Grades: Adult   808.81
1. Poetry and society 2. Literary criticism 3. Arts and Entertainment — Writing and Publishing — Literary criticism 4. Poetry — Collections

LC 2005026890

A collection of revised and expanded writings culled from the author's popular Washington Post Book World "Poet's Choice" column demonstrates how poetry responds to world challenges and introduces the work of more than 130 writers.

Includes bibliographical references and index.

808.88 Collections of miscellaneous writings

Bartlett, John
Bartlett's Familiar Quotations, 19th Ed.: A Collection of Passages, Phrases, and Proverbs Traced to Their Sources in Ancient and Modern Literature. John Bartlett; Geoffrey O'Brien, general editor. Little, Brown, and Co. 2022. LVII, 1446 p.
ISBN 9780316375306
Grades: 8 9 10 11 12 Adult   808.88
1. Quotations 2. Reference — Quotations

LC 2012019870

From ancient Egypt to today, enjoy a sweeping survey of world history through its most memorable words in this completely revised and updated nineteenth edition.

"Like the best reference collections, it has been thoughtfully weeded in order to keep it timely and relevant. An essential purchase for all reference collections." —*Booklist*

Includes indexes.

809 History, description, critical appraisal of more than two literatures

Bloom, Harold
The **Western** Canon: The Books and School of the Ages. Harold Bloom. Harcourt Brace 1994. VIII, 578 p.
ISBN 9780151957477
Grades: Adult   809
1. Books and reading 2. Literary criticism 3. Books 4. Arts and Entertainment — Writing and Publishing

LC 93043542

Booklist Editors' Choice, 1994.

A study of twenty-six canonical writers details the qualities that make them literary essentials, and includes Shakespeare, Chaucer, Milton, Beckett, Tolstoy, and Freud.

"The book succeeds not as a polemic but as a passionate, erudite and highly idiosyncratic series of essays about the literature dearest to one of America's most influential academics." —*Publishers Weekly*

Includes index.

Corbett, Emily
In Transition: Young Adult Literature and Transgender Representation. Emily Corbett. University Press of Mississippi 2024. 224 p.
ISBN 9781496852601

PUBLIC LIBRARY CORE COLLECTION: NONFICTION
Twentieth Edition

Grades: Adult Professional   **809**

1. Young adult literature 2. Books and reading 3. Authors 4. Transgender people 5. Transgender children 6. LGBTQIA+ people 7. Publishers and publishing 8. Social norms 9. Gender identity 10. Transphobia 11. Awareness 12. Characters and characteristics in literature 13. Arts and Entertainment — Writing and Publishing 14. Debut title 15. Society and culture — Gender

LC 2024002727

The first book-length work of its kind, In Transition examines the shift in the young adult book market towards increased representation of transgender characters and authors. Through a comprehensive exploration of historical conventions, genres, character diversity, and ideologies of trans representation, Emily Corbett traces the roots of trans literature from its beginnings in a cisgender-dominated publishing world to the recent rise in trans creators, characters, and implied readers. In Transition contributes new perspectives on the intersections of adolescence and trans-ness and sheds light on a dynamic subset of YA literature that has yet to receive sustained analysis.

"Corbett, editor of the International Journal of Young Adult Literature, debuts with an enlightening study of how depictions of trans characters in YA novels have changed since the early 2000s…This perceptive inquiry enthralls." —*Publishers Weekly*

Includes bibliographical references and index.

Crase, Douglas
On Autumn Lake: Collected Essays. Douglas Crase. Nightboat Books 2022. 344 p.

ISBN 9781643621432

Grades: Adult   **809**

1. Poetry writing 2. Literary criticism 3. Poets, American 4. Essays 5. Arts and Entertainment — Writing and Publishing — Literary criticism 6. Arts and Entertainment — Writing and Publishing

Douglas Crase's prose is rich with conviction and desire, inspiring as John Yau wrote, "the kind of attention usually reserved for poetry." His essays, written as rhythmically as poems, take a personal rather than abstract approach, offering committed and sometimes intimate portraits of John Ashbery, James Schuyler, Lorine Niedecker, and others. With generosity of spirit, Crase shares his devotion to poetry, democracy, and landscape in this handsome volume that greatly enlarges the available body of his work and will be seen as the essential complement to his collected poems.

"Astute observations on literature and art….Gracefully wrought essays imbued with a rare intimacy." —*Kirkus*

Damrosch, David
Around the World in 80 Books. David Damrosch. Penguin Press 2021. 384 p.

ISBN 9780593299883

Grades: Adult   **809**

1. Books and reading 2. Literary criticism 3. Authors 4. Poets 5. Fiction writing 6. Voyages and travels 7. Cross-cultural studies 8. Imagination 9. Arts and Entertainment — Writing and Publishing — Literary criticism

Following a literary itinerary from London to Venice, Tehran and points beyond, and via authors from Woolf and Dante to Nobel prizewinners Orhan Pamuk, Wole Soyinka, Mo Yan and Olga Tokarczuk, David Damrosch explores how these works have shaped our idea of the world, and the ways the world bleeds into literature. To chart the expansive landscape of world literature today, Damrosch explores how writers live in two very different worlds—the world of their personal experience, and the world of books that have enabled great writers to give shape and meaning to their lives. Around the World in 80 Books is a global invitation to look beyond ourselves and our surroundings, and to see our world and its literature in new ways.

"Damrosch's richly conceived survey offers readers a colorful map for an illuminating, enlivening tour of their own libraries. Travel fans and literature lovers alike will find something to savor." —*Publishers Weekly*

Danticat, Edwidge
The Art of Death: Writing the Final Story. Edwidge Danticat. Graywolf 2017. 160 p.

ISBN 9781555977771

Grades: Adult   **809**

1. Danticat, Edwidge, 1969- 2. Death 3. Coping 4. Grief 5. Loss 6. Death of mothers 7. Family and death 8. Authors 9. People with terminal illnesses 10. Women 11. Autobiographies and memoirs 12. Family and Relationships — Aging and Death 13. Life stories — Facing adversity — Coping with death 14. Arts and Entertainment — Writing and Publishing

LC 2016951195

Edwidge Danticat's The Art of Death: Writing the Final Story is at once a personal account of her mother dying from cancer and a deeply considered reckoning with the ways that other writers have approached death in their own work.

This slim volume wraps literary criticism, philosophy, and memoir into a gracefully circling whole, echoing the nature of grief as 'circles and circles of sorrow.' —*Publishers Weekly*

Ferrante, Elena
In the Margins: On the Pleasures of Reading and Writing. Elena Ferrante; translated by Ann Goldstein. Europa Editions 2022. 176 p.

ISBN 9781609457372

Grades: Adult   **809**

1. Ferrante, Elena 2. Literary criticism 3. Language and languages 4. Reading 5. Writing 6. Influence (Literary, artistic, etc.) 7. Women authors 8. Translations — Italian to English 9. Arts and Entertainment — Writing and publishing 10. Life stories — Arts and culture — Writing — Authors

In 2020, Claire Luchette in O, the Oprah Magazine described the beloved Italian novelist Elena Ferrante as "an oracle among authors." Here, in these four crisp essays, Ferrante offers a rare look at the origins of her literary powers. She writes about her influences, her struggles, and her formation as both a reader and a writer; she describes the perils of "bad language" and suggests ways in which it has long excluded women's truth; she proposes a choral fusion of feminine talent as she brilliantly discourses on the work of Emily Dickinson, Gertrude Stein, Ingeborg Bachmann, and many others.

"These brilliant essays not only provide insights into other great writers and their work but into Ferrante's own work as well, and will be appreciated by her many followers as well as scholars and general readers." —*Library Journal*

Ghosh, Amitav
The Great Derangement: Climate Change and the Unthinkable. Amitav Ghosh. The University of Chicago Press 2016. 176 p.

ISBN 9780226323039

Grades: Adult   **809**

1. Environmental protection 2. Climate change 3. Global warming 4. Skeptics 5. Denial (Psychology) 6. Environmental policy 7. Arts 8. Environmental degradation 9. Literary criticism 10. Effect of environment on humans 11. Public opinion 12. Politics and global affairs — Environmental issues and policies 13. Arts and Entertainment — Writing and Publishing 14. Nature Writing — Environmental Issues 15. Arts and Entertainment — Writing and Publishing — Literary criticism

LC 2016018232

Are we deranged? The acclaimed Indian novelist Amitav Ghosh argues that future generations may well think so. How else to explain our imaginative failure in the face of global warming? In his first major book of nonfiction since In an Antique Land, Ghosh examines our inability—at the level of literature, history, and politics—to grasp the scale and violence of climate change.

"A slim but certainly significant contribution to the climate crisis dialogue sure to provoke discussion and increased awareness about our imperiled planet." —*Kirkus*

James, Henry
Literary Criticism; Vol. 1. Henry James. Literary Classics of the United States 1984. 1484 p; (The Library of America)

ISBN 9780940450226

Grades: Adult   **809**

1. Literature 2. Literary criticism 3. 19th century 4. Arts and Entertainment — Writing and Publishing — Literary criticism

LC 84011241

ESSENTIAL AND RECOMMENDED TITLES
809 History, description, critical appraisal of more than two literatures

Gathers James essays about fiction, literary criticism, and the works of Alcott, Emerson, Hawthorne, Howells, Stowe, Arnold, Browning, Byron, Trollope, and Stevenson.

Includes bibliographies and indexes.

Kirsch, Adam
*The **Blessing** and the Curse: The Jewish People and Their Books in the Twentieth Century*. Adam Kirsch. W.W. Norton & Company 2020. xiv, 279 pages

ISBN 9780393652406

Grades: Adult   **809**

1. Judaism 2. 20th century 3. History writing — Jewish history 4. Spirituality and Religion — Judaism — History 5. History writing — United States

LC 2020013974

An erudite and accessible survey of Jewish life and culture in the twentieth century, as reflected in seminal texts. Following The People and the Books, which 'covers more than 2,500 years of highly variegated Jewish cultural expression' (Robert Alter, New York Times), formidable and perceptive literary critic Adam Kirsch now turns to the salient works of modern Jewish thought. From the vast emigration of Jews out of Eastern Europe to the Holocaust to the creation of Israel, the twentieth century transformed Jewish life. This was true, also, of writing: the novels, plays, poems, and memoirs of Jewish writers provided intimate access to new worlds of experience. Here Kirsch navigates four themes that shaped the twentieth century in Jewish literature and culture: Europe, America, Israel, and the endeavor to reconfigure Judaism as a modern faith. Reading writers ranging from Franz Kafka to Philip Roth, Anne Frank to Tony Kushner, Hannah Arendt to Judith Plaskow, Kirsch's scope is wide and his observations diverse. Insightful and engaging, The Blessing and the Curse brings the Jewish experience vividly to life."

"The focus throughout this illuminating and invaluable study is on secular modern Jewish writers from Central and Eastern Europe and their descendants. For all Jewish literature collections, and for informed general readers interested in modern Jewish secular literary culture." —*Library Journal*

Includes bibliographical references (pages 259-262) and index.

★ *The **People** and the Books: 18 Classics of Jewish Literature*. Adam Kirsch. W.W. Norton & Company 2016. 432 p.

ISBN 9780393241761

Grades: Adult   **809**

1. Judaism 2. Jewish people 3. Jewish way of life 4. Spirituality and religion — Judaism — History 5. History writing — Jewish history

LC 2016024818

New York Times Notable Book, 2016.

An anthology of Jewish literary classics stands as an essential exploration of a rich literary tradition spanning biblical through modern times and includes such entries as the books of Deuteronomy and Esther, the philosophy of Maimonides, the autobiography of Gluckel of Hameln and the Zionist manifestos of Theodor Herzl.

Includes bibliographical references and index.

Kundera, Milan
Encounter. Milan Kundera; translated from the French by Linda Asher. Harper 2010. 176 p.

ISBN 9780061894411

Grades: Adult   **809**

1. Modern literature 2. Music history and criticism 3. Painting 4. Humanism 5. Art 6. Aesthetics 7. Memory 8. Literary criticism 9. 20th century 10. Essays 11. Arts and Entertainment — General 12. Arts and Entertainment — Writing and Publishing — Literary criticism

LC 2010004908

New York Times Notable Book, 2010.

A collection of essays from the Franco-Czech novelist provides a defense for art during an era that he says no longer puts value on art or beauty and discusses works and artists that are important to him.

"Of specific interest are chapters comparing Francis Bacon to Samuel Beckett; Kundera's devilish mixing up of Roland Barthes with the dour theologian Karl Barth in a chance conversation; several discussions on the virtues of Rabelais as well as a restoration to prominence of Anatole France, who had been given the French intellectualist bum's rush; a powerful coupling of the bright birth of film with the sad death of Fellini; a scholar's relishing of Bertolt Brecht's body odor; the music of his fellow Czech Leos Janacek. Like the proverbial meal at the Chinese restaurant, the delicious musings of this book are filling at first. Two hours later, one craves more." —*Publishers Weekly*

Manglik, Gauri
★ *Muslims in Story: Expanding Multicultural Understanding Through Children's and Young Adult Literature*. Gauri Manglik and Sadaf Siddique. ALA Editions 2018. xvi, 248 pages : Illustration

ISBN 9780838917411

Grades: Professional   **809**

1. Islam 2. Muslims 3. Children 4. Books and reading 5. Children's literature writing 6. Literary criticism 7. Professional materials — Readers' advisory 8. Professional materials — Collection development

LC 2018023567

The authors, who are associated with a literary organization that spreads awareness about South Asian children's literature in the US, explain strategies for expanding multicultural understanding using children's and young adult literature featuring Muslims and Islam. They discuss the history of Muslims in America, understanding Islamophobia and its impact on children, and using literature to create long-term systemic change, then present book lists related to Muslim kids as heroes, inspiring Muslim leaders and thinkers, religious practices and traditions in Islam, and folk tales from Islamic traditions, with book descriptions, discussion questions, ideas for further engagement, and quotes for interpretation. They include author interviews throughout.

"This timely and essential purchase for public and school libraries humanizes Muslims and gives Muslim children authentic mirrors while creating important windows for non-Muslim readers." —*School Library Journal*

"Designed to build bridges, the book offers librarians and educators a rich list of relevant and engaging current titles on which to draw…No comparable bibliography exists, so this book is a required resource for those who study children's literature or serve children in libraries and classrooms." —*Choice*

Includes index; Includes bibliographical references.

Manguel, Alberto
*The **Dictionary** of Imaginary Places*. Alberto Manguel & Gianni Guadalupi; illustrated by Graham Greenfield; with additional illustrations by Eric Beddows; maps and charts by James Cook. Harcourt Brace 2000. xvi, 755 p. : Illustration; Map

ISBN 9780151005413

Grades: Adult   **809**

1. Geomythology 2. Imaginary places 3. Reference books — Literature 4. Arts and Entertainment — Writing and Publishing 5. Reference — Dictionaries

LC 99046994

"This resource contains entries for more than 1,200 imaginary places from literature and folklore. Each entry describes the place, its locale, and history and provides citations to the source work or tale. More than 220 maps and illustrations are included." —*Booklist*

Includes bibliographical references and index.

McKee, Robert
Dialogue: The Art of Verbal Action for Page, Stage, Screen. Robert McKee. Twelve 2016. xviii, 312 pages

ISBN 9781455591916

Grades: Adult   **809**

1. Playwriting 2. Screenplay writing 3. Fiction writing 4. Television 5. Arts and Entertainment — Movies and Television 6. Reference — Writing

LC 2016001679

In a much anticipated follow-up to the best-selling writers' guide Story, a leading authority on story creation and design analyzes how characters speak on the screen, on the stage and on the page, and applies a framework of incisive thinking to instruct the prospective writer on how to create artful, impactful speech.

Includes bibliographical references (page 297-299) and index.

PUBLIC LIBRARY CORE COLLECTION: NONFICTION
Twentieth Edition

Morrison, Toni
★ *The Origin of Others.* Toni Morrison; foreword by Ta-Nehisi Coates. Harvard University Press 2017. 116 pages
ISBN 9780674976450
Grades: Adult   **809**
1. Racism 2. Difference 3. Identity 4. Literary criticism 5. Racism in literature 6. Slavery 7. White privilege 8. United States history 9. 19th century 10. Essays 11. Society and culture — Race 12. Society and culture — Psychology and human behavior 13. Arts and Entertainment — Writing and Publishing — Literary criticism

LC Bl2017036607

What is race and why does it matter? Why does the presence of Others make us so afraid? America's foremost novelist reflects on themes that preoccupy her work and dominate politics: race, fear, borders, mass movement of peoples, desire for belonging. Ta-Nehisi Coates provides a foreword to Toni Morrison's most personal work of nonfiction to date.

"Nobel laureate Morrison, long known for her penetrating exploration of race in the U.S, continues that examination with essays derived from a lecture series at Harvard." —*Booklist*

Nafisi, Azar
Read Dangerously: The Subversive Power of Literature in Troubled Times. Azar Nafisi. Dey Street Books 2022. 256 p.
ISBN 9780062947369
Grades: Adult   **809**
1. Nafisi, Azar 2. Books and reading 3. Resistance (Psychology) 4. Politics and literature 5. Fathers and daughters 6. Political persecution 7. Intellectual freedom 8. Social justice 9. Literary criticism 10. Arts and Entertainment — Writing and Publishing — Literary criticism 11. Life stories — Arts and culture — Writing 12. Politics and global affairs — Civil and human rights

What is the role of literature in an era when one political party wages continual war on writers and the press? What is the connection between political strife in our daily lives, and the way we meet our enemies on the page in fiction? How can literature, through its free exchange, affect politics? In this galvanizing guide to literature as resistance, Nafisi seeks to answer these questions. Drawing on her experiences as a woman and voracious reader living in the Islamic Republic of Iran, her life as an immigrant in the United States, and her role as literature professor in both countries, she crafts an argument for why, in a genuine democracy, we must engage with the enemy, and how literature can be a vehicle for doing so.

"This excellent collection provokes and inspires at every turn." —*Publishers Weekly*

Poe, Edgar Allan
Essays and Reviews. Edgar Allan Poe. Literary Classics of the U.S. 1984. 1544 p. : Illustration (The Library of America)
ISBN 9780940450196
Grades: Adult   **809**
1. Literature 2. Books 3. Arts and Entertainment — Writing and Publishing

LC 83019923

Gathers Poe's essays on the theory of poetry, the art of fiction, the role of the critic, leading nineteenth-century writers, and the New York literary world.

G.R. Thompson wrote the notes and selected the texts for this volume—Prelim. p; Includes bibliographical references and index.

Puchner, Martin
The Written World: The Power of Stories to Shape People, History, Civilization. Martin Puchner. Random House 2017. 416 p.
ISBN 9780812998931
Grades: Adult   **809**
1. Literature and society 2. Literary criticism 3. Books and reading 4. Literature and history 5. History of civilization 6. Arts and Entertainment — Writing and Publishing 7. History writing — Microhistory 8. Arts and Entertainment — Writing and Publishing — Literary criticism

LC 2017002438

Massachusetts Book Awards, Nonfiction Award, 2018.

The story of literature in sixteen acts, from Alexander the Great and the Iliad to ebooks and Harry Potter, this engaging book brings together remarkable people and surprising events to show how writing shaped cultures, religions, and the history of the world.

"By providing snapshots of key moments in the written words evolution, Puchner creates a gripping intellectual odyssey." —*Publishers Weekly*
Includes index.

Roiphe, Katie
The Violet Hour: Great Writers at the End. Katie Roiphe. The Dial Press 2016. 320 p.
ISBN 9780385343596
Grades: Adult   **809**
1. Death of authors 2. Death of artists 3. Death 4. Writing 5. Authors 6. Artists 7. Psychology 8. Family and Relationships — Aging and Death 9. Arts and Entertainment — Writing and Publishing — Literary criticism

LC 2015014085

Examining the final days of five great writers and artist—Susan Sontag, Sigmund Freud, John Updike, Dylan Thomas and Maurice Sendak—a thought-provoking volume helps readers look boldly at death and be less afraid, in a wholly original meditation on mortality.

Tatar, Maria
The Heroine with 1001 Faces. Maria Tatar. Liveright Publishing 2021. 304 p.
ISBN 9781631498817
Grades: Adult   **809**
1. Heroes and heroines 2. Feminism 3. Femininity 4. Archetype (Psychology) 5. Women in literature 6. Women in popular culture 7. Characters and characteristics in literature 8. Characters and characteristics in mythology 9. Society and culture — Gender — Women 10. Society and culture — Pop culture 11. Arts and Entertainment — Writing and Publishing

World-renowned folklorist Maria Tatar reveals an astonishing but long buried history of heroines, taking us from Cassandra and Scheherazade to Nancy Drew and Wonder Woman.

"A necessary and compelling read for scholars, activists, and storytellers interested in inclusive revisions to the hero's canon." —*Library Journal*

Wilde, Oscar
The Artist as Critic: Critical Writings of Oscar Wilde. Edited by Richard Ellmann. University of Chicago Press 1982. xxviii, 446 p.
ISBN 9780226897646
Grades: Adult   **809**
1. Criticism 2. Books 3. Arts and Entertainment — Writing and Publishing — Literary criticism

LC 82013361

Presents a collection of Oscar Wilde's book reviews.
Reprint. Originally published: New York : Random House, [1969]; Includes index.

809.1 Poetry — History and criticsm

Carey, John
A Little History of Poetry. John Carey. Yale University Press 2020. 288 p.
ISBN 9780300232226
Grades: Adult   **809.1**
1. Poetry

Presents a guide to poetry, from ancient times to the present, by one of our greatest champions of literature.

"In this clever, wide-ranging history, British literary critic Carey (The Essential Paradise Lost) provides a tour of Western poetry, from Homer to Maya Angelou. Those looking for a shrewdly condensed and accessible history of poetry could not ask for a better guide." —*Publishers Weekly*

ESSENTIAL AND RECOMMENDED TITLES
809.3 Fiction — History and criticism

Sato, Hiroaki
On Haiku. Hiroaki Sato. New Directions Publishing Corporation 2018. 320 p.
ISBN 9780811227414
Grades: Professional   **809.1**
1. Japanese poetry 2. American poetry 3. Poetry writing 4. Essays 5. History writing — Arts and culture 6. Arts and Entertainment — Writing and Publishing
LC 2018021511

A collection of essays, some previously published, some given as speeches by the first president of the American Haiku Society, and including many haiku translated from the Japanese.

"An expert illumination of a poetic form, to read and reread." —*Booklist*

I would like to thank Jeffrey Yang for patiently, meticulously, editing these essays — Preface.

809.3 Fiction — History and criticism

Nevala-Lee, Alec
Astounding: John W. Campbell, Isaac Asimov, Robert A. Heinlein, L. Ron Hubbard, and the Golden Age of Science Fiction. Alec Nevala-Lee. Dey Street Books 2018. 320 p.
ISBN 9780062571946
Grades: Adult   **809.3**
1. Campbell, John Wood, 1910-1971 2. Asimov, Isaac, 1920-1992 3. Heinlein, Robert A. (Robert Anson), 1907-1988 4. Hubbard, L. Ron (La Fayette Ron), 1911-1986 5. Science fiction writing 6. Authors, American 7. Literary criticism 8. 20th century 9. Biographies 10. Science fiction 11. Arts and Entertainment — Writing and Publishing 12. History writing — Arts and culture 13. Arts and Entertainment — Writing and Publishing — Literary criticism
LC 2018275384

A comprehensive account of the creative partnership shared among literary visionaries Campbell, Heinlein, Asimov and Hubbard discusses how they invented modern science fiction and indelibly transformed world culture.

"The golden age of science fiction, spanning the years 1939 to 1950, gets an authoritative examination in this fascinating appraisal of its key players. The primary focus is John W. Campbell, editor of Astounding Science Fiction magazine, and the three very different writers who served him best: Isaac Asimov, Robert A. Heinlein, and L. Ron Hubbard." —*Publishers Weekly*

809.7 Humor — Criticism

Dauber, Jeremy Asher
Jewish Comedy: A Serious History. Jeremy Dauber. W W Norton & Company 2017. xviii, 364 p.
ISBN 9780393247879
Grades: Adult   **809.7**
1. Jewish people 2. Jokes 3. Comedy writing 4. History writing — Jewish history 5. History writing — Arts and culture
LC 2017017864

An account of Jewish humor describes its nature, its development, and its vital role in the history of the Jewish people.

"Dauber takes in a wide swath of intellectual territory—from Kafka to Mad magazine—but he delicately mixes scholarship with comedy in what is an entertaining and even profound book." —*Booklist*

Jennings, Ken
Planet Funny: How Comedy Took Over Our Culture. Ken Jennings. Simon & Schuster 2018. 336 pages
ISBN 9781501100581
Grades: Adult   **809.7**
1. Comedians 2. Jokes 3. Laughter 4. Social history 5. Human behavior 6. Literary criticism 7. Society and culture — Pop culture 8. Humor writing — General 9. History writing — Arts and culture 10. Arts and Entertainment — Comedy

LC BI2018063558

From the witty and exuberant New York Times best-selling author comes a history of humor—from fart jokes on clay Sumerian tablets all the way up to the latest Twitter memes—that tells the story of how comedy came to rule the modern world.

810 American literature in English

Cohen, Leonard
The Flame: Poems and Selections from Notebooks. Leonard Cohen; edited by Robert Faggen and Alexandra Pleshoyano. Farrar Straus & Giroux 2018. 275 p. : Illustration
ISBN 9780374156060
Grades: Adult   **810**
1. Singers 2. Songwriters 3. Life 4. Canadian poetry 5. Poetry

An eloquent valedictory collection of lyrics, poems, notebook sketches and self-portraits maps the Rock and Roll Hall of Fame inductee's singular creative journey through the weeks just prior to his death.

"Poignant and brave, lit up with flashes of anger, this is a luminous collection and classic Cohen." —*Booklist*

Poems; Originally published by Penguin Random House Canada, 2018.

Eliot, T. S.
★ *Complete Poems and Plays.: 1909-1950.* T. S. Eliot. Harcourt, Brace 1952. VII, 392 p.
ISBN 9780151211852
Grades: 11 12 Adult   **810**
1. American poetry 2. 20th century 3. Poetry
LC 52011346

This omnibus collection includes all of the author's early poetry as well as The Four Quartets, Old Possum's Book of Practical Cats, and the plays Murder in the Cathedral, The Family Reunion, and The Cocktail Party.

Poe, Edgar Allan
Complete Poems. Edgar Allan Poe; edited by Thomas Ollive Mabbott. University of Ill. Press 2000. xxx, 627 p. : Illustration
ISBN 9780252069215
Grades: 11 12 Adult   **810**
1. Poetry 2. Arts and Entertainment — Writing and Publishing — Literary criticism
LC 00038639

101 poems by Edgar Allan Poe, as well as uncollected poems, fragments, and other content attributed to him. Illustrated and containing context and biographical background.

"Massive and important." —*American Literature*

Includes bibliographical references (583-594) and indexes; Originally published as v. 1 of: Collected works of Edgar Allan Poe. Cambridge, Mass. : Belknap Press of Harvard University Press, 1978.

810.9 American literature (English) — History and criticism

Bader, Philip
African-American Writers. Philip Bader; revised by Catherine Reef. Facts on File 2011. xii, 340 p. : Illustration
ISBN 9780816081417
Grades: Adult   **810.9**
1. African Americans 2. African American authors 3. African Americans in literature 4. Authors, American 5. Intellectual life 6. Literary criticism 7. American literature 8. Society and culture — Ethnic studies 9. History writing — United States
LC 2010005463

"Otherwise, African-American Writers does a good job in serving as a general resource and is recommended for high-school, public, and undergraduate libraries." —Booklist

Includes bibliographical references and index.

Gilbert, Sandra M.
★ *Still* Mad: American Women Writers and the Feminist Imagination. Sandra M. Gilbert and Susan Gubar. W.W. Norton & Company 2021. 368 p.
ISBN 9780393651713
Grades: Adult   810.9

1. Women authors, American 2. Feminist criticism 3. Feminism 4. Women and politics 5. Women's Movement 6. Women in mass media 7. Intersectionality 8. Women and literature 9. Literary criticism 10. American literature 11. United States 12. 21st century 13. 20th century 14. Society and culture — Gender — Women 15. Arts and Entertainment — Writing and Publishing — Literary criticism 16. History writing — Women's history

LC 2021012937

From its stirrings in the midcentury to a resurgence in the new millennium, Gilbert and Gubar trace the evolution of feminist literature. They offer lucid, compassionate, and piercing readings of major works by writers including Adrienne Rich, Ursula K. Le Guin, Maxine Hong Kingston, Susan Sontag, Gloria Anzaldua, and Toni Morrison. Activists and theorists like Nina Simone, Gloria Steinem, Andrea Dworkin, Eve Kosofsky Sedgwick, and Judith Butler also populate these pages as Gilbert and Gubar examine the overlapping terrain of literature and politics in a comprehensive portrait of an expanding movement.

"Highly recommended for anyone interested in American literature or women's studies." —Library Journal

Includes bibliographical references and index.

Ginsberg, Allen
Best Minds of My Generation: A Literary History of the Beats. Allen Ginsberg; edited by Bill Morgan; introduction by Anne Waldman. Grove Press 2017. 496 p.
ISBN 9780802126498
Grades: Adult   810.9

1. Beat generation 2. Beat poets 3. Literary movements 4. Poets, American 5. Authors, American 6. Arts and Entertainment — Writing and Publishing 7. Arts and Entertainment — Writing and Publishing — Literary criticism

LC 2017003026

A unique and compelling history of the Beats, in the words of the movement's most central member, Allen Ginsberg, based on a seminal series of his lectures.

Griffin, Farah Jasmine
Read Until You Understand: The Profound Wisdom of Black Life and Literature. Farah Jasmine Griffin. W.W. Norton & Company 2021. 240 p.
ISBN 9780393651904
Grades: Adult   810.9

1. Griffin, Farah Jasmine 2. African American college teachers 3. African American art 4. African American artists 5. Intellectual life 6. African Americans 7. Democracy 8. Social justice 9. African American authors 10. Literary criticism 11. American literature 12. Race relations 13. United States history 14. United States 15. Life stories — Identity — Race and ethnicity 16. Life stories — Arts and culture 17. History writing — African American — United States 18. Arts and Entertainment — General 19. Antiracist literature

LC 2021011719

Finalist for the Hurston/Wright Legacy Awards for Nonfiction, 2022.

Farah Jasmine Griffin has taken to her heart the phrase "read until you understand," a line her father, who died when she was nine, wrote in a note to her. She has made it central to this book about love of the majestic power of words and love of the magnificence of Black life. Here, she shares a lifetime of discoveries: the ideas that inspired the stunning oratory of Frederick Douglass and Malcolm X, the soulful music of Marvin Gaye and Stevie Wonder, the daring literature of Phillis Wheatley and Toni Morrison, the inventive artistry of Romare Bearden, and many more. Griffin entwines memoir, history, and art while she keeps her finger on the pulse of the present, asking us to grapple with the continuing struggle for Black freedom and the ongoing project that is American democracy.

"Part-memoir, part-literary study, this book has something for everyone. Griffin (English, comparative literature, and African American studies, Columbia Univ; Harlem Nocturne: Women Artists and Progressive Politics During World War II) tells her own history, intertwined with analyses of Toni Morrison's novels, Barack Obama's autobiography, and other Black literature." —Library Journal

Includes bibliographical references and index.

Hart, James David
The Oxford Companion to American Literature. James D. Hart; with revisions and additions by Phillip W. Leininger. Oxford University Press 1995. IX, 779 p.
ISBN 9780195065480
Grades: 11 12 Adult   810.9

1. Authors, American 2. Literary criticism 3. American literature 4. Arts and Entertainment — Writing and Publishing — Literary criticism 5. Reference books — Literature 6. Reference — Biographical dictionaries

LC 94045727

A completely revised edition of a standard reference work covers the movements, authors, genres, critics, awards, and many other aspects of American literature, and includes nearly two hundred new entries, many covering female and ethnic writers.

Covers the movements, authors, genres, critics, awards, and many other aspects of American literature.

Includes index.

Morrison, Toni
Playing in the Dark: Whiteness and the Literary Imagination. Toni Morrison. Harvard University Press 1992. xiii, 91 p.
ISBN 9780674673779
Grades: Adult   810.9

1. Race relations 2. African Americans in literature 3. Human skin color 4. Race (Social sciences) 5. European Americans 6. Essays 7. Arts and Entertainment — Writing and Publishing 8. History writing — African American — United States

LC 91039671

Examines the effect of a racially divided society on ninteenth century American writings, and discusses works by Poe, Hawthorne, Melville, and Twain.

"Novelist Morrison takes a turn as a literary critic, examining the American literary imagination and finding it obsessed with the white/Black polarity." —Publishers Weekly

Includes bibliographical references.

Showalter, Elaine
★ A *Jury* of Her Peers: American Women Writers from Anne Bradstreet to Annie Proulx. by Elaine Showalter. Alfred A. Knopf 2009. 608 p.
ISBN 9781400041237
Grades: 11 12 Adult   810.9

1. Women authors, American 2. Intellectual life 3. Women in literature 4. Women and literature 5. Women 6. Literary criticism 7. American literature 8. United States 9. Biographies 10. Arts and Entertainment — Writing and Publishing 11. Adult books for young adults 12. Arts and Entertainment — Writing and Publishing — Literary criticism

LC 2008042312

A comprehensive history of American women writers explores the contributions of more than 250 female authors—both famous and little-known—to every field of literary endeavor and reflects on their role in the evolution of our American literary heritage.

Includes bibliographical references and index.

---

811 American poetry

Abdurraqib, Hanif
A *Fortune* for Your Disaster. Hanif Abdurraqib. Tin House Books 2019. 120 p.

ESSENTIAL AND RECOMMENDED TITLES
811 American poetry

ISBN 9781947793439
Grades: Adult   811
1. Violence 2. Racism 3. African Americans 4. Interpersonal relations 5. Friendship 6. Poetry
    LC 2019013318

In this follow-up to The Crown Ain't Worth Much, a poet, essayist, biographer and music critic presents a poetry collection about how one rebuilds oneself after heartbreak.

"This resonant second collection from cultural critic, essayist, and poet Abdurraqib grapples with physical and emotional acts of violence and their political context." —*Booklist*

Akbar, Kaveh

Calling a Wolf a Wolf: Poems. Kaveh Akbar. Alice James Books 2017. 89 p.
ISBN 9781938584671
Grades: Adult   811
1. Alcoholism 2. Alcoholics 3. American poetry 4. Rehabilitation 5. Poetry
    LC 2017015979

Poems confront craving, control, the constant battle of alcoholism and sobriety, and the questioning of the self and its instincts within the context of this never-ending fight.

Includes bibliographical references.

Pilgrim Bell: Poems. Kaveh Akbar. Graywolf Press 2021. 80 p.
ISBN 9781644450598
Grades: Adult   811
1. Language and languages 2. Families 3. Faith 4. Addiction 5. Identity 6. Power 7. Poetry

With formal virtuosity and ruthless precision, Kaveh Akbar's second collection takes its readers on a spiritual journey of disavowal, fiercely attendant to the presence of divinity where artifacts of self and belonging have been shed. How does one recover from addiction without destroying the self-as-addict? And if living justly in a nation that would see them erased is, too, a kind of self-destruction, what does one do with the body's question, "what now shall I repair?"

"Recently appointed poetry editor at The Nation, Iranian American poet/scholar Akbar follows up his corrosively beautiful debut, Calling a Wolf a Wolf, with Pilgrim Bell, a courageous spiritual journey that captures the addict's ongoing struggle and the challenges of being Muslim in an Islamophobic nation." —*Library Journal*

Alexander, Elizabeth

Crave Radiance: New and Selected Poems, 1990-2010. Elizabeth Alexander. Graywolf Press 2010. 255 p.
ISBN 9781555975685
Grades: Adult   811
1. American poetry 2. Women authors 3. African American poetry 4. Poetry 5. Poetry — African American authors
    LC Bl2010033551

Features a collection of previously published poetry from the author along with some new material, including "Praise Song for the Day," which the author read during President Obama's inauguration.

Alexander, Will

Refractive Africa: Ballet of the Forgotten. Will Alexander. New Directions Publishing 2021. xi, 106 pages
ISBN 9780811230278
Grades: Adult   811
1. African diaspora 2. Colonialism 3. African American poetry 4. Poetry
    LC 2021031345

"The poet is endemic with life itself," Will Alexander once said, and in this searing pas de trois, Refractive Africa: Ballet of the Forgotten, he has exemplified this vital candescence with a transpersonal amplification worthy of the Cambrian explosion. "This being the ballet of the forgotten," he writes as diasporic witness, "of refracted boundary points as venom." The volume's opening poem pays homage to the innovative Nigerian-Yoruban author Amos Tutuola; it ends with an encomium to the modernist Malagasy poet Jean-Joseph Rabearivelo—two writers whose luminous art suffered "colonial wrath through refraction." A tribute to the Congo forms the bridge and brisé vole of the book: the Congo as "charged aural colony" and "primal interconnection," a "subliminal psychic force" with a colonial and postcolonial history dominated by the Occident. Will Alexander's improvisatory cosmicity pushes poetic language to the point of most resistance—incantatory and swirling with magical laterality and recovery."

"Densely lyrical, Alexander's expansive poetry captures the psychic toll of colonial barbarity while suggesting the possibility of spiritual renewal and transcendence." —*Publishers Weekly*

A New Directions Paperbook Original; NDP1515—Spine.

Alvarez, Julia

The Woman I Kept to Myself: Poems. by Julia Alvarez. Algonquin Books of Chapel Hill 2004. 155 p.
ISBN 9781565124066
Grades: 11 12 Adult   811
1. Dominican American women 2. Sisters 3. Women 4. Adult books for young adults 5. Poetry
    LC 2003070807

School Library Journal Best Books: Best Adult Books 4 Teens, 2004.

Offers a collection of autobiographical poems, each comprising three ten-line stanzas.

"This collection of 75 poems is divided into three sections, and each poem has three stanzas, exactly . . . The poet, who is from the Dominican Republic, writes about being raised with her sisters in New York. The subjects are personal—love, marriage, rejection, divorce, death, religion—but also universal." —*School Library Journal*

Alyan, Hala

The Moon That Turns You Back. Hala Alyan. HarperCollins Publishers 2024. 96 pages
ISBN 9780063317475
Grades: Adult   811
1. Loss 2. Memory 3. Families 4. Refugees 5. Home (Concept) 6. Family and war 7. Southwest Asian (Middle Eastern) people 8. Southwest Asia and North Africa (Middle East) 9. Poetry
    LC 2023934550

From the author of The Arsonists' City and The Twenty-Ninth Year, a new collection of poetry that traces the fragmentation of memory, archive, and family-past, present, future-in the face of displacement and war.

"The formally inventive and devastatingly evocative latest from Alyan (The Twenty-Ninth Year) reckons with grief, displacement, and enduring kinship." —*Publishers Weekly*

Angelou, Maya

The Complete Poetry. Maya Angelou. Random House 2015. xvii, 308 pages
ISBN 9780812997873
Grades: Adult   811
1. American poetry 2. African American poetry 3. Poetry
    LC 2014043508

An updated collection of the inspirational late writer's complete body of poetry includes her reflections on African-American life in Just Give Me a Cool Drink of Water 'Fore I Diiie and her tribute to Nelson Mandela, His Day Is Done.

Armantrout, Rae

Versed. Rae Armantrout. Wesleyan University Press 2009. IX, 121 p.
ISBN 9780819568793
Grades: Adult   811
1. American poetry 2. Women authors 3. Poetry
    LC 2008043809

Provides an expanded view of the arc of the author's writing, collecting poems dealing with the perversity of human consciousness and the confrontation of the invisible experienced during the author's bout with cancer.

Wobble. Rae Armantrout. Wesleyan University Press 2018. 128 p.
ISBN 9780819578235
Grades: Adult   811

PUBLIC LIBRARY CORE COLLECTION: NONFICTION
Twentieth Edition

1. Language and languages 2. Communication 3. Consciousness 4. Technology 5. Poetry

LC 2018002974

Library Journal Best Books, 2018.

A collection of poems explores the human failings, both personal and societal, that have led to Earth's devastation.

"This volume is marked by wry humor and striking self-awareness when considering writerly craft." —*Publishers Weekly*

Asghar, Fatimah

If They Come for Us: Poems. Fatimah Asghar. One World 2018. x, 106 p.
ISBN 9780525509783

Grades: Adult — 811

1. American poetry 2. Intergenerational trauma 3. 21st century 4. Poetry

LC 2019296383

ALA Notable Book, 2019.

In a debut poetry collection, the co-creator of the Emmy-nominated web series Brown Girls openly shares her experiences of being a young Pakistani Muslim woman in America by weaving together personal and marginalized people's histories.

Ashbery, John

Commotion of the Birds: New Poems. John Ashbery. Ecco 2016. 100 pages
ISBN 9780062565099

Grades: Adult — 811

1. American poetry 2. Poetry

LC 2017275703

A crackling, moving new collection from one of America's greatest living poets. In over twenty-six original books, the poems of John Ashbery have long served as signposts guiding us through the delights, woes, hypocrisies, and uncertainties of living in the modern world. With language harvested from everyday speech, fragments of pop culture, objects and figures borrowed from art and literature, his work makes light out of darkness, playing with tone and style to show how even the seemingly frivolous stuff of existence can be employed to express the deepest levels of feeling. Commotion of the Birds showcases once again Ashbery's mastery of a staggering range of voices and his singular lyric agility: wry, frank, contemplative, resigned, bemused, and ecstatic. The poet in this new collection is at once removed from and immersed in the terrain of his examination. Disarmingly conversational, he invites the reader to join him in looking out onto the future with humor, curiosity, and insight. The lines of these poems achieve a low-humming, thrilling point of vibration, a jostling of feathers before flight.

John Ashbery: Collected Poems, 1956-1987. John Ashbery. Library of America 2008. xx, 1042 p. : Illustration
ISBN 9781598530285

Grades: Adult — 811

1. American poetry 2. 20th century 3. Poetry

LC Bl2008033577

A definitive volume of works by the preeminent American poet includes Some Trees, as well as the complete texts of such collections as Rivers and Mountains, Self-Portrait in a Convex Mirror, and Houseboat Days.
Includes index.

Notes from the Air: Selected Later Poems. John Ashbery. Ecco 2007. xv, 364 p.
ISBN 9780061367175

Grades: Adult — 811

1. American poetry 2. Poetry

LC 2008270813

A selection of key works from ten major collections by the influential American poet as written throughout the past two decades includes pieces from the critically acclaimed "April Galleons" and "Flow Chart," as well as the 2005 National Book Award finalist "Where Shall I Wander."
Includes indexes.

Selected Poems. John Ashbery. Penguin Books 1986. 349 p.
ISBN 9780140585537

Grades: Adult — 811

1. American poetry 2. 20th century 3. Poetry

LC 86009521

A collection of works by the Pulitzer Prize-winning poet that includes "Some Trees," "The Tennis Court Oath," "The Double Dream of Spring," "Self Portrait in a Convex Mirror," and "A Wave."
Elisabeth Sifton books; Includes index.

Atwood, Margaret

Dearly: New Poems. Margaret Eleanor Atwood. McClelland & Stewart 2020. 136 p.
ISBN 9780063032491

Grades: Adult — 811

1. Nature 2. Reality 3. Memories 4. Everyday life 5. Pollution 6. Loss 7. Canadian poetry 8. Poetry

Loan Stars Favourites, 2020.

The internationally acclaimed, award-winning and bestselling author presents her first collection of poetry in over a decade that addresses themes such as love, loss, the passage of time, nature—and zombies.

"Atwood (The Testaments) returns with a sardonic and sagacious masterpiece to add to her significant oeuvre.... Combining dignified vulnerability, lyrical whimsy, and staunch realism, Atwood offers a memorable collection that emboldens readers to welcome disillusionment." —*Publishers Weekly*

Auden, W. H.

Collected Poems. W.H. Auden; edited by Edward Mendelson. Modern Library 2007. xxxi, 928 p.
ISBN 9780679643500

Grades: 11 12 Adult — 811

1. British poetry 2. 20th century 3. Poetry

LC 2006047163

In honor of the centennial of the poet's birth, a definitive anthology of works collects all of the poems Auden wished to preserve, in the versions he approved as final, providing the full range of the great poet's work between 1930 and 1974.
Includes indexes.

Baca, Jimmy Santiago

Selected Poems: = Poemas Selectos. Jimmy Santiago Baca. New Directions 2009. 285 p.
ISBN 9780811218160

Grades: Adult — 811

1. American poetry 2. Bilingual materials — English/Spanish 3. Translations — Spanish to English 4. Poetry

LC 2009015089

The best of the award-winning Chicano poet is available for the first time in a completely bilingual edition, in a book with poems that draw on the author's experiences as a father and a prisoner and on the lush, and sometimes stark, landscape of the Rio Grande valley.
Translated from the English, Spanish.

Baer, Kate

What Kind of Woman: Poems. Kate Baer. Harper Perennial 2020. 93 p.
ISBN 9780063087330

Grades: Adult — 811

1. Women 2. Femininity 3. Motherhood 4. Marriage 5. Sexuality 6. Gender role 7. Vulnerability 8. Power 9. Self-acceptance 10. Identity 11. Poetry 12. Book club best bets

Through poems that are as unforgettably beautiful as they are accessible, Kate Baer proves herself to truly be an exemplary voice in modern poetry. Her words make women feel seen in their own bodies, in their own marriages, and in their own lives. Her poems are those you share with your mother, your daughter, your sister, and your friends.

"Baer debuts with a meditative exploration of her identity as a woman, wife, and mother, disrupting mainstream assumptions about femininity.... In these confident and fearless poems, Baer suggests that the deepest and most vulnerable love is found in life's imperfections." —*Publishers Weekly*

ESSENTIAL AND RECOMMENDED TITLES
811 American poetry

Bailey, Desiree C.
What Noise Against the Cane. Desiree C. Bailey; foreword by Carl Phillips. Yale Univ Pr 2021. 96 p. (Yale series of younger poets)
ISBN 9780300256543
Grades: Adult 811
1. African diaspora 2. Caribbean Americans 3. Belonging 4. Poetry 5. Book club best bets

A lyric quest for belonging and freedom, weaving political resistance, Caribbean folklore, immigration, and the realities of Black life in America.

Bang, Mary Jo
The Bride of E: Poems. Mary Jo Bang. Graywolf Press 2009. 90 p.
ISBN 9781555975395
Grades: Adult 811
1. American poetry 2. Women authors 3. Poetry
LC 2009926850

Presents one or more poems for every letter of the alphabet that deal with human existential problems.

A latest collection by the National Book Critics Circle-winning author of Elegy explores the notion of solitude and being in its first poem, "Cosmic Aloneness Is the Bride of Existence," and continues with pieces that incorporate wild and rapturous language while evincing the experience of longing.

A Doll for Throwing: Poems. Mary Jo Bang. Graywolf Press 2017. 76 p. : Illustration
ISBN 9781555977818
Grades: Adult 811
1. American poetry 2. Poetry
LC 2016951417

The author's eighth poetry collection explores the concepts of nostalgia, xenophobia, misogyny, and political extremism through the voice of a person who was once part of the German Bauhaus school, only to see it shuttered by the Nazis.

"With rich metaphors and abundant irony, these difficult prose poems serve as a portrait of the artist as a young woman whose work and reputation were stolen." —*Library Journal*

Elegy: Poems. Mary Jo Bang. Graywolf Press 2007. 92 p.
ISBN 9781555974831
Grades: Adult 811
1. Elegiac poetry 2. American poetry 3. Women authors 4. Poetry
LC 2007924768

Provides a collection of poems examining grief and loss of an adult child.

Baraka, Amiri
S O S: Poems 1961-2013. Amiri Baraka; selected by Paul Vangelisti. Grove Press 2014. xxviii, 531 pages
ISBN 9780802123350
Grades: Adult 811
1. American poetry 2. African American poetry 3. Poetry 4. Poetry — African American authors
LC Bl2015008497

Collects some of the author's poetry, spanning his decades-long career as an outspoken advocate against opression.

Includes index.

Barot, Rick
The Galleons: Poems. Rick Barot. Milkweed Editions 2020. 71 pages
ISBN 9781571315236
Grades: Adult 811
1. Identity 2. Postcolonialism 3. Immigrants 4. Poetry
LC 2019022928

For almost twenty years, Rick Barot has been writing some of the most stunningly crafted lyric poems in America, paying careful, Rilkean attention to the layered world that surrounds us. In The Galleons, he widens his scope, contextualizing the immigrant journey of his Filipino-American parents in the larger history and aftermath of colonialism.

"Important reading, especially for those interested in the issues of colonialism and immigration." —*Library Journal*

Berry, Wendell
New Collected Poems. Wendell Berry. Counterpoint 2012. xvii, 391 pages
ISBN 9781582438153
Grades: Adult 811
1. American poetry 2. Poetry
LC 2016296610

This volume reprints the nearly two hundred pieces from his earlier Collected Poems, together with the poems from his most recent collections: Entries, Given, and Leavings, to create an expanded compilation. It contains all the poems from previous collections Mr. Berry wishes to collect, except no selections have been made from his ongoing sequence published as The Sabbath Poems.

Includes index.

A Timbered Choir: The Sabbath Poems, 1979-1997. Wendell Berry. Counterpoint 1998. xviii, 216 p.
ISBN 9781887178686
Grades: Adult 811
1. Nature 2. American poetry 3. Poetry
LC 98004925

A collection of poems written outdoors on Sunday mornings over a span of more than two decades explores the beauty and spirituality of the natural world.

"Berry has continued periodically to write poems out-of-doors on days of little other work. This book reprints Sabbaths, a collection of that writing, adding to it about one and a half times as much new work. Few other poets have such chaste and precise diction or manage line and stanza with such unaffected serenity." —*Booklist*

Berryman, John
Collected Poems, 1937-1971. John Berryman; edited and introduced by Charles Thornbury. Noonday Press 1991. LXVII, 347 p.
ISBN 9780374522810
Grades: Adult 811
1. American poetry 2. Poetry
LC BL 99718107

Presents Berryman's seven collections of short poems and offers a brief overview of his life, his career, and his poetics.

Includes index; Originally published: New York : Farrar Straus Giroux, c1989.

Berssenbrugge, Mei-mei
A Treatise on Stars. Mei-mei Berssenbrugge. New Directions Books 2020. 96 p.
ISBN 9780811229388
Grades: Adult 811
1. Poetry of places 2. Poetry
LC 2019047008

Mei-mei Berssenbrugge's a Treatise on Stars extends the intensely phenomenological poetics of 'The Star Field' in Empathy, which appeared over thirty years ago. The book is structured as a continuous enfolding of poems, each made up of numbered serial parts, their presiding poetic consciousness moving from the desert arroyo of New Mexico to the white-tailed deer of Maine and between conversations with daughter, husband, friends, pets (corn snake and poodle), and a woman, or star-visitor, beneath a tree who calls 'Any spirit in matter ... star-walking.' These are poems of deep listening and patient waiting, open to the channeling of daily experience, to gestalt and angel, dolphins and extraterrestrials. Here, family is a type of constellation and 'Thought is a form of organized light.' All our senses are activated by Berssenbrugge's light absorbing lines, lines that map a geography of interconnected intelligence-interdimensional intelligence-that exists in all sentient objects and sustains us. This is not new age poetry but poetry for a new age, rigorous of thought and grounded in the physical world where 'Days fill with splendor, and earth offers its pristine beauty to an expanding present.'.

PUBLIC LIBRARY CORE COLLECTION: NONFICTION
Twentieth Edition

"Lovers of the constellations and abstraction, however, will find themselves at home in the lyrical language." —*Publishers Weekly*

A New Directions book.

Betts, Reginald Dwayne
Felon: Poems. Reginald Dwayne Betts. W. W. Norton & Co. 2019. 95 p.
ISBN 9780393652147
Grades: Adult 811
1. Imprisonment 2. Prisons 3. Prison-industrial complex 4. Social perception 5. Identity 6. Prejudice 7. Former convicts 8. Criminals 9. African American poetry 10. Poetry 11. Society and culture — Violence and crime — Criminal justice system
LC 2019026008
New York Times Notable Book, 2020.

Tells the story of the effects of incarceration, touching upon a vast array of emotions and experiences through homelessness, underemployment, love, drug abuse, domestic violence, fatherhood and grace, creating a travelogue for an imagined life.

"In visually arresting poems, Betts exposes systematic prejudices, legal disparities, and the emotional strain of raising two sons in a country accustomed to assuming the worst about Black males… the importance of Betts' collection cannot be overstated as current events shed light on ongoing injustices." —*Booklist*

Bidart, Frank
★ *Half-light: Collected Poems 1965-2016.* Frank Bidart. Farrar Straus Giroux 2017. 718 pages
ISBN 9780374125950
Grades: Adult 811
1. American poetry 2. Poetry
LC 2015038552
The collected poems of the award winning American poet Frank Bidart.

"This collected poems is an almost overwhelming bounty, a permanent book." —*Publishers Weekly*

Bishop, Elizabeth
★ *Poems.* Elizabeth Bishop. Farrar, Straus and Giroux 2011. 352 p.
ISBN 9781480630734
Grades: Adult 811
1. American poetry 2. Nature 3. Human behavior 4. Poetry

Elizabeth Bishop is one of America's greatest writers, and her art is loved and admired by readers and fellow poets alike. The poems that make up Bishop's small and select body of work display honesty and humor, grief and acceptance, observing nature and human nature with painstaking accuracy. Her poems often start outwardly, with geography and landscape—from New England and Nova Scotia, where she grew up, to Florida and Brazil, where she later lived—and move inexorably toward "the interior," exploring as they do fundamental questions of knowledge and perception, love and solitude, and the ability or inability of form to control chaos.

Poems includes the complete text of what is for many a lifelong bedside companion, the 1983 Complete Poems, plus selections from the drafts and poems in progress from Bishop's archive, first published as Edgar Allan Poe and the Juke-box… this new edition is the most loving treatment of her poetic output, the best place to start and perhaps all one needs in the end. Publisehrs Weekly.

Bitsui, Sherwin
Dissolve. Sherwin Bitsui. Copper Canyon Press 2019. VII, 67 pages
ISBN 9781556595455
Grades: Adult 811
1. Navajo (Diné) (North American people) 2. Indigenous men 3. Language and languages 4. Identity 5. Alienation 6. Indigenous reservations 7. Rural life 8. Spirituality 9. Southwest (United States) 10. Canadian poetry 11. Poetry
LC 2018016188
Drawing upon Navajo traditions and language, Sherwin Bitsui composes a brutal and catastrophic passage through the American Southwest.

Blanco, Richard
How to Love a Country: Poems. by Richard Blanco. Beacon Press 2019. 112 p.
ISBN 9780807025918
Grades: Adult 811
1. Group identity 2. National characteristics, American 3. Toleration 4. Hope 5. Political culture 6. United States 7. Poetry
LC 2018050554
Booklist Editors' Choice, 2019.

As presidential inaugural poet, memoirist, public speaker, educator, and advocate, Richard Blanco has crisscrossed the nation inviting communities to connect to the heart of human experience and our shared identity as a country. In this new collection of poems, his first in over seven years, Blanco continues to invite a conversation with all Americans. Through an oracular yet intimate and accessible voice, he addresses the complexities and contradictions of our nationhood and the unresolved sociopolitical matters that affect us all.

Blount, Tommye
Fantasia for the Man in Blue. Tommye Blount. Four Way Books 2020. 139 p.
ISBN 9781945588495
Grades: Adult 811
1. African Americans 2. LGBTQIA+ people 3. Identity 4. American poetry 5. Poetry 6. Debut title
LC 2019031755
Finalist for the Hurston/Wright Legacy Awards for Poetry, 2021.

In his debut collection Fantasia for the Man in Blue, Tommye Blount orchestrates a chorus of distinct, unforgettable voices that speak to the experience of the Black, queer body as a site of desire and violence.

"A captivating, unrelenting collection of poetry composed of sharp-edged truths and beautiful complexities." —*Booklist*

Bly, Robert
Collected Poems. Robert Bly. W. W. Norton & Company 2018. 528 p.
ISBN 9780393652444
Grades: Adult 811
1. Transcendentalism 2. Mysticism 3. Imagery (Psychology) 4. Intellectual life 5. Authenticity (Philosophy) 6. Poetry
LC 2018028547
An extraordinary culmination for Robert Bly's lifelong intellectual adventure, Collected Poems presents the full magnitude of his body of work for the first time. Influenced by Emerson and Thoreau alongside spiritual traditions from Sufism to Gnosticism, he is a poet moved by mysteries, speaking the language of images.

Includes index.

Boruch, Marianne
Eventually One Dreams the Real Thing. Marianne Boruch. Copper Canyon Press 2016. 127 pages
ISBN 9781556594915
Grades: Adult 811
1. American poetry 2. Poetry of places 3. Women authors 4. Poetry
LC 2015032450
Marianne Boruch's generous and gathering mind wanders through her poems—taking in, then turning around, a curious world.

"In her meditative new collection, Boruch (Cadaver, Speak) writes at once with and against the cascade of information and fevered, restless attention that mark contemporary daily life." —*Publishers Weekly*

Borzutzky, Daniel
Lake Michigan. Daniel Borzutzky. University of Pittsburgh Press 2018. 81 pages
ISBN 9780822965220
Grades: Adult 811
1. Prisons 2. American poetry 3. Poetry
LC Bl2018187827

ESSENTIAL AND RECOMMENDED TITLES
811 American poetry

An imagined prison camp located on the beaches of Chicago is explored through nineteen lyrical poems that show the ways in which economic policy, racism, and militarized policing combine to shape the city.

*The **Performance** of Becoming Human.* Daniel Borzutzky. Brooklyn Arts Press 2016. 89 pages
ISBN 9781936767465
Grades: Adult   811
1. American poetry 2. Poetry
LC 2015028529

The bay of Valparaiso merges into the western shore of Lake Michigan, where Borzutzky continues his poetic investigation into the political and economic violence shared by Chicago and Chile, two places integral to his personal formation.

"This is one of contemporary poetry's most cogent documents of humanity and suffering in the 21st century, one born out of an impossible but necessary struggle to reconcile existence with destruction, excess with deprivation, and alienation with proximity." —*Publishers Weekly*

Brock-Broido, Lucie
*Stay, **Illusion***. Lucie Brock-Broido. Alfred A. Knopf 2013. VIII, 100 pages
ISBN 9780307962027
Grades: Adult   811
1. American poetry 2. Women authors 3. Poetry
LC 2013023978

Presents a collection of poems which explore imagination, myth, violence, the treatment of animals, and the death penalty in America.

The award-winning author of Trouble in Mind presents a latest collection of poetic works that raise the parameters of her literary oeuvre to a new level, sharing insight into her use of unflinching, ironic language while describing the disparities between the perceived allure of her inner world and the compelling visible world.

Includes bibliographical references (page 97).

Brooks, Gwendolyn
★ *The **Essential** Gwendolyn Brooks: Selected Poems.* Gwendolyn Brooks, Elizabeth Alexander, editor. Library of America 2005. xxvi, 148 p. : Illustration (American poets project, 19)
ISBN 9781931082877
Grades: Adult   811
1. American poetry 2. Women authors 3. African American poetry 4. Poetry — African American authors 5. Poetry
LC 2005044162

A selection of the influential African-American poet's works reflects her modernist style and includes numerous definitive World War II poems as well as pieces about the social and political upheavals of the 1960s.

*In **Montgomery**, and Other Poems.* Gwendolyn Brooks. Third World Press 2003. IX, 147 p.
ISBN 9780883782323
Grades: Adult   811
1. African Americans 2. American poetry 3. Women authors 4. African American poetry 5. Poetry 6. Poetry — African American authors
LC 2003050749

Presents a collection of poems that provide monologues of a variety of voices, including urban children, Winnie Mandela, and Alabama civil rights workers.

Brown, Jericho
★ *The **Tradition**.* Jericho Brown. Copper Canyon Press 2019. xiii, 77 p.
ISBN 9781556594861
Grades: Adult   811
1. Race (Social sciences) 2. Violence 3. Vulnerability 4. Anger 5. Sexuality 6. Sex differences 7. African Americans 8. Identity 9. Poetry
LC 2018048965

ALA Notable Book, 2020; Library Journal Best Books, 2019; New York Times Notable Book, 2019.

The Tradition details the normalization of evil and its history at the intersection of the past and the personal. Brown's poetic concerns are both broad and intimate, and at their very core a distillation of the incredibly human: What is safety? Who is this nation? Where does freedom truly lie? Brown makes mythical pastorals to question the terrors to which we've become accustomed, and to celebrate how we survive. Poems of fatherhood, legacy, Blackness, queerness, worship, and trauma are propelled into stunning clarity by Brown's mastery, and his invention of the duplex—a combination of the sonnet, the ghazal, and the blues—is testament to his formal skill.

"Brown's third collection (after the New Testament) pulsates with the acute anxieties of racial and sexual difference, the psychologically complex intersections of personal intimacy with social responsibility." —*Library Journal*

Includes bibliographical references.

Brown, Molly McCully
*The **Virginia** State Colony for Epileptics and Feebleminded: Poems.* Molly McCully Brown. Persea Books 2017. 77 pages
ISBN 9780892554782
Grades: Adult   811
1. State Colony for Epileptics and Feeble-Minded (Va.) 2. People with epilepsy 3. People with developmental disabilities 4. American poetry 5. Poetry
LC 2016037960

These poems explore the haunted legacy of the Virginia State Colony for Epileptics and Feebleminded, an medical institution at the heart of the eugenics movement in the first half of the twentieth century in America. The author, who has cerebral palsy, grew up in the shadow of the former Colony in southwestern Virginia, aware that, had she been born fifty years earlier, she would quite possibly been admitted there, and exposed to a variety of inhumane treatments, including forced sterilization. Her poems give voice to the Colony's chorus of residents, reclaiming for them elements of their humanity.

Burt, Stephanie
*Don't **Read** Poetry: A Book About How to Read Poems.* Stephanie Burt. Basic Books 2019. IX, 306 p.
ISBN 9780465094509
Grades: Adult   811
1. Books and reading 2. Literary criticism 3. Poetry writing 4. Arts and Entertainment — Writing and Publishing 5. Arts and Entertainment — Writing and Publishing — Literary criticism
LC 2018054504

Award-winning poet and literary critic Stephanie Burt offers an accessible introduction to the seemingly daunting task of reading, understanding, and appreciating poetry. Burt dispels preconceptions about poetry and explains how poems speak to one another—and how they can speak to our lives. She shows readers how to find more poems once they have some poems they like, and how to connect the poetry of the past to the poetry of the present. Burt moves seamlessly from Shakespeare and other classics to the contemporary poetry circulated on Tumblr and Twitter. She challenges the assumptions that many of us make about "poetry," whether we think we like it or think we don't, in order to help us cherish—and distinguish among—individual poems.

"Burt's sweeping, insightful survey makes a great case that with wider exposure, people will discover how poems can be relevant to anyone who has 'Ever felt unique, or confused, or confusing to others.'." —*Publishers Weekly*

Includes index.

Byas, Taylor
*I **Done** Clicked My Heels Three Times.* Taylor Byas. Soft Skull Press 2023. 128 p.
ISBN 9781593767419
Grades: Adult   811
1. Self-discovery 2. Adulthood 3. African American women 4. Femininity 5. Sexuality 6. Body image 7. Family relationships 8. Alcoholism 9. Chicago, Illinois 10. Poetry

"Frontier Poetry Award winner Byas examines coming of age, family relationships, self-discovery, and homecoming in this stellar, bildungsroman-style debut." —*Booklist*

PUBLIC LIBRARY CORE COLLECTION: NONFICTION
Twentieth Edition

Carson, Anne
Autobiography of Red: A Novel in Verse. Anne Carson. A. A. Knopf 1998. 149 p.
ISBN 9780375401336
Grades: Adult 811
1. Love triangles 2. Crushes 3. Young men 4. Red (Color) 5. Hercules (Roman mythology) 6. Monsters 7. Interpersonal attraction 8. Wings 9. Identity 10. Photographers 11. Novels in verse 12. Canadian fiction 13. Adult books for young adults
Booklist Editors' Choice: Adult Books for Young Adults, 1998; New York Times Notable Book, 1998.
An award-winning poet bridges the gap between modernity and classism, prose and poetry, with an evocative journey into the soul of a winged red monster named Geryon, who retreats into the world of photography after losing a male lover.

The Beauty of the Husband: A Fictional Essay in 29 Tangos. Anne Carson. Alfred a Knopf 2001. 147 p.
ISBN 9780375408045
Grades: Adult 811
1. Romantic love 2. Marriage 3. Interpersonal relations 4. Desire 5. Breaking up (Interpersonal relations) 6. Poetry
The Beauty of the Husband is an essay on Keats's idea that beauty is truth, and is also the story of a marriage. It is told in 29 tangos. A tango (like a marriage) is something you have to dance to the end.
"Here the tango provides inspiration for lashingly precise yet sultry and graceful poems that depict the eroticism and possessiveness, competition and resentment of a marriage in dissolution, a process envisioned as both an elaborate dance and vicious warfare." —*Booklist*

Red Doc. Anne Carson. Alfred A. Knopf 2013. 167 p.
ISBN 9780307960580
Grades: Adult 811
1. Stesichorus 2. Monsters 3. Canadian poetry 4. Epic poetry 5. Poetry
LC 2012032322
G navigates the complex labyrinths of the modern age at the side of his war veteran lover Sad and the artist Ida while attending the death of his mother and tempering his hunger for flight with his longing for family and home.
This is a Borzoi book.

Carver, Raymond
All of Us: the Collected Poems. Raymond Carver. Vintage Contemporaries 2000. xxx, 386 p.
ISBN 9780375703805
Grades: Adult 811
1. American poetry 2. Poetry
LC BL 00011534
A comprehensive anthology of more than three hundred poems, organized chronologically in order of their publication, features works from Fires, Where the Water Comes Together with Other Water, and A New Path to the Waterfall.
Includes bibliographical references and indexes; Originally published in hardcover in Great Britain by the Harvill Press, London, in 1996—T.P. verso.

A New Path to the Waterfall: Poems. Raymond Carver; introduction by Tess Gallagher. Atlantic Monthly Press 1989. xxxi, 126 p.
ISBN 9780871133748
Grades: Adult 811
1. American poetry 2. Poetry
LC 88034989
Poems deal with memories, loss of identity, childhood innocence, the past, and mortality.

Chang, Tina
Hybrida: Poems. Tina Chang. W.W. Norton & Company 2019. 133 p.
ISBN 9781324002482
Grades: Adult 811
1. Multiracial children 2. Motherhood 3. Violence 4. Ethnic identity 5. Characters and characteristics in fairy tales 6. Race relations 7. United States 8. Poetry
LC 2018056723
A timely, stirring, and confident examination of mixed-race identity, violence, and history skillfully rendered through the lens of motherhood. In Hybrida, Tina Chang confronts the complexities of raising a mixed-race child during an era of political upheaval in the United States. She ruminates on the relationship between her son's Blackness and his safety, exploring the dangers of childhood in a post-Trayvon Martin era by invoking racialized roles in fairy tales. Meditating on the lives of Michael Brown, Leiby Kletzky, and Noemi Alvarez Quillay—lost at the hands of individuals entrusted to protect them—Chang creates hybrid poetic forms that mirror her investigation of racial tensions.
"For academic holdings and public collections that include a political or own voices element." —*Library Journal*

Chang, Victoria
Obit: Poems. Victoria Chang. Copper Canyon Press 2020. x, 113 pages
ISBN 9781556595745
Grades: Adult 811
1. Obituaries 2. Poetry
LC 2019043837
New York Times Notable Book, 2020.
After her mother died, poet Victoria Chang refused to write elegies. Rather, she distilled her grief during a feverish two weeks by writing scores of poetic obituaries for all she lost in the world. In Obit, Chang writes of "the way memory gets up aftersomeone has died and starts walking." These poems reinvent the form of newspaper obituary to both name what has died ("civility," "language," "the future," "Mother's blue dress") and the cultural impact of death on the living. Whereas elegy attempts to immortalize the dead, an obituary expresses loss, and the love for the dead becomes a conduit for self-expression. In this unflinching and lyrical book, Chang meets her grief and creates a powerful testament for the living."
"Often incorporating short declarative sentences, Chang's poems can veer toward being list-like but move forward quickly to endings that surprise and even amaze as they burrow deep into those grieving places all of us have experienced." —*Library Journal*
Includes bibliographical references (pages 107, 108-110).

Charles, Jos
Feeld. Jos Charles. Milkweed Editions 2018. 64 pages
ISBN 9781571315052
Grades: Adult 811
1. Gender identity 2. American poetry 3. Poetry
LC 2017058971
Poetic exploration in Middle English about the body, physical space, ownership of space, gender, and transitioning genders.

Choi, Don Mee
Hardly War. Don Mee Choi. Wave Books 2016. 97 pages : Illustration
ISBN 9781940696232
Grades: Adult 811
1. Families 2. Poetry — Asian American authors 3. Poetry
LC 2015025698
"Far from lackadaisical, Choi's poetry operates within a tradition of Korean-American experimental poets that includes Theresa Hak Kyung Cha and Myung Mi Kim. Choi's zany take on militarism and the Korean diaspora may seem absurdist, but it is an inventive and daring waltz that upends what is commonly understood as the Forgotten War.'" —*Publishers Weekly*

Choi, Franny
The World Keeps Ending, and the World Goes On. Franny Choi. HarperCollins 2022. 224 p.
ISBN 9780063240087
Grades: Adult 811

ESSENTIAL AND RECOMMENDED TITLES
811 American poetry

1. Marginalized people 2. Dystopias 3. End of the world 4. Intergenerational trauma 5. Poetry

Choi's third book features poems about historical and impending apocalypses, alongside musings on our responsibilities to each other and visions for our collective survival.

"The urgent and lyrically dynamic third collection from Choi (Soft Science) addresses intergenerational trauma and the anxieties of living in a world skating on the precipice of apocalypse….Choi's electrifying language grips the reader from the first poem and never lets go."—*Publishers Weekly*

Clark, Tiana

I Can't Talk About the Trees Without the Blood. Tiana Clark. University of Pittsburgh Press 2018. 112 p.
ISBN 9780822965589
Grades: Adult   811
1. African Americans 2. Race (Social sciences) 3. Memory 4. Identity 5. Violence 6. Poetry

For prize-winning poet Tiana Clark, trees will never be just trees. They will also and always be a row of gallows from which Black bodies once swung. This is an image that she cannot escape, but one that she has learned to lean into as she delves into personal and public histories, explicating memories and muses around race, elegy, family, and faith by making and breaking forms as well as probing mythology, literary history, her own ancestry, and, yes, even Rihanna.

Clifton, Lucille

How to Carry Water: Selected Poems of Lucille Clifton. Edited by Aracelis Girmay. BOA Editions 2020. xxii, 256 pages
ISBN 9781950774142
Grades: Adult   811
1. African American women 2. Femininity 3. Motherhood 4. Racism 5. Injustice 6. Survival 7. Independence 8. Poetry
LC 2020019710

These poems celebrating Black womanhood and resilience shimmer with intellect, insight, humor, and joy, all in Clifton's characteristic style—a voice that the late Toni Morrison described as "seductive with the simplicity of an atom, which is to say highly complex, explosive underneath an apparent quietude." Selected and introduced by award-winning poet Aracelis Girmay, this volume of Clifton's poetry is simultaneously timeless and fitting for today's tumultuous moment.

"The life work of Clifton (1936-2010) forms an incandescent prayer for self-determination in this vital selected volume featuring 10 previously uncollected poems. . . . Clifton's poems are profound and powerful to behold."—*Publishers Weekly*

Includes index.

Mercy: Poems. Lucille Clifton. BOA Editions 2004. 79 p.
ISBN 9781929918546
Grades: 11 12 Adult   811
1. African American poets 2. 20th century 3. Poetry 4. Arts and Entertainment — Writing and Publishing
LC 2004010396

A collection of poems by the African American poet focus on the stratification of American society, the power of Western materialism, and her concern for the world's children.

Codjoe, Ama

Bluest Nude: Poems. Ama Codjoe. Milkweed Editions 2022. 88 p.
ISBN 9781571315427
Grades: Adult   811
1. Women artists 2. Creation (Literary, artistic, etc.) 3. Gender role 4. Femininity 5. Expectation 6. Self-perception 7. Disorientation 8. Poetry 9. Debut title

Ama Codjoe's highly anticipated debut collection brings generous light to the inner dialogues of women as they bathe, create art, make and lose love. Each poem rises with the urgency of a fully awakened sensual life. Codjoe's poems explore how the archetype of the artist complicates the typical expectations of women: Be gazed upon, be silent, be selfless, reproduce. Dialoguing with and through art, Bluest Nude considers alternative ways of holding and constructing the self.

"The hotly burning poems in Codjoe's debut collection collapse themes of color and body into a lyrical supernova, with reiterated questions about the role of women and art at its center."—*Booklist*

Cody, Anthony

Borderland Apocrypha. Anthony Cody. Omnidawn Publishing 2020. 159 p.
ISBN 9781632430762
Grades: Adult   811
1. Lynching 2. Poetry
LC 2019049154

Borderland Apocrypha is centered around the collective histories of Mexican lynchings following the signing of the Treaty of Guadalupe Hidalgo in 1848, and the subsequent erasures, traumas, and state-sanctioned violences committed towards communities of color in the present day. Cody's debut collection responds to the destabilized, hostile landscapes and silenced histories via an experimental poetic that invents and shapeshifts in both form and space across the margin, the page, and the book's axis in aresistance, a reclamation and a re-occupation of what has been omitted. Part autohistoria, part docupoetic, part visual monument, part myth-making, Borderland Apocrypha exhumes the past in order to work toward survival, reckoning, and future- building."

Collins, Billy

Aimless Love: New and Selected Poems. Billy Collins. Random House Trade Paperbacks 2014. xix, 261 pages
ISBN 9780812982671
Grades: Adult   811
1. American poetry 2. Poetry
LC 2014498724

A two-time U.S. Poet Laureate presents a volume of more than 50 new poems accompanying a generous gathering from his collections of the past decade to lend insight into his overall poetic achievements and his use of playful, ironic and melodic language.

"Some poems are funny from the opening gambit to the closing flourish. But Collins' droll wit is often a diversionary tactic, so that when he strikes you with the hard edge of his darker visions, you reel."—*Booklist*

Sailing Alone Around the Room: New and Selected Poems. Billy Collins. Random House 2001. 171 p.
ISBN 9780375503801
Grades: Adult   811
1. American poetry 2. Poetry
LC 99052861

A definitive anthology of new and selected poetry by the acclaimed author of Questions About Angels and The Art of Drowning offers unexpected, sometimes humorous, sometimes serious insights into life, love, and human existence in such works as "Fishing on the Susquehanna in July," "Life of Riley," and "Forgetfulness."

"On every delectable page, Collins performs nimble feats of the imagination and gives voice to an emotion we foolishly trivialize and condemn: Pure pleasure."—*Booklist*

The Trouble with Poetry and Other Poems. Billy Collins. Random House 2005. 88 p.
ISBN 9780375503825
Grades: Adult   811
1. American poetry 2. Poetry
LC 2005046562

An all-new collection of poetry by America's former Poet Laureate features witty, insightful, and simple poems dealing with the themes of jazz, the passage of time, love, boyhood, and writing.

Whale Day: And Other Poems. Billy Collins. Random House 2020. 160 pages
ISBN 9780399589751
Grades: Adult   811
1. Mortality 2. Interpersonal relations 3. Poetry

LC 2020003903

The latest collection by the former Poet Laureate of the United States gathers more than 50 new poems that reflect the writer's signature mix of playful and serious language.

"As in his previous, beloved poetry collections, Collins (The Rain in Portugal, 2016) encapsulates life with both bonhomie and mordancy.... Collins delights, skewers, and enlightens." —Booklist

Collins, Martha

Admit One: An American Scrapbook. Martha Collins. University of Pittsburgh Press 2016. 89 pages
ISBN 9780822964056
Grades: Adult   811
1. Racism 2. Eugenics 3. American poetry 4. Women authors 5. Poetry

LC 2018276885

In this collection of poetry, Martha Collins relentlessly traces the history of scientific racism from the 1904 St. Louis World's Fair through the eugenics movement of the 1920s.

Includes bibliographical references (pages 86-89).

Cummings, E. E.

★ *Complete Poems, 1904-1962.* E.E. Cummings; edited by George J. Firmage. Liveright 1994. xxxii, 1102 p.
ISBN 9780871401526
Grades: 9 10 11 12 Adult   811
1. American poetry 2. 20th century 3. Poetry

LC BL 99789950

A collection of the modern poet's work shows his use of satire and sentiment in unconventional verse styles.

"This volume has been prepared directly from the poet's original manuscripts, preserving the original typography and format. It includes all the previously published works, from Tulips (1922) to Etcetera (1983), as well as 36 uncollected poems that originally appeared in little magazines or anthologies." —Library Journal

Includes bibliographical references and index; Originally published: New York : W.W. Norton, c1991.

Derricotte, Toi

I: New and Selected Poems. Toi Derricotte. University of Pittsburgh Press 2019. 298 p.
ISBN 9780822945666
Grades: Adult   811
1. Derricotte, Toi, 1941- 2. African American women 3. Wisdom 4. Purpose in life 5. Poetry

LC Bl2020006994

The acclaimed author of "The Black Notebooks" offers a collection of poetry that spans 50 years of life experience.

"Derricotte's attention lingers on places of struggle where life is at its most vibrant, urgent, and surprising." —Publishers Weekly

Diaz, Natalie

★ *Postcolonial Love Poem.* Natalie Diaz. Graywolf Press 2020. 105 p.
ISBN 9781644450147
Grades: Adult   811
1. Indigenous peoples 2. Hope 3. Colonialism 4. Indigenous peoples of North America 5. American poetry 6. Desire 7. Sexuality 8. Beauty in nature 9. 21st century 10. Poetry

LC 2019933473

ALA Notable Book, 2021.

Postcolonial Love Poem is an anthem of desire against erasure. Natalie Diaz's brilliant second collection demands that every body carried in its pages—bodies of language, land, rivers, suffering brothers, enemies, and lovers—be touched and held as beloveds.

"In this exquisite, electrifying collection, Diaz . . . continues to demonstrate her masterful use of language while reinventing narratives about desire." —Publishers Weekly

Dickinson, Emily

Dickinson: Selected Poems and Commentaries. Helen Vendler. The Belknap Press of Harvard University Press 2010. xiv, 535 p.
ISBN 9780674048676
Grades: Adult   811
1. Dickinson, Emily, 1830-1886 2. American poetry 3. Arts and Entertainment — Writing and Publishing — Literary criticism 4. Poetry

LC 2010007090

Presents 150 selected poems of Emily Dickinson along with commentary on both the stylistic and imaginative features of the poems.

Includes bibliographical references (p. 527) and index.

Doty, Mark

Deep Lane: Poems. Mark Doty. 2015. 93 p.
ISBN 9780393070231
Grades: Adult   811
1. American poetry 2. Poetry

LC 2015000660

A new collection of poems from the National Book Award-winning author features works that describe a series of descents before moving on to more uplifting possibilities.

"A somber, struggling, honest collection for Doty's many fans." —Library Journal

Winner of the National Book Award—Jacket.

Fire to Fire: New and Selected Poems. Mark Doty. Harper 2008. x, 326 p.
ISBN 9780060752477
Grades: Adult   811
1. American poetry 2. Poetry

LC 2007044646

A collection of top-selected works and new poems by the author of Dog Years features pieces that meditate on such topics as mortality, the instructive presence of animals, and art's ability to give shape to human life.

Includes bibliographical references (p. 319-321).

What Is the Grass: Walt Whitman in My Life. Mark Doty. W. W. Norton & Company 2020. 272 p.
ISBN 9780393070224
Grades: Adult   811
1. Doty, Mark 2. Whitman, Walt, 1819-1892 3. Poets, American 4. Influence (Literary, artistic, etc.) 5. Homosexuality 6. Gay men 7. Identity 8. Poetry writing 9. Life stories — Identity — LGBTQIA+ 10. Life stories — Arts and culture — Writing — Poets 11. Arts and Entertainment — Writing and Publishing

LC 2019044569

The National Book Award-winning poet explores Walt Whitman's poetic themes of love, death and queer sexuality while reflecting on Whitman's complicated impact on his own work, his sense of self and the American imagination.

"Fans of Whitman will surely enjoy Doty's extensive passages of exegesis, and many readers will admire the author's occasional descriptions of his own revisions of his ideas about Whitman's diction and poetic design. Throughout, the author exudes an exuberance about life and words that rivals that of his subject. Also informative (and necessary) are Doty's evocations of 19th-century Brooklyn and New York City. A captivating paean to Whitman combined with an unblinking self-examination." —Kirkus

Dove, Rita

Playlist for the Apocalypse: Poems. Rita Dove. W.W. Norton & Company 2021. 114 pages
ISBN 9780393867770
Grades: Adult   811
1. African American poetry 2. Poetry

LC 2021011714

In her first volume of new poems in twelve years, Rita Dove investigates the vacillating moral compass guiding America's, and the world's, experiments in democracy. Whether depicting the first Jewish ghetto in sixteenth-century Venice or Black Lives Matter, this extraordinary poet never fails to connect history's grand exploits to the triumphs and tragedies of individual lives—the simmering

ESSENTIAL AND RECOMMENDED TITLES
811 American poetry

resentment of an elevator operator, an octogenarian's exuberant mambo, the mordant humor of a philosophizing cricket. Audaciously playful yet grave, alternating poignant meditations on mortality and acerbic observations of injustice, Playlist for the Apocalypse takes us from the smallest moments of redemption to apocalyptic failures of the human soul.

"This is Dove's first new collection in a dozen years,…and it is a potent and many-chambered volume showcasing the highly awarded former U.S. Poet Laureate's signature gift for historical illumination, especially in sharp and poignant portraits of marginalized figures." —*Booklist*

★ *Selected Poems*. Rita Dove. Vintage Books 1993. xxvi, 210 p.
ISBN 9780679750802
Grades: 11 12 Adult   811
1. American poetry 2. Women authors 3. African American poetry 4. Poetry 5. Poetry — African American authors
LC 93026112

Gathers poems about slavery and freedom, home and family, and the past by America's youngest poet laureate.

"This volume places three previous collections under one cover.... The selection begins with The Yellow House on the Corner, Dove's first book, most notable for its poems derived from slave narratives. Museum, her second book, offers a potpourri of work that ranges over several continents and many millenia; Dove's tirelessly exact language illuminates the lives of saints, contemporary lifestyles, and Greek myths." —*Booklist*
Includes index.

Sonata Mulattica: A Life in Five Movements and a Short Play : Poems. Rita Dove. W. W. Norton & Co. 2009. 231 p.
ISBN 9780393070088
Grades: Adult   811
1. Bridgetower, George Augustus Polgreen 2. Multiracial men 3. Musicians 4. American poetry 5. Women authors 6. African American poetry 7. Poetry 8. Poetry — African American authors
LC 2008054281

A lyric narrative by a Pulitzer Prize-winning former U.S. poet laureate, inspired by the life of a nineteenth-century virtuoso violinist, traces the early years of George Polgreen Bridgetower as a son of a white woman and an "African prince," his acclaim in Vienna, and his break with Beethoven after a dispute over a woman.

Duncan, Robert
Selected Poems. Robert Duncan; edited by Robert J. Bertholf. New Directions 1993. xi, 147 p.
ISBN 9780811212274
Grades: Adult   811
1. American poetry 2. 20th century 3. Poetry
LC 92035812

A collection of poetry deals with such topics as love, death, revelation, religion, humanity, and war.

"Duncan was one of the true masters of contemporary American poetry. His oeuvre is by turns lyrical, experimental, archaic, visionary and political. In Bertholf's brief, insightful introduction, he makes necessary connections between the often-neglected early work and the later masterpieces." —*Publishers Weekly*
Includes index.

Dunn, Stephen
Local Visitations: Poems. Stephen Dunn. Norton 2003. 96 p.
ISBN 9780393052008
Grades: Adult   811
1. American poetry 2. Poetry
LC 2002014204

A twelfth collection by the 2000 Pulitzer Prize winner for poetry finds a temporarily freed Sisyphus struggling through twenty-first century America and nineteenth-century novelists visiting the author's South Jersey towns.

New & Selected Poems: 1974-1994. Stephen Dunn. W.W. Norton 1995. xvii, 296 p.
ISBN 9780393313000
Grades: Adult   811
1. American poetry 2. 20th century 3. Poetry
LC BI2007001363

Sixteen new poems and poems selected from the author's previous collections focus on the nuances of family and domestic life, as well as philosophical and metaphysical concerns.
Includes index.

Ellis, Thomas Sayers
Skin, Inc.: Identity Repair Poems. Thomas Sayers Ellis. Graywolf Press 2010. 181 pages
ISBN 9781555975678
Grades: Adult   811
1. American poetry 2. African American poetry 3. Poetry
LC 2010922920

Presents a collection of poetry that looks at the American identity.

Emerson, Ralph Waldo
★ *Collected Poems and Translations*. Ralph Waldo Emerson; [compiled by Harold Bloom and Paul Kane]. Library of America : 1994. 637 p; (The library of America, 70)
ISBN 9780940450288
Grades: 11 12 Adult   811
1. Translations 2. Poetry 3. Arts and Entertainment — Writing and Publishing
LC 93040245

A comprehensive new volume that includes all of the poetry that Emerson published during his lifetime, demonstrates his skill and depth as a poet, and reveals his private, meditative, emotional side—a portrait of a freer, more unconventional Emerson.

Contains Emerson's published poetry, plus selections of his unpublished poetry from journals and notebooks, and some of his translations of poetry from other languages, notably Dante's La vita nuova; Includes bibliographical references (p. 590) and index.

Erdrich, Heid E.
★ *Little Big Bully*. Heid E. Erdrich. Penguin Books 2020. xii, 94 p.
ISBN 9780143135920
Grades: Adult   811
1. Oppression (Psychology) 2. Indigenous peoples 3. Violence against marginalized women 4. Misogyny 5. Genocide 6. Environmental degradation 7. Psychic trauma 8. Truth 9. Poetry

Little Big Bully begins with a question asked of a collective and troubled we—how did we come to this? In answer, this book offers personal myth, American and Native American contexts, and allegories driven by women's resistance to narcissists, stalkers, and harassers. These poems are immediate, personal, political, cultural, even futuristic object lessons. What is truth now? Who are we now? How do we find answers through the smoke of human destructiveness? The past for Indigenous people, ecosystem collapse from near-extinction of bison, and the present epidemic of missing and murdered Indigenous women underlie these poems. Here, survivors shout back at useless cautionary tales with their own courage and visions of future worlds made well.

"As a Native American, as a woman, Erdrich knows how oppressors operate, preying on the seemingly weak or quiet ones, shouting louder and pushing hardest. She tackles different forms of bullying in these timely poems by interweaving the personal, public, and cultural." —*Booklist*

National Poetry series winner, chosen by Amy Gerstler for Penguin Books.

Espada, Martin
★ *Floaters: Poems*. Martin Espada. W.W. Norton & Company 2021. 96 p.
ISBN 9780393541038
Grades: Adult   811
1. Hispanic Americans 2. Latin American people 3. Immigrants 4. Racism 5. Prejudice 6. Social marginality 7. Social justice 8. Poetry 9. Antiracist literature

PUBLIC LIBRARY CORE COLLECTION: NONFICTION
Twentieth Edition

LC 2020027736

From the winner of the Ruth Lilly Poetry Prize come masterfully crafted narratives of protest, grief, and love. In this collection, Martin Espada bears witness to confrontation with anti-immigrant bigotry as a tenant lawyer years ago, and now sings the praises of Central American adolescents playing soccer in an internment camp founded on that same bigotry. He knows that times of hate also call for poems of love—even in the voice of a Galapagos tortoise. Whether celebrating the visions of fallen dreamers and poets or condemning the devastation of Hurricane Maria and official negligence in his father's Puerto Rico, Espada invokes ferocious, incandescent spirits.

"This impressive collection is unique for the way it captures the world-weary voice of a poet and political activist who doesn't simply call for change, but offers a sense of the long, difficult struggle toward justice." —*Publishers Weekly*

Evans, William
We Inherit What the Fires Left: Poems. William Evans. Simon & Schuster 2020. 149 p.
ISBN 9781982127398
Grades: Adult   811
1. Poetry

LC 2019028078

William Evans, the award-winning poet and cofounder of the popular culture website Black Nerd Problems, offers an emotionally vulnerable poetry collection exploring the themes of inheritances, dreams, and injuries that are passed down from one generation to the next and delving into the lived experience of a Black man in the American suburbs today.

"This is a powerful, transformative book." —*Booklist*

Ewing, Eve L.
1919. Eve L. Ewing. Haymarket Books 2019. 74 p.
ISBN 9781608466023
Grades: Adult   811
1. Race Riots 2. Violence against African Americans 3. African American communities 4. Racism 5. United States history 6. Chicago, Illinois 7. United States 8. 20th century 9. Poetry

Ewing uses speculative and Afrofuturist lenses to recast history, and illuminates the thin line between the past and the present.

"These clarion and haunting poems—some psalm-like, others percussive, even concussive, all technically brilliant and sure to galvanize adults and teens alike—incisively and resoundingly evoke the promise and betrayal of the Great Migration and the everyday struggles of Chicago's Black community against vicious and violent racism." —*Booklist*

Includes bibliographical references.

Faizullah, Tarfia
Registers of Illuminated Villages: Poems. Tarfia Faizullah. Graywolf Press 2018. 96, 98 pages
ISBN 9781555978006
Grades: Adult   811
1. American poetry 2. Women authors 3. 21st century 4. Poetry

LC 2017938024

Faizullah's new work extends and transforms her powerful accounts of violence, war, and loss into poems of many forms and voices—elegies, outcries, self-portraits, and larger-scale confrontations with discrimination, family, and memory.

"More than this collection's almost eponymous opener, "Register of Eliminated Villages" is also the title of a sinister war document detailing the destruction of 397 Kurdish villages. And Faizullah's second collection—following the award-winning Seam (2014)—is itself a mesmerizing inventory." —*Booklist*

Includes bibliographical references (pages 95-96, [97-98]).

Felix, Camonghne
Build Yourself a Boat. Camonghne Felix. Haymarket Books 2019. 96 p.
ISBN 9781608466160
Grades: Adult   811
1. Race (Social sciences) 2. Poverty 3. Injustice 4. Poetry

Booklist Editors' Choice, 2019.

This is about what grows through the wreckage. This is an anthem of survival and a look at what might come after. A view of what floats and what, ultimately, sustains. Build Yourself a Boat redefines the language of collective and individual trauma through lyric and memory.

Ferlinghetti, Lawrence
These Are My Rivers: New & Selected Poems, 1955-1993. Lawrence Ferlinghetti. New Directions 1994. V, 308 p. : Illustration
ISBN 9780811212731
Grades: 11 12 Adult   811
1. American poetry 2. 20th century 3. African American poetry 4. Poetry 5. Poetry — African American authors

LC BL 99756912

Gathers poems from each period of the poet's career, including poems dealing with fame, memory, politics, love, travel, and poetry.

"Reading this hefty selection from 12 previous volumes, plus 50 pages of new poems, we realize how accurately the poet described himself in 1979: a man who 'thinks he's Dylan Thomas and Bob Dylan rolled together with Charlie Chaplin thrown in.' His style is recognizable throughout—phlegmatic poems running several pages, often lacking stanza breaks, with short lines at the left margin or moving across the page as hand follows eye… Essential." —*Library Journal*

Includes index; Originally published: 1993.

Finney, Nikky
Love Child's Hotbed of Occasional Poetry: Poems & Artifacts. Nikky Finney. Triquarterly Books 2020. xvi, 237 p.
ISBN 9780810142015
Grades: Adult   811
1. African American history 2. Memories 3. Social history 4. Social marginality 5. African American women 6. African American children 7. Girls 8. Poetry

LC 2019042370

National Book Award winner Nikky Finney's fifth collection contains light house poems, prosaic hot beds, and personal artifacts, copper coins struck from a new matrix for American poetry, one that testifies from the witness stand and punctuates the occasional lyric within a new language of "docu-poetry." the tenderness of a father's handwritten notes shadows the collection like a ghost, while the treasured, not-for-sale interiority of a Black girl's fountainhead takes over every page. "One yellow gal with an all-black tongue has gone missing." Finney has composed a new Black spiritual, and one of the great voices of our time again stamps her singular sound into the new day.

"Finney's skillful, sweeping epic ambitiously connects personal and public history." —*Publishers Weekly*

Flynn, Nick
The Captain Asks for a Show of Hands: Poems. Nick Flynn. Graywolf Press 2011. 94 pages
ISBN 9781555975746
Grades: Adult   811
1. American poetry 2. Poetry

LC 2010937512

A meditation on love disintegrates into a collage of voices derived from media reports, overheard conversations, childhood memories, and other sources to highlight the storm of noise that permeates society.

Forche, Carolyn
Blue Hour. Carolyn Forche. Perennial 2004. 73 p.
ISBN 9780060099138
Grades: Adult   811
1. American poetry 2. Women authors 3. Poetry

LC Bl2008019681

A volume of poetry by the award-winning author of The Angel of History includes works that demonstrate her use of imagery, application of the elegy form, and considerable moral principles.

Originally published: New York : HarperCollins, 2003.

ESSENTIAL AND RECOMMENDED TITLES
811 American poetry

In the Lateness of the World: Poems. Carolyn Forche. Penguin Press 2020. 77 pages
ISBN 9780525560401
Grades: Adult   811
1. Voyages and travels 2. Life 3. Death 4. Interpersonal relations 5. Poetry
LC 2019037457

Over four decades, Carolyn Forche's visionary work has reinvigorated poetry's power to awaken the reader. Her groundbreaking poems have been testimonies, inquiries, and wonderments. They daringly map a territory where poetry asserts our inexhaustible responsibility to one another. Her first new collection in seventeen years, In the Lateness of the World is a tenebrous book of crossings, of migrations across oceans and borders, but also between the present and the past, life and death. The poems call to the reader from the end of the world where they are sifting through the aftermath of history.

"Throughout her career, Forché has forged poems of witness, and she does so here with beauty and lyricism." —*Library Journal*

Forsythe, Kelly
Perennial. Kelly Forsythe. Coffee House Press 2018. 66 pages
ISBN 9781566895170
Grades: Adult   811
1. American poetry 2. Poetry of places 3. Elegiac poetry 4. Women authors 5. 21st century 6. Poetry
LC 2018000107

The events of 1999's Columbine shooting preoccupy Forsythe in these poems, refracting her vision to encompass killer, victim, and herself as a girl, suddenly aware of the precarity of her own life and the porousness of her body to others' gaze, demands, violence.

"Forsythe's moving catalogue of a horrific event becomes a diagram of senselessness where minutiae take on a stark and eerie resonance when read beside today's headlines." —*Publishers Weekly*

Includes bibliographical references.

Gallagher, Tess
Dear Ghosts,: Poems. Tess Gallagher. Graywolf Press 2006. 140 p.
ISBN 9781555974435
Grades: Adult   811
1. American poetry 2. Poetry
LC 2005938149

Conjures the spirits of the author's deceased parents, Holocaust victims, and others as relevant members of the present, in a volume in which the writer confronts her own illness and mortality while celebrating love and friendship.

A new collection by the author of Moon Crossing Bridge and Amplitude conjures the spirits of the author's deceased parents, holocaust victims, and others as relevant members of the present, in a volume in which the writer confronts her own illness and mortality while celebrating love and friendship.

Is, Is Not: Poems. Tess Gallagher. Graywolf Press 2019. 147 p.
ISBN 9781555978419
Grades: Adult   811
1. Poetry
LC 2018958155

Is, Is Not upends our notions of linear time, evokes the spirit and sanctity of place, and hovers daringly at the threshold of what language can nearly deliver while offering alternative corollaries as gifts of its failures. Tess Gallagher's poems reverberate with the inward clarity of a bell struck on a mountaintop. Guided by humor, grace, and a deep inquiry into the natural world, every poem nudges us toward moments of awe. How else except by delight and velocity would we discover the miracle within the ordinary?

"Readers of quiet, thoughtful poetry will find much to savor." —*Library Journal*

Gander, Forrest
★ *Be With.* Forrest Gander; with six photographs by Michael Flomen. New Directions Publishing Corporation 2018. 92 pages : Illustration
ISBN 9780811226059
Grades: Adult   811
1. John of the Cross, Saint, 1542-1591 2. Death of mothers 3. Mexican-American Border Region 4. Poetry
LC 2018002148

Drawing from his experience as a translator, Forrest Gander includes in the first, powerfully elegiac section a version of a poem by the Spanish mystical poet St. John of the Cross. He continues with a long multilingual poem examining the syncretic geological and cultural history of the U.S. border with Mexico. The poems of the third section—a moving transcription of Gander's efforts to address his mother dying of Alzheimer's—rise from the page like hymns, transforming slowly from reverence to revelation. Gander has been called one of our most formally restless poets, and these new poems express a characteristically tensile energy and, as one critic noted, "the most eclectic diction since Hart Crane."

"In the depths of grief, Gander conceives of a realm more real than life. ... Throughout, he traverses literal and figurative boundaries, probing languages limits in regards to aging, loss, and violence." —*Publishers Weekly*

First published as a New Directions Paperback (NDP1408) — Verso title page; a New Directions Book; Includes bibliographical references (pages 91-92).

Gay, Ross
★ *Catalog of Unabashed Gratitude.* Ross Gay. University of Pittsburgh Press 2015. 102 pages
ISBN 9780822963318
Grades: Adult   811
1. American poetry 2. Poetry
LC 2018276408

National Book Critics Circle Award for Poetry, 2015.

Catalog of Unabashed Gratitude is a sustained meditation on that which goes away—loved ones, the seasons, the earth as we know it—that tries to find solace in the processes of the garden and the orchard.

Geter, Hafizah
Un-American. Hafizah Geter. Wesleyan University Press 2020. 96 p.
ISBN 9780819579805
Grades: Adult   811
1. Immigrants 2. Belonging 3. Racism 4. African Americans 5. Homosexuality 6. Muslims 7. Loss 8. Grief 9. Cultural differences 10. Violence against marginalized people 11. Alienation 12. Poetry
LC 2020022331

Poetry that investigates definitions of belonging in relation to migration, religion, language, and loss, tracing a family history between Nigeria and the United States.

"An eye-opening story of immigration—and of America; for most collections." —*Library Journal*

Gibran, Kahlil
And the Prophet Said: Kahlil Gibran's Classic Text with Newly Discovered Writings. Kahlil Gibran; edited by Dalton Hilu Einhorn; with a foreword by Daniel Ladinsky. Hampton Roads Publishing 2020. xxv, 147 p.
ISBN 9781642970166
Grades: Adult   811
1. Prophets 2. Prophecy 3. Wisdom 4. Immigrants 5. Mysticism 6. Anthologies 7. Classics 8. Poetry
LC 2019052619

Originally published in 1923 by Knopf, The Prophet is a teaching fable that is essentially a little book of life for all people at all times. In it, the author explores all of life's important issues—including love, marriage, the human condition, friendship, prayer, beauty, death, and much more. This edition is especially exciting because of the inclusion of newly discovered material—over 150 Kahlil Gibran poems, aphorisms, and sayings that have never been published.

"A rich collection for all interested in the work and ongoing legacy of Gibran." —*Library Journal*

The Collected Works: With Eighty-Four Illustrations by the Author. Kahlil Gibran. Alfred A. Knopf 2007. VIII, 880 p. : Illustration
ISBN 9780307267078
Grades: 11 12 Adult   811

PUBLIC LIBRARY CORE COLLECTION: NONFICTION
Twentieth Edition

1. Poetry

LC 2007028736

A collection of the major works of the celebrated poet, artist, and mystic features an array of stories, parables, prose poems, and essays that include "The Prophet," "The Wanderer," "Jesus the Son of Man," "Spirits Rebellious," and "The Gardens of the Prophet."

★ *The Prophet.* Kahlil Gibran. Knopf 1995. 105 p.
ISBN 9780679440673
Grades: 11 12 Adult   811
1. Prophets 2. Prophecy 3. Wisdom 4. Immigrants 5. Page to screen 6. Anthologies 7. Poetry

Presents the Lebanese poet and philosopher's inspirational essays on love, marriage, work, joy, sorrow, freedom, pain, teaching, friendship and death.

This book inspired the 2014 animated film The Prophet.

Gilbert, Jack

Collected Poems. Jack Gilbert. Alfred A. Knopf 2012. xviii, 408 p.
ISBN 9780307269683
Grades: Adult   811
1. American poetry 2. Poetry

LC 2011025743

The Pulitzer Prize-nominated author presents a complete collection of his poetry as written over the course of more than 50 years including the periods when he withdrew from the literary world to establish his signature fierce and declarative style, in a volume that also features several previously unpublished works.

Includes indexes.

Gimenez Smith, Carmen

Be Recorder: Poems. Carmen Gimenez Smith. Graywolf Press 2019. 88 p.
ISBN 9781555978488
Grades: Adult   811
1. Self 2. Individuality 3. Signs and symbols 4. Personality 5. Identity 6. Poetry

Offers readers a blazing way forward into an as yet unmade world; investigates the precariousness of personhood; and turns the increasingly pressing urge to cry out into a dream of rebellion—against compromise, against inertia, against self-delusion, and against the ways the media dream up our complacency in an America that depends on it.

Gioia, Dana

99 Poems: New & Selected. Dana Gioia. Graywolf Press 2016. 194 pages
ISBN 9781555977320
Grades: Adult   811
1. American poetry 2. Poetry

LC 2015953592

99 Poems: New & Selected for the first time gathers work from across his career, including a dozen remarkable new poems. Gioia has not ordered this selection chronologically. Instead, his great subjects organize this volume into broad themes of mystery, remembrance, imagination, place, stories, songs, and love. The result is a book we might live our lives alongside, and a reminder of the deep and abiding pleasures and reassurances that poetry provides us.

Includes index.

Giovanni, Nikki

★ *The Collected* Poetry of Nikki Giovanni, 1968-1998. Chronology and notes by Virginia C. Fowler. William Morrow 2003. xliii, 452 p.
ISBN 9780060541330
Grades: Adult   811
1. American poetry 2. Women authors 3. African American women poets 4. African American poetry 5. Poetry

LC 2004302269

An omnibus of early works by the author of the award-winning Blues and Quilting the Black-Eyed Pea features pieces written between 1969 and 1983 and includes the contents of five previously published volumes.

Includes bibliographical references and index.

A Good Cry: What We Learn from Tears and Laughter. Nikki Giovanni. William Morrow 2017. xi, 111 pages
ISBN 9780062399458
Grades: Adult   811
1. American poetry 2. Women authors 3. 21st century 4. African American poetry 5. Poetry 6. Poetry — African American authors

LC 2017275349

A celebrated American poet offers an intimate, affecting and revealing look at her personal history and the mysteries of her own heart, taking us into her confidence as she ruminates on her life and the people who have helped shape her into the woman she has become.

Make Me Rain: Poems & Prose. Nikki Giovanni. William Morrow and Company 2020. 144 p.
ISBN 9780062995285
Grades: Adult   811
1. Racism 2. White nationalism 3. Aging 4. Memories 5. Legacies 6. Childhood 7. African Americans 8. Poetry

In Make Me Rain, Giovanni celebrates her loved ones and unapologetically declares her pride in her Black heritage, while exploring the enduring impact of the twin sins of racism and white nationalism.

"Giovanni's latest collection is her finest to date. Imbued with the classic, accessible, and deeply empathetic style of this venerated American poet, these works touch on topics ranging from aging, memories of childhood, elegies for loved ones who have passed, and pride in Black heritage." —*Booklist*

Quilting the Black-Eyed Pea: Poems and Not Quite Poems. Nikki Giovanni. William Morrow 2002. xii, 110 p.
ISBN 9780060099527
Grades: 11 12 Adult   811
1. African American women 2. Poetry

LC 2002066025

A collection of poems, sketches, and meditations on popular culture and life in America includes the author's writings on her personal battle with illness, the relationships between mothers and their children, the South, and other topics.

Fifty poems, sketches, and meditations on popular culture and life in America include the author's writings on her personal battle with illness, the relationships between mothers and their children, legendary historical figures, the south, terrorism, and her childhood.

Girmay, Aracelis

The Black Maria: Poems. Aracelis Girmay. BOA Editions Ltd. 2016. 120 p.
ISBN 9781942683025
Grades: Adult   811
1. American poetry 2. African American poetry 3. Poetry

LC 2015043256

Taking its name from the moon's dark plains, misidentified as seas by early astronomers, the Black Maria investigates African diasporic histories, the consequences of racism within American culture, and the question of human identity. Central to this project is a desire to recognize the lives of Eritrean refugees who have been made invisible by years of immigration crisis, refugee status, exile, and resulting statelessness.

Gluck, Louise

Averno. Louise Gluck. Farrar, Straus and Giroux 2006. VIII, 79 p.
ISBN 9780374107420
Grades: Adult   811
1. Persephone (Greek deity) 2. American poetry 3. Women authors 4. Poetry

LC 2005042658

A collection of works by the Pulitzer Prize and National Book Critics Circle Award-winning writer takes its inspiration from a small crater lake in southern It-

ESSENTIAL AND RECOMMENDED TITLES
811 American poetry

aly and is an extended lamentation that evaluates Averno's existence in a winter landscape and role as a doorway between worlds.

★ *Poems 1962-2012.* Louise Gluck. Ecco Press 2012. xvii, 634 p.
ISBN 9780374126087
Grades: Adult 811
1. American poetry 2. Poetry
LC 2011051349

The collected works of the Pulitzer Prize and National Book Critics Circle Award-winning writer explores her transfigured landscapes and offers insight into her unique form created to reflect the human drive to release the past in order to realize the yet-unimagined.
Includes index.

Winter Recipes from the Collective: Poems. Louise Glück. Farrar, Straus and Giroux 2021. 80 p.
ISBN 9780374604103
Grades: Adult 811
1. Aging 2. Loss 3. Mortality 4. Memory 5. Poetry
LC 2021021485

The 2020 Nobel Prize winner's haunting new book is the voice containing all of our lifetimes—all the worlds, each more beautiful than the last.
"In her first new collection since being awarded the Nobel Prize for Literature in 2020, Gluck returns to themes of mortality and nature; she also addresses ageing.... The Nobel committee praised the 'austere beauty' of Gluck's poems; this marvelous collection adds warmth and wit." —*Booklist*

Gorman, Amanda

★ *Call Us What We Carry: Poems.* Amanda Gorman. Viking 2021. 80 p.
ISBN 9780593465066
Grades: Adult 811
1. Freedom 2. Identity 3. Grief 4. Pain 5. Memory 6. Hope 7. Poetry
Loan Stars Favourites, 2021.

The presidential inaugural poet—and unforgettable new voice in American poetry—presents a collection of poems that includes the stirring poem read at the inauguration of the 46th President of the United States.
"Poems for teenagers and adults that cast a scrutinizing eye on United States history and current events while being hopeful about the future.... The collection overflows with teachable moments you can imagine quoted at graduation ceremonies and special events for years to come." —*Kirkus*

Graham, Jorie

The Dream of the Unified Field: Selected Poems 1974-1994. Jorie Graham. Ecco Press 1995. 199 p.
ISBN 9780880014380
Grades: Adult 811
1. American poetry 2. Women authors 3. 20th century 4. Poetry
LC 95016572

A major collection of poetry brings together works from the poet's first five works: Hybrids of Plants and Ghosts, Erosion, The End of Beauty, Region of Unlikeness, and Materialism.
"Combining great vision like Blake's, a Dickinsonian philosophical introspection, and a richly modern sensuality, this selection demonstrates the full range of Graham's poetic gifts." —*Booklist*

Fast. Jorie Graham. ECCO 2017. 84 pages
ISBN 9780062663481
Grades: Adult 811
1. American poetry 2. Women authors 3. 21st century 4. Poetry
LC 2017299626

In her first new collection in five years—her most exhilarating, personal, and formally inventive to date—Graham explores the limits of the human and the uneasy seductions of the post-human. Conjuring an array of voices and perspectives—from bots, to the holy shroud, to the ocean floor, to a medium transmitting from beyond the grave—these poems give urgent form to the ever-increasing pace of transformation of our planet and ourselves. As it navigates cyber life, 3D-printed "life," life after death, biologically, chemically, and electronically modified life, Fast lights up the border of our new condition as individuals and as a species on the brink—Book jacket.

From the New World: Poems, 1976-2014. Jorie Graham. Ecco 2015. 359 pages
ISBN 9780062315403
Grades: Adult 811
1. Poetry of places 2. Nature 3. American poetry 4. Women authors 5. Poetry
LC Bl2015005706

Offers poems selected from almost forty years of the author's works, as well as several new and revised poems, touching on a broad variety of topics explored during her career.

Overlord: Poems. Jorie Graham. Ecco 2005. xii, 93 p.
ISBN 9780060745653
Grades: Adult 811
1. American poetry 2. Women authors 3. Poetry
LC 2004053681

A collection of the Pulitzer Prize-winning writer's most personal and passionate works considers such themes as the meaning of being fully present in a human life, one's vulnerability to mortal and transcendent forces, and the human capacity for being oneself. By the author of The Dream of the Unified Field.

To 2040. Jorie Graham. Copper Canyon Press 2023. 80 p.
ISBN 9781556596773
Grades: Adult 811
1. Nature 2. Climate change 3. Loss 4. Mortality 5. Forecasting 6. Poetry
LC 2022045410

A collection of poems by Jorie Graham.
"Pulitzer Prize winner Graham's 15th collection is perhaps her finest and most profound work yet, revealing such astonishing individuality in the idiosyncratic, elliptical style she has perfected over more than 40 years that fellow poets may feel tempted to throw up their hands in despair." —*Library Journal*

greathouse, torrin a

Wound from the Mouth of a Wound: Poems. Torrin a. greathouse. Milkweed Editions 2021. 96 p.
ISBN 9781571315274
Grades: Adult 811
1. Gender identity 2. Disabilities 3. Transgenderism 4. Vulnerability 5. Strength and weakness 6. Poetry 7. Debut title
LC 2020028619

Wound from the Mouth of the Wound was selected by Aimee Nezhukumatathil as the winner of the 2020 Ballard Spahr Prize for Poetry.
"The glittering, energetic debut from greathouse seeks to honor and give voices to all bodies." —*Publishers Weekly*

H. D.

Collected Poems, 1912-1944. H.D; edited by Louis L. Martz. New Directions Book 1986. xxxvi, 629 p.
ISBN 9780811209717
Grades: 11 12 Adult 811
1. Poetry
LC BL 99958483

Gathers poems from each period of Hilda Doolittle's career and includes background information on her major works.
"The editor's textual notes offer valuable and illuminating scholarly commentary and present the most important of the textual variants. An informative and sensitively written introduction discusses aspects of the interpenetration of H.D.'s biography with her poetic sensibility. This volume is an impressive scholarly work." —*Choice*
Includes bibliographical references and index; Previously published: 1983.

Hacker, Marilyn

Selected Poems, 1965-1990: 1965-1990. Marilyn Hacker. W.W. Norton 1994. xii, 250 p.
ISBN 9780393036756

Grades: Adult **811**
1. Lesbians 2. Mothers and daughters 3. Women 4. African American poetry 5. Poetry
LC 94027507

Poems from five previous collections deal with feminism, politics, and human sexuality.

"Few poets have been as successful as Hacker in negotiating the boundary of the feminist and lesbian canon while generating a buzz around their early work. Iambic and readable, the pieces in Selected Poems—taken from five previous volumes use unique inversions to explore self and other through changing situations between friends, lovers, family, and one's surroundings. Often, these are poems of loss, of desire delayed, of pleasure deferred." —Library Journal
Includes index.

*A **Stranger's** Mirror: New and Selected Poems, 1994-2014.* Marilyn Hacker. W. W. Norton & Company 2015. xiv, 288 pages
ISBN 9780393244649
Grades: Adult **811**
1. American poetry 2. Women authors 3. Poetry
LC 2014037031

Draws on two decades of poetry by the author in a collection of twenty-five pieces that span different forms to explore international dilemmas while engaging poets from different ages.
Includes index.

Hall, Donald
*The **Back** Chamber.* Donald Hall. Houghton Mifflin Harcourt 2011. 82 p.
ISBN 9780547645858
Grades: Adult **811**
1. American poetry 2. Poetry
LC 2011009152

The first full-length volume of poems in a decade by former poet laureate of the United States Donald Hall.

*The **Selected** Poems of Donald Hall.* Donald Hall. Houghton Mifflin Harcourt 2015. x, 148 pages
ISBN 9780544555600
Grades: Adult **811**
1. American poetry 2. Elegiac poetry 3. Poetry
LC 2015004341

A collection of signature works by the former poet laureate reflects the evolution of his literary career and shares insight into his use of humor, eros and engaging simple language. By the author of White Apples and The Taste of Stone.

White Apples and the Taste of Stone: Selected Poems, 1946-2006. Donald Hall. Houghton Mifflin Co. 2007. xv, 431 p.
ISBN 9780618919994
Grades: Adult **811**
1. American poetry 2. Poetry
LC Bl2007029407

Spanning the entire career of the celebrated American poet, a collection of 226 works represents sixty years of poetic endeavor, including recent poems that appeared in the New Yorker, as well as verses from Without and a CD containing readings by the author.
A Mariner book; Reprint. Originally published: 2006.

Hardwick, Elizabeth
*The **Dolphin** Letters, 1970-1979: Elizabeth Hardwick, Robert Lowell and Their Circle.* Edited by Saskia Hamilton. Farrar, Straus and Giroux 2019. 560 pages
ISBN 9780374141264
Grades: Adult **811**
1. Hardwick, Elizabeth 2. Lowell, Robert, 1917-1977 3. Bishop, Elizabeth, 1911-1979 4. Blackwood, Caroline 5. McCarthy, Mary, 1912-1989 6. Rich, Adrienne, 1929-2012 7. Poets 8. Authors 9. Letter writing 10. Marital conflict 11. Friendship 12. Intellectuals 13. Art 14. Interpersonal relations 15. Letters 16. Life stories — Arts and culture — Writing — Poets 17. Life stories — Arts and culture — Writing — Authors 18. Arts and Entertainment — Writing and Publishing 19. Life stories — Relationships — Couples
LC 2019016287

Collects correspondence between the famous literary couple and their circle of friends—including Elizabeth Bishop, Mary McCarthy and Adrienne Rich—during a time of personal crisis and the creation of Lowell's controversial poem The Dolphin.
Includes bibliographical references and index.

Harjo, Joy
*An **American** Sunrise: Poems.* Joy Harjo. W. W. Norton & Company 2019. xiii, 116 pages : Map
ISBN 9781324003861
Grades: Adult **811**
1. Creek (Muskogee) (North American people) 2. Indigenous peoples of North America — History 3. Poetry
LC 2019021562

"Newly named poet laureate and Ruth Lilly prize-winner Harjo (Conflict Resolution for Holy Beings) intertwines verse with prose vignettes, oral histories, and flash memoirs in this expressive and generous book." —Publishers Weekly

*A **Map** to the Next World: Poetry and Tales.* Joy Harjo. W.W. Norton 2001. 137 p.
ISBN 9780393320961
Grades: Adult **811**
1. American poetry 2. Women authors 3. Poetry — Native American authors 4. Poetry
LC Bl2010034450

The poet draws on her own Native American heritage in a collection of lyrical poetry that explores the cruelties and tragedies of history and the redeeming miracles of human kindness.

The poet author of The Woman Who Fell from the Sky draws on her own Native American heritage in a collection of lyrical poetry that explores the cruelties and tragedies of history and the redeeming miracles of human kindness.

Harrison, Jim
*The **Essential** Poems of Jim Harrison: The Essential Poems.* Edited by Joseph Bednarik. Copper Canyon Press 2019. 200 p.
ISBN 9781556595288
Grades: Adult **811**
1. Poetry
LC 2018049116

The Essential Poems of Jim Harrison is distilled from nearly 1,000 poems that appeared in fourteen volumes—from visionary lyrics and meditative suites to shape-shifting ghazals and prose-poem letters. Teeming throughout these pages are Harrison's legendary passions and appetites, his meditations, rages, and love-songs to the natural world. The New York Times concluded a review from early in Harrison's career with a provocative quote: 'This is poetry worth loving, hating, and fighting over, a subjectivemirror of our American days and needs.' That sentiment still holds true, as Jim Harrison's essential poems continue to call for our fiercest attention.

"Reading this essential volume, one might imagine that the gods are, indeed, staying up late, reading lights on, turning the pages." —Booklist
Includes indexes.

Songs of Unreason. Jim Harrison. Copper Canyon Press 2011. xi, 143 p.
ISBN 9781556593895
Grades: Adult **811**
1. American poetry 2. Poetry
LC 2011025560

Jim Harrison's compelling and provocative Songs of Unreason explores what it means to inhabit the world in atavistic, primitive, and totemistic ways.

"Most readers of contemporary poetry will enjoy this work." —Library Journal

ESSENTIAL AND RECOMMENDED TITLES
811 American poetry

Harrison, Leslie
The Book of Endings. Leslie Harrison. The University of Akron Press 2017. 88 pages
ISBN 9781629220628
Grades: Adult   811
1. Elegiac poetry 2. American poetry 3. Women authors 4. Poetry
LC 2016026149

The poems in The Book of Endings try to make sense of, or at least come to some kind of reckoning with absence—the death of the author's mother, the absence of the beloved, the absence of an accountable god, cicadas, the dead stars arriving, the dead moon aglow in the night sky.

"Harrison (Displacement) reveals a psyche made strange through grieving in this luminous and musical collection. Here, the self is seen as other, an art object to behold at some degree of remove." —*Publishers Weekly*

Includes bibliographical references (pages 87-88).

Hass, Robert
The Apple Trees at Olema: New and Selected Poems. Robert Hass. Ecco 2010. xv, 352 p.
ISBN 9780061923821
Grades: Adult   811
1. American poetry 2. Poetry
LC 2010281516

From the National Book Award-winning author of Time and Materials comes 20 new and selected poems, grounded in the beauty of the physical world, in the smaller details of natural, human life.

Hayden, Robert
Collected Poems. Robert Hayden; edited by Frederick Glaysher. Liveright 1996. xxxiv, 205 p.
ISBN 9780871401595
Grades: Adult   811
1. American poetry 2. African American poetry 3. Poetry
LC 96142645

Enhanced by a biographical portrait and a critical analysis of Hayden's poetry, an anthology featuring the work of one of the most important African-American poets of the twentieth century contemplates the Black experience and deals with such themes as dreams, mortality, nature, travel, and memory.

Includes bibliographical references (p. 197) and indexes; Originally published: New York : Liveright, c1985. With a new introduction by Arnold Rampersad.

Hayes, Terrance
★ *American Sonnets for My Past and Future Assassin.* Terrance Hayes. Penguin Poets 2018. 91 pages
ISBN 9780143133186
Grades: Adult   811
1. American poetry 2. 21st century 3. Poetry
Hurston/Wright Legacy Award: Poetry, 2019; ALA Notable Book, 2019.

One of America's most acclaimed poets presents 70 poems bearing the same title that, written during the first 200 days of the Trump presidency, are haunted by the country's past and future eras and errors, its dreams and nightmares.

How to Be Drawn. Terrance Hayes. Penguin Books 2015. IX, 99 pages
ISBN 9780143126881
Grades: Adult   811
1. American poetry 2. 21st century 3. African American poetry 4. Poetry
LC 2014045785

"Hayes writes far-reaching yet intimate monologues that are simultaneously subtle and hard-hitting; he unearths shards of shameful antebellum history and takes measure of the current state of moral and political paralysis." —*Booklist*

★ *Lighthead.* Terrance Hayes. Penguin Books 2010. IX, 95 p.
ISBN 9780143116967
Grades: Adult   811
1. American poetry 2. 21st century 3. African American poetry 4. Poetry
LC 2009053319

Investigates through verse how humans construct experience and combines the loftiness of dreams and the reality of everyday life into poetry that is both dark and buoyant.

"This collection is a celebration and castigation of American culture, one worthy of the term Americanist. The title references the light of inspiration and the fire that pours from the heads of two teenage lynching victims in one of the opening poems. The fact that the title can do both inspiration and elegy is indicative of how meaning is contested terrain in Hayes' work. [He] deftly quilts together different textures of language. Rants move into love poems and biting humor butts up against meditations. Sound is of primary importance to Mr. Hayes. Throughout the book he borrows from hip-hop, jazz, slang, lists, and T-shirt slogans. Content aside, his poems are full of pure pleasure of sound in his startling and sonically dense images." —*Pittsburgh Post-Gazette*

So to Speak. Terrance Hayes. Penguin Books 2023. 112 p. (Penguin poets)
ISBN 9780143137726
Grades: Adult   811
1. Thought and thinking 2. Fatherhood 3. African Americans 4. African American poetry 5. Poetry
LC 2022055375

In this seventh collection from the 2010 National Book Award winner, the author maps the strange and lyrical grammar of thinking and feeling while exploring themes of fatherhood, history and longing with remarkable openness and humanity.

"Across three various and virtuosic sections, Hayes (American Sonnets for My Past and Future Assassin) examines the personal and public, from fatherhood to the murder of George Floyd, in his muscular and meditative seventh collection." —*Publishers Weekly*

Herrera, Juan Felipe
Every Day We Get More Illegal. Juan Felipe Herrera. City Lights Books 2020. 77 p.
ISBN 9780872868281
Grades: Adult   811
1. Immigrants 2. Political culture 3. Identity 4. United States 5. Poetry
LC 2019056674

In this collection of poems, written during and immediately after two years on the road as United States Poet Laureate, Juan Felipe Herrera reports back on his travels through contemporary America. Poems written in the heat of witness, and later, in quiet moments of reflection, coalesce into an urgent, trenchant, and yet hope-filled portrait. The struggle and pain of those pushed to the edges, the shootings and assaults and injustices of our streets, the lethal border game that separates and divides, and then: a shift of register, a leap for peace and a view onto the possibility of unity. Every Day We Get More Illegal is a jolt to the conscience-filled with the multiple powers of the many voices and many textures of every day in America.

"The author of more than 20 titles, including many recent books for young readers, Herrera returns to his poetic roots for another captivating entry in his wide oeuvre." —*Booklist*

Hill, DaMaris B.
Breath Better Spent: Living Black Girlhood. DaMaris B. Hill. Bloomsbury 2022. 192 p.
ISBN 9781635576474
Grades: Adult   811
1. African American women 2. Childhood 3. Violence against African americans 4. Psychic trauma 5. African American children 6. Girls 7. Race relations 8. United States 9. Poetry
LC 2021044376

From the award-winning and critically acclaimed author of A Bound Woman Is a Dangerous Thing comes a new book of narrative in verse that takes a personal and historical look at the experience of Black girlhood. In the American imagination the contrasts between visibility and invisibility for Black girlhood are glaring. A recent report by the African American Policy Forum states that while Black girls make up only 16% of the female students in schools, they make up half of school-related arrests, and further studies show that Black girls are the fastest growing population in the juvenile justice system. And when Black girls are not viewed as criminal, their visibility seems to be eroding or disappearing. Through the eyes and stories of prominent Black female figures from Zora Neale Hurston to Riley Curry and Michelle Obama, and with an homage to Toni Morrison's Beloved, Breath Better Spent beautifully and trenchantly captures the culture of Black girlhood and its changing relationship to American culture, exploring the highly visible and invisible spaces that Black girls occupy, from school, to home, to others' imaginations, and proceeds to question the disappearance—metaphorically and literally—of Black girls from the American imagination. Powerfully drawing on both history and her own experiences, Hill brings to life the vitality, creativity, and strength of Black girlhood while shining a light on a crisis we cannot ignore.

"Poems and essays on Black girlhood, as seen through the lens of the author's personal experiences and reflections.... The book is validating in its intentions and may be useful in further study of the complexities and traumas of being Black in America." —*Kirkus*

Hirsch, Edward

Gabriel: A Poem. Edward Hirsch. Alfred A. Knopf 2014. 78 p.
ISBN 9780385353571
Grades: Adult   811
1. Children 2. Grief 3. American poetry 4. Poetry
LC 2013049301

A poignant volume of works inspired by the author's son's tragic early death reflects on the young man's boisterous youth, his rebellious early adulthood, and the author's experiences of grief.

The Living Fire: New and Selected Poems, 1975-2010. Edward Hirsch. Alfred A. Knopf 2010. xii, 237 p.
ISBN 9780375415227
Grades: Adult   811
1. American poetry 2. Poetry
LC 2009024452

A volume of more than 100 definitive and original pieces by the National Book Critics Circle Award-winning writer includes poems that critically assess his own works and explore such topics as insomnia, culture and the arts.

Special Orders: Poems. Edward Hirsch. Alfred A. Knopf 2008. VIII, 64 p.
ISBN 9780307266811
Grades: Adult   811
1. American poetry 2. Poetry
LC 2007040336

A new, deeply personal anthology of poetry by the award-winning author of Wild Gratitude and Earthly Measures provides a profound, often painful, self-examination in such works as "Self-Portrait," "The Sweetness," and "I Wish I Could Paint You."

Stranger by Night: Poems. Edward Hirsch. Alfred A. Knopf 2020. 62 pages
ISBN 9780525657781
Grades: Adult   811
1. American poetry 2. Elegiac poetry 3. Poetry of places 4. Poetry
LC 2019022482

Prose that reflects on the distinctly beautiful moments in life and also acts as a lamentation for the dead appears side by side in this new collection of poems from the prolific and award-winning poet and MacArthur Fellow.

Hirshfield, Jane

After: Poems. Jane Hirshfield. HarperCollins 2006. 97 p.
ISBN 9780060779160
Grades: Adult   811
1. American poetry 2. Poetry
LC 2005050260

Collects poetry that explores such diverse topics as global warming, sneezing, and our relationship to certainty, possibility, judgment, and grief, while reflecting on the influence of time on human life.

The Beauty: Poems. Jane Hirshfield. Alfred A. Knopf 2015. 107 pages
ISBN 9780385351072
Grades: Adult   811

1. American poetry 2. Women authors 3. Poetry
LC 2014025831

A collection of original poems by Jane Hirshfield exploring the profundities and quirks of existence.

This is a Borzoi Book—Title page verso.

Ledger: Poems. Jane Hirshfield. Alfred A. Knopf 2020. 128 p.
ISBN 9780525657804
Grades: Adult   811
1. Social responsibility 2. Environmentalism 3. Poetry
LC 2019022480

The internationally renowned power named "among the modern masters," in this book of personal, ecological and political reckoning, shares a collection of indispensable poems that are tuned toward issues of consequence to all who share this world's current and future fate.

"In her ninth book of poetry, Hirshfield, avidly read and justly celebrated with numerous prestigious awards, seeks to balance what we take with what we give, what we seek with what we find, what we observe with what we comprehend." —*Booklist*

Hoagland, Tony

Priest Turned Therapist Treats Fear of God: Poems. Tony Hoagland. Graywolf Press 2018. 74 p.
ISBN 9781555978075
Grades: Adult   811
1. American poetry 2. 20th century 3. Poetry
LC 2017953461

Tony Hoagland's poems interrogate human nature and contemporary culture with an intimate and wild urgency, located somewhere between outrage, stand-up comedy, and grief. His new poems are no less observant of the human and the worldly, no less skeptical, and no less amusing, but they have drifted toward the greater depths of open emotion. Over six collections, Hoagland's poetry has gotten bigger, more tender, and more encompassing. The poems in Priest Turned Therapist Treats Fear of God turn his clear-eyed vision toward the hidden spaces—and spaciousness—in the human predicament.

Unincorporated Persons in the Late Honda Dynasty: Poems. Tony Hoagland. Graywolf Press 2010. 90 p.
ISBN 9781555975494
Grades: Adult   811
1. American poetry 2. Poetry
LC 2009933818

"Hoagland (What Narcissism Means to Me) has fun in these poems but always in service to a smart and insightful notion." —*Library Journal*

Hong, Cathy Park

Engine Empire. Cathy Park Hong. W.W. Norton & Co. 2012. 95 p.
ISBN 9780393082845
Grades: Adult   811
1. Poetry — Asian American authors 2. Poetry
LC 2012000596

A trilogy of three interconnected poems addresses prosperity in a nineteenth-century California mining town, present-day Shenzhen, China, and the far future.

Poems.

Howe, Fanny

Second Childhood. Fanny Howe. Graywolf Press 2014. 77 pages
ISBN 9781555976828
Grades: Adult   811
1. American poetry 2. Poetry
LC 2013958013

"Recipient of the 2009 Ruth Lilly Poetry Prize for lifetime achievement, Howe (Come and See) is masterfully lyrical in her newest collection, one marbled throughout with musings over identity." —*Publishers Weekly*

ESSENTIAL AND RECOMMENDED TITLES
811 American poetry

Hughes, Langston
★ *Selected* Poems of Langston Hughes. Langston Hughes. Vintage Books 1990. 297 p; (Vintage classics)
ISBN 9780679728184
Grades: Adult   811
1. American poetry 2. African American poetry 3. Poetry — African American authors
LC 90050179
A collection of the author's favorite poetry from published books, private publications, and unpublished manuscripts.

Hutchinson, Ishion
House of Lords and Commons. Ishion Hutchinson. Farrar, Straus and Giroux 2016. 81 p.
ISBN 9780374173029
Grades: Adult   811
1. American poetry 2. Poetry — African American authors 3. Poetry
LC 2015045801
A stunning collection that traverses the borders of culture and time.

Jackson, Major
Razzle Dazzle: New and Selected Poems 2002-2022. Major Jackson. W W Norton & CO Inc 2023. 266 p.
ISBN 9781324064909
Grades: Adult   811
1. Perspective 2. Social conflict 3. Social justice 4. Race relations 5. Dignity 6. African American poetry 7. Anthologies 8. Poetry

Equally attuned to sensuous connection, metaphysical inquiries, the natural world, and ever-changing urban landscapes, Jackson possesses a sensibility at once global and personal, driven by an enduring conviction in the possibilities of art and language to mark our lives with meaning. Whether addressing racial conflict and the ongoing struggle for human dignity in America, bearing witness to the plight of refugees, or grieving the contradictory nature of humankind, these dexterous poems proclaim the remarkable power of renewal, justice, and accountability.

"This welcome gathering of new and selected poems honors Jackson's generous poetic imagination. Beginning with a selection of new poems, the collection primarily highlights Jackson's five previous books (The Absurd Man being the most recent)." —*Publishers Weekly*

Jarrell, Randall
★ *The* Complete Poems. Randall Jarrell. Farrar, Strauss & Giroux 1981. xvi, 507 pages
ISBN 9780374513054
Grades: 11 12 Adult   811
1. American poetry 2. 20th century 3. Poetry
LC Bl2013032386
A definitive anthology represents four decades of writing and includes new poems and previously published ones.
Originally published: 1969.

Jeffers, Honorée Fanonne
The Age of Phillis. Honorée Fanonne Jeffers. Wesleyan University Press 2020. 213 p. (Wesleyan Poetry)
ISBN 9780819579492
Grades: Adult   811
1. Wheatley, Phillis, 1753-1784 2. African American women authors 3. Enslaved women 4. Slavery 5. United States history 6. Massachusetts 7. 18th century 8. Poetry
LC 2019040204
A collection of original poems speaking to the life and times of Phillis Wheatley, a Colonial America-era poet brought to Boston as a slave.
"A true and rounded life, told in elegant, sometimes ravishing verse." —*Library Journal*
Includes bibliographical references.

Jeffers, Robinson
The Selected Poetry of Robinson Jeffers. Edited by Tim Hunt. Stanford University Press 2001. 758 p. : Portrait
ISBN 9780804741088
Grades: Adult   811
1. American poetry 2. Poetry
LC 00048490
To accompany his five-volume collected poetry of the American poet, to be completed this year, Hunt (English, Washington State U.) offers a one-volume selection.
"A volume for the core of American literature collections." —*Booklist*
Includes indexes.

Johnson, James Weldon
Complete Poems. James Weldon Johnson; edited with an introduction by Sondra Kathryn Wilson. Penguin Books 2000. xxxiii, 202 p.
ISBN 9780141185453
Grades: Adult   811
1. African Americans 2. American poetry 3. African American poetry 4. Poetry 5. Poetry — African American authors
LC 00039969
The important African-American poet's complete works are collected here in the centenary year of "Lift Every Voice and Sing," his most important work.
Includes bibliographical references (p. xxiii-xxvii); Works by James Weldon Johnson: P. xxiii.

Jones, Saeed
Alive at the End of the World: Poems. Saeed Jones; foreword by D. A. Powell. Coffeehouse Press 2022. 104 p.
ISBN 9781566896511
Grades: Adult   811
1. African Americans 2. Everyday life 3. End of the world 4. Grief 5. Pain 6. Collective memory 7. Psychic trauma 8. Racism 9. Environmental degradation 10. Threat (Psychology) 11. United States 12. Poetry

In haunted poems glinting with laughter, Saeed Jones explores the public and private betrayals of life as we know it. With verve, wit, and elegant craft, Jones strips away American artifice in order to reveal the intimate grief of a mourning son and the collective grief bearing down on all of us. Drawing from memoir, fiction, and persona, Jones confronts the everyday perils of white supremacy with a finely tuned poetic ear, identifying moments that seem routine even as they open chasms of hurt.

"In his bristling second poetry collection, Jones focuses on simmering tensions in American society and returns to his relationship with his deceased mother and his identity as a gay Black man, themes he explored in his widely acclaimed memoir, How We Fight for Our Lives (2019)." —*Booklist*

Prelude to Bruise: Poetry. Saeed Jones. Coffee House Press 2014. xii, 103 pages
ISBN 9781566893749
Grades: Adult   811
1. American poetry 2. Romantic love 3. African American poetry 4. Poetry — LGBTQIA 5. Poetry
LC 2014008086
Offers a collection of poems that explore questions of masculinity, sexuality, race, and shifting identity.

Jordan, June
★ *The Essential* June Jordan. Edited by Jan Heller Levi and Christoph Keller; afterword by Jericho Brown. Copper Canyon Press 2021. 256 p.
ISBN 9781556596209
Grades: Adult   811
1. Human behavior 2. Violence 3. Colonialism 4. Police brutality 5. Racism 6. Empathy 7. Love 8. Poetry
LC 2020053902
The Essential June Jordan honors the enduring legacy of a poet fiercely dedicated to building a better world. In this definitive volume, introduced by Pulitzer

Prize winner Jericho Brown, June Jordan's generous body of poetry is distilled and curated to represent the very best of her works. Written over the span of several decades—from Some Changes in 1971 to Last Poems in 2001—Jordan's poems are at once of their era and tragically current, with subject matter including racist police brutality, violence against women, and the opportunity for global solidarity amongst people who are marginalized or outside of the norm.

"Wide in scope and singular in their articulation of atrocities, Jordan's poems shine in this thoughtfully curated volume." —*Publishers Weekly*

Kaminsky, Ilya
★ *Deaf Republic: Poems*. Ilya Kaminsky. Graywolf Press 2019. 96 pages
ISBN 9781555978310
Grades: Adult　　　　　　　　　　　　　　　　　811
1. Resistance to government 2. Deafness 3. Sign language 4. Political violence 5. Child murders 6. Military occupation 7. Poetry
LC 2018947088
ALA Notable Book, 2020; Library Journal Best Books, 2019; New York Times Notable Book, 2019.

Deaf Republic opens in an occupied country in a time of political unrest. When soldiers breaking up a protest kill a deaf boy, Petya, the gunshot becomes the last thing the citizens hear—they all have gone deaf, and their dissent becomes coordinated by sign language. The story follows the private lives of townspeople encircled by public violence. At once a love story, an elegy, and an urgent plea, these poems confronts our time's vicious atrocities and our collective silence in the face of them.

Karr, Mary
Tropic of Squalor: Poems. Mary Karr. Harper, an imprint of HarperCollins Publishers 2018. xiv, 75 pages
ISBN 9780062699824
Grades: Adult　　　　　　　　　　　　　　　　　811
1. American poetry 2. Women authors 3. Religious poetry 4. Poetry
LC 2017279116

Long before she earned accolades for her genre-defining memoirs, Mary Karr was winning poetry prizes. Now the beloved author returns with a collection of bracing poems as visceral, deeply felt, and hilarious as her memoirs. In Tropic of Squalor, Karr dares to address the numinous—that mystery some of us hope toward in secret, or maybe dare to pray to. The "squalor" of meaninglessness that every thoughtful person wrestles with sits at the core of human suffering, and Karr renders it with power—illness, death, love's agonized disappointments. Her brazen verse calls us out of our psychic swamplands and into that hard-won awareness of the divine hiding in the small moments that make us human. In a single poem she can generate tears, horror, empathy, laughter, and peace. She never preaches. But whether you're an adamant atheist, a pilgrim, or skeptically curious, these poems will urge you to find an inner light in the most baffling hours of darkness.

The New York Times best-selling author of The Liar's Club and Lit presents a collection of bracing poems as primitive and raw and hilarious as her memoirs that urges readers to find an inner light in the most inexplicable hours of darkness.

Kasischke, Laura
Space, in Chains. Laura Kasischke. Copper Canyon Press 2011. xi, 113 p.
ISBN 9781556593338
Grades: Adult　　　　　　　　　　　　　　　　　811
1. American poetry 2. 21st century 3. Poetry
LC 2010040037

Space, in Chains speaks in ghostly voices, fractured narratives, songs, prayers, and dark riddles as it moves through contemporary tragedies of grief and the complex succession of generations. In her eighth book of poetry, Laura Kasischke has pared theconstruction of her verse to its bones, leaving haunting language and a visceral strangeness of imagery. by turns mournful and celebratory, Kasischke's poetry insists upon asking hard questions that are courageously left unanswered.

Kaur, Rupi
Milk and Honey. Rupi Kaur. Andrews McMeel Publishing 2015. 208 p.
ISBN 9781449496364
Grades: Adult　　　　　　　　　　　　　　　　　811
1. Psychological growth 2. Coping 3. Self-fulfillment 4. Canadian literature 5. Poetry
LC Bl2018181271

Presents poems that deal with the bitter aspects of love, loss, abuse, violence, and trauma, and celebrates the unstoppable power of grace, healing, and feminine strength.

Kearney, Douglas
Sho. Douglas Kearney. Wave Books 2021. 88 pages
ISBN 9781950268160
Grades: Adult　　　　　　　　　　　　　　　　　811
1. Poetry
LC 2020038258
Finalist for the Hurston/Wright Legacy Awards for Poetry, 2022.

An experiment and experience in language, surveying the junction of violence, entertainment, race, and folklore.

Keene, John
★ *Punks: New & Selected Poems*. John Keene. The Song Cave 2021. x, 215 pages : Illustration
ISBN 9781737277521
Grades: Adult　　　　　　　　　　　　　　　　　811
1. African Americans 2. AIDS (Disease) 3. Gay men 4. American poetry 5. United States 6. 21st century 7. African American poetry 8. Poetry
LC Bl2023005362

A generous treasury in seven sections that spans decades and includes previously unpublished and brand-new work. With depth and breadth, Punks weaves together historic narratives of loss, lust, and love. The many voices that emerge in these poems—from historic Black personalities, both familial and famous, to the poet's friends and lovers in gay bars and bedrooms—form a cast of characters capable of addressing desire, oppression, AIDS, and grief through sorrowful songs that 'we sing as hard as we live.'.

Kelly, Donika
The Renunciations: Poems. Donika Kelly. Graywolf Press 2021. 72 p.
ISBN 9781644450536
Grades: Adult　　　　　　　　　　　　　　　　　811
1. Resilience 2. Families 3. Childhood 4. Child abuse 5. Psychic trauma 6. Healing 7. Marriage 8. Survival 9. Memory 10. Poetry 11. Book club best bets

A book of resilience, survival, and the journey to radically shift one's sense of self in the face of trauma. Moving between a childhood marked by love and abuse and the breaking marriage of that adult child, Donika Kelly charts memory and the body as landscapes to be traversed and tended. These poems construct life rafts and sanctuaries even in their most devastating confrontations with what a person can bear, with how families harm themselves.

"Kelly (Bestiary) explores in her powerful latest the tenuous line between desire and trauma in poems that ache with memory and revelation." —*Publishers Weekly*

Kendall, Tim
The Art of Robert Frost. Tim Kendall. Yale University Press 2012. xvi, 392 p.
ISBN 9780300118131
Grades: Adult　　　　　　　　　　　　　　　　　811
1. American poetry 2. Arts and Entertainment — Writing and Publishing — Literary criticism 3. Poetry
LC 2011041416

Offers detailed accounts of sixty-five poems that span Frost's writing career and assesses the particular nature of the poet's style, discussing how it changes over time and relates to the works of contemporary poets and movements.

Includes the entirety of Frost's North of Boston (1914); selections from a boy's will (1913); generous selections from Mountain Interval (1916) and New Hampshire (1923); and a selection of lyrics in the section titled Later poems,

ESSENTIAL AND RECOMMENDED TITLES
811 American poetry

from West-running brook(1928), a further range (1936), a witness tree (1942), and Steeple bush (1947); Includes bibliographical references (p. 385-388) and index.

Kenner, Hugh
The Pound Era. Hugh Kenner. University of California Press 1973. xiv, 606 p. : Illustration
ISBN 9780520024274
Grades: Adult   811
1. Pound, Ezra, 1885-1972 2. Arts and Entertainment — Writing and Publishing — Literary criticism
LC BL 00003890

Hugh Kenner's The Pound Era could as well be known as the Kenner era, for there is no critic who has more firmly established his claim to valuable literary property than has Kenner to the first three decades of the 20th century in England.

Reprint. Originally published: 1971; Includes bibliographical references (p. 563-591) and index.

Kerouac, Jack
Book of Blues. Jack Kerouac; [introduction by Robert Creeley]. Penguin 1995. xiii, 273 p.
ISBN 9780140587005
Grades: Adult   811
1. American poetry 2. Poetry
LC 94045902

"Like all of Kerouac's work, these choruses live or die with the poet's enthusiasm, sometimes sunk in navel-gazing, sometimes stunning in their inspired leaps between images or thoughts." —*Publishers Weekly*

Scattered Poems. Jack Kerouac. City Lights Books 1971. 76 p.
ISBN 9780872860643
Grades: Adult   811
1. American poetry 2. Poetry
LC 71028511

Spontaneous poetry by the author of On the Road, gathered from underground and ephemeral publications; including "San Francisco Blues," the variant texts of "Pull My Daisy," and "American Haiku."

Kinnell, Galway
Collected Poems. Galway Kinnell; introduction by Edward Hirsch. Houghton Mifflin Harcourt 2017. xliv, 591 pages : Illustration
ISBN 9780544875210
Grades: Adult   811
1. American poetry 2. Poetry
LC 2017044904

The first complete showcase of "one of the true master poets of his generation," Galway Kinnell (1927-2014): a lifetime's work and a deeply lived life reflected in over two hundred poems.
Includes index.

A New Selected Poems. Galway Kinnell. Houghton Mifflin 2001. xi, 179 p.
ISBN 9780618154456
Grades: Adult   811
1. American poetry 2. Poetry
LC 2001039523

The Pulitzer Prize- and National Book Award-winning author selects poetry from his eight collections spanning 1960 to 1994 for inclusion in this sweeping survey of his work.
A Mariner book.

Strong Is Your Hold. Galway Kinnell. Houghton Mifflin 2006. 69 p.
ISBN 9780618224975
Grades: Adult   811
1. American poetry 2. Poetry
LC 2006011292

Presents a new collection of poetry by the winner of the Pulitzer Prize and the National Book Award, including "When the Towers Fell," his requiem for the victims of the September 11 attacks.

Komunyakaa, Yusef
The Chameleon Couch: Poems. Yusef Komunyakaa. Farrar, Straus and Giroux 2011. 115 p. : Illustration
ISBN 9780374120382
Grades: Adult   811
1. Poetry
LC 2010033148

A collection of poems by Yusef Komunyakaa that explores the complexities of culture and its relation to artifact and place.

"In this collection, the author shares unusually personal reflections steeped in his intimacy with ancestors, gods, and monsters. These finely formed lyrics are timeless in their shadows and wounds, and startlingly fresh in mood, metaphor, image, and such pairings as gargoyles and power lines, sugar and salt." —*Booklist*

★ *Everyday Mojo Songs of Earth: New and Selected Poems, 2001-2021.* Yusef Komunyakaa. Farrar, Straus & Giroux 2021. 288 p.
ISBN 9780374600136
Grades: Adult   811
1. War 2. Violence 3. Love 4. Beauty 5. African American music 6. Racism 7. United States 8. Poetry
LC 2020042798

Finalist for the Hurston/Wright Legacy Awards for Poetry, 2022.
Everyday Mojo Songs of Earth brings together selected poems from the past twenty years of Yusef Komunyakaa's work, as well as new poems from the Pulitzer Prize winner. Komunyakaa's masterful, concise verse conjures arresting images of peace and war, the natural power of the earth and of love, his childhood in the American South and his service in Vietnam, the ugly violence of racism in America, and the meaning of power and morality.

"With 140 poems, including 12 new works, this dazzling collection makes a definitive case for the Pulitzer Prize-winning Komunyakaa as a monumental and singular American voice." —*Publishers Weekly*
Includes index.

Warhorses: Poems. Yusef Komunyakaa. Farrar, Straus and Giroux 2008. VIII, 86 p.
ISBN 9780374286439
Grades: Adult   811
1. American poetry 2. Romantic love 3. African American poetry 4. Poetry
LC 2007051760

A collection of poems evaluates themes of war and conflict as demonstrated by global battles, social uprisings, and sexual confrontations, in a volume that explores lengthier poetic forms and includes such works as "The Autobiography of My Alter Ego."
Poems reflecting on love and war.

Kooser, Ted
Delights & Shadows: Poems. Ted Kooser. Copper Canyon Press 2004. xii, 87 p.
ISBN 9781556592010
Grades: Adult   811
1. American poetry 2. Poetry
LC 2003018447

Presents a collection of poems that celebrate everyday life.

Kunitz, Stanley
★ *The Collected Poems.* Stanley Kunitz. Norton 2000. 285 p.
ISBN 9780393050301
Grades: 11 12 Adult   811
1. American poetry 2. Poetry
LC 00041130

The author celebrates a life in poetry, sharing his work—published and unpublished—in this single volume of his life's accomplishment.

"What makes this collection of a lifetime's work so valuable is the way it allows us to perceive the interconnectedness of all Kunitz has written. Each poem stands alone, but each also enriches the others." —*New York Times Book Review*
Includes bibliographical references (p. [267]-277) and index.

Laux, Dorianne
Only as the Day Is Long: New and Selected Poems. Dorianne Laux. W. W. Norton & Company 2019. 128 p.
ISBN 9780393652338
Grades: Adult   811
1. Mothers and daughters 2. Dysfunctional families 3. Conflict in families 4. Men-women relations 5. Poetry
LC 2018038026
A collection of new and selected works from a prize-winning poet known to bear compassionate and ruthless witness to the quotidian.
Includes index.

Le Guin, Ursula K.
So Far So Good: Poems, 2014-2018. Ursula K. Le Guin. Copper Canyon Press 2018. 80 p.
ISBN 9781556595387
Grades: Adult   811
1. Aging 2. Memory 3. Identity 4. Poets 5. Authors 6. Self 7. Soul 8. Time 9. Eternity 10. Poetry
LC 2018016185
Redolent of myths, history, nursery rhymes, and the natural world, LeGuin bookends a long, daring, and prolific career.

Ursula K. Le Guin: Collected Poems. Harold Bloom, editor. The Library of America 2023. LII, 824 pages : Illustration (Library of America)
ISBN 9781598537369
Grades: Adult   811
1. Poetry
LC Bl2023013634
Ursula K. Le Guin's career began and ended with poetry. This sixth volume in the definitive Library of America edition of her works gathers, for the first time, her collected poems—from her earliest collection Wild Angels (1974) through her final publication, the collection So Far So Good, which she delivered to her editor just a week before her death in 2018.
"This imaginative and insightful collection is a worthy tribute to the poetic life's work of an important American writer." —*Publishers Weekly*
Includes bibliographical references (pages 756-803) and index.

Lee, Li-Young
The Undressing: Poems. Li-Young Lee. W. W. Norton & Company 2018. 95 pages
ISBN 9780393065435
Grades: Adult   811
1. Poetry — Asian American authors
LC 2017051768
Drawing from different sources—including the Old Testament, the Dao De Jing and the music of the Wu Tang Clan—a collection of poems attempts to uncover things hidden since the dawn of the world, investigating human violence and dispossession increasingly prevalent around the world, as well as the horrors the poet grew up with as a child of refugees.
Includes bibliographical references (page 95).

Levertov, Denise
Selected Poems. Denise Levertov; with a preface by Robert Creeley; edited and with an afterword by Paul A. Lacey. New Directions Books 2003. xvi, 220 pages
ISBN 9780811215541
Grades: 11 12 Adult   811
1. Poetry
LC Bl2015032377

Presents a collection of poems that reflect the author's childhood inspiration by T.S. Eliot, her experiences as a newcomer to post-World War II America, and her beliefs as an anti-war activist and environmentalist.
Includes bibliographical references and index.

Levine, Philip
The Simple Truth: Poems. Philip Levine. Knopf 1995. VIII, 69 p.
ISBN 9780679765844
Grades: Adult   811
1. American poetry 2. Families 3. Poetry
LC Bl 99778002
Offers thirty-three poems that interweave a complex web of myth, public and private history, family, memory, and invention as they explore the timeless truths of human existence.

Lewis, Robin Coste
To the Realization of Perfect Helplessness. Robin Coste Lewis. Alfred A. Knopf 2022. 400 p.
ISBN 9781524732585
Grades: Adult   811
1. African Americans 2. Photographs 3. Race relations 4. African American communities 5. African American community life 6. American people 7. North American people 8. United States history 9. 20th century 10. African American poetry 11. Poetry 12. Life stories — Identity — Race and ethnicity 13. Society and culture — Race
LC 2022001933
Finalist for the Hurston/Wright Legacy Awards for Poetry, 2023.
From the National Book Award-winning poet who changed the way we see the Black female figure, a continuation of that journey in a genre-bending coming together of poem and photography, toward a new definition of human migration. Twenty-five years ago, after her grandmother's death, Robin Coste Lewis discovered a stunning collection of photographs under her bed. The poetry that she marries to these vivid daily images of 20th-century Black joy and survival stands forth as an alternative to the usual way we frame the story of "race" and "the great migration"—as she puts it, "all those other clever ways we've created not to talk about Black culture."
"Shining with Lewis's trademark lyricism and fueled by resonant and inspired juxtapositions, this exquisite book makes an impact worth sharing widely and rereading." —*Publishers Weekly*

Limon, Ada
Bright Dead Things: Poems. Ada Limon. Milkweed Editions 2015. 105 pages
ISBN 9781571314710
Grades: Adult   811
1. Identity 2. Memories 3. Loss 4. Mortality 5. American poetry 6. 21st century 7. Poetry
LC 2015000088
Bright Dead Things examines the chaos that is life, the dangerous thrill of living in a world you know you have to leave one day, and the search to find something that is ultimately "disorderly, and marvelous, and ours.
"Recurring instances of anxiety about mortality in Limon's poems complicate experiences so richly written and felt." —*Publishers Weekly*
Includes bibliographical references (pages 103-105).

★ *The Carrying: Poems.* Ada Limon. Milkweed Editions 2018. 95 p.
ISBN 9781571315120
Grades: Adult   811
1. American poetry 2. 21st century 3. Poetry
LC 2017061361
ALA Notable Book, 2019.
The Carrying continues further and deeper into the bloodstream, following the hard-won truth of what it means to live in an imperfect world.

★ *The Hurting Kind: Poems.* Ada Limon. Milkweed Editions 2022. 112 p.
ISBN 9781639550494
Grades: Adult   811

ESSENTIAL AND RECOMMENDED TITLES
811 American poetry

1. Pain 2. Loss 3. Beauty 4. Family relationships 5. Nature 6. Sense of wonder 7. Poetry

LC 2021050271

"I have always been too sensitive, a weeper / from a long line of weepers," writes Ada Limón. "I am the hurting kind." What does it mean to be the hurting kind? with Limón's remarkable ability to trace thought, The Hurting Kind explores those questions—incorporating others' stories and ways of knowing, making surprising turns, and always reaching a place of startling insight. These poems slip through the seasons, teeming with horses and kingfishers and the gleaming eyes of fish. And they honor parents, stepparents, and grandparents: the sacrifices made, the separate lives lived, the tendernesses extended to a hurting child; the abundance, in retrospect, of having two families.

"The tender, arresting sixth collection from Limón (The Carrying) is an ode to the cycle of birth, death, and rebirth that characterizes the natural world....Limón's crystalline language is a feast for the senses, bringing monumental significance to the minuscule and revealing life in every blade of grass."
—*Publishers Weekly*

Long Soldier, Layli
★ *Whereas: Poems.* Layli Long Soldier. Graywolf Press 2019. 101 p.
ISBN 9781555979614
Grades: Adult   811
1. Indigenous peoples of North America, Treatment of 2. Lakota (North American people) 3. Government relations with indigenous peoples 4. Language and languages 5. Poetry

LC OC2018009514

Whereas confronts the coercive language of the United States government in its responses, treaties, and apologies to Native American peoples and tribes, and reflects that language in its officiousness and duplicity back on its perpetrators. Through a virtuosic array of short lyrics, prose poems, longer narrative sequences, resolutions, and disclaimers, Layli Long Soldier has created a brilliantly innovative text to examine histories, landscapes, her own writing, and her predicament inside national affiliations.

"A wickedly smart, necessarily solemn, and unmistakably urgent addition to a continually burgeoning canon of Native poetry." —*Booklist*

Lowell, Robert
Collected Poems. Robert Lowell; edited by Frank Bidart and David Gewanter; with the editorial assistance of DeSales Harrison. Farrar, Straus and Giroux 2003. xvii, 1186 p. : Illustration
ISBN 9780374126179
Grades: Adult   811
1. American poetry 2. Poetry

LC BL2003013769

The first full collection of Robert Lowell's work introduces readers to the literary genius of the nation's most important postwar poet, including several never-before-anthologized poems.
Includes bibliographical references (p. 1169-1170) and index.

Macfarlane, Robert
The Lost Spells. Robert Macfarlane; illustrated by Jackie Morris. House of Anansi Press 2020. 120 p.
ISBN 9781487007799
Grades: Adult   811
1. Nature 2. Wildlife 3. Words 4. Sense of wonder 5. Beauty in nature 6. Illustrated books 7. Poetry

The follow-up to the internationally bestselling sensation The Lost Words, The Lost Spells is a beautiful collection of poems and illustrations that evokes the wonder of everyday nature, conjuring up red foxes, birch trees, jackdaws, and more in words and images that flow between the pages and into readers' minds. Robert Macfarlane's spell-poems and Jackie Morris's watercolour illustrations are musical and magical: These are summoning spells, words of recollection, charms of protection.

"Combining poetic words (somewhat reminiscent of Mary Oliver's poetry in their passion for the natural world) with truly stunning illustrations, this unusually beautiful book brings to readers the magic and wonder of nature." —*Kirkus*

Mackey, Nathaniel
Splay Anthem. Nathaniel Mackey. New Directions Book 2006. xvi, 126 p.
ISBN 9780811216524
Grades: Adult   811
1. American poetry 2. African American poetry 3. Poetry — African American authors 4. Poetry

LC 2005035051

A new collection of poetry is divided into three sections including "Braid," "Fray," and "Nub" and features two ongoing serial poems that have evolved throughout more than twenty years, such as a West African spirit song and an exploration of a lost "we" tribe.

Mans, Jasmine
Black Girl, Call Home. Jasmine Mans. Penguin Group USA 2021. 256 p.
ISBN 9780593197141
Grades: Adult   811
1. Growing up 2. Daughters 3. Home (Concept) 4. African American women 5. Race (Social sciences) 6. Identity 7. LGBTQIA+ people 8. Feminism 9. Families 10. Fame 11. Sexual violence 12. Gender role 13. Communities 14. Childhood 15. African American children 16. Girls 17. Book club best bets 18. Poetry

LC 2020036788

A literary coming-of-age poetry collection, an ode to the places we call home, and a piercingly intimate deconstruction of daughterhood, Black Girl, Call Home is a love letter to the wandering Black girl and a vital companion to any woman on a journey to find truth, belonging, and healing.

"Delving into heartbreak, community, family, race, queer identity, sexual violence, feminism, and celebrity (including the blistering 'Footnotes for Kanye West' and an astounding elegy for Whitney Houston), Mans' poems are startling and unforgettable." —*Booklist*
Includes bibliographical references.

Mansbach, Adam
I Had a Brother Once: A Poem, a Memoir. Adam Mansbach. One World 2021. 176 p.
ISBN 9780593134795
Grades: Adult   811
1. Grief 2. Brothers 3. Suicide 4. Loss 5. Memory 6. Forgiveness 7. Families 8. Family relationships 9. Poetry

LC 2020031115

This epic poem tells the story of a young man grappling with the death of his beloved and troubled older brother—but more than that, trying to understand the nature of love, family, and mortality itself.

"In this heartbreaking, brutally candid memoir, Mansbach employs long stanzas of free verse to recount events surrounding his brother's death, struggling through anger, sorrow, and confusion.... This courageous and devastating memoir in verse stands out." —*Booklist*

Mao, Sally Wen
Oculus. Sally Wen Mao. Graywolf Pr 2019. 96 p.
ISBN 9781555978259
Grades: Adult   811
1. Exiles 2. Technology and civilization 3. Technology 4. Human nature 5. Poetry

In this magnificent second collection of poems, the author explores exile not just as a matter of distance and displacement, but as a migration through time and a reckoning with technology.

Marshall, Nate
Finna: Poems. by Nate Marshall. One World 2020. 112 p.
ISBN 9780593132456
Grades: Adult   811
1. Racism 2. Violence against African Americans 3. Language and languages 4. Identity 5. Social marginality 6. Love 7. Survival 8. Hope 9. Poetry

LC 2020006231

Definition of Finna, created by the author: Fin na /ˈfīnē/ contraction: (1) going to; intending to. rooted in African American Vernacular English. (2) eye dialect spelling of "fixing to." (3) Black possibility; Black futurity; Blackness as tomorrow. These poems consider the brevity and disposability of Black lives and other oppressed people in our current era of emboldened white supremacy, and the use of the Black vernacular in America's vast reserve of racial and gendered epithets. Finna explores the erasure of peoples in the American narrative; asks how gendered language can provoke violence; and finally, how the Black vernacular, expands our notions of possibility, giving us a new language of hope.

"Finna,' a contraction of 'fixing to' that salts the Black vernacular from that of southern grandmas to hip-hop artists, is the perfect title for multiple-award-winning Marshall's second collection.... Marshall's poems rip language open and reassemble it as an homage to its impact and potential." —Booklist

McCrae, Shane

In the Language of My Captor. Shane McCrae. Wesleyan University Press 2017. 86 pages

ISBN 9780819577115

Grades: Adult 811

1. American poetry 2. Poetry

LC 2016035696

In the book's three sequences, McCrae explores the role mass entertainment plays in oppression, he confronts the myth that freedom can be based upon the power to dominate others, and, in poems about the mixed-race child adopted by Jefferson Davis in the last year of the Civil War, he interrogates the infrequently examined connections between racism and love.

"With a raw honesty, McCrae refuses to shy away from the effects of oppression and faces up to those not willing to acknowledge their part in a history many want to forget." —Publishers Weekly

McGrath, Campbell

Nouns & Verbs: New and Selected Poems. Campbell McGrath. HarperCollins 2019. 288 p.

ISBN 9780062854148

Grades: Adult 811

1. United States 2. Poetry

LC 2018278470

Deeply personal but also expansive in its imaginative scope, Nouns & Verbs brings together thirty-five years of writing from Campbell McGrath, one of America's most highly lauded poets. Offering a hint of where he's headed while charting the territory already explored, McGrath gives us startlingly inventive new poems while surveying his previous work—lyric poems, prose poems, and a searing episodic personal epic, "An Odyssey of Appetite," exploring America's limitless material and spiritual hungers.

"McGrath is intelligent company, his poems exhibiting a curious, sometimes furious mind tuning into the literal noise of our culture, both violent and beautiful." —Publishers Weekly

McHugh, Heather

Muddy Matterhorn: Poems 2009-2019. Heather McHugh. Copper Canyon Press 2020. 104 p.

ISBN 9781556595967

Grades: Adult 811

1. Poetry

LC 2019043664

Heather McHugh's first book in a decade, Muddy Matterhorn, reclaims the mix of high and low that is her sensibility's signature, in matters practical and philosophical, semantic and stylistic, mortal and transitory, amorous and political, hilarious and heartbreaking. With fierce attacks on technology and social structures, McHugh finds a way to enjoy and empathize with humanity on her own terms. Ever the outsider, McHugh combines a strong sense of self with a determination to love people and the worlds they build without losing her biting criticism or witty rejection of societal norms and expectations. She is both pragmatic and theorizing, esoteric and identifiable. The joy and anger in these poems join to form an empowered and impassioned declaration of self in a chaotic time.

"McHugh's wordplay is peerless.... This is a high-impact book that is impossible to exhaust." —Booklist

Melville, Herman

Complete Poems:Battle-Pieces and Aspects of the War; Clarel: A Poem and Pilgrimage in the Holy Land; John Marr And Other Sailors with Some Sea Pieces; Timoleon Etc; Weeds and Wildings Chiefly: With a Rose Or Two; Parthenope; Uncol. Herman Melville; Hershel Parker, editor; [notes, Robert A. Sandberg]. The Library of America 2019. 990 pages : Map

ISBN 9781598536188

Grades: Adult 811

1. Pilgrims and pilgrimages, Christian 2. Sailing 3. United States history 4. American Civil War era (1861-1865) 5. Poetry

Published to coincide with Herman Melville's bicentennial, a single volume contains all four books of poetry he published in his lifetime plus uncollected poems and the poems from two projects left unfinished at the time of his death. Battle-Pieces and Aspects of the War is both a deeply philosophical work of mourning for the Civil War dead and a fascinating record of campaigns and battles and the war's immediate aftermath. With a cast of characters to rival Moby-Dick, the epic poem Clarel, about a young American divinity student's pilgrimage to the Holy Land, plumbs the profound existential and religious questions that haunted Melville throughout his life. In two late privately issued books, the retrospective John Marr and Other Sailors and Timoleon Etc, the aging poet returns to the nautical scenes and reading of his youth. Many of the poems in the two manuscripts left unfinished at Melville's death, Weeds and Wildings and Parthenope, have not been previously available in a reliable trade edition.

Merwin, W. S.

The Shadow of Sirius. W.S. Merwin. Copper Canyon Press 2008. xii, 117 p.

ISBN 9781556592843

Grades: Adult 811

1. American poetry 2. Poetry

LC 2008014578

Presents a collection of poems reflecting the author's life.

Poems.

Millay, Edna St. Vincent

Collected Poems. Edna St. Vincent Millay. Harper & Row 1981. 757 p.

ISBN 9780060908898

Grades: 11 12 Adult 811

1. American poetry 2. Women authors 3. 20th century 4. Poetry

LC BL 99753230

A selection of poems which demonstrates Millay's technical ability and directness.

"The poems in this collection are divided into two separate sections of lyrics and sonnets, arranged chronologically and printed in groups under the titles of the original volumes, ranging from Renascence of 1917 to Mine the harvest, published in 1954, four years after the poet's death." —Booklist

Selected Poems. Edna St. Vincent Millay; J.D. McClatchy, editor. The Library of America 2003. xxxiii, 231 p.

ISBN 9781931082358

Grades: Adult 811

1. American poetry 2. Women authors 3. Poetry

LC 2002032126

Offers new insights into Millay's career, presenting both familiar favorites and lesser-known pieces including translations, a verse play, songs from her opera libretto "The King's Henchmen," and the complete sonnet sequence of "Fatal Interview."

A lively collection offers new insights into Millay's career, presenting both familiar favorites and lesser-known pieces including translations, a verse play, songs from her opera libretto The King's Henchmen, and the complete sonnet sequence of Fatal Interview.

Includes index.

Miranda, Lin-Manuel

Gmorning, Gnight!: Little PEP Talks for Me & You. Lin-Manuel Miranda; Illustrations by Jonny Sun. Random House 2018. 208 p.

ISBN 9781984854278

ESSENTIAL AND RECOMMENDED TITLES
811 American poetry

Grades: Adult **811**
1. Self-esteem 2. Personal conduct 3. Motivation 4. Maxims 5. Proverbs 6. Salutations 7. Enthusiasm 8. Humor writing — General 9. Society and culture — Psychology and human behavior 10. Adult books for young adults
LC 2018029526

The creator and star of "Hamilton" presents an illustrated book of affirmations to provide inspiration at the beginning and end of each day.

Momaday, N. Scott
★ *The Death of Sitting Bear: New and Selected Poems.* N. Scott Momaday. Harper 2020. 224 p.
ISBN 9780062961150
Grades: Adult **811**
1. Sitting Bear Kiowa Chief, 1810-1871 2. Indigenous peoples of North America 3. Poetry
LC 2019034730

One of the most important and unique voices in American letters, distinguished poet, novelist, artist, teacher, and storyteller N. Scott Momaday was born into the Kiowa tribe and grew up on Indian reservations in the Southwest. The customs and traditions that influenced his upbringing-most notably the Native American oral tradition-are the centerpiece of his work. This luminous collection demonstrates Momaday's mastery and love of language and the matters closest to his heart. To Momaday, words are sacred; language is power. Spanning nearly fifty years, the poems gathered here illuminate the human condition, Momaday's connection to his Kiowa roots, and his spiritual relationship to the American landscape. The title poem, "The Death of Sitting Bear" is a celebration of heritage and a memorial to the great Kiowa warrior and chief. "I feel his presence close by in my blood and imagination," Momaday writes, "and I sing him an honor song." Here, too, are meditations on mortality, love, and loss, as well as reflections on the incomparable and holy landscape of the Southwest. The Death of Sitting Bear evokes the essence of human experience and speaks to us all.

"This accessible compendium allows readers to savor the life's work of an unparalleled poet." —*Booklist*

Moore, Marianne
New Collected Poems. Marianne Moore; edited by Heather Cass White. Farrar, Straus and Giroux 2017. xxvi, 453 pages
ISBN 9780374221041
Grades: Adult **811**
1. American poetry 2. Women authors 3. Poetry
LC 2017003857

The definitive collected edition of one of our most innovative and beloved poets, Marianne Moore.

Nezhukumatathil, Aimee
Oceanic. Aimee Nezhukumatathil. Copper Canyon Press 2018. VII, 73 pages
ISBN 9781556595264
Grades: Adult **811**
1. American poetry 2. Nature 3. Poetry of places 4. Women authors 5. Poetry 6. Poetry — Asian American authors
LC 2017030676

Nguyen, Diana Khoi
Ghost of. Diana Khoi Nguyen. Omnidawn Publishing 2018. 83 pages
ISBN 9781632430526
Grades: Adult **811**
1. American poetry 2. Women authors 3. Poetry — Asian American authors 4. Poetry
LC 2017051224

A collection of poems focuses on the photographs the author's brother left behind before his death in which he cut himself out, detailing her experiences dealing with memory, physical voids, and her family captured around an empty space.

Includes bibliographical references.

Nguyen, Hieu Minh
Not Here. Hieu Minh Nguyen. Coffee House Press 2018. 73 pages
ISBN 9781566895095
Grades: Adult **811**
1. American poetry 2. Families 3. Romantic love 4. Poetry — LGBTQIA 5. Poetry 6. Poetry — Asian American authors
LC 2017040746

"Nguyen follows up his debut, This Way to the Sugar (2014), with a collection that astounds in its intensity. Through elastic, creative form, Nguyen, a child of Vietnamese immigrants, explores Asian American identity and queer identity with acerbic wit and an open heart." —*Booklist*

Nguyen, Hoa
A Thousand Times You Lose Your Treasure. Hoa Nguyen. Wave Books 2021. 118 p. : Illustration
ISBN 9781950268177
Grades: Adult **811**
1. Mothers and daughters 2. Vietnam War, 1961-1975 3. Ghosts 4. Vietnam 5. Poetry
LC 2020038254

A new collection of poetry by Hoa Nguyen.

"Readers new to Nguyen's poems will find that they as much about the blank spaces as they are about what is written on the page, brilliantly playing on language and conversation itself." —*Library Journal*

Notley, Alice
Certain Magical Acts. Alice Notley. Penguin Books 2016. 147 pages
ISBN 9780143108160
Grades: Adult **811**
1. American poetry 2. Women authors 3. Poetry
LC 2016012657

Nye, Naomi Shihab
The Tiny Journalist: Poems. Naomi Shihab Nye. Consortium Book Sales & Dist 2019. 128 p.
ISBN 9781942683728
Grades: Adult **811**
1. Arab-Israeli conflict 2. Social justice 3. Protests, demonstrations, vigils, etc. 4. Journalism 5. Seven-year-old girls 6. Palestinian people 7. Ethnic identity 8. West Bank (Jordan River) 9. Palestine 10. Poetry
LC 2018050933

Internationally beloved poet Naomi Shihab Nye places her Palestinian American identity center stage in her latest full-length poetry collection for adults. The collection is inspired by the story of Janna Jihad Ayyad, the 'Youngest Journalist in Palestine,' who at age 7 began capturing videos of anti-occupation protests using her mother's smartphone. Nye draws upon her own family's roots in a West Bank village near Janna's hometown to offer empathy and insight to the young girl's reporting. Long an advocate for peaceful communication across all boundaries, Nye's poems in The Tiny Journalist put a human face on war and the violence that divides us from each other.

"Incisive and unsparing, Nye's caring poems will buzz in readers' brains long after reading them." —*Booklist*

Includes index.

You & Yours: Poems. Naomi Shihab Nye. BOA Editions 2005. 87 p; (American poets continuum series, no. 93)
ISBN 9781929918690
Grades: 11 12 Adult **811**
1. Poetry
LC 2005011360

A collection of poems by the Palestinian-American poet looks at life in her inner-city Texas neighborhood, as well as the daily rituals of Jews and Palestinians who live in the war-torn Middle East.

"Part one covers Nye's personal experience, at home with her child in San Antonio or as a Frequent Frequent Flyer enjoying the sights of Scotland.... Part two covers the Middle East." —*Publishers Weekly*

O'Hara, Frank
Lunch Poems. Frank O'Hara. Kraus Reprint Co. 1973. 74 p.
ISBN 9780872860353
Grades: Adult 811
1. American poetry 2. Poetry

LC 73012671

Essential poems by the late New York poet.

"The collection broadcasts snark, exuberance, lonely earnestness, and minute-by-minute autobiography to a wide, vague audience—much like today's Twitter and Facebook feeds." —*The Atlantic*

Reprint of the ed. published by City Lights Books, San Francisco, 1964.

Oates, Joyce Carol
American Melancholy: Poems. Joyce Carol Oates. Ecco Press 2021. 128 p.
ISBN 9780063035263
Grades: Adult 811
1. Loss 2. Political science 3. Racism 4. Poverty 5. Love 6. Memory 7. Social change 8. Poetry

A latest poetry collection by the National Book Award-winning author observes the human heart and mind while exploring subjects ranging from politics and racism to poverty and loss.

"Oates's high profile as a novelist should not discourage avid poetry readers from seeking out this volume, which aptly demonstrates the writer's gifts in the genre and includes several poems of the highest quality." —*Library Journal*

Olds, Sharon
Arias. by Sharon Olds. Random House Inc 2019. 208 pages
ISBN 9780525656937
Grades: Adult 811
1. Families 2. Social life and customs 3. Popular culture 4. Poetry

LC 2019007458

Following her recent Odes, the Pulitzer Prize-winning poet gives us a new collection of poems that sing of a woman's intimate life and political conscience.

"Arias offers hard-earned comfort well worth the effort." —*Booklist*

Odes. Sharon Olds. Alfred A. Knopf 2016. xii, 108 pages
ISBN 9780451493620
Grades: Adult 811
1. Sexuality 2. Desire 3. Interpersonal relations 4. Poetry

LC 2015049910

Olds addresses and embodies, in this age-old poetic form, many aspects of love and gender and sexual politics in a collection that is centered on the body and its structures and pleasures.

"Her new collection—and what a bit of alliterative pleasure Olds' Odes is—is a rampaging, rollicking play on this venerated form and a retrospective look at her signature themes." —*Booklist*

Stag's Leap. by Sharon Olds. Alfred A. Knopf 2012. x, 89 p.
ISBN 9780375712258
Grades: Adult 811
1. Marriage 2. Breaking up (Interpersonal relations) 3. Poetry

LC 2012004426

A poignant sequence of poems traces the evolution of a divorce while exploring themes of love, sex, sorrow, memory and freedom as reflected by everyday familiarities and the poignancy of former lovers parting, in a collection by the National Book Critics Circle Award-winning author of The Dead and the Living.

"Beautiful, well-crafted poems that map the end of a marriage; the poet's talent and wisdom are on display in poems that arrow to the heart over a route that is word- and image-rich." —*Library Journal*

Olivarez, Jose
Promises of Gold = Promesas De Oro. José Olivarez; translated to the Spanish by David Ruano González. Henry Holt and Company 2023. 144 p.
ISBN 9781250878496
Grades: Adult 811
1. Mexican Americans 2. Colonialism 3. Love 4. Loss 5. Friendship 6. Identity 7. Culture 8. Belonging 9. Bilingual materials — English/Spanish 10. Poetry

LC 2022047763

A groundbreaking collection of poems addressing how every kind of love—self, brotherly, romantic, familial, cultural—is birthed, shaped, and complicated by the invisible forces of gender, capitalism, religion, migration, and so on. Written in English and combined with a Spanish translation by poet David Ruano, Promises of Gold explores many forms of love and how "a promise made isn't always a promise kept," as Olivarez grapples with the contradictions of the American Dream laying bare the ways in which "love is complicated by forces larger than our hearts."

"In this moving second collection, Olivarez (Citizen Illegal) reflects on his Mexican identity through poems that explore platonic and romantic love, the joys of friendship and food, and the pain and loss at the heart of capitalist society." —*Publishers Weekly*

Poetry collection in English and translation into Spanish, bound tête-bêche.

Oliver, Mary
★ *Devotions: The Selected Poems of Mary Oliver.* Mary Oliver. Penguin Press 2017. xx, 455 pages
ISBN 9780399563249
Grades: Adult 811
1. American poetry 2. Nature 3. Poetry

LC 2017025254

The Pulitzer Prize-winning poet offers a carefully curated selection of her definitive writings in a volume spanning more than five decades of her esteemed literary career.

Includes index of titles and first lines.

Dream Work. Mary Oliver. Atlantic Monthly Press 1986. 90 p.
ISBN 9780871130693
Grades: Adult 811
1. American poetry 2. Poetry

LC 86007956

Presents poems that explore such themes as joy, self-awareness, and mankind's connection to the natural world.

New and Selected Poems; Vol. 1. Mary Oliver. Beacon Press 2004. 272 p.
ISBN 9780807068779
Grades: 11 12 Adult 811
1. American poetry 2. Women authors 3. 20th century 4. Poetry

LC 92007767

A collection of poems covering such topics as nature, writing, and art.

A Thousand Mornings. Mary Oliver. Penguin Press 2012. 82 p.
ISBN 9781594204777
Grades: Adult 811
1. American poetry 2. Poetry

LC 2012027310

Presents a collection of poems that explore such themes as the wonder of nature, the power of attention, and the mysteries of the daily experience.

Ondaatje, Michael
A Year of Last Things: Poems. Michael Ondaatje. Alfred A. Knopf 2024. 96 p.
ISBN 9780593801567
Grades: Adult 811
1. Memory 2. Authors 3. Celebrations 4. Place (Philosophy) 5. Aging 6. Reminiscing in old age 7. Loss 8. Poetry

LC 2023024604

Moving from a Sri Lankan boarding school to Molière's chair during his last stage performance, to Bulgarian churches and their icons, to the California coast and his beloved Canadian rivers, Michael Ondaatje casts a brilliant eye that merges memory with the present, in the way memory as the distant shores of art and lost friends continue to influence everything that surrounds him.

"The dazzling latest by Ondaatje (The Story) brings his formidable literary gifts and imagination to bear on questions of memory and artistic process." —*Publishers Weekly*

ESSENTIAL AND RECOMMENDED TITLES
811 American poetry

Padgett, Ron
Collected Poems. Ron Padgett. Coffee House Press 2013. 810 p.
ISBN 9781566893428
Grades: Adult 811
1. American poetry 2. Poetry
LC 2013017190

Gathering the work of more than fifty years, Ron Padgett's Collected Poems is the record of one of the most dynamic careers in twentieth-century American poetry.
Includes indexes.

Pardlo, Gregory
Spectral Evidence. Gregory Pardlo. Alfred a Knopf 2024. 128 p.
ISBN 9781524731786
Grades: Adult 811
1. Beauty 2. Art 3. Crime 4. African Americans 5. Justice 6. Identity 7. Racism 8. Popular culture 9. African American poetry 10. Poetry

A beloved Pulitzer Prize-winning poet forces us to consider how we think about devotion beauty and art; about the criminalization and death of Black lives; about justice and how these have been inscribed into our present, our history and the Western canon.

"Complex, linguistically rich, and unsparing in its analysis of both the current national psyche as well as the poet's own, Pardlo's poetry dares to ask: 'What if we didn't define ourselves according to our ability to know ourselves, but by our capacity to relate to others?'." —*School Library Journal*

Parker, Morgan
Magical Negro: Poems. Morgan Parker. W W Norton & CO Inc 2018. 112 p.
ISBN 9781947793187
Grades: Adult 811
1. African Americans 2. Civil Rights Movement 3. Racism 4. Poetry
LC 2018041653

A latest collection by the prizewinning author of There Are More Beautiful Things Than Beyoncé explores Black American womanhood through evocative themes ranging from self-conception and loneliness to objectification and ancestral trauma.

"A searing indictment, an irreverent lampoon, and a desperately urgent work of poetry, to be read alongside the work of Eve L. Ewing, Tiana Clark, and Nicole Sealey." —*Booklist*

There Are More Beautiful Things Than Beyonce. Morgan Parker. Tin House Books 2017. 85 pages
ISBN 9781941040539
Grades: Adult 811
1. American poetry 2. Women authors 3. African American poetry 4. Poetry
LC 2016049158

Morgan Parker stands at the intersections of vulnerability and performance, of desire and disgust, of tragedy and excellence. Unrelentingly feminist, tender, ruthless, and sequined, these poems are an altar to the complexities of Black American womanhood in an age of non-indictments and deja vu, and a time of wars over bodies and power.

"Cheeky and luscious yet ever aching, this collection from Pushcart Prize winner Parker (Other People's Comfort Keeps Me up at Night) uses a tough vernacular to unfold the story of a Black woman." —*Library Journal*

Perillo, Lucia
On the Spectrum of Possible Deaths. Lucia Perillo. Copper Canyon Press 2012. x, 81 p.
ISBN 9781556593970
Grades: Adult 811
1. American poetry 2. Poetry
LC 2011050110

Collects a series of poems with subjects ranging from coyotes and Scotch broom to local elections and family history.

"In her sixth collection, this Pulitzer Prize finalist and winner of the Library of Congress' Rebekah Johnson Bobbitt Award stealthily combines earthy intimacy, wry deprecation, metaphysics, and acute observations expressed in exuberant yet piercing images." —*Booklist*

Time Will Clean the Carcass Bones: Selected and New Poems. Lucia Perillo. Copper Canyon Press 2016. IX, 239 pages
ISBN 9781556594731
Grades: Adult 811
1. American poetry 2. Poetry
LC 2015034497

A retrospective of the poet's work, as well as some new poems.

"With this volume that spans more than 20 years and six poetry collections, Perillo (On the Spectrum of Possible Deaths), a poet, fiction writer, and MacArthur Fellow, exhibits her range and depth in exquisite yet unfussy poems." —*Publishers Weekly*

Petrosino, Kiki
White Blood: A Lyric of Virginia. Kiki Petrosino. Sarabande Books 2020. 107 p.
ISBN 9781946448545
Grades: Adult 811
1. African American women 2. Women 3. Slavery 4. Discrimination 5. Injustice 6. Loss 7. Genealogy 8. Family history 9. Identity 10. Virginia 11. Southern States 12. Poetry
LC 2019032278

Kiki Petrosino turns her gaze to Virginia, where she digs into her genealogical and intellectual roots, while contemplating the knotty legacies of slavery and discrimination in the Upper South. Speaking to history, loss, and injustice with wisdom, innovation, and a scientific determination to find the poetic truth, White Blood plants Petrosino's name ever more firmly in the contemporary canon.

"The result of deep historical research, impressive formal dexterity, and savvy storytelling, this volume of poetry combines genealogy, history, and verse in a way that reflects many American experiences." —*ForeWord Magazine*

Includes bibliographical references.

Phillips, Carl
★ *Then the War: And Selected Poems, 2007-2020.* Carl Phillips. Farrar, Straus and Giroux 2022. 240 p.
ISBN 9780374603762
Grades: Adult 811
1. Self-discovery 2. Intimacy 3. Ethics 4. African American poets 5. Poetry
LC 2021042469

Then the War sees Carl Phillips turn his sharp and subtle gaze inward, charting the changing landscapes of his life and work in a collection of new and selected poems.

"With an entirely new collection of poetry from Phillips bundled together with a selection of his multifarious work from across his 30-year career, this is a master class in his deceptively gentle voice and striking depictions of raw humanity. . . . An important milestone in the still flourishing career of a most brilliant poet." —*Booklist*

Includes bibliographical references and index.

Pico, Tommy
Feed. Tommy Pico. Tin House Books 2019. 78 pages
ISBN 9781947793576
Grades: Adult 811
1. American poetry 2. Romantic love 3. Poetry — Native American authors 4. Poetry — LGBTQIA 5. Poetry
LC 2019013806

New York Times Notable Book, 2020.

The American Book Award-winning author of IRL and Junk presents a conclusion to the Teebs Cycle in an irreverent epistolary collection that examines existential questions and the wild inconsistencies of life.

Junk. Tommy Pico. Tin House Books 2018. 72 pages
ISBN 9781941040973
Grades: Adult 811

PUBLIC LIBRARY CORE COLLECTION: NONFICTION
Twentieth Edition

1. American poetry 2. Romantic love 3. Breaking up (Interpersonal relations) 4. Indigenous peoples of North America 5. Gay men 6. Popular culture 7. Poetry

LC 2018002485

The third book in Tommy Pico's Teebs trilogy, Junk is a breakup poem in couplets: Ice floe and hot lava, a tribute to Janet Jackson and nacho cheese. In the static that follows the loss of a job or an apartment or a boyfriend, what can you grab onto fororientation? The narrator wonders what happens to the sense of self when the illusion of security has been stripped away. And for an indigenous person, how do these lost markers of identity echo larger cultural losses and erasures in a changing political landscape?

"Pico (Nature Poem) concludes his stellar "Teebs" trilogy in this frenetic book-length poem, a visceral exorcism of personal and collective demons." —Publishers Weekly

Nature Poem. Tommy Pico. Tin House Books 2017. 74 pages
ISBN 9781941040638
Grades: Adult   811
1. American poetry 2. Poetry — LGBTQIA 3. Poetry 4. Poetry — Native American authors

LC 2016056390

"Pico (IRL) centers his second book-length poem on the trap of conforming to identity stereotypes as he ponders his reluctance to write about nature as a Native American." —Publishers Weekly

Pinsky, Robert
The **Figured** Wheel: New and Collected Poems, 1966-1996. Robert Pinsky. Noonday Press 1997. x, 308 p.
ISBN 9780374525064
Grades: Adult   811
1. American poetry 2. Poetry

LC BL 00006276

Brings together the complete works from four previous books of poetry—Sadness and Happiness, An Explanation of America, History of My Heart, and The Want Bone—along with a dozen new poems and some of Pinsky's notable translations.

Includes bibliographical references and index; Originally published: New York : Farrar, Straus and Giroux, 1996.

Plath, Sylvia
★ *Ariel:* The Restored Edition. Sylvia Plath; foreword by Frieda Hughes. HarperCollins Publishers 2004. xxi, 211 p.
ISBN 9780060732592
Grades: Adult   811
1. Plath, Sylvia 2. American poetry 3. Women authors 4. Poetry

LC 2004047703

Seeking to restore the selection and arrangement originally intended by Plath at the time of her death, this edition of her final works features a facsimile of her complete working drafts of the title poem provided to offer insight into her creative process.

★ The **Collected** Poems. Sylvia Plath; edited by Ted Hughes. Harper Perennial Modern Classics 2008. 351, 32 p. : Illustration
ISBN 9780061558894
Grades: Adult   811
1. American poetry 2. Poetry

LC BI2009032381

Brings together a collection of all Plath's mature poetry, published and unpublished, together with a large selection of her juvenile works.

Includes index; Originally published: New York : Harper & Row, c1981. With additional material.

Pound, Ezra
★ *Poems* and Translations. Ezra Pound. Library of America 2003. xxiii, 1363 p; (The Library of America, 144)
ISBN 9781931082419
Grades: Adult   811
1. American poetry 2. Poetry

LC 2003040142

A collected edition of the modernist writer's works includes previously out-of-print pieces and demonstrates his contributions to the Imagist and Vorticist movements, in a volume that includes "Hilda's Book" and "Lustra."

A collected edition of the modernist writer's works includes dozens of previously out-of-print pieces and demonstrates his contributions to the Imagism and Vorticism movements, in a volume that includes Hilda's Book, Cathay, Lustra, and Hugh Selwyn Mauberley.

Includes index.

Powell, D. A.
Useless Landscape,: Or, a Guide for Boys. D.A. Powell. Graywolf Press 2012. 108 pages
ISBN 9781555976057
Grades: Adult   811
1. American poetry 2. Poetry

LC 2011942041

Collects the author's newest poems in his fifth tome that explores the darker side of divisions and developments.

Rasmussen, Matt
Black Aperture: Poems. Matt Rasmussen. Louisiana State University Press 2013. 64 pages
ISBN 9780807150863
Grades: Adult   811
1. American poetry 2. Poetry

LC 2012038045

Destructive and redemptive, Black Aperture opens to the complicated entanglements of mourning: Damage and healing, sorrow and laughter, and torment balanced with moments of relief.

Reed, Ishmael
New and Collected Poems, 1964-2007. Ishmael Reed. Thunder's Mouth Press 2007. xix, 490 p.
ISBN 9781568583419
Grades: Adult   811
1. American poetry 2. Poetry

LC 2008270117

First poetry collection in nearly twenty years. In language that is pointed, innovative and profoundly optimistic, Reed weaves politics and war with Nigerian poetry and jazz all in the service of his continual redefinition of American culture.

Reed, Justin Phillip
Indecency. Justin Phillip Reed. Coffee House Press 2018. 70 pages
ISBN 9781566895149
Grades: Adult   811
1. American poetry 2. Romantic love 3. African American poetry 4. Poetry — LGBTQIA 5. Poetry

LC 2017039180

A collection of poems explores inequity and injustice while critiquing the culture of white supremacy and the dominant social order.

Includes bibliographical references (page 69).

The *Malevolent* Volume: Poems. Justin Phillip Reed. Coffee House Press 2020. 93 p.
ISBN 9781566895767
Grades: Adult   811
1. African diaspora 2. Injustice 3. Race (Social sciences) 4. Avatars (Religion) 5. Characters and characteristics in mythology 6. Popular culture 7. Poetry

LC 2019041995

Subverting celebrated classics of poetry and mythology and examining horrors from contemporary film and cultural fact, National Book Award winner Justin Phillip Reed engages darkness as an aesthetic to conjure the revenant animus that lurks beneath the exploited civilities of marginalized people. In these poems, Reed finds agency in the other-than-human identities assigned to those

ESSENTIAL AND RECOMMENDED TITLES
811 American poetry

assaulted by savageries of the state. In doing so, he summons a retaliatory, counterviolent Black spirit to revolt and to inhabit the revolting.

"Winner of the 2018 National Book Award, Reed (Indecency) cyclones through a dreamscape full of sorrow and protest in his enchanting and enigmatic second collection. Weaving mythology and scripture with literature, film, music, and political speech." —*Publishers Weekly*

Includes index.

Rekdal, Paisley

Nightingale. Paisley Rekdal. Copper Canyon Press 2019. xi, 97 p.
ISBN 9781556595677
Grades: Adult   811
1. Grief 2. Transformations, Personal 3. Transformations (Magic) 4. Sexual violence 5. Poetry
LC 2018048966

West: A Translation. Paisley Rekdal. Copper Canyon Press 2023. 176 p.
ISBN 9781556596568
Grades: Adult   811
1. Chinese Americans 2. Transcontinental railroad (United States) 3. Railroad workers 4. Immigration and emigration law 5. Immigration and emigration 6. United States history 7. The West (United States) 8. Poetry
LC 2022047265

Punctuated by historical images and told through multiple voices, languages, literary forms and documents, West: A Translation explores what unites and divides America, drawing a powerful, necessary connection between the completion of the transcontinental railroad and the Chinese Exclusion Act (1882-1943).

"The powerful latest poetry and essay collection by Utah poet laureate Rekdal tells the story of the transcontinental railroad through the voices of the workers who built it." —*Booklist*

Rich, Adrienne

Collected Early Poems, 1950-1970. Adrienne Rich. W. W. Norton 1995. xxi, 435 p.
ISBN 9780393313857
Grades: Adult   811
1. American poetry 2. Women authors 3. 20th century 4. Poetry
LC BL 99768405

More than two hundred poems—including her first poem, published in the Yale Younger Poets—culled from Rich's earlier collections.

Includes bibliographical references (p. [423]-426) and index.

Collected Poems: 1950-2012. Adrienne Rich. W.W. Norton & Company 2016. LI, 1164 pages
ISBN 9780393285116
Grades: Adult   811
1. American poetry 2. Women authors 3. Poetry
LC 2016009163

The collected poems of the American poet highlights how she brought discussions of gender, race, and class to the forefront of poetical discourse.

Later Poems: Selected and New, 1971-2012. Adrienne Rich. W.W. Norton & Co. 2013. xiii, 530 p.
ISBN 9780393089561
Grades: Adult   811
1. American poetry 2. Women authors 3. Poetry
LC 2012035461

Presents a selection of poetry that draws from twelve volumes of the late author's published work as well as a manuscript posthumously left behind.

Poems; Includes bibliographical references and index.

The School Among the Ruins: Poems, 2000-2004. Adrienne Rich. W. W. Norton 2004. 113 p.
ISBN 9780393059830
Grades: Adult   811
1. American poetry 2. Women authors 3. Poetry
LC 2004008370

A collection of poetic works considers the impact of the twenty-first century's dislocations, upheavals, and public crises on individual lives, conveying in the title poem a young schoolteacher's evocation of the lessons learned by her students amid violence and hatred.

Ritvo, Max

The Final Voicemails. Max Ritvo; edited by Louise Gluck. Milkweed Editions 2018. 81 p.
ISBN 9781571315113
Grades: Adult   811
1. Death 2. Mortality 3. Identity 4. Poetry
LC 2017058089

Diagnosed with terminal cancer at sixteen, Ritvo spent the next decade of his life writing with frenetic energy, culminating in the publication of Four Reincarnations. As with his debut, The Final Voicemails brushes up against the pain, fear, and isolation that accompany a long illness, but with all the creative force of an artist in full command of his craft and the teeming affection of a human utterly in love with the world.

"The Final Voicemails may conclude Ritvo's literary legacy, but it will stand as a testament to the salvation that is poetry, how it lives beyond the page and the poet." —*Booklist*

Four Reincarnations: Poems. Max Ritvo. Milkweed Editions 2016. 79 pages
ISBN 9781571314901
Grades: Adult   811
1. American poetry 2. Elegiac poetry 3. Poetry
LC 2016030740

When Max Ritvo was diagnosed with cancer at age sixteen, he became the chief war correspondent for his body. The poems of Four Reincarnations are dispatches from chemotherapy beds and hospitals and the loneliest spaces in the home. They are relentlessly embodied, communicating pain, violence, and loss.

"Slippery and terrifyingly urgent, funny yet despairingly so, Ritvo (1990—2016) hits all the right notes in an accomplished, surprising, and bizarrely erotic debut made more poignant by his death weeks before publication." —*Publishers Weekly*

Roethke, Theodore

The Collected Poems of Theodore Roethke. Theodore Roethke. Anchor Books 1991. xiii, 272 p.
ISBN 9780385086011
Grades: 11 12 Adult   811
1. American poetry 2. 20th century 3. Poetry
LC 90048811

Contains selections from Open House, The Lost Son and Other Poems, Praise to the End, Words for the Wind, The Waking, I Am! Says the Lamb, and The Far Field in addition to sixteen previously unpublished poems.

Includes index; Originally published in hardcover by Doubleday in 1966—T.P. verso.

Rogers, Pattiann

Quickening Fields. Pattiann Rogers. Penguin Books 2017. 114 pages
ISBN 9780143131328
Grades: Adult   811
1. American poetry 2. Nature 3. Women authors 4. Poetry
LC 2016053786

A new collection by an award-winning poet. Quickening Fields gathers fifty-three poems that focus on the wide variety of life forms present on earth and their unceasing zeal to exist, their constant "push against the beyond" and the human experience among these lives.

"Rogers's poems flourish as essential experiences of wonder, as prayers." —*Publishers Weekly*

Roripaugh, Lee Ann

Tsunami vs. the Fukushima 50: Poems. Lee Ann Roripaugh. Milkweed Editions 2019. 98 p.
ISBN 9781571314857

Grades: Adult 811
1. Fukushima Nuclear Disaster, Japan, 2011 2. Nuclear power plants 3. Tsunamis 4. Natural disasters 5. Nature and civilization 6. Accidents 7. Poetry
LC 2018033636

In March 2011, a tsunami caused by an earthquake collided with nearby power plant Fukushima Daiichi, causing the only nuclear disaster in history to rival Chernobyl in scope. Those who stayed at the plant to stabilize the reactors, willing to sacrifice their lives, became known internationally as the Fukushima 50. In tsunami vs. the fukushima 50, Lee Ann Roripaugh takes a piercing, witty, and ferocious look into the heart of the disaster. Here we meet its survivors and victims, from a pearl-catcher to a mild-mannered father to a drove of mindless pink robots. And then there is Roripaugh's unforgettable Tsunami: a force of nature, femme fatale, and "annihilatrix." as humanity rebuilds in disaster's wake, Tsunami continues to wreak her own havoc, battling humans' self-appointed role as colonizer of Earth and its life-forms.

"From origin tale to glossary, anime battle to leisure ocean cruise, barbed wire that interns her to shoes that pinch and jeans that ride, Roripaughs wave rises above tragedy and the shock of a real-life nightmare." —*Publishers Weekly*

Ruefle, Mary
Dunce. Mary Ruefle. Wave Books 2019. 104 pages
ISBN 9781940696850
Grades: Adult 811
1. Poetry

A stunning new collection of poems from Mary Ruefle inviting the many readers of her prose to discover the central form of her literary imagination.

Selected Poems. Mary Ruefle. Wave Books 2010. 154 p.
ISBN 9781933517452
Grades: Adult 811
1. American poetry 2. Poetry
LC 2010005808

A career-defining retrospective by a much-beloved contemporary master.

"This first retrospective collection from Ruefle, which selects from her nine previous books of poetry, the earliest of which first appeared in 1982, shows her to be a poet of visionary imagination, abiding sensitivity, and melancholy humor." —*Publishers Weekly*

Includes index.

Ruhl, Sarah
Letters from Max: A Book of Friendship. Sarah Ruhl and Max Ritvo. Milkweed Editions 2018. 336 p.
ISBN 9781571313690
Grades: Adult 811
1. Ritvo, Max, 1990-2016 2. Ruhl, Sarah, 1974- 3. Poets 4. People with cancer 5. Friendship 6. Women playwrights 7. Teachers 8. Students 9. Mortality 10. People with terminal illnesses 11. Men 12. Letters 13. Life stories — Facing adversity — Medical issues — Physical illness 14. Life stories — Facing adversity — Coping with death 15. Arts and Entertainment — Writing and Publishing
LC 2018007328

Correspondence between playwright-teacher Sarah Ruhl and poet-cancer patient Max Ritvo, in which the student becomes the teacher.

"This companion volume to the Final Voicemails (2018), a moving compilation of the late Ritvo's incandescent poems, takes readers behind the curtain of his writing to expose his hard-won, well-lived, if sadly brief life, including his painful struggle with cancer, evolving love and marriage, and the tree-bud-to-redwood maturation of an intimate friendship with award-winning playwright Ruhl." —*Booklist*

Rukeyser, Muriel
Selected Poems. Muriel Rukeyser; Adrienne Rich, editor. Library of America 2004. xxv, 180 p. : Portrait
ISBN 9781931082587
Grades: Adult 811
1. American poetry 2. Women authors 3. Poetry
LC 2003060484

The poet, translator, and political activist is given full expression through poems selected by Adrienne Rich that feature musings on politics, geography, sexuality, and mythology, as well as observations of her own life.

The poet, translator, and political activist is given full expression through poems selected by Adrienne Rich that feature musings on politics, geography, sexuality, and mythology, as well as observations of her own life.

Includes bibliographical references (p. 169) and index.

Ryan, Kay
The Best of It: New and Selected Poems. Kay Ryan. Grove Press 2010. xiv, 270 p.
ISBN 9780802119148
Grades: Adult 811
1. American poetry 2. Poetry
LC Bl2010014718

Presents a selection of more than two hundred poems from his previous works along with a collection of new poems.

Includes index.

Salter, Mary Jo
The Surveyors: Poems. Mary Jo Salter. Alfred A. Knopf 2017. VIII, 89 pages
ISBN 9781524732660
Grades: Adult 811
1. American poetry 2. Romantic love 3. Women authors 4. Poetry
LC 2016042321

A beautiful new collection from Mary Jo Salter brings us poems of puzzlement and acceptance in the face of life's surprises.

"Essential not only for Salter's fans but for readers of poetry in general; Salter provides sane and long-lasting rewards." —*Library Journal*

Includes bibliographical references (page 89).

Sanchez, Erika L.
Lessons on Expulsion: Poems. Erika L. Sanchez. Graywolf Press 2017. 73 pages
ISBN 9781555977788
Grades: Adult 811
1. Immigrants 2. Women 3. Poetry 4. Poetry — Hispanic American
LC 2016951419

What is life but a cross / over rotten water?" Poet, novelist, and essayist Erika L. Sanchez powerful debut poetry collection explores what it means to live on both sides of the border—the border between countries, languages, despair and possibility, and the living and the dead. Sanchez tells her own story as the daughter of undocumented Mexican immigrants and as part of a family steeped in faith, work, grief, and expectations. The poems confront sex, shame, race, and an America roiling with xenophobia, violence, and laws of suspicion and suppression. With candor and urgency, and with the unblinking eyes of a journalist, Sanchez roves from the individual life into the lives of sex workers, narco-traffickers, factory laborers, artists, and lovers. What emerges is a powerful, multifaceted portrait of survival. Lessons on Expulsion is the first book by a vibrant, essential new writer now breaking into the national literary landscape.

Sanchez, Sonia
Homegirls & Handgrenades. Sonia Sanchez. Beacon Press 2023. 97 pages
ISBN 9780807012956
Grades: Adult 811
1. Love 2. Communities 3. Poetry
LC 2022053701

Originally published in 1984, this collection of prose, prose poems, and lyric verses is as fresh and radical today as it was then. Sonia Sanchez, the premiere poet of the Black Arts Movement, shows the "razor blades" clenched in her teeth in these powerful pieces.

Originally published in 1984.

ESSENTIAL AND RECOMMENDED TITLES
811 American poetry

Sandburg, Carl
★ *The Complete* Poems of Carl Sandburg. Carl Sandburg. Harcourt 2003. xxxi, 797 p.
ISBN 9780151009961
Grades: 11 12 Adult   **811**
1. American poetry 2. Poetry
LC BI2005019694

A compilation of the American poet's works includes the contents of such acclaimed anthologies as "Chicago Poems," "Cornhuskers," and "Smoke and Steel."
Originally published: New York : Harcourt Brace Jovanovich, 1970.

Santos Perez, Craig
From Unincorporated Territory [amot]. Craig Santos Perez. Omnidawn Publishing 2023. 160 p.
ISBN 9781632431189
Grades: Adult   **811**
1. Culture 2. Indigenous peoples 3. Colonialism 4. Militarism 5. Migration, Internal 6. Identity 7. Environmentalism 8. Guam 9. Poetry
LC 2022057633

This book is the fifth collection in Craig Santos Perez's ongoing from unincorporated territory series about the history of his homeland, the western Pacific island of Guåhan (Guam), and the culture of his indigenous Chamoru people. "Åmot" is the Chamoru word for "medicine," and commonly refers to medicinal plants. Through experimental and visual poetry, Perez explores how storytelling can become a symbolic form of åmot, offering healing from the traumas of colonialism, militarism, migration, environmental injustice, and the death of elders.

"Perez's ongoing project is one of the longest-running and most rewarding literary engagements with Pacific Islander and Indigenous poetics of the twenty-first century." —*Booklist*
Includes bibliographical references; in English with some text in Chamorro.

Sarton, May
Selected Poems of May Sarton. Edited and with an introd. by Serena Sue Hilsinger and Lois Brynes. Norton 1978. 206 p.
ISBN 9780393045123
Grades: Adult   **811**
1. Poetry
LC 78014850

Ranging from pastoral and lyrical to polemical and dissonant, Sarton's poems written over a period of forty years explore private moments of erotic love, public events, and sources of the creative process.

"What May Sarton does is to follow the round of a woman's life. Her verse is traditional, warm, ripe with the wisdom of her years as a poet, novelist, autobiographer. She draws on the artifacts of the past for images to live by in the here and now." —*Christian Science Monitor*
Includes index.

Scenters-Zapico, Natalie
Lima : Limon. Natalie Scenters-Zapico. Copper Canyon Press 2019. 75 p.
ISBN 9781556595318
Grades: Adult   **811**
1. Boundaries 2. Gender identity 3. Femininity 4. Masculinity 5. Immigrants 6. Political culture 7. Dualism 8. Poetry
LC 2018048964

In her striking second collection, Natalie Scenters-Zapico sets her unflinching gaze once again on the borders of things. Lima : Limon illuminates both the sweet and the sour of the immigrant experience, of life as a woman in the U.S. and Mexico, and of the politics of the present day. Drawing inspiration from the music of her childhood, her lyrical poems focus on the often-tested resilience of women. Scenters-Zapico writes heartbreakingly about domestic violence and its toxic duality of macho versus hembra, of masculinity versus femininity, and throws into harsh relief the all-too-normalized pain that women endure. Her sharp verse and intense anecdotes brand her poems into the reader; images like the Virgin Mary crying glass tears and a border fence that leaves never-healing scars intertwine as she stares down femicide and gang violence alike. Unflinching, Scenters-Zapico highlights the hardships and stigma immigrants face on both sides of the border, her desire to create change shining through in every line. Lima : Limon is grounding and urgent, a collection that speaks out against violence and works toward healing.

"A dazzling collection, it punches like spiked limonada; to be read alongside writers like Marcelo Hernandez Castillo and Angel Garcia." —*Booklist*
Includes bibliographical references.

Schiff, Robyn
A Woman of Property. Robyn Schiff. Penguin Books 2016. 81 pages
ISBN 9780143128274
Grades: Adult   **811**
1. Poetry
LC 2015048702

A new book from a poet whose work is "wild with imagination, unafraid, ambitious, inventive" (Jorie Graham) Located in a menacing, gothic landscape, the poems that comprise A Woman of Property draw formal and imaginative boundaries against boundless mortal threat, but as all borders are vulnerable, this ominous collection ultimately stages an urgent and deeply imperiled boundary dispute where haunting, illusion, the presence of the past, and disembodied voices only further unsettle questions of material and spiritual possession. This is a theatrical book of dilapidated houses and overgrown gardens, of passageways and thresholds, edges, prosceniums, unearthings, and root systems. The unstable property lines here rove from heaven to hell, troubling proportion and upsetting propriety in the name of unfathomable propagation. Are all the gates in this book folly? Are the walls too easily scaled to hold anything back or impose self-confinement? What won't a poem do to get to the other side?

"Few collections this year are likely to match the subtle intelligence in this third outing from Schiff." —*Publishers Weekly*

Schuyler, James
Collected Poems. James Schuyler. Farrar, Straus, Giroux 1993. 429 p.
ISBN 9780374524036
Grades: Adult   **811**
1. American poetry 2. Poetry
LC 92040977

Gathers all of the late writer's published poetry, and includes unpublished poems written in the last few years before his death.
Includes index.

Seidel, Frederick
★ *Frederick Seidel Selected Poems*. Frederick Seidel. Farrar, Straus and Giroux 2020. xii, 274 p.
ISBN 9780374260811
Grades: Adult   **811**
1. American poetry 2. Life 3. Mortality 4. Poetry
LC 2020028195

Showing the evolution of a master poet's craft, this collection contains the revolutionary poet's most powerful work, which has mystified and captured critics, poets and readers for decades.

"This book offers a slice of Seidel's life: the amorous, the dark, the indulgent, and the restless mind captured by a master of craft." —*Publishers Weekly*
Includes index.

Seuss, Diane
★ *Frank: Sonnets*. Diane Seuss. Graywolf Press 2021. 152 p.
ISBN 9781644450451
Grades: Adult   **811**
1. Alienation 2. American poetry 3. Poetry

A resplendent life in sonnets from the author of Four-Legged Girl, a finalist for the Pulitzer Prize.

"It's hard to pin down the meaning of a Seuss poem, which adds a certain pleasing sense of mystery to the best work here." —*Library Journal*

PUBLIC LIBRARY CORE COLLECTION: NONFICTION
Twentieth Edition

Sexton, Anne
Selected Poems of Anne Sexton. Edited with an introduction by Diane Wood Middlebrook and Diana Hume George. Houghton Mifflin 2000. xxvi, 266 p.
ISBN 9780618057047
Grades: Adult   811
1. American poetry 2. Poetry
LC BL2001008875

This selection, which is drawn from Anne Sexton's ten published volumes of poems as well as from representative early and last work, is an ideal introduction to a great American poet.
Originally published: 1988.

Shanahan, Charif
Trace Evidence: Poems. Charif Shanahan. Tin House 2023. 94 p.
ISBN 9781953534668
Grades: Adult   811
1. Identity 2. Multiracial people 3. Arab Americans 4. Black people 5. Gay men 6. Desire 7. Mortality 8. Psychic trauma 9. Belonging 10. Poetry
LC 2022054122

Charif Shanahan continues his piercing meditations on the intricacies of mixed-race identity, queer desire, time, mortality, and the legacies of anti-Blackness in the US and abroad.

"In this exquisite and affecting collection, Shanahan (Into Each Room We Enter Without Knowing) explores longing and alienation in queer and mixed-race contexts." —*Publishers Weekly*

Shapiro, Karl
Selected Poems. Karl Shapiro; John Updike, editor. Library of America 2003. xxxi, 197 p. : Illustration
ISBN 9781931082341
Grades: Adult   811
1. American poetry 2. Poetry
LC 2002032123

A reassessment of the Pulitzer Prize-winning poet explores the range of his work and considers his role as a key writer of the postwar period. Edited by the author of Rabbit at Rest.
Includes bibliographical references (p. 185-186) and index.

Sharif, Solmaz
Customs: Poems. Solmaz Sharif. Graywolf Press 2022. 72 p.
ISBN 9781644450796
Grades: Adult   811
1. Culture 2. English language 3. Identity 4. Language and languages 5. Social life and customs 6. United States 7. Poetry

A second collection of poems from the National Book Award finalist and author of Look that examine and critique the culture and social skills of American life and the English language.

"Sharif demonstrates remarkable talent in her ability to so deftly portray the traumatizing balance required to live in the West with deep roots in Iran." —*Booklist*

Look: Poems. Solmaz Sharif. Graywolf Press 2016. 98 pages
ISBN 9781555977443
Grades: Adult   811
1. American poetry 2. Women authors 3. Poetry 4. Poetry — Arab American authors
LC 2015953717

A collection of poems uses words and phrases lifted from the "Department of Defense Dictionary of Military and Associated Terms" to highlight the cost of ongoing war and the dehumanization of conflict.

Shaughnessy, Brenda
The *Octopus* Museum: Poems. Brenda Shaughnessy. Knopf 2019. 68 p.
ISBN 9780525655657
Grades: Adult   811
1. Uncertainty 2. Mother and child 3. Child safety 4. Violence 5. Environmental disasters 6. Fear 7. Poetry
LC 2018036768

Library Journal Best Books, 2019; New York Times Notable Book, 2019.

This collection of bold and scathingly beautiful feminist poems imagines what comes after our current age of environmental destruction, racism, sexism, and divisive politics. Informed by Brenda Shaughnessy's craft as a poet and her worst fears as a mother, the poems in The Octopus Museum blaze forth from her pen: in these pages, we see that what was once a generalized fear for our children (car accidents, falling from a tree) is now hyper-reasonable, specific, and multiple: school shootings, nuclear attack, loss of health care, a polluted planet. As Shaughnessy conjures our potential future, she movingly (and often with humor) envisions an age where cephalopods might rule over humankind, a fate she suggests we may just deserve after destroying their oceans. These heartbreaking, terrified poems are the battle cry of a woman who is fighting for the survival of the world she loves, and a stirring exhibition of who we are as a civilization.

"With an unparalleled ear for language, Shaughnessy excels at making the tragic transcendent." —*Publishers Weekly*

Shockley, Evie
The New Black. Evie Shockley. Wesleyan University Press 2011. 104 p. : Illustration
ISBN 9780819571403
Grades: Adult   811
1. American poetry 2. African American poetry 3. Poetry 4. Society and culture — Ethnic studies
LC 2010046345

Smart, grounded, and lyrical, Evie Shockley's The New Black integrates powerful ideas about "Blackness," past and present, through the medium of beautifully crafted verse.

"Full of surprising turnabouts and shaped by a deep quest for knowledge and understanding, Shockley's inviting and invigorating collection shimmers with positive creative energy." —*Booklist*

Semiautomatic. Evie Shockley. Wesleyan University Press 2017. 110 pages
ISBN 9780819577443
Grades: Adult   811
1. American poetry 2. African American poetry 3. Poetry
LC 2016059299

Poetry by Evie Shockley, critiquing daily life as well as responding to race- and gender-based violence.
Includes bibliographical references.

Suddenly We. Evie Shockley. Wesleyan University Press 2023. 106 p.
ISBN 9780819500236
Grades: Adult   811
1. African Americans 2. African diaspora 3. Identity 4. Expectation 5. Individuality 6. Intimacy 7. African American poetry 8. Poetry
LC 2022053758

In her new poetry collection, Evie Shockley mobilizes visual art, sound, and multilayered language to chart routes towards openings for the collective dreaming of a more capacious "we." How do we navigate between the urgency of our own becoming and the imperative insight that whoever we are, we are in relation to each other?

"This collection is a welcome companion for that ride as it celebrates the collective, the "we" that is vital to survival." —*Publishers Weekly*

Simic, Charles
Come Closer and Listen: Poems. Charles Simic. Ecco 2019. xiii, 75 pages
ISBN 9780062908469
Grades: Adult   811
1. American poetry 2. Elegiac poetry 3. Poetry
LC Bl2019019054

A new collection of poems from the Pulitzer Prize-winning poet of The World Doesn't End offer modern reflections on love, grief, the wonders of nature with a pithy, wry and cutting edge.

The Lunatic: Poems. Charles Simic. Ecco 2015. xi, 84 pages

ESSENTIAL AND RECOMMENDED TITLES
811 American poetry

ISBN 9780062364746
Grades: Adult   811
  1. American poetry 2. Poetry

LC Bl2015014919

A collection of the author's poetry features a mix of wry melancholy and sardonic wit.

New and Selected Poems: 1962-2012. Charles Simic. Houghton Mifflin Harcourt 2013. 355 pages
ISBN 9780547928289
Grades: Adult   811
  1. American poetry 2. Poetry

LC 2012042188

Collects four hundred of the American writer's poems about such topics as folktales, marriage, war, life, and American blues.

"But, until now, Simic's body of work was split between two publishers and two separate 'Selected Poems' volumes. This books brings together, for the first time, poems from Simic's entire career." —*Publishers Weekly*

The Voice at 3:00 A.M.: Selected Late & New Poems. Charles Simic. Harcourt 2003. 177 p.
ISBN 9780151008421
Grades: 11 12 Adult   811
  1. American poetry 2. Poetry

LC 2002038715

Offers a new collection of poems that plumbs the ordinary American experience for spiritual insights, wit, and historical relevance.

"This volume collects outstanding poems from six previous books ... and presents a sterling set of new poems, each moody, surprising, and tonic." —*Booklist*

Sinclair, Safiya
Cannibal. Safiya Sinclair. University of Nebraska Press 2016. x, 111 pages
ISBN 9780803290631
Grades: Adult   811
  1. Women 2. Human body 3. Women authors 4. Poetry

LC 2016007774

Colliding with and confronting The Tempest and postcolonial identity, the poems in Safiya Sinclair's Cannibal explore Jamaican childhood and history, race relations in America, womanhood, otherness, and exile. She evokes a home no longer accessible and a body at times uninhabitable, often mirrored by a hybrid Eve/Caliban figure. Blooming with intense lyricism and fertile imagery, these full-blooded poems are elegant, mythic, and intricately woven. Here the female body is a dark landscape; the female body is cannibal. Sinclair shocks and delights her readers with her willingness to disorient and provoke, creating a multitextured collage of beautiful and explosive poems.

Framed by "The Tempest" and calling on historical, cultural, and biological sources, "Cannibal" is a provocative poetic exploration of the female body, identity, and race.

Smith, Clint
★ *Above Ground.* Clint Smith. Little Brown & Company 2023. 107 p.
ISBN 9780316543033
Grades: Adult   811
  1. Fatherhood 2. Family history 3. Identity 4. Sense of wonder 5. Grief 6. Climate change 7. Childhood 8. Race (Social sciences) 9. Race relations 10. United States 11. African American poetry 12. Poetry

Clint Smith's vibrant and compelling new collection traverses the vast emotional terrain of fatherhood, and explores how becoming a parent has recalibrated his sense of the world. Above Ground wrestles with how we hold wonder and despair in the same hands, how we carry intimate moments of joy and a collective sense of mourning in the same body. Smith's lyrical, narrative poems bring the reader on a journey not only through the early years of his children's lives, but through the changing world in which they are growing up—through the changing world of which we are all a part.

"In candid lyric poems often written in direct address to his son and daughter, Smith exquisitely captures the anxiety, love, uncertainty, and joy that accompany the challenge of nurturing nascent human lives, all the while casting a nervous eye on the unstable natural, social, and political environments they'll inherit." —*Library Journal*

Smith, Danez
★ *Homie: Poems.* Danez Smith. Graywolf Press 2020. 96 p.
ISBN 9781644450109
Grades: Adult   811
  1. Friendship 2. Communities 3. Prejudice 4. Racism 5. Intersectionality 6. HIV (Viruses) 7. African Americans 8. Gender-nonconforming people 9. Poetry

LC Bl2020045532

Rooted in the loss of one of Smith's close friends, this book comes out of the search for joy and intimacy within a nation where both can seem scarce and getting scarcer. In poems of rare power and generosity, Smith acknowledges that in a country overrun by violence, xenophobia, and disparity, and in a body defined by race, queerness, and diagnosis, it can be hard to survive, even harder to remember reasons for living. But then the phone lights up, or a shout comes up to the window, and family—blood and chosen—arrives with just the right food and some redemption.

"Smith is a visionary polyglot with a fearless voice." —*Publishers Weekly*

Smith, Patricia
Blood Dazzler: Poems. Patricia Smith. Coffee House Press 2008. VIII, 77 p.
ISBN 9781566892186
Grades: Adult   811
  1. Hurricane Katrina, 2005 2. American poetry 3. Poetry

LC 2008012528

Shoulda Been Jimi Savannah: Poems. Patricia Smith. Coffee House Press 2012. 115 p.
ISBN 9781566892995
Grades: Adult   811
  1. American poetry 2. African American poetry 3. Poetry

LC 2011029282

A collection of poems explores the second wave of the Great Migration.

Unshuttered: Poems. Patricia Smith. TriQuarterly Books/Northwestern University Press 2023. 112 p.
ISBN 9780810145634
Grades: Adult   811
  1. African Americans 2. Slavery 3. Freedom 4. Grief 5. Identity 6. Happiness 7. United States 8. 19th century 9. Poetry

LC 2022051834

In this poetry collection, an award-winning author presents a portrait of nineteenth-century Black America. This masterful and haunting mosaic is a search for lost histories, both personal and inherited.

"In her evocative latest, Smith (Incendiary Art) combines photographs of Black Americans taken in the 19th century with poems written from the perspective of each image's subject to construct a wrenching tapestry of the effects of enslavement and promises of Reconstruction." —*Publishers Weekly*

Smith, Tracy K.
Duende: Poems. Tracy K. Smith. Graywolf Press 2007. 87 p.
ISBN 9781555974756
Grades: Adult   811
  1. American poetry 2. African American poetry 3. Poetry

LC 2006938264

Calls on "duende," the source of artistic power described by Federico Garcia Lorca, in thirty poems that explore identity, marginalization, and the sources of pain in a variety of geographical and historical situations.

★ *Life on Mars: Poems.* Tracy K. Smith. Graywolf Press 2011. 75 pages
ISBN 9781555975845
Grades: Adult   811
  1. American poetry 2. African American poetry 3. Poetry

LC 2011920674

With allusions to David Bowie and interplanetary travel, Life on Mars imagines a soundtrack for the universe to accompany the discoveries, failures, and oddities of human existence.

"Hypnotic and brimming with irony, the poems in Smith's latest volume aren't so much about outer space as the interior life and the search for the divine." —Library Journal

★ *Such Color: New and Selected Poems*. Tracy K. Smith. Graywolf Press 2021. 256 p.
ISBN 9781644450673
Grades: Adult 811
1. Racism 2. Injustice 3. History 4. Grief 5. Loss 6. Love 7. Poetry

Celebrated for its extraordinary intelligence and exhilarating range, the poetry of Tracy K. Smith opens up vast questions. Such Color: New and Selected Poems, her first career-spanning volume, traces an increasingly audacious commitment to exploring the unknowable, the immense mysteries of existence. Such Color collects the best poems from Smith's previous books and culminates in thirty pages of brilliant, excoriating new poems. These new works confront America's historical and contemporary racism and injustices, while they also rise toward the registers of the ecstatic, the rapturous, and the sacred—urging us toward love as a resistance to everything that impedes it.

"Smith offers her first retrospective with Such Color, selecting works from four previous volumes while continuing to push boundaries with her new poems." —Library Journal

Snyder, Gary
No Nature: New and Selected Poems. Gary Snyder. Pantheon Books 1993. xv, 390 p.
ISBN 9780679742524
Grades: Adult 811
1. American poetry 2. Poetry
LC BL 00003305

Presents selections from the author's eight previous collections of poetry, as well as previously unpublished works.

A collection of poetry ranging from Riprap to the present, this anthology integrates an ethical and spiritual vision of planet Earth as it celebrates life and the beauty of the natural world. National Book Award finalist.

Includes index.

Som, Brandon
Tripas: Poems. by Brandon Som. The University of Georgia Press 2023. 93 pages
ISBN 9780820363509
Grades: Adult 811
1. American poetry 2. Interracial families 3. Interethnic families 4. Families 5. Poetry
LC BI2024009857

With Tripas, Brandon Som follows up his award-winning debut with a book of poems built out of a multicultural, multigenerational childhood home, in which he celebrates his Chicana grandmother, who worked nights on the assembly line at Motorola, and his Chinese American father and grandparents, who ran the family corner store.

Spicer, Jack
My Vocabulary Did This to Me: The Collected Poetry of Jack Spicer. Edited by Peter Gizzi and Kevin Killian. Wesleyan University Press 2008. xxxi, 465 p. : Illustration
ISBN 9780819568878
Grades: Adult 811
1. American poetry 2. Poetry
LC 2008024997

Presents a collection of poems taken from a variety of the author's books along with poems published for the first time.

Includes bibliographical references (p. 455-456) and indexes.

Stanford, Frank
What About This: Collected Poems of Frank Stanford. Edited by Michael Wiegers. Copper Canyon Press 2015. xvi, 747 pages : Illustration
ISBN 9781556594687
Grades: Adult 811
1. American poetry 2. Poetry
LC 2014045989

Readers have dreamed about this collection for nearly four decades—an energized presentation of Frank Stanford's raw-genius ungovernable oeuvre.

"In this comprehensive and essential retrospective, the body of work left behind by Stanford—who took his own life in 1978, at age 29—more than makes good on his insistence that "poetry busts guts."" —Publishers Weekly

Includes index.

Stevens, Wallace
Collected Poetry and Prose. Wallace Stevens. Library of America 1997. xxii, 1032 p; (The library of America, 96)
ISBN 9781883011451
Grades: Adult 811
1. American poetry 2. 20th century 3. Poetry
LC 97007023

Selected works celebrate the writer's poetic response to life.

The only complete anthology of the twentieth-century American modernist's poetry includes more than fifty poems not previously collected, early versions of famous poems, and the most comprehensive selection of his prose writings yet published.

"Having all of Stevens' poems—especially all the late poems—in one volume is a great thing (previously, one had to seek them out in three different books); the Adagia and his replies to questionnaires are marvelous; and even in the somewhat turgid prose pieces, he sometimes expresses himself with exemplary force and concision." —New York Times Book Review

Includes indexes.

Strand, Mark
Collected Poems. Mark Strand. Alfred A. Knopf 2014. xviii, 520 pages
ISBN 9780385352512
Grades: Adult 811
1. Poetry
LC 2013049034

A collection of all of the poet Mark Strand's previously published poems.

For all the streamlined sadness of his dreamlike domain, Strand remains aware of other poets, which is particularly evident in his homages, translations, and elegies. His recent string of short sardonic prose poems are all quite distinct from one another, but all are instantly, recognizably Strand, 'Erasing the world and leaving instead/ the invisible lines of its calling: Out there, out there.' —Publishers Weekly

Includes bibliographical references and index.

Swenson, May
Collected Poems. May Swenson; Langdon Hammer, editor. The Library of America 2013. xxi, 759 pages
ISBN 9781598532104
Grades: Adult 811
1. American poetry 2. Poetry
LC 2012945847

A centennial celebration of the acclaimed 20th-century poet's literary life collects her entire body of poetry in a single volume that includes Another Animal, Iconographs and In Other Words as well as a selection of previously uncollected pieces, in an anthology that offers insight into her explorations of the natural world, eroticism and culture.

Includes bibliographical references and index of titles and first lines.

Sze, Arthur
Sight Lines. Arthur Sze. Copper Canyon Press 2019. VIII, 69 pages
ISBN 9781556595592
Grades: Adult 811

ESSENTIAL AND RECOMMENDED TITLES
811 American poetry

1. Poetry

LC 2018052007

Sze, in drawing connections between the pastoral and the catastrophic, speaks to a contemporary condition in which we are constantly fragmented and made whole again as we are presented with a saturation of narratives. In his scenes of the quotidian, musings on life and death, and traversals between the natural and the artificial, Sze opens us to multitudinous lines of sight.

"Finely crafted and philosophical, this is a book that rewards multiple careful readings." —*Publishers Weekly*

Tapahonso, Luci
  A Radiant Curve: Poems and Stories. Luci Tapahonso. University of Arizona Press 2008. x, 93 p.
  ISBN 9780816527083
  Grades: Adult   811
  1. Navajo (Diné) (North American people) 2. American poetry 3. Poetry

LC 2008027223

In this sixth collection of stories and verse, award-winning writer Luci Tapahonso finds sacredness in everyday life.

"In 2006, Tapahonso received a Lifetime Achievement Award from the Native Writers Circle of the Americas." —*Library Journal*

An American Indian literary series.

Thom, Kai Cheng
  Falling Back in Love with Being Human: Letters to Lost Souls. Kai Cheng Thom. The Dial Press 2023. 160 p.
  ISBN 9780593594988
  Grades: Adult   811
  1. Letter writing 2. Trans women 3. Hope 4. Forgiveness 5. love 6. Poetry 7. Self-Help — Personal growth

An award-winning writer, performance artist and community healer presents a collection of tender and poetic love letters that guide readers towards cultivating empathy, forgiving others and embracing oneself while teaching readers to fall back in love with being human.

"This fierce and tender volume leaves a mark." —*Publishers Weekly*

Tran, Paul
  All the Flowers Kneeling. Paul Tran. Penguin 2022. 96 p.
  ISBN 9780143136842
  Grades: Adult   811
  1. Psychic trauma 2. Resilience 3. Healing 4. Persistence 5. Intergenerational relations 6. Sexual violence 7. Imperialism, American 8. Love 9. Asian Americans 10. Intergenerational trauma 11. Poetry

LC 2021027962

A collection of poetry from an award-winning poet whose work has appeared in the New Yorker that celebrates rediscovering and reconfiguring one's self after suffering great trauma and showcases the human capacity for resilience, endurance and love.

"This much-anticipated debut from Tran (the first Asian American since 1993 and the first transgender poet ever to win the Nuyorican Poets Cafe Grand Slam) investigates American imperialism, sexual assault, intergenerational trauma, and the complexities of trauma recovery.... Readers will be sure to find connection and refuge within Tran's standout collection." —*Library Journal*

Trethewey, Natasha D.
  ★ *Monument: Poems : New and Selected*. Natasha Trethewey. Houghton Mifflin Harcourt 2018. 224 p.
  ISBN 9781328507846
  Grades: Adult   811
  1. African Americans 2. Interracial families 3. Race relations 4. Family history 5. Mississippi 6. Poetry

LC 2018012255

The two-term U.S. Poet Laureate and Pulitzer Prize-winning author of Native Guard poetically links the human struggles and resilience of African-American women throughout history to the collective trauma of national wounds.

"Monument is an essential volume of piercing wit, elegiac beauty, profound insights intimate and cultural, and the sustaining power of remembrance." —*Booklist*

  ★ *Native Guard*. Natasha Trethewey. Houghton Mifflin 2006. 51 p.
  ISBN 9780618604630
  Grades: Adult   811
  1. American poetry 2. Women authors 3. Poetry

LC 2005010649

A compilation of poetry addresses the complex history of the American South, offering a lyrical tribute to the Native Guard, one of the first Black regiments in service during the Civil War and paying tribute to the author's mother and her illegal interracial marriage.

A third compilation of poetry by the author of Bellocq's Ophelia and Domestic Work addresses the complex history of the American South, offering a lyrical tribute to the Native Guard, one of the first Black regiments in service during the Civil War and paying tribute to the author's mother and her illegal interracial marriage.

Includes bibliographical references (p. 47-49).

Valentine, Jean
  Door in the Mountain: New and Collected Poems, 1965-2003. Jean Valentine. Wesleyan University Press 2004. xv, 285 p; (Wesleyan poetry)
  ISBN 9780819567123
  Grades: Adult   811
  1. American poetry 2. Women authors 3. Poetry

LC 2004016019

Presents a collection of the author's established works in addition to new poems, which deal with such topics as death, aging, and the passage of time.

"The defiant, angular, yet propulsively emotional recent poems that occupy the first and last parts of the book should please both fans of Valentine's earliest poetry and fans of her strongly feminist middle period." —*Publishers Weekly*

Includes bibliographical references and index.

Vang, Mai Der
  Afterland: Poems. Mai Der Vang. Graywolf Press 2017. 94 pages
  ISBN 9781555977702
  Grades: Adult   811
  1. Refugees 2. American poetry 3. Laos 4. Poetry

LC 2016938843

Mai Der Vang is telling the story of her own family, and by doing so, she also provides an essential history of the Hmong culture's ongoing resilience in exile. Many of these poems are written in the voices of those fleeing unbearable violence after U.S. forces recruited Hmong fighters in Laos in the Secret War against communism, only to abandon them after that war went awry.

"Yet, amid bullets and bees, cyanide and stars, humpbacks and harvests, Vang imbues her imagery not only with loss but also with the remarkable resilience and crystalline spirituality of Hmong lore and language." —*Booklist*

Vuong, Ocean
  ★ *Time Is a Mother*. Ocean Vuong. Penguin Press 2022. 96 pages
  ISBN 9780593300237
  Grades: Adult   811
  1. Death of mothers 2. Memory 3. Time 4. Mortality 5. Vietnamese Americans 6. Psychic trauma 7. Loss 8. Mothers and sons 9. Families 10. Southeast Asian Americans 11. Southeast Asian people 12. Grief 13. Poetry

In this deeply intimate second poetry collection, Ocean Vuong searches for life among the aftershocks of his mother's death, embodying the paradox of sitting within grief while being determined to survive beyond it. Shifting through memory, Vuong contends with personal loss and the meaning of family. At once vivid, brave, and propulsive, Vuong's poems circle fragmented lives to find both restoration as well as the epicenter of the break.

"In this second collection of poetry by breakout star Vuong, following his first novel, on Earth We're Briefly Gorgeous (2019), he focuses on the complicated relationship with his mother in quiet, astonishing lyrics." —*Booklist*

PUBLIC LIBRARY CORE COLLECTION: NONFICTION
Twentieth Edition

Walcott, Derek
Omeros. Derek Walcott. Farrar, Straus and Giroux 1992. 325 p.
ISBN 9780374523503
Grades: Adult   **811**
1. Poetry
LC BI2005011953

A poem in five books, of circular narrative design, titled with the Greek name for Homer, which simultaneously charts two currents of history: the visible history charted in events—the tribal losses of the American Indian, the tragedy of African enslavement—and the interior, unwritten epic fashioned from the suffering of the individual in exile.

"If you can buy only one Walcott title, get this Carribean epic." —*Library Journal*

The Poetry of Derek Walcott 1948-2013. Derek Walcott; selected by the poet Glyn Maxwell. Farrar, Straus and Giroux 2014. xiii, 617 pages
ISBN 9780374125615
Grades: Adult   **811**
1. Poetry
LC 2013034997

A collection spanning the range of the Nobel Prize-winning writer's career includes his first published poem, "In My Eighteenth Year"; his first widely celebrated verses on the violence in Africa; his mature work from the Star-Apple Kingdom; and his late masterpieces from White Egrets.

Includes index.

Waldrop, Keith
Transcendental Studies: A Trilogy. Keith Waldrop. University of California Press 2009. 201 p.
ISBN 9780520258785
Grades: Adult   **811**
1. American poetry 2. Poetry
LC 2008025958

Presents a selection of recent work by the poet, including three related poem sequences that use collaged words out of context to take on new meanings.

Walker, Alice
Hard Times Require Furious Dancing: New Poems. Alice Walker; foreword and illustrations by Shiloh McCloud. New World Library 2010. xvi, 165 p. : Illustration
ISBN 9781577319306
Grades: 11 12 Adult   **811**
1. American poetry 2. Women authors 3. African American poetry 4. Poetry 5. Poetry — African American authors
LC 2010029972

Presents a collection of poems that focus on both the joys and sorrows of life.

"In this poetry collection, the author writes of loss and disappointment, and the strength that rises from meeting them unflinchingly... These are powerful anthems of womanhood and age, although just as likely to be empowering to men and to the not-yet-old." —*Booklist*

A Palm of Her Hand project; Includes index.

We Are the Ones We Have Been Waiting For: Inner Light in a Time of Darkness : Meditations. Alice Walker. New Press : 2006. xii, 257 p.
ISBN 9781595581372
Grades: 11 12 Adult   **811**
1. Happiness 2. Contentment 3. Spirituality 4. Spirituality and Religion — General

A book of spiritual ruminations with a progressive political edge, from the Pulitzer Prize-winner who has devoted her life to befriending the earth. Walker has long been a force for sanity in a chaotic world. Here she draws on her deep spiritual grounding, her political conviction and experience, and her literary gifts to offer a series of meditations filled with wisdom, hope, encouragement, and, at times, serenity to a world in need of all these things. "Happiness ... comes from the simple belief that what one is feeling and doing is right. That it is right to protect rather than terrorize others; right to feed people rather than withhold food (and medicine); right to want the freedom and joyful existence of all human kind... a deep knowing that we are the earth—our separation from Earth perhaps our greatest illusion—and that we stand, with gratitude and love, by our planetary Self.

Wang, Jackie
The Sunflower Cast a Spell to Save Us from the Void. Jackie Wang and illustrated by Kalan Sherrard. Nightboat Books 2021. 131 p.
ISBN 9781643620367
Grades: Adult   **811**
1. Wang, Jackie 2. Thought and thinking 3. Dreams 4. Interpersonal relations 5. Poetry

The poems in The Sunflower Cast a Spell to Save Us from the Void read like dispatches from the dream world, with Jackie Wang acting as our trusted comrade reporting across time and space. By sharing her personal index of dreams with its scenes of solidarity and resilience, interpersonal conflict and outlaw jouissance, Wang embodies historical trauma and communal memory. Here, the all-too-familiar interplay between crisis and resistance becomes first distorted, then clarified and refreshed.

"A cross between Mei-mei Berssenbrugge's elliptical poetic treatises and Marosa di Giorgio's fevered fables, Wang tells stories that begin in clarity but unfurl into complex landscapes, exploring the role of projection and imagination in our relationships." —*Publishers Weekly*

Wheatley, Phillis
The Poems of Phillis Wheatley. Edited with an introduction by Julian D. Mason, Jr. University of North Carolina Press 1989. xvi, 235 p.
ISBN 9780807842454
Grades: Adult   **811**
1. American poetry 2. African American poetry 3. Poetry
LC 88023280

Collects poems by the young Black slave with critical commentaries on her short career.

Includes bibliographical references.

Whitman, Walt
★ *Leaves of Grass*. Walt Whitman. William Collins 2015. IX, 162 p.
ISBN 9780008110604
Grades: 11 12 Adult   **811**
1. American poetry 2. 19th century 3. Poetry

Walt Whitman (1819—92) was an influential American poet and essayist, and is credited with being the founding father of free verse. He first published his culturally significant poetry collection 'Leaves of Grass' in 1855 from his own pocket, and revised and expanded it over thirty years. It is an essential element of America's literary tradition, much taught in schools and universities around the world.

First published: 1855.

★ *Poetry and Prose*. Walt Whitman. Library of America 1996. 1407 p.
ISBN 9781883011352
Grades: 11 12 Adult   **811**
1. American poetry 2. 19th century 3. Poetry 4. Arts and Entertainment — Writing and Publishing
LC 95052466

Gathers the original 1855 edition of "Leaves of Grass," the 1891-92 edition—the last published in Whitman's lifetime—his writings on New York history and the Civil War, and other works, with a chronology and information on his work.

Rev. ed. of: Complete poetry and collected prose. New York, N.Y. : Literary Classics of the United States, c1982; Includes bibliographical references and index.

★ *Selected Poems*. Walt Whitman; Harold Bloom, editor. The Library of America 2003. xxxi, 221 p.
ISBN 9781931082327
Grades: Adult   **811**
1. American poetry 2. Poetry
LC 2002032124

ESSENTIAL AND RECOMMENDED TITLES
811 American poetry

Surveys Walt Whitman's significant poetic works, from early notebook fragments of "Song of Myself" to the late poems of "Good-bye my Fancy."

The author of The Western Canon surveys Walt Whitman's significant poetic works, from early notebook fragments of Song of Myself to the late poems of Good-bye my Fancy.

Includes bibliographical references and index.

Wicker, Marcus
Silencer. Marcus Wicker. Mariner Books/Houghton Mifflin Harcourt 2017. 73 pages
ISBN 9781328715548
Grades: Adult   811
1. American poetry 2. Poetry of places 3. African American poetry 4. Religious poetry 5. Poetry
LC 2017014165

Welcome to Marcus Wicker's Midwest, where the muzzle is always on and where silence and daily microaggressions can chafe away at the faith of a young man grieved by images of gun violence and police brutality in twenty-first-century America. Precisely contradictory, bittersweet, witty, and heartbreaking, Silencer is where the political and the personal collide. Driven by the sounds of hip-hop and reimagined forms and structures, Wicker's explosive second book is composed of poems at war with themselves, verses in which the poet questions his own faith in God, in hope, in the American Dream, and in himself. Pushing our ideas of traditions and expectations, these poems and queries work in concert towards creating a new dialectic.

Wilbur, Richard
Anterooms: New Poems and Translations. Richard Wilbur. Houghton Mifflin Harcourt 2010. 63 p.
ISBN 9780547358116
Grades: Adult   811
1. American poetry 2. Poetry
LC 2010005772

Celebrates the human condition through reflections on nature and love, while a series of translations bring other authors' poems and riddles into a new light.

★ *Collected Poems, 1943-2004*. Richard Wilbur. Harcourt 2004. xvi, 585 p. : Illustration
ISBN 9780151011056
Grades: Adult   811
1. American poetry 2. Poetry
LC 2004009228

A comprehensive collection of works written throughout the course of the National Book Award and two-time Pulitzer Prize-winning poet's more than sixty-year career includes "In Trackless Woods" and several new and previously unpublished pieces.

Includes index.

Williams, C. K.
★ *Collected Poems*. C.K. Williams. Farrar, Straus and Giroux 2006. xx, 682 p.
ISBN 9780374126520
Grades: Adult   811
1. Poetry
LC 2005051867

Collects nearly four decades of the author's work, featuring peoms from "Tar," "With Ignorance," "Flesh and Blood," "A Dream of Mind," "Repair," and "The Singing."

"This weighty, even daunting, tome shows new and old readers the long arc of this Pulitzer Prize and National Book Award winner's career, from the morbid sanguinities of his apprentice work to the careful, moving, stanzaic focus evident in 21 new poems." —*Publishers Weekly*

Includes indexes.

Falling Ill: Last Poems. C.K. Williams. Farrar Straus Giroux 2017. 54 pages
ISBN 9780374152208
Grades: Adult   811

1. Death 2. Mortality 3. American poetry 4. Elegiac poetry 5. Poetry
LC 2016025612

Shares poems related to "the burden of being alive."

Williams, William Carlos
Paterson. William Carlos Williams. New Directions Books 1995. xv, 311 pages
ISBN 9780811212984
Grades: Adult   811
1. Poetry of places 2. American poetry 3. New Jersey 4. 20th century 5. Poetry
LC Bl2015032612

Presents the American poet's extended lyrical work in which the life and history of a city become the symbol of humanity.

Includes bibliographical references.

Wright, C. D.
One with Others: [a Little Book of Her Days]. C.D. Wright. Copper Canyon Press 2010, 168 p. : Illustration
ISBN 9781556593246
Grades: Adult   811
1. Civil rights demonstrations 2. Civil Rights Movement 3. American poetry 4. 20th century 5. Poetry
LC 2010016789

Presents a collection of poems, along with a historical account, describing the 1969 "walk against fear" through a small Arkansas by a group of African Americans.

Wright, James Arlington
Above the River: The Complete Poems. James Wright; with an introduction by Donald Hall. Noonday Press 1992. xxxvii, 387 p.
ISBN 9780374522827
Grades: Adult   811
1. American poetry 2. Poetry
LC BL 99726841

Poems deal with love, travel, myth, friendship, the past, the seasons, mortality, and language.

Includes indexes.

Xie, Jenny
Eye Level: Poems. Jenny Xie. Graywolf Press 2018, 79 pages
ISBN 9781555978020
Grades: Adult   811
1. American poetry 2. Identity 3. Voyages and travels 4. 21st century 5. Poetry
LC 2017938013

Winner of the Walt Whitman Award of the Academy of American Poets, selected by Juan Felipe Herrera.

"Xie, winner of the 2017 Walt Whitman Award, strives to develop a poetics of observation in her debut, subtly reworking the documentary impulse familiar in much contemporary writing to create an alternative way to interrogate the experience of cultural otherness, outside the fraught framework of the lyric." —*Publishers Weekly*

Young, Kevin
Ardency: A Chronicle of the Amistad Rebels. Compiled from authentic sources by Kevin Lowell Young. Alfred A. Knopf 2011. xiii, 249 p. : Illustration; Map
ISBN 9780307267641
Grades: Adult   811
1. Enslaved people 2. Enslaved people's resistance and revolts 3. Mutiny 4. Slave trade 5. Anti-slavery movements 6. United States history 7. 19th century 8. Poetry 9. History writing — African American — Enslavement — United States 10. Adult books for young adults
LC 2010030007

A poetic epic written over the course of 20 years chronicles the story of the Africans who mutinied on board the slave ship Amistad through different voices, from an interpreter for the rebels to inmates in a New Haven jail who appealed to John Quincy Adams. By the National Book Award finalist author of Jelly Roll.

"This poetry collection chronicles the slave mutiny aboard the schooner Amistad in 1839. This three-part book focuses on the 53 Africans who rebelled against their would-be slave owners. Young expertly blends cultural and social history as well as religion to dramatize the lives of the rebels. His evocative use of language—punctuated with stunning metaphors—keeps the historical context clear while moving the gripping true story forward." —*Library Journal*

Being an epic account of the capture of the Spanish schooner Amistad, by the Africans on board; their voyage and capture near Long Island, New York; with phrenological studies of several of the surviving Africans.

★ *The Art of Losing: Poems of Grief and Healing.* Edited by Kevin Young. Bloomsbury USA 2010. xxiv, 311 p.
ISBN 9781608190331
Grades: Adult 811
1. Grief 2. Poetry
LC 2009028888

A book that includes contributions from such poets as Dylan Thomas, John Ashbery, Emily Dickinson, Rita Dove, Anne Sexton, Robert Pinsky, and many more collects 150 contemporary elegies that embrace the pain, heartbreak, and healing stages of mourning.

"This book will provide solace for the bereaved. Both clergy and family members will use it to create meaningful memorial services, and all poetry lovers will find much to celebrate and ponder here." —*Library Journal*

Includes bibliographical references (p. 293-305) and index.

Book of Hours. Kevin Young. Alfred A. Knopf 2014. xii, 185 pages
ISBN 9780307272249
Grades: Adult 811
1. American poetry 2. African American poetry 3. Poetry
LC 2013019328

Presents a collection of poems with themes of bereavement and celebration, as the author deals with the unexpected death of his father and the birth of his daughter.

An award-winning poet presents a searing collection of emotional poems that acknowledges life's passages, including the tragic death of his father and the birth of his son.

Brown: Poems. Kevin Young; photographs by Melanie Dunea. Alfred A. Knopf 2018. VII, 161 pages : Illustration
ISBN 9781524732547
Grades: Adult 811
1. African Americans 2. Injustice 3. Race relations 4. Racism 5. United States 6. Poetry
LC 2017029270

New York Times Notable Book, 2018; Library Journal Best Books, 2018.

James Brown. John Brown's raid. Brown v. the Topeka Board of Ed.: the recently National Book Award-longlisted author of Blue Laws meditates on all things "brown" in this powerful new collection. A testament to Young's own—and our collective—experience, Brown offers beautiful, sustained harmonies from a poet whose wisdom deepens with time.

This is a Borzoi book—Title page verso; Includes bibliographical references (pages [159]-161).

Stones: Poems. Kevin Young. Alfred A. Knopf 2021. 96 p.
ISBN 9781524732561
Grades: Adult 811
1. Loss 2. Places 3. Home (Concept) 4. Families 5. African American authors 6. Southern States 7. Poetry
LC 2020057384

A book of elegy, loss, and what binds us to life, by a towering poetic talent. Whether it's the Louisiana summer's fireflies in a mason jar (doomed by their collection), or his grandmother, Mama Annie, who latches the screen door when someone steps out for just a moment, all that comprises our flickering precarious joy, all that we want to protect, is lifted into the light in this moving book. Stones becomes an ode to Young's home places and his dear departed, and to what of them—of us—poetry can save.

"With superbly crafted poems that engage the past and the present, Young (Brown: Poems) delivers another ambitious collection across seven lyrically powerful sections.... These elegant, measured poems offer insight into the troubled moment through an exhumation of the past, while giving the reader plenty of depth and beauty to carry into the future." —*Publishers Weekly*

Zapruder, Matthew
Come on All You Ghosts. Matthew Zapruder. Copper Canyon Press 2010. xi, 111 p.
ISBN 9781556593222
Grades: Adult 811
1. American poetry 2. Poetry
LC 2010016787

A third collection of poems mixes humor with themes of love and loss and draws upon past personal experiences in a search for self-revelation.

811.4 American poetry — 1861-1899

Dickinson, Emily
★ *The Complete Poems.* Edited by Thomas H. Johnson. Little, Brown 1960. xiii, 770 p.
ISBN 9780316184137
Grades: Adult 811.4
1. American poetry 2. Poetry
LC 60011646

This volume, containing all of Emily Dickinson's lyrics, presents biographical data about the poet and information about previous collections of her works.

"Complete is the keyword here as this is the only edition currently available that contains all of Dickinson's poems. The works were originally gathered by editor Johnson and published in a three-volume set in 1955." —*Library Journal*

811.54 American poetry — 1945-1999

Ginsberg, Allen
★ *Howl: And Other Poems.* Allen Ginsberg. City Lights Books 1959. 57 p.
ISBN 9780872860179
Grades: Adult 811.54
1. Beat generation 2. American poetry 3. 20th century 4. Poetry
LC 56008587

Ginsberg's love for a man with whom he shared some of life's worst experiences is celebrated in poems which were once the subject of a prolonged court trial.

Gregg, Linda
All of It Singing: New and Selected Poems. Linda Gregg. Graywolf Press 2008. 213 p.
ISBN 9781555975074
Grades: Adult 811.54
1. American poetry 2. Poetry
LC 2008928247

A single-volume anthology of definitive pieces reflects the career of the PEN/Voelcker Award-winning poet and combines pieces from her six previous collections with thirty new works.

A Jane Kenyon book—T.P. verso.

Myles, Eileen
I Must Be Living Twice: New & Selected Poems, 1975-2014. Eileen Myles. Ecco 2015. xii, 356 pages
ISBN 9780062389084
Grades: Adult 811.54
1. American poetry 2. Women authors 3. Poetry 4. Poetry — LGBTQIA
LC 2016297462

ESSENTIAL AND RECOMMENDED TITLES
811.6 American poetry — 2000-

"Readers will be thrilled not only that this old work is available again, but that the new work is as impressive as ever." —*Publishers Weekly*

Plath, Sylvia
The Letters of Sylvia Plath: Volume 1: 1940-1956. Sylvia Plath; edited by Peter K. Steinberg and Karen V. Kukil. Harper 2017. 800 pages
ISBN 9780062740434
Grades: Adult — 811.54
1. Plath, Sylvia 2. Women poets 3. Women authors 4. Women college students 5. Marriage 6. Letters 7. Arts and Entertainment — Writing and Publishing 8. Life stories — Arts and culture — Writing — Poets

While her renown as one of the twentieth century's most influential poets is beyond dispute, Plath was also one of its most captivating correspondents. The Letters of Sylvia Plath is the breathtaking compendium of this prolific writer's correspondence with more than 120 people, including family, friends, contemporaries, and colleagues.

The Letters of Sylvia Plath: Volume 2: 1956-1963. Sylvia Plath; edited by Peter K. Steinberg and Karen V. Kukil. Harper 2018. 1280 p.
ISBN 9780062740588
Grades: Adult — 811.54
1. Plath, Sylvia 2. Women poets 3. Women authors 4. Women college students 5. Marriage 6. Motherhood 7. Interpersonal relations 8. Writing 9. Letters 10. Arts and Entertainment — Writing and Publishing 11. Life stories — Arts and culture — Writing — Poets

One of the most talented and beloved poets, Sylvia Plath continues to fascinate and inspire the modern literary imagination. The tragedy of her untimely death at age thirty, almost fifty-five years ago, has left much unknown about her creative and personal life. In this remarkable second volume of the iconic poet and writer's collected letters, the full range of Plath's ambitions, talents, fears, and perspective is made visible through her own powerful words.

Smith, Patricia
★ *Incendiary Art: Poems.* Patricia Smith. TriQuarterly Books/Northwestern University Press 2017. 132 p.
ISBN 9780810134331
Grades: Adult — 811.54
1. Till, Emmett, 1941-1955 2. African Americans 3. American poetry 4. Women authors 5. African American poetry 6. Poetry — African American authors 7. Poetry

LC 2016036601

A National Book Award finalist and the author of six critically acclaimed volumes of poetry presents a compelling new collection that envisions, re-envisions and ultimately reinvents the role of witness with an incendiary fusion of forms, including prose poems, ghazals, sestinas and sonnets.

Includes bibliographical references (pages 131-132).

811.6 American poetry — 2000-

Alexander, Kwame
Light for the World to See. Kwame Alexander. Houghton Mifflin Harcourt 2020. 1 volume (unpaged) : Illustration
ISBN 9780358539414
Grades: Adult — 811.6
1. Floyd, George, 1974-2020 2. Kaepernick, Colin, 1987- 3. Obama, Barack 4. Police brutality 5. Institutional racism 6. Racism 7. Black Lives Matter movement 8. African American civil rights 9. Social advocacy 10. Protests, demonstrations, vigils, etc. 11. African Americans 12. Race relations 13. United States history 14. 21st century 15. Poetry 16. Politics and global affairs — Civil and human rights 17. Society and culture — Race 18. Antiracist literature

Presents a collection of three powerful poems that take on racism and Black resistance in America.

"Alexander turns his poetic attention to three milestones in recent U.S. history: the murder of George Floyd by police officers in Minneapolis, the kneeling protests of Colin Kaepernick during the national anthem before NFL games, and the election of Barack Obama.... A brave intervention by a talented writer of conviction." —*Booklist*

A thousand words on race on race and hope—Cover; American bullet points, Take a knee, and the undefeated were originally performed for ESPN's theundefeated.Com.

Browne, Mahogany L.
★ *Black Girl Magic: A Poem.* Mahogany L. Browne; art by Jess X. Snow. Roaring Brook Press 2018. 40 p.
ISBN 9781250173720
Grades: Adult — 811.6
1. Expectation 2. Success (Concept) 3. Values 4. Personal conduct 5. African American women 6. Teenage girls 7. African American teenagers 8. African American children 9. Girls 10. African American poetry 11. Poetry 12. Book club best bets

LC 2017944500

Amelia Bloomer List, 2019.

Much of what twenty-first century culture tells Black girls is not pretty: Don't wear this; don't smile at that. Don't have an opinion; don't dream big. And most of all, don't love yourself. In response to such destructive ideas, internationally recognized poet Mahogany Browne challenges the conditioning of society by crafting an anthem of strength and magic undeniable in its bloom for all beautiful Black girls.

"These dense, entrancing, necessary works by more than 60 Black women poets create a Black-girl-centric world of their own…a well-rounded look at what it means to be a Black woman and in the process serves as a platform for our voices and bodies, revealing our maneuvers through the world as deeply relevant to and deserving of literary space." —*Chicago Reader*

Corral, Eduardo C.
Guillotine: Poems. Eduardo C. Corral. Graywolf Press 2020. 81 pages
ISBN 9781644450307
Grades: Adult — 811.6
1. Borderlands 2. Immigrants 3. Grief 4. Rejection 5. Hispanic Americans 6. LGBTQIA+ people 7. Poetry

LC 2019949953

Guillotine traverses desert landscapes cut through by migrants, the grief of loss, betrayal's lingering scars, the border itself—great distances in which violence and yearning find roots. Through the voices of undocumented immigrants, border patrol agents, and scorned lovers, award-winning poet Eduardo C. Corral writes dramatic portraits of contradiction, survival, and a deeply human, relentless interiority. With extraordinary lyric imagination, these poems wonder about being unwanted or renounced.

"In his latest, corruscatingly brilliant collection, Yale Younger Poet Corral (Slow Lightning) communicates a sense of loss and betrayal along the Mexican-American border in a multivoiced narrative that becomes a single story, a single low wail.... The images rushing down these pages in tightly paced cadence take readers on a haunting journey, with Corral's impressionism delivering more than taut realism ever could." —*Library Journal*

Hass, Robert
Summer Snow: New Poems. Robert Hass. Ecco Press 2020. 192 p.
ISBN 9780062950024
Grades: Adult — 811.6
1. Nature 2. Imperfection 3. Loss 4. Poetry writing 5. Poetry 6. Adult books for young adults

Hass's trademark careful attention to the natural world, his subtle humor, and the delicate but wide-ranging eye he casts on the human experience are fully on display in his masterful collection. Touching on subjects including the poignancy of loss, the serene and resonant beauty of nature, and the mutability of desire, Hass exhibits his virtuosic abilities, expansive intellect, and tremendous readability in one of his most ambitious and formally brilliant collections to date.

Kaur, Rupi
The Sun and Her Flowers. Rupi Kaur. Andrews McMeel Publishing 2017. 256 p.

ISBN 9781449486792
Grades: Adult 811.6
1. Grief 2. Loss 3. Coping 4. Self-fulfillment 5. Poetry 6. Adult books for young adults

A collection of poetry about growth and healing, ancestry and honoring one's roots and expatriation and rising up to find a home within yourself, augmented by the author's own illustrations.

Seuss, Diane
Still Life with Two Dead Peacocks and a Girl: Poems. Diane Seuss. Graywolf Press 2018. 108 p. : Illustration
ISBN 9781555978068
Grades: Adult 811.6
1. Painting 2. American poetry 3. Art 4. Poetry
LC 2017953321

This volume of poetry takes its title from Rembrandt's painting, a dark emblem of femininity, violence, and the viewer's troubled gaze. The collection shatters the notion of a still life, and presents the painting in pieces. With invention and irreverence, the poems escape their gilded frames and overturn traditional representations of gender, class, and luxury. Details from this gallery of lives in shards hide more than they reveal, like fragmented memories, waiting until they are reassembled into a whole.

First Graywolf Printing.

Skaja, Emily
Brute. Emily Skaja. Graywolf Press 2019. 74 p.
ISBN 9781555978358
Grades: Adult 811.6
1. Gender identity 2. Femininity 3. Violence 4. Self-discovery 5. Self-perception 6. Poetry
LC 2018947085

Emily Skaja's debut collection is a fiery, hypnotic book that confronts the dark questions and menacing silences around gender, sexuality, and violence. Brute arises, brave and furious, from the dissolution of a relationship, showing how such endings necessitate self-discovery and reinvention. The speaker of these poems is a sorceress, a bride, a warrior, a lover, both object and agent, ricocheting among ways of knowing and being known. Each incarnation squares itself up against ideas of feminine virtue and sin, strength and vulnerability, love and rage, as it closes in on a hard-won freedom.

"With relentless, driving energy, Skaja's poems seek brutal truths while searching for meaningful transformation. The mythological allusions and imagery, the violence, the honest and painful reflectionsall travel toward an awakening achieved by being fully rooted in dark, human soil." —*Publishers Weekly*

Smith, Danez
★ *Don't Call Us Dead: Poems.* Danez Smith. Graywolf Press 2017. 88 pages
ISBN 9781555977856
Grades: Adult 811.6
1. Identity 2. African Americans 3. Gay men 4. Racism 5. Violence 6. Race relations 7. United States 8. Poetry
LC 2017930111

An awarding-winning poet presents a collection of works that opens with a heartrending sequence that imagines an afterlife for Black men shot by police—a place where suspicion, violence and grief are forgotten and replaced with the safety, love and longevity they deserved here on earth.

"Poised at the bruising intersection of Black and queer identity, poems such as "dear white america" ("I tried to love you, but you spent my brother's funeral making plans for brunch") lose no impact moving from spoken-word stage to page." —*Publishers Weekly*

Includes bibliographical references (page 85).

Smith, Tracy K.
★ *Wade in the Water: Poems.* Tracy K. Smith. Graywolf Press 2018. 83 pages
ISBN 9781555978136

Grades: Adult 811.6
1. Inequality 2. Social classes 3. Race relations 4. United States 5. Poetry
LC 2017951515

New York Times Notable Book, 2018.

A Pulitzer Prize-winning poet, using her signature voice—inquisitive, lyrical and wry—mulls over what it means to be a citizen, a mother and an artist in a culture arbitrated by wealth, men and violence, boldly tying America's modern moment both to our nation's fraught founding history and to a sense of the spirit, the everlasting.

"The sacred and the malevolent are astutely juxtaposed in this beautifully formed, deeply delving, and caring volume." —*Booklist*

Includes bibliographical references (pages 77-81).

Youn, Monica
Blackacre. Monica Youn. Graywolf Press 2016. 85 pages
ISBN 9781555977504
Grades: Adult 811.6
1. American poetry 2. Women authors 3. Poetry 4. Poetry — Asian American authors
LC 2016931136

In the title sequence, the poet gleans a second crop from the field of Milton's great sonnet on his blindness: a lyric meditation on her barrenness, on her own desire—her own struggle—to conceive a child. What happens when the transformative imagination comes up against the limits of unalterable fact?

"Throughout, Youn's lawyerly analyses—of life, of herself, her feelings, and of language—cut through the poetic to a place that lies triangulated between poetry, lyric memoir, and textual analysis." —*Publishers Weekly*

Includes bibliographical references (page 83).

812 American drama in English

Albee, Edward
★ *Who's Afraid of Virginia Woolf?* Edward Albee. Scribner Classics 2003. 243 p.
ISBN 9780743255257
Grades: 11 12 Adult 812
1. College teachers 2. Married people 3. Drama 4. New England 5. Arts and Entertainment — Theater — Plays
LC 2003054206

A social event becomes a personal challenge for two faculty members and their wives at a small New England college as their inner fears and desires are exposed.

Originally published: New York : Atheneum, 1962.

Auburn, David
Proof: A Play. David Auburn. Faber and Faber 2001. 83 p.
ISBN 9780571199976
Grades: 11 12 Adult 812
1. Death of fathers 2. Mathematicians 3. Men-women relations 4. Drama 5. Arts and Entertainment — Theater — Plays
LC 00050284

In a play portraying the uncertainties of trust, integrity, and genius, a woman claims authorship of a mathematical proof found among her late father's papers by one of his former students, who doubts her claim.

"Twenty-five-year-old Catherine, who sacrificed college to care for her mentally ill father (once a brilliant, much-admired mathematician), is left in a kind of limbo after his death. Socially awkward and a bit of a shut-in, she is gruff with Hal, a former student who shows up even before the funeral wanting to root through the countless notebooks her father kept in the years of his decline, hoping to find mathematical gold. On the heels of his arrival comes Claire, Catherine's cosmopolitan, blandly successful, and pushy sister, with plans to sell their father's house and take Catherine . with her back to New York." —*School Library Journal*

ESSENTIAL AND RECOMMENDED TITLES
812 American drama in English

Butler, Isaac
The World Only Spins Forward: The Ascent of Angels in America. Isaac Butler and Dan Kois. St Martins Pr 2018. 304 p.
ISBN 9781635571769
Grades: Adult   **812**
1. Kushner, Tony 2. Drama 3. Musicals 4. Homosexuality 5. LGBTQIA+ rights 6. Public opinion 7. Broadway, New York City 8. Arts and Entertainment — Theater 9. Society and culture — LGBTQIA+
LC 2018003632

Commemorating the 25th anniversary of the show's Broadway premiere, an oral history of Angels in America, a generation-defining classic and moving account of the AIDS era, is told through nearly 200 voices in vibrant conversation and debate and is both a rollicking theater saga and an uplifting testament to one of the great works of art of the past century.

"Highly recommended for anyone interested in performance, cultural history, and theater." —*Library Journal*

Edson, Margaret
Wit: A Play. Margaret Edson. Faber and Faber 1999. 85 p.
ISBN 9780571198771
Grades: Adult   **812**
1. Women college teachers 2. Arts and Entertainment — Theater — Plays
LC 99011921

The Pulitzer Prize-winning drama explores the role of nurses in the care of terminally ill patients, as Professor Vivian Bearing endures eight months of experimental chemotherapy in a grueling effort to fight ovarian cancer.

Gibson, William
★ *The Miracle Worker.* William Gibson. Scribner 2008. 112 p.
ISBN 9781416590842
Grades: 11 12 Adult   **812**
1. Keller, Helen, 1880-1968 2. Sullivan, Annie, 1866-1936 3. Women teachers 4. Drama 5. Arts and Entertainment — Theater — Plays
LC 2008275273

A text of the television play, intended for reading, of Anne Sullivan Macy's attempts to teach her pupil, Helen Keller, to communicate.

Goodrich, Frances
The Diary of Anne Frank. Frances Goodrich and Albert Hackett; newly adapted by Wendy Kesselman. Dramatists Play Service 2000. 72 p. : Illustration
ISBN 9780822217183
Grades: Adult   **812**
1. Frank, Anne, 1929-1945 2. Holocaust (1933-1945) 3. Drama 4. German occupation, World War II 5. European history 6. Netherlands 7. Arts and Entertainment — Theater — Plays
LC BI2006027516

A two-act play based on the diary of a Jewish girl who died in a Nazi concentration camp at the age of fifteen.

Based upon 'Anne Frank: the diary of a young girl'—T.P. verso.

Hansberry, Lorraine
★ *A Raisin in the Sun.* by Lorraine Hansberry; with a new introduction by Robert Nemiroff. New American Library 1988. 151 pages, [8] pages of plates : Illustration
ISBN 9780679601722
Grades: 11 12 Adult   **812**
1. Racism 2. African American families 3. Greed 4. Money 5. Poverty 6. Poor families 7. African Americans 8. Family relationships 9. African American neighborhoods 10. American people 11. North American people 12. Race relations 13. United States 14. Chicago, Illinois 15. Arts and Entertainment—Theater—Plays 16. Classics
LC 2001553309

An African-American family is united in love and pride as they struggle to overcome poverty and harsh living conditions.

A Signet book; the complete original version ... with an 8-page photo insert ... from the American Playhouse TV production starring Danny Glover and Esther Rolle. — from cover; Originally published: New York : The New American Library, 1951.

Kushner, Tony
Angels in America: A Gay Fantasia on National Themes. Tony Kushner. Theatre Communications Group 2003. 289 p.
ISBN 9781559362313
Grades: 11 12 Adult   **812**
1. Cohn, Roy M. 2. AIDS (Disease) 3. Angels 4. Gay men 5. Mormons 6. National characteristics, American 7. Passing (Identity) 8. Sexual orientation 9. Drama 10. Arts and Entertainment — Theater — Plays
LC 2003017904

Dramatizes the effects of AIDS on the United States through the experiences of lawyer Roy Cohn, a Mormon couple, and a young man called Prior Walter.

Rankine, Claudia
The White Card: A Play in One Act. Claudia Rankine. Graywolf Press 2019. IX, 89 pages : Illustration
ISBN 9781555978396
Grades: Adult   **812**
1. African Americans 2. Artists 3. Race relations 4. Drama 5. Arts and Entertainment — Theater — Plays
LC 2018947087

A revealing drama about racial divisions is experienced in the white spaces of the living room, the art gallery, the theater and the imagination itself.

A play about the imagined fault line between Black and white lives by Claudia Rankine, the author of Citizen. The White Card stages a conversation that is both informed and derailed by the Black/White American drama. The scenes in this one-act play, for all the characters' disagreements, stalemates, and seeming impasses, explore what happens if one is willing to stay in the room when it is painful to bear the pressure to listen and the obligation to respond.

"Each act in this fast-paced, thought-provoking play reads like a swift conversation, inviting readers to experience the power of whiteness from Charlotte's perspective." —*Library Journal*

Rose, Reginald
Twelve Angry Men. Reginald Rose; introduction by David Mamet. Penguin Books 2006. xi, 73 p.
ISBN 9780143104407
Grades: 9 10 11 12 Adult   **812**
1. Arts and Entertainment — Theater — Plays
LC 2006046006

A new edition of the landmark American play presents a compelling courtroom drama revolving around the trial of a boy accused of killing his father, where one man, a single hold-out juror, stands between the accused and capital punishment.

Presents a courtroom drama revolving around the trial of a boy accused of killing his father, where one man, a single hold-out juror, stands between the accused and capital punishment.

Originally published: U.S.A. :Dramatic Pub, 1955.

Shanley, John Patrick
Doubt: A Parable. John Patrick Shanley. Theatre Communications Group 2005. x, 58 p.
ISBN 9781559362764
Grades: Adult   **812**
1. Nuns 2. Clergy 3. Catholics 4. Child sexual abuse 5. Arts and Entertainment — Theater — Plays
LC 2005005284

Set in a Bronx Catholic school in 1964, a nun is faced with uncertainty as she has grave concerns for a male colleague.

Wilder, Thornton
Our Town: A Play in Three Acts. Thornton Wilder. HarperCollins 2003. xx, 181 p. : Illustration
ISBN 9780060535254

Grades: 11 12 Adult   **812**
1. Death 2. Young women 3. City life 4. Drama 5. New Hampshire 6. Arts and Entertainment — Theater — Plays
LC 2004274063

An illustrated hardcover edition of the Pulitzer Prize-winning drama, first produced in 1938, follows the changes that gradually occur in the lives of two early-twentieth-century New Hampshire families and their neighbors.
The author's Pulitzer Prize-winning drama portrays life in a small New Hampshire town during the early 1900s.
Contains a foreword by Donald Margulies.

Thornton Wilder: Collected Plays & Writings on Theater. [J.D. McClatchy, selected the texts and wrote the notes for this volume]. Library of America : 2007. x, 871 p; (The library of America, 172)
ISBN 9781598530032
Grades: Adult   **812**
1. Arts and Entertainment — Theater — Plays
LC 2006048620

A volume of approximately three dozen plays includes "The Alcestiad," "Our Town," and a previously unpublished Alfred Hitchcock screenplay, "Shadow of a Doubt," in a collection that also restores to print a key selection of Wilder's theatrical essays.
A volume of approximately three dozen plays includes The Alcestiad, Our Town, and a previously unpublished Alfred Hitchcock screenplay, Shadow of a Doubt, in a collection that also restores to print a key selection of Wilder's theatrical essays.
Includes bibliographical references (p. 835-871).

Williams, Tennessee

Plays, 1937-1955. Tennessee Williams. Library of America 2000. 975 p; (The Library of America, 119-120)
ISBN 9781883011864
Grades: Adult   **812**
1. Arts and Entertainment — Theater 2. Arts and Entertainment — Theater — Plays
LC 00030190

"Editors Gussow (drama critic, New York Times) and Holditch (founder/editor, The Tennessee Williams Journal) have added detailed notes on the texts and a newly researched chronology of Williams's life. Highly recommended for public and academic American drama collections." —*Library Journal*
Selection and notes by Mel Gussow and Kenneth Holditch.

Plays, 1957-1980. Tennessee Williams. Library of America 2000. 975 p; (The Library of America, 119-120)
ISBN 9781883011871
Grades: Adult   **812**
1. Arts and Entertainment — Theater 2. Arts and Entertainment — Theater — Plays
LC 00030190

A second compilation of plays focuses on the dramatist's later works, icnluding The Night of the Iguana, Sweet Bird of Youth, Orpheus Descending, Suddenly Last Summer, The Eccentricities of a Nightingale, and the autobiographical Vieux Carré.
Selection and notes by Mel Gussow and Kenneth Holditch.

★ *A Streetcar Named Desire.* Tennessee Williams; with an introduction by Arthur Miller. New Directions 2004. xv, 192 p.
ISBN 9780811216029
Grades: 11 12 Adult   **812**
1. Married people 2. Rape 3. Sisters 4. Widows 5. Women teachers 6. Drama 7. Arts and Entertainment — Theater — Plays
LC 2004011654

Tennessee Williams' classic drama studies the emotional disintegration of a Southern woman whose last chance for happiness is destroyed by her vindictive brother-in-law.

Wilson, August

Fences: A Play. August Wilson; introduction by Lloyd Richards. Plume 1986. xviii, 101 p.
ISBN 9780452264014
Grades: 11 12 Adult   **812**
1. African American history 2. 20th century 3. Arts and Entertainment — Theater — Plays
LC BL 99006429

During the 1950s Troy Maxson struggles against racism and tries to preserve his feelings of pride in himself.
Originally published: New York : New American Library, c1986.

King Hedley II. August Wilson. Theatre Communications Group 2005. xi, 103 p.
ISBN 9781559362603
Grades: Adult   **812**
1. African American men 2. Former convicts 3. Drama 4. Arts and Entertainment — Theater — Plays
LC 2005012535

King Hedley II is the eighth work in playwright August Wilson's 10-play cycle chronicling the history of the African American experience in each decade of the twentieth century. It's set in 1985 and tells the story of an ex-con in post-Reagan Pittsburgh trying to rebuild his life.

Ma Rainey's Black Bottom: A Play. August Wilson. New American Library 1985. xvi, 111 p.
ISBN 9780452261136
Grades: Adult   **812**
1. Arts and Entertainment — Theater — Plays
LC BL 99701783

MA Rainey, the legendary blues singer, is due to arrive with her entourage to cut new sides of old favorites. Waiting for her are her Black musician sidemen, the white owner of the record company, and her white manager. What goes down in the session to come is more than music.

The Piano Lesson. August Wilson. Plume 1990. 108 p.
ISBN 9780452265349
Grades: 11 12 Adult   **812**
1. African Americans 2. Arts and Entertainment — Theater — Plays
LC 90038735

When Boy Willie wants to sell the family's prized upright piano to purchase some land, the family must re-evaluate the piano's true worth.
"Feisty, ebullient, exuberant...Wilson is a consummate storyteller." —*Los Angeles Times*

Two Trains Running: 1969. August Wilson; foreword by Laurence Fishburne. Theatre Communications Group 2007. IX, 99 p.
ISBN 9781559363037
Grades: Adult   **812**
1. African American neighborhoods 2. African Americans 3. Drama 4. Arts and Entertainment — Theater — Plays
LC 2007022095

Set during the civil rights movement, at the lunch counter of Memphis Lee's diner.

813 American fiction in English

Atwood, Margaret

In Other Worlds: SF and the Human Imagination. Margaret Atwood. Nan A. Talese/Doubleday 2011. 208 p.
ISBN 9780385533966
Grades: Adult   **813**
1. Atwood, Margaret, 1939- 2. Science fiction writing 3. Literary criticism 4. Essays 5. Biographies 6. Canadian literature 7. Science fiction 8. Arts and Entertainment — Writing and Publishing 9. Life stories — Arts and culture — Writing — Authors 10. Arts and Entertainment — Writing and Publishing — Literary criticism

ESSENTIAL AND RECOMMENDED TITLES
813 American fiction in English

LC 2011013776

In this collection of essays Margaret Atwood contemplates the nature and history of science fiction and her relationship with it.

"A clever, thoughtful investigation that will appeal to science fiction readers and Atwood's loyal fans." —*Library Journal*

Includes bibliographical references.

Bergstein, Rachelle
The **Genius** of Judy: How Judy Blume Rewrote Childhood for All of Us. Rachelle Bergstein. One Signal 2024. 288 p.
ISBN 9781668010907
Grades: Adult   813
1. Blume, Judy 2. Women authors 3. Women children's literature authors 4. Fame 5. Books and reading 6. Teenagers 7. Puberty 8. Censorship 9. Banned books 10. Influence (Psychology) 11. American people 12. Biographies 13. Life stories — Arts and culture — Writing — Authors 14. Arts and Entertainment — Writing and Publishing — Literary criticism

LibraryReads Favorites, 2024.

Everyone knows Judy Blume. Her books have garnered her fans of all ages for decades and sold tens of millions of copies. But why were people so drawn to them? And why are we still talking about them now in the 21st century? In The Genius of Judy, her remarkable story is revealed as never before, beginning with her as a mother of two searching for purpose outside of her home in 1960s suburban New Jersey. This is the story of how a housewife became a groundbreaking artist, and how generations of empowered fans are her legacy, today more than ever.

"Journalist Bergstein (Brilliance and Fire) delivers a satisfying tribute to YA author Blume that emphasizes her novels' feminist bona fides and traces her life story against the backdrop of cultural shifts around women's sexuality and place in society." —*Publishers Weekly*

Bibbins, Mark
13th Balloon. Mark Bibbins. Copper Canyon Press 2020. 80 p.
ISBN 9781556595776
Grades: Adult   813
1. AIDS (Disease) 2. Loss 3. Lovers 4. Grief 5. United States 6. Poetry

LC 2019019606

"The scope of this darkly humorous and always tender book paints a portrait of grief as a fellow traveler that morphs but loses none of its power over time—a power readers will be lucky to experience." —*Publishers Weekly*

Bradbury, Ray
★ **Remembrance:** Selected Correspondence of Ray Bradbury. Ray Bradbury, edited by Jonathan R. Eller. Simon & Schuster 2023. 608 p.
ISBN 9781668016978
Grades: Adult   813
1. Bradbury, Ray, 1920-2012 2. Authors, American 3. Science fiction authors 4. Letter writing 5. Mentoring 6. Advice 7. Creation (Literary, artistic, etc.) 8. Friendship 9. Interpersonal relations 10. North American people 11. American people 12. Letters 13. Life stories — Arts and culture — Writing — Authors 14. Life stories — Relationships 15. Arts and Entertainment — Writing and Publishing

From the iconic author of Fahrenheit 451, The Martian Chronicles and Something Wicked This Way Comes comes a collection of his letters that illuminate the story of his life in new ways.

"Eller has gathered a marvelous compendium of Bradbury's extensive correspondence…Remembrance is a true labor of love and belongs in any library that has a Ray Bradbury collection." —*Booklist*

Britt, Ryan
★ The **Spice** Must Flow: The Story of Dune, from Cult Novels to Visionary Sci-Fi Movies. Ryan Britt. Plume 2023. 288 p.
ISBN 9780593472996
Grades: Adult   813
1. Herbert, Frank 2. Science fiction authors 3. Science fiction writing 4. Science fiction films 5. Influence (Psychology) 6. Popular culture 7. Literary criticism 8. Film history and criticism 9. Dune (Imaginary place) 10. Arts and Entertainment — Writing and Publishing — Literary criticism 11. Arts and Entertainment — Movies and Television

LC 2023022264

Touching upon the far-reaching influence of the science fiction phenomenon, from award-winning novelists to NASA engineers, this essential guide to one of the most visionary movies of all time uses original, deep access reporting, extensive research and commentary to bring the popularity of Dune out into the open.

"Britt brings a superfan's zeal to the proceedings, and the detailed account of Dune's journey to publication enlightens. The result is a riveting testament to the saga's enduring appeal." —*Publishers Weekly*

Includes bibliographical references and index.

Brown, David S.
Paradise Lost: A Life of F. Scott Fitzgerald. David S. Brown. The Belknap Press of Harvard University Press 2017. 330 p.
ISBN 9780674504820
Grades: Adult   813
1. Fitzgerald, F. Scott (Francis Scott), 1896-1940 2. Fitzgerald, Zelda, 1900-1948 3. Authors, American 4. Social classes 5. Nostalgia 6. Married men 7. Literary criticism 8. American literature 9. 20th century 10. Biographies 11. Life stories — Arts and culture — Writing — Authors

LC 2016048811

Pigeonholed as a Jazz Age epicurean and an emblem of the Lost Generation, Fitzgerald was at heart a moralist struck by the nation's shifting mood and manners after WWI. Placing him among Progressives such as Charles Beard, Randolph Bourne, and Thorstein Veblen, David Brown reveals Fitzgerald as a writer with an encompassing historical imagination.

Includes bibliographical references and index.

Cott, Jonathan
There's a Mystery There: The Primal Vision of Maurice Sendak. Jonathan Cott. Doubleday 2017. 256 p. : Illustration
ISBN 9780385540438
Grades: Adult   813
1. Sendak, Maurice 2. Children's literature authors 3. Children's book illustrators 4. Creativity 5. Imagination 6. Men 7. Children's literature writing 8. Authors 9. Psychology 10. Biographies 11. Interviews 12. Life stories — Arts and culture — Writing — Authors 13. Arts and entertainment — Writing and publishing 14. Adult books for young adults 15. Arts and Entertainment — Writing and Publishing — Literary criticism

LC 2016050812

A penetrating examination of the creative inspirations and legacy of children's book genius Maurice Sendak draws on the author's masterful 1976 Rolling Stone interview to reveal the torments and formative life experiences that shaped Sendak's complicated body of work.

Ellison, Ralph
The **Selected** Letters of Ralph Ellison. Edited by John F. Callahan and Marc C. Conner; with introductory essays by John F. Callahan. Random House 2019. 512 p.
ISBN 9780812998528
Grades: Adult   813
1. Ellison, Ralph 2. Authors, American 3. African American authors 4. Letter writing 5. Interpersonal relations 6. Intellectual life 7. Literary criticism 8. 20th century 9. Letters 10. Life stories — Arts and culture — Writing — Authors 11. Arts and Entertainment — Writing and Publishing 12. History writing — African American — United States 13. Arts and Entertainment — Writing and Publishing — Literary criticism

LC 2018020868

New York Times Notable Book, 2020.

Over six decades (1933 to 1993), Ralph Ellison's extensive and revealing correspondence remarkably details his aspirations and anxieties, confidence and uncertainties throughout his personal and professional life. From early notes to his mother, as an impoverished college student; to debates with the most distinguished American writers and thinkers of his time, including Romare Bearden, Saul Bellow, Robert Penn Warren, Richard Wright, and Alfred Kazin, among others; to exchanges with friends and family from his hometown of Oklahoma City, whose influence would always be paramount, these letters communicate the immense importance of Ellison's life and work.

Includes bibliographical references and index.

Frangello, Gina
Blow Your House Down: A Story of Family, Feminism, and Treason. Gina Frangello. Counterpoint 2021. 304 p.

ISBN 9781640093164

Grades: Adult   813

1. Frangello, Gina 2. Middle-aged women 3. Gender role 4. Motherhood 5. Extramarital affairs 6. Divorce 7. Cancer 8. Misogyny 9. Families 10. Desire 11. Secrets 12. Forgiveness 13. Feminism 14. Autobiographies and memoirs 15. Life stories — Identity — Gender 16. Life stories — Facing adversity 17. Life stories — Relationships 18. Family and Relationships — Divorce

Gina Frangello spent her early adulthood trying to outrun a youth marked by poverty and violence. Now a long-married wife and devoted mother, the better life she carefully built is emotionally upended by the death of her closest friend. Soon, awakened to fault lines in her troubled marriage, Frangello is caught up in a recklessly passionate affair, leading a double life while continuing to project the image of the perfect family. When her secrets are finally uncovered, both her home and her identity will implode, testing the limits of desire, responsibility, love, and forgiveness.

"Uncompromisingly fearless in its candor, this memoir/feminist manifesto is a powerful account of a woman's self-acceptance that deserves a place among the best literary memoirs of the last decade." —*Library Journal*

Gary, Amy
In the Great Green Room: The Brilliant and Bold Life of Margaret Wise Brown. Amy Gary; introduction by James Stillman Rockefeller Jr. Flatiron Books 2017. 288 p.

ISBN 9781250065360

Grades: Adult   813

1. Brown, Margaret Wise, 1910-1952 2. Children's literature writing 3. Children's literature authors 4. Women children's literature authors 5. Authors, American 6. Women authors, American 7. 20th century 8. Biographies 9. Arts and Entertainment — Writing and Publishing 10. Life stories — Arts and culture — Writing — Authors

LC 2016037634

Captures the exceptional life, imagination and passion of the author of Goodnight Moon, in a book that draws from unpublished manuscripts, songs, personal letters and diaries that the author discovered in Margaret Wise Brown's sister's attic.

"Brown's complicated personal life included numerous romantic adventures, most notably a ten-year relationship with poet/playwright/actress Blanche Oelrichs, former wife of John Barrymore." —*Library Journal*

Gillespie, Carmen
Critical Companion to Toni Morrison: A Literary Reference to Her Life and Work. Carmen Gillespie. Facts on File 2008. xi, 484 p. : Illustration

ISBN 9780816062768

Grades: Adult   813

1. Morrison, Toni, 1931-2019 2. Arts and Entertainment — Writing and Publishing — Literary criticism

LC 2006038231

A comprehensive guide to the American novelist includes a chronology of her life, summaries of each of her works, and entries on major characters, important places, and relevant literary terms.

Includes bibliographical references (p. 440-467) and index; Selected bibliography of Toni Morrison's works: P. 438-439.

Gorra, Michael Edward
The Saddest Words: William Faulkner's Civil War. Michael Gorra. Liveright Publishing Corporation 2020. 400 pages

ISBN 9781631491702

Grades: Adult   813

1. Faulkner, William, 1897-1962 2. Literary criticism 3. African Americans in literature 4. Southern States in literature 5. Race relations in literature 6. United States Civil War, 1861-1865 7. Race relations 8. United States history 9. American Civil War era (1861-1865) 10. Biographies 11. Arts and Entertainment — Writing and Publishing 12. Life stories — Arts and culture — Writing — Authors 13. Society and culture — Race 14. History writing — Wars and conflicts — American Civil War

LC 2020014188

New York Times Notable Book, 2020.

How do we read William Faulkner in the twenty-first century? asks Michael Gorra, in this reconsideration of Faulkner's life and legacy.

"A magisterial, multidisciplinary study of Faulkner that shakes the dust off his canonization." —*Kirkus*

Includes bibliographical references and index.

Handler, Daniel
★ *And Then? And Then? What Else?* Daniel Handler aka Lemony Snicket. Liveright Publishing 2024. 240 p.

ISBN 9781324090601

Grades: Adult   813

1. Handler, Daniel 2. Authors 3. Children's literature authors 4. Writing 5. Experience 6. Inspiration 7. American people 8. Autobiographies and memoirs 9. Life stories — Arts and culture — Writing — Authors 10. Arts and Entertainment — Writing and Publishing

The author of the popular Lemony Snicket books discusses his love of strange literature and reflects on his life experiences in an entertaining memoir that also serves as inspiration for aspiring writers.

"Thought-provoking, deeply personal, and like few other memoirs in the range of topics covered, Handler's mix of the personal and the literary is as compelling as his gloriously off-beat fiction." —*Booklist*

Hemingway, Ernest
Dear Papa: The Letters of Patrick and Ernest Hemingway. Foreward and epilogue by Patrick Hemingway; edited by Brendan Hemingway and Stephen Adams. Scribner 2022. 240 p.

ISBN 9781982196868

Grades: Adult   813

1. Hemingway, Ernest, 1899-1961 2. Hemingway, Patrick 3. Authors, American 4. Letter writing 5. Fathers and sons 6. Family relationships 7. 20th century 8. Letters 9. Life stories — Arts and culture — Writing — Authors 10. Life stories — Relationships — Parent and child 11. Arts and Entertainment — Writing and publishing

LC 2022002400

An intimate and illuminating glimpse at Ernest Hemingway as a father, revealed through a selection of letters he and his son Patrick exchanged over the span of twenty years. In the public imagination, Ernest Hemingway looms larger than life. But the actual person behind the legend has long remained elusive. Now, his son Patrick shares the letters they exchanged over two decades, offering a glimpse into how one of America's most iconic writers interacted with his children. These letters reveal a father who wished for his children to share his interests—hunting, fishing, travel—and a son who was receptive to the experiences his father offered. Edited by and including an introduction by Patrick Hemingway's nephew Brendan Hemingway and his grandson Stephen Adams, and featuring a prologue and epilogue by Patrick reflecting on his father's legacy, Dear Papa is a loving and collaborative family project and a nuanced, fascinating portrait of a father and son.

"Hardcore Hemingway fans will appreciate this view of the writer as a father." —*Publishers Weekly*

Includes index.

Jackson, Shirley
★ *The Letters of Shirley Jackson.* Shirley Jackson; edited by Laurence Jackson Hyman in consultation with Bernice M. Murphy. Random House 2021. 640 p.

ISBN 9780593134641

Grades: Adult   813

ESSENTIAL AND RECOMMENDED TITLES
813 American fiction in English

1. Jackson, Shirley, 1916-1965 2. Authors, American 3. Women authors 4. Writing 5. Families 6. Family relationships 7. Marriage 8. Everyday life 9. 20th century 10. Letters 11. Life stories — Arts and culture — Writing — Authors 12. Arts and Entertainment — Writing and Publishing

LC 2020045797

Shirley Jackson is one of the most important American authors of the last hundred years and among our greatest writers of the female experience. This extraordinary compilation of personal correspondence has all the hallmarks of Jackson's beloved fiction, and also features family photographs and Shirley's own illustrations. Written over the course of nearly three decades, from Jackson's college years to three months before her premature death at the age of forty-eight, these letters become the autobiography Shirley Jackson never wrote, full of subversive wit, vivid imagination, and gorgeous prose.

"At turns hysterical and heartbreaking, this collection is an entertaining and intriguing read even for those who are just discovering Jackson's many literary gifts." —*Library Journal*

Includes index.

Jamison, Leslie

The Empathy Exams: Essays. Leslie Jamison. Graywolf Press 2014. 256 p.
ISBN 9781555976712
Grades: Adult 813
1. Jamison, Leslie, 1983- 2. Pain 3. Empathy 4. Caring 5. Medical care 6. Essays 7. Autobiographies and memoirs 8. Life stories — Relationships 9. Family and relationships — General

LC 2013946927

New York Times Notable Book, 2014.

A collection of essays explores empathy, using topics ranging from street violence and incarceration to reality television and literary sentimentality to ask questions about people's understanding of and relationships with others.

"Jamison exhibits at once a journalist's courage to bear witness to acts and conditions that test human limits—incarceration, laboring in a silver mine, ultramarathoning, the loss of a child, devastating heartbreak, suffering from an unacknowledged illness—and a poet's skepticism at her own motives for doing so." —*Kirkus*

Jones, Sharon L.

Critical Companion to Zora Neale Hurston: A Literary Reference to Her Life and Work. Sharon L. Jones. Facts on File 2009. xvi, 288 p. : Illustration
ISBN 9780816068852
Grades: 11 12 Adult 813
1. Hurston, Zora Neale 2. African American authors 3. African Americans in literature 4. Biographies 5. Reference books — Handbooks, manuals, etc. 6. Arts and Entertainment — Writing and Publishing

LC 2008010052

An encyclopedic guide to the American author's life and works presents a brief biography, synopses of her writings, critical analysis of her characters and themes, and discusses important people, places, and topics in her life.

Bibliography of Zora Neale Hurston's works: P. 253-256; Includes bibliographical references (p. 257-266) and index.

Kenan, Randall

Black Folk Could Fly: Selected Writings. Randall Kenan; introduction by Tayari Jones. W.W. Norton & Company 2022. 272 p.
ISBN 9780393882162
Grades: Adult 813
1. Kenan, Randall 2. African American authors 3. Gay men 4. Growing up 5. Culture 6. Race (Social sciences) 7. Identity 8. Social life and customs 9. Southern States 10. Essays 11. Life stories — Arts and culture — Writing — Authors 12. Arts and entertainment — Writing and publishing 13. Society and culture — Race

Virtuosic in his use of literary forms, nurtured and unbounded by his identities as a Black man, a gay man, an intellectual, and a Southerner, Randall Kenan was known for his groundbreaking fiction. Less visible were his extraordinary nonfiction essays, published as introductions to anthologies and in small journals, revealing countless facets of Kenan's life and work. Flying under the radar, these writings were his most personal and autobiographical: Memories of the three women who raised him—a grandmother, a schoolteacher great-aunt, and the great-aunt's best friend—and of the eastern North Carolina lowlands where he grew up.

"Fans and new readers alike will appreciate this opportunity to take in Kenan's remarkable talent." —*Publishers Weekly*

Kerouac, Jack

Selected Letters, 1940-1956. Jack Kerouac; edited with an introduction and commentary by Ann Charters. Penguin Books 1996. xxvi, 629 p.
ISBN 9780140234442
Grades: Adult 813
1. Kerouac, Jack, 1922-1969 2. Authors, American 3. Beat generation 4. 20th century 5. Arts and Entertainment — Writing and Publishing

LC BL 99776024

The letters in this volume, written between 1940, when Kerouac was a freshman at college, and 1956, immediately before his breathless leap into celebrity with the publication of On the Road, offer invaluable insights into Kerouac's family life, his friendships with Neal and Carolyn Cassady, Allen Ginsberg, Gary Snyder, and William S. Burroughs, his travels, love affairs, and literary apprenticeship.

"Throughout, Kerouac comes across as a sincere and honest soul who was fiercely devoted to friends, family, and the search for passionate experience and art. Its value for scholars shouldn't obscure this terrific volume's broader appeal." —*Kirkus*

Includes bibliographical references (p. 611) and index; Originally published: New York : Viking, 1995.

Koh, EJ

The Magical Language of Others: A Memoir. E.J. Koh. Tin House Books 2020. 203 pages
ISBN 9781947793385
Grades: Adult 813
1. Koh, EJ, 1988- 2. Mothers and daughters 3. Generation gap 4. Teenage girls 5. Asian Americans 6. Intergenerational relations 7. Children of immigrants 8. Mother-deserted children 9. Father-deserted children 10. Family relationships 11. Intergenerational communication 12. Letter writing 13. Translating and interpreting 14. Forgiveness 15. Family history 16. Grandmothers 17. United States 18. South Korea 19. Japan 20. Autobiographies and memoirs 21. Letters 22. Life stories — Relationships — Parent and child 23. Life stories — Relationships — Growing up 24. Family and Relationships — Families 25. Adult books for young adults

LC 2019031239

Left behind when work requires her parents to return to Korea, a teen poet reconnects with family history to manage the impact of absent caregivers on her sense of self. By the award-winning author of A Lesser Love.

"Both creative tribute and personal reckoning, this is a finely wrought, linguistically rich, provocative memoir." —*Booklist*

English and Korean.

McDowell, Marta

The World of Laura Ingalls Wilder: The Frontier Landscapes That Inspired the Little House Books. by Marta McDowell. Timber Press 2017. 390 pages
ISBN 9781604697278
Grades: Adult 813
1. Wilder, Laura Ingalls, 1867-1957 2. Women authors, American 3. Pioneer women 4. Frontier and pioneer life 5. Family farms 6. Gardening 7. Nature in literature 8. Middle West 9. United States 10. Biographies 11. Life stories — Arts and culture — Writing — Authors 12. Life stories — People in history — Pioneers 13. Nature Writing — Natural Landscapes 14. Nature Writing — Gardens

LC 2016057864

Complemented by historical and contemporary photos, a celebration of Wilder's unique relationship with the American frontier reflects on the pioneer spirit of her time and the natural world that was integral to her stories.

"McDowell's warm descriptions of the author, her times, and the plants she loved provide a wonderful companion to Wilder's books, while instructions on

Millet, Lydia

We Loved It All: A Memory of Life. Lydia Millet. W.W. Norton & Company 2024. 256 p.

ISBN 9781324073659

Grades: Adult   813

1. Millet, Lydia, 1968- 2. Authors, American 3. Everyday life 4. Family relationships 5. Friendship 6. Anxiety 7. Climate change 8. Environmental degradation 9. Extinction 10. Threat (Psychology) 11. Human-animal relationships 12. Environmentalism 13. Hope 14. Life stories — Arts and culture — Writing — Authors 15. Life stories — Relationships 16. Nature Writing — Environmental Issues

LC 2023043166

An anti-memoir from a celebrated novelist explores the pain and joy of being a parent, child and human at a moment when the richness of the planet's life is deeply threatened.

"Novelist Millet (Dinosaurs), also a creative director at the Center for Biological Diversity, ruminates in this profoundly affecting meditation on what it means to live through climate change." —*Publishers Weekly*

Moore, Susanna

Miss Aluminum: A Memoir. Susanna Moore. Farrar, Straus and Giroux 2020. 240 pages

ISBN 9780374279714

Grades: Adult   813

1. Moore, Susanna 2. Authors, American 3. Celebrities 4. Death of mothers 5. Fashion models 6. Disguises 7. Rape 8. Self-discovery 9. California 10. Los Angeles, California 11. Hollywood, California 12. 1950s 13. 1960s 14. 1970s 15. Autobiographies and memoirs 16. Life stories — Arts and culture — Performing arts — Entertainers and celebrities 17. Life stories — Arts and culture — Writing — Authors

LC 2019046741

The author of The Life of Objects describes how she used a friend's trunk of expensive clothing to establish a career in 1963 Hollywood before embarking on a determined effort to uncover the truth about her mother's death.

"Moore was perched at the periphery of Hollywood's fast lane, which makes for a tantalizing tale, told in a seductive and provocative voice." —*Booklist*

Parini, Jay

Borges and Me: An Encounter. Jay Parini. Doubleday 2020. 320 p.

ISBN 9780385545822

Grades: Adult   813

1. Parini, Jay 2. Borges, Jorge Luis, 1899-1986 3. Authors 4. Authors, Argentine 5. American people in Europe 6. Vocation 7. Influence (Literary, artistic, etc.) 8. Voyages and travels 9. Scotland 10. 1970s 11. 20th century 12. Autobiographies and memoirs 13. Life stories — Arts and culture — Writing — Authors 14. Arts and Entertainment — Writing and Publishing

LC 2019038775

In 1971 Jay Parini was an aspiring poet and graduate student of literature at University of St Andrews in Scotland. One day his friend and mentor, Alastair Reid, asked Jay if he could play host for a "visiting Latin American writer" while he attended to business in London. That "writer" turned out to be the blind and aged and eccentric master of literary compression and metaphysics, Jorge Luis Borges.

"Essential for Borges's legions of fans, as well as those who enjoy literary memoirs by experimental writers whose works play a bit more loosely with the facts." —*Library Journal*

Philbrick, Nathaniel

Why Read Moby-Dick? Nathaniel Philbrick. Viking 2011. 144 p.

ISBN 9780670022991

Grades: Adult   813

1. Melville, Herman, 1819-1891 2. Characters and characteristics in literature 3. Literary criticism 4. History writing — General 5. Arts and Entertainment — Writing and Publishing — Literary criticism

LC 2011019766

Shares expert guidelines on how to read and appreciate Herman Melville's classic work, offering insight into its history, characters, and themes while explaining its literary relevance in the modern world.

Pitzer, Andrea

The Secret History of Vladimir Nabokov. Andrea Pitzer. Pegasus Books : 2013. xv, 432 p, 16 p. of plates : Illustration

ISBN 9781605984117

Grades: Adult   813

1. Nabokov, Vladimir Vladimirovich, 1899-1977 2. Authors, American 3. Authors, Russian 4. Refugees 5. Political persecution 6. Art and politics 7. Literary criticism 8. 20th century 9. Biographies 10. Life stories — Arts and culture — Writing — Authors 11. Life stories — Facing adversity — War and oppression — Refugees 12. Arts and Entertainment — Writing and Publishing — Literary criticism

LC 2014427844

Argues that the famous Russian-American novelist, accused of turning a blind eye to the horrors of history, hid this disturbing information within his fiction.

Drawn from newly declassified intelligence and recovered military history, this book argues that the novelist, who was repeatedly accused of turning a blind eye to human suffering to write artful takes of depravity, managed to hide disturbing history in his fiction—history that has gone unnoticed for decades.

"Drawing on new biographical material and her sharp critical senses, Pitzer reveals the tightly woven subtext of the novels, always keen to shine a light where the deception is not obvious. Though no substitute for Brian Boyd's definitive two-volume biography, this is a brilliant examination that adds to the understanding of an inspiring and enigmatic life." —*Kirkus*

Includes bibliographical references (p. 361-421) and index.

Rehak, Melanie

Girl Sleuth: Nancy Drew and the Women Who Created Her. Melanie Rehak. Harcourt 2005. xviii, 364 p, 8 p. of plates : Illustration

ISBN 9780151010417

Grades: 11 12 Adult   813

1. Wirt, Mildred A. (Mildred Augustine), 1905-2002 2. Adams, Harriet Stratemeyer 3. Keene, Carolyn (Publisher pseudonym) 4. Women authors, American 5. Girls 6. Publishers and publishing 7. Social history 8. Drew, Nancy (Fictitious character) 9. Women and literature 10. Books and reading 11. Literary criticism 12. Teenagers 13. United States 14. 20th century 15. Mysteries 16. Arts and Entertainment — Writing and Publishing 17. History writing — Women's history 18. Adult books for young adults

LC 2005009129

Agatha Award for Best Nonfiction, 2005; Macavity Award for Best Non-Fiction, 2006; Edgar Allan Poe Award for Best Critical/Biographical, 2006; Amelia Bloomer List, 2006.

An examination of the Nancy Drew stories and their influence on American girlhood since the 1930s explores mysteries related to the character's creators, and her role in shaping the modern American woman's identity.

"Packed with revealing anecdotes, Rehak's meticulously researched account of the publishing phenomenon that survived the Depression and WWII ... will delight fans of the beloved gumshoe whose gumption guaranteed that every reprobate got his due." —*Booklist*

Includes bibliographical references (p. [351]-354) and index.

Reynolds, David S.

Mightier Than the Sword: Uncle Tom's Cabin and the Battle for America. David S. Reynolds. W W Norton & CO Inc 2011. 352 p.

ISBN 9780393081329

Grades: Adult   813

1. Stowe, Harriet Beecher, 1811-1896 2. Books 3. Reading 4. Civil war 5. United States Civil War, 1861-1865 6. United States history 7. 1860s 8. American Civil War era (1861-1865) 9. History writing — Wars and conflicts —

ESSENTIAL AND RECOMMENDED TITLES
813 American fiction in English

American Civil War 10. Arts and Entertainment — Writing and Publishing 11. History writing — Antebellum America — United States 12. Society and culture — Race

LC 2011000702

Discusses the impact of Stowe's cultural and historical landmark, "Uncle Tom's Cabin," not only on the abolitionist movement and the American Civil War, but on events worldwide, including the end of serfdom in Russia and twentieth-century events.

"The powerful antislavery message of Uncle Tom's Cabin fueled the flames leading to the Civil War, making it the most influential novel in American history. Stowe claimed the novel came to her in a vision and God was its true author. Accordingly, her book is weighted with religious symbolism, which Reynolds interprets with typical English professor's zeal. He also examines its impacts not just on public attitudes toward slavery, but on women's rights, temperance, capitalism, minstrel shows, sexual customs and other aspects of mid-19th century American life. Reynolds dissects dozens of imitative novels, plays and minstrel shows—some against, others for slavery or segregation—and traces the influence of Stowe's novel into modern times, including film spin-offs. .[This is] not easy reading, but it offers virtually everything you ever wanted to know about Uncle Tom's Cabin—and probably a lot more." —*Seattle Times*

Rioux, Anne Boyd
Meg, Jo, Beth, Amy: The Story of Little Women and Why It Still Matters. Anne Boyd Rioux. W. W. Norton & Company 2018. 352 p.
ISBN 9780393254730
Grades: Adult   813
1. Alcott, Louisa May, 1832-1888 2. Influence (Literary, artistic, etc.) 3. Women authors, American 4. Women in literature 5. Books and reading 6. Literary criticism 7. American literature 8. Arts and Entertainment — Writing and Publishing 9. History writing — Arts and culture 10. Adult books for young adults 11. Arts and Entertainment — Writing and Publishing — Literary criticism

LC 2018006602

Library Journal Best Books, 2018.

A 150th anniversary tribute describes the cultural significance of Louisa May Alcott's classic, exploring how its relatable themes and depictions of family resilience, community and female resourcefulness have inspired generations of writers.

Includes bibliographical references and index.

Row, Jess
White Flights: Race, Fiction, and the American Imagination. Jess Row. Graywolf Press 2019. 320 p.
ISBN 9781555978327
Grades: Adult   813
1. Row, Jess 2. European Americans 3. Race (Social sciences) 4. Race awareness 5. Marginalized people 6. Race relations 7. Segregation 8. Music history and criticism 9. Literary criticism 10. Identity 11. American literature 12. Film history and criticism 13. Arts and Entertainment — Writing and Publishing 14. Society and culture — Race 15. Arts and Entertainment — Writing and Publishing — Literary criticism

LC 2018958158

White Flights is a meditation on whiteness in American fiction and culture from the end of the civil rights movement to the present. At the heart of the book, Jess Row ties "white flight"—the movement of white Americans into segregated communities, whether in suburbs or newly gentrified downtowns—to white writers setting their stories in isolated or emotionally insulated landscapes, from the mountains of Idaho in Marilynne Robinson's Housekeeping to the claustrophobic households in Jonathan Franzen's The Corrections. Row uses brilliant close readings of work from well-known writers to examine the ways these and other writers have sought imaginative space for themselves at the expense of engaging with race.

Includes bibliographical references.

Scottoline, Lisa
I See Life Through Rose-Colored Glasses: True Stories and Confessions. Lisa Scottoline and Francesca Serritella. St. Martin's Press 2018. 320 p.
ISBN 9781250163059
Grades: Adult   813
1. Mothers and daughters 2. Family relationships 3. Women and pets 4. Families 5. Women 6. Life 7. Autobiographies and memoirs 8. Life stories — Relationships — Parent and child 9. Humor writing — Family and relationship humor

LC 2017059642

The best-selling mother-daughter duo are back in this hilarious and heartfelt collection of stories that will strike a chord with every woman.

Shraya, Vivek
I'm Afraid of Men. Vivek Shraya. Penguin Canada 2018. 96 p.
ISBN 9780735235939
Grades: Adult   813
1. Shraya, Vivek, 1981- 2. Transgender people 3. Gender identity 4. Gender role 5. Masculinity 6. Autobiographies and memoirs 7. Canadian literature 8. Life stories — Identity — Gender 9. Society and culture — Gender

LC 2019410566

Loan Stars Favourites, 2018; Amelia Bloomer List, 2019.

A trans artist explores how masculinity was imposed on her as a boy and continues to haunt her as a girl—and how we might reimagine gender for the twenty-first century.

Souder, William
Mad at the World: A Life of John Steinbeck. William Souder. W. W. Norton & Company 2020. xiv, 446 pages
ISBN 9780393292268
Grades: Adult   813
1. Steinbeck, John, 1902-1968 2. Authors, American 3. Misanthropy 4. Injustice 5. Empathy 6. Biographies 7. Impartial writing 8. Life stories — Arts and culture — Writing — Authors 9. Arts and Entertainment — Writing and Publishing

LC 2020017019

Los Angeles Times Book Prize for Biography, 2020.

Explores how John Steinbeck's complicated persona and firsthand struggles through the depths of the Great Depression gave him deeply empathic perspectives that shaped his politics and his evocative characters and themes.

"Steinbeck fans could not ask for a more nuanced account of this troubled giant of American literature." —*Publishers Weekly*

Includes bibliographical references and index.

Thoreau, Henry David
★ *Walden, Or, Life in the Woods*. Henry David Thoreau; with an introduction by Verlyn Klinkenborg. Knopf : Distributed by Random House 1992. xxxi, 295 p.
ISBN 9780679418962
Grades: 11 12 Adult   813
1. Thoreau, Henry David, 1817-1862 2. Authors, American 3. Natural history 4. Solitude 5. Wilderness areas 6. 19th century 7. Biographies 8. Nature writing — General

LC 92054444

Presents Thoreau's reflections on his experience living alone in the woods surrounding Walden Pond as well as his philosophy concerning man's need to reevaluate life and commune with nature.

Includes bibliographical references (p. xxiii); Originally published: Boston, Ticknor and Fields, 1854.

Vonnegut, Kurt
Kurt Vonnegut: Letters. Edited and with an introduction by Dan Wakefield. Delacorte 2012. 464 p.
ISBN 9780385343756
Grades: Adult   813
1. Vonnegut, Kurt 2. Authors, American 3. Social life and customs 4. United States 5. 20th century 6. 21st century 7. Letters 8. Biographies 9. Arts and Entertainment — Writing and Publishing

LC 2012001544

PUBLIC LIBRARY CORE COLLECTION: NONFICTION
Twentieth Edition

A compilation of personal correspondence written over a sixty-year period offers insight into the iconic American author's literary personality, his experiences as a German POW, his struggles with fame, and the inspirations for his famous books.

813.009 American fiction — History and criticism

Cart, Michael
Young Adult Literature: From Romance to Realism. Michael Cart. ALA Neal-Schuman 2022. 280 p.
ISBN 9780838947470
Grades: Professional   813.009
1. Young adult literature 2. Teenagers 3. Books and reading 4. Literary criticism 5. Professional materials — Collection development 6. Reference — Bibliographies and indexes
LC 2021051390

Cart returns with a sweeping update of his classic text. His book surveys the landscape of YA lit; closely examines teen demographics, literacy, audiobooks, and the future of print; provides updated coverage of perennially popular genre fiction, including horror, sci fi, and dystopian fiction; delves deeply into multicultural and LGBTQIA+ literature, substantially updated in this edition; and more.

"This fourth edition of Cart's seminal work on the history of and trends in young adult literature is even more impressive than the three previous editions and includes 35 percent more content…[It is] a near-perfect text for either an introductory undergraduate or graduate course in the genre." —*Choice*
Includes bibliographical references and index.

Moss, Gabrielle
Paperback Crush: The Totally Radical History of '80s and '90s Teen Fiction. Gabrielle Moss. Quirk Books 2018. 256 p.
ISBN 9781683690788
Grades: Adult   813.009
1. Books and reading 2. Popular culture 3. Young adults 4. Teenagers 5. Social life and customs 6. United States 7. 1980s 8. 1990s 9. 20th century 10. Society and culture — Pop culture 11. Arts and Entertainment — Writing and Publishing 12. Adult books for young adults 13. Arts and Entertainment — Writing and Publishing — Literary criticism
LC 2017961245

This rollicking ride through the history of paperback pre-teen series of the 80s and 90s reveals the stories behind the best-known books, including Pen Pals, Dear Diary, the Pink Parrots, Cheerleaders and many others.

Town, Caren J.
LGBTQ Young Adult Fiction: A Critical Survey, 1970s-2010s. Caren J. Town. McFarland & Company 2017. VII, 197 pages
ISBN 9780786496945
Grades: Adult   813.009
1. Homosexuality and literature 2. Homosexuality in literature 3. Queer theory 4. LGBTQIA+ teenagers 5. Literary criticism 6. Lesbians 7. Gender identity 8. Teenage literature writing 9. Arts and Entertainment — Writing and Publishing — Literary criticism 10. Reference — Bibliographies and indexes
LC 2017023518

The author explores a selection of recent novels—many of which may be new to readers—and places them in the wider contexts of LGBTQ literature and history. Chapters discuss a range of topics, including the relationship of Queer Theory to literature, LGBTQ families, and recent trends in utopian and dystopian science fiction.
Includes bibliographical references (pages 187-193) and index.

813.54 American fiction — 1945-1999

Harkness, Deborah E.
The World of All Souls: The Complete Guide to a Discovery of Witches, Shadow of Night, and the Book of Life. Deborah Harkness, with Claire Baldwin, Lisa Halttunen, and Jill Hough; illustrated by Colleen Madden. Vikings Press 2018. IX, 484 pages : Illustration
ISBN 9780735220744
Grades: Adult   813.54
1. Witches 2. Vampires 3. Magic 4. Alchemy 5. Contemporary fantasy 6. Arts and Entertainment — Writing and Publishing

In The World of All Souls, Harkness shares the rich sources of inspiration behind her bewitching novels. She draws together synopses, character bios, maps, recipes, and even the science behind creatures, magic, and alchemy—all with her signature historian's touch. Bursting with fascinating facts and dazzling artwork, this essential handbook is a must-have for longtime fans and eager newcomers alike.

814 American essays in English

Acocella, Joan Ross
★ *The Bloodied Nightgown: And Other Essays.* Joan Acocella. Farrar, Straus and Giroux 2024. 304 p.
ISBN 9780374608095
Grades: Adult   814
1. Books and reading 2. Authors 3. Artists 4. Culture 5. Literary criticism 6. Essays 7. Anthologies 8. Arts and Entertainment — Writing and Publishing — Literary criticism 9. Life stories — Arts and culture
LC 2023038961

Joan Acocella has the rare ability to examine literature and unearth the lives contained within it—its authors, its subjects, and the communities from which it sprung. In her hands, arts criticism becomes a celebration and an investigation, and her essays pulse with unadulterated enthusiasm. The Bloodied Nightgown: And Other Essays gathers twenty-four essays from the past decade and a half of Acocella's career, as well as an introduction that frames her simple preoccupations, "life and art."

"The pieces brim with erudition and playfulness, offering approachable insights into literary masterpieces both new and old. Smart and accessible, this is a blast." —*Publishers Weekly*
Includes index.

Angelou, Maya
Letter to My Daughter. Maya Angelou. Random House 2008. 176 p.
ISBN 9781400066124
Grades: 9 10 11 12 Adult   814
1. Angelou, Maya 2. Growing up 3. Quality of life 4. Essays 5. Arts and Entertainment — Writing and Publishing 6. Adult books for young adults
LC Bl2008017958

A collection of short essays includes personal reminiscences, hard-won wisdom, and inspirational ideas.
"A slim volume packed with nourishing nuggets of wisdom." —*Kirkus*

Wouldn't *Take Nothing for My Journey Now.* Maya Angelou. Random House 1993. xiii, 141 p.
ISBN 9780679427438
Grades: 11 12 Adult   814
1. Understanding (Personal quality) 2. Meditations 3. Reminiscing in old age 4. Essays 5. Family and Relationships — Aging and Death
LC 93005904

A collection of wise and inspirational messages from the author distills her thoughtful insights into such topics as Friendship, Grace, Spirit, Family, and Healing.

ESSENTIAL AND RECOMMENDED TITLES
814 American essays in English

"Angelou's prose is brisk, fluid, and entrancing. This work will provide a taste of wisdom to all who read it." —*Library Journal*

A portion of this work was originally published in the December 1992 issue of Essence magazine—T.P. verso.

Atwood, Margaret
Burning Questions: Essays and Occasional Pieces, 2004 to 2021. Margaret Atwood. Doubleday 2022. 448 p.
ISBN 9780385547482
Grades: Adult   814
1. Culture 2. Climate change 3. Social change 4. Financial crises 5. COVID-19 Pandemic, 2020- 6. World leaders 7. 21st century 8. 2000s (Decade) 9. 2010s 10. 2020s 11. Essays 12. Society and culture — General 13. History writing — General 14. Arts and Entertainment — Writing and publishing

A new collection of essays and pieces from Margaret Atwood.

"Recent essays by the acclaimed novelist on art, feminism, censorship, inspirations, and her own work. Atwood's third collection of essays, reviews, speeches, and book introductions covers work from 2004 to 2021, during which time she cemented her place as a literary legend." —*Kirkus*

Baldwin, James
★ *Collected Essays.* James Baldwin. Library of America 1998. 869 p.
ISBN 9781883011529
Grades: 11 12 Adult   814
1. Racism 2. Civil rights 3. Civil Rights Movement 4. Intersectionality 5. Race relations 6. United States history 7. United States 8. 1960s 9. Essays 10. History writing — African American — Civil rights — United States 11. Antiracist literature
LC 97023496

A comprehensive compilation of Baldwin's previously published, nonfiction writings encompasses essays on America's racial divide, the social and political turbulence of his time, and his insights into the poetry of Langston Hughes and the music of Earl Hines.

"Novelist Morrison's editing of this omnibus, which includes a chronology and notes, should help rekindle interest in Baldwin, whose recurrent themes—the African American search for identity, the hypocrisy of white America, the urgent necessity for love—make his work timely and challenging." —*Publishers Weekly*

Berry, Wendell
Imagination in Place: Essays. Wendell Berry. Counterpoint ; 2010. VIII, 196 p.
ISBN 9781582435626
Grades: Adult   814
1. Literary criticism 2. Essays 3. Arts and Entertainment — Writing and Publishing
LC 2009038104
Booklist Editors' Choice, 2010.

Features essays that express the author's thoughts on subjects ranging from his former mentor, Wallace Stregner, and Shakespeare to religion, adversity, and the Civil War.

"For those who've already come to admire Berry's moral clarity and closely argued critiques of contemporary society, Imagination in Place is a welcome chance to continue the conversation." —*Christian Science Monitor*

Includes bibliographical references.

Capote, Truman
★ *Portraits and Observations: The Essays of Truman Capote.* Truman Capote. Random House 2007. x, 518 p.
ISBN 9781400066612
Grades: Adult   814
1. Capote, Truman, 1924-1984 2. Authors, American 3. Social life and customs 4. United States 5. 20th century 6. Essays 7. Biographies 8. Arts and Entertainment — Writing and Publishing
LC 2007036624

A definitive anthology containing all of the author's essays encompasses his early travel sketches of Brooklyn, New Orleans, and Hollywood; portraits of Isak Dinesen, Mae West, Humphrey Bogart, and Marilyn Monroe; accounts of the filming of "In Cold Blood;" autobiographical musings; and the recently discovered "Remembering Willa Cather."

"The featured works cover the artist's interests in travel, celebrities, the artsboth visual and literarycrimes of passion, and himself. This collection offers the highest quality of writing from a genuine American stylist." —*Library Journal*

Includes index.

Crosley, Sloane
I Was Told There'd Be Cake. Sloane Crosley. Riverhead Books 2008. 320 p.
ISBN 9781594483066
Grades: Adult   814
1. Crosley, Sloane 2. Autobiographies and memoirs 3. Essays 4. Humor writing — Social humor 5. Life stories — General
LC 2007033228

A debut compilation of literary essays offers a revealing and humorous look at human fallibility and the vagaries of modern urban life as the author details the despoiling of an exhibit at the Natural History Museum, the provocation of her first boss, siccing the cops on her mysterious neighbor, and other offbeat situations.

★ *Look Alive Out There: Essays.* Sloane Crosley. MCD/Farrar, Straus and Giroux 2018. 272 p.
ISBN 9780374279844
Grades: Adult   814
1. Crosley, Sloane 2. Women authors 3. Everyday life 4. Misadventures 5. Middle-age 6. Essays 7. Autobiographies and memoirs 8. Life stories — General 9. Humor writing — Social humor 10. Society and culture — General
LC 2017038323

A collection of essays shares the author's trademark observations on subjects ranging from scaling active volcanoes and crashing shivas to assisted fertility and playing herself on "Gossip Girl."

"A smart, droll essay collection that is all over the map but focused by Crosley's consistently sharp eye." —*Kirkus*

Cusk, Rachel
Coventry: Essays. Rachel Cusk. Farrar, Straus and Giroux 2019. 288 p.
ISBN 9780374126773
Grades: Adult   814
1. Cusk, Rachel, 1967- 2. Women authors, English 3. Family relationships 4. Writing 5. Creation (Literary, artistic, etc.) 6. Gender role 7. Literary criticism 8. Marriage 9. Motherhood 10. Essays 11. Arts and Entertainment — Writing and Publishing 12. Life stories — Arts and culture — Writing — Authors
LC 2019020202

A collection of essays by the author of A Life's Work explores themes ranging from family and gender to politics and art, discussing her fictional stories while exploring the work of such writers as D. H. Lawrence and Elena Ferrante.

"An eloquent and engrossing selection of nonfiction writing that will enhance Cusk's stature in contemporary literature." —*Kirkus*

Didion, Joan
★ *Let Me Tell You What I Mean.* Joan Didion; foreword by Hilton Als. Alfred A. Knopf 2021. 192 p.
ISBN 9780593318485
Grades: Adult   814
1. Didion, Joan 1934-2021 2. Women authors 3. Writing 4. Political science 5. Self-doubt 6. Press 7. Women 8. Essays 9. Arts and Entertainment — Writing and Publishing 10. Life stories — Arts and culture — Writing — Authors
LC 2020016867

A volume of 12 previously uncollected early pieces shares insights into the author's evolving literary style and includes reflections on such topics as a Gamblers Anonymous meeting, a Vegas WWI veteran reunion and a visit to San Simeon.

PUBLIC LIBRARY CORE COLLECTION: NONFICTION
Twentieth Edition

"This wide-ranging essay collection from Didion (South and West: From a Notebook) showcases her strengths as a short form writer. Organized chronologically from 1968 to 2000, the pieces trace Didion's development as an essayist and offer glimpses of late-20th-century social history." —*Publishers Weekly*

Dillard, Annie
The Abundance: Narrative Essays Old and New. Annie Dillard. Ecco Press 2016. 224 p.
ISBN 9780062432971
Grades: Adult 814
1. Nature 2. Women and nature 3. Life 4. Spirituality 5. Essays 6. Society and culture — General
LC Bl2016003136

A landmark collection of author-curated pieces celebrates the master essayist's celebrated career and offers insight into her establishment of the "novelized nonfiction" form.

"This collection is an excellent entry point into Dillard's writing and would especially appeal to new readers, although Dillard devotees will also enjoy this kaleidoscopic retrospective, this new way of 'seeing' her prose." —*Library Journal*

Dubus, Andre
Ghost Dogs: On Killers and Kin. Andre Dubus III.. W W Norton & CO Inc 2024. 352 p.
ISBN 9781324000440
Grades: Adult 814
1. Masculinity 2. Fatherhood 3. Bounty hunters 4. Gun ownership 5. Privilege (Social psychology) 6. American people 7. New York City 8. Essays 9. Life stories — Identity

This new collection of essays from the best-selling author of Townie: A Memoir and House of Sand and Fog reflects on his successes, failures and struggles with traditional and modern masculinity.

"Dubus's sinewy prose strengthens his probing meditations on the inextricable relationship between love and loss. Readers will be moved." —*Publishers Weekly*

Ehrenreich, Barbara
Had I Known: Collected Essays. Barbara Ehrenreich. Twelve 2020. 352 p
ISBN 9781455543670
Grades: Adult 814
1. Social justice 2. United States 3. 20th century 4. 21st century 5. Essays 6. Society and culture — General
LC Bl2020004777

A selection of the best-selling writer and political activist's most provocative signature writings includes her groundbreaking undercover investigations, op-ed pieces, essays and reviews, including the award-winning "Welcome to Cancerland."

"A rewarding, illuminating tour de force." —*Booklist*

Ellis, Bret Easton
White. by Bret Easton Ellis. Alfred A. Knopf 2019. 272 p.
ISBN 9780525656302
Grades: Adult 814
1. Ellis, Bret Easton 2. Social media 3. Online social networks 4. Interpersonal relations 5. Censorship 6. Social acceptance 7. Competition 8. Communication 9. Internet 10. White privilege 11. Essays 12. Society and culture — Media and technology 13. Society and culture — Pop culture
LC 2018050947

The author of Less Than Zero and American Psycho combines personal reflection and social observation in a first work of nonfiction that explores such subjects as self-inflicted censorship and the cult of likeability that has overshadowed the social-media age.

"Regardless of their opinions about social media, readers will be captivated by these provocative essays and then move on to rereading Less Than Zero and American Psycho." —*Library Journal*

Published in the UK by Pan Macmillan, 2019.

Ellis, Helen
Bring Your Baggage and Don't Pack Light: Essays. Helen Ellis. Doubleday 2021. 192 p.
ISBN 9780385546157
Grades: Adult 814
1. Ellis, Helen 2. Middle-aged women 3. Friendship 4. Women 5. Aging 6. Femininity 7. Marriage 8. Essays 9. Humor Writing — Family and relationship humor 10. Family and Relationships — Aging and Death 11. Family and Relationships — Dating and Marriage

The best-selling author of American Housewife and Southern Lady Code returns with a collection of comic essays that reflect on the middle-aged experience of modern women, with characters such as 50-year-old new moms and garage sale swindlers.

"Novelist Ellis (Southern Lady Code) shines in this collection of essays that lovingly underscores the importance of having a circle of close friends.... The result is a candid, funny reminder that one need not take life too seriously." —*Publishers Weekly*

Southern Lady Code: Essays. Helen Ellis. Doubleday 2019. 224 p.
ISBN 9780385543897
Grades: Adult 814
1. Ellis, Helen 2. Social life and customs 3. Popular culture 4. Growing up 5. Women 6. Interpersonal relations 7. Southern States 8. Essays 9. Autobiographies and memoirs 10. Humor writing — Family and relationship humor 11. Life stories — Relationships — Growing up
LC 2018019774

LibraryReads Favorites, 2019.

The best-selling author presents a riotous collection of essays on the art of living as a "Southern Lady" that explores subjects ranging from marriage and manners to women's health and entertaining.

"In nearly two-dozen essays filled with belly laughs and bits of hard-won wisdom, Ellis self-deprecating wit and tongue-in-cheek charm provide the perfect antidote to bad-hair, or bad-news, days." —*Booklist*

Ellison, Ralph
★ *The Collected Essays of Ralph Ellison.* Ralph Ellison, edited and with an introduction by John F. Callahan, preface by Saul Bellow. Modern Library 2024. 912 p.
ISBN 9780593730065
Grades: Adult 814
1. Quality of life 2. African American history 3. Race relations 4. Marginalized people 5. Social life and customs 6. African Americans 7. Literary criticism 8. Culture 9. United States 10. Anthologies 11. Essays 12. Interviews 13. Society and culture — Race 14. Society and culture — General

Compiled, edited, and newly revised by Ralph Ellison's literary executor, John F. Callahan, this definitive volume includes posthumously discovered reviews, criticism, and interviews, as well as the essay collections Shadow and Act (1964), and Going to the Territory (1986), an exploration of literature and folklore, jazz and culture, and the nature and quality of lives that Black Americans lead. With newly discovered essays and speeches, The Collected Essays reveals a more vulnerable, intimate side of Ellison than what we've previously seen. "Raph Ellison," wrote Stanley Crouch, "reached across race, religion, class and sex to make us all Americans."

"In this potent compendium, Callahan, Ralph Ellison's literary executor, updates his 1995 collection of Ellison's short nonfiction…The result is an intellectual feast." —*Publishers Weekly*

Ephron, Nora
The Most of Nora Ephron. by Nora Ephron. Alfred A. Knopf 2013. 576 p.
ISBN 9780385350839
Grades: Adult 814
1. Ephron, Nora 2. Women screenwriters 3. Women authors 4. Women journalists 5. Everyday life 6. Women 7. Essays 8. Anthologies 9. Autobiographies and memoirs 10. Arts and Entertainment — Writing and Publishing 11. Life stories — Arts and culture — Writing — Authors
LC 2013016426

ESSENTIAL AND RECOMMENDED TITLES
814 American essays in English

A celebration of the work of the late Academy Award-nominated author and screenwriter collects her writings on topics ranging from journalism and feminism to food and aging, in a volume complemented by her notorious Wellesley commencement address and her recent blogs about death.

"Whether Ephron is writing about politics or purses, sexism or soufflé, her appeal is her intelligent, incisive sense of humor." —*Library Journal*

Franzen, Jonathan
The End of the End of the Earth: Essays. Jonathan Franzen. Farrar, Straus and Giroux 2018. 288 p.
ISBN 9780374147938
Grades: Adult   814
1. Climate change 2. Interpersonal relations 3. Family relationships 4. Observation (Psychology) 5. Essays 6. Family and Relationships — General
LC 2018017731

A provocative new essay collection by the award-winning author of Freedom and the Corrections includes an exploration of his complex relationship with his uncle, an assessment of the global seabird crisis and his young adulthood in New York.

"Whether observing the eerie beauty of Antarctica ('far from having melted,' he reports) or dispensing 'Ten Rules for the Novelist,' Franzen makes for an entertaining, sometimes prickly, but always quotable companion." —*Publishers Weekly*

Farther Away: Essays. Jonathan Franzen. Farrar, Straus and Giroux 2012. 272 p.
ISBN 9780374153571
Grades: Adult   814
1. Self 2. Literature 3. Essays 4. Speeches, addresses, etc. 5. Arts and Entertainment — Writing and Publishing
LC 2011046067

A collection of speeches and essays on a wide variety of topics.
Also published in large print format.

Frazier, Ian
Hogs Wild: Selected Reporting Pieces. Ian Frazier. Farrar, Straus and Giroux 2016. 368 p.
ISBN 9780374298524
Grades: Adult   814
1. Essays 2. Society and culture — General
LC 2015036372

A generous selection of Frazier's most sophisticated and uproarious feature stories.

"His celebrated humor glows rather than erupts in these more expository pieces. Pieces that show Frazier's ranging curiosity, lucent style, and capacious heart." —*Kirkus*

Fumudoh, Ziwe
★ *Black Friend: Essays.* Ziwe Fumudoh. Harry N Abrams Inc 2023. 240 p.
ISBN 9781419756344
Grades: Adult   814
1. Women comedians 2. Entertainment industry and trade 3. Interracial friendship 4. Identity 5. Personal conduct 6. Popular culture 7. Race relations 8. Racism 9. Discrimination 10. African American women 11. American people 12. North American people 13. Essays 14. Autobiographies and memoirs 15. Life stories — Identity — Race and ethnicity 16. Humor writing — Social humor 17. Society and culture — Race

Ziwe made a name for herself by asking guests like Alyssa Milano, Fran Lebowitz, and Chet Hanks direct questions. In Black Friend, she turns her incisive perspective on both herself and the culture at large. Throughout the book, Ziwe combines pop-culture commentary and personal stories, which grapple with her own (mis)understanding of identity. From a hilarious case of mistaken identity via a jumbotron to a terrifying fight-or-flight encounter in the woods, Ziwe raises difficult questions for comedic relief.

"Ziwe's fans will appreciate the energetic mix of comedy and personal reflection." —*Publishers Weekly*

Gabbert, Elisa
Any Person Is the Only Self: Essays. Elisa Gabbert. FSG Originals / Farrar, Straus and Giroux 2024. 240 p.
ISBN 9780374605896
Grades: Adult   814
1. Gabbert, Elisa 2. Women poets 3. Books and reading 4. Writing 5. Diary writing 6. Intellectual life 7. Creation (Literary, artistic, etc.) 8. Inspiration 9. Literary criticism 10. Essays 11. Arts and Entertainment — Writing and Publishing — Literary criticism
LC 2023051859

Contagiously curious essays on reading, art, and the life of the mind from the acclaimed author of The Unreality of Memory.

"Gabbert is an original thinker, and the literary analysis is refreshingly unstuffy. Bookworms will appreciate these intelligent essays." —*Publishers Weekly*

Includes bibliographical references.

Gaffigan, Jim
Dad Is Fat. Jim Gaffigan. Crown Publications 2013. 208 p.
ISBN 9780385349055
Grades: Adult   814
1. Gaffigan, Jim 2. Parenthood 3. Fatherhood 4. Families 5. Fathers 6. Father and child 7. Parent and child 8. Autobiographies and memoirs 9. Humor writing — Family and relationship humor 10. Life stories — Relationships — Parent and child 11. Family and Relationships — Parenting
LC 2013012076

The popular comedian shares his misadventures as an unlikely father of five, from his formative years in a large Irish-Catholic family, to his middle-of-the-night diaper-changing foibles, to his struggles to lull tyrannical tots to sleep.

Gay, Ross
The Book of (more) Delights: Essays. Ross Gay. Algonquin Books of Chapel Hill 2023. 288 p.
ISBN 9781643753096
Grades: Adult   814
1. Gay, Ross, 1974- 2. Life 3. Joy and sorrow 4. Hope 5. Everyday life 6. Gratitude 7. Autobiographies and memoirs 8. Essays 9. Life stories — Personal growth 10. Life stories — Identity — Race and ethnicity
LC 2023015049

In this new collection of genre-defying stories, again written over the course of a year, the New York Times best-selling author explores the meaning of "delight," revealing how small, daily wonders connect us and give us meaning in these unsettling times.

"Keenly observed and delivered with deftness, these essays are a testament to the artfulness of attention and everyday joy." —*Kirkus*

Includes bibliographical references.

Inciting Joy: Essays. Ross Gay. Algonquin Books of Chapel Hill 2022. 288 p.
ISBN 9781643753041
Grades: Adult   814
1. Gay, Ross, 1974- 2. Life 3. Joy and sorrow 4. Loss 5. Family relationships 6. Grief 7. Fear 8. Multiracial people 9. Identity 10. Nature 11. Autobiographies and memoirs 12. Essays 13. Life stories — General
LC 2022021254

Hurston/Wright Legacy Award: Nonfiction, 2023.

A collection of long-form essays on joy, in which the author turns his curious and poetic mind to everything from skateboarding and cover songs, basketball and race, dancing and academia, death and laughter, and, always, the garden and the natural world.

"A pleasingly digressive and intimate memoir in essays." —*Kirkus*

Gay, Roxane
Bad Feminist. Roxane Gay. HarperCollins 2014. Films
ISBN 9780062282712

PUBLIC LIBRARY CORE COLLECTION: NONFICTION
Twentieth Edition

Grades: Adult   **814**
1. Feminism 2. Race relations 3. Culture 4. Intersectionality 5. Essays 6. Arts and Entertainment — General 7. Society and culture — Gender — Women
LC 2014498210

A cultural examination of the ways in which the media influences self-perception, and discusses how society still needs to do better.

"Writing about race, politics, gender, feminism, privilege, and popular media, [Gay] highlights how deeply misogyny is embedded in our culture, the careless language used to discuss sexual violence (seen in news reports of sexual assault), Hollywood's tokenistic treatment of race, the trivialization of literature written by women, and the many ways American society fails women and African-Americans." —*Publishers Weekly*

★ **Opinions**: *A Decade of Arguments, Criticism, and Minding Other People's Business*. Roxane Gay. Harper 2023. 304 p.
ISBN 9780063341463
Grades: Adult   **814**
1. Gay, Roxane 2. Women authors 3. Race (Social sciences) 4. Gender identity 5. Feminism 6. Sexuality 7. Political culture 8. Social criticism 9. Identity 10. Editorials 11. Advice 12. Periodical writing 13. Essays 14. Liberal writing 15. Society and culture — General 16. Arts and Entertainment — Writing and Publishing 17. Life stories — Identity

Opinions is a collection of Roxane Gay's best nonfiction pieces from the past ten years. Covering a wide range of topics—politics, feminism, the culture wars, civil rights, and much more—with an all-new introduction in which she reflects on the past decade in America, this sharp, thought-provoking anthology will delight Roxane Gay's devotees and draw new readers to this inimitable talent.

"This is a must-read for not only fans of Gay's work, but for everyone interested in reading intellectual, accessible, and important takes on timely topics." —*Booklist*

Gerard, Sarah
Sunshine State: *Essays*. Sarah Gerard. Harper Perennial 2017. 208 p.
ISBN 9780062434876
Grades: Adult   **814**
1. Gerard, Sarah 2. Intimacy 3. Addiction 4. Obsession 5. Homelessness 6. Imprisonment 7. Religions 8. Florida 9. Essays 10. Autobiographies and memoirs 11. Life stories — General
LC 2017296465

Rising literary star and Los Angeles Times First Fiction Award finalist Sarah Gerard uses her experiences growing up on Florida's gulf coast to illuminate the struggles of modern human survival—physical, emotional, environmental—through a collection of essays exploring intimacy, addiction, obsession, religion, homelessness, and incarceration.

"An intimate journey reveals a Florida few visitors would ever discover." —*Kirkus*

Gluck, Louise
American *Originality: [essays]*. Louise Gluck. Farrar, Straus and Giroux 2017. 208 p.
ISBN 9780374299552
Grades: Adult   **814**
1. Creation (Literary, artistic, etc.) 2. Poets 3. Intellectual life 4. Poetry writing 5. Essays 6. Arts and Entertainment — Writing and Publishing
LC 2016026993

A luminous collection of essays from one of our most original and influential poets. Five decades after her debut poetry collection, Firstborn, Louise Gluck is a towering figure in American letters. Written with the same probing, analytic control that has long distinguished her poetry, American Originality is Gluck's second book of essays—her first, Proofs and Theories, won the 1993 PEN/Martha Albrand Award for First Nonfiction. Gluck's moving and disabusing lyricism is on full display in this decisive new collection. From its opening pages, American Originality forces readers to consider contemporary poetry and its demigods in radical, unconsoling, and ultimately very productive ways. Determined to wrest ample, often contradictory meaning from our current literary discourse, Gluck comprehends and destabilizes notions of "narcissism" and "genius" that are unique to the American literary climate. This includes erudite analyses of the poets who have interested her throughout her own career, such as Rilke, Pinsky, Chiasson, and Dobyns, and introductions to the first books of poets like Dana Levin, Peter Streckfus, Spencer Reece, and Richard Siken. Forceful, revealing, challenging, and instructive, American Originality is a seminal critical achievement.

"A love of poetry—of the poet's life—infuses these essays and brings a glow to the theoretical and a bright flame to the personal." —*Kirkus*

Griffin, Farah Jasmine
★ **In Search of a Beautiful Freedom**: *New and Selected Essays*. Farah Jasmine Griffin. W.W. Norton & Company 2023. 320 p.
ISBN 9780393355772
Grades: Adult   **814**
1. African Americans 2. African American women 3. Feminism 4. Art 5. Political culture 6. Race (Social sciences) 7. Gender identity 8. Literary criticism 9. Social criticism 10. Essays 11. Society and culture — Race 12. Society and culture — Gender — Women 13. Arts and Entertainment — Writing and Publishing — Literary criticism

"Griffin draws inspiration from many named creative heroes, as well as the writing and work of a long lineage of earlier Black artists and intellectuals. An excellent, thought-provoking collection." —*Booklist*

Gutowitz, Jill
Girls *Can Kiss Now: Essays*. Jill Gutowitz. Atria Books 2022. 240 p.
ISBN 9781982158507
Grades: Adult   **814**
1. Gutowitz, Jill 2. Lesbians 3. Popular culture 4. Homosexuality 5. Homophobia 6. Coming out (Sexual or gender identity) 7. Self-acceptance 8. Essays 9. Life stories — Identity — LGBTQIA+ 10. Life stories — Relationships — Growing up 11. Society and culture — Pop culture 12. Society and culture — LGBTQIA+
LC 2021037696

Jill Gutowitz's life—for better and worse—has always been on a collision course with pop culture. There's the time the FBI showed up at her door because of something she tweeted about Game of Thrones. The pop songs that have been the soundtrack to the worst moments of her life. And of course, the pivotal day when Orange Is the New Black hit the airwaves and broke down the door to Jill's own sexuality. In these honest examinations of identity, desire, and self-worth, Jill explores perhaps the most monumental cultural shift of our lifetimes: the mainstreaming of lesbian culture. Dusting off her own personal traumas and artifacts of her not-so-distant youth she examines how pop culture acts as a fun house mirror reflecting and refracting our values—always teaching, distracting, disappointing, and revealing us.

"Journalist Gutowitz debuts with an incisive and funny collection of essays on coming of age as a queer woman in the early 2000s." —*Publishers Weekly*

Harrison, Jim
The **Search** *for the Genuine: Nonfiction, 1970-2015*. Jim Harrison. Grove Press 2022. 336 p.
ISBN 9780802157218
Grades: Adult   **814**
1. Harrison, Jim, 1937-2016 2. Authors 3. Periodical writing 4. Voyages and travels 5. Hunting 6. Fishing 7. Nature 8. Wilderness survival 9. Dinners and dining 10. Drinking 11. Gastronomy 12. Wanderers and wandering 13. Adventure 14. Essays 15. Life stories — Arts and culture — Writing — Authors 16. Adventure writing — Adventure travel 17. Travel Writing — General

Author Jim Harrison was a writer with a poet's economy of style and trencherman's appetites and ribald humor. In The Search for the Genuine, a collection of new and previously published essays, the author muses on everything from grouse hunting to Zen Buddhism and matters of the spirit, including reported pieces on Yellowstone and shark-tagging in the open ocean, commentary on writers from Bukowski to Neruda to Peter Matthiessen, and a heartbreaking essay on life and death on the US/Mexico border. Written with Harrison's trademark humor, compassion, and full-throated zest for life, this chronicle of a modern bon vivant is a feast for fans who may think they know Harrison's nonfiction.

ESSENTIAL AND RECOMMENDED TITLES
814 American essays in English

"Forthright, perpetually curious, and compassionate, Harrison remains wholly compelling and readers will be grateful that this buoyant, observant, and caring writer took time away from his sublime poetry to create these enriching essays." —*Booklist*

Hemon, Aleksandar
My Parents: An Introduction. Aleksandar Hemon. MCD, Farrar, Straus and Giroux 2019. 168, 182 pages
ISBN 9780374217433
Grades: Adult   814
1. Hemon, Aleksandar, 1964- 2. Immigrants 3. Refugees, Bosnian 4. Memories 5. Loss 6. Resilience 7. Yugoslav War, 1991-1995 8. Bosnian Americans 9. Power 10. Identity 11. Journalists 12. Sieges 13. European history 14. Bosnia and Hercegovina 15. Sarajevo (Bosnia and Hercegovina) 16. 1990s 17. Autobiographies and memoirs 18. Biographies 19. Life stories — Arts and culture — Writing — Authors 20. Family and Relationships — Families 21. Arts and Entertainment — Writing and Publishing
LC 2018056429

The author shares a two-in-one volume documenting his parents' immigration from Bosnia to Canada and offering a selection of short memories about his family life and childhood friendships in Sarajevo.

"An incisive combination of literature that addresses the function of literature and memories that explore the meaning of memory." —*Kirkus*

Includes bibliographical references and index.

Holt, Jim
★ *When Einstein Walked with Godel: Excursions to the Edge of Thought.* Jim Holt. Farrar Straus & Giroux 2018. 368 p.
ISBN 9780374146702
Grades: Adult   814
1. Quantum theory 2. Mathematics 3. Logic 4. Essays 5. Science writing — General

An accessible guide introduces readers to some of science's least understood ideas, including the mysteries of quantum mechanics, the foundations of mathematics and the nature of logic and truth.

"A collection of incisive essays that make learning about science fun." —*Kirkus*

Includes index.

Houston, Pam
Deep Creek: Finding Hope in the High Country. Pam Houston. W.W. Norton & Company 2019. 288 p.
ISBN 9780393241020
Grades: Adult   814
1. Ranches 2. Women authors 3. Nature 4. Land stewardship 5. Effect of environment on humans 6. Effect of humans on nature 7. Human ecology 8. Colorado 9. Rocky mountains 10. Essays 11. Life stories — Arts and culture — Writing — Authors 12. Life stories — Nature and outdoors 13. Nature Writing — Personal Responses
LC 2018037969

The author of Contents May Have Shifted draws on her travels and homestead life in the Colorado Rockies in an essay collection on her ties to nature that explores the symbiotic relationship between humans and the earth.

Hurston, Zora Neale
★ *You Don't Know Us Negroes and Other Essays.* Zora Neale Hurston; edited and with an introduction by Genevieve West and Henry Louis Gates Jr. Amistad Press 2022. 320 p.
ISBN 9780063043855
Grades: Adult   814
1. African Americans 2. Race (Social sciences) 3. Racism 4. Culture 5. Gender identity 6. Social marginality 7. Social criticism 8. Race relations 9. United States history 10. 20th century 11. Essays 12. Society and culture — Race 13. History writing — African American — United States 14. Life stories — Identity — Race and ethnicity 15. Arts and Entertainment — Writing and Publishing
LC 2021028395

One of the most acclaimed artists of the Harlem Renaissance, Zora Neale Hurston was a gifted novelist, playwright, and essayist. Drawn from three decades of her work, this anthology showcases her development as a writer, from her early pieces expounding on the beauty and precision of African American art to some of her final published works, covering the sensational trial of Ruby McCollum, a wealthy Black woman convicted in 1952 for killing a white doctor. Among the selections are Hurston's well-known works such as "How It Feels to be Colored Me" and "My Most Humiliating Jim Crow Experience." the essays in this essential collection are grouped thematically and cover a panoply of topics, including politics, race and gender, and folkloric study from the height of the Harlem Renaissance to the early years of the Civil Rights movement.

"In this newly compiled essay collection covering 35 years of life and writing, Hurston's eye turns to language, race, gender, art, and much more. . . . This is an invaluable nonfiction companion to the collection of Hurston's short stories, Hitting a Straight Lick with a Crooked Stick (2020)." —*Booklist*

Includes bibliographical references.

Hustvedt, Siri
Mothers, Fathers, and Others: Essays. Siri Hustvedt. Simon & Schuster 2021. 320 p.
ISBN 9781982176396
Grades: Adult   814
1. Family relationships 2. Women 3. Women authors 4. Women artists 5. Books and reading 6. Patriarchy 7. Misogyny 8. Boundaries (Interpersonal relations) 9. Political culture 10. Essays 11. Life stories — Relationships — Family 12. Society and culture — Gender — Women 13. Life stories — Arts and culture — Writing — Authors

Feminist philosophy meets family memoir in this new essay collection, which is an exploration of the shifting borders that define human experience, including boundaries we usually take for granted—between ourselves and others, nature and nurture, viewer and artwork—which turn out to be far less stable than we imagine.

"Hustvedt is a mind-revving investigative thinker and a commanding essayist who stirs the waters, overturns stones, opens curtains, and lifts veils with authority, refinement, and cogency." —*Booklist*

Ikpi, Bassey
I'm Telling the Truth, but I'm Lying: Essays. Bassey Ikpi. Perennial 2019. 304 pages
ISBN 9780062698346
Grades: Adult   814
1. Ikpi, Bassey 2. Immigrants 3. African American women authors 4. African American women poets 5. People with Bipolar disorder 6. Bipolar disorder 7. Anxiety disorders 8. Mental health 9. Mental illness 10. Growing up 11. New York City 12. Oklahoma 13. Nigeria 14. Essays 15. Autobiographies and memoirs 16. Life stories — Facing adversity — Medical issues — Mental illness 17. Society and culture — Illness and disease 18. Life stories — Identity 19. Life stories — Arts and culture — Performing arts
LC 2019457394

A deeply personal collection of essays by the Nigerian-American writer and creator of #NoShameDay explores how her childhood move from Nigeria to Oklahoma was complicated by Bipolar II and anxiety disorders.

"People struggling with mental-health issues will appreciate Ikpi as a talented kindred spirit as she raises such universal questions as: What does it mean to be crazy anyway? Haunting and affirming." —*Booklist*

Irby, Samantha
★ *Quietly Hostile: Essays.* Samantha Irby. Vintage Books 2023. 256 p.
ISBN 9780593315699
Grades: Adult   814
1. Irby, Samantha 2. Women authors 3. Everyday life 4. African American women 5. Women comedians 6. Lesbians 7. COVID-19 Pandemic, 2020- 8. Social media 9. Family relationships 10. Loss 11. Coping 12. Popular culture 13. Humorous writing 14. Essays 15. Autobiographies and memoirs 16. Life stories — Identity 17. Humor writing — Social humor
LC 2022042843

PUBLIC LIBRARY CORE COLLECTION: NONFICTION
Twentieth Edition

LibraryReads Favorites, 2023.

In this much-anticipated new collection of hilarious essays, the beloved author takes us on another outrageously funny tour of all the gory details that make up the true portrait of a life behind the screenshotted depression memes.

"Essayist Irby shows off her wit, empathy, and self-deprecating humor in this animated collection….Irby's fans will be glad to find her in top form." —*Publishers Weekly*

We Are Never Meeting in Real Life: Essays. Samantha Irby. Vintage Books 2017. 256 pages

ISBN 9781101912195

Grades: Adult   814

1. Irby, Samantha 2. Everyday life 3. Misadventures 4. African American women 5. Bloggers 6. Frustration 7. Online identities 8. Essays 9. Autobiographies and memoirs 10. Life stories — General 11. Humor writing — Social humor

LC 2017002278

Sometimes you just have to laugh, even when life is a dumpster fire. With We Are Never Meeting in Real Life, blogger and comedian Samantha Irby turns the serio-comic essay into an art form.

"In her new book of essays, Irby . Is once again the inimitably candid, ber-confessional friend readers will happily spend a few hundred pages with." —*Booklist*

Jamison, Leslie

★ *Make It Scream, Make It Burn: Essays.* Leslie Jamison. Little, Brown & Company 2019. 272 p.

ISBN 9780316259637

Grades: Adult   814

1. Jamison, Leslie, 1983- 2. Identity 3. Loneliness 4. Belonging 5. Women authors 6. Journalism 7. Journalistic ethics 8. Interpersonal relations 9. Motherhood 10. Essays 11. Life stories — Arts and culture — Writing — Authors 12. Arts and Entertainment — Writing and Publishing 13. Society and culture — General

LC 2019931414

With the virtuosic synthesis of memoir, criticism, and journalism for which she has become known, Leslie Jamison offers us fourteen new essays that are by turns ecstatic, searching, staggering, and wise. In its kaleidoscopic sweep, Make It Scream, Make It Burn creates a profound exploration of the oceanic depths of longing and the reverberations of obsession.

"Jamison's observational skills, genuine empathy, and lack of sentimentality create an intelligent blending of journalism, scholarship (she directs the graduate nonfiction program at Columbia Univ.), and memoir." —*Library Journal*

Krakauer, Jon

Classic Krakauer: Essays on Wilderness and Risk. by Jon Krakauer. Anchor Books, a division of Penguin Random House LLC 2019. 160 p.

ISBN 9781984897695

Grades: Adult   814

1. Mountaineering 2. Extreme sports 3. Mountaineers 4. Eccentrics and eccentricities 5. Risk-taking 6. Wilderness survival 7. Men and nature 8. Essays 9. Nature writing — General 10. Sports and Competition — Mountaineering

LC 2019018697

The gripping articles collected in Classic Krakauer—originally published in magazines such as the New Yorker, Outside, and Smithsonian—show why he is considered a standard-bearer of modern journalism. Spanning an extraordinary range of subjects and locations, these pieces take us from a horrifying avalanche on Mount Everest to a volcano poised to obliterate a big chunk of Seattle; from a wilderness teen-therapy program run by apparent sadists to an otherworldly cave in New Mexico, studied by NASA to better understand Mars; from the notebook of one Fred Beckey, who catalogued the greatest unclimbed mountaineering routes on the planet, to the last days of legendary surfer Mark Foo. Rigorously researched and vividly written, marked by an unerring instinct for storytelling and scoop, these pieces are unified by the author's ambivalent love affair with unruly landscapes and his relentless search for truth.

Lamott, Anne

★ *Somehow: Thoughts on Love.* Anne Lamott. Riverhead Books 2024. 192 p.

ISBN 9780593714416

Grades: Adult   814

1. Love 2. Authors, American 3. Personal conduct 4. Psychological growth 5. Compassion 6. Transformations, Personal 7. Spirituality 8. Essays 9. Spirituality and Religion — Body, mind, and spirit

LC 2023033482

Full of her trademark compassion and humanity, the New York Times best-selling author explores the transformative power of love in our lives: how it surprises us, forces us to confront uncomfortable truths, reminds us of our humanity and guides us forward.

"Ultimately, this is a testimony to love and hope in an often painful world. Lamott's many readers are loyal, and this will be an easy sell. But pass it on, too, to people who may not even realize that they are searching for ways to connect with and love others." —*Booklist*

LaPointe, Sasha taqwseblu

Thunder Song: Essays. Sasha taqwseblu LaPointe. Counterpoint 2024. 256 p.

ISBN 9781640096356

Grades: Adult   814

1. LaPointe, Sasha taqwseblu 2. Salishan women 3. Indigenous women 4. Indigenous peoples of North America 5. Coast Salish (North American people) 6. Marginalized people 7. Colonialism 8. Ethnic identity 9. Ancestors 10. Two-spirit people 11. LGBTQIA+ people 12. Punk culture 13. Creation (Literary, artistic, etc.) 14. Social advocacy 15. Essays 16. Life stories — Identity — Race and ethnicity 17. Society and culture — Ethnic studies 18. History writing — Indigenous peoples — United States

LC 2023041698

Drawing on a rich family archive as well as the anthropological work of her late great-grandmother, Sasha taqwseblu LaPointe explores themes ranging from indigenous identity and stereotypes to cultural displacement and environmental degradation to understand what our experiences teach us about the power of community, commitment, and conscientious honesty. Unapologetically punk, the essays in Thunder Song segue between the spiritual and the physical, as they examine the role of art—in particular music—and community in helping a new generation of indigenous people claim the strength of their heritage while defining their own path in the contemporary world.

"In this affecting collection, Coast Salish poet LaPointe (Red Paint) explores how she has navigated colonized spaces as a light-skinned Indigenous woman, and the strength she draws from ancestral knowledge." —*Publishers Weekly*

Lavery, Daniel M.

Something That May Shock and Discredit You. Daniel M. Lavery. Atria Books 2020. 256 pages

ISBN 9781982105228

Grades: Adult   814

1. Popular culture 2. Identity 3. Transgender people 4. Essays 5. Autobiographies and memoirs 6. Humor writing — Social humor 7. Life stories — Identity

LC Bl2020000422

The writer of Slate 'S "Dear Prudence" column presents an irreverent collection of essays and observations on all things pop culture, from a sinister reimagining of HGTV's House Hunters to the beauty of William Shatner.

"You'll laugh, you'll cry, often both at once. Everyone should read this extraordinary book." —*Kirkus*

Originally published under the author name Daniel Mallory Ortberg.

Le Guin, Ursula K.

No Time to Spare: Thinking About What Matters. Ursula K. Le Guin; introduction by Karen Joy Fowler. Houghton Mifflin Harcourt 2017. 192 p.

ISBN 9781328661593

Grades: Adult   814

ESSENTIAL AND RECOMMENDED TITLES
814 American essays in English

1. Aging 2. Literature 3. Belief and doubt 4. Cats 5. Personal conduct 6. Ethics 7. Civilization 8. United States 9. Essays 10. Society and culture — Philosophy

LC 2017019808

Hugo Award for Best Related Non-Fiction Book, 2018; Loan Stars Favourites, 2017.

Drawing on her blog, the author shares a collection of thoughts on aging, belief, the state of literature, and the state of the nation.

"Spirited, wry reflections on aging, literature, and America's moral life." —*Kirkus*

Leopold, Aldo

★ *A Sand County Almanac & Other Writings on Ecology and Conservation*: *A Sand County Almanac & Other Writings on Conservation and Ecology*. Aldo Leopold; Curt Meine, editor. The Library of America 2013. xv, 931 p. : Illustration; Map

ISBN 9781598532067

Grades: Adult **814**

1. Ecology 2. Nature conservation 3. United States 4. Essays 5. Nature writing — General

LC Bl2013009940

A volume of essential writings by the environmental pioneer includes previously unpublished and hard-to-find pieces and provides a relevant blueprint to environmental ethics, in a collection complemented by more than 100 letters and original images.

Presents a selection of the essential writings of the environmental pioneer, including previously unpublished and hard-to-find pieces, as well as more than one hundred letters and original images.

"The volume also includes a chronology of Leopold's life; extensive notes; an index to plants/Animals, with a mixture of common and scientific nomenclature; and a general index." —*Choice*

Includes bibliographical references and indexes.

Lepore, Jill

★ *The Deadline: Essays*. Jill Lepore. Liveright Publishing 2023. xxii, 617 p.

ISBN 9781631496127

Grades: Adult **814**

1. Lepore, Jill, 1966- 2. Women historians 3. Periodical writing 4. History 5. Political culture 6. Writing 7. Intellectual life 8. Essays 9. Life stories — Arts and culture — Writing 10. Arts and Entertainment — Writing and Publishing

Arriving at the New Yorker in 2005, Jill Lepore brought a transporting freshness and a literary vivacity to everything from profiles of long-dead writers to urgent constitutional analysis to an unsparing scrutiny of the woeful affairs of the nation itself. The astonishing essays collected in the Deadline offer a prismatic portrait of Americans' techno-utopianism, frantic fractiousness, and unprecedented—but armed—aimlessness. From lockdowns and race commissions to Bratz dolls and bicycles, to the losses that haunt Lepore's life, these essays again and again cross what she calls the deadline, the "river of time that divides the quick from the dead."

"Lepore's galvanized readers will acquire new perspectives and new knowledge as she addresses complex matters with vigor, wit, and clarity." —*Booklist*

Includes index.

Lorde, Audre

★ *The Selected Works of Audre Lorde*. Edited and with an introduction by Roxane Gay. W. W. Norton & Company 2020. 382 p.

ISBN 9781324004615

Grades: Adult **814**

1. Femininity 2. Queer theory 3. African American women 4. Intersectionality 5. Injustice 6. Race (Social sciences) 7. Racism 8. Feminism 9. Love 10. Essays 11. Poetry

LC 2020020850

A definitive selection of prose and poetry from the self-described "Black, lesbian, mother, warrior, poet," for a new generation of readers. Audre Lorde is an unforgettable voice in twentieth-century literature, one of the first to center the experiences of Black, queer women. Her incisive essays and passionate poetry-alive with sensuality, vulnerability, and rage-remain indelible contributions to intersectional feminism, queer theory, and critical race studies.

"Readers new to Lorde's work couldn't ask for a better introduction, and those already familiar will find this an ideal collection of her greatest hits." —*Publishers Weekly*

Includes index.

Sister Outsider: Essays and Speeches. by Audre Lorde; [new foreword by Cheryl Clarke]. Crossing Press 2007. 190 p.

ISBN 9781580911863

Grades: Adult **814**

1. Feminism 2. Lesbianism 3. Social justice 4. Sexism 5. Racism 6. Homophobia 7. African American women 8. Intersectionality 9. Essays 10. Society and culture — General 11. Antiracist literature

LC 2008540402

The leader of contemporary feminist theory discusses such issues as racism, self-acceptance, and mother- and woman-hood.

"With her poet's command of language, she addresses sexism, racism, Black women, Black lesbians, eroticism, and more. Still powerful." —*Library Journal*

Includes bibliographical references; Originally published in 1984.

Madden, T Kira

Long Live the Tribe of Fatherless Girls: A Memoir. T Kira Madden. Bloomsbury 2019. 309 p.

ISBN 9781635571851

Grades: Adult **814**

1. Madden, T Kira 2. Growing up 3. Dysfunctional families 4. Upper class 5. Women authors, American 6. Lesbian authors 7. Adult children of drug abusers 8. Death of fathers 9. Intersectionality 10. Fathers and daughters 11. Multiracial women 12. Alcoholic men 13. Children of alcoholics 14. Coping 15. Boca Raton, Florida 16. Autobiographies and memoirs 17. Life stories — Relationships — Growing up 18. Life stories — Relationships — Family 19. Adult books for young adults

LC 2018016519

Booklist Editors' Choice, 2019; National Book Critics Circle Award: John Leonard Prize finalist, 2019.

An acclaimed literary essayist presents this raw and redemptive debut memoir about coming of age and reckoning with desire as a queer, biracial teenager in Boca Raton, Florida, where she, the only child of parents continually battling drug and alcohol addictions, found loving friendships with fatherless girls.

"A searing, lyrical debut memoir about addiction, abuse, race, and the sexualization and objectification of young women. This coming-of-age work of forgiveness, family, and love will leave an indelible mark on all who read it." —*Library Journal*

McDermott, Alice

What About the Baby?: Some Thoughts on the Art of Fiction. Alice McDermott. Farrar, Straus and Giroux 2021. 256 p.

ISBN 9780374130626

Grades: Adult **814**

1. Writing 2. Fiction writing 3. Literature 4. Authors 5. Literary criticism 6. Books and reading 7. Essays 8. Arts and Entertainment — Writing and Publishing

LC 2021011633

A collection of essays, lectures, and observations on the art of writing fiction from Alice McDermott, winner of the National Book Award and unmatched "virtuoso of language and image" (Rebecca Steinitz, the Boston Globe).

"Exceptionally knowledgeable and passionate. . . . McDermott recalculates and reinvigorates our appreciation for the high demands and deep resonance of fiction at its most profound." —*Booklist*

Miller, Kei

Things I Have Withheld: Essays. Kei Miller. Grove Press 2021. 224 p.

ISBN 9780802158956

Grades: Adult **814**

1. Miller, Kei 2. Authors 3. Men 4. Privilege (Social psychology) 5. Identity 6. Racism 7. Belonging 8. Sexism 9. Gender role 10. Discrimination 11. Alien-

ation 12. Families 13. Essays 14. Autobiographies and memoirs 15. Life stories — Identity

LC 2021032053

In this moving, critical, and lyrical collection of essays, by the acclaimed Forward Prize winner, Kei Miller explores the silences in which so many important things are kept. Miller examines the experience of discrimination through this silence and what it means to breach it-to risk words, to risk truth; and through the body and the histories those bodies inherit-the crimes that haunt them, and how the meanings of our bodies can shift as we move through the world, variously assuming privilege or victimhood.

"In 15 thoughtful and impassioned essays, prizewinning Jamaican novelist, poet, and essayist Miller reflects on race, gender, family, language, and, most pointedly, the body. . . . A spirited collection from a significant voice of both fiction and nonfiction." —Kirkus

Momaday, N. Scott

Earth Keeper: Reflections on the American Land. N. Scott Momaday. HarperCollins Publishers 2020. 96 p.

ISBN 9780063009332

Grades: Adult   814

1. Kiowa (North American people) 2. Indigenous peoples of North America 3. Effect of environment on humans 4. Nature 5. Environmentalism 6. Conservation of natural resources 7. North America 8. Nature Writing — Environmental Issues 9. Nature Writing — Personal Responses

LC 2020025782

A Pulitzer Prize-winning novelist and poet celebrates the oral tradition of his Native American culture as he recalls the stories of his childhood, passed down for generations, and their profound and sacred connection to the natural world.

"Widely acclaimed for his poetry, fiction, and folklore, Native American writer Momaday (The Death of Sitting Bear, 2020) delivers a profound reflection on humanity's relationship with its terrestrial home, the planet Earth. . . . Even readers unfamiliar with Momaday will appreciate the timeliness of this important call to care and revel in its poetry." —Booklist

Mooallem, Jon

Serious Face: Essays. Jon Mooallem. Random House 2022. 304 p.

ISBN 9780525509943

Grades: Adult   814

1. Humans 2. Personal conduct 3. Errors 4. Vulnerability 5. Resilience 6. Everyday life 7. Essays 8. Life stories — General 9. Society and culture — General

One of our most acclaimed practitioners of narrative journalism, through this collection of brilliant and profound essays, investigates hope, heartbreak, crime, punishment, idealism and catharsis across the world and within himself.

"Readers will laugh and tear up as Mooallem makes us care about his subjects and feel better off for knowing their stories." —Booklist

Morrison, Toni

★ *The Source of Self-regard: Selected Essays, Speeches, and Meditations.* Toni Morrison. Alfred A. Knopf 2019. 336 p.

ISBN 9780525521037

Grades: Adult   814

1. Race (Social sciences) 2. Power 3. Literature and society 4. Identity 5. Human rights 6. Immigrants 7. Gender role 8. Responsibility 9. Art and society 10. Language and languages 11. Critical thinking 12. Essay writing 13. Speeches, addresses, etc. 14. Arts and Entertainment — Writing and Publishing 15. Politics and global affairs — Civil and human rights

LC 2018023690

Booklist Editors' Choice, 2019.

One of the most celebrated and revered writers of our time now gives us a new nonfiction collection—a rich gathering of her essays, speeches, and meditations on society, culture, and art, spanning four decades.

"Morrison is a master of the luminous thought, of the sense of outrage or compassion that makes readers feel as if they are in the presence of an author who deeply cares about literature and the themes that engage her. Topics include the author developing the openings of her novels and deciding what tone or turn of phrase was the perfect vehicle to convey her insights about humanity." —Library Journal

Nelson, Maggie

★ *Like Love: Essays and Conversations.* Maggie Nelson. Graywolf Press 2024. 336 p.

ISBN 9781644452813

Grades: Adult   814

1. Nelson, Maggie, 1973- 2. Women authors 3. Essayists 4. Art 5. Culture 6. Queer theory 7. Creation (Literary, artistic, etc.) 8. Inspiration 9. Social criticism 10. Essays 11. Arts and Entertainment — General 12. Society and culture — General

Like Love is a momentous, raucous collection of essays drawn from twenty years of Maggie Nelson's brilliant work. These profiles, reviews, remembrances, tributes, and critical essays, as well as several conversations with friends and idols, bring to life Nelson's passion for dialogue and dissent. The range of subjects is wide, but certain themes recur: Intergenerational exchange; love and friendship; feminist and queer issues; subversion, transgression, and perversity; the roles of the critic and of language in relation to visual and performance arts; forces that feed or impede certain bodies and creators; and the fruits and follies of a life spent devoted to making.

"A revelatory gathering of beloved art and artists presented with distinctive prose." —Kirkus

O'Gieblyn, Meghan

God, Human, Animal, Machine: Technology, Metaphor, and the Search for Meaning. Meghan O'Gieblyn. Doubleday 2021. 304 p.

ISBN 9780385543828

Grades: Adult   814

1. O'Gieblyn, Meghan 2. Artificial intelligence 3. Technological innovations 4. Identity 5. Technology and civilization 6. Posthumanism 7. Philosophy 8. Human-computer interaction 9. Autobiographies and memoirs 10. Society and culture — Media and technology 11. Science Writing — Computing, the Internet, and Technology

The author of the critically-acclaimed Interior States returns with a look at the rise of artificial intelligence, how it will affect our identities and how can still be authentically human in the face of this technology revolution.

"A melancholy, well-researched tour of faith and tech and the dissatisfactions of both." —Kirkus

Oliver, Mary

★ *Upstream: Selected Essays.* Mary Oliver. Penguin Press 2016. 256 p.

ISBN 9781594206702

Grades: Adult   814

1. Oliver, Mary, 1935-2019 2. Poets 3. Nature 4. Women and nature 5. Creativity 6. Nature and culture 7. Essays 8. Nature Writing — Personal Responses 9. Arts and Entertainment — Writing and Publishing

LC 2016043612

A collection of essays with a new piece on Provincetown, follows the author as she contemplates the pleasure of artistic labor; her boundless curiosity for the flora and fauna that surround her; and the responsibility she has inherited from the great thinkers and writers of the past, to live thoughtfully, intelligently and to observe with passion.

"A lyrical, tender essay collection." —Kirkus

Orner, Peter

Am I Alone Here?: Notes on Living to Read and Reading to Live. Peter Orner. Catapult 2016. 276 p.

ISBN 9781936787258

Grades: Adult   814

1. Orner, Peter 2. Books and reading 3. Authors, American 4. Personal conduct 5. Autobiographies and memoirs 6. Life stories — Arts and culture — Writing — Authors 7. Arts and entertainment — Writing and publishing 8. Arts and Entertainment — Writing and Publishing — Literary criticism

LC Bl2016045831

A collection of 41 short essays about reading and life reflects the acclaimed writer's beliefs about the role of stories in shaping his identity and includes entries on the censoring of the works of Isaac Babel and Zora Neale Hurston, the paradoxical loneliness of Franz Kafka and the dubious insanity of Robert Walser.

ESSENTIAL AND RECOMMENDED TITLES
814 American essays in English

Oyler, Lauren
No Judgment: Essays. Lauren Oyler. HarperOne 2024. 272 p.
ISBN 9780063235359
Grades: Adult **814**
1. Oyler, Lauren 2. Women authors 3. Gossips and gossiping 4. Writing 5. Communication 6. Judgment 7. Social criticism 8. Essays 9. Society and culture — General 10. Arts and Entertainment — Writing and Publishing 11. Life stories — Arts and culture — Writing — Authors

In her writing for Harper's, the London Review of Books, the New Yorker, and elsewhere, Lauren Oyler has emerged as one of the most trenchant and influential critics of her generation, a talent whose judgments on works of literature—whether celebratory or scarily harsh—have become notorious. But what is the significance of being a critic and consumer of media in today's fraught environment? Bringing to mind the works of such iconic writers as Susan Sontag, Pauline Kael, and Terry Castle, No Judgment is a testament to Lauren Oyler's inimitable wit and her quest to understand how we shape the world through culture.

"Oyler is frank, fierce, funny, and brilliant; her brainy, passionate criticism exhilarating." —*Booklist*

Painter, Nell Irvin
★ *I Just Keep Talking: A Life in Essays.* Nell Irvin Painter. Doubleday 2024. 464 p.
ISBN 9780385548908
Grades: Adult **814**
1. United States history 2. Political science 3. Racism 4. Race relations 5. Art 6. United States 7. Essays 8. History Writing — United States

The New York Times best-selling author of the History of White People and Old in Art School presents a series of essays that span the subjects of art, politics and the legacy of racism in America.

"This affirms Painter's reputation as a historian and political commentator par excellence." —*Publishers Weekly*

Patchett, Ann
★ *These Precious Days: Essays.* Ann Patchett. Harper 2021. 320 p.
ISBN 9780063092785
Grades: Adult **814**
1. Patchett, Ann 2. Women authors, American 3. Friendship 4. Family relationships 5. Books and reading 6. Art 7. Writing 8. Creation (Literary, artistic, etc.) 9. Personal conduct 10. Purpose in life 11. Essays 12. Arts and Entertainment — Writing and Publishing 13. Life stories — Arts and culture — Writing — Authors 14. Life stories — Relationships 15. Book club best bets

Turning her writer's eye on her own experiences, the brilliant author transforms the private into the universal, providing us all a way to look at our own worlds anew, and reminds how fleeting and enigmatic life can be.

"For the author's many fans and anyone who loves beautiful writing." —*Library Journal*

Raboteau, Emily
Lessons for Survival: Mothering Against the Apocalypse. Emily Raboteau. Henry Holt and Company 2024. 320 p.
ISBN 9781250809766
Grades: Adult **814**
1. Raboteau, Emily 2. Families 3. Race (Social sciences) 4. Climate change 5. Environmentalism 6. Social justice 7. Protectiveness 8. African American women 9. Mothers 10. African Americans 11. Race relations 12. Parenting 13. Art 14. Violence 15. New York State 16. United States 17. Autobiographies and memoirs 18. Book club best bets 19. Life stories — Relationships — Parent and child 20. Life stories — Identity — Race and ethnicity

LC 2023054865

An award-winning author and critic crafts a moving meditation on race, climate, environmental justice—and what it takes to find shelter.

"Raboteau (Searching for Zion: The Quest for Home in the African Diaspora, 2013) meditates on climate change, motherhood, and injustice in this lyrical essay collection." —*Booklist*

Rankine, Claudia
★ *Citizen: An American Lyric.* Claudia Rankine. Graywolf Press 2014. 169 pages : Illustration; Color
ISBN 9781555976903
Grades: Adult **814**
1. Racism 2. Justice 3. African Americans 4. Violence 5. Race relations 6. United States 7. Essays 8. Poetry 9. Society and culture — Race 10. Antiracist literature 11. Book club best bets

LC 2014935702

Collects essays, poetry, and images that expose the racial tensions in twenty-first century life, highlighting the slights, slips of the tongue, and intentional offensives that pervade the home, school, and popular media.

"Accounts of racially charged interactions, insidious and flagrant, transpiring in private and in the public eye, distill the immediate emotional intensity of individual experience with tremendous precision while allowing ambiguity, ambivalence, contradiction, and exhaustion to remain in all their fraught complexity…Once again Rankine inspires sympathy and outrage, but most of all a will to take a deep look at ourselves and our society." —*Publishers Weekly*

Includes bibliographical references (pages 167-168).

Rich, Adrienne
Essential Essays: Culture, Politics, and the Art of Poetry. Adrienne Cecile Rich. W W Norton & CO Inc 2018. 352 p.
ISBN 9780393652369
Grades: Adult **814**
1. Essays 2. Society and culture — General

LC 2018013156

Presents 25 essays—culled from the works of an award-winning poet, influential essayist, radical feminist and major intellectual voice of her generation—that unite the political, personal and poetical and demonstrate her revolutionary views on social justice.

Richardson, Robert D.
Emerson: The Mind on Fire: A Biography. by Robert D. Richardson, Jr; with a frontispiece by Barry Moser. University of California Press 1995. xiii, 671 p, [16] p. of plates : Illustration
ISBN 9780520088085
Grades: Adult **814**
1. Emerson, Ralph Waldo, 1803-1882 2. Authors, American 3. Social life and customs 4. United States 5. 19th century 6. Biographies 7. Arts and Entertainment — Writing and Publishing 8. Life stories — Arts and culture — Writing — Authors

LC 94036008

National Book Critics Circle Award for Biography finalist, 1995.

Challenges popular stereotypes of Ralph Waldo Emerson and reveals his many identities as a grieving widower, an affectionate father, a spokesman for individualism, and an intellectual adventurer.

"Richardson focuses principally on his subject's inner life, the life of his mind and spirit. But in this subtle portrayal of Emerson the thinker, the reader also sees the clearly limned portrait of Emerson the social activist. A masterful work, this biography will attract the attention of scholars and serious general readers for decades." —*Booklist*

A centennial book—Half t.P; Includes bibliographical references (p. 585-656) and index.

Rothfeld, Becca
★ *All Things Are Too Small: Essays in Praise of Excess.* Becca Rothfeld. Metropolitan Books 2024. 288 p.
ISBN 9781250849915
Grades: Adult **814**
1. Excess (Philosophy) 2. Life 3. Art 4. Desire 5. Social history 6. Personal conduct 7. Culture 8. Essays 9. Society and culture — General

The author issues a call to throw off restraint and balance in favor of excess, abandon and disproportion, in essays ranging from such topics as decluttering, mindfulness, David Cronenberg, sadomasochism and women who wait.

"Rothfeld has a knack for aphorism, and it's an absolute pleasure to watch her idiosyncratic arguments unfold. This is a triumph." —*Publishers Weekly*

Russo, Richard
The Destiny Thief: Essays on Writing, Writers, and Life. by Richard Russo. Alfred A. Knopf 2018. 224 p.
ISBN 9781524733513
Grades: Adult   814
1. Authors 2. Books and reading 3. Writing 4. Friendship 5. Transgender people 6. Purpose in life 7. Essays 8. Arts and Entertainment — Writing and Publishing 9. Society and culture — General
LC 2017024819

A collection of personal essays from the Pulitzer Prize-winning author of Everybody's Fool describes his broad interests and experiences, from an analysis on the value of Mark Twain, to accompanying a good friend on her pursuit of gender reassignment surgery.

"For aspiring writers, Russo's musings on the art and craft of the novel are a trove of knowledge and guidance. For adoring readers, they are a window into the imagination and inspiration for Russos beloved novels, screenplays, and short stories." —*Booklist*

Sabatini Sloan, Aisha
Dreaming of Ramadi in Detroit: Essays. Aisha Sabatini Sloan. Graywolf Press 2024. 160 p.
ISBN 9781644452714
Grades: Adult   814
1. Sabatini Sloan, Aisha 2. Women authors 3. Creative writing teachers 4. Multiracial women 5. LGBTQIA+ people 6. Art 7. Writing 8. Race (Social sciences) 9. Identity 10. Social marginality 11. Creation (Literary, artistic, etc.) 12. Voyages and travels 13. United States 14. Essays 15. Life stories — Arts and culture — Writing — Authors 16. Life stories — Identity 17. Arts and Entertainment — General 18. Society and culture — Race

This collection of innovative, penetrating, and lively essays features swimming pools and poets, road trips and museums, family dinners and celebrity sightings. Sabatini Sloan's lively style is perfectly suited to the way she circles a subject or an idea before cinching it tight. The curiosity that guides each essay, focusing on the period between the 2016 election and the onset of the pandemic, is rooted in the supposition that there is an intrinsic relationship between the way we conceptualize darkness and our collective opportunity for awakening.

"For this penetrating collection, Sloan brings together reflections about art, race, and teaching…Readers will be spellbound." —*Publishers Weekly*
Includes bibliographical references.

Sedaris, David
Calypso. David Sedaris. Little Brown & Company 2018. 288 p.
ISBN 9780316392389
Grades: Adult   814
1. Sedaris, David 2. Families 3. Autobiographies and memoirs 4. Essays 5. Life stories — Arts and culture — Writing — Authors 6. Humor writing — General
LC 2017950359
New York Times Notable Book, 2018.

A latest collection of personal essays by the best-selling author of Let's Explore Diabetes with Owls and Me Talk Pretty One Day shares even more revealing and intimate memories from his upbringing and family life.

"The authors fans and newcomers alike will be richly rewarded by this side-splitting collection." —*Publishers Weekly*

★ *Happy-Go-Lucky.* David Sedaris. Little, Brown & Company 2022. 304 p.
ISBN 9780316392457
Grades: Adult   814
1. Sedaris, David 2. Authors 3. Humorists 4. Everyday life 5. Family relationships 6. COVID-19 (Disease) 7. Death of fathers 8. Loss 9. Social criticism 10. Humorous writing 11. Essays 12. Life stories — Arts and culture — Writing — Authors 13. Life stories — Relationships 14. Humor writing — Social humor

The author of Calypso and regular contributor to the New Yorker is back with a whole new collection of satirical and humorous essays that chronical his own life and ordinary moments that turn beautifully absurd.

"The first new original collection from Sedaris in four years (after Calypso) contains essays that range far and wide in subject matter, from the 2020 presidential election to the protests surrounding the killing of George Floyd, and the pandemic lockdowns….This is Sedaris at his best, provocative and hysterical." —*Library Journal*

Shapland, Jenn
★ *Thin Skin: Essays.* Jenn Shapland. Pantheon Books 2023. 288 p.
ISBN 9780593317457
Grades: Adult   814
1. Shapland, Jenn, 1987- 2. Self 3. Work 4. Desire 5. Capitalism 6. Gender role 7. Identity 8. Human body 9. Vulnerability 10. Need 11. Human-animal relationships 12. Essays 13. Society and culture — General 14. Life stories — Identity — LGBTQIA+

Weaving together historical research, interviews and her everyday life in New Mexico, a National Book Award finalist and powerful literary mind probes the lines between self and work, human and animal, need and desire as she examines capitalism's toxic creep into the land, our bodies and our thinking.

"It's hard not to marvel at how the author draws unexpected conclusions from a diverse array of anecdotes, illuminating the profound ways in which individuals and the world shape each other. This is a gem." —*Publishers Weekly*

So, Anthony Veasna
★ *Songs on Endless Repeat: Essays and Outtakes.* Anthony Veasna So. Ecco 2023. 240 p.
ISBN 9780063049963
Grades: Adult   814
1. So, Anthony Veasna, 1992-2020 2. Family relationships 3. LGBTQIA+ people 4. Desire 5. Popular culture 6. Asian Americans 7. Cambodian people 8. Southeast Asian people 9. American people 10. Ethnic identity 11. Identity 12. Essays 13. Life stories — Identity 14. Arts and entertainment — Writing and publishing
LC 2023020569

Gathering together the late author's comic, soulful essays along with previously unpublished fiction, this astonishing final expression explores family, queer desire, pop culture and race.

"So's essays resonate with vulnerable eloquence, but his potency lies in storytelling, effortlessly creating immersive worlds animated by familiar, vital characters, their vibrancy further magnifying the poignant loss of what could have been." —*Booklist*

Solnit, Rebecca
The Faraway Nearby. Rebecca Solnit. Viking 2013. 272 p.
ISBN 9780670025961
Grades: Adult   814
1. Empathy 2. Storytelling 3. Books and reading 4. Death 5. Mortality 6. Literature 7. Interpersonal relations 8. Mothers and daughters 9. Family relationships 10. Arts and Entertainment — Writing and Publishing 11. Family and Relationships — General
LC 2013001563
New York Times Notable Book, 2013; ALA Notable Book, 2014; National Book Critics Circle Award for Autobiography/Memoir finalist.

A companion to a Field Guide for Getting Lost explores the ways that people construct lives from stories and connect to each other through empathy, narrative and imagination, sharing illustrative anecdotes about historical figures and members of her own family.

Sontag, Susan
At the Same Time: Essays and Speeches. Susan Sontag; edited by Paolo Dilonardo and Anne Jump; foreword by David Rieff. Farrar, Straus, and Giroux 2007. xvii, 235 p.

ESSENTIAL AND RECOMMENDED TITLES
814 American essays in English

ISBN 9780374100728
Grades: Adult — 814
1. Literature 2. Political activists 3. Social justice 4. Injustice 5. Politics and government 6. United States 7. Essays 8. Speeches, addresses, etc. 9. Politics and global affairs — General
LC 2006031179

A powerful compilation of sixteen essays, written in the last years of the author's life, offers a series of reflections on her commitment to the power of literature, political activism, the resistance to injustice as an ethical duty, the problems of post-9/11 America, and the work of such diverse writers as Soviet novelist Leonid Tsypkin and Nobel laureate Nadine Gordimer.

Styron, William
My Generation: Collected Nonfiction. William Styron; edited by James L. W. West III.. Random House 2015. 624 p.
ISBN 9780812997057
Grades: Adult — 814
1. Styron, William, 1925-2006 2. Authors, American 3. Social life and customs 4. United States 5. Essays 6. Autobiographies and memoirs 7. Life stories — Arts and culture — Writing — Authors 8. Arts and Entertainment — Writing and Publishing
LC 2014038029

Including significant previously uncollected material, My Generation is the definitive gathering of the fruits of this beloved writer's five decades of public life. Here is the William Styron unafraid to peer into the darkest corners of the 20th century or to take on the complex racial legacy of the United States. But here too is Styron writing about his daily walk with his dog, musing on the Modern Library's "100 Greatest Books," and offering personal insight into the extraordinary array of noted contemporary figures he interacted with over the course of an illustrious career. These are the people and events, tragic and joyful, historical and intimate, that aroused Styron's unrivalled curiosity.

"Elegant and entertaining, the writings in My Generation compose a definitive volume that will appeal to a broad audience. Summing Up: Highly recommended. Lower-division undergraduates through faculty; general readers." —*Choice*

Includes index.

Thurman, Judith
★ *A Left-Handed Woman: Essays.* Judith Thurman. Farrar, Straus and Giroux 2022. 240 p.
ISBN 9780374607166
Grades: Adult — 814
1. Gender role 2. Literature 3. History 4. Political science 5. Humans 6. Women authors 7. Fashion 8. Women 9. Art 10. Essays 11. Society and culture — General
LC 2022023786

Judith Thurman, a prolific staff writer at the New Yorker for more than two decades, has gathered a selection of her essays and profiles in a Left-Handed Woman. They consider our culture in all its guises: Literature, history, politics, gender, fashion, and art, though their paramount subject is the human condition.

"Because of the breadth of their topics, Thurman's well-written culture essays in this collection will appeal to many readers, particularly those interested in fashion." —*Library Journal*

V
★ *Reckoning.* V, formerly Eve Ensler. Bloomsbury 2023. 304 p.
ISBN 9781635579048
Grades: Adult — 814
1. Ensler, Eve, 1953- 2. Women authors 3. women playwrights 4. Women political activists 5. Feminists 6. Diary writing 7. Sexism 8. Misogyny 9. Sexual violence 10. Atrocities 11. Social change 12. Psychic trauma 13. Survival 14. Essays 15. Life stories — Arts and culture — Writing 16. Life stories — Facing adversity — Abuse survivors 17. Society and culture — Gender — Women 18. Society and culture — Social activism and philanthropy

The newest book from v. (formerly Eve Ensler) Reckoning invites you to travel the journey of a writer's and activist's life and process over forty years, representing both the core of ideas that have become global movements and the methods through which v. survived abuse and self-hatred. Seamlessly moving from the internal to the external, the personal to the political, Reckoning is a moving and inspiring work of prose, poetry, dreams, letters, and essays drawn from V's lifetime journals that takes readers from Berlin to Oklahoma to Congo, from climate disaster, homelessness, and activism to family.

"This far-reaching, deeply affecting collection will garner avid attention and ignite passionate discussion." —*Booklist*

Villarreal, Vanessa Anglica
Magical/Realism: Essays on Music, Memory, Fantasy, and Borders. Vanessa Anglica Villarreal. Tiny Reparations 2024. 368 p.
ISBN 9780593187142
Grades: Adult — 814
1. Memories 2. Working class 3. Interpersonal relations 4. Fantasy 5. Nostalgia 6. Popular culture 7. Colonialism 8. Children of musicians 9. Mexican Americans 10. Essays 11. Autobiographies and memoirs 12. Life stories — Identity 13. Society and culture — Pop culture 14. Life stories — Identity — Immigrants

A poet and essayist intimately and fearlessly explores the many complicated girlhoods of being a working-class, first-generation, Mexican American daughter of cumbia musician, in this brilliant collection that examines migration, violence and colonial erasure through the lens of music and pop culture.

"Villareal expertly reclaims those narratives here. A wondrous book that will change the way you think about fantasy and magic." —*Kirkus*

Wainaina, Binyavanga
★ *How to Write About Africa: Collected Works.* Binyavanga Wainaina; edited by Achal Prabhala. One World 2023. x, 347 p.
ISBN 9780812989656
Grades: Adult — 814
1. Wainaina, Binyavanga, 1971-2019 2. Journalists 3. Political activists 4. Satirists 5. Gay men 6. Social classes 7. Racism 8. Colonialism 9. Social criticism 10. Identity 11. Journalism 12. East African people 13. Kenyan people 14. Africa 15. Kenya 16. South Africa 17. Essays 18. Anthologies 19. Life stories — Arts and culture — Writing — Journalists 20. Life stories — Identity 21. Politics and global affairs — World politics — Africa 22. Society and culture — General

A trailblazing collection of writing on contemporary Africa from across Binyavanga Wainaina's extraordinary life, ranging from musings on politics & culture to deeply personal introspections Binyavanga Wainaina was a seminal author and activist, remembered as one of the greatest chroniclers of contemporary African life. After his death in 2019, this ground-breaking collection brings together his pioneering writing on the African continent for the first time. A rule-breaker full of wry satire and piercing wisdom, this collection includes many of Binyavanga's most critically acclaimed pieces, including the viral satirical sensation 'How to Write About Africa'.

"This fittingly sums up the considerable abilities of a talent lost too soon." —*Publishers Weekly*

Originally published in the UK by Hamish Hamilton, London, in 2022.

Walker, Alice
The Cushion in the Road: Meditation and Wandering as the Whole World Awakens to Being in Harm's Way. Alice Walker. The New Press 2013. 336 p.
ISBN 9781595588722
Grades: Adult — 814
1. Humanitarianism 2. Injustice 3. Intersectionality 4. Essays 5. Autobiographies and memoirs 6. Life stories — Arts and culture — Writing — Authors 7. Society and culture — Social activism and philanthropy
LC 2012041852

A collection of essays addresses topics ranging from the spiritual to the political, including racism, Africa, Barack Obama's presidency, Palestinian solidarity, and healthcare.

Wallace, David Foster
Consider the Lobster: And Other Essays. David Foster Wallace. Little, Brown 2005. 343 p. : Illustration
ISBN 9780316156110
Grades: Adult — 814

PUBLIC LIBRARY CORE COLLECTION: NONFICTION
Twentieth Edition

1. Essays 2. Trivia and miscellaneous facts 3. Arts and Entertainment — Writing and Publishing

LC 2005010886

New York Times Notable Book, 2006.

A collection of essays shares whimsical and biting observations about such topics as the Bush-Kerry presidential race, the pain experienced by lobsters while they are being prepared for the feast, and Franz Kafka's questionable sense of humor.

"Wallace's complex essays are written, and rightfully so, to be read more than once." —*Booklist*

Includes bibliographical references.

Waters, John
Mr. Know-it-all: The Tarnished Wisdom of a Filth Elder. John Waters. Farrar, Straus and Giroux 2019. 288 p.

ISBN 9780374214968

Grades: Adult   814

1. Waters, John, 1946- 2. Aging 3. Nonconformists 4. Fame 5. Celebrities 6. Film producers and directors 7. United States 8. Autobiographies and memoirs 9. Essays 10. Biographies 11. Life stories — Arts and culture — Performing arts — Directors and producers 12. Arts and entertainment — Movies and television

LC 2018057165

The newest essay collection from the New York Times-bestselling John Waters, reflecting on how to overcome newfound responsibility and rebel in the autumn of your years.

"In this delightful hybrid memoir/Advice book, film director Waters shares highlights from his 40-year career and musings on a random assortment of subjects, including music, architecture, and the best vacation spots." —*Publishers Weekly*

Wayne, Tiffany K.
Critical Companion to Ralph Waldo Emerson: A Literary Reference to His Life and Work. Tiffany K. Wayne. Facts on File 2010. xii, 444 p. : Illustration

ISBN 9780816073580

Grades: 11 12 Adult   814

1. Emerson, Ralph Waldo, 1803-1882 2. Authors, American 3. 19th century 4. Arts and Entertainment — Writing and Publishing — Literary criticism 5. Reference books — Literature 6. Reference books — Handbooks, manuals, etc.

LC 2009024809

"This reference book examines the life and works of a central thinker in American history.... It begins with Emerson's biography for context. Part 2 focuses on 140 significant (in the view of scholars) individual works, including 60 poems (most with one to three pages of synopses, critical commentary, and further reading). Part 3 covers related people, places, and topics.... The final appendixes offer a chronology of Emerson's life and times, bibliographies of both his works and relevant secondary sources." —*Choice*

Includes bibliographical references (p. 408-420) and index.

White, E. B.
Essays of E.B. White. E.B. White. Perennial Classics 1999. xi, 364 p. : Portrait

ISBN 9780060932237

Grades: Adult   814

1. Essays 2. Humor writing — Classic humorists

LC 98056019

Presents essays written during all stages of the author's illustrious career that range in scope from his thoughts on the city of New York and its inhabitants to his preference for brown eggs over white eggs.

Collects over 30 essays.

Williams, Terry Tempest
Erosion: Essays of Undoing. Terry Tempest Williams. Sarah Crichton Books/Farrar, Straus and Giroux 2019. 320 p.

ISBN 9780374280062

Grades: Adult   814

1. Erosion 2. Environmentalism 3. Identity 4. Nature conservation 5. Deserts 6. Political culture 7. Bears Ears National Monument (Utah) 8. The West (United States) 9. United States 10. Essays 11. Nature Writing — Environmental Issues 12. Nature Writing — Natural Landscapes 13. Nature Writing — Personal Responses

LC 2019017871

Timely essays by the aconservationist and author of the Hour of Land explore the concept of erosion, the paradox of desert landscapes and the environmental hazards of present-day American politics.

Includes bibliographical references and index.

Wiman, Christian
He Held Radical Light: The Art of Faith and the Faith of Art. Christian Wiman. Farrar, Straus and Giroux 2018. 128 p.

ISBN 9780374168469

Grades: Adult   814

1. Faith 2. Poets 3. Art and religion 4. Death 5. Poetry writing 6. People with cancer 7. Memory 8. Eternity 9. Religions 10. Autobiographies and memoirs 11. Spirituality and Religion — Christianity 12. Life stories — Religion and spirituality — Personal faith 13. Life stories — Arts and culture — Writing — Poets 14. Arts and Entertainment — Writing and Publishing

Explores the relationships between art and faith, death and fame, heaven and oblivion, in a love letter to poetry, filled with moving, surprising, and sometimes funny encounters with the poets Wiman has known.

"Readers who allow themselves to be swept along by Wimans beautiful style and oblique considerations will come away with fresh strategies for unpacking faith in the contemporary world." —*Publishers Weekly*

814.6 American essays — 2000-

Evans, William
Black Nerd Problems: Essays. William Evans and Omar Holmon. Gallery Books 2021. 288 p.

ISBN 9781982150235

Grades: Adult   814.6

1. African Americans 2. Podcasts 3. Intellectual life 4. Race (Social sciences) 5. Popular culture 6. Social criticism 7. Media fandom 8. African Americans in popular culture 9. Essays 10. Society and culture — Race 11. Society and culture — Pop culture

LC 2020057023

When William Evans and Omar Holmon founded Black Nerd Problems, they had no idea whether anyone beyond their small circle of friends would be interested in their little corner of the internet. But soon after launching, they were surprised to find out that there was a wide community of people who hungered for fresh perspectives on all things nerdy, from the perspective of #OwnedVoices. In the years since, Evans and Holmon have built a large, dedicated fanbase eager for their brand of cultural critique, whether in the form of a laugh-out-loud, raucous Game of Thrones episode recap or an eloquent essay on dealing with grief through stand-up comedy. Now, they are ready to take the next step with this vibrant and hilarious essay collection, which covers everything from X-Men to Breonna Taylor with insight and intelligence.

"This hugely entertaining, eminently thoughtful collection is a master class in how powerful—and fun—cultural criticism can be." —*Publishers Weekly*

Laymon, Kiese
How to Slowly Kill Yourself and Others in America: Essays. Kiese Laymon. Scribner 2020. 160 p.

ISBN 9781982170820

Grades: Adult   814.6

1. Racism 2. African American men 3. Race relations 4. Growing up 5. African American families 6. Mississippi 7. Southern States 8. Essays 9. Society and culture — Race

A collection of essays on family, race, violence, celebrity, music, writing, and other topics.

ESSENTIAL AND RECOMMENDED TITLES
817 American humor and satire in English

"A timely and disquieting contribution to urgent conversations about race."
—*Kirkus*

Renkl, Margaret
The Comfort of Crows: A Backyard Year. Margaret Renkl. Spiegel & Grau 2023. 288 p.
ISBN 9781954118461
Grades: Adult   **814.6**
1. Renkl, Margaret 2. Backyard animals 3. Backyard birds 4. Effect of environment on humans 5. Seasons 6. Nature 7. Memories 8. American people 9. North American people 10. Tennessee 11. Southern States 12. 2020s 13. Essays 14. Autobiographies and memoirs 15. Book club best bets 16. Nature Writing — Personal responses 17. Life stories — Nature and outdoors
LibraryReads Favorites, 2023.

The beloved New York Times opinion writer and best-selling author presents this stunning literary devotional that follows the creatures and plants in her backyard over the course of the year, tracing the passing of the seasons, personal and natural.

"New York Times columnist Renkl (Late Migrations) invites readers along on a year of loving outdoor observations in this gently moving memoir." —*Publishers Weekly*

Stone, Lillian
★ *Everybody's Favorite: Tales from the World's Worst Perfectionist.* Lillian Stone. Dey Street Books 2023. 210 p.
ISBN 9780063241039
Grades: Adult   **814.6**
1. Stone, Lillian 2. Growing up 3. OCD in teenagers 4. Compulsive behavior 5. Evangelicalism 6. Body image 7. Perfection 8. Self-improvement 9. Interpersonal relations 10. Self-acceptance 11. Essays 12. Autobiographies and memoirs 13. Life stories — Relationships — Growing up 14. Life stories — Personal growth 15. Humor writing — Social humor 16. Debut title

Lillian Stone—childhood evangelical, AOL girlfriend, and professional nail biter is always living on the edge of anxiety. In this laugh-out-loud essay collection, replete with cringe-inducing touchstones of an early-aughts girlhood, Lillian recounts her quest to be everybody's favorite.

"Stone's painfully sharp observations will draw readers in, and her honesty will keep them enthralled. This will go a long way toward helping readers feel less alone." —*Publishers Weekly*

817 American humor and satire in English

Petri, Alexandra
Alexandra Petri's US History: Important American Documents I Made Up. Alexandra Petri. W W Norton & Company 2023. 356 p.
ISBN 9781324006435
Grades: Adult   **817**
1. United States history 2. Essays 3. History Writing — United States 4. Humor writing — Social humor

"This intriguing collection will definitely keep audiences entertained, whether they read through cover to cover or dip in for the occasional treat."
—*Booklist*

818 American miscellaneous writings in English

Alexie, Sherman
You Don't Have to Say You Love Me: A Memoir. Sherman Alexie. Little, Brown & Company 2017. 320 pages
ISBN 9780316270755
Grades: Adult   **818**
1. Alexie, Sherman, 1966- 2. Growing up 3. Indigenous reservations 4. Mothers and sons 5. Dysfunctional families 6. Indigenous families 7. Siblings 8. Children of mothers 9. Poverty 10. Death of mothers 11. Memories 12. Familial love 13. Indigenous peoples of North America 14. Washington (State) 15. 1970s 16. 1980s 17. Autobiographies and memoirs 18. Life stories — Arts and culture — Writing — Authors 19. Life stories — Relationships — Parent and child 20. Life stories — Facing adversity 21. Adult books for young adults
LC 2016958327
ALA Notable Book, 2018; Booklist Editors' Choice, 2017; Library Journal Best Books, 2017.

The author of the Absolutely True Diary of a Part-Time Indian presents a literary memoir of poems, essays and intimate family photos that reflect his complicated feelings about his disadvantaged childhood on a Native American reservation with his siblings and alcoholic parents.

"Presented as a series of vignettes, some in prose, others in poetry, about Alexie's life and family, the narrative transitions between styles, which feels natural as Alexie searches for the best way to present complex memories and stories." —*Library Journal*

Berry, Wendell
★ *The World-ending Fire: The Essential Wendell Berry.* Selected and introduced by Paul Kingsnorth. Counterpoint Press 2018. 368 p.
ISBN 9781640090286
Grades: Adult   **818**
1. Berry, Wendell, 1934- 2. Agriculture 3. Farm life 4. Authors, American 5. Sustainable agriculture 6. Rural life 7. Social life and customs 8. United States 9. Essays 10. Diaries 11. Nature Writing — Environmental Issues 12. Society and culture — General
LC 2017060544

Celebrating our cultural heritage, our history and our home, an essayist, novelist and poet presents a collection of writings of a life spent farming the fields of rural Kentucky with mules and horses, and of the deeply personal knowledge of the land cultivated by this work.

"A great place to start for those who are not familiar with Berry's work; for those who are, it will be a nostalgic stroll down a rural, wooded Memory Lane. In this day and age, his writings are must-reads." —*Kirkus*

Carson, Anne
Decreation: Poetry, Essays, Opera. Anne Carson. Knopf 2005. xi, 245 p.
ISBN 9781400043491
Grades: Adult   **818**
1. Women authors 2. Canadian poetry 3. Poetry
LC 2004063367

A compilation of literary writings explores the nature and mechanics of the human acts of undoing of self and of form, as revealed in the lives of Sappho, Simone Weil, and Virginia Woolf.

A remarkable compilation of literary writings by the critically acclaimed author of Autobiography of Red features an array of original poetry, essays, a screenplay, and a libretto that explores the nature and mechanics of the human act of decreation as revealed in the lives of Sappho, Marguerite Porete, Simone Weil, Virginia Woolf, and her own relationship with her mother.

This is a Borzoi book—T.P. verso.

Chabon, Michael
Bookends: Collected Intros and Outros. Michael Chabon. Harper Perennial 2019. 224 p.
ISBN 9780062851291
Grades: Adult   **818**
1. Literary criticism 2. Literature 3. Books and reading 4. Essays 5. Arts and Entertainment — Writing and Publishing 6. Arts and Entertainment — Writing and Publishing — Literary criticism
LC Bl2019001547

The Pulitzer Prize-winning author of Moonglow presents an idiosyncratic compilation of introductions, afterwords and liner notes from classic works of literature to explore how they influenced his literary life.

Choi, Don Mee
Dmz Colony. Don Mee Choi. Wave Books 2020. 132 pages : Illustration; Color
ISBN 9781940696966

PUBLIC LIBRARY CORE COLLECTION: NONFICTION
Twentieth Edition

Grades: Adult   818
1. Korean War, 1950-1953 2. Poetry

LC 2019030061

Woven from poems, prose, photographs, and drawings, Don Mee Choi's DMZ Colony is a tour de force of personal and political reckoning set over eight acts."

"Virtuosic in its range and empathy, this is a book that shifts the reader's understanding of historical narrative from one of war to one of flight." —Publishers Weekly

Diaz, Jaquira
Ordinary Girls: A Memoir. Jaquira Díaz. Algonquin Books of Chapel Hill 2019. 256 p.
ISBN 9781616209131

Grades: Adult   818
1. Diaz, Jaquira 2. Multiracial women 3. Families 4. Family problems 5. Mental illness 6. Sexual violence victims 7. Lesbians 8. Women authors 9. Self-discovery 10. Puerto Rico 11. Miami, Florida 12. Autobiographies and memoirs 13. Life stories — Relationships — Growing up 14. Life stories — Arts and culture — Writing — Authors 15. Life stories — Identity — LGBTQIA+ 16. Life stories — Facing adversity — Abuse survivors 17. Adult books for young adults

LC 2019009593

Library Journal Best Books, 2019; LibraryReads Favorites, 2019.

Traces the author's upbringing in the housing projects of Puerto Rico, her mother's battle with schizophrenia, her personal struggles with sexual assault and her efforts to pursue a literary career.

"Her skillful weaving-in of several harrowing deaths that made national headlines, including the Casey Anthony case and the Baby Lolliipops Murder, illuminates some eerie similarities and connections to her life. While the story of a typical displaced girl's life could have been tragic, Daz takes charge, changes her trajectory, and tells a tale of an individual who ultimately triumphs." —Booklist

Febos, Melissa
Girlhood. Melissa Febos. St. Martin's Press 2021. 320 p. : Illustration
ISBN 9781635572520

Grades: Adult   818
1. Febos, Melissa 2. Growing up 3. Gender role 4. Girls 5. Women 6. Femininity 7. Self 8. Interpersonal relations 9. Desire 10. Sexuality 11. Identity 12. Feminism 13. Self-awareness 14. United States 15. Autobiographies and memoirs 16. Essays 17. Life stories — Identity — Gender 18. Society and culture — Gender — Women

The acclaimed author looks back on her experiences growing up as a female and how the values that she and other women learned in girlhood failed to prioritize their personal safety, happiness and freedom.

"An acclaimed nonfiction writer gathers essays embracing the pleasure, pain, and power of growing up as a girl and woman." —Kirkus

Gregory, Dick
★ *The Essential Dick Gregory.* Dick Gregory, edited by Christian Gregory. HarperCollins 2022. 320 p.
ISBN 9780062879202

Grades: Adult   818
1. Discrimination 2. Political activists 3. Comedians 4. Autobiographies and memoirs 5. Anthologies 6. Essays 7. Life stories — Identity — Race and ethnicity 8. Life stories — Politics — Activists and reformers

This generation-defining collection of thought-provoking, agitating and liberating writings takes readers on a breathtaking tour through the life of one of America's most prophetic and relevant cultural icons who gave up a lucrative entertainment career to fight injustice on the front line of battle.

"Sharp, funny, and often inspiring, this is a must-read for Gregory's fans, and a perfect entry point for the uninitiated." —Publishers Weekly

Harjo, Joy
Catching the Light. Joy Harjo. Yale University Press 2022. 128 p.
ISBN 9780300257038

Grades: Adult   818
1. Harjo, Joy, 1951- 2. Indigenous women 3. Indigenous poets 4. Poetry writing 5. Creation (Literary, artistic, etc.) 6. Inspiration 7. Motherhood 8. Identity 9. Indigenous peoples of North America 10. Life stories — Arts and culture — Writing — Poets 11. Arts and Entertainment — Writing and Publishing

United States Poet Laureate and winner of the 2022 Academy of American Poets Leadership Award Joy Harjo examines the power of words and how poetry summons us toward justice and healing.

"This highly recommended book is a comforting island for writers who enjoy reading about how authors succeed." —Library Journal

The 2021 Windham-Campbell lecture — t.P.

Heti, Sheila
Alphabetical Diaries. Sheila Heti. Farrar, Straus and Giroux 2024. 224 p.
ISBN 9780374610784

Grades: Adult   818
1. Heti, Sheila, 1976- 2. Women authors 3. Diary writing 4. Confession 5. Hope 6. Fear 7. Intimacy 8. Thought and thinking 9. Writing 10. Experiments 11. North American people 12. Canadian people 13. Autobiographies and memoirs 14. Canadian literature 15. Life stories — Arts and culture — Writing — Authors 16. Arts and Entertainment — Writing and Publishing

Sheila Heti kept a record of her thoughts over a ten-year period, then arranged the sentences from A to Z. Passionate and reflective, joyful and despairing, these are her alphabetical diaries.

"Playful yet disciplined, Heti's latest book is an experiment in literature…This will be a particularly suitable offering for readers who enjoy the intimacy of memoir but wish to delve into more experimental work." —Booklist

Highsmith, Patricia
★ *Patricia* Highsmith's Diaries and Notebooks: The New York Years, 1941-1950. Patricia Highsmith; edited by Anna Von Planta with a foreword by Joan Schenkar. Liveright Publishing 2023. 560 p.
ISBN 9781324092940

Grades: Adult   818
1. Highsmith, Patricia, 1921-1995 2. Women authors 3. Lesbians 4. Diary writing 5. Fiction writing 6. Sexuality 7. Books and reading 8. Interpersonal relations 9. 20th century 10. 1940s 11. 1950s 12. Diaries 13. Life stories — Arts and culture — Writing — Authors 14. Arts and Entertainment — Writing and Publishing

"A great read for aspiring writers, devotees of LGBTQ history, and those who enjoy reading about an artist's evolution." —Library Journal

Jackson, Shirley
Let Me Tell You: New Stories, Essays, and Other Writings. Shirley Jackson; edited by Laurence Jackson Hyman and Sarah Hyman DeWitt. Random House Inc. 2015. 496 p.
ISBN 9780812997668

Grades: Adult   818
1. Families 2. Family relationships 3. Short stories 4. Essays

LC 2014036656

This volume of unpublished and uncollected works brings together Shirley Jackson's deliciously eerie short stories along with frank lectures on writing, comic essays about her large, boisterous family, and whimsical drawings. Jackson's landscape here is most frequently domestic, but this familiar setting is also her most subversive: She wields humor, terror, and the uncanny to explore the real challenges of marriage, parenting, and community—the pressure of social norms, the veins of distrust in love, the constant lack of time and space.

Kerouac, Jack
Book of Sketches, 1952-57. Jack Kerouac; introduction by George Condo. Penguin Poets 2006. 496 p.
ISBN 9780142002155

Grades: 11 12 Adult   818
1. Kerouac, Jack, 1922-1969 2. Notebooks 3. Beat culture 4. Beat authors 5. Voyages and travels 6. American people 7. Observation (Psychology) 8. Sponta-

ESSENTIAL AND RECOMMENDED TITLES
818 American miscellaneous writings in English

neity 9. Men-women relations 10. 1950s 11. Autobiographical fiction 12. Adult books for young adults 13. Poetry

LC 2005044535

Records Jack Kerouac's wanderings around America, offering observations, meditations, and travelogues in a series of prose poems that discuss his travels while reflecting on art and life.

"Somewhere between diary, verbal sketchbook and play-by-play account of whatever passed before his eyes, this collection of poems transcribed from notebooks Kerouac kept in his pocket between 1952 and 1954 turns out to rank with his most interesting work. . . . Kerouac hits all the notes for which he and his fellow beats are known. While not everything here is golden, the immediacy and unpretentiousness of this off-the-cuff writing makes it an intimate glimpse into the consciousness of a man who simply couldn't stop observing." —*Publishers Weekly*

Knight, Sarah
*The **Life-changing** Magic of Not Giving a F*ck: How to Stop Spending Time You Don't Have with People You Don't Like Doing Things You Don't Want to Do*. Sarah Knight. Little, Brown and Company 2015. xi, 208 pages
ISBN 9780316270724
Grades: Adult **818**
1. Kondo, Marie 2. Self-help techniques 3. Humor writing — General 4. Self-Help — General 5. Self-Help — Personal growth — Happiness

LC Bl2015056603

A parody of the Life-Changing Magic of Tidying up explains how to rid yourself of mental clutter—unwanted obligations, shame and guilt, and instead give your attention to people and things that make you happy.

Explains how to rid yourself of mental clutter, unwanted obligations, shame, and guilt, and instead give your attention to people and things that make you happy.

Includes index.

Le Guin, Ursula K.
Words Are My Matter: Writings About Life and Books, 2000-2016 with a Journal of a Writer's Week. Ursula K. Le Guin. Small Beer Press 2016. 352 p.
ISBN 9781618731340
Grades: Adult **818**
1. Le Guin, Ursula K, 1929-2018 2. Writing 3. Creative writing 4. Narration (Rhetoric) 5. Science fiction writing 6. Literary criticism 7. Essays 8. Science fiction 9. Arts and Entertainment — Writing and Publishing 10. Arts and Entertainment — Writing and Publishing — Literary criticism

LC 2016029895

Hugo Award for Best Related Non-Fiction Book, 2017.

A brilliant collection showcases the essays, reviews, talks, book reviews and more from the National Book Foundation Medalist author and one of our foremost public literary intellectuals.

"The wide-ranging collection includes essays, lectures, introductions, and reviews, all informed by Le Guins erudition, offered without academic mystification, and written (or spoken) with an inviting grace." —*Publishers Weekly*

Includes bibliographical references.

McPhee, John
Tabula Rasa; V.1. John McPhee. Farrar, Straus and Giroux 2023. 208 p.
ISBN 9780374603601
Grades: Adult **818**
1. McPhee, John, 1931- 2. Journalists 3. Creative writing teachers 4. Essay writing 5. Voyages and travels 6. Finishing things 7. Reminiscing in old age 8. Mortality 9. Curiosity 10. 20th century 11. Life stories — Arts and culture — Writing 12. Arts and Entertainment — Writing and Publishing

LC 2023007081

Looking back at his career from the vantage point of his desk drawer, and reflecting on projects he never got around to—people to profile, regions he meant to portray—a literary legend presents a collection of vignettes and a "reminiscent montage" from a writing life.

"It's a revealing compendium of curios from a first-rate writer." —*Publishers Weekly*

Poe, Edgar Allan
★ *Poetry and Tales: Poetry and Tales*. Edgar Allan Poe. Literary Classics of the U.S. : 1984. 1408 p; (The Library of America)
ISBN 9780940450189
Grades: Adult **818**
1. Arts and Entertainment — Writing and Publishing

LC 83019931

Gathers all of Poe's poetry, tales, short stories, and general essays in chronological order.

Patrick F. Quinn wrote the notes and selected the texts for this volume—Prelim. p; Includes bibliographical references and index.

Robinson, Phoebe
Please Don't Sit on My Bed in Your Outside Clothes: Essays. Phoebe Robinson. Tiny Reparations Books 2021. 320 p.
ISBN 9780593184905
Grades: Adult **818**
1. Robinson, Phoebe 2. American wit and humor 3. Women comedians 4. Dating 5. African American women 6. Race (Social sciences) 7. Hair 8. Interpersonal relations 9. Excellence 10. Voyages and travels 11. Essays 12. Autobiographies and memoirs 13. Life stories — Identity — Race and ethnicity 14. Life stories — Relationships 15. Humor Writing — Social humor

LC 2021022661

A New York Times best-selling author, comedian, actress, and producer is back with a new essay collection that is equal parts thoughtful, hilarious, and sharp about human connection, race, hair, travel, dating, Black excellence, and more.

"2 Dope Queens comedian and actor Robinson (Everything's Trash but It's Okay) serves up, in her characteristic laugh-out-loud voice, what it means to be a young, Black success story in this inimitable, comedic tell-all." —*Publishers Weekly*

Salter, James
Don't Save Anything: The Uncollected Writing of James Salter. James Salter. Counterpoint Press 2017. 320 p.
ISBN 9781619029361
Grades: Adult **818**
1. Voyages and travels 2. Writing 3. Books and reading 4. Essays 5. Arts and Entertainment — Writing and Publishing 6. Arts and Entertainment — Writing and Publishing — Literary criticism

LC 2017017393

The late award-winning author of Dusk and Other Stories presents a collection of literary essays gathering his thoughts on such topics as the writers who shaped his literary world, America's changing military life, mountain climbing and his travels to Europe and Asia.

"Crisp and razor sharp, Salters work peels away illusions to reveal the matter-of-fact nuances of his and our lives." —*Publishers Weekly*

Sedaris, David
★ *The Best of Me*. David Sedaris. Little Brown & Company 2020. IX, 388 p.
ISBN 9780316628242
Grades: Adult **818**
1. Sedaris, David 2. Family relationships 3. Siblings 4. Families 5. Childhood 6. Interpersonal relations 7. Essays 8. Autobiographies and memoirs 9. Life stories — Arts and culture — Writing — Authors 10. Humor Writing — Family and relationship humor 11. Family and Relationships — Families

LC 2020942220

The American humorist, author and radio contributor presents shares his most memorable work in a collection of stories and essays that feature him shopping for rare taxidermy, hitchhiking with a quadriplegic and hand-feeding a carnivorous bird.

"This is the perfect introduction for the uninitiated, while Sedaris's fans will enjoy rediscovering old favorites." —*Publishers Weekly*

★ *A Carnival of Snackery: Diaries 2003-2020*. David Sedaris. Little, Brown & Company 2021. 566 p.
ISBN 9780316558792

PUBLIC LIBRARY CORE COLLECTION: NONFICTION
Twentieth Edition

Grades: Adult   818
1. Sedaris, David 2. Authors 3. Humorists 4. Observing things 5. Personal conduct 6. Everyday life 7. Cultural differences 8. Voyages and travels 9. Family relationships 10. Diaries 11. Life stories — Arts and culture — Writing — Authors 12. Humor writing — General

There's no right way to keep a diary, but if there's an entertaining way, David Sedaris seems to have mas tered it. These diaries remind you that you once really hated George W. Bush, and that not too long ago, Donald Trump was just a harm less laughingstock, at least on French TV. Time marches on, and Sedaris, at his desk or on planes, in hotel dining rooms and odd Japanese inns, records it. At its best, a Carnival of Snackery is a sort of sampler: the bitter and the sweet. Some entries are just what you wanted. Others you might want to spit discreetly into a napkin.

"The celebrated humorist returns with more offhand observations on the weird and tiresome in these sparkling diary excerpts." —*Publishers Weekly*

Seinfeld, Jerry
Is This Anything? Jerry Seinfeld. Simon & Schuster 2020. 480 p.
ISBN 9781982112691
Grades: Adult   818
1. Seinfeld, Jerry 2. Stand-up comedians 3. Stand-up comedy 4. Comedy writing 5. Humorous writing 6. Celebrities 7. Autobiographies and memoirs 8. Life stories — Arts and culture — Performing arts — Entertainers and celebrities 9. Arts and Entertainment — Comedy 10. Humor writing — Social humor
LC Bl2020022074

Since his first performance at the legendary New York nightclub "Catch a Rising Star" as a twenty-one-year-old college student in fall of 1975, Jerry Seinfeld has written his own material and saved everything. For this book, Seinfeld has selected his favorite material, organized decade by decade. In page after hilarious page, one brilliantly crafted observation after another, readers will witness the evolution of one of the great comedians of our time and gain new insights into the thrilling but unforgiving art of writing stand-up comedy.

"This sharply observed, life-in-gags treasure trove offers essential reading for comedy fans, from a master of the form." —*Publishers Weekly*

Shange, Ntozake
★ *Sing a Black Girl's Song: The Unpublished Works.* Ntozake Shange; edited by Imani Perry; foreword by Tarana Burke. Legacy Lit 2023. 464 p.
ISBN 9780306828515
Grades: Adult   818
1. Shange, Ntozake 2. Fiction writing 3. African American women 4. Communities 5. Sexism 6. Violence 7. Psychic trauma 8. Mental health 9. Essays 10. Anthologies 11. Poetry 12. Arts and Entertainment — Writing and publishing 13. Society and culture — Race
LC 2023016033

This posthumous collection of never-before-published poems, essays and plays—a love letter to Black women and girls, and the community at large—by the award-winning American literary icon establishes her as one of the most highly celebrated artists of our time.

"The literary value of these works extends far beyond the insight they offer into Shange's life and artistic career." —*Kirkus*

Smith, Tracy K.
★ *To Free the Captives: A Plea for the American Soul.* Tracy K. Smith. Alfred A. Knopf 2023. 256 p.
ISBN 9780593534762
Grades: Adult   818
1. African American women authors 2. African American families 3. African American history 4. Race relations 5. Social conflict 6. Freedom 7. Memories 8. African Americans 9. American people 10. United States history 11. Autobiographies and memoirs 12. Life stories — Identity — Race and ethnicity 13. Life stories — Relationships — Family 14. History writing — United States
LC 2023001898

In this thought-provoking personal manifesto on memory, family and history, the author, heartsick from constant assaults on Black life, finds herself soul-searching and digging into the historical archive to understand who we are as a nation and what we might hope to mean to one another.

"The juxtaposition of [Smith's] family's stories with the Black experience in the U.S. feels like a journey toward a greater understanding." —*Booklist*

Stein, Gertrude
Writings, 1903-1932. Gertrude Stein. Library of America : 1998. x, 941 p. : Illustration (The library of America, 99)
ISBN 9781883011406
Grades: Adult   818
1. Arts and Entertainment — Writing and Publishing — Literary criticism
LC 97028915

The first in a two-volume set of works combines fiction with the author's personal experiences in Paris and includes the play Four Saints in Three Acts and Lifting Belly, in which she documents her wonderful relationship with Alice B. Toklas.

Writings, 1932-1946. Gertrude Stein. Library of America 1998. 844 p.
ISBN 9781883011413
Grades: 11 12 Adult   818
1. Essays 2. Arts and Entertainment — Writing and Publishing
LC 97028916

The second in a two-volume set furnishes Stein's later literary masterpieces, including Stanzas in Meditation, Lectures in America, and the Geographical History of America, and details her relationship with Picasso and the public figures that inspired her works.

"In addition to theater pieces, fiction, and poetry memoir, philosophical speculation, literary criticism and theory, all sorts of briefer forms that are hard to account for but easy to marvel at and even to delight in, pack these volumes, and constitute, as the editors surely intended us to discover, the most consistently achieved representation of new ways of responding to life and new possibilities of getting experience into words that American literature has to show." —*New York Times Book Review*

Thoreau, Henry David
★ *Collected Essays and Poems.* Henry David Thoreau. Library of America 2001. xiv, 703 p.
ISBN 9781883011956
Grades: 11 12 Adult   818
1. Essays 2. Arts and Entertainment — Writing and Publishing 3. Poetry
LC 00046234

A collection of essential writings features Thoreau's poetry and essays on nature, materialism, conformity, and politics; including such works as "Slavery in Massachusetts," "Civil Disobedience," "A Winter Walk," and "Life Without Principle."

Includes bibliographical references and index.

Thursby, Jacqueline S.
Critical Companion to Maya Angelou: A Literary Reference to Her Life and Work. Jacqueline S. Thursby. Facts on File 2011. x, 430 p.
ISBN 9780816080939
Grades: Adult   818
1. Angelou, Maya 2. African Americans in literature 3. Arts and Entertainment — Writing and Publishing — Literary criticism 4. Reference — General
LC 2010032716

Critical Companion to Maya Angelou is a comprehensive and up-to-date resource for students interested in this prolific poet.

The opening biography gives a clear, concise overview that references a number of secondary and primary works; these also are listed in valuable bibliographies contained in the appendixes. The section titled "Works" divides Angelou's oeuvre into "Autobiographies," "Essay Collections," "Poetry," "Children's Books," and "Major Essays." —*Choice*

Includes bibliographical references (pages 404-411) and index.

V
The Apology. V (formerly Eve Ensler). Bloomsbury Publishing 2019. 208 pages
ISBN 9781635574388
Grades: Adult   818

ESSENTIAL AND RECOMMENDED TITLES
821 English poetry

1. Ensler, Eve, 1953- 2. Adult child sexual abuse victims 3. Fathers and daughters 4. Abusive men 5. Incest victims 6. Child abuse 7. Healing 8. Apologizing 9. Dysfunctional families 10. Sexually abused children 11. Girls 12. Autobiographies and memoirs 13. Life stories — Facing adversity — Abuse survivors 14. Family and Relationships — Abuse

LC 2019002247

Examines the themes of abuse and atonement via the author's own experience being both physically and sexually abused.

"This is a powerful and disturbing story that Ensler writes with grace an aplomb." —*Publishers Weekly*

Vonnegut, Kurt
★ *A Man Without a Country*. Kurt Vonnegut; edited by Daniel Simon. Seven Stories Press 2005. IX, 146 p. : Illustration
ISBN 9781583227138
Grades: Adult **818**

1. Vonnegut, Kurt 2. Authors, American 3. Politics and government 4. United States 5. 20th century 6. 2000s (Decade) 7. Autobiographies and memoirs 8. Essays 9. Biographies 10. Arts and Entertainment — Writing and Publishing 11. Life stories — Arts and culture — Writing — Authors

LC 2005014967

In a collection of brief autobiographical essays, the renowned novelist offers his views on art, politics, and everyday life in America.

"The author discusses politics, human nature, and other topics in this collection of articles written over the last five years, many from the alternative magazine in These Times." —*Publishers Weekly*

West, Lindy
Shrill: Notes from a Loud Woman. Lindy West. Hachette Books 2016. 272 p.
ISBN 9780316348409
Grades: Adult **818**

1. West, Lindy 2. Women journalists 3. Feminists 4. Women 5. Personal conduct 6. United States 7. Page to screen 8. Biographies 9. Humor writing — Social humor 10. Society and culture — Gender — Women 11. Adult books for young adults

LC 2016001577

Amelia Bloomer List, 2017; Booklist Editors' Choice: Adult Books for Young Adults, 2016.

The Guardian columnist and This American Life social commentator presents a series of essays about the qualities of a comedic feminist and her experiences of coming of age in a popular culture that is hostile to plus-sized women who speak their minds.

Wiman, Christian
Zero at the Bone: Fifty Entries Against Despair. Christian Wiman. Farrar, Straus and Giroux 2023. 320 p.
ISBN 9780374603458
Grades: Adult **818**

1. Wiman, Christian, 1966- 2. Faith 3. Despair 4. Ethics 5. Family relationships 6. God 7. Belief and doubt 8. Essays 9. Autobiographies and memoirs 10. Poetry 11. Life stories — Facing adversity 12. Arts and Entertainment — Writing and publishing 13. Spirituality and religion — General

LC 2023026123

In this intricately woven tapestry of poetry, memoir, theology and criticism, an award-winning poet, through 50 brief pieces, framed by two more, unravels the seductive appeal of despair.

"It's a gorgeous ode to the power of poetry to grapple with life's most anguished moments." —*Publishers Weekly*

821 English poetry

Auden, W. H.
Selected Poems. W.H. Auden; edited by Edward Mendelson. Vintage International 2007. xxx, 344 p.
ISBN 9780307278081

Grades: Adult **821**

1. British poetry 2. 20th century 3. Poetry

LC 2007540115

Restores the original versions of poems that Auden had revised and includes such works as "Will You Turn a Deaf Ear," "This Lunar Beauty," "Noon," and "First Things First."
Includes index.

Blake, William
★ *The Complete Poetry and Prose of William Blake*. Edited by David V. Erdman. University of California Press 2008. xxviii, 990 pages : Illustration
ISBN 9780520256378
Grades: Adult **821**

1. Arts and Entertainment — Writing and Publishing — Literary criticism

LC 2008275592

Critical commentary illuminating Blake's allusions and references accompanies the texts of his poetic and prose works.
Includes bibliographical references and index.

Boland, Eavan
The Historians: Poems. Eavan Boland. W.W. Norton & Company 2020. IX, 67 pages
ISBN 9781324006879
Grades: Adult **821**

1. Women 2. Memory 3. Freedom 4. Anger 5. Love 6. Poetry

LC 2020017149

Boland returns to her signature themes, exploring the ways in which the hidden, sometimes all-but-erased, stories of women's lives can powerfully revise our sense of the past. Two women burning letters in a back garden. A poet who died too young. A mother's parable to her daughter. These narratives cling to the future through memory, anger, and love in ways that rebuke the official record we call history.

"Boland's final book is both a perfect introduction and retrospective, offering a profound and restorative reading experience." —*Publishers Weekly*

New Collected Poems. Eavan Boland. W.W. Norton 2008. 320 p.
ISBN 9780393065794
Grades: Adult **821**

1. Poets, Irish 2. Women authors 3. Ireland 4. Poetry

LC 2007042554

A new volume of works by the author of An Origin Like Water blends chronologically arranged material from subsequent collections with key poems from her early years, in an anthology that offers insight into the author's use of critical dialogue to free herself from conventions and stereotypes.
Includes indexes.

A Woman Without a Country: Poems. Eavan Boland. W.W. Norton & Company 2014. xii, 81 pages
ISBN 9780393244441
Grades: Adult **821**

1. Poetry

LC 2014030073

A collection by "one of the finest and boldest poets of the last half century" explores themes of mother, daughter and generation and how, even without country or settled identity, a legacy of love can endure.

Browning, Robert
★ *Robert Browning's Poetry: Authoritative Texts, Criticism*. Selected and edited by James F. Loucks and Andrew M. Stauffer. W. W. Norton & Co. 2007. x, 689 p.
ISBN 9780393926002
Grades: 11 12 Adult **821**

1. Browning, Robert, 1812-1889 2. British poetry 3. Literary criticism 4. 19th century 5. Poetry 6. Arts and Entertainment — Writing and publishing — Literary criticism

LC 2006047308

Works by modern and Victorian critics are presented together with poems from each stage of Browning's literary career.

Bunting, Basil

Complete Poems. Basil Bunting; associate editor, Richard Caddel. New Directions Books 2003. 239 p.

ISBN 9780811215633

Grades: Adult   821

1. British poetry 2. Poetry

LC 2003015465

As well as "Briggflatts" (long out of print in the US, and now only available in this edition), this new Complete Poems includes Bunting's other great sonatas, most notably Villon (1925) and the Spoils (1951), along with his two books of Odes, his vividly realized "Overdrafts" (as he called his free translations of Horace, Rudaki, and others), and his brilliantly condensed Japanese adaptation, Chomei at Toyama (1932).

Includes bibliographic references (p. 15) and index.

Burns, Robert

Burns: Poems. Edited and introduced by Gerard Carruthers. Alfred A. Knopf 2007. 255 p.

ISBN 9780307266163

Grades: Adult   821

1. Poetry

LC 2006047299

A selection of poetry and lyrics by Scotland's most famous poet features Tam o' Shanter, "Holy Willie's Prayer," "Auld Lang Syne," "To a Mouse," "A Red, Red Rose," and many others.

Includes index.

Byron, George Gordon Byron

Selected Poetry of Lord Byron. Edited by Leslie A. Marchand; introduction by Thomas Disch; notes by Jeffrey Vail. Modern Library 2001. xv, 745 p.

ISBN 9780375758140

Grades: Adult   821

1. British poetry 2. Poetry

LC 2001042771

Presents a collection of Lord Byron's poetry, including "Manfred," "Childe Harold," and "Don Juan."

Includes index.

Chaucer, Geoffrey

★ *The* **Complete** *Poetry and Prose of Geoffrey Chaucer.* Edited by John H. Fisher. Holt, Rinehart, and Winston 1989. xiii, 1040 p. : Illustration

ISBN 9780030286124

Grades: Adult   821

1. Chaucer, Geoffrey, d. 1400 2. Arts and Entertainment — Writing and Publishing — Literary criticism

LC 88029400

This edition is intended to make Chaucer's texts accessible with a minimum of scholarly interference. The critical, biographical, and linguistic essays are grouped at the end so as not to impede the approach to the text.

Includes bibliographical references (p. 975-1019) and index.

Coleridge, Samuel Taylor

The **Complete** *Poems.* Samuel Taylor Coleridge; edited by William Keach. Penguin Books 1997. xxx, 626 p.

ISBN 9780140423532

Grades: Adult   821

1. British poetry 2. Romanticism in poetry 3. 18th century 4. 19th century 5. Poetry

LC 97208514

Contains all the poems published in the poet's lifetime, arranged chronologically, and includes important earlier versions of such poems as "The Eolian Harp" and "The Rime of the Ancient Mariner."

Includes bibliographical references (p. [xxvii]-xxx) and index.

Day-Lewis, Cecil

The **Complete** *Poems of C. Day Lewis.* Cecil Day Lewis. Stanford University Press 1995. 745 p.

ISBN 9780804725859

Grades: Adult   821

1. British poetry 2. 20th century 3. Poetry

LC 91068076

"The still lively fascination of his verse seems to depend on the variety of tones [Day Lewis] could pick up, change, and discard at will. His modesty was genuine and profound, giving his verse texture its winning versatility, its air that 'Tenure is not for me.'. Nothing that Day Lewis wrote is lacking its own sort of ephemeral though rediscoverable effectiveness. He was well aware of this, and it was a part of his modesty, as Jill Balcon points out in her thoughtful and sensitive introduction. For anyone who likes poetry there is real interest here in [this] complete record." —*New York Review of Books*

Dunmore, Helen

Inside the Wave. Helen Dunmore. Bloodaxe Books 2017. 63 p.

ISBN 9781780373584

Grades: Adult   821

1. British poetry 2. 21st century 3. Poetry

LC 2017296582

To be alive is to be inside the wave, always travelling until it breaks and is gone. These poems are concerned with the borderline between the living and the dead—the underworld and the human living world—and the exquisitely intense being of both. They possess a spare, eloquent lyricism as they explore the bliss and anguish of the voyage.

Fenton, James

Selected Poems. James Fenton. Farrar, Straus and Giroux 2006. VII, 196 p.

ISBN 9780374260651

Grades: Adult   821

1. British poetry 2. Poetry

LC 2006002691

Features selected poems from all of the author's published works and a few new, uncollected poems.

Originally published: London : Penguin Books, 2006.

Gunn, Thom

Boss Cupid: Poems. Thom Gunn. Farrar, Straus, Giroux 2000. VII, 111 p.

ISBN 9780374115579

Grades: Adult   821

1. Poetry

LC 99057739

"Boss Cupid offers a splendid introduction for the uninitiated. Almost all of Gunn's virtues are on display here: His playful, metrical dexterity, his unflinching celebration both of beauty and of transience. Advancing age and the AIDS-related deaths of friends—my everpresent dead—figure prominently in these poems, but so does Gunn's humorous touch." —*Time*

★ *The* **Letters** *of Thom Gunn.* Selected and edited by August Kleinzahler, Michael Nott, Clive Wilmer. Farrar, Straus and Giroux 2022. 800 p.

ISBN 9780374605698

Grades: Adult   821

1. Gunn, Thom 2. Poets, English 3. Gay men 4. British people in the United States 5. Letter writing 6. Creation (Literary, artistic, etc.) 7. Sexuality 8. Loss 9. Friendship 10. Interpersonal relations 11. 20th century 12. Letters 13. Life stories — Arts and culture — Writing — Poets 14. Life stories — Identity — LGBTQIA+ 15. Arts and Entertainment — Writing and Publishing

LC 2021059964

I write about love, I write about friendship," remarked Thom Gunn: "I find that they are absolutely intertwined." the Letters of Thom Gunn, edited by August Kleinzahler, Michael Nott, and Clive Wilmer, reveals the evolution of Gunn's work and illuminates the fascinating life that informed his poems: His struggle to come to terms with his mother's suicide; his changing relationship with his life partner, Mike Kitay; the LSD trips that led to his celebrated collec-

ESSENTIAL AND RECOMMENDED TITLES
821 English poetry

tion Moly (1971); and the deaths of friends from AIDS that inspired the powerful, unsparing elegies of the Man with Night Sweats (1992).

"Gunn's letters are a testament to his vitality and enthusiasm for a cornucopia of experiences embraced with gusto and eloquently shared." —*Booklist*

Originally published in the UK by Faber & Faber, London, in 2021; Includes bibliographical references and index.

Hardy, Thomas
Thomas Hardy: The Complete Poems. Edited by James Gibson. Palgrave 2001. xxxvi, 1003 p. : Illustration; Map
ISBN 9780333949290
Grades: Adult — 821
1. Arts and Entertainment — Writing and Publishing — Literary criticism 2. Poetry
LC 2001032732

The Complete Poems, edited by James Gibson, includes all of Hardy's prolific output of more than nine hundred poems, complemented by a detailed notes section. Collected in this single volume are his eight books of verse, all the uncollected poems, 'Domicilium' and the songs from the Dynasts.

Includes bibliographical references (p. [956]-972) and indexes.

Heaney, Seamus
District and Circle. Seamus Heaney. Farrar, Straus and Giroux 2006. 78 p.
ISBN 9780374140922
Grades: Adult — 821
1. Rural families 2. Rural life 3. Childhood 4. Poets 5. Poetry
LC 2005044687

A collection by the Nobel Prize-winning writer contains pieces that evince a childhood spent safe from the horrors of World War II, a journey on the Underground, and a melting glacier, in a volume that includes a number of prose poems and translations.

Human Chain. Seamus Heaney. Farrar, Straus and Giroux 2010. VIII, 85 p.
ISBN 9780374173517
Grades: Adult — 821
1. Poets, Irish 2. Ireland 3. Poetry
LC 2010010274

Heaney's collection elicits continuities and solidarities, between husband and wife, child and parent, then and now, inside an intently remembered present—the stepping stones of the day, the weight and heft of what is passed from hand to hand, lifted and lowered.

Opened Ground: Selected Poems, 1966-1996. Seamus Heaney. Farrar, Straus and Giroux 1998. 443 p.
ISBN 9780374526788
Grades: Adult — 821
1. Ireland 2. Arts and Entertainment — Writing and Publishing — Literary criticism 3. Poetry
LC 98004331

Selected poems by the Nobel Prizewinning Irish poet are taken from Heaney's twelve previous collections and includes work published since 1987.

The Nobel laureate's definitive selection of his poems captures the unique qualities of down-to-earth and concrete imagery, lilting rhythms, and artistic eloquence of one of the century's leading poets.

Includes index.

Hill, Geoffrey
Selected Poems. Geoffrey Hill. Yale University Press 2009. 276 p.
ISBN 9780300121568
Grades: Adult — 821
1. British poetry 2. 21st century 3. 20th century 4. Poetry
LC 2008930384

"After four decades with just five books, the past 10 years have seen Hill offer six more, including a trio of long works some liken to Dante and Blake. This first selected since 1994 … should get instant critical attention (and sustained academic adoption) even though it contains no new work. Here, entire, is Mercian Hymns, with its gorgeously medievalized evocation of a rural English upbringing. Here, complete, are all three recent long poems, with their erudite mix of elegy and jeremiad. Here, too, are the descriptive beauties that sparkle through even Hill's most rebarbative works." —*Publishers Weekly*

Hollis, Matthew
The Waste Land: A Biography of a Poem. Matthew Hollis. W. W. Norton & Company, Inc. 2022. 352 p.
ISBN 9780393240252
Grades: Adult — 821
1. Eliot, T. S, (Thomas Stearns), 1888-1965 2. Poets, Irish 3. Writing 4. Interpersonal relations 5. Poetry writing 6. 20th century 7. Biographies 8. Life stories — Arts and culture — Writing — Poets 9. Arts and Entertainment — Writing and Publishing

"Highly recommended for readers interested in the details behind the creation of this literary landmark and the times in which it was composed." —*Library Journal*

Keats, John
★ *The Complete Poems of John Keats*. John Keats. Modern Library 1994. xiv, 398 p.
ISBN 9780679601081
Grades: Adult — 821
1. British poetry 2. Poetry
LC 94004339

Presents all of the English poet's verse, including his sonnets and odes, the allegorical romance "Endymion," and the five-act poetic tragedy "Otho the Great."

Includes index.

Poems. Keats; [selected by Peter Washington]. A.A. Knopf 1994. 253 p.
ISBN 9780679433194
Grades: 11 12 Adult — 821
1. British poetry 2. Romanticism in poetry 3. Poetry
LC 94002495

A selection of poems by the English Romantic poet.
Cover Title: Keats; Includes index.

Kipling, Rudyard
Complete Verse: Definitive Edition. Rudyard Kipling. Anchor Press 1989. xiv, 850 p.
ISBN 9780385260893
Grades: 11 12 Adult — 821
1. British poetry 2. Poetry
LC 88007364

A complete collection of Kipling's poetry.
Includes index.

Larkin, Philip
★ *Collected Poems*. Philip Larkin; edited and with an introduction by Anthony Thwaite. Farrar, Straus and Giroux 2004. 218 p.
ISBN 9780374529208
Grades: Adult — 821
1. British poetry 2. Poetry
LC 2003060846

A new collection of Phillip Larkin's poetry combines all of his published collections—North Ship, the Less Deceived, the Whitsun Weddings, and High Windows—with his uncollected poems from 1940-1984.

Includes index.

The Complete Poems. Philip Larkin; edited and with an introduction and commentary by Archie Burnett. Farrar, Straus and Giroux 2012. xxx, 729 p.
ISBN 9780374126964
Grades: Adult — 821
1. British poetry 2. 20th century 3. Poetry
LC 2011945978

This entirely new edition brings together all of Philip Larkin's poems. In addition to those that appear in Collected Poems (1988) and Early Poems and

Juvenilia (2005), some unpublished pieces from Larkin's typescripts and workbooks are included, as well as verse—by turns scurrilous, satirical, affectionate, and sentimental—that had been tucked away in his letters. For the first time, Larkin's poems are given a comprehensive commentary. This draws critically upon, and substantially extends, the accumulated scholarship on Larkin, and covers closely relevant historical contexts, persons and places, allusions and echoes, and linguistic usage. Prominence is given to the poet's comments on his own poems, which often outline the circumstances that gave rise to a poem or state what he was trying to achieve. Larkin often played down his literariness, but his poetry enrichingly alludes to and echoes the writings of many others; Archie Burnett's commentary establishes him as a more complex and more literary poet than many readers have suspected.

Includes bibliographical references and index.

Lear, Edward

The Complete Verse and Other Nonsense: The Complete Verse and Other Nonsense. Edward Lear; compiled and edited with an introduction and notes by Vivien Noakes. Penguin Books 2002. LI, 566 p. : Illustration
ISBN 9780142002278
Grades: Adult   821
1. Poetry

LC 2002028998

A comprehensive collection of Lear's poetry and other nonsense writings features an array of limericks, stories, letters, illustrated alphabets, and previously unpublished material, all accompanied by the poet's own line drawings and a detailed introduction to Lear's work.

Includes bibliographical references (p. [xlv]-xlvii) and indexes.

Lowell, Amy

Selected Poems. Amy Lowell; Honor Moore, editor. Library of America 2004. xxxiii, 156 p. : Portrait
ISBN 9781931082709
Grades: Adult   821
1. American poetry 2. Women authors 3. Poetry

LC 2004048505

A selection of foremost works seeks to explore the writer's full formal range from cadenced verse and polyphonic prose to narrative poetry and Chinese adaptations, in a volume that offers insight into Lowell's open rebellion against her prestigious Boston lineage, her sophisticated feminist and anti-war stances, and her erotic themes.

Includes bibliographical references (p. 145-146) and index.

Miller, Lucasta

★ *Keats:* A Brief Life in Nine Poems and One Epitaph. Lucasta Miller. Alfred A. Knopf 2022. 368 p.
ISBN 9780525655831
Grades: Adult   821
1. Keats, John, 1795-1821 2. Poets, English 3. Creation (Literary, artistic, etc.) 4. Literary criticism 5. Poetry writing 6. 19th century 7. Biographies 8. Life stories — Arts and culture — Writing — Poets 9. Arts and Entertainment — Writing and Publishing — Literary criticism

LC 2021020620

An acclaimed biography takes nine of the best-known poems by one of the greatest lyric poets of the English language and reveals how they came to be, and what in Keats' life led to their creation, exploring his imagination in the context of his world and experience.

"Subtly intertwining biographical detail with crisp readings of the poetry, Miller creates an insightful, vibrant portrait." —*Kirkus*

This is a Borzoi Book published by Alfred A. Knopf; Includes bibliographical references and index.

Morrissey, Sinead

Parallax: And Selected Poems. Sinead Morrissey. Farrar, Straus and Giroux 2015. 211 pages
ISBN 9780865478299
Grades: Adult   821
1. Poetry

LC 2014043835

This edition of Parallax also includes Morrissey's own selection of her favorite poems from her previous collections, published for the first time in the United States.

"Consisting of Morrissey's T.S. Eliot Prize-winning Parallax (2013) as well as selections from the latest three of her four other collections, this is a sprawling volume characterized by restlessness." —*Booklist*

Muldoon, Paul

Maggot: Poems. Paul Muldoon. Farrar, Straus and Giroux 2010. 134 p.
ISBN 9780374200329
Grades: Adult   821
1. Poets, Irish 2. Poetry

LC 2010005700

"This first full-length outing since he took the poetry editorship at the New Yorker will certainly hold the attention of devotees, and individual poems, as always, shine: Sestinas, monorhymed works and especially sonnets (including a fine translation of Baudelaire's "The Albatross" and a diptych entitled "Nope" and "Yup") make Muldoon's acrobatic technique serve his strikingly playful—yet grim—sensibility." —*Publishers Weekly*

Selected Poems 1968-2014. Paul Muldoon. Farrar, Straus and Giroux 2016. 228 pages
ISBN 9780374260828
Grades: Adult   821
1. Poetry

LC 2016033242

Drawing from 2 individual collections spanning 45 years, the Pulitzer Prize-winning poet presents an array of poems that serves as an indispensable introduction to his trademark combination of intellectual hijinks and emotional honesty.

Includes index.

Oswald, Alice

Falling Awake: Poems. Alice Oswald. W. W. Norton & Company 2016. 81 pages
ISBN 9780393285284
Grades: Adult   821
1. British poetry 2. Women authors 3. Poetry

LC 2016012940

"In an era in which most poetry is concerned with personality, prizewinning Oswald takes a different approach in her attention to phenomena. In the best known of her previous six collections, Memorial (2011), a brilliant, inimitable rendering of Homer's Iliad, the similes are as vivid as the heroes." —*Booklist*

Pope, Alexander

Selected Poetry. Alexander Pope; edited with an introduction and notes by Pat Rogers. Oxford University Press 1998. xxiii, 226 p.
ISBN 9780192834942
Grades: Adult   821
1. Poetry

LC 98230887

Though critical opinion on Alexander Pope has frequently been divided, he is now regarded as the most important poet of the early eighteenth century. His greatest works—which exhibit Pope's astonishing human insight, his wide sympathies, and powers of social observation (displayed to greatest effect in his talent for satire)—are included in this selection of his poetry. It has been compiled by the distinguished Pope scholar and editor Pat Rodgers, who also provides an indispensable introduction that offers a new interpretation of Pope's poetry, and the philosophical ideas behind it.

Includes bibliographical references (p. [225]-226) and indexes.

Satyamurti, Carole

Mahabharata: A Modern Retelling. by Carole Satyamurti. W. W. Norton & Company 2015. 1200 p.
ISBN 9780393081756

ESSENTIAL AND RECOMMENDED TITLES
821.009 English poetry — History and criticism

Grades: Adult **821**
1. Feuds 2. Rulers 3. Hinduism 4. Spiritualism 5. Gods and goddesses, Hindu 6. Indian history 7. Epic poetry 8. Translations — Sanskrit to English 9. Poetry
LC 2014033595

An English retelling of the 2,000-year-old epic Hindu poem that includes the Bhagavad Gita recounts the story of the feud over a kingdom ruled by royalty descended from the gods.

"Satyamurtis exquisitely lucid and involving retelling is bookended with expert commentary by Wendy Doniger (The Hindus: An Alternative History, 2009) and translator and scholar Vinay Dharwadker." —*Booklist*

Includes bibliographical references; Translated from the Sanskrit.

Shelley, Percy Bysshe
Shelley's Poetry and Prose: Authoritative Texts, Criticism. Selected and edited by Donald H. Reiman and Neil Fraistat. Norton 2002. xxii, 786 p. : Illustration
ISBN 9780393977523
Grades: Adult **821**
1. Shelley, Percy Bysshe, 1792-1822 2. British poetry 3. Poetry
LC 2001030903

Annotated definitive texts of all of Shelley's greatest poetry as well as other poems frequently discussed and three prose works are combined with general critical studies of his art and thought and scholarly writings analyzing specific poems.

Includes bibliographical references (p. 775-783) and index.

Shelley: Poems. Percy Bysshe Shelley. Knopf 1993. 250 p.
ISBN 9780679429098
Grades: Adult **821**
1. British poetry 2. Poetry
LC 93078335

A classicist, a headlong visionary, a social radical, and a poet of serene artistry with a lyric touch second to none, Shelley personified the richly various—and contradictory—energies of his time. This compact yet comprehensive collection showcases all the extraordinary facets of Shelley's art.

Includes index.

Tennyson, Alfred
Poems. Tennyson. Alfred A. Knopf 2004. 255 p.
ISBN 9781400041879
Grades: Adult **821**
1. British poetry 2. 19th century 3. Poetry
LC 2003049505

A collection of narrative and short lyrical works by the poet favored by Queen Victoria includes "The Lady of Shalott," extracts from "Idylls of the King," and the complete text of "Ulysses."

Thomas, Dylan
The Poems of Dylan Thomas. Edited with an introduction and notes by Daniel Jones; with a preface by Dylan Thomas. New Directions 2003. xxix, 320 p. : Illustration
ISBN 9780811215411
Grades: 11 12 Adult **821**
1. 20th century 2. Poetry
LC 2002155790

Thomas' lyrical prologue introduces this collection of his complete and unfinished poems and early works.

Includes bibliographical references and index.

Tibble, Tayi
Poukahangatus: Poems. Tayi Tibble. Alfred A. Knopf 2022. 96 pages
ISBN 9780593534601
Grades: Adult **821**
1. Popular culture 2. Interpersonal relations 3. Family relationships 4. Identity 5. Social life and customs 6. New Zealand 7. New Zealand poetry 8. Poetry

The American debut of an acclaimed New Zealand poet as she explores her identity as a 21st-century indigenous woman.

"In Tibble's seismic debut, the young poet's rollicking, indignant, and invigorating narratives contend with history and navigate what it means to be millennial, female, and of Maori descent." —*Publishers Weekly*

Originally published in New Zealand by Victoria University Press, Wellington, in 2018.

Yeats, W. B.
The Collected Poems of W.B. Yeats. Edited by Richard J. Finneran. Scribner Paperback Poetry 1996. xxv, 544 p.
ISBN 9780684807317
Grades: Adult **821**
1. Poets, Irish 2. Poetry
LC 96023314

Newly revised, a collection of every poem the Irish poet approved for publication during his lifetime, grouped according to the work in which each first appeared, includes a preface and notes by a world-renowned Yeats scholar.

Includes bibliographical references and indexes.

821.009 English poetry — History and criticism

Paglia, Camille
★ *Break, Blow, Burn.* Camille Paglia. Pantheon Books 2005. xvii, 247 p.
ISBN 9780375420849
Grades: 11 12 Adult **821.009**
1. Literary criticism 2. Poetry writing 3. Poetry 4. Adult books for young adults
LC 2004056573

New York Times Notable Book, 2005.

Celebrates the great poetry of the Western tradition, looking at diverse works by poets ranging from Shakespeare and Dickinson to Plath, Hughes, and other unconventional poets.

"This work is vintage Paglia: Bracing, opinionated, and deliciously enjoyable." —*National Review*

Contains 43 poems with criticism; Includes bibliographical references (p. [241]-242).

821.709 English poetry — 1800-1837 — history and criticism

Nicolson, Adam
The Making of Poetry: Coleridge, the Wordsworths, and Their Year of Marvels. Adam Nicolson; with woodcuts and paintings by Tom Hammick. Farrar, Straus and Giroux 2020. 390 pages : Illustration; Color
ISBN 9780374200213
Grades: Adult **821.709**
1. Coleridge, Samuel Taylor, 1772-1834 2. Wordsworth, Dorothy, 1771-1855 3. Wordsworth, William, 1770-1850 4. Poets, English 5. Romanticism in poetry 6. Nature (Aesthetics) 7. Creation (Literary, artistic, etc.) 8. Poetry writing 9. Literary criticism 10. England 11. 18th century 12. Collective biographies 13. Life stories — Arts and culture — Writing — Poets 14. Arts and Entertainment — Writing and Publishing 15. Poetry
LC 2019951670

Celebrates the poems that the two English poets composed within a space of one year in which they challenged the accepted ideas of their time and presented a new vision of hope and possibility.

"An astonishingly rich re-creation of the months that the Wordsworths and Coleridges lived near each other in southwest England." —*Kirkus*

Includes bibliographical references and index; Originally published: London : William Collins, 2019.

821.8 English poetry — 1837-1899

Browning, Robert
Robert Browning: The Major Works. Edited with notes by Adam Roberts; with an introduction by Daniel Karlin. Oxford University Press 2005. xxxii, 828 p.
ISBN 9780192806260
Grades: Adult   821.8
1. British poetry 2. Poetry
LC 2006277696
A comprehensive selection includes over eighty shorter poems, the complete text of many longer poems, three books, critical writing, and correspondence.
Including Pippa passes and courtship correspondences —Cover; Includes bibliographical references (p. 822-824) and indexes; This selection and notes originally published: 1997.

Rossetti, Christina Georgina
Christina Rossetti: The Complete Poems. Text [edited] by R.W. Crump; notes and introduction by Betty S. Flowers. Penguin 2001. LV, 1221 p.
ISBN 9780140423662
Grades: Adult   821.8
1. British poetry 2. Women authors 3. Poetry
LC 2002281810
Presents a complete collection of poems by the English author along with a chronology, further reading, and notes.
Includes bibliographical references (p. [lii]-lv) and indexes.

821.912 English poetry — 1900-1945

Eliot, T. S.
Collected Poems, 1909-1962. T. S. Eliot. Harcourt, Brace & World 1963. 221 p.
ISBN 9780151189786
Grades: Adult   821.912
1. Poetry
LC 63021424
This volume contains the works Eliot personally selected to be preserved.

822 English drama

Bolt, Robert
A Man for All Seasons: A Play in Two Acts. Robert Bolt. Vintage Books 1990. xxv, 163 p.
ISBN 9780679728221
Grades: 11 12 Adult   822
1. More, Thomas, Saint, 1478-1535 2. Henry VIII, King of England, 1491-1547 3. British history 4. Drama 5. Arts and Entertainment — Theater — Plays
LC 89040518
Consciences of Sir Thomas More and Henry VIII are poles apart in the religious conflict over the king's marriage to Anne Boleyn.

Coward, Noel
Three Plays: Blithe Spirit, Hay Fever, Private Lives. Noel Coward; introduction by Philip Hoare. Vintage Books 1999. 254 p.
ISBN 9780679781790
Grades: Adult   822
1. Arts and Entertainment — Theater — Plays
LC 98047414
Filled with languid aristocrats trading witticisms as they wait for martinis, this collection of three Noel Coward plays encapsulates the qualities that made him one of the most popular playwrights of the 1930s and '40s and one of the great personalities of the century.

Fugard, Athol
★ *"master Harold"—and the Boys.* Athol Fugard. Vintage Books 2009. 60 p.
ISBN 9780307475206
Grades: 11 12 Adult   822
1. Race relations 2. Drama 3. South Africa 4. Arts and Entertainment — Theater — Plays
LC 2010292381
An argument between Master Harold, a seventeen-year-old South African, and Sam, the Black man employed at Harold's mother's restaurant, makes them reevaluate their friendship.

Marlowe, Christopher
The Complete Plays. Christopher Marlowe; edited by Frank Romany and Robert Lindsey. Penguin Books 2003. xliv, 702 p.
ISBN 9780140436334
Grades: 11 12 Adult   822
1. Tragedy 2. Arts and Entertainment — Theater — Plays
LC 2004268858
Accompanied by a critical introduction, a biographical chronology, incisive commentary, and a glossary, this definitive dramatic collection features all seven of the plays written by Christopher Marlowe—including Dido, Queen of Carthage, the Jew of Malta, Doctor Faustus, and the Massacre at Paris.
Includes bibliographical references (p. [xxxvi]-xlii).

Osborne, John
Look Back in Anger. John Osborne. Penguin 1982. 96 p.
ISBN 9780140481754
Grades: Adult   822
1. Arts and Entertainment — Theater — Plays
LC 82009144
The text of the play, first performed in London in 1956, depicts the despair of post-war youth.
Reprint. Originally published: New York : Criterion Books, 1957.

Shaffer, Peter
★ *Equus.* Peter Shaffer. Scribner 2005. x, 112 p.
ISBN 9780743287302
Grades: 11 12 Adult   822
1. Psychotherapist and patient 2. OCD 3. Horses 4. Teenage boys 5. Drama 6. Arts and Entertainment — Theater
LC 2005051600
The Tony Award-winning drama deals with a psychiatrist's exploration of the psyche of a troubled seventeen-year-old boy who senselessly and systematically blinds six horses.
Originally published: Great Britain: Andre Deutsch, 1973.

Peter Shaffer's Amadeus. with an introduction by the director Sir Peter Hall and a wholly new preface by the author. Perennial 2001. xxxiv, 124 p.
ISBN 9780060935498
Grades: Adult   822
1. Mozart, Wolfgang Amadeus, 1756-1791 2. Salieri, Antonio, 1750-1825 3. Arts and Entertainment — Theater — Plays
LC 2001278382
Originating at the National Theatre of Great Britain, Amadeus was the recipient of both the Evening Standard Drama Award and the Theatre Critics Award. In the United States, the play won the coveted Tony Award and went on to become a critically acclaimed major motion picture winning eight Oscars, including Best Picture.

Shaw, Bernard
Heartbreak House: A Fantasia in the Russian Manner on English Themes. Bernard Shaw; definitive text under the editorial supervision of Dan H. Laurence; with an introduction by David Hare. Penguin Books 2000. xii, 160 p. : Illustration
ISBN 9780140437874

ESSENTIAL AND RECOMMENDED TITLES
822.33 William Shakespeare

Grades: Adult   **822**
1. Arts and Entertainment — Theater — Plays
     LC 2001266517

Written at the height of the first World War in Europe, an impassioned satire of the late nineteenth and early twentieth-century bourgeoisie offers a scathing portrait of a household of independent eccentrics.
Includes bibliographical references.

Major Barbara. Bernard Shaw; definitive text under the editorial supervision of Dan H. Laurence; with an introduction by Margery Morgan. Penguin Books 2000. 156 p.
ISBN 9780140437904
Grades: Adult   **822**
1. Crime 2. Fathers and daughters 3. Drama 4. Arts and Entertainment — Writing and Publishing
     LC 2002275028

An enthusiastic young woman in the Salvation Army is contrasted by her wealthy and greedy father who despises poverty.
Bibliography: P. 151-152.

Man and Superman: A Comedy and a Philosophy. Bernard Shaw; definitive text under the editorial supervision of Dan H. Laurence; with an introduction by Stanley Weintraub. Penguin 2000. xiv, 264 p.
ISBN 9780140437881
Grades: Adult   **822**
1. Arts and Entertainment — Theater — Plays
     LC 2001266518

In Shaw's classic battle of the sexes, John Tanner flees when Ann Whitefield declares her intention to marry him.

★ *Pygmalion: A Romance in Five Acts.* George Bernard Shaw. And My fair lady, based on Shaw's Pygmalion / adaptation and lyrics by Alan Jay Lerner; music by Frederick Loewe. Signet Classics 2006. xiii, 219 p.
ISBN 9780451530097
Grades: Adult   **822**
1. Arts and Entertainment — Theater — Plays
     LC Bl2007001519

Accompanied by the adaptation and lyrics of the Broadway play "My Fair Lady," this play follows Professor Henry Higgins as he transforms a rough-hewn girl into a sophisticated lady of society.
Accompanied by the adaptation and lyrics of the Broadway play My Fair Lady, this fiftieth anniversary edition of Shaw's celebrated play, drawn from the Greek legend of Pygmalion, follows Professor Henry Higgins as he transforms a rough-hewn Cockney girl into a sophisticated lady of society.

Saint Joan: A Chronicle Play in Six Scenes and an Epilogue. Bernard Shaw; definitive text under the editorial supervision of Dan H. Laurence; with 'On playing Joan' by Imogene Stubbs; and an introduction by Joley Wood. Penguin Books 2001. 163 p.
ISBN 9780140437911
Grades: Adult   **822**
1. Joan of Arc, Saint, 1412-1431 2. French history 3. Drama 4. 15th century 5. Arts and Entertainment — Writing and Publishing
     LC 2002275027

Dramatizes the trial, career, and execution of Joan of Arc.
Bibliography: P. xxv-xxix.

Sheridan, Richard Brinsley

The School for Scandal and Other Plays. Richard Brinsley Sheridan; edited with an introduction and notes by Eric Rump. Penguin Books 1988. 284 p.
ISBN 9780140432404
Grades: Adult   **822**
1. Arts and Entertainment — Theater — Plays
     LC 89132729

Offers three plays featuring witty repartee, farcical situations and flamboyant characters by the nineteenth-century playwright known for satirizing the manners of his age.
A Penguin original—Label on cover; Bibliography: P. 280-281.

Stoppard, Tom

Arcadia. Tom Stoppard. Faber and Faber 1993. 97 p.
ISBN 9780571169344
Grades: Adult   **822**
1. Drama 2. Arts and Entertainment — Theater — Plays
     LC 94103754

Arcadia takes us back and forth between the nineteenth and twentieth centuries, ranging over the nature of truth and time, the difference between the Classical and the Romantic temperament, and the disruptive influence of sex on our orbits in life.

The Invention of Love. Tom Stoppard. Grove Press 1998. V, 102 p.
ISBN 9780802135810
Grades: Adult   **822**
1. Housman, A. E. (Alfred Edward), 1859-1936 2. Arts and Entertainment — Theater — Plays
     LC 98028331

It is 1936 and A. E. Housman is being ferried across the river Styx, glad to be dead at last. The river that flows through Tom Stoppard's the Invention of Love connects Hades with the Oxford of Housman's youth: High Victorian morality is under siege from the Aesthetic movement, and an Irish student named Wilde is preparing to burst onto the London scene.

★ *Rosencrantz & Guildenstern Are Dead.* Tom Stoppard. Grove Press 1991. 126 p.
ISBN 9780802130334
Grades: 11 12 Adult   **822**
1. Hamlet (Legendary character) 2. Families of murder victims 3. Death of fathers 4. Princes 5. Revenge 6. Tragedy 7. Denmark 8. Arts and Entertainment — Theater — Plays

Presents the play of Hamlet as seen through the eyes of Rosencrantz and Guildenstern.

Wilde, Oscar

★ *The Importance of Being Earnest and Other Plays: And Other Plays.* Oscar Wilde; introduction by Terrence McNally; notes by Michael F. Davis. Modern Library 2003. xvi, 257 p.
ISBN 9780812967142
Grades: 11 12 Adult   **822**
1. Arts and Entertainment — Theater — Plays
     LC 2003044566

The Importance of Being Earnest is a farce, playing with love, religion, and truth as it tells the tale of two men, Jack Worthing and Algernon Moncrieff, who bend the truth in order to add excitement to their lives.

822.33 William Shakespeare

Bloom, Harold

Lear: The Great Image of Authority. Harold Bloom. Scribner 2018. xi, 160 pages
ISBN 9781501164194
Grades: Adult   **822.33**
1. Shakespeare, William, 1564-1616 2. Lear, King (Legendary character) 3. Arts and Entertainment — Writing and Publishing — Literary criticism
     LC 2017061767

A Sterling Professor of Humanities at Yale University and noted Shakespeare scholar presents a portrait of King Lear, who is a classic example of the fall from majesty, and explores his own personal relationship with the character.
"Bloom's short, superb book has a depth of observation acquired from a lifetime of study, and the author knows when to let Shakespeare and his play speak for themselves." —*Publishers Weekly*

Shakespeare: The Invention of the Human. Harold Bloom. Riverhead Books 1998. xx, 745 p.
ISBN 9781573221207
Grades: 11 12 Adult   **822.33**

1. Shakespeare, William, 1564-1616 2. Human nature 3. Characters and characteristics in literature 4. Drama 5. Arts and Entertainment — Writing and Publishing

LC 98021325

Booklist Editors' Choice, 1998; New York Times Notable Book, 1998; National Book Award for Nonfiction finalist, 1998.

Presents an analysis of each one of the Bard's plays, designed to show that Shakespeare invented human nature and personality as we understand it today.

"The passion and obsessiveness of Bloom's approach are its greatest recommendation." —*New York Review of Books*

Karim-Cooper, Farah
★ *The Great White Bard: How to Love Shakespeare While Talking About Race.* Farah Karim-Cooper. Viking 2023. 336 p.
ISBN 9780593489376
Grades: Adult 822.33

1. Shakespeare, William, 1564-1616 2. Race (Social sciences) 3. Difference (Philosophy) 4. Racism 5. Literary criticism 6. Drama 7. Theater 8. Arts and Entertainment — Theater 9. Arts and Entertainment — Writing and publishing 10. Society and culture — Race

LC 2023026890

Combining piercing analyses of race, gender and otherness in famous plays with a radical reappraisal of Elizabethan London, a professor who has dedicated her career to the Bard sets out to unveil a Shakespeare for the 21st century, inviting new perspectives and interpretations to prolong and enrich his extraordinary legacy.

"Karim-Cooper's evenhanded approach refuses to excuse Shakespeare's racism while insisting that his plays still have much to offer modern audiences. This is a vital contribution to the shelf on Shakespeare." —*Publishers Weekly*

Includes bibliographical references and index.

Norwich, John Julius
Shakespeare's Kings: The Great Plays and the History of England in the Middle Ages, 1337-1485. John Julius Norwich. Scribner 2000. 401 p. : Color illustration; Map
ISBN 9780684814346
Grades: Adult 822.33

1. Shakespeare, William, 1564-1616 2. Drama 3. Literature and history 4. England in literature 5. Film history and criticism 6. British history 7. Great Britain 8. Medieval period (476-1492) 9. Renaissance (1300-1600) 10. History writing — Arts and culture 11. History writing — Medieval — Europe 12. History writing — Renaissance — Europe 13. Arts and Entertainment — Theater 14. Arts and Entertainment — Writing and Publishing

LC 99058271

New York Times Notable Book, 2000.

Compares the historical kings with their portrayal in Shakespeare's plays.

"The author offers overviews of Edward III; Richard II; Henry IV, parts 1 and 2; Henry V; Henry VI, parts 1, 2, and 3; and Richard III, examining each play through the lens of history. In addition to providing the necessary historical commentary, he also fills in the gaps between the plays, enabling readers to thoroughly comprehend the entire series in the proper historical context." —*Booklist*

Includes bibliographical references (p. 379-382) and index; Originally published: London : Viking, 1999.

Nuttall, A. D.
Shakespeare the Thinker. A.D. Nuttall. Yale University Press 2007. xi, 428 p.
ISBN 9780300119282
Grades: Adult 822.33

1. Shakespeare, William, 1564-1616 2. Intellectual life 3. England 4. 16th century 5. Arts and Entertainment — Writing and Publishing — Literary criticism

LC 2006035179

Offers a critical analysis of the themes, ideas, and preoccupation exemplified in the body of Shakespeare's work, including the nature of motive, cause, personal identity and relation, the status of imagination, ethics and subjectivity, and language and its capacity to occlude and communicate, in a study that emphasizes the link between great literature and its social and historical matrix.

Includes bibliographical references and index.

Shakespeare, William
★ *The Complete Works: The Complete Works.* General editors, Stanley Wells and Gary Taylor; editors Stanley Wells ... [et al.]; with introductions by Stanley Wells. Clarendon Press; 2005. LXXV, 1344 p. : Illustration
ISBN 9780199267170
Grades: Adult 822.33

1. Arts and Entertainment — Theater — Plays 2. Arts and Entertainment — Writing and Publishing — Literary criticism

LC 2005047272

Presents the works of William Shakespeare, along with an analysis of the nature and authority of the early documents, a list of the canon and chronological order of composition, an essay on Shakespeare's language, and a bibliography.

Includes bibliographical references (p. 1311-1326) and index.

Shapiro, James
Contested Will: Who Wrote Shakespeare? James Shapiro. Simon & Schuster 2010. 384 p.
ISBN 9781416541622
Grades: Adult 822.33

1. Shakespeare, William, 1564-1616 2. Writing 3. Literary forgeries and hoaxes 4. Arts and Entertainment — Writing and Publishing 5. Arts and Entertainment — Writing and Publishing — Literary criticism

LC 2009032710

New York Times Notable Book, 2010.

Examines current debates about the actual authors of Shakespeare's plays, citing challenges from famous historical figures while discussing the sources of modern doubts and the author's own beliefs.

"A thorough, engaging work whose arguments would prove more persuasive were we not living in an era of such fierce anti-intellectualism and pervasive conspiracy theory." —*Kirkus*

Includes bibliographical references and index.

Shakespeare in a Divided America: What His Plays Tell Us About Our Past and Future. James Shapiro. Penguin Press 2020. 320 p.
ISBN 9780525522294
Grades: Adult 822.33

1. Shakespeare, William, 1564-1616 2. Influence (Literary, artistic, etc.) 3. Literature and society 4. Theater and society 5. Politics and literature 6. Inspiration 7. Translating and interpreting 8. Theater 9. United States 10. History writing — United States 11. Arts and entertainment — Writing and publishing 12. Arts and entertainment — Theater

LC 2019026000

New York Times Notable Book, 2020; National Book Critics Circle Award for Nonfiction finalist, 2020.

The award-winning author of the Year of Lear presents a scholarly examination of how American leaders have found wisdom in the works of Shakespeare, revealing the lessons that the Bard's plays can teach about the political turbulence of today.

"Written with broad appeal and expert insight, this sparkling account deserves to be widely read." —*Publishers Weekly*

Includes bibliographical references and index.

The Year of Lear: Shakespeare in 1606. James Shapiro. Simon & Schuster 2015. 384 p.
ISBN 9781416541646
Grades: Adult 822.33

1. Shakespeare, William, 1564-1616 2. Gunpowder Plot, 1605 3. Religious persecution 4. Literature and society 5. Drama 6. English history 7. 17th century 8. Biographies 9. History writing — Europe — United Kingdom 10. Life stories — Arts and culture — Writing 11. Arts and Entertainment — Writing and Publishing — Literary criticism

LC 2015031731

James Tait Black Memorial Prize for Biography, 2015.

ESSENTIAL AND RECOMMENDED TITLES
822.91 English drama — 20th century

Looks at the year 1606, in which Shakespeare created three of his great tragedies, examining how the tumultuous events and cultural conflicts of that year helped shape these works, and affected Shakespeare on a personal level.

"His well-written, scholarly exploration will stand as a n influential work that is a joy to read." —*Kirkus*

Published in Great Britain under the title: 1606: William Shakespeare and the Year of Lear.

Smith, Emma
This Is Shakespeare. Emma Smith. Pantheon Books 2020. 349 p.
ISBN 9781524748548
Grades: Adult   822.33
1. Shakespeare, William, 1564-1616 2. Drama 3. Theater and society 4. Film history and criticism 5. Social life and customs 6. England 7. 17th century 8. Essays 9. Arts and Entertainment — Theater 10. History writing — Europe — United Kingdom
LC 2019028316

A genius and prophet whose timeless works encapsulate the human condition like no other. A writer who surpassed his contemporaries in vision, originality, and literary mastery. A man who wrote like an angel, putting it all so much better than anyone else. Is this Shakespeare? Well, sort of. But it doesn't tell us the whole truth. So much of what we say about Shakespeare is either not true, or just not relevant. In This Is Shakespeare, Emma Smith takes us into a world of politicking and copycatting, as we watch Shakespeare emulating the blockbusters of Christopher Marlowe and Thomas Kyd (the Spielberg and Tarantino of their day), flirting with and skirting around the cutthroat issues of succession politics, religious upheaval, and technological change.

"Smith wears her learning lightly and writes in an accessible, conversational style, making this an excellent work for those eager to brush up their Shakespeare, forsooth." —*Library Journal*

Includes bibliographical references and index; Originally published: London : Pelican Books, 2019.

Winkler, Elizabeth
Shakespeare Was a Woman & Other Heresies: How Doubting the Bard Became the Biggest Taboo in Literature. Elizabeth Winkler. Simon & Schuster 2023. 400 p.
ISBN 9781982171261
Grades: Adult   822.33
1. Shakespeare, William, 1564-1616 2. Playwrights, English 3. Literary criticism 4. Theories 5. Writing 6. 16th century 7. Arts and Entertainment — Writing and Publishing 8. Life stories — Arts and culture — Writing — Authors 9. History writing — Europe — United Kingdom
LC 2022047288

Interviewing scholars and skeptics, a journalist and literary critic investigates the Shakespeare authorship question, taking readers from London to Stratford-upon-Avon to Washington, DC, showing how the forces of nationalism and empire, religion and mythmaking, gender and class have shaped our admiration for Shakespeare across the centuries.

"Journalist and literary critic Winkler makes her book debut with a witty, irreverent inquiry into a fraught question: Who wrote Shakespeare's plays?…A shrewd, entertaining journey into a literary quagmire." —*Kirkus*

Includes bibliographical references and index.

822.91 English drama — 20th century

Thomas, Dylan
Under Milk Wood: A Play for Voices. Dylan Thomas. New Directions 1954. xiv, 107 p. Illustration
ISBN 9780811202091
Grades: 11 12 Adult   822.91
1. Drama 2. Wales 3. Arts and Entertainment — Theater — Plays
LC 54009641

The inhabitants of a small Welsh town must defend their sanity in a court case.

Music for the songs: P. 100-107.

823 English fiction

Ackroyd, Peter
The Death of King Arthur: The Immortal Legend. Sir Thomas Malory; a retelling by Peter Ackroyd. Viking 2011. 336 p.
ISBN 9780670023073
Grades: 11 12 Adult   823
1. Arthur, King 2. Grail 3. Knights and knighthood 4. Rulers 5. Love triangles 6. Merlin (Legendary character) 7. Wizards 8. Magic 9. Betrayal 10. Quests 11. British history 12. Anglo-Saxon period (449-1066) 13. Arthurian legends
LC 2011021800

A modern adaptation of the legendary epic by the author of the Canterbury Tales: A Retelling adds vivid dimensions to Malory's 15th-century work using contemporary prose that makes such events as the romance between Guinevere and Lancelot, the search for the Holy Grail and the treacherous betrayal of Mordred accessible to today's audiences.

"Ackroyd takes the daunting Middle English verse and retells the ancient legends in modern English prose. He also omits most of Malorys medieval tales as perhaps too creaky for modern minds, or maybe simply to make his retelling a niftier little book. All the essential stories are here … Ackroyd tells these stories in such simple, vivid language that they seem as new as they must have when first heard around the peat fires of cold and gloomy England perhaps 1,000 years ago. And theyre still a lot of fun." —*Dallas Morning News*

Attwell, David
J. M. Coetzee and the Life of Writing: Face-to-face with Time. David Attwell. Viking Press 2015. 256 p.
ISBN 9780525429616
Grades: Adult   823
1. Coetzee, J. M, 1940- 2. Authors, South African 3. Nobel Prize winners 4. Authors, Australian 5. Fiction writing 6. South African people 7. 20th century 8. Biographies 9. Life stories — Arts and culture — Writing — Authors
LC 2016479778

An authoritative biography of the Nobel Prize-winning author traces the passage from confession to detachment in each of his novels, shedding new light on his personal papers that reveal him to be more autobiographical than readers would have imagined.

Briggs, Julia
Virginia Woolf: An Inner Life. Julia Briggs. Harcourt, Inc. 2005. xiv, 527 p. : Illustration
ISBN 9780151011438
Grades: Adult   823
1. Woolf, Virginia, 1882-1941 2. Self in literature 3. Women and literature 4. Social life and customs 5. England 6. 20th century 7. Essays 8. Biographies 9. Arts and Entertainment — Writing and Publishing 10. Life stories — Arts and culture — Writing — Authors 11. Arts and Entertainment — Writing and Publishing — Literary criticism
LC 2005016048

A portrait of the twentieth-century writer reveals how her life was centered on her writing; drawing on letters, diaries, and essays to explain how her written works reflect her formative experiences and creative philosophies.

"That this book is a must for Woolf fans goes without saying, but it is also a must for anyone interested in the nature of female consciousness at its most self-aware and the workings of artistic sensibility at their most illuminating." —*Publishers Weekly*

Originally published: London : Allen Lane, 2005; Includes bibliographical references and index.

PUBLIC LIBRARY CORE COLLECTION: NONFICTION
Twentieth Edition

Feder, Rachel
The Darcy Myth: How Romantic Leads Got Mixed up with Scary Monsters, and Why It Matters. Rachel Feder. Quirk Books 2023. 256 p.
ISBN 9781683693574
Grades: Adult   823
1. Austen, Jane, 1775-1817 2. Literary criticism 3. Women authors 4. Romance authors 5. Monsters 6. Popular culture 7. Darcy, Fitzwilliam (Fictitious character) 8. 19th century 9. Arts and Entertainment — Writing and Publishing — Literary criticism
LC 2023005040

An examination of how the romantic narrative from Pride and Prejudice was born out of Gothic horror, how it influenced pop culture since its publishing, and how it has reinforced harmful cultural concepts of real-life romance.—.

"Feder's study is a readable, entertaining contemporary analysis that is suitable for students new to Austen's work and for discussion groups looking for a fresh approach to many readers' favorite novel." —*Library Journal*

Includes bibliographical references and index.

Greene, Graham
Graham Greene: A Life in Letters. Edited by Richard Greene. W.W. Norton 2008. xxxiv, 446 p, 8 p. of plates : Illustration; Portrait
ISBN 9780393066425
Grades: Adult   823
1. Greene, Graham, 1904-1991 2. Authors, English 3. 20th century 4. Letters 5. Life stories — Arts and culture — Writing
LC 2008040452

An autobiographical account in letters offers insight into the late-twentieth-century author's political influence, espionage activities, and personal life, in a volume that also covers how his work was influenced by his humanitarian visits to Mexico, Vietnam, and Cuba.

"Greene is presented in these letters through the five main preoccupations of his life: Roman Catholicism, politics, love, travel and . the processes of writing and publishing. This well-thought-out collection newly reveals a remarkable activist-writer." —*Publishers Weekly*

Includes bibliographical references and index; First published: London : Little, Brown, 2007.

Hardy, Thomas
The Collected Letters of Thomas Hardy: Further Letters 1861-1927. Edited by Michael Millgate and Keith Wilson. Clarendon Press 2012. 317 p.
ISBN 9780199607754
Grades: Adult   823
1. Hardy, Thomas, 1840-1928 2. Authors, English 3. 19th century 4. 20th century 5. Letters 6. Arts and Entertainment — Writing and Publishing — Literary criticism 7. Arts and Entertainment — Writing and Publishing
LC 77030355

Contains previously unpublished letters from all periods of Hardy's career, his earliest known letter among them. It introduces important new correspondents, throws fresh light on existing correspondences, and richly enhances the reader's understanding of both familiar and hitherto unfamiliar aspects of Hardy's life and work and of the times in which he lived.

Includes indexes.

Huxley, Aldous
★ *Brave New World Revisited.* Aldous Huxley. Harper Perennial Modern Classics 2006. 123, 14 p.
ISBN 9780060898526
Grades: Adult   823
1. Culture 2. Propaganda 3. Brainwashing 4. Arts and Entertainment — Writing and Publishing
LC Bl2007012306

Written thirty years after his epic novel "Brave New World," a thoughtprovoking sequel describes the shocking scientific devices and techniques available to any group in a position to manipulate society.

Originally published: New York : Harper, 1958. With additional material.

James, P. D.
Talking About Detective Fiction. P.D. James. Alfred A. Knopf 2009. VIII, 198 p. : Illustration
ISBN 9780307592828
Grades: Adult   823
1. Characters and characteristics in literature 2. Detectives in literature 3. Mystery writing 4. Mystery authors 5. Literary criticism 6. Arts and Entertainment — Writing and Publishing
LC 2009038501

Anthony Award for Best Critical/Nonfiction, 2010; Macavity Award for Best Non-Fiction, 2010.

To judge by the worldwide success of Arthur Conan Doyle's Sherlock Holmes and Agatha Christie's Poirot, it is not only the Anglo-Saxons who have an appetite for mystery and mayhem. Talking about the craft of detective writing and sharing her personal thoughts and observations on one of the most popular and enduring forms of literature, P.D. James examines the challenges, achievements and potential of a genre which has fascinated her for nearly fifty years as a novelist.

Includes bibliographical references (p. 197-198).

Kelly, Helena
Jane Austen, the Secret Radical. Helena Kelly. New York 2017. 352 p.
ISBN 9781524732103
Grades: Adult   823
1. Austen, Jane, 1775-1817 2. Literature and society 3. Social change 4. Feminism 5. Books and reading 6. Radicalism 7. Social problems 8. Arts and entertainment — Writing and publishing 9. Society and culture — General 10. Arts and Entertainment — Writing and Publishing — Literary criticism
LC 2016042656

An authority on Jane Austen invites readers to look deeper into the author's work and see her true, subversive nature which brought to life radical subjects including slavery, poverty, feminism, the Church and evolution between the pages of her demure drawing rooms.

"A fine-grained study that shows us how to read between the lines to discover the remarkable woman who helped transform the novel from trash to an absolute art form." —*Kirkus*

Includes bibliographical references and index.

Lessing, Doris May
Under My Skin: My Autobiography to 1949. Doris Lessing. Harper Collins 1994. 419 p. : Illustration
ISBN 9780060926649
Grades: 11 12 Adult   823
1. Lessing, Doris May, 1919-2013 2. Women communists 3. British people in foreign countries 4. British people 5. Growing up 6. Marriage 7. Authors, English 8. Men-women relations 9. Zimbabwe 10. England 11. 20th century 12. Autobiographies and memoirs 13. Biographies 14. Life stories — Arts and culture — Writing — Authors 15. Arts and Entertainment — Writing and Publishing
LC 94020051

Booklist Editors' Choice, 1994; James Tait Black Memorial Prize for Biography, 1994; Los Angeles Times Book Prize for Biography, 1995.

The author recounts her childhood in Persia and Southern Rhodesia, difficult adolescence, two marriages, political activity, and growth as a writer.

"In this immediate, vivid, beautifully paced memoir, Doris Lessing sets the individual against history, the personal against the general, and shows, by the example of her own life set down honestly, how biography and fiction mesh, how fiction transmutes the personal to the general, how the particular experience illuminates the universe." —*London Review of Books*

Sequel: Walking in the shade.

Lynskey, Dorian
The Ministry of Truth: The Biography of George Orwell's 1984. Dorian Lynskey. Doubleday 2019. 256 p.
ISBN 9780385544054
Grades: Adult   823

ESSENTIAL AND RECOMMENDED TITLES
823 English fiction

1. Orwell, George, 1903-1950 2. Authors, English 3. Literary criticism 4. Influence (Literary, artistic, etc.) 5. Political culture 6. Cold War 7. 20th century 8. Arts and Entertainment — Writing and Publishing 9. Life stories — Arts and culture — Writing — Authors 10. History writing — Arts and culture 11. Arts and Entertainment — Writing and Publishing — Literary criticism

LC 2019937137

The Ministry of Truth is the first book that fully examines the epochal and cultural event that is 1984 in all its aspects: Its roots in the utopian and dystopian literature that preceded it; the personal experiences in wartime Great Britain that Orwell drew on as he struggled to finish his masterpiece in his dying days; and the political and cultural phenomena that the novel ignited at once upon publication and that far from subsiding, have only grown over the decades.

"Lynskey maps the vast influence of Nineteen Eighty-Four in discussions of its stage and screen adaptations, its language, from doublethink to Newspeak, thoughtcrime, unperson, and Big Brother, and the many novels it inspired, including.." —*Booklist*

Malory, Thomas
Le Morte Darthur, Or, the Hoole Book of Kyng Arthur and of His Noble Knyghtes of the Rounde Table: Authoritative Text, Sources and Backgrounds, Criticism. Sir Thomas Malory; edited by Stephen H.A. Shepherd. Norton 2004. LII, 954 p.

ISBN 9780393974645

Grades: Adult **823**

1. Malory, Thomas, Sir, 15th cent 2. Knights and knighthood 3. Rulers 4. Arthurian legends 5. Arts and Entertainment — Writing and Publishing — Literary criticism

LC 2002026534

A primary and secondary source to the 15th-century prose saga for students of English literature. The text includes footnotes explaining terms and references, and marginal references to manuscript pages.

Includes bibliographical references (p. 945-954).

Mead, Rebecca
My Life in Middlemarch. Rebecca Mead. Crown 2014. 304 p.

ISBN 9780307984760

Grades: Adult **823**

1. Eliot, George, 1819-1880 2. Mead, Rebecca 3. Books and reading 4. Reading 5. Readers 6. Women journalists 7. Marriage 8. Creation (Literary, artistic, etc.) 9. Autobiographies and memoirs 10. Arts and Entertainment — Writing and Publishing 11. Life stories — Arts and culture — Writing

LC 2013011477

Library Journal Best Books 2014.

In this memoir, journalist and New Yorker staff writer Rebecca Mead, draws out the intricate ways in which the themes of George Eliot's Middlemarch—"one of the few English novels written for grown-up people," according to Virginia Woolf—have run through her own life. Mead also draws an uncanny portrait of the ways in which Eliots's life resonates with her own through a fascinating reading of Eliot's biography. For those who wonder about the power of literature to shape our lives, this book is a must-read.

"A rare and remarkable fusion of techniques that draws two women together across time and space." —*Kirkus*

Includes bibliographical references; Published by the Text Publishing Company; Melbourne, Victoria in 2014 under the title: The road to Middlemarch: My life with George Eliot.

Montillo, Roseanne
The Lady and Her Monsters: A Tale of Dissections, Attempts to Reanimate Dead Tissue, and the Writing of Mary Shelley's Frankenstein. Roseanne Montillo. Willam Morrow 2013. 320 p.

ISBN 9780062025814

Grades: Adult **823**

1. Shelley, Mary Wollstonecraft, 1797-1851 2. Women authors, English 3. Frankenstein's monster (Fictitious character) 4. Monsters in literature 5. Women and literature 6. Scientists 7. England 8. 19th century 9. Biographies 10. Arts and Entertainment — Writing and Publishing 11. Life stories — Arts and culture — Writing — Authors 12. Arts and Entertainment — Writing and Publishing — Literary criticism

LC 2012021509

Blending grotesque 19th-century science with literary creation, this fascinating volume, tracing the origins of the greatest horror story of all time, explores how Shelley and her contemporaries were intrigued by the occultists and scientists who risked everything to advance our understanding of human anatomy and medicine.

"Fraught with suicides, superstitions, natural disasters, and love affairs, the life of Mary Shelley shares much emotionally with the harrowing tale of her great protagonist, Victor Frankenstein. A delicious and enticing journey into the origins of a masterpiece." —*Publishers Weekly*

Includes bibliographical references.

Skal, David J.
Something in the Blood: The Untold Story of Bram Stoker, the Man Who Wrote Dracula. David J. Skal. Liveright 2015. 448 p.

ISBN 9781631490101

Grades: Adult **823**

1. Stoker, Bram, 1847-1912 2. Theatrical managers 3. Horror writing 4. Dracula, Count (Fictitious character) 5. Authors, English 6. 19th century 7. Biographies 8. Life stories — Arts and culture — Writing — Authors 9. Arts and Entertainment — Writing and Publishing — Literary criticism

LC 2016028093

A groundbreaking biography reveals the haunted origins of the man who created Dracula and traces the psychosexual contours of late Victorian society.

"An engagingly written, well-documented biography of a famous writer we all think we know, even if we really dont." —*Booklist*

Thomson, Jennifer
Josephine Tey: A Life. Jennifer Morag Henderson. Dufour Editions 2016. 420 p.

ISBN 9781910124703

Grades: Adult **823**

1. Tey, Josephine, 1896 or 1897-1952 2. Women authors, Scottish 3. Authors, Scottish 4. 20th century 5. Life stories — Arts and culture — Writing

Josephine Tey was the pen-name of Elizabeth MacKintosh (1896-1952). Born in Inverness, MacKintosh lived several 'Lives': Best known as Golden Age Crime Fiction writer 'Josephine Tey', she was also successful novelist and playwright 'Gordon Daviot'.

Includes bibliographical references and index; Originally published: Dingwall, Scotland : Sandstone Press, 2015.

Wilson, A. N.
C.S. Lewis: A Biography. A.N. Wilson. Norton 1990. xviii, 334 p, [8] p. of plates : Illustration

ISBN 9780393028133

Grades: 11 12 Adult **823**

1. Lewis, C. S. (Clive Staples), 1898-1963 2. Anglicans 3. Authors, English 4. 20th century 5. Biographies 6. Arts and Entertainment — Writing and Publishing 7. Life stories — Arts and culture — Writing — Authors

LC 89027361

Chronicles the personal struggle for wisdom of renowned inspirational and children's book writer C.S. Lewis, his conversion to Christianity, and some of his problematic relationships with women, including his clandestine marriage to a divorcee.

"The mixture presented in Wilson's biography of the life of learning, the college life at Magdalen where he taught, of domestic drama and bad temper, religion, and sex, is irresistible." —*New York Review of Books*

Includes bibliographical references (p. 322-325) and index; First published in Great Britain 1990—T.P. verso.

The Mystery of Charles Dickens. A. N. Wilson. HarperCollins 2020. 384 p.

ISBN 9780062954947

Grades: Adult **823**

1. Dickens, Charles, 1812-1870 2. Creation (Literary, artistic, etc.) 3. Fame 4. Suffering 5. Sexuality 6. Marriage 7. Family relationships 8. Extramarital af-

fairs 9. Authors 10. Literary criticism 11. Characters and characteristics in literature 12. Authors, English 13. Psychology 14. 19th century 15. Biographies 16. Life stories — Arts and culture — Writing — Authors 17. Arts and Entertainment — Writing and Publishing

LC Bl2020046150

A lively and insightful biographical celebration of the imaginative genius of Charles Dickens, published in commemoration of the 150th anniversary of his death. Charles Dickens was a superb public performer, a great orator and one of the most famous of the Eminent Victorians. Slight of build, with a frenzied, hyper-energetic personality, Dickens looked much older than his fifty-eight years when he died—an occasion marked by a crowded funeral at Westminster Abbey, despite his waking wishes for a small affair. Experiencing the worst and best of life during the Victorian Age, Dickens was not merely the conduit through whom some of the most beloved characters in literature came into the world. He was one of them.

"Wilson is the perfect choice to write about this complicated soul, showing how reading Dickens, one emerges with a new appreciation of the people one encounters. Even 150 years after his death, Dickens's life and works continue to fascinate." —*Library Journal*

Woolf, Virginia

The Virginia Woolf Reader. Edited by Mitchell A. Leaska. Harcourt Brace Jovanovich 1984. IX, 371 p.
ISBN 9780156935906
Grades: Adult   823
1. Arts and Entertainment — Writing and Publishing — Literary criticism
LC 84004478

Presents five short stories, essays, correspondence, and selections from four novels by the prominent British author.

A Harvest/HBJ book.

---

824 English essays

Amis, Martin

*The **Rub** of Time: Bellow, Nabokov, Hitchens, Travolta, Trump: Essays and Reportage, 1986-2017.* by Martin Amis. Alfred A. Knopf 2018. 336 p.
ISBN 9781400044535
Grades: Adult   824
1. Literary journalism 2. Essays 3. Society and culture — General 4. Arts and Entertainment — Writing and Publishing — Literary criticism
LC 2017017321

The definitive collection of essays and reportage written during the past thirty years from one of most provocative and widely read writers—with new commentary by the author. For more than thirty years, Amis has turned his keen intellect and unrivaled prose loose on an astonishing range of topics—politics, sports, celebrity, America, and, of course, literature. Now, at last, these incomparable essays have been gathered together.

"Amis writes with buoyant and cutting authority. His vocabulary, cross-pollinated by his trans-Atlantic reading and life, is pinpoint and peppery; his syntax supple and ensnaring. The pleasure Amis takes in observation, cogitation, and composition is palpable, and he is acidly funny." —*Booklist*

This is a Borzoi book; Includes index.

Coetzee, J. M.

Late Essays, 2006-2017. J.M. Coetzee. Viking Press 2018. 297 pages
ISBN 9780735223912
Grades: Adult   824
1. Literary criticism 2. Books and reading 3. Writing 4. Authors 5. Essays 6. Arts and Entertainment — Writing and Publishing

A provocative collection of 23 pieces showcases the writings of the Nobel Prize-winning author as he examines the work of some of the world's greatest writers, including Daniel Defoe, Samuel Beckett, Irene Nemirovsky and Goethe.

"Continuing in the vein of his earlier essay collections, including Inner Workings (2007), Nobel laureate Coetzee again demonstrates his range and precision as a literary critic and his gift for rendering challenging material accessible. His interest is in probing the Western canon for works that are praiseworthy, but also those that fall short in interesting ways." —*Booklist*

Collects 23 literary essays; Originally published: North Sydney, NSW : Knopf Australia, 2017.

Gaiman, Neil

The View from the Cheap Seats: Selected Non-fiction. Neil Gaiman. William Morrow & Co 2016. 256 p.
ISBN 9780062262264
Grades: Adult   824
1. Authors 2. Writing 3. Psychology 4. Essays 5. Autobiographies and memoirs 6. Life stories — Arts and culture — Writing — Authors 7. Arts and Entertainment — Writing and Publishing
LC 2015046480

Presents a collection of nonfiction essays on a myriad of topics—from art and artists to dreams, myths, and memories—observed in the author's distinctive, probing, and amusing style.

"With this volume, Gaiman has shown that his nonfiction rivals his much-lauded fiction." —*Publishers Weekly*

Olds, Sally

★ *People Who Lunch: On Work, Leisure, and Loose Living.* Sally Olds. Little, Brown Spark 2024. 220 pages
ISBN 9780316565714
Grades: Adult   824
1. Work 2. Intimacy 3. Work environment 4. Technology 5. Work-life balance 6. Leisure 7. Essays 8. Australian literature 9. Debut title 10. Society and culture — General

With both drollness and acuity, Sally Olds takes us into worlds we may not have ever visited before. In these sometimes alien spaces she explores and reports on everyday intimacies and vulnerabilities. Across a series of essays, Sally Olds probes the ambivalent utopias of polyamory, cryptocurrency, clubbing, communes, a secret fraternity, and the essay form itself. Curiosity drives each of these adventures into projected worlds, where Olds explores how living with precariousness changes expectations of how a life can be lived in this thrilling appraisal of the state of things.

"A set of challenging, intermittently illuminating essays on the nature of work and relationships." —*Kirkus*

Originally published in Australia by Upswell, Perth, in 2022.

Pratchett, Terry

*A **Slip** of the Keyboard: Collected Nonfiction.* Terry Pratchett; introduction by Neil Gaiman. Doubleday 2014. 336 p.
ISBN 9780385538305
Grades: Adult   824
1. Pratchett, Terry 2. Life 3. Popular culture 4. Animal welfare 5. Alzheimer's disease 6. Medical research 7. People with Alzheimer's disease 8. Fantasy fiction writing 9. Autobiographies and memoirs 10. Essays 11. Humor writing — General 12. Life stories — Arts and culture — Writing — Authors 13. Adult books for young adults
LC 2014011949

A collection of essays and other non fiction from Terry Pratchett, spanning the whole of his writing career from his early years to the present day. Terry Pratchett has earned a place in the hearts of readers the world over with his bestselling Discworld series—but in recent years he has become equally well-known and respected as an outspoken campaigner for causes including Alzheimer's research and animal rights. A Slip of the Keyboard brings together for the first time the finest examples of Pratchett's non fiction writing, both serious and surreal: from musings on mushrooms to what it means to be a writer (and why banana daiquiris are so important); from memories of Granny Pratchett to speculation about Gandalf's love life, and passionate defences of the causes dear to him. With all the humour and humanity that have made his novels so enduringly popular, this collection brings Pratchett out from behind the scenes of the Discworld to speak for himself—man and boy, bibliophile and computer geek, champion of hats, orangutans and Dignity in Dying.

"The essays, letters, speeches, and articles feature all the wit and charm of his beloved novels and allow readers a more personal look at Pratchett's life and be-

ESSENTIAL AND RECOMMENDED TITLES
824.914 English Essays – 1945-1990

liefs. In a mere 336 pages, Pratchett ruminates on the underappreciated role of fantasy fiction and its importance in the literary world; the trick to becoming a successful author (hint: There isn't one); the care and feeding of authors while on book tours; and his work with fellow writer and friend Neil Gaiman." —*Booklist*

Rushdie, Salman
Languages of Truth: Essays 2003-2020. Salman Rushdie. Random House 2021. 384 p.
ISBN 9780593133170
Grades: Adult   824
1. Rushdie, Salman 2. Writing 3. Storytelling 4. Multiculturalism 5. Authors 6. Censorship 7. Creativity 8. Migration, Internal 9. Language and languages 10. Essays 11. Arts and Entertainment — Writing and Publishing

A collection of nonfiction from the Booker Prize-winning, internationally best-selling author of the Satanic Verses brings together his thoughts and insights in essays, criticism, and speeches written between 2003 and 2020 that focus on his relationship with the written word.

"Collecting pieces he wrote in the first two decades of the 21st century, some never before published, Booker Prize winner Rushdie surveys issues of migration, multiculturalism, and censorship in a tumultuous time." —*Library Journal*

Smith, Zadie
★ *Feel Free: Essays.* Zadie Smith. Penguin Press 2018. 448 p.
ISBN 9781594206252
Grades: Adult   824
1. Social media 2. Race relations 3. Political culture 4. Essays 5. Society and culture — General 6. Politics and global affairs — General
LC 2017478938
New York Times Notable Book, 2018.

In a collection of essays arranged into five sections—In the World, in the Audience, in the Gallery, on the Bookshelf, and Feel Free—the best-selling author discusses important questions about our world that readers will immediately recognize.

"In this collection of conversational essays, novelist Smith (Swing Time) brings her precise observations and distinct voice to an expansive range of topics." —*Publishers Weekly*

Intimations: Six Essays. Zadie Smith. Penguin Books 2020. 97 p.
ISBN 9780593297612
Grades: Adult   824
1. Smith, Zadie 2. Social isolation 3. Epidemics 4. Current events 5. Violence against marginalized people 6. Police brutality 7. Racism 8. Injustice 9. Riots 10. Disasters 11. Work 12. Household activities 13. Creation (Literary, artistic, etc.) 14. Women authors 15. Essays 16. Society and culture — Illness and disease — Epidemics 17. Society and culture — Violence and crime 18. Society and culture — Race 19. Life stories — Arts and culture — Writing — Authors
LC 2020027444

Written during the early months of lockdown, Intimations explores ideas and questions prompted by an unprecedented situation. What does it mean to submit to a new reality—or to resist it? How do we compare relative sufferings? What is the relationship between time and work? In our isolation, what do other people mean to us? What is the ratio of contempt to compassion in a crisis? When an unfamiliar world arrives, what does it reveal about the world that came before it? Suffused with a profound intimacy and tenderness in response to these extraordinary times, Intimations is a slim, suggestive volume with a wide scope, in which Zadie Smith clears a generous space for thought, open enough for each reader to reflect on what has happened—and what should come next.

"In just under 100 pages, Smith intimately captures the profundity of our current historical moment. Quietly powerful, deftly crafted essays bear witness to the contagion of suffering." —*Kirkus*

824.914 English Essays – 1945-1990

Mantel, Hilary
Mantel Pieces: Royal Bodies and Other Writing from the London Review of Books. Hillary Mantel. Fourth Estate 2020. 304 pages

ISBN 9780008429973
Grades: Adult   824.914
1. Literary criticism 2. Book reviews 3. Modern literature 4. Book reviewing 5. Books and reading 6. Essays 7. Autobiographies and memoirs 8. Arts and Entertainment — Writing and Publishing 9. Life stories — Arts and culture — Writing — Authors

From the twice Booker Prize winner and internationally best-selling Hilary Mantel comes a collection of writing—essays, book reviews, memoir—from over 30 years contributing to the London Review of Books.

All pieces previously published in London review of books.

828 English miscellaneous writings

Barker, Elspeth
★ *Notes from the Henhouse: On Marrying a Poet, Raising Children and Chickens, and Writing.* Elspeth Barker; with an introduction by Raffaella Barker. Scribner 2024. 256 p.
ISBN 9781668022153
Grades: Adult   828
1. Barker, Elspeth 2. Authors, Scottish 3. Motherhood 4. Parenthood 5. Farm life 6. Women authors 7. Journalists 8. Scottish people 9. Loss 10. Rural life 11. Autobiographies and memoirs 12. Essays 13. Life stories — Relationships — Family 14. Life stories — Arts and culture — Writing — Authors 15. Arts and Entertainment — Writing and publishing
LC 2023046382

A sharp and witty collection of autobiographical essays by the late Elspeth Barker—acclaimed journalist and author of the beloved modern classic O Caledonia.

"The personal reminiscences are the real attraction, showcasing Barker's lyrical prose and frank introspection. Poignant and poetic, this enchants." —*Publishers Weekly*

Originally published in the UK by Orion Publishing Group, London, in 2023.

Orwell, George
Diaries. George Orwell; edited by Peter Davison; introduction by Christopher Hitchens. Liveright 2012. 608 p.
ISBN 9780871404107
Grades: Adult   828
1. Orwell, George, 1903-1950 2. Authors 3. Writing 4. Diaries 5. Arts and Entertainment — Writing and Publishing
LC 2012009895

Collects the diaries of George Orwell, chronicling the major events of his life, including the rise of totalitarianism and the death of his first wife, that influenced his writing.

"The diaries will appeal to all—literary scholars, historians, and students of 20th-century literature—seeking the inner life of this profoundly influential writer. Strongly recommended." —*Library Journal*

Includes bibliographical references and index.

830.9 German literature — history and criticism

Wulf, Andrea
Magnificent Rebels: The First Romantics and the Invention of the Self. Andrea Wulf. Alfred A. Knopf 2022. 416 p.
ISBN 9780525657118
Grades: Adult   830.9
1. Romanticism 2. Romanticism in art 3. Authors 4. Poets 5. Philosophers 6. Philosophy 7. Self 8. Free will and determinism 9. Art movements 10. Intellectual life 11. Germany 12. 18th century 13. 19th century 14. History writing — Arts and culture 15. Life stories — Philosophy 16. Life stories — Arts and culture 17. Life stories — Education — Philosophers

In 1790s Germany, an extraordinary group of young rebels—poets, novelists and philosophers—incited a revolution of the mind that launched Romanticism, transforming our world forever, in this inspiring book that explores the extremely modern tension between the dangers of selfishness and the thrilling possibilities of free will.

"Historian Wulf (The Invention of Nature) delivers an engrossing group biography of the late-18th-century German intellectuals whose 'Obsession with the free self' initiated the Romantic movement and led to the modern conception of self-determination." —Publishers Weekly

831 German poetry

Celan, Paul

Breathturn into Timestead: The Collected Later Poetry : A Bilingual Edition. Paul Celan; translated from the German and with commentary by Pierre Joris. Farrar, Straus and Giroux 2014. LXXVIII, 654 pages
ISBN 9780374125981
Grades: Adult 831
1. Translations — German to English 2. Bilingual materials — English/German 3. Poetry
LC 2014020543

A collection of the late poems of German-language poet Paul Celan.

"Celan's poetry focuses on a new (and very ancient) kind of light: the light of 'The other's Other,' the dark, invisible light beyond all fictions of the abyssal non-origin of being, time, and space. Poetry suffers from what Celan calls Lichtzwang, light duress, which has prevented poetry from 'Darkening over' to its essence. Summing Up: Highly recommended. Upper-division undergraduates through faculty." —Choice

Includes bibliographical references (pages 629-642) and index.

★ *Memory* Rose into Threshold Speech: The Collected Earlier Poetry. Paul Celan; translated by Pierre Joris. Farrar Straus & Giroux, 2020. 548 p.
ISBN 9780374298371
Grades: Adult 831
1. Poetry

"This admirable translation presents the early work of an eminent German language postwar poet to a new audience." —Publishers Weekly

Goethe, Johann Wolfgang von

Selected Poetry. Johann Wolfgang von Goethe; translated with an introduction and notes by David Luke. Penguin Books 2005. xliv, 283 p.
ISBN 9780140424560
Grades: Adult 831
1. Translations — German to English 2. Poetry
LC Bl2007011896

Presents a collection of Goethe's best and most famous poems, in the original German with English translation.

Arranged chronologically, David Luke's verse translations are set alongside the German originals to give a picture of Goethe's poetic development.

Includes bibliographical references and index; Originally published: London : Libris, 1999.

Rilke, Rainer Maria

Ahead of All Parting: The Selected Poetry and Prose of Rainer Maria Rilke. Edited and translated by Stephen Mitchell. Modern Library 1995. xiii, 615 p.
ISBN 9780679601616
Grades: Adult 831
1. Rilke, Rainer Maria, 1875-1926 2. Translations — German to English 3. Poetry
LC 94043917

Presents a collection of the twentieth-century German poet's collected and uncollected works, as well as passages from his novel, "The Notebooks of Malte Laurids Brigge."

Includes indexes; English and German.

★ *Duino* Elegies. Rainer Maria Rilke; translated from the German by David Young; with an introduction and commentary. W. W. Norton 2006. 202 p.
ISBN 9780393328844

Grades: Adult 831
1. Rilke, Rainer Maria, 1875-1926 2. Translations — German to English 3. Poetry
LC 2006009872

One of the literary masterpieces of the century, this translation is now presented with facing-page German.

Includes bibliographical references; This translation was originally published in Field, Contemporary Poetry and Poetics, issues 5 through 9. Reissued in Norton paperback editions 1992, 2006; English and German on facing pages.

★ *Letters* to a Young Poet: With the Letters to Rilke from The. Rainer Maria Rilke, Franz Xaver Kappus; translated and with an introduction and afterword by Damion Searls. Liveright Publishing Corporation 2021. 256 p.
ISBN 9781631497674
Grades: Adult 831
1. Rilke, Rainer Maria, 1875-1926 2. Kappus, Franz Xaver, 1883-1966 3. Authors 4. Poets 5. Authors, German 6. Poets, German 7. 1900s (Decade) 8. 20th century 9. Letters 10. Arts and Entertainment — Writing and Publishing
LC 2020022621

Nearly a century after the publication of Rilke's inspirational work, the missing letters of the young poet himself finally appear in this canonical edition. For more than ninety years, eager writers and young poets, even those simply looking for a purpose in life, have embraced the wisdom of Rainer Maria Rilke's Letters to a Young Poet, first published in 1929. Most readers and scholars assumed that the letters from young poet were forever lost to posterity. Yet, shockingly, the letters were recently discovered by Erich Unglaub, a Rilke scholar, and published in German in 2019.

Includes bibliographical references; Originally published in German as Briefe an einen jungen Dichter: Mit den Briefen von Franz Xaver Kappus.

New Poems. Rainer Maria Rilke; selected and translated by Edward Snow. North Point Press 2001. xii, 329 p.
ISBN 9780865476127
Grades: Adult 831
1. Translations — German to English 2. Poetry
LC 2001042714

Originally published in two volumes in 1907 and 1908, this collection of poetry, now available in a superlative new translation, by the acclaimed poet includes such works as "The Panther" and "Archaic Torso of Apollo."

The translations in this book were originally published in two separate volumes: New poems (Neue Gedichte) in 1984 and New poems: the other part ((Der neuen Gedichte anderer Teil) in 1987—Pref; Includes indexes.

★ *Sonnets* to Orpheus. Rainer Maria Rilke; translated from the German by M.D. Herter Norton. W.W. Norton 2006. 160 p.
ISBN 9780393328851
Grades: Adult 831
1. Translations — German to English 2. Poetry
LC Oc2007045642

German and English on opposite pages.

832 German drama

Goethe, Johann Wolfgang von

Goethe's Faust. Translated by by Walter Kaufmann. Anchor Books 1989. 503 p.
ISBN 9780385031141
Grades: 11 12 Adult 832
1. Faustian bargains 2. Devil 3. Contracts 4. Temptation 5. Men-women relations 6. Classics
LC 89018328

The best translation of Faust available, this volume provides the original German text and its English counterpart on facing pages.

Part one and sections from part two; in the original German and a new translation and introduction by Walter Kaufmann.

ESSENTIAL AND RECOMMENDED TITLES
838 German miscellaneous writings

838 German miscellaneous writings

Grass, Gunter
Of All That Ends. Gunter Grass; translated from the German by Breon Mitchell. Houghton Mifflin Harcourt 2016. 192 p.
ISBN 9780544785380
Grades: Adult   838
1. Grass, Gunter, 1927-2015 2. Aging 3. Writing 4. Essays 5. Translations — German to English 6. Arts and Entertainment — Writing and Publishing 7. Poetry
LC Bl2016047482

A final major collection by the late Nobel Prize-winning author of the Tin Drum is comprised of lighthearted and elegiac meditations on writing, aging and the world.

"Fractured but elegant musings on dying and, most poignantly, living." —*Kirkus*

Contains fiction, poetry, and original artwork by the author.

839.71 Swedish poetry

Transtromer, Tomas
The Great Enigma: New Collected Poems. Tomas Transtromer; translated from the Swedish by Robin Fulton. New Directions Pub. 2006. xxii, 262 p; (New Directions paperback, 1050)
ISBN 9780811216722
Grades: Adult   839.71
1. Transtromer, Tomas, 1931-2015 2. Translations — Swedish to English 3. Poetry
LC 2006022551

Firmly rooted in the natural world, his work falls between dream and dream; it probes "the great unsolved love" with the opening up, through subtle modulations, of "concrete words."

"The major contemporary poet of Scandinavia, and a perennial Nobel Prize candidate (so rumor has it), Transtrmer and his compact, sometimes grim lyricism have long enjoyed a serious following in the United States. This version from the Scot Fulton (whose first Transtrmer selection appeared in 1987) contains everything Transtrmer has published in book form." —*Publishers Weekly*

A New Directions paperback original, NDP1050—P. [4] of cover; Includes index.

841 French poetry

Baudelaire, Charles
Les Fleurs Du Mal: The Complete Text of the Flowers of Evil. Charles Baudelaire; in a new translation by Richard Howard; illustrated with nine original monotypes by Michael Mazur. D.R. Godine 1982. xxxii, 365 p. : Illustration
ISBN 9780879234621
Grades: Adult   841
1. Poets, French 2. 19th century 3. Translations — French to English 4. Poetry
LC 81013283

Presents the first American translation of the complete text of Baudelaire's 1857 masterwork and includes the complete original French texts for easy comparison.

"Howard puts the original's rhymed alexandrines primarily into iambic pentameter blank verse, which allows him to capture the immediate, concrete, visceral quality of Baudelaire's imagery." —*Choice*

Includes index; Translated from the French.

Poems. Baudelaire. A.A. Knopf 1993. 256 p.
ISBN 9780679429104
Grades: 11 12 Adult   841
1. Baudelaire, Charles, 1821-1867 2. Poets, French 3. 19th century 4. Translations — French to English 5. Poetry
LC 93014363

Modern poetry begins with Charles Baudelaire (1821-67), who employed his unequalled technical mastery to create the shadowy, desperately dramatic urban landscape—populated by the addicted and the damned—which so compellingly mirrors our modern condition. Deeply though darkly spiritual, titanic in the changes he wrought, Baudelaire looms over all the work, great and small, created in his wake.

Cover title: Baudelaire; Includes index.

Beckett, Samuel
Collected Poems in English and French. Samuel Beckett. Grove Press 1977. IX, 147 p.
ISBN 9780802130969
Grades: Adult   841
1. Poets, Irish 2. Translations — French to English 3. Poetry
LC 77077855

Gathers together the Nobel Prize-winning writer's English verses, English translations of poems by Eluard, Rimbaud, Apollinaire, and Chamfort, and poems in French, several of which are presented in translation.

Contains poems written by Beckett in English, and by Beckett in French, with translations in some cases, and bilingual versions of poems by Eluard, Rimbaud, Apollinaire, and Chamfort in Beckett's translations.

Rimbaud, Arthur
The Illuminations. Arthur Rimbaud; translated from the French by Donald Revell. Omnidawn Pub. 2009. 119 p.
ISBN 9781890650360
Grades: Adult   841
1. Rimbaud, Arthur, 1854-1891 2. Poets, French 3. Translations — French to English 4. Poetry
LC 2009015569

Presents a new translation of the author's collection of prose poems, rendered for a contemporary audience.

Includes bibliographical references and indexes; with French on the verso pages and English on the recto pages.

Villon, Francois
The Poems of Francois Villon. Translated with an introduction and notes by Galway Kinnell. University Press of New England 1982. xxiii, 246 p.
ISBN 9780874512366
Grades: Adult   841
1. Villon, Francois, 1431-1463 2. Translations — French to English 3. Poetry 4. Arts and Entertainment — Writing and Publishing — Literary criticism
LC 81071907

"Using standard academic texts of the medieval French poet, Kinnell exceeds a transliteration of the originals. Villon's ribaldry and humorous despair sparkle throughout." —*Booklist*

Text of poems in English and French; Bibliography: P. 243-246.

842 French drama

Camus, Albert
Caligula & Three Other Plays. Translated from the French by Stuart Gilbert. With a pref. written specially for this ed, and translated by Justin O'Brien. Knopf 1958. x, 302 p.
ISBN 9780394702070
Grades: Adult   842
1. Caligula, Emperor of Rome, 12-41 2. Arts and Entertainment — Theater — Plays
LC 58011227

Contains four plays.

Sartre, Jean-Paul
★ *No Exit, and Three Other Plays*. Jean-Paul Sartre. Vintage International 1989. 275 p.

ISBN 9780679725169
Grades: Adult **842**
1. Sartre, Jean-Paul, 1905-1980 2. Arts and Entertainment — Theater
LC 89040097

English translations of four plays which dramatize the theme of man's responsibility for his own actions, by the leader of French existentialism.
Translated from the French.

843 French fiction

Bellos, David
The Novel of the Century: The Extraordinary Adventure of Les Miserables. David Bellos. Farrar, Straus & Giroux 2017. 352 pages
ISBN 9780374223236
Grades: Adult **843**
1. Hugo, Victor, 1802-1885 2. Authors 3. Writing 4. Books 5. Literary criticism 6. Social problems 7. Poverty 8. Exile (Punishment) 9. French history 10. 19th century 11. Arts and Entertainment — Writing and Publishing 12. History writing — Arts and culture 13. Arts and Entertainment — Writing and Publishing — Literary criticism
LC 2016049133

A narrative account of the story behind Victor Hugo's literary masterpiece describes how he wrote the book under violent conditions and during exile, the considerable measures that were required for its publication and its various stage and screen interpretations.

"Anyone who loves Hugo, France, and the French language will revel in this delightful book that explains all the intimacies of 19th-century French life." —*Kirkus*

Shattuck, Roger
Proust's Way: A Field Guide to in Search of Lost Time. Roger Shattuck. W.W. Norton 2000. xxiv, 290 p.
ISBN 9780393049145
Grades: Adult **843**
1. Proust, Marcel, 1871-1922 2. Literary criticism 3. Arts and Entertainment — Writing and Publishing
LC 99058472

New York Times Notable Book, 2000.

A critical evaluation of Proust's "In Search of Lost Time" which is most traditionally translated as "Remembrance of Things Past."

"Shattuck is most helpful in placing Proust and the work in the context of his time, giving a balanced treatment to the novel as a whole. Written in a style that will appeal to both the scholar and the lay reader, Shattuck's field guide should be a standard for years to come." —*Library Journal*

Includes bibliographical references (p. 269-270) and index.

844 French essays

Camus, Albert
The Myth of Sisyphus and Other Essays. Albert Camus; translated from the French by Justin O'Brien. Vintage Books 1991. VI, 212 p.
ISBN 9780679733737
Grades: Adult **844**
1. Essays 2. Translations — French to English 3. Society and culture — Philosophy
LC 90050476

Essays deal with nihilism and the problem of suicide.
Originally published: New York : Knopf, 1955.

Resistance, Rebellion, and Death. Albert Camus; translated from the French and with an introduction by Justin O'Brien. Vintage International 1995. VIII, 272 p.
ISBN 9780679764014
Grades: Adult **844**

1. Good and evil 2. Politics and government 3. Europe 4. Arts and Entertainment — Writing and Publishing
LC 95215592

The author's personal beliefs and his reactions to the major issues of his lifetime are reflected in these selected writings.
Essays selected by the author from his Actuelles and other works; Originally published: New York : Knopf, 1960.

Frampton, Saul
When I Am Playing with My Cat, How Do I Know She Is Not Playing with Me?: Montaigne and Being in Touch with Life. Saul Frampton. Pantheon Books 2011. 288 p.
ISBN 9780375424717
Grades: Adult **844**
1. Montaigne, Michel de, 1533-1592 2. European Renaissance 3. Grief 4. Philosophers 5. Authors 6. Renaissance (1300-1600) 7. Family and Relationships — Aging and Death 8. History writing — Renaissance — Europe
LC 2010043642

An introduction to the life and works of the 16th-century literary master traces the impact of personal tragedies and war on such pieces as Les Essais, discussing the writer's reflections on myriad subjects and his enduring legacy.

"The author renders a rigorous history of ideas in this engaging account of the life and the work of Michel de Montaigne (1533-1592). Frampton tucks a good deal of biography into his tour of the evolution of the essays and the events that inspired them, but his extraordinary achievement is in conveying—and inviting the reader to commune with—Montaigne's unique sensibility and his take on death, sex, travel, friendship, kidney stones, the human thumb, and above all, the power of the ordinary and the unremarkable, the value of the here-and-now. This scholarly romp through the Renaissance is a jewel." —*Publishers Weekly*

Includes bibliographical references and index.

848 French miscellaneous writings

Beckett, Samuel
The Letters of Samuel Beckett. Editors, Martha Dow Fehsenfeld, Lois More Overbeck; associate editors, George Craig, Daniel Gunn. Cambridge University Press 2009. 782 p. (Letters of Samuel Beckett, 1)
ISBN 9780521867931
Grades: Adult **848**
1. Beckett, Samuel, 1906-1989 2. Authors, Irish 3. Authors, French 4. 20th century 5. Letters 6. Arts and Entertainment — Writing and Publishing
LC 2008025530

SUPERANNO Offers a collection of letters written by the author (1929 through 1940) that provide insight into his feelings about his work, chosen profession, death of his father, and views on the world in which he lived.

"This is an extraordinary work of scholarship on the part of its main editors. What Fehsenfeld and Overbeck have produced is a revelatory triumph." —*Los Angeles Times Book Review*

Correspondence chiefly written in English; letters written in French and German are accompanied by English translations; Includes bibliographical references and indexes.

Burger, Ariel
Witness: Lessons from Elie Wiesel's Classroom. Ariel Burger. 2018. 256 p.
ISBN 9781328802699
Grades: Adult **848**
1. Wiesel, Elie, 1928-2016 2. Teacher-student relationships 3. Teachers 4. Holocaust survivors 5. Holocaust (1933-1945) 6. Authors, French 7. Humanism 8. 20th century 9. Autobiographies and memoirs 10. Biographies 11. Life stories — Education — Scholars and educators 12. Social issues — Education 13. Life stories — Relationships — Friendship
LC 2018006868

National Jewish Book Award, 2018.

Ariel Burger first met Elie Wiesel at age fifteen. They studied together and taught together. Witness chronicles the intimate conversations between these

ESSENTIAL AND RECOMMENDED TITLES
851 Italian poetry

two men over decades, as Burger sought counsel on matters of intellect, spirituality, and faith, while navigating his own personal journey from boyhood to manhood, from student and assistant to rabbi and, in time, teacher. In this profoundly hopeful, thought-provoking, and inspiring book, Burger takes us into Elie Wiesel's classroom, where the art of listening and storytelling conspire to keep memory alive. As Wiesel's teaching assistant, Burger gives us a front-row seat witnessing these remarkable exchanges in and out of the classroom. The act of listening, of sharing these stories, makes us, the readers, witnesses.

Coffin, Judith G.
Sex, Love, and Letters: Writing Simone De Beauvoir. Judith G. Coffin. Cornell University Press 2020. xiv, 310 p.
ISBN 9781501750540
Grades: Adult   **848**
1. Beauvoir, Simone de, 1908-1986 2. Women authors, French 3. Letter writing 4. Authors and readers 5. Public opinion 6. Women philosophers 7. Intellectual life 8. Salons 9. Postwar life 10. 20th century 11. Letters 12. Life stories — Arts and culture — Writing — Authors 13. Life stories — Education — Philosophers 14. Arts and Entertainment — Writing and Publishing 15. History writing — Arts and culture

LC 2020005876

When Judith G. Coffin discovered a virtually unexplored treasure trove of letters to Simone de Beauvoir from her international readers, it inspired her to explore the intimate bond between the famed author and her reading public. This correspondence, at the heart of Sex, Love, and Letters, immerses us in the tumultuous decades from the late 1940s to the 1970s—from the painful aftermath of World War Two to the horror and shame of French colonial brutality in Algeria through the dilemmas and exhilarations of the early gay liberation and feminist movements. It also provides a glimpse into the power of reading and the power of readers to seduce the authors of their favorite books.

"This beautifully written, frequently moving book is a crucial addition to the scholarship on Simone de Beauvoir." —*Kirkus*

Includes bibliographical references and index.

Sartre, Jean-Paul
We Have Only This Life to Live: Selected Essays, 1939/1975. by Jean-Paul Sartre; edited by Ronald Aronson and Adrian van den Hoven. New York Review Books 2013. 600 p.
ISBN 9781590174937
Grades: Adult   **848**
1. Sartre, Jean-Paul, 1905-1980 2. Essays 3. Autobiographies and memoirs 4. Life stories — Arts and culture — Writing — Authors 5. Spirituality and Religion — General

LC 2013001043

This is the first gathering of Sartre's essays in English to draw on all ten volumes of Situations, the title under which Sartre collected his essays during his life, while also featuring previously uncollected work, including the reports Sartre filed during his 1945 trip to America. Here Sartre writes about Faulkner, Bataille, Giacometti, Fanon, the liberation of France, torture in Algeria, existentialism and Marxism, friends lost and found, and much else. We Have Only This Life to Live provides an indispensable, panoramic view of the world of Jean-Paul Sartre.

Includes bibliographical references.

---
851 Italian poetry

Ariosto, Lodovico
Orlando Furioso =: The Frenzy of Orlando : A Romantic Epic. Ludovico Ariosto; translated with an introduction by Barbara Reynolds. Penguin 1975. 268 p. : Illustration; Table
ISBN 9780140443110
Grades: Adult   **851**
1. Roland (Legendary character) 2. Poetry

LC 75327748

One of the greatest epic poems of the Italian Renaissance, Orlando Furioso is an intricate tale of love and enchantment set at the time of the Holy Roman Emperor Charlemagne's conflict with the Moors.

Includes bibliographical references and index.

Dante Alighieri
★ *The Divine Comedy: Inferno, Purgatorio, Paradiso.* Dante Alighieri; translated by Allen Mandelbaum; with an introduction by Eugenio Montale and notes by Peter Armour. Alfred A. Knopf 1995. 798 p. : Illustration
ISBN 9780679433132
Grades: Adult   **851**
1. Epic poetry 2. Translations — Italian to English 3. Poetry

LC BL98005712

Dante Alighieri's epic poem travels through the endless agony of Hell, up the treacherous slopes of Purgatory, and on to the wondrous kingdom of Paradise—the realm of universal unity and eternal salvation.

Includes bibliographical references.

Inferno. Dante Alighieri; translated by Robert & Jean Hollander; introduction & notes by Robert Hollander. Anchor Books 2002. xl, 694 pages : Illustration
ISBN 9780385496988
Grades: 11 12 Adult   **851**
1. Hell 2. Life after death 3. Arts and Entertainment — Writing and Publishing 4. Poetry

LC Bl2015010141

In a new translation of the first part of Dante's epic poem about the Christian afterlife, presented with the original Italian and the English version on facing pages, Virgil leads a spiritual pilgrim through the circles of Hell.

The most cogent English translation of Dante's classic poem in years brings the epic poem of hell into the modern English language with subtle shadings of meaning intact.

"The heart of the Hollanders' edition is the translation itself, which nicely balances the precision required for a much-interpreted allegory and the poetic qualities that draw most readers to the work. The result is a terse, lean Dante with its own kind of beauty. The Hollanders' lines will satisfy both the poetry lover and scholar; they are at once literary, accessible and possessed of the seeming transparence that often characterizes great translations. The Italian text is included on the facing page for easy reference, along with notes drawing on some 60 Dante scholars, several indexes, a list of works cited and an introduction by Robert Hollander." —*Publishers Weekly*

Includes bibliographical references (pages 657-694) and indexes.

The Paradiso. Dante Alighieri; translated by John Ciardi; with an introduction by John Freccero and an afterword by Edward M. Cifelli. New American Library 2009. 365 p. : Illustration
ISBN 9780451531414
Grades: Adult   **851**
1. Christianity 2. Life after death 3. Heaven 4. Paradise 5. Epic poetry 6. Translations — Italian to English 7. Poetry

LC 2010668194

The final canticle of Dante's "The Divine Comedy" shares the ultimate goal of human striving: the merging of individual destiny with universal order. One of the towering creations of world literature, Dante's vision of universal harmony and eternal salvation is an immortal hymn to God, Nature, Eternity, and Love.

Includes bibliographical references.

Paradiso. Dante Alighieri; a verse translation by Robert & Jean Hollander; introduction & notes by Robert Hollander. Anchor Books 2008. xxix, 989 pages : Illustration
ISBN 9781400031153
Grades: Adult   **851**
1. Hell 2. Paradise 3. Life after death 4. Epic poetry 5. Translations — Italian to English 6. Poetry

LC Bl2015010149

Follows the spiritual pilgrim as he puts behind him the horrors of Hell and the trials of Pugatory to ascend to Paradise, where he encounters his beloved Beatrice and meets the Heavenly Court and the Lord.

PUBLIC LIBRARY CORE COLLECTION: NONFICTION
Twentieth Edition

A new translation of the classic third installment in the Divine Comedy follows the spiritual pilgrim as he puts behind him the horrors of Hell and the trials of Pugatory to ascend to Paradise, where he encounters his beloved Beatrice and meets the Heavenly Court and the Lord.

Includes bibliographical references (pages 957-989) and index.

Purgatorio. Dante Alighieri; a verse translation from the Italian by Jean Hollander & Robert Hollander; introduction & notes by Robert Hollander. Doubleday 2003. xxiv, 742 p.

ISBN 9780385496995

Grades: 11 12 Adult   851

1. Sin 2. Repentance 3. Salvation 4. Purgatory 5. Dead 6. Suffering 7. Epic poetry 8. Translations — Italian to English 9. Poetry

LC 2002067100

A verse translation of the second section of Dante's monumental epic, the Divine Comedy, chronicles the poet-narrator's odyssey, with the poet Virgil as his guide, up the Mount of Purgatory toward Paradise, in a version that includes a detailed introduction, extensive notes, and commentaries on each canto.

"These translations, honed over Robert Hollander's 35 years teaching Dante at Princeton, are touted as the U.S. English standard for rendering Dante's layered meanings." —*Publishers Weekly*

Includes bibliographical references (p. 716-742) and indexes.

Raffa, Guy P.

Dante's Bones: How a Poet Invented Italy. Guy P. Raffa. Harvard Univ Pr 2020. 304 p.

ISBN 9780674980839

Grades: Adult   851

1. Dante Alighieri, 1265-1321 2. Relics 3. Burial 4. Forensic anthropology 5. National characteristics, Italian 6. History writing — Europe — Italy 7. Life stories — Arts and culture — Writing — Poets

LC 2019049287

Dante, whose Divine Comedy gave the world its most vividly imagined story of the afterlife, endured an extraordinary afterlife of his own. Exiled in death as in life, the Florentine poet has hardly rested in peace over the centuries. Like a saint's relics, his bones have been stolen, recovered, reburied, exhumed, examined, and, above all, worshiped. Actors in this graveyard history range from Lorenzo de' Medici, Michelangelo, and Pope Leo X to the Franciscan friar who hid the bones, the stone mason who accidentally discovered them, and the opportunistic sculptor who accomplished what princes, popes, and politicians could not: Delivering to Florence a precious relic of the native son it had banished. In Dante's Bones, Guy Raffa narrates for the first time the complete course of the poet's hereafter, from his death and burial in Ravenna in 1321 to a computer-generated reconstruction of his face in 2006.

"In tracing the history of Dante's bones, Raffa also provides an illuminating exploration of Italian nationalism and political thought." —*Publishers Weekly*

Includes bibliographical references and index.

854 Italian essays

Calvino, Italo

Collection of Sand. Italo Calvino; translated by Martin McLaughlin. Mariner Books 2014. 240 p.

ISBN 9780544146464

Grades: Adult   854

1. Calvino, Italo 2. Essays 3. Translations — Spanish to English 4. Arts and entertainment — Writing and publishing 5. Arts and Entertainment — Writing and Publishing — Literary criticism

LC 2014001373

Published for the first time in English, a final collection of essays by the renowned fabulist writer tours the visual world through explorations of subjects ranging from cuneiform and antique maps to Mexican temples and Japanese gardens.

858 Italian miscellaneous writings

Levi, Primo

The Periodic Table. Primo Levi; translated from the Italian by Raymond Rosenthal; with an introduction by Neal Ascherson. Alfred A. Knopf 1996. xxv, 241 p. : Illustration

ISBN 9780805210415

Grades: Adult   858

1. Levi, Primo 2. Chemists 3. Chemical elements 4. Periodic table of the elements 5. Jewish men 6. Scientists 7. Dissenters 8. Memory 9. Purpose in life 10. World War II 11. Holocaust (1933-1945) 12. Italy 13. Germany 14. Second World War era (1939-1945) 15. 20th century 16. Autobiographies and memoirs 17. History writing — Wars and conflicts — Holocaust — World War II 18. Life stories — Facing adversity — War and oppression — Holocaust 19. Life stories — Science, technology, and medicine — Scientists and inventors

LC 96008920

One of Italy's leading men of letters, a chemist by profession, writes about incidents in his life in which one or another of the elements figured in such a way as to become a personal preoccupation.

"This curious memoir, organized in 21 chapters from Argon to Zinc, ransacks the periodic table of the elements for strained metaphors as it traces one adolescent's search for identity. Levi ironically portrays himself as a young aspiring chemist eager to fathom nature's secrets." —*Publishers Weekly*

Includes bibliographical references (p. xvii); Originally published in the U.S, in translation : New York : Schocken Books, 1984.

861 Spanish poetry

Aleixandre, Vicente

A Longing for the Light: Selected Poems of Vicente Aleixandre. Edited by Lewis Hyde. Copper Canyon Press 2007. xxi, 279 p.

ISBN 9781556592546

Grades: Adult   861

1. Aleixandre, Vicente, 1898-1984 2. Translations — Spanish to English 3. Poetry

LC 2007000992

A comprehensive collection spans the entirety of Nobel Laureate Aleixandre's career, from his early surrealist work to his complex and fascinating "dialogues," as well as prose interludes.

Includes bibliographical references and indexes.

Borges, Jorge Luis

★ *Selected Poems.* Jorge Luis Borges; edited by Alexander Coleman. Penguin Books 2000. xii, 483 p.

ISBN 9780140587210

Grades: 11 12 Adult   861

1. Borges, Jorge Luis, 1899-1986 2. Latin American poetry 3. 19th century 4. Translations — Spanish to English 5. Poetry

LC Bl2011001811

A bilingual collection presents two hundred of the Argentine author's poems.

"Poetry is the heart of Borges' metaphysical, mythical, and cosmopolitan oeuvre. Editor Coleman commissioned a wealth of new translations for this unprecedented and invaluable collection, and the roster of translators includes such luminaries as Robert S. Fitzgerald, W.S. Merwin, Mark Strand, and John Updike." —*Booklist*

Originally published: New York : Viking, 1999; English and Spanish on facing pages.

Cardenal, Ernesto

Pluriverse: New and Selected Poems. Ernesto Cardenal; edited by Jonathan Cohen; with a foreword by Lawrence Ferlinghetti; translations from the Spanish by Jonathan Cohen ... [et al.]. New Directions Pub. 2009. xxii, 249 p.

ISBN 9780811218092

Grades: Adult   861

ESSENTIAL AND RECOMMENDED TITLES
861 Spanish poetry

    1. Cardenal, Ernesto, 1925-2020 2. Translations — Spanish to English 3. Poetry
    LC 2008040582
"Cardenal is political, of course, and much of the work presented here (translated by many illustrious hands, including Jonathan Cohen, Thomas Merton and Kenneth Rexroth) deals with the struggle and history of his country and Latin America at large. But he can sing lyrically too. Beautiful." —*Los Angeles Times Book Review*
    Includes bibliographical references and index.

Garcia Lorca, Federico
    Collected *Poems.* Federico Garcia Lorca; revised edition, with an introduction and notes by Christopher Maurer; translated from the Spanish by Catherine Brown … [et al.]. Farrar, Straus and Giroux 2002. LXIV, 990 p. : Illustration
    ISBN 9780374526917
Grades: Adult   861
    1. Garcia Lorca, Federico, 1898-1936 2. 19th century 3. Translations — Spanish to English 4. Poetry
    LC 2001018779
Spain's greatest twentieth-century poet and most influencial modernist speaks to a new generation of readers in this revised edition of his complete poetical works.
    Rev. ed. of: Collected poems / Federico Garcia Lorca. 1991. (Poetical works of Federico Garcia Lorca; v. 2); Includes bibliographical references (p. 953-962) and indexes.

    Poet *in New York: A Bilingual Edition.* Federico Garcia Lorca; translated from the Spanish by Greg Simon and Steven F. White; edited and with an introduction and notes by Christopher Maurer. The Noonday Press 1998. xxxv, 303 p. : Illustration
    ISBN 9780374525408
Grades: Adult   861
    1. Garcia Lorca, Federico, 1898-1936 2. 19th century 3. Translations — Spanish to English 4. Poetry
    LC 97049953
A collection of surrealistic poems with English translations reflect Lorca's response to New York City during a prolonged visit in 1930.

Juana Ines de la Cruz, Sister
    Selected *Works.* Sor Juana Ines de la Cruz; translated by Edith Grossman; introduction by Julia Alvarez. W. W. Norton & Company 2014. xxiv, 216 pages
    ISBN 9780393241754
Grades: Adult   861
    1. 17th century 2. Translations — Spanish to English 3. Poetry
    LC 2014025634
A collection of best-known works from the seventeenth-century feminist poet showcases her intellect and range and highlights her belief in a woman's right to study and write.
    Includes bibliographical references.

Neruda, Pablo
    All *the Odes.* Pablo Neruda; edited by Ilan Stavans. Farrar, Straus and Giroux 2013. xxiii, 861 p.
    ISBN 9780374115289
Grades: Adult   861
    1. Neruda, Pablo, 1904-1973 2. Chilean poetry 3. Latin American poetry 4. 20th century 5. Translations — Spanish to English 6. Poetry
    LC 2012009146
A career-spanning volume charting the Nobel laureate's work in the ode form is published in a dual-language format and includes English-language renderings by such accomplished translators as Philip Levine, Paul Muldoon and Mark Strand.
    Includes index; Text in English and Spanish.

    Then *Come Back: The Lost Neruda Poems.* Pablo Neruda; translated from the Spanish by Forrest Gander. Copper Canyon Press 2016. xx, 165 pages
    ISBN 9781556594946

Grades: Adult   861
    1. Neruda, Pablo, 1904-1973 2. Chilean poetry 3. Latin American poetry 4. 20th century 5. Translations — Spanish to English 6. Poetry
    LC 2015048546
In a Spanish-English edition, the lost poems of one of the world's most beloved and best-selling poets—which were originally composed on napkins, playbills, receipts and notebooks—have been translated for the first time.
    Includes bibliographical references.

    ★ ***Twenty*** *Love Poems and a Song of Despair.* Pablo Neruda; translated by W.S. Merwin; introduction by Cristina Garcia; illustrations by Pablo Picasso. Penguin Books 2004. xviii, 94 p. : Illustration
    ISBN 9780142437704
Grades: 9 10 11 12   861
    1. Love 2. Passion 3. Romantic love 4. Chilean poetry 5. Latin American poetry 6. Poetry
    LC 2003067611
Presents a bilingual edition of the Nobel Prize-winning Chilean poet's collection of poems celebrating the beauty and nature of love and the passions, fears, pain, and anguish of human existence.
    "This bilingual collection presents a series of poems that contains sea and nature imagery that associates woman with the productive forces of Mother Earth." —*Choice*
    Includes bibliographical references (p. 93-94); Originally published: Great Britain : Jonathan Cape Ltd, 1969. With new introd.

    World's *End.* Pablo Neruda; translated from the Spanish by William O'Daly. Copper Canyon Press 2009. xxvii, 303 p.
    ISBN 9781556592829
Grades: Adult   861
    1. Neruda, Pablo, 1904-1973 2. Chilean poetry 3. Latin American poetry 4. 20th century 5. Translations — Spanish to English 6. Poetry
    LC 2008034637
Offers a collection of the Nobel prize-winning Chilean author's poems from 1969, in which he condemns the hypocrisy and violence of the twentieth century and praises those who work for change, accompanied by a new English translation.

Paz, Octavio
    ★ *The* ***Collected*** *Poems of Octavio Paz, 1957-1987.* Edited and translated by Eliot Weinberger; with additional translations by Elizabeth Bishop … [et al.]. New Directions 1991. xvii, 669 p. : Illustration
    ISBN 9780811210379
Grades: 11 12 Adult   861
    1. Paz, Octavio, 1914-1998 2. Translations — Spanish to English 3. Bilingual materials — English/Spanish 4. Poetry
    LC BI2006006081
Poems, in both English translation and the original Spanish, deal with fate, nature, language, intimacy, love, friendship, and the senses.
    "Dense, weighty, and miraculous, this bilingual edition compresses into one volume all the poems published in book form since 1957. Nearly 200 poems, some newly translated, many new to an English-language edition, conclusively demonstrate Paz's power." —*Library Journal*
    Includes bibliographical references (p. 657-659) and indexes.

    The ***Poems*** *of Octavio Paz.* Edited and translated by Eliot Weinberger with additional translations by Elizabeth Bishop, Paul Blackburn, Denise Levertov, Muriel Rukeyser, and Charles Tomlinson. New Directions 2012. xiii, 606 p.
    ISBN 9780811220439
Grades: Adult   861
    1. Paz, Octavio, 1914-1998 2. Translations — Spanish to English 3. Poetry
    LC 2012016228
Collects the author's poetry spanning his entire writing career, including his first published poem as well as his last, along with a biographical note and notes on the poems taken from interviews with the author.
    Includes bibliographical references and index.

PUBLIC LIBRARY CORE COLLECTION: NONFICTION
Twentieth Edition

864 Spanish essays

Borges, Jorge Luis
Selected Non-Fictions. Jorge Luis Borges; edited by Eliot Weinberger; translated by Esther Allen, Suzanne Jill Levine & Eliot Weinberger. Viking 1999. xvi, 559 p.
ISBN 9780670849475
Grades: Adult **864**
1. Borges, Jorge Luis, 1899-1986 2. Literature 3. Lectures and lecturing 4. Time 5. Eternity 6. Infinity 7. Essays 8. Translations — Spanish to English 9. Arts and Entertainment — Writing and Publishing
LC 99012386

A third and last volume in a centenary edition of the collected works in English of one of the century's most respected literary figures offers new translations of more than 150 of Borges's nonfiction works.

"Shifting effortlessly from Homer to Hitler, from Kafka to King Kong, these hundred and sixty-one essays, appreciations, prologues, and philosophical investigations are dizzying in scope and dazzling in execution. But it is Borges's dogged pursuit of familiar themes infinity and eternity, reflexivity and recurrence which gives this collection its unusual unity and depth." —*The New Yorker*

Includes bibliographical references (p. [523]-548) and index.

868 Spanish miscellaneous writings

Cercas, Javier
Lord of All the Dead: A Nonfiction Novel. by Javier Cercas; translated from the Spanish by Anne McLean. Alfred A. Knopf 2019. 288 p.
ISBN 9780525520900
Grades: Adult **868**
1. Cercas, Javier, 1962- 2. Family history 3. Shame 4. War 5. Forgiveness 6. Collective memory 7. Memories 8. Dictators 9. Political parties 10. Fascism 11. Spanish history 12. 20th century 13. Translations — Spanish to English 14. Autobiographies and memoirs 15. Life stories — Arts and culture — Writing — Authors 16. Life stories — People in history 17. History writing — Wars and conflicts — Civil Wars 18. History writing — Europe — Spain
LC 2019016660

The award-winning author of Soldiers of Salamis explores the life of his enigmatic great-uncle, a Spanish Civil War soldier whose early battlefield death shaped family perspectives on heroism, morality, legacy and the historical relevance of everyday individuals.

"Cercas is a marvelous writer, and his character studies of the elusive Mena are masterly." —*Kirkus*

A Borzoi book—Title page verso; Originally published in the Spanish language as El monarca de las sombras by Javier Cercas, Penguin Random House Grupo Editorial, S. A. U. in 2017.

Vargas Llosa, Mario
The Call of the Tribe. Mario Vargas Llosa, translated by John King. Farrar Straus & Giroux 2023. 288 p.
ISBN 9780374118051
Grades: Adult **868**
1. Vargas Llosa, Mario, 1936- 2. Influence (Literary, artistic, etc.) 3. Authors 4. Peruvian people 5. Thought and thinking 6. Intellectual life 7. Autobiographies and memoirs 8. Life stories — Arts and culture — Writing — Authors 9. Life stories — Politics — Politicians 10. Arts and Entertainment — Writing and publishing

"Vargas Llosa reveals with enthusiasm and aplomb the political and social beliefs that have found homes in his work." —*Kirkus*

Conversation at Princeton. Mario Vargas Llosa with Rubén Gallo; translated from the Spanish by Anna Kushner. Farrar, Straus and Giroux 2023. 272 p.
ISBN 9780374129019
Grades: Adult **868**
1. Literature 2. Politics and literature 3. Journalism 4. Writing 5. Translations — Spanish to English 6. Arts and Entertainment — Writing and publishing
LC 2022041851

A series of talks Mario Vargas Llosa gave at Princeton in a class he cotaught with Rubén Gallo, covering the history of the novel, journalism, terrorism, and all of Vargas Llosa's best-known books.

"An indispensable volume for fans of Vargas Llosa, Latin American literature, and the art of great writing." —*Kirkus*

Translated from the Spanish.

871 Latin poetry

Virgil
The Eclogues of Virgil: A Translation. David Ferry. Farrar Straus & Giroux 1999. xv, 101 pages; 21 cm
ISBN 9780374146344
Grades: Adult **871**
1. Pastoral poetry 2. Translations 3. Poetry
LC 98052547

"English translators of Virgil traditionally prize what they call "accuracy" over preserving the text's elegance and readability. Ferry, an American poet and translator (his 1997 rendering of Horace's Odes garnered critical acclaim), comes very close to the best of both worlds: His complete, bilingual edition captures the verbal texture of the original while retaining its deliberately archaic feel, sensitivity and wit, surpassing his recent predecessors (such as Paul Alpers and Guy Lee) in polish and faithfulness." —*Publishers Weekly*

Text in Latin and English on facing pages.

873 Latin epic poetry and fiction

Ovid
Tales from Ovid. [translated by] Ted Hughes. Farrar, Straus and Giroux 1997. x, 257 p.
ISBN 9780374228415
Grades: 11 12 Adult **873**
1. Metamorphosis 2. Epic poetry 3. Translations — Latin to English 4. Classics 5. Poetry
LC 97036061

New York Times Notable Book, 1998.

A translation of Ovid's narrative collection of tales from ancient Greek and Roman mythology tells the stories of Theseus, King Midas, Hercules, Daedalus, Icarus, and the Trojan War, among other legends.

"This is an inspired act of translation that stands as vigorous poetry in its own right." —*New York Times Book Review*

Comprises 24 stories from Metamorphoses.

Virgil
★ *The Aeneid.* Virgil; translated by Robert Fagles; introduction by Bernard Knox. Viking 2006. 496 p.
ISBN 9780670038039
Grades: 11 12 Adult **873**
1. Aeneas (Legendary character) 2. Heroes and heroines, Roman 3. Gods and goddesses, Roman 4. Warriors 5. Trojan War 6. Adventurers 7. Voyages and travels 8. Troy (Extinct city) 9. Carthage (Extinct city) 10. Ancient Rome 11. Italy 12. Bronze and Iron Ages (3500-27 B.C.E.) 13. Epic poetry 14. Classics 15. Poetry
LC 2006047220

Robert Fagles is a highly celebrated poet and translator of ancient texts. He makes Virgil's wondrous epic feel utterly relevant and modern with this stunning treatment. It is the tale of Aeneas, who flees the smoldering ashes of Troy to found a new civilization—Rome.

Previously published: Glasgow : J. Aitken & Co, 1826.

The Aeneid. Virgil; translated from the Latin by Robert Fitzgerald. Knopf 1992. xxvii, 483 p.

ESSENTIAL AND RECOMMENDED TITLES
874 Latin lyric poetry

ISBN 9780679413356
Grades: Adult **873**
1. Aeneas (Legendary character) 2. Epic poetry 3. Classics 4. Translations — Latin to English 5. Poetry

LC 91058698

Virgil's poem about the adventures of Aeneas after the fall of Troy. Includes bibliographical references (p. xxii-xxiii).

874 Latin lyric poetry

Catullus, Gaius Valerius
The Poems of Catullus. Translated by Charles Martin. Johns Hopkins University Press 1990. xxv, 181 p.
ISBN 9780801839269
Grades: Adult **874**
1. Catullus, Gaius Valerius 2. Ancient Rome 3. Arts and Entertainment — Writing and Publishing — Literary criticism

LC 89045486

Lyric poems, often inspired by the joy, pain, or disillusionment brought about by his love for Lesbia, demonstrate the evocative and satirical talents of the ancient Roman poet.

"The introduction ranges through Martin's observations on Catullus' place among Roman lyricists, his virtuosity, acuity, irony, and appeal to modern poets. The translations themselves, while open to inevitable quibbling among Latinists, are remarkably true to the versification, denotations, and connotations of the original texts. Martin is particularly adept at shaping the English into approximations of the Latin meters." —*Choice*

A limited edition of these poems was published by Abattoir Editions, the University of Nebraska at Omaha, in 1979—T.P. verso; Includes index.

Horace
Odes and Epodes. Horace; edited and translated by Niall Rudd. Harvard University Press 2004. IX, 350 p; (The Loeb classical library, 33)
ISBN 9780674996090
Grades: Adult **874**
1. Horace 2. Ancient Rome 3. Arts and Entertainment — Writing and Publishing — Literary criticism 4. Poetry

LC 2003065236

The poetry of Horace (born 65 BCE) is richly varied, its focus moving between public and private concerns, urban and rural settings, Stoic and Epicurean thought. Here is a new Loeb Classical Library edition of the great Roman poet's Odes and Epodes, a fluid translation facing the Latin text.
Includes index.

875 Latin speeches

Cicero, Marcus Tullius
Selected Works. Cicero; translated with an introduction by Michael Grant. Penguin 2004. 272 p.
ISBN 9780140440997
Grades: Adult **875**
1. Cicero, Marcus Tullius 2. History writing — Ancient — Rome 3. Society and culture — Anthropology

LC Bl2012019000

Offers a selection of writings from the Roman orator and statesman.

880.09 Classical literatures (Greek and Latin) — History

Jenkyns, Richard
Classical Literature: An Epic Journey from Homer to Virgil and Beyond. Richard Jenkyns. Basic Books, a member of the Perseus Books Group 2016. xi, 270 pages
ISBN 9780465097975

Grades: Adult **880.09**
1. Literary criticism 2. Arts and Entertainment — Writing and Publishing — Literary criticism 3. History writing — Ancient — Greece 4. History writing — Ancient — Rome

LC Bl2016007791

Introduces and discusses thousands of years of Greek and Roman literature, including Homer and the birth of epic poetry, how Aeschylus developed tragedy, and the love poems of Catullus.

Offers a dynamic and comprehensive introduction to a thousand years of Greek and Roman literature.

"A rich, witty, perceptive, and brief account of the Greek and Latin classics and their importance, both in themselves and in their enduring influence on the Western world. One of the best introductions available to the general reader." —*Library Journal*

Includes bibliographical references (pages 247-259) and index.

881 Classical Greek poetry

Hesiod
Works and Days; and Theogony. Hesiod; translated by Stanley Lombardo; with introduction, notes, and glossary by Robert Lamberton. Hackett Pub. Co. 1993. 128 p.
ISBN 9780872201798
Grades: Adult **881**
1. Hesiod 2. Agriculture 3. Translations — Greek to English 4. Poetry

LC 93024545

"This is a translation of two ancient Greek poems. Theogony is a genealogy of the Greek gods and some of their myths, and the Works and Days is a meditation on work, justice, and the gods, together with a farmer's almanac of the ancient agricultural year. For a literal rendition of the Greek, readers should turn elsewhere, but those who want a translation that captures something of the spirit of an ancient Greek poetic voice and its cultural milieu and transmits it in an appealing, lively, and accessible style will now turn to Lombardo." —*Choice*

Includes bibliographical references.

882 Classical Greek dramatic poetry and drama

Aeschylus
The Oresteia. Aeschylus; translated by Alan Shapiro and Peter Burian. Oxford University Press 2003. IX, 285 p.
ISBN 9780195135923
Grades: Adult **882**
1. Aeschylus 2. Agamemnon (Greek mythology) 3. Orestes (Greek mythology) 4. Electra (Greek mythology) 5. Drama 6. Arts and Entertainment — Writing and Publishing

LC 2002066272

"The collaboration of poet and scholar... produces a language that is easy to read and easy to speak." —*Library Journal*

Includes bibliographical references (p. 281-285).

883 Classical Greek epic poetry and fiction

Alexander, Caroline
The War That Killed Achilles: The True Story of Homer's Iliad. Caroline Alexander. Viking 2009. 320 p.
ISBN 9780670021123
Grades: Adult **883**
1. Homer 2. War in literature 3. Trojan War 4. Achilles (Greek mythology) 5. Mythology 6. Literary criticism 7. Ancient Greece 8. Bronze and Iron Ages (3500-27 B.C.E.) 9. History writing — Ancient — Greece 10. Arts and Entertainment — Writing and Publishing — Literary criticism

LC 2009020160

Many have forgotten that the subject of the "Illiad" was war—not merely the poetical romance of the war at Troy, but war, in all its enduring devastation. This groundbreaking reading of Homer's epic poem restores the poet's vision of the tragedy of war, addressing many of the central questions that define the war experience of every age.

"In its bones and sinews, the book is a nobly bold, even rousing, venture, a read-through of the Iliad, from beginning to end, always with a sharp eye to half a century of revealing scholarship, by great Hellenists like Gregory Nagy, Jasper Griffin, M.L. West and many others. The book's best ideas won't be new to readers versed in this work, but it would be hard to find a faster, livelier, more compact introduction to such a great range of recent Iliadic explorations." —*New York Times Book Review*

Includes bibliographical references and index.

Homer

The Iliad. Homer; translated by Robert Fagles; introduction and notes by Bernard Knox. Viking 1990. xvi, 683 p.
ISBN 9780670835102
Grades: 8 9 10 11 12 Adult   883
1. Achilles (Greek mythology) 2. Trojan War 3. Classics 4. Epic poetry 5. Translations — Greek to English 6. Epics and hero tales — Greece 7. Mythology — Classical — Greek 8. Poetry
LC 89070695

The centuries-old epic about the wrath of Achilles is rendered into modern English verse by a renowned translator.

"Fagles offers a new verse rendering of the Iliad. Maneuvering between the literal and the literary, he tries with varying degrees of success to suggest the vigor and manner of the original while producing readable poetry in English." —*Library Journal*

Includes bibliographical references (p. 635-637).

The Iliad. Homer; translated by Robert Fitzgerald; with an introduction by Gregory Nagy. Knopf 1992. xxv, 594 p.
ISBN 9780679410751
Grades: 11 12 Adult   883
1. War 2. Achilles (Greek mythology) 3. Trojan War 4. Ancient Aegean civilizations (3000-1000 B.C.E.) 5. Classics 6. Epic poetry 7. Translations — Greek to English 8. Page to screen 9. Poetry
LC 91053222

Recounts the triumphs and defeats of the Greek and Trojan heroes during the Trojan War and the destruction of Troy by combined Greek armies.

"Fitzgerald has solved virtually every problem that has plagued translators of Homer. The narrative runs, the dialogue speaks, the military action is clear, and the repetitive epithets become useful text rather than exotic relics. Aside from the ability to write poetry, which is basic to the undertaking, Mr. Fitzgerald's success derives from the use of a predominantly Anglo-Saxon vocabulary, a concentration on specific meanings, and an occasional arbitrary, but highly effective, substitution of implication for literal sense." —*The Atlantic*

Later film version: Troy; Translated by Robert Fitzgerald with an introduction by Gregory Nagy; Includes bibliographical references (p. xxiii-xxv).

Iliad. Homer; translated by Stanley Lombardo; introduction by Sheila Murnaghan. Hackett Pub. Co. 1997. LVII, 516 p. : Map
ISBN 9780872203525
Grades: 11 12 Adult   883
1. Achilles (Greek mythology) 2. Trojan War 3. Classics 4. Epic poetry 5. Translations — Greek to English 6. Epics and hero tales — Greece 7. Mythology — Classical — Greek 8. Poetry
LC 96053368

"Lombardo manages to be respectful of Homer's dire spirit while providing on nearly every page some wonderfully fresh refashioning of his Greek. The result is a vivid and sometimes disarmingly hard-bitten reworking of a great classic. Not all of Lombardo's gambles pay off, and his attention-grabbing colloquialisms sometimes undermine the force of the original. Still, the success of so many of Lombardo's choices more than makes up for the false notes." —*New York Times Book Review*

Includes bibliographical references (p. 514-516) and index.

★ *The Iliad*. Homer; translated by Emily Wilson. W.W. Norton & Company 2023. 760 p.
ISBN 9781324001805
Grades: Adult   883
1. Trojan War 2. Oracles, Greek 3. Warriors 4. Generals 5. Heroes and heroines 6. Gods and goddesses 7. Jealousy 8. Men-women relations 9. Death 10. Grief 11. Fate and fatalism 12. Achilles (Greek mythology) 13. Helen of Troy (Greek mythology) 14. Agamemnon (Greek mythology) 15. Hector (Legendary character) 16. Troy (Extinct city) 17. Ancient Greece 18. Ancient Aegean civilizations (3000-1000 B.C.E.) 19. Epic poetry 20. Translations — Greek to English 21. Page to screen 22. Poetry

The greatest literary landmark of antiquity masterfully rendered by the most celebrated translator of our time.

"A bloody tale of ancient war and grief comes to vibrant life in modern-day English." —*Kirkus*

Includes bibliographical references.

The Odyssey. Homer; translated by Robert Fitzgerald; introduction by D.S. Carne-Ross. Farrar, Straus and Giroux 1998. LXX, 515 pages : Map
ISBN 9780374525743
Grades: 9 10 11 12 Adult   883
1. Heroes and heroines, Greek 2. Gods and goddesses, Greek 3. Voyages and travels 4. Odysseus (Greek mythology) 5. Ancient Aegean civilizations (3000-1000 B.C.E.) 6. Epic poetry 7. Page to screen 8. Classics 9. Poetry
LC 98-73703

Presents the classic poem concerning the wanderings of the hero Odysseus and his miraculous return to Ithaca and a faithful wife.

The 2000 film entitled O brother, where art thou? is loosely based on this book; Includes bibliographical references (pages 511-512).

The Odyssey. Homer; translated by Robert Fagles; introduction and notes by Bernard Knox. Viking 1996. x, 541 p.
ISBN 9780670821624
Grades: 8 9 10 11 12 Adult   883
1. Heroes and heroines, Greek 2. Adventurers 3. Voyages and travels 4. Odysseus (Greek mythology) 5. Gods and goddesses, Greek 6. Trojan War 7. Troy (Extinct city) 8. Ancient Greece 9. Ancient Aegean civilizations (3000-1000 B.C.E.) 10. Epic poetry 11. Page to screen 12. Classics 13. Poetry
LC 96017280

New York Times Notable Book, 1997.

A new verse translation of the Greek classic describes the wanderings of Odysseus after the fall of Troy.

"Fagles' Odyssey is the one to put into the hands of younger, first-time readers, not least because of its paucity of notes, which, though sometimes frustrating, is a sign that translation has been used to do the work of explanation. Altogether, an outstanding piece of work." —*Booklist*

The 2000 film entitled O brother, where art thou? is loosely based on this book; Includes bibliographical references.

Odyssey. Homer; translated by Stanley Lombardo; introduction by Sheila Murnaghan. Hackett Pub. Co. 2000. LXIV, 414 p. : Illustration; Map
ISBN 9780872204850
Grades: 11 12 Adult   883
1. Adventurers 2. Gods and goddesses, Greek 3. Voyages and travels 4. Odysseus (Greek mythology) 5. Heroes and heroines, Greek 6. Monsters 7. Romantic love 8. Ancient Aegean civilizations (3000-1000 B.C.E.) 9. Epic poetry 10. Page to screen 11. Classics 12. Epics and hero tales — Greece 13. Poetry
LC 99054175

New York Times Notable Book, 2000.

"Lombardo has brought his laconic wit and love of the ribald, as well as his clever use of idiomatic American slang, to his version of the Odyssey. His carefully honed syntax gives the narrative energy and a whirlwind pace. The lines,

ESSENTIAL AND RECOMMENDED TITLES
884 Classical Greek lyric poetry

rhythmic and clipped, have the tautness and force of Odysseus' bow." —*New York Times Book Review*

The 2000 film entitled O brother, where art thou? is loosely based on this book; Includes bibliographical references (p. 412-414) and index; Translated from the Greek.

★ *The Odyssey*. Homer; translated by Emily Wilson. W. W. Norton & Co. 2018. 582 pages
ISBN 9780393089059
Grades: Adult   883
1. Heroes and heroines, Greek 2. Adventurers 3. Ocean travel 4. Seafaring life 5. Civilization, Ancient 6. Veterans 7. Husband and wife 8. Gods and goddesses, Greek 9. Odysseus (Greek mythology) 10. Ancient Greece 11. Ancient Aegean civilizations (3000-1000 B.C.E.) 12. Epic poetry 13. Classics 14. Translations — Greek to English 15. Page to screen 16. Poetry
LC 2017027185

New York Times Notable Book, 2018.

A new translation of the epic poem, and the first by a woman, brings alive Homer's tale of shipwrecks, monsters, and magic, and provides an introductory overview of the poem's major themes, controversial origin, and the scope of its influence.

"Wilson's goal is for the work to sound natural to the modern reader without falling into contemporizing anachronisms, such as those found in the translation of Stanley Lombardo." —*Library Journal*

The Odyssey. Homer; translated, with an introduction and notes, by Stephen Mitchell. Atria Books 2013. xlv, 375 pages : Map
ISBN 9781451674170
Grades: Adult   883
1. Epic poetry 2. Translations — Greek to English 3. Poetry
LC 2012050572

A new translation of Homer's epic adventure endeavors to instill the poetic nature of its original language while retaining accuracy, readability, and character vibrancy.

Includes bibliographical references.

Manguel, Alberto
Homer's the Iliad and the Odyssey: A Biography. Alberto Manguel. Atlantic Monthly Press 2007. x, 285 p.
ISBN 9780871139764
Grades: Adult   883
1. Homer 2. Odysseus, King of Ithaca (Mythological character) 3. Trojan War 4. Arts and Entertainment — Writing and Publishing 5. Poetry
LC 2013443263

An insightful analysis of the two great epic poems that have served as the cornerstone of Western literature traces the history of the Iliad and the Odyssey from their earliest origins, the colorful characters and events chronicling the Trojan War and its aftermath, and their important legacy for Western culture.

Examines "The Iliad" and "The Odyssey" from their origins, the colorful characters and events chronicling the Trojan War and its aftermath, and their legacy for Western culture.

"A study of the influence of the Iliad and the Odyssey on Western literature. First describing the two epics and the Homer question, Manguel then compares various translations in English, Spanish, French, and German, a move that brings out the complexities and richness of Homer's language. Does the poet sing of the rage, wrath, anger, rancor, or mania of Achilles? Then, following a more or less chronological progression, Manguel surveys the various shifting interpretations of the epics from Plato and Virgil to the present, including extended discussions of Derek Walcott, Timothy Findley, and Jorge Luis Borges. Highly recommended for general readers." —*Library Journal*

Includes bibliographical references and index.

Nicolson, Adam
Why Homer Matters. by Adam Nicolson. Henry Holt and Company 2014. 288 p.
ISBN 9781627791793
Grades: Adult   883

1. Homer 2. Poets 3. Europe 4. Arts and Entertainment — Writing and publishing 5. History writing — Ancient — Greece 6. Arts and Entertainment — Writing and Publishing — Literary criticism
LC 2014006763

Taking readers on an extraordinary journey through mythical and modern landscapes, the author of a celebrated column for the Sunday Telegraph explores the places forever haunted by their Homeric heroes and reveals the real roots of Homeric consciousness.

"Nicholson writes in a clear, fluid prose with apparently effortless ease; his vivid descriptions of landscapes and archaeological remains and his passionate engagement with history make this book a page-turner. Classicists will no doubt find fault with some of Nicholson's statements, but they will also be grateful to the author for explaining to the larger public in such an appealing fashion why Homer is not only unique but also relevant and necessary today. Summing Up: Highly recommended. General readers." —*Choice*

A John Macrae book; Includes bibliographical references and index.

884 Classical Greek lyric poetry

Sappho
If Not, Winter: Fragments of Sappho. Translated by Anne Carson. Vintage Books 2003. xiii, 397 p.
ISBN 9780375724510
Grades: Adult   884
1. Translations — Greek to English 2. Poetry
LC Bl2013026362

A critically acclaimed poet and classicist presents a dramatic new translation of the poetry of Sappho, presenting all the extant fragments that exist of the ancient poet's works in both English and the original Greek and furnishing an incisive introduction to Sappho's life and times.

"Much of what survives of Sappho are fragments, often just a stray word, phrase, or even a few letters. Like many modern poets, Carson deploys these on the blank page, letting their suggestiveness fill the gaps and create whole lyrics in the imagination of the readers." —*Library Journal*

Originally published: New York : Alfred A. Knopf, 2002; Includes bibliographical references (p. 357-383); Translated from the Ancient Greek.

889 Modern Greek literature

Cavafy, Constantine
The Collected Poems. C.P. Cavafy; translated by Evangelos Sachperoglou; Greek text edited by Anthony Hirst; with an introduction by Peter Mackridge. Oxford University Press 2007. xlviii, 238 p.
ISBN 9780199212927
Grades: Adult   889
1. Cavafy, Constantine, 1863-1933 2. Translations — Greek to English 3. Poetry
LC 2007015833

The only bilingual edition of Cavafy's collected poems currently available, this volume presents the most authentic Greek text of every poem he ever published, together with a new English translation that beautifully conveys the accent and rhythm of Cavafy's individual tone of voice.

Includes bibliographical references (p. [xlii]-xliv) and indexes; Poems in Greek and in English translation.

891 East Indo-European and Celtic literatures

Hafiz
★ *The Gift: Poems by the Great Sufi Master*. Hafiz; translated from the Persian by Daniel James Ladinsky. Arkana 1999. xvi, 333 p.
ISBN 9780140195811
Grades: Adult   891
1. Translations — Persian to English 2. Religious poetry 3. Poetry

Celebrates one of Islam's greatest poetic voices and renowned spiritual leaders with a collection of 250 mystical healing poems.

Firdawsi
Shahnameh: *The Persian Book of Kings.* Abolqasem Ferdowsi; translated by Dick Davis; with a foreword by Azar Nafisi. Viking 2006. xxxvii, 886 p. : Illustration
ISBN 9780670034857
Grades: Adult 891
1. Rulers 2. Fathers and sons 3. Heroes and heroines 4. Inheritance and succession 5. Southwest Asia and North Africa (Middle East) history 6. Iran 7. Bronze and Iron Ages (3500-27 B.C.E.) 8. Translations — Persian to English
LC 2005042352

A new translation of the late-tenth-century Persian epic follows its story of pre-Islamic Iran's mythic time of creation through the seventh-century Arab invasion, tracing ancient Persia's incorporation into an expanding Islamic empire. Includes index.

Jalal al-Din Rumi
The ***Essential*** *Rumi.* Translated by Coleman Barks, with John Moyne, A.A. Arberry, Reynold Nicholson. Harper 1995. 302 p.
ISBN 9780062509598
Grades: Adult 891
1. Jalal al-Din Rumi, Maulana, 1207-1273 2. Translations — Persian to English 3. Poetry
LC 94044995

A collection of poetry by the thirteenth century Sufi saint cover topics ranging from emptiness and silence to elegance and majesty.

A Sufi poet's comprehensive work is translated here in a volume designed to bring all the magic, mysticism, and wisdom of the great Sufi poet's work to an English-speaking audience.

Includes bibliographical references (p. 297-302) and index.

Rumi: *Bridge to the Soul : Journeys into the Music and Silence of the Heart.* Translations by Coleman Barks, with A.J. Arberry and Nevit Ergin. HarperOne 2007. x, 148 p. : Illustration
ISBN 9780061338168
Grades: Adult 891
1. Religious poetry 2. Spirituality and Religion — Islam
LC 2007018384

A new collection of poems by the great Sufi mystic, the majority of which have never been published previously, is in celebration of the master writer's eight hundredth birthday and is accompanied by a description of the interpreter's culturally rich visit to Iran at the side of the poet Robert Bly.

Includes bibliographical references (p. 147-148).

Rumi: *The Big Red Book : The Great Masterpiece Celebrating Mystical Love and Friendship.* the collected translations of Coleman Barks, based on the work of John Moyne … [et al.]. HarperOne 2010. 492 p.
ISBN 9780061905827
Grades: Adult 891
1. Jall al-Dn Rm, Maulana, 1207-1273 2. Translations — Persian to English 3. Poetry
LC 2010007895

Rumi's "Divani Shamsi Tabriz" ("The Works of Shams of Tabriz"—Named in honor of Rumi's spiritual teacher and friend) is a collection of lyric poems that contain more than 40,000 verses by America's bestselling poet, and is a classic of Persian literature. Its most familiar form is as a big red book, hence the name. Coleman Barks is famous for his renderings of Rumi's poetry and his work on these particular poems has never been published anywhere. This book represents over thirty-three years on Rumi's seminal classic.

A volume of seminal renderings of previously unpublished poems by the medieval Sufi mystic compiles more than three decades of work by Barks and offers insight into Rumi's use of lyrical language and the influence of historical Persian culture on his achievements.

Odes and Quatrains from the Shams; Includes bibliographical references and index; Translated from the Persian.

Rumi: *Unseen Poems.* Translated and edited by Brad Gooch and Maryam Mortaz. Alfred A. Knopf 2019. 224 pages
ISBN 9781101908105
Grades: Adult 891
1. Rumi, Jalal al-Din, 1207-1273 2. Love 3. Spiritual life 4. Islam 5. Sufism 6. Mysticism 7. Faith (Islam) 8. Translations — Persian to English 9. Poetry
LC 2019013642

A collection of never-before-translated poems by the widely beloved medieval Persian poet Rumi.

Translated from the Persian.

Omar Khayyam
Rubaiyat *of Omar Khayyam.* Rendered into English verse by Edward Fitz-Gerald; with illustrations by Edmund J. Sullivan. St. Martin's Press 1983. 75 p. : Illustration
ISBN 9780312695279
Grades: 11 12 Adult 891
1. Poetry
LC 83009767

Contains the English edition of the eleventh-century Persian poet's quatrains that express his philosophy of love and life.

Translation of: Rubaiyat.

Tagore, Rabindranath
Selected *Poems.* Rabindranath Tagore; translated from the Bengali by William Radice. Penguin Books 2005. 202 p.
ISBN 9780140449884
Grades: Adult 891
1. Tagore, Rabindranath, 1861-1941 2. Translations — Bengali to English 3. Poetry
LC Oc2007026863

Poems such as 'Earth' and 'In the Eyes of a Peacock' present a picture of natural processes unaffected by human concerns, while others, as in 'Recovery—14', convey the poet's bewilderment about his place in the world.

Includes bibliographical references (p. 10-13); Translated from the Bengali.

891.7 Russian literature and related East Slavic literatures

Batuman, Elif
The ***Possessed:*** *Adventures with Russian Books and the People Who Read Them.* Elif Batuman. Farrar, Straus and Giroux 2010. 304 p.
ISBN 9780374532185
Grades: Adult 891.7
1. Authors, Russian 2. Writing 3. Books and reading 4. Readers 5. Reading 6. Essays 7. Arts and Entertainment — Writing and Publishing 8. Arts and Entertainment — Writing and Publishing — Literary criticism
LC 2009025416

New York Times Notable Book, 2010.

An award-winning Stanford University literary professor documents the stories of individuals who have dedicated their lives in occasionally absurd ways to pay tribute to Russian classics.

"In this book, the author makes you look at Russian literature from a fresh perspective, using an unusual blend of memoir and travelogue as she delves into the lives and personalities of such Russian literary giants as Isaac Babel, Fyodor Dostoevsky and Leo Tolstoy. … in a sense, the details of Batuman's essays are less significant than the tone. She cruises through minor crises with an air of detached amusement, eye focused on the little absurdities that make travel—and people—fun." —*Cleveland Plain Dealer*

ESSENTIAL AND RECOMMENDED TITLES
891.71 Russian poetry

Blaisdell, Robert
Creating Anna Karenina: Tolstoy and the Birth of Literature's Most Enigmatic Heroine. Bob Blaisdell. Pegasus Books 2020. xxiii, 389 pages, 8 unnumbered pages of plates : Illustration; Color
ISBN 9781643134628
Grades: Adult   891.7
1. Tolstoy, Leo, graf, 1828-1910 2. Characters and characteristics in literature 3. Authors, Russian 4. Creation (Literary, artistic, etc.) 5. Fiction writing 6. Women in literature 7. Family relationships 8. Marriage 9. Interpersonal relations 10. Suicidal behavior 11. Literary criticism 12. Biographies 13. Life stories — Arts and culture — Writing — Authors 14. Arts and Entertainment — Writing and Publishing

The story behind the origins of Anna Karenina and the turbulent life and times of Leo Tolstoy.

"Tolstoy comes to life as a complex individual defying easy classification. Tolstoy's fans will relish learning from, and, occasionally, arguing with Blaisdell's opinions. This passionate book is almost impossible to put down." —Publishers Weekly

Includes bibliographical references (pages [375]-377) and index.

Saunders, George
★ *A Swim* in a Pond in the Rain: In Which Four Russians Give a Master Class on Writing, Reading, and Life. George Saunders. Random House 2021. 432 p.
ISBN 9781984856029
Grades: Adult   891.7
1. Gogol, Nikolai Vasilievich, 1809-1852 2. Chekhov, Anton Pavlovich, 1860-1904 3. Turgenev, Ivan Sergeevich, 1818-1883 4. Tolstoy, Leo, graf, 1828-1910 5. Fiction writing 6. Short story writing 7. Creative writing 8. Short stories 9. Arts and Entertainment — Writing and Publishing
LC 2020031045

In A Swim in a Pond in the Rain, George Saunders guides the reader through seven classic Russian short stories he's been teaching for twenty years as a professor in the prestigious Syracuse University graduate MFA creative writing program. Paired with stories by Chekhov, Turgenev, Tolstoy, and Gogol, these essays are intended for anyone interested in how fiction works and why it's more relevant than ever in these turbulent times. Funny, frank, and rigorous, a Swim in a Pond in the Rain ultimately shows how great fiction can change a person's life and become a benchmark of one's moral and ethical beliefs.

"An invaluable and uniquely pleasurable master course and a generous celebration of reading, writing, and all the ways literature enriches our lives." —Booklist

Includes texts of seven short stories; Includes bibliographical references.

891.71 Russian poetry

Akhmatova, Anna Andreevna
★ *The* **Complete** *Poems of Anna Akhmatova*. Translated by Judith Hemschemeyer; edited by Roberta Reeder. Zephyr Press; 1992. 908 p. : Illustration
ISBN 9780939010271
Grades: Adult   891.71
1. Russian people 2. Translations — Russian to English 3. Arts and Entertainment — Writing and Publishing — Literary criticism 4. Poetry
LC 92062648

The present edition adds 80 new poetic texts which came to light at the end of 1990, as well as numerous photographs, and a 16-page portfolio portraying the poet through the eyes of painters, sculptors, and other artists.

Includes bibliographical references (p. 907-908) and index.

Poems: Poems. Akhmatova; translated from the Russian by D.M. Thomas. Knopf 2006. 256 p.
ISBN 9780307264244
Grades: Adult   891.71
1. Akhmatova, Anna Andreevna, 1889-1966 2. Women authors 3. 20th century 4. Translations — Russian to English 5. Poetry

LC 2006297217

A definitive body of work by one of the great Russian poets of the twentieth century includes poetry from all of her major collections, including "Requiem," a memorial to the victims of Stalin's terror, as well as twenty poems that have been newly translated for this collection.

This selection first published, under the title You will hear thunder, in Great Britain by Martin Secker & Warburg Ltd, 1985—T.P. verso.

Pushkin, Aleksandr Sergeevich
Eugene Onegin: And Other Poems. Pushkin; translated from the Russian by Charles Johnston. Knopf 1999. 240 p.
ISBN 9780375406720
Grades: Adult   891.71
1. Translations — Russian to English 2. Poetry
LC BL 99006547

Two brief poems accompany a long narrative poem about a heartless fop who is the object of an ardent young woman's selfless love.

TSvetaeva, Marina
Selected Poems. Marina TSvetayeva; translated from the Russian and introduced by Elaine Feinstein; with literal versions provided by Angela Livingstone ... [et al.]. Penguin Books 1994. xviii, 131 p.
ISBN 9780140187595
Grades: Adult   891.71
1. TSvetaeva, Marina, 1892-1941 2. Women authors 3. Translations — Russian to English 4. Poetry
LC BL 00003448

An admired contemporary of Rilke, Akhmatova, and Mandelstam, Marina Tsvetaeva was a witness to the political turmoil and the social devastation wrought by the Russian Revolution and a powerfully inspired chronicler of a difficult life and exile sustained by poetry.

Originally published: Oxford; New York : Oxford University Press, 1993. (Oxford poets).

891.72 Russian drama

Chekhov, Anton Pavlovich
Chekhov: The Four Major Plays. in new translations by Curt Columbus. Ivan R. Dee 2005. 294 p.
ISBN 9781566636261
Grades: Adult   891.72
1. Chekhov, Anton Pavlovich, 1860-1904 2. Arts and Entertainment — Writing and Publishing — Literary criticism
LC 2004048612

Curt Columbus endows these timeless dramas, Seagull, Uncle Vanya, Three Sisters and Cherry Orchard, with dialogue that is faithful to the Russian original but dazzlingly attuned to contemporary audiences.

The **Complete** *Plays.* Anton Chekhov; translated, edited, and annotated by Laurence Senelick. W.W. Norton 2007. LX, 1060 p.
ISBN 9780393330694
Grades: Adult   891.72
1. Chekhov, Anton Pavlovich, 1860-1904 2. Arts and Entertainment — Theater — Plays
LC Bl2008007029

A single-volume, English-language collection of all of Chekhov's plays includes previously untranslated pieces including the Power of Hypnosis, a first version of Ivanov, and early humorous dialogues.

Includes bibliographical references; Reprint. Originally published: C2006.

Malcolm, Janet
Reading Chekhov: A Critical Journey. Janet Malcolm. Random House 2001. 209 p.
ISBN 9780375506680
Grades: 11 12 Adult   891.72

1. Chekhov, Anton Pavlovich, 1860-1904 2. Voyages and travels 3. Russia 4. Arts and Entertainment — Writing and Publishing 5. Travel Writing — Europe

LC 2001019585

New York Times Notable Book, 2002.

A biographical study of the Russian literary master and his works is set against the backdrop of a modern-day journey to Russia and the various places where Anton Chekhov lived and worked, reflecting on the characters and ideas her created in his remarkable short stories and plays. 25,000 first printing.

"The author's pilgrimage to Chekhov's Russia—Moscow, St. Petersburg, the gardens of his villa in Yalta—is a reunion with this most reticent of literary fathers. Malcolm analyzes the transformations that Chekhov grants his redeemable rogues and guileless heroines, and illuminates the hidden surreality and waywardness of his realism." —The New Yorker

Includes bibliographical references (p. [207]-[210]).

891.73 Russian fiction

Finn, Peter
The Zhivago Affair: The Kremlin, the Cia, and the Battle Over a Forbidden Book. Peter Finn and Petra Couvee. Pantheon Books 2014. 352 pages
ISBN 9780307908001
Grades: Adult 891.73
1. Pasternak, Boris Leonidovich, 1890-1960 2. Authors, Russian 3. Dissenters 4. Cold War 5. Banned books 6. Politics and literature 7. International relations 8. Politics and government 9. Soviet Union 10. United States 11. 20th century 12. History writing — Cold War 13. History writing — Europe — Russia 14. Arts and Entertainment — Writing and Publishing

LC 2013033875

National Book Critics Circle Award for Nonfiction finalist, 2014.

Doctor Zhivago, a novel published in translation during the late 1950s by Russian author Boris Pasternak, created a sensation in the West with its negative depiction of the Russian Revolution. The CIA recognized that the book could promote anti-Communist sentiment within the Soviet Union, so they arranged to produce copies of the original Russian text and sneak them into Russia. The Zhivago Affair relates the exciting story of how the book-smuggling was accomplished, the severe consequences the Kremlin imposed on Pasternak and his family, and the international controversy aroused by the novel.

"Drawing on recently declassified CIA documents, Finn and Couve present an engaging thriller, in which bureaucratic obstructions and Cold War politics threaten the publication of a controversial masterpiece of world literature." —Booklist

Includes bibliographical references (pages 325-335) and index.

891.8 Slavic (Slavonic) literatures

Herbert, Zbigniew
The Collected Poems, 1956-1998. Zbigniew Herbert; translated and edited by Alissa Valles; with additional translations by Czeslaw Milosz and Peter Dale Scott; introduction by Adam Zagajewski. Ecco 2007. xviii, 600 p.
ISBN 9780060783907
Grades: Adult 891.8
1. 19th century 2. Translations — Polish to English 3. Poetry

LC 2006040856

A new translation of poetic works by the Polish Nobel Prize candidate includes pieces from his entire body of work, from String of Light to Epilogue of the Storm, in a volume that offers insight into his perspectives on such topics as imagination, art, and exile.

Includes index.

Milosz, Czeslaw
★ *Milosz's Abc's.* Czeslaw Milosz; translated from the Polish by Madeline G. Levine. Farrar, Straus and Giroux 2001. 313 p.
ISBN 9780374199777

Grades: Adult 891.8
1. Milosz, Czeslaw 2. Authors, Polish 3. Poland 4. 20th century

LC 00042176

New York Times Notable Book, 2001.

Presents a collection of musings on a variety of subjects, listed alphabetically, including literary characters, historical figures, and real and imagined places.

"The short prose entries in this quiet book take note of some of the people and places and ideas that contributed to the making of Milosz. The subjects of his sketches range from Alchemy and Curiosity to Rimbaud and Whitman, from childhood friends to Polish intellectuals little known in the West. But what could have been no more than a light memory work becomes almost a registry of gratitude: a meditation on the obligations of having lived a life and the responsibilities inherent in its particulars." —The New Yorker

Translation of selections from the author's Abecadlo Milosza and Inne abecadlo.

Sosnowski, Andrzej
Lodgings: Selected Poems, 1987-2010. Andrzej Sosnowski; translated from the Polish by Benjamin Paloff. Open Letter 2011. xi, 163 p.
ISBN 9781934824320
Grades: Adult 891.8
1. Translations — Polish to English 2. Poetry

LC 2010052054

First collection in English of the foremost Polish poet of his generation.

Szymborska, Wislawa
Here. Wislawa Szymborska; translated from the Polish by Clare Cavanagh and Stanislaw Baraczak. Houghton Mifflin Harcourt 2010. 85 p.
ISBN 9780547364612
Grades: Adult 891.8
1. Translations — Polish to English 2. Poetry

LC 2010018889

A collection of poems covering aspects of life as varied as Vermeer's "Milkmaid," miniseries, and the apocalypse.

"Szymborska writes pithy, mischievous, and wise poems that disarm, delight, and enlighten in a flash even as they illuminate hidden dimensions of existence. She writes of her teenage self, the earth's astounding bounty, accidents, nature's innocence, and time. Szymborska is sharply ironic and lithely philosophical, pondering the phenomenal precision of dreams and the elusiveness of meaning. The neat, prancing lyrics collected in this slender, piercing book are delectable and profound." —Booklist

Polish and English.

Map: Collected and Last Poems. Wislawa Szymborska; translated from the Polish by Clare Cavanagh and Stanislaw Baraczak; edited by Clare Cavanagh. Houghton Mifflin Harcourt 2015. xiv, 447 pages
ISBN 9780544126022
Grades: Adult 891.8
1. Translations — Polish to English 2. Poetry

LC 2015297265

Collects translations of poems from throughout the author's career, including several new translations, including her entire final collection in English for the first time.

"Throughout, Szymborska considers loss and fragility, as when former lovers walk past each other and an aging professor is no longer allowed his vodka and cigarettes. She writes, too, of the imprecision of memory, and in the title poem, the discovery that maps 'Give no access to the vicious truth.' This is a brilliant and important collection." —Booklist

Includes index; Translated from the Polish.

Zagajewski, Adam
Eternal Enemies. Adam Zagajewski; translated from the Polish by Clare Cavanagh. Farrar, Straus and Giroux 2008. 116 p.
ISBN 9780374216344
Grades: Adult 891.8

ESSENTIAL AND RECOMMENDED TITLES
892 Afro-Asiatic literatures

1. Zagajewski, Adam, 1945-2021 2. Translations — Polish to English 3. Poetry
LC 2007042855

An anthology of poetry reflects on place, language, and history in a collection that includes tributes to such writers as Milosz, Sebald, Brodsky, and Blake, as well as portraits of family members and other loved ones.

892 Afro-Asiatic literatures

Darwish, Mahmoud
★ *Unfortunately, It Was Paradise: Selected Poems.* Mahmoud Darwish; translated and edited by Munir Akash and Carolyn Forche; with Sinan Antoon and Amira El-Zein. University of California Press 2003. xix, 191 p.
ISBN 9780520237544
Grades: Adult   892
1. Translations — Arabic to English 2. Poetry
LC 2002068454

Mahmoud Darwish is a literary rarity: at once critically acclaimed as one of the most important poets in the Arabic language, and beloved as the voice of his people. He is a living legend whose lyrics are sung by fieldworkers and schoolchildren. He has assimilated some of the world's oldest literary traditions at the same time that he has struggled to open new possibilities for poetry. This collection spans Darwish's entire career, nearly four decades, revealing an impressive range of expression and form. A splendid team of translators has collaborated with the poet on these new translations, which capture Darwish's distinctive voice and spirit.

892.4 Hebrew literature

Amichai, Yehuda
Open Closed Open: Poems. Yehuda Amichai; translated from the Hebrew by Chana Bloch and Chana Kronfeld. Harcourt 2000. VI, 184 p.
ISBN 9780151003785
Grades: Adult   892.4
1. Amichai, Yehuda 2. Translations — Hebrew to English 3. Poetry
LC 00023537

A new anthology of poetry by Israel's leading poet offers meditative, lyrical, and playful observations on the language of love, Jerusalem, beauty, and the Jewish experience.

Qashu, Sayed
Native: Dispatches from an Israeli-palestinian Life. Sayed Kashua; translated from the Hebrew by Ralph Mandel. Grove Press 2016. 304 p.
ISBN 9780802124555
Grades: Adult   892.4
1. Qashu, Sayed, 1975- 2. Arab-Israeli conflict 3. Prejudice 4. Historiography 5. Palestinian people 6. Israel 7. Essays 8. Autobiographies and memoirs 9. Translations — Hebrew to English 10. Life stories — Arts and culture — Writing — Authors 11. Politics and global affairs — World politics — Southwest Asia and North Africa (Middle East) — Israel and Palestine
LC B12016000992

Collects translations of the the author's weekly columns written for the Israeli newspaper, Haaretz, that offer a nuanced exploration of the life of an Israeli-Palestinian and the contradictions of modern Israel.

"A wickedly ironic but humane collection." —*Kirkus*

Translation from the Hebrew of: Ben haaretz.

892.7 Arabic and Maltese literatures

Adunis
Concerto Al-quds. Adonis; translated from the Arabic by Khaled Mattawa. Yale University Press 2017. 85 p.
ISBN 9780300197648

Grades: Adult   892.7
1. Jerusalem, Israel 2. Translations — Arabic to English 3. Poetry
LC 2017941088

"In this stunning volume about Jerusalem (al-Quds in Arabic), Syrian poet Adonis, who has been hailed as a founding voice in Arabic-language modernism, envisions the poem as a space for dialogue between traditions, nations, and historical milieux." —*Publishers Weekly*

Includes bibliographical references (pages 69-83); Translated from the Arabic.

Darwish, Mahmoud
If I Were Another. Mahmoud Darwish; translated from the Arabic by Fady Joudah. Farrar, Straus and Giroux 2009. xxviii, 201 p.
ISBN 9780374174293
Grades: Adult   892.7
1. Translations — Arabic to English 2. Poetry
LC 2009011521

Contains translations of the popular Palestinian poet's work focusing on themes including loss and exile.

Includes bibliographical references.

895 Literatures of East and Southeast Asia

Rexroth, Kenneth
One Hundred Poems from the Japanese. Kenneth Rexroth. New Directions 1955. 143 p.
ISBN 9780811201810
Grades: Adult   895
1. Japanese poetry 2. Translations — Japanese to English 3. Poetry — Collections
LC 56002557

A collection of Japanese poems accompanied by their English translations.

895.6 Japanese literature

Keene, Donald
The Pleasures of Japanese Literature. Donald Keene. Columbia University Press 1988. xii, 133 p, 4 p. of plates : Color illustration
ISBN 9780231067362
Grades: Adult   895.6
1. Theater 2. Aesthetics, Japanese 3. Japan 4. Arts and Entertainment — Writing and Publishing — Literary criticism
LC 88018069

Introduces Japanese culture, and discusses the aesthetics, poetry, fiction, and theater of Japan.

"If your library has no other introduction to the Japanese classics, nor any need for another, this is the one it ought to include." —*Booklist*

Includes index; Bibliography: P. [123]-126.

895.64 Japanese essays (Literature)

Murakami, Haruki
★ *Novelist as a Vocation.* Haruki Murakami; translated from the Japanese by Philip Gabriel and Ted Goossen. Alfred A. Knopf 2022. 224 p.
ISBN 9780451494641
Grades: Adult   895.64
1. Murakami, Haruki, 1949- 2. Writing 3. Authors 4. Creativity 5. Inspiration 6. Creation (Literary, artistic, etc.) 7. Essays 8. Autobiographies and memoirs 9. Translations — Japanese to English 10. Life stories — Arts and culture — Writing — Authors 11. Arts and Entertainment — Writing and publishing
LC 2022021694

In this highly personal look at the craft of writing, an internationally best-selling author and famously reclusive writer shares his own creative process as well as his thoughts on the sparks of creativity that inspire other writers, artists and musicians.

"Although this is a concrete and practical guide, as Murakami intended, it is also a fascinating personal and professional memoir." —*Library Journal*

Originally publishing in Japanese under the title Shokugyoto shite no Shosetsuka in 2015.

901 Philosophy and theory of history

Graeber, David

The Dawn of Everything: A New History of Humanity. David Graeber and David Wengrow. Farrar, Straus & Giroux 2021. 608 p.

ISBN 9780374157357

Grades: Adult   901

1. History of civilization 2. Civilization 3. Social history 4. Social evolution 5. History 6. Sociocultural anthropology 7. Philosophy 8. History writing — Archaeology 9. History writing — General 10. Society and culture — General

LC 2021025790

An activist and public intellectual teams up with a professor of comparative archaeology to deliver an account of human history, challenging our most fundamental assumptions about social evolution—from the development of agriculture and cities to the emergence of "the state," political violence and social inequality—and revealing new possibilities for human emancipation.

"A fascinating, intellectually challenging big book about big ideas." —*Kirkus*

Includes bibliographical references and index.

Tyson, Neil deGrasse

Starry Messenger: Cosmic Perspectives on Civilization. Neil deGrasse Tyson. Henry Holt & Company 2022. 272 p.

ISBN 9781250861504

Grades: Adult   901

1. Cosmology 2. Astrophysics 3. Civilization 4. Polarization (Social sciences) 5. Social conflict 6. Science 7. Reason 8. Belief and doubt 9. Common sense 10. Perspective 11. Science writing — Astronomy 12. Society and culture — General

Bringing his cosmic perspective to civilization on Earth, an astrophysicist discusses the scientific palette that sees and paints the world differently, sharing insights on resolving global conflict to reminders of how precious it is to be alive in a universe, stimulating a deeper sense of unity for us all.

"Astrophysicist Tyson unabashedly wades into the political and cultural fray, using a 'Cosmic perspective' to weigh in on some of the topics that consume the majority of Americans today." —*Booklist*

Includes bibliographical references and index.

902 Miscellany of history

Grun, Bernard

★ *The Timetables of History: A Historical Linkage of People and Events.* Bernard Grun. Simon & Schuster 2005. 835 p.

ISBN 9780743270038

Grades: 11 12 Adult   902

1. Chronology, Historical 2. Reference books — History

LC 2005049766

Updated to cover the years 1990 through 2004, this detailed historical reference provides a chronology of seven thousand years of significant moments in history, religion, science, technology, culture, and the arts in an accessible format designed for quick reference.

"This chronology includes material from 4500 BCE to 2004. . . . The information is listed by year in seven columns labeled History, Politics, Literature, Theater, Religion, Philosophy, Learning, Visual Arts, Music, Science, Technology, Growth, and Daily Life. . . . This work is an excellent chronological tool, and should be found in all libraries." —*Choice*

A Touchstone book; Based on Werner Stein's Kulturfahrplan; Includes index.

903 Dictionaries, encyclopedias, concordances of history

Znamierowski, Alfred

The World Encyclopedia of Flags: An Illustrated Guide to International Flags, Banners, Standards and Ensigns. Alfred Znamierowski. Lorenz Books 2019. 256 pages : Color; Illustration

ISBN 9780754834809

Grades: 5 6 7 8 9 10 11 12 Adult   903

1. Flags 2. Reference books — Encyclopedias

A comprehensive reference to flags including a fascinating history, with over 1400 illustrations and newly updated in a special large-format edition.

904 Collected accounts of events

Cassidy, Cody

How to Survive History: How to Outrun a Tyrannosaurus, Escape Pompeii, Get off the Titanic, and Survive the Rest of History's Deadliest Catastrophes. Cody Cassidy. Penguin Books 2023. 240 p.

ISBN 9780143136408

Grades: Adult   904

1. Disasters 2. Civilization 3. Survival 4. History 5. Threat (Psychology) 6. History Writing — General 7. Humor Writing — General

LC 2022051160

Using hindsight and modern science for surviving history's most challenging threats, including dinosaurs, the Donner Party, the Titanic, the Black Death and the lava flows of Pompeii, this detailed resource is guaranteed to make sure you make it out alive.

"A crisp blend of humor, history, and science, this is a crowd pleaser." —*Publishers Weekly*

Includes bibliographical references.

908 History with respect to groups of people

Gates, Henry Louis

The Black Box: Writing the Race. Henry Louis Gates. Penguin Group USA 2024. 272 p.

ISBN 9780593299784

Grades: Adult   908

1. African Americans 2. African American communities 3. Communities 4. African American history 5. United States history 6. Race relations 7. Racism 8. Literary criticism 9. Ethnic identity 10. Black people 11. United States 12. Anthologies 13. Society and culture — Race

Through essays and speeches, novels, plays and poems, this epic story of Black self-definition in America is told through the myriad of writers who've led the way and who have used words to create a livable world—a "home"—for Black people destined to live out their lives in a racist society.

"Clear, revealing commentary on Black America's literary achievements." —*Kirkus*

909 World history

Boccaletti, Giulio

Water: A Biography. Giulio Boccaletti. Pantheon Books 2021. 416 p.

ISBN 9781524748234

Grades: Adult   909

ESSENTIAL AND RECOMMENDED TITLES
909 World history

1. Water 2. Civilization 3. Effect of environment on humans 4. Bodies of water 5. Water and civilization 6. Natural resources 7. Irrigation 8. Nature 9. History writing — Microhistory 10. Nature Writing — Environmental Issues
LC 2020037044

Spanning millennia and continents, here is a stunningly revealing history of how the distribution of water has shaped human civilization.

"Climate scientist Boccaletti (Sch. of Enterprise and the Environment, Oxford Univ.) weaves a detailed tapestry describing the social, economic, and political history of water, primarily in the form of rivers.... A fascinating analysis that will bridge the interests of environmentalists and historians, political scientists, or economists." —*Library Journal*

Includes bibliographical references and index.

Cahill, Thomas
Sailing the Wine-dark Sea: Why the Greeks Matter. Thomas Cahill. Nan A. Talese, Doubleday 2003. xiv, 304 p, 32 p. of plates : Illustration (Hinges of history, 4)
ISBN 9780385495530
Grades: 11 12 Adult   909
1. Civilization, Western 2. Philosophy, Ancient 3. Greek civilization 4. Ancient Greece 5. Ancient Greece (800 B.C.E.-640 C.E.) 6. History writing — Ancient — Greece 7. Adult books for young adults
LC 2003050725

Examines the remarkable legacy of the ancient Greeks, from the origins of Greek culture to the development of Western literature, drama, poetry, and philosophy to the Greek influence on human science, mathematics, and logic.

"This author begins with a discussion of Homer's Iliad and Odyssey and how these two epic poems relate to the history of Greece. He then focuses on such themes as the Greek alphabet, literature, and political system, and its playwrights, philosophers, and artists. A final chapter examines the effects that Greco-Roman and Judeo-Christian traditions had on each other." —*Booklist*

Includes bibliographical references and index.

Christian, David
Origin Story: A Big History of Everything. David Christian. Little Brown & Company 2018. 320 p.
ISBN 9780316392006
Grades: Adult   909
1. Scientific discoveries 2. Cosmology 3. Science 4. Science — General
LC 2017952230

Offers a captivating history of the universe—from before the dawn of time through the far reaches of the distant future.

Cliff, Nigel
Holy War: How Vasco Da Gama's Epic Voyages Turned the Tide in a Centuries-old Clash of Civilizations. by Nigel Cliff. Harper 2011. 480 p.
ISBN 9780061735127
Grades: Adult   909
1. Gama, Vasco da, 1469-1524 2. East and West 3. Discoveries (in geography) 4. Christianity 5. Interfaith relations 6. Explorers 7. Exploration 8. Islam 9. Africa 10. India 11. History writing — Exploration
LC 2011021331

New York Times Notable Book, 2011.

This radical new interpretation of Vasco da Gama's revolutionary voyages, which were seen as a turning point in the struggle between Christianity and Islam, presents the epic story of da Gama and his crew of adventurers that explores the tragic collision of cultures.

Later published as the last crusade: New York : HarperCollins, 2012.

Davis, Jack E.
★ *The Gulf: The Making of an American Sea.* Jack E. Davis. Liveright Publishing Corporation 2017. x, 592 pages : Illustration; Map
ISBN 9780871408662
Grades: Adult   909

1. Coastal ecology 2. Coasts 3. Effect of environment on humans 4. Environmentalism 5. United States 6. Gulf of Mexico 7. Nature Writing — Environmental Issues
LC 2016051692

Booklist Editors' Choice, 2017; Kirkus Prize for Nonfiction, 2017; New York Times Notable Book, 2017; Pulitzer Prize for History, 2018; Longlisted for the Andrew Carnegie Medal for Excellence in Non-Fiction, 2018; National Book Critics Circle Award for Nonfiction finalist, 2017.

A comprehensive history of the Gulf of Mexico and its identity as a region marked by hurricanes, oil fields and debates about population growth and the environment demonstrates how its picturesque ecosystems have inspired and reflected key historical events.

"An elegant narrative braced by a fierce, sobering environmental conviction." —*Kirkus*

Includes bibliographical references (pages 559-564) and index.

Elkins, Caroline
Legacy of Violence: A History of the British Empire. Caroline Elkins. Alfred A. Knopf 2022. 448 p.
ISBN 9780307272423
Grades: Adult   909
1. State-sponsored terrorism 2. Punishment 3. Liberalism 4. Imperialism 5. Violence 6. Politics and government 7. Colonies 8. British history 9. Great Britain 10. 20th century 11. History writing — Colonialism — Europe
LC 2021018550

Drawing on more than a decade of research on four continents, and covering 200 years of history, a Pulitzer Prize-winning historian shows how the British Empire's pervasive use of violence throughout the 20th century was exported, modified and institutionalized in colonies around the world. Map(s).

"Elkins's intricate but immersive account is a feat of scholarship that elucidates the bureaucratic and legal machinery of oppression, dissects the intellectual justifications for it, and explores in gripping, sometimes grisly detail the suffering that resulted." —*Publishers Weekly*

This is a Borzoi Book published by Alfred A. Knopf; Includes bibliographical references and index.

Frankopan, Peter
The Silk Roads: A New History of the World. Peter Frankopan. Alfred A. Knopf 2016. xix, 645 pages, 16 unnumbered pages of plates : Illustration
ISBN 9781101946329
Grades: Adult   909
1. Commerce 2. Historic sites 3. Trade routes 4. Asian history 5. Asia 6. Silk Road 7. Central Asia 8. History writing — Ancient 9. History writing — Asia
LC 2015013264

Looks at how the Asian Silk Roads have acted as a crucible of culture throughout history, capturing the importance of these networks that linked the Atlantic with the Pacific, the Mediterranean with India, and America with the Persian Gulf.

"A timely challenge to conventional thinking about a pivotal part of the globe." —*Booklist*

Includes bibliographical references and index.

Gibbins, David J. L.
A History of the World in Twelve Shipwrecks. David Gibbins. St. Martin's Press 2024. 384 p.
ISBN 9781250325372
Grades: Adult   909
1. Shipwrecks 2. Underwater archaeology 3. History 4. Underwater exploration 5. History writing — Natural disasters and tragedies 6. History Writing — Archaeology
LC 2023056206

From renowned underwater archaeologist David Gibbins comes an exciting and rich narrative of human history told through the archaeological discoveries of twelve shipwrecks across time.

"Gibbins' remarkable research will grant both maritime and general historians a deeper perspective on how our world developed." —*Booklist*

Includes bibliographical references and index.

PUBLIC LIBRARY CORE COLLECTION: NONFICTION
Twentieth Edition

Hansen, Valerie
The Year 1000: When Globalization Began. Valerie Hansen. Scribner 2020. xi, 308 pages
ISBN 9781501194108
Grades: Adult   909
1. Millennium (Christian eschatology) 2. International trade 3. Civilization 4. Cultural relations 5. Globalization (Economics) 6. Explorers 7. Rulers 8. Geopolitics 9. Trade routes 10. Trading and swapping 11. Silk Road 12. Asia 13. 10th century 14. History writing — Exploration 15. Business and economics — Economics — History
LC 2019045048
The author draws on extensive research in a groundbreaking history of the explorations and trade commissions that connected the world's most advanced societies for the first time 1,000 years ago.
"The author covers a vast amount of territory in a concise, readable manner, making for a welcome contribution to the popular literature on early global trade and geopolitics. A thoroughly satisfying history of a distant era and people." —*Kirkus*
Includes bibliographical references and index.

Harari, Yuval N.
★ *Sapiens: A Brief History of Humankind.* Yuval Noah Harari. Harper 2015. 352 p.
ISBN 9780062316097
Grades: Adult   909
1. Humans 2. Evolution 3. Biology 4. Memory 5. Cognition 6. Thought and thinking 7. Cognition and culture 8. Physiology 9. Science Writing — Biology 10. History writing — General 11. Society and culture — Psychology and human behavior
LC 2014028418
Booklist Editors' Choice, 2015.
A narrative history of humanity's creation and evolution explores how biology and history have defined understandings of what it means to be human and details the role of modern cognition in shaping the ecosystem and civilizations.
"Although Harari's ideas may be controversial for some readers, those who are interested in history, anthropology, and evolution will find his work a fascinating, hearty read." —*Library Journal*

Horn, Dara
★ *People Love Dead Jews: Reports from a Haunted Present.* Dara Horn. W. W. Norton & Company 2021. 224 p.
ISBN 9780393531565
Grades: Adult   909
1. Horn, Dara, 1977- 2. Jewish people 3. Antisemitism 4. Death 5. History writing — Jewish history 6. Society and culture — Ethnic studies 7. Spirituality and Religion — Judaism
LC 2021012209
Kirkus Prize for Nonfiction finalist, 2021.
A startling and profound exploration of how Jewish history is exploited to comfort the living.
"A moving, meditative, well-written book that will be of profound interest to anyone concerned with Jewry and Jewish literature. Horn's writing is personable and engaging from start to finish." —*Library Journal*
Includes bibliographical references and index.

Mac Sweeney, Naoíse
The West: A New History in Fourteen Lives. Naoíse Mac Sweeney. Dutton 2023. 416 p.
ISBN 9780593472170
Grades: Adult   909
1. Civilization, Western 2. Historiography 3. History 4. Civilization 5. Europe 6. History Writing — General
LC 2022055501
A prize-winning historian presents a story-driven retelling of Western civilization by profiling 14 figures who each played a role in the creation of the Western idea and who each tell us something unexpected about the age in which it was lived and why we've misunderstood it for so long.
"A highly readable, vigorous repudiation of the Western-centric school of history." —*Kirkus*
Includes bibliographical references and index.

Marozzi, Justin
Islamic Empires: The Cities That Shaped Civilization—from Mecca to Dubai. Justin Marozzi. W W Norton & CO Inc 2020. 512 p.
ISBN 9781643133065
Grades: Adult   909
1. Civilization, Islamic 2. Islam 3. Cities and towns 4. Civilization 5. Voyages and travels 6. Southwest Asia and North Africa (Middle East) 7. Islamic countries 8. History writing — Southwest Asia and North Africa (Middle East) 9. Spirituality and Religion — Islam 10. Travel Writing — Southwest Asia and North Africa (Middle East)
LC Bl2019037183
Takes readers on a tour of the defining moments, diverse civilizations and the greatest cities in Islamic history over fifteen centuries, from Mecca in the seventh century to the rise of Doha in the twenty-first century.
"A rich foray into the history of Islam and the emergence of key cities as capitals of commerce, culture, and conquest." —*Kirkus*
Originally published in the UK as Islamic empire : Fifteen cities that define a civilization, Allen Lane, 2019.

Sanghera, Sathnam
Empireworld: How British Imperialism Shaped the Globe. Sathnam Sanghera. PublicAffairs 2024. 464 p.
ISBN 9781541704978
Grades: Adult   909
1. Colonialism 2. Colonies 3. Colonization 4. Imperialism 5. Exploitation 6. Industrialization 7. Slavery 8. Forced relocations 9. Influence (Psychology) 10. Civilization 11. Geopolitics 12. British history 13. Great Britain 14. History writing — Europe — United Kingdom 15. History writing — Colonialism — Europe 16. Politics and global affairs — General
2.6 billion people are inhabitants of former British colonies. The empire's influence upon the quarter of the planet it occupied, and its gravitational influence upon the world outside it, has been profound: from the spread of Christianity by missionaries to the shaping of international law. Yet Britain's idea of its imperial history and the world's experience of it are two very different things. Sathnam Sanghera ultimately shows how the largest empire in world history still exerts influence over planet Earth in all sorts of silent and unsilent ways.
"Like its predecessor, Empireworld is a smart, illuminating exploration of how England exercised global power to create the world we know today." —*Booklist*
Includes bibliographical references.

Schama, Simon
★ *The Story of the Jews; Volume Two :: Belonging, 1492-1900.* Simon Schama. Ecco Press 2017. 790 p.
ISBN 9780062339577
Grades: Adult   909
1. Jewish history 2. Judaism 3. History 4. Media tie-ins 5. History writing — Jewish history 6. Spirituality and Religion — Judaism — History
LC Bl2017034048
A second volume of a sumptuously illustrated companion to the PBS and BBC series spans centuries and continents from the Iberian Peninsula and the shtetls of Russia to the streets of early Hollywood and the poetry written in concentration camps.
"This is a wonderful chronicle spanning centuries in the development of an enduring people." —*Booklist*

★ *The Story of the Jews; Volume One :: Finding the Words, 1000 Bc-1492 Ad.* Simon Schama. Ecco Press 2014. 496 pages, 24 unnumbered pages of plates : Illustration; Color; Map
ISBN 9780060539184
Grades: Adult   909

ESSENTIAL AND RECOMMENDED TITLES
909.04 History with respect to ethnic and national groups

1. Jewish history 2. Judaism 3. History 4. Media tie-ins 5. History writing — Jewish history 6. Spirituality and Religion — Judaism — History

LC 2014466181

Booklist Editors' Choice, 2014.

Acclaimed author and historian Simon Schama explores the Jewish sense of identity, art, and religious teachings from 1000 B.C. to 1492 A.D, when Portugal expelled Jewish residents. Focusing on a specific object at the beginning of each chapter, Schama explores the item's context and its significance to the people associated with it, broadening his discussion to examine the Jewish community at each relevant geographical location and historical period. Schama's engaging approach draws readers into the settings and provides insight into the history of Jews and Judaism through the millennia.

"Schama has written an unconventional but masterful and deeply felt history of his people, which seamlessly integrates themes of art, religion, and ethnicity as he illustrates how Jews both influenced and were influenced by the other people they lived among for more than 1,500 years." —*Booklist*

Includes bibliographical references (pages 431-465) and index.

Winchester, Simon
Pacific: Silicon Chips and Surfboards, Coral Reefs and Atom Bombs, Brutal Dictators, Fading Empires, and the Coming Collision of the World's Superpowers. Simon Winchester. HarperCollins 2015. 480 p.
   ISBN 9780062315410
Grades: Adult   **909**

1. Oceans 2. Geopolitics 3. Geography 4. Pacific Ocean 5. History writing — General

LC 2015020468

Library Journal Best Books, 2015; Kirkus Prize for Nonfiction finalist, 2015.

The New York Times best-selling author of the Men Who United the States traces the geological history of the Pacific Ocean to assess its relationship with humans and indelible role in the modern world.

"Winchester . does not do the expected: There is no chapter about the geological history of the ocean, followed by a slow chronology. Instead, realizing the difficulty of his own task, the author focuses on 10 aspects of the ocean and its inhabitants—islanders, those on the shores—and uses them to illustrate some historical points." —*Kirkus*

Worth, Robert Forsyth
★ *A Rage for Order: The Middle East in Turmoil, from Tahrir Square to Isis*. Robert F. Worth. Farrar, Straus and Giroux 2016. 400 p.
   ISBN 9780374252946
Grades: Adult   **909**

1. Arab Spring, 2010-2012 2. Civil rights 3. Social movements 4. Human rights 5. Democratization 6. Politics and government 7. Southwest Asia and North Africa (Middle East) 8. Arab countries 9. 21st century 10. Politics and global affairs — World politics — Southwest Asia and North Africa (Middle East) 11. Politics and global affairs — Civil and human rights

LC 2015041559

New York Times Notable Book, 2016; Lionel Gelber Prize (Canada), 2017.

A New York Times former Beirut bureau chief chronicles the events of the Arab Spring and its troubled aftermath, discussing the uprising of Middle Eastern revolutionaries whose efforts to end tyranny, corruption and poverty eventually succumbed to prior divisions under the oppression of terrorists and dictators.

"General readers and policymakers will find this timely volume enlightening." —*Library Journal*

909.04 History with respect to ethnic and national groups

Mackintosh-Smith, Tim
Arabs: A 3,000-year History of Peoples, Tribes and Empires. Tim Mackintosh-Smith. Yale University Press 2019. xxvi, 630 pages : Color; Illustration; Map
   ISBN 9780300180282
Grades: Adult   **909.04**

1. Civilization, Arabic 2. Arabic language 3. Language and languages 4. Nomads 5. Kinship-based society 6. Ethnic groups 7. Islam 8. History writing — Southwest Asia and North Africa (Middle East) 9. History writing — Ancient 10. Society and culture — Ethnic studies

This kaleidoscopic book covers almost 3,000 years of Arab history and shines a light on the footloose Arab peoples and tribes who conquered lands and disseminated their language and culture over vast distances. Tracing this process to the origins of the Arabic language, rather than the advent of Islam, Tim Mackintosh-Smith begins his narrative more than a thousand years before Muhammad and focuses on how Arabic, both spoken and written, has functioned as a vital source of shared cultural identity over the millennia.

"Over the course of an extensive, consistently fascinating history, Mackintosh-Smith expertly picks and chooses his details and analyses, providing an admirably complete picture of a consistently misunderstood part of world history and culture." —*Kirkus*

Includes bibliographical references (pages 602-608) and index.

909.07 General historical periods

Asbridge, Thomas S.
★ *The Crusades: The Authoritative History of the War for the Holy Land*. Thomas Asbridge. Ecco Press 2010. 640 p.
   ISBN 9780060787288
Grades: Adult   **909.07**

1. Crusades 2. Christianity 3. Interfaith relations 4. Civilization, Medieval 5. Religious tolerance 6. Aggressiveness 7. International relations 8. Church history 9. Southwest Asia and North Africa (Middle East) history 10. Islamic Empire 11. Europe 12. Medieval period (476-1492) 13. History writing — Wars and conflicts — Crusades

LC Bl2010006562

Drawing on both European and Arabic sources, a magisterial, narrative history tells the full story of this brutal struggle for dominion of the Holy Land from both the Christian and Muslim perspective for the first time, revealing the full horror, passion, and barbaric grandeur of the Crusades.

"Covering the 200-year period of the Crusades in a single volume is a monumental task, but Asbridge . handles it well, presenting an evenhanded view of the actions of Christian and Muslim forces and paying particular attention to the larger-than-life figures of Richard the Lionheart and Saladin. In addition to relating the facts of the expeditions, he explores both the motivations of the Crusaders . and the reasons that Christians eventually failed to retain any hold on conquered territory." —*Library Journal*

Gertsman, Elina
The Middle Ages in 50 Objects. Elina Gertsman, Barbara H. Rosenwein. Cambridge University Press 2018. xvii, 233 pages : Color; Illustration; Map
   ISBN 9781107150386
Grades: Adult   **909.07**

1. Civilization, Medieval 2. History writing — Europe

LC 2017037848

Complex and varied, vibrant and intense, medieval objects demand to be examined closely, to be thought about deeply, to be approached kinesthetically. Extraordinary in the multiplicity of meanings that it harbors and engenders, the material culture of the Middle Ages offers its beholders a rich experience of looking, often multisensory, always rewarding. It offers, too, a glimpse of an equally rich society, or rather the many societies that were in constant flux and in intermittent conversations (and, at times, screaming matches) with one another. And yet, each object has its own history. So how do we write history through objects?

Includes bibliographical references (pages 214-221) and index.

Jones, Dan
Crusaders: An Epic History of the Wars for the Holy Lands. Dan Jones. Viking 2019. 448 p.
   ISBN 9780525428312
Grades: Adult   **909.07**

1. Crusades 2. War 3. Christianity 4. Islam 5. Interfaith relations 6. Fanaticism 7. Military history 8. Civilization, Medieval 9. European history 10. Europe 11. Medieval period (476-1492) 12. History writing — Wars and conflicts — Crusades 13. History writing — Medieval — Europe

LC 2019017922

The author presents a wide-ranging, narrative history of the Crusades that examines 8th-century Christian-Muslim relations from the perspectives of diverse people on all sides of the wars.

Includes bibliographical references and index.

909.08 Modern history, 1450/1500

Tuchman, Barbara W.
March of Folly: From Troy to Vietnam. Barbara W. Tuchman. Ballantine Books 1985. xvi, 447 p. : Illustration; Color
ISBN 9780345308238
Grades: Adult **909.08**
1. Modern history 2. History 3. Power 4. Judgment 5. History writing — General 6. Reference books — History

LC 84045672

Examines the irrationalities of governments through analysis of four crises of history—the fall of Troy, the Renaissance popes' provocation of the Protestant Reformation, Britain's loss of the American colonies, and America's involvement in Vietnam.

Includes bibliographical references (p. [391]-428) and index.

909.8 World history — 1800

Mishra, Pankaj
Age of Anger: A History of the Present. Pankaj Mishra. Farrar Straus & Giroux 2017. 192 p.
ISBN 9780374274788
Grades: Adult **909.8**
1. Colonialism 2. Nationalism 3. Globalization 4. Xenophobia 5. Domestic terrorism 6. North-South relations 7. Computers and civilization 8. North-South economic relations 9. Demagoguism and demagogues 10. Politics and global affairs — World politics 11. History writing — Colonialism — Europe 12. Business and economics — Economics — Socioeconomics

LC 2016050813

New York Times Notable Book, 2017.

A columnist explores the rising tide of paranoid hatred in modern times and attributes it to our inability to fulfill the promises of a globalized economy.

909.82 World history — 20th century, 1900-1999

Harari, Yuval N.
★ *21 Lessons for the 21st Century.* Yuval Noah Harari. Spiegel & Grau 2018. 240 p.
ISBN 9780525512172
Grades: Adult **909.82**
1. Civilization, Western 2. Technology and civilization 3. World politics 4. Forecasting 5. 21st century 6. Politics and global affairs — World politics

LC 2018013856

Shares insights into such present-day issues as the role of technology in transforming humanity, the epidemic of false news, and the modern relevance of nations and religion.

"Magnificently combining historical, scientific, political, and philosophical perspectives, Harari (Sapiens and Homo Deus), a Hebrew University of Jerusalem history professor, explores 21 of what he considers to be todays greatest challenges." —*Publishers Weekly*

Includes bibliographical references and index.

Hochschild, Adam
Lessons from a Dark Time: And Other Essays. Adam Hochschild. University of California Press 2018. 303 p.
ISBN 9780520297241
Grades: Adult **909.82**
1. Social advocacy 2. Social justice 3. Political activists 4. Political persecution 5. Despotism 6. Essays 7. Anthologies 8. Politics and global affairs — Civil and human rights 9. Society and culture — Social activism and philanthropy 10. Politics and global affairs — World politics

LC 2018009384

Hochschild shares the stories of people who took a stand against despotism, spoke out against unjust wars and government surveillance, and dared to dream of a better and more just world.

Includes index.

Junger, Sebastian
Fire. Sebastian Junger. W.W. Norton 2001. xv, 224 p.
ISBN 9780393010466
Grades: Adult **909.82**
1. Disasters 2. Survival 3. World politics 4. Terrorism 5. Forest fires 6. Diamond industry and trade 7. Low-intensity conflicts (Military science) 8. 20th century 9. Essays 10. Adventure writing — General 11. Adult books for young adults

LC 2001045236

New York Times Notable Book, 2001.

Junger brings his heart-pounding prose to bear on forest fires, terrorism, and war, in a collection of pieces that span a decade's worth of journalism. Junger's firsthand acounts of how people handle danger reveals both the awe and the terror evoked by desperate situations.

"The stories are all told with Junger's unfailing eye for detail, which often lends the pieces a disturbing authenticity." —*Library Journal*

Contains previously published magazine articles.

Kennedy, Paul M.
The Rise and Fall of the Great Powers: Economic Change and Military Conflict from 1500 to 2000. Paul Kennedy. Vintage Books 1989. xxv, 677 p. : Map
ISBN 9780679720195
Grades: Adult **909.82**
1. Economic history 2. Balance of power 3. Modern history 4. Business and economics — Economics — History 5. History writing — General

LC 88040123

Surveys global politics over the past five hundred years and discusses current problems facing the major powers.

Includes index; Bibliography: P. 625-662.

Kurlansky, Mark
1968: The Year That Rocked the World. Mark Kurlansky. Ballantine 2004. xx, 441 p. : Illustration
ISBN 9780345455819
Grades: Adult **909.82**
1. King, Martin Luther, Jr, 1929-1968 2. Kennedy, Robert Francis, 1925-1968 3. Modern history 4. Insurgency 5. Vietnam War, 1961-1975 6. Student movements 7. Protest movements 8. Tet Offensive, 1968 9. Political violence 10. Radicalism 11. Massacres 12. United States 13. 1960s 14. 20th century 15. History writing — Wars and conflicts — Vietnam War 16. History writing — 1960s — United States

LC 2004299128

ALA Notable Book, 2005.

Provides a detailed look at 1968, a pivotal year in the history of the twentieth century, exploring the turbulent events, politics, culture, economics, and social changes that marked a volatile year.

"This is an account of the global, social, and political upheaval, warfare, and assassinations that define one year in a tumultuous decade." —*Booklist*

Includes bibliography (p. [405]-412) and index.

ESSENTIAL AND RECOMMENDED TITLES
909.825 World history, 1950-1959

Phillips, Timothy
Retracing the Iron Curtain: A 3,000-mile Journey Through the End and Afterlife of the Cold War. Dr. Timothy Phillips. The Experiment, LLC 2023. 480 p.
ISBN 9781615199648
Grades: Adult   909.82
1. Phillips, Timothy 2. Iron Curtain 3. Communism 4. Borderlands 5. Cold War 6. Voyages and travels 7. Europe 8. Western Europe 9. Russia 10. Soviet Union 11. History writing — Wars and conflicts 12. History Writing — Communism — Europe — Russia 13. Travel Writing — Europe

An epic people's history of life in the shadow of the Iron Curtain, from an intrepid reporter who traveled all 3,000 miles of the former East-West barrier to investigate the deep and lingering aftermath of the Cold War.

"Knowledgeable and engrossing, this is an illuminating portrait of post-communist life." —*Publishers Weekly*

Service, Robert
The End of the Cold War 1985-1991. Robert Service. Public Affairs 2015. 464 p.
ISBN 9781610394994
Grades: Adult   909.82
1. Cold War 2. World politics 3. International relations 4. East-West relations 5. Soviet Union 6. United States 7. 20th century 8. History writing — Cold War
LC 2015942161

A British historian and author investigates the final years of the Cold War from both sides of the Iron Curtain, discussing the relationship between Reagan and Gorbachev whose unprecedented, historic cooperation worked against the odds to end the arms race.

"A wholly satisfying, likely definitive, but not triumphalist account of the end of an era." —*Kirkus*

Tuchman, Barbara W.
The Proud Tower: A Portrait of the World Before the War, 1890-1914. Barbara W. Tuchman. Ballantine Books 1996. xiii, 528 p. : Illustration
ISBN 9780345405012
Grades: 11 12 Adult   909.82
1. Modern history 2. Social history 3. European history 4. Europe 5. 20th century 6. History writing — General
LC 96096511

Looks at the history of society and culture in the years leading up to World War I.

Includes bibliographical references (p. 465-510) and index; Originally published: New York : Macmillan, 1966.

Von Tunzelmann, Alex
Blood and Sand: Suez, Hungary, and Eisenhower's Campaign for Peace. Alex Von Tunzelmann. HarperCollins 2016. 432 p.
ISBN 9780062249241
Grades: Adult   909.82
1. Eisenhower, Dwight D. (Dwight David), 1890-1969 2. International relations 3. Cold War 4. Diplomatic negotiations in international disputes 5. Balance of power 6. Decision-making 7. Arab-Israeli conflict 8. Political leadership 9. Presidents 10. Southwest Asia and North Africa (Middle East) history 11. Egypt 12. Suez Canal (Egypt) 13. Hungary 14. United States 15. 1950s 16. 20th century 17. History writing — Presidency — 20th century — United States 18. History writing — Nationalism — Southwest Asia and North Africa (Middle East) 19. History writing — Cold War 20. Nonfiction that reads like fiction
LC Bl2016043983

Describes the twin crises in 1956 involving Suez and Hungary that brought the world to the brink of nuclear war and discusses both events in the context of the resulting global Cold War, the ongoing Arab-Israeli conflict and the dangerous politics of oil.

"This is an outstanding reexamination of these sad, history-altering events." —*Booklist*

909.825 World history, 1950-1959

Westad, Odd Arne
The Cold War: A World History. Odd Arne Westad. Basic Books 2017. 800 p.
ISBN 9780465054930
Grades: Adult   909.825
1. Cold War 2. World politics 3. International relations 4. Socialism 5. Capitalism 6. Communism 7. Democracy 8. Arms race 9. Politics and government 10. Soviet Union 11. United States 12. 20th century 13. Politics and global affairs — Political philosophy 14. History writing — Cold War
LC 2017939229

The immediate historical roots of the Cold War sprouted after World War II, when Soviet-led countries faced off against the U.S. and its allies. Though the division of Germany into East and West, the Iron Curtain cutting off Eastern Europe, and the American anticommunist frenzy of the 1940s and '50s come readily to mind, award-winning historian Odd Arne Westad traces the Cold War's origins to the Industrial Revolution and illuminates its effects throughout the world.

"He ably synthesizes contemporary scholarship to produce an accessible narrative that provides a fresh perspective on the conflicts pervasive global influence." —*Publishers Weekly*

909.83 World history — 21st century, 2000-2099

Bergen, Peter L.
The Longest War: The Enduring Conflict Between America and Al-qaeda. Peter L. Bergen. Free Press 2011. xx, 473 p, 8 p. of plates : Illustration; Map
ISBN 9780743278935
Grades: Adult   909.83
1. War on Terrorism, 2001-2009 2. Antiterrorist policy 3. Terrorists 4. Terrorism prevention 5. Iraq War, 2003-2011 6. United States 7. Politics and global affairs — Terrorism
LC 2010015268

A forefront expert on al Qaeda draws on his unique first-hand interviews with Osama bin Laden, top-level jihadists and Washington officials to offer insight the war on terror from both sides. By the author of the Osama bin Laden I Know.

"This is a broad, almost stereoscopic account that brings an array of sources together into an illuminating synthesis. . If you want a solid, readable history of the Long War, this is a great place to start." —*Washington Monthly*

Includes bibliographical references and index.

Harari, Yuval N.
Homo Deus: A Brief History of Tomorrow. Yuval Noah Harari; translated by the author. Harper 2017. 449 p.
ISBN 9780062464316
Grades: Adult   909.83
1. Forecasting 2. Humans 3. Ethics 4. Evolution 5. Biology 6. Translations — Hebrew to English 7. Science Writing — Biology 8. Society and culture — Philosophy
LC Bl2017000348

The best-selling author of Sapiens examines the civilized world's phenomenal achievements in the areas of famine, disease and war while making provocative predictions about the evolutionary goals of the 21st century. philosophy and every discipline in between.

"A relentlessly fascinating book that is sure to become and deserves to be a bestseller." —*Kirkus*

First published as the History of Tomorrow in Hebrew in Israel in 2015 by Kinneret Zmora-Bitan Dvir. Previously published in Great Britain in 2016 by Harvill Secker, a division of Penguin Random House Group Ltd.—Title page verso.

Klosterman, Chuck
But What If We're Wrong: Thinking About the Present as If It Were the Past. Charles Klosterman. Blue Rider Press 2016. 288 p.

ISBN 9780399184123

Grades: Adult **909.83**

1. Popular culture 2. National characteristics, American 3. 21st century 4. Essays 5. Society and culture — Pop culture

LC 2016023103

The best-selling author of Sex, Drugs, and Cocoa Puffs explores the idea that today's mainstream beliefs about the world are fundamentally incorrect, drawing on original interviews with forefront intellectuals and experts to consider how the music, sports, literature and other present-day conventions may be perceived in future centuries.

McKibben, Bill
Falter: Has the Human Game Begun to Play Itself Out? Bill McKibben. Henry Holt and Co. 2019. 291 p.
ISBN 9781250178268

Grades: Adult **909.83**

1. Civilization, Western 2. Effect of humans on nature 3. Technology and civilization 4. Human ecology 5. Climate change 6. Global warming 7. Artificial intelligence 8. Gene editing 9. 21st century 10. Politics and global affairs — Environmental issues and policies 11. Science Writing — Computing, the Internet, and Technology

LC 2018046452

Shares cautionary insights into how emerging technologies, including artificial intelligence and robotics, are being developed through fervent ideologies that are threatening the diversity of human experience.

Includes bibliographical references and index.

910 Geography and travel

Butler, Daniel Allen
"unsinkable": The Full Story of the Rms Titanic. Daniel Allen Butler. Da Capo Press 2003. xii, 292 p. : Illustration
ISBN 9780306811104

Grades: 11 12 Adult **910**

1. Shipwrecks 2. North Atlantic Ocean 3. 1910s 4. History writing — Natural disasters and tragedies

LC BL2003016651

Describes the construction and maiden voyage of the "unsinkable" Titanic, which sank after colliding with an iceberg in the North Atlantic in April 1912.

Includes bibliographical references (p. 279-283) and index; Originally published: Mechanicsburg, PA : Stackpole Books, 1998.

Lord, Walter
★ *A Night to Remember.* Walter Lord. Henry, Holt, and Co. 2005. xx, 182 p. : Illustration
ISBN 9780805077643

Grades: 11 12 Adult **910**

1. Shipwrecks 2. North Atlantic Ocean 3. Page to screen 4. History writing — Natural disasters and tragedies 5. Nonfiction that reads like fiction

LC 2004059509

Recounts the demise of the "unsinkable" Titanic, the massive luxury liner that housed extravagances such as a French "sidewalk cafe" and a grand staircase, but failed to provide enough lifeboats for the 2,207 passengers on board.

"A detailed account of the tragic drama of that terrible night—April 4, 1912—when the Titanic, the unsinkable ship, struck an iceberg and went down in the icy waters of the Atlantic." —*Library Journal*

A Owl Book; First published in hardcover in 1955 by Henry, Holt, and Company—T.P. verso.

910.4 Accounts of travel and facilities for travelers

Cordingly, David
Under the Black Flag: The Romance and the Reality of Life Among the Pirates. David Cordingly. Random House Trade Paperbacks 2006. xxi, 296 p. : Illustration; Map
ISBN 9780812977226

Grades: 11 12 Adult **910.4**

1. Pirates 2. Seafaring life 3. Pirate ships 4. Piracy 5. History writing — Pirates

LC Bl2006011709

A revisionist history of the golden age of piracy draws on original archive records to provide a realistic study of pirates and their lives that refutes many of the myths about the era.

"This succinct history is full of unexpected revelations about the facts and myths of piracy; a typical seventeenth-century Western pirate vessel, for example, was run democratically long before the French Revolution, and one of the most successful pirates of all time was a nineteenth-century Chinese woman who controlled some fifty thousand seagoing outlaws." —*The New Yorker*

Includes bibliographical references (p. [255]-283) and index; Originally published: New York : Random House, 1996.

Dana, Richard Henry
Two Years Before the Mast: A Personal Narrative of Life at Sea. Richard Henry Dana; introduction by Gary Kinder; notes by Duncan Hasell. Modern Library 2001. xxiv, 516 p. : Illustration
ISBN 9780375757945

Grades: 11 12 Adult **910.4**

1. Dana, Richard Henry 1815-1882 2. Seafaring life 3. Sailors 4. Personal diaries 5. Voyages and travels 6. California 7. Cape Horn 8. 19th century 9. Autobiographies and memoirs 10. History writing — Exploration 11. Life stories — People in history — Explorers

LC 2001031243

A personal narrative of life aboard an American merchant ship in the 1830s.

Johnson, Steven
Enemy of All Mankind: A True Story of Piracy, Power, and History's First Global Manhunt. Steven Johnson. Riverhead Books 2020. 288 p.
ISBN 9780735211605

Grades: Adult **910.4**

1. Avery, John, active 1695 2. Pirates 3. Corporations 4. Merchant ships 5. International trade 6. Piracy 7. Mutiny 8. Ocean travel 9. Raids (Military science) 10. Colonialism 11. British history 12. Indian Ocean 13. 17th century 14. History writing — Pirates 15. True Crime — Historical Crime

LC 2019022493

Henry Every was the seventeenth century's most notorious pirate. The press published wildly popular—and wildly inaccurate—reports of his nefarious adventures. The British government offered enormous bounties for his capture, alive or (preferably) dead. But Steven Johnson argues that Every's most lasting legacy was his inadvertent triggering of a major shift in the global economy. Enemy of All Mankind focuses on one key event—the attack on an Indian treasure ship by Every and his crew—and its surprising repercussions across time and space. It's the gripping tale one of the most lucrative crimes in history, the first international manhunt, and the trial of the seventeenth century.

"Consummate popular history: Fast-paced, intelligent, and entertaining." —*Library Journal*

Includes bibliographical references and index.

Kois, Dan
How to Be a Family: The Year I Dragged My Kids Around the World to Find a New Way to Be Together. Dan Kois. Little, Brown & Company 2019. 320 p.
ISBN 9780316552622

Grades: Adult **910.4**

1. Kois, Dan 2. Journalists 3. Families 4. Voyages and travels 5. Family travel 6. Cultural differences 7. Happiness 8. Purpose in life 9. Autobiographies and

ESSENTIAL AND RECOMMENDED TITLES
910.41 Trips around the world

memoirs 10. Family and Relationships — Families 11. Travel Writing — General 12. Life stories — Relationships — Family

LC Bl2019028227

A father humorously recounts the year his family spent trying to get out of the rut of their busy, overscheduled East Coast lives by living in New Zealand, the Netherlands, Costa Rica and small-town Kansas.

Sides, Hampton

★ *In the Kingdom of Ice: The Grand and Terrible Polar Voyage of the U.S.S. Jeannette.* Hampton Sides. Doubleday 2014. 384 p.

ISBN 9780385535373

Grades: Adult   910.4

1. Bennett, James Gordon, 1841-1918 2. De Long, George W. (George Washington), 1844-1881 3. Shipwrecks 4. Survival (after airplane accidents, shipwrecks, etc.) 5. Polar expeditions 6. Survival 7. Arctic Ocean 8. 1870s 9. 19th century 10. Adventure writing — Survival

LC 2014004367

ALA Notable Book, 2015; Booklist Editors' Choice, 2014; Library Journal Best Books, 2014.

On his first Polar voyage in 1873, nothing in the frigid north appealed to Lieutenant George De Long, but he soon became obsessed. A few years later, leading an 1879 Arctic expedition and tasked with finding a mythical open-sea passage, De Long and his crew faced deadly trouble when their ship became trapped in the ice. Using letters, diaries, expedition records, newspaper reports, and other documents, bestselling author Hampton Sides provides a dramatic account of what happened to De Long and his crew in this gripping nautical tale.

"Sides . tapped amazing archival material, including diaries, letters, and the ship logs, to render a completely thrilling saga of survival in unbelievably harsh conditions." —*Booklist*

Includes bibliographical references.

Thomson, Keith

Born to Be Hanged: The Epic Story of the Gentlemen Pirates Who Raided the South Seas, Rescued a Princess, and Stole a Fortune. Keith Thomson. Little, Brown, & CO 2022. 400 pages : Illustration; Map

ISBN 9780316703611

Grades: Adult   910.4

1. Pirates 2. Rescues 3. Princesses 4. Privateering 5. Seafaring life 6. Piracy 7. Colonialism 8. Ocean travel 9. Personal diaries 10. Panama 11. South America 12. 17th century 13. History writing — Latin America 14. History writing — Pirates

Charts a legendary two-year expedition by 300 pirates in the year 1680 to wreak havoc on the Pacific coastline, raiding cities, mines and merchant ships as well as their sensational trial back in England.

"Novelist Thomson (Once a Spy) follows a motley crew of English pirates on a voyage of plunder along the Pacific coast of South America in this rollicking historical account drawing on the contemporary journals of seven participants." —*Library Journal*

910.41 Trips around the world

Foer, Joshua

Atlas Obscura. Joshua Foer, Dylan Thuras & Ella Morton. Workman Publishing 2016. 480 p.

ISBN 9780761169086

Grades: Adult   910.41

1. Voyages and travels 2. Curiosities and wonders 3. Trivia and miscellaneous facts 4. Travel Writing — General

LC 2016041548

Booklist Editors' Choice: Adult Books for Young Adults, 2016.

Atlas Obscura is the bucket-list guide to over 700 of the most unusual, curious, bizarre, and mysterious places on earth.

"Featuring full-color illustrations, this hefty and gorgeously produced tome will be eagerly pored over by readers of many ages and fans of the original website." —*Booklist*

★ *Atlas Obscura 2nd Ed.: An Explorer's Guide to the World's Hidden Wonders.* Joshua Foer, Dylan Thuras & Ella Morton. Workman Pub CO 2019. 480 pages

ISBN 9781523506484

Grades: Adult   910.41

1. Voyages and travels 2. Curiosities and wonders 3. Trivia and miscellaneous facts 4. Travel Writing — General

LC Bl2019023904

A completely revised and updated second edition of the best-selling guide to the planet's most unusual and mysterious locations incorporates 120 new entries and a full-color gatefold road trip map outlining an itinerary for ultimate enthusiasts.

Second edition, revised & updated.

910.452 Shipwrecks

Mearns, David L.

The Shipwreck Hunter: A Lifetime of Extraordinary Discovery and Adventure in the Deep Seas. David L. Mearns. W W Norton & Company 2018. xiii, 400 pages, 32 unnumbered pages of plates : Illustration; Color; Portrait

ISBN 9781681777603

Grades: Adult   910.452

1. Mearns, David L. 2. Treasure troves 3. Underwater exploration 4. Shipwrecks 5. Oceanography 6. Oceanographers 7. Australian literature 8. Adventure writing — Exploration

David Mearns, the man who discovered the wreck of HMAS Sydney, takes us on an extraordinary voyage through his amazing career as one of the world's most successful shipwreck hunters.

Originally published Australia, 2017; Includes bibliographical references (pages 387-392) and index.

910.9 History, geographic treatment, biography

Adams, Simon

Journey: An Illustrated History of Travel. Foreword, Michael Collins; contributors, Simon Adams, R.G. Grant, Andrew Humphreys. DK 2017. 440 p. : Illustration; Color; Map; Portrait

ISBN 9781465464149

Grades: Adult   910.9

1. Voyages and travels 2. History writing — Exploration 3. Life stories — People in history — Explorers

LC 2017297217

An account of human travel, from the earliest migrations to great explorations, features biographies of conquerors, explorers, and travelers; stories of technological innovation; literary journals; and works of art.

"Each short chapter presents the people who made the trip, where they went, how they traveled, and the importance of that journey to our understanding of the world." —*Booklist*

Includes index; at head of cover title: Smithsonian.

910.91 Geography of and travel in areas, regions, places in general

Brandt, Anthony

The Man Who Ate His Boots: The History of the Search for the Northwest Passage. Anthony Brandt. Alfred A. Knopf 2010. 464 p.

ISBN 9780307263926

Grades: Adult   910.91

1. Survival 2. Explorers 3. North American history 4. Arctic regions 5. 19th century 6. History writing — Exploration

LC 2009038835

Documents the experiences of nineteenth-century adventurers who searched for the Northwest Passage, describing the sixteenth-century myths that inspired their pursuits and the ways in which many met tragic ends when confronting the harsh Arctic elements.

"Often witty in his approach, Brandt makes the absurdity of Arctic exploration and the quest for the Northwest Passage entertaining for the general reader. Highly recommended for fans of British or Arctic exploration history." —*Library Journal*

A Borzoi book; Includes bibliographical references and index.

Dean, Josh
The Taking of K-129: How the CIA Used Howard Hughes to Steal a Russian Sub in the Most Daring Covert Operation in History. Josh Dean. E.P. Dutton 2017. 384 p.
ISBN 9781101984437
Grades: Adult 910.91
1. Hughes, Howard, 1905-1976 2. Submarine disasters 3. Nuclear warfare 4. Submarines, Soviet 5. Intelligence service 6. United States 7. History writing — Cold War

LC 2017011991

A true story of Cold War espionage and engineering reveals how the CIA, the U.S. Navy and an eccentric billionaire spent six years and nearly a billion dollars to steal a nuclear-armed Soviet submarine after it sank in the Pacific Ocean.

"Dean delivers an engaging rendition of the high-profile espionage effort." —*Booklist*

Fairbanks, Amanda M.
The Lost Boys of Montauk: The True Story of the Wind Blown, Four Men Who Vanished at Sea, and the Survivors They Left Behind. Amanda M. Fairbanks. Gallery Books 2021. 352 p.
ISBN 9781982103231
Grades: Adult 910.91
1. Boating accidents 2. Storms 3. Fishing boat captains 4. Fishers 5. Loss 6. Brotherhoods 7. Families 8. Fishing 9. Shipwrecks 10. North Atlantic Ocean 11. Montauk, New York 12. New York (state) 13. 1980s 14. History writing — Natural disasters and tragedies 15. History writing — Regional history — United States

This immersive account of the 1984 tragedy of the fishing boat Wind Blown at sea whose repercussions haunt its survivors to this day explores one of the most important questions we face as humans: How do memories of the dead inform the lives of those left behind?

"A memorable lost-at-sea narrative focusing on a Montauk-based commercial fishing boat.... The author's genuine desire to provide an accurate account of the history of the Wind Blown and the lives of its crew members is evident in her extensive research and attention to detail, making this a no-brainer for fans of the Perfect Storm and similar books." —*Kirkus*

Franklin, Jonathan
438 Days: An Extraordinary True Story of Survival at Sea. Jonathan Franklin. Atria Books 2015. 304 p.
ISBN 9781501116292
Grades: Adult 910.91
1. Alvarenga, Salvador, approximately 1977 2. Marine accidents 3. Sea survival 4. Shipwrecks 5. Fishers 6. Fishing boats 7. Fisheries 8. Undocumented immigrants 9. Chiapas, Mexico (State) 10. Biographies 11. Life stories — Facing adversity — Disasters and tragedies

LC 2015030740

Based on interviews with the man who survived alone and adrift at sea longer than anyone in recorded history and interviews with his colleagues, an epic tale of survival chronicles Salvador Alvarenga's 14 months at sea during which he imagined a method of survival that kept his body and mind intact until he was rescued.

"Franklin sprinkles the story with expert opinions to give it depth and context, but the most striking details are those offered by Alvarenga himself about the challenges he faced day in and day out. A spectacular triumph of grit over adversity, 438 Days is an intense, immensely absorbing read." —*Booklist*

Grann, David
★ *The Wager: A Tale of Shipwreck, Mutiny and Murder.* David Grann. Doubleday 2023. 352 p.
ISBN 9780385534260
Grades: Adult 910.91
1. Sailors 2. Shipwrecks 3. Shipwreck victims 4. Ship captains 5. Mutiny 6. Survival (after airplane accidents, shipwrecks, etc.) 7. Murder 8. Courts-martial and courts of inquiry 9. Patagonia (Argentina and Chile) 10. 18th century 11. History writing — Historical mysteries 12. True Crime — Historical crime

LC 2022028630

In this tale of shipwreck, survival and savagery, the #1 New York Times bestselling author of Killers of the Flower Moon recounts the events on His Majesty's Ship the Wager, a British vessel that left England in 1740 on a secret mission, resulting in a court martial that revealed a shocking truth.

"A new account of the Wager Mutiny, in which a shipwrecked and starving British naval crew abandoned their captain on a desolate Patagonian island, emphasizes the extreme hardships routinely faced by eighteenth-century seafarers as well as the historical resonance of the dramatic 1741 event." —*Booklist*

Includes bibliographical references and index.

Kurson, Robert
Pirate Hunters: Treasure, Obsession, and the Search for a Legendary Pirate Ship. Robert Kurson. Random House Inc 2015. 336 p.
ISBN 9781400063369
Grades: Adult 910.91
1. Pirate ships 2. Voyages and travels 3. Underwater exploration 4. Explorers 5. Deep diving 6. Adventure writing — Exploration

LC 2014020225

LibraryReads Favorites, 2015.

Traces the high-stakes quest of John Mattera and Shadow Divers' Chatterton to find the lost pirate ship of Joseph Bannister, discussing their teamwork with technology-eschewing Tracy Bowden and the story behind Bannister's elusive treasure.

"An enjoyable read, especially if you've got a thing for pirates." —*Kirkus*

Levy, Buddy
Labyrinth of Ice: The Triumphant and Tragic Greely Polar Expedition. Buddy Levy. St. Martin's Press 2019. 336 p.
ISBN 9781250182197
Grades: Adult 910.91
1. Greely, A. W. (Adolphus Washington), 1844-1935 2. Voyages and travels 3. Adventure 4. Scientists 5. Explorers 6. Rescues 7. Starvation 8. Exploration 9. Arctic regions 10. Polar regions 11. History writing — Exploration 12. Adventure writing — Exploration 13. Life stories — People in history — Explorers

LC 2019034039

National Outdoor Book Award for History/Biography, 2020.

In July 1881, Lt. A.W. Greely and his crew of 24 scientists and explorers were bound for the last region unmarked on global maps. Their goal: Farthest North. What would follow was one of the most extraordinary and terrible voyages ever made. Labyrinth of Ice tells the true story of the heroic lives and deaths of these voyagers hell-bent on fame and fortune—at any cost—and how their journey changed the world.

Includes bibliographical references.

Russell, Gareth
The Ship of Dreams: The Sinking of the Titanic and the End of the Edwardian Era. Gareth Russell. Atria Books 2019. 423 p.
ISBN 9781501176722
Grades: Adult 910.91
1. Shipwrecks 2. Ship passengers 3. Social classes 4. Social change 5. Edwardian era (1901-1914) 6. History writing — Natural disasters and tragedies

LC 2019005535

Booklist Editors' Choice, 2019.

ESSENTIAL AND RECOMMENDED TITLES
910.911 Frigid zones — Travel

A narrative history links the Titanic tragedy to unprecedented social, technological, political and economic changes in England and the United States.

Includes bibliographical references and index; Originally published in Great Britain in 2019 as the Darksome Bounds of a Failing World by William Collins— T.P. verso.

Slade, Rachel
Into the Raging Sea: Thirty-three Mariners, One Megastorm, and the Sinking of El Faro. Rachel Slade. Ecco Press 2018. xiv, 391 p.
ISBN 9780062699701
Grades: Adult   910.91
1. Ships 2. Hurricanes 3. Shipwrecks 4. Sailors 5. Accidents 6. Disasters 7. Merchant marine 8. Shipping industry and trade 9. Atlantic Ocean 10. Caribbean Sea 11. Adventure writing — Natural disaster 12. Nature Writing — Natural Disaster
LC 2018002800

New York Times Notable Book, 2018.

On October 1, 2015, Hurricane Joaquin barreled into the Bermuda Triangle and swallowed the container ship El Faro whole, resulting in the worst American shipping disaster in thirty-five years. A richly reported account of a singular tragedy, into the Raging Sea takes us into the heart of an age-old American industry, casting new light on the hardworking men and women who paid the ultimate price in the name of profit.

"A pulse-pounding, Perfect Storm-style tale of a shipping disaster. A taut, chilling, and emotionally charged retelling of a doomed ship's final days." —*Kirkus*

Includes bibliographical references and index.

Stone, Daniel
Sinkable: Obsession, the Deep Sea, and the Shipwreck of the Titanic. Daniel Stone. E P Dutton 2022. 416 p.
ISBN 9780593329375
Grades: Adult   910.91
1. Shipwrecks 2. Obsession 3. Underwater archaeology 4. History writing — Natural disasters and tragedies

In this fascinating work of personal journalism, the author discusses the Titanic as a shipwreck, exploring generations of eccentrics who attempted to raise it, and then turns inward to his own obsession with the Titanic and shipwrecks in general.

"Journalist Stone (The Food Explorer) examines in this incisive and entertaining history how the sinking of the Titanic in 1912 has captured the public's imagination….Colorful personalities, astute cultural analysis, and fascinating details about the science of shipwrecks and the mechanics of salvage operations make this a must-read for Titanic buffs." —*Publishers Weekly*

910.911 Frigid zones — Travel

Welky, David
★ *A Wretched and Precarious Situation: In Search of the Last Arctic Frontier*. David Welky. W.W. Norton & Company 2016. 480 p.
ISBN 9780393254419
Grades: Adult   910.911
1. MacMillan, Donald Baxter, born 1874 2. Borup, George, 1885-1912 3. Explorers 4. North Pole 5. Arctic regions 6. Adventure writing — Exploration
LC 2016023022

In 1906, from atop a snow-swept hill in the ice fields northwest of Greenland, Commander Robert E. Peary spotted a heretofore unknown land looming in the distance. He called it "Crocker Land." Scientists and explorers agreed that Peary had found a new continent. Several years later, two of Peary's disciples, George Borup and Donald MacMillan—with the sponsorship of the American Museum of Natural History—assembled a team of amateurs to investigate.

Includes bibliographical references and index.

910.92 Geographers, travelers, explorers regardless of country of origin

Bellows, Amanda Brickell
The Explorers: A New History of America in Ten Expeditions. Amanda Bellows. William Morrow, an Imprint of HarperCollins Publishers 2024. 400 p.
ISBN 9780063227408
Grades: Adult   910.92
1. Explorers 2. Women explorers 3. Adventurers 4. Missionaries 5. African Americans 6. Indigenous peoples of North America 7. Freed people 8. Discoveries (in geography) 9. Voyages and travels 10. American people 11. Collective biographies 12. Life stories — People in history — Explorers 13. History writing — Exploration 14. Adventure writing — Exploration
LC 2023054991

Told through the stories of a diverse group of ten extraordinary, yet often overlooked, adventurers, including Sacagawea, James Beckwourth, Harriet Chalmers Adams and Sally Ride, this exhilarating new history of American exploration brings to life the people who took on great risk in unfamiliar territory to exercise personal freedom.

"Bellows…considers 10 figures—explorers of all types—who have shaped the identity of the United States, from an enslaved person who forged his freedom as a mountain man to astronaut Sally Ride." —*Library Journal*

Includes bibliographical references and index.

Sides, Hampton
★ *The Wide Wide Sea: Imperial Ambition, First Contact and the Fateful Final Voyage of Captain James Cook*. Hampton Sides. Doubleday 2024. 432 p.
ISBN 9780385544764
Grades: Adult   910.92
1. Cook, James, 1728-1779 2. Ship captains 3. Explorers 4. Islands 5. Voyages and travels 6. Cartography 7. Indigenous peoples 8. First contact of indigenous peoples with Europeans 9. First contact (Anthropology) 10. Exploration 11. Imperialism 12. Violence 13. Islands of the Pacific 14. North America 15. Pacific Ocean 16. Life stories — People in history — Explorers 17. History writing — Exploration 18. Adventure writing — Exploration 19. Travel Writing — Historic Journeys

Part high-seas adventure, part examination of the Age of Exploration, this account of Captain James Cook's last voyage in 1776 charts how his overt and covert missions came to a head on the island of Hawaii and left behind a complex and controversial legacy still debated to this day.

"With an admirably light touch, Sides teases out his convincing thesis amid a riveting day-by-day narrative of the voyage and fascinating asides…This exquisitely crafted and novelistic portrait of the mercurial captain enthralls." —*Publishers Weekly*

911 Historical geography

Hayes, Derek
Historical Atlas of the American West: With Original Maps. Derek Hayes. University of Calif. Press 2009. 1 atlas (288 p.) : Illustration; Color; Map
ISBN 9780520256521
Grades: 11 12 Adult   911
1. Maps 2. The West (United States) history 3. The West (United States) 4. History writing — Regional history — United States 5. Reference — Atlases
LC Oc2010000799

Presents a collection of more than six hundred maps that depict the history of the American West.

"More than 600 maps have been carefully selected and beautifully reproduced in full color. They provide the primary-source documentation for the historical narrative, written for the general reader, tracing the development of the Western United States from its indigenous inhabitants to European exploration, the migration of settlers, and 20th-century events.... A high quality publication

at an amazingly low price, this atlas is highly recommended for all public and academic libraries, history buffs, and map enthusiasts." —*Library Journal*
Includes bibliographical references (p. 278-279) and index.

Historical *Atlas of the United States: With Original Maps.* Derek Hayes. University of Calif. Press 2007. 1 atlas (280 p.) : Illustration; Color; Map
ISBN 9780520250369
Grades: Adult 911
1. Maps 2. Geography 3. United States 4. Atlases 5. History writing — United States 6. Science writing — Geography
LC Bl2008002456

Presents a collection of more than five hundred historical maps covering more than half a millennium and ranging from the earliest days of exploration to the transformation of the Gulf Coast following hurricane Katrina.

The evolution of geographical knowledge is presented, along with a fascinating chronicle of the expansion and development of the U.S, in a collection of more than five hundred historical maps covering more than half a millennium and ranging from the earliest days of exploration to the transformation of the Gulf Coast following hurricane Katrina.

Includes bibliographical references (p. 270-271) and index; Originally published: Vancouver : Douglas & McIntyre, 2006.

---

912 Graphic representations of surface of earth and of extraterrestrial worlds

Carballo, David M.
America: The Atlas. Contributors: David M. Carballo, Jon Chandler, Clarissa Confer, Celso A. Mendoza, Ben Railton [and 2 others]. Thunder Bay Press 2023. 384 pages : Illustration; Color (Smithsonian)
ISBN 9781645178422
Grades: Adult 912
1. History 2. Geography 3. Maps 4. United States 5. North America 6. Atlases 7. Visual nonfiction 8. Adult books for young adults 9. History writing — United States 10. Society and culture — General 11. Reference — Atlases
LC Bl2023111868

Smithsonian America: The Atlas is a superb depiction of the history of North America and the United States told through extensive photographs and maps, both old and new. In collaboration with experts from the Smithsonian Institution, every corner of the continent is explored in detail—from the early people who first settled the land thousands of years ago to the diversity of the present day. This edition also includes 32 pages of bonus material, including a timeline of American history and a guide to all 50 U.S. states, as well as a large foldout page featuring two detailed full-color maps.

"This noteworthy atlas effectively invites readers into the interpretive process and, in an approachable academic style, shares with them the historical role of geography in making the country of today." —*Booklist*

At head of title: Smithsonian; Includes: Foldout Lewis & Clark track map and railroad track map on the back side; Includes bibliographical references (pages 372-374) and indexes.

912.19 Specific areas, regions, places in general

Sluglett, Peter
Atlas of Islamic History. Peter Sluglett with Andrew Currie. Routledge, Taylor & Francis Group 2014. 1 atlas (112 pages) : Color; Illustration; Map
ISBN 9781138821286
Grades: Adult 912.19
1. Islam 2. Maps 3. Civilization, Islamic 4. Geography 5. Atlases 6. Reference — Atlases

This Atlas gives the main outlines of Islamic history from the immediately pre-Islamic period until the First World War, that is, before most parts of the Muslim world became sovereign nation states. Each map is accompanied by a text that contextualises, explains, and expands upon the map. All the maps are in full colour: 18 of them are double-page spreads, and 25 are single page layouts. This is an atlas of Islamic, not simply Arab or Middle Eastern history; hence it covers the entire Muslim world, including Spain, North, West and East Africa, the Indian sub-continent, Central Asia and Southeast Asia.—Page 4 of cover.
Includes bibliographical references and index.

---

914 Geography of and travel in Europe

Bryson, Bill
Notes from a Small Island. Bill Bryson. Morrow 1996. 324 p. : Map
ISBN 9780688147259
Grades: Adult 914
1. Bryson, Bill 2. Travelers 3. National characteristics, British 4. Civilization 5. Voyages and travels 6. Civilization, Medieval 7. England 8. 20th century 9. Medieval period (476-1492) 10. Travel Writing — Europe 11. Humor writing — Classic humorists
LC 95043437

The author of Made in America combines social commentary and travel notes, irreverent wit and fond appreciation, in an account of life in and the land of Great Britain, his adopted home for the past two decades.

The Road *to Little Dribbling: Adventures of an American in Britain.* Bill Bryson. Doubleday, an Imprint of Penguin Random House 2016. 400 p.
ISBN 9780385539289
Grades: Adult 914
1. Bryson, Bill 2. Travelers 3. National characteristics, British 4. American people in Great Britain 5. Cultural differences 6. Civilization 7. Voyages and travels 8. Civilization, Medieval 9. England 10. 21st century 11. Medieval period (476-1492) 12. Travel Writing — Europe 13. Humor writing — Classic humorists
LC 2015027450

LibraryReads Favorites, 2016.

A sequel to "Notes from a Small Island" stands as the author's tribute to his adopted country of England and describes his riotous return visit two decades later to rediscover the country, its people, and its culture.

"Anglophiles will find Bryson's field notes equally entertaining and educational." —*Kirkus*

Eichar, Donnie
Dead *Mountain: The True Story of the Dyatlov Pass Incident.* by Donnie Eichar. Chronicle Books 2013. 288 p.
ISBN 9781452112749
Grades: Adult 914
1. Eichar, Donnie 2. Hiking 3. Mountaineering accidents 4. Mountaineering 5. Tragedy 6. 1950s 7. 20th century 8. History writing — Natural disasters and tragedies 9. Sports and Competition — Mountaineering
LC 2013014843

The author attempts to unravel the mystery behind a group of nine hikers whose baffling deaths in the Russina Ural Mountains has led to decades of speculation on what happened to them.

"Eichar marries the short story of the students' lives with the procedural tale of the official investigation and then integrates his own amateur investigation. [A] well-told and accurate whodunit." —*Kirkus*

Greene, David
Midnight *in Siberia: A Journey into the Heart of Russia.* David Greene. W W Norton & CO Inc 2014. 320 p.
ISBN 9780393239959
Grades: Adult 914
1. Greene, David, 1976- 2. Railroad travel 3. Russia 4. Travel Writing — Europe
LC 2014029382

The co-host of NPR's "Morning Edition" describes his travels along the Trans-Siberian Railroad, from Moscow to Vladivostok, describing the people he met, from singing babushkas to entrepreneurial teens to political activists, and discusses the challenges faced by 21st-century Russia.

ESSENTIAL AND RECOMMENDED TITLES
914.1 British Isles — Geography

"With abundant interpersonal detail, Greene delivers a lively, tangible feeling of meeting modern Russians on one of the worlds famous railroads." —*Booklist*

914.1 British Isles — Geography

Banville, John
Time Pieces: A Dublin Memoir. John Banville; photographs by Paul Joyce. Alfred A. Knopf 2018. 224 p.
ISBN 9781524732837
Grades: Adult   914.1
1. Banville, John 2. Authors, Irish 3. Dublin, Ireland 4. Autobiographies and memoirs 5. Life stories — Arts and culture — Writing — Authors 6. History writing — Europe — Ireland
LC Bl2017050209

Presents a memoir of the author's life near Dublin, a city that inspired his imagination and literary life and served as a backdrop for the dissatisfactions of adult years shaped by Dublin's cultural, political, architectural, and social history.

"Featuring excellent photographs by Paul Joyce, the short tome resembles a whimsical, funnier version of W. G. Sebalds meditative style. A richly rewarding and personal work of Irish history and culture." —*Booklist*

Originally published by Hachette Books Ireland, 2016.

914.5 Italy — Geography

Mayes, Frances
See You in the Piazza: New Places to Discover in Italy. Frances Mayes. Crown Publishing 2019. xvii, 429 pages : Map
ISBN 9780451497697
Grades: Adult   914.5
1. Mayes, Frances 2. Women travelers 3. Recipes 4. Culture 5. American people in Italy 6. Voyages and travels 7. Italy 8. Travel Writing — Europe 9. Food writing — Memoirs and biographies
LC 2018289932

Presents an evocative, recipe-complemented travel narrative through Italy's 20 regions, from Friuli to Calabria, that identifies the lesser-known cultural and historical gems enjoyed by locals.

"Accompanied by her husband, Ed, and sometimes by her precocious grandson, William, or by various friends, Mayes enthusiastically seeks out the highlights of small towns, usually in the off season." —*Booklist*

Includes indexes.

915 Geography of and travel in Asia

Belliveau, Denis
In the Footsteps of Marco Polo: A Companion to the Public Television Film. Denis Belliveau and Francis O'Donnell. Rowman & Littlefield Publishers : 2008. 256 p.
ISBN 9780742556836
Grades: 9 10 11 12 Adult   915
1. Polo, Marco, 1254-1323? 2. Belliveau, Denis, 1964- 3. O'Donnell, Francis 4. Explorers 5. Adventurers 6. Voyages and travels 7. Asia 8. Travel Writing — Retracing Historic Journeys 9. Travel Writing — Asia and the South Pacific 10. Adult books for young adults
LC 2008023411

An illustrated companion volume to a PBS documentary traces the authors' two-year expedition to answer the question about Marco Polo's alleged visit to China, a venture that was fraught with the perils and turmoil of the Middle East and natural threats. TV tie-in.

Includes bibliographical references.

Feiler, Bruce
Walking the Bible: A Journey by Land Through the Five Books of Moses. Bruce Feiler. Harper Perennial 2005. 451 p. : Map
ISBN 9780060838638
Grades: Adult   915
1. Feiler, Bruce, 1964- 2. Pilgrims and pilgrimages 3. Travelers 4. Voyages and travels 5. Southwest Asia and North Africa (Middle East) 6. Spirituality and Religion — Christianity 7. Spirituality and Religion — Judaism 8. Travel Writing — Southwest Asia and North Africa (Middle East)
LC Oc2007124492

The author recounts his ten-thousand-mile journey across the Middle East in search of the roots of the Bible to discover whether it was an abstraction or a living, breathing entity.

"Determined to connect more deeply with his religious roots, Feiler joined an archaeologist in a trek through the Middle East, visiting the sites mentioned in the Pentateuch, the first five books of the Hebrew Bible. A book full of wonder and awe and personal enlightenment." —*Booklist*

Includes bibliographical references and index.

Theroux, Paul
The Great Railway Bazaar: By Train Through Asia. Paul Theroux. Houghton Mifflin 2006. 342 p.
ISBN 9780618658947
Grades: Adult   915
1. Theroux, Paul 2. American people in Asia 3. Travelers 4. Railroad travel 5. Railroads 6. Authors, American 7. Voyages and travels 8. Asia 9. 1970s 10. 20th century 11. Travel Writing — Modes of Transportation — by Train 12. Travel Writing — Asia and the South Pacific
LC 2006287162

I have seldom heard a train go by and not wished I was on it," confesses the author. Take the train with him through Europe and Asia.

"The author took a four-month solitary lecture tour of Asia in 1973, traveling by train wherever possible. His route was through Turkey, Iran, India, Southeast Asia, Japan, and back to London via the Soviet Union. He writes of conversations and impressions of the people encountered." —*Library Journal*

Reprint. Previously published: Boston : Houghton Mifflin, 1975.

Riding the Iron Rooster: By Train Through China. Paul Theroux. Houghton Mifflin 2006. 528 p.
ISBN 9780618658978
Grades: 11 12 Adult   915
1. Theroux, Paul 2. American people in Asia 3. Railroad travel 4. Authors, American 5. Trains 6. National characteristics, Chinese 7. Voyages and travels 8. China 9. 20th century 10. Travel Writing — Modes of Transportation — by Train 11. Travel Writing — Asia and the South Pacific
LC 2006028745

Thomas Cook Travel Book Award, 1989.

The author of the Great Railway Bazaar recounts his experiences while traveling throughout Communist China by train, offering observations on the scenery and recalling conversations with Chinese citizens and other fellow travelers. Reprint.

"This is an account of the author's yearlong rail journey through China. For Theroux, traveling is both about people—their thoughts, customs, and peculiarities—and a form of autobiography, and here we learn as much about his own quirks and fancies as we do about the intriguing world of contemporary China." —*Library Journal*

Originally published: New York : Putnam's, 1988.

Thubron, Colin
Shadow of the Silk Road. Colin Thubron. Harper Collins 2007. 363 p. : Map
ISBN 9780061231728
Grades: Adult   915
1. Thubron, Colin, 1939- 2. Travelers 3. Roads 4. Voyages and travels 5. Silk Road 6. Travel Writing — Asia and the South Pacific
LC 2006052142

The author recounts his ambitious and dangerous trek along the legendary Silk Road, during which he ventured from the heart of China to the mountains of

Central Asia, through northern Afghanistan, across the plains of Iran, and into Kurdish Turkey.

"An illuminating account of a breathtaking journey." —*Booklist*

Includes index; Originally published: London : Chatto & Windus, 2006.

915.804 Central Asia — Travel

Harris, Kate

Lands of Lost Borders: A Journey on the Silk Road. Kate Harris. Dey Street Books 2018. 320 p. : Illustration; Map

ISBN 9780062839343

Grades: Adult   **915.804**

1. Harris, Kate, 1982- 2. Women travelers 3. Bicycling 4. Bicycle touring 5. Voyages and travels 6. Silk Road 7. Autobiographies and memoirs 8. Canadian literature 9. Travel writing — Asia and the South Pacific 10. Travel Writing — Modes of Transportation — Cycling

Charles Taylor Prize for Literary Non-Fiction (Canada), 2019; Edna Staebler Award for Creative Non-Fiction, 2019.

An Oxford-trained scientist and award-winning writer presents an evocative travelogue and memoir of her journey by bicycle along the Silk Road and how it became synonymous with humanity's exploration of boundaries.

Includes bibliographical references and Internet addresses.

916 Geography of and travel in Africa

Theroux, Paul

The Last Train to Zona Verde: My Ultimate African Safari. Paul Theroux. Houghton Mifflin Harcourt 2013. 353 p. : Map

ISBN 9780618839339

Grades: Adult   **916**

1. Voyages and travels 2. American people in Africa 3. Travel Writing — Africa

Booklist Editors' Choice, 2013.

An acclaimed travel writer and novelist describes his journey across Africa, from Cape Town to Cape Province and into Namibia, riding elephants, meeting Bushmen and discussing the changes that have taken place since his first visit 50 years ago.

"The acclaimed travel writer and novelist chronicles his journey through Africa as tourist, adventure-seeker, thinker and hopeful critic... Reading this enlightening book won't only open a window into Theroux's mind, it will also impart a deeper understanding of Africa and travel in general." —*Kirkus*

916.204 Egypt — Travel

Millard, Candice

★ *River of the Gods: Genius, Courage, and Betrayal in the Search for the Source of the Nile.* Candice Millard. Doubleday 2022. 320 p.

ISBN 9780385543101

Grades: Adult   **916.204**

1. Burton, Richard Francis, Sir, 1821-1890 2. Speke, John Hanning, 1827-1864 3. Bombay, Sidi Mubarak 4. Explorers 5. Rivers 6. Expeditions 7. Discoveries (in geography) 8. Guides (People) 9. Competition 10. Betrayal 11. British people in Africa 12. Colonialism 13. Aristocracy 14. Nile River 15. Egypt 16. Sudan 17. Great Britain 18. Life stories — People in history — Explorers 19. Adventure writing — Exploration 20. History writing — Colonization — Africa 21. History writing — Exploration

LC 2021044497

Set against the backdrop of the race to exploit Africa by the colonial powers, a story of courage and adventure brings to life the rivalry between two enemies—a decorated soldier and a young aristocrat/Army officer—as they set out to find the mysterious headwaters of the Nile River.

"Millard's lushly detailed adventure story keeps a steady eye on the racial power dynamics involved in this imperialist endeavor and brilliantly illuminates the characters of Burton, Speke, and Bombay." —*Publishers Weekly*

Includes bibliographical references and index.

917 Geography of and travel in North America

Bryson, Bill

★ *A Walk in the Woods: Rediscovering America on the Appalachian Trail.* Bill Bryson. Broadway Books 1998. 276 p.

ISBN 9780767902519

Grades: 11 12 Adult   **917**

1. Bryson, Bill 2. Natural history 3. Hiking 4. Travelers 5. Voyages and travels 6. Appalachian Trail 7. 20th century 8. Page to screen 9. Nature Writing — Personal Responses 10. Travel Writing — Modes of Transportation — on Foot 11. Travel Writing — United States 12. Adult books for young adults 13. Humor writing — Classic humorists 14. Nonfiction that reads like fiction

LC 97032627

Bryson shares his breath-taking adventures and the fascinating history of the 2,100-mile Appalachian Trail, as he travels slowly on foot.

"Bryson's breezy, self-mocking tone may turn off readers who hanker for another into Thin Air or Seven Years in Tibet. Others, however, may find themselves turning the pages with increasing amusement and anticipation as they discover that they're in the hands of a satirist of the first rank, one who writes (and walks) with Chaucerian brio." —*New York Times Book Review*

Later published in an omnibus entitled: Walkabout; the 2015 film a Walk in the Woods: Rediscovering America on the Appalachian Trail is based on this memoir; Includes bibliographical references (p. [275]-276).

Buck, Rinker

Life on the Mississippi: An Epic American Adventure. Rinker Buck. Avid Reader Press 2022. 320 p.

ISBN 9781501106378

Grades: Adult   **917**

1. Buck, Rinker, 1950- 2. Brothers 3. Voyages and travels 4. Rivers 5. Mississippi river 6. United States 7. Travel Writing — Retracing Historic Journeys 8. Travel Writing — Modes of Transportation 9. History writing — Regional history — United States

The author of the New York Times best-seller the Oregon Trail, building an authentic wooden flatboat from a bygone era, casts off down the Mississippi river, charting his own geographical and emotional journey, while providing a satisfying work of history.

"Journalist Buck, who documented his travels by covered wagon in the Oregon Trail, returns with a captivating and occasionally cantankerous account of the 2,000-mile, four-month flatboat journey he made in 2016 down the Ohio and Mississippi rivers from Pittsburgh to New Orleans." —*Publishers Weekly*

Horwitz, Tony

Spying on the South: An Odyssey Across the American Divide. Tony Horwitz. Penguin Press 2019. 496 p.

ISBN 9781101980286

Grades: Adult   **917**

1. Olmsted, Frederick Law, 1822-1903 2. Horwitz, Tony, 1958- 3. Travelers 4. Cultural differences 5. Race relations 6. Social life and customs 7. Voyages and travels 8. Southern States 9. Travel Writing — Retracing Historic Journeys 10. History writing — Regional history — United States

LC 2018056912

The Pulitzer Prize-winning New Yorker writer and author of Confederates in the Attic retraces Frederick Law Olmstead's epic journey across the pre-Civil War American South in search of common ground in today's dangerously divided nation.

Includes bibliographical references and index.

ESSENTIAL AND RECOMMENDED TITLES
917.286 Costa Rica — Geography

Perry, Imani
★ *South* to America: A Journey Below the Mason-dixon to Understand the Soul of a Nation. Imani Perry. Ecco Press 2022. 336 p.
ISBN 9780062977403
Grades: Adult   917
1. Perry, Imani, 1972- 2. African American women 3. Multiracial women 4. Homecomings 5. African American families 6. Culture 7. History 8. Regionalism 9. Group identity 10. Race relations 11. Social life and customs 12. Voyages and travels 13. Southern States 14. 21st century 15. Book club best bets 16. Life stories — Identity 17. Travel Writing — United States 18. History writing — Regional history — United States 19. Society and culture — Urban and regional studies
LC 2021047476
National Book Award for Nonfiction, 2022.

We all think we know the South. Even those who have never lived there can rattle off a list of signifiers: the Civil War, Gone with the Wind, the Ku Klux Klan, plantations, football, Jim Crow, slavery. But the idiosyncrasies, dispositions, and habits of the region are stranger and more complex than much of the country tends to acknowledge. In South to America, Imani Perry shows that the meaning of American is inextricably linked with the South, and that our understanding of its history and culture is the key to understanding the nation as a whole. This is the story of a Black woman and native Alabaman returning to the region she has always called home and considering it with fresh eyes. Her journey is full of detours, deep dives, and surprising encounters with places and people.

"Perry, professor of African American studies at Princeton, melds memoir, travel narrative, and history in an intimate, penetrating journey through the South, from the Mason-Dixon Line to Florida, West Virginia, and the Bahamas. . . . A graceful, finely crafted examination of America's racial, cultural, and political identity." —*Kirkus*
Includes index.

Theroux, Paul
On the Plain of Snakes: A Mexican Journey. Paul Theroux. Houghton Mifflin Harcourt 2019. 448 pages
ISBN 9780544866478
Grades: Adult   917
1. Theroux, Paul 2. Social life and customs 3. Travelers 4. Boundaries 5. Voyages and travels 6. Mexico 7. Mexican-American Border Region 8. Travel Writing — Central and South America
LC 2019004920

Legendary travel writer Paul Theroux fearlessly drives the entire length of the US-Mexico border, then goes deep into the hinterland, on the back roads of Chiapas and Oaxaca, to uncover the rich, layered world behind today's brutal headlines.

"This is a personal book, and Theroux does not hesitate to articulate his point of view on a number of topics, allowing for no sacred cows [cuidado con el realismo mgico!] as he unapologetically takes into consideration context, anecdotal evidence, and his on-the-road experiences to arrive at his prescription for improving the Mexican situation." —*Booklist*
Includes index.

Thoreau, Henry David
The Maine Woods. by Henry David Thoreau; introduction by Edward Hoagland. Penguin Books 1988. xxxiii, 442 p.
ISBN 9780140170139
Grades: Adult   917
1. Thoreau, Henry David, 1817-1862 2. Authors, American 3. Natural history 4. Nature 5. Logging 6. Indigenous peoples of North America 7. Voyages and travels 8. Maine 9. 19th century 10. Nature Writing — Personal Responses 11. Travel Writing — United States
LC 88003644

Thoreau's narratives of his journeys into the Maine wilderness are presented.
Includes index; Reprint, with new introd. Originally published: Boston : Ticknor & Fields, 1864.

Watson, Paul
Ice Ghosts: The Epic Hunt for the Lost Franklin Expedition. Paul Watson. W W Norton & CO Inc 2017. 384 p.
ISBN 9780393249385
Grades: Adult   917
1. Explorers 2. Salvage 3. Shipwrecks 4. Exploration 5. Arctic regions 6. Northwest Passage 7. History writing — Exploration 8. History writing — Historical mysteries
LC 2016054683

A Pulitzer Prize-winning journalist and expedition member describes how an unlikely combination of marine science and Inuit knowledge helped solve the mystery of the lost Franklin expedition of 1845.

"A keen, entertaining chronicle of the various attempts to locate a sensationally doomed expedition." —*Kirkus*

917.286 Costa Rica — Geography

Dial, Roman
The Adventurer's Son: A Memoir. Roman Dial. William Morrow & Co 2020. 368 pages
ISBN 9780062876607
Grades: Adult   917.286
1. Dial, Roman 2. Fathers and sons 3. Adventurers 4. Rain forests 5. Wilderness areas 6. Missing men 7. Searching 8. Memories 9. Grief 10. Costa Rica 11. Autobiographies and memoirs 12. Life stories — Relationships — Parent and child 13. Family and relationships — Parenting
LC Bl2020000030

An Alaska Pacific University scientist and National Geographic Explorer recounts his two-year effort to uncover the fate of his adventurer son, who in 2014 disappeared into the untracked rainforest of Corcovado National Park.

"In its emotional restraint and careful descriptions of the wild, this is a slow-burning tribute. A poignant, highly moving memoir of tragic circumstances and a lifelong love of exploring." —*Kirkus*

917.3 Geography of and travel in United States

Heat Moon, William Least
Roads to Quoz: An American Mosey. William Least Heat-Moon. Little, Brown 2008. 592 p.
ISBN 9780316110259
Grades: Adult   917.3
1. Heat Moon, William Least 2. Small town life 3. Small towns 4. U.S. states 5. American people 6. Travelers 7. Voyages and travels 8. United States 9. Travel Writing — United States 10. Travel Writing — Small Town Life 11. Adult books for young adults
LC 2008019375

Recounts the author's series of journeys into small-town America, visits during which he performed life-enhancing investigations into some of the nation's most incongruous regions.

"The author's journey is as meandering as the Ouachita itself, and readers will relish the experiences he and . [his wife] describe along their trip." —*Library Journal*

917.304 Geography of and travel in United States — Travel

Hall, Alvin D.
Driving the Green Book: A Road Trip Through the Living History of Black Resistance. Alvin Hall, with Karl Weber. HarperOne, an imprint of HarperCollins 2023. 288 p.
ISBN 9780063271968
Grades: Adult   917.304
1. Hall, Alvin D. 2. African American authors 3. Voyages and travels 4. Tourism 5. Segregation 6. Racism 7. Marginalized people 8. Cross-country automo-

bile trips 9. African American history 10. Race relations 11. United States history 12. 20th century 13. History writing — African American — United States 14. Life stories — Identity — Race and ethnicity 15. Travel Writing — United States 16. Travel Writing — Modes of Transportation — Road Trips

LC Bl2022038517

A broadcaster and educator presents the vivid stories of African-Americans who traveled the country during the age of segregation, using the Green Book, a guide which helped Black people travel safely.

"This well-written account will appeal to readers interested in civil rights, Black history, and travel literature." —*Library Journal*

Includes bibliographical references.

Heat Moon, William Least
Blue Highways: *A Journey into America*. William Least Heat-Moon; photographs by the author; with a new afterword by the author. Back Bay Books 1999. 429 p. : Illustration
ISBN 9780316353298
Grades: 11 12 Adult   917.304
1. Heat Moon, William Least 2. Cross-country automobile trips 3. Travelers 4. Freeways 5. Automobile travel 6. Automobiles 7. Voyages and travels 8. United States 9. 20th century 10. Travel Writing — Modes of Transportation — Road Trips 11. Travel Writing — United States

LC 00265444

Hailed as a masterpiece of American travel writing, Blue Highways is an unforgettable journey along our nation's backroads. William Least Heat-Moon set out with little more than the need to put home behind him and a sense of curiosity about "those little towns that get on the map-if they get on at all-only because some cartographer has a blank space to fill: Remote, Oregon; Simplicity, Virginia; New Freedom, Pennsylvania; New Hope, Tennessee; Why, Arizona; Whynot, Mississippi." His adventures, his discoveries, and his recollections of the extraordinary people he encountered along the way amount to a revelation of the true American experience.

Includes index; Originally published: Boston : Little, Brown, c1982.

Jenkins, Peter
A Walk Across America. Peter Jenkins. Perennial 2001. x, 290 p. : Color illustration; Map
ISBN 9780060959555
Grades: 11 12 Adult   917.304
1. Jenkins, Peter, 1951- 2. Travelers 3. Walking 4. Adventure travel 5. Self-fulfillment 6. Voyages and travels 7. United States 8. Biographies 9. Travel Writing — Modes of Transportation — on Foot 10. Travel Writing — United States

LC BL2004001132

A young New Englander celebrates a rarely seen and almost forgotten America as he recalls the people he met and the situations he experienced during a journey in search of his country and himself.

Sequel: The walk west; Originally published: New York : Morrow, 1979.

Waterman, Jonathan
National Geographic Atlas of the National Parks. Jon Waterman; foreword by Gary Knell, Chairman, National Geographic Partners. National Geographic 2019. 431 pages : Illustration; Color
ISBN 9781426220579
Grades: Adult   917.304
1. National parks and reserves 2. United States 3. Nature Writing — Natural Landscapes 4. Reference — Atlases 5. Reference — Travel guides 6. Adult books for young adults

LC 2019009040

Profiles of 60 parks—from battlefields to national seashores—administered by the National Park Service, highlighting their diverse appeal and available outdoor activities. A brief glimpse is given of 29 additional parks, including the newly created Indiana Sand Dunes."

Includes indexes.

917.47 Geography of and travel in United States — New York

Satow, Julie
The Plaza: The Secret Life of America's Most Famous Hotel. Julie Satow. 2019. 352 p.
ISBN 9781455566679
Grades: Adult   917.47
1. Architecture 2. Hotels 3. Historic buildings 4. Architecture, American 5. New York City history 6. History writing — Regional history — United States 7. Arts and Entertainment — Architecture 8. Adult books for young adults

LC 2018048170

Recounts the wealthy history of the Plaza hotel, covering major scandals, tragedies, and some of the celebrities who have graced the rooms of the establishment.

"Readers will happily soak up period details and take notes on how the stalwart staff dealt with class snobbery, prohibition and gangsters, wartime privations, the turbulent 1960s, wealthy dowagers, blushing debutantes, persistent groupies, omnipresent prostitutes, and brawling Indian billionaires. This is social history at its best: Thoughtful, engaging, and lots of fun." —*Booklist*

Includes bibliographical references and index.

917.53 Washington (D.C.) — geography

Souza, Pete
The West Wing and Beyond: What I Saw Inside the Presidency. Pete Souza. Voracious, Little, Brown and Company 2022. 253 pages : Color; Illustration
ISBN 9780316383370
Grades: Adult   917.53
1. Obama, Barack 2. Presidents 3. Photography 4. 21st century 5. Visual nonfiction 6. History writing — Presidency — 21st century — United States 7. Life stories — Politics — Politicians

LC Bl2022029872

Pete Souza has spent more time in the Oval Office than almost any person in history. During the Obama administration alone, Souza was inside the presidential bubble for more than 25,000 hours and made nearly two million photographs. The result is an unprecedented view of how our democracy really works. Now Souza invites you into the inner sanctum of the American presidency, sharing rarely seen photographs and untold stories of life and work in the White House and traveling with the President around the world."

"This unique offering is bound to be popular, so expect demand—and have the Obama book standing by." —*Booklist*

917.64 Texas — Geography

Wright, Lawrence
God Save Texas: *A Journey into the Soul of the Lone Star State*. Lawrence Wright. Alfred A. Knopf 2018. 304 p.
ISBN 9780525520108
Grades: Adult   917.64
1. Wright, Lawrence, 1947- 2. U.S. states 3. Culture 4. Social life and customs 5. Politics and government 6. Voyages and travels 7. Texas 8. Autobiographies and memoirs 9. Life stories — Identity 10. History writing — Regional history — United States 11. Travel Writing — United States

LC 2017031324

New York Times Notable Book, 2018; National Book Critics Circle Award for Nonfiction finalist, 2018.

The Pulitzer Prize-winning author of the Looming Tower explores the history, culture and politics of Texas while challenging popular stereotypes, offering insight into how the state boasts some of the highest rates of diversity, technology exports and growth as well as the lowest tax models and government regulations.

"Wrights large-scale portrait, which reveals how Texas is only growing in influence, is comprehensive, insightful, and compulsively entertaining." —*Publishers Weekly*

ESSENTIAL AND RECOMMENDED TITLES
917.804 Geography of and travel in United States — West (U.S.) — Travel

917.804 Geography of and travel in United States — West (U.S.) — Travel

Ambrose, Stephen E.
★ *Undaunted Courage: Meriwether Lewis, Thomas Jefferson, and the Opening of the American West.* Stephen E. Ambrose. Simon & Schuster 1996. 511 p. : Illustration; Map
ISBN 9780684811079
Grades: 11 12 Adult   917.804
1. Lewis, Meriwether, 1774-1809 2. Clark, William, 1770-1838 3. Jefferson, Thomas, 1743-1826 4. Explorers 5. Overland journeys to the Pacific 6. Voyages and travels 7. Exploration 8. The West (United States) 9. United States 10. 19th century 11. History writing — Westward expansion — United States 12. History writing — Early America — United States 13. Adult books for young adults
LC 95037146
ALA Notable Book, 1997; School Library Journal Best Books: Best Adult Books 4 Teens, 1996; Spur Award for Historical Nonfiction, 1997.
  In 1803 President Thomas Jefferson selected his personal secretary, Captain Merriwether Lewis, to lead a voyage up the Missouri River to the Rockies, over the mountains, down the Columbia River to the Pacific Ocean and back. Lewis and his partner, Captain William Clark, endured incredible hardships and saw incredible sights.
  "This treatment of the Lewis and Clark Expedition is essentially a biography of Lewis, although the bulk of it is a lively retelling of the journey of the two captains—together with their party of soldiers and frontiersmen, Clark's Black slave, York, and the legendary Shoshone Indian woman, Sacagawea, and her infant son—conveyed with passionate enthusiasm by Mr. Ambrose and sprinkled liberally with some of the most famous and vivid passages from the travelers' journals." —*New York Times Book Review*
  Includes bibliographical references (p. 493-496) and index.

Grant, Will
The Last Ride of the Pony Express: My 2,000-mile Horseback Journey into the Old West. Will Grant. Little Brown & Company 2023. 336 p.
ISBN 9780316422314
Grades: Adult   917.804
1. Grant, Will, (journalist) 2. Cowboys 3. Journalists 4. Equestrianism 5. Pony Express 6. Voyages and travels 7. The West (United States) 8. United States 9. Autobiographies and memoirs 10. Life stories — Nature and outdoors 11. Travel Writing — Modes of transportation 12. Travel Writing — Retracing historic journeys 13. History writing — Regional history — United States 14. Debut title
  Inspired by the likes of Mark Twain, Sir Richard Burton and Horace Greeley, a cowboy and journalist takes us an epic and authentic horseback journey across the American West as he rides the Pony Express trail from one end to the other.
  "Journalist Grant debuts with a thoughtful and entertaining account of his five-month trip along the length of the 19th-century overland mail route from St. Joseph, Mo, to Sacramento, Calif....Enriched by Grant's deep knowledge of the West, matter-of-fact prose, and colorful character sketches, this is a rewarding ride." —*Publishers Weekly*

Schmidt, Thomas
The Saga of Lewis & Clark: Into the Uncharted West. Thomas Schmidt and Jeremy Schmidt. DK Pub. 1999. 210 p. : Illustration; Color; Map
ISBN 9780789480767
Grades: Adult   917.804
1. Exploration 2. The West (United States) 3. Illustrated books 4. Biographies 5. History writing — Early America — United States 6. Life stories — People in history — Explorers
LC 99025606
YALSA Best Books for Young Adults, 2000.
  Provides an illustrated account of the expedition of Lewis and Clark from Missouri, through vast uncharted territories, to Oregon.
  A Tehabi book; Includes index.

Wallis, Michael
Route 66: The Mother Road. Michael Wallis. St. Martin's Griffin 2001. xi, 276 p. : Illustration; Color; Map
ISBN 9780312281670
Grades: Adult   917.804
1. Roads 2. United States Highway 66 3. Voyages and travels 4. The West (United States) 5. History writing — Regional history — United States
LC BL 00005386
  Updated and revised to coincide with the seventy-fifth anniversary of this American icon, a fascinating social history of Route 66, which spurred a revival of the dying American road, evokes the magic of the people and landscapes that surround it. A cultural history of America's most famous highway chronicles the road from its founding to its demise and unprecedented revival, and celebrates the many sites and stops along its 2,400-mile route.
  75th anniversary edition; Includes bibliographical references (p. 270-271).

917.91 Geography of and travel in United States — Arizona

Fedarko, Kevin
A Walk in the Park: The True Story of a Spectacular Misadventure in the Grand Canyon. Kevin Fedarko. Scribner 2024. 560 p.
ISBN 9781501183058
Grades: Adult   917.91
1. Fedarko, Kevin 2. McBride, Peter (Photographer) 3. Voyages and travels 4. Hiking 5. Grand Canyon National Park 6. Colorado River 7. The West (United States) 8. Nature Writing — Natural Landscapes 9. Travel Writing — United States
LC 2023056196
  The author of the Emerald Mile discusses chronicles his dangerous, life-changing, year-long 750-mile trek along the length of the Grand Canyon, living in the vertical wilderness between the caprock along the rims and the Colorado River.
  "An immersive account of the challenges of a grueling 750-mile hike through the Grand Canyon." —*Kirkus*
  Includes bibliographical references.

Owen, David
Where the Water Goes: Life and Death Along the Colorado River. David Owen. Riverhead Books 2017. 272 p.
ISBN 9781594633775
Grades: Adult   917.91
1. Owen, David, 1955- 2. Water-supply 3. Stream ecology 4. Colorado River 5. Travel writing — United States 6. Nature writing — Natural landscapes
LC 2016039410
  The author of the Conundrum presents a revelatory account of where our water comes from and where it goes, examining the complicated human-made ecosystem of waterways, reservoirs, power plants, fracking sites and farms that contribute to shortage issues in the western United States.
  "With water shortages looming across the globe, Owens work provides invaluable lessons on the rewards and pitfalls involved in managing an essential natural resource." —*Booklist*
  Includes bibliographical references and index.

Ross, John F.
The Promise of the Grand Canyon: John Wesley Powell's Perilous Journey and His Vision for the American West. John F. Ross. Viking Press 2018. 400 p.
ISBN 9780525429876
Grades: Adult   917.91
1. Powell, John Wesley, 1834-1902 2. Naturalists 3. Explorers 4. National parks and reserves 5. Geologists 6. Nature conservation 7. Land Stewardship 8. Water conservation 9. Grand Canyon 10. Colorado River 11. American Westward Expansion (1803-1899) 12. Biographies 13. Adventure writing — Exploration 14. Nature Writing — Natural Landscapes 15. Nature Writing — Environmental Issues 16. Life stories — People in history — Explorers 17. Life stories — Nature and outdoors

LC Bl2018125383

When John Wesley Powell became the first person to navigate the entire Colorado River, through the Grand Canyon, he completed what Lewis and Clark had begun nearly 70 years earlier—the final exploration of continental America. The son of an abolitionist preacher, a Civil War hero (who lost an arm at Shiloh), and a passionate naturalist and geologist, in 1869 Powell tackled the vast and dangerous gorge carved by the Colorado River and known today (thanks to Powell) as the Grand Canyon.

"If you've ever used a topographic map, thank Powell. His legacy deserves more attention, and Ross's biography stands to correct this. For all readers, especially lovers of science, history, and adventure." —*Library Journal*

917.94 Geography of and travel in United States — California

Robinson, Kim Stanley
The High Sierra: A Love Story. Kim Stanley Robinson. Little, Brown & Company 2022. 560 p.
ISBN 9780316593014
Grades: Adult   917.94
1. Robinson, Kim Stanley 2. Authors 3. Mountains 4. Landforms 5. Outdoor life 6. Hiking 7. Camping 8. Natural history 9. Naturalists 10. Nature conservation 11. Sierra Nevada Mountains 12. Nature Writing — Natural Landscapes 13. Nature Writing — Personal Responses 14. Travel Writing — United States 15. Life stories — Nature and outdoors

In this stunning tribute to the Sierra Nevada mountains, a writer explores what makes this span of mountains one of the most compelling places on Earth and shares his own personal experiences to inspire other travel readers to prepare for a life-changing adventure.

"Novelist Robinson (the Mars trilogy) vividly conveys his passion for the Sierra mountains in this enthralling blend of memoir, history, and science." —*Publishers Weekly*

917.9804 Geography of and travel in United States — Alaska — Travel

Adams, Mark
Tip of the Iceberg: My 3,000-mile Journey Around Wild Alaska, the Last Great American Frontier. Mark Adams. Dutton 2018. 336 p.
ISBN 9781101985106
Grades: Adult   917.9804
1. Adams, Mark, 1967- 2. Voyages and travels 3. Alaska 4. Autobiographies and memoirs 5. Travel writing — Retracing historic journeys

LC 2017039007

A fascinating and funny journey into Alaska, America's last frontier, retracing the historic 1899 Harriman Expedition.

"Tourists will certainly enjoy reading about both the past and the present, and the breezy, self-deprecating tone makes for an obvious vacation diversion." —*Booklist*

Krakauer, Jon
Into the Wild. Jon Krakauer. Villard Books 1996. 207 p. : Map
ISBN 9780679428503
Grades: 11 12 Adult   917.9804
1. McCandless, Christopher Johnson, 1968-1992 2. Wilderness survival 3. Adventurers 4. Young men 5. Travelers 6. Hitchhiking 7. Adventure 8. Voyages and travels 9. Asceticism 10. Death 11. Nature 12. Men and nature 13. Idealism 14. Alaska 15. The West (United States) 16. Biographies 17. Page to screen 18. Life stories — Facing adversity — Disasters and tragedies 19. Sports and Competition — Mountaineering 20. Adventure writing — Survival 21. Adult books for young adults 22. Nonfiction that reads like fiction 23. Book club best bets

LC 95020008

Garden State Teen Book Award (New Jersey), Nonfiction, 1999; YALSA Best Books for Young Adults, 1997.

Christopher Johnson McCandless, a young man from a well-to-do family, hitchhikes to Alaska in April of 1992. He had given his savings to charity, abandoned his car and his possessions, burned all his cash, and invented a new life for himself. Four months later, his decomposed body was found by a moose hunter.

"Christopher McCandless was a disaffected, idealistic young man who trekked into the Alaskan wilderness in search of transcendence and perished there. This narrative, which ponders his journey and inner life with sympathy and imagination, has YA appeal on many levels." —*Booklist*

918.1 Brazil — Geography

Grann, David
The Lost City of Z: A Tale of Deadly Obsession in the Amazon. David Grann. Doubleday 2008. 352 p.
ISBN 9780385513531
Grades: Adult   918.1
1. Fawcett, Percy Harrison, 1867-1925? 2. Grann, David 3. El Dorado (Legendary land) 4. Exploration 5. Expeditions 6. Explorers 7. Voyages and travels 8. Amazon River 9. Latin America 10. Page to screen 11. History writing — Historical mysteries 12. History writing — Latin America 13. Nonfiction that reads like fiction 14. Debut title

LC 2008017432

Indies' Choice Book Awards, Adult Nonfiction, 2010; ALA Notable Book, 2010; New York Times Notable Book, 2009.

Interweaves the story of British explorer Percy Fawcett, who vanished during a 1925 expedition into the Amazon to find an ancient civilization, with the author's own adventure-filled quest into the uncharted wilderness to uncover the mysteries surrounding Fawcett's final journey and the secrets of what really lies deep in the Amazon jungle.

"A colorful tale of true adventure, marked by satisfyingly unexpected twists, turns and plenty of dark portents." —*Kirkus*

Title adapted into a film by the same name in 2017; Includes bibliographical references.

Millard, Candice
River of Doubt: Theodore Roosevelt's Darkest Journey. Candice Millard. Doubleday 2005. IX, 416 p, 16 p. of plates : Illustration
ISBN 9780385507967
Grades: Adult   918.1
1. Roosevelt, Theodore, 1858-1919 2. Natural history 3. Presidents 4. Rain forests 5. Voyages and travels 6. Amazon Valley 7. United States 8. Biographies 9. History writing — Latin America — South America 10. Adventure writing — Exploration 11. Nonfiction that reads like fiction

LC 2005046541

New York Times Notable Book, 2005.

Chronicles the 1914 expedition of Theodore Roosevelt into the unexplored heart of the Amazon basin to explore and map the region surrounding a tributary called the River of Doubt, detailing the perilous conditions they faced.

"The author turns this incredible story into one that easily matches an Indiana Jones screen adventure." —*Library Journal*

Includes bibliographical references (p. [395]-402) and index.

919 Geography of and travel in Australasia, Pacific Ocean islands, Atlantic Ocean islands, Arctic islands, Antarctica and on extraterrestrial worlds

Bell, Jim
The Interstellar Age: Inside the Forty-year Voyager Mission. Jim Bell. Dutton 2015. x, 324 pages : Illustration; Color
ISBN 9780525954323
Grades: Adult   919
1. Project Voyager 2. Space exploration 3. Space probes 4. Space flight 5. Planets 6. Astronautics 7. Exploration 8. Aviation 9. United States 10. Science Writing — Space and Flight

ESSENTIAL AND RECOMMENDED TITLES
919.8 Arctic islands — Geography

LC 2014031706
ALA Notable Book, 2016.

The story of the men and women who drove the Voyager spacecraft mission told by a scientist who was there from the beginning.

"A highly enjoyable read for anyone with an interest in popular science." —*Library Journal*

Includes bibliographical references (pages 297-308) and index.

Bryson, Bill

In a Sunburned Country. Bill Bryson. Broadway Books 2000. x, 307 p. : Illustration; Map

ISBN 9780767903851

Grades: Adult   919

1. Bryson, Bill 2. Travelers 3. National characteristics, Australian 4. Voyages and travels 5. Australia 6. Travel Writing — Asia and the South Pacific 7. Humor writing — Classic humorists 8. Nonfiction that reads like fiction

LC 00025566

Booklist Editors' Choice, 2000.

Bryson shares accounts of his travels in Australia, which has the friendliest inhabitants, the hottest weather, and the most peculiar and lethal wildlife on the planet.

"In this book, Bryson chronicles his exploration of Australia, he introduces us to a town that went without electricity until the early 1990s, a former high-ranking politician who hawks his own autobiography to passersby, an assortment of coffee shops and restaurants, . a type of giant worm, and the world's most poisonous creature, the box jellyfish." —*Booklist*

Also published as: Down under: Travels in a sunburned country; Later published in an omnibus entitled: Walkabout; Includes bibliographical references (p. [305]-307).

Sagan, Carl

Pale Blue Dot: A Vision of the Human Future in Space. Carl Sagan. Random House 1994. xviii, 429 p. : Illustration; Color; Map

ISBN 9780679438410

Grades: Adult   919

1. Space exploration 2. Space 3. Science Writing — Space and Flight

LC 94018121

Examines humankind's changing awareness of its place in the universe and the rich potential of human ventures into the world beyond Earth.

"In a tour of our solar system, galaxy and beyond . Sagan meshes a history of astronomical discovery, a cogent brief for space exploration and an overview of life. His exploration of our place in the universe is illustrated with photographs, relief maps and paintings, including high-resolution images made by Voyager 1 and 2, as well as photos taken by the Galileo spacecraft, the Hubble Space Telescope and satellites orbiting Earth." —*Publishers Weekly*

Includes bibliographical references (p. [406]-411) and index.

919.8 Arctic islands — Geography

Alexander, Caroline

The Endurance: Shackleton's Legendary Antarctic Expedition. Caroline Alexander. Knopf 1998. 211 p. : Illustration; Map

ISBN 9780375404030

Grades: 11 12 Adult   919.8

1. Shackleton, Ernest Henry, Sir, 1874-1922 2. Explorers 3. Survival (after airplane accidents, shipwrecks, etc.) 4. Photographs 5. Exploration 6. Antarctica 7. 1910s 8. 20th century 9. History writing — Exploration 10. Adventure writing — Survival 11. Adult books for young adults

Alex Award, 1999; Booklist Editors' Choice: Adult Books for Young Adults, 1998; YALSA Best Books for Young Adults, 2000.

Recounts Sir Ernest Shackleton's expedition to cross Antarctica and the harrowing fight to survive for twenty months in freezing Antarctic conditions.

"Alexander, relying extensively on journals by crew members, some never published, as well as on myriad other sources, delivers a spellbinding story of human courage. . . . What makes this book especially exciting, however, are the 170 previously unpublished photos by the expedition's photographer, Frank Hurley." —*Publishers Weekly*

In association with the American Museum of Natural History.

Larson, Edward J.

An Empire of Ice: Scott, Shackleton, and the Heroic Age of Antarctic Science. Edward J. Larson. Yale University Press 2011. 360 p.

ISBN 9780300154085

Grades: Adult   919.8

1. Scott, Robert Falcon, 1868-1912 2. Shackleton, Ernest Henry, Sir, 1874-1922 3. Explorers 4. Scientific expeditions 5. Voyages and travels 6. Discoveries (in geography) 7. Expeditions 8. Exploration 9. Antarctica 10. 20th century 11. Biographies 12. Adventure writing — Exploration 13. History writing — Exploration 14. Life stories — People in history — Explorers

LC 2010044396

Examines the pioneering Antarctic expeditions of the early twentieth century within their larger scientific, social, and geopolitical context.

Includes bibliographical references and index.

919.89 Antarctica — Geography

Wood, Gillen D'Arcy

Land of Wondrous Cold: The Race to Discover Antarctica and Unlock the Secrets of Its Ice. Gillen D'Arcy Wood. Princeton University Press 2020. 304 p.

ISBN 9780691172200

Grades: Adult   919.89

1. Ice caps 2. Explorers 3. Expeditions 4. Polar expeditions 5. Exploration 6. Climate change 7. Antarctica 8. Nature Writing — Natural Landscapes 9. History writing — Exploration

LC 2019029836

A history of the first race to Antarctica that weaves the great polar discoveries of the nineteenth century with scientific breakthroughs of the modern era. Antarctica, the ice kingdom hosting the South Pole, looms large in the human imagination. The secrets of this vast frozen desert have long tempted explorers, but its brutal climate and glacial shores notoriously resist human intrusion. Land of Wondrous Cold tells a gripping story of the pioneer nineteenth-century voyages, when British, French, and American commanders raced to penetrate Antarctica's glacial rim for unknown lands beyond. These intrepid Victorian explorers-James Ross, Dumont D'Urville, and Charles Wilkes-laid the foundation for our current understanding of Terra Australis Incognita. Today, the white continent poses new challenges, as scientists race to uncover Earth's climate history recorded in the south polar ice and ocean floor, and to monitor the increasing instability of the Antarctic ice cap, which threatens inundation of coastalcities worldwide. Interweaving the breakthrough research of the modern Ocean Drilling Program with the dramatic discovery tales of their Victorian-era forerunners, Gillen D'Arcy Wood describes Antarctica's role in a planetary drama of plate tectonics, climate change, and species evolution stretching back more than thirty million years. An original, multifaceted portrait of the polar continent emerges, illuminating our profound connection to Antarctica in its past, present, and future incarnations. A deep-time history of monumental scale, Land of Wondrous Cold brings the remotest of worlds within close reach-an Antarctica vital to both planetary history and human fortunes.

"Outstanding history accompanied by outstanding popular science." —*Kirkus*

Includes bibliographical references and index.

919.8904 Antarctica — Travel

Bound, Mensun

The Ship Beneath the Ice: The Discovery of Shackleton's Endurance. Mensun Bound. Mariner Books 2023. 416 p.

ISBN 9780063297401

Grades: Adult   919.8904

PUBLIC LIBRARY CORE COLLECTION: NONFICTION
Twentieth Edition

1. Shackleton, Ernest Henry, Sir, 1874-1922 2. Bound, Mensun 3. Discoveries (in geography) 4. Ships 5. Shipwrecks 6. Underwater archaeologists 7. Archaeological expeditions 8. Explorers 9. Exploration 10. Antarctica 11. Debut title 12. Life stories — People in history — Explorers 13. History Writing — Archaeology 14. History Writing — Exploration

A renowned marine biologist presents this extraordinary firsthand account of the discovery of Ernest Shackleton's Endurance a century to the day after Shackleton's death that captures the intrepid spirit that joins two mariners across the centuries—both of whom accomplished the impossible.

"Throughout, Bound nicely interweaves the fascinating history of Shackleton's expedition into his own. An entertaining true-life adventure tale perfect for naval aficionados and armchair expeditioners." —*Kirkus*

Originally published in the UK by Macmillan, London, in 2022.

O'Brady, Colin

★ *The Impossible First: From Fire to Ice - Crossing Antarctica Alone.* Colin O'Brady. Scribner 2020. 288 pages

ISBN 9781982133115

Grades: Adult   919.8904

1. O'Brady, Colin 2. Quests 3. Voyages and travels 4. Goals and objectives 5. Competition 6. Expeditions 7. Wilderness survival 8. Exploration 9. Antarctica 10. Arctic regions 11. Autobiographies and memoirs 12. Adventure writing — Exploration 13. Travel Writing — Polar Regions 14. Travel Writing — Modes of Transportation — on Foot 15. Adult books for young adults

LC Bl2020000113

Alex Award, 2021.

A multiple world-record holder and premier endurance athlete recounts his triumphant recovery from a disabling burn accident in early adulthood and his inspiring 932-mile solo crossing of Antarctica.

"An unforgettable memoir of perseverance, survival, daring to dream big, and showing the world how to make the impossible possible." —*Booklist*

Roberts, David

Alone on the Ice: The Greatest Survival Story in the History of Exploration. David Roberts. W W Norton & CO Inc 2013. 352 p.

ISBN 9780393083712

Grades: Adult   919.8904

1. Explorers 2. Survival 3. Exploration 4. Antarctica 5. Biographies 6. History writing — Exploration 7. Adventure writing — Survival 8. Life stories — People in history — Explorers 9. Life stories — Facing adversity — Disasters and tragedies

LC 2012037677

Describes the epic and heroic journey undertaken by Douglas Mawson, who suffered starvation, the loss of his entire team, and a massive foot injury as he resorted to ultimately crawling back to base camp during the Australasian Antarctic Expedition of 1913.

Sancton, Julian

Madhouse at the End of the Earth: The Belgica's Journey into the Dark Antarctic Night. Julian Sancton. Crown 2021. 384 p.

ISBN 9781984824332

Grades: Adult   919.8904

1. Gerlache de Gomery, A. de (Adrien), commandant, 1866-1934 2. Cook, Frederick Albert, 1865-1940 3. Amundsen, Roald, 1872-1928 4. South Pole expeditions 5. Ships 6. Survival 7. Explorers 8. Diseases 9. Voyages and travels 10. Polar expeditions 11. Expeditions 12. Exploration 13. Antarctica 14. Polar regions 15. 1890s 16. 19th century 17. Adventure Writing — Exploration 18. Adventure Writing — Survival 19. History writing — Exploration 20. Life stories — People in history — Explorers 21. Nonfiction that reads like fiction

Drawing on the Belgica 'S crew's diaries and journals and exclusive access to the ship's logbook, this epic tale of a polar expedition that went terribly awry follows the crew, as they, condemned to months of endless night and plagued by a mysterious illness, descend into madness.

"Journalist Sancton debuts with a riveting account of the first polar expedition to spend the winter south of the Antarctic Circle. . . . This is a well-researched and enthralling portrait of endurance and escape." —*Publishers Weekly*

Includes bibliographical references and index.

920 Collective biographies

Abbott, Karen

Liar, Temptress, Soldier, Spy: Four Women Undercover in the Civil War. Karen Abbott. Harper 2014. 368 pages

ISBN 9780062092892

Grades: Adult   920

1. Boyd, Belle, 1844-1900 2. Greenhow, Rose O'Neal, 1814-1864 3. Van Lew, Elizabeth L, 1818-1900 4. Bowser, Mary Elizabeth, approximately 1840- 5. Women spies 6. Women and war 7. Disguises 8. Deception 9. United States Civil War, 1861-1865 10. United States history 11. American Civil War era (1861-1865) 12. Collective biographies 13. History writing — Women's history 14. History writing — Wars and conflicts — American Civil War 15. History writing — Spies and spying 16. Life stories — Law and order — Spies and secret agents

LC 2014013602

Library Journal Best Books 2014.

Draws from primary source material and interviews to weave together the adventures of four courageous women who risked everything to become spies during the most tumultuous years of the Civil War.

"Remarkable, brave lives rendered in a fluidly readable, even romantic history lesson." —*Kirkus*

Ackmann, Martha

The Mercury 13: The Untold Story of Thirteen American Women and the Dream of Space Flight. Martha Ackmann. Random House 2003. 239 p. : Illustration

ISBN 9780375507441

Grades: 11 12 Adult   920

1. Project Mercury 2. Women astronauts 3. Sexism 4. Space flight 5. Sexism in science 6. Sex discrimination 7. Astronautics 8. United States history 9. United States 10. 20th century 11. Collective biographies 12. History writing — Women's history 13. Science Writing — Space and Flight 14. Life stories — Science, technology, and medicine — Astronauts and pilots 15. Adult books for young adults 16. Debut title

LC 2002037118

Profiles the thirteen women, all pilots who passed the same battery of tests as the Mercury 7 astronauts, who were chosen as America's first female astronauts but who were refused the opportunity to participate.

"Mercury 13 is both an outstanding work of research and an exceptionally readable and well-told story. Readers will gain new perspectives on space, medicine, women, and American culture, and will appreciate the magnitude of what was lost when the women were grounded." —*School Library Journal*

Includes bibliographical references (p. [219]-227) and index.

Ahamed, Liaquat

Lords of Finance: The Bankers Who Broke the World. Liaquat Ahamed. Penguin Press 2009. 576 p.

ISBN 9781594201820

Grades: Adult   920

1. Capitalists and financiers 2. Bankers 3. Economic history 4. Gold standard 5. Banks and banking 6. International finance 7. Depressions 8. Economics 9. United States 10. 20th century 11. Biographies 12. Collective biographies 13. History writing — Great Depression — United States 14. Life stories — Business — Business leaders 15. Business and economics — Economics — History

LC Bl2008029148

Pulitzer Prize for History, 2010; New York Times Notable Book, 2009.

With penetrating insights for today, this vital history of the world economic collapse of the late 1920s offers unforgettable portraits of four men—Montagu Norman, Amile Moreau, Hjalmar Schacht, and Benjamin Strong—whose personal and professional actions as heads of their respective central banks changed the course of the twentieth century.

"A grand, sweeping narrative of immense scope and power." —*New York Times Book Review*

ESSENTIAL AND RECOMMENDED TITLES
920 Collective biographies

Ambrose, Stephen E.
★ *Band* of Brothers: E Company, 506th Regiment, 101st Airborne : From Normandy to Hitler's Eagle's Nest. Stephen E. Ambrose. Simon & Schuster 1992. 335 p. : Map
ISBN 9780743224543
Grades: 11 12 Adult   920
1. Soldiers 2. World War II 3. Military campaigns 4. Airborne troops 5. Normandy Invasion, June 6, 1944 6. Western Front (World War II) 7. Courage 8. Western Europe 9. Collective biographies 10. Page to screen 11. History writing — Wars and conflicts — World War II — European Theater 12. Life stories — Law and order — Armed forces personnel
LC 91047684
Describes E Company's contributions to the campaigns in western Europe.
"Here is the story of the daring E Company, which began the war by parachuting into France on D-Day and ended it by capturing Eagle's Nest, Hitler's outpost in Bavaria." —*Library Journal*
Includes bibliographical references and index.

Avrich, Paul
Sasha and Emma: The Anarchist Odyssey of Alexander Berkman and Emma Goldman. Paul Avrich and Karen Avrich. Belknap Press of Harvard University Press 2012. 528 p.
ISBN 9780674065987
Grades: Adult   920
1. Berkman, Alexander, 1870-1936 2. Goldman, Emma, 1869-1940 3. Anarchists 4. Political activists 5. Anarchism 6. United States 7. Collective biographies 8. True Crime — Historical Crime 9. Life stories — Law and order — Criminals and law-breakers
LC 2012008659
Offers a glimpse into the intertwined lives of the anarchist movement leaders who remained comrades despite separations caused by Berkman's fourteen-year imprisonment and Goldman's fame as the champion of revolutionary causes.
Includes bibliographical references and index.

Bakewell, Sarah
★ *At* the Existentialist Cafe: Freedom, Being, and Apricot Cocktails. Sarah Bakewell. Other Press 2016. 304 p.
ISBN 9781590514887
Grades: Adult   920
1. Philosophers 2. Existentialism 3. Philosophy 4. Freedom 5. Ontology 6. Collective biographies 7. Biographies 8. Life stories — Education — Philosophers 9. Society and culture — Philosophy
LC 2015047824
ALA Notable Book, 2017; New York Times Notable Book, 2016; Kirkus Prize for Nonfiction finalist, 2016.
Featuring not only philosophers, but also playwrights, anthropologists, convicts, and revolutionaries, at the Existentialist Cafe follows the existentialists' story, from the first rebellious spark through the Second World War, to its role in postwar liberation movements such as anticolonialism, feminism, and gay rights.
With Jean-paul Sartre, Simone De Beauvoir, Albert Camus, Martin Heidegger, Maurice Merleau-ponty and others.

Barr, Luke
Ritz & Escoffier: The Hotelier, the Chef, and the Rise of the Leisure Class. Luke Barr. Clarkson Potter 2018. 288 p.
ISBN 9780804186292
Grades: Adult   920
1. Ritz, Cesar, 1850-1918 2. Escoffier, A. (Auguste), 1846-1935 3. Hospitality industry and trade 4. Leisure class 5. Luxury 6. Hotels 7. Rich people 8. Collective biographies 9. Life stories — Business — Business leaders 10. History writing — Arts and culture
LC 2017015344
Transports readers to turn-of-the-century London and Paris to discover how celebrated hotelier César Ritz and famed chef Auguste Escoffier joined forces at the Savoy Hotel to spawn the modern luxury hotel and restaurant, where women and American Jews mingled with British high society, signaling a new social order and the rise of the middle class.
"A well-researched, glitzy, and flawed history of conspicuous consumption." —*Kirkus*
Includes bibliographical references and index.

Barrett, Duncan
Gi Brides: The Wartime Girls Who Crossed the Atlantic for Love. Duncan Barrett & Nuala Calvi. William Morrow Paperbacks 2014. 592 p.
ISBN 9780062328052
Grades: Adult   920
1. World War II 2. War brides 3. Women immigrants 4. British Americans 5. Women's participation in wars 6. Collective biographies 7. Life stories — People in history — Witness to history 8. Life stories — Identity — Immigrants 9. History writing — Wars and conflicts — World War II
LC 2014010526
Worn down by years of war and hardship, girls like Sylvia, Margaret, and Gwendolyn were thrilled when American GI's arrived in Britain with their exotic accents, handsome uniforms and aura of Hollywood glamor. Others, like Rae, who distrusted the Yanks, were eventually won over by their easy charm. So when VE Day finally came, for the 70,000 women who'd become GI brides, it was tinged with sadness—it meant leaving their homeland behind to follow their husbands across the Atlantic. Adapting to a new culture thousands of miles from home, often with a man they barely knew, was difficult—but these women survived the Blitz and could cope with anything. GI BRIDES shares the sweeping, compelling, and moving true stories of four women who gave up everything and crossed an ocean for love.
"Alternating among the women, the authors bring to light the joys and sorrows of each woman, but readers may find it easier to read each story in its entirety before switching to another one. Entertaining stories about four women who embraced life with American soldiers after the end of World War II." —*Kirkus*
Includes bibliographical references and index.

Becker, Adam
What Is Real?: The Unfinished Quest for the Meaning of Quantum Physics. Adam Becker. Basic Books 2018. 288 p.
ISBN 9780465096053
Grades: Adult   920
1. Quantum theory 2. Physicists 3. Physics 4. Collective biographies 5. History writing — Science, technology, and medicine 6. Science writing — Physics
LC 2017043844
Describes how a long line of physicists, beginning in the 1920s, persisted in seeking the true meaning of quantum mechanics despite the scientific community's favoring of Niels Bohr's Copenhagen interpretation that dismissed it as solipsism and poor reasoning.
"With his crisp voice, Becker lucidly relates the complicated history of quantum foundations." —*Publishers Weekly*
Includes bibliographical references and index.

Bell-Scott, Patricia
The Firebrand and the First Lady: Portrait of a Friendship : Pauli Murray, Eleanor Roosevelt, and the Struggle for Social Justice. Patricia Bell-Scott. Alfred A. Knopf 2016. 480 p.
ISBN 9780679446521
Grades: Adult   920
1. Roosevelt, Eleanor, 1884-1962 2. Murray, Pauli, 1910-1985 3. Women social reformers 4. African American women civil rights workers 5. African American intellectuals 6. Feminists 7. Female friendship 8. Social justice 9. Presidents' spouses 10. United States 11. Collective biographies 12. Life stories — Politics — Activists and reformers 13. History writing — Women's history
LC 2015033959
ALA Notable Book, 2017; Booklist Editors' Choice, 2016; Andrew Carnegie Medal for Excellence in Non-Fiction Finalist, 2017.
Describes the unlikely friendship between First Lady Eleanor Roosevelt and Pauli Murray, a lawyer and civil rights pioneer whose grandfather was a mixed

race slave, and the important work they each did, taking stands for justice and freedom.

"Bell-Scott's groundbreaking portrait of these two tireless and innovative champions of human dignity adds an essential and edifying facet to American history." —*Booklist*

Bennett, Jackie
The Writer's Garden: How Gardens Inspired Our Best-Loved Authors. Jackie Bennett; photography by Richard Hanson. Frances Lincoln 2014. 176 p. : Illustration
ISBN 9780711234949
Grades: Adult   920
1. Authors 2. Rural life 3. Gardens 4. Gardening 5. Great Britain 6. Collective biographies 7. Life stories — Arts and culture — Writing — Authors 8. Nature Writing — Gardens

In this book of 18 gardens and 20 writers, the author examines how the poet, writer, novelist derived a creative spirit from their private garden, how they tended and enjoyed their gardens, and how they managed their outdoor space.

Bernstein, Andrea
American Oligarchs: The Kushners, the Trumps, and the Marriage of Money and Power. Andrea Bernstein. W W Norton & CO Inc 2020. 484 pages
ISBN 9781324001874
Grades: Adult   920
1. Kushner family 2. Trump family 3. Kushner, Jared, 1981- 4. Trump, Ivanka, 1981- 5. Trump, Donald, 1946- 6. Rich people 7. Ambition 8. Scandals 9. Rich families 10. Family businesses 11. Real estate developers 12. Corruption 13. Collective biographies 14. Business and economics — Corruption and scandal 15. Politics and global affairs — Political figures
LC Bl2019038547

Bernstein traces how the two families ruthlessly harnessed New York and New Jersey machine politics to gain valuable tax breaks and grew rich on federal programs that bolstered the middle class.

"The author, who conducted hundreds of interviews and read more than 100,000 documents to create this damning portrait of two clearly unscrupulous families . . . [offers a] painstaking documentation of a relentless culture of corruption." —*Kirkus*

Includes bibliographical references and index.

Borman, Tracy
Anne Boleyn and Elizabeth I: The Mother and Daughter Who Forever Changed British History. Tracy Borman. Atlantic Monthly Press 2023. 320 p.
ISBN 9780802162069
Grades: Adult   920
1. Elizabeth I, Queen of England, 1533-1603 2. Anne Boleyn, Queen, consort of Henry VIII, King of England, 1507-1536 3. Tudor, House of 4. Henry VIII, King of England, 1491-1547 5. Women rulers 6. Monarchy 7. Mothers and daughters 8. Influence (Psychology) 9. Women's role 10. British people 11. English people 12. British history 13. Leadership 14. Elizabethan era (1558-1603) 15. Collective biographies 16. Life stories — Politics — Royalty 17. History writing — Europe — United Kingdom 18. History writing — Women's history
LC 2023003688

The future Queen Elizabeth was not yet three when her mother, Anne Boleyn, was beheaded on May 19, 1536, on King Henry VIII's order, incensed that she had not given him a son and tired of her contentious nature. Elizabeth had been raised away from court, rarely even seeing Anne; and after her death, Henry tried in every way to erase Anne's presence and memory. At that moment in history, few could have predicted that mother and daughter would each leave enduring, and interlocked, legacies. Yet as Tracy Borman reveals in this first-ever joint portrait, both women broke the mold for British queens and for women in general at the time.

"Beautifully envisioned and full of insight, this is a must-read for Tudor history buffs." —*Publishers Weekly*

Includes bibliographical references and index.

Elizabeth's Women: Friends, Rivals and Foes Who Shaped the Virgin Queen. by Tracy Borman. Bantam Books 2010. 496 p.
ISBN 9780553806984
Grades: Adult   920
1. Elizabeth I, Queen of England, 1533-1603 2. Royal houses 3. Nobility 4. Women rulers 5. Rulers 6. Courts and courtiers 7. British history 8. Great Britain 9. 16th century 10. Tudor period (1485-1603) 11. Renaissance (1300-1600) 12. Elizabethan era (1558-1603) 13. Biographies 14. History writing — Europe — United Kingdom 15. Life stories — Politics — Royalty
LC 2010009333

Examines Queen Elizabeth I through the eyes of the women who shaped her life—from her bewitching mother to her dangerously obsessive sister, and from the rivals to her throne to her rivals in love.

Includes bibliographical references and index; Originally published: London : Jonathan Cape, 2009.

The Private Lives of the Tudors: Uncovering the Secrets of Britain's Greatest Dynasty. Tracy Borman. Grove Press 2016. 464 p.
ISBN 9780802125996
Grades: Adult   920
1. Tudor, House of 2. Royal houses 3. Monarchy 4. Nobility 5. Rulers 6. British history 7. Great Britain 8. 15th century 9. 16th century 10. Tudor period (1485-1603) 11. Renaissance (1300-1600) 12. Collective biographies 13. Life stories — Politics — Royalty 14. Life stories — People in history — Famous families 15. History writing — Renaissance — Europe 16. History writing — Europe — United Kingdom
LC 2017275637

An in-depth examination behind the public faces of the Tudor monarchs draws on original material from their most intimate courtiers to illuminate lesser-known details about their private worlds, from what they ate and the clothes they wore to how they practiced their faith and how they were treated while sick.

"This Downton Abbey-like peek into the everyday lives of these privileged yet cloistered rulers and their households will appeal to both serious scholars and Tudor enthusiasts." —*Booklist*

Bram, Christopher
Eminent Outlaws: The Gay Writers Who Changed America. Christopher Bram. Twelve 2012. 320 p.
ISBN 9780446563130
Grades: Adult   920
1. Authors, American 2. Gay authors 3. 20th century 4. Collective biographies 5. Arts and Entertainment — Writing and Publishing 6. Life stories — Arts and culture — Writing 7. Society and culture — LGBTQIA+ 8. Arts and Entertainment — Writing and Publishing — Literary criticism
LC 2011029910

Describes the trailblazing, post-war gay literary figures, including Tennessee Williams, Gore Vidal, Truman Capote and Allen Ginsberg, who paved the way for newer generations including Armistead Maupin, Edmund White and Edward Albee.

Branch, John
The Last Cowboys: A Pioneer Family in the New West. John Branch. W W Norton & Company 2018. 304 p.
ISBN 9780393292343
Grades: Adult   920
1. Wright family 2. Ranchers 3. Rodeo performers 4. Cowboys 5. Cattle ranchers 6. Cattle ranches 7. Rodeos 8. Utah 9. Collective biographies 10. Life stories — Nature and outdoors — Farmers and ranchers
LC 2017061611

The Pulitzer Prize-winning reporter and award-winning author of Boy on Ice presents a portrait of the Wright family of Smith Mesa and their generations-long achievements as some of the world's most successful cattle ranchers and rodeo champions, tracing three generations of their battles against natural obstacles, federal regulation and injuries and how the changes of the 21st century are challenging their future.

ESSENTIAL AND RECOMMENDED TITLES
920 Collective biographies

Brands, H. W.
★ *The Zealot and the Emancipator: John Brown, Abraham Lincoln and the Struggle for American Freedom.* H.W. Brands. Doubleday 2020. 464 p.
ISBN 9780385544009
Grades: Adult   **920**
1. Brown, John, 1800-1859 2. Lincoln, Abraham, 1809-1865 3. Abolitionists 4. History of anti-slavery movements 5. Presidents 6. Causes of war 7. Harpers Ferry, Battle of, Harpers Ferry, W. Va, 1862 8. United States history 9. United States 10. West Virginia 11. 19th century 12. American Civil War era (1861-1865) 13. 1860s 14. Collective biographies 15. History writing — Antebellum America — United States 16. Life stories — Politics — Politicians 17. Life stories — Politics — Activists and reformers 18. History writing — Presidency — 19th century — United States
LC 2019036370

Follows the epic struggle over slavery as embodied by John Brown and Abraham Lincoln—two men moved to radically different acts to confront our nation's gravest sin.

"A fascinating and wonderfully readable portrayal of the tensions between fiery militancy and determined but measured devotion in working toward a goal. Excellent for general readers, especially those with an interest in the Civil War." —*Library Journal*

Includes bibliographical references and index.

Brickell, Francesca Cartier
The Cartiers: The Untold Story of the Family Behind the Jewelry Empire. Francesca Cartier Brickell. Ballantine Books 2019. 352 p.
ISBN 9780525621614
Grades: Adult   **920**
1. Cartier family 2. Jewelers 3. Rich families 4. Jewelry making 5. Luxury 6. Fame 7. Success in business 8. Trademarks 9. Paris, France 10. London, England 11. New York City 12. Life stories — Arts and culture — Fashion 13. Arts and Entertainment — Fashion 14. History writing — Arts and culture 15. Life stories — People in history — Famous families 16. Adult books for young adults
LC Bl2019029788

A Cartier great-granddaughter with exclusive access to long-lost family archives tells the story of the three brothers who turned their grandfather's humble Parisian jewelry store into a global luxury icon.

Brower, Kate Andersen
First in Line: Presidents, Vice Presidents, and the Pursuit of Power. Kate Andersen Brower. HarperCollins 2018. 400 p.
ISBN 9780062668943
Grades: Adult   **920**
1. Presidents 2. Vice presidents 3. Politicians 4. Politics and government 5. Washington, D.C. 6. United States 7. Collective biographies 8. Impartial writing 9. History writing — Presidency — United States 10. Life stories — Politics — Politicians
LC 2018655046

From the author of the New York Times best-sellers First Women and the Residence comes an intimate, news-making look at the men who are next in line to the most powerful office in the world—the vice presidents of the modern era—from Richard Nixon to Joe Biden to Mike Pence.

"Notwithstanding the famous assessment that the vice presidency is not worth a bucket of warm spit, 14 of the 47 U.S. vice presidents have gone on to the presidency. CNN contributor Brower interviewed 200 people, including VPs and their families, to find out what the job is really like." —*Library Journal*

First Women: The Grace and Power of America's Modern First Ladies. Kate Andersen Brower. HarperCollins 2016. 352 p.
ISBN 9780062439659
Grades: Adult   **920**
1. Women and politics 2. Presidents' spouses 3. Washington, D.C. 4. United States 5. Collective biographies 6. Impartial writing 7. History writing — Presidency — United States 8. Life stories — Politics — Politicians
LC 2016440928

The author of the Residence presents an intimate examination of the true influences of White House First Ladies from Jackie Kennedy to Michelle Obama, which draws on previous untapped and candid sources to document their stories.

"Brower writes with grace and ease and finely outlines the lives of these influential figures, providing deep insights into the experiences of each." —*Library Journal*

Includes bibliographies and index.

Brown, Craig
150 Glimpses of the Beatles. Craig Brown. Farrar, Straus and Giroux 2020. 574 p.
ISBN 9780374109318
Grades: Adult   **920**
1. Lennon, John, 1940-1980 2. McCartney, Paul 3. Starr, Ringo, 1940- 4. Harrison, George, 1943-2001 5. Bands (Music) 6. Rock music 7. Popular culture 8. Biographies 9. Collective biographies 10. Life stories — Arts and culture — Performing arts — Musicians and composers 11. Arts and Entertainment — Music — Rock
LC 2020022500

Baillie Gifford Prize for Non-Fiction, 2020.

The author draws on previously unexamined lore and celebrity testimony in a kaleidoscopic group portrait of the Fab Four that reveals lesser-known examples of their indelible and enduring cultural impact.

"Brown presents a fresh take on a seemingly inexhaustible subject—Beatles people, you know you should be glad." —*Library Journal*

Includes bibliographical references; Originally published in 2020 by 4th Estate, Great Britain.

Brown, Tina
★ *The Palace Papers: Inside the House of Windsor - the Truth and the Turmoil.* Tina Brown. Crown 2022. 400 p.
ISBN 9780593138090
Grades: Adult   **920**
1. Windsor, House of 2. Royal houses 3. Marriage 4. Childbirth 5. Death 6. Scandals 7. Monarchy 8. British history 9. Great Britain 10. 20th century 11. 21st century 12. Collective biographies 13. Life stories — Politics — Royalty 14. Life stories — People in history — Famous families 15. History writing — Scandals 16. History writing — Europe — United Kingdom

Picking up where Tina Brown's masterful the Diana Chronicles left off, the Palace Papers reveals how the royal family reinvented itself after the traumatic years when Diana's blazing celebrity ripped through the House of Windsor like a comet. Brown takes readers on a tour de force journey through the scandals, love affairs, power plays, and betrayals that have buffeted the House of Windsor over the last twenty-five years, and her sweeping account is full of powerful revelations, colorful details, and searing insight gleaned from remarkable access to royal insiders.

"Brown (the former Tatler and Vanity Fair editor in chief, and author of the Diana Chronicles and the Vanity Fair Diaries) uses research and interviews to chronicle the events of the British monarchy since Princess Diana's 1997 death." —*Library Journal*

Browne, David
Crosby, Stills, Nash and Young: The Wild, Definitive Saga of Rock's Greatest Supergroup. David Browne. Da Capo Press 2019. xiii, 465 p.
ISBN 9780306903281
Grades: Adult   **920**
1. Rock groups 2. Rock musicians 3. Fame 4. Artistic collaboration 5. Interpersonal conflict 6. Rock music 7. Collective biographies 8. Life stories — Arts and culture — Performing arts — Musicians and composers 9. Arts and Entertainment — Music — Rock
LC 2018968044

Even in the larger-than-life world of rock and roll, it was hard to imagine four more different men. David Crosby, the opinionated hippie guru. Stephen Stills, the perpetually driven musician. Graham Nash, the tactful pop craftsman. Neil Young, the creatively restless loner. But together, few groups were as in sync with their times as Crosby, Stills, Nash and Young. But their story would rarely be as harmonious as their legendary and influential vocal blend. In the years that followed, these four volatile men would continually break up, reunite, and disband again—all against a backdrop of social and musical change, recurring disagreements and jealousies, and self-destructive tendencies that threatened to cripple them both as a group and as individuals.

Includes bibliographical references and index.

Cadbury, Deborah

Princes at War: The Bitter Battle Inside Britain's Royal Family in the Darkest Days of Wwii. Deborah Cadbury. Public Affairs 2015. 320 p.
ISBN 9781610394031

Grades: Adult   **920**

1. Windsor, Edward, Duke of, 1894-1972 2. George VI, King of Great Britain, 1895-1952 3. Windsor, House of 4. Princes 5. Royal houses 6. War and society 7. World War II 8. Competition 9. Monarchy 10. Rulers 11. British history 12. Great Britain 13. 20th century 14. 1930s 15. Collective biographies 16. History writing — Europe — United Kingdom 17. Life stories — Politics — Royalty

LC 2014957933

British author Cadbury explores the many layers involved in the abdication crisis of 1936, which ceded the British crown to the seemingly least prepared of the four sons of George V, George VI, aka Bertie, who revealed himself in the subsequent crisis of war to be the most suitable and stalwart of all.

"Bias aside, this is an engaging, well-told history of England and its royals during its most fragile period; conveying wartime tensions, worldwide scandals, and familial devotions and rivalries with equal vividness." —*Library Journal*

Carter, Alice A.

The Red Rose Girls: An Uncommon Story of Art and Love. by Alice A. Carter. H.N. Abrams 2000. 216 p. : Illustration; Color
ISBN 9780810944374

Grades: Adult   **920**

1. Smith, Jessie Willcox, 1863-1935 2. Elliott, Elizabeth Shippen Green 3. Oakley, Violet, 1874- 4. Women artists 5. Artists 6. Artists' studios 7. Lesbians 8. United States 9. Biographies 10. Arts and Entertainment — General

LC 99039866

"Three of the first American women artists to achieve fame and fortune in the Victorian era—Jessie Willcox Smith, Elizabeth Shippen Green and Violet Oakley—lived unconventional lives marked by a remarkable degree of collaboration. In this study, Carter explores the trio's internecine artistic and romantic relations." —*Publishers Weekly*

Includes bibliographical references (p. 208-212) and index.

Cheever, Susan

American Bloomsbury: Louisa May Alcott, Ralph Waldo Emerson, Margaret Fuller, Nathaniel Hawthorne, and Henry David Thoreau : Their Lives, Their Loves, Their Work. Susan Cheever. Simon & Schuster 2006. xvi, 223 p, 8 p. of plates : Illustration
ISBN 9780743264617

Grades: Adult   **920**

1. Authors, American 2. Intellectual life 3. Literary landmarks 4. Concord, Massachusetts 5. 19th century 6. Collective biographies 7. Arts and Entertainment — Writing and Publishing 8. Life stories — Arts and culture — Writing — Authors 9. Arts and Entertainment — Writing and Publishing — Literary criticism

LC 2006045015

A portrait of five Concord, Massachusetts, writers whose works were at the center of mid-nineteenth-century American thought and literature evaluates their interconnected relationships, influence on each other's works, and complex beliefs.

Includes bibliographical references (p. [211]-214) and index.

Chivers, C. J.

The Fighters: Americans in Combat in Afghanistan and Iraq. C.J. Chivers. Simon & Schuster 2018. xxiii, 374 p. : Map
ISBN 9781451676648

Grades: Adult   **920**

1. Iraq War, 2003-2011 2. Afghan War, 2001-2021 3. Soldiers 4. Pilots 5. War on Terrorism, 2001-2009 6. Military history 7. Armed Forces 8. United States 9. 21st century 10. Collective biographies 11. Life stories — Law and order — Armed forces personnel 12. History writing — Wars and conflicts — War in Afghanistan 13. History writing — Wars and conflicts — Iraq War

LC 2018003987

The Pulitzer Prize-winning author traces the wars in Afghanistan and Iraq through its most at-risk participants, offering insights into such events as the hunt for bin Laden and counterguerilla warfare in the mountains of the Korengal Valley.

"Civilians will gain understanding of the military world. Prospective recruits will get an unvarnished look at what may await them: the challenges, the hardships, the glory, the camaraderie, and some of the things recruiters dont talk about." —*Booklist*

Clavin, Thomas

The Dimaggios: Three Brothers, Their Passion for Baseball, Their Pursuit of the American Dream. Tom Clavin. HarperCollins 2013. 288 p.
ISBN 9780062183774

Grades: Adult   **920**

1. DiMaggio, Joe, 1914-1999 2. DiMaggio, Vince 3. DiMaggio, Dom 4. Professional baseball players 5. Professional baseball 6. Brothers 7. Baseball players 8. Baseball teams 9. Baseball 10. Popular culture 11. United States history 12. 20th century 13. Collective biographies 14. Biographies 15. Sports and Competition — Baseball 16. Family and Relationships — Siblings 17. Life stories — Sports — Athletes

LC 2013443409

Drawing from a vast of array of source materials, interviews with family members and teammates, and in-depth reporting, this Great American Story traces the DiMaggio brothers' rise to fame in American sports and popular culture.

Clinton, Hillary Rodham

The Book of Gutsy Women: Favorite Stories of Courage and Resilience. Hillary Rodham Clinton and Chelsea Clinton. Simon & Schuster 2019. 464 pages
ISBN 9781501178412

Grades: Adult   **920**

1. Courage 2. Women social reformers 3. Women social advocates 4. Women's rights 5. Women scientists 6. Women authors 7. Women athletes 8. Women physicians 9. Women politicians 10. Women environmentalists 11. Women teachers 12. Women 13. Determination 14. Persistence 15. Resilience 16. Collective biographies 17. Essays 18. Biographies 19. History writing — Women's history 20. Society and culture — Gender — Women

LC Bl2019028632

Hillary Rodham Clinton and her daughter, Chelsea, share the stories of the gutsy women who have inspired them&;women with the courage to stand up to the status quo, ask hard questions, and get the job done.

"A book to savor over multiple sittings, allowing readers to revisit well-known heroines or discover new ones among the pages." —*Library Journal*

Includes index.

Coll, Steve

The Bin Ladens: An Arabian Family in the American Century. Steve Coll. Penguin Press 2008. 671 p, 8 p. of plates : Illustration
ISBN 9781594201646

Grades: 11 12 Adult   **920**

1. Bin Laden, Osama, 1957-2011 2. Bin Laden family 3. Terrorism 4. International relations 5. September 11 Terrorist Attacks, 2001 6. Southwest Asia and North Africa (Middle East) history 7. Saudi Arabia 8. 20th century 9. Collective biographies 10. History writing — Nationalism — Southwest Asia and North Africa (Middle East) 11. Family and Relationships — Families 12. Life stories — People in history — Famous families

LC 2007042748

ALA Notable Book, 2009; National Book Critics Circle Award for Biography finalist, 2008; Pulitzer Prize for Biography or Autobiography finalist, 2009.

ESSENTIAL AND RECOMMENDED TITLES
920 Collective biographies

Traces the Bin Laden family's rise to power and privilege, describes the diverse lifestyles of the generation to which Osama bin Laden belongs, and discusses their attempts to recover from the effects of September 11.

Includes bibliographical references and index.

Cooney, Kara
When Women Ruled the World: Six Queens of Egypt. Kara Cooney. National Geographic 2018. 400 p.
ISBN 9781426219771
Grades: Adult   920
1. Women rulers 2. Gender role 3. Patriarchy 4. Civilization, Ancient 5. Rulers 6. Civilization 7. Leadership 8. Ancient Egypt 9. Egypt 10. Ancient Egypt (3100 B.C.E.-640 C.E.) 11. Collective biographies 12. History writing — Women's history 13. History writing — Ancient — Egypt 14. Life stories — Politics — Royalty 15. Life stories — Identity — Gender 16. Adult books for young adults
LC 2018377472

A professor of Egyptology at UCLA explores the lives of the queens of Egypt, including Hatshepsut, Nefertiti, and Cleopatra, who transcended traditional patriarchal obstacles and describes what the modern world can learn from example.

"Not since Leonard Cottrell's Lady of the Two Lands (1966) has such an engrossing, well-researched collective study of Egyptian power queens been available." —*Library Journal*

Cooper, Anderson
Vanderbilt: The Rise and Fall of an American Dynasty. Anderson Cooper and Katherine Howe. Harper 2021. 384 p.
ISBN 9780062964618
Grades: Adult   920
1. Vanderbilt family 2. Cooper, Anderson 3. Rich families 4. Railroad owners 5. Capitalists and financiers 6. Patriarchs 7. Wealth 8. Family fortunes 9. Inheritance and succession 10. Sibling rivalry 11. Conflict in families 12. Tragedy 13. Family history 14. United States history 15. Collective biographies 16. Life stories — People in history — Famous families 17. History writing — United States

When eleven-year-old Cornelius Vanderbilt began to work on his father's small boat ferrying supplies in New York Harbor at the beginning of the nineteenth century, no one could have imagined that one day he would, through ruthlessness, cunning, and a pathological desire for money, build two empires—one in shipping and another in railroads—that would make him the richest man in America. By 2018, when the last Vanderbilt was forced out of the Breakers—the seventy-room summer estate in Newport, Rhode Island—the family would have been unrecognizable to the tycoon who started it all. Now, the Commodore's great-great-great-grandson Anderson Cooper joins with historian Katherine Howe to explore the story of his legendary family and their outsized influence.

"CNN anchor Cooper (The Rainbow Comes and Goes) and novelist Howe (The Daughters of Temperance Hobbes) tell the story of 'The greatest American fortune ever squandered' in this juicy portrait of Cooper's forebears, the Vanderbilts.... Marked by meticulous research and deep emotional insight, this is a memorable chronicle of American royalty." —*Publishers Weekly*

Also published in large print format.

Cornejo Villavicencio, Karla
★ *The Undocumented Americans.* Karla Cornejo Villavicencio. One World 2020. xvii, 185 pages
ISBN 9780399592683
Grades: Adult   920
1. Cornejo Villavicencio, Karla 2. Undocumented immigrants 3. Undocumented workers 4. Immigrant families 5. Hispanic Americans 6. Immigrants 7. Children of undocumented immigrants 8. Work 9. Poverty 10. Everyday life 11. Discrimination 12. Immigration and emigration 13. United States 14. Collective biographies 15. Life stories — Identity — Immigrants 16. Life stories — Facing adversity 17. Society and culture — Immigration
LC 2018039595

New York Times Notable Book, 2020; National Book Critics Circle Award: John Leonard Prize finalist, 2020; National Book Award for Nonfiction finalist, 2020.

An Ivy League-educated DACA beneficiary reveals the hidden lives of her fellow undocumented Americans, from the volunteers recruited for the 9/11 Ground Zero cleanup to the homeopathy botanicas of Miami that provide limited health care to non-citizens.

"A must-read indictment on what it means to be undocumented and what it means to be American." —*Library Journal*

Includes bibliographical references (pages 177-185).

Cozzens, Peter
Tecumseh and the Prophet: The Shawnee Brothers Who Defied a Nation. Peter Cozzens. Alfred A. Knopf 2020. 560 p.
ISBN 9781524733254
Grades: Adult   920
1. Tecumseh, Shawnee Chief, 1768-1813 2. Tenskwatawa, Shawnee Prophet 3. Shawnee (North American people) 4. Indigenous peoples of North America — Wars 5. Alliances 6. Resistance to government 7. Government relations with indigenous peoples 8. Indigenous peoples of North America — History 9. Spiritual life 10. Indigenous peoples of North America — Religion 11. Great Lakes region 12. Ohio River Valley 13. Revolutionary America (1775-1783) 14. 18th century 15. Collective biographies 16. Biographies 17. History writing — Indigenous peoples — United States 18. Life stories — People in history — Indigenous peoples
LC 2019052436

Spur Award for Biography, 2021.

The first biography of the great Shawnee leader in more than 20 years, and the first to make clear that his misunderstood younger brother, Tenskwatawa, was an equal partner in the last great pan-Indian alliance against the United States. Detailed research of Native American society and customs provides a window into a world often erased from history books and reveals how both men came to power in different but no less important ways.

"Tecumseh's life and the wider struggle for the Great Lakes and Ohio River valley now has a current, solid work by an accomplished author." —*Library Journal*

This is a Borzoi book—Title page verso; Includes bibliographical references and index.

Crowther, Gail
Three-martini Afternoons at the Ritz: The Rebellion of Sylvia Plath and Anne Sexton. by Gail Crowther. Gallery Books 2021. 304 p.
ISBN 9781982138394
Grades: Adult   920
1. Plath, Sylvia 2. Sexton, Anne, 1928-1974 3. Competition 4. Female friendship 5. Poets, American 6. Mental illness 7. Suicide 8. Gender role 9. Women poets 10. United States 11. 20th century 12. Collective biographies 13. Life stories — Arts and culture — Writing — Poets 14. History writing — Women's history 15. Arts and Entertainment — Writing and Publishing
LC 2020029091

A dual biography of poets, friends, and rivals Sylvia Plath and Anne Sexton.

Crowther (The Haunted Reader and Sylvia Plath) places poets Sylvia Plath and Anne Sexton side by side in this solid study that illuminates two 'Hugely ambitious women in a cultural moment that did not know how to deal with ambitious women.' —*Publishers Weekly*

Includes bibliographical references.

Damrosch, Leopold
The Club: Johnson, Boswell, and the Friends Who Shaped an Age. Leo Damrosch. Yale University Press 2019. 472 p.
ISBN 9780300217902
Grades: Adult   920
1. Johnson, Samuel, 1709-1784 2. Boswell, James, 1740-1795 3. Intellectuals 4. Authors 5. Clubs 6. Conversation 7. Artists 8. Political culture 9. London, England history 10. British history 11. 18th century 12. Collective biographies 13. Life stories — Arts and culture — Writing 14. History writing — Europe —

PUBLIC LIBRARY CORE COLLECTION: NONFICTION
Twentieth Edition

United Kingdom 15. History writing — Arts and culture 16. Arts and Entertainment — Writing and Publishing — Literary criticism

LC 2018952381

New York Times Notable Book, 2019.

Brings to life a brilliant and eccentric cast of characters known simply as "the Club," a group of extraordinary writers, artists and thinkers who gathered weekly at a London tavern, whose friendship with Samuel Johnson and James Boswell stand at the heart of the narrative, conjuring the exciting, often brutal world of late 18th-century Britain.

"Enriched with well-chosen color plates and black-and-white illustrations, this is an excellent introduction to Johnson and his world for the novice and a pleasant retelling for the initiated." —Library Journal

Davenport, Christian

The **Space** Barons: Jeff Bezos, Elon Musk, and the Quest to Colonize the Cosmos. Christian Davenport. PublicAffairs 2018. 320 p.

ISBN 9781610398299

Grades: Adult   920

1. Bezos, Jeffrey 2. Musk, Elon 3. Space exploration 4. Industrialists 5. Entrepreneurs 6. Aerospace engineers 7. Aerospace industry and trade 8. Space industrialization 9. Space 10. Collective biographies 11. Biographies 12. Science Writing — Space and Flight 13. Life stories — Science, technology, and medicine

LC 2017053089

Library Journal Best Books, 2018.

Traces the historic quest to rekindle the human exploration of space as navigated by billionaire entrepreneurs, sharing insights into how professional rivalry and Silicon Valley innovations are lowering the cost of space travel and exceeding the achievements of NASA.

Includes bibliographical references and index.

Davis, William C.

Crucible of Command: Ulysses S. Grant and Robert E. Lee : The War They Fought, the Peace They Forged. William C. Davis. Da Capo Pr. 2015. 448 p.

ISBN 9780306822452

Grades: Adult   920

1. Grant, Ulysses S, 1822-1885 2. Lee, Robert E. (Robert Edward), 1807-1870 3. Generals 4. Civil War 5. Command of troops 6. Military strategy 7. Military history 8. Leadership 9. Peace 10. United States Civil War, 1861-1865 11. United States history 12. American Civil War era (1861-1865) 13. Collective biographies 14. Biographies 15. Life stories — Law and order — Military leaders 16. History writing — Wars and conflicts — American Civil War

LC 2013497767

A dual biography sheds new light of the two iconic leaders|who determined the outcome of the Civil War and cast competing styles for the reunited nation|by exploring their personalities, character and their ethical, moral and political worlds.

De Courcy, Anne

The **Husband** Hunters: American Heiresses Who Married into the British Aristocracy. Anne De Courcy. St. Martin's Press 2018. 368 p.

ISBN 9781250164599

Grades: Adult   920

1. American people in Great Britain 2. Nouveaux riches 3. Heirs and heiresses 4. Courtship 5. Mate selection 6. Aristocracy 7. Great Britain 8. 19th century 9. 20th century 10. Collective biographies 11. Life stories — People in history 12. History writing — Europe — United Kingdom 13. Life stories — Relationships — Couples

LC 2018013474

Describes the years between 1874 and 1904, a period that saw an unprecedented amount of young, American heiresses marrying into the British peerage, trading their New World wealth for Old World titles and sophistication.

Includes bibliographical references and index; Originally published: London : Weidenfeld & Nicolson, 2017.

De Semlyen, Nick

Wild and Crazy Guys: How the Comedy Mavericks of the '80s Changed Hollywood Forever. Nick De Semlyen. Random House Inc 2019. 336 p.

ISBN 9781984826640

Grades: Adult   920

1. Aykroyd, Dan, 1952- 2. Belushi, John, 1949-1982 3. Candy, John, 1950-1994 4. Chase, Chevy, 1943- 5. Martin, Steve, 1945- 6. Murphy, Eddie, 1961- 7. Murray, Bill, 1950 September 21- 8. Comedians 9. Comedy films 10. Actors and actresses 11. Film industry and trade 12. Entertainment industry and trade 13. 1980s 14. Collective biographies 15. Life stories — Arts and culture — Performing arts — Entertainers and celebrities 16. Arts and Entertainment — Movies and Television

LC Bl2019014657

Featuring icons like Bill Murray, Steve Martin and Eddie Murphy—and covering films like Animal House, Caddyshack and Ghostbusters—the author tells the behind-the-scenes story of the comedy misfits who ruled 1980s Hollywood and the beloved films that made them famous.

"Children of the 1980s, take note: This is a fond, engrossing look back at the making of movies that became cultural touchstones, with plenty of behind-the-scenes details about the key male performers who brought them to life." —Booklist

Demick, Barbara

★ **Nothing** to Envy: Ordinary Lives in North Korea. Barbara Demick. Spiegel & Grau 2009. 336 p.

ISBN 9780385523905

Grades: Adult   920

1. Kim, Chong-il, 1942-2011 2. Kim, Il-song, 1912-1994 3. Government services 4. Dictatorship 5. Totalitarianism 6. North Korea 7. 20th century 8. Collective biographies 9. Life stories — Facing adversity — War and oppression 10. Life stories — People in history — Witness to history 11. History writing — Asia — North and South Korea 12. Nonfiction that reads like fiction

LC Bl2009000139

ALA Notable Book, 2011; BBC Samuel Johnson Prize for Non-Fiction, 2010; National Book Award for Nonfiction finalist, 2010; National Book Critics Circle Award for Nonfiction finalist, 2010.

Follows the lives of six North Koreans over fifteen years, a chaotic period that saw the rise to power of Kim Jong IL and the devastation of a famine that killed one-fifth of the population, illustrating what it means to live under the most repressive totalitarian regime today.

"Strongly written and gracefully structured, Demicks potent blend of personal narratives and piercing journalism vividly and evocatively portrays courageous individuals and a tyrannized state within a saga of unfathomable suffering punctuated by faint glimmers of hope." —Booklist

DePalma, Anthony

The **Cubans**: Ordinary Lives in Extraordinary Times. Anthony DePalma. Penguin Group USA 2020. 368 p.

ISBN 9780525522447

Grades: Adult   920

1. Everyday life 2. Island life 3. Resilience 4. Poverty 5. Neighborhoods 6. Caribbean history 7. Havana, Cuba 8. Cuba 9. 20th century 10. 21st century 11. Collective biographies 12. History writing — Latin America — Cuba 13. Life stories — General

LC 2019052262

A foreign correspondent for the New York Times creates a snapshot of modern Cuba by focusing on a single neighborhood near Old Havana and describing their optimism towards the future as well as the huge challenges they still face.

"Overall, a rich, intimate, evenhanded narrative that reveals the Cuban people's resilience and resourcefulness amid oppression." —Library Journal

Includes index.

Doherty, Maggie

The **Equivalents**: A Story of Art, Female Friendship, and Liberation in the 1960s. Maggie Doherty. Alfred A. Knopf 2020. 352 p.

ISBN 9781524733056

ESSENTIAL AND RECOMMENDED TITLES
920 Collective biographies

Grades: Adult **920**

1. Women artists 2. Feminism 3. Scholarships and fellowships 4. Female friendship 5. Creation (Literary, artistic, etc.) 6. Gender role 7. Women authors 8. Women poets 9. Women intellectuals 10. Women scholars and academics 11. Women 12. Self-fulfillment 13. Cambridge, Massachusetts 14. 1960s 15. 20th century 16. Collective biographies 17. Life stories — Arts and culture — Artists 18. Life stories — Identity — Gender 19. Arts and Entertainment — General 20. History writing — Women's history 21. History writing — Arts and culture

LC 2019036686

National Book Critics Circle Award for Biography finalist, 2020.

The timely, never-before-told story of five brilliant, passionate women who, in the early 1960s, converged at the newly founded Radcliffe Institute for Independent Study and became friends as well as artistic collaborators, and who went on to shape the course of feminism in ways that are still felt today. Poets Anne Sexton and Maxine Kumin, painter Barbara Swan, sculptor Mariana Pineda, and writer Tillie Olsen—quickly formed deep bonds with one another that would inspire and sustain their most ambitious work. They called themselves "the Equivalents."

"Harvard University lecturer Doherty debuts with an elegant, novelistic history of the Radcliffe Institute for Independent Study and its influence on the lives and careers of five female artists and the women's movement at large. . . . This empathetic, wide-angled portrait will resonate with fans of the individual artists as well as feminists and readers of women's history." —*Publishers Weekly*

Includes bibliographical references and index.

Duberman, Martin B.
Hold Tight Gently: Michael Callen, Essex Hemphill, and the Battlefield of AIDS. Martin Duberman. New Press, the 2014. 368 pages

ISBN 9781595589453

Grades: Adult **920**

1. Callen, Michael, 1955-1993 2. Hemphill, Essex 3. Gay men 4. AIDS (Disease) 5. People with AIDS 6. AIDS activists 7. African American gay men 8. People with HIV 9. Gay activists 10. Collective biographies 11. Life stories — Identity — LGBTQIA+ 12. Society and culture — LGBTQIA+

LC 2013039158

Lambda Literary Award for LGBT Nonfiction.

In December 1995, the FDA approved the release of protease inhibitors, the first effective treatment for AIDS. For countless people, the drug offered a reprieve from what had been a death sentence; for others, it was too late. In the United States alone, over 318,000 people had died from AIDS-related complications—among them were the singer Michael Callen and the poet Essex Hemphill. Meticulously researched and evocatively told, Two Lives, Two Deaths is historian Martin Duberman's poignant memorial to those lost to AIDS and to two of the great unsung heroes of the early years of the epidemic. Callen, a white gay Midwesterner who moved to New York, became a leading figure in the movement to increase awareness of AIDS in the face of willful neglect; Hemphill, an African American gay man, contributed to the Black gay and lesbian flowering in Washington, D.C, with poetry of searing intensity and introspection. A profound exploration of the intersection of race, sexuality, class, and identity and the politics of AIDS activism beyond ACT-UP, Two Lives, Two Deaths captures both a generation struggling to cope with the deadly disease and the extraordinary refusal of two men to give in to despair.

"This combination of cautionary tale, history, and dual biography of compelling, if obscure, artist-activists is fluidly written." —*Library Journal*

Includes bibliographical references and index.

Eder, Mari K.
The Girls Who Stepped Out of Line: Untold Stories of the Women Who Changed the Course of World War II. Major General Mari K. Eder, U.S. Army, Retired. Sourcebooks 2021. 400 p.

ISBN 9781728230924

Grades: Adult **920**

1. World War II 2. Refugees 3. Heroes and heroines 4. Postwar life 5. Women's participation in wars 6. United States history 7. 20th century 8. Collective biographies 9. History writing — Women's history 10. Life stories — Facing adversity — War and oppression 11. History writing — Wars and conflicts — World War II 12. Life stories — Law and order — Armed forces personnel

LC 2021001192

The Girls Who Stepped Out of Line takes you inside the lives and experiences of 15 unknown women heroes from the Greatest Generation, the women who served, fought, struggled, and made things happen during WWII-in and out of uniform, for theirs is a legacy destined to embolden generations of women to come.

"Eder's engaging writing makes these compelling histories read like a suspense novel." —*Library Journal*

Includes bibliographical references.

Eilenberger, Wolfram
Time of the Magicians: Wittgenstein, Benjamin, Cassirer, Heidegger, and the Decade That Reinvented Philosophy. Wolfram Eilenberger; translated by Shaun Whiteside. Penguin Press 2020. 432 p.

ISBN 9780525559665

Grades: Adult **920**

1. Wittgenstein, Ludwig, 1889-1951 2. Cassirer, Ernst, 1874-1945 3. Benjamin, Walter, 1892-1940 4. Heidegger, Martin, 1889-1976 5. Philosophers 6. Intellectuals 7. Philosophy, Modern 8. Scholars and academics 9. World War I 10. Ethics 11. Semiotics 12. Phenomenology 13. Social change 14. 1920s 15. Between the Wars (1918-1939) 16. Collective biographies 17. Translations — German to English 18. Life stories — Education — Philosophers 19. Society and culture — Philosophy 20. History writing — Arts and culture

LC 2019050893

A grand narrative of the intertwining lives of Walter Benjamin, Martin Heidegger, Ludwig Wittgenstein, and Ernst Cassirer, major philosophers whose ideas shaped the twentieth century. The year is 1919. The horror of the First World War is still fresh for the protagonists, each of whom finds himself at a crucial juncture. The stage is set for a great intellectual drama, which will unfold across the next decade. The lives and ideas of this extraordinary philosophical quartet will converge as they become world historical figures. But as the Second World War looms on the horizon, their fates will be very different.

"A readable, expert introduction to some of the most abstruse yet influential philosophical thought of the 20th century. . . . The book's special value lies in greatly advancing accessibility to these men's works and thought." —*Kirkus*

Originally published: Stuttgart : Klett-Cotta, 2018; Translated from the German.

Eisen, Norman L.
The Last Palace: Europe's Turbulent Century in Five Lives and One Legendary House. Norman Eisen. Crown Publishing 2018. 368 p.

ISBN 9780451495785

Grades: Adult **920**

1. Eisen, Norman L, 1961- 2. Palaces 3. Mansions 4. Diplomatic and consular service 5. War 6. Communism 7. Diplomats 8. Ambassadors 9. Industrialists 10. Women Holocaust survivors 11. Generals 12. European history 13. Eastern Europe 14. Prague, Czech Republic 15. Czechoslovakia 16. 20th century 17. Collective biographies 18. Life stories — People in history — Witness to history 19. History writing — Europe — Eastern Europe 20. Book club best bets

LC 2018014382

A former U.S. ambassador describes the prior occupants of his residence in Prague, including a Jewish financial baron and a Nazi general who carved swastikas into the furniture, and in the process creates a detailed history of Central Europe in the 20th century.

Evans, Claire Lisa
Broad Band: The Untold Story of the Women Who Made the Internet. Claire L. Evans. Portfolio 2018. 272 p.

ISBN 9780735211759

Grades: Adult **920**

1. Women computer scientists 2. Internet 3. Women computer programmers 4. Computer scientists 5. Computer programmers 6. Women in technology 7. Collective biographies 8. Life stories — Science, technology, and medicine 9.

Society and culture — Media and technology 10. History writing — Women's history 11. Adult books for young adults

LC 2017054620

Amelia Bloomer List, 2019.

The YACHT lead singer and VICE reporter celebrates the lesser-known contributions of women to the history of technology, sharing brief profiles of such boundary-breaking innovators as Ada Lovelace, Grace Hopper, Elizabeth "Jake" Feinler and Stacy Horn.

"From COBOL and ARPANET to Silicon Valley and cyberfeminism, women have always played a major role in developing computer technology. Now their collective stories are finally being shared in Evans fascinating and inspiring work of womens history." —*Booklist*

Includes index.

Eyman, Scott

Hank and Jim: The Fifty-year Friendship of Henry Fonda and James Stewart. Scott Eyman. Simon & Schuster 2017. 416 pages

ISBN 9781501102172

Grades: Adult 920

1. Fonda, Henry, 1905-1982 2. Stewart, James, 1908-1997 3. Friendship 4. Interpersonal relations 5. Family relationships 6. Films 7. Actors and actresses 8. New York City 9. Hollywood, California 10. 20th century 11. Collective biographies 12. Life stories — Arts and culture — Performing arts — Actors and actresses 13. Life stories — Relationships — Friendship 14. Arts and Entertainment — Movies and Television

LC 2017011527

Scott Eyman tells the story of the remarkable friendship of two Hollywood legends who, though different in many ways, maintained a close friendship that endured all of life's twists and turns. A fascinating portrait of an extraordinary friendship that lasted through war, marriages, children, careers, and everything else.

"An entertaining, richly documented biography that will be appreciated by film and theater scholars as well as fans of these memorable actors." —*Kirkus*

Includes bibliographical references and index.

Fehrman, Craig

Author in Chief: The Untold Story of Our Presidents and the Books They Wrote. Craig Fehrman. Avid Reader Press 2020. 416 pages

ISBN 9781476786391

Grades: Adult 920

1. Authors 2. Books 3. Autobiography 4. Politicians 5. Writing 6. Letter writing 7. Books and reading 8. Presidents 9. United States 10. Collective biographies 11. History writing — Presidency — United States 12. Life stories — Arts and culture — Writing — Authors 13. Life stories — Politics — Politicians 14. Arts and Entertainment — Writing and Publishing 15. History writing — Politicians — United States

LC Bl2020000504

In Craig Fehrman's groundbreaking work of history, Author in Chief, the story of America's presidents and their books opens a rich new window into presidential biography. From volumes lost to history—Calvin Coolidge's Autobiography, which was one of the most widely discussed titles of 1929—to ones we know and love—Barack Obama's Dreams from My Father, which was very nearly never published—Fehrman unearths countless insights about the presidents through their literary works.

"Illustrations grace the text, and extensive bibliographic notes brim with intriguing facts. Both history buffs and politics enthusiasts will relish this." —*Booklist*

Includes bibliographical references and index.

Figes, Orlando

The Europeans: Three Lives and the Making of a Cosmopolitan Culture. Orlando Figes. Metropolitan Books 2019. xix, 562 pages, 16 unnumbered pages of plates : Illustration; Map

ISBN 9781627792141

Grades: Adult 920

1. Turgenev, Ivan Sergeevich, 1818-1883 2. Viardot, Louis, 1800-1883 3. Viardot-García, Pauline, 1821-1910 4. Culture and globalization 5. Cosmopolitanism 6. Art and culture 7. Globalization 8. Railroad travel 9. Authors 10. Opera singers 11. Love triangles 12. Music 13. Literature 14. Social life and customs 15. Intellectual life 16. Europe 17. 19th century 18. Collective biographies 19. History writing — Europe 20. Life stories — People in history 21. Society and culture — General 22. Arts and Entertainment — General

LC 2019035029

Using documents, letters and archival materials an acclaimed historian and author describes the first age of cultural globalization in the 1800s that led to heightened cosmopolitanism across a Europe that freely shared ideas and artistic creations between nations.

Includes bibliographical references and index.

Finkel, David

Thank You for Your Service. David Finkel. Sarah Crichton Books 2013. 256 pages : Illustration

ISBN 9780374180669

Grades: Adult 920

1. Veterans 2. Iraq War, 2003-2011 3. Homecomings 4. Post-traumatic stress disorder 5. Family relationships 6. Depression 7. War and society 8. Soldiers 9. Military dependents 10. Families of military personnel 11. Veterans' families 12. War 13. Social life and customs 14. United States 15. 21st century 16. Essays 17. Collective biographies 18. Page to screen 19. History writing — Military — Military Today 20. Life stories — Law and order — Armed forces personnel 21. History writing — Wars and conflicts — Iraq War 22. Book club best bets

LC 2013021990

Booklist Editors' Choice, 2013; New York Times Notable Book, 2013; National Book Critics Circle Award for Nonfiction finalist, 2013.

An award-winning staff writer for the Washington Post discusses the hardships faced by soldiers who have come home from service by following the men of the 2-16 Infantry Battalion originally depicted in his book the Good Soldiers.

"It is impossible not to be moved, outraged, and saddened by these stories, and Finkel's deeply personal brand of narrative journalism is both heartbreaking and gut-wrenching in its unflinching honesty." —*Booklist*

Adapted into a film by the same name in 2017; Includes bibliographical references and index.

Finkelstein, Daniel

Two Roads Home: Hitler, Stalin and the Miraculous Survival of My Family. Daniel Finkelstein. Doubleday 2023. 448 p.

ISBN 9780385548557

Grades: Adult 920

1. Finkelstein, Mirjam, 1933-2017 2. Finkelstein, Ludwik, 1929-2011 3. Wiener family 4. Finkelstein family 5. Holocaust survivors 6. Children of Holocaust survivors 7. World War II 8. Holocaust (1933-1945) 9. Refugees, Jewish 10. Jewish families 11. Forced relocations 12. Survival 13. War crimes 14. Archives 15. Western European people 16. Eastern European people 17. German people 18. Polish people 19. British people 20. English people 21. Poland 22. Germany 23. Netherlands 24. Soviet Union 25. Collective biographies 26. Life stories — Facing adversity — War and oppression — Holocaust 27. Life stories — Relationships — Family 28. History writing — Wars and conflicts — Holocaust — World War II

LC 2022058846

In this edge-of-your-seat story of narrow escapes, forged passports, ingenuity, bravery and luck, a beloved British journalist, drawing on personal testimony, letters, diaries and years of historical research, chronicles his family's WWII history of resistance that spans Europe and brings to life the near-miraculous stories of his parents' survival.

"Two progenitors survive the Holocaust, against all the odds, in this extraordinary narrative." —*Kirkus*

Published in the UK under the title Hitler, Stalin, Mum and Dad; Includes bibliographical references and index.

Fox, Margalit

The Riddle of the Labyrinth: The Quest to Crack an Ancient Code. Margalit Fox. HarperCollins 2013. 400 p.

ISBN 9780062228833

Grades: Adult 920

ESSENTIAL AND RECOMMENDED TITLES
920 Collective biographies

1. Kober Alice, 1906-1950 2. Ventris, Michael, 1922-1956 3. Evans, Arthur, Sir, 1851-1941 4. Women linguists 5. Writing methods and systems 6. Excavations (Archaeology) 7. Archaeology 8. Translating and interpreting 9. Language and languages 10. Women scientists 11. Linguistics 12. Research 13. Antiquities 14. Crete 15. Ancient Greece 16. Bronze and Iron Ages (3500-27 B.C.E.) 17. Collective biographies 18. History writing — Archaeology 19. History writing — Women's history 20. Life stories — Science, technology, and medicine — Scientists and inventors

LC 2013404394

ALA Notable Book, 2014; New York Times Notable Book, 2013; William Saroyan International Prize for Writing, Nonfiction category, 2014.

An award-winning journalist presents a gripping, intellectual detective story set in the 1900s that follows the three men who were driven to unlock one of the great secrets of human history—the decipherment of an unknown script from the Aegean Bronze Age.

This exciting linguistic adventure, intended for the nonspecialist, is recommended to anyone interested in archaeological mysteries—and even to crossword puzzle enthusiasts! —*School Library Journal*

Freeman, Sally Mott
*The **Jersey** Brothers: A Missing Naval Officer in the Pacific and His Family's Quest to Bring Him Home.* Sally Mott Freeman. Simon & Schuster 2017. 576 p.
ISBN 9781501104145
Grades: Adult   920

1. Cross, Barton, 1918-1945 2. Brothers 3. Missing in action 4. Soldiers 5. Prisoners of war 6. World War II 7. Philippines 8. Second World War era (1939-1945) 9. Biographies 10. Collective biographies 11. Life stories — Law and order — Armed forces personnel 12. Life stories — Facing adversity — War and oppression — Hostages and POWs 13. History writing — Wars and conflicts — World War II — Pacific Theater 14. Nonfiction that reads like fiction

LC 2016021592

Documents the extraordinary story of three brothers in World War II who found themselves at the epicenter of three of the war's most crucial moments, describing the rescue mission launched by the elder two when their youngest brother was declared missing in action in the Philippines. A first book.

"A grieving family ultimately finds closure in this meticulously researched and compelling history." —*Kirkus*

Funk, Mason
*The **Book** of Pride: LGBTQ Heroes Who Changed the World.* Mason Funk. HarperOne 2019. 288 pages
ISBN 9780062571700
Grades: Adult   920

1. LGBTQIA+ rights 2. Gay activists 3. Gay and Lesbian Movement 4. Gay men 5. Lesbians 6. Bisexual people 7. Transgender people 8. LGBTQIA+ people 9. Human rights 10. Civil rights 11. Collective biographies 12. History writing — LGBTQIA+ 13. Life stories — Identity — LGBTQIA+ 14. Society and culture — LGBTQIA+ 15. Politics and global affairs — Civil and human rights 16. Adult books for young adults

LC 2019006758

Paying tribute to more than 50 extraordinarily and influential leaders who sparked the worldwide LGBTQ-rights movement, this important volume tells stories of dedication and triumph through never-before-published original interviews.

"Funk serves up a generous offering of 75 interviews with individuals whom the books subtitle accurately calls LGBTQ Heroes Who Changed the World. Culled from the Outwords Archive, an oral-history project, these interviews represent an invaluable contribution to American LGBTQ+ history." —*Booklist*

Gabriel, Mary
Love and Capital: Karl and Jennie Marx and the Birth of a Revolution. Mary Gabriel. Little, Brown and Company 2011. 800 p.
ISBN 9780316066112
Grades: Adult   920

1. Marx, Karl, 1818-1883 2. Marx, Jenny, 1814-1881 3. Revolutionaries 4. Socialists 5. Communists 6. Husband and wife 7. Intellectual life 8. Collective biographies 9. History writing — Europe 10. Family and Relationships — Dating and Marriage 11. Life stories — People in history

LC 2010044021

National Book Award for Nonfiction finalist, 2011; National Book Critics Circle Award for Biography finalist, 2011; Pulitzer Prize for Biography or Autobiography finalist, 2012.

An acclaimed biographer tells the story of the Karl and Jenny Marx's marriage, painting a unique and human picture of the revolutionary German socialist as a protective father, loving husband and a jokester.

Includes bibliographical references and index.

Ninth Street Women: Lee Krasner, Elaine De Kooning, Grace Hartigan, Joan Mitchell, and Helen Frankenthaler: Five Painters and the Movement That Changed Modern Art. Mary Gabriel. Little Brown & CO 2018. 568 p.
ISBN 9780316226189
Grades: Adult   920

1. Women artists 2. Abstract expressionism 3. Nonconformists 4. Social change 5. Avant-garde (Aesthetics) 6. Social life and customs 7. Creativity 8. New York City 9. United States 10. 20th century 11. Collective biographies 12. Life stories — Arts and culture — Artists 13. Life stories — Identity — Gender

LC Bl2018185097

A National Book Award finalist describes the lives and careers of five pioneering women artists who entered the male-dominated world of mid-20th century abstract painting and changed their field and American society in the process.

"Biographer Gabriel corrects long-standing misperceptions about New Yorks abstract-expressionism movement by telling the dramatic, often traumatic stories of the five gifted and courageous women painters at the center of that radical flowering." —*Booklist*

Garcia, Mayte
*The **Most** Beautiful: My Life with Prince.* Mayte Garcia. Hachette Books 2017. 304 p.
ISBN 9780316468978
Grades: Adult   920

1. Prince 2. Garcia, Mayte, 1973- 3. Dancers 4. Couples 5. Love 6. Marriage 7. Creativity 8. Marital conflict 9. Loss 10. Interpersonal attraction 11. Rock musicians 12. United States 13. Collective biographies 14. Autobiographies and memoirs 15. Biographies 16. Life stories — Relationships — Couples 17. Arts and Entertainment — Music — Rock 18. Family and Relationships — Dating and Marriage

LC 2016054437

A candid assessment of the iconic musician's personal and professional life by his first wife traces their long-distance courtship, marriage, and creative partnership as well as the challenges that compromised their romance.

"A genial, candid portrait of Prince's ill-fated turn as a family man." —*Kirkus*

Also published in large print format.

Garrett, Kent
*The **Last** Negroes at Harvard: The Class of 1963 and the 18 Young Men Who Changed Harvard Forever.* Kent Garrett and Jeanne Ellsworth. Houghton Mifflin Harcourt 2020. 288 pages
ISBN 9781328879974
Grades: Adult   920

1. Garrett, Kent 2. African American college students 3. African American men 4. Discrimination in universities and colleges 5. Racism 6. Civil Rights Movement 7. African Americans 8. Affirmative action in education 9. Identity 10. Education 11. Inequality 12. Race relations 13. Social life and customs 14. United States history 15. United States 16. Cambridge, Massachusetts 17. 1960s 18. 20th century 19. Autobiographies and memoirs 20. Collective biographies 21. Interviews 22. Society and culture — Education — Higher education 23. Society and culture — Race 24. Life stories — Identity — Race and ethnicity 25. History writing — African American — Civil rights — United States 26. Life stories — Education

LC 2019014973

PUBLIC LIBRARY CORE COLLECTION: NONFICTION
Twentieth Edition

A Harvard graduate who attended as one of 18 African-American recruits in an early affirmative-action program describes how he reconnected with his fellow graduates half a century later to learn their remarkable stories.

"Essential reading for those interested in civil rights, racial identity, and higher education." —*Library Journal*

Includes bibliographical references and index.

Gelwicks, Andrew
The Queer Advantage: Conversations with LGBTQ+ Leaders on the Power of Identity. Andrew Gelwicks. Hachette Go 2020. 528 pages
ISBN 9780306874628
Grades: Adult   920
1. LGBTQIA+ people 2. Identity 3. Success (Concept) 4. Gay men 5. Lesbians 6. Bisexual people 7. Transgender people 8. Gender identity 9. Leadership 10. Ambition 11. Resilience 12. Collective biographies 13. Interviews 14. Life stories — Identity — LGBTQIA+ 15. Life stories — Business — Business leaders 16. Society and culture — LGBTQIA+

LC 2020940814

Collecting incisive, deeply personal conversations with LGBTQ+ trailblazers about how they leveraged the challenges and insights they had as relative outsiders to succeed in the worlds of business, tech, politics, Hollywood, sports and beyond, the QueerAdvantage celebrates the unique, supercharged power of queerness.

"The result is a book that is both informative and inspirational." —*Booklist*

Goldstone, Nancy Bazelon
Daughters of the Winter Queen: Four Remarkable Sisters, the Crown of Bohemia, and the Enduring Legacy of Mary, Queen of Scots. Nancy Goldstone. Little, Brown and Company 2018. 464 p.
ISBN 9780316387910
Grades: Adult   920
1. Elizabeth, Queen, consort of Frederick I, King of Bohemia, 1596-1662 2. Elisabeth, Countess Palatine, 1618-1680 3. Louise Hollandine, Countess Palatine, Abbess of Maubuisson, 1622-1709 4. Sophia, Electress, consort of Ernest Augustus, Elector of Hanover, 1630-1714 5. Women rulers 6. Princesses 7. 17th century 8. Collective biographies 9. Life stories — Politics — Royalty 10. History writing — Europe

LC Bl2018003653

Documents how a betrayed Elizabeth Stuart, the daughter of James I, raised her four daughters in exile during the Dutch Golden Age, tracing how their stories shaped a three-decade war and fulfilled the promises of their great-grandmother, Mary Queen of Scots.

In the Shadow of the Empress: The Defiant Lives of Maria Theresa, Mother of Marie Antoinette, and Her Daughters. Nancy Goldstone. Little, Brown & Company 2021. 608 p.
ISBN 9780316449335
Grades: Adult   920
1. Maria Theresa, Empress of Austria, 1717-1780 2. Marie Antoinette, Queen, consort of Louis XVI, King of France, 1755-1793 3. Maria Christine, consort of Albrecht Kasimir, Duke of Saxe-Teschen, 1742-1798 4. Maria Carolina, Queen, consort of Ferdinand I, King of the Two Sicilies, 1752-1814 5. Habsburg, House of 6. Women rulers 7. Mothers and daughters 8. Sisters 9. Royal houses 10. Marriage 11. Courts and courtiers 12. Revolutions 13. European history 14. 18th century 15. Collective biographies 16. Life stories — Politics — Royalty 17. Life stories — Relationships — Family 18. History writing — Europe

Out of the thrilling and tempestuous eighteenth century comes the sweeping family saga of beautiful Maria Theresa, a sovereign of uncommon strength and vision, the only woman ever to inherit and rule the vast Habsburg Empire in her own name, and three of her remarkable daughters: Lovely, talented Maria Christina, governor-general of the Austrian Netherlands; spirited Maria Carolina, the resolute queen of Naples; and the youngest, Marie Antoinette, the glamorous, tragic queen of France, and perhaps the most famous princess in history. Unfolding against an irresistible backdrop of brilliant courts from Vienna to Versailles, embracing the exotic lure of Naples and Sicily, this epic history of Maria Theresa and her daughters is a tour de force of desire, adventure, ambition, treachery, sorrow, and glory.

"Historian Goldstone (Daughters of the Winter Queen) recounts in this fascinating saga the personalities and power struggles of Maria Theresa, ruler of the Habsburg Empire, and three of her daughters, each of whom served as official or de facto rulers of their own realms during periods of upheaval.... This mesmerizing history isn't to be missed." —*Publishers Weekly*

Includes bibliographical references and index.

Good, Cassandra A.
First Family: George Washington's Heirs and the Making of America. Cassandra A. Good. Hanover Square Press 2023. 320 p.
ISBN 9781335449511
Grades: Adult   920
1. Washington, George, 1732-1799 2. Washington, Martha, 1731-1802 3. Custis family 4. Presidents 5. Children of presidents 6. Stepchildren 7. Families 8. Slaveholders 9. Influence (Psychology) 10. Wealth 11. Power 12. United States history 13. Early America (1784-1819) 14. Collective biographies 15. Impartial writing 16. Life stories — People in history — Famous families 17. History writing — Early America — United States

While it's widely known in America that George and Martha Washington never had children of their own, few are aware that they raised numerous children together. In First Family, we see Washington as a father figure, as well as meet the children he helped raise and trace their complicated roles in American history. The children of Martha Washington's son by her first marriage—Eliza, Patty, Nelly and Wash Custis—were born into life in the public eye. Raised in the country's first "first family," they remained well-known as Washington's family and keepers of his legacy throughout their lives.

"With wit and a careful eye for detail, Good capably balances the book's three narrative tracks: the lives of the Custis clan; the wars, politics, and society around them; and the lives of enslaved and free African Americans in the antebellum era." —*Booklist*

Goodwin, Doris Kearns
No Ordinary Time: Franklin and Eleanor Roosevelt : The Home Front in World War II. Doris Kearns Goodwin. Simon & Schuster 1994. 759 p, 32 p. of plates : Illustration
ISBN 9780671642402
Grades: 11 12 Adult   920
1. Roosevelt, Franklin D. (Franklin Delano), 1882-1945 2. Roosevelt, Eleanor, 1884-1962 3. Women and politics 4. Husband and wife 5. Marriage 6. Presidents' spouses 7. Presidents 8. World War II 9. Men-women relations 10. United States history 11. United States 12. 20th century 13. Collective biographies 14. Biographies 15. History writing — Presidency — 20th century — United States 16. History writing — Wars and conflicts — Homefront — World War II 17. Family and Relationships — Dating and Marriage 18. Life stories — Law and order — Armed forces personnel 19. Life stories — Politics — Politicians

LC 94028565

ALA Notable Book, 1995; Booklist Editors' Choice, 1994; Pulitzer Prize for History, 1995.

Presents a social history of the United States in 1940, along with a moment-by-moment account of Roosevelt's leadership and the private lives of the president and first lady.

Includes bibliographical references (p. [715]-725) and index.

Gopal, Anand
No Good Men Among the Living: America, the Taliban, and the War Through Afghan Eyes. Anand Gopal. Metropolitan Books/Henry Holt and Company 2014. 272 p. (American Empire Project)
ISBN 9780805091793
Grades: Adult   920
1. Afghan War, 2001-2021 2. Soldiers 3. Warlords 4. Homemakers 5. Unconventional warfare 6. Peace-building 7. Internal security 8. Military policy 9. Afghanistan 10. United States 11. Collective biographies 12. Life stories — Facing adversity — War and oppression — War survivors 13. History writing — Wars and conflicts — War in Afghanistan

LC 2014001384

ESSENTIAL AND RECOMMENDED TITLES
920 Collective biographies

New York Times Notable Book, 2014; Pulitzer Prize for General Nonfiction finalist, 2015; National Book Award for Nonfiction finalist, 2014.

Following three Afghans—a Taliban commander, a US-backed warlord and a housewife trapped in the middle of the fighting—through years of US missteps, this dramatic narrative reveals the workings of America's longest war and the truth behind its prolonged agony.

"Policymakers and informed readers will benefit immensely from this illuminating book." —*Library Journal*

Includes index.

Gordon, Charlotte
Romantic Outlaws: The Extraordinary Lives of Mary Wollstonecraft and Her Daughter Mary Shelley. by Charlotte Gordon. Random House 2015. 640 p.
ISBN 9781400068425
Grades: Adult   920
1. Wollstonecraft, Mary, 1759-1797 2. Shelley, Mary Wollstonecraft, 1797-1851 3. Authors, English 4. Women authors, English 5. Feminists 6. Mothers and daughters 7. Women authors 8. 18th century 9. 19th century 10. Biographies 11. Collective biographies 12. Arts and Entertainment — Writing and Publishing 13. Life stories — Arts and culture — Writing — Authors
LC 2014014841

ALA Notable Book, 2016; National Book Critics Circle Award for Biography, 2015.

Mary Wollstonecraft and her daughter Mary Shelley were ardent feminists long before feminism was cool—actually, it was considered morally suspect. In Romantic Outlaws, author Charlotte Gordon relates their lives in alternating chapters, demonstrating the parallels between their philosophical and socially conscious outlooks. Wollstonecraft, who penned the revolutionary Vindication of the Rights of Women, died just two weeks after her daughter's 1797 birth, but Shelley (author ofFrankenstein), who led a similarly tumultuous life, found inspiration in her mother's writings. Viewing the remarkable women's biographies in parallel provides unexpected insights and enriched appreciation of their achievements.

"Gordon's prose is compelling and her scholarship meticulous; her contention that both women led 'Lives as memorable as the words they left behind' is brilliantly supported." —*Library Journal*

Includes bibliographical references and index.

Gordon-Reed, Annette
★ *The Hemingses of Monticello: An American Family.* Annette Gordon-Reed. W.W. Norton & Co. 2008. 608 p.
ISBN 9780393064773
Grades: 10 11 12 Adult   920
1. Hemings family 2. Hemings, Sally, 1773-1835? 3. Jefferson, Thomas, 1743-1826 4. African American families 5. Multiracial people 6. Enslaved people 7. Slaveholders 8. Slavery 9. African Americans 10. United States history 11. Virginia 12. 19th century 13. Collective biographies 14. Biographies 15. Family and Relationships — Families 16. Life stories — Facing adversity — War and oppression — Enslaved people 17. Adult books for young adults 18. History writing — African American — United States
LC 2008014642

ALA Notable Book, 2009; National Book Award for Nonfiction, 2008; New York Times Notable Book, 2008; Pulitzer Prize for History, 2009; National Book Critics Circle Award for Biography finalist, 2008.

Traces the history of the Hemings family from early eighteenth-century Virginia to their dispersal after Thomas Jefferson's death in 1826, and describes their family ties to the third president against a backdrop of Revolutionary America and the French Revolution.

Includes bibliographical references and index.

Gray, Charlotte
★ *Reluctant* Genius: Alexander Graham Bell and the Passion for Invention. Charlotte Gray. Arcade Pub. : 2006. 466 p. : Illustration; Map
ISBN 9781559708098
Grades: 11 12 Adult   920
1. Bell, Alexander Graham, 1847-1922 2. Bell, Mabel Hubbard, 1857-1923 3. Hearing 4. Telephones 5. Husband and wife 6. Inventors 7. Experiments 8. Social life and customs 9. United States 10. 19th century 11. 20th century 12. Collective biographies 13. Canadian literature 14. Biographies 15. Science Writing — Great Engineering Feats 16. Life stories — Science, technology, and medicine — Scientists and inventors 17. Adult books for young adults
LC 2005029609

Ottawa Book Award for English Non-Fiction, 2007.

Draws on new research to offer insight into the inventor's private life, as well as his passionate drive for new innovations, discussing the influence of his speech therapist father and deaf mother on his work, his tempestuous relationship with his wife,and his avoidance of fame and fortune.

"The author recounts both the inventor of the telephone's creation of the device and the projects he pursued once his future was secured.... Combining the household history of the Bells with that of Alexander's successive enthusiasms (Helen Keller, kites, airplanes, hydrocraft), Gray fairly portrays the attractions and exasperations of Bell's life." —*Booklist*

Includes bibliographical references and index.

Groom, Winston
The Aviators: Eddie Rickenbacker, Jimmy Doolittle, Charles Lindbergh, and the Epic Age of Flight. Winston Groom. National Geographic 2013. 448 p.
ISBN 9781426211560
Grades: Adult   920
1. Rickenbacker, Eddie, 1890-1973 2. Doolittle, James Harold, 1896-1993 3. Lindbergh, Charles A. (Charles Augustus), 1902-1974 4. Military pilots 5. Heroes and heroines, American 6. Adventurers 7. Military aviation 8. Aviation history 9. Pilots 10. Military history 11. United States 12. 20th century 13. Collective biographies 14. Biographies 15. History writing — Military — Aviation History 16. Life stories — Law and order — Armed forces personnel
LC 2013015171

Interweaves the adventures during wartime and beyond, of three remarkable aviators—Charles Lindbergh, Eddie Rickenbacker, and Jimmy Doolittle—who defined aviation during the great age of flight.

"A gripping document of a brilliant era in our history and a few of the men who helped make it so." —*Kirkus*

Includes bibliographical references and index.

The Generals: Patton, MacArthur, Marshall, and the Winning of World War II. Winston Groom. National Geographic 2015. 464 p.
ISBN 9781426215490
Grades: Adult   920
1. MacArthur, Douglas, 1880-1964 2. Marshall, George C, (George Catlett), 1880-1959 3. Patton, George S, 1885-1945 4. World War II 5. Military campaigns 6. Military strategy 7. Leadership 8. Command of troops 9. Military officers 10. Generals 11. Military history 12. United States 13. Second World War era (1939-1945) 14. 20th century 15. Collective biographies 16. Biographies 17. History writing — Military — Military leadership 18. History writing — Wars and conflicts — World War II 19. Life stories — Law and order — Military leaders 20. Nonfiction that reads like fiction
LC 2015021562

Traces the intertwined, uniquely American tales of three men-of-arms who became prominent World War II generals and redefined the nation's ideas about military leadership.

"There is much material on the battle tactics of both World Wars, which should appeal to military buffs, while general readers will welcome a review of the facts about these men conveyed through felicitous prose." —*Library Journal*

The Patriots: Alexander Hamilton, Thomas Jefferson, John Adams, and the Making of America. Winston Groom. National Geographic 2020. 464 p.
ISBN 9781426221491
Grades: Adult   920
1. Adams, John, 1735-1826 2. Hamilton, Alexander, 1757-1804 3. Jefferson, Thomas, 1743-1826 4. Politicians 5. Founding Fathers of the United States 6. Revolutionaries 7. Politics and government 8. United States history 9. United States 10. Revolutionary America (1775-1783) 11. Early America (1784-1819) 12. 1780s 13. Collective biographies 14. Life stories — Politics — Politicians 15. History writing — Early America — United States
LC 2020015016

When the Revolutionary War ended in victory, there remained the stupendous problem of how to establish a workable democratic government in the vast, newly independent country. Three key Founding Fathers played significant roles: John Adams, Thomas Jefferson, and Alexander Hamilton. Their lives and policies could not have been more different; their relationships with each other were complex and often rife with animosity. And yet these three men led the charge-two of them creating and signing the Declaration of Independence, and the third establishing a national treasury and the earliest delineation of a Republican party. They managed to shoulder the heavy mantle of creating the United States of America, putting aside their differences to make a great country, once and always.

"Historian and novelist Groom (The Allies) delivers an entertaining group portrait of founding fathers Alexander Hamilton, Thomas Jefferson, and John Adams and their disputes over how to balance federal and state power in the American system of government. . . . This solid history reveals that the art of compromise is an essential ingredient in American democracy." —*Publishers Weekly*

Includes bibliographical references and index.

Gwynne, S. C.

*The **Perfect** Pass: American Genius and the Reinvention of Football.* S. C. Gwynne. Scribner 2016. 320 p.
ISBN 9781501116193
Grades: Adult   920
1. Mumme, Hal 2. Leach, Mike, 1961- 3. Football coaches 4. Football 5. Collective biographies 6. Life stories — Sports — Coaches, managers, and owners 7. Sports and competition — Football

LC 2016012980

As brutal as football can be today, it was much worse in the past—and one of the reasons was that forward passing was not permitted. When it was eventually legalized thanks to the efforts of those looking to make the game safer, it was still rarely used, as passing continued to be seen as a sissy move. In the 1980s, football coaches Hal Mumme and Mike Leach started developing a pass-centric strategy that came to be known as the Air Raid—and transformed the sport into a faster, more dynamic game.

"That makes his subtitle all the more fitting, for undeniably, the two coaches changed the game and brought glory to their institutions. A superb treat for all gridiron fans." —*Kirkus*

Harris, M. A.

*The **Black** Book: 35th Anniversary Edition.* Middleton A. Harris; with the assistance of Morris Levitt, Roger Furman, Ernest Smith; with a new foreword by Toni Morrison; including the original introduction by Bill Cosby. Random House 2009. 198 p. : Illustration; Color; Map; Portrait; Facsimile
ISBN 9781400068487
Grades: Adult   920
1. African American history 2. Society and culture — Ethnic studies 3. History writing — General 4. History writing — United States

LC 2010292662

Now in a deluxe 35th anniversary hardcover edition, The Black Book remains a breathtaking testament to the legendary wisdom, strength, and perseverance of Black men and women intent on freedom; features a new foreword and original poem by Toni Morrison.

35th anniversary ed; Originally published in hardcover and trade paperback in the United States by Random House ... in 1974—T.P. verso.

Hazelgrove, William Elliott

Wright Brothers, Wrong Story: How Wilbur Wright Solved the Problem of Manned Flight. by William Hazelgrove. Random House Inc. 2018. 288 p.
ISBN 9781633884588
Grades: Adult   920
1. Wright, Orville, 1871-1948 2. Wright, Wilbur, 1867-1912 3. Haskell, Katharine Wright, 1874-1929 4. Inventors 5. Flight 6. Aviation 7. Collective biographies 8. Biographies 9. Life stories — Science, technology, and medicine — Scientists and inventors 10. History writing — Science, technology, and medicine

LC 2018031181

Analyzes the myth of the Wright Brothers and their accomplishments in the world of aviation and makes a convincing case that Wilbur, and not Orville, did most of the work on the first successful airplane.

Includes bibliographical references and index.

Hibbert, Christopher

*The **Borgias** and Their Enemies: 1431-1519.* Christopher Hibbert. Harcourt, Inc. 2008. 336 p.
ISBN 9780151010332
Grades: Adult   920
1. Borgia family 2. Nobility 3. European Renaissance 4. Italian history 5. Italy 6. Renaissance (1300-1600) 7. 15th century 8. Age of exploration (1419-1610) 9. Collective biographies 10. History writing — Europe — Italy 11. History writing — Renaissance — Europe 12. Life stories — People in history 13. Life stories — People in history — Famous families

LC 2008003076

A biography of the Borgia family looks at the dynasty's rise to power from its Spanish roots, while profiling its powerful patriarch, Pope Alexander VI; his daughter, Lucrezia; and his ruthless son Cesare, the model for Machiavelli's "The Prince."

"Lucrezia Borgia, on hearing that her father, Pope Alexander VI, was choosing her third husband, noted that her first two had been very unlucky. Luck had little to do with it, as Hibbert shows in this vivid chronicle of the notoriously corrupt Renaissance family. One husband was killed on the orders of her brother Cesare, whose ruthlessness made him the model for Machiavelli's the Prince; the other was discarded after ceasing to be politically useful to the Pope. Hibbert ably traces the web of alliances through which the Spanish-born Alexander hoped to secure his hold on Italy and his family's place in power." —*The New Yorker*

Includes bibliographical references and index.

*The **House** of Medici: Its Rise and Fall.* Christopher Hibbert. Morrow Quill Paperbacks 1980. 364 p, 12 leaves of plates : Illustration
ISBN 9780688053390
Grades: Adult   920
1. Medici, House of 2. Italian history 3. Florence, Italy 4. Renaissance (1300-1600) 5. Collective biographies 6. History writing — Renaissance — Europe 7. History writing — Europe — Italy 8. Life stories — People in history — Famous families

LC 79026508

An account of the fortunes and influences of the great Florentine banking family, covering over three hundred years of soldiers, art patrons, collectors, builders, popes, statesmen, and scholars.

"This book is concerned with heads of the Medici family {who directed the government of the Florentine state from 1434, with Cosimo's return from exile, until the death of the Grand Duke Giovanni Gastone in 1737." —*Times Literary Supplement*

First published in 1974 under title: The rise and fall of the House of Medici; Includes index; Bibliography: P. 338-345.

Holley, Santi Elijah

*An **Amerikan** Family: The Shakurs and the Nation They Created.* Santi Elijah Holley. Mariner Books 2023. 320 p.
ISBN 9780358588764
Grades: Adult   920
1. Shakur, Afeni 2. Shakur family 3. Shakur, Tupac, 1971-1996 4. Shakur, Lumumba Abdul, 1943-1985 5. African American families 6. African American political activists 7. Political activists 8. African American revolutionaries 9. North American people 10. American people 11. Collective biographies 12. Life stories — Politics — Activists and reformers 13. Life stories — Identity — Race and ethnicity 14. Society and culture — Race

LC 2022051479

A history of the rise and lasting impact of Black liberation groups in America, as seen through the Shakurs, one of the movement's most prominent and fiercely creative families, home to Tupac and Assata, and a powerful incubator for today's activism, scholarship, and artistry.

ESSENTIAL AND RECOMMENDED TITLES
920 Collective biographies

"Holley's riveting, detailed history is essential reading for understanding modern America and the Shakurs' enduring legacy."—*Booklist*
Includes bibliographical references and index.

Holt, Nathalia
The Queens of Animation: The Untold Story of the Women Who Transformed the World of Disney and Made Cinematic History. Nathalia Holt. Little, Brown and Company 2019. xiv, 379 pages, 8 unnumbered pages of plates : Illustration; Color; Portrait
ISBN 9780316439152
Grades: Adult   920
1. Gender role 2. Women artists 3. Animated films 4. Women cartoonists 5. Women animators 6. Sexism 7. Animated film industry and trade 8. Film history and criticism 9. Collective biographies 10. Arts and Entertainment — Comics, Cartoons, and Animation 11. Life stories — Arts and culture — Artists 12. History writing — Women's history 13. Arts and Entertainment — Movies and Television

The best-selling author draws on extensive research to trace the role of women employees at Walt Disney Studios, who endured sexism, domestic abuse and workplace intimidation to create iconic films.

"This groundbreaking work laments the discrimination these artists endured while celebrating the verve, creativity, and resiliency they drew on to bring beautiful art and three-dimensional characters to the big screen."—*Booklist*

Hope, Clover
The Motherlode: 100+ Women Who Made Hip-hop. Clover Hope; illustrations by Rachelle Baker. Abrams Image 2021. 272 p.
ISBN 9781419742965
Grades: Adult   920
1. Rap music 2. African American rap musicians 3. Rap musicians 4. African American women singers 5. Women musicians 6. Hip-hop culture 7. Gender role 8. Arts and Entertainment — Music — Rap and R&B 9. History writing — Women's history 10. History writing — Arts and culture

Accompanied by vibrant illustrations, this book profiles more than 100 women in rap, including pioneers like Roxanne Shante, and game changers like Lauryn Hill and Missy Elliott, who have helped shape the genre and eschewed gender norms in the process.

"An appealing survey that highlights many unsung heroines along with the superstars."—*Library Journal*

Ice-T
Split Decision: Life Stories. Ice-T and Spike and Douglas Century. Gallery Books 2022. 320 p.
ISBN 9781982148775
Grades: Adult   920
1. Ice-T (Musician) 2. Spike, 1962- 3. Rap musicians 4. Gangsters 5. African American men 6. Criminals 7. Crime 8. Jewelry theft 9. Fame 10. Success (Concept) 11. Imprisonment 12. Social advocacy 13. At-risk youth 14. Options, alternatives, choices 15. Consequences 16. Collective autobiographies and memoirs 17. Life stories — Law and order — Criminals and law-breakers 18. Life stories — Law and order — Prisoners and inmates 19. Life stories — Arts and culture — Performing arts — Entertainers and celebrities 20. Society and culture — Violence and crime 21. Society and culture — Social activism and philanthropy
LC 2022003438

Award-winning actor, rapper, and producer Ice-T unveils a compelling and astonishing memoir of his early life robbing jewelry stores until he found fame and fortune—while a handful of bad choices sent his former crime partner down an incredibly different path.

"With the help of journalist Century, rapper Ice-T and his former, literal partner-in-crime Spike deliver a propulsive chronicle of the choices that shaped their lives, beginning with the smash-and-grab jewelry robberies that brought the two together in L.A. in their early 20s in the early 1980s."—*Publishers Weekly*

Ignotofsky, Rachel
Women in Science: 50 Fearless Pioneers Who Changed the World. Written and illustrated by Rachel Ignotofsky. Ten Speed Press 2016. 127 p.
ISBN 9781607749769
Grades: Adult   920
1. Women scientists 2. Scientists 3. Collective biographies 4. Illustrated books 5. Biographies 6. Biographies — Science and medicine — Scientists and inventors
LC 2015050246

A collection of artworks inspired by the lives and achievements of fifty famous women in science, technology, engineering, and mathematics, from the ancient world to the present, profiles each notable individual.
Illustrated by the author.

Isay, David
Callings: A Celebration of Lives of Purpose and Passion. Dave Isay. Penguin Press 2016. 266 pages
ISBN 9781594205187
Grades: Adult   920
1. Vocation 2. Personal conduct 3. Oral histories 4. Collective autobiographies and memoirs 5. Life stories — Personal growth
LC Bl2016005261

The founder of StoryCorps describes the amazing, true stories of people who are doing what they love and making a difference.

"These wonderful stories reveal that work becomes meaningful to those who chooseor are in some cases chosen bythe calling that motivates, energizes, and inspires them."—*Publishers Weekly*

Jeal, Tim
Explorers of the Nile: The Triumph and Tragedy of a Great Victorian Adventure. Tim Jeal. Yale University Press 2011. 592 p.
ISBN 9780300149357
Grades: Adult   920
1. Burton, Richard F, 1821-1890 2. Speke, John Hanning, 1827-1864 3. Explorers 4. Exploration 5. Nile River 6. Central Africa 7. Congo (Democratic Republic) 8. 19th century 9. Collective biographies 10. Biographies 11. History writing — Exploration 12. Adventure writing — Exploration 13. Life stories — People in history — Explorers
LC 2011933872

Examines the journeys of the six men and one woman, who risked their lives, to solve the mystery of the source of the White Nile, between 1856 and 1876, and discusses the consequences the search has had on Uganda and the Sudan.

Kalb, Claudia
Andy Warhol Was a Hoarder: Inside the Minds of History's Great Personalities. Claudia Kalb. National Geographic Books 2016. 288 p.
ISBN 9781426214660
Grades: Adult   920
1. Fame 2. Celebrities 3. Mental illness 4. Eccentrics and eccentricities 5. Compulsive behavior 6. Deviant behavior 7. Addiction 8. Collective biographies 9. Life stories — Facing adversity — Medical issues — Mental illness 10. Science Writing — Medicine and health — Mental health
LC 2015024370

In this surprising, inventive, and meticulously researched look at the evolution of mental health, acclaimed health and science journalist Claudia Kalb gives readers a glimpse into the lives of high-profile historic figures through the lens of modern psychology, weaving groundbreaking research into biographical narratives that are deeply embedded in our culture.

"In all, Kalbs well-written exercise in applying modern psychiatric theory to historical figures, from Marilyn Monroe to Albert Einstein to Charles Darwin, certainly makes for some very entertaining armchair speculation."—*Booklist*
Includes bibliographical references.

Kaplan, James
3 Shades of Blue: Miles Davis, John Coltrane, Bill Evans, and the Lost Empire of Cool. James Kaplan. Penguin Press 2024. 480 p.
ISBN 9780525561002
Grades: Adult   920

1. Davis, Miles 2. Coltrane, John, 1926-1967 3. Evans, Bill, 1929-1980 4. Jazz music 5. Jazz trumpeters 6. African American jazz musicians 7. Music, American 8. Jazz musicians 9. Music history and criticism 10. United States 11. 20th century 12. Collective biographies 13. Arts and Entertainment — Music — Jazz and the Blues 14. Life stories — Arts and culture — Performing arts — Musicians and composers

LC 2023026564

The story of how three legends—Miles Davis, John Coltrane and Bill Evans—came together in 1959 to create Kind of Blue, which is widely considered the great jazz album of time.

"A compulsively readable book about three jazz legends who came together for one glorious moment to produce one of the best, most influential jazz records ever." —*Library Journal*

Includes bibliographical references and index.

Kaplan, Janice

The **Genius** *of Women: From Overlooked to Changing the World.* Janice Kaplan. E.P. Dutton 2020. 320 p.

ISBN 9781524744212

Grades: Adult 920

1. Genius 2. Gifted women 3. Intellectuals 4. Gender role 5. Creativity 6. Collective biographies 7. History writing — Women's history 8. Society and culture — Gender — Women 9. Life stories — Education — Scholars and educators 10. Life stories — Science, technology, and medicine 11. Life stories — Identity — Gender 12. Adult books for young adults

LC 2019027361

A look at the history of women geniuses and how they have historically not been recognized to the same degree as their male counterparts in a variety of fields including science and the performing arts.

"Expect this well-reasoned account to generate a lot of interest and conversation." —*Booklist*

Karbo, Karen

In **Praise** *of Difficult Women: Life Lessons from 29 Heroines Who Dared to Break the Rules.* Karen Karbo, foreword by Cheryl Strayed. National Geographic Society 2018. 288 p.

ISBN 9781426217746

Grades: Adult 920

1. Feminism 2. Women 3. Personal conduct 4. Quality of life 5. Collective biographies 6. Life stories — People in history 7. History writing — Women's history 8. Society and culture — Gender — Women 9. Adult books for young adults

The internationally best-selling author of the "Kick-Ass Women" series shines a spotlight on female rule-breakers, including Amelia Earhart, Helen Gurley Brown, Frida Kahlo, Nora Ephron and Carrie Fisher, providing inspiration and instruction for the new age of feminism.

Kashner, Sam

The **Fabulous** *Bouvier Sisters: The Tragic and Glamorous Lives of Jackie and Lee.* Sam Kashner and Nancy Schoenberger. Harper, an imprint of HarperCollinsPublishers 2018. 400 p.

ISBN 9780062364982

Grades: Adult 920

1. Onassis, Jacqueline Kennedy, 1929-1994 2. Radziwill, Lee Bouvier, 1933- 3. Sisters 4. Celebrities 5. Sibling rivalry 6. Sisterhood 7. Presidents' spouses 8. United States 9. Collective biographies 10. Biographies 11. Life stories — Relationships — Family 12. Family and Relationships — Siblings

LC Bl2018134487

Draws on candid interviews with Jackie Kennedy Onassis' sister, Lee, to share dramatic insights into the complicated relationship the two shared, discussing their artistic interests and the rivalries that complicated their bond.

Katz, Catherine Grace

The **Daughters** *of Yalta: The Churchills, Roosevelts, and Harrimans: A Story of Love and War.* Catherine Grace Katz. Houghton Mifflin Harcourt 2020. 400 p.

ISBN 9780358117858

Grades: Adult 920

1. Roosevelt, Anna, 1906-1975 2. Churchill, Sarah, 1914-1982 3. Mortimer, Kathleen Lanier Harriman, 1917-2011 4. World War II 5. Alliances 6. Summit meetings 7. Women and politics 8. Heads of state 9. Children of politicians 10. Women war correspondents 11. Armed forces 12. Fathers and daughters 13. Diplomacy 14. Military officers 15. Women's participation in wars 16. Collective biographies 17. Life stories — Politics 18. Life stories — Relationships — Family 19. History writing — Wars and conflicts — World War II 20. History writing — Women's history 21. Nonfiction that reads like fiction

LC 2020004935

The story of the fascinating and fateful "daughter diplomacy" of Anna Roosevelt, Sarah Churchill, and Kathleen Harriman, three glamorous young women who accompanied their famous fathers to the Yalta Conference with Stalin in the waning days of World War II.

"Katz effectively shows how these three often overlooked women proved to be indispensable in a variety of ways. Engaging, multilayered history of the best kind, grounded in telling detail and marvelous personalities." —*Kirkus*

Includes bibliographical references and index.

Kearse, Bettye

The **Other** *Madisons: The Lost History of a President's Black Family.* Bettye Kearse. Houghton Mifflin Harcourt 2020. x, 253 p.

ISBN 9781328604392

Grades: Adult 920

1. Kearse, Bettye 2. Madison, James, 1751-1836 3. Madison family 4. Mandy, active 18th century 5. Coreen, active 18th century 6. African American families 7. Multiracial people 8. Founding fathers of the United States 9. Family history 10. Oral history projects 11. Genealogy 12. Matriarchs 13. Family secrets 14. Enslaved people 15. Freed people 16. Racism 17. Families 18. Presidents 19. Virginia 20. Texas 21. United States 22. 18th century 23. 19th century 24. Collective biographies 25. Life stories — Identity — Race and ethnicity 26. Life stories — Relationships — Family 27. History writing — African American — United States 28. History writing — Presidency — 19th century — United States

LC 2019024941

For thousands of years, West African griots (men) and griottes (women) have recited the stories of their people. Without this tradition Bettye Kearse would not have known that she is a descendant of President James Madison and his slave, and half-sister, Coreen. In 1990, Bettye became the eighth-generation griotte for her family. Their credo—"Always remember—you're a Madison. You come from African slaves and a president"—was intended to be a source of pride, but for her, it echoed with abuses of slavery, including rape and incest. Confronting those abuses, Bettye embarked on a journey of discovery—of her ancestors, the nation, and herself.

"Poignant and eye-opening, this is a must-read." —*Booklist*

Includes bibliographical references.

Keene, Adrienne

Notable **Native** *People: 50 Indigenous Leaders, Dreamers, and Changemakers from Past and Present.* Adrienne Keene; illustrations by Ciara Sana. Ten Speed Press 2021. 143 pages

ISBN 9781984857941

Grades: Adult 920

1. Indigenous peoples of North America 2. Native Hawaiians 3. Indigenous peoples 4. Collective biographies 5. Life stories — Identity — Race and ethnicity

LC 2021003418

American Indian Youth Literature Awards Honor Book, Young Adult Book, 2022.

Perfect for readers of all ages, this celebration of lives, stories and contributions of 50 notable Native American people highlights the vital impact indigenous dreamers and leaders have made on the world.

"This is a well-composed, highly readable introduction to significant Native people ... the entries serve to inform readers, while broadening their knowledge of and appreciation for the myriad ways in which Native populations work to en-

ESSENTIAL AND RECOMMENDED TITLES
920 Collective biographies

sure rights for their people, protect the environment, and preserve their heritage."
—*Booklist*

Includes index.

Kelly, Kate
Ordinary Equality: The Fearless Women and Queer People Who Shaped the U.S. Constitution and the Equal Rights Amendment. Kate Kelly; illustrated by Nicole Larue. Gibbs Smith 2022. 256 p.

ISBN 9781423658726

Grades: Adult   920

1. Constitutional history 2. Civil rights 3. Equal rights amendments 4. Equality 5. Constitutional amendments 6. Social advocates 7. Feminists 8. Gender equity 9. United States history 10. History writing — Women's history

We are all living through modern constitutional history in the making, and Ordinary Equality helps teach about the past, present, and future of the Equal Rights Amendment (ERA) through the lives of the bold, fearless women and queer people who have helped shape the U.S. Constitution.

"Lawyer and podcaster Kelly focuses this breezy and inspiring history of the fight against gender and sex discrimination on 12 women who pushed for 'Constitutional equality' for women and other marginalized groups." —*Publishers Weekly*

Kennedy, John F.
Profiles in Courage. John F. Kennedy. Harper Collins 2003. xxii, 245 p.

ISBN 9780060530624

Grades: 7 8 9 10 11 12 Adult   920

1. Politicians 2. Legislators 3. Politics and government 4. Courage 5. United States 6. Collective biographies 7. Biographies 8. History writing — Politicians — United States 9. Life stories — Politics — Politicians

LC 2003040676

Jane Addams Book Award, General Category, 1964; Pulitzer Prize for Biography or Autobiography, 1957.

Profiles eight historical figures who demonstrated particular integrity in the face of opposition, including John Quincy Adams, Daniel Webster, Thomas Hart Benton, and Robert A. Taft.

We have evaluated this title and no longer recommend it for purchase.

Includes bibliographical references (p. 227-237) and index; Originally published: New York : Harper & Brothers, 1956.

Kerrison, Catherine
Jefferson's Daughters: Three Sisters, White and Black, in a Young America. Catherine Kerrison. Ballantine Books 2018. 432 p.

ISBN 9781101886243

Grades: Adult   920

1. Randolph, Martha Jefferson, 1772-1836 2. Eppes, Maria, 1778-1804 3. Hemings, Harriet, 1801- 4. Jefferson, Thomas, 1743-1826 5. Fathers and daughters 6. Gender role 7. Women and politics 8. Half sisters 9. Multiracial children 10. Enslaved people 11. Early America (1784-1819) 12. Collective biographies 13. Life stories — People in history 14. History writing — Early America — United States 15. History writing — Women's history

LC 2017043540

A portrait of the divergent lives of Thomas Jefferson's three daughters reveals how his white daughters struggled with the realities of lives they were ill-prepared to manage, while the daughter he fathered with a slave did not achieve freedom until adulthood.

"Incisive and elegant, Kerrisons book is at once a fabulous family story and a stellar work of historical scholarship." —*Publishers Weekly*

Includes bibliographical references and index.

Khilnani, Sunil
Incarnations: A History of India in Fifty Lives. Sunil Khilnani. Farrar, Straus and Giroux 2016. 384 p.

ISBN 9780374175498

Grades: Adult   920

1. Human geography 2. Intellectual life 3. Social life and customs 4. Civilization 5. Indian history 6. India 7. Collective biographies 8. Biographies 9. History writing — Asia — South Asia — India 10. Life stories — People in history

LC 2016007101

The author of the Idea of Indian presents an entertaining and provocative account of India's past via a series of portraits of emperors, warriors, philosophers, film stars and corporate titans—some famous, some unjustly forgotten, but all important in the country's rich history.

Khilnanis essays are provocative and serious, a worthy rebuttal to the image of Indian history as 'Curiously unpeopled.' —*Publishers Weekly*

Includes notes and index; Originally published, in somewhat different form, in 2016 by Allen Lane, an imprint of Penguin Books, Great Britain—Title page verso.

King, Charles
★ *Gods of the Upper Air: How a Circle of Renegade Anthropologists Reinvented Race, Sex, and Gender in the Twentieth Century.* Charles King. Doubleday 2019. xii, 431 p.

ISBN 9780385542197

Grades: Adult   920

1. Boas, Franz, 1858-1942 2. Anthropologists 3. Sociocultural anthropology 4. Women anthropologists 5. Non-industrial societies 6. Dissenting opinions 7. Teacher-student relationships 8. Collective biographies 9. Life stories — Education — Scholars and educators 10. Society and culture — Ethnic studies 11. History writing — Arts and culture

LC 2019014081

National Book Critics Circle Award for Biography finalist, 2019.

A dazzling group portrait of Franz Boas, the founder of cultural anthropology, and his circle of women scientists, who upended American notions of race, gender, and sexuality in the 1920s and 1930s—a sweeping chronicle of how our society began to question the basic ways we understand other cultures and ourselves.

"Rich in ideas, the book also abounds in absorbing accounts of friendships, animosities, and rivalries among these early anthropologists. This superb narrative of debunking scientists provides timely reading for our great-again era." —*Kirkus*

Includes bibliographical references and index.

Koch, Bea
Mad and Bad: Real Heroines of the Regency. Bea Koch. Grand Central Publishing 2020. VIII, 261 p.

ISBN 9781538701010

Grades: Adult   920

1. Women's history 2. Women intellectuals 3. Lesbians 4. Marginalized women 5. Jewish women 6. Women 7. Social life and customs 8. British history 9. England 10. 19th century 11. Regency period (1811-1820) 12. Georgian era (1714-1837) 13. Collective biographies 14. History writing — Women's history 15. History writing — Europe — United Kingdom 16. Life stories — Identity — Gender 17. Life stories — People in history 18. Adult books for young adults

LC 2019049246

A feminist pop history explores the achievements of iconoclastic women from the Regency era, from Dido Elizabeth Belle and Caroline Herschel to Anne Lister and Judith Montefiore, who broke barriers to live on their own terms.

"This fun and informative account will be treasured by readers of Jane Austen and contemporary Regency romance novelists, as well as fans of feminist history." —*Publishers Weekly*

Includes bibliographical references and index.

Kolker, Robert
★ *Hidden Valley Road: Inside the Mind of an American Family.* Robert Kolker. Doubleday 2020. 352 p.

ISBN 9780385543767

Grades: Adult   920

1. Galvin family 2. People with schizophrenia 3. Schizophrenia 4. People with mental illnesses 5. Family problems 6. Family violence 7. Family secrets 8. Treatment 9. Family relationships 10. Genetics 11. Collective biographies 12. Life stories — Facing adversity — Medical issues — Mental illness 13. Sci-

ence writing — Medicine and health — Mental health 14. Family and relationships — Illness and the family 15. Life stories — Relationships — Family 16. Book club best bets

LC 2019028466

ALA Notable Book, 2021; New York Times Notable Book, 2020.

Tells the heartrending story of a midcentury American family with 12 children, 6 of them diagnosed with schizophrenia, that became science's great hope in the quest to understand the disease.

"An exceptional, unforgettable, and significant work that must not be missed." —*Booklist*

Includes bibliographical references and index.

Koppel, Lily

The Astronaut Wives Club: A True Story. Lily Koppel. Grand Central Publishing 2013. 288 p.

ISBN 9781455503254

Grades: Adult   920

1. Women in public life 2. Astronauts 3. Married women 4. Women celebrities 5. Extramarital affairs 6. Female friendship 7. Marital conflict 8. Astronautics 9. Public opinion 10. Social life and customs 11. Houston, Texas 12. United States 13. 20th century 14. Collective biographies 15. Page to screen 16. Biographies 17. Life stories — Science, technology, and medicine — Astronauts and pilots 18. History writing — Women's history

LC 2012045976

With selection of the first crew members of the Mercury space program in 1959, a small group of women who had been ordinary military wives became celebrities. As role models and representatives of the space program, NASA demanded their perfection, from their clothing to the meals they served at home. This intimate, informative group portrait chronicles how they formed a support group (ater extending it to the wives of the Gemini and Apollo astronauts) which became an essential resource behind the scenes of the space program's early years.

Book adapted into a TV series for ABC in 2015.

Krist, Gary

The Mirage Factory: Illusion, Imagination, and the Invention of Los Angeles. Gary Krist. Crown Publishing 2018. 432 p.

ISBN 9780451496386

Grades: Adult   920

1. Mulholland, William, 1855-1935 2. Griffith, D. W. (David Wark), 1875-1948 3. McPherson, Aimee Semple, 1890-1944 4. Social history 5. Los Angeles, California 6. Collective biographies 7. History writing — Regional history — United States 8. Life stories — People in history

LC 2017049682

Describes how the visions of three people: William Mulholland, an engineer; D.W. Griffith, an early filmmaker; and Aimee Semple McPherson, an evangelist and faith healer combined to turn sleepy, near-desert farmland into the city of Los Angeles.

Kroger, Lisa

Monster, She Wrote: The Women Who Pioneered Horror and Speculative Fiction. Lisa Kroger and Melanie R. Anderson. Qurik Books 2019. 352 p.

ISBN 9781683691389

Grades: Adult   920

1. Women authors 2. Books and reading 3. Science fiction authors 4. Fantasy fiction authors 5. Women horror authors 6. Literary criticism 7. Television programs 8. Film history and criticism 9. Women 10. Collective biographies 11. Arts and entertainment — Writing and publishing 12. Life stories — Arts and culture — Writing — Authors 13. History writing — Women's history 14. Society and culture — Pop culture 15. Arts and Entertainment — Writing and Publishing — Literary criticism

LC 2019930321

Booklist Editors' Choice, 2019; Bram Stoker Award for Superior Achievement in Non-Fiction, 2019; Locus Award for Best Nonfiction/Related/Reference Book, 2020.

Frankenstein was just the beginning: Horror stories and other weird fiction wouldn't exist without the women who created it. From Gothic ghost stories to psychological horror to science fiction, women have been primary architects of speculative literature of all sorts. And their own life stories are as intriguing as their fiction. Part biography, part reader's guide, the engaging write-ups and detailed reading lists will introduce you to more than a hundred authors and over two hundred of their mysterious and spooky novels, novellas, and stories.

"Straddling the divide between highly useful reference and compulsively readable stories about the writing lives of the women of horror, this book will keep you up all night (one way or another)." —*Booklist*

Landdeck, Katherine Sharp

The Women with Silver Wings: The Inspiring True Story of the Women Airforce Service Pilots of World War II. Katherine Sharp Landdeck. Crown 2020. 368 p.

ISBN 9781524762810

Grades: Adult   920

1. World War II 2. Military pilots 3. Women pilots 4. Sexism 5. Women's participation in wars 6. Ambition 7. Second World War era (1939-1945) 8. Collective biographies 9. History writing — Women's history 10. History writing — Wars and conflicts — World War II 11. Life stories — Law and order — Armed forces personnel

LC 2019059114

Tells the true story of the daring female aviators who helped the United States win World War II—only to be forgotten by the country they served.

"Based on hundreds of oral histories with surviving WASP women, along with letters, diaries, and government documents, Landdeck explains the women's vital role ferrying planes, the group's disbandment, and their fight decades later to be rightfully recognized as veterans … a must-read for those interested in women's and World War II history." —*Library Journal*

Includes index.

Leamer, Laurence

The Kennedy Men: 1901-1963 : The Laws of the Father. Laurence Leamer. Wm. Morrow 2001. 882 p. : Illustration

ISBN 9780688163150

Grades: Adult   920

1. Kennedy, Joseph P. (Joseph Patrick), 1888-1969 2. Kennedy, John F. (John Fitzgerald), 1917-1963 3. Kennedy family 4. Politicians 5. United States 6. Collective biographies 7. Biographies 8. History writing — Politicians — United States 9. Family and Relationships — Families 10. Life stories — Politics — Politicians 11. Life stories — People in history — Famous families

LC 2001031689

Presents a multigenerational portrait of the Kennedy men and their rise to the heights of American politics, beginning in 1901 with twelve-year-old Joseph P. Kennedy and ending in 1963 with the assassination of President John F. Kennedy.

"Leamers writing is impressive throughout, regularly catching the reader up with a felicitous phrase or a surprising insight." —*Booklist*

Includes bibliographical references (p. [829]-845) and index.

Levingston, Steven

Kennedy and King: The President, the Pastor, and the Battle Over Civil Rights. Steven Levingston. Hachette Books 2017. 352 p.

ISBN 9780316267397

Grades: Adult   920

1. King, Martin Luther, Jr, 1929-1968 2. Kennedy, John F. (John Fitzgerald), 1917-1963 3. Civil Rights Movement 4. Civil rights workers 5. Political science 6. Politicians 7. African American civil rights 8. Presidents 9. United States 10. Collective biographies 11. Biographies 12. Life stories — Politics — Activists and reformers — Civil Rights leaders 13. Life stories — Politics — Politicians 14. History writing — African American — Civil rights — United States

LC Bl2017015720

A revelatory account of the contentious relationship between the 35th President and Martin Luther King, Jr. throughout the tumultuous early years of the Civil Rights movement shares insights into their profound influence on one another and the important decisions that were inspired by their rivalry.

"A dual biography chronicles three years of upheaval in the civil rights movement." —*Kirkus*

ESSENTIAL AND RECOMMENDED TITLES
920 Collective biographies

Lewis, Michael
★ *The Undoing Project: A Friendship That Changed Our Minds.* Michael Lewis. W W Norton & Company 2016. 362 pages
ISBN 9780393254594
Grades: Adult   **920**
1. Kahneman, Daniel, 1934-2024 2. Tversky, Amos 3. Cognitive neuroscience 4. Neuroscience 5. Decision-making 6. Male friendship 7. Nobel Prize winners 8. Psychologists 9. Neuropsychology 10. Collective biographies 11. Science Writing — Biology 12. Life stories — Science, technology, and medicine — Healthcare professionals
New York Times Notable Book, 2017.

Examines the history of behavioral economics, discussing the theory of Israeli psychologists who wrote the original studies undoing assumptions about the decision-making process and the influence it has had on evidence-based regulation.

Louvin, Charlie
Satan Is Real: The Ballad of the Louvin Brothers. Charlie Louvin and Benjamin Whitmer. HarperCollins 2012. 297 p.
ISBN 9780062069030
Grades: Adult   **920**
1. Louvin, Charlie, 1927-2011 2. Louvin, Ira, 1924-1965 3. Country music 4. Family relationships 5. Country music industry and trade 6. Popular culture 7. United States history 8. 20th century 9. Autobiographies and memoirs 10. Life stories — Relationships — Family 11. Arts and Entertainment — Music — Country 12. Life stories — Arts and culture — Performing arts — Musicians and composers
LC 2012563500

The story of musical brothers Charlie and Ira Louvin—the first a church-going gospel singer, the second a hard drinking, mandolin-smashing hellraiser who was banned from performing at the Grand Ole Opry after his wife shot him for trying to choke her.

Lownie, Andrew
Traitor King: The Scandalous Exile of the Duke & Duchess of Windsor. Andrew Lownie. Pegasus Books 2022. 432 p.
ISBN 9781639361410
Grades: Adult   **920**
1. Windsor, Edward, Duke of, 1894-1972 2. Windsor, Wallis Warfield, Duchess of, 1896-1986 3. Scandals 4. Dukes and duchesses 5. Betrayal 6. Rulers 7. British history 8. Great Britain 9. Collective biographies 10. History writing — Europe — United Kingdom 11. Life stories — Politics — Royalty

Drawing upon newly released archives, bestselling biographer Andrew Lownie tells the story of the Duke and Duchess of Windsor's glittering lives after Edward abdicated the throne—a world that was riddled with treachery and betrayal.

"Although numerous books have been written about the Duke and Duchess of Windsor (Edward VIII and Wallis Simpson), Lownie's (The Mountbattens) well-researched and comprehensive book proves there's more to learn about the couple." —*Library Journal*

Originally published in the UK by Blink Publishing, London, in 2021.

Lucey, Donna M.
Sargent's Women: Four Lives Behind the Canvas. Donna M. Lucey. W.W. Norton & Company 2017. 320 p.
ISBN 9780393079036
Grades: Adult   **920**
1. Myers, Elsie Palmer, 1872-1955 2. Fuller, Lucia Fairchild, 1872-1924 3. Chapman, Elizabeth Winthrop Chanler, 1866-1937 4. Gardner, Isabella Stewart, 1840-1924 5. Sargent, John Singer, 1856-1925 6. Upper class 7. Gender role 8. Portraits 9. Artists 10. Women 11. Independence 12. United States history 13. United States 14. 19th century 15. 20th century 16. Collective biographies 17. Biographies 18. Life stories — Arts and culture 19. History writing — Women's history 20. Arts and entertainment — Painting, drawing, and sculpture
LC 2017013987

Describes the lives of four high-society women who were immortalized in portraits done by the iconic artist, John Singer Sargent, each one incredibly wealthy, beautiful and commanding who experienced numerous mysteries, passions and tragedies during the Gilded Age.

"Perceptive biographies of a quartet of Gilded Age women." —*Kirkus*

Includes bibliographical references and index.

Mahoney, Richard D.
Sons & Brothers: The Days of Jack and Bobby Kennedy. Richard D. Mahoney. Arcade Pub. 1999. xvii, 441 p. : Illustration
ISBN 9781559704809
Grades: Adult   **920**
1. Kennedy, John F. (John Fitzgerald), 1917-1963 2. Kennedy, Robert Francis, 1925-1968 3. Kennedy family 4. Brothers 5. Presidents 6. Legislators 7. Politics and government 8. United States 9. 1960s 10. Collective biographies 11. Biographies 12. History writing — Politicians — United States 13. Family and Relationships — Families 14. Life stories — Politics — Politicians 15. Life stories — People in history — Famous families
LC 99025681

An intimate and powerful portrait of the Kennedy brothers details their extraordinary bond based on their shared belief of tragic destiny.

"Writing in a steady, almost relentlessly elegiac tone, Mahoney proves that the lives and deaths of John F. and Robert F. Kennedy remain as compelling now as they were throughout the turbulent 1960s." —*Publishers Weekly*

Includes bibliographical references (p. 379-424) and index.

Makos, Adam
Devotion: An Epic Story of Heroism, Friendship, and Sacrifice. Adam Makos. Ballantine Books 2015. 400 p.
ISBN 9780804176583
Grades: Adult   **920**
1. Brown, Jesse Leroy 2. Hudner, Tom 3. Korean War, 1950-1953 4. African American men 5. Racism in the military 6. Search and rescue operations 7. Page to screen 8. Collective biographies 9. Life stories — Law and order — Armed forces personnel 10. History writing — Wars and conflicts — Korean War
LC 2015023955

Traces the inspirational story of famous Navy aviator duo Tom Hudner and Jesse Brown, recounting how they defied period conventions to serve their country, overcome racial barriers and protect one another on a daring Korean War mission.

Made into a movie released in theaters in October 2022.

Mann, William J.
Bogie & Bacall: The Surprising True Story of Hollywood's Greatest Love Affair. William J. Mann. Harper 2023. 448 p.
ISBN 9780063026391
Grades: Adult   **920**
1. Bogart, Humphrey, 1899-1957 2. Bacall, Lauren, 1924-2014 3. Actors and actresses 4. Couples 5. Relationships between young women and older men 6. Husband and wife 7. Celebrities 8. Marriage 9. Interpersonal relations 10. North American people 11. American people 12. Collective biographies 13. Life stories — Arts and culture — Performing arts — Actors and actresses 14. Life stories — Relationships — Couples 15. Arts and Entertainment — Movies and Television

In Bogie & Bacall, William Mann offers a deep and comprehensive look at Lauren Bacall, Humphrey Bogart, and the unlikely love they shared. Mann details their early years—Bogart's effete upbringing in New York City; Bacall's rise as a model and actress. He paints a vivid portrait of their courtship and twelve-year marriage: the fights, the reconciliations, the children, the affairs, Bogie's illness and Bacall's steadfastness until his death. Surpassing previous biographies, Mann digs deep into the celebrities' personal lives and considers their relationship from surprising angles.

"Biographer Mann (The Contender) spotlights screen legends Humphrey Bogart (1899-1957) and Lauren Bacall (1924-2014) in this engrossing examination of the couple's intertwined careers and mythologized romance." —*Publishers Weekly*

Markham, Lauren

★ *The Far Away Brothers: Two Young Migrants and the Making of an American Life*. Lauren Markham. Crown Publishing 2017. 352 pages
ISBN 9781101906187
Grades: Adult   920

1. Flores, Ernesto, 1997- 2. Flores, Raul, 1997- 3. Twin brothers 4. Undocumented immigrants 5. Teenagers 6. Immigration policy 7. Immigration and emigration law 8. Immigrants 9. Unaccompanied immigrant children 10. Violence in gangs 11. Salvadoran Americans 12. El Salvador 13. Oakland, California 14. California 15. Collective biographies 16. Life stories — Identity — Immigrants 17. Life stories — Facing adversity 18. Politics and global affairs — Immigration 19. Adult books for young adults

LC 2017000952

Author Lauren Markham was working as a counselor in an Oakland, California school district when she met identical twins Raúl and Ernesto Flores. The teenagers had fled El Salvador to escape deadly gang violence, knowing no English and unprepared for American society. Markham traces their harrowing journey to the U.S. and their struggles to survive in a strange land, illuminating the difficulties of undocumented minors; she also offers details on migrant shelters, the Texas border wall, and court proceedings in immigration cases.

"This is a timely and thought-provoking exploration of a international quagmire. Markham provides a sensitive and eye-opening take on whats at stake for young immigrants with nowhere else to go." —*Publishers Weekly*

Martin, Justin

Rebel Souls: Walt Whitman and America's First Bohemians. Justin Martin. Da Capo Press 2014. 368 pages
ISBN 9780306822261
Grades: Adult   920

1. Whitman, Walt, 1819-1892 2. Ward, Artemus, 1834-1867 3. Booth, Edwin, 1833-1893 4. Ludlow, Fitz Hugh, 1836-1870 5. Menken, Adah Isaacs, 1839?-1868 6. Bohemianism 7. Beat culture 8. Intellectual life 9. Bars (Drinking establishments) 10. New York City 11. Collective biographies 12. History writing — Arts and culture 13. Life stories — Arts and culture 14. History writing — United States

LC 2014008822

In the shadow of the Civil War, a circle of radicals in a rowdy saloon changed American society and helped set Walt Whitman on the path to poetic immortality. Rebel Souls is the first book ever written about the colorful group of artists—regulars at Pfaff's Saloon in Manhattan—rightly considered America's original Bohemians. Besides a young Whitman, the circle included actor Edwin Booth; trailblazing stand-up comic Artemus Ward; psychedelic drug pioneer and author Fitz Hugh Ludlow; and brazen performer Adah Menken, famous for her Naked Lady routine. Central to their times, the artists managed to forge connections with Ralph Waldo Emerson, Mark Twain, and even Abraham Lincoln. This vibrant tale, packed with original research, offers the pleasures of a great group biography like the Banquet Years or the Metaphysical Club. Justin Martin shows how this first bohemian culture—imported from Paris to a dingy Broadway saloon—seeded and nurtured an American tradition of rebel art that thrives to this day.

"This book is a lively and entertaining read for students of American literature, history, and culture." —*Choice*

Includes bibliographical references and index.

Marton, Kati

The Great Escape: Nine Jews Who Fled Hitler and Changed the World. Kati Marton. Simon & Schuster 2006. 271 p. : Illustration; Map
ISBN 9780743261159
Grades: 11 12 Adult   920

1. Jewish people 2. Refugees, Jewish 3. Exiles 4. European history 5. Budapest, Hungary 6. 20th century 7. Collective biographies 8. Biographies 9. History writing — Jewish history 10. Life stories — Identity — Immigrants

LC 2006049162

Traces the early twentieth century journey of nine prominent men from Budapest who fled fascism to seek sanctuary in America, where they made pivotal contributions to science, film, and photojournalism.

"By looking at these nine lives salvaged, and crucial—Marton provides a moving measure of how much was lost." —*The New Yorker*

Includes bibliographical references (p. [245]-254) and index.

Massing, Michael

Fatal Discord: Erasmus, Luther, and the Fight for the Western Mind. Michael Massing. HarperCollins 2018. 800 p.
ISBN 9780060517601
Grades: Adult   920

1. Erasmus, Desiderius, died 1536 2. Luther, Martin, 1483-1546 3. Theologians 4. Academic rivalry 5. Religious reformers 6. Christian philosophy 7. Christian humanism 8. Evangelicalism 9. Humanism 10. Theology 11. Renaissance (1300-1600) 12. Collective biographies 13. Biographies 14. Life stories — Religion and spirituality — Religious and spiritual leaders 15. History writing — Renaissance — Europe

LC Bl2017051782

New York Times Notable Book, 2018; Library Journal Best Books, 2018.

The Harvard-educated author of Now They Tell Us presents an intellectual assessment of the rivalry between Desiderius Erasmus and Martin Luther that examines their respective characters and belief systems, sharing insights into their enduring influence and proper historical roles in western tradition.

"As we commemorate the 500th anniversary of the Protestant Reformation, this engaging tale of the contentious relationship between two precursors of the modern world—one who remained a Catholic, the other whose teaching spawned the various Protestant denominations—provides much-needed historical background and reflection on a major period in church and world history." —*Library Journal*

Matteson, John

Eden's Outcasts: The Story of Louisa May Alcott and Her Father. John Matteson. W.W. Norton 2007. 528 p.
ISBN 9780393059649
Grades: Adult   920

1. Alcott, Louisa May, 1832-1888 2. Authors, American 3. Fathers and daughters 4. Transcendentalism (New England) 5. Family relationships 6. Social life and customs 7. United States 8. 20th century 9. Collective biographies 10. Arts and Entertainment — Writing and Publishing 11. Life stories — Arts and culture — Writing — Authors

LC 2007013707

Pulitzer Prize for Biography or Autobiography, 2008.

Evaluates the relationship between Louisa May Alcott and her idealistic father, discussing how Louisa's exuberant personality often challenged Bronson's child-rearing philosophies and how Louisa eventually came to support her family through writing.

"Matteson's lucid, commanding biography casts new light on an unusual father-daughter bond and a new land at war with itself." —*Booklist*

Includes bibliographical references and index.

McCalman, George

Illustrated Black History: Honoring the Iconic and the Unseen. George McCalman with April Reynolds. Harper One, an imprint of HarperCollinsPublishers 2022. xxxii, 345 pages : Illustration; Color
ISBN 9780062913234
Grades: Adult   920

1. African Americans 2. Collective biographies 3. Life stories — General

LC Bl2022027614

Profiling 145 Black heroes, both famous and unsung, in politics, science, literature, music and more, this illuminating, informative, vibrant and timely compendium showcases the depth and breadth of Black genius.

"Graphic designer McCalman expands on his project to paint one 'Black history pioneer' every day for a month in this vibrant and stylish portrait collection....This vivid survey of Black history leaps off the page." —*Publishers Weekly*

ESSENTIAL AND RECOMMENDED TITLES
920 Collective biographies

McCullough, David G.
The Greater Journey: Americans in Paris, 1830-1900. David McCullough. Simon & Schuster 2011. 544 p.
ISBN 9781416571766
Grades: Adult 920
1. Intellectual life 2. American people in France 3. Intellectuals 4. Artists 5. Authors, American 6. Physicians 7. Paris, France 8. France 9. United States 10. 19th century 11. History writing — Europe — France 12. Arts and Entertainment — General
LC 2010053001
Booklist Editors' Choice, 2011.
Relates the story of the American artists, writers, and doctors who traveled to Paris in the nineteenth century, fell in love with the city and its people, and changed America through what they learned there.
"An account of young Americans, driven by wanderlust, setting out in search of greener Parisian pastures. Well-known figures such as James Fenimore Cooper, Oliver Wendell Holmes Sr, and Mary Cassat, and long-forgotten entities like Elizabeth Blackwell and William Wells Brown, all walked along the Avenue des Champs-lyses, went to the Muse du Louvre, ate wonderful meals, and became inspired. Their life-changing adventures played a vital role in transforming the course of US history." —*Christian Science Monitor*
Includes bibliographical references and index.

The Pioneers: The Heroic Story of the Settlers Who Brought the American Ideal West. by David McCullough. Simon & Schuster 2019. 320 p.
ISBN 9781501168680
Grades: Adult 920
1. Pioneers 2. Pioneer families 3. Frontier and pioneer life 4. Territorial expansion 5. United States history 6. Ohio River Valley 7. United States 8. 18th century 9. Early America (1784-1819) 10. Collective biographies 11. History writing — Early America — United States 12. Life stories — People in history — Pioneers
LC 2018057066
Best-selling author David McCullough chronicles the lesser-known settling of the Northwest Territory by dauntless pioneers whose community ideals shaped a fledgling America.
"Drawing on little-known archives, acclaimed popular historian McCullough offers a unique chronicle of the settlement of the Ohio River Valley that emphasizes the courage and tenacity of early pioneers and the precedents they set for further westward expansion." —*Booklist*
Simon & Schuster nonfiction original hardcover; Includes bibliographical references and index.

McDonald, Greg (Producer)
Elvis and the Colonel: An Insider's Look at the Most Legendary Partnership in Show Business. Greg McDonald and Marshall Terrill. St. Martin's Press 2023. 304 p.
ISBN 9781250287496
Grades: Adult 920
1. Parker, Tom, 1909-1997 2. Presley, Elvis, 1935-1977 3. Singers 4. Rock musicians 5. Impresarios 6. Concert agents 7. Music agents 8. Executives 9. Interpersonal relations 10. Marketing 11. Music industry and trade 12. Western European people 13. Dutch people 14. North American people 15. American people 16. Collective biographies 17. Life stories — Arts and culture — Performing arts 18. Life stories — Business 19. Arts and Entertainment — Music — Rock
LC 2023016804
A fresh biography of legendary entertainment manager Colonel Tom Parker, with a contrarian and corrective point of view.
"This book successfully explodes the myth of Parker as a manipulative puppeteer by portraying him as a shrewd but fair, loyal, and hardworking marketing innovator." —*Library Journal*
Includes bibliographical references and index.

McNeur, Catherine
Mischievous Creatures: The Forgotten Sisters Who Transformed Early American Science. Catherine McNeur. Basic Books 2023. IX, 418 p.
ISBN 9781541674172
Grades: Adult 920
1. Morris, Margaretta Hare, 1797-1867 2. Morris, Elizabeth Carrington, 1795-1865 3. Women scientists 4. Women biologists 5. Sisters 6. Botanists 7. Entomologists 8. Sexism in science 9. Marginalized women 10. North American people 11. American people 12. Collective biographies 13. Life stories — Science, technology, and medicine — Scientists and inventors 14. Life stories — Identity — Gender 15. Science Writing — Biology 16. History writing — Women's history 17. History writing — Science, technology, and medicine
LC 2023010253
In Mischievous Creatures, historian Catherine McNeur uncovers the lives and work of Margaretta Hare Morris and Elizabeth Carrington Morris, sisters and scientists in early America. Together, their discoveries helped fuel the growth and professionalization of science in antebellum America. But these very developments confined women in science to underpaid and underappreciated roles for generations to follow, erasing the Morris sisters' contributions along the way.
"Lively biography of two sisters who made substantial contributions to 19th-century natural history…A welcome addition to intellectual history that restores two gifted women to the scholarly record." —*Kirkus*
Includes bibliographical references and index.

Mehr, Bob
Trouble Boys: The True Story of the Replacements. Bob Mehr. Da Capo Press 2015. 304 p.
ISBN 9780306818790
Grades: Adult 920
1. Rock groups 2. Rock musicians 3. Alternative rock music 4. United States 5. Collective biographies 6. Life stories — Arts and culture — Performing arts — Musicians and composers 7. Arts and entertainment — Music — Rock
LC 2015026791
Trouble Boys: The True Story of the Replacements is the definitive boigraphy of one of the last great rock 'N' roll bands of the twentieth century. Written with the participation of the group's key members, including reclusive singer-songwriter Paul Westerberg, bassist Tommy Stinson, and the family of late guitarist Bob Stinson, Trouble Boys is a deeply intimate and nuanced portrait, exposing the primal factors and forces—addiction, abuse, fear—that would shape one of the most brilliant and notoriously self-destructive bands of all time.
Includes bibliographical references and index.

Meyer, G. J.
The Borgias: The Hidden History. G.J. Meyer. Bantam Books 2013. 560 p.
ISBN 9780345526915
Grades: Adult B
1. Borgia family 2. Nobility 3. European Renaissance 4. Italian history 5. Italy 6. Renaissance (1300-1600) 7. 15th century 8. Age of exploration (1419-1610) 9. Collective biographies 10. History writing — Europe — Italy 11. History writing — Renaissance — Europe 12. Family and Relationships — Families 13. Life stories — People in history — Famous families
LC 2012037777
Published to coincide with the upcoming new season of the Showtime series, the Borgias, the acclaimed author of the Tudors introduces the members of one of the most notorious families in European history during an era of unparalleled beauty, terror and intrigue.
Includes bibliographical references and index.

The Tudors: The Complete Story of England's Most Notorious Dynasty. G.J. Meyer. Delacorte Press 2010. 640 p.
ISBN 9780385340762
Grades: Adult 920
1. Tudor, House of 2. Royal houses 3. Rulers 4. Monarchy 5. British history 6. Great Britain 7. 16th century 8. Tudor period (1485-1603) 9. Collective biographies 10. History writing — Europe — United Kingdom 11. Life stories — Politics — Royalty 12. Life stories — People in history — Famous families
LC 2009040032
Goodreads Choice Award, 2010.

PUBLIC LIBRARY CORE COLLECTION: NONFICTION
Twentieth Edition

A single-volume history of Henry VIII and his three heirs offers new insights into the dynasty's precarious position in world politics and culture while evaluating the role of religion in 16th-century government.

Includes bibliographical references and index.

Mulley, Clare
The Women Who Flew for Hitler: A True Story of Soaring Ambition and Searing Rivalry. Clare Mulley. St. Martin's Press 2017. 400 pages
ISBN 9781250063670
Grades: Adult   **920**

1. Reitsch, Hannah 2. Stauffenberg, Melitta, Grafin, 1903-1945 3. Women pilots 4. World War II 5. Gender role 6. Aeronautical engineers 7. Military aircraft 8. Women's role 9. Third Reich, 1933-1945 10. Courage 11. Second World War era (1939-1945) 12. Collective biographies 13. Biographies 14. History writing — Wars and conflicts — World War II 15. History writing — Women's history 16. History writing — Europe — Germany

LC 2017011483

A dual biography of the first two women flight captains for the Nazis describes how, in spite of Hitler's dictates against women in the military, Aryan poster girl Hanna Reitsch and Jewish aeronautical engineer Melitta Schenk Gräfin von Stauffenger were awarded the Iron Cross.

"Absolutely gripping, Mulleys double portrait is a reminder that there are many more stories to tell from this oft-examined time." —*Booklist*

Myers, Paul
The Kids in the Hall: One Dumb Guy. Paul Myers. House of Anansi Press 2017. 320 p.
ISBN 9781487001834
Grades: Adult   **920**

1. McCulloch, Bruce 2. Foley, Dave, 1963- 3. McDonald, Kevin, 1961- 4. McKinney, Mark, 1963- 5. Thompson, Scott, 1959- 6. Comedians 7. Television writing 8. Television comedies 9. Television industry and trade 10. Collective biographies 11. Life stories — Arts and culture — Performing arts — Entertainers and celebrities 12. Arts and entertainment — Comedy 13. Arts and Entertainment — Movies and Television

LC Oc2017014199

The definitive, authorized story of legendary sketch comedy troupe the Kids in the Hall by critically acclaimed biographer and comedy aficionado Paul Myers.

"A terrific account of a truly unique sensation, best accompanied by pulling up corresponding sketches on YouTube." —*Kirkus*

Napoli, Lisa
Susan, Linda, Nina & Cokie: The Extraordinary Story of the Founding Mothers of Npr. Lisa Napoli. Harry N Abrams 2021. 288 p.
ISBN 9781419750403
Grades: Adult   **920**

1. Stamberg, Susan, 1938- 2. Wertheimer, Linda 3. Totenberg, Nina 4. Roberts, Cokie, 1943-2019 5. Women journalists 6. Public radio 7. Radio programs 8. Sexism 9. Journalism 10. Radio 11. Collective biographies 12. History writing — Women's history 13. Life stories — Arts and culture — Writing — Journalists 14. Arts and Entertainment — Radio

A group biography of four beloved women who fought sexism, covered decades of American news, and whose voices defined NPR.

"Journalist and author Napoli (Up All Night) weaves a fascinating, highly readable account of the women of National Public Radio. . . . Readers interested in feminism, women's history, and biography will be rewarded with a great story that deserves to be widely known." —*Library Journal*

Nimura, Janice P.
Daughters of the Samurai: A Journey from East to West and Back. Janice P. Nimura. W W Norton & CO Inc 2015. 352 p.
ISBN 9780393077995
Grades: Adult   **920**

1. Japanese people in the United States 2. Cultural differences 3. Culture conflict 4. 19th century 5. Collective biographies 6. Life stories — Identity — Immigrants 7. History writing — Reconstruction — United States 8. Adult books for young adults

LC 2014046933

New York Times Notable Book, 2015.

In the years after 1853, when Japan opened its harbors to trade with the U.S, the Japanese government realized that its citizens would need to understand Western culture as it pursued commerce with the rest of the world. Since they viewed women as essential to the preparation of future leaders, they decided to send some girls to the U.S. so they could learn American ways and return to Japan as educators. Daughters of the Samurai presents complete biographies of three of the five girls who were chosen, tracing their foreign experiences and following their adult lives in Japan.

Nutt, Amy Ellis
Becoming Nicole: The Transformation of an American Family. Amy Ellis Nutt. Random House 2015. 336 p.
ISBN 9780812995411
Grades: 11 12 Adult   **920**

1. Identical twins 2. Transgender people 3. Adoption 4. LGBTQIA+ rights 5. Identity 6. Families 7. Human rights 8. Civil rights 9. Collective biographies 10. Life stories — Identity — LGBTQIA+ 11. Society and culture — LGBTQIA+

LC 2015031162

New York Times Notable Book, 2015; Stonewall Non-Fiction Honor Book, 2016.

The inspiring true story of a transgender girl, her identical twin brother, and an ordinary American family's extraordinary journey to understand, nurture, and celebrate the right to be different—from the Pulitzer Prize-winning science reporter for the Washington Post.

"This poignant account of a transgender girl's transition offers a heartfelt snapshot of a family whose only objective is to protect their daughter. Tackling the subject from a biological, social, and psychological viewpoint, Pulitzer-winning reporter Nutt weaves complex elements of what being transgender means into a compelling narrative about a young woman who has identified as female since early childhood. Writing in a very journalistic tone, Nutt succeeds in placing Nicole's individual story within the more general narrative of transgender rights in the United States and humanizes the issues currently at play." —*Publishers Weekly*

O'Brien, Keith
Fly Girls: How Five Daring Women Defied All Odds and Made Aviation History. Keith O'Brien. Houghton Mifflin Harcourt 2018. xiv, 338 pages
ISBN 9781328876645
Grades: Adult   **920**

1. Elder, Ruth, 1902-1977 2. Earhart, Amelia, 1897-1937 3. Nichols, Ruth, 1901-1960 4. Thaden, Louise McPhetridge, 1905-1979 5. Klingensmith, Florence 6. Aviation 7. Women pilots 8. Airplane racing 9. Air shows 10. Between the Wars (1918-1939) 11. Biographies 12. Collective biographies 13. Life stories — Science, technology, and medicine — Astronauts and pilots 14. History writing — Women's history 15. History writing — Military — Aviation History

New York Times Notable Book, 2018.

An award-winning journalist traces the lesser-known story of five women, including Amelia Earhart, who successfully fought to compete against men in the high-stakes national air races of the 1920s and 1930s.

"Highly recommended for readers with an interest in aviation history, women's history, cultural history, and 20th-century history." —*Library Journal*

Includes bibliographical references and index.

Pappu, Sridhar
The Year of the Pitcher: Bob Gibson, Denny McLain, and the End of Baseball's Golden Age. Sridhar Pappu. Houghton Mifflin Harcourt 2017. 320 p.
ISBN 9780547719276
Grades: Adult   **920**

1. Gibson, Bob, 1935-2020 2. McLain, Denny 3. Pitching (Baseball) 4. Pitchers (Baseball) 5. Baseball 6. Baseball players 7. Collective biographies 8. Sports and Competition — Baseball 9. Life stories — Sports — Athletes

LC Bl2017039163

ESSENTIAL AND RECOMMENDED TITLES
920 Collective biographies

The story of the remarkable 1968 baseball season: an epic battle of pitchers, Bob Gibson and Denny McClain, which culminated in one of the greatest World Series of all time.

"The author effectively interweaves the stories of McLain and Gibson in an engaging fashion, engrossing readers with the rivalry of Detroit and St. Louis." —*Library Journal*

Paranque, Estelle
Blood, Fire & Gold: The Story of Elizabeth I & Catherine De Medici. Estelle Paranque. Hachette Books 2022. 400 p.
ISBN 9780306830518
Grades: Adult   920
1. Elizabeth I, Queen of England, 1533-1603 2. Catherine de Medicis, Queen, consort of Henry II, King of France, 1519-1589 3. Women rulers 4. Women's power 5. Tudor period (1485-1603) 6. Renaissance (1300-1600) 7. Elizabethan era (1558-1603) 8. 16th century 9. Collective biographies 10. History writing — Renaissance — Europe 11. History writing — Women's history 12. Life stories — Politics — Royalty

"Historian Paranque examines female power in sixteenth-century Europe, using the relationship between Queen Elizabeth I and Catherine de Medici as her focal point....Drawing on new research and private correspondence, Paranque paints a vivid picture of two formidable women whose rivalry motivated their respective choices and accomplishments." —*Booklist*

Patterson, James
Walk in My Combat Boots: True Stories from America's Bravest Warriors. James Patterson and Matt Eversmann with Chris Mooney. Little Brown & Company 2021. 416 p.
ISBN 9780316429092
Grades: Adult   920
1. Soldiers 2. Veterans 3. Military service 4. War 5. Combat 6. Self-sacrifice 7. Loss 8. Armed Forces 9. United States 10. Collective biographies 11. Interviews 12. Life stories — Law and order — Armed forces personnel 13. History writing — Military — Military Today

The decorated war hero who inspired the movie, Black Hawk Down, shares firsthand wartime accounts describing the courageous battlefield sacrifices of men and women from every branch and operational specialty of the U.S. military.

"Bestseller Patterson (Deadly Cross) and retired U.S. Army Ranger Eversmann gather firsthand accounts from veterans, most of whom served in Iraq or Afghanistan, to deliver a vivid and authentic portrait of life in the modern military." —*Publishers Weekly*

Walk the Blue Line: No Right, No Left—just Cops Telling Their True Stories to James Patterson. James Patterson, and Matt Eversmann; with Chris Mooney. Little, Brown and Company 2023. 352 p.
ISBN 9780316406604
Grades: Adult   920
1. Police 2. Sheriffs 3. United States 4. Life stories — Law and order — Police and law officers
LC Bl2022038034

Presents the dramatic true stories, told in their own words, of the patrol officers and K9 handlers, sheriffs and detectives who risk their lives every day to protect and serve, revealing what it's really like to wear the uniform and carry the weight of the responsibility they've been given.

"Walk the Blue Line is an oral history collection of open-ended interviews, this time chronicling a variety of stories from a diverse sample of law enforcement officers....This collection is well-organized; the stories are compelling and authentic and flow from the page with ease and impact." —*Booklist*

What Really Happens in Vegas: True Stories of the People Who Make Vegas, Vegas. James Patterson, Mark Seal. Little, Brown and Company 2023. 400 p.
ISBN 9780316406901
Grades: Adult   920
1. Celebrities 2. Entertainment industry and trade 3. Social life and customs 4. Las Vegas, Nevada 5. Nevada 6. HIstory Writing — Regional history — United States 7. Arts and Entertainment — General 8. Life stories — Arts and culture — Performing arts
Loan Stars Favourites, 2023.

Revealing the real Vegas, this dazzling journey through stories of excess, drama and hope transports readers from the thrill of adrenaline-fueled vice to the glitter of A-list celebrity and entertainment.

"Focusing primarily on Horatio Alger-like rags-to-riches stories, the authors downplay the city's dark side but keep things uptempo, vivid, and fun." —*Publishers Weekly*

Paul, Richard
We Could Not Fail: The First African Americans in the Space Program. by Richard Paul and Steven Moss. University of Texas Press 2015. 274 p.
ISBN 9780292772496
Grades: Adult   920
1. African American engineers 2. African American astronauts 3. Discrimination in employment 4. Racism 5. Collective biographies 6. Life stories — Science, technology, and medicine — Astronauts and pilots 7. Life stories — Identity — Race and ethnicity 8. Society and culture — Race
LC 2014030513

Profiles ten pioneer African American space workers whose stories illustrated the role NASA and the space program played in promoting civil rights.

"Vital and of interest to all Americans, from history and space buffs to students, researchers, and casual readers." —*Library Journal*
Includes bibliographical references and index.

Pawel, Miriam
The Browns of California: The Family Dynasty That Transformed a State and Shaped a Nation. Miriam Pawel. St Martins Pr 2018. 400 p.
ISBN 9781632867339
Grades: Adult   920
1. Brown family 2. Brown, Jerry, 1938- 3. Brown, Edmund G. (Edmund Gerald), 1905-1996 4. Families 5. Governors 6. State governments 7. U.S. states 8. United States history 9. California 10. Collective biographies 11. Biographies 12. Life stories — People in history — Famous families 13. History writing — Regional history — United States
LC 2018011464

The Pulitzer Prize-winning author of the Crusades of Cesar Chavez presents a panoramic history of California and its impact on the nation from the Gold Rush to Silicon Valley, told through the lens of Governor Jerry Brown's family dynasty.

Popova, Maria
Figuring. Maria Popova. Pantheon Books 2019. 544 p.
ISBN 9781524748135
Grades: Adult   920
1. Artists 2. Authors 3. Women scientists 4. Scientists 5. Purpose in life 6. Truth 7. Successful people 8. Happiness 9. Music 10. Feminism 11. Religions 12. Collective biographies 13. Life stories — Science, technology, and medicine 14. History writing — Science, technology, and medicine
LC 2018027009

Booklist Editors' Choice, 2019; Los Angeles Times Book Prize for Science and Technology, 2019; Andrew Carnegie Medal for Excellence in Non-Fiction Finalist, 2020.

Explores the search for truth and meaning through the interconnected lives of historical figures from four centuries—artists, writers, and scientists, most of them women, who changed the way humans understand, experience, and appreciate the universe.

"Writing with an ardor for language and musing on chance, affinity, and our fear of change, Popova constructs an intricate biographical cosmos that is intellectually scintillating, artistically wondrous, and deeply affecting." —*Booklist*
Includes bibliographical references and index.

Quinn, Bridget

Broad Strokes: 15 Women Who Made Art and Made History, in That Order. Bridget Quinn; with illustrations by Lisa Congdon. Chronicle Books 2017. 192 p.

ISBN 9781452152363

Grades: Adult 920

1. Women artists 2. Art history 3. Collective biographies 4. Biographies 5. Biographies — Arts — Visual arts — Painters

LC 2016023856

Amelia Bloomer List, 2018.

Shares the lives and careers of fifteen female artists, including Artemisia Gentileschi, Edmonia Lewis, and Susan O'Malley.

"Quinn skillfully examines the lives of an eclectic group of artists and the treatment of their work over time, mixing in comments from art historians and her own personal anecdotes." —*Publishers Weekly. Annex*

Includes bibliographical references.

Rappaport, Helen

The Romanov Sisters: The Lost Lives of the Daughters of Nicholas and Alexandra. Helen Rappaport. St. Martin's Press 2014. 512 p.

ISBN 9781250020208

Grades: Adult 920

1. Nicholas II, Emperor of Russia, 1868-1918 2. Romanov, House of 3. Anastasia Nikolaevna, Grand Duchess, daughter of Nicholas II, Emperor of Russia, 1901-1918 4. Olga, Grand Duchess of Russia, 1895-1918 5. Mariia Nikolaevna, Grand Duchess, daughter of Nicholas II, Emperor of Russia, 1899-1918 6. Tatiana Nikolaevna, Grand Duchess, daughter of Nicholas II, Emperor of Russia, 1897-1918 7. Alexandra, Empress, consort of Nicholas II, Emperor of Russia, 1872-1918 8. Princesses 9. Sisters 10. Royal houses 11. Russian history 12. Russia 13. Romanov Dynasty (1613-1917) 14. 20th century 15. Collective biographies 16. History writing — Europe — Russia 17. History writing — Historical mysteries 18. Life stories — Politics — Royalty 19. Life stories — People in history — Famous families

LC 2014003159

Goodreads Choice Award, 2014.

Draws on personal writings and private sources to challenge common misperceptions and illuminate the daily lives and vibrant personalities of the four Russian Grand Duchesses from their own perspectives, revealing their awareness of family turmoil and the approach of the Russian Revolution.

"A gossipy, revealing story of the doomed Russian family's fairy tale life told by an expert in the field." —*Kirkus*

Also published in large print format.

Reid, Joy-Ann Lomena

★ *Medgar and Myrlie: Medgar Evers and the Love Story That Awakened America.* Joy-Ann Reid. Mariner Books 2024. 368 p.

ISBN 9780063068797

Grades: Adult 920

1. Evers, Myrlie 2. Evers, Medgar Wiley, 1925-1963 3. Civil rights Movement 4. African American civil rights 5. African American civil rights workers 6. Civil rights workers 7. Civil Rights Movement 8. Couples 9. 20th century 10. 1950s 11. 1960s 12. Collective biographies 13. History writing — African American — Civil rights — United States 15. History writing — 1960s — United States 16. Life stories — Politics — Activists and reformers

Tracing the extraordinary lives and legacy of two civil rights icons, this gripping account of Medgar and Myrlie Evers is told through their relationship and the work that went into winning basic rights for Black Americans, and the repercussions that still resonate today.

"Acclaimed for her cogent analysis and spirited commentary on matters of social justice, MSNBC host Reid focuses her keen appreciation on the legacy of the marriage of iconic civil rights activists Medgar and Myrlie Evers." —*Booklist*

Ricks, Thomas E.

Churchill and Orwell: The Fight for Freedom. Thomas E. Ricks. Penguin Group USA 2017. 320 p.

ISBN 9781594206139

Grades: Adult 920

1. Orwell, George, 1903-1950 2. Churchill, Winston, 1874-1965 3. Authors, English 4. Anti-fascism 5. Politicians 6. Ideology 7. Leadership 8. Democracy 9. Political leadership 10. Second World War era (1939-1945) 11. Collective biographies 12. Biographies 13. History writing — Wars and conflicts — Homefront — World War II 14. Life stories — Politics — Politicians 15. Life stories — Arts and culture — Writing — Authors

LC 2016056757

New York Times Notable Book, 2017.

A dual portrait of Winston Churchill and George Orwell focuses on the pivotal years from the mid-1930s through the 1940s, describing how both suffered nearly fatal injuries before their vision and campaigns inspired action to preserve democracy throughout the world.

"In vivid prose, Ricks entwines the biographies of two figures who fought in strikingly different ways to achieve similar goals." —*Publishers Weekly*

Roberts, Andrew

Leadership in War: Essential Lessons from Those Who Made History. Andrew Roberts. Viking 2019. 256 p.

ISBN 9780525522386

Grades: Adult 920

1. Leadership 2. Command of troops 3. World leaders 4. Military strategy 5. War 6. Military history 7. Collective biographies 8. History writing — Military — Military leadership 9. Life stories — Law and order — Military leaders 10. History writing — Wars and conflicts 11. Life stories — Politics — Politicians

LC 2019025070

Taking us from the French Revolution to the Cold War, Andrew Roberts presents us with a bracingly honest and deeply insightful look at nine major figures in modern history: Napoleon Bonaparte, Horatio Nelson, Winston Churchill, Adolf Hitler, Joseph Stalin, George C. Marshall, Charles de Gaulle, Dwight D. Eisenhower, and Margaret Thatcher.

Includes bibliographical references.

Roberts, Cokie

Capital Dames: The Civil War and the Women of Washington, 1848-1868. Cokie Roberts. HarperCollins 2015. 400 p.

ISBN 9780062002761

Grades: Adult 920

1. Women and war 2. Women and politics 3. Women 4. United States Civil War, 1861-1865 5. Political participation 6. Independence 7. United States history 8. American Civil War era (1861-1865) 9. Collective biographies 10. History writing — Women's history 11. History writing — Wars and conflicts — American Civil War

LC 2015001049

Documents the experiences, influence and contributions of women during the American Civil War.

"An enlightening account detailing how the Civil War changed the nation's capital while expanding the role of women in politics, health care, education, and social services." —*Kirkus*

Founding Mothers: The Women Who Raised Our Nation. Cokie Roberts. William Morrow 2004. xx, 359 p. : Illustration

ISBN 9780060090258

Grades: 11 12 Adult 920

1. Women and politics 2. Women's history 3. American Revolution, 1775-1783 4. Revolutions 5. Women 6. Political participation 7. Women's participation in wars 8. United States history 9. United States 10. 18th century 11. 19th century 12. Early America (1784-1819) 13. Colonial America (1600-1775) 14. Revolutionary America (1775-1783) 15. Collective biographies 16. Biographies 17. History writing — Women's history 18. History writing — Early America — United States 19. Adult books for young adults

Explores the lives of women who helped shape the United States, profiling such key figures as Abigail Adams, Eliza Pinkney, Dolley Payne Madison, Deborah Read Franklin, and Catherine Littlefield Greene.

ESSENTIAL AND RECOMMENDED TITLES
920 Collective biographies

"In addition to telling wonderful stories, Roberts also presents a very readable, serviceable account of politics—male and female—in early America. If only our standard history textbooks were written with such flair!." —*Publishers Weekly*

Includes bibliographical references and index.

Ladies *of Liberty: The Women Who Shaped Our Nation.* Cokie Roberts. HarperCollins 2007. 336 p.
ISBN 9780060782344
Grades: 11 12 Adult **920**
1. Women and politics 2. Women 3. Political participation 4. United States history 5. 18th century 6. 19th century 7. Collective biographies 8. History writing — Women's history 9. History writing — United States
LC 2008298367

A sequel to Founding Mothers shares the stories of remarkable women who shaped American history between 1796 and 1828, including Dolley Madison, Theodosia Burr, and Sacajawea.

"While Roberts' aim is to see the period from her subjects' point of view, she is not uncritical; for instance, Roberts casts blame on Mrs. Adams's uncompromising partisanship in the undoing of her husband. With a little-seen perspective and fascinating insight into the culture of the day, this is popular history done right." —*Publishers Weekly*

Roberts, Randy
Blood *Brothers: The Fatal Friendship Between Muhammad Ali and Malcolm X.* Randy Roberts, Johnny Smith. Basic Books 2016. 400 p.
ISBN 9780465079704
Grades: Adult **920**
1. Malcolm X, 1925-1965 2. Ali, Muhammad, 1942-2016 3. Male friendship 4. Boxers (Sports) 5. Political activists 6. Former friends 7. Black Muslims 8. Attitude change 9. Civil Rights Movement 10. Islam 11. United States 12. Collective biographies 13. Biographies 14. Life stories — Relationships — Friendship 15. Life stories — Politics — Activists and reformers
LC 2015043982

Booklist Editors' Choice, 2016.

Draws on previously untapped sources to illuminate the secret friendship and disastrous estrangement between Cassius Clay and Malcolm X, sharing insights into Malcolm's alleged role in shaping Clay's double life as a patriotic athlete and Islamic reformer.

"A page-turning tale from the 1960s about politics and sports and two proud, extraordinary men whose legacies endure." —*Kirkus*

Rocca, Mo
Mobituaries: *Great Lives Worth Reliving.* MO Rocca and Jonathan Greenberg. Simon & Schuster 2019. 384 p.
ISBN 9781501197628
Grades: Adult **920**
1. Obituaries 2. Biography writing 3. Humorous writing 4. Celebrities 5. Social life and customs 6. Collective biographies 7. Media tie-ins 8. Life stories — General 9. Humor writing — General
LC 2019949306

A popular TV correspondent and writer offers an irreverent and rigorously researched book that celebrates the dead people who made life worth living.

Based on a podcast; Includes bibliographical references.

Roe, Sue
In *Montmartre: Picasso, Matisse and the Birth of Modernist Art.* Sue Roe. Penguin Group USA 2015. 352 p.
ISBN 9781594204951
Grades: Adult **920**
1. Picasso, Pablo, 1881-1973 2. Matisse, Henri, 1869-1954 3. Derain, Andre, 1880-1954 4. Vlaminck, Maurice de, 1876-1958 5. Braque, Georges, 1882-1963 6. Modigliani, Amedeo, 1884-1920 7. Brancusi, Constantin, 1876-1957 8. Stein, Gertrude, 1874-1946 9. Modernism (Art) 10. Artists 11. Paris, France 12. Montmartre, Paris, France 13. 1900s (Decade) 14. 20th century 15. Collective biographies 16. Life stories — Arts and culture — Artists 17. Arts and entertainment — Painting, drawing, and sculpture
LC BI2015009983

Beginning about 1900, the Paris suburb of Montmartre became one of the trendiest artists' enclaves in history. Pablo Picasso, Georges Braque, Amedeo Modigliani, Constantin Brancusi, Gertrude Stein, and many other painters, sculptors, writers, musicians, and dancers lived and worked there. Author Sue Roe engagingly and vividly creates a portrait of the time, place, and people while exploring modernist movements such as Fauvism and Cubism.

The Private *Lives of the Impressionists.* Sue Roe. Harper Collins Publishers 2006. VIII, 356 p, 8 p. of plates : Illustration; Color; Map
ISBN 9780060545581
Grades: Adult **920**
1. Painters 2. Artists 3. Impressionism (Art) 4. France 5. 19th century 6. Collective biographies 7. Arts and Entertainment — Painting, Drawing, and Sculpture 8. Life stories — Arts and culture — Artists
LC 2006043621

A group portrait of the Impressionist artists traces how the movement's early leaders met in the studios of Paris and lived and worked together closely for several years, supporting one another through a series of emotional and financial difficulties.

Includes bibliographical references (p. [315]-322) and index.

Rose, Alexander
Empires *of the Sky: Zeppelins, Airplanes, and Two Men's Epic Duel to Rule the World.* Alexander Rose. Random House 2020. 592 p.
ISBN 9780812989977
Grades: Adult **920**
1. Eckener, Hugo, 1868-1954 2. Trippe, J. T. (Juan Terry), 1899-1981 3. Zeppelin, Ferdinand, Graf von, 1838-1917 4. Aviation history 5. Inventors 6. Competition 7. Commercial aviation 8. Air travel 9. Airplanes 10. Airships 11. Technological innovations 12. Collective biographies 13. Biographies 14. Life stories — Science, technology, and medicine — Scientists and inventors 15. History writing — Technological innovations 16. Science Writing — Space and Flight 17. Science Writing — Great Engineering Feats
LC 2019024115

At the dawn of the twentieth century, when human flight was still considered an impossibility, Germany's Count Ferdinand von Zeppelin vied with the Wright Brothers to build the world's first successful flying machine. As the Wrights labored to invent the airplane, Zeppelin fathered the remarkable airship, sparking a bitter rivalry between the two types of aircraft and their innovators that would last for decades, in the quest to control one of humanity's most inspiring achievements.

"A dense yet exhilarating history of the dawn of modern air travel." —*Publishers Weekly*

Includes bibliographical references and index.

Samaha, Albert
Never *Ran, Never Will: Boyhood and Football in a Changing American Inner City.* Albert Samaha. PublicAffairs 2018. xiv, 343 p.
ISBN 9781610398688
Grades: Adult **920**
1. Football 2. African American neighborhoods 3. Inner city 4. Sports 5. Children and sports 6. Football teams 7. Football coaches 8. Poverty 9. Violence 10. Gentrification of cities 11. Community organization 12. Identity 13. Persistence 14. Teenage boys 15. African American teenagers 16. Brooklyn, New York City 17. Collective biographies 18. Life stories — Facing adversity 19. Sports and Competition — Football 20. Life stories — Identity — Race and ethnicity 21. Society and culture — Urban and regional studies
LC 2018000983

Describes the history and impact of the MO Better Jaguars, a football team in a poor Brooklyn neighborhood and the people who have had their lives shaped for the better by playing and participating. Football isn't everybody's ideal way to find the American dream, but for some kids it's the surest road there is.

Includes bibliographical references and index.

PUBLIC LIBRARY CORE COLLECTION: NONFICTION
Twentieth Edition

Sankovitch, Nina
American Rebels: How the Hancock, Adams, and Quincy Families Fanned the Flames of Revolution. Nina Sankovitch. St. Martin's Press 2020. 384 pages
ISBN 9781250163288
Grades: Adult   920
1. Hancock family 2. Adams family 3. Quincy family 4. Quincy, Josiah, 1744-1775 5. Adams, John, 1735-1826 6. Adams, Abigail, 1744-1818 7. Hancock, John, 1737-1793 8. Hancock, Dorothy Quincy, 1747-1830 9. Revolutionaries 10. Founding Fathers of the United States 11. Families 12. Friendship 13. Communities 14. Freedom 15. American Revolution, 1775-1783 16. United States history 17. Massachusetts 18. 18th century 19. Revolutionary America (1775-1783) 20. Collective biographies 21. History writing — Wars and conflicts — Revolutionary War (America) 22. History writing — Colonial America — United States 23. Life stories — Politics — Politicians 24. Life stories — People in history — Famous families
LC 2019043211
Explores, for the first time, the intertwined lives of the Hancock, Quincy, and Adams families, and the role each person played in sparking the American Revolution.
"Sankovitch has woven a compelling, potent chronicle of members of three principal American families that will be valued by readers of American history at all levels." —*Library Journal*
Includes bibliographical references and index.

Schatz, Kate
Rad Women Worldwide: Artists and Athletes, Pirates and Punks, and Other Revolutionaries Who Shaped History. by Kate Schatz; illustrated by Miriam Klein Stahl. Ten Speed Press 2016. 112 p.
ISBN 9780399578861
Grades: 6 7 8 9 10 11 12 Adult   920
1. Women 2. History of women's rights 3. Intersectionality 4. Collective biographies 5. Biographies — Politics — Activists and reformers — Women's rights 6. Biographies — People in history
LC 2016012179
Amelia Bloomer List, 2017.
From the authors of the New York Times bestselling book Rad American Women A-Z, comes a bold new collection of 40 biographical profiles, each accompanied by a striking illustrated portrait, showcasing extraordinary women from around the world.
"Readers of either gender could well find a role model in the India-born U.S. astronaut Kalpana Chawla, or in Wangari Maathai, whose Green Belt Movement in Africa resulted in the planting of more than 30 million environment-reviving trees." —*Booklist*
Includes bibliographical references and index.

Schell, Orville
Wealth and Power: China's Long March to the Twenty-first Century. Orville Schell & John Delury. Random House 2013. 288 p.
ISBN 9780679643470
Grades: Adult   920
1. Economic development 2. Political science 3. Intellectual life 4. Politics and government 5. Chinese history 6. China 7. 20th century 8. 21st century 9. Collective biographies 10. Politics and global affairs — World politics — Asia 11. Life stories — General 12. History writing — Asia — China
LC 2013002596
Two leading experts on China evaluate its rise throughout the past one hundred fifty years, sharing portraits of key intellectual and political leaders to explain how China transformed from a country under foreign assault to a world giant.
"An astute, knowledgeable and nicely accessible history and assessment of China for all readers." —*Kirkus*
Includes bibliographical references and index.

Schultz, Kevin Michael
Buckley and Mailer: The Difficult Friendship That Shaped the Sixties. Kevin M. Schultz. W. W. Norton & Company, Inc. 2015. 400 p.
ISBN 9780393088717
Grades: Adult   920
1. Buckley, William F. (William Frank), 1925-2008 2. Mailer, Norman 3. Authors, American 4. Journalists 5. United States history 6. United States 7. 1960s 8. 20th century 9. Collective biographies 10. Biographies 11. Life stories — Arts and culture — Writing 12. Life stories — Relationships — Friendship 13. History writing — 1960s — United States
LC 2015001553
A lively chronicle of the 1960s through the incredibly contentious and surprisingly close friendship of its two most colorful characters. Norman Mailer and William F. Buckley, Jr, were towering figures who argued publicly about every major issue of the1960s: the counterculture, Vietnam, feminism, civil rights, the Cold War. Behind the scenes, the two were close friends and trusted confidantes who lived surprisingly parallel lives. In Buckley and Mailer, historian Kevin M. Schultz delves into their personal archives to tell the rich story of their friendship, arguments, and the tumultuous decade they did so much to shape.
"By contextualizing the friendship, this volume, in addition to its considerable virtues as quasi-biography, is also a provocative and thorough, if not quite comprehensive (it's pretty much all East Coast, and there's no music), social and political history of the sixties, among the very best we have had." —*Booklist*
Includes bibliographical references and index.

Sears, Stephen W.
Lincoln's Lieutenants: The High Command of the Army of the Potomac. Stephen W. Sears. Houghton Mifflin Harcourt 2017. 640 p.
ISBN 9780618428250
Grades: Adult   920
1. Lincoln, Abraham, 1809-1865 2. Civil War 3. Command of troops 4. Generals 5. Armies 6. Soldiers 7. Military history 8. Military officers 9. American Civil War era (1861-1865) 10. Collective biographies 11. Biographies 12. History writing — Military — Military units 13. History writing — Wars and conflicts — American Civil War 14. Life stories — Law and order — Military leaders
LC 2017288442
The award-winning author of Landscape Turned Red presents a multilayered group portrait of the commanders who led the Army of the Potomac to explore how interpersonal tensions and their disagreements with Washington politics rendered them pawns to a vindictive Congress.
"A staggering work of research by a masterly historian." —*Kirkus*

Sigmund, Karl
Exact Thinking in Demented Times: The Vienna Circle and the Epic Quest for the Foundations of Science. Karl Sigmund. Basic Books 2017. 384 p.
ISBN 9780465096954
Grades: Adult   920
1. Science 2. Intellectual life 3. Philosophy 4. Between the Wars (1918-1939) 5. Collective biographies 6. Life stories — Science, technology, and medicine 7. Science writing — General
LC 2017037770
A group portrait of the early 20th-century intellectuals who transformed the way the world regarded math and science examines the collective stories of such forefront minds as Kurt Gödel, Rudolph Carnap, Ludwig Wittgenstein and Karl Popper.
"Many readers will agree that we are currently living in demented times, and Sigmund adeptly lays out a history that has great relevance for today."—*Kirkus*
Includes bibliographical references and index.

Smith, Sally Bedell
George VI and Elizabeth: The Marriage That Saved the Monarchy. Sally Bedell Smith. Random House 2023. 720 p.
ISBN 9780525511632
Grades: Adult   920
1. George VI, King of Great Britain, 1895-1952 2. Elizabeth, Queen, consort of George VI, King of Great Britain, 1900-2002 3. Windsor, House of 4. Royal houses 5. Rulers 6. Marriage 7. Family relationships 8. Leadership 9. British people 10. English people 11. Scottish people 12. British history 13. Collective

ESSENTIAL AND RECOMMENDED TITLES
920 Collective biographies

biographies 14. Life stories — Politics — Royalty 15. History writing — Europe — United Kingdom

A revelatory account of the loving marriage of King George VI and Queen Elizabeth. Granted special access by Queen Elizabeth II to her parents' letters and diaries and to the papers of their close friends and family, Sally Bedell Smith brings the love story of this iconic royal couple to vibrant life. This deeply researched and revealing book shows how a loving and devoted marriage helped the King and Queen meet the challenges of World War II, lead a nation, solidify the public's faith in the monarchy, and raise their daughters, Princess Elizabeth and Princess Margaret.

"Biographer Smith (Prince Charles) spotlights the partnership between Queen Elizabeth II's parents in this exhaustive yet intimate chronicle." —*Publishers Weekly*

Snyder, Laura J.
Eye of the Beholder: Johannes Vermeer, Antoni Van Leeuwenhoek, and the Reinvention of Seeing. Laura J. Snyder. W.W. Norton & Company 2015. 416 p.
ISBN 9780393077469
Grades: Adult   920
1. Vermeer, Johannes, 1632-1675 2. Leeuwenhoek, Anthony van, 1632-1723 3. Science and art 4. Painters 5. Art 6. Science 7. Scientists 8. European history 9. Netherlands 10. 17th century 11. Collective biographies 12. Biographies 13. Life stories — Science, technology, and medicine — Scientists and inventors 14. Life stories — Arts and culture — Artists 15. History writing — Europe
LC 2014038143

Taking readers to 17th-century Holland, where artists and scientists gathered, an extraordinary story reveals how two geniuses—a self-taught natural philosopher and an artist—transformed the way we see the world by coming to the realization that there is more than meets the eye.

"Though it is only speculation that these great thinkers knew each other personally, Snyder expertly brings to life their shared social milieu of artists and scientists, all seeking new ways to investigate nature. These intertwined biographies weave a story of two men whose insistence on daring to see revolutionized our understanding of perception itself." —*Booklist*

Includes bibliographical references and index.

Taraborrelli, J. Randy
Jackie, Janet & Lee: The Secret Lives of Janet Auchincloss and Her Daughters, Jacqueline Kennedy Onassis and Lee Radziwill. J. Randy Taraborrelli. St. Martin's Press 2018. 544 pages
ISBN 9781250128010
Grades: Adult   920
1. Onassis, Jacqueline Kennedy, 1929-1994 2. Auchincloss, Janet Lee, 1907-1989 3. Radziwill, Lee Bouvier, 1933- 4. Mothers and daughters 5. Presidents' spouses 6. Celebrities 7. Marriage 8. Rich families 9. Competition 10. Collective biographies 11. Life stories — People in history — Famous families 12. History writing — Women's history
LC 2017036190

A portrait of Jacqueline Bouvier Kennedy Onassis; her mother, Janet Lee Auchincloss; and her sister, Princess Lee Radziwill, discusses their ambitions, status-seeking marriages, illicit liaisons and psychological profiles as based on interviews with close friends and family members.

Includes bibliographical references and index.

The Kennedy Heirs: John, Caroline, and the New Generation; a Legacy of Triumph and Tragedy. J. Randy Taraborrelli. St. Martin's Press 2019. 480 p.
ISBN 9781250174062
Grades: Adult   920
1. Kennedy family 2. Politicians' families 3. Children of politicians 4. Rich families 5. Fame 6. Family relationships 7. Collective biographies 8. Life stories — People in history — Famous families
LC 2018055445

Explores the lives of the third generation of Kennedys, from undisclosed facts about the deaths of John Kennedy, Jr. and Carolyn Bessette to Joseph Kennedy III's compelling response to Trump's State of the Union.

Includes bibliographical references.

Teitel, Amy Shira
Fighting for Space: Two Pilots and Their Historic Battle for Female Spaceflight. Amy Shira Teitel. Grand Central Publishing 2020. 448 p.
ISBN 9781538716045
Grades: Adult   920
1. Cochran, Jacqueline 2. Cobb, Jerrie 3. Women pilots 4. Women astronauts 5. Gender equity 6. Gender role 7. Space flight 8. Flight 9. Aviation history 10. Space programs 11. United States history 12. United States 13. Collective biographies 14. Life stories — Science, technology, and medicine — Astronauts and pilots 15. History writing — Women's history 16. History writing — Military — Aviation History 17. Life stories — Identity — Gender
LC BI2020000072

The spaceflight historian and creator of YouTube's "Vintage Space" traces the engaging story of female pilots Jackie Cochran and Jerrie Cobb, who battled personal and patriarchal challenges to pursue their dream of becoming astronauts.

"A well-researched contribution to women's and aviation history." —*Kirkus*

Terkel, Studs
Hope Dies Last: Keeping the Faith in Difficult Times. Studs Terkel. New Press 2003. xxix, 326 p.
ISBN 9781565848375
Grades: 11 12 Adult   920
1. Hope 2. Coping 3. Faith 4. Social action 5. Social life and customs 6. United States 7. Oral histories 8. Interviews 9. Spirituality and Religion — General 10. History writing — United States 11. Adult books for young adults
LC 2003050989

Explores the theme of hope in the midst of challenging times in a collection of oral histories that link hope with a spirit of activism, commitment, and the determination.

"As a collector of true stories and a guardian of free speech, Terkel ensures that grass-root alternatives to the official word are heard from sea to shining sea." —*Booklist*

Includes bibliographical references.

Working: People Talk About What They Do All Day and How They Feel About What They Do. Studs Terkel. The New Press 1997. xlix, 589 p.
ISBN 9781565843424
Grades: Adult   920
1. Occupations 2. Work 3. Working class 4. Employees 5. United States 6. Collective biographies 7. Life stories — Business — Working life
LC 73018037

Men and women representing a variety of occupations, describe the daily routine of their jobs and express their grievances, aims, and dreams.

Originally published: New York : Pantheon Books, 1974.

Thomas, Dana
Gods and Kings: The Rise and Fall of Alexander McQueen and John Galliano. Dana Thomas. Penguin Books 2014. 384 pages
ISBN 9781594204944
Grades: Adult   920
1. Galliano, John 2. McQueen, Alexander, 1969-2010 3. Fashion designers 4. Couture clothing 5. Clothing industry and trade 6. Luxury 7. Collective biographies 8. Life stories — Arts and culture — Fashion 9. Arts and entertainment — Fashion
LC 2015460559

In her groundbreaking work, Gods and Kings, acclaimed journalist Dana Thomas tells the true story of McQueen and Galliano. In so doing, she reveals the relentless world of couture—and the price it demanded of the very ones who saved it.

Thomas, Gordon
Defying Hitler: The Germans Who Resisted Nazi Rule. Gordon Thomas, Greg Lewis. Dutton 2019. 560 p.
ISBN 9780451489043
Grades: Adult   920

PUBLIC LIBRARY CORE COLLECTION: NONFICTION
Twentieth Edition

1. Scholl, Sophie, 1921-1943 2. Harnack-Fish, Mildred, 1902-1943 3. Bonhoeffer, Dietrich, 1906-1945 4. Gerstein, Kurt, 1905-1945 5. Baum, Herbert, 1912-1942 6. Oster, Hans 7. Stauffenberg, Claus von 1907-1944 8. Schulze-Boysen, Harro, 1909-1942 9. Nazism 10. Anti-Nazis 11. Anti-Nazi movement 12. World War II 13. White Rose (Anti-Nazi group) 14. Third Reich, 1933-1945 15. Politics and government 16. Germany 17. 1940s 18. 1930s 19. Collective biographies 20. History writing — Wars and conflicts — World War II 21. Life stories — Facing adversity — War and oppression — Holocaust

LC 2018021073

A vivid chronicle of the underground resistance efforts of everyday Germans who thwarted Nazi rule shares the stories of heroes who risked or lost their lives to speak out, smuggle intelligence, defy wrongful laws and help Jewish escapees.

"Highly recommended for those wishing to comprehend life in Nazi Germany and what courage it took not to surrender to authority."—*Library Journal*

Thompson-Hernandez, Walter

The **Compton** *Cowboys: The New Generation of Cowboys in America's Urban Heartland.* Walter Thompson-Hernandez. William Morrow & Co 2020. 304 pages

ISBN 9780062910608

Grades: Adult   920

1. African Americans 2. Cowboys 3. Horses 4. Ranch life 5. Equestrian therapy 6. Identity 7. Post-traumatic stress disorder 8. California 9. Collective biographies 10. Life stories — Identity — Race and ethnicity 11. Life stories — Nature and outdoors — Farmers and ranchers 12. History writing — African American — United States

LC Bl2020011729

Tells the story of the Compton Cowboys, a group of African-American men and women who defy stereotypes and continue the proud, centuries-old tradition of Black cowboys.

"A year in the lives of 10 inner-city men fighting to keep Black cowboy culture alive and well even as their personal lives are in disarray… a gritty and somber chronicle of an often overlooked community."—*Kirkus*

Todd, Kim

Sensational: *The Hidden History of America's Girl Stunt Reporters.* Kim Todd. HarperCollins 2021. 304 p.

ISBN 9780062843616

Grades: Adult   920

1. Women journalists 2. Newspapers 3. Undercover operations 4. Journalism 5. News media 6. Sensationalism in journalism 7. Investigative journalism 8. Women's rights 9. Sensationalism in newspapers 10. Disguises 11. Journalists 12. United States 13. Gilded Age (1865-1898) 14. 19th century 15. Collective biographies 16. Life stories — Arts and culture — Writing — Journalists 17. History writing — Gilded Age — United States 18. Arts and Entertainment — Writing and Publishing

A vivid social history of the Gilded Age that examines the stories of women journalists who went undercover to champion women's rights and expose corruption and abuse in America.

"Todd (Sparrow), a professor of creative writing at the University of Minnesota, offers a spirited survey of the muckraking female journalists of the Gilded Age."—*Publishers Weekly*

Toibin, Colm

Mad, *Bad, Dangerous to Know: The Fathers of Wilde, Yeats and Joyce.* Colm Toibin. Scribner 2018. 240 p.

ISBN 9781476785172

Grades: Adult   920

1. Wilde, Oscar, 1854-1900 2. Yeats, W. B. (William Butler), 1865-1939 3. Joyce, James, 1882-1941 4. Family relationships 5. Poets, Irish 6. Authors, Irish 7. Fathers and sons 8. Ireland 9. Collective biographies 10. Life stories — Arts and culture — Writing — Authors 11. Life stories — Relationships — Family

LC 2018037024

The New York Times best-selling author of Brooklyn offers an intimate study of Irish culture, history and literature told through the lives of William Wilde, John Butler Yeats and John Stanislaus Joyce—and the complicated relationships they had with their literary-legend sons.

Weir, Alison

Queens *of the Age of Chivalry.* Alison Weir. Ballantine Books 2022. 448 p. (England's medieval queens, 3)

ISBN 9781101966723

Grades: Adult   920

1. Isabella, Queen, consort of Edward II, King of England, 1292-1358 2. Margaret, Queen, consort of Edward I, King of England, 1279?-1318 3. Philippa, Queen, consort of Edward III, King of England, -1369 4. Anne, Queen, consort of Richard II, King of England, 1366-1394 5. Isabella, of Valois, Queen, consort of Richard II, King of England 6. Plantagenet, House of 7. Women rulers 8. Marriage 9. Duty 10. Intrigue 11. Western European people 12. British people 13. French people 14. English people 15. British history 16. Plantagenet period (1154-1485) 17. Collective biographies 18. Life stories — Politics — Royalty 19. History writing — Europe — United Kingdom 20. History writing — Women's history 21. History writing — Medieval — Europe

LC 2022038992

This epic narrative of the Age of Chivalry, a period of high drama in English history, which included the toppling of two kings, the Hundred Years' War, the Black Death and the Peasants' Revolt, focuses on the lives and reigns of five extraordinary queen consorts.

"Five consorts of 14th-century British kings, hitherto obscure, come vividly to life."—*Kirkus*

Includes bibliographical references.

Queens *of the Conquest.* Alison Weir. Ballantine Books 2017. 448 p. (England's medieval queens, 1)

ISBN 9781101966662

Grades: Adult   920

1. Plantagenet, House of 2. Women rulers 3. Rulers 4. Civilization, Medieval 5. English history 6. Medieval period (476-1492) 7. Plantagenet period (1154-1485) 8. Norman period (1066-1154) 9. Collective biographies 10. History writing — Medieval — Europe 11. History writing — Europe — United Kingdom

LC 2018303412

Vivid profiles of five powerful Norman queens examine their enduring influence and the myths and prejudices that obscured their achievements, in a first joint biography that includes portraits of Matilda of Flanders; William the Conqueror's wife; and Empress Matilda, the mother of King Henry II.

West, Cornel

Black *Prophetic Fire.* in dialogue with and edited by Christa Buschendorf. Beacon Press 2014. 248 pages

ISBN 9780807003527

Grades: Adult   920

1. Douglass, Frederick, 1818-1895 2. Du Bois, W. E. B. (William Edward Burghardt), 1868-1963 3. King, Martin Luther, Jr, 1929-1968 4. Baker, Ella, 1903-1986 5. Malcolm X, 1925-1965 6. Wells, Ida B, 1862-1931 7. West, Cornel, 1953- 8. African Americans 9. Political activists 10. Revolutionaries 11. United States 12. Collective biographies 13. Society and culture — Race 14. Life stories — Politics — Activists and Reformers 15. Life stories — Identity — Race and ethnicity 16. History writing — African American — United States

LC 2014010359

A prominent activist and democratic thinker along with a distinguished scholar examine the legacies of African American leaders from the past two centuries and discuss their passion, vision and commitment.

Includes bibliographical references and index.

Whipple, Chris

The **Spymasters**: *How the CIA Directors Shape History and the Future.* Chris Whipple. Scribner 2020. 384 pages

ISBN 9781982106409

Grades: Adult   920

1. Directors of Central Intelligence 2. Intelligence service 3. Presidents 4. United States 5. Collective biographies 6. History writing — United States

ESSENTIAL AND RECOMMENDED TITLES
920 Collective biographies

7. History writing — Spies and spying 8. Life stories — Law and order — Spies and secret agents

LC Bl2020045525

The best-selling author of the Gatekeepers presents a behind-the-scenes tour of the inner workings of the CIA and how it often operates as an essential counterforce against presidents who would overstep the powers of the executive office.

"Whipple makes excellent use of insider accounts and provides enough color to keep readers turning the pages. This well-written and accessible survey illuminates a neglected role in American history." —*Publishers Weekly*

Wickenden, Dorothy

The Agitators: Three Friends Who Fought for Abolition and Women's Rights. Dorothy Wickenden. Scribner 2021. 400 p.

ISBN 9781476760735

Grades: Adult   920

1. Tubman, Harriet, 1820?-1913 2. Seward, Frances Adeline, 1805-1865 3. Wright, Martha Coffin, 1806-1875 4. Women abolitionists 5. History of women's rights 6. Anti-slavery movements 7. Underground railroad 8. Civil War 9. New York (State) 10. United States 11. 19th century 12. American Civil War era (1861-1865) 13. Collective biographies 14. History writing — Women's history 15. History writing — United States 16. Life stories — Politics — Activists and reformers 17. History writing — African American — United States

From the intimate perspective of three friends and neighbors in mid-nineteenth century Auburn, New York, author Dorothy Wickenden tells the fascinating and crucially American stories of abolition, the underground railroad, the early women's rights movement, and the Civil War.

"New Yorker executive editor Wickenden (Nothing Daunted) expertly weaves together the biographies of 'Co-conspirators and intimate friends' Harriet Tubman, Martha Wright, and Frances Seward in this novelistic history. . . . This is an essential addition to the history of American progressivism." —*Publishers Weekly*

Wides-Munoz, Laura

The Making of a Dream: How a Group of Young Undocumented Immigrants Helped Change What It Means to Be American. Laura Wides-Munoz. HarperCollins 2018. 304 pages

ISBN 9780062560124

Grades: Adult   920

1. Immigration and emigration 2. Undocumented immigrants 3. Child immigrants 4. Teenagers 5. Social movements 6. Public opinion 7. Human rights 8. Deportation 9. Immigrants 10. Discrimination 11. Collective biographies 12. Life stories — Facing adversity — War and oppression 13. Politics and global affairs — Immigration 14. Society and culture — General 15. Adult books for young adults

LC Bl2017048622

Library Journal Best Books, 2018.

A journalist chronicles the next chapter in civil rights—the story of a movement and a nation, witnessed through the poignant and inspiring experiences of five young undocumented activists who are transforming society's attitudes toward one of the most contentious political matters roiling America today: Immigration.

"This inspiring, well-written, well-documented account is an important read for Americans on all sides of this lingering issue." —*Library Journal*

Wills, Shomari

Black Fortunes: The Story of the First Six African Americans Who Escaped Slavery and Became Millionaires. Shomari Wills. Amistad Press 2018. 320 p.

ISBN 9780062437594

Grades: Adult   920

1. African Americans 2. Freed people 3. Millionaires 4. Success (Concept) 5. Rich people 6. Race relations 7. United States 8. Collective biographies 9. Life stories — People in history 10. History writing — African American — United States

LC Bl2018002424

The astonishing untold history of America's first Black millionaires—former slaves who endured incredible challenges to amass and maintain their wealth for a century, from the Jacksonian period to the Roaring Twenties—self-made entrepreneurs whose unknown success mirrored that of American business heroes such as Henry Ford, John D. Rockefeller, and Thomas Edison.

"Wills storytelling is infectious, his subjects are irresistible, and his broad coverage invites readers to venture further into the events and historical context he so vividly introduces." —*Booklist*

Wolff, Daniel J.

Grown-up Anger: The Connected Mysteries of Bob Dylan, Woody Guthrie, and the Calumet Massacre of 1913. Daniel Wolff. Harper 2017. 304 p.

ISBN 9780062451699

Grades: Adult   920

1. Dylan, Bob, 1941- 2. Guthrie, Woody, 1912-1967 3. Popular music 4. Folk music 5. Injustice 6. Strikes 7. Mass murder 8. Copper miners 9. Musicians 10. Memory 11. Social change 12. Loss 13. Social life and customs 14. Anger 15. United States 16. 20th century 17. Collective biographies 18. Life stories — Arts and culture — Performing arts — Musicians and composers 19. History writing — United States

LC 2017003018

After researching a 1913 tragedy described in a Woody Guthrie song, a lifelong Bob Dylan fan discusses the historical details of the event and how rage at the injustice inspired both musicians to create art from loss and fury.

"Wolff has crafted a fascinating and relevant whirlwind examination of music, economic injustice, and two American icons." —*Booklist*

Includes bibliographical references and index.

Woo, Ilyon

★ *Master Slave Husband Wife: An Epic Journey from Slavery to Freedom*. Ilyon Woo. Simon & Schuster 2023. 288 p.

ISBN 9781501191053

Grades: Adult   920

1. Craft, William 2. Craft, Ellen 3. Disguises 4. Freedom seekers 5. Secret identity 6. Passing (Identity) 7. Freedom 8. Couples 9. Slavery 10. Antebellum America (1820-1861) 11. Collective biographies 12. Life stories — Facing adversity — War and oppression — Enslaved people 13. History Writing — African American — Enslavement — United States 14. History writing — Antebellum America — United States 15. Life stories — People in history 16. Nonfiction that reads like fiction

Pulitzer Prize for Biography, 2024.

The remarkable true story of Ellen and William Craft, who escaped slavery through daring, determination, and disguise, with Ellen passing as a wealthy, disabled White man and William posing as "his" slave.

"Throughout, Woo's narrative is suspenseful and wonderfully told. A captivating tale that ably captures the determination and courage of a remarkable couple." —*Kirkus*

Wood, Gordon S.

Friends Divided: John Adams and Thomas Jefferson. Gordon S. Wood. Penguin Press 2017. 512 p.

ISBN 9780735224711

Grades: Adult   920

1. Jefferson, Thomas, 1743-1826 2. Adams, John, 1735-1826 3. Politicians 4. Male friendship 5. Political parties 6. Presidents 7. Politics and government 8. United States 9. Collective biographies 10. History writing — Early America — United States 11. Life stories — Politics — Politicians 12. Life stories — Relationships — Friendship

LC 2017025116

New York Times Notable Book, 2017.

A dual portrait of the second and third U.S. presidents shares insights into their disparate backgrounds, the partnership decisions that helped establish America's foundation and the unexpected ways their subsequent falling out and reconciliation corrected the course of a young republic.

"Wood glides through the political intricacies and intrigues of the times, offering incisive analyses, especially of the ongoing debate over slavery, finely illuminating the minds of Adams and Jefferson." —*Publishers Weekly*

Wulf, Andrea
The Brother Gardeners: Botany, Empire, and the Birth of an Obsession. Andrea Wulf. Knopf 2009. 368 p.

ISBN 9780307270238

Grades: Adult   920

1. Horticulturists 2. Plant collectors 3. Gardening 4. Plant collecting 5. Gardens 6. Gardeners 7. English history 8. British history 9. Great Britain 10. 18th century 11. Collective biographies 12. Biographies 13. Nature Writing — Gardens 14. Life stories — People in history

LC Bl2009000183

Follows the lives of six men who shared a passion for plants and a love of gardening in eighteenth-century London, who made Britain the epicenter of horticulture, and transformed gardening from an aristocratic pastime to a national obsession.

"A garden will never look quite the same after you've read this book. Wulf's book will be of interest to anyone with a garden, even if it's on a windowsill." —*Library Journal*

Originally published: London : William Heinemann, 2008; Includes bibliographical references and index.

Yaffa, Joshua
Between Two Fires: Truth, Ambition, and Compromise in Putin's Russia. Joshua Yaffa. Tim Duggan Books 2020. 356 p.

ISBN 9781524760595

Grades: Adult   920

1. Putin, Vladimir Vladimirovich, 1952- 2. Power 3. Investigative journalism 4. Dissenters 5. Public opinion 6. Political culture 7. Presidents 8. Political persecution 9. Political leadership 10. Political corruption 11. Politics and government 12. Russia 13. Collective biographies 14. Politics and global affairs — World politics — Europe 15. Politics and global affairs — Political figures 16. History writing — Europe — Russia 17. Life stories — Politics

LC 2019025918

Orwell Prize, 2021.

Between Two Fires chronicles the lives of eight ambitious Russians—from politicians and entrepreneurs to artists and historians—who have built their careers and constructed their identities in the shadow of the Putin system, where astonishingly, Putin's approval rating remains at 80%. Torn between their own ambitions and the omnipresent demands of the state, some muster cunning and cynicism to extract privileges from those in power while others are broken or demoralized. For each, the question of compromise—where to bend, how much, and in the service of what goal—is ever-present. The result is an intimate and probing portrait of the way citizens shape their lives around the demands of a capricious and repressive state, which offers urgent lessons about the nature of modern authoritarianism.

"This superb portrait of contemporary Russia is full of insight and moral drama." —*Publishers Weekly*

Zwonitzer, Mark
Will You Miss Me When I'm Gone?: The Carter Family and Their Legacy in American Music. Mark Zwonitzer with Charles Hirshberg. Simon & Schuster 2002. xii, 417 p. : Illustration

ISBN 9780684857633

Grades: Adult   920

1. Country musicians 2. Music, American 3. Music history and criticism 4. Virginia 5. United States 6. Collective biographies 7. Biographies 8. Life stories — Arts and culture — Performing arts — Musicians and composers 9. Arts and Entertainment — Music — Country 10. Adult books for young adults

LC 2002022395

Booklist Editors' Choice, 2002; New York Times Notable Book, 2002; National Book Critics Circle Award for Biography finalist, 2002.

Traces the bluegrass country music achievements of the Carter family, from their discovery by a New York record maker to their rise to stardom and eventual breakup, noting their influence on the careers of top performers.

"The author follows the Carter family's history from the 1891 birth of A.P. Carter, the musical founder, up through the late 1970s, offering background on the social, economic and technological developments that spawned American folk, country and rock music. Zwonitzer writes with flair, weaving anecdotes into a compelling study that will intrigue historians and music lovers alike." —*Publishers Weekly*

Includes index.

920.72 Biography — Women

Ditum, Sarah
Toxic: Women, Fame, and the Tabloid 2000s. Sarah Ditum. Harry N Abrams Inc 2024. 304 p.

ISBN 9781419763113

Grades: Adult   920.72

1. Women 2. Fame 3. Celebrities 4. Sexism 5. Tabloid newspapers 6. Culture 7. Popular culture 8. 2000s (Decade) 9. Society and culture — Pop culture 10. Life stories — Arts and culture — Performing arts — Entertainers and celebrities 11. Society and culture — Gender — Women

Reexamining the lives of nine women who defined the hell of celebrity in the 2000s, this book reveals how their portrayal has shaped the way all women are viewed today as their stories intersect with our current political, social and cultural climate.

"Top-notch pop-culture commentary—a smart and entertaining look at female celebrity during a decade of immense change." —*Kirkus*

Originally published in the UK under the title Toxic: Women, fame and the Noughties, by Fleet Publishing, London, in 2023.

Lovell, Mary S.
The Sisters: The Saga of the Mitford Family. Mary S. Lovell. Norton 2002. 611 p, 24 p. of plates : Illustration

ISBN 9780393010435

Grades: Adult   920.72

1. Mitford family 2. Mitford, Nancy, 1904-1973 3. Mitford, Jessica, 1917-1996 4. Mitford, Unity, 1914-1948 5. Sisters 6. Women and politics 7. European history 8. Great Britain 9. 20th century 10. Collective biographies 11. Biographies 12. Life stories — People in history — Famous families 13. History writing — Europe — United Kingdom

LC 2001044942

New York Times Notable Book, 2002.

A portrait of the Mitford sisters follows Jessica, a communist; Debo, the Duchess of Devonshire; Nancy, a best-selling novelist; Diana, who was the most hated woman in England; and Unity, who was obsessed with Adolf Hitler.

"The story of the six high-spirited, aristocratic, amusing and amusable sisters who did as they pleased, mostly, and captured the imagination of Britain for about half the 20th century; the author takes no sides and, what is truly remarkable, keeps track of all six lives at once." —*New York Times Book Review*

Originally published as the Mitford girls: London : Little, Brown, 2001; Includes bibliographical references (p. [581]-584) and index.

921 Philosophers and psychologists

Cooper, Helene
The House at Sugar Beach: A Memoir. Helene Cooper. Simon & Schuster 2008. 320 p.

ISBN 9780743266246

Grades: 11 12 Adult   921

1. Cooper, Helene 2. African history 3. Liberia 4. Autobiographies and memoirs 5. Life stories — Facing adversity — War and oppression — War survivors 6. History writing — Wars and conflicts — Civil Wars 7. Family and Relationships — Families 8. Adult books for young adults 9. History writing — Civil wars and genocide — Africa

LC 2008277249

New York Times Notable Book, 2008; National Book Critics Circle Award for Autobiography/Memoir finalist.

The author traces her childhood in war-torn Liberia and her reunion with a foster sister who had been left behind when her family fled the region.

ESSENTIAL AND RECOMMENDED TITLES
929 Genealogy, names, insignia

"A coming-of-age story told with unremitting honesty. With her pedigree and her freedom from internalized racism, Cooper is liberated to enjoy a social universe that is a fluid mix of all things American and African. . . . While Cooper's memoir is mesmerizing in its portrayal of a Liberia rarely witnessed, its description of the psychological devastationand coping mechanismsbrought on by profound loss is equally captivating." —*New York Times Book Review*

O'Meara, Mallory
The Lady from the Black Lagoon: Hollywood Monsters and the Lost Legacy of Milicent Patrick. Mallory O'Meara. Hanover Sqaure Press 2019. 307 pages : Illustration
ISBN 9781335937803
Grades: Adult   921
1. Patrick, Milicent, 1915-1998 2. O'Meara, Mallory 3. Filmmaking 4. Women animators 5. Special effects (Cinematography) 6. Women artists 7. Sexism 8. Sexism in employment 9. Monster films 10. Horror films 11. Film industry and trade 12. Film history and criticism 13. Life stories — Arts and culture — Artists 14. History writing — Women's history 15. Arts and Entertainment — Movies and Television 16. Adult books for young adults
LC 2019299927
Booklist Editors' Choice, 2019; Library Journal Best Books, 2019.

The story of Millicent Patrick, a feminist trailblazer in the horror film industry who never received proper credit for creating the classic monster from Creature from the Black Lagoon.

"This is a fascinating slice of Hollywood history with a feminist slant, correcting a sexist wrong from decades ago and restoring Patrick to her rightful place of esteem." —*Publishers Weekly*

Includes bibliographical references and index.

929 Genealogy, names, insignia

Franklin, John Hope
In Search of the Promised Land: A Black Family and the Old South. John Hope Franklin, Loren Schweninger. Oxford University Press 2006. xvii, 286 p. : Illustration; Map
ISBN 9780195160871
Grades: Adult   929
1. Thomas, Sally, 1787-1850 2. Thomas family 3. Rapier family 4. Enslaved people 5. African Americans 6. African American families 7. Slavery 8. Race relations 9. Nashville, Tennessee 10. Southern states 11. Biographies 12. Family and Relationships — Families 13. Life stories — People in history 14. History writing — African American — United States 15. Book club best bets
LC 2004061666

Focuses on the experiences of the Thomas-Rapier family to analyze race relations in the antebellum South, as well as to provide an in-depth look at the turbulent nature of American society in the era that followed.

"The authors trace the history of the Thomas-Rapier family during the antebellum and Civil War eras. Starting with matriarch Sally Thomas, born a slave in 1787, the book enables readers to distinguish the various complex modes within which slavery operated. The resulting family history also traces the evolution of race relations in diverse locations from New Orleans to New York City, Canada, Minnesota, and the Caribbean." —*Library Journal*

Includes bibliographical references (p. 281-282) and index.

McCourt, Frank
★ *Angela's Ashes: A Memoir*. Frank McCourt. Scribner 1996. 364 p. : Illustration
ISBN 9780684874357
Grades: 11 12 Adult   929
1. McCourt family 2. McCourt, Frank 3. Growing up 4. Poor families 5. Children of alcoholics 6. Irish Americans 7. American people in Ireland 8. Hunger 9. Childhood 10. Poverty 11. Limerick, Ireland 12. Autobiographies and memoirs 13. Page to screen 14. Biographies 15. Family and Relationships — Growing up 16. Life stories — Relationships — Growing up 17. Nonfiction that reads like fiction

LC 96005335
ALA Notable Book, 1997; Book Sense Book of the Year Adult Trade, 1997; Library Journal Best Books, 1996.

The author recounts his childhood in Depression-era Brooklyn as the child of Irish immigrants who decide to return to worse poverty in Ireland when his infant sister dies.

"An extraordinary work in every way. McCourt magically retrieves love, dignity, and humor from a childhood of hunger, loss, and pain." —*Kirkus*

Sequel: 'Tis.

Neighbors, Joy
The Family Tree Cemetery Field Guide: How to Find, Record, & Preserve Your Ancestors' Graves. Joy Neighbors. Family Tree Books 2017. 239 pages : Illustration
ISBN 9781440352126
Grades: Adult   929
1. Cemeteries 2. Genealogy 3. United States 4. Reference — Genealogy 5. Reference books — Handbooks, manuals, etc.
LC 2017276788

Unearth clues to your past. Not all research can be done from home—sometimes you have to head into the field. Cemeteries are crucial for any genealogist's search, and this book will show you how to search for and analyze your ancestors' graves. Discover tools for locating tombstones, tips for traipsing through cemeteries, an at-a-glance guide to frequently used gravestone icons, and practical strategies for on-the-ground research. And once you've returned home, learn how to incorporate gravestone information into your research, as well as how to upload grave locations to BillionGraves and record your findings in memorial pages on Find a Grave. The Family Tree Cemetery Field Guide features: Detailed step-by-step guides to finding ancestor's cemeteries using websites like Find a Grave, plus how to record and preserve death and burial information; Tips and strategies for navigating cemeteries and finding individual tombstones in the field, plus an at-a-glance guide to tombstone symbols and iconography;Resources and techniques for discovering other death records and incorporating information from cemeteries into genealogical research.

Not all research can be done from home—sometimes you have to head into the field. Cemeteries are crucial for any genealogist's search, and this book will show you how to search for and analyze your ancestors' graves. Discover tools for locating tombstones, tips for traipsing through cemeteries, an at-a-glance guide to frequently used gravestone icons, and practical strategies for on-the-ground research.

"Cemeteries are crucial for genealogy research, and this solid, compact, one-stop book shows how to search for and analyze ancestors graves." —*Booklist*

Includes bibliographical references (pages 226-231) and index.

Samaha, Albert
Concepcion: An Immigrant Family's Fortunes. Albert Samaha. Riverhead Books 2021. 320 p.
ISBN 9780593086087
Grades: Adult   929
1. Concepcion family 2. Samaha, Albert 3. Filipino Americans 4. Journalists 5. Immigrant families 6. Ethnic identity 7. Colonialism 8. Inequality 9. Family history 10. Southeast Asian Americans 11. Southeast Asian people 12. Immigration and emigration 13. Asian history 14. San Francisco, California 15. Philippines 16. United States 17. Autobiographies and memoirs 18. Life stories — Identity — Immigrants 19. Life stories — Facing adversity 20. Society and culture — Immigration 21. Society and culture — Ethnic studies
LC 2021013641

National Book Critics Circle Award for Autobiography/Memoir finalist, 2021.

A journalist's powerful and incisive account of the forces steering the fate of his sprawling Filipinx-American family reframes how we comprehend the immigrant experience. Nearing the age at which his mother had migrated to the U.S, part of the wave of non-Europeans who arrived after immigration quotas were relaxed in 1965, Albert Samaha began to question the ironclad belief in a better future that had inspired her family to uproot themselves from their birthplace. Excavating his family's history back to the region's unique geopolitical roots in Spanish colonialism, Japanese occupation, and American intervention, Samaha fits his family's arc into the wider story of global migration as determined by chess moves among superpowers.

"Journalist Samaha (Never Ran, Never Will) presents a wide-angle view of immigration, particularly showing how its history, economics, and culture have shaped the lives of his Filipino American family in the United States. . . . Samaha's memoir of his family's experience is a clear, moving, and powerful rumination on what it means to be an immigrant." —*Library Journal*

Includes bibliographical references.

929.1 Genealogy

Jacobs, A. J.

It's All Relative: Adventures up and Down the World's Family Tree. A.J. Jacobs. Simon & Schuster 2017. 416 p.

ISBN 9781476734491

Grades: Adult   929.1

1. Jacobs, A. J, 1968- 2. Jacobs family 3. Genealogy 4. Ancestors 5. Families 6. Genetic genealogy 7. Extended families 8. Humor writing — Family and relationship humor

LC Bl2017036988

Traces the author's three-year investigation into what constitutes family, describing how, after receiving an e-mail from a stranger who claimed to be a distant cousin, he embarked on an effort to build the biggest family tree in history.

"A delightful, easy-to-read, informative book." —*Kirkus*

Pennavaria, Katherine

Genealogy for Beginners. Katherine Pennavaria. Rowman & Littlefield 2020. 241 p.

ISBN 9781538125489

Grades: Adult   929.1

1. Genealogy 2. Reference — Genealogy

LC 2019043515

This book covers everything you need to get started researching your family history or continue a project you've already started. It offers practical suggestions from an experienced genealogist, and detailed, step-by-step instructions for carrying out aquality family history research.

"For youth or adults, this guide simplifies the massive effort of analyzing family and clan roots. Recommended for public and high school libraries." —*Booklist*

Includes bibliographical references and index.

929.2 Family histories

Teege, Jennifer

My Grandfather Would Have Shot Me: A Black Woman Discovers Her Family's Nazi Past. Jennifer Teege and Nikola Sellmair, translated by Carolin Sommer. The Experiment 2015. 288 p.

ISBN 9781615192533

Grades: Adult   929.2

1. Teege, Jennifer, 1970- 2. Goth, Amon, 1908-1946 3. Grandfather and granddaughter 4. Multiracial women 5. Nazis 6. Life change events 7. Family secrets 8. Coping 9. Concentration camp commandants 10. World War II 11. Autobiographies and memoirs 12. Translations — German to English 13. Life stories — Identity 14. Life stories — Relationships

LC 2014046242

A German-Nigerian woman discovers, while examining a library book, that her grandfather, Amon Goeth, was portrayed in Schindler's List as the central villain of the Plaszów concentration camp, responsible for brutally murdering thousands of people.

"Originally published in German as Amon: Mein Grossvater htte mich erschossen, Teege's account is an important addition to narratives written by descendants of war criminals. A gripping read, highly recommended for anyone interested in history, memoirs, and biography." —*Library Journal*

Originally published under the title Amon : Mein Grossvater hätte mich erschossen, 2013.

Wills, Clair

★ *Missing Persons: Or, My Grandmother's Secrets.* Clair Wills. Farrar, Straus and Giroux 2024. 208 p.

ISBN 9780374611866

Grades: Adult   929.2

1. Wills, Clair 2. Women 3. Irish people 4. Single mothers 5. Unplanned pregnancy 6. Families 7. Maternity homes 8. Social history 9. Irish people in England 10. Family secrets 11. Ireland 12. 20th century 13. Autobiographies and memoirs 14. Life stories — Relationships — Family 15. Family and relationships — Families 16. History writing — Europe — Ireland

LC 2023041345

Blending memoir with social history, Clair Wills movingly explores the gaping holes in the fabric of modern Ireland, and in her own family story.

"Frank, self-aware, and deeply moving, Missing Persons draws attentions to what (and who) gets forgotten and left out of history." —*Booklist*

Originally published in 2024 by Allen Lane, Great Britain.

929.7 Royal houses, peerage, orders of knighthood

Sebag-Montefiore, Simon

★ *The World: A Family History of Humanity.* Simon Sebag Montefiore. Alfred A. Knopf 2023. 1296 p.

ISBN 9780525659532

Grades: Adult   929.7

1. Royal houses 2. Families 3. Rulers 4. Women rulers 5. Upper class 6. War 7. Betrayal 8. Violence 9. Power 10. History 11. Civilization 12. History writing — General 13. Life stories — People in history — Famous families 14. Life stories — Politics

LC 2022033250

Capturing the whole human story in a single, masterful narrative, an award-winning historian, by chronicling the world's great dynasties throughout history, which features a cast of extraordinary diversity, shows the one commonality—families.

"History buffs and novices will appreciate this extensive, accessible, highly recommended work; it may inspire them to dig into lesser-known areas of global history." —*Library Journal*

Includes bibliographical references and index.

930.1 Archaeology

Ceram, C. W.

Gods, Graves & Scholars: The Story of Archaeology. C.W. Ceram; translated from the German by E.B. Garside and Sophie Wilkins. Wings Books 1994. xiv, 441, xiv p. : Illustration; Map

ISBN 9780517119815

Grades: 11 12 Adult   930.1

1. Archaeology 2. Archaeologists 3. Archaeological expeditions 4. Archaeological sites 5. Historians 6. Treasure hunters 7. Bronze and Iron Ages (3500-27 B.C.E.) 8. History writing — Archaeology 9. History writing — Ancient

LC 94015215

A highly readable introduction to archeology that details the expeditions and work of individuals who made such important discoveries as Troy, Pompeii, Teotihuacan, and the Tower of Babel.

Includes bibliographical references (p. 435-441) and index; Originally published: New York : Knopf, 1951.

MacGregor, Neil

A History of the World in 100 Objects. Neil MacGregor. Allen Lane 2010. xxvi, 707 p. : Color illustration; Map

ESSENTIAL AND RECOMMENDED TITLES
932 Egypt to 640

ISBN 9781846144134
Grades: Adult 930.1
1. Civilization 2. Material culture 3. Antiquities 4. Antiquities, Prehistoric 5. Ancient history 6. Modern history 7. Social history 8. Civilization, Classical 9. Civilization, Medieval 10. History writing — Arts and culture 11. History writing — General

Neil MacGregor's radio series 'A History of the World in 100 Objects' has been a unique event that has set a benchmark for public service broadcasting in the UK and across the world. This book is the tie-in to that event, reproducing the scripts describing the objects that made us who we are.

Based on the celebrated BBC Radio 4 series - front cover; Includes bibliographical references and index.

Preston, Douglas J.
The Lost Tomb: And Other Real-life Stories of Bones, Burials, and Murder. Douglas Preston; foreword by David Grann. GCP 2023. 320 p.
ISBN 9781538741221
Grades: Adult 930.1
1. Preston, Douglas J. 2. Archaeology 3. Civilization, Ancient 4. Curiosities and wonders 5. History writing — Archaeology 6. True Crime — General 7. History Writing — Exploration
LC 2023026359

From the haunted country of Italy to the largest tomb in Egypt's Valley of the Kings, the #1 New York Times bestselling author of the Lost City of the Monkey God presents extraordinary and enthralling true stories of Egyptian burial chambers, lost treasure, mysterious murders, strange crimes and more.

"Bestseller Preston (The Lost City of the Monkey God), who coauthors the Aloysius Pendergast series with Lincoln Child, shares the inspirations for many of those procedurals in this gripping compendium of his journalistic work, much of which was previously published in the New Yorker." —*Publishers Weekly*

932 Egypt to 640

Darnell, John Coleman
Egypt's Golden Couple: When Akhenaten and Nefertiti Were Gods on Earth. John Darnell and Colleen Darnell. St. Martin's Press 2022. 384 p.
ISBN 9781250272874
Grades: Adult 932
1. Akhenaten, King of Egypt 2. Nefertiti, Queen of Egypt, 14th cent. B.C.E 3. Rulers 4. Husband and wife 5. Monotheism 6. Social change 7. Egyptology 8. Antiquities 9. Civilization 10. Egypt 11. Ancient Egypt 12. Ancient Egypt (3100 B.C.E.-640 C.E.) 13. History writing — Ancient — Egypt 14. History writing — Archaeology
LC 2022023810

Akhenaten has been the subject of radically different, even contradictory, biographies. The king has achieved fame as the world's first individual and the first monotheist, but others have seen him as an incestuous tyrant who nearly ruined the kingdom he ruled. The gold funerary mask of his son Tutankhamun and the painted bust of his wife Nefertiti are the most recognizable artifacts from all of ancient Egypt. But who are Akhenaten and Nefertiti? And what can we actually say about rulers who lived more than three thousand years ago? From clue to clue, renowned Egyptologists John and Colleen Darnell reconstruct an otherwise untold story of the magnificent reign of Akhenaten and Nefertiti.

"In this innovative and detailed study, husband-and-wife Egyptologists John and Colleen Darnell (Tutankhamun's Armies) explore the 14th-century BCE reign of Pharaoh Akhenaten and Queen Nefertiti, the parents of Tutankhamun." —*Publishers Weekly*

Includes bibliographical references and index.

Mertz, Barbara
Temples, Tombs, & Hieroglyphs: A Popular History of Ancient Egypt. Barbara Mertz. William Morrow 2007. xxvi, 324 p. : Illustration; Color; Map
ISBN 9780061252761
Grades: 9 10 11 12 Adult 932

1. Egyptian hieroglyphics 2. Temples 3. Tombs 4. Egypt 5. Ancient Egypt 6. Ancient Egypt (3100 B.C.E.-640 C.E.) 7. History writing — Ancient — Egypt
LC 2007029118

An updated classic history of ancient Egypt draws on archaeological reporting, historical speculation, and other sources, in an account that provides coverage of professional discoveries from the past quarter century.

"This is an introduction to the history of ancient Egypt and Egyptology. . . . Mertz gives special attention to such topics as the kingship (yes) of Queen Hatshepsut, the exploits of Thutmose III, and the Amarna Period with its intriguing players Akhenaten, Nefertiti, and Tutankhamen. Presenting both pros and cons of current theories, Mertz also explains in simple language archaeological techniques such as carbon 14 dating and historical chronology. . . . [This is] an excellent introduction for patrons interested in the land of the pharaohs." —*Library Journal*

Includes bibliographical references (p. [309]-311) and index.

Romer, John
A History of Ancient Egypt: From the First Farmers to the Great Pyramid. John Romer. Thomas Dunne Books 2013. 512 p.
ISBN 9781250030115
Grades: Adult 932
1. Ancient history 2. Civilization, Ancient 3. Ancient Egypt 4. Ancient Egypt (3100 B.C.E.-640 C.E.) 5. History writing — Ancient — Egypt
LC 2013012485

A first volume of a history of the earliest days of ancient Egypt challenges popular archaeological understandings to chronicle the ancient world's first agricultural practices through the construction of the pyramids.

Includes bibliographical references and index.

Shaw, Ian
The Princeton Dictionary of Ancient Egypt. Ian Shaw and Paul Nicholson. Princeton University Press 2008. 368 p. : Illustration; Color; Map
ISBN 9780691137629
Grades: Adult 932
1. Antiquities 2. Civilization 3. Civilization, Ancient 4. Ancient Egypt 5. Egypt 6. Ancient Egypt (3100 B.C.E.-640 C.E.) 7. Dictionaries 8. Reference — Dictionaries 9. History writing — Ancient — Egypt
LC 2008927831

More than six hundred entries explain the major ideas, events, and personalities that shaped ancient Egypt and identify major tombs and archaeological sites.

In association with the British Museum; Also published under title: British Museum dictionary of ancient Egypt (London : British Museum, 2008); Previous ed.: Dictionary of ancient Egypt (New York: Harry N. Abrams, 1995); previous British ed.: British Museum dictionary of ancient Egypt; Includes bibliographical references and index.

Wilkinson, Toby A. H.
★ *The Rise and Fall of Ancient Egypt.* Toby Wilkinson. Random House 2011. 656 p.
ISBN 9780553805536
Grades: Adult 932
1. Ancient history 2. Civilization, Ancient 3. Ancient Egypt 4. Ancient Egypt (3100 B.C.E.-640 C.E.) 5. History writing — Ancient — Egypt
LC 2009047322

An authoritative history of a 3,000-year period from the birth of the world's first nation-state to its absorption into the Roman Empire includes comprehensive coverage of such topics as its government, the influence of religion and the roles of women.

"The author offers a revisionist view of the ugly life hidden by the splendors and dazzling treasures of pharaonic Egypt. He shows in rich detail that it was a brutal society where life was cheap, royal power absolute and established through fear and coercion. This is a penetrating and authoritative overview of a violent ancient civilization often revered by contemporary scholars and enthusiasts." —*Publishers Weekly*

Includes bibliographical references and index.

PUBLIC LIBRARY CORE COLLECTION: NONFICTION
Twentieth Edition

A **World** *Beneath the Sands: The Golden Age of Egyptology.* Toby Wilkinson. W.W. Norton & Company 2020. 528 p.
ISBN 9781324006893
Grades: Adult 932
1. Egyptology 2. Egyptologists 3. Archaeologists 4. Adventurers 5. International competition 6. Exploration 7. Exploitation 8. Civilization, Ancient 9. Excavations (Archaeology) 10. Antiquities 11. Southwest Asia and North Africa (Middle East) history 12. Nile Valley 13. Egypt 14. 19th century 15. History writing — Archaeology 16. History writing — Ancient — Egypt 17. History writing — Colonization — Africa 18. Life stories — People in history — Explorers 19. History writing — Exploration
LC 2020010916

From the decipherment of hieroglyphics in 1822 to the discovery of Tutankhamun's tomb by Howard Carter and Lord Carnarvon a hundred years later, the uncovering of Egypt's ancient past took place in an atmosphere of grand adventure and international rivalry. In A World Beneath the Sands, the acclaimed Egyptologist Toby Wilkinson chronicles the ruthless race between the British, French, Germans and Americans to lay claim to its mysteries and treasures.

The result is an essential portrait of how the rediscovery of 'Ancient past paved the way for its modern rebirth.' —*Publishers Weekly*

Includes bibliographical references and index.

933 Palestine to 70

Garfinkel, Yosef
In the Footsteps of King David: Revelations from an Ancient Biblical City. Yosef Garfinkel, Saar Ganor, Michael G. Hasel. Thames & Hudson 2018. 240 p.
ISBN 9780500052013
Grades: Adult 933
1. David, King of Israel 2. Extinct cities 3. Archaeology 4. Excavations (Archaeology) 5. Anthropology 6. Material culture 7. Civilization, Ancient 8. Israel 9. History writing — Archaeology 10. History writing — Southwest Asia and North Africa (Middle East) 11. Spirituality and Religion — Judaism — History 12. Spirituality and Religion — Christianity — History 13. History writing — Ancient
LC Bl2018087239

Offers an account of how years of investigating the excavation of Khirbet Qeiyafa in the Valley of Elah have uncovered a city dating back to the time of the Biblical King David, and how these findings shed light on his kingdom and defend the historicity of the Bible.

"This is a worthwhile work on a number of counts. Though sometimes a bit technical, the book is a fascinating glimpse into the methods, rigors, and rewards of archaeology. On another level, the authors add to a larger conversation about the historicity of the Bible while describing a find of true significance. An engaging glimpse into the ancient past." —*Kirkus*

935 Mesopotamia to 637 and Iranian Plateau to 637

Kriwaczek, Paul
Babylon: Mesopotamia and the Birth of Civilization. Paul Kriwaczek. Thomas Dunne Books/St. Martin's Press 2012. 320 p.
ISBN 9781250000071
Grades: Adult 935
1. Hammurabi, King of Babylonia 2. Ancient cities and towns 3. Civilization, Ancient 4. Civilization 5. Southwest Asia and North Africa (Middle East) history 6. Mesopotamia 7. Iraq 8. Babylonia 9. Bronze and Iron Ages (3500-27 B.C.E.) 10. History writing — Ancient
LC 2012003104

A history of the ancient city credited with establishing the foundations of modern civilization documents its rise and fall over thousands of years and includes coverage of its politics, social systems and technical innovations. By the award-winning author of Yiddish Civilisation.

Includes bibliographical references and index.

936 Europe north and west of Italian Peninsula to ca. 499

Higgins, Charlotte
Under Another Sky: Journeys in Roman Britain. Charlotte Higgins. The Overlook Press 2015. 304 p.
ISBN 9781468310894
Grades: Adult 936
1. Roman people in Great Britain 2. British history 3. Roman Britain (55 B.C.E.-449 C.E.) 4. History writing — Europe — United Kingdom 5. History writing — Ancient — Rome

What does Roman Britain mean to us now? How were its physical remains rediscovered and made sense of? How has it been reimagined, in story and song and verse? Sometimes on foot, sometimes in a magnificent, if not entirely reliable, VW camper van, Charlotte Higgins sets out to explore the ancient monuments of Roman Britain. She explores the land that was once Rome's northernmost territory and how it has changed since the years after the empire fell. Under Another Sky invites us to see the British landscape, and British history, in an entirely fresh way: as indelibly marked by how the Romans first imagined and wrote, these strange and exotic islands, perched on the edge of the known world, into existence.

"A thoroughly researched, elegantly written history." —*Kirkus*

Originally published in 2013 (London : Jonathan Cape, 2013).

936.2 England to 410 and Wales to 410

Parker Pearson, Michael
Stonehenge: A New Understanding : Solving the Mysteries of the Greatest Stone Age Monument. by Mike Parker Pearson and the Stonehenge Riverside Project. The Experiment 2013. 410 pages : Illustration; Color
ISBN 9781615190799
Grades: Adult 936.2
1. Megalithic monuments 2. Archaeology 3. Antiquities 4. English history 5. England 6. Stonehenge, England 7. Prehistoric era (Stone Age) 8. History writing — Europe — United Kingdom 9. History writing — Archaeology
LC 2012047688

An archaeologist who participated in a seven-year excavation at the historic monument describes recent findings that correct previously-held notions about the site, including the dating and significance of the structure as well as how the builders lived.

"Renowned archaeologist Pearson...presents the findings of the most ambitious and scientifically informed investigation of Stonehenge thus far. Filled with maps, drawings, photographs and diagrams, the book details the group's findings in a well-organized, absorbing manner." —*Kirkus*

Includes bibliographical references (pages 371-386) and index; First published in Great Britain in 2012 as Stonehenge : Exploring the greatest stone age mystery by Simon & Schuster, a division of Simon & Schuster UK Ltd.—T.P. verso.

Pryor, Francis
★ *Stonehenge:* The Story of a Sacred Landscape. Francis Pryor. Pegasus Books 2018. 207 p.
ISBN 9781681776408
Grades: Adult 936.2
1. Megalithic monuments 2. Prehistoric humans 3. Monuments 4. Archaeology 5. England 6. Stonehenge, England 7. History writing — Europe — United Kingdom 8. History writing — Ancient

Describes the nature and history of one of the world's most well-known and mysterious places, discussing how it was constructed in phases over 1,500 years and examining the enigmatic prehistoric monument in a wider cultural context.

"A renowned archaeologist chronicles the remarkable changes in our knowledge of the builders of Stonehenge and other, equally important and connected henges throughout Britain." —*Kirkus*

ESSENTIAL AND RECOMMENDED TITLES
937 Italian Peninsula to 476 and adjacent territories to 476

937 Italian Peninsula to 476 and adjacent territories to 476

Beard, Mary
★ *Emperor of Rome*. Mary Beard. Liveright Publishing 2023. 512 p.
ISBN 9780871404220
Grades: Adult   937
1. Roman emperors 2. Rulers 3. Leadership 4. Power 5. Inheritance and succession 6. Social life and customs 7. Lifestyles 8. Civilization, Ancient 9. Civilization 10. Ancient Rome 11. Roman Empire (27 B.C.E.-476 C.E.) 12. Life stories — Politics — Royalty 13. History writing — Ancient — Rome 14. History writing — Archaeology

A sweeping account of the social and political world of the Roman emperors. Along the way, author Mary Beard explores Roman fictions of imperial power, overturning many of the assumptions that we hold as gospel. With its finely nuanced portrayal of sex, class, and politics, Emperor of Rome goes directly to the heart of Roman fantasies (and our own) about what it was to be Roman at its richest, most luxurious, most extreme, and most powerful.

"For readers who want to see for themselves where these emperors held sway, Beard offers an itinerary of locations to visit as well as a comprehensive list of additional readings." —*Booklist*

The Fires of Vesuvius: Pompeii Lost and Found. Mary Beard. Belknap Press of Harvard University Press 2008. 360 p, 16 p. of plates : Illustration; Color; Map
ISBN 9780674029767
Grades: Adult   937
1. City life 2. Ancient cities and towns 3. Social life and customs 4. Pompeii (Extinct city) 5. Ancient Rome 6. History writing — Ancient — Rome
LC 2008027513
New York Times Notable Book, 2009.

From its political and religious systems to slavery and attitudes toward sex, the ruins of this ancient Roman city are explored in a study that brings to light new facts about the way the people of Pompeii lived prior to meeting their devastating end in 79 CE.

Includes bibliographical references (p. 317-335) and index.

★ *S.P.Q.R.: A History of Ancient Rome*. Mary Beard. Liveright 2015. 512 p.
ISBN 9780871404237
Grades: Adult   937
1. Ancient history 2. Romans 3. Civilization, Classical 4. Citizenship 5. Civilization, Greco-Roman 6. Enslaved people 7. Women 8. Philosophy 9. Legislation 10. Ancient Rome 11. History writing — Ancient — Rome
LC 2015036060
Library Journal Best Books, 2015; New York Times Notable Book, 2015; National Book Critics Circle Award for Nonfiction finalist.

A prominent classicist explores ancient Rome and how its citizens adapted the notion of imperial rule, invented the concepts of citizenship and nation, and made laws about those traditionally overlooked in history, including women, slaves, and criminals.

"Since the author is a well-known popularizer of classical studies, it is no surprise that this is a humorous and accessible work, but it is also extremely rigorous in its questioning of standard conclusions and methods. At all points, her approaches are easy to follow." —*Library Journal*

Berry, Joanne
The Complete Pompeii. Joanne Berry. Thames & Hudson 2007. 256 p. : Illustration; Color; Map
ISBN 9780500051504
Grades: 11 12 Adult   937
1. Pompeii (Extinct city) 2. History writing — Ancient — Rome
LC 2007922095

A comprehensive visual survey of the ancient city draws on cutting-edge architectural research to reconstruct the latest beliefs about Pompeii's history, discussing such topics as the lives and deaths of its citizens, its political and religious structures, and its destruction by the eruption of AD 79.

"This book covers the origins and evolution of the city, the daily life of its residents, the geography of the region, and the eruption of Mt. Vesuvius, as well as a history of the excavation of the site. Easy to read and with full color pictures of the excavation, along with maps, time lines, diagrams, and vivid art reproductions, this book gives a broad and comprehensive introduction to the Pompeian world.... High school libraries should be advised that there is a section on eroticism that contains visually and verbally explicit sexual material." —*Library Journal*

Includes bibliographical references (p. 245-250) and index.

Cline, Eric H.
After 1177 B.C.: The Survival of Civilizations. Eric H. Cline. 2024. 352 p.
ISBN 9780691192130
Grades: Adult   937
1. Civilization, Ancient 2. Bronze age 3. Archaeology 4. Civilization 5. Inventions 6. Mediterranean Region 7. Aegean Sea region 8. Bronze and Iron Ages (3500-27 B.C.E.) 9. History writing — Ancient 10. History writing — Archaeology

In this gripping sequel to his bestselling 1177 B.C, Eric Cline tells the story of what happened after the Bronze Age collapsed—why some civilizations endured, why some gave way to new ones, and why some disappeared forever.

"Historian Cline follows up 1177 B.C, his bestselling study of the end of the Bronze Age, with a sweeping account of what came next." —*Publishers Weekly*

Sequel to 1177 B.C.: the year civilization collapsed.

Everitt, Anthony
The Rise of Rome: The Making of the World's Greatest Empire. Anthony Everitt. Random House 2012. 416 p.
ISBN 9781400066636
Grades: Adult   937
1. Romans 2. Imperialism 3. Civilization, Classical 4. Civilization, Ancient 5. Political culture 6. Ancient history 7. Social classes 8. Civil war 9. Ancient Rome 10. Roman Empire (27 B.C.E.-476 C.E.) 11. History writing — Ancient — Rome
LC 2011048318

The best-selling author of Cicero traces the rise of Rome as an unlikely evolution from a market village to the world's most powerful empire, offering insight into its political clashes, military strategies, leading figures and internal corruptions.

Gibbon, Edward
★ *The Decline and Fall of the Roman Empire*. Edward Gibbon; edited, abridged, and with a critical introduction by Hans-Friedrich Mueller; introduction by Daniel J. Boorstin; illustrations by Giovanni Battista Piranesi. Modern Library 2003. xxxvii, 1258 p. : Illustration; Map
ISBN 9780375758119
Grades: Adult   937
1. Civilization, Ancient 2. Ancient Rome 3. Byzantine Empire 4. Byzantine Empire (330-1453) 5. Roman Empire (27 B.C.E.-476 C.E.) 6. Medieval period (476-1492) 7. History writing — Ancient — Rome
LC 2002032585

Recounts the events that led to the fall of the Roman Empire, from the second century A.D. to the fifteenth century A.D.

Includes bibliographical references (p. xxxvi-xxxvii).

Goldsworthy, Adrian Keith
Antony and Cleopatra. Adrian Goldsworthy. Yale University Press 2010. VI, 470 p, 16 p. of plates : Col. ill, maps; 24 cm.
ISBN 9780300165340
Grades: 11 12 Adult   937
1. Antonius, Marcus, 83-30 B.C.E 2. Cleopatra, Queen of Egypt, 69-30 B.C.E 3. Generals 4. Suicide 5. Women rulers 6. Politicians 7. Romans 8. Civilization, Ancient 9. Politics and government 10. Ancient Egypt 11. Ancient Rome 12. Egypt 13. Ancient Egypt (3100 B.C.E.-640 C.E.) 14. Roman Republic (509-27 B.C.E.) 15. Biographies 16. History writing — Ancient — Egypt 17. Life stories — People in history

PUBLIC LIBRARY CORE COLLECTION: NONFICTION
Twentieth Edition

In this dual biography of the two great lovers of antiquity, historian Adrian Goldsworthy goes beyond myth and romance to create a portrait of his subjects—who were first and foremost political animals.

"Narrating [Antony] and Cleopatra's parts in the tumultuous end of the Roman Republic, Goldsworthy skillfully integrates the partial and partisan source material into an accessible presentation of a classic tale from classical times." —*Booklist*

Includes bibliographical references (p. 418-454) and index.

Pax Romana: War, Peace and Conquest in the Roman World. Adrian Goldsworthy. Yale University Press 2016. 528 pages

ISBN 9780300178821

Grades: Adult 937
1. Ancient history 2. Civilization, Ancient 3. Military history 4. Culture 5. Civilization 6. Ancient Rome 7. Roman Empire (27 B.C.E.-476 C.E.) 8. History writing — Ancient — Rome

LC 2016941493

Best-selling author Adrian Goldsworthy turns his attention to the Pax Romana, the famous peace and prosperity brought by the Roman Empire at its height in the first and second centuries AD. Yet the Romans were conquerors, imperialists who took by force avast empire stretching from the Euphrates to the Atlantic coast. Ruthless, Romans won peace not through coexistence but through dominance; millions died and were enslaved during the creation of their empire. Pax Romana examines how the Romans came to control so much of the world and asks whether traditionally favorable images of the Roman peace are true. Goldsworthy vividly recounts the rebellions of the conquered, examining why they broke out, why most failed, and how they became exceedingly rare. He reveals that hostility was just one reaction to the arrival of Rome and that from the outset, conquered peoples collaborated, formed alliances, and joined invaders, causing resistance movements to fade away.

"An engrossing account of how the Roman Empire grew and operated." —*Kirkus*

Harper, Kyle

The **Fate** *of Rome: Climate, Disease, and the End of an Empire.* Kyle Harper. Princeton University Press 2017. 420 pages

ISBN 9780691166834

Grades: Adult 937
1. Climate change 2. Droughts 3. Diseases 4. Regression (Civilization) 5. Effect of environment on humans 6. Civilization 7. Ancient Rome 8. Roman Empire (27 B.C.E.-476 C.E.) 9. History writing — Ancient — Rome 10. History writing — Natural disasters and tragedies

LC 2017952241

A sweeping chronicle of the role of climate change and disease in the fall of the Roman Empire interweaves historical narrative with cutting-edge climate science and genetic discoveries to trace 500 years of volcanic eruptions, solar cycles, climate instability and devastating illnesses that combined in catastrophic ways.

"There is much to absorb in this significant scholarly achievement, which effectively integrates natural, social, and humanistic sciences to show how the fall of the empire caused the decline of Rome." —*Kirkus*

Includes bibliographical references and index.

O'Connell, Robert L.

The **Ghosts** *of Cannae: Hannibal and the Darkest Hour of the Roman Republic.* Robert L. O'Connell. Random House 2010. 320 p.

ISBN 9781400067022

Grades: Adult 937
1. Hannibal, 247-182 B.C.E 2. Scipio, Africanus 236?-183 B.C.E 3. Punic Wars, 264-146 B.C.E 4. Military campaigns 5. Military strategy 6. Military history 7. Armed Forces 8. Carthage (Extinct city) 9. Ancient Rome 10. Bronze and Iron Ages (3500-27 B.C.E.) 11. Roman Republic (509-27 B.C.E.) 12. History writing — Ancient 13. History writing — Wars and conflicts — Battles

LC 2009040006

An account of the slaughter at Cannae traces the massive defeat of the huge but inexperienced Roman army by Hannibal's forces, interpreting the larger course of the Second Punic War and the often-disastrous ways in which the battle has been imitated throughout history.

"The distinctive edge of the Ghosts of Cannae is Robert L. O'Connell's consistently professional instinct for the behavior of men and units on the battlefield. He is able to put himself and his reader on the ground at Cannae, gagging in the heat of a southern Italian midsummer, assailed by an overload from every one of the five senses." —*New York Times Book Review*

Includes bibliographical references and index.

Strauss, Barry S.

The **Death** *of Caesar: The Story of History's Most Famous Assassination.* Barry Strauss. Simon & Schuster 2015. 352 p.

ISBN 9781451668797

Grades: Adult 937
1. Caesar, Julius, 100-44 B.C.E 2. Assassination 3. Rulers 4. Civilization, Ancient 5. Ancient history 6. Politics and government 7. Ancient Rome 8. Roman Republic (509-27 B.C.E.) 9. Biographies 10. Life stories — Politics 11. True Crime — Historical Crime 12. History writing — Ancient — Rome

LC 2014032045

Thanks to William Shakespeare, the death of Julius Caesar is the most famous assassination in history. But what actually happened on March 15, 44 BC is even more gripping than Shakespeare's play. In this thrilling new book, Barry Strauss tells the real story.

"The author explains how Caesar's funeral was even more dramatic than Shakespeare's versionespecially Mark Antony's eulogy. Once again, Strauss takes us deep into the psyche of ancient history in an exciting, twisted tale that is sure to please." —*Kirkus*

Ten **Caesars**: *Roman Emperors from Augustus to Constantine.* Barry Strauss. Simon & Schuster 2019. 384 p.

ISBN 9781451668834

Grades: Adult 937
1. Roman emperors 2. Rulers 3. Politics and government 4. Civilization 5. Ancient Rome 6. Roman Empire (27 B.C.E.-476 C.E.) 7. Collective biographies 8. History writing — Ancient — Rome 9. Life stories — Politics — Royalty

LC 2018036261

The classical historian and author of the Death of Caesar chronicles three and a half centuries of the Roman Empire through the lives of 10 forefront emperors, from Augustus to Constantine.

Includes bibliographical references and index.

★ *The* **War** *That Made the Roman Empire: Antony, Cleopatra, and Octavian at Actium.* Barry Strauss. Simon & Schuster 2021. 304 p.

ISBN 9781982116675

Grades: Adult 937
1. Cleopatra, Queen of Egypt, 69-30 B.C.E 2. Antonius, Marcus, 83-30 B.C.E 3. Augustus, Emperor of Rome, 63 B.C.E.-14 C.E 4. Civil war 5. Military campaigns 6. Generals 7. Women rulers 8. Naval battles 9. Ancient Rome 10. Roman Republic (509-27 B.C.E.) 11. History writing — Ancient — Rome 12. History writing — Military 13. History writing — Wars and conflicts — Battles 14. Life stories — Law and order — Military leaders

LC 2021007113

Following Caesar's assassination and Mark Antony's defeat of the conspirators who killed Caesar, two powerful men remained in Rome—Antony and Caesar's chosen heir, young Octavian, the future Augustus. When Antony fell in love with the most powerful woman in the world, Egypt's ruler Cleopatra, and thwarted Octavian's ambition to rule the empire, another civil war broke out. In 31 BC one of the largest naval battles in the ancient world took place—more than 600 ships, almost 200,000 men, and one woman—the Battle of Actium. Octavian prevailed and subsequently defeated Antony and Cleopatra, who eventually committed suicide. In this riveting and exciting history, Barry Strauss describes this consequential battle with the drama and expertise that it deserves.

"Historian Strauss (The Caesars) delivers a gripping account of the war for control of the Roman Empire that culminated in Octavian's decisive victory over Mark Antony and Cleopatra at the Battle of Actium in western Greece in 31 BCE." —*Publishers Weekly*

Includes bibliographical references and index.

ESSENTIAL AND RECOMMENDED TITLES
938 Greece to 323

Woolf, Greg
Rome: An Empire's Story. Greg Woolf. Oxford University Press 2012. 384 p.
ISBN 9780199775293
Grades: Adult **937**
1. Imperialism 2. Roman emperors 3. Civilization, Classical 4. Rulers 5. Battles 6. Conquerors 7. Military strategy 8. Civilization, Ancient 9. Religion and politics 10. Conversion to Christianity 11. Gods and goddesses, Roman 12. Ancient Rome 13. Roman Empire (27 B.C.E.-476 C.E.) 14. History writing — Ancient — Rome

Describes how the Roman Empire was created, how it was sustained during crises, and how it shaped the world.

Includes bibliographic references and index.

938 Greece to 323

Everitt, Anthony
The Rise of Athens: The Story of the World's Greatest Civilization. Anthony Everitt. Random House 2016. 512 p.
ISBN 9780812994582
Grades: Adult **938**
1. Greek civilization 2. Architecture, Greek 3. Mythology 4. Literary criticism 5. Ancient Greece 6. Athens, Greece 7. Ancient Greece (800 B.C.E.-640 C.E.) 8. History writing — Ancient — Greece
LC 2016014843

Presents a magisterial account of how Athens became the world's most influential civilization, charting the characteristics, flaws and unique intellectual accomplishments of the ambitious city-civilization and how it helped establish the foundations of today's world.

"Everitt has a gift for making ancient history accessible. Highly recommended to anyone with an interest in world history, Western civilization, philosophy, or political science." —*Library Journal*

Includes bibliographical references and index.

Herodotus
The Histories. Herodotus; translated by Tom Holland; introduction and notes by Paul Cartledge. Viking 2014. xxxix, 833 pages : Illustration
ISBN 9780670024896
Grades: Adult **938**
1. Ancient history 2. Civilization, Ancient 3. Persian Wars, 500-449 B.C.E 4. Ancient Greece 5. Ancient Greece (800 B.C.E.-640 C.E.) 6. Translations — Greek to English 7. History writing — Ancient
LC Bl2014020136

Recounts the causes and history of the wars between the Greek city-states and Persia.

"This ancient Greek historian could easily be called the father of humor; he irreverently describes events, players and their countless harebrained schemes." —*Kirkus*

Includes bibliographical references (pages 745-746) and indexes.

Kagan, Donald
The Peloponnesian War. by Donald Kagan. Viking 2003. xxvii, 511 p. : Illustration; Map
ISBN 9780670032112
Grades: Adult **938**
1. Peloponnesian War, 431-404 B.C.E 2. Military history 3. Ancient Greece 4. Sparta (Extinct city) 5. Athens, Ancient Greece 6. Ancient Greece (800 B.C.E.-640 C.E.) 7. History writing — Ancient — Greece 8. History writing — Wars and conflicts — Peloponnesian War
LC 2002193377

The classical scholar takes a new look at the war between Athens and Sparta, examining the conflict that devastated Ancient Greece in the fifth century B.C.E.

"This is a study of the conflict between Athens and Sparta in the fifth century B.C. {Kagan's primary source is, of course, Thucydides' epic history, but {he draws on Aristotle, Xenophon, and others to provide an objective, nuanced perspective on the military drama. And it's quite a drama: the clash of democracy and oligarchy, the testing of great leaders, the innovative military tactics, and the unprecedented human cost." —*Booklist*

Includes bibliographical references and index.

Thucydides: *The Reinvention of History.* by Donald Kagan. Viking 2009. 272 p.
ISBN 9780670021291
Grades: Adult **938**
1. Thucydides, 460?-395? B.C.E 2. Historians 3. Civilization, Ancient 4. Intellectual life 5. Ancient history 6. Peloponnesian War, 431-404 B.C.E 7. Athens, Ancient Greece 8. Ancient Greece 9. Ancient Greece (800 B.C.E.-640 C.E.) 10. Biographies 11. History writing — Ancient — Greece 12. Life stories — Education — Scholars and educators
LC 2009008368

A Yale professor's reassessment of the life and contributions of the ancient revisionist historian places him in a context of his time, citing the pivotal influence of his refusal to credit the gods or individuals with the societal events documented in the Peloponnesian War.

Includes bibliographical references and index.

Roberts, Jennifer Tolbert
The Plague of War: Athens, Sparta, and the Struggle for Ancient Greece. Jennifer T. Roberts. Oxford University Press 2017. 448 pages
ISBN 9780199996643
Grades: Adult **938**
1. Peloponnesian War, 431-404 B.C.E 2. City-states 3. War and society 4. Strategic alliances (Military) 5. Ancient military history 6. Greece 7. Ancient Greece 8. Athens, Ancient Greece 9. Sparta (Extinct city) 10. Ancient Greece (800 B.C.E.-640 C.E.) 11. History writing — Ancient — Greece 12. History writing — Wars and conflicts — Peloponnesian War
LC 2016012098

Tracing the conflict among the city-states of Greece over several generations, this book argues that the Peloponnesian War did not entirely end in 404 with the capture of the Athenian fleet at Aegospotami in 404 B.C. but rather continued in one form or another well into the fourth century.

"Literate and lucida fine complement and corrective to the ancient sources." —*Kirkus*

Includes bibliographical references and index.

940 History of Europe

Dwork, Deborah
★ *Holocaust: A History.* Deborah Dwork, Robert Jan van Pelt. Norton 2002. xx, 444 p. : Illustration
ISBN 9780393051889
Grades: 11 12 Adult **940**
1. Holocaust (1933-1945) 2. Antisemitism 3. Nazis 4. World War II 5. Jewish people 6. Religious persecution 7. Causes of war 8. Interethnic relations 9. Third Reich, 1933-1945 10. Politics and government 11. Germany 12. History writing — Wars and conflicts — Holocaust — World War II 13. Adult books for young adults
LC 2002023565

A chronicle of events beginning in the Middle Ages through the modern era reveals the unfolding of Nazism and how it brought about the Holocaust, negotiating the division between the histories of its perpetrators and the victims and their families.

"The authors examine such issues as the historic relationship between Jews, gentiles, and Germans; World War I and its consequences; National Socialism in the Weimar Republic; the Third Reich and its anti-Semitic measures; worldwide refugee policies that became a disaster for the Jews; and Jewish and gentile life under German occupation. They also examine the efforts by Allied nations to help the Jews. This is a monumental work of impeccable scholarship." —*Booklist*

Includes bibliographical references (p. 389-428) and index.

PUBLIC LIBRARY CORE COLLECTION: NONFICTION
Twentieth Edition

Hirst, J. B

The Shortest History of Europe: How Conquest, Culture, and Religion Forged a Continent — a Retelling for Our Times. John Hirst; afterword by Filip Slaveski, PhD.. The Experiment 2022. 218 p.

ISBN 9781615199143

Grades: Adult   **940**

1. History 2. Christianity 3. Culture 4. Civilization 5. European history 6. Europe 7. History writing — Europe

The Shortest History of Europe begins with a rapid overview of European civilisation, describing its birth from an unlikely mixture of classical learning, Christianity and German warrior culture. Over the centuries, this unstable blend produced highly distinctive characters—pious knights and belligerent popes, romantics spouting folklore and revolutionaries imitating Rome and its coming apart provided the dynamic of European history in modern times.

"Written in easily approachable style and resonating like the lectures of a beloved and provocative undergraduate history professor, this summary of European history holds broad appeal." —*Booklist*

Originally published in Australia by Black Inc, Collingwood, in 2012; Includes index.

940.1 History of Europe — Early history to 1453

Gies, Joseph

Life in a Medieval Castle. Joseph Gies and Frances Gies. Harper & Row 2015. xv, 272 p. : Illustration

ISBN 9780060906740

Grades: 11 12 Adult   **940.1**

1. Castles 2. Courts and courtiers 3. Medieval military history 4. Military history 5. Civilization, Medieval 6. British history 7. Great Britain 8. Europe 9. Wales 10. Medieval period (476-1492) 11. History writing — Medieval — Europe

LC 79103901

Describes the evolution, architecture, and historical function of the medieval castle and the daily life, habits, and relationships of its inhabitants through a detailed study of England's thirteenth-century Chepstow Castle.

"Using Chepstow Castle on the Welsh border as a model, the authors provide descriptions of the medieval world where the castle was household, feudal center, and military target, and by concentrating on Anglo-Norman examples illustrate what existence was like as the dark ages began to brighten." —*Booklist*

Newly reissued in 2015; Includes bibliographical references (p. 249-261) and index.

Ramirez, Janina

Femina: A New History of the Middle Ages, Through the Women Written Out of It. Janina Ramirez. Hanover Square Press 2023. 320 p.

ISBN 9781335498526

Grades: Adult   **940.1**

1. Femininity 2. Women 3. Civilization, Medieval 4. Europe 5. Medieval period (476-1492) 6. History Writing — Women's history 7. History writing — Medieval — Europe

Through examination of artefacts, writings and possessions, this reappraisal of medieval femininity presents countless cases of influential women such Jadwiga, the only female King in Europe, whose names were struck from history.

"A well-documented study of several significant women of the medieval era….Extensive, well-researched, and readable, this book invites us to reassess the historical record." —*Kirkus*

Originally published in the UK by W.H. Allen, London, in 2022.

Reston, James

The Last Apocalypse: Europe at the Year 1000 A.D. James Reston, Jr. Anchor Books 1999. 299 p. : Illustration; Map

ISBN 9780385483360

Grades: Adult   **940.1**

1. European history 2. Medieval period (476-1492) 3. History writing — Europe

LC BL 99002813

Traces the victories of the kings and popes of Christendom against the seemingly invincible Vikings, Moors, and Hungarian Magyars, shaking the world and confirming the popular belief that history was about to end.

Includes bibliographical references (p. 282-287) and index; Originally published: New York : Doubleday, c1998.

Wickham, Chris

The Inheritance of Rome: Illuminating the Dark Ages, 400-1000. Chris Wickham. Viking 2009. 400 p.

ISBN 9780670020980

Grades: Adult   **940.1**

1. Civilization, Medieval 2. History 3. Culture 4. European history 5. Ancient Rome 6. Medieval period (476-1492) 7. History writing — Europe — Italy

LC 2009015169

Historian Chris Wickham defies conventional views of the "Dark Ages" in European history with a work of rigorous yet accessible scholarship. Drawing on a wealth of new material and featuring a thoughtful synthesis of historical and archaeological approaches, Wickham argues that these centuries were critical in the formulation of European identity. Far from being a "middle" period between more significant epochs, this age has much to tell us in its own right about the progress of culture and the development of political thought. Wickham focuses on a world still profoundly shaped by Rome, which encompassed peoples ranging from Goths, Franks, and Vandals to Arabs, Anglo-Saxons, and Vikings. Digging deep into each culture, Wickham constructs a vivid portraitof a vast and varied world stretching from Ireland to Constantinople, the Baltic to the Mediterranean—the crucible in which Europe would ultimately be created.

"Wickham's achievement contributes richly to our picture of this often narrowly understood period." —*Publishers Weekly*

Includes bibliographical references and index.

940.2 History of Europe — 1453-

Barzun, Jacques

From Dawn to Decadence: 500 Years of Western Cultural Life : 1500 to the Present. Jacques Barzun. Harper Collins 2000. xviii, 877 p.

ISBN 9780060175863

Grades: 11 12 Adult   **940.2**

1. Civilization, Western 2. Learning and scholarship 3. Intellectual life 4. Civilization 5. European history 6. Europe 7. History writing — Europe

LC 99016194

ALA Notable Book, 2001; Booklist Editors' Choice, 2000; Library Journal Best Books, 2000; New York Times Notable Book, 2000; National Book Award for Nonfiction finalist, 2000.

Showcases the triumphs and defeats of five hundred years of Western cultural history, highlighting the contributions of women and arguing that decadance is required in order to spark creativity in the next era.

"Encyclopedic without being discontinuous, the book hardly seems as long, as carefully constructed or as densely packed as it is. Though the ideas it explains are often complicated, the explanations it offers are limpidly clear, sparkling with biographical anecdote and counter-canonical observations." —*New York Times Book Review*

Includes bibliographical references (p. [803]-828) and indexes.

Cornwell, Bernard

Waterloo: The History of Four Days, Three Armies, and Three Battles. Bernard Cornwell. HarperCollins 2015. 352 p.

ISBN 9780062312051

Grades: Adult   **940.2**

1. Napoleon I, Emperor of the French, 1769-1821 2. Wellington, Arthur Wellesley, Duke of, 1769-1852 3. Waterloo, Battle of, 1815 4. Napoleonic Wars, 1800-1815 5. Military campaigns 6. Military history 7. French Revolution, 1789-1799 8. Belgium 9. Germany 10. France 11. 19th century 12. History writing — Wars and conflicts — Napoleonic Wars 13. History writing — Wars and conflicts — Battles

ESSENTIAL AND RECOMMENDED TITLES
940.3 History of Europe — World War I, 1914-1918

LC 2015487235

In his first work of nonfiction, Bernard Cornwell combines his storytelling skills with a meticulously researched history to give a riveting chronicle of every dramatic moment, from Napoleon's daring escape from Elba to the smoke and gore of the three battlefields and their aftermath. Through quotes from the letters and diaries of Emperor Napoleon, the Duke of Wellington, and the ordinary officers and soldiers, he brings to life how it actually felt to fight those famous battles—as well as the moments of amazing bravery on both sides that left the actual outcome hanging in the balance until the bitter end.

Evans, Richard J.
The Pursuit of Power: Europe 1815-1914. Richard J. Evans. Viking 2016. 928 p.
ISBN 9780670024575
Grades: Adult **940.2**
1. World War I 2. Causes of war 3. Politics and government 4. Europe 5. 19th century 6. History writing — Europe

LC 2016044050

Covers the century between the fall of Napoleon to the outbreak of World War I, discussing events ranging from the crumbling of the Spanish, Ottoman and Mughal empires and the rise of British imperial ambition to the violent revolution in Spain and the unifications of Germany and Italy.

"An immensely readable work that considers incremental continental developments up to the outbreak of war in 1914." —*Kirkus*

Grayling, A. C.
The Age of Genius: The Seventeenth Century and the Birth of the Modern Mind. A.C. Grayling. Bloomsbury USA 2016. 352 p.
ISBN 9781620403440
Grades: Adult **940.2**
1. Intellectual life 2. Individualism 3. Human rights 4. Europe 5. 17th century 6. History writing — Europe

LC 2016429801

The Age of Genius explores the eventful intertwining of outward event and inner intellectual life to tell, in all its richness and depth, the story of the 17th century in Europe. It was a time of creativity unparalleled in history before or since, from science to the arts, from philosophy to politics. Acclaimed philosopher and historian A.C. Grayling points to three primary factors that led to the rise of vernacular (popular) languages in philosophy, theology, science, and literature; the rise of the individual as a general and not merely an aristocratic type; and the invention and application of instruments and measurement in the study of the natural world.

"Grayling does a fantastic job of proving his assertion that the 17th century saw a dramatic shift in Western thought. Readers with an interest in the history of philosophy and scientific discovery will enjoy this highly engaging book." —*Library Journal*

Greenblatt, Stephen
★ *The Swerve: How the World Became Modern.* Stephen Greenblatt. W. W. Norton & Co. 2011. 320 p.
ISBN 9780393064476
Grades: Adult **940.2**
1. European Renaissance 2. Humanism (14th-16th centuries) 3. Intellectual life 4. Intellectuals 5. Civilization, Western 6. European history 7. Renaissance (1300-1600) 8. 15th century 9. 16th century 10. 17th century 11. 18th century 12. History writing — Renaissance — Europe

LC 2011019765

ALA Notable Book, 2012; National Book Award for Nonfiction, 2011; New York Times Notable Book, 2011; Pulitzer Prize for General Nonfiction, 2012.

A humanities professor describes the impact had by the translation of the last remaining manuscript of on the Nature of Things by Roman philosopher Lucretius, which fueled the Renaissance and inspired artists, great thinkers and scientists.

"A fascinating, intelligent look at what may well be the most historically resonant book-hunt of all time." —*Booklist*

Also published in large print format.

Manchester, William
A World Lit Only by Fire: The Medieval Mind and the Renaissance : Portrait of an Age. William Manchester. Little, Brown 1993. xvii, 322 p. : Illustration; Map
ISBN 9780316545563
Grades: Adult **940.2**
1. European Renaissance 2. Civilization, Medieval 3. European history 4. Medieval period (476-1492) 5. Renaissance (1300-1600) 6. History writing — Medieval — Europe 7. History writing — Renaissance — Europe

LC BL 99738239

Chronicles the historical transition from the Middle Ages to the Renaissance, profiling the age's leading figures and noting key events and accomplishments.

"The author covers the tumultuous span from the Dark Ages to the dawn of the Renaissance. He delineates an age when invisible spirits infested the air, when tolerance was seen as treachery and 'A mafia of profane popes desecrated Christianity.' Besides re-creating the arduous lives of ordinary people, . . {Manchester peoples his tapestry with such figures as Leonardo, Machiavelli, Lucrezia Borgia, Erasmus, Luther, Henry VIII and Anne Boleyn." —*Publishers Weekly*

Originally published: Boston, MA : Little, Brown, 1992; Includes bibliographical references (p. [297]-306) and index.

O'Keeffe, Paul
Waterloo: The Aftermath. Paul O'Keeffe. Overlook Press 2015. 400 p.
ISBN 9781468311303
Grades: Adult **940.2**
1. Waterloo, Battle of, 1815 2. Napoleonic Wars, 1800-1815 3. Military campaigns 4. War and society 5. European history 6. 19th century 7. History writing — Wars and conflicts — Napoleonic Wars

LC 2015010800

A 200th anniversary account of the last days of the Napoleonic Wars traces the events and aftermath of the battle of Waterloo, as well as the perspective of Napoleon as he considered his surrender, exile and captivity.

Wilson, Ellen Judy
Encyclopedia of the Enlightenment. Peter Hanns Reill, consulting editor; Ellen Judy Wilson, principal author. Facts on File 2004. xvii, 670 p. : Illustration
ISBN 9780816053353
Grades: Adult **940.2**
1. Philosophy 2. Encyclopedias 3. Reference books 4. History writing — Renaissance — Europe

LC 2003022973

Presents a comprehensive introduction to the period, covering such topics as science, education, art and architecture, aesthetics, and music, as well as the key terms, individuals, locations, and significant works.

Includes bibliographical references (p. 643-646) and index.

940.3 History of Europe — World War I, 1914-1918

Carter, Miranda
George, Nicholas and Wilhelm: Three Royal Cousins and the Road to World War I. by Miranda Carter. Alfred A. Knopf 2010. xxv, 498 p, 32 p. of plates : Illustration; Map
ISBN 9781400043637
Grades: 11 12 Adult **940.3**
1. William II, German Emperor, 1859-1941 2. Edward VII, King of Great Britain, 1841-1910 3. Nicholas II, Emperor of Russia, 1868-1918 4. World War I 5. Rulers 6. World politics 7. Causes of war 8. Politics and government 9. German history 10. British history 11. Russian history 12. Europe 13. Edwardian era (1901-1914) 14. Romanov Dynasty (1613-1917) 15. History writing — Europe 16. History writing — Wars and conflicts — World War I

LC 2009037690

Booklist Editors' Choice, 2010.

Draws on correspondence and diaries to trace the parallel stories of monarchs William II of Germany, George v. Of Britain, and Nicholas II of Russia, who at the onset of World War I wrongly counted on their shared family relationship to safeguard European interests.

Includes bibliographical references (p. [469]-478) and index; Originally published as the three emperors: London : Fig Tree, 2009.

Grant, R. G.
World War I: The Definitive Visual History : From Sarajevo to Versailles. R.G Grant. DK Publishing 2018. 372 pages : Illustration; Color
ISBN 9781465470010
Grades: Adult   940.3
1. World War I 2. World War I 3. History writing — Wars and conflicts — World War I 4. History writing — General 5. Reference books — History
LC Bl2018004158

A guide to the first World War features timelines, maps, and accounts of the action to bring to life the world leaders, key players, and soldiers who fought the battles with weapons and new technologies that changed history.

At head of title: DK Smithsonian; Includes index.

Hastings, Max
Catastrophe 1914: Europe Goes to War. by Max Hastings. Alfred A. Knopf 2013. 640 p.
ISBN 9780307597052
Grades: Adult   940.3
1. World War I 2. Military history 3. Causes of war 4. European history 5. 1910s 6. History writing — Wars and conflicts — World War I
LC 2013027865

New York Times Notable Book, 2013.

A history of the early phase of World War I traces the breakdown of diplomatic measures and the dramatic battles that occurred throughout the first year.

"Readers accustomed to Hastings' vivid battle descriptions, incisive anecdotes from all participants, and shrewd, often unsettling opinions will not be disappointed. Among the plethora of brilliant accounts of this period, this is one of the best." —*Kirkus*

Herman, Arthur
1917: Lenin, Wilson, and the Birth of the New World Disorder. Arthur Herman. Harper 2017. 256 p.
ISBN 9780062570888
Grades: Adult   940.3
1. Wilson, Woodrow, 1856-1924 2. Lenin, Vladimir Il'ich, 1870-1924 3. World War I 4. Social change 5. World politics 6. International relations 7. Soviet Union history 8. United States 9. 1910s 10. Russian Revolution and Civil War (1917-1921) 11. History writing — General
LC 2017021669

Chronicles the intertwined stories of Woodrow Wilson and Vladimir Lenin, revealing how their crucial decisions changed world politics and spread disruptive ideologies that continue to influence the modern world.

"Mixing both real events and a few moments of speculation, a fine account of a climacteric year." —*Kirkus*

Includes bibliographical references and index.

Keegan, John
The First World War. John Keegan. Knopf 1999. xvi, 475 p. : Illustration; Map
ISBN 9780375400520
Grades: 11 12 Adult   940.3
1. War 2. Soldiers 3. World War I 4. Military campaigns 5. Causes of war 6. European history 7. 1910s 8. 20th century 9. History writing — Wars and conflicts — World War I
LC 9831826

Booklist Editors' Choice, 1999; Library Journal Best Books, 1999.

A history of the Great War chronicles the events of the conflict from early diplomatic efforts to avert war, through the nightmarish campaigns and battles, to the end of the war and its repercussions.

"This history is elegantly written, clear, detailed and omniscient. As a narrative it is outstanding." —*New York Times Book Review*

Includes bibliographical references (p. 449-455) and index; Originally published: London : Hutchinson, 1998.

MacMillan, Margaret
Paris 1919: Six Months That Changed the World. Margaret MacMillan. Random House 2002. xxxi, 570 p, 16 p. of plates : Illustration
ISBN 9780375508264
Grades: 11 12 Adult   940.3
1. Wilson, Woodrow, 1856-1924 2. Lloyd George, David, 1863-1945 3. Clemenceau, Georges, 1841-1929 4. World War I 5. Treaties 6. Nationalism 7. Reparations 8. Peace 9. Paris, France history 10. German history 11. European history 12. Germany 13. 1910s 14. 20th century 15. Between the Wars (1918-1939) 16. Impartial writing 17. History writing — Wars and conflicts — World War I
LC 2002023707

CBA Libris Award for Non-Fiction Book of the Year, 2003; Governor General's Literary Award for English-Language Nonfiction, 2003; Samuel Johnson Prize for Nonfiction, 2002.

Describes the six months following the end of the First World War when leaders of the great powers, as well as men and women from all over the world, all with their own agendas, converged on Paris to shape the peace.

"MacMillan's lucid prose brings her participants to colorful and quotable life, and the grand sweep of her narrative encompasses all the continents the peacemakers vainly carved up." —*Publishers Weekly*

Includes bibliographical references and index; Originally published as Peacemakers : the Paris Peace Conference of 1919 and its attempt to end war: London : J. Murray, 2001.

McMeekin, Sean
July 1914: Countdown to War. Sean McMeekin. Basic Books 2013. xviii, 461 p. : Illustration; Map
ISBN 9780465031450
Grades: Adult   940.3
1. Militarism 2. Diplomacy 3. World War I 4. Causes of war 5. Political intrigue 6. International intrigue 7. Great powers 8. International relations 9. Politicians 10. European history 11. 20th century 12. History writing — Europe 13. History writing — Wars and conflicts — World War I
LC 2012049777

The award-winning author of the Russian Origins of the First World War traces the efforts of a small group of influential statesmen who used the largely ignored assassination of Archduke Franz Ferdinand to trigger World War I, drawing on new archival evidence to reveal the roles of duplicitous figures in Russia and France in setting the stage for the conflict.

"McMeekin's work is a fine diplomatic history of the period, a must-read for serious students of WWI, and a fascinating story for anyone interested in modern history." —*Publishers Weekly*

Includes bibliographical references and index.

Rogan, Eugene L.
The Fall of the Ottomans: The Great War in the Middle East. Eugene Rogan. Basic Books 2015. 448 p.
ISBN 9780465023073
Grades: Adult   940.3
1. World War I 2. Military history 3. Southwest Asia and North Africa (Middle East) history 4. Turkey 5. Ottoman Empire (1299-1922) 6. 1910s 7. 20th century 8. Impartial writing 9. History writing — Wars and conflicts — World War I 10. History writing — Southwest Asia and North Africa (Middle East)
LC 2015300788

Evaluates the impact of World War I on the Ottoman Empire and the Middle East, while explaining the region's less-understood but essential contributions to the war and the establishment of present-day conflicts.

ESSENTIAL AND RECOMMENDED TITLES
940.309 History of Europe — History, geographic treatment, biography

940.309 History of Europe — History, geographic treatment, biography

Englund, Peter
The Beauty and the Sorrow: An Intimate History of the First World War. by Peter Englund. Alfred A. Knopf 2011. 560 p.
ISBN 9780307593863
Grades: Adult   940.309
1. World War I 2. Military history 3. History 4. 20th century 5. History writing — Wars and conflicts — World War I
LC 2011020828

A revelatory narrative history of World War I explores its impact on everyday men and women, drawing on diaries and letters by 20 individuals from various countries to present an international mosaic of less-represented perspectives.

"Mr. Englund's book is a deviation from standard history books. It is a corrective too to the notion that World War I was only about the dire trench warfare on the Western Front. [It] expertly pans across other theaters of war: the Alps, the Balkans, the Eastern Front, Mesopotamia, East Africa." —*New York Times Book Review*

Includes index; Originally published in Sweden as Stridens Skonhet Och Sorg by Atlantis, Stockholm, in 2009 [i.e. 2008].—T.P. verso.

940.4 Military history of World War I

Bascomb, Neal
The Escape Artists: A Band of Daredevil Pilots and the Grandest Escape of the Great War. Neal Bascomb. Houghton Mifflin Harcourt 2018. 320 p.
ISBN 9780544937116
Grades: Adult   940.4
1. Prisoners of war 2. Escaped prisoners of war 3. World War I 4. Airmen 5. Soldiers 6. Military pilots 7. Courage 8. Escapes 9. First World War era (1914-1918) 10. 1910s 11. History writing — Wars and conflicts — World War I
LC 2017058527

Presents the story of a group of downed Allied airmen who masterminded a courageous and ingenious breakout from Germany's Holzminden POW camp.
Includes bibliographical references and index.

Carroll, Andrew
My Fellow Soldiers: General John Pershing and the Americans Who Helped Win the Great War. Andrew Carroll. Penguin Group USA 2017. 400 p.
ISBN 9781594206481
Grades: Adult   940.4
1. Pershing, John Joseph, 1860-1948 2. American participation in wars 3. World War I 4. Soldiers 5. War and society 6. First World War era (1914-1918) 7. History writing — Wars and conflicts — World War I
LC 2016056754

The best-selling author of War Letters presents a 100th anniversary account of the American experience during World War I, centering on an intimate portrait of General Pershing while drawing on a rich trove of newly uncovered letters to convey the grassroots realities of everyday workers, soldiers, medics and families.

"Carroll uses the personal correspondence of Gen. Pershing . as a means of establishing the war timeline. Varied American perspectives of the war are included, and the letters of African-Americans and women figure prominently in the work." —*Publishers Weekly*

Davenport, Matthew J.
First Over There: The Attack on Cantigny, America's First Battle of World War I. Matthew J. Davenport. Thomas Dunne Books, St. Martin's Press 2015. 360 p.
ISBN 9781250056443
Grades: Adult   940.4
1. World War I 2. Military campaigns 3. Soldiers 4. France 5. 1910s 6. History writing — Wars and conflicts — World War I
LC 2015012154

Relying on letters, diaries and reports by the "doughboys" themselves, the author describes the events that took place on May 28, 1918, when the United States fought and won its first battle of World War I in Cantigny.

"From the 'Creeping barrage' of artillery to the eventual American victory, the reader will hear every explosion, feel each bullet whiz past, and sometimes cry at the loss of a comrade." —*Library Journal*

Includes bibliographical references and index.

Fox, Margalit
The Confidence Men: How Two Prisoners of War Engineered the Most Remarkable Escape in History. Margalit Fox. Random House 2021. 352 p.
ISBN 9781984853844
Grades: Adult   940.4
1. Jones, E. H. (Elias Henry), 1883-1942 2. Hill, C. W. (Cedric Waters), 1891-1975 3. World War I 4. Prisoners of war 5. Escaped prisoners of war 6. Prisoner-of-war escapes 7. Prisoner-of-war camps 8. Soldiers 9. Magicians 10. Swindlers and swindling 11. Hoaxes 12. Spiritualism 13. Friendship 14. Southwest Asia and North Africa (Middle East) history 15. Turkey 16. 20th century 17. History writing — Wars and conflicts — World War I 18. Life stories — Law and order — Prisoners and inmates 19. Nonfiction that reads like fiction
LC 2020044276

Imprisoned in a remote Turkish prison camp during World War I, having survived a two-month forced march and a terrifying shootout in the desert, two British officers, Harry Jones and Cedric Hill, join forces to bamboozle their iron-fisted captors. To stave off despair and boredom, Jones takes a handmade Ouija board and fakes elaborate séances for his fellow prisoners. Word gets around camp, and one day, a Turkish officer approaches Jones with a query: Could Jones contact the spirit world to find a vast treasure rumored to be buried nearby? Jones, a trained lawyer, and Hill, a brilliant magician, use the Ouija board—and their keen understanding of the psychology of deception—to build a trap for the Turkish officers that will ultimately lead them to freedom.

"Fox (Conan Doyle for the Defense), a former obituary writer for the New York Times, recounts in this marvelous history how two British army officers in WWI orchestrated 'The most singular prison break ever recorded.' . . . Readers will be mesmerized by this rich and rewarding tale." —*Publishers Weekly*

Includes bibliographical references and index.

Hynes, Samuel
The Unsubstantial Air: American Fliers in the First World War. Samuel Hynes. Farrar, Straus and Giroux 2014. 352 p.
ISBN 9780374278007
Grades: Adult   940.4
1. World War I 2. Fighter pilots 3. Aviation history 4. Aerial operations 5. History writing — Wars and conflicts — World War I
LC 2014008673

The Unsubstantial Air is the gripping story of the Americans who fought and died in the aerial battles of World War I, told through the words and voices of the aviators themselves.

"The reader quickly becomes aware of the acute danger pilots faced the narratives Haynes utilizes to tell the story often end abruptly with a terse account of a death due to a training accident, mechanical failure, or combat. It is a must read for anyone interested in aviation history, military history, and the American experience in the Great War." —*Publishers Weekly*

Includes bibliographical references and index.

Korda, Michael
Muse of Fire: World War I as Seen Through the Lives of the Soldier Poets. Michael Korda. Liveright Publishing Corporation 2024. 352 p.
ISBN 9781631496882
Grades: Adult   940.4
1. Soldiers 2. Poets 3. World War I 4. Poetry writing 5. War 6. First World War era (1914-1918) 7. Collective biographies 8. Life stories — Law and order — Armed forces personnel 9. Arts and Entertainment — Writing and publishing 10. Life stories — Arts and culture — Writing — Poets 11. History writing — Wars and conflicts — World War I

"The lives and legacies of the young British men known as the 'War poets' of WWI are explored in this agile literary study from biographer Korda (Ulysses S. Grant)." —*Publishers Weekly*

Larson, Erik
★ *Dead Wake: The Last Crossing of the Lusitania.* by Erik Larson. Crown Publishers 2015. 464 p.
ISBN 9780307408860
Grades: Adult   940.4
1. World War I 2. Shipping 3. Passenger ships 4. Naval history 5. Cruise ships 6. Shipwrecks 7. Naval operations 8. Military history 9. Europe 10. North Atlantic Ocean 11. 1910s 12. 20th century 13. History writing — Wars and conflicts — World War I 14. History writing — Natural disasters and tragedies 15. Nonfiction that reads like fiction
LC 2014034182
LibraryReads Favorites, 2015; Library Journal Best Books, 2015; ALA Notable Book, 2016.

The author of in the Garden of Beasts presents a 100th-anniversary chronicle of the sinking of the Lusitania that discusses the factors that led to the tragedy and the contributions of such figures as President Wilson, bookseller Charles Lauriat and architect Theodate Pope Riddle.

"Reader engrossment is tightly sustained as we move back and forth between the Lusitania on its return from New York City to its home port of Liverpool under a black cloud of warnings that the imperial German government considered the waters around Britain to be a war zone, and the rapacious German submarine U-20, stalking the seas for prey like a lion on the Serengeti. Factual and personal to a high degree, the narrative reads like a grade-A thriller." —*Booklist*

Also published in large print format; Includes bibliographical references and index.

Lawrence, T. E.
Seven Pillars of Wisdom: A Triumph. T.E. Lawrence. Anchor Books 1991. 784 p.
ISBN 9780385418959
Grades: 11 12 Adult   940.4
1. Lawrence, T. E. (Thomas Edward), 1888-1935 2. World War I 3. Military campaigns 4. Soldiers 5. British people in Southwest Asia and North Africa (Middle East) 6. Imperialism, British 7. Bedouins 8. Arab people 9. Arabian Peninsula 10. 20th century 11. Autobiographies and memoirs 12. Page to screen 13. History writing — Wars and conflicts — World War I 14. Life stories — Law and order — Armed forces personnel 15. Travel Writing — Southwest Asia and North Africa (Middle East) 16. History writing — Southwest Asia and North Africa (Middle East)

The classic account of the Arab tribes' guerrilla warfare against Turkish forces during World War I and of Lawrence's part in and reflections on that warfare.

Originally published in a private edition by the George Doran Publishing Company in 1926—T.P. verso; Title of film adaptation: Lawrence of Arabia.

Lloyd, Nick
The Western Front: A History of the Great War, 1914-1918. Nick Lloyd. Liveright Publishing Corporation 2021. 640 p.
ISBN 9781631497940
Grades: Adult   940.4
1. World War I 2. Military tactics 3. Western front (World War I) 4. Military engineering 5. Military campaigns 6. War 7. Technological innovations 8. 1910s 9. First World War era (1914-1918) 10. History writing — Wars and conflicts — World War I 11. History writing — Military — Weapons
LC 2020050473

A panoramic history of the savage combat on the Western Front between 1914 and 1918 that came to define modern warfare.

"A rising-star military historian at King's College London, Lloyd ambitiously covers the Western Front from 1914 to 1918, providing intimate detail and showing how the war led to significant technological and tactical advances." —*Library Journal*

Includes bibliographical references and index.

Massie, Robert K.
Castles of Steel: Britain, Germany, and the Winning of the Great War at Sea. Robert K. Massie. Random House 2003. xii, 865 p, 16 p. of plates : Illustration; Map
ISBN 9780679456711
Grades: Adult   940.4
1. Naval history 2. Jutland, Battle of, 1916 3. World War I 4. Military strategy 5. Naval operations 6. North Sea 7. 1910s 8. 20th century 9. History writing — Wars and conflicts — World War I
LC 2003041373
New York Times Notable Book, 2003.

The author continues his study of early twentieth-century military and naval history in an analysis of the confrontation between the two most powerful navies in the world as the British and Germans clashed at sea during World War I.

"The author makes a coherent if long narrative out of a sequence of events familiar to students of naval history but probably not to many other potential readers." —*Publishers Weekly*

Sequel to: Dreadnought; Includes bibliographical references (p. [821]-829) and index.

Moore, Wendy
No Man's Land: The Trailblazing Women Who Ran Britain's Most Extraordinary Military Hospital During World War I. Wendy Moore. Basic Books 2020. 336 p.
ISBN 9781541672727
Grades: Adult   940.4
1. Women physicians 2. World War I 3. Suffragists 4. Women's rights 5. British history 6. First World War era (1914-1918) 7. 20th century 8. History writing — Wars and conflicts — World War I 9. History writing — Women's history 10. History writing — Europe — United Kingdom
LC 2019041778

Documents the story of how two pioneering suffragette doctors transformed modern medicine, broke boundaries and raised standards for patient care in World War I-era London before founding Endell Street's highly respected Suffragette's Hospital.

"Drawing on diaries, letters, and newspaper accounts, Moore narrates with verve and precision, highlighting the pressures and obstacles these women and their staff faced. Readers interested in medical, military, and women's histories will savor this sterling account." —*Publishers Weekly*

Preston, Diana
A Higher Form of Killing: Six Weeks in World War I That Forever Changed the Nature of Warfare. Diana Preston. Bloomsbury Press 2015. 340 p.
ISBN 9781620402122
Grades: Adult   940.4
1. World War I 2. Weapons of mass destruction 3. Airships 4. Torpedoes 5. Poisonous gases 6. Chemical weapons 7. History writing — Wars and conflicts — World War I
LC 2014019999

An acclaimed historian chronicles the birth of weapons of mass destruction during World War I, including the use of poison gas by the Germans at Ypres, the torpedoes that sunk the Lusitania and an aerial bombardment of London by a zeppelin.

"In what is often difficult but necessary reading, Preston provides haunting descriptions of the effects of poison gas. A harrowingand, in this era of drones, absolutely pertinentlook at the rapacious reaches of man's murderous imagination." —*Kirkus*

Tuchman, Barbara W.
★ *The Guns of August.* Barbara W. Tuchman; with a new foreword by Robert K. Massie. Ballantine 1994. xxiv, 511 p. : Illustration; Map
ISBN 9780345386236
Grades: 11 12 Adult   940.4
1. World War I 2. Military campaigns 3. Western Front (World War I) 4. European history 5. 1910s 6. History writing — Wars and conflicts — World War I
LC 93090461

ESSENTIAL AND RECOMMENDED TITLES
940.5 Europe — 1918

Pulitzer Prize for General Nonfiction, 1963.

Barbara Tuchman has brought to life again the people and events that led up to World War I. With attention to fascinating detail, and an intense knowledge of her subject and its characters, Ms. Tuchman reveals, for the first time, just how the war started, why, and why it could have been stopped but wasn't.

Includes bibliographical references (p. 441-455) and index; Originally published: New York : Macmillan, 1962.

940.5 Europe — 1918

Talty, Stephan
Agent Garbo: How a Brilliant, Eccentric Spy Tricked Hitler and Saved D-Day. Stephan Talty. Houghton Mifflin Harcourt 2012. 320 p.
ISBN 9780547614816
Grades: Adult   940.5
1. Pujol, Juan 2. World War II 3. Spies 4. Espionage 5. Secret service 6. Intelligence service 7. Third Reich, 1933-1945 8. Politics and government 9. London, England history 10. Germany 11. Great Britain 12. 20th century 13. Biographies 14. Life stories — Law and order — Spies and secret agents 15. History writing — Wars and conflicts — World War II — European Theater 16. History writing — Spies and spying
LC 2012005470

Describes the life of Juan Pujol, a poultry farmer who opposed the Nazis and concocted a series of staggering lies that lead to his becoming one of Germany's most valued spies, while actually acting as a double-agent for the Allies.

940.53 World War II, 1939-1945

Ackerman, Diane
★ *The Zookeeper's Wife: A War Story*. Diane Ackerman. W.W. Norton 2007. 288 p.
ISBN 9780393061727
Grades: 11 12 Adult   940.53
1. Jewish people 2. Righteous Gentiles in the Holocaust 3. World War II 4. Rescues 5. Zoo keepers 6. Holocaust (1933-1945) 7. Polish people 8. Interethnic relations 9. European history 10. Warsaw, Poland 11. Poland 12. 20th century 13. Biographies 14. Page to screen 15. History writing — Wars and conflicts — Homefront — World War II 16. History writing — Wars and conflicts — Holocaust — World War II 17. Life stories — Politics — Activists and reformers 18. Adult books for young adults
LC 2007012635

ALA Notable Book, 2008; Booklist Editors' Choice, 2007; Library Journal Best Books, 2007.

Documents the true story of Warsaw Zoo keepers and resistance activists Jan and Antonina Zabinski, who in the aftermath of Germany's invasion of Poland saved the lives of hundreds of Jewish citizens by smuggling them into empty cages and their home villa.

"An exemplary work of scholarship and an ecstasy of imagining, Ackerman's affecting telling of the heroic Zabinskis' dramatic story illuminates the profound connection between humankind and nature, and celebrates life's beauty, mystery, and tenacity." —*Booklist*

Also published in large print format; Includes bibliographical references and index.

Aleksievich, Svetlana
Last Witnesses: An Oral History of the Children of World War II. Svetlana Alexievich; translated by Richard Pevear and Larissa Volokhonsky. Random House 2019. 320 pages
ISBN 9780399588754
Grades: Adult   940.53
1. Children and war 2. Child soldiers 3. Child war victims 4. World War II 5. Child witnesses 6. Children 7. Soviet Union history 8. European history 9. Second World War era (1939-1945) 10. 20th century 11. Translations — Russian to English 12. History writing — Wars and conflicts — World War II — European Theater
LC 2018034984

A Nobel Prize-winning author presents an oral history of children's experiences in WWII across Europe and Russia, providing a kaleidoscopic portrait of the human consequences of the war.

"As usual, Alexievich shines a bright light on those who were there; an excellent book but not for the faint of heart." —*Kirkus*

Translation of: Poslednie svideteli : Kniga nedetskikh rasskazov; Originally published: Moscow : Molodaia gvardiia, 1985; Translated from the Russian.

★ *The Unwomanly Face of War: An Oral History of Women in World War II*. Svetlana Alexievich. Random House 2017. 384 p.
ISBN 9780399588723
Grades: Adult   940.53
1. World War II 2. Women soldiers 3. Women's role 4. Women's participation in wars 5. Soviet Union history 6. European history 7. Second World War era (1939-1945) 8. 1940s 9. 20th century 10. Translations — Russian to English 11. History writing — Women's history 12. History writing — Wars and conflicts — World War II — European Theater
LC 2016036099

This absorbing oral history, a Nobel Prize-winning author compiles firsthand reports of Russian women in military service during World War II. Many were reluctant to discuss their experiences; while they often performed similar duties as men (for example, as snipers or tank drivers) their perceptions and experiences differed significantly. Weaving their accounts into a vivid tapestry, the Unwomanly Face of War spotlights previously unnoticed ordeals and historical achievements.

"A worldwide best seller when it was originally published in Russian in 1985, this work by Nobel Prize winner Alexievich . combines hundreds of oral history accounts with the author's own reflections. Alexievich conducted these interviews between 1978 and 1985, intending to capture 'Women's history of war.'" —*School Library Journal*

Originally published by Mastatskaya litaratura in 1985.

Allport, Alan
Britain at Bay: The Epic Story of the Second World War, 1938-1941. Alan Allport. Alfred A. Knopf 2020. xviii, 590 p.
ISBN 9780451494740
Grades: Adult   940.53
1. Military campaigns 2. World War II 3. Politics and government 4. Great Britain 5. 1930s 6. 1940s 7. Second World War era (1939-1945) 8. 20th century 9. History writing — Europe — United Kingdom 10. History writing — Wars and conflicts — World War II — European Theater
LC 2020028530

Here is the many-faceted, world-historically significant story of Britain at war. In looking closely at the military and political dimensions of the conflict's first crucial years, Alan Allport tackles questions such as: Could the war have been avoided? Could it have been lost? Were the strategic decisions the rights ones? How well did the British organize and fight? How well did the British live up to their own values? What difference did the war make in the end to the fate of the nation?

"Expertly researched and marvelously written, this sterling history casts an oft-studied subject in a new light." —*Publishers Weekly*

Includes bibliographical references and index.

Andrews, Lena S.
★ *Valiant Women: The Extraordinary American Servicewomen Who Helped Win World War II*. Lena S. Andrews. Mariner Books 2023. 400 p.
ISBN 9780063088337
Grades: Adult   940.53
1. Women 2. Women and war 3. War 4. World War II 5. Women soldiers 6. American people 7. Second World War era (1939-1945) 8. History Writing — Women's History 9. History Writing — Wars and conflicts — World war II 10. History Writing — United States

In this groundbreaking new history of the role of American women in WWII, a top military analyst for the CIA presents the inspiring, shocking and heartbreaking stories of these servicewomen that reveal a fundamental misunderstanding of the nature of combat in WWII and Illustrates important realities about modern warfighting.

"Binge-able and easily approachable for those new to the subject, this book is perfect for WWII buffs and readers of history, military history, women's history, and feminist nonfiction." —*Booklist*

Batalion, Judith

*The **Light** of Days: The Untold Story of Women Resistance Fighters in Hitler's Ghettos.* Judy Batalion. William Morrow 2022. 352 p.
ISBN 9780062874214
Grades: Adult   940.53
1. Jewish women 2. Jewish resistance and revolts 3. Warsaw Ghetto uprising, 1943 4. Jewish people 5. Female friendship 6. Holocaust survivors 7. Holocaust (1933-1945) 8. Sabotage 9. Espionage 10. Guerrilla warfare 11. World War II 12. Polish people 13. Resistance to military occupation 14. Courage 15. European history 16. Poland 17. Second World War era (1939-1945) 18. Impartial writing 19. History writing — Wars and conflicts — Resistance — World War II 20. History writing — Jewish history 21. History writing — Women's history 22. History writing — Wars and conflicts — Holocaust — World War II

Canadian Jewish Book Award, 2021.

Documents the essential World War II contributions of Jewish-Polish female resistance fighters, sharing the stories of courageous women who risked their lives to work against the Nazis as fighters, intelligence agents and saboteurs.

"A welcome addition to the literature of the Shoah and of anti-Nazi resistance." —*Kirkus*

Berenbaum, Michael

*The **World** Must Know: The History of the Holocaust as Told in the United States Holocaust Memorial Museum.* Michael Berenbaum; Arnold Kramer, editor of photographs. United States Holocaust Memorial Museum 2006. xxi, 250 p. : Illustration; Color
ISBN 9780801883583
Grades: Adult   940.53
1. Holocaust (1933-1945) 2. History writing — Wars and conflicts — Holocaust — World War II 3. Arts and Entertainment — Museums and Collections
LC Bl2006005031

Draws on eyewitness accounts, artifacts, and photographs to tell the story of the perpetrators, bystanders, rescuers, and victims of the Holocaust.

Includes bibliographical references (p. 227-239) and index.

Beschloss, Michael R.

*The **Conquerors**: Roosevelt, Truman, and the Destruction of Hitler's Germany, 1941-1945.* Michael Beschloss. Simon & Schuster 2002. xiv, 377 p, 16 p. of plates : Illustration
ISBN 9780684810270
Grades: Adult   940.53
1. Roosevelt, Franklin D. (Franklin Delano), 1882-1945 2. Truman, Harry S, 1884-1972 3. Morgenthau, Henry, 1891-1967 4. Churchill, Winston, 1874-1965 5. Stalin, Joseph, 1879-1953 6. Reconstruction (1939-1951) 7. Geopolitics 8. World War II 9. Diplomacy 10. International relations 11. Politics and government 12. Germany 13. United States 14. 1940s 15. Second World War era (1939-1945) 16. History writing — Wars and conflicts — World War II
LC 2002030331

New York Times Notable Book, 2002.

Based on recently released documents, one of the nation's most celebrated historians reveals one of the little-known secrets of World War II—FDR's and Truman's sometimes shocking plans for a postwar Germany.

"As German forces were driven back in 1943-45, American leaders were anxious that in 20 years, just as it had done after its defeat in 1918, a vengeful Germany would start another world war. To prevent this, two schools of thought flowed through DC's salons of power: Punishment or rehabilitation. Beschloss covers the meeting-by-meeting, memo-by-memo political battle between the two approaches. Beschloss' comprehensive research and narration into every nuance opens a significant perspective on bureaucratic politics' effect on the Germany that eventually formed in the early cold war." —*Booklist*

Includes bibliographical references (p. 297-314) and index.

Blau, Magda Hellinger

*The **Nazis** Knew My Name: A Remarkable Story of Survival and Courage in Auschwitz.* Magda Hellinger, and Maya Lee; with David Brewster. Atria Books 2021. 352 p.
ISBN 9781982181222
Grades: Adult   940.53
1. Blau, Magda Hellinger, 1916-2006 2. World War II 3. Jewish people 4. Holocaust (1933-1945) 5. Holocaust survivors 6. Prisons 7. Slovakia 8. Autobiographies and memoirs 9. Life stories — Facing adversity — War and oppression — Holocaust 10. History writing — Wars and conflicts — Holocaust — World War II
LC 2021019898

Based on Magda Hellinger's personal account and completed by her daughter's extensive research, this awe-inspiring tale follows Magda, a prisoner selected for leadership, as she secretly saved lives while avoiding suspicion by the SS and risking execution.

"A Holocaust survivor's daughter chronicles how her mother used her influence as a prisoner functionary to save lives at Auschwitz." —*Kirkus*

Cadbury, Deborah

*The **School** That Escaped from the Nazis: The True Story of the Schoolteacher Who Defied Hitler.* Deborah Cadbury. Public Affairs 2022. 320 p.
ISBN 9781541751194
Grades: Adult   940.53
1. Essinger, Anna 2. School principals 3. Schools 4. Jewish people 5. Children 6. World War II 7. Women teachers 8. Nazis 9. Kent, England 10. Germany 11. 1930s 12. 20th century 13. Biographies 14. Life stories — Education — Scholars and educators 15. History writing — Wars and conflicts — Holocaust — World War II 16. History writing — Europe — United Kingdom 17. Life stories — Facing adversity — War and oppression — Holocaust

The true story of a courageous school principal, Anna Essinger, who saw the dangers of Nazi Germany and took drastic steps to save those in harm's way.

"In 1933, to escape the darkness descending over Europe, one teacher transported her entire boarding school from south Germany to Britain's Kent countryside....Cadbury (Princes at War, 2015) tells the story of this remarkable school and its courageous leader as she details the lives of many of the children who made their way out of horror to a safe haven." —*Booklist*

Cahan, Richard

Un-american: The Incarceration of Japanese Americans During World War II. Richard Cahan and Michael Williams; images by Dorothea Lange, Ansel Adams, and other government photographers. CityFiles Press 2016. 240 pages : Illustration
ISBN 9780991541867
Grades: Adult   940.53
1. World War II 2. East Asian Americans 3. Concentration camps 4. Japanese American forced removal and incarceration 5. Second World War era (1939-1945) 6. History writing — United States 7. Society and culture — Ethnic studies
LC Bl2016055107

Photographs captured by U.S. government photographers relate the experiences of Japanese Americans and those of Japanese ancestry throughout their internment during World War II.

Includes bibliographical references (pages 233-238) and index.

Churchill, Winston

*The **Grand** Alliance.* Winston S. Churchill. Houghton Mifflin 1985. xxii, 818 p, 3 leaf of plates : Illustration
ISBN 9780395410578
Grades: 11 12 Adult   940.53
1. Churchill, Winston, 1874-1965 2. Eastern Front (World War II) 3. Strategic alliances (Military) 4. International relations 5. Military campaigns 6. World War II 7. Diplomacy 8. European history 9. Africa 10. Atlantic Ocean 11. 1940s 12. 20th century 13. History writing — Wars and conflicts — World War II
LC 86144261

ESSENTIAL AND RECOMMENDED TITLES
940.53 World War II, 1939-1945

An account of World War II and the union formed between the United States, Great Britain, and the Soviet Union.
Includes index.

Their *Finest Hour.* Winston S. Churchill. Houghton Mifflin 1985. xxiii, 683 p, 3 leaves of plates : Illustration
ISBN 9780395410561
Grades: 11 12 Adult   940.53
1. Churchill, Winston, 1874-1965 2. World War II 3. Diplomacy 4. Military strategy 5. Britain, Battle of, 1940 6. Military campaigns 7. French history 8. European history 9. 1940s 10. 20th century 11. History writing — Europe — United Kingdom 12. History writing — Wars and conflicts — World War II — European Theater
LC 86144253
The former British prime minister describes his first year in office in 1940 and the problems he faced with World War II.
Includes bibliographical references and index.

Triumph and Tragedy. Winston S. Churchill. Houghton Mifflin 1985. xxii, 716 p, 11 leaves of plates : Illustration
ISBN 9780395410608
Grades: 11 12 Adult   940.53
1. Churchill, Winston, 1874-1965 2. Diplomacy 3. International relations 4. World War II 5. Military campaigns 6. European history 7. 1940s 8. 20th century 9. History writing — Wars and conflicts — World War II — European Theater
LC 86144270
The British statesman's account of the political and military theories and events which culminated World War II and solidified East-West conflicts.
Includes index.

Clark, Lloyd
The **Commanders:** *The Leadership Journeys of George Patton, Bernard Montgomery and Erwin Rommel.* Lloyd Clark. Atlantic Monthly Press 2022. 432 p.
ISBN 9780802160225
Grades: Adult   940.53
1. Patton, George S, 1885-1945 2. Montgomery of Alamein, Bernard Law Montgomery, Viscount, 1887-1976 3. Rommel, Erwin, 1891-1944 4. World War II 5. Generals 6. Command of troops 7. Ambition 8. Self-confidence 9. Military campaigns 10. Battles 11. Collective biographies 12. Life stories — Law and order — Military leaders 13. History writing — Wars and conflicts — World War II 14. History writing — Military — Military leadership
LC 2022026989
Born in the two decades prior to World War I, George Patton, Bernard Montgomery, and Erwin Rommel became among the most recognized and successful military leaders of the twentieth century. However, as acclaimed military historian Lloyd Clark reveals in his penetrating and insightful braided chronicle of their lives, they each charted very different, often interrupted, paths to leadership positions commanding hundreds of thousands of American, British, and German troops during World War II. Ultimately, however, their unique abilities to bridge the space between leader and led cemented their legendary reputations.
"Military historian Clark (modern war studies, Univ. of Buckingham; Blitzkrieg) intertwines the lives of Erwin Rommel, George Patton, and Bernard Montgomery in this engaging book....Military history buffs and those wanting to learn about leadership and management styles from three important men of the 20th century will likely eagerly consume this tremendous work." —*Library Journal*
Includes bibliographical references and index.

Cooke, Alistair
The **American** *Home Front, 1941-1942.* Alistair Cooke. Atlantic Monthly Press : 2006. xx, 327 p. : Illustration; Map
ISBN 9780871139399
Grades: Adult   940.53
1. Cooke, Alistair, 1908-2004 2. World War II 3. Social life and customs 4. United States history 5. United States 6. 1940s 7. Depression era (1929-1941) 8. History writing — Wars and conflicts — Homefront — World War II
LC 2005058860
The famed BBC correspondent furnishes an incisive, firsthand portrait of America on the homefront during the early days of World War II, describing the dramatic changes that were occurring throughout the nation during the period as it was transformed from a civilian society to a wartime one, as seen through the eyes of ordinary citizens.
"Crisscrossing the American continent from east to west and north to south, stopping in diners and bus stations and newly humming industrial plants, Mr. Cooke brings to life an America stepping into the unknown, committing its muscle and blood to an enterprise that most citizens could barely articulate, in places most of them had never heard of." —*New York Times*
Includes index; Map on lining papers.

Daniels, Roger
Prisoners Without Trial: Japanese Americans in World War II. Roger Daniels. Hill and Wang 2004. 162 p. : Illustration (A Critical issue)
ISBN 9780809078967
Grades: 11 12 Adult   940.53
1. World War II 2. East Asian Americans 3. Japanese American forced removal and incarceration 4. United States 5. 20th century 6. Second World War era (1939-1945) 7. History writing — Wars and conflicts — World War II 8. History writing — United States
LC 2004047328
Part of Hill and Wang's Critical Issues Series and well established on college reading lists, Prisoners Without Trial presents a concise introduction to a shameful chapter in American history: the incarceration of nearly 120,000 Japanese Americans during World War II. With a revised final chapter and expanded recommended readings, Roger Daniels's updated [2004] edition examines a tragic event in our nation's past and thoughtfully asks if it could happen again.
"An account of the relocation of Japanese Americans during World War II, an injustice prompted not by military necessity but by political and racial motivations. The purpose of this volume is to tell the story in light of the redress legislation enacted in 1988." —*Library Journal [review of 1993 edition]*
Includes bibliographical references (p. [139]-143) and index.

Debreczeni, Jozsef
Cold Crematorium: Reporting from the Land of Auschwitz. József Debreczeni; translated from the Hungarian by Paul Olchváry; with a foreword by Jonathan Freedland. St. Martin's Press 2023. 256 p.
ISBN 9781250290533
Grades: Adult   940.53
1. Debreczeni, Jozsef, 1905-1978 2. Holocaust (1933-1945) 3. World War II 4. Jewish people 5. Hungarian people 6. Concentration camps 7. Serbia 8. Translations — Hungarian to English 9. Autobiographies and memoirs 10. Life stories — Facing adversity — War and Oppression — Holocaust 11. History Writing — Jewish history 12. History Writing — Wars and conflicts — Holocaust — World War II
LC 2023027451
This lost memoir from a Holocaust survivor, translated into English for the first time, provides an eyewitness account of his twelve horrifying months of incarceration and slave labor in World War II Nazi concentration camps. 60,000 first printing.
"An unforgettable testimonial to the terror of the Holocaust and the will to endure." —*Kirkus*
Translated from the Hungarian.

Edsel, Robert M.
The **Monuments** *Men: Allied Heros, Nazi Thieves, and the Greatest Treasure Hunt in History.* Robert M. Edsel with Bret Witter. Center Street 2009. 496 p.
ISBN 9781599951492
Grades: Adult   940.53
1. Art thefts 2. World War II 3. Nazi plunder 4. Art and war 5. Art treasures in war 6. Cultural property 7. Pillage 8. German history 9. Europe 10. 1940s 11. 20th century 12. Page to screen 13. History writing — Wars and conflicts —

World War II 14. True Crime — Heists and Robbery 15. Arts and Entertainment — Painting, Drawing, and Sculpture

LC 2009012255

The previously untold story of a little-known WWII Allied division whose mission was to track down European art and treasures that had been looted by the Nazis at Hitler's command.

Film adaptation by the same name (2013); Includes bibliographical references and index.

Englund, Peter

November 1942: An Intimate History of the Turning Point of World War II. Peter Englund; translated by Peter Graves. Alfred A. Knopf 2023. 464 p.

ISBN 9781524733315

Grades: Adult   940.53

1. World War II 2. Months 3. Battles 4. Geopolitics 5. Soldiers 6. Prisoners of war 7. World War II home front 8. Diary writing 9. Letter writing 10. Second World War era (1939-1945) 11. Diaries 12. Letters 13. Translations — Swedish to English 14. History writing — Wars and conflicts — World War II — European Theater 15. History writing — Wars and conflicts — Homefront — World War II 16. History writing — Wars and conflicts — World War II — Pacific Theater 17. Life stories — People in history — Witness to history

Taking readers back to the most important month of WWII, November 1942, this hugely innovative and gripping history is based solely on the remarkable, deeply personal diaries, letters and memoirs that tell the stories of those who lived through it.

"This gripping and propulsive account, expertly translated by Graves in lyrical prose, recreates the daily uncertainty of war as experienced by regular people with limited information and few resources." —*Publishers Weekly*

Originally published in Swedish as Onda nätters drömmar : November 1942 och andra världskrigets vändpunkt i 360 korta kapitel, by Natur & Kultur, Stockholm, in 2022.

Evans, Richard J.

The Third Reich at War. Richard J. Evans. Penguin Press 2008. 800 p.

ISBN 9781594202063

Grades: Adult   940.53

1. Military history 2. War 3. World War II 4. Third Reich, 1933-1945 5. Armed Forces 6. German history 7. Germany 8. 1940s 9. 1930s 10. Second World War era (1939-1945) 11. History writing — Wars and conflicts — World War II — European Theater 12. History writing — Europe — Germany

LC 2008044765

Booklist Editors' Choice, 2009; New York Times Notable Book, 2009.

A final volume in a trilogy on the history of Nazi Germany traces the rise and fall of the military, the ways in which the Nazis gained compliance and support from the private sector, and Hitler's campaign of racial subjugation and genocide. By the author of The Coming of the Third Reich.

"Perhaps the best of an impressive series, this book is recommended for all libraries." —*Library Journal*

Includes bibliographical references and index.

Fishman, David E.

The Book Smugglers: Partisans, Poets, and the Race to Save Jewish Treasures from the Nazis. David E. Fishman. ForeEdge, an imprint of University Press of New England 2017. 312 p.

ISBN 9781512600490

Grades: Adult   940.53

1. Holocaust (1933-1945) 2. Art thefts 3. World War II 4. Antique thefts 5. Art treasures in war 6. Nazis 7. Cultural property 8. European history 9. 1940s 10. 20th century 11. History writing — Wars and conflicts — Holocaust — World War II

LC 2017018923

National Jewish Book Award, 2017.

"Fishman engagingly tells the astonishing story of a group of dedicated bibliophiles and religious and cultural caretakers determined to save a massive number of Jewish manuscripts and books and other artifacts from the Nazis ." —*Kirkus*

Includes bibliographical references and index.

Frank, Anne

★ *The Diary of a Young Girl: The Definitive Edition.* Anne Frank; edited by Otto H. Frank and Mirjam Pressler; translated by Susan Massotty. Doubleday 1995. 340 p.

ISBN 9780385473781

Grades: 5 6 7 8 9 10 11 12 Adult   940.53

1. Frank, Anne, 1929-1945 2. Holocaust (1933-1945) 3. Hidden children (Holocaust) 4. World War II 5. Jewish people 6. Religious persecution 7. Teenage girls 8. Jewish teenagers 9. Interethnic relations 10. Amsterdam, Netherlands 11. Page to screen 12. Autobiographies and memoirs 13. Biographies — Jewish 14. History books — Wars — Holocaust — World War II 15. Biographies — Identity — Children and teenagers 16. Biographies — People in history — Holocaust

LC 9441379

YALSA Best Books for Young Adults, 1996.

An uncut edition of Anne Frank's diary includes entries originally omitted by her father and provides insight into Anne's relationship with her mother.

"This new translation of Frank's famous diary includes material about her emerging sexuality and her relationship with her mother that was originally excised by Frank's father, the only family member to survive the Holocaust." —*Library Journal*

The diary of a young girl has been closely adapted to a television mini-series in 2009 and into film in 1959 under the title the Diary of Anne Frank. A 1980 television movie of that same name was loosely adapted from the 1959 film.

Frankel, Rebecca

Into the Forest: A Holocaust Story of Survival, Triumph, and Love. Rebecca Frankel. St. Martin's Press 2021. 352 p.

ISBN 9781250267641

Grades: Adult   940.53

1. Rabinowitz family 2. Rabinowitz, Miriam Dworetsky, 1908-1981 3. Rabinowitz, Morris, 1906-1982 4. Lazowski, Philip 5. Jewish families 6. Survival 7. World War II 8. Holocaust survivors 9. Jewish people 10. Polish people 11. Collective biographies 12. Life stories — Facing adversity — War and oppression — Holocaust 13. History writing — Jewish history 14. History writing — Wars and conflicts — Holocaust — World War II

LC 2021016349

The inspiring story of a Polish family who narrowly escaped the Holocaust by fleeing to the Bialowieza Forest, surviving two years of brutal winters, disease and Nazi raids until their 1944 rescue by the Red Army.

"Frankel, author of the best-selling War Dogs (2014), tells the extraordinary story of Miriam and Morris Rabinowitz's enduring love and their determined struggle to survive in eastern Poland during the Holocaust." —*Booklist*

Includes bibliographical references and index.

Freedland, Jonathan

★ *The Escape Artist: The Man Who Broke Out of Auschwitz to Warn the World.* Jonathan Freedland. HarperCollins 2022. 304 p.

ISBN 9780063112339

Grades: Adult   940.53

1. Vrba, Rudolf 2. Concentration camps 3. Jewish men 4. Teenagers 5. Holocaust (1933-1945) 6. World War II 7. Escapes 8. History writing — Wars and conflicts — Holocaust — World War II 9. History writing — Jewish history 10. Life stories — People in history

National Jewish Book Award, 2022.

Tells the incredible story of Rudolf Vrba, a brilliant, yet troubled young man—and gifted "escape artist," whose became the first Jew to break out of Auschwitz to reveal the truth of the death camp to the world, earning his place in the annals of World War II.

"Guardian columnist Freedland debuts with a harrowing account of Rudolf Vrba's escape from Auschwitz and his quest to hold Jewish leaders accountable for failing to prevent more people from dying in the Holocaust….The result is a noteworthy contribution to the history of the Holocaust." —*Publishers Weekly*

ESSENTIAL AND RECOMMENDED TITLES
940.53 World War II, 1939-1945

Friedlander, Saul
Nazi Germany and the Jews: The Years of Persecution, 1933-1939. Saul Friedlander. HarperCollins 1997. xii, 436 p.
ISBN 9780060190422
Grades: Adult   **940.53**
1. Jewish people 2. Holocaust (1933-1945) 3. Western European people 4. German people 5. Religious persecution 6. Interethnic relations 7. Germany 8. 1930s 9. History writing — Wars and conflicts — Holocaust — World War II 10. History writing — Europe — Germany
New York Times Notable Book, 1997.

Examines the anti-Semitism that led to Nazi Germany's attempts to exterminate Europe's Jewish population, focusing on the people and events from the Nazi accession to power in 1933 to the onset of World War II.

"Not the least impressive aspect of Friedlnder's book is the skill with which he juxtaposes different levels of reality within an overall chronological frame, moving from high-level Nazi debates on Jewish policy to the routine brutalities of the SA and SS, and from the perceptions of the average German citizen to those of the victims." —*New York Review of Books*

Includes bibliographical references and index.

Nazi Germany and the Jews: The Years of Extermination, 1939-1945. Saul Friedlander. Harper 2007. 896 p.
ISBN 9780060190439
Grades: Adult   **940.53**
1. Jewish people 2. World War II 3. Holocaust (1933-1945) 4. Religious persecution 5. Germany 6. History writing — Wars and conflicts — Holocaust — World War II
Pulitzer Prize for General Nonfiction, 2008.

An authoritative account of the Holocaust goes beyond usual historical studies to include coverage of the reactions of period world authorities, religious groups, and social groups, in a volume that draws on more than thirty years of research.

Includes bibliographical references and index.

Gilbert, Martin
The Second World War: A Complete History. Martin Gilbert. H. Holt 1991. xviii, 846 p, [64] p. of plates : Illustration; Map
ISBN 9780805017885
Grades: 11 12 Adult   **940.53**
1. World War II 2. Military history 3. European history 4. 20th century 5. History writing — Wars and conflicts — World War II
LC 91028255

A striking new edition of the most authoritative account of the Second World War by one of the greatest living military historians.

"The author begins this study with the invasion of Poland. Gilbert's flowing narrative is spiced with anecdotal details culled from diaries, memoirs and official documents. He is especially skillful at interweaving summaries of military strategy with vignettes of civilian suffering—the genocide of the Jews is never far from view." —*Newsweek*

First owl book revised edition—T.P. verso; an owl book—P. [4] of cover; Includes bibliographical references (p. 749-764) and index.

Goldhagen, Daniel Jonah
Hitler's Willing Executioners: Ordinary Germans and the Holocaust. Daniel Jonah Goldhagen. Vintage Books 1997. x, 634 p. : Illustration; Map
ISBN 9780679772682
Grades: 11 12 Adult   **940.53**
1. Holocaust (1933-1945) 2. Antisemitism 3. War criminals 4. Nazism 5. Psychology 6. Causes of war 7. Germany 8. History writing — Wars and conflicts — Holocaust — World War II
LC BL 99782641

National Book Critics Circle Award for Nonfiction finalist, 1996.

A revisionist study of Nazi Germany and the Holocaust reveals why ordinary Germans from all walks of life participated willingly in the extermination of the Jews.

"The author endeavors to show that the common apologia for the Germans—that Hitler brainwashed them—is nonsense and that most Germans gave their active assent to genocide. An ordinary German commander, for example, might feel himself bound by a strict code of conduct yet not be at all averse to murdering Jews. The book ends with a detailed notes section and an appendix that explains the correct methodology for studying the Nazi period." —*Library Journal*

Includes bibliographical references (p. [487]-613) and index; Originally published: New York : Knopf, 1996.

Goodman, Simon
The Orpheus Clock: The Search for My Family's Art Treasures Stolen by the Nazis. Simon Goodman. Scribner 2015. 352 p.
ISBN 9781451697636
Grades: Adult   **940.53**
1. Goodman, Simon 2. World War II 3. Art thefts 4. Nazis 5. Trials 6. Art treasures in war 7. Art and war 8. Nazi plunder 9. German history 10. 20th century 11. Autobiographies and memoirs 12. History writing — Wars and conflicts — World War II 13. True Crime — Heists and Robbery 14. Arts and Entertainment — Painting, Drawing, and Sculpture 15. Life stories — Facing adversity — War and oppression
LC 2015017171

The author presents a passionate, gripping, true story of his single-minded quest to reclaim what the Nazis stole from his family, their beloved art collection, and to restore their legacy.

Grose, Peter
A Good Place to Hide: How One French Village Saved Thousands of Lives in World War II. Peter Grose. Norton 2015. xxviii, 323 pages : Illustration
ISBN 9781605986920
Grades: Adult   **940.53**
1. World War II 2. Compassion 3. Jewish people 4. Rescues 5. Hiding 6. Nazis 7. Holocaust (1933-1945) 8. Villages 9. Western European people 10. French people 11. Religious persecution 12. German occupation, World War II 13. French history 14. France 15. Australian literature 16. History writing — Wars and conflicts — Holocaust — World War II 17. History writing — Wars and conflicts — Homefront — World War II
LC 2014432733

Describes how the residents of an isolated village in the Loire Valley of France banded together during World War II to provide shelter and sanctuary to 3,500 Jews, hiding them from the Nazis.

Originally published in Sydney (Allen & Unwin, 2014); Includes bibliographical references (pages 315-323).

Gross, Jan Tomasz
Neighbors: The Destruction of the Jewish Community in Jedwabne, Poland. Jan T. Gross. Princeton University Press 2001. x, 261 p. : Illustration; Map
ISBN 9780691086675
Grades: Adult   **940.53**
1. Jewish people 2. Interethnic relations 3. World War II 4. Nazi collaborators 5. Holocaust (1933-1945) 6. Polish people 7. Religious persecution 8. Atrocities 9. Poland 10. History writing — Wars and conflicts — Holocaust — World War II
LC 2003286412

Library Journal Best Books, 2001; National Book Award for Nonfiction finalist, 2001; National Book Critics Circle Award for Nonfiction finalist, 2001.

Documents the brutal 1941 massacre of 1,600 Jewish men, women, and children by their own neighbors in the Polish town of Jedwabne, offering additional examinations of the period's Jewish-Polish relations, the Holocaust, and human responses to occupation and totalitarianism.

Includes bibliographical references and index.

Hayes, Peter
Why?: Explaining the Holocaust. Peter Hayes. W. W. Norton & Company, independent publishers since 1923 2017. 400 p.
ISBN 9780393254365
Grades: Adult   **940.53**

PUBLIC LIBRARY CORE COLLECTION: NONFICTION
Twentieth Edition

1. Holocaust (1933-1945) 2. Jewish people 3. Religious persecution 4. Genocide 5. Persecution by Nazis 6. Antisemitism 7. Causes of war 8. Interethnic relations 9. Third Reich, 1933-1945 10. Germany 11. 20th century 12. History writing — Wars and conflicts — Holocaust — World War II

LC 2016031588

A timely exploration of the most commonly asked questions about the Holocaust challenges common misconceptions and discusses how no single theory fully explains the tragedy, drawing on a wealth of scholarly research and experience to offer new insights to future generations.

Includes bibliographical references and index.

Helm, Sarah
Ravensbruck: Life and Death in Hitler's Concentration Camp for Women. Sarah Helm. Nan A. Talese/Doubleday 2014. 656 p.

ISBN 9780385520591

Grades: Adult   940.53

1. World War II 2. Women internment camp inmates 3. Concentration camps 4. History writing — Wars and conflicts — World War II

LC 2014014974

Traces the sobering history of World War II's largest female concentration camp, revealing the torturous experiences and deaths of thousands of women prisoners of more than twenty nationalities.

"This book deserves significant attention, both for Helm's notable interviews of aging witnesses and as a beautifully written history of events that offers additional insight into Nazism and those caught in its path." —*Publishers Weekly*

Includes index.

Henderson, Bruce B.
Bridge to the Sun: The Secret Role of the Japanese Americans Who Fought in the Pacific in World War II. Bruce Henderson. Alfred A. Knopf 2022. 448 p.

ISBN 9780525655817

Grades: Adult   940.53

1. World War II 2. Japanese American forced removal and incarceration 3. Children of immigrants 4. Volunteer army 5. Undercover operations 6. Combat 7. Translating and interpreting 8. Military intelligence 9. Concentration camps 10. Prisoners of war 11. East Asian Americans 12. Military history 13. United States 14. Second World War era (1939-1945) 15. History writing — Wars and conflicts — World War II — Pacific Theater 16. History writing — Immigration — United States 17. Life stories — Law and order — Armed forces personnel 18. Life stories — Identity — Race and ethnicity 19. History writing — Military

After Japan's surprise attack on Pearl Harbor, the U.S. military was desperate to find Americans who spoke Japanese to serve in the Pacific war. They soon turned to the Nisei—first-generation U.S. citizens whose parents were immigrants from Japan. Eager to prove their loyalty to America, several thousand Nisei—many of them volunteering from the internment camps where they were being held behind barbed wire—were selected by the Army for top-secret training, then were rushed to the Pacific theater. These Japanese American soldiers operated in elite intelligence teams alongside Army infantrymen and Marines on the front lines of the Pacific war.

"This exceptional history documents the crucial part played by Japanese American soldiers and interpreters in the Pacific theater of WWII." —*Publishers Weekly*

Sons and Soldiers: The Untold Story of the Jews Who Escaped the Nazis and Returned with the U.S. Army to Fight Hitler. Bruce Henderson. William Morrow 2017. 384 p.

ISBN 9780062419095

Grades: Adult   940.53

1. World War II 2. Jewish history 3. Military interrogation 4. Refugees 5. Intelligence officers 6. European history 7. United States history 8. Second World War era (1939-1945) 9. 1940s 10. 20th century 11. History writing — Wars and conflicts — World War II — European Theater 12. History writing — Jewish history 13. History writing — Military — Special Forces

LC Bl2017020900

Drawing on veteran interviews and archival research, an account of the lesser-known contributions of the German-born Jewish-American soldiers known as the Ritchie Boys describes how they risked their lives to join major combat units and gather crucial intelligence from German POWs.

"A gripping addition to the literature of the period and an overdue tribute to these unique Americans." —*Kirkus*

Herman, Arthur
Freedom's Forge: How American Business Built the Arsenal of Democracy That Won World War II. Arthur Herman. Random House 2012. 400 p.

ISBN 9781400069644

Grades: Adult   940.53

1. World War II 2. Industrial mobilization 3. Industrial management 4. Manufacturing industry and trade 5. Economic policy 6. Economics 7. United States 8. 20th century 9. History writing — Wars and conflicts — World War II 10. Business and economics — Economics — History

LC 2011040661

Herman pens this look at how two businessmen turned the U.S. into a military powerhouse during World War II. In 1940, FDR asked General Motors CEO William Knudsen to oversee the production of guns, tanks, and planes needed for the war. Meanwhile, industrialist Henry J. Kaiser presided over the building of "Liberty ships"—vessels that came to symbolize America's great wartime output.

Includes bibliographical references and index.

Holden, Wendy
★ *Born Survivors: Three Young Mothers and Their Extraordinary Story of Courage, Defiance, and Hope.* Wendy Holden. HarperCollins 2015. 320 p.

ISBN 9780062370259

Grades: Adult   940.53

1. Holocaust survivors 2. Jewish women 3. Concentration camps 4. Pregnant women 5. Survival 6. Holocaust (1933-1945) 7. World War II 8. History writing — Wars and conflicts — Holocaust — World War II 9. History writing — Wars and conflicts — World War II 10. Adult books for young adults

LC Bl2015016220

In a true account, three pregnant women meet in Auschwitz where they, managing to conceal their pregnancies from the infamous Nazi doctor Josef Mengele, fight for their survival as well as the survival of their newborns as they embark on a treacherous journey to freedom.

"An engrossing, intense, and highly descriptive narrative chronicling the ghastly conditions three pregnant women suffered through at the hands of the Nazis." —*Kirkus*

Holland, James
The Savage Storm: The Battle for Italy 1943. James Holland. Atlantic Monthly Press 2023. 480 p.

ISBN 9780802161604

Grades: Adult   940.53

1. World War II 2. Military campaigns 3. Battles 4. Command of troops 5. Soldiers 6. Military history 7. Italy 8. Second World War era (1939-1945) 9. History writing — Wars and conflicts — World War II — European Theater 10. History writing — Military 11. Life stories — Law and order — Armed forces personnel

LC 2023034790

Following victory in Sicily, while the central command planned the spring 1944 invasion of France, Allied troops crossed into southern Italy in September 1943, expecting to drive Axis forces north and liberate Rome by Christmas. Italy quickly surrendered but German divisions fiercely resisted, and the hoped-for quick victory descended into one of the most challenging and protracted battles of the entire war. Putting readers vividly in the moment as events unfolded, with characters made unforgettable by their own words, James Holland's the Savage Storm is a defining account of the pivotal months leading to Monte Cassino, and a landmark in the writing about war.

"A riveting, often appalling look at an under-recognized part of the fight against Hitler." —*Kirkus*

Includes bibliographical references and index.

ESSENTIAL AND RECOMMENDED TITLES
940.53 World War II, 1939-1945

Hurowitz, Richard
In the Garden of the Righteous: The Heroes Who Risked Their Lives to Save Jews During the Holocaust. Richard Hurowitz. HarperCollins 2022. 320 p.
ISBN 9780063037236
Grades: Adult   940.53
1. Holocaust (1933-1945) 2. Anti-Nazi movement 3. World War II 4. Righteous Gentiles in the Holocaust 5. Jewish people 6. Undercover operations 7. Collective biographies 8. Life stories — People in history 9. Life stories — Facing adversity — War and oppression 10. History Writing — Wars and conflicts — Holocaust — World War II 11. History Writing — Wars and conflicts — Resistance — World War II

A collection of inspiring profiles pay tribute to the incredible deeds of the Righteous Among the Nations, little-known heroes who saved countless lives during the Holocaust.

"A deep dive into the lives of 10 heroic individuals who rescued Jews during the Holocaust....A fresh, engrossing contribution to the literature on the Holocaust, focusing on heroics rather than despair." —*Kirkus*

Iperen, Roxane van
★ *The Sisters of Auschwitz: The True Story of Two Jewish Sisters' Resistance in the Heart of Nazi Territory.* Roxane Van Iperen. HarperCollins 2021. 352 p.
ISBN 9780063097629
Grades: Adult   940.53
1. Brilleslijper, Lien 2. Brilleslijper, Janny 3. Sisters 4. Jewish women 5. Jewish resistance and revolts 6. Resistance to military occupation 7. Jewish people 8. Survival 9. Holocaust (1933-1945) 10. Dutch people 11. Western European people 12. German occupation, World War II 13. European history 14. Amsterdam, Netherlands 15. Netherlands 16. Second World War era (1939-1945) 17. Collective biographies 18. History writing — Wars and conflicts — Holocaust — World War II 19. Life stories — Facing adversity — War and Oppression — Holocaust 20. History writing — Wars and conflicts — World War II — European Theater 21. History writing — Jewish history

The unforgettable story of two unsung heroes of World War II: Sisters Janny and Lien Brilleslijper who joined the Dutch Resistance, helped save dozens of lives, were captured by the Nazis, and ultimately survived the Holocaust.

"Dutch lawyer and novelist van Iperen weaves a spellbinding story of resistance and survival during WWII.... Offering fascinating insights into Amsterdam's Jewish Quarter, the fate of the Frank family, and the bonds of sisterly devotion, this standout history isn't to be missed." —*Publishers Weekly*

Kaiser, Menachem
Plunder: A Memoir of Family Property and Nazi Treasure. Menachem Kaiser. Houghton Mifflin Harcourt 2020. 288 p.
ISBN 9781328508034
Grades: Adult   940.53
1. Kaiser, Meir Menachem, 1921-1977 2. Kaiser family 3. Inheritance and succession 4. Nazi plunder 5. Jewish property 6. reparations 7. Holocaust survivors 8. World War II 9. Treasure troves 10. Pillage 11. German occupation, World War II 12. European history 13. Poland 14. 20th century 15. Autobiographies and memoirs 16. Life stories — Facing adversity — War and oppression — Holocaust 17. History writing — Wars and conflicts — Holocaust — World War II 18. Nonfiction that reads like fiction
LC 2020033851
Canadian Jewish Book Award, 2021.

From a gifted young writer, the story of his quest to reclaim his family's apartment building in Poland-and of the astonishing entanglement with Nazi treasure hunters that follows.

"Fulbright fellow Kaiser invites the reader to share his journey to reclaim family property lost during the Holocaust.... This exceptional book will deeply engage readers interested in Jewish, Polish, and WWII history, especially the Holocaust and its aftermath, including the redemptive hunt for family treasures stolen by the Nazis." —*Booklist*

Karski, Jan
Story of a Secret State: My Report to the World. Jan Karski; foreword by Madeleine Albright. Georgetown University Press 2013. xxxi, 414 p.
ISBN 9781589019836
Grades: Adult   940.53
1. Karski, Jan, 1914-2000 2. World War II 3. Prisoners of war, Polish 4. Concentration camps 5. German occupation, World War II 6. European history 7. Poland 8. 1940s 9. Autobiographies and memoirs 10. Life stories — Facing adversity — War and oppression — War survivors 11. History writing — Wars and conflicts — World War II — European Theater 12. History writing — Europe — Eastern Europe
LC 2012037549

Karski, who was posthumously awarded the Presidential Medal of Freedom in 2012, served as a liaison officer and courier of the Polish Underground during WWII and brought the first eyewitness accounts of the Nazi death camps to the outside world. Full of alternate identities, daring escapes, and heroism, his memoir details the operations of the Polish government in exile as part of a larger network of clandestine resistance organizations. The book was a bestseller when it was first published in 1944. This reprint of the 2010 edition follows the text of the original 1944 US edition, supplemented with translations of additional material provided by the author in 1999 for the Polish edition. This edition includes previously unpublished b&w historical photos, documents, and letters, plus a glossary. This edition also includes a foreword by Madeleine Albright, a biographical essay by a Yale historian, and an afterword by Zbigniew Brzezinski.

"Briskly paced, this is a gripping and immediate account of Nazi brutality from a brave leader of the resistance. Karski, who died in 2000, was awarded a posthumous Presidential Medal of Freedom in 2012." —*Publishers Weekly*

Originally published: 1944; Includes bibliographical references and index.

Keegan, John
The Second World War. John Keegan. Viking 1990. 608 p. : Illustration; Map
ISBN 9780670823598
Grades: Adult   940.53
1. World War II 2. Military history 3. Military strategy 4. History writing — Wars and conflicts — World War II
LC 89016682

Marking the sixtieth anniversary of the end of World War II, this landmark history of the conflict surveys the events, strategies, campaigns, and personalities of World War II, and covers in depth five key battles, weapons production, espionage, and the Resistance, among other topics.

"An informed and informative accounting of a horrific war that, the author suggests in an affecting epilogue, might just have saved the world from wider-ranging hostilities. The text is profusely illustrated, with dramatic photographs and helpful maps throughout." —*Kirkus*

Includes bibliographical references (p. 596-598); First published London : Hutchinson, c1989.

Kershaw, Alex
Avenue of Spies: A True Story of Terror, Espionage, and One American Family's Heroic Resistance in Nazi-occupied Paris. Alex Kershaw. Crown 2015. 304 p.
ISBN 9780804140034
Grades: Adult   940.53
1. Jackson, Sumner Waldron 2. French Resistance (World War II) 3. World War II 4. Resistance to military occupation 5. Spies 6. Physicians 7. American people in France 8. Intelligence service 9. Nazism 10. Surgeons 11. Families 12. Nazi collaborators 13. Secrets 14. Military pilots 15. Military history 16. German occupation, World War II 17. Courage 18. French history 19. Paris, France 20. 20th century 21. Biographies 22. History writing — Spies and spying 23. Life stories — Law and order — Spies and secret agents 24. History writing — Wars and conflicts — World War II — European Theater 25. History writing — Wars and conflicts — Resistance — World War II
LC 2015016861
Booklist Editors' Choice, 2015.

Documents the story of American doctor Sumner Jackson in Nazi-occupied Paris and his life-risking espionage contributions to the French resistance during World War II.

"Kershaw tells their story in an intense, moving account that also serves to vividly describe the life of ordinary Parisians under the occupation." —*Booklist*

PUBLIC LIBRARY CORE COLLECTION: NONFICTION
Twentieth Edition

Kertzer, David I.
The Pope at War: The Secret History of Pius XII, Mussolini, and Hitler. David I. Kertzer. Random House 2022. 672 p.
ISBN 9780812989946
Grades: Adult 940.53
1. Pius XII, Pope, 1876-1958 2. World War II 3. Popes 4. Judaism 5. Interfaith relations 6. Holocaust (1933-1945) 7. Jewish people 8. Church history 9. European people 10. Religious persecution 11. Diplomacy 12. International relations 13. Italian history 14. Vatican City 15. Life stories — Religion and spirituality — Religious and spiritual leaders 16. Spirituality and Religion — Christianity — Catholicism 17. History writing — Wars and conflicts — Holocaust — World War II 18. History writing — Europe

LC 2022000861

Based on newly opened Vatican archives, a Vatican scholar paints a new, dramatic portrait of what Pope Pius XII, one of the most controversial popes in Church history, did and did not do during WWII as the Nazis began their systematic mass murder of Europe's Jews.

"Drawing on recently unsealed documents from the Vatican archives, Pulitzer winner Kertzer (The Pope and Mussolini) delivers a devastating look at how Pope Pius XII put the preservation of the Catholic Church ahead of 'Courageous moral leadership' during WWII." —*Publishers Weekly*

Includes bibliographical references and index.

Kinstler, Linda
Come to This Court and Cry: How the Holocaust Ends. Linda Kinstler. Public Affairs 2022. 304 p.
ISBN 9781541702592
Grades: Adult 940.53
1. War crimes 2. World War II 3. Holocaust (1933-1945) 4. Holocaust survivors 5. Trials 6. Justice 7. Memory 8. Criminal investigation 9. History writing — Wars and conflicts — Holocaust — World War II

An author investigates both her family story and the archives of ten nations in this story of the post-Holocaust era in Europe and how that legacy extends into the present.

"Journalist Kinstler debuts with a captivating investigation into 'How the memory of the Holocaust extends into the present and acts upon it.'…The result is a fascinating and often troubling account of how the past haunts the present." —*Publishers Weekly*

Kix, Paul
The Saboteur: The Aristocrat Who Became France's Most Daring Anti-nazi Commando. Paul Kix. HarperCollins 2017. 416 p.
ISBN 9780062322524
Grades: Adult 940.53
1. French Resistance (World War II) 2. Spies 3. Sabotage 4. Espionage 5. International intrigue 6. Subversive activities 7. Unconventional warfare 8. World War II 9. Intelligence officers 10. Special forces 11. Aristocracy 12. German occupation, World War II 13. French history 14. European history 15. Second World War era (1939-1945) 16. 20th century 17. Biographies 18. Life stories — Law and order — Spies and secret agents 19. History writing — Wars and conflicts — Resistance — World War II 20. History writing — Wars and conflicts — World War II — European Theater

LC 2017276823

The senior editor of ESPN the Magazine presents a first book in which he illuminates the life and exploits of British Special Operations Executive and French Resistance hero Robert de la Rochefoucald, tracing his privileged upbringing, his elite military training and the missions he conducted as an Allied spy.

"This thoroughly sourced account is highly readable and effectively showcases the life of a fascinating, complex man whose too-little-known role in the Resistance will be of great interest to followers of WWII history." —*Booklist*

Larman, Alexander
The Windsors at War: The King, His Brother, and a Family Divided. Alexander Larman. St. Martin's Press 2023. 352 p.
ISBN 9781250284587
Grades: Adult 940.53
1. Windsor, House of 2. George VI, King of Great Britain, 1895-1952 3. Windsor, Edward, Duke of, 1894-1972 4. Rulers 5. Royal houses 6. Families 7. World War II 8. Politics and government 9. Great Britain 10. 20th century 11. Biographies 12. History writing — Europe — United Kingdom 13. Life stories — Politics — Royalty 14. History Writing — Wars and conflicts — World War II

LC 2022052677

The next volume in the author's chronicle of the Windsor family follows the royals as they go to war with Adolf Hitler—and each other.

"The second in a series about the Windsor family follows the hand-wringing over Edward VIII's perfidy courting the Nazis during World War II—and official attempts to contain him." —*Kirkus*

Includes bibliographical references and index.

Levi, Primo
★ *The Drowned and the Saved.* Primo Levi; translated from the Italian by Raymond Rosenthal. Vintage International 1989. 203 p.
ISBN 9780679721864
Grades: Adult 940.53
1. Levi, Primo 2. Holocaust (1933-1945) 3. Authors, Italian 4. 20th century 5. History writing — Wars and conflicts — Holocaust — World War II

LC 88040375

A meditation on the meaning of the Nazi exterminations after the passing of forty years reveals how memories of the Holocaust have been filtered and rearranged by both the oppressor and the victims.

"If the unending tragedy of the Holocaust can ever be said to make sense, then it does so in these pages." —*The New Yorker*

Translation of: I Sommersi e i salvati; Reprint. Originally published: New York : Summit Books, 1988.

Lipstadt, Deborah E.
History on Trial: My Day in Court with David Irving. Deborah E. Lipstadt. Ecco 2006. xxi, 346 p. : Illustration
ISBN 9780060593766
Grades: 11 12 Adult 940.53
1. Irving, David, 1938- 2. Lipstadt, Deborah E, 1947- 3. Trials (Libel) 4. Holocaust (1933-1945) 5. Holocaust denial 6. Historiography 7. London, England 8. Page to screen 9. History writing — Wars and conflicts — Holocaust — World War II 10. Adult books for young adults

LC 2004057533

National Jewish Book Award, 2005.

Chronicles the author's legal battle with David Irving, a prolific supporter of Holocaust denial, and describes how the author and a team of experts defended against Irving's libel suit while exposing his distortions of history.

"No one who cares about historical truth, freedom of speech or the Holocaust will avoid a sense of triumph from Gray's decision—or a sense of dismay that British libel laws allowed such intimidation by Irving of a historian and a publisher in the first place." —*Publishers Weekly*

History on Trial inspired the 2016 film Denial, directed by Mick Jackson and starring Rachel Weisz, Andrew Scott, and Timothy Spall; Includes bibliographical references (p. [311]-328) and index.

Loftis, Larry
★ *The Watchmaker's* Daughter: The True Story of World War II Heroine Corrie Ten Boom. Larry Loftis. William Morrow and Company 2023. 384 p.
ISBN 9780063234581
Grades: Adult 940.53
1. Ten Boom, Corrie 2. Clock and watch makers 3. Survival 4. World War II 5. Concentration camps 6. Missionaries 7. Righteous Gentiles in the Holocaust 8. Holocaust (1933-1945) 9. Christian women 10. Faith (Christianity) 11. Dutch people 12. Faith 13. Biographies 14. Life stories — Facing adversity — War and oppression — War survivors 15. History Writing — Wars and conflicts — World War II 16. Life stories — Religion and spirituality — Personal faith 17. History writing — Wars and conflicts — Holocaust — World War II

A New York Times best-selling author writes the first major biography of Corrie ten Boom, a Dutch watchmaker who saved the lives of hundreds of Jews

ESSENTIAL AND RECOMMENDED TITLES
940.53 World War II, 1939-1945

during World War II—at the cost of losing her family and being sent to a concentration camp, only to survive, forgive her captors and live the rest of her life as a Christian missionary.

"Historian Loftis (The Princess Spy) brings to life the first major biography about Corrie ten Boom (1892?1983) while also illuminating the Nazi resistance movement in the Netherlands....A haunting and inspiring tale of moral courage." —*Library Journal*

Lower, Wendy
Hitler's Furies: German Women in the Nazi Killing Fields. Wendy Lower. Houghton Mifflin Harcourt 2013. 288 p.
ISBN 9780547863382
Grades: Adult   940.53
1. World War II 2. Nazism 3. Women 4. Holocaust (1933-1945) 5. War criminals 6. Women's participation in wars 7. Europe 8. History writing — Wars and conflicts — Holocaust — World War II 9. History writing — Wars and conflicts — World War II
LC 2013026081

National Book Award for Nonfiction finalist, 2013.

A revelatory history of the role of German women in the Holocaust reveals their lesser-known roles as plunderers, witnesses and actual executioners on the Eastern front, describing how period nurses, teachers, secretaries and wives responded to what they believed to be Nazi opportunities only to perform brutal duties.

"Lower, a consultant for the Holocaust Memorial Museum in Washington, D.C, sheds some much-needed light on an aspect of WWII history that has remained in the shadows for decades. The consensus in Holocaust and genocide studies, the author writes, is that the systems that make mass murder possible would not function without the broad participation of society, and yet nearly all histories of the Holocaust leave out half of those who populated that society, as if women's history happens somewhere else. Based on two decades of research and interviews, the book looks at the role of women in Nazi Germany, in particular women who participated in the Nazi extermination of the Jews...Lower writes about horribly violent female concentration-camp guards; of young girls trained in the use of firearms; of brutality that would rival anything perpetrated by their male counterparts. Surprising and deeply unsettling, the book is a welcome addition to the literature on the Holocaust." —*Booklist*

Lukacs, John
Five Days in London, May 1940. John Lukacs. Yale University Press 1999. xvi, 236 p. : Illustration
ISBN 9780300080308
Grades: Adult   940.53
1. Halifax, Edward Frederick Lindley Wood, Earl of, 1881-1959 2. Churchill, Winston, 1874-1965 3. World War II 4. Diplomacy 5. Military history 6. Politics and government 7. Great Britain 8. 20th century 9. History writing — Wars and conflicts — World War II — European Theater
LC 99027583

"This work focuses on the chaotic few days during which, according to the author, Hitler came closest to winning the war. Lukacs concentrates on the struggle within the British War Cabinet, which pitted the Prime Minister, Winston Churchill, against the Foreign Secretary, Lord Halifax, a Tory idol and a friend of the King. The point of contention was Halifax's belief that England should attempt to negotiate a general European settlement with Hitler. Churchill's stubborn refusal won out. The author's equally stubborn digging uncovered a stunning amount of defeatism and intrigue against Churchill by contemporary statesmen." —*The New Yorker*

Includes bibliographical references (p. 221-227) and index.

Macadam, Heather Dune
999: The Extraordinary Young Women of the First Official Jewish Transport to Auschwitz. Heather Dune Macadam; foreword by Caroline Moorehead. Citadel Press 2019. xxv, 438 pages, [32] pages of plates : Illustration
ISBN 9780806539362
Grades: Adult   940.53
1. Jewish women 2. Single women 3. Concentration camps 4. Holocaust (1933-1945) 5. Persecution by Nazis 6. Atrocities 7. Courage 8. Poland 9. Slovakia 10. Second World War era (1939-1945) 11. 1940s 12. History writing — Jewish history 13. History writing — Wars and conflicts — Holocaust — World War II
LC 2019944522

Reveals the poignant stories of the 999 women on the first official transport to Auschwitz, drawing on extensive interviews with survivors, and consulting with historians, witnesses and relatives of those first deportees.

"This careful, sympathetic history illuminates an incomprehensible human tragedy." —*Publishers Weekly*

Includes bibliographical references (pages 409-417) and index.

Mazower, Mark
Hitler's Empire: How the Nazis Ruled Europe. Mark Mazower. Penguin Press 2008. 768 p.
ISBN 9781594201882
Grades: Adult   940.53
1. Nazis 2. Political leadership 3. Nazism 4. Antisemitism 5. World War II 6. Third Reich, 1933-1945 7. European history 8. Germany 9. 20th century 10. History writing — Wars and conflicts — World War II 11. History writing — Europe — Germany
LC 2008026997

Los Angeles Times Book Prize for History, 2008.

Profiles the Reich's pre-World War II plans for transforming Eastern Europe, describing the considerable resources that were amassed for the endeavor while explaining how Nazi brutality and short-sightedness ultimately cost Germany its victories.

Includes bibliographical references and index.

McConahay, Mary Jo
The Tango War: The Struggle for the Hearts, Minds and Riches of Latin America During World War II. Mary Jo McConahay. St. Martin's Press 2018. 320 p.
ISBN 9781250091239
Grades: Adult   940.53
1. World War II 2. International relations 3. Political intrigue 4. War and society 5. South American history 6. Latin America 7. History writing — Wars and conflicts — World War II 8. History writing — Latin America
LC 2018011523

Traces the lesser-known story of the fight for the allegiance of Latin America during World War II, tracing the region's essential role in supplying important materials, providing military support and negotiating prisoner exchanges.

Includes bibliographical references and index.

McDougall, Christopher
Natural Born Heroes: How a Daring Band of Misfits Mastered the Lost Secrets of Strength and Endurance. Christopher McDougall. Alfred A. Knopf 2015. 368 p.
ISBN 9780307594969
Grades: Adult   940.53
1. Pheidippides, fl. 490 B.C.E 2. Marathon, Battle of, Greece, 490 B.C.E 3. Marathon running 4. Endurance sports 5. Running 6. Sports and competition — General
LC 2014047459

The author of the best-selling Born to Run describes his investigation into ancestral training techniques that have enabled Mediterranean athletes to achieve extraordinary levels of strength and fitness.

McKean, David
Watching Darkness Fall: FDR, His Ambassadors, and the Rise of Adolf Hitler. David McKean. St. Martin's Press 2021. 416 p.
ISBN 9781250206961
Grades: Adult   940.53
1. Roosevelt, Franklin D. (Franklin Delano), 1882-1945 2. Kennedy, Joseph P. (Joseph Patrick), 1888-1969 3. Dodd, William, 1869-1940 4. Long, Breckinridge, 1881-1958 5. Bullitt, William C. (William Christian), 1891-1967 6. Ambassadors 7. Fascism 8. Aggression (International relations) 9. Military

occupation 10. Diplomacy 11. Presidents 12. World War II 13. International relations 14. United States 15. Europe 16. Second World War era (1939-1945) 17. 20th century 18. Collective biographies 19. Life stories — Politics — Politicians 20. History writing — Presidency — 20th century — United States 21. History writing — Wars and conflicts — World War II — European Theater 22. Life stories — People in history — Witness to history

A gripping new history of the years leading up to and the beginning of WWII in Europe told through the lives of five well-educated and mostly wealthy men all vying for the attention of the man in the Oval Office.

"McKean (Suspected of Independence), the former U.S. ambassador to Luxembourg, delivers a perceptive group biography of four American diplomats as they witnessed—and struggled to handle—the rise of fascism in Europe from 1933 to 1941.... This is a lively, immersive history of a pivotal time." —*Publishers Weekly*

Includes bibliographical references and index.

McMeekin, Sean

Stalin's War: A New History of World War II. Sean McMeekin. Basic Books 2021. 864 p.

ISBN 9781541672796

Grades: Adult   940.53

1. Stalin, Joseph, 1879-1953 2. World War II 3. Communism 4. Diplomacy 5. Soviet Union 6. Second World War era (1939-1945) 7. 20th century 8. History writing — Europe — Russia 9. History writing — Wars and conflicts — World War II

LC 2020038843

This history of World II as seen through the prism of Josef Stalin examines how he influenced the conflicts that emerged after the war and how it helped the Soviets conquer most of Eurasia.

"Soviet leader Josef Stalin cleverly manipulated the U.S. and Great Britain during WWII, sowing the seeds for Communist expansion throughout Europe and Asia, according to this richly detailed account.... Packed with incisive character sketches and illuminating analyses of military and diplomatic maneuvers, this is a skillful and persuasive reframing of the causes, developments, and repercussions of WWII." —*Publishers Weekly*

Includes bibliographical references and index.

Meacham, Jon

Franklin and Winston: An Intimate Portrait of an Epic Friendship. Jon Meacham. Random House 2003. xx, 490 p. : Illustration

ISBN 9780375505003

Grades: Adult   940.53

1. Roosevelt, Franklin D. (Franklin Delano), 1882-1945 2. Churchill, Winston, 1874-1965 3. World War II 4. Command of troops 5. Political leadership 6. Politicians 7. Diplomacy 8. International relations 9. Great Britain 10. United States 11. 20th century 12. History writing — Presidency — 20th century — United States 13. History writing — Wars and conflicts — World War II 14. History writing — Europe — United Kingdom 15. Family and Relationships — Friendship

LC 2003041300

Examines the complex relationship between Franklin Roosevelt and Winston Churchill and its influence on the course of World War II, examining their individual attempts to manage and influence each other.

"The book focuses on the relationship between two giants of the 20th century. Both were democrats, but FDR leaned heavily in a progressive direction, whereas Churchill remained bound to the past as a conservative. Meacham . skillfully, elegantly, and fairly captures the essence of the relationship as well as that with their top associates, by balancing original research and the use of secondary sources. An exceptionally enjoyable read, this is sure to be a public hit in all general and academic collections." —*Library Journal*

Includes bibliographical references (p. [449]-467) and index.

Meltzer, Brad

★ *The Nazi Conspiracy: The Secret Plot to Kill Roosevelt, Stalin, and Churchill.* Brad Meltzer, and Josh Mensch. Flatiron Books 2023. 352 p.

ISBN 9781250777263

Grades: Adult   940.53

1. Roosevelt, Franklin D. (Franklin Delano), 1882-1945 2. Stalin, Joseph, 1879-1953 3. Churchill, Winston, 1874-1965 4. World War II 5. Nazis 6. Conspiracies 7. Germany 8. Iran 9. History Writing — Wars and conflicts — World War II 10. History Writing — Spies and Spying

LC 2022022939

In this gripping true story of daring rescues, body doubles and political intrigue, the New York Times best-selling authors of the First Conspiracy and the Lincoln Conspiracy reveal the Nazi's plans to kill FDR, Joseph Stalin and Winston Churchill—an assassination plot that would've changed history.

"Meltzer and Mensch follow up the Lincoln Conspiracy with an action-packed account of the German plan to assassinate the leaders of the U.S, Britain, and the Soviet Union in Tehran in 1943....Meltzer and Mensch acknowledge doubts about the plot's actual existence yet convincingly argue that it was real, and provide necessary historical context while setting a brisk, thriller-like pace." —*Publishers Weekly*

Includes bibliographical references and index.

Moorehead, Caroline

A House in the Mountains: The Women Who Liberated Italy from Fascism. Caroline Moorehead. HarperCollins 2020. 432 pages

ISBN 9780062686350

Grades: Adult   940.53

1. Gobetti, Ada, 1902-1968 2. Malan, Frida 3. Pons, Silvia, 1919-1958 4. Guidetti Serra, Biana 5. World War II 6. Resistance to military occupation 7. Anti-Nazi movement 8. Women political activists 9. Women soldiers 10. Women and war 11. Gender role 12. German occupation, World War II 13. Italian history 14. Turin, Italy 15. Second World War era (1939-1945) 16. 20th century 17. History writing — Wars and conflicts — World War II 18. History writing — Europe — Italy 19. History writing — Wars and conflicts — Resistance — World War II 20. History writing — Women's history

LC Bl2019037375

Drawing on previously untranslated sources, a prize-winning historian tells the little-known story of the women of the Italian-partisan movement and their fight for freedom against fascism in all its forms, while Europe collapsed in ruins around them.

A Train in Winter: An Extraordinary Story of Women, Friendship, and Resistance in Occupied France. Caroline Moorehead. Harpercollins 2011. 352 p.

ISBN 9780061650703

Grades: Adult   940.53

1. Women and war 2. Concentration camps 3. French Resistance (World War II) 4. World War II 5. Resistance to military occupation 6. German occupation, World War II 7. French history 8. 1940s 9. History writing — Wars and conflicts — World War II 10. History writing — Europe — France 11. History writing — Wars and conflicts — Resistance — World War II

LC Bl2011033120

New York Times Notable Book, 2011.

In January 1943, the Gestapo hunted down 230 women of the French Resistance and sent them to Auschwitz. This is their story, told in full for the first time—a searing and unforgettable chronicle of terror, courage, defiance, survival, and the power of friendship to transcend evil that is an essential addition to the history of World War II.

Moorhouse, Roger

The Devils' Alliance: Hitler's Pact with Stalin, 1939-1941. Roger Moorhouse. Basic Books 2014. 432 p.

ISBN 9780465030750

Grades: Adult   940.53

1. Nazi-Soviet Pact, 1939 2. World War II 3. Treaties 4. Diplomacy 5. International relations 6. Germany 7. Soviet Union 8. History writing — Wars and conflicts — World War II

LC 2012278241

In The Devils' Alliance, acclaimed historian Roger Moorhouse explores the causes and implications of the Nazi-Soviet Pact, an unholy covenant whose creation and dissolution were crucial turning points in World War II. Forged by the German foreign minister, Joachim von Ribbentrop, and his Soviet counterpart, Vyacheslav Molotov, the nonaggression treaty briefly united the two powers in a

ESSENTIAL AND RECOMMENDED TITLES
940.53 World War II, 1939-1945

brutally efficient collaboration. Together, the Germans and Soviets quickly conquered and divided central and eastern Europe—Poland, the Baltic States, Finland, and Bessarabia—and the human cost was staggering: During the two years of the pact hundreds of thousands of people in central and eastern Europe caught between Hitler and Stalin were expropriated, deported, or killed. Fortunately for the Allies, the partnership ultimately soured, resulting in the surprise June 1941 German invasion of the Soviet Union. Ironically, however, the powers' exchange of materiel, blueprints, and technological expertise during the period of the Pact made possible a far more bloody and protracted war than would have otherwise been conceivable.

"Moorhouse's accessible prose and clear explication make this a great story for history readers, and his extensive research and documentation help create a critical text for academics focusing on World War II, German history, and Soviet history." —*Library Journal*

The Forgers: The Forgotten Story of the Holocaust's Most Audacious Rescue Operation. Roger Moorhouse. Basic Books 2023. 384 p.
ISBN 9781541619852
Grades: Adult   940.53
1. World War II 2. Holocaust (1933-1945) 3. Identification cards 4. Forgery 5. Diplomatic and consular service 6. Rescues 7. Poland 8. Switzerland 9. Second World War era (1939-1945)
LC 2023016628

Roger Moorhouse unfolds this never-before-told history Holocaust resistance, illuminating the remarkable story of Polish diplomats, Jewish activists, Japanese bureaucrats, and ordinary people who systematically forged as many as 10,000 passports and saved hundreds, potentially thousands, of Jewish lives. Drawing upon first-hand accounts and survivor testimony with new research and revelations about the Lados Group, Moorhouse unspools the lives, work, and valor of Aleksander Lados, Stefan Ryniewicz, Konstanty Rokicki, Juliusz Kuhl, Chaim Eiss, Abraham Silberschein, six members of the Polish government-in-exile who seized an opportunity to do good in the face of a world at war.—.

"The result is a captivating narrative of heroism and an illuminating account of the international diplomatic response to the Holocaust." —*Publishers Weekly*
Includes bibliographical references and index.

Nagorski, Andrew
Saving Freud: The Rescuers Who Brought Him to Freedom. Andrew Nagorski. Simon & Schuster 2022. 352 p.
ISBN 9781982172831
Grades: Adult   940.53
1. Freud, Sigmund, 1856-1939 2. Psychoanalysts 3. Jewish men 4. Friendship 5. Threat (Psychology) 6. World War II 7. Vienna, Austria 8. London, England 9. 20th century 10. Biographies 11. Life stories — Science, technology, and medicine — Healthcare professionals 12. Science Writing — Medicine and health — Mental health 13. Family and Relationships — Friendship

Part incisive new biography of Freud, part group biography of the extraordinary friends who saved his life, this riveting story shows how a group of those closest to Freud persuaded him to escape to London following the German annexation of Austria.

"Sigmund Freud's vibrant life in Vienna and narrow escape from the Gestapo are recounted in this entertaining history." —*Publishers Weekly*

Nasaw, David
The Last Million: Europe's Displaced Persons from World War to Cold War. David Nasaw. Penguin Press 2020. 651 p.
ISBN 9781594206733
Grades: Adult   940.53
1. Concentration camp survivors 2. Prisoners of war 3. Political prisoners 4. Refugees 5. Refugees, Jewish 6. Political refugees 7. Humanitarianism 8. World War II 9. Jewish people 10. Immigration and emigration 11. Europe 12. United States 13. 20th century 14. History writing — Wars and conflicts — World War II 15. History writing — Europe
LC 2020016888

Documents the experiences and fates of the one million concentration camp survivors, POWs, slave laborers and political prisoners left in Germany after World War II who spent years as displaced refugees in unsupported, segregated, and poorly converted buildings while the world's nations refused shelter.

"A thought-provoking, highly recommended perspective on a complex and largely overlooked people and period of modern history." —*Library Journal*
Includes bibliographical references and index.

Novick, Peter
The Holocaust in American Life. Peter Novick. Houghton Mifflin 1999. 373 p.
ISBN 9780395840092
Grades: Adult   940.53
1. Holocaust (1933-1945) 2. Jewish Americans 3. Public opinion 4. Historiography 5. United States 6. History writing — Wars and conflicts — Holocaust — World War II
LC 99020074

New York Times Notable Book, 1999.
Examines the shift in American focus on the Jewish Holocaust, from avoiding the issue to embracing it politically and socially.

"A measured, thorough investigation of the process by which the collective memory of the Holocaust has evolved, and a plea to more consciously shape that memory in the future, Novick's study will be a benchmark in Holocaust studies for years to come." —*Publishers Weekly*
Includes bibliographical references (p. [285]-352) and index.

O'Reilly, Bill
Killing the Ss: The Hunt for the Worst War Criminals in History. Bill O'Reilly and Martin Dugard. Henry Holt & CO 2018. 304 p.
ISBN 9781250165541
Grades: Adult   940.53
1. Nazis 2. War criminals 3. War crime trials 4. Nazi hunters 5. History writing — Wars and conflicts — World War II
LC 2018017242

Traces the daring of Nazi hunters after World War II, revealing the contributions of legal experts, intelligence agents and concentration-camp survivors in tracking down and capturing high-profile Nazis. By the #1 New York Times best-selling authors of Killing the Rising Sun.

Ohler, Norman
The Bohemians: The Lovers Who Led Germany's Resistance Against the Nazis. Norman Ohler; translated from the German by Tim Mohr and Marshall Yarbrough. Houghton Mifflin Harcourt 2020. 320 pages
ISBN 9781328566300
Grades: Adult   940.53
1. Schulze-Boysen, Harro, 1909-1942 2. Schulze-Boysen, Libertas, 1913-1942 3. World War II 4. Military intelligence 5. Spies 6. War 7. Espionage 8. Married people 9. Bohemianism 10. Anti-Nazi movement 11. Resistance to military occupation 12. Third Reich, 1933-1945 13. Germany 14. Soviet Union 15. Between the Wars (1918-1939) 16. Second World War era (1939-1945) 17. 20th century 18. Translations — German to English 19. History writing — Wars and conflicts — Resistance — World War II 20. Life stories — Politics — Activists and reformers 21. History writing — Europe — Germany 22. History writing — Wars and conflicts — World War II — European Theater
LC 2019057794

The best-selling author draws on unpublished diaries, letters and Gestapo files to trace the remarkable story of idealistic lovers Harro Schulze-Boysen and Libertas Haas-Heye, the leaders of the anti-Nazi resistance in 1930s Berlin's bohemian underworld.

"This deeply researched and stylishly written account unearths an appealing yet overlooked chapter in WWII history. Espionage enthusiasts will be riveted." —*Publishers Weekly*
Translation of: Harro & Libertas; Includes bibliographical references and index; Originally published: Koin : Kiepenheuer & Witsch, 2019; Translated from the German.

PUBLIC LIBRARY CORE COLLECTION: NONFICTION
Twentieth Edition

Olson, Lynne
Last Hope Island: Britain, Occupied Europe, and the Brotherhood That Helped Turn the Tide of War. Lynne Olson. Random House 2016. 576 p.
ISBN 9780812997354
Grades: Adult   940.53
1. Heads of state 2. Political refugees 3. World War II 4. Resistance to government 5. Persecution by Nazis 6. Europeans 7. Exiles 8. Diplomacy 9. Politics and government 10. Europe 11. Great Britain 12. History writing — Wars and conflicts — Resistance — World War II 13. History writing — Europe
LC 2016019187
Chronicles how Britain became an island of refuge for Europeans who escaped the Nazi juggernaut, exploring how royals, soldiers, government leaders, and resistance fighters found safety and established bases of operations to reclaim their homelands.
"The many individuals are finely drawn, major developments... are well covered, and the book provides an unusual and very insightful angle on the war." —*Booklist*
Includes bibliographical references and index.

Those Angry Days: Roosevelt, Lindbergh, and America's Fight Over World War II, 1939-1941. by Lynne Olson. Random House 2013. 608 p.
ISBN 9781400069743
Grades: Adult   940.53
1. Roosevelt, Franklin D. (Franklin Delano), 1882-1945 2. Lindbergh, Charles A. (Charles Augustus), 1902-1974 3. World War II 4. Isolationism 5. Intervention (International law) 6. Political culture 7. Diplomacy 8. International relations 9. Politics and government 10. Military policy 11. United States 12. 20th century 13. Second World War era (1939-1945) 14. History writing — Wars and conflicts — World War II
LC 2012025381
New York Times Notable Book, 2013.
From the acclaimed author of Citizens of London comes the definitive account of the debate over American intervention in World War II—a bitter, sometimes violent clash of personalities and ideas that divided the nation and ultimately determined the fate of the free world.
Includes bibliographical references and index.

Overy, R. J.
Why the Allies Won. Richard Overy. W.W. Norton 1995. xiv, 396 p, 16 p. of plates : Illustration; Map
ISBN 9780393316193
Grades: 11 12 Adult   940.53
1. World War II 2. Strategy 3. History writing — Wars and conflicts — World War II
LC 95052444
Explains how the Allies regained military superiority after 1942, and discusses important campaigns, naval battles, industrial strength, fighting ability, leadership, and moral issues.
"Eschewing the belief that the Allies won solely because of their prodigious production of weapons and equipment, Mr. Overy points out that in the early stages of the war, before the Allies were fully mobilized, the Axis countries held the production advantage, yet failed to achieve victory because Germany's management of supply logistics was far inferior to that of the Alliesfrequently as a result of Hitler's wrongheaded interference. . . . Assiduously researched and concisely written, this is a highly perceptive study." —*New York Times Book Review*
Includes bibliographical references (p. [367]-379) and index.

Parkin, Simon
The Island of Extraordinary Captives: A Painter, a Poet, an Heiress, and a Spy in a World War II British Internment Camp. Simon Parkin. Scribner 2022. 448 p.
ISBN 9781982178529
Grades: Adult   940.53
1. Midgley, Peter, 1921-1991 2. Refugees, Jewish 3. Orphans 4. Prisoners of war 5. Spies 6. Forced relocations 7. Concentration camps 8. Heirs and heiresses 9. Intellectuals 10. Expatriates 11. Communities 12. British history 13. Isle of Man 14. Second World War era (1939-1945) 15. 20th century 16. Life stories — Facing adversity — War and oppression — Hostages and POWs 17. Life stories — Facing adversity — War and oppression — Refugees 18. History writing — Wars and conflicts — World War II 19. History writing — Europe — United Kingdom
LC 2021056257
Offers the untold story of a Jewish orphan who fled Nazi Germany for London, only to be arrested there by the British government and sent to an internment camp for suspected foreign agents on the Isle of Man, alongside a renowned group of refugee musicians, intellectuals, artists and—possibly—genuine spies.
"Parkin (A Game of Birds and Wolves) illuminates the long ignored injustices of Britain's World War II concentration camp policies by focusing on some of the prominent individuals confined at Hutchinson Camp on the Isle of Man....A deeply effective look at an important but rarely discussed aspect of World War II history." —*Library Journal*
Includes bibliographical references and index.

Plokhy, Serhii
Yalta: The Price of Peace. S.M. Plokhy. Viking 2010. 448 p.
ISBN 9780670021413
Grades: Adult   940.53
1. World politics 2. Military history 3. Peace 4. International relations 5. World War II 6. Diplomacy 7. 1940s 8. 20th century 9. History writing — Wars and conflicts — World War II
LC 2009026833
A history of the eight-day peace conference in 1945 between FDR, Churchill, and Stalin offers insight into the strained political forces that influenced peace talks, challenging popular opinions about Yalta's role in triggering the Cold War.
"Plokhy has produced a colorful and gripping portrait of the three aging leaders at their historic encounter." —*Wall Street Journal*
Includes bibliographical references and index.

Pomerantsev, Peter
★ *How to Win an Information War: The Propagandist Who Outwitted Hitler.* Peter Pomerantsev. PublicAffairs 2024. 304 p.
ISBN 9781541774728
Grades: Adult   940.53
1. Delmer, Sefton, 1904-1979 2. World War II 3. Journalists 4. Propaganda 5. War propaganda 6. Anti-Nazi movement 7. Misinformation 8. Radio personalities 9. Influence (Psychology) 10. Resistance to military occupation 11. Second World War era (1939-1945) 12. History writing — Wars and conflicts — Resistance — World War II 13. Life stories — Arts and culture — Writing — Journalists 14. Life stories — Arts and culture — Performing arts — Entertainers and celebrities
LC 2023028347
In the summer of 1941, Hitler ruled Europe from the Atlantic to the Black Sea. Britain was struggling to combat his powerful propaganda machine, his frequent radio speeches blasted out on loudspeakers and into homes. British claims that Hitler was dangerous had little impact against this wave of disinformation. Except for the broadcasts of someone called Der Chef, a German who questioned Nazi doctrine. His listeners included German soldiers and citizens, as well as politicians in Washington DC who were debating getting into the war. And—most importantly—Der Chef was a fiction. He was a character created by the British propagandist Thomas Sefton Delmer, a unique weapon in the war.
"This profile of the nearly forgotten genius of propaganda deepens our perception of disinformation as a vile and dangerous weapon." —*Booklist*
Includes bibliographical references and index.

Pressman, Steven
50 Children: One Ordinary American Couple's Extraordinary Rescue Mission into the Heart of Nazi Germany. Steven Pressman. HarperCollins 2014. 256 p.
ISBN 9780062237477
Grades: Adult   940.53
1. Kraus, Gilbert, 1897-1975 2. Kraus, Eleanor, 1903-1989 3. Jewish children 4. Nazism 5. Husband and wife 6. Rescues 7. American people in foreign

ESSENTIAL AND RECOMMENDED TITLES
940.53 World War II, 1939-1945

countries 8. Nazis 9. Antisemitism 10. Austria 11. Media tie-ins 12. History writing — Wars and conflicts — Holocaust — World War II

Based on the HBO documentary of the same name, this remarkable true story of personal courage and heroism follows one Jewish-American couple as they, risking their own lives, travel to Nazi-controlled Vienna and Berlin to rescue 50 Jewish children.

Preston, Diana
Eight Days at Yalta: How Churchill, Roosevelt and Stalin Shaped the Post-war World. Diana Preston. Atlantic Monthly Press 2020. 416 pages
ISBN 9780802147653
Grades: Adult   940.53
1. Churchill, Winston, 1874-1965 2. Roosevelt, Franklin D. (Franklin Delano), 1882-1945 3. Stalin, Joseph, 1879-1953 4. World politics 5. Military history 6. World War II 7. International relations 8. Peace 9. Diplomacy 10. Europe 11. United States 12. 1940s 13. 20th century 14. History writing — Wars and conflicts — World War II

LC 2019045231

Presents a 75th-anniversary account of the historic conference, discussing its role in strategizing the end of World War II, the restructuring of Germany and the constitution of a nascent United Nations.

"Colorful personalities, piquant details, and a diverse array of perspectives make this a satisfying introduction to the subject." —*Publishers Weekly*

Includes bibliographical references and index.

Rajchman, Chil
The Last Jew of Treblinka: A Memoir. Chil Rajchman; foreword by Elie Wiesel. W W Norton & CO Inc 2011. 208 p.
ISBN 9781605981390
Grades: Adult   940.53
1. Holocaust (1933-1945) 2. Genocide 3. Jewish people 4. World War II 5. Concentration camps 6. Poland 7. 1940s 8. History writing — Wars and conflicts — Holocaust — World War II 9. History writing — Wars and conflicts — World War II

Why do some live while so many others perish? Tiny children, old men, beautiful girls; in the gas chambers of Treblinka, all are equal. The Nazis kept the fires of Treblinka burning night and day, a central cog in the wheel of the Final Solution. There was no pretense of work here like in Auschwitz or Birkenau, only a train platform and a road covered with sand. A road that led only to death. But not for the author, a young man who survived working as a "barber" and "dentist," heartsick with witnessing atrocity after atrocity. Yet he managed to survive so that somehow he could tell the world what he had seen. How he found the dress of his little sister abandoned in the woods. How he was forced to extract gold teeth from the corpses. How every night he had to cover the body pits with sand. How every morning the blood of thousands still rose to the surface. Many have courageously told their stories, and in the tradition of Elie Wiesel's "Night" and Primo Levi's "Survival at Auschwitz" and "The Drowned and the Saved," the author provides the only survivor's record of Treblinka. Originally written in Yiddish in 1945 without hope or agenda other than to bear witness, this tale shows that sometimes the bravest and most painful act of all is to remember.

Rees, Laurence
Auschwitz: A New History. Laurence Rees. Public Affairs 2005. xxii, 327 p.
ISBN 9781586483036
Grades: Adult   940.53
1. Eichmann, Adolf, 1906-1962 2. Nazis 3. Holocaust survivors 4. War criminals 5. World War II 6. Concentration camp survivors 7. Death 8. Sadism 9. Genocide 10. Jewish people 11. Concentration camps 12. Holocaust (1933-1945) 13. European people 14. Religious persecution 15. Atrocities 16. European history 17. Poland 18. 1930s 19. 1940s 20. Interviews 21. Biographies 22. History writing — Wars and conflicts — Holocaust — World War II

LC 2004043196

British Book Award for History Book of the Year, 2006.

Insights gleaned from more than one hundred original interviews shed new light on history's most notorious death camp, with the testimonies of survivors providing a detailed portrait of the camp's inner workings.

"For this history of the concentration camp, the author interviewed 100 former Nazi perpetrators and survivors from the camp and drew on hundreds of interviews conducted for his previous research on the Third Reich, many with former members of the Nazi Party. This is a significant contribution to our understanding of the intricacies of Nazi racial and ethnic policy that resulted in this ultimate abomination." —*Booklist*

Includes bibliographical references (p. [301]-312) and index.

Hitler and Stalin: The Tyrants and the Second World War. Laurence Rees. Public Affairs 2021. 544 p.
ISBN 9781610399647
Grades: Adult   940.53
1. Hitler, Adolf, 1889-1945 2. Stalin, Joseph, 1879-1953 3. World War II 4. Dictatorship 5. Political leadership 6. Dictators 7. Soviet Union 8. Germany 9. Eastern Europe 10. 20th century 11. Collective biographies 12. History writing — Communism — Europe — Russia 13. Life stories — Politics — Politicians 14. History writing — Europe — Germany 15. History writing — Wars and conflicts — World War II — European Theater

A dual portrait of Adolph Hitler and Josef Stalin that explores how they casually used human suffering as a tool, impacting millions of lives in sweeping power-grab campaigns.

A dual biography of two of history's most notorious dictators from a master historian who has 'Spent the last thirty years making documentaries and writing books about the Third Reich, Stalinism and the Second World War.' —*Kirkus*

The Holocaust: A New History. Laurence Rees. Public Affairs 2017. xv, 509 p.
ISBN 9781610398442
Grades: Adult   940.53
1. Holocaust (1933-1945) 2. Jewish people 3. Persecution by Nazis 4. Political persecution 5. Religious persecution 6. History writing — Wars and conflicts — Holocaust — World War II

LC 2017933355

A historian who has an unrivaled archive of firsthand testimony from both the perpetrators and victims of the Holocaust presents almost all of this evidence for the first time in an authoritative and accessible account of the greatest crime against humanity.

"Historian Rees ... combines thorough scholarship of the Nazi era with his own vast archive of interviews with survivors, perpetrators, and bystanders to create a comprehensive, chilling, and readable history of the Holocaust." —*Library Journal*

Includes index.

Reeves, Richard
Infamy: The Shocking Story of the Japanese American Internment in World War II. Richard Reeves. Henry Holt and Company 2015. 384 p.
ISBN 9780805094084
Grades: Adult   940.53
1. Japanese American forced removal and incarceration 2. World War II 3. Concentration camps 4. East Asian Americans 5. Second World War era (1939-1945) 6. History writing — Wars and conflicts — Homefront — World War II 7. History writing — United States

LC 2014033329

In Infamy, the story of this appalling chapter in American history is told more powerfully than ever before. Acclaimed historian Richard Reeves has interviewed survivors, read numerous private letters and memoirs, and combed through archives to deliver a sweeping narrative of this atrocity. Men we usually consider heroes—FDR, Earl Warren, Edward R. Murrow—were in this case villains, but we also learn of many Americans who took great risks to defend the rights of the internees. Most especially, we hear the poignant stories of those who spent years in "war relocation camps," many of whom suffered this terrible injustice with remarkable grace.

"Reeves mixes intimate narratives with historical documents to give an authoritative account of one of the darkest periods in American history." —*Library Journal*

Includes bibliographical references and index.

PUBLIC LIBRARY CORE COLLECTION: NONFICTION
Twentieth Edition

Rhodes, Richard
Masters of Death: The SS-Einsatzgruppen and the Invention of the Holocaust. Richard Rhodes. A.A. Knopf 2002. xii, 335 p, 16 p. of plates : Illustration; Map
ISBN 9780375409004
Grades: Adult   940.53
1. Genocide 2. Executions and executioners 3. Holocaust (1933-1945) 4. World War II 5. Secret service 6. Third Reich, 1933-1945 7. Soviet Union 8. Poland 9. History writing — Wars and conflicts — Holocaust — World War II 10. History writing — Wars and conflicts — World War II — European Theater
LC 2001038898

Examines the role of the Einsatzgruppen, task forces deployed in Eastern Europe by the SS, whose job was to slaughter Eastern European Jews, and discusses Hitler's eventual plans to annihilate members of other ethnic groups.

"This is a grotesquely fascinating chronicle. Reading this book is an ordeal, but it is a necessary trial if one is to grasp the full scope of the war against the Jews." —*Booklist*

Includes bibliographical references (p. [305]-319) and index.

Ronald, Susan
Hitler's Aristocrats: The Secret Power Players in Britain and America Who Supported the Nazis, 1923-1941. Susan Ronald. St. Martin's Press 2023. 432 p.
ISBN 9781250276551
Grades: Adult   940.53
1. Hitler, Adolf, 1889-1945 2. World War II 3. Nazism 4. Fascists 5. Nazi collaborators 6. Spies 7. Elite (Social sciences) 8. Aristocracy 9. Influence (Psychology) 10. Nazi propaganda 11. International relations 12. Germany 13. History writing — Europe — Germany 14. History writing — Wars and conflicts — Homefront — World War II 15. History writing — Spies and spying 16. Life stories — Law and order — Spies and secret agents
LC 2022051604

Hitler said, "I am convinced that propaganda is an essential means to achieve one's aims." Enlisting Europe's aristocracy, international industrialists, and the political elite in Britain and America, Hitler spun a treacherous tale everyone wanted to believe: He was a man of peace. Hitler's aristocrats became his eyes, listening posts, and mouthpieces in the drawing rooms, cocktail parties, and weekend retreats of Europe and America. Distrustful of his own Foreign Ministry, Hitler used his aristocrats to open the right doors in Great Britain and the United States, creating a formidable fifth column within government and financial circles.

"A character-driven chronicle of the numerous British and American elites who abetted Hitler's efforts to seize and maintain power." —*Kirkus*

Includes bibliographical references and index.

Rose, Sarah
D-Day Girls: The Untold Story of the Female Spies Who Helped Win World War Two. by Sarah Rose. Random House Inc 2019. 320 p.
ISBN 9780451495082
Grades: Adult   940.53
1. Odette, 1912-1995 2. Baissac, Lise de, 1905-2004 3. Borrel, Andree, 1919-1944 4. Women spies 5. Secret service 6. Spies 7. Espionage 8. French Resistance (World War II) 9. Nazis 10. Intelligence service 11. Great Britain 12. Collective biographies 13. Biographies 14. Life stories — Law and order — Spies and secret agents 15. History writing — Spies and spying 16. History writing — Wars and conflicts — World War II 17. Adult books for young adults
LC 2018038372

The dramatic, inspiring story of the extraordinary women recruited by Britain's elite spy agency to sabotage the Nazis, shore up the Resistance, and pave the way for Allied victory in World War II."

"Thoroughly researched and written as smoothly as a good thriller, this is a mesmerizing story of creativity, perseverance, and astonishing heroism." —*Publishers Weekly*

Includes bibliographical references.

Rosner, Elizabeth
Survivor Cafe: The Legacy of Trauma and the Labyrinth of Memory. Elizabeth Rosner. Counterpoint 2017. 304 p.
ISBN 9781619029545
Grades: Adult   940.53
1. Collective memory 2. Psychic trauma 3. Social history 4. Pain 5. Loss 6. Survival 7. War and society 8. Violence 9. Intergenerational trauma 10. History writing — General

As firsthand survivors of many of the twentieth century's most monumental events—the Holocaust, Pearl Harbor, the Killing Fields—begin to pass away, Survivor Café addresses urgent questions: How do we carry those stories forward? How do we collectively ensure that the horrors of the past are not forgotten?

"A thoughtful, probing meditation on the fragility of memory and the indelible inheritance of pain." —*Kirkus*

Russell, Jan Jarboe
The Train to Crystal City: FDR's Secret Prisoner Exchange Program and America's Only Family Internment Camp During World War II. Jan Jarboe Russell. Scribner 2015. 416 p.
ISBN 9781451693669
Grades: Adult   940.53
1. Italian Americans 2. Japanese American forced removal and incarceration 3. World War II 4. Forced relocations 5. German Americans 6. Prisoners of war 7. Family and war 8. Immigrants, Japanese 9. Immigrants, German 10. Immigrants, Italian 11. East Asian Americans 12. Prisons 13. United States history 14. 1940s 15. Second World War era (1939-1945) 16. 20th century 17. History writing — Wars and conflicts — Homefront — World War II
LC 2014030862

A little-known episode in World War II history appears in the Train to Crystal City, which details how the U.S. incarcerated thousands of civilians in a Texas facility. Italian, Japanese, and German immigrants were sent there with their spouses and children, many of whom were U.S. citizens. Relying in part on personal interviews, author Jan Russell portrays life in the camp, the struggles of those who were sent abroad in prisoner exchanges, and post-war expulsion of foreign nationals.

"Based in part on interviews with camp survivors, Russell documents in chilling detail a shocking story of national betrayal." —*Kirkus*

Sakamoto, Pamela Rotner
Midnight in Broad Daylight: A Japanese American Family Caught Between Two Worlds. Pamela Rotner Sakamoto. Harper 2016. 400 p.
ISBN 9780062351937
Grades: Adult   940.53
1. Fukuhara, Harry K, 1920-2015 2. Fukuhara, Pierce, 1922-2008 3. Fukuhara, Frank, 1924-2015 4. Pearl Harbor, Attack on, 1941 5. Japanese American families 6. Translators 7. Soldiers 8. Japanese Americans 9. Nuclear weapons 10. Nuclear warfare 11. Atomic bomb 12. World War II 13. Hiroshima, Japan 14. 1940s 15. Second World War era (1939-1945) 16. Collective biographies 17. Life stories — People in history 18. History writing — Wars and conflicts — World War II
LC 2015017943

Describes the true story of three Japanese American brothers, two of whom move to their mother's ancestral home in Hiroshima after their father's death, and find themselves on opposite sides of the world and the war as Pearl Harbor unfolds.

"A beautifully rendered work wrought with enormous care and sense of compassionate dignity." —*Kirkus*

Samet, Elizabeth D.
Looking for the Good War: American Amnesia and the Violent Pursuit of Happiness. Elizabeth D. Samet. Farrar, Straus and Giroux 2021. 354 p.
ISBN 9780374219925
Grades: Adult   940.53
1. Collective memory 2. Postwar life 3. Memory 4. National characteristics, American 5. War in literature 6. War and society 7. World War II 8. United States

ESSENTIAL AND RECOMMENDED TITLES
940.53 World War II, 1939-1945

9. History writing — Post World War II - 1959 — United States 10. History writing — Wars and conflicts 11. Society and culture — General

LC 2021028289

n Looking for the Good War, Elizabeth D. Samet reexamines the literature, art, and culture that emerged after World War II, bringing her expertise as a professor of English at West Point to bear on the complexity of the postwar period in national life. Samet finds the war's ambivalent legacy in some of its most heavily mythologized figures: the war correspondent epitomized by Ernie Pyle, the character of the erstwhile G.I. turned either cop or criminal in the pulp fiction and feature films of the late 1940s, the disaffected Civil War veteran who looms so large on the screen in the Cold War Western, and the resurgent military hero of the post-Vietnam period. Taken together, these figures reveal key elements of postwar attitudes toward violence, liberty, and nation—attitudes that have shaped domestic and foreign policy and that respond in various ways to various assumptions about national identity and purpose established or affirmed by World War II.

"In her latest book, Samet (English, West Point; No Man's Land) argues that many of the myths about the Second World War, especially the notion of the 'Greatest generation,' have a negative influence on the American psyche. . . . A thought-provoking, thoroughly researched work that asks readers to reconsider World War II mythology." —*Library Journal*

Includes bibliographical references.

Schwarz, Geraldine
Those Who Forget: My Family's Story in Nazi Europe—a Memoir, a History, a Warning. Geraldine Schwarz; translated from the French by Laura Marris. Scribner 2020. 320 p.

ISBN 9781501199080

Grades: Adult   940.53

1. Schwarz, Geraldine 2. Schwarz family 3. Holocaust (1933-1945) 4. Journalists 5. Postwar life 6. Guilt 7. Denial (Psychology) 8. Social responsibility 9. Memory 10. World War II 11. Family history 12. German occupation, World War II 13. French history 14. Third Reich, 1933-1945 15. German history 16. Europe 17. 20th century 18. Autobiographies and memoirs 19. Translations — French to English 20. Life stories — People in history 21. History writing — Europe 22. History writing — Wars and conflicts — Homefront — World War II

LC 2020004934

Offers an account of the author's German and French grandparents' lives during World War II, an in-depth history of Europe's post-war reckoning with fascism, and an urgent appeal to remember as a defense against today's rise of far-right nationalism.

"In searing yet engaging prose, Schwarz makes her case for the need for memory work in this highly recommended read for fans of memoirs and World War II history." —*Library Journal*

Originally published: Paris : Flammarion, 2017; Translated from the French.

Snyder, Timothy
Black Earth: The Holocaust as History and Warning. Timothy Snyder. Crown 2015. 464 p.

ISBN 9781101903452

Grades: Adult   940.53

1. Genocide 2. World War II 3. Holocaust (1933-1945) 4. Jewish people 5. Causes of war 6. History writing — Wars and conflicts — Holocaust — World War II 7. History writing — Wars and conflicts — World War II

LC 2015016818

The award-winning author of Bloodlands presents a history of the Holocaust that offers insights into Hitler's genocidal views and the partisan groups who supported Jewish targets, arguing that wrong conclusions about the Holocaust are compromising the world's future. Map(s).

"Snyder brings two fresh elements to his dizzying, harrowing tale. The first is his extraordinarily wide and deep research into the remarkable stories, many unknown, of individual Holocaust survivors, the subject of the last half of his book. The second element, likely to be controversial, is his argument, asserted and reasserted, that, at its roots, the Holocaust was made possible by the failure of national states." —*Publishers Weekly*

Stargardt, Nicholas
The German War: A Nation Under Arms. Nicholas Stargardt. Basic Books 2015. 768 p.

ISBN 9780465018994

Grades: Adult   940.53

1. Hitler, Adolf, 1889-1945 2. World War II 3. German people 4. Military history 5. Third Reich, 1933-1945 6. Politics and government 7. Germany 8. 20th century 9. Impartial writing 10. History writing — Wars and conflicts — World War II

LC 2015945013

New York Times Notable Book, 2015.

Drawing on a range of primary source materials—personal diaries, court records and military correspondence—the author explores the German psyche during World War II, specifically why they prolonged the war when their defeat was all but assured as early as 1941.

"A well-researched, unsettling social history of war that will prove deeply thought-provoking—even worrying—for readers who wonder what they might have done under the same circumstances." —*Kirkus*

Includes bibliographical references and index.

Stone, Dan
★ *The Holocaust: An Unfinished History.* Dan Stone. Mariner Books 2024. 416 p.

ISBN 9780063349032

Grades: Adult   940.53

1. Holocaust (1933-1945) 2. 20th century 3. Second World War era (1939-1945) 4. History Writing — Jewish history 5. History writing — Wars and conflicts — Holocaust — World War II

A leading scholar offers an authoritative, revelatory new history of the Holocaust.

"Concluding with a dire warning that the modern nation-state is a catalyst for racist and genocidal thinking that is today often targeted at migrants, Muslims, and other marginalized groups, this is an urgent new perspective on a much-studied calamity." —*Publishers Weekly*

Originally published in the UK by Pelican, London, in 2023.

Strauss, Gwen
The Nine: The True Story of a Band of Women Who Survived the Worst of Nazi Germany. Gwen Strauss. St. Martin's Press 2021. 336 p.

ISBN 9781250239297

Grades: Adult   940.53

1. Podliasky, Hélène, 1920-2012 2. World War II 3. Women political prisoners 4. Women internment camp inmates 5. Prisoner-of-war escapes 6. Prisoners of war, German 7. Guerrillas 8. Anti-Nazi movement 9. Prisons 10. Resistance to military occupation 11. Germany 12. France 13. 20th century 14. Second World War era (1939-1945) 15. Collective biographies 16. History writing — Wars and conflicts — World War II 17. History writing — Women's history 18. Life stories — Facing adversity — War and oppression

LC 2020053539

The powerful, previously untold WWII story of nine female resistance fighters who banded together to survive the camps and ultimately escaped from a final death march across war-torn Germany.

"With this work of nonfiction, poet and author Strauss tells the story of a group of nine French Resistance prisoners, all women, who escaped the Nazis during a death march from a sub-camp of the Buchenwald concentration camp. . . . A fast-paced account that is strongly recommended for lovers of action-oriented narrative nonfiction, and for women's history collections." —*Library Journal*

Includes bibliographical references.

Sullivan, Rosemary
The Betrayal of Anne Frank: A Cold Case Investigation. Rosemary Sullivan. HarperCollins 2022. 400 p.

ISBN 9780062892355

Grades: Adult   940.53

1. Frank, Anne, 1929-1945 2. Jewish people 3. Cold cases (Criminal investigation) 4. Nazi collaborators 5. Betrayal 6. Holocaust (1933-1945) 7. Dutch peo-

ple 8. Western European people 9. Netherlands 10. Canadian Literature 11. History writing — Wars and conflicts — Holocaust — World War II 12. History writing — Jewish history 13. True Crime — Forensic Sciences

Crime Writers of Canada Awards of Excellence Best Nonfiction Book, 2023.

Using a new technology, recently discovered documents, and sophisticated investigative techniques, a retired FBI agent and a Cold Case Team painstakingly pieced together the months leading to the infamous arrest of Anne Frank and her family—and came to a shocking conclusion.

"An extraordinary tale of modern science and old-fashioned gumshoe work applied to a world-renowned crime 80 years after the fact....Every reader of Anne Frank's Diary will want to have this superbly rendered tale of scholarly detection at hand." —Kirkus

Takaki, Ronald T.
Double Victory: A Multicultural History of America in World War II. Ronald Takaki. Back Bay Books 2001. VI, 281 p. : Illustration
ISBN 9780316831567
Grades: 11 12 Adult   940.53
1. Racism 2. World War II 3. Race relations 4. United States 5. History writing — Wars and conflicts — Homefront — World War II 6. Adult books for young adults

LC BL2001013368

Arguing that many Americans fought in World War II for a "double victory"—one against fascism abroad, the other against racism at home—the author captures the voices of people who are often overlooked in traditional narratives of the conflict.

Includes bibliographical references (p. 237-269) and index; Originally published: Boston : Little, Brown, 2000.

Taylor, Fred
1939: A People's History of the Coming of the Second World War. Frederick Taylor. W. W. Norton & Company 2020. 448 p.
ISBN 9781324006794
Grades: Adult   940.53
1. World War II 2. Public opinion 3. Causes of war 4. Politics and government 5. European history 6. Europe 7. 1930s 8. 20th century 9. History writing — Wars and conflicts — World War II

LC 2020000207

The best-selling author of Dresden draws on contemporary sources in an account of the fateful months between the Munich Agreement and Hitler's invasion of Poland that offers insight into the decisions of key leaders and the experiences of everyday citizens.

"For World War II buffs, an illuminating study of a depressing year." —Kirkus

Published in England as: 1939: a people's history : 'The war nobody wanted.'; Includes bibliographical references and index.

Van De Perre, Selma
My Name Is Selma: The Remarkable Memoir of a Jewish Resistance Fighter and Ravensbruck Survivor. Selma Van De Perre. Scribner 2021. 256 p.
ISBN 9781982164676
Grades: Adult   940.53
1. Van De Perre, Selma 2. Jewish women 3. Anti-Nazi movement 4. Jewish resistance and revolts 5. Survival (in concentration camps, prisons, etc.) 6. Concentration camps 7. Political prisoners 8. Netherlands 9. Autobiographies and memoirs 10. Life stories — Facing adversity — War and oppression — Holocaust 11. History books — Wars — Holocaust — World War II 12. History writing — Jewish history

This memoir from a 98-year-old Jewish Resistance fighter and concentration camp survivor tells the story of how she took on an assumed identity fighting Nazi occupation in the Netherlands before being sent to a women's prison camp.

"Van de Perre . . . movingly recounts her work with Dutch resistance organizations and the people she met along the way. . . . The author's voice, strength, and pain are palpable throughout; everyone can benefit from reading her story." —Library Journal

Van Wijk-voskuijl, Joop
The Last Secret of the Secret Annex: The Untold Story of Anne Frank, Her Silent Protector, and a Family Betrayal. Joop Van Wijk-voskuijl, Jeroen De Bruyn. Simon & Schuster 2023. 288 p.
ISBN 9781982198213
Grades: Adult   940.53
1. Frank, Anne, 1929-1945 2. Voskuijl, Bep 3. Frank family 4. Betrayal 5. Family secrets 6. Holocaust (1933-1945) 7. Holocaust victims 8. Jewish families 9. Amsterdam, Netherlands 10. Netherlands 11. History Writing — Wars and conflicts — Holocaust — World War II 12. Life stories — People in history

"The result is a superbly well-written, intimate, engrossing, and heartrending reckoning with the endless damage done by genocide." —Booklist

Wachsmann, Nikolaus
KL: A History of the Nazi Concentration Camps. Nikolaus Wachsmann. Farrar, Straus and Giroux 2015. 896 p.
ISBN 9780374118259
Grades: Adult   940.53
1. Internment camp inmates 2. Concentration camps 3. World War II 4. Holocaust (1933-1945) 5. Prisons 6. Atrocities 7. Germany 8. History writing — Wars and conflicts — Holocaust — World War II

LC 2014031269

Mark Lynton History Prize, 2016.

While many accounts of Nazi concentration camps have focused on particular facilities or described the effects on prisoners, historian Nicolaus Wachsmann is the first to analyze the entire system of labor camps and extermination centers. This gripping, revelatory study draws on massive collections of documents, some of which have only become available over the past 25 years. KL doesn't just detail Nazi Germany's methodology of slave labor and genocide: It reveals how it was integral to the Third Reich's economic and political system.

"A comprehensive, encyclopedic work that should be included in the collections of libraries, schools and other institutions." —Kirkus

Includes bibliographical references and index.

White, Elizabeth B.
★ *The Counterfeit Countess: The Jewish Woman Who Rescued Thousands of Poles During the Holocaust.* Elizabeth B. White & Joanna Sliwa. Simon & Schuster 2024. 336 p.
ISBN 9781982189129
Grades: Adult   940.53
1. Melhberg, Josephine Janina, 1905-1969 2. Women mathematicians 3. Resistance to military occupation 4. World War II 5. Jewish resistance and revolts 6. False personation 7. Holocaust (1933-1945) 8. Polish people 9. Jewish people 10. Poland 11. Second World War era (1939-1945) 12. Biographies 13. History Writing — Jewish history 14. History Writing — Wars and conflicts — Holocaust — World War II 15. Life stories — People in history

Tells the story of Dr. Josephine Janina Mehlberg—a Jewish mathematician who saved thousands of lives in Nazi-occupied Poland by masquerading as a Polish aristocrat—drawing on Mehlberg's own unpublished memoir.

"A full portrait of a woman who saved thousands in Nazi-occupied Poland, with broad appeal for readers interested in Holocaust and eastern European history and survivor's stories." —Library Journal

Winik, Jay
1944: FDR and the Year That Changed History. Jay Winik. Simon & Schuster 2015. 512 p.
ISBN 9781439114087
Grades: Adult   940.53
1. Roosevelt, Franklin D. (Franklin Delano), 1882-1945 2. World War II 3. Holocaust (1933-1945) 4. Presidents 5. Command of troops 6. Political leadership 7. United States 8. 1940s 9. History writing — Wars and conflicts — World War II 10. History writing — United States

LC 2015013912

The best-selling author of April 1865 chronicles the events of 1944 to reveal how nearly the Allies lost World War II, citing the pivotal contributions of FDR, Churchill and Stalin.

ESSENTIAL AND RECOMMENDED TITLES
940.5309 World War II, 1939-1945 — History, geographic treatment, biography

"An accomplished popular historian unpacks the last full year of World War II and the excruciatingly difficult decisions facing Franklin Roosevelt. A complex history rendered with great color and sympathy." —*Kirkus*
Includes bibliographical references and index.

Yellin, Emily
Our Mothers' War: American Women at Home and at the Front During World War II. Emily Yellin. Free Press 2004. xiv, 447 p. : Illustration
ISBN 9780743245142
Grades: 11 12 Adult   940.53
1. Women's history 2. Women 3. World War II 4. Women's participation in wars 5. United States 6. 20th century 7. History writing — Wars and conflicts — Homefront — World War II 8. History writing — Women's history 9. Adult books for young adults
LC 2004040496
Examines how World War II transformed traditional women's roles, describing the experiences of nurses, factory employees, the military's first women soldiers, and female prisoners of war.
"Yellin reveals all of the responsibilities held by women, including helping to manufacture aircraft, ships, and other munitions; and, in the process, outproducing all of America's allies and enemies, by far. Readers see war brides who worked hard to maintain the morale of their husbands while surviving long separation, fear, and shortages of virtually everything necessary to support a family. . . . [This book] is an important book because the role played by women in World War II has been regularly ignored." —*School Library Journal*
Includes bibliographical references (p. 415-428) and index.

940.5309 World War II, 1939-1945 — History, geographic treatment, biography

Groom, Winston
The Allies: Roosevelt, Churchill, Stalin, and the Unlikely Alliance That Won World War II. Winston Groom. National Geographic 2018. 464 p.
ISBN 9781426219665
Grades: Adult   940.5309
1. Roosevelt, Franklin D. (Franklin Delano), 1882-1945 2. Churchill, Winston, 1874-1965 3. Stalin, Joseph, 1879-1953 4. World War II 5. Heads of state 6. Strategic alliances (Military) 7. Political leadership 8. Military strategy 9. Collective biographies 10. Biographies 11. History writing — Wars and conflicts — World War II 12. Life stories — Law and order — Military leaders 13. Life stories — Politics — Politicians
LC 2018027574
Using details from the letters sent between them to paint a more thorough picture of their personal and military lives, describes how three very different men came to control World War II in Europe and the Pacific.
Includes bibliographical references and index.

940.5318 World War II, 1939-1945 — Holocaust

Eisen, Max
By Chance Alone: A Remarkable True Story of Courage and Survival at Auschwitz. Max Eisen. HarperCollins 2016. xii, 276 pages : Illustration; Map
ISBN 9781443449281
Grades: Adult   940.5318
1. Eisen, Max 2. Internment camp inmates 3. Holocaust survivors 4. Jewish people 5. Holocaust (1933-1945) 6. Czech people 7. Eastern European people 8. Canadian literature 9. Autobiographies and memoirs 10. Life stories — Facing adversity — War and oppression — Holocaust 11. History writing — Wars and conflicts — Holocaust — World War II
Shortlisted for the Charles Taylor Prize for Literary Non-Fiction, 2017.
This autobiography of Canadian Max Eisen details the rural Hungarian deportations to Auschwitz-Birkenau, back-breaking slave labour in Auschwitz I, the infamous 'Death march' of January 1945, the painful aftermath of liberation, and a journey of physical and psychological healing.

"In the vein of Holocaust memoirs such as Elie Wiesel's Night and Primo Levi's Survival in Auschwitz, this significant new entry offers further documentation of a dark period in history. It will be a solid addition to all World War II collections." —*Library Journal*
Includes bibliographical references.

Pivnik, Sam
Survivor: Auschwitz, the Death March, and My Fight for Freedom. Sam Pivnik. St. Martin's Press 2013. 320 p.
ISBN 9781250029522
Grades: Adult   940.5318
1. Pivnik, Sam, 1926-2017 2. Holocaust (1933-1945) 3. Holocaust survivors 4. Jewish people 5. Concentration camps 6. Survival 7. Polish people 8. Autobiographies and memoirs 9. Biographies 10. History writing — Wars and conflicts — Holocaust — World War II 11. History writing — Wars and conflicts — World War II 12. Life stories — Facing adversity — War and oppression — Holocaust
LC 2012474461
Documents the extraordinary story of the author's survival of the Holocaust, relating his harrowing endurance of ghetto establishments in his home town of Bedzin after the Nazi invasion of Poland, his torturous six-month imprisonment at Auschwitz and his near escapes from subsequent wartime brutalities.

940.5322 World War II, 1939-1945 — Diplomatic history — Allies

Roberts, Andrew
Masters and Commanders: How Four Titans Won the War in the West, 1941-1945. Andrew Roberts. Harper 2009. xl, 673 p. : Illustration; Map
ISBN 9780061228575
Grades: Adult   940.5322
1. Roosevelt, Franklin D. (Franklin Delano), 1882-1945 2. Churchill, Winston, 1874-1965 3. Marshall, George C. (George Catlett), 1880-1959 4. Alanbrooke, Viscount, 1883-1963 5. World War II 6. Command of troops 7. Military history 8. Diplomacy 9. History writing — Wars and conflicts — World War II
A joint profile of Winston Churchill, Franklin D. Roosevelt, and their armed forces commanders Alan Brooke and George C. Marshall evaluates the pivotal ways in which they determined the strategies of allied forces during World War II, in an account that reveals their divergent agendas and tense efforts to collaborate or outmaneuver each other.
Previous ed. has subtitle: How Roosevelt, Churchill, Marshall, and Alanbrooke won the war in the West; Includes bibliographical references (p. 615-624) and index; Originally published: London : Allen Lane, 2008.

940.54 Military history of World War II

Alexander, Caroline
Skies of Thunder: A Forgotten Epic of World War II. Caroline Alexander. Viking 2024. 496 p.
ISBN 9781984879233
Grades: Adult   940.54
1. World War II 2. Military campaigns 3. Military occupation 4. Japanese occupation, World War II 5. Aerial operations 6. Burma 7. Himalaya Mountains 8. China 9. India 10. Second World War era (1939-1945) 11. History Writing — Military 12. History Writing — Wars and conflicts — World War II 13. History Writing — Asia — Southeast Asia
LC 2023026939
The New York Times best-selling author presents this masterpiece of modern war history in which she, drawing on obscure memoirs and long-ignored records, gives us the World War II pilots' and soldiers' eye views of flying and combat, probing at what it takes to survive extreme circumstances. Map(s).
"In this soaring account, bestseller Alexander (The Endurance) spotlights a group of American airmen stationed in Burma who flew the 'Hump' over the Hi-

malayas to deliver supplies to Chinese allies during WWII." —*Publishers Weekly*
Includes bibliographical references and index.

Ambrose, Stephen E.
Citizen Soldiers: The U.S. Army from the Normandy Beaches to the Bulge to the Surrender of Germany, June 7, 1944-May 7, 1945. Stephen E. Ambrose. Simon & Schuster 1997. 512 p. : Illustration; Map
ISBN 9780684815251
Grades: 11 12 Adult   940.54
1. Western Front (World War II) 2. Soldiers 3. Military campaigns 4. Battles 5. World War II 6. European history 7. 1940s 8. 20th century 9. Second World War era (1939-1945) 10. History writing — Wars and conflicts — World War II — European Theater
LC 97023876
New York Times Notable Book, 1998.
Citizen Soldiers opens on June 7, 1944, on the Normandy beaches, and ends on May 7, 1945. From the high command on down to the enlisted men, Stephen E. Ambrose draws on hundreds of interviews and oral histories from men on both sides who were there. He recreates the experiences of the individuals who fought the battles, the women who served, and the Germans who fought against us.
"These events have all been well documented, but in Ambrose's capable hands, the bloody and dramatic battles fought in northwest Europe in 1944-45 come alive as never before." —*New York Times Book Review*
Includes bibliographical references (p. 493-498) and index.

D-Day, June 6, 1944: The Climactic Battle of World War II. Stephen E. Ambrose. Simon & Schuster 1995. 655 p. : Illustration; Map
ISBN 9780684801377
Grades: 11 12 Adult   940.54
1. World War II 2. Normandy Invasion, June 6, 1944 3. Military campaigns 4. Battles 5. Military history 6. Normandy 7. France 8. 1940s 9. 20th century 10. History writing — Wars and conflicts — World War II — European Theater 11. History writing — Wars and conflicts — Battles
LC BL 99763163
Chronicles the events, politics, and personalities of this pivotal day in World War II, shedding light on the strategies of commanders on both sides and the ramifications of the battle.
"Mr. Ambrose wonderfully illuminates the mind of the very young soldier of any nation anywhere who has never been in fighting before." —*New York Times Book Review*
A Touchstone book; Appendix A: Veterans who contributed oral histories or written memoirs to the Eisenhower Center as of August 13, 1993: P. 617-632; Includes bibliographical references (p. 613-616) and index; Originally published: New York : Simon & Schuster, 1994.

The Victors: Eisenhower and His Boys : The Men of World War II. Stephen E. Ambrose. Simon & Schuster 1998. 396 p. : Illustration; Map
ISBN 9780684856285
Grades: 11 12 Adult   940.54
1. Eisenhower, Dwight D. (Dwight David), 1890-1969 2. Western Front (World War II) 3. Soldiers 4. Command of troops 5. World War II 6. Military campaigns 7. Generals 8. United States history 9. United States 10. 1940s 11. 20th century 12. Biographies 13. History writing — Wars and conflicts — World War II — European Theater 14. Life stories — Law and order — Military leaders 15. Adult books for young adults
LC 98037808
New York Times Notable Book, 1998.
To re-create the last year of WWII, the author tells the soldiers' stories, drawn from interviews and oral histories from government and private archives.
"The author is a master of letting his subjects tell the story, of standing back and allowing the large lessons to unfold. The result is history with lasting impact." —*School Library Journal*
Includes bibliographical references (p. 372-379) and index.

The Wild Blue: The Men and Boys Who Flew the B-24s Over Germany. Stephen E. Ambrose. Simon & Schuster 2001. 299 p, 8 p. of plates : Illustration
ISBN 9780743203395
Grades: Adult   940.54
1. McGovern, George S, 1922-2012 2. B-24 bomber 3. World War II 4. Bomber pilots 5. Bombers (Airplanes) 6. Air warfare 7. Aerial bombing 8. Flight crews 9. Aerial operations 10. Germany 11. 1940s 12. History writing — Wars and conflicts — World War II — European Theater 13. History writing — Military — Aviation History 14. History writing — Military — Military units
LC 2001020563
New York Times Notable Book, 2001.
The stories of the Army Air Forces' B24 pilots and crews who were stationed in Italy and flew combat missions over Germany during World War II.
"Ambrose's narrative flows smoothly, even as he manages to cover each man's story." —*Library Journal*
Includes bibliographical references (p. 279-281) and index.

Atkinson, Rick
An Army at Dawn: The War in North Africa, 1942-1943. Rick Atkinson. Henry Holt & Co. 2002. xiii, 681 p, 32 p. of plates : Illustration; Map (Liberation trilogy, 1)
ISBN 9780805062885
Grades: Adult   940.54
1. World War II 2. Military campaigns 3. Armed forces 4. Military history 5. Southwest Asia and North Africa (Middle East) history 6. Southwest Asia and North Africa (Middle East) 7. Tunisia 8. 1940s 9. 20th century 10. History writing — Wars and conflicts — World War II
LC 2002024130
Pulitzer Prize for History, 2003.
Atkinson tells the story of the war in North Africa in this first volume of a trilogy about the liberation of Europe in World War II.
"This volume covers the conception of Operation Torch through the German surrender in Tunisia in May 1943. An exemplary work that feeds anticipation of the succeeding volumes." —*Booklist*
Includes bibliographical references (p. [626]-654) and index.

The Day of Battle: The War in Sicily and Italy, 1943-1944. Rick Atkinson. H. Holt 2007. 816 p. (Liberation trilogy, 2)
ISBN 9780805062892
Grades: Adult   940.54
1. World War II 2. Military campaigns 3. Armed forces 4. Battles 5. Military history 6. European history 7. Italy 8. 1940s 9. 20th century 10. History writing — Wars and conflicts — World War II — European Theater
LC 2007007653
New York Times Notable Book, 2007.
The second volume in a trilogy chronicling the liberation of Europe during World War II focuses on the Allied campaigns in Sicily and Italy, detailing the bloody battles at Salerno, Anzio, and Monte Cassino, as well as the June 1944 liberation of Rome.
"The second volume of . [the author's] Liberation trilogy, which began with the Pulitzer Prizewinning an Army at Dawn: The War in North Africa, 1942-1943, this is probably the most eagerly awaited World War II book of the year. Atkinson's clear prose, perceptive analysis, and grasp of the personalities and nuances of the campaigns make his book an essential purchase." —*Library Journal*
Includes bibliographical references and index.

The Guns at Last Light: The War in Western Europe, 1944-1945. Rick Atkinson. Henry Holt and Co. 2013. 896 p. (Liberation trilogy, 3)
ISBN 9780805062908
Grades: Adult   940.54
1. Western Front (World War II) 2. Military history 3. World War II 4. Military campaigns 5. Normandy Invasion, June 6, 1944 6. Military tactics 7. Battle history 8. 1940s 9. History writing — Wars and conflicts — World War II
LC 2012034312
New York Times Notable Book, 2013.
The final volume of the trilogy chronicling the Allied victory in Western Europe brings to life the brutal struggles in Normandy and at the Battle of the Bulge to the freeing of Paris, as experienced by participants from every level of the military.

ESSENTIAL AND RECOMMENDED TITLES
940.54 Military history of World War II

"[L]ively, occasionally lyric prose brings the vast theater of battle, from the beaches of Normandy deep into Germany, brilliantly alive." —*Publishers Weekly*

Includes bibliographical references and index.

Barrett, David Dean
140 Days to Hiroshima: The Story of Japan's Last Chance to Avert Armageddon. David Dean Barrett. Diversion Books 2020. 351 p.
ISBN 9781635765816
Grades: Adult   940.54
1. Togo, Shigenori, 1882-1950 2. Military strategy 3. Politicians 4. Generals 5. Negotiation 6. Conventional warfare 7. Diplomatic negotiations in international disputes 8. Nuclear weapons 9. Nuclear warfare 10. Atomic bomb 11. World War II 12. Japanese history 13. Hiroshima, Japan 14. Nagasaki, Japan 15. Japan 16. United States 17. 20th century 18. Second World War era (1939-1945) 19. History writing — Asia — Japan 20. History writing — Wars and conflicts — Atomic Bomb — World War II 21. History writing — Military

A military historian, taking us inside the cabinets of the US and Japan leading to the atomic bombing of Hiroshima, then Nagasaki, and ultimately to Japan's surrender, presents this nearly day-by-day account of the struggle to end the most destructive conflict in history.

"A nonrevisionist, reflective, opinionated, intensely researched WWII history." —*Kirkus*

Bascomb, Neal
The Winter Fortress: The Epic Mission to Sabotage Hitler's Atomic Bomb. Neal Bascomb. Houghton Mifflin Harcourt 2016. 352 p.
ISBN 9780544368057
Grades: Adult   940.54
1. Commando operations 2. Sabotage 3. World War II 4. Resistance to military occupation 5. Atomic bomb 6. Germany 7. Norway 8. History writing — Wars and conflicts — Resistance — World War II
LC 2015042716

Documents the Allied raid against occupied Norway's Vermork hydroelectric plant, the world's only supplier of an essential ingredient needed by the Nazis to build an atomic bomb, citing the teamwork of British Special Ops, a brilliant scientists and refugee Norwegian commandos that foiled Hitler's nuclear ambitions.

"Parts of the book read like an adventure novel, others like straightforward history, but the combination will appeal to readers of both WWII fiction and nonfiction." —*Booklist*

Includes bibliographical references and index.

Beevor, Antony
Ardennes 1944: Hitler's Last Gamble. Antony Beevor. Viking 2015. xix, 451 pages
ISBN 9780670025312
Grades: Adult   940.54
1. Ardennes, Battle of the, 1944-1945 2. World War II 3. Battles 4. Military history 5. 1940s 6. History writing — Wars and conflicts — World War II
LC 2015490442

Reconstructs the Battle of the Bulge in riveting detail to discuss the surprise counter-offensive by German forces, the numerous casualties on both sides and the strategies that enabled an Allied victory.

"Beevor skewers the pretensions and weaknesses of generals and details atrocities and mistreatment of both civilians and surrendering enemies by both sides. The author takes for granted more knowledge of the battle, the terrain, and the German language than general readers may possess, and he occasionally repeats information attentive readers will recall from previous mentions. But these are small quibbles. On the whole, this is a treasure of memorable portraits, striking details, fascinating revelations, and broad insights likely to be the definitive account of the battle for years to come. Essential reading for anyone interested in World War II." —*Kirkus*

The Battle of Arnhem: The Deadliest Airborne Operation of WWII, 1944. Antony Beevor. Viking 2018. 480 p.
ISBN 9780525429821

Grades: Adult   940.54
1. Arnhem, Battle of, 1944 2. Military campaigns 3. Parachute troops 4. Airborne troops 5. Military defeat 6. Command of troops 7. Military strategy 8. World War II 9. Netherlands 10. Second World War era (1939-1945) 11. History writing — Wars and conflicts — World War II — European Theater

The prize-winning historian and author of "D-Day" reconstructs the devastating airborne battle of Arnhem.

Includes bibliographical references and index.

D-Day: The Battle for Normandy. Antony Beevor. Viking 2009. 608 p.
ISBN 9780670021192
Grades: 9 10 11 12 Adult   940.54
1. World War II 2. Normandy Invasion, June 6, 1944 3. Military history 4. Military campaigns 5. Battles 6. French history 7. Normandy 8. 1940s 9. History writing — Wars and conflicts — World War II 10. History writing — Wars and conflicts — Battles
LC 2009023574

Presents an account of the Normandy invasion that offers insight into the experiences of soldiers and French civilians, documenting the heavy casualties suffered on all fronts and the ways in which the war influenced relations between America and Europe.

"This is a vibrant work of history that honors the sacrifice of tens of thousands of men and women." —*Time*

Includes bibliographical references and index.

The Fall of Berlin, 1945. Antony Beevor. Viking 2002. xxxvii, 489 p, 24 p. of plates : Illustration; Map; Portrait
ISBN 9780670030415
Grades: Adult   940.54
1. Berlin, Battle of, 1945 2. World War II 3. Pillage 4. German history 5. Germany 6. Berlin, Germany 7. Berlin, Germany 8. History writing — Wars and conflicts — World War II — European Theater 9. History writing — Wars and conflicts — Battles
LC 2002510674

Chronicles the horror of Berlin's fall to the Soviets in 1945, recalling the starvation, exposure, artillery fire, rape, and mass destruction that marked the Red Army's final push on Germany's capital.

"The author relies on material from American, German, British, French, and Swedish archives and documents from former Soviet files, making the book an invaluable and meticulous account." —*Booklist*

Includes bibliographical references (p. 466-475) and index.

The Second World War. Antony Beevor. Little, Brown and Co. 2012. 704 p.
ISBN 9780316023740
Grades: Adult   940.54
1. World War II 2. War and society 3. War 4. 1940s 5. 20th century 6. History writing — Wars and conflicts — World War II
LC 2012007028

The British historian and author presents a single volume history of the world's largest conflict, from Manchuria in 1939 to the Soviet invasion of northern China six years later, describing the human drama of soldiers, civilians and political leaders.

Includes bibliographical references and index.

Stalingrad. Antony Beevor. Viking 1998. xvii, 493 p, 16 p. of plates : Illustration; Map
ISBN 9780670870950
Grades: Adult   940.54
1. Stalingrad, Battle of, 1942-1943 2. Operation Barbarossa 3. Soviet Union history 4. 1940s 5. History writing — Wars and conflicts — World War II — European Theater
LC 98019346

Samuel Johnson Prize for Nonfiction, 1999; Hawthornden Prize, 1999.

With the benefit of Russian documents never before seen by Western scholars, German transcripts, and private letters and diaries, the author offers a narrative of the battle of Stalingrad, which broke the back of the Nazi army during the Second World War.

PUBLIC LIBRARY CORE COLLECTION: NONFICTION
Twentieth Edition

"Beevor has composed a history of Stalingrad unlikely to be bettered." —*Booklist*

Includes bibliographical references (p. 477-485) and index.

Blume, Lesley M. M.
Fallout: The Hiroshima Cover-Up and the Reporter Who Revealed It to the World. Lesley M. M. Blume. Simon & Schuster 2020. 288 p.

ISBN 9781982128517

Grades: Adult   940.54

1. Hersey, John, 1914-1993 2. Hibakusha 3. Radioactive fallout 4. War correspondents 5. Military cover-ups 6. War propaganda 7. Public opinion 8. Nuclear weapons policy 9. Journalists 10. Journalism 11. Nuclear weapons 12. Nuclear warfare 13. Atomic bomb 14. World War II 15. Japanese history 16. Hiroshima, Japan 17. Japan 18. United States 19. 20th century 20. Second World War era (1939-1945) 21. Biographies 22. Life stories — Arts and culture — Writing — Journalists 23. History writing — Wars and conflicts — Atomic Bomb — World War II 24. History writing — Asia — Japan

LC 2020000055

New York Times Notable Book, 2020.

Just days after the United States decimated Hiroshima and Nagasaki with nuclear bombs, the Japanese surrendered unconditionally. But even before the surrender, the US government and military had begun a secret propaganda and information suppression campaign to hide the devastating nature of these experimental weapons. The cover-up intensified as Occupation forces closed the atomic cities to Allied reporters, preventing leaks about the horrific long-term effects of radiation which would kill thousands during the months after the blast. For nearly a year the cover-up worked—until New Yorker journalist John Hersey got into Hiroshima and managed to report the truth to the world. When the magazine published "Hiroshima" in August 1946, it became an instant global sensation, and inspired pervasive horror about the hellish new threat that America had unleashed.

"Journalist Blume (Everybody Behaves Badly) delivers a thrilling behind-the-scenes account of John Hersey's seminal 1946 report on the atomic bombing of Hiroshima.... This enthralling, fine-grained chronicle reveals what it takes to cut through 'Dangerously anesthetizing' statistics and speak truth to power." —*Publishers Weekly*

Includes bibliographical references and index.

Bradley, James
Flags of Our Fathers. James Bradley with Ron Powers. Bantam Books 2000. 376 p. : Illustration; Map

ISBN 9780440229209

Grades: 11 12 Adult   940.54

1. Rosenthal, Joe, 1911-2006 2. Iwo Jima, Battle of, 1945 3. Military campaigns 4. Photographs 5. Marines 6. Soldiers 7. World War II 8. Military history 9. Pacific Area 10. United States 11. Japan 12. 1940s 13. Second World War era (1939-1945) 14. Biographies 15. Page to screen 16. History writing — Wars and conflicts — World War II — Pacific Theater 17. Life stories — Law and order — Armed forces personnel 18. Adult books for young adults

LC 00025803

Alex Award, 2001.

Chronicles one of the bloodiest battles of World War II, focusing on the men who raised the flag at Iwo Jima.

"This is the story of the most famous photograph to come out of World War II, the flag-raising on Mount Suribachi during the Battle of Iwo Jima in February 1945. Bradley is the son of one of the six men immortalized in that remarkable photo, and his gripping narrative, vivid descriptions, and heartfelt style make this a powerful story of courage, humility, and tragedy." —*Library Journal*

Includes bibliographical references (p. [365]-366) and index.

Flyboys: A True Story of Courage. James Bradley. Little, Brown 2003. 398 p, 32 p. of plates : Illustration

ISBN 9780316105842

Grades: Adult   940.54

1. Military pilots 2. Prisoners of war 3. War crime trials 4. World War II 5. Prisons 6. Atrocities 7. Military history 8. 20th century 9. Biographies 10. History writing — Wars and conflicts — World War II — Pacific Theater 11. Life stories — Law and order — Armed forces personnel

LC 2003044725

Relates the story of eight American airmen who were shot down over Chichi Jima during World War II, one of whom was rescued and later became president of the United States, and the other seven who were captured by Japanese troops.

Includes bibliographical references (p. 371-378) and index.

Brotherton, Marcus
A Bright and Blinding Sun: A World War II Story of Survival, Love, and Redemption. Marcus Brotherton. Little Brown & Company 2022. 320 p.

ISBN 9780316318914

Grades: Adult   940.54

1. Johnson, Joe, Jr, 1926-2017 2. World War I 3. Soldiers 4. Teenage boys 5. Prisoners of war 6. Survival 7. War 8. Prostitutes 9. Redemption 10. United States 11. Philippines 12. Japan 13. Biographies 14. History writing — Wars and conflicts — World War I 15. Life stories — Law and order — Armed forces personnel 16. Nonfiction that reads like fiction

The New York Times best-selling author tells the true story of an underage solder who joined the Army at age 14 and was sent to the Philippines after Pearl Harbor, where he became a prisoner of war.

"Full of near-death escapes and unlikely twists of fate, this will appeal to fans of Laura Hillenbrand's Unbroken." —*Publishers Weekly*

Brown, Daniel James
★ *Facing the Mountain: A True Story of Japanese American Heroes in World War II.* Daniel James Brown. Viking 2021. 560 p.

ISBN 9780525557401

Grades: Adult   940.54

1. Military campaigns 2. Japanese Americans 3. Japanese American families 4. Soldiers 5. Racism 6. World War II 7. East Asian Americans 8. Military history 9. American participation in wars 10. United States 11. Second World War era (1939-1945) 12. 20th century 13. History writing — Wars and conflicts — World War II 14. Life stories — Law and order — Armed forces personnel 15. History writing — Military — Military units

LC 2020053098

Based on extensive interviews with the families of the protagonists as well as deep archival research, the New York Times bestselling author of the Boys in the Boat chronicles the special Japanese-American Army unit that overcame brutal odds in Europe.

"While the Japanese American 442nd Regimental Combat Team continues to produce admiring histories, this definitive account tells a larger story.... An insightful portrait of exceptional heroism amid deeply embedded racism." —*Publishers Weekly*

Includes bibliographical references and index.

Bruning, John R.
The Race of Aces: WWII's Elite Airmen and the Epic Battle to Become the Masters of the Sky. John R. Bruning. Hachette Books 2020. 320 p.

ISBN 9780316508629

Grades: Adult   940.54

1. World War II 2. Fighter pilots 3. Military history 4. Fighter planes 5. Aviation history 6. Aerial operations 7. Japanese history 8. United States history 9. Second World War era (1939-1945) 10. 20th century 11. Biographies 12. Life stories — Law and order — Armed forces personnel 13. History writing — Military — Aviation History 14. History writing — Wars and conflicts — World War II — Pacific Theater

LC 2019020760

Documents the challenge presented by ace pilot Eddie Rickenbacker and General George Kenney to five U.S. fighter pilots who contended for personal glory at the lead of a resurgent World War II air force.

"General readers may find Bruning's descriptions of dogfights too repetitive, and the minutia of wartime record keeping threatens to bury the action under facts and figures. Military aviation buffs, however, will relish the level of detail." —*Publishers Weekly*

Includes bibliographical references and index.

ESSENTIAL AND RECOMMENDED TITLES
940.54 Military history of World War II

Budiansky, Stephen
Blackett's War: The Men Who Defeated the Nazi U-boats and Brought Science to the Art of Warfare. Stephen Budiansky. Alfred A. Knopf 2013. 336 p.
ISBN 9780307595966
Grades: Adult   940.54
1. Blackett, P. M. S. (Patrick Maynard Stuart), Baron Blackett, 1897-1974 2. Submarines, German 3. World War II 4. Radar 5. Naval tactics 6. Scientists 7. Naval operations 8. Submarine warfare 9. Second World War era (1939-1945) 10. History writing — Wars and conflicts — World War II 11. History writing — Military — Naval history
LC 2012025272

Documents the lesser-known story of a small group of British and American scientists who applied intellectual strategies to battle techniques and revolutionized the process of how wars are waged and won, citing the particular contributions of operational research founder and future Nobel winner Patrick Blackett.
Includes bibliographical references and index.

Caddick-Adams, Peter
Sand and Steel: The D-Day Invasions and the Liberation of France. Peter Caddick-Adams. Oxford University Press 2019. 1072 p.
ISBN 9780190601898
Grades: Adult   940.54
1. Normandy Invasion, June 6, 1944 2. World War II 3. Operation Overlord 4. Military campaigns 5. Raids (Military science) 6. Military planning 7. Battle history 8. Normandy 9. France 10. 20th century 11. History writing — Wars and conflicts — World War II — European Theater 12. History writing — Military
LC 2018055471

Sand and Steel gives us D-Day, arguably the greatest and most consequential military operation of modern times, beginning with the years of painstaking and costly preparation, through to the pitched battles fought along France's northern coast, from Omaha Beach to the Falaise and the push east to Strasbourg.
Includes bibliographical references and index.

Campbell, James
The Ghost Mountain Boys: Their Epic March and the Terrifying Battle for New Guinea, the Forgotten War of the South Pacific. James Campbell. Crown Publishers 2007. xv, 378 p. : Illustration; Map
ISBN 9780307335968
Grades: Adult   940.54
1. World War II 2. Military campaigns 3. Military history 4. Papua New Guinea 5. United States 6. History writing — Wars and conflicts — World War II — Pacific Theater
LC 2007013140

RR Donnelley Literary Award (Wisconsin), 2008.
Chronicles a little-known episode of World War II in which America's "Ghost Mountain Boys" endured hardship, malnutrition, disease, and harsh conditions in a forty-two-day march from New Guinea's south coast to the north coast battlefields of Buna.
Includes bibliographical references (p. 347-357) and index.

Chrisinger, David
The Soldier's Truth: Ernie Pyle and the Story of World War II. David Chrisinger. Penguin 2023. 400 p.
ISBN 9781984881311
Grades: Adult   940.54
1. Pyle, Ernie, 1900-1945 2. Chrisinger, David, 1986- 3. Journalists 4. War correspondents 5. World War II 6. People with depression 7. War 8. Battles 9. Combat 10. Civilians in war 11. Journalism 12. Military life 13. North American people 14. American people 15. Biographies 16. Life stories — Arts and culture — Writing — Journalists 17. History writing — Wars and conflicts — World War II 18. Travel Writing — Retracing Historic Journeys
LC 2022041989

Drawing on access to all of Pyle's personal correspondences, an acclaimed writer paints a vivid portrait of the life and world of legendary journalist Ernie Pyle, an ordinary American hero who gave WWII a human face for millions of Americans, and interweaves his own travels searching for the landmarks Pyle wrote about.
"Displaying Pyle's detailed snapshots of victory, levity, fatigue, death, and grief, Chrisinger leaves his readers free to form their own conclusions about Pyle's journalistic achievements." —*Kirkus*
Includes bibliographical references and index.

Clavin, Thomas
Lightning Down: A World War II Story of Survival. Tom Clavin. St. Martin's Press 2021. 320 p.
ISBN 9781250151261
Grades: Adult   940.54
1. Moser, Joseph F. 2. World War II 3. Prisoners of war 4. Prisoners of war, American 5. Concentration camps 6. Survival (in concentration camps, prisons, etc.) 7. Fighter pilots 8. Prisons 9. Biographies 10. Life stories — Facing adversity — War and Oppression — Hostages and POWs 11. History writing — Wars and conflicts — World War II
LC 2021027076

This real-life thriller recounts the story of fighter pilot Joe Moser, who beat insurmountable odds to escape the most brutal of Nazi concentration camps right before he was to be executed.
"The journalist and bestselling popular historian returns with the story of an American soldier who survived Nazi terror. . . . A fast-paced account of a little-known POW experience." —*Kirkus*
Includes bibliographical references and index.

Clavin, Tom
The Last Hill: The Epic Story of a Ranger Battalion and the Battle That Defined Wwii. Tom Clavin, and Bob Drury. St. Martin's Press 2022. 336 p.
ISBN 9781250247162
Grades: Adult   940.54
1. World War II 2. Soldiers 3. Military history 4. History Writing — Wars and conflicts — World War II 5. History Writing — United States 6. History Writing — Military — Military Units
LC 2022021367

Offers the untold story of one Ranger battalion's heroism and courage in World War II.
"Frequent collaborators Drury and Clavin (Blood and Treasure) revisit the 1944 Battle of Hürtgen Forest in this exhaustive history." —*Publishers Weekly*
Includes bibliographical references and index.

Conant, Jennet
The Lotus Eaters: The Adventures of Julia Child and Paul Child in the Oss. Jennet Conant. Simon & Schuster 2011. 448 p.
ISBN 9781439163528
Grades: Adult   940.54
1. Child, Julia 2. Child, Paul, 1902-1994 3. McCarthy, Joseph, 1908-1957 4. Spies 5. World War II 6. Secret service 7. Intelligence officers 8. Anti-communist movements 9. Intelligence service 10. United States history 11. United States 12. 1940s 13. 20th century 14. History writing — Spies and spying
LC 2011002875

Chronicles the iconic chef's contributions as a member of the OSS during World War II and her efforts at the side of her husband to support an agent accused of being a spy, describing how their wartime experiences shaped their characters, relationships, and ambitions.
Also published as a Covert Affair.

Delmont, Matthew F.
Half American: The Epic Story of African Americans Fighting World War II at Home and Abroad. Matthew Delmont. Viking 2022. 400 p.
ISBN 9781984880390
Grades: Adult   940.54
1. World War II 2. African American civil rights 3. Racism 4. Racism in the military 5. American participation in wars 6. Race relations 7. African American soldiers 8. Armed Forces 9. United States history 10. United States 11. 20th cen-

tury 12. History writing — African American — United States 13. History writing — Wars and conflicts — World War II 14. Society and culture — Race

LC 2022010535

This history of World War II as told from the African American perspective looks at the bravery and patriotism of the one million Black men and women who served in the face of unfathomable racism.

"Civil rights expert Delmont (history, Dartmouth; Why Busing Failed) has written what is sure to become the standard text on the experience of Black U.S. soldiers—enrolled in segregated units of all the military branches—who fought in World War II." —*Library Journal*

Includes bibliographical references and index.

Dickson, Paul
The **Rise** of the G.I. Army 1940-1941: The Forgotten Story of How America Forged a Powerful Army Before Pearl Harbor. Paul Dickson. Atlantic Monthly Press 2020. 384 p.
ISBN 9780802147677
Grades: Adult   940.54
1. World War II 2. Soldiers 3. Military education 4. Infantry 5. Armies 6. Military history 7. United States history 8. United States 9. 1940s 10. Second World War era (1939-1945) 11. 20th century 12. History writing — Wars and conflicts — World War II 13. History writing — United States 14. History writing — Military

LC BI2020019435

This important addition to American history presents the gripping, untold story of the extraordinary transformation of America's military in a little more than 18 months, which turned them into a disciplined and mobile fighting force that helped win World War II.

"One of the best treatments to date of America's rapid transition from the Depression to the wartime power it became." —*Kirkus*

Dimbleby, Jonathan
The **Battle** of the Atlantic: How the Allies Won the War. Jonathan Dimbleby. Oxford University Press 2016. 560 p.
ISBN 9780190495855
Grades: Adult   940.54
1. World War II 2. Military campaigns 3. Submarine warfare 4. Naval battles 5. Atlantic Ocean 6. History writing — Wars and conflicts — World War II

LC 2015032726

Though often overlooked, the Battle of the Atlantic was crucial to both sides. Had Germany succeeded in cutting off the supply of American ships, England would have likely not held out; the outcome of the war—as well as the future of Europe and the world—would have been remarkably different.

"The history of the battle for the Atlantic is well documented, but Dimbleby's work, with its emphasis on the strategic importance of the battle, is an excellent addition to the story, and expert historians as well as general readers can enjoy this effort." —*Publishers Weekly*

Includes bibliographical references and index.

Drabkin, Ronald
Beverly Hills Spy: The Double-agent War Hero Who Helped Japan Attack Pearl Harbor. Ronald Drabkin. William Morrow 2024. 288 p.
ISBN 9780063310070
Grades: Adult   940.54
1. Rutland, Frederick, 1887-1949 2. Espionage 3. Pearl Harbor, Attack on, 1941 4. World War II 5. World War I veterans 6. Pilots 7. Expatriates 8. Spies 9. Double agents 10. Military intelligence 11. Bribery 12. Betrayal 13. Western European people 14. British people 15. American people 16. Hollywood, California 17. Hawaii 18. Japan 19. Second World War era (1939-1945) 20. Biographies 21. Life stories — Law and order — Spies and secret agents 22. History writing — Wars and conflicts — World War II 23. History writing — Spies and spying 24. Nonfiction that reads like fiction

LC 2023046767

Tells the story of how a debonair British World War I hero, flying ace, fixture of Los Angeles society and friend of Golden Age Hollywood stars flipped to become a spy for Japan in the lead-up to the attack on Pearl Harbor.

"Drawing on recently declassified files, historian Drabkin debuts with a riveting account of Frederick Rutland (1886-1949), a British WWI hero who spied for the Japanese on the eve of WWII." —*Publishers Weekly*

Includes bibliographical references and index.

Dugard, Martin
Taking Berlin: The Bloody Race to Defeat the Third Reich. Martin Dugard. Dutton Caliber, an imprint of Penguin Random House 2022. xi, 332 p.
ISBN 9780593187425
Grades: Adult   940.54
1. World War II 2. Military campaigns 3. Alliances 4. Heads of state 5. Armies 6. Battles 7. International competition 8. Berlin, Germany 9. Europe 10. Second World War era (1939-1945) 11. History writing — Wars and conflicts — World War II — European Theater 12. History writing — Europe 13. Life stories — People in history

LC 2022017499

Recounts the race between the Allies and Soviets to conquer the heart of Nazi Germany in the final, desperate months of WWII, chronicling a moment in history when allies become adversaries.

"Bestseller Dugard follows Taking Paris with a kaleidoscopic account of the Allies' campaign to capture Berlin in the final months of WWII....This fast-paced history is well worth the read." —*Publishers Weekly*

Includes index.

Taking Paris: The Epic Battle for the City of Lights. by Martin Dugard. Dutton Caliber 2021. 400 p.
ISBN 9780593183083
Grades: Adult   940.54
1. World War II 2. Military campaigns 3. Military occupation 4. Battles 5. Espionage 6. French Resistance (World War II) 7. Resistance to military occupation 8. German occupation, World War II 9. Paris, France history 10. French history 11. History writing — Wars and conflicts — World War II — European Theater 12. History writing — Europe — France

LC 2021017300

From Martin Dugard, coauthor of the Killing series with Bill O'Reilly, comes the spellbinding story of the Allied liberation of Paris from the grip of the Nazis during World War II.

"Dugard's book retells the familiar history with notable skill." —*Library Journal*

Includes index.

Frank, Richard B.
Downfall: The End of the Imperial Japanese Empire. Richard B. Frank. Random House 1999. 484 p. : Illustration; Map
ISBN 9780679414247
Grades: 11 12 Adult   940.54
1. World War II 2. Military campaigns 3. Air warfare 4. B-29 bomber 5. Aerial bombing 6. Bombardment 7. Japanese history 8. Second World War era (1939-1945) 9. History writing — Wars and conflicts — World War II — Pacific Theater

LC 99011838

A chronicle of the months leading up to the dropping of the atomic bomb in 1945 includes information from recently declassified documents and offers insight into the reasons behind the decision.

Includes bibliographical references (p. [445]-459) and index.

Tower of Skulls: A History of the Asia-pacific War July 1937-may 1942. Richard B. Frank. W.W. Norton & Company 2020. 751 p.
ISBN 9781324002109
Grades: Adult   940.54
1. Battles 2. Military occupation 3. Colonialism 4. Nationalism 5. Sovereignty 6. Military history 7. World War II 8. Pacific area 9. Pacific Ocean 10. History writing — Wars and conflicts — World War II — Pacific Theater 11. History writing — Military 12. Life stories — Law and order — Military leaders

LC 2019033200

ESSENTIAL AND RECOMMENDED TITLES
940.54 Military history of World War II

In 1937, the swath of the globe east from India to the Pacific Ocean enclosed half the world's population, all save a fraction enduring under some form of colonialism. Japan's onslaught into China that year unleashed a tidal wave of events that fundamentally transformed this region and killed about twenty-five million people. This extraordinary World War II narrative vividly describes in exquisite detail the battles across this entire region and links those struggles on many levels with their profound twenty-first-century legacies. In this first volume of a trilogy, historian Richard B. Frank draws on rich archival research and recently discovered documentary evidence to tell an epic story that gave birth to the world we live in now.

"A painful yet riveting history, especially valuable for historians and military buffs." —*Kirkus*

First in a proposed 3-volume series; Includes bibliographical references and index.

Garrett, Leah
X Troop: The Secret Jewish Commandos of World War II. Leah Garrett. Houghton Mifflin Harcourt 2021. 368 p.
ISBN 9780358172031
Grades: Adult 940.54
1. Masters, Peter, 1922-2005 2. Gans, Manfred 3. Anson, Colin Edward, 1922-2016 4. World War II 5. Refugees, Jewish 6. Commando troops 7. Military intelligence 8. Secret service 9. Jewish people 10. Military campaigns 11. Great Britain 12. History writing — Wars and conflicts — World War II — European Theater 13. History writing — Jewish history 14. Life stories — Law and order — Armed forces personnel 15. Life stories — Facing adversity — War and oppression — Refugees
LC 2020044747

June 1942. The shadow of the Third Reich has fallen across the European continent. In desperation, Winston Churchill and his chief of staff form an unusual plan: a new commando unit made up of Jewish refugees who have escaped to Britain. The resulting volunteers are a motley group of intellectuals, artists, and athletes, most from Germany and Austria. Many have been interned as enemy aliens, and have lost their families, their homes—their whole worlds. They will stop at nothing to defeat the Nazis.

"Garrett (Young Lions), a professor of Jewish studies at Hunter College, recounts in this dramatic and deeply researched history the WWII exploits of X Troop, a British commando unit made up of Jewish refugees from Austria, Germany, and Hungary." —*Publishers Weekly*

Includes bibliographical references and index.

Geroux, William
The Ghost Ships of Archangel: The Arctic Voyage That Defied the Nazis. William Geroux. Viking 2019. 368 p.
ISBN 9780525557463
Grades: Adult 940.54
1. Naval convoys 2. Military missions 3. World War II 4. Submarines, German 5. Military supplies 6. Navigation 7. Freighters 8. Survival 9. Naval operations 10. Arctic ocean 11. History writing — Military — Naval history 12. History writing — Wars and conflicts — World War II
LC 2018049389

Documents the extraordinary journey of four Allied ships who in 1942 became separated from their convoy and navigated a perilous maze of Arctic ice, Nazi bombers and U-boats to deliver much-needed supplies to the Soviet war effort.

"Drawing on diaries, firsthand interviews (with, for example, merchant mariner Jim North, who was on the Troubadour), and several memoirs, Geroux focuses on multiple first-person perspectives to shed light on everything from boredom in the Icelandic port to the sailors new reality of life as prey susceptible to German attacks." —*Publishers Weekly*

Includes bibliographical references and index.

Giangreco, D. M.
Hell to Pay: Operation Downfall and the Invasion of Japan, 1945-47. D.M. Giangreco. Naval Institute Press 2009. xxiii, 362 p. : Illustration; Map
ISBN 9781591143161
Grades: Adult 940.54
1. Military campaigns 2. Military history 3. World War II 4. Armed Forces 5. United States history 6. Japan 7. 1940s 8. Second World War era (1939-1945) 9. History writing — Wars and conflicts — World War II
LC 2009027766

Discusses the United States' 1943 plan to launch a two-year invasion of Japan, using newly declassified American and Japanese internal documents that provide specifics of the military tactics and weaponry meant to be used.

"Illustrative of just how much the war with Japan was a close-run thing, this is essential reading." —*Library Journal*

Includes bibliographical references and index.

Gladwell, Malcolm
★ *The Bomber Mafia: A Dream, a Temptation, and the Longest Night of the Second World War*. Malcolm Gladwell. Little, Brown & Company 2021. 288 p.
ISBN 9780316296618
Grades: Adult 940.54
1. LeMay, Curtis E, 1906-1990 2. Aerial bombing 3. Bombardment 4. Military strategy 5. Generals 6. Decision-making 7. World War II 8. Tokyo, Japan 9. Japan 10. Second World War era (1939-1945) 11. History writing — Wars and conflicts — World War II — Pacific Theater 12. History writing — Military — Aviation History 13. Life stories — Law and order — Military leaders

Most military thinkers in the years leading up to World War II saw the airplane as an afterthought. But a small band of idealistic strategists had a different view. This "Bomber Mafia" asked: What if precision bombing could, just by taking out critical choke points—industrial or transportation hubs—cripple the enemy and make war far less lethal? Malcolm Gladwell examines the bombing of Tokyo on the deadliest night of the war and asks, "Was it worth it?".

"Gladwell (Talking to Strangers) delivers a ruminative, anecdotal account of what led up to the deadliest air raid of WWII: the firebombing of Tokyo by U.S. forces in March 1945." —*Publishers Weekly*

Graff, Garrett M.
★ *When the Sea Came Alive: An Oral History of D-Day*. Garrett M. Graff. Avid Reader Press 2024. 384 p.
ISBN 9781668027813
Grades: Adult 940.54
1. Normandy Invasion, June 6, 1944 2. World War II 3. Military history 4. Military campaigns 5. Aerial operations 6. Naval operations 7. Battles 8. French history 9. United States history 10. Normandy 11. Second World War era (1939-1945) 12. Anthologies 13. History writing — Wars and conflicts — World War II 14. History writing — Wars and conflicts — Battles

D-Day is one of history's greatest and most unbelievable military and human triumphs. Though the full campaign lasted just over a month, the surprise landing of over 150,000 Allied troops on June 6, 1944, is considered the moment that turned the tide for the Allied forces and ultimately led to the defeat of the Axis powers in World War II. Historian Garrett M. Graff explores the full impact of this world-changing event—from the secret creation of landing plans by top government and military officials and organization of troops, to the moment the boat doors opened to reveal the beach where men fought for their lives and the future of the free world.

"Graff draws from more than 700 eyewitness accounts for this gripping and propulsive history of the D-Day invasion…Readers will be spellbound." —*Publishers Weekly*

Grayling, A. C.
Among the Dead Cities: The History and Moral Legacy of the Wwii Bombing of Civilians in Germany and Japan. A.C. Grayling. Walker & Co. 2006. xii, 361 p. : Illustration; Map
ISBN 9780802714718
Grades: 11 12 Adult 940.54
1. Bombardment 2. Aerial operations 3. War casualties 4. World War II 5. Military history 6. Germany 7. Japan 8. 20th century 9. Second World War era (1939-1945) 10. History writing — Wars and conflicts — World War II 11. Adult books for young adults

Presents an analysis of the miltary rationale used by Britain and the United States for bombing civilian targets in Germany and Japan during World War II, discussing the reasons why such tactics were both largely ineffective and morally reprehensible.

"Was it wrong for the Allies to bomb German and Japanese civilians in World War II? In this book, . . . [the author] attends to one of the twentieth-century's largest unexploded moral conundrums. . . . Grayling's book builds careful, generous cases for and against the bombing, admitting as evidence both the experience of the bombed as well as the bombers." —*Booklist*

Includes bibliographical references (p. [345]-348) and index.

Ham, Paul

Hiroshima Nagasaki: The Real Story of the Atomic Bombings and Their Aftermath. Paul Ham. Thomas Dunne Books, St. Martin's Press 2014. IX, 629 p, 8 unnumbered p. of plates : Illustration

ISBN 9781250047113

Grades: Adult   940.54

1. Hibakusha 2. Atrocities 3. Nuclear weapons 4. Nuclear warfare 5. Atomic bomb 6. World War II 7. Hiroshima, Japan 8. Nagasaki, Japan 9. Second World War era (1939-1945) 10. Australian literature 11. History writing — Wars and conflicts — Atomic Bomb — World War II 12. History writing — Wars and conflicts — World War II — Pacific Theater

LC 2014008489

A comprehensive history drawn from eyewitness accounts challenges the belief that the nuclear attacks on Hiroshima and Nagasaki brought the war in the Pacific to an end, arguing that the bombings were unnecessary to the war's outcome, especially because they cost tens of thousands of human lives.

"A valuable contribution to the literature of World War II that asks its readers to rethink much of what theyve been taught about America's just cause." —*Kirkus*

Includes bibliographical references (pages 581-601) and index; Originally published: Pymble, N.S.W. : HarperCollins, 2011.

Hamilton, Nigel

The Mantle of Command: FDR at War, 1941/1942. Nigel Hamilton. Houghton Mifflin Harcourt 2014. 528 pages

ISBN 9780547775241

Grades: Adult   940.54

1. Roosevelt, Franklin D. (Franklin Delano), 1882-1945 2. Command of troops 3. World War II 4. International relations 5. United States 6. Great Britain 7. History writing — Wars and conflicts — World War II

LC 2013045586

An in-depth analysis of FDR's leadership during the Second World War reveals how he assumed control over key decisions to launch a successful trial landing in North Africa to shift the war in favor of Allied forces.

"Though it's a weighty tome, and is based extensively on Roosevelt's own notes, Hamilton keeps a brisk pace throughout to produce what will likely be seen as a definitive volume on this aspect of Roosevelt's career." —*Publishers Weekly*

Includes bibliographical references and index.

Hampton, Dan

Operation Vengeance: The Astonishing Aerial Ambush That Changed World War II. Dan Hampton. William Morrow and Company 2020. 448 p. : Illustration; Map

ISBN 9780062938091

Grades: Adult   940.54

1. Mitchell, John W, 1914-1995 2. Yamamoto, Isoroku, 1884-1943 3. Fighter pilots 4. Admirals 5. World War II 6. Enemies 7. Assassination 8. Aerial operations 9. 1940s 10. Second World War era (1939-1945) 11. History writing — Wars and conflicts — World War II — Pacific Theater 12. History writing — Military

LC Bl2020015968

The best-selling author of Viper Pilot presents a narrative account of America's secret World War II mission to assassinate Isoroku Yamamoto, the Japanese commander who masterminded the Pearl Harbor attacks.

"Although this history is well documented in World War II literature, the accessible storytelling by Hampton will likely be of interest for aficionados of the period." —*Library Journal*

Hanson, Victor Davis

The Second World Wars: How the First Global Conflict Was Fought and Won. Victor Davis Hanson. Basic Books, an imprint of Perseus Books, LLC, a subsidiary of Hachette Book Group, Inc. 2017. 688 p.

ISBN 9780465066988

Grades: Adult   940.54

1. World War II 2. War and civilization 3. Military power 4. Weapons 5. Battles 6. Second World War era (1939-1945) 7. History writing — Wars and conflicts — World War II

LC 2017024227

A noted military historian presents a definitive account of World War II and a dramatic reinterpretation the most lethal conflict in human history.

"An ingenious, always provocative analysis of history's most lethal war." —*Kirkus*

Includes bibliographical references and index.

Harmon, Mark

Ghosts of Honolulu: A Japanese Spy, a Japanese American Spy Hunter, and the Untold Story of Pearl Harbor. Mark Harmon and Leon Carroll, Jr. Harper Select 2023. 272 p.

ISBN 9781400337019

Grades: Adult   940.54

1. World War II 2. Pearl Harbor, Attack on, 1941 3. Espionage 4. Spies 5. Counterintelligence 6. United States 7. Pearl Harbor, Hawaii 8. Second World War era (1939-1945) 9. History writing — Wars and conflicts — World War II — Pacific Theater

Scrutinizing long-buried historical documents, a NCIS star and a former NCIS Special Agent, have brought forth a true-life NCIS story of deception, discovery and danger, depicting the incredible high stakes game of naval intelligence and the need to define what is real and what only appears to be real.

"NCIS star Harmon and Carroll, the show's technical adviser, spotlight in their fast-paced debut how the historical precursor of the Naval Criminal Investigative Service dueled with Japanese spies in Hawaii during WWII." —*Publishers Weekly*

Hastings, Max

Armageddon: The Battle for Germany, 1944-45. Max Hastings. A.A. Knopf 2004. xxiii, 584 p. : Illustration; Map

ISBN 9780375414336

Grades: Adult   940.54

1. World War II 2. Military campaigns 3. Third Reich, 1933-1945 4. 1940s 5. History writing — Wars and conflicts — World War II — European Theater

LC 2004046468

New York Times Notable Book, 2005.

A sweeping history of the final eight months of World War II on the European front draws on interviews with survivors and the archives of the major combatants to raise provocative questions about the pact between the Allies and the Soviet Union, the role of strategic bombing, the combat abilities of soldiers on all sides of the conflict, and the roles of such leaders as Eisenhower, Roosevelt, Churchill, Montgomery, and others.

"The author tells the grim tale of the final collapse of the Third Reich. It does so from the viewpoints of the upper millstone (the Western Allies), the lower millstone (the Russians) and the grain being ground in between (the Germans). The research includes previously untapped Russian archives (particularly in the accounts of Soviet veterans) and leads to a gripping and horrifying story that serious students of military history will find almost impossible to put down." —*Publishers Weekly*

Includes bibliographical references and index.

Inferno: The World at War, 1939-45. by Max Hastings. Alfred A. Knopf 2011. 672 p.

ISBN 9780307273598

Grades: Adult   940.54

1. World War II 2. Soldiers 3. 1940s 4. 20th century 5. History writing — Wars and conflicts — World War II

LC 2011013890

New York Times Notable Book, 2011.

ESSENTIAL AND RECOMMENDED TITLES
940.54 Military history of World War II

Here, for the first time, Max Hastings gives us a magnificent, single-volume history of World War II in its entirety. Through his strikingly detailed stories of everyday people, he provides an intimate portrait of the world at war. Remarkably informed and wide-ranging, Inferno is both elegantly written and cogently argued. Above all, it is a new and essential understanding of one of the greatest and bloodiest events of the twentieth century.

Includes bibliographical references and index; Originally published: London : HarperPress, 2010.

Operation Chastise: *The Raf's Most Brilliant Attack of World War II*. Max Hastings. HarperCollins 2020. 416 pages
ISBN 9780062953636
Grades: Adult   940.54
1. World War II 2. Air warfare 3. Bombers (Airplanes) 4. Dams 5. Military pilots 6. Aerial bombing 7. Airmen 8. Military aviation 9. Military strategy 10. Military campaigns 11. Floods 12. Aviation history 13. Military history 14. German history 15. Europe 16. Second World War era (1939-1945) 17. 1940s 18. 20th century 19. History writing — Wars and conflicts — World War II — European Theater 20. History writing — Military — Aviation History
LC Bl2020000366

One of the most lauded historians of our time returns to the Second World War in this magnificent retelling of the awe-inspiring raid on German dams conducted by the Royal Army Force's 617 Squadron.

"The master of military history takes on Britain's celebrated May 1943 Dam Buster air attack . . . showing once again that the preparations, participants, and consequences of a military action are as fascinating as the fireworks."—*Kirkus*

Operation Pedestal: *The Fleet That Battled to Malta, 1942*. Max Hastings. Harper 2021. 416 p.
ISBN 9780062980151
Grades: Adult   940.54
1. World War II 2. Islands 3. Bombardment 4. Naval battles 5. Naval convoys 6. Merchant ships 7. Intelligence service 8. Aerial operations 9. Naval operations 10. Malta 11. Mediterranean Sea 12. Great Britain 13. History writing — Wars and conflicts — World War II — European Theater 14. History writing — Wars and conflicts — Battles 15. History writing — Military — Naval history 16. Nonfiction that reads like fiction

Over the fall of 1941, the Royal Navy and RAF, aided by British intelligence, used the island of Malta to launch a punishing campaign against the Germans, sinking more than 75 percent of their supply ships destined for North Africa. But by spring 1942, the British lost their advantage. In April and May, the Luftwaffe dropped more bombs on Malta than London received in the Blitz. British submarines and surface warships were withdrawn, and the remaining forces were on the brink of starvation. Operation Pedestal chronicles the ensuing British mission to save those troops. Over twelve days in August, German and Italian forces faced off against British air and naval fleets in one of the fiercest battles of the war. As historian Max Hastings makes clear, while the Germans claimed victory, it was the British who ultimately prevailed, for Malta remained a crucial asset that helped lead to the Nazis' eventual defeat.

"Buoyed by prodigious research and vivid prose, this is a brilliant illumination of one of WWII's most dramatic episodes."—*Publishers Weekly*

Overlord: *D-Day and the Battle for Normandy*. Max Hastings. Vintage Books 2006. 368 p. : Illustration; Map
ISBN 9780307275714
Grades: 11 12 Adult   940.54
1. World War II 2. Military campaigns 3. Normandy Invasion, June 6, 1944 4. Military history 5. Normandy 6. 1940s 7. 20th century 8. History writing — Wars and conflicts — World War II — European Theater 9. History writing — Wars and conflicts — Battles
LC 2006271018

Recounts in detail the 1944 Allied invasion of Europe and analyzes the strategies followed by the American and British invaders and the German defenders.

"Hastings' reportage of the battle is not unworthy to stand with that of the best journalists and writers who witnessed it. He has managed to recreate what it was like for almost everyone who was there."—*New York Times Book Review*

Includes bibliographical references (p. [350]-353) and index; Originally published: New York : Simon and Schuster, 1984.

Retribution: *The Battle for Japan, 1944-45*. by Max Hastings. Alfred A. Knopf 2008. xxv, 615 p, 32 p. of plates : Illustration; Map
ISBN 9780307263513
Grades: Adult   940.54
1. World War II veterans 2. World War II 3. Military campaigns 4. Military history 5. Japanese history 6. Japan 7. Pacific Area 8. 20th century 9. History writing — Wars and conflicts — World War II — Pacific Theater 10. Adult books for young adults
LC 2007034202

Booklist Editors' Choice, 2008; New York Times Notable Book, 2008.

A definitive chronicle of the final year in the Pacific war of World War II offers insightful portraits of key figures in the efforts to defeat Japan—MacArthur, Nimitz, Mountbatten, Mao, and Chiang Kai-shek—and discusses such topics as the road to Allied victory, the war's bloody campaigns, Japan's war against China, and the decision to bomb Hiroshima and Nagasaki.

"Encompassing the British, Chinese, and Soviet roles in vanquishing Japan, Hastings is both comprehensive and finely acute in this masterful interpretive narrative."—*Booklist*

Includes bibliographical references.

The Secret War: *Spies, Ciphers, and Guerrillas, 1939-1945*. Max Hastings. HarperCollins 2016. 640 pages
ISBN 9780062259271
Grades: Adult   940.54
1. Secret service 2. Commando operations 3. World War II 4. Military intelligence 5. History writing — Wars and conflicts — World War II 6. History writing — Spies and spying
LC Bl2016012661

A sweeping examination of one of the most important yet underexplored aspects of World War II—intelligence—showing how espionage successes and failures by the United States, Britain, Russia, Germany and Japan influenced the course of the war and its final outcome.

"This wide-ranging account is filled with compelling characters, some admirable, others morally dubious. Hastings also illustrates that even great intelligence coups can be wasted by politicians who fail to properly utilize the information."—*Booklist*

Hemming, Henry
Agents *of Influence: A British Campaign, a Canadian Spy, and the Secret Plot to Bring America into World War II*. Henry Hemming. PublicAffairs 2019. 352 p.
ISBN 9781541742147
Grades: Adult   940.54
1. World War II 2. Undercover operations 3. Public opinion 4. Propaganda 5. Intelligence service 6. Espionage 7. Secrecy 8. United States history 9. Second World War era (1939-1945) 10. 1940s 11. History writing — Wars and conflicts — Homefront — World War II 12. History writing — Spies and spying
LC 2019946472

Tells the story of Canadian-born MI6 officer William Stephenson who came to New York during World War II in order to persuade the Americans to join the war. His main opponent was Charles Lindbergh who had no interest in participating in the war.

Hersey, John
★ ***Hiroshima***. John Hersey. Vintage Books 1989. 152 p.
ISBN 9780679721031
Grades: 11 12 Adult   940.54
1. Bombs 2. Aerial bombing 3. Nuclear weapons 4. Nuclear warfare 5. Atomic bomb 6. World War II 7. Hiroshima, Japan 8. 1940s 9. Second World War era (1939-1945) 10. History writing — Wars and conflicts — Atomic Bomb — World War II

LC 88040016

The classic tale of the day the first atom bomb was dropped offers a haunting evocation of the memories of survivors and an appeal to the conscience of humanity.

A new edition with a final chapter written forty years after the explosion; Reprint. Originally published: New York : A.A. Knopf, 1985.

Hervieux, Linda
Forgotten: The Untold Story of D-Day's Black Heroes, at Home and at War. Linda Hervieux. HarperCollins Publishers 2015. 368 p.
ISBN 9780062313799
Grades: Adult   940.54
1. World War II 2. African American soldiers 3. Normandy Invasion, June 6, 1944 4. Race relations 5. Military campaigns 6. Military history 7. American participation in wars 8. Normandy 9. United States 10. History writing — Wars and conflicts — World War II 11. History writing — African American — United States

LC 2015017941

Drawing on newly uncovered military records and original interviews with surviving members of the 320th Barrage Balloon Battalion—a unit of African-American soldiers that has been overlooked by history—and their families, the author tells the story of these heroic men charged with manning armed balloons meant to deter enemy aircraft on D-Day.

"Recommended for aviation buffs, chroniclers of World War II, and anyone who wants a nondense military read." —*Library Journal*

Includes bibliographical references and index.

Hindley, Meredith
Destination Casablanca: Exile, Espionage, and the Battle for North Africa in World War II. Meredith Hindley. PublicAffairs 2017. 432 p.
ISBN 9781610394055
Grades: Adult   940.54
1. Military campaigns 2. Espionage 3. Intelligence service 4. World War II 5. Spies 6. Political intrigue 7. Diplomacy 8. Battles 9. International relations 10. Southwest Asia and North Africa (Middle East) history 11. Southwest Asia and North Africa (Middle East) 12. Morocco 13. France 14. United States 15. 20th century 16. History writing — Wars and conflicts — World War II

LC 2017018911

Filled with rogue soldiers, power grabs and diplomatic intrigue, a captivating and untold story of Casablanca, the glamorous city memorialized in the classic film, 'shows how this exotic travel destination became a crucial logistical hub in the fight against Germany.

Includes bibliographical references and index.

Hogan, William R.
Task Force Hogan: The World War II Tank Battalion That Spearheaded the Liberation of Europe. William R. Hogan. William Morrow 2023. 320 p.
ISBN 9780063272026
Grades: Adult   940.54
1. Hogan, Samuel Mason, 1915-2005 2. Combat 3. Military campaigns 4. Tank warfare 5. Military history 6. Military officers 7. American participation in wars 8. World War II 9. Tanks (Military science) 10. Self-sacrifice 11. United States history 12. Germany 13. France 14. Belgium 15. Second World War era (1939-1945) 16. Letters 17. Interviews 18. Biographies 19. History writing — Wars and conflicts — World War II — European Theater 20. Life stories — Facing adversity — War and oppression 21. History writing — Military — Military units

LC 2023024271

Aided by never-before-seen letters, military dispatches, journal entries and interviews with surviving family members, a fourth-generation US Army officer tells the story of his father Sam Hogan's tank battalion, the "Spearhead," as they battled on the front lines of some of World War II's toughest fights against impossible odds.

"Former U.S. Army officer and fourth-generation soldier Hogan debuts with a fast-paced and immersive chronicle of the wartime exploits of his father, Samuel Hogan, who fought in WWII as a member of the Third Armored Division." —*Publishers Weekly*

Includes bibliographical references and index.

Holland, James
Battle of Britain: Five Months That Changed History, May-october 1940. James Holland. St. Martin's Press 2011. 704 p.
ISBN 9780312675004
Grades: Adult   940.54
1. Britain, Battle of, 1940 2. Battles 3. World War II 4. Military history 5. Armed forces 6. 1940s 7. History writing — Wars and conflicts — World War II

LC 2010040646

The historian author of Italy's Shadow presents an account of the pivotal World War II battle based on extensive interviews with people on both sides, offering insight into how the fight was won and the potential of alternate scenarios.

"This massive volume is informative, enthralling, and movingoften all three at once. It effectively combines narrative and analysis to tell the story of the confrontation between the Luftwaffe and RAF Fighter Command from May through October 1940." —*Booklist*

First published in Great Britain by Bantam Press—T.P. verso; Includes bibliographical references and index.

Big Week: The Biggest Air Battle of World War II. James Holland. Atlantic Monthly 2018. 400 p.
ISBN 9780802128393
Grades: Adult   940.54
1. World War II 2. Normandy Invasion, June 6, 1944 3. Air warfare 4. Military campaigns 5. Military aircraft 6. Military aviation 7. Air power 8. European history 9. Second World War era (1939-1945) 10. 20th century 11. History writing — Wars and conflicts — World War II — European Theater 12. History writing — Military — Aviation History

Tells the vivid and largely untold story of the dramatic Allied air campaign against Germany that was a turning point in World War II and ultimately crucial to the success of D-Day and the Allied invasion of Europe.

Brothers in Arms: One Legendary Tank Regiment's Bloody War from D-Day to V-e Day. James Holland. Atlantic Monthly Press 2021. 592 p.
ISBN 9780802159083
Grades: Adult   940.54
1. Tank warfare 2. Tanks (Military science) 3. Normandy Invasion, June 6, 1944 4. Military campaigns 5. Battles 6. War casualties 7. World War II 8. Military history 9. European history 10. Great Britain 11. Germany 12. France 13. 20th century 14. History writing — Military — Military units 15. History writing — Wars and conflicts — World War II — European Theater 16. History writing — Europe — United Kingdom 17. Life stories — Law and order — Armed forces personnel

LC 2021041408

In the annals of World War II, certain groups of soldiers stand out, and among the most notable were the Sherwood Rangers. Originally a cavalry unit in the last days of horses in combat, whose officers were landed gentry leading men who largely worked for them, they were switched to the "mechanized cavalry" of tanks in 1942. Winning acclaim in the North African campaign, the Sherwood Rangers then spearheaded one of the D-Day landings in Normandy on June 6, 1944, led the way across France, were the firstBritish troops to cross into Germany, and contributed mightily to Germany's surrender in May 1945. Inspired by Stephen Ambrose's Band of Brothers, WWII historian James Holland memorably profiles an extraordinary group of citizen soldiers constantly in harm's way.

"Military historian Holland (Sicily '43) turns his keen storytelling skill to the Sherwood Rangers, a British tank unit that had, by the end of the Second World War, amassed more battlefield honors than any other unit in British army history. ... An excellent addition to other World War II unit histories and a must-read for anybody interested in military history and the Second World War." —*Library Journal*

Includes bibliographical references and index.

ESSENTIAL AND RECOMMENDED TITLES
940.54 Military history of World War II

★ *Burma '44: The Battle That Turned World War II in the East.* James Holland. Atlantic Monthly Press 2024. 448 p.
ISBN 9780802160584
Grades: Adult   940.54
1. World War II 2. Military campaigns 3. Strategic alliances (Military) 4. Battles 5. Jungle warfare 6. Burma 7. Second World War era (1939-1945) 8. History writing — Wars and conflicts — World War II — Pacific Theater 9. History writing — Wars and conflicts — Battles 10. History writing — Military
LC 2024004886
The celebrated World War II historian recounts the remarkable Allied triumph at the fifteen-day Battle of the Admin Box in Burma (currently Myanmar), a pivotal moment in the Far East conflict.
"A thrilling account of a little-known but vital battle, for readers interested in World War II history, especially the Pacific Theater of Operations." —*Library Journal*
Includes bibliographical references and index.

Normandy '44: D-Day and the Epic 77-day Battle for France. James Holland. Atlantic Monthly 2019. 649 p.
ISBN 9780802129420
Grades: Adult   940.54
1. Normandy Invasion, June 6, 1944 2. World War II 3. Operation Overlord 4. Military campaigns 5. Raids (Military science) 6. Military planning 7. Battle history 8. Normandy 9. France 10. 20th century 11. History writing — Wars and conflicts — World War II — European Theater
LC Bl2019016622
Uses archival knowledge and eyewitness testimonies to reexamine D-Day, including the extraordinary planning, the brutal landings, and the strategic decisions of the commanders.
"From Omaha Beach to the Falaise Gap, this is thoughtful, crisply written military history." —*Booklist*

The Rise of Germany, 1939-1941; Vol. 1 /: The War in the West. James Holland. Grove/Atlantic 2015. 512 p.
ISBN 9780802123978
Grades: Adult   940.54
1. World War II 2. Nazis 3. World politics 4. Germany 5. 1930s 6. 1940s 7. History writing — Wars and Conflicts — World War II
LC Bl2015034780
The first segment in a three-part history of World War II in Europe, North Africa, and the Atlantic draws on original testimony and new research to discuss events from the outbreak of war in 1939 to the eve of the invasion of the Soviet Union.
"Holland skillfully integrates the broad political, diplomatic, economic, and military narrative with stories of individuals, civilians, and soldiers from all the belligerents." —*Library Journal*

Sicily '43: The First Assault on Fortress Europe. James Holland. Atlantic Monthly Press 2020. 592 p.
ISBN 9780802157188
Grades: Adult   940.54
1. World War II 2. Military campaigns 3. Military history 4. Military strategy 5. Italian history 6. Sicily, Italy 7. 1940s 8. Second World War era (1939-1945) 9. History writing — Wars and conflicts — World War II — European Theater 10. History writing — Wars and conflicts — Battles
LC 2020038631
Based on his own battlefield studies in Sicily and on much new research, James Holland's Sicily '43 offers a vital new perspective on a major turning point in World War II and a chronicle of a multi-pronged campaign in a uniquely diverse and contained geographical location.
"An excellent and accessible telling of the invasion that will be enjoyed by military history and World War II enthusiasts alike." —*Library Journal*

Hornfischer, James D.
Neptune's Inferno: The U.S. Navy at Guadalcanal. James D. Hornfischer. Bantam Books 2011. 528 p.
ISBN 9780553806700
Grades: Adult   940.54
1. Guadalcanal, Battle of, 1942-1943 2. Naval battles 3. World War II 4. Military campaigns 5. World War II veterans 6. Military history 7. Guadalcanal Island 8. Solomon Islands 9. United States 10. 1940s 11. 20th century 12. History writing — Wars and conflicts — World War II — Pacific Theater
Draws on interviews with veterans and primary sources to present a narrative account of the pivotal World War II campaign, chronicling the three-month effort to gain control of Guadalcanal as a battle that taught the U.S. Navy and Marines new approaches to warfare.

Hotta, Eri
Japan 1941: Countdown to Infamy. Eri Hotta. Alfred A. Knopf 2013. 320 p.
ISBN 9780385350518
Grades: Adult   940.54
1. Military planning 2. War 3. Pearl Harbor, Attack on, 1941 4. Military policy 5. World War II 6. Japan 7. 20th century 8. History writing — Wars and conflicts — World War II 9. History writing — Asia — Japan
LC 2013014781
A history of the attack on Pearl Harbor from a Japanese perspective argues that the nation's leaders largely understood they were destined to lose the war, offering insight into the tradition-obscured belief system that prompted the country to place its citizens in harm's way.
Includes bibliographical references and index.

Iredale, Will
The Kamikaze Hunters: Fighting for the Pacific: 1945. Will Iredale. Pegasus Books 2016. 456 p.
ISBN 9781681771670
Grades: Adult   940.54
1. World War II 2. Soldiers 3. Military history 4. Pacific Area 5. History writing — Wars and conflicts — World War II — Pacific Theater
Follows a group of young men who fought towards the end of World War II, from their enlistment and initial training to the terrifying and unexpected reality of fighting against pilots who would rather choose death than a dishonorable defeat.

Isserman, Maurice
The Winter Army: The World War II Odyssey of the 10th Mountain Division, America's Elite Alpine Warriors. Maurice Isserman. Houghton Mifflin Harcourt 2019. 320 p.
ISBN 9781328871435
Grades: Adult   940.54
1. Mountain warfare 2. Battles 3. Soldiers 4. Skiing 5. Western Front (World War II) 6. Military campaigns 7. World War II 8. Military history 9. United States 10. Italy 11. Second World War era (1939-1945) 12. 1940s 13. 20th century 14. History writing — Wars and conflicts — World War II — European Theater
LC 2019009836
The epic story of the U.S. Army's 10th Mountain Division, whose elite soldiers broke the last line of German defenses in Italy's mountains in 1945, spearheading the Allied advance to the Alps and final victory.
Includes bibliographical references and index.

Jacobsen, Annie
★ *Operation Paperclip: The Secret Intelligence Program to Bring Nazi Scientists to America.* Annie Jacobsen. Little Brown & CO 2013. 680 p.
ISBN 9780316221047
Grades: Adult   940.54
1. World War II 2. Nazis 3. Scientists 4. Physicians 5. Military research 6. Cold War 7. War criminals 8. German Americans 9. Intelligence service 10. United States 11. 20th century 12. History writing — Immigration — United States 13. History writing — Wars and conflicts — World War II
LC 2013028255
Details how the U.S. government embarked on a covert operation to recruit and employ Nazi scientists in the years following World War II in an effort to prevent their knowledge and expertise from falling into the hands of the Soviet Union.

"Built upon archival records, court transcripts, declassified documents, and interviews, Jacobsen's impressive book plumbs the dark depths of this postwar recruiting and shows the historical truths behind the space race and postwar U.S. dominance." —*Library Journal*

Includes bibliographical references and index.

Jordan, Jonathan W.

***Brothers**, Rivals, Victors: Eisenhower, Patton, Bradley, and the Partnership That Drove the Allied Conquest in Europe*. Jonathan W. Jordan. New American Library 2011. 672 p.

ISBN 9780451232120

Grades: Adult   **940.54**

1. Eisenhower, Dwight D. (Dwight David), 1890-1969 2. Patton, George S. (George Smith), 1885-1945 3. Bradley, Omar Nelson, 1893-1981 4. World War II 5. Military campaigns 6. Male friendship 7. Generals 8. Military history 9. United States 10. Europe 11. 20th century 12. Biographies 13. History writing — Wars and conflicts — World War II

LC 2010034841

Describes the complex friendship between Dwight D. Eisenhower, George S. Patton, and Omar Bradley that began decades before the war and was shaped by shifting allegiances, jealousy, insecurity, and ambition.

Kempowski, Walter

***Swansong** 1945: A Collective Diary of the Last Days of the Third Reich*. Walter Kempowski; translated from the German by Shaun Whiteside. W W Norton & CO Inc. 2015. 512 p.

ISBN 9780393248159

Grades: Adult   **940.54**

1. Military capitulations 2. Military defeat 3. World War II 4. Public opinion 5. German history 6. Germany 7. 20th century 8. Translations — German to English 9. Collective biographies 10. Diaries 11. Letters 12. History writing — Wars and conflicts — World War II 13. Life stories — Facing adversity — War and oppression — War survivors

Chronicles the end of Nazi Germany and World War II in Europe through hundreds of letters, diaries, and autobiographical accounts.

Translation of DAS Echolot Fuga furiosa : Ein kollektives Tagebuch Winter 1945 Bd. 2 21. bis 28. Januar 1945; Previously published in the UK: Swansong 1945: a collective diary from Hitler's last birthday to VE Day.

Kennedy, Paul

***Engineers** of Victory: The Problem Solvers Who Turned the Tide in the Second World War*. Paul Kennedy. Random House Inc 2013. 224 p.

ISBN 9781400067619

Grades: Adult   **940.54**

1. Military strategy 2. Military tactics 3. Soldiers 4. World War II 5. History writing — Wars and conflicts — World War II

LC 2012024284

The renowned historian analyzes previously unexplored strategic factors he believes to be responsible for the Allied victory in World War II, sharing behind-the-scenes assessments of ambitious goals successfully pursued by FDR, Churchill and other attendees at the Casablanca Conference.

Kershaw, Alex

***Against All Odds**: A True Story of Ultimate Courage and Survival in World War II*. Alex Kershaw. Dutton Caliber 2022. 432 p.

ISBN 9780593183748

Grades: Adult   **940.54**

1. Britt, Maurice Lee 2. Daly, Michael J, 1924-2008 3. Murphy, Audie, 1924-1971 4. Ware, Keith L. 5. Medal of Honor 6. Medal of Honor recipients 7. Military campaigns 8. Western Front (World War II) 9. World War II 10. Soldiers 11. Military history 12. Courage 13. Europe 14. United States 15. Collective biographies 16. Biographies 17. Life stories — Law and order — Armed forces personnel 18. History writing — Wars and conflicts — World War II — European Theater 19. History writing — Military — Military units

LC 2021035935

As the Allies raced to defeat Hitler, four men, all in the same unit, earned medal after medal for battlefield heroism. Maurice "Footsie" Britt, a former professional football player, became the very first American to receive every award for valor in a single war. Michael Daly was a West Point dropout who risked his neck over and over to keep his men alive. Keith Ware would one day become the first and only draftee in history to attain the rank of general before serving in Vietnam. In WWII, Ware owed his life to the finest soldier he ever commanded, a baby-faced Texan named Audie Murphy. In the campaign to liberate Europe, each would gain the ultimate accolade, the Congressional Medal of Honor. Tapping into personal interviews and a wealth of primary source material, Alex Kershaw has delivered his most gripping account yet of American courage, spanning more than six hundred days of increasingly merciless combat, from the deserts of North Africa to the dark heart of Nazi Germany.

"Kershaw describes his subjects' heroic acts with earthy exuberance and lucidly explains military strategy." —*Publishers Weekly*

Includes bibliographical references and index.

***The Few**: The American*. Alex Kershaw. Da Capo Press 2006. xi, 301 p. : Illustration; Map

ISBN 9780306813030

Grades: Adult   **940.54**

1. Air warfare 2. Military pilots 3. Military aircraft 4. World War II 5. American people in foreign countries 6. American people 7. Aerial operations 8. Great Britain 9. 1940s 10. 20th century 11. History writing — Wars and conflicts — World War II — European Theater

LC Bl2006025886

Tells the story of the few Americans who decided that they could not remain neutral during World War Two and joined Britain's Royal Air Force to defend the country from Hitler.

Includes bibliographical references (p. 245-288) and index.

***The First Wave**: The D-Day Warriors Who Led the Way to Victory in World War II*. by Alex Kershaw. Dutton Caliber 2019. 464 p.

ISBN 9780451490056

Grades: Adult   **940.54**

1. Normandy Invasion, June 6, 1944 2. Combat 3. Soldiers 4. Commando troops 5. Amphibious warfare 6. Military campaigns 7. World War II 8. History writing — Wars and conflicts — World War II — European Theater 9. Life stories — Law and order — Armed forces personnel 10. History writing — Military

LC 2018057388

Beginning in the predawn darkness of June 6, 1944, the First Wave follows the remarkable men who carried out D-Day's most perilous missions. The first to fight when the stakes were highest and the odds longest, these men would determine the fate of the invasion of Hitler's Fortress Europe—and the very history of the twentieth century.

"Kershaw presents war in all of its ugliness and horror even as he emphasizes the commitment of the young fighters to their comrades. The First Wave, a welcome and fresh take on one of the greatest and most significant of WWII missions, marks D-Day's 75th anniversary." —*Booklist*

Includes bibliographical references and index.

Korda, Michael

***Alone**: Britain, Churchill, and Dunkirk : Defeat into Victory*. Michael Korda. Liveright Publishing Company, a division of W. W. Norton & Company 2017. 564 p.

ISBN 9781631491320

Grades: Adult   **940.54**

1. Korda, Michael, 1933- 2. Dunkirk, France, Battle of, 1940 3. War and society 4. Morale 5. World War II 6. Great Britain 7. France 8. History writing — Wars and conflicts — World War II — European Theater

LC 2017017244

Author and former editor-in-chief of Simon & Schuster Michael Korda was born in England in 1933; his family went to the US in 1941 for the duration of World War II. In Alone, Korda weaves his childhood memories of Britain with a thoroughly researched history of the early months of the war up through the 1940 evacuation from Dunkirk. This detailed history presents an engaging review of military tactics and international politics, illuminated by Korda's personal recollections.

ESSENTIAL AND RECOMMENDED TITLES
940.54 Military history of World War II

"Korda succeeds in infusing straight history with the accessible tone of narrative nonfiction." —*Booklist*
Includes bibliographical references and index.

With *Wings Like Eagles: A History of the Battle of Britain.* Michael Korda. Harper 2009. 336 p.
ISBN 9780061125355
Grades: Adult   940.54
1. Britain, Battle of, 1940 2. World War II 3. Battles 4. Military history 5. Aerial operations 6. British history 7. 1940s 8. 20th century 9. Impartial writing 10. History writing — Wars and conflicts — World War II — European Theater
LC 2008009293

An in-depth history of the Battle of Britain draws on the firsthand perspectives of pilots, ground crews, and commanders on both sides, and places the campaign against a backdrop of the political forces that shaped it.

"This is a skillful, absorbing, often moving contribution to the popular understanding of one of the few episodes in history to live on untarnished and undiminished in the collective memory and to deserve the description heroic." —*Washington Post*
Includes bibliographical references.

Lance, Rachel
Chamber Divers: The Untold Story of the D-Day Scientists Who Changed Special Operations Forever. Rachel Lance. Dutton 2024. 448 p.
ISBN 9780593184936
Grades: Adult   940.54
1. Haldane, J. B. S. (John Burdon Sanderson), 1892-1964 2. Strategic alliances (Military) 3. Special operations (Military science) 4. Normandy Invasion, June 6, 1944 5. Scientists 6. Military research 7. Amphibious warfare 8. Underwater warfare 9. Deep diving 10. Submarines 11. Submersibles 12. London, England 13. Great Britain 14. Second World War era (1939-1945) 15. History writing — Military — Special Forces 16. History writing — Wars and conflicts — World War II — European Theater 17. Life stories — Law and order — Armed forces personnel 18. Life stories — Science, technology, and medicine — Scientists and inventors

This story of the men and women who provided invaluable submarine and underwater breathing reconnaissance that led to the Allies' dramatic and history-making success during D-Day is based on top secret documents only recently declassified.

"Propulsively narrated and full of moments of astonishing sacrifice, this brings a remarkable history to light." —*Publishers Weekly*

Larson, Erik
★ *The* **Splendid** *and the Vile: A Saga of Churchill, Family, and Defiance During the Blitz.* Erik Larson. Crown 2020. 464 p.
ISBN 9780385348713
Grades: Adult   940.54
1. Churchill, Winston, 1874-1965 2. Prime ministers 3. World War II 4. Aerial bombing 5. Bombardment 6. London, England history 7. British history 8. English history 9. Great Britain 10. 20th century 11. Second World War era (1939-1945) 12. History writing — Wars and conflicts — World War II 13. Life stories — Politics — Politicians 14. Nonfiction that reads like fiction
LC 2019045028

New York Times Notable Book, 2020; LibraryReads Favorites, 2020.

Draws on personal diaries, archival documents and declassified intelligence in a portrait of Winston Churchill that explores his day-to-day experiences during the Blitz and his role in uniting England.

"Blending a gripping narrative and a well-researched examination of personal and news archives, Larson's distinctive history of Britain's 'Darkest hour' offers a new angle for those already familiar with this era, while attracting readers who wish to learn more about the notable leader." —*Library Journal*
Includes bibliographical references and index.

Letts, Elizabeth
The **Perfect** *Horse: The Daring U.S. Mission to Rescue the Priceless Stallions Kidnapped by the Nazis.* Elizabeth Letts. Ballantine 2016. 368 p.
ISBN 9780345544803
Grades: Adult   940.54
1. Patton, George S, 1885-1945 2. Thoroughbred horses 3. Lipizzaner horse 4. Nazi propaganda 5. Horse breeding 6. History writing — Wars and conflicts — World War II — European Theater 7. Nature writing — Animal studies
LC 2016010501

Traces the lesser-known efforts of Hitler to build a master race of the finest purebred horses and the heroic achievements of American soldiers to rescue imperiled stolen equines from a hidden Czechoslovakian farm during a 1945 battle between Third Reich and Allied forces.

"The author's elegant narrative conveys how the love for these amazing creatures transcends national animosities." —*Kirkus*

Lewis, Damien
Churchill's **Hellraisers:** *The Secret Mission to Storm a Forbidden Nazi Fortress.* Damien Lewis. Citadel Press 2020. 400 p.
ISBN 9780806540740
Grades: Adult   940.54
1. Lees, Michael 2. Farren, Roy 3. World War II 4. Military campaigns 5. Parachute troops 6. Soldiers 7. Raids (Military science) 8. Special operations (Military science) 9. German occupation, World War II 10. Military occupation 11. Italian history 12. Italy 13. Second World War era (1939-1945) 14. 20th century 15. History writing — Wars and conflicts — World War II — European Theater

An award-winning historian, war reporter and bestselling author tells the untold story of the heroic hellraisers—two brave paratroopers and the team they recruited—who stormed a Nazi fortress in one of the most daring raids of World War II.

"Successful niche military history for a popular audience." —*Kirkus*

The **Dog** *Who Could Fly: The Incredible True Story of a Wwii Airman and the Four-legged Hero Who Flew at His Side.* Damien Lewis. Atria Books 2014. 304 p.
ISBN 9781476739144
Grades: Adult   940.54
1. Lewis, Damien 2. Dogs 3. Military pilots 4. World War II 5. German shepherd dog 6. Dog heroes 7. Bombers (Airplanes) 8. Loyalty 9. Friendship 10. Animals in war 11. Human-animal relationships 12. British history 13. 1930s 14. 20th century 15. Autobiographies and memoirs 16. Life stories — Law and order — Armed forces personnel 17. Life stories — Relationships — Pets and Owners 18. Adult books for young adults
LC 2014015567

A U.S. release of a popular UK account by the best-selling co-author of Sergeant Rex documents the true story of a World War II Royal Air Force service dog who aided missions and survived close calls before saving the life of his closest human companion.

"A heartwarming and well-paced man-and-his-dog story. Lewis has captured the spirit of the era and told the story using Bozdech's manuscript as source material without making it maudlin or sentimental." —*Publishers Weekly*

Lineberry, Cate
The **Secret** *Rescue: An Untold Story of American Nurses and Medics Behind Nazi Lines.* Cate Lineberry. Little, Brown and Co. 2013. 288 p.
ISBN 9780316220224
Grades: Adult   940.54
1. World War II 2. Airplane accidents 3. Survival 4. Nurses 5. Nazis 6. Courage 7. History writing — Wars and conflicts — World War II 8. Adventure writing — Survival
LC 2013934814

Recounts how the passengers and crew of an American medical evacuation plane, including thirteen nurses and thirteen medics, survived after it crashed in Nazi-controlled Albania in November, 1943, until they could be rescued.

Lisle, John
The **Dirty** *Tricks Department: Stanley Lovell, the Oss, and the Masterminds of World War II Secret Warfare.* John Lisle. St. Martin's Press 2023. 384 p.
ISBN 9781250280244
Grades: Adult   940.54

PUBLIC LIBRARY CORE COLLECTION: NONFICTION
Twentieth Edition

1. Lovell, Stanley P. 2. Intelligence service 3. Ethics 4. Drugs 5. Human experimentation in medicine 6. Medical ethics 7. Scientists 8. Espionage 9. Research 10. United States 11. 20th century 12. Second World War era (1939-1945) 13. History Writing — Wars and conflicts — World War II 14. History Writing — United States 15. History Writing — Spies and spying 16. History writing — Science, technology, and medicine 17. Debut title

LC 2022039367

Drawing on extensive archival research and personal interviews, this previously untold story of the OSS Research and Development Branch, a secret group of scientists who invented deadly items, forged documents and performed truth drug experiments during WWII, explores the moral dilemmas they faced and reveals their dark legacy.

"Using recently declassified documents, Lisle has composed an absolutely engaging chronicle of the founding and WWII heyday of the OSS, the precursor of today's CIA." —*Booklist*

Includes bibliographical references and index.

Lowe, Keith
Prisoners of History: What Monuments to World War II Tell Us About Our History and Ourselves. Keith Lowe. St. Martin's Press 2020. 384 p.

ISBN 9781250235022

Grades: Adult   940.54

1. World War II 2. Memorialization 3. War memorials 4. Collective memory 5. War and society 6. Second World War era (1939-1945) 7. History writing — Wars and conflicts — World War II

LC 2020030034

A look at how our monuments to World War II shape the way we think about the war by an award-winning historian.

Includes bibliographical references.

MacGregor, Iain
The Lighthouse of Stalingrad: The Hidden Truth at the Heart of the Greatest Battle of World War II. Iain MacGregor. Scribner 2022. 352 p.

ISBN 9781982163587

Grades: Adult   940.54

1. Stalingrad, Battle of, 1942-1943 2. World War II 3. Urban warfare 4. Battles 5. Military occupation 6. Nazis 7. Russian people 8. German people 9. Soviet Union history 10. Soviet Union 11. Germany 12. Second World War era (1939-1945) 13. History writing — Wars and conflicts — World War II 14. History writing — Europe — Russia 15. History writing — Wars and conflicts — Battles

LC 2022017235

A thrilling, vivid and highly detailed account of the epic siege during one of World War II's most important battles, told by the brilliant British editor-turned-historian and author of Checkpoint Charlie.

"Historian MacGregor (Checkpoint Charlie) delivers a brisk and dramatic account of a much mythologized episode in the Battle for Stalingrad during WWII....Meticulous yet action-packed, this will thrill WWII buffs." —*Publishers Weekly*

Includes bibliographical references and index.

Macintyre, Ben
Double Cross: The True Story of the D-Day Spies. Ben Macintyre. Crown 2012. 384 p.

ISBN 9780307888754

Grades: Adult   940.54

1. Espionage 2. Spies 3. Military campaigns 4. World War II 5. Secret service 6. Military history 7. Third Reich, 1933-1945 8. Politics and government 9. Normandy 10. Germany 11. 20th century 12. Biographies 13. Life stories — Law and order — Spies and secret agents 14. History writing — Wars and conflicts — World War II — European Theater 15. History writing — Spies and spying

LC 2012003089

Traces the sophisticated D-Day operation through which extraordinary spies deceived the Nazis about the location of the Allied attack, profiling the successful Double Cross System and the remarkable individuals who used the program to save thousands of lives.

Includes bibliographical references and index.

★ *Operation Mincemeat: How a Dead Man and a Bizarre Plan Fooled the Nazis and Assured an Allied Victory.* Ben MacIntyre. Harmony Books 2010. x, 400 p, [16] p. of plates : Illustration; Plan

ISBN 9780307453273

Grades: Adult   940.54

1. Montagu, Ewen, 1901-1985 2. Military deception 3. Military intelligence 4. World War II 5. Secret service 6. English history 7. Deception 8. Great Britain 9. 1940s 10. 20th century 11. Page to screen 12. History writing — Wars and conflicts — World War II

LC 2009047562

New York Times Notable Book, 2010.

Chronicles World War II's pivotal deception by two British naval officers who successfully fed false intelligence to the Nazis about where Allied forces were planning an attack in southern Europe.

"A true WWII tale that reads like something by Ian Fleming. In fact, two of Fleming's fellow British intelligence officers hatched the title operation. They dressed a corpse in uniform and arranged for it to wash up on a Nazi-friendly stretch of the Spanish coast bearing a suitcase with false war plans. Against all odds, Operation Mincemeat succeeded and helped convince the Germans that the Allies planned to invade Sardinia and Greece in 1943 instead of their real target, Sicily. Relying on a cache of once-classified documents, Macintyre provides the fullest account yet of this curious episode and enlivens his yarn with quirky details." —*Entertainment Weekly*

Made into a movie in May 2022 on Netflix; Includes bibliographical references (p. [385]-387) and index.

★ *Prisoners of the Castle: An Epic Story of Survival and Escape from Colditz, the Nazis' Fortress Prison.* Ben Macintyre. Crown 2022. 368 p.

ISBN 9780593136331

Grades: Adult   940.54

1. World War II 2. Castles 3. Prisoners of war 4. Prisoner-of-war escapes 5. Military intelligence 6. Prisons 7. German history 8. History writing — Wars and conflicts — World War II — European Theater 9. Life stories — Facing adversity — War and oppression — Hostages and POWs

LC 2022026350

A look at the German prison at Colditz Castle, and the defiant Allied prisoners who tried relentlessly to escape.

"In this riveting history of Nazi Germany's most notorious POW camp, bestseller Macintyre (Agent Sonya) spotlights the indomitable will and creativity of the inmates who tried to escape from it." —*Publishers Weekly*

Includes bibliographical references and index.

★ *Rogue Heroes: The History of the Sas, Britain's Secret Special Forces Unit That Sabotaged the Nazis and Changed the Nature of War.* Ben MacIntyre. Crown 2016. 352 p.

ISBN 9781101904169

Grades: Adult   940.54

1. Special forces 2. Commando troops 3. World War II 4. Sabotage 5. Military history 6. Military art and science 7. Second World War era (1939-1945) 8. History writing — Wars and conflicts — World War II 9. History writing — Military — Special Forces

LC Bl2016035969

A history of Great Britain's Special Air Service or SAS that fought against the Nazis during World War II.

"He demonstrates that even in a global war, a few uniquely talented, imaginative, and bold individuals of relatively junior rank can have a major impact. Macintyre delivers a solid history and an enjoyable read that will appeal to those interested in military history as well as readers who enjoy real-life tales of adventure." —*Publishers Weekly*

Magida, Arthur J.
Code Name Madeleine: A Sufi Spy in Nazi-occupied Paris. Arthur J. Magida. W.W. Norton & Company 2020. 324 p.

ISBN 9780393635188

ESSENTIAL AND RECOMMENDED TITLES
940.54 Military history of World War II

Grades: Adult   **940.54**

1. Khan, Noor Inayat, 1914-1944 2. French Resistance (World War II) 3. Women spies 4. Espionage 5. Radio operators 6. Indian people 7. Sufism 8. Resistance to military occupation 9. Concentration camps 10. World War II 11. Intelligence service 12. Prisons 13. Women's participation in wars 14. German occupation, World War II 15. Courage 16. French history 17. Great Britain 18. Biographies 19. Life stories — Law and order — Spies and secret agents 20. History writing — Wars and conflicts — Resistance — World War II 21. History writing — Women's history 22. History writing — Spies and spying

LC 2019053511

Documents the story of artist Noor Inayat Khan, the daughter of an Indian Sufi mystic who joined the British SOE during World War II and became an only wireless operator in Paris during the crucial months leading up to D-Day.

"Magida delivers a gripping account of a tenacious young woman who demonstrated bravery in the face of extreme evil." —*Booklist*

Includes bibliographical references and index.

Makos, Adam

★ *A Higher Call.* by Adam Makos with Larry Alexander. Berkley Books 2013. 400 p.

ISBN 9780425252864

Grades: Adult   **940.54**

1. Brown, Charlie, 1912-2008 2. Stigler, Franz, 1916-2008 3. Bomber pilots 4. Fighter pilots 5. Life change events 6. Air warfare 7. Pilots 8. World War II 9. Aerial bombing 10. Aerial operations 11. 1940s 12. History writing — Wars and conflicts — World War II

LC 2012015546

Relates the true story of two World War II airmen, one American and one German, who put aside the conflict and helped each other to safety in the wake of a damaged aircraft, and describes their meeting again forty-seven years later.

Maurer, Kevin

Damn Lucky: One Man's Courage During the Bloodiest Military Campaign in Aviation History. Kevin Maurer. St. Martin's Press 2022. 384 p.

ISBN 9781250274380

Grades: Adult   **940.54**

1. Luckadoo, John, 1922- 2. Bomber pilots 3. Military campaigns 4. Bombardment 5. Combat survival 6. World War II 7. Aerial operations 8. Europe 9. Biographies 10. Life stories — Law and order — Armed forces personnel 11. History writing — Military — Aviation History 12. History writing — Wars and conflicts — World War II — European Theater

LC 2021051080

The story of a young American B-17 Flying Fortress pilot who survived 25 of the deadliest bombing missions as part of the Eighth Air Force's 100th Bomb Group during World War II.

"Journalist Maurer (coauthor, No Easy Day) delivers a comprehensive account of bomber pilot John 'Lucky' Luckadoo's experiences during WWII." —*Publishers Weekly*

Includes index.

McKay, Sinclair

The Fire and the Darkness: The Bombing of Dresden, 1945. Sinclair McKay. St Martins Pr 2020. 400 p.

ISBN 9781250258014

Grades: Adult   **940.54**

1. Fires 2. Death 3. Civilians in war 4. World War II 5. Aerial operations 6. Third Reich, 1933-1945 7. Aerial bombing 8. Dresden, Germany 9. Germany 10. Second World War era (1939-1945) 11. Impartial writing 12. History writing — Natural disasters and tragedies 13. History writing — Wars and conflicts — World War II — European Theater 14. History writing — Military 15. Life stories — People in history — Witness to history

LC 2019044455

On February 13th, 1945 at 10:03 PM, British bombers began one of the most devastating attacks of WWII: the bombing of Dresden. The first contingent killed people and destroyed buildings, roads, and other structures. The second rained down fire, turning the streets into a blast furnace, the shelters into ovens, and whipping up a molten hurricane in which the citizens of Dresden were burned, baked, or suffocated to death. Early the next day, American bombers finished off what was left. Sinclair McKay's the Fire and the Darkness is a pulse-pounding work of history that looks at the life of the city in the days before the attack, tracks each moment of the bombing, and considers the long period of reconstruction and recovery.

"McKay's extensive research and animated prose capture the terror and tragedy of the bombing. Readers won't soon forget this devastating account." —*Publishers Weekly*

Published in the UK as Dresden: the fire and the darkness; Includes bibliographical references and index.

The Secret Lives of Codebreakers: The Men and Women Who Cracked the Enigma Code at Bletchley Park. Sinclair McKay. Penguin Group 2012. 352 p.

ISBN 9780452298712

Grades: Adult   **940.54**

1. World War II 2. Cryptography 3. Intelligence service 4. Military intelligence 5. England 6. History writing — Wars and conflicts — World War II — European Theater

LC 2012018408

A remarkable look at the day-to-day lives of the codebreakers whose clandestine efforts helped win World War II.

Includes bibliographical references and index; Previous ed.: The secret life of Bletchley Park : the WWII codebreaking centre and the men and women who worked there / Sinclair McKay, 2010.

McManus, John C.

Fire and Fortitude: The Us Army in the Pacific War 1941-1943. John C. McManus. Dutton Caliber 2019. 640 pages

ISBN 9780451475046

Grades: Adult   **940.54**

1. MacArthur, Douglas, 1880-1964 2. Military campaigns 3. Soldiers 4. Generals 5. Military strategy 6. World War II 7. Military history 8. Pacific Area 9. United States 10. Pacific Ocean 11. Second World War era (1939-1945) 12. 20th century 13. History writing — Wars and conflicts — World War II — Pacific Theater

The award-winning author of September Hope presents an epic chronicle of the U.S. Army's role in the Pacific during World War II, offering insight into military transformations under the leadership of generals MacArthur, Eichelberger, Stillwell and Krueger.

"Clearly written in an engaging style, this book will appeal to general readers of military history." —*Library Journal*

Sequel: Island infernos; First of three volumes; Includes bibliographical references and index.

Island Infernos: The Us Army's Pacific War Odyssey, 1944. John C. McManus. Dutton Caliber 2021. 576 p.

ISBN 9780451475060

Grades: Adult   **940.54**

1. MacArthur, Douglas, 1880-1964 2. Military campaigns 3. Generals 4. Command of troops 5. Military strategy 6. Combat 7. Amphibious warfare 8. Racism in the military 9. World War II 10. Military history 11. Pacific Area 12. United States 13. Pacific Ocean 14. 20th century 15. History writing — Wars and conflicts — World War II — Pacific Theater 16. History writing — Military 17. Life stories — Law and order — Armed forces personnel

LC 2021009801

In this second volume of a trilogy, military historian John McManus continues the US Army's epic crusade in the Pacific War, from the battle of Saipan to the occupation of Japan, climaxing with the American return to the Philippines.

"Historian McManus follows Fortitude and Fire with an outstanding second volume in his planned trilogy on the Pacific theater of WWII.... Distinguished by informative deep dives into logistical and strategic issues and McManus's storytelling prowess, this is an excellent study of how the U.S. turned the tide of the war in the Pacific." —*Publishers Weekly*

Sequel to Fire and fortitude; Sequel: To the end of the earth; Includes bibliographical references and index.

To the End of the Earth: The Us Army and the Downfall of Japan, 1945. John C. McManus. Dutton Caliber 2023. 576 p.

ISBN 9780593186886
Grades: Adult 940.54
1. World War II 2. Military campaigns 3. Command of troops 4. Combat 5. Military capitulations 6. Resistance to military occupation 7. Japanese history 8. Pacific Area 9. History writing — Wars and conflicts — World War II — Pacific Theater 10. History writing — Military 11. History writing — Asia — Japan 12. Life stories — Law and order — Armed forces personnel
LC 2022055494

The dawn of 1945 finds a US Army at its peak in the Pacific. Allied victory over Japan is all but assured. The only question is how many more months—or years—of fight does the enemy have left. John C. McManus's series returns with this brilliant final volume.

"Historian McManus (Island Infernos) concludes his trilogy on the U.S. Army in the Pacific theater of WWII with a dramatic account of the period from the recapture of the Philippines through the invasion of Okinawa and Japan's surrender." —Publishers Weekly

Sequel to Island infernos; Third of three volumes; Includes bibliographical references and index.

Merridale, Catherine
Ivan's War: Life and Death in the Red Army, 1939-1945. Catherine Merridale. Metropolitan Books 2006. xii, 462 p. : Illustration; Map
ISBN 9780805074550
Grades: Adult 940.54
1. Eastern Front (World War II) 2. World War II 3. Military campaigns 4. Soldiers 5. Military history 6. Soviet Union 7. 20th century 8. History writing — Wars and conflicts — World War II — European Theater
LC 2005050457

Drawing on previously closed military and secret police archives and interviews with veterans, a comprehensive history of the Red Army rank and file follows the soldiers from the shock of the German invasion to their costly triumph in Stalingrad.

Includes bibliographical references (p. [433]-439) and index.

Miller, Donald L.
★ *Masters of the Air: America's Bomber Boys Who Fought the Air War Against Nazi Germany.* Donald L. Miller. Simon & Schuster 2006. VIII, 671 p, 24 p. of plates : Illustration; Map
ISBN 9780743235440
Grades: Adult 940.54
1. Air warfare 2. Western Front (World War II) 3. Bomber pilots 4. World War II 5. Military campaigns 6. Germany 7. Page to screen 8. History writing — Wars and conflicts — World War II — European Theater
LC 2006050461

Traces the story of the Eighth Air Force crewmen who fought Nazi forces during World War II, setting their story against a backdrop of wartime England and Nazi Germany while drawing on oral histories, diaries, and government documents to recreate their missions.

Television series adaptation released on Apple TV+ in 2024; Includes bibliographical references (p. [609]-642) and index.

Milton, Giles
Churchill's Ministry of Ungentlemanly Warfare: The Mavericks Who Plotted Hitler's Defeat. Giles Milton. Picador USA 2017. 368 p.
ISBN 9781250119025
Grades: Adult 940.54
1. Churchill, Winston, 1874-1965 2. World War II 3. Subversive activities 4. Special forces 5. Guerrilla warfare 6. Spies 7. History writing — Wars and conflicts — World War II — European theater
LC 2016039180

Documents the top-secret guerilla campaign founded in London to orchestrate spectacular acts of sabotage against Hitler's war machine, profiling the six remarkable men behind the campaign and how they changed the course of World War II.

"An exciting, suspenseful tale of international intrigue." —Kirkus

Soldier, Sailor, Frogman, Spy, Airman, Gangster, Kill or Die: How the Allies Won on D-Day. Giles Milton. Henry Holt & Company 2019. 489 p.
ISBN 9781250134929
Grades: Adult 940.54
1. Normandy Invasion, June 6, 1944 2. Military campaigns 3. World War II 4. Battles 5. Raids (Military science) 6. Combat 7. Western Front (World War II) 8. Second World War era (1939-1945) 9. History writing — Military 10. History writing — Wars and conflicts — World War II — European Theater 11. Life stories — People in history — Witness to history
LC Bl2019001163

A chronicle of the first 24 hours of the D-Day invasion shares the perspectives of a diverse range of Allied, German and French contributors to explore the conflict's strategic mastery and human realities. Map(s).

"Highly recommended for World War II aficionados and those seeking a great read in military history." —Library Journal

Includes bibliographical references and index.

Mundy, Liza
Code Girls: The Untold Story of the American Women Code Breakers Who Helped Win World War II. Liza Mundy. Hachette Books 2017. 500 p.
ISBN 9780316439893
Grades: Adult 940.54
1. World War II 2. Women 3. Cryptographers 4. Electronic intelligence 5. Cryptography 6. Work 7. Women's participation in wars 8. History writing — Wars and conflicts — World War II 9. History writing — Spies and spying 10. Society and culture — Gender — Women
LC 2017020069

Booklist Editors' Choice, 2017.

Recruited by the U.S. Army and Navy from small towns and elite colleges, more than ten thousand women served as codebreakers during World War II. While their brothers and boyfriends took up arms, these women moved to Washington and learned the meticulous work of code-breaking. Their efforts shortened the war, saved countless lives, and gave them access to careers previously denied to them. A strict vow of secrecy nearly erased their efforts from history; now, through dazzling research and interviews with surviving code girls, best-selling author Liza Mundy brings to life this riveting and vital story of American courage, service, and scientific accomplishment.

"A well-researched, compellingly written, crucial addition to the literature of American involvement in World War II." —Kirkus

Includes bibliographical references and index.

Murphy, Brian
81 Days Below Zero: The Incredible Survival Story of a World War II Pilot in Alaska's Frozen Wilderness. Brian Murphy. Da Capo Press 2015. 256 p.
ISBN 9780306823282
Grades: Adult 940.54
1. Crane, Leon, 1919-2002 2. Military pilots 3. World War II 4. Airplane accidents 5. Survival (after airplane accidents, shipwrecks, etc.) 6. Wilderness survival 7. B-24 bomber 8. Aerial operations 9. Alaska 10. Biographies 11. Adventure writing — Survival 12. Life stories — Law and order — Armed forces personnel
LC 2015003484

Shortly before Christmas in 1943, five Army aviators left Alaska's Ladd Field on a test flight. Only one ever returned: Leon Crane, a city kid from Philadelphia with little more than a parachute on his back when he bailed from his B-24 Liberator before it crashed into the Arctic. Alone in subzero temperatures, Crane managed to stay alive in the dead of the Yukon winter for nearly twelve weeks and, amazingly, walked out of the ordeal intact. Murphy recounts, for the first time, the full story of Crane's remarkable saga.

Includes bibliographical references and index.

Nelson, Craig
Pearl Harbor: From Infamy to Greatness. Craig Nelson. Scribner, an imprint of Simon & Schuster 2016. 384 p.
ISBN 9781451660494
Grades: Adult 940.54

ESSENTIAL AND RECOMMENDED TITLES
940.54 Military history of World War II

1. Pearl Harbor, Attack on, 1941 2. Military history 3. United States 4. 20th century 5. History writing — Wars and conflicts — World War II
LC 2016018490

Published to commemorate the 75th anniversary of the attack, an account based on years of research and new information illuminates less-understood aspects of how and why Japan targeted America, sharing additional details about the experiences of survivors.

"Nelsons well written history of Pearl Harbor will be enjoyed by the general reader and appropriately highlights the battles historical significance." —*Publishers Weekly*

Includes bibliographical references.

Norman, Elizabeth M.
We Band of Angels: The Untold Story of American Nurses Trapped on Bataan by the Japanese. Elizabeth M. Norman. Random House 1999. xv, 327 p. : Illustration; Map
ISBN 9780375502453
Grades: Adult   940.54

1. Prisoners of war 2. Nurses 3. Women prisoners 4. Medical care 5. Prisons 6. World War II 7. United States history 8. Philippines 9. United States 10. 20th century 11. Second World War era (1939-1945) 12. History writing — Wars and conflicts — World War II — Pacific Theater 13. History writing — Women's history
LC 98045998

Celebrates the heroism of the Army and Navy nurses imprisoned for three years in a Japanese prisoner-of-war camp.

"Norman (nursing, New York Univ.) tells their harrowing story through survivor interviews as well as letters and journals kept by the nurses during this time. Her book is a well-written account of an obscure piece of World War II history." —*Library Journal*

Includes bibliographical references (p. [283]-292) and index.

Norman, Michael
Tears in the Darkness: The Story of the Bataan Death March and Its Aftermath. Michael Norman and Elizabeth M. Norman. Farrar, Straus, and Giroux 2009. 480 p.
ISBN 9780374272609
Grades: Adult   940.54

1. Bataan Death March, 1942 2. World War II 3. Prisoners of war 4. Military history 5. Atrocities 6. Prisons 7. 1940s 8. History writing — Wars and conflicts — World War II — Pacific Theater
LC 2008047163

ALA Notable Book, 2010.

Following the U.S. surrender to the Japanese on the peninsula of Bataan in 1942, 76,000 American and Filipino POWs began the infamous Death March. This gripping narrative, told in unsparing but sympathetic detail, focuses intermittently on American POW Ben Steele, whose sketches adorn the book, and the hell of Japanese prison and labor camps that introduced these captives to the starvation, dehydration and murderous Japanese brutality that would become routine for the next three years.

"This book is authoritative history. Ten years in the making, it is based on hundreds of interviews with American, Filipino and Japanese combatants. But it is also a narrative achievement. The book seamlessly blends a wide-angle view with the stories of many individual participants." —*New York Times*

Includes bibliographical references and index.

Paradis, Michel
The Light of Battle: Eisenhower, D-Day, and the Birth of the American Superpower. Michel Paradis. Mariner Books 2024. 320 p.
ISBN 9780358682370
Grades: Adult   940.54

1. Eisenhower, Dwight D. (Dwight David), 1890-1969 2. World War I 3. Normandy Invasion, June 6, 1944 4. Diplomacy 5. Soldiers 6. Command of troops 7. Generals 8. Military campaigns 9. Armed Forces 10. France 11. Normandy 12. Biographies 13. History writing — Presidency — 20th century — United States 14. Life stories — Politics — Politicians 15. History writing — Wars and conflicts — World War II 16. Life stories — Law and order — Armed forces personnel
LC 2023054999

Drawing on meticulous research and newly discovered records, letters, diaries and first-hand accounts from three continents, a leading human rights lawyer, historian and national security law scholar chronicles the rise of Dwight Eisenhower in the months leading up to D-Day, which was integral to America's rise as a global superpower.

"Dwight Eisenhower's steady wartime leadership is limned in this meticulous account of the planning of D-Day." —*Publishers Weekly*

Includes bibliographical references and index.

Parkin, Simon
A Game of Birds and Wolves: The Ingenious Young Women Whose Secret Board Game Helped Win World War II. Simon Parkin. Little Brown & CO 2020. 320 pages
ISBN 9780316492096
Grades: Adult   940.54

1. Women and war 2. Military strategy 3. Submarines, German 4. Young women 5. War games 6. Board games 7. Second World War era (1939-1945) 8. History writing — Wars and conflicts — World War II 9. History writing — Military — Naval history 10. History writing — Women's history 11. Adult books for young adults 12. Nonfiction that reads like fiction
LC Bl2020000334

Tells the triumphant story of a group of young women who helped devised a winning strategy to defeat the Nazi U-boats and deliver a decisive victory in the Battle of the Atlantic.

"An informative, satisfying, and overall great read." —*Booklist*

Pellegrino, Charles R.
To Hell and Back: The Last Train from Hiroshima. Charles Pellegrino. Rowman & Littlefield 2015. 424 p.
ISBN 9781442250581
Grades: Adult   940.54

1. Hibakusha 2. Radiation victims 3. Nuclear weapons 4. Nuclear warfare 5. Atomic bomb 6. World War II 7. Japanese history 8. Hiroshima, Japan 9. 1940s 10. 20th century 11. Second World War era (1939-1945) 12. Essays 13. History writing — Wars and conflicts — Atomic Bomb — World War II
LC 2015014341

Draws on the voices of atomic-bomb survivors and the science of forensic archaeology to describe the events and aftermath of two days in August 1945 when nuclear devices detonated over Japan changed life on Earth forever.

"This is horrifying, painful, and necessary reading." —*Kirkus*

Originally published under title: The last train from Hiroshima. New York : Henry Holt and Co, 2010; Includes bibliographical references and index.

Porter, Carolyn
Marcel's Letters: A Font and the Search for One Man's Fate. Carolyn Porter. Skyhorse Publishing 2017. 352 pages
ISBN 9781510719330
Grades: Adult   940.54

1. Porter, Carolyn 2. Heuzé, Marcel, 1912-1992 3. Father-separated families 4. Historical research 5. Letter writing 6. Graphic designers 7. Families 8. War 9. Translating and interpreting 10. Type and type-founding 11. Graphic design 12. Handwriting 13. Paleography 14. Genealogy 15. German occupation, World War II 16. French history 17. Third Reich, 1933-1945 18. Minnesota 19. Second World War era (1939-1945) 20. Biographies 21. Life stories — People in history — Witness to history 22. Life stories — Relationships — Family 23. History writing — Wars and conflicts — Homefront — World War II 24. Life stories — Arts and culture
LC 2017001221

A graphic designer's search for inspiration leads to a cache of letters and the mystery of one man's fate during World War II.

"Porters captivating memoir describes her journey to find answers, noting how her fascination with Marcel proved infectious as she faces obstacle after obstacle and enlists the help of experts to discover the fate that awaited him." —*Booklist*

PUBLIC LIBRARY CORE COLLECTION: NONFICTION
Twentieth Edition

Prange, Gordon W.
At Dawn We Slept: The Untold Story of Pearl Harbor. Gordon W. Prange in collaboration with Donald M. Goldstein and Katherine V. Dillon. Penguin Books 2001. xvi, 889 p. : Illustration
ISBN 9780140157345
Grades: Adult   940.54
1. Pearl Harbor, Attack on, 1941 2. World War II 3. Hawaii 4. 1940s 5. History writing — Wars and conflicts — World War II
LC 2001276551
Records the planning and execution of the Japanese attack on Pearl Harbor, and looks at what it reveals about American leadership.
"The author offers a comprehensive account of Japanese preparations for the attack, the origins and extent of American unpreparedness, and the aftermath of the attack on both sides." —*Booklist*
Includes bibliographical references (p. 843-854) and index; Originally published: New York : McGraw-Hill, 1981.

Price, David A.
Geniuses at War: Bletchley Park, Colossus, and the Dawn of the Digital Age. by David A. Price. Alfred A. Knopf 2021. 224 p.
ISBN 9780525521549
Grades: Adult   940.54
1. Flowers, T. H. (Thomas Harold), 1905-1998 2. Newman, Max 3. Turing, Alan Mathison, 1912-1954 4. Computers 5. World War II 6. Computer scientists 7. Engineers 8. Cryptography 9. Military intelligence 10. English history 11. Second World War era (1939-1945) 12. 20th century 13. History writing — Wars and conflicts — World War II 14. History writing — Spies and spying 15. History writing — Wars and conflicts — World War II — European Theater 16. History writing — Science, Technology, and medicine 17. Nonfiction that reads like fiction
LC 2020050887
Tells the story of how an English engineer's team decoded the Nazi high command's infamous Enigma code during a pivotal moment in World War II by building the world's first digital electronic computer.
"Journalist Price (The Pixar Touch) delivers a solid history of how Allied codebreakers at Bletchley Park developed 'The first operational digital computers' to defeat Germany's vaunted Lorenz SZ cipher machines. . . . Those looking for an entertaining introduction to Bletchley Park and the era's technological innovations would do well to start here." —*Publishers Weekly*
A Borzoi book.—Title page verso; Includes bibliographical references and index.

Read, Anthony
The Fall of Berlin. Anthony Read and David Fisher. Da Capo Press 1995. 513 p. : Illustration; Map
ISBN 9780306806193
Grades: 11 12 Adult   940.54
1. Berlin, Battle of, 1945 2. Nazism 3. World War II 4. Third Reich, 1933-1945 5. German history 6. Berlin, Germany 7. Germany 8. History writing — Wars and conflicts — World War II — European Theater 9. History writing — Wars and conflicts — Battles
LC 94047798
A narrative of the fall of Berlin chronicles the history of the city from the pomp and glitter of the 1936 Olympic games, through the rise of the Nazis, to World War II and the Allied conquest.
"The result is a highly readable and, at the same time, sophisticated and reliable narrative history." —*Library Journal*
Includes bibliographical references (p. 469-478) and index; Originally published: London : Hutchinson, 1992.

Reid, Anna
Leningrad: The Epic Siege of World War II, 1941-1944. Anna Reid. Walker & Co. 2011. xv, 492 p, 16 p. of plates : Illustration; Map
ISBN 9780802715944
Grades: Adult   940.54
1. Siege warfare 2. Operation Barbarossa 3. Bombardment 4. World War II 5. Sieges 6. St. Petersburg, Russia 7. 1940s 8. History writing — Wars and conflicts — World War II
LC Bl2011021728
A narrative account of the siege of Leningrad reveals the Nazi decision to starve Leningrad into surrender and related Soviet leadership failures, describing the harrowing experiences of residents within the blockaded city.
Includes bibliographical references (p. [459]-471) and index.

Reynolds, Nicholas E.
Need to Know: World War II and the Rise of American Intelligence. Nicholas Reynolds. Mariner Books 2022. 400 p.
ISBN 9780062967473
Grades: Adult   940.54
1. Intelligence service 2. Military intelligence 3. Administrative agencies 4. World War II 5. Cold War 6. Espionage 7. Surveillance 8. Spies 9. Life stories — Law and order — Spies and secret agents 10. History writing — United States
A historian and former CIA officer explores the birth, infancy and adolescence of modern American intelligence, combining little-known history and gripping spy stories to illuminate its key role in securing Allied victory, which laid the foundation for all other conflicts to come.
"Former CIA officer Reynolds (Writer, Sailor, Soldier, Spy) delivers an exhaustively researched critical history of American military intelligence from 1940 to the beginning of the Cold War." —*Publishers Weekly*

Roberts, Andrew
The Storm of War: A New History of the Second World War. Andrew Roberts. Harpercollins 2011. 608 p.
ISBN 9780061228599
Grades: Adult   940.54
1. Hitler, Adolf, 1889-1945 2. World War II 3. Military campaigns 4. Military strategy 5. Second World War era (1939-1945) 6. History writing — Wars and conflicts — World War II — European Theater
LC Bl2011011949
New York Times Notable Book, 2011.
Analyzing the factors that affected the war's outcome and presenting stories of many little-known individuals whose experiences are the epitome of remarkable courage and self-sacrifice, the New York Times best-selling author of Masters and Commanders tells the story of World War II like never before.

Rogoyska, Jane
Surviving Katyn: Stalin's Polish Massacre and the Search for Truth. Jane Rogoyska. Oneworld Publications 2021. 400 p.
ISBN 9781786078926
Grades: Adult   940.54
1. Katyn Forest Massacre, 1940 2. World War II 3. Prisoners of war, Polish 4. Massacres 5. Prisons 6. Atrocities 7. Russia 8. History writing — Wars and conflicts — World War II
Mark Lynton History Prize, 2022.
Committed in utmost secrecy in April-May 1940 by the NKVD on the direct orders of Joseph Stalin, for nearly fifty years the Soviet regime succeeded in maintaining the fiction that Katyn was a Nazi atrocity, their story unchallenged by Western governments fearful of upsetting a powerful wartime ally and Cold War adversary. Surviving Katyn explores the decades-long search for answers, focusing on the experience of those individuals with the most at stake—the few survivors of the massacre and the Polish wartime forensic investigators—whose quest for the truth in the face of an inscrutable, unknowable, and utterly ruthless enemy came at great personal cost.
"The Katyn Massacre was the opening salvo to a war defined by unimaginable horrors. Here, its story is told clearly and passionately with allegiance only to the truth." —*Kirkus*

Scott, James
Black Snow: Curtis Lemay, the Firebombing of Tokyo, and the Road to the Atomic Bomb. James M. Scott. W.W. Norton & Company 2022. 448 p.
ISBN 9781324002994

ESSENTIAL AND RECOMMENDED TITLES
940.54 Military history of World War II

Grades: Adult 940.54
1. LeMay, Curtis E, 1906-1990 2. Generals 3. World War II 4. Aerial bombing 5. Firebombing 6. B-29 bomber 7. Tragedy 8. Civilians in war 9. War 10. Japanese history 11. Tokyo, Japan 12. 20th century 13. History writing — Wars and conflicts — World War II — Pacific Theater 14. History writing — Military — Aviation History 15. History writing — Asia — Japan 16. Life stories — Law and order — Military leaders

Seven minutes past midnight on March 10, 1945, nearly 300 American B-29s thundered into the skies over Tokyo. Their payloads of incendiaries ignited a firestorm that reached up to 2,800 degrees, liquefying asphalt and vaporizing thousands; sixteen square miles of the city were flattened and more than 100,000 men, women, and children were killed. Drawing on first-person interviews with American pilots and bombardiers and Japanese survivors, air force archives, and oral histories never before published in English, Scott delivers a harrowing and gripping account, and his most important and compelling work to date.

"In this immersive, meticulously researched history, Pulitzer finalist Scott (Target Tokyo) contends that the 1945 firebombing campaign against Japan marked a moral shift in U.S. military strategy and paved the way to the use of the atomic bomb....Full of vivid action scenes and sharp character observations, this riveting WWII history reveals the staggering cost of obtaining peace." —*Publishers Weekly*

Rampage: Macarthur, Yamashita, and the Battle of Manila. James M. Scott. W.W. Norton & Company 2018. 635 pages, 16 unnumbered pages of plates : Illustration; Map
ISBN 9780393246940
Grades: Adult 940.54
1. MacArthur, Douglas, 1880-1964 2. Yamashita, Tomobumi, 1885-1946 3. Atrocities 4. Military occupation 5. Violence 6. World War II 7. Manila, Philippines 8. Philippines 9. Second World War era (1939-1945) 10. 1940s 11. History writing — Wars and conflicts — World War II — Pacific Theater
LC 2018289656

Presents a history of the Battle of Manila that traces the capture of the Philippine capital by Japanese forces, the massacre of an estimated 100,000 civilians and liberation campaign that ultimately destroyed the city.

Includes bibliographical references (pages 599-607) and index.

Target Tokyo: Jimmy Doolittle and the Raid That Avenged Pearl Harbor. James M. Scott. W.W. Norton & Company 2015. 640 p.
ISBN 9780393089622
Grades: Adult 940.54
1. Doolittle, James Harold, 1896-1993 2. World War II 3. Aerial bombing 4. Air defenses 5. Military history 6. Aerial operations 7. Tokyo, Japan 8. 1940s 9. Second World War era (1939-1945) 10. History writing — Wars and conflicts — World War II
LC 2014043257

Pulitzer Prize for History finalist, 2016.

Presents a gripping account of the Doolittle Raid, a top-secret bombing mission and ambitious counterstrike against Tokyo in 1941, that was led by daredevil Lieutenant Colonel Jimmy Doolittle and turned the tide of the war|but came at a horrific cost.

"This popular history will appeal to fans of Laura Hillebrand's Unbroken and is comparable to other histories of the Tokyo Raid including Craig Nelson's the First Heroes and Carroll V. Glines's the Doolittle Raid." —*Library Journal*
Includes bibliographical references and index.

Sides, Hampton
★ *Ghost Soldiers: The Forgotten Epic Story of World War II's Most Dramatic Mission.* Hampton Sides. Doubleday 2001. 342 p, 16 p. of plates : Illustration; Color; Map
ISBN 9780385495646
Grades: 11 12 Adult 940.54
1. Military campaigns 2. Concentration camps 3. World War II 4. Atrocities 5. Prisoners of war, American 6. Prisoners of war, British 7. Prisons 8. Military history 9. 20th century 10. History writing — Wars and conflicts — World War II — Pacific Theater 11. Adult books for young adults
LC 2001017337

Chronicles the daring mission of the elite U.S. Army Sixth Ranger Battalion to slip behind enemy lines in the Phillipines and rescue the 513 American and British POWs who had spent over three years in a hellish, Japanese-run camp near Cabanatuan.

"The author's excellent grasp of human emotions and bravery makes this a compelling book hard to put down." —*Publishers Weekly*
Maps of Route of death march and Ranger raid on Cabanatuan on end pages; Includes bibliographical references.

Siegal, Nina
The Diary Keepers: World War II in the Netherlands, as Written by the People Who Lived Through It. Nina Siegal. Ecco Press 2023. 304 p.
ISBN 9780063070653
Grades: Adult 940.54
1. Dutch people 2. Personal diaries 3. World War II 4. Resistance to military occupation 5. Memory 6. War 7. German occupation, World War II 8. European history 9. Netherlands 10. Second World War era (1939-1945) 11. Diaries 12. Life stories — Facing adversity — War and oppression 13. History writing — Wars and conflicts — World War II 14. History writing — Europe

Based on select writings from a collection of more than 2,000 Dutch diaries written during World War II, this remarkable book seeks to understand the nature of resistance, the workings of memory and the ways we reflect on, commemorate and re-envision the past.

"This diverse and enlightening collection of excerpts from journals kept during the Nazi occupation of the Netherlands is an essential contribution to the history of WWII....Even those well versed in the subject will find much to discover in this treasure trove of firsthand perspectives." —*Publishers Weekly*

Simms, Brendan
The Silver Waterfall: How America Won the War in the Pacific at Midway. Brendan Simms and Steven McGregor. PublicAffairs 2022. 304 p.
ISBN 9781541701373
Grades: Adult 940.54
1. Midway, Battle of, 1942 2. Military aircraft 3. Bomber pilots 4. Air warfare 5. Naval battles 6. German Americans 7. Command of troops 8. Military engineering 9. Weapons industry and trade 10. World War II 11. Pacific Ocean 12. History writing — Wars and conflicts — World War II — Pacific Theater 13. History writing — Wars and conflicts — Battles 14. Life stories — Law and order — Armed forces personnel 15. History writing — Military
LC 2021041953

The stunning and decisive battle of Midway was perhaps the most crucial naval battle in the Pacific theater during World War II. Walter Lord explained away the US victory at Midway against a numerically superior and apparently more skilled Japanese fleet due to 'Lady Luck.' in the Silver Waterfall acclaimed historian Brendan Simms and historian and military veteran Steve McGregor show it was no such thing. Instead the authors show how the forces of industrial dynamism and innovation were central to the US being able to win the war in the Pacific. Equally important, the Navy drew on the skills of a wide variety of immigrants or descendants of immigrants—especially those from Germany, the principal hostile power. The engineer who designed the plane which decided the Battle of Midway was Ed Heinemann, the strategist who decided America would defend Midway Island was Chester Nimitz; and the pilot who symbolized American performance on the day was Dusty Kleiss. Without these men, America could not have designed, planned, or done what was needed to win.

"The U.S. Navy's victory at the Battle of Midway in June 1942 was the result of the skills of its veteran pilots and 'The effectiveness of their equipment,' according to this immersive account from biographer Simms (coauthor, Hitler's American Gamble) and U.S. Army veteran McGregor." —*Publishers Weekly*
Includes bibliographical references and index.

Smith, Jim B.
The Last Mission: The Secret Story of World War II's Final Battle. Jim B. Smith and Malcolm McConnell. Broadway Books 2003. xix, 349 p. : Illustration; Map
ISBN 9780767907798
Grades: Adult 940.54

1. B-29 bomber 2. Aerial operations 3. Politics and government 4. Nuclear weapons 5. Nuclear warfare 6. Atomic bomb 7. World War II 8. Hiroshima, Japan 9. Nagasaki, Japan 10. Japan 11. 20th century 12. Second World War era (1939-1945) 13. History writing — Wars and conflicts — World War II — Pacific Theater 14. History writing — Wars and conflicts — Battles

LC Bl2004119939

Traces the events surrounding the final American bombing mission of World War II, identifying a Japanese rebel plot for a massive coup that would have kept Japan in the war and prevented its surrender to Allied forces in August 1945.

"Smith was a radio operator on the crew of the B-29 bomber Boomerang in the Pacific theater of World War II. His plane, along with the others in the 315th Bomb Wing, 20th Air Force, was assigned to bomb strategic targets in the Japanese home islands. On their return from one mission, they passed three Superforts flying toward Japan and learned only later that one was the Enola Gay on its mission to drop the first atomic bomb on Hiroshima. More than a fascinating firsthand report of the last bombing mission over Japan, this book is an account of the last days of World War II in the Pacific." —*Library Journal*

Reprint. Originally published: 2002; Includes bibliographical references (p. [327]-333) and index.

Snyder, Steve

Shot Down: The True Story of Pilot Howard Snyder and the Crew of the B-17 Susan Ruth. Steve Snyder. Sea Breeze Publishing 2015. Iv, 360 pages : Illustration; Map

ISBN 9780986076008

Grades: Adult   940.54

1. Snyder, Howard, 1915-2007 2. B-17 bomber 3. World War II 4. Aerial operations 5. History writing — Military — Aviation history 6. History writing — Wars and conflicts — World War II

LC 2010904344

Set within the larger framework of World War II in Europe, the story is about the experiences of each member of a B-17 crew after their plane was knocked out of the sky by German fighters over Belgium and about the courageous Belgian patriots who risked their lives to help them. The book includes more than 200 period photographs of the people who were involved and the places where the events took place.

Includes bibliographical references (pages 343-350) and index.

Snyder, Timothy

★ *Bloodlands: Europe Between Hitler and Stalin.* Timothy Snyder. Basic Books 2010. 432 p.

ISBN 9780465002399

Grades: Adult   940.54

1. Stalin, Joseph, 1879-1953 2. Hitler, Adolf, 1889-1945 3. Genocide 4. Massacres 5. Holocaust (1933-1945) 6. World War II 7. Dictators 8. Dictatorship 9. Atrocities 10. Third Reich, 1933-1945 11. Soviet Union history 12. European history 13. Eastern Europe 14. History writing — Wars and conflicts — World War II 15. History writing — Wars and conflicts — Holocaust — World War II

LC 2010016816

Cundill Prize in Historical Literature finalist.

Describes how fourteen million people were murdered by Hitler's and Stalin's regimes in the area between Germany and Russia during the time when both men were in power and examines the motives and methods behind the mass murders.

"Mr. Snyder's book is revisionist history of the best kind: in spare, closely argued prose, with meticulous use of statistics, he makes the reader rethink some of the best-known episodes in Europe's modern history." —*The Economist*

Includes bibliographical references and index.

Southard, Susan

Nagasaki: Life After Nuclear War. Susan Southard. Viking Press 2015. 416 p.

ISBN 9780670025626

Grades: Adult   940.54

1. Radiation victims 2. Hibakusha 3. Nuclear weapons 4. Nuclear warfare 5. Atomic bomb 6. World War II 7. Hiroshima, Japan 8. Nagasaki, Japan 9. Japan 10. 1940s 11. Second World War era (1939-1945) 12. History writing — Wars and conflicts — Atomic Bomb — World War II

ALA Notable Book, 2016; J. Anthony Lukas Book Prize, 2016.

Published to coincide with the 70th anniversary of the bombing of Nagasaki, a riveting narrative of human resilience, told through first-hand experiences of five survivors, reveals the physical, emotional and social challenges of post-atomic life.

Stanton, Doug

In Harm's Way: The Sinking of the Uss Indianapolis and the Extraordinary Story of Its Survivors. Doug Stanton. H. Holt 2003. xxvi, 339 p. : Illustration; Map

ISBN 9780805073669

Grades: 11 12 Adult   940.54

1. World War II 2. Survival 3. Naval history 4. Naval operations 5. Shipwrecks 6. Pacific Ocean 7. History writing — Wars and conflicts — World War II — Pacific Theater 8. Adult books for young adults

LC BL2003007405

Chronicles the worst disaster in U.S. naval history, describing heroism in the face of persistant shark attacks and hypothermia after the sinking of the U.S.S. Indianapolis in the South Pacific in the final days of World War II.

"Illuminating and emotional without being maudlin, Stanton's book helps explain what many have long considered an inexplicable catastrophe." —*Publishers Weekly*

An Owl book; Includes bibliographical references (p. 289-317) and index; Originally published: 2001. With a new afterword by the author.

Stevenson, William

A Man Called Intrepid: The Secret War. William Stevenson. Lyons Press 2000. xxv, 486 p. : Illustration

ISBN 9781585741540

Grades: Adult   940.54

1. Stephenson, William Samuel, 1896-1989 2. World War II 3. Secret service 4. Canadian literature 5. History writing — Wars and conflicts — World War II 6. History writing — Spies and spying

LC 00712424

Offers an account of the intelligence activities of William Stephenson, code name Intrepid, and of the world's first integrated intelligence network, established in 1940 by Stephenson under the joint aegis of Churchill and Roosevelt.

Includes index; Originally published: New York : Harcourt, Brace, Javanovich, c1976.

Sullivan, James

Unsinkable: Five Men and the Indomitable Run of the Uss Plunkett. James Sullivan. Scribner 2020. 352 p.

ISBN 9781982147631

Grades: Adult   940.54

1. Naval battles 2. Destroyers (Warships) 3. World War II 4. Normandy Invasion, June 6, 1944 5. Second World War era (1939-1945) 6. 1940s 7. History writing — Military — Naval history 8. History writing — Wars and conflicts — World War II — European Theater

Documents the true story of a U.S. Navy destroyer that inspired the writings of John Ford and Herman Wouk, drawing on the journals and other writings of five shipmates who witnessed the Anzio attacks and D-Day invasion.

Symonds, Craig L.

The Battle of Midway. Craig L. Symonds. Oxford University Press 2011. 448 p.

ISBN 9780195397932

Grades: 10 11 12 Adult   940.54

1. Midway, Battle of, 1942 2. World War II 3. Naval battles 4. Battles 5. War 6. Naval operations 7. Pacific Ocean 8. Midway Islands 9. 1940s 10. History writing — Wars and conflicts — World War II — Pacific Theater 11. History writing — Wars and conflicts — Battles

LC 2011010648

ESSENTIAL AND RECOMMENDED TITLES
940.54 Military history of World War II

A close-up look at the battle of Midway Island analyzes this crucial naval victory, which marked the turning point for the American fleet in the Pacific theater of World War II.
Includes bibliographical references and index.

World *War II at Sea: A Global History.* Craig L. Symonds. Oxford University Press 2018. 792 p.
ISBN 9780190243678
Grades: Adult   940.54
1. Naval art and science 2. Naval history 3. Sailors 4. World War II 5. Naval operations 6. 20th century 7. History writing — Military — Naval history
LC 2017032532

Craig L. Symonds' World War II at Sea offers a definitive naval history of the Second World War presenting the chronology of the naval war, from the London Conference of 1930 to the surrender in Tokyo Bay in 1945, on a global scale for the first time.
"A veteran maritime historian delivers a satisfying one-volume history of 'The impact of sea services from all nations on the overall trajectory and even the outcome' of World War II." —*Kirkus*

Terkel, Studs
The **Good** *War: An Oral History of World War Two.* Studs Terkel. Pantheon Books 1984. 587 p.
ISBN 9781565843431
Grades: 11 12 Adult   940.54
1. War and society 2. World War II 3. United States history 4. Second World War era (1939-1945) 5. Oral histories 6. History writing — Wars and conflicts — World War II

Pulitzer Prize for General Nonfiction, 1985.
Oral history evokes the innocent idealism, as well as the terror and horror, of ordinary Americans at home and abroad during World War II.

Thomas, Evan
Sea *of Thunder: Four Commanders and the Last Great Naval Campaign, 1941-1945.* Evan Thomas. Simon & Schuster 2006. 415 p. : Illustration; Map
ISBN 9780743252218
Grades: Adult   940.54
1. Halsey, William Frederick, 1882-1959 2. Evans, Ernest Edwin, 1908-1944 3. Kurita, Takeo, 1889-1977 4. Ugaki, Matome, 1890-1945 5. Leyte Gulf, Battle of, 1944 6. Naval battles 7. Command of troops 8. World War II 9. Military campaigns 10. Military history 11. Philippines 12. Pacific Ocean 13. United States 14. 20th century 15. History writing — Wars and conflicts — World War II — Pacific Theater 16. History writing — Wars and conflicts — Battles
LC 2006047511

An account of the Battle of Leyte Gulf in October 1944 is told through the commands of four naval leaders, including two American commanders and two Japanese admirals, and offers insight into how the war reflected profound cultural differences.
"This is an account of the Battle of Leyte Gulf, October 1944, one of history's largest naval battles, where Admiral William Bull Halsey, the commander of the U.S. Third Fleet, and his commander, Ernest Evans, met the forces of Japanese admirals Takeo Kurita and Matome Ugaki. Thomas paints compelling portraits of these men, offering insight into their characters and actions throughout the war in the Pacific." —*Library Journal*
Includes bibliographical references (p. 391-402) and index.

Toll, Ian W.
The **Conquering** *Tide: War in the Pacific Islands, 1942/1944.* Ian W. Toll. W. W. Norton & Company 2015. 672 p.
ISBN 9780393080643
Grades: Adult   940.54
1. Naval tactics 2. Naval battles 3. World War II 4. Military campaigns 5. Naval history 6. Battles 7. Military strategy 8. Military history 9. Pacific Area 10. 1940s 11. History writing — Wars and Conflicts — World War II 12. History writing — Military — Naval history
LC 2015009591

Presents an account of the Allied effort to reclaim thousands of Japanese-occupied islands, detailing the campaign's technical innovations, logistic complications, and human and economic costs.
Includes bibliographical references and index.

Pacific *Crucible: War at Sea in the Pacific, 1941-1942.* Ian W. Toll. W W Norton & CO Inc. 2011. 544 p.
ISBN 9780393068139
Grades: Adult   940.54
1. Naval tactics 2. Naval battles 3. World War II 4. Military campaigns 5. Pacific Ocean 6. 1940s 7. History writing — Wars and conflicts — World War II — European Theater 8. History writing — Military — Naval history
LC 2011028907

Draws on eyewitness accounts and primary sources to describe the first months of World War II in the Pacific, after the U.S. Navy suffered the worst defeat in its history at Pearl Harbor.
"The author makes vast quantities of technological and tactical concepts intelligible to all but the rankest beginnerfor whom this book is not remotely suitable. A particular gift of the author is intelligent character portraits: Yamamoto, MacArthur, Halsey, and Nimitz (clearly one of the author's favorites). Add to all these other attributes a thorough scholarly apparatus, and it is difficult to think of a recent book on this subject that is of such consistently outstanding value."
—*Booklist*

Twilight *of the Gods: War in the Western Pacific, 1944-1945.* Ian W. Toll. W. W. Norton & Company 2020. 864 p.
ISBN 9780393080650
Grades: Adult   940.54
1. MacArthur, Douglas, 1880-1964 2. Naval battles 3. Military campaigns 4. World War II 5. Military strategy 6. Atomic bomb 7. Military history 8. Naval history 9. Pacific Area 10. 1940s 11. History writing — Wars and Conflicts — World War II 12. History writing — Military — Naval history
LC 2020009619

A conclusion to the trilogy that began with Pacific Crucible is based on the final year of World War II and follows MacArthur's pledge to the Philippines, the kamikaze attacks on Allied fleets and the bombing of Hiroshima and Nagasaki.
"Written with flair and chock-full of stories both familiar and fresh, this monumental history fires on all cylinders. WWII aficionados will be enthralled."
—*Publishers Weekly*
Includes bibliographical references and index.

Trimble, Lee
Beyond *the Call: The True Story of One World War II Pilot's Covert Mission to Rescue Pows on the Eastern Front.* Lee Trimble, Jeremy Dronfield. Penguin Group USA 2015. 352 p.
ISBN 9780425276044
Grades: Adult   940.54
1. Trimble, Robert M. 2. Bomber pilots 3. World War II 4. Military missions 5. Secrecy in government 6. International relations 7. Military intelligence 8. Prisoners of war 9. Espionage 10. Suspicion 11. Rescues 12. Prisons 13. United States 14. Soviet Union 15. Second World War era (1939-1945) 16. Biographies 17. History writing — Wars and conflicts — World War II — European Theater 18. Life stories — Law and order — Armed forces personnel

An account of bomber pilot Captain Robert M. Trimble's secret rescue mission, co-written by his son, details the strained tensions between America and Russia and the daunting challenges he faced trying to save hundreds of abandoned POWs.

Twomey, Steve
Countdown *to Pearl Harbor: The Twelve Days to the Attack.* Steve Twomey. Simon & Schuster 2016. 416 p.
ISBN 9781476776460
Grades: Adult   940.54
1. Pearl Harbor, Attack on, 1941 2. World War II 3. Hawaii 4. 1940s 5. Second World War era (1939-1945) 6. History writing — Wars and conflicts — World War II — Pacific Theater
LC 2016019080

A Pulitzer Prize-winning reporter chronicles the 12 days leading up to the Japanese attack on Pearl Harbor, examining the miscommunications, clues, missteps and racist assumptions that may have been behind America's failure to safeguard against the tragedy.

"A well-researched study of an infamous moment that is still fascinating and controversial." —Kirkus

Vincent, Lynn
Indianapolis: The True Story of the Worst Sea Disaster in U.S. Naval History and the Fifty-year Fight to Exonerate an Innocent Man. Lynn Vincent and Sara Vladic. Simon & Schuster 2018. 320 p.
ISBN 9781501135941
Grades: Adult   940.54
1. McVay, Charles Butler, III, 1898-1968 2. Shipwrecks 3. Government cover-ups 4. World War II 5. Courts-martial and courts of inquiry 6. Malicious accusation 7. Naval operations 8. History writing — Military — Naval history
LC 2018015537
Loan Stars Favourites, 2018.

An account of the sinking of the USS "Indianapolis" during World War II draws on original research and new reporting to trace the half-century battle to exonerate Captain Charles McVay after a wrongful court martial.

"Recommended for readers interested in the final days of World War II, particularly naval activity in the Pacific theater, and anyone curious about McVay and his vessel." —*Library Journal*

Includes bibliographical references and index.

Wallace, Chris
Countdown 1945: The Extraordinary Story of the Atomic Bomb and the 116 Days That Changed the World. Chris Wallace, with Mitch Weiss. Avid Reader Press 2020. 312 p.
ISBN 9781982143343
Grades: Adult   940.54
1. Truman, Harry S, 1884-1972 2. Generals 3. Command of troops 4. Military pilots 5. Nuclear physicists 6. Bombing victims 7. Girls 8. Presidents 9. Aerial operations 10. Nuclear weapons 11. Nuclear warfare 12. Atomic bomb 13. World War II 14. United States history 15. Japanese history 16. Hiroshima, Japan 17. Nagasaki, Japan 18. United States 19. Japan 20. Second World War era (1939-1945) 21. 20th century 22. Impartial writing 23. History writing — Wars and conflicts — Atomic Bomb — World War II 24. History writing — Presidency — 20th century — United States 25. History writing — Asia — Japan 26. History writing — Wars and conflicts — World War II — Pacific Theater
LC Bl2020012971

April 12, 1945: After years of bloody conflict in Europe and the Pacific, America is stunned by news of President Franklin D. Roosevelt's death. In an instant, Vice President Harry Truman, who has been kept out of war planning and knows nothing of the top-secret Manhattan Project to develop the world's first atomic bomb, must assume command of a nation at war on multiple continents—and confront one of the most consequential decisions in history. Countdown 1945 tells the gripping true story of the turbulent days, weeks, and months to follow, leading up to August 6, 1945, when Truman gives the order to drop the bomb on Hiroshima.

"A brisk work of history that weaves together the various factions responsible for the deployment of the first nuclear bombs." —*Kirkus*

Weale, Adrian
Army of Evil: A History of the Ss. Adrian Weale. New American Library 2012. 496 p.
ISBN 9780451237910
Grades: Adult   940.54
1. Nazism 2. World War II 3. Military history 4. Third Reich, 1933-1945 5. Politics and government 6. Germany 7. History writing — Wars and conflicts — World War II 8. History writing — Europe — Germany
LC 2012014170

Describes how the Nazi enforcers of the Third Reich began as a small group of politically-motivated thugs and grew to take control of all the police and security positions in Germany and ultimately became the Waffen SS with more than 800,000 members.

Includes bibliographical references and index.

Weintraub, Robert
No Better Friend: One Man, One Dog, and Their Extraordinary Story of Courage and Survival in Wwii. Robert Weintraub. Little, Brown and Company 2015. 288 p.
ISBN 9780316337069
Grades: Adult   940.54
1. Prisoners of war 2. Pointer (Dog breed) 3. Internment camp inmates 4. Concentration camps 5. World War II 6. Prisons 7. Human-animal relationships 8. Biographies 9. Life stories — Relationships — Pets and owners 10. Life stories — Facing adversity — War and oppression — Hostages and POWs
LC 2015932606

Describes the story of the unbreakable bond that developed between a Royal Air Force technician and a fiercely loyal purebred pointer named Judy, who met in an internment camp during World War II, where the pair became a symbol of hope to the other prisoners.

"By mutual trust and aid, dog and man survived several brutal Japanese camps together, braving hunger, sadistic guards, snakes, and tigers. Weintraub's research on the prisoners' experiences in the camps is remarkable as he narrates Judy and Frank's heroic tale." —*Kirkus*

Wheelan, Joseph
Midnight in the Pacific: Guadalcanal: The World War II Battle That Turned the Tide of War. Joseph Wheelan. Da Capo Press 2017. 356 pages
ISBN 9780306824593
Grades: Adult   940.54
1. Guadalcanal, Battle of, 1942-1943 2. World War II 3. Military campaigns 4. Battles 5. Naval battles 6. Air battles 7. Combat 8. Marines 9. Soldiers 10. Sailors 11. Guadalcanal Island 12. Second World War era (1939-1945) 13. History writing — Wars and conflicts — World War II — Pacific Theater 14. History writing — Military

Published to coincide with the 75th anniversary of the battle, a sweeping narrative recounts America's first major offensive in World War II—the brutal, no-quarter-given campaign to take Japanese-occupied Guadacanal between August 7, 1942, and February 10, 1943.

"Current-day readers, accustomed to an era of perpetual war with no end in sight, will find this expert, nuts-and-bolts history of a famous victory thoroughly satisfying." —*Kirkus*

Includes bibliographical references and index.

Wukovits, John F.
Lost at Sea: Eddie Rickenbacker's Twenty-four Days Adrift on the Pacific—a World War II Tale of Courage and Faith. John Wukovits. Dutton Caliber 2023. 464 p.
ISBN 9780593184844
Grades: Adult   940.54
1. Rickenbacker, Eddie, 1890-1973 2. Search and rescue operations 3. World War II 4. Airplane accidents 5. Survival 6. War 7. United States 8. Pacific Area 9. 20th century 10. History writing — Wars and conflicts — World War II — Pacific Theater 11. Life stories — Law and order — Armed forces personnel 12. History Writing — Military
LC 2022038131

Drawing on survivors' accounts and contemporary records, a military expert recounts American war hero Eddie Rickenbacker's crash landing in the Pacific during World War II and his incredible 23-day fight to keep his crew alive, in this gripping story of survival, leadership and faith in a time of crisis.

"Drawing largely from survivors' accounts, Wukovits viscerally describes their ordeal and conveys the miraculous nature of the outcome." —*Publishers Weekly*

Includes index.

ESSENTIAL AND RECOMMENDED TITLES
940.54012 Military history of World War II — Strategy — Allies

Zuckoff, Mitchell
Lost in Shangri-la: The Epic True Story of a World War II Plane Crash into the Stone Age. Mitchell Zuckoff. HarperCollins 2011. 448 p.
ISBN 9780061988349
Grades: Adult   940.54
1. Search and rescue operations 2. Survival (after airplane accidents, shipwrecks, etc.) 3. Airplane accidents 4. World War II 5. Non-industrial societies 6. Aerial operations 7. Missing in action 8. New Guinea 9. History writing — Wars and conflicts — World War II 10. Adventure writing — Survival
LC 2010034508

L. L. Winship/PEN New England Award for Nonfiction, 2012.

Award-winning former Boston Globe reporter Mitchell Zuckoff unleashes the exhilarating, untold story of an extraordinary World War II rescue mission, where a plane crash in the South Pacific plunged a trio of U.S. military personnel into the jungle-clad land of New Guinea.

"On May 13, 1945, an American transport plane carrying 24 servicemen and women crashed into a mountain in the tropical jungles of Dutch New Guinea (now Papua), leaving three survivors. Learning about the event while researching another subject, the author recognized the ingredients of a terrific tale: a beautiful young WAC, a hidden valley reminiscent of the Shangri-La in James Hilton's Lost Horizon, primitive tribal people and a daring air rescue. In this well-crafted book, Zuckoff turns the long-forgotten episode into an unusually exciting narrative. Drawing on the young WAC survivor Margaret Hastings' diary as well as journals and interviews, the author hones in on life at the U.S. military base in Hollandia, on the northern coast of uncharted New Guinea; a soldier's chance discovery a year earlier of Baliem Valley, a verdant area about 150 miles into the interior, with its hundreds of native villages surrounded by gardens; and the doomed flight of officers and enlisted personnel out on a joy ride to view this much-talked-about land of Stone Age people from the air." —*Kirkus*

Includes bibliographical references and index.

940.54012 Military history of World War II — Strategy — Allies

Olson, Lynne
Citizens of London: The Americans Who Stood with Britain in Its Darkest, Finest Hour. Lynne Olson. Random House 2010. 448 p.
ISBN 9781400067589
Grades: Adult   940.54012
1. Murrow, Edward R, 1908-1965 2. Harriman, W. Averell (William Averell), 1891-1986 3. Churchill, Winston, 1874-1965 4. World War II 5. Strategic alliances (Military) 6. Military history 7. Diplomacy 8. International relations 9. Great Britain 10. United States 11. History writing — Wars and conflicts — World War II
LC 2010278653

ALA Notable Book, 2011.

The behind-the-scenes story of how the United States forged its wartime alliance with Britain, told from the perspective of three key American players in London: Edward R. Murrow, Averell Harriman, and John Gilbert Winant.

"A nuanced history that captures the intensity of life in a period when victory was not a foregone conclusion." —*Kirkus*

940.55 History of Europe — 1945-1999

Judt, Tony
Postwar: A History of Europe Since 1945. Tony Judt. Penguin Press 2005. xv, 878 p, 24 p. of plates : Illustration; Map
ISBN 9781594200656
Grades: Adult   940.55
1. Postwar life 2. World War II 3. International relations 4. Cold War 5. Social life and customs 6. Politics and government 7. Economics 8. European history 9. Europe 10. 20th century 11. History writing — Europe
LC 2005052126

Library Journal Best Books, 2005; New York Times Notable Book, 2005; Pulitzer Prize for General Nonfiction finalist.

A history of contemporary Europe includes coverage of thirty-four countries and draws on a wide range of newly available sources to document the region's economic development, culture, politics, and more, in a volume complemented by maps, photos, and cartoon illustrations.

"This is the best history we have of Europe in the postwar period and not likely to be surpassed for many years." —*Publishers Weekly*

Includes bibliographical references and index.

Kershaw, Ian
The Global Age: Europe 1950-2017. Ian Kershaw. Penguin Group 2019. 656 p.
ISBN 9780735223981
Grades: Adult   940.55
1. World politics 2. Economic development 3. International cooperation 4. Peace 5. Prosperity 6. Financial crises 7. Globalization 8. Cold War 9. Berlin Wall 10. Energy policy 11. Global Financial Crisis, 2008-2009 12. Oil industry and trade 13. 20th century 14. 21st century 15. Business and economics — Economics — World economy 16. Politics and global affairs — World politics — Europe 17. History writing — Europe
LC 2019023176

Traces the latter half of the twentieth century to the present and covers the impact of nuclear threat, accelerating globalization, and the post-2008 financial crises.

"The second installment of the eminent English historian's comprehensive overview of modern European history." —*Kirkus*

Lowe, Keith
Savage Continent: Europe in the Aftermath of World War Two. Keith Lowe. St. Martin's Press 2012. 400 p.
ISBN 9781250000200
Grades: Adult   940.55
1. World War II 2. Winning and losing 3. Reconstruction (1939-1951) 4. Crime 5. Murder 6. Hunger 7. Forced relocations 8. Recession (Economics) 9. Antisemitism 10. European history 11. Europe 12. 20th century 13. History writing — Europe 14. History writing — Wars and conflicts — World War II
LC 2011279703

An account of the period of violent disorder that racked Europe after World War II describes the brutal acts against Germans and collaborators, the anti-Semitic beliefs that reemerged and the Allied-tolerated expulsions of millions of citizens from their ancestral homelands. By the author of Inferno.

940.56 History of Europe — 2000-

Friedman, George
Flashpoints: The Emerging Crisis in Europe. George Friedman. Random House Inc. 2015. 320 p.
ISBN 9780385536332
Grades: Adult   940.56
1. Geopolitics 2. Forecasting 3. Politics and culture 4. Culture conflict 5. Social prediction 6. Politics and government 7. European history 8. Europe 9. 21st century 10. Politics and global affairs — World politics — Europe

Examines key geopolitical flashpoints in Europe and their potential for future conflicts, discussing the failure of the European Union to minimize cultural conflict and geopolitical tensions and exploring how events in Europe will affect the rest of the world.

941 British Isles

Borman, Tracy
Crown & Sceptre: A New History of the British Monarchy, from Willam the Conqueror to Elizabeth II. Tracy Borman. Atlantic Monthly Press 2022. 576 p.
ISBN 9780802159106

PUBLIC LIBRARY CORE COLLECTION: NONFICTION
Twentieth Edition

Grades: Adult   **941**

1. Royal houses 2. Sovereignty 3. Leadership 4. Monarchy 5. Rulers 6. British history 7. Great Britain 8. Collective biographies 9. Biographies 10. Impartial writing 11. Life stories — Politics — Royalty 12. History writing — Europe — United Kingdom

This sweeping history of the British monarchy looks at the 41 kings and queens, from William I to Queen Elizabeth II, who have sat on the throne and set helped set the course of history.

"Borman, best-selling historical biographer and novelist, traces the evolution of the British monarchy through the lives of the forty-one men and women who have reigned since 1066.... Crown and Sceptre will delight history buffs. Crisp, clear writing, insightful character sketches, and unifying themes keep the narrative moving along." —*Booklist*

Fowler, Corinne

★ *The* **Countryside:** *Ten Rural Walks Through Britain and Its Hidden History of Empire.* Corinne Fowler. Scribner 2024. 240 p.

ISBN 9781668003978

Grades: Adult   **941**

1. Walking 2. Historic sites 3. Rural lands 4. Economic development 5. Macroeconomics 6. Social classes 7. Colonies 8. Colonialism 9. Slavery 10. Imperialism 11. British history 12. Great Britain 13. History writing — Europe — United Kingdom 14. History writing — Colonialism — Europe 15. Travel Writing — Europe

LC 2024006722

Through ten walks through the green fields, rugged highlands and rolling hills of England, Scotland and Wales, the author explores the history of these countryside locations and the people who lived and worked in them, encountering people with ties to these places who transform our understanding of British landscapes, colonialism and heritage.

"A deftly critical, readable contribution to the historiography of empire." —*Kirkus*

Published in Great Britain under the title Our island stories: Country walks through colonial Britain, by Allen Lane, London, in 2024; Includes bibliographical references and index.

Lacey, Robert

Great Tales from English History 1: The Truth About King Arthur, Lady Godiva, Richard the Lionheart, and More. Robert Lacey. Little, Brown 2004. xvi, 254 p. : Map

ISBN 9780316109109

Grades: Adult   **941**

1. Civilization, Medieval 2. British history 3. Medieval period (476-1492) 4. History writing — Europe — United Kingdom

LC 2003115660

Vivid retellings of forty-three classic English tales include the 7150 BC life and death of Cheddar Man, the infamous adventures of Hobbehod, and the Peasants' Revolt of 1381.

Includes bibliographical references (p. 223-240) and index; First published in Great Britain by Little, Brown, 2003—T.P. verso.

Great Tales from English History 2: Joan of Arc, the Princes in the Tower, Bloody Mary, Oliver Cromwell, Sir Isaac Newton, and More. Robert Lacey. Little, Brown and Co. 2005. xvi, 271 p. : Illustration; Map

ISBN 9780316109246

Grades: Adult   **941**

1. British history 2. Stuart period (1603-1714) 3. Medieval period (476-1492) 4. Norman period (1066-1154) 5. Plantagenet period (1154-1485) 6. Tudor period (1485-1603) 7. History writing — Europe — United Kingdom

LC 2004063351

A second collection of historical accounts from the England of Chaucer and Shakespeare covers the period between 1387 and 1687, and features influential figures including Henry VIII, Mary, Queen of Scots, and Sir Francis Drake.

"The author's second volume on English history opens in 1348, the year of the Black Plague, which wiped out half of England's five million people, and proceeds through the astonishing scientific discoveries of Sir Isaac Newton in 1687. Lacey's animated prose, energetic storytelling and spirited approach to British history bring the past to life." —*Publishers Weekly*

First published in Great Britain by Little, Brown and Company, 2004—T.P. verso; Includes bibliographical references (p. 241-256) and index.

Great Tales from English History 3: Captain Cook, Samuel Johnson, Queen Victoria, Charles Darwin, Edward the Abdicator, and More. Robert Lacey. Little, Brown 2006. IX, 305 p. : Illustration

ISBN 9780316114592

Grades: Adult   **941**

1. Social life and customs 2. British history 3. Great Britain 4. History writing — Europe — United Kingdom

LC 2006931723

A third compilation of historical accounts covers English history from 1690 to 1953 and captures the pivotal events and characters of England's modern age, including Samuel Johnson, Mary Wollstonecraft, Charles Darwin, and Winston Churchill.

"The third volume in Lacey's series of edifying and entertaining stories from English history abounds in fascinating profiles. Industrial and agricultural pioneers such as Jethro Tull, James Hargreaves and Isambard Kingdom Brunel abide alongside human rights protestors such as Thomas Clarkson, who founded the British antislavery movement; feminist philosopher Mary Wollstonecraft; and journalist Annie Besant, who initiated a successful 1888 match girls' strike." —*Publishers Weekly*

First published in Great Britain by Little, Brown and Company, 2006—T.P. verso; Includes bibliographical references (p. 267-287) and index.

Morris, Ian

Geography Is Destiny: Britain and the World: A 10,000-year History. Ian Morris. Farrar, Straus and Giroux 2022. 544 p.

ISBN 9780374157272

Grades: Adult   **941**

1. International trade 2. Imperialism 3. Power 4. Economic development 5. Geography 6. Immigration and emigration 7. International relations 8. Great Britain 9. Europe 10. History writing — Europe — United Kingdom 11. Politics and global affairs — World politics — Europe

LC 2021061234

When Britain voted to leave the European Union in 2016, the 48 percent who wanted to stay and the 52 percent who wanted to go each accused the other of stupidity, fraud, and treason. In reality, the Brexit debate merely reran a script written eight thousand years earlier, when the rising seas physically separated the British Isles from the European continent. Ever since, geography has been destiny—yet it is humans who get to decide what that destiny means. Ian Morris, the critically acclaimed author of Why the West Rules—for Now, describes how technology and organization have steadily enlarged Britain's arena, and how its people have tried to turn this to their advantage.

"England's fateful geographical adjacency to Europe drives a millennia-long love-hate relationship in this sparkling history....Written with verve and wit, this compulsively readable overview of British history is full of fascinating lore and incisive analysis." —*Publishers Weekly*

Includes bibliographical references and index.

Sanghera, Sathnam

★ **Empireland:** *How Imperialism Has Shaped Modern Britain.* Sathnam Sanghera; foreword by Marlon James. Pantheon Books 2023. 384 p.

ISBN 9780593316672

Grades: Adult   **941**

1. Imperialism 2. Colonialism 3. Postcolonialism 4. Racism 5. Multiculturalism 6. British people 7. Great Britain 8. History writing — Europe — United Kingdom

British Book Award for Narrative Nonfiction of the Year, 2022.

An award-winning journalist tracks the roots of the British empire and how imperial domination still continues to shape the modern-day United Kingdom as well as their former colonies, including the United States.

"Imperialism is not something that can be erased with a few statues being torn down or a few institutions facing up to their dark pasts,' according to this

ESSENTIAL AND RECOMMENDED TITLES
941.03 Great Britain — 1154-1399

pointed and wide-ranging survey of how Britain's imperialist past informs its present." —*Publishers Weekly*

Originally published in Great Britain by Viking, 2021.

Schama, Simon
A History of Britain; 2. Simon Schama. Hyperion 2001. 544 p. : Illustration; Color; Map
ISBN 9780786867523
Grades: Adult **941**
1. International relations 2. Civilization 3. British history 4. Great Britain 5. History writing — Europe — United Kingdom
LC 00061442

A comprehensive history of Britain chronicles battles waged by the British, both at home and abroad, details its role as a global power, and examines key events and personalities that shaped more than two centuries of history.

"Schama writes wonderfully, in an easygoing yet elegant manner, with an eye for the telling aesthetic detail, and throughout brimming with intelligence and passion." —*New York Times Book Review*

Includes bibliographical references and index.

941.03 Great Britain — 1154-1399

Green, Matthew
Shadowlands: A Journey Through Britain's Lost Cities and Vanished Villages. Matthew Green. W W Norton & CO Inc 2022. 336 p.
ISBN 9780393635348
Grades: Adult **941.03**
1. Extinct cities 2. Local history 3. Voyages and travels 4. British history 5. Great Britain 6. Travel Writing — Europe 7. Debut title

From an Orkney settlement buried in sand five thousand years ago to a medieval city mouldering beneath the waves of the North Sea, Britain's landscape is scarred with the haunting and romantic remains; these shadowlands that were once filled with life are now just spectral echoes.

"First-time author Green's haunting travelogue through Britain's disappeared places is both an examination of the historical forces that led to their abandonment and a meditation on the presence of absence in physical and emotional landscapes." —*Library Journal*

941.06 House of Stuart and Commonwealth periods, 1603-1714

Healey, Jonathan
The Blazing World: A New History of Revolutionary England, 1603-1689. Jonathan Healey. Alfred A. Knopf 2023. 384 p.
ISBN 9780593318355
Grades: Adult **941.06**
1. Politics and government 2. British history 3. Great Britain 4. Stuart period (1603-1714) 5. History Writing — Europe — United Kingdom
LC 2022038721

A noted historian transports us back to 17th-century England, painting a vivid portrait of a country in the midst of a revolutionary age where new ideas were forged that were angry, populist, and almost impossible for monarchs to control, and where wealth, creativity and daring curiosity heralded a new world. Map(s).

"Healey's elegant narrative provides a sure guide through the century's labyrinthine political intrigues while analyzing deeper social dynamics that he crystallizes in dramatic scenes of hierarchies being suddenly upended." —*Publishers Weekly*

This is a Borzoi book; Includes bibliographical references and index.

Mortimer, Ian
The Time Traveler's Guide to Restoration Britain: A Handbook for Visitors to the Seventeenth Century: 1660-1699. Ian Mortimer. Pegasus Books 2017. 416 p.
ISBN 9781681773544

Grades: Adult **941.06**
1. Charles II, King of England, 1630-1685 2. Civilization, Western 3. History 4. British history 5. Stuart period (1603-1714) 6. 17th century 7. Restoration England (1660-1688) 8. History writing — Europe — United Kingdom
LC Bl2017013557

An up-close-and-personal look at Britain between the Restoration of King Charles II in 1660 and the end of the century delves into the nuances of daily life to paint a vibrant and detailed picture of society at the dawn of the modern world. By the author of the Time Traveler's Guide to Medieval England.

"This is a sure bet for history lovers and readers with a penchant for unusual travelogues." —*Booklist*

941.07 Period of House of Hanover, 1714-1837

Ackroyd, Peter
Revolution: The History of England from the Battle of the Boyne to the Battle of Waterloo. Peter Ackroyd. Thomas Dunne Books/St. Martin's Press 2017. 416 p. (History of England, 4)
ISBN 9781250003645
Grades: Adult **941.07**
1. William III King of Great Britain 1650-1702 2. Mary II, Queen of Great Britain, 1662-1694 3. Anne, Queen of Great Britain, 1665-1714 4. George I, King of Great Britain, 1660-1727 5. George II King of Great Britain 1683-1760 6. George III, King of Great Britain, 1738-1820 7. George IV, King of Great Britain, 1762-1830 8. Stuart, House of 9. Hanover, House of 10. Industrial revolution 11. Economic development 12. Napoleonic Wars, 1800-1815 13. Royal houses 14. English history 15. Stuart period (1603-1714) 16. Georgian era (1714-1837) 17. 17th century 18. 18th century 19. 19th century 20. History writing — Europe — United Kingdom
LC 2017027329

The award-winning novelist, broadcaster, biographer and historian behind Thames: Sacred River offers the fourth volume in his sweeping history of England, covering the events from William of Orange's accession to the defeat of Napoleon at Waterloo.

Originally published: 2016.

Morrison, Robert
The Regency Years: During Which Jane Austen Writes, Napoleon Fights, Byron Makes Love, and Britain Becomes Modern. Robert Morrison. 2019. 416 p.
ISBN 9780393249057
Grades: Adult **941.07**
1. National characteristics, English 2. English literature 3. Arts 4. Modern arts 5. Literary criticism 6. Social life and customs 7. Civilization 8. Civilization, Medieval 9. British history 10. England 11. Great Britain 12. Regency period (1811-1820) 13. 19th century 14. Georgian era (1714-1837) 15. Medieval period (476-1492) 16. Arts and Entertainment — General 17. History writing — Europe — United Kingdom
LC 2018053659

Examines the complex history of the Regency era, exploring the social, religious, scientific, and artistic movements of the period that helped shape the modern world.

"An intriguing discussion on the finer and more fascinating aspects of the Regency period that will appeal to history buffs, particularly those curious about European and British history." —*Library Journal*

Also published in the UK under the title, the regency revolution; Includes bibliographical references and index.

941.081 Reign of Victoria, 1837-1901

Cadbury, Deborah
Queen Victoria's Matchmaking: The Royal Marriages That Shaped Europe. Deborah Cadbury. PublicAffairs 2017. 320 pages
ISBN 9781610398466

PUBLIC LIBRARY CORE COLLECTION: NONFICTION
Twentieth Edition

Grades: Adult 941.081
1. Victoria, Queen of Great Britain, 1819-1901 2. Women rulers 3. Matchmaking 4. Marriage 5. Arranged marriage 6. Royal houses 7. Power 8. Scandals 9. Royal weddings 10. Victorian era (1837-1901) 11. Biographies 12. Life stories — Politics — Royalty 13. History writing — Europe — United Kingdom 14. History writing — Europe

LC 2017952726

Booklist Editors' Choice, 2017.

An exploration of the role in which Queen Victoria exerted the most international power and influence: as a matchmaking grandmother.

"British historian and documentarian Cadbury (Princes at War) energetically reveals the extent of Queen Victorias meddling in the marriage arrangements of her grandchildren in order to create the familys ideal British-German alliance." —Publishers Weekly

Gill, Gillian

We Two: Victoria and Albert : Rulers, Partners, Rivals. Gillian Gill. Ballantine Books 2009. 384 p.

ISBN 9780345484055

Grades: Adult 941.081
1. Victoria, Queen of Great Britain, 1819-1901 2. Albert, Prince Consort, consort of Victoria, Queen of Great Britain, 1819-1861 3. Husband and wife 4. Princes 5. Women rulers 6. British history 7. Great Britain 8. Victorian era (1837-1901) 9. History writing — Europe — United Kingdom

Gillian Gill offers a revolutionary portrait of a queen and her prince, revealing at once both an intimate but far-from-idyllic relationship that succeeded against all odds as the strong, feisty queen and the brilliant, fragile prince worked together to build a family based on support, trust, and fidelity.

Goodman, Ruth

How to Be a Victorian: A Dawn-to-dusk Guide to Victorian Life. Ruth Goodman. Liveright Publishing Corporation, a division of W. W. Norton & Company 2014. 464 pages

ISBN 9780871404855

Grades: Adult 941.081
1. Social life and customs 2. Historical reenactments 3. British history 4. Great Britain 5. Victorian era (1837-1901) 6. 19th century 7. History writing — Europe — United Kingdom

LC 2014023719

Describes the details of everyday life in the Victorian period, from leisure activities and fashion, to education, and contraception, including doing calisthenics, putting on a corset, and giving opium to the children before bedtime.

First published in Great Britain in 2013 by Penguin Books Ltd.—T.P. verso; Includes index.

941.083 Reign of George V, 1910-1936

Nicolson, Juliet

*The **Great** Silence: Britain from the Shadow of the First World War to the Dawn of the Jazz Age.* Juliet Nicolson. Grove Press 2009. xvi, 302 p, 16 p. of plates : Illustration

ISBN 9780802119445

Grades: Adult 941.083
1. Social change 2. Social structure 3. Social classes 4. World War I 5. British history 6. Great Britain 7. 20th century 8. History writing — Europe — United Kingdom

A social history of the first two years in Britain following World War I covers topics ranging from the development of skin grafting procedures by surgeon Harold Gillies and the passage of the women's vote to the state funeral of the Unknown Soldier.

Includes bibliographical references and index.

941.084 Great Britain — 1936-1945

McCarten, Anthony

Darkest Hour: How Churchill Brought England Back from the Brink. Anthony McCarten. HarperCollins 2017. 256 pages

ISBN 9780062749512

Grades: Adult 941.084
1. Churchill, Winston, 1874-1965 2. World War II 3. Diplomacy 4. Military strategy 5. Britain, Battle of, 1940 6. Military campaigns 7. European history 8. 1940s 9. 20th century 10. New Zealand literature 11. Biographies 12. Page to screen 13. Life stories — Politics — Politicians 14. History writing — Wars and conflicts — World War II — European Theater 15. History writing — Europe — United Kingdom

LC Bl2017034059

Presents an account of the period immediately following Winston Churchill's ascendancy to Prime Minister and how he met the challenges of the Blitzkrieg.

"A fresh, readable look at events and players that, though well-known to history, deserve to be studied for some time to come." —*Kirkus*

Morton, Andrew

17 Carnations: The Royals, the Nazis and the Biggest Cover-up in History. Andrew Morton. Grand Central Publishing 2015. 368 p.

ISBN 9781455527113

Grades: Adult 941.084
1. Windsor, Edward, Duke of, 1894-1972 2. Windsor, Wallis Warfield, Duchess of, 1896-1986 3. World War II 4. Nazis 5. Royal houses 6. Government cover-ups 7. Secrecy 8. History writing — Wars and conflicts — World War II 9. History writing — Europe — United Kingdom

LC 2014957815

A meticulously researched account of the scandalous collaboration between Edward VIII and Hitler draws on hidden correspondence to reveal how the Duke of Windsor's wife, Wallis Simpson, embroiled him in a German plot to take over the British Empire.

"This tale of British history, cover-ups, and surprising connections to the Nazi party truly intrigues. It provides a closer look into the world of royals during the first half of the 20th century when there was still so much being kept secret." —*Library Journal*

Olson, Lynne

Troublesome Young Men: The Rebels Who Brought Churchill to Power and Helped Save England. Lynne Olson. Farrar, Straus and Giroux 2007. 426 p. : Illustration

ISBN 9780374179540

Grades: Adult 941.084
1. Churchill, Winston, 1874-1965 2. Chamberlain, Neville, 1869-1940 3. Politics and government 4. Great Britain 5. History writing — Europe — United Kingdom

LC 2006017905

Describes how, in 1940, a group of rebellious Tory members of Parliament defied the appeasement policies of British Prime Minister Neville Chamberlain to force his resignation and bring to power Winston Churchill.

Includes bibliographical references (p. [365]-411) and index.

Spicer, Charles

Coffee with Hitler: The Untold Story of the Amateur Spies Who Tried to Civilize the Nazis. Charles Spicer. Pegasus Books 2022. 520 p.

ISBN 9781639362264

Grades: Adult 941.084
1. Hitler, Adolf, 1889-1945 2. Spies 3. Nazis 4. World War II 5. Nazism 6. Friendship 7. International relations 8. Great Britain 9. Germany 10. History writing — Europe — United Kingdom 11. History writing — Europe — Germany 12. History writing — Wars and conflicts — World War II

The fascinating story of how an eccentric group of intelligence agents used amateur diplomacy to penetrate the Nazi high command in an effort to prevent the start of World War II.

ESSENTIAL AND RECOMMENDED TITLES
941.085 Great Britain — 1945-1999

941.085 Great Britain — 1945-1999

Charter, David
Royal Audience: 70 Years, 13 Presidents — One Queen's Special Relationship with America. David Charter. Putnam 2024. 352 p.
ISBN 9780593712870
Grades: Adult   941.085
1. Elizabeth II, Queen of Great Britain, 1926-2022 2. Women rulers 3. Monarchy 4. Presidents 5. Alliances 6. Diplomacy 7. International relations 8. Interpersonal relations 9. Politics and government 10. British people 11. English people 12. Great Britain 13. United States 14. Biographies 15. Life stories — Politics — Royalty 16. Life stories — Relationships 17. History writing — Europe — United Kingdom 18. History writing — Presidency — United States

This fascinating, in-depth look at the extraordinary and varied personal bonds Queen Elizabeth II forged with 13 presidents over her 70-year reign charts her distinctive brand of one-to-one diplomacy through the eyes of those who experienced it firsthand and shows how, throughout the years, her sense of duty and service remained steadfast.

"It adds up to a perceptive, if highly burnished, overview of diplomatic relations between two countries' heads of state." —*Publishers Weekly*

Holmes, Elizabeth
HRH: So Many Thoughts on Royal Style. Elizabeth Holmes. Celadon Books 2020. 327 p. Illustration
ISBN 9781250625083
Grades: Adult   941.085
1. Diana, Princess of Wales, 1961-1997 2. Catherine, Princess of Wales, 1982- 3. Meghan, Duchess of Sussex, 1981- 4. Elizabeth II, Queen of Great Britain, 1926-2022 5. Clothing 6. Fashion 7. Princesses 8. Women rulers 9. Great Britain 10. Illustrated books 11. Biographies 12. Life stories — Politics — Royalty 13. Arts and Entertainment — Fashion
LC 2020024954

The veteran fashion journalist blends commentary, essays and hundreds of photographs in an expansion of her award-winning "So Many Thoughts" Instagram series to reveal the political statements within the style, branding and positioning of prominent British royals.

"Royal watchers will delight in this breezy survey of Windsor family fashions." —*Publishers Weekly*

Larman, Alexander
★ *Power and Glory: Elizabeth II and the Rebirth of Royalty.* Alexander Larman. St. Martin's Press 2024. 352 p.
ISBN 9781250289599
Grades: Adult   941.085
1. Elizabeth II, Queen of Great Britain, 1926-2022 2. Philip, Prince, consort of Elizabeth II, Queen of Great Britain, 1921-2021 3. Windsor, House of 4. Royal houses 5. Marriages of royalty and nobility 6. Monarchy 7. British history 8. Rulers 9. Great Britain 10. Collective biographies 11. Life stories — Politics — Royalty
LC 2023056126

A master chronicler of the House of Windsor brings his acclaimed trilogy to a dramatic and poignant conclusion.

"Larman makes all this history accessible even to those unfamiliar with palace protocols and hierarchies, cementing this as a must-read for royal watchers and Anglophiles of all sorts." —*Booklist*

Includes bibliographical references and index.

Moore, Charles
Margaret Thatcher: The Authorized Biography, from Grantham to the Falklands. Charles Moore. Alfred A. Knopf 2013. 859 p. (Margaret Thatcher: the authorized biographies, 1)
ISBN 9780307958945
Grades: Adult   941.085
1. Thatcher, Margaret 2. Women politicians 3. Political leadership 4. Prime ministers 5. Women prime ministers 6. Politics and government 7. Great Britain 8. 20th century 9. Biographies 10. History writing — Europe — United Kingdom 11. Life stories — Politics — Politicians
LC 2013020670

Elizabeth Longford Prize for Historical Biography, 2014.

With unequaled authority and dramatic detail, the first volume of Charles Moore's authorized biography of Margaret Thatcher reveals as never before the early life, rise to power, and first years as prime minister of the woman who transformed Britain and the world in the late twentieth century.

941.1 Scotland

Herman, Arthur
How the Scots Invented the Modern World: The True Story of How Western Europe's Poorest Nation Created Our World & Everything in It. Arthur Herman. Crown Publishers 2001. VIII, 392 p.
ISBN 9780609606353
Grades: Adult   941.1
1. Civilization, Western 2. National characteristics, Scottish 3. Scottish people in foreign countries 4. Enlightenment (European intellectual movement) 5. Intellectual life 6. Civilization 7. Scotland 8. History writing — Europe — United Kingdom
LC 2001028951

Explores the seminal contributions of Scotland to the development of modern Western civilization, discussing the impact of such ideals as democracy, freedom of speech, equal opportunity, and a commitment to education.

"This is a worthwhile book for the general reader." —*Publishers Weekly*

Includes bibliographical references (p. 362-376) and index.

Nicolson, Adam
Sea Room: An Island Life in the Hebrides. Adam Nicolson. North Point Press 2002. 391 p. : Illustration; Map
ISBN 9780865476363
Grades: Adult   941.1
1. Nicolson, Adam, 1957- 2. Natural history 3. Voyages and travels 4. Hebrides 5. Scotland 6. Travel Writing — Europe
LC 2002019816

Booklist Editors' Choice, 2002.

Documents the author's experiences with and love for three Outer Hebrides islands he inherited as a young man, tracing the area's rich and sometimes violent history of hermits, legendary ghosts, farmers, fishermen, and Bronze Age gold.

"Magnificent and poetic, this is a literary and ecological masterpiece." —*Booklist*

Includes bibliographical references (p. 381-386) and index; Originally published: London, HarperCollins Publishers, 2001.

941.105 Scotland — Reformation period, 1542-1603

Weir, Alison
Mary, Queen of Scots, and the Murder of Lord Darnley. Alison Weir. Ballantine Books 2003. xvii, 670 p, [16] p. of plates; Color illustration; Map
ISBN 9780345436580
Grades: Adult   941.105
1. Darnley, Henry Stuart, Lord, 1545-1567 2. Mary, Queen of Scots, 1542-1587 3. Murder 4. Women rulers 5. Scottish history 6. Scotland 7. Renaissance (1300-1600) 8. 16th century 9. Scottish Stewart period (1371-1603) 10. History writing — Europe — United Kingdom 11. History writing — Renaissance — Europe 12. History writing — Historical mysteries 13. True Crime — Murder 14. True Crime — Historical Crime
LC 2002034467

The best-selling author of Henry VIII reexamines an array of source material to describe the relationship between Mary, Queen of Scots, and her ambitious second husband, Lord Darnley, and to investigate the 1567 murder of Lord Darnley, to assess the potential involvement of Mary, and to provide a solution to this four-hundred-year-old mystery.

"No stone is left unturned in {Weir's investigation, and despite its detail, her book is as dramatic as witnessing firsthand the most riveting court case." —*Booklist*

Includes bibliographical references (p. [580]-649) and index.

941.3 Southeastern Scotland

Robb, Graham
The Debatable Land: The Lost World Between Scotland and England. Graham Robb. Picador 2018. x, 334 pages, 16 unnumbered pages of plates : Illustration; Color; Map
ISBN 9780393285321
Grades: Adult   941.3
1. Ptolemy, active 2nd century 2. Robb, Graham, 1958- 3. Maps 4. Archaeology 5. Boundaries 6. Borderlands 7. Extinct cities 8. Law 9. Scottish history 10. British history 11. Great Britain 12. Scottish Borders (England and Scotland) 13. Roman Britain (55 B.C.E.-449 C.E.) 14. Medieval period (476-1492) 15. History writing — Europe — United Kingdom
LC 2017054854

A biographer and historian describes his firsthand investigation into the 2,000-year-old map of Ptolemy, which led him to more than one discovery of major historical significance in the once-hotly contested Debatable Land territory.

Stewart, Rory
The Marches: A Borderland Journey Between England and Scotland. Rory Stewart. Houghton Mifflin Harcourt 2016. 304 p.
ISBN 9780544108882
Grades: Adult   941.3
1. Borderlands 2. Landscape 3. Walking 4. Boundaries 5. British history 6. England 7. Scotland 8. Travel writing — Europe
LC Bl2016030217

The New York Times best-selling author of the Places in Between explores the landscape of his home on the borderland between England and Scotland—known as the Marches—and the history, people and conflicts that have shaped it.

941.5 Ireland

Kavanagh, Julie
The Irish Assassins: Conspiracy, Revenge and the Phoenix Park Murders That Stunned Victorian England. Julie Kavanagh. Grove Press 2021. 320 p.
ISBN 9780802149367
Grades: Adult   941.5
1. Murder 2. Conspiracies 3. Assassination 4. Murder investigation 5. Political persecution 6. Irish history 7. Victorian era (1837-1901) 8. 19th century 9. History writing — Europe — Ireland 10. True Crime — Historical Crime

A brilliant work of historical true crime charting a pivotal event in the 19th century, the Phoenix Park murders in Dublin, that gripped the world and forever altered the course of Irish history, from renowned journalist, former New Yorker London editor, and Costa Biography Award finalist Julie Kavanagh.

"A historical true-crime tale revisits three notorious Victorian-era murders that shocked Britain and dealt a body blow to the cause of Home Rule for Ireland. . . . A cinematic, multilayered revenge tragedy centered on Ireland's fraught quest for independence." —*Kirkus*

941.501 Ireland — Early history to 1086

Cahill, Thomas
How the Irish Saved Civilization: The Untold Story of Ireland's Heroic Role from the Fall of Rome to the Rise of Medieval Europe. Thomas Cahill. Nan A. Talese, Doubleday 1995. x, 246 p. : Illustration; Map (Hinges of history, 1)
ISBN 9780385418485

Grades: 11 12 Adult   941.501
1. Learning and scholarship 2. Manuscripts 3. Books 4. Civilization, Medieval 5. Civilization 6. Ireland 7. Europe 8. Medieval period (476-1492) 9. History writing — Medieval — Europe
LC 94028130

Presents an accessible and revealing portrait of medieval times. As Europe reaches intellectual stagnation and decline, Ireland bursts forth as a vigorous haven of scholarship.

"Highly literate and affectionate, if somewhat rambling and indulgent. As a freewheeling, witty popular history of Irish Christianity in the Dark Ages, this will amuse and enlighten." —*Library Journal*

Includes bibliographical references and index.

941.5081 Ireland — 1800-1899

Kelly, John
The Graves Are Walking : The Great Famine and the Saga of the Irish People. John Kelly. Henry Holt and Co. 2012. 304 p.
ISBN 9780805091847
Grades: Adult   941.5081
1. Famines 2. Nation-building 3. British people in Ireland 4. Hunger 5. Social conflict 6. Political corruption 7. Immigrants, Irish 8. Immigration and emigration 9. Political culture 10. Economic policy 11. Irish history 12. 19th century 13. Irish Potato Famine (1845-1852) 14. History writing — Plague and famine 15. History writing — Europe — Ireland 16. History writing — Europe — United Kingdom
LC 2012011493

Describes the Great Irish Potato Famine that began in 1845 and discusses how the combined forces of bacterial infection, political greed and religious intolerance started a disaster that killed twice as many people as died during the American Civil War.

941.7 Republic of Ireland (Eire)

Gibney, John
A Short History of Ireland, 1500-2000. John Gibney. Yale University Press 2017. xiv, 281 pages : Map
ISBN 9780300208511
Grades: Adult   941.7
1. Irish history 2. History writing — Europe — Ireland
LC 2017941374

A brisk, concise, and readable overview of Irish history from the Protestant Reformation to the dawn of the twenty-first century.

Includes bibliographic references (pages 261-265) and index.

O'Toole, Fintan
★ *We Don't Know Ourselves: A Personal History of Modern Ireland.* Fintan O'Toole. Liveright Publishing Corporation 2022. 336 p.
ISBN 9781631496530
Grades: Adult   941.7
1. O'Toole, Fintan, 1958- 2. Technology 3. Financial crises 4. The Troubles, 1968-1998 5. Violence 6. Corruption 7. British history 8. Northern Ireland 9. Ireland 10. 20th century 11. 21st century 12. History writing — Europe — Ireland 13. Life stories — Arts and culture — Writing — Journalists
LC 2021058515

A celebrated Irish writer's magisterial, brilliantly insightful chronicle of the wrenching transformations that dragged his homeland into the modern world. Fintan O'Toole was born in the year the revolution began. It was 1958, and the Irish government—in despair, because all the young people were leaving—opened the country to foreign investment and popular culture. So began a decades-long, ongoing experiment with Irish national identity. In We Don't Know Ourselves, O'Toole, one of the Anglophone world's most consummate stylists, weaves his own experiences into Irish social, cultural, and economic change, showing how Ireland, in just one lifetime, has gone from a reactionary

ESSENTIAL AND RECOMMENDED TITLES
942 England and Wales

"backwater" to an almost totally open society-perhaps the most astonishing national transformation in modern history.

"In O'Toole's case, sharp reporting makes good history."—*Library Journal*

Originally published in the UK by Head of Zeus, London, in 2021.

942 England and Wales

Ackroyd, Peter
Rebellion: The History of England from James I to the Glorious Revolution. Peter Ackroyd. St Martins Pr. 2014. 528 p. (History of England, 3)
ISBN 9781250003638
Grades: Adult 942
1. James I, King of England, 1566-1625 2. Charles I, King of England, 1600-1649 3. Cromwell, Oliver, 1599-1658 4. Civil war 5. Regicide 6. Royal houses 7. English Civil War, 1642-1649 8. Resistance to government 9. British history 10. England 11. 17th century 12. Stuart period (1603-1714) 13. History writing — Europe — United Kingdom 14. History writing — Wars and conflicts — Civil Wars
LC 2014026045

A latest volume in the award-winning author's series covers the Stuart dynasty during a turbulent 17th century marked by three civil wars, citing the roles of such figures as James VI, Charles I and Oliver Cromwell.

"Although general readers in the U.S. may find some of the names and places unfamiliar, this masterful work of popular history will remind them that the ideas that launched our own revolution were forged during this seminal period of English history."—*Booklist*

Foundation: The History of England from Its Earliest Beginnings to the Tudors. Peter Ackroyd. Thomas Dunne Books 2012. 496 p. (History of England, 1)
ISBN 9781250003614
Grades: Adult 942
1. Civilization, Medieval 2. British history 3. Tudor period (1485-1603) 4. Medieval period (476-1492) 5. History writing — Europe — United Kingdom
LC 2012028305

The first entry in a six-volume epic traces the birth of England, documenting the region's primeval origins through the death of Henry VII and covering the construction of Stonehenge, the establishment of common law, and the roles of successive invasions.

First published in Great Britain by Macmillan—T.P. verso; Includes bibliographical references and index.

Castor, Helen
She-wolves: The Women Who Ruled England Before Elizabeth. Helen Castor. Harpercollins 2011. 480 p.
ISBN 9780061430763
Grades: Adult 942
1. Women rulers 2. Rulers 3. Great Britain 4. England 5. History writing — Europe — United Kingdom 6. History writing — Women's history
LC 2010013263

Explores women and power in England, as witnessed through the lives of six females who exercised power against the odds—and one who never got the chance.

"The author recounts the lives of six women who exercised—or tried to exercise—political power in England prior to Elizabeth I: Matilda, granddaughter of William the Conqueror; Eleanor of Aquitaine; Isabella of France; Margaret of Anjou; Jane Grey; and Mary Tudor. Readers of popular history of British royals will enjoy their immensely human stories and applaud the indomitable will of these strong protofeminists."—*Library Journal*

Tombs, Robert
The **English** *and Their History.* by Robert Tombs. Alfred A. Knopf 2015. 1024 p.
ISBN 9781101874769
Grades: Adult 942
1. History 2. National characteristics, British 3. British history 4. History writing — Europe — United Kingdom
LC 2014048390

New York Times Notable Book, 2016.

Presents the story of England, examining the language, literature, law, religion, politics, and more while investigating the sources of England's collective memory and belief.

"All readers will benefit from a history that reveals the connections and disconnections, the continuities and discontinuities that make the English who they think they are. Summing Up: Essential. All levels/Libraries."—*Choice*

This is a Borzoi Book.

942.01 England — Early history to 1066

Morris, Marc
★ *The* **Anglo-saxons:** *A History of the Beginnings of England: 400-1066.* Marc Morris. Pegasus Books 2021. 452 p.
ISBN 9781643133126
Grades: Adult 942.01
1. Anglo-Saxons 2. Civilization, Anglo-Saxon 3. Civilization, Medieval 4. British history 5. England 6. Anglo-Saxon period (449-1066) 7. Medieval period (476-1492) 8. History writing — Medieval — Europe 9. History writing — Europe — United Kingdom

Sixteen hundred years ago, Britain left the Roman Empire and fell swiftly into ruin. Grand cities and luxurious villas were deserted and left to crumble&;and civil society collapsed into chaos. Into this violent and unstable world came foreign invaders from across the sea, and established themselves as its new masters. Tracing the turbulent history of these people across the next six centuries, Morris explains how their earliest rulers fought relentlessly against each other for glory and supremacy, and then were almost destroyed by the onslaught of the vikings. It explores how they abandoned their old gods for Christianity, established hundreds of churches, and created dazzlingly intricate works of art. Marc Morris illuminates a period of history that is only dimly understood, separates the truth from the legend, and tells the extraordinary story of how the foundations of England were laid.

"Historian Morris (The Norman Conquest) delivers a character-driven history of how the Anglo-Saxons developed England in the centuries between the end of Roman rule and the Norman conquest."—*Publishers Weekly*

942.02 England — Norman period, 1066-1154

The **Norman** *Conquest: The Battle of Hastings and the Fall of Anglo-saxon England.* Marc Morris. Pegasus Books 2013. 440 p.
ISBN 9781605984513
Grades: Adult 942.02
1. William I, King of England, 1027 or 1028-1087 2. Hastings, Battle of, England, 1066 3. Normans 4. Battles 5. British history 6. Norman period (1066-1154) 7. 11th century 8. Anglo-Saxon period (449-1066) 9. Medieval period (476-1492) 10. History writing — Medieval — Europe 11. History writing — Europe — United Kingdom
LC 2013431768

Explains why the Norman conquest was the most significant event in English history, assessing the historical circumstances of the battle and how language, law, philosophy, and other aspects of society were permanently altered by the conquest.

Also published in large print format; Originally published: London : Hutchinson, 2012.

942.03 England — Period of House of Plantagenet, 11541399

Asbridge, Thomas S.
The **Greatest** *Knight: The Remarkable Life of William Marshal, the Power Behind Five English Thrones.* Thomas Asbridge. Ecco Press 2014. 256 p.

ISBN 9780062262059
Grades: Adult							942.03
1. Pembroke, William Marshal, Earl of, 1144?-1219 2. Knights and knighthood 3. English history 4. British history 5. 12th century 6. Medieval period (476-1492) 7. Norman period (1066-1154) 8. Plantagenet period (1154-1485) 9. Biographies 10. Life stories — Law and order — Armed forces personnel 11. History writing — Europe — United Kingdom

LC 2015431306

A renowned scholar brings to life medieval England's most celebrated knight, William Marshal—who served under such rulers as Queen Eleanor of Aquitaine, Richard the Lionheart and his infamous brother, John—providing an unprecedented and intimate view of this age and the legendary warrior class that shaped it.

"Matters did not improve after Henry's death, so Marshal's career comes across as a relentless series of intrigues, battles, atrocities, truces quickly broken, internal revolts and treason that often included Marshal for reasons the author must guess because historical evidence is lacking. A valuable biography of an important figure in a distant, violent, barely comprehensible era." —*Kirkus*

942.03092 England — Period of House of Plantagenet, 1154-1399 — Biography

Jones, Dan
★ *The Plantagenets: The Warrior Kings and Queens Who Made England.* Dan Jones. Viking 2013. 560 p.
ISBN 9780670026654
Grades: Adult							942.03092
1. Plantagenet, House of 2. Civilization, Medieval 3. Royal houses 4. Rulers 5. British history 6. Great Britain 7. Plantagenet period (1154-1485) 8. Medieval period (476-1492) 9. History writing — Medieval — Europe

LC 2012039998

An epic history of the Plantagenet royal dynasty traces its first king's inheritance of a violence-stricken realm through the family's growth of a powerful empire that stretched from Scotland to Jerusalem, citing the enduring influences of such figures as Eleanor of Aquitaine, Richard II and King John.

"The great battles against the Scots and French and the subjugation of the Welsh make for thrilling reading but so do the equally enthralling struggles over succession, the Magna Carta, and the Provisions of Oxford…Written with prose that keeps the reader captivated throughout accounts of the span of centuries and the not-always-glorious trials of kingship, this book is at all times approachable, academic, and entertaining." —*Booklist*

Includes bibliographical references and index.

942.033 Reign of John, 1199-1216

Morris, Marc
King John: Treachery and Tyranny in Medieval England: The Road to Magna Carta. Marc Morris. Pegasus 2015. 400 p.
ISBN 9781605988856
Grades: Adult							942.033
1. John, King of England, 1167-1216 2. Civilization, Medieval 3. Political leadership 4. Command of troops 5. Rulers 6. British history 7. 13th century 8. Plantagenet period (1154-1492) 9. Medieval period (476-1492) 10. Biographies 11. Life stories — Politics — Royalty 12. History writing — Medieval — Europe

LC 2015452049

An authoritative and dramatic new biography paints a vivid picture of the real King John through two interwoven stories, which reveal a dynamic, inventive, relentless and terribly flawed man whose rejection of the Magna Carta led to civil war, foreign invasion and his own demise. By the national best-selling author of the Norman Conquest.

"Describing the kings exactions, Morris shows how they provoked opposition from Englands magnates. Despite Magna Cartas subsequent renown as the foundation of constitutional law, at the time it was a truce surrounded by civil war. That the war ended quickly after John died in 1216 points, suggests Morris, to his personal shortcomings as significant causes of the disasters of his reign. Balanced and dramatic, Morris riveting account will effortlessly attract history readers." —*Booklist*

942.04 England — Period of Houses of Lancaster and York, 1399-1485

Jones, Dan
★ *The Wars of the Roses: The Fall of the Plantagenets and the Rise of the Tudors.* Dan Jones. Viking 2014. 416 p.
ISBN 9780670026678
Grades: Adult							942.04
1. Tudor, House of 2. Plantagenet, House of 3. Margaret of Anjou, Queen of England, 1430-1482 4. Beaufort, Margaret, Countess of Richmond and Derby, 1443-1509 5. Elizabeth, Queen, consort of Edward IV, King of England, 1437?-1492 6. Wars of the Roses, 1455-1485 7. British history 8. 15th century 9. Plantagenet period (1154-1485) 10. History writing — Europe — United Kingdom 11. History writing — Wars and conflicts

LC 2014010099

Traces the fifteenth-century civil wars that irrevocably shaped the British crown, particularly evaluating the roles of strong women including Margaret of Anjou, Elizabeth Woodville, and Margaret Beaufort in shifting power between two ruling families.

"This excellent and fairly accessible contribution to the history of the Wars of the Roses serves as a helpful corrective to previous mythologized versions. It is highly recommended for studies of British royal history and for readers of popular narrative nonfiction." —*Library Journal*

Includes bibliographical references and index.

Penn, Thomas
The Brothers York: A Royal Tragedy. Thomas Penn. Simon & Schuster 2020. xxiii, 660 p.
ISBN 9781451694178
Grades: Adult							942.04
1. York, House of 2. Edward IV, King of England, 1442-1483 3. Richard III, King of England, 1452-1485 4. Clarence, George, Duke of, 1449-1478 5. Royal houses 6. Political corruption 7. Wars of the Roses, 1455-1485 8. Rulers 9. British history 10. Great Britain 11. 15th century 12. Plantagenet period (1154-1485) 13. Biographies 14. Life stories — Politics — Royalty 15. History writing — Europe — United Kingdom 16. Life stories — People in history — Famous families 17. Nonfiction that reads like fiction

LC 2019045050

Fascinating, dramatic, and filled with vivid historical detail, the Brothers York is a brilliant account of a conflict that fractured England for a generation. Riven by internal rivalries, jealousy, and infighting, the three York brothers failed to sustain their power and instead self-destructed. It is a rich and bloody tale as gripping as any historical fiction.

"Penn's latest is a treat for dedicated readers of English history who know the outlines of the story covered but wish to learn more." —*Library Journal*

Includes bibliographical references and index; Originally published in Great Britain in 2019 by Penguin Random House UK.

Weir, Alison
The Wars of the Roses. Alison Weir. Ballantine Books 1995. xvii, 462 p, 12 p. of plates : Illustration; Portrait
ISBN 9780345391179
Grades: 11 12 Adult						942.04
1. Richard II, King of England, 1367-1400 2. Henry VI, King of England, 1421-1471 3. Wars of the Roses, 1455-1485 4. British history 5. 15th century 6. Plantagenet period (1154-1485) 7. Tudor period (1485-1603) 8. Medieval period (476-1492) 9. Renaissance (1300-1600) 10. History writing — Medieval — Europe 11. History writing — Renaissance — Europe

Booklist Editors' Choice, 1995.

ESSENTIAL AND RECOMMENDED TITLES
942.04092 England — Period of Houses of Lancaster and York, 1399-1485 — Biography

Chronicles the struggles of the Lancaster and York families to control the British monarchy, while offering profiles of such figures as Katherine of Valois, Elizabeth Wydville, and Margaret of Anjou.

"No history collection should do without this perfectly focused and beautifully unfolded account." —*Booklist*

Includes bibliographical references (p. [431]-441) and index; Originally published: London : J. Cape, 1995.

942.04092 England — Period of Houses of Lancaster and York, 1399-1485 — Biography

Gristwood, Sarah
Blood Sisters: The Women Behind the Wars of the Roses. Sarah Gristwood. Basic Books, a Member of the Perseus Books Group 2013. 384 p.
ISBN 9780465018314
Grades: Adult   942.04092
1. Plantagenet, House of 2. Margaret of Anjou, Queen of England, 1430-1482 3. York, Cecily, Duchess of, 1415-1495 4. Elizabeth, Queen, consort of Edward IV, King of England, 1437-1492 5. Anne, Queen, consort of Richard III, King of England, 1456-1485 6. Margaret, of York, Duchess, consort of Charles the Bold, Duke of Burgundy, 1446-1503 7. Elizabeth, Queen, consort of Henry VII, King of England, 1465-1503 8. Beaufort, Margaret, Countess of Richmond and Derby, 1443-1509 9. Wars of the Roses, 1455-1485 10. Inheritance and succession 11. Rulers 12. Civil war 13. British history 14. 15th century 15. Plantagenet period (1154-1485) 16. Tudor period (1485-1603) 17. Medieval period (476-1492) 18. History writing — Europe — United Kingdom 19. History writing — Medieval — Europe 20. History writing — Women's history
LC 2012044813

A historian describes the drama and family feuding within the Plantagenets, England's fifteenth-century ruling family, from the perspective of the mothers, wives and daughters who wove a web of loyalty and betrayal that ultimately gave way to the Tudors.

Includes bibliographical references and index.

942.046 Reign of Richard III, 1483-1485

Pitts, Mike
Digging for Richard III: The Search for the Lost King. Mike Pitts. Thames & Hudson 2014. 207 p.
ISBN 9780500252000
Grades: Adult   942.046
1. Richard III, King of England, 1452-1485 2. Excavations (Archaeology) 3. Human remains (Archaeology) 4. Rulers 5. England 6. Biographies 7. History writing — Archaeology 8. Life stories — Politics — Royalty

In August 2012 a search began and on February 4, 2013 a team from Leicester University delivered its verdict to a mesmerized press room, watched by media studios around the world: They had found the remains of Richard III, whose history is perhaps the most contested of all British monarchs.History offers a narrow range of information about Richard III which mostly has already been worked to destruction. Archaeology creates new data, new stories, with a different kind of material: Physical remains from which modern science can wrest a surprising amount, and which provide a direct, tangible connection with the past.

Includes bibliographical references and index.

942.05 England — Period of House of Tudor, 1485-1603

Ackroyd, Peter
Tudors: The History of England from Henry VIII to Elizabeth I. Peter Ackroyd. Thomas Dunne Books/St. Martin's Press 2013. 512 p. (History of England, 2)
ISBN 9781250003621
Grades: Adult   942.05

1. Royal houses 2. Reformation 3. British history 4. England 5. Tudor period (1485-1603) 6. History writing — Europe — United Kingdom
LC 2013024573

A chronicle of the English Reformation, the making of the Anglican Church, and the age of the Tudors follows Henry VIII's relentless pursuit of both the perfect wife and the perfect heir, the brief reign of teenage king Edward VI, and the long reign of Elizabeth I.

Includes bibliographical references and index; Originally published: London : Macmillan, 2012.

Bordo, Susan
The Creation of Anne Boleyn: A New Look at England's Most Notorious Queen. Susan Bordo. Houghton Mifflin Harcourt 2013. xvii, 343 p. : Illustration
ISBN 9780547328188
Grades: Adult   942.05
1. Anne Boleyn, Queen, consort of Henry VIII, King of England, 1507-1536 2. Henry VIII, King of England, 1491-1547 3. Henry VII, King of England, 1491-1547 4. Rulers' spouses 5. Women rulers 6. Women in popular culture 7. Perception 8. Character 9. Image 10. Popular culture 11. British history 12. Tudor period (1485-1603) 13. Biographies 14. Life stories — Politics — Royalty 15. History writing — Europe — United Kingdom 16. Arts and Entertainment — General
LC 2012039119

Reconstructs the life of the second wife of Henry VIII, drawing on scholarly studies and critical analysis to define an English queen who has been alternately viewed as a whore, martyr, feminist icon, and cautionary tale.

Includes bibliographical references and index.

Borman, Tracy
Henry VIII and the Men Who Made Him. Tracy Borman. Grove Press 2018. 320 p.
ISBN 9780802128430
Grades: Adult   942.05
1. Henry VIII, King of England, 1491-1547 2. Henry VII, King of England, 1491-1547 3. Rulers 4. Power 5. Royal houses 6. Courts and courtiers 7. Politics and government 8. British history 9. Great Britain 10. Tudor period (1485-1603) 11. Biographies 12. Life stories — Politics — Royalty 13. History writing — Europe — United Kingdom
LC 2018049543

From acclaimed historian Tracy Borman, a penetrating new portrait of Henry VIII and the men who greatly impacted his life and historic reign.

"A thorough read for all interested in the Tudor era, the Reformation, and the British monarchy." —*School Library Journal*

Includes bibliographical references and index.

Fraser, Antonia
★ *The Wives of Henry VIII.* Antonia Fraser. Knopf 1992. IX, 479 p, 48 p. of plates : Illustration; Color
ISBN 9780394585383
Grades: Adult   942.05
1. Catharine, of Aragon, Queen, consort of Henry VIII, King of England, 1485-1536 2. Anne Boleyn, Queen, consort of Henry VIII, King of England, 1507-1536 3. Jane Seymour, Queen, consort of Henry VIII, King of England, 1509-1537 4. Anne, of Cleves, Queen, consort of Henry VIII, King of England, 1515-1557 5. Catherine Howard, Queen, consort of Henry VIII, King of England, d. 1542 6. Catharine Parr, Queen, consort of Henry VIII, King of England, 1512-1548 7. Henry VIII, King of England, 1491-1547 8. Marriages of royalty and nobility 9. Monarchy 10. Women rulers 11. British history 12. Great Britain 13. 16th century 14. Renaissance (1300-1600) 15. Collective biographies 16. Biographies 17. Life stories — Politics — Royalty 18. History writing — Europe — United Kingdom 19. History writing — Renaissance — Europe
LC 92052950

Presents a provocative study of the diverse and complex characters of the six wives of Henry VIII and their impact on the world.

Includes bibliographical references (p. 448-458) and index; Originally published in Great Britain in 1992 as: The six wives of Henry VIII by George Weidenfeld and Nicholson Limited—T.P. verso.

PUBLIC LIBRARY CORE COLLECTION: NONFICTION
Twentieth Edition

Goodman, Ruth
How to Be a Tudor: A Dawn-to-dusk Guide to Tudor Life. Ruth Goodman. Liveright Publishing Corporation 2016. 464 p.
ISBN 9781631491399
Grades: Adult   942.05
1. Tudor, House of 2. Social life and customs 3. Historical reenactments 4. British history 5. Great Britain 6. 16th century 7. Tudor period (1485-1603) 8. Renaissance (1300-1600) 9. History writing — Europe — United Kingdom 10. History writing — Renaissance — Europe
LC 2015038420

On the heels of her triumphant How to Be a Victorian, Ruth Goodman travels even further back in English history to the era closest to her heart, the dramatic period from the crowning of Henry VII to the death of Elizabeth I. Drawing on her own adventures living in re-created Tudor conditions, Goodman serves as our intrepid guide to sixteenth-century living.

"Throughout, Goodmans palpable enthusiasm and clear appreciation for the resourcefulness of the eras people make these men and women entirely relatable and yet full of surprises." —*Publishers Weekly*

Includes bibliographical references and index.

How to Behave Badly in Elizabethan England: A Guide for Knaves, Fools, Harlots, Cuckolds, Drunkards, Liars, Thieves, and Braggarts. Ruth Goodman. Liveright Publishing, a Division of W. W. Norton & Company 2018. 320 p.
ISBN 9781631495113
Grades: Adult   942.05
1. Etiquette 2. Social life and customs 3. Great Britain 4. Elizabethan era (1558-1603) 5. Stuart period (1603-1714) 6. 16th century 7. History writing — Renaissance — Europe 8. History writing — Europe — United Kingdom 9. History writing — Arts and culture
LC 2018032705

Drawing from period-specific advice manuals, court cases, and sermons the author celebrates one of the naughtiest eras of British history through the troublemakers, drunkards, snooty needlers and boors present in Elizabethan England.

First published in Great Britain under the title How to behave badly in Renaissance Britain; Includes bibliographical references and index.

Gristwood, Sarah
The Tudors in Love: Passion and Politics in the Age of England's Most Famous Dynasty. Sarah Gristwood. St. Martin's Press 2022. 400 pages
ISBN 9781250271426
Grades: Adult   942.05
1. Tudor, House of 2. Women rulers 3. Courtly love 4. Power 5. Political intrigue 6. Marriage 7. Obsession 8. International relations 9. Rulers 10. Men-women relations 11. Politics and government 12. British history 13. Great Britain 14. Tudor period (1485-1603) 15. 15th century 16. 16th century 17. 17th century 18. Biographies 19. Life stories — Politics — Royalty 20. Family and Relationships — Dating and Marriage 21. History writing — Europe — United Kingdom
LC 2022034905

Loan Stars Favourites, 2022.

Offers a brilliant history of the Tudor dynasty, showing how the rules of romantic courtly love irrevocably shaped the politics and international diplomacy of the period.

"Historian Gristwood (The Queen's Mary) offers an engrossing look at how the Tudor dynasty employed the 'Stylish and stylised game' of courtly love....The result is a fresh and tantalizing look at a much-scrutinized dynasty." —*Publishers Weekly*

Originally published in the UK by Oneworld, London, in 2021; Includes bibliographical references and index.

Kaufmann, Miranda
Black Tudors: The Untold Story. Miranda Kaufmann. Oneworld Publications 2017. 352 p.
ISBN 9781786071842
Grades: Adult   942.05
1. African people in foreign countries 2. African people 3. Tudor period (1485-1603) 4. Renaissance (1300-1600) 5. 17th century 6. History writing — Europe — United Kingdom 7. History writing — Renaissance — Europe

Drawing from long-forgotten records, the author provides insight into how Africans came to be in Tudor England, what they did there and how they were treated, forcing readers to re-examine the 17th century to determine what caused perceptions to change so radically.

Mortimer, Ian
The Time Traveler's Guide to Elizabethan England. Ian Mortimer. Viking 2013. 384 p.
ISBN 9780670026074
Grades: Adult   942.05
1. European Renaissance 2. Civilization, Western 3. Social life and customs 4. British history 5. England 6. 16th century 7. Tudor period (1485-1603) 8. Renaissance (1300-1600) 9. Elizabethan era (1558-1603) 10. History writing — Renaissance — Europe 11. History writing — Europe — United Kingdom
LC 2013001566

Mortimer explores the reign of Queen Elizabeth I. A golden age of maritime heroes like Sir Walter Raleigh and writers such as Shakespeare, Elizabethan England was also an era of violence, famine, and religious persecution. But for all these trials, Elizabeth's subjects settled America, circumnavigated the globe, and laid the groundwork for the modern world.

Includes bibliographical references and index.

Starkey, David
Six Wives: The Queens of Henry VIII. David Starkey. Harper Collins Publishers 2003. xxvii, 852 p. : Color illustration
ISBN 9780694010431
Grades: 11 12 Adult   942.05
1. Henry VIII, King of England, 1491-1547 2. Catharine, of Aragon, Queen, consort of Henry VIII, King of England, 1485-1536 3. Anne Boleyn, Queen, consort of Henry VIII, King of England, 1507-1536 4. Anne, of Cleves, Queen, consort of Henry VIII, King of England, 1515-1557 5. Henry VII, King of England, 1457-1509 6. Marriages of royalty and nobility 7. Divorce 8. Women rulers 9. British history 10. England 11. Great Britain 12. 16th century 13. Tudor period (1485-1603) 14. Renaissance (1300-1600) 15. Biographies 16. History writing — Renaissance — Europe 17. History writing — Europe — United Kingdom 18. Life stories — Politics — Royalty 19. Adult books for young adults
LC 2004556138

Booklist Editors' Choice, 2003.

Profiles the six marriages of King Henry VIII against the political drama of the Tudor era, tracing his twenty-four-year first marriage to Catherine of Aragon and subsequent whirlwind decade of new brides.

"Solidly researched and delightfully told, this is highly recommended." —*Library Journal*

Includes bibliographical references (p. [766]-818) and index.

Weir, Alison
The Six Wives of Henry VIII. Alison Weir. Grove Weidenfeld 1991. xii, 643 p. : Illustration
ISBN 9780802136831
Grades: 11 12 Adult   942.05
1. Henry VIII, King of England, 1491-1547 2. Marriages of royalty and nobility 3. Married women 4. Women rulers 5. British history 6. Great Britain 7. Tudor period (1485-1603) 8. Renaissance (1300-1600) 9. 16th century 10. Biographies 11. History writing — Europe — United Kingdom 12. History writing — Renaissance — Europe 13. Nonfiction that reads like fiction
LC 91029522

Profiles each of Henry VIII's six wives, describing their backgrounds, personalities, relationship to the king, and ultimate demise, and shows how each reflected the perceptions of women and marriage at the time.

"Wonderfully detailed, extensively researched. The narrative is free flowing, humorous, informative, and readable." —*School Library Journal*

Includes bibliographical references (p. 573-610) and index; Originally published: London : Bodley Head, 1991.

ESSENTIAL AND RECOMMENDED TITLES
942.06 England — House of Stuart and Commonwealth periods to present, 1603

942.06 England — House of Stuart and Commonwealth periods to present, 1603

Fraser, Antonia
Faith and Treason: The Story of the Gunpowder Plot. Antonia Fraser. Doubleday 1996. xxxv, 347 p. : Illustration; Color
ISBN 9780385471909
Grades: Adult   942.06
1. Fawkes, Guy, 1570-1606 2. Gunpowder Plot, 1605 3. Insurgency 4. Conspiracy theories 5. Rebels 6. Religion and politics 7. Politics and government 8. British history 9. Great Britain 10. 17th century 11. Stuart period (1603-1714) 12. Renaissance (1300-1600) 13. History writing — Europe — United Kingdom 14. History writing — Renaissance — Europe
Gold Dagger Award for Best Nonfiction of the Year, 1996.
Recounts one of the most famous conspiracies in British history, the attempt in 1605, led by Guy Fawkes, to blow up the House of Parliament and King James I.
"The Gunpowder Plot was both cruel and crackpot, but Fraser does a wonderful job of conveying to the modern reader just why a few Catholics felt that it was justified and also was likely to succeed." —*The New Yorker*
Later republished in England as the Gunpowder Plot : Terror & faith in 1605; Includes bibliographical references (p. [318]-329) and index.

942.082 England — 1901-1999

Ackroyd, Peter
Innovation. Peter Ackroyd. St. Martin's Press 2021. 400 p. (History of England, 6)
ISBN 9781250003669
Grades: Adult   942.082
1. Royal houses 2. War and society 3. Social life and customs 4. Battles 5. Rulers 6. Women rulers 7. World War II 8. World War I 9. British history 10. 20th century 11. History writing — Europe — United Kingdom
LC 2021017799
This final volume in the History of England series examines the period from the Boer War until the end of the twentieth century, covering two world wars, four monarchs and the end of the post-war slump.
"Novelist/Historian Ackroyd's Innovation wraps up his long-running history of England, starting with the Boer War, then moving through the Bloomsbury Group, World War II, the rise of Labour, and the Swinging Sixties to Tony Blair and the Millennial Dome." —*Library Journal*
Includes bibliographical references and index.

942.1 London (England)

London: The Biography. Peter Ackroyd. Nan A. Talese 2000. xxvi, 801 p. : Illustration; Color; Map
ISBN 9780385497701
Grades: 11 12 Adult   942.1
1. Social life and customs 2. London, England history 3. London, England 4. History writing — Europe — United Kingdom
LC 2001326868
Booklist Editors' Choice, 2001; New York Times Notable Book, 2002.
Bestselling British author Peter Ackroyd draws upon everything from ballads and folk tales to court records and newspaper accounts to create a book about London that's as diverse and enthralling as the city itself. Ackroyd portrays this amazing place as a living entity and organizes his chapters thematically, writing about such topics as the city's inhabitants, crime, theater, street life, and waste disposal practices over time.
"A sweeping, highly readable account of London's colorful and complicated history." —*Library Journal*
Includes bibliographical references (p. 781-793) and index; Originally published: London : Chatto & Windus, 2000.

Asher, Zain E.
Where the Children Take US: How One Family Achieved the Unimaginable. Zain E. Asher. Amistad Press 2022. 288 p.
ISBN 9780063048836
Grades: Adult   942.1
1. Ejiofor, Obiajulu 2. Black British people 3. Nigerian people in foreign countries 4. Immigrant families 5. Single mothers 6. Widows 7. Tragedy 8. Poverty 9. Racism 10. Discrimination 11. Ambition 12. Student achievement 13. Success (Concept) 14. Family relationships 15. London, England 16. Biographies 17. Life stories — Identity — Immigrants 18. Life stories — Relationships — Parent and child 19. Life stories — Facing adversity
LC 2021037878
Living in Brixton and awaiting the return of her husband and young son from Nigeria, Obiajulu Ejiofor received shattering news. There had been a fatal car crash, and one of them was dead. In Where the Children Take Us, Obiajulu's daughter, Zain Asher, tells the story of her family and her mother's deeply personal fight to protect her children from the daily pressures of poverty, crime, and racism in 1980s and '90s South London as a widowed emigrant. The story of a woman who survived genocide, famine, poverty, and crushing grief to rise from war torn Africa to the streets of Brixton and eventually the drawing rooms of Buckingham Palace, Where the Children Take Us is an unforgettable portrait of strength, tenacity, love, and perseverance embodied in one towering woman.
"Asher, a CNN International news anchor and sister of Oscar-nominated actor Chiwetel Ejiofor, has written a moving and inspiring memoir about her mother, Obiajulu Ejiofor." —*Library Journal*

Flanders, Judith
The Victorian City: Everyday Life in Dickens' London. Judith Flanders. St. Martins Press 2014. 544 p.
ISBN 9781250040213
Grades: Adult   942.1
1. Street life 2. Social life and customs 3. England 4. 19th century 5. History writing — Europe — United Kingdom
LC 2014007566
A meticulously researched portrait of everyday life in Dickensian London evaluates the Victorian era as a time of unprecedented transformation marked by rapid construction, railways, street lighting and a population boom at every economic level.
"This is a superb portrait of an exciting, thriving, and dangerous city." —*Booklist*

Russell, Gareth
★ *The Palace: From the Tudors to the Windsors, 500 Years of British History at Hampton Court.* Gareth Russell. Atria Books 2023. 448 p; Illustration
ISBN 9781982169060
Grades: Adult   942.1
1. Architecture 2. Architecture and society 3. Palaces 4. Social life and customs 5. London, England 6. History writing — Europe — United Kingdom 7. Arts and Entertainment — Architecture
Takes us into every room of Hampton Court Palace—the stage of some of the most important events in British history, such as the commissioning of King James's version of the Bible and Queen Elizabeth II's coronation ball, illustrating what was at play politically, socially and economically at the time.
"An entertaining journey into the past." —*Kirkus*

Woolf, Virginia
The London Scene: Six Essays on London Life. Virginia Woolf. Ecco 2006. xv, 77 p. : Illustration; Map
ISBN 9780060881283
Grades: Adult   942.1
1. City life 2. Social life and customs 3. Voyages and travels 4. London, England 5. Essays 6. Arts and Entertainment — Writing and publishing
LC 2005054170
Map on endpapers.

942.3 West Country (England)

Ash, Lamorna
Dark, Salt, Clear: The Life of a Fishing Town. Lamorna Ash. Bloomsbury Publishing 2020. 336 p.
ISBN 9781635576153
Grades: Adult 942.3
1. Ash, Lamorna 2. Fishing villages 3. Fishers 4. Fisheries 5. Small towns 6. Coasts 7. Fishing industry and trade 8. Social life and customs 9. Voyages and travels 10. Cornwall, England 11. England 12. Life stories — Business — Working life 13. Nature Writing — Animal Studies — Fish and Fishing 14. Society and culture — Urban and regional studies

LC 2020008659

Somerset Maugham Award, 2021.

Before arriving in Newlyn, a Cornish fishing village at the end of the railway line, Lamorna Ash was told that no fisherman would want a girl joining an expedition. Weeks later, the only female on board a trawler called the Filadelfia, she is heading out to sea with the dome of the sky above and the black waves below. Determined to know the community on its own terms, Ash lodges in a spare room by the harbor and lets the village wash over her in all of its clamoring unruliness, thumping machinery, and tangled nets—its history, dialect, and centuries-old industry. Moving between Ash's surprising, transformational journey aboard the Filadelfia and her astute observations of Newlyn's landscape and people, Dark, Salt, Clear is an assured work of indelible characters and a multilayered travelogue through a landscape both lovely and merciless.

942.7 Northern England

Rebanks, James
The Shepherd's Life: Modern Dispatches from an Ancient Landscape. James Rebanks. Flatiron Books 2015. xviii, 292 pages : Illustration
ISBN 9781250060242
Grades: Adult 942.7
1. Rebanks, James 2. Shepherds 3. Rural life 4. Lake District (England) 5. Autobiographies and memoirs 6. Life stories — Nature and outdoors

A shepherd in the Lake District of northern England shares his way of life in this memoir about living and farming in a storied landscape.

Originally published in Canada (Toronto : Doubleday Canada, 2015).

942.9 Wales

Morris, Jan
A Writer's House in Wales. Jan Morris. National Geographic 2002. 143 p. : Map
ISBN 9780792265238
Grades: Adult 942.9
1. Morris, Jan, 1926-2020 2. Home (Concept) 3. Villages 4. Social life and customs 5. Wales 6. Autobiographies and memoirs 7. Arts and Entertainment — Writing and Publishing 8. Life stories — Arts and culture — Writing — Authors

LC 2001044731

The author describes Trefan Morys, her country house in Wales, and looks at Welsh culture, history, and symbols.

"The author reflects on her home in Wales, its beautiful setting and the nature of being Welsh. This slim and charming volume offers a crisp account of the turbulent history of the Welsh and their battle to maintain their language and culture in the shadow of their more powerful neighbor." —*Publishers Weekly*

942.901 Wales — Early history to 1066

Charles-Edwards, T. M.
Wales and the Britons, 350-1064. T.M. Charles-Edwards. Oxford University Press 2013. xx, 795 p. : Illustration; Map
ISBN 9780198217312
Grades: Adult 942.901
1. Civilization, Medieval 2. British history 3. Wales 4. Medieval period (476-1492) 5. History writing — Medieval — Europe 6. History writing — Europe — United Kingdom

LC 2012376060

This, the first volume in the History of Wales, provides a detailed history of Wales in the period in which it was created out of the remnants of Roman Britain. It thus begins in the fourth century, with accelerating attacks from external forces, and ends shortly before the Norman Conquest of England.

Includes bibliographical references (p. [680]-739) and index.

943 Germany and neighboring central European countries

Donner, Rebecca
All the Frequent Troubles of Our Days: The American Woman at the Heart of the German Resistance to Hitler. Rebecca Donner. Little Brown & Company 2021. 336 p.
ISBN 9780316561693
Grades: Adult 943
1. Harnack-Fish, Mildred, 1902-1943 2. Executions and executioners 3. Secret service 4. Resistance to military occupation 5. World War II 6. American people in Europe 7. Anti-Nazi movement 8. Soviet Union 9. Germany 10. 20th century 11. Biographies 12. History writing — Wars and conflicts — World War II — European Theater 13. Life stories — Politics — Activists and reformers 14. History writing — Wars and conflicts — Resistance — World War II

National Book Critics Circle Award for Biography, 2021; Finalist for the Governor General's Literary Award for English-Language Nonfiction, 2022.

Part biography, part political thriller, part scholarly detective story that draws on letters, diary entries, notes smuggled out of a Berlin prison, and other documents, this true story chronicles the life and brutal death of the American leader of one of the largest underground resistance groups in Germany.

"Historical biography of an American woman who led resistance groups against the Nazis before Hitler personally ordered her execution in 1943.... This is a welcome contribution to the history of the anti-Nazi underground." —*Kirkus*

Finalist for the Governor General's Literary Award for English-Language Nonfiction, 2022.

Harding, Thomas
The House by the Lake: One House, Five Families, and a Hundred Years of German History. Thomas Harding. Picador 2016. 464 p. : Illustration; Map
ISBN 9781250065063
Grades: Adult 943
1. Houses 2. Families 3. Communities 4. War and society 5. Social life and customs 6. German history 7. Germany 8. 20th century 9. History writing — Europe — Germany

LC 2015044339

Tells the story of Germany through the inhabitants of one small wooden building: a nobleman farmer, a prosperous Jewish family, a renowned Nazi composer, a widow and her children, a Stasi informant.

"This personal saga centered on a family home will appeal to enthusiasts of German history, especially post-World War II division and reunification." —*Library Journal*

Originally published: London : William Heinemann, 2015.

MacGregor, Neil
Germany: Memories of a Nation. Neil MacGregor. Alfred A. Knopf 2015. 644 p.
ISBN 9781101875667
Grades: Adult 943
1. Culture 2. National characteristics, German 3. Civilization 4. German history 5. Germany 6. History writing — Europe — Germany

LC 2014048396

Germany is unlike any other country in the world. But how much do we really know about it, and how do its people understand themselves? In Germany: Memories of a Nation, Neil MacGregor—director of the British Museum and

ESSENTIAL AND RECOMMENDED TITLES
943 Germany and neighboring central European countries

author of a History of the World in 100 Objects—presents the stories of a nation through a collection of thirty objects and touchstones. From coins and crowns to fairytales and philosophers, MacGregor presents the inventions, ideas, and icons that comprise the many identities of the German people. Germany: Memories of a Nation is a view of this complex and fascinating country like no other.

"Most importantly, the author finds post-World War II Germany hyperattuned to the need for memorials to victims of terror and oppression—e.g., via the work of painter and printmaker Kathe Kollwitz. A comprehensive record jam-packed with visuals." —*Kirkus*

Includes bibliographical references and index.

McKay, Sinclair
Berlin: Life and Death in the City at the Center of the World. Sinclair McKay. St. Martin's Press 2022. 368 p.
ISBN 9781250277503
Grades: Adult   943
1. Cities and towns 2. World War II 3. Cold War 4. Culture 5. German history 6. Berlin, Germany 7. 20th century 8. 21st century 9. History writing — Europe — Germany 10. History writing — Wars and conflicts — World War II
LC 2022009052

This history of Berlin from 1919 to the present looks at how the city survived the destruction of two world wars, being divided in two and its subsequent rise to a pinnacle of culture and political importance.

"Journalist McKay (The Fire and the Darkness: The Bombing of Dresden) traces the spirit and history of Berlin from the end of World War I through the fall of the Berlin Wall in 1989." —*Library Journal*

Includes bibliographical references and index.

Merriman, Helena
★ *Tunnel 29: The True Story of an Extraordinary Escape Beneath the Berlin Wall.* Helena Merriman. Public Affairs 2021. 256 p.
ISBN 9781541788848
Grades: Adult   943
1. Berlin Wall 2. Communism 3. Escapes 4. Refugees 5. Tunnels 6. Cold War 7. German history 8. Berlin, Germany 9. 1960s 10. History writing — Europe — Germany

In a book based on the podcast series, a broadcast journalist tells the unbelievable true story of 22-year-old Joachim Rudolph, who, in 1961, set out to build an escape tunnel under the Berlin Wall and was faced with many obstacles before freeing 29 people.

The inside story of a daring episode by a group of German students who dug into East Berlin to help their friends and families escape. . . . An entertaining real-life Cold War thriller following a group of students who escaped under 'The Wall of all walls.' —*Kirkus*

Milton, Giles
Checkmate in Berlin: The Cold War Showdown That Shaped the Modern World. Giles Milton. Henry Holt and Company 2021. 352 p.
ISBN 9781250247568
Grades: Adult   943
1. Cold War 2. World War II 3. German history 4. Berlin, Germany 5. Germany 6. 20th century 7. History writing — Europe — Germany 8. History writing — Cold War
LC 2021002362

The lively, immersive story of the race to seize Berlin in the aftermath of World War II that fired the starting gun for the Cold War.

"Historian Milton (Soldier, Sailor, Frogman, Spy) captures in this immersive account the drama and intrigue of Berlin in the immediate aftermath of WWII. . . . Full of vivid details and intriguing personalities, this is a page-turning chronicle of a noteworthy period in world history." —*Publishers Weekly*

Includes bibliographical references and index.

Moorhouse, Roger
Berlin at War. Roger Moorhouse. Basic Books 2010. 432 p.
ISBN 9780465005338
Grades: Adult   943
1. Bombardment 2. Sieges 3. Rationing 4. Survival 5. Berlin, Battle of, 1945 6. War 7. World War II 8. Third Reich, 1933-1945 9. German history 10. Berlin, Germany 11. 1940s 12. 20th century 13. Between the Wars (1918-1939) 14. History writing — Wars and conflicts — Homefront — World War II 15. History writing — Europe — Germany
LC BI2010027837

Drawing on diaries, memoirs, and interviews, the author provides a first-hand account of life and death on the home front in the Nazi capital of Berlin, including some Berliners' efforts to help the city's remaining Jews.

"Election results in the fading days of the Weimar Republic indicate that Berliners were not particularly sympathetic to Hitler or his movement. Yet Berlin endured horrible physical destruction, deprivation, and death. This included intense Allied bombings by day and night, and a siege and eventual ravaging by the Russian army. [Moorhouse] begins with an almost idyllic scene as huge crowds in Berlin witness the celebration of Hitler's birthday in April 1939; at the time, of course, Germany seemed to have achieved its foreign-policy goals without firing a shot. As the fortunes of Germany and Berlin deteriorate, Moorhouse uses the testimonies of a variety of Berliners to describe some memorable scenes and struggles. This is a hard, unrelenting saga of the effects of total warfare on citizens just hoping to survive." —*Booklist*

Rady, Martyn C.
The Middle Kingdoms: A New History of Central Europe. Martyn Rady. Basic Books 2023. 656 p.
ISBN 9781541619784
Grades: Adult   943
1. History 2. Culture 3. Art 4. Religions 5. War 6. Civilization 7. European history 8. Central Europe 9. Eastern Europe 10. History writing — Europe 11. Life stories — People in history

Central Europe has long been infamous as a region beset by war, a place where empires clashed and world wars began. In The Middle Kingdoms, Martyn Rady offers the definitive history of the region, demonstrating that Central Europe has always been more than merely the fault line between West and East. Even as Central European powers warred with their neighbors, the region developed its own cohesive identity and produced tremendous accomplishments in politics, society, and culture.

"Historian Rady (The Hapsburgs) offers an ambitious survey of Central Europe from antiquity to the present day….He covers a vast swath of geographical and chronological ground, and his evocative prose renders this complex history accessible." —*Publishers Weekly*

Includes bibliographical references and index.

Roth, Joseph
What I Saw: Reports from Berlin, 1920-1933. Joseph Roth; translated with an introduction by Michael Hofmann; German selection by Michael Bienert. Norton 2003. 227 p. : Illustration; Map
ISBN 9780393051674
Grades: Adult   943
1. Crime 2. Nazism 3. Social life and customs 4. Politics and government 5. Berlin, Germany 6. Germany 7. 1920s 8. 1930s 9. 20th century 10. Between the Wars (1918-1939) 11. History writing — Europe — Germany
LC 2002014211

Offers the poet and journalist's political and impressionistic essays for the first time in English, providing a glimpse into the social and political environment of the Weimar Republic.

Includes index.

Smith, Helmut Walser
Germany, a Nation in Its Time: Before, During, and After Nationalism, 1500-2000. Helmut Walser Smith. Liveright Publishing Corporation 2020. xvi, 590 pages
ISBN 9780871404664
Grades: Adult   943
1. Nationalism 2. National characteristics 3. German history 4. Third Reich, 1933-1945 5. Germany 6. 20th century 7. 19th century 8. History writing — Europe — Germany
LC 2019050560

PUBLIC LIBRARY CORE COLLECTION: NONFICTION
Twentieth Edition

The first major history of Germany in a generation, a work that presents a five-hundred-year narrative that challenges our traditional perceptions of Germany's conflicted past.

"This new perspective on German history should be welcomed by all libraries." —*Library Journal*

Includes bibliographical references and index.

Taylor, Fred
The Berlin Wall: A World Divided, 1961-1989. Frederick Taylor. Harper Perennial 2008. xxi, 486 p. : Illustration; Map
ISBN 9780060786144
Grades: Adult   943
1. Berlin Wall 2. German reunification 3. Cold War 4. Opposition (Political science) 5. Symbolism in politics 6. Communism 7. Capitalism 8. Politics and government 9. German history 10. East Germany 11. Germany 12. Berlin, Germany 13. West Germany 14. 1980s 15. 20th century 16. History writing — Europe — Germany 17. History writing — Cold War
LC Bl2008016829

A history of the 103-mile wall between East and West Germany discusses its geopolitical ramifications, its representation of the struggle between Soviet communism and American capitalism, and the internal and external pressures that led to its dismantling.

First published in Great Britain in 2006 by Bloomsbury Publishing—T.P. verso; Includes bibliographical references (p. [469]-472) and index; Originally published: London : Bloomsbury Publishing, 2006.

Watson, Peter
The German Genius: Europe's Third Renaissance, the Second Scientific Revolution, and the Twentieth Century. Peter Watson. Harper 2010. xix, 964 p.
ISBN 9780060760229
Grades: Adult   943
1. Intellectual life 2. Civilization 3. German history 4. Germany 5. History writing — Europe — Germany
LC 2010006738

A virtuosic cultural history of German ideas and influence, from 1750 to the present day.

"This is a panoramic review of German cultural and intellectual development from 1750 to the present. Examining the contributions of literally hundreds of German thinkers and doers and mapping the conceptual connections between them, the author demonstrates the breadth, volume, and influence of German output in philosophy, science, industry, art, literature, and all forms of scholarly activity. But Watson's true focus is the cultural crucible, forged in the eighteenth and nineteenth centuries and informed by notions of Bildung and inwardness, that gave rise to such accomplishments but also set the stage for the evil actions of the Third Reich. To some extent an effort to untether our understanding of German history from the conflicts of the twentieth century, this study is also a reminder that our modern Western worldview has deep German roots." —*Booklist*

Includes bibliographical references and index.

Wilson, Peter H.
Heart of Europe: A History of the Holy Roman Empire. Peter H. Wilson. The Belknap Press of Harvard University Press 2016. 1008 p.
ISBN 9780674058095
Grades: Adult   943
1. European history 2. Holy Roman Empire 3. History writing — Europe
LC 2015037932

The Holy Roman Empire lasted a thousand years, far longer than ancient Rome. Yet this formidable dominion never inspired the awe of its predecessor. Voltaire distilled the disdain of generations when he quipped it was neither holy, Roman, nor an empire. Yet as Peter Wilson shows, the Holy Roman Empire tells a millennial story of Europe better than the histories of individual nation-states. And its legacy can be seen today in debates over the nature of the European Union. Heart of Europe traces the Empire from its origins within Charlemagne's kingdom in 800 to its demise in 1806.

First published in the United Kingdom as the Holy Roman Empire: A Thousand Years of Europe's History by Penguin Books Ltd. 2015.—Title page verso; Includes bibliographical references and index.

943.004 Germany and neighboring central European countries — Ethnic and National Groups

The *Warburgs: The Twentieth-century Odyssey of a Remarkable Jewish Family.* Ron Chernow. Random House 1993. xvii, 820 p. : Illustration
ISBN 9780679418238
Grades: Adult   943.004
1. Warburg family 2. Jewish people 3. Jewish Americans 4. Bankers 5. Jewish American families 6. Western European people 7. German people 8. Biographies 9. History writing — Jewish history 10. Family and Relationships — Families 11. Business and economics — Business leaders and entrepreneurs 12. Life stories — Business — Business leaders
LC 93016599

ALA Notable Book, 1994.

Presents a monumental portrait of the powerful Warburg banking dynasty, tracing this remarkable Jewish family's odyssey from post-World War I Germany through the rise of Hitler and beyond.

Includes bibliographical references (p. [729]-739) and index.

943.08 Germany since 1866

Evans, Richard J.
The Coming of the Third Reich. Richard J. Evans. The Penguin Press 2004. xi, 622 p. : Illustration; Map
ISBN 9781594200045
Grades: Adult   943.08
1. Hitler, Adolf, 1889-1945 2. Nazism 3. German history 4. Between the Wars (1918-1939) 5. History writing — Europe — Germany
LC 2003063205

A history of Adolf Hitler's rise to power and the collapse of democracy in Nazi Germany explains why Nazism's ideology of hatred flourished in a country embittered by military defeat and economic disaster following World War I.

"This is a first-rate narrative history that informs and educates and may inspire readers to delve even deeper into the subject." —*Booklist*

Includes bibliographical references (p. [335]-584) and index.

Hoyer, Katja
Blood and Iron: The Rise and Fall of the German Empire. Katja Hoyer. Pegasus Books 2021. 272 p.
ISBN 9781643138374
Grades: Adult   943.08
1. International relations 2. German history 3. Germany 4. 19th century 5. 20th century 6. History writing — Europe — Germany

In this vivid fifty-year history of Germany from 1871-1918—which inspired events that forever changed the European continent—here is the story of the Second Reich from its violent beginnings and rise to power to its calamitous defeat in the First World War.

"Historian Hoyer debuts with an accessible if abbreviated chronicle of Germany's Second Reich focused on its two most important leaders.... The result is a solid introduction to how modern Germany came into being." —*Publishers Weekly*

Trentmann, Frank
Out of the Darkness: The Germans, 1942-2022. Frank Trentmann. Alfred A. Knopf 2024. 784 p.
ISBN 9781524732912
Grades: Adult   943.08
1. Countries 2. National characteristics 3. Dictatorship 4. Democracy 5. War 6. Genocide 7. Immigration and emigration 8. Civilization 9. Culture 10. Politics and government 11. Social change 12. German history 13. European history 14. Germany 15. 20th century 16. 21st century 17. History writing — Europe — Germany 18. Politics and global affairs — World politics — Europe

A new history of the people at the center of Europe, from the Second World War to today. In 1945, Germany lay in ruins, morally and materially. The German people stood condemned by history, responsible for a horrifying genocide and a

ESSENTIAL AND RECOMMENDED TITLES
943.085 Period of Weimar Republic, 1918-1933

war of extermination. But by 2015 Germany looked to many to be the moral voice of Europe, welcoming over one million refugees. At the same time, it pursued a controversially rigid fiscal discipline and made energy deals with a dictator. Many have asked how Germany descended into the darkness of the Nazis, but this book asks another vital question: How, and how far, have the Germans since reinvented themselves?

"Fascinating insights on how a country of poets, philosophers, and scientists emerged from totalitarianism and genocide." —*Kirkus*

Originally published in the UK by Penguin, London, in 2023.

943.085 Period of Weimar Republic, 1918-1933

Haffner, Sebastian
Defying Hitler: A Memoir. Sebastian Haffner; translated from the German by Oliver Pretzel. Farrar, Straus and Giroux 2002. 309 p. : Illustration
ISBN 9780374161576
Grades: Adult   943.085
1. Haffner, Sebastian, 1907- 2. Historians 3. Nazism 4. German history 5. Between the Wars (1918-1939) 6. Autobiographies and memoirs 7. Biographies 8. History writing — Wars and conflicts — Homefront — World War II 9. Life stories — Law and order — Armed forces personnel
LC 2002017058

A memoir on the rise of Nazism in Germany and the lives of ordinary German citizens between the two world wars find the author witnessing such developments as the rise of the First Free Corps, the Hitler Youth movement, the Stresemann years, and Hitler's coming to power.

"This is a small masterpiece." —*Booklist*
Translation of : Geschichte eines Deutschen.

Hett, Benjamin Carter
The *Death* of Democracy: Hitler's Rise to Power and the Downfall of the Weimar Republic. Benjamin Carter Hett. Henry Holt & Company 2018. 288 p.
ISBN 9781250162502
Grades: Adult   943.085
1. Hitler, Adolf, 1889-1945 2. Politicians 3. Nazism 4. Between the Wars (1918-1939) 5. 1920s 6. History writing — Europe — Germany 7. Life stories — Politics — Politicians
LC Bl2018003982

A timely account of how the Nazi party came to power argues that failures throughout the Weimar Republic and the shortsightedness of German politicians who were trying to co-opt populist insurgencies inadvertently secured the tools that Hitler needed to get elected and establish a genocidal dictatorship.

Ullrich, Volker
Germany 1923: Hyperinflation, Hitler's Putsch, and Democracy in Crisis. Volker Ullrich; translated by Jefferson Chase. Liveright Publishing 2023. xiv, 432 p.
ISBN 9781324093466
Grades: Adult   943.085
1. Political culture 2. Democracy 3. Political stability 4. Inflation 5. Poverty 6. Insurgency 7. Border disputes 8. Right-wing extremists 9. Social change 10. Germany 11. 1920s 12. Translations — German to English 13. History writing — Europe — Germany 14. Life stories — People in history

As the great Austrian writer Stefan Zweig confided in his autobiography, written in exile, "I have a pretty thorough knowledge of history, but never, to my recollection, has it produced such madness in such gigantic proportions." He was referring to the situation in Germany in 1923. It was a "year of lunacy," defined by hyperinflation, a political system on the verge of collapse, and separatist movements that threatened Germany's territorial integrity. Most significantly, Adolf Hitler launched his infamous Beer Hall Putsch in Munich—a failed coup that nonetheless drew international attention and demonstrated the Nazis' ruthless determination to seize power.

"This captivating account sheds much light on a complex and consequential era." —*Publishers Weekly*

Originally published in German as Deutschland 1923, by Verlag C.H. Beck, Munich, in 2022; Includes bibliographical references and index.

943.086 Germany — Period of the Third Reich, 1933-1945

Bailey, Catherine
A *Castle* in Wartime: One Family, Their Missing Sons, and the Fight to Defeat the Nazis. Catherine Bailey. Viking 2019. IX, 461 pages, 16 unnumbered pages of plates : Illustration; Map
ISBN 9780525559290
Grades: Adult   943.086
1. Pirzio-Biroli, Detalmo, 1916-2006 2. Hassell, Ulrich von, 1881-1944 3. Anti-Nazi movement 4. World War II 5. Husband and wife 6. Diplomatic and consular service 7. Families 8. Sons 9. Prisoners 10. Anti-fascism 11. Castles 12. Undercover operations 13. German people in Italy 14. Resistance to military occupation 15. German people in foreign countries 16. Italian history 17. Between the Wars (1918-1939) 18. History writing — Wars and conflicts — Resistance — World War II 19. History writing — Europe — Italy 20. Life stories — Facing adversity — War and oppression

The author documents the experiences of ambassador's daughter Fey von Hassell, whose family made the brave decision to forfeit their privileged existences to resist the Nazis during the occupation of northern Italy.

Includes bibliographical references and index; Originally published in Great Britain as the lost boys: a family ripped apart by war by Viking, London, 2019.

Bascomb, Neal
Hunting Eichmann: How a Band of Survivors and a Young Spy Agency Chased Down the World's Most Notorious Nazi War Criminal. Neal Bascomb. Houghton Mifflin Harcourt 2009. 400 p.
ISBN 9780618858675
Grades: Adult   943.086
1. Eichmann, Adolf, 1906-1962 2. War criminals 3. Fugitives 4. Nazis 5. Spies 6. Secret service 7. Israel 8. History writing — Spies and spying 9. History writing — Arab-Israeli relations — Southwest Asia and North Africa (Middle East) 10. True Crime — Investigations and Trials
LC 2008035757

Based on groundbreaking new information and featuring never-before-published surveillance photographs, a narrative of the pursuit and capture of Adolf Eichmann recounts how the Nazi managed to slip out of the country and build a new life in Argentina while an international manhunt spent fifteen years tracking him down and bringing him to justice.

"The author recounts the pursuit, capture, and abduction of Nazi war criminal Adolf Eichmann. Bascomb spread a wide net in researching the 15-year hunt, and he fills his book with previously unknown or neglected details, utilizing the remembrances of former Mossad agents, German and American intelligence operatives, and Argentine Nazi sympathizers who tried to find Eichmann after his seizure. This is an outstanding account of a sustained and worthy manhunt." —*Booklist*

Childers, Thomas
The *Third* Reich: A History of Nazi Germany. Thomas Childers. Simon & Schuster 2017. 651 pages : Illustration; Map
ISBN 9781451651133
Grades: Adult   943.086
1. Nazis 2. World War II 3. Holocaust (1933-1945) 4. Atrocities 5. Crimes against humanity 6. Totalitarianism 7. Causes of war 8. Third Reich, 1933-1945 9. Politics and government 10. Germany 11. 1940s 12. Second World War era (1939-1945) 13. History writing — Wars and conflicts — World War II — European Theater
LC 2016019506

Based in part on documents seldom used by previous historians, this history of the Third Reich shows how the dramatic, improbable rise of the Nazis happened because of tragic miscalculations and blunders, then documents what life was like for ordinary Germans as the Nazis precipitated the horrors of World War II and the Holocaust.

"A riveting study delves deeply into the conditions of the perfect storm that allowed Hitler and his Nazi party to seize and wield unprecedented power." —*Kirkus*

Includes bibliographical references and index.

Crasnianski, Tania
*The **Children** of Nazis: The Sons and Daughter of Himmler, Goring, Hoss, Mengele, and Others — Living with a Father's Monstrous Legacy*. Tania Crasnianski; translated by Molly Grogan. Arcade Publishing 2018. 235 p.

ISBN 9781628728057

Grades: Adult **943.086**

1. Children of Nazis 2. Nazis 3. Family relationships 4. War crime trials 5. World War II 6. Legacies 7. Postwar life 8. Holocaust (1933-1945) 9. Stigmatization 10. European history 11. 20th century 12. Collective biographies 13. Translations — French to English 14. History writing — Europe — Germany 15. Life stories — People in history — Witness to history 16. Life stories — Relationships — Family 17. History writing — Wars and conflicts — Holocaust — World War II 18. History writing — Wars and conflicts — Homefront — World War II

LC 2017035834

Describes how the offspring of the leaders of the Third Reich, born into privilege and unaware of their fathers' occupations, dealt with the aftermath of the war and examines the unique experiences of these descendants as they grappled with their fathers' monstrous legacies.

Originally published: Paris : Editions Grasset & Fasquelle, 2016; Translated from the French.

Dumbach, Annette E.
*Sophie **Scholl** and the White Rose*. Annette Dumbach, Jud Newborn. Natl Book Network 2018. 238 p.

ISBN 9781851685363

Grades: 11 12 Adult **943.086**

1. Scholl, Sophie, 1921-1943 2. White Rose (Anti-Nazi group) 3. World War II 4. Resistance to military occupation 5. Anti-Nazi movement 6. Third Reich, 1933-1945 7. Germany 8. History writing — Europe — Germany 9. History writing — Wars and conflicts — Homefront — World War II 10. History writing — Wars and conflicts — Resistance — World War II

From its inception to end, this title offers an account of German resistance to the Third Reich. It presents the story of 5 university students and their professor, who, as the White Rose group, launched a clandestine campaign against the Third Reich. It takes the reader from the early days of their crusade through their arrest and interrogation.

"This revised edition contains a ton of new information, a reworked introduction, a foreword by Studs Terkel, additional photos, and much more, expanding this remarkable tale." —*Library Journal*

First released in 1986 as Shattering the German Night.

Evans, Richard J.
*The **Third** Reich in Power, 1933-1939*. Richard J. Evans. Penguin Press 2005. xvii, 941 p. : Illustration

ISBN 9781594200748

Grades: Adult **943.086**

1. Hitler, Adolf, 1889-1945 2. State-sponsored terrorism 3. Jewish people 4. Nazism 5. Religious persecution 6. Third Reich, 1933-1945 7. Politics and government 8. Germany 9. 20th century 10. History writing — Europe — Germany 11. History writing — Wars and conflicts — World War II

LC 2005052128

Documents the radical transformation of Germany under Nazi rule, exploring how virtually every area of life was reordered to comply with the regime's preparations for war, and describes the increasing brutality towards marginalized groups.

"This is a major achievement. No other recent synthetic history has quite the range and narrative power of Evans's work." —*Publishers Weekly*

Includes bibliographical references (p. [827]-900) and index.

Fritzsche, Peter
*Life and **Death** in the Third Reich*. Peter Fritzsche. Belknap Press of Harvard University Press 2008. VIII, 368 p.

ISBN 9780674027930

Grades: Adult **943.086**

1. Nazism 2. Collective memory 3. Ideology 4. Holocaust (1933-1945) 5. World War II 6. Causes of war 7. Interethnic relations 8. Third Reich, 1933-1945 9. Politics and government 10. German history 11. Germany 12. 20th century 13. Between the Wars (1918-1939) 14. History writing — Europe — Germany

LC 2007040552

Cundill Prize in Historical Literature finalist.

A scholar deciphers the puzzle of Nazism's ideological grip in a critical analysis that examines the efforts of Germans to adjust to new racial identities, to believe in the necessity of war, and to accept the dynamic of unconditional destruction.

Includes bibliographical references (p. 309-357) and index.

McDonough, Frank
*The **Hitler** Years: Triumph, 1933-1939*. Frank McDonough. St. Martin's Press 2021. 488 p.

ISBN 9781250275103

Grades: Adult **943.086**

1. Hitler, Adolf, 1889-1945 2. World leaders 3. Nazism 4. Dictatorship 5. Militarism 6. Antisemitism 7. Military campaigns 8. World War II 9. Third Reich, 1933-1945 10. Politics and government 11. Germany 12. History writing — Europe — Germany 13. History writing — Wars and conflicts — World War II — European Theater 14. Life stories — Politics — Politicians

LC 2021001876

On January 30th, 1933, Adolf Hitler was appointed the German Chancellor of a coalition government by President Hindenburg. Within a few months he had installed a dictatorship, jailing and killing his leftwing opponents, terrorizing the rest of the population and driving Jews out of public life. Over the course of the years from 1933 to 1939, Hitler won over most of the population to his vision of a renewed Reich. In these years of domestic triumph, cunning maneuvers, pitting neighboring powers against each other and biding his time, we see Hitler preparing for the moment that would realize his ambition. But what drove Hitler's success was also to be the fatal flaw of his regime: a relentless belief in war as the motor of greatness, a dream of vast conquests in Eastern Europe and an astonishingly fanatical racism.

"McDonough provides an expert, disheartening account of the first seven years of Hitler's chancellorship, during which he seemed to have the golden touch. . . . Hitler biographies are not in short supply, but this one is worthy of study." —*Kirkus*

Includes bibliographical references and index; Originally published: London : Head of Zeus, 2019.

O'Donnell, Svenja
*Inge's **War**: A German Woman's Story of Family, Secrets, and Survival Under Hitler*. Svenja O'Donnell. Viking 2020. 256 p.

ISBN 9781984880215

Grades: Adult **943.086**

1. Single mothers 2. Soldiers 3. Refugees 4. Grandmothers 5. Survival 6. Antisemitism 7. Psychic trauma 8. Identity 9. Nationalism 10. Secrets 11. Family relationships 12. World War II 13. Paris, France 14. Second World War era (1939-1945) 15. Life stories — Facing adversity — War and oppression — Refugees 16. Life stories — People in history — Witness to history 17. History writing — Wars and conflicts — Homefront — World War II

LC Bl2020007326

An award-winning political correspondent shares the long-secret story of her German grandmother, who endured the brutal Nazi regime and postwar years before the advancing Red Army separated her from the father of her baby.

"The author, a graceful, eloquent writer, follows a trail that sometimes takes her through deeply troubling terrain, and she amply reveals the cruelty and compassion that characterize times of war. Haunting family stories that serve as a metaphor for human suffering everywhere." —*Kirkus*

ESSENTIAL AND RECOMMENDED TITLES
943.087 Germany — 1945-1990

Ryback, Timothy W.
Takeover: Hitler's Final Rise to Power. Timothy W. Ryback. Alfred A. Knopf 2024. 368 p.
ISBN 9780593537428
Grades: Adult   943.086
1. Hitler, Adolf, 1889-1945 2. Germany 3. 20th century 4. History writing — Europe — Germany 5. History writing — Wars and conflicts — World War II
LC 2023020412

Drawing on previously inaccessible archival materials, the internationally acclaimed author of Hitler's Private Library provides a new perspective and insights into Hitler's personal and professional lives during the six critical months before he seized power as chancellor of Germany and dismantled democracy.

"Informed by diaries, newspapers, meeting minutes, and other archival sources, Ryback offers a discerning play-by-play of this 'Devils' dance' and reminds readers of the many missed opportunities for individuals to have chosen differently. He makes no reference to the present, but its relevance is obvious." —*Booklist*

Includes bibliographical references and index.

Shirer, William L.
★ *The Rise and Fall of the Third Reich: A History of Nazi Germany.* by William L. Shirer. Simon & Schuster 1981. xii, 1249 p.
ISBN 9780671728687
Grades: 11 12 Adult   943.086
1. Hitler, Adolf, 1889-1945 2. Nazism 3. Third Reich, 1933-1945 4. Germany 5. History writing — Wars and conflicts — World War II 6. History writing — Europe — Germany
LC BL 99788949

National Book Award for Nonfiction, 1961.

The rise and fall of the Third Reich offers an examination of how Adolf Hitler nearly succeeded in conquering the world. Shirer's account of the pivotal characters and events of that critical era benefits from his many years as a reporter and his own personal recollections, as well as from the mass of historical documents retrieved from the German Foreign Office. The result is this account of how Hitler wrested political control of Germany and managed to take the country with him on his mad six-year quest for world domination, only to see it go down in flames in the end.

A Touchstone book; Includes bibliographical references (p. 1185-1195) and index; Originally published: New York : Simon and Schuster, 1960.

Ullrich, Volker
★ *Eight Days in May: The Final Collapse of the Third Reich.* Volker Ullrich; translated by Jefferson Chase. Liveright Publishing Corporation, a division of W. W. Norton & Company 2021. 336 p.
ISBN 9781631498275
Grades: Adult   943.086
1. Hitler, Adolf, 1889-1945 2. Nazis 3. World War II 4. Third Reich, 1933-1945 5. Politics and government 6. Germany 7. 1940s 8. Second World War era (1939-1945) 9. Translations — German to English 10. History writing — Wars and conflicts — World War II — European Theater 11. History writing — Europe — Germany
LC 2021027618

On April 30, 1945, in a bunker deep beneath the Old Reich Chancellery, Adolf Hitler and his newly wedded wife, Eva Braun, killed themselves. But Nazi Germany lived on, however briefly. The subsequent eight days were among the most turbulent in history, witnessing not only the final battles of World War II and the collapse of the Wehrmacht, but the near-total disintegration of the once-mighty Third Reich. In a taut, propulsive narrative, eminent historian Volker Ullrich depicts the final days of the Nazi empire through the eyes of Germans, both famous and ordinary, who experienced them. He takes us inside the phantomlike regime of Hitler's chosen successor, Admiral Karl Dönitz, while capturing the drama of a society in its death throes—from mass suicides to fanatics calling for one last stand.

"German journalist and historian Ullrich (Hitler: A Biography) examines the chaotic week between Adolf Hitler's death on April 30, 1945, and Nazi Germany's Second World War surrender on May 7-8. . . . Less magisterial than Ullrich's two-volume Hitler biography, this slimmer work is still expertly researched and written." —*Library Journal*

Originally published in German as Acht Tage im Mai: Die letzte Woche des Dritten Reiches; Includes bibliographical references and index; Translated from the German.

943.087 Germany — 1945-1990

Hoyer, Katja
★ *Beyond the Wall: A History of East Germany.* Katja Hoyer. Basic Books 2023. 475 p.
ISBN 9781541602571
Grades: Adult   943.087
1. Countries 2. Boundaries 3. Berlin Wall 4. Communism 5. Cold War 6. Identity 7. Culture 8. Modernization (Social sciences) 9. Nation-building 10. German reunification 11. East Germany 12. History writing — Europe — Germany 13. History writing — Cold War 14. Society and culture — Urban and regional studies

In 1990, a country disappeared. When the iron curtain fell, East Germany simply ceased to be. For over forty years, from the ruin of the Second World War to the cusp of a new millennium, the GDR presented a radically different German identity to anything that had come before, and anything that exists today. Socialist solidarity, secret police, central planning, barbed wire—this was a Germany forged on the fault lines of ideology and geopolitics. In Beyond the Wall, acclaimed historian Katja Hoyer offers a kaleidoscopic new vision of this vanished country.

"A historian discards the Cold War caricature of East Germany to deliver a compelling historical study...The definitive history of 'The other Germany, beyond the Wall.' —*Kirkus*

Jahner, Harald
★ *Aftermath: Life in the Fallout of the Third Reich, 1945-1955.* Harald Jahner; translated by Shaun Whiteside. Alfred A. Knopf 2022. 400 p.
ISBN 9780593319734
Grades: Adult   943.087
1. Postwar life 2. Postwar reconstruction 3. Social change 4. German history 5. Germany 6. 20th century 7. Translations — German to English 8. History writing — Europe — Germany 9. History writing — Wars and conflicts — Homefront — World War II 10. Life stories — Facing adversity — War and oppression — War survivors 11. Life stories — People in history — Witness to history
LC 2021020610

The years 1945 to 1955 were a raw, wild decade that found many Germans politically, economically, and morally bankrupt. Victorious Allied forces occupied the four zones that make up present-day Germany. More than half the population was displaced; 10 million newly released forced laborers and several million prisoners of war returned to an uncertain existence. Using major global political developments as a backdrop, Harald Jahner weaves a series of life stories into a nuanced panorama of a nation undergoing monumental change. Poised between two eras, this decade is portrayed by Jahner as a period that proved decisive for Germany's future—and one starkly different from how most of us imagine it today.

"An illuminating study of the decade following the defeat of the Third Reich. In his engrossing first book, Jahner, the former editor of the Berlin Times, examines how and why Germany was capable of radically transforming from a sinister fascist mindset toward a modern democratic state." —*Kirkus*

This is a Borzoi Book; Originally published in German as Wolfszeit by Rowohlt, Berlin, in 2019; English translation originally published in the United Kingdom by WH Allen in 2021; Includes bibliographical references and index.

Sarotte, M. E
The Collapse: The Accidental Opening of the Berlin Wall. Mary Elise Sarotte. Basic Books 2014. 320 p.
ISBN 9780465064946
Grades: Adult   943.087

1. Berlin Wall 2. Cold War 3. German reunification 4. Bureaucracy 5. Politics and government 6. German history 7. Germany 8. Berlin, Germany 9. 20th century 10. History writing — Cold War 11. History writing — Europe — Germany

LC 2014026435

In The Collapse historian Mary Elise Sarotte shows that the opening of the Berlin Wall on November 9, 1989, was not, as is commonly believed, the East German government's deliberate concession to outside influence. It was an accident. A carelessly worded memo written by mid-level bureaucrats, a bumbling press conference given by an inept member of the East German Politburo, the negligence of government leaders, the bravery of ordinary people in East and West Berlin—these combined to bring about the end of nearly forty years of oppression, fear, and enmity in divided Berlin. Drawing on evidence from archives in multiple countries and languages, along with dozens of interviews with key actors, the Collapse is the definitive account of the event that brought down the East German Politburo and came to represent the final collapse of the Cold War order.

"Amply researched and emotive, this work shares the full narrative of events leading to the fall of the Berlin Wall in a way that both academics and lay readers will appreciate. Those already familiar with the subjects and time frames involved will definitely benefit from the author's extensive research and emphasis on personal narratives." —Library Journal

Includes bibliographical references and index.

943.155 Berlin (Germany)

MacLean, Rory
Berlin: Portrait of a City Through the Centuries. Rory MacLean. St. Martin's Press 2014. VIII, 421 pages : Illustration
ISBN 9781250051868
Grades: Adult   943.155
1. German history 2. Berlin, Germany 3. Germany 4. History writing — Europe — Germany

The history of Berlin told through the lives of numerous residents over the last 500 years.

Includes bibliographical references and index; Originally published in the UK (London: Weidenfeld & Nicolson, 2014.).

943.6 Austria and Liechtenstein

Judson, Pieter M.
The Habsburg Empire: A New History. Pieter M. Judson. The Belknap Press of Harvard University Press 2016. 480 p.
ISBN 9780674047761
Grades: Adult   943.6
1. Habsburg, House of 2. Nationalism 3. Imperialism 4. Central Europe 5. History writing — Europe

LC 2015036845

Moving beyond older approaches to the history of the Habsburgs in Central Europe in which nations are the main actors and nationalist conflict the inevitable moving force in the monarchy's trajectory, Pieter Judson offers an alternate narrative framework for the history of Habsburg Central Europe from the eighteenth century to the demise of the empire in World War I. He investigates how shared imperial institutions, administrative practices, and cultural programs helped to shape local society in every region of the empire. He shows how all of these elements gave imperial citizens fundamentally common experiences that crossed linguistic, confessional, and regional divides—experiences that even shaped nationalists' understandings of nationhood. And he traces what happened to the common or shared elements of imperial practice when the Habsburg monarchy formally ceased to exist in 1918.

Includes bibliographical references and index.

King, Greg
Twilight of Empire: The Tragedy at Mayerling and the End of the Habsburgs. Greg King and Penny Wilson. St. Martin's Press 2017. 368 p.

ISBN 9781250083029
Grades: Adult   943.6
1. Rudolf, Crown Prince of Austria, 1858-1889 2. Vetsera, Mary, Baroness, 1871-1889 3. Habsburg, House of 4. Princes 5. Mistresses 6. Scandals 7. Suicide pacts 8. Royal houses 9. Family secrets 10. Politics and government 11. Austria 12. Belle Epoque (1871-1914) 13. 19th century 14. 20th century 15. Collective biographies 16. Life stories — Politics — Royalty 17. History writing — Europe — Eastern Europe 18. History writing — Scandals

LC 2017024874

Presents an account of the murder-suicide credited with triggering the end of the Habsburg monarchy by examining the facts behind the heavily romanticized story.

943.64 Western Austria, and Liechtenstein

Schindler, Meriel
The Lost Cafe Schindler: One Family, Two Wars, and the Search for Truth. Meriel Schindler. W.W. Norton & Company 2021. 400 p.
ISBN 9780393881622
Grades: Adult   943.64
1. Schindler, Meriel, 1964- 2. Schindler, Kurt, 1925-2017 3. Schindler, Hugo, 1888-1952 4. Schindler family 5. Jewish families 6. Restaurants 7. Family businesses 8. Father and adult daughter 9. Swindlers and swindling 10. Conflict in families 11. Genealogy 12. Antisemitism 13. Nazism 14. Holocaust (1933-1945) 15. Jewish people 16. World War II 17. Family history 18. Religious persecution 19. Refugees 20. European history 21. Austria 22. 19th century 23. 20th century 24. Autobiographies and memoirs 25. Life stories — Facing adversity — War and oppression — Holocaust 26. Life stories — Relationships — Parent and child 27. History writing — Wars and conflicts — Holocaust — World War II 28. Nonfiction that reads like fiction

LC 2021027800

An extraordinary memoir of a Jewish family spanning two world wars and its flight from Nazi-occupied Austria. Meriel Schindler spent her adult life trying to keep her father, Kurt, at bay. But when he died in 2017, he left behind piles of Nazi-era documents related to her family's fate in Innsbruck, Austria, and a treasure trove of family albums reaching back to before World War I. Meriel was forced to confront not only their fractured relationship, but also the truth behind their family history. This is a story of tragic loss, but ultimately of reclamation and reconciliation.

"A powerful account of the divergent fortunes of a prominent Austrian Jewish family.... Throughout, Schindler writes vividly about representation, memory, and the aftermath of atrocity. A significant addition to the literature on the Holocaust." —Kirkus

Includes bibliographical references.

943.71 Czech Republic

Albright, Madeleine Korbel
Prague Winter: A Personal Story of Remembrance and War, 1937-1948. Madeleine Albright. Harper 2012. 352 p.
ISBN 9780062030313
Grades: 9 10 11 12 Adult   943.71
1. Albright, Madeleine Korbel, 1937-2022 2. World War II 3. Jewish families 4. Childhood 5. Memories 6. European history 7. Czechoslovakia 8. Prague, Czech Republic 9. Prague (Czech Republic) 10. 20th century 11. Second World War era (1939-1945) 12. Autobiographies and memoirs 13. Life stories — Facing adversity — War and oppression — War survivors 14. History writing — Wars and conflicts — Holocaust — World War II

LC 2011049416

Booklist Editors' Choice, 2012.

Set against the backdrop of occupied Czechoslovakia and World War II, the former Secretary of State paints a vivid portrait of her early life from 1937 to 1948 during which she witnessed the Nazi invasion of her native Prague, the Ho-

ESSENTIAL AND RECOMMENDED TITLES
943.9 Hungary

locaust, the defeat of fascism, the rise of communism and the onset of the Cold War."
Includes bibliographical references and index.

943.9 Hungary

Michener, James A.
The **Bridge** at Andau. James A. Michener. Random House 1957. 270 p. Illustration
ISBN 9780449210505
Grades: 11 12 Adult   943.9
1. Refugees, Hungarian 2. Revolutions 3. European history 4. Hungary 5. 1950s 6. History writing — Europe — Eastern Europe 7. History writing — Wars and conflicts — Revolutions
LC 57008158

By a trick of fate, the Andau Bridge becomes a lifeline to freedom for Hungarians fleeing the Russians in 1956.

943.912 Budapest (Hungary)

Sebestyen, Victor
Budapest: Portrait of a City Between East and West. Victor Sebestyen. Pantheon Books 2023. 432 pages
ISBN 9780593317563
Grades: Adult   943.912
1. Culture 2. Hungary 3. Budapest, Hungary 4. Central Europe 5. History writing — Europe

Throughout history the centre of gravity in Budapest and among Hungarians has shifted between East and West culturally, politically, emotionally. The shifts have sometimes been violent. Victor Sebestyen describes revolutions, bloody battles, the Uprising of 1956 and wars of conquest: Some won, some lost. Others were more peaceful, although the repercussions were no less significant: for example, the fall of Soviet-style Communism. The story of Budapest is dramatic, and full of extraordinary, colourful personalities.

"Historian Sebestyen (Lenin the Dictator) delivers a sweeping and insightful chronicle of Budapest from its origins as a first-century Roman settlement on the Danube to the present…The result is a comprehensive account of one of Europe's great cities." —*Publishers Weekly*

Originally published in the UK under the title Budapest: Between East and West, by Weidenfeld & Nicolson, London, in 2022; Includes bibliographical references and index.

944 France and Monaco

Barker, Juliet R. V.
Agincourt: Henry v. and the Battle That Made England. Juliet Barker. Little, Brown and Co. 2006. xiii, 445 p, 16 p. of plates : Illustration; Color; Map
ISBN 9780316015035
Grades: Adult   944
1. Henry V, King of England, 1387-1422 2. Agincourt, Battle of, 1415 3. Hundred Years' War, 1339-1453 4. Battles 5. Military strategy 6. Military history 7. Civilization, Medieval 8. British history 9. Great Britain 10. France 11. 15th century 12. Medieval period (476-1492) 13. History writing — Wars and conflicts — Hundred Years War 14. History writing — Wars and conflicts — Battles 15. History writing — Medieval — Europe
LC 2006002034

An examination of the ongoing legacy of the Battle of Agincourt draws on a wide range of sources and refutes popular beliefs to offer insight into how the conflict's outnumbered English archers succeeded against more heavily armed French knights.

Includes bibliographical references (p. [413]-423) and index; Originally published: London, 2005.

Darnton, Robert
*The **Revolutionary** Temper: Paris, 1748-1789.* Robert Darnton. W W Norton & CO Inc 2023. 608 p.
ISBN 9781324035589
Grades: Adult   944
1. Louis XVI, King of France, 1754-1793 2. Louis XV, King of France, 1710-1774 3. Revolutions 4. French history 5. European history 6. Politics and government 7. Power 8. Social life and customs 9. French Revolution, 1789-1799 10. Rulers 11. French people 12. France 13. 18th century 14. Collective biographies 15. History writing — Europe — France 16. Life stories — Politics — Royalty 17. History writing — Wars and conflicts — French Revolution

A groundbreaking account of the coming of the French Revolution from a historian of worldwide acclaim.

"A page-turner on the 40 years before the fall of the Bastille…The run-up to the French Revolution in expert hands." —*Kirkus*

DeJean, Joan E.
How Paris Became Paris: The Invention of the Modern City. Joan DeJean. Bloomsbury USA 2014. 288 p.
ISBN 9781608195916
Grades: Adult   944
1. Henry IV, King of France, 1553-1610 2. Louis XIV, King of France, 1638-1715 3. Urban planning 4. Urban planners 5. Social life and customs 6. Voyages and travels 7. Paris, France history 8. Paris, France 9. 17th century 10. History writing — Europe — France 11. Arts and Entertainment — Architecture
LC 2013031527

Explains how Paris became a modern city, from the urban designs of the seventeenth century, to its transformation to a city of parks and boulevards, to its emergence as a cultural center of art and wealth by the mid-nineteenth century.

Includes bibliographical references and index.

Goldstone, Nancy Bazelon
*The **Rival** Queens: Catherine De' Medici, Her Daughter Marguerite De Valois, and the Betrayal That Ignited a Kingdom.* Nancy Goldstone. Little Brown & CO 2015. 432 p.
ISBN 9780316409650
Grades: Adult   944
1. Catherine de Medicis, Queen, consort of Henry II, King of France, 1519-1589 2. Marguerite, Queen, consort of Henry IV, King of France, 1553-1615 3. Women rulers 4. Rulers 5. Ambition 6. Competition 7. Royal houses 8. Manipulation (Social sciences) 9. Inheritance and succession 10. Heirs and heiresses 11. Courts and courtiers 12. Mothers and daughters 13. French history 14. Renaissance (1300-1600) 15. 16th century 16. Biographies 17. History writing — Renaissance — Europe 18. History writing — Women's history 19. Life stories — Politics — Royalty 20. History writing — Europe — France
LC 2014955135

The author of the Maid and the Queen documents the turbulent mother-daughter relationship between Catherine de' Medici and Marguerite de Valois to explore the court politics, assassinations, espionage and betrayals that shaped their time.

"This highly accessible account is recommended for general but serious readers interested in European history and royal biography." —*Library Journal*

Horne, Alistair
Seven Ages of Paris. Alistair Horne. A.A. Knopf 2002. xvii, 458 p, 24 p. of plates : Illustration; Color
ISBN 9780679454816
Grades: Adult   944
1. Paris, France history 2. History writing — Europe — France
LC 2002029653

New York Times Notable Book, 2003.

In this luminous portrait of Paris, the celebrated historian gives us the history, culture, disasters, and triumphs of one of the world's truly great cities. While Paris may be many things, it is never boring. With a keen eye for the telling anecdote and pivotal moment, he portrays an array of vivid incidents to show us how

Paris endures through each age, is altered but always emerges more brilliant and beautiful than ever.

"The author traces the history of Paris through seven periods, beginning in the 12th century and ending with the death of Charles de Gaulle in 1969. Each section includes fascinating insights into the social and cultural life of the age, fashions in clothing, architectural developments, leading personalities, and lifestyles of rich and poor alike. With the verve of a master storyteller, Horne captures Parisians' zest for living." —*Library Journal*

Includes bibliographical references (p. 428-436) and index.

Mayle, Peter

Encore Provence: New Adventures in the South of France. Peter Mayle. Knopf 1999. 226 p. : Illustration
ISBN 9780679441243

Grades: Adult　　　　　　　　　　　　　　　　　　　　944

1. Mayle, Peter 2. British people in France 3. Voyages and travels 4. Tourists 5. Tourism 6. Social life and customs 7. France 8. Provence, France 9. Travel Writing — Living Abroad 10. Travel Writing — Europe

LC 99062335

The author continues his celebration of Provence in a new collection of culinary delights, profiles of colorful Gallic characters, and personal observations.

"Mayle's book is all about the renewal of his acquaintance with the land he so loves. Essays range widely over Provecal life. His observations and commentaries are laced with humor but encompass true respect and admiration for his adopted homeland." —*Booklist*

Provence A-z. Peter Mayle. Knopf 2006. xi, 286 p. : Illustration; Map
ISBN 9781400044429

Grades: Adult　　　　　　　　　　　　　　　　　　　　944

1. Tourism 2. Tourists 3. Social life and customs 4. Voyages and travels 5. France 6. Provence, France 7. Travel Writing — Europe

LC 2006040885

An informative resource on Provence includes nearly two hundred alphabetically organized entries on such subjects as architecture, expatriates, Aix-en-Provence, Provencal linguistic oddities, and local legends and lore.

★ *A Year in Provence.* Peter Mayle; illustrations by Judith Clancy. Knopf 1990. 207 p.
ISBN 9780394572307

Grades: Adult　　　　　　　　　　　　　　　　　　　　944

1. Mayle, Peter 2. Voyages and travels 3. British people in France 4. Moving to a new home 5. Moving to a new country 6. Social life and customs 7. France 8. Provence, France 9. Travel Writing — Living Abroad 10. Travel Writing — Europe 11. Nonfiction that reads like fiction

LC 89038475

The author describes his experiences when he and his wife moved to a two-hundred-year-old French farmhouse, and shares his observations on the people and culture of Provence.

Originally published in Great Britain by Hamish Hamilton, Ltd, London, in 1989—T.P. verso.

Moorehead, Caroline

Village of Secrets: Defying the Nazis in Vichy France. Caroline Moorehead. HarperCollins 2014. 384 p.
ISBN 9780062202475

Grades: Adult　　　　　　　　　　　　　　　　　　　　944

1. French Resistance (World War II) 2. Anti-Nazi movement 3. Righteous Gentiles in the Holocaust 4. Hidden children (Holocaust) 5. Holocaust (1933-1945) 6. German occupation, World War II 7. French history 8. Le Chambon-sur-Lignon, France 9. History writing — Wars and conflicts — World War II 10. History writing — Wars and conflicts — Holocaust — World War II 11. History writing — Europe — France 12. History writing — Wars and conflicts — Resistance — World War II

LC 2014497785

A small mountain village in France, Le Chambon-sur-Lignon, has a long heritage of dealing with religious persecution because of its Huguenot roots. During World War II, Protestant Pastor Andre Trocme inspired the villagers to shelter Resistance fighters, Jews, and escaped POWs. Their efforts included such activities as forging ration books (so the hidden population could eat), warning of the arrival of Nazi officials, and guiding refugees through the mountains into Switzerland. Author Caroline Moorehead draws on interviews with survivors as well as archival records to bring this heroic tale to life, producing a riveting account of World War II survival.

"Moorehead not only recounts the heroics but also the everyday ordinariness of those involved, busting the embellished mythology while emphasizing the essential humanity of the entire operation." —*Booklist*

Includes bibliographical references and index; Originally published in Canada (Toronto : Random House Canada, 2014).

Norwich, John Julius

A History of France. John Julius Norwich. Atlantic Monthly Press 2018. 400 p.
ISBN 9780802128904

Grades: Adult　　　　　　　　　　　　　　　　　　　　944

1. Rulers 2. Political intrigue 3. Politicians 4. Battles 5. French history 6. European history 7. Gaul 8. History writing — Europe — France

LC 2018026531

With his trademark stylistic panache and expert command of detail, a world-renowned historian presents this ode to France, filled with heroes and villains, battles and rebellion.

Poirier, Agnes

Left Bank: Art, Passion, and the Rebirth of Paris, 1940-50. Agnes Poirier. Henry Holt and Company 2018. 320 p.
ISBN 9781627790246

Grades: Adult　　　　　　　　　　　　　　　　　　　　944

1. Intellectual life 2. Intellectuals 3. Politics and literature 4. Left bank, Paris France 5. Paris, France 6. Collective biographies 7. Life stories — Arts and culture 8. History writing — Europe — France 9. Arts and Entertainment — General

LC 2017023902

Explores the lives of the poets, writers, artists and politicians who mingled in Paris between 1940 and 1950 and gave the world some of the most celebrated works of the past century, including Richard Wright, Albert Camus, James Joyce and Saul Bellow.

Includes bibliographical references and index.

Puhak, Shelley

The Dark Queens: The Bloody Rivalry That Forged the Medieval World. Shelley Puhak. Bloomsbury Publishing Place 2022. 304 p.
ISBN 9781635574913

Grades: Adult　　　　　　　　　　　　　　　　　　　　944

1. Brunhild 2. Fredegund, Queen, consort of Chilperic I, King of Neustria,?-597 3. Women rulers 4. Visigoths 5. Women's power 6. Rulers 7. Sisters in law 8. 6th century 9. Medieval period (476-1492) 10. Collective biographies 11. Life stories — Politics — Royalty 12. History writing — Medieval — Europe 13. History writing — Women's history

The remarkable, little-known story of two trailblazing women in the Early Middle Ages who wielded immense power, only to be vilified for daring to rule.

"Poet Puhak (Guinevere in Baltimore) delivers a lyrical and astute assessment of the political maneuvers, battlefield strategies, and resilience of medieval queens and rivals Fredegund and Brunhild.... The resulting is deeply fascinating portrait of the early Middle Ages that vigorously reclaims two powerhouse women from obscurity." —*Publishers Weekly*

Rappaport, Helen

After the Romanovs: Russian Exiles in Paris from the Belle Epoque Through Revolution and War. Helen Rappaport. St. Martin's Press 2022. 400 p.
ISBN 9781250273109

Grades: Adult　　　　　　　　　　　　　　　　　　　　944

1. Russian people in foreign countries 2. Exiles 3. Political refugees 4. Aristocracy 5. Intellectual life 6. Soviet Union history 7. Paris, France 8. 20th century

ESSENTIAL AND RECOMMENDED TITLES
944 France and Monaco

9. Russian Revolution and Civil War (1917-1921) 10. History writing — Europe — Russia 11. History writing — Europe — France

LC 2021044046

This is the story of the Russian aristocrats, artists, and intellectuals who sought freedom and refuge in the City of Light. Paris has always been a city of cultural excellence, but it has also been a place of refuge for those fleeing persecution, never more so than before and after the Russian Revolution and the fall of the Romanov dynasty. For years, Russian aristocrats had enjoyed all Belle Epoque Paris had to offer. But the brutality of the Bolshevik takeover forced Russians of all types to flee their homeland, sometimes leaving with only the clothes on their backs. This is their story.

"Noted historian Rappaport (The Romanov Sisters, 2014) presents a a thorough and extremely well-researched examination of the Russian experience in Paris before and after the Bolshevik uprising of 1917." —*Booklist*

Includes bibliographical references and index.

Robb, Graham

The Discovery of France: A Historical Geography from the Revolution to the First World War. Graham Robb. Norton 2007. xvii, 454 p, 16 p. of plates : Illustration; Color; Map

ISBN 9780393059731

Grades: Adult   944

1. Cities and towns 2. Prehistoric religion 3. Imperialism, French 4. Voyages and travels 5. French history 6. France 7. 19th century 8. 20th century 9. History writing — Europe — France

LC 2007018529

Booklist Editors' Choice, 2007; New York Times Notable Book, 2007; RSL Ondaatje Prize, 2008.

An exploration of France's rural landscapes and inhabitants celebrates the country's ancient tribes, prehistoric networks, and early religions, offering insight into how France was explored, charted, and colonized outside of regions under imperial influence.

"Drawing on his own travels and research, Robb provides a guide to the variety of Frances in the century or so after the Revolution. New Statesman (Engl), Mr. Robb has accomplished quite a feat. He has reintroduced France to itself." —*New York Times*

Also published in large print format; Includes bibliographical references (p. 395-427) and indexes.

France: An Adventure History. Graham Robb. W.W. Norton & Company 2022. 448 p.

ISBN 9781324002567

Grades: Adult   944

1. Robb, Graham, 1958- 2. Authors 3. Historic sites 4. Bicycle touring 5. Voyages and travels 6. French history 7. France 8. Travel Writing — Europe 9. History writing — Europe — France 10. Travel Writing — Modes of Transportation — Cycling

LC 2022017487

Graham Robb's own adventures and discoveries while living, working, and traveling in France connect this tour through space and time with on-the-ground experience. There are scenes of wars and revolutions from the plains of Provence to the slums and boulevards of Paris. Robb conveys with wit and precision what it felt like to look over the shoulder of a young Louis XIV as he planned the vast garden of Versailles, and the dangerous thrill of having a ringside seat at the French revolution. Some of the protagonists may be familiar, but appear here in a very different light—Caesar, Charlemagne, Louis XIV, Napoleon Bonaparte, General Charles de Gaulle. This extraordinary narrative is the fruit of decades of research and thirty thousand miles on a self-propelled, two-wheeled time machine (a bicycle). Even seasoned Francophiles will wonder if they really know that terra incognita on the edge of Europe that is currently referred to as "France."

"Melding memoir, travelogue, and history, British biographer and cultural historian Robb offers a sweeping, spirited, and refreshingly unsentimental portrait of France, from the Bronze Age to the present." —*Kirkus*

Includes bibliographical references and index.

Parisians: An Adventure History of Paris. Graham Robb. W. W. Norton & Co. 2010. 496 p.

ISBN 9780393067248

Grades: Adult   944

1. Cities and towns 2. City dwellers 3. Social history 4. Paris, France history 5. History writing — Europe — France

LC 2009054279

New York Times Notable Book, 2010.

Reveals the historical secrets of the City of Light from the Revolution to the present, including how Marie Antoinette was unable to flee the city because she lacked a reliable map.

"Robb has the passion of a naturalist displaying a wall of rare butterflies or a cabinet of exotic corals, but his specimens are all human and walked the streets of Paris at some point between the French revolution and now. [A] generous and humane book." —*Times (London)*

Includes bibliographical references and indexes.

Sciolino, Elaine

The Only Street in Paris: Life on the Rue Des Martyrs. Elaine Sciolino. W. W. Norton & Co, Inc. 2015. 256 p.

ISBN 9780393242379

Grades: Adult   944

1. Culture 2. American people in France 3. Cities and towns 4. France 5. Travel Writing — Europe 6. Society and culture — Urban and regional studies

Part memoir, part travelogue, part love letter to the people who live and work on a magical street in Paris, Elaine Sciolino, the former Paris bureau chief for the New York Times, invites us on a tour of her favorite Parisian street, offering an homage to street life and the pleasures of Parisian living. 'I can never be sad on the Rue des Martyrs,' Sciolino explains, as she celebrates the neighborhood's rich history and vibrant lives. While many cities suffer from the leveling effects of globalization, the Rue des Martyrs maintains its distinct allure. On this street, the patron saint of France was beheaded and the Jesuits took their first vows. It was here that Edgar Degas and Pierre-Auguste Renoir painted circus acrobats, Emile Zola situated a lesbian dinner club in his novel Nana, and Francois Truffaut filmed scenes from The 400 Blows. Sciolino reveals the charms and idiosyncrasies of this street and its longtime residents—the Tunisian greengrocer, the husband-and-wife cheesemongers, the showman who's been running a transvestite cabaret for more than half a century, the owner of a hundred-year-old bookstore, the woman who repairs eighteenth-century mercury barometers—bringing Paris alive in all of its unique majesty. The Only Street in Paris will make readers hungry for Paris, for cheese and wine, and for the kind of street life that is all too quickly disappearing.

The Seine: The River That Made Paris. Elaine Sciolino. W.W. Norton & Company, Inc. 2019. 304 pages

ISBN 9780393609356

Grades: Adult   944

1. Sciolino, Elaine 2. Rivers 3. River life 4. History 5. Harbors 6. Waterways 7. Boating 8. Cities and towns 9. National characteristics, French 10. Culture 11. Voyages and travels 12. Paris, France history 13. Seine River 14. Paris, France 15. France 16. Autobiographies and memoirs 17. Travel Writing — Europe 18. History writing — Europe — France

LC 2019025988

The former New York Times Paris bureau chief and author of the best-selling the Only Street in Paris presents a vibrant tour of the Seine that traces its rich history and the stories of contributors from all walks of life.

Includes bibliographical references and index.

Tuchman, Barbara W.

★ *A Distant Mirror: The Calamitous 14th Century.* Barbara W. Tuchman. Ballantine Books 1979. xx, 677 p, 20 leaves of plates : Illustration; Color; Map

ISBN 9780345349576

Grades: 11 12 Adult   944

1. Coucy, Enguerrand de, 1340-1397 2. Civilization, Medieval 3. French history 4. France 5. 14th century 6. Medieval period (476-1492) 7. History writing — Medieval — Europe

LC BL 99917028

National Book Critics Circle Award for Nonfiction finalist, 1978.

The prize-winning historian traces the major currents of the fourteenth century, revealing the century's great historical rhythms and events and the texture of daily life at all levels of European society.

"The author traces the history of the fourteenth century by following the career of a feudal lord, Enguerrand de Coucy VII, the seigneur of some 150 towns and villages in Picardy. He was born in 1340, and he died in captivity in 1397, having been made a prisoner by the Turks." —*Time*

Includes bibliographical references (p. [599]-617) and index.

White, Edmund
The Flaneur: A Stroll Through the Paradoxes of Paris. Edmund White. Bloomsbury 2001. 211 p. : Map
ISBN 9781582341354
Grades: Adult   944
1. White, Edmund, 1940- 2. Travelers 3. Social life and customs 4. Voyages and travels 5. Paris, France 6. Travel Writing — Europe
LC 00046812
New York Times Notable Book, 2001.

A collection of essays by the acclaimed author of a Boy's Own Story explores the unfamiliar byways of the City of Lights, taking readers into virtually unknown sections of Paris as he shares his observations and meditations on the city's bookshops and boutiques, monuments and palaces, eateries and history. 20,000 first printing.

"White is richly informed, and his evocative writing should appeal to both armchair travelers and visitors to Paris." —*Library Journal*

Winder, Simon
Lotharingia: A Personal History of Europe's Lost Country. Simon Winder. Farrar, Straus and Giroux 2019. xi, 504 pages
ISBN 9780374192181
Grades: Adult   944
1. Lothair II, King of Lorraine, approximately 825-869 2. Rulers 3. Material culture 4. Civilization, Medieval 5. European history 6. German history 7. Belgium 8. Netherlands 9. Switzerland 10. 9th century 11. Medieval period (476-1492) 12. History writing — Europe
LC 2018052632

Retraces the various powers that have tried to overtake the land that stretches from the mouth of the Rhine to the Alps and the might of the peoples who have lived there for centuries.

Originally published in 2019 by Picador, an imprint of Pan Macmillan, Great Britain—Title page verso; Includes bibliographical references and index.

944.026 Reigns of Charles VI and Charles VII, 1380-1461

Jager, Eric
Blood Royal: A True Tale of Crime and Detection in Medieval Paris. Eric Jager. Little, Brown and Company 2014. 352 p.
ISBN 9780316224512
Grades: Adult   944.026
1. Orleans, Louis, duc d', 1372-1407 2. Regicide 3. Assassination 4. Conspiracies 5. Political intrigue 6. Murder investigation 7. Crime 8. French history 9. 15th century 10. Medieval period (476-1492) 11. History writing — Medieval — Europe 12. History writing — Scandals 13. True Crime — Historical Crime
LC 2013028257
ALA Notable Book, 2015.

In this medieval true crime story set in 15th century Paris, one of history's first detectives uncovers a shocking conspiracy while he investigates the murder of Louis of Orleans, brother to King Charles, by a band of masked assailants.

Includes bibliographical references and index.

944.04 France since 1789

Burke, Edmund
Reflections on the Revolution in France. Edmund Burke. Oxford University Press 2009. 352 p.
ISBN 9780199539024
Grades: Adult   944.04
1. Revolutions 2. French Revolution, 1789-1799 3. Military history 4. Public opinion 5. Politics and government 6. French history 7. France 8. 18th century 9. Revolutionary France (1789-1799) 10. History writing — Wars and conflicts — French Revolution 11. Arts and Entertainment — Writing and Publishing — Literary criticism
LC Oc2009000560

Reflections on the Revolution in France is a slashing attack on the French Revolution by one of Britain's most famous statesmen. Liberty and social order, Burke argues, are maintained by the traditional rights and duties embedded in custom and law. And when these traditions are overthrown in revolutions, society is threatened with chaos, bloodshed and despotism.

Includes bibliographical references and index; This ed. originally published: 1999.

Davidson, Ian
The French Revolution: From Enlightenment to Tyranny. Ian Davidson. Pegasus Books 2016. 336 p.
ISBN 9781681772509
Grades: Adult   944.04
1. French history 2. Revolutionary France (1789-1799) 3. 18th century 4. History writing — Wars and conflicts — French Revolution

An assessment of the French Revolution explores its immensely complicated and multifaceted dynamics and how it became weighted with political, social and moral values.

Includes index.

Popkin, Jeremy D.
A New World Begins: The History of the French Revolution. Jeremy D. Popkin. Basic Books 2019. 640 p.
ISBN 9780465096664
Grades: Adult   944.04
1. French Revolution, 1789-1799 2. Social change 3. Political violence 4. Regime change 5. Revolutions 6. Revolutionaries 7. Political science 8. French history 9. Revolutionary France (1789-1799) 10. History writing — Wars and conflicts — French Revolution 11. History writing — Europe — France
LC 2019019101

A comprehensive analysis of the principles, events and influences of the French Revolution examines the roles of such contributors as Mirabeau and Robespierre while explaining the violent debates that led to modernism and the rise of Napoleon.

Includes bibliographical references and index.

Schama, Simon
Citizens: A Chronicle of the French Revolution. Simon Schama. Alfred A. Knopf 1989. xx, 948 p. : Illustration
ISBN 9780394559483
Grades: 11 12 Adult   944.04
1. Louis XVI, King of France, 1754-1793 2. Revolutionaries 3. Nationalism 4. Revolutions 5. French history 6. France 7. 18th century 8. Revolutionary France (1789-1799) 9. History writing — Wars and conflicts — French Revolution
LC 88045320

Explores the roots and fruition of the French Revolution in terms of the vitality and infatuation with technology that motivated French citizenry toward change and the conflicting strained economics frustrating their visions for France.

ESSENTIAL AND RECOMMENDED TITLES
944.05 Period of First Empire, 1804-1815

"The author offers a narrative in the form of a nineteenth-century chronicle that delves into the events and meaning of that momentous series of historical events." —*Booklist*

Includes bibliographical references (p. 879-906) and index.

944.05 Period of First Empire, 1804-1815

Broers, Michael
Napoleon: The Decline and Fall of an Empire: 1811-1821. Michael Broers. Pegasus Books 2022. 496 p.
ISBN 9781639361779
Grades: Adult   944.05
1. Napoleon I, Emperor of the French, 1769-1821 2. Rulers 3. Napoleonic Wars, 1800-1815 4. Command of troops 5. Imperialism 6. Alliances 7. Military defeat 8. Exile (Punishment) 9. French history 10. European history 11. 19th century 12. Biographies 13. Life stories — Politics — Politicians 14. Life stories — Law and order — Military leaders 15. History writing — Wars and conflicts — Napoleonic Wars 16. History writing — Europe — France

In 1811, Napoleon stood at his zenith. He had defeated all his continental rivals, come to an entente with Russia, and his blockade of Britain seemed, at long last, to be a success. The emperor had an heir on the way with his new wife, Marie-Louise, the young daughter of the Emperor of Austria. It was a moment of unprecedented peace and hope. But in less than two years, all of this was in peril. In four years, it was gone, swept away by the tides of war against the most powerful alliance in European history.

"Oxford University historian Broers (Napoleon) delivers a granular history of Napoleon's final decade." —*Publishers Weekly*

944.0816 Period of World War II, 1939-1945

Rosbottom, Ronald C.
When Paris Went Dark: The City of Light Under German Occupation, 1940-1944. Ronald C. Rosbottom. Little Brown 2014. 352 p.
ISBN 9780316217446
Grades: Adult   944.0816
1. Military occupation 2. Nazi collaborators 3. French Resistance (World War II) 4. World War II 5. Military history 6. German occupation, World War II 7. French history 8. France 9. 1940s 10. 20th century 11. History writing — Wars and conflicts — World War II — European Theater 12. History writing — Wars and conflicts — Resistance — World War II

Describes what life was like in Paris after June 1940, when the Nazis occupied France, juxtaposing the eerie sense of normalcy felt by many Parisians with the passion of the strong resistance movement that rose around Charles de Gaulle.

944.9 Provence-Cote d'Azur, Monaco, Corsica

De Courcy, Anne
Chanel's Riviera: Glamour, Decadence, and Survival in Peace and War, 1930-1944. Anne de Courcy. St. Martin's Press 2020. 304 p.
ISBN 9781250177070
Grades: Adult   944.9
1. Chanel, Coco, 1883-1971 2. Socialites 3. World War II 4. Women fashion designers 5. Fashion designers 6. Social life and customs 7. French Riviera 8. France 9. 1930s 10. 20th century 11. Biographies 12. History writing — Europe — France 13. Arts and Entertainment — Fashion 14. Life stories — Arts and culture — Fashion 15. Adult books for young adults

In this captivating narrative, Chanel's Riviera explores the fascinating world of the Cote d'Azur during a period that saw the deepest extremes of luxury and terror in the twentieth century. The Cote d'Azur in 1938 was a world of wealth, luxury, and extravagance, inhabited by a sparkling cast of characters including the Duke and Duchess of Windsor, Joseph P. Kennedy, Gloria Swanson, Colette, the Mitfords, Picasso, Cecil Beaton, and Somerset Maugham. The elite flocked to the Riviera each year to swim, gamble, and escape from the turbulence plaguing the rest of Europe. At the glittering center of it all was Coco Chanel, whose very presence at her magnificently appointed villa, La Pausa, made it the ultimate place to be. Born an orphan, her beauty and formidable intelligence allured many men, but it was her incredible talent, relentless work ethic, and exquisite taste that made her an icon. But this wildly seductive world was poised on the edge of destruction. In a matter of months, the Nazis swooped down and the glamour of the pre-war parties and casinos gave way to the horrors of evacuation and the displacement of thousands of families during World War II. From the bitter struggle to survive emerged powerful stories of tragedy, sacrifice, and heroism. Enriched by original research and de Courcy's signature skill, Chanel's Riviera brings the experiences of both rich and poor, protected and persecuted, to vivid life.

"This will be popular with royal watchers, fashionistas, and readers who relish the international social scene, and should cover new territory for most." —*Booklist*

Includes bibliographical references and index; Originally published: London : Weidenfeld & Nicolson, 2019.

Mayle, Peter
My Twenty-five Years in Provence: Reflections on Then and Now. Peter Mayle. Alfred A. Knopf 2018. VI, 179 p.
ISBN 9780451494528
Grades: Adult   944.9
1. Villages 2. Rural life 3. Small town life 4. British people in France 5. Expatriates 6. Voyages and travels 7. Provence, France 8. France 9. Autobiographies and memoirs 10. Travel Writing — Living Abroad 11. Travel Writing — Europe
LC 2018001245

The late award-winning author of a Year in Provence presents a final collection of all-new writings that vividly describe the 25 years his wife and he shared in an increasingly modern but still-beloved south of France.

945 Italy, San Marino, Vatican City, Malta

Berendt, John
The City of Falling Angels. John Berendt. Penguin Press 2005. 414 p.
ISBN 9781594200588
Grades: Adult   945
1. Fires 2. Fire investigation 3. Opera houses 4. Arson 5. Arson investigation 6. Social life and customs 7. Voyages and travels 8. Venice, Italy 9. Italy 10. 1990s 11. History writing — Europe — Italy 12. History writing — Natural disasters and tragedies 13. Travel Writing — Europe
LC 2005047661

Traces the aftermath of the 1996 Venice opera house fire, an event that devastated Venetian society and was investigated by the author, who through interviews with local figures learned about the region's rich cultural history.

"Berendt delivers an urbane, beautifully fashioned book with much exotic charm. [The author] makes erudite, inquisitive, nicely skeptical company as he leads the reader through the shadows of what was heretofore better known as a tourist attraction." —*New York Times*

Map of Venice on endpapers; Also published in large print format.

Crowley, Roger
City of Fortune: How Venice Ruled the Seas. by Roger Crowley. Random House 2011. xxix, 432 p. : Illustration; Map
ISBN 9781400068203
Grades: Adult   945
1. Sea power 2. Military history 3. International trade 4. Merchants 5. Commerce 6. Naval history 7. Merchant ships 8. War 9. International economic relations 10. Civilization, Medieval 11. Italian history 12. Venice, Italy 13. Mediterranean Region 14. Medieval period (476-1492) 15. History writing — Europe — Italy 16. History writing — Military — Naval history
LC 2011005529

Draws on firsthand accounts of pitched sea battles, skillful negotiations, and diplomatic maneuvers to offer a complete history of Venice's centuries-long reign as a naval power and maritime trading empire.

"An action-packed political and military history that will remind readers of the Italian sea power that prevailed for centuries before Western European nations arrived on the scene." —*Kirkus*

Includes bibliographical references and index.

Duggan, Christopher
The Force of Destiny: A History of Italy Since 1796. Christopher Duggan. Houghton Mifflin 2008. 688 p.

ISBN 9780618353675

Grades: Adult   945

1. Italian history 2. 19th century 3. 21st century 4. 20th century 5. History writing — Europe — Italy

A history of Italy describes the turbulent birth of a unified modern nation during the first half of the nineteenth century, its destructive role during World War I, the rise of Mussolini and authoritarianism in the 1920s and 1930s, its defeat during World War II, and the legacy of its tempestuous history for modern-day Italy.

Includes bibliographical references and index.

Leon, Donna
My Venice and Other Essays. Donna Leon. Atlantic Monthly Press 2013. 240 pages

ISBN 9780802120366

Grades: Adult   945

1. Leon, Donna 2. Everyday life 3. American people 4. American people in foreign countries 5. Venice, Italy 6. Essays 7. Autobiographies and memoirs 8. Life stories — Arts and culture — Writing — Authors

LC 2015295832

The author of the international best-selling Commissario Guido Brunetti series, which is set in Italy, presents more than 50 humorous, passionate and insightful essays about her life in Venice that also explore her family history, her former life in New Jersey and the idea of the Italian man.

Madden, Thomas F.
Venice: Islands of Honor and Profit : A New History. Thomas F. Madden. Viking 2012. 480 p.

ISBN 9780670025428

Grades: Adult   945

1. Architecture, Italian 2. Civilization, Western 3. Art, Renaissance (Europe) 4. Performing arts 5. Artists 6. Capitalism 7. Cities and towns 8. Canals 9. Naval power 10. Italian history 11. Venice, Italy 12. History writing — Europe — Italy

LC 2012005304

An all-encompassing history of Venice draws on rare archival material and newly translated documents to chronicle the city's rise from a humble lagoon refuge, to its apex as a maritime empire and Renaissance epicenter, to its rebirth as a modern tourist hub.

Includes bibliographical references and index.

Mayes, Frances
Bella Tuscany: The Sweet Life in Italy. Frances Mayes. Broadway Books 1999. xiv, 286 p.

ISBN 9780767902830

Grades: Adult   945

1. Mayes, Frances 2. American people in Italy 3. Remarriage 4. Building conservation and restoration 5. Divorced women 6. Women authors 7. Houses 8. Social life and customs 9. Voyages and travels 10. Tuscany, Italy 11. Autobiographies and memoirs 12. Biographies 13. Travel Writing — Living Abroad 14. Travel Writing — Europe

LC 99024880

The author explores life in the idyllic Italian countryside, offering authentic Tuscan recipes and intimately portraying the local people and the environment.

"This book follows Under the Tuscan Sun, Mayes's popular account of falling in love with Tuscany and purchasing an old villa for her summer vacations. Now Mayes, on sabbatical from her teaching position in San Francisco, is experiencing Italy in the early spring with her friend and soon-to-be-spouse, Ed." —*Library Journal*

Sequel to: Under the Tuscan sun.

Under the Tuscan Sun: At Home in Italy. Frances Mayes. Chronicle Books 1996. 280 p.

ISBN 9780811808422

Grades: Adult   945

1. Mayes, Frances 2. American people in Italy 3. Women travelers 4. Divorced women 5. Cooking, Italian 6. Houses 7. Renovation (Architecture) 8. Design and construction 9. Social life and customs 10. Voyages and travels 11. Tuscany, Italy 12. Autobiographies and memoirs 13. Page to screen 14. Travel Writing — Living Abroad 15. Travel Writing — Europe 16. Food writing — Memoirs and biographies 17. Life stories — Personal growth

LC 96015137

The poet and travel writer describes her experiences in Tuscany during the restoration of her countryside villa.

"Casual and conversational, [Ms. Mayes's] chapters are filled with craftsmen and cooks, with exploratory jaunts into the countryside—but what they all boil down to is an intense celebration of what she calls 'The voluptuousness of Italian life.' Occasionally, this leads to the sort of gushy observations you might expect from a besotted lover. But more often it produces an appealing and very vivid snapshot imagery." —*New York Times Book Review*

Excerpts from this book appeared in the New York Times, Ploughshares, and House Beautiful; Sequel: Bella Tuscany.

Norwich, John Julius
A History of Venice. John Julius Norwich. Vintage Books 1989. xxvi, 673 p, 32 p. of plates : Illustration; Map

ISBN 9780679721970

Grades: Adult   945

1. European Renaissance 2. Art history 3. Architecture 4. Cities and towns 5. Italian history 6. Venice, Italy 7. Italy 8. Renaissance (1300-1600) 9. History writing — Renaissance — Europe 10. History writing — Europe — Italy

LC 88082393

An incisive account of the history of the Venetian Republic chronicles its fifth-century origins, development as a commercial and maritime power, Renaissance era, long decline, and termination in 1797.

Originally published in 2 v. under title: Venice; Originally published: New York : Knopf : Distributed by Random House, 1982; Includes bibliographical references (p. 643-649) and index.

Parks, Tim
The Hero's Way: Walking with Garibaldi from Rome to Ravenna. Tim Parks. W. W. Norton & Company 2021. 352 p.

ISBN 9780393866841

Grades: Adult   945

1. Parks, Tim 2. Garibaldi, Giuseppe, 1807-1882 3. Revolutionaries 4. Walking 5. Voyages and travels 6. Italian history 7. Italy 8. 19th century 9. Travel Writing — Europe 10. Travel Writing — Historic Journeys 11. Travel Writing — Modes of Transportation — on Foot

LC 2021013011

Beloved guide to Italian culture and history Tim Parks traces Garibaldi's famous journey across the Apennines in search of the country's past and present. Tim Parks, the author of four best-selling accounts of Italian life, retraced Garibaldi's steps in the summer of 2019. In The Hero's Way he delivers a superb travelogue that combines a memorable portrait of Garibaldi and the country before unification with Parks's own fine observations of contemporary Italian people, politics, customs, food, and landscape.

"This gripping account of Italy's visionary past serves as a revealing window into its clouded present." —*Publishers Weekly*

Strathern, Paul
The Florentines: From Dante to Galileo: The Transformation of Western Civilization. Paul Strathern. Pegasus Books 2021. 400 p.

ISBN 9781643137322

ESSENTIAL AND RECOMMENDED TITLES
945.06 Italy, San Marino, Vatican City, Malta — 1494-1527

Grades: Adult **945**

1. Dante Alighieri, 1265-1321 2. Galilei, Galileo, 1564-1642 3. Machiavelli, Niccolo, 1469-1527 4. Leonardo, da Vinci, 1452-1519 5. Civilization, Western 6. Art and society 7. Intellectuals 8. European Renaissance 9. Civilization 10. Italian history 11. Florence, Italy 12. Italy 13. Renaissance (1300-1600) 14. Medieval period (476-1492) 15. History writing — Renaissance — Europe 16. History writing — Europe — Italy

A sweeping and magisterial four-hundred-year history of both the city and the people who gave birth to the Renaissance.

"Novelist and historian Strathern (The Borgias) paints an accessible portrait of Renaissance-era Florence as a city of 'Revolutionary' ideas where geography, a burgeoning banking industry, and luck contributed to the evolution of humanism, artistic breakthroughs, and the scientific revolution." —*Publishers Weekly*

945.06 Italy, San Marino, Vatican City, Malta — 1494-1527

The **Borgias**: *Power and Fortune*. Paul Strathern. Pegasus Books 2019. xvi, 383 pages : Illustration; Color; Map
ISBN 9781643130835
Grades: Adult **945.06**

1. Borgia family 2. Alexander VI, Pope, 1431-1503 3. Borgia, Lucrezia, 1480-1519 4. Borgia, Cesare, 1476?-1507 5. Political corruption 6. Ambition 7. Power 8. Popes 9. Siblings 10. Art, Italian 11. Family fortunes 12. European Renaissance 13. Nobility 14. Italian history 15. Italy 16. Renaissance (1300-1600) 17. 15th century 18. 16th century 19. Age of exploration (1419-1610) 20. History writing — Renaissance — Europe 21. History writing — Europe — Italy 22. Life stories — People in history — Famous families

LC 2020275788

Corruption, incest, ruthless megalomania, avarice and vicious cruelty—all have been associated with the name Borgia. But the family which produced corrupt popes, depraved princes and poisoners would also produce a saint. Strathern believes that, in order to understand the Borgias, one must understand the world which enabled them to flourish: the Renaissance.—adapted from jacket.

"Highly recommended for readers interested in the drama surrounding the Borgias that spurred a number of scandalous rumors that continue to circulate today." —*Library Journal*

Includes bibliographic sources (pages 343-361) and index.

945.091 Reign of Victor Emmanuel III, 1900-1946

Mazzeo, Tilar J.
Sisters in Resistance: How a German Spy, a Banker's Wife, and Mussolini's Daughter Outwitted the Nazis. Tilar J. Mazzeo. Grand Central Publishing 2022. 352 p.
ISBN 9781538735268
Grades: Adult **945.091**

1. Ciano, Edda Mussolini, Contessa 2. Purwin, Hilde, 1919-2010 3. Ciano, Galeazzo, conte, 1903-1944 4. Espionage 5. Intelligence service 6. Women spies 7. Political prisoners 8. Anti-Nazi movement 9. Married men 10. Undercover operations 11. Diary writing 12. War crimes 13. Fascism 14. World War II 15. Politics and government 16. German occupation, World War II 17. Italian history 18. Italy 19. Between the Wars (1918-1939) 20. Life stories — Law and order — Spies and secret agents 21. Life stories — Facing adversity — War and oppression — Hostages and POWs 22. History writing — Wars and conflicts — Resistance — World War II

LC 2021053690

In 1944, Benito Mussolini's daughter, Edda, gave Hitler and her father an ultimatum: Release her husband, Galeazzo Ciano, from prison, or risk her leaking her husband's journals to the press. To avoid the peril of exposing Nazi lies, Hitler and Mussolini hunted for the diaries for months, determined to destroy them. Hilde Beetz, a German spy, was deployed to seduce Ciano to learn the diaries' location and take them from Edda. As the seducer became the seduced, Hilde converted as a double agent, joining forces with Edda to save Ciano from execution.

When this failed, Edda fled to Switzerland with Hilde's daring assistance to keep Ciano's final wish: to see the diaries published for use by the Allies.

"New York Times best-selling author Mazzeo (Irena's Children) reveals that three Sisters in Resistance—a German spy, an American socialite, and Mussolini's daughter—risked their lives to hand over the secret diaries of Italy's jailed former foreign minister, Galeazzo Ciano, to the Allies." —*Library Journal*

Includes bibliographical references and index.

945.093 Italy, San Marino, Vatican City, Malta — 2000-

Hooper, John
The **Italians**. John Hooper. Viking Press 2015. 336 p.
ISBN 9780525428077
Grades: Adult **945.093**

1. Italian people 2. National characteristics, Italian 3. Italy 4. History writing — Europe — Italy

LC 2014038474

If you love all things Italian and wish you knew more about the country and its people, the Italians makes an offer you can't refuse. This entertaining book explains what makes Italians unique, and it covers a wide range of topics well, from Italy's storied beginnings, ties to religion, and the roots of the mafia to its beautiful land, delicious food, and intriguing regional differences. Written by British journalist John Hooper, who's lived in Italy for years, this book may prove especially intriguing for those of Italian ancestry.

"Few countries,' writes the author, 'Are as comprehensively associated with happiness as Italy. Just the mention of its name brings to mind sunny days, blue skies, glittering seas; delicious, comforting food; good-looking, well-dressed people; undulating hills topped with cypress trees; museums crammed with much of the best of Western art.' What's not to love? A thoroughly researched, well-written, ageless narrative of a fascinating people." —*Kirkus*

945.5 Tuscany

Strathern, Paul
The **Medici**: *Power, Money, and Ambition in the Italian Renaissance*. Paul Strathern. Pegasus Books 2016. 464 p.
ISBN 9781605989662
Grades: Adult **945.5**

1. Medici, House of 2. European Renaissance 3. Art patrons 4. Art, Italian 5. Artists 6. Power 7. Renaissance (1300-1600) 8. History writing — Renaissance — Europe 9. History writing — Europe — Italy 10. Life stories — People in history — Famous families

LC 2017304214

One of the most influential families in history, the Medici dominated Florence and much of Europe for several generations, promoting the arts and sciences at the height of the Renaissance and transforming the economy through their banking system. In this detailed and engaging book, author Paul Strathern traces the origins, rise, and eventual collapse of this dynasty. He recounts the lives of individual family members, both great and inconsequential, as well as the artists and scientists they sponsored. If you enjoy fiction or nonfiction about the Renaissance, give this enthralling history a try.

"A fantastically comprehensive history covering the breadth of the great learning, art, politics, and religion of the period." —*Kirkus*

945.6 Central Italy and Vatican City

Addis, Ferdinand
The **Eternal City**: *A History of Rome*. Ferdinand Addis. Pegasus Books 2018. 648 p.
ISBN 9781681775425
Grades: Adult **945.6**

1. Capitals (Cities) 2. Civilization 3. Ancient Rome 4. History writing — Ancient — Rome 5. History writing — Europe — Italy

PUBLIC LIBRARY CORE COLLECTION: NONFICTION
Twentieth Edition

LC Bl2018188542

A historian describes the history of Rome through its most dramatic moments, including the city's mythic founding in 753 BC, the murder of Caesar, the coronation of Charlemagne and the painting of the Sistine Chapel.

"The author's methodical yet swiftly flowing presentation yields an excellent and valuable one-volume treatment of the many-faceted tale of the Eternal City, a widely appealing achievement that deserves a place in all public libraries." —Booklist

Hughes, Robert
Rome: A Personal, Visual and Cultural History. Robert Hughes. Weidenfeld & Nicolson 2011. 534 p, 32 p. of plates : Illustration; Color; Portrait
ISBN 9780297844648
Grades: Adult   945.6
1. Civilization 2. Rome, Italy 3. Ancient Rome 4. History writing — Europe — Italy 5. Adult books for young adults

LC Oc2009059681

Prizewinning writer and critic's dazzling biography of the Eternal City.

"The author gives us a guided tour through the city in its many incarnations, excavating the geologic layers of its cultural past and creating an indelible portrait of a city in love with spectacle and power . The reader need not agree with Mr. Hughes's acerbic assessments or even be interested in Rome as a destination on the map to relish this volume, so captivating is his narrative. Although his book is a biography of Rome, it is also an acutely written historical essay informed by his wide-ranging knowledge of art, architecture and classical literature, and a thought-provoking meditation on how gifted artists (like Bernini and Michelangelo) and powerful politicians and church leaders (like Augustus, Mussolini and Pope Sixtus V) can reshape the map and mood of a city." —*New York Times Book Review*

Includes bibliographical references (p. [488]-498) and index.

Kneale, Matthew
Rome: A History in Seven Sackings. Matthew Kneale. Simon & Schuster 2018. 432 p.
ISBN 9781501191091
Grades: Adult   945.6
1. Military art and science 2. Natural disasters 3. Military campaigns 4. Battles 5. Armies 6. Military strategy 7. Military history 8. Italian history 9. Rome, Italy 10. History writing — Wars and conflicts

LC 2017045287

A novelist offers a nonfiction history of the Eternal City by focusing on seven moments of crisis and catastrophe, including fires, floods, earthquakes and most epically, attacks and invasions from roving armies.

945.8 Sicily and adjacent islands

Norwich, John Julius
Sicily. John Julius Norwich. Random House 2015. 416 p.
ISBN 9780812995176
Grades: Adult   945.8
1. Italian history 2. Sicily, Italy 3. History writing — Europe — Italy

LC 2015007371

A history of Sicily analyzes its influence on world events and culture, profiling its remarkable leaders, its Crusades-era rise to a multicultural trading hub and the evolution of the Mafia.

"This excellent, informative source on natural features, art and architecture, and regional lifestyles is not to be missed by armchair travelers, history lovers, and fans of Norwich's previous works." —*Library Journal*

Includes bibliographical references and index.

946 Spain, Andorra, Gibraltar, Portugal

Fuentes, Carlos
The Buried Mirror: Reflections on Spain and the New World. Carlos Fuentes. Houghton Mifflin 1992. 399 p. : Illustration; Color
ISBN 9780395924990
Grades: 11 12 Adult   946
1. Culture 2. Colonies 3. Civilization 4. Spain 5. Latin America 6. History writing — Latin America

LC 91034312

An exploration of Spanish culture in Spain and the Americas traces the social, political, and economic forces that created that culture.

"Every page in this lapidary essay offers profound insight into the Spanish American psyche." —*Library Journal*

Includes bibliographical references (p. 366-384) and index.

Hughes, Robert
Barcelona. Robert Hughes. Knopf 1992. xi, 573 p. : Illustration
ISBN 9780394580272
Grades: Adult   946
1. Arts 2. Architecture 3. Spain 4. Barcelona, Spain 5. Arts and Entertainment — Architecture 6. History writing — Europe — Spain

LC 91053179

The author of the Fatal Shore links 1,500 years of Catalan history with the architecture, painting, sculpture, music, and poetry of Barcelona to pay tribute to the intense accomplishments of the Catalunya culture.

Links 1,500 years of Catalan history with the architecture, painting, sculpture, music, and poetry of Barcelona to pay tribute to the accomplishments of Catalunya culture.

"Hughes's lengthy and thoroughly researched narrative lucidly delineates those historical factors generating the intense cultural nationalism of Spain's Catalonia and its great metropolis." —*Library Journal*

Includes bibliographical references (p. 543-552) and index.

Kurlansky, Mark
The Basque History of the World. Mark Kurlansky. Walker 1999. xii, 387 p. : Illustration; Map
ISBN 9780802713490
Grades: Adult   946
1. Basques 2. Ethnic groups 3. Basque Provinces 4. Spain 5. History writing — Europe — Spain 6. History writing — Microhistory

LC 99026808

Booklist Editors' Choice, 1999; Library Journal Best Books, 1999.

A history of the Basque people of Spain speculates on the origins of this enigmatic group of Europeans whose language and culture have long baffled anthropologists.

"This book traces the history of the Basques from their mysterious origins to their politically fraught existence in this century. Kurlansky shows how Basques, famed for their geographic and linguistic isolation, have played significant roles in world history-as mercenaries in ancient Greece, whalers in the Middle Ages, explorers in the Americas, and even cautious supporters of modern European integration." —*The New Yorker*

Includes bibliographical references (p. 362-372) and index.

Preston, Paul
A People Betrayed: A History of Corruption, Political Incompetence and Social Division in Modern Spain. Paul Preston. Liveright Publishing Corporation 2020. 752 p.
ISBN 9780871408686
Grades: Adult   946
1. Franco, Francisco, 1892-1975 2. Political corruption 3. Fascism 4. Politics and government 5. Spanish history 6. Spain 7. 20th century 8. History writing — Europe — Spain

LC 2020012133

ESSENTIAL AND RECOMMENDED TITLES
946.08 Spain — 1931-

Nowhere does the ceaseless struggle to maintain democracy in the face of political corruption come more alive than in Paul Preston's magisterial history of modern Spain.

"Likely to be the go-to history of modern Spain for many years to come." —*Kirkus*

Includes bibliographical references and index.

Stewart, Chris
Driving Over Lemons: An Optimist in Spain. Chris Stewart. Vintage Departures 2001. 249 p. : Illustration; Map (Driving over lemons, 1)
ISBN 9780375709159
Grades: Adult   **946**
1. Stewart, Chris, 1951- 2. Rural life 3. Sheep ranches 4. Families 5. Interpersonal relations 6. Expatriates 7. Farm life 8. Social life and customs 9. Spain 10. Travel Writing — Living Abroad 11. Travel Writing — Europe
LC Bl2006027328

A bestseller in England, this warm, funny account of a British family's attempt to make a home in southern Spain follows the first drummer for the rock band Genesis as he heads for Andalucia with his wife and kids.

"The ability to write hilarious travelogues featuring excruciating scenes of discomfort may well be a {British national characteristic. It's certainly possessed by Chris Stewart." —*New York Times Book Review*

Originally published: New York : Pantheon Books, c1999.

946.08 Spain — 1931-

Tremlett, Giles
Ghosts of Spain: Travels Through Spain and Its Silent Past. Giles Tremlett. Walker & Co. 2007. 386 p.
ISBN 9780802715746
Grades: Adult   **946.08**
1. Tremlett, Giles 2. Social life and customs 3. Voyages and travels 4. Spanish history 5. Spain 6. 20th century 7. History writing — Europe — Spain
LC Bl2006029008

An odyssey through Spain's painful recent past examines the causes and consequences of the Spanish Civil War, as well as its repercussions in the lives of modern-day Spaniards, and offers observations on other elements of Spanish life.

Includes index; Originally published: London : Faber and Faber, 2006.

946.081 Spain — Period of Second Republic, 1931-1939

Hochschild, Adam
Spain in Our Hearts: Americans in the Spanish Civil War, 1936/1939. Adam Hochschild. Houghton Mifflin Harcourt 2016. 448 p.
ISBN 9780547973180
Grades: Adult   **946.081**
1. Revolutions 2. Dictatorship 3. Democracy 4. American people in Europe 5. Civil war 6. Social change 7. Spanish Civil War, Spain, 1936-1939 8. Politics and government 9. Spanish history 10. Spain 11. 1930s 12. History writing — Wars and conflicts — Civil Wars 13. History writing — Europe — Spain
LC 2015037244

From 1936-39, news about the Spanish Civil War fired the imaginations of young men and women in other parts of the world, especially the U.S. and Britain. Thousands went to Spain to fight with the underdog Republicans, who were backed by the Soviet Union but ill-equipped and underfunded. Germany, Italy, and anti-Communist businessmen guaranteed the eventual success of Generalissimo Francisco Franco's Nationalists. In Spain in Our Hearts, acclaimed historian Adam Hochschild highlights the war's complexities and explores the personal perspectives of Americans who participated in the fighting.

Preston, Paul
The Spanish Holocaust: Inquisition and Extermination in Twentieth-century Spain. Paul Preston. W. W. Norton & Co, Inc. 2012. 464 p.
ISBN 9780393064766
Grades: Adult   **946.081**
1. Franco, Francisco, 1892-1975 2. Revolutionaries 3. Revolutions 4. Coups d'etat 5. Resistance to government 6. Armed forces and politics 7. Dictatorship 8. Democracy 9. Social change 10. Spanish Civil War, Spain, 1936-1939 11. Politics and government 12. Spanish history 13. Spain 14. 1930s 15. History writing — Wars and conflicts — Civil Wars 16. History writing — Europe — Spain

Describes the atrocities committed during the reign of General Francisco Franco, who executed tens of thousands of "non-persons" and abused women and children under a belief system comprised of eugenics, terror, domination and mind control.

Watling, Sarah
Tomorrow Perhaps the Future: Writers, Outsiders, and the Spanish Civil War. Sarah Watling. Alfred A. Knopf 2023. 320 p.
ISBN 9780593319666
Grades: Adult   **946.081**
1. Civil war 2. Women authors 3. Women artists 4. Women political activists 5. Anti-fascism 6. Volunteers 7. Expatriate women 8. Marginalized women 9. Freedom 10. Literary criticism 11. Spanish history 12. History writing — Wars and conflicts — Revolutions 13. Life stories — Arts and culture 14. Life stories — Identity — Gender 15. Arts and Entertainment — Writing and Publishing — Literary criticism
LC 2022049910

It was the Spanish Civil War of 1936, surprisingly, that Sarah Watling found herself drawn to when confounded by the tumultuous politics of our present day. This was a conflict that galvanized tens of thousands of volunteers from around the world to join the fight. Watling sifts through archives for lost journals, letters, and manifestos, discovering a trove of work by women writers and outsiders who had often been relegated to the shadows of history. From a variety of backgrounds and beliefs, these women saw history coming, and they went out to meet it. Yet the reality was far from simple.

"British historian Watling, author of the Olivier Sisters (2019), illuminates a varied group of women who devoted their talents and passion—and, in some cases, gave their lives—to telling the world about what was happening during the Spanish Civil War." —*Booklist*

Includes bibliographical references and index.

947 Russia and neighboring east European countries

Applebaum, Anne
Iron Curtain: The Crushing of Eastern Europe, 1945-1956. Anne Applebaum. Doubleday 2012. 640 p.
ISBN 9780385515696
Grades: Adult   **947**
1. Political culture 2. Political persecution 3. Communist countries 4. Communism 5. International relations 6. Politics and government 7. Soviet Union 8. Eastern Europe 9. 20th century 10. History writing — Europe — Eastern Europe 11. History writing — Communism — Europe — Russia
LC 2012022086

Cundill Prize in History, 2013; New York Times Notable Book, 2012; National Book Award for Nonfiction finalist, 2012.

Discusses the creation of the Communist regimes that took hold in Eastern Europe at the end of World War II and describes what daily life was like in these countries.

"A dark but hopeful chronicle that shows how even humanity's worst can fracture and fall." —*Kirkus*

Includes bibliographical references and index.

Figes, Orlando
The Crimean War: A History. Orlando Figes. Metropolitan Books/Henry Holt and Co. 2011. 592 p.
ISBN 9780805074604
Grades: Adult   **947**

1. Crimean War, 1853-1856 2. War 3. 19th century 4. History writing — Wars and conflicts — Crimean War

LC 2010023152

From "the great storyteller of modern Russian historians" comes the definitive account of the Crimean War, a forgotten war that shaped the modern age. Figes reconstructs the first full conflagration of modernity, a global industrialized struggle fought with unusual ferocity and incompetence.

"This is a complex tale, told vividly by Mr Figes. Perhaps it should serve as a healthy cold shower for any modern civilisational warrior who sets out to present the course of history as a simple tug-of-war between Christianity and Islam." —*The Economist*

Published simultaneously in the United Kingdom by Penguin Books, London—T.P. verso; Includes bibliographical references and index.

★ *The Story of Russia*. Orlando Figes. Metropolitan Books 2022. 320 p.
ISBN 9781250796899
Grades: Adult   947

1. Ideology 2. Political culture 3. Aristocracy 4. Despotism 5. Russia 6. Soviet Union 7. History writing — Europe — Russia

Based on a lifetime of scholarship, this fresh approach to the thousand years of Russia's history discusses the national mythologies and imperial ideologies that have shaped how Russians think about their past and how the country thinks and acts today.

"A lucid, astute text that unpacks the myths of Russian history to help explain present-day motivations and actions." —*Kirkus*

Garrels, Anne

Putin Country: A Journey into the Real Russia. Anne Garrels. Farrar, Straus and Giroux 2015. 288 p.
ISBN 9780374247720
Grades: Adult   947

1. Garrels, Anne, 1951-2022 2. Putin, Vladimir Vladimirovich, 1952- 3. Political culture 4. Subcultures 5. Social life and customs 6. Voyages and travels 7. Russia 8. Interviews 9. History writing — Europe — Russia 10. Politics and global affairs — World politics — Europe

LC 2015034644

What is life in Russia really like and why do Russians love Vladimir Putin? Anne Garrels, formerly an NPR correspondent based in Moscow, answers these complicated questions using a variety of people (from taxi drivers to doctors) in the Chelyabinsk region as a microcosm. Having visited the area (which is located far from Moscow) for two decades, she not only offers a journalistic collection that documents the differences in everyday lives over time, but also describes how growing freedoms have not always been beneficial, and shares what Russians really think of the West.

"This book will be of interest to general readers seeking to learn more about the country that exists beyond Moscow and St. Petersburg, as well as those wanting to gain better insight into its interior political and social conditions." —*Library Journal*

Massie, Robert K.

The Romanovs: The Final Chapter. Robert K. Massie. Random House 1995. 308 p. : Illustration
ISBN 9780394580487
Grades: 11 12 Adult   947

1. Nicholas II, Emperor of Russia, 1868-1918 2. Alexandra, Empress, consort of Nicholas II, Emperor of Russia, 1872-1918 3. Romanov, House of 4. Olga, Grand Duchess of Russia, 1895-1918 5. Mariia Nikolaevna, Grand Duchess, daughter of Nicholas II, Emperor of Russia, 1899-1918 6. Tatiana Nikolaevna, Grand Duchess, daughter of Nicholas II, Emperor of Russia, 1897-1918 7. Anastasia Nikolaevna, Grand Duchess, daughter of Nicholas II, Emperor of Russia, 1901-1918 8. Royal pretenders 9. Royal houses 10. Russian history 11. Romanov Dynasty (1613-1917) 12. History writing — Europe — Russia 13. History writing — Historical mysteries

LC 95004718

The story behind the Romanov murders and the investigation to find their hidden bodies describes Lenin's cover-up and the roles played by such figures as James Baker, Boris Yeltsin, and Prince Philip.

"With memorable sketches of the main participants and a skillful discussion of the scientific evidence, Massie pulls together a sprawling theme and infuses it with quiet drama." —*Kirkus*

Includes bibliographical references and index.

Mikanowski, Jacob

★ *Goodbye, Eastern Europe: An Intimate History of a Divided Land*. Jacob Mikanowski. Pantheon Books 2023. 368 p.
ISBN 9781524748500
Grades: Adult   947

1. Mikanowski, Jacob 2. Countries 3. National characteristics 4. Regionalism 5. Imperialism 6. Geopolitics 7. Sovereignty 8. Civilization 9. Culture 10. Multiculturalism 11. European history 12. Eastern Europe 13. History writing — Europe — Eastern Europe 14. Society and culture — Ethnic studies 15. Life stories — People in history 16. Debut title

LC 2022037756

This history and celebration of the cultures of Eastern Europe chronicles a thousand years of war, strife and bloodshed, from pre-Christianity to the fall of Communism and the birth of modern nation-states.

Eastern Europe, the moniker, has gone out of fashion since the fall of the Soviet Union. Ask someone now, and they might tell you that Eastern Europe is a place that barely exists at all, except in cultural memory. Yet it remains a powerful marker of identity for many, with a fragmented and wide history, defined by memories of hardship and suffering. Jacob Mikanowski presents a masterful narrative about a place that has survived the brink of being forgotten, offering a kaleidoscopic tour recounting the rise and fall of great empires, the dawn of the modern era, the ravages of Fascism and Communism, as well as Capitalism, the birth of the modern nation-state, and more.

"An informative study of a part of the world too often ignored, told with vigor, color, and authority." —*Kirkus*

Includes bibliographical references and index.

Miles, Jonathan

St. Petersburg: Madness, Murder, and Art on the Banks of the Neva. Jonathan Miles. Pegasus Books 2018. 560 p.
ISBN 9781681776767
Grades: Adult   947

1. Cities and towns 2. Political intrigue 3. Social classes 4. Russian history 5. St. Petersburg, Russia 6. History writing — Europe — Russia

From Peter the Great to Putin, this is the unforgettable story of St Petersburg—one of the most magical, menacing, and influential cities in the world.

Plokhy, Serhii

Lost Kingdom: The Quest for Empire and the Making of the Russian Nation, from 1470 to the Present. Serhii Plokhy. Basic Books 2017. 400 p.
ISBN 9780465098491
Grades: Adult   947

1. Nationalism 2. Imperialism 3. Russian history 4. Soviet Union history 5. European history 6. Russia 7. Soviet Union 8. Ukraine 9. Belarus 10. History writing — Europe — Russia

LC 2017021215

Examines the history of Russian imperialism and nationalism from the end of the Mongol rule to today.

"A timely work of impeccable research that elucidates the Russian impulse toward regaining lost lands under a powerful myth of origins." —*Kirkus*

Includes bibliographical references and index.

Riasanovsky, Nicholas V.

A History of Russia. Nicholas V. Riasanovsky, Mark D. Steinberg. Oxford University Press 2018. xx 658 p. : Illustration; Map; Color
ISBN 9780190645588
Grades: 11 12 Adult   947

1. Social life and customs 2. Russian history 3. Soviet Union history 4. Russia 5. History writing — Europe — Russia

LC 98056640

ESSENTIAL AND RECOMMENDED TITLES
947.08 Russia since 1855

Now extensively revised in this ninth edition, a History of Russia covers the entire span of the country's history, from ancient times to the post-communist present. Keeping with the hallmark of the text, Riasanovsky and Steinberg examine all aspects of Russia's history—political, international, military, economic, social, and cultural—with a commitment to objectivity, fairness, and balance, and to reflecting recent research and new trends in scholarly interpretation.

Maps on lining papers; Includes bibliographical references (pages B-1-B-34) and index.

Sebag-Montefiore, Simon
The Romanovs: 1613-1918. by Simon Sebag Montefiore. Alfred A. Knopf 2016. 816 p.
ISBN 9780307266521
Grades: Adult   947
1. Romanov, House of 2. Royal houses 3. Monarchy 4. Rulers 5. Russian history 6. Russia 7. Biographies 8. History writing — Europe — Russia
LC 2015046026

The acclaimed author of Young Stalin and Jerusalem gives readers an accessible, lively account—based in part on new archival material—of the extraordinary men and women who ruled Russia for three centuries.

"Montefiore's compassionate and incisive portraits of the Romanov rulers and their retinues, his liberal usage of contemporary diaries and correspondence, and his flair for the dramatic produce a narrative that effortlessly holds the reader's interest and attention despite its imposing length." —*Publishers Weekly*

This is a Borzoi Book; Includes bibliographical references.

947.08 Russia since 1855

Figes, Orlando
A People's Tragedy: The Russian Revolution, 1891-1924. Orlando Figes. Viking 1997. 960 p.
ISBN 9780140243642
Grades: 11 12 Adult   947.08
1. Lenin, Vladimir Il'ich, 1870-1924 2. Kerensky, Alexander, 1881-1970 3. Revolutions 4. Revolutionaries 5. Social change 6. Russian history 7. Soviet Union history 8. 1910s 9. 1920s 10. Russian Revolution and Civil War (1917-1921) 11. Romanov Dynasty (1613-1917) 12. History writing — Wars and conflicts — Russian Revolution
LC 96036761
ALA Notable Book, 1998; Los Angeles Times Book Prize for History, 1997; New York Times Notable Book, 1997.

Covers Russian history from the end of the nineteenth century to the death of Lenin, and explores how Russian pre-revolution social forces were violently erased and replaced.

"The author has produced an engagingly written and well-researched book that will leave few readers with any doubts that the Bolsheviks, and especially their leader, Lenin, were ruthless killers, willing to sacrifice millions of lives for the sake of power and their own personal ambitions." —*New York Times Book Review*

Includes bibliographical references and index.

Rappaport, Helen
The Race to Save the Romanovs: The Truth Behind the Secret Plans to Rescue the Russian Imperial Family. Helen Rappaport. St Martins Pr 2018. 464 p.
ISBN 9781250151216
Grades: Adult   947.08
1. Romanov, House of 2. Royal houses 3. Massacres 4. Rescues 5. Murder 6. Revolutions 7. Assassination 8. Political violence 9. True Crime — Historical Crime 10. History writing — Europe — Russia
LC 2018005136

Published to mark the 100th anniversary of the massacre, a heavily researched investigation into the international efforts to save the Romanov family explores why every measure failed and who was responsible.

"Relying on fresh archival material, Rappaport dispels some mystery about secret Western rescue plans—that is to say, she clarifies that they were nonexistent. Regarding myriad Russian monarchist rescue plots, she admits that rumors and misinformation make unraveling the truth an impossible task. This is a well-researched account of a colorful, suspenseful, and tragic series of events." —*Publishers Weekly*

Zygar, Mikhail
The Empire Must Die: Russia's Revolutionary Collapse, 1900-1917. Mikhail Zygar. PublicAffairs 2017. 256 pages
ISBN 9781610398312
Grades: Adult   947.08
1. Romanov, House of 2. Liberalism 3. Intellectual life 4. Financial crises 5. Elite (Social sciences) 6. Freedom 7. Inequality 8. Class struggle 9. Politics and government 10. Russian history 11. Russia 12. Belle Epoque (1871-1914) 13. First World War era (1914-1918) 14. Russian Revolution and Civil War (1917-1921) 15. Romanov Dynasty (1613-1917) 16. History writing — Europe — Russia
LC Bl2017045807

A vivid portrayal of Russia's brief and exotic experiment with liberalism and cultural openness in the years before the Communist Revolution and the deaths of the Tsar and his family reveals how the period marked a blossoming of artistic expression and open political views.

"A vivid, character-driven reconstruction of the period leading up to the overthrow of the Romanovs and the birth of modern Russia." —*Kirkus*

947.084 Russia — 1914-1991

Amis, Martin
Koba the Dread: Laughter and the Twenty Million. Martin Amis. Vintage International 2003. VIII, 306 p. : Illustration
ISBN 9781400032204
Grades: Adult   947.084
1. Terrorism 2. State-sponsored terrorism 3. Political persecution 4. Politics and government 5. Soviet Union 6. 20th century 7. History writing — Europe — Russia
LC 2003053764

The author describes the role of communism in mid-twentieth-century thought and its influence on his own family as he reflects on Stalin, his impact on the Soviet Union, and his legacy.

Amis create{s a compelling narrative, summarizing vast amounts of information and presenting it in a lucid, accessible form.New York Times.

Includes index; Originally published: New York : Talk Miramax Books, 2002.

Beevor, Antony
Russia: Revolution and Civil War, 1917-1921. Antony Beevor. Viking Press 2022. 592 p.
ISBN 9780593493878
Grades: Adult   947.084
1. Civil war 2. Revolutions 3. War 4. Soviet Union history 5. Russian history 6. Russia 7. 20th century 8. 1910s 9. 1920s 10. Russian Revolution and Civil War (1917-1921) 11. Romanov Dynasty (1613-1917) 12. History writing — Wars and conflicts — Civil Wars 13. History writing — Europe — Russia 14. History writing — Europe — Eastern Europe

Drawing upon the most up-to-date scholarship and archival research, this gripping narrative forms the complete picture of the conflict that reshaped Eastern Europe between 1917 and 1921, a struggle that became a world war by proxy, as told through the eyes of those individuals who experienced it firsthand. Map(s).

"Czar Nicholas II's abdication in 1917 created a 'Sudden vacuum of power' that enabled the Bolshevik takeover of Russia, according to this tart history....Fine-grained yet fluidly written, this sweeping portrait illuminates the chaos and tragedy of Russian civil war." —*Publishers Weekly*

PUBLIC LIBRARY CORE COLLECTION: NONFICTION
Twentieth Edition

Hochschild, Adam
The Unquiet Ghost: Russians Remember Stalin. Adam Hochschild. Viking 1994. xxvii, 304 p. : Illustration; Map
ISBN 9780670840915
Grades: Adult   947.084
1. Stalin, Joseph, 1879-1953 2. Disappeared people 3. Soviet Union history 4. 20th century 5. History writing — Communism — Europe — Russia
LC 93027473

Explores how Russians—prison survivors, historians, concentration camp guards, and others—are healing the wounds inflicted by long-repressed memories of the former leader and recounts the efforts of many to locate or find out what happened to relatives who disappeared during Stalin's tyrannical tenure.

"In this look at Stalin's legacy the author visits the ruins of the old prison camps of Kazakhstan and Kolyma, digs through the K.G.B. archives and spends a night at Stalin's seaside retreat. Most important, he interviews camp survivors, camp guards and the children of both. The questions he asks are of universal significance. By asking these questions while traveling through today's Russia, Mr. Hochschild effectively places Stalinism in a modern context." —*New York Times Book Review*

Includes bibliographical references (p. 289-296) and index.

Longo, Matthew
The Picnic: A Dream of Freedom and the Collapse of the Iron Curtain. Matthew Longo. W W Norton & CO Inc 2023. 288 p.
ISBN 9780393540772
Grades: Adult   947.084
1. Iron Curtain 2. Cold War 3. Freedom 4. Boundaries 5. Borderlands 6. Picnicking 7. Defectors 8. Political refugees 9. Hungary 10. East Germany 11. 1980s 12. Oral histories 13. History Writing — Cold War
Orwell Prize, 2024.

Chronicles and examines the collective passion for freedom that shook the world toward the end of the Cold War.

"This captivating narrative brings an underreported Cold War turning point into focus." —*Publishers Weekly*

McMeekin, Sean
The Russian Revolution: A New History. Sean McMeekin. Basic Books 2017. 384 p.
ISBN 9780465039906
Grades: Adult   947.084
1. Revolutions 2. Communism 3. Social classes 4. Marxism 5. War 6. Peasantry 7. Class struggle 8. Social change 9. Soviet Union history 10. Russian Revolution and Civil War (1917-1921) 11. History writing — Communism — Europe — Russia 12. History writing — Wars and conflicts — Russian Revolution
LC 2016058361

Discusses how the Russian Revolution changed the course of world history in the early part of the 20th century, describing how the Bolsheviks came into power, ending Romanov rule and killing over 20 million Russians in the process.

"McMeekin effectively shows how easily one man could undermine the foundations of a nation, and he makes the revolution comprehensible as he exposes the deviousness of its leader." —*Kirkus*

Includes bibliographical references and index.

Medvedev, Roy Aleksandrovich
Let History Judge: The Origins and Consequences of Stalinism. Roy Medvedev. Columbia University Press 1989. xxi, 903 p.
ISBN 9780231063500
Grades: 11 12 Adult   947.084
1. Stalin, Joseph, 1879-1953 2. Political atrocities 3. Politics and government 4. Soviet Union 5. 20th century 6. History writing — Communism — Europe — Russia
LC 89000758

A translation of the Soviet scholar's definitive study of Stalin and his era.

"Never have Stalin's crimes against humanity been more forcefully or more thoroughly documented than in . {this book, which distills firsthand testimonies of the mass arrests, torture, imprisonment and executions that befell millions of innocent Soviet citizens." —*Publishers Weekly*

Includes bibliographical references and index.

Mieville, China
October: The Story of the Russian Revolution. China Mieville. Verso 2017. 304 p.
ISBN 9781784782771
Grades: Adult   947.084
1. Lenin, Vladimir Il'ich, 1870-1924 2. Trotsky, Leon, 1879-1940 3. Kerensky, Alexander, 1881-1970 4. Kornilov, Lavr Georgievich, 1870-1918 5. Revolutionaries 6. Communism 7. Socialists 8. Rebels 9. Coups d'etat 10. Political science 11. Soviet Union history 12. Russian history 13. Russian Revolution and Civil War (1917-1921) 14. 20th century 15. History writing — Wars and conflicts — Russian Revolution
LC 2016051217

A new account of the Russian Revolution explores how the ongoing consequences of the political event created a story of drama, passion, and strangeness.

"Miville is an ideal guide through this complex historical moment, giving agency to obscure and better-known participants alike, and depicting the revolution as both a tragically lost opportunity and an ongoing source of inspiration." —*Publishers Weekly*

Pipes, Richard
A Concise History of the Russian Revolution. Richard Pipes. Knopf 1995. xvii, 431 p. : Illustration; Map
ISBN 9780679422778
Grades: 11 12 Adult   947.084
1. Revolutions 2. War 3. World politics 4. Soviet Union history 5. Russian history 6. 1910s 7. 1920s 8. Russian Revolution and Civil War (1917-1921) 9. Romanov Dynasty (1613-1917) 10. History writing — Wars and conflicts — Russian Revolution
LC 95003127

Looks at the decay of the tsarist empire and the causes of the Revolution, discusses the aims of the Bolshevik party, and recounts the major events of the conflict.

"Forcefully showing why the 70-year-old Communist experiment failed {Pipes provides the nonacademic reader with accurate historical events in a highly readable format." —*Library Journal*

Abridged version of the Russian Revolution; Includes bibliographical references (p. [415]-416) and index.

The Russian Revolution. Richard Pipes. Vintage Books 1991. xxiv, 944 p. : Illustration; Map
ISBN 9780679736608
Grades: Adult   947.084
1. Russian history 2. Soviet Union history 3. Russian Revolution and Civil War (1917-1921) 4. Romanov Dynasty (1613-1917) 5. History writing — Europe — Russia
LC 91050008

Looks at the decay of the Czarist regime and the causes of the Revolution, discusses the aims of the Bolshevik party, and recounts the major events of the conflict.

Includes index; Originally published: New York : Knopf, 1990.

Radzinskii, Edvard
Stalin: The First In-depth Biography Based on Explosive New Documents from Russia's Secret Archives. Edvard Radzinsky; translated by H.T. Willetts. Doubleday 1997. xii, 607 p. : Illustration
ISBN 9780385479547
Grades: 11 12 Adult   947.084
1. Stalin, Joseph, 1879-1953 2. Heads of state 3. Soviet Union history 4. 20th century 5. Biographies 6. History writing — Europe — Russia 7. Life stories — Politics — Politicians
LC BL 99794376

Presents a new version of the life of the Soviet dictator based on recently recovered documents.

ESSENTIAL AND RECOMMENDED TITLES
947.085 Russia — 1953-1991

"For this biography of the Soviet ruler the author has examined mountains of rare archival sources and interviewed many who lived through decades of Stalinist (mis)rule. The result is the best general biography of Stalin to date. Radzinsky strips away layer after layer of myth, falsehood, and enigma to produce a riveting portrait of a man whose primary role model was Ivan the Terrible." —*Library Journal*

Anchor Books imprint on spine; Reprint. Originally published: C1996; Includes bibliographical references (p. [585]-594) and index.

Reed, John
Ten Days That Shook the World. John Reed. Penguin Books 2007. xix, 351 p.
ISBN 9780141442129
Grades: Adult   **947.084**
1. Soviet Union history 2. Russian Revolution and Civil War (1917-1921) 3. History writing — Wars and conflicts — Russian Revolution
LC 78305844

Chronicles the events in Petrograd in November 1917, when Lenin and the Bolsheviks finally seized power, including speeches by leaders and quotes from everyday bystanders.

Originally published: New York : Boni & Liveright, 1919.

Slezkine, Yuri
The House of Government: A Saga of the Russian Revolution. Yuri Slezkine. Princeton University Press 2017. 1096 p.
ISBN 9780691176949
Grades: Adult   **947.084**
1. Communists 2. Apartment dwellers 3. Victims of state-sponsored terrorism 4. Political purges 5. Torture 6. Communities 7. Communism 8. Politics and government 9. Russia 10. Moscow, Russia 11. Soviet Union 12. 20th century 13. History writing — Communism — Europe — Russia
LC 2016049071

New York Times Notable Book, 2017.

On the 100th anniversary of the Russian Revolution, the epic story of an enormous apartment building where Communist true believers lived before their destruction.

"Slezkine aggregates mountains of detail for an enthralling account of the rise and fall of the revolutionary generation." —*Publishers Weekly*

Smith, Douglas
The Russian Job: The Forgotten Story of How America Saved the Soviet Union from Ruin. Douglas Smith. Farrar Straus & Giroux 2019. 320 p.
ISBN 9780374252960
Grades: Adult   **947.084**
1. Food relief 2. Famines 3. Humanitarian assistance 4. International relations 5. Soviet Union history 6. Soviet Union 7. United States 8. 1920s 9. History writing — Europe — Russia
LC 2019017677

The award-winning historian and author of Rasputin traces the little-known story of Herbert Hoover's American Relief Administration and its 1921 effort to save the newly formed Soviet Union from a devastating famine.

947.085 Russia — 1953-1991

Carlson, Peter
K Blows Top: A Cold War Comic Interlude Starring Nikita Khrushchev, America's Most Unlikely Tourist. Peter Carlson. PublicAffairs 2009. 352 p.
ISBN 9781586484972
Grades: Adult   **947.085**
1. Khrushchev, Nikita Sergeevich, 1894-1971 2. Cold War 3. Voyages and travels 4. Russian people in the United States 5. International relations 6. Soviet Union 7. United States 8. 1950s 9. History writing — Cold War
LC 2008039090

Recounts Khrushchev's 1959 trip across America against the backdrop of the Cold War and a capitalist America living under the shadow of the hydrogen bomb.

"Drawing on contemporary news reports, modern interviews, and memoirs written by some of the participants, [this is] . a story about a poorly educated but extraordinarily powerful man who became, for a brief time, a pop-culture icon. A fine example of popular history at its most engaging—anecdotal but informative and written with great feeling for the comedic side of current events." —*Booklist*

Includes bibliographical references and index.

Gorbachev, Mikhail
On My Country and the World. Mikhail Gorbachev. Columbia University Press 2000. 300 p.
ISBN 9780231115148
Grades: Adult   **947.085**
1. Gorbachev, Mikhail, 1931-2022 2. World politics 3. Russian history 4. Soviet Union history 5. 20th century 6. History writing — Europe — Eastern Europe
LC 99031273

Looks at the October Revolution, the Cold War, Lenin, Stalin, Yeltsin, and the future of Russia, and argues that the development of socialism was cut short by Stalin.

Includes index.

Remnick, David
Lenin's Tomb: The Last Days of the Soviet Empire. David Remnick. Random House 1993. xii, 576 p, 16 p. of plates : Illustration
ISBN 9780679751250
Grades: 11 12 Adult   **947.085**
1. Gorbachev, Mikhail, 1931-2022 2. Yeltsin, Boris Nikolayevich, 1931-2007 3. Sakharov, Andrei, 1921-1989 4. Glasnost 5. Perestroika 6. Economic policy 7. Governmental reform 8. Politics and government 9. Soviet Union 10. 1980s 11. 1990s 12. 20th century 13. History writing — Communism — Europe — Russia
LC 92056841

ALA Notable Book, 1994; Pulitzer Prize for General Nonfiction, 1994; National Book Critics Circle Award for Nonfiction finalist, 1993.

The Washington Post's Moscow correspondent chronicles the collapse of the Soviet empire, from the rise of glasnost, through the final lowering of the Soviet flag, to the start of the post-Communist age.

"This book is a record of almost four years beginning in 1988 when David Remnick, a Washington Post reporter, was assigned to Moscow. He argues convincingly that what did in the old Soviet leadership, right down through Mikhail Gorbachev, was its unending assault not only on people but on memory. By making a secret of history, it made its people increasingly distracted, and desperate, until they overthrew it." —*New York Times Book Review*

Sequel: Resurrection; Includes bibliographical references (p. [549]-552) and index.

Sebestyen, Victor
Revolution 1989: The Fall of the Soviet Empire. Victor Sebestyen. Pantheon Books 2009. 480 p.
ISBN 9780375425325
Grades: Adult   **947.085**
1. Cold War 2. Democracy 3. Socialism 4. Communism 5. Politics and government 6. Soviet Union 7. 1980s 8. 1990s 9. History writing — Communism — Europe — Russia 10. History writing — Cold War
LC 2009023045

Documents the collapse of the Soviet Union's European empires and the transition of each to independent states, drawing on interviews with everyday people and newly uncovered archival material to offer insight into 1989's rapid changes and the USSR's minimal resistance.

"Numerous books have come out that attempt to synthesize the compelling story of the fall of communism, but Revolution 1989 comes closest to being the essential volume. Sebestyen's elegant narrative lays out in crisp episodes what was happening in Russia, Bulgaria, East Germany, Hungary, Czechoslovakia, and Afghanistan throughout the tumultuous 1980s. His portrait of Gorbachev is particularly sharp and asks us to reconsider the Soviet leader's surprising role 20 years ago. As a refugee from Hungary in 1956, Sebestyen brings a personal touch to these historic moments." —*Daily Beast*

947.086 Russia — 1991-

Aleksievich, Svetlana
★ *Secondhand Time: The Last of the Soviets.* Svetlana Alexievich; translated by Bela Shayevich. Random House 2016. 512 p.
ISBN 9780399588808
Grades: Adult   947.086
1. Communism 2. Post-communism 3. Soviet Union 4. Russia 5. Oral histories 6. Translations — Russian to English 7. History writing — Communism — Europe — Russia 8. History writing — Europe — Eastern Europe
LC 2016005925
Booklist Editors' Choice, 2016; Los Angeles Times Book Prize for Current Interest, 2016; New York Times Notable Book, 2016.

Though it's too late to travel to the Soviet Union, which broke up in 1991, you can still visit via this moving oral history collection that provides an eye-opening look at the (pre- and post-) Soviet soul. Sharing the stories of a wide variety of people from across the vast country—ranging from before the end of communism to the beginnings of the new Russia and the rise of Putin—2015 Nobel Prize winner Svetlana Aleksievich provides a thorough, fascinating look at war, freedom, family, and more, giving voice to those who've seen so much upheaval.

"Journalist Alexievich (Voices from Chernobyl), who won the 2015 Nobel Prize in Literature, captures the heartache, excitement, and harsh realities of life at the end of the Soviet era and the birth of modern Russia. A collection of oral histories linked by topic, theme, and the author's own musings, this impassioned and critical study, originally published in Russian in 2013, documents the immense changes the Russian people underwent in the 1990s and 2000s. A must for historians, lay readers, and anyone who enjoys well-curated personal narratives. All readers will appreciate the revelations about Russia's turbulent transition and present cultural and political status." —*Library Journal*

First published in Russian in 2013.

Conradi, Peter J.
Who Lost Russia?: How the World Entered a New Cold War. Peter Conradi. Oneworld Publications Ltd. 2017. 400 p.
ISBN 9781786070418
Grades: Adult   947.086
1. Political culture 2. Ideology 3. Diplomacy 4. Diplomatic negotiations in international disputes 5. International relations 6. Russia 7. United States 8. Impartial writing 9. Politics and global affairs — World politics — Europe

When the Soviet Union collapsed on December 26, 1991, it looked like the start of a remarkable new era of peace and co-operation. Some even dared to declare the end of history, assuming all countries would converge on enlightenment values and liberal democracy. Nothing could be further from the truth. Russia emerged from the 1990s battered and humiliated; the parallels with Weimar Germany are striking.

"In this balanced and timely work, Sunday Times foreign editor Conradi (The Great Survivors) charts the complex and turbulent course of U.S.-Russia relations since the collapse of the U.S.S.R." —*Publishers Weekly*

Includes biliographical references and index.

Galeotti, Mark
A Short History of Russia: How the World's Largest Country Invented Itself, from the Pagans to Putin. Mark Galeotti. Hanover Square Press 2020. 224 p.
ISBN 9781335145703
Grades: Adult   947.086
1. Nationalism 2. Identity 3. International relations 4. Politics and government 5. Russian history 6. Russia 7. History writing — Europe — Russia 8. Politics and global affairs — World politics — Europe

Explores the epic and dramatic history of Russia through two intertwined issues—the way successive influences from beyond its borders have shaped the country and the way Russians came to terms with this influence.

"This is an accessible and illuminating summary of how modern Russia came to be." —*Publishers Weekly*

Gessen, Masha
The Future Is History: How Totalitarianism Reclaimed Russia. Masha Gessen. Riverhead Books 2017. 400 p.
ISBN 9781594634536
Grades: Adult   947.086
1. Despotism 2. Totalitarianism 3. Political persecution 4. Politics and government 5. Russia 6. History writing — Europe — Russia 7. Politics and global affairs — World politics — Europe
LC 2017014363
New York Times Notable Book, 2017; National Book Award for Nonfiction, 2017; Booklist Editors' Choice, 2017; National Book Critics Circle Award for Nonfiction finalist, 2017.

The award-winning Russian-American journalist and author of the best-selling the Man Without a Face traces how within the space of a generation, Russia has succumbed to a more virulent and resistant strain of autocracy as demonstrated by the experiences of four prototype individuals born at the once-presumed dawn of Russian democracy.

"A superb, alarming portrait of a government that exercises outsize influence in the modern world, at great human cost." —*Kirkus*

Includes bibliographical references and index.

Kasparov, Gary
Winter Is Coming: Why Vladimir Putin and the Enemies of the Free World Must Be Stopped. Garry Kasparov. PublicAffairs 2015. 208 p.
ISBN 9781610396202
Grades: Adult   947.086
1. Putin, Vladimir Vladimirovich, 1952- 2. World politics 3. Political leadership 4. International relations 5. Russia 6. United States 7. Politics and global affairs — World politics — Europe 8. History writing — Europe — Russia

A Russian former #1 ranked chess player explains why he has opposed Russian president Vladimir Putin all along and issues a call for taking a diplomatic and economic stand against him.

Khodorkovsky, Mikhail
The Russia Conundrum: How the West Fell for Putin's Power Gambit—and How to Fix It. Mikhail Khodorkovsky, with Martin Sixsmith. St. Martin's Press 2022. 352 p.
ISBN 9781250285591
Grades: Adult   947.086
1. Putin, Vladimir Vladimirovich, 1952- 2. International relations 3. World leaders 4. Political corruption 5. Geopolitics 6. Politics and government 7. Russia 8. History Writing — Europe — Russia 9. Politics and global affairs — World politics — Europe
LC 2022036635

Working as a pro-democracy campaigner in enforced exile, a former Kremlin insider, who was stripped of his wealth and imprisoned for speaking out against the corruption of Putin's regime, brings us the insider's battle to save his country's soul in order to pave the way for a better future.

"Authoritative, essential reading for anyone who wants to understand the frightening breadth and depth of Putin's methods." —*Kirkus*

Includes bibliographical references and index.

Politkovskaya, Anna
A Russian Diary: A Journalist's Final Account of Life, Corruption, and Death in Putin's Russia. Anna Politkovskaya; translated by Arch Tait; foreword by Scott Simon. Random House 2007. 369 p.
ISBN 9781400066827
Grades: Adult   947.086
1. Putin, Vladimir Vladimirovich, 1952- 2. Journalists 3. Political corruption 4. Politics and government 5. Russia 6. History writing — Europe — Russia 7. Politics and global affairs — World politics — Europe
LC Bl2007014787
National Book Critics Circle Award for Autobiography/Memoir finalist.

Written in the form of a diary, a stark account of life in twenty-first-century Russia offers an unflinching account of the plight of millions of Russian citizens

ESSENTIAL AND RECOMMENDED TITLES
947.7 Ukraine

and the corruption of the Putin presidency, in a final work by the acclaimed Russian journalist, murdered in October 2006.

Satter, David
The Less You Know, the Better You Sleep: Russia's Road to Terror and Dictatorship Under Yeltsin and Putin. David Satter. Yale Univ Pr 2016. 224 p.
ISBN 9780300211429
Grades: Adult   947.086
1. Atrocities 2. Nationalism 3. Conspiracies 4. Communism 5. Politics and government 6. Russia 7. Soviet Union 8. History writing — Europe — Russia

In December 2013, David Satter became the first American journalist to be expelled from Russia since the Cold War. The Moscow Times said it was not surprising that he was expelled, "it was surprising it took so long." Satter is known in Russia for havingwritten that the apartment bombings in 1999, which were blamed on Chechens and brought Putin to power, were actually carried out by the Russian FSB security police. In this book, Satter tells the story of the apartment bombings and how Boris Yeltsin presided over the criminalization of Russia, why Vladimir Putin was chosen as his successor, and how Putin has suppressed all opposition while retaining the appearance of a pluralist state. As the threat represented by Russia becomes increasingly clear, Satter's description of where Russia is and how it got there will be of vital interest to anyone concerned about the dangers facing the world today.

Seierstad, Asne
Angel of Grozny: Orphans of a Forgotten War. Asne Seierstad. Perseus Books Group 2008. 384 p.
ISBN 9780465011223
Grades: Adult   947.086
1. Orphans 2. War and society 3. Abandonment (Psychology) 4. Loss 5. Civil war 6. Russian history 7. Chechnya, Russia 8. 21st century 9. 20th century 10. History writing — Wars and conflicts — Civil Wars 11. History writing — Europe — Eastern Europe 12. Adult books for young adults
LC 2008925222

After reporting on the war in Chechnya over ten years ago, the author describes her return visit to the country, its future, and the long-term effects of war on the generation of orphans left behind.

"Seierstad's searing, evocative recounting brings Chechnya to life, especially the unimaginable suffering and strength of the Chechen people. Powerful, painful, and raw, . [this] is essential reading." —*Booklist*

Szablowski, Witold
Dancing Bears: True Stories of People Nostalgic for Life Under Tyranny. Witold Szablowski; translated by Antonia Lloyd-Jones. Penguin Books 2018. 233 p.
ISBN 9780143129745
Grades: Adult   947.086
1. Post-communism 2. Social change 3. Former Communists 4. Bulgaria 5. Eastern Europe 6. Cuba 7. Translations — Polish to English 8. Society and culture — General 9. Politics and global affairs — Political philosophy
LC 2017043107

An award-winning Polish journalist, in the tradition of Ryszard Kapuscinski, presents the extraordinary stories of people throughout Eastern Europe and in Cuba who, like Bulgaria's dancing bears, are now free but who seem nostalgic for the time when they were not.

"A surprising look at societies grappling with profound change." —*Kirkus*
Originally published: Warsaw : Agora S.A, 2014; Translated from the Polish.

Walker, Shaun
The Long Hangover: Putin's New Russia and the Ghosts of the Past. Shaun Walker. Oxford University Press 2017. 288 p.
ISBN 9780190659240
Grades: Adult   947.086
1. Putin, Vladimir Vladimirovich, 1952- 2. Presidents 3. Political culture 4. International relations 5. Post-communism 6. Politics and government 7. Russia 8. Politics and global affairs — World politics — Europe
LC 2017015739

In The Long Hangover, Shaun Walker provides a deeply reported, bottom-up explanation of Russia's resurgence under Putin. By cleverly exploiting the memory of the Soviet victory over fascism in World War II, Putin's regime has made ordinary Russians feel that their country is great again.

"Intelligent and ambitious, Walkers book succeeds in providing insight into the recent history of a nation at the center of world attention." —*Publishers Weekly*

Zygar, Mikhail
All the Kremlin's Men: Inside the Court of Vladimir Putin. Mikhail Zygar. PublicAffairs 2016. 336 p.
ISBN 9781610397391
Grades: Adult   947.086
1. Putin, Vladimir Vladimirovich, 1952- 2. Political consultants 3. Charismatic political leadership 4. Manipulation (Social sciences) 5. Politics and government 6. Russia 7. Politics and global affairs — Political figures 8. Politics and global affairs — World politics — Europe 9. History writing — Europe — Russia
LC 2016018443

In an account based on first-hand interviews with Vladimir Putin's inner circle, the author asserts that Putin is actually a weary leader controlled by the many men who advise and deceive him and that many of the Kremlin's decisions have been nothing more than tactical responses to external events, devoid of logic or objective.

"This excellent book contains a continuous account of Putin's years in power seasoned with details that are poorly known to most readers, if known at all." —*Library Journal*

947.7 Ukraine

Harding, Luke
Invasion: The Inside Story of Russia's Bloody War and Ukraine's Fight for Survival. Luke Harding. Vintage 2022. 336 pages
ISBN 9780593685174
Grades: Adult   947.7
1. Harding, Luke, 1968- 2. Putin, Vladimir Vladimirovich, 1952- 3. Zelensky, Volodymyr, 1978- 4. War correspondents 5. War 6. Russo-Ukrainian War, 2014- 7. Aggression (International relations) 8. Military occupation 9. Armies 10. Civilians in war 11. Survival 12. World leaders 13. Resilience 14. International relations 15. Geopolitics 16. European history 17. Russia 18. Ukraine 19. Politics and global affairs — World politics — Europe 20. Politics and global affairs — Political figures 21. History writing — Wars and conflicts 22. History writing — Europe — Eastern Europe

For months, the omens had pointed in one scarcely believable direction: Russia was about to invade Ukraine. And yet, the world was stunned by the epochal scale of the assault that began in February 2022. It was an attempt by one nation to devour another. The Kremlin wanted nothing less than a new world order. Invasion is Luke Harding's gripping chronicle of the war that changed everything. Reporting on the ground through the initial months of shock and heartbreak, Harding shares unheard human stories behind the headlines, while also excavating the compelling narrative of two very different leaders.

"Guardian foreign correspondent Harding (Shadow State) delivers a comprehensive and riveting account of Russia's February 2022 invasion of Ukraine....Enriched by Harding's deep knowledge of the region and impressive access, this is a valuable report on an ongoing geopolitical crisis." —*Publishers Weekly*

King, Charles
Odessa: Genius and Death in a City of Dreams. Charles King. W.W. Norton & Co. 2011. 352 p.
ISBN 9780393070842
Grades: Adult   947.7
1. Multiculturalism 2. Cosmopolitanism 3. Cities and towns 4. Genius 5. Jewish people 6. Social change 7. Cruelty 8. Death 9. History writing — Europe — Eastern Europe

Describes the vibrant Black Sea port city of Odessa and the thriving Jewish population that included Alexander Pushkin, Isaac Babel, Zionist activist Vladimir Jabotinsky and immunologist Ilya Mechnikov and the mass murders of the Romanian occupation during World War II.

"This is a finely written and evocative portrait of the city. [Its] detail, coupled with a fine feel for the sweep of history…makes this book a worthy tribute to one of Europe's greatest and least-known cities." —The Economist

Includes bibliographical references and index.

Kurtz, Glenn
Three Minutes in Poland: Discovering a Lost World in a 1938 Family Film. Glenn Kurtz. Farrar, Straus and Giroux 2014. 288 p.
ISBN 9780374276775
Grades: Adult   947.7
1. Kurtz, Glenn 2. Jewish people 3. Holocaust (1933-1945) 4. Small towns 5. Amateur films 6. Holocaust survivors 7. Polish people 8. European history 9. Poland 10. 20th century 11. Autobiographies and memoirs 12. History writing — Wars and conflicts — Holocaust — World War II 13. Life stories — Facing adversity — War and oppression — Holocaust

LC 2014008516

The author's search for the annihilated Polish community captured in his grandfather's 1938 home movie. From this brief film, Glenn Kurtz creates a riveting exploration of memory, loss, and improbable survival—a monument to a lost world.

"Engrossing detective work and chance encounters—one casual online viewer recognized a 13-year-old boy in the film as her still-living grandfather—allowed Kurtz to assemble a vibrant portrait of Jewish Nasielsk, its homely shops, proud synagogue, quarreling Hasidim and Zionists, impish kids, and, not least, of its harrowing war-time dissolution. He also explores the resurrection of the communitys history, as survivors find images of loved ones lost for generations and forge new bonds." —Publishers Weekly

Miller, Christopher
The War Came to US: Life and Death in Ukraine. Christopher Miller. Bloomsbury Continuum 2023. 288 p.
ISBN 9781399406857
Grades: Adult   947.7
1. Miller, Christopher 2. Journalists 3. War correspondents 4. Aggression (International relations) 5. Resistance to military occupation 6. Volunteer army 7. Combat 8. War casualties 9. Civilians in war 10. Survival 11. Russo-Ukrainian War, 2014- 12. European history 13. Ukraine 14. Politics and global affairs — World politics — Europe 15. History writing — Wars and conflicts 16. History writing — Europe — Eastern Europe 17. Debut title

When Russian President Vladimir Putin launched his unprovoked, full-scale invasion of Ukraine just before dawn on 24 February 2022, it marked his latest and most overt attempt to brutally conquer the country, and reshaped the world order. Christopher Miller, the Ukraine correspondent for the Financial Times and the foremost journalist covering the country, was there on the ground when the first Russian missiles struck and troops stormed over the border. This is the definitive, inside story of its long fight for freedom.

"A penetrating account of the reality of Putin's war on Ukraine…With powerful stories and insightful background, Miller provides a human dimension to a bloody conflict." —Kirkus

Plokhy, Serhii
★ *The Gates of Europe: A History of Ukraine.* Serhii Plokhy. Basic Books 2021. 352 p.
ISBN 9781541675643
Grades: Adult   947.7
1. European history 2. Eastern Europe 3. Former Soviet republics 4. Ukraine 5. History writing — Europe — Eastern Europe 6. Politics and global affairs — World politics — Europe

LC 2015015256

A history of the Ukraine including its current fight with Russia to preserve its political independence.

Includes bibliographical references and index.

★ *The Russo-ukrainian War: The Return of History.* Serhii Plokhy. W W Norton & CO 2023. 384 p.
ISBN 9781324051190
Grades: Adult   947.7
1. Putin, Vladimir Vladimirovich, 1952- 2. Zelensky, Volodymyr, 1978- 3. Russo-Ukrainian War, 2014- 4. Military campaigns 5. Military history 6. War 7. Ukrainian people 8. Politics and government 9. Russian history 10. European history 11. Ukraine 12. 21st century 13. Politics and global affairs — World politics — Europe 14. History writing — Wars and conflicts

Despite repeated warnings from the White House, Russia's invasion of Ukraine in February 2022 shocked the world. Why did Putin start the war—and why has it unfolded in previously unimaginable ways? Ukrainians have resisted a superior military; the West has united, while Russia grows increasingly isolated. Serhii Plokhy, a leading historian of Ukraine and the Cold War, offers a definitive account of this conflict, its origins, course, and the already apparent and possible future consequences.

"Imperial nostalgia and miscalculation precipitated the war in Ukraine, according to this wide-ranging study….The result is an essential account of the conflict that manages to make sense of its obscure and tangled origins." —Publishers Weekly

Trofimov, Yaroslav
★ *Our Enemies Will Vanish: The Russian Invasion and Ukraine's War of Independence.* Yaroslav Trofimov. Penguin Press 2024. 400 p.
ISBN 9780593655184
Grades: Adult   947.7
1. Military occupation 2. Russo-Ukrainian War, 2014- 3. Independence 4. War 5. European history 6. Ukraine 7. Russia 8. Government and politics — Europe — Ukraine 9. History Writing — Wars and conflicts 10. History Writing — Europe — Eastern Europe

"This tour de force covers the first year of war in Ukraine and a solid second draft of history, as the author intended." —Booklist

Zelensky, Volodymyr
A Message from Ukraine: Speeches, 2019-2022. Volodymyr Zelensky. Crown 2022. xix, 118 pages
ISBN 9780593727171
Grades: Adult   947.7
1. Zelensky, Volodymyr, 1978- 2. Presidents 3. Russo-Ukrainian War, 2014- 4. War 5. Resistance to military occupation 6. Political leadership 7. Politics and government 8. European history 9. Ukraine 10. Speeches, addresses, etc. 11. Translations — Ukrainian to English 12. Politics and global affairs — World politics — Europe 13. History writing — Wars and conflicts 14. Politics and global affairs — Political figures

LC BI2022037662

An urgent call to arms from the Ukrainian leader whose unwavering courage in the face of the Russian invasion has inspired the world and turned him overnight into a global beacon of democracy. Bringing together a new introduction by Volodymyr Zelensky with his most powerful war speeches, this book recounts Ukraine's story through the words of its president. The only book officially authorized by President Zelensky, a Message from Ukraine includes speeches he has personally selected to tell the story of the Ukrainian people.

The speeches featured in this book have been abridged and edited for clarity—Title page verso.

947.708 Ukraine — 1855-

Applebaum, Anne
★ *Red Famine: Stalin's War on Ukraine.* Anne Applebaum. Doubleday 2017. 384 p.
ISBN 9780385538855
Grades: Adult   947.708

ESSENTIAL AND RECOMMENDED TITLES
948 Scandinavia and Finland

1. Famines 2. Atrocities 3. Genocide 4. Soviet Union history 5. European history 6. Ukraine 7. Eastern Europe 8. 1930s 9. History writing — Communism — Europe — Russia

LC 2017029952

Lionel Gelber Prize (Canada), 2018.

According to Pulitzer Prize-winning historian Anne Applebaum, Soviet dictator Joseph Stalin deliberately created famine conditions in Ukraine as an act of genocide from 1931-34. Making effective use of previously published and newly available sources, Red Famine documents the effects of collectivization, removal of food to other regions, and other oppressive measures that resulted in the deaths of four million Ukrainians. Applebaum concludes that Stalin aimed to replace ethnic Ukrainians with Russians to achieve a more compliant populace. Though her analysis may be controversial, it sheds light on current tensions between Russia and Ukraine.

"An authoritative history of national strife from a highly knowledgeable guide." —*Kirkus*

948 Scandinavia and Finland

Brown, Nancy Marie

The Real Valkyrie: The Hidden History of Viking Warrior Women. Nancy Marie Brown. St. Martin's Press 2021. VIII, 320 p.

ISBN 9781250200846

Grades: Adult   948

1. Viking women 2. Women warriors 3. Women chiefs (Political anthropology) 4. Vikings 5. Civilization, Viking 6. Excavations (Archaeology) 7. Mythology, Norse 8. Gender role 9. Sexism 10. Civilization, Medieval 11. European history 12. Scandinavia 13. Medieval period (476-1492) 14. History writing — Archaeology 15. History writing — Medieval — Europe 16. History writing — Women's history

LC 2021006973

In 2017, DNA tests revealed that a Viking warrior in a high-status grave in Birka, Sweden was actually a woman. The Real Valkyrie weaves together archaeology, history, and literature to imagine her life and times, showing that Viking women had more power and agency than historians have imagined. Nancy Marie Brown uses science to link the Birka warrior to Viking trading towns and to their great trade route east to Byzantium and beyond.

"According to this passionate and well-researched account, Viking men who murdered, looted, burned, and ravaged across Europe were often accompanied by equally murderous women who have been written out of history.... Giving archaeology and history equal time with folklore, Brown makes a convincing case that Viking women played a prominent public role." —*Kirkus*

Includes bibliographical references and index.

Herman, Arthur

The Viking Heart: How Scandinavians Conquered the World. Arthur Herman. Houghton Mifflin Harcourt 2021. 448 p.

ISBN 9781328595904

Grades: Adult   948

1. Civilization, Viking 2. Vikings 3. Northmen and Northwomen 4. Warriors 5. Scandinavian Americans 6. European history 7. Scandinavia 8. History writing — General

LC 2020057689

Arthur Herman melds a compelling historical narrative with cutting-edge archaeological and DNA research to trace the epic story of this remarkable and diverse people. He shows how the Scandinavian experience has universal meaning, and how we can still be inspired by their indomitable spirit.

"Herman ... offers both an overview of Viking history and a microcosmic account of some Scandinavian descendants of Vikings, and their contributions to American life." —*Library Journal*

Includes bibliographical references and index.

Price, Neil S.

★ *Children of Ash and Elm: A History of the Vikings*. Neil Price. Basic Books 2020. 608 p.

ISBN 9780465096985

Grades: Adult   948

1. Vikings 2. Northmen and Northwomen 3. Civilization, Viking 4. Antiquities 5. History writing — Europe

LC 2020001863

A distinguished archaeologist with decades of expertise offers a full history of the Vikings—from arts and culture to politics and cosmology.

"Readers interested in Viking culture should consider this monumental history a must-read." —*Publishers Weekly*

Includes bibliographical references and index.

Winroth, Anders

The Age of the Vikings. Anders Winroth. Princeton University Press 2014. 304 p.

ISBN 9780691149851

Grades: Adult   948

1. Vikings 2. Civilization, Viking 3. Northmen and Northwomen 4. European history 5. Medieval period (476-1492) 6. History writing — Medieval — Europe 7. Adult books for young adults

LC 2014006488

Dispels common myths about Vikings and their civilization, and uses archaeological and written evidence to explore their contributions to art, literature, religious thought, commerce, and politics.

Includes bibliographical references and index.

948.071 Scandinavia and Finland — 2000-2019

Booth, Michael

The Almost Nearly Perfect People: Behind the Myth of the Scandinavian Utopia. Michael Booth. Picador 2015. 448 p.

ISBN 9781250061966

Grades: Adult   948.071

1. National characteristics 2. Social policy 3. Economic policy 4. Taxation 5. Scandinavia 6. Norway 7. Denmark 8. Sweden 9. Finland 10. Travel Writing — Europe

LC 2015413295

Journalist Michael Booth has lived among the Scandinavians for more than ten years, and he has grown increasingly frustrated with the rose-tinted view of this part of the world offered up by the Western media. In this timely book he leaves his adopted home of Denmark and embarks on a journey through all five of the Nordic countries to discover who these curious tribes are, the secrets of their success, and, most intriguing of all, what they think of one another.

"Thanks to Booths good-natured description of his adventuresand his honest admirationwe may head for Scandinavia after all (bringing some elf-off spray, just in case)." —*Booklist*

949.12 Iceland

Bjarnason, Egill

How Iceland Changed the World: The Big History of a Small Island. Egill Bjarnason. Penguin 2021. 272 p.

ISBN 9780143135883

Grades: Adult   949.12

1. European history 2. Iceland 3. History writing — Europe

Provides a tour of the history of Iceland, from the time a Viking captain ran aground there 1,200 years ago to the pivotal role it placed during the French Revolution, the Moon Landing, and the foundation of Israel.

"Journalist Bjarnason debuts with an insightful and fawning history of his native Iceland.... Rich with entertaining anecdotes and helpful pronunciation guides, this is a winning introduction to a unique and fascinating culture." —*Publishers Weekly*

949.2 Netherlands

Schama, Simon
The Embarrassment of Riches: An Interpretation of Dutch Culture in the Golden Age. Simon Schama. Alfred A. Knopf 1987. xiii, 698 p. : Illustration
ISBN 9780394510750
Grades: 11 12 Adult   949.2
1. Identity 2. Nationalism 3. European history 4. Netherlands 5. 17th century 6. History writing — Europe
LC 86045418

The author of Citizens presents an exhaustive, lively history of life in seventeenth-century Holland, the height of Dutch influence, culture, and affluence, accompanied by more than one hundred black-and-white reproductions and illustrations.

"Delving into customs, beliefs, popular art and quirks of behavior, Schama has fashioned a tour de force, a profound, unconventional and rewarding portrait of a people." —*Publishers Weekly*

Includes bibliographical references and index.

Shorto, Russell
Amsterdam: A History of the World's Most Liberal City. Russell Shorto. Doubleday 2013. 357 pages, [24] pages of plates : Illustration; Color; Map
ISBN 9780385534574
Grades: Adult   949.2
1. Liberalism 2. City life 3. Canals 4. Coasts 5. Amsterdam, Netherlands 6. History writing — Europe
LC 2013003544

A historical portrait of Amsterdam and the ideas that make it unique explores the ongoing efforts of its citizens to navigate its seaside challenges and democratic philosophies, revealing the influence of the liberal ideals that evolved there.

Includes bibliographical references (pages 333-343) and index.

949.5 Greece

Brownworth, Lars
Lost to the West: The Forgotten Byzantine Empire That Rescued Western Civilization. Lars Brownworth. Random House 2009. 352 p.
ISBN 9780307407955
Grades: Adult   949.5
1. Byzantine civilization 2. Civilization, Medieval 3. Civilization, Ancient 4. Social life and customs 5. Civilization 6. Ancient Rome 7. Byzantine Empire 8. Byzantine Empire (330-1453) 9. Medieval period (476-1492) 10. History writing — Medieval — Europe 11. History writing — Southwest Asia and North Africa (Middle East) 12. History writing — Ancient — Rome
LC 2009279520

A portrait of the lesser-known Byzantine Empire reveals how it endured as Christianity's capital for a long period following the fall of the Roman Empire and shaped the Renaissance in the west, in an account that includes vivid coverage of the deliverance of numerous adversaries to Constantinople's throne.

Herrin, Judith
Byzantium: The Surprising Life of a Medieval Empire. Judith Herrin. Princeton University Press 2008. 304 p.
ISBN 9780691131511
Grades: Adult   949.5
1. Civilization, Medieval 2. European history 3. Southwest Asia and North Africa (Middle East) 4. Byzantine Empire 5. Byzantine Empire (330-1453) 6. Medieval period (476-1492) 7. History writing — Medieval — Europe 8. History writing — Southwest Asia and North Africa (Middle East)

Explores the rise and fall of the Byzantine Empire, including important figures who shaped its history and the role it played in protecting Christianity from Islam's expansion across western Europe.

Mazower, Mark
The Greek Revolution: 1821 and the Making of Modern Europe. Mark Mazower. Penguin Press 2021. 560 p.
ISBN 9781591847335
Grades: Adult   949.5
1. Revolutions 2. Modernization (Social sciences) 3. Insurgency 4. War 5. Freedom 6. Military history 7. European history 8. Europe 9. Greece 10. 19th century 11. 1820s 12. History writing — Europe 13. History writing — Wars and conflicts — Revolutions
LC 2021029233

One of our great historians, in this definitive new history, shows us myths about the Greek War of Independence outpaced the facts from the very beginning, and for good reason.

"Mazower (history, Columbia Univ; the Balkans) provides a detailed examination of the Greek quest for independence from the Ottoman Empire during the first portion of the 19th century.... Mazower contextualizes a major transformation in 19th-century Eastern Europe for readers of European history and provides a solid background of modern Greece for students of ancient history." —*Library Journal*

Includes bibliographical references and index.

Salonica, City of Ghosts: Christians, Muslims, and Jews, 1430-1950. Mark Mazower. Alfred A. Knopf 2005. xv, 490 p, 32 p. of plates : Illustration; Color; Map
ISBN 9780375412981
Grades: Adult   949.5
1. European history 2. Greece 3. History writing — Europe — Eastern Europe
LC 2004057690

National Jewish Book Award, 2005.

Presents a history of Salonica, from its heyday as a Byzantine port, through its role as a progressive center of the Ottoman Empire, to its occupation during World War II by the Nazis and their deportation of its Jewish inhabitants.

"The author's graceful, evocative prose, his deft attention to details and his empathetic presentation of all sides of the story add up to a magnificent tale of this unique city." —*Publishers Weekly*

Includes bibliographical references (p. 441-468) and index; Originally published: London : HarperCollins, 2004.

Norwich, John Julius
Byzantium: The Apogee. John Julius Norwich. Knopf 1992. xxiv, 389 p. : Illustration; Color; Map
ISBN 9780394537795
Grades: Adult   949.5
1. European history 2. Byzantine Empire 3. Byzantine Empire (330-1453) 4. Medieval period (476-1492) 5. History writing — Europe — Eastern Europe
LC 91053119

Describes Byzantium's battles against foreign threats, its internal conflicts, the return of iconoclasm in the ninth century, and the struggles between Anatolia's military aristocracy and the eunuchs of the capital.

Includes bibliographical references (p. 370-[375]) and index; Originally published in the United Kingdom by Viking Penguin, London—T.P. verso.

Byzantium: The Decline and Fall. John Julius Norwich. Knopf 1996. xxxvii, 488 p. : Illustration; Map
ISBN 9780679416500
Grades: Adult   949.5
1. European history 2. Byzantine Empire 3. Byzantine Empire (330-1453) 4. Medieval period (476-1492) 5. History writing — General
LC BL 99788137

The third and final volume of a trilogy that also includes Byzantium: The Early Centuries and Byzantium: The Apogee describes the final days of the city of Constantinople and its fall in May 1453.

Includes bibliographical references (p. 455-461) and index.

Byzantium: The Early Centuries. John Julius Norwich. Knopf 1989. 407 p, 32 unnumbered pages of plates : Illustration; Map
ISBN 9780394537788

ESSENTIAL AND RECOMMENDED TITLES
949.6 Balkan Peninsula

Grades: Adult   **949.5**
1. European history 2. Byzantine history 3. Byzantine Empire (330-1453) 4. Medieval period (476-1492) 5. History writing — Europe — Eastern Europe
LC 88045508

Relates the history of the Byzantine Empire, from its beginnings up to the emergence of its rival, the Holy Roman Empire, in 800 AD.

Includes bibliographical references and indexes; Originally published in Great Britain by Viking, London, 1988—T.P. verso, v. [1].

A Short History of Byzantium. John Julius Norwich. Vintage Books 1999. xl, 430 p. : Illustration; Map
ISBN 9780679772699
Grades: 11 12 Adult   **949.5**
1. Byzantine civilization 2. Civilization, Medieval 3. European history 4. Byzantine Empire 5. Medieval period (476-1492) 6. Byzantine Empire (330-1453) 7. History writing — Medieval — Europe 8. Adult books for young adults
LC Bl2004107967

A history of the most powerful nation in Europe for over 1000 years during the Dark and Middle Ages recaps its intrigue, madmen, conquests, religious schism, and eventual decline, and profiles the major personalities.

"In his shorter telling of the history between the founding of Constantinople in 330 and its fall in 1453, Lord Norwich has sacrificed none of the virtues of the longer work: Lively narration and a taste for the eccentric anecdote and revelatory detail." —*New York Times Book Review*

Abridgment of the author's three-vol. work Byzantium; Includes bibliographical references (p. 392-[404]) and index; Originally published: New York : Knopf, 1997.

949.6 Balkan Peninsula

Mazower, Mark
The Balkans: A Short History. Mark Mazower. Modern Library 2000. xliii, 188 p. : Map
ISBN 9780679640875
Grades: 11 12 Adult   **949.6**
1. Interethnic relations 2. European history 3. Balkan Peninsula 4. History writing — Europe — Eastern Europe 5. Adult books for young adults
LC 00056244

Examines the causes of ethnic conflict in the Balkans, discussing how the meeting of European and Asian cultural influences and the blending of Christian and Muslim populations have created a complex and divisive situation.

"This is an excellent primer on the region's history, especially the growth of the nation-state in the 19th century." —*The Economist*
Includes bibliographical references and index.

949.61 Turkey in Europe (Eastern Thrace)

Crowley, Roger
1453: The Holy War for Constantinople and the Clash of Islam and the West. Roger Crowley. Hyperion 2006. 328 p. : Illustration; Map
ISBN 9781401308506
Grades: Adult   **949.61**
1. Civilization, Islamic 2. Civilization, Western 3. East and West 4. Islam and world politics 5. International relations 6. Civilization, Medieval 7. Southwest Asia and North Africa (Middle East) history 8. Istanbul, Turkey 9. Turkey 10. Islamic Empire 11. Europe 12. Ottoman Empire (1299-1922) 13. Byzantine Empire (330-1453) 14. Medieval period (476-1492) 15. History writing — Southwest Asia and North Africa (Middle East)

A comprehensive account of the fall of Constantinople to the Ottoman Turks in 1453 examines the end of the Byzantine Empire and of the medieval era in light of the rise of two separate worlds—the West and the Middle East—as well as the implications of the siege for the relationship between the West and Islam.

Includes bibliographical references and index.

Hughes, Bettany
Istanbul: A Tale of Three Cities. Bettany Hughes. Da Capo Press 2017. 416 pages
ISBN 9780306825842
Grades: Adult   **949.61**
1. Cities and towns 2. Capitals (Cities) 3. Geopolitics 4. Commerce 5. Anthropology 6. Social history 7. East and West 8. Religions 9. Istanbul, Turkey 10. History writing — Southwest Asia and North Africa (Middle East) 11. History writing — Asia 12. History writing — Archaeology
LC 2017937000

A historian describes the history of one of the world's greatest and oldest cities, which has held three different names and has played host to Phoenicians, Genoese, Venetians, Jews, Vikings and Azeris who all called it home.

"Hughes balances especially well a study of one city with the commentary of greater time periods and historic events taking place simultaneously around the world; the rich, cultural, religious, and social presence of Istanbul's complex tale lends itself as an excellent focus." —*Library Journal*
Includes bibliographical references and index.

King, Charles
Midnight at the Pera Palace: The Birth of Modern Istanbul. Charles King. W.W. Norton and Company 2014. 480 pages
ISBN 9780393089141
Grades: Adult   **949.61**
1. City life 2. Social change 3. Cosmopolitanism 4. Intellectual life 5. Exiles 6. Southwest Asia and North Africa (Middle East) history 7. Istanbul, Turkey 8. Turkey 9. 20th century 10. History writing — Nationalism — Southwest Asia and North Africa (Middle East)
LC 2014012360

Brings to life a remarkable era after the 1925 establishment of the Turkish Republic, when the storied city of Istanbul stumbled into the modern world and reshaped the meaning of cosmopolitanism via its ethnically diverse population and importance in the key historical events and cultural movements of the early 20th century.

Includes bibliographical references and index.

Madden, Thomas F.
Istanbul: City of Majesty at the Crossroads of the World. Thomas F. Madden. Viking Press 2016. 448 p.
ISBN 9780670016600
Grades: Adult   **949.61**
1. Civilization, Islamic 2. Cities and towns 3. Southwest Asia and North Africa (Middle East) history 4. Istanbul, Turkey 5. Turkey 6. Ottoman Empire (1299-1922) 7. Byzantine Empire (330-1453) 8. History writing — Southwest Asia and North Africa (Middle East)

This biography of the 2,000-year-old city, founded by Greeks and eventually ruled by the Macedonians, the Romans and the Ottomans, details the rich history, traditions and changing populace of a city that is a key to understanding modern civilization.

Pamuk, Orhan
Istanbul: Memories and the City. Orhan Pamuk; translated from the Turkish by Maureen Freely. Knopf 2005. xii, 384 p. : Illustration
ISBN 9781400040957
Grades: Adult   **949.61**
1. Pamuk, Orhan, 1952- 2. Art and society 3. Architecture and society 4. Civilization, Islamic 5. Voyages and travels 6. Southwest Asia and North Africa (Middle East) history 7. Turkey 8. Istanbul, Turkey 9. Ottoman Empire (1299-1922) 10. Translations — Turkish to English 11. Autobiographies and memoirs 12. Life stories — Arts and culture — Writing — Authors 13. History writing — Southwest Asia and North Africa (Middle East)
LC 2004061537

National Book Critics Circle Award for Autobiography/Memoir finalist.

A portrait of one of the world's most complex and diverse cities interweaves the history of Istanbul with observations and reflections on the city's landmarks, art, people, institutions, and great spaces.

"The author mingles personal memoir with cultural history, and a fascinating read it is too for anyone who has even the slightest acquaintance with this fabled bridge between east and west." —*The Economist*

949.702 Yugoslavia, 1918-1991

Maass, Peter
Love Thy Neighbor: A Story of War. Peter Maass. Alfred A. Knopf 1996. 305 p. : Map
ISBN 9780679444336
Grades: 11 12 Adult   **949.702**
1. Maass, Peter, 1960- 2. Milosevic, Slobodan, 1941-2006 3. Serbian people 4. Muslims 5. Genocide 6. Interethnic relations 7. Yugoslav War, 1991-1995 8. European history 9. Bosnia and Hercegovina 10. 1990s 11. History writing — Wars and conflicts — Civil Wars

LC 95039250

Los Angeles Times Book Prize for Current Interest, 1996.

A foreign correspondent offers a portrait of the conflict in Bosnia, from the battlefield of Sarajevo, to the atrocities that have been reported, to the lives of those caught in the crossfire.
Includes bibliographical references (p. [291]-292) and index.

949.703 Period as sovereign nations, 1991

Rohde, David
Endgame: The Betrayal and Fall of Srebrenica, Europe's Worst Massacre Since World War II. David Rohde. Westview Press 1998. xvi, 450 : Illustration
ISBN 9780813335339
Grades: Adult   **949.703**
1. Yugoslav War, 1991-1995 2. Atrocities 3. Military history 4. History writing — General

LC 98026127

Pulitzer Prize-winning author David Rohde follows the experiences of seven central characters—three Muslims in Srebrenica, two Dutch peacekeepers charged with defending the surrounded town, and two Serb Army soldiers attacking it—through the ten-day period that changed the course of the war in Bosnia and was arguably the darkest hour in United Nations history.
Includes bibliographical references (p. [403]-434) and index.

949.9 Bulgaria

Kassabova, Kapka
Border: A Journey to the Edge of Europe. Kapka Kassabova. Granta 2017. xviii, 379 pages : Map
ISBN 9781555977863
Grades: Adult   **949.9**
1. Borderlands 2. Boundaries 3. Refugees 4. Culture 5. Culture conflict 6. Border security 7. National territory 8. Immigration and emigration 9. Balkan Peninsula 10. Mediterranean Region 11. Bulgaria 12. Greece 13. Turkey 14. History writing — Europe — Eastern Europe 15. History writing — Southwest Asia and North Africa (Middle East) 16. Travel Writing — Europe 17. Life stories — Identity

LC 2016436902

National Book Critics Circle Award for Nonfiction finalist, 2017.

Bulgarian-born poet and writer Kapka Kassabova lives in Scotland, but in Border she describes return visits to Eastern Europe between 2013-2015. In the complex, magical area where Bulgaria, Turkey, and Greece meet, Kassabova traveled through mountains, villages, and forests and spoke with former border guards, people who tried to escape Communist Bulgaria, villagers who live near the countries' edges, and incoming refugees fleeing Syria. Clever, lyrical, and acutely observed, this book is a fascinating examination of Eastern European borderlands.

"Wild animals abound, myths mingle with reality, and Kassabova proves to be a penetrating and contemplative guide through rough terrain." —*Publishers Weekly*
Includes bibliographical references (pages 377-379).

950.2 Period of Mongol and Tartar empires 1162-1480

Marozzi, Justin
Tamerlane: Sword of Islam, Conqueror of the World. Justin Marozzi. Perseus Books Group 2006. 368 p.
ISBN 9780306814655
Grades: Adult   **950.2**
1. Tamerlane, 1336-1405 2. Mongols 3. Conquerors 4. Rulers 5. Asian history 6. Biographies 7. Life stories — Politics — Politicians 8. Life stories — Law and order — Armed forces personnel 9. History writing — Asia

Offers a powerful account of the life of Tamerlane the Great (1336-1405), the Mongol successor to Genghis Khan, ruler of a vast empire, and one of history's most brutal tyrants who imposed an iron rule from the steppes of Asia to the Syrian coastline, torturing conquered inhabitants without mercy. 25,000 first printing.

McLynn, Frank
Genghis Khan: His Conquests, His Empire, His Legacy. Frank McLynn. Da Capo Press 2015. 512 p.
ISBN 9780306823954
Grades: Adult   **950.2**
1. Genghis Khan, 1162-1227 2. Conquerors 3. Command of troops 4. Mongols 5. Military history 6. Rulers 7. Mongolia 8. Biographies 9. History writing — Military — Military leadership 10. Life stories — Law and order — Armed forces personnel 11. History writing — Asia

A portrait of the conqueror traces his rise to power, blending details of his life with that of the Mongol people's culture to show how Khan was able to unite a collection of fractious tribes into one cohesive group that could dominate any settlement they chose.

950.4 History of Asia — 1905-

Mishra, Pankaj
From the Ruins of Empire: The Intellectuals Who Remade Asia. Pankaj Mishra. Farrar Straus & Giroux 2012. 320 p.
ISBN 9780374249595
Grades: Adult   **950.4**
1. Intellectuals 2. Intellectual life 3. Social life and customs 4. Asia 5. History writing — Asia

LC 2012940483

Provides an overview of the great thinkers and philosophical leaders from across Asia who helped change and shape the modern continent, including Tagore and Gandhi in India, Liang Qichao in China and Abdurreshi al Ibrahim in the Ottoman Empire.

951 China and adjacent areas

Demick, Barbara
Eat the Buddha: Life and Death in a Tibetan Town. Barbara Demick. Random House 2020. 352 p.
ISBN 9780812998757
Grades: Adult   **951**
1. Tibetan people 2. Resistance to government 3. Culture conflict 4. Social change 5. Tibetan Buddhism 6. Political persecution 7. Refugees, Tibetan 8. Chinese history 9. Tibet 10. China 11. Society and culture — Ethnic studies 12. Society and culture — Urban and regional studies 13. Life stories — Facing adversity — War and oppression 14. History writing — Asia — China

LC 2019044133

ESSENTIAL AND RECOMMENDED TITLES
951 China and adjacent areas

New York Times Notable Book, 2020.

Eat the Buddha spans decades of modern Tibetan and Chinese history, as told through the private lives of Demick's subjects, among them a princess whose family is wiped out during the Cultural Revolution, a young Tibetan nomad who becomes radicalized in the storied monastery of Kirti, an upwardly mobile entrepreneur who falls in love with a Chinese woman, a poet and intellectual who risks everything to voice his resistance, and a Tibetan schoolgirl forced to choose at an early age between her family and the elusive lure of Chinese money. All of them face the same dilemma: Do they resist the Chinese, or do they join them? Do they adhere to Buddhist teachings of compassion and nonviolence, or do they fight?

"Taking a compelling approach to documenting Ngaba's history through the eyes of its own people, this wonderfully written book will leave readers with a stronger appreciation for why the movement to support the Tibetan people deserves so much more attention." —Library Journal

Hessler, Peter
Oracle Bones: A Journey Between China's Past and Present. Peter Hessler. HarperCollins 2006. xi, 491 p. : Illustration; Map
ISBN 9780060826581
Grades: Adult 951
1. Language and culture 2. Economic development 3. East and West 4. Social life and customs 5. Civilization 6. Voyages and travels 7. China 8. Travel Writing — Asia and the South Pacific
LC 2005052607

ALA Notable Book, 2007; New York Times Notable Book, 2006; National Book Award for Nonfiction finalist, 2006.

Chronicles the author's 7,000-mile drive across northern China, following the Great Wall, during which he investigated a historically important rural region being abandoned as young people migrate to jobs in the southeast; his five-year stay in a small farming village; and his three years of research in Lishui, a small city slated to become a major industrial center.

"The author has a marvelous sense of the intonations and gestures that give life to the moment; he knows when to join in the action and when simply to wait for things to happen." —New York Times Book Review

Includes bibliographical references (p. 459-467) and index.

Kaufman, Jonathan
The Last Kings of Shanghai: The Rival Jewish Dynasties That Helped Create Modern China. Jonathan Kaufman. Penguin Group USA 2020. 384 p.
ISBN 9780735224414
Grades: Adult 951
1. Sassoon, David, 1792-1864 2. Sassoon family 3. Kadoorie, Elly, 1865-1944 4. Kadoorie family 5. Jewish families 6. Rich families 7. Businesspeople 8. Entrepreneurs 9. Business competition 10. Chinese history 11. Shanghai, China 12. Hong Kong 13. 19th century 14. 20th century 15. Collective biographies 16. Life stories — People in history 17. History writing — Asia — China 18. Life stories — Business
LC 2019052103

An epic, multigenerational story of two rival dynasties who flourished in Shanghai and Hong Kong as twentieth-century China surged into the modern era, from the Pulitzer Prize-winning journalist.

"This richly detailed account illuminates an underexamined overlap between modern Jewish and Chinese history." —Publishers Weekly

Includes bibliographical references and index.

Platt, Stephen R.
Autumn in the Heavenly Kingdom: China, the West, and the Epic Story of the Taiping Civil War. by Stephen R. Platt. Alfred A. Knopf 2012. 480 p.
ISBN 9780307271730
Grades: Adult 951
1. Interethnic conflict 2. Civil war 3. Visitors 4. European people 5. American people 6. Interethnic relations 7. International relations 8. Chinese history 9. Western hemisphere 10. China 11. 19th century 12. Qing dynasty (1644-1912) 13. History writing — Wars and conflicts — Civil Wars 14. History writing — Asia — China
LC 2011035137

Cundill Prize in History, 2012.

A narrative history of China's 19th-century Taiping Rebellion traces an 1850s revolution led by a failed civil servant who claimed divine ties, citing the roles played by the United States and Britain as well as the contributions of such figures as military strategist Zeng Guofan and Taiping leader Hong Rengan.

This is a Borzoi book—T.P. verso; Includes bibliographical references.

Imperial Twilight: The Opium War and the End of China's Last Golden Age. Stephen R. Platt. Alfred A. Knopf 2018. 592 p.
ISBN 9780307961730
Grades: Adult 951
1. International trade 2. Colonialism 3. East and West 4. Opium industry and trade 5. Power 6. Chinese history 7. 19th century 8. Qing dynasty (1644-1912) 9. History writing — Imperial China — Asia — China 10. History writing — Wars and conflicts
LC 2017028172

Describes how 19th-century British efforts to "open" China to trade set in motion the fall of the Qing dynasty and started a war that allowed for the rise of nationalism and communism in the 20th century.

A Borzoi book; Includes bibliographical references.

Schmitz, Rob
Street of Eternal Happiness: Big City Dreams Along a Shanghai Road. Rob Schmitz. Crown Publishers 2016. 336 p.
ISBN 9780553418088
Grades: Adult 951
1. Streets 2. Neighborhoods 3. City life 4. China 5. Shanghai, China 6. Society and culture — Ethnic studies
LC 2015041162

A narrative account profiling the ordinary men and women who live, work, and dream on the author's street in Shanghai, inspired by his enormously popular Marketplace series of the same name.

"Probing human-interest stories that mine the heart of today's China." —Kirkus

Spence, Jonathan D.
God's Chinese Son: The Taiping Heavenly Kingdom of Hong Xiuquan. Jonathan D. Spence. W.W. Norton 1997. xxvii, 400 p. : Illustration; Color; Map
ISBN 9780393315561
Grades: Adult 951
1. Hung, Hsiu-Chuan, 1814-1864 2. Revolutions 3. Religions 4. Chinese history 5. East Asia 6. China 7. 19th century 8. History writing — Wars and conflicts — Revolutions 9. History writing — Imperial China — Asia — China
LC BL 99783519

A history of the Taiping Heavenly Kingdom in mid-nineteenth-century China profiles a period of extreme violence, during which a massive uprising, led by religious visionary Hong Xiuquan, cost some twenty million lives.

"In 1836, twenty-two-year-old Hong Xiuquan failed the civil-service examinations in Canton and came across some Christian tracts. When he later fell sick and had visions, he became convinced that he was the Christian God's second son, destined to rule a 'Heavenly kingdom' on earth. Many were attracted to Hong's egalitarian policies—despite his enforced separation of the sexes—and his sect prospered. But its attempts to overthrow the Qing dynasty resulted in unprecedented bloodshed: Twenty million people died before the uprising was defeated, in 1864. Spence's present-tense narrative is riveting." —The New Yorker

Reprint. Originally published: 1996; Includes bibliographical references (p. [373]-388) and index.

The Search for Modern China. Jonathan D. Spence. Norton 1990. xxv, 876 p, 136 p. of plates : Illustration; Color; Map
ISBN 9780393307801
Grades: 11 12 Adult 951
1. Chinese history 2. 20th century 3. Qing dynasty (1644-1912) 4. History writing — Asia — China
LC 89009241

Lionel Gelber Prize (Canada), 1990.

PUBLIC LIBRARY CORE COLLECTION: NONFICTION
Twentieth Edition

Covering more than four centuries of Chinese history, this work chronicles the various dynasties, the ideas of reformist Confucian scholars, and China's poets, novelists, artists, students, and leaders.

"Beginning with the decline of the Ming dynasty and ending with the Tiananmen Square massacre, Spence chronicles the cultural and social transformations of the country, concentrating on the many wars and rebellions."—*Booklist*

Includes bibliographical references (p. 749-788) and index.

Wood, Michael
The Story of China: The Epic History of a World Power from the Middle Kingdom to Mao and the China Dream. Michael Wood. St Martins Press 2020. 384 p.
ISBN 9781250202574
Grades: Adult   951

1. History 2. International relations 3. Civilization 4. Economics 5. Chinese history 6. China 7. History writing — Asia — China 8. Politics and global affairs — World politics — Asia

A narrative history of China by the documentary historian and best-selling author of Conquistadors draws on newly opened archives and extensive travels to examine the nation's past dominance and potential as a future world ruler.

Includes bibliographical references and index.

951.04 China — Period of Republic, 1912-1949

Chang, Iris
★ *The Rape of Nanking: The Forgotten Holocaust of World War II.* Iris Chang. BasicBooks 1997. xi, 290 p. : Illustration; Map
ISBN 9780465068357
Grades: 11 12 Adult   951.04

1. Rabe, John, 1882-1950 2. Nanking Massacre, Nanjing, Jiangsu Sheng, China, 1937 3. Massacres 4. Genocide 5. Sino-Japanese Conflict, 1937-1945 6. Chinese history 7. 1930s 8. History writing — Wars and conflicts — World War II — Pacific Theater 9. Adult books for young adults

LC 97024137

New York Times Notable Book, 1998.

Relates an account of the 1937 massacre of 250,000 Chinese civilians in Nanking by the invading Japanese military, a carnage for which the Japanese government has never admitted responsibility.

"Chang's book is a memorial to the victims of Nanking, a damning indictment of Japanese political historiography, a valuable addition to Pacific war literature, and a literary model of how to speak about the unspeakable."—*Booklist*

Includes bibliographical references (p. 231-283) and index.

Chang, Jung
Big Sister, Little Sister, Red Sister: Three Women at the Heart of Twentieth-century China. Jung Chang. Knopf 2019. 384 p.
ISBN 9780451493507
Grades: Adult   951.04

1. Song, Qingling, 1893-1981 2. Chiang, May-ling Soong, 1897-2003 3. Soong, Ai-ling, 1890-1973 4. Sisters 5. Communism 6. Political culture 7. Women and politics 8. Chinese women 9. Chinese history 10. China 11. 20th century 12. Biographies 13. History writing — Women's history 14. Life stories — People in history — Witness to history 15. History writing — Asia — China

As China battled through a hundred years of wars and seismic transformations, the three Soong sisters from Shanghai were at the center of power, and each of them left an indelible mark on history.

Kurtz-Phelan, Daniel
The China Mission: George Marshall's Unfinished War, 1945-1947. Daniel Kurtz-Phelan. W W Norton & CO Inc 2018. 416 p.
ISBN 9780393240955
Grades: Adult   951.04

1. Marshall, George C. (George Catlett), 1880-1959 2. Political leadership 3. Communism 4. World politics 5. International relations 6. Chinese Civil War, 1945-1949 7. Civil war 8. China 9. United States 10. 1940s 11. History writing — Post World War II - 1959 — United States 12. History writing — Communist China — Asia — China

LC 2017053909

Presents a narrative account of General George Marshall's high-stakes mission to broker peace among rival Chinese leaders, establish a Chinese democracy and prevent a Communist takeover while navigating threats of another war.

LI, Zhuqing
Daughters of the Flower Fragrant Garden: Two Sisters Separated by China's Civil War. Zhuqing Li. W.W. Norton & Company, Inc 2022. 336 p.
ISBN 9780393541779
Grades: Adult   951.04

1. Chen, Wenjun, 1923-2014 2. Chen, Hong (Pseudonym) 3. Chen family 4. Sisters 5. Families 6. Refugees 7. Identity 8. Chinese Civil War, 1945-1949 9. Civil war 10. China 11. Taiwan 12. 20th century 13. Biographies 14. Collective biographies 15. Life stories — Identity 16. Life stories — Relationships — Family 17. Life stories — Facing adversity — War and oppression 18. History writing — Asia — China

LC 2022007374

The story of two Chinese sisters separated by the Chinese Civil War during the 1930s by a quirk of timing, as one sister settled in Taiwan and the other remained on the mainland.

"A saga of the author's two Chinese aunts that mirrors the convulsive history of 20th-century China….Beautifully woven family memories coalesce into a vivid history of two very different Chinas."—*Kirkus*

Mitter, Rana
Forgotten Ally: China's World War II, 1937-1945. Rana Mitter. Houghton Mifflin Harcourt 2013. 464 p.
ISBN 9780547840567
Grades: Adult   951.04

1. Chiang, Kai-shek, 1887-1975 2. Mao, Zedong, 1893-1976 3. Wang, Jingwei, 1883-1944 4. Nanking Massacre, Nanjing, Jiangsu Sheng, China, 1937 5. World War II 6. International relations 7. Sino-Japanese Conflict, 1937-1945 8. Chinese history 9. China 10. Japan 11. 1930s 12. 1940s 13. History writing — Wars and conflicts — World War II — Pacific Theater 14. History writing — Communist China — Asia — China

LC 2013026746

Made possible through access to newly unsealed Chinese archives, this riveting book tells the untold story of China's devastating eight-year-war of resistance against Japan in World War II, rewriting the larger history of the war in the process.

Zia, Helen
Last Boat Out of Shanghai: The Epic Story of the Chinese Who Fled Mao's Revolution. Helen Zia. Ballantine Books 2019. 496 p.
ISBN 9780345522320
Grades: Adult   951.04

1. Refugees 2. Immigration and emigration 3. Exiles 4. Political refugees 5. Decision-making 6. Courage 7. Resilience 8. Panic 9. Communists 10. Chinese Civil War, 1945-1949 11. Civil war 12. Chinese history 13. Shanghai, China 14. 20th century 15. History writing — Communist China — Asia — China 16. Life stories — Facing adversity — War and oppression — Refugees

LC 2018036197

A rare English-language account traces the dramatic true stories of four young people caught up in the mass exodus of Shanghai in the wake of China's 1949 Communist Revolution.

"In this enthralling, heartfelt narrative, journalist Zia (Asian American Dreams) tells the stories of four people during the 1949 mass exodus from Shanghai following Chinas Communist takeover."—*Publishers Weekly*

Includes bibliographical references and index.

ESSENTIAL AND RECOMMENDED TITLES
951.05 China — Period of People's Republic, 1949

951.05 China — Period of People's Republic, 1949

Branigan, Tania
Red Memory: The Afterlives of China's Cultural Revolution. Tania Branigan. W.W. Norton & Company 2023. 288 p.
ISBN 9781324051954
Grades: Adult   951.05
1. Revolutions 2. Communism 3. Ideology 4. Class struggle 5. Political persecution 6. Political violence 7. Brainwashing 8. Social control 9. Betrayal 10. Psychic trauma 11. Hysteria (Social psychology) 12. Totalitarianism 13. Political culture 14. Memory 15. History 16. Chinese history 17. 1960s 18. 1970s 19. Chinese Cultural Revolution (1966-1976) 20. Oral histories 21. History writing — Communist China — Asia — China 22. Life stories — Facing adversity — War and oppression
Cundill Prize in History, 2023.
More than fifty years afterwards, the Cultural Revolution's scar runs through the heart of Chinese society, and through the souls of its citizens. Stationed in Beijing for the Guardian, Tania Branigan came to realise that this brutal and turbulent decade continues to propel and shape China to this day. Yet official suppression and personal trauma have conspired in national amnesia: It exists, for the most part, as an absence. Red Memory explores the stories of those who are driven to confront the era, fearing or yearning its return.
"Journalist Branigan debuts with a visceral history of the Cultural Revolution and a probing look at how the modern-day Chinese Communist Party has sought to erase this chapter from its past….This is essential reading for China watchers." —*Publishers Weekly*

Chen, Da
Colors of the Mountain. Da Chen. Random House 1999. 310 p.
ISBN 9780375502880
Grades: 11 12 Adult   951.05
1. Chen, Da, 1962-2019 2. Chinese history 3. China 4. Chinese Cultural Revolution (1966-1976) 5. Autobiographies and memoirs 6. Biographies 7. Life stories — Facing adversity — War and oppression 8. History writing — Communist China — Asia — China
LC 00698913
A Chinese American lawyer shares his memories of growing up in rural China during Mao's Cultural Revolution, describing how he struggled to overcome persecution and adversity to achieve an education, both in China and the U.S.
"Despite the devastating circumstances of his childhood and adolescence, Chen recounts his coming of age with arresting simplicity." —*Publishers Weekly*

Dikotter, Frank
China After Mao: The Rise of a Superpower. Frank Dikötter. Bloomsbury 2022. 352 p.
ISBN 9781639730513
Grades: Adult   951.05
1. Countries 2. Culture 3. Economic development 4. Communism 5. Industrial policy 6. Monetary policy 7. Great powers 8. Politics and government 9. Economics 10. Chinese history 11. China 12. Politics and global affairs — World politics — Asia 13. History writing — Communist China — Asia — China
Through decades of direct experience of the People's Republic combined with extraordinary access to hundreds of hitherto unseen documents in communist party archives, the author of the People's Trilogy offers a riveting account of China's rise from the disaster of the Cultural Revolution. He takes us inside the country's unprecedented four-decade economic transformation—from rural villages to industrial metropoles and elite party conclaves—that vaulted the nation from 126t largest economy in the world to second largest. A historian at the pinnacle of his field, Dikötter challenges much of what we think we know about how this happened.
"A richly informative, disquieting history." —*Kirkus*

Mao's Great Famine: The History of China's Most Devastating Catastrophe, 1958-1962. Frank Dikotter. Walker & Co. 2010. 448 p.
ISBN 9780802777683
Grades: Adult   951.05
1. Famines 2. Forced labor 3. Agricultural policy 4. Industrial policy 5. Food supply 6. China 7. History writing — Communist China — Asia — China
LC 2010013141
BBC Samuel Johnson Prize for Non-Fiction, 2011.
"Between 1958 and 1962, China descended into hell. Mao Zedong threw his country into a frenzy with the Great Leap Forward, an attempt to catch up with and overtake Britain in less than fifteen years. The experiment ended in the greatest catastrophe the country had ever known, destroying tens of millions of lives." so opens Frank Dikotter's astonishing, riveting, magnificently detailed chronicle of an era in Chinese history much speculated about but never before fully documented because access to Communist Party archives has long been restricted to all but the most trusted historians. However, a new archive law has opened up thousands of central and provincial documents that "fundamentally change the way one can study the Maoist era." "Dikotter makes clear, as nobody has before, that far from being the program that would lift the country among the world's superpowers and prove the power of communism, as Mao imagined, the Great Leap Forward propelled the country in the other direction. It became not only one of the most deadly mass killings in human history—at least 45 million people were worked, starved, or beaten to death—but also the greatest demolition of real estate in history, as up to one third of all housing was turned into rubble. The experiment was a catastrophe for the natural world as well, as the land was savaged in the maniacal pursuit of steel and other industrial accomplishments."
"In a powerful meshing of exhaustive research in Chinese archives and narrative drive, Dikotter for the first time links up what happened in the corridors of power—the vicious backstabbing and bullying tactics that took place among party leaders—with the everyday experiences of ordinary people, giving voice to the dead and disenfranchised. His magisterial account recasts the history of the People's Republic of China.
"The author parses this study of the Great Leap Forward into three components: Mao Zedong's bloody-minded resolve to implement the accelerated collectivization of the countryside, and the stifling of all opposition; the effects of these devastating policies on agriculture, industry, trade, housing and nature; and the catastrophic human toll (at least 45 million people died unnecessarily between 1958 and 1962)." —*Kirkus*
Includes bibliographical references and index.

Liao, Yiwu
Bullets and Opium: Real-life Stories of China After the Tiananmen Square Massacre. Liao Yiwu; translated by David Cowhig, Jessie Cowhig, and Ross Perlin. Atria Books 2019. 304 p.
ISBN 9781982126643
Grades: Adult   951.05
1. Tiananmen Square Massacre, Beijing, China, June 3-4, 1989 2. State-sponsored terrorism 3. Political prisoners 4. Political persecution 5. Massacres 6. Politics and government 7. Chinese history 8. China 9. 20th century 10. Translations — German to English 11. History writing — Communist China — Asia — China 12. Politics and global affairs — Civil and human rights
LC 2019009011
For over seven years, Liao Yiwu—a master of contemporary Chinese literature, imprisoned and persecuted as a counter-revolutionary until he fled the country in 2011—secretly interviewed survivors of the devastating 1989 Tiananmen Square massacre. Tortured, imprisoned, and forced into silence and the margins of Chinese society for thirty years, their harrowing stories are now finally revealed in this gripping and masterful work of investigative journalism.
Originally published: Die Kugel Und DAS Opium : Leben und Tod am Platz des Himmlischen Friedens. Germany : Fischer, 2012; Includes bibliographical references and index; Translated from the Chinese by David and Jessie Cowhig and Ross Perlin.

Lim, Louisa
The People's Republic of Amnesia: Tiananmen Revisited. Louisa Lim. Oxford University Press, USA 2014. 240 p.
ISBN 9780199347704
Grades: Adult   951.05
1. Tiananmen Square Massacre, Beijing, China, June 3-4, 1989 2. Democracy 3. World politics 4. State-sponsored terrorism 5. Politics and government

6. Chinese history 7. China 8. 20th century 9. History writing — Communist China — Asia — China

LC 2013044312

Explains how the Tiananmen Square massacre changed China and how China changed the events of that day by rewriting its own history.

Includes bibliographical references and index.

Xue, XInran
The Book of Secrets: A Personal History of Betrayal in Red China. XInran Xue. Continuum International Publishing Group 2024. 288 p.
ISBN 9781399406680
Grades: Adult   951.05
1. Spies 2. Military intelligence 3. Communism 4. Marriage 5. Secrets 6. Families 7. Betrayal 8. China 9. 20th century 10. History Writing — Communist China — Asia — China 11. History writing — Spies and spying 12. Politics and global affairs — World politics — Asia

The spellbinding story of the secret life of a spy in modern China, drawn from an extraordinary archive of personal diaries and letters.

"The surreal lyricism of a spymaster's secret diary coupled with the behind-the-scenes look at China's intelligence apparatus makes for addictive reading. Readers will be hooked." —*Publishers Weekly*

Yang, Jisheng
The World Turned Upside Down: A History of the Chinese Cultural Revolution. Yang Jisheng; translated from the Chinese and edited by Stacy Mosher and Guo Jian. Farrar, Straus and Giroux 2021. 768 p.
ISBN 9780374293130
Grades: Adult   951.05
1. Political culture 2. Communism and culture 3. Revolutions 4. Chinese history 5. China 6. 20th century 7. 1960s 8. 1970s 9. Chinese Cultural Revolution (1966-1976) 10. Translations — Chinese to English 11. History writing — Communist China — Asia — China

LC 2020039387

The only complete history of the Cultural Revolution by an independent scholar based in mainland China, 'The World Turned Upside Down' makes a crucial contribution to understanding the Cultural Revolution and its lasting influence today.

Includes bibliographical references and index; Originally published in Chinese by Cosmos Books, Hong Kong, 2016; Translated from the Chinese.

951.056 China, 1960-1969

Dikotter, Frank
The Cultural Revolution: A People's History, 1962-1976. Frank Dikotter. St. Martin's Press 2016. 400 p.
ISBN 9781632864215
Grades: Adult   951.056
1. Political leadership 2. Communism 3. World politics 4. Revolutions 5. Chinese history 6. China 7. Chinese Cultural Revolution (1966-1976) 8. History writing — Communist China — Asia — China

LC 2019303176

Drawing on hundreds of previously classified party documents, from secret police reports to unexpurgated versions of leadership speeches, the author sheds new light on China's most tumultuous era, during which the country descended into violent purges and entrenched fear.

"Dikotter tells a harrowing tale of unbelievable suffering. A potent combination of precise history and moving examples, plus a useful chronology of events." —*Kirkus*

951.06 China and adjacent areas — 2000-

Juan, Li
Winter Pasture: One Woman's Journey with China's Kazakh Herders. LI Juan. Astra House 2021. 320 p.
ISBN 9781662600333
Grades: Adult   951.06
1. Juan, LI 2. Herders 3. Women 4. Rural families 5. Kazakhs 6. Livestock 7. Nomads 8. Voyages and travels 9. China 10. Autobiographies and memoirs 11. Travel Writing — Asia and the South Pacific

An award-winning travel memoir from China documents how the author, a girl from the Altai Mountains, joined a Kazakh family of camel, sheep and cattle herders during their winter pasture migration from the Ulungur River to the Heavenly Mountains.

"Chinese journalist Juan makes her stateside debut with a magnificent tale about traveling through the freezing tundra of northern China." —*Publishers Weekly*

Osnos, Evan
Age of Ambition: Chasing Fortune, Truth, and Faith in the New China. Evan Osnos. Farrar, Straus and Giroux 2014. 416 p.
ISBN 9780374280741
Grades: Adult   951.06
1. Economic development 2. Individualism 3. Authoritarianism 4. Social change 5. Politics and government 6. China 7. 21st century 8. Politics and global affairs — World politics — Asia

LC 2013041338

National Book Award for Nonfiction, 2014; Pulitzer Prize for General Nonfiction finalist.

A Beijing correspondent for the New Yorker documents the political, economic and cultural changes occurring in today's China, examining a transition from Communist to personal power while addressing key questions about national freedom, generational identity and the influence of the West.

"Osnos combines scintillating reportage with an eye for telling ironies that illuminate broader trends; without downplaying the uniqueness of Chinese society, he makes its tensions feel achingly familiar for Western readers." —*Publishers Weekly*

Includes index.

Wong, Chun Han
Party of One: The Rise of XI Jinping and China's Superpower Future. Chun Han Wong. Avid Reader Press 2023. 400 p.
ISBN 9781982185732
Grades: Adult   951.06
1. XI, Jinping 2. Political leadership 3. Power 4. Political parties 5. Political science 6. International relations 7. Politics and government 8. China 9. 21st century 10. Biographies 11. History writing — Communist China — Asia — China 12. Life stories — Politics — Politicians

Drawing on his years of first-hand reporting across China, including insights from scholars and diplomats and analyses of official speeches and documents, a the Wall Street Journal correspondent provides a broad, lucid account of China's leader and how he inspires fear and fervor in his Party, his nation and beyond.

"A penetrating and timely unraveling of the personality and impact of a strongman president." —*Kirkus*

951.25 Hong Kong

Cheung, Karen
The Impossible City: A Hong Kong Memoir. Karen Cheung. Random House 2022. 288 p.
ISBN 9780593241431
Grades: Adult   951.25
1. Cheung, Karen, 1993- 2. Journalists 3. Democracy 4. Depression 5. Growing up 6. Protests, demonstrations, vigils, etc. 7. Family relationships 8. Social life and customs 9. Hong Kong 10. Autobiographies and memoirs 11. Life stories — People in history — Witness to history 12. Politics and global affairs — World politics — Asia

LC 2021027512

Weaving together memoir, cultural criticism and reportage, and drawing from her own experiences as well as the experiences of others, a journalist gives

ESSENTIAL AND RECOMMENDED TITLES
951.904 Korea — 1945-1999

us an insider's view of Hong Kong at a critical moment in history—both for this city and democracies around the world.

"An intimate look at Hong Kong by an 'Ambivalent' native who never appreciated it until the incremental seizure of freedoms by mainland China.... A powerful memoir of love and anguish in a cold financial capital with an underbelly of vibrant, freedom-loving youth." —*Kirkus*

Lim, Louisa
Indelible City: Dispossession and Defiance in Hong Kong. Louisa Lim. Riverhead 2022. 320 p.
ISBN 9780593191811
Grades: Adult **951.25**
1. Protest movements 2. Social movements 3. Dissenters 4. Politics and government 5. Asian history 6. Hong Kong 7. History writing — Asia — China 8. Politics and global affairs — World politics — Asia
LC 2021039690

An award-winning journalist and Hong Kong resident examines the unique city, from the British takeover in 1842, its "return" to China in 1997 and current protest amongst crackdowns from Beijing.

"Journalist Lim (The People's Republic of Amnesia) mixes memoir and reportage in this riveting portrait of Hong Kong....The result is a vivid and vital contribution to postcolonial history." —*Publishers Weekly*

Includes bibliographical references.

Mahtani, Shibani
Among the Braves: Hope, Struggle, and Exile in the Battle for Hong Kong and the Future of Global Democracy. Shibani Mahtani & Timothy McLaughlin. Hachette Books 2023. 336 p.
ISBN 9780306830365
Grades: Adult **951.25**
1. Political activists 2. Politics and government 3. Democracy 4. Citizen participation in government 5. Dissenters 6. Civil rights 7. International relations 8. Hong Kong 9. China 10. 2010s 11. Politics and global affairs — Civil and human rights 12. Politics and global affairs — Political philosophy 13. History writing — Asia

Two journalists tell the story of the Hong Kong pro-democracy movement, focusing on a group of activists and how a draconian 2019 law led to them to the streets and resulted in a brutal crackdown.

"Citizen activists stoutly resist an encroaching tyranny in this powerful and moving debut...The result is a gripping account of one of the great political tragedies of our time." —*Publishers Weekly*

951.904 Korea — 1945-1999

Cumings, Bruce
The Korean War: A History. Bruce Cumings. Modern Library 2010. xix, 288 p. : Illustration; Map
ISBN 9780679643579
Grades: Adult **951.904**
1. Korean War, 1950-1953 2. United States history 3. 1950s 4. 20th century 5. History writing — Wars and conflicts — Korean War
LC 2010005629

A revisionist account of the controversial war examines perspectives on both sides of the conflict while assessing its cultural contradictions and lasting influence, placing particular focus on the roles of McCarthyism and the media.

Includes bibliographical references (p. [247]-275) and index.

Halberstam, David
The Coldest Winter: America and the Korean War. David Halberstam. Hyperion 2007. 736 p.
ISBN 9781401300524
Grades: Adult **951.904**
1. Soldiers 2. Military policy 3. War 4. Korean War, 1950-1953 5. United States history 6. United States 7. 1950s 8. 20th century 9. History writing — Wars and conflicts — Korean War 10. Book club best bets

LC 2007001635
Booklist Editors' Choice, 2007; Pulitzer Prize for History finalist, 2008.

Explores the lesser-known elements of heroism and pathos that marked the Korean War and evaluates political decisions and miscalculations on both sides of the conflict.

Hutton, Robin L.
Sgt. Reckless: America's War Horse. Robin Hutton. Regnery Publishing 2014. 256 p.
ISBN 9781621572633
Grades: Adult **951.904**
1. Sergeant Reckless (War horse), approximately 1948-1968 2. Korean War, 1950-1953 3. Military campaigns 4. Horses 5. Humans and horses 6. War horses 7. Human-animal relationships 8. Korea 9. 20th century 10. History writing — Wars and conflicts — Korean War
LC 2014019750

Describes the small Mongolian mare and celebrated hero of the Korean War who helped the American war effort by carrying wounded soldiers and making multiple trips across combat zones to deliver supplies.

"Hutton's passion and admiration for her subject (she also heads an effort to create a monument to Reckless) shines through in this sparkling and engaging portrait of a most remarkable and courageous animal." —*Publishers Weekly*

Includes bibliographical references and index.

Oberdorfer, Don
The Two Koreas 3rd Ed.: A Contemporary History. Don Oberdorfer. Basic Books 2013. 519 p. : Illustration
ISBN 9780201409277
Grades: Adult **951.904**
1. Asian history 2. South Korea 3. North Korea 4. History writing — Asia — North and South Korea
LC 97019302

A revised overview of contemporary Korean history incorporates recent events and chronicles the last three decades, placing the tensions between the northern and southern regions within a historical context while considering the influences of outside powers.

Includes bibliographical references (p. 423-458) and index.

Sides, Hampton
On Desperate Ground: The Marines at the Reservoir, the Korean War's Greatest Battle. Hampton Sides. Doubleday 2018. 368 p.
ISBN 9780385541152
Grades: Adult **951.904**
1. Korean War, 1950-1953 2. Military campaigns 3. Marines 4. Military history 5. Courage 6. Asian history 7. United States 8. Korea 9. 1950s 10. History writing — Wars and conflicts — Korean War 11. History writing — Wars and conflicts — Battles
LC 2018010543

A chronicle of the extraordinary feats of heroism by Marines called on to do the impossible during the greatest battle of the Korean War.

"The result is a masterpiece of storytelling about a war that is often given short shrift in American history. Readers will feel the fierce cold, the constant threat of death, and the desperation of being trapped and under siege felt by the U.S. Marines in Sides' vivid and invaluable history." —*Booklist*

Includes bibliographical references and index.

951.93 North Korea (People's Democratic Republic of Korea)

Jeppesen, Travis
See You Again in Pyongyang: A Journey into Kim Jong Un's North Korea. Travis Jeppesen. Hachette Books 2018. 304 p.
ISBN 9780316509152
Grades: Adult **951.93**
1. Jeppesen, Travis, 1979- 2. Kim, Chong-un, 1984- 3. Fascism 4. Dictatorship 5. Isolationism 6. International relations 7. Politics and government 8. Asian

history 9. North Korea 10. Autobiographies and memoirs 11. Essays 12. Politics and global affairs — World politics — Asia 13. History writing — Asia — North and South Korea

LC Bl2018079962

The author, the first American to study at a North Korean university, recounts his experiences living, traveling, and studying in the country to create a multifaceted portrait of Pyongyang in the Kim Jong Un era.

Lee, Sung-yoon
The Sister: North Korea's Kim Yo Jong, the Most Dangerous Woman in the World. Sung-yoon Lee. Public Affairs 2023. 304 p.
ISBN 9781541704121
Grades: Adult   951.93
1. Kim, Yo-jong 2. Kim, Chong-un, 1984- 3. Women politicians 4. Power 5. Families 6. Politics and government 7. North Korea 8. Asia 9. Biographies 10. Life stories — Politics 11. History writing — Asia — North and South Korea

A specialist on North Korea offers this authoritative account of Kim Yo Jong, the sister of North Korea's Supreme Leader, takes readers into a murderous dynasty whose lust for power entails the brutal suppression of civilians, a missile program that can reach the continental U.S. and the constant threat of global destruction.

"Lee is a U.S.-based academic who has been studying and writing about North Korea and the Kim family for many years, so he is perfectly situated to provide a detailed examination of Kim Yo Jong (b. 1987), the younger sister of Supreme Leader Kim Jong Un and the likely heir apparent." —*Kirkus*

Tudor, Daniel
North Korea Confidential: Private Markets, Fashion Trends, Prison Camps, Dissenters and Defectors. Daniel Tudor, James Pearson. Tuttle Publishing 2015. 192 p.
ISBN 9780804844581
Grades: Adult   951.93
1. Totalitarianism 2. Dictatorship 3. North Korea 4. 21st century 5. Politics and global affairs — World politics — Asia

LC 2016469265

Private Markets, Fashion Trends, Prison Camps, Dissenters and Defectors. North Korea is one of the most troubled societies on earth. The country's 24 million people live under a violent dictatorship led by a single family, which relentlessly pursues the development of nuclear arms, which periodically incites risky military clashes with the larger, richer, liberal South, and which forces each and every person to play a role in the "theater state" even as it pays little more than lip service to the wellbeing of the overwhelming majority. With this deeply anachronistic system eventually failed in the 1990s, it triggered a famine that decimated the countryside and obliterated the lives of many hundreds of thousands of people. However, it also changed life forever for those who survived. A lawless form of marketization came to replace the iron rice bowl of work in state companies, and the Orwellian mind control of the Korean Workers' Party was replaced for many by dreams of trade and profit. A new North KoreaSociety was born from the horrors of the era one that is more susceptible to outside information than ever before with the advent of k-pop and video-carrying USB sticks. This is the North Korean society that is described in this book. In seven fascinating chapters the authors explore what life is actually like in modern North Korea today for the ordinary "man and woman on the street." They interview experts and tap a broad variety of sources to bring a startling new insider's view of North Korean societyfrom members of Pyongyang's ruling families to defectors from different periods and regions, to diplomats and NGOs with years of experience in the country, to cross-border traders from neighboring China, and textual accounts appearing in English, Korean and Chinese sources. The resulting stories reveal the horror as well as the innovation and humor which abound in this fascinating country.

"Rather than describing a gray, economically stagnant, and totalitarian society dominated by dictator Kim Jong Un, veteran journalists and coauthors Tudor and Pearson paint a vivid portrait of how North Korea functions by opportunistic entrepreneurism abetted by bribery." —*Library Journal*

951.9304 North Korea (People's Democratic Republic of Korea) — 1945-1994

Lankov, A. N.
The Real North Korea: Life and Politics in the Failed Stalinist Utopia. Andrei Lankov. Oxford University Press 2013. 304 p.
ISBN 9780199964291
Grades: Adult   951.9304
1. Kim, Il-song, 1912-1994 2. Kim, Chong-un, 1984- 3. Communism 4. Political culture 5. Social forecasting 6. Dictators 7. Social change 8. Totalitarianism 9. Stalinism 10. Economic forecasting 11. Politics and government 12. North Korea 13. Politics and global affairs — World politics — Asia 14. History writing — Asia — North and South Korea

LC 2012046992

After providing an accessible history of the nation, the author turns his focus to what North Korea is, what its leadership thinks and how its people cope with living in such an oppressive and poor place, arguing that North Korea is not irrational, but rather a nation that has survived against all odds.

Includes bibliographical references and index.

951.9305 North Korea (People's Democratic Republic of Korea) — 1994-

Palin, Michael
North Korea Journal. Michael Palin. Random House Canada 2019. 176 p.
ISBN 9780735279827
Grades: Adult   951.9305
1. Palin, Michael 2. Voyages and travels 3. North Korea 4. Media tie-ins 5. Travel Writing — Asia and the South Pacific

Former Monty Python member Michael Palin shares the journal he kept when he visited North Korea in 2018 to film a documentary, describing experiences in a country unlike any other he has visited.

952 Japan

Gordon, Andrew
A Modern History of Japan: From Tokugawa Times to the Present. Andrew Gordon. Oxford University Press 2003. xiv, 384 p. : Illustration
ISBN 9780195110609
Grades: Adult   952
1. Japanese history 2. 19th century 3. Tokugawa period (1600-1868) 4. History writing — Asia — Japan

LC 2002070916

Gordon (history and Japanese studies, Harvard U.) begins his history in about 1800, looking at how particularly the industrial revolution had changed the balance of global economic and military power, and the pressures that caused the Tokugawa military lords to fall from power.

"The author examines Japan's political, economic, social, and cultural inventions of its modernity in evolving international contexts, incorporating inside viewpoints and debates. Beyond identifying the national stages (feudalism, militarism, democracy), the author innovatively emphasizes how labor unions, cultural figures, and groups in society (especially women) have been affected over time and have responded." —*Library Journal*

Includes bibliographical references (p. 363-370) and index.

Iyer, Pico
The Lady and the Monk: Four Seasons in Kyoto. Pico Iyer. Vintage Books 1992. 337 p.
ISBN 9780679738343
Grades: Adult   952
1. Iyer, Pico 2. Monasteries 3. Buddhism 4. Women 5. Voyages and travels 6. Japan 7. Kyoto, Japan 8. Travel Writing — Asia and the South Pacific

LC 92050071

ESSENTIAL AND RECOMMENDED TITLES
952.03 Japan — 1868-1945

An account of the author's stay in a monastery in Kyoto, Japan, in order to learn about Zen Buddhism, introduces readers to Sachiko—a well-educated, English-speaking, Japanese housewife locked in a traditional marriage but drawn to the author and to Western culture.

"British born and Harvard educated, Iyer arrived in Japan in 1987 with no organized plans, contacts, or living arrangements. This poetic account of his year-long sojourn offers fascinating insight into Japanese culture and the people he met."—*Booklist*

Originally published: New York : Knopf, 1991.

Jansen, Marius
The Making of Modern Japan. Marius B. Jansen. Belknap Press of Harvard University Press 2000. 871 p. : Illustration; Map
ISBN 9780674003347
Grades: 11 12 Adult   952
1. Meiji, Emperor of Japan, 1852-1912 2. Japanese history 3. Tokugawa period (1600-1868) 4. History writing — Asia — Japan
LC 00041352

A sweeping history of modern Japan begins in 1600 and retraces the three major upheavals in Japanese history that have helped shape it into a modern Asian nation.

"Jansen has produced what is sure to become the standard narrative history of modern Japan. In every way this is a remarkable book . and no reference collection on Japan can pretend to be complete without it."—*Choice*

Includes bibliographical references (p. [795]-840) and index.

Sherman, Anna
The Bells of Old Tokyo: Meditations on Time and a City. Anna Sherman. Picador 2019. 337 pages
ISBN 9781250206404
Grades: Adult   952
1. Sherman, Anna (Anne Katherine), 1970- 2. Time 3. Bells 4. Change 5. Social life and customs 6. Japanese history 7. Tokyo, Japan 8. Japan 9. Autobiographies and memoirs 10. Travel Writing — Asia and the South Pacific 11. History writing — Asia — Japan 12. Life stories — Personal growth
LC 2019016492

Explores the history and culture of Tokyo as the author searches for eight lost bells that used to mark neighborhoods and time before Western-style clocks were common and introduces readers to residents both past and present and their contributions.

"Highly recommended for anyone who has visited or is planning to visit Tokyo. Readers will gain insight into the history, culture, and language of Japan as well as ideas on city hot spots."—*Library Journal*

Includes bibliographical references (pages 317-332).

952.03 Japan — 1868-1945

Buruma, Ian
Inventing Japan, 1853-1964. Ian Buruma. The Modern Library 2003. 194 p.
ISBN 9780679640851
Grades: 11 12 Adult   952.03
1. Japanese history 2. 19th century 3. History writing — Asia — Japan
LC 2002026346

New York Times Notable Book, 2003.

Traces the history of Japan from the country's nineteenth-century feudal isolation, to its rise to military power and defeat during World War II, to its rebirth as a global economic and working democracy in the postwar era.

"Buruma traces the remarkable metamorphosis that transformed an isolated island shogunate into an expansive military empire and then into a pacified and prosperous democracy. . . . An excellent introductory study."—*Booklist*

A Modern Library chronicles book; Includes bibliographical references (p. [183]-187) and index.

Keene, Donald
Emperor of Japan: Meiji and His World, 1852-1912. Donald Keene. Columbia University Press 2002. xiii, 922 p. : Illustration
ISBN 9780231123402
Grades: Adult   952.03
1. 1852-1912 2. Meiji, Emperor of Japan, 1852-1912 3. Rulers 4. Japanese history 5. Japan 6. Biographies 7. Life stories — Politics — Royalty 8. History writing — Asia — Japan
LC 2001028826

Even Japanese who consider Meiji the greatest ruler of all time, points out Keene (Japanese literature, Columbia U.), can rarely name anything he actually did. He searches for the elusive human who was born into a country that had refused almost all contact with the West for centuries, but saw Japan transformed during his lifetime into a world power and a members of the community of nations.

"This is a biography-cum-history of Emperor Meiji and his times. Meiji's reign saw Japan become fully industrialized under a brand new constitution, and with new economic and educational systems adopted. Despite the book's massive scale, Keene's graceful writing holds the reader's interest throughout."—*Booklist*

Includes bibliographical references (p. [867]-879) and index.

Kemper, Steve
Our Man in Tokyo: An American Ambassador and the Countdown to Pearl Harbor. Steve Kemper. Mariner Books 2022. 352 p.
ISBN 9780358064749
Grades: Adult   952.03
1. World War II 2. Ambassadors 3. Personal diaries 4. Economic policy 5. Diplomacy 6. American people 7. North American people 8. Japanese people 9. East Asian people 10. International relations 11. United States 12. Japan 13. Between the Wars (1918-1939) 14. Second World War era (1939-1945) 15. Biographies 16. History writing — United States
LC 2022026045

Drawing on the diary of the ambassador to Japan in 1932, as well as U.S. embassy correspondence, diplomatic dispatches and firsthand Japanese accounts, this gripping book recounts his time in Tokyo during the volatile decade that led to WWII—and how he risked everything to avert another world war.

"Expertly marshaled from Grew's diaries and reports, this is a poignant and profound look at diplomacy in action."—*Publishers Weekly*

Includes bibliographical references and index.

McClain, James
Japan: A Modern History. James L. McClain. W.W. Norton & Co. 2002. xxiii, 632, 92 p. : Illustration; Map
ISBN 9780393041569
Grades: 11 12 Adult   952.03
1. Japanese history 2. 19th century 3. Tokugawa period (1600-1868) 4. History writing — Asia — Japan
LC 2001034545

A definitive and compelling history of Japan details the tumultuous political, economic, and social change, over four centuries, that molded Japan into a modern world power by bringing to life the many historical figures who helped build a successful and strong nation.

"This is a well-written, well-researched, and easily readable survey of the modern history of a fascinating and important nation."—*Booklist*

Includes bibliographical references (p.[34] 3rd group) and index.

952.04 Japan — 1945-1999

Bass, Gary Jonathan
★ *Judgment at Tokyo: World War II on Trial and the Making of Modern Asia.* Gary J. Bass. Alfred A. Knopf 2023. 800 p.
ISBN 9781101947104
Grades: Adult   952.04

PUBLIC LIBRARY CORE COLLECTION: NONFICTION
Twentieth Edition

1. Trials 2. War crime trials 3. World War II 4. War crimes 5. Atrocities 6. Military officers 7. Pearl Harbor, Attack on, 1941 8. Tokyo, Japan 9. Japan 10. Pacific Area 11. 20th century 12. 1940s 13. History Writing — Wars and conflicts — World War II 14. History Writing — Asia — Japan 15. History Writing — Military

LC 2022061519

The product of 10 years of research and writing, this riveting story of wartime action, dramatic courtroom battles and the epic formative years that set the stage for the Asian postwar era recounts the trial of Japan's leaders as war criminals to create a legal framework to prosecute war crimes.

"This magisterial history delves into the two-year trial of Japan's military leaders, held before a panel of judges from China, India, the Philippines, Australia, Europe, and Americas, a counterpart to the trial at Nuremberg…A massive history that captures a pivotal moment in Asian history that would affect the latter half of the 20th century." —*Library Journal*

Includes bibliographical references and index.

Dower, John W.

Embracing Defeat: Japan in the Wake of World War II. John W. Dower. W.W. Norton & Co. 1999. 676 p. : Illustration; Map

ISBN 9780393046861

Grades: Adult   952.04

1. Hirohito, Emperor of Japan, 1901-1989 2. Tojo, Hideki, 1884-1948 3. MacArthur, Douglas, 1880-1964 4. War crime trials 5. World War II 6. Social life and customs 7. Politics and government 8. Military occupation 9. Japanese history 10. Japan 11. 1940s 12. 20th century 13. Second World War era (1939-1945) 14. History writing — Asia — Japan

LC 98022133

ALA Notable Book, 2000; L. L. Winship/PEN New England Award, 2000; Library Journal Best Books, 1999; Los Angeles Times Book Prize for History, 1999; Mark Lynton History Prize, 2000; National Book Award for Nonfiction, 1999; New York Times Notable Book, 1999; Pulitzer Prize for General Nonfiction, 2000; National Book Critics Circle Award for Nonfiction finalist, 1999.

Dower illuminates how shattering defeat, followed by years of American military occupation, affected every level of Japanese society in ways that neither the victor nor the vanquished could anticipate. The book vividly portrays the countless ways the Japanese met the challenge of starting over.

"Dower demonstrates an impressive mastery of voluminous sources, both American and Japanese, and he deftly situates the political story within a rich cultural context." —*Publishers Weekly*

Includes bibliographical references and index.

952.05 Japan — 2000-

Iyer, Pico

A Beginner's Guide to Japan: Observations and Provocations. Pico Iyer. Alfred A. Knopf 2019. 240 pages

ISBN 9780451493958

Grades: Adult   952.05

1. Iyer, Pico 2. Social life and customs 3. Culture 4. Voyages and travels 5. Japan 6. Essays 7. Travel Writing — Asia and the South Pacific 8. History writing — Asia — Japan

LC 2018038539

A lyrical guide to the enigma of contemporary Japan by the author of the Art of Stillness draws on more than three decades of residence and his local friendships to share unexpected, incisive glimpses into Japan's regional culture and landmarks.

Parry, Richard Lloyd

Ghosts of the Tsunami: Death and Life in Japan's Disaster Zone. Richard Lloyd Parry. Farrar, Straus and Giroux 2017. 352 p.

ISBN 9780374253974

Grades: Adult   952.05

1. Tsunamis 2. Natural disasters 3. Tohoku Earthquake and Tsunami, Japan, 2011 4. Fukushima Nuclear Disaster, Japan, 2011 5. Japanese history 6. 21st century 7. Politics and global affairs — World politics — Asia 8. Nature Writing — Natural Disaster 9. History writing — Natural disasters and tragedies

LC 2017021678

The award-winning correspondent and author of in the Time of Madness presents an account of the events and fallout of the 2011 tsunami in Japan that explores reports of ghosts and hauntings in a community tormented by devastating secrets.

"A sobering and compelling narrative of calamity." —*Kirkus*

952.0512 Japan — 2010-2019

Pilling, David

Bending Adversity: Japan and the Art of Survival. David Pilling. Penguin 2014. 400 p.

ISBN 9781594205842

Grades: Adult   952.0512

1. Economic policy 2. National characteristics, Japanese 3. Natural disasters 4. Tsunamis 5. Tohoku Earthquake and Tsunami, Japan, 2011 6. Fukushima Nuclear Disaster, Japan, 2011 7. Globalization (Economics) 8. Politics and government 9. Japanese history 10. Japan 11. 21st century 12. Politics and global affairs — World politics — Asia

An illuminating portrait of contemporary Japan by the Asia editor of the Financial Times bases his observations on a cross-section of Japanese citizenry while evaluating such major events as the World War II atom bombings, the 1990 economic recession and the earthquake, tsunami and nuclear meltdown disasters of 2011.

953 Arabian Peninsula and adjacent areas

Al Samawi, Mohammed

The Fox Hunt: A Refugee's Memoir of Coming to America. Mohammed Al Samawi. William Morrow & Company 2018. 352 p.

ISBN 9780062678195

Grades: Adult   953

1. Al Samawi, Mohammed, 1986- 2. Muslim men 3. Civil war 4. Escapes 5. Interfaith friendship 6. Religious persecution 7. Social media 8. Online friendship 9. Yemen (Republic) 10. Arabian Peninsula 11. Autobiographies and memoirs 12. Life stories — Facing adversity — War and oppression — Refugees 13. Adult books for young adults

LC Bl2018003717

The son of middle-class Shiite doctors in Yemen shares his moving story of love, war and hope that describes his harrowing escape from regional fanaticism and civil unrest through a daring plan engineered on social media by a small group of Western interfaith activists.

"Gracious and generous, this personal account of a remarkable life is a reminder of how peace comes in small increments as the result of the work of committed individuals." —*Kirkus*

953.805 Saudi Arabia — 1926-

Lacey, Robert

Inside the Kingdom: Kings, Clerics, Modernists, Terrorists, and the Struggle for Saudi Arabia. Robert Lacey. Viking 2009. 432 p.

ISBN 9780670021185

Grades: Adult   953.805

1. Lacey, Robert 2. Islam 3. Royal houses 4. Civilization 5. Southwest Asia and North Africa (Middle East) history 6. Saudi Arabia 7. Southwest Asia and North Africa (Middle East) 8. History writing — Nationalism — Southwest Asia and North Africa (Middle East)

LC 2009008367

ESSENTIAL AND RECOMMENDED TITLES
954 India and neighboring south Asian countries

Tracing a path through the Persian Gulf War and the events of 9/11 to the oil market convulsions of today, this gives readers a modern history of the Saudis in their own words, revealing a people attempting to reconcile life under religious law with the demands of a rapidly changing world.

"The author's eye for sweeping trends and the telling detail combined with the depth, breadth and evenhandedness of his research makes for an indispensable guide." —*Publishers Weekly*

Sequel to: The Kingdom: New York : Harcourt Brace Jovanovich, 1982, c1981; Includes bibliographical references and index.

Trofimov, Yaroslav
The Siege of Mecca: The Forgotten Uprising in Islam's Holiest Shrine and the Birth of Al Qaeda. Yaroslav Trofimov. Doubleday 2007. xii, 301 p, 16 p. of plates : Illustration; Map
ISBN 9780385519250
Grades: Adult   953.805
1. Islam 2. Mosques 3. Terrorism 4. Southwest Asia and North Africa (Middle East) history 5. Southwest Asia and North Africa (Middle East) 6. 20th century 7. Spirituality and Religion — Islam 8. History writing — Nationalism — Southwest Asia and North Africa (Middle East)
LC 2007007520

On November 20, 1979, the first morning of a new Muslim century, hundreds of gunmen stunned the world by seizing Islam's holiest shrine, the Grand Mosque in Mecca. These men came from more than a dozen countries, launching the first operation of global jihad in modern times. They believed that the Saudi royal family had become a craven servant of American infidels, and sought a return to the glory of uncompromising Islam. With nearly 100,000 worshippers trapped inside the holy compound, the bloody siege lasted two weeks, inflaming Muslim rage against the U.S. and causing hundreds of deaths. The desperate Saudis finally enlisted the help of French commandos, who prepared the final assault. The Saudi royal family ultimately compromised with the rebels' supporters, helping to set free the forces that produced the attacks of 9/11 and the harrowing circumstances that surround us today.

Includes bibliographical references (p. [265]-289) and index.

954 India and neighboring south Asian countries

Dalrymple, William
White Mughals: Love and Betrayal in the Eighteenth-century India. William Dalrymple. Viking 2003. xlvii, 459 p. : Illustration; Map
ISBN 9780670031849
Grades: Adult   954
1. British people in India 2. Interethnic relations 3. Men-women relations 4. Social life and customs 5. Indian history 6. India 7. British Raj (1858-1947) 8. 18th century 9. History writing — Asia — South Asia — India
LC 2002191082

Shortlisted for the James Tait Black Memorial Prize for Biography, 2003.

Traces the practice by British colonizers in India to assume local customs and religious practices, offering a particular focus on James Kirkpatrick, who converted to Islam and spied on the East India Company while having an affair with the great-niece of the region's prime minister.

"This book, ambitious in scope and rich in detail, demonstrates that a century before Kipling's never the twain shall meet two centuries before neocons and radical Islamists trumpeted the clash of civilizationsthe story of the Westerner in Muslim India was one not of conquest but of appreciation, adaptation, and seduction." —*The New Yorker*

Includes bibliographical references (p. 441-448) and index.

Goodheart, Adam
The Last Island: Discovery, Defiance, and the Most Elusive Tribe on Earth. Adam Goodheart. Godine 2023. 136 p.
ISBN 9781567926828
Grades: Adult   954
1. Journalists 2. Islands 3. Indigenous peoples 4. Suspicion 5. Hostility (Psychology) 6. Resistance (Psychology) 7. History 8. Civilization 9. Voyages and travels 10. Culture conflict 11. Andaman and Nicobar Islands (India) 12. Society and culture — Ethnic studies 13. Adventure writing — Exploration 14. Travel Writing — Asia and the South Pacific
LC 2023002219

In November 2018, a zealous American missionary was killed while attempting to visit an island he called "Satan's last stronghold," a small patch of land known as North Sentinel in the Andaman Islands, a remote archipelago in the Indian Ocean. News of the tragedy fascinated people around the world. Most were unaware such a place still existed in our time. Twenty years before the missionary's ill-fated visit, a historian and journalist named Adam Goodheart also traveled to the waters off North Sentinel. The Last Island is a work of history as well as travel, showing how the web of modernity is drawing ever closer to the island's shores.

"A thrilling book that will leave you contemplating the concept of civilization." —*Kirkus*

Includes bibliographical references.

Keay, John
India: A History : From the Earliest Civilisations to the Boom of the Twenty-first Century. John Keay. Grove Press 2010. xxvii, 658 p, (32 p. of plates) : Illustration; Color; Map
ISBN 9780802137975
Grades: 11 12 Adult   954
1. Social life and customs 2. Indian history 3. India 4. History writing — Asia — South Asia — India
LC BL2001005574

Offers an in-depth look at the history of India through a chronological review of the major events that transformed its diverse cultures and traditions.

"This history ranges from the ancient brick cities of Mohenjo-daro and Harappa, built in the Indus Valley around 2000 B.C, to modern India's urban middle class." —*Publishers Weekly*

Includes bibliographical references (p. 619-632) and index; Originally published: New York : Atlantic Monthly Press, 2000.

Lapierre, Dominique
The City of Joy. Dominique Lapierre; translated from the French by Kathryn Spink. Warner Books 1986. 464 p.
ISBN 9780446355568
Grades: Adult   954
1. Personal conduct 2. Altruism 3. Refugees 4. Calcutta, India 5. Page to screen 6. Society and culture — Wealth and class
LC BL 99963471

Depicts the efforts of four people to improve the harsh conditions of life in the impoverished and over-populated area of Calcutta, India.

Translation of: La Cite de la joie; Originally published: Garden City, N.Y. : Doubleday, 1985.

Mehta, Suketu
Maximum City: Bombay Lost and Found. Suketu Mehta. Vintage Books 2005. xii, 542 p. : Map
ISBN 9780375703409
Grades: Adult   954
1. Mehta, Suketu 2. City life 3. Social life and customs 4. Mumbai, India 5. India 6. History writing — Asia — South Asia — India
LC Bl2005021325

Kiriyama Prize for Nonfiction, 2005; Library Journal Best Books, 2004; Pulitzer Prize for General Nonfiction finalist.

A portrait of Bombay, India, and its people chronicles the everday life of the city and its inhabitants, from the criminal underworld of rival Muslim and Hindu gangs to the diverse people who come from the villages in search of a better life.

"The author explores various aspects of Bombay life, from setting up residence to exploring the hugely successful domestic film industry; from detailing Bombay's sex industry to profiling the reasons behind India's own September 11, the 1993 riots and bombings that exposed a vast enmity between extremist Hindus and Muslims. Mehta delivers a fresh and unblinking look at contemporary Bombay." —*Booklist*

Originally published: New York : Alfred A. Knopf, 2004.

PUBLIC LIBRARY CORE COLLECTION: NONFICTION
Twentieth Edition

Roy, Arundhati
Walking with the Comrades. Arundhati Roy. Penguin Group USA 2011. 240 p.
ISBN 9780143120599
Grades: Adult   954
1. Insurgency 2. Civil rights 3. International trade 4. Guerrillas 5. Indigenous peoples 6. Democracy 7. Industrialization 8. Economic development 9. Mines and mineral resources 10. Politics and government 11. India 12. 21st century 13. Politics and global affairs — World politics — Asia 14. Society and culture — Social activism and philanthropy

LC 2011039307

In early 2010, Roy traveled into the forests of Central India, homeland to millions of indigenous people, dreamland to some of the world's biggest mining corporations. The result is this… report from the heart of an unfolding revolution.

"The author exposes the violent contradictions of India's economic miracle in this blistering critique of the Indian government's campaign against the Maoist insurgents in the country's central tribal lands encompassing several states. Roy, who recounts time spent on the move with a cadre of rebels, argues forcefully that Operation Green Huntlaunched by the state under the rubric of the threat of terrorismis an all-out war to remove indigenous communities from lands already promised to corporations eager to exploit their extremely valuable resources. Informed, impassioned, at times strident, and fleet and fascinating when describing life on the ground among the rebels, Roy's prose will both rouse and ruffle." —*Publishers Weekly*

Sen, Amartya
The Argumentative Indian: Writings on Indian History, Culture, and Identity. Amartya Sen. Farrar, Straus and Giroux 2005. xx, 409 p. : Illustration
ISBN 9780374105839
Grades: Adult   954
1. Social life and customs 2. Civilization 3. India 4. History writing — Asia — South Asia — India

LC 2005049460

In a collection of sixteen interlinked essays, the Nobel Prize-winning economist shares his observations on India's intellectual and political heritage, revealing how the country's argumentative tradition is vital for the continuing success of its democracy and secular politics.

"Sen's lucid reasoning and thoroughgoing humanism . ensure a lively and commanding defense of diversity and dialogue."—*Publishers Weekly*

Includes bibliographical references and index.

954.03 India — Period of British rule, 1785-1947

Dalrymple, William
★ *The Anarchy: The Relentless Rise of the East India Company.* William Dalrymple. Bloomsbury Publishing 2019. xxxv, 522 p.
ISBN 9781635573954
Grades: Adult   954.03
1. Corporations 2. Colonialism 3. Exploitation 4. Capitalists and financiers 5. Armies 6. Corporate power 7. Indian history 8. Mughal Empire 9. Great Britain 10. 18th century 11. History writing — Asia — South Asia — India 12. History writing — Europe — United Kingdom

In August 1765, the East India Company defeated the young Mughal emperor and set up, in his place, a government run by English traders who collected taxes through means of a private army. The Anarchy tells one of history's most remarkable stories: How the Mughal Empire—which dominated world trade and manufacturing and possessed almost unlimited resources—fell apart and was replaced by a multinational corporation based thousands of miles overseas, and answerable to shareholders, most of whom had never even seen India and no idea about the country whose wealth was providing their dividends.

Cover title: The anarchy : the East India Company, corporate violence, and the pillage of an empire; Includes bibliographical references and index.

Guha, Ramachandra
Rebels Against the Raj: Western Fighters for India's Freedom. Ramachandra Guha. Alfred A. Knopf 2022. 384 p.
ISBN 9781101874837
Grades: Adult   954.03
1. Colonialism 2. European people in foreign countries 3. American people in India 4. Dissenters 5. Resistance to government 6. Political participation 7. Social advocates 8. Political prisoners 9. East and West 10. National liberation movements 11. Indian history 12. India 13. British Raj (1858-1947) 14. Collective biographies 15. Life stories — Politics — Activists and reformers 16. History writing — Asia — South Asia — India

LC 2021047324

Elizabeth Longford Prize for Historical Biography, 2023.

Rebels Against the Raj tells the story of seven people who chose to struggle for a country other than their own: Foreigners to India who across the late 19th to late 20th century arrived to join the freedom movement fighting for independence from British colonial rule. Of the seven, four were British, two American, and one Irish. Four men, three women. Before and after being jailed or deported they did remarkable and pioneering work in a variety of fields: Journalism, social reform, education, the emancipation of women, environmentalism. This book tells their stories, each renegade motivated by idealism and genuine sacrifice; each one leaving a profound impact on the region in which they worked, their legacies continuing through the institutions they founded and the generations and individuals they inspired.

"Brits and Americans who joined India's struggle against British rule are remembered in this vibrant historical study. . . . Guha's elegantly written group portrait ably conveys the passion and idealism of the Gandhian independence movement and its hold over the Western imagination." —*Publishers Weekly*

Includes bibliographical references and index.

954.04 India and neighboring south Asian countries — 1947-1971

Guha, Ramachandra
India After Gandhi: The History of the World's Largest Democracy. Ramachandra Guha. Ecco 2007. xviii, 893 p. : Illustration; Map
ISBN 9780060198817
Grades: Adult   954.04
1. Social life and customs 2. Indian history 3. India 4. 20th century 5. History writing — Asia — South Asia — India

LC 2006052180

Documents the conflicts that have shaped modern India while evaluating the factors that have helped maintain stability and democracy throughout the region.

Includes bibliographical references and index (p. [765]-857).

Hajari, Nisid
Midnight's Furies: The Deadly Legacy of India's Partition. Nisid Hajari. Houghton Mifflin Harcourt 2015. 304 p.
ISBN 9780547669212
Grades: Adult   954.04
1. Jinnah, Mahomed Ali, 1876-1948 2. Nehru, Jawaharlal, 1889-1964 3. World politics 4. Colonialism 5. Indian Partition, 1947 6. Indian history 7. Asian history 8. Pakistan 9. 1940s 10. 20th century 11. Impartial writing 12. History writing — Wars and conflicts 13. History writing — Asia — South Asia — Pakistan

LC 2014034426

The author describes how a few bloody months in South Asia during the summer of 1947—the Partition of India, which led to the creation of Pakistan—largely explain the world that troubles us today.

Includes bibliographical references and index.

Malhotra, Aanchal
Remnants of Partition: 21 Objects from a Continent Divided. Aanchal Malhotra. Hurst & Company 2019. xxi, 371 p.
ISBN 9781787381209
Grades: Adult   954.04

ESSENTIAL AND RECOMMENDED TITLES
954.91 Pakistan

1. Refugees 2. Loss 3. Memories 4. Heirlooms 5. Immigration and emigration 6. Violence 7. Murder 8. Boundaries 9. Partition, Territorial 10. Family history 11. Indian Partition, 1947 12. Indian history 13. Asian history 14. Pakistan 15. 20th century 16. Oral histories 17. Life stories — Facing adversity — War and oppression — Refugees 18. History writing — Asia — South Asia — India 19. History writing — Asia — South Asia — Pakistan

Seventy years on, the Partition of India fades from memory. Can it be restored? Despite being born into a family affected by the great divide, artist and oral historian Aanchal Malhotra had thought little about it until she encountered the objects her own great-grandparents had saved as they fled their homes. Remnants of Partition is a unique revisiting of Partition through dozens of personal belongings carried between the new India and Pakistan, amid the chaos of communal killings and mass displacement. Hidden in these objects is the memory of a time and place, a story of migration, and a life that once was.

Includes bibliographical references.

954.91 Pakistan

Shackle, Samira
Karachi Vice: *Life and Death in a Divided City.* Samira Shackle. Melville House 2021. 272 p.
ISBN 9781612199429
Grades: Adult   954.91
1. Cities and towns 2. Overpopulation 3. Urban problems 4. City dwellers 5. Corruption 6. Organized crime 7. Violence 8. Social conflict 9. City life 10. Karachi, Pakistan 11. Society and culture — Urban and regional studies 12. Society and culture — Violence and crime 13. Life stories — Facing adversity

Karachi. Pakistan's largest city is a sprawling metropolis of twenty million people, twice the size of New York City. It is a place of political turbulence in which those who have power wield it with brutal and partisan force. It takes an insider to know where is safe, who to trust, and what makes Karachi tick. In this powerful debut, Samira Shackle explores the city of her mother's birth in the company of a handful of Karachiites. Among them is Safdar the ambulance driver, who knows the city's streetsand shortcuts intimately and will stop at nothing to help his fellow citizens. There is Parveen, the activist whose outspoken views on injustice repeatedly lead her towards danger. And there is Zille, the hardened journalist whose commitment to getting the best scoops puts him at increasing risk. Their individual experiences unfold and converge, as Shackle tells the bigger story of Karachi over the past decade as it endures a terrifying crime wave: a period in which the Taliban arrive in Pakistan, addingto the daily perils for its residents and pushing their city into the international spotlight.

"Karachi Vice paints a vivid and compassionate picture of a metropolis struggling with poverty, ethnic tensions, corruption, and the scars of colonialism." —*Booklist*

Walsh, Declan
The Nine *Lives of Pakistan: Dispatches from a Precarious State.* Declan Walsh. W. W. Norton & Company 2020. 360 p.
ISBN 9780393249910
Grades: Adult   954.91
1. Walsh, Declan 2. Extremism 3. Identity 4. Faith 5. Politics and government 6. Voyages and travels 7. Asian history 8. Pakistan 9. Politics and global affairs — World politics — Southwest Asia and North Africa (Middle East) 10. Travel Writing — Southwest Asia and North Africa (Middle East)
LC 2020008294

On assignment for the New York Times and other outlets, Walsh traveled from the raucous port of Karachi to the salons of Lahore, and from Baluchistan to the mountains of Waziristan. He met a diverse cast of extraordinary Pakistanis-a chieftain readying for war at his desert fort, a retired spy skulking through the borderlands, and a crusading lawyer risking death for her beliefs, among others.

Includes bibliographical references and index.

954.9105 Pakistan — 1971-

Lieven, Anatol
Pakistan: A Hard Country. Anatol Lieven. Perseus Books Group 2011. 560 p.
ISBN 9781610390217
Grades: Adult   954.9105
1. Politics and culture 2. International relations 3. Pakistan 4. Politics and global affairs — World politics — Asia
LC 2011921821

Explores nearly every facet of Pakistan—from its regions, ethnicities and religious traditions to its violent history and political tensions, as well as its periods of surprising stability. By the author of Chechnya: Tombstone of Russian Power?

"Lieven breaks down his study by specific region; considers the structures of justice, religion, the military and politics in turn; and, finally, in a skillful, insightful synthesis, addresses the history of and issues concerning the Taliban, both Pakistani and Afghani. A well-reasoned, welcome resource for Western experts and lay readers alike." —*Kirkus*

954.92 Bangladesh

Carney, Scott
The Vortex: A True Story of History's Deadliest Storm, an Unspeakable War, and Liberation. Scott Carney and Jason Miklian. Ecco Press 2022. 464 p.
ISBN 9780062985415
Grades: Adult   954.92
1. Cyclones 2. Genocide 3. Coups d'etat 4. Atrocities 5. Violence against women 6. India-Pakistan Conflict, 1971 7. Geopolitics 8. Cold War 9. Revolutions 10. Pakistan 11. Bangladesh 12. 1970s 13. History writing — Cold War 14. History writing — Asia — South Asia — Pakistan 15. History writing — Natural disasters and tragedies

The deadliest storm in modern history ripped Pakistan in two and led the world to the brink of nuclear war when American and Soviet forces converged in the Bay of Bengal.

"Shot through with colorful character sketches and lucid explanations of South Asian politics, this is an urgent warning about the links between global warming and geopolitical turmoil." —*Publishers Weekly*

954.9303 1948-

Mohan, Rohini
The Seasons of Trouble: Life Amid the Ruins of Sri Lanka's Civil War. Rohini Mohan. Verso Books 2014. 256 p.
ISBN 9781781686003
Grades: Adult   954.9303
1. Tamil (Indic people) 2. Interethnic conflict 3. Nationalism 4. Child soldiers 5. National liberation movements 6. Survival 7. Psychic trauma 8. Disappeared people 9. Violence 10. Refugees 11. Civil war 12. Asian history 13. Sri Lanka 14. 1980s 15. 1990s 16. 2000s (Decade) 17. History writing — Wars and conflicts — Civil Wars 18. History writing — Asia — South Asia
LC 2014026813

Follows the lives of Sarvam, his middle-aged mother, Indra, and a girl named Mugil revealing the struggles they face after the Sri Lanka Civil War.

Subramanian, Sammanth
This Divided Island: Life, Death, and the Sri Lankan War. Sammanth Subramanian. Thomas Dunne Books 2015. 352 p.
ISBN 9781250069740
Grades: Adult   954.9303
1. Interethnic conflict 2. Civil war 3. Violence 4. Tamil (Indic people) 5. Sri Lankan people 6. Sri Lanka 7. South Asia 8. History writing — Wars and Conflicts — Civil Wars 9. History writing — Asia — South Asia

A New Delhi-based writer and journalist who has written stories for the New Yorker and the New York Times presents an extraordinary account of the Sri Lankan war and the lives it changed, and, through travels and conversations, examines how people reconcile themselves to violence.

954.96 NEPAl

Kirkby, Bruce
Blue Sky Kingdom: An Epic Family Journey to the Heart of the Himalaya. Bruce Kirkby. Pegasus Books 2020. 295 p.
ISBN 9781643135687
Grades: Adult   954.96
1. Kirkby, Bruce, 1968- 2. Television personalities 3. Families 4. Voyages and travels 5. Family travel 6. Hiking 7. Wilderness areas 8. Mountains 9. Buddhist monasteries 10. Tibetan Buddhism 11. Canadian people 12. Autistic children 13. Boys 14. Neurodivergent people 15. Himalaya Mountains 16. Tibet 17. Autobiographies and memoirs 18. Canadian literature 19. Travel Writing — Asia and the South Pacific 20. Adventure writing — Adventure travel 21. Life stories — Relationships — Family

Bruce Kirkby had fallen into a pattern of looking mindlessly at his phone for hours, flipping between emails and social media, ignoring his children and wife, when a thought struck him. This wasn't living; this wasn't him. This moment of clarity started a chain reaction which ended with a grand plan: He was going to take his wife and two young sons, jump on a freighter and head for the Himalayas. Bruce and his family had a remarkable three months journey, where they would end up living amongst the Lamas of Zanskar Valley, one of the last places on earth where Himalayan Buddhism is still practiced freely in its original setting.

"A breathtaking journey, both geographical and internal, Kirkby's blending of travelog of an already fascinatingly remote locale and personal family experience is unique and luminous. Will appeal to a wide range of readers." —*Library Journal*

Includes bibliographical references.

955 Iran

Amanat, Abbas
Iran: A Modern History. Abbas Amanat. Yale University Press 2017. 1000 p.
ISBN 9780300112542
Grades: Adult   955
1. Southwest Asia and North Africa (Middle East) history 2. Iran 3. Southwest Asia and North Africa (Middle East) 4. History writing — Southwest Asia and North Africa (Middle East)

This history of modern Iran is not a survey in the conventional sense but an ambitious exploration of the story of a nation. It offers a revealing look at how events, people, and institutions are shaped by currents that sometimes reach back hundreds of years. The book covers the complex history of the diverse societies and economies of Iran against the background of dynastic changes, revolutions, civil wars, foreign occupation, and the rise of the Islamic Republic.

"A stately, scholarly study of Iran's modern development, emphasizing themes of Iranian distinctness from Arab and Western cultures and traditions." —*Kirkus*

Includes index.

Follett, Ken
On Wings of Eagles. Ken Follett. New American Library 1984. 416 p. : Illustration
ISBN 9780451163530
Grades: Adult   955
1. Perot, H. Ross, 1930- 2. Iran Hostage Crisis, 1979-1981 3. Hostages 4. American people in Southwest Asia and North Africa (Middle East) 5. Escapes 6. Hostage negotiations 7. Businesspeople 8. Contractors 9. Hostage rescue units 10. Hostage taking 11. Military history 12. Iran 13. United States 14. 1970s 15. 20th century 16. History writing — 1970s — United States 17. Nonfiction that reads like fiction
LC BL 99942027

Recreates the harrowing, real-life adventure of the successful prison break engineered by Col. Bull Simons, a World War II and Vietnam commando, who rescued two Texans imprisoned in a Teheran jail.

"The author recounts the efforts of successful Texas industrialist Ross Perot to rescue from a Teheran jail two senior corporate executives arrested during the anti-American and revolutionary period in Iran in 1979." —*Library Journal*

A Signet book; Originally published: New York : W. Morrow, 1983.

Housden, Roger
Saved by Beauty: An American Romantic in Iran. Roger Housden. Broadway Books 2011. 320 p.
ISBN 9780307587732
Grades: Adult   955
1. Housden, Roger 2. Rumi, Jalal al-Din, 1207-1273 3. Hafiz, 1320-1389 4. American people in Southwest Asia and North Africa (Middle East) 5. Intellectual life 6. Travelers 7. Social life and customs 8. Voyages and travels 9. Iran 10. Travel Writing — Southwest Asia and North Africa (Middle East)
LC 2011003323

The author of Ten Poems to Change Your Life challenges popular misconceptions about Iran's youth culture, describing his visits to regions that inspired Rumi and Hafez, where he learned about the rich histories, cuisines and arts that comprise everyday life.

"The author documents his travels to Iran in late 2008 and early 2009. The narrative flows seamlessly as the author visits Tehran, paradise gardens in Shiraz, the Pasargadae archaeological site where Cyrus the Great is buried, Persepolis, the Jewish quarter in Yazd, Esfaha-n, Sanandaj, Mashhad, Neysha-bur, Tu-s, Kermanshah, Ahvaz, and Turkey's Bursa and Konya, as well as surrounding settlements, plains, deserts, and mountainous areas. Poetry lovers and adventurers alike will appreciate this work." —*Library Journal*

Navai, Ramita
City of Lies: Love, Sex, Death, and the Search for Truth in Tehran. Ramita Navai. Public Affairs 2014. 320 p.
ISBN 9781610395199
Grades: Adult   955
1. Political persecution 2. Women's role 3. Social life and customs 4. Women 5. Sharia (Islamic religious practice) 6. Islamic law 7. Politics and government 8. Tehran, Iran 9. Iran 10. Southwest Asia and North Africa (Middle East) 11. 21st century 12. Spirituality and Religion — Islam 13. History writing — Nationalism — Southwest Asia and North Africa (Middle East)

Rich, absorbing, and exotic, City of Lies travels up and down Vali Asr Street, Tehran's pulsing thoroughfare, from the lavish shopping malls of Tajrish through the smog that lingers over the alleyways and bazaars of the city's southern districts. RamitaNavai gives voice to ordinary Iranians forced to live extraordinary lives: the porn star, the aging socialite, the assassin and enemy of the state who ends up working for the Republic, the dutiful housewife who files for divorce, and the old-time thug running a gambling den.

955.05 Iran — 1906-2005

Abrahamian, Ervand
The Coup: 1953, the Cia, and the Roots of Modern U.S.-iranian Relations. Ervand Abrahamian. The New Press 2013. 304 p.
ISBN 9781595588265
Grades: Adult   955.05
1. Intervention (International relations) 2. Coups d'etat 3. Oil industry and trade 4. International relations 5. Southwest Asia and North Africa (Middle East) history 6. Great Britain 7. Iran 8. United States 9. 1950s 10. 20th century 11. History writing — Nationalism — Southwest Asia and North Africa (Middle East)
LC 2012031402

A history of the CIA's 1953 coup in Iran and its aftermath.
Includes bibliographical references and index.

ESSENTIAL AND RECOMMENDED TITLES
955.06 Iran — 2005-

Bowden, Mark
Guests of the Ayatollah: The First Battle in America's War with Militant Islam. Mark Bowden. Atlantic Monthly Press 2006. 680 p. : Illustration; Map
ISBN 9780871139252
Grades: Adult   955.05
1. Iran Hostage Crisis, 1979-1981 2. Hostages 3. American people in Southwest Asia and North Africa (Middle East) 4. Fundamentalism 5. Theocracy 6. Islam 7. International relations 8. Iran 9. United States 10. 1970s 11. 1980s 12. History writing — 1970s — United States 13. History writing — Nationalism — Southwest Asia and North Africa (Middle East)
LC 2005058862

Provides an account of the Iran hostage crisis during which fifty-two Americans were held hostage for 444 days, offering insights from the hostages, soldiers sent to free them, the radical captors, and diplomats trying to end the crisis.
Includes bibliographical references and index.

Ghattas, Kim
Black Wave: The Saudi-iran Wars on Religion and Culture That Destroyed the Middle East. by Kim Ghattas. Henry Holt and Co. 2020. 368 p.
ISBN 9781250131201
Grades: Adult   955.05
1. Social conflict 2. Sunni Islam 3. Shiites 4. International relations 5. Religion and politics 6. Islam and politics 7. Iranian revolution, 1979-1997 8. Southwest Asia and North Africa (Middle East) history 9. Iraq 10. Iran 11. Saudi Arabia 12. Southwest Asia and North Africa (Middle East) 13. Politics and global affairs — Religion and politics 14. Politics and global affairs — World politics — Southwest Asia and North Africa (Middle East) 15. History writing — Nationalism — Southwest Asia and North Africa (Middle East) 16. Spirituality and Religion — Islam
LC 2019024945

New York Times Notable Book, 2020.
Chronicles decades of rivalry between Saudia Arabia and Iran, linking the 1979 Iranian revolution, American policy changes, distortions in religious expression and the rise of sectarian violence to present-day perceptions about the Middle East.
"Essential for all who follow world events." —*Kirkus*
Includes bibliographical references and index.

Kinzer, Stephen
★ *All the Shah's Men: An American Coup and the Roots of Middle East Terror.* Stephen Kinzer. J. Wiley & Sons 2003. xiv, 258 p, 8 p. of plates : Illustration; Map
ISBN 9780471265177
Grades: Adult   955.05
1. Mosaddeq, Mohammad, 1880-1967 2. World politics 3. International relations 4. Political leadership 5. Iran 6. United States 7. History writing — Post World War II - 1959 — United States 8. History writing — Nationalism — Southwest Asia and North Africa (Middle East) 9. Nonfiction that reads like fiction
LC 2003009968

New York Times Notable Book, 2003.
Traces the events leading to the 1953 coup in Iran and its consequences, discussing the covert operations under the joint authority of Eisenhower and Churchill involving prime minister Mossadegh and CIA officer Roosevelt.
"This comprehensive . account of the nationalization of the Anglo-Iranian Oil Company under the leadership of Mohammad Mossadegh in 1951 ... is a valuable and informative work." —*Choice*
Includes bibliographical references (p. 244-249) and index.

Mendez, Antonio J.
Argo: How the CIA and Hollywood Pulled off the Most Audacious Rescue in History. Antonio J. Mendez and Matt Baglio. Viking 2012. 352 p.
ISBN 9780670026227
Grades: Adult   955.05
1. Mendez, Antonio J. 2. Former CIA agents 3. Iran Hostage Crisis, 1979-1981 4. Diplomats 5. Undercover operations 6. International relations 7. Canada 8. Iran 9. 1970s 10. Page to screen 11. History writing — Spies and spying
LC 2012014991

An account of the Iran Hostage Crisis and how the United States Central Intelligence Agency and the Government of Canada rescued six American diplomats.

955.06 Iran — 2005-

Orth, Stephan
Couchsurfing in Iran: Revealing a Hidden World. Stephan Orth. Greystone Books 2018. 240 p.
ISBN 9781771642804
Grades: Adult   955.06
1. Culture 2. European people in foreign countries 3. Stereotypes 4. Religion and culture 5. Hospitality 6. Travelers 7. Voyages and travels 8. Southwest Asia and North Africa (Middle East) 9. Iran 10. Translations — German to English 11. Travel Writing — Southwest Asia and North Africa (Middle East)
LC Bl2018179650

The author recounts the sixty-two days he spent traveling around Iran, providing a behind-the-scenes look at life in one of the world's most closed societies, including what he calls the "two Irans" that coexist side by side.
Originally published in 2015 by Malik; Translated from the German Couchsurfing im Iran by Jamie McIntosh.

956 Middle East

Barr, James
A Line in the Sand: The Anglo-french Struggle for the Middle East, 1914-1948. James Barr. W. W. Norton & Co. 2011. 352 p.
ISBN 9780393070651
Grades: Adult   956
1. Balfour Declaration 2. Zionism 3. Imperialism 4. International relations 5. Politics and government 6. France 7. Southwest Asia and North Africa (Middle East) 8. Great Britain 9. 20th century 10. History writing — Nationalism — Southwest Asia and North Africa (Middle East)
LC 2011038037

Uses recently declassified French and British government documents to describe how the two countries secretly divided the Middle East during World War I and the effect these mandates had on local Arabs and Jews.

Lords of the Desert: The Battle Between the United States and Great Britain for Supremacy in the Modern Middle East. James Barr. Basic Books 2018. 432 p.
ISBN 9780465050635
Grades: Adult   956
1. World politics 2. Colonialism 3. International competition 4. Political intrigue 5. Oil industry and trade 6. International relations 7. Southwest Asia and North Africa (Middle East) 8. Arab countries 9. United States 10. Great Britain 11. 20th century 12. Politics and global affairs — World politics — Southwest Asia and North Africa (Middle East) 13. History writing — Southwest Asia and North Africa (Middle East)

Using recently declassified documents, a historian describes how the United States argued with Great Britain over their colonial rule of the Arab world, ultimately forcing them out, taking their place and earning widespread resentment.

Collins, Larry
O Jerusalem! Larry Collins and Dominique Lapierre. Simon & Schuster 1988. 635 p. : Illustration; Map
ISBN 9780671662417
Grades: Adult   956
1. Israel-Arab War, 1948-1949 2. Southwest Asia and North Africa (Middle East) history 3. Jerusalem, Israel 4. 20th century 5. History writing — Arab-Israeli relations — Southwest Asia and North Africa (Middle East) 6. History writing — Wars and conflicts — Arab-Israeli conflict
LC 87038121

An account of the bitter 1948 dispute between the Arabs and Jews over Jerusalem, highlights the role of the British as well as prominent individuals in the struggle.

Includes bibliographical references (p. 595-604) and index.

Frankopan, Peter
The First Crusade: The Call from the East. Peter Frankopan. Belknap Press of Harvard University Press 2012. xxiii, 262 p. : Illustration

ISBN 9780674059948

Grades: Adult   956

1. Alexius I Comnenus, Emperor of the East, 1048-1118 2. First Crusade, 1096-1099 3. War 4. Islam 5. Christianity 6. Interfaith relations 7. Crusades 8. European history 9. Southwest Asia and North Africa (Middle East) history 10. Byzantine Empire 11. Medieval period (476-1492) 12. Byzantine Empire (330-1453) 13. History writing — Wars and conflicts — Crusades

LC 2011050722

Argues that the true instigator of the First Crusade was not Pope Urban II, as widely believed, but was in fact Emperor Alexios I Komnenos of the Christian Byzantine Empire, who in 1095, with his realm under siege from the Turks and on the point of collapse, begged the pope for military support.

Also published in large print format; Includes bibliographical references and index; First published in Great Britain in 2011 by the Bodley Head.

Lambert, Malcolm
God's Armies: Crusade and Jihad: Origins, History, Aftermath. Malcolm Lambert. WW Norton & CO Inc. 2016. 352 p.

ISBN 9781681772240

Grades: Adult   956

1. Jihad 2. Crusades 3. War 4. Islam 5. Christianity 6. Interfaith relations 7. Civilization, Medieval 8. Politics and war 9. Sacred space 10. Religions 11. Southwest Asia and North Africa (Middle East) history 12. History writing — Wars and conflicts — Crusades 13. Spirituality and Religion — Christianity — History 14. Spirituality and Religion — Islam — History

LC 2017275409

Chronicling the Christian and Islamic struggle to control the sacred places of Palestine and the Middle East between the 7th and 13th century, a dynamic new history, placing equal emphasis on the inner histories of Christianity and Islam, traces the origins and development of the crusade and jihad.

"An all-encompassing introduction to the Christian-Islamic struggle for the armchair history buff." —*Kirkus*

Lewis, Bernard
The Middle East: A Brief History of the Last 2,000 Years. Bernard Lewis. Simon & Schuster 1997. xii, 433 p. : Illustration; Map

ISBN 9780684832807

Grades: 11 12 Adult   956

1. Southwest Asia and North Africa (Middle East) history 2. History writing — Southwest Asia and North Africa (Middle East)

LC BL 99790901

National Book Critics Circle Award for Nonfiction finalist, 1996.

A popular history of the Middle East traces the rise and spread of Islam throughout this volatile region, the impact of Western ideas and technology, and Islamic fundamentalism and its struggle to control the spread of Western thought.

"Lewis has chosen to accentuate the social, economic, and cultural changes that have occurred over 20 centuries. He ranges from seemingly trivial concerns (changes in dress and manners in an Arab coffeehouse) to earth-shaking events (the Mongol conquest of Mesopotamia) in painting a rich, varied, and fascinating portrait of a region that is steeped in traditionalism while often forced by geography and politics to accept change." —*Booklist*

A Touchstone book; Includes bibliographical references (p. 394-396) and index; Originally published: New York : Scribner, 1995.

Morris, Benny
Righteous Victims: A History of the Zionist-arab Conflict, 1881-1999. Benny Morris. Knopf 1999. xiv, 751 p.

ISBN 9780679421207

Grades: Adult   956

1. Arab-Israeli conflict 2. Arab-Israeli relations 3. Israeli-Palestinian relations 4. Oslo Accords, 1993 5. Zionism 6. Southwest Asia and North Africa (Middle East) history 7. Israel 8. Palestine 9. 20th century 10. History writing — Arab-Israeli relations — Southwest Asia and North Africa (Middle East) 11. History writing — Wars and conflicts — Arab-Israeli conflict

LC 98042774

New York Times Notable Book, 1999.

Drawing on Israeli, Western, U.N, Arab, and Palestinian archives to present an objective analysis of the Arab-Israeli conflict and the fragile inner workings of the peace process.

"The author displays a remarkable grasp of the history of the Zionist-Arab conflict and an analytical style that is devoid of the polemics that have characterized so many books on this subject." —*Library Journal*

Includes bibliographical references (p. 711-725) and index.

956.04 Middle East — 1945-1980

Carter, Jimmy
Palestine: Peace Not Apartheid. Jimmy Carter. Simon & Schuster 2006. xiv, 264 p. : Map

ISBN 9780743285025

Grades: Adult   956.04

1. Carter, Jimmy, 1924- 2. Arab-Israeli conflict 3. Peace movements 4. Interethnic relations 5. Jewish people 6. Muslims 7. Islam 8. Peace 9. Judaism 10. Southwest Asian (Middle Eastern) people 11. Israeli people 12. Israel 13. Palestine 14. Southwest Asia and North Africa (Middle East) 15. 21st century 16. 20th century 17. Politics and global affairs — World politics — Southwest Asia and North Africa (Middle East) — Israel and Palestine 18. History writing — Wars and conflicts — Arab-Israeli conflict 19. Adult books for young adults

LC 2006050997

The former president draws on his understanding of Middle East history and his personal relationships with regional leaders to share an assessment of what he believes is necessary to bring lasting peace to Israel while preserving Palestinian dignity.

Includes bibliographical references and index.

Fisk, Robert
The Great War for Civilisation: The Conquest of the Middle East. Robert Fisk. Alfred A. Knopf 2005. xxii, 1107 p. : Map

ISBN 9781400041510

Grades: Adult   956.04

1. War and society 2. International relations 3. Military history 4. Colonization 5. Southwest Asia and North Africa (Middle East) 6. United States 7. 21st century 8. 20th century 9. History writing — Nationalism — Southwest Asia and North Africa (Middle East)

LC 2005049813

National Book Critics Circle Award for Nonfiction finalist, 2005.

A journalist in the Middle East for more than thirty years brings his intimate knowledge of the region to address the recent historical and political events in Iraq, Iran, Afghanistan, Algeria, Israel, and Lebanon.

Includes bibliographical references (p. [1061]-1067) and index.

Friedman, Thomas L.
★ *From Beirut to Jerusalem: Updated with a New Chapter.* Thomas L. Friedman. Anchor Books 1995. xv, 588 p.

ISBN 9780385413725

Grades: 11 12 Adult   956.04

1. Friedman, Thomas L. 2. Arab-Israeli conflict 3. Jewish people 4. Historiography 5. Palestinian people 6. International relations 7. Politics and government 8. Southwest Asia and North Africa (Middle East) history 9. Arab countries 10. Israel 11. Lebanon 12. Southwest Asia and North Africa (Middle East)

ESSENTIAL AND RECOMMENDED TITLES
956.04 Middle East — 1945-1980

13. 1990s 14. 1980s 15. 20th century 16. History writing — Arab-Israeli relations — Southwest Asia and North Africa (Middle East)

LC 95001665

ALA Notable Book, 1990; National Book Award for Nonfiction, 1989.

The New York Times Middle East correspondent profiles this troubled region, describing the everyday horrors of Beirut, the intricacies of Arab politics, Arab-Israeli relations, and American perceptions of the region.

"When recounting his frequently harrowing experiences in that troubled region, Friedman can be absolutely riveting; similarly, his historical insights, his explanation of the root causes of the Arab-Israeli conflict, and his impressions of people and places in the Holy Land never fail to fascinate." —*Booklist*

Includes index; Originally published: New York : Farrar, Straus, Giroux, 1989.

Goodman, Micah
Catch-67: The Left, the Right, and the Legacy of the Six-day War. Micah Goodman; translated by Eylon Levy. Yale Univ Pr 2018. 224 p.

ISBN 9780300236743

Grades: Adult   956.04

1. Israel-Arab War, 1967 2. Israeli-Palestinian relations 3. Arab-Israeli conflict 4. Political culture 5. Israel 6. Translations — Hebrew to English 7. Politics and global affairs — World politics — Southwest Asia and North Africa (Middle East) — Israel and Palestine

A controversial examination of the internal Israeli debate over the Israeli-Palestinian conflict from a best-selling Israeli author.

Originally published in Israel by Kinneret Zmora-Bitan Dvir, 2017; Translated from the Hebrew Milkud 67: Ha-ra'aionot me-achorei ha-machloket she-kora'at et Yisrael.

Kaufmann, Uri R.
Eighteen Days of October: The Yom Kippur War and How It Created the Modern Middle East. Uri Kaufman. St. Martin's Press 2023. 448 p.

ISBN 9781250281883

Grades: Adult   956.04

1. Israel-Arab War, 1973 2. Arab-Israeli relations 3. Military history 4. Israel-Arab War, 1967 5. Israel 6. Southwest Asia and North Africa (Middle East) 7. 20th century 8. 1970s 9. History Writing — Wars and conflicts — Arab-Israeli conflict 10. History writing — Arab-Israeli relations — Southwest Asia and North Africa (Middle East)

LC 2023015094

This major new history of the Yom Kippur War draws on formerly classified records to tell the story of the 1973 war that shaped the modern Middle East.

"If the 1967 Six Day War was an unmitigated triumph for Israel, the 1973 Yom Kippur War was very nearly a total disaster, argues real estate developer Kaufman in his deeply researched debut." —*Publishers Weekly*

Includes bibliographical references and index.

Morris, Benny
1948: A History of the First Arab-israeli War. Benny Morris. Yale University Press 2008. xiv, 524 p, 16 p. of plates : Illustration; Map

ISBN 9780300126969

Grades: 11 12 Adult   956.04

1. Arab-Israeli conflict 2. Israel-Arab War, 1948-1949 3. International relations 4. Military history 5. Politics and government 6. Southwest Asia and North Africa (Middle East) history 7. Palestine 8. Israel 9. Arab countries 10. 20th century 11. History writing — Arab-Israeli relations — Southwest Asia and North Africa (Middle East) 12. History writing — Wars and conflicts — Arab-Israeli conflict

National Jewish Book Award, 2008.

Presents an analysis of the causes, battles, and outcome of the Israel-Arab War.

Includes bibliographical references (p. 421-505) and index.

Oren, Michael B.
Six Days of War: June 1967 and the Making of the Modern Middle East. Michael B. Oren. Oxford University Press 2002. xv, 446 p, 16 p. of plates : Illustration

ISBN 9780195151749

Grades: Adult   956.04

1. Arab-Israeli relations 2. Israel-Arab War, 1967 3. Military occupation 4. Politics and government 5. Southwest Asia and North Africa (Middle East) history 6. West Bank (Jordan River) 7. Gaza Strip 8. Israel 9. 1960s 10. 20th century 11. History writing — Arab-Israeli relations — Southwest Asia and North Africa (Middle East) 12. History writing — Wars and conflicts — Arab-Israeli conflict

LC 2001058823

Los Angeles Times Book Prize for History, 2002.

Relates the events of the six-day Arab-Israeli War of June, 1967, discussing it in the context of regional and international politics and examining its consequences for the Middle East.

"What makes this book important is the breadth and depth of the research. Oren draws on archives, newly declassified documents, memoirs and interviews from Israel, America, Britain and what was then the Soviet Union." —*New York Times Book Review*

Includes bibliographical references (p. [402]-419) and index.

Shlaim, Avi
The Iron Wall: Israel and the Arab World. Avi Shlaim. W.W. Norton 2000. xxv, 670 p. : Illustration; Map

ISBN 9780393048162

Grades: 11 12 Adult   956.04

1. Arab-Israeli conflict 2. International relations 3. Southwest Asia and North Africa (Middle East) history 4. Israel 5. History writing — Arab-Israeli relations — Southwest Asia and North Africa (Middle East)

LC 99023121

Challenging the consequences of the political, social, and military miracles of the modern State of Israel, the author argues that the "Iron Wall" strategy of making Israel the dominant state in the region has not produced large-scale peace or prosperity in the Middle East.

"A thorough analysis of Israel's relationships with the West as well as its neighbors from a controversial but thoughtful point of view." —*Booklist*

Includes bibliographical references (p. [633]-642) and index.

Wright, Lawrence
Thirteen Days in September: Carter, Begin, and Sadat at Camp David. Lawrence Wright. Alfred A. Knopf 2014. 360 p.

ISBN 9780385352031

Grades: Adult   956.04

1. Carter, Jimmy, 1924- 2. Begin, Menachem, 1913-1992 3. Sadat, Anwar, 1918-1981 4. Arab-Israeli conflict 5. Israel-Arab War, 1973 6. History writing — Wars and conflicts — Arab-Israeli conflict 7. History writing — Arab-Israeli relations — Southwest Asia and North Africa (Middle East)

LC 2013497329

Booklist Editors' Choice, 2014; New York Times Notable Book, 2014; Andrew Carnegie Medal for Excellence in Non-Fiction finalist, 2015.

In September 1978, President Jimmy Carter brought representatives of Israel and Egypt together at Camp David (the U.S. president's retreat in Maryland) and persuaded them to sign a peace treaty. This detailed, authoritative account provides a compelling day-by-day chronicle of the two weeks in which President Carter, Israeli Prime Minister Menachem Begin, and Egyptian President Anwar Sadat negotiated a historic agreement that paved the way for subsequent progress toward Middle Eastern peace. Character profiles of the participants and commentary on how Judaism, Islam, and Christianity influenced the negotiations, this study vividly dramatizes and humanizes the momentous conference.

956.05 Middle East (Near East) — 1980-

Bacevich, Andrew J.
America's War for the Greater Middle East: A Military History. Andrew J. Bacevich. Random House 2016. 480 p.
ISBN 9780553393934
Grades: Adult   956.05
1. Military policy 2. International relations 3. Intervention (International relations) 4. Military history 5. Southwest Asia and North Africa (Middle East) 6. United States 7. History writing — Military 8. History writing — Nationalism — Southwest Asia and North Africa (Middle East)
LC 2015038868
A critical assessment of America's foreign policy in the Middle East throughout the past four decades evaluates and connects regional engagements since 1990 while revealing their massive costs.
Includes bibliographical references and index.

Engel, Richard
And Then All Hell Broke Loose: Two Decades in the Middle East. Richard Engel. Simon & Schuster 2016. 400 p.
ISBN 9781451635119
Grades: Adult   956.05
1. Engel, Richard, 1973- 2. Foreign correspondents 3. War correspondents 4. Politics and government 5. Southwest Asia and North Africa (Middle East) 6. 21st century 7. Autobiographies and memoirs 8. Life stories — Arts and culture — Writing — Journalists 9. Politics and global affairs — World politics — Southwest Asia and North Africa (Middle East)
LC 2015030898
Over two decades Engel has been under fire, blown out of hotel beds, taken hostage. He has watched Mubarak and Morsi in Egypt arrested and condemned, reported from Jerusalem, been through the Lebanese war, covered the whole shooting match in Iraq, interviewed Libyan rebels who toppled Gaddafi, reported from Syria as Al-Qaeda stepped in, was kidnapped in the Syrian crosscurrents of fighting. He goes into Afghanistan with the Taliban and to Iraq with ISIS.
"Clear, candid, and concise, Engels overview of the ongoing battleground should be required reading for anyone desiring a thorough and informed portrait of what the past has created and what the future holds for the Middle East and the world at large." —*Booklist*
Includes index.

Shavit, Ari
My Promised Land: The Triumph and Tragedy of Israel. Ari Shavit. Spiegel & Grau 2013. 480 p.
ISBN 9780385521703
Grades: Adult   956.05
1. Arab-Israeli conflict 2. Zionism 3. Arab-Israeli relations 4. Jewish people 5. International relations 6. Political science 7. Southwest Asian (Middle Eastern) people 8. Israeli people 9. Interethnic relations 10. Politics and government 11. Israel 12. History writing — Arab-Israeli relations — Southwest Asia and North Africa (Middle East)
LC 2012046122
New York Times Notable Book, 2013; National Jewish Book Award, 2013.
Presents an examination of Israel that traces the events that led the country to its current state of conflict through the stories of everyday citizens to illuminate the importance of lesser-known historical events.

Thrall, Nathan
★ *A Day in the Life of Abed Salama: Anatomy of a Jerusalem Tragedy.* Nathan Thrall. Metropolitan Books, Henry Holt and Company 2023. xiii, 255 p.
ISBN 9781250854971
Grades: Adult   956.05
1. Salama, Abed 2. Palestinian men 3. Traffic accidents 4. Fathers and sons 5. Military occupation 6. Bureaucracy 7. Tragedy 8. Marginalized people 9. Injustice 10. Arab-Israeli relations 11. Jerusalem, Israel 12. West Bank (Jordan River) 13. Life stories — Facing adversity — War and oppression 14. History writing — Arab-Israeli relations — Southwest Asia and North Africa (Middle East)
LC 2023017070
Pulitzer Prize for General Nonfiction, 2024.
Five-year-old Milad Salama is excited for a school trip to a theme park on the outskirts of Jerusalem. On the way, his bus collides with a semitrailer. His father, Abed, gets word of the crash and rushes to the site. The scene is chaos—the children have been taken to different hospitals in Jerusalem and the West Bank. Abed sets off on an odyssey to learn Milad's fate. It is every parent's worst nightmare, but for Abed it is compounded by the maze of physical, emotional, and bureaucratic obstacles he must navigate because he is Palestinian.
"A moving, often maddening portrait of the dire life straits of Palestinians in Israel." —*Kirkus*
Includes bibliographical references and index.

956.1 Turkey

Finkel, Caroline
Osman's Dream: The Story of the Ottoman Empire, 1300-1923. Caroline Finkel. Basic Books 2006. xix, 660 p. : Illustration; Map
ISBN 9780465023967
Grades: Adult   956.1
1. Osman I, Sultan of the Turks, 1258-1326 2. Rulers 3. Civilization, Islamic 4. Southwest Asia and North Africa (Middle East) history 5. Turkey 6. Ottoman Empire (1299-1922) 7. History writing — Southwest Asia and North Africa (Middle East)
LC Bl2006029375
An account of the epic story of the Ottoman empire, from its origins in the thirteenth century through its destruction on the battlefields of World War I.
"This history makes a riveting and enjoyable read for all audiences." —*Publishers Weekly*
Includes bibliographical references (p. 573-641) and index; Originally published: London : John Murray Publishers, 2005.

956.6 Eastern Turkey

Akcam, Taner
A Shameful Act: The Armenian Genocide and the Question of Turkish Responsibility. Taner Akcam; translated by Paul Bessemer. Metropolitan Books 2006. x, 483 p. : Map
ISBN 9780805079326
Grades: Adult   956.6
1. Armenian genocide, 1915-1923 2. Genocide 3. War crimes 4. Southwest Asia and North Africa (Middle East) history 5. Turkey 6. 1910s 7. 20th century 8. Society and culture — Violence and crime — Genocide 9. Life stories — Facing adversity — War and oppression — War survivors 10. History writing — Southwest Asia and North Africa (Middle East)
LC 2005058401
Minnesota Book Award for General Nonfiction, 2007.
A study of the Armenian genocide draws on Ottoman sources, including parliamentary minutes, letters, military and court records, and eyewitness accounts, to lay responsibility for the event on Turkish authorities, revealing a systematic orchestration of the killings by the military, ruling political parties, and the Ottoman state.
Originally published in Turkey in 1999 under the title Insan haklari ve Ermeni sorunu : Ittihat ve Terakki'den Kurtulus Savasi'n—T.P. verso; Includes bibliographical references (p. [377]-464) and index.

Balakian, Peter
The Burning Tigris: The Armenian Genocide and America's Response. Peter Balakian. Harper Collins 2003. xx, 475 p. : Illustration
ISBN 9780060198404
Grades: Adult   956.6

ESSENTIAL AND RECOMMENDED TITLES
956.62 Northeastern Turkey

1. Genocide 2. Human rights 3. Armenian genocide, 1915-1923 4. Armenian people 5. Southwest Asia and North Africa (Middle East) history 6. Turkey 7. 1910s 8. 20th century 9. Society and culture — Violence and crime — Genocide 10. Life stories — Facing adversity — War and oppression — War survivors 11. History writing — Southwest Asia and North Africa (Middle East)

LC 2003044986

New York Times Notable Book, 2003.

A history of the Armenian massacres of the 1890s and the genocide of 1915 also traces America's effort to assist the Armenian people, citing the contributions of such figures as Julia Ward Howe, Theodore Roosevelt, and Mark Twain.

"The book's real power derives from the eyewitness accounts of the genocide itself. The sheer volume of outsiders' testimony that Balakian compiles, and the horrifying similarity of their observations of men, women and children beaten, tortured, burned to death in churches or sent out into the desert to starve, is an overwhelmingly convincing retort to genocide deniers." —*New York Times Book Review*

Includes bibliographical references (p. [441]-453) and index.

Mackeen, Dawn Anahid
The Hundred-Year Walk: An Armenian Odyssey. Dawn Anahid Mackeen. Houghton Mifflin Harcourt 2015. 288 p.
ISBN 9780618982660
Grades: Adult   956.6

1. Miskjian, Stepan, 1886-1974 2. Mackeen, Dawn Anahid 3. Armenian genocide, 1915-1923 4. Crimes against humanity 5. Refugees, Armenian 6. Armenian genocide survivors 7. Deportation 8. Atrocities 9. Genocide 10. World War I 11. Armenian people 12. Southwest Asia and North Africa (Middle East) history 13. Turkey 14. 1910s 15. 20th century 16. Biographies 17. Society and culture — Violence and crime — Genocide 18. Life stories — Facing adversity — War and oppression — War survivors 19. History writing — Southwest Asia and North Africa (Middle East)

LC 2015016713

During and after World War I, the Ottoman government killed over a million Armenians in one of the first modern genocides. One survivor was Stepan Miskjian; he escaped from a caravan leading him to slaughter, walked 1,000 miles across Turkey and Syria, and later wrote journals about his experiences. Using those journals as a starting point, his granddaughter, journalist Dawn Anahid MacKeen retraced his footsteps, learning about her grandfather, her roots, herself, and the Middle East in the process. Deftly combining history and travelogue, MacKeen provides a harrowing and inspirational tale.

"Powerful, terrible stories about what people are willing to do to other peoplebut leavened with hope and, ultimately, forgiveness." —*Kirkus*

956.62 Northeastern Turkey

Bogosian, Eric
Operation Nemesis: The Assassination Plot That Avenged the Armenian Genocide. Eric Bogosian. Little, Brown & Co. 2015. 288 p.
ISBN 9780316292085
Grades: Adult   956.62

1. Armenian genocide, 1915-1923 2. Revenge 3. Assassination plots 4. Assassins 5. Refugees, Armenian 6. Southwest Asia and North Africa (Middle East) history 7. Turkey 8. 20th century 9. History writing — Europe — Eastern Europe 10. History writing — Wars and conflicts — World War I

In 1921, a small group of self-appointed patriots set out to avenge the deaths of almost one million victims of the Armenian Genocide. They named their operation Nemesis after the Greek goddess of retribution. Over several years, the men tracked down and assassinated former Turkish leaders. The story of this secret operation has never been fully told until now. Eric Bogosian goes beyond simply telling the story of this cadre of Armenian assassins to set the killings in context by providing a summation of the Ottoman and Armenian history as well as the history of the genocide itself.

956.7044 Iraq — 1979-

Abdul-Ahad, Ghaith
A Stranger in Your Own City: Travels in the Middle East's Long War. Ghaith Abdul-Ahad. Alfred A. Knopf 2023. 320 p.
ISBN 9780593536889
Grades: Adult   956.7044

1. Abdul-Ahad, Ghaith 2. Iraq War, 2003-2011 3. War 4. Voyages and travels 5. Baghdad, Iraq 6. Iraq 7. Debut title 8. Life stories — Identity 9. History writing — Southwest Asia and North Africa (Middle East) 10. History Writing — Wars and conflicts — Iraq War

LC 2022048464

An award-winning journalist's powerful portrait of his native Baghdad, the people of Iraq, and twenty years of war.

"Journalist Abdul-Ahad's kaleidoscopic and incisive debut recounts the 20 years since U.S.-led coalition forces took control of Baghdad....It's a master class in reporting." —*Publishers Weekly*

Bardenwerper, William
The Prisoner in His Palace: Saddam Hussein, His American Guards, and What History Leaves Unsaid. Will Bardenwerper. Scribner 2017. 272 p.
ISBN 9781501117831
Grades: Adult   956.7044

1. Hussein, Saddam, 1937-2006 2. Soldiers 3. Prison guards 4. Trials (Crimes against humanity) 5. Capital punishment 6. Former presidents 7. Military prisons 8. Imprisonment 9. Compassion 10. Prisoners 11. Dictators 12. Trials 13. Impartial writing 14. History writing — Wars and conflicts — Iraq War 15. Life stories — Law and order — Criminals and law-breakers

Documents the story of twelve young American soldiers deployed to Iraq in the summer of 2006 who were assigned to guard Saddam Hussein in the months before his execution, a responsibility that raised life-changing questions about their beliefs and Hussein's character.

"Bardenwerpers engrossing history reveals that everybody has the capacity for good, and, more disturbingly, that every good person has the capacity for great evil." —*Publishers Weekly*

Chandrasekaran, Rajiv
Imperial Life in the Emerald City: Inside Iraq's Green Zone. Rajiv Chandrasekaran. Alfred A. Knopf 2006. x, 320 p. : Map
ISBN 9781400044870
Grades: 11 12 Adult   956.7044

1. Postwar reconstruction 2. Iraq War, 2003-2011 3. Political corruption 4. Politics and government 5. Southwest Asia and North Africa (Middle East) history 6. Iraq 7. United States 8. 2000s (Decade) 9. 21st century 10. Page to screen 11. History writing — Wars and conflicts — Iraq War

LC 2006041014

New York Times Notable Book, 2007; Samuel Johnson Prize for Nonfiction, 2007; National Book Award for Nonfiction finalist, 2006.

A journalist and former Baghdad bureau chief for the Washington Post furnishes a revealing look at life in Baghdad's Green Zone, the headquarters for the American occupation in Iraq, criticizing the follies and foibles of L. Paul Bremer and others in the invasion and reconstruction of Iraq.

"This is a clearly written, blessedly undidactic book. It should be read by anyone who wants to understand how things went so badly wrong in Iraq." —*New York Times Book Review*

Book made into a movie called Green zone; Includes bibliographical references (p. [303]-306) and index.

Coker, Margaret
The Spymaster of Baghdad: A True Story of Bravery, Family, and Patriotism in the Battle Against Isis. Margaret Coker. Dey Street Books 2020. 320 p.
ISBN 9780062947420
Grades: Adult   956.7044

1. Intelligence service 2. Espionage 3. Terrorism prevention 4. Terrorism 5. Patriotism 6. Spies 7. Southwest Asia and North Africa (Middle East) history 8. Iraq 9. 21st century 10. Politics and global affairs — Terrorism 11. History

writing — Spies and spying 12. History writing — Wars and conflicts 13. Nonfiction that reads like fiction

LC 2020034098

From the former New York Times bureau chief in Baghdad comes the gripping and heroic story of an elite, top-secret team of unlikely spies who triumphed over ISIS.

"Coll's book is an important addition to the history of the Iraq War, and shows how Iraqi security and intelligence agencies made significant contributions in restoring order during and especially since the end of the conflict." —Library Journal

Includes bibliographical references and index.

Coll, Steve
★ The *Achilles Trap: Saddam Hussein, the C.I.A, and the Origins of America's Invasion of Iraq.* Steve Coll. Penguin Press 2024. 576 p.
ISBN 9780525562269
Grades: Adult   956.7044
1. Hussein, Saddam, 1937-2006 2. Iraq War, 2003-2011 3. Politics and government 4. International relations 5. International security 6. Political corruption 7. Military secrets 8. Iraq 9. United States 10. 2000s (Decade) 11. History writing — Wars and conflicts — Iraq War 12. Politics and global affairs — World politics — Southwest Asia and North Africa (Middle East)

LC 2023022034

From bestselling and Pulitzer Prize-winning author Steve Coll, the definitive story of the decades-long relationship between the United States and Saddam Hussein, and a deeply researched and news-breaking investigation into how human error, cultural miscommunication, and hubris led to one of the costliest geopolitical conflicts of our time.

"The Pulitzer Prize-winning author returns with a tour de force examination of the events leading up to the 2003 invasion of Iraq." —*Kirkus*

Includes bibliographical references and index.

Draper, Robert
To Start a War: How the Bush Administration Took America into Iraq. Robert Draper. Penguin Press 2020. xiv, 480 p.
ISBN 9780525561040
Grades: Adult   956.7044
1. Bush, George W. (George Walker), 1946- 2. Iraq War, 2003-2011 3. Cabinet officers 4. Military intelligence 5. Decision-making 6. September 11 Terrorist Attacks, 2001 7. War on Terrorism, 2001-2009 8. Conspiracies 9. International relations 10. Military policy 11. Presidents 12. Causes of war 13. Politics and government 14. United States history 15. United States 16. 21st century 17. 2000s (Decade) 18. Impartial writing 19. History writing — Wars and conflicts — Iraq War 20. History writing — Presidency — 21st century — United States 21. Life stories — Politics

LC 2020001715

From the author of Dead Certain comes the definitive, revelatory reckoning with arguably the most consequential decision in the history of American foreign policy—the decision to invade Iraq. Even now, after more than fifteen years, it is hard to see the these events through the cool, considered gaze of history. For too many people, the damage is still too palpable, and still unfolding. Robert Draper's prodigious reporting has yielded scores of consequential new revelations, from the important to the merely absurd. As a whole, the book paints a vivid and indelible picture of a decision-making process that was fatally compromised by a combination of post-9/11 fear and paranoia, rank naivete, craven groupthink, and a set of actors who gamed the process relentlessly.

"Although exhaustive details might discourage general audiences, informed readers and foreign policy specialists will be engaged in what is likely the definitive contemporary account of the origins of the War in Iraq." —*Library Journal*

Includes bibliographical references and index.

Filkins, Dexter
The Forever War. Dexter Filkins. Alfred A. Knopf 2008. 384 p.
ISBN 9780307266392
Grades: Adult   956.7044
1. Iraq War, 2003-2011 2. War on Terrorism, 2001-2009 3. World politics 4. Terrorism 5. War 6. Politics and government 7. Southwest Asia and North Africa (Middle East) 8. Politics and global affairs — Terrorism 9. History writing — Wars and conflicts 10. Spirituality and Religion — Islam — Political Aspects

LC 2008011761

National Book Critics Circle Award for Non-Fiction, 2008; ALA Notable Book, 2009; New York Times Notable Book, 2008.

Provides a firsthand account of the battle against Islamic fundamentalism, from the rise of the Taliban in the 1990s, to the terrorist attacks of 9/11, to the wars in Afghanistan and Iraq, offering a study of the people involved from all sides of the conflict.

Finkel, David
The Good Soldiers. by David Finkel. Farrar, Straus and Giroux 2009. 304 p.
ISBN 9780374165734
Grades: 11 12 Adult   956.7044
1. Iraq War, 2003-2011 2. Military campaigns 3. Battles 4. Unconventional warfare 5. Soldiers 6. Southwest Asia and North Africa (Middle East) history 7. Iraq 8. United States 9. 21st century 10. Biographies 11. History writing — Military — Military Today 12. Adult books for young adults 13. History writing — Wars and conflicts — Iraq War

LC 2009019391

Alex Award, 2010; J. Anthony Lukas Book Prize, 2010; ALA Notable Book, 2010; New York Times Notable Book, 2009.

Relates the author's experiences as an embedded reporter with Battalion 2-16, telling the story of the surge from the perspective of the someone who worked with the soldiers every day.

Frederick, Jim
Black Hearts: One Platoon's Plunge into Madness in the Triangle of Death and the American Struggle in Iraq. Jim Frederick. Harmony Books 2010. 352 p.
ISBN 9780307450753
Grades: Adult   956.7044
1. War crimes 2. Murder 3. Rape 4. Iraq War, 2003-2011 5. Soldiers 6. Iraq War veterans 7. Atrocities 8. Psychology 9. Social life and customs 10. Iraq 11. 21st century 12. Impartial writing 13. History writing — Wars and conflicts — Iraq War 14. History writing — Military — Special Forces 15. True Crime — Sex Crimes

LC 2009035537

Documents the events surrounding the tragic rape of a 14-year-old Iraqi girl and the executions of her family members by members of the 502nd Infantry Regiment, citing contributing factors while examining the event's relevance in shaping future military initiatives.

Includes bibliographical references and index.

Gallego, Ruben
They Called Us. Ruben Gallego, with Jim DeFelice. Custom House 2021. 304 p.
ISBN 9780063045811
Grades: Adult   956.7044
1. Gallego, Ruben, 1979- 2. Iraq War, 2003-2011 3. Marines 4. Iraq War veterans 5. Hispanic Americans 6. Military campaigns 7. Battles 8. Terrorism 9. Combat 10. War casualties 11. Post-traumatic stress disorder 12. Adjustment 13. Postwar life 14. Legislators 15. Iraq 16. United States 17. Autobiographies and memoirs 18. Biographies 19. Life stories — Law and order — Armed forces personnel 20. Life stories — Politics — Politicians 21. History writing — Wars and conflicts — Iraq War 22. History writing — Military — Military units

LC 2021038045

Opening up for the first time about his combat experience, Congressman Ruben Gallego (D, AZ) delivers a moving and unforgettable memoir of the eternal bonds forged between the Marines of Lima Company, the hardest-hit unit of the Iraq War.

Serving as a tribute to his fallen comrades, who made the ultimate sacrifice for their country, Congressman and former infantryman Ruben Gallego presents a memoir in which he shares the eternal bonds forged between the Marines of Lima Company, the hardest-hit unit of the Iraq War.

ESSENTIAL AND RECOMMENDED TITLES
956.7044 Iraq — 1979-

"Arizona congressman Gallego and DeFelice (coauthor, American Sniper) deliver a powerful, grunt's-eye view of modern combat and the struggle to readjust to life back home.... This searing autobiography leaves a mark." —*Kirkus*

Includes bibliographical references.

King, Charles Monroe
A Journal for Jordan: Hopes, Prayers, and Life Lessons from a Fallen Soldier and the Woman He Loved for the Son He Left Behind. Charles Monroe King with Dana Canedy. Crown Publishers 2008. 288 p.
ISBN 9780307395795
Grades: Adult   956.7044
1. King, Charles Monroe, d. 2006 2. Iraq War, 2003-2011 3. Soldiers 4. Death 5. Advice 6. Fathers and sons 7. Fatherhood 8. Autobiographies and memoirs 9. Life stories — Law and order — Armed forces personnel 10. Family and Relationships — Parenting
LC 2008034135

In a poignant memoir of love and war, a Pulitzer Prize-winning journalist presents the journal of her fiance, a dedicated career soldier killed in Iraq, in which he records the events of the war, his grief over losing men in battle, and advice to his infant son on every aspect of life.

Luttrell, Marcus
Service: A Navy SEAL at War. Marcus Luttrell, with James D. Hornfischer. Little Brown & Co. 2012. 352 p.
ISBN 9780316185363
Grades: Adult   956.7044
1. Iraq War, 2003-2011 2. Special forces 3. Military service 4. Navy SEALs 5. Soldiers 6. United States 7. Autobiographies and memoirs 8. Biographies 9. Life stories — Law and order — Armed forces personnel
LC 2012904468

A combat trained Navy SEAL shares dramatic stories from his Special Operations assignments throughout the world while highlighting the contributions of remarkable soldiers.

Mikhaiil, Dunya
The Beekeeper: Saving the Stolen Women of Iraq. Dunya Mikhail; translated by Max Weiss. New Directions Publishing Corporation 2018. 211 p.
ISBN 9780811226127
Grades: Adult   956.7044
1. Yezidis 2. Escapes 3. Beekeepers 4. Women refugees 5. Human trafficking 6. Survival 7. Social advocacy 8. Sexual slavery 9. Genocide 10. Collective biographies 11. Translations — Arabic to English 12. History writing — Southwest Asia and North Africa (Middle East) 13. Life stories — Facing adversity — War and oppression

Describes the harrowing stories of women who escaped the Islamic State, all of whom said their hero was a beekeeper who used his knowledge of local terrain and a wide network of helpers and smugglers to get them to safety.

Translation of: Fi Suq Al-sabaya; Originally published: Manshurat al-Mutawassit, 2017; Translated from the Arabic.

Mills, Dan
Sniper One: On Scope and Under Siege with a Sniper Team in Iraq. Dan Mills. St. Martin's Press 2008. 352 p.
ISBN 9780312531263
Grades: Adult   956.7044
1. Mills, Dan, 1968- 2. Iraq War, 2003-2011 3. Snipers 4. British people in Southwest Asia and North Africa (Middle East) 5. Soldiers 6. Armed Forces 7. Iraq 8. Great Britain 9. Autobiographies and memoirs 10. Life stories — Law and order — Armed forces personnel 11. History writing — Military — Special Forces 12. Adult books for young adults
LC 2008020438

A decorated member of the Princess of Wales' Royal Regiment recounts his 2004 tour of duty in Iraq, a six-month service of peaceful intentions that were violently altered by hostile attacks by the people of AL Amarah.

"When a battalion of the Princess of Wales' Royal Regiment landed in Iraq in 2004, Mills commanded the 18 men of the sniper platoon. His gripping combat narrative covers how the platoon did more than its share of the fighting during the months when the Iraqis virtually besieged the battalion." —*Booklist*

Nixon, John
Debriefing the President: The Interrogation of Saddam Hussein. John Nixon. Blue Rider Press 2016. 242 pages
ISBN 9780399575815
Grades: Adult   956.7044
1. Hussein, Saddam, 1937-2006 2. Nixon, John (Middle East expert) 3. Dictators 4. War criminals 5. Military interrogation 6. Iraq War, 2003-2011 7. Causes of war 8. Politics and government 9. Iraq 10. 21st century 11. Politics and global affairs — World politics — Southwest Asia and North Africa (Middle East)
LC 2016047934

The first man to conduct a prolonged interrogation of Saddam Hussein after his capture explains why preconceived ideas about the dictator led Washington policymakers and the Bush White House astray.

Packer, George
The Assassins' Gate: America in Iraq. George Packer. Farrar, Straus and Giroux 2005. 467 p.
ISBN 9780374299637
Grades: Adult   956.7044
1. Military policy 2. Iraq War, 2003-2011 3. Insurgency 4. Civil war 5. American people in Southwest Asia and North Africa (Middle East) 6. International relations 7. Politics and government 8. Iraq 9. United States 10. 2000s (Decade) 11. Impartial writing 12. Adult books for young adults 13. History writing — Wars and conflicts — Iraq War
LC 2005011521

ALA Notable Book, 2006; New York Times Notable Book, 2005; Pulitzer Prize for General Nonfiction finalist.

The Assassins' Gate, dubbed so by American soldiers, is the entrance to the American zone in the city of Baghdad. In 2003, the United States blazed into Iraq to depose dictator Saddam Hussein. But after three years and unknown thousands killed, that country faces an escalating civil war and an uncertain fate. How did it get to this point? George Packer describes the players and ideas behind the Bush administration's war policy. He also provides first-hand accounts of the men and women—both civilian and military, coalition and Iraqi—who are caught in the middle of the conflict.

"This book rests on three main pillars: Analysis of the intellectual origins of the Iraq war, summary of the political argument that preceded and then led to it, and firsthand description of the consequences on the ground. The Iraq debate has long needed someone who is both tough-minded enough, and sufficiently sensitive, to register all its complexities. In George Packer's work, this need is answered." —*Publishers Weekly*

Includes bibliographical references and index.

Philipps, David
Alpha: Eddie Gallagher and the War for the Soul of the Navy SEALs. David Philipps. Crown 2021. 480 p.
ISBN 9780593238387
Grades: Adult   956.7044
1. Gallagher, Eddie, 1979- 2. Courts-martial and courts of inquiry 3. War crime trials 4. Iraq War, 2003-2011 5. Military discipline 6. Trials (Murder) 7. United States 8. Mosul, Iraq 9. Biographies 10. Life stories — Law and order — Armed forces personnel 11. History writing — Military — Special forces 12. History writing — Wars and conflicts — Iraq war
LC 2021012804

Pulitzer Prize-winning reporter David Philipps uncovers the shocking rise and fall of Eddie Gallagher, the decorated Navy SEAL accused of war crimes during his deployment to Mosul, the fellow SEALs who turned him in, and the court martial that captivated the nation.

"New York Times reporter Philipps (Lethal Warriors) presents an enthralling, blow-by-blow account of the 2019 court-martial of U.S. Navy SEAL platoon chief Eddie Gallagher for stabbing a wounded ISIS prisoner to death...."

This is the definitive portrait of a saga that exposed deep fault lines within an elite fighting force." —*Publishers Weekly*

Includes index.

Ricks, Thomas E.

Fiasco: The American Military Adventure in Iraq. Thomas E. Ricks. Penguin Press 2006. xiv, 482 pages, 16 unnumbered pages of plates : Illustration; Map

ISBN 9780143038917

Grades: Adult 956.7044

1. Iraq War, 2003-2011 2. Military strategy 3. Decision-making 4. International relations 5. Armed Forces 6. Iraq 7. United States 8. 21st century 9. History writing — Wars and conflicts — Iraq War

New York Times Notable Book, 2006; Pulitzer Prize for General Nonfiction finalist.

An assessment of America's role in the Iraq War as viewed from the perspectives of senior military officers argues that the guerrilla insurgency after the fall of Saddam Hussein was avoidable and that officers who spoke against the war did so at the cost of their careers.

"The author critically assesses the Bush administration's decision to invade Iraq and its management of the war and the occupation." —*New York Times*

"This book is not a political rant nor is it shrill. But in its low-key, extraordinarily well-sourced, highly-detailed portrait of the run-up to and conduct of the war it is devastating." —*Christian Science Monitor*

Includes bibliographical references (p. [452]-473) and index.

Stewart, Rory

The Prince of the Marshes: And Other Occupational Hazards of a Year in Iraq. Rory Stewart. Harvest Books 2007. 432 p.

ISBN 9780156032797

Grades: Adult 956.7044

1. Stewart, Rory 2. British people in Southwest Asia and North Africa (Middle East) 3. Iraq War, 2003-2011 4. Governors 5. Strategic alliances (Military) 6. Voyages and travels 7. Iraq 8. Autobiographies and memoirs 9. Life stories — Politics — Politicians 10. Adult books for young adults 11. History writing — Wars and conflicts — Iraq War

LC Bl2007009349

Recounts how the author, a British diplomat, was named deputy governor of Amarah and Nasiriya in southern Iraq at the end of 2003, an appointment during which he negotiated hostage releases, held elections, and worked to organize a social infrastructure for millions of beleaguered Iraqi citizens.

"In 2003, Stewart, a former British diplomat, joined the Coalition Provisional Authority in Iraq and was posted to the southern province of Maysan, where he found himself the de-facto governor of a restive populace whose allegiances were split among fifty-four political parties, twenty major tribes, and numerous militias. Stewart's account of his attempts to placate the various local figures who continually threaten to kill each other, or him, is both shrewd and self-deprecating." —*The New Yorker*

Originally published: Orlando, FL : Harcourt, 2006.

Swofford, Anthony

Jarhead: A Marine's Chronicle of the Gulf War and Other Battles. Anthony Swofford. Scribner 2003. 260 p.

ISBN 9780743235358

Grades: 11 12 Adult 956.7044

1. Swofford, Anthony 2. Snipers 3. Persian Gulf War, 1991 4. Marines 5. Soldiers 6. United States 7. Autobiographies and memoirs 8. Page to screen 9. Biographies 10. History writing — Wars and conflicts — Persian Gulf War 11. Life stories — Law and order — Armed forces personnel

LC 2002030866

New York Times Notable Book, 2003.

Swofford weaves his experience of the Gulf War in the early 1990s with vivid accounts of boot camp, reflections on the mythos of the marines, and remembrances of battles with lovers and family.

"This book offers an unflinching portrayal of the loneliness and brutality of modern warfare and sophisticated analyses of—and visceral reactions to—its politics." —*Publishers Weekly*

Verini, James

They Will Have to Die Now: Mosul and the Fall of the Caliphate. James Verini. W.W. Norton & Company, Inc. 2019. 277 pages : Map

ISBN 9780393652475

Grades: Adult 956.7044

1. War correspondents 2. Soldiers 3. Antiterrorists 4. Terrorism 5. Extremism 6. Urban warfare 7. Military occupation 8. Politics and government 9. Mosul, Iraq 10. Iraq 11. 21st century 12. Politics and global affairs — Terrorism 13. History writing — Wars and conflicts 14. History writing — Southwest Asia and North Africa (Middle East) 15. Life stories — Arts and culture — Writing — Journalists

LC 2019014781

An award-winning journalist documents his firsthand witness to the events of the Battle of Mosul in Iraq, describing the conflict's harrowing violence and improbable humanity through the experiences of Middle East soldiers and civilians.

Wright, Evan

Generation Kill: Devil Dogs, Iceman, Captain America, and the New Face of American War. Evan Wright. G.P. Putnam's Sons 2004. 354 p. : Illustration; Map

ISBN 9780399151934

Grades: Adult 956.7044

1. Marines 2. Guerrilla warfare 3. War 4. Soldiers 5. Iraq War, 2003-2011 6. Psychology 7. Southwest Asia and North Africa (Middle East) history 8. Iraq 9. 21st century 10. Adult books for young adults 11. History writing — Wars and conflicts — Iraq War

LC 2004044682

Los Angeles Times Book Prize for Current Interest, 2004; J. Anthony Lukas Book Prize, 2005.

Wright rode into Iraq on March 20, 2003, with a platoon of First Reconnaissance Battalion Marines, the Marine Corps' special operations unit whose motto is "Swift, Silent, Deadly." These highly trained and highly motivated First Recon Marines were the leading unit of the American-led invasion force. Wright wrote about that experience in a three-part series in Rolling Stone that was hailed for its evocative, accurate war reporting.

"This account is a personality-driven, readable and insightful look at the Iraq War's first month from the Marine grunt's point of view." —*Publishers Weekly*

956.70443 Iraq — 1991-

Seierstad, Asne

A Hundred and One Days: A Baghdad Journal. Asne Seierstad; translated by Ingrid Christophersen. Basic Books 2005. 321 p. : Illustration; Map

ISBN 9780465076000

Grades: 11 12 Adult 956.70443

1. Seierstad, Asne, 1970- 2. Journalists 3. Iraq War, 2003-2011 4. Iraq 5. 21st century 6. Adult books for young adults 7. History writing — Wars and conflicts — Iraq War

Provides a narrative of life in Iraq just before, during, and after the American invasion of March 2003, presenting the opinions and experiences of ordinary Iraquis attempting to carry on some semblance of normal life.

"The author writes about her stay as a reporter for Scandinavian, Dutch, and German media in Baghdad in the days before the war in Iraq through the fall of Baghdad.... Seierstad puts a human face to and provides insight into the mosaic of the people of Iraq, the Bath party supporters, the dissidents, and the average person caught in the nightmare of the Saddam regime and the horrors of war." —*School Library Journal*

Originally published in Norwegian as Hundre og en dag: Oslo, Norway : J.W. Cappelen, 2003.

ESSENTIAL AND RECOMMENDED TITLES
956.9104 Syria — 1920-

956.9104 Syria — 1920-

Abouzeid, Rania
No Turning Back: Life, Loss, and Hope in Wartime Syria. Rania Abouzeid. W. W. Norton & Company 2018. 384 p.
ISBN 9780393609493
Grades: Adult   956.9104
1. Abouzeid, Rania 2. Assad, Bashar, 1965- 3. Civil war 4. Revolutions 5. Insurgency 6. Jihad 7. Military government 8. Southwest Asia and North Africa (Middle East) history 9. Syria 10. Southwest Asia and North Africa (Middle East) 11. 2010s 12. 2020s 13. Autobiographies and memoirs 14. Life stories — Facing adversity — War and oppression 15. Life stories — Law and order — Armed forces personnel 16. Politics and global affairs — World politics — Southwest Asia and North Africa (Middle East)
LC 2017052698
Booklist Editors' Choice, 2018; New York Times Notable Book, 2018; Shortlisted for the RSL Ondaatje Prize, 2019.

Chronicles the tragedy of the Syrian War through the dramatic stories of four young people, including a creator of online video protests, a father who hides his radical beliefs, an unlikely poet commander in a Free Syrian Army militia and a child who opened her family's door to a military raid that forced her father to flee.

"A brilliant, detailed work on a devastating topic. For readers interested in narrative nonfiction, the Syrian war, the Middle East, and personal accounts." —Library Journal

Dagher, Sam
Assad or We Burn the Country: How One Family's Lust for Power Destroyed Syria. Sam Dagher. Little, Brown & Company 2019. xxvi, 564 p.
ISBN 9780316556729
Grades: Adult   956.9104
1. Assad, Bashar, 1965- 2. Rulers 3. Protest movements 4. Political violence 5. Dictatorship 6. Arab Spring, 2010-2012 7. Civil war 8. World politics 9. Politics and government 10. Southwest Asia and North Africa (Middle East) history 11. Syria 12. 2010s 13. 2020s 14. Politics and global affairs — World politics — Southwest Asia and North Africa (Middle East) 15. History writing — Nationalism — Southwest Asia and North Africa (Middle East)

In spring 2011, Syrian President Bashar al-Assad turned to his friend and army commander, Manaf Tlass, for advice about how to respond to Arab Spring-inspired protests. Tlass pushed for conciliation but Assad decided to crush the uprising—an act which would catapult the country into an eight-year long war, killing almost half a million and fueling terrorism and a global refugee crisis. Assad or We Burn the Country examines Syria's tragedy through the generational saga of the Assad and Tlass families, once deeply intertwined and now estranged in Bashar's bloody quest to preserve his father's inheritance. By drawing on his own reporting experience in Damascus and exclusive interviews with Tlass, Dagher takes readers within palace walls to reveal the family behind the destruction of a country and the chaos of an entire region.

Includes bibliographical references and index.

DI Giovanni, Janine
The Morning They Came for US: Dispatches from Syria. Janine di Giovanni. Liveright Publishing 2016. 288 p.
ISBN 9780871407139
Grades: Adult   956.9104
1. Political violence 2. Civil war 3. Arab Spring, 2010-2012 4. Southwest Asia and North Africa (Middle East) history 5. Syria 6. 21st century 7. 2010s 8. 2020s 9. Collective autobiographies and memoirs 10. Life stories — Facing adversity — War and oppression 11. History writing — Nationalism — Southwest Asia and North Africa (Middle East)
LC 2016007537

Right now, Syria isn't so much a place that people jet off to as it is a place they escape from. Even so, armchair travelers can visit via award-winning foreign correspondent Janine di Giovanni's latest book. Taking readers on an eye-opening journey to the troubled country ruled by a dictator and riven by civil war, di Giovanni describes the brutality of post-Arab Spring life here. Having been based in the Middle East for over two decades, she knows Syria and evocatively shows it to readers through the stories of everyday people, including doctors, nuns, activists, a baker, a musician, and a student.

"DI Giovanni presents a devastating picture of the horrors of civil war and the disintegration of Syrian society. Her vivid depictions of suffering may be overwhelming for some readers." —Library Journal

Includes bibliographical references and index.

Fleming, Melissa
A Hope More Powerful Than the Sea: One Refugee's Incredible Story of Love, Loss, and Survival. Melissa Fleming. Flatiron Books 2017. 320 p.
ISBN 9781250105998
Grades: 11 12 Adult   956.9104
1. Zamel, Doaa Al, 1995- 2. Refugees 3. Immigration and emigration 4. Resilience 5. Families 6. Refugees, Syrian 7. Syria 8. Biographies 9. Life stories — Facing adversity — War and oppression — Refugees 10. Society and culture — Immigration 11. Adult books for young adults
LC 2016044107
Alex Award, 2018; Amelia Bloomer List, 2018.

Recounts the powerful experiences of Syrian refugee Doaa Zamel, who was cast adrift in a frigid sea with the children of drowned parents after their dangerously overcrowded ship sank, in an account that details what their experiences reveal about an ongoing international crisis.

"This book amply demonstrates why she has since become a symbol of hope for other refugees. Fleming should be congratulated for bringing AL Zamels inspiring and illuminating story to the page." —Publishers Weekly

Lemmon, Gayle Tzemach
The Daughters of Kobani: A Story of Rebellion, Courage, and Justice. Gayle Tzemach Lemmon. Penguin Press 2021. 288 p.
ISBN 9780525560685
Grades: Adult   956.9104
1. Kurds 2. Women soldiers 3. Special operations (Military science) 4. Insurgency 5. Revolutions 6. Women and war 7. Southwest Asia and North Africa (Middle East) history 8. Syria 9. 21st century 10. 2010s 11. 2020s 12. History writing — Southwest Asia and North Africa (Middle East) 13. History writing — Women's history 14. History writing — Military — Special Forces 15. Life stories — Law and order — Armed forces personnel
LC 2020027506

The story of how an all-female Kurdish militia drove ISIS from the Syrian town of Kobani, empowering the women of that region and earning the respect and support of U.S. Special Operations Forces.

"National security analyst Lemmon (Ashley's War) delivers a fascinating portrait of Kurdish female fighters and their role in the Syrian civil war and the fight against the Islamic State." —Publishers Weekly

Includes bibliographical references and index.

Levin, Daniel
Proof of Life: Twenty Days on the Hunt for a Missing Person in the Middle East. Daniel Levin. Algonquin Books of Chapel Hill 2021. 288 p.
ISBN 9781643750989
Grades: Adult   956.9104
1. Levin, Daniel, 1963- 2. Blocher, Paul (Missing person) 3. Missing persons 4. Negotiators 5. Missing men 6. Missing persons investigation 7. Southwest Asia and North Africa (Middle East) history 8. Syria 9. 2010s 10. 2020s 11. Autobiographies and memoirs 12. History writing — Southwest Asia and North Africa (Middle East) 13. Life stories — Law and order 14. History writing — Spies and spying
LC 2020048421

A fast-paced thriller wrapped in a memoir follows a lawyer turned armed-conflict negotiator as he searches for a missing person in Syria over 20 tense days, delving deep into a shadowy world where few have access to find the truth.

"Levin's story is not an easy one to experience, but it is an important one." —Booklist

PUBLIC LIBRARY CORE COLLECTION: NONFICTION
Twentieth Edition

McCann, Colum
American Mother. Colum McCann with Diane Foley. Etruscan Press 2024. 200 p.
ISBN 9798985882452
Grades: Adult   956.9104
1. Foley, Diane Marie, 1956- 2. Mothers 3. Mothers and sons 4. Terrorism 5. Hostages 6. Sons 7. War correspondents 8. Death of sons 9. War 10. Autobiographies and memoirs 11. Life stories — Facing adversity — War and oppression 12. History Writing — Wars and conflicts

"It is hard to call such a tragic story a thing of beauty, and yet that is what McCann has created here." —*Booklist*

Pearlman, Wendy
We Crossed a Bridge and It Trembled: Voices from Syria. Wendy Pearlman. HarperCollins Publishers 2017. 224 p.
ISBN 9780062654618
Grades: Adult   956.9104
1. Protest movements 2. Refugees 3. Human rights 4. Religious persecution 5. Political violence 6. Southwest Asia and North Africa (Middle East) history 7. Syria 8. 2010s 9. 2020s 10. Collective autobiographies and memoirs 11. Life stories — Facing adversity — War and oppression — Refugees 12. History writing — Nationalism — Southwest Asia and North Africa (Middle East)
LC 2016049210
Longlisted for the Andrew Carnegie Medal for Excellence in Non-Fiction, 2018.

Chronicles the lives of ordinary Syrians during the 2011 Arab Spring through the ensuing civil war and resulting humanitarian catastrophe, based on the first-hand testimonies of displaced citizens who face their uncertain future with hope, courage and conviction.

"This powerfully edifying work of witness is essential reading." —*Booklist*

Samer
The Raqqa Diaries: Escape From. Samer; edited by Mike Thomson and John Neal, translated by Ibrahim Nader, illustrated by Scott Coelho. Interlink Books 2017. 106 p.
ISBN 9781566560054
Grades: Adult   956.9104
1. Samer, 1992 or 1993- 2. Atrocities 3. Refugees, Syrian 4. Southwest Asia and North Africa (Middle East) history 5. Syria 6. 2010s 7. 2020s 8. Autobiographies and memoirs 9. Diaries 10. Translations — Arabic to English 11. Life stories — Facing adversity — War and oppression — Refugees 12. Politics and global affairs — World politics — Southwest Asia and North Africa (Middle East)
LC BI2017032381

A young activist chronicles his experience in Raqqa following its capture by Daesh and describes how he eventually fled to a refugee camp in northern Syria.

Samer (a pseudonym) is twenty-four years old. Having escaped Raqqa, he is living in a refugee camp in northern Syria. — from book jacket; This diary was smuggled out of Syria and translated from the Arabic; Translated from the Arabic.

Seierstad, Asne
Two Sisters: A Father, His Daughters, and Their Journey into the Syrian Jihad. Asne Seierstad; translated from the Norwegian by Sean Kinsella. Farrar, Straus and Giroux 2018. VI, 418 pages
ISBN 9780374279677
Grades: Adult   956.9104
1. Teenagers 2. Runaways 3. Fathers and daughters 4. Women terrorists 5. Immigrants 6. Muslims 7. Siblings 8. Social media 9. Civil war 10. Radicalism 11. Norway 12. Syria 13. Politics and global affairs — Terrorism 14. Life stories — Relationships — Family 15. Politics and global affairs — Religion and politics 16. Life stories — Facing adversity — War and oppression
LC 2017047949

Describes the true story of how two Somali immigrants living in Norway discovered that their teenage twin daughters had been radicalized and had run away to Syria to join the Islamic State and recounts their harrowing attempt to find them.

"Seierstad's scrupulous reporting shines a revealing new light on the phenomenon of young Westerners becoming fervent supporters of terror." —*Publishers Weekly*
Includes bibliographical references.

Thomson, Mike
Syria's Secret Library: Reading and Redemption in a Town Under Siege. Mike Thomson. PublicAffairs 2019. 305 pages, 16 unnumbered pages of plates : Color; Illustration
ISBN 9781541767621
Grades: Adult   956.9104
1. Libraries 2. Books and reading 3. Communities 4. Libraries and society 5. Civilians in war 6. Resilience 7. Secrets 8. Civil war 9. Southwest Asia and North Africa (Middle East) history 10. Syria 11. Damascus, Syria 12. 2010s 13. 2020s 14. History writing — Southwest Asia and North Africa (Middle East) 15. Society and culture — General
Booklist Editors' Choice, 2019.

Describes how the people of Darayya risked their lives to read in a small, secret, makeshift basement library filled with thousands of rescued books during a devastating four-year siege at the height of the Syrian Civil War.

Includes bibliographical references; Originally published in the United Kingdom in 2019 by Weidenfeld & Nicolson, an imprint of the Orion Publishing Group, Ltd.—Colophon.

Warrick, Joby
Black Flags: The Rise of ISIS. Joby Warrick. Doubleday 2015. 416 p.
ISBN 9780385538213
Grades: Adult   956.9104
1. Fundamentalism 2. Terrorists 3. Islam 4. Terrorism 5. Politics and government 6. Southwest Asia and North Africa (Middle East) 7. 21st century 8. Politics and global affairs — World politics — Southwest Asia and North Africa (Middle East) 9. Politics and global affairs — Terrorism
LC 2015020949
Pulitzer Prize for General Nonfiction, 2016.

The Pulitzer Prize-winning author of the Triple Agent traces how the strain of militant Islam behind ISIS first arose in a remote Jordanian prison and spread with the unwitting aid of two American presidents.

"The author focuses on dramatic flashpoints and the roles of key players, creating an exciting tale with a rueful tone, emphasizing how the Iraq invasion's folly birthed ISIS and created many missed opportunities to stop al-Zarqawi quickly. Warrick stops short of offering policy solutions, but he provides a valuable, readable introduction to a pressing international security threat." —*Kirkus*

Red Line: The Unraveling of Syria and America's Race to Destroy the Most Dangerous Arsenal in the World. Joby Warrick. Doubleday 2021. xv, 346 p.
ISBN 9780385544467
Grades: Adult   956.9104
1. Chemical weapons 2. Terrorism prevention 3. Antiterrorist policy 4. Spies 5. Chemical warfare 6. Atrocities 7. Weapons of mass destruction 8. International relations 9. Southwest Asia and North Africa (Middle East) history 10. Syria 11. United States 12. 2010s 13. 2020s 14. Politics and global affairs — World politics — Southwest Asia and North Africa (Middle East) 15. History writing — Southwest Asia and North Africa (Middle East) 16. History writing — Wars and conflicts — Civil Wars 17. Nonfiction that reads like fiction
LC 2020017981

In August 2012, Syrian president Bashar al-Assad was clinging to power in a vicious civil war. When secret intelligence revealed that the dictator might resort to using chemical weapons, President Obama warned that doing so would cross "a red line." Assad did it anyway, bombing the Damascus suburb of Ghouta with sarin gas, killing hundreds of civilians and forcing Obama to decide if he would mire America in another unpopular Middle Eastern war. When Russia offered to broker the removal of Syria's chemical weapons, Obama leapt at the out. So begins an electrifying race to find, remove, and destroy 1,300 tons of chemical weapons in the midst of a raging civil war. As America's ability to control events in Syria shrinks, the White House learns that ISIS, building its caliphate in

ESSENTIAL AND RECOMMENDED TITLES
956.9204 Lebanon — 1926-

Syria's war-tossed territory, is seeking chemical weapons for itself, with an eye to attacking the West.

"Pulitzer winner Warrick (Black Flags) explores America's scramble to neutralize war-torn Syria's chemical weapons in this vigorous true-life thriller.... Espionage fans and military history buffs will be enthralled." —*Publishers Weekly*

Includes bibliographical references and index.

956.9204 Lebanon — 1926-

Blanford, Nicholas
Warriors of God: How Hezballah Became the Middle East's Most Powerful Armed Group. by Nicholas Blanford. Random House 2011. 304 p.
ISBN 9781400068364
Grades: Adult   956.9204
1. Shiah Islam 2. Militants 3. Fundamentalists 4. Islam 5. Muslims 6. Lebanon 7. Israel 8. History writing — Arab-Israeli relations — Southwest Asia and North Africa (Middle East) 9. Spirituality and Religion — Islam — Political aspects
                                              LC 2011012620
Hezbollah is the most powerful Islamist group operating in the Middle East today, and no other Western journalist has penetrated as deeply inside this secretive organization as Nicholas Blanford. Now Blanford has written the first comprehensive inside account of Hezbollah and its enduring struggle against Israel.

Includes bibliographical references and index.

956.94 Palestine; Israel

Armstrong, Karen
Jerusalem: One City, Three Faiths. Karen Armstrong. Ballantine Books 2005. xxi, 482 p. : Illustration; Color; Map
ISBN 9780345391681
Grades: 11 12 Adult   956.94
1. Monotheism 2. Christianity 3. Judaism 4. Islam 5. Religions 6. Interethnic relations 7. Interfaith relations 8. Politics and government 9. Southwest Asia and North Africa (Middle East) history 10. Jerusalem, Israel 11. History writing — Arab-Israeli relations — Southwest Asia and North Africa (Middle East) 12. Spirituality and Religion — Christianity 13. Spirituality and Religion — Islam 14. Spirituality and Religion — Judaism
                                              LC 2005281886
A comprehensive history of Jerusalem, the holy city venerated by the Christian, Jewish, and Muslim faiths, explains how the city became a defining site for the three religions, following its development from its earliest origins to the present day.

"Armstrong's overarching theme, that Jerusalem has been central to the experience and sacred geography of Jews, Muslims and Christians and thus has led to deadly struggles for dominance, is a familiar one, yet she brings to her sweeping, profusely illustrated narrative a grasp of sociopolitical conditions seldom found in other books." —*Publishers Weekly*

Includes bibliographical references (p. [446]-457) and index; Originally published: New York : A.A. Knopf, 1996.

Gordis, Daniel
Impossible Takes Longer: 75 Years After Its Creation, Has Israel Fulfilled Its Founders Dreams? Daniel Gordis. Ecco Press 2023. 224 p.
ISBN 9780063239449
Grades: Adult   956.94
1. Israel 2. History writing — Arab-Israeli relations — Southwest Asia and North Africa (Middle East) 3. Politics and global affairs — World politics — Southwest Asia and North Africa (Middle East) — Israel and Palestine

On Israel's seventy-fifth anniversary comes a nuanced examination of the country's past, present, and future, from the two-time National Jewish Book Award-winning author of Israel.

"On the 75th anniversary of the creation of Israel, Gordis, a two-time winner of the National Jewish Book Award, offers a nuanced assessment of its successes and challenges....A thoughtful, well-informed analysis." —*Publishers Weekly*

Hoffman, Bruce
Anonymous Soldiers: The Struggle for Israel, 1918-1947. Bruce Hoffman. Alfred A. Knopf 2015. 532 p.
ISBN 9780307594716
Grades: Adult   956.94
1. Jewish people 2. World War II 3. Unconventional warfare 4. Zionism 5. Terrorism 6. Political science 7. Politics and government 8. Southwest Asia and North Africa (Middle East) history 9. Palestine 10. Southwest Asia and North Africa (Middle East) 11. Great Britain 12. 20th century 13. History writing — Arab-Israeli relations — Southwest Asia and North Africa (Middle East)
                                              LC 2014018177
Draws on newly available documents from the National Archives in Britain to chronicle the historical events and key campaigns that led to the creation of Israel. By the author of Inside Terrorism.

"A must-read for anyone interested in the origins of the State of Israel." —*Library Journal*

Kimmerling, Baruch
The Palestinian People: A History. Baruch Kimmerling, Joel S. Migdal. Harvard University Press 2003. xxix, 568 p. : Map
ISBN 9780674011298
Grades: Adult   956.94
1. Arab-Israeli conflict 2. Historiography 3. Palestinian people 4. Southwest Asia and North Africa (Middle East) history 5. History writing — Arab-Israeli relations — Southwest Asia and North Africa (Middle East)
                                              LC 2002191281
Chronicles the modern history of the Palestinian people from the Arab revolt of 1834 through the founding of Israel and continues up to the Oslo peace process.

An earlier version of this book was published in 1994 as Palestinians: The Making of a People—T.P. verso; Includes bibliographical references (p. 457-545) and index.

Lawler, Andrew
Under Jerusalem: The Buried History of the World's Most Contested City. Andrew Lawler. Doubleday 2021. 448 p. : Illustration; Map
ISBN 9780385546850
Grades: Adult   956.94
1. Excavations (Archaeology) 2. Tunnels 3. Tombs 4. Explorers 5. Politics and government 6. Southwest Asia and North Africa (Middle East) history 7. Jerusalem, Israel 8. History writing — Southwest Asia and North Africa (Middle East)

Bringing to life the unforgettable characters who have investigated this subterranean landscape, an acclaimed journalist takes readers into the tombs, tunnels and trenches of the Holy City, in this saga of biblical treasures, intrepid explorers and political upheaval.

"Journalist Lawler (The Secret Token) explores in this sweeping account the complicated history of archaeological digs in Jerusalem.... Richly detailed, sensitively argued, and entertainingly written, this immersive history casts Jerusalem in a new light and reveals the tensions that meet at the intersection of science, politics, religion, and history." —*Publishers Weekly*

LeBor, Adam
City of Oranges: An Intimate History of Arabs and Jews in Jaffa. Adam LeBor. Norton & Company 2007. 384 p.
ISBN 9780393329841
Grades: Adult   956.94
1. Jewish way of life 2. Jewish people 3. Arab people 4. Southwest Asia and North Africa (Middle East) history 5. Tel Aviv, Israel 6. Israel 7. 20th century 8. History writing — Arab-Israeli relations — Southwest Asia and North Africa (Middle East)
                                              LC 2007002389

An account of the Israeli-Palestinian conflict through the perspectives of three Arab and three Jewish families is drawn from personal interviews, generations-old memoirs, letters, and diaries, and offers insight into the intersection of Muslim, Jewish, and Christian communities in Tel Aviv.

Includes bibliographical references and index.

Sebag-Montefiore, Simon
Jerusalem: The Biography. by Simon Sebag Montefiore. Alfred A. Knopf 2011. 672 p.

ISBN 9780307266514

Grades: Adult   956.94

1. Interfaith relations 2. Jewish people 3. Civilization, Islamic 4. Religion and culture 5. Culture conflict 6. Causes of war 7. Cities and towns 8. Southwest Asia and North Africa (Middle East) history 9. Jerusalem, Israel 10. History writing — Arab-Israeli relations — Southwest Asia and North Africa (Middle East) 11. Spirituality and Religion — Judaism — History 12. Spirituality and Religion — Islam — History 13. Spirituality and Religion — Christianity — History

LC 2011020827

Booklist Editors' Choice, 2011; New York Times Notable Book, 2011.

An epic history of the holy city at the heart of Judaism, Christianity, and Islam is presented through the lives of its creators and conquerors, in a chronicle that draws on new archival materials, current scholarship, and the author's own family records.

"If, as some have maintained, the word Jerusalem means city of peace, it is a grand historical irony. For, as this beautifully written, absorbing, but often grim account shows, there are few stones of the city that have not been stained with the blood of its inhabitants during the past 3,000 years. Acclaimed historian and biographer Montefiore views Jerusalem as a living, breathing organism bearing the genetic imprint of many conquerors, including Jews, Greeks, Arabs, crusading Franks, Turks, and the British. While sometimes painful to read, this is an essential book for those who wish to understand a city that remains a nexus of world affairs." —*Booklist*

This Is a Borzoi Book—T.P. verso; Includes bibliographical references and index.

956.9405 Israel — 1948-

Bennis, Phyllis
Understanding the Palestinian-israeli Conflict: A Primer. Phyllis Bennis. Olive Branch Press 2007. IX, 196 p. : Map

ISBN 9781566566858

Grades: Adult   956.9405

1. Arab-Israeli conflict 2. International relations 3. Southwest Asia and North Africa (Middle East) 4. United States 5. History writing — Arab-Israeli relations — Southwest Asia and North Africa (Middle East) 6. Politics and global affairs — World politics

LC 2006100376

DI Cintio, Marcello
Pay No Heed to the Rockets: Palestine in the Present Tense. Marcello DI Cintio. Counterpoint 2018. 272 p.

ISBN 9781640090811

Grades: Adult   956.9405

1. DI Cintio, Marcello, 1973- 2. Literature and society 3. Palestinian people 4. Intellectual life 5. Authors 6. Poets 7. War 8. Arab-Israeli conflict 9. Intergenerational trauma 10. Jerusalem, Israel 11. West Bank (Jordan River) 12. Gaza Strip 13. Canadian literature 14. Travel Writing — Southwest Asia and North Africa (Middle East) 15. Life stories — Facing adversity — War and oppression 16. Arts and Entertainment — Writing and Publishing 17. History writing — Southwest Asia and North Africa (Middle East)

LC 2018007702

Marcello DI Cintio first visited Palestine in 1999, and as with most outsiders, the narrative he knew was one defined by unending struggle, a near-Sisyphean curse of stories of oppression, exile, and occupation. In Pay No Heed to the Rockets, he reveals a more complex story—the Palestinian experience as seen through the lens of authors, books, and literature. Using the form of a political-literary travelogue, he explores what literature means to modern Palestinians and how Palestinians make sense of the conflict between a rich imaginative life and the daily tedium and violence of survival.

"Interweaving history and politics, the book introduces Western readers to the modern Palestinian literary scene while celebrating the rich diversity of voices that comprise it." —*Kirkus*

Includes bibliographical references.

Ephron, Dan
Killing a King: The Assassination of Yitzhak Rabin and the Remaking of Israel. Dan Ephron. W.W. Norton & Company 2015. 352 p.

ISBN 9780393242096

Grades: Adult   956.9405

1. Rabin, Yitzhak, 1922-1995 2. Amir, Yigal 3. Assassination 4. Political violence 5. Right-wing extremists 6. Orthodox Judaism 7. Politics and government 8. Israel 9. History writing — Arab-Israeli relations — Southwest Asia and North Africa (Middle East)

LC 2015025695

Los Angeles Times Book Prize for History, 2015; New York Times Notable Book, 2015.

Traces the parallel stories of Israeli Prime Minister Yitzhak Rabin and his stalker, Yigal Amir, to explore the assassination's fundamental and wrenching impact on the conflict between Israel and Palestine.

"Fascinating characterizations of real people and intrigue make this book appealing to readers of both fiction and nonfiction thrillers and anyone interested in the history of Israel." —*Library Journal*

Includes bibliographical references and index.

Gordis, Daniel
Israel: A Concise History of a Nation Reborn. Daniel Gordis. Ecco Press 2016. 256 p.

ISBN 9780062368744

Grades: Adult   956.9405

1. Jewish history 2. Arab-Israeli conflict 3. Israel 4. Southwest Asia and North Africa (Middle East) 5. 20th century 6. History writing — Arab-Israeli relations — Southwest Asia and North Africa (Middle East)

LC 2017303760

Presenting a brief but thorough account of the cultural, economic and political history of the state of Israel, a public intellectual sheds light on the past of this complex nation, one rife with conflict, so that readers can understand its future.

"A readable, concise history that effectively captures the sense of grand ideas in Israels identity." —*Kirkus*

Kershner, Isabel
The Land of Hope and Fear: Israel's Battle for Its Inner Soul. Isabel Kershner. Alfred A. Knopf 2023. 384 p.

ISBN 9781101946763

Grades: Adult   956.9405

1. Countries 2. Sovereignty 3. Citizenship 4. Human rights 5. Jewish people 6. Arab people 7. Social life and customs 8. Political culture 9. Polarization (Social sciences) 10. Social conflict 11. Everyday life 12. Politics and government 13. Israel 14. Politics and global affairs — World politics — Southwest Asia and North Africa (Middle East) 15. Society and culture — Urban and regional studies

Drawing on her 30 years of working in Israel—the last 15 for the New York Times—a correspondent, in this moving narrative and with on-the-ground reporting, decodes Israel today at its 75th anniversary, examining the ways in which the country has both exceeded and failed the ideals and expectations of its founders.

"Nuanced and persuasive, this is a valuable dispatch from a country in turmoil." —*Publishers Weekly*

This is a Borzoi Book published by Alfred A. Knopf — t.P. verso; Includes bibliographical references and index.

ESSENTIAL AND RECOMMENDED TITLES
956.94054 Palestine; Israel — 1974-2001

Khalidi, Rashid
★ *The Hundred Years' War on Palestine: A History of Settler Colonialism and Resistance, 1917-2017.* Rashid Khalidi. Metropolitan Books 2019. 352 p.
ISBN 9781627798556
Grades: Adult   956.9405
1. Arab-Israeli conflict 2. Arab-Israeli relations 3. Military occupation 4. Southwest Asia and North Africa (Middle East) history 5. Palestine 6. History writing — Arab-Israeli relations — Southwest Asia and North Africa (Middle East) 7. Politics and global affairs — World politics — Southwest Asia and North Africa (Middle East) — Israel and Palestine
LC 2019008933

A history of the Israeli/Palestinian conflict told from the Palestinian perspective, arguing the period since the Balfour Declaration of 1917 has amounted to a hundred years of colonial war against the Palestinians.

"Highly recommended as a valuable and accurate presentation of a century of struggle between Jews and Palestinians seeking to build a nation on the same territory, vastly unequal in resources and efficacy." —*Library Journal*

Includes bibliographical references and index.

Mitchell, George J.
A Path to Peace: A Brief History of Israeli-palestinian Negotiations and a Way Forward in the Middle East. George J. Mitchell, Alon Sachar. Simon & Schuster 2016. 192 p.
ISBN 9781501153914
Grades: Adult   956.9405
1. Arab-Israeli conflict 2. Peace 3. Politics and government 4. Palestine 5. Israel 6. Southwest Asia and North Africa (Middle East) 7. Impartial writing 8. History writing — Arab-Israeli relations — Southwest Asia and North Africa (Middle East) 9. Politics and global affairs — World politics — Southwest Asia and North Africa (Middle East) — Israel and Palestine
LC 2016027278

A former Democratic senator from Maine and the primary architect of the 1998 Good Friday Agreement for peace in Northern Ireland offers an insider's account of how the Palestinians and Israelis have progressed and regressed in their talks for peace in the region.

"Mitchells careful statements may simply seem inconclusive to the more casual reader, but this is only a testament to the level of nuance in this scrupulous book." —*Publishers Weekly*

Includes bibliographical references and index.

Pappe, Ilan
The Biggest Prison on Earth: A History of the Occupied Territories. Ilan Pappe. BOneworld 2017. 400 p.
ISBN 9781851685875
Grades: Adult   956.9405
1. Israeli-Palestinian relations 2. Military occupation 3. Arab-Israeli conflict 4. Genocide 5. Palestinian people 6. Civil rights 7. Interethnic relations 8. Southwest Asia and North Africa (Middle East) history 9. West Bank (Jordan River) 10. Israeli-occupied territories 11. Israel 12. Gaza Strip 13. History writing — Arab-Israeli relations — Southwest Asia and North Africa (Middle East)

In a follow-up to his critically acclaimed investigation of the ethnic cleansing of Palestine in the 1940s, a renowned Israeli historian—drawing on groundbreaking archival research, NGO records and eyewitness accounts—turns his attention to the annexation and occupation of Gaza and the West Bank.

"A grim, hard-hitting look at the nuts and bolts of Israeli occupation." —*Kirkus*

Shehadeh, Raja
Where the Line Is Drawn: A Tale of Crossings, Friendships, and Fifty Years of Occupation in Israel-palestine. Raja Shehadeh. New Press, the 2017. 288 p.
ISBN 9781620972915
Grades: Adult   956.9405
1. Shehadeh, Raja, 1951- 2. Arab-Israeli conflict 3. Interethnic friendship 4. National territory 5. Authors 6. Political activists 7. Boundaries 8. Military occupation 9. Male friendship 10. Palestine 11. Israel 12. Israeli-occupied territories 13. Politics and global affairs — World politics — Southwest Asia and North Africa (Middle East) — Israel and Palestine 14. History writing — Nationalism — Southwest Asia and North Africa (Middle East) 15. History writing — Arab-Israeli relations — Southwest Asia and North Africa (Middle East)
LC 2017007627

Shehadeh explores how occupation has affected him personally, chronicling the various crossings that he undertook into Israel over a period of forty years to visit friends and family, to argue before the Israeli courts, and to negotiate failed peace agreements; and provides an anatomy of his friendship with Henry, a Canadian Jew who immigrated to Israel, and an exploration of whether it is possible for bonds to transcend political divisions.

"Shehadeh—a Ramallah-based human-rights activist and lawyer—writes a gentle, hopeful book of what could and should be. His belief in 'we will'—have a sovereign state, lasting peace, and mutual forgiveness —inspires, exemplifies, and leads." —*Booklist*

Sokatch, Daniel
Can We Talk About Israel?: A Guide for the Curious, Confused, and Conflicted. Daniel Sokatch; illustrated by Christopher Noxon. Bloomsbury Publishing Place USA 2021. 256 p; Illustration
ISBN 9781635573879
Grades: Adult   956.9405
1. Arab-Israeli conflict 2. Politics and government 3. Southwest Asia and North Africa (Middle East) history 4. Israel 5. Palestine 6. Impartial writing 7. History writing — Arab-Israeli relations — Southwest Asia and North Africa (Middle East) 8. History writing — Wars and conflicts — Arab-Israeli conflict 9. Politics and global affairs — World politics — Southwest Asia and North Africa (Middle East) — Israel and Palestine

An expert on the Israeli-Palestinian conflict explains the century-long struggle in a digestible but thorough format, along with illustrations which help explain the history of the most complicated conflict the world.

"New Israel Fund CEO Sokatch debuts with an accessible and balanced survey of the Israeli-Palestinian conflict.... Readers will welcome this informative and fair-minded primer on one of the world's most fiercely debated issues." —*Publishers Weekly*

956.94054 Palestine; Israel — 1974-2001

Halevi, Yossi Klein
★ *Letters to My Palestinian Neighbor.* Yossi Klein Halevi. HarperCollins 2018. 224 p.
ISBN 9780062844910
Grades: Adult   956.94054
1. Arab-Israeli conflict 2. Arab-Israeli relations 3. Palestinian people 4. Diplomatic negotiations in international disputes 5. Politics and government 6. Israel 7. Letters 8. Politics and global affairs — World politics — Southwest Asia and North Africa (Middle East) — Israel and Palestine

Attempting to break the agonizing impasse between Israelis and Palestinians, the Israeli commentator and award-winning author of Like Dreamers directly addresses his Palestinian neighbors in this taut and provocative book, empathizing with Palestinian suffering and longing for reconciliation as he explores how the conflict looks through Israeli eyes.

956.95 Jordan and West Bank

Ehrenreich, Ben
The Way to the Spring : Life and Death in Palestine. Ben Ehrenreich. Penguin 2016. 352 p.
ISBN 9781594205903
Grades: Adult   956.95
1. Arab-Israeli conflict 2. Israeli West Bank Barrier 3. Farmers 4. Palestinian people 5. Boundaries 6. West Bank (Jordan River) 7. Israel 8. History writing — Arab-Israeli relations — Southwest Asia and North Africa (Middle East)
LC 2016287137

The award-winning journalist and author of the Suitors describes his immersion into the lives and struggles of everyday Palestinians along the West Bank, sharing firsthand insights into their resistance and resilience in the face of occupation by the Israeli military.

"Ehrenreichs journal conveys how the Israeli-Palestinian conflict truly plays out at ground level, where normal might include the sounds of screaming, being arrested and questioned for hours, or simply being shot at." —*Booklist*

Grossman, David
The Yellow Wind. David Grossman; translated from the Hebrew by Haim Watzman. Picador USA/Farrar, Straus and Giroux 2002. xii, 222 p. : Map
ISBN 9780312420987

Grades: Adult   956.95
1. Grossman, David 2. Arab-Israeli conflict 3. Israeli-Palestinian relations 4. Historiography 5. Palestinian people 6. Israeli people 7. Voyages and travels 8. West Bank (Jordan River) 9. 1980s 10. History writing — Arab-Israeli relations — Southwest Asia and North Africa (Middle East)

LC 2002067325

A prominent Israeli writer's report on the Israeli-Arab situation describes what he observed on the West Bank in early 1987, from the miserable condition of the Palestinian refugees and their hatred of the Israelis to the costs of occupation for both occupier and occupied.

"Grossman was assigned to report for a weekly newspaper on life for both occupied and occupier on the West Bank during the 20th anniversary of its conquest. With an eye and ear for revealing detail, he argues that the Jews are now doing to Palestinians what has been done to them through the ages." —*Library Journal*

957 Siberia (Asiatic Russia)

Frazier, Ian
Travels in Siberia. Ian Frazier. Farrar, Straus and Giroux 2010. 560 p.
ISBN 9780374278724

Grades: Adult   957
1. Frazier, Ian 2. Travelers 3. Social life and customs 4. Voyages and travels 5. Soviet Union history 6. Siberia 7. Travel Writing — Asia and the South Pacific

LC 2010005784

ALA Notable Book, 2011; New York Times Notable Book, 2010.

Did you know that Siberia doesn't officially exist? or that there's a city that was once known as the "Paris of Siberia"? or that…well, we could go on and on. And you'll be able to, too, if you read author and humorist Ian Frazier's Travels in Siberia. Frazier's taken five trips to the region, and he describes his various travels across the vast, remote area (including long road trips in both winter and summer) and discusses Siberian geography, people, culture, and history.

"A dense, challenging, dazzling work that will leave readers exhausted but yearning for more." —*Kirkus*

Includes bibliographical references.

Thubron, Colin
In Siberia. Colin Thubron. Harper Collins 1999. 286 p.
ISBN 9780060195434

Grades: Adult   957
1. Thubron, Colin, 1939- 2. Travelers 3. Russian people 4. Eastern European people 5. Social life and customs 6. Voyages and travels 7. Siberia 8. Travel Writing — Asia and the South Pacific

LC 99041346

ALA Notable Book, 2001; Library Journal Best Books, 2000; New York Times Notable Book, 2000.

The author describes his tours of Russian regions that have long captured the Western imagination revealing the breathtaking natural beauty, tragic history, and vast spaces that make up Siberia.

"Thubron elegantly encompasses both awe-inspiring landscapes and their dark histories as well as immersing himself in local eccentricities." —*Times Literary Supplement*

Includes index.

958.1 Afghanistan

Ansary, Mir Tamim
Games Without Rules: The Often-interrupted History of Afghanistan. Tamim Ansary. PublicAffairs 2012. 336 p.
ISBN 9781610390941

Grades: Adult   958.1
1. Military occupation 2. Great powers 3. American people in Asia 4. Causes of war 5. Kinship-based society 6. Imperialism 7. Modernization (Social sciences) 8. British people in foreign countries 9. Asian history 10. Afghanistan 11. Islamic countries 12. History writing — Asia — South Asia — Afghanistan

LC 2012025651

Traces the history of Afghanistan and the power conflicts that have interrupted its ongoing struggle to combine a democracy with Islamist fanaticism and meld the modern world with the tribal village republics that populate the countryside.

Includes bibliographical references and index.

Dalrymple, William
The Return of a King: The Battle for Afghanistan, 1839-42. William Dalrymple. Alfred A. Knopf 2013. 384 p.
ISBN 9780307958280

Grades: Adult   958.1
1. Shah Shuja, Amir of Afghanistan, 1780?-1842 2. Colonialism 3. Imperialism, British 4. Intervention (International relations) 5. Military defeat 6. International relations 7. Culture conflict 8. Rulers 9. British people in foreign countries 10. Asian history 11. Afghanistan 12. 19th century 13. History writing — Asia — South Asia — Afghanistan 14. History writing — Europe — United Kingdom 15. History writing — Colonialism — Europe 16. History writing — Wars and conflicts

LC 2012040998

Examines the mid-19th-century Afghan war as a tragic result of neocolonial ambition, cultural collision and hubris, drawing on previously untapped primary sources to explore such topics as the reestablishment of a puppet-leader Shah, the conflict's brutal human toll and the similarities between the war and present-day challenges.

Includes bibliographical references and index.

Loyn, David
In Afghanistan: 200 Years of British, Russian and American Occupation. David Loyn. Palgrave Macmillan 2009. 288 p.
ISBN 9780230614031

Grades: Adult   958.1
1. Military occupation 2. British people in foreign countries 3. British people 4. Russian people 5. American people in foreign countries 6. American people in Asia 7. Armed Forces 8. Military history 9. Politics and government 10. Asian history 11. Afghanistan 12. History writing — Asia — South Asia — Afghanistan

LC 2008051653

An award-winning BBC foreign correspondent chronicles the military conflicts of Afghanistan throughout the past two centuries, evaluating the roles of misunderstanding and broken agreements as well as the author's perspectives on how foreign occupiers underestimated Afghani capabilities.

Includes bibliographical references and index.

Richardson, Edmund
The King's Shadow: Obsession, Betrayal, and the Deadly Quest for the Lost City of Alexandria. Edmund Richardson. St. Martin's Press 2022. VIII, 328 p.
ISBN 9781250278593

Grades: Adult   958.1
1. Masson, Charles, 1800-1853 2. Archaeologists 3. Extinct cities 4. Deserters 5. Secret identity 6. Espionage 7. Colonialism 8. Civilization, Ancient 9. Antiquities 10. Indian history 11. Asian history 12. Afghanistan 13. 19th century 14. Biographies 15. Life stories — People in history — Explorers 16. Adventure writing — Exploration 17. History writing — Asia — South Asia 18. History writing — Archaeology 19. Nonfiction that reads like fiction

ESSENTIAL AND RECOMMENDED TITLES
958.104 Afghanistan — 1919

LC 2021048595

For centuries the city of Alexandria Beneath the Mountains was a meeting point of East and West. Then it vanished. In 1833 it was discovered in Afghanistan by the unlikeliest person imaginable: Charles Masson, deserter, pilgrim, doctor, archaeologist, spy, one of the most respected scholars in Asia, and the greatest of nineteenth-century travelers. This is a wild journey through nineteenth-century India and Afghanistan, with impeccably researched storytelling that shows us a world of espionage and dreamers, ne'er-do-wells and opportunists, extreme violence both personal and military, and boundless hope. At the edge of empire, amid the deserts and the mountains, it is the story of an obsession passed down the centuries.

"A British historian resurrects the life of a self-taught archaeologist who discovered a lost civilization on the plains of Afghanistan....Captivating biography of an archaeological pioneer sure to please history fans and students of the spy game." —*Kirkus*

Originally published in Great Britain under the title Alexandria: the quest for the lost city by Bloomsbury Publishing, London, in 2021; Includes bibliographical references and index.

Seierstad, Asne
*The **Bookseller** of Kabul.* Asne Seierstad; translated from the Norwegian by Ingrid Christophersen. Back Bay Books/Little, Brown 2004. xvi, 288 p.
ISBN 9780316159418
Grades: 11 12 Adult   958.1
1. Khan family 2. Seierstad, Asne, 1970- 3. Booksellers 4. Kabul, Afghanistan 5. Biographies 6. Life stories — Facing adversity — War and oppression 7. Adult books for young adults

LC 2006274444

Capturing the harsh realities of life in modern-day Afghanistan and plight of Afghan women, the Norwegian journalist provides a portrait of a committed Muslim man, a bookseller, and his family living in post-Taliban Kabul, Afghanistan.

"The author entered Kabul with Northern Alliance soldiers after they ousted the Taliban. She took the rare opportunity to live with and write a book about the extended family of Sultan Khan, bookseller and entrepreneur. The result, organized around events in the lives of individual members of Khan's large clan . . . provides appropriate information about recent Afghani history, a glimpse from the inside at an Islamic family, and an understanding of the harshness and difficulty of the daily grind in Afghanistan—both under the Taliban and after the U.S. antiterrorist campaign." —*Booklist*

958.104 Afghanistan — 1919

Ackerman, Elliot
*The **Fifth** Act: America's End in Afghanistan.* Elliot Ackerman. Penguin Press 2022. 304 p.
ISBN 9780593492048
Grades: Adult   958.104
1. Ackerman, Elliot 2. Afghan War, 2001-2021 3. Paramilitary forces 4. Military strategy 5. Evacuation of civilians 6. Afghanistan 7. History writing — Wars and conflicts — War in Afghanistan

LC 2022007217

Using the dramatic rescue efforts in Kabul as his framework, a New York Times best-selling author presents this powerful and dramatic eyewitness account in which he weaves a personal history of the war's long progression, beginning with the initial invasion in the months after 9/11.

"A veteran ponders America's 'Harried withdrawal' from Afghanistan in this haunting memoir....Ackerman provides a clear-eyed indictment of America's failures in Afghanistan while paying homage to the soldiers who fought there." —*Publishers Weekly*

Bergen, Peter L.
*The **Rise** and Fall of Osama Bin Laden.* Peter Bergen. Simon & Schuster 2021. 320 p.
ISBN 9781982170523
Grades: Adult   958.104
1. Bin Laden, Osama, 1957-2011 2. Extremists 3. Terrorists 4. Jihad 5. September 11 Terrorist Attacks, 2001 6. War on Terrorism, 2001-2009 7. Terrorism 8. Antiterrorist policy 9. Geopolitics 10. Fugitives 11. Assassination 12. Biographies 13. Life stories — Law and order — Criminals and law-breakers 14. Politics and global affairs — Terrorism 15. Politics and global affairs — World politics — United States

In The Rise and Fall of Osama bin Laden, Peter Bergen provides the first re-evaluation of the man responsible for precipitating America's long wars with al-Qaeda and its descendants, capturing bin Laden in all the dimensions of his life: as a family man, as a zealot, as a battlefield commander, as a terrorist leader, and as a fugitive. In the end, bin Laden died in a squalid suburban compound, far from the front lines of his holy war. And yet despite that unheroic denouement, his ideology lives on. Thanks to exclusive interviews with family members and associates, and documents unearthed only recently, Bergen's portrait of Osama will reveal for the first time who he really was and why he continues to inspire a new generation of jihadists.

"CNN national security analyst Bergen (Trump and His Generals) adds intriguing new details to the story of Osama bin Laden in this solid, well-sourced biography." —*Publishers Weekly*

Chesney, Will
No Ordinary Dog: My Partner from the Seal Teams to the Bin Laden Raid. Will Chesney, with Joe Layden. St. Martin's Press 2019. 352 p.
ISBN 9781250176950
Grades: Adult   958.104
1. Cairo (Dog) 2. Chesney, Will, 1984- 3. Dogs 4. Afghan War, 2001-2021 5. Afghan War veterans 6. Service dogs 7. Navy SEALs 8. Brain injury 9. Post-traumatic stress disorder 10. Animals in war 11. People with disabilities 12. Veterans 13. Human-animal relationships 14. United States 15. Autobiographies and memoirs 16. Life stories — Law and order — Armed forces personnel 17. Life stories — Relationships — Pets and owners 18. Family and relationships — Pets and owners 19. Life stories — Facing adversity — Medical issues — Mental illness 20. Life stories — Facing adversity — Medical issues — Living with disabilities

LC 2019031697

No Ordinary Dog is the powerful true story of a SEAL Team Operator and military dog handler, and the dog that saved his life.

"Touching on the power of the human-animal bond, the effects of PTSD, and the legacy of the 'War on terror,' this earnest account delivers many memorable moments. Dog lovers and fans of military history will be enthralled." —*Publishers Weekly*

Coll, Steve
***Directorate** S: The C.I.A. And America's Secret Wars in Afghanistan and Pakistan.* Steve Coll. Penguin Press 2018. xxiii, 757 pages, 8 unnumbered pages of plates : Illustration; Map
ISBN 9781594204586
Grades: Adult   958.104
1. International relations 2. Terrorism 3. Afghanistan 4. Pakistan 5. 2000s (Decade) 6. Politics and global affairs — Terrorism 7. History writing — Asia — South Asia — Afghanistan 8. History writing — Asia — South Asia — Pakistan

National Book Critics Circle Award for Non-Fiction, 2018.

A follow-up to the Pulitzer Prize-winning Ghost Wars traces America's intelligence, military and diplomatic efforts to defeat AL Qaeda and the Taliban in Afghanistan and Pakistan in the years since 9/11.

"With his evenhanded approach, gift for limning character, and dazzling reporting skills, he has created an essential work of contemporary history." —*Booklist*

Includes bibliographical references (pages 729-736) and index.

★ *Ghost Wars: The Secret History of the Cia, Afghanistan, and Bin Laden, from the Soviet Invasion to September 10, 2001.* Steve Coll. Penguin Press 2004. xvii, 695 p. : Map
ISBN 9781594200076
Grades: Adult   958.104

1. Bin Laden, Osama, 1957-2011 2. International relations 3. Terrorism 4. Politics and government 5. Asian history 6. Afghanistan 7. United States 8. 1980s 9. 1990s 10. 1970s 11. History writing — Asia — South Asia — Afghanistan

LC 2003058593

Lionel Gelber Prize (Canada), 2004; Pulitzer Prize for General Nonfiction, 2005; New York Times Notable Book, 2004.

To what extent did America's best intelligence analysts grasp the rising threat of Islamist radicalism? Who tried to stop bin Laden and why did they fail? Comprehensively and for the first time, this Pulitzer Prize-winning work by journalist Steve Coll recounts the history of the covert wars in Afghanistan that fueled Islamic militancy and sowed the seeds of the September 11 attacks. Based on scrupulous research and firsthand accounts by key government, intelligence, and military personnel both foreign and American, Ghost Wars details the secret history of the CIA's role in Afghanistan, the rise of the Taliban, the emergence of bin Laden, and the efforts by US forces to find and assassinate bin Laden in Afghanistan.

"The author has given us what is certainly the finest historical narrative so far on the origins of AL Qaeda in the post-Soviet rubble of Afghanistan." —*New York Times Book Review*

Includes bibliographical references (p. [653]-664) and index.

Feifer, Gregory
The Great Gamble: The Soviet War in Afghanistan. Gregory Feifer. Harper 2009. 336 p.
ISBN 9780061143182
Grades: Adult   958.104

1. Military occupation 2. Military history 3. Asian history 4. Afghanistan 5. Soviet Union 6. 1980s 7. 1970s 8. History writing — Wars and conflicts 9. History writing — Asia — South Asia — Afghanistan

LC 2008022594

The Soviet war in Afghanistan was a grueling debacle that has striking lessons for the 21st century. Parallels between the Soviet invasion of Afghanistan and the U.S. invasions of Afghanistan and Iraq are impossible to ignore. The Soviet Union sent some of its most elite troops to unfamiliar lands to fight a vaguely defined enemy, which eventually defeated their superior numbers with unconventional tactics. Although the Soviet leadership initially saw the invasion as a victory, many Russian soldiers came to view the war as a demoralizing and devastating defeat, the consequences of which had a substantial impact on the Soviet Union and its collapse. NPR Moscow correspondent Gregory Feifer examines the conflict from the perspective of the soldiers on the ground. His extensive research includes eye-opening interviews with participants from both sides of the conflict, vividly depicting the invasion of a volatile country that no power has ever successfully conquered.

Includes bibliographical references.

Golembesky, Michael
Level Zero Heroes: The Story of U.S. Marine Special Operations in Bala Murghab, Afghanistan. Michael Golembesky with John R. Bruning. St. Martin's Press 2014. 320 pages
ISBN 9781250030405
Grades: Adult   958.104

1. Golembesky, Michael 2. Marines 3. Afghan War, 2001-2021 4. Afghanistan 5. 21st century 6. Autobiographies and memoirs 7. Life stories — Law and order — Armed forces personnel 8. History writing — Military — Special Forces 9. History writing — Wars and conflicts — War in Afghanistan

LC 2014016597

Follows the members of U.S. Marine Special Operations Team 8222 on their assignment to the remote and isolated Taliban stronghold known as Bala Murghab as they tried to break the Taliban's grip on the valley.

"Readers who enjoy first-person accounts of battles laced with nonstop action will have a tough time putting this one down." —*Library Journal*

Includes bibliographical references.

Junger, Sebastian
War. Sebastian Junger. Twelve 2010. 320 p.
ISBN 9780446556248
Grades: Adult   958.104

1. War 2. Soldiers 3. Battles 4. Coping 5. Afghan War, 2001-2021 6. Military campaigns 7. American people in Asia 8. Afghanistan 9. Adult books for young adults 10. History writing — Wars and conflicts — War in Afghanistan

LC 2009049493

Offers an on-the-ground account of a single platoon during its fifteen-month tour of duty in the most dangerous outpost in Afghanistan's Korengal Valley.

"The war in Afghanistan contains brutal trauma but also transcendent purpose in this riveting combat narrative. Junger spent 14 months in 2007-2008 intermittently embedded with a platoon of the 173rd Airborne brigade in Afghanistan's Korengal Valley, one of the bloodiest corners of the conflict. Junger experiences everything they do—nerve-racking patrols, terrifying roadside bombings and ambushes, stultifying weeks in camp when they long for a firefight to relieve the tedium. The result is an unforgettable portrait of men under fire." —*Publishers Weekly*

Includes index.

Kesling, Ben
Bravo Company: An Afghanistan Deployment and Its Aftermath. Ben Kesling. Harry N Abrams 2022. 320 p.
ISBN 9781419751158
Grades: Adult   958.104

1. Soldiers 2. Afghan War, 2001-2021 3. Postwar life 4. War 5. Veterans 6. Military campaigns 7. Homecomings 8. Adjustment 9. History Writing — Wars and conflicts — War in Afghanistan 10. History Writing — Military — Military Units

Drawing on extensive interviews and original reporting, a Wall Street Journal correspondent tells the story of a parachute infantry regiment in Afghanistan and its members' struggles to return to civilian life.

"Journalist and Marine Corps veteran Kesling's gut-wrenching debut documents the physical and psychological tolls of the war in Afghanistan through the story of one U.S. Army unit's deployment….Devastating yet cautiously hopeful, this is an essential study of combat trauma." —*Publishers Weekly*

Loyn, David
The Long War: The Inside Story of America and Afghanistan Since 9/11. David Loyn. St. Martin's Press 2021. 320 p.
ISBN 9781250128423
Grades: Adult   958.104

1. Afghan War, 2001-2021 2. Generals 3. War 4. Military campaigns 5. Command of troops 6. Strategic alliances (Military) 7. Diplomacy 8. Insurgency 9. Military occupation 10. Military policy 11. International relations 12. Asian history 13. Afghanistan 14. United States 15. 21st century 16. Impartial writing 17. History writing — Wars and conflicts — War in Afghanistan 18. History writing — Early 21st century — United States 19. Politics and global affairs — World politics — Asia

LC 2021026568

Just as U. S. soldiers and diplomats pulled out of Afghanistan, supposedly concluding their role and responsibility in the two-decade conflict, the country fell to the Taliban. In The Long War, BBC foreign correspondent David Loyn uncovers the political and military strategies—and failures—that prolonged America's longest war.

"Loyn (In Afghanistan), a former BBC correspondent and Afghan government adviser, ranges from the front lines to the halls of power in this deeply reported chronicle of America's 'Forever war.' . . . Distinguished by its granular detail and insider access, this is an authoritative study of where things went wrong." —*Publishers Weekly*

Includes bibliographical references and index.

Luttrell, Marcus
Lone Survivor: The Eyewitness Account of Operation Redwing and the Lost Heroes of Seal Team 10. Marcus Luttrell with Patrick Robinson. Little, Brown 2007. 390 p, 8 p. of plates : Illustration; Map
ISBN 9780316067591
Grades: Adult   958.104

1. Luttrell, Marcus 2. Afghan War, 2001-2021 3. Soldiers 4. Military campaigns 5. Survival 6. War 7. Battles 8. Navy SEALs 9. Afghanistan 10. Autobi-

ESSENTIAL AND RECOMMENDED TITLES
958.104 Afghanistan — 1919

ographies and memoirs 11. Page to screen 12. History writing — Wars and conflicts — War in Afghanistan 13. History writing — Military — Special Forces 14. Life stories — Law and order — Armed forces personnel

LC 2007921207

The leader, and only survivor, of a team of U.S. Navy SEALs sent to northern Afghanistan to capture a well-known al Qaeda leader chronicles the events of the battle that killed his teammates and offers insight into the training of this elite group of warriors.

Title adapted into a film by the same name (2013).

Meyer, Dakota
Into the Fire: A Firsthand Account of the Most Extraordinary Battle in the Afghan War. Dakota Meyer, with Bing West. Random House Inc. 2012. 336 p.
ISBN 9780812993400
Grades: Adult   958.104

1. Battles 2. American people in Asia 3. Afghan War, 2001-2021 4. Infantry 5. Combat 6. Snipers 7. Marines 8. Soldiers 9. Asian history 10. Afghanistan 11. United States 12. Autobiographies and memoirs 13. Biographies 14. Life stories — Law and order — Armed forces personnel 15. History writing — Wars and conflicts — War in Afghanistan

A Marine sniper shares the story of his heroism facing a Taliban ambush during which he saved Afghan soldiers and Marine advisors, a victory that resulted from him disobeying orders and assuming command without reinforcements or artillery support.

Morgan, Wesley
The Hardest Place: The American Military Adrift in Afghanistan's Pech Valley. Wesley Morgan. Random House 2020. 304 p.
ISBN 9780812995060
Grades: Adult   958.104

1. Afghan War, 2001-2021 2. Soldiers 3. Asian history 4. Afghanistan 5. 21st century 6. History writing — Wars and conflicts — War in Afghanistan

LC 2020011937

A deeply reported history of the American war in Afghanistan told through the infantry battalions and commando teams who fought in one of the country's most violent regions: the Pech valley.

"Journalist Morgan debuts with an exhaustive and deeply reported history of U.S. military presence in Afghanistan's. . . . The result is a definitive portrait of the epicenter of America's longest war." —*Publishers Weekly*

Rashid, Ahmed
Taliban: Militant Islam, Oil and Fundamentalism in Central Asia. Ahmed Rashid. Yale University Press 2010. xvii, 319 p. : Map
ISBN 9780300163681
Grades: 11 12 Adult   958.104

1. Fundamentalism 2. Islam and state 3. Islam and politics 4. Terrorism 5. Islam 6. Fundamentalists 7. Muslims 8. Afghanistan 9. Politics and global affairs — Terrorism

LC 2009938249

Rashid brings the shadowy world of the Taliban into sharp focus. He explains its rise to power, its impact on Afghanistan and the region, its role in oil and gas company decisions, and the effects of changing American attitudes toward the Taliban.

Includes bibliographical references (p. [284]-304) and index.

Romesha, Clinton
Red Platoon: A True Story of American Valor. Clinton Romesha. E P Dutton 2016. 368 p.
ISBN 9780525955054
Grades: Adult   958.104

1. Romesha, Clinton 2. Battles 3. Afghan War, 2001-2021 4. Military campaigns 5. Unconventional warfare 6. Soldiers 7. Afghanistan 8. History writing — Wars and conflicts — War in Afghanistan

LC 2016498127

A comprehensive account of the 13-hour firefight at the Battle of Keating by a Medal of Honor recipient describes the harrowing events of the October 3, 2009 attack and how the sacrifices and victories of heroic men raised questions about whether the strategically vulnerable outpost should ever have been built.

Slahi, Mohamedou Ould
The Mauritanian. Mohamedou Ould Slahi; edited by Larry Siems. Back Bay Books 2015. 400 p.
ISBN 9780316282543
Grades: Adult   958.104

1. Slahi, Mohamedou Ould 2. Prisoners of war 3. Detention of people 4. Torture victims 5. War on Terrorism, 2001-2009 6. Politics and government 7. Guantanamo Bay Naval Base, Cuba 8. United States 9. Autobiographies and memoirs 10. Life stories — Facing adversity — War and oppression 11. History writing — Wars and conflicts

LC 2014023763

New York Times Notable Book, 2015.

Since 2002, Mohamedou Slahi has been imprisoned at the detention camp at Guantanamo Bay, Cuba. In all these years, the United States has never charged him with a crime. A federal judge ordered his release in March 2010, but the U.S. government fought that decision, and there is no sign that the United States plans to let him go. Three years into his captivity Slahi began a diary, recounting his life before he disappeared into U.S. custody, "his endless world tour" of imprisonment and interrogation, and his daily life as a Guantanamo prisoner.

Republished in 2021 as the Mauritanian with additonal content that was previously redacted; Originally published as Guantanamo Diary by Little, Brown and Company in 2015.

Stanton, Doug
12 Strong: The Declassified True Story of the Horse Soldiers. Doug Stanton. Pocket Books 2017. 534 p.
ISBN 9781501178511
Grades: Adult   958.104

1. Special forces 2. Afghan War, 2001-2021 3. Unconventional warfare 4. Armed Forces 5. Soldiers 6. Urban warfare 7. Military history 8. United States 9. Afghanistan 10. 21st century 11. Page to screen 12. History writing — Wars and conflicts — War in Afghanistan 13. History writing — Military — Special Forces

New York Times Notable Book, 2009.

Documents the post-September 11 mission during which a small band of Special Forces soldiers captured the strategic Afghan city of Mazar-e-Sharif as part of an effort to defeat the Taliban.

Previously published as Horse soldiers, Simon and Schuster, 2009; Adapted into a film entitled 12 Strong in 2018; Includes bibliographical references.

Wallace, Chris
Countdown Bin Laden: The Untold Story of the 247-day Hunt to Bring the Mastermind of 9/11 to Justice. Chris Wallace, with Mitch Weiss. Avid Reader Press 2021. 320 p.
ISBN 9781982176525
Grades: Adult   958.104

1. Bin Laden, Osama, 1957-2011 2. Panetta, Leon E, 1938- 3. McRaven, William H. (William Harry), 1955- 4. Terrorists 5. Fugitives 6. Intelligence officers 7. Special operations (Military science) 8. Navy SEALs 9. Elite operatives 10. Antiterrorists 11. Raids (Military science) 12. Assassination 13. United States 14. Pakistan 15. 21st century 16. History writing — Military — Special forces 17. History writing — Early 21st century — United States 18. Life stories — Law and order — Armed forces personnel 19. Life stories — Law and order — Spies and secret agents

On August 27, 2010, three CIA officers ask for a private meeting with CIA Director Leon Panetta. During that secret session, they tell Panetta that agents have tracked a courier with deep AL Qaeda ties to a three-story house at the end of a dead-end street in Abbottabad, Pakistan. But they say it's more than a house—it's a heavily protected fortress. No one in the meeting says the name bin Laden. They don't have to. Everyone understands that finally, after nearly a decade, maybe, just maybe, they've found the world's most wanted man. Published on the twentieth anniversary of 9/11, Countdown bin Laden is a historical thriller filled with intrigue, cinematic action, and fresh reporting about the race to apprehend and bring to justice the mastermind of the most consequential terrorist attack in American history.

"The latest in the Fox News host's Countdown series tells the inside story of the CIA operation to kill Osama bin Laden.... A highly readable, vividly detailed account of one of the most dramatic intelligence victories in recent history." —*Kirkus*

Whitlock, Craig
The **Afghanistan** *Papers: A Secret History of the War.* Craig Whitlock. Simon & Schuster 2021. 416 p.
ISBN 9781982159009
Grades: Adult   **958.104**
1. Afghan War, 2001-2021 2. Military campaigns 3. World leaders 4. Terrorism 5. Presidents 6. International relations 7. Politics and government 8. Asian history 9. United States 10. Afghanistan 11. History writing — Asia — South Asia — Afghanistan 12. History writing — Wars and conflicts — War in Afghanistan 13. Politics and global affairs — World politics — Asia
LC 2021016683

The groundbreaking investigative story of how three successive presidents and their military commanders deceived the public year after year about the longest war in American history.

Rigorously detailed and relentlessly pessimistic, this is a heartbreaking look at how America's leaders 'Chose to bury their mistakes and let the war drift.' —*Publishers Weekly*

Includes bibliographical references and index.

Wise, Beau
Three Wise Men: A Navy SEAL, a Green Beret, and How Their Marine Brother Became a War's Sole Survivor. Beau Wise and Tom Sileo. St. Martin's Press 2021. 320 p.
ISBN 9781250253446
Grades: Adult   **958.104**
1. Wise, Beau, 1984- 2. Wise, Benjamin B, 1977-2012 3. Wise, Jeremy J, 1974-2009 4. Wise family 5. Afghan War, 2001-2021 6. Iraq War, 2003-2011 7. Families of military personnel 8. Brothers 9. Military service 10. Arkansas 11. Autobiographies and memoirs 12. Life stories — Law and order — Armed forces personnel 13. Family and Relationships — Siblings
LC 2020035341

From Beau Wise and Tom Sileo comes Three Wise Men, an incredible memoir of family, service and sacrifice by a Marine who lost both his brothers in combat—becoming the only "Sole Survivor" during the war in Afghanistan. Shortly after the 9/11 attacks, three brothers by blood became brothers in arms when each volunteered to defend their country. No military family has sacrificed more during the ensuing war, which has become the longest ever fought by America's armed forces. While serving in Afghanistan, US Navy SEAL veteran and CIA contractor Jeremy Wise was killed in an al Qaeda suicide bombing that devastated the US intelligence community. Less than three years later, US Army Green Beret sniper Ben Wise was fatally wounded after volunteering for a dangerous assignment during a firefight with the Taliban. Ben was posthumously awarded the Silver Star, while Jeremy received the Intelligence Star-one of the rarest awards bestowed by the U.S. government-and also a star on the CIA's Memorial Wall. United States Marine Corps combat veteran Beau Wise is the only known American service member to be pulled from the battlefield after losing two brothers in Afghanistan. Told in Beau's voice, Three Wise Men is an American family's historic true story of service andsacrifice.

"It's a gripping read and an exemplary collaboration between a participant and a professional writer.... More than that, it's a consistently absorbing story of the 9/11 generation and of America's response to global terror, a topic still relevant today." —*Kirkus*

Zuckoff, Mitchell
The **Secret** *Gate: A True Story of Courage and Sacrifice During the Collapse of Aghanistan.* Mitchell Zuckoff. Random House 2023. 320 p.
ISBN 9780593594841
Grades: Adult   **958.104**
1. Qaderi, Homeira, 1979 or 1980- 2. Aronson, Sam 3. Women authors 4. Mothers and sons 5. Afghan War, 2001-2021 6. Evacuation of civilians 7. Diplomats 8. Afghan people 9. Afghanistan 10. Life stories — Facing adversity — War and oppression 11. Politics and global affairs — World politics — Southwest Asia and North Africa (Middle East) 12. History writing — Southwest Asia and North Africa (Middle East)
LC 2022034906

The #1 New York Times best-selling author of 13 Hours tells the incredible true story of American diplomat Sam Aronson, who, in the final hours of the U.S. evacuation of Afghanistan, helped Homeira Qaderi, a celebrated author, academic and women's liberation champion, and her 8-year-old son escape. Map(s).

"Drawing on extensive interviews with Aronson and Qaderi, Zuckoff reveals the human side of geopolitics. Readers won't be able to put this down." —*Publishers Weekly*

Includes bibliographical references and index.

959.105 Myanmar — 1948-

Thant Myint-U
The **Hidden** *History of Burma: Race, Capitalism, and the Crisis of Democracy in the 21st Century.* Thant Myint-U.. W. W. Norton & Company 2020. 272 p.
ISBN 9781324003298
Grades: Adult   **959.105**
1. Aung San Suu Kyi 2. War crimes 3. Crimes against humanity 4. Genocide 5. Refugees 6. Political corruption 7. Rohingya (Burmese people) 8. Violence against marginalized people 9. Asian history 10. Burma 11. 20th century 12. History writing — Asia — Southeast Asia 13. Politics and global affairs — World politics — Asia
LC 2019026007

The award-winning historian, former diplomat and presidential advisor shares first-person insights into the recent election of Nobel Laureate Aung San Suu Kyi and the war crimes, inequalities and expulsions that have decimated Burma in less than a decade.

Includes bibliographical references and index.

959.604 Cambodia — 1949-

Ung, Loung
First They Killed My Father: A Daughter of Cambodia Remembers. Loung Ung. Harper Perennial 2006. 238 p. : Illustration; Map
ISBN 9780060856267
Grades: 11 12 Adult   **959.604**
1. Ung, Loung 2. Refugees, Cambodian 3. Women refugees 4. Refugees 5. Genocide 6. Atrocities 7. Politics and government 8. Cambodia 9. 1970s 10. Autobiographies and memoirs 11. History writing — Wars and conflicts — Civil Wars 12. Life stories — Facing adversity — War and oppression — War survivors 13. Adult books for young adults 14. History writing — Asia — Southeast Asia
LC Bl2006011138

Booklist Editors' Choice, 2000; School Library Journal Best Books: Best Adult Books 4 Teens, 2000; YALSA Best Books for Young Adults, 2001.

Chronicles the brutality of the Khmer Rouge in Cambodia, from the author's forced "evacuation" of Phnom Penh in 1975 to her family's subsequent movements from town to town and eventual separation.

Sequel: Lucky child; Originally published: New York : HarperCollinsPublishers, 2000.

959.704 Vietnam — 1945-

Albracht, William
Abandoned in Hell: The Fight for Vietnam's Fire Base Kate. Captain William Albracht (Ret.) and Captain Marvin J. Wolf (Ret.).. NAL Caliber 2015. 400 p.

ESSENTIAL AND RECOMMENDED TITLES
959.704 Vietnam — 1945-

ISBN 9780451468086

Grades: Adult **959.704**

1. Albracht, William 2. Vietnam War, 1961-1975 3. Escapes 4. Heroes and heroines, American 5. Command of troops 6. Courage 7. Special forces 8. Soldiers 9. Vietnam 10. United States 11. Autobiographies and memoirs 12. Biographies 13. History writing — Wars and conflicts — Vietnam War 14. Life stories — Law and order — Armed forces personnel

LC 2014028501

In October 1969, William Albracht, the youngest Green Beret captain in Vietnam, took command of a remote hilltop outpost called Fire Base Kate, held by only 27 American soldiers and 150 Montagnard militiamen. At dawn the next morning, three North Vietnamese Army regiments—some 6,000 men—crossed the Cambodian border and attacked. Albracht's men held off repeated ground assaults with fierce hand-to-hand fighting, air support and a dangerously close B-52 strike. After five days, Kate's defenders were out of ammo and water. Albracht led his troops, including many wounded, off the hill and on a daring night march through enemy lines.

"This fast-paced narrative encapsulates Vietnam War themes, significantly the bravery of grunts and company grade officers and their loyalty to one another, and also bureaucratic mistakes with tragic consequences made by inexperienced officers and government officials too far removed from front-line action. Ultimately, Firebase Kate, as Albracht says, was built in a vulnerable location and its men were written off when they could no longer defend it. Readers of such excellent battlefield works as Harold Moore and Joseph Galloway's We Were Soldiers Once And Young will delve into this one." —*Library Journal*

Appy, Christian G.
American Reckoning: The Vietnam War and Our National Identity. Christian G. Appy. Viking 2015. 416 p.

ISBN 9780670025398

Grades: Adult **959.704**

1. Nationalism 2. Popular culture 3. Political culture 4. Vietnam War, 1961-1975 5. International relations 6. Civilization 7. United States 8. 20th century 9. History writing — Wars and conflicts — Vietnam War 10. History writing — 1970s — United States 11. History writing — 1960s — United States

LC 2014038477

The critically acclaimed author of Patriots draws on sources ranging from movies and songs to official documents and news stories to analyze the role of the Vietnam War in shaping America's national identity, popular culture and post-war foreign policy.

"Appy paints with a broad brush and may interpret our national security needs too narrowly. Still, his assertion that our current policies could guarantee constant warfare deserves to be seriously considered." —*Booklist*

Black, George
★ *The Long Reckoning: A Story of War, Peace, and Redemption in Vietnam.* George Black. Alfred A. Knopf 2023. 496 p.

ISBN 9780593534106

Grades: Adult **959.704**

1. Vietnam War, 1961-1975 2. Vietnam veterans 3. Scientists 4. War casualties 5. Agent Orange 6. Land mines 7. Environmental degradation 8. Diseases 9. Psychic trauma 10. War memorials 11. Postwar life 12. Redemption 13. International relations 14. Asian history 15. United States 16. Vietnam 17. History writing — Wars and conflicts — Vietnam War 18. Life stories — Facing adversity — War and oppression — War survivors

LC 2022023618

This inspirational story follows a small group of veterans, scientists and Quaker-inspired pacifists and their Vietnamese partners as they used their moral authority, scientific and political ingenuity and sheer persistence to heal the horrors left in the wake of the military engagement in Southeast Asia.

"One of the best recent books on a war that ended half a century ago but that still reverberates." —*Kirkus*

This is a Borzoi book; Includes bibliographical references and index.

Bowden, Mark
★ *Hue 1968: The Turning Point of the American War in Vietnam.* Mark Bowden. Atlantic Monthly Press 2017. 394 pages

ISBN 9780802127006

Grades: Adult **959.704**

1. Tet Offensive, 1968 2. Urban warfare 3. Vietnam War, 1961-1975 4. Military campaigns 5. International relations 6. Asian history 7. United States 8. Vietnam 9. 1960s 10. History writing — Wars and conflicts — Vietnam War 11. History writing — Wars and conflicts — Battles

LC 2017022809

ALA Notable Book, 2018; Longlisted for the Andrew Carnegie Medal for Excellence in Non-Fiction, 2018.

Interviews with participants from both sides of the conflict and materials from Vietnamese and American archives provide multiple points of view on each stage of the Battle of Hue.

"One of the best books on a single action in Vietnam, written by a tough, seasoned journalist who brings the events of a half-century past into sharp relief." —*Kirkus*

Brokhausen, Nick
Whispers in the Tall Grass. Nick Brokhausen. Casemate 2019. xiv, 199 pages

ISBN 9781612007755

Grades: Adult **959.704**

1. Espionage 2. Vietnam War, 1961-1975 3. Special forces 4. Soldiers 5. Vietnam 6. 1970s 7. Autobiographies and memoirs 8. History writing — Wars and conflicts — Vietnam War 9. Life stories — Law and order — Armed forces personnel

The previously unpublished second volume of Nick Brokhausen's vivid and riveting memoir of his experiences in MACV-SOG in Vietnam.

"A great read for military history buffs immersed in Vietnam as well as anyone interested in the life and perceptions of a distinguished soldier." —*Booklist*

Sequel to: We Few.

Caputo, Philip
A Rumor of War. Philip Caputo. Henry Holt and Co. 1996. xxi, 356 p.

ISBN 9780708958643

Grades: 11 12 Adult **959.704**

1. Caputo, Philip, 1941- 2. Vietnam War, 1961-1975 3. Marines 4. Soldiers 5. United States 6. Autobiographies and memoirs 7. Biographies 8. History writing — Wars and conflicts — Vietnam War 9. Life stories — Law and order — Armed forces personnel 10. Adult books for young adults

LC 96019314

A personal memoir of the war in Vietnam, in which the author first served as a Marine and which he later covered as a reporter.

"These are the combat recollections of a very young Marine officer in Vietnam in 1965-1966. Caputo later became a newspaperman. . . . He remembers himself as a patriotic youngster, eager to prove his manhood, and then . . . he takes us through his step-by-step discovery that war and manhood and their interrelation are more complicated than he had dreamed." —*The New Yorker*

An Owl book; Reprinted in 2017 as a 40th anniversary edition; Originally published: New York : Holt, Rinehart and Winston, 1977.

Clarke, Thurston
Honorable Exit: How a Few Brave Americans Risked All to Save Our Vietnamese Allies at the End of the War. Thurston Clarke. Doubleday 2019. 448 p.

ISBN 9780385539647

Grades: Adult **959.704**

1. Vietnam War, 1961-1975 2. Evacuation of civilians 3. Refugees 4. Rescues 5. Diplomats 6. International relations 7. United States 8. Vietnam 9. History writing — Wars and conflicts — Vietnam War 10. History writing — Military

LC 2018029232

A revisionist history of the end of the Vietnam War reveals how American evacuees helped more than 100,000 South Vietnamese civilians to escape execution or concentration-camp incarceration by North Vietnamese invaders. By the author of the Last Campaign.

"Fans of military and U.S. history will revel in Clarke's expert storytelling, well-crafted re-creations, and research." —*Library Journal*

Includes bibliographical references and index.

PUBLIC LIBRARY CORE COLLECTION: NONFICTION
Twentieth Edition

FitzGerald, Frances
Fire in the Lake: The Vietnamese and the Americans in Vietnam. Frances Fitzgerald; [with a new afterword by the author]. Little, Brown 2002. xii, 500 p. : Map
ISBN 9780316159197
Grades: 11 12 Adult   959.704
1. Vietnam War, 1961-1975 2. International relations 3. United States 4. Vietnam 5. 1960s 6. 1970s 7. History writing — Wars and conflicts — Vietnam War
LC 2003543944
Pulitzer Prize for General Nonfiction, 1973.
Presents a study of Vietnamese society and politics and the effects of American intervention, based on the journalist's stay in South Vietnam from February through November of 1966.
Includes bibliographical references (p. [479]-485) and index; Originally published: Boston, MA : Little, Brown, 1972.

Hastings, Max
★ *Vietnam: An Epic Tragedy, 1945-1975.* Max Hastings. HarperCollins 2018. 512 p.
ISBN 9780062405661
Grades: Adult   959.704
1. Vietnam War, 1961-1975 2. War and society 3. War 4. Military history 5. Atrocities 6. Vietnam 7. History writing — Wars and conflicts — Vietnam War
LC Bl2018168524
The best-selling author of the Secret War draws on survivor interviews from both sides in a modern history of the Vietnam War that discusses its hotly debated political divides, major and lesser-known battles and brutal human costs.
"This isn't an easy read, but it is an essential one to comprehend the totality of the wars in that long-besieged country." —*Booklist*

Hendrickson, Paul
The Living and the Dead: Robert McNamara and Five Lives of a Lost War. Paul Hendrickson. Alfred A. Knopf 1996. IX, 427 p. : Illustration
ISBN 9780679427612
Grades: 11 12 Adult   959.704
1. McNamara, Robert S, 1916-2009 2. Vietnam War, 1961-1975 3. Politics and government 4. Military policy 5. United States 6. 20th century 7. History writing — Wars and conflicts — Vietnam War 8. History writing — Politicians — United States
LC 96007445
Booklist Editors' Choice, 1996; National Book Award for Nonfiction finalist, 1996.
A critical study of Secretary of Defense Robert McNamara and his role in the Vietnam War focuses on the lives of five people who become intertwined in the resulting storm.
"Exhaustively researched, probing, important contribution to the annals of American history." —*Publishers Weekly*
Includes bibliographical references (p.409-415) and index.

Karnow, Stanley
Vietnam, a History. Stanley Karnow. Penguin Books 1997. xv, 768 p. : Illustration; Map
ISBN 9780140265477
Grades: 11 12 Adult   959.704
1. Vietnam War, 1961-1975 2. United States history 3. Asian history 4. Vietnam 5. United States 6. 20th century 7. 19th century 8. History writing — Wars and conflicts — Vietnam War
LC 97197160
A study of American involvement in Vietnam, from French domination to the final withdrawal of American forces, discusses the historical background, politics, military campaigns, participants, and consequences of American involvement.
"A summation of over two centuries of conflict in Indochina. Chronicling a tragic history, Karnow presents a balanced and sympathetic view of Vietnamese aspirations and the mishaps that led to American involvement in a war nobody won." —*Voice of Youth Advocates.* [review of 1983 edition]
Includes bibliographical references (p. 721-741) and index; Originally published: New York : Viking, 1983.

Kissinger, Henry
Ending the Vietnam War: A History of America's Involvement in and Extrication from the Vietnam War. Henry Kissinger. Simon & Schuster 2003. 635 p. : Map
ISBN 9780743215329
Grades: Adult   959.704
1. Vietnam War, 1961-1975 2. United States 3. History writing — Wars and conflicts — Vietnam War
LC 2002017996
The former Secretary of State describes America's involvement in Southeast Asia, the events of the war, the peace negotiations, the domestic unrest over the war, and the diplomats, politicians, military leaders, and others who became part of history.
"Readers interested in the Vietnam period but unfamiliar with Kissinger's previous books will find this new volume worthwhile. Kissinger's account of America's venture in Vietnam and his role in that shipwreck is factually accurate, eminently informed and masterfully crafted." —*Publishers Weekly*
Includes bibliographical references and index.

Lee, Heath Hardage
★ *The League of Wives: The Untold Story of the Women Who Took on the U.S. Government to Bring Their Husbands Home.* Heath Hardage Lee. St. Martin's Press 2019. 288 p.
ISBN 9781250161109
Grades: Adult   959.704
1. Military spouses 2. Prisoners of war, American 3. Missing in action 4. Vietnam War, 1961-1975 5. Military pilots 6. Imprisonment 7. Families of military personnel 8. Codes (Communication) 9. Prisons 10. Politics and government 11. Determination 12. Hanoi, Vietnam 13. United States 14. 1960s 15. 1970s 16. History writing — Wars and conflicts — Vietnam War
LC 2018041164
Describes how a fierce band of military wives transformed themselves from convention-ruled married women into national lobbyists, advocates, international human-rights figures, and spies in their efforts to bring their POW husbands home from Vietnam.
"Lee addresses the stringent societal constraints the wives struggled under, rules that demanded they defer to the military in all matters regarding threats to their husbands careers and livelihoods." —*Booklist*

Logevall, Fredrik
Embers of War: The Fall of an Empire and the Making of America's Vietnam. Fredrik Logevall. Random House 2012. 880 p.
ISBN 9780375504426
Grades: Adult   959.704
1. Imperialism, French 2. Cold War 3. International relations 4. Colonies 5. Chinese history 6. Indochina 7. France 8. United States 9. Vietnam 10. History writing — Wars and conflicts — Vietnam War 11. History writing — Asia — Southeast Asia
LC 2011034971
Pulitzer Prize for History, 2013; Cundill Prize in Historical Literature finalist.
A history of the four decades leading up to the Vietnam War offers insights into how the U.S. became involved, identifying commonalities between the campaigns of French and American forces while discussing relevant political factors.
"Logevall's exhaustive study shows chapter and verse why not—and why the ensuing American war was doomed to fail." —*Kirkus*
Includes bibliographical references and index.

ESSENTIAL AND RECOMMENDED TITLES
959.704 Vietnam — 1945-

Maraniss, David
They Marched into Sunlight: War and Peace, Vietnam and America, October 1967. David Maraniss. Simon & Schuster 2003. xvii, 572 p, 16 p. of plates : Illustration; Map
ISBN 9780743217804
Grades: 11 12 Adult   959.704
1. Vietnam War, 1961-1975 2. Protest movements 3. Ambushes and surprises 4. Politics and government 5. United States 6. Madison, Wisconsin 7. 1960s 8. History writing — Wars and conflicts — Protests — Vietnam War 9. History writing — 1960s — United States 10. Adult books for young adults
LC 2003052885
J. Anthony Lukas Book Prize, 2004; New York Times Notable Book, 2003; Pulitzer Prize for History finalist, 2004.

The epic story of Vietnam and the sixties is told through the events of a few tumultuous days in 1967, bringing that catastrophic time back to life while examining questions about the meaning of dissent and the official manipulation of the truth.

"This is a narrative by a reporter who juxtaposes a ghastly little battle in Vietnam with an antiwar and anti-Dow demonstration at the University of Wisconsin, Madison, on the same day; it captures moral ambiguity everywhere, without stereotyping or condescension." —*New York Times Book Review*
Includes bibliographical references (p. 555-557) and index.

McNamara, Robert S.
In Retrospect: The Tragedy and Lessons of Vietnam. Robert S. McNamara with Brian VanDeMark. Times Books 1995. xviii, 414 p. : Illustration; Map
ISBN 9780812925234
Grades: Adult   959.704
1. Military history 2. Vietnam War, 1961-1975 3. Politics and government 4. Military policy 5. United States 6. 1960s 7. History writing — Wars and conflicts — Vietnam War
LC 94040088
Booklist Editors' Choice, 1995.

The Secretary of Defense for the Kennedy and Johnson administrations provides an account of how and why America became involved in Vietnam and discusses the legacy of decisions made during the 1960s.

"Former defense secretary McNamara seeks to put Vietnam in context and counter the cynicism and even contempt with which so many people view our political institutions and leaders. He identifies eleven major causes for our disaster in Vietnam and six points when the U.S. could legitimately have withdrawn. Certainly not the last word on this still-controversial subject but an essential acquisition for most libraries." —*Booklist*
Maps on lining papers; Includes bibliographical references (p. [381]-385) and index.

Moore, Harold G.
We Are Soldiers Still: A Journey Back to the Battlefields of Vietnam. Harold G. Moore, Joseph L. Galloway. Harper 2008. 304 p.
ISBN 9780061147760
Grades: Adult   959.704
1. Moore, Harold G, 1922-2017 2. Galloway, Joseph L. 3. Vietnam veterans 4. Vietnam War, 1961-1975 5. Military campaigns 6. Military history 7. Voyages and travels 8. Vietnam 9. 20th century 10. History writing — Wars and conflicts — Vietnam War
LC 2008011034
To honor fallen comrades, a journalist and a soldier return to Vietnam battlefields more than 30 years later.

We Were Soldiers Once—and Young: Ia Drang, the Battle That Changed the War in Vietnam. Harold G. Moore and Joseph L. Galloway. Random House 1992. xvi, 412 p, 20 p. of plates : Illustration
ISBN 9780679411581
Grades: 11 12 Adult   959.704
1. Vietnam War, 1961-1975 2. Battles 3. Soldiers 4. Military history 5. 1960s 6. Page to screen 7. History writing — Wars and conflicts — Vietnam War 8. History writing — Wars and conflicts — Battles
LC 92053642

A definitive study of the 1965 battle of Ia Drang, in the central highlands of South Vietnam, provides a blow-by-blow account of the battle and the implications of this key confrontation.

"On Nov. 14, 1965, the 1st Battalion of the 7th Cavalry, commanded by Col. Moore and accompanied by UPI reporter Galloway, helicoptered into Vietnam's remote Ia Drang Valley and found itself surrounded by a numerically superior force of North Vietnamese regulars. Moore and Galloway here offer a detailed account, based on interviews with participants and on their own recollections, of what happened during the four-day battle." —*Publishers Weekly*
Includes bibliographical references (p. [398]-402) and index.

Nguyen, Viet Thanh
Nothing Ever Dies: Vietnam and the Memory of War. Viet Thanh Nguyen. Harvard University Press 2016. 310 p.
ISBN 9780674660342
Grades: Adult   959.704
1. Vietnam War, 1961-1975 2. Memory 3. War and society 4. Art and war 5. Art 6. Identity 7. History writing — Wars and conflicts — Vietnam War
LC 2015037444
National Book Critics Circle Award for Nonfiction finalist, 2016.

Nothing Ever Dies, Viet Thanh Nguyen writes. All wars are fought twice, the first time on the battlefield, the second time in memory. From the author of the bestselling novel The Sympathizer comes a searching exploration of a conflict that lives on in the collective memory of both the Americans and the Vietnamese.

"Essentially a critical study, Nguyen's work is a powerful reflection on how we choose to remember and forget." —*Kirkus*
Includes bibliographical references and index.

Sheehan, Neil
A Bright Shining Lie: John Paul Vann and America in Vietnam. Neil Sheehan. Random House 1989. 861 p.
ISBN 9780679724148
Grades: 11 12 Adult   959.704
1. Vann, John Paul, 1924-1972 2. Vietnam War, 1961-1975 3. Soldiers 4. United States 5. 1960s 6. Biographies 7. History writing — Wars and conflicts — Vietnam War 8. Life stories — Law and order — Armed forces personnel
National Book Award for Nonfiction, 1988; Pulitzer Prize for General Nonfiction, 1989; Robert F. Kennedy Book Award, 1989; National Book Critics Circle Award for Nonfiction finalist, 1988; Pulitzer Prize for Biography or Autobiography finalist, 1989; Pulitzer Prize for History finalist, 1989.

When he came to Vietnam in 1962, Lieutenant Colonel John Paul Vann was the one clear-sighted participant in an enterprise riddled with arrogance and self-deception, a charismatic soldier who put his life and career on the line in an attempt to convince his superiors that the war should be fought another way. By the time he died in 1972, Vann had embraced the follies he once decried. He died believing that the war had been won. In this book, a monument of history and biography ... a journalist tells the story of John Vann ... and of the tragedy which destroyed the country and squandered so much of America's young manhood and resources.

"The author tells the story of the war through the focus of John Paul Vann, an army officer who faced down South Vietnamese politicians and American generals to expose the corruption that undermined our efforts and later was President Nixon's civilian adviser in Vietnam until he was killed in a helicopter crash in 1972. It is a dramatic device that lets Mr. Sheehan bring the very palpable feel of the war to us with passionate power." —*New York Times Book Review*

Shultz, Richard H.
The Secret War Against Hanoi: The Untold Story of Spies, Saboteurs, and Covert Warriors in North Vietnam. Richard H. Shultz, Jr. Perennial 2000. xvii, 408 p. : Illustration; Map
ISBN 9780060932534
Grades: 11 12 Adult   959.704
1. Spies 2. Psychological warfare 3. Deception 4. Espionage 5. Vietnam War, 1961-1975 6. Politics and government 7. Undercover operations 8. United States 9. Vietnam 10. 1960s 11. History writing — Wars and conflicts — Vietnam War 12. History writing — Spies and spying
LC BL2001000308

The largest covert operation of the Cold War is laid bare in this fascinating account of the eight-year Pentagon-run espionage campaign against North Vietnam—a program initiated in 1963 by JFK to replace the CIA's ineffectual effort.

"Schultz was given access to SOG archives and veterans and has produced a professional volume on how SOG originated and operated over its eight-year existence." —Booklist

Includes bibliographical references (p. [355]-394) and index; Originally published: New York : HarperCollins, 1999.

Stanton, Doug

The Odyssey of Echo Company: The 1968 Tet Offensive and the Epic Battle to Survive the Vietnam War. Doug Stanton. Scribner 2017. 416 p.

ISBN 9781476761916

Grades: Adult   959.704

1. Vietnam War, 1961-1975 2. Military campaigns 3. Guerrilla warfare 4. Tet Offensive, 1968 5. Soldiers 6. Survival 7. Military reconnaissance 8. Postwar life 9. United States history 10. Asian history 11. Vietnam 12. 1960s 13. 20th century 14. History writing — Military — Military units 15. History writing — Wars and conflicts — Vietnam War

LC Bl2017030704

A portrait of the American recon platoon of the 101st Airborne Division describes their 60-day fight for survival during the early 1968 attack by North Vietnamese soldiers on dozens of South Vietnam cities, tracing their postwar difficulties with acclimating into a peacetime America that did not want to hear their story.

Talty, Stephan

Saving Bravo: The Greatest Rescue Mission in Navy SEAL History. Stephan Talty. Houghton Mifflin Harcourt 2018. 304 p.

ISBN 9781328866721

Grades: Adult   959.704

1. Hambleton, Gene (Iceal Eugene), 1918-2004 2. Search and rescue operations 3. Vietnam War, 1961-1975 4. Military history 5. Vietnam 6. United States 7. 20th century 8. History writing — Wars and conflicts — Vietnam War 9. History writing — Military — Special Forces

LC 2018006365

The untold story of the most important rescue mission not just of the Vietnam War, but the entire Cold War: One American aviator, who knew our most important secrets, crashed behind enemy lines and was sought by the entire North Vietnamese and Russian military machines. One Navy SEAL and his Vietnamese partner had to sneak past them all to save him.

Includes bibliographical references and index.

Ward, Geoffrey C.

★ *The Vietnam War: An Intimate History.* Geoffrey C. Ward; based on a documentary film by Ken Burns & Lynn Novick; with a preface by Ken Burns & Lynn Novick. Alfred A. Knopf 2017. 528 p.

ISBN 9780307700254

Grades: Adult   959.704

1. Vietnam War, 1961-1975 2. War 3. Military history 4. United States history 5. Asian history 6. Vietnam 7. 20th century 8. Media tie-ins 9. History writing — Wars and conflicts — Vietnam War 10. Adult books for young adults

LC 2017015686

More than forty years after it ended, the Vietnam War continues to haunt our country. We still argue over why we were there, whether we could have won, and who was right and wrong in their response to the conflict. When the war divided the country, it created deep political fault lines that continue to divide us today.

"Accompanying the PBS series to be aired in September 2017, this is an outstanding, indispensable survey of the Vietnam War." —Kirkus

Includes bibliographical references and index.

Warren, James A.

Year of the Hawk: America's Descent into Vietnam, 1965. James A. Warren. Scribner 2021. 352 p.

ISBN 9781982122942

Grades: Adult   959.704

1. Vietnam War, 1961-1975 2. Communism 3. Insurgency 4. Colonialism 5. Military occupation 6. Anti-Communism 7. Cold War 8. Battles 9. Military policy 10. International relations 11. United States 12. Vietnam 13. History writing — 1960s — United States 14. History writing — Wars and conflicts — Vietnam War 15. History writing — Asia — Southeast Asia

The Vietnam War was the greatest disaster in the history of American foreign policy. The conflict shook the nation to its foundations, exacerbating already deep cleavages in American society, and left the country baffled and ambivalent about its role in the world. Year of the Hawk is a military and political history of the war in Vietnam during 1965—the pivotal first year of the American conflict, when the United States decided to intervene directly with combat units in a struggle between communist and pro-Western forces in South Vietnam that had raged on and off for twenty years.

"Historian Warren's (God, War, and Providence) account of the Vietnam War delivers valuable lessons about the United States' escalation in Southeast Asia in 1965, and more generally about the lengthy wars that have often entangled U.S. foreign policy. . . . Highly recommended as a concise study of the United States' entrance into the Vietnam War." —Library Journal

White, Ralph

Getting Out of Saigon: How a 27-year-old American Banker Saved 113 Vietnamese Civilians. Ralph White. Simon & Schuster 2023. 320 p.

ISBN 9781982195175

Grades: Adult   959.704

1. White, Ralph 2. Vietnam War, 1961-1975 3. Bankers 4. Military occupation 5. Bank employees 6. Families 7. Evacuation of civilians 8. Civilians in war 9. Bureaucracy 10. Rescues 11. Escapes 12. Immigration and emigration 13. North American people 14. American people 15. Ho Chi Minh City, Vietnam 16. Autobiographies and memoirs 17. Life stories — People in history 18. History writing — Wars and conflicts — Vietnam War 19. History writing — Asia — Southeast Asia

The gripping and remarkable true story of author Ralph White's desperate effort to save the entire staff of the Saigon branch of Chase Manhattan bank and their families before the city fell to the North Vietnamese Army. Getting Out of Saigon is the remarkable story of a city on the eve of destruction and the colorful characters who respond differently to impending doom. It's about one man's quest to save innocent lives not because it was ordered but because it was the right thing to do.

"In this stirring debut, White recounts his extraordinary mission rescuing civilians during the fall of South Vietnam." —Publishers Weekly

Wright, James Edward

★ *Enduring Vietnam: An American Generation and Its War.* James Wrigh. Thomas Dunne Books, an imprint of St. Martin's Press 2017. 352 p.

ISBN 9781250092489

Grades: Adult   959.704

1. Vietnam War, 1961-1975 2. Soldiers 3. Families of military personnel 4. War 5. History writing — Wars and conflicts — Vietnam War

LC 2016038762

Depicts the cruelty of the Vietnam war through interviews with those who served and the families of those who served and never returned, discussing why they joined the military, what they thought of the war and what it was like to serve.

"Wrights worthy effort is a tribute to Americans who saw the worst that the Vietnam War offered, combined with a broad look at the domestic and geopolitical factors that led to the U.S. getting involved in the long, controversial conflict." —Publishers Weekly

Includes bibliographical references and index.

959.9 Philippines

Resendez, Andres

Conquering the Pacific: An Unknown Mariner and the Final Great Voyage of the Age of Discovery. Andres Resendez. Houghton Mifflin Harcourt 2021. 304 p. Illustration; Map

ESSENTIAL AND RECOMMENDED TITLES
960 History of Africa

ISBN 9781328515971
Grades: Adult **959.9**
1. Legazpi, Miguel Lopez de, 1510?-1572 2. Martin, Lope 3. Sailors 4. Expeditions 5. Multiracial men 6. Explorers 7. Naval history 8. Exploration 9. Philippines 10. Pacific Ocean 11. Mexico 12. Biographies 13. History writing — Europe — Spain 14. Life stories — People in history — Explorers 15. History writing — Exploration
LC 2021004112

The story of an uncovered voyage as colorful and momentous as any on record for the Age of Discovery—and of the Black mariner whose stunning accomplishment has been until now lost to history.

"A vivid tale of adventure and discovery that will draw in all history lovers."
—*Library Journal*

Includes bibliographical references and index.

960 History of Africa

French, Howard W.
Born in Blackness: Africa, Africans, and the Making of the Modern World, 1471 to the Second World War. Howard W. French. Liveright Publishing 2021. 464 p.
ISBN 9781631495823
Grades: Adult **960**
1. Slave trade 2. African diaspora 3. Modern history 4. African civilization 5. Colonialism 6. Genocide 7. Historiography 8. African history 9. European history 10. History writing — Colonization — Africa 11. History writing — Colonialism — Europe 12. History writing — African American — Enslavement — United States 13. Society and culture — Race
LC 2021025763

Hurston/Wright Legacy Award: Nonfiction, 2022.

Revealing the central yet intentionally obliterated role of Africa in the creation of modernity, Born in Blackness vitally reframes our understanding of world history. In a sweeping narrative that traverses 600 years, one that eloquently weaves precise historical detail with poignant personal reportage, Howard W. French retells the story of medieval and emerging Africa, demonstrating how the economic ascendancy of Europe, the anchoring of democracy in America, and the fulfillment of so-called Enlightenment ideals all grew out of Europe's dehumanizing engagement with the "darkest" continent. Born in Blackness dramatically retrieves the lives of major African historical figures whose stories have been repeatedly etiolated and erased over centuries.

"A Black journalist reframes modern history by restoring Africa to its rightful place at the center of the story. . . . French's underlying argument and accompanying cogent analysis make for essential reading for anyone looking to decolonize their understanding of the Western world." —*Kirkus*

Includes bibliographical references and index.

Meredith, Martin
The **Fortunes** *of Africa: A 5000-year History of Wealth, Greed, and Endeavor.* Martin Meredith. Public Affairs 2014. 784 p.
ISBN 9781610394598
Grades: Adult **960**
1. African civilization 2. Social life and customs 3. Africa 4. History writing — Africa
LC 2014939816

In this vast and vivid panorama of history, Martin Meredith follows the fortunes of Africa over a period of 5,000 years. With compelling narrative, he traces the rise and fall of ancient kingdoms and empires; the spread of Christianity and Islam; the enduring quest for gold and other riches; the exploits of explorers and missionaries; and the impact of European colonization. He examines, too, the fate of modern African states and concludes with a glimpse of their future.

"A gripping tale of insatiable greed—personal and collective." —*Booklist*

Soyinka, Wole
Of Africa. Wole Soyinka. Yale University Press 2012. 224 p.
ISBN 9780300140460

Grades: Adult
1. Postcolonialism 2. Religion and politics 3. Culture 4. Civil rights 5. Theocracy 6. Totalitarianism 7. Humanism 8. International relations 9. Nationalism 10. African civilization 11. African history 12. Africa 13. Essays 14. History writing — Africa
LC 2012013544

The first African recipient of a Nobel Prize in Literature offers a thought-provoking analysis of Africa's current crises while making recommendations for cultural and political renewal, exploring the region's history as it relates to the histories of other nations and critically assessing Africa's stances on race and religious tolerance.

960.33 History of Africa — 2000-

Faloyin, Dipo
★ *Africa Is Not a Country: Notes on a Bright Continent.* Dipo Faloyin. W.W. Norton & Company 2022. 400 p.
ISBN 9780393881530
Grades: Adult **960.33**
1. Continents 2. National characteristics 3. Multiculturalism 4. Democracy 5. Dictatorship 6. Colonialism 7. Stereotypes 8. Social life and customs 9. Politics and government 10. Africa 11. Politics and global affairs — World politics — Africa 12. Society and culture — Ethnic studies
LC 2022017536

So often, Africa has been depicted simplistically as a uniform land of famines and safaris, poverty and strife, stripped of all nuance. In this bold and insightful book, Dipo Faloyin offers a much-needed corrective, weaving a vibrant tapestry of stories that bring to life Africa's rich diversity, communities, and histories. Witty and insightful, Africa is Not a Country is an idiosyncratic and entertaining exploration of a diverse continent that deserves to finally be understood, respected, and celebrated.

"With clarity and incisive wit, journalist Faloyin explores the origins of the 54 countries of Africa and invites readers to look beyond the stereotypes that remain at the forefront of the rest of the world's portrayals of the continent."
—*Booklist*

Originally published in the UK under the title Africa is not a country: Breaking stereotypes of modern Africa by Harvill Secker, London, in 2022; Includes bibliographical references.

962 Egypt, Sudan, South Sudan

Wilkinson, Toby A. H.
The **Nile:** *A Journey Downriver Through Egypt's Past and Present.* by Toby Wilkinson. Alfred A. Knopf 2014. xv, 332 pages, 16 unnumbered pages of plates : Illustration; Color; Map
ISBN 9780385351553
Grades: Adult **962**
1. Rivers 2. Civilization, Ancient 3. Religions 4. African history 5. Nile River 6. Egypt 7. Ancient Egypt (3100 B.C.E.-640 C.E.) 8. Travel Writing — Southwest Asia and North Africa (Middle East) 9. History writing — Ancient — Egypt 10. History writing — Southwest Asia and North Africa (Middle East)
LC 2013045874

Traces the history of the famous river to illuminate the civilizations it renewed and sustained, documenting the stories of real and fabled characters whose experiences were intertwined with the Nile.

Originally published by Bloomsbury, London, in 2014; Includes bibliographical references and index.

962.05 Egypt since 1922

Hessler, Peter
The **Buried:** *An Archaeology of the Egyptian Revolution.* Peter Hessler. Penguin Press 2019. 463 pages : Illustration; Map

ISBN 9780525559566

Grades: Adult 962.05

1. Hessler, Peter, 1969- 2. Journalists 3. Ancient Cities and towns 4. Revolutions 5. Social change 6. City life 7. Antiquities 8. American people in Africa 9. Excavations (Archaeology) 10. Arab Spring, 2010-2012 11. Social life and customs 12. Politics and government 13. Cairo, Egypt 14. Egypt 15. 21st century 16. Politics and global affairs — World politics — Southwest Asia and North Africa (Middle East) 17. Society and culture — Urban and regional studies 18. Life stories — Arts and culture — Writing — Journalists

LC 2018050659

National Book Critics Circle Award for Nonfiction finalist, 2019.

Drawn by a fascination with Egypt's rich history and culture, Peter Hessler moved with his wife and twin daughters to Cairo in 2011. He wanted to learn Arabic, explore Cairo's neighborhoods, and visit the legendary archeological digs of Upper Egypt. After his years of covering China for the New Yorker, friends warned him that Egypt would be a much quieter place. But not long before he arrived, the Egyptian Arab Spring had begun, and now the country was in chaos. In the midst of the revolution, he attached himself to an important archeological dig at a site rich in royal tombs known in as al-Madfuna, or "The Buried." He and his wife set out to master Arabic, striking up a friendship with their instructor, a cynical political sophisticate. A different kindof friendship was formed with the neighborhood garbage collector, an illiterate but highly perceptive man named Sayyid, whose access to the trash of Cairo would be its own kind of archeological excavation. Hessler also met a family of Chinese small-business owners in the lingerie trade; their view of the country proved a bracing counterpoint to the West's conventional wisdom. Through the lives of these and other ordinary people at a time of tragedy and heartache, and through connections between contemporary Egypt and its ancient past, Hessler creates an astonishing portrait of a country and its people.

"This is writing at its best and highly recommended for anyone interested in Egypt, modern or ancient." —*Library Journal*

Includes bibliographical references and index.

962.404 Sudan — 1956-

Mahjoub, Jamal

A Line in the River: Khartoum, City of Memory. Jamal Mahjoub. Bloomsbury Publishing 2018. 401 p. : Illustration; Map

ISBN 9781408885468

Grades: Adult 962.404

1. Mahjoub, Jamal, 1960- 2. Social life and customs 3. Identity 4. Homecomings 5. Authors 6. Cultural differences 7. Social classes 8. Religious persecution 9. Politics and government 10. Self-discovery 11. Southwest Asia and North Africa (Middle East) 12. Sudan 13. Autobiographies and memoirs 14. History writing — Africa 15. Travel Writing — Africa 16. Life stories — Arts and culture — Writing — Authors

LC 2019300509

Traces the author's early memories of Khartoum and his studies into Sudan's past as well as the factors that triggered and perpetuated the civil war after it gained independence in 1956.

Includes index.

965 Algeria

Evans, Martin

Algeria: France's Undeclared War. Martin Evans. Oxford University Press 2012. xxi, 457 p. : Illustration; Map

ISBN 9780192803504

Grades: Adult 965

1. Colonialism 2. War 3. Colonies 4. International relations 5. Revolutions 6. Southwest Asia and North Africa (Middle East) history 7. Africa 8. France 9. Algeria 10. 1950s 11. 1960s 12. History writing — Africa 13. History writing — Europe — France

Drawing upon previously classified archival sources as well as new oral testimonies, this book underlines the conflict of values between the Republican Front and Algerian nationalism, explaining how this clash produced patterns of thought and action, such as the institutionalization of torture and the raising of pro-French Muslim militias, which tragically polarized choices and framed all subsequent stages of the conflict.

Includes bibliographical references (p. [415]-429) and index.

Shatz, Adam

The Rebel's Clinic: The Revolutionary Lives of Frantz Fanon. Adam Shatz. Farrar, Straus and Giroux 2024. 448 p.

ISBN 9780374176426

Grades: Adult 965

1. Fanon, Frantz, 1925-1961 2. Intellectuals 3. Revolutionaries 4. Psychiatrists 5. Racism 6. Algerian people 7. Psychology 8. Human rights 9. Algeria 10. Biographies 11. Life stories — Politics — Activists and reformers 12. Life stories — Education — Scholars and educators

LC 2023030996

This eye-opening new biography of the intellectual activist of the postcolonial era whose writings about race, revolution and the psychology of power continue to shape radical movements across the world offers a dramatic reconstruction of his extraordinary life.

"Shatz's thoroughly researched biography of Frantz Fanon, psychiatrist turned revolutionary intellectual and activist, focuses on a complex man who lived a brief but adventurous life and left a significant legacy." —*Booklist*

Includes bibliographical references and index.

966.62 Liberia

Cooper, Helene

Madame President: The Incredible Journey of Ellen Johnson Sirleaf. Helene Cooper. Simon & Schuster 2017. 352 pages

ISBN 9781451697353

Grades: Adult 966.62

1. Johnson-Sirleaf, Ellen, 1938- 2. Women presidents 3. Politicians 4. Sex discrimination against women 5. Gender role 6. Women's role 7. Women politicians 8. Family violence victims 9. Exile (Punishment) 10. Political corruption 11. Civil war 12. Leadership 13. African history 14. Liberia 15. Central Africa 16. 20th century 17. Biographies 18. Life stories — Politics — Politicians 19. History writing — Women's history 20. History writing — Civil wars and genocide — Africa

LC 2016042087

The harrowing, but triumphant story of Ellen Johnson Sirleaf, leader of the Liberian women's movement, winner of the Nobel Peace Prize, and the first democratically elected female president in African history.

"A brisk chronicle of a strong-willed, tireless, and determined leader." —*Kirkus*

966.68 Cote d'Ivoire (Ivory Coast)

Erdman, Sarah

Nine Hills to Nambonkaha: Two Years in the Heart of an African Village. Sarah Erdman. Henry Holt 2003. xi, 322 p.

ISBN 9780805073812

Grades: Adult 966.68

1. Erdman, Sarah 2. Villages 3. Cote d'Ivoire 4. Africa 5. Autobiographies and memoirs 6. Travel writing — Living abroad 7. Life stories — General 8. Adult books for young adults

LC 2003044955

A Peace Corps worker offers a portrayal of an African village that stands on the brink of modernity, caught between ancient superstitions and the era of the cell phone as they struggle with AIDS and other life-threatening problems.

"This is an engrossing, well-told tale certain to appeal to armchair travelers and to anyoneespecially womenconsidering international volunteer work." —*Publishers Weekly*

ESSENTIAL AND RECOMMENDED TITLES
967.51 Democratic Republic of the Congo

967.51 Democratic Republic of the Congo

Hochschild, Adam
King Leopold's Ghost: A Story of Greed, Terror, and Heroism in Colonial Africa. Adam Hochschild. Houghton Mifflin 1998. 366 p. : Illustration; Map
ISBN 9780395759240
Grades: 11 12 Adult   967.51
1. Leopold II, King of the Belgians, 1835-1909 2. Forced labor 3. Indigenous peoples 4. Human rights 5. Mass murder 6. Slavery 7. Colonies 8. Race relations 9. Politics and government 10. African history 11. Africa 12. Congo (Democratic Republic) 13. Belgium 14. 19th century 15. 1910s 16. History writing — Colonization — Africa
LC 98016813
ALA Notable Book, 1999; Booklist Editors' Choice, 1998; Lionel Gelber Prize (Canada), 1999; Mark Lynton History Prize, 1999; New York Times Notable Book, 1998; National Book Critics Circle Award for Nonfiction finalist, 1998.
A provocative study of King Leopold II of Belgium's genocidal plunder of the Congo in the 1880s, as the European powers were colonizing Africa, reveals the heroic efforts that led to the first international human rights movement.
"Hochschild's impressively researched history records the roles of the famous and obscure, missionaries, journalists, opportunists, politicians, and royalty in this long-forgotten drama." —*Booklist*
Includes bibliographical references (p. 338-350) and index.

Reid, Stuart A.
The Lumumba Plot: The Secret History of the CIA and a Cold War Assassination. Stuart A. Reid. Alfred A. Knopf 2023. 320 p.
ISBN 9781524748814
Grades: Adult   967.51
1. Lumumba, Patrice, 1925-1961 2. Civil war 3. International relations 4. Assassination 5. Politics and government 6. African history 7. Congo (Democratic Republic) 8. United States 9. 1960s 10. History Writing — Civil wars and genocide — Africa 11. Politics and global affairs — World politics — Africa
LC 2023003992
Reading like a Cold War spy thriller, this engrossing work of history recounts the U.S.-sanctioned plot in 1960 to assassinate Patrice Lumumba, the leader of the newly independent Congo, to forestall the spread of communism in Africa, which represented the opening chapter of a long horror story.
"An evenhanded work of deep scholarship that clearly elucidates a largely hidden piece of U.S. foreign policy." —*Kirkus*
Includes bibliographical references and index.

967.5103 Democratic Republic of the Congo — 1960-

Prendergast, John
Congo Stories: Battling Five Centuries of Exploitation and Greed. Text by John Prendergast and Fidel Bafilemba; foreword by Soriya Aziz Souleymane; postscript by Dave Eggers; afterword by Chouchou Namegabe; illlustrations by Sam Ilus; photographs by Ryan Gosling. Grand Central Publishing, a division of Hachette Book Group 2018. 320 p.
ISBN 9781455584642
Grades: Adult   967.5103
1. Exploitation 2. Colonialism 3. Humanitarianism 4. Mines and mineral resources 5. African history 6. Congo (Democratic Republic) 7. Politics and global affairs — World politics — Africa 8. Society and culture — Social activism and philanthropy
LC 2018021726
The humanitarian co-author of Beyond Mindfulness investigates the role of western prosperity on 500 years of Congolese history, sharing the poignant experiences of everyday people whose lives have been upended by regional violence.

967.57104 Rwanda — 1962-

Hatzfeld, Jean
Machete Season: The Killers in Rwanda Speak : A Report. by Jean Hatzfeld; translated from the French by Linda Coverdale; preface by Susan Sontag. Farrar, Straus and Giroux 2005. xiv, 253 p. : Illustration; Map
ISBN 9780374280826
Grades: 11 12 Adult   967.57104
1. Tutsi (African people) 2. Genocide 3. Hutu (African people) 4. Interethnic relations 5. Atrocities 6. Rwandan Civil War, 1994 7. African history 8. Rwanda 9. 20th century 10. History writing — Wars and conflicts — Civil Wars 11. History writing — Civil wars and genocide — Africa
LC 2004061600
A veteran foreign correspondent shares a collection of interviews with ten Hutu men—all tried, convicted and sentenced for the genocidal killings of their Tutsi neighbors—as they describe their participation in the heinous crimes and their reasons for the murders, in a study that considers the roots of human morality and ethics.
"Steering clear of politics, this important book succeeds in offering the reader some grasp of how such unspeakable acts unfolded." —*Publishers Weekly*
Originally published in French as Saison de machettes: Paris : Seuil, 2003.

967.5710431 Rwanda — Civil War of 1994

Blood *Papa: Rwanda's New Generation.* Jean Hatzfeld; translated from the French by Joshua David Jordan. Farrar, Straus and Giroux 2018. 240 p.
ISBN 9780374279783
Grades: Adult   967.5710431
1. Tutsi (African people) 2. Genocide 3. War 4. Memory 5. Psychic trauma 6. Postwar life 7. Intergenerational relations 8. Atrocities 9. Rwandan Civil War, 1994 10. Intergenerational trauma 11. African history 12. Rwanda 13. Interviews 14. Translations — French to English 15. Life stories — Facing adversity — War and oppression — War survivors 16. Life stories — People in history — Witness to history 17. Society and culture — Violence and crime — Genocide
LC 2018007632
Provides first-person accounts of what life is like for today's Rwandan teenagers and what they have learned from their parents, one generation removed from the ethnic-based genocide in 1994 when the Hutu killed 800,000 Tutsis.
"This book, more of an ethnography than a history, exposes the effects of the genocides stubborn legacy on the next generation, but is not an introduction to the events of 1994. Readers approaching it without prior knowledge of the genocide or Hutu-Tutsi relations will have a hard time fully understanding it, but those who have context will find this an illuminating update." —*Publishers Weekly*
Originally published: Paris : Gallimard, 2015; Translated from the French.

967.62 Kenya

Anderson, David
Histories of the Hanged: The Dirty War in Kenya and the End of Empire. David Anderson. W.W. Norton 2005. VIII, 406 p, 16 p. of plates : Illustration; Map; Portrait
ISBN 9780393059861
Grades: Adult   967.62
1. Mau Mau Movement and Revolt, 1946-1960 2. African history 3. Kenya 4. History writing — Colonization — Africa
LC 2004024804
A history of the war between the colonial government and the insurrectionist Mau Mau between 1952 and 1960 casts Gikuyu rebels in a more sympathetic light and profiles the British as the conflict's aggressors, in a volume that also discusses the contributions of such figures as Winston Churchill and Harold MacMillan.

"This is vital reading for any student of British colonial and African history."
—*Publishers Weekly*
Includes bibliographical references (p. 357-387) and index.

Dinesen, Isak
Out of Africa. Isak Dinesen. Modern Library 1992. xv, 399 p.
ISBN 9780679600213
Grades: Adult   967.62
1. Dinesen, Isak, 1885-1962 2. Rural life 3. British people in Africa 4. Authors, Danish 5. Intellectual life 6. Colonialism 7. Human-animal relationships 8. Social life and customs 9. Voyages and travels 10. Kenya 11. 20th century 12. 19th century 13. Autobiographies and memoirs 14. Page to screen 15. Classics 16. Travel Writing — Africa 17. Travel Writing — Living Abroad
                                                 LC 92050213
In describing her experiences managing a coffee plantation in Kenya, the author provides insight into the nature of African life.
Originally published: London : Putnam, 1937. With new biographical note.

967.7305 Somalia — 1960-

Bowden, Mark
Black Hawk Down: A Story of Modern War. Mark Bowden. Atlantic Monthly Press 1999. 386 p. : Illustration; Map
ISBN 9780871137388
Grades: Adult   967.7305
1. Aidid, Mohammed Farah, 1934-1996 2. Rescue work 3. Military strategy 4. Adventure 5. Operation Restore Hope, 1992-1993 6. Somalia 7. Mogadishu, Somalia 8. 1990s 9. Page to screen 10. History writing — Military — Special Forces 11. Adventure writing — Survival
                                                 LC 98046688
ALA Notable Book, 2000; New York Times Notable Book, 1999; National Book Award for Nonfiction finalist, 1999.
A group of elite U.S. soldiers is sent into Mogadishu in 1993 on a U.N. peacekeeping operation, and for eighteen harrowing hours they are trapped, facing overwhelming odds in hostile territory.
"The author describes both sides of the October 1993 raid into the heart of Mogadishu, Somalia, a raid that quickly became the most intensive close combat Americans have engaged in since the Vietnam War. But Bowden's gripping narrative of the fighting is only a framework for an examination of the internal dynamics of America's elite forces and a critique of the philosophy of sending such high-tech units into combat with minimal support." —*Publishers Weekly*
Portions of this book were originally published as a series in the Philadelphia inquirer.

Rawlence, Ben
City of Thorns: Nine Lives in the World's Largest Refugee Camp. Ben Rawlence. Picador 2016. 400 pages
ISBN 9781250067630
Grades: Adult   967.7305
1. Refugee camps 2. Refugees, Somali 3. Human rights 4. Interpersonal relations 5. Deserts 6. Political corruption 7. Civil war 8. Southwest Asia and North Africa (Middle East) history 9. Somalia 10. Kenya 11. 20th century 12. Society and culture — Violence and crime — Genocide 13. Adult books for young adults 14. History writing — Civil wars and genocide — Africa
                                                 LC 2015029505
A researcher for Human Rights Watch describes the refugee camp in Dabaab, home to those fleeing civil war in Somalia, and highlights the life of various residents, including a former child soldier, a schoolgirl and a youth leader.

968.04 Republic of South Africa — 1814-1910

Millard, Candice
★ *Hero of the Empire: The Boer War, a Daring Escape, and the Making of Winston Churchill*. Candice Millard. Doubleday, a division of Penguin Random House LLC 2016. 352 p.
ISBN 9780385535731
Grades: Adult   968.04
1. Churchill, Winston, 1874-1965 2. Prisoners of war 3. Boer War, 1899-1902 4. Escaped prisoners of war 5. Survival 6. Escapes 7. Colonialism 8. Imperialism, British 9. British people in South Africa 10. Journalists 11. Politicians 12. International relations 13. Great Britain 14. South Africa 15. 19th century 16. Biographies 17. Life stories — Politics — Politicians 18. History writing — Wars and conflicts
                                                 LC 2015049806
New York Times Notable Book, 2016.
The best-selling author of Destiny of the Republic presents a narrative account of Churchill's lesser-known heroics during the Boer War, describing his daring escape from rebel captors, trek through hundreds of miles with virtually no supplies and eventual return to South Africa to liberate the soldiers captured with him.
"Here the author documents the equally risky adventures of Winston Churchill (1874-1965) during the Second Boer War, in which Churchill and his fellow soldiers were captured upon arriving in South Africa. Churchill managed an escape, eventually returning to South Africa to free the men with whom he was imprisoned. Enjoyable for all readers, especially fans of Churchill, military and world history, narrative nonfiction, and survival stories." —*Library Journal*

968.06 South Africa — Period as Republic, 1961

Carlin, John
Playing the Enemy: Nelson Mandela and the Game That Made a Nation. John Carlin. Penguin Group 2008. 304 p.
ISBN 9781594201745
Grades: 11 12 Adult   968.06
1. Mandela, Nelson, 1918-2013 2. Postcolonialism 3. Rugby football 4. Sports 5. Race relations in sports 6. Presidents 7. Segregation 8. Race relations 9. Politics and government 10. African history 11. South Africa 12. 20th century 13. Page to screen 14. Sports and Competition — Teams 15. Adult books for young adults 16. History writing — Africa — South Africa 17. Sports and competition — Rugby
                                                 LC 2008298721
Documents the anti-apartheid advocate's ten-year effort to unite his country, during which he worked with proponents of apartheid from his jail cell, won the presidency, and helped South Africa's national rugby team host the World Cup as part of a unifying campaign.
"Deftly sketched characters make up both an audience for the big game and a gallery of South Africa, through which Carlin will recount the absorbing story of a country emerging from its cruelly absurd racist experiment." —*New York Times Book Review*
Book made into a movie called Invictus.

968.06092 South Africa — 1961 — Biography

Mandela, Nelson
The Prison Letters of Nelson Mandela. Nelson Mandela; edited by Sahm Venter, with foreword by Zamaswazi DLamini-Mandela. Liveright Publishing Corporation 2018. 592 p.
ISBN 9781631491177
Grades: Adult   968.06092
1. Mandela, Nelson, 1918-2013 2. Human rights 3. Justice 4. Anti-apartheid activists 5. Politicians 6. Social advocates 7. Presidents 8. Politics and government 9. South Africa 10. 20th century 11. Letters 12. Life stories — Politics — Activists and reformers 13. History writing — Africa — South Africa

ESSENTIAL AND RECOMMENDED TITLES
968.07 South Africa — 1994-

LC 2018009933

Published on the centenary of his birth, a selection of 255 of the anti-apartheid champion's letters, written during his incarceration, convey his intimate perspectives on such subjects as his wife's imprisonment, the death of his son and human rights.

968.07 South Africa — 1994-

Malala, Justice
The Plot to Save South Africa: The Week Mandela Averted Civil War and Forged a New Nation. Justice Malala. Simon & Schuster 2023. 352 p.
ISBN 9781982149734
Grades: Adult   968.07
1. Mandela, Nelson, 1918-2013 2. De Klerk, F. W, 1936-2021 3. Assassination 4. Political leadership 5. White supremacists 6. Civil war 7. Apartheid 8. Race relations 9. Violence 10. Peace 11. South African people 12. Southern African people 13. Politics and government 14. South Africa 15. 20th century 16. Politics and global affairs — Political figures 17. Politics and global affairs — World politics — Africa

LC 2022027751

A riveting, kaleidoscopic account of nine days in the life of a country on the edge, as the assassination of Nelson Mandela's protégé by a white supremacist threatens to derail South Africa's democratic transition and plunge the nation into civil war.

"A suspenseful nonfiction thriller featuring valuable firsthand observation." —*Kirkus*

Includes bibliographical references and index.

968.91 Zimbabwe

Lamb, Christina
House of Stone: The True Story of a Family Divided in War-torn Zimbabwe. Christina Lamb. Lawrence Hill Books 2007. 320 p.
ISBN 9781556527357
Grades: 11 12 Adult   968.91
1. Hough, Nigel 2. Aqui, 1962- 3. Land tenure 4. European people in foreign countries 5. Race relations 6. Politics and government 7. African history 8. Zimbabwe 9. Autobiographies and memoirs 10. Family and Relationships — Families 11. Life stories — Facing adversity — War and oppression — War survivors 12. Adult books for young adults 13. History writing — Civil wars and genocide — Africa

LC 2007019814

Describes the lives of two very different Zimbabweans—Nigel Hough, a wealthy white farmer, and Aqui, his poor Black nanny—from the 1970s to 2002, focusing how both were affected by Zimbabwe's brutal civil war and its aftermath.

"Through the parallel accounts of two people in Zimbabwe, one a poor Black maid, one a rich white farmer, . . . Lamb tells the compelling story of a country ravaged first by colonial settlers and now by brutal civil war. . . . The anguished personal detail, true to the changing viewpoints, makes for a gripping read." —*Booklist*

970.004 Ethnic and national groups

Dodds Pennock, Caroline
★ *On Savage Shores: How Indigenous Americans Discovered Europe.* Caroline Dodds Pennock. Alfred A. Knopf 2023. 352 p.
ISBN 9781524749262
Grades: Adult   970.004
1. Indigenous peoples of North America 2. Indigenous peoples of Mexico 3. Indigenous peoples of South America 4. Indigenous peoples of Central America 5. Transatlantic voyages 6. Voyages and travels 7. Exploration 8. Commerce 9. Diplomacy 10. Slavery 11. Marginalized people 12. Cultural differences 13. Influence (Psychology) 14. European history 15. North American history 16. South American history 17. Central American history 18. Western Hemisphere 19. Age of exploration (1419-1610) 20. History writing — Renaissance — Europe 21. History writing — Exploration 22. History writing — Indigenous peoples — Latin America 23. History writing — Indigenous peoples — United States 24. History writing — Indigenous peoples — Canada

LC 2022046208

We have long been taught to presume that modern global history began when the "Old World" encountered the "New," when Christopher Columbus "discovered" America in 1492. But, as Caroline Dodds Pennock conclusively shows in this groundbreaking book, for tens of thousands of Aztecs, Maya, Totonacs, Inuit and others—enslaved people, diplomats, explorers, servants, traders—the reverse was true: They discovered Europe. The story of these Indigenous Americans abroad is a story of abduction, loss, cultural appropriation, and, as they saw it, of apocalypse—a story that has largely been absent from our collective imagination of the times.

"The exploration, colonization, and exploitation of the Americas flowed from Europe to the so-called New World, but historian Pennock cleverly and capably reveals that some Indigenous people reversed the flow, traveling to Europe and changing that continent." —*Booklist*

Includes bibliographical references and index.

Dunbar-Ortiz, Roxanne
★ *An Indigenous Peoples' History of the United States.* Roxanne Dunbar-Ortiz. Beacon Press 2014. 296 pages
ISBN 9780807000403
Grades: Adult   970.004
1. Indigenous peoples of North America 2. Indigenous peoples of North America, Treatment of 3. Intersectionality 4. Colonialism 5. Colonized peoples 6. Colonization 7. United States 8. History writing — Indigenous peoples — United States 9. Society and culture — Race 10. Antiracist literature

LC 2013050262

Challenges the founding myth of the United States and shows how policy against the indigenous peoples was genocidal and imperialist, designed to crush the original inhabitants. Spanning more than 300 years, a classic bottom-up history significantly reframes how we view our past. Told from the viewpoint of the indigenous, it reveals how Native Americans, for centuries, actively resisted expansion of the U.S. empire.

Includes bibliographical references and index.

DuVal, Kathleen
★ *Native Nations: A Millennium of Indigenous Change and Persistence.* Kathleen DuVal. Random House 2024. 752 p.
ISBN 9780525511038
Grades: Adult   970.004
1. Indigenous peoples of North America 2. Indigenous peoples of North America — Politics and government 3. First contact of indigenous peoples with Europeans 4. Civilization, Indigenous 5. Indigenous peoples relations with missionaries, traders, etc. 6. Politics and government 7. Civilization 8. History 9. Social history 10. Indigenous peoples 11. United States 12. North America 13. History writing — Indigenous peoples — United States

LC 2023011941

An award-winning historian tells the story of the Native nations, from the rise of ancient cities to the present, reframing North American history with Indigenous power and sovereignty at its center and showing how the influence of Native peoples remained a constant and will continue far into the future.

"In this impressive history, DuVal...offers a long-term view of how Indigenous peoples in North America flourished both before and long after the arrival of Europeans, leveraging their power and negotiating their place alongside or within settler culture amid increasing existential threats." —*Kirkus*

Includes bibliographical references and index.

Gulbrandsen, Don
Edward Sheriff Curtis: Visions of the First Americans. Don Gulbrandsen. Chartwell Books 2010. 256 pages : Illustration; Color
ISBN 9780785826507
Grades: Adult   970.004

1. Curtis, Edward S, 1868-1952 2. Indigenous peoples of North America — Social life and customs 3. Indigenous peoples of North America 4. Portraits 5. Arts and Entertainment — Photography

LC Bl2017008407

Presents photographs selected from each volume of Edward Sheriff Curtis' "The North American Indian" that provide insight into the lifestyles of numerous Native American tribes.

Includes index.

Hamalainen, Pekka
★ *Indigenous* Continent: The Epic Contest for North America. Pekka Hämäläinen. Liveright Publishing Company, a division of W.W. Norton & Company 2022. 576 p.
ISBN 9781631496998
Grades: Adult 970.004

1. Indigenous peoples of North America — History 2. Indigenous peoples of North America 3. European Americans 4. Race relations 5. Government relations with indigenous peoples 6. History writing — Indigenous peoples — United States

LC 2022009104

Pekka Hämäläinen overturns the traditional, Eurocentric narrative, demonstrating that, far from being weak and helpless "victims" of European colonialism, Indigenous peoples controlled North America well into the 19th century. Native empires frequently decimated white newcomers in battle, forcing them to accept and even adopt Native ways. Indigenous peoples flourished due to sophisticated diplomacy and flexible leadership structures. In our myth-busting era, this restoration of Native Americans to their rightful place at the very center of American history will be seen as one of the most important correctives yet.

"Reorienting the history of the Western Hemisphere away from 'European ambitions, European perspectives, and European sources,' [Hämäläinen] focuses instead on the 'Overwhelming and persistent Indigenous power' that lasted in North America from 10000 BCE until the end of the 19th century....This top-notch history casts the story of America in an astonishing new light." —*Publishers Weekly*

Includes bibliographical references and index.

Hogeland, William
Autumn of the Black Snake: The Creation of the U.S. Army and the Invasion That Opened the West. William Hogeland. Farrar Straus & Giroux 2017. 448 p.
ISBN 9780374107345
Grades: Adult 970.004

1. Wayne, Anthony, 1745-1796 2. Indigenous peoples of North America — Wars 3. Military history 4. United States 5. History writing — Military

LC 2016052193

An account of how the U.S. Army was created to fight a crucial Native American war describes how George Washington and other early leaders organized the Legion of the United States under General "Mad" Anthony Wayne in response to a 1791 militia defeat in the Ohio River Valley.

"This is a scrupulously balanced account of a formative period in westward expansion." —*Booklist*

Nesteroff, Kliph
We Had a Little Real Estate Problem: The Unheralded Story of Native Americans & Comedy. by Kliph Nesteroff. Simon & Schuster 2021. 336 p.
ISBN 9781982103033
Grades: Adult 970.004

1. Indigenous peoples of North America 2. Indigenous peoples of North America — Social conditions 3. Comedians 4. Literary criticism 5. United States 6. Canada 7. Arts and Entertainment — Comedy 8. History writing — Indigenous peoples — United States 9. Life stories — Arts and culture — Performing arts — Entertainers and celebrities 10. Life stories — People in history — Indigenous peoples

LC 2020020301

An acclaimed comedy historian explores how Native Americans have influenced and advanced the entertainment industry, tracing the achievements of performers ranging from Will Rogers and Adrianne Chalepah to Hill and the 1491s.

"Comedian Nesteroff (The Comedians) delivers a veritable who's who of Native American comedy from 'The rez' to New York City in this sometimes disturbing yet beautiful history.... This sharp collection addresses the politics, history, and merits of Native comedy in a way that's never been done before." —*Publishers Weekly*

Includes index.

Treuer, David
★ *The* **Heartbeat** of Wounded Knee: Native America from 1890 to the Present. David Treuer. Riverhead Books 2019. 512 pages : Illustration; Map
ISBN 9781594633157
Grades: Adult 970.004

1. Indigenous peoples of North America — History 2. Indigenous peoples of North America, Treatment of 3. Indigenous resistance and revolts 4. Assimilation (Sociology) 5. Identity 6. 20th century 7. History writing — Indigenous peoples — United States 8. Society and culture — Ethnic studies

Booklist Editors' Choice, 2019; Library Journal Best Books, 2019; Minnesota Book Award for General Nonfiction, 2020; New York Times Notable Book, 2019; National Book Award for Nonfiction finalist, 2019; Andrew Carnegie Medal for Excellence in Non-Fiction Finalist, 2020.

An anthropologist's chronicle of Native American life from the Wounded Knee massacre to the present traces the unprecedented resourcefulness and reinvention of distinct tribe cultures that assimilated into mainstream life to preserve Native identity.

"Treuer takes on a bold task: a history of Native America from the Paleolithic to the Standing Rock Reservation protest against the Dakota Access Pipeline in 2017. Peoples from all regions of North America are included. Unlike other works that depict the 'Vanishing Indian' narrative, Treuer's does not end at the 1890 Wounded Knee massacre. Rather, he uses Wounded Knee as a springboard to discuss the Native American experience as it has adapted and persisted since." —*Library Journal*

Includes bibliographical references and index.

Wilbur, Matika
Project 562: Changing the Way We See Native America. Matika Wilbur. Ten Speed Press 2023. 416 p.
ISBN 9781984859525
Grades: Adult 970.004

1. Indigenous peoples of North America 2. Portrait photography 3. Ethnic identity 4. Culture 5. Lifestyles 6. Traditional ecological knowledge 7. Environmental stewardship 8. Community activism 9. Social advocacy 10. Oral histories 11. Life stories — Identity — Race and ethnicity 12. Life stories — People in history — Indigenous peoples 13. Society and culture — Ethnic studies

In this visually stunning celebration of contemporary Native American life and cultures, a critically acclaimed social documentarian and photographer presents compelling personal narratives of Native people and the issues they face that will inspire, educate and truly change the way we see Native America.

"An essential purchase for all libraries; as the people and places pictured here span Turtle Island, the book will be relevant to patrons everywhere." —*Library Journal*

970.00497 American native peoples

Johnson, Michael
Encyclopedia of Native Tribes of North America. Michael Johnson; illustrator, Richard Hook. Compendium 2007. 320 p. : Illustration; Color; Map
ISBN 9781905573745
Grades: Adult 970.00497

1. Indigenous peoples of North America 2. History writing — United States 3. Reference — Encyclopedias

LC 2008360036

Respected researcher Michael G. Johnson meticulously details every aspect of each American Indian tribe's history, arts, crafts and material culture.

ESSENTIAL AND RECOMMENDED TITLES
970.01 North America — Early history to 1599

"The maps, photographs, and beautiful illustrations by Hook, combined with concise, accurate entries, make this volume a good purchase, especially for libraries that lack the 2007 edition." —*Choice*

Previous ed.: Oxford: Compendium, 2001.

970.01 North America — Early history to 1599

Cervantes, Fernando
Conquistadores: A New History of Spanish Discovery and Conquest. Fernando Cervantes. Viking 2021. 496 p.

ISBN 9781101981269

Grades: Adult   970.01

1. Conquistadors 2. Conquerors 3. Aztec (Mexican people) 4. Inca (South American people) 5. Indigenous peoples of Mexico 6. Indigenous peoples of South America 7. First contact of indigenous peoples with Europeans 8. Religious conversion 9. Colonialism 10. Atrocities 11. Spanish history 12. South American history 13. Latin America 14. 16th century 15. History writing — Exploration 16. History writing — Colonialism — Europe 17. History writing — Indigenous peoples — Latin America 18. Life stories — People in history — Explorers

LC 2021029480

Over the few short decades that followed Christopher Columbus's first landing in the Caribbean in 1492, Spain conquered the two most formidable civilizations of the Americas: the Aztecs of Mexico and the Incas of Peru. But centuries later, the men leading these conquests have become the stuff of nightmares. In their own time, they were glorified as heroic adventurers, spreading Christian culture and helping to build an empire unlike any the world had ever seen. Today, they stand condemned for their cruelty and exploitation as men who decimated ancient civilizations and carried out horrific atrocities in their pursuit of gold and glory. In Conquistadores, acclaimed Mexican historian Fernando Cervantes—himself a descendent of one of the conquistadors—cuts through the layers of myth and fiction to help us better understand the context that gave rise to the conquistadors' actions.

"This robust reconsideration of the Spaniards who conquered the New World emphasizes the brutality of their tactics but also the religious and intellectual trade winds that filled their sails. . . . Cervantes, a historian at the University of Bristol, isn't out to redeem the conquistadors, so much as to explain them in context, and the result is a nuanced, compelling narrative that cuts against the historical grain." —*Booklist*

Includes bibliographical references and index.

Horwitz, Tony
★ *A Voyage Long and Strange: Rediscovering the New World.* Tony Horwitz. Henry Holt and Co. 2008. 448 p.

ISBN 9780805076035

Grades: 11 12 Adult   970.01

1. Explorers 2. Exploration 3. Western Hemisphere 4. North America 5. Travel Writing — Retracing Historic Journeys 6. History writing — Exploration 7. Adult books for young adults

LC 2007045883

ALA Notable Book, 2009; New York Times Notable Book, 2008.

A chronicle of the period in American history between Columbus's discovery of the new world and Jamestown's founding evaluates the voyages and first-contact experiences of numerous European adventurers.

"Realizing that his knowledge of American history between Columbus's discovery and Plymouth Rock over 100 years later was sketchy at best, . . . [the author] sets out to educate himself with his own explorations. He intertwines his experiences retracing the early conquistadors, adventurers, and entrepreneurs through such regions as Newfoundland, the Dominican Republic, and the American South, Southwest, and New England with thoroughly researched accounts of the territories themselves, the natives who were historically affected, and the motives of the explorers. . . . This readable and vastly entertaining history travelog is highly recommended for public libraries." —*Library Journal*

Includes bibliographical references and index.

Mann, Charles C.
★ *1491: New Revelations of the Americas Before Columbus.* Charles C. Mann. Knopf 2005. xii, 465 p. : Illustration; Map

ISBN 9781400040063

Grades: 11 12 Adult   970.01

1. Civilization, Pre-Columbian 2. Indigenous peoples of Central America 3. Indigenous peoples of South America 4. Indigenous peoples of North America 5. Archaeology 6. Anthropology 7. Antiquities 8. United States 9. History writing — Archaeology 10. Adult books for young adults 11. History writing — Indigenous peoples — Latin America

LC 2004061547

Booklist Editors' Choice, 2005; National Academies Communication Award, 2006; New York Times Notable Book, 2005.

An analysis of America prior to 1492 describes how the research of archaeologists and anthropologists has transformed myths about the Americas, revealing that the cultures were far older and more advanced than previously known.

"Mann navigates adroitly through the controversies. He approaches each in the best scientific tradition, carefully sifting the evidence, never jumping to hasty conclusions, giving everyone a fair hearingthe experts and the amateurs; the accounts of the Indians and their conquerors. And rarely is he less than enthralling." —*New York Times Book Review*

Includes bibliographical references (p. [403]-449) and index.

970.1 North American native peoples

Treuer, Anton
Everything You Wanted to Know About Indians but Were Afraid to Ask. Anton Treuer. Borealis Books 2012. 184 p.

ISBN 9780873518611

Grades: 9 10 11 12 Adult   970.1

1. Indigenous peoples of North America — History 2. Ojibwe (North American people) 3. Race relations 4. Interethnic relations 5. Indigenous peoples of North America in popular culture 6. History writing — Indigenous peoples — United States 7. Society and culture — Race

LC 2011053026

Treuer, an Ojibwe scholar and cultural preservationist, answers the most commonly asked questions about American Indians, both historical and modern. He gives a frank, funny, and personal tour of what's up with Indians, anyway.

"Overall, this is a thoughtful and thought-provoking overview that serves to alleviate misconceptions and bridge knowledge gaps among cultures." —*School Library Journal*

Includes bibliographical references and index.

970.5 Government relations with North American native peoples

Redniss, Lauren
★ *Oak Flat: A Fight for Sacred Land in the American West.* Lauren Redniss. Random House 2020. 281 pages : Illustration; Color

ISBN 9780399589720

Grades: 11 12 Adult   970.5

1. Apache (North American people) 2. Government relations with indigenous peoples 3. Nature conservation 4. Indigenous peoples of North America — Land rights 5. Indigenous peoples of North America 6. Indigenous reservations 7. Sacred space 8. Copper 9. Mines and mineral resources 10. Arizona 11. Illustrated books 12. Politics and global affairs — Environmental issues and policies 13. Society and culture — Race 14. Adult books for young adults

ALA Notable Book, 2021.

Three generations of an Apache family struggle to protect sacred land from a multinational mining corporation.

"As a work of advocacy, the book is compelling and convincing; as a work of art, it is masterful." —*Kirkus*

"Redniss, a recipient of Guggenheim and MacArthur fellowships, forges an enthralling convergence of oral history and narrative to tell with precision and empathy the dramatic story of the still unresolved battle over Oak Flat." —*Booklist*

Includes bibliographical references (pages 262-281).

971.6 Nova Scotia

Bacon, John U.

The Great Halifax Explosion: A World War I Story of Treachery, Tragedy, and Extraordinary Heroism. John U. Bacon. William Morrow & Co. 2017. IX, 418 pages, 16 unnumbered pages of plates : Illustration; Map

ISBN 9780062666536

Grades: Adult **971.6**

1. Halifax Explosion, December 6, 1917 2. Explosions 3. World War I 4. Canadian history 5. Halifax, Nova Scotia 6. 20th century 7. History writing — Natural disasters and tragedies 8. History writing — Regional history — Canada

LC 2017276263

An account of the world's largest man-made explosion before the atomic bomb describes the events that led to the catastrophic igniting of the French freighter Mont-Blanc in 1917 Halifax, killing and wounding thousands while leading to advances in medicine and weapons science.

"An absorbing history of disaster and survival." —*Kirkus*

Also published in large print format; Includes bibliographical references (pages 393-397) and index.

971.9 Northern territories

Castner, Brian

Stampede: *Gold Fever and Disaster in the Klondike.* Brian Castner. Doubleday 2021. 336 p.

ISBN 9780385544504

Grades: Adult **971.9**

1. Gold miners 2. Gold mines and mining 3. Pioneers 4. Frontier and pioneer life 5. Mines and mineral resources 6. Canadian history 7. United States history 8. Yukon River Valley (Yukon and Alaska) 9. Klondike River Valley, Yukon Territory 10. 19th century 11. History writing — Exploration 12. History writing — Canada

LC 2020055497

A gripping account of the Klondike Gold Rush of 1897-1898 sets the experiences of tens of thousands of desperate people against a backdrop of the period's economic depression while tracing the stories of the era's most iconic characters.

Journalist Castner (Disappointment River) paints a dramatic and frequently gruesome portrait of the Klondike gold rush.... Packed with evocative details and colorful personalities, this immersive history captures the tragic consequences of 'Gold fever.' —*Publishers Weekly*

Includes bibliographical references.

972 Mexico, Central America, West Indies, Bermuda

Bobrow-Strain, Aaron

*The **Death** and Life of Aida Hernandez: A Border Story.* Aaron Bobrow-Strain. Farrar, Straus and Giroux 2019. 352 p.

ISBN 9780374191979

Grades: Adult **972**

1. Hernandez, Aida 2. Immigrants 3. Undocumented immigrants 4. Mexican people in the United States 5. Immigrants, Mexican 6. Immigration policy 7. Child immigrants 8. Borderlands 9. Deportation 10. Immigration and emigration 11. Mexican-American Border Region 12. United States 13. Biographies 14. Life stories — Identity — Immigrants 15. Politics and global affairs — Immigration 16. Society and culture — Immigration

LC 2018044062

"Bobrow-Strain crafts a gripping narrative that is highly recommended for anyone looking for a better understanding of the policies and emotions surrounding the current debate over immigration and border security." —*Library Journal*

Includes bibliographical references.

Coe, Michael D.

The Maya. Michael D. Coe. Thames & Hudson 2015. 320 pages : Illustration; Map

ISBN 9780500291887

Grades: Adult **972**

1. Indigenous peoples of Central America — Antiquities 2. Indigenous peoples of Mexico — Antiquities 3. Maya (Central American People) 4. Antiquities 5. Mexico 6. Central America 7. History writing — Archaeology 8. History writing — Latin America — Mexico

LC 2014951100

Includes bibliographical references (pages 308-313) and index.

Crutchfield, James A.

Revolt *at Taos: The New Mexican and Indian Insurrection of 1847.* James A. Crutchfield. Westholme Publishing 2015. 400 p.

ISBN 9781594162237

Grades: Adult **972**

1. Indigenous peoples of North America 2. Mexican-American War, 1846-1848 3. Insurgency 4. Manifest destiny 5. New Mexico 6. 1840s 7. 19th century 8. History writing — Wars and conflicts — American Indigenous Wars 9. History writing — Indigenous peoples — United States

LC 2015451017

"This broad treatment of the Taos Revolt is a sincere attempt to view events and consequences from the perspectives of all peoples involved. Recommended for the examination of civil rights during the forced Americanization of established residents of New Mexico territory." —*Library Journal*

Diaz del Castillo, Bernal

*The **Discovery** and Conquest of Mexico, 1517-1521.* by Bernal Díaz del Castillo; edited from the only exact copy of the original MS (and published in Mexico) by Genaro García; translated with an introduction and notes by A.P. Maudslay; new introduction by Hugh Thomas. Da Capo Press 1996. xxxi, 478 p. : Illustration; Map

ISBN 9780306806971

Grades: Adult **972**

1. Cortes, Hernan, 1485-1547 2. Mexican history 3. Conquest of Mexico (1519-1540) 4. History writing — Latin America — Mexico

LC 95045871

"The memoirs of an old man, who began to write of his experiences half a century after they occurred and completed his account at the age of 84, they are not free from minor inaccuracies, but they are the most reliable narrative that exists." —*Chicago Sunday Tribune*

Originally published: New York : Farrar, Straus, and Cudahy, 1956; Includes index.

Foster, Lynn V.

*A **Brief** History of Mexico.* Lynn V. Foster. Facts on File 2009. 336 p. (Brief history (Facts on File))

ISBN 9780816074051

Grades: 9 10 11 12 Adult **972**

1. History 2. Culture 3. Mexican history 4. Central American history 5. History books — Central and South America — Mexico

LC 2009018298

An introduction to the history of Mexico covers such topics as indigenous peoples, the environment, the North American Free Trade Agreement, and current law enforcement efforts against the drug cartels.

Includes bibliographical references and index.

Hernandez, Kelly Lytle

★ ***Bad*** *Mexicans: Race, Empire, and Revolution in the Borderlands.* Kelly Lytle Hernandez. W.W. Norton & Company 2022. 352 p.

ESSENTIAL AND RECOMMENDED TITLES
972.08 Mexico since 1867

ISBN 9781324004370
Grades: Adult **972**
1. Flores Magon, Ricardo, 1873-1922 2. Revolutions 3. Political violence 4. Imperialism 5. Revolutionaries 6. Mexican Americans 7. International relations 8. Mexican history 9. North American history 10. Mexico 11. Mexican-American Border Region 12. United States 13. 20th century 14. History writing — Wars and conflicts — Revolutions 15. History writing — Latin America — Mexico 16. History writing — Early 20th century — United States
LC 2022007616

National Book Critics Circle Award for Nonfiction finalist, 2022.

Rebel historian" Kelly Lytle Hernandez reframes our understanding of U.S. history in this groundbreaking narrative of revolution in the borderlands. Bad Mexicans tells the dramatic story of the magonistas, the migrant rebels who sparked the 1910 Mexican Revolution from the United States. Led by a brilliant but ill-tempered radical named Ricardo Flores Magon, the magonistas were a motley band of journalists, miners, migrant workers who organized thousands of Mexican workers—and American dissidents—to their cause. Determined to oust Mexico's dictator, Porfirio Diaz, who encouraged the plunder of his country by U.S. imperialists such as Guggenheim and Rockefeller, the rebels had to outrun and outsmart the swarm of U. S. authorities vested in protecting the Diaz regime. Taking readers to the frontlines of the magonista uprising and the counterinsurgency campaign that failed to stop them, Kelly Lytle Hernandez puts the magonista revolt at the heart of U.S. history.

"An astute historical analysis of how Mexican resistance to longtime authoritarian President Porfirio Di az resonated on both sides of the U.S.-Mexico border....A beautifully crafted, impressively inclusive history of the Mexican Revolution." —*Kirkus*

Includes bibliographical references and index.

Restall, Matthew
When Montezuma Met Cortes: The True Story of the Meeting That Changed History. Matthew Restall. Ecco 2018. 256 p.
ISBN 9780062427267
Grades: Adult **972**
1. Montezuma II, Emperor of Mexico, ca. 1480-1520 2. Cortes, Hernan, 1485-1547 3. Aztec (Mexican people) 4. Indigenous peoples of Mexico — History 5. Mexican history 6. Conquest of Mexico (1519-1540) 7. 16th century 8. History writing — Indigenous peoples — Latin America 9. History writing — Latin America — Mexico
LC Bl2018002433

An extensively researched account of the early 16th-century encounter between Montezuma and Hernando Cortes that overturns what is popularly understood about the natures of both men and the Spanish conquest of the Americas.

"Blending erudition with enthusiasm, Restall has achieved a rare kind of workserious scholarship that is impossible to put down." —*Publishers Weekly*

Townsend, Richard F.
The Aztecs. Richard F. Townsend. Thames & Hudson 2009. 256 p. : Illustration; Color; Map
ISBN 9780500287910
Grades: 11 12 Adult **972**
1. Aztec (Mexican people) 2. Indigenous peoples of Mexico 3. Civilization, Ancient 4. Indigenous peoples of Mexico — History 5. Civilization 6. Mexico 7. History writing — Indigenous peoples — Latin America
LC 2010549825

Examines the history of these accomplished people through a review of the monuments and artifacts they left behind; exploring how their water-control projects worked, the purposes of their ceremonial centers, and the way they built their incredible ancient structures that still stand today.

Includes bibliographical references (p. 246-252) and index.

972.08 Mexico since 1867

Guinn, Jeff
★ *War on the Border: Villa, Pershing, the Texas Rangers, and an American Invasion.* Jeff Guinn. Simon & Schuster 2021. 368 p.
ISBN 9781982128869
Grades: Adult **972.08**
1. Pershing, John Joseph, 1860-1948 2. Villa, Pancho, 1878-1923 3. Borderlands 4. Revolutionaries 5. Generals 6. Battles 7. Military campaigns 8. Mexican history 9. North American history 10. Mexican-American Border Region 11. 20th century 12. Mexican Revolution (1910-1920) 13. History writing — Latin America — Mexico 14. History writing — Early 20th century — United States 15. History writing — Wars and conflicts 16. Nonfiction that reads like fiction
LC 2020049279

A riveting account of the "Punitive Expedition" of 1916 between Pancho Villa and Gen. John J. Pershing and how this violent conflict still reverberates in the Southwestern U.S. to this day as the US-Mexico border remains as vexed and volatile as ever.

"Guinn (The Vagabonds) brings the U.S.-Mexico conflicts of the early 20th century to vibrant life in this superior history.... The result is a riveting introduction to a lesser-known chapter in American history." —*Publishers Weekly*

Includes bibliographical references and index.

972.85 Nicaragua

Preston, Douglas J.
★ *The Lost City of the Monkey God: A True Story.* Douglas Preston. Grand Central Publishing 2017. 336 pages
ISBN 9781455540006
Grades: Adult **972.85**
1. Preston, Douglas J. 2. Extinct cities 3. Jungles 4. Excavations (Archaeology) 5. Wildlife 6. Diseases 7. Rain forests 8. Indigenous peoples of Central America 9. Jungle survival 10. Honduras 11. Autobiographies and memoirs 12. Adventure writing — Exploration 13. Travel Writing — Central and South America 14. History writing — Indigenous peoples — Latin America
LC 2016037247

New York Times Notable Book, 2017.

Though he's probably better known as the co-author of the suspenseful Pendergast novels, Douglas Preston also writes thrilling nonfiction. In his latest real-life adventure tale, he gives us a compelling, high-octane account of his travels in Honduras' Mosquitia area, where he's part of a team looking for evidence of the fabled Ciudad Blanca (The White City) aka "The Lost City of the Monkey God"—but the group has to deal with unfriendly soldiers, parasites, jaguars, snakes, insects, and more.

Includes bibliographical references and index.

972.87 Panama

McCullough, David G.
The Path Between the Seas: The Creation of the Panama Canal, 1870-1914. David McCullough. Simon and Schuster 1999. 698 p. : Illustration
ISBN 9780743262132
Grades: 11 12 Adult **972.87**
1. Lesseps, Ferdinand Marie, comte de, 1805-1894 2. Roosevelt, Theodore, 1858-1919 3. Canals 4. Imperialism, American 5. Civil engineering 6. Design and construction 7. Central American history 8. Panama 9. Panama Canal 10. 19th century 11. History writing — Technological innovations 12. History writing — Latin America
LC 00266235

National Book Critics Circle Award for Nonfiction finalist.

Describes all the events and personalities involved in the monumental undertaking which precipitated revolution, scandal, economic crisis, and a new Central American republic.

"Not only is this a well-told story of the building of the Panama Canal but it also supplies welcome background for the . . . debate on the canal's role in inter-American relations." —*Booklist*

Includes bibliographical references (p. 655-669) and index.

Parker, Matthew
Panama Fever: The Epic History of One of the Greatest Engineering Triumphs of All Time. Matthew Parker. Doubleday 2008. 560 p.
ISBN 9780385515344
Grades: Adult 972.87
1. Canals 2. Building 3. Engineering 4. Central American history 5. Panama Canal 6. History writing — Technological innovations 7. Science Writing — Great Engineering Feats 8. History writing — Latin America
LC 2007017995

Traces the four-century dream to build a canal linking tha Atlantic and Pacific Oceans, the triumphant construction of the waterway and its opening in 1914, and the appalling human cost of the project in terms of harsh working conditions and epidemics.

Includes bibliographical references and index.

972.9 West Indies (Antilles) and Bermuda

Kritzler, Ed
Jewish Pirates of the Caribbean: How a Generation of Swashbuckling Jews Carved Out an Empire in the New World in Their Quest for Treasure, Religious Freedoms and Revenge. Ed Kritzler. Doubleday 2008. 336 p.
ISBN 9780385513982
Grades: 11 12 Adult 972.9
1. Jewish people 2. Marranos 3. Buccaneers 4. Pirates 5. Interethnic relations 6. Caribbean history 7. 17th century 8. History writing — Pirates 9. History writing — Jewish history
LC 2008015790

Describes how Jews fleeing the Spanish Inquisition took to the high seas as pirates and attacked and plundered the Spanish treasure fleet while forming alliances with other European countries to protect the safety of other Jews in hiding.

"Though Kritzler tends to leap from topic to topic, he covers an impressive interdisciplinary range-combining politics, economics and religion-that should satisfy fans of religious history and swashbuckling true stories." —*Publishers Weekly*

Includes bibliographical references and index.

972.91 Cuba

Ferrer, Ada
★ *Cuba:* An American History. Ada Ferrer. Scribner 2021. xi, 560 p.
ISBN 9781501154553
Grades: Adult 972.91
1. Islands 2. Colonialism 3. Slavery 4. Revolutions 5. Communism 6. Cultural differences 7. Social change 8. International relations 9. Caribbean history 10. Cuba 11. United States 12. Impartial writing 13. History writing — Latin America — Cuba 14. History writing — United States
LC 2021020533

Los Angeles Times Book Prize for History, 2021; Pulitzer Prize for History, 2022.

In 1961, at the height of the Cold War, the United States severed diplomatic relations with Cuba, where a momentous revolution had taken power three years earlier. For more than half a century, the stand-off continued—through the tenure of ten American presidents and the fifty-year rule of Fidel Castro. His death in 2016, and the retirement of his brother and successor Raul Castro in 2021, have spurred questions about the country's future. Meanwhile, politics in Washington—Barack Obama's opening to the island, Donald Trump's reversal of that policy, and the election of Joe Biden—have made the relationship between the two nations a subject of debate once more. Historian Ada Ferrer delivers an ambitious and moving chronicle written for a moment that demands a new reckoning with both the island's past and its relationship with the United States. Spanning more than five centuries, Cuba: An American History provides us with a front-row seat as we witness the evolution of the modern nation, with its dramatic record of conquest and colonization, of slavery and freedom, of independence and revolutions made and unmade.

"A fluid, consistently informative history of the long, inextricable link between Cuba and the U.S., well rendered by a veteran Cuban American historian. . . . A wonderfully nuanced history of the island nation and its often troubled dealings with its gigantic and voracious neighbor." —*Kirkus*

Includes bibliographical references and index.

Kurlansky, Mark
Havana: A Subtropical Delirium. Mark Kurlansky. Bloomsbury USA 2017. 224 p.
ISBN 9781632863911
Grades: Adult 972.91
1. Kurlansky, Mark 2. American people in Cuba 3. City life 4. Voyages and travels 5. Caribbean history 6. Havana, Cuba 7. History writing — Latin America — Cuba 8. Travel Writing — Central and South America
LC 2016041072

Award-winning author Mark Kurlansky, who wrote the bestsellers Salt and Cod, here turns his keen eye to the beloved city he's been visiting for 30 years: Havana, Cuba. In this adoring travelogue/History, Kurlansky shares personal stories and offers details about the 500-year-old Caribbean city's past and present, people, culture, sports, and music, as well as its appearances in art and literature (yes, Hemingway is discussed). Havana is a complex place, and if you want a talented guide to help you understand this elegant yet downtrodden city, pick up Havana, which includes not only recipes but pen-and-ink drawings by the talented author.

"An affectionate, richly detailed, brief biography of a unique city." —*Kirkus*

Includes bibliographical references.

Sallah, Michael
The Yankee Comandante: The Untold Story of Courage, Passion, and One American's Fight to Liberate Cuba. Michael Sallah, Mitch Weiss. Lyons Press, an imprint of Rowman & Littlefield 2015. 304 p.
ISBN 9780762792870
Grades: Adult 972.91
1. Morgan, William, 1928-1961 2. Revolutionaries 3. Communism 4. Double agents 5. Political prisoners 6. Political intrigue 7. Revolutions 8. Caribbean history 9. Cuba 10. 1950s 11. Biographies 12. Life stories — Law and order — Military leaders 13. Life stories — Politics — Political prisoners 14. History writing — Latin America — Cuba
LC 2014033720

"Olga lives today in the U.S, and Sallah and Weiss interviewed her extensively. They also make clear Morgan's flaws: He had at least three wives and several children by them; was court martialed by the U.S. Army, serving time in prison; and was employed by and associated with known mobsters. Though the tale does not end happily, it's a romantic and entertaining read." —*Publishers Weekly*

972.9106 Cuba — 1899-

Guillermoprieto, Alma
Dancing with Cuba: A Memoir of the Revolution. Alma Guillermoprieto; translated from the Spanish by Esther Allen. Pantheon Books 2004. 290 p.
ISBN 9780375420931
Grades: Adult 972.9106
1. Guillermoprieto, Alma, 1949- 2. Modern dance 3. Dance teachers 4. Revolutions 5. Voyages and travels 6. Caribbean history 7. Cuba 8. 1970s 9. 20th century 10. Autobiographies and memoirs 11. Biographies 12. Arts and Entertainment — Dance 13. Life stories — Arts and culture — Performing arts — Dancers and choreographers 14. Life stories — Politics 15. History writing — Latin America — Cuba
LC 2003044200

ESSENTIAL AND RECOMMENDED TITLES
972.91063 Cuba — 1933-1958

New York Times Notable Book, 2004.

Traces the period spent by the author in 1970 Cuba, a time during which she worked as a dance instructor, came to understand the idealism of the Castro-adoring locals, and formed the belief system that set the tone for her career.

"Guillermoprieto vividly and purposefully recounts her acute discomfort with the strained and ludicrous rhetoric of the revolution, her sorrow over Castro's catastrophic failures, her astonishment at the great valor of Cuba's people, and her gradual recognition of her true calling as a journalist." —*Booklist*

Hastings, Max
The Abyss: Nuclear Crisis Cuba 1962. Max Hastings. HarperCollins 2022. 480 p.

ISBN 9780062980137

Grades: Adult   972.9106

1. Cuban Missile Crisis, 1962 2. Ballistic missiles 3. Missiles 4. International relations 5. Soviet Union 6. United States 7. 1960s 8. History writing — Cold War 9. History writing — 1960s — United States 10. History writing — Latin America — Cuba

An award-winning journalist reevaluates the Cuban Missile Crisis, one of the most gripping and tense international events in modern history, seeking to explain the attitudes and conduct of the Soviets, Cubans and Americans, and recreate the heightened fears of countless innocent bystanders whose lives hung in the balance. Map(s).

"One of the greatest living historians tackles the Cuban missile crisis....The definitive account of a brief yet frightening period in global history." —*Kirkus*

Plokhy, Serhii
★ *Nuclear Folly: A History of the Cuban Missile Crisis*. Serhii Plokhy. W.W. Norton & Company 2021. 464 p.

ISBN 9780393540819

Grades: Adult   972.9106

1. Cuban Missile Crisis, 1962 2. Cold War 3. International relations 4. Nuclear warfare 5. Cuba 6. Soviet Union 7. United States 8. 20th century 9. History writing — Cold War 10. History writing — Military — Weapons 11. Nonfiction that reads like fiction

LC 2020033221

A dramatic re-creation and urgent examination of the Cuban Missile Crisis. Nearly thirty years after the end of the Cold War, today's world leaders are abandoning disarmament treaties, building up their nuclear arsenals, and exchanging threats of nuclear strikes. To survive this new atomic age, we must return to the lessons of the most dangerous moment of the Cold War: the Cuban Missile Crisis. Nuclear Folly offers an international perspective on the crisis, tracing the tortuous decision-making that produced and then resolved it, involving John Kennedy and his advisers, Nikita Khrushchev and Fidel Castro, and their commanders on the ground.

"Harvard history professor Plokhy (Forgotten Bastards) offers a comprehensive study of the 1962 Cuban missile crisis focused on the 'Misjudgments and misunderstandings' that nearly led to nuclear war. . . . History buffs will savor this balanced and richly detailed look at both sides of the crisis." —*Publishers Weekly*

Includes bibliographical references and index.

Rasenberger, Jim
The Brilliant Disaster: JFK, Castro, and America's Doomed Invasion of Cuba's Bay of Pigs. Jim Rasenberger. Simon & Schuster 2011. 352 p.

ISBN 9781416596509

Grades: Adult   972.9106

1. Kennedy, John F. (John Fitzgerald), 1917-1963 2. Castro, Fidel, 1926-2016 3. Bay of Pigs Invasion, 1961 4. Communism 5. International relations 6. Cuba 7. United States 8. 1960s 9. History writing — 1960s — United States 10. History writing — Cold War

LC 2011004178

Rasenberger delivers the definitive account of one of the most ill-fated blunders in U.S. history. Trained by the CIA, 1,400 Cuban expats planned to invade Cuba, trigger a popular revolt, and topple Castro's communist regime. But when Castro was tipped off and U.S. air support was cancelled, the would-be liberators were sacrificed in a crossfire of betrayal.

"On Apr. 17, 1961, a CIA-trained brigade of 1,400 Cuban exiles, mostly students and former soldiers, made an unsuccessful amphibious assault on the Bay of Pigs, in southern Cuba, hoping to spur a popular revolt and overthrow the Castro regime. Fifty years later, Rasenberger succeeds admirably in offering a nuanced view of the entire botched operation, from its planning in two U.S. administrations to the Cuban armed forces' quick defeat of the exiles, whose attack lacked air cover and the element of surprise." —*Kirkus*

Sherwin, Martin J.
Gambling with Armageddon: Nuclear Roulette from Hiroshima to the Cuban Missile Crisis, 1945-1962. Martin J. Sherwin. Alfred A. Knopf 2020. 624 p.

ISBN 9780307266880

Grades: Adult   972.9106

1. Kennedy, John F. (John Fitzgerald), 1917-1963 2. Cuban Missile Crisis, 1962 3. Arms race 4. World politics 5. Nuclear warfare 6. 20th century 7. History writing — Military — Weapons 8. History writing — Cold War

LC 2019057322

In this groundbreaking look at the Cuban Missile Crisis, Martin Sherwin not only gives us a riveting sometimes hour-by-hour explanation of the crisis itself, but also explores the origins, scope, and consequences of the evolving place of nuclear weapons in the post-World War II world.

"Intricately detailed, vividly written, and nearly Tolstoyan in scope, Sherwin's account reveals just how close the Cold War came to boiling over. History buffs will be enthralled." —*Publishers Weekly*

A Borzoi Book; Includes bibliographical references and index.

972.91063 Cuba — 1933-1958

Guevara, Che
Diary of a Combatant: From the Sierra Maestra to Santa Clara, Cuba, 1956-58. Ernesto Che Guevara; edited by Maria del Carmen Ariet. Ocean Press 2013. 358 p, 40 p. of plates : Illustration; Map; Facsimile

ISBN 9780987077943

Grades: Adult   972.91063

1. Guevara, Che, 1928-1967 2. Politics and government 3. Caribbean history 4. Cuba 5. 20th century 6. Autobiographies and memoirs 7. History writing — Wars and conflicts — Revolutions 8. History writing — Latin America

LC 2011943989

This never-before-published diary (comprising a dozen small notebooks) Ernesto Che Guevara kept during the guerrilla war in Cuba when he joined the struggle to overthrow the Batista dictatorship that led to the 1959 revolution has now been meticulously transcribed by his widow, Aleida March.

"Aken alone the volume is valuable; as a part of Che's extensive writings it is indispensable." —*Library Journal*

Translation of: Diario de un combatiente : De la Sierra Maestra a Santa Clara, 1956-1958; Includes bibliographical references.

972.9107 Cuba — 2008-

Craig, William
Yankee Come Home: On the Road from Guantanamo to San Juan Hill. William Craig. Walker & Co. 2011. 288 p.

ISBN 9780802710932

Grades: Adult   972.9107

1. Spanish-American War, 1898 2. Imperialism, American 3. Family history 4. International relations 5. Cuba 6. United States 7. 19th century 8. Family and Relationships — General 9. History writing — Latin America — Cuba

LC Bl2012027963

Contends that events from the Spanish-American war set the stage for troubled present-day relations between the United States and Cuba, arguing that America's 1898 intervention was an act of hubris and avarice that has culminated in a regional abandonment of defining ideals.

973 United States

Andersen, Kurt
★ *Fantasyland: How America Went Haywire: A 500-year History.* Kurt Andersen. Random House 2017. 480 pages
ISBN 9781400067213
Grades: Adult   973
1. Reality 2. Empiricism 3. Belief and doubt 4. Public opinion 5. Conspiracy theories 6. Pseudoscience 7. Gullibility 8. Dishonesty 9. United States 10. History writing — United States 11. Society and culture — Psychology and human behavior
LC 2017016052

The author of Heyday explains how the influences of dreamers, zealots, hucksters and superstitious groups shaped America's tendency toward a rich fantasy life, citing the roles of contributors ranging from P. T. Barnum and Billy Graham to Disney and Donald Trump in perpetuating conspiracy theories, self-delusion and magical thinking.

Anderson, Fred
The Dominion of War: Empire and Liberty in North America, 1500-2000. Fred Anderson and Andrew Cayton. Penguin Books 2005. xxiv, 520 p. : Illustration; Map
ISBN 9780143036517
Grades: Adult   973
1. Imperialism 2. Republicanism 3. War and society 4. National characteristics, American 5. Military history 6. Territorial expansion 7. United States 8. North America 9. History writing — Wars and conflicts
LC Bl2006007432

A reinterpretation of the development of the United States argues that warfare has played a leading role in shaping North America throughout the past five hundred years, in a history that focuses on the lives of eight men, including George Washington, Ulysses S. Grant, and Colin Powell.

"The authors provide an account of the U.S. rise to global preeminence over five centuries. Central to their thesis is the assertion that military conflict has been essential in determining the cultural and political evolution of North America. Anderson and Cayton have provided a well-written and important reinterpretation of our past." —*Booklist*

Originally published: New York : Viking, 2005; Includes bibliographical references (p. [425]-501) and index.

Arana, Marie
★ *Latinoland: A Portrait of America's Largest and Least Understood Minority.* Marie Arana. Simon & Schuster 2024. 352 p.
ISBN 9781982184896
Grades: Adult   973
1. Hispanic Americans 2. Latin American people 3. American people 4. Identity 5. United States 6. Society and culture — Ethnic studies

This wide-ranging overview of the turbulent and little-known history of the diverse Latino experience in America is based on hundreds of interviews and research about the fastest-growing minority in America.

"Arana has a fascinating, complex, and deeply personal story to tell, and she narrates it with abundant verve and intelligence." —*Kirkus*

Berlin, Ira
The Making of African America: The Four Great Migrations. Ira Berlin. Viking 2010. 320 p.
ISBN 9780670021376
Grades: Adult   973
1. African American history 2. Migration, Internal 3. Immigrants 4. Slave trade 5. Race relations 6. African Americans 7. Immigration and emigration 8. United States history 9. Atlantic Ocean 10. History writing — African American — United States
LC 2009028366

A 400-year history of the African-American experience traces four pivotal migrations including the violent relocation of one million slaves to the antebellum South, the movement of millions to industrial cities a century later and the arrivals of Black immigrants since the 1960s.

"Berlin's neat synthesis offers the sharp insights and provocative commentary of one of the foremost historians of Black America. Essential for library collections, general readers, and scholars of African American history." —*Library Journal*

Includes bibliographical references and index.

Boorstin, Daniel J.
The Americans: The Democratic Experience. Daniel J. Boorstin. Cardinal 1988. 717 p.
ISBN 9780394710112
Grades: 11 12 Adult   973
1. Democracy 2. Americanization 3. Civilization 4. Economics 5. United States history 6. United States 7. 19th century 8. Gilded Age (1865-1898) 9. History writing — Gilded Age — United States
LC 95152524

Pulitzer Prize for History, 1974.
Winner of the Pulitzer Prize. A study of the last 100 years of American history.

Sequel to: The Americans: the national experience; Includes bibliographical references and index; Originally published: New York : Random House, 1973.

The Americans: The National Experience. by Daniel J. Boorstin. Random House 1965. 517 p.
ISBN 9780394703589
Grades: 11 12 Adult   973
1. National characteristics, American 2. Social life and customs 3. Civilization 4. United States history 5. United States 6. History writing — United States
LC 95153525

A view of American life and dominant figures from the Revolution to the Civil War.

"A cultural interpretation of American history, this book traces the roots of contemporary American life to the years between the Revolution and the Civil War." —*Booklist*

Sequel to: The Americans: the colonial experience; Sequel: The Americans: the democratic experience; Bibliographical notes: P. 433-495.

Branch, Taylor
Parting the Waters: America in the King Years, 1954-63. Taylor Branch. Simon and Schuster 1988. xii, 1064 p, 32 p. of plates : Illustration (America in the King years, 1)
ISBN 9780671687427
Grades: 11 12 Adult   973
1. King, Martin Luther, Jr, 1929-1968 2. African American civil rights 3. Racism 4. Prejudice 5. Civil Rights Movement 6. United States history 7. United States 8. 1950s 9. 1960s 10. Biographies 11. History writing — African American — Civil rights — United States 12. History writing — 1960s — United States 13. Life stories — Politics — Activists and Reformers — Civil Rights Leaders
LC 88024033

ALA Notable Book, 1990; Los Angeles Times Book Prize for Current Interest, 1989; National Book Critics Circle Award for Non-Fiction, 1988; National Book Award for Nonfiction finalist, 1989.

Focuses on Martin Luther King, Jr, and the key moments that defined his rise to the forefront of the civil rights movement in America, from Rosa Parks' arrest in Montgomery to King's imprisonment in Birmingham and his triumphant march on Washington.

"The author has searched out the hidden reality and often tragic human drama of the King years. On his best pages, the past, miraculously, seems to spring back to life. King himself appears human, all too human. Yet when the reader is done, his remarkable virtues and ordinary vices seem of a piece, the component parts of a coherent, towering personality." —*Newsweek*

Sequel: Pillar of Fire; Includes bibliographical references.

ESSENTIAL AND RECOMMENDED TITLES
973 United States

Burns, Ken
★ *Our America: A Photographic History.* Ken Burns, with Susanna Steisel, Brian Lee, and David Blistein. Alfred A. Knopf 2022. 334 pages : Illustration; Color
ISBN 9780385353014
Grades: Adult   973
1. Photography 2. Social life and customs 3. United States history 4. United States 5. Visual nonfiction 6. History writing — United States
LC 2021057411

Assembling images that best embody 200 years of the American experience, some from renowned photographers and by others who worked in obscurity, an Academy Award-nominated filmmaker shares images of our country's natural beauty, of war and civil conflict and of communities drawing together across lines of race and class.

"Documentarian Burns (Country Music: An Illustrated History) presents a stunning collection of photographs chronicling American history from 1839 to 2019....Visually arresting and expertly curated, this is a must-have for fans of Burns's documentaries." —*Publishers Weekly*

This is a Borzoi book published by Alfred A. Knopf—Title page verso.

Choy, Catherine Ceniza
★ *Asian American Histories of the United States.* Catherine Ceniza Choy. Beacon Press 2022. 288 p.
ISBN 9780807050798
Grades: Adult   973
1. Asian Americans 2. Ethnic identity 3. Immigration and emigration 4. United States history 5. Asia 6. Society and culture — Race 7. History writing — United States
LC 2022001429

An inclusive and landmark history emphasizes how essential Asian American experiences are to any understanding of U.S. history.

"Readers of ethnic studies and U.S. history will find this an essential and illuminating resource on the impact and legacies of colonialism, imperialism, violence, and resistance that Asian Americans have experienced." —*Booklist*

Includes bibliographical references and index.

Davis, Thomas J.
History of African Americans: Exploring Diverse Roots. Thomas J. Davis. Greenwood, an imprint of ABC-CLIO, LLC 2016. xxxiii, 271 pages : Illustration
ISBN 9780313385407
Grades: Adult   973
1. African American history 2. African Americans 3. Ethnic identity 4. Racism 5. United States 6. Society and culture — Ethnic studies
LC 2016025200

Over the centuries Black peoples in America have nurtured distinctive attitudes, beliefs, characters, folkways, and manners. They have shared common circumstances and conditions that have distinguished them in America beyond reference to the continent of their ancestral origins or their physical appearance. Yet African Americans have never been singular in experience or outlook. They have ever been diverse peoples. Time, temperament, talents, opportunities, place, and interpersonal relations, among myriad elements of life, have invariably set Blacks apart from one another as individuals and as groups, even as pronounced racial distinction and discrimination have invariably set Blacks as a group apart from others in America. African American history is thus not singular or simple; it has many facets and layers; it spreads across time and place and personalities.

"Daviss book is mandatory reading for undergraduates and the general public, who tend to have only the most superficial understanding of African American history." —*Choice*

Includes bibliographical references (pages 247-257) and index.

Du Bois, W. E. B.
★ *The Souls of Black Folk.* W.E.B. Du Bois; edited with an introduction and notes by Brent Hayes Edwards. Oxford University Press 2007. 223 p.
ISBN 9780192806789

Grades: 11 12 Adult   973
1. African Americans 2. Intersectionality 3. Racism 4. Race relations 5. United States 6. Essays 7. History writing — African American — Civil rights — United States
LC 2006035193

Personal recollections are included in this work depicting the spirit, status, and problems of African Americans since emancipation and reflecting on the history of race and democracy in America.

Published together with up from slavery and the autobiography of an ex-colored man, as Three negro classics, 1965; Includes bibliographical references; Originally published: Chicago, IL : A.C. McClurg & Co, 1903.

★ *Writings:* The Suppression of the African Slave-trade : The Souls of Black Folk : Dusk of Dawn : Essays : Articles from the Crisis. W.E.B. Du Bois; [Nathan Huggins, editor]. Library of America : 1996. 1334 p.
ISBN 9781883011314
Grades: Adult   973
1. African Americans 2. Arts and Entertainment — Writing and Publishing
LC BL 00016300

Gathers writings, articles, and essays revealing Du Bois's views on racial inequality and oppression.

Includes bibliographical references (p. 1314-1334) and index; Originally published: New York, N.Y. : Literary Classics of the United States, 1986.

Dutta, Sunil
Stealing Green Mangoes: Two Brothers, Two Fates, One Indian Childhood. Sunil Dutta. Ecco 2019. 238 pages
ISBN 9780062795854
Grades: Adult   973
1. Dutta, Sunil 2. Brothers 3. Indian Americans 4. Refugees 5. Police 6. Criminal behavior 7. Loss 8. Growing up 9. Cancer survivors 10. Family violence 11. Coping 12. Indian Partition, 1947 13. Indian history 14. Autobiographies and memoirs 15. Life stories — Relationships — Family 16. Life stories — Facing adversity — War and oppression — Refugees 17. Society and culture — Violence and crime
LC 2020275911

An Indian refugee-turned-LAPD terrorism expert describes his complicated relationship with his brother, a fugitive and terrorist who the author sought to understand in the wake of a terminal cancer diagnosis.

"An insightful read about the strength of individuals to overcome adversity, reminding us that while our past and family do contribute to our identity, they do not define who we become." —*Library Journal*

Fernandez-Armesto, Felipe
Our America: A Hispanic History of the United States. Felipe Fernandez-Armesto. W W Norton & CO Inc 2014. 416 p.
ISBN 9780393239539
Grades: Adult   973
1. Historical revisionism 2. Hispanic Americans 3. International relations 4. United States history 5. United States 6. Latin America 7. Spain 8. History writing — United States

While the majority of history textbooks in the U.S. emphasize English colonization and the English-speaking heritage of North America, large portions of what is now the U.S. were first settled by the Spanish. In Our America, historian Felipe Fernndez-Armesto paints a more complete portrait of early colonists, including Dutch and French as well as British and Spanish settlers. Spanish cultural influences, the possible identity of the real Zorro, and details of major and minor Anglo-Spanish conflicts emerge in this engaging though potentially controversial work that argues for inclusion of the U.S. in Latin America.

Fischer, David Hackett
★ *African Founders: How Enslaved People Expanded American Ideals.* David Hackett Fischer. Simon & Schuster 2022. 800 p.
ISBN 9781982145095
Grades: Adult   973
1. African American history 2. European Americans 3. African people in the United States 4. Enslaved people 5. Freed people 6. Slavery 7. Intercultural com-

munication 8. Regionalism 9. African people in foreign countries 10. African Americans 11. Civilization 12. United States history 13. United States 14. History writing — African American — Enslavement — United States 15. History writing — Regional history — United States 16. Life stories — People in history

LC 2021020168

African Founders explores the little-known history of how enslaved people from different regions of Africa interacted with colonists of European origins to create new regional cultures in the colonial United States. The Africans brought with them linguistic skills, novel techniques of animal husbandry and farming, and generations-old ethical principles, among other attributes. This startling history reveals how much our country was shaped by these African influences in its early years, producing a new, distinctly American culture. Drawing on decades of research, some of it in western Africa, Fischer recreates the diverse regional life that shaped the early American republic.

"In his latest sweeping, scholarly history, Pulitzer Prize-winning historian Fischer delivers an exhaustive, multidimensional work about the waves of enslaved Africans brought forcibly to America and how their cultural elements interacted with White-controlled society to create a variety of unique American regions." —*Kirkus*

Includes bibliographical references and index.

Franklin, John Hope

★ *From Slavery to Freedom: A History of African Americans.* John Hope Franklin, Evelyn Higginbotham. McGraw-Hill 2011. xxv, 710 p. : Illustration; Color; Map

ISBN 9780072963786

Grades: 11 12 Adult   973

1. African American history 2. Slavery 3. Enslaved people 4. Free African Americans 5. Interethnic relations 6. United States history 7. History writing — African American — United States 8. Antiracist literature

LC 2005299886

Documents the African American experience, from their origin in Africa to slavery in the Western Hemisphere and their successful struggle for freedom.

Includes bibliographical references (p. 640-676) and index.

Gates, Henry Louis

100 Amazing Facts About the Negro. Henry Louis Gates. Pantheon Books 2017. 288 p.

ISBN 9780307908711

Grades: Adult   973

1. African American history 2. Racism 3. Race relations 4. History writing — African American — United States 5. Society and culture — Race

LC 2016024453

The first edition of Joel Augustus Rogers's now legendary 100 Amazing Facts About the Negro with Complete Proof, published in 1957, was billed as "A Negro 'Believe It or Not.'" Rogers's little book was priceless because he was delivering enlightenment and pride, steeped in historical research, to a people too long starved on the lie that they were worth nothing. For African Americans of the Jim Crow era, Rogers's was their first Black history teacher. But Rogers was not always shy about embellishing the "facts" and minimizing ambiguity; neither was he above shock journalism now and then. With élan and erudition—and with winning enthusiasm—Henry Louis Gates, Jr. gives us a corrective yet loving homage to Rogers's work.

In Search of Our Roots: How 19 Extraordinary African Americans Reclaimed Their Past. Henry Louis Gates, Jr. Crown Publishers 2008. 448 p.

ISBN 9780307382405

Grades: 11 12 Adult   973

1. African Americans 2. Genealogy 3. Generations 4. Families 5. Identity 6. United States 7. Africa 8. Adult books for young adults 9. History writing — African American — Civil rights — United States

LC 2008011860

The distinguished scholar examines the origins and history of African-American ancestry as he profiles nineteen noted African Americans and illuminates their individual family sagas throughout U.S. history.

Includes bibliographical references and index.

★ *Life Upon These Shores: Looking at African American History, 1513-2008.* Henry Louis Gates, Jr. Knopf 2011. 416 p.

ISBN 9780307593429

Grades: 11 12 Adult   973

1. African American history 2. African Americans 3. Civilization 4. United States 5. History writing — African American — Civil rights — United States

LC 2011014277

A director of the W. E. B. Du Bois Institute at Harvard presents a sumptuously illustrated chronicle of more than 500 years of African-American history that focuses on defining events, debates and controversies as well as important achievements of famous and lesser-known figures, in a volume complemented by reproductions of ancient maps and historical paraphernalia.

"With nearly 900 illustrations (formal portraits, news photos, historic lithographs, broadsides, flyers, posters, newspaper clippings, advertisements) complemented by a succinct but informing text, Harvard professor Gates (Black in Latin America) provides a visual sojourn through African-American history, a generally upbeat march from Juan Garrido, accompanying Corts in 1519, to Barack Obama taking the presidential oath in 2008. Gathered in this chronologically arranged compendium, with its focus on the accomplishments and moments of achievement in the African-American community, is a wealth of materials about the historical, political, social, literary, and scientific events influencing American social and political culture." —*Publishers Weekly*

Includes bibliographical references and index.

★ *Stony the Road: Reconstruction, White Supremacy, and the Rise of Jim Crow.* Henry Louis Gates, Jr. Penguin Press 2019. 320 p.

ISBN 9780525559535

Grades: Adult   973

1. Racism 2. African Americans 3. Reconstruction (United States history) 4. African American history 5. White supremacy movements 6. Racism in popular culture 7. Inequality 8. Prejudice 9. Visual communication 10. Segregation 11. Race relations 12. United States 13. 19th century 14. 20th century 15. Media tie-ins 16. Society and culture — Race 17. History writing — African American — Civil rights — United States

LC 2018056211

New York Times Notable Book, 2019.

The NAACP Image Award-winning creator of the African Americans: Many Rivers to Cross presents a revisionist chronicle of America's post-Civil War struggle for racial equality and the violent counterrevolution that resubjugated Black Americans throughout the 20th century.

"This fresh, much-needed inquiry into a misunderstood yet urgently relevant era will appear in conjunction with Gates new PBS documentary, Reconstruction: America after the Civil War, scheduled for broadcast in April." —*Booklist*

This book is published with the companion PBS documentary, Reconstruction: America after the Civil War; Includes bibliographical reference and index.

Glass, Brent D

50 Great American Places: Essential Historic Sites Across the U.S. Brent D. Glass; foreword by David McCullough. Simon & Schuster Paperbacks 2016. xxiv, 293 pages : Illustration

ISBN 9781451682038

Grades: Adult   973

1. Historic sites 2. United States 3. Travel Writing — United States 4. Reference — Travel guides 5. Reference — General

LC 2015031714

A one-of-a-kind guide to 50 of the most important cultural and historic sites in the United States is guaranteed to fascinate, educate and entertain, and is selected and described by the former director of the Smithsonian's National Museum of American History.

Profiles fifty sites across the United States that trace the cultural history of the country, discussing the people and events that led to each site's importance, from the National Mall in D.C. to Pearl Harbor in Hawaii.

ESSENTIAL AND RECOMMENDED TITLES
973 United States

"This book will whet the appetite of history buffs interested in possible destinations, or anybody who would like to learn American history through the places where it happened." —*Library Journal*

Includes bibliographical references (pages 263-274) and index.

Grande, Reyna
★ *The Distance Between US: a Memoir.* Reyna Grande. Atria Books 2012. 320 p.
ISBN 9781451661774
Grades: Adult   973

1. Grande, Reyna 2. Mexican Americans 3. Immigrants 4. Growing up 5. Child abuse victims 6. Mexican American women 7. Dysfunctional families 8. Women authors 9. Immigration and emigration 10. Mexico 11. United States 12. Los Angeles, California 13. Autobiographies and memoirs 14. Biographies 15. Life stories — Relationships — Growing up 16. Arts and Entertainment — Writing and Publishing 17. Adult books for young adults 18. Life stories — Facing adversity — Abuse survivors

LC 2012001634

School Library Journal Best Books: Best Adult Books 4 Teens, 2012; National Book Critics Circle Award for Autobiography/Memoir finalist.

Traces the author's experiences as an illegal child immigrant, describing her father's violent alcoholism, her efforts to obtain a higher education, and the inspiration of Latina authors.

Grandin, Greg
The End of the Myth: From the Frontier to the Wall in the Mind of America. Greg Grandin. Metropolitan Books 2019. 224 p.
ISBN 9781250179821
Grades: Adult   973

1. Turner, Frederick Jackson, 1861-1932 2. Populism 3. National characteristics, American 4. Frontier thesis 5. Borderlands 6. Boundaries 7. National territory 8. Frontier and pioneer life 9. Self-reliance 10. International trade 11. Social problems 12. Nationalism 13. Independence 14. United States history 15. United States 16. History writing — Westward expansion — United States 17. Society and culture — Immigration

LC 2018027790

Pulitzer Prize for General Nonfiction, 2020; Pulitzer Prize for History finalist, 2020; Longlisted for the National Book Award for Nonfiction, 2019.

Examines how the identity-shaping idea of an open and ever-expanding American frontier has evolved from early westward expansion into the reactionary populism of Donald Trump's border-wall proposals.

"In a broad and sweeping history stretching from the founding of the nation through the election of Donald Trump, Bancroft Prize winner Grandin . . . examines what he calls the 'Expansionist imperative' of the frontier and what happens when that expansion comes to a halt." —*Library Journal*

Includes bibliographical references and index.

Gregory, Dick
Defining Moments in Black History: Reading Between the Lies. Dick Gregory. Amistad Press 2017. 240 pages
ISBN 9780062448699
Grades: Adult   973

1. African American history 2. African Americans 3. Race (Social sciences) 4. Racism 5. Civil rights 6. Social advocacy 7. Social change 8. Race relations 9. United States 10. Essays 11. History writing — African American — United States 12. Society and culture — Race

LC Bl2017036957

The activist and social satirist who trail-blazed a new form of racial commentary in the 1960s examines 100 key events in Black History through this collection of essays which examine Middle Passage, the creation of Jheri Curl and the Black Lives Matter movement.

"Gregory's devotion to civil rights and his global recognition add to his appealing writing style and clever sense of humor to make this a book for a wide audience." —*Kirkus*

Harriot, Michael
★ *Black AF History: The Un-Whitewashed Story of America.* Michael Harriot. Dey Street Books 2023. 432 p.
ISBN 9780358439165
Grades: Adult   973

1. Harriot, Michael 2. African Americans 3. African American history 4. African American families 5. Growing up 6. Racism 7. Colonialism 8. Marginalized people 9. Misinformation 10. United States history 11. Essays 12. History writing — African American — United States 13. Life stories — Identity — Race and ethnicity 14. Society and culture — Race 15. Debut title

BCALA Literary Award for First Novelist, 2024.

The acclaimed columnist and political commentator presents a sharp and often hilarious retelling of American history that focuses on the overlooked contribution of Black Americans and corrects the idea that American history is white history.

"With blunt, entertaining, irreverent, sarcastic, and sometimes laugh-out-loud statements, Herriot provocatively explains how the United States came to be and how money-focused, self-serving intentions made it what it is today." —*Library Journal*

Includes bibliographical references and index.

Immerwahr, Daniel
How to Hide an Empire: A History of the Greater United States. Daniel Immerwahr. Farrar, Straus and Giroux 2019. 560 p.
ISBN 9780374172145
Grades: Adult   973

1. Imperialism 2. Globalization 3. Citizenship 4. Civil rights 5. Colonialism 6. Colonies 7. United States history 8. Philippines 9. Puerto Rico 10. Guam 11. Virgin Islands of the United States 12. United States 13. History writing — United States 14. Politics and global affairs — World politics — United States

LC 2018020388

Traces the stories of the U.S. territories outside the mainland, including the Guano Islands, the Philippines, and Puerto Rico, to offer insights into how America has transitioned from colonialism to technological innovation.

Includes bibliographical references and index.

Lee, Erika
The Making of Asian America: A History. Erika Lee. Simon & Schuster 2015. 416 p.
ISBN 9781476739403
Grades: Adult   973

1. Asian Americans 2. Immigrants 3. Interethnic relations 4. Intersectionality 5. Racism 6. Asian people 7. Race relations 8. Immigration and emigration 9. United States history 10. Asian history 11. South Asia 12. United States 13. Society and culture — Ethnic studies 14. History writing — Immigration — United States

LC 2015010372

Asian Pacific American Award for Literature: Adult Nonfiction, 2016.

Describes the lasting impact and contributions Asian immigrants have had on America, beginning with sailors who crossed the Pacific in the 16th century, through the ordeal of internment during World War II and to their current status as |model minorities.|.

"An impressive work that details how this diverse population has both swayed and been affected by the United States." —*Library Journal*

Lepore, Jill
★ *These Truths: A History of the United States.* Jill Lepore. W. W. Norton & Co. 2018. xx, 932 pages : Illustration; Map
ISBN 9780393635249
Grades: Adult   973

1. Political values 2. Slavery 3. Nation-building 4. Founding Fathers of the United States 5. Nationalism 6. Social values 7. United States history 8. United States 9. History writing — United States

Massachusetts Book Awards, Nonfiction Award, 2019; New York Times Notable Book, 2018.

PUBLIC LIBRARY CORE COLLECTION: NONFICTION
Twentieth Edition

In the most ambitious one-volume American history in decades, award-winning historian and New Yorker writer Jill Lepore offers a magisterial account of the origins and rise of a divided nation, an urgently needed reckoning with the beauty and tragedy of American history.

"Lepore is a historian with wide appeal, and this comprehensive work will answer readers questions about who we are as a nation." —*Booklist*

Includes bibliographical references and index.

Mays, Kyle

★ *An Afro-Indigenous History of the United States.* Kyle T. Mays. Beacon Press 2021. 280 p.

ISBN 9780807011683

Grades: Adult   973

1. African Americans 2. Indigenous peoples of North America 3. Social conflict 4. Colonialism 5. Slavery 6. Racism 7. Injustice 8. Identity 9. Race relations 10. United States history 11. United States 12. History writing — African American — United States 13. History writing — Indigenous peoples — United States 14. Society and culture — Race 15. Society and culture — Ethnic studies

LC 2021020880

Mays explores the relationship and differences between the Black American quest for freedom and the Native American struggle for sovereignty in the U.S.

"A Saginaw Chippewa writer and scholar analyzes the unacknowledged, sometimes fraught relationships between the African American and Indigenous communities.... This book reveals uncomfortable truths about the dehumanizing legacies of both capitalism and colonialism while forging a path of reconciliation between the Black and Native communities." —*Kirkus*

Includes bibliographical references and index.

McCullough, David G.

★ *The American Spirit: Who We Are and What We Stand for.* David McCullough. Simon & Schuster 2017. 176 p.

ISBN 9781501174216

Grades: Adult   973

1. National characteristics, American 2. American dream 3. Citizenship 4. Patriotism 5. Civilization 6. United States 7. Essays 8. Society and culture — General

LC 2017002640

A timely collection of speeches by David McCullough, the most honored historian in the United States—winner of two Pulitzer Prizes, two National Book Awards, and the Presidential Medal of Freedom, among many others—that reminds us of fundamental American principles.

"Historian McCullough . presents this collection of 15 inspiring speeches in which he celebrates America's talent for curiosity, intelligence, goodwill, and humanity." —*Library Journal*

McLoughlin, William Gerald

After the Trail of Tears: The Cherokees' Struggle for Sovereignty, 1839-1880. William G. McLoughlin. University of North Carolina Press 1993. xv, 439 p. : Map

ISBN 9780807821114

Grades: Adult   973

1. Cherokee (North American people) 2. Trail of Tears, 1838-1839 3. Government relations with indigenous peoples 4. Indigenous peoples of North America — Politics and government 5. Indigenous peoples of North America — History 6. 19th century 7. History writing — Indigenous peoples — United States

LC 93018532

"The author recounts the tragedy that continued to afflict the Cherokee Nation after their forced removal from their traditional home to Oklahoma during the 1820s and 1830s. In Oklahoma the Cherokee Nation set out to reconstruct their society, reestablishing their newspaper, which published in the Cherokee language, and governing themselves according to a constitution modeled on that of the United States. McLoughlin vividly depicts the conflicts between full-bloods, who sought to live by more traditional ways, and Cherokees of mixed ancestry who favored assimilation into the dominant culture." —*Publishers Weekly*

Includes bibliographical references (p. 381-434) and index.

Meacham, Jon

★ *The Soul of America: The Battle for Our Better Angels.* Jon Meacham. Random House 2018. xii, 402 pages : Illustration

ISBN 9780399589812

Grades: Adult   973

1. National characteristics, American 2. Democracy 3. Presidents 4. Politics and government 5. United States history 6. United States 7. History writing — United States 8. History writing — Presidency — United States

LC 2018010451

While the American story has not always been heroic, we have been sustained by a belief in progress even in the gloomiest of times. In this inspiring book, Meacham reassures us, "The good news is that we have come through such darkness before"—as, time and again, Lincoln's better angels have found a way to prevail.

"An excellent work by a skilled historian and worthy of all library collections." —*Library Journal*

Includes bibliographical references (pages 277-377) and index.

Proenza-Coles, Christina

American Founders: How People of African Descent Established Freedom in the New World. Christina Proenza-Coles; Foreword by Edward L. Ayers. NewSouth Books 2019. 450 p.

ISBN 9781588383310

Grades: Adult   973

1. African American history 2. Multiculturalism 3. Equality 4. Freedom 5. Race relations 6. Nation-building 7. Colonialism 8. United States history 9. Society and culture — Race 10. History writing — African American — United States

LC 2018047640

Examines American history as inexorably intertwined with its Black and white counterparts contributing equally to the development and freedom of the nation.

"Lucid prose and straightforward structure make this easy to read, and the unearthing of so many lesser-known figures offers new perspectives to those with deeper knowledge of American history." —*Publishers Weekly*

Includes bibliographical references and index.

Prothero, Stephen R.

The American Bible: How Our Words Unite, Divide, and Define a Nation. Stephen Prothero. HarperCollins 2012. 480 p.

ISBN 9780062123435

Grades: Adult   973

1. National characteristics, American 2. Rhetoric 3. Literature and society 4. Language and culture 5. Nationalism 6. United States 7. Speeches, addresses, etc. 8. History writing — United States 9. Spirituality and Religion — General

LC 2012005054

The New York Times best-selling author of Religious Literacy identifies the most crucial texts written by Americans and published in America, which have profoundly shaped our national identity, including the speeches of Lincoln, Kennedy and Reagan, and the novels of Melville, Salinger and Rand."

Prud'homme, Alex

★ *Dinner with the President: Food, Politics, and a History of Breaking Bread at the White House.* Alex Prud'homme. Alfred A. Knopf 2023. 416 p.

ISBN 9781524732219

Grades: Adult   973

1. Presidents 2. Food 3. Food habits 4. United States 5. Food Writing — General 6. Life stories — Politics — Politicians 7. History Writing — Presidency — United States

LC 2022018067

The coauthor of Julia Child's best-selling memoir My Life in France looks at the history of presidential tastes in food and how it can have significant impact on politics, history and global trade.

ESSENTIAL AND RECOMMENDED TITLES
973 United States

"An entertaining, well-researched, politically tinged gastronomic history." —*Kirkus*

This is a Borzoi Book published by Alfred A. Knopf; Includes bibliographical references and index.

Puglionesi, Alicia
In Whose Ruins: Power, Possession, and the Landscapes of American Empire. Alicia Puglionesi. Scribner 2022. 320 p.

ISBN 9781982116750

Grades: Adult   973

1. Historic sites 2. Indigenous peoples 3. Exploitation 4. Memory 5. National characteristics, American 6. Anthropology 7. United States 8. History writing — United States

LC 2021055729

Popular narratives of American history conceal as much as they reveal. They present a national identity based on harvesting the treasures that lay in wait for European colonization. In Whose Ruins tells another story: Winding through the US landscape, from Native American earthworks in West Virginia to the Manhattan Project in New Mexico, this history is a tour of sites that were mined for an empire's power. Showing the hidden costs of ruthless economic growth, particularly to Indigenous people and ways of understanding, this book illuminates the myth-making intimately tied to place.

"This narrative history from poet, professor, and scholar Puglionesi delves into how white settlers found resources on Native land and overtook it for capitalistic gain, focusing on four geographic areas....Dense with research, Puglionesi's book ought to be widely studied." —*Booklist*

Includes bibliographical references.

Rubenstein, David M.
The American Experiment: Dialogues on a Dream. David M. Rubenstein. Simon & Schuster 2021. 416 p.

ISBN 9781982165734

Grades: Adult   973

1. American Dream 2. Democracy 3. Culture 4. Ideas (Philosophy) 5. Social change 6. Equality 7. Politics and government 8. United States history 9. United States 10. History writing — United States

American icons and historians explore the grand American experiment in democracy, culture, innovation, and ideas, featuring Ken Burns, Madeleine Albright, Billie Jean King, Henry Louis Gates Jr, and many more.

"Rubenstein follows the American Story with another stimulating collection of interviews with prominent historians and public figures. . . . Enriched by the diversity of its interviewees and Rubenstein's simple yet illuminating prompts ('Explain the Tet Offensive'; 'When there were just thirteen colonies, did any let women vote?'), this is a rewarding survey of what makes America tick." —*Publishers Weekly*

Sexton, Jared Yates
American Rule: How a Nation Conquered the World but Failed Its People. Jared Yates Sexton. Dutton 2020. 355 p.

ISBN 9781524745714

Grades: Adult   973

1. Collective memory 2. Corruption 3. National characteristics, American 4. Democracy 5. Inequality 6. Politics and government 7. United States 8. History writing — United States 9. Politics and global affairs — World Politics — United States

LC 2020005155

In recent years, Americans have faced a deluge of horrifying developments in politics and culture: Stolen elections, fascist rallies, families torn apart and locked away. A common refrain erupts at each new atrocity: This isn't who we are. In American Rule, Jared Yates Sexton upends those convenient fictions by laying bare the foundational myths at the heart of our collective American imagination. Working through each era of American growth and change, Sexton weaves together the origins and perpetuation of these narratives still in the public memory, and the acts we have chosen to forget.

"Sexton's survey of American political history is taut and tart, but his prescriptions for recapturing the better angels of the American spirit and renewing faith in science and reason gloss over the heavy lifting involved. Still, this is an unflinching and well-crafted takedown of the nationalist rhetoric that fueled Trump's rise." —*Publishers Weekly*

Includes bibliographical references and index.

Smith, Clint
★ *How the Word Is Passed: A Reckoning with the History of Slavery Across America.* Clint Smith. Little, Brown & Company 2021. 336 p.

ISBN 9780316492935

Grades: Adult   973

1. Slavery 2. African Americans 3. Enslaved people 4. Historiography 5. Historic sites 6. National monuments 7. Collective memory 8. Historical revisionism 9. Denial (Psychology) 10. United States history 11. History writing — African American — Enslavement — United States 12. Society and culture — General 13. Life stories — People in history 14. Life stories — Identity — Race and ethnicity

National Book Critics Circle Award for Non-Fiction, 2021.

Beginning in his hometown of New Orleans, Clint Smith leads the reader on an unforgettable tour of monuments and landmarks—those that are honest about the past and those that are not—that offer an intergenerational story of how slavery has been central in shaping our nation's collective history, and ourselves. A deeply researched and transporting exploration of the legacy of slavery and its imprint on centuries of American history, How the Word Is Passed illustrates how some of our country's most essential stories are hidden in plain view, ensuring the brutal history of the trade in enslaved men, women, and children has been deeply imprinted.

"Poet and Atlantic staff writer Smith debuts with a moving and perceptive survey of landmarks that reckon, or fail to reckon, with the legacy of slavery in America. . . . Suffused with lyrical descriptions and incisive historical details . . . this is an essential consideration of how America's past informs its present." —*Publishers Weekly*

Sullivan, Patricia
Lift Every Voice: The Naacp and the Making of the Civil Rights Movement. Patricia Sullivan. New Press : 2009. xii, 514 p, 16 p. of plates : Illustration

ISBN 9781595585110

Grades: Adult   973

1. Civil Rights Movement 2. Segregation 3. Civil rights 4. African American history 5. Race relations 6. United States 7. 20th century 8. History writing — African American — Civil rights — United States

LC 2009009473

Delivers a solidly researched examination of the NAACP's growth and influence, from its inception in 1909 to the present.

Includes bibliographical references (p. [435]-497) and index.

Weingarten, Gene
★ *One Day: The Extraordinary Story of an Ordinary 24 Hours in America.* Gene Weingarten. Blue Rider Press 2019. 384 p.

ISBN 9780399166662

Grades: Adult   973

1. Days 2. Life change events 3. Social life and customs 4. United States 5. 1980s 6. Biographies 7. Life stories — People in history 8. History writing — United States 9. Society and culture — General 10. Adult books for young adults

LC 2019001936

On New Year's Day 2013, two-time Pulitzer Prize-winner Gene Weingarten asked three strangers to, literally, pluck a day, month, and year from a hat. That day—chosen completely at random—turned out to be Sunday, December 28, 1986, by any conventional measure a most ordinary day. Weingarten spent the next six years proving that there is no such thing. One Day asks and answers the question of whether there is even such a thing as "ordinary" when we are talking about how we all lurch and stumble our way through the daily, daunting challenge of being human.

Winchester, Simon
The Men Who United the States: America's Explorers, Inventors, Eccentrics and Mavericks, and the Creation of One Nation, Indivisible. Simon Winchester. HarperCollins 2013. 512 p.

PUBLIC LIBRARY CORE COLLECTION: NONFICTION
Twentieth Edition

ISBN 9780062079602
Grades: Adult 973
1. Progress 2. Explorers 3. Technological innovations 4. Economic development 5. Infrastructure 6. Territorial expansion 7. United States history 8. United States 9. History writing — Exploration

Winchester illuminates the men who toiled fearlessly to discover, connect, and bond the citizenry and geography of the U.S.A. from its beginnings and ponders whether the historic work of uniting the States has succeeded, and to what degree.

Yang, Jeff
★ *Rise: A Pop History of Asian America from the Nineties to Now.* by Jeff Yang, Phil Yu, and Philip Wang. HarperCollins 2022. 288 p.
ISBN 9780358508090
Grades: Adult 973
1. Asian Americans 2. Popular culture 3. Social life and customs 4. United States history 5. United States 6. 20th century 7. 21st century 8. 1990s 9. 2000s (Decade) 10. 2010s 11. Society and culture — Pop culture 12. History writing — United States 13. Society and culture — Ethnic studies

A love letter to and for Asian Americans offers a vivid scrapbook of voices, emotions and memories from an era in which our culture was forged and transformed, and a way to preserve both the headlines and the intimate conversations that have shaped our community into who we are today.

"This rich, balanced collection provides a dazzling history of late 20th and early 21st century pop culture in the United States, and the lasting impact of Asian Americans. With a visually stunning layout, the book is an essential read." —*Library Journal*

Yip-Williams, Julie
★ *The Unwinding of the Miracle: A Memoir of Life, Death, and Everything That Comes After.* by Julie Yip-Williams. Random House 2019. 256 p.
ISBN 9780525511359
Grades: Adult 973
1. Yip-Williams, Julie, 1976-2018 2. Vietnamese Americans 3. Colon cancer 4. Boat people (Southeast Asian refugees) 5. Refugees, Vietnamese 6. Southeast Asian Americans 7. Southeast Asian people 8. People with cancer 9. Women 10. Autobiographies and memoirs 11. Life stories — Facing adversity — Coping with death 12. Life stories — Facing adversity — War and oppression — Refugees 13. Book club best bets
LC 2018031944
New York Times Notable Book, 2019.

An unconventional memoir by a young mother with Stage IV metastatic cancer describes her experiences as a blind Vietnamese political refugee-turned-Harvard-educated lawyer before terminal illness inspired her blog to share the real-world guidance she wished she had.

"Her writing is honest and, by turns, angry, humorous, and heart-breaking, especially when she talks about her two little girls, who are just starting elementary school. Even though readers know the ending—the prologue indicates that if theyre reading this, she's already gone—every bit of new bad news hits like a blow to the gut." —*Booklist*

Zinn, Howard
★ *A People's History of the United States: 1492-present.* Howard Zinn. Harper Perennial Modern Classics 2005. 729, 16 p.
ISBN 9780060838652
Grades: Adult 973
1. Resistance to government 2. Protest movements 3. Social movements 4. Imperialism, American 5. Historians 6. United States history 7. Liberal writing 8. History writing — United States
LC BI2005016609

Presents the history of the United States from the point of view of those who were exploited in the name of American progress.

Includes bibliographical references (p. [689]-708) and index; Originally published: New York : HarperCollins, 2003.

973.04 United States — Ethnic and national groups

Blackhawk, Ned
★ *The Rediscovery of America: Native Peoples and the Unmaking of U.S. History.* Ned Blackhawk. Yale University Press 2023. 576 p.
ISBN 9780300244052
Grades: Adult 973.04
1. Indigenous peoples of North America 2. Indigenous peoples of North America, Treatment of 3. Imperialism, American 4. Colonialism 5. United States 6. History writing — Indigenous peoples — United States

National Book Award for Nonfiction, 2023; Western Heritage Award for Outstanding Nonfiction Book, 2024; Mark Lynton History Prize, 2024.

A sweeping and overdue retelling of U.S. history that recognizes that Native Americans are essential to understanding the evolution of modern America.

"Striking a masterful balance between the big picture and crystal-clear snapshots of key people and events, this is a vital new understanding of American history." —*Publishers Weekly*

Bruchac, Joseph
Our Stories Remember: American Indian History, Culture, & Values Through Storytelling. Joseph Bruchac. Fulcrum Pub. 2003. 192 p.
ISBN 9781555911294
Grades: 11 12 Adult 973.04
1. Indigenous peoples of North America — History 2. Indigenous peoples of North America — Social life and customs 3. Folklore, Indigenous — History and criticism 4. History writing — Indigenous peoples — United States 5. Adult books for young adults
LC 2002151236

Retells traditional Native American stories drawn from throughout the country, providing insights into Native American history, culture, values, and wisdom.

"This important volume includes a wealth of traditional stories and solid information." —*School Library Journal*

Includes bibliographical references.

973.07202 Historians — United States

Rubenstein, David M.
The American Story: Conversations with Master Historians. Edited by David M. Rubenstein; foreword by Carla Hayden. Simon & Schuster 2019. 416 p.
ISBN 9781982120252
Grades: Adult 973.07202
1. Historians 2. Founding Fathers of the United States 3. Presidents 4. Social reformers 5. Leadership 6. United States history 7. Interviews 8. History writing — United States

The philanthropist and co-founder of the Carlyle Group shares lively dialogues with leading historians on the subjects they most understand, from Ron Chernow's views on Alexander Hamilton to Doris Kearns Goodwin's insights into Abraham Lincoln.

973.09 United States — History, geographic treatment, biography

Cohen, Jared
Accidental Presidents: Eight Men Who Changed America. Jared Cohen. Simon & Schuster 2019. 416 p.
ISBN 9781501109829
Grades: Adult 973.09
1. Tyler, John, 1790-1862 2. Fillmore, Millard, 1800-1874 3. Johnson, Andrew, 1808-1875 4. Arthur, Chester Alan, 1829-1886 5. Roosevelt, Theodore, 1858-1919 6. Coolidge, Calvin, 1872-1933 7. Truman, Harry S, 1884-1972 8. Johnson, Lyndon B, 1908-1973 9. Vice presidents 10. Presidents 11. United States 12. History writing — Presidency — United States

Illuminates the evolution of American presidential power through the unique lens of the eight successors to presidents who died in office, sharing insights into

ESSENTIAL AND RECOMMENDED TITLES
973.2 United States — Colonial period, 1607-1775

the significant historical contributions of leaders who came to the office indirectly.

***Life** After Power: Seven Presidents and Their Search for Purpose Beyond the White House*. Jared Cohen. Simon & Schuster 2024. 384 p.
ISBN 9781982154547
Grades: Adult   973.09
1. Presidents 2. Former presidents 3. Retirement 4. Leadership 5. Power 6. Influence (Psychology) 7. Politics and government 8. United States history 9. North American people 10. American people 11. United States 12. Collective biographies 13. Life stories — Politics — Politicians 14. History writing — Presidency — United States

Former presidents have an unusual place in American life. King George III believed that George Washington's departure after two terms made him "the greatest character of the age." but Alexander Hamilton worried former presidents might "[wander] among the people like ghosts." They were both right. In Life After Power, Jared Cohen tells the stories of seven former presidents, from the Founding to today, exploring the untold stories in the final chapters of their lives, and offering a gripping and illuminating account of how they went from President of the United States one day to ordinary citizens the next.

"The author packs this expansive sweep of presidential history with enough storytelling verve and grounded research to legitimize these presidents' underrepresented post-term stories." —*Kirkus*

Goodwin, Doris Kearns
★ ***Leadership** in Turbulent Times*. Doris Kearns Goodwin. Simon & Schuster 2018. 352 p.
ISBN 9781476795928
Grades: Adult   973.09
1. Lincoln, Abraham, 1809-1865 2. Roosevelt, Theodore, 1858-1919 3. Roosevelt, Franklin D. (Franklin Delano), 1882-1945 4. Johnson, Lyndon B, 1908-1973 5. Character 6. Crisis management 7. Resilience 8. Political culture 9. Political leadership 10. Presidents 11. Politics and government 12. United States 13. Life stories — Politics — Politicians 14. History writing — Presidency — United States 15. Politics and global affairs — Political figures
LC 2018020283

Draws on five decades of scholarship to offer an illuminating exploration of the early development, growth, and exercise of leadership as demonstrated by Presidents Abraham Lincoln, Theodore Roosevelt, Franklin Roosevelt, and Lyndon Johnson.

"Goodwin draws on 50 years of scholarship in this strong and resonant addition to the literature of the presidency." —*Booklist*

Includes bibliographical references and index.

Ricks, Thomas E.
★ ***First** Principles: What America's Founders Learned from the Greeks and Romans and How That Shaped Our Country*. Thomas E. Ricks. Harper 2020. xxiv, 386 p.
ISBN 9780062997456
Grades: Adult   973.09
1. Washington, George 1732-1799 2. Adams, John, 1735-1826 3. Jefferson, Thomas, 1743-1826 4. Madison, James, 1751-1836 5. Founding fathers of the United States 6. Politicians 7. Philosophy, Ancient 8. Philosophy 9. Political science 10. Greek civilization 11. Presidents 12. Literary criticism 13. Politics and government 14. Civilization 15. Ancient Rome 16. United States 17. Ancient Greece (800 B.C.E.-640 C.E.) 18. Life stories — Politics — Politicians 19. Politics and global affairs — Political philosophy 20. History writing — Presidency — United States

The author of Fiasco examines how the educations of America's founders, and in particular their scholarly devotion to ancient Greek and Roman classics, informed the beliefs and ideals that shaped the nation's constitution and government.

"With incisive selections from primary sources and astute cultural and political analysis, this lucid and entertaining account is a valuable take on American history." —*Publishers Weekly*

Rogers, Katie
★ ***American** Woman: The Transformation of the Modern First Lady, from Hillary Clinton to Jill Biden*. Katie Rogers. Crown Publishing 2024. 304 p.
ISBN 9780593240564
Grades: Adult   973.09
1. Politicians 2. Women 3. Presidents' spouses 4. United States 5. Collective biographies 6. Life stories — Politics — Politicians 7. History Writing — Women's history 8. History Writing — Presidency — United States

Focusing on Hillary Clinton, Michelle Obama and Jill Biden, a White House correspondent for the New York Times looks at the twenty-first century's transformation of the First Lady's role from a ceremonial symbol to a political operator.

"Rogers's easily digestible analysis is focused on outlining the first ladies' own perceptions and reminiscences. Readers will be rewarded by this feminist personal history of celebrity and power." —*Publishers Weekly*

Stephanopoulos, George
★ *The **Situation** Room: The Inside Story of Presidents in Crisis*. George Stephanopoulos with Lisa Dickey. Grand Central Publishing 2024. 368 p.
ISBN 9781538740767
Grades: Adult   973.09
1. Crisis management in government 2. Crisis management 3. Domestic terrorism 4. Governmental investigations 5. Politics and government 6. United States history 7. International relations 8. Military intelligence 9. Presidents 10. Special operations (Military science) 11. Decision-making 12. Executive power 13. Political leadership 14. United States 15. 20th century 16. 21st century 17. Politics and global affairs — National security 18. Politics and global affairs — World politics — United States 19. History writing — United States
LC 2023041729

A former senior advisor to President Clinton, and for more than 20 years, the anchor of This Week and the co-anchor of Good Morning America, takes us into the White House Situation Room, the epicenter of crisis management where decisions are made that affect the lives of every person on this planet.

"Famed ABC broadcaster and former White House senior advisor Stephanopoulos examines the room where it happens, the inner sanctum where presidents make their most consequential decisions." —*Library Journal*

Includes bibliographical references and index.

973.2 United States — Colonial period, 1607-1775

Demos, John
*The **Unredeemed** Captive: A Family Story from Early America*. John Demos. Vintage Books 1995. xiii, 315 p. : Illustration; Map
ISBN 9780679759614
Grades: Adult   973.2
1. Williams, Eunice, 1696-1786 2. Williams, John, 1664-1729 3. Williams family 4. Captivity 5. Mohawk (North American people) 6. Indigenous peoples of North America — History 7. French and Indian War, 1754-1763 8. United States history 9. Massachusetts 10. History writing — Colonial America — United States
LC Bl2006000155

Describes the 1704 French and Indian attack on Deerfield, Massachusetts, and the capture of Puritan minister John Williams and his five children.

"This is a lively introduction to an authentically multicultural colonial North America." —*New York Times Book Review*

Includes bibliographical references (p. [253-310]) and index; Originally published: New York : Alfred A. Knopf, 1994.

Dolin, Eric Jay
***Black** Flags, Blue Waters: The Epic History of America's Most Notorious Pirates*. Eric Jay Dolin. Liveright Publishing 2018. 416 p.
ISBN 9781631492105
Grades: Adult   973.2
1. Pirates 2. Piracy 3. Criminals 4. Colonists 5. Colonial administrators 6. United States history 7. Great Britain 8. Atlantic Ocean 9. Colonial America

(1600-1775) 10. History writing — Pirates 11. History writing — Colonial America — United States 12. Life stories — Law and order — Criminals and law-breakers

A chronicle of America's lesser-known "Golden Age" of piracy describes how exploration-era colonists initially supported, and then violently opposed, pirates that targeted the North American coast, citing the contributions of such figures as Blackbeard, John Winthrop and Benjamin Franklin.

Franklin, Benjamin
★ *Autobiography, Poor Richard, and Later Writings: Letters from London, 1757-1775, Paris, 1776-1785, Philadelphia, 1785-1790, Poor Richard's Almanack, 1733-1758, the Autobiography.* Benjamin Franklin. Library of America 1997. 816 p.
ISBN 9781883011536
Grades: 11 12 Adult   973.2
1. Franklin, Benjamin, 1706-1790 2. Politicians 3. Politics and government 4. United States 5. 18th century 6. 19th century 7. Biographies 8. Life stories — People in history

LC 97021611

Collects Benjamin Franklin's best-known writings, both personal and public, arranged by period and place, and includes scholarly notes.

J.A. Leo Lemay wrote the notes and selected the texts for this volume—Prelim. paging; Includes bibliographical references and index.

Lepore, Jill
The Name of War: King Philip's War and the Origins of American Identity. Jill Lepore. Knopf 1998. xxviii, 337 p. : Illustration; Map
ISBN 9780679446866
Grades: Adult   973.2
1. King Philip's War, 1675-1676 2. Indigenous peoples of North America — Wars 3. Wampanoag (North American people) 4. Indigenous peoples of North America — History 5. Colonies 6. Great Britain 7. North America 8. United States 9. 17th century 10. Colonial America (1600-1775) 11. History writing — Wars and conflicts — American Indigenous Wars 12. History writing — Indigenous peoples — United States 13. History writing — Colonial America — United States

LC 97002820

Examines how the American colonists interpreted the brutal war that erupted between them and Native Americans in New England in 1675, showing how they looked to it during the Revolution and used it to justify nineteenth-century Indian removals.

"This is a powerful book that doesn't shy away from depicting the sheer horror of what must be termed a race war." —*Booklist*

Includes bibliographical references (p. 247-326) and index.

Philbrick, Nathaniel
★ *Mayflower: A Story of Courage, Community, and War.* Nathaniel Philbrick. Viking 2006. xvii, 461 p. : Illustration; Map
ISBN 9780670037605
Grades: 11 12 Adult   973.2
1. Bradford, William, 1590-1657 2. Church, Benjamin, 1639-1718 3. Massasoit, Wampanoag Chief, 1590?-1661 4. Pilgrims (New England settlers) 5. Indigenous peoples of North America — Wars 6. Colonists 7. Wampanoag (North American people) 8. Indigenous peoples relations with missionaries, traders, etc. 9. Indigenous peoples of North America — History 10. United States history 11. Massachusetts 12. Plymouth, Massachusetts 13. Colonial America (1600-1775) 14. 17th century 15. History writing — Colonial America — United States 16. Adult books for young adults

LC 2005058470

ALA Notable Book, 2007; Booklist Editors' Choice, 2006; Massachusetts Book Awards, Nonfiction Award, 2007; New York Times Notable Book, 2006; Pulitzer Prize for History finalist, 2007.

A history of the Pilgrim settlement of New England discusses such topics as the diseases of European origin suffered by the Wampanoag tribe, the relationship between the Pilgrims and their Native American neighbors, and the impact of King Philip's War.

"The author has written a judicious, fascinating work of revisionist history. Mayflower is a surprise-filled account of what are supposed to be some of the best-known events in this country's past but are instead an occasion for collective amnesia." —*New York Times*

Includes bibliographical references (p. [415]-443) and index.

Schultz, Eric B.
King Philip's War: The History and Legacy of America's Forgotten Conflict. Eric B. Schultz, Michael J. Tougias. Countryman Press 1999. xv, 416 p. : Illustration
ISBN 9780881504347
Grades: Adult   973.2
1. King Philip's War, 1675-1676 2. Indigenous peoples of North America 3. Government relations with indigenous peoples 4. Wampanoag (North American people) 5. Indigenous peoples of North America — History 6. New England history 7. 17th century 8. Colonial America (1600-1775) 9. History writing — Colonial America — United States 10. History writing — Indigenous peoples — United States 11. History writing — Wars and conflicts — American Indigenous Wars

LC 99023481

Describes King Philip and the causes of the war.

"The first part of this volume provides a chronological retelling of the war. The second part, organized geographically and the heart of the volume, takes readers through New England to various sites associated with the conflict. The third part offers three contemporary narratives reflecting the significance of the war on the people of the era. Useful maps assist the reader throughout." —*Library Journal*

Includes bibliographical references (p. 399-408) and index.

973.3 United States — Periods of Revolution and Confederation, 1775-1789

Atkinson, Rick
★ *The British Are Coming: The War for America, Lexington to Princeton, 1775-1777.* Rick Atkinson. Henry Holt & Company 2019. 800 p.
ISBN 9781627790437
Grades: Adult   973.3
1. American Revolution, 1775-1783 2. War 3. Revolutionaries 4. Armies 5. Militias and irregular armies 6. Raids (Military science) 7. Military history 8. Colonies 9. United States history 10. United States 11. Great Britain 12. Revolutionary America (1775-1783) 13. History writing — Wars and conflicts — Revolutionary War (America) 14. History writing — United States 15. History writing — Military

LC 2018029510

New York Times Notable Book, 2019.

The Pulitzer Prize-winning author of the Liberation Trilogy presents the first volume in a new series on the American Revolution that draws on perspectives from both sides to chronicle the first 21 months of America's violent war for independence.

"This graphic account will especially appeal to military history enthusiasts but is accessible for all readers seeking to experience the realities of the revolution." —*Library Journal*

Includes bibliographical references and index.

Beeman, Richard R.
Our Lives, Our Fortunes and Our Sacred Honor: The Forging of American Independence, 1774-1776. Richard R. Beeman. Basic Books, a Member of the Perseus Books Group 2013. 384 p.
ISBN 9780465026296
Grades: Adult   973.3
1. American Revolution, 1775-1783 2. Revolutionaries 3. Politicians 4. Politics and government 5. United States history 6. United States 7. 18th century 8. Revolutionary America (1775-1783) 9. 19th century 10. Biographies 11. History writing — Wars and conflicts — Revolutionary War (America) 12. History writing — Wars and conflicts — Battles

ESSENTIAL AND RECOMMENDED TITLES
973.3 United States — Periods of Revolution and Confederation, 1775-1789

LC 2013001875

Describes the political, diplomatic, and military challenges faced by the delegates from the 13 colonies at the Continental Congress and how they came together to agree to free themselves from British rule and forge independence for America.

Includes bibliographical references and index.

Bobrick, Benson

Angel in the Whirlwind: The Triumph of the American Revolution. Benson Bobrick. Simon & Schuster 1997. 553 p. : Map

ISBN 9780684810607

Grades: Adult   **973.3**

1. Colonists 2. Revolutionaries 3. American Revolution, 1775-1783 4. Revolutions 5. United States history 6. United States 7. 18th century 8. Revolutionary America (1775-1783) 9. History writing — Wars and conflicts — Revolutionary War (America)

LC 97011320

Explores the frequently overlooked fact that, despite charismatic leadership and eventual success, the revolutionary movement never garnered the support of more than half of the American colonists.

"Many of the stories are familiar—Paul Revere's ride, Arnold's descent into infamy—but the book's strength lies in its many lesser-known details on the battlefield and beyond. Though the format demands only brief treatment of complicated issues, what emerges is a highly impressive show of exhaustive research and engaging storytelling." —*Publishers Weekly*

Includes bibliographical references (p. [527]-531) and index.

Brands, H. W.

★ *Founding Partisans: Hamilton, Madison, Jefferson, Adams and the Brawling Birth of American Politics.* H. W. Brands. Doubleday 2023. 464 p.

ISBN 9780385549240

Grades: Adult   **973.3**

1. Hamilton, Alexander, 1757-1804 2. Madison, James, 1751-1836 3. Adams, John, 1735-1826 4. Jefferson, Thomas, 1743-1826 5. Founding Fathers of the United States 6. Political culture 7. Political parties 8. Polarization (Social sciences) 9. Politics and government 10. United States history 11. United States 12. Early America (1784-1819) 13. History writing — Early America — United States 14. History writing — Politicians — United States 15. Life stories — Politics — Politicians

LC 2023020138

To the framers of the Constitution, political parties were a fatal threat to republican virtues. They had suffered the consequences of partisan politics in Britain before the American Revolution, and they wanted nothing similar for America. Yet parties emerged even before the Constitution was ratified, and they took firmer root in the following decade. In Founding Partisans, master historian H. W. Brands has crafted a fresh and lively narrative of the early years of the republic as the Founding Fathers fought one another with competing visions of what our nation would be.

"Brands employs his agreeable approach of largely permitting the principals to tell the story while deftly weaving his own balanced analysis within an enlightening, contextually clear narrative. The result is a cogent history of how partisanship and faction shaped the early U.S. and a valuable repository of some of the most important speeches, letters, and declarations produced by serious men who wrestled with serious ideas." —*Kirkus*

Includes bibliographical references and index.

★ *Our First Civil War: Patriots and Loyalists in the American Revolution.* H.W. Brands. Doubleday 2021. 496 p.

ISBN 9780385546515

Grades: Adult   **973.3**

1. American Revolution, 1775-1783 2. Loyalists (United States history) 3. Opposition (Political science) 4. Colonists 5. Social conflict 6. Revolutionaries 7. Causes of war 8. Politics and government 9. United States history 10. United States 11. Revolutionary America (1775-1783) 12. History writing — Colonial America — United States 13. History writing — Wars and conflicts — Revolutionary War (America) 14. Life stories — Politics 15. Life stories — People in history

LC 2020043860

Historian H. W. Brands offers a fresh and riveting narrative of the American Revolution that shows it to be more than a fight against the British, but also a violent battle among neighbors forced to choose sides, Loyalist and Patriot.

"This engaging book, which includes often-neglected Indigenous and Black perspectives of the war, reads like the story of a contentious extended family, as opposed to a traditional military history." —*Library Journal*

Includes index.

Dolin, Eric Jay

★ *Rebels at Sea: Privateering in the American Revolution.* Eric Jay Dolin. Liveright Publishing Corporation 2022. 352 p.

ISBN 9781631498251

Grades: Adult   **973.3**

1. Privateering 2. Privateers 3. American Revolution, 1775-1783 4. Naval history 5. Revolutions 6. United States history 7. United States 8. 18th century 9. Revolutionary America (1775-1783) 10. History writing — Wars and conflicts — Revolutionary War (America)

LC 2021060796

Presenting the nation's first war as we have rarely seen it before, along with tales of daring maneuvers and deadly encounters, a best-selling historian reveals how privateers were in fact critical to America winning the Revolutionary War.

"Dolin's valuable achievement in recognizing and honoring these sailors' oft-ignored contributions to American independence more fully fleshes out American naval history." —*Booklist*

Includes bibliographical references and index.

Drury, Bob

Valley Forge. Bob Drury and Tom Clavin. Simon & Schuster 2018. 432 p.

ISBN 9781501152719

Grades: Adult   **973.3**

1. Washington, George, 1732-1799 2. American Revolution, 1775-1783 3. Generals 4. Command of troops 5. Military defeat 6. Military discipline 7. Military campaigns 8. Military history 9. Determination 10. United States history 11. Valley Forge, Pennsylvania 12. United States 13. Pennsylvania 14. 18th century 15. Revolutionary America (1775-1783) 16. History writing — United States 17. History writing — Wars and conflicts — Revolutionary War (America) 18. History writing — Military — Military leadership 19. Life stories — Law and order — Military leaders

LC 2018022453

An account of Valley Forge, the Continental Army winter camp where George Washington turned the tide of the American Revolution.

"A fluent, readable story that corrects mythmaking errors and provides a more nuanced narrative in their place." —*Kirkus*

Includes bibliographical references and index.

Ellis, Joseph J.

American Creation: Triumphs and Tragedies at the Founding of the Republic. by Joseph J. Ellis. A. A. Knopf 2007. 304 p.

ISBN 9780307263698

Grades: 11 12 Adult   **973.3**

1. Politicians 2. Federal government 3. National characteristics 4. American people 5. American Revolution, 1775-1783 6. Political culture 7. Revolutions 8. Politics and government 9. United States history 10. United States 11. 18th century 12. Early America (1784-1819) 13. Revolutionary America (1775-1783) 14. 19th century 15. History writing — Early America — United States 16. History writing — Wars and conflicts — Revolutionary War (America)

LC 2007005273

Booklist Editors' Choice, 2007; New York Times Notable Book, 2007.

An examination of the early years of the American Republic analyzes the eventful last quarter of the eighteenth century, the accomplishments of the American founders, and the triumphs and failures that shaped the early nation and the American character.

PUBLIC LIBRARY CORE COLLECTION: NONFICTION
Twentieth Edition

"The author selects certain propitious moments from the American Revolution and early republic, dramatizes them, and analyzes their crucial ramifications for America's future.... A history bound for phenomenal popularity."—*Booklist*

This is a Borzoi book—T.P. verso; Includes bibliographical references and index.

★ *American Dialogue: The Founders and Us.* Joseph J. Ellis. Alfred A. Knopf 2018. 304 p.
ISBN 9780385353427
Grades: Adult   **973.3**
1. Founding Fathers of the United States 2. Law 3. Political science 4. Political culture 5. Philosophy 6. Politics and government 7. United States 8. 18th century 9. 21st century 10. Politics and global affairs — Political philosophy 11. History writing — Early America — United States 12. Life stories — Politics — Politicians

LC 2017050340
New York Times Notable Book, 2018.

The story of history is a ceaseless conversation between past and present, and in American Dialogue, Joseph Ellis uses the perspective of the present to shed light on the views of the Founding Fathers. Examining four of the most seminal historical figures through the prism of particular topics, he makes clear how their now centuries-old ideas illuminate the disturbing impasse of today's political conflicts. Through these juxtapositions—and in his hallmark dramatic and compelling narrative voice—Ellis illuminates the obstacles and pitfalls paralyzing contemporary discussions of these fundamentally important issues.

"Drawing from his intimate knowledge of the Founding Fathers, Ellis addresses four 21st-century obstacles to reveal truths from their writings that should infuse wisdom into present-day debate: Thomas Jefferson's inconsistency on slavery and race; John Adams's warnings about financial aristocracy and economic inequality; James Madison's politically expedient concessions and the idea of original intent; and George Washington's approach to national and foreign policy, and the incompatibility of American imperialism with revolutionary ideals." —*Library Journal*

The Cause: The American Revolution and Its Discontents, 1773-1783. Joseph J. Ellis. Liveright Publishing 2021. 320 p.
ISBN 9781631498985
Grades: Adult   **973.3**
1. American Revolution, 1775-1783 2. Colonists 3. Revolutionaries 4. Countries 5. Slavery 6. Colonies 7. Politics and government 8. North American history 9. United States history 10. Great Britain 11. United States 12. Revolutionary America (1775-1783) 13. 18th century 14. 19th century 15. History writing — Wars and conflicts — Revolutionary War (America) 16. History writing — Early America — United States

LC 2021028335
A culminating work on the American Founding by one of its leading historians, the Cause rethinks the American Revolution as we have known it. George Washington claimed that anyone who attempted to provide an accurate account of the war for independence would be accused of writing fiction. At the time, no one called it the "American Revolution": Former colonists still regarded themselves as Virginians or Pennsylvanians, not Americans, while John Adams insisted that the British were the real revolutionaries, for attempting to impose radical change without their colonists' consent. With The Cause, Ellis takes a fresh look at the events between 1773 and 1783, discovering a strange breed of "prudent" revolutionaries, whose prudence proved wise yet tragic when it came to slavery, the original sin that still haunts our land.

"With his characteristically graceful prose, Ellis offers a short, straightforward history of a critical decade in the nation's youth.... It's hard to imagine a better-told brief history of the key years of the American Revolution." —*Kirkus*

Includes bibliographical references and index.

★ *Revolutionary Summer: The Birth of American Independence.* by Joseph J. Ellis. Alfred A. Knopf 2013. 240 p.
ISBN 9780307701220
Grades: Adult   **973.3**
1. Colonies 2. Battles 3. Politicians 4. American Revolution, 1775-1783 5. United States history 6. 18th century 7. Revolutionary America (1775-1783) 8. History writing — Colonial America — United States

LC 2012026140
Presents a revelatory account of America's declaration of independence and the political and military responses on both sides throughout the summer of 1776 that influenced key decisions and outcomes.

"This thought-provoking, well-documented historical narrative is packed with insightful analysis. It will attract general and academic readers." —*Library Journal*

Includes bibliographical references and index.

Ferling, John E.
Winning Independence: The Decisive Years of the Revolutionary War, 1778-1781. John Ferling. Bloomsbury 2021. 528 p.
ISBN 9781635572766
Grades: Adult   **973.3**
1. Washington, George, 1732-1799 2. Clinton, Henry, Sir, 1738?-1795 3. American Revolution, 1775-1783 4. Generals 5. Alliances 6. Military strategy 7. Revolutions 8. Military campaigns 9. Military history 10. United States history 11. United States 12. 18th century 13. Revolutionary America (1775-1783) 14. History writing — Wars and conflicts — Revolutionary War (America) 15. Life stories — Law and order — Military leaders 16. History writing — Military — Military leadership

It was 1778, and the recent American victory at Saratoga had netted the U.S a powerful ally in France. Many, including General George Washington, presumed France's entrance into the war meant independence was just around the corner. Meanwhile, having lost an entire army at Saratoga, Great Britain pivoted to a "southern strategy." Britain would henceforth seek to regain its southern colonies, Virginia, North Carolina, South Carolina, and Georgia, a highly profitable segment of its pre-war American empire. Deep into 1780 Britain's new approach seemed headed for success as the U.S. economy collapsed and morale on the home front waned. Winning Independence is the dramatic story of how and why Great Britain ultimately failed to win the war, exploring the choices and decisions made by Clinton, Washington, and others that led the French and American allies to clinch the pivotal victory at Yorktown that secured American independence.

"Ferling's lengthy, comprehensive, and essential work has staying power and should become one of the leading resources on the Revolutionary War." —*Library Journal*

Fischer, David Hackett
Paul Revere's Ride. David Hackett Fischer. Oxford University Press 1994. xviii, 445 p. : Illustration; Map
ISBN 9780195088472
Grades: Adult   **973.3**
1. Revere, Paul, 1735-1818 2. Lexington, Battle of, 1775 3. Concord, Battle of, 1775 4. Revolutionaries 5. American Revolution, 1775-1783 6. Revolutions 7. United States history 8. United States 9. Massachusetts 10. 18th century 11. Revolutionary America (1775-1783) 12. History writing — Wars and conflicts — Revolutionary War (America)

LC 93025739
Discusses the events leading up to Paul Revere's ride, and reinforces his importance in the history of the Revolutionary War.

"Fischer's solid study of Paul Revere and his infamous ride debunks the myths surrounding the event, reconstructing the circumstances leading to the Battle of Lexington and Concord. Fischer's extensive use of primary sources affords an intimate glimpse of the participants' thoughts and feelings." —*Booklist*

Includes bibliographical references (p. 373-421) and index.

Washington's Crossing. David Hackett Fischer. Oxford University Press 2004. x, 564 p. : Illustration; Map
ISBN 9780195170344
Grades: 11 12 Adult   **973.3**
1. Washington, George, 1732-1799 2. Generals 3. Military strategy 4. Command of troops 5. Soldiers 6. Battles 7. Trenton, Battle of, 1776 8. War 9. American Revolution, 1775-1783 10. Revolutions 11. Military campaigns 12. United States history 13. Trenton, New Jersey 14. United States 15. Pennsylvania 16. New Jersey 17. 18th century 18. Revolutionary America (1775-1783)

ESSENTIAL AND RECOMMENDED TITLES
973.3 United States — Periods of Revolution and Confederation, 1775-1789

19. History writing — Wars and conflicts — Revolutionary War (America) 20. Adult books for young adults

LC 2003019858

ALA Notable Book, 2005; Booklist Editors' Choice, 2004; New York Times Notable Book, 2004; Pulitzer Prize for History, 2005; School Library Journal Best Books: Best Adult Books 4 Teens, 2004; National Book Award for Nonfiction finalist, 2004.

Provides a colorful and dramatic account of a pivotal moment in American history—the Christmas night crossing of the Delaware River to mount a sneak attack on British and Hessian troops at Trenton, New Jersey—an event that marked a turning point in America's battle for independence.

"This is Fischer's strong suit: He tells stories and gives details that bring history alive. In the hands of such a thorough researcher and talented writer, this is powerful stuff." —*School Library Journal*

Includes bibliographical references (p. 459-486) and index.

Hogeland, William
Declaration: The Nine Tumultuous Weeks When America Became Independent, May 1-July 4, 1776. William Hogeland. Simon & Schuster 2010. 320 p.

ISBN 9781416584094

Grades: Adult 973.3

1. American Revolution, 1775-1783 2. Revolutions 3. Revolutionaries 4. Causes of war 5. Politics and government 6. United States history 7. United States 8. Great Britain 9. 18th century 10. Colonial America (1600-1775) 11. Revolutionary America (1775-1783) 12. 19th century 13. Georgian era (1714-1837) 14. History writing — Colonial America — United States 15. History writing — Wars and conflicts — Revolutionary War (America)

LC 2010003239

Looks at the history of the United States during the period before, during, and after the Revolutionary War, especially focusing on the circumstances in colonial life that led Americans to fight for their independence from Britain.

"The author forges a compelling narrative from the dozens of intricate political imbroglios that culminated with the signing of the Declaration of Independence. By casting a light on the daily interests of colonial Americans, particularly those whose homes and businesses patterned the spaces of bustling 18th-century Philadelphia, the author animates the discontents of the soon-to-be independent citizenry. With charming detail, the narrative brings together the diverse political players working during the nine weeks prior to the signing of the Declaration." —*Kirkus*

Includes bibliographical references and index.

Holton, Woody
Liberty Is Sweet: The Hidden History of the American Revolution. Woody Holton. Simon & Schuster 2021. 800 p.

ISBN 9781476750378

Grades: Adult 973.3

1. American Revolution, 1775-1783 2. Marginalized people 3. Revolutions 4. Freedom 5. Slavery 6. Inequality 7. Social history 8. Documentary evidence 9. Women's participation in wars 10. United States history 11. Revolutionary America (1775-1783) 12. History writing — Wars and conflicts — Revolutionary War (America) 13. History writing — Colonial America — United States 14. Life stories — People in history

LC 2020049257

Using more than a thousand eyewitness accounts, Liberty Is Sweet explores countless connections between the Patriots of 1776 and other Americans whose passion for freedom often brought them into conflict with the Founding Fathers. "It is all one story," historian Woody Holton writes. Holton describes the origins and crucial battles of the Revolution from Lexington and Concord to the British surrender at Yorktown, always focusing on marginalized Americans—enslaved Africans and African Americans, Native Americans, women, and dissenters—and on overlooked factors such as weather, North America's unique geography, chance, misperception, attempts to manipulate public opinion, and disease. Offering surprises at every turn, this majestic history revivifies a story we thought we already knew.

"A thoroughgoing work of scholarship that debunks many myths about the American Revolution by incorporating the full story involving Native Americans, African Americans, and women as participants. . . . A rich, multifaceted work showing how the U.S. has always been a multiracial nation." —*Kirkus*

Includes bibliographical references and index.

Hoock, Holger
Scars of Independence: America's Violent Birth. Holger Hoock. Random House Inc 2017. 480 p.

ISBN 9780804137287

Grades: Adult 973.3

1. Violence 2. War crimes 3. American Revolution, 1775-1783 4. Political violence 5. Rape in war 6. Atrocities 7. Slavery 8. Torture 9. Cruelty 10. Pillage 11. United States history 12. Revolutionary America (1775-1783) 13. History writing — Wars and conflicts — Revolutionary War (America)

LC 2016031348

According to historian Holger Hoock, the American Revolution wasn't only a conflict over principles, but also a violent civil war whose legacy historians have only recently recognized. In Scars of Independence, he carefully assesses how this violence affected everyone: Patriot and Loyalist civilians, military personnel on all sides, Native Americans, and free and enslaved Blacks. Hoock's balanced and accessible historical analysis includes explicit descriptions of atrocities, which may be disturbing to some readers.

"An accomplished, powerful presentation of the American Revolution as it was, rather than as we might wish to remember it." —*Kirkus*

Jefferson, Thomas
Writings: Autobiography Notes on the State of Virginia Public and Private Papers Addresses Letters. Thomas Jefferson. Literary Classics of the U.S. 1984. 1600 p. : Map (The Library of America, 17)

ISBN 9780940450165

Grades: 11 12 Adult 973.3

1. Jefferson, Thomas, 1743-1826 2. Politics and government 3. Virginia 4. United States 5. Early America (1784-1819) 6. 18th century 7. 19th century 8. Letters 9. Essays 10. History writing — Colonial America — United States 11. History writing — Early America — United States

LC 83019917

Gathers Jefferson's letters to politicians, scientists, and family members, public speeches, travel essays, and political writings.

"This is the largest and most skillfully edited single-volume Jefferson ever published." —*New York Times Book Review*

Merrill D. Peterson wrote the notes and selected the texts for this volume—Prelim. p. 5; Folded map in pocket; Includes bibliographical references and index.

Ketchum, Richard M.
Saratoga: Turning Point of America's Revolutionary War. Richard M. Ketchum. H. Holt 1997. xii, 545 p. : Illustration

ISBN 9780805046816

Grades: 11 12 Adult 973.3

1. Saratoga Campaign, 1777 2. American Revolution, 1775-1783 3. Revolutions 4. Military campaigns 5. United States history 6. Saratoga Springs, New York 7. United States 8. New York (State) 9. 1770s 10. Revolutionary America (1775-1783) 11. History writing — Wars and conflicts — Revolutionary War (America)

LC 97002773

New York Times Notable Book, 1997.

The diaries and letters of soldiers under General Horatio Gates offer a view of the pivotal victory against the British in the Saratoga campaign.

"A narrative account of the Saratoga campaign of 1777. Ketchum provides the full political context within which the fighting took place while penning dozens of colorful portraits of the principal characters. The author also succeeds in his goal of telling the story from the perspective of the participants, illustrating what the American Revolution in upstate New York meant for soldiers and civilians alike." —*Library Journal*

Includes bibliographical references and index.

Maier, Pauline
American Scripture: Making the Declaration of Independence. Pauline Maier. Knopf 1997. xxi, 304 p. : Illustration
ISBN 9780679454922
Grades: 11 12 Adult   973.3
1. Jefferson, Thomas, 1743-1826 2. American Revolution, 1775-1783 3. Revolutions 4. Causes of war 5. Politics and government 6. United States history 7. United States 8. 1770s 9. 1780s 10. Revolutionary America (1775-1783) 11. 18th century 12. 19th century 13. History writing — Colonial America — United States

LC 97002769

ALA Notable Book, 1998; National Book Critics Circle Award for Nonfiction finalist.

Reveals the origins of the Declaration's ideas and phrases, unravels the story of its drafting, and explores the implications of its treatment as a sacred text.

"In the spring of 1776, with a British invasion fleet on its way, the Second Continental Congress appointed a committee to compose a statement explaining America's decision to seek independence. Thomas Jefferson was the principal drafter of the statement, but Maier makes it clear that his task was to express the sentiments of the Congress, not his personal views, and she shows that when the congressmen edited his draft they improved it greatly (rather than mangling it, as Jefferson ever after maintained). The Declaration of Independence is, she argues, a profoundly collective document, both in its origins and in our still-evolving interpretation of its self-evident truths." —*The New Yorker*

Includes bibliographical references (p. [243]-285) and index.

McCullough, David G.
★ *1776.* David McCullough. Simon & Schuster 2005. 386 p. : Illustration; Color; Map
ISBN 9780743287708
Grades: Adult   973.3
1. Washington, George, 1732-1799 2. George III, King of Great Britain, 1738-1820 3. Militias and irregular armies 4. Rebels 5. American Revolution, 1775-1783 6. Revolutions 7. Revolutionaries 8. Causes of war 9. United States history 10. United States 11. Revolutionary America (1775-1783) 12. 1770s 13. History writing — Wars and conflicts — Revolutionary War (America) 14. Adult books for young adults

LC 2005042505

Booklist Editors' Choice, 2005; New York Times Notable Book, 2005.

Draws on personal correspondence and period diaries to present a history of the American Revolution that ranges from the siege of Boston, to the American defeat at Brooklyn and retreat across New Jersey, to the American victory at Trenton.

"This is a narrative tour de force, exhibiting all the hallmarks the author is known for: Fascinating subject matter, expert research and detailed, graceful prose." —*Publishers Weekly*

Includes bibliographical references (p. 347-371) and index.

Middlekauff, Robert
The Glorious Cause: The American Revolution, 1763-1789. Robert Middlekauff. Oxford University Press 2005. xiv, 736 p. : Illustration; Map
ISBN 9780195162479
Grades: Adult   973.3
1. American Revolution, 1775-1783 2. Revolutions 3. United States history 4. United States 5. Revolutionary America (1775-1783) 6. 1780s 7. History writing — Wars and conflicts — Revolutionary War (America)

LC 2004016295

Pulitzer Prize for History finalist, 1983.

A panoramic history of the conflict between England and America highlights the political and personal aspects of the colonial struggle for independence, provides a definitive overview of the events leading up to the Revolution, and discusses the major leaders, campaigns, battles, and repercussions of the war.

"This is narrative history at its best, written in a conversational and engaging style." —*Library Journal*

Previous ed. published as v. 2 in series: The Oxford history of the United States; Includes bibliographical references and index; Originally published: New York : Oxford University Press, 1982.

Norton, Mary Beth
1774: The Long Year of Revolution. Mary Beth Norton. Random House Inc 2020. 400 pages
ISBN 9780385353366
Grades: Adult   973.3
1. Boston Tea Party, 1773 2. Lexington, Battle of, 1775 3. Concord, Battle of, 1775 4. Loyalists (United States history) 5. Colonialism 6. Taxation 7. Revolutions 8. United States history 9. United States 10. Revolutionary America (1775-1783) 11. 1770s 12. Colonial America (1600-1775) 13. History writing — Wars and conflicts — Revolutionary War (America) 14. History writing — Colonial America — United States

LC 2019021556

A book on the American Revolution that looks at the critical "long year" of 1774, and the revolutionary change that took place from December 1773 to mid-April 1775, from the Boston Tea Party and the first Continental Congress to the Battle of Lexington and Concord.

"Norton makes a good case for considering 1774 and not 1776 to be the foundational year of the new republic." —*Kirkus*

This is a Borzoi book; Includes bibliographical references and index.

O'Donnell, Patrick K.
The Indispensables: The Diverse Soldier-mariners Who Shaped the Country, Formed the Navy, and Rowed Washington Across the Delaware. Patrick K. O'Donnell. Atlantic Monthly Press 2021. 464 p.
ISBN 9780802156891
Grades: Adult   973.3
1. American Revolution, 1775-1783 2. Soldiers 3. Military history 4. Sailors 5. African American soldiers 6. Indigenous soldiers 7. United States history 8. Massachusetts 9. 18th century 10. Revolutionary America (1775-1783) 11. History writing — Military — Military units 12. History writing — Wars and conflicts — Revolutionary War (America) 13. History writing — United States

In an addition to the literature of the American Revolution, a best-selling historian dramatically recounts how and why the Marblehead Regiment, led by John Glover, was truly indispensable.

"Historian O'Donnell (Washington's Immortals) offers a comprehensive look at the 'Indispensable' role of the Marblehead Regiment in the Revolutionary War.... Revolutionary War buffs will delight in the copious details and vivid battle scenes." —*Publishers Weekly*

Philbrick, Nathaniel
★ *Bunker Hill: A City, a Siege, a Revolution.* Nathaniel Philbrick. Viking 2013. 400 p.
ISBN 9780670025442
Grades: Adult   973.3
1. Bunker Hill, Battle of, 1775 2. Military history 3. Military tactics 4. Siege warfare 5. Battle history 6. American Revolution, 1775-1783 7. United States history 8. Massachusetts 9. 1770s 10. 1780s 11. Revolutionary America (1775-1783) 12. History writing — Colonial America — United States 13. History writing — Wars and conflicts — Revolutionary War (America)

LC 2013001534

Traces the experiences of Patriot leader Dr. Joseph Warren, a newly recruited George Washington, and British General William Howe.

Includes bibliographical references and index.

★ *In the Hurricane's Eye: The Genius of George Washington and the Victory at Yorktown.* Nathaniel Philbrick. Penguin Group USA 2018. 448 p.
ISBN 9780525426769
Grades: Adult   973.3
1. Washington, George, 1732-1799 2. Lafayette, Marie Joseph Paul Yves Roch Gilbert Du Motier, marquis de, 1757-1834 3. American Revolution, 1775-1783 4. Command of troops 5. Naval battles 6. Strategic alliances (Mili-

ESSENTIAL AND RECOMMENDED TITLES
973.3 United States — Periods of Revolution and Confederation, 1775-1789

tary) 7. Military history 8. United States history 9. France 10. Revolutionary America (1775-1783) 11. History writing — Wars and conflicts — Revolutionary War (America)

LC 2018029041

A narrative chronicle of the Battle of the Chesapeake traces the maneuvers by Lafayette and Washington that are credited with America's Revolutionary War victory.

"All readers interested in the Revolutionary War, and especially fans of naval history, will find Philbrick's fresh account rewarding, right through the epilogue describing what happened to many of the key figures going forward." —*Booklist*

Phillips, Kevin
1775: A Good Year for Revolution. Kevin Phillips. Viking 2012. 640 p.
ISBN 9780670025121
Grades: Adult   973.3

1. Paine, Thomas, 1737-1809 2. Lexington, Battle of, 1775 3. Concord, Battle of, 1775 4. American Revolution, 1775-1783 5. Revolutions 6. Politics and government 7. United States history 8. United States 9. Massachusetts 10. Revolutionary America (1775-1783) 11. 18th century 12. 19th century 13. History writing — Wars and conflicts — Revolutionary War (America) 14. History writing — Wars and conflicts — Battles

LC 2012001786

An unconventional assessment of the American Revolution by the author of the Pulitzer Prize finalist the Cousins' War assesses the events, politics, economic factors and military preparations of 1775 that he believes ignited the war and established patriot control over American governance and key territories.

Includes bibliographical references and index.

Rakove, Jack N.
Revolutionaries: A New History of the Invention of America. Jack Rakove. Houghton Mifflin Harcourt 2010. 487 p.
ISBN 9780618267460
Grades: Adult   973.3

1. Politicians 2. Nation-building 3. Intellectual life 4. Diplomats 5. American Revolution, 1775-1783 6. Revolutions 7. Revolutionaries 8. Politics and government 9. United States history 10. United States 11. 1770s 12. 18th century 13. Revolutionary America (1775-1783) 14. 19th century 15. History writing — Wars and conflicts — Revolutionary War (America)

LC 2009047557

Spans the most crucial decades of the country's birth, from 1772 to 1792, using the stories of famous (and not-so-famous) men to capture the intensely creative period of the Republic's founding.

"The author reflects on how a group of lawyers and planters came to wage the American Revolution. Instead of focusing on the battlefield, the author examines what might be called a revolution of the mindthat is, how the early Founding Fathers' ideas developed and took hold. An ambitious, intelligent exploration into the intellectual underpinnings of the Revolution." —*Kirkus*

Includes bibliographical references and index.

Randall, Willard Sterne
The Founders' Fortunes: How Money Shaped the Birth of America. Willard Sterne Randall. E.P. Dutton 2022. 336 p.
ISBN 9781524745929
Grades: Adult   973.3

1. Founding Fathers of the United States 2. Constitutional history 3. Constitutional law 4. Wealth 5. Politics and government 6. Economics 7. United States history 8. United States 9. Revolutionary America (1775-1783) 10. Early America (1784-1819) 11. 18th century 12. Politics and global affairs — Political philosophy 13. History writing — Early America — United States 14. History writing — Antebellum AMerica — United States

A financial history of the Founding Fathers reveals how their personal finances shaped the Constitution and the new nation.

"A detailed look at the economic roots of the American Revolution and the early republic.... Like Randall's previous works, especially Unshackling America, the narrative is well written and packed with human interest, providing a valuable update to the Revolutionary-era history many readers may not have studied since high school." —*Kirkus*

Raphael, Ray
*A **People's** History of the American Revolution: How Common People Shaped the Fight for Independence.* Ray Raphael. Perennial 2002. xiv, 506 p.
ISBN 9780060004408
Grades: 11 12 Adult   973.3

1. American Revolution, 1775-1783 2. Revolutions 3. United States history 4. United States 5. Revolutionary America (1775-1783) 6. History writing — Wars and conflicts — Revolutionary War (America)

LC 2002016992

Presents a history of the American Revolution from the perspective of farmers, soldiers, laborers, and other common folk by using personal letters, diaries, and other primary source material.

"Moving from broad overviews to stories of small groups or individuals, Raphael's study is impressive in both its sweep and its attention to the particular." —*Publishers Weekly*

Includes bibliographical references (p. [401]-487) and index; Originally published: New York : The New Press, 2001.

Rosen, Jeffrey
*The **Pursuit** of Happiness: How Classical Writers on Virtue Inspired the Lives of the Founders and Defined America.* Jeffrey Rosen. Simon & Schuster 2024. 368 p.
ISBN 9781668002476
Grades: Adult   973.3

1. Founding Fathers of the United States 2. Literature and history 3. Literature 4. Books and reading 5. Literature and society 6. United States history 7. Influence (Literary, artistic, etc.) 8. 18th century 9. Early America (1784-1819) 10. Revolutionary America (1775-1783) 11. History Writing — Early America — United States 12. History writing — Colonial America — United States

In this interpretation of the Declaration of Independence's famous phrase, the president of the National Constitution Center profiles six of the most influential founders to show what pursuing happiness meant in their lives and how it became the foundation of our democracy.

"Rosen's noteworthy book offers a better understanding of philosophy and American history." —*Booklist*

Taylor, Alan
American Republics: A Continental History of the United States, 1783-1850. Alan Taylor. W. W. Norton & Company 2021. 592 p.
ISBN 9781324005797
Grades: Adult   973.3

1. Race relations 2. Territorial expansion 3. United States history 4. United States 5. 18th century 6. Early America (1784-1819) 7. Antebellum America (1820-1861) 8. 19th century 9. History writing — United States

LC 2021003043

American History Book Prize, 2022.

From a Pulitzer Prize-winning historian, the powerful story of a fragile nation as it expands across a contested continent. In this beautifully written history of America's formative period, a preeminent historian upends the traditional story of a youngnation confidently marching to its continent-spanning destiny.

"The newest volume in Taylor's U.S. history series, after American Revolutions, covers the post-revolutionary period through the Compromise of 1850.... This insightful and engaging survey is essential reading for scholars as well as casual readers of history." —*Library Journal*

Includes bibliographical references and index.

American Revolutions: A Continental History, 1750-1804. Alan Taylor. W. W. Norton & Company 2016. xvii, 681 pages : Illustration; Map
ISBN 9780393082814
Grades: Adult   973.3

1. American Revolution, 1775-1783 2. Founding Fathers of the United States 3. Slavery 4. Postcolonialism 5. Revolutions 6. United States history 7. United States 8. 18th century 9. Early America (1784-1819) 10. Revolutionary America (1775-1783) 11. Colonial America (1600-1775) 12. History writing — Colonial America — United States 13. History writing — Antebellum America — United States 14. History writing — Wars and conflicts — Revolutionary War (America)

An authoritative, revisionist history of America's founding period by a two-time Pulitzer Prize winner challenges views about the Revolution's orderly conduct to illuminate the violence and corruption that prompted national leaders to ratify a frame of government that would consolidate power and restrain unruly state democracies.

"A clear, authoritative, well-organized look at the messy Colonial march toward revolution and self-rule." —*Kirkus*

Includes bibliographical references (pages 497-663) and index.

Thompson, Bob
Revolutionary Roads: Searching for the War That Made America Independent...and All the Places It Could Have Gone Terribly Wrong. Bob Thompson. Twelve 2023. 432 p.
ISBN 9781455565153
Grades: Adult   973.3
1. Thompson, Bob, 1950 August 28- 2. American Revolution, 1775-1783 3. Revolutions 4. Monuments 5. Voyages and travels 6. United States history 7. United States 8. Revolutionary America (1775-1783) 9. Travel Writing — United States 10. History Writing — Wars and conflicts 11. History writing — Antebellum America — United States
LC 2022042073

An American Revolution book like no other, this time-traveling adventure takes readers through the crucial places American independence was won and might have been lost, revisiting the pivotal figures and key turning points during this 8-year epic battle that transformed the world.

"Journalist Thompson...mixes playful imagination and solid research in this episodic romp through the Revolutionary War....The result is an eclectic yet cogent and cohesive account of the American Revolution." —*Publishers Weekly*

Includes bibliographical references and index.

Unger, Harlow G.
American Tempest: How the Boston Tea Party Sparked a Revolution. Harlow Giles Unger. Da Capo Press 2011. 288 p.
ISBN 9780306819629
Grades: 11 12 Adult   973.3
1. Boston Tea Party, 1773 2. Protests, demonstrations, vigils, etc. 3. Revolutionaries 4. American Revolution, 1775-1783 5. Revolutions 6. Causes of war 7. United States history 8. Boston, Massachusetts 9. United States 10. Massachusetts 11. 18th century 12. Revolutionary America (1775-1783) 13. History writing — Colonial America — United States
LC 2010047734

Describes the events of the Boston Tea Party on December 16, 1773, the turmoil it initiated in Boston and other cities, and the social, political, and economic consequences that eventually led to the Declaration of Independence and the birth of the United States.

"As Unger makes clear, the true impact of the Boston Tea Party came from Britain's ill-advised overreaction to the symbolic act of vandalism. It was exactly the response [Sam] Adams had dreamed of, with an enraged British government closing the port of Boston, sending more troops, imposing martial law, and requiring permits for any large Boston meetings. These Coercive Acts, along with Adams's constant drumbeat of anti-British propaganda, helped unify the colonies around the idea of independence. Unger ends the book with British soldiers marching out to Lexington and Concord hoping to arrest Adams and Hancock (who, tipped off by Paul Revere, had fled). The rest, as they say, is history, and Unger has brought it brilliantly to life." —*Boston Globe*

Includes bibliographical references and index.

Weintraub, Stanley
Iron Tears: America's Battle for Freedom, Britain's Quagmire, 1775-1783. Stanley Weintraub. Free Press 2005. xviii, 375 p, 16 p. of plates : Illustration; Map
ISBN 9780743226875
Grades: Adult   973.3
1. Public opinion 2. Soldiers 3. War and society 4. Military strategy 5. Political corruption 6. Winning and losing 7. Command of troops 8. Military officers 9. Politicians 10. American Revolution, 1775-1783 11. Revolutions 12. United States history 13. Great Britain 14. United States 15. 18th century 16. History writing — Wars and conflicts — Revolutionary War (America) 17. History writing — Europe — United Kingdom
LC 2004056363

A dual-sided history of the Revolutionary War examines the conflict from both the colonial and British sides.

"Weintraub's fast-paced narrative and impeccable historical research provide a stimulating challenge to conventional histories of the Revolutionary War that focus exclusively on the heroism of American forces." —*Publishers Weekly*

Includes bibliographical references (p. [347]-361) and index.

973.4 United States — Constitutional period, 1789-1809

Adams, Abigail
Abigail Adams: Letters. Edith Gelles, editor. The Library of America 2016. xxxix, 1180 pages
ISBN 9781598534658
Grades: Adult   973.4
1. Adams, Abigail, 1744-1818 2. Presidents' spouses 3. Letter writing 4. United States history 5. United States 6. Early America (1784-1819) 7. Revolutionary America (1775-1783) 8. History writing — Early America — United States 9. Arts and Entertainment — Writing and Publishing
LC 2015935694

Chronicles the life of the first lady through her correspondence with her husband and other notable figures, covering her courtship and marriage, the American Revolution, her travels in Europe, and her time in the White House.

Includes index.

Adams, John
My Dearest Friend: Letters of Abigail and John Adams. Edited by Margaret A. Hogan and C. James Taylor. Belknap Press of Harvard University Press 2007. xx, 508 p, [20] p. of plates : Illustration; Color; Map
ISBN 9780674026063
Grades: Adult   973.4
1. Adams, John, 1735-1826 2. Adams, Abigail, 1744-1818 3. Married people 4. Couples 5. American Revolution, 1775-1783 6. Presidents' spouses 7. Presidents 8. Revolutions 9. United States history 10. United States 11. 18th century 12. Early America (1784-1819) 13. Revolutionary America (1775-1783) 14. Love letters 15. Letters 16. History writing — Presidency — 18th century — United States 17. Family and Relationships — Dating and Marriage 18. History writing — Early America — United States
LC 2007004380

Presents a collection of letters between John and Abigail Adams that chronicle their lives and the events that surrounded them.

"This is a treasure, for general readers and scholars alike." —*Booklist*

Includes index.

Avlon, John P.
Washington's Farewell: The Founding Father's Warning to Future Generations. by John Avlon. Simon & Schuster 2017. 320 p.
ISBN 9781476746463
Grades: Adult   973.4
1. Washington, George, 1732-1799 2. National characteristics, American 3. Political leadership 4. Political parties 5. Presidents 6. United States history 7. United States 8. Early America (1784-1819) 9. 18th century 10. Biographies 11. History writing — Presidency — 18th century — United States 12. Life stories — Politics — Politicians
LC 2016045258

In Washington's Farewell, Avlon offers important insight into Washington's final public days, presenting not only a startling description of the perilous state of the new nation but a rare view of the man behind the usual face of a tranquil First Father.

"A solid analysis of our first president and his farewell to the American people." —*Library Journal*

Includes bibliographical references and index.

ESSENTIAL AND RECOMMENDED TITLES
973.4 United States — Constitutional period, 1789-1809

Baier, Bret
To Rescue the Constitution: George Washington and the Fragile American Experiment. Bret Baier. Mariner Books 2023. 400 p.
ISBN 9780063039582
Grades: Adult   973.4
1. Washington, George, 1732-1799 2. Generals 3. Presidents 4. Founding Fathers of the United States 5. Revolutionaries 6. Command of troops 7. Politicians 8. Leadership 9. Constitutional history 10. North American people 11. American people 12. United States history 13. Revolutionary America (1775-1783) 14. Early America (1784-1819) 15. Biographies 16. Impartial writing 17. Life stories — Politics — Politicians 18. Life stories — Law and order — Military leaders 19. History writing — Presidency — 18th century — United States 20. History writing — Early America — United States 21. History writing — Wars and conflicts — Revolutionary War (America)

A sweeping narrative ranging from the unsettled early American frontier and the battlefields of the Revolution to the history-making clashes within Philadelphia's Independence Hall, Bret Baier's To Rescue the Constitution dramatically reveals the life of George Washington, the Founder who did more than perhaps any other individual to secure the future of the United States.

"In To Rescue the Constitution, Baier, the chief political anchor for Fox News, charts George Washington's return from retirement post-Revolutionary War to lead the Constitutional Convention that bound together the United States." —*Library Journal*

Burstein, Andrew
Madison and Jefferson. Andrew Burstein and Nancy Isenberg. Random House 2010. xxvii, 809 p, 8 p. of plates : Illustration; Map
ISBN 9781400067282
Grades: Adult   973.4
1. Jefferson, Thomas, 1743-1826 2. Madison, James, 1751-1836 3. Founding Fathers of the United States 4. Politicians 5. Politics and culture 6. Presidents 7. Politics and government 8. United States 9. 18th century 10. 19th century 11. Biographies 12. History writing — Presidency — 18th century — United States 13. Life stories — Politics — Politicians
LC 2010005884

A provocative analysis of the historically pivotal friendship between the third and fourth presidents offers insight into their complex characters while presenting a sobering assessment of how politics were conducted in the country's early years.

"This dual biography promotes Madison from junior partner to full-fledged colleague of the more magnetic Jefferson. According to the authors, Madison's popular image peaked in 1789 as father of the Constitution. But Burstein—and Isenberg—see him as a canny, effective politician for four decades, from the Continental Congress through his two terms as America's fourth president. An important, thoughtful, and gracefully written political history from the viewpoint of the young nation's two most intellectual founding fathers." —*Publishers Weekly*

Includes bibliographical references (p. [755]-780) and index.

Ellis, Joseph J.
American Sphinx: The Character of Thomas Jefferson. Joseph J. Ellis. Alfred A. Knopf 1997. xiv, 365 p.
ISBN 9780679444909
Grades: 11 12 Adult   973.4
1. Jefferson, Thomas, 1743-1826 2. Intellectuals 3. Intellectual life 4. Presidents 5. Politicians 6. Politics and government 7. Idealism 8. United States history 9. United States 10. 19th century 11. Biographies 12. Impartial writing 13. History writing — Presidency — 19th century — United States 14. History writing — Early America — United States 15. History writing — Colonial America — United States 16. Life stories — Politics — Politicians
LC 96026171

Booklist Editors' Choice, 1997; National Book Award for Nonfiction, 1997; New York Times Notable Book, 1997; National Book Critics Circle Award for Biography finalist, 1997.

A character study of Thomas Jefferson.

"Penetrating Jefferson's placid, elegant facade, this extraordinary biography brings the sage of Monticello down to earth without either condemning or idolizing him." —*Publishers Weekly*

Includes bibliographical references and index.

First Family: Abigail and John. Joseph J. Ellis. Alfred A. Knopf 2010. 320 p.
ISBN 9780307269621
Grades: 11 12 Adult   973.4
1. Adams, John, 1735-1826 2. Adams, Abigail, 1744-1818 3. Founding Fathers of the United States 4. Married people 5. Husband and wife 6. Presidents' spouses 7. Presidents 8. Politics and government 9. United States 10. 18th century 11. Early America (1784-1819) 12. Biographies 13. History writing — Presidency — 18th century — United States 14. History writing — Early America — United States
LC 2010016837

Massachusetts Book Awards, Nonfiction Award, 2011.

John and Abigail Adams left a remarkable portrait of their lives together in their personal correspondence: Both were prolific letter writers (although John conceded that Abigail was the more gifted), and over the years they exchanged more than twelve hundred letters. Joseph J. Ellis distills them to give us an account both intimate and panoramic; part biography, part political history, and part love story. Ellis describes their first meeting as inauspicious—John was twenty-four, Abigail just fifteen, and each was entirely unimpressed. But they soon began a passionate correspondence that resulted in their marriage five years later. Over the next decades, the couple were separated nearly as much as they were together. When John became president, Abigail's health led to reservations about moving to the swamp on the Potomac, but he persuaded her that he needed his closest advisor by his side. Here, John and Abigail's relationship unfolds in the context of America's birth as a nation.

Includes bibliographical references and index.

Founding Brothers: The Revolutionary Generation. by Joseph J. Ellis. Alfred A. Knopf 2000. xi, 288 p.
ISBN 9780375405440
Grades: 11 12 Adult   973.4
1. Federal government 2. Revolutionaries 3. Presidents 4. Politicians 5. Politics and government 6. United States history 7. United States 8. 18th century 9. Early America (1784-1819) 10. Biographies 11. History writing — Early America — United States 12. Adult books for young adults
LC 99059304

New York Times Notable Book, 2001; Pulitzer Prize for History, 2001.

An analysis of the intertwined careers of the founders of the American republic documents the lives of John Adams, Aaron Burr, Benjamin Franklin, Alexander Hamilton, Thomas Jefferson, James Madison, and George Washington.

"Ellis' essays are angled, fascinating, and perfect for general-interest readers." —*Booklist*

Includes bibliographical references (p. 249-278) and index.

Flexner, James Thomas
George Washington and the New Nation, 1783-1793. James Thomas Flexner. Little, Brown 1970. xi, 466 p. : Illustration; Facsimile; Footnotes; Map; Plan; Portrait
ISBN 9780316286008
Grades: Adult   973.4
1. Washington, George, 1732-1799 2. Presidents 3. Politics and government 4. United States history 5. United States 6. 18th century 7. Early America (1784-1819) 8. Biographies 9. History writing — Presidency — 18th century — United States 10. History writing — Early America — United States 11. Life stories — Politics — Politicians
LC 78117042

Detailed narrative of Washington's career from his return to Mount Vernon following the Revolutionary War through his first term as president.

Includes bibliographical references (p. 431-437).

PUBLIC LIBRARY CORE COLLECTION: NONFICTION
Twentieth Edition

Gordon-Reed, Annette
★ *Most Blessed of the Patriarchs: Thomas Jefferson and the Empire of the Imagination.* Annette Gordon-Reed and Peter S. Onuf. Liveright Pub Corp 2016. 320 p.
ISBN 9780871404428
Grades: Adult   973.4
1. Jefferson, Thomas, 1743-1826 2. Political participation 3. Political values 4. Presidents 5. Politics and government 6. United States history 7. United States 8. 18th century 9. Early America (1784-1819) 10. 1780s 11. Biographies 12. History writing — Presidency — 18th century — United States 13. History writing — Early America — United States 14. Life stories — Politics — Politicians

LC 2016000927

A noted historian and a leading Jefferson scholar clarify philosophical questions about the Founding Father to trace his youth and development through the inconsistencies attributed to his character and his old age.

"An elegant, astute study that is both readable and thematically rich." —*Kirkus*

Isenberg, Nancy
The Problem of Democracy: The Presidents Adams Confront the Cult of Personality. Nancy Isenberg and Andrew Burstein. Viking 2019. 544 p.
ISBN 9780525557500
Grades: Adult   973.4
1. Adams, John, 1735-1826 2. Adams, John Quincy, 1767-1848 3. Elite (Social sciences) 4. Populism 5. Democracy 6. Presidents 7. Politics and government 8. Philosophy 9. United States 10. 18th century 11. 19th century 12. Biographies 13. History writing — Presidency — 18th century — United States 14. History writing — Presidency — 19th century — United States 15. Life stories — Politics — Politicians

LC 2018039232

A recasting of the second and sixth presidents, father and son John and John Quincy Adams, explores how they worked to partially protect a fledgling American democracy from its vulnerabilities to popularity-driven elections and an elite ruling class.

"To make sense of Americas twenty-first-century political discontents, Isenberg and Burstein turn to the nations second and sixth presidents, a father-son pair of one-term chief executives often dismissed as elitists, out of touch with their countrys democratic spirit." —*Booklist*

Includes bibliographical references and index.

Kilmeade, Brian
★ *George Washington's Secret Six: The Spy Ring That Saved the American Revolution.* Brian Kilmeade and Don Yaeger. Sentinel 2013. 288 p.
ISBN 9781595231031
Grades: Adult   973.4
1. Washington, George, 1732-1799 2. Townsend, Robert, 1753-1838 3. Secret service 4. Spies 5. American Revolution, 1775-1783 6. United States history 7. New York (State) 8. 18th century 9. Revolutionary America (1775-1783) 10. History writing — Spies and spying 11. History writing — Wars and conflicts — Revolutionary War (America)

LC 2013032285

The co-host of Fox & Friends shares the true story of an anonymous group of spies who played lesser-known, important roles in winning the Revolutionary War, documenting how they risked their lives to obtain crucial intelligence for General Washington using sophisticated tactics and complex codes.

"While Kilmeade and Yaeger don't provide deep analysis, the narrative should please enthusiastic fans of the upheaval surrounding the founding of the United States. In a slim, quick-moving book, the authors bring attention to a group that exerted an enormous influence over events during the Revolutionary War." —*Kirkus*

Includes bibliographical references and index.

★ *Thomas Jefferson and the Tripoli Pirates: The Forgotten War That Changed American History.* Brian Kilmeade and Don Yaeger. Sentinel 2015. 256 p.
ISBN 9781591848066

Grades: Adult   973.4
1. Jefferson, Thomas, 1743-1826 2. Piracy 3. Naval battles 4. War 5. Pirates 6. Hijacking of ships 7. Tripolitan War, 1801-1805 8. Southwest Asia and North Africa (Middle East) history 9. Libya 10. Early America (1784-1819) 11. 1800s (Decade) 12. History writing — Wars and conflicts — Tripolitan War 13. History writing — Military — Naval history 14. History writing — Pirates

The authors of George Washington's Secret Six present a pop-history narrative that illuminates a lesser-known confrontation between the recently inaugurated third President and Pasha of Tripoli pirates who openly challenged his leadership by attacking American ships.

"This work will appeal to all history readers." —*Library Journal*

Meltzer, Brad
★ *The First Conspiracy: The Secret Plot to Kill George Washington.* Brad Meltzer and Josh Mensch. Flatiron Books 2019. 432 p.
ISBN 9781250130334
Grades: Adult   973.4
1. Washington, George, 1732-1799 2. Assassination plots 3. Treason 4. Military intelligence 5. Conspiracies 6. Bodyguards 7. Traitors 8. Spies 9. Assassination 10. Presidents 11. United States history 12. United States 13. 18th century 14. Revolutionary America (1775-1783) 15. History writing — Presidency — 18th century — United States 16. History writing — Early America — United States 17. History writing — Wars and conflicts — Revolutionary War (America)

LC 2018037886

The author of the Inner Circle presents the lesser-known story of an assassination attempt against pre-Revolutionary War George Washington by some of his own bodyguards, exploring how the plot catalyzed the creations of the CIA and FBI.

"What Meltzer and Mensch do bring out is how the scheme helped to inspire American innovations in defensive spycraft, eventually known as counterintelligence, by their juxtaposing the Hickey attempt with the ad hoc nature of the political and military leadership seeking to control the city and prosecute the war. Readers who like their histories full of twists, turns, and cliff-hangers will enjoy this romp through the Revolution." —*Booklist*

Includes bibliographical references and index.

Philbrick, Nathaniel
Travels with George: In Search of Washington and His Legacy. Nathaniel Philbrick. Viking 2021. 368 p.
ISBN 9780525562177
Grades: Adult   973.4
1. Washington, George, 1732-1799 2. Philbrick, Nathaniel 3. Historical reenactments 4. Presidents 5. Politics and government 6. Voyages and travels 7. United States history 8. United States 9. 18th century 10. Travel Writing — Retracing Historic Journeys 11. History writing — Early America — United States 12. History writing — Presidency — 18th century — United States

LC 2020054623

Written at a moment when America's founding figures are under increasing scrutiny, the author, retracing George Washington's journey as a new president through all thirteen former colonies, paints a picture of 18th-century America as divided and fraught as it is today.

"Philbrick (In the Hurricane's Eye) retraces George Washington's presidential travels from 1789 to 1791 in this entertaining mix of history, travelogue, and memoir that takes a page from John Steinbeck's Travels with Charley." —*Publishers Weekly*

Includes bibliographical references and index.

Sedgwick, John
War of Two: Alexander Hamilton, Aaron Burr, and the Duel That Stunned the Nation. John Sedgwick. Berkley Books 2015. 432 p.
ISBN 9781592408528
Grades: Adult   973.4
1. Hamilton, Alexander, 1757-1804 2. Burr, Aaron, 1756-1836 3. Burr-Hamilton Duel, Weehawken, N.J, 1804 4. Dueling 5. Politicians 6. Enemies 7. Politics and government 8. United States 9. 1800s (Decade) 10. 19th century 11. History writing — Early America — United States

ESSENTIAL AND RECOMMENDED TITLES
973.5 United States — 1809-1845

LC 2015014275

In the summer of 1804, two of America's most eminent statesmen squared off, pistols raised, on a bluff along the Hudson River. That two such men would risk not only their lives but the stability of the young country they helped forge is almost beyond comprehension. Yet we know that it happened. The question is why. In War of Two, John Sedgwick explores the long-standing conflict between Founding Father Alexander Hamilton and Vice President Aaron Burr.

"A fine rendition of a storied episode in American history." —*Booklist*

Includes bibliographical references and index.

Stewart, David O.

George Washington: The Political Rise of America's Founding Father. David O. Stewart. Dutton 2021. 576 p.

ISBN 9780451488985

Grades: Adult   973.4

1. Washington, George, 1732-1799 2. Generals 3. Political leadership 4. Founding Fathers of the United States 5. Presidents 6. Politics and government 7. United States history 8. United States 9. 18th century 10. Early America (1784-1819) 11. Revolutionary America (1775-1783) 12. 19th century 13. Biographies 14. Life stories — Politics — Politicians 15. History writing — Presidency — 18th century — United States 16. History writing — Colonial America — United States 17. Life stories — Law and order — Military leaders

LC 2020036458

Historian David O. Stewart unveils the political education that made Washington a master politician, and America's most essential leader. From Virginia's House of Burgesses, where Washington learned the craft and timing of a practicing politician, to his management of local government as a justice of the Fairfax County Court to his eventual role in the Second Continental Congress and his grueling generalship in the American Revolution, Washington perfected the art of governing and service, earned trust, and built bridges. The lessons in leadership he absorbed along the way would be invaluable during the early years of the republic as he fought to unify the new nation.

"This is a readable and revealing contemporary look at an oft-studied personality." —*Booklist*

Includes bibliographical references and index.

Wiencek, Henry

Master of the Mountain: Thomas Jefferson and His Slaves. Henry Wiencek. Farrar, Straus and Giroux 2012. 416 p.

ISBN 9780374299569

Grades: Adult   973.4

1. Jefferson, Thomas, 1743-1826 2. Hemings, Sally, 1773-1835 3. Enslaved people 4. Slavery 5. Plantation life 6. United States history 7. Virginia 8. 18th century 9. History writing — Presidency — 18th century — United States 10. History writing — Early America — United States 11. History writing — African American — Enslavement — United States

LC 2011052231

A controversial reassessment of the third President draws on new archaeological studies and previously disregarded personal records, assessing his contradictory views on slavery while examining what is revealed by his monetary records.

"Wiencek's insightful and engaging account is recommended to both the illustrious Virginian's detractors and to his devotees." —*Library Journal*

Includes bibliographical references and index.

Wood, Gordon S.

Empire of Liberty: A History of the Early Republic, 1789-1815. Gordon S. Wood. Oxford University Press 2009. xix, 778 p, 32 p. of plates : Illustration; Map

ISBN 9780195039146

Grades: 11 12 Adult   973.4

1. Politicians 2. Presidents 3. Politics and government 4. Civilization 5. United States 6. 19th century 7. Early America (1784-1819) 8. Antebellum America (1820-1861) 9. History writing — Early America — United States

LC 2009010762

American History Book Prize, 2009; New York Times Notable Book, 2009; Pulitzer Prize for History finalist, 2010.

Integrating all aspects of life, from politics and law to the economy and culture, "Empire of Liberty" offers a marvelous account of this pivotal era when America took its first unsteady steps as a new and rapidly expanding nation.

Includes bibliographical references and index.

973.5 United States — 1809-1845

Ayers, Edward L.

American Visions: The United States, 1800-1860. Edward L. Ayers. W.W. Norton & Company 2023. xii, 351 p.

ISBN 9780393881264

Grades: Adult   973.5

1. Culture 2. Politics and government 3. Power 4. Racism 5. Slavery 6. Sexism 7. Xenophobia 8. Inequality 9. Marginalized people 10. Dissenters 11. Abolitionists 12. Social reformers 13. Social change 14. United States history 15. 19th century 16. History writing — Early America — United States 17. History writing — Antebellum America — United States 18. Life stories — Politics — Activists and reformers

A celebrated historian turns his distinctive sensibility to a formative period of American history defined by competing strains of innovation and dissent that continues to echo in our society today.

"Ayers' accurate, balanced, and compelling history proves that progress is possible and that patriotism can be rooted in the complicated truths about the past." —*Booklist*

Includes bibliographical references and index.

Brands, H. W.

★ *Heirs of the Founders: The Epic Rivalry of Henry Clay, John Calhoun and Daniel Webster, the Second Generation of American Giants.* H. W. Brands. Doubleday, a division of Penguin Random House LLC 2018. 432 p.

ISBN 9780385542531

Grades: Adult   973.5

1. Calhoun, John C, 1782-1850 2. Clay, Henry, 1777-1852 3. Webster, Daniel, 1782-1852 4. Constitutional history 5. Nation-building 6. Politicians 7. Politics and government 8. United States 9. 19th century 10. Biographies 11. History writing — Early America — United States

LC 2018010542

Chronicles the efforts of three second-generation political giants who at the beginning of the nineteenth century battled to complete the unfinished initiatives of the Founding Fathers.

"Requiring of readers no prior knowledge of the period or the players, this fascinating history illuminates rifts that still plague the country today." —*Publishers Weekly*

Includes bibliographical references and index.

Cook, Jane Hampton

American Phoenix: John Quincy and Louisa Adams, the War of 1812, and the Exile That Saved American Independence. Jane Hampton Cook. Thomas Nelson 2013. 496 p.

ISBN 9781595555410

Grades: Adult   973.5

1. Adams, John Quincy, 1767-1848 2. Adams, Louisa Catherine, 1775-1852 3. Diplomats 4. Husband and wife 5. War of 1812 6. Presidents' spouses 7. Presidents 8. International relations 9. Russia 10. United States 11. 19th century 12. Biographies 13. History writing — Presidency — 19th century — United States 14. Life stories — Politics — Politicians

LC 2012039898

Draws from diaries and correspondence to chronicle John Quincy Adams's experience serving as U.S. envoy to Russia and his role in ending the War of 1812, while also detailing his wife Louisa's trials as a diplomatic spouse.

Includes bibliographical references and index.

Cozzens, Peter

A Brutal Reckoning: Andrew Jackson, the Creek Indians, and the Epic War for the American South. Peter Cozzens. Random House Inc 2023. 480 p.

PUBLIC LIBRARY CORE COLLECTION: NONFICTION
Twentieth Edition

ISBN 9780525659457
Grades: Adult　　　　　　　　　　　　　　　　　　　973.5
1. Jackson, Andrew, 1767-1845 2. Indigenous peoples of North America 3. Creek War, 1813-1814 4. Creek (Muskogee) (North American people) 5. Government relations with indigenous peoples 6. Trail of Tears, 1838-1839 7. War 8. Race relations 9. Leadership 10. United States history 11. 19th century 12. History writing — Indigenous peoples — United States 13. History writing — Wars and conflicts — American Indigenous Wars 14. History writing — Presidency — 19th century — United States

The acclaimed historian chronicles the brutal Creek War of 1813-1814, where Andrew Jackson shattered Native American control of the Deep South which led to the infamous Trail of Tears and set the stage for the Civil War.

"An authoritative account of a disturbing chapter in the relations between the U.S. military and Indigenous peoples." —*Kirkus*

Greenidge, Kerri
★ *The Grimkes: The Legacy of Slavery in an American Family.* Kerri K. Greenidge. Liveright Publishing 2022. 416 p.
ISBN 9781324090847
Grades: Adult　　　　　　　　　　　　　　　　　　　973.5
1. Grimke, Angelina Emily, 1805-1879 2. Grimke, Sarah Moore, 1792-1873 3. Quaker women 4. Feminists 5. Abolitionists 6. Anti-slavery movements 7. Freed people 8. Interracial families 9. Slavery 10. Racism 11. Hypocrisy 12. North American people 13. American people 14. Race relations 15. Guilt 16. United States history 17. Philadelphia, Pennsylvania 18. Collective biographies 19. History writing — Antebellum America — United States 20. Life stories — Politics — Activists and reformers 21. History writing — African American — Enslavement — United States 22. Society and culture — Race

National Book Critics Circle Award for Biography finalist, 2022.

Sarah and Angelina Grimke—the Grimke sisters—are revered figures in American history, famous for rejecting their privileged lives on a plantation in South Carolina to become firebrand activists in the North. Their antislavery pamphlets, among the most influential of the antebellum era, are still read today. Yet retellings of their epic story have long obscured their Black relatives. In The Grimkes, award-winning historian Kerri Greenidge presents a parallel narrative, indeed a long-overdue corrective, shifting the focus from the white abolitionist sisters to the Black Grimkes and deepening our understanding of the long struggle for racial and gender equality.

A multigenerational history of an American family that grappled with racism and reform….The author's discoveries reveal both 'White reformers' disavowal of their complicity in America's racial project' and 'The limits of interracial alliances.' —*Kirkus*

Includes bibliographical references and index.

Gutzman, Kevin R. C.
The Jeffersonians: The Visionary Presidencies of Jefferson, Madison, and Monroe. Kevin R. C. Gutzman. St. Martin's Press 2022. 608 p.
ISBN 9781250135452
Grades: Adult　　　　　　　　　　　　　　　　　　　973.5
1. Jefferson, Thomas, 1743-1826 2. Madison, James, 1751-1836 3. Monroe, James, 1758-1831 4. Presidents 5. Republicanism 6. North American people 7. American people 8. Politics and government 9. United States 10. 19th century 11. Collective biographies 12. Life stories — Politics — Politicians 13. History writing — Presidency — 19th century — United States 14. History writing — Early America — United States

LC 2022035070

Before the consecutive two-term administrations of Presidents Bill Clinton, George W. Bush, and Barack Obama, there had only been one other trio of its type: Thomas Jefferson, James Madison, and James Monroe. Kevin R. C. Gutzman's the Jeffersonians is a complete chronicle of the men, known as the Virginia Dynasty, who served as president from 1801 to 1825 and implemented the foreign policy, domestic, and constitutional agenda of the radical wing of the American Revolution, setting guideposts for later American liberals to follow.

"Political histories are rarely page-turners, but Gutzman, clearly a scholar who has read everything on his subjects, writes lively prose and displays a refreshingly opinionated eye for a huge cast of characters and their often unfortunate actions." —*Kirkus*

Includes bibliographical references and index.

Howe, Daniel Walker
What Hath God Wrought: The Transformation of America, 1815-1848. Daniel Walker Howe. Oxford University Press 2007. xviii, 904 p, 16 p. of plates : Illustration; Map
ISBN 9780195078947
Grades: Adult　　　　　　　　　　　　　　　　　　　973.5
1. Social change 2. International relations 3. Politics and government 4. Economics 5. United States history 6. United States 7. 19th century 8. History writing — Antebellum America — United States

LC 2007012370

American History Book Prize, 2007; Pulitzer Prize for History, 2008; National Book Critics Circle Award for Nonfiction finalist, 2007.

A panoramic history of the United States ranges from the 1815 Battle of New Orleans to the end of the Mexican-American War and chronicles the dramatic changes that took place in America during the period, interweaving political and military events with social, economic, and cultural history to address such issues as women's rights, religion, slavery and abolition, education, literature, and more.

"The author narrates a crucial period in U.S. history a time of territorial growth, religious revival, booming industrialization, a recalibrating of American democracy and the rise of nationalist sentiment. Supported by engaging prose, Howe's achievement will surely be seen as one of the most outstanding syntheses of U.S. history published this decade." —*Publishers Weekly*

Includes bibliographical references (p. [856]-878) and index.

Kilmeade, Brian
★ *Andrew Jackson and the Miracle of New Orleans: The Battle That Shaped America's Destiny.* Brian Kilmeade and Don Yaeger. Sentinel, an imprint of Penguin Random House 2017. 256 p.
ISBN 9780735213234
Grades: Adult　　　　　　　　　　　　　　　　　　　973.5
1. Jackson, Andrew, 1767-1845 2. New Orleans, Battle of, 1815 3. Generals 4. War of 1812 5. Military campaigns 6. Battles 7. United States history 8. New Orleans, Louisiana 9. 19th century 10. History writing — Wars and conflicts — War of 1812

LC 2017027754

A high-energy portrait of the seventh American president focuses on his formative military prowess during the War of 1812 and his pivotal contributions to the capturing of New Orleans from the British.

Includes bibliographical references and index.

Lincoln, Abraham
Speeches and Writings, 1832-1858: Speeches, Letters, and Miscellaneous Writings, the Lincoln-douglas Debates. Abraham Lincoln. Literary Classics of the United States : 1989. xix, 898 p; (The Library of America, 45)
ISBN 9780940450431
Grades: Adult　　　　　　　　　　　　　　　　　　　973.5
1. Lincoln, Abraham, 1809-1865 2. Politics and government 3. Illinois 4. United States 5. 19th century 6. History writing — United States 7. Arts and Entertainment — Writing and Publishing

LC 88082723

The President's writings trace his involvement in Illinois politics, his opposition to slavery, and his political debates with Stephen Douglas.

First printing—P. [iv]; the texts are selected (from the collected works of Abraham Lincoln / edited by Roy Basler, c1953 and its supplement, c1974) and annotated by Don E. Fehrenbacher; Don E. Fehrenbacher wrote the notes and selected the texts for this volume; Includes index; Bibliography: P. 858-876.

May, Gregory
A Madman's Will: John Randolph, Four Hundred Slaves, and the Mirage of Freedom. Gregory May. Liveright Publishing Corporation 2023. 384 p.
ISBN 9781324092216

ESSENTIAL AND RECOMMENDED TITLES
973.56 Administration of Andrew Jackson, 1829-1837

Grades: Adult **973.5**
1. Randolph, John 2. Wills 3. Slaveholders 4. Freedom 5. Slavery 6. Enslaved people 7. African Americans 8. Southern States history 9. Virginia 10. 19th century 11. Antebellum America (1820-1861) 12. Biographies 13. History writing — African American — Enslavement — United States 14. Life stories — People in history 15. Life stories — Politics — Politicians

"Lawyer-turned-historian May (Jefferson's Treasure) offers a fascinating account of Virginia senator John Randolph's posthumous efforts to free nearly 400 enslaved people and provide for their resettlement." —*Publishers Weekly*

Paul, Joel R.
Indivisible: Daniel Webster and the Birth of American Nationalism. Joel Richard Paul. Riverhead Books 2022. 448 p.
ISBN 9780593189047
Grades: Adult **973.5**
1. Webster, Daniel, 1782-1852 2. Politicians 3. Speakers 4. Nationalism 5. National characteristics 6. Group identity 7. Politics and government 8. United States 9. 19th century 10. Life stories — Politics — Politicians 11. History writing — Antebellum America — United States
LC 2022003812

A historian and law professor examines how Daniel Webster rose to national prominence by planting the seeds of American nationalism and arguing that the U.S. Constitution was an agreement made by the states but an expression of the will of all Americans.

"Historian Paul (Without Precedent) examines in this intriguing study the role that 19th-century lawyer, congressman, and orator Daniel Webster played in promoting the idea of American nationalism based on the Constitution....Full of fascinating digressions and astute analysis, this is a rewarding look at one of America's most enduring fault lines." —*Publishers Weekly*

Includes bibliographical references and index.

Taylor, Alan
The Civil War of 1812: American Citizens, British Subjects, Irish Rebels, and Indian Allies. Alan Taylor. Alfred A. Knopf 2010. 640 p.
ISBN 9781400042654
Grades: Adult **973.5**
1. Nationalism 2. Loyalty 3. Border disputes 4. National territory 5. War of 1812 6. Impressment 7. Canadian history 8. United States 9. Ontario 10. Northern boundary of the United States 11. 1810s 12. Early America (1784-1819) 13. 19th century 14. History writing — Wars and conflicts — War of 1812 15. History writing — Early America — United States
LC 2010012783

In a world of double identities, slippery allegiances, and porous borders, the leaders of the American Republic and the British Empire struggled to control their own diverse peoples. Taylor's narrative of an often brutal—sometimes farcical—war reveals much about the tangled origins of the United States and Canada.

"Instead of a traditional narrative of the war from its beginnings in June 1812 to its end in early 1815, [this] book is structured topically. Such a neat and methodical organization helps Taylor bring the confused and chaotic events of the war under control. It also allows him to present an enormous amount of materialon persons, events, and storieswithout overwhelming the reader. And the amount of material is enormous." —*New York Review of Books*

Includes bibliographical references and index.

Trask, Kerry A.
Black Hawk: The Battle for the Heart of America. Kerry A. Trask. Henry Holt 2006. 368 p. : Map
ISBN 9780805077582
Grades: Adult **973.5**
1. Black Hawk, Sauk chief, 1767-1838 2. Sauk (North American people) 3. Fox (Meskwaki) (North American people) 4. Black Hawk War, 1832 5. Indigenous peoples of North America 6. Indigenous peoples of North America — History 7. History writing — Wars and conflicts — American Indigenous Wars 8. History writing — Indigenous peoples — United States
LC 2005050283

An account of the Black Hawk War illuminates the violent history of frontier America from the perspective of the Native Americans forced from their ancestral lands to make way for settlers' insatiable need for additional land.

A John Macrae book; Includes bibliographical references (p. [339]-350) and index.

973.56 Administration of Andrew Jackson, 1829-1837

Inskeep, Steve
Jacksonland: President Andrew Jackson, Cherokee Chief John Ross, and a Great American Land Grab. Steve Inskeep. Penguin Group 2015. 480 p.
ISBN 9781594205569
Grades: Adult **973.56**
1. Jackson, Andrew, 1767-1845 2. Ross, John, 1790-1866 3. Government relations with indigenous peoples 4. Cherokee (North American people) 5. Creek War, 1813-1814 6. Creek (Muskogee) (North American people) 7. Indigenous peoples of North America 8. Indigenous peoples of North America — History 9. Indigenous peoples of North America — Forced removal 10. Race relations 11. Politics and government 12. United States 13. Alabama 14. 19th century 15. Impartial writing 16. History writing — Presidency — 19th century — United States 17. History writing — Indigenous peoples — United States 18. History writing — Wars and conflicts — American Indigenous Wars
LC 2015300789

A renowned journalist and cohost of NPR's Morning Edition presents a thrilling narrative history of President Andrew Jackson and Cherokee Chief John Ross—two heroic yet tragically opposed men whose actions decided the fate of states and Indian nations in America at a moment of transition.

"This superb book is highly recommended for readers interested in Native American studies or Southern history. For more on Catherine Beecher and her movement, see Alisse Portnoy's Their Right to Speak: Women's Activism in the Indian and Slave Debates." —*Library Journal*

973.6 United States — 1845-1861

Achorn, Edward
The Lincoln Miracle: Inside the Republican Convention That Changed History. Edward Achorn. Atlantic Monthly Press 2023. 512 p.
ISBN 9780802160621
Grades: Adult **973.6**
1. Lincoln, Abraham, 1809-1865 2. Presidential election, 1860 3. Politics and government 4. United States 5. 19th century 6. History Writing — Presidency — 19th century — United States 7. Politics and global affairs — Political figures 8. Politics and global affairs — Civil and human rights 9. History writing — Wars and conflicts — American Civil War
LC 2022042883

Bringing to life arguably the most consequential political story in America's history, a Pulitzer Prize finalist for Commentary chronicles Abraham Lincoln's nomination to lead the Republican Party in the 1860 presidential election, showing how a seemingly impossible long shot prevailed to the nation's benefit.

"Lincoln's victory at the 1860 Republican national convention was one of the most improbable in American political history, according to this comprehensive and often riveting account....The result is a dramatic and well-informed study of political sausage-making." —*Publishers Weekly*

Includes bibliographical references and index.

Bordewich, Fergus M.
America's Great Debate: Henry Clay, Stephen A. Douglas, and the Compromise That Preserved the Union. Fergus M. Bordewich. Simon & Schuster 2012. 448 p.
ISBN 9781439124604
Grades: Adult **973.6**
1. Clay, Henry, 1777-1852 2. Douglas, Stephen A. (Stephen Arnold), 1813-1861 3. Slavery 4. Debates and debating 5. United States Civil War, 1861-1865 6. Causes of war 7. Politics and government 8. United States history

9. United States 10. 19th century 11. American Civil War era (1861-1865) 12. History writing — United States

LC 2011029547

Los Angeles Times Book Prize for History, 2012.

Chronicles the heated debates surrounding the 1850s appeals of California and other territories to join the Union as slave or free states, profiling tenacious period balances in the Senate, Henry Clay's attempts at compromise and the explosive boundary crisis between New Mexico and Texas.

Includes bibliographical references and index.

Guelzo, Allen C.

Lincoln and Douglas: The Debates That Defined America. Allen C. Guelzo. Simon & Schuster 2008. 416 p.

ISBN 9780743273206

Grades: 11 12 Adult 973.6

1. Lincoln, Abraham, 1809-1865 2. Douglas, Stephen A. (Stephen Arnold), 1813-1861 3. Politicians 4. Debates and debating 5. Presidential elections 6. Politics and government 7. United States 8. Illinois 9. 19th century 10. History writing — Presidency — 19th century — United States 11. History writing — Antebellum America — United States 12. Adult books for young adults

LC 2007044254

An account of the famous open-air 1858 Senate election debates between Stephen A. Douglas and Abraham Lincoln provides insight into their political rivalry while gauging mid-nineteenth-century issues and how they affected local and presidential campaigns.

"This Lincoln-Douglas rendition will engage every interest in Civil War and Black history." —*Booklist*

Includes bibliographical references and index.

Lincoln, Abraham

Speeches and Writings, 1859-1865: Speeches, Letters, and Miscellaneous Writings, Presidential Messages and Proclamations. Abraham Lincoln. Literary Classics of the United States 1989. xxxiii, 787 p; (The Library of America, 46)

ISBN 9780940450639

Grades: Adult 973.6

1. Politics and government 2. United States 3. 19th century 4. American Civil War era (1861-1865) 5. Speeches, addresses, etc. 6. History writing — Presidency — 19th century — United States

LC 89045349

The President's writings trace his opposition to slavery, share his appraisal of the presidential election, and document his leadership during the Civil War.

The texts are selected (from the collected works of Abraham Lincoln / edited by Roy Basler, c1953 and its supplement, c1974) and annotated by Don E. Fehrenbacher; Don E. Fehrenbacher wrote the notes and selected the texts for this volume—P. [v]; Includes index.

Wineapple, Brenda

Ecstatic Nation: Confidence, Crisis, and the End of Compromise, 1848-1877. Brenda Wineapple. Harper 2013. 544 p.

ISBN 9780061234576

Grades: Adult 973.6

1. Slavery 2. Reconstruction (United States history) 3. United States Civil War, 1861-1865 4. Anti-slavery movements 5. Causes of war 6. Territorial expansion 7. United States history 8. 19th century 9. American Civil War era (1861-1865) 10. History writing — Reconstruction — United States 11. History writing — Wars and conflicts — American Civil War 12. History writing — African American — Enslavement — United States

LC 2012051538

New York Times Notable Book, 2013.

Documents the rise of America during the heart of the 19th century, starting with the end of the Mexican-American War and moving through the complexities of Reconstruction and women's equality, the displacement of the Indians and the transformation of a confederation into one nation.

Includes bibliographical references and index.

973.7 Administration of Abraham Lincoln, 1861-1865

Ash, Stephen V.

Firebrand of Liberty: The Story of Two Black Regiments That Changed the Course of the Civil War. Stephen V. Ash. W.W. Norton & Co. 2008. 320 p.

ISBN 9780393065862

Grades: Adult 973.7

1. African American soldiers 2. Military history 3. United States Civil War, 1861-1865 4. Union soldiers 5. Civil war 6. Military campaigns 7. United States history 8. Florida 9. 19th century 10. American Civil War era (1861-1865) 11. History writing — Wars and conflicts — American Civil War 12. History writing — Military 13. History writing — African American — United States

LC 2008002503

Traces the March 1863 invasion of African-American Union troops in Jacksonville, Florida, in a campaign led by prominent abolitionist Thomas Wentworth Higginson that was mysteriously called off but still influenced Lincoln's full-scale recruitment of free Black soldiers.

"The titular firebrand in this revealing history is not an individual but a curious and ambitious project: the establishment, in March 1863, of a permanent Union outpost in Florida to serve as a haven for fugitive slaves and to help ignite the destruction of Southern slavery from within. In readable prose and relying exclusively on primary sources, historian Ash . tells the little-known but crucial story of how 900 newly freed slaves, under the leadership of white abolitionist officers, captured Jacksonville." —*Publishers Weekly*

Includes bibliographical references and index.

Avlon, John P.

Lincoln and the Fight for Peace. John Avlon. Simon & Schuster 2022. 384 p.

ISBN 9781982108120

Grades: Adult 973.7

1. Lincoln, Abraham, 1809-1865 2. Social advocates 3. Civil rights 4. Human rights 5. Civil Rights Movement 6. Race relations 7. Social advocacy 8. Peace 9. United States history 10. American Civil War era (1861-1865) 11. Society and culture — Social activism and philanthropy 12. History writing — Wars and conflicts — American Civil War

LC 2021042304

This groundbreaking history shows how Abraham Lincoln's plan to secure a just and lasting peace after the Civil War inspired future presidents as well as the world's most famous peacemakers, including Nelson Mandela, Mahatma Gandhi and Martin Luther King, Jr.

Vividly told and expertly researched, this inspiring history draws on Lincoln's example to chart 'A path away from violent polarization and toward reconciliation in defense of democracy.' —*Publishers Weekly*

Includes bibliographical references and index.

Berg, Scott W.

★ *38 Nooses: Lincoln, Little Crow, and the Beginning of the Frontier's End.* Scott W. Berg. Pantheon Books 2012. 336 p.

ISBN 9780307377241

Grades: Adult 973.7

1. Lincoln, Abraham, 1809-1865 2. Little Crow, died 1863 3. Dakota (North American people) 4. Indigenous peoples of North America — Forced removal 5. Battles 6. Executions and executioners 7. Indigenous peoples of North America — Wars 8. United States history 9. 1860s 10. 19th century 11. History writing — Wars and conflicts — American Indigenous Wars 12. History writing — Indigenous peoples — United States

LC 2012002807

Placing a seminal moment in American history in the larger context of the Civil War, this account revisits the little-known Dakota War of 1862, an uprising on the Minnesota frontier which resulted in the forced relocation of the Dakota and the hanging of thirty-eight Dakota warriors.

"A captivating tale of an oft-overlooked, morally ambiguous moment in American history." —*Kirkus*

Includes bibliographical references and index.

ESSENTIAL AND RECOMMENDED TITLES
973.7 Administration of Abraham Lincoln, 1861-1865

Blanton, DeAnne
They Fought Like Demons: Women Soldiers in the American Civil War. DeAnne Blanton and Lauren M. Cook. Louisiana State University Press 2002. xiii, 277 p. : Illustration
ISBN 9780807128060
Grades: Adult   973.7
1. Women soldiers 2. Union soldiers 3. Civil war 4. United States Civil War, 1861-1865 5. Women's participation in wars 6. United States history 7. American Civil War era (1861-1865) 8. History writing — Wars and conflicts — American Civil War 9. History writing — Women's history
LC 2002004441

A study of the hundreds of women who disguised themselves as male soldiers to fight on both sides of the Union and Confederate conflict chronicles the stories of Jennie Hodgers, Frances Clayton, and Loreta Velazquez, among others.

"The authors reconstruct the reasons why women entered the armed forces: Many were simply patriotic, while others followed their husbands or lovers and yet others yearned to break free from the constraints that Victorian society had laid on them as women. Blanton and Cook detail women soldiers in combat, on the march, in camp and in the hospital, where many were discovered after getting sick. Some even wound up in grim prisons kept by both sides, while a few hid pregnancies and were only discovered after giving birth. Solid research by the authors, including a look at the careers of a few women soldiers after the war, makes this a compelling book that belongs in every Civil War library." —*Publishers Weekly*

Includes bibliographical references (p. [215]-230) and index.

Bordewich, Fergus M.
Bound for Canaan: The Underground Railroad and the War for the Soul of America. Fergus M. Bordewich. Amistad 2005. xv, 540 p, 16 p. of plates : Illustration; Map
ISBN 9780060524302
Grades: Adult   973.7
1. Underground railroad 2. Anti-slavery movements 3. Freedom seekers 4. Abolitionists 5. 19th century 6. History writing — African American — Enslavement — United States
LC 2004052082

ALA Notable Book, 2006; Great Lakes Book Awards, General category, 2005.

Offers insight into the Underground Railroad and the role played by westward expansion, the spiritual beliefs that motivated each side of the conflict, and the efforts of Black and white citizens to save tens of thousands of lives.

"The men and women of this remarkable account will remain with readers for a long time to come." —*Publishers Weekly*

Includes bibliographical references (p. [508]-519).

Brewster, Todd
Lincoln's Gamble: The Tumultuous Six Months That Gave America the Emancipation Proclamation and Changed the Course of the Civil War. Todd Brewster. Scribner 2014. 320 p.
ISBN 9781451693867
Grades: Adult   973.7
1. Lincoln, Abraham, 1809-1865 2. History of anti-slavery movements 3. Political leadership 4. United States Civil War, 1861-1865 5. Presidents 6. Freed people 7. Politics and government 8. United States history 9. United States 10. 19th century 11. American Civil War era (1861-1865) 12. History writing — Reconstruction — United States 13. History writing — African American — Enslavement — United States
LC 2013497336

On July 12, 1862, Abraham Lincoln spoke for the first time of his intention to free the slaves. On January 1, 1863, Lincoln signed the Emancipation Proclamation, doing precisely that. In between, however, was perhaps the most tumultuous six months of his presidency, an episode during which the sixteenth president fought bitterly with his generals, disappointed his cabinet, and sank into painful bouts of clinical depression. Most surprising, the man who would be remembered as "The Great Emancipator" did not hold firm to his belief in emancipation. He agonized over the decision and was wracked by private doubts almost to the moment when he inked the decree that would change a nation.

"Featuring vignettes of figures who met Lincoln during his formulation of the proclamation, Brewsters work illuminates Lincolns lines of thought during this turning point in American history." —*Booklist*

Burlingame, Michael
The Black Man's President: Abraham Lincoln, African Americans, and the Pursuit of Racial Equality. Michael Burlingame. Pegasus Books 2021. 452 p.
ISBN 9781643138138
Grades: Adult   973.7
1. Lincoln, Abraham, 1809-1865 2. Anti-slavery movements 3. Abolitionists 4. Slavery 5. Freed people 6. United States history 7. 19th century 8. History writing — Presidency — 19th century — United States 9. History writing — African American — Enslavement — United States 10. History writing — Wars and conflicts — American Civil War

Frederick Douglass called the martyred president "emphatically the Black man's president" as well as "the first who rose above the prejudice of his times and country." This narrative history of Lincoln's personal interchange with Black people over the course his career reveals a side of the sixteenth president that, until now, has not been fully explored or understood.

"Historian Burlingame (Abraham Lincoln: A Life) defends Abraham Lincoln against charges of racism in this provocative and extensively documented account.... This is a resolute and well-researched vindication of Lincoln's progressive credentials." —*Publishers Weekly*

Colaiaco, James A.
Frederick Douglass and the Fourth of July. James A. Colaiaco. Palgrave Macmillan 2006. 247 p.
ISBN 9781403970336
Grades: 11 12 Adult   973.7
1. Douglass, Frederick, 1818-1895 2. African American abolitionists 3. Fourth of July 4. Constitutional history 5. Anti-slavery movements 6. African American history 7. Civil rights 8. United States history 9. 19th century 10. History writing — Antebellum America — United States 11. History writing — African American — United States
LC 2005051520

An account of America's pre-Civil War conflict between its ideals and practices evaluates Douglass's famous Fourth of July speech and considers his lifelong dedication to refuting misconceptions about the Constitution's alleged support of slavery and the rights granted to Black Americans by the phrase, "all men are created equal."

"Colaiaco's careful study recaptures Douglass' reputation as one of America's greatest orators." —*Booklist*

Includes bibliographical references (p. [229]-238) and index.

Davis, Burke
Sherman's March. Burke Davis. Vintage Books 1988. VIII, 335 p. : Map
ISBN 9780394757636
Grades: 11 12 Adult   973.7
1. Sherman, William Tecumseh, 1820-1891 2. Sherman's March to the Sea 3. Sherman's March through the Carolinas 4. History writing — Wars and conflicts — American Civil War
LC 87045927

Weaving together hundreds of eyewitness accounts, a noted historian recreates Sherman's devastating sweep through Georgia and the Carolinas in 1864 and 1865 and narrates the experiences of soldiers and civilians.

"The author reconstructs Sherman's infamous, but vastly consequential march through Georgia and the Carolinas, which sent the Confederacy into its death throes. Basing his narrative on eyewitness accounts, Davis brings the event down to a personal level." —*Booklist*

Includes index; Bibliography: P. [303]-317; Originally published: New York : Random House, 1980.

1135

PUBLIC LIBRARY CORE COLLECTION: NONFICTION
Twentieth Edition

Delbanco, Andrew
The War Before the War: Fugitive Slaves and the Struggle for America's Soul from the Revolution to the Civil War. Andrew Delbanco. Penguin Press 2018. 384 p.
ISBN 9781594204050
Grades: Adult   973.7
1. Enslaved people 2. Freedom seekers 3. Civil war 4. Constitutional history 5. Dred Scott Case 6. Abolitionists 7. Racism in law 8. Causes of war 9. United States Civil War, 1861-1865 10. Slavery 11. Legislation 12. United States history 13. 19th century 14. American Civil War era (1861-1865) 15. History writing — African American — Enslavement — United States 16. History writing — Antebellum America — United States 17. History writing — Wars and conflicts — American Civil War
LC 2018419007
Mark Lynton History Prize, 2019; New York Times Notable Book, 2019.
Argues that issues surrounding fugitive slaves is what truly drove the North and South to Civil War and explains the history behind how this happened.
"This well-documented and valuable work makes clear how slavery shaped the early American experience with effects that reverberate today." —*Publishers Weekly*

Egerton, Douglas R.
Thunder at the Gates: The Black Civil War Regiments That Redeemed America. Douglas R. Egerton. Basic Books 2016. 448 p.
ISBN 9780465096640
Grades: Adult   973.7
1. African American soldiers 2. African American history 3. Civil war 4. United States Civil War, 1861-1865 5. Military campaigns 6. United States history 7. Massachusetts 8. American Civil War era (1861-1865) 9. 1860s 10. 19th century 11. History writing — Wars and conflicts — American Civil War
LC 2016032057
Illuminates the public responses, debates and dangers that shaped the entry of Black regiments into the Civil War after the 1863 Emancipation Proclamation, chronicling the formation and battlefield triumphs of key regiments while discussing their role in shaping public opinion and promoting full citizenship for Blacks.
Includes bibliographical references and index.

Faust, Drew Gilpin
Mothers of Invention: Women of the Slaveholding South in the American Civil War. Drew Gilpin Faust. University of North Carolina Press 1996. xvi, 326 p. : Illustration (The Fred W. Morrison series in Southern studies)
ISBN 9780807822555
Grades: 11 12 Adult   973.7
1. Women's history 2. Women's participation in wars 3. United States history 4. American Civil War era (1861-1865) 5. History writing — Antebellum America — United States 6. Society and culture — Gender — Women
LC 95008896
Details how well-bred Confederate women tried to retain their social standing.
"Faust's provocative analysis of a complex subject merits a place in all collections of U.S. history." —*Publishers Weekly*
Includes bibliographical references (p. 259-312) and index.

This Republic of Suffering: Death and the American Civil War. Drew Gilpin Faust. Alfred A. Knopf 2008. 346 p. : Illustration
ISBN 9780375404047
Grades: 11 12 Adult   973.7
1. Death 2. Burial 3. Civil war 4. Loss 5. Grief 6. United States Civil War, 1861-1865 7. United States history 8. American Civil War era (1861-1865) 9. Page to screen 10. History writing — Wars and conflicts — American Civil War 11. Adult books for young adults
LC 2007014658
ALA Notable Book, 2009; American History Book Prize, 2008; Library Journal Best Books, 2008; New York Times Notable Book, 2008; National Book Award for Nonfiction finalist, 2008; National Book Critics Circle Award for Nonfiction finalist, 2008; Pulitzer Prize for History finalist, 2009.
Assesses the impact of the enormous carnage of the Civil War on every aspect of American life from a material, political, intellectual, cultural, social, and spiritual perspective.
"The result is an insightful, often moving portrait of a people torn by grief." —*Publishers Weekly*
The TV movie Death and the Civil War is based on this book; Includes bibliographical references (p. [273]-322) and index.

Feldman, Noah
The Broken Constitution: Lincoln, Slavery, and the Refounding of America. Noah Feldman. Farrar, Straus and Giroux 2021. 448 p.
ISBN 9780374116644
Grades: Adult   973.7
1. Lincoln, Abraham, 1809-1865 2. Slavery 3. Federal government 4. Freed people 5. Legislation 6. Politics and government 7. United States 8. 19th century 9. 18th century 10. History writing — Presidency — 19th century — United States 11. History writing — African American — Enslavement — United States 12. History writing — Antebellum America — United States
LC 2021025293
In this gripping narrative of legal dilemmas and moral courage, a celebrated legal scholar, in this groundbreaking study, tells the story of how Lincoln broke the Constitution in order to remake it.
Harvard law professor Feldman (The Arab Winter) analyzes in this probing study how Abraham Lincoln, in justifying the Civil War and signing the Emancipation Proclamation, transformed the Constitution from 'A compromise that preserved slavery' to a 'Moral compact—a higher law that embodies an ideal form of government.' —*Publishers Weekly*
Includes bibliographical references and index.

Fields-Black, Edda L.
Combee: Harriet Tubman, the Combahee River Raid, and Black Freedom During the Civil War. Edda L. Fields-Black. Oxford University Press 2024. 368 p.
ISBN 9780197552797
Grades: Adult   973.7
1. Tubman, Harriet, 1820?-1913 2. Enslaved people 3. Spies 4. Freed people 5. United States Civil War, 1861-1865 6. Raids (Military science) 7. Civil war 8. Union soldiers 9. African American women 10. Women and war 11. South Carolina 12. United States 13. American Civil War era (1861-1865) 14. 19th century 15. History Writing — African American — United States 16. History Writing — Regional history — United States 17. History writing — Wars and conflicts — American Civil War
LC 2023032481
This book offers the first full account of Harriet Tubman's Civil War service and the Combahee River Raid. It details how Tubman commanded a ring of spies, scouts, and pilots and participated in military expeditions behind Confederate lines. It also recounts the story of enslaved families living in bondage and fighting for their freedom, using their own distinct and individual voices. The book uses more than 175 US Civil War pension files of the regiments of Second South Carolina Volunteers, including Tubman's. It is based on original documentation and written by a descendent of the enslaved men and women who fought in it, and in the process liberated themselves.
"Sprawling and kaleidoscopic, this is a marvel of deep research." —*Publishers Weekly*
Includes bibliographical references and index.

Foner, Eric
★ *Gateway to Freedom: The Hidden History of the Underground Railroad.* Eric Foner. W. W. Norton & Co. 2015. 288 p.
ISBN 9780393244076
Grades: Adult   973.7
1. Underground Railroad 2. Slavery 3. Freedom seekers 4. Anti-slavery movements 5. Abolitionists 6. African American history 7. United States history 8. 19th century 9. History writing — African American — Enslavement — United States

ESSENTIAL AND RECOMMENDED TITLES
973.7 Administration of Abraham Lincoln, 1861-1865

LC 2014036993

American History Book Prize, 2015.

Traces the workings of the underground railroad in slave-dependent New York by three lesser-known heroes who coordinated with Black dockworkers and counterparts in other states to help thousands of fugitive slaves between 1830 and 1860.

"The author eschews the common approach of documenting the phenomenon from the South, instead centering his monograph on New York City. Through individuals such as abolitionist Sydney Howard Gay and minister Charles Ray, he demonstrates that ferrying escaped slaves from the city's waterfront to other locales throughout the North was fraught with extreme danger."
—*Library Journal*

Foote, Shelby
The Civil War: A Narrative. by Shelby Foote. Vintage Books 1986. 3 v. : Map; Color
ISBN 9780394746234
Grades: Adult   973.7
1. Civil war 2. United States Civil War, 1861-1865 3. United States history 4. 1860s 5. American Civil War era (1861-1865) 6. History writing — Wars and conflicts — American Civil War

LC 86040135

Follows the course of the war from 1862 to 1864, discusses the strategies of both sides in major battles, and assesses the performance of the Union generals.
Includes bibliographies and indexes.

Stars in Their Courses: The Gettysburg Campaign, June-july 1863. Shelby Foote. Modern Library 1994. VIII, 290 p. : Map
ISBN 9780679601128
Grades: Adult   973.7
1. Gettysburg Campaign, 1863 2. History writing — Antebellum America — United States

LC 94196068

Recreates the Battle of Gettysburg from both the Confederate and Union perspectives.
Series statement from jacket; Originally published by Random House, Inc, as volume II of the Civil War, a narrative : Fredericksburg to Meridian—T.P. verso.

Ford, Lacy K.
Deliver Us from Evil: The Slavery Question in the Old South, 1787-1840. Lacy K. Ford. Oxford University Press 2009. 688 p.
ISBN 9780195118094
Grades: Adult   973.7
1. Slavery 2. European Americans 3. Slaveholders 4. Southern States history 5. 18th century 6. 19th century 7. History writing — Antebellum America — United States 8. History writing — African American — Enslavement — United States

LC 2008047533

Illuminates the white South's efforts to justify slavery, focusing on the period from the drafting of the federal constitution in 1787 through the age of Jackson. Draws heavily on primary sources, including newspapers, government documents, legislative records, pamphlets, and speeches.

"This book provides an intricate, textured argument about the intellectual, social, and political interests shaping the slavery question, as well as a reminder that Southern white commitment to a hardened proslavery position was not preordained or one-dimensional. Essential for all students of this subject." —*Library Journal*
Includes bibliographical references and index.

Freeman, Joanne B.
The Field of Blood: Violence in Congress and the Road to Civil War. Joanne B. Freeman. Farrar, Straus & Giroux 2018. 384 p.
ISBN 9780374154776
Grades: Adult   973.7
1. Legislators 2. Politicians 3. Violence 4. Hand-to-hand fighting 5. Dueling 6. Debates and debating 7. Democracy 8. Disagreement 9. Feuds 10. Slavery 11. Anti-slavery movements 12. Polarization (Social sciences) 13. Political journalism 14. Politics and government 15. United States 16. History writing — Politicians — United States 17. History writing — Antebellum America — United States

LC 2018010176

New York Times Notable Book, 2018.

Documents the lesser-known violence that marked legislative sessions in the decades before the American Civil War, detailing acts of physical fighting, duels and mortal threats over disagreements about key issues, particularly slavery. By the award-winning author of Affairs of Honor. Bibliography. Appendix. Index.

Goodheart, Adam
1861: The Civil War Awakening. Adam Goodheart. Alfred A. Knopf 2011. 496 p. : Illustration
ISBN 9781400040155
Grades: 11 12 Adult   973.7
1. War 2. Military history 3. Slavery 4. Civil war 5. United States Civil War, 1861-1865 6. Intellectual life 7. Causes of war 8. Politics and government 9. United States history 10. United States 11. 1860s 12. 19th century 13. American Civil War era (1861-1865) 14. History writing — Wars and conflicts — American Civil War

LC 2010051326

New York Times Notable Book, 2011.

Chronicles the revolution of ideas that preceded—and led to—the start of the Civil War, looking at a diverse cast of characters and the actions of citizens throughout the country in their efforts to move beyond compromise and end slavery.

"Goodheart leads us on a journey through the frenzied, frightening months between Abraham Lincoln's election to the presidency in 1860 followed with breakneck speed by the secession of the Confederate States and the outbreak of war and July 4, 1861, when President Lincoln delivered his first message to Congress, laying out the case not only for the necessity of war, but for a more democratic vision of the United States. The election of Lincoln and the secession crisis is, of course, familiar terrain. But Goodheart's version is at once more panoramic and more intimate than most standard accounts, and more inspiring. This is fundamentally a history of hearts and minds, rather than of legislative bills and battles." —*New York Times Book Review*
Includes index.

Grinspan, Jon
Wide Awake: The Forgotten Force That Elected Lincoln and Spurred the Civil War. Jon Grinspan. Bloomsbury 2024. 368 p.
ISBN 9781639730643
Grades: Adult   973.7
1. Abolitionists 2. Anti-slavery movements 3. Influence (Psychology) 4. Presidential election, 1860 5. Presidents 6. Slavery 7. Militarism 8. Protests, demonstrations, vigils, etc. 9. Social conflict 10. United States Civil War, 1861-1865 11. United States history 12. United States 13. Antebellum America (1820-1861) 14. American Civil War era (1861-1865) 15. History writing — Antebellum America — United States 16. History writing — Wars and conflicts — American Civil War

At the start of the 1860 presidential campaign, a handful of fired-up young Northerners appeared as bodyguards to defend anti-slavery stump speakers from frequent attacks. The group called themselves the Wide Awakes. Soon, hundreds of thousands of young White and Black men, and a number of women, were organizing boisterous, uniformed, torch-bearing brigades of their own. To some, it looked like a paramilitary force training to invade the South. Smithsonian historian Jon Grinspan examines how exactly our nation crossed the threshold from a political campaign into a war.

"[Grinspan] shines attention on the 1860s anti-enslavement movement that played a key role in starting the U.S. Civil War, illuminating how that political campaign, which grew to include hundreds of thousands, pushed the nation from rhetoric to war." —*Library Journal*

Groom, Winston
Shiloh, 1862: The First Great and Terrible Battle of the Civil War. Winston Groom. Random House Inc 2012. 512 p.
ISBN 9781426208744

Grades: Adult 973.7
1. Shiloh, Battle of, 1862 2. Battles 3. Civil war 4. United States Civil War, 1861-1865 5. Military campaigns 6. United States history 7. 1860s 8. American Civil War era (1861-1865) 9. History writing — Wars and conflicts — American Civil War 10. History writing — Wars and conflicts — Battles
LC 2012372339

Offers a detailed account of the Battle of Shiloh, a turning point when both the Union and the Confederacy realized the grand scale of the conflict, the large number of casualties to be expected, and that the war would not end quickly.

Guelzo, Allen C.
Gettysburg: The Last Invasion. by Allen C. Guelzo. Alfred A. Knopf 2013. 688 p.
ISBN 9780307594082
Grades: Adult 973.7
1. Gettysburg, Battle of, 1863 2. Civil war 3. Battle history 4. United States Civil War, 1861-1865 5. United States history 6. American Civil War era (1861-1865) 7. History writing — Wars and conflicts — American Civil War
LC 2012047013

The award-winning author of Lincoln's Emancipation Proclamation presents a vivid 150th anniversary account of the legendary Civil War battle from the perspectives of ordinary soldiers to offer insight into 19th-century military practices, the pivotal influence of politics on the battle's course and the unique characters of artillery units.

This is a Borzoi book—Title page verso; Includes bibliographical references and index.

Gwynne, S. C.
Hymns of the Republic: The Story of the Final Year of the American Civil War. S.C. Gwynne. Scribner 2019. 352 p.
ISBN 9781501116223
Grades: Adult 973.7
1. Grant, Ulysses S, 1822-1885 2. Lee, Robert E. (Robert Edward), 1807-1870 3. Lincoln, Abraham, 1809-1865 4. Barton, Clara, 1821-1912 5. Military strategy 6. United States Civil War, 1861-1865 7. Civil war 8. United States history 9. American Civil War era (1861-1865) 10. History writing — Wars and conflicts — American Civil War
LC 2019017038

An epic account of the dramatic conclusion of the American Civil War.

Holzer, Harold
Brought Forth on This Continent: Abraham Lincoln and American Immigration. Harold Holzer. E.P. Dutton 2024. 448 p.
ISBN 9780451489012
Grades: Adult 973.7
1. Lincoln, Abraham, 1809-1865 2. Presidents 3. Immigration and emigration 4. Immigrants 5. Public opinion 6. Prejudice 7. Demography 8. United States Civil War, 1861-1865 9. Social change 10. Politics and government 11. United States history 12. United States 13. 19th century 14. Biographies 15. Life stories — Politics — Politicians 16. History writing — Immigration — United States 17. History writing — Presidency — 19th century — United States

An acclaimed Lincoln historian presents a groundbreaking examination of how immigration in the decades before the civil led to enormous changes in the political landscape, destroyed the Whig party and exacerbated tensions in the country.

"An outstanding and important book on Lincoln and immigration. A must for readers of American history and immigration studies." —*Library Journal*

Horwitz, Tony
Confederates in the Attic: Dispatches from the Unfinished Civil War. Tony Horwitz. Pantheon Books 1998. IX, 406 p. : Map
ISBN 9780679439783
Grades: 11 12 Adult 973.7
1. Horwitz, Tony, 1958- 2. Historical reenactments 3. Civil war 4. United States Civil War, 1861-1865 5. Military campaigns 6. United States history 7. Confederate States of America 8. American Civil War era (1861-1865) 9. History writing — Wars and conflicts — American Civil War 10. Adult books for young adults
LC 97026759

New York Times Notable Book, 1998.

A journalist leads readers on a journey through the Old South, tangling with the forces of white rage, rebel grit, and regional pride in places where the Civil War is more than a memory.

"This is the work of a skilled journalist looking at how and why the War Between the States continues to live in so many issues still with us." —*Library Journal*

Includes index.

★ *Midnight Rising: John Brown and the Raid That Sparked the Civil War.* Tony Horwitz. Henry Holt and Co. 2011. 384 p.
ISBN 9780805091533
Grades: 11 12 Adult 973.7
1. Brown, John, 1800-1859 2. Abolitionists 3. Anti-slavery movements 4. Militants 5. Harpers Ferry, Battle of, Harpers Ferry, W. Va, 1862 6. United States history 7. West Virginia 8. 19th century 9. 1860s 10. Biographies 11. History writing — Antebellum America — United States 12. History writing — African American — Enslavement — United States 13. Life stories — Politics — Activists and reformers 14. Book club best bets
LC 2011015659

Library Journal Best Books, 2011; New York Times Notable Book, 2011.

Chronicles the 1859 raid by radical abolitionist John Brown on Harpers Ferry, revealing how his acts, deemed terrorism by the South, prompted a counterattack by Robert E. Lee and galvanized Northern supporters during Lincoln's election campaign.

"The author presents a narrative of Brown and the raid on Harpers Ferry that in many ways set the stage for Southern secession and civil war. . . . Horwitz's Brown did not die in vain. By recalling the drama that fired the imagination and fears of Brown's time, Midnight Rising calls readers to account for complacency about social injustices today. This is a book for our time." —*Library Journal*

Includes bibliographical references and index.

Keegan, John
The American Civil War: A Military History. by John Keegan. Alfred A. Knopf 2009. 416 p.
ISBN 9780307263438
Grades: Adult 973.7
1. Military history 2. Military strategy 3. Civil war 4. War 5. United States Civil War, 1861-1865 6. Military campaigns 7. Geography 8. United States history 9. United States 10. 1860s 11. 19th century 12. American Civil War era (1861-1865) 13. History writing — Wars and conflicts — American Civil War
LC 2009019469

Booklist Editors' Choice, 2009.

Analyzes many puzzling aspects of the Civil War, from its mismatched sides to the absence of decisive outcomes for dozens of skirmishes, and offers insight into the war's psychology, ideology, and economics while discussing the pivotal roles of leadership and geography.

"The author provides the single best one-volume assessment of the military character and conduct of America's ordeal by fire." —*Library Journal*

Includes bibliographical references and index.

Lance, Rachel
In the Waves: My Quest to Solve the Mystery of a Civil War Submarine. Rachel Lance. Dutton 2020. 400 pages
ISBN 9781524744151
Grades: Adult 973.7
1. Lance, Rachel 2. Submarines 3. Shipwrecks 4. Excavations (Archaeology) 5. Underwater archaeology 6. United States Civil War, 1861-1865 7. Women scientists 8. Naval operations 9. Antiquities 10. United States history 11. Charleston, South Carolina 12. 19th century 13. American Civil War era (1861-1865) 14. Autobiographies and memoirs 15. History writing — Wars and conflicts — American Civil War 16. History writing — Military — Naval history 17. Life stories — Science, technology, and medicine — Scientists and inventors

ESSENTIAL AND RECOMMENDED TITLES
973.7 Administration of Abraham Lincoln, 1861-1865

LC 2019021230

An inventive woman scientist recounts the 1864 sinking of the Confederate submarine, H.L. Hunley, recounting her efforts to uncover what actually happened when the sub was discovered 131 years later with its hull and victims still intact.

"Lance delivers a lively, if often technical, description of the many experiments, models, calculations, and explosions that persuaded her and her doctoral committee that this is what happened to the Hunley. An entertaining account of research that solved a historical mystery." —*Kirkus*

Includes bibliographical references and index.

Larson, Erik
★ *The Demon of Unrest: A Saga of Hubris, Heartbreak, and Heroism at the Dawn of the Civil War.* Erik Larson. Crown Publishing 2024. 608 p.
ISBN 9780385348744
Grades: Adult   973.7

1. Lincoln, Abraham, 1809-1865 2. United States Civil War, 1861-1865 3. Secession 4. United States history 5. Presidents 6. United States 7. American Civil War era (1861-1865) 8. History writing — Wars and conflicts — American Civil War 9. Life stories — Politics — Politicians

Drawing on diaries, secret communiques, slave ledgers and plantation ledgers, the #1 New York Times best-selling author of the Splendid and the Vile offers a gripping account of the months between Lincoln's election and the start of the Civil War, which tore a deeply divided nation in two.

"Compelling details, fresh perspectives, and lively writing make this a standout view of the antebellum and Civil War eras." —*Booklist*

Levine, Bruce C.
The Fall of the House of Dixie: How the Civil War Remade the American South. Bruce Levine. Random House 2013. 464 p.
ISBN 9781400067039
Grades: Adult   973.7

1. Elite (Social sciences) 2. Slavery 3. War and society 4. Social classes 5. Social change 6. Plantation life 7. United States Civil War, 1861-1865 8. Civil war 9. Change 10. United States history 11. United States 12. Confederate States of America 13. 19th century 14. American Civil War era (1861-1865) 15. History writing — Reconstruction — United States

LC 2011048310

Told in the words of the people who lived it, the Fall of the House of Dixie illuminates the radical transformation of the American South during and after the Civil War. Award-winning author Bruce Levine employs a wealth of primary sources—diaries, letters, newspaper articles, government documents, and more—to vividly bring to life the perspectives of slaves, shopkeepers, soldiers, and others in a stellar history of the South's social, political and economic deconstruction and rebuilding.

Lowenstein, Roger
Ways and Means: Lincoln and His Cabinet and the Financing of the Civil War. Roger Lowenstein. Penguin Press 2022. 432 p.
ISBN 9780735223554
Grades: Adult   973.7

1. Lincoln, Abraham, 1809-1865 2. United States Civil War, 1861-1865 3. Cost of war 4. Income tax 5. Paper money 6. Monetary policy 7. Presidents 8. Politics and government 9. Economics 10. United States history 11. United States 12. 19th century 13. American Civil War era (1861-1865) 14. History writing — Presidency — 19th century — United States 15. History writing — Wars and conflicts — American Civil War 16. Business and economics — Economics — History

LC 2021029398

In Ways and Means, journalist Roger Lowenstein reveals the unlikely story of how Abraham Lincoln used the urgency of financing the Civil War to transform a union of states into one united nation. Through a financial lens, he explores how this second American revolution, led by Lincoln, his cabinet, and his congress, changed the direction of the country.

"Journalist Lowenstein (The End of Wall Street) argues in this masterful history that the financing of the Civil War was as crucial to the shaping of American history as the Emancipation Proclamation and the defeat of the Confederacy.... Full of fascinating historical tidbits and clear explanations of complex financial and political matters, this is a must-read for American history buffs." —*Publishers Weekly*

Includes bibliographical references and index.

Manning, Chandra
Troubled Refuge: Struggling for Freedom in the Civil War. Chandra Manning. Alfred A. Knopf 2016. 416 p.
ISBN 9780307271204
Grades: Adult   973.7

1. Freed people 2. African American civil rights 3. United States Civil War, 1861-1865 4. African American soldiers 5. United States history 6. American Civil War era (1861-1865) 7. 1860s 8. History writing — Wars and conflicts — American Civil War

LC 2015039724

In a riveting examination of the escaped-slave refugee camps at the end of the Civil War, the author, drawing on first-hand accounts, reveals what these camps were really like and how former slaves and Union soldiers warily united there, shaping the course of emancipation and Black citizenship.

"An essential contribution to the history of the Civil War and its aftermath." —*Booklist*

Includes bibliographical references.

Masur, Louis P.
The Civil War: A Concise History. Louis P. Masur. Oxford University Press 2011. xiv, 118 p. : Illustration; Map
ISBN 9780199740482
Grades: 11 12 Adult   973.7

1. United States history 2. American Civil War era (1861-1865) 3. History writing — Wars and conflicts — American Civil War

LC 2010019460

A year-by-year chronicle of the Civil War, highlighting major political, social, and military events, and looking at the causes and consequences of the conflict.

"The author provides a concise but compelling narrative of the Civil War era, packing in the critical information to track the trajectory of secession, war, emancipation, and Reconstruction. He focuses on the political and the military, with Lincoln, Jefferson Davis, and the generals especially getting their due." —*Library Journal*

Includes bibliographical references (p. [107]-109) and index.

McPherson, James M.
Battle Cry of Freedom: The Civil War Era. James M. McPherson. Oxford University Press 1988. xix, 904 p, 16 p. of plates : Illustration
ISBN 9780195038637
Grades: 11 12 Adult   973.7

1. Civil war 2. Military history 3. United States Civil War, 1861-1865 4. Causes of war 5. Military campaigns 6. United States history 7. 1860s 8. American Civil War era (1861-1865) 9. History writing — Wars and conflicts — American Civil War

LC 87011045

Pulitzer Prize for History, 1989; National Book Critics Circle Award for Nonfiction finalist, 1988.

Abraham Lincoln wondered whether "in a free government the minority have the right to break up the government." Jefferson Davis felt "forced to take up arms" to guarantee his states' rights. McPherson merges the words of these men and other political luminaries, housewives, and soldiers from both armies with his own concise analysis of the war to create a story as compelling as any novel.

"This volume is comprehensive yet succinct, scholarly without being pedantic, eloquent but unrhetorical. It is compellingly readable." —*New York Times Book Review*

Includes index; Bibliography: P. 865-882.

Drawn with the Sword: Reflections on the American Civil War. James M. McPherson. Oxford University Press 1996. xiv, 258 p.
ISBN 9780195096798

PUBLIC LIBRARY CORE COLLECTION: NONFICTION
Twentieth Edition

Grades: 11 12 Adult **973.7**
1. Lincoln, Abraham, 1809-1865 2. Civil war 3. Military history 4. United States Civil War, 1861-1865 5. United States history 6. 1860s 7. American Civil War era (1861-1865) 8. Essays 9. History writing — Wars and conflicts — American Civil War

LC 95038107

Shares a collection of thought-provoking essays on the Civil War, discussing the leaders of the era, the international impact of the war, slavery, the problems with the modern study of history, and other topics.

"These pieces provide a lively reminder that the best scholarship is also often a pleasure to read." —*New York Times Book Review*

For Cause and Comrades: Why Men Fought in the Civil War. James M. McPherson. Oxford University Press 1997. xviii, 237 p.
ISBN 9780195090239
Grades: 11 12 Adult **973.7**
1. Combat 2. Military history 3. United States Civil War, 1861-1865 4. Civil war 5. Confederate soldiers 6. Union soldiers 7. United States history 8. 1860s 9. 19th century 10. American Civil War era (1861-1865) 11. History writing — Wars and conflicts — American Civil War 12. Adult books for young adults

LC 96024760

Drawing on thousands of letters and diaries by soldiers on both sides, the Pulitzer Prize-winning author shows how the soldiers remained firmly committed to their ideals throughout the Civil War.

"Volumes have been written on the causes of the Civil War, but less has been written on what caused soldiers to risk their lives on the battlefield. McPherson . . . fills the gap. After studying thousands of letters and diaries, he discusses what really led soldiers to enlist, what kept them in the army, and what led them to the front lines." —*Library Journal*

Includes bibliographical references (p. 189-232) and index.

Hallowed Ground: A Walk at Gettysburg. James M. McPherson. Crown Journeys 2003. 141 p. : Map
ISBN 9780609610237
Grades: Adult **973.7**
1. Gettysburg, Battle of, 1863 2. Walking 3. Civil war 4. Battles 5. Military history 6. United States Civil War, 1861-1865 7. Military campaigns 8. United States history 9. American Civil War era (1861-1865) 10. History writing — Wars and conflicts — American Civil War 11. History writing — Wars and conflicts — Battles 12. Travel Writing — United States 13. Adult books for young adults

LC 2002035154

The author takes a tour around one of America's most hallowed battlefields, describing the events and personalities of the bloody three-day 1863 conflict at Gettysburg and shedding light on the significance of the battle.

"If it were only a pointer to the physical ground and commemorative markers, this guide would be ordinary, but McPherson so articulately injects reminders—as of a free Black farmer who fled the approaching battle lest Confederates enslave him—of what the Civil War was about as to display the crystalline style that has made him one of our finest Civil War historians." —*Booklist*

★ *Tried by War: Abraham Lincoln as Commander in Chief.* James M. McPherson. Penguin Press 2008. 384 p.
ISBN 9781594201912
Grades: 11 12 Adult **973.7**
1. Lincoln, Abraham, 1809-1865 2. Executive power 3. Political leadership 4. Civil war 5. United States Civil War, 1861-1865 6. Presidents 7. Politics and government 8. United States history 9. United States 10. 19th century 11. American Civil War era (1861-1865) 12. Biographies 13. History writing — Presidency — 19th century — United States 14. History writing — Wars and conflicts — American Civil War 15. Adult books for young adults

LC 2008025229

Evaluates Lincoln's talents as a commander in chief in spite of limited military experience, tracing the ways in which he worked with, or against, his senior commanders to defeat the Confederacy and reshape the presidential role.

Includes bibliographical references and index.

Meyer, Eugene L.
Five for Freedom: The African American Soldiers in John Brown's Army. Eugene L. Meyer. Lawrence Hill Books 2018. 304 p.
ISBN 9781613735718
Grades: Adult **973.7**
1. Anderson, Osborne P. (Osborne Perry), 1830-1872 2. Copeland, John A. (John Anthony), 1834-1859 3. Green, Shields, approximately 1836-1859 4. Leary, Lewis Sheridan, 1835-1859 5. Newby, Dangerfield, 1815-1859 6. Brown, John, 1800-1859 7. African American abolitionists 8. History of anti-slavery movements 9. Race relations 10. Abolitionists 11. Militants 12. Slavery 13. Harpers Ferry, Battle of, Harpers Ferry, W. Va, 1862 14. United States history 15. West Virginia 16. 19th century 17. 1860s 18. History writing — Antebellum America — United States 19. History writing — African American — Enslavement — United States

LC 2017045333

On October 16, 1859, John Brown and his integrated band of raiders descended on Harpers Ferry attempting to incite a slave insurrection; they seized the federal arsenal, took hostages, and retreated to a fire engine house where they barricaded themselves until soldiers forced their way in two days later. One of the few survivors later published an insider account of the event that was a catalyst to the catastrophic American Civil War that followed.

Includes bibliographical references and index.

Miller, Donald L.
Vicksburg: Grant's Campaign That Broke the Confederacy. Donald L. Miller. Simon & Schuster 2019. 640 p.
ISBN 9781451641370
Grades: Adult **973.7**
1. Grant, Ulysses S, 1822-1885 2. Strategy 3. Civil war 4. Gettysburg, Battle of, 1863 5. United States Civil War, 1861-1865 6. Sieges 7. United States history 8. Vicksburg, Mississippi 9. United States 10. Mississippi 11. American Civil War era (1861-1865) 12. History writing — Wars and conflicts — American Civil War 13. History writing — Wars and conflicts — Battles

LC 2019010269

The author of Masters of the Air presents an account of the decisive Civil War military campaign that split the Confederacy, freed tens of thousands of slaves and rendered Grant the war's most celebrated general.

Includes bibliographical references and index.

O'Donnell, Patrick K.
The Unvanquished: The Untold Story of Lincoln's Special Forces, the Manhunt for Mosby's Rangers, and the Shadow War That Forged America's Special Operations. Patrick K. O'Donnell. Atlantic Monthly Press 2024. 448 p.
ISBN 9780802162861
Grades: Adult **973.7**
1. Guerrillas 2. Special operations (Military science) 3. United States Civil War, 1861-1865 4. Secret service 5. Commando operations 6. United States history 7. United States 8. American Civil War era (1861-1865) 9. History writing — Wars and conflicts — Civil Wars 10. History writing — Military — Special Forces

LC 2023056573

An expert on special operations tells the epic story of Lincoln's special forces, the Jessie Scouts, in its entirety for the first time, taking readers into the action as the Jessie Scouts led the Union Army to a final victory, in this full chronicle of the shadow war between North and South.

"A revealing history of the largely unknown role of irregular forces and undercover agents in the Civil War." —*Kirkus*

Includes bibliographical references and index.

Oakes, James
Freedom National: The Destruction of Slavery in the United States, 1861-1865. James Oakes. W W Norton & CO Inc 2012. 384 p.
ISBN 9780393065312
Grades: Adult **973.7**
1. Slavery 2. Freedom 3. Abolitionists 4. Civil war 5. United States Civil War, 1861-1865 6. United States history 7. American Civil War era (1861-1865)

ESSENTIAL AND RECOMMENDED TITLES
973.7 Administration of Abraham Lincoln, 1861-1865

8. History writing — Wars and conflicts — American Civil War 9. History writing — African American — Enslavement — United States
LC 2012035601

Traces the history of emancipation and its impact on the Civil War, discussing how Lincoln and the Republicans fought primarily for freeing slaves throughout the war, not just as a secondary objective in an effort to restore the country.

Raines, Howell
Silent Cavalry: How Union Soldiers from Alabama Helped Sherman Burn Atlanta, and Then Got Written Out of History. Howell Raines. Crown 2023. 528 p.
ISBN 9780593137758
Grades: Adult   973.7
1. Military history 2. Soldiers 3. Alabama 4. Southern States 5. United States 6. American Civil War era (1861-1865) 7. History writing — Wars and conflicts — American Civil War 8. History Writing — United States 9. History Writing — Military
LC 2023021001

Part American history, part family saga, part scholarly detective story, a Pulitzer Prize-winning journalist brings to life the little-known story of the First Alabama Cavalry—renegade Southerners who played a decisive role in the Civil War but who were scrubbed from the history books.

"A much-needed addition to the demythologizing literature of the Civil War." —*Kirkus*

Includes bibliographical references and index.

Sears, Stephen W.
★ *Chancellorsville.* Stephen W. Sears. Houghton Mifflin 1998. x, 593 p. : Illustration; Map
ISBN 9780395877449
Grades: 11 12 Adult   973.7
1. Chancellorsville, Battle of, 1863 2. Military campaigns 3. Civil war 4. United States Civil War, 1861-1865 5. United States history 6. Virginia 7. American Civil War era (1861-1865) 8. History writing — Wars and conflicts — American Civil War 9. History writing — Wars and conflicts — Battles
LC BL 98006846

Recounts the Civil War battle at Chancellorsville where Robert E. Lee scored his greatest victory.

"In this history of the campaign that ended in Chancellorsville, the author argues that a chain of errors, assumptions, and communications failures combined with the genuine brilliance and good luck of the Confederates to lead to a stinging if indecisive Union defeat." —*Booklist*

A Mariner book; Includes bibliographical references (p. 564-577) and index; Originally published: Boston, MA : Houghton Mifflin, 1996.

Gettysburg. Stephen W. Sears. Houghton Mifflin 2003. xiv, 623 p. : Illustration; Map
ISBN 9780395867617
Grades: 11 12 Adult   973.7
1. Gettysburg, Battle of, 1863 2. Civil war 3. United States Civil War, 1861-1865 4. Military campaigns 5. United States history 6. Pennsylvania 7. 1860s 8. American Civil War era (1861-1865) 9. History writing — Wars and conflicts — American Civil War 10. History writing — Wars and conflicts — Battles
LC 2002191259

New York Times Notable Book, 2003.

Drawing on years of research, Sears focuses on the big picture, capturing the entire essence of the momentous three-day struggle while offering fresh insights that will surprise even the best-versed Civil War buffs, from Robert E. Lee's decision to bring the war north, to Joshua L. Chamberlain's brilliant defense of Little Round Top, to George Pickett's fateful charge.

"This is an assessment of the battle of Gettysburg and the events leading up to it. . . . Sears examines several turning points during the battle's buildup and three-day duration. The resulting insights add to the excellent and dramatic narrative flow. . . . For all Civil War collections and academic libraries." —*Library Journal*

Includes bibliographical references (p. 590-600) and index.

★ *Landscape Turned Red: The Battle of Antietam.* Stephen W. Sears. Houghton Mifflin 2003. xii, 431 p. : Illustration; Map
ISBN 9780618344192
Grades: Adult   973.7
1. Antietam, Battle of, MD, 1862 2. Military campaigns 3. Civil war 4. United States Civil War, 1861-1865 5. United States history 6. Virginia 7. American Civil War era (1861-1865) 8. History writing — Wars and conflicts — American Civil War 9. History writing — Wars and conflicts — Battles
LC BL2003011305

A definitive study of the climactic and pivotal battle of Antietam offers a vivid account of the two armies, the soldiers and officers, and the bitter, bloody campaign and analyzes the impact of Antietam on the Civil War as a whole.

"This account of the Battle of Antietam, the bloodiest day of the Civil War, is wide-ranging, detailed, and copiously documented. Stephen Sears . describes the tension-filled days preceding September 17, 1862, especially the political climate of Union pessimism and Confederate optimism. The battle itself is then exhaustively recounted." —*Booklist*

Originally published: New Haven, CT : Ticknor & Fields, 1983; a Mariner book; Includes bibliographical references (p. [375]-414) and index.

Seidule, Ty
Robert E. Lee and Me: A Southerner's Reckoning with the Myth of the Lost Cause. Ty Seidule. St. Martin's Press 2021. 304 p.
ISBN 9781250239266
Grades: Adult   973.7
1. Lee, Robert E. (Robert Edward), 1807-1870 2. Seidule, Ty 3. Racism 4. Slavery 5. European Americans 6. United States Civil War, 1861-1865 7. Historical revisionism 8. Historians 9. Identity 10. Race relations 11. Teaching 12. United States history 13. Southern States 14. United States 15. American Civil War era (1861-1865) 16. History writing — Wars and conflicts — American Civil War 17. Society and culture — Race 18. Life stories — Education — Scholars and educators
LC 2020035324

Ty Seidule grew up revering Robert E. Lee. From his southern childhood to his service in the U.S. Army, every part of his life reinforced the Lost Cause myth: That Lee was the greatest man who ever lived, and that the Confederates were underdogs who lost the Civil War with honor. Now, as a retired brigadier general and Professor Emeritus of History at West Point, his view has radically changed. From a soldier, a scholar, and a southerner, Ty Seidule believes that American history demands a reckoning.

"West Point history professor emeritus Seidule (coeditor, West Point History of the American Revolution) delivers a ruminative and carefully researched look at how the Confederacy is understood and memorialized a century and a half after its defeat." —*Publishers Weekly*

Includes bibliographical references.

Shane, Scott
★ *Flee North: A Forgotten Hero and the Fight for Freedom in Slavery's Borderland.* Scott Shane. Celadon Books 2023. VIII, 340 p.
ISBN 9781250843210
Grades: Adult   973.7
1. Smallwood, Thomas, 1801-1883 2. Torrey, Charles T. (Charles Turner), 1813-1846 3. Slatter, Hope H. (Hope Hull), 1790-1853 4. African American abolitionists 5. Abolitionists 6. African American men 7. European American men 8. Freed people 9. Essayists 10. Anonymous letters 11. Underground Railroad 12. Freedom seekers 13. Slave trade 14. Anti-slavery movements 15. North American people 16. American people 17. Canadian people 18. Baltimore, Maryland 19. Boston, Massachusetts 20. Toronto, Ontario 21. Antebellum America (1820-1861) 22. Collective biographies 23. History writing — African American — Enslavement — United States 24. Life stories — Politics — Activists and reformers 25. Life stories — Identity — Race and ethnicity 26. Nonfiction that reads like fiction
LC 2023012436

A riveting account of the extraordinary abolitionist, liberator, and writer Thomas Smallwood, who bought his own freedom, led hundreds out of slavery, and popularized the term "underground railroad," from author and journalist Scott Shane. Flee North tells the story for the first time of an American hero all but lost to history.

"A forgotten chapter in abolitionist history is restored to history in a lively, readable narrative." —*Kirkus*

Includes bibliographical references and index.

Snodgrass, Mary Ellen

The **Underground** *Railroad: An Encyclopedia of People, Places, and Operations.* Mary Ellen Snodgrass. M.E. Sharpe 2008. 746 p; Illustration; Map
ISBN 9780765680938
Grades: 7 8 9 10 11 12 Adult   973.7
1. Abolitionists 2. Freedom seekers 3. Slavery 4. Underground Railroad 5. Anti-slavery movements 6. United States history 7. 19th century 8. Reference — Encyclopedias 9. History writing — African American — Enslavement — United States
LC 2007009199

Offers more than fifteen hundred alphabetically arranged entries covering the key people, routes, events, documents, organizations, and publications related to slave liberation, along with genealogical histories of participating families, passenger data, and detailed passenger maps.

"The author has compiled an important and extensively researched encyclopedia of the Underground Railroad. Beginning with a concise, informative general introduction, this ambitious two-volume set neatly identifies the key people, places, documents, organizations, and publications of the Underground Railroad movement, along with significant actions, events, and ideas underlying it in the US and Canada. Offering photographs, bookplates, sketches, and handbills, the set is visually attractive." —*Choice*

Includes bibliographical references and index.

Taylor, Alan

American Civil Wars: A Continental History, 1850-1873. Alan Taylor. W W Norton & CO Inc 2024. 672 p.
ISBN 9781324035282
Grades: Adult   973.7
1. United States Civil War, 1861-1865 2. Power 3. Political corruption 4. Idealism 5. Civil war 6. Abolitionists 7. Freed people 8. North American history 9. Mexican history 10. Canadian history 11. United States history 12. 19th century 13. American Civil War era (1861-1865) 14. History writing — Wars and conflicts — Civil Wars 15. History writing — Wars and conflicts — American Civil War

A two-time Pulitzer Prize winner provides a masterful historical account of the twenty-year period from 1850-1873 during which the United States, Mexico and Canada underwent significant transformations and evolved into the nations we know today.

"This sweeping account from Pulitzer winner Taylor (American Republics) examines the Civil War in a wider North American context." —*Publishers Weekly*

Tobin, Jacqueline

From Midnight *to Dawn: The Last Tracks of the Underground Railroad.* Jacqueline Tobin with Hettie Jones. Doubleday 2007. xi, 272 p. : Illustration; Map
ISBN 9780385514316
Grades: 11 12 Adult   973.7
1. Underground railroad 2. Freedom seekers 3. African Americans 4. Land settlement 5. Canadian history 6. Ontario 7. 19th century 8. History writing — African American — Enslavement — United States 9. Adult books for young adults 10. History writing — Early Canada to Confederation (1867) — Canada
LC 2006046304

A history of the Underground Railroad brings together portraits of the men and women who established the escape organization for runaway slaves, as well as the people who traveled it to find new lives in Canada.

"There's an enlightening portrait of Josiah Henson (the model for Stowe's Uncle Tom) as a political activist, a fascinating look at the pioneering journalist and early feminist Mary Ann Shadd and an intriguing section on the deep Canadian connection to Harpers Ferry, as John Brown meets with the fugitives in Chatham. Accessible and fluidly written, the book will appeal to general readers." —*Publishers Weekly*

Map on lining papers; Includes bibliographical references (p. 255-264) and index.

Hidden *in Plain View: The Secret Story of Quilts and the Underground Railroad.* Jacqueline L. Tobin and Raymond G. Dobard. Doubleday 1999. x, 208 p. : Illustration; Color; Map
ISBN 9780385491372
Grades: 11 12 Adult   973.7
1. Underground Railroad 2. Freedom seekers 3. African American quilts 4. Codes (Communication) 5. United States history 6. 19th century 7. History writing — African American — Enslavement — United States 8. Arts and Entertainment — Crafts and hobbies
LC 98049804

Reveals the secret codes woven by African American slaves into quilts they used to navigate their escape on the Underground Railroad.

"This is a needed and valuable contribution to the literature of African American culture." —*Library Journal*

Includes bibliographical references (p. [193]-208).

Toler, Pamela D.

Heroines *of Mercy Street.* Pamela D. Toler. Little Brown & CO 2016. 320 p.
ISBN 9780316392075
Grades: Adult   973.7
1. Nurses 2. Medical care 3. United States Civil War, 1861-1865 4. United States history 5. American Civil War era (1861-1865) 6. Media tie-ins 7. History writing — Wars and conflicts — American Civil War

Reveals the true stories of the nurses at Mansion House, the mansion-turned-wartime hospital in Alexandria, Virginia, during the Civil War, the setting for the PBS series "Mercy Street."

"Accessible and well researched, Toler's book coincides with the recent PBS series Mercy Street and successfully illustrates the beginnings of nursing as a designated field of medical practice." —*Library Journal*

Waller, Douglas C.

Lincoln's *Spies: Their Secret War to Save a Nation.* Douglas Waller. Simon & Schuster 2019. 624 p.
ISBN 9781501126840
Grades: Adult   973.7
1. Van Lew, Elizabeth L, 1818-1900 2. Lincoln, Abraham, 1809-1865 3. Sharpe, George H. (George Henry), 1828-1900 4. Baker, La Fayette C. (La Fayette Curry), 1826-1868 5. Pinkerton, Allan, 1819-1884 6. Espionage 7. Spies 8. Intelligence service 9. Women spies 10. Political intrigue 11. United States history 12. American Civil War era (1861-1865) 13. History writing — Wars and conflicts — American Civil War 14. History writing — Spies and spying
LC 2018277647

Describes the lives of three men and one woman who served as secret agents for the North who informed Lincoln's generals with crucial information on enemy positions and helped foil assassination attempts during the Civil War.

"For those wanting to see spying through both a wide-angle lens in terms of patterns of espionage and a microscopic one in terms of personalities, Waller's book is the one to read." —*Library Journal*

Ward, Andrew

★ *The Slaves' War: The Civil War in the Words of Former Slaves.* Andrew Ward. Houghton Mifflin Co. 2008. 400 p.
ISBN 9780618634002
Grades: 11 12 Adult   973.7
1. Enslaved people 2. Freed people 3. Civil war 4. United States Civil War, 1861-1865 5. African Americans 6. African American soldiers 7. African American history 8. United States history 9. American Civil War era (1861-1865) 10. Biographies 11. History writing — Wars and conflicts — American Civil War 12. History writing — African American — Enslavement — United States
LC 2008001532

ESSENTIAL AND RECOMMENDED TITLES
973.7 Administration of Abraham Lincoln, 1861-1865

The Slaves' War delivers an unprecedented vision of the nation's bloodiest conflict, told from the perspective of those whose destiny it decided. Woven together from interviews, diaries, letters, and memoirs, here is the Civil War as seen not only from battlefields and camps but also from slave quarters, kitchens, roadsides, and fields. Speaking in a quintessentially American language of biblical power and intensity, body servants, army cooks and launderers, runaways, teamsters, and gravediggers bring the war to life—from theories about the war's causes to frank assessments of such figures as Lincoln, Davis, Lee, and Grant; from searing memories of the carnage of battle to often startling attitudes toward masters and liberators alike; and from initial jubilation at the Yankee invasion of the slave South to the crushing disappointment of freedom's promise unfulfilled.

"The author has provided a . . . narrative that gives voice to the experiences and attitudes of slaves who endured the conflict. Ward utilizes testimonials, diaries, and letters, and organizes them in chronological order from the months before the commencement of hostilities to the aftermath of the surrender at Appomattox. . . . This is a work that will interest both scholars and general readers." —*Booklist*

Includes index.

Ward, Geoffrey C.
The Civil War: An Illustrated History. Narrative by Geoffrey C. Ward; based on a documentary filmscript by Geoffrey C. Ward, Ric Burns, and Ken Burns; with contributions by Don E. Fehrenbacher [et al.]. Knopf 1990. xix, 425 p. : Illustration; Color; Map
ISBN 9780394562858
Grades: 11 12 Adult   973.7
1. Civil war 2. Slavery 3. Military history 4. Race relations 5. United States Civil War, 1861-1865 6. United States history 7. American Civil War era (1861-1865) 8. History writing — Wars and conflicts — American Civil War
LC 89043475

Portrays the lives of politicians, soldiers, and slaves during the Civil War.

"A companion to a nine-part Public Broadcasting System documentary, this superbly designed book easily stands on its own." —*New York Times Book Review*

Includes bibliographical references and index.

Williams, David
Bitterly Divided: The South's Inner Civil War. David Williams. New Press 2008. 352 p.
ISBN 9781595581082
Grades: 11 12 Adult   973.7
1. Social conflict 2. Social classes 3. Secession 4. Public opinion 5. Unionists (United States Civil War) 6. Civil war 7. Race relations 8. United States Civil War, 1861-1865 9. Southern States history 10. United States history 11. Southern States 12. Confederate States of America 13. 1860s 14. 19th century 15. American Civil War era (1861-1865) 16. History writing — Wars and conflicts — American Civil War 17. History writing — Confederacy — United States
LC 2007045285

Booklist Editors' Choice, 2008.

A revisionist account of the American Confederacy's lesser-known internal divisions reveals how Civil War-era white southerners were divided about the issue of secession, in a volume that considers how southern resistance was significantly responsible for the Confederacy's ultimate collapse.

"Williams marshals abundant evidence to demonstrate that the Confederacy also lost an internal civil war during 1861-65. This firm repudiation of the myth of the solid Confederate South is absolutely essential Civil War reading." —*Booklist*

Includes bibliographical references and index.

Willis, Deborah
★ *The Black Civil War Soldier: A Visual History of Conflict and Citizenship.* Deborah Willis. New York University Press 2021. 240 p. : Illustration
ISBN 9781479809004
Grades: Adult   973.7
1. African american soldiers 2. African Americans 3. United States Civil War, 1861-1865 4. Union soldiers 5. Photography 6. Portraits 7. Civil war 8. Citizenship 9. Race relations 10. United States history 11. 19th century 12. American Civil War era (1861-1865) 13. Illustrated books 14. History writing — Wars and conflicts — American Civil War 15. History writing — African American — United States 16. History writing — Wars and conflicts — Civil Wars 17. Society and culture — Race

Though both the Union and Confederate armies excluded African American men from their initial calls to arms, many of the men who eventually served were Black. Simultaneously, photography culture blossomed—marking the Civil War as the first conflict to be extensively documented through photographs. In The Black Civil War Soldier, Deb Willis explores the crucial role of photography in (re)telling and shaping African American narratives of the Civil War, pulling from a dynamic visual archive that has largely gone unacknowledged.

"The carefully constructed text, often incorporating letters and diary entries, is a winning complement to this superb collection of documentary images. Essential to any Civil War collection and a book that invites rereading." —*Kirkus*

Envisioning Emancipation: Black Americans and the End of Slavery. Deborah Willis and Barbara Krauthamer. Temple University Press 2013. 248 p.
ISBN 9781439909850
Grades: Adult   973.7
1. African American history 2. Documentary photography 3. Historiography 4. Enslaved people 5. Free African Americans 6. United States Civil War, 1861-1865 7. United States history 8. United States 9. 1860s 10. 19th century 11. American Civil War era (1861-1865) 12. Visual nonfiction 13. History writing — Wars and conflicts — American Civil War 14. History writing — African American — Civil rights — United States
LC 2012032600

What freedom looked like for Black Americans in the Civil War era.

"Their very learned analysis brings to the reader many significant glimpses into the true nature of Black people's evolving status during the late slavery period, during emancipation itself, and during the often confusing days of their first taste of freedom." —*Booklist*

Includes bibliographical references and index.

Wills, Garry
Lincoln at Gettysburg: The Words That Remade America. Garry Wills. Simon & Schuster 1992. 317 p.
ISBN 9780671769567
Grades: Adult   973.7
1. Lincoln, Abraham, 1809-1865 2. Rhetoric 3. Political leadership 4. Civil war 5. United States Civil War, 1861-1865 6. Presidents 7. United States history 8. United States 9. Gettysburg, Pennsylvania 10. 19th century 11. American Civil War era (1861-1865) 12. Speeches, addresses, etc. 13. History writing — Presidency — 19th century — United States 14. History writing — Wars and conflicts — American Civil War
LC 92003546

Pulitzer Prize for General Nonfiction, 1993; ALA Notable Book, 1993; National Book Award for Nonfiction finalist, 1992; Pulitzer Prize for History finalist, 1993.

An account of Lincoln's revolutionary speech describes how, in the space of 272 words, the President brought to bear the rhetoric of the Greek Revival, the categories of transcendentalism, and the imagery of the Rural Cemetary Movement.

"This is a tour de force that will cause much discussion and argument." —*Library Journal*

Includes bibliographical references (p. 267-304) and indexes.

Winik, Jay
April 1865: The Month That Saved America. Jay Winik. Harper Collins 2001. xviii, 461 p. Illustration; Map
ISBN 9780060187231
Grades: 11 12 Adult   973.7
1. Lincoln, Abraham, 1809-1865 2. Appomattox Campaign, 1865 3. Civil war 4. United States Civil War, 1861-1865 5. Peace 6. United States history 7. Richmond, Virginia 8. American Civil War era (1861-1865) 9. 19th century 10. History writing — Wars and conflicts — American Civil War 11. History writing — Wars and conflicts — Battles
LC 2001336531

Jay Winik explores the end of the Civil War in a panoramic narrative that takes readers on a journey through the tumultuous month of April 1865, showing that America's future rested on a few crucial decisions and twists of fate.

"Winik has written a provocative account.... He suggests that the assassination of Lincoln could have triggered a coup in the North, and his insights into the on-again, off-again 'Peace' negotiations are incisive. Scholars and Civil War buffs may disagree with some of his assertions, but this fast moving, well-written chronicle will highlight obscure aspects of the war and stimulate further controversy." —*Booklist*

Includes bibliographical references (p. [389]-448) and index.

973.7092 United States — 1861-1865 — Biography

Craughwell, Thomas J.
Stealing Lincoln's Body. Thomas J. Craughwell. Harvard University Press 2007. IX, 250 p. : Illustration
ISBN 9780674024588
Grades: 9 10 11 12 Adult   973.7092
1. Lincoln, Abraham, 1809-1865 2. Grave robbing 3. Body snatching 4. Crime and the press 5. Dead 6. Stealing 7. Ransom 8. Counterfeits and counterfeiting 9. Presidents 10. Irish Americans 11. United States history 12. Illinois 13. United States 14. 19th century 15. History writing — Presidency — 19th century — United States 16. History writing — Scandals

LC 2006050842

Details a bizarre, little-known historical event in which a gang of Chicago counterfeiters attempted to steal the entombed, embalmed body of Abraham Lincoln on the night of the 1876 presidential election, discussing the planning and execution of the crime, the resulting investigation, the reaction of Lincoln's family, and the aftermath.

"Summoning the raw spirit of crime novels and horror stories, as well as the forensic detail of a coroner's inquest, Thomas J. Craughwell has turned the eerie final chapter of the Lincoln story into a guilty pleasure." —*Washington Post Book World*.

Includes bibliographical references and index.

Foner, Eric
The *Fiery Trial: Abraham Lincoln and American Slavery*. Eric Foner. W. W. Norton & Co. 2010. xxi, 426 p, 16 p. of plates : Illustration; Map
ISBN 9780393066180
Grades: Adult   973.7092
1. Lincoln, Abraham, 1809-1865 2. Slavery 3. Racism 4. Politicians 5. Race relations 6. Abolitionists 7. Presidents 8. Politics and government 9. United States 10. 1860s 11. 19th century 12. American Civil War era (1861-1865) 13. History writing — Presidency — 19th century — United States 14. History writing — Wars and conflicts — American Civil War

LC 2010023425

Pulitzer Prize for History, 2011; New York Times Notable Book, 2010.

In this landmark work of deep scholarship and insight, Eric Foner gives the definitive history of Abraham Lincoln and the end of slavery in America. Foner's Lincoln emerges as a leader, one whose greatness lies in his capacity for moral and political growth through real engagement with allies and critics alike. This powerful work will transform our understanding of the nation's greatest president and the issue that mattered most.

In the vast library on Lincoln, Foner's book stands out as the most sensitive and sensible reading of Lincoln's lifetime involvement with slavery and the most insightful assessment of Lincoln's—and indeed America's—imperative to move toward freedom lest it be lost. An essential work for all Americans.

Includes bibliographical references (p. 349-406) and index.

Holzer, Harold
A *Just* and Generous Nation: Abraham Lincoln and the Fight for American Opportunity. Harold Holzer and Norton Garfinkle. Basic Books, a member of the Perseus Books Group 2015. 288 p.
ISBN 9780465028306
Grades: Adult   973.7092

1. Lincoln, Abraham, 1809-1865 2. Equality 3. Economic development 4. Social mobility 5. United States Civil War, 1861-1865 6. Causes of war 7. Politics and government 8. United States history 9. United States 10. 19th century 11. American Civil War era (1861-1865) 12. Biographies 13. History writing — Presidency — 19th century — United States 14. Life stories — Politics — Politicians

LC 2015022842

In A Just and Generous Nation, the eminent historian Harold Holzer and the noted economist Norton Garfinkle present a groundbreaking new account of the beliefs that inspired our sixteenth president to go to war when the Southern states seceded from the Union. Rather than a commitment to eradicating slavery or a defense of the Union, they argue, Lincoln's guiding principle was the defense of equal economic opportunity. Lincoln firmly believed that the government's primary role was to ensure that all Americans had the opportunity to better their station in life. As president, he worked tirelessly to enshrine this ideal within the federal government. He funded railroads and canals, supported education, and, most importantly, issued the Emancipation Proclamation, which opened the door for former slaves to join white Americans in striving for self-improvement.

"This review of Lincoln's thoughts and actions and examination of subsequent administrations' willingness to promote and secure the American Dream will generate much-needed debate on the history, efficacy, and morality of government's role and responsibility in shaping an economy of fairness and growth. The future of America depends on that question." —*Library Journal*

Includes bibliographical references and index.

Kaplan, Fred
Lincoln and the Abolitionists: John Quincy Adams, Slavery, and the Civil War. Fred Kaplan. HarperCollins 2017. 352 p.
ISBN 9780062440006
Grades: Adult   973.7092
1. Adams, John Quincy, 1767-1848 2. Lincoln, Abraham, 1809-1865 3. Abolitionists 4. Slavery 5. Equality 6. Racism in politics and government 7. African Americans 8. Presidents 9. Race relations 10. United States 11. 19th century 12. History writing — Presidency — 19th century — United States 13. History writing — African American — Enslavement — United States

LC Bl2017017854

Explores how the differing experiences and viewpoints of two Presidents shaped slavery and race relations in America for more than a century.

"A fresh look at John Quincy Adams, Abraham Lincoln, the Civil War, abolitionism, and other related American history." —*Kirkus*

Meltzer, Brad
The *Lincoln* Conspiracy: The Secret Plot to Kill America's 16th President—and Why It Failed. Brad Meltzer and Josh Mensch. Flatiron Books 2020. 416 p.
ISBN 9781250317476
Grades: Adult   973.7092
1. Lincoln, Abraham, 1809-1865 2. Pinkerton, Allan, 1819-1884 3. Proslavery movements 4. Assassination plots 5. Conspiracies 6. Political crimes and offenses 7. Presidents 8. Attempted assassination 9. United States history 10. Baltimore, Maryland 11. United States 12. 1860s 13. 19th century 14. American Civil War era (1861-1865) 15. History writing — Presidency — 19th century — United States 16. History writing — Antebellum America — United States

LC 2020006774

The best-selling authors of the First Conspiracy share the lesser-known story of the 1861 assassination attempt on the 16th President by a secret pro-Southern society that organized an elaborate plot targeting a newly elected Lincoln on his inaugural train journey.

"In short, energetic chapters, Meltzer and Mensch . . . fashion a brisk political thriller centered on a nefarious plot to murder Lincoln before his inauguration." —*Kirkus*

Includes bibliographical references and index.

Mitchell, Elizabeth
Lincoln's Lie: A True Civil War Caper Through Fake News, Wall Street, and the White House. Elizabeth Mitchell. Counterpoint 2020. xii, 288 pages

ESSENTIAL AND RECOMMENDED TITLES
973.8 United States — Reconstruction period, 1865-1901

ISBN 9781640092822
Grades: Adult **973.7092**

1. Lincoln, Abraham, 1809-1865 2. Presidents 3. Journalism 4. Press and politics 5. Censorship 6. Journalists 7. Mass media 8. United States history 9. 19th century 10. American Civil War era (1861-1865) 11. History writing — Wars and conflicts — American Civil War 12. Society and culture — Media and technology

LC 2020006260

In 1864, during the bloodiest days of the Civil War, two newspapers published a call, allegedly authored by President Lincoln, for the immediate conscription of 400,000 more Union soldiers. New York streets erupted in pandemonium. Wall Street markets went wild. When Lincoln sent troops to seize the newspaper presses and arrest the editors, it became clear: the proclamation was a lie. Who put out this fake news? Was it a Confederate spy hoping to incite another draft riot? a political enemy out to ruin the president in an election year? or was there some truth to the proclamation-far more truth than anyone suspected?

"This thrilling account of a nearly forgotten chapter of Civil War history echoes present-day political controversies." —*Booklist*

Includes bibliographical references (pages 253-279) and index.

Pryor, Elizabeth Brown

***Six** Encounters with Lincoln: A President Confronts Democracy and Its Demons.* Elizabeth Brown Pryor. Viking Press 2017. 400 pages
ISBN 9780670025909
Grades: Adult **973.7092**

1. Lincoln, Abraham, 1809-1865 2. Character 3. Ideology 4. Conversation 5. Social behavior 6. American Civil War era (1861-1865) 7. 19th century 8. Biographies 9. History writing — Presidency — 19th century — United States 10. Life stories — Politics — Politicians 11. History writing — Wars and conflicts — American Civil War

LC 2016042837

Explores the psychology, character and leadership of the 16th President as evidenced by six lesser-known encounters with his constituents, from an awkward meeting with Army officers on the eve of the Civil War to a White House conversation with a fierce abolitionist.

"Deeply researched, telling moments in the life of arguably the most written-about man in American history." —*Kirkus*

973.8 United States — Reconstruction period, 1865-1901

Bordewich, Fergus M.

***Klan** War: Ulysses S. Grant and the Battle to Save Reconstruction.* Fergus M. Bordewich. Alfred A. Knopf 2023. 448 p.
ISBN 9780593317815
Grades: Adult **973.8**

1. Grant, Ulysses S, 1822-1885 2. Reconstruction (United States history) 3. Domestic terrorism 4. Race relations 5. United States 6. 19th century 7. History Writing — Reconstruction — United states

LC 2022058874

In this bold and bracing record of America's past, a celebrated historian transports us to the front lines of President Grant's war on the Ku Klux Klan, reviving an unsung generation of grassroots Black leaders and key figures, while discussing the present-day battles to stamp out resurgent white supremacist ideologies.

"A critically important revisionist history." —*Kirkus*

Includes bibliographical references and index.

Brands, H. W.

*The **Last** Campaign: Sherman, Geronimo, and the War for America.* H. W. Brands. Doubleday 2022. 416 p.
ISBN 9780385547284
Grades: Adult **973.8**

1. Geronimo, Apache chief, 1829-1909 2. Sherman, William Tecumseh, 1820-1891 3. Indigenous peoples of North America — Wars 4. Indigenous peoples of North America — Forced removal 5. Generals 6. Apache (North American people) 7. Rulers 8. Military strategy 9. Frontier and pioneer life 10. Race relations 11. Battles 12. The West (United States) 13. History Writing — Indigenous peoples — United States 14. History Writing — Westward Expansion — United States 15. History Writing — Wars and conflicts — American Indigenous Wars

LC 2021051025

A best-selling historian and Pulitzer Prize finalist follows the lives of two war chiefs—General William Tecumseh Sherman and Geronimo—over the course of the 1870s and 1880s during which they confronted each other in the final battle for the American West would be.

"Historian Brands (Our First Civil War) takes a fine-grained yet somewhat lopsided look at the final military battles fought between the U.S. government and the Apache, Lakota, Nez Perce, and other Native American tribes." —*Publishers Weekly*

Includes bibliographical references and index.

Connell, Evan S.

Son of the Morning Star. Evan S. Connell. North Point Press 1984. 441 p. : Illustration
ISBN 9780865475106
Grades: 11 12 Adult **973.8**

1. Custer, George A. (George Armstrong), 1839-1876 2. Little Bighorn, Battle of the, 1876 3. Cheyenne (North American people) 4. Dakota (North American people) 5. Arapaho (North American people) 6. Indigenous peoples of North America 7. Indigenous peoples of North America — History 8. Generals 9. United States history 10. Montana 11. United States 12. 1870s 13. 19th century 14. Page to screen 15. Biographies 16. History writing — Wars and conflicts — American Indigenous Wars

LC 84060681

Los Angeles Times Book Prize for History, 1985; National Book Critics Circle Award for Nonfiction finalist, 1984.

Portrays the life of General Custer and describes the massacre of him and his forces by the Indians at the Little Bighorn.

"This book is impressive in its massive presentation of information, and in the conclusions it draws about the probable events that led to the fracas on the banks of the Little Bighorn. But its strength lies in the way the author has shaped his material." —*New York Times Book Review*

Maps on lining papers; Includes index; Bibliography: P. [425]-437.

Cwiklik, Robert

Sheridan's Secret Mission: How the South Won the War After the Civil War. Robert Cwiklik. HarperCollins 2023. 288 p.
ISBN 9780062950642
Grades: Adult **973.8**

1. Sheridan, Philip Henry, 1831-1888 2. Reconstruction (United States history) 3. Civil war 4. United States Civil War, 1861-1865 5. Oppression (Psychology) 6. Racism 7. American Civil War era (1861-1865) 8. History writing — Wars and conflicts — American Civil War 9. History Writing — Regional history — United States

Recounts the late-Reconstruction Era mission of General Philip Sheridan, a Union hero dispatched to the South 10 years after the Civil War to protect the rights of newly freed Black men, who were under siege by violent paramilitary groups like the White league intent on erasing their postwar gains.

"In the months leading up to the 1874 midterm elections, the White League, a racist vigilante organization, terrorized Louisiana, recounts former Wall Street Journal editor Cwiklik (House Rules) in this meticulous and propulsive blow-by-blow chronicle of the political violence and the federal government's response." —*Publishers Weekly*

Donovan, Jim

*A **Terrible** Glory: Custer and the Little Bighorn : The Last Great Battle of the American West.* James Donovan. Little, Brown and Co. 2008. 544 p.
ISBN 9780316155786
Grades: 11 12 Adult **973.8**

1. Custer, George A. (George Armstrong), 1839-1876 2. Little Bighorn, Battle of the, 1876 3. Indigenous peoples of North America 4. Government relations

with indigenous peoples 5. Military history 6. Military policy 7. The West (United States) 8. United States 9. 19th century 10. History writing — Wars and conflicts — American Indigenous Wars 11. History writing — Wars and conflicts — Battles

LC 2007026156

In June of 1876, on a desolate hill above a winding river called "the Little Bighorn," George Armstrong Custer and all 210 men under his command were annihilated by almost 2,000 Sioux and Cheyenne. The news caused a public uproar, and those in positions of power promptly began to point fingers in order to avoid responsibility. Custer, who was conveniently dead, took the brunt of the blame. The truth, however, was far more complex.

"The author collects the multiple threads that led to the 1876 massacre at Little Big Horn. . . . Exhaustive research, lively prose and fresh interpretation make for a valuable addition to literature on this otherwise well-trodden historical event." —Publishers Weekly

Includes bibliographical references and index.

Douglass, Frederick

★ *Frederick Douglass: Selected Speeches and Writings*. Edited by Philip S. Foner; abridged and adapted by Yuval Taylor. Lawrence Hill Books 1999. xviii, 789 p; (The library of Black America)

ISBN 9781556523526

Grades: Adult   973.8

1. Enslaved people 2. African American history 3. Civil rights 4. Anti-slavery movements 5. United States history 6. 19th century 7. History writing — Antebellum America — United States

LC 99023180

Collects the abolitionist's ideas on slavery, feminism, electoral politics, and peace.

Includes bibliographical references and index.

The Portable Frederick Douglass. Frederick Douglass; edited with an introduction and notes by John Stauffer and Henry Louis Gates, Jr; general editor: Henry Louis Gates, Jr… Penguin Books 2016. xxxvi, 579 pages

ISBN 9780143106814

Grades: Adult   973.8

1. Douglass, Frederick, 1818-1895 2. African American abolitionists 3. African American history 4. Enslaved people 5. Anti-slavery movements 6. United States history 7. 19th century 8. Biographies 9. Arts and Entertainment — Writing and Publishing 10. Society and culture — Ethnic studies

LC 2016006199

Presents a newly edited collection of the seminal writings and speeches of a legendary writer, orator and civil rights leader.

Includes bibliographical references (pages 555-579).

Dray, Philip

Capitol Men: The Epic Story of Reconstruction Through the Lives of the First Black Congressmen. Philip Dray. Houghton Mifflin Co. 2008. 480 p.

ISBN 9780618563708

Grades: 11 12 Adult   973.8

1. Reconstruction (United States history) 2. African American legislators 3. African American politicians 4. Racism 5. Social justice 6. Race relations 7. Politics and government 8. Southern States 9. United States 10. 19th century 11. Biographies 12. History writing — Reconstruction — United States 13. Adult books for young adults 14. History writing — African American — Civil rights — United States

LC 2008011292

New York Times Notable Book, 2008.

A history of the Reconstruction era viewed from the perspective of America's first Black members of Congress examines their key role in promoting such reforms as public education for all children, equal rights, and protection from Klan violence.

Includes bibliographical references and index.

Foner, Eric

Forever Free: The Story of Emancipation and Reconstruction. Eric Foner; illustrations edited and with commentary by Joshua Brown. Knopf 2005. xxx, 268 p. : Illustration; Portrait

ISBN 9780375402593

Grades: 11 12 Adult   973.8

1. Reconstruction (United States history) 2. Civil war 3. United States Civil War, 1861-1865 4. Freed people 5. African American soldiers 6. Race relations 7. Politics and government 8. United States history 9. United States 10. 19th century 11. American Civil War era (1861-1865) 12. History writing — Reconstruction — United States 13. Adult books for young adults 14. History writing — African American — Civil rights — United States

LC 2005040706

Analyzes the post-Civil War era of emancipation and Reconstruction with an emphasis on discovering the larger political and cultural meaning for contemporary America of the lives of the newly freed slaves and the rise of the Ku Klux Klan.

Forever Free project : Stephen B. Brier, Peter O. Almond, executive editors/Producers; Christine Doudna, editor; Includes bibliographical references (p. 239-244) and index.

★ *Reconstruction: America's Unfinished Revolution, 1863-1877*. Eric Foner. Harper & Row 1988. xxvii, 690 p, 16 p. of plates : Illustration

ISBN 9780060158514

Grades: Adult   973.8

1. Reconstruction (United States history) 2. African American history 3. Democracy 4. Civil rights 5. Political corruption 6. African Americans 7. Political participation 8. Politics and government 9. United States history 10. United States 11. 1860s 12. 1870s 13. 19th century 14. History writing — Reconstruction — United States

LC 87045615

Los Angeles Times Book Prize for History, 1988; National Book Award for Nonfiction finalist, 1988; National Book Critics Circle Award for Nonfiction finalist, 1988; Pulitzer Prize for History finalist, 1989.

Describes the changes brought about by the Civil War, discusses the impact of slavery's end, and looks at the political, economic, and social aspects of Reconstruction.

"This invaluable, definitive history re-creates the post-Civil War period as a pivotal drama in which ordinary people get equal billing with politicians and wheelers and dealers." —Publishers Weekly

Includes index and bibliographical references (p. 615-641).

Langguth, A. J.

After Lincoln: How the North Won the Civil War and Lost the Peace. A. J. Langguth. Simon & Schuster 2014. 464 p.

ISBN 9781451617320

Grades: Adult   973.8

1. African American history 2. Reconstruction (United States history) 3. Politics and government 4. United States 5. 1860s 6. 1870s 7. 19th century 8. History writing — Reconstruction — United States

LC 2013051340

A latest historical chronicle by the author of Patriots examines the Reconstruction era, covering such topics as the impeachment of Andrew Johnson, Ulysses Grant's efforts to quash a rising KKK and Rutherford Hayes' agreement to remove troops from the South.

"The power of the Ku Klux Klan to strike fear was very real, no matter how foreign it seems today. This is a cogent, well-researched, well-told history of that important period. Langguth shows rather than explains, and the result is a rich history of an understudied period of American history." —Kirkus

Includes bibliographical references and index.

Levine, Robert S.

★ *The Failed Promise: Reconstruction, Frederick Douglass, and the Impeachment of Andrew Johnson*. Robert S. Levine. W.W. Norton & Company 2021. 256 p.

ISBN 9781324004752

Grades: Adult   973.8

ESSENTIAL AND RECOMMENDED TITLES
973.8 United States — Reconstruction period, 1865-1901

1. Douglass, Frederick, 1818-1895 2. Johnson, Andrew, 1808-1875 3. Reconstruction (United States history) 4. African American civil rights 5. Freed people 6. Opposition (Political science) 7. Racism 8. Presidents 9. Race relations 10. Politics and government 11. United States history 12. United States 13. 19th century 14. American Civil War era (1861-1865) 15. History writing — African American — Civil rights — United States 16. History writing — Reconstruction — United States 17. History writing — Presidency — 19th century — United States 18. Life stories — Politics — Activists and Reformers — Civil Rights Leaders

LC 2021005132

Drawing on letters, articles and the most important African American newspaper of the time, the author recreates the conflicts that brought Frederick Douglass and the wider Black community to reject President Andrew Johnson and call for a guilty verdict in his impeachment trial.

"University of Maryland English professor Levine (The Lives of Frederick Douglass) foregrounds in this enlightening and timely history the efforts of Frederick Douglass to persuade President Andrew Johnson and congressional Republicans to deliver 'Dignity and equality for Black people' in the years after the Civil War." —*Publishers Weekly*

Includes bibliographical references and index.

Millard, Candice
***Destiny** of the Republic: A Tale of Madness, Medicine and the Murder of a President.* Candice Millard. Doubleday 2011. 368 p.

ISBN 9780385526265

Grades: Adult   973.8

1. Garfield, James Abram, 1831-1881 2. History of medicine 3. Assassination 4. Political corruption 5. Presidents 6. United States history 7. United States 8. 19th century 9. Biographies 10. History writing — Presidency — 19th century — United States 11. Life stories — Politics — Politicians 12. Nonfiction that reads like fiction

LC 2011001549

ALA Notable Book, 2012; Booklist Editors' Choice, 2011; Edgar Allan Poe Award for Best Fact Crime, 2012; New York Times Notable Book, 2011.

A narrative account of James Garfield's political career offers insight into his background as a scholar and Civil War hero, his battles against the corrupt establishment, and Alexander Graham Bell's failed attempt to save him from an assassin's bullet.

Miller, Scott
*The **President** and the Assassin: McKinley, Terror, and Empire at the Dawn of the American Century.* Scott Miller. Random House Inc. 2011. 464 p.

ISBN 9781400067527

Grades: Adult   973.8

1. McKinley, William, 1843-1901 2. Czolgosz, Leon F, 1873?-1901 3. Anarchism 4. Blue collar workers 5. Assassination 6. Presidents 7. Politics and government 8. United States 9. 19th century 10. Biographies 11. History writing — Presidency — 19th century — United States 12. History writing — Gilded Age — United States 13. History writing — Wars and conflicts — Spanish-American War 14. Life stories — Law and order — Armed forces personnel

LC 2010038857

An account of the 25th President's assassination places events against a backdrop of a rapidly changing, newly industrial nation that McKinley regarded as increasingly great while his assassin, Czolgosz, became obsessed with his views on poverty, injustice and social revolution.

Philbrick, Nathaniel
★ *The **Last** Stand: Custer, Sitting Bull, and the Battle of the Little Bighorn.* by Nathaniel Philbrick. Viking 2010. 480 p.

ISBN 9780670021727

Grades: Adult   973.8

1. Sitting Bull, 1831-1890 2. Custer, George A. (George Armstrong), 1839-1876 3. Little Bighorn, Battle of the, 1876 4. Dakota (North American people) 5. Indigenous peoples of North America — Wars 6. Indigenous resistance and revolts 7. Cheyenne (North American people) 8. Battles 9. Chiefs (Political anthropology) 10. Indigenous peoples of North America 11. Government relations with indigenous peoples 12. Generals 13. United States history 14. Montana 15. United States 16. 1870s 17. 19th century 18. Biographies 19. History writing — Wars and conflicts — American Indigenous Wars 20. History writing — Indigenous peoples — United States 21. History writing — Wars and conflicts — Battles

LC 2009047209

ALA Notable Book, 2011; New York Times Notable Book, 2010.

Analyzes the characters and contributions of the Plains Indians leader and one of the Union's greatest cavalry officers while explaining how the conflict forged a Native American alliance and set the stage for the confinement of major tribal leaders on reservations.

"The author writes a lively narrative that brushes away the cobwebs of mythology to reveal the context and realities of Custer's unexpected 1876 defeat at the hands of his Indian enemies under Sitting Bull, and the character of each leader. Judicious in his assessments of events and intentions, Philbrick offers a rounded history of one of the worst defeats in American military history, a story enhanced by his minute examination of the battle's terrain and interviews with descendants in both camps." —*Publishers Weekly*

Includes bibliographical references and index.

Sinha, Manisha
★ *The **Rise** and Fall of the Second American Republic: Reconstruction, 1860-1920.* Manisha Sinha. Liveright Publishing Corporation, a division of W.W. Norton & Company 2024. 544 p.

ISBN 9781631498442

Grades: Adult   973.8

1. Reconstruction (United States history) 2. Democracy 3. United States 4. Gilded Age (1865-1898) 5. 19th century 6. 20th century 7. History writing — Reconstruction — United States

From 1860, when the election Abraham Lincoln triggered the secession of the Deep South states and ending in 1920 when women were granted the right to vote, an acclaimed historian narrates the major episodes of the era and introduces the key individuals who helped remake American democracy, or whose actions spelled its doom.

"A strong addition to modern studies of Reconstruction, bringing feminist and internationalist elements to the fore." —*Kirkus*

Tuccille, Jerome
*The **Roughest** Riders: The Untold Story of the Black Soldiers in the Spanish-American War.* Jerome Tuccille. Chicago Review Press 2015. 304 p.

ISBN 9781613730461

Grades: Adult   973.8

1. Spanish American War, 1898 2. African American soldiers 3. American participation in wars 4. 19th century 5. History writing — Wars and conflicts — Spanish-American War 6. History writing — Military — Military units 7. History writing — African American — United States

LC 2015001414

Americans have long heard the story of Teddy Roosevelt and the Rough Riders charging up San Juan Hill during the Spanish-American War. But often forgotten in the great swamp of history is that Roosevelt's success was ensured by a dedicated corps of Black soldiers—the so-called Buffalo Soldiers—who fought by Roosevelt's side during his legendary campaign. Roosevelt admitted that the Black troops actually spearheaded the charge, beating him to the top of Kettle Hill ahead of San Juan Hill, but later changed his story, claiming their performance was due to the superior white officers under whom the Black troops served.

"Tuccille's excellent descriptions give readers a graphic feel for the vicissitudes of jungle warfare and the grim racial and social realities that these men endured." —*Publishers Weekly*

Includes bibliographical references and index.

Williams, Kidada E.
*I **Saw** Death Coming: A History of Terror and Survival in the War Against Reconstruction.* Kidada E. Williams. Bloomsbury 2023. xxv, 351 p.

ISBN 9781635576634

Grades: Adult   973.8

1. African Americans 2. Reconstruction (United States history) 3. Freed people 4. Racism 5. White supremacists 6. Violence against African Americans

7. Domestic terrorism 8. Civil rights 9. Survival 10. Psychic trauma 11. Resilience 12. Southern States history 13. 19th century 14. History writing — Reconstruction — United States 15. History writing — African American — United States 16. Life stories — Facing adversity — Victims of crime — Terrorism 17. Debut title

The story of Reconstruction is often told from the perspective of the politicians, generals, and journalists whose accounts claim an outsized place in collective memory. But this pivotal era looked very different to African Americans in the South transitioning from bondage to freedom after 1865. They were besieged by a campaign of white supremacist violence that persisted through the 1880s and beyond. For too long, their lived experiences have been sidelined, impoverishing our understanding of the obstacles post-Civil War Black families faced, their inspiring determination to survive, and the physical and emotional scars they bore because of it.

"A deeply researched work that exposes the shameful legacy of the neo-Confederacy, one that lingers to this day." —*Kirkus*

Includes bibliographical references and index.

Wineapple, Brenda
The Impeachers: The of Trial of Andrew Johnson and the Dream of a Just Nation. Brenda Wineapple. Random House 2019. 512 p.
ISBN 9780812998368
Grades: Adult   973.8
1. Johnson, Andrew, 1808-1875 2. Trials (Impeachment) 3. Reconstruction (United States history) 4. Impeachments 5. Politics and government 6. United States 7. 19th century 8. History writing — Presidency — 19th century — United States 9. History writing — Reconstruction — United States
LC 2018034980
ALA Notable Book, 2020; New York Times Notable Book, 2019.

An account of the impeachment of Andrew Johnson shares insights into the 17th President's disregard of Congress, opposition to civil rights and anti-Reconstruction stance, exploring the roles of such impeachment contributors as Ulysses S. Grant and Thaddeus Stevens.

"Complementing but not replacing David Stewart's Impeached, this volume offers a skillfully crafted and useful history." —*Library Journal*

Includes bibliographical references and index.

973.9 United States — 1901-

Allen, Frederick Lewis
Only Yesterday: An Informal History of the 1920's. Frederick Lewis Allen. Perennial Classics 2000. x, 338 p. : Illustration
ISBN 9780060956653
Grades: 11 12 Adult   973.9
1. Economics 2. United States history 3. 1920s 4. 20th century 5. Between the Wars (1918-1939) 6. Depression era (1929-1941) 7. 1930s 8. History writing — Roaring 20s — United States
LC 00028345

Recreates the social, political, and economic scene of the 1920s in America. Sequel: Since yesterday; Includes bibliographical references (p. [311]-315) and index; Originally published: Harper & Row, 1931.

Churchwell, Sarah Bartlett
Behold, America: The Entangled History Of. Sarah Churchwell. Basic Books 2018. VIII, 348 p.
ISBN 9781541673403
Grades: Adult   973.9
1. National characteristics, American 2. American Dream 3. Isolationism 4. Slogans 5. Propaganda 6. Social change 7. Nationalism 8. United States history 9. United States 10. 20th century 11. History writing — United States 12. Politics and global affairs — General 13. Society and culture — General
LC 2018020585

Discusses the history of the "America First" movement, which was linked with white supremacy, and compares it with the "American Dream," which promotes economic equality, through the various historical events of the twentieth century.

Includes bibliographical references and index.

973.91 United States — 1901-1953

Bryson, Bill
One Summer: America, 1927. Bill Bryson. Doubleday 2013. 544 p.
ISBN 9780767919401
Grades: Adult   973.91
1. Popular culture 2. Social life and customs 3. United States history 4. United States 5. 1920s 6. 20th century 7. Between the Wars (1918-1939) 8. Depression era (1929-1941) 9. 1930s 10. History writing — Roaring 20s — United States 11. Humor writing — Classic humorists
LC 2013016041
Booklist Editors' Choice, 2013.

Recounts the story of a pivotal cultural year in the United States when mainstream pursuits and historical events were marked by contributions by such figures as Charles Lindbergh, Babe Ruth, and AL Capone.

Fraser, Steve
The Age of Acquiescence: The Life and Death of American Resistance to Organized Wealth and Power. Steve Fraser. Little, Brown and Company 2015. 432 p.
ISBN 9780316185431
Grades: Adult   973.91
1. Elite (Social sciences) 2. Social conflict 3. Income inequality 4. Protest movements 5. Power 6. Social psychology 7. Politics and government 8. United States 9. 20th century 10. History writing — United States 11. Business and economics — Economics — History
LC 2014020466
Booklist Editors' Choice, 2015.

Investigates how and why, from the 18th century to the present day, Americans' resistance to their ruling elites has vanished.

Hochschild, Adam
American Midnight: The Great War, a Violent Peace, and Democracy's Forgotten Crisis. Adam Hochschild. Mariner Books 2022. 384 p.
ISBN 9780358455462
Grades: Adult   973.91
1. World War I 2. Labor movement 3. Political violence 4. Violence 5. Democracy 6. Politics and government 7. United States history 8. United States 9. 20th century 10. First World War era (1914-1918) 11. 1910s 12. 1920s 13. History writing — United States
LC 2022012762
NPR.

The award-winning New York Times best-selling historian examines America during World War I and its troubled aftermath, which included torture, censorship, racial-motivated killings and threats to democracy.

"President Woodrow Wilson's call for the U.S. to enter WWI to make the world 'Safe for democracy' ironically set the stage for an unprecedented attack on Americans' civil liberties, according to this expert and eye-opening account....Meticulously researched, fluidly written, and frequently enraging, this is a timely reminder of the 'Vigilant respect for civil rights and Constitutional safeguards' needed to protect democracy and forestall authoritarianism." —*Publishers Weekly*

Includes bibliographical references and index.

Kennedy, David M.
★ *Freedom from Fear: The American People in Depression and War, 1929-1945.* David M. Kennedy. Oxford University Press 1999. xviii, 936 p, 32 p. of plates : Illustration; Map
ISBN 9780195038347

ESSENTIAL AND RECOMMENDED TITLES
973.91092 United States — 1901-1953 — Biography

Grades: 11 12 Adult **973.91**
1. Depressions, 1929-1941 2. New Deal, 1933-1939 3. Stock market crash, October 1929 4. World War II 5. United States history 6. United States 7. 1930s 8. 1940s 9. 1920s 10. History writing — Great Depression — United States 11. History writing — Wars and conflicts — Homefront — World War II
LC 98049580
Pulitzer Prize for History, 2000; New York Times Notable Book, 1999.
Examines the forces and people that shaped United States history between the Great Depression and the end of World War II.
"Rarely does a work of historical synthesis combine such trenchant analysis and elegant writing. For its scope, its insight and its purring narrative engine, Kennedy's book will stand for years to come as the definitive account of the critical decades of the American century." —*Publishers Weekly*
Includes bibliographical references (p. 859-871) and index.

Mirski, Sean A.
We May Dominate the World: Ambition, Anxiety, and the Rise of the American Colossus. Sean A. Mirski. PublicAffairs 2023. 512 p.
ISBN 9781541758438
Grades: Adult **973.91**
1. International relations 2. Military policy 3. Great powers 4. Intervention (International relations) 5. Geopolitics 6. Hegemony 7. United States history 8. 19th century 9. 20th century 10. History writing — United States 11. History writing — Wars and conflicts
The cutthroat world of international politics has always been dominated by great powers. Yet no great power in the modern era has ever managed to achieve the kind of invulnerability that comes from being completely supreme in its own neighborhood. No great power, that is, except one—the United States. In We May Dominate the World, Sean A. Mirski tells the riveting story of how the United States became a regional hegemon in the century following the Civil War. Mirski reveals the surprising reasons behind U.S. foreign policy in a narrative full of colorful characters and original accounts of the bloody interventions that turned the fledgling republic into a global superpower.
"In this penetrating study, Hoover Institution foreign policy scholar Mirski argues that the international order established by the U.S. after WWII was prefigured by well-intentioned but abusive and bloody imperialism in Latin America, the Caribbean, and the Pacific." —*Publishers Weekly*

Shlaes, Amity
The Forgotten Man: A New History of the Great Depression. Amity Shlaes. Harper Collins Publishers 2007. x, 464 p, 16 p. of plates : Illustration
ISBN 9780066211701
Grades: Adult **973.91**
1. Depressions, 1929-1941 2. New Deal, 1933-1939 3. Economics 4. United States history 5. United States 6. 20th century 7. Depression era (1929-1941) 8. 1920s 9. 1930s 10. Conservative writing 11. History writing — Great Depression — United States 12. History writing — Politicians — United States 13. Business and economics — Economics — History 14. Business and economics — Economics — Socioeconomics
LC 2006049761
A reinterpretation of the Great Depression seeks to demonstrate how the failures of Hoover and Roosevelt to understand the prosperity of the 1920s directly contributed to massive national burdens that marginalized everyday citizens, in an account that shares the survival stories of lesser-known historical figures from the period.
"Reminding readers that the reputedly do-nothing Hoover pulled hard on the fiscal levers (raising tariffs, increasing government spending), Shlaes nevertheless emphasizes that his enthusiasm for intervention paled against the ebullient FDR's glee in experimentation. She focuses closely on the influence of his fabled Brain Trust, her narrative shifting among Raymond Moley, Rexford Tugwell, and other prominent New Dealers. Businesses that litigated their resistance to New Deal regulations attract Shlaes' attention, as do individuals who coped with the despair of the 1930s through self-help, such as Alcoholics Anonymous cofounder Bill Wilson. The book culminates in the rise of Wendell Willkie, and Shlaes' accent on personalities is an appealing avenue into her skeptical critique of the New Deal." —*Booklist*
Includes bibliographical references (p. [415]-433) and index.

Terkel, Studs
★ *Hard Times: An Oral History of the Great Depression*. Studs Terkel. New Press 2000. xvii, 462 p.
ISBN 9781565846562
Grades: 11 12 Adult **973.91**
1. Depressions, 1929-1941 2. United States history 3. United States 4. 1920s 5. 1930s 6. Oral histories 7. History writing — Great Depression — United States
LC 2003389318
Recreates the character and atmosphere of this dramatic era in a collage of recollections by both well-known and obscure Americans.
"Persons of all ages, occupations, and classes scattered across the U.S. remember what they experienced or were told about the economic crisis of the 1930's. The result is a social document of immense interest." —*Booklist*
Originally published: New York : Pantheon Books, 1970.

973.91092 United States — 1901-1953 — Biography

Schlesinger, Arthur M.
Journals, 1952-2000. Arthur M. Schlesinger, Jr; edited by Andrew Schlesinger and Stephen Schlesinger. Penguin Press 2007. xvi, 894 p.
ISBN 9781594201424
Grades: Adult **973.91092**
1. Schlesinger, Arthur M. (Arthur Meier), 1917-2007 2. Historians 3. Authors, American 4. Politics and culture 5. Personal diaries 6. Social life and customs 7. Politics and government 8. United States history 9. United States 10. 21st century 11. 20th century 12. History writing — Politicians — United States
LC Bl2007021482
The distinguished political historian's journals provide an intimate history of post-war America, the writer's contributions to multiple presidential administrations, and his relationships with numerous cultural and intellectual figures.
"This book contains juicy morsels on every one of its [pages]. The book contains not just his witty apercus, but those of hundreds of A-list friends, some of whom are still alive and will blanch at seeing private lunches in print. The presidential scuttlebutt is prime. The private score-settling is fun reading." —*Newsweek*
Includes index.

973.911 Administration of Theodore Roosevelt, 1901-1909

Berfield, Susan
The Hour of Fate: Theodore Roosevelt, J.P. Morgan, and the Battle to Transform American Capitalism. Susan Berfield. Bloomsbury Publishing 2020. 304 p.
ISBN 9781635572490
Grades: Adult **973.911**
1. Roosevelt, Theodore, 1858-1919 2. Morgan, John Pierpont, 1837-1913 3. Capitalists and financiers 4. Antitrust law 5. Capitalism 6. Labor disputes 7. Strikes 8. Economic history 9. Labor organizers 10. Coal miners 11. Economics 12. Presidents 13. United States 14. 20th century 15. History writing — Early 20th century — United States 16. History writing — Presidency — 20th century — United States
LC Bl2020046911
Describes how J.P. Morgan's domination of Wall Street screeched to a halt after the assassination of business-friendly President McKinley put Theodore Roosevelt in charge and his subsequent implementation of policies of government checks on big business in the early 1900s.
"An extremely readable work that will engage American history and business readers everywhere." —*Library Journal*
Includes bibliographical references (pages 287-310) and index.

Egan, Timothy
★ *The Big Burn: Teddy Roosevelt and the Fire That Saved America*. Timothy Egan. Houghton Mifflin Harcourt 2009. 336 p.

PUBLIC LIBRARY CORE COLLECTION: NONFICTION
Twentieth Edition

ISBN 9780618968411
Grades: Adult   **973.911**

1. Roosevelt, Theodore, 1858-1919 2. Pinchot, Gifford, 1865-1946 3. Forest fires 4. Forest conservation 5. Environmentalists 6. Political leadership 7. National parks and reserves 8. Nature conservation 9. Presidents 10. United States 11. Montana 12. Idaho 13. 20th century 14. Biographies 15. History writing — Presidency — 20th century — United States 16. Nature Writing — General

LC 2009021881

Narrates the struggles of the overmatched rangers against the implacable fire of August, 1910, and Teddy Roosevelt's pioneering conservation efforts that helped turn public opinion permanently in favor of the forests, though it changed the mission of the forest service with consequences felt in the fires of today.

Includes bibliographical references and index.

Gardner, Mark L.
Rough Riders: Theodore Roosevelt, His Cowboy Regiment, and the Immortal Charge up San Juan Hill. Mark Lee Gardner. William Morrow 2016. 320 p.

ISBN 9780062312082
Grades: Adult   **973.911**

1. Roosevelt, Theodore, 1858-1919 2. Spanish-American War, 1898 3. Command of troops 4. Military history 5. History writing — Wars and conflicts — Spanish-American War 6. Adult books for young adults

LC 2015046230

From the author of to Hell on a Fast Horse comes a definitive account of this legendary U.S. fighting force during the Spanish-American War and its extraordinary leader, Theodore Roosevelt.

"Gardner provides some terrifying, exhilarating stories of the battle, including the valiant charge up San Juan Hill through enemy gunfire. Throughout, Gardner celebrates Roosevelt, who as a postwar commander-in-chief never forgot the lesson of war and the heroic sacrifices of the fighters." —*Publishers Weekly*

Goodwin, Doris Kearns
★ The *Bully* Pulpit: Theodore Roosevelt, William Howard Taft, and the Golden Age of Journalism. Doris Kearns Goodwin. Simon & Schuster 2013. 848 p.

ISBN 9781416547860
Grades: Adult   **973.911**

1. Roosevelt, Theodore, 1858-1919 2. Taft, William H. (William Howard), 1857-1930 3. Progressivism (United States politics) 4. Press and politics 5. Presidents 6. Politics and government 7. United States 8. 20th century 9. 1900s (Decade) 10. History writing — Presidency — 20th century — United States 11. History writing — Early 20th century — United States

LC 2013032709

Andrew Carnegie Medal for Excellence in Non-Fiction, 2014; Booklist Editors' Choice, 2013; New York Times Notable Book, 2013.

Focusing on the broken friendship between Teddy Roosevelt and his chosen successor, William Howard Taft, a Pulitzer Prize-winning historian revisits the Progressive Era during which Roosevelt wielded the Bully Pulpit to challenge and triumph over abusive monopolies, political bosses and corrupt money brokers only to see it compromised by Taft.

"By shining a light on a little-discussed President and a much-discussed one, Goodwin manages to make history very much alive and relevant." —*Publishers Weekly*

Includes bibliographical references and index.

Morris, Edmund
★ *Theodore* Rex. Edmund Morris. Random House 2001. x, 772 p. : Illustration; Map

ISBN 9780394555096
Grades: 11 12 Adult   **973.911**

1. Roosevelt, Theodore, 1858-1919 2. Conservation of natural resources 3. Nobel Prize winners 4. Presidents 5. Politicians 6. Imperialism, American 7. Politics and government 8. Central American history 9. United States 10. Panama Canal 11. Philippines 12. 1910s 13. 20th century 14. 1900s (Decade) 15. Biographies 16. History writing — Presidency — 20th century — United States 17. History writing — Early 20th century — United States 18. Life stories — Politics — Politicians

LC 2001019366

ALA Notable Book, 2003; Booklist Editors' Choice, 2001; Library Journal Best Books, 2001; Los Angeles Times Book Prize for Biography, 2001; New York Times Notable Book, 2002.

Describes Theodore Roosevelt's presidency as he faced the challenges of a new century in which the United States would become a world power, and discusses his accomplishments and failures, the enemies he made, and his family life.

"Morris excels at placing TR in the context of his time, showing how he out maneuvered powerful but ossified opponents from the Gilded Age and trumped isolationists by averting war, in the process winning the first Nobel Peace Prize." —*Library Journal*

Sequel to: The Rise of Theodore Roosevelt; Sequel: Colonel Roosevelt; Includes bibliographical references (p. [563]-571) and index.

973.917 Administration of Franklin Delano Roosevelt, 1933-1945

Katznelson, Ira
Fear Itself: The New Deal and the Origins of Our Time. Ira Katznelson. Liveright Publishing Corporation, a Division of W.W. Norton & Company 2013. 512 p.

ISBN 9780871404503
Grades: Adult   **973.917**

1. Roosevelt, Franklin D. (Franklin Delano), 1882-1945 2. New Deal, 1933-1939 3. World politics 4. Depressions, 1929-1941 5. Recession (Economics) 6. Political culture 7. Politics and government 8. United States 9. 1930s 10. 1940s 11. 20th century 12. History writing — Great Depression — United States

LC 2012041794

Brings to life the New Deal era of American history, highlighting the politicians and pundits of the time, many of whom argued for positions that modern citizens would find questionable, including advocating for separation of the races and an American dictatorship.

Includes bibliographical references and index.

Michaelis, David
★ *Eleanor:* A Life. David Michaelis. Simon & Schuster 2020. xx, 698 pages, 32 unnumbered pages of numbered plates; Illustration

ISBN 9781439192016
Grades: Adult   **973.917**

1. Roosevelt, Eleanor, 1884-1962 2. Roosevelt, Franklin D. (Franklin Delano), 1882-1945 3. Women social advocates 4. Feminism 5. Presidents' spouses 6. Independence 7. United States history 8. United States 9. 20th century 10. Biographies 11. History writing — Presidency — 20th century — United States 12. Life stories — Politics — Politicians

Presents a breakthrough portrait of Eleanor Roosevelt, America's longest-serving First Lady, an avatar of democracy whose ever-expanding agency as diplomat, activist, and humanitarian made her one of the world's most widely admired and influential women.

"Biographer Michaelis (Schulz and Peanuts) presents a compulsively readable and exhaustively researched portrait of one of the most admired women of the 20th century.... This jam-packed biography is a must-read for 20th-century history buffs." —*Publishers Weekly*

Includes bibliographical references (pages 637-667) and index.

Nelson, Craig
★ *V Is for Victory: Franklin Roosevelt's American Revolution and the Triumph of World War II.* Craig Nelson. Scribner 2023. 448 p.

ISBN 9781982122911
Grades: Adult   **973.917**

1. Roosevelt, Franklin D. (Franklin Delano), 1882-1945 2. World War II 3. Industrial mobilization 4. Politics and government 5. Economics 6. United States 7. Second World War era (1939-1945) 8. 20th century 9. History Writing —

ESSENTIAL AND RECOMMENDED TITLES
973.917092 United States — 1933-1945 — Biography

Wars and conflicts — World War II 10. History Writing — Presidency — 20th century — United States

LC 2023000177

A New York Times bestselling historian, in this fascinating and meticulously researched account, chronicles how, under Franklin D. Roosevelt's resolute leadership, America's top industrialists and the American people joined in the war effort, building "the arsenal of democracy" that won World War II.

"Deeply researched and fluidly written, this is a rousing portrait of the partnership between America's public and private sectors firing on all cylinders." —Publishers Weekly

Includes bibliographical references and index.

973.917092 United States — 1933-1945 — Biography

Burns, Eric
Someone to Watch Over Me: A Portrait of Eleanor Roosevelt and the Tortured Father Who Shaped Her Life. Eric Burns. Pegasus Books 2017. 304 p.
ISBN 9781681773285
Grades: Adult   973.917092
1. Roosevelt, Eleanor, 1884-1962 2. Roosevelt, Elliot Bulloch, 1860-1894 3. Fathers and daughters 4. Presidents' spouses 5. Independence 6. United States 7. Biographies 8. Life stories — Relationships — Parent and child 9. Life stories — Politics — Politicians

LC 2017276796

A fresh and sensitive examination of Eleanor Roosevelt—one of the most remarkable Americans in history—and the tortured father who would inspire and shape her future leadership and advocacy.

"Using personal letters and the little information that is known of his relationship with Eleanor . the author underscores the crucial connection between her success and idolization of her father." —Library Journal

Fullilove, Michael
Rendezvous with Destiny: How Franklin D. Roosevelt and Five Extraordinary Men Took America into the War and into the World. Michael Fullilove. The Penguin Press 2013. 480 p.
ISBN 9781594204357
Grades: Adult   973.917092
1. Roosevelt, Franklin D. (Franklin Delano), 1882-1945 2. Welles, Sumner, 1892-1961 3. Donovan, William J. (William Joseph), 1883-1959 4. Hopkins, Harry L. (Harry Lloyd), 1890-1946 5. Willkie, Wendell L. (Wendell Lewis), 1892-1944 6. Harriman, W. Averell (William Averell), 1891-1986 7. International relations 8. Diplomacy 9. World War II 10. United States 11. 1940s 12. 20th century 13. Second World War era (1939-1945) 14. Australian literature 15. History writing — Presidency — 20th century — United States 16. History writing — Wars and conflicts — World War II

LC 2012047003

NSW Premier's Literary Awards, Douglas Stewart Prize for Non Fiction, 2014.

Documents the lesser-known role of the 32nd President and five influential diplomats in overturning American isolationist beliefs and pulling the country into World War II, citing the pivotal reports that led to America's support of an inundated Great Britain and Russia.

Includes bibliographical references and index.

Persico, Joseph E.
Franklin and Lucy: An Intimate Portrait of Franklin D. Roosevelt, Mrs. Rutherfurd, and the Other Remarkable Women Who Shaped FDR's Life. Joseph E. Persico. Random House 2008. 576 p.
ISBN 9781400064427
Grades: Adult   973.917092
1. Roosevelt, Franklin D. (Franklin Delano), 1882-1945 2. Rutherfurd, Lucy Mercer 3. Roosevelt, Eleanor, 1884-1962 4. Social secretaries 5. Presidents' spouses 6. Presidents 7. United States 8. 20th century 9. Biographies 10. History writing — Presidency — United States 11. Family and Relationships — Dating and Marriage 12. History writing — Presidency — 20th century — United States

LC 2007036851

Examines Franklin Delano Roosevelt's relationships with the women around him, from his devoted secretary Missy Lehand and wife Eleanor to Lucy Mercer Rutherfurd, the woman with whom he shared a long, secret, and life-altering relationship until his death.

"The author engagingly and eloquently narrates the tangled relationships between Franklin and the various women to whom he became close. Persico offers what will prove an important, lasting addition to the literature of the Roosevelts." —Publishers Weekly

Includes bibliographical references and index.

Simon, James F.
FDR and Chief Justice Hughes: The President, the Supreme Court, and the Epic Battle Over the New Deal. by James F. Simon. Simon & Schuster 2012. 368 p.
ISBN 9781416573289
Grades: Adult   973.917092
1. Roosevelt, Franklin D. (Franklin Delano), 1882-1945 2. Hughes, Charles Evans, 1862-1948 3. New Deal, 1933-1939 4. Executive power 5. Depressions, 1929-1941 6. Political questions and judicial power 7. Politics and government 8. United States 9. 20th century 10. History writing — Great Depression — United States 11. History writing — Judicial branch — United States

LC 2011028825

Documents the political clashes between the 32nd President and the Supreme Court under Chief Justice Hughes regarding the New Deal, providing coverage of the President's proposed legislative remedies, the constitutional challenges posed by a conservative bloc on the Court and FDR's efforts to undermine the abilities of opposing justices.

Includes bibliographical references and index.

973.918 Administration of Harry S Truman, 1945-1953

Frank, Jeffrey
The Trials of Harry S. Truman: The Extraordinary Presidency of an Ordinary Man, 1945-1953. Jeffrey Frank. Simon & Schuster 2022. 544 p.
ISBN 9781501102899
Grades: Adult   973.918
1. Truman, Harry S, 1884-1972 2. Political leadership 3. Presidents 4. International relations 5. Politics and government 6. United States 7. 20th century 8. 1940s 9. Biographies 10. Life stories — Politics — Politicians 11. History writing — Presidency — 20th century — United States

Drawing on archival discoveries and meticulous research, the best-selling author of Ike and Dick turns his attention to Harry S. Truman, revealing a portrait of an ordinary man suddenly forced to shoulder extraordinary responsibilities as he led America through the pivotal years of the mid-20th century.

"An absorbing reexamination of Harry Truman's two-term presidency and the critical years during which he held office.... A well-researched, engagingly human portrait of this complex mid-20th-century political leader." —Kirkus

Roll, David L.
Ascent to Power: How Truman Emerged from Roosevelt's Shadow and Remade the World. David L. Roll. Dutton 2024. 480 p.
ISBN 9780593186442
Grades: Adult   973.918
1. Truman, Harry S, 1884-1972 2. Presidents 3. Duty 4. World War II 5. Postwar life 6. Peace-building 7. Alliances 8. Geopolitics 9. Nuclear weapons 10. Civil rights 11. Anti-Communism 12. Leadership 13. American people 14. Biographies 15. Life stories — Politics — Politicians 16. History writing — Presidency — 20th century — United States 17. History writing — Post World War II - 1959 — United States

The story of how Harry Truman transcended the legacy of Franklin Roosevelt to lead America through the tumultuous post-war period of 1944-1948, which saw the revival of Western Europe, the reform of Japan and the birth of Israel.

PUBLIC LIBRARY CORE COLLECTION: NONFICTION
Twentieth Edition

"This is an engrossing account of post-WWII history and a thrilling portrait of a humble man who did much to shape history." —*Booklist*

973.918092 United States — 1945-1953 — Biography

Brands, H. W.
The General vs. the President: Macarthur and Truman at the Brink of Nuclear War. H.W. Brands. Doubleday 2016. 416 p.
ISBN 9780385540575
Grades: Adult   973.918092
1. Truman, Harry S, 1884-1972 2. MacArthur, Douglas, 1880-1964 3. Nuclear warfare 4. Presidents 5. Generals 6. World War II 7. Cold War 8. Reconstruction (1939-1951) 9. Korean War, 1950-1953 10. Military policy 11. China 12. United States 13. Impartial writing 14. History writing — Post World War II - 1959 — United States
LC 2016021412
Traces the story of how President Harry Truman and General Douglas MacArthur confronted each other's oppositional stances for America's future in the aftermath of World War II.
"An exciting, well-written comparison study of two American leaders at loggerheads during the Korean War crisis." —*Kirkus*
Includes bibliographical references and index.

973.92 United States — 1953-2001

Halberstam, David
The Best and the Brightest. David Halberstam; foreword by John McCain. Modern Library 2001. xxviii, 780 p.
ISBN 9780679640998
Grades: 11 12 Adult   973.92
1. Military policy 2. Politicians 3. Presidents 4. Vietnam War, 1961-1975 5. Politics and government 6. United States 7. 1960s 8. 1970s 9. History writing — Wars and conflicts — Vietnam War
LC 2001031261
An account of American power and politics in the 1950s and 1960s highlights the political and military figures who shaped domestic and foreign policy and who orchestrated America's involvement in Vietnam.
"The author describes analytically rather than narratively, how the Kennedy-Johnson intellectual (McNamara, Bundy, Rusk, Ball, Taylor, et al.) men praised as 'The best and the brightest' men of this century, became the architects of the disastrous American policy of Indochina." —*Library Journal*
Includes bibliographical references (p. [767]-772) and index; Originally published: New York : Random House, 1972.

The Fifties. David Halberstam. Villard Books 1993. xi, 800 p. : Illustration
ISBN 9780449909331
Grades: 11 12 Adult   973.92
1. Popular culture 2. Social life and customs 3. Politics and government 4. Economics 5. United States history 6. United States 7. 1950s 8. 20th century 9. History writing — Post World War II - 1959 — United States
LC 92056815
The Pulitzer Prize-winning journalist examines the social, political, economic, and cultural history of the 1950s, from McCarthy to I Love Lucy.
"The author's sources are secondary and derivative, but his instinct for the revealing anecdote, his ear for the memorable quote, and his awesome powers of organization add up to a variegated overview that moves seamlessly between the serious shenanigans of Chief Justice Earl Warren and the frivolous ones of . Grace Metalious." —*National Review*
Includes bibliographical references (p. [737]-745) and index.

Kennedy, Robert Francis
Rfk: His Words for Our Times. Robert F. Kennedy Jr; edited by C. Richard Allen and Edwin O. Guthman. William Morrow 2018. 304 p.
ISBN 9780062834102
Grades: Adult   973.92
1. Kennedy, Robert Francis, 1925-1968 2. Civil rights 3. Social justice 4. Politicians 5. Social change 6. Speeches, addresses, etc. 7. Politics and global affairs — World politics — United States 8. History writing — Politicians — United States 9. History writing — 1960s — United States
LC Bl2018045295
Published to commemorate the 50th anniversary of his assassination and featuring commentary by notable historians and public figures, an inspiring collection of Bobby Kennedy's most famous speeches shares intimate perspectives into his views on such subjects as civil rights, social justice, foreign policy, poverty and the Vietnam War.
"Rich background information on policy and historical context introduces each chapter and frames each speech, which reveal Kennedy's appeal to Democrats and Republicans, minorities and the middle class." —*Library Journal*

Kruse, Kevin Michael
Fault Lines: A History of the United States Since 1974. Kevin M. Kruse, Julian E. Zelizer. W.W. Norton & Company 2019. 400 p.
ISBN 9780393088663
Grades: Adult   973.92
1. Political culture 2. Polarization (Social sciences) 3. Right and left (Political science) 4. Income inequality 5. Racism 6. Political parties 7. Gender role 8. Mass media 9. United States history 10. Liberal writing 11. History writing — United States 12. Politics and global affairs — General 13. Society and culture — General
LC 2018035645
Two historians trace the origins of today's divided America to pivotal events in 1974, from Watergate to the energy crisis, to explore how long-standing disputes over income inequality, racial division, and gender roles fueled a polarized political landscape.
"Their survey constitutes a valuable road map for readers seeking to understand why the U.S. Is the way it is and ends with the hopeful message that the wear-and-tear inflicted on the country has inspired new institutions before and may do so again." —*Booklist*
Includes bibliographical references and index.

Risen, James
★ *The Last Honest Man: The CIA, the FBI, the Mafia, and the Kennedys — and One Senator's Fight to Save Democracy.* James Risen, with Thomas Risen. Little, Brown & Company 2023. 464 p.
ISBN 9780316565134
Grades: Adult   973.92
1. Church, Frank 2. Legislators 3. Ambition 4. Governmental investigations 5. Intelligence service 6. Administrative agencies 7. Political corruption 8. Assassination 9. Political surveillance 10. Organized crime 11. International relations 12. National security 13. North American people 14. American people 15. United States history 16. 20th century 17. Biographies 18. Life stories — Politics — Politicians 19. History writing — Scandals 20. History writing — 1970s — United States 21. True Crime — Investigations and Trials 22. Nonfiction that reads like fiction
Senator Frank Church of Idaho was an unlikely hero. He led congressional opposition to the Vietnam War and had become a scathing, radical critic of what he saw as American imperialism around the world. But he was still politically ambitious, privately yearning for acceptance from the foreign policy establishment that he hated and eager to run for president. Despite his flaws, Church would show historic strength in his greatest moment, when in the wake of Watergate he was suddenly tasked with investigating abuses of power in the intelligence community.
"A welcome restoration of a largely forgotten politician who navigated issues that continue to reverberate." —*Kirkus*
Includes bibliographical references and index.

Schulman, Bruce J.
The Seventies: The Great Shift in American Culture, Society, and Politics. Bruce J. Schulman. Free Press 2001. xvii, 334 p, 8 p. of plates : Illustration
ISBN 9780684828145
Grades: Adult   973.92

ESSENTIAL AND RECOMMENDED TITLES
973.92092 United States — 1953-2001 — Biography

1. Social life and customs 2. Politics and government 3. Civilization 4. United States 5. 1970s 6. 20th century 7. History writing — 1970s — United States

LC 2001023238

New York Times Notable Book, 2001.

Arguing that the 1970s were a formative decade in American history, the author probes the period between 1968 and 1984 for lessons about culture and politics.

"This is an important contribution to modern American social history and the literature of popular culture." —*Publishers Weekly*

Includes bibliographical references (p. 259-316) and index.

Thompson, Nicholas
The Hawk and the Dove: Paul Nitze, George Kennan, and the History of the Cold War. Nicholas Thompson. Henry Holt 2009. 416 p.

ISBN 9780805081428

Grades: 11 12 Adult   **973.92**

1. Nitze, Paul H. 2. Kennan, George F. (George Frost), 1904-2005 3. Cold War 4. Anti-communist movements 5. Ambassadors 6. National security 7. International relations 8. Government employees 9. United States 10. 20th century 11. Biographies 12. History writing — Politicians — United States 13. History writing — Cold War

LC 2009009225

ALA Notable Book, 2010; Library Journal Best Books, 2009.

Only two Americans held positions of great influence throughout the Cold War; ironically, they were the chief advocates for the opposing strategies in that harrowing conflict. Both came to power during World War II, reached their professional peaks during the Cold War's most frightening moments, and fought epic political battles that spanned decades. Yet despite their very different views, Paul Nitze and George Kennan remained good friends all their lives. Nitze—the hawk—believed that the best way to avoid a nuclear clash was to prepare to win one. More than any other American, he was responsible for the arms race. Kennan—the dove—persuasively argued that we should contain the Soviet Union while waiting for it to collapse from within. In following these two rivals and friends from the beginning of the Cold War to its end, Nicholas Thompson tells the story of our nation during the most dangerous half century in history.

"This book does an inspired job of telling the story of the Cold War through the careers of two of its most interesting and important figures." —*Washington Monthly*

Woodward, Bob
Shadow: Five Presidents and the Legacy of Watergate. Bob Woodward. Simon & Schuster 1999. 592 p. : Illustration

ISBN 9780684852621

Grades: Adult   **973.92**

1. Nixon, Richard M. (Richard Milhous), 1913-1994 2. Ford, Gerald R, 1913-2006 3. Carter, Jimmy, 1924- 4. Reagan, Ronald 5. Bush, George, 1924-2018 6. Clinton, Bill, 1946- 7. Mass media 8. Politicians 9. Watergate Scandal 10. Scandals 11. Impeachments 12. Presidents 13. Politics and government 14. Washington, D.C. 15. United States 16. 20th century 17. 21st century 18. History writing — Presidency — 20th century — United States

LC 99037045

New York Times Notable Book, 1999.

Examines the legacy of Watergate in terms of how Nixon's disgrace forever altered American politics and culture.

Includes bibliographical references (p. [518]-572) and index.

973.92092 United States — 1953-2001 — Biography

Whipple, Chris
The Gatekeepers: How the White House Chiefs of Staff Define Every Presidency. Chris Whipple. Crown 2017. 384 p.

ISBN 9780804138246

Grades: Adult   **973.92092**

1. White House chiefs of staff 2. Political culture 3. Presidential staff 4. Politics and government 5. United States 6. 20th century 7. History writing — Presidency — 20th century — United States

LC 2016046233

Examines how the American presidency has hinged on the effectiveness of the White House chiefs of staff, drawing on interviews with all seventeen living chiefs of staff and two former presidents to reveal how their decisions have influenced the nation.

"In this page-turner of a history, readers will discover new facets of historical events that they felt they already knew." —*Publishers Weekly*

973.921092 United States — 1953-1961 — Biography

Hitchcock, William I.
The Age of Eisenhower: America and the World in the 1950s. William I. Hitchcock. Simon & Schuster 2018. 512 p.

ISBN 9781439175668

Grades: Adult   **973.921092**

1. Eisenhower, Dwight D. (Dwight David), 1890-1969 2. Presidents 3. Cold War 4. International relations 5. United States 6. 1950s 7. 20th century 8. Biographies 9. Life stories — Politics — Politicians 10. History writing — Post World War II - 1959 — United States 11. History writing — Presidency — 20th century — United States

LC 2017026867

Citing the enduring popularity of America's 34th President, an original and penetrating assessment of Eisenhower analyzes his considerable influence on the Cold War, today's America and the nature of the presidency itself. By the Pulitzer Prize-finalist author of the Bitter Road to Freedom.

Includes bibliographical references and index.

Thomas, Evan
Ike's Bluff: President Eisenhower's Secret Battle to Save the World. Evan Thomas. Little, Brown and Co. 2012. 432 p.

ISBN 9780316091046

Grades: Adult   **973.921092**

1. Eisenhower, Dwight D. (Dwight David), 1890-1969 2. Presidents 3. Cold War 4. Nuclear weapons 5. Nuclear warfare 6. National security 7. International relations 8. United States 9. 1950s 10. 20th century 11. History writing — Presidency — United States 12. History writing — Post World War II - 1959 — United States 13. History writing — Cold War 14. History writing — Presidency — 20th century — United States

LC 2012019640

Examines the White House years of Dwight Eisenhower and reveals the former president, often viewed as a doddering lightweight, as a brilliant, intellectual tactician who could be patient and ruthless, and generous and self-serving.

Includes bibliographical references and index.

973.922 Administration of John Fitzgerald Kennedy, 1961-1963

Abrams, Dan
Kennedy's Avenger: Assassination, Conspiracy, and the Forgotten Trial of Jack Ruby. Dan Abrams and David Fisher. Hanover Square Press 2021. 320 p.

ISBN 9781335914033

Grades: Adult   **973.922**

1. Kennedy, John F. (John Fitzgerald), 1917-1963 2. Ruby, Jack, 1911-1967 3. Oswald, Lee Harvey, 1939-1963 4. Kennedy, Joseph P. (Joseph Patrick), 1888-1969 5. Trials 6. Organized crime 7. Nightclub owners 8. Assassins 9. Assassination 10. Conspiracy theories 11. Presidents 12. United States history 13. United States 14. 1960s 15. 20th century 16. History writing — 1960s — United States 17. True Crime — Investigations and trials 18. History writing — Conspiracy theories

Two New York Times best-selling authors examine the story behind the bizarre trial of Jack Ruby, a Dallas nightclub owner who murdered Lee Harvey

Oswald, the accused assassin of President John F. Kennedy, live on national television.

"Journalists Abrams and Fisher take a fresh, detailed look at Jack Ruby and his trial, a spectacle that riveted the nation in 1963-64.... Followers of all things regarding the JFK assassination will be fascinated by this account of one of the most unique trials of the twentieth century." —*Booklist*

Cohen, Andrew
Two Days in June: John F. Kennedy and the 48 Hours That Made History. Andrew Cohen. McClelland & Stewart 2014. 404 p.
ISBN 9780771023873
Grades: Adult   **973.922**
1. Kennedy, John F. (John Fitzgerald), 1917-1963 2. Political oratory 3. Presidents 4. Politics and government 5. United States 6. 20th century 7. 1960s 8. Biographies 9. Canadian literature 10. History writing — Presidency — 20th century — United States 11. History writing — 1960s — United States 12. Life stories — Politics — Politicians
LC Bl2014049755

Recounts forty-eight hours in John F. Kennedy's presidency in which he delivered two addresses to the public that would result in the Limited Nuclear Test Ban Treaty of 1963 and the Civil Rights Act of 1964.

"This book is a page-turner. Undoubtedly, Kennedy supporters will love it. More important, it serves as a first-rate introduction to why the president made such a significant impression on the nation and the world despite his brief tenure." —*Library Journal*

Matthews, Christopher
Kennedy & Nixon: The Rivalry That Shaped Postwar America. Christopher Matthews. Simon & Schuster 1996. 377 p. : Illustration
ISBN 9780684810300
Grades: 11 12 Adult   **973.922**
1. Kennedy, John F. (John Fitzgerald), 1917-1963 2. Nixon, Richard M. (Richard Milhous), 1913-1994 3. Politics and government 4. United States 5. 20th century 6. History writing — Presidency — 20th century — United States 7. History writing — 1960s — United States
LC 96015677

Traces the rivalry between John Kennedy and Richard Nixon, whose 1960 presidential contest set America's Cold War political course.

Includes bibliographical references and index.

973.922092 United States — 1961-1963 — Biography

Coleman, David G.
The Fourteenth Day: JFK and the Aftermath of the Cuban Missile Crisis. David G. Coleman. W.W. Norton & Co. 2012. 192 p.
ISBN 9780393084412
Grades: Adult   **973.922092**
1. Kennedy, John F. (John Fitzgerald), 1917-1963 2. Khrushchev, Nikita Sergeevich, 1894-1971 3. Cuban Missile Crisis, 1962 4. Nuclear weapons 5. Ballistic missiles 6. Missiles 7. International relations 8. Politics and government 9. Cuba 10. United States 11. Soviet Union 12. 1960s 13. History writing — Cold War 14. History writing — 1960s — United States 15. History writing — Latin America — Cuba
LC 2012025397

Describes what was going on in the Oval Office as the highly-charged events leading up the Cuban Missile Crisis unfolded, as well as the immediate aftermath, based on secret recordings made by President Kennedy.

Includes bibliographical references and index.

Hill, Clint
Five Days in November. Clint Hill and Lisa McCubbin. Gallery Books 2013. 256 p.
ISBN 9781668035757
Grades: Adult   **973.922092**
1. Kennedy, John F. (John Fitzgerald), 1917-1963 2. Onassis, Jacqueline Kennedy, 1929-1994 3. Assassination 4. Presidents 5. Secret service 6. United States history 7. United States 8. 20th century 9. Autobiographies and memoirs 10. History writing — Presidency — 20th century — United States 11. Life stories — Law and order — Police and law officers 12. True Crime — Murder
LC 2013019272

The retired United States Secret Service agent who is remembered for his courageous actions in the presidential motorcade after JFK was shot shares his memories of the five days leading up to, and after, that tragic day in November 1963.

Mrs. Kennedy and Me: An Intimate Memoir. Clint Hill; with Lisa McCubbin. Gallery Books 2012. 320 p.
ISBN 9781451648447
Grades: Adult   **973.922092**
1. Hill, Clint 2. Onassis, Jacqueline Kennedy, 1929-1994 3. Secret service 4. Charisma 5. Presidents' spouses 6. United States history 7. United States 8. 1960s 9. Autobiographies and memoirs 10. History writing — Presidency — 20th century — United States 11. History writing — 1960s — United States 12. Life stories — Politics 13. Life stories — Law and order 14. Life stories — Relationships
LC 2011051017

From 1960 to 1964, Clint Hill was the Secret Service agent assigned to First Lady Jacqueline Kennedy. Telling his story for the first time, Hill recounts Mrs. Kennedy's unfailing grace, intelligence, and spirit during times both joyful and tragic—from the birth of her children to her husband's assassination.

Lattin, Don
The Harvard Psychedelic Club: How Four Visionaries Killed the Fifties and Ushered in a New Age for America. by Don Lattin. HarperCollins Publishers 2010. 272 p.
ISBN 9780061655937
Grades: Adult   **973.922092**
1. Smith, Huston, 1919-2016 2. Ram Dass 3. Weil, Andrew 4. Leary, Timothy, 1920-1996 5. Hallucinogenic drug use 6. Research 7. Spirituality 8. Counterculture 9. Hallucinogenic drugs 10. Religions 11. United States 12. 1960s 13. 1970s 14. History writing — 1960s — United States 15. True Crime — Drugs
LC 2009026323

A Pulitzer Prize-nominated author explains how three brilliant scholars and one ambitious freshman crossed paths in Cambridge, Massachusetts, in the winter of 1960-61, and how their experiences in a psychedelic drug-research project transformed their lives and much of American culture in the 60s and 70s.

"Mr. Lattin does a lovely, gently humorous job of setting the scene and bringing these men together. This groovy story unfurls . like a ready-made treatment for a sprawling, elegiac and crisply comic movie, let's say Robert Altman by way of Wes Anderson." —*New York Times*

Includes bibliographical references and index.

Minutaglio, Bill
Dallas 1963: Politics, Treason, and the Assassination of JFK. Bill Minutaglio, Steven L. Davis. Grand Central Pub 2013. 272 p.
ISBN 9781455522095
Grades: Adult   **973.922092**
1. Kennedy, John F. (John Fitzgerald), 1917-1963 2. Hate groups 3. Right and left (Political science) 4. Extremists 5. Assassination 6. Presidents 7. United States history 8. Dallas, Texas 9. United States 10. 1960s 11. 20th century 12. History writing — Presidency — 20th century — United States 13. History writing — 1960s — United States
LC 2013939303

Presents an explosive and unsettling account of the radicals, reactionaries and extremists who turned Dallas into a city infamous for the assassination of JFK.

Oliphant, Thomas
★ *The Road to Camelot: Inside JFK's Five-year Campaign.* Thomas Oliphant and Curtis Wilkie. Simon & Schuster 2017. 432 p.

ESSENTIAL AND RECOMMENDED TITLES
973.923 Administration of Lyndon Baines Johnson, 1963-1969

ISBN 9781501105562
Grades: Adult **973.922092**
1. Kennedy, John F. (John Fitzgerald), 1917-1963 2. Presidential election, 1960 3. Presidential candidates 4. Political campaigns 5. Elections 6. Politics and government 7. United States 8. 1960s 9. 20th century 10. 1950s 11. Biographies 12. History writing — Presidency — United States 13. History writing — 1960s — United States
LC 2016050682

A behind-the-scenes account of the 35th President's journey to the White House includes coverage of his failed vice presidential nomination in 1956, the ways his Catholic faith challenged his campaigns and the successful efforts of his team of young advisors to reinvent the traditional party.

"The authors add a new perspective to literature on Kennedy by focusing on his electioneering efforts rather than his persona and policy outcomes." —*Library Journal*

Simon & Schuster nonfiction original hardcover—Title page verso; Includes bibliographical references and index.

Sherman, Casey
Above and Beyond: John F. Kennedy and America's Most Dangerous Cold War Spy Mission. Casey Sherman and Michael Tougias. PublicAffairs 2018. 352 p.

ISBN 9781610398046
Grades: Adult **973.922092**
1. Kennedy, John F. (John Fitzgerald), 1917-1963 2. Cold war 3. Cuban Missile Crisis, 1962 4. Spy planes 5. Military pilots 6. Ballistic missiles 7. Nuclear weapons 8. Military aviation 9. U-2 (Jet reconnaissance plane) 10. Fear of nuclear war 11. Presidents 12. United States 13. Soviet Union 14. Cuba 15. 1960s 16. 20th century 17. History writing — Cold War 18. History writing — Spies and spying 19. History writing — Presidency — 20th century — United States
LC 2018002748

The New York Times best-selling authors of the Finest Hours presents the gripping firsthand account of three war heroes|President John F. Kennedy and two U-2 pilots, Rudy Anderson and Chuck Maultsby|who were all brought together during Cuban Missile Crisis and risked their lives to save the United States.

Swanson, James L.
End of Days: The Assassination of John F. Kennedy. James L. Swanson. HarperCollins 2013. 304 p.

ISBN 9780062083487
Grades: Adult **973.922092**
1. Kennedy, John F. (John Fitzgerald), 1917-1963 2. Assassination 3. Presidents 4. Politics and government 5. United States history 6. Dallas, Texas 7. United States 8. 1960s 9. 20th century 10. History writing — Presidency — 20th century — United States 11. True Crime — Murder 12. History writing — 1960s — United States

The New York Times best-selling author of Manhunt: The 12-Day Chase for Lincoln's Killer presents a complete account of the day Kennedy was killed, following the event hour-by-hour, from the Kennedys' arrival in Texas through the shooting in Dealey Plaza to the shocking aftermath.

"Drawing on the decades of technological advances that have deepened the knowledge of the assassination, the author presents the stunning unfolding of the event in punchy, poignant vignettes, following one character after another to the inexorable conclusion." —*Kirkus*

Zapruder, Alexandra
Twenty-six Seconds: A Personal History of the Zapruder Film. Alexandra Zapruder. Twelve 2016. 272 p.

ISBN 9781455574810
Grades: Adult **973.922092**
1. Kennedy, John F. (John Fitzgerald), 1917-1963 2. Zapruder, Abraham 3. Ethical problems 4. Public interest 5. Memory 6. Films and history 7. Conspiracy theories 8. Fair use (Copyright) 9. Collective memory 10. Amateur films 11. 20th century 12. Biographies 13. History writing — Presidency — 20th century — United States 14. Life stories — General
LC 2016025786

The lesser-known family story behind Abraham Zapruder's film footage of the Kennedy assassination and its lasting impact, told by Zapruder's granddaughter, draws on personal records and previously sealed archives to trace the film's role in the media, courts, government and arts community.

"This well-written exploration of conspiracy, propriety, copyright, and public good versus private gain is seen through the prism of the worlds most famous home movie." —*Publishers Weekly*

Also published in large print format; Includes bibliographical references and index.

973.923 Administration of Lyndon Baines Johnson, 1963-1969

Boyle, Kevin
The Shattering: America in the 1960s. Kevin Boyle. W. W. Norton & Company 2021. 464 p.

ISBN 9780393355994
Grades: Adult **973.923**
1. Civil rights movement 2. Vietnam War, 1961-1975 3. Women's rights 4. War 5. Gender role 6. Race relations 7. United States history 8. United States 9. 20th century 10. 1960s 11. History writing — 1960s — United States
LC 2021022377

A National Book Award winner, covering the late 1950s through the early 1970s, focuses on the period's fierce conflicts over race, sex and war, capturing the inspiring and brutal events of this passionate time with a remarkable empathy that restores the humanity in those making this history.

"A concise, beautifully written history of the 'Long' 1960s, bringing the most important events and developments of that tumultuous decade to vivid life. . . . Ultimately, this is a standout example of narrative analytical history. A brilliantly achieved history of some unusually fraught years of American history." —*Kirkus*

Includes bibliographical references and index.

Johnson, Lyndon B.
Taking Charge: The Johnson White House Tapes, 1963-1964. Edited and with commentary by Michael R. Beschloss. Simon & Schuster 1997. 592 p.

ISBN 9780684804071
Grades: 11 12 Adult **973.923**
1. Johnson, Lyndon B, 1908-1973 2. Presidents 3. Tape recorders and players 4. Politics and government 5. United States 6. 1960s 7. 20th century 8. History writing — Presidency — 20th century — United States 9. History writing — 1960s — United States

New York Times Notable Book, 1997.

Portrays the thirty-sixth president as a man who struggled to surpass JFK on civil rights, guided the country into Vietnam, and twisted the arms of friends and enemies alike.

"There are no stunning revelations and no recorded moments of epochal importance. But Taking Charge is a riveting book nevertheless. This is partly because it has been superbly edited and annotated by the historian Michael R. Beschloss, who has made everything—even the most arcane references—accessible to ordinary readers." —*New York Times Book Review*

Includes bibliographical references and index.

Whitaker, Mark
★ *Saying It Loud: 1966—the Year Black Power Challenged the Civil Rights Movement*. Mark Whitaker. Simon & Schuster 2023. 400 p.

ISBN 9781982114121
Grades: Adult **973.923**
1. Black power 2. Civil Rights Movement 3. African American history 4. Revolutions 5. Radicalism 6. African American political activists 7. Antiracism 8. Power 9. Social justice 10. Race relations 11. United States history 12. United States 13. 1960s 14. 20th century 15. History writing — 1960s — United States 16. History writing — African American — Civil rights — United States 17. Life stories — Politics — Activists and Reformers — Civil Rights Leaders 18. Antiracist literature

In gripping, novelistic detail, Saying It Loud tells the story of how the Black Power phenomenon began to challenge the traditional civil rights movement in the turbulent year of 1966. Deeply researched and widely reported, Saying It Loud offers brilliant portraits of the major characters in the yearlong drama, and provides new details and insights from key players and journalists who covered the story. It also makes a compelling case for why the lessons from 1966 still resonate in the era of Black Lives Matter and the fierce contemporary battles over voting rights, identity politics, and the teaching of Black history.

Throughout, Whitaker elevates the movement's lesser-known figures, analyzes how internal and external forces splintered the movement, and contextualizes cultural developments including the free jazz of John Coltrane and Charles Mingus and the emergence of the Afro as a symbol of Black liberation. It adds up to a comprehensive and character-driven portrait of the 'First Black Power generation.' —Publishers Weekly

Includes bibliographical references and index.

Woods, Randall Bennett
Prisoners of Hope: Lyndon B. Johnson, the Great Society, and the Limits of Liberalism. Randall B. Woods. Basic Books 2016. 432 p.
ISBN 9780465050963
Grades: Adult   973.923
1. Johnson, Lyndon B, 1908-1973 2. Antipoverty programs 3. Social change 4. Liberalism 5. Politics and government 6. Social policy 7. United States 8. 20th century 9. 1960s 10. Biographies 11. History writing — Presidency — 20th century — United States 12. History writing — 1960s — United States
LC 2015040042

Offers a nuanced look at America's most ambitious—and controversial—domestic policy agenda since the New Deal, as well as an intriguing portrait of the president behind it.

"A sympathetic but also gimlet-eyed scholar's look at a towering physical and political presence who learned, to his sorrow, that good intentions were insufficient." —Kirkus

Includes bibliographical references and index.

Zeitz, Joshua
Building the Great Society: Inside Lyndon Johnson's White House. Joshua Zeitz. Viking 2018. xviii, 378 pages
ISBN 9780525428787
Grades: Adult   973.923
1. Johnson, Lyndon B, 1908-1973 2. Presidents 3. Liberalism 4. Social change 5. Cabinet officers 6. Civil rights 7. School integration 8. Race relations 9. Vietnam War, 1961-1975 10. Politics and government 11. United States 12. 1960s 13. 20th century 14. Biographies 15. Life stories — Politics — Politicians 16. History writing — Presidency — 20th century — United States 17. History writing — 1960s — United States
LC Bl2017046094

An analysis of the Johnson administration reveals how the Great Society programs were put into practice, profiling major figures in the liberal reforms of the 1960s and how they made Johnson's ambitious vision a reality.

"Zeitzs lucid account yields engrossing insights into one of Americas most hopeful, productive, and tragic political eras." —Publishers Weekly. Annex

Includes bibliographical references (pages 353-361) and index.

973.924 Administration of Richard Milhous Nixon, 1969-1974

Dobbs, Michael
King Richard: Nixon and Watergate—an American Tragedy. Michael Dobbs. Alfred A. Knopf 2021. 416 p.
ISBN 9780385350099
Grades: Adult   973.924
1. Nixon, Richard M. (Richard Milhous), 1913-1994 2. Watergate Scandal 3. Political corruption 4. Presidential tapes 5. Government cover-ups 6. Scandals 7. Politics and government 8. United States 9. 20th century 10. 1970s 11. 1960s 12. History writing — Scandals 13. History writing — Presidency — 20th century — United States 14. History writing — 1970s — United States
LC 2020028534

In January 1973, Richard Nixon had just been inaugurated after winning re-election in a historic landslide. But by April 1973, his presidency had fallen apart as the Watergate scandal metastasized into what White House counsel John Dean called "a full-blown cancer." King Richard is the intimate, utterly absorbing narrative of the tension-packed hundred days when the Watergate burglars and their handlers in the administration turned on one another, revealing their direct connection ties to the White House.

"Dobbs, former Washington Post reporter and author of a trilogy of nonfiction books about the Cold War, delivers a spellbinding account of the 100 days following Richard Nixon's second inaugural. . . . A riveting portrait of ambition, hubris, betrayal, and the downfall of an American president." —Kirkus

Includes bibliographical references and index.

Ferguson, Niall
Kissinger: The Idealist, 1923-1968. Niall Ferguson. Penguin Group USA 2015. 560 p.
ISBN 9781594206535
Grades: Adult   973.924
1. Kissinger, Henry, 1923-2023 2. National security advisors 3. Negotiation 4. Jewish men 5. Immigrants 6. Historians 7. Politicians 8. International relations 9. United States history 10. United States 11. 20th century 12. Biographies 13. History writing — Politicians — United States 14. Life stories — Politics — Politicians
LC 2015373204

A definitive portrait of the American statesman, based on unprecedented access to his private papers, challenges common misconceptions to trace Kissinger's beliefs to philosophical idealism.

"It will surprise many readers how quickly Kissinger finds his principles incompatible with the Kennedy-Johnson policy in Vietnam, and how reluctant he is to serve under the devious Nixon. A sophisticated portrait, certain to stir debate—and to heighten expectations for the sequel." —Booklist

Graff, Garrett M.
Watergate: A New History. Garrett M. Graff. Avid Reader Press 2022. 448 p.
ISBN 9781982139162
Grades: Adult   973.924
1. Nixon, Richard M. (Richard Milhous), 1913-1994 2. Watergate Scandal 3. Conspiracies 4. Cabinet officers 5. Political campaigns 6. Scandals 7. Political corruption 8. Government cover-ups 9. Governmental investigations 10. Impeachments 11. Presidents 12. Politics and government 13. United States 14. 20th century 15. 1960s 16. 1970s 17. History writing — Presidency — 20th century — United States 18. History writing — Scandals 19. History writing — 1970s — United States 20. Politics and global affairs — Political figures 21. Nonfiction that reads like fiction

Pulitzer Prize for History finalist, 2023.

In the early hours of June 17, 1972, a security guard named Frank Wills entered six words into the log book of the Watergate office complex that would change the course of history: "1:47 AM Found tape on doors; call police." Over the next two years, that single thwarted break-in would lead to dozens more arrests, an alleged kidnapping, FBI and congressional investigations, a Senate hearing, and bombshell testimonies from the highest levels of political power that ultimately would reveal a cover-up, sink a vice-president and a half-dozen Cabinet officials, lead to the jailing of an FBI director, end a presidency, and alter our views of moral authority and leadership. And yet, recent revelations like the release of more Nixon tapes and the identity of "Deep Throat" himself, means that the full story has never been told from start to finish. Now, in Watergate, journalist and author Garrett M. Graff explores the full sweep of the scandal that would come to define all others.

"Journalist Graff (The Only Plane in the Sky) sheds new light on the Watergate scandal in this exhaustive history. . . . Expertly researched and assembled, this is a valuable introduction to one of history's greatest political scandals." —Publishers Weekly

Morley, Jefferson
Scorpions' Dance: The President, the Spymaster, and Watergate. Jefferson Morley. St. Martin's Press 2022. 320 p.

ESSENTIAL AND RECOMMENDED TITLES
973.924092 United States — 1969-1974 — Biography

ISBN 9781250275837
Grades: Adult **973.924**
1. Helms, Richard 2. Nixon, Richard M. (Richard Milhous), 1913-1994 3. Watergate Scandal 4. Enemies 5. Secrets 6. Political intrigue 7. Intelligence service 8. Presidents 9. CIA agents 10. Politics and government 11. United States 12. 20th century 13. 1960s 14. 1970s 15. History writing — Scandals 16. History writing — Presidency — 20th century — United States 17. History writing — Spies and spying 18. Life stories — Politics

LC 2022002311

Jefferson Morley reveals the Watergate scandal in a completely new light: as the culmination of a concealed, deadly power struggle between President Richard Nixon and CIA Director Richard Helms. Nixon and Helms went back decades; both were 1950s Cold Warriors, and both knew secrets about the disastrous Bay of Pigs invasion of Cuba as well as off-the-books American government and CIA plots to remove Fidel Castro and other leaders in Latin America. Both had enough information on each other to ruin their careers. After the Watergate burglary on June 17, 1972, Nixon was desperate to shut down the FBI's investigation. He sought Helms' support and asked that the CIA intervene—knowing that most of the Watergate burglars were retired CIA agents with deep knowledge of the Agency's most sensitive secrets. The two now circled each other like scorpions, defending themselves with the threat of lethal attack. The loser would resign his office in disgrace; the winner, however, would face consequences for the secrets he had kept.

"With a complex cast of characters, Cold War espionage, and tense courtroom drama, Morley's timely book will appeal to readers seeking an in-depth understanding of both Watergate and CIA history." —*Library Journal*

Includes bibliographical references and index.

Packer, George
★ *The Unwinding: An Inner History of the New America*. George Packer. Farrar, Straus and Giroux 2013. 432 p.
ISBN 9780374102418
Grades: Adult **973.924**
1. National characteristics, American 2. Middle class 3. Economic policy 4. Social problems 5. Politics and government 6. United States history 7. United States 8. 21st century 9. 20th century 10. Politics and global affairs — World politics — United States

LC 2013004431

Booklist Editors' Choice, 2013; National Book Award for Nonfiction, 2013; New York Times Notable Book, 2013; National Book Critics Circle Award for Nonfiction finalist, 2013.

Through an examination of the lives of several Americans and leading public figures over the past three decades, Packer portrays a superpower in danger of coming apart at the seams, its elites no longer elite, its institutions no longer working, its ordinary people left to improvise their own schemes for success and salvation.

Perlstein, Rick
The Invisible Bridge: The Fall of Nixon and the Rise of Reagan. Rick Perlstein. Simon & Schuster 2014. 800 p.
ISBN 9781476782416
Grades: Adult **973.924**
1. Nixon, Richard M. (Richard Milhous), 1913-1994 2. Reagan, Ronald 3. Ideology 4. Conservatism 5. Presidents 6. United States history 7. United States 8. 1970s 9. 20th century 10. Biographies 11. History writing — 1970s — United States 12. History writing — Presidency — United States 13. History writing — Presidency — 20th century — United States

LC 2014381509

New York Times Notable Book, 2014.

The best-selling author of Nixonland presents a portrait of the United States during the turbulent political and economic upheavals of the 1970s, covering events ranging from the Arab oil embargo and the era of Patty Hearst to the collapse of the South Vietnamese government and the rise of Ronald Reagan.

"Although the book only goes up to Reagan's loss of the 1976 Republican nomination to President Gerald Ford, the scope of the work never feels limited. A compelling, astute chronicle of the politics and culture of late-20th-century America." —*Kirkus*

★ *Nixonland: America's Second Civil War and the Divisive Legacy of Richard Nixon, 1965-1972*. Rick Perlstein. Scribner 2008. 640 p.
ISBN 9780743243025
Grades: Adult **973.924**
1. Nixon, Richard M. (Richard Milhous), 1913-1994 2. Elections 3. Presidents 4. United States history 5. United States 6. 1960s 7. 20th century 8. Biographies 9. History writing — Presidency — 20th century — United States 10. History writing — 1960s — United States

LC 2008273706

New York Times Notable Book, 2008.

An account of the thirth-seventh presidency sets Nixon's administration against a backdrop of the tumultuous civil rights movement while offering insight into how key events in the 1960s set the stage for today's political divides.

973.924092 United States — 1969-1974 — Biography

Dean, John W.
The Nixon Defense: What He Knew and When He Knew It. John W. Dean. Viking 2014. 416 p.
ISBN 9780670025367
Grades: Adult **973.924092**
1. Nixon, Richard M. (Richard Milhous), 1913-1994 2. Watergate Scandal 3. Political corruption 4. Presidents 5. United States 6. 20th century 7. Biographies 8. History writing — Presidency — 20th century — United States 9. History writing — 1970s — United States

LC 2014020821

A former White House Counsel and one of the last surviving major figures from Watergate uses his own transcripts from hundreds of conversations as well as documents in the archives to definitively determine what Nixon knew and when he knew it.

"[O]ne of the best and fullest accounts of the Watergate cover-up, one that conveys in Nixon's own voice the casual criminality of his troubled presidency." —*Publishers Weekly*

Feldstein, Mark Avrom
Poisoning the Press: Richard Nixon, Jack Anderson, and the Rise of Washington's Scandal Culture. Mark Feldstein. Farrar, Straus and Giroux 2010. 480 p.
ISBN 9780374235307
Grades: Adult **973.924092**
1. Nixon, Richard M. (Richard Milhous), 1913-1994 2. Anderson, Jack, 1922-2005 3. Press and politics 4. Mass media 5. Political culture 6. Political corruption 7. Presidents 8. Journalists 9. Politics and government 10. United States 11. 20th century 12. 1960s 13. 1970s 14. Biographies 15. History writing — Presidency — 20th century — United States 16. History writing — Presidency — United States 17. Arts and Entertainment — Writing and Publishing 18. History writing — 1970s — United States

LC 2010010272

Profiles the relationship between the 37th president and a reviled Pulitzer Prize-winning columnist, citing Anderson's shady investigative pursuits of revelatory information and Nixon's retaliatory campaign of bogus evidence and discrediting smears.

Includes bibliographical references and index.

Reston, James
The Conviction of Richard Nixon: The Untold Story of the Frost/Nixon Interviews. James Reston, Jr. Harmony Books 2007. 207 p.
ISBN 9780307394200
Grades: Adult **973.924092**
1. Nixon, Richard M. (Richard Milhous), 1913-1994 2. Frost, David 3. Reston, James, Jr, 1941-2023 4. Former presidents 5. Watergate Scandal 6. Presidents 7. Politics and government 8. United States 9. 20th century 10. 1960s 11. 1970s 12. Interviews 13. History writing — Presidency — 20th

century — United States 14. History writing — 1970s — United States 15. History writing — Scandals

LC 2007001238

Drawing on his experiences spearheading the research team that prepared David Frost for his 1977 interviews with former president Richard Nixon, offers a dramatic perspective of the Watergate scandal and its aftermath.

"In 1977, three years after his resignation, Richard Nixon returned to the public eye in a series of interviews with British television journalist David Frost, for which Nixon received $1 million." —*Publishers Weekly*

973.925092 United States — 1974-1977 — Biography

Rumsfeld, Donald
When the Center Held: Gerald Ford and the Rescue of the American Presidency. Donald Rumsfeld. Free Press 2018. 352 p.
ISBN 9781501172939
Grades: Adult   **973.925092**
1. Ford, Gerald R, 1913-2006 2. Rumsfeld, Donald, 1932-2021 3. Politicians 4. Watergate Scandal 5. Legislators 6. Presidents 7. Politics and government 8. United States 9. 1970s 10. 20th century 11. Life stories — Politics — Politicians 12. Politics and global affairs — Political figures 13. History writing — Presidency — 20th century — United States 14. History writing — 1970s — United States

LC 2018001411

A revealing political memoir of the presidency of Gerald Ford is seen through the eyes of Donald Rumsfeld, a New York Times best-selling author and Ford's former secretary of defense, chief of staff and longtime personal confidant.

"A few flaws aside, this is an engrossing and informative tribute to a man whom Jimmy Carter rightfully thanked in his inaugural address for all he has done to heal our land." —*Kirkus*

Smith, Richard Norton
On His Own Terms: A Life of Nelson Rockefeller. Richard Norton Smith. Random House Inc. 2014. 640 p. : Illustration
ISBN 9780375505805
Grades: Adult   **973.925092**
1. Rockefeller, Nelson Aldrich, 1908-1979 2. Republicans 3. Philanthropists 4. Vice-presidents 5. Politicians 6. Businesspeople 7. Politics and government 8. United States 9. 20th century 10. Biographies 11. Life stories — Politics — Politicians

LC 2013497351

A Pulitzer Prize finalist offers a sweeping portrait of one of the 20th century's most significant politicians, businessmen and philanthropists. Illustrations. Tour. Family tree provided online.

973.926 Administration of Jimmy (James Earl) Carter, 1977-1981

Bird, Kai
The Outlier: The Unfinished Presidency of Jimmy Carter. KAI Bird. Crown 2021. 832 p.
ISBN 9780451495235
Grades: Adult   **973.926**
1. Carter, Jimmy, 1924- 2. Presidents 3. International relations 4. Politics and government 5. United States 6. 20th century 7. 1970s 8. 1980s 9. Biographies 10. Life stories — Politics — Politicians 11. History writing — Presidency — 20th century — United States 12. Politics and global affairs — Political figures

LC 2021004350

An expert biographer and author of American Prometheus, drawing on interviews with members of Carter's administration as well as recently unclassified documents from his presidential library, reevaluates the complex triumphs and tragedies of Jimmy Carter's presidential legacy.

"In this latest book, Bird (American Prometheus) draws heavily from personal accounts to present a thorough understanding of Jimmy Carter (b. 1924) and his presidency.... This engaging political biography, similar in scope to Jonathan Alter's His Very Best, will introduce Carter to a new generation, and will remind other readers of a truly transitional time in U.S. politics." —*Library Journal*

Includes bibliographical references and index.

Carter, Jimmy
Sharing Good Times. Jimmy Carter. Simon & Schuster 2005. xii, 174 p.
ISBN 9780743270687
Grades: Adult   **973.926**
1. Carter, Jimmy, 1924- 2. Sharing 3. Families 4. Family relationships 5. Interpersonal relations 6. Personal conduct 7. Presidents 8. United States 9. 20th century 10. Autobiographies and memoirs 11. Biographies 12. History writing — Presidency — 20th century — United States 13. Life stories — Politics — Politicians 14. Life stories — Relationships — Family 15. History writing — 1970s — United States

LC 2004051351

The former president recalls some of the simple joys that he has experienced throughout the years, especially those that he has shared with members of his family, friends, and colleagues.

"The author recalls various occasions in his life that became lasting sources of pleasure. [These remembrances] include his personal reasons for seeing his father as a hero, watching minor and major-league baseball games growing up, his days in the navy, road trips with his wife and children, his entry into politics, taking vacations while in the White House, his famous volunteer work, and even his hobbies." —*Booklist*

Includes index.

White House Diary. Jimmy Carter. Farrar, Straus and Giroux 2010. xv, 570 p, 24 p. of plates : Illustration
ISBN 9780374280994
Grades: Adult   **973.926**
1. Carter, Jimmy, 1924- 2. Presidents 3. Personal diaries 4. Executive power 5. Politicians 6. Political leadership 7. Politics and government 8. United States 9. 20th century 10. 1970s 11. 1980s 12. Autobiographies and memoirs 13. History writing — Presidency — 20th century — United States 14. Life stories — Politics — Politicians 15. History writing — 1970s — United States 16. History writing — 1980s — United States

LC 2010015544

The edited, annotated diary of President Jimmy Carter—filled with insights into his presidency, his relationships with friends and foes, and his lasting impact on issues that still preoccupy America and the world.

"That the language is blunt and occasionally a little un-Christian may come as a surprise. But the writings here reflect the Mr. Carter we know: Boastful and painfully confessional, sanctimonious and callous, insightful and un-self-aware. These are the thoughts of a secular preacher and calculating politician, surrounded by friends and yet often alone." —*New York Times*

Includes index.

Perlstein, Rick
★ *Reaganland: America's Right Turn 1976-1980.* Rick Perlstein. Simon & Schuster 2020. 1120 p.
ISBN 9781476793054
Grades: Adult   **973.926**
1. Reagan, Ronald 2. Carter, Jimmy, 1924- 3. Right and left (Political science) 4. Elections 5. Conservatism 6. Presidents 7. Politics and government 8. United States history 9. United States 10. 1970s 11. 1980s 12. 20th century 13. History writing — Presidency — 20th century — United States 14. History writing — 1970s — United States

LC Bl2020016082

New York Times Notable Book, 2020.

Backed by a reenergized conservative Republican base, Reagan ran on the campaign slogan "Make America Great Again," and prevailed. Reaganland is the story of how that happened, tracing conservative's cutthroat strategies to gain power and explaining why they endure four decades later.

"Political historian Perlstein (The Invisible Bridge) concludes the saga of right-wing insurgency he started in Before the Storm, his magisterial account of

ESSENTIAL AND RECOMMENDED TITLES
973.927092 United States — 1981-1989 — Biography

the 1964 Goldwater presidential campaign, with this chronicle of intensifying 1970s political clashes.... The result is an insightful and entertaining analysis of a watershed era in American politics." —*Publishers Weekly*

973.927092 United States — 1981-1989 — Biography

Mann, Jim
The Rebellion of Ronald Reagan: A History of the End of the Cold War. James Mann. Viking 2009. 432 p.
ISBN 9780670020546
Grades: Adult
973.927092
1. Reagan, Ronald 2. Nixon, Richard M. (Richard Milhous), 1913-1994 3. Massie, Suzanne 4. Cold War 5. International relations 6. Diplomacy 7. Political leadership 8. Presidents 9. United States 10. Soviet Union 11. 20th century 12. 1980s 13. Biographies 14. History writing — Presidency — 20th century — United States 15. History writing — 1980s — United States 16. History writing — Cold War
LC 2008029029

Analyzes the fortieth president's role in ending the Cold War, in a report that challenges popular beliefs, reveals lesser-known aspects of the Reagan administration's foreign policy, and cites the contributions of such figures as Nixon, Kissinger, and Gorbachev.

"Ronald Reagan did not win the Cold War, nor was he just historically lucky, as two contrasting viewpoints would sometimes have it. Instead, . [the author writes,] after a career of hard line anticommunism Reagan proved more flexible and visionary than many other leaders of American foreign policy and more opportunistic and insightful into the motives of Mikhail Gorbachev when the Soviet leader signaled change in the USSR's own conventional hard-line position. Mann bases his argument upon impressive original research, including interviews with principals who range from George Shultz, to Colin Powell, to Helmut Kohl, to Nancy Reagan." —*Library Journal*

Includes bibliographical references and index.

973.928 Administration of George Bush, 1989-1993

Bush, George
All the Best, George Bush: My Life in Letters and Other Writings. George Bush. Scribner 1999. 640 p. : Illustration
ISBN 9780684839585
Grades: Adult
973.928
1. Bush, George, 1924-2018 2. Presidents 3. United States 4. 20th century 5. History writing — Presidency — 20th century — United States 6. History writing — 1990s — United States
LC 99040440

The former president shares his life in correspondence, diary entries, memos, and other writings, from his letter home as an eighteen-year-old Navy pilot during World War II to one written to his children on the eve of Desert Storm.

"This work is refreshing and, in many ways, will shed more light on the man's personal character and public persona than any memoir or biography could. It offers an intriguing picture of a man who takes fierce pride in his modesty." —*Publishers Weekly*

George Bush in the title appears as his signature; a Lisa Drew book; Includes index.

Updegrove, Mark K.
The Last Republicans: Inside the Extraordinary Relationship Between George H.W. Bush and George W. Bush. Mark K. Updegrove. Harper 2017. 304 p.
ISBN 9780062654120
Grades: Adult
973.928
1. Bush, George, 1924-2018 2. Bush, George W. (George Walker), 1946- 3. Bush family 4. Fathers and sons 5. Presidents 6. Politicians 7. Politics and government 8. United States 9. 20th century 10. 21st century 11. Biographies 12. History writing — Presidency — 20th century — United States

LC 2017034575

Written with the full cooperation of Presidents George H. W. Bush and George W. Bush, a major biographical examination of their relationship as presidents and as father and son draws on exclusive interviews with the pair and close family members.

"A thoughtful political biography of two dynasts of a now-receding generation of politicians." —*Kirkus*

Includes bibliographical references.

973.929 Administration of Bill Clinton, 1993-2001

Branch, Taylor
The Clinton Tapes: Wrestling History with the President. Taylor Branch. Simon & Schuster 2009. x, 707 p, 8 p. of plates : Illustration; Portrait
ISBN 9781416543336
Grades: Adult
973.929
1. Clinton, Bill, 1946- 2. Politicians 3. Presidents 4. Politics and government 5. Leadership 6. United States history 7. United States 8. 1990s 9. 20th century 10. 21st century 11. Biographies 12. History writing — Presidency — 20th century — United States 13. Life stories — Politics — Politicians 14. History writing — 1990s — United States
LC 2009502213

Recounts the intimate talks the author shared with the forty-second president during the latter's two terms in office, sharing his perspective on Clinton's private torments, family life at the White House, and presidential challenges.

"Not everyone who begins it will finish Branch's book, yet Clinton's remarks contribute critically to the historical record and accordingly merit a place in most library collections." —*Booklist*

Includes bibliographical references and index.

Gates, Robert Michael
★ *Exercise of Power: American Failures, Successes, and a New Path Forward in the Post-cold War World.* Robert M. Gates. Random House Inc 2020. 256 p.
ISBN 9781524731885
Grades: Adult
973.929
1. International relations 2. Great powers 3. Military policy 4. Geopolitics 5. World politics 6. Diplomacy 7. Politics and government 8. United States 9. 20th century 10. 21st century 11. Politics and global affairs — World politics
LC 2019057305

New York Times Notable Book, 2020.

The former Secretary of Defense and author of the best-selling Duty offers a candid, sweeping examination of American executive powers and how they have been exercised with positive and negative results by American Presidents throughout the post-Cold War era.

"This important work dives deep into the past three decades of American foreign policy to provide a realistic picture of how key policy decisions were crafted. Highly recommended for those wanting an examination of America's role within the global community." —*Library Journal*

Includes bibliographical references and index.

973.93 United States — 2001-

Gill, A. A.
To America with Love. A. A. Gill. Simon & Schuster 2013. 272 p.
ISBN 9781416596219
Grades: Adult
973.93
1. Gill, A. A, 1954- 2. Social life and customs 3. Voyages and travels 4. United States 5. Travel Writing — General
LC Bl2013031371

Presents a tribute to America that traces the history and logic of the nation's habits while sharing illuminating anecdotes reflecting the nation's diverse culture as experienced by everyday people.

Originally published in Great Britain in 2012 by Weidenfeld & Nicolson under title: The Golden door.

Offerman, Nick
Where the Deer and the Antelope Play: The Pastoral Observations of One Ignorant American Who Loves to Walk Outside. Nick Offerman. E.P. Dutton 2021. 320 p.

ISBN 9781101984697

Grades: Adult   973.93

1. Offerman, Nick, 1970- 2. Actors and actresses 3. Hiking 4. Nature walks 5. Male friendship 6. Outdoor recreation 7. Wilderness areas 8. Rural life 9. Nature conservation 10. National characteristics, American 11. Natural history 12. Voyages and travels 13. Glacier National Park 14. The West (United States) 15. England 16. United States 17. Life stories — Arts and culture — Performing arts — Actors and actresses 18. Life stories — Nature and outdoors 19. Travel Writing — United States 20. Society and culture — General

In July 2019, Nick took a hiking trip to Glacier National Park with his friends Jeff Tweedy and George Saunders. The trip, and the conversations between the three men, began a study and exploration of both the American West and its National Parks that addresses so many of the important issues that affect America today. With wit, heartwarming stories and a keen insight into new and exciting ways to see both the past and the future of the country, the actor, writer and woodworker takes a literary journey to America's frontier to celebrate the people and landscape that have made it great.

"A great mix of wit and perceptive observation from travels in the United States and the United Kingdom just before and during the COVID-19 pandemic, with a surprising amount of history, nature, and ecology thrown in." —*Library Journal*

Osnos, Evan
Wildland: The Making of America's Fury. Evan Osnos. Farrar, Straus & Giroux 2021. 464 p.

ISBN 9780374286675

Grades: Adult   973.93

1. Osnos, Evan, 1976- 2. Identity 3. Everyday life 4. Economics 5. Inequality 6. Polarization (Social sciences) 7. American dream 8. Political culture 9. American people 10. Politics and government 11. Civilization 12. Voyages and travels 13. United States 14. 21st century 15. Impartial writing 16. Society and culture — Urban and regional studies 17. Politics and global affairs — General 18. Travel Writing — United States

LC 2021022114

Evan Osnos moved to Washington, D.C, in 2013 after a decade away from the United States. While abroad, he often found himself making a case that even though America had made grave mistakes throughout its history, it aspired to some foundational moral commitments: the rule of law, the power of truth, the right of equal opportunity for all. But when he returned to the United States, he found each of these principles under assault. In search of an explanation for the crisis that reached an unsettling crescendo in 2020—a year of pandemic, civil unrest, and political turmoil—he focused on three places he knew firsthand: Greenwich, Connecticut; Clarksburg, West Virginia; and Chicago, Illinois. Reported over the course of six years, Wildland follows ordinary individuals as they navigate the varied landscapes of twenty-first-century America. Through their powerful, often poignant stories, Osnos traces the sources of America's political dissolution.

"The National Book Award-winning journalist examines the ideological gaps that have widened between 9/11 and the Jan. 6, 2021 assault on the U.S. Capitol. . . . As an overview of a fractious ideological landscape, this skillful treatment is hard to beat. An elegant survey of the causes and effects of polarization in America." —*Kirkus*

Includes index.

Packer, George
Last Best Hope: America in Crisis and Renewal. George Packer. Farrar Straus & Giroux 2021. 240 p.

ISBN 9780374603663

Grades: Adult   973.93

1. Inequality 2. Democracy 3. Civics 4. Income inequality 5. National characteristics, American 6. Equality 7. Identity 8. Injustice 9. Politics and government 10. Civilization 11. United States 12. 21st century 13. Society and culture — Wealth and class 14. Politics and global affairs — World politics — United States

An acclaimed National Book Award-winning author diagnoses America's descent into a failed state and envisions a path toward overcoming our injustices, paralyses and divides.

"National Book Award-winner Packer explains our current political tensions as the collision of four incompatible narratives about what makes the U.S. special." —*Booklist*

Tolentino, Jia
★ *Trick Mirror: Reflections on Self-delusion.* Jia Tolentino. Random House 2019. 256 p.

ISBN 9780525510543

Grades: Adult   973.93

1. Social networks 2. Internet 3. Identity 4. Self-deception 5. Life 6. Social change 7. Reality television programs 8. Capitalism 9. Swindlers and swindling 10. Culture 11. Social media 12. Civilization 13. United States 14. 21st century 15. Essays 16. Society and culture — Media and technology 17. Society and culture — Pop culture 18. Arts and Entertainment — Writing and Publishing — Literary criticism 19. Book club best bets

LC 2019000446

New York Times Notable Book, 2019; National Book Critics Circle Award: John Leonard Prize finalist, 2019.

Presents nine original essays examining the fractures at the center of culture today, offering insights into the conflicts, contradictions, incentives, and changes related to the rise of toxic social networking.

"Tolentino brings a preternaturally aware millennial sensibility and exceptional literary skills to her keenly inquisitive and complexly involving essays." —*Booklist*

973.931 Administration of George W. Bush, 2001-2009

Ackerman, Spencer
Reign of Terror: How the 9/11 Era Destabilized America and Produced Trump. Spencer Ackerman. Viking 2021. 384 p.

ISBN 9781984879776

Grades: Adult   973.931

1. War on Terrorism, 2001-2009 2. September 11 Terrorist Attacks, 2001 3. Nativism 4. Authoritarianism 5. National security 6. International relations 7. Politics and government 8. Military policy 9. United States 10. 21st century 11. 2000s (Decade) 12. 2010s 13. Politics and global affairs — National security 14. Politics and global affairs — World politics — United States

LC 2021015357

An examination of the profound impact that the War on Terror had in pushing American politics and society in an authoritarian direction for an entire generation, at home and abroad. The United States has waged an endless conflict known as the War on Terror. In addition to multiple ground wars, it has pioneered drone strikes and industrial-scale digital surveillance, as well as detaining people indefinitely and torturing them. These conflicts have yielded neither peace nor victory, but they have transformed America.

"National-security reporter Ackerman delivers a tour-de-force about the transformation of the United States in the two decades since the September 11 attacks, that thoroughly and comprehensively examines how the post-9/11 security state has engulfed society. . . . An essential work that encapsulates the trajectory of American politics in the first two decades of the 21st century, and the lasting impact on everyday life." —*Library Journal*

Includes bibliographical references and index.

ESSENTIAL AND RECOMMENDED TITLES
973.931 Administration of George W. Bush, 2001-2009

Farmer, John J.
The Ground Truth: The Untold Story of America Under Attack on 9/11. John Farmer. Riverhead Books 2009. 384 p.
ISBN 9781594488948
Grades: 9 10 11 12 Adult   973.931
1. September 11 Terrorist Attacks, 2001 2. National security 3. Bureaucracy 4. Terrorists 5. Political science 6. Terrorism 7. United States history 8. United States 9. 21st century 10. History writing — September 11, 2001 — United States
LC 2009023297
New York Times Notable Book, 2009.

A senior counsel to the 9/11 Commission draws on recordings, transcripts, and recently declassified records to reveal aspects of the attacks that have not been previously disclosed, arguing that the day's events were predictable and that the nation is still at risk.
Includes bibliographical references and index.

Graff, Garrett M.
★ *The Only Plane in the Sky: An Oral History of 9/11*. Garrett M. Graff. Avid Reader Press 2019. 512 p.
ISBN 9781501182204
Grades: Adult   973.931
1. September 11 Terrorist Attacks, 2001 2. Witnesses 3. Tragedy 4. First responders 5. Public officials 6. Victims of terrorism 7. Search and rescue operations 8. Terrorism 9. United States history 10. New York City 11. Washington, D.C. 12. 21st century 13. Oral histories 14. Impartial writing 15. Life stories — Facing adversity — Victims of crime — Terrorism 16. Life stories — People in history — Witness to history 17. History writing — September 11, 2001 — United States 18. History writing — Natural disasters and tragedies
LC Bl2019021009

A panoramic oral history of the September 11 attacks draws on hundreds of interviews with government officials, first responders, survivors, friends and family members to recount events from the perspectives of firsthand witnesses.
"This excellent oral history provides a much-needed perspective of the events and aftermath." —*Library Journal*
Includes bibliographical references and index.

Khan, Mahvish Rukhsana
My Guantanamo Diary: The Detainees and the Stories They Told Me. Mahvish Khan. PublicAffairs 2008. xv, 302 p.
ISBN 9781586484989
Grades: Adult   973.931
1. Detention of people 2. Prisoners of war 3. Combatants and noncombatants (International law) 4. Due process of law 5. Prisoners 6. Prisons 7. Prisoner abuse 8. Military prisons 9. Legislation 10. Human rights 11. Civil rights 12. War on Terrorism, 2001-2009 13. Guantanamo Bay Naval Base, Cuba 14. Biographies 15. Life stories — Facing adversity — War and oppression 16. History writing — Wars and conflicts
LC Bl2008011526
Library Journal Best Books, 2008.

An American attorney born to immigrant Afghan parents describes her outrage over the detainments at Guantanamo, her volunteer role as an interpreter for prisoners, and the plight of those who have been detained for years without trial.

Mayer, Jane
The Dark Side: The Inside Story of How the War on Terror Turned into a War on American Ideals. Jane Mayer. Doubleday 2008. 392 p. : Illustration
ISBN 9780385526395
Grades: Adult   973.931
1. Torture 2. Terrorists 3. War on Terrorism, 2001-2009 4. Terrorism 5. Confession (Law) 6. Antiterrorist policy 7. National security 8. Presidents 9. Politics and government 10. United States 11. 21st century 12. Politics and global affairs — Terrorism
ALA Notable Book, 2009; J. Anthony Lukas Book Prize, 2009; New York Times Notable Book, 2008; Robert F. Kennedy Book Award, 2009; National Book Award for Nonfiction finalist, 2008; National Book Critics Circle Award for Nonfiction finalist, 2008.

Examines how the U.S. made self-destructive decisions in pursuit of terrorism in the wake of 9/11 and reveals how these actions violated the Constitution, hampered efforts to bring down AL Qaeda, and damaged the nation's moral and political standing in the world.
"This is a brilliantly researched and deeply unsettling book." —*New York Times Book Review*
Includes bibliographical references (p. [361]-369) and index.

Pfeifer, Joseph
Ordinary Heroes: A Memoir of 9/11. Joseph Pfeifer. Portfolio/Penguin 2021. 272 p.
ISBN 9780593330258
Grades: Adult   973.931
1. Pfeifer, Joseph, 1956- 2. September 11 Terrorist Attacks, 2001 3. Fire fighters 4. Grief 5. Resilience 6. Search and rescue operations 7. Heroes and heroines 8. New York city 9. Autobiographies and memoirs 10. Life stories — Facing adversity — Victims of crime — Terrorism 11. History writing — September 11, 2001 — United States
LC 2021024461

Ordinary Heroes is the unforgettable and intimate account of what Chief Pfeifer witnessed at Ground Zero, on that day and the days that followed. Through his eyes, we see the horror of the attack and the courage of the firefighters who ran into the burning towers to save others. We see him send his own brother up the stairs of the North Tower, never to return. And we walk with him and his fellow firefighters through weeks of rescue efforts and months of numbing grief, as they wrestle with the real meaning of heroism and leadership. This gripping narrative gives way to resiliency and a determination that permanently reshapes Pfeifer, his fellow firefighters, NYC, and America.
"A heartfelt, affecting book that sheds new light on one of the darkest moments in recent history." —*Kirkus*
Includes bibliographical references.

Smith, Jean Edward
Bush. Jean Edward Smith. Simon & Schuster 2016. 816 p.
ISBN 9781476741192
Grades: Adult   973.931
1. Bush, George W. (George Walker), 1946- 2. Presidents 3. Faith (Christianity) 4. Decision-making 5. Politics and government 6. United States 7. 21st century 8. 2000s (Decade) 9. Biographies 10. History writing — Presidency — 21st century — United States 11. Life stories — Politics — Politicians
LC 2015034690

Examines the role of the forty-third president's deep religious faith in his controversial decisions, exploring his inclinations to ignore advisors and make fateful independent decisions, most significantly the invasion of Iraq, in ways that have had profound consequences.
"This is a superb recap and critical analysis of Bush's controversial administration." —*Publishers Weekly*
Includes bibliographical references and index.

Wright, Lawrence
★ *The Looming Tower: Al-qaeda and the Road to 9/11*. Lawrence Wright. Knopf 2006. 469 p, 16 p. of plates : Illustration; Map
ISBN 9780375414862
Grades: Adult   973.931
1. September 11 Terrorist Attacks, 2001 2. Militants 3. Islam 4. Radicalism 5. Antiterrorist policy 6. Intelligence service 7. Terrorism 8. United States 9. 20th century 10. Page to screen 11. History writing — September 11, 2001 — United States
LC 2006041032

Pulitzer Prize for General Nonfiction, 2007; Los Angeles Times Book Prize for History, 2006; J. Anthony Lukas Book Prize, 2007; Lionel Gelber Prize (Canada), 2007; New York Times Notable Book, 2006; National Book Award for Nonfiction finalist, 2006.

Explores both the American and Arab sides of the September 11th terrorist attacks in an account of the people, ideas, events, and intelligence failures that led to the attacks.

"This book is not just a detailed, heart-stopping account of the events leading up to 9/11, written with style and verve, and carried along by villains and heroes that only a crime novelist could dream up. It's an education, too . a thoughtful examination of the world that produced the men who brought us 9/11, and of their progeny who bedevil us today." —*New York Times Book Review*

This title was adapted into a 10-episiode TV miniseries of the same name airing on Hulu. This miniseries stars Alec Baldwin, Jeff Daniels, Tahar Rahim, and Peter Sarsgaard; Includes bibliographical references (p. 429-438) and index.

Zuckoff, Mitchell

★ *Fall and Rise: The Story of 9/11.* Mitchell Zuckoff. HarperCollins 2019. 592 p.

ISBN 9780062275646

Grades: Adult   **973.931**

1. September 11 Terrorist Attacks, 2001 2. United Airlines Flight 93 Hijacking Incident, 2001 3. Terrorism 4. United States 5. History writing — September 11, 2001 — United States

LC Bl2019008366

Weaves together the events in New York, at the Pentagon, and in Shanksville, Pennsylvania to create a complete narrative of the terrorist attacks of September 11, 2001, offering stories of the people most affected by the attacks and their immediate aftermath.

"Though difficult to read, this emotional compilation will find a place with other 9/11 histories for its thorough recounting of the human cost of political violence." —*Library Journal*

973.932 Administration of Barack Obama, 2009-2017

Balz, Daniel J.

*The **Battle** for America, 2008: The Extraordinary Election of 2008.* Dan Balz and Haynes Johnson. Viking 2009. 432 p.

ISBN 9780670021116

Grades: Adult   **973.932**

1. Obama, Barack 2. McCain, John, 1936-2018 3. Presidential candidates 4. Presidential election, 2008 5. Political campaigns 6. Elections 7. Practical politics 8. Political journalism 9. Political parties 10. Political science 11. Politics and government 12. United States 13. 21st century 14. 2000s (Decade) 15. Politics and global affairs — Elections

LC 2009017129

In an account of an election during a most critical time, two political journalists cover the whole saga, from the earliest stages of the nominees' campaigns through a thorough analysis of what actually happened at the polls and why.

"Although we all know how things turned out, the authors know how to work a cliffhanger, and, as they effectively demonstrate, things could have turned out differently at any number of turns. Essential for watchers of politics and a model for similar electoral analyses in the future." —*Kirkus*

A James H. Silberman book; Includes bibliographical references and index.

Chait, Jonathan

Audacity: How Barack Obama Defied His Critics and Transformed America. Jonathan Chait. Custom House 2017. 256 p.

ISBN 9780062426970

Grades: Adult   **973.932**

1. Obama, Barack 2. Political leadership 3. Presidents 4. International relations 5. Politics and government 6. United States 7. 21st century 8. History writing — Presidency — 21st century — United States 9. Politics and global affairs — Political figures

LC 2016038527

An analysis of Barack Obama's considerable accomplishments in the face of critics from both parties explains why the author believes he will be considered one of history's greatest leaders on major policy fronts ranging from economics and the environment to health care and civil rights.

Keenan, Cody

Grace: President Obama, His Speechwriter, and Ten Remarkable Days in the Battle for America. Cody Keenan. Mariner Books 2022. 304 p.

ISBN 9780358651895

Grades: Adult   **973.932**

1. Keenan, Cody 2. Obama, Barack 3. Speechwriters 4. Presidents 5. Racism 6. Massacres 7. Mass shootings 8. Speech writing 9. Autobiographies and memoirs 10. Life stories — Arts and culture — Writing 11. Life stories — Politics 12. Politics and global affairs — General

The former chief speechwriter for President Obama provides an account of 10 days in his presidency in June 2015 in the shadow of a racist massacre in Charleston and two impending Supreme Court decisions.

"Keenan, former White House Director of Speechwriting under President Barack Obama, writes a compelling memoir of his tenure in the West Wing." —*Library Journal*

Mayer, Jane

★ *Dark Money: The Hidden History of the Billionaires Behind the Rise of the Radical Right.* Jane Mayer. Doubleday 2016. xii, 449 pages

ISBN 9780385535595

Grades: Adult   **973.932**

1. Koch, David H, 1940-2019 2. Koch, Charles G. (Charles de Ganahl), 1935- 3. Conservatism 4. Political culture 5. Radicalism 6. Politics and government 7. United States 8. 2000s (Decade) 9. 2010s 10. Politics and global affairs — Political parties

LC Bl2016000369

New York Times Notable Book, 2016; National Book Critics Circle Award for Nonfiction finalist, 2016.

An investigation into the growing radical right reveals a network of wealthy people with extreme Libertarian views, led by the Koch brothers, that has been systematically influencing and controlling academic institutions, the courts, and the United States government.

Includes bibliographical references (pages 381-425) and index.

Rhodes, Benjamin J.

The World as It Is: A Memoir of the Obama White House. Ben Rhodes. Random House 2018. xx, 450 pages, 8 unnumbered pages of plates : Illustration

ISBN 9780525509356

Grades: Adult   **973.932**

1. Rhodes, Benjamin J, 1977- 2. Political science 3. Political culture 4. Presidential staff 5. Social life and customs 6. Politics and government 7. Washington, D.C. 8. United States 9. 21st century 10. 2000s (Decade) 11. 2010s 12. Autobiographies and memoirs 13. Life stories — Politics 14. History writing — Presidency — 21st century — United States

From one of Barack Obama's closest aides comes a behind-the-scenes account of his presidency—and how idealism can confront harsh reality and still survive.

Souza, Pete

Obama: An Intimate Portrait. Pete Souza; foreword by Barack Obama. Little, Brown and Company 2017. 349 pages : Illustration; Color

ISBN 9780316512589

Grades: Adult   **973.932**

1. Obama, Barack 2. Presidents 3. United States history 4. United States 5. 21st century 6. Arts and Entertainment — Photography 7. Life stories — Politics — Politicians 8. Politics and global affairs — General

LC Bl2017044934

A visual biography of Barack Obama's historic presidency, captured in unprecedented detail by his White House photographer, includes images documenting the most consequential hours of the Obama administration as well as the 44th President's encounters with world leaders, cultural figures and family members. (This book was listed in a previous issue of Forecast.).

Showcases iconic photographs from President Obama's two terms as president, sharing both classified and candid pictures, including an image of the president and his advisors during the bin Laden mission, family photographs, and his interactions with world leaders.

ESSENTIAL AND RECOMMENDED TITLES
973.933 Administration of Donald Trump, 2017-2021

"In addition to being a collection of masterfully crafted images, the volume is a time capsule, capturing an era in pictures—one still fresh in collective memory." —*Publishers Weekly*

Shade: *A Tale of Two Presidents*. Pete Souza. Little, Brown and Company 2018. 235 pages : Illustration; Portrait
ISBN 9780316421829
Grades: Adult   973.932
1. Obama, Barack 2. Trump, Donald, 1946- 3. Political leadership 4. Presidents 5. United States 6. Arts and Entertainment — Photography 7. History writing — African American — United States 8. Life stories — Politics — Politicians
LC 2018946890

The former official White House photographer compares the most recent two administrations via photos of Barack Obama side-by-side with tweets, headlines and quotes from the Trump administration.

973.933 Administration of Donald Trump, 2017-2021

Baker, Peter
The Divider: Trump in the White House, 2017-2021. Peter Baker and Susan Glasser. Doubleday 2022. 384 p.
ISBN 9780385546539
Grades: Adult   973.933
1. Trump, Donald, 1946- 2. Political leadership 3. Presidents 4. Politics and government 5. United States 6. 21st century 7. 2010s 8. 2020s 9. Politics and global affairs — Political figures 10. History writing — Early 21st century — United States

Based on unprecedented access to key players, two top journalists and the best-selling authors of the Man Who Ran Washington tell the inside story of the four years when Donald Trump went to war with Washington, from the chaotic beginning to the violent finale.

"Married journalists Baker and Glasser follow up the Man Who Ran Washington with a comprehensive and scathing chronicle of the Trump administration….The result is the most encyclopedic account of the Trump presidency yet published." —*Publishers Weekly*

Bender, Michael C.
"frankly, We Did Win This Election": The Inside Story of How Trump Lost. Michael C. Bender. Twelve 2021. xi, 417 p.
ISBN 9781538734803
Grades: Adult   973.933
1. Trump, Donald, 1946- 2. Presidential election, 2020 3. Political campaigns 4. Presidents 5. Politics and government 6. United States 7. 21st century 8. Politics and global affairs — Political figures 9. Politics and global affairs — Elections 10. History writing — Early 21st century — United States
LC Bl2021016502

Beginning with President Trump's first impeachment and ending with his second, journalist Michael C. Bender chronicles the inside-the-room deliberations between Trump and his campaign team as they opened 2020 with a sleek political operation built to harness a surge of momentum from a bullish economy, a unified Republican Party, and a string of domestic and foreign policy successes—only to watch everything unravel when fortunes suddenly turned. Bender brings readers into the arena for an epic election-year convergence of COVID, economic collapse, and civil rights upheaval—and an unorthodox president's attempt to battle it all.

"Wall Street Journal senior White House reporter Bender turns in an engaging fly-on-the-wall account of the losing Trump 2020 campaign. . . . A thoroughly revealing account of a spectacularly inept presidential campaign that politics junkies will eat up." —*Kirkus*
Includes bibliographical references.

Bowden, Mark
The Steal: The Attempt to Overturn the 2020 Election and the People Who Stopped It. Mark Bowden & Matthew Teague. Atlantic Monthly Press 2022. 304 p.
ISBN 9780802159953
Grades: Adult   973.933
1. Biden, Joseph R. 1942- 2. Trump, Donald, 1946- 3. Presidential election, 2020 4. Voting 5. Presidential candidates 6. Election corruption 7. Political corruption 8. Political parties 9. Elections 10. Politics and government 11. United States 12. 21st century 13. Politics and global affairs — Elections

Two veteran journalists offer a week-by-week, state-by-state account of the effort to overturn the 2020 presidential election.

"Rousing, infuriating, sobering, and instructive, this page-turning account of the election debacle exposes the legal, political, and, sadly, even physical attacks on those civic-minded individuals trusted with upholding democracy's foundations and those committed to destroying that trust." —*Booklist*

Carpenter, Amanda B.
Gaslighting America: Why We Love It When Trump Lies to Us. Amanda Carpenter. Harper 2018. 224 p.
ISBN 9780062748003
Grades: Adult   973.933
1. Trump, Donald, 1946- 2. Deception 3. Communication in politics 4. Mass media 5. Social media 6. Press and politics 7. Presidential election, 2016 8. Political campaigns 9. Journalism 10. Politics and government 11. United States 12. 21st century 13. 2010s 14. 2020s 15. Liberal writing 16. Politics and global affairs — Mass media and politics 17. History writing — Presidency — 21st century — United States
LC 2017047193

A CNN political commentator and former senior staffer to Senator Ted Cruz breaks down the formula behind Trump's fake narratives and conspiracy theories, which seem to enthrall his supporters and play his victims and detractors.
Includes bibliographical references and index.

Frum, David
Trumpocracy: The Corruption of the American Republic. David Frum. Harper, an imprint of HarperCollinsPublishers 2018. 240 p.
ISBN 9780062796738
Grades: Adult   973.933
1. Trump, Donald, 1946- 2. Authoritarianism 3. Political culture 4. Politics and government 5. United States 6. 2010s 7. 2020s 8. Canadian literature 9. Politics and global affairs — World politics — United States
LC Bl2017046357

Builds on the author's March 2017 "How to Build an Autocracy" column in "The Atlantic" to explain how Donald Trump has undermined America's most important institutions as part of a carefully crafted plan to institute authoritarianism.

"Highly recommended for anyone who cares about the republic and its future." —*Library Journal*

Gessen, Masha
Surviving Autocracy. Masha Gessen. Riverhead Books 2020. xvi, 270 p.
ISBN 9780593188934
Grades: Adult   973.933
1. Trump, Donald, 1946- 2. Presidential election, 2016 3. Leadership 4. Social criticism 5. Democracy 6. Political culture 7. Social change 8. Politics and government 9. United States 10. 2010s 11. 2020s 12. 21st century 13. Politics and global affairs — Political figures 14. History writing — Presidency — 21st century — United States
LC 2020003180

An analysis of the destruction the Trump administration has waged on our institutions, the cultural norms we hoped would save us, and our very sense of identity. This incisive book provides an indispensable overview of the calamitous trajectory of the past few years. Gessen not only highlights the corrosion of the media, the judiciary, and the cultural norms we hoped would save us but also tells us the story of how a short few years have changed us, from a people who saw ourselves as a nation of immigrants to a populace haggling over a border wall, heirs to a degraded sense of truth, meaning, and possibility.

"Many writers have chronicled the Trump administration's missteps and crimes, but few as concisely as Gessen, and her book belongs on the shelf alongside Timothy Snyder's On Tyranny and Amy Siskind's The List as a record of how far we have fallen." —Kirkus

Includes bibliographical references.

Hennessey, Susan
Unmaking the Presidency: Donald Trump's War on the World's Most Powerful Office. Susan Hennessey and Benjamin Wittes. Farrar, Straus and Giroux 2020. VIII, 418 p.

ISBN 9780374175368

Grades: Adult 973.933

1. Trump, Donald, 1946- 2. Political leadership 3. Foreign interference in elections 4. Executive power 5. Presidents 6. Politics and government 7. United States 8. 21st century 9. Politics and global affairs — Political figures 10. Life stories — Politics — Politicians 11. History writing — Presidency — 21st century — United States

LC 2019028858

The extraordinary authority of the U.S. presidency has no parallel in the democratic world. Today that authority resides in the hands of one man, Donald J. Trump. But rarely if ever has the nature of a president clashed more profoundly with the nature of the office. Unmaking the Presidency tells the story of the confrontation between a person and the institution he almost wholly embodies. By setting Trump in the light of history, Hennessey and Wittes provide a crucial and durable account of a presidency like no other.

"Serious political readers and presidential studies scholars will derive much from this cogent appraisal." —Library Journal

Includes bibliographical references and index.

Hoffman, Carl
Liar's Circus: A Strange and Terrifying Journey into the Upside-down World of Trump's MAGA Rallies. Carl Hoffman. Custom House 2020. xii, 249 p.

ISBN 9780063009769

Grades: Adult 973.933

1. Trump, Donald, 1946- 2. Personality and politics 3. Identity 4. Political culture 5. Social psychology 6. Politics and government 7. United States 8. 21st century 9. 2010s 10. 2020s 11. Politics and global affairs — Elections 12. History writing — Presidency — 21st century — United States

LC 2020017022

Fear and Loathing on the Campaign Trail meets a work of daring and immersive contemporary anthropology: Carl Hoffman, who has written about the most dangerous and remote corners of the world, journeys deep inside President Trump's rallies, seeking to understand the strange and powerful tribe that forms the president's base.

"A valuable portrait of authoritarianism in action and its more-than-willing adherents." —Kirkus

Includes bibliographical references and index.

Isikoff, Michael
Russian Roulette: The Inside Story of How Vladimir Putin Attacked a U.S. Election and Shaped the Trump Presidency. Michael Isikoff and David Corn. Twelve 2018. 352 p.

ISBN 9781538728758

Grades: Adult 973.933

1. Trump, Donald, 1946- 2. Putin, Vladimir Vladimirovich, 1952- 3. Election corruption 4. Political corruption 5. International relations 6. Russia 7. United States 8. Politics and global affairs — Elections

LC 2018300042

Explains how Vladimir Putin and Russia hacked an American election as part of a covert operation to subvert the United States' democracy and help Donald Trump win the presidency.

"The way the text builds from the 2016 election to the presentcovering how those in the Obama administration and the intelligence services dealt with the interference issue (or, in some cases, didn't) makes for thought-provoking reading. A smart, solid, even-handed book that future historians will use as a starting point." —Booklist

Johnston, David Cay
The Big Cheat: How Donald Trump Fleeced America and Enriched Himself and His Family. David Cay Johnston. Simon & Schuster 2021. 320 p.

ISBN 9781982178031

Grades: Adult 973.933

1. Trump, Donald, 1946- 2. Trump family 3. Corporations 4. Business corruption 5. Profit 6. Political corruption 7. Fraud 8. Misconduct in office 9. Presidents 10. United States 11. 21st century 12. History writing — Presidency — 21st century — United States 13. Politics and global affairs — Political figures

Investigative reporter David Cay Johnston takes readers on a guided tour of how money flowed in and out of Trump's hundreds of enterprises, showing in simple terms how his family and courtiers used his presidency to enrich themselves, even putting national security at risk. Johnston details the four most recent years of the corruption that has defined the Trump family since 1885 and reveals the costs of Trump's extravagant lifestyle for American taxpayers.

"Johnston . . . delivers a damning portrait of how 'Donald Trump, his extended family, and his cronies . . . used his presidency to get richer, to set up lucrative future opportunities, and to escape their own financial quagmires.' . . . The result is a devastating roundup of malfeasance." —Publishers Weekly

It's Even Worse Than You Think: What the Trump Administration Is Doing to America. David Cay Johnston. Simon & Schuster 2018. 320 p.

ISBN 9781501174162

Grades: Adult 973.933

1. Trump, Donald, 1946- 2. Presidents 3. Political culture 4. Politics and government 5. United States 6. 2010s 7. 2020s 8. Politics and global affairs — World politics — United States

LC Bl2017046348

Examines the Trump administration's policies in its first one hundred days to reveal how its policies are affecting the daily lives of Americans and how the actions of federal government agencies have been quietly approved by the administration without drawing attention from the media.

"Thoroughly depressing—but urgent, necessary reading, at least for those who aren't true believers in the Trumpite cause." —Kirkus

Includes bibliographical references and index.

Karl, Jonathan
Betrayal: The Final Act of the Trump Show. Jonathan Karl. E.P. Dutton 2021. xix, 362 p.

ISBN 9780593186329

Grades: Adult 973.933

1. Trump, Donald, 1946- 2. Regime change 3. Presidents 4. Politics and government 5. United States history 6. United States 7. 21st century 8. Politics and global affairs — Political figures 9. History writing — Presidency — 21st century — United States

The author and chief Washington correspondent for ABC News examines the turbulent final weeks and months of the Trump presidency and what it means for the future of the Republican Party.

"In the follow-up to Front Row at the Trump Show, the ABC News political correspondent delivers fresh news on the last months of the Trump presidency. . . . Karl's message is clear: Trump was bad news, but it could have been much worse." —Kirkus

Front Row at the Trump Show. Jonathan Karl. Dutton 2020. xxvi, 340 pages : Illustration

ISBN 9781524745622

Grades: Adult 973.933

1. Trump, Donald, 1946- 2. Karl, Jonathan, 1968- 3. Political journalists 4. Presidential election, 2016 5. Presidents 6. Press and politics 7. Deception 8. Corruption 9. Politics and government 10. United States 11. 21st century 12. 2010s 13. 2020s 14. Politics and global affairs — World politics — United States 15. History writing — Presidency — United States

LC 2019046582

The ABC News chief White House correspondent and host of the Powerhouse Politics podcast reveals how Donald Trump wages a public campaign against the truth and orchestrates deliberate attacks against people and organizations that disagree with him.

ESSENTIAL AND RECOMMENDED TITLES
973.933 Administration of Donald Trump, 2017-2021

"No one's mind will be changed by Karl's book, but it's a valuable report from the scene of an ongoing train wreck." —*Kirkus*
Includes bibliographical references and index.

Tired of Winning: Donald Trump and the End of the Grand Old Party. Jonathan Karl. Dutton 2023. 384 p.
ISBN 9780593473986
Grades: Adult   973.933
1. Trump, Donald, 1946- 2. Former presidents 3. Police charges 4. Public opinion 5. Political parties 6. Elections 7. Political campaigns 8. Politics and government 9. United States 10. Politics and global affairs — Political figures 11. Politics and global affairs — Elections

From his exile in Mar-a-Lago, Donald Trump has become more extreme, vengeful, and divorced from reality than he was on January 6, 2021. His meddling damaged the GOP's electoral prospects for a third consecutive election in 2022. His legal troubles are mounting. Yet he's re-emerged as the frontrunner for the 2024 Republican presidential nomination. Jonathan Karl covered every day of Trump's administration as ABC News's chief White House correspondent. No one is in a better position to detail the former president's quest for retribution and provide a glimpse at what the GOP would be signing up for if it once again chooses him as its standard bearer.

"Drawing on his own meticulous reporting and interviews with Trump and his associates, Karl's portrait is uncompromising in its negativity." —*Publishers Weekly*

Kurtz, Howard
Media Madness: Donald Trump, the Press, and the War Over the Truth. Howard Kurtz. Regnery Publishing 2018. 256 p.
ISBN 9781621577263
Grades: Adult   973.933
1. Trump, Donald, 1946- 2. Mass media bias 3. Political culture 4. Journalists 5. Mass media 6. Television news 7. Politicians 8. Radical journalists 9. Presidents 10. Politics and government 11. United States 12. 2010s 13. 2020s 14. Society and culture — Media and technology 15. Politics and global affairs — World politics — United States
LC 2018286477

A former media critic for the Washington Post argues that Donald Trump's criticism is, at least partially, justified and explains how he believes most journalists have gone from neutral truth-tellers to pure pundits.

"Alongside Kurtz's lively, entertaining narrative of vitriolic news cycles is a penetrating critique of a liberal news establishment that, he contends, has abandoned objectivity for a hysterical partisanship that galvanizes Trumps support among the conservative voters it disdains." —*Publishers Weekly*

Leonnig, Carol
I Alone Can Fix It: Donald J. Trump's Catastrophic Final Year. Carol Leonnig, Philip Rucker. Penguin Group 2021. 578 pages
ISBN 9780593298947
Grades: Adult   973.933
1. Trump, Donald, 1946- 2. Political corruption 3. COVID-19 (Disease) 4. Recession (Economics) 5. Coronavirus infections 6. Epidemics 7. Political leadership 8. Presidents 9. Politics and government 10. United States 11. 21st century 12. 2010s 13. 2020s 14. Politics and global affairs — Political figures 15. History writing — Early 21st century — United States

The true story of what took place in Donald Trump's White House during a disastrous 2020 has never before been told in full. What was really going on around the president, as the government failed to contain the coronavirus and over half a million Americans perished? Who was influencing Trump after he refused to concede an election he had clearly lost and spread lies about election fraud? to answer these questions, Phil Rucker and Carol Leonnig reveal a dysfunctional and bumbling presidency's inner workings in unprecedented, stunning detail.

A hard-hitting expose of the last year of the Trump regime packed with appalling revelations. This book, write Washington Post reporters Leonnig and Rucker in their sequel to a Very Stable Genius (2020), recounts 'How Trump stress-tested the republic, twisting the country's institutions for personal gain and then pushing his followers too far.' —*Kirkus*

Martin, Jonathan
This Will Not Pass: Trump, Biden, and the Battle for America's Future. Jonathan Martin, Alexander Burns. Simon & Schuster 2022. 480 p.
ISBN 9781982172480
Grades: Adult   973.933
1. Trump, Donald, 1946- 2. Biden, Joseph R, 1942- 3. Presidential election, 2020 4. Two-party systems 5. Polarization (Social sciences) 6. Political science 7. Democracy 8. Presidents 9. Politics and government 10. United States 11. 21st century 12. History writing — Presidency — 21st century — United States 13. Politics and global affairs — Elections 14. Politics and global affairs — Political parties 15. Politics and global affairs — Political figures

This is the authoritative account of an eighteen-month crisis in American democracy that will be seared into the country's political memory for decades to come. With stunning, in-the-room detail, New York Times reporters Jonathan Martin and Alexander Burns show how both our political parties confronted a series of national traumas, including the coronavirus pandemic, the January 6 attack on the Capitol, and the political brinksmanship of President Biden's first year in the White House. More than at any time in recent history, the long-established traditions and institutions of American politics are under siege as a set of aging political leaders struggle to hold together a changing country.

"New York Times reporters Martin and Burns debut with an impressively sourced and consistently revealing chronicle of America's 'Political emergency' in the months between the onset of the coronavirus pandemic and the start of President Biden's second year in office." —*Publishers Weekly*

Mogelson, Luke
The Storm Is Here: An American Crucible. Luke Mogelson. Penguin 2022. 336 p.
ISBN 9780593489215
Grades: Adult   973.933
1. Mogelson, Luke 2. Political culture 3. COVID-19 Pandemic, 2020- 4. Capitol Riot, Washington, D.C, 2021 5. Protests, demonstrations, vigils, etc. 6. Polarization (Social sciences) 7. Social conflict 8. Political violence 9. Politics and government 10. United States 11. 21st century 12. Liberal writing 13. History writing — Early 21st century — United States 14. Society and culture — Violence and crime 15. Politics and global affairs — General
LC 2022008423

An award-winning war correspondent, after years of living abroad, returns to the U.S, presenting an eyewitness account of how—during a season of sickness, economic uncertainty and violence—Americans started to break down, in this unique record of a pivotal moment in history and an urgent warning about those to come.

"A war correspondent provides a crucial account of the events leading up to the Jan. 6, 2021, coup attempt....Essential for understanding the right-wing rage that boils across America." —*Kirkus*
Includes bibliographical references and index.

Nance, Malcolm W.
The Plot to Betray America: How Team Trump Embraced Our Enemies, Compromised Our Security, and How We Can Fix It. Malcolm Nance. Hachette Books 2019. IX, 358 pages
ISBN 9780316535762
Grades: Adult   973.933
1. Trump, Donald, 1946- 2. Putin, Vladimir Vladimirovich, 1952- 3. Democracy 4. Treason 5. Hacking 6. Spies 7. International crime 8. Political corruption 9. International relations 10. Russia 11. United States 12. Politics and global affairs — World politics — United States 13. Politics and global affairs — National security
LC BI2019027708

The counterterrorism analyst, whistleblower and best-selling author of The Plot to Hack America presents a searing investigation into the American officials who he believes have been complicit in the Trump-Russia conspiracy.

Neus, Nora
24 Hours in Charlottesville: An Oral History of the Stand Against White Supremacy. Nora Neus. Beacon Press 2023. 192 p.

ISBN 9780807011928
Grades: Adult   973.933
1. White supremacy movements 2. Antiracism 3. Right-wing extremists 4. White nationalism 5. Racism 6. Race relations 7. Charlottesville, Virginia 8. 21st century 9. Society and culture — Race 10. Politics and global affairs — Terrorism 11. History Writing — Regional history — United States
LC 2023014301

A gripping oral history of the white nationalist riots that shook the nation and signaled the arrival of a galvanizing new era, told from the perspective of the anti-racist activists who fought back.

"Not just a visceral portrayal of political violence, but also a major addition to our understanding of right-wing terrorism." —*Kirkus*

Petri, Alexandra
Nothing Is Wrong and Here Is Why: Essays. Alexandra Petri. W. W. Norton & Company 2020. 240 p.
ISBN 9781324006459
Grades: Adult   973.933
1. Trump, Donald, 1946- 2. Political corruption 3. Current events 4. Foreign interference in elections 5. Presidents 6. Politics and government 7. United States 8. 2010s 9. 2020s 10. Essays 11. Satire and parodies 12. Society and culture — General
LC 2020007461

Adapted from the author's viral Post columns, a riotous essay collection on the normalized horrors of today's world outlines logical and reassuring reasons behind the seemingly inexplicable changes in American politics and culture throughout the past four years.

"Acidic and spot-on, Petri's work captures the surreal quality of Trump's tenure as perhaps no other book has." —*Publishers Weekly*

Rohde, David
In Deep: The FBI, the CIA, and the Truth About America's. David Rohde. W.W. Norton & Company 2020. 352 p.
ISBN 9781324003540
Grades: Adult   973.933
1. Politicians 2. Secrecy in government 3. Government conspiracies 4. Separation of powers 5. Suspicion 6. Foreign interference in elections 7. Political culture 8. Presidents 9. Politics and government 10. United States 11. Impartial writing 12. Politics and global affairs — General 13. History writing — Scandals 14. History writing — United States
LC Bl2020007688

A revelatory investigation into the alleged "deep state" that draws on dozens of interviews with career spymasters, covert CIA operatives and FBI agents to determine if they are working in America's democratic best interests.

"Pulitzer Prize-winner Rohde (Beyond War) delivers an illuminating history of the often tense relationship between U.S. presidents and the career civil servants who enact—or, by some accounts, thwart—their policies. . . . Political junkies and generalists alike will relish this deeply informed account." —*Publishers Weekly*

Rothkopf, David J.
American Resistance: The Inside Story of How the Deep State Saved the Nation. David Rothkopf. PublicAffairs 2022. 275 p.
ISBN 9781541700635
Grades: Adult   973.933
1. Trump, Donald, 1946- 2. Presidents 3. Public officials 4. Political consultants 5. Resistance to government 6. Democracy 7. Despotism 8. Misconduct in office 9. Political corruption 10. Politics and government 11. United States 12. 21st century 13. Politics and global affairs — Political figures 14. History writing — Presidency — 21st century — United States 15. Life stories — Politics

Each federal employee takes an oath to "support and defend the Constitution of the United States against all enemies foreign and domestic," but none had imagined that enemy might be the Commander-in-Chief. American Resistance is the first book to chronicle the unprecedented role so many in the government were forced to play and the consequences of their actions during the Trump administration. David Rothkopf chronicles how each person came to realize that they were working for an administration that threatened to wreak havoc in an intense drama in which a few good men and women stood up to the tyrant in their midst.

"This book is a worthy companion to recent books by Marie Yovanovitch (Lessons from the Edge) and Alexander Vindman (Here, Right Matters). It is an unrelenting indictment of Donald Trump's abuse of the presidency." —*Library Journal*

Rothschild, Mike
The **Storm** *Is Upon US: How Qanon Became a Movement, Cult, and Conspiracy Theory of Everything.* Mike Rothschild. Melville House 2021. xviii, 301 pages
ISBN 9781612199290
Grades: Adult   973.933
1. Conspiracy theories 2. Extremism 3. Social psychology 4. Right-wing extremists 5. Politics and government 6. United States 7. 21st century 8. Politics and global affairs — World politics — United States
LC Bl2021014430

A journalist who specializes in conspiracy theories draws on interviews with QAnon converts and victims, as well as psychologists, sociologists, and academics to explain the origin and growth of the movement, its embrace by right-wing media and politicians, and why it is important to understand it rather than mock it.

"Journalist Rothschild (The World's Worst Conspiracies) provides an enlightening history of the QAnon conspiracy theory. . . . This is a disturbing and well-informed look at the darker side of modern American politics." —*Publishers Weekly*

Includes bibliographical references (pages 253-292) and index.

Schmidt, Michael S.
★ **Donald** Trump V. The United States: Inside the Struggle to Stop a President. Michael S. Schmidt. Random House 2020. 432 p.
ISBN 9781984854667
Grades: Adult   973.933
1. Trump, Donald, 1946- 2. Cabinet officers 3. Executive power 4. Power 5. Political corruption 6. Presidents 7. Politics and government 8. United States 9. 21st century 10. 2010s 11. 2020s 12. History writing — Presidency — 21st century — United States 13. Politics and global affairs — Political figures

New York Times reporter Michael S. Schmidt, drawing on secret FBI and White House documents and confidential sources inside federal law enforcement and the West Wing, chronicles the clash between a president and the officials of his own government who tried to stop him.

"A detailed, deeply reported portrait of a president willfully obstructing justice—with plenty of help." —*Kirkus*

Includes bibliographical references.

Sharpton, Al
Rise Up: Confronting a Country at the Crossroads. Reverend AL Sharpton; foreword by Michael Eric Dyson. Hanover Square Press 2020. 304 p.
ISBN 9781335966629
Grades: Adult   973.933
1. Sharpton, AL 2. African American political activists 3. Baptists 4. African American politicians 5. Progressivism (United States politics) 6. Antiracist action 7. Social action 8. Multiculturalism 9. Social responsibility 10. Protests, demonstrations, vigils, etc. 11. African American civil rights 12. Voter suppression 13. Clergy 14. Politics and government 15. United States 16. Liberal writing 17. Politics and global affairs — General 18. Life stories — Politics — Activists and Reformers — Civil Rights Leaders 19. Adult books for young adults
LC Bl2020018644

A rousing call to action for today's turbulent political moment, drawing on lessons learned from Reverend Sharpton's unique experience as a politician, television and radio host, and civil rights leader. In Rise Up, Sharpton revisits the highlights of the Obama administration, the 2016 election and Trump's subsequent hold on the GOP, and draws on his decades-long experience with other key players in politics and activism, including Shirley Chisholm, Hillary Clinton, Dr. Martin Luther King Jr. and more.

ESSENTIAL AND RECOMMENDED TITLES
973.933 Administration of Donald Trump, 2017-2021

"The outspoken civil rights leader sees a nation in peril. Baptist minister, former presidential candidate, and founder of the National Action Network, Sharpton mounts an impassioned call for activism." —*Kirkus*

Smith, Mychal Denzel
Stakes Is High: Life After the American Dream. Mychal Denzel Smith. Bold Type Books 2020. 208 p.
ISBN 9781568588735
Grades: Adult   973.933
1. American dream 2. Patriotism 3. Social justice 4. Police misconduct 5. Criminal justice system 6. Identity 7. Racism 8. Ideology 9. Hypocrisy 10. Social change 11. Equality 12. Civil rights 13. Prisons 14. Politics and government 15. United States 16. Essays 17. Politics and global affairs — General 18. Society and culture — Wealth and class 19. Society and culture — Race
LC 2020001915
Kirkus Prize for Nonfiction, 2020.

Growth only happens when we confront our deceptions and our own complicity in them. In Stakes Is High, Smith exposes the contradictions at the heart of American life—between patriotism and justice, between freedom and inequality, incarceration, police violence. In a series of incisive essays, Smith holds us to account individually and as a nation. He examines his own shortcomings, grapples with the anxiety of feeling stuck, and looks in new directions for the tools to build a just America.

"This is not always easy book, but it is one that sees the United States for what it is. A searing combination of memoir and commentary that makes for essential reading." —*Library Journal*

Sommer, Will
★ *Trust the Plan: The Rise of Qanon and the Conspiracy That Unhinged America*. Will Sommer. HarperCollins 2023. 320 p.
ISBN 9780063114487
Grades: Adult   973.933
1. Republicans 2. Radicalism 3. Conspiracy theories 4. White supremacy movements 5. Social movements 6. Politics and government 7. United States 8. 21st century 9. Society and culture — General 10. Politics and global affairs — General
LC Bl2022038963

A journalist who has followed the rise of QAnon explains what it is, how it has gained a mainstream following among Republican lawmakers and ordinary citizens, the threat it poses to democracy, and how we can reach those who have embraced the conspiracy and are disseminating its lies.

"This is an absolutely fascinating and deeply troubling book. Rage-inducing and heartbreaking, it's a rigorously researched, energetically written examination of a phenomenon laughed off for too long as fringe silliness." —*Booklist*

Toobin, Jeffrey
True Crimes and Misdemeanors: The Investigation of Donald Trump. Jeffrey Toobin. Doubleday 2020. 432 p.
ISBN 9780385536738
Grades: Adult   973.933
1. Trump, Donald, 1946- 2. Misconduct in office 3. Political corruption 4. Scandals 5. Conspiracies 6. Justice 7. Foreign interference in elections 8. Impeachments 9. Presidents 10. Politics and government 11. United States 12. 2010s 13. 2020s 14. 21st century 15. Liberal writing 16. Politics and global affairs — Political figures 17. History writing — Presidency — 21st century — United States 18. History writing — Scandals
LC 2020017608

The CNN chief legal analyst and author presents a behind-the-scenes account of the Mueller investigation to explain how in spite of associate convictions and an impeachment, Donald Trump has survived to run for reelection.

"CNN legal analyst Toobin (American Heiress) delivers a vivid and doggedly reported rundown of special counsel Robert Mueller's investigation into Russian interference in the 2016 election and the impeachment of Donald Trump over the Ukraine affair.... The result is a definitive behind-the-scenes portrait of what these investigations accomplished, and why they didn't bring Trump down." —*Publishers Weekly*

Wilson, Rick
Running Against the Devil: A Plot to Save America from Trump — and Democrats from Themselves. Rick Wilson. Crown Forum 2020. 272 pages
ISBN 9780593137581
Grades: Adult   973.933
1. Trump, Donald 1946- 2. Presidential election, 2020 3. Political campaigns 4. Strategy 5. Democrats 6. Political parties 7. Political science 8. Politics and government 9. United States 10. 21st century 11. 2000s (Decade) 12. 2010s 13. 2020s 14. Politics and global affairs — Elections 15. History writing — Presidency — 21st century — United States 16. Politics and global affairs — Political parties
LC 2019042005

The veteran Republican strategist and best-selling author of Everything Trump Touches Dies outlines the mistakes made by both parties during throughout the 2016 presidential campaign, identifying the challenges that must be overcome to prevent Trump's reelection.

"A caustically funny, outraged, and deadly serious analysis." —*Kirkus*

Wolff, Michael
Fire and Fury: Inside the Trump White House. Michael Wolff. Henry Holt & CO 2018. 321 p.
ISBN 9781250158062
Grades: Adult   973.933
1. Trump, Donald, 1946- 2. Political leadership 3. Political culture 4. Political intrigue 5. Presidents 6. Washington, D.C. 7. United States 8. 21st century 9. History writing — Presidency — 21st century — United States 10. Politics and global affairs — Political figures
LC 2017050324

Reveals the chaos of Donald Trump's first nine months in office, detailing why Comey was really fired, how to communicate with the president, and who is directing the administration following Bannon's dismissal.

"While Wolff's use of anonymous 'Deep background' sources may give readers reservations about the accuracy of every detail, this explosive account will undoubtedly remain a topic of conversation for the near future." —*Publishers Weekly*

Landslide: The Final Days of the Trump White House. Michael Wolff. Henry Holt & Company 2021. 312 p.
ISBN 9781250830012
Grades: Adult   973.933
1. Trump, Donald, 1946- 2. Political leadership 3. Political intrigue 4. Misconduct in office 5. Executive power 6. Presidents 7. Politics and government 8. Washington, D.C. 9. United States 10. 21st century 11. 2010s 12. 2020s 13. History writing — Presidency — 21st century — United States 14. Politics and global affairs — Political figures

Wolff closes the story of Trump's four years in office and his tumultuous last months at the helm of the country, based on Wolff's extraordinary access to White House aides and to the former president himself, yielding a wealth of new information and insights about what really happened inside the highest office in the land, and the world.

"The veteran journalist delivers an in-the-bunker account of the disastrous end of the Trump administration.... A satisfying neck-craning look at the raging dumpster fire of Trump's final months in office." —*Kirkus*

Woodward, Bob
Fear: Trump in the White House. Bob Woodward. Simon & Schuster 2018. xxii, 420 pages, 16 unnumbered pages of plates : Color; Illustration
ISBN 9781501175510
Grades: Adult   973.933
1. Trump, Donald, 1946- 2. Political culture 3. Presidents 4. Political leadership 5. Political intrigue 6. Politics and government 7. Washington, D.C. 8. United States 9. 21st century 10. 2010s 11. 2020s 12. Politics and global affairs — World politics — United States 13. History writing — Presidency — 21st century — United States
LC 2019462344

Draws on interviews with firsthand sources, meeting notes, personal diaries, and other documents to depict life in the Trump White House, focusing on Trump's decision-making process for foreign and domestic policies.

"The title of the book comes from an interview in which the president states that true power comes through fear. Well, this look inside the Trump White House is pretty scary." —*Booklist*

Includes bibliographical references and index.

Peril. Bob Woodward, Robert Costa. Simon & Schuster 2021. xxviii, 482 pages, 16 unnumbered pages of plates : Illustration
ISBN 9781982182915
Grades: Adult 973.933

1. Biden, Joseph R, 1942- 2. Trump, Donald, 1946- 3. Political culture 4. Political leadership 5. Political intrigue 6. Presidents 7. National security 8. Political corruption 9. Elections 10. Politics and government 11. United States 12. Washington, D.C. 13. 2020s 14. 21st century 15. Biographies 16. History writing — Presidency — 21st century — United States 17. History writing — Early 21st century — United States 18. Politics and global affairs — Political figures

Bob Woodward and Robert Costa cover the end of the Trump presidency and the early months of the Biden presidency.

"An account of the last gasps of the Trump administration, completing a trilogy begun with Fear (2018) and Rage (2020).... A solid work of investigation that, while treading well-covered ground, offers plenty of surprises." —*Kirkus*

Includes bibliographical references and index.

Yovanovitch, Marie
Lessons from the Edge. Marie Yovanovitch. Houghton Mifflin Harcourt 2021. 256 p.
ISBN 9780358457541
Grades: Adult 973.933

1. Yovanovitch, Marie 2. Women ambassadors 3. Women politicians 4. Ambassadors 5. International relations 6. Diplomats 7. Politics and government 8. United States 9. Autobiographies and memoirs 10. History writing — Politicians — United States 11. Life stories — Politics — Politicians

In a new memoir, the U.S. Ambassador to the Ukraine, whose life and work have taught her the preciousness of democracy as well as the dangers of corruption, details her involvement in President Trump's impeachment inquiry and her response to his smear campaign.

"The former U.S. ambassador to Ukraine, who got unwillingly caught up in Donald Trump's first impeachment, examines corruption abroad and at home in this stinging memoir....Full of shrewd insights and bitter ironies, Yovanovitch's saga offers a revealing insider's take on the labyrinth of foreign policy and on one of the most sordid episodes of Trump's presidency." —*Publishers Weekly*

973.934 Administration of Joseph R. Biden, Jr, 2021-

Foer, Franklin
★ *The Last Politician: Inside Joe Biden's White House and the Struggle for America's Future*. Franklin Foer. Penguin 2023. 414 p.
ISBN 9781101981146
Grades: Adult 973.934

1. Biden, Joseph R, 1942- 2. Presidents 3. Regime change 4. Political culture 5. North American people 6. American people 7. Politics and government 8. United States 9. Politics and global affairs — Political figures 10. History writing — Presidency — 21st century — United States

LC Bl2023026258

With unparalleled access to the tight inner circle of advisers who have surrounded Biden for decades, Franklin Foer dramatizes in forensic detail the first two years of the Biden presidency, concluding with the historic midterm elections. The result is a gripping and high-definition portrait of a major president at a time when democracy itself seems imperiled. With his back to the wall, Biden resorted to old-fashioned politics: Deal-making and compromise.

"Overall, the author creates a respectful portrait of a savvy, dedicated politician. A deeply researched political history and biography." —*Kirkus*

Includes bibliographical references (pages 379-397) and index.

Whipple, Chris
The Fight of His Life: Inside Joe Biden's White House. Chris Whipple. Scribner 2023. 384 p.
ISBN 9781982106430
Grades: Adult 973.934

1. Biden, Joseph R, 1942- 2. Presidents 3. Political leadership 4. Politics and government 5. United States 6. 21st century 7. Politics and global affairs — Political figures 8. History writing — Presidency — 21st century — United States

Taking readers behind the scenes of one of America's most consequential presidencies, a prizewinning journalist, with unprecedented access to the White House, reveals how President Joe Biden and his seasoned team have battled to achieve their agenda, delivering a surprising portrait of politics on the edge.

"Journalist Whipple follows up the Spymasters with a fascinating insider's account of the first two years of the Biden administration....Distinguished by Whipple's impressive access and incisive character sketches, this is a valuable first draft of history." —*Publishers Weekly*

974.1 Maine

Georges, Gigi
Downeast: Five Maine Girls and the Unseen Story of Rural America. Gigi Georges. Harper 2021. 240 p.
ISBN 9780062984456
Grades: Adult 974.1

1. Teenage girls 2. Young women 3. Everyday life 4. Poverty 5. Unemployment 6. Ambition 7. Adulthood 8. Gender role 9. Identity 10. Options, alternatives, choices 11. Home (Concept) 12. Rural life 13. Maine 14. Society and culture — Gender — Women 15. Life stories — Relationships — Growing up 16. Life stories — Facing adversity 17. Society and culture — Urban and regional studies

Nestled in Maine's far northeast corner, Washington County sits an hour's drive from the heart of famed and bustling Acadia National Park. Yet it's a world away. For Willow, Vivian, McKenna, Audrey, and Josie—five teenage girls caught between tradition and transformation in this remote region—it is home. Downeast follows their journeys of heartbreak and hope in uncertain times, creating a nuanced and unique portrait of rural America with women at its center.

"Georges' lovely book will appeal to readers seeking memoirs, understanding of rural worlds, feminist values, or even travel writing." —*Booklist*

974.4 Massachusetts

Bunker, Nick
★ *Making Haste from Babylon: The Mayflower Pilgrims and Their World : A New History*. by Nick Bunker. Alfred A. Knopf 2010. 400 p.
ISBN 9780307266828
Grades: Adult 974.4

1. Pilgrims (New England settlers) 2. Colonists 3. Colonies 4. Evangelicalism 5. United States history 6. Massachusetts 7. Plymouth, Massachusetts 8. 17th century 9. Colonial America (1600-1775) 10. History writing — Colonial America — United States

LC 2009038520

Explores the complexities of Pilgrim character from their radical sectarian beliefs to their entrepreneurial capabilities, drawing on previously untapped sources to offer insight into how they established a thriving New Plymouth settlement in spite of formidable circumstances.

Includes bibliographical references.

Fraser, Rebecca
The Mayflower: The Families, the Voyage, and the Founding of America. Rebecca Fraser. St. Martin's Press 2017. 384 pages
ISBN 9781250108562
Grades: Adult 974.4

1. Winslow, Edward, 1595-1655 2. Winslow, Josiah, 1629?-1680 3. Winslow family 4. Pilgrims (New England settlers) 5. Colonists 6. Survival 7. Trading

ESSENTIAL AND RECOMMENDED TITLES
974.5 Rhode Island

companies 8. Wampanoag (North American people) 9. Interethnic relations 10. Colonies 11. Women colonists 12. United States history 13. Massachusetts 14. Colonial America (1600-1775) 15. Biographies 16. History writing — Colonial America — United States 17. Life stories — People in history — Witness to history

LC 2017026873

With the aid of contemporary documents, the author brings to life an ordinary family, the Winslows, made less ordinary by their responses to the challenges of the New World after their passage on the Mayflower, in a book that looks at the First Thanksgiving and the Winslows conflicted relationship with the Wampanoag Indians.

Includes bibliographical references and index.

Junger, Sebastian
The Perfect Storm: A True Story of Men Against the Sea. Sebastian Junger. Norton 1997. xii, 227 p. : Map

ISBN 9780393040166

Grades: 11 12 Adult 974.4

1. Storms 2. Natural disasters 3. Fishers 4. Shipwrecks 5. North Atlantic Ocean 6. Northeastern States 7. Atlantic Ocean 8. 1990s 9. Page to screen 10. Adventure writing — Natural disaster 11. Nature Writing — Natural Disaster 12. Adult books for young adults 13. Nonfiction that reads like fiction

LC 96042412

ALA Notable Book, 1998; Alex Award, 1998; New York Times Notable Book, 1997; School Library Journal Best Books: Best Adult Books 4 Teens, 1997.

Presents a vivid account of a history-making storm that hit the New England coast in October 1991 and the lives it changed, weaving together the history of the fishing industry, the science of storms, and personal accounts.

"Junger's fine dramatic style is complemented by a wealth of details that flesh out the story: Wave physics and water thermoclines; what it means if you see whitewater outside your porthole; where the terms mayday, ill-wind, and down East came from. Reading this gripping book is likely to make the would-be sailor feel both awed and a little frightened by nature's remorseless power." —*Kirkus*

Manegold, Catherine S.
Ten Hills Farm: The Forgotten History of Slavery in the North. C.S. Manegold. Princeton University Press 2010. 344 p.

ISBN 9780691131528

Grades: Adult 974.4

1. Slavery 2. Slave trade 3. Enslaved people 4. Race relations 5. United States history 6. Massachusetts 7. History writing — African American — Enslavement — United States

LC 2009030875

Ten Hills Farm tells the powerful saga of five generations of slave owners in colonial New England. Settled in 1630 by John Winthrop, governor of the Massachusetts Bay Colony, Ten Hills Farm, a six-hundred-acre estate just north of Boston, passed from the Winthrops to the Ushers, to the Royalls—all prominent dynasties tied to the Native American and Atlantic slave trades. In this mesmerizing narrative, C. S. Manegold exposes how the fortunes of these families—and the fate of Ten Hills Farm—were bound to America's most tragic and tainted legacy. Manegold follows the compelling tale from the early seventeenth to the early twenty-first century, from New England, through the South, to the sprawling slave plantations of the Caribbean. John Winthrop, famous for envisioning his 'City on the hill' and lauded as a paragon of justice, owned slaves on that ground and passed the first law in North America condoning slavery. Each successive owner of Ten Hills Farm—from John Usher, who was born into money, to Isaac Royall, who began as a humble carpenter's son and made his fortune in Antigua—would depend upon slavery's profits until the 1780s, when Massachusetts abolished the practice. In time, the land became a city, its questionable past discreetly buried, until now. Challenging received ideas about America and the Atlantic world, Ten Hills Farm digs deep to bring the story of slavery in the North full circle—from concealment to recovery.

Includes bibliographical references and index.

Pestana, Carla Gardina
The World of Plymouth Plantation. Carla Gardina Pestana. The Belknap Press of Harvard University Press 2020. 232 p.

ISBN 9780674238510

Grades: Adult 974.4

1. Pilgrims (New England settlers) 2. United States history 3. Massachusetts 4. 17th century 5. Colonial America (1600-1775) 6. History writing — Colonial America — United States

LC 2020003452

Published to coincide with the 400th anniversary of the Mayflower landing and the establishment of the colony, this revealing account of life in Plymouth Plantation goes beyond familiar founding myths to portray real life in the settlement.

"Readers will give thanks for this cogent study of the real people and events behind this 'Foundational moment' in American history." —*Publishers Weekly*

Includes bibliographical references and index.

Silverman, David J.
★ *This Land Is Their Land: The Wampanoag Indians, Plymouth Colony, and the Troubled History of Thanksgiving.* David J. Silverman. Bloomsbury Publishing 2019. 432 pages

ISBN 9781632869241

Grades: Adult 974.4

1. Rowlandson, Mary White, approximately 1635-1711 2. Thanksgiving Day 3. Wampanoag (North American people) 4. Pilgrims (New England settlers) 5. Alliances 6. King Philip's War, 1675-1676 7. Indigenous peoples of North America 8. First contact of indigenous peoples with Europeans 9. First contact (Anthropology) 10. Government relations with indigenous peoples 11. United States history 12. Plymouth, Massachusetts 13. Colonial America (1600-1775) 14. History writing — Indigenous peoples — United States 15. History writing — Colonial America — United States

LC 2019022966

Ahead of the 400th anniversary of the first Thanksgiving, a new look at the Plymouth colony's founding events, told for the first time with Wampanoag people at the heart of the story.

"Silverman's reconstruction of the world of the Wampanoag provides fascinating insights for both general readers and scholars into the early years of the colonization of Massachusetts, situating not only Thanksgiving within the nation's history but also the tragedy of King Philip's War." —*Library Journal*

Includes bibliographical references and index.

Whittock, Martyn
Mayflower Lives: Pilgrims in a New World and the Early American Experience. Martyn Whittock. Pegasus Books 2019. 416 pages

ISBN 9781643131320

Grades: Adult 974.4

1. Bradford, William, 1590-1657 2. Standish, Myles, 1584?-1656 3. Howland, John, 1592?-1672 4. Hopkins, Stephen, 1581-1644 5. Squanto 6. Pilgrims (New England settlers) 7. Colonists 8. United States history 9. Massachusetts 10. Plymouth, Massachusetts 11. 17th century 12. Colonial America (1600-1775) 13. History writing — Colonial America — United States

LC Bl2019021741

A 400th anniversary tribute to the Mayflower voyage draws on the lives of 14 diverse individuals, from Myles Standish and Squanto to Mary Chilton and Stephen Hopkins, to illuminate the human realities of one of America's most seminal events.

"This accessible book, among several that have demythologized Mayflower history, will appeal to readers at all levels." —*Library Journal*

Includes bibliographical references and index.

974.5 Rhode Island

Barry, John M.
Roger Williams and the Creation of the American Soul: Church, State, and the Birth of Liberty. John M. Barry. Viking 2012. 464 p. : Map

PUBLIC LIBRARY CORE COLLECTION: NONFICTION
Twentieth Edition

ISBN 9780670023059
Grades: Adult   974.5
1. Williams, Roger, 1604?-1683 2. Christian theologians 3. Baptists 4. Freedom of religion 5. Christian history 6. United States history 7. Rhode Island 8. Colonial America (1600-1775) 9. Biographies 10. Spirituality and Religion — Christianity 11. Life stories — Religion and spirituality — Religious and spiritual leaders 12. History writing — Colonial America — United States
LC 2011032995

Barry explores the development of the fundamental ideas of church and state through the story of Roger Williams. The first to link religious freedom to individual liberty, Williams helped shape the balance of religion and politics seen in America today.

Includes bibliographical references and index.

Warren, James A.

God, War, and Providence: The Epic Struggle of Roger Williams and the Narragansett Indians Against the Puritans of New England. James A. Warren. Scribner 2018. 352 p.
ISBN 9781501180415
Grades: Adult   974.5
1. Williams, Roger, 1604?-1683 2. Indigenous peoples of North America — Wars 3. Narragansett (North American people) 4. Colonists 5. Puritans 6. Clergy 7. Exile (punishment) 8. Freedom of religion 9. Government relations with indigenous peoples 10. Indigenous peoples — Land rights 11. New England history 12. Colonial America (1600-1775) 13. History writing — Indigenous peoples — United States 14. History writing — Colonial America — United States 15. Life stories — Politics — Activists and reformers 16. Life stories — People in history — Indigenous peoples
LC Bl2018100313

The tragic and fascinating history of the first epic struggle between white settlers and Native Americans in the early seventeenth century: a fresh look at the aggressive expansionist Puritans in New England and the determined Narragansett Indians, who refused to back down and accept English authority over people and their land.

974.7 New York

Anbinder, Tyler

★ *City of Dreams: The 400-year Epic History of Immigrant New York.* Tyler Anbinder. Houghton Mifflin Harcourt 2016. 672 p.
ISBN 9780544104655
Grades: Adult   974.7
1. Immigration and emigration 2. Immigrants 3. City life 4. New York City 5. History writing — Immigration — United States
LC 2016286135

Mark Lynton History Prize, 2017; New York Times Notable Book, 2016.

A history of immigration in New York shares the poignant stories of individuals ranging from bodybuilder Charles Atlas to couture artist Oscar de la Renta to trace the essential role of foreign-born innovators and revolutionaries in the city's evolution.

Brenwall, Cynthia S

The Central Park: Original Designs for New York's Greatest Treasure. Cynthia S. Brenwall, New York City Municipal Archives; foreword by Martin Filler. Abrams 2019. 229 pages : Illustration; Color
ISBN 9781419732324
Grades: Adult   974.7
1. Landscape architecture 2. Gardens 3. Design and construction 4. Central Park, New York City 5. Visual nonfiction 6. Arts and Entertainment — Architecture 7. Arts and Entertainment — Painting, Drawing, and Sculpture 8. NAture writing — Gardens
LC Bl2019029377

Drawing on the unparalleled collection of original designs for Central Park in the New York City Municipal Archives, Cynthia S. Brenwall tells the story of the creation of New York's great public park, from its conception to its completion.

"A stunning collection of architectural drawings that detail the original vision of New York City's Central Park and offer a history of its evolution." —*Kirkus*

Includes bibliographical references (pages 223-227) and index.

Burns, Cherie

The Great Hurricane—1938. Cherie Burns. Atlantic Monthly Press 2005. 238 p. : Illustration; Map; Plate
ISBN 9780871138934
Grades: Adult   974.7
1. New England Hurricane, 1938 2. Natural disasters 3. Hurricanes 4. New England history 5. United States history 6. Long Island, New York 7. 1930s 8. 20th century 9. History writing — Great Depression — United States 10. Nature Writing — Natural Disaster 11. Adventure writing — Natural disaster 12. History writing — Natural disasters and tragedies
LC 2005041211

Examines one of the worst natural disasters in the nation's history—the 1938 Hurricane that struck the coast of New England at 186 miles per hour causing devastation throughout the region—and the personal stories of survivors of the catastrophe.

Includes bibliographical references (p. 215-217) and index.

Chin, Ava

★ *Mott Street: A Chinese American Family's Story of Exclusion and Homecoming.* Ava Chin. Penguin Press 2023. 384 p.
ISBN 9780525557371
Grades: Adult   974.7
1. Chinese people 2. Immigrants 3. Chinese Americans 4. Chinese American families 5. Family history 6. Immigration and emigration 7. Racism 8. Chinatown, New York City 9. China 10. Life stories — People in history
LC 2022040793

Beautifully written, meticulously researched and tremendously resonant, this sweeping narrative history of the Chinese Exclusion Act traces the story of her pioneering family members' epic journey to lay down roots in America, piecing together how they bore and resisted the weight of the Exclusion laws.

"This richly narrated family history starts in Chinatown, then amplifies the broader experience of Chinese Americans across two centuries of hardship and opportunity." —*Booklist*

Includes bibliographical references and index.

Daughan, George C.

Revolution on the Hudson: New York City and the Hudson River Valley in the American War of Independence. George C. Daughan. W. W. Norton & Co. 2016. 432 p.
ISBN 9780393245721
Grades: Adult   974.7
1. American Revolution, 1775-1783 2. Revolutions 3. United States history 4. Hudson Valley 5. United States 6. New York (State) 7. Revolutionary America (1775-1783) 8. History writing — Wars and conflicts — Revolutionary War (America)
LC 2016007017

Traces the lesser-known story of the fight for the Hudson River Valley during the American Revolution, explaining the conflict's essential role in the outcome of the war and the political, military, economic and social strategies that influenced both sides.

"A stimulating look at the American Revolution by a diligent historian and talented writer." —*Kirkus*

Includes bibliographical references and index.

Dwyer, Jim

102 Minutes: The Unforgettable Story of the Fight to Survive Inside the Twin Towers. Jim Dwyer and Kevin Flynn. Times Books 2011. xxiv, 353 p.
ISBN 9780805094213
Grades: 11 12 Adult   974.7

ESSENTIAL AND RECOMMENDED TITLES
974.7 New York

1. September 11 Terrorist Attacks, 2001 2. Victims of terrorism 3. Buildings 4. Rescue work 5. Self-preservation 6. New York City 7. 21st century 8. History writing — September 11, 2001 — United States 9. Adult books for young adults

LC 2006272620

New York Times Notable Book, 2005; National Book Award for Nonfiction finalist, 2005.

Traces the hours following the September 11 attacks on the World Trade Center to reveal the first-hand experiences of survivors, in a volume that draws on oral reports, e-mails, radio transcripts, and cell-phone conversations.

"Dwyer and Flynn have given us a fitting tribute to the people caught up in one of the great dramas of our time. And for people still haunted by the events of that day, reading 102 Minutes provides a cathartic release." —*New York Times Book Review*

Originally published: New York : Times Books, 2005; Includes index.

Friend, David

Watching the World Change: The Stories Behind the Images of 9/11. David Friend. Farrar, Straus and Giroux 2006. xix, 435 p, 24 p. of plates : Illustration; Color

ISBN 9780374299330

Grades: Adult   974.7

1. September 11 Terrorist Attacks, 2001 2. Documentary photography 3. Terrorism 4. New York City 5. History writing — September 11, 2001 — United States

LC 2005036158

Tells the stories behind the photographs of 9/11, discusses the controversy over whether the images are exploitative or redemptive, and shows how photographs help us witness, grieve, and understand the unimaginable.

"In this analysis of how images of 9/11 and the war on terror have altered our understanding of power, world politics, religion and identity, . [the author] successfully merges reportage and analysis as he interprets the images of falling towers, panic in Manhattan streets and prisoners at Abu Ghraib that have been burned into our brains." —*Publishers Weekly*

Includes bibliographical references (p. [349]-413) and index.

Gage, Beverly

The Day Wall Street Exploded: A Story of America in Its First Age of Terror. Beverly Gage. Oxford University Press 2009. VIII, 400 p, 16 p. of plates : Illustration

ISBN 9780195148244

Grades: 10 11 12 Adult   974.7

1. Terrorism 2. Bombings 3. Bombing investigation 4. New York City history 5. New York City 6. Wall Street, New York City 7. 1920s 8. 20th century 9. History writing — Early 20th century — United States

LC 2008022074

Offers a factual account of the worst terrorist act in United States history up until 1920 when a cart packed with dynamite blew up on a corner near Wall Street, killing many, injuring hundreds, and putting in motion a four-year global manhunt to track down the perpetrators.

Includes bibliographical references (p. 339-385) and index.

Gill, Jonathan

Harlem: The Four Hundred Year History from Dutch Village to Capital of Black America. Jonathan Gill. Grove Press 2011. 448 p.

ISBN 9780802119100

Grades: Adult   974.7

1. Community life 2. African American history 3. New York City history 4. Harlem, New York City 5. 20th century 6. History writing — African American — United States

LC 2011283059

Harlem is perhaps the most famous, iconic neighborhood in the United States. A bastion of freedom and the capital of Black America, Harlem's twentieth century renaissance changed our arts, culture, and politics forever. But this is only one of the many chapters in its history. In this work the author, a historian presents a chronicle of this remarkable place. From Henry Hudson's first contact with native Harlemites, through Harlem's years as a colonial outpost on the edge of the known world, he traces the neighborhood's story, marshaling a wealth of detail and a host of figures from George Washington to Langston Hughes. Harlem was an agricultural center under British rule and the site of a key early battle in the Revolutionary War. Later, wealthy elites including Alexander Hamilton built great estates there for entertainment and respite from the epidemics ravaging downtown. In the nineteenth century, transportation urbanized Harlem and brought waves of immigrants from Germany, Italy, Ireland, and elsewhere. Harlem's mix of cultures, extraordinary wealth and extreme poverty was electrifying and explosive. This work is the history of the Manhattan neighborhood of Harlem, beginning with Hudson's first experiences in the area, through its early growth as a Dutch village and colonial agricultural center, to its transformation into a modern neighborhood.

"Comprehensive and compassionate—an essential text of American history and culture." —*Kirkus*

Griswold, Mac K.

The Manor: Three Centuries at a Slave Plantation on Long Island. Mac Griswold. Farrar, Straus and Giroux 2013. 304 p.

ISBN 9780374266295

Grades: Adult   974.7

1. Slavery 2. Plantations 3. Plantation life 4. Excavations (Archaeology) 5. Plantation owners 6. United States history 7. New York (State) 8. Long Island, New York 9. History writing — African American — Enslavement — United States

LC 2013005463

A compelling history of a Long Island plantation, spanning three centuries and eleven generations, reveals the extensive but little-known story of Northern slavery.

Includes bibliographical references and index.

Khan, Yasmin Sabina

Enlightening the World: The Creation of the Statue of Liberty. Yasmin Sabina Khan. Cornell University Press 2010. 240 p.

ISBN 9780801448515

Grades: 11 12 Adult   974.7

1. Bartholdi, Frederic Auguste, 1834-1904 2. Statues 3. Sculptors 4. Symbolism in architecture 5. Design 6. Statue of Liberty (New York, N.Y.) 7. Monuments 8. International relations 9. Buildings 10. New York City history 11. United States 12. France 13. 20th century 14. Arts and Entertainment — Architecture 15. History writing — Gilded Age — United States

LC 2009035711

The State of Liberty has been a symbol of US democratic ideals since 1886. Based on extensive research including travels to France where Liberty Enlightening the World was created, an independent scholar chronicles the story behind its conception, construction, and gifting to the US in the wake of the Civil War. Khan showcases sculptor Auguste Bertholdi, engineer Gustave Eiffel, poet Emma Lazarus, and fundraiser/publisher Joseph Pulitzer, among the many individuals involved. The book features new details about Liberty's design and b&w images.

"This is a lucid account connecting France's widespread grief over Abraham Lincoln's 1865 assassination with that country's own struggles to establish a lasting democracy. Khan shows how Edouard-Reen Lefebvre de Laboulaye, a legal scholar and celebrant of French-American friendship, led others to design and construct what was officially called Liberty Enlightening the World. . . . An important book for general audiences." —*Publishers Weekly*

Includes bibliographical references and index.

Langewiesche, William

American Ground: Unbuilding the World Trade Center. William Langewiesche. North Point Press 2002. 205 p.

ISBN 9780865475823

Grades: Adult   974.7

1. September 11 Terrorist Attacks, 2001 2. Wrecking 3. Skyscrapers 4. Structural engineering 5. Underground construction 6. Disaster relief 7. Design and construction 8. Manhattan, New York City 9. New York City 10. United States 11. History writing — September 11, 2001 — United States

LC 2002075153

New York Times Notable Book, 2002; National Book Critics Circle Award for Nonfiction finalist, 2002.

American Ground is the story—until now untold—of the people who responded to the destruction of the World Trade Center on September 11, 2001. Within days, William Langewiesche made his way into the innermost recesses of the collapse. By virtue of the integrity and excellence of his previous work, he quickly secured unique, unrestricted, around-the-clock access to the site, the rescue workers and laborers there, and the meetings of city officials, engineers, construction companies, and consultants.

"This is a genuinely monumental story, told without melodrama, an intimate depiction of ordinary Americans reacting to grand-scale tragedy at their best—and sometimes their worst." —*Publishers Weekly*

Lepore, Jill
New York Burning: Liberty, Slavery, and Conspiracy in Eighteenth-century Manhattan. Jill Lepore. Alfred A. Knopf 2005. xx, 323 p. : Illustration; Map
ISBN 9781400040292

Grades: Adult   974.7

1. Enslaved people's resistance and revolts 2. Fires 3. African American history 4. Race relations 5. New York City history 6. New York City 7. 18th century 8. Colonial America (1600-1775) 9. History writing — African American — Enslavement — United States

LC 2004057625

ALA Notable Book, 2006; Booklist Editors' Choice, 2005; Pulitzer Prize for History finalist, 2006.

The untold story of the little-known Manhattan slave rebellion of 1741 and the white hysteria that resulted in thirty Black men hanged or burned at the stake, over a hundred Black men and women thrown into the dungeon beneath City Hall, and many more shipped into bone-crushing slavery on Caribbean plantations. Was this a brutal and audacious rebellion prevented just in time or a far more horrible and unjust version of the Salem witch trials?

"In this first-rate social history, Lepore not only adroitly examines the case's travesty, questioning whether such a conspiracy ever existed, but also draws a splendid portrait of the struggles, prejudices and triumphs of a very young New York City in which fully one in five inhabitants was enslaved." —*Publishers Weekly*

Includes bibliographical references (p. 275-308) and index.

MacColl, Gail
To Marry an English Lord. Gail MacColl and Carol McD. Wallace. Workman Pub. 1989. x, 403 p. : Illustration
ISBN 9780894809392

Grades: Adult   974.7

1. Marriage 2. Wealth 3. Upward mobility 4. Nouveaux riches 5. Heirs and heiresses 6. Aristocracy 7. Nobility 8. Upper class 9. Social life and customs 10. New York City 11. England 12. United States 13. Great Britain 14. Victorian era (1837-1901) 15. 19th century 16. History writing — Europe — United Kingdom 17. Family and Relationships — Dating and Marriage

LC 85040529

Tells the stories of wealthy nineteenth-century American heiresses who married British noblemen.

Includes bibliographical references (p. 367-370) and index.

Martin, Wednesday
Primates of Park Avenue: A Memoir. Wednesday Martin, Ph.D.. Simon & Schuster 2015. 256 p.
ISBN 9781476762623

Grades: Adult   974.7

1. Martin, Wednesday 2. Primates 3. Interpersonal relations 4. Social classes 5. Mothers 6. City life 7. Animal behavior 8. Social life and customs 9. Upper East Side, New York City 10. New York City 11. Autobiographies and memoirs 12. Impartial writing 13. Life stories — Relationships 14. Society and culture — Wealth and class

LC 2014041481

Library Journal Best Books, 2015.

The author, a professional anthropologist, compares the behavior of the wealthy mothers of the Upper East Side in New York City that she lived among to primate social behavior, with its rules and rituals about dominance, display, hierarchy, mating practices, physical adornment, and anxiety.

"This anthropological journey into the wilds of New York City's most exclusive zip code could have easily devolved into condescension, but instead it proves that mothers everywhere want the same thing: Health and happiness for their progeny." —*Library Journal*

Includes bibliographical references.

Miller, Donald L.
Supreme City: How Jazz Age Manhattan Gave Birth to Modern America. Donald L. Miller. Simon & Schuster 2014. 672 pages
ISBN 9781416550198

Grades: Adult   974.7

1. Ambition 2. City life 3. Social life and customs 4. New York City history 5. Manhattan, New York City 6. New York City 7. 1920s 8. 20th century 9. History writing — Roaring 20s — United States

LC 2013020154

Miller surveys the astonishing cast of characters who helped turn Manhattan into the world capital of commerce, communication and entertainment.

"Conveying the panoramic sweep of the era with wit, illuminating details, humor, and style, Miller illustrates how Midtown Manhattan became the nation's communications, entertainment, and commercial epicenter." —*Publishers Weekly*

Includes bibliographical references and index.

Reid, David
The Brazen Age: New York City and the American Empire : Politics, Art, and Bohemia. David Reid. Pantheon Books 2016. 384 p.
ISBN 9780394572376

Grades: Adult   974.7

1. Bohemianism 2. New York City history 3. Manhattan, New York City 4. Greenwich Village, New York City 5. 1940s 6. 20th century 7. 19th century 8. History writing — Regional history — United States 9. Arts and Entertainment — Writing and Publishing — Literary criticism

LC 2015024900

Chronicles the vibrant and thriving history, culture and politics of mid-1900s Manhattan and the effect that Thomas Dewey, Henry Wallace, Harry Truman and James Forrestal had on focusing the attention of the world on the city.

"Reid delivers his opinion in a score of unrelated but brilliant chapters on iconic New York individuals (Berenice Abbott, Weegee), groups (returning soldiers, homosexuals), politics (the 1948 elections, leftist magazines), and bohemia (Greenwich village again and again). A historical tour de force." —*Kirkus*

Includes bibliographical references and index.

Smith, Dennis
Report from Ground Zero: The Story of the Rescue Efforts at the World Trade Center. Dennis Smith. Viking 2002. VII, 366 p, 16 p. of plates : Illustration; Map
ISBN 9780670031160

Grades: Adult   974.7

1. September 11 Terrorist Attacks, 2001 2. Fire departments 3. Rescue work 4. Building failures 5. History writing — September 11, 2001 — United States

LC 2002019840

In a tribute to the fallen heroes of September 11, 2001, a former firefighter provides an eyewitness record of events at Ground Zero and the extraordinary efforts of police, fire, and emergency medical teams.

Taylor, Alan
The Divided Ground: Indians, Settlers and the Northern Borderland of the American Revolution. Alan Taylor. Alfred A. Knopf 2006. 542 p. : Illustration; Map
ISBN 9780679454717

Grades: Adult   974.7

1. Brant, Joseph, Mohawk chief, 1742-1807 2. Iroquois (Haudenosaunee) (North American people) 3. Property rights 4. Land tenure 5. Indigenous soldiers 6. Interethnic relations 7. Government relations with indigenous peoples 8. Indigenous peoples of North America 9. First Nations (Canada) 10. American

ESSENTIAL AND RECOMMENDED TITLES
974.8 Pennsylvania

Revolution, 1775-1783 11. Indigenous peoples of North America — History 12. Revolutions 13. Canadian history 14. New York (State) 15. Ontario 16. United States 17. 18th century 18. 19th century 19. Revolutionary America (1775-1783) 20. History writing — Indigenous peoples — United States 21. History writing — Wars and conflicts — Revolutionary War (America) 22. Adult books for young adults

LC 2005043582

The changing relationship of Joseph Brant, a young Mohawk, and Samuel Kirkland, the son of a colonial clergyman is set against the role of the Native American peoples in North America during the American Revolution.

"Taylor's exquisite writing and thorough research in both Canadian and US archives and manuscript collections make this a major work."—*Choice*

Includes bibliographical references (p. [505]-525) and index.

Von Drehle, Dave

★ *Triangle: The Fire That Changed America*. David Von Drehle. Atlantic Monthly Press 2003. 340 p. : Illustration

ISBN 9780871138743

Grades: 11 12 Adult   **974.7**

1. Fires 2. Factories 3. Labor laws and legislation 4. Safety 5. New York City history 6. New York City 7. 1910s 8. 20th century 9. 19th century 10. Biographies 11. History writing — Early 20th century — United States 12. History writing — Natural disasters and tragedies 13. Adult books for young adults

LC 2003041835

ALA Notable Book, 2004; New York Times Notable Book, 2003.

Describes the 1911 fire that destroyed the Triangle Shirtwaist factory in New York's Greenwich Village, the deaths of 146 workers in the fire, and its implications for twentieth-century politics and labor relations.

"Von Drehle's engrossing account, which emphasizes the humanity of the victims and the theme of social justice, brings on of the pivotal and most shocking episodes of American labor history to life."—*Publishers Weekly*

Includes bibliographical references (p. [321]-325) and index.

Wallace, Mike

Greater Gotham: A History of New York City from 1898 to 1919. Mike Wallace. Oxford University Press 2018. 1200 p.

ISBN 9780195116359

Grades: Adult   **974.7**

1. City life 2. New York City history 3. Wall Street, New York City 4. Broadway, New York City 5. History writing — Regional history — United States

LC 2017005224

New York Times Notable Book, 2017.

In Greater Gotham Mike Wallace, co-author of GOTHAM, picks up the story of New York at the critical juncture of 1898 and carries it forward during the period when it became not just the country's greatest urban center but a megapolis on an international scale, and with global reach. Between consolidation and the end of World War One, New York was transformed and transforming, mirroring the juggernauting dynamism of the country at large—and largely fueling it. The names of two its streets encapsulate the degree of the city's preeminence: Wall Street and Broadway.

"Wallace shapes this sprawl into a coherent, engrossing narrative thats nicely balanced between historical sweep and colorful detail. The result sets a standard for urban history, capturing both New Yorks particularities and its protean dynamism."—*Publishers Weekly*

Includes bibliographical references and index.

974.8 Pennsylvania

Longman, Jere

Among the Heroes: United Flight 93 and the Passengers and Crew Who Fought Back. Jere Longman. Harper Collins 2002. xiv, 288 p. : Illustration

ISBN 9780060099084

Grades: 11 12 Adult   **974.8**

1. September 11 Terrorist Attacks, 2001 2. Victims of terrorism 3. Airplane accident victims 4. Heroes and heroines, American 5. Hijacking of aircraft 6. United States 7. History writing — September 11, 2001 — United States 8. Adult books for young adults

LC 2002068530

New York Times Notable Book, 2002.

An account of Flight 93's heroic final moments describes phone calls between passengers and their loved ones, their decision to fight the hijackers, and their heroic sacrifices to prevent a greater tragedy.

"This book gives us an incredibly detailed and personal tale of that horrific episode."—*Booklist*

Includes bibliographical references (p. [275]-280) and index.

Roker, Al

Ruthless Tide: The Tragic Epic of the Johnstown Flood. Al Roker. William Morrow 2018. 320 p.

ISBN 9780062445513

Grades: Adult   **974.8**

1. Natural disasters 2. Floods 3. Dams 4. United States history 5. Pennsylvania 6. 1880s 7. 19th century 8. Nature Writing — Natural Disaster 9. History writing — Regional history — United States 10. Nonfiction that reads like fiction

LC Bl2018045324

The Emmy Award-winning NBC host and weather authority presents a gripping narrative history of the 1889 Johnstown Flood to chronicle key events, the damage that rendered the flood one of America's worst disasters and the pivotal contributions of key period figures, from dam engineer John Parke to American Red Cross founder Clara Barton.

"Roker is especially adept at focusing on key individuals—residents, politicians, movers and shakers, rescue workers—and letting their stories represent the myriads of others. An exciting, tragic story seasoned with sensitive social analysis and criticism."—*Kirkus*

975 Southeastern United States (South Atlantic states)

Bragg, Rick

Where I Come From: Stories from the Deep South. Rick Bragg. Alfred A. Knopf 2020. 256 p.

ISBN 9780593317785

Grades: Adult   **975**

1. Bragg, Rick 2. Identity 3. Men 4. Social life and customs 5. Southern States 6. Essays 7. Society and culture — Ethnic studies 8. Life stories — Identity

LC 2020005021

From his love of Tupperware ("My Affair with Tupperware") to the decline of country music, from the legacy of Harper Lee to the metamorphosis of the pick-up truck, the best way to kill fire ants, the unbridled excess of Fat Tuesday, and why any self-respecting Southern man worth his salt should carry a good knife, Where I Come from is an ode to the stories and the history of the deep south, written with tenderness, wit, and deep affection—a book that will be treasured by fans old and new.

"Bragg's longtime fans will enjoy the piquant one-liners they've come to expect, but new readers looking for meaningful insight into the South should look to his previous works."—*Publishers Weekly*

Crawford, Alan Pell

This Fierce People: The Untold Story of America's Revolutionary War in the South. Alan Pell Crawford. Alfred A. Knopf 2024. 352 p.

ISBN 9780593318508

Grades: Adult   **975**

1. Greene, Nathanael, 1742-1786 2. Morgan, Daniel, 1736-1802 3. American Revolution, 1775-1783 4. Battles 5. Generals 6. Command of troops 7. Guerrilla warfare 8. Colonists 9. Insurgency 10. Loyalists (United States history) 11. Militias and irregular armies 12. Social conflict 13. Violence 14. United States history 15. Southern States 16. Revolutionary America (1775-1783) 17. History writing — Wars and conflicts — Revolutionary War (America) 18. History writ-

ing — Regional history — United States 19. Life stories — Law and order — Military leaders

LC 2023050429

A groundbreaking, important recovery of history; the overlooked story of the critical aspect of America's Revolutionary War that was fought in the South, showing that the British surrender at Yorktown was the direct result of the southern campaign, and that the battles that emerged south of the Mason-Dixon line between loyalists to the Crown and patriots who fought for independence were, in fact, America's first civil war.

"A clear, coherent, and even suspenseful account of the American Revolution." —*Kirkus*

This is a Borzoi book; Includes bibliographical references and index.

Genovese, Eugene D.
Roll, Jordan, Roll: The World the Slaves Made. Eugene D. Genovese. Vintage Books 1976. xxii, 823 p.
ISBN 9780394716527
Grades: Adult   975
1. Enslaved people 2. Slavery 3. United States history 4. 19th century 5. History writing — African American — United States

LC 75026906

A definitive account of slave life in the Old South and the role of the slaves in fashioning a Black national culture.

"The most profound, learned, and detailed analysis of slavery to appear since World War II. It covers an incredible range of topics and offers fresh insights on nearly every page.... Genovese's great gift is his ability to penetrate the minds of both slaves and masters, revealing not only how they viewed themselves and each other, but also how their contradictory perceptions interacted." —*New York Times*

Includes bibliographical references and indexes.

Hahn, Steven
A Nation Under Our Feet: Black Political Struggles in the Rural South, from Slavery to the Great Migration. Steven Hahn. Belknap Press of Harvard University Press 2003. 610 p, 16 p. of plates : Illustration
ISBN 9780674011694
Grades: Adult   975
1. African Americans 2. Freed people 3. Slavery 4. Political participation 5. Politics and culture 6. Race relations 7. Politics and government 8. Southern States 9. 19th century 10. 20th century 11. Antebellum America (1820-1861) 12. History writing — African American — Civil rights — United States

LC 2003045326

Pulitzer Prize for History, 2004.

Emphasizing the role of kinship, labor, and networks in the African-American community, the author retraces six generations of Black struggles since the end of the Civil War, revealing a "nation" under construction throughout this entire period.

Includes bibliographical references (p. [481]-593) and index.

Lemann, Nicholas
Redemption: The Last Battle of the Civil War. Nicholas Lemann. Farrar, Straus and Giroux 2006. xi, 257 p.
ISBN 9780374248550
Grades: Adult   975
1. Ames, Adelbert, 1835-1933 2. Segregation 3. Violence against African Americans 4. Racism 5. Reconstruction (United States history) 6. African American history 7. Civil rights 8. Race relations 9. Politics and government 10. Southern States history 11. Southern States 12. 19th century 13. History writing — Wars and conflicts — American Civil War 14. History writing — African American — United States

LC 2006000091

New York Times Notable Book, 2006.

A study of the campaign of organized racial violence that followed the Civil War describes efforts on the part of white Southern Democrats to prevent the rise of Black political power.

"This book offers a vigorous, necessary reminder of how racist reaction bred an American terrorism that suppressed Black political activity and crushed Reconstruction in the South." —*New York Times Book Review*

Includes bibliographical references (p. [211]-236) and index.

Theroux, Paul
Deep South: Four Seasons on Back Roads. Paul Theroux. Houghton Mifflin Harcourt 2015. 384 p.
ISBN 9780544323520
Grades: Adult   975
1. Theroux, Paul 2. Seasons 3. Social life and customs 4. Voyages and travels 5. Southern States 6. Travel Writing — United States

LC 2015006631

For over 50 years, acclaimed novelist and travel writer Paul Theroux has traveled all over the world. But in his latest journey, he turned his eyes to a region of his home country he wanted to know better. Traveling to various Southern states (including Alabama, Arkansas, Mississippi, Louisiana, Georgia, and South Carolina) on a variety of road trips, Theroux bypassed the big cities and gleaming towns. Instead, he focused his keen eye on smaller, rural towns, where he visited with people in churches, restaurants, corner stores, farms, and gun shows, and explored the culture and paradoxes of the region.

"Therouxs books always appear on the best-seller list, and his latest may prove to be his most popular book yet." —*Booklist*

Includes bibliographical references and index.

975.004 Southeastern United States — Ethnic and national groups

Gayle, Caleb
We Refuse to Forget: A True Story of Black Creeks, American Identity, and Power. Caleb Gayle. Riverhead Books 2022. 288 p.
ISBN 9780593329580
Grades: Adult   975.004
1. Race (Social sciences) 2. Ethnic identity 3. Creek (Muskogee) (North American people) 4. Freed people 5. Elders (Indigenous leaders) 6. African Americans 7. Indigenous peoples of North America 8. Race relations 9. Interethnic relations 10. Racism 11. Colonialism 12. History writing — African American — United States 13. History writing — Indigenous peoples — United States 14. Society and culture — Race 15. Society and culture — Ethnic studies 16. Life stories — Identity — Race and ethnicity

LC 2021053867

Finalist for the Hurston/Wright Legacy Awards for Nonfiction, 2023.

In this paradigm-shattering work of American history, Caleb Gayle tells the extraordinary story of the Creek Nation, a Native tribe that two centuries ago both owned slaves and accepted Black people as full members. Thanks to the leadership of a chief named Cow Tom—a Black former slave—a treaty with the U.S. government recognized Creek citizenship for its Black members. Yet this equality was shredded in the 1970s when Creek leaders revoked the citizenship of Black Creeks, even those who could trace their tribal history back generations. Why did this happen? What led to this reversal? How was the U.S. government involved? and how can marginalized people today defend themselves? These are some of the questions that journalist Caleb Gayle explores in this provocative examination of racial and ethnic identity.

Sharp character sketches, incisive history lessons, and Gayle's autobiographical reflections as a Jamaican American transplant to Oklahoma make this a powerful portrait of how 'White supremacy divides marginalized groups and pits them against each other.' —*Publishers Weekly*

Includes bibliographical references and index.

Sedgwick, John
Blood Moon: An American Epic of War and Splendor in the Cherokee Nation. by John Sedgwick. Simon and Schuster 2018. 416 p.
ISBN 9781501128714
Grades: Adult   975.004

ESSENTIAL AND RECOMMENDED TITLES
975.2 Maryland

1. Ridge, Major, approximately 1771-1839 2. Ross, John, 1790-1866 3. Cherokee (North American people) 4. Trail of Tears, 1838-1839 5. Government relations with indigenous peoples 6. Forced relocations 7. History writing — Indigenous peoples — United States

LC 2017041911

A history of the nineteenth-century rivalry between Cherokee chiefs The Ridge and John Ross contends that though initially allies, they and their followers became divided on key tenets of peace talks and devastated the Cherokee Nation with division, war, and forced migrations.

Includes bibliographical references and index.

975.2 Maryland

Giorgione, Michael
Inside Camp David: The Private World of the Presidential Retreat. Michael Giorgione. Little, Brown and Company 2017. 320 p.

ISBN 9780316509619

Grades: Adult   975.2

1. Presidents 2. Retreat centers 3. Camp David, Maryland 4. History writing — Presidency — United States

LC 2017936280

Celebrates the 75th anniversary of the president's peaceful country retreat with an insider's account of how the leaders of the free world spent their time there, from horseback riding to jumping on a trampoline with their children and hosting diplomatic summits.

Swarns, Rachel L.
The 272: The Families Who Were Enslaved and Sold to Build the American Catholic Church. Rachel L. Swarns. Random House Inc 2023. 288 p.

ISBN 9780399590863

Grades: Adult   975.2

1. Slavery 2. Enslaved people 3. Forced labor 4. Slaveholders 5. United States 6. 19th century 7. History Writing — African American — Enslavement — United States 8. Spirituality and Religion — Christianity — History

Following one family through nearly two centuries of indentured servitude and enslavement, this powerful account illustrates how the Catholic Church relied on slave labor and slave sales to help finance its expansion, bringing to light the people whose forced labor helped to build the largest denomination in the nation.

"Both lively and scrupulously documented, the book brings to light a previously unknown piece of the history of slavery in the U.S." —*Kirkus*

975.3 District of Columbia (Washington)

Bordewich, Fergus M.
Washington: Making the American Capital. by Fergus M. Bordewich. Harper Collins Publishers 2008. 320 p.

ISBN 9780060842383

Grades: Adult   975.3

1. Urban planning 2. Local government 3. Metropolitan government 4. Municipal government 5. Planning 6. United States history 7. Washington, D.C 8. 18th century 9. History writing — Regional history — United States

LC 2007052053

A history of the nation's capital city reveals the role of slavery in its construction, the political and financial obstacles that were faced by the founding fathers, and the back-room deals and shifting alliances that were to shape the region's influence.

"The author explains how the city's site was chosen and how political scheming, personal conflicts, and greed almost doomed the project of designing and constructing a capital city from scratch. Two themes are woven throughout his narrative: the important but often overlooked role played by slaves and former freed slaves and the constant North-South debate at the root of the bitter dispute over the capital's locale." —*Library Journal*

Includes bibliographical references and index.

Brower, Kate Andersen
The Residence: Inside the Private World of the White House. Kate Andersen Brower. Harper 2015. 320 p.

ISBN 9780062305190

Grades: Adult   975.3

1. Presidents' spouses 2. Children of presidents 3. Household employees 4. Presidents 5. Families 6. United States history 7. United States 8. History writing — Presidency — United States

LC 2014040404

An intimate account of White House life from the perspectives of the service staffs of the Kennedys through the Obamas details their friendships, marriages, everyday activities and elaborate state dinners.

"Fans of Downton Abbey will find this look into the secret world of the White House fascinating. History buffs who would like to learn more about the personal lives of the presidents and their families will definitely enjoy all the intriguing vignettes." —*Library Journal*

Euchner, Charles C.
Nobody Turn Me Around: A People's History of the 1963 March on Washington. Charles Euchner. Beacon Press 2010. 256 p.

ISBN 9780807000595

Grades: 11 12 Adult   975.3

1. March on Washington for Jobs and Freedom, 1963 2. Civil Rights Movement 3. Civil rights demonstrations 4. Human rights activists 5. African American history 6. Civil rights 7. United States history 8. 1960s 9. 20th century 10. History writing — African American — Civil rights — United States

LC 2009046943

Draws on the oral histories of more than one hundred participants to provide a behind-the-scenes look at the historic 1963 March on Washington that culminated in Martin Luther King Jr.'s "I Have a Dream" speech.

Includes bibliographical references and index.

Kendrick, Kathleen M
Official Guide to the Smithsonian National Museum of African American History & Culture. National Museum of African American History and Culture; writer: Kathleen M. Kendrick. Smithsonian Books 2017. 175 pages : Illustration; Color

ISBN 9781588345936

Grades: Adult   975.3

1. History writing — African American — United States 2. Travel writing — General 3. Travel Writing — United States

LC 2016038059

A colorful guide introducing the newest Smithsonian museum, the National Museum of African American History and Culture.

Lusane, Clarence
The Black History of the White House. by Clarence Lusane. City Lights Books 2011. 200 p.

ISBN 9780872865327

Grades: 11 12 Adult   975.3

1. African American history 2. Slavery 3. African Americans 4. Presidents 5. Race relations 6. United States 7. Biographies 8. History writing — Presidency — United States

LC 2010036925

Presents a history of the White House from an African American perspective, with information on such topics as slavery, the abolitionist movement, and African-American White House staff.

Includes bibliographical references and index.

Mead, Corey
The Hidden History of the White House: Power Struggles, Scandals, and Defining Moments. Corey Mead; foreword by Kate Anderse Brower. William Morrow & Company 2024. 320 p. : Illustration

ISBN 9780063343382

Grades: Adult   975.3

1. Scandals 2. Social life and customs 3. United States 4. Illustrated books 5. History Writing — United States

Equal parts social, political and cultural history, and inspired by Wondery's hit podcast American History Tellers, this entertaining book places us in the point of view of the historical figures who lived through the fierce power struggles, world-altering decisions, shocking scandals and unforgettable meetings in an iconic American landmark.

"This accessible, well-researched, and generously illustrated book will appeal not only to history buffs, but to anyone interested in the colorful stories—and characters—associated with America's most storied structure." —*Kirkus*

Smith, Michael S.
Designing History: The Extraordinary Art & Style of the Obama White House. Michael S. Smith with Margaret Russell; foreword by Michelle Obama. Rizzoli International Publications 2020. 303 pages : Color; Illustration
ISBN 9780847864799
Grades: Adult   975.3
1. Obama, Barack 2. Obama, Michelle, 1964- 3. Presidents 4. United States 5. House and Home — Interior Decorating and Furnishings 6. Arts and Entertainment — Architecture

Created for design enthusiasts, political aficionados, and students of Americana, Designing History documents Michael Smith's extraordinary collaboration with President Barack Obama and First Lady Michelle Obama. Not since Jacqueline Kennedy's iconic work on the White House has a designer of Michael Smith's stature been commissioned to bring a new design spirit to the mansion. Through extensive photography, behind-the-scenes stories, and rich archival material, the book places the Obama White House within the context of the building's storied past and its evolution over the past two centuries. The book beautifully documents the process of updating the country's most symbolic residence, revealing how Smith's collaboration on the decoration, showcasing of artworks, and style of entertaining reflected the youthful spirit of the First Family and their vision of a more progressive, inclusive American society.

Snow, Peter
When Britain Burned the White House: The 1814 Invasion of Washington. Peter Snow. Thomas Dunne Books, St. Martin's Press 2014. 320 p.
ISBN 9781250048288
Grades: Adult   975.3
1. War of 1812 2. Military history 3. Military campaigns 4. United States history 5. Washington (D.C.) 6. Maryland 7. 19th century 8. 1810s 9. Early America (1784-1819) 10. History writing — Wars and conflicts — War of 1812 11. History writing — Early America — United States
LC 2014010743

A 200th anniversary tribute chronicles the burning of a fledgling America's capital through the anthem-inspiring Battle of Fort McHenry, documenting the near-escape of the First Family while sharing eyewitness perspectives by forefront figures on both sides of the conflict.

"Although the author ultimately tells a riveting true story, he offers little new about the campaign, which is disappointing. Summing Up: Recommended. Public libraries/General collections." —*Choice*

Includes bibliographical references and index.

975.5 Virginia

Ayers, Edward L.
★ *The Thin Light of Freedom: The Civil War and Emancipation in the Heart of America.* Edward L. Ayers. W. W. Norton & Company 2017. xxiii, 576 pages : Illustration; Map
ISBN 9780393292633
Grades: Adult   975.5
1. War and society 2. Postwar life 3. Civilians in war 4. War 5. Reconstruction (United States history) 6. United States Civil War, 1861-1865 7. United States history 8. American Civil War era (1861-1865) 9. 1860s 10. 1870s 11. History writing — Wars and conflicts — American Civil War 12. History writing — Reconstruction — United States
LC 2017021653

A landmark Civil War history told from a fresh, deeply researched ground-level perspective.

"Ayers focuses on the thoughts, fears, and hopes of normal people struggling to stay alive and make sense of the murderous events taking place around them. The result is a superb, readable work of history." —*Publishers Weekly*

Horn, James P. P.
Land as God Made It: Jamestown and the Birth of America. James P. P. Horn. Perseus Books Group 2006. 337 p.
ISBN 9780465030958
Grades: Adult   975.5
1. Smith, John, 1580-1631 2. Powhatan (North American people) 3. Indigenous peoples of North America 4. European Americans 5. Race relations 6. United States history 7. Jamestown, Virginia 8. 17th century 9. Colonial America (1600-1775) 10. History writing — Colonial America — United States
LC Bl2010021668

Chronicles the experiences of the first English settlers that colonized the future United States, and explains how Jamestown set the precedent for North American slavery, Native American conflicts, and representative government.

"Possessing Jamestown's inherent drama, this is a solid rendition of the saga." —*Booklist*

Kelly, Joseph
Marooned: Jamestown, Shipwreck, and the Epic Story of the First Americans. Joseph Kelly. Bloomsbury Publishing 2018. 400 p.
ISBN 9781632867773
Grades: Adult   975.5
1. Hopkins, Stephen, 1581-1644 2. Frontier and pioneer life 3. Colonists 4. Colonies 5. Democracy 6. Social classes 7. United States history 8. Jamestown, Virginia 9. Virginia 10. Colonial America (1600-1775) 11. History writing — Colonial America — United States 12. History writing — Colonialism — Europe
LC 2018003587

A revisionist account of the history of Jamestown challenges popular beliefs to reveal how the Jamestown colonists were essentially marooned by the British caste system and were arguably responsible for America's founding beliefs about government by the people.

Discovering seeds of democracy in Massachusetts' zealots or Virginia's autocratic patricians has never been easy, but Kelly's lively, heavily researched, frequently gruesome account gives a slight nod to Jamestown as the 'Better place to look for the genesis of American ideals.' —*Kirkus*

Includes bibliographical references.

McElya, Micki
The Politics of Mourning: Death and Honor in Arlington National Cemetery. Micki McElya. Harvard University Press 2016. 395 p.
ISBN 9780674737242
Grades: Adult   975.5
1. Memorials 2. Cemeteries 3. Funerals 4. Military service 5. National cemeteries 6. Tomb of the Unknowns (Va.) 7. Nationalism 8. Military history 9. Arlington, Virginia 10. United States 11. History writing — Military
LC 2016008043

Pulitzer Prize for General Nonfiction finalist, 2017.

Shares the history of Arlington National Cemetery and discusses its place in American culture and self-conception.

"McElya diligently unravels the American desire to honor the dead, preserve history and custom, and devise symbols of what the cemetery should represent in the minds of its citizens." —*Library Journal*

Includes bibliographical references and index.

Poole, Robert M.
Section 60: Arlington National Cemetery : Where War Comes Home. Robert M. Poole. Bloomsbury 2014. 304 p.

ESSENTIAL AND RECOMMENDED TITLES
975.6 North Carolina

ISBN 9781620402931
Grades: Adult **975.5**
1. Families of military personnel 2. Memorial Day 3. Afghan War, 2001-2021 4. Iraq War, 2003-2011 5. Burial 6. War casualties 7. Memorialization 8. Cemeteries 9. National cemeteries 10. Military cemeteries 11. United States 12. Arlington, Virginia 13. History writing — Military — Military Today
LC 2014017528

The acclaimed author of On Hallowed Ground, using Section 60 of the Arlington National Cemetery as a window into the latest wars, recounts stories of courage and sacrifice by fallen heroes and how they are honored and remembered by those they left behind.

"Nonfiction enthusiasts will appreciate this work; it will especially satisfy those with an interest in the human condition. It is a book that will linger in the reader's mind." —*Library Journal*

Includes bibliographical references and index.

Price, David A.
★ *Love and Hate in Jamestown: John Smith, Pocahontas, and the Heart of a New Nation*. David A. Price. Knopf 2003. 305 p. : Map
ISBN 9780375415418
Grades: Adult **975.5**
1. Smith, John, 1580-1631 2. Pocahontas, d. 1617 3. Race relations 4. Indigenous peoples of North America 5. First contact of indigenous peoples with Europeans 6. Powhatan (North American people) 7. Enslaved people 8. Culture conflict 9. Class conflict 10. Resourcefulness 11. Survival 12. First contact (Anthropology) 13. United States history 14. Jamestown, Virginia 15. Virginia 16. 17th century 17. Colonial America (1600-1775) 18. History writing — Colonial America — United States 19. History writing — Indigenous peoples — United States 20. Adult books for young adults
LC 2002043437

New York Times Notable Book, 2003; School Library Journal Best Books: Best Adult Books 4 Teens, 2004.

Retells the events of the first permanent English settlement in the new world drawing on letters, chronicles, and records which depict daily experiences, and cites the contributions of John Smith, Pocahontas, and Chief Powhatan.

"For those general readers who wish to move beyond the myths and obtain a better understanding of them and the early years of the colony, this book will be an enjoyable and valuable tool." —*Booklist*

Includes bibliographical references (p. 283-290) and index.

Smith, Lee
Dimestore: A Writer's Life. Lee Smith. Algonquin Books of Chapel Hill 2016. 224 p.
ISBN 9781616205027
Grades: Adult **975.5**
1. Smith, Lee, 1944- 2. Growing up 3. Authors, American 4. Women authors 5. Virginia 6. Autobiographies and memoirs 7. Life stories — Arts and culture — Writing — Authors 8. Life stories — Relationships — Growing up
LC 2015023739

LibraryReads Favorites, 2016.

In her first work of nonfiction, the author recounts her early days in the small coal town of Grundy, Virginia—and beyond.

"In this candid, wistful, appreciative, and beguiling memoir, Smith offers a distinctive and intimate look at one writers beginnings." —*Booklist*

Taylor, Alan
★ *The Internal Enemy: Slavery and War in Virginia, 1772-1832*. Alan Taylor. W. W. Norton & Company 2013. 624 p.
ISBN 9780393073713
Grades: Adult **975.5**
1. Slavery 2. Enslaved people 3. Freed people 4. African American soldiers 5. Plantation life 6. War of 1812 7. United States history 8. Virginia 9. Early America (1784-1819) 10. 1810s 11. History writing — African American — Enslavement — United States 12. History writing — Wars and conflicts — War of 1812 13. History writing — Early America — United States
LC 2013009643

Pulitzer Prize for History, 2014; National Book Award for Nonfiction finalist, 2013.

Drawn from new sources, a Pulitzer Prize-winning historian presents a gripping narrative that recreates the events that inspired hundreds of slaves to pressure British admirals into becoming liberators by using their intimate knowledge of the countryside to transform the war.

"This is a well-written and scrupulously researched examination of an important aspect of the struggle against American slavery." —*Booklist*

Includes bibliographical references and index.

975.6 North Carolina

Horn, James P. P.
A Kingdom Strange: The Brief and Tragic History of the Lost Colony of Roanoke. James Horn. Basic Books 2010. 304 p.
ISBN 9780465004850
Grades: 11 12 Adult **975.6**
1. Colonies 2. Colonists 3. Indigenous peoples of North America 4. Interethnic marriage 5. Colonialism 6. United States history 7. Roanoke Island, North Carolina 8. Roanoke Colony 9. 16th century 10. History writing — Colonial America — United States 11. History writing — Historical mysteries
LC 2010000563

In this gripping account based on new archival material, colonial historian James Horn tells for the first time the complete story of what happened to the Roanoke colonists and their descendants.

",The author creates an engaging, you-are-there feel to the narrative, with rich descriptions of European politics, colonists' daily struggles and the vagaries of relations between Native American tribes. A satisfying recounting of some of the earliest American history." —*Kirkus*

Kiernan, Denise
The Last Castle: The Epic Story of Love, Loss, and American Royalty in the Nation's Largest Home. Denise Kiernan. Touchstone 2017. 384 p.
ISBN 9781476794044
Grades: Adult **975.6**
1. Vanderbilt family 2. Mansions 3. Rich people 4. Architecture 5. Buildings 6. United States history 7. North Carolina 8. 19th century 9. History writing — Gilded Age — United States 10. Arts and Entertainment — Architecture
LC 2017015229

Documents the story of the Gilded Age mansion Biltmore, George Vanderbilt's construction of his spectacular European-style estate with the help of two famed architects and the efforts of his bride, Edith Stuyvesant Dresser, to become its mistress and protector in the face of changing fortunes and times.

"Kiernan (The Girls of Atomic City) presents an intriguing history of the largest private U.S. residence: the Biltmore House." —*Library Journal*

Includes bibliographical references.

Lawler, Andrew
The Secret Token: Myth, Obsession, and the Search for the Lost Colony of Roanoke. by Andrew Lawler. Doubleday 2018. 352 p.
ISBN 9780385542012
Grades: Adult **975.6**
1. Dare, Virginia, 1587- 2. Colonialism 3. Colonies 4. Colonists 5. Archaeology and history 6. Immigrants 7. Public opinion 8. United States history 9. Roanoke Colony 10. Roanoke Island, North Carolina 11. North Carolina 12. 16th century 13. Colonial America (1600-1775) 14. History writing — Historical mysteries 15. History writing — Colonial America — United States
LC 2017045395

Documents the events surrounding the unsolved 1587 disappearance of the Roanoke Island colony, tracing major investigations from the past 400 years as well as the author's own findings about how the Lost Colony is tied to today's America.

"This detailed historical inquiry will powerfully intrigue early American history buffs." —*Booklist*

Includes bibliographical references.

PUBLIC LIBRARY CORE COLLECTION: NONFICTION
Twentieth Edition

Tyson, Timothy B.
Blood Done Sign My Name: A True Story. Timothy B. Tyson. Crown Publishers 2004. VII, 355 p.
ISBN 9780609610589
Grades: 11 12 Adult   975.6
1. Tyson, Timothy B. 2. Crimes against African Americans 3. Murder 4. Trials (Murder) 5. Riots 6. European Americans 7. African Americans 8. Race riots 9. Race relations 10. 20th century 11. Autobiographies and memoirs 12. History writing — African American — Civil rights — United States 13. True Crime — Murder 14. Life stories — Facing adversity — Victims of crime 15. True Crime — Investigations and Trials

LC 2003019804

National Book Critics Circle Award for Nonfiction finalist, 2004.

Thirty years after the murder of a Black man by a Klansman and his acquittal by an all-white jury, the author returns to his hometown of Oxford, North Carolina, to make sense of what happened, interweaving his own childhood memories and the real world of modern-day Oxford with interviews with participants on both sides, shedding new light on the struggle for racial justice.

"A significant work of memoir and social history; for public and academic libraries." —*Library Journal*

Includes bibliographical references (p. 326-344).

975.7 South Carolina

Ball, Edward
Slaves in the Family. Edward Ball. Farrar, Straus and Giroux 1998. 504 p. : Illustration; Map
ISBN 9780374265823
Grades: Adult   975.7
1. Ball family 2. Interracial families 3. Enslaved people 4. Slaveholders 5. Plantation life 6. African American history 7. Race relations 8. United States history 9. Charleston, South Carolina 10. Family and Relationships — Families 11. History writing — African American — Enslavement — United States 12. Adult books for young adults

LC 97034640

Booklist Editors' Choice, 1998; National Book Award for Nonfiction, 1998; New York Times Notable Book, 1998.

Explores the slave-holding dynasty of Elias Ball, a South Carolina plantation owner, the history of slave uprisings, and the memories of the descendants of those slaves.

"For nearly a hundred and seventy years before the Civil War, members of the Ball family owned a string of plantations worked by slaves along South Carolina's Cooper River. After the war, the author's ancestors lost or sold their land and scattered to make new lives, but he wondered what happened to the slaves. This book, a brilliant blend of archival research and oral history, tells what he found." —*The New Yorker*

Includes bibliographical references (p. [457]-484) and index.

Kytle, Ethan J.
Denmark Vesey's Garden: Slavery and Memory in the Cradle of Confederacy. Ethan J. Kytle and Blain Roberts. The New Press 2018. 384 p.
ISBN 9781620973653
Grades: Adult   975.7
1. Vesey, Denmark, approximately 1767-1822 2. Slavery 3. Memory 4. Collective memory 5. United States history 6. Charleston, South Carolina 7. 19th century 8. Antebellum America (1820-1861) 9. History writing — Antebellum America — United States 10. History writing — African American — Enslavement — United States

LC 2017041546

Striking at the heart of the recent flare-ups over Confederate symbols in Charlottesville, New Orleans and elsewhere, the authors reveal the deep roots of these controversies and trace them to the heart of slavery in the U.S.—Charleston, South Carolina—providing competing of histories of how slavery is remembered in this city.

Includes bibliographical references and index.

975.8 Georgia

Berendt, John
Midnight in the Garden of Good and Evil: A Savannah Story. John Berendt. Random House 1994. 388 p.
ISBN 9780679429227
Grades: Adult   975.8
1. Williams, Jim, d. 1990 2. Trials (Murder) 3. Eccentrics and eccentricities 4. Murder 5. Murderers 6. Social life and customs 7. United States history 8. Southern States 9. Savannah, Georgia 10. 1980s 11. Page to screen 12. True Crime — Murder 13. Nonfiction that reads like fiction

LC 93003955

Lambda Literary Award for Gay Men's Mystery, 1994; Pulitzer Prize for General Nonfiction finalist.

Tells the true story of the murder of the local bad boy in the opulent mansion of a gay antiques dealer in charming Old South Savannah, Georgia.

"Berendt has fashioned a Baedeker to Savannah that, while it flirts with condescension, is always contagiously affectionate. Few cities have been introduced more seductively." —*Newsweek*

Finkel, David
An American Dreamer: Life in a Divided Country. David Finkel. Random House 2024. 256 p.
ISBN 9780593597064
Grades: Adult   975.8
1. Cummings, Brent 2. Iraq War veterans 3. Families 4. Political culture 5. Small town life 6. Polarization (Social sciences) 7. Extremism 8. Disillusionment 9. Loss 10. Social change 11. North American people 12. American people 13. Georgia 14. United States 15. 2010s 16. 2020s 17. History writing — Early 21st century — United States 18. Life stories — People in history — Witness to history 19. History writing — United States 20. Nonfiction that reads like fiction

Brent Cummings finds himself coping with the feeling that the country he loves is fracturing in front of his eyes. An Iraq war veteran, raised to believe in a vision of America that values fairness, honesty, and respect for others, Cummings is increasingly surprised by the behavior and beliefs of others, and engulfed by the fear, anger, and confusion that is sweeping through his beloved country as he tries to hold on to his hope for America's future. David Finkel spent fourteen years deep inside Brent Cummings's world to create this intimate portrait of a man's life, his work, family, community, and his quest for connection, as America becomes ever more divided.

"An intimate look at American lives in fraught times." —*Kirkus*

Jones, Jacqueline
Saving Savannah: The City and the Civil War. by Jacqueline Jones. Alfred A. Knopf 2008. 528 p.
ISBN 9781400042937
Grades: Adult   975.8
1. Freed people 2. Elite (Social sciences) 3. Social classes 4. Slavery 5. African American history 6. Civil war 7. United States Civil War, 1861-1865 8. Race relations 9. United States history 10. Georgia 11. Savannah, Georgia 12. 19th century 13. American Civil War era (1861-1865) 14. History writing — Wars and conflicts — Homefront — American Civil War 15. History writing — Confederacy — United States 16. History writing — African American — United States

LC 2008011508

Drawing on diaries, letters, newspaper articles, memoirs, and military records, an in-depth study of the city of Savannah before, during, and in the aftermath of the Civil War describes the African-American struggle for equality and freedom in the midst of war, political turmoil, and social upheaval.

"Synthesizing the perspectives of the mercantile elite, the aristocratic upper crust and the downtrodden, . [the author has] fashioned a compelling social and political history." —*Washington Post Book World*

Includes bibliographical references and index.

ESSENTIAL AND RECOMMENDED TITLES
975.9 Florida

Pressly, Paul M.
On the Rim of the Caribbean: Colonial Georgia and the British Atlantic World. Paul M. Pressly. University of Georgia Press 2013. xii, 354 p. : Illustration; Map
ISBN 9780820335674
Grades: Adult **975.8**
1. Plantations 2. United States history 3. Georgia 4. 18th century 5. History writing — Latin America 6. History writing — Colonial America — United States
LC 2012033964

"This richly documented, analytically complex, and well-written book is a major contribution to the study of Colonial Georgia and the 18th-century Atlantic world." —*Choice*

Includes bibliographical references (p. [301]-335) and index.

975.9 Florida

Douglas, Marjory Stoneman
The Everglades: River of Grass. by Marjory Stoneman Douglas; illustrated by Robert Fink; [update by Michael Grunwald]. Pineapple Press 2007. 447 p. : Illustration; Map
ISBN 9781561643943
Grades: 11 12 Adult **975.9**
1. Natural history 2. Wilderness areas 3. Nature 4. United States history 5. Everglades, Florida 6. Florida 7. Nature Writing — Natural Landscapes 8. Nature Writing — Environmental Issues
LC 2007028384

This edition includes the complete text of the 1947 and an extended afterword by journalist Grunwald which explains what happened after Douglas alerted the country about the situation of the Everglades, including successful efforts to create the Everglades National Park and the unsuccessful efforts of the Army Corps of Engineers to remake it.

Includes bibliographical references (p. 426-433) and indexes; Original ed.: New York : Rinehart, 1947.

976.1 Alabama

Agee, James
★ *Cotton Tenants: Three Families.* James Agee; [photographs by] Walker Evans; edited by John Summers; preface by Adam Haslett. Melville House 2013. 224 p. : Illustration
ISBN 9781612192123
Grades: Adult **976.1**
1. Depressions, 1929-1941 2. Sharecropping 3. Sharecroppers 4. Families 5. Rural life 6. Rural families 7. Poor families 8. Poor people 9. Poverty 10. Economics 11. United States 12. 20th century 13. History writing — Great Depression — United States
LC 2013370909

On assignment for "Fortune" magazine in 1936, Agee and Evans set out to explore the plight of sharecroppers during the Great Depression. Published for the first time, Agee's original dispatch (accompanied by 25 of Evans' historic photographs) is an unsparing record of three families at a desperate time.

"Accessible, hard-hitting, moving, and still thematically relevant. Highly recommended for all collections." —*Library Journal*

Let Us Now Praise Famous Men: Three Tenant Families. James Agee, Walker Evans; with an introduction to the new edition by John Hersey. Houghton Mifflin 1988. Liv, 471 p, 61 p. of plates : Illustration
ISBN 9780395489017
Grades: 11 12 Adult **976.1**
1. Agee, James, 1909-1955 2. Farm life 3. Poverty 4. Tenant farmers 5. Depressions, 1929-1941 6. Rural conditions 7. Alabama 8. History writing — United States
LC 88018110

An illustrated portrayal of three Alabama sharecropper families in 1936, examining their everyday existence in poverty.

Originally published: Boston, MA : Houghton Mifflin, 1941.

Kix, Paul
★ *You Have to Be Prepared to Die Before You Can Begin to Live: Ten Weeks in Birmingham That Changed America.* Paul Kix. Celadon Books 2023. 400 p.
ISBN 9781250807694
Grades: Adult **976.1**
1. King, Martin Luther, Jr, 1929-1968 2. Abernathy, Ralph, 1926-1990 3. Shuttlesworth, Fred L, 1922-2011 4. Bevel, James L. (James Luther), 1936-2008 5. Civil Rights Movement 6. African Americans 7. Protests, demonstrations, vigils, etc. 8. Civil rights organizations 9. Racism 10. Police brutality 11. Violence in mass media 12. United States history 13. Birmingham, Alabama 14. 1960s 15. History writing — African American — Civil rights — United States 16. History writing — 1960s — United States 17. Life stories — Politics — Activists and Reformers — Civil Rights Leaders 18. Nonfiction that reads like fiction
LC 2022055913

In You Have to Be Prepared to Die Before You Can Begin to Live, Paul Kix takes the reader behind the scenes as he tells the story of the Southern Christian Leadership Conference's pivotal 10 week campaign in 1963 to end segregation in Birmingham, Alabama. At the same time, he also provides a window into the minds of the four extraordinary men who led the campaign—Martin Luther King, Jr, Wyatt Walker, Fred Shuttlesworth, and James Bevel.

"Journalist Kix (The Saboteur) delivers a gripping, novelistic account of the Southern Christian Leadership Conference's campaign to desegregate Birmingham, Ala, in 1963….Kix makes a persuasive case that Birmingham saved a floundering organization and galvanized the Kennedy administration to commit to civil rights." —*Publishers Weekly*

Includes bibliographical references and index.

McWhorter, Diane
Carry Me Home: Birmingham, Alabama, the Climactic Battle of the Civil Rights Revolution. Diane McWhorter. Simon & Schuster 2001. 701 p, 16 p. of plates : Illustration; Map
ISBN 9780684807478
Grades: 11 12 Adult **976.1**
1. Wallace, George, 1919-1998 2. Connor, Eugene, 1897-1973 3. Freedom Riders (Civil rights movement) 4. White supremacists 5. Civil Rights Movement 6. Racism 7. Prejudice 8. Segregation in education 9. African American history 10. Civil rights 11. Race relations 12. Alabama 13. Birmingham, Alabama 14. 1960s 15. 20th century 16. History writing — African American — Civil rights — United States
LC 00053827

J. Anthony Lukas Book Prize, 2002; Library Journal Best Books, 2001; Pulitzer Prize for General Nonfiction, 2002; New York Times Notable Book, 2001.

A journalist chronicles the peak of the civil rights movement, focusing on the African American freedom fighters who stood firm on issues of civil rights and segregation during the movement's eventful climax in Birmingham.

"A daughter of Birmingham's privileged elite, McWhorter weaves a personal narrative through this startling account of the history, events, and major players on both sides of the civil rights battle in that city." —*Booklist*

Maps on lining papers; Includes bibliographical references (p. [661]-669) and index.

Tabor, Nick
Africatown: America's Last Slave Ship and the Community It Created. Nick Tabor. St. Martin's Press 2023. 320 p.
ISBN 9781250766540
Grades: Adult **976.1**
1. African Americans 2. West African people 3. Slavery 4. Enslaved people 5. United States history 6. Alabama 7. Mobile, Alabama 8. 19th century 9. History writing — African American — Enslavement — United States
LC 2022035463

Tells the story of the enslaved people brought over on America's last slave ship, and the community they established outside Mobile, Alabama, that still exists today.

"Journalist Tabor debuts with an eye-opening and often gripping history of more than 100 enslaved West Africans brought to America aboard the Clotilda in 1860 and the Alabama community they created....Exhaustive research, pointed analysis, and poignant character sketches make this an essential study of racism in America." —*Publishers Weekly*

Includes bibliographical references and index.

976.2 Mississippi

Grant, Richard
The Deepest South of All: True Stories from Natchez, Mississippi. Richard Grant. Simon & Schuster 2020. 288 pages
ISBN 9781501177828
Grades: Adult   976.2
1. Cities and towns 2. Race relations 3. Inequality 4. Eccentrics and eccentricities 5. Racism 6. Princes 7. Slavery 8. Natchez, Mississippi 9. History writing — Regional history — United States 10. Travel Writing — United States 11. Society and culture — Race 12. Society and culture — Wealth and class 13. Nonfiction that reads like fiction

LC Bl2020018825

An engaging portrait of Natchez, Mississippi traces its rich cultural heritage and remarkable contradictions, sharing the stories of history-shaping locals, from FBI informant and brothel madam Nellie Jackson to enslaved West African prince Abd al Rahman Ibrahima.

"Readers will be enthralled by Grant's lively prose and the colorful contradictions of this unique and haunted place." —*Publishers Weekly*

Welty, Eudora
One Time, One Place: Mississippi in the Depression : A Snapshot Album. Eudora Welty. University Press of Mississippi 1996. xiv, 115 p. : Illustration
ISBN 9780878058662
Grades: Adult   976.2
1. Depressions 2. Documentary photography 3. Mississippi 4. Arts and Entertainment — Photography

LC 95046057

Collects photographs of Mississippians that Welty took in the 1930s when she worked for the Works Progress Administration.

"This is a collection of photographs of Mississippians that Welty took in the 1930s, when she worked for the Works Progress Administration (WPA). This Silver Anniversary Edition contains a great foreword by William Maxwell that absolutely nails the importance of the book for many readers." —*Booklist*

Originally published: New York : Random House, 1971.

976.3 Louisiana

Berry, Jason
City of a Million Dreams: A History of New Orleans at Year 300. Jason Berry. The University of North Carolina Press 2018. 424 p.
ISBN 9781469647142
Grades: Adult   976.3
1. United States history 2. New Orleans, Louisiana 3. History writing — Arts and culture 4. History writing — Regional history — United States

LC 2018020837

Jason Berry delivers a character-driven history of New Orleans at its tricentennial. Chronicling cycles of invention, struggle, death, and rebirth, Berry reveals the city's survival as a triumph of diversity, its map-of-the-world neighborhoods marked by resilience despite hurricanes, epidemics, fires, and floods.

Includes bibliographical references and index.

Brinkley, Douglas
The Great Deluge: Hurricane Katrina, New Orleans, and the Mississippi Gulf Coast. Douglas Brinkley. Morrow 2006. xix, 716 p. : Illustration; Color
ISBN 9780061124235
Grades: 11 12 Adult   976.3
1. Hurricane Katrina, 2005 2. Hurricanes 3. Disaster victims 4. Emergency planning 5. Floods 6. Disaster relief 7. New Orleans, Louisiana 8. United States 9. 21st century 10. Nature Writing — Natural Disaster 11. History writing — Natural disasters and tragedies 12. History writing — Early 21st century — United States

LC 2006043338

New York Times Notable Book, 2006; Robert F. Kennedy Book Award, 2007.

A deeply personal account of hurricane Katrina and the devastation it left in New Orleans and across the Gulf Coast documents the events and repercussions of the tragedy and its aftermath, the historical roots of the terrible storm, and the ongoing crisis confronting the region.

"The author captures the human toll of Katrina as graphically as the most vivid newspaper and television accounts did, and by pulling together a huge, choral portrait of what happened during that first week of havoc and distress ... he gives the reader a richly detailed timeline of disaster—a timeline in which the sheer cumulative power of details impresses upon us, again, just how abysmally inept relief efforts were on every level, from FEMA to the Red Cross to the New Orleans police department, from the federal government to state and local authorities." —*New York Times*

Includes bibliographical references and index.

Dyson, Michael Eric
Come Hell or High Water: Hurricane Katrina and the Color of Disaster. Michael Eric Dyson. Basic Civitas 2006. xii, 258 p.
ISBN 9780465017614
Grades: 11 12 Adult   976.3
1. Bush, George W. (George Walker), 1946- 2. African American civil rights 3. Hurricane Katrina, 2005 4. African Americans 5. Poor people 6. Racism 7. Classism 8. Floods 9. Emergency planning 10. Race relations 11. United States 12. 21st century 13. Nature Writing — Natural Disaster

A searing assessment of the meaning of Hurricane Katrina combines interviews with survivors of the disaster and the author's knowledge of Black migrations and government policy over decades, and explores the legacy of Black suffering in America since slavery.

"This book on Hurrican Katrina not only chronicles what happened when, it also argues that the nation's failure to offer timely aid to Katrina's victims indicates deeper problems in race and class relations. . . . [The author's] contention that Katrina exposed a dominant culture pervaded not only by active malice toward poor Blacks but also by a long history of passive indifference to their problems is both powerful and unsettling." —*Publishers Weekly*

Includes bibliographical references (p. 213-244) and index.

Horne, Jed
Breach of Faith: Hurricane Katrina and the Near Death of a Great American City. Jed Horne. Random House 2006. 432 p.
ISBN 9781400065523
Grades: 11 12 Adult   976.3
1. Hurricane Katrina, 2005 2. Disasters 3. Hurricanes 4. Floods 5. Disaster victims 6. Levees 7. Emergency planning 8. Disaster relief 9. New Orleans, Louisiana 10. United States 11. Nature Writing — Natural Disaster 12. History writing — Natural disasters and tragedies 13. Adult books for young adults

LC 2006046468

ALA Notable Book, 2007.

A journalist and resident of New Orleans offers a firsthand, eyewitness account of Hurricane Katrina, its devastating impact on New Orleans, and its terrifying aftermath, arguing that the origins of the disaster lie in the culture and politics of a troubled city and in the national politics of poverty, homeland security, and race relations.

"The New Orleans Times-Picayune's staff (including metro editor Horne) won Pulitzer Prizes for its coverage of Katrina. Such esteem is deserved, as

ESSENTIAL AND RECOMMENDED TITLES
976.4 Texas

Horne here demonstrates. His on-the-ground narrative emphasizes his ear for local idiom and his sharp eye for compelling detail." —*Library Journal*

Johnson, Walter
Soul by Soul: Life Inside the Antebellum Slave Market. Walter Johnson. Harvard University Press 1999. 283 p. ; Illustration
ISBN 9780674821484
Grades: Adult 976.3
1. Enslaved people 2. Slave trade 3. African Americans 4. Slaveholders 5. Race relations 6. New Orleans, Louisiana 7. 19th century 8. History writing — African American — Enslavement — United States

LC 99046696

"This is an examination of the antebellum slave market. Using slave narratives, court records, planters' letters, and more, Johnson enters the slave pens and showrooms of the New Orleans slave market to observe how slavery turned men and women into merchandise and how slaves resisted such efforts to steal their humanity." —*Library Journal*

Includes bibliographical references (p. [223]-273) and index.

Krist, Gary
Empire of Sin: A Story of Sex, Jazz, Murder, and the Battle for Modern New Orleans. Gary Krist. Crown 2014. 432 pages
ISBN 9780770437060
Grades: Adult 976.3
1. Anderson, Thomas Charles, 1858-1931 2. Political corruption 3. Police chiefs 4. Race relations 5. Crime 6. Murder 7. Jazz music 8. Sex customs 9. Prostitution 10. Immigrants, Italian 11. Organized crime 12. United States history 13. New Orleans, Louisiana 14. Storyville (New Orleans, Louisiana) 15. 20th century 16. True Crime — Historical Crime 17. History writing — Early 20th century — United States

LC 2014003191

Library Journal Best Books 2014.

Describes the internal struggle in early-twentieth-century New Orleans between the city's upper crust and the underworld, focusing on the head of the red light district, who fought to keep his vice business at the top in a wicked city.

"Krist's lively book is only marred by an overlong section devoted to a series of axe murders that plagued the city. A wild, well-told tale." —*Kirkus*

Lane, Charles
The Day Freedom Died: The Colfax Massacre, the Supreme Court, and the Betrayal of Reconstruction. Charles Lane. Henry Holt 2008. 352 p.
ISBN 9780805083422
Grades: Adult 976.3
1. Beckwith, James, 1832-1912 2. Crimes against African-Americans 3. Massacres 4. Violence 5. Racism 6. Reconstruction (United States history) 7. Lawyers 8. Trials (Murder) 9. Race relations 10. United States 11. 19th century 12. History writing — Judicial branch — United States 13. True Crime — Investigations and Trials 14. History writing — African American — Civil rights — United States

LC 2007037514

Describes the 1873 Colfax, Louisiana, massacre of sixty former slaves by former Confederate soldiers, and the efforts to bring the perpetrators to justice that ended with a Supreme Court verdict that left Southern Blacks at the mercy of violent racists for generations.

"The Colfax Massacre . took place on an Easter Sunday afternoon in 1873. Within four hours, at least eighty Black American men had been brutally murdered by white vigilantes in Colfax, LA. Journalist Lane's groundbreaking and persuasive work illustrates this pivotal event in the political and constitutional history of post-Civil War America and its social, political and judicial aftermath. Students of American and African-American history will find it particularly valuable; fans of American history will find it a moving and instructive drama." —*Publishers Weekly*

Includes bibliographical references and index.

Rasmussen, Daniel
American Uprising: The Untold Story of America's Largest Slave Revolt. Daniel Rasmussen. Harper 2011. 288 p.
ISBN 9780061995217
Grades: Adult 976.3
1. Enslaved people's resistance and revolts 2. Slavery 3. Revolutions 4. African Americans 5. Race relations 6. United States history 7. New Orleans, Louisiana 8. 19th century 9. History writing — African American — Enslavement — United States 10. History writing — Early America — United States

LC 2010017855

The author, a historian reveals the long forgotten history of America's largest slave uprising, the New Orleans slave revolt of 1811 that nearly toppled New Orleans and changed the course of American history.

"This is an account of a large-scale, three-day slave revolt on the sugar plantations near New Orleans during the 1811 Carnival (Mardi Gras) season. The author argues that the slave-rebels, who had learned warfare tactics in their native Africa, were inspired by the successful Haitian revolution. This is a welcome addition to popular history and an engaging read for anyone interested in this important chapter in the tragic story of American slavery." —*Library Journal*

Includes bibliographical references and index.

Rivlin, Gary
Katrina: After the Flood. Gary Rivlin. Simon & Schuster 2015. 416 p.
ISBN 9781451692228
Grades: Adult 976.3
1. Hurricane Katrina, 2005 2. Urban renewal 3. Urban planning 4. City life 5. Natural disasters 6. New Orleans, Louisiana 7. History writing — Natural disasters and tragedies 8. History writing — Regional history — United States

LC 2015431412

New York Times Notable Book, 2015.

Ten years after Hurricane Katrina made landfall in southeast Louisiana—on August 29, 2005—journalist Gary Rivlin traces the storm's immediate damage, the city of New Orleans's efforts to rebuild itself, and the storm's lasting effects not just on the city's geography and infrastructure—but on the psychic, racial, and social fabric of one of this nation's great cities.

Rivlin captures the snark, the bellyaching, and the outright denial of those in charge—and many aimed to be in charge (while many dodged responsibility as well). A fascinating lesson in urban planning in the face of calamity and financial shenanigans about what has been deemed 'The most expensive disaster in history.' —*Booklist*

976.4 Texas

Burrough, Bryan
Forget the Alamo: The Rise and Fall of an American Myth. Bryan Burrough, Chris Tomlinson, and Jason Stanford. Penguin Press 2021. 416 p.
ISBN 9781984880093
Grades: Adult 976.4
1. Revolutions 2. Battles 3. Slavery 4. Anti-slavery movements 5. White supremacy movements 6. Historical revisionism 7. United States history 8. San Antonio, Texas 9. Texas 10. 19th century 11. Impartial writing 12. History writing — Regional history — United States 13. History writing — Wars and conflicts — Battles 14. Life stories — People in history

LC 2020044815

There's no piece of history more important to Texans than the Battle of the Alamo, when Davy Crockett and a band of rebels went down in a blaze of glory fighting for independence from Mexico, losing the battle but setting Texas up to win the war. However, that version of events owes more to fantasy than reality. Just as the site of the Alamo was left in ruins for decades, its story was forgotten and twisted over time, with the contributions of Tejanos, Texans of Mexican origin who fought alongside the Anglo rebels, scrubbed from the record, and the origin of the conflict over Mexico's push to abolish slavery papered over. Forget the Alamo provocatively explains the true story of the battle against the backdrop of Texas's struggle for independence, then shows us how the sausage of myth got made in the Jim Crow South of the late 19th and early 20th century.

PUBLIC LIBRARY CORE COLLECTION: NONFICTION
Twentieth Edition

"A zesty, journalistic, half history, half sendup about the battle of the Alamo and the myths that cling to it. Setting out to distinguish ascertainable fact from Texas tub-thumping, Burrough, Tomlinson, and Stanford, all Texans, succeed brilliantly in their intent." —*Kirkus*

Includes bibliographical references and index.

Donovan, Jim
The Blood of Heroes: The 13-day Struggle for the Alamo — and the Sacrifice That Forged a Nation. James Donovan. Little, Brown and Co. 2012. 544 p.
ISBN 9780316053747
Grades: Adult   976.4
1. Sieges 2. Battles 3. Courage 4. United States history 5. Texas 6. 19th century 7. History writing — Wars and conflicts — Battles 8. History writing — Wars and conflicts — Mexican-American War 9. History writing — Westward expansion — United States

LC 2011050067

The author describes the valiant fight by 200 Americans in an abandoned mission near San Antonio, Texas, against the Mexican army.

Includes bibliographical references and index.

Fields, Micah
★ *We Hold Our Breath: A Journey to Texas Between Storms.* Micah Fields. W.W. Norton & Company 2023. 192 p.
ISBN 9781324003793
Grades: Adult   976.4
1. Fields, Micah 2. Cities and towns 3. Homecomings 4. Economic development 5. Urban sprawl 6. Hurricanes 7. Storms 8. Floods 9. Rescues 10. Oil industry and trade 11. Chemical industry and trade 12. Environmental degradation 13. Pollution 14. Land use 15. Natural disasters 16. Loss 17. Houston, Texas 18. Society and culture — Urban and regional studies 19. Nature Writing — Environmental Issues 20. Life stories — Facing adversity — Disasters and tragedies

Part reportage, part history, part memoir, this portrait of Houston, whose story has always been one of war waged relentlessly against water, investigates the conflicting facets of Texan identity that are resilient as they are catastrophic, steeped in racial subjugation, environmental collapse and capitalist greed.

"With eloquence and grace, the author investigates the interconnectedness of place, history, and identity. A thoughtfully elegant, reflective work." —*Kirkus*

Johnson, Kirk W.
The Fishermen and the Dragon: Fear, Greed, and a Fight for Justice on the Gulf Coast. Kirk Wallace Johnson. Viking 2022. 368 p.
ISBN 9781984880123
Grades: Adult   976.4
1. Fisheries 2. Fishers 3. Refugees 4. Vietnamese Americans 5. Asian Americans 6. Environmental disasters 7. White supremacists 8. Racism 9. Competition 10. Blame 11. Violence 12. Oil spills 13. Marine pollution 14. Women environmentalists 15. Class actions (Civil procedure) 16. Southeast Asian Americans 17. Southeast Asian people 18. Galveston, Texas 19. Texas 20. Gulf of Mexico 21. 20th century 22. Nature Writing — Environmental Issues 23. Society and culture — Race 24. Society and culture — Violence and crime 25. History writing — Regional history — United States

LC 2021060150

A gripping, twisting account of a small town set on fire by hatred, xenophobia, and ecological disaster—a story that weaves together corporate malfeasance, a battle over shrinking natural resources, a turning point in the modern white supremacist movement, and one woman's relentless battle for environmental justice.

"[Johnson's] fascinating and disturbing narrative is a winning mix of biography, true crime, and ecological study." —*Kirkus*

Includes bibliographical references and index.

976.6 Oklahoma

Anderson, Sam
Boom Town: The Fantastical Saga of Oklahoma City, Its Chaotic Founding... Its Purloined Basketball Team, and the Dream of Becoming a World-class Metropolis. Sam Anderson. Crown 2018. 304 p.
ISBN 9780804137317
Grades: Adult   976.6
1. Social history 2. Urban planning 3. Sports 4. Cities and towns 5. Human geography 6. Basketball 7. Population 8. Oklahoma City, Oklahoma 9. Society and culture — Urban and regional studies

LC 2017054583

Booklist Editors' Choice, 2018; New York Times Notable Book, 2018.

An award-winning journalist documents the idiosyncratic mix of history, sports, urban studies and more reflected in Oklahoma City, tracing its chaotic origins through the near-instant metropolis of today through the stories of creative innovators.

"Andersons lively and empathetic saga captures the outsize ambitions, provincial realities, and vibrant history of a quintessentially American city." —*Publishers Weekly*

Ellsworth, Scott
The Ground Breaking: An American City and Its Search for Justice. Scott Ellsworth. Dutton 2021. 352 p. : Illustration
ISBN 9780593182987
Grades: Adult   976.6
1. Tulsa Race Massacre, Tulsa, Oklahoma, 1921 2. Racism 3. Violence against African Americans 4. African Americans 5. African American neighborhoods 6. Reparations 7. Race relations 8. United States history 9. Tulsa, Oklahoma 10. Oklahoma 11. 1920s 12. 20th century 13. 21st century 14. Society and culture — Race 15. History writing — Regional history — United States 16. History writing — African American — United States 17. True Crime — Historical Crime

LC 2020057916

Part true-crime murder mystery, part narrative history, a New York Times bestselling author, 100 years after the Tulsa Race Massacre,—the worst single incident of racial violence in all of American history—returns to his hometown in search of answers.

"Historian Ellsworth (Death in a Promised Land) delivers a riveting investigation into the origins and aftermath of the 1921 Tulsa race massacre.... This eloquent, deeply moving history isn't to be missed." —*Publishers Weekly*

Includes bibliographical references and index.

Hirsch, James S.
Riot and Remembrance: America's Worst Race Riot and Its Legacy. James S. Hirsch. Houghton Mifflin 2002. VIII, 358 p. ; Illustration
ISBN 9780618108138
Grades: Adult   976.6
1. African American history 2. Racism 3. Riots 4. Violence 5. Neighborhoods 6. Social conflict 7. Race riots 8. Race relations 9. Tulsa, Oklahoma 10. 20th century 11. Society and culture — Race 12. History writing — African American — Civil rights — United States

LC 2001051615

Drawing on period documents and interviews with survivors and their descendants, the author of Hurricane offers a definitive account of the 1921 race riot that destroyed the Greenwood section of Tulsa, Oklahoma, leaving hundreds of Black residents dead, and describes the battle for belated justice and reparations to the victims.

"Hirsch unearths an important episode in U.S. history with verve, intelligence and compassion." —*Publishers Weekly*

Includes bibliographical references (p. [333]-339) and index.

Luckerson, Victor
Built from the Fire: The Epic Story of Tulsa's Greenwood District, America's Black Wall Street: One Hundred Years in the Neighborhood That Refused to Be Erased. Victor Luckerson. Random House 2023. 560 p.

ESSENTIAL AND RECOMMENDED TITLES
976.6004 Oklahoma — Ethnic and national groups

ISBN 9780593134375
Grades: Adult **976.6**
1. Goodwin family 2. African Americans 3. African American families 4. Tulsa Race Massacre, Tulsa, Oklahoma, 1921 5. Violence against marginalized people 6. Urban renewal 7. African American neighborhoods 8. African American-owned businesses 9. Newspapers 10. Gentrification of cities 11. Family history 12. Resilience 13. Tulsa, Oklahoma 14. Life stories — Identity — Race and ethnicity 15. Life stories — Facing adversity — Victims of crime — Terrorism 16. History writing — African American — United States 17. History writing — Regional history — United States 18. Antiracist literature 19. Debut title

LC 2022055077

A multigenerational saga of a family and a community in Tulsa's Greenwood district, or "Black Wall Street," that in one century survived the 1921 Tulsa Race Massacre, urban renewal, and gentrification.

"It's a comprehensive and impassioned portrait of a community fighting for its survival." —*Publishers Weekly*

Includes bibliographical references and index.

Madigan, Tim

*The **Burning**: The Tulsa Race Massacre of 1921.* Tim Madigan. Thomas Dunne Books/St. Martin's Griffin 2021. xix, 297 p; Illustration
ISBN 9781250800725
Grades: Adult **976.6**
1. African American history 2. Neighborhoods 3. Riots 4. Violence 5. Racism 6. Race riots 7. Race relations 8. Tulsa, Oklahoma 9. 20th century 10. History writing — Roaring 20s — United States 11. Adult books for young adults 12. History writing — African American — Civil rights — United States

LC BL2003000282

An account of the massacre at Greenwood recreates this destruction of a prosperous African American southern community near Tulsa, Oklahoma.

"Madigan's skill at description, dialogue and pacing keeps the reader's interest at peak levels, and he does not gloss over brutal scenes of murder, arson and torture." —*Publishers Weekly*

Includes bibliographical references (p. 271-287) and index; Originally published as the burning : Massacre, destruction, and the Tulsa race riot of 1921. New York : Thomas Dunne Books, 2001.

976.6004 Oklahoma — Ethnic and national groups

Grann, David

★ *Killers of the Flower Moon: The Osage Murders and the Birth of the FBI.* David Grann. Doubleday 2017. x, 338 pages : Illustration; Map
ISBN 9780385534246
Grades: 11 12 Adult **976.6004**
1. Osage (North American people) 2. Serial murders 3. Racism 4. Oil wells 5. Indigenous peoples of North America 6. Murder investigation 7. Discrimination 8. Oklahoma 9. 1920s 10. Page to screen 11. True Crime — Historical Crime 12. True Crime — Murder 13. True Crime — Investigations and Trials 14. History writing — Indigenous peoples — United States 15. Nonfiction that reads like fiction 16. Adult books for young adults 17. Book club best bets

LC 2016021407

ALA Notable Book, 2018; Anthony Award for Best Critical/Nonfiction, 2018; Booklist Editors' Choice, 2017; Edgar Allan Poe Award for Best Fact Crime, 2018; Indies' Choice Book Awards, Adult Nonfiction, 2018; Library Journal Best Books, 2017; LibraryReads Favorites, 2017; Loan Stars Favourites, 2017; New York Times Notable Book, 2017; Oklahoma Book Award for Nonfiction, 2018; School Library Journal Best Books: Best Adult Books 4 Teens, 2017; Spur Award for Historical Nonfiction, 2018; Andrew Carnegie Medal for Excellence in Non-Fiction finalist, 2018; National Book Award for Nonfiction finalist, 2017.

Presents a true account of the early 20th-century murders of dozens of wealthy Osage and law-enforcement officials, citing the contributions and missteps of a fledgling FBI that eventually uncovered one of the most chilling conspiracies in American history.

"Grann employs you-are-there narrative effects to set readers right in the action, and he relays the humanity, evil, and heroism of the people involved. His riveting reckoning of a devastating episode in American history deservedly captivates." —*Booklist*

Maps on endpapers; Made into a movie in 2023 directed by Martin Scorsese; Includes bibliographical references (pages 301-336).

976.7 Arkansas

Hill, David

*The **Vapors**: A Southern Family, the New York Mob, and the Rise and Fall of Hot Springs, America's Forgotten Capital of Vice.* David Hill. Farrar, Straus & Giroux 2020. 368 p.
ISBN 9781250086112
Grades: Adult **976.7**
1. Hill, David 2. Madden, Owney, 1891-1980 3. Organized crime 4. Resort towns 5. Casinos 6. Gangsters 7. Bootleggers 8. Mafia 9. Single mothers 10. Casino employees 11. Gambling 12. Prostitution 13. Tourism 14. Political corruption 15. Small towns 16. United States history 17. Hot Springs, Arkansas 18. Arkansas 19. 20th century 20. True Crime — Organized Crime, Mafia, and Gangs 21. True Crime — Historical Crime 22. History writing — Regional history — United States 23. Life stories — Law and order — Criminals and law-breakers 24. Life stories — People in history — Witness to history 25. Nonfiction that reads like fiction

LC Bl2020019326

New York Times Notable Book, 2020.

Back in the days before Vegas was big, when the Mob was at its peak and neon lights were but a glimmer on the horizon, a little Southern town styled itself as a premier destination for the American leisure class. Hot Springs, Arkansas was home to healing waters, Art Deco splendor, and America's original national park—as well as horse racing, nearly a dozen illegal casinos, and some of the country's most bald-faced criminals. It was a place where small-town hustlers and bigtime high-rollers could make their fortunes, and hide from the law. The Vapors is the extraordinary story of three individuals—spanning the golden decades of Hot Springs, from the 1930s through the 1960s—and the lavish casino whose spectacular rise and fall would bring them together before blowing them apart.

"More than a simple crime story, this is a forgotten history of Arkansas in the mid-20th century. Recommended for readers interested in antiheroes, self-made men, and survivor stories." —*Library Journal*

Includes bibliographical references and index.

976.8 Tennessee

Kiernan, Denise

*The **Girls** of Atomic City: The Untold Story of the Women Who Helped Win World War II.* Denise Kiernan. Simon & Schuster 2013. 320 p.
ISBN 9781451617528
Grades: Adult **976.8**
1. World War II 2. Women and war 3. Atomic bomb 4. Secrecy 5. Research 6. War and society 7. Cities and towns 8. Military research 9. Women's participation in wars 10. United States history 11. Tennessee 12. Oak Ridge, Tennessee 13. History writing — Women's history 14. History writing — Wars and conflicts — Homefront — World War II 15. History writing — Wars and conflicts — Atomic Bomb — World War II

LC 2013431175

The town of Oak Ridge, Tennessee, boomed on U.S military-owned acreage between 1942-1944. Its electricity usage matched that of New York City, and its population reached 75,000—yet it didn't appear on a single map during World War II. Many new residents were women, recruited at top-dollar wages for positions from chemists to couriers. Sworn to strict secrecy protocols, they were told only that their work would ensure a swift, final World War II victory. The nuclear blast at Hiroshima at last revealed their hidden roles. The Girls of Atomic City brilliantly illuminates a long-overlooked chapter of both World War II and women's history.

Lauterbach, Preston
Beale Street Dynasty: Sex, Song, and the Struggle for the Soul of Memphis. Preston Lauterbach. W. W. Norton & Co. Inc. 2015. 320 p.
ISBN 9780393082579
Grades: Adult 976.8
1. Church, Robert Reed, 1839-1912 2. Cities and towns 3. African American families 4. Multiracial men 5. Race relations 6. Memphis, Tennessee 7. History writing — Regional history — United States
LC 2014039928

Documents the rise and fall of the legendary Memphis thoroughfare that indelibly shaped American culture, documenting its story through the life of former slave and first Black millionaire Robert Church. By the award-winning author of the Chitlin' Circuit.

"While sex and song (as promised in the book's subtitle) are present at times, this account is really about politics and power in a major Southern city. Recommended for all readers interested in Memphis or in African American history." —*Library Journal*

976.9 Kentucky

Snyder, Christina
Great Crossings: Indians, Settlers, and Slaves in the Age of Jackson. Christina Snyder. Oxford Univ Pr. 2017. 408 p.
ISBN 9780199399062
Grades: Adult 976.9
1. Jackson, Andrew, 1767-1845 2. Social history 3. African Americans 4. Indigenous peoples of North America 5. Racism 6. Slavery 7. Race relations 8. Interracial families 9. Indigenous residential schools 10. Political culture 11. United States history 12. Kentucky 13. United States 14. American Westward Expansion (1803-1899) 15. 19th century 16. History writing — Indigenous peoples — United States 17. History writing — African American — Enslavement — United States 18. History writing — Westward expansion — United States
LC 2016024418

Great Crossings features Indians from across the continent seeking new ways to assert anciently-held rights, and people of African descent who challenged the United States to live up to its ideals. These diverse groups met in an experimental community in central Kentucky called Great Crossings, home to the first federal Indian school and a famous interracial family.

"This is a well-researched, engagingly written, and remarkable work of scholarship." —*Publishers Weekly*

977 North central United States

Barry, John M.
Rising Tide: The Great Mississippi Flood of 1927 and How It Changed America. John M. Barry. Simon & Schuster 1997. 524 p. : Illustration; Map
ISBN 9780684810461
Grades: Adult 977
1. Humphreys, Andrew Atkinson, 1810-1883 2. Eads, James Buchanan, 1820-1887 3. Percy family 4. Floods 5. Flood control 6. Survival (after floods) 7. Race relations 8. United States history 9. Mississippi Valley 10. Mississippi River 11. 1920s 12. 20th century 13. 19th century 14. History writing — Roaring 20s — United States 15. Nature Writing — Natural Disaster 16. History writing — Natural disasters and tragedies
LC 96040077

New York Times Notable Book, 1997.

In 1927, the Mississippi River swept across an area roughly equal in size to Massachusetts, Connecticut, New Hampshire, and Vermont combined, leaving water as deep as thirty feet on the land stretching from Illinois and Missouri south to the Gulf of Mexico. Close to a million people—in a nation of 120 million—were forced out of their homes. Some estimates place the death toll in the thousands. The Red Cross fed nearly 700,000 refugees for months. Rising Tide tells how the flood changed the face of American and laid the groundwork for the New Deal.

"This is the story of human defeat by a savage, unpredictable river. The flood of 1927, three times greater than the flood of 1993, was an unprecedented disaster that spurred a political innovation. Congress's agreement to rebuild the Mississippi's shattered flood-control system marked the federal government's first assumption of full financial responsibility for a regional calamity. Much of the book recounts how the greed of New Orleans bankers and Delta planters increased the sufferings of the rural poor. Barry's book is a virtuoso piece of exposition." —*The New Yorker*

Includes bibliographical references (p. 481-496) and index.

Cox, Anna-Lisa
The Bone and Sinew of the Land: America's Forgotten Black Pioneers and the Struggle for Equality. Anna-Lisa Cox. PublicAffairs 2018. 336 p.
ISBN 9781610398107
Grades: Adult 977
1. African American history 2. Race relations 3. Racism 4. Frontier and pioneer life 5. African Americans 6. United States history 7. Ohio 8. Indiana 9. 19th century 10. 18th century 11. History writing — African American — United States 12. Society and culture — Race
LC 2017056938

A revealing story of America's Black pioneers discusses how thousands of free African Americans built hundreds of settlements in the Northern Territory, where slavery was banned and equal voting rights to all men were guaranteed.

"Cox provides a moving and necessary corrective to American pioneer history." —*Booklist*

Includes bibliographical references and index.

Dennis, Jerry
The Living Great Lakes: Searching for the Heart of the Inland Seas. Jerry Dennis. Thomas Dunne Books 2003. VIII, 296 p. : Illustration; Map
ISBN 9780312251932
Grades: 11 12 Adult 977
1. Dennis, Jerry, 1954- 2. Natural history 3. Marine biology 4. Lake ecology 5. United States history 6. United States 7. Great Lakes region 8. Great Lakes 9. Nature Writing — Natural Landscapes 10. Adult books for young adults
LC 2002032500

Provides a history of the Great Lakes as told by the biologists, fishermen, sailors, and others who have experienced them firsthand and traces the author's experiences as a local resident and schooner crewperson.

Map on lining papers; Includes bibliographical references (p. [265]-286) and index.

Erdrich, Louise
Books and Islands in Ojibwe Country. Louise Erdrich. National Geographic 2003. 143 p. : Illustration; Map
ISBN 9780792257196
Grades: Adult 977
1. Erdrich, Louise 2. Ojibwe (North American people) 3. Island life 4. Indigenous peoples of North America — Rites and ceremonies 5. Mothers and daughters 6. Authors, American 7. Voyages and travels 8. Minnesota 9. Ontario 10. 20th century 11. Biographies 12. Travel Writing — United States 13. Travel Writing — Canada 14. History writing — Indigenous peoples — United States 15. History writing — Indigenous peoples — Canada
LC 2003045906

The critically acclaimed author describes her evocative odyssey back to the islands of her ancestors in southern Ontario, offering a compelling portrait of Ojibwe language, culture, spirits, traditions, and art as she visits centuries-old rock paintings and recalls her own family and contemporary life.

"Fans of Erdrich's bestselling fiction will recognize her signature combination of the sacred and the ordinary in this lively traveler's memoir, and many will enjoy the rare glimpse of her personal life as well as the physical facts of her journey from her home in Minneapolis to the lakes and islands of her Ojibwe ancestors in Ontario and Minnesota." —*Booklist*

ESSENTIAL AND RECOMMENDED TITLES
977.1 Ohio

Laskin, David
The Children's Blizzard. David Laskin. Harper Perennial 2005. IX, 307, 16 p. : Illustration; Map
ISBN 9780060520762
Grades: 11 12 Adult   **977**
1. Blizzards 2. Prairies 3. Death of children 4. Hypothermia 5. Pioneers 6. Immigrants 7. Frontier and pioneer life 8. Midwest (United States) history 9. Middle West 10. 19th century 11. Biographies 12. History writing — Natural disasters and tragedies 13. History writing — Westward expansion — United States 14. Adult books for young adults
LC Bl2006029012

Describes the deadly 1888 snowstorm in the Great Plains that killed more than five hundred people including numerous schoolchildren, describing how the storm devastated immigrant families and dramatically affected pioneer advancement.

Includes bibliographical references (p. 273-289) and index; Originally published: New York : HarperCollins, 2004.

977.1 Ohio

Gup, Ted
A Secret Gift: How One Man's Kindness—and a Trove of Letters—revealed the Hidden History of the Great Depression. Ted Gup. Penguin Press 2010. 368 p.
ISBN 9781594202704
Grades: Adult   **977.1**
1. Stone, Samuel, 1887-1981 2. Benefactors 3. Benevolence 4. Depressions, 1929-1941 5. Rich men 6. Kindness 7. 1930s 8. 20th century 9. History writing — Great Depression — United States
LC 2010017302

The author explains how the discovery of a cache of letters revealed his grandfather's offer of cash gifts to seventy-five families in distress in Depression-scarred Canton, Ohio, in 1933, and explores the profound effects the gifts had on their recipients.

977.311 Chicago (Ill.)

Berg, Scott W.
The Burning of the World: The Great Chicago Fire and the War for a City's Soul. Scott W. Berg. Pantheon Books 2023. 464 p.
ISBN 9780804197847
Grades: Adult   **977.311**
1. Great Fire, Chicago, Ill, 1871 2. Cities and towns 3. Fires 4. Disasters 5. Disaster victims 6. Homeless people 7. Social classes 8. Elite (Social sciences) 9. Working class 10. Racism 11. Classism 12. Municipal government 13. United States history 14. Chicago, Illinois 15. History writing — Natural disasters and tragedies 16. History writing — United States
LC 2023000507

Recounting one of the most infamous natural disasters in history—the 1871 Great Chicago Fire—this gripping book traces the fire's devastating path and its aftermath during which a new political order rose out of the ashes, causing a power struggle over the city's future.

"As Berg traces the battles between public and private interests that played out in the years after the fire, he astutely observes how the city was transformed…This impressively researched account fascinates." —*Publishers Weekly*

Includes bibliographical references and index.

Dyja, Tom
The Third Coast: When Chicago Built the American Dream. Thomas Dyja. The Penguin Press 2013. 384 p.
ISBN 9781594204326
Grades: Adult   **977.311**

1. City life 2. Cities and towns 3. United States history 4. Chicago, Illinois 5. Illinois 6. History writing — Regional history — United States
LC 2012039710

New York Times Notable Book, 2013.

A cultural history of mid-20th-century Chicago traces the development of mass-marketing practices, technological advances and artistic development that profoundly influenced modern America, offering additional insight into the role of racial divisions, housing projects and migration.

"A readable, richly detailed history of America's second city." —*Kirkus*

Includes bibliographical references and index.

Miller, Donald L.
City of the Century: The Epic of Chicago and the Making of America. Donald Miller. Simon & Schuster 1997. 704 p. : Illustration; Map
ISBN 9780684831381
Grades: Adult   **977.311**
1. United States history 2. Chicago, Illinois 3. History writing — Gilded Age — United States
LC BL 99785489

A chronicle of the coming of the Industrial Age to one American city traces the explosive entrepreneurial, technological, and artistic growth that converted Chicago from a trading post to a modern industrial metropolis by the 1890s.

"In this account of Chicago's history in the nineteenth century Miller tells of Chicago's historical and literary figures, reform leaders, architects, industrialists, and entrepreneurs." —*Library Journal*

A Touchstone book; Originally published: New York : Simon & Schuster, 1996; Includes bibliographical references (p. [639]-682) and index.

Trice, Dawn Turner
★ *Three Girls from Bronzeville: A Uniquely American Memoir of Race, Fate, and Sisterhood.* Dawn Turner. Simon & Schuster 2021. 304 p.
ISBN 9781982107703
Grades: Adult   **977.311**
1. Trice, Dawn Turner 2. Turner, Kim, 1968-1994 3. Trice, Debra 4. African American women 5. Journalists 6. Female friendship 7. Sisterhood 8. Fate and fatalism 9. Growing up 10. Resilience 11. Loss 12. Racism 13. Social classes 14. Chicago, Illinois 15. Illinois 16. Autobiographies and memoirs 17. Life stories — Relationships — Friendship 18. Life stories — Facing adversity 19. Family and Relationships — Friendship

A memoir about three Black girls from the storied Bronzeville section of Chicago that offers a penetrating exploration of race, opportunity, friendship, sisterhood, and the powerful forces at work that allow some to flourish -and others to falter.

"Novelist and former Chicago Tribune columnist Turner brings to the fore three wildly different, profoundly connected girls who lived at the heart of the African American hub in Chicago known as Bronzeville during the 1970s…. Turner's candid memoir of entwined yet divergent lives is a probing inquiry into fate, frailty, tenacity, and ultimately, redemption." —*Booklist*

977.4 Michigan

Bomey, Nathan
Detroit Resurrected: To Bankruptcy and Back. Nathan Bomey. W.W. Norton & Company, Inc. 2016. 320 p.
ISBN 9780393248913
Grades: Adult   **977.4**
1. Bankruptcy 2. Financial crises 3. Urban economics 4. Urban economic development 5. Cities and towns 6. Detroit, Michigan 7. 21st century 8. Business and economics — Economics — Contemporary U.S. economy
LC 2016001681

Drawing on exclusive interviews, insider sources and thousands of records, an insider's account of financial ruin, backroom intrigue and political rebirth reveals the tricky path to rescuing a city facing a legacy of broken promises from $18 billion in debt and giving new hope to its citizens.

Includes bibliographical references and index.

PUBLIC LIBRARY CORE COLLECTION: NONFICTION
Twentieth Edition

Boyd, Herb
Black Detroit: A People's History of Self-determination. Herb Boyd. Amistad 2017. 352 p.
ISBN 9780062346629
Grades: Adult   977.4
1. African Americans 2. Urban economics 3. Urban economic development 4. Cities and towns 5. Detroit, Michigan 6. History writing — Regional history — United States
LC Bl2017021396

The author of Baldwin's Harlem looks at the evolving culture, politics, economics, and spiritual life of Detroit—a blend of memoir, love letter, history, and clear-eyed reportage that explores the city's past, present, and future and its significance to the African American legacy and the nation's fabric.

"An inspiring, illuminating book that will interest students of urban history and the Black experience." —*Kirkus*

LeDuff, Charlie
Detroit: An American Autopsy. Charlie LeDuff. Penguin Press 2013. 272 p.
ISBN 9781594205347
Grades: Adult   977.4
1. LeDuff, Charlie 2. Journalists 3. Investigative journalism 4. Local government 5. Inner city 6. Street life 7. Social justice 8. Cities and towns 9. Political corruption 10. Detroit, Michigan 11. Autobiographies and memoirs 12. Biographies 13. History writing — Regional history — United States 14. Life stories — Arts and culture — Writing — Journalists 15. Life stories — Identity — Race and ethnicity 16. Society and culture — Urban and regional studies
LC 2012030924

The Pulitzer Prize-winning author presents an expose of bureaucratic corruption and systemic arson in his home city of Detroit, tracing his work with a local fire brigade and his investigations into the daily lives of politicians, police officials, businesspeople and homeowners who are working to save the troubled city.

McDonnell, Michael
Masters of Empire: Great Lakes Indians and the Making of America. Michael McDonnell. Hill & Wang Pub. 2015. 336 p.
ISBN 9780809029532
Grades: Adult   977.4
1. Indigenous peoples of North America 2. European Americans 3. Race relations 4. Odawa (North American people) 5. Kinship-based society 6. United States history 7. Great Lakes region 8. Colonial America (1600-1775) 9. History writing — Indigenous peoples — United States
LC 2015022331

Describes and chronicles the important historical role the native people of the Great Lakes had in the history of North America, highlighting the Anishinaabeg tribe's experiences with other native Americans, as well as with the newcomer Europeans.

"McDonnell's scholarly yet compelling history will be a valuable addition to American history and Native American collections." —*Booklist*

Miles, Tiya
The Dawn of Detroit: A Chronicle of Slavery and Freedom in the City of the Straits. Tiya Miles. The New Press 2017. 288 p.
ISBN 9781620972311
Grades: Adult   977.4
1. Slavery 2. Slave trade 3. Race relations 4. Fur industry and trade 5. United States history 6. Detroit, Michigan 7. History writing — Regional history — United States 8. History writing — African American — Enslavement — United States
LC 2017018381

Booklist Editors' Choice, 2017; Hurston/Wright Legacy Award: Nonfiction, 2018.

From the MacArthur genius grant winner, a beautifully written and revelatory look at the slave origins of a major northern American city.

"Diligently researched and well written, this provocative exploration of slavery in frontier-era Detroit proves illuminating." —*Choice*

Includes bibliographical references and index.

978 Western United States

Akins, Damon B.
★ *We Are the Land: A History of Native California.* Damon B. Akins, William J. Bauer. University of California Press 2021. 345 p.
ISBN 9780520280496
Grades: Adult   978
1. Indigenous peoples of North America 2. Social advocacy 3. Imperialism 4. Historic sites 5. California 6. United States 7. History writing — Indigenous peoples — United States 8. Society and culture — Race

We Are the Land is the first and most comprehensive text of its kind, centering the long history of California around the lives and legacies of the Indigenous people who shaped it. Beginning with the ethnogenesis of California Indians, We Are the Land recounts the centrality of the Native presence from before European colonization through statehood; paying particularly close attention to the persistence and activism of California Indians in the late twentieth and early twenty-first centuries.

"A welcome contribution to Native studies and the rich literature of California's first peoples." —*Kirkus*

Brands, H. W.
Dreams of El Dorado: A History of the American West. H. W. Brands. Basic Books 2019. 544 p.
ISBN 9781541672529
Grades: Adult   978
1. Pioneers 2. Indigenous peoples of North America — History 3. Frontier and pioneer life 4. Businesspeople 5. Culture conflict 6. American dream 7. The West (United States) history 8. United States history 9. American Westward Expansion (1803-1899) 10. History writing — Westward expansion — United States 11. Life stories — People in history — Indigenous peoples 12. Life stories — People in history — Pioneers 13. Adult books for young adults
LC 2018048887

H. W. Brands tells the thrilling, panoramic story of the settling of the American West. He takes us from John Jacob Astor's fur trading outpost in Oregon to the Texas Revolution, from the California gold rush to the Oklahoma land rush. He shows how the migrants' dreams drove them to feats of courage and perseverance that put their stay-at-home cousins to shame-and how those same dreams also drove them to outrageous acts of violence against indigenous peoples and one another. The West was where riches would reward the miner's persistence, the cattleman's courage, the railroad man's enterprise; but El Dorado was at least as elusive in the West as it ever was in the East.

"This broad but clearly structured study, with its many well-chosen illustrations, is likely to have wide appeal." —*Publishers Weekly*

Includes bibliographical references and index.

Brown, Dee
The American West. Dee Brown; photos edited by Martin F. Schmitt. Scribner 1994. 448 p.
ISBN 9780025174214
Grades: 11 12 Adult   978
1. Pioneers 2. Ranches 3. The West (United States) in literature 4. Wild West shows 5. The West (United States) history 6. 19th century 7. History writing — Westward expansion — United States
LC 94037444

Booklist Editors' Choice, 1994.

An epic account of the American West depicts the tragic destruction of the Native American way of life and covers major events and key figures.

"This narrative history of westward expansion paints a vivid portrait of the settlers, pioneers, entrepreneurs, and Native Americans of the old West. Useful as collateral research material and for recreational reading." —*Booklist*

Includes bibliographical references (p.) and index.

ESSENTIAL AND RECOMMENDED TITLES
978 Western United States

★ *Bury* My Heart at Wounded Knee: An Indian History of the American West. by Dee Brown. H. Holt 2001. xix, 487 p. : Illustration
ISBN 9780805066340
Grades: 8 9 10 11 12 Adult   978
1. Battles 2. Indigenous peoples of North America 3. Indigenous peoples of North America — History 4. The West (United States) history 5. 19th century 6. Page to screen 7. History writing — Indigenous peoples — United States 8. History writing — Wars and conflicts — American Indigenous Wars
LC 00040958
The systematic destruction of the American Indians, told in the words of those who were there.
Includes bibliographical references (p. 465-473) and index; Originally published: New York : Holt, Rinehart & Winston, 1971.

Calloway, Colin G.
One Vast Winter Count: The Native American West Before Lewis and Clark. Colin G. Calloway. University of Nebraska Press 2003. xvii, 631 p. : Illustration; Map
ISBN 9780803215306
Grades: Adult   978
1. Indigenous peoples of North America 2. Government relations with indigenous peoples 3. Race relations 4. History writing — Indigenous peoples — United States
LC 2003044757
Spur Award for Historical Nonfiction, 2004.
A professor of history offers a sweeping new history of the Native American West before the Lewis and Clarke expedition opened it to exploration, focusing particular attention on the period of conflict that preceded this period. (History)
"Calloway concentrates on the Indian experience from the Appalachians to the Pacific, in a time frame from prehistory to the 18th century. The scope is staggering, but Calloway masters it, demonstrating a remarkable command of a broad spectrum of historical, ethnographic and archeological sources including printed material and oral traditions." —*Publishers Weekly*
Includes bibliographical references (p. 569-596) and index.

Cozzens, Peter
The Earth Is Weeping: The Indian Wars for the American West, 1866-1891. by Peter Cozzens. Alfred A. Knopf 2016. 576 p.
ISBN 9780307958044
Grades: Adult   978
1. Indigenous peoples of North America — Wars 2. Government relations with indigenous peoples 3. Interethnic relations 4. Race relations 5. United States history 6. The West (United States) 7. United States 8. American Westward Expansion (1803-1899) 9. 19th century 10. Impartial writing 11. History writing — Indigenous peoples — United States 12. History writing — Westward expansion — United States
LC 2015044077
Booklist Editors' Choice, 2016.
A history of the struggle between white forces and Native Americans over the fate of the post-Civil War West details the deconstruction of tribal culture to establish the modern U.S, covering such topics as the conditions endured by frontier soldiers and the ethical quandaries of military officials who sympathized with Native adversaries.
This is a Borzoi Book; Includes bibliographical references.

Egan, Timothy
The Worst Hard Time: The Untold Story of Those Who Survived the Great American Dust Bowl. Timothy Egan. Houghton Mifflin Co. 2006. x, 340 p. : Illustration; Map
ISBN 9780618346974
Grades: 11 12 Adult   978
1. Depressions, 1929-1941 2. Dust Bowl Era, 1931-1939 3. Farms 4. Droughts 5. Dust storms 6. Economics 7. United States history 8. United States 9. Great Plains (United States) 10. Middle West 11. Dust Bowl (South Central United States) 12. 1930s 13. 20th century 14. Depression era (1929-1941) 15. History writing — Great Depression — United States 16. Adult books for young adults 17. Book club best bets
LC 2005008057
ALA Notable Book, 2007; National Book Award for Nonfiction, 2007; New York Times Notable Book, 2006; Oklahoma Book Award for Nonfiction, 2006; Western Heritage Award for Outstanding Nonfiction Book, 2007.
Presents an oral history of the dust storms that devastated the Great Plains during the Depression, following several families and their communities in their struggle to persevere despite the devastation.
Includes bibliographical references (p. 315-327) and index.

Hickman, Katie
Brave Hearted: The Women of the American West. Katie Hickman. Spiegel & Grau 2022. 400 p.
ISBN 9781954118171
Grades: Adult   978
1. Women 2. Violence 3. Resilience 4. Marginalized women 5. The West (United States) 6. United States 7. American Westward Expansion (1803-1899) 8. Collective biographies 9. Life stories — Identity — Gender 10. History writing — United States 11. History writing — Women's history 12. History writing — Westward expansion — United States
WILLA Literary Awards: Creative Nonfiction, 2023.
Drawing on letters, diaries and contemporary accounts, this history of women's experiences in the Wild West focuses tells the stories of both the women who were brutally exploited as well as those fought incredible odds to forge home and identities.
"Historian and novelist Hickman (Daughters of Britannia) delivers a painstakingly researched and fluidly written study of the women who helped settle the American West....Full of heartrending accounts of courage and tragedy, this is a vital contribution to the history of America's frontier." —*Publishers Weekly*

Hyde, Anne Farrar
★ *Born* of Lakes and Plains: Mixed-descent Peoples and the Making of the American West. Anne F. Hyde. W. W. Norton & Company 2022. 480 p.
ISBN 9780393634099
Grades: Adult   978
1. Multiracial people 2. Indigenous peoples of North America 3. European Americans 4. Indigenous peoples of North America — History 5. Fur traders 6. Indigenous families 7. Interracial families 8. Marginalized people 9. The West (United States) 10. 18th century 11. 19th century 12. History writing — Indigenous peoples — United States
LC 2021037131
A revealing history of the West that pivots on Native peoples and the mixed families they made with European settlers.
"University of Oklahoma history professor Hyde, author of the Bancroft Prize-winning Empires, Nations, and Families: A New History of the North American West, 1800-1860, turns her attention to an overlooked aspect of the peopling of North America: the union of Native Americans with people from other continents, their descendants often derided as 'Half-breeds' and worse.... A necessary contribution to American studies for all the shameful episodes it recounts." —*Kirkus*
Includes bibliographical references and index.

Empires, Nations, and Families: A New History of the North American West, 1800-1860. Anne F. Hyde. University of Nebraska Press 2011. xv, 628 p. : Illustration; Map
ISBN 9780803224056
Grades: Adult   978
1. Exploration 2. Families 3. Frontier and pioneer life 4. Pioneers 5. Kinship-based society 6. The West (United States) history 7. History writing — Westward expansion — United States
Pulitzer Prize for History finalist, 2012.
Empires, Nations, and Families shows how the world of river and maritime trade effectively shifted political power away from military and diplomatic circles into the hands of local people.
"This innovative study examines the vast area of the Trans-Mississippi West during the first half of the 19th century." —*Choice*
Includes bibliographical references (p. 563-596) and index.

PUBLIC LIBRARY CORE COLLECTION: NONFICTION
Twentieth Edition

Morgan, Robert
Lions of the West: Heroes and Villains of the Westward Expansion. Robert Morgan. Algonquin Books of Chapel Hill 2011. 508 p.
ISBN 9781565126268
Grades: Adult   978
1. Pioneers 2. Explorers 3. Presidents 4. Territorial expansion 5. The West (United States) history 6. United States 7. Biographies 8. History writing — Westward expansion — United States
LC 2011023832
Chronicles the lives of Americans who influenced the development of the Western frontier, including Thomas Jefferson, Kit Carson, and Sam Houston.
"This is a collection of biographical sketches of 10 men largely limited to the pivotal roles each played in America's westward expansion. Included are four U.S. presidents, Thomas Jefferson, Andrew Jackson, James K. Polk, and John Quincy Adams; orchardist and naturalist John Johnny Appleseed Chapman; frontier legends Davy Crockett and Kit Carson; statesmen Sam Houston and Nicholas Trist; and General Winfield Scott. This collective biography provides a digestible introduction to American expansion, Manifest Destiny, and the larger-than-life men who led the inexorable charge westward." —*Booklist*
A Shannon Ravenel Book; Includes bibliographical references and index.

Nelson, Megan Kate
The Three-cornered War: The Union, the Confederacy, and Native Peoples in the Fight for the West. Megan Kate Nelson. Simon & Schuster 2019. 320 pages
ISBN 9781501152542
Grades: Adult   978
1. Federal government 2. Indigenous peoples of North America 3. Government relations with indigenous peoples 4. Indigenous peoples of North America — Wars 5. Apache (North American people) 6. Navajo (Diné) (North American people) 7. Frontier and pioneer life 8. Migration, Internal 9. Military history 10. Military policy 11. The West (United States) history 12. United States 13. New Mexico (Territory) 14. The West (United States) 15. American Civil War era (1861-1865) 16. 19th century 17. History writing — Wars and conflicts — American Indigenous Wars 18. History writing — Wars and conflicts — American Civil War 19. History writing — Indigenous peoples — United States 20. History writing — Westward expansion — United States
LC 2019018824
Pulitzer Prize for History finalist, 2021.
A deeply-researched, dramatic, and character-driven narrative account of the violent struggle between Union and Confederate forces to claim the American West during the Civil War.
"Nelson effectively blends military history with a fresh look at a region typically obscured in accounts of the Civil War. American history buffs will relish this entertaining and eye-opening portrait." —*Publishers Weekly*
Includes bibliographical references.

Raban, Jonathan
Bad Land: An American Romance. Jonathan Raban. Pantheon Books 1996. 324p. : Map
ISBN 9780679442547
Grades: 11 12 Adult   978
1. Homesteaders 2. Homesteading 3. Prairie life 4. Farmers 5. Frontier and pioneer life 6. Voyages and travels 7. The West (United States) history 8. United States history 9. Dakota Territory 10. Montana 11. North Dakota 12. South Dakota 13. The West (United States) 14. 19th century 15. 20th century 16. History writing — Westward expansion — United States 17. Travel Writing — Historic Journeys
LC 96013432
ALA Notable Book, 1998; Booklist Editors' Choice, 1996; National Book Critics Circle Award for Non-Fiction, 1996.
Journeys beyond the myth of the American West to reveal the harsh and desperate realities of the homesteaders' lives, offering an incisive portrait of the American heartland that redefines the essence of the American dream.

Sides, Hampton
Blood and Thunder: An Epic of the American West. Hampton Sides. Doubleday 2006. xi, 460 p. : Illustration
ISBN 9780385507776
Grades: Adult   978
1. Carson, Kit, 1809-1868 2. Military history 3. Indigenous peoples of North America — Wars 4. Indigenous peoples of North America 5. Navajo (Diné) (North American people) 6. Frontier and pioneer life 7. Indigenous peoples of North America — History 8. Territorial expansion 9. The West (United States) history 10. United States history 11. Southwest (United States) 12. United States 13. The West (United States) 14. 19th century 15. History writing — Westward expansion — United States 16. History writing — Indigenous peoples — United States
LC 2006016579
New York Times Notable Book, 2006; Spur Award for Historical Nonfiction, 2007.
Examines America's westward expansion, describing the forcible subjugation of Native American tribes, including the fierce battles against the Navajo which ended with a brutal siege at Canyon de Chelly and the "Long Walk" migration.
"This book will surely capture readers, and it ought to. It's a riveting account of a vast swath of history with which few Americans are familiar." —*The New Yorker*
Maps on endpapers; Includes bibliographical references (p. [427]-440) and index.

Wallis, Michael
The Best Land Under Heaven: The Donner Party in the Age of Manifest Destiny. Michael Wallis. Liveright Publishing Corporation 2017. 320 p.
ISBN 9780871407696
Grades: Adult   978
1. Donner Party 2. Frontier and pioneer life 3. Overland journeys to the Pacific 4. Pioneers 5. Survival 6. Voyages and travels 7. The West (United States) 8. American Westward Expansion (1803-1899) 9. History writing — Westward expansion — United States
LC 2017012937
Longlisted for the Andrew Carnegie Medal for Excellence in Non-Fiction, 2018.
An account of the 1846 Donner-Reed Party expedition parses fact from fiction to reveal the true events surrounding the tragedy, profiling the adventurous, business-savvy and adventurous characters who shaped the group and how various interpersonal factors led to their harrowing experiences.
"Solid Western history that enhances the understanding of a tragic tale by highlighting the strong human dimension through the accounts of participants before, during, and after the expedition." —*Kirkus*

Ward, Geoffrey C.
The West: An Illustrated History. Narrative by Geoffrey C. Ward; based on a documentary film script by Geoffrey C. Ward and Dayton Duncan; with a preface by Stephen Ives and Ken Burns; and contributions by Dayton Duncan … [et al.]. Back Bay Books 2003. xvii, 445 p. : Illustration; Color; Map
ISBN 9780316735896
Grades: 11 12 Adult   978
1. Pioneers 2. Indigenous peoples of North America 3. Frontier and pioneer life 4. The West (United States) 5. 19th century 6. History writing — Westward expansion — United States
LC 96004323
Based on the popular PBS-television series, the narrative from the landmark chronicle of the American West is accompanied by essays from seven renowned writers and historians on various aspects of western history.
"The book's eight chapters, each written by a different historian, are arranged according to the corresponding PBS series. Beginning with Western America in the 1500s, the work presents all aspects of Western culture from the reality to the myth, moving chronologically from the Spanish exploration of the West, Native Americans, Hispanic Westerners, women in the West, and the Gold Rush, and ending with Buffalo Bill's Wild West Show. If one is looking for an in-depth,

ESSENTIAL AND RECOMMENDED TITLES
978.004 Western United States — Ethnic and national groups

comprehensive history of the westward movement, this is not it, but as an introduction, this work is an enjoyable and interesting place to start." —*Library Journal*

Includes bibliographical references (p. 435) and index; Originally published: Boston : Little, Brown, 1996.

978.004 Western United States — Ethnic and national groups

Estes, Nick
Our History Is the Future: Standing Rock Versus the Dakota Access Pipeline, and the Long Tradition of Indigenous Resistance. Nick Estes. Verso Books 2019. 310 pages : Illustration; Map
ISBN 9781786636720
Grades: Adult   978.004
1. Indigenous peoples 2. Indigenous peoples of North America, Treatment of 3. Resistance to government 4. Protests, demonstrations, vigils, etc. 5. Indigenous reservations 6. Water rights 7. Water conservation 8. Environmental protection 9. Oil industry and trade 10. Social action 11. Indigenous peoples of North America 12. Society and culture — Social activism and philanthropy 13. Nature Writing — Environmental Issues 14. History writing — Indigenous peoples — United States

Traces the traditions of indigenous resistance that led to the #NoDAPL movement.

"An honest and passionate voice of Indigenous power that needs to be included in contemporary political discourse." —*Library Journal*

Includes bibliographical references and index.

Gardner, Mark L.
The Earth Is All That Lasts: Crazy Horse, Sitting Bull, and the Last Stand of the Great Sioux Nation. Mark Lee Gardner. Mariner Books 2022. 560 p.
ISBN 9780062669896
Grades: Adult   978.004
1. Sitting Bull, 1831-1890 2. Crazy Horse, approximately 1842-1877 3. Lakota (North American people) 4. Chiefs (Political anthropology) 5. Warriors 6. Medicine people (Indigenous religions) 7. Resistance to government 8. Little Bighorn, Battle of the, 1876 9. Indigenous peoples of North America — Wars 10. Indigenous peoples of North America 11. Race relations 12. United States history 13. Great Plains (United States) 14. 19th century 15. Collective biographies 16. Life stories — People in history — Indigenous peoples 17. History writing — Indigenous peoples — United States 18. History writing — Wars and conflicts — American Indigenous Wars

Crazy Horse and Sitting Bull: Their names are iconic, their significance in American history undeniable. Together, these two Lakota chiefs, one a fabled warrior and the other a revered holy man, crushed George Armstrong Custer's vaunted Seventh Cavalry. Yet their legendary victory at the Little Big Horn has overshadowed the rest of their rich and complex lives. Now, based on years of research and drawing on a wealth of previously ignored primary sources, author Mark Lee Gardner delivers the definitive chronicle, thrillingly told, of these extraordinary Indigenous leaders.

"Spirited history of the great Sioux war leaders of the late 19th century and their valiant stand against White encroachment….A strong work of Western history that strives to bring the Native American view to center stage." —*Kirkus*

Jackson, Joe
Black Elk: The Life of an American Visionary. Joe Jackson. Farrar, Straus and Giroux 2016. 576 p.
ISBN 9780374253301
Grades: Adult   978.004
1. Black Elk, 1863-1950 2. Indigenous men 3. Spiritual life 4. Healers 5. Oglala (North American people) 6. Lakota (North American people) 7. Visions 8. Visionaries 9. Indigenous peoples of North America — History 10. Indigenous peoples of North America — Religion 11. Indigenous peoples of North America 12. 19th century 13. Biographies 14. Life stories — People in history — Indigenous peoples 15. History writing — Indigenous peoples — United States

LC 2016016695

Booklist Editors' Choice, 2016; Spur Award for Biography, 2017; National Book Critics Circle Award for Biography finalist, 2016.

Describes the life of the Native American holy man who fought at Little Big Horn, witnessed the death of his cousin Crazy Horse, traveled to Europe as part of Buffalo Bill's Wild West show and became a traditionalist in the Ghost Dance movement.

Includes bibliographical references and index.

978.02 Western United States — 1800-1899

Gallagher, Winifred
New Women in the Old West: From Settlers to Suffragists. Winifred Gallagher. Penguin Press 2021. 304 p.
ISBN 9780735223257
Grades: Adult   978.02
1. Pioneer women 2. Marginalized women 3. History of women's rights 4. Suffragist movement 5. Women 6. Frontier and pioneer life 7. Suffrage 8. Social life and customs 9. The West (United States) 10. 19th century 11. 20th century 12. American Westward Expansion (1803-1899) 13. Life stories — People in history 14. History writing — Regional history — United States 15. History writing — Westward expansion — United States 16. History writing — Women's history

LC 2020055750

Drawing on an extraordinary collection of research, this book paints a vibrant picture of the little known and under-reported women who played monumental roles in the history of the Old West—and in the women's rights movement, forever redefining the "American woman."

"The catchy title of this survey of women's history in the American West more than explains many roles—social, economic, and political—that women took on and mastered during the pivotal years of 1840 through the early 20th century…. Gallagher's emphasis on the diversity of her subjects makes the book exceptional." —*Library Journal*

Includes bibliographical references and index.

978.1 Kansas

Clavin, Thomas
Dodge City: Wyatt Earp, Bat Masterson, and the Wickedest Town in the American West. Tom Clavin. St. Martin's Press 2017. 384 p.
ISBN 9781250071484
Grades: Adult   978.1
1. Earp, Wyatt, 1848-1929 2. Masterson, Bat, 1853-1921 3. Peace officers 4. Outlaws 5. Frontier and pioneer life 6. United States history 7. Dodge City, Kansas 8. Kansas 9. American Westward Expansion (1803-1899) 10. 19th century 11. Biographies 12. Life stories — People in history 13. History writing — Westward expansion — United States 14. Life stories — Law and order — Police and law officers

LC 2016038741

Well known as an inspiration for many of Hollywood's Wild West shoot-em-ups, 1870s Dodge City, Kansas was a supply center, a railhead, and a host to gigantic stockyards. Attracting characters of all types, it existed on the fuzzy boundary between law and lawlessness, where tough and fearless men, among them Bat Masterson and Wyatt Earp, kept order. In this vivid portrait of the city and its denizens, award-winning journalist Tom Clavin traces Masterson's and Earp's careers, culminating with the final battle, called the Dodge City War, between lawmen and desperados. Wild West aficionados will find Dodge City un-put-downable.

"This is an enjoyable saga, appealing to both Old West aficionados and general readers." —*Booklist*

978.3 South Dakota

Mort, T. A.
Thieves' Road: The Black Hills Betrayal and Custer's Path to Little Bighorn. Terry Mort. Random House 2015. 340 p.
ISBN 9781616149604
Grades: Adult   978.3
1. Culture conflict 2. Gold rush 3. Dakota (North American people) 4. Gold mines and mining 5. Gold prospecting 6. Sacred space 7. Indigenous peoples of North America 8. European-Americans 9. Race relations 10. Revenge 11. Mines and mineral resources 12. United States history 13. Black Hills 14. South Dakota 15. 1870s 16. Gilded Age (1865-1898) 17. 19th century 18. History writing — Westward expansion — United States 19. History writing — Indigenous peoples — United States

LC 2014035457

Describes a little-known exploratory mission by General Custer in 1874, who took 1,000 troops deep into the Black Hills of South Dakota where he found gold and started a chain of events that led up to the end of Sioux territorial independence.

"This highly readable and insightful work is recommended as an essential backstory to Custer's subsequent downfall at the aforementioned battle." —*Library Journal*

978.7 Wyoming

Black, George
Empire of Shadows: The Epic Story of Yellowstone. George Black. St. Martin's Press 2012. 576 p.
ISBN 9780312383190
Grades: Adult   978.7
1. National parks and reserves 2. Wilderness areas 3. Natural areas 4. United States history 5. Yellowstone National Park 6. Nature Writing — Natural Landscapes

LC 2011041351

A reinterpretation of the 19th-century West documents the exploration of an uninhabited Yellowstone region after the Civil War, evaluating the roles of key contributors while providing coverage of the pioneer era, the Indian wars and period efforts to "civilize" the frontier. By the author of the Trout Pool Paradox.

Includes bibliographical references.

978.9 New Mexico

Childs, Craig
House of Rain: Tracking a Vanished Civilization Across the American Southwest. Craig Childs. Little, Brown and Co. 2007. xiv, 496 p. : Illustration; Map
ISBN 9780316608176
Grades: Adult   978.9
1. Pueblo (North American people) 2. Anasazi Culture 3. Indigenous peoples of North America 4. Indigenous peoples of North America — History 5. Antiquities 6. Voyages and travels 7. Chaco Culture National Historical Park, New Mexico 8. Southwest (United States) 9. New Mexico 10. History writing — Indigenous peoples — United States 11. History writing — Archaeology

LC 2006019112

The greatest unsolved mystery of the American Southwest is the fate of the Anasazi, the native peoples who in the eleventh century converged on Chaco Canyon (in today's northwestern New Mexico) and built a flourishing cultural center that attracted pilgrims from far and wide, a vital crossroads of the prehistoric world. The Anasazis' accomplishments—in agriculture, art, commerce, architecture, and engineering—were astounding, as remarkable in their way as those of Mayans in distant Central America. By the thirteenth century, however, the Anasazi were gone from the region. What brought about the rapid collapse of their civilization? Was it drought? pestilence? war? Naturalist Childs draws on the latest scholarly research, as well as on a lifetime of adventure and exploration in the most forbidding landscapes of the American Southwest, to shed new light on this compelling mystery.

"Beginning at the monumental cultural center of Chaco Canyon, where the Anasazi flourished, Childs's quest to understand their apparent disappearance leads him to the numerous great houses of New Mexico, such as Pueblo Bonito, to the Four Corners area of northeastern Arizona, southern Colorado and Utah, and beyond to northern Mexico. In these places, he identifies features that had not appeared prior to the apparent abandonment of Chaco (thus implying that the Anasazi migrated to these areas). Childs vividly weaves his personal narrative, imbued with a deep respect for the geography and cultural landscape, with scientific research and numerous interactions with foremost scholars." —*Library Journal*

Includes bibliographical references (p. 461-482) and index.

979 Great Basin and Pacific Slope region of United States

Hutton, Paul Andrew
The Apache Wars: The Hunt for Geronimo, the Apache Kid, and the Captive Boy Who Started the Longest War in American History. Paul Andrew Hutton. Crown 2016. 400 p.
ISBN 9780770435813
Grades: Adult   979
1. Mickey Free 2. Geronimo, Apache chief, 1829-1909 3. Apache Kid, approximately 1860- 4. Apache (North American people) 5. Multiracial men 6. Indigenous peoples of North America 7. War 8. Battles 9. Fugitives 10. Indigenous peoples of North America — Wars 11. United States history 12. Southwest (United States) 13. 19th century 14. History writing — Indigenous peoples — United States 15. Nonfiction that reads like fiction

LC 2015050712

Spur Award for Historical Nonfiction, 2017.

Describes the violent history between the frontiersmen and the Native Americans in the Southwestern borderlands by following Mickey Free, a mixed-blood warrior who played a pivotal role in the fighting as he pursued the Apache Kid.

"What happened to Felix Ward is less important to the larger historical picture than how the situation with the Apaches was resolved, but Hutton provides an unexpected twist that keeps the story fresh until the end." —*Publishers Weekly*

979.1004 Arizona — Ethnic and national groups

Brooks, James
Mesa of Sorrows: A History of the Awat'ovi Massacre. James F. Brooks. W.W. Norton & Company 2016. 224 p.
ISBN 9780393061253
Grades: Adult   979.1004
1. Indigenous peoples of North America 2. Massacres 3. Hopi (North American people) 4. Excavations (Archaeology) 5. Pueblo Revolt, 1680 6. Pueblo (North American people) 7. Violence 8. Indigenous peoples of North America — History 9. Indigenous peoples of North America — Religion 10. United States history 11. Arizona 12. Southwest (United States) 13. 18th century 14. 1700s (Decade) 15. History writing — Indigenous peoples — United States

LC 2015037504

Draws on oral traditions, archival accounts and archaeological research to investigate the reasons behind the 1700 slaughter of the Hopi community of Awat'ovi by their kinsmen, examining theories about their welcome of Franciscan missionaries, sorcery practices, political crises and beliefs about ritual bloodshed.

Includes bibliographical references and index.

Iverson, Peter
Dine: A History of the Navajos. Peter Iverson; featuring photographs by Monty Roessel. University of New Mexico Press 2002. xii, 386 p. : Illustration; Color; Map
ISBN 9780826327147

ESSENTIAL AND RECOMMENDED TITLES
979.2 Utah

Grades: 11-12 Adult **979.1004**
1. Navajo (Diné) (North American people) 2. Indigenous peoples of North America 3. Indigenous peoples of North America — History 4. Indigenous peoples of North America — Social life and customs 5. Identity 6. Southwest (United States) 7. History writing — Indigenous peoples — United States
LC 2002006407

Spur Award for Contemporary Nonfiction, 2003.

In this general narrative history of the Navajo (DinT) people, Iverson (History, Arizona State U.) explores the origins and history of the Native American group through the first years of the 21st century.

"Perhaps owing to Iverson's lengthy relationship with the tribe, this history stands out among the many other books on the subject, which pale by comparison. His well-organized, thoughtful, and informative book offers a vivid and detailed account of Navajo culture and history." —Choice

Includes bibliographical references (p. 365-376) and index.

Pasternak, Judy
Yellow Dirt: An American Story of a Poisoned Land and a People Betrayed. Judy Pasternak. Free Press 2010. 336 p.
ISBN 9781416594826
Grades: Adult **979.1004**
1. Navajo (Diné) (North American people) 2. Government relations with indigenous peoples 3. Radiation 4. Radiation victims 5. Environmental degradation 6. Pollution 7. Indigenous peoples of North America 8. Uranium 9. Mines and mineral resources 10. United States history 11. Navajo Reservation 12. Southwest (United States) 13. 20th century 14. History writing — Indigenous peoples — United States
LC 2010005546

Describes how the Navajo worked for the U.S. government unprotected in the uranium mines that fueled the Cold War, and how the abandoned mines remained on the Navajo reservation, causing cancer rates and birth defects to soar.

Includes bibliographical references.

979.2 Utah

Roberts, David
The Bears Ears: A Human History of America's Most Endangered Wilderness. David Roberts. W.W. Norton & Company 2021. 352 p.
ISBN 9781324004813
Grades: Adult **979.2**
1. Roberts, David, 1943- 2. Indigenous peoples of North America 3. Sacred space 4. Cliff-dwellings 5. Archaeological sites 6. National parks and reserves 7. Conservation of natural resources 8. Bears Ears National Monument (Utah) 9. Utah 10. Nature Writing — Natural Landscapes
LC 2020042614

A personal and historical exploration of the Bears Ears country and the fight to save a national monument.

"One last fond look at a favorite place? a swan song of a prolific author? Roberts adds inviting details throughout this must-read book, adding poignancy to an already fascinating read." —Library Journal

Includes bibliographical references and index.

Walker, Ronald W.
★ *Massacre at Mountain Meadows.* Ronald W. Walker, Richard E. Turley, Jr, Glen M. Leonard. Oxford University Press 2008. xvi, 430 p. : Illustration; Map; Portrait
ISBN 9780195160345
Grades: Adult **979.2**
1. Mountain Meadows Massacre, 1857 2. Mormons 3. Massacres 4. Violence 5. Religious persecution 6. Crimes against immigrants 7. United States history 8. Utah 9. 19th century 10. History writing — Westward expansion — United States 11. True Crime — Murder 12. Spirituality and Religion — Christianity — Mormonism 13. True Crime — Historical Crime
LC 2008014451

Booklist Editors' Choice, 2008.

This account of the most infamous event in Mormon history, the tragic massacre of the overland emigrants at Mountain Meadow, Utah, paints finely drawn portraits of the key players in the drama and their roles in the tragedy.

Map on lining papers; Includes bibliographical references (p. [281]-408) and index.

979.3 Nevada

D'Agata, John
About a Mountain. John D'Agata. W.W. Norton 2010. 236 p.
ISBN 9780393068184
Grades: Adult **979.3**
1. Radioactive waste sites 2. Radioactive wastes 3. Suicide 4. Conservation of natural resources 5. Wrecking 6. Anthropology 7. Social life and customs 8. Las Vegas, Nevada 9. Society and culture — Urban and regional studies
LC 2009039295

The author's investigation into all facets of Yucca Mountain, a desert range near Las Vegas slated to be a federal nuclear waste storage facility, turns personal when his research unearths a report of a teenager's suicidal plunge off the roof of the Stratosphere Hotel, a boy the author believes he spoke with before his suicide.

"D'Agata uses the federal government's highly controversial (and recently rejected) proposal to entomb the U.S.'s nuclear waste located in Yucca Mountain, near Las Vegas, as his way into a spiraling and subtle examination of the modern city, suicide, linguistics, Edvard Munch's the Scream, ecological and psychic degradation, and the gulf between information and knowledge. Acting as a counterpoint to Yucca is the story of a teenager named Levi who leapt to his death off Las Vegas' Stratosphere Motel. A sublime reading experience, aesthetically rewarding and marked by moral courage and humility." —Publishers Weekly

Includes bibliographical references.

979.4 California

Atleework, Kendra
Miracle Country: A Memoir. Kendra Atleework. Algonquin Books of Chapel Hill 2020. 368 p.
ISBN 9781616209988
Grades: Adult **979.4**
1. Atleework, Kendra, 1989- 2. Growing up 3. Deserts 4. Death of mothers 5. Climate change 6. Effect of environment on humans 7. Coping 8. California 9. Southern California 10. Sierra Nevada Mountains 11. Autobiographies and memoirs 12. Nature Writing — Personal Responses 13. Life stories — Facing adversity — Coping with death 14. Nature Writing — Environmental Issues
LC 2019053878

WILLA Literary Awards: Creative Nonfiction, 2021.

Describes how the author's thriving childhood in the natural desert landscape of the Eastern Sierra Nevada was upended by her mother's tragic early death and how the region of her youth has been ravaged by climate change.

"Essayist Atleework recalls her family roots and explores the history of California's arid Eastern Sierras in her ambitious, beautiful debut.... Atleework's remarkable prose renders the ordinary wondrous and firmly puts this overlooked region of California onto the map." —Publishers Weekly

Brands, H. W.
The Age of Gold: The California Gold Rush and the New American Dream. H.W. Brands. Doubleday 2002. 547 p, [16] p. of plates : Illustration; Map
ISBN 9780385502160
Grades: Adult **979.4**
1. Gold rush 2. Prospectors 3. Social change 4. Consequences 5. Gold mines and mining 6. Frontier and pioneer life 7. Migration, Internal 8. U.S. states 9. Mines and mineral resources 10. Territorial expansion 11. United States history 12. United States 13. California 14. 19th century 15. History writing — Westward expansion — United States

PUBLIC LIBRARY CORE COLLECTION: NONFICTION
Twentieth Edition

LC 2002023776

A history of the people and commercial imperatives that contributed to the California gold rush discusses the massive influx of hundreds of thousands of people to the area, which became a state in record time, in a volume set against the political climate and national issues of the period.

"Combining this wealth of ideas with vivid biographies of actors great and small in the expansionist drama, Brands has produced a work that stands far above the tide of mostly forgettable titles that accompanied the 150th anniversary of the Gold Rush three years ago. A lucid, literate survey of events that transformed the nation, for better and worse." —*Kirkus*

Includes bibliographical references (p. [509]-527) and index.

Chude-Sokei, Louis Onuorah

Floating in a Most Peculiar Way: A Memoir. Louis Chude-Sokei. Houghton Mifflin Harcourt 2021. 240 p.
ISBN 9781328841582
Grades: Adult   979.4

1. Chude-Sokei, Louis Onuorah, 1967- 2. Nigerian Americans 3. Jamaican Americans 4. Immigrants 5. Identity 6. Growing up 7. Childhood 8. Ethnic identity 9. Los Angeles, California 10. Nigeria 11. Autobiographies and memoirs 12. Life stories — Identity — Race and ethnicity 13. Life stories — Identity — Immigrants

LC 2020023320

A prominent African-American scholar discusses his childhood displacement from the short-lived African nation of Biafra to a relative's strictly religious Jamaican household before arriving in his mother's California home on the eve of the L.A. Riots.

"This absorbing memoir from Chude-Sokei, director of Boston University's African American studies program, chronicles his personal journey through the African diaspora." —*Booklist*

Davenport, Matthew J.

The **Longest** *Minute: The Great San Francisco Earthquake and Fire of 1906.* Matthew J. Davenport. St. Martin's Press 2023. 336 p.
ISBN 9781250279279
Grades: Adult   979.4

1. San Francisco Earthquake and Fire, Calif, 1906 2. Earthquakes 3. Fires 4. Natural disasters 5. San Francisco, California 6. 20th century 7. History Writing — Regional history — United States 8. History Writing — Natural disasters and tragedies

LC 2023025153

Meticulously researched and gracefully written, the Longest Minute is both a harrowing chronicle of devastation and the portrait of a city's resilience in the burning aftermath of greed and folly. Drawing on the letters and diaries and unpublished memoirs of survivors and previously unearthed archival records, Matthew Davenport combines history and science to tell the dramatic true story of one of the greatest disasters in American history.

"Davenport brings fresh insights to the 1906 earthquake and devastating, citywide fires in San Francisco...A tale both captivating and cautionary." —*Booklist*

Includes bibliographical references and index.

Didion, Joan

Where I Was from. Joan Didion. Knopf 2003. 226 p.
ISBN 9780679433323
Grades: Adult   979.4

1. Didion, Joan 1934-2021 2. National characteristics, American 3. California in literature 4. Self-reliance 5. Independence 6. United States history 7. California 8. Autobiographies and memoirs 9. Life stories — General 10. Society and culture — Urban and regional studies

LC 2002043325

New York Times Notable Book, 2003.

The essayist explores American ideals of independence and self-reliance by probing her own life and those of her relatives, discussing how the character of California's settlers created the state as it exists today.

"This is a complex and challenging memoir, difficult to enter into but just as difficult to put down. Those who have long admired the clarity and precision of her prose will not be disappointed with this partly autobiographical, partly historical, but fully engrossing account." —*Library Journal*

Hahn, Emanuel

Koreatown Dreaming: Stories & Portraits of Korean Immigrant Life. Emanuel Hahn. Running Press 2023. 256 pages : Color; Illustration
ISBN 9780762484584
Grades: Adult   979.4

1. Korean Americans 2. Social life and customs 3. Ethnic neighborhoods 4. Immigrants, Korean 5. Immigrants 6. Businesspeople 7. Small business 8. Portrait photography 9. Street photography 10. American people 11. Korean people 12. Los Angeles, California 13. California 14. United States 15. Visual nonfiction 16. Society and culture — Ethnic studies 17. Arts and Entertainment — Photography

LC 2022050391

A successful self-published project, now in a new and expanded trade package, Koreatown Dreaming offers readers an intimate look into the lives of shopkeepers and small business owners in Los Angeles Koreatown. A touching homage to Korean immigrants everywhere, this book will resonate with the growing audience of people interested in Korean culture.

"Hahn uses his images as a vehicle to shed light on the broader experiences of the Korean diaspora in the United States...Readers will appreciate the beautiful and poignant photographs included throughout." —*Library Journal*

Includes index.

Lunenfeld, Peter

City at the Edge of Forever: Los Angeles Reimagined. Peter Lunenfeld. Viking 2020. 336 p.
ISBN 9780525561934
Grades: Adult   979.4

1. Cities and towns 2. Community development 3. Popular culture 4. Architecture 5. Local history 6. Social change 7. Urban economics 8. Entertainment industry and trade 9. Social life and customs 10. Civilization 11. United States history 12. Los Angeles, California 13. 20th century 14. Society and culture — Urban and regional studies 15. History writing — Regional history — United States 16. History writing — Arts and culture

LC 2020013210

How did Los Angeles start the 20th century as a dusty frontier town and end up a century later as one of the globe's supercities—with unparalleled cultural, economic, and technological reach? in City at the Edge of Forever, Peter Lunenfeld constructs an urban portrait, layer by layer, from serendipitous affinities, historical anomalies, and uncanny correspondences. Lunenfeld weaves together the city's art, architecture, and design, juxtaposes its entertainment and literary histories, and moves from restaurant kitchens to recording studios to ultra-secret research and development labs. In the process, he reimagines Los Angeles as simultaneously an exemplar and cautionary tale for the 21st century.

"UCLA digital media scholar Lunenfeld (coauthor, Digital_Humanities) draws surprising links between the artistic, economic, and political milieus of Los Angeles in this immersive cultural history. . . . Richly detailed and evocatively written, this highly original account unearths L.A. stories." —*Publishers Weekly*

Includes bibliographical references and index.

Menuez, Doug

Fearless Genius: The Digital Revolution in Silicon Valley, 1985-2000. Doug Menuez; foreword by Elliott Erwitt; introduction by Kurt Andersen. Atria Books 2014. xix, 171 pages : Illustration
ISBN 9781476752693
Grades: Adult   979.4

1. Documentary photography 2. High technology 3. Santa Clara Valley, California 4. Arts and Entertainment — Photography 5. Business and economics — Industries — Technology

LC 2013045228

An award-winning documentary photographer presents a striking visual history of the Silicon Valley technology boom that reflects key moments in the careers of Steve Jobs, Bill Gates and other leading innovators.

ESSENTIAL AND RECOMMENDED TITLES
979.5 Oregon

Offers a pictorial chronicle of the Silicon Valley technology boom, beginning with Steve Jobs' NeXT Computer company in 1985 and expending to other innovative companies in the region up to the bursting of the dot com bubble.

"Menuez even makes the innovators' solitude—sequestered behind drawn blinds for days or cordoned off from the rest of the pack in lonely cubicles—surprisingly compelling. The accompanying text is both complementary and instructive." —*Kirkus*

Muir, John
The Yosemite. John Muir; [foreword by David Brower]. Sierra Club Books 1988. xx, 215 p.
ISBN 9780871567826
Grades: Adult   **979.4**
1. Yosemite National Park 2. Yosemite Valley 3. Nature writing — Natural Landscapes
LC 87023573

The naturalist and founder of the Sierra Club recounts his experiences exploring Yosemite Valley and shares his observations on the local wildlife.

Includes index; Reprint. Originally published: Boston : Houghton Mifflin, 1914.

Ross, Steven Joseph
★ *Hitler in Los Angeles: How Jews Foiled Nazi Plots Against Hollywood and America*. Steven J. Ross. Bloomsbury Press 2017. 320 p.
ISBN 9781620405628
Grades: Adult   **979.4**
1. Nazis 2. Films, American 3. Spies 4. Jewish people 5. Antisemitism 6. Los Angeles, California 7. Second World War era (1939-1945) 8. History writing — Spies and spying 9. History writing — Wars and conflicts — Homefront — World War II
LC 2017012324

Pulitzer Prize for History finalist, 2018.

An acclaimed historian presents a gripping, little-known story of the rise of Nazism in Los Angeles during which attorney Leon Lewis ran a spy operation to stop the Nazis from killing the city's Jews and sabotaging the nation's military installations.

"Ross puts his experience in film history to good use, and he creates lively portraits of the men and women whom Lewis recruited as spies and who succeeded in putting some dangerous Nazis behind bars." —*Kirkus*

Includes bibliographical references.

Stein, Jean
West of Eden: An American Place. Jean Stein. Random House 2016. 320 p.
ISBN 9780812998405
Grades: Adult   **979.4**
1. Oral history projects 2. Popular culture 3. Social life and customs 4. United States history 5. Hollywood, California 6. California 7. Los Angeles, California 8. 20th century 9. Arts and entertainment — General
LC 2015022411

An oral history of five outsider families who rose to power and fortune in Hollywood and Los Angeles traces their humble origins, the dreams that inspired their ambitions, the setbacks that challenged their achievements and their enduring legacies.

"Steins exhaustive research and brand-new interviews make this an invaluable resource for any student of pop culture, or indeed of 20th-century American history." —*Publishers Weekly*

Winchester, Simon
A Crack in the Edge of the World: America and the Great California Earthquake of 1906. Simon Winchester. Harper Collins 2005. xiv, 462 p. : Illustration; Map
ISBN 9780060571993
Grades: Adult   **979.4**
1. Disasters 2. Natural disasters 3. San Francisco Earthquake and Fire, Calif, 1906 4. Earthquakes 5. Fires 6. United States history 7. California 8. San Francisco, California 9. 1900s (Decade) 10. 20th century 11. Nature Writing — Natural Disaster 12. History writing — Early 20th century — United States
LC 2005046009

The definitive account of the San Francisco earthquake and a fascinating exploration of a legendary event that changed the way we look at the planet on which we live.

"In this brawny page-turner, . [the author] has crafted a magnificent testament to the power of planet Earth and the efforts of humankind to understand her." —*Publishers Weekly*

Includes bibliographical references and index.

979.5 Oregon

Sharfstein, Daniel J.
★ *Thunder in the Mountains: Chief Joseph, Oliver Otis Howard, and the Nez Perce War*. Daniel J. Sharfstein. W.W. Norton & Company 2017. 384 p.
ISBN 9780393239416
Grades: Adult   **979.5**
1. Howard, O. O. (Oliver Otis), 1830-1909 2. Joseph, Nez Perce Chief, 1840-1904 3. Nez Perce (Nimíipuu) (North American people) 4. Government relations with indigenous peoples 5. Indigenous peoples of North America 6. European-Americans 7. Indigenous peoples of North America — Civil rights 8. Political culture 9. Civil rights 10. Indigenous peoples of North America — Wars 11. Race relations 12. The West (United States) history 13. United States 14. 1870s 15. 19th century 16. History writing — Indigenous peoples — United States 17. History writing — Wars and conflicts — American Indigenous Wars
LC 2016055352

Booklist Editors' Choice, 2017.

Chronicles the epic clash between General Oliver Otis Howard, who took on a mission in the Pacific Northwest to force Native Americans onto reservations, and the Nez Perce leader Chief Joseph, who refused to leave his ancestral land.

"Sharfstein has provided a scrupulously researched and detailed revisiting of one of the most moving and saddest sagas in American history." —*Booklist*

Includes bibliographical references and index.

Stark, Peter
Astoria: John Jacob Astor and Thomas Jefferson's Lost Pacific Empire: A Story of Wealth, Ambition, and Survival. Peter Stark. Ecco Press 2014. 384 p.
ISBN 9780062218292
Grades: Adult   **979.5**
1. Astor, John Jacob, 1763-1848 2. Expeditions 3. Overland journeys to the Pacific 4. Ocean travel 5. Fur industry and trade 6. Capitalists and financiers 7. Wilderness survival 8. Ambition 9. 19th century 10. History writing — Early America — United States 11. History writing — Exploration
LC Bl2014004837

Drawing on original source material, this gripping true story, filled with high adventure and incredible hardship, documents the 3-year expedition, from 1810 to 1813, to establish Fort Astoria, a trading post on the Columbia River in the Pacific Northwest.

"A fast-paced, riveting account of exploration and settlement, suffering and survival, treachery and death." —*Kirkus*

979.7 Washington

Krist, Gary
The White Cascade: The Great Northern Railway Disaster and America's Deadliest Avalanche. Gary Krist. Henry Holt and Company 2007. xii, 315 p, 16 p. of plates : Illustration; Map
ISBN 9780805077056
Grades: Adult   **979.7**
1. Avalanches 2. Railroad accidents 3. Railroad travel 4. Blizzards 5. United States history 6. Washington (State) 7. 20th century 8. History writing — Natural disasters and tragedies 9. Nature Writing — Natural Disaster
LC 2006049047

In February 1910, a monstrous blizzard hit Washington State. High in the Cascade Mountains near the tiny town of Wellington, two trainloads of cold, hungry passengers and their crews found their railcars buried in rising drifts, parked precariously on the edge of a steep ravine. An army of the Great Northern Railroad's men worked round-the-clock to rescue the trains, but the storm was unrelenting. Suddenly the earth shifted and a colossal avalanche tumbled, sweeping the trains and their sleeping passengers over the steep slope and down the mountainside.

"This is a tale in which snow falls, a mountain looms, and most of the protagonists simply sit. The outcome is predetermined. Mr. Krist does wonders with this unpromising material, however. Adopting a restrained, documentary tone, he slowly builds a picture of massing natural forces and helpless humanity, brought closer and closer to catastrophe with each tick of the clock. The pacing is expertly judged, and the potentially confusing narrative threads, involving multiple actors in scattered locations, are tied together neatly." —*New York Times*

Includes bibliographical references (p. [291]-297) and index.

Sone, Monica Itoi
Nisei Daughter. Monica Sone. University of Washington Press 2014. xvii, 238 p.
ISBN 9780295993553
Grades: Adult   **979.7**
1. Sone, Monica Itoi, 1919-2011 2. Japanese Americans 3. Japanese American forced removal and incarceration 4. East Asian Americans 5. Seattle, Washington 6. Second World War era (1939-1945) 7. Autobiographies and memoirs 8. History writing — Wars and conflicts — Homefront — World War II 9. Family and Relationships — Growing up 10. Life stories — Relationships — Growing up
LC 79004921

Tells the story of a Japanese-American woman growing up in Seattle in the 1930s who was subjected to relocation during World War II.

Sullivan, Randall
Graveyard of the Pacific: Shipwreck and Survival on America's Deadliest Waterway. Randall Sullivan. Atlantic Monthly Press 2023. 272 p.
ISBN 9780802162403
Grades: Adult   **979.7**
1. Sullivan, Randall 2. Shipwrecks 3. Identity 4. Psychic trauma 5. Adult child abuse victims 6. United States history 7. Columbia River region 8. Columbia River 9. United States 10. Autobiographies and memoirs 11. Life stories — General 12. History Writing — Regional history — United States 13. Travel Writing — United States 14. Travel Writing — Modes of transportation
LC 2023003700

A man who successfully crossed the Columbia River Bar with a friend in a two-man kayak reflects on the experience of battling one of the most notorious stretches of water in the world and reflects on those who went before him.

"Vividly evoking Sullivan's deep fascination with the Pacific Northwest and thirst for friendship and adventure, this is a thrill ride." —*Publishers Weekly*

Includes bibliographical references.

979.8 Alaska

Borneman, Walter R.
Alaska: Saga of a Bold Land. Walter R. Borneman. Harper Collins 2003. xiv, 608 p. : Illustration; Map
ISBN 9780060503062
Grades: 11 12 Adult   **979.8**
1. Frontier and pioneer life 2. United States history 3. Alaska 4. History writing — Regional history — United States
LC 2002027271

A comprehensive history of Alaska provides coverage of such topics as the area's native culture, its exploration and mountaineering, the mining rushes, its railroads and aviation, its military operations, the conservation versus development conflict, and the ANWR oil drilling debate.

"Separated into nine chronologically based chapters, the text explores a recurring theme in Alaska's development: Conflict among disparate groups over how the land would be used for personal enrichment. Engaging chapters detail the important events and those who helped shape Alaska's history. This expansive, comprehensive history is recommended for all libraries." —*Library Journal*

Includes bibliographical references and index.

Heacox, Kim
Rhythm of the Wild: A Life Inspired by Alaska's Denali National Park. Kim Heacox. Lyons Press 2015. 256 p.
ISBN 9781493003891
Grades: Adult   **979.8**
1. Heacox, Kim 2. Natural history 3. Nature conservation 4. Landscape protection 5. Wildlife conservation 6. Climate change 7. National parks and reserves 8. Voyages and travels 9. United States history 10. Alaska 11. Nature Writing — Natural Landscapes 12. Nature Writing — Personal Responses
LC 2014048442

A compelling memoir about Kim Heacox's more than thirty-year relationship with the most iconic landscape in Alaska.

"The park's wildlife—moose, eagles, red fox, sandhill cranes, grizzly bears, porcupines and wolves—share the stage with human actors in Heacox's chronicle. Top-notch environmental writing to shelve alongside George Perkins Marsh, Aldo Leopold, Robert Marshall and Barry Lopez." —*Kirkus*

Includes bibliographical references and index.

Jenkins, Peter
Looking for Alaska. Peter Jenkins. St. Martin's Press 2001. 434 p. : Illustration; Color; Map
ISBN 9780312261788
Grades: Adult   **979.8**
1. Jenkins, Peter, 1951- 2. Indigenous peoples of North America 3. Adventure travel 4. Travelers 5. Indigenous peoples of North America — Social life and customs 6. Social life and customs 7. Voyages and travels 8. Alaska 9. Travel Writing — United States 10. Adult books for young adults
LC 2001048871

The author's chronicle of his year-long trek through Alaska introduces the people and places of the nation's "last frontier."

"This book sparkles with adventure, quirky characters, unbelievable hardships, and indescribable beauty." —*Library Journal*

Van Hemert, Caroline
The Sun Is a Compass: A 4,000-mile Journey into the Alaskan Wilds. Caroline Van Hemert. Little, Brown Spark 2019. 320 p.
ISBN 9780316414425
Grades: Adult   **979.8**
1. Women scientists 2. Husband and wife 3. Voyages and travels 4. Wilderness areas 5. Bird migration 6. Transformations, Personal 7. Animal migration 8. Arctic regions 9. Alaska 10. Autobiographies and memoirs 11. Life stories — Nature and outdoors 12. Nature Writing — Personal Responses 13. Life stories — Science, technology, and medicine — Scientists and inventors
LC Bl2019002450

Documents the biologist adventurer's treks in the vast wilderness region spanning the Pacific rainforest through the Alaskan Arctic, where her husband and she tested their physical boundaries while making profound natural-world connections and discoveries about animal survival.

980 History of South America

Chasteen, John Charles
Americanos: Latin America's Struggle for Independence. John Charles Chasteen. Oxford University Press 2008. 240 p.
ISBN 9780195178814
Grades: 11 12 Adult   **980**

ESSENTIAL AND RECOMMENDED TITLES
980.03 South America — 1830-1999

1. National liberation movements 2. South American history 3. Latin America 4. 19th century 5. History writing — Latin America
LC 2007028595

"This is a beautiful, vibrant...book; it may also be one of the more socially important books to appear in some time." —*Booklist*

Includes bibliographical references and index.

Born in Blood and Fire: A Concise History of Latin America. John Charles Chasteen. W.W. Norton & Company 2016. xiii, 356, A50 pages : Illustration; Color; Map
ISBN 9780393283051
Grades: 11 12 Adult **980**
1. History 2. Latin American people 3. South American history 4. Latin America 5. History writing — Latin America
LC 2016014210

A concise, chronological history of Latin America spans six centuries and encompasses twenty countries as it discusses the people, events, and factors that shaped Latin America—including colonization, revolution, ethnic diversity, and the struggle for economic growth and political and social equality.

"Chasteen focuses on major political, social and economic topics and trends that helped shape Latin America, including liberalism, the caste system, the mixing of races, nationalism and the Western notion of Progress; he also examines the role that Europe and the United States played in the development of these phenomena. Also refreshing is Chasteen's examination of the periods he covers from the perspective of women." —*Publishers Weekly.* [review of 2000 edition]
Includes index.

Thomas, Hugh
Rivers of Gold: The Rise of the Spanish Empire, from Columbus to Magellan. Hugh Thomas. Random House 2003. xxi, 696 p. : Illustration; Color; Map
ISBN 9780375502040
Grades: Adult **980**
1. Colonies 2. Colonialism 3. Exploration 4. Spanish people 5. Spanish history 6. Western Hemisphere 7. Caribbean area 8. 16th century 9. Age of exploration (1419-1610) 10. History writing — Europe — Spain 11. History writing — Colonialism — Europe 12. History writing — Latin America
LC 2003069316

New York Times Notable Book, 2004.

A history of Spain's first thirty years in the Americas traces Columbus's pioneering voyage through Magellan's first circumnavigation of the earth.

"Engagingly presented, this book clearly shows the author's passion for his subject." —*Booklist*

Includes bibliographical references (p. [555]-574) and index.

980.03 South America — 1830-1999

Vargas Llosa, Mario
Sabers and Utopias: Visions of Latin America. Mario Vargas Llosa; translated from the Spanish by Anna Kushner. Farrar, Straus and Giroux 2018. xxiii, 275 p.
ISBN 9780374253738
Grades: Adult **980.03**
1. Literary criticism 2. Latin American people 3. Politics and government 4. Latin America 5. Essays 6. Translations — Spanish to English 7. History writing — Latin America 8. Politics and global affairs — World Politics — Latin America
LC 2017038306

A collection of essays from the winner of the 2010 Nobel Prize in Literature offers criticisms and meditations on issues affecting Latin America, including recent history with political groups like FARC and Sendero Luminoso and also the legacies of Papa Doc Duvalier and Fidel Castro.

"After nearly a half century of literary output, Vargas Llosa still has few equals when it comes to power of expression and clearheaded conviction." —*Booklist*

Includes index; Originally published in Spanish in 2009 by Santillana Ediciones Generales, Spain, as Sables y Utopías; Translated from the Spanish.

981 Brazil

Reel, Monte
The Last of the Tribe: The Epic Quest to Save a Lone Man in the Amazon. Monte Reel. Scribner 2010. IX, 273 p. : Illustration; Map
ISBN 9781416594741
Grades: Adult **981**
1. Indigenous peoples of South America 2. Wild men 3. Indigenous peoples of South America — Social conditions 4. Brazil 5. Adventure writing — Survival 6. History writing — Indigenous peoples — Latin America
LC 2009037974

Recounts the story of the men who ventured deep into the Amazon to find and protect the last Brazilian Indian and explains how businesspersons, politicians, territorial farmers, and the Indian himself marred an effort to save the Indian.

"In the opening scene of Monte Reel's the Last of the Tribe, Brazilian government workers approach the deep jungle hideout of an Amazonian Indian they suspect to be the last living member of his tribe. The Indian sits in his hut, cornered, an arrow drawn on his bow, and waits. After two hours, the standoff ends. The government workers leave; the Indian disappears into the jungle. Again. The Last of the Tribe is the story of the 20-year pursuit of that solitary Indian by aid workers who want to contact and protect him, and by loggers and miners who want him dead or moved before he gives the government a reason to protect more land from resource extraction. Reel's tale is expertly told: Perfectly timed, thoroughly researched and descriptively written." —*San Francisco Chronicle*

Includes bibliographical references and index.

Skidmore, Thomas E.
Brazil: Five Centuries of Change. Thomas E. Skidmore. Oxford University Press 2010. xv, 285 p. : Illustration; Map
ISBN 9780195374551
Grades: Adult **981**
1. South American history 2. Brazil 3. History writing — Latin America
LC 2009011669

Revised and updated in this second edition, Brazil: Five Centuries of Change vividly traces the development of Brazil over the last 500 years.

Includes bibliographical references (p. 257-269) and index.

Wallace, Scott
The Unconquered: In Search of the Amazon's Last Uncontacted Tribes. Scott Wallace. Crown Publishers 2011. 512 p.
ISBN 9780307462961
Grades: Adult **981**
1. Wallace, Scott 2. Indigenous peoples of South America — Social life and customs 3. Expeditions 4. Voyages and travels 5. Indigenous peoples of South America 6. Rain forests 7. Wilderness survival 8. Jungle survival 9. Amazon River Region 10. Travel Writing — Central and South America
LC 2011006717

A "National Geographic" writer describes his journey with thirty-four other people into the depths of the Amazon rain forest in an attempt to track one of the last uncontacted tribes on the planet, the "People of the Arrow."

Includes bibliographical references.

982 Argentina

Parrado, Nando
★ *Miracle in the Andes: 72 Days on the Mountain and My Long Trek Home.* Nando Parrado with Vince Rause. Crown Publishers 2006. 291 p, 32 p. of plates : Illustration; Map
ISBN 9781400097678
Grades: 11 12 Adult **982**
1. Parrado, Nando, 1949- 2. Airplane accidents 3. Cannibalism 4. Airplane accident victims 5. Rugby football players 6. Survival (after airplane accidents, shipwrecks, etc.) 7. Andes 8. Andes Region 9. 1970s 10. Adventure writing — Survival 11. Adult books for young adults 12. Book club best bets

PUBLIC LIBRARY CORE COLLECTION: NONFICTION
Twentieth Edition

Booklist Editors' Choice: Adult Books for Young Adults, 2006.

A survivor of the horrific 1972 plane crash that stranded his rugby team in the Andes for seventy-two days—popularized in the best-selling Alive—provides his own chilling account of the ordeal and of his desperate expedition across seventy miles of frozen wilderness to find help.

"Rugby team member Parrado has written a beautiful story of friendship, tragedy and perseverance." —*Publishers Weekly*

Read, Piers Paul
★ *Alive: The Story of the Andes Survivors*. Piers Paul Reed. Avon Books 2002. xiv, 398 p. : Illustration
ISBN 9780380003211
Grades: 11 12 Adult   **982**

1. Rugby football players 2. Survival (after airplane accidents, shipwrecks, etc.) 3. Airplane accidents 4. Cannibalism 5. Andes 6. Andes Region 7. 1970s 8. Page to screen 9. Adventure writing — Survival 10. Adult books for young adults

LC 2003269866

Records the struggles and sufferings of the young Uruguayans during the ten weeks following an airplane crash in the Andes.

Originally published: Philadelphia, PA : Lippincott, 1974.

Salama, Jordan
★ *Stranger in the Desert: A Family Story*. Jordan Salama. Catapult 2024. 240 p.
ISBN 9781646221653
Grades: Adult   **982**

1. Salama, Jordan 2. Authors 3. Family history 4. Genealogy 5. Arab people 6. Jewish people 7. Great-grandfathers 8. Immigrants 9. Traveling sales personnel 10. Voyages and travels 11. Extended families 12. Family relationships 13. Identity 14. Self-discovery 15. Southwest Asian (Middle Eastern) people 16. Syrian people 17. South American people 18. Argentine people 19. American people 20. Syria 21. Argentina 22. Andes Region 23. Autobiographies and memoirs 24. Life stories — Relationships — Family 25. Travel Writing — Central and South America 26. Family and Relationships — Families 27. Society and culture — Ethnic studies

Combining travelog, history, memoir and reportage, a young writer, after discovering a large binder filled with 500 years of wandering history of his Arab-Jewish family, embarks on an epic quest through the Argentine Andes in search of his heritage, while grappling with his own Jewish, Arab and Latin American identities.

"A nonchronological personal narrative rather than a standard travel memoir, Stranger in the Desert is a reflection on family history, identity, and storytelling." —*Booklist*

985 Peru

Adams, Mark
Turn Right at Machu Picchu: Rediscovering the Lost City One Step at a Time. Mark Adams. Dutton 2011. 352 p.
ISBN 9780525952244
Grades: Adult   **985**

1. Adams, Mark, 1967- 2. Bingham, Hiram, 1875-1956 3. Cultural property 4. Voyages and travels 5. Exploration 6. Material culture 7. Machu Picchu, Peru 8. Peru 9. Travel Writing — Retracing Historic Journeys 10. Travel Writing — Central and South America

LC 2011010211

ALA Notable Book, 2012.

Traces the author's recreation of Hiram Bingham III's discovery of an ancient Andes Mountains cloud city, describing the author's struggles with rudimentary survival tools and his experiences at the sides of local guides. By the author of Mr. America.

"While some readers may prefer a more straightforward version of Bingham's exploits , those favoring a quirkier retelling will relish Mr. Adams's wry, revealing romp through the Andes." —*Wall Street Journal*

Includes index.

Bingham, Hiram
★ *Lost City of the Incas: The Story of Machu Picchu and Its Builders*. Hiram Bingham. Greenwood Press 1981. xviii, 263 p, 64 p. of plates : Illustration
ISBN 9780313229503
Grades: 11 12 Adult   **985**

1. Bingham, Hiram, 1875-1956 2. Inca (South American people) 3. Indigenous peoples of South America 4. Indigenous peoples of South America — Antiquities 5. Antiquities 6. Voyages and travels 7. Machu Picchu, Peru 8. Peru 9. Latin America 10. History writing — Indigenous peoples — Latin America 11. History writing — Latin America — South America

LC 81007196

An historian and explorer recounts his 1911 discovery of the long-lost Incan city of Machu Picchu.

"In 1911 Bingham, an American explorer, found the Inca city of Machu Picchu, which had been lost for 300 years. In this volume he tells of its origin, how it came to be lost and how it was finally discovered." —*Library Journal*

Includes bibliographical references (p. 253-255) and index; Originally published: New York : Duell, Sloan and Pearce, 1948.

986.1 Colombia

Davis, Wade
Magdalena: River of Dreams. Wade Davis. Alfred A. Knopf 2020. 433 pages
ISBN 9780375410994
Grades: Adult   **986.1**

1. Rivers 2. River travel 3. River life 4. Voyages and travels 5. South American history 6. Colombia 7. Canadian literature 8. Nature writing — Natural landscapes 9. Travel writing — Modes of transportation — Boating 10. Travel writing — Central and South America

LC 2019022605

The award winning writer, photographer, filmmaker, and ethnographer—a longtime Explorer-in-Residence at the National Geographic Society—recounts an enthralling journey down Colombia's Magdalena River that illuminates the country's rebirth after decades of political violence, drug cartels, and guerrilla warfare.

"In this deeply inquisitive, dazzlingly fluent scientific, cultural, and spiritual investigation, Davis illuminates the natural and human history of Río Magdalena, 'The Mississippi River of Colombia'. . . . A far-reaching, centuries-encompassing river biography." —*Booklist*

Includes bibliographical references and index.

994 Australia

Hughes, Robert
The Fatal Shore. Robert Hughes. Vintage Books 1988. xviii, 628 p, 40 p. of plates : Illustration; Map; Portrait
ISBN 9780394753669
Grades: Adult   **994**

1. Exiles 2. Penal colonies 3. Australian history 4. Australia 5. 19th century 6. 18th century 7. Australian literature 8. History writing — Early Australia — Australia

LC 87040089

Age Non Fiction Award, 1987.

Draws on diverse original materials to recount the European settlement of Australia, from the 1788 landing of the first prison fleet to 1868.

"This epic account chronicles the history of Australia during the 80 years (1788-1868) of England's convict transportation system, when some 160,000 convicts reached 'The fatal shore.' Interweaving his own lucid narrative with un-

ESSENTIAL AND RECOMMENDED TITLES
995.1 Western New Guinea (Irian Barat)

tapped original sources—including the diaries and letters of the prisoners themselves—Hughes shows the evolution of the system and of the fledgling nation that emerged from the brutal penal colony." —*Library Journal*

Includes bibliographical references (p. 656-670) and index.

Keneally, Thomas
A Commonwealth of Thieves: The Improbable Birth of Australia. Thomas Keneally. Nan A. Talese, Doubleday 2006. 385 p. : Map
ISBN 9780385514590
Grades: Adult   994
1. Phillip, Arthur, 1738-1814 2. Prisoners 3. Convict ships 4. Governors 5. Frontier and pioneer life 6. Penal colonies 7. Australian history 8. Australia 9. 18th century 10. 19th century 11. Biographies 12. Australian literature 13. Life stories — People in history 14. History writing — Early Australia — Australia
LC 2006044470

A history of the European settlement of Australia tells the story of Captain Arthur Phillip, who was empowered to govern a colony comprised primarily of unskilled criminals and petty thieves, disgruntled military men, and a sometimes hostile native population.

"This book offers an engaging treatment of a subject which over the years has provoked a long and sometimes heated debate." —*Times Literary Supplement*

Includes bibliographical references (p. [363]-367) and index; Originally published: Milson Point, N.S.W. : Random House Australia, 2005.

995.1 Western New Guinea (Irian Barat)

Hoffman, Carl
★ *Savage Harvest: A Tale of Cannibals, Colonialism, and Michael Rockefeller's Tragic Quest for Primitive Art.* Carl Hoffman. HarperCollins 2014. 304 p.
ISBN 9780062116154
Grades: Adult   995.1
1. Rockefeller, Michael Clark 2. Missing persons 3. Cannibalism 4. Ethnology 5. Art collectors and collecting 6. Villages 7. Folk art 8. Conspiracies 9. Colonialism 10. New Guinea 11. Travel writing — Asia and the South Pacific
LC 2015452225

In 1961, a scion of the powerful Rockefeller family, 23-year-old Michael, disappeared during an expedition to Dutch New Guinea where'd he planned to study a primitive tribe and gather art for a museum that his father—the governor of New York—had founded. Michael's body was never found, and officials ruled that he had drowned…but rumors swirled that he was actually killed and eaten by natives. In search of the truth, avid traveler and author Carl Hoffman recently retraced Michael's path, immersing himself in the world of former headhunters and cannibals to solve this historical whodunit.

"[An] unforgettable story of a soothing and politically expedient cover-up and a brutal and tragic collision of cultures." —*Booklist*

996.1 Southwest central Pacific, and isolated islands of southeast Pacific

Alexander, Caroline
The Bounty: The True Story of the Mutiny on the Bounty. Caroline Alexander. Viking 2003. 491 p. : Illustration; Color; Map
ISBN 9780670031337
Grades: 11 12 Adult   996.1
1. Bligh, William, 1754-1817 2. Christian, Fletcher, 1764-1793 3. Courts-martial and courts of inquiry 4. Mutiny 5. Bounty Mutiny, 1789 6. Navigation 7. Voyages and travels 8. Oceania 9. 18th century 10. History writing — Military — Naval history 11. Adventure writing — General 12. Adult books for young adults
LC 2003050158

Library Journal Best Books, 2003; National Book Critics Circle Award for Nonfiction finalist, 2003.

An account of the events surrounding the conflict aboard the HMS Bounty focuses on the court-martial of its ten mutineers, citing the breakdown and exile of Fletcher Christian and Lieutenant Bligh's navigation talents.

"A rollicking sea adventure told with enormous confidence and style." —*Booklist*

Includes bibliographical references (p. 449-467) and index.

Severin, Timothy
In Search of Robinson Crusoe. Tim Severin. Basic Books 2002. 333 p.
ISBN 9780465076987
Grades: Adult   996.1
1. Defoe, Daniel, 1661?-1731 2. Selkirk, Alexander, 1676-1721 3. Wafer, Lionel, 1660?-1705? 4. Pitman, Henry 5. Survival (after airplane accidents, shipwrecks, etc.) 6. Literature and history 7. Castaways 8. Voyages and travels 9. Great Britain 10. Travel Writing — Retracing Historic Journeys 11. History writing — Exploration 12. Arts and Entertainment — Writing and Publishing 13. Adult books for young adults
LC 2002071661

Retraces the journeys of castaways and pirates to discover the inspiration for Daniel Defoe's classic, describing his undertaking of a perilous sea voyage and search for the Miskutu Indians in Nicaragua and Honduras.

"The work is energetic and Severin is an ideal guide to the world behind the word. This will surely appeal to the lovers of maritime history." —*Publishers Weekly*

996.18 Isolated islands of southeast Pacific

Preston, Diana
Paradise in Chains: The Bounty Mutiny and the Founding of Australia. Diana Preston. Bloomsbury USA 2017. xii, 333 p.
ISBN 9781632866103
Grades: Adult   996.18
1. Bligh, William, 1754-1817 2. Bounty Mutiny, 1789 3. Transportation of prisoners 4. Prisoners 5. Escapes 6. Ocean travel 7. Sea survival 8. Australian history 9. Colonial Australia (1788-1901) 10. History writing — Early Australia — Australia 11. History writing — Exploration
LC 2017002518

Celebrated historian Diana Preston presents betrayals, escapes, and survival at sea in her account of the mutiny of the Bounty and the flight of convicts from the Australian penal colony. The story of the mutiny of the Bounty and William Bligh and his men's survival on the open ocean for 48 days and 3,618 miles has become the stuff of legend. But few realize that Bligh's escape across the seas was not the only open-boat journey in that era of British exploration and colonization. Indeed, 9 convicts from the Australian penal colony, led by Mary Bryant, also traveled 3,250 miles across the open ocean and some uncharted seas to land at the same port Bligh had reached only months before.

"A wonderful look into the beginnings of Australia and the remarkable strength of the survivors of these dangerous voyages." —*Kirkus*

Treister, Kenneth
Easter Island's Silent Sentinels: The Sculpture and Architecture of Rapa Nui. Kenneth Treister, Patricia Vargas Casanova, and Claudio Cristino; foreword by Daniel Libeskind; maps and illustrations by Roberto Izaurieta and Kenneth Treister. University of New Mexico Press 2013. xv, 144 pages : Color; Illustration
ISBN 9780826352644
Grades: Adult   996.18
1. Antiquities 2. South American history 3. Easter Island 4. History writing — Archaeology 5. Society and culture — Anthropology 6. Arts and Entertainment — Architecture
LC 2013013728

This richly illustrated book of the history, culture, and art of Easter Island is the first to examine in detail the island's vernacular architecture, often overshadowed by its giant stone statues.

Includes bibliographical references (pages 123-132) and index.

PUBLIC LIBRARY CORE COLLECTION: NONFICTION
Twentieth Edition

996.9 Hawaii and neighboring north central Pacific Ocean islands

Haley, James L.
Captive Paradise: The United States and Hawai'i. James L. Haley. St. Martin's Press 2014. 448 p.
ISBN 9780312600655
Grades: Adult 996.9
1. Territorial expansion 2. United States history 3. Hawaii 4. United States 5. 20th century 6. History writing — Early 20th century — United States
LC 2014026108

A narrative history of Hawaii profiles its former state as a royal kingdom, recounting the wars fought by European powers for control of its position, its adoption of Christianity and its eventual annexation by the United States. By the author of Passionate Nation.

"Haley underscores how remarkable it was that the islands were able to withstand coercion by French, British and American forces for as long as they did. A pertinent work of keen understanding of the complex Hawaiian story." —*Kirkus*

Includes bibliographical references and index.

Moore, Susanna
Paradise of the Pacific: Approaching Hawaii. Susanna Moore. Farrar, Straus and Giroux 2015. 352 p.
ISBN 9780374298777
Grades: Adult 996.9
1. Social change 2. Culture conflict 3. Acculturation 4. Legends 5. United States history 6. Hawaii 7. 18th century 8. History writing — Regional history — United States
LC 2015002967

The history of Hawaii may be said to be the story of arrivals—from the eruption of volcanoes on the ocean floor 18,000 feet below, the first hardy seeds that over millennia found their way to the islands, and the confused birds blown from their migratory routes, to the early Polynesian adventurers who sailed across the Pacific in double canoes, the Spanish galleons en route to the Philippines, and the British navigators in search of a Northwest Passage, soon followed by pious Protestant missionaries, shipwrecked sailors, and rowdy Irish poachers escaped from Botany Bay—all wanderers washed ashore, sometimes by accident. This is true of many cultures, but in Hawaii, no one seems to have left. And in Hawaii, a set of myths accompanied each of these migrants—legends that shape our understanding of this mysterious place.

"Moore's background in storytelling radiates throughout this work, creating a quick- paced and well-crafted narrative. Highly recommended for the armchair historian and those intrigued by Hawaiian history, maritime exploration, and the history of Christian missionaries. For readers with a continued fascination with the development of the Hawaiian Islands, perusing Julia Flynn Siler's Lost Kingdom might also prove a rewarding endeavor." —*Library Journal*

Includes bibliographical references and index.

998 Arctic islands and Antarctica

Hartman, Darrell
Battle of Ink and Ice: A Sensational Story of News Barons, North Pole Explorers, and the Making of Modern Media. Darrell Hartman. Viking 2023. 400 p.
ISBN 9780593297162
Grades: Adult 998
1. Peary, Robert E. (Robert Edwin), 1856-1920 2. Cook, Frederick Albert, 1865-1940 3. Explorers 4. North Pole expeditions 5. Newspapers 6. Newspaper publishers and publishing 7. Competition 8. Business competition 9. Benefactors 10. Publicity 11. Journalism 12. Conflict of interests 13. Misinformation 14. Exploration 15. Mass media 16. North Pole 17. Arctic regions 18. 1900s (Decade) 19. Adventure writing — Exploration 20. Arts and Entertainment — Writing and Publishing 21. Life stories — People in history — Explorers 22. Life stories — Arts and culture — Writing 23. Nonfiction that reads like fiction 24. Debut title

National Outdoor Book Award for Outdoor Literature, 2023.

In the fall of 1909, a pair of bitter contests captured the world's attention. The American explorers Robert Peary and Frederick Cook both claimed to have discovered the North Pole, sparking a vicious feud that was unprecedented in international scientific and geographic circles. At the same time, the rivalry between two powerful New York City newspapers—the storied Herald and the ascendant Times—fanned the flames of the so-called polar controversy, as each paper financially and reputationally committed itself to an opposing explorer and fought desperately to defend him.

"A thorough account of the unexpected connection between American media and Arctic exploration at the turn of the 20th century….This is an engrossing and readable account of polar exploration, the birth of the modern newspaper, and media wars that feel all too familiar to modern readers." —*Kirkus*

Turney, Chris
1912: The Year the World Discovered Antarctica. Chris Turney. Counterpoint Press 2012. 320 p.
ISBN 9781582437897
Grades: Adult 998
1. Discoveries (in geography) 2. Explorers 3. Expeditions 4. Exploration 5. Antarctica 6. Polar regions 7. Australian literature 8. History writing — Exploration 9. Science Writing — Geology
LC Bl2012038688

Shares the stories behind the sensational newspaper headlines about the expeditions and discoveries in Antarctica a century ago, tracing the scientific achievements of five international teams who also made painful sacrifices to establish foundations for modern exploration.

Includes bibliographical references and index.

998.2 Greenland

Ehrlich, Gretel
This Cold Heaven: Seven Seasons in Greenland. Gretel Ehrlich. Pantheon Books 2001. xv, 377 p. : Illustration; Map
ISBN 9780679442004
Grades: Adult 998.2
1. Ehrlich, Gretel 2. Rasmussen, Knud Johan Victor, 1879-1933 3. Women and nature 4. Men and nature 5. Loneliness 6. Inuit (North American people) 7. Explorers 8. Voyages and travels 9. Greenland 10. 20th century 11. Travel Writing — Living Abroad 12. Adult books for young adults
LC 00069277

Booklist Editors' Choice, 2001; New York Times Notable Book, 2001.

The author describes her seven-year odyssey back and forth to Greenland to explore the culture, society, and lifestyle of the polar Eskimos and to learn about the lives of others who had chosen to live in a land dominated by ice.

"Ehrlich began traveling to Greenland during her recovery from a nearly fatal lightning strike, and her keen, often poetic responses to the beauty of the frigid landscape and the warmth of Inuit families, combined with a profound immersion in Greenland history, infuse her captivating account with both drama and reflection." —*Booklist*

Includes bibliographical references (p. 359-361) and index.

Zuckoff, Mitchell
Frozen in Time: An Epic Story of Survival and a Modern Quest for Lost Heroes of World War II. Mitchell Zuckoff. HarperCollins 2013. 432 p.
ISBN 9780062133434
Grades: Adult 998.2
1. Search and rescue operations 2. World War II 3. Survival (after airplane accidents, shipwrecks, etc.) 4. Airplane accidents 5. Aerial operations 6. Arctic regions 7. 1940s 8. History writing — Wars and conflicts — World War II 9. Adventure writing — Survival 10. Adult books for young adults
LC 2012532376

School Library Journal Best Books: Best Adult Books 4 Teens, 2013.

Drawing on intensive research and a firsthand account of the dangerous 2012 expedition, this thrilling true story of survival, which moves between World War

ESSENTIAL AND RECOMMENDED TITLES
Biography

II and today, follows the survivors of a U.S. cargo plane crash in 1942 and their 148 days spent fighting for their lives during a brutal Arctic winter.

"Zuckoff's…complex narrative involves the fates of three downed missions to Greenland in late 1942, juxtaposed with the events of the modern-day search effort, led by an exploration company in August 2012 and joined by the author. As a result of the many competing strands and characters, some confusion in the details ensues—though maps and a cast of characters are included to help orient readers… an exhaustively layered but exciting account involving characters of enormous courage and stamina." —*Kirkus*

Biography

Abbott, Karen
American Rose: A Nation Laid Bare : The Life and Times of Gypsy Rose Lee. by Karen Abbott. Random House 2010. 320 p.
ISBN 9781400066919
Grades: Adult   B
1. Lee, Gypsy Rose, 1914-1970 2. Stripteasers 3. Burlesque 4. Authors, American 5. 1920s 6. 20th century 7. Biographies 8. History writing — Roaring 20s — United States 9. Life stories — Arts and culture — Performing arts — Entertainers and celebrities

LC 2010015081

Chronicles the life of the controversial striptease entertainer to reveal her intelligence, representation of American values, and achievements against a backdrop of the vaudeville and burlesque circuits.

"Imaginative and engaging, Abbott's biography of the celebrated stripper, who died in 1970 at age 59, also proves a well-informed look at the evolution of musical theater in the early 20th century." —*Publishers Weekly*

Abdelmahmoud, Elamin
Son of Elsewhere: A Memoir in Pieces. Elamin Abdelmahmoud. Ballantine Books 2022. 176 p.
ISBN 9780593496855
Grades: Adult   B
1. Abdelmahmoud, Elamin 2. Immigrants 3. Families 4. Black Canadians 5. Teenage immigrants 6. Growing up 7. Race (Social sciences) 8. Intergenerational relations 9. Ethnic identity 10. Culture shock 11. Identity 12. Belonging 13. Essays 14. Autobiographies and memoirs 15. Canadian literature 16. Life stories — Identity — Immigrants 17. Life stories — Identity — Race and ethnicity 18. Society and culture — Race

Covering such topics as Blackness, faith, and pop culture, this debut collection of essays from a culture writer for Buzzfeed News explores how our experiences and our environments help us in the continuous task of defining who we really are.

"BuzzFeed culture writer Abdelmahmoud debuts with an enthralling meditation on the joys and challenges of coming-of-age as an immigrant." —*Publishers Weekly*

Abdul-Jabbar, Kareem
Coach Wooden and Me: Our 50-year Friendship on and off the Court. Kareem Abdul-Jabbar. Grand Central Publishing 2017. 288 p.
ISBN 9781455542277
Grades: Adult   B
1. Abdul-Jabbar, Kareem, 1947- 2. Wooden, John, 1910-2010 3. Basketball coaches 4. Mentoring 5. Personal conduct 6. Athletic coaches 7. Friendship 8. Autobiographies and memoirs 9. Life stories — Relationships — Friendship 10. Life stories — Sports — Coaches, managers, and owners 11. Sports and competition — Basketball

LC 2018459432

In 1965, 18-year old Lew Alcindor played basketball for Coach John Wooden at UCLA. It was the beginning of what was to become a 50-year long relationship. On the court, they broke basketball records. Off the court, they transcended their athletic achievements to gain even wider recognition and tremendous national respect.

"Abdul-Jabbar and Wooden shared a priceless friendship, and this sensitive, sharply written account brings it to full, vivid life." —*Booklist*

Abramovic, Marina
Walk Through Walls: A Memoir. Marina Abramovic. Crown Publishing 2016. 304 p.
ISBN 9781101905043
Grades: Adult   B
1. Abramovic, Marina 2. Performance artists 3. Women performance artists 4. Performance art 5. Autobiographies and memoirs 6. Life stories — Arts and culture — Performing arts — Entertainers and celebrities
Booklist Editors' Choice, 2016.

A celebrated performance artist details her remarkable life—from her dark childhood in postwar Yugoslavia and her formative relationships to her rise to worldwide fame and her creative efforts to test and overcome the limits of pain and fear to achieve authentic, distinctive expressions.

Abrams, Stacey
Lead from the Outside: How to Build Your Future and Make Real Change. Stacey Abrams. Picador, Henry Holt and Company 2019. xxx, 226 pages
ISBN 9781250214805
Grades: Adult   B
1. Abrams, Stacey 2. African American women politicians 3. Politicians 4. Legislators 5. African American legislators 6. Political participation 7. Political leadership 8. Social action 9. Social change 10. Self-Help — Personal growth — Motivation 11. Politics and global affairs — Elections 12. Politics and global affairs — Civil and human rights

LC Bl2019009214

The Georgia politician describes her own experiences working in business and politics and offers guidance for people outside of traditional social groups to pursue success by recognizing their passion and pursuing it with their special perspective and strengths.

"Abrams offers a handbook for the dispossessed, disenfranchised, and underrepresented for rising to our rightful place at the table, in the boardroom, and eventually, in office. Calling her book the outsider's version of the Art of War, the author reveals herself to be a worthy successor to Sun Tzu." —*Kirkus*
Includes index.

Abu Sayf, Atif
The Drone Eats with Me: A Gaza Diary. Atef Abu Saif. Beacon Press 2016. 256 p.
ISBN 9780807049105
Grades: Adult   B
1. Abu Sayf, Atif 2. Palestinian people 3. Arab-Israeli conflict 4. War 5. Politics and government 6. Gaza Strip 7. Autobiographies and memoirs 8. Life stories — Facing adversity — War and oppression 9. Politics and global affairs — World politics — Southwest Asia and North Africa (Middle East) — Israel and Palestine

LC 2015044062

A writer and teacher from Jabalia refugee camp presents a first-hand account from the 50-day Israel-Gaza conflict that began in early July 2014 and left more than 2,000 people dead, offering an intimate glimpse of life during wartime as he, his wife and two young children attempt to live their lives with a sense of normalcy in spite of ever-present danger.
Includes bibliographical references.

Abuelaish, Izzeldin
I Shall Not Hate: A Gaza Doctor's Sacrifice on the Road to Peace and Human Dignity. Izzeldin Abuelaish. Walker & Co. 2010. 224 p.
ISBN 9780802779175
Grades: Adult   B
1. Abuelaish, Izzeldin 2. Physicians 3. Palestinian people 4. Obstetricians 5. Gynecologists 6. Arab-Israeli conflict 7. Politics and government 8. Gaza Strip 9. Israel 10. 20th century 11. Canadian literature 12. Autobiographies and memoirs 13. Politics and global affairs — World politics — Southwest Asia and North Africa (Middle East) — Israel and Palestine 14. Life stories — Facing ad-

versity — War and oppression — War survivors 15. History writing — Arab-Israeli relations — Southwest Asia and North Africa (Middle East)
LC 2010024513

Harvard-trained Palestinian doctor Izzeldin Abuelaish recounts his extraordinary life of devotion to medicine and reconciliation between Israelis and Palestinians.

Originally published: Toronto : Random House Canada, 2010.

Achebe, Chinua

The Education of a British-protected Child: Essays. Chinua Achebe. Alfred A. Knopf 2009. 208 p.

ISBN 9780307272553

Grades: 11 12 Adult B

1. Achebe, Chinua 2. Authors, Nigerian 3. Writing 4. Nigeria 5. 20th century 6. Autobiographies and memoirs 7. Essays 8. Arts and Entertainment — Writing and Publishing 9. Life stories — Arts and culture — Writing — Authors
LC 2009017480

A latest volume of autobiographical essays by the Man Booker International Prize-winning author of Things Fall Apart includes such pieces as "African-American Visitations," "What Is Nigeria to Me?" and "Politics of the Politicians of Language."

"With African literature emerging as a world force, it's good to have Achebe back after more than 20 years, offering 17 sterling essays." —*Library Journal*

There Was a Country: A Personal History of Biafra. Chinua Achebe. Penguin Press 2012. 352 p.

ISBN 9781594204821

Grades: Adult B

1. Achebe, Chinua 2. Authors, Nigerian 3. Civil war 4. African history 5. Nigeria 6. 20th century 7. 1960s 8. Autobiographies and memoirs 9. Life stories — Arts and culture — Writing — Authors 10. History writing — Civil wars and genocide — Africa
LC 2012005603

A world-renowned novelist describes what it was like living through the Biafran War in Nigeria from 1967-1970, detailing the horror of those terrible years and discussing what that time has come to mean for him as a writer.

Includes bibliographical references and index.

Ackerman, Elliot

Places and Names: On War, Revolution, and Returning. Elliot Ackerman. Penguin Press 2019. 256 pages

ISBN 9780525559962

Grades: Adult B

1. Ackerman, Elliot 2. Iraq War, 2003-2011 3. Afghan War, 2001-2021 4. War 5. Marines 6. War correspondents 7. World politics 8. Combat 9. War casualties 10. Friendship 11. Courage 12. Refugee camps 13. Turkey 14. Iraq 15. Afghanistan 16. Autobiographies and memoirs 17. Essays 18. History writing — Military — Military Today 19. Life stories — Law and order — Armed forces personnel
LC 2018041429

The decorated Marine and author of the National Book Award finalist, Dark at the Crossing, draws on five tours of duty to assess the nature of combat and the human cost of the wars in Iraq, Afghanistan and Syria.

"Any fan of Ackerman's previous novels (Waiting for Eden), memoirs on the Iraq or Afghanistan wars, and valuable outlooks on the nature of war and its combatants will find this phenomenal." —*Library Journal*

Ackmann, Martha

★ *These Fevered Days: Ten Pivotal Moments in the Making of Emily Dickinson.* Martha Ackmann. W. W. Norton & Company 2020. 288 p.

ISBN 9780393609301

Grades: Adult B

1. Dickinson, Emily, 1830-1886 2. Poets, American 3. Women poets 4. Writing 5. Women and literature 6. Creativity 7. United States history 8. United States 9. Massachusetts 10. 19th century 11. Biographies 12. Life stories — Arts and culture — Writing — Poets 13. Arts and entertainment — Writing and publishing 14. Nonfiction that reads like fiction

LC 2019044493

Shares remarkable insights into the mythologized world of Emily Dickinson through 10 decisive episodes that marked her evolution as a poet, from her religious crisis as a student at Mount Holyoke through her relationship with sister-in-law first reader, Susan.

"Radiant prose, palpable descriptions, and deep empathy for the poet's sensibility make this biography extraordinary." —*Kirkus*

Includes bibliographical references and index.

Ackroyd, Peter

Charlie Chaplin: A Brief Life. Peter Ackroyd. Doubleday 2014. 304 p.

ISBN 9780385537377

Grades: Adult B

1. Chaplin, Charlie, 1889-1977 2. Comedians 3. Films 4. Actors and actresses 5. United States 6. Biographies 7. Arts and Entertainment — Movies and Television 8. Arts and Entertainment — Comedy 9. Life stories — Arts and culture — Performing arts — Entertainers and celebrities
LC 2014013009

Booklist Editors' Choice, 2014.

A concise portrait of the iconic film star traces his humble theatrical beginnings through his honorary Academy Award win, sharing engaging anecdotes about his lesser-known antics and associations. By the award-winning author of Albion: The Origins of the English Imagination.

"Readers are left with an understanding of Chaplin's background, the biographical details of his long and troubled life, and some idea of the hellish conditions on the exacting filmmaker's sets, but conclusions about his significance as an artist, his work's relationship to the culture at large, and the internal forces that engendered such personal misery and creative transcendence fail to cohere. A comprehensive look at Chaplin the man but lacking as a portrait of the artist and his legacy." —*Kirkus*

Adams, John

Hallelujah Junction: Composing an American Life. John Adams. Farrar, Straus and Giroux 2008. 352 p.

ISBN 9780374281151

Grades: Adult B

1. Adams, John, 1947- 2. Composers 3. Music 4. Creativity 5. Social life and customs 6. United States 7. 20th century 8. Autobiographies and memoirs 9. Biographies 10. Arts and Entertainment — Music 11. Life stories — Arts and culture — Performing arts — Musicians and composers
LC 2008017922

New York Times Notable Book, 2008.

An eminent composer shares the story of his life, from his childhood and early studies in classical composition to his minimalist and "docu-opera" achievements, in an account that evaluates his professional relationships and the social movements that inspired his creative process.

"Readers will enjoy the candor and completeness of the book, which serves as a gateway to an accomplished body of work. Like the author's music: Carefully considered, deliberate and often exciting, gathering together many disparate elements of American life." —*Kirkus*

Includes index.

Adayfi, Mansoor

Don't Forget Us Here: Lost and Found at Guantanamo. Mansoor Adayfi; edited by Antonio Aiello. Hachette Books 2021. 336 p.

ISBN 9780306923869

Grades: Adult B

1. Adayfi, Mansoor 2. Detention of people 3. Imprisonment 4. War on Terrorism, 2001-2009 5. Prisoners 6. Prisoner abuse 7. Human rights 8. Civil rights 9. Prisoners of war 10. Civil rights 11. Guantanamo Bay Naval Base, Cuba 12. Autobiographies and memoirs 13. Life stories — Facing adversity — War and oppression 14. Society and culture — Violence and crime — Criminal justice system 15. Politics and global affairs — Civil and human rights
LC 2021006356

In the Margins Book Awards: Advocacy and Social Justice, 2023.

The moving, eye-opening memoir of an innocent man detained at Gauntanamo Bay for 15 years: a story of humanity in the unlikeliest of places

ESSENTIAL AND RECOMMENDED TITLES
Biography

and an unprecedented look at life at Guantanamo on the eve of its 20th anniversary.

"Adayfi debuts with a searing look at the brutal conditions he endured during his 14 years at the U.S. military's Guantanamo Bay detention camp." —*Publishers Weekly*

Addario, Lynsey
It's What I Do: A Photographer's Life of Love and War. Lynsey Addario. The Penguin Press 2015. 384 p.
ISBN 9781594205378
Grades: Adult **B**
1. Addario, Lynsey 2. Women and war 3. Women photojournalists 4. Women war correspondents 5. Photojournalists 6. War photographers 7. September 11 Terrorist Attacks, 2001 8. Women war photographers 9. Autobiographies and memoirs 10. Life stories — Identity — Gender 11. Life stories — Arts and culture

LC 2014036653

Wisconsin Library Association Literary Award, 2016.

If you've ever wondered why war photographers risk their lives for photos, this heartfelt, powerful memoir will provide some insight. Pulitzer Prize-winning photojournalist Lynsey Addario touches on her quirky childhood in Connecticut before diving into how she went from taking pictures as a hobby to shooting in conflict zones for days on end, including Afghanistan just after 9/11, Lebanon, Iraq, Sudan, Congo, and Libya (where she was kidnapped).

"A brutally real and unrelentingly raw memoir that is as inspiring as it is horrific." —*Kirkus*

Includes index.

Agassi, Andre
Open: An Autobiography. Andre Agassi. Alfred A. Knopf 2009. 400 p.
ISBN 9780307268198
Grades: Adult **B**
1. Agassi, Andre, 1970- 2. Tennis players 3. Professional tennis 4. Tennis 5. Professional tennis players 6. Self-acceptance 7. Self-discovery 8. Autobiographies and memoirs 9. Sports and Competition — Tennis 10. Life stories — Sports — Athletes 11. Sports and Competition — Individual Athlete

LC 2009024004

New York Times Notable Book, 2009.

A stunning memoir by one of the world's most beloved athletes—a nuanced self-portrait, an intensely candid account of a remarkable life, and a thrilling inside view of the pro tennis tour.

"By sharing an unvarnished, at times inspiring story in an arresting, muscular style, Agassi may have just penned one of the best sports autobiographies of all time. Check it's one of the better memoirs out there, period. Fans will devour Agassi's juicy revelations about both himself and other tennis luminaries." —*Time*

Borzoi Book.

Ahmad, Aeham
The Pianist from Syria: A Memoir. Aeham Ahmad, as told to Sandra Hetzl and Ariel Hauptmeier; translated by Emanuel Bergmann. Atria Books 2019. 276 pages : Illustration; Map
ISBN 9781501173493
Grades: Adult **B**
1. Ahmad, Aeham, 1988- 2. Pianists 3. Refugees, Palestinian 4. War 5. Arab-Israeli conflict 6. Piano music 7. Civil war 8. Music 9. Southwest Asia and North Africa (Middle East) history 10. Damascus, Syria 11. Syria 12. Germany 13. Palestine 14. 2010s 15. 2020s 16. Autobiographies and memoirs 17. Life stories — Facing adversity — War and oppression — Refugees 18. Life stories — Arts and culture — Performing arts — Musicians and composers

The prize-winning human-rights activist and celebrated pianist traces the story of his escape from war-torn Syria, drawing on first-person perspectives to offer urgent insights into the Palestinian refugee crisis.

"Well-rendered and affecting, this is a fine delineation of the plight of an unwitting protagonist in the Syrian conflagration." —*Kirkus*

Originally published in the UK as the Pianist of Damascus.

Al-Maria, Sophia
The Girl Who Fell to Earth: A Memoir. Sophia Al-maria. HarperCollins 2012. 320 p.
ISBN 9780061999758
Grades: 9 10 11 12 Adult **B**
1. Growing up 2. Arab Americans 3. Filmmakers 4. Filmmaking 5. Voyages and travels 6. Autobiographies and memoirs 7. Life stories — Relationships — Growing up

LC 2012285305

Middle East Book Award, Youth Literature Winner, 2013.

An award-winning young filmmaker and writer's funny and wry coming-of-age memoir about growing up in between the American and Arab cultures.

"Al-Maria's narrative is laced with keen observations on Bedouin culture, class distinctions, sexual rules, and everyday life in the Middle East and America. Her story is a satisfying trek through a complex cross-cultural landscape toward a creative and satisfying life." —*Publishers Weekly*

Albers, Patricia
Joan Mitchell: Lady Painter. by Patricia Albers. Alfred A. Knopf 2011. 544 p.
ISBN 9780375414374
Grades: Adult **B**
1. Mitchell, Joan, 1926-1992 2. Abstract expressionism 3. Abstract expressionists 4. Women painters 5. Painters 6. Expressionism (Art) 7. United States 8. Biographies 9. Arts and Entertainment — Painting, Drawing, and Sculpture 10. Life stories — Arts and culture — Artists

LC 2011000457

A reconstruction of the major Abstract Expressionist's life includes coverage of her debutante years in the Midwest, her marriage to Barney Rosset, Jr, and her pioneering achievements as a woman in male-dominated artistic circles.

"This is a biography of Joan Mitchell (192592), a major 20th-century American artist. This significant biography covers all aspects of Mitchell's life, including her synesthesia, eidetic memory, alcoholism, troubled relationships, and art. Filled with intimate details of her complex personality and unconventional lifestyle, this is a conscientiously objective yet sympathetic portrait of the lady painter and the social and cultural contexts in which she became a successful artist in the male-dominated Parisian and New York art worlds." —*Library Journal*

A Borzoi book; Includes bibliographical references and index.

Albertine, Viv
Clothes, Clothes, Clothes. Music, Music, Music : Boys, Boys, Boys: A Memoir. Viv Albertine. Thomas Dunne Books 2015. 432 p.
ISBN 9781250065995
Grades: Adult **B**
1. Albertine, Viv, 1954- 2. Vicious, Sid 3. Jones, Mick 4. Punk rock musicians 5. Women musicians 6. Self esteem 7. Gender role 8. Punk rock music 9. Music history and criticism 10. Popular culture 11. English history 12. Great Britain 13. 20th century 14. Autobiographies and memoirs 15. Arts and Entertainment — Music — Rock 16. Life stories — Arts and culture — Performing arts — Musicians and composers 17. Life stories — Identity — Gender

LC 2014029971

As lead guitarist and songwriter for the seminal band the Slits, she influenced a future generation of artists including Kurt Cobain and Carrie Brownstein. She formed a band with Sid Vicious and was there the night he met Nancy Spungeon. She tempted Johnny Thunders, toured America with the Clash, dated Mick Jones, and inspired the classic Clash anthem "Train in Vain." but Albertine was no mere muse. In Clothes, Clothes, Clothes. Music, Music, Music. Boys, Boys, Boys, Albertine delivers a unique and unfiltered look at a traditionally male-dominated scene.

"This pioneer and pivotal punk rocker discusses her relationships/Friendships with fellow musicians Joe Strummer, Johnny Rotten, Sid Vicious, and Johnny Thunders in this fascinating insiders look at the punk scene from a female perspective." —*Booklist*

PUBLIC LIBRARY CORE COLLECTION: NONFICTION
Twentieth Edition

Albom, Mitch
Finding Chika: A Little Girl, an Earthquake, and the Making of a Family. Mitch Albom. HarperCollins 2019. 256 p.
ISBN 9780062952394
Grades: Adult B
1. Jeune, Chika 2. Albom, Mitch, 1958- 3. Orphans 4. Survival (after earthquakes) 5. Children with terminal illnesses 6. Families 7. Adoption 8. Child care 9. Haiti 10. United States 11. Life stories — Facing adversity — Disasters and tragedies 12. Family and Relationships — Parenting — Adoption 13. Life stories — Facing adversity — Medical issues — Physical illness 14. Life stories — Relationships — Parent and child 15. Family and Relationships — Illness and the Family

LC Bl2019025255

The author traces the inspirational story of a child from the Have Faith Haiti Orphanage, whose short life of poverty and incurable illness prompted her loving adoption into his family.

Tuesdays with Morrie: An Old Man, a Young Man, and Life's Greatest Lesson. Mitch Albom. Doubleday 1997. 192 p.
ISBN 9780385484510
Grades: 11 12 Adult B
1. Schwartz, Morris S. 2. Death 3. Friendship 4. Purpose in life 5. People with amyotrophic lateral sclerosis 6. College teachers 7. Teacher-student relationships 8. People with terminal illnesses 9. Men 10. Social life and customs 11. United States 12. Page to screen 13. Autobiographies and memoirs 14. Life stories — Relationships 15. Family and Relationships — Aging and Death 16. Family and Relationships — Friendship

LC 96052535

A sportswriter conveys the wisdom of his late mentor, professor Morrie Schwartz, recounting their weekly conversations as Schwartz lay dying.

"As a student at Brandeis University in the late 1970s, Albom was especially drawn to his sociology professor, Morris Schwartz. On graduation he vowed to keep in touch with him, which he failed to do until 1994, when he saw a segment about Schwartz on the TV program Nightline, and learned that he had just been diagnosed with Lou Gehrig's disease. By then a sports columnist for the Detroit Free Press . Albom was idled by the newspaper strike in the Motor City and so had the opportunity to visit Schwartz in Boston every week until the older man died. Their dialogue is the subject of this moving book." —*Publishers Weekly*

Albright, Madeleine Korbel
Hell and Other Destinations: A 21st-century Memoir. Madeleine Albright. HarperCollins 2020. xi, 370 p.
ISBN 9780062802255
Grades: Adult B
1. Albright, Madeleine Korbel 1937-2022 2. Women cabinet officers 3. Women politicians 4. Diplomatic and consular service 5. Political consultants 6. Aging 7. Diplomacy 8. International relations 9. United States 10. 21st century 11. Autobiographies and memoirs 12. Life stories — Politics — Politicians 13. Politics and global affairs — World politics 14. History writing — Early 21st century — United States

LC Bl2020007191

The bestselling author and former Secretary of State—one of the world's most admired and tireless public servants—reflects on the final stages of her career and how she has blazed her own trail in her later years.

"This passionately told account of Albright's 'Afterlife' will inspire readers to become involved in the issues meaningful to them. Recommended for all interested in politics, leadership, and women's studies." —*Library Journal*

Also published in large print format.

Alden, Ginger
Elvis and Ginger: Elvis Presley's Fiancee and Last Love Finally Tells Her Story. Ginger Alden. Berkley Publishing Group 2014. 400 pages
ISBN 9780425266335
Grades: Adult B
1. Presley, Elvis, 1935-1977 2. Alden, Ginger 3. Relationships between young women and older men 4. Engaged people 5. Rock music 6. Singers 7. Rock musicians 8. Men-women relations 9. United States 10. Biographies 11. Life stories — Arts and culture — Performing arts — Musicians and composers 12. Arts and entertainment — Music — Rock 13. Life stories — Relationships — Couples

LC 2014009089

Breaking her thirty-year silence, the former fiancee to Elvis Presley tells the story of her whirlwind romance with the King and what it was like being in Graceland when fifty thousand mourners arrived to pay their respects.

"Its an outpouring of affection for a man who has stayed in the authors mind all these years, a way for her to show the world the Elvis she knew. The book has a pretty much guaranteed readership, as many Elvis fans will read anything and everything that appears in print about their idol." —*Booklist*

Alderton, Dolly
Everything I Know About Love: A Memoir. Dolly Alderton. HarperCollins 2020. 360 p.
ISBN 9780062968784
Grades: Adult B
1. Alderton, Dolly 2. Women journalists 3. Growing-up 4. Interpersonal relations 5. Friendship 6. Dating 7. Family relationships 8. Job hunting 9. Adulthood 10. Love 11. Women 12. Men-women relations 13. Self-acceptance 14. England 15. Autobiographies and memoirs 16. Biographies 17. Page to screen 18. Life stories — Relationships — Growing up 19. Life stories — Arts and culture — Writing — Journalists 20. Family and Relationships — Growing Up

The award-winning Sunday Times columnist and co-host of the High Low podcast presents a U.S. release of her internationally best-selling memoir about growing up, aging and learning to navigate relationships and a career.

"A poignant breath of fresh air for those who struggled—or are struggling—with the dramedy of early adulthood." —*Kirkus*

Made into a television show on Peacock, 2022; First published in 2018 by Fig Tree, an imprint of Penguin Random House UK.

Aldrin, Buzz
No Dream Is Too High. Buzz Aldrin with Ken Abraham. National Geographic Society 2016. 223 pages
ISBN 9781426216497
Grades: Adult B
1. Aldrin, Buzz 2. Astronauts 3. Space flight to the moon 4. Apollo 11 (Spacecraft) 5. Space exploration 6. Aviation history 7. United States 8. Autobiographies and memoirs 9. Biographies 10. Life stories — Science, technology, and medicine — Astronauts and pilots

LC 2015037069

The American astronaut shares the wisdom and guiding principles he has gleaned throughout his historical career, sharing accompanying anecdotes and memories on such topics as his initial rejection as an astronaut and his eightieth-birthday Galapagos dive.

"Aldrin's journey will engage space exploration enthusiasts, and his motivational advice will connect especially well with young adults." —*Library Journal*

Alekhina, Mariija
Riot Days. Maria Alyokhina. Metropolitan Books 2017. 195 p.
ISBN 9781250164926
Grades: Adult B
1. Alekhina, Mariija, 1988- 2. Punk rock musicians 3. Resistance to government 4. Protest movements 5. Imprisonment 6. Moscow, Russia 7. Autobiographies and memoirs 8. Life stories — Politics — Activists and reformers 9. History writing — Europe — Russia 10. Life stories — Arts and culture — Performing arts — Musicians and composers

LC 2017035437

In February 2012, Maria Alyokhina and other members of the radical collective Pussy Riot took on the Orthodox church and its support for Vladimir Putin's authoritarian regime. For this, they were charged with "organized hooliganism" and were tried while confined in a cage and guarded by Rottweilers. The trial and Alyokhina's subsequent imprisonment became an international cause; her two-year sentence launched a bitter struggle against the Russian prison system and an iron-willed refusal to be deprived of her humanity.

Also published: London : Allen Lane, 2017.

ESSENTIAL AND RECOMMENDED TITLES
Biography

Alexander, Kwame
Why Fathers Cry at Night: A Memoir in Love Poems, Letters, Recipes, and Remembrances. Kwame Alexander. Little, Brown & Company 2023. 256 p.
ISBN 9780316417228
Grades: Adult   B
1. Alexander, Kwame 2. Authors 3. African American families 4. Growing up 5. Marriage 6. Divorce 7. Fatherhood 8. Fathers and daughters 9. Intergenerational relations 10. Death of mothers 11. Grief 12. Loss 13. Vulnerability 14. Identity 15. Recipes 16. Hope 17. Unconditional love 18. North American people 19. American people 20. Autobiographies and memoirs 21. Life stories — Relationships — Family 22. Life stories — Identity 23. Life stories — Facing adversity — Coping with death 24. Family and Relationships — Families

In a powerfully intimate and non-traditional (or "new-fashioned") memoir, Kwame Alexander shares snapshots of a man learning how to love. He attempts to deal with the unravelling of his marriage and the grief of his mother's recent passing while sharing the solace he found in learning how to perfect her famous fried chicken dish. With an open heart, Alexander weaves together memories of his past to try and understand his greatest love: His daughters. Why Fathers Cry at Night inspires bravery and vulnerability in every reader who has experienced the reckless passion, heartbreak, failure, and joy that define the whirlwind woes and wonders of love.

"A poetic and epistolary collage focused on familial, romantic, and nourishing love....This magnanimous hybrid-form memoir is rich with solace and wisdom." —*Kirkus*

Alexander, Larry
Biggest Brother: The Life of Major D. Winters, the Man Who Led the Band of Brothers. Larry Alexander. NAL Caliber 2005. xxii, 287 p. : Illustration
ISBN 9780451215109
Grades: Adult   B
1. Winters, Richard D. 2. Soldiers 3. World War II 4. Military history 5. Military campaigns 6. United States 7. Biographies 8. History writing — Wars and conflicts — World War II 9. Life stories — Law and order — Armed forces personnel
LC 2004027330

A tribute complemented by the insights of family, friends, and fellow veterans chronicles the war-time accomplishments of Major Richard D. Winters, the skillful leader of the Band of Brothers, the legendary fighting unit of World War II.

Complemented by never-before-seen photographs and insights by family, friends, and fellow veterans, this inspirational chronicle pays tribute to the war-time accomplishments of Major Richard D. Winters, the skillful leader of the Band of Brothers, the legendary fighting unit of World War II.

"This is the story of what distinguished Easy Company from other first-class field units: Its leadership, in the person of Major Richard Winters, its commander. Alexander is especially good at showing how Winters' sense of responsibility developed as a student, an enlistee, in OCS, and as an officer. He also gives a detailed picture of the army of 60-plus years ago, and the process that turned thousands of young civilians into the men who beat the Germans." —*Booklist*

Includes bibliographical references p. (p. 290) and index.

Alexander, Paul
Bitter Crop: The Heartache and Triumph of Billie Holiday's Last Year. Paul Alexander. Alfred A. Knopf 2024. 304 p.
ISBN 9780593315903
Grades: Adult   B
1. Holiday, Billie, 1915-1959 2. Jazz singers 3. Blues musicians 4. African American women 5. African American singers 6. American people 7. United States 8. Biographies 9. Arts and Entertainment — Music — Jazz and the Blues 10. Life stories — Arts and culture — Performing arts — Musicians and composers
LC 2023017461

An acclaimed biographer examines the final tumultuous year of the legendary jazz singer's life and her continued artistic brilliance despite drug abuse, relationships with violent men and run-ins with the law.

"A portrait as affecting and indelible as Holiday's exquisite performances." —*Booklist*

Alford, Terry
Fortune's Fool: The Life of John Wilkes Booth. Terry Alford. Oxford University Press 2015. 454 pages : Illustration
ISBN 9780195054125
Grades: Adult   B
1. Booth, John Wilkes, 1838-1865 2. Lincoln, Abraham, 1809-1865 3. Biographies 4. True Crime — Murder 5. True Crime — Historical Crime 6. Life stories — Law and order — Criminals and law-breakers

National Book Critics Circle Award for Biography finalist, 2015.

In Fortune's Fool, Terry Alford provides the first comprehensive look at the life of an enigmatic figure whose life has been overshadowed by his final, infamous act.

Ali, Fatima
★ *Savor: A Chef's Hunger for More.* Fatima Ali with Tarajia Morrell; foreword by Farezeh Durrani. Ballantine Books, an imprint of Random House, a division of Penguin Random House LLC 2022. 352 p.
ISBN 9780593355190
Grades: Adult   B
1. Ali, Fatima, -2019 2. Women cooks 3. Cooks 4. Bone cancer 5. Food 6. Identity 7. LGBTQIA+ people 8. Pakistani Americans 9. Families 10. Resilience 11. Sexuality 12. Mortality 13. South Asian Americans 14. South Asian people 15. People with terminal illnesses 16. Women 17. Autobiographies and memoirs 18. Life stories — Identity — LGBTQIA+ 19. Food Writing — Memoirs and biographies
LC 2022000429

James Beard Foundation Book Awards, Writing and Literature, 2023.

In this triumphant memoir, a young, boundary-breaking culinary star, diagnosed with a rare form of bone cancer, spends her final year savoring the world, delicious food and her loved ones, as she reflects on her life and her identity as a chef, a daughter and a queer woman butting up against traditional views.

"This portrait of a remarkable talent whose life was cut short is a tough one to forget." —*Publishers Weekly*

Ali, Wajahat
Go Back to Where You Came From: And Other Helpful Recommendations on How to Become American. Wajahat Ali. W. W. Norton & Company 2022. 256 p.
ISBN 9780393867978
Grades: Adult   B
1. Ali, Wajahat 2. Children of immigrants 3. Pakistani Americans 4. Political activists 5. Identity 6. Playwrights 7. Immigrants 8. Racism 9. Islamophobia 10. Journalists 11. South Asian Americans 12. South Asian people 13. Interethnic relations 14. United States 15. Autobiographies and memoirs 16. Biographies 17. Life stories — Identity — Immigrants
LC 2021037426

A rollercoaster ride of a memoir, by turns hilarious and heartbreaking, by the journalist, playwright, and political activist Wajahat Ali. "Go back to where you came from, you terrorist!" This is just one of the many warm, lovely, and helpful tips that Wajahat Ali and other children of immigrants receive on a daily basis. Go back where exactly? His hometown in the San Francisco Bay Area, where he can't afford rent? Awkward, left-handed, suffering from OCD, and wearing Husky pants, Ali grew up on the margins of the American mainstream, devoid of Brown superheroes, where people like him were portrayed as goofy sidekicks, shop owners with funny accents, sweaty terrorists, or aspiring sweaty terrorists. Driven by his desire to expand the American narrative to include protagonists who look like him, he became a writer, and in the aftermath of the 9/11 terror attacks, an accidental activist and ambassador of all things Muslim-y. He uses his pen with turmeric-stained fingernails to fill in missing narratives, challenge the powerful, and booby trap racist stereotypes. In his bold, hopeful and hilarious memoir, Ali offers indispensable lessons and strategies to help cultivate a more compassionate America.

"A Pakistani American memoir that shines with passion, intelligence, and humor." —*Kirkus*

Includes bibliographical references.

PUBLIC LIBRARY CORE COLLECTION: NONFICTION
Twentieth Edition

Alinder, Mary Street
Ansel Adams: A Biography. Mary Street Alinder. H. Holt 1996. xx, 489 p, [32] p. of plates : Illustration
ISBN 9780805041163
Grades: Adult B
1. Adams, Ansel, 1902-1984 2. Photographers 3. Environmentalists 4. Nature photography 5. Yosemite Valley 6. Biographies 7. Life stories — Arts and culture — Artists
LC 95044741

Traces the life and career of Ansel Adams, including his early years in San Francisco, his relationship with the Native Americans of Yosemite, and the influences on his photography and painting of western landscapes.

"As Alinder traces the straightforward course of Adams' dazzling career . she emphasizes the connection between his stunning landscape photography and his zealous work with the Sierra Club. Alinder is as lucid on the topic of Adams' technical mastery as on his environmentalism and aesthetics, and she also tackles the muddle of his contentious private life with aplomb and candor." —*Booklist*

Includes bibliographical references (p. 459-469) and index.

Alinizhad, Masih
The Wind in My Hair: My Fight for Freedom in Modern Iran. Masih Alinejad. Little Brown & Company 2018. 352 p.
ISBN 9780316548915
Grades: Adult B
1. Alinizhad, Masih, 1976- 2. Social advocates 3. Hijab (Islamic clothing) 4. Women journalists 5. Women exiles 6. Women's resistance and revolts 7. Women and oppression (Psychology) 8. Iran 9. Autobiographies and memoirs 10. Life stories — Politics — Activists and reformers 11. Society and culture — Gender — Women
LC Bl2018029726

An Iranian journalist in exile discusses leaving her country, challenging tradition and sparking an online movement against compulsory hijab.

"Alinejad's journey both within and outside of Iran depicts her resilience and determination to lead a full life amid an often repressive society. For all readers interested in women's memoirs and women's rights." —*Library Journal*

Allende, Isabel
My Invented Country: A Nostalgic Journey Through Chile. Isabel Allende; translated from the Spanish by Margaret Sayers Peden. Perennial 2004. 224 p.
ISBN 9780060545673
Grades: Adult B
1. Allende, Isabel 2. Exiles 3. Immigrants 4. Writing 5. September 11 Terrorist Attacks, 2001 6. Authors 7. Chilean people 8. South American history 9. Chile 10. 20th century 11. Autobiographies and memoirs 12. Arts and Entertainment — Writing and Publishing 13. Life stories — Arts and culture — Writing — Authors 14. Adult books for young adults 15. History writing — Regimes and political violence — Latin America
LC Bl2004004873

The author explores the landscapes and people of her native country; recounts the 1973 assassination of her uncle, which caused her to go into exile; and shares her experiences as an immigrant in post-September 11 America.

"In this memoir-cum-study of her home ground, the author delves into the history, social mores and idiosyncrasies of Chile, where she was raised, showing, in the process, how that land has served as her muse. This is a reflective book, lacking the pull of Allende's fiction but unearthing intriguing elements of the author's captivating history." —*Publishers Weekly*

Originally published: New York : HarperCollins, 2003.

★ *Paula.* Isabel Allende; translated from the Spanish by Margaret Sayers Peden. Harper Collins 1995. 330 p.
ISBN 9780060927219
Grades: 11 12 Adult B
1. Allende, Isabel 2. Allende family 3. Mother and adult daughter 4. Death 5. Death of daughters 6. Family relationships 7. Authors 8. Chilean people 9. Coping 10. South American history 11. Chile 12. Venezuela 13. California 14. 20th century 15. Autobiographies and memoirs 16. Family and Relationships — Parenting 17. Family and Relationships — Illness and the Family 18. Life stories — Facing adversity — Coping with death 19. Life stories — Relationships — Parent and child
LC 95002452

ALA Notable Book, 1996; Booklist Editors' Choice, 1995.

Written next to the hospital bedside of her critically ill daughter, the acclaimed author presents the story of her ancestors and youth, reflecting on the challenges and achievements of one family during a turbulent era in Chilean history.

"Allende interweaves the story of her own life with the slow dying of her 28-year-old daughter, Paula." —*Publishers Weekly*

Originally published in Spanish with the same title: Barcelona : Plaza & Janes, 1994.

The Sum of Our Days: A Memoir. Isabel Allende; translated from the Spanish by Margaret Sayers Peden. Harper Collins 2007. 320 p.
ISBN 9780061551833
Grades: 11 12 Adult B
1. Allende, Isabel 2. Writing 3. Authors 4. Chilean people 5. Coping 6. 20th century 7. Autobiographies and memoirs 8. Arts and Entertainment — Writing and Publishing 9. Life stories — Arts and culture — Writing — Authors
LC 2007033251

A narrative memoir of the author's life in the wake of her daughter's tragic death describes the idiosyncratic network of friends she has gathered around herself and the realizations she has formed about such topics as love, parenthood, and addiction.

"In this sequel to her memoir Paula (1995), about the yearlong coma suffered by her daughter, Chilean novelist Allende tells of the difficult years following Paula's death. . . . Surprisingly candid, frequently funny, and highly aware of her own failings, Allende is a person fully engaged in life, and readers will find her eloquent memoir inspirational reading." —*Booklist*

Translation of : Suma de los dias; Sequel to: Paula.

Allgor, Catherine
A Perfect Union: Dolley Madison and the Creation of the American Nation. Catherine Allgor. Henry Holt & Co. 2006. x, 493 p. : Illustration; Portrait
ISBN 9780805073270
Grades: Adult B
1. Madison, Dolley, 1768-1849 2. Women and politics 3. Presidents' spouses 4. Men-women relations 5. Politics and government 6. United States 7. 19th century 8. 18th century 9. Biographies 10. History writing — Presidency — 19th century — United States 11. History writing — Early America — United States 12. History writing — Women's history 13. Life stories — Politics — Politicians
LC 2005055127

Booklist Editors' Choice, 2006.

An in-depth study of the early days of the American republic offers an intriguing portrait of the life of a remarkable American woman, profiling the seminal role played by Dolley Madison amid the turbulent and complex political, social, and cultural world of the early nineteenth century.

Includes bibliographical references (p. [409]-470) and index.

Alter, Jonathan
His Very Best: Jimmy Carter, a Life. Jonathan Alter. Simon & Schuster 2020. 672 p.
ISBN 9781501125485
Grades: Adult B
1. Carter, Jimmy, 1924- 2. Political leadership 3. Social advocacy 4. Presidents 5. United States 6. 20th century 7. Biographies 8. Life stories — Politics — Politicians 9. History writing — Presidency — 20th century — United States

An intimate portrait of the 39th President draws on fresh archival material to trace Jimmy Carter's improbable rise from a humble peanut farmer and complex man of faith to an American President and Nobel Prize-winning humanitarian.

"Alter's fluidly written account adds depth and nuance to the popular understanding of Carter's presidency, yet his post-White House career gets short shrift. Still, this is an illuminating and persuasive reevaluation of Carter's legacy." —*Publishers Weekly*

ESSENTIAL AND RECOMMENDED TITLES
Biography

Alvis-Walker, Marcie
Everybody Come Alive: A Memoir in Essays. Marcie Alvis-Walker. Convergent 2023. 288 p.
ISBN 9780593443729
Grades: Adult   B
1. Alvis-Walker, Marcie 2. African American women 3. Spiritual life 4. Identity 5. Race relations 6. African Americans 7. United States 8. Essays 9. Life stories — Facing adversity 10. Society and culture — Race
LC 2022026401
A dazzling memoir that explores what it means to become fully alive and holy when we embrace the silenced stories we've inherited—from the creator of Black Coffee with White Friends.

"Everybody Come Alive is an appropriate fit for a diversity, equity, and inclusion book collection, and will challenge readers to create their own stories by looking within, considering the people who shape them, and questioning the world around them." —*Booklist*

Includes bibliographical references.

Ambroz, David
A Place Called Home: A Memoir. David Ambroz. Legacy Lit 2022. 256 p.
ISBN 9780306903540
Grades: Adult   B
1. Ambroz, David 2. Homeless children 3. Foster children 4. Homelessness 5. Poverty 6. Lawyers 7. Gay men 8. Psychic trauma 9. New York city 10. Autobiographies and memoirs 11. Life stories — Facing adversity 12. Life stories — Politics — Activists and reformers 13. Society and culture — Wealth and class — Poverty
LC 2022019466
A national poverty and child welfare expert who was raised homeless in New York City discusses how he escaped poverty to become a powerful child welfare advocate for the Obama administration and major U.S. companies.

"The heart of this first memoir is both a raw account of Ambroz's journey to adulthood and a powerful, uncompromising call to action for significant change." —*Booklist*

Amos, Tori
Resistance: A Songwriter's Story of Hope, Change, and Courage. Tori Amos. Atria 2020. 176 p.
ISBN 9781982104153
Grades: Adult   B
1. Amos, Tori, 1963- 2. Patriarchy 3. Social advocacy 4. Feminism 5. Environmentalism 6. Social change 7. Musicians 8. Me Too movement 9. Music and society 10. Songwriters 11. Autobiographies and memoirs 12. Society and culture — General 13. Life stories — Arts and culture — Performing arts — Musicians and composers
LC Bl2020011939
The Grammy-nominated music artist reflects on how her career has reflected her political views on toxic patriarchal power structures, urging readers for active engagement in protecting the environment and supporting the #MeToo movement.

"In this thoughtful book, Amos shares the inspiration for many of her songs, beginning with her teenage gig playing piano at a gay bar in Washington, DC, and weaving through years of touring, writing, successes, and setbacks." —*Booklist*

Anand, Anita
The Patient Assassin: A True Tale of Massacre, Revenge, and India's Quest for Independence. Anita Anand. Simon & Schuster 2019. 320 p.
ISBN 9781501195709
Grades: Adult   B
1. Udham Singh, 1899-1940 2. Massacres 3. Revolutionaries 4. Revenge 5. Atrocities 6. Colonialism 7. National liberation movements 8. India 9. Biographies 10. Life stories — Politics — Activists and reformers 11. History writing — Asia — South Asia — India

The dramatic true story of a celebrated young survivor of a 1919 British massacre in India, and his ferocious twenty-year campaign of revenge that made him a hero to hundreds of millions—and spawned a classic legend.

Andersen, Christopher P.
The Good Son: JFK Jr. And The Mother He Loved. Christopher Andersen. Simon & Schuster 2014. 320 p.
ISBN 9781476775562
Grades: Adult   B
1. Kennedy, John F. Jr, 1960-1999 2. Kennedy family 3. Onassis, Jacqueline Kennedy, 1929-1994 4. Children of presidents 5. Mothers and sons 6. Interpersonal relations 7. Biographies 8. Life stories — Relationships — Parent and child 9. Life stories — People in history — Famous families 10. Life stories — Politics — Politicians
LC 2014024249
At the heart of The Good Son is the most important relationship in JFK Jr.'s life: that with his mother, the beautiful and mysterious Jackie Kennedy Onassis. Andersen explores his reactions to his mother's post-Dallas suicidal depression and growing dependence on prescription drugs (as well as men); how Jackie felt about the women in her son's life, from Madonna and Sarah Jessica Parker, to Daryl Hannah and Carolyn Bessette, to his turbulent marriage; the senseless plane crash the took his life; the aftermath of shock, loss, grief, and confusion; and much more. Offering new insights into the intense, tender, often stormy relationship between this iconic mother and son, The Good Son is a riveting, bittersweet biography for lovers of all things Kennedy.

Sensitive and astute, Andersen's book offers an intriguing look at a fraught mother-son dynamic that, years after the deaths of both Jackie and John Jr, still has the power to mesmerize. An intimate and compelling look at 'the most brilliant star in the Kennedy firmament.' —*Kirkus*

Andersen, Jens
Astrid Lindgren: The Woman Behind Pippi Longstocking. Jens Andersen; translated from the Swedish by Caroline Waight. Yale University Press 2018. 360 p.
ISBN 9780300226102
Grades: Adult   B
1. Lindgren, Astrid, 1907-2002 2. Children's literature authors 3. Authors, Swedish 4. Longstocking, Pippi (Fictitious character) 5. Biographies 6. Translations — Swedish to English 7. Life stories — Arts and culture — Writing — Authors 8. Arts and Entertainment — Writing and Publishing — Literary criticism
LC 2017940326
The first English-language biography of Astrid Lindgren provides a moving and revealing portrait of the beloved Scandinavian literary icon whose adventures of Pippi Longstocking have influenced generations of young readers all over the world.

"Andersen incisively and resonantly chronicles the evolution of Lindgrens progressive work and its impact, along with her influence as a childrens-book editor and environmental activist, bringing to new light a writer as empowered and exhilarating as her most cherished creation." —*Booklist*

Originally published: Sweden : Nordstedts, 2014; Translated from the Swedish.

Anderson, Jon Lee
Che Guevara: A Revolutionary Life. Jon Lee Anderson. Grove Press 1997. xv, 814 p. : Illustration; Map
ISBN 9780802116000
Grades: 11 12 Adult   B
1. Guevara, Che, 1928-1967 2. Guerrillas 3. Revolutions 4. Revolutionaries 5. South American history 6. Latin America 7. 20th century 8. Biographies 9. Life stories — Politics — Activists and reformers
LC 97003993
Booklist Editors' Choice, 1997; New York Times Notable Book, 1997; Shortlisted for the James Tait Black Memorial Prize for Biography, 1997.

A thorough biography, based on unique access to government documents and extensive interviews with those close to the infamous Latin American rebel, traces Che Guevara's life from its privileged roots to struggles in Cuba and Bolivia.

Includes bibliographical references (p. 777-787) and index.

Anderson, Scott
Lawrence in Arabia: War, Deceit, Imperial Folly and the Making of the Modern Middle East. Scott Anderson. Doubleday 2013. 577 p.

ISBN 9780385532921

Grades: Adult   B

1. Lawrence, T. E. (Thomas Edward), 1888-1935 2. World War I 3. Soldiers 4. Military campaigns 5. Southwest Asia and North Africa (Middle East) history 6. Turkey 7. 1910s 8. History writing — Wars and conflicts — World War I 9. History writing — Nationalism — Southwest Asia and North Africa (Middle East) 10. Nonfiction that reads like fiction

LC 2012049719

ALA Notable Book, 2014; Booklist Editors' Choice, 2013; New York Times Notable Book, 2013; National Book Critics Circle Award for Biography finalist, 2013.

A narrative chronicle of World War I's Arab Revolt explores the pivotal roles of a small group of adventurers and low-level officers who orchestrated a secret effort to control the Middle East, demonstrating how they instigated jihad against British forces, built an elaborate intelligence ring and forged ties to gain valuable oil concessions.

Includes bibliographical references.

Andrews, Julie
Home Work: A Memoir of My Hollywood Years. Julie Andrews, with Emma Walton Hamilton. Hachette Books 2019. 352 p.

ISBN 9780316349253

Grades: Adult   B

1. Andrews, Julie 2. Actors and actresses 3. Fame 4. Marriage 5. Family relationships 6. Musicals 7. Entertainment industry and trade 8. Films 9. Autobiographies and memoirs 10. Life stories — Arts and culture — Performing arts — Actors and actresses 11. Arts and Entertainment — Movies and Television

LC 2019947243

In a follow-up to the critically acclaimed Home, the beloved performing artist reflects on her Hollywood career and the creations of three of her most iconic films, Mary Poppins, the Sound of Music and Victor/Victoria.

Home: A Memoir of My Early Years. by Julie Andrews. Hyperion 2008. 352 p.

ISBN 9780786865659

Grades: Adult   B

1. Andrews, Julie 2. Singers 3. Women singers 4. Growing up 5. Films 6. Actors and actresses 7. Autobiographies and memoirs 8. Arts and Entertainment — Movies and Television 9. Life stories — Arts and culture — Performing arts — Actors and actresses

LC Bl2008001661

A personal account of the iconic actress's pre-fame life traces the time between her birth in 1935 and her discovery by Walt Disney during her 1962 Broadway performance in "Camelot."

"Spanning events from her 1935 birth to the early 1960s, . [the author] covers her rise to fame and ends with Walt Disney casting her in Mary Poppins (1963). The heart of her book documents the rehearsals, tryouts and smash 1956 opening of My Fair Lady. Readers will rejoice, since Andrews is an accomplished writer who holds back nothing while adding a patina of poetry to the antics and anecdotes throughout this memoir of bittersweet backstage encounters and theatrical triumphs." —*Publishers Weekly*

Andrews-Dyer, Helena
Reclaiming Her Time: The Power of Maxine Waters. Helena Andrews-Dyer and R. Eric Thomas; with illustrations by Sabrina Dorsainvil. Dey Street Books 2020. 256 p.

ISBN 9780062992031

Grades: Adult   B

1. Waters, Maxine 2. African American women legislators 3. Social justice 4. African American women politicians 5. Women legislators 6. Biographies 7. Life stories — Politics — Politicians 8. Life stories — Identity — Race and ethnicity 9. Politics and global affairs — Political figures

LC 2020008250

To millions nationwide, Congresswoman Maxine Waters is a hero of the resistance and an icon, serving eye rolls, withering looks, and sharp retorts to any who dare waste her time on nonsense. But behind the Auntie Maxine meme is a seasoned public servant and she's not here to play. Throughout her forty years in public service and eighty years on earth, U.S. Representative for California's 43rd district has been a role model, a crusader for justice, a game-changer, a trailblazer, and an advocate for the marginalized who has long defied her critics, including her most vocal detractor, Donald J. Trump. And she's just getting started. Featuring inspiring highlights from her personal life and political career, beloved memes, and testimonies from her many friends and fans, Reclaiming Her Time is a funny, warm, and admiring portrait of a champion who refuses to stay silent in the face of corruption and injustice.

"Their buoyant and zesty portrait of the woman known as 'Auntie Maxine' is perfect for the vivacious, unconventional, tireless, and essential Waters." —*Booklist*

Includes bibliographical references and index.

Angelou, Maya
★ *I Know Why the Caged Bird Sings.* Maya Angelou. Bantam Books 1993. 289 p.

ISBN 9780553279375

Grades: 11 12 Adult   B

1. Angelou, Maya 2. African American authors 3. African American women authors 4. Intersectionality 5. Authors, American 6. Social life and customs 7. United States 8. 20th century 9. Autobiographies and memoirs 10. Arts and Entertainment — Writing and Publishing 11. Life stories — Arts and culture — Writing — Authors

LC Bl 00012436

This is a 1969 autobiography about the early years of American writer and poet Maya Angelou. The first in a seven-volume series, it is a coming-of-age story that illustrates how strength of character and a love of literature can help overcome racism and trauma. Maya transforms from a victim of racism with an inferiority complex into a self-possessed, dignified young woman capable of responding to prejudice.

"Angelou is a skillful writer; her language ranges from beautifully lyrical prose to earthy metaphor, and her descriptions have power and sensitivity." —*Library Journal*

Sequel: Gather Together in My Name; Originally published: New York : Random House, 1970.

A Song Flung up to Heaven. Maya Angelou. Random House 2002. 212 p.

ISBN 9780375507472

Grades: 11 12 Adult   B

1. Angelou, Maya 2. African American women authors 3. Civil Rights Movement 4. African American authors 5. Women civil rights workers 6. Authors, American 7. Social life and customs 8. United States 9. 20th century 10. Autobiographies and memoirs 11. Biographies 12. Arts and Entertainment — Writing and Publishing 13. Life stories — Arts and culture — Writing — Authors 14. Adult books for young adults

LC 2001034914

In a sixth memoir, the author and poet describes her return from Africa to the U.S, her work with the civil rights movement, and the writing of her first autobiographical work, "I know Why the Caged Bird Sings."

"This sixth installment in Angelou's autobiographical works begins in 1964 as Angelou returned to the U.S. from Ghana. She worked in Watts at the time of the riots, and Malcolm X and Martin Luther King Jr. were both assassinated just before she was to begin working with them. She moved to New York, where she rejoined a vibrant group of famous writers, intellectuals, and friends; worried about her young-adult son; and understood the humor and heartache of a painful love affair. Spiced with her mother's aphorisms, her often-poetic prose is best at the end, as she muses on the condition of Black women and sitting at her mother's table, begins to write I Know Why the Caged Bird Sings." —*Booklist*

Sequel to: All God's Children Need Traveling Shoes.

ESSENTIAL AND RECOMMENDED TITLES
Biography

Anolik, Lili
Hollywood's Eve: Eve Babitz and the Secret History of L.A. Lili Anolik. Scribner 2019. x, 277 pages : Illustration
ISBN 9781501125799
Grades: Adult **B**
1. Babitz, Eve 2. Women artists 3. Women authors, American 4. Social life and customs 5. Hollywood, California 6. 20th century 7. Biographies 8. Arts and Entertainment — Writing and Publishing 9. Life stories — Arts and culture — Artists
LC 2018035881

A portrait of the Hollywood artist details the iconic photograph that catapulted Eve Babitz to notoriety, her high-profile affairs, her unheralded literary achievements, her years in seclusion and her recent re-emergence.

Anthony, Carl Sferrazza
Camera Girl: The Coming of Age of Jackie Bouvier Kennedy. Carl Sferrazza Anthony. Gallery Books 2023. 368 p.
ISBN 9781982141875
Grades: Adult **B**
1. Onassis, Jacqueline Kennedy, 1929-1994 2. Celebrities 3. Women editors 4. Women photographers 5. Presidents' spouses 6. Intellectual life 7. United States 8. 1940s 9. 1950s 10. Biographies 11. Life stories — Politics — Politicians 12. Arts and Entertainment — Writing and Publishing

An illuminating new biography of the young Jackie Bouvier Kennedy that covers her formative adventures abroad in Paris; her life as a writer and photographer at a Washington, DC, newspaper; and her romance with a dashing, charismatic Massachusetts congressman who shared her intellectual passion.

"Prior to her marriage to John F. Kennedy, Jacqueline Bouvier (1929-1994) was an ambitious journalist and photographer, a remarkable period of her life captured in this engaging coming-of-age biography." —*Kirkus*

Nellie Taft: The Unconventional First Lady of the Ragtime Era. Carl Sferrazza Anthony. William Morrow 2005. x, 534 p. : Illustration
ISBN 9780060513825
Grades: Adult **B**
1. Taft, Helen Herron, 1861-1943 2. Taft, William H. (William Howard), 1857-1930 3. Presidents' spouses 4. United States 5. 20th century 6. Biographies 7. History writing — Presidency — 20th century — United States 8. History writing — Women's history 9. Life stories — Politics — Politicians
LC 2004052553

A portrait of the early twentieth-century First Lady describes her bold determination to fulfill a then-untraditional political and public role at the side of her husband, noting her part in the emergence of the Progressive era.

"This lively biography provides an illuminating glimpse into the life of an until-now underappreciated First Lady." —*Booklist*

Includes bibliographical references (p. [509]-513) and index.

Anthony, Carmelo
Where Tomorrows Aren't Promised: A Memoir of Survival and Hope. Carmelo Anthony, with D. Watkins. Gallery Books 2021. 224 p.
ISBN 9781982160593
Grades: Adult **B**
1. Anthony, Carmelo, 1984- 2. Professional basketball players 3. African American men 4. Growing up 5. Street life 6. Poverty 7. Violence 8. Loss 9. Determination 10. Survival 11. Brooklyn, New York City 12. Baltimore, Maryland 13. Autobiographies and memoirs 14. Life stories — Facing adversity 15. Life stories — Sports — Athletes 16. Sports and Competition — Basketball 17. Sports and Competition — Individual Athlete
LC 2021019923

For a long time, Carmelo Anthony's world wasn't any larger than the view of the hoopers and hustlers he watched from the side window of his family's first-floor project apartment in Red Hook, Brooklyn. He faced palpable dangers growing up in the housing projects in Red Hook and West Baltimore's Murphy Homes. He navigated an education system that ignored, exploited, or ostracized him. He suffered the untimely deaths of his closely held loved ones. He struggled to survive physically and emotionally. But with the strength of family and the guidance of key mentors on the streets and on the court, he pushed past lethal odds to endure and thrive. By the time Carmelo found himself at the NBA Draft at Madison Square Garden in 2003 preparing to embark on his legendary career, he wondered: How did a kid who'd had so many hopes, dreams, and expectations beaten out of him by a world of violence, poverty, and racism make it here at all?

"In his debut, NBA All-Star Anthony shoots and scores with a gripping account of how he went from being 'A Black kid from the bottom' to being a world-renowned pro athlete.... Those in search of inspiration will find no shortage of it here." —*Publishers Weekly*

Aptowicz, Cristin O'Keefe
Dr. Mutter's Marvels: A True Tale of Intrigue and Innovation at the Dawn of Modern Medicine. by Cristin O'Keefe Aptowicz. Gotham Books 2014. 371 pages : Illustration
ISBN 9781592408702
Grades: Adult **B**
1. Mutter, Thomas D. (Thomas Dent), 1811-1859 2. Humanists 3. Surgeons 4. Physicians 5. Surgery 6. Pathology 7. Compassion 8. Medical innovations 9. Medical care 10. Philosophy 11. Biographies 12. Life stories — Science, technology, and medicine — Healthcare professionals 13. Science Writing — Medicine and health — Doctors and nurses 14. Adult books for young adults
LC 2014014747

School Library Journal Best Books: Best Adult Books 4 Teens, 2014.

A portrait of the brilliant and eccentric medical innovator who revolutionized American surgery and founded America's most famous medical oddities museum describes his advocacy for clean and compassionate patient care in spite of his numerous detractors.

"In her deftly crafted narrative, the author provides an absorbing account of the charismatic surgeon's life and career as well as a vivid look at the medical practices and prejudices of his time." —*Kirkus*

Includes bibliographical references and index.

Arana, Marie
American Chica: Two Worlds, One Childhood. Marie Arana. Dial Press 2001. 309 p.
ISBN 9780385319621
Grades: 11 12 Adult **B**
1. Arana, Marie 2. Growing up 3. Journalists 4. Multiracial children 5. United States 6. Peru 7. 20th century 8. Autobiographies and memoirs 9. Biographies 10. Family and Relationships — Growing up 11. Life stories — Relationships — Growing up 12. Life stories — Arts and culture — Writing — Journalists 13. Adult books for young adults
LC 00047529

ALA Notable Book, 2002; Library Journal Best Books, 2001; New York Times Notable Book, 2001; National Book Award for Nonfiction finalist, 2001.

A journalist describes her efforts to come to terms with her dual heritage as a Hispanic American and offers a portrait of her family members, including her talented American mother and her brilliant Peruvian father.

"Arana blends a journalist's dedication to research with a style that sings with humor. Her memoir is an outstanding contribution to the growing shelf of Latina literature." —*Publishers Weekly*

Bolivar: American Liberator. Marie Arana. Simon & Schuster 2013. 603 p, 8 p. of plates : Illustration; Color; Map; Portrait
ISBN 9781439110195
Grades: Adult **B**
1. Bolivar, Simon, 1783-1830 2. Leadership 3. Heads of state 4. Revolutionaries 5. National liberation movements 6. Revolutions 7. Command of troops 8. Freedom 9. Equality 10. South American history 11. 19th century 12. Biographies 13. Life stories — Law and order — Armed forces personnel 14. Life stories — Politics — Politicians 15. History writing — Wars and conflicts — Revolutions 16. History writing — Latin America
LC 2012034661

Booklist Editors' Choice, 2013; Los Angeles Times Book Prize for Biography, 2013.

An authoritative portrait of the Latin-American warrior-statesman draws on a wealth of primary documents to set his life against a backdrop of the explosive tensions of 19th-century South America, providing coverage of such topics as his role in the 1813 campaign for Colombian and Venezuelan independence, his legendary love affairs and his achievements as a strategist, abolitionist and diplomat.

"Drawing on Bolvar's voluminous correspondence and political writings, Arana assembles a chronological narrative that does justice to both Bolvar's august achievements and his human imperfections. This well-rounded work reveals not just an accomplished military tactician but also an able statesman." —*Library Journal*

Includes bibliographical references and index.

Archibald, John

Shaking the Gates of Hell: A Search for Family and Truth in the Wake of the Civil Rights Revolution. John Archibald. Alfred A. Knopf 2021. 320 p.
ISBN 9780525658115
Grades: Adult   B

1. Archibald, John, 1963- 2. European American men 3. Civil Rights Movement 4. Christian church and race relations 5. Childhood 6. Children of clergy 7. Fathers 8. Family relationships 9. Social justice 10. Religious ethics 11. Race relations 12. United States history 13. Alabama 14. Autobiographies and memoirs 15. Life stories — Religion and spirituality 16. Life stories — Relationships — Parent and child 17. History writing — 1960s — United States 18. Spirituality and Religion — Christianity 19. Antiracist literature

LC 2020002918

On growing up in the American South of the 1960s—an all-American white boy—son of a long line of Methodist preachers, in the midst of the civil rights revolution, and discovering the culpability of silence within the church.

"A powerful reflection on the influences of family and community and the ability to act justly in tumultuous times." —*Library Journal*

Includes index; Borzoi book.

Arkin, Alan

An Improvised Life: A Memoir. Alan Arkin. Da Capo Press 2011. 224 p.
ISBN 9780306819667
Grades: 11 12 Adult   B

1. Arkin, Alan 2. Film industry and trade 3. Filmmaking 4. Actors and actresses 5. Films 6. United States 7. Autobiographies and memoirs 8. Biographies 9. Arts and Entertainment — Movies and Television 10. Life stories — Arts and culture — Performing arts — Actors and actresses

LC 2010045034

An Improvised Life" is Oscar winner Alan Arkin's wise and unpretentious recollection of the process—artistic and personal—of becoming an actor, and a revealing look into the creative mind of one of the best practitioners on stage or screen.

"Arkin looks back on his career as an actor, but this memoir forgoes the backstage gossip and star-studded anecdotes readers might expect. In fact, the author largely ignores his accomplishments in favor of charting his inner evolution as an artist, focusing on intellectual and spiritual epiphanies that have shaped his approach to acting. . . . Earnest, intelligent and well-observedless a celebrity memoir than a serious consideration of the principles of acting and improvisation." —*Kirkus*

Includes index.

Armstrong, Karen

Buddha. Karen Armstrong. Penguin Books 2004. 240 p.
ISBN 9780143034360
Grades: 11 12 Adult   B

1. Gautama Buddha 2. Enlightenment (Buddhism) 3. Buddhism 4. Spiritual leaders 5. Biographies 6. Spirituality and Religion — Buddhism 7. Spirituality and Religion — Religious Leaders 8. Life stories — Religion and spirituality — Religious and spiritual leaders

LC Bl2004114688

A portrait of the Buddha explores his identities both as an archetypal religious icon and as a man, chronicling his journey from his decision to leave a life of ease and power to his attainment of spiritual enlightenment.

"Armstrong interprets the mythologized story of the Buddha's abandonment of his life of comfort and privilege; commitment to practicing advanced forms of yoga and nearly fatal asceticism; enlightenment beneath a bodhi tree; and 45 years of wandering and teaching until his death in 483. And as she does so, she lucidly explains his revelations and influence." —*Booklist*

Includes bibliographical references; Originally published: New York : Viking, 2001.

Muhammad: A Prophet for Our Time. Karen Armstrong. Atlas Books; Harper Collins 2006. 249 p. : Map (Eminent lives)
ISBN 9780060598976
Grades: 11 12 Adult   B

1. Muhammad, Prophet, d. 632 2. Islam 3. Religious leaders 4. Muslims 5. 21st century 6. Biographies 7. Spirituality and Religion — Islam 8. Spirituality and Religion — Religious Leaders 9. Life stories — Religion and spirituality — Religious and spiritual leaders

LC 2006045864

A meticulously researched account of the works and lasting influence of the prophet Muhammad discusses his life at the end of the sixth and beginning of the seventh centuries, offering insight into his establishment of a faith that was to have a profound impact on world history.

"Readers of these pages cannot escape the genius of Muhammad and his aim for peace and compassion among nations and among Muslims themselves. . . . Recommended for all libraries." —*Library Journal*

Includes bibliographical references (p. 231-249).

The Spiral Staircase: My Climb Out of Darkness. Karen Armstrong. Alfred A. Knopf 2004. xxii, 305 p.
ISBN 9780375413186
Grades: 11 12 Adult   B

1. Armstrong, Karen, 1944- 2. Former nuns 3. People with depression 4. Women 5. Religious life 6. Faith 7. Coping 8. England 9. 21st century 10. Autobiographies and memoirs 11. Spirituality and Religion — Christianity 12. Adult books for young adults 13. Life stories — Religion and spirituality — Leaving religion

LC 2003047550

The author relates her decision to leave her convent after failing to find religious fulfillment, her struggles with depression and epilepsy, her realization of her calling, and her career working with sacred texts.

"Even among readers who embrace doctrines Armstrong dismisses (such as the reality of a personal God), this candid memoir will clarify thinking about the search for the sacred." —*Booklist*

Armstrong, Louis

Louis Armstrong, in His Own Words: Selected Writings. Louis Armstrong; edited and with an introduction by Thomas Brothers. Oxford University Press 1999. xxvii, 255 p. : Illustration
ISBN 9780195119589
Grades: Adult   B

1. Armstrong, Louis, 1901-1971 2. African American jazz musicians 3. Jazz music 4. Jazz musicians 5. Music history and criticism 6. Social life and customs 7. New Orleans, Louisiana 8. Biographies 9. Arts and Entertainment — Music — Jazz and the Blues 10. Life stories — Arts and culture — Performing arts — Musicians and composers

LC 99017040

Contains letters, magazine articles, autobiographical writings, and essays by the jazz musician.

"In this collection Armstrong recounts episodes from his childhood in New Orleans, pays tribute to other musicians, and extolls the virtues of marijuana, laxatives, and rice and beans while speaking candidly about race relations, the music business, and his extramarital affairs. The joy he took in expressing himself on paper is abundantly evident." —*The New Yorker*

Includes bibliographical references (p. 225-227) and index.

Aron, Nina Renata

Good Morning, Destroyer of Men's Souls: A Memoir of Women, Addiction, and Love. Nina Renata Aron. Crown 2020. 288 p.
ISBN 9780525576679
Grades: Adult   B

ESSENTIAL AND RECOMMENDED TITLES
Biography

1. Aron, Nina Renata 2. Codependency 3. Drug addiction 4. Enabling (Psychology) 5. Drug addicts 6. Addiction 7. Extramarital affairs 8. Drug abuse 9. Obsession 10. California 11. Autobiographies and memoirs 12. Life stories — Facing adversity — Medical issues — Addiction

LC 2020003061

A woman vividly recounts her love affair with an ex-addict who began using again and tries to make sense of drug abuse, codependency and obsession in this intense memoir of love and addiction.

"Aron's dark, gorgeously narrated memoir of destructive codependency will captivate readers." —*Publishers Weekly*

Arrington, Leonard J.
***Brigham** Young: American Moses.* Leonard J. Arrington. Knopf 1985. xvii, 522, 16 p. of plates : Illustration

ISBN 9780394510224

Grades: Adult   B

1. Young, Brigham, 1801-1877 2. Religious leaders 3. Mormons 4. Biographies 5. Life stories — Religion and spirituality — Religious and spiritual leaders 6. Spirituality and Religion — Religious Leaders

LC 84048650

National Book Critics Circle Award for Biography finalist, 1985.

An historian of the Mormon Church draws on diaries and letters not available to previous biographers to profile the controversial church leader.

Includes bibliographical references (p. [500]-509) and index.

Arsenault, Kerri
***Mill** Town: Reckoning with What Remains.* Kerri Arsenault. St. Martin's Press 2020. 368 p.

ISBN 9781250155931

Grades: Adult   B

1. Arsenault, Kerri 2. Paper mills 3. Small towns 4. Blue collar workers 5. Blue collar families 6. Water pollution 7. Air pollution 8. People with cancer 9. Industries 10. Labor-management relations 11. Business corruption 12. Environmentalism 13. Social life and customs 14. Maine 15. Autobiographies and memoirs 16. Life stories — Facing adversity 17. Society and culture — Urban and regional studies 18. Business and economics — Corruption and scandal 19. Nature Writing — Environmental Issues

LC 2020019303

National Book Critics Circle Award: John Leonard Prize finalist, 2020.

Kerri Arsenault grew up in the rural working class town of Mexico, Maine. For over 100 years the community orbited around a paper mill that employs most townspeople, including three generations of Arsenault's own family. Years after she moved away, Arsenault realized the price she paid for her seemingly secure childhood. The mill, while providing livelihoods for nearly everyone, also contributed to the destruction of the environment and the decline of the town's economic, physical, and emotional health in a slow-moving catastrophe, earning the area the nickname "Cancer Valley."

"She writes urgently about the dire effects the mill's toxic legacy had on Mexico's residents and the area's ecology while evocatively mining the emotional landscape of caretaking for aging parents and rediscovering the roots of her childhood. Bittersweet memories and a long-buried atrocity combine for a heartfelt, unflinching, striking narrative combination." —*Kirkus*

Includes bibliographical references.

Arsenault, Raymond
***John** Lewis: In Search of the Beloved Community.* Raymond Arsenault. Yale University Press 2024. 552 p.

ISBN 9780300253757

Grades: Adult   B

1. Lewis, John, 1940-2020 2. African American politicians 3. Civil Rights Movement 4. African American civil rights workers 5. African American legislators 6. Freedom Riders (Civil rights movement) 7. Protests, demonstrations, vigils, etc. 8. Nonviolence 9. Race relations 10. Social justice 11. American people 12. Biographies 13. Life stories — Politics — Activists and Reformers — Civil Rights Leaders 14. Life stories — Politics — Politicians 15. History writing — African American — Civil rights — United States 16. History writing — Politicians — United States

For six decades John Robert Lewis (1940-2020) was a towering figure in the U.S. struggle for civil rights. As an activist and progressive congressman, he was renowned for his unshakable integrity, indomitable courage, and determination to get into "good trouble." In this first book-length biography of Lewis, Raymond Arsenault traces Lewis's upbringing in rural Alabama, his activism as a Freedom Rider and leader of the Student Nonviolent Coordinating Committee, his championing of voting rights and anti-poverty initiatives, and his decades of service as the "conscience of Congress."

"An exemplary biography of an exemplary person, essential to the history of the Civil Rights Movement." —*Kirkus*

Includes bibliographical references and index.

Asbrink, Elisabeth
***And** in the Vienna Woods the Trees Remain: The Heartbreaking True Story of a Family Torn Apart by War.* Elisabeth Asbrink; translated from the Swedish by Saskia Vogel. Other Press 2020. 320 p.

ISBN 9781590519172

Grades: Adult   B

1. Ullmann, Otto, 1925-2005 2. Refugees, Jewish 3. World War II 4. Holocaust (1933-1945) 5. Antisemitism 6. Refugees 7. European history 8. Sweden 9. 20th century 10. Second World War era (1939-1945) 11. Biographies 12. Translations — Swedish to English 13. Life stories — Facing adversity — War and oppression — Holocaust 14. History writing — Wars and conflicts — Holocaust — World War II

LC 2019019275

Winner of the August Prize, an intricate weave of documents, substantive narrative, and emotional commentary that centers on a young Jewish refugee's friendship with the future founder of IKEA.

"Top-notch microcosmic World War II history and an excellent illustration of the immense power of the written word." —*Kirkus*

Includes bibliographical references.

Askwith, Richard
Unbreakable: *The Woman Who Defied the Nazis in the World's Most Dangerous Horse Race.* Richard Askwith. Pegasus Books 2019. 408 p.

ISBN 9781643132105

Grades: Adult   B

1. Lata Brandisova 2. Horse racing 3. Nazis 4. Women athletes 5. Steeplechasing 6. Horses 7. Women jockeys 8. Competition 9. Military occupation 10. Nationalism 11. European history 12. Czechoslovakia 13. Second World War era (1939-1945) 14. Biographies 15. Life stories — Sports — Athletes 16. Sports and Competition — Racing — Horses 17. History writing — Women's history 18. History writing — Europe — Eastern Europe

LC Bl2019024651

Traces the story of the courageous Czech countess who defied the Nazis in a legendary horse race, describing her achievement and the retaliation of the Nazis against a backdrop of the death of Tomás Masaryk and the Third Reich invasion.

Assael, Shaun
*The **Murder** of Sonny Liston: Las Vegas, Heroin, and Heavyweights.* Shaun Assael. Blue Rider Press 2016. 352 p.

ISBN 9780399169755

Grades: Adult   B

1. Liston, Sonny, 1932-1970 2. Heroin 3. Boxers (Sports) 4. Police cover-ups 5. Organized crime 6. Murder 7. Boxing 8. Sports corruption 9. Las Vegas, Nevada 10. True crime — Murder

LC 2016016232

An investigation into the unsolved death of Heavyweight Champion Sonny Liston is set against a backdrop of the Vegas mob battles, drug wars and boxing glory days of the early 1970s and shares the insights of close associates who doubted official rulings that his death was due to a drug overdose.

Includes index.

PUBLIC LIBRARY CORE COLLECTION: NONFICTION
Twentieth Edition

Atria, Travis
Better Days Will Come Again: The Life of Arthur Briggs, Jazz Genius of Harlem, Paris, and a Nazi Prison Camp. Travis Atria. Chicago Review Press 2020. 336 p.
ISBN 9780914090106
Grades: Adult   B
1. Briggs, Arthur, 1901-1991 2. Internment camp inmates 3. World War II 4. Jazz musicians 5. Paris, France history 6. 1930s 7. Second World War era (1939-1945) 8. 20th century 9. Biographies 10. Life stories — Facing adversity — War and oppression — War survivors 11. Life stories — Arts and culture — Performing arts — Musicians and composers 12. History writing — Wars and conflicts — Holocaust — World War II
LC 2019029238

Describes the life story of the legendary jazz musician who was regarded as the greatest trumpeter in Europe, but who failed to heed warnings to leave Paris before the Nazi takeover and was sent to a prison camp.

"A fascinating story and valuable reclamation of an overlooked musician." —*Booklist*

Includes bibliographical references and index.

Attas, Amy
Pets and the City: True Tales of a Manhattan House Call Veterinarian. Dr. Amy Attas, Founder of City Pets. G.P. Putnam's Sons 2024. 336 p.
ISBN 9780593715673
Grades: Adult   B
1. Attas, Amy 2. Veterinarians 3. Women veterinarians 4. Veterinary medicine 5. Pets 6. Celebrities 7. New York city 8. Life stories — Science, technology, and medicine — Healthcare professionals 9. Family and relationships — Pets and owners
LC 2024007477

New York City's premier "house call veterinarian" takes you into the exclusive penthouses and four-star hotel rooms of the wealthiest New Yorkers and shows that, when it comes to their pets, they are just as neurotic as any of us.

"A sure hit for pet lovers and anyone looking to peek into the lives and homes of the Manhattan elite." —*Library Journal*

Attenborough, David
Adventures of a Young Naturalist: The Zoo Quest Expeditions. David Attenborough. Quercus 2018. 400 p.
ISBN 9781635060690
Grades: Adult   B
1. Attenborough, David, 1926- 2. Wildlife 3. Nature study 4. Zoology 5. Zoos 6. Captive wild animals 7. Wild animal collecting 8. Autobiographies and memoirs 9. Life stories — Nature and outdoors 10. Nature Writing — Animal Studies
LC 2017048329

In 1954, David Attenborough, a young television presenter was offered the opportunity of a lifetime—to travel the world finding rare and elusive animals for London Zoo's collection, and to film the expedition for the BBC for a new show called Zoo Quest.

Originally published: London: Hodder & Stoughton, 2017.

Au-Yeung, Angel
Wonder Boy: Tony Hsieh, Zappos, and the Myth of Happiness in Silicon Valley. Angel Au-Yeung and David Jeans. Henry Holt and Company 2023. 320 p.
ISBN 9781250829092
Grades: Adult   B
1. Hsieh, Tony 2. Businesspeople 3. Shoe industry and trade 4. Success in business 5. Clothing industry and trade 6. Electronic commerce 7. Mental illness 8. Venture capitalists 9. Drug abuse 10. Biographies 11. Life stories — Business — Business leaders 12. Business and economics — Business leaders and entrepreneurs 13. Business and economics — Industries 14. Nonfiction that reads like fiction
LC 2023005568

A riveting investigation into the turbulent life of Zappos visionary Tony Hsieh, whose radical business strategies revolutionized both the tech world and corporate culture, based on rigorous research and reporting by two seasoned journalists.

"Journalists Au-Yeung and Jeans debut with a nuanced, sympathetic biography of Zappos founder Tony Hsieh, tracing his life from Silicon Valley wunderkind through his spiraling addiction and death in 2020....Au-Yeung and Jeans's empathetic portrait is as enthralling as it is achingly sad, combining rich research with a propulsive novelistic style." —*Publishers Weekly*

Includes bibliographical references and index.

Augustine
Confessions. Saint Augustine; translated from the Latin by Henry Chadwick. Oxford University Press 2008. xxviii, 311 p; (Oxford world's classics (Oxford University Press))
ISBN 9780199537822
Grades: Adult   B
1. Augustine, Saint, Bishop of Hippo 2. Christianity 3. Faith (Christianity) 4. Christian saints 5. Bishops 6. Religions 7. Autobiographies and memoirs 8. Biographies 9. Life stories — Religion and spirituality — Religious and spiritual leaders 10. Spirituality and Religion — Christianity — History 11. Spirituality and Religion — Religious Leaders
LC 2008491261

Henry Chadwick, an eminent scholar of early Christianity, has given us the first new English translation in thirty years of this classic spiritual journey. Chadwick renders the details of Augustine's conversion in clear, modern English.

Includes bibliographical references (p. [xxvii]-xxviii) and index; Translated from the Latin.

Auletta, Ken
Media Man: Ted Turner's Improbable Empire. Ken Auletta. Norton 2004. 205 p. : Illustration
ISBN 9780393051681
Grades: Adult   B
1. Turner, Ted 2. Sports team owners 3. Telecommunication 4. Businesspeople 5. Social life and customs 6. United States 7. 21st century 8. Biographies 9. Arts and Entertainment — Movies and Television 10. Business and economics — Business leaders and entrepreneurs 11. Life stories — Business — Business leaders 12. Life stories — Sports — Coaches, managers, and owners 13. Business and economics — Industries — Entertainment and media
LC 2004012215

Traces the rise and fall of the cable network mogul, relating his transformation of a small Atlanta network into a national cable superstation, invention of the first twenty-four-hour CNN news channel, and eventual ousting after selling his company to Time Warner.

Includes bibliographical references and index.

Auster, Paul
Burning Boy: The Life and Work of Stephen Crane. Paul Auster. Henry Holt & CO 2021. 800 p.
ISBN 9781250235831
Grades: Adult   B
1. Crane, Stephen, 1871-1900 2. Authors, American 3. Journalists 4. Literary criticism 5. 19th century 6. Biographies 7. Arts and Entertainment — Writing and Publishing 8. Life stories — Arts and culture — Writing — Authors

Los Angeles Times Book Prize for Biography, 2021.

With Burning Boy, celebrated novelist Paul Auster tells the extraordinary story of Stephen Crane, best known as the author of the Red Badge of Courage, who transformed American literature through an avalanche of original short stories, novellas, poems, journalism, and war reportage before his life was cut short by tuberculosis at age twenty-eight.

"Auster's sprawling narrative combines punchy writing and shrewd analysis with an exuberant passion for his subject. The result is a definitive biography of a great writer." —*Publishers Weekly*

ESSENTIAL AND RECOMMENDED TITLES
Biography

Austin, Nefertiti
Motherhood so White: A Memoir of Race, Gender, and Parenting in America. Nefertiti Austin. Sourcebooks 2019. 304 p.
ISBN 9781492679011
Grades: Adult B
1. Austin, Nefertiti 2. African American single mothers 3. Adoptive mothers 4. Adoption 5. African American parents 6. Prejudice 7. Racism 8. Boys 9. Adopted children 10. Autobiographies and memoirs 11. Life stories — Relationships — Parent and child 12. Family and Relationships — Parenting — Adoption 13. Society and culture — Race 14. Life stories — Identity — Race and ethnicity

A literary diversity activist draws on her personal experiences as an African-American adoptive mother to reveal the virtual absence of Black representation in today's parenting culture and the challenges that diverse families encounter from the adoption community.

Auvinen, Karen
Rough Beauty: Forty Seasons of Mountain Living. Karen Auvinen. Simon & Schuster 2018. 320 p.
ISBN 9781501152283
Grades: Adult B
1. Auvinen, Karen 2. Mountain life 3. Solitude 4. Cabins 5. Poets 6. Fires 7. Community life 8. Dysfunctional families 9. Rocky Mountains 10. Autobiographies and memoirs 11. Essays 12. Life stories — Nature and outdoors
LC 2017061755

A memoir by an award-winning poet describes her retreats to a wilderness cabin to write in solitude and find answers to life's big questions, describing how a catastrophic fire forced her to reconcile her conflicting needs for isolation and community.

"This breathtaking memoir honors the wildness of the Rockies and shows readers how they might come to rely on their animal companions." —*Publishers Weekly*

Azad
Long Shot: The Inside Story of the Snipers Who Broke Isis. Azad. Atlantic Monthly Press 2019. 412 p.
ISBN 9780802129079
Grades: Adult B
1. Azad, 1983- 2. Snipers 3. Kurds 4. Militias and irregular armies 5. Military desertion 6. Deserters 7. Conscientious objectors 8. Southwest Asia and North Africa (Middle East) history 9. Iran 10. Syria 11. 2010s 12. 2020s 13. History writing — Nationalism — Southwest Asia and North Africa (Middle East)
LC 2018047580

A gripping narrative by an Iran-born Kurdish journalist who joined the ranks of the Kurdish army as a sniper in the fight against ISIS.

First published in Great Britain in 2018 by Weidenfeld & Nicolson, an imprint of Orion Publishing Group.

Babb, Valerie Melissa
The Book of James: The Power, Politics, and Passion of Lebron. Valerie Babb. PublicAffairs 2023. 280 p.
ISBN 9781541702042
Grades: Adult B
1. James, LeBron 2. Basketball players 3. Professional athletes 4. African American men 5. Basketball 6. Fame 7. African Americans in mass media 8. Public opinion 9. Racism 10. Racism in sports 11. Social advocacy 12. North American people 13. American people 14. Biographies 15. Life stories — Sports — Athletes 16. Life stories — Identity — Race and ethnicity 17. Sports and Competition — Basketball 18. Sports and Competition — Individual Athlete 19. Society and culture — Race
LC 2023018620

This unique social, cultural and political look at the life of LeBron James shows how he uses his celebrity not to transcend Blackness, but to give it a place of cultural prominence, exposing the frictions between Blackness and a country not fully comfortable with its presence.

"This is a valuable contribution to the growing literature examining the intersection of professional sports and race in America." —*Publishers Weekly*
Includes bibliographical references and index.

Bacall, Lauren
By Myself and Then Some. Lauren Bacall. Harper 2006. 506 p. : Color illustration
ISBN 9780061127915
Grades: Adult B
1. Bacall, Lauren, 1924-2014 2. Celebrities 3. Film acting 4. Entertainment industry and trade 5. Films 6. Actors and actresses 7. United States 8. Autobiographies and memoirs 9. Biographies 10. Arts and Entertainment — Movies and Television 11. Arts and Entertainment — Theater 12. Life stories — Facing adversity — Coping with death 13. Life stories — Arts and culture — Performing arts — Actors and actresses
LC Bl2007014842

The star's memoir chronicles events since her story's original publication, from her appearances on Broadway to her latest film achievements and relationships with such individuals as Katharine Hepburn and Humphrey Bogart.

"Certainly more intelligently written than your average celebrity autobiography, this memoir tells a fascinating story of one woman's journey through life with an intimacy that's sure to engage legions of readers." —*Booklist*

Rev. ed. of: Lauren Bacall by myself. 1st ed. 1979; Originally published: New York : HarperEntertainment, c2005.

Backman, Fredrik
Things My Son Needs to Know About the World. Fredrik Backman; translated by Alice Menzies. Atria Books 2019. 208 p.
ISBN 9781501196867
Grades: Adult B
1. Backman, Fredrik, 1981- 2. Authors, Swedish 3. Fatherhood 4. Fathers and sons 5. Advice 6. Love 7. Family relationships 8. Essays 9. Translations — Swedish to English 10. Life stories — Relationships — Parent and child 11. Family and Relationships — Parenting
LC 2018054900

Things My Son Needs to Know About the World collects the personal dispatches from the front lines of one of the most daunting experiences any man can experience: Fatherhood. As he conveys his profound awe at experiencing all the "firsts" that fill him with wonder and catch him completely unprepared, Fredrik Backman doesn't shy away from revealing his own false steps and fatherly flaws, tackling issues both great and small, from masculinity and mid-life crises to practical jokes and poop. In between the sleep-deprived lows and wonderful highs, Backman shares the true story of learning to live a life that revolves around the people you care about unconditionally.

"Each chapter is filled with Backmans dry wit and brutal honesty, but behind all of the humor is real, heartfelt sentiment and poignant advice." —*Booklist*

Includes bibliographical references and index; Originally published: Stockholm : Forum, 2012; Translated from the Swedish.

Baier, Bret
Three Days in January: Dwight Eisenhower's Final Mission. Bret Baier with Catherine Whitney. William Morrow 2017. 320 p.
ISBN 9780062569035
Grades: Adult B
1. Eisenhower, Dwight D. (Dwight David), 1890-1969 2. Kennedy, John F. (John Fitzgerald), 1917-1963 3. Politicians 4. Presidents 5. Generals 6. Politics and government 7. United States 8. 20th century 9. 1950s 10. 1960s 11. Biographies 12. History writing — Presidency — 20th century — United States 13. History writing — Post World War II - 1959 — United States
LC Bl2016051650

Fox News Channel's chief political anchor and the host of the #1 rated Special Report with Bret Baier explores the Presidency of Dwight D. Eisenhower through the lens of his last three days in office in January 1961, revealing Ike to be a model of strong yet principled leadership that is desperately missing in America today.

"A focused and timely study of Eisenhower's significant speech and the sticky transition to JFK's inherited new world." —*Kirkus*

1211

PUBLIC LIBRARY CORE COLLECTION: NONFICTION
Twentieth Edition

Bailey, Lily
Because We Are Bad: Ocd and a Girl Lost in Thought. Lily Bailey. HarperCollins 2018. 320 p.
ISBN 9780062696168
Grades: Adult   B
1. Bailey, Lily 2. OCD 3. Mental illness 4. Teenagers with mental illnesses 5. Autobiographies and memoirs 6. Life stories — Facing adversity — Medical issues — Mental illness 7. Adult books for young adults
LC Bl2018053368

By the age of thirteen, Lily Bailey was convinced she was bad. She had killed someone with a thought, spread untold disease, and ogled the bodies of other children. Only by performing an exhausting series of secret routines could she make up for what she'd done. But no matter how intricate or repetitive, no act of penance was ever enough.

Baime, A. J.
The Accidental President: Harry S. Truman and the Four Months That Changed the World. A. J. Baime. Houghton Mifflin Harcourt 2017. 352 p.
ISBN 9780544617346
Grades: Adult   B
1. Truman, Harry S, 1884-1972 2. Political leadership 3. Cold War 4. Presidents 5. International relations 6. Politics and government 7. United States 8. 1940s 9. 20th century 10. Biographies 11. Life stories — Politics — Politicians 12. History writing — Presidency — 20th century — United States 13. History writing — Post World War II - 1959 — United States
LC 2017044086

A suspenseful chronicle of the 33rd president's first four months in office traces his unlikely rise to the Oval Office and his pivotal contributions to major decisions, from the founding of the United Nations and the Nazi surrender to the liberation of concentration camps and the decision to drop the bomb.

White Lies: The Double Life of Walter White and America's Darkest Secret. A. J. Baime. Mariner Books 2022. 384 p.
ISBN 9780358447757
Grades: Adult   B
1. White, Walter, 1893-1955 2. Civil rights 3. African American men 4. Passing (Identity) 5. Journalists 6. Social advocates 7. Race (Social sciences) 8. Race relations 9. United States 10. 20th century 11. Autobiographies and memoirs 12. Life stories — Politics — Activists and reformers 13. History writing — African American — United States

This first character study of a little-known Black civil rights leader who passed for white reveals a man fraught by internal and external conflict as he leveraged this ambiguity as a reporter, changing the racial identity of America forever.

"Historian Baime (Dewey Defeats Truman) delivers a captivating portrait of civil rights activist and novelist Walter White (1893-1955) and the fight to end anti-Black violence and racial discrimination in the U.S. . . . Filled with vibrant period details and lucid explanations of legal and political matters, this is a riveting portrait of a complex and courageous crusader for racial equality." —*Publishers Weekly*

Bair, Deirdre
Al Capone: His Life, Legacy, and Legend. Deirdre Bair. Nan A. Talese 2016. 432 p.
ISBN 9780385537155
Grades: Adult   B
1. Capone, Al, 1899-1947 2. Organized crime 3. Crime bosses 4. Criminals 5. Gangsters 6. Income tax 7. Prohibition 8. Family relationships 9. United States history 10. Chicago, Illinois 11. 20th century 12. Biographies 13. True Crime — Organized Crime, Mafia, and Gangs 14. Life stories — Law and order — Criminals and law-breakers
LC 2016009367

This complete biography of the legendary gangster begins with his birth in 1899 Brooklyn, New York, to poor, Italian immigrant parents to becoming the head of a multimillion-dollar gambling, bootlegging and prostitution operation during the height of Prohibition in Chicago.

"Bair has written perhaps the last word on Capone. Highly recommended." —*Library Journal*

Saul Steinberg: A Biography. Deirdre Bair. Nan A. Talese/Doubleday 2012. 752 p.
ISBN 9780385524483
Grades: Adult   B
1. Steinberg, Saul, 1914-1999 2. Cartoonists 3. Immigrants 4. World War II 5. Artists 6. Biographies 7. Life stories — Arts and culture — Artists
LC 2011050601

New York Times Notable Book, 2012.

A definitive portrait of one of the New Yorker's most iconic artists includes coverage of his education in Milan, extensive service during World War II, marriage to artist Hedda Sterne and relationships with such contemporaries as Saul Bellow, Vladimir Nabokov and Le Corbusier. By the National Book Award-winning author of Samuel Beckett.

Baird, Julia
★ *Victoria the Queen: An Intimate Biography of the Woman Who Ruled an Empire.* Julia Baird. Random House 2016. 704 p.
ISBN 9781400069880
Grades: Adult   B
1. Victoria, Queen of Great Britain, 1819-1901 2. Husband and wife 3. Women's role 4. Loss 5. Identity 6. Industrial revolution 7. Women rulers 8. British history 9. Great Britain 10. Victorian era (1837-1901) 11. Australian literature 12. Biographies 13. History writing — Europe — United Kingdom 14. Life stories — Politics — Royalty
LC 2015025297

LibraryReads Favorites, 2016.

An account of the life of the longtime English monarch offers insight into the passionate and sensuous aspects of her character, placing her reign against a backdrop of dynamic world events while sharing insights into her relationship with Albert and her pivotal role in building the British empire.

"Baird does not turn a blind eye on Victorias darker sides, including her willfulness, selfishness, and self-pity. But that simply adds dimensions to a significant character." —*Booklist*

Includes bibliographical references and index.

Baker, Deborah
The Convert: A Parable of Islam and America. Deborah Baker. Farrar Straus & Giroux 2011. 224 p.
ISBN 9781555975821
Grades: 11 12 Adult   B
1. Muslim women 2. Converts to Islam 3. Fundamentalism 4. Islam 5. Fundamentalists 6. Muslims 7. Pakistan 8. 1960s 9. Biographies 10. Spirituality and Religion — Islam 11. Life stories — Religion and spirituality — Spiritual journeys
LC 2011920617

National Book Award for Nonfiction finalist, 2011.

The Pulitzer Prize-finalist author of in Extremis documents the conversion of New York Jewish suburbanite Margaret Marcus to Islam's Maryam Jameelah of Lahore, drawing on personal correspondence and the author's investigation into Maryam's adoptive father to resolve questions about the legitimacy and significance of her decision.

Baker, Nicholson
Finding a Likeness: How I Got Somewhat Better at Art. Nicholson Baker. Penguin Press 2024. 352 p.
ISBN 9781984881397
Grades: Adult   B
1. Baker, Nicholson, 1957- 2. Art 3. Creativity 4. Painting 5. Authors 6. Creativity in art 7. Creation (Literary, artistic, etc.) 8. Art history 9. Autobiographies and memoirs 10. Illustrated books 11. Life stories — Arts and culture 12. Arts and Entertainment — Painting, Drawing, and Sculpture

Finding a Likeness is Baker's record of the years he worked to improve his artistic skills, beginning with his first, humble attempts to set paintbrush to paper. Driven by a natural curiosity and a strong desire to paint faces, clouds, and land-

ESSENTIAL AND RECOMMENDED TITLES
Biography

scapes that actually resemble faces, clouds, and landscapes, he attends classes from local artists, watches YouTube tutorials, and seeks out master painters from the past and present in the hopes of uncovering their secrets. In his inimitable voice, Baker recounts the highs and lows of the creative process, reflects on memories of growing up as the son of two painters, and learns what it means to really see.

"The understated and art-filled latest from novelist Baker (Baseless) chronicles how he learned to paint and draw." —*Publishers Weekly*

Baker, Peter
The Man Who Ran Washington: The Life and Times of James A. Baker III. Peter Baker and Susan Glasser. Doubleday 2020. 688 p.
ISBN 9780385540551
Grades: Adult **B**
1. Baker, James Addison, 1930- 2. Cabinet officers 3. Negotiation 4. Power 5. Politicians 6. Politics and government 7. Ambition 8. United States 9. 20th century 10. 1980s 11. 21st century 12. Biographies 13. Life stories — Politics — Politicians 14. History writing — Presidency — 20th century — United States
LC 2019038715

New York Times Notable Book, 2020.

A portrait of the influential White House Chief of Staff and Secretary of State includes coverage of the family tragedy that spurred his political career, his brokering of the reunification of Germany and his indelible role in the Gulf War.

"The authors interviewed Baker, and talked with numerous friends and associates to present a well-documented, engaging read.... Indispensable reading for anyone interested in late 20th-century U.S. politics." —*Library Journal*

Includes bibliographical references and index.

Bakewell, Sarah
How to Live—or—a Life of Montaigne : In One Question and Twenty Attempts at an Answer. Sarah Bakewell. Other Press 2010. IX, 389 p. : Illustration; Map
ISBN 9781590514252
Grades: Adult **B**
1. Montaigne, Michel de, 1533-1592 2. Authors, French 3. Life 4. Intellectuals 5. Philosophy 6. French history 7. 16th century 8. Biographies 9. Life stories — Education — Philosophers 10. History writing — Renaissance — Europe 11. Politics and global affairs — Political philosophy 12. Life stories — Politics
LC 2010026896

Library Journal Best Books, 2010; National Book Critics Circle Award for Biography, 2010.

Examines the essays of Michel de Montaigne that explored the search for the meaning of life, and profiles the philosopher using the questions he posed and the answers he explored.

"In a wide-ranging intellectual career, Michel de Montaigne found no knowledge so hard to acquire as the knowledge of how to live this life well. By casting her biography of the writer as 20 chapters, each focused on a different answer to the question How to live? Bakewell limns Montaigne's ceaseless pursuit of this most elusive knowledge. Embedded in the 20 life-knowledge responses, readers will find essential factswhen and where Montaigne was born, and whom he married, how he became mayor of Bordeaux, how he managed a public life in a time of lethal religious and political passions. Because Montaigne's capacious mirror still captivates many, this insightful life study will win high praise from both scholars and general readers." —*Booklist*

Includes bibliographical references (p. [369]-372) and index; Originally published: London : Chatto & Windus, 2010.

Balf, Todd
Major: A Black Athlete, a White Era, and the Fight to Be the World's Fastest Human Being. Todd Balf. Crown Publishers 2008. 320 p.
ISBN 9780307236586
Grades: Adult **B**
1. Taylor, Marshall Walter, 1878-1932 2. Bicyclists 3. Bicycle racing 4. United States history 5. 20th century 6. Biographies 7. Sports and Competition — Racing — Cycling 8. Sports and Competition — Individual Athlete 9. Life stories — Sports — Athletes 10. Adult books for young adults
LC 2007020747

A portrait of turn-of-the-twentieth-century cyclist Major Taylor, the first great African-American sports celebrity, describes his remarkable sports career, his virtuous and devout lifestyle, and his competition with such white rivals as Floyd McFarland.

"The author chronicles the life of the unlikeliest of stars in the early years of cycling: Marshall Major Taylor. Taylor was an incomparable athlete, poet and celebrity, but he was also a Black man living during a time when the scars of the Civil War and slavery were still fresh in the minds of Americans. Balf . . . does great work presenting the complex nature of Taylor's life, including his upbringing in poverty in Indianapolis, the years he was treated as a son by a rich white family, the fans who both worshipped and vilified him and his close relationships with his white trainer and promoter." —*Publishers Weekly*

Includes index.

Ball, Lucille
Love, Lucy. Lucille Ball with Betty Hannah Hoffman; foreword by Lucie Arnaz. G. P. Putnam's Sons 1996. xiv, 286 p, 32 p. of plates : Illustration
ISBN 9780399142055
Grades: Adult **B**
1. Ball, Lucille, 1911-1989 2. Arnaz, Desi, 1917-1986 3. Actors and actresses 4. Social life and customs 5. United States 6. 20th century 7. Autobiographies and memoirs 8. Biographies 9. Arts and Entertainment — Movies and Television 10. Arts and Entertainment — Comedy 11. Life stories — Arts and culture — Performing arts — Actors and actresses 12. Life stories — Arts and culture — Performing arts — Entertainers and celebrities
LC 96020751

The comedienne's recently discovered memoirs, penned more than thirty years ago, recounts her career, including her marriage to Desi Arnaz and their life on and off the TV screen.

Ball, Molly
★ *Pelosi*. Molly Ball. Henry Holt & Comapny 2020. 345 p.
ISBN 9781250252869
Grades: 10 11 12 Adult **B**
1. Pelosi, Nancy, 1940- 2. Women legislators 3. Women politicians 4. Influence (Psychology) 5. Politics and government 6. Leadership 7. United States 8. Biographies 9. Life stories — Politics — Politicians 10. Politics and global affairs — Political figures 11. History writing — Women's history
LC 2020930617

She's the iconic leader who puts Donald Trump in his place, the woman with the toughness to take on a lawless president and defend American democracy. Ever since the Democrats took back the House in the 2018 midterm elections, Nancy Pelosi has led the opposition with strategic mastery and inimitable elan. It's a remarkable comeback for the veteran politician who for years was demonized by the right and taken for granted by many in her own party. Ball's portrait takes readers inside the life and times of this historic and underappreciated figure. Based on exclusive interviews with the Speaker and deep background reporting, Ball shows Pelosi through a thoroughly modern lens to explain how this extraordinary woman has met her moment.

"A cradle-to-today portrait of a master politician. . . . A top-notch political biography." —*Kirkus*

Bamberger, Michael
The Second Life of Tiger Woods. Michael Bamberger. Avid Reader Press 2020. 288 pages
ISBN 9781982122829
Grades: Adult **B**
1. Woods, Tiger 2. Golfers 3. Athletes 4. Personal conduct 5. Scandals 6. Health 7. Mental health 8. African American men 9. Asian American men 10. Celebrities 11. Golf 12. Biographies 13. Impartial writing 14. Life stories — Sports — Athletes 15. Sports and Competition — Golf
LC Bl2020004900

Presents an intimate account of Tiger Woods's comeback that discusses the golf champion's high-risk back surgery, 2017 DUI arrest, rehabilitation and triumphant 2019 Masters victory.

"In all, this may be the most insightful and evenhanded book written yet about one of the signature athletes of the last 25 years." —*Booklist*

PUBLIC LIBRARY CORE COLLECTION: NONFICTION
Twentieth Edition

Bamford, Maria
Sure, I'll Join Your Cult: A Memoir of Mental Illness and the Quest to Belong Anywhere. Maria Bamford. Gallery Books 2023. 288 p.
ISBN 9781982168568
Grades: Adult   B
1. Bamford, Maria, 1970- 2. Comedians 3. People with mental illnesses 4. Belonging 5. Mental health 6. Communities 7. Autobiographies and memoirs 8. Life stories — Facing adversity — Medical issues — Mental illness 9. Life stories — Arts and culture — Performing arts — Entertainers and celebrities
LC 2023008307

In Bamford's signature voice, Sure, I'll Join Your Cult, brings us on a quest to participate in something. With sincerity and transparency, she recounts every anonymous fellowship she has joined (including but not limited to: Debtors Anonymous, Sex and Love Addicts Anonymous, and Overeaters Anonymous), every hypomanic episode (from worrying about selling out under capitalism to enforcing union rules on her Netflix TV show set to protect her health), and every easy 1-to-3-step recipe for fudge in between.

"Bamford creates an effective mix of introduction (or reintroduction) to a fascinating comedian, a guide to the self-help industry, and an encouragingly lighthearted, respectful assessment of mental health, reminding readers that they are not alone." —*Kirkus*

Barbree, Jay
Neil Armstrong: A Life of Flight. Jay Barbree. Thomas Dunne Books 2014. 320 p.
ISBN 9781250040718
Grades: Adult   B
1. Armstrong, Neil, 1930-2012 2. Astronauts 3. Space flight to the moon 4. Space programs 5. Pilots 6. Aviation history 7. United States 8. Biographies 9. Science Writing — Space and Flight 10. Life stories — Science, technology, and medicine — Astronauts and pilots
LC 2014008696

Published to coincide with the 45th anniversary of the Apollo 11 launch, a definitive portrait of the pioneering astronaut draws on personal notes and interviews with the Armstrong family and includes previously unshared photos and mission details.

"The author paints a detailed and colorful picture of his subject and an unbiased depiction of the period in which he lived, while also demonstrating reverence for Armstrong as a confidant." —*Library Journal*

Bard, Elizabeth
Lunch in Paris: A Love Story, with Recipes. Elizabeth Bard. Little, Brown and Co. 2010. 336 p.
ISBN 9780316042796
Grades: Adult   B
1. Bard, Elizabeth 2. Cooking, French 3. American people in France 4. Husband and wife 5. Marriage 6. Recipes 7. Food habits 8. Men-women relations 9. Social life and customs 10. Voyages and travels 11. Paris, France 12. France 13. Autobiographies and memoirs 14. Food writing — Memoirs and biographies 15. Family and Relationships — Dating and Marriage 16. Life stories — Relationships — Couples
LC 2009022064

Documents how the author fell in love and discovered the excellence of French cuisine during a life-changing lunch, recounting her decision to leave her fast-paced New York life to build a life abroad marked by bustling marketplaces, bad-tempered butchers and decadent chocolate shops."

"Falling in love with a Frenchman was not in Elizabeth Bard's master plan, but then he took her to a local canteen: Not to minimize Gwendal's many charms, but he was halfway to home base as soon as I cut into that marvelous steak, she writes. Culture shock set in as she learned to shop and cook in Paris, standing in line here for the best green beans, going there for the best walnuts. I thought the recipes were a cutesy touch until I made a few of them: Chicken tagine with two kinds of lemon, spiced apricots, chouquettes. Forget the narrative you could just buy this as a cookbook." —*Entertainment Weekly*

Picnic in Provence: A Memoir with Recipes. Elizabeth Bard. Little Brown & Co. 2015. 336 p.
ISBN 9780316246163
Grades: Adult   B
1. Bard, Elizabeth 2. American people in France 3. Marriage 4. Cooking, French 5. Small town life 6. Family relationships 7. Husband and wife 8. Recipes 9. Food habits 10. Provence, France 11. France 12. Food writing — Memoirs and biographies 13. Family and Relationships — Dating and Marriage 14. Life stories — Relationships — Couples

If you enjoyed Lunch in Paris, get ready for a Picnic in Provence. American author Elizabeth Bard's second memoir traces her and her French husband's impulsive move from Paris to a small town in Southern France…when she's six months pregnant. Having bought the charming former home of French Resistance leader and poet René Char, the couple settled in, met their new neighbors, enjoyed nature, savored delicious foods, and opened an artisan ice cream shop. Oh, and they welcomed their new bébé! Bring both your literary and your gastronomic appetite—this delightful, food-centric book (recipes are included) will have you salivating.

Barkan, Ady
Eyes to the Wind: A Memoir of Love and Death, Hope and Resistance. Ady Barkan; foreword by Alexandria Ocasio-Cortez. Atria Books 2019. 304 p.
ISBN 9781982111540
Grades: Adult   B
1. Barkan, Ady 2. Political activists 3. Political participation 4. People with amyotrophic lateral sclerosis 5. Grassroots movement 6. Citizen participation in government 7. Lawyers 8. People with terminal illnesses 9. Men 10. Autobiographies and memoirs 11. Liberal writing 12. Life stories — Politics — Activists and reformers 13. Life stories — Facing adversity — Medical issues — Physical illness 14. Society and culture — Social activism and philanthropy 15. Politics and global affairs — General
LC 2019019264

In this inspirational and moving memoir, activist Ady Barkan explores his life with ALS and how his diagnosis gave him a profound new understanding of his commitment to social justice for all.

"Barkans powerful narrative gives great insight into the nuts and bolts of political activism at work." —*Publishers Weekly*

Barnes, Cinelle
Monsoon Mansion: A Memoir. Cinelle Barnes. Little a 2018. 252 p.
ISBN 9781542046138
Grades: Adult   B
1. Barnes, Cinelle 2. Growing up 3. Rich families 4. Dysfunctional families 5. Coping 6. Father-deserted families 7. Mansions 8. Philippines 9. Autobiographies and memoirs 10. Life stories — Relationships — Growing up 11. Life stories — Facing adversity 12. Adult books for young adults

Told with a lyrical, almost-dreamlike voice as intoxicating as the moonflowers and orchids that inhabit this world, Monsoon Mansion is a harrowing yet triumphant coming-of-age memoir exploring the dark, troubled waters of a family's rise and fall from grace in the Philippines. It would take a young warrior to survive it.

Barnes, Julian
The Man in the Red Coat. Julian Barnes. Alfred A. Knopf 2020. 265 p. : Illustration; Color; Portrait
ISBN 9780525658771
Grades: Adult   B
1. Pozzi, Samuel, 1846-1918 2. Gynecologists 3. Surgeons 4. History of medicine 5. Culture 6. Art 7. Portraits 8. Counts and countesses 9. Princes 10. Voyages and travels 11. Shopping 12. Civilization 13. France 14. Paris, France 15. London, England 16. Belle Epoque (1871-1914) 17. 19th century 18. 20th century 19. Biographies 20. Life stories — Science, technology, and medicine — Healthcare professionals 21. History writing — Europe — France
LC 2019028764

A tour of Belle Epoque Paris, via the remarkable life story of the pioneering surgeon, Samuel Pozzi.

"Finely honed biographical intuition and a novelist's sensibility make for a stylish, engrossing narrative." —*Kirkus*

Originally published: London : Jonathan Cape, 2019.

ESSENTIAL AND RECOMMENDED TITLES
Biography

Barnett, Brittany K.
★ *A Knock at Midnight: A Story of Hope, Justice, and Freedom*. Brittany K. Barnett. Crown 2020. 304 p.
ISBN 9781984825780
Grades: Adult **B**
1. Barnett, Brittany K. 2. Jones, Sharanda 3. African American women defense attorneys 4. Criminal justice system 5. Racism in the criminal justice system 6. Judicial system 7. Criminal justice policy 8. Criminal justice reform 9. African American women 10. Women lawyers 11. Prisoners 12. Judicial error 13. Injustice 14. Clemency 15. Legislation 16. Texas 17. United States 18. Autobiographies and memoirs 19. Society and culture — Violence and crime — Criminal justice system 20. Politics and global affairs — Civil and human rights 21. History writing — African American — United States 22. Life stories — Law and order — Judges and lawyers
LC 2020007214
ALA Notable Book, 2021.
Presents an urgent call for justice-system reform in the story of a disadvantaged, African-American single mother from the rural South who was separated from her young daughter and sentenced to life in prison for a first-time offense.
"Recommended for readers who enjoyed Bryan Stevenson's Just Mercy, this is an essential read for anyone seeking to understand the devastating effects of mandatory drug sentencing and looking for inspiration to seek change." —*Library Journal*

Barnett, Erica C.
Quitter: A Memoir of Drinking, Relapse, and Recovery. Erica C. Barnett. Viking 2020. 322 p.
ISBN 9780525522324
Grades: Adult **B**
1. Barnett, Erica C. 2. Alcoholic women 3. Addicts 4. Alcoholism 5. Drug abuse 6. Women journalists 7. Alcoholism treatment centers and clinics 8. Failure 9. Denial (Psychology) 10. Sobriety 11. Treatment 12. Autobiographies and memoirs 13. Life stories — Facing adversity — Medical issues — Addiction 14. Life stories — Arts and culture — Writing — Journalists
LC 2019052898
An award-winning political reporter and recovering alcoholic shares her story, describing her repeated recoveries and lapses, discussing how Alcoholics Anonymous didn't correspond to her experience and actually was detrimental and highlighting the lack of rehabilitation options available to addicts.
"Emotionally devastating and self-aware, this cautionary tale about substance abuse is a worthy heir to Cat Marnell's How to Murder Your Life." —*Publishers Weekly*

Barra, Allen
Inventing Wyatt Earp: His Life and Many Legends. Allen Barra. Carroll & Graf Publishers 1998. V, 426 p. : Illustration
ISBN 9780786705627
Grades: Adult **B**
1. Earp, Wyatt, 1848-1929 2. Peace officers 3. United States marshals 4. Frontier and pioneer life 5. United States history 6. Southwest (United States) 7. 19th century 8. Biographies 9. History writing — Westward expansion — United States 10. Life stories — Law and order — Police and law officers
LC 00268780
Tells the entire story of Earp's amazing life, explaining why he became a legend among his contemporaries and how Hollywood reinvented him first as a hero and then as a scoundrel.
"Barra is at his best in describing the efforts of assorted Hollywood icons, including John Ford, John Sturges, and Kevin Costner, to depict the real Earp." —*Booklist*
Includes bibliographical references (p. 406-412) and index.

★ *The Last Coach: A Life of Paul*. Allen Barra. W. W. Norton & Co. 2005. xxix, 546 p. : Illustration
ISBN 9780393059823
Grades: Adult **B**
1. Bryant, Paul W. 2. Football coaches 3. Childhood 4. College football coaches 5. Football coaching 6. College football 7. Philosophy 8. Statistics 9. Social life and customs 10. United States 11. 20th century 12. Biographies 13. Sports and Competition — Football 14. Sports and Competition — Coaches 15. Life stories — Sports — Athletes 16. Life stories — Sports — Coaches, managers, and owners
LC 2005014609
Traces the life and career of the college football coach, describing his coming of age during the Depression, work with such teams as Texas A&M and Alabama, contributions to college football integration, and relationships with players and coaches.
"Anyone who loves football will further enjoy this book for its glimpse into the game before it became the multimillion-dollar business it is today." —*Library Journal*
Includes bibliographical references (p. [544]-546).

★ *Yogi Berra: Eternal Yankee*. Allen Barra. W. W. Norton & Co. 2009. 480 p.
ISBN 9780393062335
Grades: 11 12 Adult **B**
1. Berra, Yogi, 1925-2015 2. Baseball coaches 3. Baseball 4. Baseball players 5. Social life and customs 6. United States 7. 20th century 8. Biographies 9. Sports and Competition — Baseball 10. Sports and Competition — Individual Athlete 11. Life stories — Sports — Athletes 12. Adult books for young adults 13. Life stories — Sports — Coaches, managers, and owners
LC 2008045799
Allen Barra presents the life story of baseball's most successful player, Yogi Berra. From his rough-and-tumble childhood in St. Louis to the baseball Hall of Fame, Yogi has seen his share of triumphs, as well as defeats. As the most quoted, funniest athlete of all time, Yogi's story becomes complete in this larger-than-life biography.
"Barra brings to his sporting version of the Everyman story an encyclopedic knowledge and warm understanding of the game of baseball; meticulous research into business, sociology, and history; and a fluid writing style. Baseball biography taken to a higher level." —*Booklist*
Includes bibliographical references and index.

Barthel, Joan
American Saint: The Life of Elizabeth Seton. Joan Barthel; foreword by Maya Angelou. Thomas Dunne Books 2014. 304 pages
ISBN 9780312571627
Grades: Adult **B**
1. Seton, Elizabeth Ann, Saint, 1774-1821 2. Catholic women 3. Christian saints 4. Women's rights 5. Rich families 6. Converts to Catholicism 7. Nuns 8. Biographies 9. Life stories — Religion and spirituality — Religious and spiritual leaders 10. Spirituality and Religion — Christianity — Catholicism
LC 2013030995
Mother Elizabeth Seton was canonized by the Catholic Church in 1975, 200 years after her birth to a prominent Episcopalian family in New York City. In American Saint, Joan Barthel, a professor of American Studies at Wake Forest University, engagingly highlights the significance of Elizabeth's contributions to American education, the Catholic Church, and women's roles in the Church. Barthel relates Elizabeth's rejection by New York society after her conversion to Catholicism, her relocation to Maryland, her struggles within the Church, and her eventual triumph in founding the first American women's religious order and establishing the first parochial school.
"A biography of the first American saint. offering a rounded portrait of an ambitious woman who struggled mightily to fulfill the tenets of her faith: to be obedient, merciful and good." —*Kirkus*
Includes bibliographical references and index.

Bartlett, Rosamund
★ *Tolstoy: A Russian Life*. Rosamund Bartlett. Houghton Mifflin Harcourt 2011. 500 p.
ISBN 9780151014385
Grades: Adult **B**
1. Tolstoy, Leo, graf, 1828-1910 2. Authors, Russian 3. Intellectual life 4. Rebels 5. Authors 6. Russian history 7. 19th century 8. Biographies 9. Arts and En-

tertainment — Writing and Publishing 10. Life stories — Arts and culture — Writing — Authors

LC 2010050015

Draws on key Russian sources and extensive new materials to trace the influential 19th-century literary master's life and legacy, providing coverage of such topics as his early life, his troubled relationship with his wife and his evocative portrayals of beloved Russian landscapes.

Includes bibliographical references and index.

Basbanes, Nicholas A.

★ *Cross* of Snow: A Life of Henry Wadsworth Longfellow. Nicholas A. Basbanes. Alfred A. Knopf 2020. x, 461 p.

ISBN 9781101875148

Grades: Adult   B

1. Longfellow, Henry Wadsworth, 1807-1882 2. Poets, American 3. Translators 4. Creation (Literary, artistic, etc.) 5. Influence (Literary, artistic, etc.) 6. Intellectual life 7. Poetry writing 8. Literary criticism 9. 19th century 10. Biographies 11. Arts and Entertainment — Writing and Publishing 12. Life stories — Arts and culture — Writing — Poets

LC 2019028002

In Cross of Snow, the result of more than twelve years of research, including access to never-before-examined letters, diaries, journals, notes, Nicholas Basbanes reveals the life, the times, the work—the soul—of the man who shaped the literature of a new nation with his countless poems, sonnets, stories, essays, translations, and whose renown was so wide-reaching that his deep friendships included Charles Dickens, Nathaniel Hawthorne, Ralph Waldo Emerson, Julia Ward Howe, and Oscar Wilde.

"A revelatory exploration of Longfellow's life and art. . . . A welcome new biography of the iconic 19th-century poet." —*Kirkus*

This is a Borzoi Book — t.P. verso; Includes bibliographical references and index.

Basie, Count

Good Morning Blues: The Autobiography of Count Basie. as told to Albert Murray. Random House 1985. xiv, 399 p. : Illustration

ISBN 9780394548647

Grades: 11 12 Adult   B

1. Basie, Count, 1904-1984 2. Jazz musicians 3. Autobiographies and memoirs 4. Biographies 5. Arts and Entertainment — Music — Jazz and the Blues 6. Life stories — Arts and culture — Performing arts — Musicians and composers

LC 85002439

Presents the life and times of the great jazz musician and band leader as told by the man himself, from his early days playing pickup at local social events, through his arrival—and eventual triumph—in New York.

"Basie pays tribute to his colleagues and managers (and to John Hammond for discovering him), but does not hesitate to discuss their weaknesses and short-comings; his language is direct and earthy. Although some of the book reads more like a catalogue or itinerary than an autobiography, it will have strong appeal for jazz buffs and fans of the late bandleader." —*Publishers Weekly*

Includes index.

Bass, Rick

The Traveling Feast: On the Road and at the Table with America's Finest Writers. Rick Bass. Little Brown & Company 2018. 448 p.

ISBN 9780316381239

Grades: Adult   B

1. Bass, Rick, 1958- 2. Authors, American 3. Voyages and travels 4. Dinners and dining 5. Writing 6. Inspiration 7. Food 8. Friendship 9. Mentors 10. Misadventures 11. Divorced men 12. Gratitude 13. Autobiographies and memoirs 14. Life stories — Arts and culture — Writing — Authors 15. Life stories — Relationships — Friendship 16. Arts and Entertainment — Writing and Publishing 17. Food writing — Memoirs and biographies 18. Arts and Entertainment — Writing and Publishing — Literary criticism

LC 2018933125

A transformative journey written in gratitude to the award-winning author's mentors describes his midlife attempt to recapture the passions of his youth, an effort marked by encounters with famous contemporaries and a variety of colorful mishaps.

"Bass reflective, funny, and generous chronicle of culinary adventures and nourishing literary encounters will renew readers appreciation for stories and storytellers and how literature guides us back to some deeper, older place." —*Booklist*

Bastianich, Lidia

My American Dream: A Life of Love, Family, and Food. by Lidia Matticchio Bastianich. Alfred A. Knopf 2018. 304 p.

ISBN 9781524731618

Grades: Adult   B

1. Bastianich, Lidia 2. Cooks 3. Cooking, Italian 4. Growing up 5. Refugees 6. Autobiographies and memoirs 7. Life stories — arts and culture — Culinary arts 8. Food writing — Memoirs and biographies

LC 2017045478

The host of "Lidia's Kitchen" shares a memoir that traces her impoverished but loving upbringing under Tito's communist regime in Yugoslavia, her years as a refugee while trying to enter the United States, and her early start as a restaurant worker.

"A warm story of a life buoyed by resilience, determination, love of family, and food." —*Kirkus*

This is a borzoi book.

Bate, Jonathan

Radical Wordsworth: The Poet Who Changed theWorld. Jonathan Bate. Yale University Press 2020. xxii, 586 pages, 16 unnumbered pages of plates : Illustration; Color; Map

ISBN 9780300169645

Grades: Adult   B

1. Wordsworth, William, 1770-1850 2. Poets, English 3. Influence (Literary, artistic, etc.) 4. Romanticism in art 5. Nature (Aesthetics) 6. Intellectual life 7. Poetry writing 8. Literary criticism 9. Great Britain 10. 19th century 11. Biographies 12. Life stories — Arts and culture — Writing — Poets 13. Arts and Entertainment — Writing and Publishing

LC 2020931386

Published in time for the 250th anniversary of William Wordsworth's birth, this is the biography of a great poetic genius, a revolutionary who changed the world. He and his fellow Romantics changed forever the way we think about childhood, the sense of the self, our connection to the natural environment, and the purpose of poetry. But his was also a revolutionary life in the old sense of the word, insofar as his art was of memory, the return of the past, the circling back to childhood and youth. This beautifully written biography is purposefully fragmentary, momentary, and selective, opening up what Wordsworth called "the hiding-places of my power."

"In this energetic literary biography, Bate (Shakespeare and the English Romantic Imagination), a senior research fellow at Oxford University, places William Wordsworth's work in the context of his life. . . . Appealingly conveying his own love of and frustrations with Wordsworth, Bate demonstrates in his delightful volume how, flaws and all, the poet 'Made a difference' in the way future generations would think and feel." —*Publishers Weekly*

Includes bibliographical references and index; First published in 2020 in Great Britain by William Collins—Title page verso.

Bauermeister, Erica

House Lessons: Renovating a Life. Erica Bauermeister. Sasquatch Books 2020. 224 pages

ISBN 9781632172440

Grades: Adult   B

1. Bauermeister, Erica 2. Women authors, American 3. Building conservation and restoration 4. Families 5. Home (Concept) 6. Houses 7. Architecture 8. Identity 9. Design and construction 10. Washington (State) 11. Essays 12. Autobiographies and memoirs 13. Life stories — Personal growth 14. Arts and Entertainment — Architecture 15. Family and Relationships — General

LC 2020003113

ESSENTIAL AND RECOMMENDED TITLES
Biography

In this mesmerizing memoir-in-essays, Erica Bauermeister renovates a trash-filled house in eccentric Port Townsend, Washington, and in the process takes readers on a journey to discover the ways our spaces subliminally affect us.

"This will resonate with any readers who love words and old houses." —*Booklist*

Baum, Dan
Nine Lives: Death and Life in New Orleans. Dan Baum. Spiegel and Grau 2009. 288 p.
ISBN 9780385523196
Grades: Adult **B**
1. City dwellers 2. Hurricanes 3. Subcultures 4. Social life and customs 5. New Orleans, Louisiana 6. 21st century 7. 20th century 8. Society and culture — Pop culture
LC 2008031483

Nine Lives" explores New Orleans through the lives of nine characters over 40 years, bracketed by two epic hurricanes. It brings back to life the doomed city, its wondrous subcultures, and the rich and colorful lives that played themselves out within its borders.

"Baum's in-depth reporting (he was on scene during Katrina, even turning himself in at the Convention Center to chronicle the out-of-sight outrages) is evident on every page." —*Booklist*

Baylor, Elgin
Hang Time: My Life in Basketball. Elgin Baylor with Alan Eisenstock. Houghton Mifflin Harcourt 2018. 336 pages
ISBN 9780544617056
Grades: Adult **B**
1. Baylor, Elgin 2. Basketball players 3. African American basketball players 4. Professional basketball 5. Racism 6. Racism in sports 7. Ethnic identity 8. Autobiographies and memoirs 9. Life stories — Sports — Athletes 10. Life stories — Identity — Race and ethnicity 11. Sports and Competition — Basketball
LC 2017045607

The 11-time NBA All-Star and 2006 NBA Executive of the Year traces his career in professional basketball, touching on such subjects as the vertical-versus-horizontal strategies that shaped him as both a player and a general manager, his battles against racism and his relationship with the notorious Donald Sterling. Includes index.

Beah, Ishmael
★ *A Long Way Gone: Memoirs of a Boy Soldier.* Ishmael Beah. Farrar, Straus and Giroux 2007. 229 p. : Map
ISBN 9780374105235
Grades: 11 12 Adult **B**
1. Beah, Ishmael, 1980- 2. Child soldiers 3. Civil war 4. Soldiers 5. Violence 6. African history 7. Sierra Leone 8. 1990s 9. Autobiographies and memoirs 10. History writing — Wars and conflicts — Civil Wars 11. Life stories — Facing adversity — War and oppression — War survivors 12. Adult books for young adults 13. History writing — Civil wars and genocide — Africa
LC 2006017101

Alex Award, 2008; Booklist Editors' Choice: Adult Books for Young Adults, 2007; New York Times Notable Book, 2007; School Library Journal Best Books: Best Adult Books 4 Teens, 2007; YALSA Best Books for Young Adults, 2008; Children's Africana Book Awards Honor Book, Older Readers, 2008.

A human rights activist offers a firsthand account of war from the perspective of a former child soldier, detailing the violent civil war that wracked his native Sierra Leone and the government forces that transformed a gentle young boy into a killer as a member of the army.

"Told in clear, accessible language by a young writer with a gifted literary voice, this memoir seems destined to become a classic firsthand account of war and the ongoing plight of child soldiers in conflicts worldwide." —*Publishers Weekly*

Beam, Alex
American Crucifixion: The Murder of Joseph Smith and the Fate of the Mormon Church. Alex Beam. Public Affairs 2014. 352 p.
ISBN 9781610393133
Grades: Adult **B**
1. Smith, Joseph 1805-1844 2. Mormons 3. Polygamy 4. Assassination 5. Mormon polygamy 6. Martyrdom (Christianity) 7. Illinois 8. 19th century 9. History writing — United States 10. Spirituality and religion — Christianity — Mormonism
LC 2014004063

Journalist Alex Beam, a Boston Globe columnist and contributor to the Atlantic, examines the life of Latter Day Saints' founder Prophet Joseph Smith as well as the events that led to his group's move to Utah in the mid-1840s. While still in Illinois, Smith's ambitions grew, and he prepared to run for the U.S. presidency—but having led the Mormons to settle there after fleeing Missouri, he provoked violent backlash against his doctrines and was arrested and ultimately killed by gunfire while awaiting trial for perjury and polygamy. Beam's thoroughly researched and balanced narration of Smith's rise and fall will captivate anyone interested in American history, especially the history of religion.

"Beam offers a captivating saga of Smith's rise and fall and of a colorful cast of characters who contributed to the internal politics and rivalries that led to Smith's death and drove the Mormons forward to their destiny." —*Booklist*

Beauvais, Garcelle
Love Me as I Am. Garcelle Beauvais. Amistad Press 2022. 336 p.
ISBN 9780063099586
Grades: Adult **B**
1. Actors and actresses 2. Haitian Americans 3. African American women 4. Fashion models 5. Motherhood 6. Autobiographies and memoirs 7. Life stories — Arts and culture — Performing arts — Actors and actresses 8. Arts and entertainment — Movies and Television

Garcelle Beauvais's smart, inspiring, and raw memoir is an entertaining and unforgettable emotional rollercoaster ride that moves from her early childhood years in Haiti to her adolescence in Boston; from her heady days as a young model in New York—her first taste of real freedom—to Los Angeles and the many ups, downs, and then more ups, both personal and professional, she experienced in her three-decade acting career, including her massive fame as a star of the Real Housewives of Beverly Hills.

"One of the stars of the Real Housewives of Beverly Hills talks about real life. Haitian American actor and podcast host Beauvais (b. 1966), whose TV credits include Housewives, NYPD Blue, Family Matters, and the Mentalist, makes her adult book debut (she has published several children's books) with a disarmingly candid memoir." —*Kirkus*

Beavan, Colin
No Impact Man: The Adventures of a Guilty Liberal Who Attempts to Save the Planet, and the Discoveries He Makes About Himself and Our Way of Life in the Process. Colin Beavan. Farrar, Straus, and Giroux 2009. 288 p.
ISBN 9780374222888
Grades: Adult **B**
1. Beavan, Colin 2. Authors, American 3. Environmental protection 4. Sustainable living 5. Environmentalism 6. Environmental movement 7. Community activism 8. 21st century 9. Autobiographies and memoirs 10. Nature Writing — Environmental Issues 11. Life stories — Personal growth 12. Life stories — Nature and outdoors — Simple living
LC 2009010188

The author of Fingerprints describes his one-year experiment with minimizing his impact on the earth, an effort for which he eschewed technology, processed foods, and other negative-impact products while evaluating the plausibility and actual value of sustainable living.

"An inspiring, persuasive argument that individuals are not helpless in the battle against environmental degradation and global warming." —*Kirkus*
Includes index.

Bee, Vanessa A.
Home Bound: An Uprooted Daughter's Reflections on Belonging. by Vanessa A. Bee. Astra House 2022. 256 p.
ISBN 9781662601330
Grades: Adult **B**

PUBLIC LIBRARY CORE COLLECTION: NONFICTION
Twentieth Edition

1. Bee, Vanessa A, 1988- 2. Adoptees 3. Identity 4. West African people 5. Home (Concept) 6. Belonging 7. Faith (Christianity) 8. Social classes 9. Women lawyers 10. Essayists 11. Autobiographies and memoirs 12. Life stories — Relationships — Parent and child 13. Life stories — Identity 14. Family and relationships — Parenting — Adoption

LC 2022006629

A multifaceted global memoir reflecting on Bee's adoption from Cameroon, her childhood experiences with public housing and homelessness in rural France, Lyon, and London, her immigration as a teen to Nevada, and eventually rethinking her devotion to evangelical Christianity at Harvard Law. Home Bound touches on constructions of home, and the issues of identity that can complicate it, including class, race, education, faith, and nationality.

"A Cameroonian-born lawyer and essayist explores layers of a multiracial upbringing across cultures, continents, and economic classes….This richly tapestried memoir offers a unique perspective on identity as it restlessly probes the nature of belonging." —*Kirkus*

Includes bibliographical references.

Begley, Adam
The Great Nadar: The Man Behind the Camera. Adam Begley. Tim Duggan Books 2017. 256 pages

ISBN 9781101902608

Grades: Adult **B**

1. Nadar, Felix, 1820-1910 2. Photographers 3. Celebrities 4. Balloons (Aeronautics) 5. Ballooning 6. Aerial photography 7. Artists 8. Celebrity promotion 9. Publicity stunts 10. Portrait photography 11. Paris, France 12. 19th century 13. Belle Epoque (1871-1914) 14. Biographies 15. Life stories — Arts and culture 16. Arts and Entertainment — Photography 17. History writing — Arts and culture 18. History writing — Europe — France

LC 2016045382

A portrait of the fabled Parisian photographer, adventurer and pioneer discusses his bohemian youth, larger-than-life studio, pioneering exploits as a balloonist and photography sessions with such famed subjects as Victor Hugo, Gustave Courbet and Alexandre Dumas.

"Told in a pleasant, conversational style, this title is not only filled with curious, whimsical details about a lively figure, it is also is a very readable narrative." —*Library Journal*

Includes index.

Bego, Mark
Aretha Franklin: The Queen of Soul. Mark Bego. St. Martin's Press 1989. x, 340 p. : Illustration

ISBN 9780312028633

Grades: Adult **B**

1. Franklin, Aretha, 1942-2018 2. African American musicians 3. African American women musicians 4. Soul musicians 5. Biographies 6. Arts and Entertainment — Music — Rap and R&B 7. Life stories — Arts and culture — Performing arts — Musicians and composers

LC 88035939

Traces the life of Aretha Franklin from deserted child, to teenage mother, to Grammy winner, to inductee in the Rock & Roll Hall of Fame.

Includes index.

Belcher, Chris
Pretty Baby: A Memoir. Chris Belcher. Avid Reader Press 2022. 224 p.

ISBN 9781982175825

Grades: Adult **B**

1. Female domination (Sexuality) 2. Sexuality 3. LGBTQIA+ people 4. Desire 5. Identity 6. Social classes 7. Power 8. Femininity 9. Women 10. Autobiographies and memoirs 11. Life stories — Identity — LGBTQIA+ 12. Society and culture — Sex and sexuality

A queer teen rebel escapes small-town Appalachia and becomes Los Angeles's Renowned Lesbian Dominatrix in a darkly humorous memoir that upends our understanding of sexuality, class, and power.

"A professor of writing and gender studies reflects on the life path that led her into part-time sex work as a professional dominatrix." —*Kirkus*

Belcourt, Billy-Ray
★ *A History of My Brief Body: Essays*. Billy-Ray Belcourt. Two Dollar Radio 2020. 142 p.

ISBN 9781937512934

Grades: Adult **B**

1. Belcourt, Billy-Ray 2. Young gay men 3. First Nations (Canada) 4. Cree (Eeyou) (North American people) 5. Growing up 6. Homosexuality 7. Colonialism 8. Poets 9. Violence 10. Indigenous peoples of North America 11. Vulnerability 12. Intersectionality 13. Freedom 14. Love 15. Social justice 16. Autobiographies and memoirs 17. Essays 18. Canadian literature 19. Life stories — Identity — Race and ethnicity 20. Life stories — Identity — LGBTQIA+ 21. Society and culture — Ethnic studies 22. Society and culture — LGBTQIA+

LC Bl2020052265

BC and Yukon Book Prizes, Hubert Evans Non-Fiction Prize, 2021.

A memoir of Canadian poet Billy-Ray Belcourt from the Driftpile Cree Nation.

"At the nexus of critical race and queer thought, this should become a timeless interdisciplinary resource for students, educators, and social justice activists." —*Kirkus*

Includes bibliographical references and Internet addresses.

Bell, Julian
Van Gogh: A Power Seething. Julian Bell. New Harvest 2014. 208 p.

ISBN 9780544343733

Grades: Adult **B**

1. Gogh, Vincent van, 1853-1890 2. Painters 3. Social life and customs 4. Netherlands 5. 19th century 6. Biographies 7. Arts and Entertainment — Painting, Drawing, and Sculpture 8. Life stories — Arts and culture — Artists

LC Bl2015000972

A passionate account of the tortured life and tragic death of the greatest artist of the nineteenth century, by renowned critic and painter Julian Bell.

"Bell describes with glorious acuity the rapid artistic evolution of this self-taught genius propelled by a 'Peculiar inner seething,' celebrating with unique fluency Van Goghs 'Rapturous vision' and the 'Visual electricity' of his masterpieces. A vividly illuminating portrait both for readers versed in Van Gogh and those who are newly curious." —*Booklist*

Bell, Laura
Claiming Ground. by Laura Bell. Alfred A. Knopf 2010. 256 p.

ISBN 9780307272881

Grades: Adult **B**

1. Bell, Laura, 1954- 2. Solitude 3. Women and nature 4. Social isolation 5. Ranching 6. Shepherds 7. Young women 8. Ranch life 9. Ranches 10. Social life and customs 11. Wyoming 12. Autobiographies and memoirs 13. Nature Writing — Personal Responses 14. Life stories — Nature and outdoors

LC 2009029644

Documents the author's late-1970s experiences in various eclectic jobs in Wyoming, a journey of self-exploration during which she met numerous eccentrics, struggled to forge a home, and realized her love for someone from her past.

"After college, a Kentucky girl spends a summer in Wyoming to find herself and regroup. Thirty years later, she's still there. In this memoir, Bell vividly depicts her life out West, starting with her first job herding sheepan occupation usually done by men. She goes on to write about her life as a ranch hand, masseuse, housewife, stepmother, and forest ranger, mixing work experiences with touching and poignant accounts of family and friends. Bell here turns in satisfying reading for ranching enthusiasts, memoir fanatics, and anyone who likes to get lost in stories about rural life and nature's beauty." —*Library Journal*

Bell, Madison Smartt
Child of Light: A Biography of Robert Stone. Madison Smartt Bell. Doubleday 2020. 608 pages

ISBN 9780385541602

Grades: Adult **B**

1. Stone, Robert, 1937-2015 2. Writing 3. Drug addiction 4. Interpersonal relations 5. Families 6. Authors, American 7. 20th century 8. Biographies 9. Arts

ESSENTIAL AND RECOMMENDED TITLES
Biography

and Entertainment — Writing and Publishing 10. Life stories — Arts and culture — Writing — Authors

LC 2019022780

A portrait of American novelist Robert Stone traces his relationship with a mentally unstable mother, his military service, his Stanford education, his membership in the Merry Pranksters and the publication of such novels as the award-winning Dog Soldiers.

"Perhaps not the last word on Stone but essential for students and fans of the writer's works." —*Kirkus*

Toussaint Louverture: A Biography. Madison Smartt Bell. Pantheon Books 2007. 333 p. : Map
ISBN 9780375423376
Grades: Adult **B**
1. Toussaint Louverture, 1743-1803 2. Revolutionaries 3. Generals 4. Revolutions 5. Caribbean history 6. Haiti 7. 1790s 8. 1800s (Decade) 9. Biographies 10. Life stories — Politics — Activists and reformers 11. History writing — Latin America

LC 2006045848

Presents a biography of Toussaint Louverture that captures the frequently contradictory and complex life of the leader of the late-eighteenth-century Haitian Revolution that became the only successful slave revolt in history.

"This is the best biography of Toussaint yet, in large part because Bell does not shy away from the man's contradictions." —*New York Times Book Review*

Map on lining papers; Includes bibliographical references (p. 315-318) and index.

Bella, Timothy
Barkley: A Biography. Timothy Bella. Hanover Square Press 2022. 320 p.
ISBN 9781335484970
Grades: Adult **B**
1. Barkley, Charles, 1963- 2. African Americans 3. Professional basketball players 4. African American basketball players 5. Basketball 6. Television newscasters and commentators 7. Growing up 8. Professional athletes 9. Biographies 10. Sports and Competition — Basketball 11. Sports and Competition — Individual Athlete 12. Life stories — Sports — Athletes

A biography of basketball player Charles Barkley.

Bella, a Washington Post staff writer and editor, debuts with an brawny look at basketball star Charles Barkley, who 'Helped change not just how fans watched the game but also how they talked about it.' —*Publishers Weekly*

Benedict, Jeff
Lebron. Jeff Benedict. Simon & Schuster 2023. 480 p.
ISBN 9781982110895
Grades: Adult **B**
1. James, LeBron 2. Basketball players 3. African American basketball players 4. Professional basketball players 5. Basketball 6. African Americans 7. Success (Concept) 8. Biographies 9. Life stories — Sports — Athletes 10. Sports and competition — Basketball

From the #1 New York Times bestselling author of Tiger Woods comes a biography of LeBron James, one of the greatest athletes of all time and the figure at the center of social movements, based on three years of exhaustive research and more than 200 interviews.

"Even devoted fans will emerge with a greater understanding of the superstar." —*Publishers Weekly*

★ *Tiger Woods*. Jeff Benedict and Armen Keteyian. Simon & Schuster 2018. xix, 490 pages
ISBN 9781501126420
Grades: Adult **B**
1. Woods, Tiger 2. Golfers 3. Athletes 4. Celebrities 5. African American men 6. Asian American men 7. Biographies 8. Life stories — Sports — Athletes 9. Sports and Competition — Golf

LC Bl2018038015

A behind-the-scenes portrait of the golf star's meteoric rise and fall from grace draws on interviews from every aspect of Wood's life to reveal the true Tiger Woods.

"Journalists and coauthors Benedict and Keteyian (both, the System) have deconstructed the carefully crafted movie script that has been Tiger Woods's life." —*Library Journal*

Includes bibliographical references (pages 409-469) and index.

Benner, Erica
Be Like the Fox: Machiavelli in His World. Erica Benner. W. W. Norton & Company 2017. 384 p.
ISBN 9780393609721
Grades: Adult **B**
1. Machiavelli, Niccolo, 1469-1527 2. Intellectuals 3. Intellectual life 4. Ideology 5. Political scientists 6. Power 7. Politicians 8. Authors, Italian 9. Italian history 10. Florence, Italy 11. Renaissance (1300-1600) 12. 15th century 13. 16th century 14. Age of exploration (1419-1610) 15. Biographies 16. Life stories — Arts and culture — Writing — Authors 17. History writing — Renaissance — Europe

LC 2017000694

The dramatic, myth-shattering story of how Machiavelli, the most misunderstood thinker of all time, fought to change his corrupt world.

Bennetts, Leslie
Last Girl Before Freeway: The Life, Loves, Losses, and Liberation of Joan Rivers. Leslie Bennetts. Little, Brown and Company 2016. 304 p.
ISBN 9780316261302
Grades: Adult **B**
1. Rivers, Joan 2. Women comedians 3. Television producers and directors 4. Comedians 5. Entertainers 6. United States 7. Autobiographies and memoirs 8. Biographies 9. Life stories — Arts and culture — Performing arts — Entertainers and celebrities

LC 2016938566

A portrait of the influential comedienne explores her enduring cultural legacy, discussing subjects ranging from her husband's suicide and her feud with Johnny Carson to her numerous cosmetic surgeries and her controversial death in 2014.

Berg, A. Scott
Kate Remembered. A. Scott Berg. Berkley Books 2004. xii, 370 p. : Illustration
ISBN 9780425199091
Grades: Adult **B**
1. Hepburn, Katharine, 1907-2003 2. Berg, A. Scott (Andrew Scott) 3. Family relationships 4. Interpersonal relations 5. Film industry and trade 6. Entertainment industry and trade 7. Films 8. Actors and actresses 9. Bisexual women 10. Social life and customs 11. United States 12. 20th century 13. Biographies 14. Arts and Entertainment — Movies and Television 15. Life stories — Arts and culture — Performing arts — Actors and actresses 16. Life stories — Identity — LGBTQIA+

LC Bl2004110214

Recounts the remarkable life of leading lady Katharine Hepburn, presenting a portrait of the four-time Academy Award winner through her intimate conversations and private reflections on love, family, friendship, and show business.

"In this posthumous biography, the author reveals details about such pivotal events as the death of her brother by hanging, her relationships with powerful men like Howard Hughes and John Ford, and her slow, sad decline. Berg's writing is so intimate that readers may feel they are hiding behind a curtain as they listen to the stories he elicits from his subject. Kate herself comes across pretty much the way she did on screen: Bossy, courageous, and self-involved." —*Booklist*

Originally published: New York : G.P. Putnam's Sons, c2003.

★ *Wilson*. A. Scott Berg. G.P. Putnam's Sons 2013. 800 p.
ISBN 9780399159213
Grades: Adult **B**
1. Wilson, Woodrow, 1856-1924 2. World War I 3. Democrats 4. World politics 5. Presidents 6. Politicians 7. Politics and government 8. United States 9. 20th century 10. 1910s 11. 1920s 12. Biographies 13. History writing — Pres-

idency — 20th century — United States 14. History writing — Early 20th century — United States 15. Life stories — Politics — Politicians

LC 2013009339

Booklist Editors' Choice, 2013.

This biography of the 28th President of the United States from the Pulitzer Prize-winning author of Lindbergh includes details from recently-discovered papers that highlight the character of the scholar-leader who shepherded his country through the first World War.

"Berg portrays Wilson as an utterly new kind of chief executive, in a mold that has yet to be refilled. Readable, authoritative and, most usefully, inspiring." —Kirkus

Berg, Mary

The Diary of Mary Berg: Growing up in the Warsaw Ghetto. Mary Berg; edited by Susan Lee Pentlin. Oneworld 2006. 350 p. : Illustration; Map

ISBN 9781851684724

Grades: 11 12 Adult **B**

1. Berg, Mary, 1924-2013 2. Jewish people 3. World War II 4. Holocaust (1933-1945) 5. Personal diaries 6. Polish people 7. German occupation, World War II 8. European history 9. Warsaw, Poland 10. Poland 11. History writing — Wars and conflicts — Homefront — World War II 12. Adult books for young adults

Relates the experiences of a child prisoner of the Warsaw ghetto as recorded in her diary between 1940 and 1943, describing profound levels of suffering and her eventual rescue.

Includes bibliographical references (p. 266-272) and index; Originally published: New York : L.B. Fischer, 1945.

Berg, Ryan

No House to Call My Home: Love, Family, and Other Transgressions. Ryan Berg. Nation Books 2015. 320 p.

ISBN 9781568585093

Grades: Adult Professional **B**

1. Berg, Ryan, 1974- 2. Gay teenagers 3. Group homes for teenagers 4. Counselors 5. LGBTQIA+ children 6. LGBTQIA+ teenagers 7. Autobiographies and memoirs 8. Life stories — General 9. Society and culture — LGBTQIA+ 10. Adult books for young adults

LC 2015011424

Minnesota Book Award for General Nonfiction, 2016.

Underemployed and directionless, Ryan Berg took a job in a group home for disowned and homeless LGBTQ (lesbian, gay, bisexual, transgender and questioning) teenagers. His job was to help these teens discover their self worth, get them back on their feet, earn high school degrees, and find jobs. But he had no idea how difficult it would be, and the complexities that were involved with coaxing them away from dangerous sex work and cycles of drug and alcohol abuse, and helping them heal from years of abandonment and abuse. In No House to Call My Home, Ryan Berg tells profoundly moving, intimate, and raw stories from the frontlines of LGBTQ homelessness and foster care.

"Through their compelling stories, Berg looks at inequalities suffered by LGBTQ youth in housing, public safety, health care, prison, immigration, employment, poverty, and homelessness." —Booklist

Includes bibliographical references and index.

Berger, Eric

Liftoff: Elon Musk and the Desperate Early Days That Launched Spacex. Eric Berger. William Morrow & Company 2021. 304 p.

ISBN 9780062979971

Grades: Adult **B**

1. Musk, Elon 2. Rockets (Aviation) 3. Corporations 4. Scientists 5. Engineers 6. New businesses 7. Rocketry 8. Space flight 9. Technological innovations 10. Aerospace industry and trade 11. Science Writing — Space and Flight 12. Science Writing — Great Engineering Feats 13. Life stories — Science, technology, and medicine — Scientists and inventors

In September 2008, SpaceX's last chance for success lifted off. ... and accelerated like a dream, soaring into orbit flawlessly. That success would launch a miraculous decade for the company, in which SpaceX grew from building a single-engine rocket to one with a staggering 27 engines; created two different spacecraft, and mastered reusable-rocket descents using mobile drone ships on the open seas. It marked a level of production and achievement that has not been seen since the space race of the 1960s. But these achievements would not have been possible without SpaceX's first four flight tests. Drawing on unparalleled access and exclusive interviews with dozens of former and current employees—including Elon Musk—Eric Berger tells the complete story of this foundational generation that transformed SpaceX into the world's leading space company.

"In this page-turner, award-winning journalist Berger explores the critical early days of SpaceX, the rocket manufacturing company founded by Elon Musk." —Library Journal

Berger, William

Verdi with a Vengeance: An Energetic Guide to the Life and Complete Works of the King of Opera. William Berger. Vintage Books 2000. VIII, 497 p. : Illustration

ISBN 9780375705182

Grades: Adult **B**

1. Verdi, Giuseppe, 1813-1901 2. Classical music 3. Composers 4. Social life and customs 5. Italy 6. 19th century 7. Biographies 8. Arts and Entertainment — Music — Opera 9. Life stories — Arts and culture — Performing arts — Musicians and composers

LC 00042261

Provides background on the artist's childhood and struggle with success, scene-by-scene analyses of such operas as Aida, La traviata, and Don Carlos, and a discussion on his musical recordings.

"The author provides a brief overview of the composer's life and times and examines the connections between contemporary politics and Verdi's creative output. A glossary and recommended recordings, films, and soundtracks are included. Informative and eminently readable for the novice and scholar alike." —Library Journal

Includes discographical references (p. 431-448), bibliographical references (p. 459-463), an annotated film list (p. 464-473), and index.

Bergner, Daniel

★ *Sing for Your Life: A Story of Race, Music, and Family.* Daniel Bergner. Little Brown & CO 2016. 320 p.

ISBN 9780316300674

Grades: Adult **B**

1. Green, Ryan Speedo 2. Opera singers 3. Life change events 4. Child abuse 5. City life 6. Juvenile detention 7. Change (Psychology) 8. Growing up 9. Poverty 10. Imprisonment 11. African American men 12. Racism 13. Teenage abuse victims 14. Virginia 15. Biographies 16. Life stories — Facing adversity — Personal transformation 17. Society and culture — Race 18. Arts and entertainment — Music — Classical 19. Adult books for young adults

LC Bl2016035233

A chronicle of a young Black man's journey from violence to the world's elite opera circles describes Ryan Speedo Green's abuse-marked upbringing and struggles with racism and imprisonment before winning a New York Metropolitan Opera competition.

Bergreen, Laurence

In Search of a Kingdom: Francis Drake, Elizabeth I, and the Perilous Birth of the British Empire. Laurence Bergreen. Custom House 2021. 464 p; Illustration; Map

ISBN 9780062875358

Grades: Adult **B**

1. Drake, Francis, Sir, 1540?-1596 2. Elizabeth I, Queen of England, 1533-1603 3. Privateering 4. Trips around the world 5. Explorers 6. Admirals 7. Naval history 8. British history 9. Great Britain 10. Renaissance (1300-1600) 11. Elizabethan era (1558-1603) 12. 16th century 13. Tudor period (1485-1603) 14. Biographies 15. History writing — Exploration 16. Life stories — People in history — Explorers

LC 2020039354

An exploration narrative of the highest order: the bestselling author of Over the Edge of the World brings alive the extraordinary life and adventures of Sir Francis Drake, whose mastery of the seas during the reign of Queen Elizabeth I

ESSENTIAL AND RECOMMENDED TITLES
Biography

changed the course of history-as a pirate raiding Spanish galleons, as the first explorer to successfully circumnavigate the globe, and as a naval hero who defeated the Spanish Armada and reshaped the global order.

"With a keen sense of adventure and a sharp grasp of personalities on sea and land, Bergreen (Over the Edge of the World, 2008) details Drake's round-the-world adventures as well as political intrigues and mutinous sailors." —*Booklist*

Includes bibliographical references and index.

Marco Polo: From Venice to Xanadu. Laurence Bergreen. A.A. Knopf 2007. 415 p. : Illustration; Color; Map
ISBN 9781400043453
Grades: 9 10 11 12 Adult   **B**
1. Polo, Marco, 1254-1323? 2. Explorers 3. Voyages and travels 4. European history 5. Asia 6. Renaissance (1300-1600) 7. 13th century 8. Biographies 9. History writing — Renaissance — Europe 10. History writing — Exploration 11. Life stories — People in history — Explorers

LC 2007021860

Booklist Editors' Choice, 2007.

A portrait of the thirteenth-century explorer, adventurer, and global traveler follows Marco Polo from his youth in Venice to his journey to Asia and role in the court of Kublai Khan, to his return to Europe, and discusses his influence on the history of his era.

"The author gives a full-blooded rendition of Polo's astonishing journey. It is richly researched and vividly conveyed." —*Washington Post Book World*

Includes bibliographical references (p. [367]-391) and index.

Over the Edge of the World: Magellan's Terrifying Circumnavigation of the Globe. Laurence Bergreen. Morrow 2003. xvi, 458 p. : Illustration; Color; Map
ISBN 9780066211732
Grades: 11 12 Adult   **B**
1. Magellan, Ferdinand, 1480?-1521 2. Trips around the world 3. Explorers 4. Exploration 5. Expeditions 6. Ocean travel 7. Consequences 8. Voyages and travels 9. 16th century 10. Renaissance (1300-1600) 11. History writing — Exploration 12. History writing — Renaissance — Europe 13. Adventure writing — Exploration

LC 2003050143

A chronicle of Ferdinand Magellan's sixteenth-century voyage around the world draws on first-person accounts and describes his crew's experiences with mutiny, navigation, death, and Magellan's ruthless leadership.

"The author tells a well-rounded story of Magellan, not just that of the romanticized hero but also that of the explorer's darker side. . . . Fascinating reading for history buffs, and a great story that rivals any seagoing adventure." —*Booklist*

Colored map on endpapers; Includes bibliographical references (p. [415]-439).

Berlin, Edward A.

King of Ragtime: Scott Joplin and His Era. Edward A. Berlin. Oxford University Press 1995. xii, 334 p. : Illustration
ISBN 9780195101089
Grades: 11 12 Adult   **B**
1. Joplin, Scott, 1868-1917 2. Composers 3. United States 4. Biographies 5. Arts and Entertainment — Music — Classical

LC 96107624

The story of the popular, critically acclaimed music of Scott Joplin shares a definitive portrait of a man who was part of the first post-Civil War generation of African-American pioneers who escaped poverty and low social status through entertainment.

First published in 1994 by Oxford University Press ... First issued as an Oxford University Press paperback, 1995—T.P. verso; List of Joplin's works: P. [259]-270; Includes bibliographical references (p. [325]-327), music, and index.

Berlin, Lucia

★ *Welcome Home: A Memoir with Selected Photographs and Letters.* Lucia Berlin. Farrar, Straus and Giroux 2018. 160 p.
ISBN 9780374287597
Grades: Adult   **B**
1. Berlin, Lucia 2. Marriage 3. Voyages and travels 4. Women travelers 5. Women authors 6. Autobiographies and memoirs 7. Biographies 8. Life stories — Arts and culture — Writing — Authors

LC 2018017727

A compilation of previously unpublished sketches, photos, and letters from the late American short story writer depict and describe the places and people she met in Alaska, Argentina, Kentucky, Mexico, Chile, and New York City.

"An excellent start to understanding a writer and her work." —*Kirkus*

Bernstein, Burton

★ *Leonard Bernstein: American Original.* Burton Bernstein and Barbara B. Haws. Collins 2008. 240 p.
ISBN 9780061537868
Grades: 11 12 Adult   **B**
1. Bernstein, Leonard, 1918-1990 2. Musicians 3. Conductors (Music) 4. Composers 5. Music, American 6. Broadway, New York City 7. 20th century 8. Biographies 9. Essays 10. Arts and Entertainment — Music — Classical 11. Life stories — Arts and culture — Performing arts — Musicians and composers 12. Adult books for young adults

LC 2008013702

A visual tribute to the life and career of the pioneering conductor evaluates his role as a first American-born and trained conductor of a major orchestra, in an account that evaluates his contributions in a range of venues as well as his part in opening doors for women musicians.

"A flat-out wonderful book." —*Booklist*

Includes index.

Bernstein, Carl

★ *Chasing History: A Kid in the Newsroom.* Carl Bernstein. Henry Holt & Company 2021. 352 p.
ISBN 9781627791502
Grades: Adult   **B**
1. Bernstein, Carl, 1944- 2. Journalists 3. Investigative journalism 4. 1960s 5. Autobiographies and memoirs 6. Life stories — Arts and culture — Writing — Journalists 7. Arts and Entertainment — Writing and publishing

The Pulitzer Prize winning coauthor of All the President's Men recounts the world of the 1960s as he experienced it as a young reporter learning his craft at the Washington Star.

"Pulitzer Prize winner Bernstein (All the President's Men) looks back at his early days as a reporter, before his Watergate reporting made him a household name, in this entertaining memoir. . . . Admirers of this remarkable journalist will find much to love in this charming account." —*Publishers Weekly*

Berr, Helene

The Journal of Helene Berr. Helene Berr; translated from the French by David Bellos. Weinstein Books 2008. 307 pages : Illustration; Map
ISBN 9781602860643
Grades: 11 12 Adult   **B**
1. Berr, Helene, 1921-1945 2. Jewish people 3. Holocaust (1933-1945) 4. World War II 5. Western European people 6. French people 7. Paris, France history 8. France 9. 1940s 10. Diaries 11. Life stories — Facing adversity — War and oppression — Holocaust 12. History writing — Wars and conflicts — Holocaust — World War II 13. Adult books for young adults

LC 2009293998

Ranging from 1942 to her family's 1944 deportation, the personal journal of the daughter of a prominent Jewish family describes two years of life in war-time Paris under Nazi occupation, writing not only of the harsh realities of being a Jew in Vichy France but also of her love of literature and music, the beauty of Paris, and more.

"A worthy addition to Holocaust literature, evoking the sweetness of one life lost and reminding us with urgent clarity how inexorably it was swept under those tragic times." —*Kirkus*

Includes bibliographical references and index.

PUBLIC LIBRARY CORE COLLECTION: NONFICTION
Twentieth Edition

Berry, Mary Frances
My Face Is Black Is True: Callie House and the Struggle for Ex-slave Reparations. Mary Frances Berry. Alfred A. Knopf 2005. xiv, 314 p. : Illustration
ISBN 9781400040032
Grades: 11 12 Adult   **B**
1. House, Callie, 1861-1928 2. African American women political activists 3. Women political activists 4. African Americans 5. Reparations 6. Biographies 7. History writing — Women's history 8. Life stories — Politics — Activists and reformers 9. Adult books for young adults 10. History writing — African American — Civil rights — United States
LC 2004051330

Booklist Editors' Choice, 2005.

Offers a portrait of Callie House, a former slave, Nashville seamstress, and widowed mother of five who pioneered original efforts to seek reparations for ex-slaves, and the persecution she faced from the U.S. government for her efforts.

"The author unearths the intriguing story of Callie House (1861-1928), a Tennessee washerwoman and seamstress become activist, and the organization she led, the National Ex-Slave Mutual Relief, Bounty and Pension Association... Students and scholars of African-American history, as well as those engaged in the current reparations debates, will be deeply informed by the rise and fall of the Ex-Slave Association." —*Publishers Weekly*

This is a Borzoi Book—T.P. verso; Includes bibliographical references (p. 253-295) and index.

Bertch, Jane
The French Ingredient: Making a Life in Paris One Lesson at a Time: A Memoir. Jane Bertch. Ballantine Books 2024. 272 p.
ISBN 9780593500422
Grades: Adult   **B**
1. Bertch, Jane 2. Cooks 3. Cooking, French 4. Moving to a new country 5. Expatriates 6. Women entrepreneurs 7. New businesses 8. Cooking schools 9. Teaching 10. Determination 11. Success (Concept) 12. American people 13. Western European people 14. French people 15. Paris, France 16. Autobiographies and memoirs 17. Life stories — Arts and culture — Culinary arts 18. Food writing — Memoirs and biographies 19. Travel Writing — Living Abroad 20. Debut title
LC 2023028981

The author, an American woman who had the gall to open a cooking school in Paris in 2009, shares her true story of triumphing over French elitism to create a thriving business that welcomes international visitors to learn the care, precision, patience and beauty involved in French cooking.

"An inspiring story that will appeal to foodies and budding entrepreneurs alike." —*Kirkus*

Bertinelli, Valerie
Enough Already: Learning to Love the Way I Am Today. Valerie Bertinelli. Mariner Books 2022. 304 p.
ISBN 9780358567363
Grades: Adult   **B**
1. Bertinelli, Valerie, 1960- 2. Actors and actresses 3. Women television personalities 4. Middle age 5. Self-acceptance 6. Self-perception 7. Autobiographies and memoirs 8. Life stories — Arts and culture — Performing arts — Actors and actresses 9. Life stories — Personal growth 10. Arts and Entertainment — Movies and Television

The actress and TV personality returns with a look at turning 60 and learning to love herself the way she is despite a past spent judging herself too harshly.

"In a series of brutally frank essays, Bertinelli (Losing It), host of the Food Network show Valerie's Home Cooking, looks back on the emotional struggles and triumphs of her life.... By turns raw and inspiring, this contains a little bit of wisdom for everyone." —*Publishers Weekly*

Beyer, Kurt
Grace Hopper and the Invention of the Information Age. Kurt Beyer. MIT Press 2009. xii, 389 p. : Illustration
ISBN 9780262013109
Grades: Adult   **B**
1. Hopper, Grace Murray, 1906-1992 2. Women computer engineers 3. Computer science 4. Technological innovations 5. Computer engineers 6. Biographies 7. Science Writing — Computing, the Internet, and Technology 8. Life stories — Science, technology, and medicine — Scientists and inventors
LC 2008044229

"In Beyer's fascinating mix of biography and technological history, Grace Hopper comes vividly to life as a navy admiral who launched the art of computer programming." —*Booklist*

Includes bibliographical references and index.

Bhattacharya, Ananyo
The Man from the Future: The Visionary Life of John Von Neumann. Ananyo Bhattacharya. W.W. Norton & Company 2022. 368 p.
ISBN 9781324003991
Grades: Adult   **B**
1. VonNeumann, John, 1903-1957 2. Mathematicians 3. 20th century 4. Biographies 5. Science Writing — Mathematics 6. Life stories — Science, technology, and medicine
LC 2021050487

The smartphones in our pockets and computers like brains. The vagaries of game theory and evolutionary biology. Nuclear weapons and self-replicating spacecrafts. All bear the fingerprints of one remarkable, yet largely overlooked, man: John von Neumann. Taking us on an astonishing journey, Ananyo Bhattacharya explores how a combination of genius and unique historical circumstance allowed a single man to sweep through a stunningly diverse array of fields, sparking revolutions wherever he went. The Man from the Future is an insightful and thrilling intellectual biography of the visionary thinker who shaped our century.

"John von Neumann (1903-1957) was one of the most important scientists of the 20th century and 'Probably the smartest man on Earth,' contends journalist Bhattacharya in his knotty debut.... Those with a strong grounding in the material will be entranced." —*Publishers Weekly*

Includes bibliographical references and index.

Bialosky, Jill
Poetry Will Save Your Life: A Memoir. by Jill Bialosky. Atria Books 2017. 208 p.
ISBN 9781451693201
Grades: Adult   **B**
1. Bialosky, Jill 2. Poets, American 3. American poetry 4. Influence (Psychology) 5. Growing up 6. Personal conduct 7. Literary criticism 8. 21st century 9. Autobiographies and memoirs 10. Life stories — Arts and culture — Writing — Poets 11. Adult books for young adults
LC 2016056306

The critically acclaimed author of the Prize presents a coming-of-age memoir organized around poems by such classic writers as Robert Frost, Emily Dickinson and Sylvia Plath, pairing each poem with key events that shaped her life, from the first time she fell in love and her sister's suicide to September 11 and the birth of a child.

"With brief poet biographies, this is a resplendent and invaluable anthology and an involving, richly illuminating narrative." —*Booklist*

Biden Owens, Valerie
Growing up Biden: A Memoir. Valerie Biden Owens. Celadon Books 2022. 304 p.
ISBN 9781250821768
Grades: Adult   **B**
1. Biden Owens, Valerie, 1945- 2. Biden, Joseph R, 1942- 3. Women political consultants 4. Political consultants 5. Political campaigns 6. Presidential election, 2020 7. Siblings 8. Family relationships 9. Presidents 10. United States 11. Autobiographies and memoirs 12. Life stories — Politics 13. Life stories — Relationships — Family 14. Politics and global affairs — Political figures
LC 2021059429

A memoir from Valerie Biden Owens, Joe Biden's younger sister, trusted confidante and lifelong campaign manager. Valerie, one of the first female campaign managers in United States history, writes of the role of family, faith, and

ESSENTIAL AND RECOMMENDED TITLES
Biography

fate in shaping her life, and the power of empathy and kindness in the face of turmoil and division. Growing up Biden details Valerie's decades-long professional career in politics, and the central role she played in her brother's life as an insightful adviser, an ever-loyal advocate and best friend.

"This family memoir by Joe Biden's youngest sister, who was also his longtime campaign manager, is unusual in combining accounts of family life and of a politician's campaign and governing experiences….Owens's narrative is informative and engaging and is a perceptive firsthand account of President Biden's background." —*Library Journal*

Biden, Jill
Where the Light Enters: Building a Family, Discovering Myself. Jill Biden. Flatiron Books 2019. 224 p.
ISBN 9781250182326
Grades: Adult   B
1. Biden, Jill 2. Biden, Joseph R, 1942- 3. Family relationships 4. Marriage 5. Teachers 6. Politicians' spouses 7. Loss 8. Autobiographies and memoirs 9. Life stories — Relationships — Family 10. Life stories — Politics 11. Life stories — Education — Scholars and educators
LC 2019000561

The former Second Lady describes her marriage to Joe Biden and the role of politics in her life and teaching career, sharing intimate insights into the traditions, resilience and love that have helped her family establish balance and endure tragedy.

Biden, Joseph R.
Promise ME, Dad: A Year of Hope, Hardship, and Purpose. Joe Biden. Flatiron Books 2017. 272 p.
ISBN 9781250171672
Grades: Adult   B
1. Biden, Joseph R, 1942- 2. Biden, Beau, 1969-2015 3. Fathers and sons 4. Coping 5. People with terminal illnesses 6. Hope 7. Loss 8. Vice-presidents 9. Legislators 10. Family relationships 11. United States 12. Autobiographies and memoirs 13. Biographies 14. Life stories — Relationships — Parent and child 15. Life stories — Facing adversity — Coping with death
LC Bl2017036907

The former vice-president of the United States chronicles the difficult final year of his son's battle with cancer, his efforts to balance his responsibilities to the country and his family, and the lessons he learned.

"Written without an ounce of self-pity, it serves instead as an homage to a man Biden admired above all others and offers a passionate ray of hope to those who have suffered the loss of a loved one with the reassuring message that there is, indeed, a way through their grief." —*Booklist*

Biden, Robert Hunter
Beautiful Things: A Memoir. Hunter Biden. Gallery Books 2021. 288 p.
ISBN 9781982151119
Grades: Adult   B
1. Biden, Robert Hunter, 1970- 2. Drug addiction 3. Alcoholism 4. Loss 5. Recovering alcoholics 6. Death of mothers 7. Recovering drug abusers 8. Family relationships 9. Marital conflict 10. Grief 11. Drug abuse 12. Sobriety 13. Autobiographies and memoirs 14. Life stories — Facing adversity — Medical issues — Addiction

When he was two-years-old, Hunter Biden was badly injured in a car accident that killed his mother and baby sister. In 2015, he suffered the devastating loss of his beloved big brother, Beau, who died of brain cancer at the age of forty-six. These hardships were compounded by the collapse of his marriage and a years-long battle with drug and alcohol addiction. In Beautiful Things, Hunter recounts his descent into substance abuse and his tortuous path to sobriety. The story ends with where Hunter is today—a sober married man with a new baby, finally able to appreciate the beautiful things in life.

"President Biden's son takes a searing look at the vicissitudes of his life in this bracing warts-and-all memoir.… This courageous self-assessment makes the despair of substance abuse devastatingly palpable." —*Publishers Weekly*

Bigsby, Christopher William Edgar
Arthur Miller: 1915-1962. Christopher Bigsby. Harvard University Press 2009. 776 p.
ISBN 9780674035058
Grades: Adult
1. Miller, Arthur, 1915-2005 2. Playwrights, American 3. Social life and customs 4. United States 5. 20th century 6. Biographies 7. Arts and Entertainment — Theater 8. Life stories — Arts and culture — Artists 9. Arts and Entertainment — Writing and Publishing — Literary criticism
LC 2009002489

Shortlisted for the James Tait Black Memorial Prize for Biography, 2008.

"A richly detailed, revealing look at the making of a playwright and a man." —*Kirkus*

Includes bibliographical references and index.

Bilal, Wafaa
Shoot an Iraqi: Life, Art and Resistance Under the Gun. by Wafaa Bilal and Kari Lydersen. City Lights Books 2008. xxii, 177 p. : Illustration; Color
ISBN 9780872864917
Grades: Adult   B
1. Bilal, Wafaa 2. Artists 3. Conceptual art 4. Iraq War, 2003-2011 5. Expatriate artists 6. Computer art 7. Iraqi people 8. Southwest Asian (Middle Eastern) people 9. Social life and customs 10. United States 11. Iraq 12. 21st century 13. Autobiographies and memoirs 14. Arts and Entertainment — Painting, Drawing, and Sculpture 15. Life stories — Arts and culture — Artists 16. Life stories — Facing adversity — War and oppression 17. Adult books for young adults
LC 2008020487

Booklist Editors' Choice, 2008.

The creator of "Domestic Tension," an unsettling interactive performance piece that speaks to the horrors of life in a conflict zone, reveals his experiences growing up under Saddam Hussein's rule.

"A powerful and demanding read, that is, frankly, a literary punch to the gut." —*Booklist*

Bilger, Burkhard
Fatherland: A Memoir of War, Conscience, and Family Secrets. Burkhard Bilger. Random House 2023. 256 p.
ISBN 9780385353984
Grades: Adult   B
1. Gönner, Karl, 1899-1979 2. Bilger, Burkhard 3. Former Nazis 4. German people 5. Secrets 6. Grandfathers 7. Teachers 8. Conscience 9. Families 10. War 11. World War II 12. German occupation, World War II 13. French history 14. 20th century 15. Autobiographies and memoirs 16. Life stories — Relationships — Family 17. History Writing — Wars and conflicts — World War II
LC 2022035829

A New Yorker staff writer tells the story of his nearly ten-year quest to uncover the truth about his grandfather, a Nazi party chief, and the questions it raises about reckoning with the pasts of our families.

"Discovering that his grandfather was a Nazi imprisoned for war crimes, the author explores his life.…A moving, humane biography of a minor Nazi official who did his job without the usual horrors." —*Kirkus*

Includes bibliographical references.

Bilton, Chrysta
Normal Family: On Truth, Love, and How I Met My 35 Siblings. Chrysta Bilton. Little Brown & Company 2022. 320 p.
ISBN 9780316536547
Grades: Adult   B
1. Bilton, Chrysta 2. Families 3. Siblings 4. Truth 5. Secrets 6. Children of sperm donors 7. Childhood 8. Love 9. Children of LGBTQIA+ parents 10. Family secrets 11. Dysfunctional families 12. Loss 13. Autobiographies and memoirs 14. Family and relationships — Families 15. Life stories — Relationships — Family 16. Family and relationships — Siblings

A riveting, nuanced portrait of unforgettable characters thrown together by chance and DNA.

"Eloquently written and compulsively readable, Bilton's jaw-dropping coming-of-age memoir—and the love and survival found within its pages—is one readers won't soon forget." —*Library Journal*

Binyon, T. J.
Pushkin: A Biography. T.J. Binyon. Knopf 2003. xxix, 727 p, 16 p. of plates : Illustration; Map; Portrait
ISBN 9781400041107
Grades: Adult **B**
1. Pushkin, Aleksandr Sergeevich, 1799-1837 2. Poets, Russian 3. Marriage 4. Men-women relations 5. 19th century 6. Biographies 7. Arts and Entertainment — Writing and Publishing 8. Life stories — Arts and culture — Writing — Poets
LC 2003112113

New York Times Notable Book, 2003; Samuel Johnson Prize for Nonfiction, 2003.

Discusses the Russian poet's birth in 1799 Moscow, survival of Napoleon's invasion and other military conflicts, scrutiny and censure for his satirical writings and personal beliefs, most significant literary achievements, and death during a duel in 1837.

"The author argues that Pushkin's political views and rebellious temper were a continual source of trouble, inviting criticism and condemnation his entire life and eventually ending it in 1837 when he was fatally wounded in a duel with George D'Anthes. A stunning achievement, this thorough biography is sure to become the definitive account of Pushkin's life for years to come and will appeal to the scholar and general reader alike." —*Library Journal*

Includes bibliographical references (p. [681]-685) and index.

Birbiglia, Mike
The New One: Painfully True Stories from a Reluctant Dad. Mike Birbiglia; with poems by J. Hope Stein. Grand Central Publishing 2020. 256 p.
ISBN 9781538701515
Grades: Adult **B**
1. Birbiglia, Mike 2. Comedians 3. Fatherhood 4. Parent and child 5. Families 6. Parenting 7. Pregnancy 8. Adulthood 9. Fathers and daughters 10. Husband and wife 11. Humor writing — Family and relationship humor 12. Family and Relationships — Families 13. Life stories — Relationships — Family
LC 2019049244

The comedian and author of the memoir Sleepwalk with Me shares laugh-out-loud observations on the haphazard journey of parenting as experienced by him and his poet wife that inspired a Broadway production.

"Hilarious, relatable, cringeworthy, and effortlessly entertaining, particularly for new parents or those in contemplation." —*Kirkus*

Bird, Kai
American Prometheus: The Triumph and Tragedy of J. Robert Oppenheimer. by KAI Bird and Martin J. Sherwin. A.A. Knopf 2005. xiii, 721 p. : Illustration
ISBN 9780375726262
Grades: Adult **B**
1. Oppenheimer, J. Robert, 1904-1967 2. Physicists 3. Science 4. Physics 5. McCarthyism 6. Political persecution 7. Atomic bomb 8. United States history 9. United States 10. 20th century 11. Biographies 12. Page to screen 13. Science Writing — Physics 14. History writing — Wars and conflicts — Atomic Bomb — World War II 15. Life stories — Law and order — Armed forces personnel
LC 2004061535

Booklist Editors' Choice, 2005; National Book Critics Circle Award for Biography, 2005; New York Times Notable Book, 2005; Pulitzer Prize for Biography or Autobiography, 2006.

A portrait of scientist J. Robert Oppenheimer, the father of the atomic bomb, discusses his role in the twentieth-century scientific world, as well as his roles as family man and head of Princeton's Institute for Advanced Studies.

"The authors explore Oppenheimer's life from his youth as a child prodigy through his radical political activities in the 1930s, and on to the Manhattan Project and its political fallout. The humanity of the troubled man behind the porkpie hat emerges on every page of this unquestionably definitive account." —*Booklist*

Made into a theatrical movie called Oppenheimer, to be released in 2023; Includes bibliographical references (p. [685]-699) and index.

Birdsall, John
The Man Who Ate Too Much: The Life of James Beard. John Birdsall. W. W. Norton & Company 2020. 464 p.
ISBN 9780393635713
Grades: Adult **B**
1. Beard, James, 1903-1985 2. Cooks 3. Gay men 4. Cooking, American 5. 20th century 6. Biographies 7. Life stories — Arts and culture — Culinary arts 8. Food Writing — Memoirs and biographies
LC 2020015582

After World War II, a newly affluent United States reached for its own gourmet culture, one at ease with the French international style of Escoffier, but also distinctly American. Enter James Beard, authority on cooking and eating, his larger-than-life presence and collection of whimsical bow ties synonymous with the nation's food for decades, even after his death in 1985.

"Highly recommended, this book offers new insight into Beard's life and time. It also helps another generation of foodies appreciate how Beard shaped American cuisine and helps all of us better understand the struggles LGBQT people faced in the mid-20th century." —*Library Journal*

Includes bibliographical references and index.

Biskind, Peter
Star: How Warren Beatty Seduced America. Peter Biskind. Simon & Schuster 2010. 640 p.
ISBN 9780743246583
Grades: Adult **B**
1. Beatty, Warren, 1937- 2. Actors and actresses 3. Celebrities 4. Films 5. United States 6. Biographies 7. Arts and Entertainment — Movies and Television 8. Life stories — Arts and culture — Performing arts — Actors and actresses
LC 2009022225

Drawing on interviews with Warren Beatty's colleagues and intimates, as well as the star himself, the author offers a tell-all biography of the Hollywood legend responsible for such classics as "Bonnie and Clyde," "Heaven Can Wait," and "Reds."

Includes bibliographical references and index.

Bix, Herbert P.
Hirohito and the Making of Modern Japan. Herbert P. Bix. Harper Collins 2000. xi, 800 p, 16 p. of plates : Illustration; Map
ISBN 9780060193140
Grades: Adult **B**
1. Hirohito, Emperor of Japan, 1901-1989 2. Imperialism, Japanese 3. World War II 4. Rulers 5. Politics and government 6. Japanese history 7. Japan 8. 20th century 9. Showa period (1926-1989) 10. Biographies 11. Impartial writing 12. Life stories — Politics — Royalty 13. History writing — Asia — Japan
LC 99089427

Booklist Editors' Choice, 2000; National Book Critics Circle Award for Biography, 2000; Pulitzer Prize for General Nonfiction, 2001; New York Times Notable Book, 2000.

In this groundbreaking biography of the Japanese emperor Hirohito, Herbert P. Bix offers the first complete, unvarnished look at the enigmatic leader whose sixty-three-year reign ushered Japan into the modern world. Never before has the full life of this controversial figure been revealed with such clarity and vividness.

"In 1945, fearing that the Japanese would resist American occupation unless the Emperor ordered them to obey, General MacArthur colluded with Hirohito in maintaining that the sovereign had been powerless to control Japan's military leaders. {Bix, uses newly available sources to argue that Hirohito was a war criminal. An imperialist whose policies reflected his belief in the racial superiority of the Japanese, Hirohito governed by manipulation for almost two decades, and used the threat of Soviet Communism to justify domestic repression and

ESSENTIAL AND RECOMMENDED TITLES
Biography

soaring military budgets. The author's virtuoso scholarship and accessible narrative invite us into Hirohito's world." —*The New Yorker*
Includes bibliographical references and index.

Bjork, Daniel W.
B.F. Skinner: A Life. Daniel W. Bjork. Basic Books 1993. xiv, 298 p, 8 p. of plates : Illustration
ISBN 9780465006113
Grades: Adult **B**
1. Skinner, B. F, 1904-1990 2. Psychologists 3. Behaviorism (Psychology) 4. Psychology 5. United States history 6. 20th century 7. Biographies 8. Life stories — Science, technology, and medicine — Healthcare professionals
LC 92054522
The first major biography of the preeminent psychologist traces Skinner's life and work and places his contributions within the American tradition of utopian and social-political debate.
"Bjork places Skinner squarely in the context of the US social, technological, and political history. Although heavily documented, Bjork's book is very readable because documentation is in endnotes. A handsome, well-indexed work, with an excellent bibliography." —*Choice*
Includes bibliographical references (p. [273]-284) and index.

Black Elk
Black Elk Speaks: Being the Life Story of a Holy Man of the Oglala Sioux. John G. Neihardt; foreword by Vine Deloria, Jr; with illustrations by Standing Bear; essays by Alexis N. Petri and Lori Utecht. University of Nebraska Press 2004. xxix, 270 p. : Illustration; Color; Map
ISBN 9780803283916
Grades: 11 12 Adult **B**
1. Black Elk, 1863-1950 2. Oglala (North American people) 3. Indigenous peoples of North America 4. Healers 5. Spiritual life 6. Philosophy 7. Lakota (North American people) 8. Indigenous peoples of North America — History 9. Indigenous peoples of North America — Religion 10. 19th century 11. Autobiographies and memoirs 12. Biographies 13. History writing — Indigenous peoples — United States 14. Life stories — Religion and spirituality — Religious and spiritual leaders
LC 2004012692
Reveals the life of Lakota healer Nicholas Black Elk as he led his tribe's battle against white settlers who threatened their homes and buffalo herds, and describes the victories and tragedies at Little Bighorn and Wounded Knee.
Includes index; Originally published: New York : W. Morrow, 1932.

Black Thought
The Upcycled Self: A Memoir on the Art of Becoming Who We Are. Tariq Trotter and Jasmine Martin. One World 2023. 190 p.
ISBN 9780593446928
Grades: Adult **B**
1. Black Thought, 1973- 2. Rap musicians 3. African American men 4. Growing up 5. Orphans 6. Loss 7. Accidents 8. Guilt in children 9. Music 10. Creativity 11. Hip-hop culture 12. Communities 13. Bands (Music) 14. Friendship 15. Rap music 16. North American people 17. American people 18. Philadelphia, Pennsylvania 19. Autobiographies and memoirs 20. Life stories — Arts and culture — Performing arts — Musicians and composers 21. Life stories — Relationships — Growing up 22. Life stories — Facing adversity — Disasters and tragedies 23. Arts and Entertainment — Music — Rap and R&B 24. Debut title
Today Tariq Trotter—better known as Black Thought—is the platinum-selling, Grammy-winning co-founder of the Roots and one of the most exhilaratingly skillful and profound rappers our culture has ever produced. But his story begins with a tragedy. In The Upcycled Self, Trotter doesn't only narrate a riveting and moving portrait of the artist as a young man, he gives readers a courageous model of what it means to live an examined life. In vivid vignettes, he tells the dramatic stories of the four powerful relationships that shaped him—with community, friends, art, and family—each a complex weave of love, discovery, trauma, and loss.
"An eloquently insightful autobiography from an iconic rapper and wordsmith." —*Kirkus*

Black, Dustin Lance
Mama's Boy: A Story from Our Americas. by Dustin Lance Black. Alfred A. Knopf 2018. 336 p.
ISBN 9781524733278
Grades: Adult **B**
1. Black, Dustin Lance 2. Gay men 3. Mothers and sons 4. Growing up 5. Screenwriters 6. Mormons 7. Coming out (Sexual or gender identity) 8. Conflict in families 9. Familial love 10. LGBTQIA+ rights 11. Social advocacy 12. Resilience 13. Texas 14. California 15. Autobiographies and memoirs 16. Biographies 17. Life stories — Identity — LGBTQIA+ 18. Life stories — Relationships — Parent and child 19. Adult books for young adults
LC 2018036767
From the Academy Award-winning screenwriter and political activist, a candid, vivid, powerfully resonant memoir about growing up as a gay Mormon in Texas that is, as well, a moving tribute to the mother who taught him about surviving against all odds Dustin Lance Black wrote the Oscar-winning screenplay for Milk and helped overturn California's anti-gay marriage Proposition 8, but as an LGBTQ+ activist he has unlikely origins. Mama's Boy is a stirring celebration of the connections between mother and son, Redstates and Blue, and the spirit of optimism and perseverance that can create positive change in the world.
"Black provides a wholly en g rossing account of how a mother and son evolved beyond their potentially divisive religious and political beliefs to uncover a source of strength and unity through their enduring bond. A terrifically moving memoir of the myriad complexities of family dynamics." —*Kirkus*
This is a Borzoi book.

Blain, Keisha N.
Until I Am Free: Fannie Lou Hamer's Enduring Message to America. Keisha N. Blain. Beacon Press 2021. 181 pages
ISBN 9780807061503
Grades: Adult **B**
1. Hamer, Fannie Lou, 1917-1977 2. African American women civil rights workers 3. Civil rights 4. Civil rights workers 5. African Americans 6. Civil Rights Movement 7. Social advocates 8. United States history 9. Mississippi 10. Life stories — Politics — Activists and reformers 11. Life stories — Identity — Race and ethnicity 12. History writing — African American — Civil rights — United States
LC 2021019372
National Book Critics Circle Award for Biography finalist, 2021.
Blending together social commentary, biography and history, an award-winning historian challenges us to listen to Fannie Lou Hamer, a working-poor and disabled Black woman activist and intellectual of the civil rights movement, as we grapple with modern concerns around race, inequality and social justice.
"This excellent introduction to Hamer and her life is well-contextualized." —*Library Journal*
Includes bibliographical references and index.

Blair, Selma
Mean Baby: A Memoir of Growing up. Selma Blair. Alfred a Knopf 2022. 336 p.
ISBN 9780525659495
Grades: Adult **B**
1. Blair, Selma, 1972- 2. Actors and actresses 3. Growing up 4. Alcoholism 5. Addiction 6. Mothers 7. Families 8. Psychic trauma 9. People with multiple sclerosis 10. Women 11. Autobiographies and memoirs 12. Life stories — Arts and culture — Performing arts — Actors and actresses 13. Life stories — Facing adversity — Medical issues 14. Life stories — Relationships — Growing up 15. Arts and entertainment — Movies and television 16. Family and relationships — General
The celebrated Hollywood actress and model, in this original, intelligent and wise memoir, lays bare her addiction to alcohol, her devotion to her brilliant and complicated mother, the moments she had flirted with death and how she found surprising salvation in her multiple sclerosis diagnosis.
"This compassionate and intelligent work will leave fans floored." —*Publishers Weekly*

PUBLIC LIBRARY CORE COLLECTION: NONFICTION
Twentieth Edition

Blair, Tony
A Journey: My Political Life. Tony Blair. Alfred A. Knopf 2010. xvi, 700 p, 32 p. of plates : Illustration; Color
ISBN 9780307269836
Grades: Adult   B
1. Blair, Tony, 1953- 2. Conservatism 3. Politicians 4. Political reform 5. Conservatives 6. Political ethics 7. Prime ministers 8. International relations 9. Leadership 10. Great Britain 11. 1990s 12. 2000s (Decade) 13. Autobiographies and memoirs 14. History writing — Europe — United Kingdom 15. Life stories — Politics — Politicians
LC 2010028262
"Without delving too deeply into his personal life, . [Blair] gives the reader a good sense of his role not just as a public figure but also as a son, husband, and father. Particulars of British party politics might elude some American readers, but the narrative keeps flowing. Essential for readers of current British politics." —*Library Journal*
This is a Borzoi book—T.P. verso; Includes bibliographical references and index.

Blais, Madeleine
Queen of the Court: The Many Lives of Tennis Legend Alice Marble. Madeleine Blais. Atlantic Monthly Press 2023. 288 p.
ISBN 9780802128324
Grades: Adult   B
1. Marble, Alice, 1913-1990 2. Women tennis players 3. Women athletes 4. Women celebrities 5. Tennis 6. Actors and actresses 7. Women singers 8. Civil rights 9. Social advocacy 10. Sports history 11. Biographies 12. Life stories — Sports — Athletes 13. Sports and Competition — Individual Athlete 14. Sports and Competition — Tennis 15. History writing — Women's history
LC 2023011521
In August 1939, Alice Marble graced the cover of Life magazine, photographed by the famed Alfred Eisenstaedt. She was a glamorous worldwide celebrity, having that year won singles, women's doubles, and mixed doubles tennis titles at both Wimbledon and the US Open. Yet today one of America's greatest female athletes and most charismatic characters is largely forgotten. Queen of the Court places her back on center stage.
"An engagingly thorough biography of a dazzling woman." —*Kirkus*
Includes bibliographical references and index.

Blakinger, Keri
Corrections in Ink: A Memoir. Keri Blakinger. St. Martin's Press 2022. 288 p.
ISBN 9781250272850
Grades: Adult   B
1. Blakinger, Keri 2. Women journalists 3. Figure skaters 4. Self-destructive behavior 5. Drug addicts 6. Heroin addicts 7. Prisoners 8. Former convicts 9. Privilege (Social psychology) 10. Prisons for women 11. Investigative journalism 12. Prison reform 13. Autobiographies and memoirs 14. Society and culture — Violence and crime — Criminal justice system 15. Life stories — Facing adversity — Medical issues — Addiction 16. Life stories — Arts and culture — Writing — Journalists 17. Life stories — Law and order — Prisoners and inmates
LC 2022002306
An memoir discusses a woman's journey—from the ice rink to addiction and a prison sentence to the newsroom—and how she emerged with a fierce determination to expose the broken system she experienced.
"An investigative reporter reflects on the time she spent in the prison system for a drug crime....A gorgeously written, page-turning memoir about addiction, prison, and privilege." —*Kirkus*

Blanco, Richard
The Prince of Los Cocuyos: A Miami Childhood. Richard Blanco. Ecco Press 2014. 288 p.
ISBN 9780062313768
Grades: Adult   B
1. Blanco, Richard, 1968- 2. Poets 3. Gay men 4. Immigrants 5. Culture conflict 6. Hispanic Americans 7. Growing up 8. Autobiographies and memoirs 9. Life stories — Identity — LGBTQIA+ 10. Life stories — Relationships — Growing up 11. Life stories — Arts and culture — Writing — Poets 12. Adult books for young adults
LC 2014501685
Lambda Literary Award for Gay Memoir/Biography.
A ... memoir from the first Latino and openly gay inaugural poet, which explores his coming-of-age as the child of Cuban immigrants and his attempts to understand his place in America while grappling with his burgeoning artistic and sexual identities.
"Filled with colorful characters, often poignant and sometimes melancholy, Blancos episodic memoir is a meditation on belonging, on self-acceptance, and on his familys almost mystical connection to Cuba." —*Booklist*

Blanning, T. C. W.
Frederick the Great: King of Prussia. Tim Blanning. Random House 2016. 720 p.
ISBN 9781400068128
Grades: Adult   B
1. Frederick II, the Great, King of Prussia, 1712-1786 2. Enlightenment (European intellectual movement) 3. Social change 4. Rulers 5. Prussia 6. Biographies 7. Life stories — Politics — Royalty 8. History writing — Europe — Germany 9. History writing — Wars and conflicts
LC 2015030616
King Frederick II of Prussia, known as "the Great," brilliantly sustained the well-run state he inherited from his father, Frederick I. Yet in all other respects the younger Frederick was the opposite of his predecessor, who had physically abused him and rejected the music, art, and philosophy he loved. In this superbly written biography, historian Tim Blanning explores Frederick II's psychology while detailing his life and vividly chronicling his accomplishments. General biography lovers and fans of 18th-century European history will find this an engaging study.
"Readers both casual and scholarly will enjoy this profile for the in-depth examination of its subject, his placement in the historical events of the time, and his future in German history." —*Library Journal*
Originally published by Allen Lane in the UK—Title page verso; Includes bibliographical references and index.

Blight, David W.
★ *Frederick Douglass: Prophet of Freedom.* David W. Blight. Simon & Schuster 2018. 864 p.
ISBN 9781416590316
Grades: Adult   B
1. Douglass, Frederick, 1818-1895 2. Abolitionists 3. African American abolitionists 4. Enslaved people 5. Oratory 6. Political oratory 7. African Americans 8. Civil rights 9. Human rights 10. Philosophers 11. Thought and thinking 12. Anti-slavery movements 13. United States history 14. 19th century 15. Biographies 16. Life stories — Politics — Activists and reformers 17. History writing — African American — Enslavement — United States 18. Life stories — Facing adversity — War and oppression — Enslaved people 19. History writing — Reconstruction — United States
LC 2018007511
ALA Notable Book, 2019; Los Angeles Times Book Prize for Biography, 2018; New York Times Notable Book, 2018; Pulitzer Prize for History, 2019.
Chronicles the life of the escaped slave who became one of the greatest orators of his day and a leading abolitionist and writer.
"This magnum opus surpasses previous singular biographies in heft and depth, establishing an essential text for students and educators seeking to understand Douglass's complex and expansive narrative. It will appeal to general audiences and specialists alike." —*Library Journal*
Includes bibliographical references and index.

A Slave No More: Two Men Who Escaped to Freedom : Including Their Own Narratives of Emancipation. David W. Blight. Harcourt 2007. 320 p.
ISBN 9780151012329
Grades: 11 12 Adult   B

ESSENTIAL AND RECOMMENDED TITLES
Biography

1. Washington, John, 1838-1918 2. Turnage, Wallace, 1846-1916 3. Freedom seekers 4. Enslaved people 5. Working class 6. Civil war 7. United States Civil War, 1861-1865 8. African Americans 9. African American soldiers 10. United States history 11. United States 12. Virginia 13. North Carolina 14. 19th century 15. American Civil War era (1861-1865) 16. Collective autobiographies and memoirs 17. Biographies 18. History writing — African American — Enslavement — United States 19. Life stories — Facing adversity — War and oppression — Enslaved people 20. Adult books for young adults

LC 2007014467

Two slave narratives that document the experiences of runaway slaves who managed to reach the protection of Union forces are accompanied by biographies of both men that reconstruct their childhoods, escape, Civil War service, and successful later lives.

Includes bibliographical references and index.

Blom, Onno
Young Rembrandt: A Biography. Onno Blom; translated from the Dutch by Beverley Jackson. W. W. Norton & Company 2020. 288 p. : Illustration
ISBN 9780393531794
Grades: Adult **B**

1. Rembrandt Harmenszoon van Rijn, 1606-1669 2. Painters 3. Painting, Dutch 4. Childhood 5. Dutch people 6. Social life and customs 7. Netherlands 8. 17th century 9. Biographies 10. Translations — Dutch to English 11. Life stories — Arts and culture — Artists 12. Arts and Entertainment — Painting, Drawing, and Sculpture

LC 2020024524

A captivating exploration of the little-known story of Rembrandt's formative years by a prize-winning biographer. Rembrandt van Rijn's early years are as famously shrouded in mystery as Shakespeare's, and his life has always been an enigma. How did a miller's son from a provincial Dutch town become the greatest artist of his age? How in short, did Rembrandt become Rembrandt?

"This portrait will delight both casual art fans and connoisseurs alike." —*Publishers Weekly*

Includes bibliographical references and index; Originally published: London : Pushkin Press, 2019; Translated from the Dutch.

Bloom, Amy
In Love: A Memoir of Love and Loss. Amy Bloom. Random House 2022. 240 p.
ISBN 9780593243947
Grades: Adult **B**

1. Bloom, Amy, 1953- 2. Husband and wife 3. Women authors, American 4. Alzheimer's disease 5. Options, alternatives, choices 6. Physician-assisted suicide 7. Death 8. Love 9. Loss 10. People with terminal illnesses 11. Men 12. Autobiographies and memoirs 13. Life stories — Relationships — Couples 14. Life stories — Facing adversity — Coping with death 15. Family and Relationships — Aging and Death

Amy Bloom began to notice changes in her husband, Brian: He retired early from a new job he loved; he withdrew from close friendships; he talked mostly about the past. Suddenly, it seemed there was a glass wall between them, and their long walks and talks stopped. Their world was altered forever when an MRI confirmed what they could no longer ignore: Brian had Alzheimer's disease. Forced to confront the truth of the diagnosis and its impact on the future he had envisioned, Brian was determined to die on his feet, not live on his knees. Supporting each other in their last journey together, Brian and Amy made the unimaginably difficult and painful decision to go to Dignitas, an organization based in Switzerland that empowers a person to end their own life with dignity and peace.

"A beloved fiction writer shares the story of her husband's assisted suicide after being diagnosed with Alzheimer's disease. . . . As Alzheimer's becomes more prevalent, this shimmering love story and road map is must-read testimony." —*Kirkus*

Blount, Roy
Robert E. Lee. Roy Blount, Jr. Lipper/Viking 2003. 210 p.
ISBN 9780670032204
Grades: 11 12 Adult **B**

1. Lee, Robert E. (Robert Edward), 1807-1870 2. Generals 3. Command of troops 4. Confederate soldiers 5. Civil war 6. United States Civil War, 1861-1865 7. Military campaigns 8. Leadership 9. United States history 10. American Civil War era (1861-1865) 11. Biographies 12. History writing — Military — Military leadership 13. Life stories — Law and order — Military leaders 14. History writing — Wars and conflicts — American Civil War 15. Adult books for young adults

LC 2002032423

A portrait of the Civil War leader delves into his family history and personality to reveal the human behind the general, documenting how the lessons he learned from his elders were applied on the battlefield.

"Blount's concise writing keeps his biography trim and succinct, and his admiration for the subject allows for enjoyable reading." —*Booklist*

Includes bibliographical references (p. 207-210).

Blumenthal, Sidney
★ *All the Powers of Earth: The Political Life of Abraham Lincoln, 1856-1860.* Sidney Blumenthal. Simon & Schuster 2019. 512 p.
ISBN 9781476777283
Grades: Adult **B**

1. Lincoln, Abraham, 1809-1865 2. Politicians 3. Legislators 4. Debates and debating 5. Political oratory 6. Slavery 7. Ambition 8. United States history 9. 19th century 10. Biographies 11. Life stories — Politics — Politicians 12. History writing — Presidency — 19th century — United States

After a period of depression that he would ever find his way to greatness, Lincoln takes on the most powerful demagogue in the country, Stephen Douglas, in the debates for a senate seat. He sidelines the frontrunner William Seward, a former governor and senator for New York, to cinch the new Republican Party's nomination. All the Powers of Earth is the political story of all time. Lincoln achieves the presidency by force of strategy, of political savvy and determination. This is Abraham Lincoln, who indisputably becomes the greatest president and moral leader in the nation's history. But he must first build a new political party, brilliantly state the anti-slavery case and overcome shattering defeat to win the presidency.

Third volume of author's work on the life of Abraham Lincoln, following A Self-Made Man and Wrestling with His Angel.

A Self-made Man: The Political Life of Abraham Lincoln, 1809-1849. Sidney Blumenthal. Simon & Schuster 2016. 608 p.
ISBN 9781476777252
Grades: Adult **B**

1. Lincoln, Abraham, 1809-1865 2. Political leadership 3. Childhood 4. Books and reading 5. Lawyers 6. Presidents 7. Ambition 8. United States history 9. United States 10. 19th century 11. Biographies 12. History writing — Presidency — 19th century — United States 13. Life stories — Politics — Politicians

LC Bl2017022882

The first book in a multivolume biography of the sixteenth president follows his childhood as a "newsboy" and a voracious reader that molded him into a "free thinker," ultimately setting up his political aspirations and career in law.

"In this engrossing life-and-times study of the formative years of Abraham Lincoln (1809-65), before he became a national figure, political journalist and historian Blumenthal (The Strange Death of Republican America) takes the reader deep into Illinois and national politics to locate the character and content of Lincoln's ideas, interests, and identity, and to understand his driving ambition to succeed in law and politics. In doing so, the author makes the important point that Lincoln gained empathy and understanding of the people from his own self-awareness and need to escape his own origins of relative poverty and hard struggle. If Blumenthal sometimes loses Lincoln in his detailed accounting of patronage, politicking, and personalities, great and small, he effectively shows that the president's Illinois was a proving ground for the politics of expansion, economic development, nativism, anti-Mormonism, and slavery that both reflected and affected national concerns. Lincoln, the self-made man, is revealed as tried-and-true, ready for the troubled times that came in the years leading up to the Civil War." —*Library Journal*

Wrestling with His Angel: The Political Life of Abraham Lincoln, 1849-1856. Sidney Blumenthal. Simon & Schuster 2017. 576 p.
ISBN 9781501153785

Grades: Adult   **B**

1. Lincoln, Abraham, 1809-1865 2. Debates and debating 3. Political oratory 4. Lawyers 5. Intellectual life 6. Political science 7. Equality 8. Presidents 9. Ambition 10. United States history 11. United States 12. 19th century 13. Biographies 14. History writing — Presidency — 19th century — United States 15. Life stories — Politics — Politicians

LC Bl2017019319

The second volume of this acclaimed biography of the 16th president explores how he rebounded from the disintegration of the Whig Party and took on the anti-Immigration party in Illinois to clear a path for a new Republican Party.

"A painstakingly researched portrait of the political landscape as the country inched toward civil war." —*Kirkus*

This book follows Blumenthal's A Self-Made Man: the Political Life of Abraham Lincoln, 1809-1849, 2016.

Blunk, Jonathan

James Wright: A Life in Poetry. Jonathan Blunk. Farrar, Straus and Giroux 2017. 528 p.

ISBN 9780374178598

Grades: Adult   **B**

1. Wright, James Arlington, 1927-1980 2. Poets, American 3. Biographies 4. Life stories — Arts and culture — Writing — Poets

LC 2017003852

The sweeping authorized biography of one of America's most complex, influential, and enduring poets.

"A much-needed, engaging, and discerning biography that should help Wright find a new generation of readers." —*Kirkus*

Includes bibliographical references and index.

Boeheim, Jim

Bleeding Orange: Fifty Years of Blind Referees, Screaming Fans, Beasts of the East, and Syracuse Basketball. Jim Boeheim, with Jack McCallum. HarperCollins 2014. 288 p.

ISBN 9780062316646

Grades: Adult   **B**

1. Boeheim, Jim 2. College basketball 3. Basketball coaches 4. Basketball coaching 5. College basketball coaching 6. Autobiographies and memoirs 7. Biographies 8. Life stories — Sports — Coaches, managers, and owners 9. Sports and Competition — Basketball 10. Sports and Competition — Coaches

LC Bl2014048728

A candid personal account by the Syracuse head coach reflects on his life, teachers and game experiences, recounts the events of the competitive 1980s Big East conference and offers insight into allegations against assistant Bernie Fine.

"The tales from the Big East in its heyday mark some of the highlights of the book, as do his coaching insights. Sometimes accused of being a complainer on the court, Boeheim comes across as likable in this readable, thoughtful book about coaching college basketball." —*Kirkus*

Boessenecker, John

Gentleman Bandit: The True Story of Black Bart, the Old West's Most Infamous Stagecoach Robber. John Boessenecker. Hanover Square Press 2023. 352 p.

ISBN 9781335449429

Grades: Adult   **B**

1. Black Bart, 1835-1917 2. Thieves 3. Outlaws 4. Stagecoach robberies 5. Socialites 6. Detectives 7. Frontier and pioneer life 8. The West (United States) history 9. United States history 10. California 11. American Westward Expansion (1803-1899) 12. 19th century 13. Biographies 14. Life stories — Law and order — Criminals and law-breakers 15. History Writing — Westward expansion — United States 16. True Crime — Heists and Robbery

"A writer with a fascination for the storied crimes of the Wild West turns to the stagecoach robber of history and lore….An entertaining, well-researched foray into the life of a well-known but legend-layered outlaw." —*Kirkus*

Texas Ranger: The Epic Life of Frank Hamer, the Man Who Killed Bonnie and Clyde. John Boessenecker. Thomas Dunne Books 2016. 496 p.

ISBN 9781250069986

Grades: Adult   **B**

1. Hamer, Frank, 1884-1955 2. Barrow, Clyde, 1909-1934 3. Parker, Bonnie, 1910-1934 4. Police 5. Law enforcement 6. Texas 7. Biographies 8. Life stories — Law and order — Police and law officers

LC 2015048659

Chronicles the life of Frank Hamer, whose extraordinary career as a Texas Ranger made him one of the West's most legendary lawmen.

"Through the extraordinary experiences of this straight-shooting, honor-bound lawman, Boessenecker sets forth a critically needed look at the history of Texas lynchings and race riots while presenting evidence for the murderous nature of Bonnie and Clyde that foreordained their violent deaths." —*Library Journal*

Includes bibliographical references.

Bogus, Carl T.

Buckley: William F. Buckley Jr. And The Rise of American Conservatism. Carl T. Bogus. Bloomsbury Press 2011. x, 405 p, 8 p. of plates : Illustration

ISBN 9781596915800

Grades: Adult   **B**

1. Buckley, William F. (William Frank), 1925-2008 2. Conservatism 3. Ideology 4. Journalists 5. Politics and government 6. United States 7. 20th century 8. Biographies 9. Life stories — Arts and culture — Writing — Journalists

LC 2011012734

Documents the story and legacy of a leading architect of the American conservative movement throughout the past half century, tracing his 1955 launch of the influential National Review and his television show Firing Line as well as his role in promoting modern values about the free market, religion and an aggressive foreign policy.

"This is an insightful book that will please anyone interested in midcentury American history and politics. Anyone serious about political philosophy will learn from it. Highly recommended." —*Library Journal*

Boles, John B.

Jefferson: Architect of American Liberty. John B. Boles. Basic Books 2017. 626 p.

ISBN 9780465094684

Grades: Adult   **B**

1. Jefferson, Thomas, 1743-1826 2. Founding Fathers of the United States 3. American Revolution, 1775-1783 4. Presidents 5. Revolutions 6. Politicians 7. Politics and government 8. United States 9. Revolutionary America (1775-1783) 10. Early America (1784-1819) 11. 18th century 12. 19th century 13. Biographies 14. History writing — Presidency — 18th century — United States 15. Life stories — Politics — Politicians

LC Bl2017015381

A comprehensive biography of a Founding Father depicts him as an architect, scientist, bibliophile, paleontologist, musician and gourmet and offers new insight into his actions and thoughts about race, abolition, democracy and patriarchal responsibility.

"A fully fleshed biography of Thomas Jefferson (1743-1826) that emphasizes his creative paradoxes and accomplishments." —*Kirkus*

Bonanos, Christopher

Flash: The Making of Weegee the Famous. Christopher Bonanos. Henry Holt and Company 2018. 336 p.

ISBN 9781627793063

Grades: Adult   **B**

1. Weegee, 1899-1968 2. Photojournalists 3. Crime scenes 4. Photographers 5. Biographies 6. Life stories — People in history 7. History writing — United States

LC 2017041202

Library Journal Best Books, 2018; National Book Critics Circle Award for Biography, 2018.

Arthur Fellig's ability to arrive at a crime scene just as the cops did was so uncanny that he renamed himself "Weegee," claiming that he functioned as a human Ouija board. Weegee documented better than any other photographer the crime, grit, and complex humanity of midcentury New York City. In Flash, we get a portrait not only of the man (both flawed and deeply talented, with generous

ESSENTIAL AND RECOMMENDED TITLES
Biography

appetites for publicity, women, and hot pastrami) but also of the fascinating time and place that he occupied.

"Bonanos has meticulously researched every aspect of Weegee's life, filling this fascinating and lively account with amusing and touching anecdotes and photographs carefully selected to illustrate Weegee's work and life." —*Library Journal*

Includes index.

Bono

★ *Surrender: 40 Songs, One Story.* Bono. Alfred a Knopf 2022. 576 p.
ISBN 9780525521044
Grades: Adult   B
1. Bono, 1960- 2. Musicians 3. Growing up 4. Fame 5. AIDS activists 6. Social advocates 7. Poverty 8. Faith (Christianity) 9. Family relationships 10. Rock musicians 11. Autobiographies and memoirs 12. Life stories — Arts and culture — Performing arts — Musicians and composers 13. Life stories — Politics — Activists and reformers 14. Arts and entertainment — Music — Rock

One of the music world's most iconic artists writes about his remarkable life for the first time, from his early days growing up in Dublin, to U2's meteoric rise to fame, to his more than twenty years of activism dedicated to the fight against AIDS and extreme poverty.\

"Sometimes confessional, many times humorous, and always clever and entertaining, Bono has delivered a fascinating autobiography of a major force in popular music and world affairs for all readers." —*Library Journal*

Boot, Max

★ *The Road Not Taken: Edward Lansdale and the American Tragedy in Vietnam.* Max Boot. Liveright Publishing Corporation 2018. 784 p.
ISBN 9780871409416
Grades: Adult   B
1. Lansdale, Edward Geary, 1908-1987 2. Vietnam War, 1961-1975 3. Intelligence officers 4. Generals 5. Military intelligence 6. Military campaigns 7. 1960s 8. Biographies 9. History writing — Wars and conflicts — Vietnam War 10. Life stories — Law and order — Spies and secret agents
LC Bl2017046061

Pulitzer Prize for Biography or Autobiography finalist, 2019.

In chronicling the adventurous life of legendary CIA operative Edward Lansdale, the author aims to reframe readers' understanding of the Vietnam War.

"A probing, timely study of wrong turns in the American conduct of the Vietnam War." —*Kirkus*

Borman, Tracy

Thomas Cromwell: The Untold Story of Henry VIII's Most Faithful Servant. Tracy Borman. Atlantic Monthly Press 2015. 336 p.
ISBN 9780802123176
Grades: Adult   B
1. Cromwell, Thomas, Earl of Essex, 1485?-1540 2. Henry VIII, King of England, 1491-1547 3. Henry VII, King of England, 1491-1547 4. Prime ministers 5. Bribery 6. Politicians 7. Executions and executioners 8. Courts and courtiers 9. Reformation 10. British history 11. English history 12. Great Britain 13. England 14. Tudor period (1485-1603) 15. Medieval period (476-1492) 16. 16th century 17. Biographies 18. History writing — Medieval — Europe 19. History writing — Europe — United Kingdom 20. Life stories — Politics — Politicians
LC 2015431316

A sympathetic portrait of the architect of the English Reformation describes Cromwell's lesser-known experiences as a devoted family man, fiercely loyal servant and revolutionary who helped transform England into a modern state.

"Neglecting neither the public persona nor the private man, Borman provides an insightful biography of a much-maligned historical figure." —*Booklist*

Borneman, Walter R.

The Admirals: Nimitz, Halsey, Leahy, and King—the Five-star Admirals Who Won the War at Sea. Walter R. Borneman. Little, Brown and Co. 2012. 512 p.
ISBN 9780316097840
Grades: Adult   B
1. Nimitz, Chester W. (Chester William), 1885-1966 2. Halsey, William Frederick, 1882-1959 3. Leahy, William D. 4. King, Ernest Joseph, 1878-1956 5. Admirals 6. Naval art and science 7. Command of troops 8. World War II 9. Naval operations 10. Leadership 11. 1940s 12. 20th century 13. Biographies 14. History writing — Wars and conflicts — World War II
LC 2011032394

Evaluates the pivotal contributions of history's only five-star admirals and how their triumphs in World War II rendered the United States the world's dominant sea power.

"Borneman deftly manipulates multiple narrative strands and a wealth of detail. He vividly fleshes out the numerous vain, ambitious men vying for power at the top and examines their important decisions and lasting ramifications." —*Kirkus*

Includes bibliographical references and index.

Macarthur at War: World War II in the Pacific. Walter R. Borneman. Little, Brown and Co. 2016. VIII, 594 pages, 16 unnumbered pages of plates : Illustration; Map
ISBN 9780316405324
Grades: Adult   B
1. MacArthur, Douglas, 1880-1964 2. World War II 3. Command of troops 4. Military strategy 5. Military history 6. Generals 7. Biographies 8. History writing — Wars and conflicts — World War II 9. Life stories — Law and order — Military leaders
LC 2016931808

The author of the national best-seller the Admirals chronicles General Douglas MacArthur's amazing rise during World War II.

"An able researcher and fluent writer, Borneman holds solid appeal for the military history audience." —*Booklist*

Polk: The Man Who Transformed the Presidency and America. Walter R. Borneman. Random House 2008. 448 p.
ISBN 9781400065608
Grades: Adult   B
1. Polk, James K. (James Knox), 1795-1849 2. Politicians 3. Presidents 4. Politics and government 5. Leadership 6. United States 7. 19th century 8. Biographies 9. History writing — Presidency — United States 10. History writing — Antebellum America — United States 11. Life stories — Politics — Politicians 12. History writing — Presidency — 19th century — United States
LC 2007014040

A biography of a misunderstood and under-appreciated American president follows the political career of James K. Polk and the events of his administration, including the acceptance of Texas into the union and the expansion of presidential powers.

"The author presents a birth-death biography of Polk. Borneman has a pleasing style and makes fine use of primary sources that all demonstrate why Polk is habitually ranked as one of the ten best presidents by historians." —*Library Journal*

Includes bibliographical references and index.

Bostridge, Mark

Florence Nightingale: The Making of an Icon. Mark Bostridge. Farrar, Straus and Giroux 2008. 672 p.
ISBN 9780374156657
Grades: Adult   B
1. Nightingale, Florence, 1820-1910 2. Nurses 3. Crimean War, 1853-1856 4. British history 5. 19th century 6. Biographies 7. History writing — Europe — United Kingdom 8. History writing — Women's history 9. Science Writing — Medicine and health — Doctors and nurses 10. Life stories — Science, technology, and medicine — Healthcare professionals 11. Adult books for young adults
LC 2008031424

Elizabeth Longford Prize for Historical Biography, 2009.

A profile of the iconic Victorian social reformer evaluates her scandalous decision to break with the conventions of her privileged class to work as a nurse, the myths surrounding her, and the controversial nature of her achievements.

"Bostridge presents a well-researched, and comprehensive biography of Nightingale, drawing heavily on letters, diaries, and other primary sources in a successful effort to create a balanced and authentic portrait of the woman, not the myth. Beginning with moving depictions of Nightingale's struggles to be allowed to pursue her calling despite her family's objections, Bostridge skillfully illuminates the spiritual and philosophical motivations that drove Nightingale's impassioned and lifelong dedication to the causes of nursing and public health reform." —*Library Journal*

Includes bibliographical references.

Boswell, James

★ *The* **Life** *of Samuel Johnson*. James Boswell; with an introduction by Claude Rawson. Knopf 1992. LIII, 1278 p. : Illustration

ISBN 9780679417170

Grades: 11 12 Adult   **B**

1. Johnson, Samuel, 1709-1784 2. Authors, English 3. Lexicographers 4. 18th century 5. Biographies 6. Arts and Entertainment — Writing and Publishing — Literary criticism 7. Life stories — Arts and culture — Writing 8. Arts and Entertainment — Writing and Publishing

LC 92052915

Boswell's classic biography of the eighteenth-century English lexicographer, critic, and conversationalist.

Includes bibliographical references (p. xxxiv-xxxvii) and index.

Bourdain, Anthony

★ **Kitchen** *Confidential: Adventures in the Culinary Underbelly*. Anthony Bourdain. Bloomsbury 2000. x, 307 p.

ISBN 9781582340821

Grades: Adult   **B**

1. Bourdain, Anthony. 1956-2018 2. Cooks 3. Cooking 4. Food 5. Food industry and trade 6. Restaurants 7. Social life and customs 8. New York City 9. Autobiographies and memoirs 10. Food writing — Memoirs and biographies 11. Life stories — Arts and culture — Culinary arts

LC 2003267610

A New York City chef recounts his experiences in the restaurant business, and exposes abuses of power, sexual promiscuity, drug use, and other secrets of life behind kitchen doors.

"This is one bitter, nasty, searing, hard-to-swallow piece of work. But if you can choke the thing down, you'll probably wake up grinning in the middle of the night. In a style partaking of Hunter S. Thompson, Iggy Pop and a little Jonathan Swift, Bourdain gleefully rips through the scenery to reveal private backstage horrors little dreamed of by the trusting public. To a world infested with synthesized romance, candlelit illusions and sentimental piety, Kitchen Confidential offers a nice palate-clearing taste of poison." —*New York Times Book Review*

Medium *Raw: A Bloody Valentine to the World of Food and the People Who Cook*. Anthony Bourdain. Ecco 2010. xviii, 281 p.

ISBN 9780061718946

Grades: Adult   **B**

1. Bourdain, Anthony. 1956-2018 2. Cooks 3. Cooking 4. Food 5. Food industry and trade 6. Restaurants 7. Social life and customs 8. New York City 9. Autobiographies and memoirs 10. Food writing — Memoirs and biographies 11. Life stories — Arts and culture — Culinary arts

LC Bl2010014257

Tracking his own strange and unexpected voyage from journeyman cook to globe-traveling professional eater and drinker, and even to fatherhood, Bourdain takes no prisoners as he dissects what he's seen, pausing along the way for a series of confessions, rants, investigations, and interrogations of some of the most controversial figures in food.

"This book mixes personal memoir with travelogues and ruminations on such matters as the degradation of the American hamburger, the dumbing down of the Food Network, the tedium of multicourse tasting menus and the rise of food gurus such as David Chang. Mr. Bourdain is a vivid, bawdy and often foul-mouthed writer. He thrills in the attack, but he is also an enthusiast who writes well about things he holds dear. His detailed reporting on the backroom lives of restaurant employees is terrific." —*Wall Street Journal*

Bowdler, Michelle

★ *Is Rape a Crime?: A Memoir, an Investigation, and a Manifesto*. Michelle Bowdler. Flatiron Books 2020. 304 p.

ISBN 9781250255631

Grades: Adult   **B**

1. Bowdler, Michelle 2. Rape 3. Rape victims 4. Women social advocates 5. Violent crimes 6. Law 7. Rape investigation 8. Sexual violence 9. Psychic trauma 10. Victims of crimes 11. Social justice 12. Human rights 13. Civil rights 14. Autobiographies and memoirs 15. Life stories — Facing adversity — Victims of crime 16. Society and culture — Violence and crime — Criminal justice system 17. Society and culture — Social activism and philanthropy

LC 2019060188

Writer and public health executive Michelle Bowdler's memoir indicts how sexual violence has been addressed for decades in our society, asking whether rape is a crime given that it is the least reported major felony, least successfully prosecuted, and fewer than 3% of reported rapes result in conviction. Cases are closed before they are investigated and DNA evidence sits for years untested and disregarded. In 1984, the Boston Sexual Assault Unit was formed as a result of a series of break-ins and rapes that terrorized the city, of which Michelle's own horrific rape was the last. Twenty years later, after a career of working with victims like herself, Michelle decides to find out what happened to her case and why she never heard from the police again after one brief interview.

"This is a brilliant study of how society views rape." —*Publishers Weekly*

Includes bibliographical references.

Bowker, Gordon

★ *James Joyce: A Biography*. Gordon Bowker. Farrar, Straus and Giroux 2012. 624 p.

ISBN 9780374178727

Grades: Adult   **B**

1. Joyce, James, 1882-1941 2. Authors, Irish 3. Modernism (Literature) 4. Irish people 5. Irish people in foreign countries 6. Western European people 7. Expatriates 8. Europe 9. 20th century 10. Biographies 11. Arts and Entertainment — Writing and Publishing 12. Life stories — Arts and culture — Writing — Authors

LC 2011045954

Booklist Editors' Choice, 2012.

A revealing new biography—the first in more than fifty years—of one of the twentieth-century's towering literary figures—James Joyce, author of "Ulysses."

"The extent to which Bowker ties life events, even minor ones, to details in Joyce's works sets this book apart. This is where scholars will benefit as much as Joyce novices who are interested in learning more about this trailblazing author who changed the way fiction is written and read." —*Library Journal*

Includes bibliographical references and index.

Bowler, Kate

No Cure for Being Human: (and Other Truths I Need to Hear). Kate Bowler. Random House 2021. 240 p.

ISBN 9780593230770

Grades: Adult   **B**

1. Bowler, Kate 2. Women college teachers 3. Terminal illness 4. Time 5. Mortality 6. Death 7. Immunotherapy 8. Purpose in life 9. Loss 10. Joy and sorrow 11. Faith (Christianity) 12. People with cancer 13. Family relationships 14. Colon cancer 15. Autobiographies and memoirs 16. Canadian literature 17. Life stories — Facing adversity — Medical issues — Physical illness 18. Family and Relationships — Illness and the Family

LC 2021010350

When she discovers that she has cancer at the age of 35, the author searches for a way forward as she mines the wisdom—and absurdity—of our modern "best life now" advice industry, learning how to deal with her diagnosis on her own terms.

"In heartbreaking essays, Bowler (Everything Happens for a Reason) recounts lessons learned after being diagnosed with stage four colon cancer at the age of 35.... Those in need of a wake-up call will find it in this breathtaking narrative." —*Publishers Weekly*

ESSENTIAL AND RECOMMENDED TITLES
Biography

Boyer, Anne
*The **Undying**: Pain, Vulnerability, Mortality, Medicine, Art, Time, Dreams, Data, Exhaustion, Cancer, and Care.* Anne Boyer. Farrar, Straus and Giroux 2019. 192 p.
ISBN 9780374279349
Grades: Adult   B
1. Boyer, Anne, 1973- 2. Women authors 3. Poets 4. Breast cancer 5. Mastectomy 6. Chemotherapy 7. Medical care 8. Cancer 9. Mortality 10. Literature 11. Psychology 12. Treatment 13. People with cancer 14. Women 15. Anger 16. Life stories — Facing adversity — Medical issues — Physical illness 17. Life stories — Arts and culture — Writing — Poets 18. Society and culture — Illness and disease
LC 2019000373
Pulitzer Prize for General Nonfiction, 2020.

A week after her forty-first birthday, the acclaimed poet Anne Boyer was diagnosed with highly aggressive triple-negative breast cancer. For a single mother living paycheck to paycheck who had always been the caregiver rather than the one needing care, the catastrophic illness was both a crisis and an initiation into new ideas about mortality and the gendered politics of illness.

"Boyers gorgeous language elevates this artful, piercing narrative well above the average medical memoir." —*Publishers Weekly*

Includes bibliographical references.

Boylan, Jennifer Finney
***Good** Boy: My Life in Seven Dogs.* Jennifer Finney Boylan. Celadon Books 2020. 288 p.
ISBN 9781250261878
Grades: Adult   B
1. Boylan, Jennifer Finney, 1958- 2. Dog owners 3. Dogs 4. Women and dogs 5. Trans women 6. Unconditional love 7. Self-acceptance 8. Authors, American 9. Human-animal relationships 10. United States 11. 20th century 12. Autobiographies and memoirs 13. Biographies 14. Life stories — Identity — LGBTQIA+ 15. Life stories — Relationships — Pets and owners 16. Family and relationships — Pets and owners
LC 2019037746

The best-selling author of She's Not There, New York Times opinion columnist and human rights activist offers a memoir of the transformative power of loving dogs.

"Intimate and insightful glimpses into Boylan's life and the dogs that have helped her learn more about love." —*Kirkus*

Bradford, Sarah
***Lucrezia** Borgia: Life, Love and Death in Renaissance Italy.* Sarah Bradford. Viking 2004. xxiv, 421 p. : Illustration; Map
ISBN 9780670033539
Grades: Adult   B
1. Borgia, Lucrezia, 1480-1519 2. Alexander VI, Pope, 1431-1503 3. Nobility 4. Italian history 5. Renaissance (1300-1600) 6. 16th century 7. Age of exploration (1419-1610) 8. Biographies 9. History writing — Renaissance — Europe 10. History writing — Europe — Italy 11. History writing — Women's history 12. Life stories — Politics
LC 2004054881

Neither a vicious monster nor a seductive pawn, Lucrezia Borgia was a shrewd, determined woman who used her beauty and intelligence to secure a key role in the political struggles of her day. Drawing from a trove of contemporary documents and fascinating firsthand accounts, Bradford brings to life the art, the pageantry, and the dangerous politics of the Renaissance world Lucrezia Borgia helped to create.

"The author presents Lucrezia as an intelligent noblewoman, powerless to defy her family's patriarchal order, yet an enlightened ruler in her own right as Duchess of Ferrara. As a project designed to distinguish the historical Lucrezia Borgia from the legend, Bradford's readable biography resoundingly succeeds."
—*Publishers Weekly*

Includes bibliographical references (p. [393]-397) and index.

Bradlee, Ben
*The **Kid**: The Immortal Life of Ted Williams.* Ben Bradlee, Jr. Little, Brown, and Company 2013. 864 pages
ISBN 9780316614351
Grades: Adult   B
1. Williams, Ted, 1918-2002 2. Batting (Baseball) 3. Baseball 4. Baseball players 5. Statistics 6. United States 7. Biographies 8. Life stories — Sports — Athletes 9. Sports and Competition — Baseball 10. Sports and Competition — Individual Athlete
LC 2013028253

A biography of the baseball legend discusses his status as the best hitter in the history of the sport, his five years away from baseball to serve as a Marine pilot in WWII and Korea, and how he spent most of his life hiding his Mexican heritage.

"Sprawling, entertaining life of the baseball great, renowned as a sports hero while leading a life as checkered as Babe Ruth's or Ty Cobb's." —*Kirkus*

Includes bibliographical references and index.

Bradley, Mark A.
***Blood** Runs Coal: The Yablonski Murders and the Battle for the United Mine Workers of America.* Mark A. Bradley. W.W. Norton & Company 2020. 334 p.
ISBN 9780393652536
Grades: Adult   B
1. Boyle, William Anthony, 1904-1985 2. Yablonski, Joseph A, 1910-1969 3. Corruption 4. Labor leaders 5. Family-killing 6. Greed 7. Coal miners 8. Labor unions 9. Pennsylvania 10. United States 11. 1960s 12. True Crime — Murder
LC 2020016358

Documents the 1969 assassination of the Yablonski family amid a campaign to oust the corrupt president of the UMWA, in a timely account that reflects the violent labor movements, industrial transformations and socioeconomic realities of fossil-fuel dependency.

"An absorbing narrative of pride, greed, arrogance, and retribution that will find a place in history and true crime collections." —*Library Journal*

Includes bibliographical references and index.

Brady, Frank
***Endgame**: The Spectacular Rise and Fall of Bobby Fischer.* by Frank Brady. Crown 2010. 304 p.
ISBN 9780307463906
Grades: Adult   B
1. Fischer, Bobby, 1943-2008 2. Chess players 3. Chess 4. Biographies 5. Sports and Competition — Games 6. Life stories — Sports
LC 2010033840

From an author who wrote one of the bestselling Bobby Fischer books ever and who was himself a friend of Fischer's comes an impressively researched biography that for the first time captures the complete, remarkable arc of the life of the chess master.

"Brady's insightful biography of the legendary chess player focuses more on Fischer's life as a chess champion than on his much-publicized legal troubles and alleged psychological breakdowns. Brady first became friends with Fischer at a chess tournament when they were both children, and he combines a traditional biography with a personal memoir. Brady is uniquely qualified to write this book. Not only is he a seasoned biographer and someone who knew Fischer on a personal level; he's also an accomplished chess player himself, able to convey the game's intricacies to the reader in a clear, uncomplicated manner."
—*Booklist*

Brady, James
*The **Coldest** War: A Memoir of Korea.* James Brady. St. Martin's Griffin 2000. 256 p.
ISBN 9780312265113
Grades: 11 12 Adult   B
1. Brady, James, 1928-2009 2. Korean War, 1950-1953 3. Marines 4. Armed forces 5. Soldiers 6. United States 7. 1950s 8. Autobiographies and memoirs 9. Biographies 10. History writing — Wars and conflicts — Korean War 11. Life

stories — Law and order — Armed forces personnel 12. Adult books for young adults

LC BL 00010554

A personal account of the Korean War, as chronicled by a young Marine lieutenant, describes the harsh realities of war, the pressures of command, the struggle for survival, and the tragic impact of the war on all Americans.

"From November 1951 to July 1952, the author was a marine lieutenant who frequently found himself called upon to fight and kill Chinese and North Korean soldiers on the battlefields of Korea. His memoir of that experience is a well-crafted piece told in a voice that skillfully mixes the sardonic insight of an older man looking back on a highly extraordinary episode of his past with the naivete of the young warrior he once was." —*Booklist*

Includes index; Originally published: New York : Orion Books, 1990.

Brady, Patricia

Martha Washington: An American Life. Patricia Brady. Viking 2005. 276 p, [16] p. of plates : Illustration

ISBN 9780670034307

Grades: 11 12 Adult   B

1. Washington, Martha, 1731-1802 2. Presidents' spouses 3. United States 4. 18th century 5. Biographies 6. History writing — Presidency — 18th century — United States 7. History writing — Early America — United States 8. Life stories — Politics — Politicians

LC 2004061242

Challenges popular misconceptions to profile the nation's original first lady as the widowed mother of two children who became Washington's beloved partner and a mainstay in his powerful and stressful life, drawing on numerous sources to reveal her contributions to American character as well as her passionate commitment to her family.

Includes bibliographical references (p. [255]-266) and index.

Braitman, Laurel

What Looks Like Bravery: An Epic Journey Through Loss to Love. Laurel Braitman. Simon & Schuster 2023. 288 p.

ISBN 9781501158506

Grades: Adult   B

1. Braitman, Laurel 2. Women authors 3. Death of fathers 4. Grief 5. Denial (Psychology) 6. Purpose in life 7. Self-fulfillment 8. Loss 9. Love 10. Healing 11. North American people 12. American people 13. People with terminal illnesses 14. Men 15. Autobiographies and memoirs 16. Life stories — Facing adversity — Coping with death 17. Life stories — Arts and culture — Writing — Authors

The author shares how, in the years following her beloved father's death, she denied her suffering and lived with the constant fear of loss that left her terrified of love and intimacy until she set out on a journey to confront the grief she'd been avoiding for so long.

"Memoir of a young life punctuated by devastating grief….An affecting investigation of loss, sorrow, and the search for meaning." —*Kirkus*

Branch, John

Boy on Ice: The Life and Death of Derek Boogaard. John Branch. W.W. Norton & Company 2014. 384 p.

ISBN 9780393239393

Grades: Adult   B

1. Boogaard, Derek, 1982-2011 2. Violence in sports 3. Hockey 4. Hockey players 5. Violence 6. Canada 7. Biographies 8. Life stories — Sports — Athletes 9. Sports and competition — Hockey

LC 2014015731

The tragic death of hockey star Derek Boogaard at twenty-eight was front-page news across the country in 2011 and helped shatter the silence about violence and concussions in professional sports. Widely regarded as the toughest man in the NHL, Boogaard was a gentle man off the ice but a merciless fighter on it. But, as Branch reveals, behind the scenes Boogaard's injuries and concussions were mounting and his mental state was deteriorating, culminating in his early death from an overdose of alcohol and painkillers.

Includes bibliographical references and index.

Brand, Christo

Mandela: My Prisoner, My Friend. Christo Brand. Thomas Dunne 2014. 288 p.

ISBN 9781250055262

Grades: Adult   B

1. Mandela, Nelson, 1918-2013 2. Prison guards 3. Political prisoners 4. Civil rights workers 5. Bonding (Interpersonal relations) 6. Intergenerational relations 7. Interracial friendship 8. Friendship 9. Presidents 10. Politics and government 11. South Africa 12. Biographies 13. Life stories — Politics — Politicians 14. Life stories — Politics — Activists and reformers 15. Adult books for young adults

LC 2014026586

A tribute to the late world leader by a prison guard assigned to his maximum-security wing describes their friendship and the author's witness to Mandela's peace advocacy work and private losses.

"The author quickly recounts Mandela's general biography, including the Rivonia trial for sabotage that landed him in prison, but this is really a tale of two men and their shared humanity in an inhumane place. A worthy addition to the canon of Mandela literature that details a relationship that many knew about but few truly understood." —*Kirkus*

Brands, H. W.

★ *Andrew Jackson, His Life and Times.* H.W. Brands. Doubleday 2005. xi, 620 p. : Illustration; Map

ISBN 9780385507387

Grades: Adult   B

1. Jackson, Andrew, 1767-1845 2. Political leadership 3. Character 4. Veterans 5. Politicians 6. Democracy 7. Political culture 8. Presidents 9. Politics and government 10. United States 11. 19th century 12. Biographies 13. History writing — Presidency — 19th century — United States 14. History writing — Antebellum America — United States 15. Life stories — Politics — Politicians 16. Adult books for young adults

LC 2005042178

Explores the life of the first "common man" to become president of the United States, discussing Jackson's early days in South Carolina, his military exploits, and his contributions to the cause of democracy and Manifest Destiny.

Includes bibliographical references (p. [597]-607) and index.

The First American: The Life and Times of Benjamin Franklin. H.W. Brands. Anchor Books 2002. 765 p; 21 cm.

ISBN 9780385495400

Grades: 11 12 Adult   B

1. Franklin, Benjamin, 1706-1790 2. Founding Fathers of the United States 3. Diplomacy 4. Printers 5. Scientists 6. Political leadership 7. Politicians 8. Politics and government 9. United States 10. 18th century 11. Colonial America (1600-1775) 12. 19th century 13. Biographies 14. History writing — Colonial America — United States 15. History writing — Early America — United States 16. Life stories — Politics — Politicians 17. Life stories — Science, technology, and medicine — Scientists and inventors 18. Science Writing — General

LC 2005453313

Pulitzer Prize for Biography or Autobiography finalist.

A biography of America's first Renaissance man discusses Benjamin Franklin's diverse roles as a scientist, businessman, philosopher, writer, inventor, diplomat, politician, wit, and Founding Father.

"Brands fills in disparate pockets of history (the importance of Cotton Mather in Boston, the intellectual enthusiasms of the Royal Society in London) with readable, unobtrusive scholarship. Perhaps he took as his model his unassuming subject, who treated his extraordinary achievements in fields as diverse as science and diplomacy as if they were ordinary. Franklin emerges as a man with a passion to add to human happiness." —*The New Yorker*

Includes bibliographical references (p. [717]-747) and index.

★ *The Man Who Saved the Union: Ulysses Grant in War and Peace.* H. W. Brands. Doubleday 2012. 718 p, 16 p. of plates : Illustration; Map; Portrait

ISBN 9780385532419

Grades: Adult   B

ESSENTIAL AND RECOMMENDED TITLES
Biography

1. Grant, Ulysses S, 1822-1885 2. Presidents 3. Generals 4. United States history 5. United States 6. 19th century 7. Biographies 8. History writing — Presidency — 19th century — United States 9. Life stories — Politics — Politicians 10. History writing — Politicians — United States

LC 2011043795

An analysis of Ulysses Grant's contributions during the Civil War and his presidency covers his defense of Black civil rights, his controversial willingness to sacrifice troops to win, and the heated criticism of his Reconstruction policies.

Includes index; Map on endpapers.

Reagan: The Life. H. W. Brands. Doubleday 2015. 816 p.
ISBN 9780385536394
Grades: Adult   B
1. Reagan, Ronald 2. Presidents 3. Politics and government 4. United States 5. 20th century 6. 1980s 7. Biographies 8. History writing — Presidency — 20th century — United States 9. History writing — 1980s — United States 10. Life stories — Politics — Politicians

LC 2014038054

The two-time Pulitzer Prize nominee and author of Traitor to His Class explores the 40th president's indelible role in preserving democracy and shaping present-day America, detailing his early life, improbable rise and presidential achievements.

"This is a detailed look at a president who sparked much controversy and affection and it belongs in most collections of presidential biography."—*Booklist*

Traitor to His Class: The Privileged Life and Radical Presidency of Franklin Delano Roosevelt. H.W. Brands. Doubleday 2008. 888 p, 16 p. of plates : Illustration
ISBN 9780385519588
Grades: Adult   B
1. Roosevelt, Franklin D. (Franklin Delano), 1882-1945 2. Depressions, 1929-1941 3. New Deal (1933-1939) 4. Political leadership 5. Political science 6. Social classes 7. Social change 8. World War II 9. Radicalism 10. Political culture 11. Presidents 12. Politics and government 13. United States 14. 20th century 15. Biographies 16. History writing — Presidency — 20th century — United States 17. Life stories — Politics — Politicians 18. Adult books for young adults

LC 2008015164

Booklist Editors' Choice, 2008; Pulitzer Prize for Biography or Autobiography finalist.

A biography of Franklin Delano Roosevelt examines his political leadership in a dark time of Depression and war, his championship of the poor, his revolutionary New Deal legislation, and his legacy for the future.

"A thoroughly readable, scrupulously fair assessment of the one president who could inspire a Mt. Rushmore makeover." —*Kirkus*

Includes bibliographical references and index.

Woodrow Wilson. H.W. Brands. Times Books 2003. xvi, 169 p. : Illustration
ISBN 9780805069556
Grades: Adult   B
1. Wilson, Woodrow, 1856-1924 2. International relations 3. Causes of war 4. Political ethics 5. Military policy 6. Political leadership 7. Presidents 8. Politics and government 9. Idealism 10. United States 11. 20th century 12. 1910s 13. 1920s 14. Biographies 15. History writing — Presidency — 20th century — United States 16. History writing — Early 20th century — United States 17. Life stories — Politics — Politicians

LC 2002041393

Offers an account of the administration of Woodrow Wilson, detailing Wilson's unusual route to the White House, his campaign against corporate interests, his influential shaping of American foreign policy, and his political successes and failures.

"The author presents Wilson as a moralistic, idealistic intellectual who came to the presidency well versed in domestic policy but sadly lacking in knowledge and experience of international affairs, a leader who ultimately sacrificed his health and his presidential legacy in a doomed battle with Sen. Henry Cabot Lodge to have the League of Nations ratified. Brands's brief, skillful life of the President is recommended for all public libraries." —*Library Journal*

Includes bibliographical references (p. 153-156) and index.

Branum, Guy
My Life as a Goddess: A Memoir Through (un)popular Culture. Guy Branum; foreword by Mindy Kaling. Atria Books 2018. 272 p.
ISBN 9781501170225
Grades: Adult   B
1. Branum, Guy, 1975- 2. Comedians 3. Self-discovery 4. Actors and actresses 5. Gay men 6. Popular culture 7. Fat men 8. Self-fulfillment 9. Self-acceptance 10. Autobiographies and memoirs 11. Life stories — Arts and culture — Performing arts — Entertainers and celebrities 12. Arts and Entertainment — Comedy

LC 2018016385

Traces the author's path from a California farm town to success as a stand-up comic, and the inspiration he received from pop culture to accept himself as he truly was.

"Keenly observant and intelligent, Branum's book not only offers uproarious insights into walking paths less traveled, but also into what self-acceptance means in a world still woefully intolerant of difference. Wickedly smart, funny, and witty." —*Kirkus*

Bremer, Francis J.
John Winthrop: America's Forgotten Founding Father. Francis J. Bremer. Oxford University Press 2003. xviii, 478 p. : Illustration
ISBN 9780195149135
Grades: Adult   B
1. Winthrop, John, 1588-1649 2. Puritans 3. Colonists 4. Church history 5. Governors 6. British history 7. United States history 8. Massachusetts 9. England 10. 17th century 11. 16th century 12. Stuart period (1603-1714) 13. Tudor period (1485-1603) 14. Colonial America (1600-1775) 15. Biographies 16. History writing — Colonial America — United States 17. Life stories — Politics — Politicians

LC 2002038143

The first full-length biography of the first governor of the Massachusetts Bay Colony delves deeply into the life of this seminal figure in the formation of American society and culture.

"Bremer's definitive biography gracefully portrays Winthrop as a man of his time, whose influence in the new colony grew out of his own struggles to establish his identity before he left England." —*Publishers Weekly*

Includes bibliographical references and index.

Brennan, Thomas J.
Shooting Ghosts: A U.S. Marine, a Combat Photographer, and Their Journey Back from War. Thomas J. Brennan and Finbarr O'Reilly. Viking Press 2017. 336 p.
ISBN 9780399562549
Grades: Adult   B
1. Brennan, Thomas J. (Thomas James) 2. O'Reilly, Finbarr 3. Afghan War, 2001-2021 4. Post-traumatic stress disorder 5. Friendship 6. Marines 7. War photographers 8. Autobiographies and memoirs 9. Life stories — General 10. History writing — Wars and conflicts — War in Afghanistan

LC 2017019760

In Shooting Ghosts, Marine veteran Thomas Brennan and battle photographer Finbarr O'Reilly team up to offer insight into their experiences in Afghanistan. Both of them were psychologically traumatized by their ordeals—Brennan by his wounds from an explosion and O'Reilly's from the intensity of what he witnessed. Though civilian O'Reilly found help relatively easily, Brennan had to negotiate the complex military bureaucracy as well as the Marine culture of machismo. In this account, they defy the tradition that psychological trauma is a source of shame and make an appeal for mental health treatment for veterans.

"A courageous breaking of the code of silence to seek mental health for veterans and the war-scarred." —*Kirkus*

Brier, Bob
The Murder of Tutankhamen: A True Story. Bob Brier. G. P. Putnam's Sons 1998. xx, 264 p. : Illustration
ISBN 9780399143830
Grades: 11 12 Adult   B

PUBLIC LIBRARY CORE COLLECTION: NONFICTION
Twentieth Edition

1. Tutankhamen, King of Egypt 2. Rulers 3. Egypt 4. Ancient Egypt 5. Ancient Egypt (3100 B.C.E.-640 C.E.) 6. Biographies 7. History writing — Ancient — Egypt 8. History writing — Historical mysteries 9. True Crime — Murder 10. Life stories — Law and order — Criminals and law-breakers 11. Adult books for young adults

LC 97049193

A look at the last days of the ancient Egyptian pharaoh draws on new medical and archaeological evidence that suggests that Tutankhamen suffered a brutal, untimely death that led to subsequent palace and political intrigue.

"By combining known historical events with evidence gathered by advanced technologies, Brier has recreated the suspenseful story of religious upheaval and political intrigue that likely resulted in the murder of the teenage King Tutankhamen." —*Booklist*

"Brier obviously knows his subject and is impassioned by it. Readers who enjoy history or true-crime stories will be intrigued by this work." —*School Library Journal*

Includes bibliographical references (p.235-254) and index.

Brierley, Saroo

A Long Way Home: A Memoir. Saroo Brierley with Larry Buttrose. G.P. Putnam's Sons 2014. 272 pages

ISBN 9780399169281

Grades: Adult   **B**

1. Brierley, Saroo 2. Adopted children 3. Birthparents 4. International adoption 5. Indian people 6. Identification 7. Hobart, Tasmania 8. Kolkata, India 9. Autobiographies and memoirs 10. Page to screen 11. Life stories — Relationships — Family 12. Family and relationships — Parenting — Adoption

LC 2014003745

An account of the author's inspirational effort to find his India birthplace describes how he was accidentally separated from his family in the mid-1980s, his survival on the streets of Calcutta, his adoption by an Australian family, and his headline-making Google Earth search.

A Long Way Home inspired the 2016 film Lion, directed by Garth Davis and starring Dev Patel, Rooney Mara, and Nicole Kidman; Published in 2016 under the title Lion.

Brighton, Terry

Patton, Montgomery, Rommel: Masters of War. Terry Brighton. Crown Publishers 2009. xix, 426 p. : Illustration; Map

ISBN 9780307461544

Grades: Adult   **B**

1. Patton, George S, 1885-1945 2. Montgomery of Alamein, Bernard Law Montgomery, Viscount, 1887-1976 3. Rommel, Erwin, 1891-1944 4. World War II 5. Military campaigns 6. Military history 7. Generals 8. Southwest Asia and North Africa (Middle East) 9. Europe 10. United States 11. Biographies 12. History writing — Wars and conflicts — World War II

LC Bl2009031129

An account of World War II as it was experienced by three influential commanders draws on primary source materials to evaluate their explosive relationships with one another, their command talents, and their enthusiasm for publicity.

"Brighton shows how during the period between the wars, each refined his skills, which included reading one another's published treatises on the subject of mobile warfare. The author pulls no punches in revealing their flaws as well. Very highly recommended." —*Library Journal*

Originally published: Masters of battle. London : Viking, 2008; Includes bibliographical references (p. 407-411) and index.

Brinkley, Alan

John F. Kennedy: The 35th President, 1961-1963. Alan Brinkley. Times Books : 2012. 224 p. (American Presidents series (Times Books))

ISBN 9780805083491

Grades: Adult   **B**

1. Kennedy, John F. (John Fitzgerald), 1917-1963 2. Politicians 3. Democrats 4. Presidents 5. Politics and government 6. United States 7. 1960s 8. 20th century 9. Biographies 10. History writing — Presidency — 20th century — United States 11. Life stories — Politics — Politicians

LC 2011043747

Analyzes the contrast between Kennedy's achievements and his legend, tracing the successes and failures of such events as the Bay of Pigs and the Cuban Missile Crisis while exploring the ways in which he reshaped views of the presidency.

Includes bibliographical references and index.

★ *The Publisher: Henry Luce and His American Century.* by Alan Brinkley. Alfred A. Knopf 2010. 528 p.

ISBN 9780679414445

Grades: Adult   **B**

1. Luce, Henry Robinson, 1898-1967 2. Periodicals 3. Publishers and publishing 4. Editors 5. Journalists 6. Businesspeople 7. Literary criticism 8. United States 9. 20th century 10. Biographies 11. Business and economics — Business leaders and entrepreneurs 12. Arts and Entertainment — Writing and Publishing 13. Life stories — Arts and culture — Writing

LC 2009038834

New York Times Notable Book, 2010; Pulitzer Prize for Biography or Autobiography finalist.

A profile of the media giant founder of such magazines as "Time," "Life," and "Fortune" documents his childhood as the son of missionaries, university years, and prescient beliefs that transformed the magazine industry.

Includes bibliographical references.

Brinkley, Douglas

★ *Cronkite.* Douglas Brinkley. Harper 2012. 400 p.

ISBN 9780061374265

Grades: Adult   **B**

1. Cronkite, Walter 2. Television journalists 3. Broadcasting 4. Journalists 5. United States 6. Biographies 7. Life stories — Arts and culture — Writing — Journalists

LC 2011051467

The author of The Quiet World offers a candid look at the renowned, yet fiercely private, journalist and news anchor who reported on some of the biggest news of the 20th century.

"The best portrait of Cronkite—that legendary journalist, certainly worthy of a big biography—that we have." —*Kirkus*

Rightful Heritage: Franklin D. Roosevelt and the Land of America. Douglas Brinkley. HarperCollins 2016. 752 p.

ISBN 9780062089236

Grades: Adult   **B**

1. Roosevelt, Franklin D. (Franklin Delano), 1882-1945 2. New Deal (1933-1939) 3. Wildlife conservationists 4. Nature conservation 5. Presidents 6. United States 7. History writing — United States 8. Nature Writing — General

LC Bl2016003042

The New York Times best-selling author of the Wilderness Warrior examines the environmental legacy of FDR and the New Deal, evaluating the creation of the Civilian Conservation Corps and the dozens of State Park systems that were protected by his decisions.

"Brinkley vividly tracks Roosevelts 'Political know-how, legislative muscle, and fearlessness' from a unique and important perspective in this engrossing and richly illuminating portrait of one of the American environments most ardent and effective champions." —*Booklist*

Wheels for the World: Henry Ford, His Company, and a Century of Progress, 1903-2003. Douglas Brinkley. Viking 2003. xxii, 858 p. : Illustration

ISBN 9780670031818

Grades: Adult   **B**

1. Ford, Henry, 1863-1947 2. Model T automobile 3. Automobile designers 4. Automobile industry and trade 5. Mass production 6. Industrialists 7. United States 8. Biographies 9. History writing — United States 10. History writing — Technological innovations 11. Business and economics — Business leaders and entrepreneurs 12. Life stories — Business — Business leaders 13. Business and economics — Industries — Transportation

LC 2002033066

New York Times Notable Book, 2003.

ESSENTIAL AND RECOMMENDED TITLES
Biography

An evaluation of the impact of Henry Ford and Ford Motor Company on human civilization discusses the successes of early car models while noting specific ways in which automobile technology has affected industrial labor relations and America's middle class.

"Car lovers will appreciate this amazing account of the birth of the automobile industry, including funny anecdotes about the trusty Model T, the evolution of the V-8 engine, the artistic design of the Thunderbird, sophistication of the Lincoln Continental, and popularity of the Mustang." —*Booklist*

Includes bibliographical references (p. 769-835) and index.

*The **Wilderness** Warrior: Theodore Roosevelt and the Crusade for America.* Douglas Brinkley. Harpercollins 2009. xv, 940 p. : Illustration; Map
ISBN 9780060565282
Grades: Adult   B
1. Roosevelt, Theodore, 1858-1919 2. Wildlife conservationists 3. Environmentalists 4. Nature conservation 5. Presidents 6. United States 7. Biographies 8. History writing — Gilded Age — United States 9. Nature Writing — General 10. Life stories — Politics — Politicians
LC 2009291902

Booklist Editors' Choice, 2009; Green Prize for Sustainable Literature: Adult Nonfiction, 2010; National Outdoor Book Award for History/Biography, 2009; New York Times Notable Book, 2009.

Evaluates Theodore Roosevelt's role in launching modern conservationsim, identifying the contributions of such influences as James Audubon and John Muir while describing how Roosevelt's exposure to natural wonders in his early life shaped his environmental values.

"The author has absorbed a huge amount of research, but encyclopedic inclusiveness and repetition occasionally mar narrative movement. But this book has Rooseveltian energy. It is largehearted, full of the vitality of its subject and a palpable love for the landscape it describes." —*New York Times Book Review*

Includes bibliographical references (p. [831]-896) and index.

Broadwater, Jeff

★ *George Mason: Forgotten Founder.* Jeff Broadwater. University of North Carolina Press 2006. xii, 329 p. : Illustration; Map
ISBN 9780807830536
Grades: Adult   B
1. Mason, George, 1725-1792 2. Constitutional history 3. American Revolution, 1775-1783 4. Revolutions 5. Politicians 6. United States history 7. Virginia 8. United States 9. Colonial America (1600-1775) 10. Revolutionary America (1775-1783) 11. 18th century 12. 19th century 13. 1780s 14. Biographies 15. History writing — Early America — United States 16. History writing — Colonial America — United States 17. History writing — Wars and conflicts — Revolutionary War (America) 18. Life stories — Law and order — Armed forces personnel
LC 2006010729

Traces the life of George Mason, one of the founding fathers who played a key role in the Stamp Act crisis, American Revolution, and the drafting of Virginia's first state constitution.

"Because Mason left little evidence of his private life, there are blurred edges in the portrait that Broadwater paints, but overall this is an exemplary biography: Sympathetic but dispassionate, thorough but not cluttered, convincing in its interpretations and arguments. It leaves no doubt that Mason deserves to be returned to the esteem and reputation he enjoyed during his lifetime, but in no way is it hagiography." —*Washington Post Book World.*

Includes bibliographical references (p. [307]-322) and index.

James Madison: A Son of Virginia and a Founder of the Nation. Jeff Broadwater. University of North Carolina Press 2012. 320 p.
ISBN 9780807835302
Grades: Adult   B
1. Madison, James, 1751-1836 2. Ideology 3. Presidents 4. Politicians 5. Politics and government 6. United States 7. 19th century 8. 18th century 9. Biographies 10. History writing — Presidency — 18th century — United States 11. History writing — Early America — United States
LC 2011035946

Ragan Old North State Award Cup for Nonfiction, 2012.

Focuses on Madison's role in the battle for religious freedom in Virginia, his contributions to the adoption of the Constitution and the Bill of Rights, his place in the evolution of the party system, his relationship with Dolley Madison, his performance as commander in chief during the War of 1812 and his views on slavery.

Includes bibliographical references and index.

Broers, Michael

Napoleon: Soldier of Destiny. Michael Broers. Pegasus Books 2015. 608 p. (Napoleon (Michael Broers), 1)
ISBN 9781605988726
Grades: Adult   B
1. Napoleon I, Emperor of the French, 1769-1821 2. Generals 3. Politicians 4. Command of troops 5. Rulers 6. Politics and government 7. French history 8. France 9. 19th century 10. 18th century 11. Biographies 12. History writing — Military — Military leadership 13. Life stories — Law and order — Military leaders 14. History writing — Wars and conflicts — Napoleonic Wars 15. Life stories — Politics — Politicians
LC 2016303202

All previous lives of Napoleon have relied more on the memoirs of others than on his own uncensored words. This is the first life of Napoleon, in any language, that makes full use of his newly released personal correspondence compiled by the Napoleon Foundation in Paris.

"Highly recommended for general readers and scholars alike." —*Library Journal*

Originally published: London : Faber and Faber, 2014.

Napoleon: The Spirit of the Age 1805-1810. Michael Broers. Pegasus Books 2018. 544 p. (Napoleon (Michael Broers), 2)
ISBN 9781681776699
Grades: Adult   B
1. Napoleon I, Emperor of the French, 1769-1821 2. Generals 3. Politicians 4. Command of troops 5. Rulers 6. Politics and government 7. French history 8. France 9. 19th century 10. 18th century 11. Biographies 12. History writing — Military — Military leadership 13. Life stories — Law and order — Military leaders 14. History writing — Wars and conflicts — Napoleonic Wars 15. Life stories — Politics — Politicians
LC 2017278630

The second volume in this dynamic three-part life of Napoleon, covering the tumultuous years of 1805 to 1810—marking the zenith of Napoleon's power and military might across Europe.

Brokaw, Tom

The Fall of Richard Nixon: A Reporter Remembers Watergate. Tom Brokaw. Random House 2019. 224 p.
ISBN 9781400069705
Grades: Adult   B
1. Brokaw, Tom 2. Nixon, Richard M. (Richard Milhous), 1913-1994 3. Journalists 4. Watergate Scandal 5. Press and politics 6. Presidential tapes 7. Investigative journalism 8. Impeachments 9. Presidents 10. Public opinion 11. Politics and government 12. United States 13. 1970s 14. 20th century 15. 1960s 16. Autobiographies and memoirs 17. Biographies 18. Life stories — Arts and culture — Writing — Journalists 19. History writing — Presidency — 20th century — United States 20. History writing — 1970s — United States 21. History writing — Scandals
LC 2019029798

The last year of the Nixon presidency was filled with power politics, legal jiu-jitsu and high-stakes showdowns, with head-shaking surprises every day. Tom Brokaw, the NBC News White House correspondent during the final year of Watergate, gives us a close-up, personal account of the players, the strategies, and the highs and lows of the scandal that brought down a president.

Includes index.

Brooks, Maegan Parker

Fannie Lou Hamer: America's Freedom Fighting Woman. Maegan Parker Brooks. Rowman & Littlefield 2020. 213 p.
ISBN 9781538115947

PUBLIC LIBRARY CORE COLLECTION: NONFICTION
Twentieth Edition

Grades: 11 12 Adult **B**
1. Hamer, Fannie Lou, 1917-1977 2. African American women civil rights workers 3. African Americans 4. Civil Rights Movement 5. Civil rights workers 6. Social advocates 7. Biographies 8. Adult books for young adults 9. History writing — African American — Civil rights — United States 10. Life stories — Politics — Activists and reformers — Civil Rights leaders

LC Bl2020045808

Fannie Lou Hamer leapt to America's attention in 1964 when she delivered a stinging indictment of the American promise to the Democratic National Convention. This accessible biography underscores that Hamer's testimony was but one moment within a remarkable life that spanned fifty-nine tumultuous years in the history of American race relations.

Brooks, Mel
★ *All About Me!: My Remarkable Life in Show Business.* Mel Brooks. Ballentine Books 2021. 400 p.

ISBN 9780593159118

Grades: Adult **B**
1. Brooks, Mel, 1926- 2. Actors and actresses 3. Film producers and directors 4. Comedians 5. Filmmaking 6. Growing up 7. Film industry and trade 8. Family relationships 9. Social life and customs 10. United States 11. 20th century 12. Autobiographies and memoirs 13. Life stories — Arts and culture — Performing arts — Actors and actresses 14. Life stories — Arts and culture — Performing arts — Directors and producers 15. Arts and Entertainment — Movies and Television

The author reflects on his incredible lifetime of work, in a funny, poignant and nostalgic memoir.

"In this laugh-a-minute memoir, actor and producer Brooks (Young Frankenstein) looks back at his rise through Hollywood, gleefully doling out punch lines along the way. . . . Studded with snickering asides and rapid-fire jokes, Brooks's account of making it in show biz is just as sidesplitting as his movies." —*Publishers Weekly*

Brooks, Michael
The Quantum Astrologer's Handbook: A History of the Renaissance Mathematics That Birthed Imaginary Numbers, Probability, and the New Physics of the Universe. Michael Brooks. Scribe Publications 2019. 256 p.

ISBN 9781947534810

Grades: Adult **B**
1. Cardano, Girolamo, 1501-1576 2. Physicians 3. European Renaissance 4. Quantum theory 5. Probabilities 6. Astrologers 7. Mathematicians 8. Gamblers 9. Mathematics 10. Heretics 11. Milan, Italy 12. Biographies 13. Life stories — Science, technology, and medicine 14. Science Writing — Mathematics 15. History writing — Renaissance — Europe 16. History writing — Science, technology, and medicine

LC Bl2019029290

Who is Jerome Cardano? A gambler and blasphemer, inventor and schemer, plagued by demons and anxieties, astrologer to kings, emperors, and popes. This stubborn and unworldly man was the son of a lawyer and a brothel keeper, but also a gifted physician and the unacknowledged discoverer of the mathematical foundations of quantum physics.

Broom, Sarah M.
The Yellow House. Sarah M. Broom. Grove Press 2019. 304 pages

ISBN 9780802125088

Grades: Adult **B**
1. Broom, Sarah M. 2. African American women authors 3. African Americans 4. African American families 5. Home (Concept) 6. Identity 7. Hurricane Katrina, 2005 8. Houses 9. Racism 10. New Orleans, Louisiana 11. Autobiographies and memoirs 12. Life stories — Relationships — Growing up 13. Life stories — Identity — Race and ethnicity 14. Family and Relationships — Growing up 15. Book club best bets

LC 2019009107

National Book Critics Circle Award: John Leonard Prize, 2019; ALA Notable Book, 2020; National Book Award for Nonfiction, 2019; New York Times Notable Book, 2019.

Describes the author's upbringing in a New Orleans East shotgun house as the unruly 13th child of a widowed mother, tracing a century of family history and the impact of class, race and Hurricane Katrina on her sense of identity.

"Broom's lyrical style celebrates her family bonds, but a righteous fury runs throughout the narrative at New Orleans' injustices, from the foundation on up. A tribute to the multitude of stories one small home can contain, even one bursting with loss." —*Kirkus*

Broome, Brian
★ *Punch Me up to the Gods.* Brian Broome. Houghton Mifflin Harcourt 2021. 272 p.

ISBN 9780358439103

Grades: Adult **B**
1. Broome, Brian 2. African American authors 3. African American gay men 4. Growing up 5. Masculinity 6. Addiction 7. Identity 8. Childhood 9. Racism 10. Homophobia 11. Poets 12. Race awareness 13. Gay men 14. Authors 15. Intergenerational trauma 16. United States 17. 1970s 18. 1980s 19. Autobiographies and memoirs 20. Life stories — Identity 21. Life stories — Arts and culture — Writing — Authors 22. Life stories — Relationships — Growing up 23. Family and Relationships — Growing up 24. Debut title

LC 2020044745

Kirkus Prize for Nonfiction, 2021; Lambda Literary Award for Gay Memoir/Biography, 2022.

A coming-of-age memoir about Blackness, masculinity and addiction follows the author, a poet and screenwriter, as he recounts his experiences, revealing a perpetual outsider awkwardly squirming to find his way in.

"Broome debuts with a magnificent and harrowing memoir that digs into the traumas of growing up Black and gay in Ohio in the late 1970s and early '80s. . . . His testimony rings out as a searing critique of soul-crushing systems and stereotypes." —*Publishers Weekly*

Brothers, Thomas David
★ *Louis Armstrong, Master of Modernism.* Thomas Brothers. W. W. Norton 2014. 720 p.

ISBN 9780393065824

Grades: Adult **B**
1. Armstrong, Louis, 1901-1971 2. African American jazz musicians 3. Racism 4. Jazz music 5. Jazz musicians 6. Music history and criticism 7. New Orleans, Louisiana 8. Biographies 9. Arts and Entertainment — Music — Jazz and the Blues 10. Life stories — Arts and culture — Performing arts — Musicians and composers 11. Society and culture — Race

LC 2013037726

Pulitzer Prize for Biography or Autobiography finalist.

Picking up where "Louis Armstrong's New Orleans" left off, this biographical account of the legendary jazz trumpet virtuoso highlights the historical role Armstrong played in the creation of modern music and also his encounters with racism.

"A monumental follow-up to Louis Armstrong's New Orleans (2006). Brothers' work, covering an astonishingly creative decade, is comprehensive and firmly grounded in musicology and in the racial and cultural climate of the 1920s. It is voluminously researched, compellingly written, and supported by a valuable discography and bibliography." —*Booklist*

Includes bibliographical references and index.

Broven, John
Record Makers and Breakers: Voices of the Independent Rock 'N' Roll Pioneers. John Broven. University of Illinois Press 2008. 592 p.

ISBN 9780252032905

Grades: Adult **B**
1. Sound recording executives and producers 2. Sound recording industry and trade 3. Rock music 4. Social life and customs 5. United States 6. 20th century 7. Arts and Entertainment — Music — Rock

LC 2008027204

Describes the history of the early independent rock 'n' roll industry, from its regional beginnings in the 1940s through its peak and decline in the 1960s, celebrating its contribution to modern music history.

Includes bibliographical references and index.

ESSENTIAL AND RECOMMENDED TITLES
Biography

Brower, Kate Andersen
Elizabeth Taylor: The Grit & Glamour of an Icon. Kate Andersen Brower. HarperCollins 2022. 320 p.
ISBN 9780063067653
Grades: Adult **B**
1. Taylor, Elizabeth, 1932-2011 2. Films 3. Actors and actresses 4. United States 5. Biographies 6. Arts and Entertainment — Movies and Television 7. Life stories — Arts and culture — Performing arts — Actors and actresses

The author of the New York Times best-seller the Residence returns with the first authorized biography of the Hollywood icon, including her rise to fame at age 12, her eight marriages and her efforts to fight AIDS.

"Journalist Brower draws on the capacious archives of actor and philanthropist Elizabeth Taylor (1932-2011)—7,358 letters, diary entries, articles, and personal notes and 10,271 photographs—as well as interviews with her friends and family, to produce an appreciative biography of the iconic celebrity….A well-researched, gossipy portrait of a star." —*Kirkus*

Brown, Austin Channing
★ *I'm Still Here: Black Dignity in a World Made for Whiteness.* Austin Channing Brown. Convergent Books 2018. 185 pages
ISBN 9781524760854
Grades: Adult **B**
1. Brown, Austin Channing 2. Racism 3. African Americans 4. Race (Social sciences) 5. Microaggressions 6. Race relations 7. United States 8. Autobiographies and memoirs 9. Society and culture — Race 10. Life stories — Identity — Race and ethnicity 11. Adult books for young adults 12. Antiracist literature 13. Book club best bets

Austin Channing Brown's first encounter with a racialized America came at age 7, when she discovered her parents named her Austin to deceive future employers into thinking she was a white man. Growing up in majority-white schools, organizations, and churches, Austin writes, "I had to learn what it means to love Blackness," a journey that led to a lifetime spent navigating America's racial divide as a writer, speaker and expert who helps organizations practice genuine inclusion.

"An eloquent argument for meaningful reconciliation focused on racial injustice rather than white feelings." —*Booklist*

Brown, Carolyn
Chance and Circumstance: Twenty Years with Cage and Cunningham. Carolyn Brown. Alfred A. Knopf 2007. VI, 645 p, 40 p. of plates : Illustration
ISBN 9780394401911
Grades: Adult **B**
1. Brown, Carolyn, 1927- 2. Cunningham, Merce, 1919-2009 3. Cage, John, 1912-1992 4. Dancers 5. Choreographers 6. Dance companies 7. Interpersonal relations 8. Composers 9. Avant-garde (Aesthetics) 10. Popular culture 11. Social life and customs 12. United States 13. 20th century 14. Autobiographies and memoirs 15. Biographies 16. Arts and Entertainment — Dance 17. Life stories — Arts and culture — Performing arts — Dancers and choreographers
LC 2006048799

This long-awaited memoir is an intimate chronicle of a crucial era in modern dance: the story of Brown's own remarkable career, of the formative years of the Merce Cunningham Dance Company, and of the two brilliant, iconoclastic, and forward-thinking artists at its center—Merce Cunningham and John Cage. From its inception in the 1950s until her departure in the 1970s, Brown was a major dancer in the company and part of the vibrant artistic community of downtown New York. She describes the exhilaration—and dire financial straits—of the company's early days, when composer Cage was musical director and Robert Rauschenberg designed lighting, sets and costumes; and the struggle for acceptance of their controversial, avant-garde dance. She explores Cunningham's technique, choreography, and experimentation with compositional procedures influenced by Cage. And she probes the personalities of these two men: the reticent, moody, often secretive Cunningham, and the effusive, fun-loving, enthusiastic Cage.

"The author traces the trajectory of her modern dance career with that organization during its crawling stages in the 1950s and 1960s, when composer John Cage was musical director and artist Robert Rauschenberg was set and costume designer. Brown documents the company's early struggles for acceptance (it was considered avant-garde), various tours, and eventual world recognition. This book will appeal to modern dance buffs and memoir readers." —*Library Journal*
Includes bibliographical references (p. 612) and index.

Brown, Claude
Manchild in the Promised Land. Claude Brown. Touchstone 1999. 415 p.
ISBN 9780684864181
Grades: 11 12 Adult **B**
1. Brown, Claude, 1937- 2. African American men 3. Street life 4. African American gangs 5. African Americans 6. Drug traffic 7. Poor people 8. Poverty 9. Growing up 10. Ghettoes, African American 11. Teenage boys 12. African American teenagers 13. Harlem, New York City 14. New York City 15. 1950s 16. 1940s 17. Autobiographies and memoirs 18. Life stories — Identity — Race and ethnicity 19. Life stories — Facing adversity

Traces the author's experiences as a first-generation African American raised in the Northern ghettos of Harlem in the mid-twentieth century, an upbringing marked by violence, drugs, and devastating urban disadvantages.

Brown, Craig
Ninety-nine Glimpses of Princess Margaret. Craig Brown. Farrar, Straus and Giroux 2018. 432 p.
ISBN 9780374906047
Grades: Adult **B**
1. Margaret, Princess, Countess of Snowdon, 1930-2002 2. Reputation 3. Fame 4. Princesses 5. Great Britain 6. Biographies 7. Life stories — Politics — Royalty
LC 2018008784

James Tait Black Memorial Prize for Biography, 2017; New York Times Notable Book, 2018; National Book Critics Circle Award for Biography finalist, 2018.

Combining interviews, parodies, dreams, parallel lives, diaries, announcements, lists, catalogues and essays on Princess Margaret, the author offers a kaleidoscopic experiment in biography and a witty meditation on fame and art, snobbery and deference, bohemia and high society.

"Readers wanting a straightforward biography should look elsewhere, but those interested in a sometimes hilarious, sometimes gloomy view of Princess Margaret through a variety of lenses, or a look at how popular representation shapes our view of a public figure should snap up this book." —*Library Journal*

Originally published in 2017 by 4th Estate, an imprint of HarperCollinsPublishers, Great Britain, as Ma'am Darling: 99 Glimpses of Princess Margaret.

Brown, Daniel James
The Indifferent Stars Above: The Harrowing Saga of a Donner Party Bride. Daniel James Brown. William Morrow 2009. 320 p.
ISBN 9780061348105
Grades: Adult **B**
1. Fosdick, Sarah Graves, 1825-1871 2. Donner Party 3. Pioneer women 4. Brides 5. Overland journeys to the Pacific 6. Pioneers 7. Frontier and pioneer life 8. Voyages and travels 9. Sierra Nevada Mountains 10. The West (United States) 11. California 12. 19th century 13. History writing — Westward expansion — United States
LC 2008040646

A chronicle of the mid-nineteenth-century wagon train tragedy draws on the perspectives of one of its survivors, Sarah Graves, recounting how her new husband and she joined the Donner party on their California-bound journey and encountered violent perils, in an account that also offers insight into the scientific reasons that some died while others survived.

"In April 1846, as young newlywed Sarah Graves departed her Illinois home on a journey to California, she could not foresee the misery and horror that awaited her. After numerous delays on their difficult westward path, she and her family found themselves dangerously behind schedule as winter loomed, and they decided to join an ill-fated wagon train under the leadership of George Donner. Ending up snowbound and starving in the Sierra Nevada range, the Donner party descended into cannibalism. Never melodramatic or maudlin, Brown's work gracefully balances graphic depictions of extreme privation with humanizing glimpses of the emigrants' everyday hopes and fears." —*Library Journal*

Includes bibliographical references.

Brown, Mick
★ *Tearing* Down the Wall of Sound: The Rise and Fall of Phil Spector. Mick Brown. Alfred A. Knopf 2007. VIII, 452 p. : Illustration
ISBN 9781400042197
Grades: Adult   B
1. Spector, Phil, 1940-2021 2. Sound recording executives and producers 3. Men 4. Trials (Murder) 5. Personal conduct 6. Social life and customs 7. Los Angeles, California 8. United States 9. 21st century 10. Biographies 11. Arts and Entertainment — Music 12. Life stories — Arts and culture — Performing arts — Musicians and composers 13. Adult books for young adults
LC 2007004819

Phil Spector, born in the Bronx in 1940, grew up an outsider despised by his peers. Yet after his family moved to California, he learned everything he could about music, formed a band, and had a number-one hit with "To know him is to love him." He quickly became the top producer of early rock and roll, originator of such girl groups as the Ronettes, a millionaire by twenty-one, owner of his own label by twenty-two. Hit followed hit, and for all of them he used a new technique called the "wall of sound." but the reign of the boy-man who owned pop culture seemed doomed by the "British Invasion," and he spiraled into paranoid isolation and peculiar behavior. Though he seemed to improve for a time, even returning to the recording studio to work, it didn't last, and in 2003, the actress Lana Clarkson was found at his home, dead by gunshot.

"Stacked with incredible anecdotes, Brown's entertaining and nuanced portrait lifts the fog of myth and outright falsehood (including Spector's own) that have obscured the celebrity producer (like an enormous, gravity-defying wig) through the years." —*Publishers Weekly*

Originally published: London : Bloomsbury, 2007; Includes bibliographical references (p. [449]-452) and index.

Brown, Molly McCully
Places I've Taken My Body: Essays. Molly McCully Brown. Persea Books 2020. 215 p.
ISBN 9780892555130
Grades: Adult   B
1. Brown, Molly McCully, 1991- 2. Cerebral palsy 3. Human body 4. Body movement 5. Faith 6. Loss 7. Voyages and travels 8. Women poets 9. 21st century 10. Autobiographies and memoirs 11. Essays 12. Life stories — Facing adversity — Medical issues — Living with disabilities 13. Life stories — Arts and culture — Writing — Poets
LC 2019044336

In sixteen intimate essays, poet Molly McCully Brown explores living within and beyond the limits of a body-in her case, one shaped since birth by cerebral palsy.

"Brown is a writer to watch. Heartfelt and wrenching, a significant addition to the literature of disability." —*Kirkus*

Brown, Nancy Marie
The Abacus and the Cross: The Story of the Pope Who Brought the Light of Science to the Dark Ages. Nancy Marie Brown. Basic Books 2010. 368 p.
ISBN 9780465009503
Grades: Adult   B
1. Sylvester II, Pope, 945?-1003 2. Religion and science 3. Popes 4. Religious leaders 5. Civilization, Medieval 6. Medieval period (476-1492) 7. History writing — Medieval — Europe 8. Spirituality and Religion — Christianity — History 9. Science Writing — General
LC 2010036361

Traces the achievements of medieval Pope Sylvester II, revealing his lesser-known role in promoting scientific awareness throughout turn-of-the-first-millennium Catholicism, in a report that includes coverage of his humble origins and introduction of Arabic numerals to Europe.

"As readably knowledgeable about Gerbert's political fortunes as about his intellectual influence, Brown is a lively narrator and interesting interpreter of Gerbert's life and world. This portrait gives both the science and the history audiences something to talk about." —*Booklist*

Includes bibliographical references and index.

Brown, Robert J.
You Can't Go Wrong Doing Right: How a Child of Poverty Rose to the White House and Helped Change the World. Robert J. Brown. Convergent 2019. xiii, 237 pages
ISBN 9781524762780
Grades: Adult   B
1. Brown, Robert J. (Robert Joe), 1935-2020 2. Business consultants 3. Grandmothers 4. Grandparent and child 5. Political consultants 6. Autobiographies and memoirs 7. Self-Help — Personal growth 8. Spirituality and Religion — Christian living
LC Bl2018192314

The highly sought power broker, presidential advisor and founder of global business-management consulting firm B&C International describes how the lessons of his impoverished childhood and wise grandmother informed his perspectives about a life in service and major historical events.

Describes how the power broker and presidential advisor took lessons from his grandmother and his poverty-stricken childhood to inform his life's work.

Brown, Stephen
Glitterville's Handmade Christmas: A Glittered Guide for Whimsical Crafting. Stephen Brown. Andrews McMeel Publishing 2014. xxiii, 181 pages : Color; Illustration
ISBN 9781449414559
Grades: Adult   B
1. Handicraft 2. Christmas decorations 3. Arts and Entertainment — Crafts and hobbies — Seasonal
LC Bl2014038441

Provides step-by-step, illustrated instructions for twenty holiday craft projects, including ginger cookie kids, wacky woods felt ornaments, and a pinecone gnome.

Brown, Terence
The Life of W.B. Yeats: A Critical Biography. Terence Brown. Blackwell 1999. xiii, 410 p, [8] p. of plates : Illustration
ISBN 9780631182986
Grades: Adult   B
1. Yeats, W. B. (William Butler), 1865-1939 2. Poets, Irish 3. Ireland 4. 19th century 5. 20th century 6. Biographies 7. Life stories — Arts and culture — Writing — Poets 8. Arts and Entertainment — Writing and Publishing
LC 99028388

"In this biography Brown places Yeats's work as poet and dramatist in its political and socialas well as personal—and erotic—context." —*New York Times Book Review*

Includes bibliographical references (p. [392]-398) and index.

Brown, Tina
The Diana Chronicles. Tina Brown. Doubleday 2007. xvi, 542 p. : Illustration
ISBN 9780385517089
Grades: Adult   B
1. Diana, Princess of Wales, 1961-1997 2. Mothers and daughters 3. Female friendship 4. Princesses 5. Great Britain 6. Biographies 7. Life stories — Politics — Royalty
LC Bl2007007241

New York Times Notable Book, 2007.

A portrait of the late Princess Diana examines her relationships with the various women in her life, including her sexually charged mother, scheming grandmother, hated stepmother, competitive sisters, and the "other woman," Camilla Parker Bowles.

Ill. on lining papers; Includes bibliographical references (p. 487-524) and index.

ESSENTIAL AND RECOMMENDED TITLES
Biography

The Vanity Fair Diaries: 1983-1992. Tina Brown. Henry Holt & Co. 2017. 400 p.
ISBN 9781627791366
Grades: Adult **B**
1. Brown, Tina 2. Fashion periodicals 3. British people in the United States 4. Women periodical editors 5. New York City 6. 1980s 7. Diaries 8. Life stories — Arts and culture — Writing — Journalists 9. Arts and Entertainment — Fashion
LC 2017028578

The diaries of the author's years as editor-in-chief of "Vanity Fair" provide a portrait of the 1980s in New York and Hollywood, describing her summons from London to save Conde Nast's troubled periodical and her experiences within the cutthroat world of glamour magazines.

"High and low, perceptive and prescient (in 1987, she speculated that the American public wont be able to resist the crassness of Donald Trump), this is a wildly entertaining, essential look at print journalism before the fall. Let us all pray that Brown also kept diaries of her years in the 1990s as editor of the New Yorker." —*Booklist*

Brown-Nagin, Tomiko
Civil Rights Queen: Constance Baker Motley and the Struggle for Equality. Tomiko Brown-Nagin. Pantheon Books 2022. 400 p.
ISBN 9781524747183
Grades: Adult **B**
1. Motley, Constance Baker, 1921-2005 2. Judges 3. African American judges 4. Women judges 5. Civil Rights Movement 6. Social justice 7. Equality 8. Manhattan, New York City 9. United States 10. Biographies 11. Life stories — Law and order — Judges and lawyers

This biography of the first Black woman to argue a case in front of the Supreme Court examines how she played a critical role in vanquishing Jim Crow laws throughout the South.

"Brilliantly balancing the details of Motley's professional and personal life with lucid legal analysis, this riveting account shines a well-deserved—and long overdue—spotlight on a remarkable trailblazer." —*Publishers Weekly*

Browne, David
So Many Roads: The Life and Times of the Grateful Dead. David Browne. Da Capo Press 2015. xiii, 482 p.
ISBN 9780306821707
Grades: Adult **B**
1. Jam bands 2. Rock music 3. Rock musicians 4. United States 5. Biographies 6. Arts and Entertainment — Music — Rock
LC BI2015017032

An all-encompassing narrative portrait of the iconic mid-20th-century band draws on interviews with its surviving members to trace its origins, eclectic sound, influence and struggles in the years after Jerry Garcia's death.

"This very well-told history of the San Francisco-based band the Grateful Dead, which formed 50 years ago, contains new interviews, including with the living members of the group and some of their earliest fans and associates. This adds a freshness to the narrative." —*Library Journal*

Browne, E. J.
Charles Darwin: A Biography. Janet Browne. Knopf 1995. xiii, 605 pages, 32 unnumbered pages of plates : Illustration; Facsimile; Table; Portrait
ISBN 9780394579429
Grades: Adult **B**
1. Darwin, Charles, 1809-1882 2. Naturalists 3. Evolution 4. Family relationships 5. Natural history 6. English history 7. 19th century 8. Biographies 9. Life stories — Science, technology, and medicine — Scientists and inventors 10. Science Writing — Biology
LC 94006598

The first of a two-volume biography of Charles Darwin follows the great nineteenth-century scientist from his youth, through his scientific apprenticeship at sea, to his refinement of the ideas that he presented in Origin of Species.

"The author captures the spirit of a quietly revolutionary scientist whose ingrained Victorian prejudices were at odds with his radical ideas." —*Publishers Weekly*
Includes bibliographical references and indexes.

Charles Darwin: A Biography. Janet Browne. Knopf 2002. 591 pages, 24 unnumbered pages of plates : Illustration; Portrait
ISBN 9780679429326
Grades: Adult **B**
1. Darwin, Charles, 1809-1882 2. Naturalists 3. Evolution 4. Family relationships 5. Natural history 6. English history 7. 19th century 8. Biographies 9. Life stories — Science, technology, and medicine — Scientists and inventors 10. Science Writing — Biology

James Tait Black Memorial Prize for Biography, 2003; Library Journal Best Books, 2002; New York Times Notable Book, 2002; National Book Critics Circle Award for Biography, 2002.

The second volume in a definitive biography of Charles Darwin, following Charles Darwin: Voyaging, begins in 1858 when, against his better judgment, Darwin was forced to publicly reveal his theory of evolution in a world that held to the biblical creation ideal, and examines the fierce controversy that resulted from his work.

"This second volume of Browne's biography of Darwin begins a year before the publication of on the Origin of Species, with the arrival of a package from Alfred Russel Wallace, whose own ideas on natural selection virtually mirrored Darwin's, forcing him to go public. Browne's subject is monumental, but her writing style is never overburdened by the weight. Rather, her prose is elegant in its clarity of thought, her craftsmanship impeccable in the way it weaves a coherent whole from the innumerable threads of thought, experience and persona that comprised this colossal life." —*Publishers Weekly*
Includes bibliographical references (pages 533-568) and index.

Bruck, Connie
When Hollywood Had a King: The Reign of Lew Wasserman, Who Leveraged Talent into Power and Influence. Connie Bruck. Random House 2003. xiv, 512 p. : Illustration
ISBN 9780375501685
Grades: Adult **B**
1. Wasserman, Lew 2. Chief executive officers 3. Labor unions 4. Businesspeople 5. Chicago, Illinois 6. Hollywood, California 7. Biographies 8. Life stories — Business — Business leaders 9. Arts and Entertainment — Movies and Television
LC 2003041418

Booklist Editors' Choice, 2003; New York Times Notable Book, 2003.

A history of the Music Corporation of America traces the entertainment giant from its founding in 1924, through its rise to become the most powerful force in the film world under the visionary leadership of Lew Wasserman.

"Those who are interested in comprehensive details about the inner workings of the entertainment industryits history, business, customs, people, and gossipwill find this a fascinating read and a solid resource." —*Library Journal*
Includes bibliographical references (p. 483-494) and index.

Bruni, Frank
The Beauty of Dusk: On Vision Lost and Found. Frank Bruni. Avid Reader Press 2022. 320 p.
ISBN 9781982108571
Grades: Adult **B**
1. Bruni, Frank 2. Journalists 3. People with visual disabilities 4. Personal conduct 5. Vision 6. Aging 7. Success (Concept) 8. Priorities 9. Life change events 10. Blindness 11. Autobiographies and memoirs 12. Life stories — Facing adversity — Medical issues — Living with disabilities 13. Science Writing — Medicine and health — Disabilities and disorders

A New York Times columnist, after a rare stroke renders him blind in his right eye, learns he could lose his sight altogether and recounts his adjustment to this daunting reality—a medical and spiritual journey on which he reappraised his own priorities.

"New York Times columnist Bruni (Where You Go Is Not Who You'll Be) imparts in this generous memoir the wisdom he learned after he began to lose his eyesight.... Smartly mixing memoir and cultural criticism, this movingly speaks to an entire generation." —*Publishers Weekly*

Bruning, John R.
Indestructible: One Man's Rescue Mission That Changed the Course of Wwii. John R. Bruning. Hachette Books 2016. 288 p.
ISBN 9780316339407
Grades: Adult   B
1. Gunn, Paul Irvin, 1899-1957 2. World War II 3. Military aviation 4. American people in Asia 5. Prisoners of war 6. Rescues 7. Prisoner of war camps 8. Hostages 9. Pilots 10. Aerial operations 11. Japanese occupation, World War II 12. Asian history 13. Philippines 14. United States 15. Biographies 16. Life stories — Law and order — Armed forces personnel 17. History writing — Wars and conflicts — World War II — Pacific Theater 18. History writing — Military — Aviation History

LC 2016021715

Chronicles the story of a renegade American pilot consumed by his personal mission to rescue his family from the Japanese in World War II—a man who happened to change the war's very course along the way.

Includes bibliographical references and index.

Brunson, Quinta
She Memes Well. Quinta Brunson. Houghton Mifflin Harcourt 2021. 256 p.
ISBN 9781328638984
Grades: Adult   B
1. Brunson, Quinta 2. Internet personalities 3. Comedians 4. Humorous writing 5. African American women 6. African American comedians 7. Essays 8. Humor writing — Social humor 9. Life stories — Arts and culture — Performing arts — Entertainers and celebrities 10. Arts and Entertainment — Comedy 11. Book club best bets

LC 2020057705

Quinta Brunson is a master at breaking the internet. Before having any traditional background in media, her humorous videos were the first to go viral on Instagram's platform. Now, Brunson is bringing her comedic chops to the page in She Memes Well, an earnest, laugh-out-loud collection about this unusual road to notoriety.

"In this hilarious and poignant memoir, comedian Brunson shares her head and her heart for readers who may only know her face from the internet.... Brunson's razor-sharp wit and gratitude for her extraordinary life leap off every page." —*Booklist*

Bryant, Howard
The Last Hero: A Life of Henry Aaron. Howard Bryant. Pantheon Books 2010. xvi, 600 p, 16 p. of plates : Illustration
ISBN 9780375424854
Grades: 11 12 Adult   B
1. Aaron, Hank, 1934-2021 2. African American baseball players 3. Professional baseball players 4. Professional baseball 5. Racism 6. Race relations 7. Baseball history 8. Baseball players 9. United States 10. 20th century 11. Biographies 12. Sports and Competition — Baseball 13. Sports and Competition — Individual Athlete 14. Life stories — Sports — Athletes

LC 2009040573

New York Times Notable Book, 2010.

Chronicles the baseball star's on-field achievements and explains how the dignity and determination with which Aaron stood against racism helped transform the role and significance of the professional Black athlete and turn Aaron into a national icon.

Includes bibliographical references (p. 563-566) and index.

Rickey: The Life and Legend of an American Original. Howard Bryant. Mariner Books 2022. 420 p.
ISBN 9780358047315
Grades: Adult   B
1. Henderson, Rickey, 1958- 2. Professional baseball players 3. Baseball 4. Professional baseball 5. Baseball players 6. Biographies 7. Sports and Competition — Baseball 8. Sports and Competition — Individual Athlete 9. Life stories — Sports — Athletes

A critically acclaimed sportswriter and culture critic presents this definitive biography of the Hall of Famer—and the record holder for the most stolen bases in a single game who also stole America's heart—who played for nine different teams throughout his decades-long career.

"Bryant (The Last Hero), a senior writer for ESPN.Com, delivers a solid and comprehensive take on the life and career of Rickey Henderson, Major League Baseball's all-time stolen base leader....The book most succeeds in its rich historical context, underscoring Rickey's outsize influence in a new vanguard of 'Great Black talents' that shook up the hallowed white halls of baseball." —*Publishers Weekly*

Bryant, Kobe
The Mamba Mentality: How I Play. Kobe Bryant; photography by Andrew D. Bernstein. Farrar Straus & Giroux 2018. 208 p.
ISBN 9780374201234
Grades: Adult   B
1. Bryant, Kobe, 1978-2020 2. Professional basketball players 3. African American basketball players 4. Success (Concept) 5. Basketball 6. Basketball players 7. Professional athletes 8. Autobiographies and memoirs 9. Sports and Competition — Basketball 10. Life stories — Sports — Athletes

LC Bl2018180038

In the wake of his retirement from professional basketball, the NBA great nicknamed "The Black Mamba" has decided to share his vast knowledge and understanding of the game to take readers on an unprecedented journey to the core of his legendary "Mamba mentality."

"He offers plenty of anecdotes about teammates and opponents, which will satisfy fans interested mainly in the memoir aspect; but what sets this book apart from the competition is Bernsteins photography. It's wonderful." —*Booklist*

Bryson, Bill
The Life and Times of the Thunderbolt Kid: A Memoir. Bill Bryson. Broadway Books 2006. x, 270 p. : Illustration
ISBN 9780767919364
Grades: 11 12 Adult   B
1. Bryson, Bill 2. Travel writers 3. Growing up 4. Authors, American 5. Popular culture 6. Iowa 7. Des Moines, Iowa 8. 1950s 9. 20th century 10. Autobiographies and memoirs 11. Arts and Entertainment — Writing and Publishing 12. Life stories — Relationships — Growing up 13. Adult books for young adults 14. Humor writing — Classic humorists 15. Nonfiction that reads like fiction

LC 2006043859

The author describes his all-American childhood growing up as a member of the baby boom generation in the heart of Iowa, detailing his rich fantasy life as a superhero known as the Thunderbolt Kid and his remarkably normal 1950s family life.

Includes bibliographical references (p. [269]-270); Also published: Toronto : Anchor Canada, 2007, c2006.

Shakespeare: The World as Stage. Bill Bryson. Atlas Books; Harper Collins 2007. 208 p.
ISBN 9780060740221
Grades: 9 10 11 12   B
1. Shakespeare, William, 1564-1616 2. Playwrights, English 3. Theater 4. Authors, English 5. Social life and customs 6. England 7. 16th century 8. Biographies 9. Arts and Entertainment — Writing and Publishing 10. Arts and Entertainment — Theater 11. History writing — Europe — United Kingdom 12. Life stories — Arts and culture — Writing — Authors 13. Adult books for young adults 14. Humor writing — Classic humorists

LC 2007021647

William Shakespeare, the most celebrated poet in the English language, left behind nearly a million words of text, but his biography has long been a thicket of supposition arranged around scant facts. With his trademark wit, Bill Bryson sorts through this colorful muddle to reveal the man himself. Bryson documents the efforts of earlier scholars, and, emulating the style of his travelogues, records episodes in his own research. He celebrates Shakespeare as a writer of unimaginable talent and enormous inventiveness, a coiner of phrases ("vanish into thin air," "foregone conclusion," "one fell swoop") that even today have common

ESSENTIAL AND RECOMMENDED TITLES
Biography

currency. His Shakespeare is like no one else's—the beneficiary of Bryson's genial nature, his engaging skepticism, and an unrivaled gift for storytelling.

In this addition to the Eminent Lives series, bestselling author Bryson…does what he does best: Marshaling the usual little facts that others might overlook—for example, that in Shakespeare's day perhaps 40% of women were pregnant when they got married—to paint a portrait of the world in which the Bard lived and prospered… Bryson is a pleasant and funny guide to a subject at once overexposed and elusive—as Bryson puts it, 'He is a kind of literary equivalent of an electron—forever there and not there.' —*Publishers Weekly*

Includes bibliographical references.

Buck, Joe
Lucky Bastard: My Life, My Dad, and the Things I'm Not Allowed to Say on TV. Joe Buck, with Michael Rosenberg. Dutton 2016. 320 p.
ISBN 9781101984567
Grades: Adult **B**
1. Buck, Joe 2. Sportscasters 3. Television sportscasters 4. Autobiographies and memoirs 5. Sports and Competition — General 6. Arts and Entertainment — Movies and Television 7. Life stories — Arts and culture — Writing — Journalists
LC 2016011271

The famed Super Bowl sportscaster shares stories from his life and career, describing his work in and out of the shadow of his legendary sportscaster father Jack Buck, his marriage to sportscaster Michelle Beisner and more.

"With a comic yet reverent approach to his life and broadcasting, Buck effectively captures the merging of his career and the popularity of American sports." —*Publishers Weekly*

Budiansky, Stephen
Journey to the Edge of Reason: The Life of Kurt Godel. Stephen Budiansky. W.W. Norton & Company 2021. 384 p.
ISBN 9781324005445
Grades: Adult **B**
1. Godel, Kurt, 1906-1978 2. Logicians 3. Mathematicians 4. Mathematics 5. Philosophy 6. Biographies 7. Life stories — Science, technology, and medicine 8. Science writing — Mathematics
LC 2020054854

The first major biography of the logician and mathematician whose incompleteness theorems helped launch a modern scientific revolution.

"Historian Budiansky (Oliver Wendell Holmes) recaps the revolutionary work of mathematician and logician Kurt Gödel (1906-1978) in this probing biography…. This captivating portrait of a great if neurotic mind hits the mark." —*Publishers Weekly*

Includes bibliographical references and index.

Oliver Wendell Holmes: A Life in War, Law, and Ideas. Stephen Budiansky. W. W. Norton & Company 2019. 560 p.
ISBN 9780393634723
Grades: Adult **B**
1. Holmes, Oliver Wendell, 1841-1935 2. Judges 3. Judicial opinions 4. Judicial review 5. United States 6. 20th century 7. Biographies 8. Life stories — Law and order — Judges and lawyers 9. History writing — Judicial branch — United States 10. History writing — Early 20th century — United States
LC 2018054671

A portrait of the influential U.S. Supreme Court justice includes coverage of his achievements as a legal scholar, his Civil War service and his often-dissenting but prophetic views on free speech, criminal justice and economic reform.

"This wide-ranging examination of Holmes as an individual and of the law he helped make will appeal to those with an interest in constitutional law as well as to general readers." —*Publishers Weekly*

Includes bibliographical references and index.

Buford, Bill
★ *Dirt: Adventures in Lyon as a Chef in Training, Father, and Sleuth Looking for the Secret of French Cooking.* Bill Buford. Alfred A. Knopf 2020. 412 p.
ISBN 9780307271013
Grades: Adult **B**
1. Buford, Bill 2. Cooks 3. Cooking 4. Cooking, French 5. Gourmet cooking 6. Moving to a new country 7. Families 8. American people in France 9. Food habits 10. Lyon, France 11. France 12. Autobiographies and memoirs 13. Life stories — Arts and culture — Culinary arts 14. Food writing — Memoirs and biographies 15. Food Writing — Food and Culture 16. Travel Writing — Living Abroad 17. Food writing — Cooking and cookbooks — Chefs and restaurants
LC 2019039927

Bill Buford turns his inimitable attention from Italian cuisine to the food of France. Baffled by the language, but convinced that he can master the art of French cooking—or at least get to the bottom of why it is so revered—he begins what becomes a five-year odyssey by shadowing the esteemed French chef Michel Richard, in Washington, D.C. But when Buford (quickly) realizes that a stage in France is necessary, he goes—this time with his wife and three-year-old twin sons in tow—to Lyon, the gastronomic capital of France.

"Buford (Heat) delivers a vivid and often laugh-out-loud account of the tribulations, humblings, and triumphs he and his family endured in the five years they lived in France. . . . It's a remarkable book, and even readers who don't know a sabayon from a Sabatier will find it endlessly rewarding." —*Publishers Weekly*

Buford, Kate
Native American Son: The Life and Sporting Legend of Jim Thorpe. Kate Buford. Alfred A. Knopf 2010. 448 p.
ISBN 9780375413247
Grades: 11 12 Adult **B**
1. Thorpe, Jim, 1887-1953 2. Athletes 3. Indigenous athletes 4. Indigenous peoples of North America 5. Biographies 6. Sports and Competition — Individual Athlete 7. Life stories — Sports — Athletes 8. Adult books for young adults 9. Life stories — People in history — Indigenous peoples
LC 2010012815

Chronicles defining moments in the career of the preeminent American athlete, from his contributions to college football and gold-medal wins at the 1912 Olympics to his role in shaping professional football and baseball, in a portrait that also discusses his private struggles and political views.

Borzoi Book; Includes bibliographical references and index.

Buhle, Kathleen
If We Break: A Memoir of Marriage, Addiction, and Healing. Kathleen Buhle. Crown 2022. 288 p.
ISBN 9780593241059
Grades: Adult **B**
1. Buhle, Kathleen 2. Biden, Robert Hunter, 1970- 3. Couples 4. Marriage 5. Spouses of alcoholics 6. Addiction 7. Codependency 8. Children of politicians 9. Secrets 10. Divorce 11. Healing 12. Autobiographies and memoirs 13. Life stories — Relationships — Couples 14. Life stories — Facing adversity — Medical issues — Addiction

The former wife of Hunter Biden discusses the heartbreaking collapse of her marriage to Hunter Biden, President Joe Biden's son, which ended in 2017 amid his then-secret struggles with addiction.

"Remarkably lacking in both sensationalism and vengeance, this sad story will be familiar to anyone who has loved an addict." —*Kirkus*

Bundles, A'Lelia
On Her Own Ground: The Life and Times of Madam C.J. Walker. A'Lelia Bundles. Scribner 2001. 415 p. : Illustration
ISBN 9780684825823
Grades: 11 12 Adult **B**
1. Walker, C. J, 1867-1919 2. African American women executives 3. African American businesspeople 4. Cosmetics industry and trade 5. Hair care products 6. African Americans 7. Biographies 8. Page to screen 9. Life stories — Business — Business leaders 10. Business and economics — Business leaders and entrepreneurs
LC 00057372

New York Times Notable Book, 2001.

Written by her great-great-granddaughter, a biography of the entrepreneur and philanthropist Madam C.J. Walker is told through personal letters, records, and photographs from the family collection.

"Bundles presents a biography of her great-great-grandmother, who was born Sarah Breedlove on a Louisiana plantation in 1867 and whose name subsequently became synonymous with hair straightening and Black wealth." —Library Journal

A Lisa Drew book; This book is being made into a TV show called Self Made; Includes bibliographical references (p.296-385) and index.

Bunker, Nick

Young Benjamin Franklin: The Birth of Ingenuity. Nick Bunker. Alfred a Knopf 2018. 464 p.

ISBN 9781101874417

Grades: Adult   B

1. Franklin, Benjamin, 1706-1790 2. Founding Fathers of the United States 3. Scientists 4. Printers 5. Inventors 6. Ambition 7. United States history 8. United States 9. 18th century 10. Colonial America (1600-1775) 11. Biographies 12. History writing — Colonial America — United States 13. Life stories — Science, technology, and medicine — Scientists and inventors

LC 2017057711

The Pulitzer Prize-finalist author of "Making Haste from Babylon" presents an account of Ben Franklin's early life to share insights into the challenges he overcame in a harsh colonial world and the passion for knowledge that inspired his scientific achievements.

"This thoroughly researched examination of the development of America's earliest preeminent scientist and statesman will appeal to academics and popular history readers." —Library Journal

Bunnell, David

Good Friday on the Rez. David Hugh Bunnell. St Martins Press 2017. 320 p.

ISBN 9781250112538

Grades: Adult   B

1. Bunnell, David 2. Oglala (North American people) 3. Indigenous reservations 4. Indigenous peoples of North America — History 5. Indigenous peoples of North America, Treatment of 6. Inequality 7. Automobile travel 8. Indigenous activists 9. Indigenous peoples of North America — Social life and customs 10. South Dakota 11. Pine Ridge Indian Reservation, South Dakota 12. Great Plains (United States) 13. Autobiographies and memoirs 14. History writing — Indigenous peoples — United States 15. Society and culture — Ethnic studies 16. Life stories — Relationships — Growing up

LC 2016052536

A magnificent mix of memoir and recent Native American history is told through a 280-mile car trip around the Pine Ridge Reservation where the author lived during and after the siege at Wounded Knee, tracking the torment and miraculous resurrection of Native American pride, spirituality and culture.

"This informative account should be placed alongside all books on Native American history and culture. It deserves to be read by all, particularly in light of the recent Dakota Access Pipeline protests." —Library Journal

Bunting, Josiah

★ *The Making of a Leader: The Formative Years of George C. Marshall.* Josiah Bunting III.. Alfred A. Knopf 2024. 272 p.

ISBN 9781400042586

Grades: Adult   B

1. Marshall, George C. (George Catlett), 1880-1959 2. Generals 3. Soldiers 4. World War I 5. World War II 6. Military education 7. Duty 8. Command of troops 9. Leadership 10. Nobel Prize winners 11. North American people 12. American people 13. Biographies 14. Life stories — Law and order — Military leaders 15. History writing — Military — Military leadership

A military historian, in this portrait of one of the greatest leaders of modern history, cuts through the legend of George Catlett Marshall to the man—his frustrations, passions, loves and brilliance—to reveal a humble commander who knew not only how to lead but how to see the leader in others.

"A superb account of the early life of an unsullied American hero." —Kirkus

Ulysses S. Grant. Josiah Bunting III.. Times Books 2004. xx, 180 p. ; Illustration (American presidents series (Times Books))

ISBN 9780805069495

Grades: Adult   B

1. Grant, Ulysses S, 1822-1885 2. Presidents 3. Politics and government 4. United States 5. 19th century 6. Biographies 7. History writing — Presidency — United States 8. History writing — Gilded Age — United States 9. History writing — Reconstruction — United States 10. Life stories — Politics — Politicians 11. Adult books for young adults 12. History writing — Presidency — 19th century — United States

LC 2004047889

Traces the life and presidency of Ulyssses S. Grant and discusses why he was undervalued as a president.

"This superb book should support those who are gradually moving Grant from the lower to the upper half of rankings of chief executives." —Publishers Weekly

Includes bibliographical references (p. [161]-165) and index.

Burcaw, Shane

★ *Laughing at My Nightmare.* Shane Burcaw. Roaring Brook Press 2014. 256 p.

ISBN 9781626720077

Grades: 10 11 12 Adult   B

1. Burcaw, Shane 2. Spinal muscular atrophy 3. People with disabilities 4. Twenty-one-year-old men 5. Disabilities 6. Neuromuscular diseases 7. Wheelchairs 8. Autobiographies and memoirs 9. Biographies — Coping with challenges — Illness 10. Narrative nonfiction for kids and teens 11. Books for reluctant readers

LC 2014010634

YALSA Quick Picks for Reluctant Young Adult Readers, 2015; YALSA Award for Excellence in Nonfiction finalist, 2015.

With acerbic wit & a hilarious voice, Shane Burcaw's YA memoir describes the challenges he faces as a 20-year-old with muscular atrophy. From awkward handshakes to trying to finding a girlfriend and everything in between—.

Burgin, R. V.

Islands of the Damned: A Marine at War in the Pacific. R.V. Burgin with William Marvel. New American Library 2010. 296 p.

ISBN 9780451229908

Grades: Adult   B

1. Burgin, R. V. 2. World War II 3. Military campaigns 4. Marines 5. Pacific area 6. Autobiographies and memoirs 7. History writing — Wars and conflicts — World War II — Pacific Theater 8. Life stories — Law and order — Armed forces personnel

LC 2009040454

An eyewitness account of some of the most savage and brutal fighting in the war against Japan is told from the point of view of a young Marine who left Texas to escape life as a traveling salesman.

"As this well-written, excellently detailed personal narrative makes clear, some Marines who fought alongside him did not make it home alive. They and thousands more died amid war's confusing and unspeakable horrors. Sometimes they were killed by the enemy, sometimes by friendly fire, sometimes by accidents, and sometimes by shocking, split-second decisions where one life was sacrificed to save others. Time is thinning the ranks of America's Pacific War veterans. But Islands of the Damned is a taut, engrossing, haunting book that will help keep their accomplishments and enormous sacrifices alive." —Dallas Morning News

Burke, Carolyn

Lee Miller: A Life. Carolyn Burke. Knopf 2005. xv, 426 p. : Illustration

ISBN 9780375401473

Grades: Adult   B

1. Miller, Lee, 1907-1977 2. Photographers 3. Photojournalists 4. Women photographers 5. Fashion models 6. Muses (People) 7. Biographies 8. Australian literature 9. Arts and Entertainment — Photography 10. Life stories — Arts and culture — Artists

LC 2004043844

New York Times Notable Book, 2006; National Book Critics Circle Award for Biography finalist, 2005.

A detailed profile of Lee Miller offers a multifaceted study of the iconic model, photographer, muse, journalist, mother, sexual adventuress, and gourmet

ESSENTIAL AND RECOMMENDED TITLES
Biography

cook, documenting her love affair with artist Man Ray, her unconventional marriages, and her troubled personal life.

"This sympathetic tribute sheds further light on the lives of this highly original, often misunderstood woman."—*The Economist*

Includes bibliographical references and index.

Burke, Tarana
★ *Unbound: My Story of Liberation and the Birth of the Me Too Movement.* Tarana Burke. Flatiron Books 2021. 320 p.
ISBN 9781250621733
Grades: Adult   **B**
1. Burke, Tarana 2. Me Too movement 3. African American women 4. Sexual violence victims 5. Empathy 6. Healing 7. African American social advocates 8. Sexual harassment of women 9. Rape victims 10. Hope 11. Life stories — Politics — Activists and reformers 12. Life stories — Facing adversity — Victims of crime

Rise: A Feminist Book Project List, 2023.

The founder and activist behind the "me too" movement shares her own story of how she came to say those two words herself after being sexually assaulted, in this debut memoir that explores how to piece back together our fractured selves.

"In this powerful debut, Burke, founder of the #MeToo movement, depicts her experiences as a survivor of sexual assault and an advocate for the 'Necessary work' of collective healing. . . . Intensely moving and unapologetically frank, Burke's fearless memoir will uplift and inspire the next generation of survivors, advocates, and truth-tellers." —*Publishers Weekly*

Burkett, Elinor
Golda. Elinor Burkett. Harper 2008. 480 p.
ISBN 9780060786656
Grades: 11 12 Adult   **B**
1. Meir, Golda, 1898-1978 2. Zionists 3. Prime ministers 4. Israel 5. Biographies 6. History writing — Arab-Israeli relations — Southwest Asia and North Africa (Middle East) 7. Life stories — Politics — Politicians 8. Adult books for young adults

LC 2007048283

The first female head of state in the Western world and one of the most influential women in modern history, Golda Meir was one of the founders of the State of Israel, the architect of its socialist infrastructure, and its most tenacious international defender. Historian-journalist Burkett looks beyond Meir's well-known accomplishments to the complex motivations and ideals, personal victories and disappointments, of her charismatic public persona. Beginning with Meir's childhood in virulently anti-Semitic Russia and her family's subsequent relocation to the United States, Burkett places Meir within the framework of the American immigrant experience, the Holocaust, and the singlemindedness of a generation that carved a nation out of its own nightmares anddreams.

Includes bibliographical references.

Burlingame, Michael
Abraham Lincoln: A Life. Michael Burlingame. Johns Hopkins University Press 2008. 2 v.
ISBN 9780801889936
Grades: Adult   **B**
1. Lincoln, Abraham, 1809-1865 2. Civil war 3. United States Civil War, 1861-1865 4. Political leadership 5. Presidents 6. Politicians 7. Politics and government 8. United States history 9. United States 10. 1860s 11. 19th century 12. American Civil War era (1861-1865) 13. Biographies 14. History writing — Presidency — 19th century — United States 15. History writing — Wars and conflicts — American Civil War 16. Life stories — Politics — Politicians

LC 2007052919

Examines Abraham Lincoln's early childhood, his experiences as a boy in Indiana and Illinois, his legal training, and the political ambition that led to a term in Congress.

"The author has produced the finest Lincoln biography in more than 60 years. Future Lincoln books cannot be written without it, and from no other book can a general reader learn so much about Abraham Lincoln." —*Publishers Weekly*

Includes bibliographical references and index.

Burns, William J.
The Back Channel: A Memoir of American Diplomacy and the Case for Its Renewal. by William J. Burns. Random House 2019. 288 p.
ISBN 9780525508861
Grades: Adult   **B**
1. Burns, William J. (William Joseph), 1956- 2. Diplomacy 3. International relations 4. World politics 5. Diplomats 6. International cooperation 7. International security 8. United States 9. Autobiographies and memoirs 10. Biographies 11. Impartial writing 12. Politics and global affairs — World politics — United States 13. Life stories — Politics

LC 2018042715

America's highest-ranking Foreign Service career ambassador and president of the Carnegie Endowment for International Peace presents a memoir of his career in service while outlining an impassioned case for diplomacy in today's increasingly volatile world.

Includes bibliographical references and index.

Burroughs, Augusten
★ *Toil & Trouble.* Augusten Burroughs. St. Martin's Press 2019. 304 p.
ISBN 9781250019950
Grades: Adult   **B**
1. Burroughs, Augusten 2. Authors, American 3. Gay couples 4. Witchcraft 5. Precognition 6. Building conservation and restoration 7. Eccentrics and eccentricities 8. Houses 9. Autobiographies and memoirs 10. Life stories — Arts and culture — Writing — Authors 11. Humor writing — General

LC 2019018100

Master memoirist Augusten Burroughs delivers a hilarious and spooky account of his life as the descendant of witches. The author of Running with Scissors documents his lifelong capacity for causing impossible manifestations, exploring his mother's revelations about their witch ancestry and his efforts to understand himself and his powers.

"Although scientifically unsound, this book's allegorical evidence for the belief in witchcraft will appeal to casual memoir readers, particularly those interested in the lighter side of religion and psychology." —*Library Journal*

Burton, Susan
Becoming Ms. Burton: From Prison to Recovery to Leading the Fight for Incarcerated Women. Susan Burton & Cari Lynn with a foreword by Michelle Alexander. The New Press 2017. 228 p.
ISBN 9781620972120
Grades: Adult   **B**
1. Women former convicts 2. Former drug addicts 3. Women social reformers 4. Prison reform 5. Rehabilitation 6. Autobiographies and memoirs 7. Life stories — Politics — Activists and reformers 8. Life stories — Facing adversity — Personal transformation 9. Society and culture — Violence and crime — Criminal justice system

A South Los Angeles woman who self-medicated with drugs after her son's death and was in and out of prison for 15 years describes her struggle to get clean and how she became an advocate and supporter of women facing similar situations.

"A dramatic, honest, moving narrative of how hard life can get and how one can still overcome seemingly insurmountable adversity to do good in the world." —*Kirkus*

Burton, Susan, 1973-
Empty: A Memoir. Susan Burton. Random House Inc 2020. 288 p.
ISBN 9780812992847
Grades: Adult   **B**
1. Burton, Susan, 1973- 2. Eating disorders 3. Food 4. Food habits 5. Compulsive eating 6. Anorexia nervosa 7. Moving to a new home 8. Diary writing 9. Women journalists 10. People with eating disorders 11. Family relationships 12. Radio programs 13. Adult children of divorced parents 14. Women 15. Autobiographies and memoirs 16. Life stories — Relationships — Growing up 17. Family and Relationships — Growing Up

LC 2019037475

PUBLIC LIBRARY CORE COLLECTION: NONFICTION
Twentieth Edition

An award-winning This American Life documentary producer shares the story of her battles with anorexia and a binge-eating disorder, describing the painful compulsions that shaped her education, career and relationships.

"A powerful picture of anorexia and binge-eating disorder that would benefit from being shorter and more targeted." —*Kirkus*

Busbee, Jay
Earnhardt Nation: The Full-throttle Saga of Nascar's First Family. Jay Busbee. HarperCollins 2016. 240 p.
ISBN 9780062367716
Grades: Adult   B
1. Earnhardt family 2. Earnhardt, Dale, 1951-2001 3. Stock car racing 4. Automobile racing drivers 5. Sports and Competition — Racing — Cars
LC 2016427179

Published to commemorate the 15th anniversary of Earnhardt Sr.'s death, a profile of the influential NASCAR family is set against a backdrop of the history of the world's fastest stock-car-racing organization and traces the achievements of three generations of Earnhardt drivers.

Bush, George W.
41: A Portrait of My Father. George W. Bush. Crown Publishing 2014. 288 p.
ISBN 9780553447781
Grades: Adult   B
1. Bush, George, 1924-2018 2. Fathers and sons 3. Presidents 4. United States 5. 21st century 6. 20th century 7. Biographies 8. History writing — Presidency — 21st century — United States 9. History writing — Presidency — 20th century — United States 10. Life stories — Politics — Politicians
LC 2014469972

Forty-three men have served as President of the United States. Countless books have been written about them. But never before has a President told the story of his father, another President, through his own eyes and in his own words. A unique and intimate biography, the book covers the entire scope of the elder President Bush's life and career, including his service in the Pacific during World War II, his pioneering work in the Texas oil business, and his political rise as a Congressman, U.S. Representative to China and the United Nations, CIA Director, Vice President, and President.

Decision Points. George W. Bush. Random House Inc 2010. xii, 497 p, 32 p. of plates : Illustration; Color
ISBN 9780307590619
Grades: Adult   B
1. Bush, George W. (George Walker), 1946- 2. Republicans 3. Decision-making 4. Presidents 5. Politicians 6. Politics and government 7. United States 8. 21st century 9. 2000s (Decade) 10. Autobiographies and memoirs 11. Biographies 12. History writing — Presidency — 21st century — United States 13. History writing — Early 21st century — United States 14. Life stories — Politics — Politicians
LC 2010513034

Many readers are interested in why George W. Bush made the choices he did while in office. Here, he offers a candid journey through his decisions, discussing the hotly contested 2000 election, his selection of key appointees, 9/11, the Iraq War, and his controversial choices during the financial crisis and Hurricane Katrina. Getting personal, he also addresses his decision to quit drinking as well as his faith and relationship with his family.

"Critics on both the left and right are challenged to walk in his shoes, and may come away with a new view of the former presidentor at least an appreciation of the hard and often ambiguous choices he was forced to make. Honest, of course, but also surprisingly approachable and engaging." —*Kirkus*

Includes index.

Butcher, Amy
Mothertrucker: Finding Joy on the Loneliest Road in America. Amy Butcher. Little a 2021. 284 p.
ISBN 9781542014328
Grades: Adult   B

1. Butcher, Amy 2. Wiebe, Joy 3. Female friendship 4. Abused women 5. Women truck drivers 6. Women authors 7. Women college teachers 8. Partner abuse 9. Wilderness areas 10. Fear 11. Alaska 12. Autobiographies and memoirs 13. Life stories — Facing adversity — Abuse survivors 14. Life stories — Relationships — Friendship 15. Life stories — Personal growth

The true story of two women who found meaning, strength, and friendship in one of the most punishing and magnificent landscapes on earth.

"An acclaimed essay writer and memoirist tells the story of her life-changing meeting with a female Alaskan Artic ice road trucker. . . . A sobering reflection on verbal and psychological abuse, Butcher's book honors the healing power of female friendship and questions the nature of divinity beyond its constricting patriarchal manifestations." —*Kirkus*

Butcher, Carmen Acevedo
Man of Blessing: A Life of St. Benedict. Carmen Acevedo Butcher. Paraclete Press 2006. VI, 180 p. : Map
ISBN 9781557254856
Grades: 11 12 Adult   B
1. Benedict, Saint, Abbot Of Monte Cassino 2. Christian saints 3. Italy 4. Biographies 5. Spirituality and Religion — Christianity — History 6. Spirituality and Religion — Religious Leaders 7. Life stories — Religion and spirituality — Religious and spiritual leaders
LC 2005035827

This biography of the "patriarch of western monasticism" combines what is known about his life with information about the time in which he lived.

"This is the story of the life of St. Benedict of Nursia, who founded Western monasticism in the sixth century and later became the patron saint of Europe. . . . The book's readability will make it easy for patrons to escape into late Roman culture and find peace in a monastic simplicity." —*Library Journal*

Includes bibliographical references (p. 167-178).

Butler, Marcia
The Skin Above My Knee. Marcia Butler. Little Brown & CO 2017. 272 p.
ISBN 9780316392280
Grades: Adult   B
1. Butler, Marcia 2. Family violence 3. Musicians 4. Adult child abuse victims 5. Child prodigies 6. Music therapy 7. Women 8. Autobiographies and memoirs 9. Life stories — Facing adversity — Abuse survivors 10. Life stories — Arts and culture — Performing arts — Musicians and composers
LC 2015960626

A musical prodigy relates how she sought refuge from an abusive family by immersing herself in the oboe, describing how as an adult her memories of trauma led to dangerous relationships and self-destructive habits until she returned to music as a primary source of therapy.

Buttigieg, Pete
Shortest Way Home: One Mayor's Challenge and a Model for America's Future. Pete Buttigieg. W W Norton & CO Inc. 2019. 352 p.
ISBN 9781631494369
Grades: Adult   B
1. Buttigieg, Pete, 1982- 2. Mayors 3. Politicians 4. Urban renewal 5. Political science 6. Gay politicians 7. South Bend, Indiana 8. Indiana 9. Autobiographies and memoirs 10. Life stories — Politics — Politicians
LC 2018044991

An Afghanistan veteran and two-term mayor of South Bend, Indiana, traces the inspirational story of how the city, once an industrial wasteland, became a shining model of urban reinvention.

"First and foremost a great, engaging read, this is also an inspiring story of a millennial making a difference." —*Booklist*

Byrne, Paula
Kick: The True Story of Kick Kennedy, JFK's Forgotten Sister and the Heir to Chatsworth. Paula Byrne. Harper 2016. 352 p.
ISBN 9780062296276
Grades: Adult   B

ESSENTIAL AND RECOMMENDED TITLES
Biography

1. Kennedy, Kathleen, 1920-1948 2. Kennedy family 3. Socialites 4. American people in England 5. Young women 6. Siblings 7. Family relationships 8. Catholics 9. Aristocracy 10. Families 11. Presidents 12. Social life and customs 13. United States 14. Great Britain 15. 20th century 16. Biographies 17. Life stories — People in history — Famous families

LC 2016008270

Filled with a wealth of revealing new material and insight, the biography of the vivacious, unconventional—and nearly forgotten—young Kennedy sister who charmed American society and the English aristocracy and would break with her family for love.

"At first, the book is less a biography and more a society report of England's upper class, but it evolves into an exciting, heartbreakingly tense love story." —*Kirkus*

Includes bibliographical references and index.

Caesar, Ed
The Moth and the Mountain: A True Story of Love, War, and Everest. Ed Caesar. Avid Reader Press 2020. 320 p.

ISBN 9781501143373

Grades: Adult **B**

1. Wilson, Maurice, 1898-1934 2. World War I veterans 3. Men 4. Mountaineering 5. Solo voyages 6. Love 7. Voyages and travels 8. Adventurers 9. Airplanes 10. Men-women relations 11. Mount Everest 12. 1930s 13. Between the Wars (1918-1939) 14. Biographies 15. Adventure Writing — Adventure travel 16. Life stories — People in history 17. Travel Writing — Asia and the South Pacific

In the 1930s, as official government expeditions set their sights on conquering Mount Everest, a little-known World War I veteran named Maurice Wilson conceives his own crazy, beautiful plan: He will fly a plane from England to Everest, crash-land on its lower slopes, then become the first person to reach its summit—all utterly alone. Wilson doesn't know how to climb. He barely knows how to fly. But he has the right plane, the right equipment, and a deep yearning to achieve his goal.

Caine, Michael
Blowing the Bloody Doors Off: And Other Lessons in Life. Michael Caine. Hachette Books 2018. 304 p.

ISBN 9780316451192

Grades: Adult **B**

1. Caine, Michael 2. Film industry and trade 3. Storytelling 4. Success (Concept) 5. Actors and actresses 6. Films 7. Autobiographies and memoirs 8. Biographies 9. Arts and Entertainment — Movies and Television 10. Life stories — Arts and culture — Performing arts — Actors and actresses

LC Bl2018167870

The Hollywood legend reveals the wisdom, stories, insights and skills that life has taught him in his rise from humble origins to the pinnacle of success.

Calcaterra, Regina
Etched in Sand: A True Story of Five Siblings Who Survived an Unspeakable Childhood on Long Island. Regina Calcaterra. William Morrow & Co, 2013. 320 p.

ISBN 9780062218834

Grades: Adult **B**

1. Calcaterra, Regina 2. Child abuse 3. Siblings 4. Abandoned children 5. Childhood 6. Growing up 7. Child abuse victims 8. Birthfathers 9. Child neglect 10. Women lawyers 11. Foster care 12. Parenting by siblings 13. Foster parents 14. Identification 15. Long Island, New York 16. Autobiographies and memoirs 17. Life stories — Facing adversity — Abuse survivors 18. Family and Relationships — Abuse 19. Life stories — Relationships — Growing up 20. Family and Relationships — Growing Up

LC Bl2013035608

In this real-life rags-to-riches story, a tenacious lawyer, state official and activist recounts her childhood in foster homes and on the streets with her four siblings, revealing a life of horrible abuse in the shadows between Manhattan and the Hamptons.

Girl Unbroken: A Sister's Harrowing Story of Survival from the Streets of Long Island to the Farms of Idaho. Regina Calcaterra and Rosie Maloney. William Morrow & Co, 2016. 288 p.

ISBN 9780062412584

Grades: Adult **B**

1. Maloney, Rosie 2. Calcaterra, Regina 3. Child abuse 4. Sisters 5. Child abuse victims 6. Farm life 7. Parental kidnapping 8. Childhood 9. Growing up 10. Child neglect 11. Foster care 12. Foster parents 13. Long Island, New York 14. Idaho 15. Biographies 16. Life stories — Facing adversity — Abuse survivors 17. Family and Relationships — Abuse 18. Life stories — Relationships — Growing up 19. Family and Relationships — Growing Up

LC Bl2016044777

The authors share the experiences of youngest sister Rosie as a child of an alcoholic, abusive mother after moving into foster care in Long Island before being forced to continue living with her damaged mother in Idaho after her sisters made their escape.

"As engrossing as Etched in Sand, this book is a testament to Maloneys remarkable resilience and a moving tribute to the unbreakable bond of love she shared with her siblings. Courageous and emotionally intense." —*Kirkus*

Caldwell, Gail
Let's Take the Long Way Home: A Memoir of Friendship. Gail Caldwell. Random House 2010. 208 p.

ISBN 9781400067381

Grades: Adult **B**

1. Knapp, Caroline, 1959-2002 2. Caldwell, Gail, 1951- 3. Friendship 4. People with lung cancer 5. Women authors, American 6. Critics 7. Lung cancer 8. Female friendship 9. Best friends 10. Loss 11. Journalists 12. Grief 13. United States 14. Autobiographies and memoirs 15. Biographies 16. Life stories — Relationships — Friendship 17. Life stories — Facing adversity — Medical issues — Physical illness 18. Life stories — Arts and culture — Writing — Authors

LC 2009029384

In this gorgeous, moving memoir, Pulitzer Prize-winning author Gail Caldwell reflects on her own coming-of-age in midlife, as she learns to open herself to the power and healing of sharing her life with a best friend.

"This is a book you'll want to share with your own necessary pillars of life, as Caldwell refers to her nearest and dearest. Her memoir, a tribute to the enduring power of friendship, is a lovely gift to readers." —*Washington Post*

Calhoun, Ada
Also a Poet: Frank O'Hara, My Father, and Me. Ada Calhoun. Grove Press 2022. 272 p.

ISBN 9780802159786

Grades: Adult **B**

1. Calhoun, Ada 2. O'Hara, Frank, 1926-1966 3. Schjeldahl, Peter 4. Poets, American 5. Art critics 6. Women authors 7. Biography writing 8. Fathers and daughters 9. Adult children of dysfunctional families 10. Family relationships 11. Writing 12. Reconciliation 13. New York City 14. Autobiographies and memoirs 15. Life stories — Arts and culture — Writing — Authors 16. Life stories — Relationships — Parent and child 17. Arts and Entertainment — Writing and Publishing

When Ada Calhoun stumbled upon old cassette tapes of interviews her father, celebrated art critic Peter Schjeldahl, had conducted for his never-completed biography of poet Frank O'Hara, she set out to finish the book her father had started forty years earlier. As a lifelong O'Hara fan who grew up amid his bohemian cohort in the East Village, Calhoun thought the project would be easy, even fun, but the deeper she dove, the more she had to face not just O'Hara's past, but also her father's, and her own. In reckoning with her unique heritage, as well as providing new insights into the life of one of our most important poets, Calhoun offers a brave and hopeful meditation on parents and children, artistic ambition, and the complexities of what we leave behind.

"New York Times best-selling author Calhoun blends literary history and memoir, examining her relationship with her father, art critic and poet Peter Schjeldahl, and their shared passion for Frank O'Hara's work as she draws on taped interviews he conducted for a never-completed biography of O'Hara." —*Library Journal*

Callahan, Tom
Arnie: The Life of Arnold Palmer. Tom Callahan. HarperCollins 2017. 304 p.
ISBN 9780062439727
Grades: Adult — B
1. Palmer, Arnold, 1929-2016 2. Golfers 3. Golf 4. Professional golfers 5. Biographies 6. Sports and Competition — Golf 7. Sports and Competition — Individual Athlete 8. Life stories — Sports — Athletes

LC 2017002983

A veteran sportswriter a author of His Father's Son: Earl and Tiger Woods shines a spotlight on one of the greatest golfers ever to play the game, Arnold Palmer.

"Sportswriter Callahan breezily floats from story to story across the life of legendary golfer Arnold Palmer, describing dashing Palmers enduring appeal from the moment he burst onto the new television screens of the 1950s." —*Publishers Weekly*

Callow, Simon
★ *Orson Welles: One-man Band.* Simon Callow. Viking 2016. 466 p. : Illustration; Plate (Orson Welles (Simon Callow), 3)
ISBN 9780670024919
Grades: Adult — B
1. Welles, Orson, 1915-1985 2. Filmmakers 3. American people in Europe 4. Expatriates 5. Exiles 6. Film industry and trade 7. Actors and actresses 8. Film producers and directors 9. Hollywood, California 10. United States 11. Biographies 12. Arts and Entertainment — Movies and Television 13. Life stories — Arts and culture — Performing arts — Actors and actresses 14. Life stories — Arts and culture — Performing arts — Directors and producers

LC Bl2016013489

New York Times Notable Book, 2016.

In the third installment in his four-volume survey of Orson Welles' life and work, a celebrated British actor traces Welles' self-exile from America and his realization that he could only function to his own satisfaction as an independent film-maker, a one-man band, which committed him to a perpetual cycle of money-raising.

"Welles rightly imagined that people would never stop writing about him after he died. Callow continues to set the standard in this increasingly crowded field." —*Kirkus*

Includes bibliographical references and index; Includes filmography; Originally published: London : Jonathan Cape, 2015.

Campbell, Hayley
The Art of Neil Gaiman. Hayley Campbell; foreword by Audrey Niffenegger. Harper Design 2014. 320 pages : Illustration; Color
ISBN 9780062248565
Grades: Adult — B
1. Gaiman, Neil 2. Authors, English 3. 20th century 4. Life stories — Arts and culture — Writing

LC Bl2014015284

With unprecedented access to Neil Gaiman's personal archives, the author gives an insider's glimpse into the artistic inspirations and musings of one of the world's most visionary writers.

Includes bibliographical references and index.

Campoverdi, Alejandra
First Gen: A Memoir. Alejandra Campoverdi. Grand Central Publishing 2023. 320 p.
ISBN 9781538757185
Grades: Adult — B
1. Campoverdi, Alejandra 2. Mexican American women 3. Children of immigrants 4. Breast cancer 5. Cancer 6. American dream 7. Healing 8. Mental health 9. Belonging 10. American people 11. Success (Concept) 12. Marginalized people 13. United States 14. Autobiographies and memoirs 15. Life stories — Facing adversity 16. Life stories — Identity — Immigrants

LC 2023016024

A trailblazing women's health advocate and former Obama aide discusses her experiences as Mexican American woman raised by an immigrant single mother in Los Angeles and the challenges of navigating social mobility as a first-generation Latina.

"An inspiring story and an invaluable resource for first-generation immigrant children striving for success in America." —*Kirkus*

Includes bibliographical references.

Canellos, Peter S.
The Great Dissenter: The Story of John Marshall Harlan, America's Judicial Hero. Peter S. Canellos. Simon & Schuster 2021. 624 p.
ISBN 9781501188206
Grades: Adult — B
1. Harlan, John Marshall, 1833-1911 2. Harlan, Robert J. 3. Judges 4. Dissenters 5. African American civil rights workers 6. Half-brothers 7. Plessy Case, 1896 8. Equality 9. Civil rights 10. African Americans 11. Immigrants' rights 12. Marginalized people 13. Labor rights 14. Social advocacy 15. Social justice 16. United States 17. Biographies 18. Life stories — Law and order — Judges and lawyers 19. History writing — Judicial branch — United States 20. History writing — African American — Civil rights — United States

LC 2021003146

They say that history is written by the victors. But not in the case of the most famous dissenter on the Supreme Court. Almost a century after his death, it was John Marshall Harlan's words that helped end segregation, and gave us our civil rights and our modern economic freedom. Harlan's dissents, particularly in Plessy v. Ferguson, were widely read and a source of hope for decades. Thurgood Marshall called Harlan's Plessy dissent his "Bible"—and his legal roadmap to overturning segregation. In the end, Harlan's words built the foundations for the legal revolutions of the New Deal and Civil Rights eras. Spanning from the Civil War to the Civil Rights movement and beyond, the Great Dissenter is an epic rendering of the American legal system's greatest failures and most inspiring successes.

"Biographer Canellos (Last Lion) intertwines in this original and eye-opening biography the lives of Supreme Court justice John Marshall Harlan and his rumored half-brother, Robert Harlan, who was born a slave.... This is a masterful introduction to two fascinating figures in American history." —*Publishers Weekly*

Includes bibliographical references and index.

Cannadine, David
★ *Mellon: An American Life.* David Cannadine. A.A. Knopf 2006. xvi, 779 p, 48 p. of plates : Illustration; Color
ISBN 9780679450320
Grades: Adult — B
1. Mellon, Andrew W. (Andrew William), 1855-1937 2. Cabinet officers 3. Diplomats 4. Bankers 5. Industrialists 6. Philanthropists 7. Politicians 8. Politics and government 9. United States 10. Biographies 11. Business and economics — Business leaders and entrepreneurs 12. Life stories — Business — Business leaders

LC 2006045116

Shortlisted for the James Tait Black Memorial Prize for Biography, 2006.

A portrait of Andrew Mellon describes his rise to the heights of political and financial power, his controversial role as treasury secretary under three presidents, and his remarkable philanthropy and gift to America of the National Gallery of Art.

Includes bibliographical references (p. [633]-733) and index.

Cannell, Michael T.
A Brotherhood Betrayed: The Man Behind the Rise and Fall of Murder, Inc. Michael Cannell. Minotaur Books 2020. 336 p.
ISBN 9781250204387
Grades: Adult — B
1. Reles, Abe, 1906-1941 2. Assassins 3. Mafia 4. Mafiosi 5. Murder 6. Organized crime 7. New York City 8. 20th century 9. 1940s 10. Biographies 11. Life stories — Law and order — Criminals and law-breakers 12. True Crime — Organized Crime, Mafia, and Gangs

LC 2020017246

ESSENTIAL AND RECOMMENDED TITLES
Biography

The riveting true story of the rise and fall of Murder, Inc. and the executioner-turned-informant whose mysterious death became a turning point in Mob history.

"Readers interested in a non-sensationalized treatment of a major chapter in American crime will be riveted." —*Publishers Weekly*

Includes bibliographical references and index.

Cantu, Francisco
The Line Becomes a River: Dispatches from the Border. Francisco Cantú. Riverhead Books 2018. 256 p.
ISBN 9780735217713
Grades: Adult — **B**
1. Cantu, Francisco (Essayist) 2. Border patrol agents 3. Undocumented immigrants 4. Mexican Americans 5. Immigration and emigration 6. Border security 7. Mexican-American Border Region 8. Autobiographies and memoirs 9. Life stories — Law and order 10. Society and culture — Immigration
LC 2017014247

Los Angeles Times Book Prize for Current Interest, 2018; Booklist Editors' Choice, 2018; Library Journal Best Books, 2018; Spur Award for First Nonfiction Book, 2019; Spur Award for Contemporary Nonfiction, 2019; National Book Critics Circle Award for Nonfiction finalist, 2018; Andrew Carnegie Medal for Excellence in Non-Fiction Finalist, 2019.

A former agent for the U.S. Border Patrol describes his upbringing as the son of a park ranger and grandson of a Mexican immigrant, who upon joining the Border Patrol encountered the violence and political rhetoric that overshadows life for both migrants and the police.

"An exBorder Patrol agent finds himself on both sides of the battle over illegal immigration in this fraught memoir of his time patrolling the Arizona, New Mexico, and Texas borders from 2008 to 2012, an experience that roiled his emotions and shook his sense of his own part-Mexican identity." —*Publishers Weekly*

Capote, Truman
Too Brief a Treat: The Letters of Truman Capote. Edited by Gerald Clarke. Random House 2004. xvi, 487 p. : Illustration
ISBN 9780375501333
Grades: Adult — **B**
1. Capote, Truman, 1924-1984 2. Authors, American 3. Writing 4. Friendship 5. 20th century 6. Arts and Entertainment — Writing and Publishing
LC 2004050313

Spanning his entire life, this collection of private letters by the acclaimed author includes Capote's correspondence with such notables as David O. Selznick, Edith Sitwell, Cecil Beaton, Christopher Isherwood, and Bennett Cerf.

"Capote's untrammeled personality fairly falls off the pages of these letters, and rather than being irritating, his disregard of reticence is especially poignant in this day of sterile e-mailing. Ideal for devotees to dip into here and there instead of reading from start to finish." —*Booklist*

Includes bibliographical references and index.

Carcaterra, Lorenzo
Three Dreamers: A Memoir of Family. Lorenzo Carcaterra. Ballantine Books 2021. 240 p.
ISBN 9780593156711
Grades: Adult — **B**
1. Carcaterra, Lorenzo 2. Authors, American 3. Italian Americans 4. Women 5. Role models 6. Mothers 7. Grandmothers 8. Married women 9. Courage 10. Family relationships 11. Kindness 12. Men-women relations 13. 21st century 14. Autobiographies and memoirs 15. Life stories — Relationships 16. Family and Relationships — General 17. Life stories — Arts and culture — Writing — Authors
LC 2020025677

The best-selling author of Sleepers presents a tribute to his mother, grandmother and late wife that celebrates their accomplishments as strong women role models and survivors of history who imparted lessons in courage, kindness and the power of storytelling.

"Carcaterra (Sleepers) pays a moving tribute to his grandmother, mother, and wife in this heartfelt account of how they shaped him. . . . This emotional narrative isn't for the fainthearted, but its beauty is a thing to behold." —*Publishers Weekly*

Cardwell, Diane
Rockaway: Surfing Headlong into a New Life. Diane Cardwell. Houghton Mifflin Harcourt 2020. 272 p.
ISBN 9780358067788
Grades: Adult — **B**
1. Cardwell, Diane, 1964- 2. Women surfers 3. Surfing 4. Women journalists 5. African American journalists 6. Divorced women 7. Hurricane Sandy, 2012 8. Lifestyle change 9. Self-discovery 10. New York (State) 11. Autobiographies and memoirs 12. Life stories — Sports 13. Life stories — Personal growth 14. Sports and Competition — General
LC 2019045702

This wonderful story of one women's reinvention follows the author as she dives headlong into surfing off of New York City's eccentric Rockaway Beach, finding a true home among her fellow passionate longboarders.

"In this eloquent narrative, the author offers a moving portrait of a woman in search of herself as well as a joyful celebration of physicality, friendship, and the art of surfing. A bighearted and uplifting memoir." —*Kirkus*

Cargle, Rachel Elizabeth
A Renaissance of Our Own: A Memoir & Manifesto on Reimagining. Rachel Elizabeth Cargle. Ballantine Books 2023. 256 p.
ISBN 9780593134733
Grades: Adult — **B**
1. Cargle, Rachel Elizabeth 2. Antiracism 3. Identity 4. Individuality 5. Self-fulfillment 6. Self-discovery 7. Independence 8. Feminism 9. Personal conduct 10. Institutional racism 11. Women social advocates 12. Philanthropists 13. Race relations 14. United States 15. Autobiographies and memoirs 16. Life stories — Identity 17. Life stories — Personal growth
LC 2022047562

A modern voice in feminism and racial justice describes her own journey and approach to dismantling the frameworks and systems that no longer serve us while building liberating new ones that better affirm our individuality.

"Cargle's self-help memoir is highly recommended for DEI and LGTBQ+ collections and women of all ages who want to renew and rethink their purpose in life." —*Booklist*

Carlile, Brandi
Broken Horses: A Memoir. Brandi Carlile. Crown 2021. 320 p.
ISBN 9780593237243
Grades: Adult — **B**
1. Carlile, Brandi 2. Singers 3. Women musicians 4. Music 5. Lesbians 6. Faith (Christianity) 7. Growing up 8. Childhood 9. Identity 10. Women singers 11. LGBTQIA+ people 12. Life stories — Arts and culture — Performing arts — Musicians and composers 13. Arts and Entertainment — Music 14. Life stories — Identity — LGBTQIA+ 15. Life stories — Religion and spirituality
LC 2021004334

Brandi Carlile was born into a musically gifted, impoverished family on the outskirts of Seattle and grew up in a constant state of change, moving from house to house, trailer to trailer, fourteen times in as many years. Though imperfect in every way, her dysfunctional childhood was as beautiful as it was strange, and as nurturing as it was difficult. At the age of five, Brandi contracted bacterial meningitis, which almost took her life, leaving an indelible mark on her formative years and altering her journey into young adulthood. As an openly gay teenager, Brandi grappled with the tension between her sexuality and her faith when her pastor publicly refused to baptize her on the day of the ceremony. Shockingly, her small town rallied around Brandi in support and set her on a path to salvation where the rest of the misfits and rejects find it: Through twisted, joyful, weird, and wonderful music.

"Carlile, a multiple Grammy Award-winning musician, recalls the pivotal events that shaped her music and identity in this captivating memoir. . . . While the author's rise to fame was impressive, it is her raw emotion that resonates after the book's end." —*Publishers Weekly*

PUBLIC LIBRARY CORE COLLECTION: NONFICTION
Twentieth Edition

Carlin, Kelly
A Carlin Home Companion: Growing up with George. Kelly Carlin. St. Martin's Press 2015. 336 p.
ISBN 9781250058256
Grades: Adult   B
1. Carlin, Kelly, 1963- 2. Carlin, George 3. Television producers and directors 4. Radio broadcasters 5. Fathers and daughters 6. Family relationships 7. Fame 8. Drug abuse 9. Actors and actresses 10. Comedians 11. United States 12. Autobiographies and memoirs 13. Biographies 14. Life stories — Arts and culture — Performing arts — Entertainers and celebrities 15. Arts and entertainment — General

LC 2015017795

The popular radio host and star of the acclaimed solo show by the same name recounts her experiences as the daughter of comedian, voice actor and social critic George Carlin, describing her early tours, drug use and renaissance in the years before his death.

"A funny, honest, and compassionate account of growing up with a master of comedy." —*Kirkus*

Carlin, Peter Ames
Bruce: The Innocence, the Darkness, the Rising. Peter Ames Carlin. Simon & Schuster 2012. 416 p.
ISBN 9781439191828
Grades: 10 11 12 Adult   B
1. Springsteen, Bruce 2. Rock musicians 3. Popular music 4. Bands (Music) 5. Music industry and trade 6. Rock music 7. Singers 8. Musicians 9. Popular culture 10. United States history 11. United States 12. 20th century 13. Biographies 14. Life stories — Arts and culture — Performing arts — Entertainers and celebrities 15. Arts and Entertainment — Music — Rock 16. Adult books for young adults

LC 2012020890

Carlin has produced the definitive biography of the Boss himself—rock legend Bruce Springsteen. Drawing upon unfettered access to the singer as well as his closest friends and colleagues, Carlin examines the depths of this iconic figure and his considerable music catalog.

"The author presents his subject as a supremely gifted musician and truly heroic figure, albeit one with a lot on his troubled mind." —*Kirkus*

Carlisle, Clare
Philosopher of the Heart: The Restless Life of Soren Kierkegaard. Clare Carlisle. Farrar, Straus and Giroux 2020. 368 p.
ISBN 9780374231187
Grades: Adult   B
1. Kierkegaard, Soren, 1813-1855 2. Philosophers 3. Philosophy, Modern 4. Existentialism 5. Christianity 6. Biographies 7. Life stories — Education — Philosophers 8. Society and culture — Philosophy

LC 2019055663

A biography of the passionate and challenging philosopher known as the founder of existentialism describes how he explored the questions of existence, being human, the nature of love and Christianity in Copenhagen of the mid 1800s.

"Carlisle (On Habit), reader in philosophy and theology at King's College London, makes an intimidatingly chilly and mercurial figure relatable to readers in this admirable biography." —*Publishers Weekly*

Carlo, Philip
Gaspipe: Confessions of a Mafia Boss. Philip Carlo. William Morrow 2008. 368 p.
ISBN 9780061429842
Grades: Adult   B
1. Casso, Gaspipe, 1942-2020 2. Gangsters 3. Organized crime 4. Mafia 5. Criminals 6. Murderers 7. Police corruption 8. Police misconduct 9. Informers 10. Lifers (Prisoners) 11. Crime bosses 12. New York City 13. Autobiographies and memoirs 14. True Crime — Organized Crime, Mafia, and Gangs 15. Life stories — Law and order — Criminals and law-breakers 16. Adult books for young adults 17. Life stories — Law and order — Prisoners and inmates

LC 2008002683

A look into the world of a convicted Mafia head covers such topics as the order he received to murder John Gotti, the intricate relationship between La Cosa Nostra and the Russian mafia, and the Mafia's role in America's unions and drug networks.

"This powerful story is required reading for anyone with a yen for the Mafia, the criminal underworld and a law enforcement system struggling to keep up." —*Publishers Weekly*

Carlsen, William
Jungle of Stone: The True Story of Two Men, Their Extraordinary Journey, and the Discovery of the Lost Civilization of the Mayans. William Carlsen. William Morrow 2016. 464 p.
ISBN 9780062407399
Grades: Adult   B
1. Stephens, John L, 1805-1852 2. Catherwood, Frederick 3. Carlsen, William 1945- 4. Archaeological expeditions 5. Explorers 6. Maya (Central American people) 7. Expeditions 8. Central America 9. 1840s 10. Adventure writing — Exploration 11. Travel Writing — Retracing Historic Journeys 12. History writing — Latin America

LC 2016429951

Documents the true story of the 19th-century rediscovery of the Mayan civilization by American ambassador John Lloyd Stephens and British architect Frederick Catherwood, illuminating how their findings profoundly changed Western understandings about human history.

"A captivating history of two men who dramatically changed their contemporaries' view of the past." —*Kirkus*

Carlson, Brady
Dead Presidents: An American Adventure into the Strange Deaths and Surprising Afterlives of Our Nation's Leaders. Brady Carlson. W. W. Norton & Co. 2016. 336 p.
ISBN 9780393243932
Grades: Adult   B
1. Gravestones, mausoleums, etc. 2. Monuments 3. Historic sites 4. Presidents 5. Politics and government 6. Local history 7. Voyages and travels 8. United States 9. Biographies 10. History writing — Presidency — United States 11. Travel Writing — United States

LC 2015032329

An engaging exploration into the death stories of American presidents, and the wild ways that have been chosen to memorialize them, shares the surprising origins of landmark monuments and what they reveal about American history and culture.

"A brisk, lighthearted travelogue with an exuberant guide." —*Kirkus*
Includes bibliographical references and index.

Carlson, W. Bernard
Tesla: Inventor of the Electrical Age. W. Bernard Carlson. Princeton University Press 2013. 500 p.
ISBN 9780691057767
Grades: 11 12 Adult   B
1. Tesla, Nikola, 1856-1943 2. Electrical engineers 3. Electric power 4. Electrical engineering 5. Inventors 6. United States 7. Biographies 8. Science Writing — Great Engineering Feats 9. Life stories — Science, technology, and medicine — Scientists and inventors

LC 2012049608

Draws on original documents from Tesla's private and public life to place the engineer within the cultural and technological context of his time, focusing on his inventions as well as the creation and maintenance of his celebrity.
Includes bibliographical references and index.

Carmon, Irin
Notorious Rbg: The Life and Times of Ruth Bader Ginsburg. Irin Carmon and Shana Knizhnik. Dey Street Books 2015. 208 p.
ISBN 9780062415837
Grades: Adult   B

ESSENTIAL AND RECOMMENDED TITLES
Biography

1. Ginsburg, Ruth Bader, 1933-2020 2. Judges 3. Feminists 4. Women's rights 5. Women judges 6. Civil rights 7. United States 8. Biographies 9. Life stories — Law and order — Judges and lawyers 10. History writing — Women's history
LC 2015027547

Amelia Bloomer Lists, 2016.

In an illustrated biography of the feminist icon and legal pioneer, readers can get to know the Supreme Court Justice and fierce Jewish grandmother, who has changed the world despite our struggle with the unfinished business of gender equality and civil rights, standing as a testament to what a little chutzpah can do.

"The brief, cogent excerpts from her court opinions are annotated in plain language by prominent legal academics. Moreover, the authors successfully situate RBG's work within a larger historical context, thereby illustrating her central role in advancing equal rights for all." —*Library Journal*

Includes bibliographical references and index.

Caro, Robert A.
★ *The Passage of Power: The Years of Lyndon Johnson*. Robert A. Caro. Random House 2012. xix, 712 p.
ISBN 9780679405078
Grades: Adult   B

1. Johnson, Lyndon B, 1908-1973 2. Kennedy, John F. (John Fitzgerald), 1917-1963 3. Vice-presidents 4. Presidents 5. Politicians 6. Democrats 7. Politics and government 8. United States 9. 1960s 10. 20th century 11. Biographies 12. History writing — Presidency — 20th century — United States 13. History writing — 1960s — United States 14. Life stories — Politics — Politicians

American History Book Prize, 2012; Booklist Editors' Choice, 2012; Los Angeles Times Book Prize for Biography, 2012; Mark Lynton History Prize, 2013; National Book Critics Circle Award for Biography, 2012; New York Times Notable Book, 2012; National Book Award for Nonfiction finalist, 2012.

Examines Lyndon Johnson's volatile relationships with John and Robert Kennedy, describes JFK's assassination from Johnson's viewpoint, and recounts his accomplishments as president before they were overshadowed by the Vietnam War.

Includes bibliographical references (p. [613]-628) and index.

The Power Broker: Robert Moses and the Fall of New York. Robert A. Caro. Knopf 1974. IX, 1246 p. : Illustration
ISBN 9780394480763
Grades: Adult   B

1. Moses, Robert, 1888-1981 2. Public works 3. Political corruption 4. Roads 5. Civil service workers 6. Design and construction 7. New York City history 8. 20th century 9. Biographies 10. Life stories — Business — Business leaders
LC 73020751

Pulitzer Prize for Biography or Autobiography, 1975.

Moses is pictured as idealist reformer, and political manipulator as his rise to power and eventual domination of New York State politics is documented.

"This is a biographical critique of the man who in four decades as a public official built most of the parks, bridges and highways in and around New York City." —*Newsweek*

Include bibliographical references (p. [1170]-1177).

★ *Working: Researching, Interviewing, Writing*. by Robert A. Caro. Alfred A. Knopf 2019. 240 p.
ISBN 9780525656340
Grades: Adult   B

1. Caro, Robert A. 2. Authors 3. Biographers 4. Journalists 5. Writing 6. Historical research 7. Authors, American 8. Autobiographies and memoirs 9. Essays 10. Life stories — Arts and culture — Writing — Authors 11. Arts and Entertainment — Writing and Publishing
LC 2018055999

The author of the Power Broker and the Years of Lyndon Johnson provides an unprecedented gathering of vivid, candid and deeply revealing recollections about his experiences researching and writing his acclaimed books.

"Caro's skill as a biographer, master of compelling prose, appealing self-deprecation, and overall generous spirit shine through on every page." —*Kirkus*

This is a Borzoi book published by Alfred A. Knopf.

Carpenter, Kyle
You Are Worth It: Building a Life Worth Fighting for. Kyle Carpenter and Don Yaeger. William Morrow & Company 2019. 304 p.
ISBN 9780062898548
Grades: Adult   B

1. Carpenter, Kyle 2. Former marines 3. Medal of Honor recipients 4. Battle casualties 5. Wounds and injuries 6. Healing 7. Physical therapy 8. Courage 9. Self-sacrifice 10. Afghan War, 2001-2021 11. Determination 12. Autobiographies and memoirs 13. Life stories — Law and order — Armed forces personnel 14. Life stories — Facing adversity — War and oppression — War survivors 15. Life stories — Facing adversity — Medical issues

On November 21, 2010, U.S. Marine Lance Corporal Kyle Carpenter was posted on a rooftop in Helmand Province, Afghanistan, when an enemy grenade skittered toward Kyle and fellow Marine Nick Eufrazio. Without hesitation, Kyle chose a path of selfless heroism that few can imagine. He jumped on the grenade, saving Nick but sacrificing himself. Kyle's remarkable memoir reveals a central truth that will inspire every reader: Life is worth everything we've got. It is the story of how one man became a so-called hero who willingly laid down his life for his brother-in-arms—and equally, it is a story of rebirth, of how Kyle battled back from the gravest challenge to forge a life of joyful purpose.

Carr, C.
Candy Darling: Dreamer, Icon, Superstar. Cynthia Carr. Farrar, Straus and Giroux 2024. 384 p.
ISBN 9781250066350
Grades: Adult   B

1. Darling, Candy, 1944-1974 2. Warhol, Andy, 1928-1987 3. Actors and actresses 4. Transgender people 5. Biographies 6. Life stories — Identity — LGBTQIA+ 7. Life stories — Arts and culture — Performing arts — Actors and actresses
LC 2023040888

From an acclaimed biographer comes the first full portrait of the queer icon and Warhol superstar Candy Darling. Bibliography. Index.

"Carr resurrects a trans icon whose life, artistry, and struggle speak directly to our moment." —*Kirkus*

Includes bibliographical references and index.

Carr, Caleb
My Beloved Monster: Masha, the Half-wild Rescue Cat Who Rescued Me. Caleb Carr. Little, Brown and Company 2024. 240 p.
ISBN 9780316503600
Grades: Adult   B

1. Carr, Caleb, 1955-2024 2. Cats 3. Men and cats 4. Living alone 5. Cats as pets 6. Feral cats 7. Animal rescue 8. Pet adoption 9. Human-animal relationships 10. Sick people 11. Bonding (Human-animal) 12. Love 13. Loss 14. American people 15. Autobiographies and memoirs 16. Family and Relationships — Pets and Owners 17. Nature Writing — Animal Studies

Caleb Carr has had special relationships with cats since he was a young boy in a turbulent household. As an adult, he has had many close feline companions, but only after building a three-story home in rural, upstate New York did he enter into the most extraordinary of all of his cat pairings: Masha, a semi-feral Siberian Forest cat who had been abandoned as a kitten, and was languishing in a shelter when Caleb met her. For the seventeen years that followed, Caleb and Masha were inseparable. Theirs is a love story like no other.

"Novelist Carr (the Kreizler series) delivers a lively and moving memoir about his 17-year companionship with a Siberian forest cat named Masha." —*Publishers Weekly*

Carr, David
The Night of the Gun: A Reporter Investigates the Darkest Story of His Life, His Own. David Carr. Simon & Schuster 2008. VII, 389 p. : Illustration
ISBN 9781416541523
Grades: Adult   B

1. Carr, David, 1956-2015 2. Drug addicts 3. Cocaine abuse 4. Journalists 5. Drug abuse 6. Addiction 7. Social life and customs 8. Minneapolis, Minnesota 9. New York City 10. Autobiographies and memoirs 11. True Crime — Drugs

PUBLIC LIBRARY CORE COLLECTION: NONFICTION
Twentieth Edition

12. Science Writing — Medicine and health — Addiction 13. Life stories — Facing adversity — Medical issues — Addiction 14. Life stories — Arts and culture — Writing — Journalists 15. Adult books for young adults

LC 2008012178

Library Journal Best Books, 2008; New York Times Notable Book, 2008.

A confessional account of the author's struggles with addiction traces his rise from a crack house regular to a columnist for "The New York Times," describing his experiences with rehabilitation, cancer, and single parenthood.

"Carr takes a detailed inventory of his years of drug addiction, chronicling the slide from drinking and marijuana use during his teen years in Minneapolis to shooting cocaine and smoking crack while trying to maintain his life as a reporter and the father of twin girls. Carr is meticulous in the investigation of his past, reconstructing events with the aid of police reports, magazine rejection letters, and more than sixty interviews with friends, former dealers, and fellow-addicts. His journalistic skills are on full display as he works to excavate the truth from his often hazy memories. He evinces genuine remorse for his frequently reprehensible behavior and succeeds in creating something more than merely another entry in what he terms the growing pile of junkie memoirs." —*The New Yorker*

Carr, Erin Lee

All That You Leave Behind: A Memoir. Erin Lee Carr. Ballantine Books 2019. 272 p.

ISBN 9780399179716

Grades: Adult   B

1. Carr, David, 1956-2015 2. Carr, Erin Lee 3. Journalists 4. Recovering addicts 5. Fathers and daughters 6. Sobriety 7. Death of fathers 8. Loss 9. Autobiographies and memoirs 10. Biographies 11. Life stories — Arts and culture — Writing — Journalists 12. Life stories — Facing adversity — Medical issues — Addiction 13. Life stories — Facing adversity — Coping with death

LC 2018059597

A celebrated journalist, bestselling author (The Night of the Gun), and recovering addict, David Carr was in the prime of his career when he suffered a fatal collapse in the newsroom of the New York Times in 2015. Shattered by his death, his daughter Erin Lee Carr, at age twenty-seven an up-and-coming documentary filmmaker, began combing through the entirety of their shared correspondence—1,936 items in total—in search of comfort and support.

"Erin writes honestly about her relationship with her father…as she delivers a clear-eyed view into multigenerational substance abuse and simultaneously celebrates the redemption of a fathers love. Readers cant help but get caught up in Erins tragic and ultimately transformative story." —*Publishers Weekly*

Carretta, Vincent

Equiano, the African: Biography of a Self-made Man. Vincent Carretta. University of Georgia Press 2005. xxiv, 436 p. : Illustration; Map

ISBN 9780820325712

Grades: Adult   B

1. Equiano, Olaudah, 1745-1797 2. Enslaved people 3. Freed people 4. Slave trade 5. United States history 6. Great Britain 7. 18th century 8. 19th century 9. Biographies 10. History writing — African American — Enslavement — United States 11. Life stories — Facing adversity — War and oppression — Enslaved people

LC 2005011898

Tells the story of the former slave who was the English-speaking world's most renowned person of African descent in the 1700s and is considered the founding father of both the African and the African American literary traditions.

"This is a thoroughly rich, engrossing, and well-researched portrait of an exceptional man and the cause he championed." —*Booklist*

Includes bibliographical references (p. 395-417) and index.

Carriere, Alice

Everything/Nothing/Someone: A Memoir. Alice Carriere. Spiegel & Grau 2023. 288 p.

ISBN 9781954118294

Grades: Adult   B

1. Carriere, Alice 2. Growing up 3. Childhood 4. Dissociative disorders 5. Mental illness 6. Self-harm 7. Medical malpractice 8. Psychic trauma 9. Families 10. Mental health 11. 1990s 12. Autobiographies and memoirs 13. Book club best bets 14. Debut title 15. Life stories — Relationships — Growing up 16. Life stories — Facing adversity — Medical issues — Mental illness

This compelling literary debut tells the story of a young woman coming of age in the bohemian '90s as she navigates through the challenges of adolescence and grapples with dissociative disorder.

"Carrière's urgent, visceral debut traces the roots of her struggles with dissociative disorder to the poor boundaries of her childhood." —*Publishers Weekly*

Carroll, Rebecca

Surviving the White Gaze: A Memoir. Rebecca Carroll. Simon & Schuster 2021. 320 p.

ISBN 9781982116255

Grades: Adult   B

1. Carroll, Rebecca 2. Interracial adoption 3. Adopted children 4. Race awareness in children 5. Interracial families 6. African American women authors 7. African Americans 8. Racism 9. Birthmothers 10. Interpersonal relations 11. Identity 12. New Hampshire 13. Autobiographies and memoirs 14. Life stories — Identity — Race and ethnicity 15. Life stories — Relationships — Growing up 16. Family and Relationships — Parenting — Adoption

LC 2020029852

A woman describes growing up as the only Black person in a rural New Hampshire town, the tense relationship she had with her birth mother, her loyalty towards her adoptive parents and her search for racial identity.

Carroll's narrative, which reflects the author's 'Decades-long, self-initiated rite of passage,' is a blunt, urgent study of racial identity and an attempt to chronicle 'My ultimate arrival at the complicated depths of my own Blackness.' —*Kirkus*

Carter, Ash

Life Isn't Everything: Mike Nichols, as Remembered by 103 of His Closest Friends. Ash Carter and Sam Kashner. Henry Holt and Company 2019. 368 p.

ISBN 9781250112873

Grades: Adult   B

1. Nichols, Mike 2. Film producers and directors 3. Filmmakers 4. Biographies 5. Life stories — Arts and culture — Performing arts — Directors and producers 6. Arts and Entertainment — Movies and Television

LC 2019031319

Booklist Editors' Choice, 2019.

An up-close and personal portrait of legendary filmmaker, theater director, and comedian Mike Nichols, drawing on candid conversations with his closest friends in show business and the arts-from Dustin Hoffman and Meryl Streep to Natalie Portman and Lorne Michaels.

Includes index.

Carter, Jimmy

Everything to Gain: Making the Most of the Rest of Your Life. Jimmy and Rosalynn Carter. University of Arkansas Press 1995. xv, 176 p.

ISBN 9781557283887

Grades: Adult   B

1. Carter, Jimmy, 1924- 2. Carter, Rosalynn 3. Life skills 4. Personal conduct 5. Presidents' spouses 6. Presidents 7. United States 8. Biographies 9. History writing — United States

LC 95024257

A dual account of the former president and first lady describes their post-White House careers and highlights such topics as midlife marriage, America's health-care issues, the efforts of the Carter Center, and more.

Originally published: New York : Random House, c1987. With appropriate amendments to cover a few changed circumstances.

A Full Life: Reflections at Ninety. Jimmy Carter. Simon & Schuster 2015. 256 p.

ISBN 9781501115639

Grades: Adult   B

1. Carter, Jimmy, 1924- 2. Humanitarianism 3. Former presidents 4. Presidents 5. Politicians 6. Politics and government 7. United States 8. 20th century 9. 1970s 10. 1980s 11. Autobiographies and memoirs 12. Biographies 13. His-

ESSENTIAL AND RECOMMENDED TITLES
Biography

tory writing — Presidency — 20th century — United States 14. Life stories — Politics — Politicians

LC 2015007489

The 39th president and Nobel Peace Prize winner reflects on his full and happy life with pride, humor and a few second thoughts.

"The drawings and poems by the author add even more of a personal touch, though crises in his marriage and his estrangement from the Obama presidency offer the most noteworthy revelations. A memoir that reads like an epilogue to a life of accomplishment." —*Kirkus*

Includes index.

*An **Hour** Before Daylight: Memories of a Rural Boyhood.* Jimmy Carter. Simon & Schuster 2001. 284 p. : Illustration

ISBN 9780743211932

Grades: 11 12 Adult   B

1. Carter, Jimmy, 1924- 2. Carter family 3. Farm life 4. Growing up 5. Farmers 6. Rural life 7. Presidents 8. Georgia 9. United States 10. 20th century 11. Autobiographies and memoirs 12. Biographies 13. History writing — Presidency — 20th century — United States 14. Family and Relationships — Growing up 15. Life stories — Relationships — Growing up 16. Life stories — Politics — Politicians 17. Adult books for young adults 18. Life stories — Nature and outdoors — Farmers and ranchers

LC 00048248

Pulitzer Prize for Biography or Autobiography finalist.

In vivid detail and with "an appealingly gritty honesty" (Kirkus Reviews), former president Jimmy Carter relives his experiences growing up on a Georgia farm during the Depression in the time of segregation. In the process, he shares the difficulties of farm life and profiles the people who shaped his life, including his parents, his eccentric relatives, and his African-American friends.

"This is social and agricultural history as plain and honest as one of the tables the author makes in his workshop—an American classic." —*The New Yorker*

Includes index.

***Keeping** Faith: Memoirs of a President.* Jimmy Carter. Bantam Books 1982. xiv, 622 p. : Illustration; Map; Portrait

ISBN 9780553050233

Grades: Adult   B

1. Carter, Jimmy, 1924- 2. Presidents 3. Politics and government 4. United States 5. 1970s 6. 1980s 7. Autobiographies and memoirs 8. Biographies 9. Life stories — Politics — Politicians 10. History writing — 1970s — United States

LC 82090323

In Keeping Faith, originally published in 1982, President Carter provides a candid account of his time in the Oval Office, detailing the hostage crisis in Iran, his triumph at the Camp David Middle East peace summit, his relationships with world leaders, and even glimpses into his private world.

"These memoirs treat such matters as improving relations with China; enacting energy legislation; negotiating the second Strategic Arms Limitation treaty (SALT II); concluding the Panama Canal treaties; and convincing Menachem Begin and Anwar Sadat to reach agreement at Camp David. Carter also devotes more than a quarter of the book to the frustrations arising from the capture of hostages in Tehran." —*New York Review of Books*

Includes index.

Carter, Stephen L.

***Invisible:** The Forgotten Story of the Black Woman Lawyer Who Took Down America's Most Powerful Mobster.* Stephen L. Carter. Henry Holt and Company 2018. 336 p.

ISBN 9781250121974

Grades: Adult   B

1. Carter, Eunice Hunton, 1899-1970 2. Luciano, Lucky, 1897-1962 3. Dewey, Thomas E, (Thomas Edmund), 1902-1971 4. Carter, Stephen L, 1954- 5. African American women lawyers 6. Public prosecutors 7. Organized crime 8. African American authors 9. African American families 10. Mafia trials 11. Political activists 12. New York City 13. 1930s 14. Life stories — Law and order — Judges and lawyers 15. Society and culture — Violence and crime 16. True Crime — Organized Crime, Mafia, and Gangs 17. True Crime — Investigations and Trials 18. Antiracist literature

LC 2017050088

Finalist for the Hurston/Wright Legacy Awards for Nonfiction, 2019.

The best-selling author of the Emperor of Ocean Park traces the story of his grandmother, an African-American attorney who, in spite of period barriers, devised the strategy that sent mafia chieftain Lucky Luciano to prison in the 1930s.

"With artful storytelling and a narrative-like delivery, Carter tells Eunice's story in the best way possible, offering a compelling, unputdownable read with as much value in social history as legal appeal. Not to be missed." —*Library Journal*

Includes index.

Carwardine, Richard

***Lincoln:** A Life of Purpose and Power.* Richard Carwardine. Alfred A. Knopf 2006. xv, 394 p. : Illustration; Map

ISBN 9781400044566

Grades: 9 10 11 12 Adult   B

1. Lincoln, Abraham, 1809-1865 2. Civil war 3. United States Civil War, 1861-1865 4. Presidents 5. Politics and government 6. United States history 7. United States 8. 19th century 9. American Civil War era (1861-1865) 10. Biographies 11. History writing — Presidency — 19th century — United States 12. History writing — Wars and conflicts — American Civil War 13. Life stories — Law and order — Armed forces personnel 14. Adult books for young adults 15. Life stories — Politics — Politicians

LC 2005047230

A portrait of America's sixteenth president follows Lincoln's life and career during his rise to political power and his years in the White House, arguing that he looked beyond the political system to find support in his struggle to end slavery.

"This book is not only analytical and smart, it's also delightfully readable and it will surely emerge as one of the most important Lincoln books to be published this decade." —*Publishers Weekly*

Includes bibliographical references (p. [327]-360) and index; Originally published: London : Pearson Education, 2003.

Cash, Rosanne

★ ***Composed:*** *A Memoir.* Rosanne Cash. Viking 2010. 288 p.

ISBN 9780670021963

Grades: Adult   B

1. Cash, Rosanne 2. Songwriters 3. Country music 4. Country musicians 5. Music 6. Singers 7. United States 8. Autobiographies and memoirs 9. Biographies 10. Arts and Entertainment — Music — Country 11. Life stories — Arts and culture — Performing arts — Musicians and composers

LC 2010010327

For thirty years as a musician, Rosanne Cash has enjoyed both critical and commercial success, releasing a series of albums that are as notable for their lyrical intelligence as for their musical excellence. In this memoir, Cash writes compellingly about her upbringing in Southern California as the child of country legend Johnny Cash, and of her relationships with her mother and her famous stepmother, June Carter Cash. In her account of her development as an artist she shares memories of recording her own first album on a German label; working her way to success; her Nashville marriage to Rodney Crowell; her relationship with the country music establishment; taking a new direction in her music and moving to New York; motherhood; dealing with the deaths of her parents, in part through music; the process of songwriting; and her fulfillment with her current husband and musical collaborator, John Leventhal.

"The moving chapters about Roseanne Cash's glorious career and the moments of great tenderness and tension with her legendary family are like exquisite album tracks: Individually they are great reads, but together they add up to something cohesive and powerful. Composed provides no bombshell confessions about her failed marriage to Rodney Crowell or her wonderfully complicated relationship with her dad, Johnny. (Though she does dismiss the biopic Walk the Line as an egregious oversimplification of our family's private pain.) Instead, Cash delivers writerly meditations on what it means to be an artist and a public person and, yes, a daughter. Rare is the celebrity memoir that is so full of self-awareness and dignity." —*Entertainment Weekly*

PUBLIC LIBRARY CORE COLLECTION: NONFICTION
Twentieth Edition

Casillo, Charles
Marilyn Monroe: The Private Life of a Public Icon. Charles Casillo. St. Martin's Press 2018. 336 p.
ISBN 9781250096869
Grades: Adult   B
1. Monroe, Marilyn, 1926-1962 2. People with bipolar disorder 3. Foster children 4. Fame 5. Suicidal behavior 6. Child sexual abuse 7. Self-destructive behavior 8. Films 9. Actors and actresses 10. Biographies 11. Life stories — Arts and culture — Performing arts — Actors and actresses 12. History writing — Arts and culture

LC 2018004352

The author of the Marilyn Diaries draws on new research and interviews to reveal how Monroe's traumatic childhood contributed to her struggle with bipolar disorder and impacted her career and personal life.

"Beginning with Monroes illegitimate birth and impoverished childhood in and out of foster homes and orphanages, Casillo traces the deep roots of Monroes essential feelings of inadequacy and longing for acceptance." —*Booklist*

Includes index.

Castner, Brian
The Long Walk: A Story of War and the Life That Follows. Brian Castner. Doubleday 2012. 224 p.
ISBN 9780385536202
Grades: Adult   B
1. Castner, Brian 2. Bomb squads 3. Veterans 4. Explosives 5. Soldiers 6. Iraq War, 2003-2011 7. Autobiographies and memoirs 8. Life stories — Law and order — Armed forces personnel 9. History writing — Wars and conflicts — Iraq War

LC 2011052419

A memoir by a bomb-disposal veteran of the Iraq War traces his three tours of duty in the Middle East and his team's daily life-threatening efforts to stop roadside bombers, and shares the challenges he faced while reacclimating to civilian life.

Includes bibliographical references and index.

Castor, Helen
Joan of Arc: A History. Helen Castor. HarperCollins 2015. 352 p.
ISBN 9780062384393
Grades: Adult   B
1. Joan of Arc, Saint, 1412-1431 2. Women saints 3. Hundred Years' War, 1339-1453 4. Women soldiers 5. Christian women 6. Courage 7. French history 8. Leadership 9. European history 10. 15th century 11. Medieval period (476-1492) 12. Biographies 13. History writing — Medieval — Europe 14. History writing — Europe — France 15. Life stories — Law and order — Armed forces personnel 16. Life stories — Religion and spirituality — Religious and spiritual leaders 17. Spirituality and Religion — Christianity

LC 2014029053

Tells the story of the extraordinary peasant girl from Domremy as never told before, revealing a living, breathing woman confronting the challenges of faith and doubt and placing her actions in the context of the larger political and religious conflicts of this period in France.

Castor carefully combs the record of her interrogation then and rehabilitation 25 years later. An unorthodox yet erudite and elegant biography of this 'Massive star.' —*Kirkus*

Castro, Fidel
Fidel Castro: My Life : A Spoken Autobiography. Fidel Castro and Ignacio Ramonet; translated by Andrew Hurley. Scribner 2008. 723 p. : Illustration; Map
ISBN 9781416553281
Grades: 11 12 Adult   B
1. Castro, Fidel, 1926-2016 2. Heads of state 3. International relations 4. Revolutionaries 5. Caribbean history 6. Cuba 7. 20th century 8. Autobiographies and memoirs 9. Life stories — Politics — Politicians 10. History writing — Latin America — Cuba

LC Bl2007014874

Booklist Editors' Choice, 2008.

In a series of interviews with a European journalist and scholar, the Cuban leader describes his early life, the Cuban Revolution, and his experiences ruling Cuba, and discusses his views on socialism, international affairs, and the future.

Includes bibliographical references (p. 663-648) and index; English translation originally published in Great Britain in 2007 by Allen Lane—T.P. verso.

Cather, Willa
The Selected Letters of Willa Cather. Edited by Andrew Jewell and Janis Stout. Alfred A. Knopf 2013. xxiii, 715 p. : Illustration
ISBN 9780307959300
Grades: Adult   B
1. Cather, Willa, 1873-1947 2. Authors, American 3. Letter writing 4. 20th century 5. Life stories — Arts and culture — Writing 6. Arts and Entertainment — Writing and Publishing

LC 2012036882

A collection of the writer's personal correspondences includes teenage reports of her 1880s Red Cloud life, letters written during her early journalism years, and the exchanges penned in observation of World War II and her own struggles with aging.

A first publication of the acclaimed writer's personal correspondences includes whimsical teenage reports of her 1880s Red Cloud life, letters written during her early journalism years and the 1940s exchanges penned in observation of World War II and her own struggles with aging.

This is a Borzoi book.

Cayton-Holland, Adam
Tragedy Plus Time: A Tragi-comic Memoir. Adam Cayton-Holland. Touchstone 2018. 288 p.
ISBN 9781501170164
Grades: Adult   B
1. Cayton-Holland, Adam 2. Comedians 3. Suicide victims 4. Siblings 5. Grief 6. Depression 7. Suicidal behavior 8. Family and death 9. Survivors of suicide victims 10. Denver, Colorado 11. Autobiographies and memoirs 12. Life stories — Facing adversity — Coping with death 13. Life stories — Relationships — Family 14. Family and Relationships — Siblings

LC 2017049067

A memoir about the touring comic author's beautiful, funny and ultimately heartbreaking relationship with his younger sister describes their activist upbringing and the mental illness and depression that culminated in her suicide.

"This is Cayton-Hollands heartbreaking work of genius: His story of Lydia, his best friend and closest confidant, and her tragic suicide at 28. He writes with candor and care of Lydias bright light and his own darkest hour, making for an unforgettable read." —*Booklist*

Century, Douglas
Barney Ross. Douglas Century. Nextbook : 2006. xvii, 215 p. : Illustration
ISBN 9780805242232
Grades: Adult   B
1. Ross, Barney, 1909-1967 2. Boxers (Sports) 3. Boxing 4. Drug addiction 5. Weapons industry and trade 6. World War II 7. Social life and customs 8. Israel 9. United States 10. 20th century 11. Biographies 12. Sports and Competition — Boxing 13. Sports and Competition — Individual Athlete 14. Life stories — Sports — Athletes

LC 2005049939

A profile of one of the most colorful sports figures of the twentieth century follows the life and career of boxer Barney Ross, from his youth as the child of Eastern European immigrants in a tough Chicago neighborhood and his hardscrabble early life, to his successful boxing career, exploits as a combat Marine during World War II, campaign against drug abuse, and fervent support of a Jewish state.

Cervini, Eric
The Deviant's War: The Homosexual vs. the United States of America. Eric Cervini. Farrar, Straus and Giroux 2020. 494 p.
ISBN 9780374139797
Grades: Adult   B

ESSENTIAL AND RECOMMENDED TITLES
Biography

1. Kameny, Frank, 1925-2011 2. Gay men 3. Civil service workers 4. Discrimination in employment 5. Astronomers 6. Veterans 7. Homophobia 8. Social justice 9. Homosexuality 10. LGBTQIA+ rights 11. Legislation 12. United States 13. Biographies 14. Life stories — Identity — LGBTQIA+ 15. Life stories — Politics — Activists and reformers 16. History writing — LGBTQIA+ 17. History writing — 1960s — United States

LC 2020003415

Pulitzer Prize for History finalist, 2021.

In 1957, Frank Kameny, a rising astronomer working for the U.S. Defense Department in Hawaii, received a summons to report immediately to Washington, D.C. The Pentagon had reason to believe he was a homosexual, and after a series of humiliating interviews, Kameny, like countless gay men and women before him, was promptly dismissed from his government job. Unlike many others, though, Kameny fought back. Based on firsthand accounts, recently declassified FBI records, and forty thousand personal documents, Eric Cervini's the Deviant's War unfolds over the course of the 1960s, as the Mattachine Society of Washington, the group Kameny founded, became the first organization to protest the systematic persecution of gay federal employees.

"An absolutely indispensable, highly readable work of history that belongs in every library." —*Booklist*

Includes bibliographical references and index.

Chabon, Michael
Manhood for Amateurs: The Pleasures and Regrets of a Husband, Father, and Son. Michael Chabon. Harper 2009. 320 p.
ISBN 9780061490187
Grades: Adult   B

1. Chabon, Michael 2. Married men 3. Fathers 4. Sons 5. Fatherhood 6. Masculinity 7. Marriage 8. Authors, American 9. United States 10. 20th century 11. Autobiographies and memoirs 12. Biographies 13. Arts and Entertainment — Writing and Publishing 14. Life stories — Arts and culture — Writing — Authors

LC 2009004749

The author questions what it means to be a man today in a series of interlinked autobiographical reflections, regrets, and reexaminations, each sparked by an encounter, in the present, that holds some legacy of the past.

"For the most part in these pages [Chabon] manages to write about himself, his family and his generation with humor and introspective wisdom. As in his novels, he shifts gears easily between the comic and the melancholy, the whimsical and the serious, demonstrating once again his ability to write about the big subjects of love and memory and regret without falling prey to the Scylla and Charybdis of cynicism and sentimentality." —*New York Times*

Chafkin, Max
The Contrarian: Peter Thiel and Silicon Valley's Pursuit of Power. Max Chafkin. Penguin Press 2021. 400 p.
ISBN 9781984878533
Grades: Adult   B

1. Thiel, Peter A. 2. Capitalists and financiers 3. Power 4. Influence (Psychology) 5. Conservatives 6. High technology industry and trade 7. Silicon Valley, California 8. Biographies 9. Life stories — Business — Business leaders 10. Business and economics — Industries — Technology 11. Politics and global affairs — General

LC 2021007920

Since the days of the dot-com bubble in the late 1990s, no industry has made a greater impact on the world than Silicon Valley. And few individuals have done more to shape Silicon Valley than billionaire venture capitalist and entrepreneur Peter Thiel. From the technologies we use every day to the delicate power balance between Silicon Valley, Wall Street, and Washington, Thiel has been a behind-the-scenes operator influencing countless aspects of our contemporary way of life. But despite his power and the ubiquity of his projects, no public figure is quite so mysterious. Eye-opening and deeply reported, The Contrarian is a revelatory biography of a one-of-a-kind leader and an incisive portrait of a tech industry whose explosive growth and power is both thrilling and fraught with controversy.

"Chafkin, a features editor at Bloomberg Businessweek, brings long experience in the tech world to his book debut, a savvy biography of billionaire venture capitalist and outspoken neo-reactionary Peter Thiel (b. 1967). . . . A brisk, well-researched life of an enigmatic billionaire." —*Kirkus*

Includes bibliographical references and index.

Chan, Jackie
Never Grow up. Jackie Chan, with Zhu Mo; translated by Jeremy Tiang. Gallery Books 2018. 352 p.
ISBN 9781982107215
Grades: Adult   B

1. Chan, Jackie, 1954- 2. Martial artists 3. Celebrities 4. Film producers and directors 5. Risk-taking 6. Growing up 7. Family relationships 8. Films 9. Actors and actresses 10. Hong Kong 11. United States 12. Autobiographies and memoirs 13. Translations — Chinese to English 14. Life stories — Arts and culture — Performing arts — Actors and actresses 15. Arts and Entertainment — Movies and Television 16. Sports and Competition — Martial Arts 17. Life stories — Relationships — Family

LC 2018035059

The martial artist, actor, director and stuntman from Rush Hour and the Karate Kid reflects on his life, including his childhood at the China Drama Academy, his lucky breaks, setbacks and near death experiences both on and off movie sets.

Originally published in China in 2015 by Jiangsu Literature and Art Publishing House as Never Grow Up, Only Get Older— T.P. verso.

Empress Dowager Cixi: The Concubine Who Launched Modern China. Jung Chang. Alfred A. Knopf 2013. 352 p.
ISBN 9780307271600
Grades: Adult   B

1. Cixi, Empress dowager of China, 1835-1908 2. Women rulers 3. Mistresses 4. Politics and government 5. Chinese history 6. China 7. 19th century 8. Biographies 9. Life stories — Politics — Royalty 10. History writing — Imperial China — Asia — China

LC 2013020766

New York Times Notable Book, 2013; Shortlisted for the James Tait Black Memorial Prize for Biography, 2013.

Chosen as one of the Emperor's concubines at age 16, Empress Dowager Cixi (1835-1908) ruled China for decades and brought a medieval empire into the modern age. Upon the Emperor's death in 1861, their 5-year-old son ascended to the throne; Cixi overthrew the appointed regents, to become the true power behind the throne (a silk screen literally separated her from her all-male advisors during briefings). She abolished tortuous punishments, inaugurated women's liberation, moved China toward more egalitarian means of rulership.

"Chang uses the work of revisionist scholars to paint a largely plausible portrait of a ruthless, farsighted politician who welcomed change and restructured the state." —*Library Journal*

Includes bibliographical references and index.

Mao: The Unknown Story. Jung Chang, Jon Halliday. Knopf 2005. xiii, 814 p. : Illustration; Map
ISBN 9780679422716
Grades: Adult   B

1. Mao, Zedong, 1893-1976 2. Heads of state 3. Totalitarianism 4. Communism 5. Chinese history 6. China 7. 20th century 8. Biographies 9. Life stories — Politics — Politicians 10. History writing — Communist China — Asia — China

LC 2004063826

Booklist Editors' Choice, 2005; New York Times Notable Book, 2005.

A portrait of the late Chinese leader refutes a wide variety of myths about Mao and provides facts about the Long March, his relationship with Stalin, and the impact of his thirst for power on the Chinese people.

"This is a magisterial work. This biography supplies substantial . information and presents it all in a stylish way that will put it on bedside tables around the world." —*New York Times Book Review*

Includes bibliographical references (p. [739]-790) and index; Originally published in Great Britain by Jonathan Cape, London—T.P. verso.

★ *Wild Swans: Three Daughters of China*. Jung Chang; [with a new introduction by the author]. Touchstone 2003. 524 p, 16 p. of plates : Illustration; Map

ISBN 9780743246989
Grades: 11 12 Adult B
1. Chang, Jung, 1952- 2. Mothers and daughters 3. Communism 4. Chinese women 5. China 6. Collective autobiographies and memoirs 7. History writing — Women's history 8. Life stories — People in history — Witness to history 9. Life stories — Facing adversity — War and oppression 10. History writing — Asia — China
LC 91020696
British Book Award for Book of the Year, 1994.
Traces three generations of a family in twentieth-century China, during which a warlord's concubine, a powerful Communist Party member, and a Cultural Revolution survivor witness Mao's impact on their nation and their livelihoods.
"The author tells the harrowing life stories of her maternal grandmother, her mother, and herself. Their tales span a period of radical change in China that has touched every aspect of life." —*Booklist*
Includes index; Originally published : New York : Simon & Schuster, 1991.

Chapman, Rex
★ *It's Hard for Me to Live with Me.* Rex Chapman, Seth Davis. Simon & Schuster 2024. 288 p.
ISBN 9781982197773
Grades: Adult B
1. Basketball players 2. Professional athletes 3. Addiction 4. American people 5. Autobiographies and memoirs 6. Life stories — Sports — Athletes 7. Sports and Competition — Basketball
A memoir from the University of Kentucky basketball legend, NBA veteran and social media influencer about his recovery from addiction.
"A former basketball prodigy's blunt memoir about stardom, addiction, and American culture." —*Kirkus*

Chase, James
Acheson: The Secretary of State Who Created the Ameircan World. James Chase. Simon & Schuster 2007. 512 pages : Illustration
ISBN 9781416548652
Grades: Adult B
1. Acheson, Dean, 1893-1971 2. Cabinet officers 3. Politicians 4. International relations 5. United States 6. Biographies 7. Life stories — Politics
LC Bl2014018671
A definitive biography describes the personal and political life of Dean Acheson, who, in tandem with President Harry S. Truman, created the American force that won the Cold War and established a world order still in existence today.
Describes the personal and political life of Dean Acheson, who created the American force that won the Cold War.
"Dean Acheson was Truman's Secretary of State from 1949 to 1953, and today's world, as Chace shows in this lucid biography, was shaped in no small degree by his efforts." —*The New Yorker*
Includes bibliographical references and index.

Chaudry, Rabia
Fatty Fatty Boom Boom: A Memoir of Food, Fat, and Family. Rabia Chaudry. Algonquin Books of Chapel Hill 2022. 320 p.
ISBN 9781643750385
Grades: Adult B
1. Chaudry, Rabia 2. Women 3. Pakistani Americans 4. Food habits 5. Families 6. Body image 7. Fat people 8. Self esteem 9. Immigrant families 10. Childhood 11. Life stories — Relationships — Growing up 12. Life stories — Identity
LC 2022025653
From the best-selling author and host of the popular Undisclosed podcast comes a warm, intimate memoir about food, body image and growing up in a loving but sometimes oppressively concerned Pakistani immigrant family.
"Chaudry (Adnan's Story), a podcaster, executive producer, and lawyer most known for being an Adnan Syed advocate, pens a delightful and entertaining memoir of her childhood and early adulthood journey with her weight and nutrition habits, both gains and losses." —*Library Journal*

Chee, Alexander
★ *How to Write an Autobiographical Novel: Essays.* Alexander Chee. Mariner Books 2018. 288 p.
ISBN 9781328764522
Grades: Adult B
1. Authors 2. Writing 3. Identity 4. Gay men 5. Books and reading 6. Growing up 7. Family relationships 8. Korean American men 9. LGBTQIA+ rights 10. Political participation 11. Essays 12. Autobiographies and memoirs 13. Life stories — Arts and culture — Writing — Authors 14. Life stories — Identity — Race and ethnicity 15. Life stories — Identity — LGBTQIA+ 16. Life stories — Politics — Activists and reformers
LC 2017045808
Library Journal Best Books, 2018.
From the author of the Queen of the Night, an essay collection exploring how we form our identities in life, in politics, and in art.
"This is a beautiful book—hard to sum up, sometimes hard to digest, but a delight to read. A must for anyone interested in the craft of writing, politics, LGBTQA+ rights, AIDS activism, family, tarot, even roses." —*Library Journal*

Cheney, Lynne V.
James Madison: A Life Reconsidered. Lynne Cheney. Viking Adult 2014. 576 pages
ISBN 9780670025190
Grades: Adult B
1. Madison, James, 1751-1836 2. Founding Fathers of the United States 3. War of 1812 4. Presidents 5. Politicians 6. Politics and government 7. United States 8. 19th century 9. Biographies 10. Life stories — Politics — Politicians 11. History writing — Early America — United States
LC 2013047837
A portrait of the fourth U.S. president offers insight into his pivotal contributions as a Founding Father, covering such topics as his political philosophy and his role as the intellectual force behind the Constitution.
"Cheney conclusively demonstrates through the historical record that Madison, in word and deed, was a primary figure in shaping early American development." —*Publishers Weekly*
Includes bibliographical references and index.

The Virginia Dynasty: Four Presidents and the Creation of the American Nation. Lynne Cheney. Viking Press 2020. 576 p.
ISBN 9781101980040
Grades: Adult B
1. Washington, George, 1732-1799 2. Jefferson, Thomas, 1743-1826 3. Madison, James, 1751-1836 4. Monroe, James, 1758-1831 5. Politicians 6. Founding Fathers of the United States 7. Presidents 8. Politics and government 9. United States history 10. Virginia 11. United States 12. Early America (1784-1819) 13. 18th century 14. 19th century 15. Biographies 16. History writing — Early America — United States
LC Bl2020018419
A group portrait of America's first four Virginia Presidents focuses on a series of key historical episodes that illustrate how the myriad leadership roles of Washington, Jefferson, Madison and Monroe promoted transcendental, if contradictory, national views about freedom and equality.
"Bringing these men together as a group draws attention to how their thought and action unfolded in response to new challenges and dispels any illusion that they were a monolithic bloc. Cheney is an adept writer who makes no wrong steps. Perfect for history buffs, though little new ground is tread." —*Library Journal*

Cheng, Nien
Life and Death in Shanghai. Nien Cheng. Grove Press 1987. IX, 547 p.
ISBN 9780394555485
Grades: 11 12 Adult B
1. Cheng, Nien, 1915-2009 2. Loss 3. False imprisonment 4. Political prisoners 5. Communism 6. Intellectual life 7. Revolutions 8. Chinese history 9. China 10. Chinese Cultural Revolution (1966-1976) 11. Autobiographies and memoirs 12. Life stories — Facing adversity — War and oppression — Hostages and POWs 13. History writing — Communist China — Asia — China

ESSENTIAL AND RECOMMENDED TITLES
Biography

LC 86045254

This account of the horrors faced by the author during China's Cultural Revolution tells of her arrest, the failed attempts to make her confess to spying, her imprisonment, and the story of her survival.

"This is a volume that belongs on the shelf alongside the writings of Primo Levi, Elie Wiesel, Dith Pran, and other chroniclers of ideological fanaticism, its dehumanizing consequences, and its all too rare resisters." —*Christian Science Monitor*

Chernaik, Judith
Schumann: The Faces and the Masks. by Judith Chernaik. Alfred A. Knopf 2018. 336 p.
ISBN 9780451494467
Grades: Adult **B**
1. Schumann, Robert, 1810-1856 2. Composers 3. Classical music 4. Mental illness 5. Musicians 6. Music 7. 19th century 8. Biographies 9. Life stories — Arts and culture — Performing arts — Musicians and composers 10. Arts and entertainment — Music — Classical
LC 2017060796

Drawing on unpublished archive material, as well as more established materials, the author traces the life and music of a major composer and key figure of Romanticism, who has been the subject of major controversy since his early death in a mental asylum.

This is a Borzoi Book published by Alfred A. Knopf; Includes bibliographical references and index.

Chernow, Ron
★ *Alexander Hamilton.* Ron Chernow. Penguin Press 2004. 818 p.
ISBN 9781594200090
Grades: Adult **B**
1. Hamilton, Alexander, 1757-1804 2. Politicians 3. Politics and government 4. United States 5. 18th century 6. Early America (1784-1819) 7. Biographies 8. History writing — Politicians — United States 9. History writing — Early America — United States 10. Life stories — Politics — Politicians
LC 2003065641

ALA Notable Book, 2005; Booklist Editors' Choice, 2004; New York Times Notable Book, 2004; National Book Critics Circle Award for Biography finalist, 2004.

The personal life of Alexander Hamilton, an illegitimate, largely self-taught orphan from the Caribbean who rose to become George Washington's aide-de-camp and the first Treasury Secretary of the United States, is captured in a definitive biography.

"Chernow makes fresh contributions to Hamiltoniana: No one has discovered so much about Hamilton's illegitimate origins and harrowed youth; few have been so taken by Hamilton's long-suffering, loving wife, Eliza. This is a fine work that captures Hamilton's life with judiciousness and verve." —*Publishers Weekly*

Includes bibliographical references (p. [780]-788) and index.

★ *Grant.* Ron Chernow. Penguin Press 2017. 928 p.
ISBN 9781594204876
Grades: Adult **B**
1. Grant, Ulysses S, 1822-1885 2. Presidents 3. Generals 4. United States Civil War, 1861-1865 5. Command of troops 6. Politics and government 7. United States history 8. United States 9. American Civil War era (1861-1865) 10. 19th century 11. Biographies 12. History writing — Presidency — 19th century — United States 13. Life stories — Law and order — Military leaders
LC 2017025263

New York Times Notable Book, 2017; Booklist Editors' Choice, 2017; ALA Notable Book, 2018; Longlisted for the Andrew Carnegie Medal for Excellence in Non-Fiction, 2018.

Presents a meticulously researched portrait of the complicated Civil War general and 18th President, challenging the views of his critics while sharing insights into his prowess as a military leader, the honor with which he conducted his administration and the rise and fall of his fortunes.

"In this sympathetic biography, the author continues the revival of Grant's reputation. At nearly 1,000 pages, Chernow delivers a deeply researched, everything-you-ever-wanted-to-know biography, but few readers will regret the experience." —*Kirkus*

Washington: A Life. Ron Chernow. Penguin Press 2010. 800 p.
ISBN 9781594202667
Grades: Adult **B**
1. Washington, George, 1732-1799 2. Political leadership 3. Presidents 4. Generals 5. United States history 6. United States 7. 18th century 8. Biographies 9. History writing — Presidency — 18th century — United States 10. History writing — Colonial America — United States 11. Life stories — Politics — Politicians 12. Life stories — Law and order — Military leaders
LC 2010019154

ALA Notable Book, 2011; American History Book Prize, 2010; Booklist Editors' Choice, 2010; Pulitzer Prize for Biography or Autobiography, 2011; New York Times Notable Book, 2010.

A comprehensive account of the life of George Washington negates the stereotype of a stolid, unemotional man and instead reveals a dashing, passionate man of fiery opinions and many moods who fiercely guarded his private life.

Includes bibliographical references and index.

Chiger, Krystyna
The Girl in the Green Sweater: A Life in Holocaust's Shadow. Krystyna Chiger with Daniel Paisner. St. Martin's Press 2008. 288 p.
ISBN 9780312376567
Grades: 11 12 Adult **B**
1. Chiger, Krystyna, 1935- 2. Jewish history 3. Polish people 4. Eastern European people 5. Jewish children 6. Holocaust (1933-1945) 7. Hiding 8. Survival 9. Children 10. German occupation, World War II 11. European history 12. Ukraine 13. 1940s 14. Autobiographies and memoirs 15. History writing — Wars and conflicts — Holocaust — World War II 16. Life stories — Facing adversity — War and oppression — Hostages and POWs 17. Life stories — Facing adversity — War and oppression — War survivors 18. Adult books for young adults
LC 2008022521

The last member of a group of Jewish-Polish survivors who found refuge from Nazi persecution in the sewers of LVov traces the author's harrowing fourteen-month existence during which she was helped by Leopold Socha, a Catholic who risked his life to bring food and supplies to her struggling family.

Child, Julia
★ *My Life in France.* Julia Child with Alex Prud'homme. Alfred A. Knopf 2006. xi, 317 p. : Illustration
ISBN 9781400043460
Grades: Adult **B**
1. Child, Julia 2. Cooks 3. Cooking, French 4. American people in France 5. Cooking 6. Paris, France 7. 1950s 8. Autobiographies and memoirs 9. Food writing — Memoirs and biographies 10. Life stories — Arts and culture — Culinary arts 11. Adult books for young adults
LC 2005044727

IACP Cookbook Awards, Literary Food Writing, 2007.

A memoir begun just months before Child's death describes the legendary food expert's years in Paris, Marseille, and Provence and her journey from a young woman from Pasadena who cannot cook or speak any French to the publication of her legendary Mastering cookbooks and her winning the hearts of America as "The French Chef."

Includes index.

Chin, Curtis
Everything I Learned, I Learned in a Chinese Restaurant: A Memoir. Curtis Chin. Little, Brown & Company 2023. 304 p.
ISBN 9780316507653
Grades: Adult **B**
1. Chin, Curtis 2. Television producers and directors 3. Documentary filmmakers 4. Chinese Americans 5. Gay men 6. LGBTQIA+ people 7. Growing up 8. Chinese American families 9. Restaurateurs 10. Chinese restaurants 11. Memories 12. Neighborhoods 13. Extended families 14. Multiculturalism 15. Identity 16. East Asian people 17. Chinese people 18. North American people 19. Ameri-

can people 20. Detroit, Michigan 21. Autobiographies and memoirs 22. Life stories — Relationships — Growing up 23. Life stories — Identity 24. Food writing — Memoirs and biographies 25. Debut title

Nineteen eighties Detroit was a volatile place to live, but above the fray stood a safe haven: Chung's Cantonese Cuisine, where anyone could sit down for a warm, home-cooked meal. Here was where, surrounded by his multigenerational family, filmmaker and activist Curtis Chin came of age; where he learned to embrace his identity as a gay ABC, or American-born Chinese; where he navigated the divided city's spiraling misfortunes; and where—between helpings of almond boneless chicken, sweet-and-sour pork, and some of his own, less-savory culinary concoctions—he realized just how much he had to offer to the world, to his beloved family, and to himself.

"Chin is a born storyteller with an easy manner, and this memoir should earn him many readers." —*Kirkus*

Chisholm, Edward

A Waiter in Paris: Adventures in the Dark Heart of the City. Edward Chisholm. Pegasus Books 2022. 384 p.
ISBN 9781639362837
Grades: Adult   **B**
1. Chisholm, Edward 2. Waiters 3. Young men 4. Culture 5. Food industry and trade 6. Social life and customs 7. Paris, France 8. Autobiographies and memoirs 9. Life stories — General 10. Food Writing — Memoirs and biographies

A waiter's job is to deceive you. They want you to believe in a luxurious calm because on the other side of that door…is hell. Edward Chisholm's spellbinding memoir of his time as a Parisian waiter takes you below the surface of one of the most iconic cities in the world and right into its glorious underbelly. He inhabits a world of inhuman hours, snatched sleep and dive bars; scraping by on coffee, bread and cigarettes, often under sadistic managers with a wage so low you're fighting your colleagues for tips. Colleagues including thieves, narcissists, ex-Legionnaires, paperless immigrants, wannabe actors and drug dealers, who are the closest thing to family that you've got. It's physically demanding, frequently humiliating and incredibly competitive. But it doesn't matter because you're in Paris, the centre of the universe, and there's nowhere else you'd rather be in the world.

"A Dickensian tale of a young man's trial by fire in a French bistro gives rise to biting commentary on Parisian culture in Chisholm's intoxicating debut." —*Publishers Weekly*

Chow, Kat

Seeing Ghosts: A Memoir. Kat Chow. Grand Central 2021. 304 p.
ISBN 9781538716328
Grades: Adult   **B**
1. Chow, Kat 2. Death of mothers 3. Grief 4. Loss 5. Families 6. Chinese American women 7. Extended families 8. Immigration and emigration 9. Memories 10. Cancer 11. Chinese American families 12. People with cancer 13. Women 14. Autobiographies and memoirs 15. Life stories — Facing adversity — Coping with death 16. Family and Relationships — Aging and Death 17. Family and Relationships — Families 18. Life stories — Relationships — Family 19. Book club best bets

After her mother dies unexpectedly of cancer, a Chinese American writer and journalist weaves together the story of the fallout of grief that follows her extended family as they emigrate from China and Hong Kong to Cuba and America.

"A Chinese American writer reflects on the profound loss of her mother to cancer and how it informed her adulthood.... By uniting family memories, elements of Chinese culture, and an intimate perspective, Chow wraps tragedy and history into an affecting memorial." —*Kirkus*

Chozick, Amy

Chasing Hillary: Ten Years, Two Presidential Campaigns, and One Intact Glass Ceiling. Amy Chozick. HarperCollins 2018. 352 p.
ISBN 9780062413598
Grades: Adult   **B**
1. Clinton, Hillary Rodham 2. Presidential election, 2016 3. Elections 4. Presidential candidates 5. Political campaigns 6. Campaigning 7. Politicians 8. Politics and government 9. United States 10. 21st century 11. Biographies 12. Politics and global affairs — Elections 13. Life stories — Politics — Politicians

LC Bl2018029362

Trailing Hillary Clinton through all of the highs and lows of the most noxious and wildly dramatic presidential election in American history, the author came to understand what drove Clinton, how she accomplished what no woman had before and why she ultimately failed.

Christie, Chris

Let Me Finish: Trump, the Kushners, Bannon, New Jersey, and the Power of In-your-face Politics. Chris Christie. Hachette Books 2019. 304 p.
ISBN 9780316421799
Grades: Adult   **B**
1. Politicians 2. Conservatives 3. Former governors 4. Presidential candidates 5. Power 6. Political science 7. Politics and government 8. New Jersey 9. United States 10. Autobiographies and memoirs 11. Conservative writing 12. Life stories — Politics — Politicians 13. Politics and global affairs — Political figures

LC Bl2018192577

The controversial former governor and presidential candidate traces his rise to power through the bare-knuckle politics of New Jersey, describes his long friendship with Donald Trump and shares frank insights into the current administration.

Chung, Nicole

All You Can Ever Know. Nicole Chung. Catapult 2018. 240 p.
ISBN 9781936787975
Grades: Adult   **B**
1. Chung, Nicole 2. Adoptees 3. Korean American women 4. Interracial adoption 5. Identity 6. Birthparents 7. Families 8. Adoption reunions 9. Identification 10. Autobiographies and memoirs 11. Life stories — Identity — Race and ethnicity 12. Life stories — Relationships — Family 13. Society and culture — Race 14. Adult books for young adults

LC 2018938840

Library Journal Best Books, 2018; National Book Critics Circle Award for Autobiography/Memoir finalist, 2018.

A Korean adoptee who grew up with a white family in Oregon discusses her journey to find her identity as an Asian American woman and a writer after becoming curious about her true origins.

"Chung's clear, direct approach to her experience, which includes the birth of her daughter as well as her investigation of her family, reveals her sharp intelligence and willingness to examine difficult emotions." —*Booklist*

★ *A Living Remedy: A Memoir.* Nicole Chung. Ecco Press 2023. 288 p.
ISBN 9780063031616
Grades: Adult   **B**
1. Korean American children 2. Family relationships 3. Interracial adoption 4. Grief 5. Death of parents 6. Equality 7. Poverty 8. Income inequality 9. Working class families 10. Adoptive parents 11. Adopted children 12. American people 13. North American people 14. Oregon 15. United States 16. Autobiographies and memoirs 17. Book club best bets 18. Life stories — Relationships — Family 19. Life stories — Facing adversity — Coping with death 20. Life stories — Identity — Race and ethnicity

LC 2022038945

The best-selling author of *All You Can Ever Know* returns with a memoir of her experiences as a Korean adoptee and the challenges she faced holding on to family bonds in the face of hardship and tragedy.

"Chung…couches the evolution of the bond between parent and child in the struggles of class and loss in this melancholy memoir….Powerfully rendered scenes illuminate this quiet polemic against a dysfunctional healthcare system, hidden poverty, and racism." —*Publishers Weekly*

Chung, Vinh

Where the Wind Leads: A Refugee Family's Miraculous Story of Loss, Rescue, and Redemption. Vinh Chung with Tim Downs. Thomas Nelson 2014. 368 pages

ESSENTIAL AND RECOMMENDED TITLES
Biography

ISBN 9780849947568
Grades: Adult — **B**
1. Chung, Vinh, 1975- 2. Boat people (Southeast Asian refugees) 3. Refugees 4. Chinese people in foreign countries 5. Chinese people in the United States 6. Chinese people 7. Vietnam 8. Autobiographies and memoirs 9. Life stories — Facing adversity — War and oppression — Refugees
LC Bl2014007800

Offers the author's account of his Chinese family's flight from oppression in Vietnam, their harrowing experiences as boat people, their subsequent rescue, and the difficulties they faced after being relocated to Fort Smith, Arkansas.

Cisneros, Sandra
*A **House** of My Own: Stories from My Life.* Sandra Cisneros. Knopf 2015. 320 p.
ISBN 9780385351331
Grades: Adult — **B**
1. Cisneros, Sandra 2. Mexican Americans 3. Mexican American women 4. Authors, American 5. Women authors 6. Mexico 7. United States 8. 20th century 9. Essays 10. Autobiographies and memoirs 11. Biographies 12. Life stories — Arts and culture — Writing — Authors 13. Adult books for young adults
LC 2015007520

Booklist Editors' Choice: Adult Books for Young Adults, 2015.

In A House of My Own, award-winning Chicana author Sandra Cisneros compiles essays and lectures into her autobiography. Some of her vignettes were previously published, but have new contextual comments here. Noting that the presence of a typewriter constitutes "home," she reflects on places she's lived, the meaning of home, and how it relates to her fiction and poetry. By turns funny, poignant, and contemplative, this memoir brings the author to life, presenting a woman you're sure you've met before.

"At once righteously irreverent and deeply compassionate, Cisneros writes frankly and tenderly of independence and connection, injustice and transcendence, resilience and creativity, the meaning of home and the writer's calling." —*Booklist*

This is a Borzoi book — Verso title page.

Clapton, Eric
Clapton: The Autobiography. Eric Clapton. Broadway Books 2007. 343 p. : Illustration
ISBN 9780385518512
Grades: Adult — **B**
1. Clapton, Eric 2. Musicians 3. Guitarists 4. Rock musicians 5. England 6. Autobiographies and memoirs 7. Biographies 8. Arts and Entertainment — Music — Rock 9. Life stories — Arts and culture — Performing arts — Musicians and composers
LC 2007015482

The legendary guitarist recounts the story of his life and his career, recalling his work with the Yardbirds, Cream, and as a solo artist; years of drug and alcohol abuse; failed marriage to Patti Boyd; and the accidental death of his young son.

"As he retraces every step of his career, from the early stints with the Yardbirds and Cream to his solo successes, Clapton also devotes copious detail to his drug and alcohol addictions, particularly how they intersected with his romantic obsession with Pattie Boyd. Both the youthful excesses and the current calm state are narrated with an engaging tone that nudges Clapton's story ahead of other rock 'N' roll memoirs." —*Publishers Weekly*

Clarey, Christopher
★ *The **Master**: The Long Run and Beautiful Game of Roger Federer.* Christopher Clarey. Twelve 2021. 352 p.
ISBN 9781538719268
Grades: Adult — **B**
1. Federer, Roger, 1981- 2. Tennis players 3. Professional tennis players 4. Tennis 5. Athletes 6. Biographies 7. Life stories — Sports — Athletes 8. Sports and Competition — Tennis 9. Sports and Competition — Individual Athlete

A tennis correspondent for the New York Times sits down with Roger Federer and those closest to him to tell the story of the greatest player in men's tennis.

"Sports journalist Clarey (the New York Times tennis correspondent) takes readers inside Federer's world and provides a fascinating, complete portrait of the athlete that clearly demonstrates how and why he has become a tennis superstar." —*Library Journal*

Clark, Heather
★ *Red **Comet**: The Short Life and Blazing Art of Sylvia Plath.* Heather Clark. Alfred A. Knopf 2020. 1120 p.
ISBN 9780307961167
Grades: Adult — **B**
1. Plath, Sylvia 2. Women Poets 3. Poets, American 4. Women and literature 5. Suicide 6. Authors, American 7. Poets 8. People with depression 9. Women 10. Biographies 11. Life stories — Arts and culture — Writing — Poets 12. Arts and Entertainment — Writing and Publishing
LC 2019041635

Pulitzer Prize for Biography or Autobiography finalist, 2021; National Book Critics Circle Award for Biography finalist, 2020.

The highly anticipated new biography of Sylvia Plath that focuses on her remarkable literary and intellectual achievements, while restoring the woman behind the long-held myths about her life and art.

"Clark's in-depth scholarship and fine writing result in a superb work that will deliver fresh revelations to Plath's many devoted fans." —*Publishers Weekly*

Clark, John Lee
Touch the Future: A Manifesto in Essays. John Lee Clark. W W Norton & Company 2023. 192 p.
ISBN 9781324035367
Grades: Adult — **B**
1. Clark, John Lee, 1978- 2. People who are blind 3. People who are deaf 4. Language and languages 5. Communication 6. Touch 7. Social advocates 8. Families 9. Barrier-free design 10. Autobiographies and memoirs 11. Essays 12. Life stories — Facing adversity — Medical issues — Living with disabilities 13. Family and relationships — Disabled family members

"Clark serves up passionate meditations on the DeafBlind Protactile movement...Lucid and incisive, this is not to be missed." —*Publishers Weekly*

Clark, Liz
Swell: A Sailing Surfer's Voyage of Awakening. Liz Clark. Patagonia 2018. 256 p.
ISBN 9781938340543
Grades: Adult — **B**
1. Clark, Liz 2. Women sailors 3. Women surfers 4. Self-discovery 5. Solitude 6. Solo voyages 7. Seafaring life 8. Single-handed sailing 9. Surfing 10. Autobiographies and memoirs 11. Adventure writing — Adventure travel 12. Travel Writing — Modes of Transportation — Boating

Captain Liz Clark spent her youth dreaming of traveling the world by sailboat and surfing remote waves. When she was 22, she met a mentor who helped turn her desire into reality. Embarking on an adventure that most only fantasize about, she set sail from Santa Barbara, California, as captain of her 40-foot sailboat, Swell, headed south in search of surf, self, and the wonder and learning that lies beyond the unbroken horizon.

Clarke, Rachel
Dear Life: A Doctor's Story of Love and Loss. Rachel Clarke. Thomas Dunne Books 2020. 336 p.
ISBN 9781250764515
Grades: Adult — **B**
1. Clarke, Rachel (Physician) 2. Physicians 3. Terminal care 4. Palliative treatment 5. Quality of life 6. Death 7. Grief 8. Compassion 9. Last days 10. Hospice care 11. Death of fathers 12. Fathers and daughters 13. Autobiographies and memoirs 14. Life stories — Science, technology, and medicine — Healthcare professionals 15. Family and Relationships — Aging and death 16. Life stories — Facing adversity — Coping with death

An NHS palliative medicine expert identifies an industry gap in guidelines for qualitative end-of-life care, sharing career-based insights into how loved ones and professional caregivers can more compassionately assist patients through the final stages of life.

"Clarke's message is especially timely as we continue to face a global pandemic, and she also includes practical advice on end-of-life preparations and helpful notes about relevant resources. Death comes to all of us; these authentic stories show how it can be met with strength and grace instead of fear." —*Kirkus*

Originally published: London : Little, Brown, 2020.

Clarke, Thurston

JFK's Last Hundred Days: The Transformation of a Man and the Emergence of a Great President. Thurston Clarke. The Penguin Press 2013. 384 p.
ISBN 9781594204258
Grades: Adult B
1. Kennedy, John F. (John Fitzgerald), 1917-1963 2. Change (Psychology) 3. Political leadership 4. Presidents 5. Politics and government 6. United States 7. 20th century 8. 1960s 9. Biographies 10. History writing — Presidency — 20th century — United States 11. History writing — 1960s — United States
LC 2012047456

Clarke reexamines the last months of the President's life to show a man in the midst of great change, finally on the cusp of making good on his extraordinary promise.

Includes bibliographical references and index.

The Last Campaign: Robert F. Kennedy and 82 Days That Inspired America. Thurston Clarke. Henry Holt 2008. 272 p.
ISBN 9780805077926
Grades: Adult B
1. Kennedy, Robert Francis, 1925-1968 2. Presidential election, 1968 3. Politics and government 4. United States 5. 1960s 6. History writing — 1960s — United States 7. History writing — Politicians — United States
LC 2007045880

Documents Robert Kennedy's dramatic and ill-fated 1968 presidential campaign, outlining his positions on such issues as the Vietnam War, race, and poverty as well as his private struggles with the assassination of JFK.

"In this account of Robert F. Kennedy's run for president, Clarke follows on Bobby's heels as he plunged headlong into his campaign, from Kansas and Indiana to Oregon and California, throwing off his brother's mantle and becoming at last his own man. He spoke passionately, almost recklessly, inciting crowds to frenzy with his idealistic speeches about the moral shame of Vietnam, the needs of the poor and minorities and the responsibility of each American. Incorporating accounts by a gamut of reporters, politicians, family and Honorary Kennedys, as well as extracts from Bobby's own stunning stump speeches, Clarke compellingly recreates this huge, joyous adenture." —*Kirkus*

Includes index.

Clavin, Thomas

Wild Bill: The True Story of the American Frontier's First Gunfighter. Tom Clavin. St. Martin's Press 2019. 448 p.
ISBN 9781250173799
Grades: Adult B
1. Hickok, Wild Bill, 1837-1876 2. Calamity Jane, 1852-1903 3. Peace officers 4. Frontier and pioneer life 5. Gunfighters 6. Gunfights 7. United States Civil War, 1861-1865 8. Men-women relations 9. The West (United States) history 10. American Westward Expansion (1803-1899) 11. 19th century 12. Biographies 13. Life stories — Law and order — Police and law officers 14. History writing — Westward expansion — United States
LC 2018041162

The best-selling author of Dodge City traces the life of the true James Butler "Wild Bill" Hickok, from his service as a Union spy and lawman to his famous romances and the confrontations that shaped his gunfighter legend.

"Well written, full of vivid characters, and detailed, but built largely from existing literature, this is an accessible celebration of Hickoks life rather than a rigorous deconstruction of his romantic mythos." —*Booklist*

Includes bibliographical references.

Clay, Catrine

King, Kaiser, Tsar: Three Royal Cousins Who Led the World to War. Catrine Clay. Walker 2007. xiii, 416 p. : Illustration
ISBN 9780802716231
Grades: Adult B
1. George V, King of Great Britain, 1865-1936 2. William II, German Emperor, 1859-1941 3. Nicholas II, Emperor of Russia, 1868-1918 4. Heads of state 5. World War I 6. Rulers 7. British history 8. German history 9. Russian history 10. Europe 11. Romanov Dynasty (1613-1917) 12. History writing — Wars and conflicts — World War I 13. Book club best bets
LC Bl2007016520

Library Journal Best Books, 2007.

Profiles three royal cousins—George v. Of England, Kaiser Wilhelm II of Germany, and Tsar Nicholas II of Russia—whose actions shaped the course of twentieth-century history, drawing on hitherto unpublished diaries and letters.

"This is a biography of not one but three significant men. King George v. Of England, Kaiser Wilhelm II of Germany, and Tsar Nicholas II of Russia (familiarly known as Georgie, Willy, and Nicky) were more than just the leaders of three of the most powerful countries in the world in the early 20th centurythey were cousins who had grown up together, played together, and attended family functions together. [The author] provides an intimate look inside the lives of these boys as they grew into manhood and became king, kaiser, and tsar, bringing new pleasures and details to a well-known subject." —*Library Journal*

Includes bibliographical references (p. 388-393) and index; Originally published: London : John Murray, 2006.

Cleage, Pearl

Things I Should Have Told My Daughter: Lies, Lessons & Love Affairs. Pearl Cleage. Atria Books 2014. 320 pages
ISBN 9781451664690
Grades: Adult B
1. Cleage, Pearl 2. Women authors, American 3. Motherhood 4. Self-fulfillment 5. Autobiographies and memoirs 6. Life stories — Arts and culture — Writing — Authors 7. Arts and entertainment — Writing and publishing
LC 2013034164

When author Pearl Cleage was going through boxes full of her journals, her daughter suggested burning them. Fortunately for readers, Cleage instead drew from them to compile Things I Should Have Told My Daughter. This memoir, which presents diary excerpts without added context, provides a compelling view of the African American experience from 1970 to 1988. Cleage is a highly regarded writer who was a civil rights activist, wrote speeches for Maynard Jackson, Atlanta's first Black mayor, experimented with drugs, avidly followed cinema and popular music, and had numerous lovers.

Includes bibliographical references and index.

Cleaver, Eldridge

Soul on Ice. Eldridge Cleaver. Delta Trade Paperbacks 1999. 242 p.
ISBN 9780385333795
Grades: Adult B
1. Cleaver, Eldridge, 1935-1998 2. African American authors 3. Civil rights 4. African Americans 5. Psychology 6. Race relations 7. Social life and customs 8. United States history 9. United States 10. 20th century 11. Autobiographies and memoirs 12. Essays 13. Biographies 14. Life stories — Politics — Activists and reformers 15. History writing — African American — United States
LC BL 99004710

Eldridge Cleaver's letters from Folsom Prison in which he reveals his sensibility and his literary prowess.

Originally published: New York : McGraw-Hill, 1968.

Clemmons, Francois S.

Officer Clemmons: More Than a Song. Francois S. Clemmons. Catapult 2020. 268 pages : Illustration
ISBN 9781948226707
Grades: Adult B
1. Clemmons, Francois S. 2. Rogers, Fred 3. Television personalities 4. African American men 5. Gay men 6. Spiritual life 7. Personal conduct 8. Friendship

ESSENTIAL AND RECOMMENDED TITLES
Biography

9. Identity 10. Autobiographies and memoirs 11. Life stories — Identity — Race and ethnicity 12. Life stories — Identity — LGBTQIA+ 13. Arts and entertainment — Movies and television

LC Bl2020010609

Loan Stars Favourites, 2020.

An intimate debut memoir by the Grammy Award-winning artist who famously played "Officer Clemmons" on Mister Rogers' Neighborhood traces his Oberlin College music studies, his embrace of his sexual orientation and his life-changing chance encounter with Fred Rogers.

"Clemmons's thoroughly delightful, inspiring story will speak particularly to artists in marginalized communities." —*Publishers Weekly*

Cleveland, Pat

Walking with the Muses: A Memoir. by Pat Cleveland (with Lorraine Glennon).. 37 INK 2016. 320 p.

ISBN 9781501108228

Grades: Adult   **B**

1. Cleveland, Pat 2. Fashion 3. Fashion designers 4. Fashion shows 5. Fashion design 6. African American women 7. 1970s 8. 1960s 9. 20th century 10. Autobiographies and memoirs 11. Biographies 12. Life stories — Arts and culture — Fashion 13. Arts and Entertainment — Fashion

LC 2015041692

An exciting account of the international adventures of fashion model Pat Cleveland—one of the first Black supermodels during the wild sixties and seventies.

"Some readers will be particularly interested in her discussion of Bill Cosby, but Cleveland is the real star of her own story of passion, strength, and elegance above all." —*Publishers Weekly*

Includes bibliographical references and index.

Clinton, Bill

My Life. Bill Clinton. Knopf 2004. 957, xliii p. : Illustration

ISBN 9780375414572

Grades: Adult   **B**

1. Clinton, Bill, 1946- 2. Clinton family 3. Presidents 4. Politicians 5. Politics and government 6. Arkansas 7. Washington, D.C. 8. United States 9. 1990s 10. 20th century 11. 21st century 12. Autobiographies and memoirs 13. Biographies 14. History writing — Presidency — 20th century — United States 15. History writing — 1990s — United States 16. Life stories — Politics — Politicians

LC 2004107564

British Book Award for Biography of the Year, 2005; New York Times Notable Book, 2004.

The former president looks back on his life and career, discussing his youth and education, his early public service, his years as governor of Arkansas, and his accomplishments during two terms in the White House.

"Clinton's memoir has the raw material for a blockbuster book." —*Publishers Weekly*

Includes index.

Clinton, Catherine

Harriet Tubman: The Road to Freedom. Catherine Clinton. Little, Brown 2004. xiii, 272 p.

ISBN 9780316144926

Grades: 11 12 Adult   **B**

1. Tubman, Harriet, 1820?-1913 2. Enslaved people 3. Underground Railroad 4. History of anti-slavery movements 5. African American women 6. United States history 7. 19th century 8. Biographies 9. History writing — African American — Enslavement — United States 10. History writing — Women's history 11. Life stories — Facing adversity — War and oppression — Enslaved people 12. Life stories — Politics — Activists and reformers 13. Adult books for young adults

LC 2003056185

A biography of the fugitive slave turned "conductor" on the Underground Railroad describes Tubman's youth in the South, her escape to Philadelphia, her efforts to liberate slaves, and her work for the Union Army.

"Clinton turns sobriquets into meaningful descriptors of a unique person. In her hands, a familiar legend acquires human dimension with no diminution of its majesty and power." —*Publishers Weekly*

Includes bibliographical references (p. 251-257) and index.

Clinton, Hillary Rodham

Living History. Hillary Rodham Clinton. Simon & Schuster 2003. xi, 562 p. : Illustration

ISBN 9780743222242

Grades: 11 12 Adult   **B**

1. Clinton, Hillary Rodham 2. Clinton, Bill, 1946- 3. Women legislators 4. Women politicians 5. Presidents' spouses 6. Politicians 7. Legislators 8. Politics and government 9. United States 10. 2000s (Decade) 11. 20th century 12. 21st century 13. Autobiographies and memoirs 14. Biographies 15. Liberal writing 16. Life stories — Politics — Politicians 17. Politics and global affairs — Political figures

LC 2003276264

The author chronicles her eight years as First Lady of the United States, looking back on her husband's two administrations, the challenges she faced during the period, the impeachment crisis, and her own political work.

"This book is important not because of the history Senator Clinton records, but because of the history she doesn't record, and what that airbrushing tells us about the history she aspires to shape." —*New York Times Book Review*

Coates, Ta-Nehisi

The Beautiful Struggle: A Father, a Son, and an Unlikely Road to Manhood. Ta-Nehisi Coates. Spiegel & Grau 2008. 240 p.

ISBN 9780385520362

Grades: 11 12 Adult   **B**

1. Coates, Ta-Nehisi 2. African American authors 3. African Americans 4. Fathers and sons 5. African American young men 6. Street life 7. Growing up 8. Family relationships 9. Social life and customs 10. Baltimore, Maryland 11. 20th century 12. Autobiographies and memoirs 13. Family and Relationships — Growing up 14. Life stories — Relationships — Growing up

LC 2007052166

A memoir of growing up in the tough world of Baltimore in the 1980s chronicles the relationship between the author and his father, a Vietnam vet and Black Panther affiliate, and his campaign to keep his sons from falling victim to the temptations of the streets.

Coe, Alexis

★ *You Never Forget Your First: A Biography of George Washington.* Alexis Coe. Viking Books 2020. 320 p.

ISBN 9780735224100

Grades: Adult   **B**

1. Washington, George, 1732-1799 2. Generals 3. Political leadership 4. Command of troops 5. Founding Fathers of the United States 6. Presidents 7. United States 8. 18th century 9. Biographies 10. Impartial writing 11. Life stories — Politics — Politicians 12. History writing — Presidency — 18th century — United States

LC 2019045005

A whimsically irreverent portrait of America's first President includes coverage of Washington's entitled upbringing by a single mother, his dog "Sweetlips," his numerous military defeats and the partisan nightmares that spun from his back-stabbing cabinet.

"Evenhanded and engaging, this biography brings fresh insight to one of America's most written-about leaders." —*Kirkus*

Includes bibliographical references and index.

Coffin, Jaed

Roughhouse Friday: A Memoir. Jaed Coffin. Farrar, Straus and Giroux 2019. 256 p.

ISBN 9780374251956

Grades: Adult   **B**

1. Coffin, Jaed 2. Boxing 3. Fathers and sons 4. Masculinity 5. Identity 6. Multiracial men 7. Family relationships 8. Belonging 9. Boxers (Sports) 10.

Thai Americans 11. Southeast Asian Americans 12. Southeast Asian people 13. Self-discovery 14. Anger 15. Alaska 16. Autobiographies and memoirs 17. Life stories — Personal growth 18. Sports and Competition — Boxing 19. Life stories — Identity — Gender

LC 2018045292

While lifting weights in the Seldon Jackson College gymnasium on a rainy autumn night, Jaed Coffin heard the distinctive whacking sound of sparring boxers down the hall. That evening, Coffin joined a ragtag boxing club. Deeply honest and vulnerable, Roughhouse Friday is a meditation on violence and abandonment, masculinity, and our inescapable longing for love. It suggests that sometimes the truth of what's inside you comes only if you push yourself to the extreme.

"Coffins lyrical account of his eventful initiation into the world of amateur boxing takes readers to southeast Alaska. This is a powerful, wonderfully written exploration of ones sense of manhood." —*Publishers Weekly*

Coldstream, Catherine

★ *Cloistered: My Years as a Nun.* Catherine Coldstream. St. Martin's Press 2024. 288 p.
ISBN 9781250323514
Grades: Adult   B
1. Coldstream, Catherine 2. Catholic women 3. Death of fathers 4. Grief 5. Faith (Christianity) 6. Nuns 7. Convents 8. Monasticism and religious orders for women 9. Corruption 10. Emotional abuse 11. Disillusionment 12. British people 13. English people 14. Great Britain 15. Autobiographies and memoirs 16. Life stories — Religion and spirituality — Spiritual journeys 17. Spirituality and Religion — Christianity 18. Debut title

Provides a memoir of life inside the world of a traditional Carmelite monastery and the intense personal journey into and out of an enclosed life of poverty, chastity and obedience.

"Readers interested in spiritual memoirs and religious formation, abuse, and reform will welcome Coldstream's intelligent, unflinching writing and perceptive account of years as a cloistered nun." —*Booklist*

Cole, Jason

Elway: A Relentless Life. Jason Cole. Hachette Books 2020. 368 p.
ISBN 9780316455770
Grades: Adult   B
1. Elway, John, 1960- 2. Football players 3. Quarterbacks (Football) 4. Executives 5. Competition 6. Leadership 7. Professional football 8. Biographies 9. Life stories — Sports 10. Sports and Competition — Football 11. Sports and Competition — Individual Athlete

LC 2020013577

This biography of the Hall of Fame quarterback examines his struggles to reach the NFL, the crushing disappointment of losing three Super Bowls, and the eventual triumph of leading the Denver Broncos to two consecutive championships.

"With exclusive recollections of Elway's college football years, Cole delves into the forces that shaped the quarterback and gave him the resiliency to overcome challenges both on and off the field. Recommended for all public library collections, and especially for readers interested in the evolution of sports in the late 20th century." —*Library Journal*

Includes index.

Cole, Natalie

Angel on My Shoulder: An Autobiography. Natalie Cole; written with Digby Diehl. Warner Books 2000. IX, 353 p. : Illustration
ISBN 9780446527460
Grades: Adult   B
1. Cole, Natalie, 1950-2015 2. Women singers 3. Fathers and daughters 4. Drug use 5. Divorced women 6. Singers 7. Faith 8. United States 9. Autobiographies and memoirs 10. Biographies 11. Arts and Entertainment — Music — Jazz and the Blues 12. Life stories — Arts and culture — Performing arts — Musicians and composers

LC 00061455

The singer shares her tale of trijmph over drugs, depression, divorce, and all the worst celebrity can bring.

"Although she concentrates mostly on the good times, Cole isn't shy about the bad times, which makes this intriguing, engaging, and inspirational life story worthy of attention." —*Booklist*

Includes discography (p. [333]-345) and index.

Coleman, Rick

★ *Blue Monday: Fats Domino and the Lost Dawn of Rock 'N' Roll.* Rick Coleman. Da Capo Press 2006. xix, 364 p. : Illustration; Map
ISBN 9780306814914
Grades: Adult   B
1. Domino, Fats, 1928-2017 2. Rhythm and blues musicians 3. Rock musicians 4. United States 5. Biographies 6. Arts and Entertainment — Music — Rock 7. Adult books for young adults

LC BI2006015325

A noted R&B scholar celebrates the contributions of Fats Domino to the evolution of modern-day rock music, drawing on interviews with many early musical legends—including Lloyd Price, the Clovers, Charles Brown, and others—to examine the career of the legendary musician, the influence of New Orleans, and the impact of rock 'N' roll on the civil rights movement.

"Coleman has crafted a biography of Fats Domino, drawing on new interviews with the pianist himself. From his childhood in New Orleans through the early days of rock'n'roll, when he endured travel difficulties in the segregated South and frequent riots at his concerts, Fats remained a shy but demanding performer and personality. A homesick father who seemed to cherish his family, Fats was also a hard-drinking womanizer, and Coleman tells his story with compassion and honesty up to Fats's survival of Hurricane Katrina in his Ninth Ward home. His argument that rock'n'roll sprung from Fats and the New Orleans sound is hard to dispute, as Fats was playing long before others now credited with starting the revolution. Despite the occasional slips into fandom, this is an essential purchase for any library collecting the history of rock'n'roll." —*Library Journal*

Includes bibliographical references (p. [307]-344) and index.

Collins, Gail

William Henry Harrison: The 9th President, 1841. Gail Collins. Times Books/Henry Holt and Co. 2012. 176 p. (American presidents series (Times Books))
ISBN 9780805091182
Grades: 9 10 11 12 Adult   B
1. Harrison, William Henry, 1773-1841 2. Political campaigns 3. Politicians 4. Governors 5. Presidential elections 6. Politics and government 7. United States history 8. United States 9. 1840s 10. 19th century 11. Biographies 12. History writing — Presidency — 19th century — United States 13. History writing — Antebellum America — United States 14. Life stories — Politics — Politicians

LC 2011018976

Assesses the president's political career and month-long term in office, including his considerable contributions to the War of 1812 and his role in making permanent changes to the campaign process.

"Although more a journalist than a historian, Collins has done her homework and written a lively, opinionated portrait of early-19th-century America and the modestly talented general who briefly became president." —*Kirkus*

Includes bibliographical references and index.

Collins, Lauren

When in French: Love in a Second Language. Lauren Collins. Penguin Press 2016. 256 p.
ISBN 9781594206443
Grades: Adult   B
1. Collins, Lauren (Journalist) 2. Women journalists 3. French language 4. Husband and wife 5. American people in foreign countries 6. Cultural differences 7. Social life and customs 8. Geneva, Switzerland 9. France 10. Autobiographies and memoirs 11. Life stories — Arts and culture — Writing — Journalists 12. Family and Relationships — Dating and Marriage 13. Travel Writing — Living Abroad

LC 2016017611

New York Times Notable Book, 2016.

ESSENTIAL AND RECOMMENDED TITLES
Biography

An Anglophone American in London falls in love with a Frenchman and moves to Francophone Geneva, Switzerland. Once there, she decides to learn French; not only does she want to be able to buy things, but she wants to become closer to her new husband and, when the time comes, not be "a Borat of a mother." Chronicling her amusing adventures overseas and her attempts to communicate in a new tongue, talented New Yorker writer Lauren Collins serves up a funny, romantic, intelligent memoir.

"Throughout, the author ably weaves together the personal and the historical. A memoir filled with pleasing passages in every chapter." —*Kirkus*

Collins, Max Allan
Spillane: King of Pulp Fiction. Max Allan Collins and James L. Traylor. The Mysterious Press 2023. 400 p.
ISBN 9781613163795
Grades: Adult   B
1. Spillane, Mickey, 1918-2006 2. Fiction writing 3. Authors 4. Mystery writing 5. Mystery authors 6. Biographies 7. Life stories — Arts and culture — Writing — Authors 8. Arts and Entertainment — Writing and publishing

The first-ever biography of the most popular and most influential pulp writer of all time, written by the collaborator who knew him best.

"A thoroughly engrossing life story and an indispensable account of the rise of paperback publishing." —*Booklist*

Coltman, Leycester
The Real Fidel Castro. Leycester Coltman; with a foreword by Julia E. Sweig. Yale University Press 2003. x, 335 p. : Illustration; Map
ISBN 9780300107609
Grades: 11 12 Adult   B
1. Castro, Fidel, 1926-2016 2. Heads of state 3. Caribbean history 4. Cuba 5. 20th century 6. Biographies 7. Life stories — Politics — Politicians 8. History writing — Latin America — Cuba
LC 2003012942

The former British ambassador to Cuba provides an intimate look at the life of the Cuban dictator.

"In a remarkably evenhanded and illuminating biography, Coltman (former British ambassador to Cuba) reveals how Fidel Castro repeatedly has frustrated his foes." —*Booklist*

Includes bibliographical references (p. [323]-324) and index.

Colwell, Rita R.
A Lab of One's Own: One Woman's Personal Journey Through Sexism in Science. Rita Colwell and Sharon Bertsch McGrayne. Simon & Schuster 2020. 288 p.
ISBN 9781501181276
Grades: Adult   B
1. Colwell, Rita R, 1934- 2. Women scientists 3. Sex discrimination 4. Women microbiologists 5. Sexual harassment 6. Women and science 7. Sexism 8. Sexism in employment 9. Scientists 10. Autobiographies and memoirs 11. Life stories — Science, technology, and medicine — Scientists and inventors 12. Science Writing — Biology
LC Bl2020017518

A Lab of One's Own shares the sheer joy a scientist feels when moving toward a breakthrough, and the thrill of uncovering a whole new generation of female pioneers. But it is also the science book for the #MeToo era, offering an astute diagnosis of how to fix the problem of sexism in science and a celebration of the women pushing back.

"In this beautifully written memoir, Colwell, a leading microbiologist whose many accolades include being the first female director of the National Science Foundation, exposes 'A deep-seated bias against women in science [that] has been documented at almost every level, from Nobel Prize winners down to undergraduates.' . . . An unforgettable tell-all that's rife with details of insurrection, scientific breakthrough, and overcoming the odds." —*Kirkus*

Common
One Day It'll All Make Sense: A Memoir. by Common with Adam Bradley. Atria Books 2011. 256 p.
ISBN 9781451625875
Grades: Adult   B
1. Common (Musician) 2. Rap musicians 3. Childhood 4. Family relationships 5. Acting 6. Music industry and trade 7. Social life and customs 8. Chicago, Illinois 9. United States 10. 21st century 11. 20th century 12. Autobiographies and memoirs 13. Biographies 14. Life stories — Arts and culture — Performing arts — Musicians and composers
LC 2011021691

Street Lit Book Award Medal: Adult Non-Fiction, 2012.

The Grammy Award-winning recording artist, actor and friend to President Obama shares the story of his life, from his youth on Chicago's South side and rise in the hip-hop industry to his performances in such movies as Just Wright and the lessons he has learned as a son and a father.

Includes bibliographical references and index.

Conant, Jennet
Man of the Hour: James B. Conant, Warrior Scientist. Jennet Conant. Simon & Schuster 2017. 416 p.
ISBN 9781476730882
Grades: Adult   B
1. Conant, James, 1893-1978 2. Scientists 3. Atomic bomb 4. Educators 5. Technology and war 6. International relations 7. United States history 8. 20th century 9. Biographies 10. Life stories — Science, technology, and medicine — Scientists and inventors 11. History writing — Wars and conflicts — Atomic Bomb — World War II 12. History writing — United States
LC 2017033241

A portrait of the wartime scientist, Harvard University president and presidential advisor, written by his granddaughter, places his life against a backdrop of key historical events to offer particular insights into his oversight of the Manhattan Project and subsequent campaigns in support of atomic weapon control at the international level.

"Including frank portrayals of family situations and problems, Jennet Conants capable, informative portrait should be included in collections about the history of American science." —*Booklist*

Connolly, Ray
Being Elvis: A Lonely Life. Ray Connolly. Liveright Publishing Corporation 2016. 368 p.
ISBN 9781631492808
Grades: Adult   B
1. Presley, Elvis, 1935-1977 2. Rock music 3. Singers 4. Rock musicians 5. United States 6. Biographies 7. Life stories — Arts and culture — Performing arts — Musicians and composers
LC 2016054735

Taking a fresh look at the 20th-century icon who fundamentally transformed American culture, a veteran rock journalist, with a narrative formed by interviews over many years, explores the extravagance and irrationality inherent in the Elvis mythology, offering a thoughtful celebration of an immortal life.

"Connolly carefully and sympathetically paints the many faces of Presley, faces eventually shrouded in despair." —*Kirkus*

Being John Lennon: A Restless Life. Ray Connolly. W W Norton & CO Inc. 2018. 448 p.
ISBN 9781643130538
Grades: Adult   B
1. Lennon, John, 1940-1980 2. Musicians 3. Rock musicians 4. Celebrities 5. Popular culture 6. Great Britain 7. England 8. 20th century 9. 1960s 10. Biographies 11. Arts and Entertainment — Music — Rock 12. Life stories — Arts and culture — Performing arts — Musicians and composers
LC Bl2018188289

Provides an intimate yet unsparing biography of one of the greatest and most mythologized musicians of the 20th century.

"A welcome new perspective on an endlessly influential and compelling artist." —*Booklist*

PUBLIC LIBRARY CORE COLLECTION: NONFICTION
Twentieth Edition

Conradi, Peter J.
Iris: The Life of Iris Murdoch. Peter J. Conradi. Norton 2002. xxix, 706 p. : Illustration
ISBN 9780393324013
Grades: Adult   B
1. Murdoch, Iris 2. Philosophers 3. Authors, English 4. Social life and customs 5. Great Britain 6. 20th century 7. Biographies 8. Arts and Entertainment — Writing and Publishing 9. Life stories — Arts and culture — Writing — Authors
LC BL2002013388

Traces the life and career of the philosopher and novelist, from her student days at Oxford, through her marriage to John Bayley, to Murdoch's influence on literary England, from 1940 to the present day.

"Rich footnoting leads the reader to expansions on the narrative as well as to the authority behind the biographer's statements. Scholars need this text, but it will also intrigue lay readers." —*Library Journal*

Originally published under title: Iris Murdoch. London : HarperCollins Publishers, 2001; Includes bibliographical references (p. 599-676) and index.

Conroy, Pat
My Losing Season. Pat Conroy. Nan A. Talese 2002. 402 p.
ISBN 9780385489126
Grades: 11 12 Adult   B
1. Conroy, Pat 2. Failure 3. Basketball players 4. College sports 5. Authors, American 6. Charleston, South Carolina 7. 20th century 8. Autobiographies and memoirs 9. Biographies 10. Arts and Entertainment — Writing and Publishing 11. Sports and Competition — Basketball 12. Life stories — Arts and culture — Writing — Authors 13. Adult books for young adults
LC 2002066212

Alex Award, 2003.

The author reflects on the place of sports in his own life, describing his love of basketball, the role of the athlete for young men searching for their own identity and place in the world, his education at the Citadel, his relationship with his coach, and his journey to best-selling writer.

"A wonderfully rich, informative, and well-researched reminiscence." —*Library Journal*

Conyers, Jonathan
I Wasn't Supposed to Be Here: Finding My Voice, Finding My People, Finding My Way. Jonathan Conyers, with Lori L. Tharps. Legacy Lit 2023. xi, 302 p.
ISBN 9781538742501
Grades: Adult   B
1. Conyers, Jonathan, 1994- 2. African American men 3. Medical personnel 4. Debates and debating 5. Mentors 6. Interpersonal relations 7. Growing up 8. Dysfunctional families 9. Homelessness 10. Marginalized children 11. Teacher-student relationships 12. Self-discovery 13. North American people 14. American people 15. Autobiographies and memoirs 16. Life stories — Facing adversity 17. Life stories — Relationships 18. Life stories — Personal growth 19. Society and culture — Wealth and class — Poverty

Everybody was rooting for Jonathan Conyers after seeing his profile on Humans of New York went viral and sparked millions in donations to the Brooklyn Debate League. The kid who went from struggling to read to being a breakout star on his high school debate team, thanks to a life-changing friendship with his transgender debate coach, captured the heart of America. Jonathan's story highlights the important role teachers play in opening up worlds of opportunity for the most vulnerable students.

Inspirational but never sentimental, with many lessons on 'Adding value to the world.' —*Kirkus*

Cook, Blanche Wiesen
Eleanor Roosevelt; Volume 2. Blanche Wiesen Cook. Viking 1999. 686 p.
ISBN 9780670844982
Grades: 11 12 Adult   B
1. Roosevelt, Eleanor, 1884-1962 2. Roosevelt, Franklin D. (Franklin Delano), 1882-1945 3. Women social advocates 4. Feminism 5. Husband and wife 6. Elections 7. Presidents' spouses 8. Men-women relations 9. Independence 10. New England history 11. United States history 12. Washington, D.C. 13. United States 14. 20th century 15. Biographies 16. History writing — Presidency — 20th century — United States 17. History writing — Women's history 18. Life stories — Politics — Politicians

New York Times Notable Book, 1999.

The second volume in the best-selling biography of America's visionary First Lady examines Eleanor Roosevelt's growing influence on the history and policy of America during the White House years and the Depression, as she championed racial justice, women's rights, and more.

"Cook is unafraid to take on difficult issues . thus rendering the biography not simply a riveting read but also a profoundly moving and wise account of how history has been shaped by the intricacies of the human heart, mind and spirit." —*Publishers Weekly*

Includes bibliographical references and index.

★ *Eleanor Roosevelt; Volume 3.* Blanche Weisen Cook. Viking 2016. 720 p.
ISBN 9780670023950
Grades: Adult   B
1. Roosevelt, Eleanor, 1884-1962 2. Roosevelt, Franklin D. (Franklin Delano), 1882-1945 3. Women social advocates 4. Feminism 5. Husband and wife 6. Elections 7. Presidents' spouses 8. Men-women relations 9. Independence 10. New England history 11. United States history 12. Washington, D.C. 13. United States 14. 20th century 15. Biographies 16. History writing — Presidency — 20th century — United States 17. History writing — Women's history 18. Life stories — Politics — Politicians
LC 87040632

New York Times Notable Book, 2016.

A concluding volume to the definitive portrait of Eleanor Roosevelt traces her post-World War II years, covering subjects ranging from FDR's death and the founding of the UN through her efforts to promote key initiatives in spite of limited support and her death in 1962.

"All this makes for fascinating reading, and it highlights for students of history how the world has changed since ERs time. And how it has not." —*Booklist*

Includes bibliographical references and index.

Cooper, Alex
Saving Alex: When I Was Fifteen I Told My Mormon Parents I Was Gay, and That's When My Nightmare Began. Alex Cooper and Joanna Brooks. HarperOne 2016. 304 p.
ISBN 9780062374608
Grades: Adult   B
1. Cooper, Alex, 1994- 2. Mormons 3. Lesbian teenagers 4. Abused women 5. Lesbians 6. Homosexuality 7. Teenage girls 8. Conversion therapy 9. Utah 10. Autobiographies and memoirs 11. Life stories — Identity — LGBTQIA+ 12. Society and culture — LGBTQIA+ 13. Adult books for young adults
LC 2015031520

Booklist Editors' Choice: Adult Books for Young Adults, 2016; Rainbow List, 2017.

After 15-year-old Alex Cooper told her Mormon parents she was a lesbian, they sent her to a family in Utah who promised to reorient her to "normal" sexuality. Using a combination of physical and emotional torture and intensive lessons in Mormon orthodoxy, they abused her for eight months until she contacted closeted gay people in the community, who helped her obtain legal assistance. In this troubling but inspiring memoir, Cooper relates how she persevered in seeking the right to make her own choices while striving to maintain her personal sense of faith.

"Alexs horrifying story is one that needs to be heard, and her book is an eloquent testament to that. It is encouraging proof that, as Alex is told, things do get better." —*Booklist*

Cooper, Anderson
The Rainbow Comes and Goes: A Mother and Son Talk About Life, Love, and Loss. Anderson Cooper and Gloria Vanderbilt. HarperCollins Publishers 2016. 224 p.
ISBN 9780062454942
Grades: Adult   B
1. Cooper, Anderson 2. Vanderbilt, Gloria, 1924-2019 3. Television journalists 4. Celebrities 5. Mothers and sons 6. Aging 7. Mother and adult son 8. United

ESSENTIAL AND RECOMMENDED TITLES
Biography

States 9. Letters 10. Biographies 11. Life stories — Relationships — Family 12. Family and relationships — Families

LC 2016000369

A poignant correspondence between the CNN journalist and his iconic designer mother, exchanged in the aftermath of the latter's brief illness, shares a rare window into their relationship and the life lessons imparted by an aging mother to her adult son.

"Vanderbilt and her son, Cooper, relate the touching story of how an epistolary exchange created new emotional intimacy between them." —*Publishers Weekly*

Cooper, Andrew Scott
*The **Fall** of Heaven: The Pahlavis and the Final Days of Imperial Iran*. Andrew Scott Cooper. Henry Holt and Co. 2016. 352 p.

ISBN 9780805098976

Grades: Adult   B

1. Mohammed Reza Pahlavi, Shah of Iran, 1919-1980 2. Farah, Empress, consort of Mohammad Reza Pahlavi, Shah of Iran, 1938- 3. Southwest Asia and North Africa (Middle East) history 4. Iran 5. 20th century 6. Biographies 7. Life stories — Politics — Royalty 8. History writing — Nationalism — Southwest Asia and North Africa (Middle East)

LC 2015046095

Describes the rise and fall of the glamorous Pahlavi dynasty in Iran, which began when Mohammad Reza Pahlavi took the throne in 1941 and ended during the Iranian Revolution in 1979 led by the Ayatollah Khomeini.

"A thorough new appraisal of an enigmatic ruler who died believing his people still loved him." —*Kirkus*

Includes bibliographical references and index.

Cooper, Brittney C.
***Eloquent** Rage: A Black Feminist Discovers Her Superpower*. Brittney Cooper. St. Martin's Press 2018. 288 p.

ISBN 9781250112576

Grades: Adult   B

1. Cooper, Brittney C, 1980- 2. Feminism 3. Intersectionality 4. Autobiographies and memoirs 5. Life stories — Identity 6. Society and culture — Gender — Women 7. Society and culture — Race 8. Adult books for young adults 9. Antiracist literature

LC 2017036275

Finalist for the Hurston/Wright Legacy Awards for Nonfiction, 2019.

A leading young Black feminist illuminates how organized anger, friendship and faith can be powerful sources of positive feminist change, explaining how targeted rage has shaped the careers of such African-American notables as Serena Williams, Beyoncé and Michelle Obama.

"Deftly blending the conversational tone of a memoir with pointed critique, Cooper offers a comprehensive and accessible analysis of topics from the Bible to pop music to U.S. politics past and present." —*Library Journal*

Cooper, Christian
***Better** Living Through Birding: Notes from a Black Man in the Natural World*. Christian Cooper. Random House 2023. 288 p.

ISBN 9780593242384

Grades: Adult   B

1. Cooper, Christian 2. Bird watchers 3. Comics and graphic novel writers 4. African American men 5. Gay men 6. Bird watching 7. Nature 8. Self-acceptance 9. Social advocacy 10. North American people 11. American people 12. Autobiographies and memoirs 13. Life stories — Nature and outdoors 14. Life stories — Identity 15. Nature Writing — Animal Studies — Birds and Birding

LC 2022050405

LibraryReads Favorites, 2023.

Christian Cooper is a self-described "Blerd" (Black nerd), an avid comics fan and expert birder who devotes every spring to gazing upon the migratory birds that stop to rest in Central Park, just a subway ride away from where he lives in New York City. One morning in May 2020, Cooper was engaged in his birdwatching ritual when what might have been a routine encounter with a dog walker exploded age-old racial tensions. Cooper's viral video of the incident would send shock waves through the nation. Equal parts memoir, travelogue, and primer on the art of birding, this is Cooper's story of learning to claim and defend space for himself and others like him.

"Cooper, a Black birder who first gained media attention after sharing a video of him being falsely accused by a white woman of threatening her in Central Park in 2020, debuts with a lively, thoughtful memoir in which he defines himself by the hobby he was pursuing the afternoon he made headlines." —*Publishers Weekly*

Cooper, John Milton
***Woodrow** Wilson: A Biography*. John Milton Cooper, Jr. Alfred A. Knopf 2009. VIII, 702 p, 16 p. of plates : Illustration

ISBN 9780307265418

Grades: Adult   B

1. Wilson, Woodrow, 1856-1924 2. World War I 3. Democrats 4. World politics 5. Presidents 6. Politicians 7. Politics and government 8. United States 9. 20th century 10. 1910s 11. 1920s 12. Biographies 13. History writing — Presidency — 20th century — United States 14. History writing — Early 20th century — United States 15. Life stories — Politics — Politicians

LC 2009019097

Pulitzer Prize for Biography or Autobiography finalist.

This thoroughly researched one-volume profile of America's 28th president is universally hailed for its scholarship and insight into the life and career of one of the nation's most polarizing leaders.

"Cooper exhibits complete command of his materials, a sure knowledge of the man and a nuanced understanding of a presidency almost Shakespearean in its dimensions." —*Kirkus*

Includes bibliographical references (p. [601]-668) and index.

Copaken, Deborah
***Ladyparts**: A Memoir*. by Deborah Copaken. Random House 2020. 320 p. : Illustration

ISBN 9781984855473

Grades: Adult   B

1. Copaken, Deborah 2. Authors, American 3. Poverty 4. Women 5. Women authors 6. Women's health services 7. Harassment 8. Photojournalists 9. Interpersonal relations 10. Divorce 11. Women photographers 12. Body image 13. Health 14. 21st century 15. Life stories — Identity — Gender 16. Society and culture — Gender — Women 17. Life stories — Facing adversity — Medical issues

LC 2020055455

From bloodclots and breast exams, heart palpitations and heartbreaks, to the terror, loneliness, and empowerment of a woman fighting for her life, Copaken weaves her harrowing experiences together with insights from medical and historical research to show how many of these common health issues and disabilities merely amplify what women around the world confront on a daily basis: Warped beauty standards, workplace sexism, worries about romantic partners, and mistrust of their own bodies.

"A searing indictment of capitalism, the gig economy, and the U.S. medical system—all recounted with a sense of dark humor. Copaken's latest will engage readers of feminist memoirs." —*Library Journal*

Copeland, B. Jack
***Turing**: Pioneer of the Information Age*. Jack Copeland. Oxford University Press 2012. 300 p. : Illustration

ISBN 9780199639793

Grades: Adult   B

1. Turing, Alan Mathison, 1912-1954 2. Artificial intelligence 3. World War II 4. Mathematicians 5. Military intelligence 6. Computers 7. Codes (Communication) 8. Information technology 9. Cryptography 10. British history 11. 20th century 12. Biographies 13. Life stories — Science, technology, and medicine — Scientists and inventors 14. History writing — Technological innovations 15. History writing — Wars and conflicts — World War II 16. Science Writing — Computing, the Internet, and Technology

LC Bl2013024746

In the centenary of Alan Turing's birth, we celebrate the life and work of one of the greatest scientists of the 20th century. Best known for the role he played in cracking German secret code Enigma during World War Two, and the personal tragedy of his death aged only 41, this is an insight into to the man, his work, and his legacy.

Includes bibliographical references and index.

Copeland, Misty

★ *Life in Motion: An Unlikely Ballerina.* Misty Copeland. Touchstone Books 2014. 288 p.
ISBN 9781476737980
Grades: Adult   B
1. Copeland, Misty 2. Ballet 3. Ballet dancers 4. Women ballet dancers 5. African American ballet dancers 6. Intersectionality 7. Autobiographies and memoirs 8. Life stories — Arts and culture — Performing arts — Dancers and choreographers 9. Adult books for young adults 10. Arts and entertainment — Dance
LC 2014002922

Documents the author's emotionally dynamic effort to become the third African-American soloist in the history of the American Ballet Theatre, describing the harsh family difficulties she overcame including her mother's highly publicized custody battle to halt her career.

"Her story is an inspiration to anyone—man or woman, Black or white—who has ever chased a dream against the odds, and the grace with which she triumphs is an example for us all." —*Booklist*

The Wind at My Back: Resilience, Grace, and Other Gifts from My Mentor, Raven Wilkinson. Misty Copeland. Grand Central Publishing 2022. 336 p.
ISBN 9781538753859
Grades: Adult   B
1. Copeland, Misty 2. Wilkinson, Raven 3. African American dancers 4. Dancers 5. Mentors 6. Friendship 7. Women ballet dancers 8. Ballet dancers 9. Ballet 10. Mentoring 11. Racism 12. Persistence 13. Resilience 14. Race (Social sciences) 15. Autobiographies and memoirs 16. Life stories — Arts and culture — Performing arts — Dancers and choreographers 17. Arts and Entertainment — Dance 18. Life stories — Relationships — Friendship
LC 2022026199

The first African-American principal ballerina at the American Ballet Theatre honors her mentor, Raven Wilkinson, the only teacher who could truly understand the obstacles she faced, sharing a story of two unapologetically Black ballerinas, their friendship and how they changed each other—and the dance world—forever.

"Copeland celebrates her mentor's wisdom as she shoulders the burdens and thrills of her historic career, and aims to inspire other dancers of color who face similar barriers as they pursue their passions." —*Publishers Weekly*

Includes index.

Cordery, Stacy A.

Alice: Alice Roosevelt Longworth, American Princess and Washington Power Broker. Stacy A. Cordery. Viking 2007. 608 p.
ISBN 9780670018338
Grades: 11 12 Adult   B
1. Longworth, Alice Roosevelt, 1884-1980 2. Roosevelt, Theodore, 1858-1919 3. Children of presidents 4. Women and politics 5. Intellectual life 6. United States history 7. 20th century 8. Biographies 9. History writing — Women's history 10. History writing — Early 20th century — United States 11. Life stories — People in history — Famous families
LC 2006103087

New York Times Notable Book, 2007.

A portrait of Teddy Roosevelt's daughter relates such facts as her tempestuous teen years and flouting of social conventions in order to promote women's rights, her infidelity-tested marriage to Nicholas Longworth, and her criticism of FDR's New Deal programs.

"An authoritative, intriguing portrait of a first daughter who broke the mold." —*Publishers Weekly*

Includes bibliographical references and index.

Cornelius, Maria M.

The Final Season: The Perseverance of Pat Summitt. Maria M. Cornelius foreword by Candace Parker. The University of Tennessee Press 2016. xvii, 311 p.
ISBN 9781621902720
Grades: Adult   B
1. Summitt, Pat Head, 1952-2016 2. Basketball coaches 3. Alzheimer's disease 4. Medical care 5. People with Alzheimer's disease 6. Life stories — Sports 7. Sports and Competition — Basketball 8. Life stories — Identity — Gender
LC 2016009421

Cornelius, a writer and editor who has written about the Lady Vols basketball program since 1998, tells the story of the final season of U. of Tennessee basketball coach Pat Summitt, who established the Lady Vols as the top athletics program in the history of NCAA basketball and was the winningest coach in NCAA basketball history.

"The book is full of raw emotion, reactions, and observations from those closest to Pat." —*Choice*

Includes index.

Cornwell, John

Hitler's Pope: The Secret History of Pius XII. John Cornwell. Penguin Books 2008. xii, 430 p. : Illustration
ISBN 9780670886937
Grades: Adult   B
1. Pius XII, Pope, 1876-1958 2. World War II 3. Antisemitism 4. Religion and politics 5. Politics and government 6. European history 7. Europe 8. 1930s 9. 1940s 10. 20th century 11. History writing — Wars and conflicts — World War II 12. Spirituality and Religion — Christianity — Catholicism
LC 99028311

New York Times Notable Book, 1999.

Draws on secret archives to present a record of the career of Pope Pius XII, showing his collaboration with the Nazis and his anti-Semitism, and discusses his continuing influence.

"Relying on exclusive access to Vatican and Jesuit archives, . {the author argues that through a 1933 Concordat with Hitler, Pope Pius XII facilitated the dictator's riseand, ultimately, the Holocaust." —*Library Journal*

Includes bibliographical references (p. [413]-417) and index; Originally published: New York, N.Y. : Viking, 1999.

Corrigan, Kelly

Glitter and Glue: A Memoir. Kelly Corrigan. Ballantine Books 2014. 240 p.
ISBN 9780345532831
Grades: Adult   B
1. Corrigan, Kelly, 1967- 2. Mothers and daughters 3. Consolation 4. Motherhood 5. Nannies 6. Death of mothers 7. suburban life 8. American people in Australia 9. Grief 10. Condolence 11. Widowers 12. Australia 13. 1990s 14. Autobiographies and memoirs 15. Family and Relationships — Parenting 16. Life stories — Facing adversity — Coping with death 17. Life stories — Relationships — Parent and child
LC 2013041936

Presents an account of the author's perspectives on motherhood, which have been shaped by her job as a nanny for a grieving Australian family and her character-testing experiences with her daughters.

"Written in a breezy style with humor and heart, the book reminds us how rewarding it can be to see a parent outside the context of our own needs." —*Kirkus*

Costa, James T.

Radical by Nature: The Revolutionary Life of Alfred Russel Wallace. James T. Costa. Princeton University Press 2023. 528 p.
ISBN 9780691233796
Grades: Adult   B
1. Wallace, Alfred Russel, 1823-1913 2. Evolution 3. Natural selection 4. Scientific discoveries 5. Biologists 6. Scientists 7. English people 8. British people 9. Biographies 10. Science Writing — Biology 11. Life stories — Science, technology, and medicine — Scientists and inventors

ESSENTIAL AND RECOMMENDED TITLES
Biography

"Comprehensive and revelatory, this is a first-rate take on an overlooked figure in scientific history." —*Publishers Weekly*

Costello, Elvis
Unfaithful Music & Disappearing Ink. Elvis Costello. Blue Rider Press 2015. 674 pages : Illustration; Portrait
ISBN 9780399167256
Grades: Adult   B
1. Costello, Elvis 2. Rock music 3. Fame 4. Rock musicians 5. Musicians 6. England 7. Autobiographies and memoirs 8. Biographies 9. Arts and Entertainment — Music — Rock 10. Life stories — Arts and culture — Performing arts — Musicians and composers 11. Adult books for young adults
LC 2015032865

A personal introspective by the influential pop songwriter and performer traces his Liverpool upbringing, artistic influences, creative pursuit of original punk sounds and emergence in the MTV world.

"Costello comes across as the perennial outsider, as someone who is surprised that he has been invited to the party. A must for Costello fans everywhere." —*Booklist*

Couric, Katie
Going There. Katie Couric. Little Brown & CO 2021. 288 p.
ISBN 9780316535861
Grades: Adult   B
1. Couric, Katie, 1957- 2. Broadcast journalism 3. Women television newscasters and commentators 4. Women television journalists 5. Widows 6. Sexism 7. People with eating disorders 8. Women 9. Determination 10. Autobiographies and memoirs 11. Life stories — Arts and culture — Writing — Journalists 12. Arts and Entertainment — Movies and Television

In this memoir, the iconic media star discusses her professional and personal life, including losing her husband at a young age, her historic turn as anchor of the CBS Evening News and experiences dealing with gender inequality.

"In this eagerly anticipated memoir, Couric (b. 1957) transforms the events of her long, illustrious career into an immensely readable story—a legacy-preserving exercise, for sure, yet judiciously polished and insightful, several notches above the fray of typical celebrity memoirs.... A sharp, entertaining view of the news media from one of its star players." —*Kirkus*

Courogen, Carrie
★ *Miss May Does Not Exist: The Life and Work of Elaine May, Hollywood's Hidden Genius*. Carrie Courogen. St. Martin's Press 2024. 304 p.
ISBN 9781250279224
Grades: Adult   B
1. May, Elaine, 1932- 2. Women screenwriters 3. Women film producers and directors 4. Women comedians 5. Screenwriters 6. Film producers and directors 7. Comedians 8. United States 9. Biographies 10. Life stories — Arts and culture — Performing arts 11. Arts and Entertainment — Comedy 12. Arts and Entertainment — Movies and television
LC 2024005589

A riveting biography of comedian, director, actor and writer Elaine May, one of America's greatest comic geniuses. May began her career as one-half of the legendary comedy team known as Nichols and May, the duo that revolutionized the comedy sketch.

"The writing in this book is whip-smart and funny. It produces a fully realized portrait of a mysterious film genius." —*Library Journal*
Includes bibliographical references and index.

Cousteau, Jacques Yves
The Human, the Orchid, and the Octopus: Exploring and Conserving Our Natural World. Jacques Cousteau and Susan Schiefelbein. Bloomsbury USA : 2007. 320 p.
ISBN 9781596914179
Grades: 11 12 Adult   B
1. Cousteau, Jacques Yves 2. Oceanographers 3. Nature conservation 4. Effect of humans on nature 5. Nature 6. Nature Writing — Environmental Issues 7. Adult books for young adults

LC 2007018824
The last book by the legendary explorer, activist, filmmaker, and oceanographer offers a call for action to preserve our world, its wildlife, and its natural wonders for future generations, looking at the impact of human action on our precarious environment.

"Cousteau's reverence for life's miracles . shines through in this eloquent testimony on the importance of pursuing higher ideals, particularly the preservation of the oceans and the natural world for future generations." —*Publishers Weekly*

Cox, Lynne
Swimming to Antarctica: Tales of a Long-distance Swimmer. Lynne Cox. A.A. Knopf 2004. IX, 323 p.
ISBN 9780375415074
Grades: 11 12 Adult   B
1. Cox, Lynne, 1957- 2. Swimmers 3. Women athletes 4. Women swimmers 5. Athletes 6. Marathon swimming 7. Swimming 8. Endurance sports 9. Extreme sports 10. Training 11. Health 12. Autobiographies and memoirs 13. Sports and Competition — Swimming and Diving 14. Sports and Competition — Extreme Sports 15. Life stories — Sports — Athletes 16. Adult books for young adults
LC 2003047577

Alex Award, 2005; Booklist Editors' Choice: Adult Books for Young Adults, 2004.

noted long-distance swimmer with a love for cold water describes her eventful career in the sport, from her record-breaking English Channel crossing and her 1987 swim across the Bering Strait from America to the Soviet Union to her exploits in the Straits of Magellan, Lake Baikal, and Antarctica.

"Cox is a pleasure.... Many passages are grip-the-page exciting, whether she's dodging Antarctic icebergs or Nile River sewage." —*Booklist*

Crabapple, Molly
Drawing Blood. Molly Crabapple. HarperCollins 2015. 352 pages : Illustration
ISBN 9780062323644
Grades: Adult   B
1. Crabapple, Molly 2. Women journalists 3. Women artists 4. Autobiographies and memoirs 5. Life stories — Arts and culture — Writing — Journalists 6. Life stories — Arts and culture — Artists
LC Bl2015044785

The underground artist and journalist presents a memoir of her years between September 11 and the Occupy movement in New York City to discuss the impact of historical events on her work and her decision to become a witness journalist.

"Lavishly illustrated, the book offers a candid portrayal of an artist's journey to self-knowledge and fulfillment." —*Kirkus*

Craig, Mya-Rose
Birdgirl: Looking to the Skies in Search of a Better Future. Mya-Rose Craig. Celadon Books 2023. 320 p.
ISBN 9781250807670
Grades: Adult   B
1. Craig, Mya-Rose 2. Bird watchers 3. Women environmentalists 4. Bird watching 5. Mothers and daughters 6. Voyages and travels 7. Rare and endangered birds 8. Environmental degradation 9. Social advocacy 10. South Asian people 11. Bangladeshi people 12. Western European people 13. British people 14. People with bipolar disorder 15. Women 16. Nature Writing — Animal Studies — Birds and Birding 17. Life stories — Nature and outdoors 18. Society and culture — Social activism and philanthropy 19. Debut title
LC 2022036808

Somerset Maugham Award, 2023.

A young environmental activist shares her experiences of traveling the world in search of rare birds and astonishing landscapes and her passion for social justice and dedication to preserving our planet.

"This is a forthright and compelling chronicle by a remarkable birder, environmentalist, and advocate." —*Booklist*

Originally published in the UK by Jonathan Cape, London, in 2022.

PUBLIC LIBRARY CORE COLLECTION: NONFICTION
Twentieth Edition

Crais, Clifton C.
History Lessons: A Memoir of Madness, Memory, and the Brain. Clifton Crais. Overlook Press 2014. 288 p.
ISBN 9781468303681
Grades: Adult   B
1. Crais, Clifton C. 2. Alcoholic mothers 3. Amnesia 4. Chronic diseases 5. Child neglect victims 6. Child neglect 7. Poverty 8. Mental illness 9. Identity 10. Resilience 11. Psychic trauma 12. Neuroscience 13. New Orleans, Louisiana 14. Autobiographies and memoirs 15. Life stories — Relationships — Growing up 16. Family and Relationships — Growing Up
LC Bl2014012646
Library Journal Best Books 2014.
An Emory University professor and co-author of Sara Baartman and the Hottentot Venus draws on his expertise as a historian to better understand his traumatic early life in New Orleans, marked by an alcoholic mother who tried to drown him, an absent father, his chronic childhood amnesia and long-buried family secrets.
"The ambiguities of a life only half recalled are fully illuminated in this chronicle of trying to understand what has been forgotten." —*Library Journal*

Cramer, Richard Ben
Joe Dimaggio: The Hero's Life. Richard Ben Cramer. Simon & Schuster 2000. xi, 546 p. : Illustration
ISBN 9780684853918
Grades: 11 12 Adult   B
1. DiMaggio, Joe, 1914-1999 2. Monroe, Marilyn, 1926-1962 3. Engelberg, Morris 4. Baseball players 5. Outfielders (Baseball) 6. Batters (Baseball) 7. Personal conduct 8. Mafia 9. Men-women relations 10. Biographies 11. Sports and Competition — Baseball 12. Sports and Competition — Individual Athlete 13. Life stories — Sports — Athletes
LC 00049232
New York Times Notable Book, 2000.
A chronicle of the complex, inspiring, and sometimes tragic life of one of the century's great sports stars also examines the influence of the media and the nature of celebrity in American society.
"In this biography of the baseball player, Cramer taps every plank in the wall that DiMaggio erected around himself and that protected him from inquiry. In the wall's hollow spots, Cramer locates the girls, finds the Mob guys, and behind the legend of grace and elegance on and off the field discovers a legend who in reality was more often than not graceless and inelegant." —*The New Yorker*
Includes index.

Crawford, Bill
★ *All American: The Rise and Fall of Jim Thorpe.* Bill Crawford. John Wiley & Sons 2004. Iv, 284 p. : Illustration
ISBN 9780471557326
Grades: 11 12 Adult   B
1. Thorpe, Jim, 1887-1953 2. Athletes 3. Indigenous athletes 4. Indigenous Olympic medal winners 5. Olympic games 6. Baseball players 7. Football players 8. Social life and customs 9. United States 10. 20th century 11. Biographies 12. Life stories — Sports — Athletes 13. Sports and Competition — Individual Athlete 14. Sports and Competition — Olympic Sports 15. Adult books for young adults
LC 2004014376
A biography of Jim Thorpe, one of the greatest all-around athletes in history.
"This terse, punchy biography of sports legend Thorpe (1888-1953) illuminates the current debate over the exploitation of unpaid college athletes by moneymaking, headline-grabbing educational institutions." —*Publishers Weekly*
Includes bibliographical references (p. 251-270) and index.

Crawford, Lacy
Notes on a Silencing: A Memoir. Lacy Crawford. Little, Brown & Company 2020. 391 p.
ISBN 9780316491556
Grades: 11 12 Adult   B
1. Crawford, Lacy 2. Private schools 3. Teenage girls 4. Rape 5. Teenage sexual abuse 6. Teenage rape victims 7. Scholarly cover-ups 8. School administrators 9. Corruption 10. Conspiracies 11. Ostracism 12. Shame 13. Power 14. Injustice 15. Women authors 16. Memories 17. Psychic trauma 18. New Hampshire 19. Autobiographies and memoirs 20. Life stories — Facing adversity — Abuse survivors 21. True Crime — Sex Crimes 22. Society and culture — Wealth and class
LC 2019947036
New York Times Notable Book, 2020.
The author traces her healing journey after a traumatizing sexual assault at infamous St. Paul's boarding school, describing how she helped police uncover proof of the school's institutionalized mandate of silence.
"Crawford's teenage assault is, as she writes 'Not a remarkable story.' Teens who are ready may find powerful truths and a sympathetic perspective." —*Booklist*

Crawford, Robert
Eliot After the Waste Land. Robert Crawford. Farrar, Straus and Giroux 2022. 608 p.
ISBN 9780374279462
Grades: Adult   B
1. Eliot, T. S. (Thomas Stearns), 1888-1965 2. Poets, American 3. American people in England 4. Middle age 5. Extramarital affairs 6. Remarriage 7. Faith (Christianity) 8. Writing 9. Interpersonal relations 10. Autobiographies and memoirs 11. Life stories — Arts and culture — Writing — Poets 12. Arts and Entertainment — Writing and Publishing
LC 2022020636
After being kept from the public for more than fifty years, the letters between T. S. Eliot and his longtime love and muse Emily Hale were unsealed in 2020. Drawing on these intimate exchanges and on countless interviews and archives, as well as on Eliot's own poetry and prose, the award-winning biographer Robert Crawford completes the narrative he began in Young Eliot. Eliot After "The Waste Land", the long-awaited second volume of Crawford's magisterial, meticulous portrait of the twentieth century's most significant poet, tells the story of the mature Eliot during his years as a world-renowned writer and intellectual, including his complex interior life.
"Crawford illuminates the contradictions that make Eliot such a fascinating symbol of his times. The result is a rewarding look at a key literary figure." —*Publishers Weekly*
"The Nobel-winning poet and playwright Thomas Stearns Eliot (1888-1965) claws his way out of modernist despondency in this revelatory biography from Crawford (after Young Eliot)." —*Publishers Weekly*
Originally published in 2022 by Jonathan Cape, Great Britain; Includes bibliographical references and index.

Creamer, Robert W.
Babe: The Legend Comes to Life. Robert W. Creamer. Simon & Schuster 1992. 443 p. : Illustration
ISBN 9780671760700
Grades: 11 12 Adult   B
1. Ruth, Babe, 1895-1948 2. Baseball players 3. Biographies 4. Sports and Competition — Baseball 5. Sports and Competition — Individual Athlete 6. Life stories — Sports — Athletes
LC 91039086
The truth behind the famous Ruth stories analyzes the astounding statistics with detailed information on specific games, and describes Ruth's varied, often volatile, relations with those around him, from fellow players to fans, friends, and reporters. From Babe Ruth's early days in a Baltimore orphanage, to the glory days with the Yankees, to his final years, Robert W. Creamer has drawn an indelible portrait of a true folk hero.
A Fireside book; Includes index.

Crespino, Joseph
Atticus Finch: The Biography: Harper Lee, Her Father, and the Making of an American Icon. Joseph Crespino. Basic Books 2018. 288 p.
ISBN 9781541644946
Grades: Adult   B

ESSENTIAL AND RECOMMENDED TITLES
Biography

1. Lee, Harper 2. Authors, American 3. Women authors 4. 20th century 5. Biographies 6. Life stories — Arts and culture — Writing — Authors 7. Arts and entertainment — Writing and publishing 8. Arts and Entertainment — Writing and Publishing — Literary criticism

LC 2017056457

Who was the real Atticus Finch? the publication of Go Set a Watchman in 2015 forever changed how we think about Atticus Finch. Once seen as a paragon of decency, he was reduced to a small-town racist. How are we to understand this transformation? in Atticus Finch, historian Joseph Crespino draws on exclusive sources to reveal how Harper Lee's father provided the central inspiration for each of her books.

Includes bibliographical references and index.

Cronkite, Walter
A Reporter's Life. Walter Cronkite. A.A. Knopf 1996. VIII, 384 p. : Illustration

ISBN 9780394578798

Grades: 11 12 Adult   B

1. Cronkite, Walter 2. Journalists 3. United States 4. Autobiographies and memoirs 5. Biographies 6. Arts and Entertainment — Writing and Publishing 7. Life stories — Arts and culture — Writing — Journalists 8. Adult books for young adults

LC 96021053

New York Times Notable Book, 1997.

One of America's most trusted journalists describes his youth, his early career as a reporter, his work as a war correspondent, and his rise to the pinnacle of television news, sharing his views on the media, news, and the American condition.

"Cronkite's memoir is a short course on the flow of events in the second half of this centuryevents the world knows more about because of Walter Cronkite's work, and some of which might not have happened without it." —*New York Times Book Review*

Crosley, Sloane
Grief Is for People. Sloane Crosley. MCD/Farrar, Straus and Giroux 2024. 240 p.

ISBN 9780374609849

Grades: Adult   B

1. Crosley, Sloane 2. Women authors 3. Loss 4. Grief 5. Death of friends 6. Suicide 7. Memories 8. Interpersonal relations 9. Healing 10. North American people 11. American people 12. Autobiographies and memoirs 13. Life stories — Facing adversity — Coping with death 14. Life stories — Relationships — Friendship 15. Family and Relationships — Aging and Death 16. Family and Relationships — Friendship

LC 2023038970

Grief Is for People is a deeply moving and surprisingly suspenseful portrait of friendship, and a book about loss packed with verve for life. After the pain and confusion of losing her closest friend to suicide, Crosley looks for answers in friends, philosophy, and art, hoping for a framework more useful than the unavoidable stages of grief. Crosley's search for truth is frank, darkly funny, and gilded with a resounding empathy. Upending the "grief memoir," Grief Is for People is the category-defying story of the struggle to hold on to the past without being consumed by it.

"In this aching meditation on loss and friendship, essayist and novelist Crosley (Cult Classic) eulogizes her late literary mentor and best friend against the backdrop of the high-pressure publishing industry." —*Publishers Weekly*

Cross, Charles R.
Room Full of Mirrors: A Biography of Jimi Hendrix. Charles R. Cross. Hyperion 2005. xvi, 384 p. : Illustration

ISBN 9781401300289

Grades: 11 12 Adult   B

1. Hendrix, Jimi, 1942-1970 2. Rock musicians 3. United States 4. Biographies 5. Arts and Entertainment — Music — Rock 6. Life stories — Arts and culture — Performing arts — Musicians and composers 7. Adult books for young adults

LC 2005046362

Library Journal Best Books, 2005.

The image and lifestyle of Jimi Hendrix was larger-than-life, but beyond this was a complex man who struggled to accept his role as an idol. This sensitive, meticulously-researched biography recounts the entire arc of Hendrix's life: from his troubled childhood in Seattle's projects and the early loss of his mother, to his struggles against racial prejudice as a young musician and his rapid ascent to the top of the swinging London scene, and finally to the apex of his career headlining Woodstock in 1969, with his death a year later.

"Admirably comprehensive and well referenced, this is the Hendrix biography to acquire if you can acquire only one." —*Booklist*

Includes bibliographical references and index.

Crouch, Gregory
The Bonanza King: John Mackay and the Battle Over the Greatest Riches in the American West. Gregory Crouch. Scribner 2018. 384 p.

ISBN 9781501108198

Grades: Adult   B

1. Mackay, John William, 1831-1902 2. Gold rush 3. Prospecting 4. Prospectors 5. Irish people in the United States 6. Frontier and pioneer life 7. Gold mines and mining 8. Mines and mineral resources 9. The West (United States) 10. California 11. American Westward Expansion (1803-1899) 12. 1840s 13. Biographies 14. Life stories — People in history 15. History writing — Westward expansion — United States

LC Bl2018055915

Traces the rags-to-riches frontier story of Irish immigrant John Mackay, describing how in mid-19th-century Nevada he outmaneuvered the pernicious "Bank Ring" monopoly and thousands of rivals to take control of the nation-changing Comstock Lode.

Crouch, Stanley
Kansas City Lightning: The Rise and Times of Charlie Parker. Stanley Crouch. It Books 2013. 448 p.

ISBN 9780062005595

Grades: Adult   B

1. Parker, Charlie, 1920-1955 2. Smith, Buster, 1904-1991 3. Jazz music 4. Saxophonists 5. Heroin users 6. Heroin addiction 7. Jazz musicians 8. Musicians 9. Kansas City, Missouri 10. New York City 11. 20th century 12. Biographies 13. Arts and Entertainment — Music — Jazz and the Blues 14. Life stories — Arts and culture — Performing arts — Musicians and composers

LC 2013015773

The first of two volumes based on the life of one of the most talented and influential musicians of the 20th century reaches back past the legend to reveal Charlie Parker the wunderkind who was raised in the midst of the Depression in the wide-open town of Boss Tom Pendergast's Kansas City.

Crowell, Rodney
Chinaberry Sidewalks. by Rodney Crowell. Alfred A. Knopf 2011. 288 p.

ISBN 9780307594204

Grades: Adult   B

1. Crowell, Rodney 2. Alcoholic fathers 3. Growing up 4. Families 5. Country musicians 6. Houston, Texas 7. United States 8. Autobiographies and memoirs 9. Biographies 10. Arts and Entertainment — Music — Country 11. Life stories — Relationships — Growing up

LC 2010035996

Recounts the author's experiences growing up in Houston in the 1950s as the only child of an alcoholic father and epileptic mother, describing a coming-of-age marked by barroom brawls, apocalyptic hurricanes, and wild improvisations in the face of unpaidbills.

"Crowell is among the best storytellers to emerge from Nashville. Up to now, he told his stories in song, but with this heartfelt memoir, he can now be called a writer of the first order. Houston, where Crowell grew up in the 1950s and early 1960s, was a city full of characters found in stereotypical country songs: Hard-drinking fathers and longsuffering mothers singing along to the beer-soaked ballads of Hank Williams. But this is not fiction; Crowell actually lived the life, soaking up its exhilarating and disturbing atmosphere. Crowell is unsparingly honest, yet there is an admirable restraint here, too." —*Booklist*

PUBLIC LIBRARY CORE COLLECTION: NONFICTION
Twentieth Edition

Cullen, Kevin
Whitey Bulger: America's Most Wanted Gangster and the Manhunt That Brought Him to Justice. Kevin Cullen and Shelley Murphy. W.W. Norton & Co. 2013. VIII, 478 pages, 16 unnumbered pages of plates : Illustration; Map
ISBN 9780393087727
Grades: Adult   **B**
1. Bulger, Whitey, 1929-2018 2. Gangsters 3. Organized crime 4. Political corruption 5. Murderers 6. Fugitives 7. Biographies 8. True Crime — Organized Crime, Mafia, and Gangs 9. Life stories — Law and order — Criminals and law-breakers
LC 2012050752
National Book Critics Circle Award for Nonfiction finalist, 2013.
Chronicles the criminal career of the gangster who provided a protection racket against drug lords, ran illegal gambling, robbed banks, and served as an informant for the FBI until going into hiding for sixteen years.
Includes bibliographical references (pages 431-464) and index.

Cumming, Alan
Baggage: Tales from a Fully Packed Life. Alan Cumming. Dey Street Books 2021. 304 p.
ISBN 9780062435781
Grades: Adult   **B**
1. Cumming, Alan, 1965- 2. Actors and actresses 3. Bisexual men 4. Psychic trauma 5. Marriage 6. LGBTQIA+ people 7. Interpersonal relations 8. Acting 9. Self-acceptance 10. Autobiographies and memoirs 11. Life stories — Arts and culture — Performing arts — Actors and actresses 12. Life stories — Relationships
The acclaimed actor chronicles his work in Hollywood, his two marriages, and his journey through personal calamities, bad decisions, encounters with legends, and moments of joy to become the flawed but happy middle-aged man he is today.
"Actor Cumming (Not My Father's Son) returns with a series of revealing and witty reflections on coming to terms with his demons rather than conquering them.... Engaging and often funny, this surprisingly deep work beguiles with its sharp observations and earnest life lessons." —*Publishers Weekly*

Cummings, Elijah
★ *We're* Better Than This: My Fight for the Future of Our Democracy. Elijah Cummings, with James Dale; foreword by Speaker Nancy Pelosi. HarperCollins 2020. 272 p.
ISBN 9780062992260
Grades: Adult   **B**
1. Cummings, Elijah 2. African American legislators 3. African American politicians 4. Democracy 5. Justice 6. Equality 7. Political leadership 8. African American civil rights 9. Legislators 10. Politicians 11. Politics and government 12. Maryland 13. United States 14. Autobiographies and memoirs 15. Liberal writing 16. Life stories — Politics — Politicians 17. Politics and global affairs — Political figures 18. Life stories — Identity — Race and ethnicity
LC Bl2020012969
A memoir by the late Congressman details how his experiences as a sharecroppers' son in volatile South Baltimore shaped his life in activism, explaining how government oversight can become a positive part of a just American collective.
"Excellent political memoir by the late Democratic representative from Baltimore, one of the sitting president's most vocal opponents.... A thoughtful and inspiring exhortation to do better by a much-missed leader." —*Kirkus*

Cunningham, William J.
★ *Fashion* Climbing: A Memoir with Photographs. Bill Cunningham; preface by Hilton Als. Penguin Press 2018. 256 p.
ISBN 9780525558705
Grades: Adult   **B**
1. Cunningham, William J. 2. Fashion designers 3. Photographers 4. Fashion 5. Portrait photography 6. New York City 7. Autobiographies and memoirs 8. Life stories — Arts and culture — Fashion 9. Arts and Entertainment — Fashion 10. History writing — Arts and culture

LC 2018024955
The iconic "New York Times" photographer presents a sophisticated, visual account of his early education in New York City's high-fashion circles.
"It documents his unparalleled eye and appreciation for fashions magic, mystery, and illusions; styles potential to invent and transform. As both the very personal autobiography of an icon and a valuable social history, this wins." —*Booklist*

Curtis, James
Buster Keaton: A Filmmaker's Life. James Curtis. Alfred A. Knopf 2022. 832 p.
ISBN 9780385354219
Grades: Adult   **B**
1. Keaton, Buster, 1895-1966 2. Comedians 3. Filmmakers 4. Filmmaking 5. Films 6. Actors and actresses 7. United States 8. Autobiographies and memoirs 9. Life stories — Arts and culture — Performing arts — Actors and actresses 10. Arts and Entertainment — Movies and Television
LC 2021017984
A comprehensive account of the life and work of Buster Keaton.
This major new biography of the beloved comic artist examines how his iconic look and acrobatic brilliance often obscured the fact that behind the camera he was one of our most gifted filmmakers.
"Film historian and biographer Curtis draws on abundant archival sources as well as interviews, memoirs, and previous biographies to create a comprehensive, warmly sympathetic life of iconic entertainer Joseph Frank 'Buster' Keaton (1895-1966).... Meticulous research informs a brisk biography of an entertainment icon." —*Kirkus*
This is a Borzoi book published by Alfred A. Knopf; Includes bibliographical references and index.

Spencer Tracy: A Biography. by James Curtis. Alfred A. Knopf 2011. 1024 p.
ISBN 9780307262899
Grades: Adult   **B**
1. Tracy, Spencer, 1900-1967 2. Alcoholism 3. Celebrities 4. Actors and actresses 5. Family relationships 6. Men-women relations 7. Faith 8. United States 9. Biographies 10. Life stories — Arts and culture — Performing arts — Actors and actresses 11. Arts and Entertainment — Movies and Television
LC 2011014719
A major portrait of the revered screen actor, written with the cooperation of his daughter, draws on personal records to cover his family life, his battle with alcoholism, and his long-time affair with Katharine Hepburn.
"The author presents an exhaustive and exhausting biography of the legendary Hollywood star, famed for his uncanny naturalism and authority on camera and best remembered for the series of films he made with longtime companion Katharine Hepburn. A monumental, definitive biography of one of the finest film actors in the history of the medium." —*Kirkus*
Includes bibliographical references and index.

Cusk, Rachel
Aftermath: On Marriage and Separation. Rachel Cusk. Farrar, Straus and Giroux 2012. 160 p.
ISBN 9780374102135
Grades: Adult   **B**
1. Cusk, Rachel, 1967- 2. Marriage 3. Divorce 4. Divorced women 5. Authors, English 6. 20th century 7. Canadian literature 8. Biographies 9. Family and Relationships — Divorce
LC 2012003807
Library Journal Best Books, 2012.
aA well-known memoirist and novelist presents an intense study on divorce and its place in modern society, discussing the pain that accompanies ending a relationship but also the new opportunities it presents.

D'Antonio, Michael
The Hunting of Hillary: The Forty-year Campaign to Destroy Hillary Clinton. Michael D'Antonio. Thomas Dunne Books 2020. 336 p.
ISBN 9781250154606

ESSENTIAL AND RECOMMENDED TITLES
Biography

Grades: Adult **B**

1. Clinton, Hillary Rodham 2. Sexism in politics and government 3. Misogyny 4. Women politicians 5. Sexism 6. Presidential candidates 7. Women presidential candidates 8. Women 9. Political participation 10. Politics and government 11. United States 12. 21st century 13. 2000s (Decade) 14. 2010s 15. Politics and global affairs — Political figures 16. History writing — Presidency — 21st century — United States

LC 2020010750

The Pulitzer Prize-winning journalist and author of a Consequential President explores the right-wing conspiracy that operated for decades to continually discredit Hillary Clinton, sharing insight into the unique opposition she encountered behind the scenes.

"This galvanizing exposé will stand as a key resource in the study of sexism and politics." —*Booklist*

Includes bibliographical references and index.

Dalai Lama

Freedom in Exile: The Autobiography of the Dalai Lama. Dalai Lama XIV.. Harper Collins 1990. xiv, 288 p. : Illustration; Map

ISBN 9780060987015

Grades: 11 12 Adult **B**

1. Dalai Lama XIV, 1935- 2. Dalai lamas 3. Tibetan Buddhism 4. Buddhists 5. Tibet 6. Central Asia 7. Autobiographies and memoirs 8. Spirituality and Religion — Buddhism 9. Spirituality and Religion — Religious Leaders 10. Life stories — Religion and spirituality — Religious and spiritual leaders 11. History writing — Asia

LC 89046523

Tibet's exiled spiritual and secular leader describes his childhood, the Chinese invasion of Tibet, and how exiled Tibetans have rebuilt their lives and explains Tibetan Buddhism along with his philosophy of peace.

"The Dalai Lama's story is, in part, a chapter in the 2,500-year history of Buddhism as well as a testament to the mendacity and barbarity of Communist China. He shares the details of his amazing life, a glimpse at some of the mysteries of Tibetan Buddhism, and his unshakable belief in the basic good of humanity." —*Booklist*

A Cornelia & Michael Bessie book; Includes index.

Daley, Mark

Safe: A Memoir of Fatherhood, Foster Care, and the Risks We Take for Family. Mark Daley. Atria Books 2024. 320 p.

ISBN 9781668008782

Grades: Adult **B**

1. Daley, Mark (Foster child advocate) 2. Foster parents 3. Foster children 4. Gay men 5. Foster home care 6. Birthparents 7. Adoption 8. Bureaucracy 9. Child welfare 10. Social advocacy 11. Family relationships 12. North American people 13. American people 14. Autobiographies and memoirs 15. Life stories — Relationships — Family 16. Family and Relationships — Parenting — Adoption 17. Society and culture — General 18. Debut title

LC 2023029083

As a strategist and activist fighting for better outcomes for foster children, Mark Daley thought he had the answer. But when Ethan and Logan, an adorable infant and a precocious toddler, entered into their lives, Mark and his husband Jason quickly realized they were not remotely prepared for the uncertainty and complication of foster parenting. Every day seven hundred children enter the foster care system in the United States. Safe offers a deeply personal window into what happens when the universal longing for family crashes up against the bureaucracy of a child protection system that often fails to consider the needs of the most vulnerable parties of all—the children themselves.

"Public policy consultant Daley blends his own foster-care-to-adoption story with an informative overview of the current state of the U.S. foster care system." —*Booklist*

Includes bibliographical references and index.

Daley, Tom

Coming up for Air. Tom Daley. Hanover Square Press 2022. 240 p.

ISBN 9781335662569

Grades: Adult **B**

1. Daley, Tom, 1994- 2. Gay men 3. Olympic athletes 4. Swimmers 5. Family relationships 6. Interpersonal relations 7. Fatherhood 8. LGBTQIA+ people 9. Sports 10. Autobiographies and memoirs 11. Life stories — Sports — Athletes 12. Life stories — Identity — LGBTQIA+ 13. Sports and competition — Swimming and diving

In this deeply personal memoir, the celebrated Olympic Gold Medal diver and LGBTQ+ advocate discusses his struggles, triumphs and how he developed the mindset to compete at an elite level.

"This is an important historical account of training for the Olympics during a pandemic and an inspirational memoir of a young gay man coming into his own as an athlete, advocate, husband, and father, who is at ease whether he's executing a forward three-and-a-half somersault or knitting between competitions." —*Booklist*

Dallek, Robert

★ *Franklin D. Roosevelt: A Political Life*. Robert Dallek. Viking 2017. 704 p.

ISBN 9780525427902

Grades: Adult **B**

1. Roosevelt, Franklin D. (Franklin Delano), 1882-1945 2. Political leadership 3. Politicians 4. Presidents 5. Political science 6. Politics and government 7. United States 8. 20th century 9. Biographies 10. Impartial writing 11. History writing — Presidency — 20th century — United States 12. Life stories — Politics — Politicians

LC 2017032686

Booklist Editors' Choice, 2017.

A wide-ranging portrait of the 32nd President focuses on his career as an incomparable politician and dealmaker whose unusual skills served to unite divided factions, initiate essential reforms and transform America into an international superpower.

"The result is a comprehensive retelling of a major American life that will rank among the standard biographies of its subject." —*Publishers Weekly*

Includes bibliographical references and index.

Harry S. Truman: The 33rd President, 1945-1953. Robert Dallek; edited by Arthur M. Schlesinger and Sean Wilentz. Times Books 2008. 208 p. (American presidents series (Times Books))

ISBN 9780805069389

Grades: 11 12 Adult **B**

1. Truman, Harry S, 1884-1972 2. Presidents 3. Politicians 4. Politics and government 5. United States 6. 1940s 7. 1950s 8. 20th century 9. Biographies 10. History writing — Presidency — United States 11. History writing — Post World War II - 1959 — United States 12. Adult books for young adults 13. History writing — Presidency — 20th century — United States

LC 2008010193

Traces the thirty-third president's unlikely rise to power and his role in bringing America into the nuclear age, covering his perspectives on civil rights, his clashes with Douglas MacArthur over the conduct of the Korean War, and his re-election in 1948.

"This book is the best starting point for knowledge of Truman's life and for an astute assessment of his career." —*Publishers Weekly*

Includes bibliographical references and index.

Let Every Nation Know: John F. Kennedy in His Own Words. Robert Dallek and Terry Golway. Sourcebooks MediaFusion 2006. xii, 289 p. : Illustration

ISBN 9781402206474

Grades: 9 10 11 12 Adult **B**

1. Kennedy, John F. (John Fitzgerald), 1917-1963 2. Presidents 3. Politics and government 4. United States 5. 20th century 6. 1960s 7. Speeches, addresses, etc. 8. Biographies 9. History writing — Presidency — United States 10. History writing — 1960s — United States 11. Life stories — Politics — Politicians 12. Adult books for young adults 13. History writing — Presidency — 20th century — United States

LC 2005037973

A collection of thirty-four of John F. Kennedy's speeches, debates, and interviews offers insight into the ideals, politics, and life of the charismatic president.

"The voice of John F. Kennedy is burned into the brains of people of a certain age. But younger citizens may not be familiar with his ideas and the distinctive way in which he expressed himself. There have been past recordings of JFK's presidential speeches, but this unique package pairs a CD of the speeches with a collection of essays on them by historians Golway and Dallek (the latter wrote his own JFK book, An Unfinished Life, 2003). The result is nothing short of terrific..." —Booklist

Includes bibliographical references (p. [255]-262) and index.

Nixon and Kissinger: Partners in Power. Robert Dallek. Harper Collins Publishers 2007. xii, 740 p. : Illustration
ISBN 9780060722302
Grades: Adult   B
1. Nixon, Richard M. (Richard Milhous), 1913-1994 2. Kissinger, Henry, 1923-2023 3. Politicians 4. Presidents 5. International relations 6. United States 7. 20th century 8. History writing — Presidency — 20th century — United States 9. History writing — Cold War
LC 2006052100

Pulitzer Prize for History finalist, 2008.

A dual portrait of the late former president and the former Secretary of State describes the ambitious drives that motivated them, offering insight into the tumultuous relationship that shaped their respective foreign policy agendas.

"A look behind the scenes at this quintessential pair of power brokers and their lasting influence, for good and ill, on the political stage." —Bookmarks

Includes bibliographical references (p. [697]-700) and index.

*An **Unfinished** Life: John F. Kennedy, 1917-1963.* Robert Dallek. Little, Brown, and Co. 2003. x, 838 p, 32 p. of plates : Illustration
ISBN 9780316172387
Grades: Adult   B
1. Kennedy, John F. (John Fitzgerald), 1917-1963 2. Campaigning 3. Presidents 4. Politicians 5. Politics and government 6. United States 7. 20th century 8. 1960s 9. Biographies 10. History writing — Presidency — 20th century — United States 11. History writing — 1960s — United States 12. Life stories — Politics — Politicians
LC 2002116388

Library Journal Best Books, 2003; New York Times Notable Book, 2003.

Drawing upon previously unavailable material and never-before-opened archives to tell Kennedy's story, we learn for the first time just how sick Kennedy was, what medications he took and concealed from all but a few, and how his medical condition affected his actions as President. We learn for the first time the real story of how Bobby was selected as Attorney General. Dallek reveals what Jack's father did to help his son's election to the presidency, and he follows previously unknown evidence to show what path JFK would have taken in the Vietnam entanglement had he survived.

"The author has written the most accessible, balanced, and scholarly biography yet of JFK. It is the Kennedy biography against which others will be measured." —Library Journal

Includes bibliographical references (p. [805]-811) and index.

Dance, Stanley

★ *The **World** of Earl Hines.* Stanley Dance. Da Capo Press 1983. IX, 324 p. : Illustration; Portrait
ISBN 9780306801822
Grades: Adult   B
1. Jazz music 2. Jazz musicians 3. Biographies 4. Arts and Entertainment — Music — Jazz and the Blues 5. Life stories — Arts and culture — Performing arts — Musicians and composers
LC 82025252

The life and career of the innovative jazz pianist and bandleader as well as the rise and fall of the big bands are described in the words of such eminent jazzmen as Dizzy Gillespie, Billy Eckstine, and Budd Johnson.

"This book consists of numerous tape-recorded and edited interviews with musicians and vocalists associated with Basie, and each gets to tell his own story. Many overlap and there are interesting confirmations and disputes over details. The language has been polished (and no doubt in some cases cleaned up), but Dance does not noticeably impose his own views on others. There are good photographs." —Choice

Reprint. Originally published: New York : Scribner, 1977. (The World of swing; v. 2); Includes index; Bibliography: P. 312; Discography: P. 313-314.

Daniels, Stormy

Full Disclosure. Stormy Daniels with Kevin Carr O'Leary. St Martins Press 2018. 270 p.
ISBN 9781250205568
Grades: Adult   B
1. Daniels, Stormy, 1979- 2. Trump, Donald, 1946- 3. Extramarital affairs 4. Mistresses 5. Scandals 6. Presidential staff 7. Pornographic films 8. Actors and actresses 9. United States 10. 21st century 11. Autobiographies and memoirs 12. Life stories — Politics 13. History writing — Presidency — 21st century — United States

Adult film star Stormy Daniels tells all in Full Disclosure, a behind-the-scenes memoir sharing her childhood journey to the national stage, featuring never-before-revealed intimate details of her relationship with Donald Trump. Candid and funny, her life story shows why she has become "the hero America needs" (Rolling Stone).

Danler, Stephanie

Stray: A Memoir. Stephanie Danler. Alfred A. Knopf 2020. 240 p.
ISBN 9781101875964
Grades: Adult   B
1. Danler, Stephanie 2. Authors, American 3. Children of alcoholics 4. Children of drug abusers 5. Divorced women 6. Addiction 7. Psychic trauma 8. Children of divorced parents 9. Grief 10. Dysfunctional families 11. Coping 12. California 13. Southern California 14. 21st century 15. Autobiographies and memoirs 16. Life stories — Facing adversity — Medical issues — Addiction 17. Life stories — Relationships — Family
LC 2019055034

After selling her first novel—a dream she'd worked long and hard for—Stephanie Danler knew she should be happy. Instead, she found herself driven to face the difficult past she'd left behind a decade ago: a mother disabled by years of alcoholism, further handicapped by a tragic brain aneurysm; a father who abandoned the family when she was three, now a meth addict in and out of recovery. After years in New York City she's pulled home to Southern California by forces she doesn't totally understand, haunted by questions of legacy and trauma. Here, she works toward answers, uncovering hard truths about her parents and herself as she explores whether it's possible to change the course of her history. Lucid and honest, heart-breaking and full of hope, Stray is an examination of what we inherit and what we don't have to, of what we have to face in ourselves to move forward, and what it's like to let go of one's parents in order to find peace—and a family—of one's own.

"Danler knits together the stories of her long-divorced parents and the effects of their addictions on her self-formation.... Acknowledging both the tribute of memory and the mercy of forgetting with one distinctive voice, this is a rare and skillfully structured view of an artist's love, grief, and growth." —Booklist

Danticat, Edwidge

★ *Brother, I'm Dying.* Edwidge Danticat. Alfred A. Knopf 2007. x, 272 p.
ISBN 9781400041152
Grades: 11 12 Adult   B
1. Danticat, Edwidge, 1969- 2. Immigration and emigration 3. Family relationships 4. Uncles 5. Haitian people in the United States 6. Authors, American 7. Haiti 8. 20th century 9. Autobiographies and memoirs 10. Biographies 11. Family and Relationships — Families 12. Life stories — Relationships — Family 13. Adult books for young adults
LC 2007006887

National Book Critics Circle Award for Autobiography, 2007; Hurston/Wright Legacy Award: Nonfiction, 2008; New York Times Notable Book, 2007; National Book Award for Nonfiction finalist, 2007.

In a personal memoir, the author describes her relationships with the two men closest to her—her father and his brother, Joseph, a charismatic pastor with whom she lived after her parents emigrated from Haiti to the United States.

"The author has written a fierce, haunting book about exile and loss and family love, and how that love can survive distance and separation, loss and abandonment and somehow endure, undented and robust." —New York Times

ESSENTIAL AND RECOMMENDED TITLES
Biography

Darkshire, Oliver
Once Upon a Tome: The Misadventures of a Rare Bookseller. Oliver Darkshire. W W Norton & Company 2023. 256 p.
ISBN 9781324092070
Grades: Adult **B**
1. Darkshire, Oliver 2. Rare books 3. Antiquarian booksellers 4. Booksellers 5. Bookstores 6. Books 7. Autobiographies and memoirs 8. Life stories — Arts and culture — Writing 9. Arts and Entertainment — Writing and Publishing

Some years ago, Oliver Darkshire stepped into the hushed interior of Henry Sotheran Ltd (est. 1761) to apply for a job. Allured by the smell of old books and the temptation of a management-approved afternoon nap, Darkshire was soon unteetering stacks of first editions and placating the store's resident ghost (the late Mr. Sotheran, hit by a tram).A novice in this ancient, potentially haunted establishment, Darkshire describes Sotheran's brushes with history (Dickens, the Titanic), its joyous disorganization, and the unspoken rules of its gleefully old-fashioned staff, whose mere glance may cause the computer to burst into flames.

"In this witty and heartwarming memoir, Darkshire, a former bookseller at London's Henry Sotheran Ltd, catalogs the stories behind the books, patrons, and antiques that found their way to the shop during his apprenticeship." —*Publishers Weekly*

Darling, Ron
The Complete Game: Reflections on Baseball, Pitching, and Life on the Mound. by Ron Darling with Daniel Paisner. Alfred A. Knopf 2009. 288 p.
ISBN 9780307269843
Grades: Adult **B**
1. Darling, Ron 2. Baseball 3. Pitchers (Baseball) 4. Pitching (Baseball) 5. Baseball players 6. United States 7. Autobiographies and memoirs 8. Biographies 9. Sports and Competition — Baseball 10. Sports and Competition — Individual Athlete 11. Life stories — Sports — Athletes
LC 2008055706

The former Mets pitcher recounts memorable innings throughout his career, offering insight to the game of baseball and the techniques, tactics, and psychology of pitching.

"Darling, the stalwart ex-Mets starter and incumbent Mets broadcaster . offers pitches and outcomes (but no box scores) from ten selected games in his career, including a successful World Series start against the Red Sox at Fenway Park in 1986, a gruesome windy-day thumping suffered at Wrigley Field, and his celebrated extra-inning near-no-hitter back when he was pitching for Yale. Among them are enough oddities and thrilling turns of baseball to make a reader glad to be here andwell, not out there." —*The New Yorker*

Daugherty, Tracy
Larry McMurtry: A Life. Tracy Daugherty. St. Martin's Press 2023. 544 p.
ISBN 9781250282330
Grades: Adult **B**
1. McMurtry, Larry, 1936-2021 2. Authors, American 3. Screenwriters 4. Booksellers 5. Historical fiction writing 6. Literary criticism 7. North American people 8. American people 9. The West (United States) 10. Biographies 11. Impartial writing 12. Life stories — Arts and culture — Writing — Authors 13. Arts and Entertainment — Writing and Publishing — Literary criticism
LC 2023019859

Pulitzer Prize for Biography finalist, 2024.

In over forty books, in a career that spanned over sixty years, Larry McMurtry staked his claim as a superior chronicler of the American West, and as the Great Plains' keenest witness since Willa Cather and Wallace Stegner. Larry McMurtry: A Life traces his origins as one of the last American writers who had direct contact with this country's pioneer traditions. It follows his astonishing career as bestselling novelist, Pulitzer-Prize winner, author of the beloved Lonesome Dove, Academy-Award winning screenwriter, public intellectual, and passionate bookseller.

"The late Pulitzer Prize-winning Texas novelist receives a thoughtful yet appropriate critical treatment in the hands of literary biographer Daugherty…A definitive life of the novelist/Bookseller/Scriptwriter/Curmudgeon of interest to any McMurtry fan." —*Kirkus*

Includes bibliographical references and index.

The **Last** *Love Song: A Biography of Joan Didion.* Tracy Daugherty. St. Martin's Press 2015. 560 p.
ISBN 9781250010025
Grades: Adult **B**
1. Didion, Joan. 1934-2021 2. Authors, American 3. Women authors 4. Biographies 5. Life stories — Arts and culture — Writing — Authors
LC 2015017162

Oregon Book Awards, Frances Fuller Victor Award for General Nonfiction, 2017.

Joan Didion lived a life in the public and private eye with her late husband, writer John Gregory Dunne, whom she met while the two were working in New York City when Didion was at Vogue and Dunne was writing for Time. They became wildly successful writing partners when they moved to Los Angeles and co-wrote screenplays and adaptations together. Didion is well-known for her literary journalistic style in both fiction and non-fiction. Some of her most-notable work includes Slouching Towards Bethlehem, Run River, and the Year of Magical Thinking, a National Book Award winner and shortlisted for the Pulitzer Prize, it dealt with the grief surrounding Didion after the loss of her husband and daughter. Daugherty takes readers on a journey back through time, following a young Didion in Sacramento, through to her adult life as a writer interviewing those who know and knew her personally, while maintaining a respectful distance from the reclusive literary great.

Davidson, Mark A.
★ *Bob* **Dylan**: *Mixing up the Medicine.* Edited by Mark Davidson, Parker Fishel; with editorial assistance by Austin Short; additional essays selected by Michael Chaiken and Robert Polito. Callaway 2023. 607 pages : Illustration; Color
ISBN 9781734537796
Grades: Adult **B**
1. Dylan, Bob, 1941- 2. Rock musicians 3. Music history and criticism 4. Photographs 5. Biographies 6. Visual nonfiction 7. Arts and Entertainment — Music — Rock 8. Life stories — Arts and culture — Performing arts — Musicians and composers
LC BI2023179126

A carefully curated selection of over 600 images including never-before-circulated draft lyrics, writings, photographs, drawings and other ephemera from the Dylan archive. With an introductory essay by Sean Wilentz and epilogue by Douglas Brinkley, the book features a surprising range of distinguished writers, artists and musicians, including Joy Harjo, Greil Marcus, Michael Ondaatje, Gregory Pardlo, Amanda Petrusich, Tom Piazza, Lee Ranaldo, Alex Ross, Ed Ruscha, Lucy Sante, Greg Tate and many others. After experiencing the collection firsthand in Tulsa, each of the authors was asked to select a single item that beguiled or inspired them.

"This extraordinary book showcases the Bob Dylan Center and the artist himself. It introduces enticing new scholarship in the Dylan historiography to be studied and celebrated for generations to come." —*Library Journal*

Includes bibliographical references (pages 590-591) and indexes.

Davis, Geena
Dying of Politeness: A Memoir. Geena Davis. HarperCollins 2022. 356 p.
ISBN 9780063119130
Grades: Adult **B**
1. Davis, Geena 2. Personal conduct 3. Childhood 4. Actors and actresses 5. Etiquette 6. Gender equity 7. Hollywood, California 8. Autobiographies and memoirs 9. Life stories — Arts and culture — Performing arts — Actors and actresses 10. Arts and Entertainment — Movies and television

In this candid memoir, the Academy Award winner recalls her journey from a quiet and polite childhood to a screen icon who helped lead the way to gender parity in Hollywood.

"Academy Award winner Davis makes an engaging literary debut with a candid, appealing memoir recounting her evolution from self-effacing young woman to feisty activist." —*Kirkus*

PUBLIC LIBRARY CORE COLLECTION: NONFICTION
Twentieth Edition

Davis, Jack E.
An **Everglades** *Providence: Marjory Stoneman Douglas and the American Environmental Century.* Jack E. Davis. University of Georgia Press 2009. 616 p.
ISBN 9780820330716
Grades: Adult **B**
1. Douglas, Marjory Stoneman, 1890-1998 2. Women environmentalists 3. Feminists 4. Nature conservation 5. Environmental degradation 6. Wetland conservation 7. Environmental policy 8. Authors, American 9. Everglades, Florida 10. Florida 11. United States 12. 20th century 13. Biographies 14. Nature Writing — Environmental Issues
LC 2008049073
Tells the tale of this suffragist, feminist, and environmentalist who fought for the preservation and protection of the Everglades and, through her due diligence and skillful writing, won the battle that resulted in it becoming a national wilderness area.
"This is both a portrait of one of the 20th century's most important environmental figures and a history of Florida's Everglades. The long-lived Douglas (1890-1998) is best known for the classic the Everglades: River of Grass and her tireless efforts to preserve that region. But she was also a lifelong feminist and social activist who worked to advance human rights. In addition to the rich detail and documentation of Douglas's life, Davis offers an impressive look at America during Douglas's lifetime and the growth of America's environmental movement." —*Library Journal*
Includes bibliographical references and index.

Davis, Jennifer Pharr
Called **Again**: *A Story of Love and Triumph.* by Jennifer Pharr Davis. Beaufort Books 2013. 298 p.
ISBN 9780825306938
Grades: Adult **B**
1. Davis, Jennifer Pharr 2. Hikers 3. Hiking 4. Self-discovery 5. Christian women 6. Commitment (Psychology) 7. Women hikers 8. Appalachian Trail 9. Autobiographies and memoirs 10. Travel Writing — Modes of Transportation — on Foot 11. Travel Writing — United States
LC 2013002077
The woman who holds the overall record for hiking the Appalachian Trail shares her story discussing her love for hiking and her love for her husband.
"A serviceably written yet inspired exploration of the meaning of commitment." —*Kirkus*

Davis, Seth
Wooden: *A Coach's Life.* Seth Davis. Times Books 2014. 576 p.
ISBN 9780805092806
Grades: Adult **B**
1. Wooden, John, 1910-2010 2. Athletic coaches 3. Basketball coaching 4. College basketball 5. Basketball 6. College sports 7. Basketball teams 8. Winning and losing 9. Coaching (Athletics) 10. Universities and colleges 11. Ambition 12. Integrity 13. Biographies 14. Sports and Competition — Coaches 15. Sports and Competition — Basketball 16. Sports and Competition — Teams 17. Life stories — Sports — Athletes 18. Life stories — Sports — Coaches, managers, and owners
LC 2013020209
A provocative assessment of legendary UCLA coach John Wooden draws on hundreds of interviews from all periods of his career to offer insight into his driving ambition, divided relationships and hard-won lessons.
"Davis has avoided stultifying, game-by-game detail (but does offer genuinely exciting accounts of several key games) and has provided a multidimensional, nearly cradle-to-grave portrait of a highly successful and revered coach and teacher, in the process delivering a history of the evolution of college basketball and profiles of many of its stars." —*Booklist*
Includes index.

Davis, Stephen
Gold *Dust Woman: A Biography of Stevie Nicks.* Stephen Davis. St. Martin's Press 2017. 320 p.
ISBN 9781250032898
Grades: Adult **B**
1. Nicks, Stevie, 1948- 2. Rock groups 3. Songwriters 4. Singers 5. Rock musicians 6. United States 7. Biographies 8. Life stories — Arts and culture — Performing arts — Musicians and composers 9. Arts and Entertainment — Music — Rock
LC 2017023621
An in-depth portrait of the classic-rock artist includes coverage of such topics as her role in the stardom of Fleetwood Mac, the affairs that inspired her greatest songs, her struggles with addiction and her successful solo career.
"An entertaining rock biography, even if you're a take-it-or-leave-it fan of the singer." —*Kirkus*

Davis, Viola
★ **Finding** *Me.* Viola Davis. HarperOne 2022. 288 p.
ISBN 9780063037328
Grades: Adult **B**
1. Davis, Viola, 1965- 2. African American women 3. Growing up 4. Ambition 5. Identity 6. Self-discovery 7. Self-acceptance 8. Actors and actresses 9. Intergenerational trauma 10. Autobiographies and memoirs 11. Biographies 12. Life stories — Arts and culture — Performing arts — Actors and actresses 13. Life stories — Personal growth 14. Life stories — Identity — Race and ethnicity 15. Arts and Entertainment — Movies and Television 16. Book club best bets
A noted actress's memoir, in her own words, spans her incredible, inspiring life, from her coming-of-age in Rhode Island to her present day.
"In a starkly forthright memoir, Oscar and Tony winner Davis reflects on family, love, motherhood, and acting....An unvarnished chronicle of hard-won, well-earned success." —*Kirkus*

Davis, Wade
Into **the** **Silence**: *The Great War, Mallory, and the Conquest of Everest.* by Wade Davis. A. Knopf 2011. 672 p.
ISBN 9780375408892
Grades: 11 12 Adult **B**
1. Mallory, George, 1886-1924 2. Mount Everest Expedition, 1924 3. Mountaineers 4. World War I 5. Mountaineering 6. Explorers 7. Mount Everest 8. 1920s 9. Canadian literature 10. Sports and Competition — Mountaineering
LC 2011013888
Samuel Johnson Prize for Non-Fiction, 2012; Shortlisted for the Charles Taylor Prize for Literary Non-Fiction; Governor General's Literary Awards, English-language Non-fiction finalist.
Recounts George Mallory's attempt to scale Mount Everest in the early 1920s, and how, in the aftermath of World War I, the expedition became a symbol of national pride and hope.
A Borzoi book.

Dawidziak, Mark
A **Mystery** *of Mysteries: The Death and Life of Edgar Allan Poe.* Mark Dawidziak. St. Martin's Press 2023. 304 p.
ISBN 9781250792495
Grades: Adult **B**
1. Poe, Edgar Allan, 1809-1849 2. Authors, American 3. Authors 4. 19th century 5. Biographies 6. Life stories — Arts and culture — Writing — Authors 7. History Writing — United States 8. Arts and Entertainment — Writing and publishing
LC 2022035450
A Mystery of Mysteries is a brilliant biography of Edgar Allan Poe that examines the renowned author's life through the prism of his mysterious death and its many possible causes.
"TV and film critic Dawidziak draws on published and archival sources, including more than 50 interviews with Edgar Allan Poe scholars and other experts, to create a colorful portrait of the poet, critic, and story writer....A brisk, satisfying biography of a literary icon who still fascinates." —*Kirkus*
Includes bibliographical references and index.

ESSENTIAL AND RECOMMENDED TITLES
Biography

Dawkins, Richard
*An **Appetite** for Wonder: The Making of a Scientist.* Richard Dawkins. Ecco Press 2013. 320 p.
ISBN 9780062225795
Grades: Adult   B
1. Dawkins, Richard, 1941- 2. Biologists 3. Evolution 4. Atheism 5. Scientists 6. Autobiographies and memoirs 7. Biographies 8. Life stories — Science, technology, and medicine — Scientists and inventors 9. Science Writing — Biology
LC Bl2013035860

Famous for his radical new vision of Darwinism, Richard Dawkins paints a colorful, richly textured canvas of his early life from innocent child to charismatic world-famous scientist.

***Brief** Candle in the Dark: My Life in Science.* Richard Dawkins. Ecco 2015. 320 p.
ISBN 9780062288431
Grades: Adult   B
1. Dawkins, Richard, 1941- 2. Biologists 3. Intellectual life 4. Scientists 5. Autobiographies and memoirs 6. Biographies 7. Life stories — Science, technology, and medicine — Scientists and inventors 8. Science Writing — Biology
LC Bl2015029707

A sequel to an Appetite for Wonder candidly explores the influences of fame on the author's career, shares memories about his intellectual peers and evaluates the events and ideas that have shaped his beliefs.

"Though the narrative could have used some pruning, the author provides an entertaining portrait of his life and times, including the quaint cus t oms still in practice at Oxford. An impressive overview of Dawkins' life's work, written with the freshness of youthful vigor." —*Kirkus*

Dawson, Kate Winkler
★ *American Sherlock: Murder, Forensics, and the Birth of American Csi.* Kate Winkler Dawson. G.P. Putnam's Sons 2020. 325 pages, 8 unnumbered pages of plates : Illustration
ISBN 9780525539551
Grades: Adult   B
1. Heinrich, Edward Oscar, 1881-1953 2. Chemists 3. Crime laboratories 4. Criminal evidence 5. Forensic sciences 6. Forensic medicine 7. Criminal investigation 8. Biographies 9. Life stories — Law and order 10. Life stories — Science, technology, and medicine — Scientists and inventors 11. True Crime — Investigations and Trials 12. Nonfiction that reads like fiction
LC 2019050904

Describes the life of America's greatest, and first, forensic scientist, who invented tools that are still being used today, including blood spatter analysis, ballistics, lie-detector tests and fingerprints and solved at least two thousand cases during his forty-year career.

"A fascinating book worthy of being associated with the title's literary sleuth. Readers will want a follow-up so they can discover more of Heinrich's cases as told through Dawson's great storytelling." —*Library Journal*

Includes bibliographical references (pages 279-313) and index.

Day, Daniel R.
***Dapper** Dan: Made in Harlem : A Memoir.* by Daniel R. Day with Mikael Awake. Random House 2019. 304 p.
ISBN 9780525510512
Grades: Adult   B
1. Day, Daniel R. 2. African American fashion designers 3. Fashion 4. City life 5. Hip-hop culture 6. Growing up 7. Fashion design 8. Fashion designers 9. Harlem, New York City 10. New York City 11. Autobiographies and memoirs 12. Life stories — Arts and culture — Fashion 13. Arts and Entertainment — Fashion 14. Life stories — Facing adversity — Personal transformation
LC 2018036839
BCALA Literary Award for Nonfiction, 2020.

A memoir by the legendary designer who pioneered high-end streetwear traces his rise from an early-1980s Harlem storefront to the red carpet in Hollywood, working with such celebrities as Salt-N-Pepa and Beyonce. Illustrations.

"Day is a natural storyteller with a distinct point of view that clearly comes through in this enjoyable memoir." —*Booklist*

De Hart, Jane Sherron
★ *Ruth Bader Ginsburg: A Life.* Jane Sherron de Hart. Alfred A. Knopf 2018. 752 p.
ISBN 9781400040483
Grades: Adult   B
1. Ginsburg, Ruth Bader, 1933-2020 2. Judges 3. Women judges 4. Jurisprudence 5. Women's rights 6. Marginalized people 7. Civil rights 8. United States 9. Biographies 10. Life stories — Law and order — Judges and lawyers 11. History writing — Judicial branch — United States 12. History writing — Women's history
LC 2018004415

The first full life—private; public; legal; philosophical—of the 107th Supreme Court Justice, one of the most profound and profoundly transformative legal minds of our time; a book fifteen years in work, written with the cooperation of Ruth Bader Ginsburg herself and based on many interviews with the Justice, her husband, her children, her friends, and associates.

"This extensively documented account, incorporating more than 100 pages of chapter notes and a bibliography that cites hundreds of resources, is also quite engaging and very easy to read." —*Booklist*

Includes bibliographical references and index.

De Stefano, Cristina
*The **Child** Is the Teacher: A Life of Maria Montessori.* Cristina De Stefano; translated from the Italian by Gregory Conti. Other Press 2022. 384 p.
ISBN 9781635420845
Grades: Adult   B
1. Montessori, Maria, 1870-1952 2. Montessori method of education 3. Women educators 4. Feminists 5. Sex discrimination against women 6. Primary education 7. Individualized instruction 8. Child psychology 9. Educational innovations 10. Independence 11. Obstinacy 12. Italy 13. Biographies 14. Translations — Italian to English 15. Impartial writing 16. Life stories — Education — Scholars and educators 17. Life stories — Politics — Activists and reformers 18. Society and culture — Education
LC 2021033929

A thorough, nuanced portrait of this often-controversial woman who changed the way we look at children's minds, this first biographical work on Maria Montessori draws from original letters, diaries, notes, and texts written by Montessori herself, including an array of previously unpublished material.

"Journalist and literary scout De Stefano (Oriana Fallaci) focuses this episodic biography on childhood education pioneer Maria Montessori's tumultuous personal life and prickly personality rather than her pedagogical theory….Readers of feminist history will savor this evenhanded profile of a groundbreaking educator and businesswoman." —*Publishers Weekly*

Originally published in Italian as IL bambino e il maestro: Vita di Maria Montessori by Rizzoli, Milan, in 2020; Includes bibliographical references.

De Vise, Daniel
*The **Comeback**: Greg Lemond, the True King of American Cycling, and a Legendary Tour De France.* Daniel de Visé.. Atlantic Monthly Press 2018. 432 p.
ISBN 9780802127945
Grades: Adult   B
1. LeMond, Greg 2. Bicycle racing 3. Bicyclists 4. Bicycling 5. Biographies 6. Life stories — Sports — Athletes 7. Sports and Competition — Racing — Cycling
LC 2017061342

Traces the dramatic life story of the first American Tour de France winner, covering such topics as his complicated family life, the hunting accident that nearly ended his cycling career and his confrontation with Lance Armstrong over performance-drug allegations.

Includes bibliographical references.

PUBLIC LIBRARY CORE COLLECTION: NONFICTION
Twentieth Edition

De Waal, Edmund
The Hare with Amber Eyes. Edmund De Waal. Farrar Straus & Giroux 2010. 272 p.
ISBN 9780374105976
Grades: Adult **B**
1. Collectors and collecting 2. Rich men 3. Art patrons 4. Art patronage 5. Bankers 6. Jewish men 7. Art collectors and collecting 8. Vienna, Austria 9. Paris, France 10. 1870s 11. History writing — Europe 12. History writing — Europe — France 13. Book club best bets

LC 2010025539

ALA Notable Book, 2011; Booklist Editors' Choice, 2010; Costa Biography Award, 2010; RSL Ondaatje Prize, 2011.

Traces the parallel stories of 19th-century art patron Charles Ephrussi and his unique collection of 360 miniature netsuke Japanese ivory carvings, documenting Ephrussi's relationship with Marcel Proust and the impact of the Holocaust on his cosmopolitan family.

"From a hard and vast archival mass of journals, memoirs, newspaper clippings and art-history books, Mr de Waal has fashioned, stroke by minuscule stroke, a book as fresh with detail as if it had been written from life, and as full of beauty and whimsy as a netsuke from the hands of a master carver." —*The Economist*

Dearborn, Mary V.
Carson McCullers: A Life. Mary V. Dearborn. Alfred A. Knopf 2024. 512 p.
ISBN 9780525521013
Grades: Adult **B**
1. McCullers, Carson, 1917-1967 2. Women authors, American 3. Fame 4. Marriage 5. Chronic diseases 6. Alcoholism 7. People who have had strokes 8. Bisexual women 9. LGBTQIA+ people 10. Interpersonal relations 11. American people 12. Biographies 13. Life stories — Arts and culture — Writing — Authors 14. Life stories — Identity — LGBTQIA+ 15. Arts and Entertainment — Writing and Publishing

LC 2023007221

V. S. Pritchett called her "a genius." Tennessee Williams said, "The only real writer the South ever turned out, was Carson." While Carson McCullers's literary stature continues to endure, her private life has remained enigmatic and largely unexamined. Now, with unprecedented access to the cache of materials that has surfaced in the past decade, Mary Dearborn gives us the first full picture of this brilliant, complex artist who was decades ahead of her time, a writer who understood—and captured—the heart and longing of the outcast.

Drawing on abundant archival material, much not available to earlier biographers, Dearborn offers a thorough, passionate recounting of the life of Carson McCullers (1917-1967), a writer with an 'Unerring instinct for the outsider's life.' —*Kirkus*

Includes bibliographical references and index.

Ernest Hemingway: A Biography. Mary V. Dearborn. Knopf 2017. 752 p.
ISBN 9780307594679
Grades: Adult **B**
1. Hemingway, Ernest, 1899-1961 2. Journalists 3. Men 4. Masculinity 5. Men and success 6. Identity 7. Authors, American 8. Psychology 9. 20th century 10. Biographies 11. Arts and Entertainment — Writing and Publishing 12. Life stories — Arts and culture — Writing — Authors 13. Life stories — Arts and culture — Writing — Journalists

LC 2016015837

A full biography of Ernest Hemingway draws on a wide range of previously untapped material and offers particular insight into the private demons that both inspired and tormented his literary achievements.

"Dearborn's account shines from beginning to end, helped by Hemingway's dramatic life and charismatic personality." —*Publishers Weekly*

Includes bibliographical references.

DeCurtis, Anthony
Lou Reed: A Life. Anthony DeCurtis. Little, Brown and Company 2017. 448 p.
ISBN 9780316376556
Grades: Adult **B**
1. Reed, Lou. 1942-2013 2. Songwriters 3. Singers 4. Rock musicians 5. Biographies 6. Life stories — Arts and culture — Performing arts — Musicians and composers 7. Arts and entertainment — Music — Rock

LC 2017008817

A portrait of the lead singer and songwriter for the Velvet Underground cites his foundational role in the alternative rock genre while examining the contradictions, reinventions and extremes that marked his personal and professional endeavors.

Includes bibliographical references and index.

Delaney, Rob
★ *A Heart That Works.* Rob Delaney. Spiegel & Grau 2022. 196 p.
ISBN 9781954118317
Grades: Adult **B**
1. Delaney, Rob, 1977- 2. Parents 3. Death 4. Death of children 5. Brain tumors 6. Grief 7. Death of sons 8. Loss 9. Grief in parents 10. Autobiographies and memoirs 11. Life stories — Facing adversity — Coping with death 12. Life stories — Relationships — Parent and child 13. Family and relationships — Aging and death 14. Family and relationships — Parenting

The co-creator and co-star of the hit series Catastrophe presents a deeply personal memoir about the death of his young son from a brain tumor and takes readers through the grief and pain that followed.

"Delaney is no stranger to balancing grief and humor, and it shows in this heartbreaking yet often darkly funny recounting of how he lost his third son, Henry, to brain cancer….A heart-wrenching and impressively self-aware story of a father living through the death of his young child." —*Kirkus*

Delany, Sarah Louise
Having Our Say: The Delany Sisters' First 100 Years. Sarah and A. Elizabeth Delany; with Amy Hill Hearth. Kodansha International 1993. xiii, 210 p. : Illustration
ISBN 9781568360102
Grades: 11 12 Adult **B**
1. Delany family 2. Delany, Sarah Louise, 1889-1999 3. Delany, Annie Elizabeth, 1891-1995 4. Senior women 5. Aging 6. African American sisters 7. Seniors 8. African Americans 9. African American women 10. Race relations 11. Independence 12. United States history 13. United States 14. North Carolina 15. New York (State) 16. Autobiographies and memoirs 17. Biographies 18. Life stories — People in history — Witness to history 19. History writing — African American — United States

LC 93023890

ALA Notable Book, 1994.

Two sisters, both over one hundred years old and the daughters of a man born into slavery, recall the triumphs and tragedies of their lives together, discussing their success as African-American professional women during Harlem's golden age.

"The combination of the two voices, beautifully blended by Ms. Hearth, evokes an epic history, often cruel and brutal, but always deeply humane in their spirited telling of it." —*New York Times Book Review*

Denevi, Timothy
Freak Kingdom: Hunter S. Thompson's Manic Ten-year Crusade Against American Fascism. Timothy Denevi. PublicAffairs 2018. 416 p.
ISBN 9781541767942
Grades: Adult **B**
1. Thompson, Hunter S. 2. Nixon, Richard M. (Richard Milhous), 1913-1994 3. Presidential elections 4. Journalists 5. Political campaigns 6. Politicians 7. Political journalism 8. Politics and government 9. United States 10. 20th century 11. Biographies 12. Life stories — Arts and culture — Writing — Journalists 13. History writing — 1960s — United States 14. History writing — 1970s — United States 15. History writing — Presidency — 20th century — United States

LC 2018015549

This brilliantly told and dramatic story chronicles Hunter S. Thompson|s crusade against Richard Nixon and how his fevered effort to expose institutional in-

ESSENTIAL AND RECOMMENDED TITLES
Biography

justice hastened his own decline but led to some of the best political writing in our history.

Includes bibliographical references and index.

Deng, Alephonsion
They Poured Fire on Us from the Sky: The True Story of Three Lost Boys from Sudan. Alephonsion Deng, Benson Deng, Benjamin Ajak; with Judy A. Bernstein. Public Affairs 2005. xxiii, 311 p. : Map

ISBN 9782005042568

Grades: 11 12 Adult   B

1. Deng, Benson 2. Deng, Alephonsion 3. Ajak, Benjamin 4. Refugees, Sudanese 5. Genocide 6. Atrocities 7. Civil war 8. Southwest Asia and North Africa (Middle East) history 9. East Africa 10. Sudan 11. 20th century 12. 21st century 13. 1990s 14. 2000s (Decade) 15. 1980s 16. History writing — Wars and conflicts — Civil Wars 17. History writing — Civil wars and genocide — Africa 18. Adult books for young adults

As gunshots, flames, and screams engulfed their village, three cousins fled into the cover of the forest. Every step led the boys away from their peaceful, agrarian world—a traditional world were spear-toting fathers protected their huts from the lions that roamed by night. With each footstep they were drawn deeper into the horrific violence of Sudan's civil war: a world of bombed-out villages, mine-sown roads, and relentless desert, a world where starving adults would snatch the grain from a weak child's fingers. Across Sudan, between 1987 and 1989, tens of thousands of young boys took flight from these massacres. Their journey led them first to Ethiopia and then, driven back into Sudan, toward Kenya. They walked nearly one thousand miles, sustained only by the sheer will to live. This book is the three boys' account of that unimaginable journey.

"This collection is moving in its depictions of unbelievable courage." —*Publishers Weekly*

Dennis, David J, Jr
The Movement Made US: a Father, a Son, and the Legacy of a Freedom Ride. David J. Jr. in collaboration with David J. Dennis Sr. HarperCollins 2022. 288 p.

ISBN 9780063011427

Grades: Adult   B

1. Dennis, David J, Jr 2. Dennis, David J, Sr 3. Civil rights movement 4. Black Lives Matter movement 5. Civil rights 6. Freedom Riders (Civil rights movement) 7. Social justice 8. Social change 9. Fathers and sons 10. African American men 11. Social movements 12. Race relations 13. Autobiographies and memoirs 14. Life stories — Politics — Activists and reformers 15. History writing — African American — Civil rights — United States

A work of oral history and memoir chronicles the extraordinary story of the Civil Rights Movement of the 1960s and its living legacy embodied in Black Lives Matter.

"A young Black activist revisits his father's role in the civil rights movement of the 1960s." —*Kirkus*

Dennis, Felix
How to Get Rich: One of the World's Greatest Entrepreneurs Shares His Success Wisdom. Felix Dennis. Portfolio 2008. 288 p.

ISBN 9781591842057

Grades: Adult   B

1. Dennis, Felix, 1947-2014 2. Success in business 3. Entrepreneurship 4. Wealth 5. Autobiographies and memoirs 6. Business and economics — Business Advice 7. Life stories — Business — Business leaders 8. Adult books for young adults

The distilled wisdom of one of Britains's wealthiest self-made entrepreneurs.

Dennison, Matthew
Behind the Mask: The Life of Vita Sackville-west. Matthew Dennison. St. Martin's Press 2015. 416 p.

ISBN 9781250033949

Grades: Adult   B

1. Sackville-West, V. (Victoria), 1892-1962 2. Aristocracy 3. Eccentrics and eccentricities 4. Gardeners 5. Gardening 6. Open marriage 7. LGBTQIA+ people 8. Homosexuality 9. Authors, English 10. 20th century 11. Biographies 12. Life stories — Arts and culture — Writing — Authors 13. Life stories — Identity — LGBTQIA+

LC 2015002466

In this new biography of Vita Sackville-West, Matthew Dennison traces the triumph and contradictions of Vita's extraordinary life. His narrative charts a fascinating course from Vita's lonely childhood at Knole, through her affectionate but 'Open' marriage to Harold Nicolson (during which both husband and wife energetically pursued homosexual affairs, Vita most famously with Virginia Woolf), and through Vita's literary successes and disappointments, to the famous gardens the couple created at Sissinghurst. The book tells how, from her privileged world of the aristocracy, Sackville-West brought her penchant for costume, play-acting and rebellion to the artistic vanguard of modern Britain.

"Dennison downplays Vita's relationship with Woolf as a smoldering and significant writerly friendship. His narrative is utterly absorbing in its attention to the minutiae of property, inheritance, houses, clothing, and letters. All the while, the author extracts from Vita's writing rich autobiographical detail. A lively, vigorously written biography of a singular character that beckons readers urgently back to Sackville-West's writing." —*Kirkus*

Includes bibliographical references and index.

The Man in the Willows: The Life of Kenneth Grahame. Matthew Dennison. Pegasus Books 2019. 352 p.

ISBN 9781643130071

Grades: Adult   B

1. Grahame, Kenneth, 1859-1932 2. Authors, British 3. Children's literature authors 4. Nature in literature 5. Rural life 6. England 7. Biographies 8. Life stories — Arts and culture — Writing — Authors 9. Arts and entertainment — Writing and publishing 10. Adult books for young adults 11. Arts and Entertainment — Writing and Publishing — Literary criticism

LC 2018276650

A biography of the author of the children's classic the Wind in the Willows celebrates how the secretary of the Bank of England was inspired by his pastoral wanderings in his country house with his fanciful wife and fragile son.

"Dennisons account of all this is sympathetic but honest, psychologically acute and insightful. It is, withal, a sad story but one that Dennison tells extremely well to his and Grahames credit." —*Booklist*

Denton, Sally
The Profiteers: Bechtel and the Men Who Built the World. Sally Denton. Simon & Schuster 2016. 384 p.

ISBN 9781476706467

Grades: Adult   B

1. Bechtel family 2. Bechtel, Warren A, 1872-1933 3. Contractors 4. Building 5. Engineering 6. Infrastructure 7. Hoover Dam 8. Channel Tunnel 9. Business and economics — Industries

LC 2015510596

The tale of the Bechtel family dynasty is a classic American business story. It begins with Warren A. "Dad" Bechtel, who led a consortium that constructed the Hoover Dam. From that auspicious start, the family and its eponymous company would go on to "build the world," from the construction of airports in Hong Kong and Doha, to pipelines and tunnels in Alaska and Europe, to mining and energy operations around the globe.

"However readers view the company, Dentons extensively researched work informs readers about the firms maintenance as a privately held concern during its growth into a huge, multinational enterprise." —*Booklist*

DePastino, Todd
Bill Mauldin: A Life up Front. Todd DePastino. W.W. Norton 2008. 320 p.

ISBN 9780393061833

Grades: 11 12 Adult   B

1. Mauldin, William Henry, 1921-2003 2. Cartoonists 3. United States 4. Biographies 5. Arts and Entertainment — Comics, Cartoons, and Animation 6. Life stories — Arts and culture — Artists

LC 2007040494

Traces the World War II military service of the two-time Pulitzer Prize-winning creator of the popular "Up Front" cartoon, offering insight into his work's reflection of soldier life, in an account that features more than ninety classic cartoons and rare photographs.

"Thoroughly researched and sprightly written, DePastino's balanced biography is a solid introduction to an American original. Classic Mauldin cartoons are an entertaining bonus." —*Publishers Weekly*

Includes bibliographical references and index.

Deraniyagala, Sonali
Wave: A Memoir of Life After the Tsunami. Sonali Deraniyagala. Alfred A. Knopf 2013. 224 p.
ISBN 9780307962690
Grades: Adult   B
1. Deraniyagala, Sonali 2. Disaster victims 3. Widows 4. Indian Ocean Tsunami, 2004 5. Grief 6. Death of parents 7. Death of children 8. Tsunamis 9. Natural disasters 10. Sri Lanka 11. Autobiographies and memoirs 12. Life stories — Facing adversity — Coping with death 13. History writing — Natural disasters and tragedies 14. Life stories — Facing adversity — Disasters and tragedies
LC 2012040980

Library Journal Best Books, 2013; New York Times Notable Book, 2013; National Book Critics Circle Award for Autobiography/Memoir finalist.

A memoir of the author's experiences as a survivor of the 2004 tsunami that killed her parents, husband, and two young sons recounts her struggles with profound grief and survivor's guilt and her gradual steps toward healing.

Borzoi Books.

DeRogatis, Jim
Soulless: The Case Against R. Kelly. Jim DeRogatis. Abrams Press 2019. 306 p.
ISBN 9781419740077
Grades: Adult   B
1. Kelly, R. 2. Sexually abused teenagers 3. Child pornography 4. Trials (Sex crimes) 5. Musicians 6. Music industry and trade 7. Sexually abused children 8. Girls 9. Arts and Entertainment — Music 10. True Crime — Sex Crimes
LC 2019930879

In November 2000, Chicago journalist and music critic Jim DeRogatis received an anonymous fax that alleged R. Kelly had a problem with "young girls." Weeks later, DeRogatis broke the shocking story, publishing allegations that the R&B superstar and local hero had groomed girls, sexually abused them, and paid them off. DeRogatis thought his work would have an impact. Instead, Kelly's career flourished. DeRogatis's work tells the story of Kelly's career, DeRogatis's investigations, and the world in which the two crossed paths, and brings the story up to the moment when things finally seem to have changed. Decades in the making, this is an outrageous, darkly riveting account of the life and actions of R. Kelly, and their horrible impact on dozens of girls, by the only person to tell it.

"Individuals who have experienced abuse may want to avoid this book entirely. For readers interested in the cult of celebrity, the life of R. Kelly, true crime, journalism, and the #MeToo movement." —*Library Journal*

Dery, Mark
Born to Be Posthumous: The Eccentric Life and Mysterious Genius of Edward Gorey. Mark Dery. Little Brown & CO 2018. 496 p.
ISBN 9780316188548
Grades: Adult   B
1. Gorey, Edward, 1925-2000 2. Recluses 3. Eccentrics and eccentricities 4. Avant-garde (Aesthetics) 5. Artists 6. Authors 7. Gay culture 8. Asexuality 9. Social life and customs 10. United States 11. 20th century 12. Biographies 13. Life stories — Arts and culture — Artists 14. Life stories — Arts and culture — Writing — Authors 15. Arts and Entertainment — Painting, Drawing, and Sculpture 16. Arts and Entertainment — Writing and publishing
LC Bl2018192296

Library Journal Best Books, 2018.

The definitive biography of Edward Gorey, the eccentric master of macabre nonsense.

Devantez, Chelsea
★ *I Shouldn't Be Telling You This: But I'm Going to Anyway.* Chelsea Devantez. Hanover Square Press 2024. 336 p.
ISBN 9781335455079
Grades: Adult   B
1. Devantez, Chelsea 2. Women comedians 3. Childhood 4. Women 5. Influence (Literary, artistic, etc.) 6. Secrets 7. Life 8. Autobiographies and memoirs 9. Essays 10. Life stories — Relationships — Growing up 11. Family and relationships — Growing up

The Emmy-nominated writer, comedian and podcaster presents a memoir-in-essays that trace her path from a tumultuous childhood to Hollywood success by focusing on the women who helped shaped her journey along the way.

"Energetic and revealing, this title will surely please Devantez's listeners and fans. Aficionados of tragicomic, gossip-tinged memoirs will like it too." —*Library Journal*

DI Maio, Vincent J. M.
Morgue: A Life in Death. Dr. Vincent DI Maio and Ron Franscell; foreword by Dr. Jan Garavaglia. St. Martin's Press 2016. 304 p.
ISBN 9781250067142
Grades: Adult   B
1. DI Maio, Vincent J. M, 1941- 2. Pathologists 3. Forensic sciences 4. Autopsy 5. Criminal investigation 6. True Crime — Forensic Sciences
LC 2016001125

An award-winning writer and a renowned pathologist describe the most famous and interesting cases of the doctor's career, including the exhuming of Lee Harvey Oswald and the shooting of Trayvon Martin.

"DI Maio and Franscell deliver a well-paced, thoughtful, and absorbing work that will fascinate crime buffs and scholars alike." —*Publishers Weekly*

Diamond, Cheryl
Nowhere Girl: A Memoir of a Fugitive Childhood. Cheryl Diamond. Algonquin Books of Chapel Hill 2021. 320 p.
ISBN 9781616208202
Grades: Adult   B
1. Diamond, Cheryl 2. Families 3. Daughters 4. Growing up 5. Criminals 6. Fugitives 7. Psychic trauma 8. Missing persons 9. Exiles 10. Outlaws 11. Impersonation 12. Impostors 13. Family secrets 14. Family relationships 15. Threat (Psychology) 16. Autobiographies and memoirs 17. Life stories — Relationships — Family 18. Life stories — Law and order — Criminals and law-breakers 19. Adventure writing — General 20. Family and Relationships — Families
LC 2021002159

In this impossible-to-believe true story of self-discovery and triumph, the author, born into a family of outlaws with no proof that she even existed, shares her escape from the only people she had in the world in order to survive.

"Diamond has always been caught between the Con Man and the Cop.... The survivor of extreme psychological and physical abuse, Diamond recounts her lifelong struggle to discover her true self in a beyond-harrowing memoir." —*Booklist*

Dickinson, Amy
Strangers Tend to Tell Me Things: A Memoir of Love, Loss, and Living on. Amy Dickinson. Hachette Books 2016. 240 p.
ISBN 9780316352642
Grades: Adult   B
1. Dickinson, Amy 2. Advice columnists 3. Family relationships 4. Men-women relations 5. Family and Relationships — General 6. Life stories — Arts and culture — Writing — Journalists
LC 2016027999

The voice behind America's most popular advice column "Ask Amy" and the New York Times best-selling author of The Mighty Queens of Freeville—returns with her follow-up memoir of family, second chances and finding love.

"In this extension of her debut memoir, Dickinson remains an engagingly chatty, witty, and relatable writer with sage insights." —*Kirkus*

ESSENTIAL AND RECOMMENDED TITLES
Biography

Dickinson, Bruce
What Does This Button Do?: Iron Maiden and Other Extraordinary Rides of My Life. Bruce Dickinson. HarperCollins 2017. 448 p.
ISBN 9780062468130
Grades: Adult   B
1. Dickinson, Bruce, 1958- 2. Singers 3. Rock groups 4. Rock musicians 5. Heavy metal music 6. Screenwriters 7. Entrepreneurs 8. Cancer survivors 9. Growing up 10. Social life and customs 11. Great Britain 12. 20th century 13. Autobiographies and memoirs 14. Arts and Entertainment — Music — Rock 15. Life stories — Arts and culture — Performing arts — Musicians and composers
LC 2017568208

A highly anticipated memoir by the multifaceted lead vocalist of Iron Maiden traces his myriad experiences outside of the entertainment industry while sharing insight into his solo work, his turbulent childhood, his battle with cancer and his views on the band's enduring cultural influence.

Didion, Joan
★ *The Year of Magical Thinking.* Joan Didion. A.A. Knopf 2005. 227 p.
ISBN 9781400043149
Grades: Adult   B
1. Didion, Joan 1934-2021 2. Dunne, John Gregory, 1932-2003 3. Loss 4. Grief 5. Mothers and daughters 6. Widows 7. Marriage 8. Family relationships 9. Authors, American 10. Journalists 11. Children in comas 12. United States 13. 20th century 14. Autobiographies and memoirs 15. Biographies 16. Life stories — Facing adversity — Coping with death 17. Family and Relationships — Aging and Death 18. Family and Relationships — Illness and the Family 19. Adult books for young adults
LC 2005045132

Booklist Editors' Choice, 2005; Library Journal Best Books, 2005; National Book Award for Nonfiction, 2005; New York Times Notable Book, 2005; Pulitzer Prize for Biography or Autobiography finalist; National Book Critics Circle Award for Autobiography/Memoir finalist.

An autobiographical portrait of marriage and motherhood by the acclaimed author details her struggle to come to terms with life and death, illness, sanity, personal upheaval, and grief.

"The author chronicles the year following the death of her husband, fellow writer John Gregory Dunne, from a massive heart attack on December 30, 2003, while the couple's only daughter, Quintana, lay unconscious in a nearby hospital suffering from pneumonia and septic shock. This is an indispensable addition to Didion's body of work and a lyrical, disciplined entry in the annals of mourning literature." —*Publishers Weekly*

Dietrich, Sean
You Are My Sunshine: A Story of Love, Promises, and a Really Long Bike Ride. Sean Dietrich. Zondervan Books 2022. 256 p.
ISBN 9780310355786
Grades: Adult   B
1. Dietrich, Sean, 1982- 2. Promises 3. Life 4. Love 5. Husband and wife 6. Life change events 7. Bicycling 8. Bicyclists 9. Interpersonal relations 10. Voyages and travels 11. United States 12. Autobiographies and memoirs 13. Life stories — Relationships 14. Travel writing — Modes of transportation — Cycling
LC 2022017099

A moving story you won't be able to put down, You Are My Sunshine by master storyteller Sean Dietrich shares the true-life tale of keeping a promise—and taking the longest bike ride of his life. Through laugh-out-loud adventures and poignant moments, Sean and Jamie's story will capture your heart as it reminds you of what's most important in life.

"The zany escapades entertain, but it's the life-affirming reflections and conversations that set this apart, such as when Dietrich discusses the afterlife with a priest he meets along the trail. This inspiring volume will melt hearts." —*Publishers Weekly*

DiGiulian, Sasha
Take the Lead: Hanging On, Letting Go, and Conquering Life's Hardest Climbs. Sasha DiGiulian. St. Martin's Press 2023. 288 p.
ISBN 9781250280701
Grades: Adult   B
1. DiGiulian, Sasha 2. Women mountaineers 3. Social media 4. Persistence 5. Rock climbing 6. United States 7. Autobiographies and memoirs 8. Life stories — Sports 9. Sports and competition — Mountaineering 10. Life stories — Personal growth
LC 2023022816

World champion climber Sasha DiGiulian tells her story—from coming of age under the scrutiny of social media, navigating a male-dominated sport, and tackling her most heart-stopping climbs—and shares the power of perseverance and positivity.

"This well-written memoir combines professional rock climber DiGiulian's life story with fascinating information about an increasingly popular sport." —*Booklist*

Includes index.

Dilbeck, D. H.
Frederick Douglass: America's Prophet. D. H. Dilbeck. The University of North Carolina Press 2018. 191 p. : Illustration
ISBN 9781469636184
Grades: Adult   B
1. Douglass, Frederick, 1818-1895 2. African American abolitionists 3. Abolitionists 4. Faith (Christianity) 5. Christian life 6. Enslaved people 7. Anti-slavery movements 8. United States history 9. 19th century 10. Biographies 11. Life stories — Religion and spirituality — Personal faith 12. History writing — African American — Enslavement — United States 13. Life stories — Politics — Activists and reformers

From his enslavement to freedom, Frederick Douglass was one of America's most extraordinary champions of liberty and equality. Throughout his long life, Douglass was also a man of profound religious conviction.

"Dilbeck investigates Douglass legacy as Americas moral voice and conscience, from his teenage conversion to Christianity to his search for a church that strongly opposed slavery as stridently as he did. The result is a biography that offers an insightful new understanding of an extraordinary man." —*Booklist*

Includes bibliographical references (pages 181-198) and index.

Dillard, Annie
An American Childhood. Annie Dillard. Harper & Row 1987. 255 p. : Map
ISBN 9780060158057
Grades: Adult   B
1. Dillard, Annie 2. Growing up 3. Childhood 4. Authors, American 5. Social life and customs 6. Pittsburgh, Pennsylvania 7. 1950s 8. 20th century 9. Autobiographies and memoirs 10. Biographies 11. Family and Relationships — Growing up 12. Life stories — Relationships — Growing up
LC BL 99986231

National Book Critics Circle Award for Biography finalist, 1987.

A moving and vivid recollection of the Pulitzer Prize-winning authors childhood in Pittsburgh in the 1950s conveys the keen mind and sense of adventure with which she experienced relatives, neighbors, nature, friends, and changes.

"Dillard's luminous prose painlessly captures the pain of growing up in this wonderful evocation of childhood. The events of childhood often loom larger than life; the magic of Dillard's writing is that she sets down typical childhood happenings with their original immediacy and force." —*Publishers Weekly*

Map on lining papers.

The Writing Life. Annie Dillard. Harper & Row 1989. 111 p.
ISBN 9780060161569
Grades: Adult   B
1. Dillard, Annie 2. Authors, American 3. Social life and customs 4. United States 5. 20th century 6. Biographies 7. Arts and Entertainment — Writing and Publishing
LC 89045034

PUBLIC LIBRARY CORE COLLECTION: NONFICTION
Twentieth Edition

A best-selling, Pulizer Prize-winning author looks at her craft and, in a series of illuminating metaphors and anecdotes, paints a picture of a demanding, unpredictable, and sometimes absurd existence.

"The author probes the sorcery that levitates her own writing, discussing with clear eye and wry wit how, where and why she writes." —*Publishers Weekly*

DiMarco, Nyle
★ *Deaf Utopia: A Memoir and a Love Letter to a Way of Life.* Nyle Dimarco with Robert Siebert. William Morrow and company 2022. 288 p.
ISBN 9780063062351
Grades: Adult   B
1. DiMarco, Nyle, 1989- 2. Actors and actresses 3. Film producers and directors 4. Deaf culture 5. Social advocates 6. Italian American men 7. People who are deaf 8. Men 9. Autobiographies and memoirs 10. Life stories — Facing adversity — Medical issues — Living with disabilities 11. Family and relationships — Disabled family members 12. Life stories — Arts and culture — Performing arts 13. Arts and entertainment — General

A heartfelt and inspiring memoir and Deaf culture anthem by Nyle DiMarco, actor, producer, two-time reality show winner, and cultural icon of the international Deaf community.

"DiMarco's memoir is an eye-opening and engaging tale of what it is like to grow up in the Deaf community along with the difficult and rewarding aspects of navigating the world when everyone expects you to be able to hear everything….DiMarco's memories, told with a true gift of storytelling and filled with his big personality, are funny and enlightening for any reader." —*Library Journal*

Dochartaigh, Kerri ni
Cacophony of Bone: The Circle of a Year. Kerri ní Dochartaigh. Milkweed Editions 2023. xiii, 288 p.
ISBN 9781571311573
Grades: Adult   B
1. Dochartaigh, Kerri ni, 1983- 2. Authors, Irish 3. Couples 4. Cottages 5. Moving to a new home 6. COVID-19 Pandemic, 2020- 7. Social isolation 8. Pregnancy 9. Nature 10. Books and reading 11. Time 12. Home (Concept) 13. Western European people 14. Irish people 15. Ireland 16. Essays 17. Autobiographies and memoirs 18. Life stories — Arts and culture — Writing — Authors 19. Life stories — Relationships 20. Arts and Entertainment — Writing and Publishing
LC 2023013512

Two days after the winter solstice in 2019, Kerri and her partner moved to a remote cottage in the heart of Ireland. They were looking for a home, somewhere to settle into a stable life. Then the pandemic arrived and their secluded abode became a place of enforced isolation. What was meant to be the beginning of an enriching new chapter was instead marked by uncertainty and fear. The seasons still passed, the swallows returned, the rhythms of the natural world went on, but in many ways 2020 was unlike any year we had seen before. And for Kerri there would be one more change: a baby, longed for but utterly, beautifully unexpected.

"Dochartaigh takes readers on a yearlong journey through the unpredictable and unprecedented year of 2020…Personal, relatable, and restorative, Cacophony of Bone voices a crucial plea to have faith in humanity." —*Booklist*

Doggett, Peter
You Never Give Me Your Money: The Beatles After the Breakup. Peter Doggett. Harpercollins 2010. 320 p.
ISBN 9780061774461
Grades: Adult   B
1. Lennon, John, 1940-1980 2. McCartney, Paul 3. Harrison, George, 1943-2001 4. Starr, Ringo, 1940- 5. Rock music 6. Music history and criticism 7. Rock musicians 8. Popular culture 9. Social life and customs 10. England 11. 20th century 12. Biographies 13. Arts and Entertainment — Music — Rock 14. Life stories — Arts and culture — Performing arts — Musicians and composers

The world stopped in 1970 when Paul McCartney announced that he was through with the Beatles. His statement not only marked the end of the band's remarkable career, but also seemed to signal the demise of an era of unprecedented optimism in social history. Though the Beatles' breakup was widely viewed as a cultural tragedy, one of the most fascinating phases of their story was just about to begin. Here is the behind-the-scenes story of the personal rivalries and legal feuds that have dominated the Beatles' lives since 1969. Journalist Peter Doggett charts the Shakespearean battles between Lennon and McCartney, the conflict in George Harrison's life between spirituality and fame, and the struggle with alcoholism that threatened to take Richard Starkey's life. This is a compelling human drama and a rich and absorbing story of the Beatles' creative and financial empire, set up to safeguard their interests but destined to control their lives.

Dogon, Mondiant
Those We Throw Away Are Diamonds: A Refugee's Search for Home. Mondiant Dogon with Jenna Krajeski. Penguin Press 2021. 336 p.
ISBN 9781984881281
Grades: Adult   B
1. Dogon, Mondiant 2. Refugees, Rwandan 3. Tutsi (African people) 4. Human rights activists 5. Refugees 6. Violence 7. Refugee camps 8. Survival 9. Families 10. Autobiographies and memoirs 11. Life stories — Facing adversity — War and oppression — Refugees 12. Society and culture — Violence and crime — Genocide 13. History writing — Civil wars and genocide — Africa 14. Life stories — Politics — Activists and reformers
LC 2021004861

A Congolese author, human rights activist and refugee ambassador who has lived in refugee camps since 1996 and has faced the very worst of humanity speaks up for forever refugees everywhere, in this heartbreaking lens on the global refugee crisis.

"Human rights activist Dogon has written a searing account of the horrific violence his family endured in their native Congo, and then of living as refugees in Rwanda. . . . Those interested in international relations, immigration, and social work will find Dogon's firsthand account essential reading." —*Library Journal*

Dolby, Thomas
The Speed of Sound: Breaking the Barrier Between Music and Technology. Thomas Dolby. Flatiron Books 2016. 288 p.
ISBN 9781250071842
Grades: Adult   B
1. Dolby, Thomas 2. Composers 3. Music and technology 4. Digital music 5. Music industry and trade 6. Autobiographies and memoirs 7. Life stories — Arts and culture — Performing arts — Musicians and composers 8. Arts and entertainment — Music
LC 2016021708

The 1980s New Wave star-turned-Silicon Valley entrepreneur traces his disadvantaged early years in a London bedsit, creation of the breakout hit "She Blinded Me with Science" and role in pioneering the use of MP3s in cellphones.

"This stellar book will appeal to students, scholars, and general readers interested in modern technologys startling effects on music and popular culture." —*Kirkus*

Donald, Aida DiPace
Citizen Soldier: A Life of Harry S. Truman. Aida D. Donald. Basic Books 2012. 224 p.
ISBN 9780465031207
Grades: 9 10 11 12 Adult   B
1. Truman, Harry S, 1884-1972 2. Presidents 3. Soldiers 4. Politics and government 5. United States 6. 20th century 7. Biographies 8. History writing — Presidency — United States 9. History writing — Post World War II - 1959 — United States 10. Life stories — Politics — Politicians 11. History writing — Presidency — 20th century — United States
LC 2012025583

Depicts the life of America's 33rd president, from his impoverished start with his farming family, through enlisting in the army in 1917 and numerous failed business ventures to beginning a political career in Missouri that ultimately led to the presidency.

"With her research and historical expertise, Donald, former editor-in-chief of Harvard University Press, has succeeded in making Truman much more than a

ESSENTIAL AND RECOMMENDED TITLES
Biography

silent commander of a failed watch, into a fully formed man of sizable defects and masterful achievements." —*Publishers Weekly*
Includes bibliographical references.

Donald, David Herbert
Lincoln. David Herbert Donald. Simon & Schuster 1995. 714 p, 32 p. of plates : Illustration; Map
ISBN 9780684825359
Grades: 11 12 Adult **B**
1. Lincoln, Abraham, 1809-1865 2. Politicians 3. Civil war 4. United States Civil War, 1861-1865 5. Presidents 6. United States history 7. United States 8. 19th century 9. American Civil War era (1861-1865) 10. Biographies 11. History writing — Presidency — 19th century — United States 12. History writing — Wars and conflicts — American Civil War 13. Life stories — Law and order — Armed forces personnel 14. Life stories — Politics — Politicians
LC 95004782
ALA Notable Book, 1996; Booklist Editors' Choice, 1995.
Draws extensively on Lincoln's personal papers and legal writings to present a biography of the president.
"This biography examines: Lincoln's relationship with his father; his romance with Ann Rutledge; his bouts of hypo, which amounted at times almost to clinical depression; his marriage; his political ambition; his attitudes toward slavery and Black people; his relations with radical Republicans during the Civil War; the mistakes and successes of his wartime leadership." —*The Atlantic*
Includes bibliographical references (p. [600]-686) and index.

Dorey-Stein, Beck
From the Corner of the Oval: A Memoir. Rebecca Dorey-Stein. Random House Inc. 2018. 304 p.
ISBN 9780525509127
Grades: Adult **B**
1. Dorey-Stein, Beck 2. Stenographers 3. Office romance 4. Political culture 5. Presidential staff 6. Social life and customs 7. Politics and government 8. Washington, D.C. 9. United States 10. 21st century 11. 2000s (Decade) 12. 2010s 13. Autobiographies and memoirs 14. Life stories — Politics 15. History writing — Presidency — 21st century — United States
LC 2017053262
A behind-the-scenes memoir takes readers inside the Obama White House through the eyes of a young staffer learning the ropes, falling in love and finding her place in the world.
"Dorey-Stein relates the highs and lows of the Obama presidency intermixed with those from her personal life in a compulsively readable stylethink history lesson meets soap opera. In this poignant, brutally honest, and often-funny work of self-reflection, Dorey-Stein pulls no punches and tells all she learned from and about the president who taught me to look up." —*Booklist*

Doughty, Caitlin
Smoke Gets in Your Eyes: And Other Lessons from the Crematory. Caitlin Doughty. W. W. Norton & Company 2014. 256 p.
ISBN 9780393240238
Grades: Adult **B**
1. Doughty, Caitlin 2. Undertakers 3. Death education 4. Burial 5. Bloggers 6. Social life and customs 7. United States 8. Autobiographies and memoirs 9. Life stories — Business — Working life
LC 2014017294
Library Journal Best Books 2014; LibraryReads Favorites, 2014.
The blogger behind the popular Web series "Ask a Mortician" describes her experiences working at a crematory, including how she sometimes gets ashes on her clothes and how she cared for bodies of all shapes and sizes.
Not shying away from candid descriptions of corpses, cremation, and putrefaction, Doughty . details postmortem proceedings not to repulse but to reveal our modern society's 'Death denial.' —*Booklist*
Includes bibliographical references.

Douglas, John E.
The Killer Across the Table: Unlocking the Secrets of Serial Killers and Predators with the FBI's Original Mindhunter. John E. Douglas and Mark Olshaker. William Morrow 2019. 288 pages
ISBN 9780062910639
Grades: Adult **B**
1. Douglas, John E. 2. FBI agents 3. Criminal profiling 4. Serial murderers 5. Criminal psychology 6. Serial murder investigation 7. Psychology 8. United States 9. True Crime — Police and Lawyers 10. True Crime — Murder 11. Life stories — Law and order — Police and law officers
LC Bl2019008878
The FBI criminal profiler and inspiration for the Mindhunter series shares the stories of four of the most complex predatory killers of his career, offering previously undisclosed insights into his strategies and profiling process.
"Famous as a groundbreaking FBI criminal profiler, a prolific true-crime writer, and the catalyst for Mindhunter on Netflix, Douglas, along with coauthor Olshaker, reveals what hes discerned in the minds of notorious killers." —*Booklist*

Douglass, Frederick
My Bondage and My Freedom. Frederick Douglass; edited, with a foreword and notes, by John Stauffer. Modern Library 2003. LV, 321 p. : Illustration
ISBN 9780812970319
Grades: Adult **B**
1. Douglass, Frederick, 1818-1895 2. African American abolitionists 3. Abolitionists 4. History of anti-slavery movements 5. Freedom seekers 6. Enslaved people 7. Plantation life 8. United States history 9. Maryland 10. 19th century 11. Autobiographies and memoirs 12. Biographies 13. History writing — African American — Enslavement — United States 14. Life stories — Politics — Activists and reformers
LC 2003053976
In an autobiographical account, the great American reformer of the nineteenth century offers eyewitness insights into slavery, the anti-slavery movement, and their impact on race relations.
Originally published: New York : Miller, Orton & Mulligan, 1855; Includes bibliographical references (p. [293]-321).

Narrative of the Life of Frederick Douglass, an American Slave. Written by himself; edited with an introduction by Houston A. Baker, Jr. Penguin Books 1982. 159 p. : Portrait (The Penguin American library)
ISBN 9780140390124
Grades: Adult **B**
1. Douglass, Frederick, 1818-1895 2. Abolitionists 3. African American abolitionists 4. Life stories — Identity — Race and ethnicity 5. History writing — Antebellum America — United States
LC 82005371
The autobiography of the famous abolitionist and statesman who escaped to the North after twenty-one years of enslavement.
Portrait on lining paper; Bibliography: P. 25-27.

Downey, Kirstin
Isabella: The Warrior Queen. Kirstin Downey. Nan A. Talese/Doubleday 2014. 480 p.
ISBN 9780385534116
Grades: Adult **B**
1. Isabella I, Queen of Spain, 1451-1504 2. Women politicians 3. Christian women 4. Women 5. International relations 6. Inquisition 7. Women rulers 8. Religious life 9. Determination 10. Spanish history 11. Spain 12. 15th century 13. Renaissance (1300-1600) 14. Age of exploration (1419-1610) 15. Biographies 16. History writing — Renaissance — Europe 17. History writing — Europe — Spain 18. Life stories — Politics — Royalty 19. History writing — Women's history
LC 2014003895
Drawing on new scholarship, the Pulitzer Prize-winning author of the Woman Behind the New Deal presents a biography of Isabella of Castile, the controversial Queen of Spain who sponsored Christopher Columbus' journey to

the New World, established the Spanish Inquisition and became one of the most influential female rulers in history.

"As one of the most influential political players of the transitional era bridging the Middle Ages and the Renaissance, Isabella has earned her place in the spotlight." —*Booklist*

Includes bibliographical references and index.

Doyle, Glennon
Untamed. Dial Press 2020. 320 p.
ISBN 9781984801258
Grades: Adult   B

1. Doyle, Glennon, 1976- 2. Self-fulfillment 3. Personal conduct 4. Married women 5. Divorced women 6. Christian women 7. Blended families 8. Lesbians 9. White privilege 10. Women-women relations 11. Self-discovery 12. Independence 13. Autobiographies and memoirs 14. Life stories — Relationships 15. Book club best bets

LC 2019047945

An activist, speaker and philanthropist offers a memoir wrapped in a wake-up call that reveals how women can reclaim their true, untamed selves by breaking free of the restrictive expectations and cultural conditioning that leaves them feeling dissatisfied and lost.

"This testament to female empowerment and self-love, with an endearing coming-out story at the center, will delight readers." —*Publishers Weekly*

Doyne, Maggie
Between the Mountain and the Sky: A Mother's Story of Love, Loss, Healing, and Hope. Maggie Doyne. HarperHorizon 2022. 272 p.
ISBN 9780785240280
Grades: Adult   B

1. Doyne, Maggie 2. Women philanthropists 3. Orphanages 4. Foundations 5. Love 6. Adoption 7. Loss 8. Charities 9. Children 10. Healing 11. Hope 12. Philanthropy 13. NEPAL 14. Autobiographies and memoirs 15. Life stories — Politics — Activists and reformers 16. Life stories — Personal growth 17. Family and relationships — General

Between the Mountain and the Sky tells the story of Maggie Doyne's amazing journey from carefree New Jersey teen to mother of over fifty NEPAlese children by the age of thirty.

Doyne, founder of Kopila Valley Children's Home, traces in this affecting work the extraordinary decade in which she 'Moved to NEPAl, built a house, raised fifty-four children…and experienced the wildest love imaginable.' —*Publishers Weekly*

Drape, Joe
Black Maestro: The Epic Life of an American Legend. Joe Drape. Morrow 2006. 280 p.
ISBN 9780060537296
Grades: Adult   B

1. Winkfield, Jimmy, 1882-1974 2. African American jockeys 3. Jockeys 4. Horse racing 5. Social life and customs 6. Europe 7. United States 8. 20th century 9. Biographies 10. Sports and Competition — Racing — Horses 11. Sports and Competition — Individual Athlete 12. Life stories — Sports — Athletes

Presents the life of African-American jockey Jimmy Winkfield, who after winning the Kentucky Derby, emigrated to Europe and became a wealthy horse racer and trainer in Russia and France, until forced by circumstance to return to America and racial discrimination.

Dregni, Michael
Django: The Life and Music of a Gypsy Legend. Michael Dregni. Oxford University Press 2004. 326 p. : Illustration
ISBN 9780195167528
Grades: Adult   B

1. Reinhardt, Django, 1910-1953 2. Guitarists 3. Jazz musicians 4. Romanies 5. Music history and criticism 6. Jazz music 7. Biographies 8. Arts and Entertainment — Music — Jazz and the Blues 9. Life stories — Arts and culture — Performing arts — Musicians and composers 10. Life stories — Facing adversity — Personal transformation

LC 2004006214

The first major critical biography of the great jazz musician chronicles the colorful life of guitarist Django Reinhardt, including his long musical relationship with violinist Stephane Grapelli and his wanderings around Europe and the United States.

"This biography does its complex subject justice. And even when Dregni dallies overlong on some byways, his immersion in the period's history enriches his storytelling and our understanding. The panoramic results present Django Reinhardt as he has never been seen." —*New York Times Book Review*

Includes bibliographical references (p. [279]-315) and index.

Dresner, Amy
My Fair Junkie: A Memoir of Getting Dirty and Staying Clean. Amy Dresner. Hachette Books 2017. 240 p.
ISBN 9780316430951
Grades: Adult   B

1. Dresner, Amy 2. Drug addicts 3. Women drug abusers 4. Addiction 5. Alcoholic women 6. Women stand-up comedians 7. Rehabilitation 8. Community service (Punishment) 9. California 10. Autobiographies and memoirs 11. Life stories — Facing adversity — Medical issues — Addiction

LC 2017016499

A former stand-up comic and prolific online writer chronicles her 20-year battle with sex, drug and alcohol addiction, and what happened when she finally emerged on the other side.

"Dresner brings humility, wit, and sensitivity to a topic many readers are unfamiliar with, and those that are will recognize her truths." —*Booklist*

Driver, Minnie
Managing Expectations: A Memoir in Essays. Minnie Driver. HarperOne 2022. 352 p.
ISBN 9780063115309
Grades: Adult   B

1. Driver, Minnie 2. Actors and actresses 3. Growing up 4. Children of divorced parents 5. Ambition 6. Fame 7. Motherhood 8. Loss 9. Self-discovery 10. Autobiographies and memoirs 11. Essays 12. Life stories — Arts and culture — Performing arts — Actors and actresses 13. Arts and Entertainment — Movies and Television

In this intimate, beautifully crafted collection, Driver writes with disarming charm, candor, razor-sharp humor and grace as she explores navigating the depths of failure, fighting for success, discovering the unmatched wonder and challenge of motherhood, and wading through immeasurable grief. Effortlessly charming, deeply funny, personal, and honest, Managing Expectations reminds us of the way life works out—even when it doesn't.

A memoir in essays from actor Minnie Driver, chronicling the way life works out even when it doesn't.

"The veteran actor delivers a memoir in a series of deftly crafted essays. In her debut, Driver engagingly writes about family dramas, self-doubt, her unruly hair, unexpected motherhood, and the trajectory of her career." —*Kirkus*

Drury, Bob
Blood and Treasure: Daniel Boone and the Fight for America's First Frontier. Bob Drury and Tom Clavin. St. Martin's Press 2021. 336 p.
ISBN 9781250247131
Grades: Adult   B

1. Boone, Daniel, 1734-1820 2. Pioneers 3. Explorers 4. Indigenous peoples of North America — Wars 5. Frontier and pioneer life 6. Territorial expansion 7. United States history 8. United States 9. Kentucky 10. 18th century 11. Revolutionary America (1775-1783) 12. Biographies 13. Life stories — People in history — Pioneers 14. History writing — United States

LC 2020048552

A narrative account of the life of historical frontiersman Daniel Boone goes beyond pop-culture depictions to offer insight into his Revolutionary War heroism and nation-shaping achievements as witnessed by 18th-century colonists and Native Americans. Map(s).

ESSENTIAL AND RECOMMENDED TITLES
Biography

"Popular historians Drury and Clavin deliver a ripsnortin' tale of the early frontier and its first and most powerful legend. . . . A well-written, fast-paced account that neatly bridges the gap between historical fact and fiction." —*Kirkus*
Includes bibliographical references and index.

The Heart of Everything That Is: The Untold Story of Red Cloud, an American Legend. Bob Drury and Tom Clavin. Simon & Schuster 2013. 400 p.
ISBN 9781451654660
Grades: Adult   **B**
1. Red Cloud, 1822-1909 2. Oglala (North American people) 3. Red Cloud's War, 1866-1867 4. Government relations with indigenous peoples 5. Indigenous peoples of North America 6. 19th century 7. Biographies 8. History writing — Indigenous peoples — United States 9. History writing — Wars and conflicts — American Indigenous Wars 10. Life stories — People in history — Indigenous peoples
LC 2013003200

Draws on Red Cloud's autobiography, which was lost for nearly a hundred years, to present the story of the great Oglala Sioux chief who was the only Plains Indian to defeat the United States Army in a war.

"The authors offer a battle-and-skirmish account of Sioux leader Red Cloud's war on the whites who invaded the Great Plains, though their narrative is strong on ethnohistorical matters as well. A well-researched and -written account of an often overlooked figure in the history of the Indian Wars." —*Kirkus*

Lucky 666: The Impossible Mission. by Bob Drury and Tom Clavin. Simon & Schuster 2016. 352 p.
ISBN 9781476774855
Grades: Adult   **B**
1. Zeamer, Jay, Jr, 1918-2007 2. Bomber pilots 3. B-17 bomber 4. World War II 5. Aerial operations 6. Biographies 7. Life stories — Law and order — Armed forces personnel 8. History writing — Wars and conflicts — World War II — Pacific Theater 9. Nonfiction that reads like fiction
LC 2016017924

The authors of the #1 New York Times best-selling the Heart of Everything That Is traces the lesser-known story of a daredevil bomber pilot and his misfit crew who in 1943 engaged the Japanese in what became history's longest dogfight, changing the course of the war through their heroic acts of sacrifice.

"Drury and Clavin offer a vivid slice of war history that WWII buffs and anyone who admires true acts of heroism will find riveting." —*Booklist*
Includes bibliographical references and index.

Duberman, Martin B.

Andrea Dworkin: The Feminist as Revolutionary. Martin Duberman. The New Press 2020. 384 p.
ISBN 9781620975855
Grades: Adult   **B**
1. Dworkin, Andrea 2. Feminists 3. Women authors 4. Women radicals 5. Feminism 6. United States 7. Life stories — Arts and culture — Writing — Authors 8. Life stories — Politics — Activists and reformers 9. Arts and entertainment — Writing and publishing
LC 2020010657

Fifteen years after her death, Andrea Dworkin remains one of the most important and challenging figures in second-wave feminism. Although frequently relegated to its more radical fringes, Dworkin was without doubt a formidable and influential writer, a philosopher, and an activist-a brilliant figure who inspired and infuriated in equal measure.

"A sympathetic, cleareyed portrait that gives Dworkin her due without smoothing over her rough edges." —*Kirkus*
Includes bibliographical references and index.

Howard Zinn: A Life on the Left. Martin Duberman. New Press : 2012. 352 p.
ISBN 9781595586780
Grades: Adult   **B**
1. Zinn, Howard, 1922-2010 2. Historians 3. Political activists 4. Radicals 5. Biographies 6. Life stories — Politics — Activists and reformers
LC 2012017592

A portrait of the life and achievements of the progressive activist, author, and teacher examines his roles as an anti-war veteran, an iconic contributor to the civil rights movement, and dedicated white professor at a historically Black college.
Includes bibliographical references and index.

Dubus, Andre

Townie: A Memoir. Andre Dubus III.. W. W. Norton & Co. 2011. 352 p.
ISBN 9780393064667
Grades: 11 12 Adult   **B**
1. Dubus, Andre, III, 1959- 2. Violence 3. Growing up 4. Boxers (Sports) 5. Small town life 6. Fathers and sons 7. Writing 8. Authors, American 9. 20th century 10. Autobiographies and memoirs 11. Biographies 12. Arts and Entertainment — Writing and Publishing 13. Life stories — Facing adversity 14. Adult books for young adults
LC 2010038029
Library Journal Best Books, 2011.

Acclaimed author Andre Dubus III looks back on the dangerous path he began to take following his parents' split. Once known for his ability to speak with his fists, he shares how he turned his life around.

Duckworth, Tammy

Every Day Is a Gift. Tammy Duckworth. Twelve 2021. 320 p.
ISBN 9781538718506
Grades: Adult   **B**
1. Duckworth, Tammy, 1968- 2. Women senators 3. Iraq War veterans 4. Women politicians 5. Multiracial women 6. Thai Americans 7. Growing up 8. Politicians 9. People with disabilities 10. Patriotism 11. Veterans 12. Southeast Asian Americans 13. Southeast Asian people 14. Politics and government 15. United States 16. Autobiographies and memoirs 17. Life stories — Politics — Politicians

The U.S. senator and Iraq War veteran Tammy Duckworth presents her incredible story.

"With a breezy candor that is, by turns, intimate and assertive, Duckworth offers an affecting account of a life of sacrifice, patriotism, valor, integrity, and grace." —*Booklist*

Duggar, Jill

Counting the Cost: A Memoir. Jill Duggar, with Derick Dillard and Craig Borlase. Gallery Books 2023. 271 p.
ISBN 9781668024447
Grades: Adult   **B**
1. Duggar, Jill 2. Dillard, Derick 3. Husband and wife 4. Christian couples 5. Fame 6. Television personalities 7. Reality television programs 8. Extended families 9. Parenthood 10. Dysfunctional families 11. Family secrets 12. Honesty 13. Faith (Christianity) 14. North American people 15. American people 16. Collective autobiographies and memoirs 17. Life stories — Arts and culture — Performing arts — Entertainers and celebrities 18. Life stories — Religion and spirituality — Spiritual journeys 19. Arts and Entertainment — Movies and Television

For the first time, discover the unedited truth about the Duggars, the traditional Christian family that captivated the nation on TLC's hit show 19 Kids and Counting, as they share their story, revealing the secrets, manipulation, and intimidation behind the show that remained hidden from their fans.

Duiker, William J.

Ho Chi Minh. William J. Duiker. Hyperion 2000. xix, 695 p, 32 p. of plates : Illustration; Map
ISBN 9780786863877
Grades: 11 12 Adult   **B**
1. Ho, Chi Minh, 1890-1969 2. Vietnam War, 1961-1975 3. Communism 4. Political leadership 5. Politicians 6. Colonialism 7. Nationalism 8. Presidents 9. Politics and government 10. Vietnam 11. 20th century 12. Biographies 13. History writing — Wars and conflicts — Vietnam War 14. Life stories — Politics — Politicians 15. History writing — Asia — Southeast Asia
LC 00026757
Booklist Editors' Choice, 2000; New York Times Notable Book, 2000.

Describes Ho Chi Minh's poverty-stricken youth, his expatriate years in the U.S, France, and the Soviet Union, and his commitment to the Vietnamese revolution and reunification of Vietnam under Communist rule.

"In this biography the author examines Ho's life primarily in the context of his political activity in Paris, Moscow, southern China, and Vietnam, occasionally spiced with anecdotes of Ho's highly secretive personal life.... Duiker handles the complicated political and diplomatic issues with ease, and his narrative, though it sometimes strays from Ho's life to fill in the bigger picture, never bogs down." —*Booklist*

Map of Southeast Asia and Pacific Ocean on endpapers; Includes bibliographical references (p. [581]-670) and index.

Dunaway, David King
★ *How Can I Keep from Singing?: The Ballad of Pete Seeger*. David King Dunaway. Villard 2008. 560p.

ISBN 9780345506085

Grades: Adult **B**

1. Seeger, Pete, 1919-2014 2. Folk singers 3. Folk music, American 4. Biographies 5. Arts and Entertainment — Music — Folk 6. Life stories — Arts and culture — Performing arts — Musicians and composers

LC 2007041814

Seeger's private papers and numerous interviews with his friends, family, and fellow musicians provide material for a newly revised, detailed portrait of the famous folk singer, tracing his career and influence as a singer, surveying his political development, and including never-before-published photographs from the singer's archives.

"The focus of Seeger's life has been on using music as a force for social change. But he is perhaps best known as the major banjo-playing folksinger who pioneered the folk music revival that flowered in the 1960s. This excellent book provides a well-written and extensively researched account, not only of Seeger's life, but also of the social and political movements of the times in which he lived. An extensive bibliography and discography add to the book's usefulness." —*Library Journal*

Includes bibliographical references (p.), discography (p.), and index.

Dunbar, Erica Armstrong
★ *Never Caught: The Washingtons' Relentless Pursuit of Their Runaway Slave, Ona Judge*. Erica Armstrong Dunbar. 37 INK 2017. 256 pages

ISBN 9781501126390

Grades: Adult **B**

1. Washington, George, 1732-1799 2. Judge, Oney, 1773-1848 3. Washington, Martha, 1731-1802 4. African American history 5. Freedom seekers 6. Slavery 7. Injustice 8. Enslaved women 9. Presidents 10. Southern States history 11. Mount Vernon 12. Philadelphia, Pennsylvania 13. United States 14. Early America (1784-1819) 15. 18th century 16. History writing — African American — Enslavement — United States 17. History writing — Presidency — 18th century — United States 18. History writing — Early America — United States 19. Adult books for young adults

LC 2017932249

National Book Award for Nonfiction finalist, 2017.

A revelatory account of the actions taken by the first president to retain his slaves in spite of Northern laws profiles one of the slaves, Ona Judge, describing the intense manhunt that ensued when she ran away.

"A startling, well-researched slave narrative that seriously questions the intentions of our first president." —*Kirkus*

★ *She Came to Slay: The Life and Times of Harriet Tubman*. Erica Armstrong Dunbar. Simon & Schuster 2019. xiv, 157 pages

ISBN 9781982139599

Grades: Adult **B**

1. Tubman, Harriet, 1820?-1913 2. African American women abolitionists 3. Underground Railroad 4. Women spies 5. Suffragists 6. Freedom seekers 7. Enslaved people 8. History of anti-slavery movements 9. African American women 10. Courage 11. United States history 12. 19th century 13. Biographies 14. History writing — African American — Enslavement — United States 15. Life stories — Politics — Activists and reformers 16. Life stories — Facing adversity — War and oppression — Enslaved people 17. History writing — Women's history 18. Adult books for young adults

Rise: A Feminist Book Project List, 2021.

A lively, informative and illustrated tribute to one of the most exceptional women in American history—Harriet Tubman—looks at a heroine whose fearlessness and activism still resonates today.

"With illustrations and catchy asides enhancing the conversational style, this smoothly readable narrative tells a story kept alive through oral tradition for decades. Perfect for Tubman novices but also enjoyable historical reading for those who already know most of the stories." —*Kirkus*

Duncan, Isadora
My Life. by Isadora Duncan. Liveright 1972. 359 p, 10 leaves of plates : Illustration

ISBN 9780871409423

Grades: Adult **B**

1. Duncan, Isadora, 1877-1927 2. Dancers 3. Modern dance 4. Choreographers 5. Choreography 6. Dancing 7. Flamboyance (Personal quality) 8. Women 9. Sexuality 10. Autobiographies and memoirs 11. Arts and Entertainment — Dance 12. Life stories — Arts and culture — Performing arts — Dancers and choreographers

LC 78102483

The famous dancer and choreographer tells the story of her life, from her enchantment with music and poetry to her love affairs and personal tragedies.

Duncan, Michael
★ *Hero of Two Worlds: The Marquis De Lafayette in the Age of Revolution*. Mike Duncan. PublicAffairs 2021. 512 p.

ISBN 9781541730335

Grades: Adult **B**

1. Lafayette, Marie Joseph Paul Yves Roch Gilbert Du Motier, marquis de, 1757-1834 2. Generals 3. Politicians 4. French participation in wars 5. United States history 6. French history 7. Revolutionary America (1775-1783) 8. Revolutionary France (1789-1799) 9. Biographies 10. History writing — Wars and conflicts — Revolutionary War (America) 11. Life stories — Law and order — Military leaders 12. History writing — Europe — France

LC 2021005452

From the massively popular podcaster and New York Times bestselling author comes the story of the Marquis de Lafayette's lifelong quest to protect the principles of democracy, told through the lens of the three revolutions he participated in: the American Revolution, the French Revolution, and the Revolution of 1830.

"Best-selling author (The Storm Before the Storm) and podcast host (The History of Rome) Duncan reintroduces a celebrated hero whose name may be common knowledge but whose life story is not.... A highly readable biography of a committed liberal activist caught up in the fickle political passions of revolutionary extremism, violence, and war." —*Library Journal*

Includes bibliographical references and index.

Dunn, Harry
Standing My Ground: A Capitol Police Officer's Fight for Accountability and Good Trouble After January 6th. Harry Dunn with Ron Harris. Hachette Books 2023. IX, 244 p.

ISBN 9780306831133

Grades: Adult **B**

1. Dunn, Harry (Police officer) 2. Police 3. African American men 4. Capitol Riot, Washington, D.C, 2021 5. Presidential election, 2020 6. Insurgency 7. Democracy 8. First responders 9. Psychic trauma 10. Politics and government 11. North American people 12. American people 13. United States 14. Autobiographies and memoirs 15. Life stories — Law and order — Police and law officers 16. Life stories — Facing adversity — Victims of crime — Terrorism 17. Politics and global affairs — National security

LC 2023024764

A Capitol Police Officer on duty January 6th provides a firsthand account of the events that unfolded in the White House, becoming one of the most prominent and essential voices regarding the truth of that day and providing a backdrop for examining the political and racial divide in this country.

ESSENTIAL AND RECOMMENDED TITLES
Biography

Dunnavant, Keith
Montana: The Biography of Football's Joe Cool. Keith Dunnavant. Thomas Dunne Books 2015. 352 p.
ISBN 9781250017840
Grades: Adult **B**
1. Montana, Joe, 1956- 2. Quarterbacks (Football) 3. Football 4. Football players 5. United States 6. Biographies 7. Life stories — Sports — Athletes 8. Sports and Competition — Football
LC 2015019171

A portrait of the three-time Superbowl MVP and Pro Football Hall of Famer traces his career against a backdrop of late-20th-century America, from his working class childhood in Pennsylvania and years at Notre Dame through his remarkable achievements in San Francisco and beyond.

"Well written and researched, this title will be of interest to a wide range of sports fans." —*Library Journal*

Dunne, Griffin
★ *The Friday Afternoon Club: A Family Memoir.* Griffin Dunne. Penguin Press 2024. 400 p.
ISBN 9780593652824
Grades: Adult **B**
1. Dunne, Griffin 2. Actors and actresses 3. Families 4. Family relationships 5. Celebrities 6. Growing up 7. Childhood 8. American people 9. Autobiographies and memoirs 10. Book club best bets 11. Life stories — Relationships — Family 12. Family and relationships — Families 13. Family and relationships — Growing up 14. Life stories — Arts and culture — Performing arts — Actors and actresses
LC 2023030129

A memoir and coming-of-age story chronicling the successes and disappointments, wit and wildness of Dunne and his multigenerational family of larger-than-life characters.

"After Hours actor Griffin recounts in his bittersweet debut how movies, madness, and murder have touched his celebrated American family." —*Publishers Weekly*

Duran, Elvis
Where Do I Begin?: Stories from a Life Lived Out Loud. Elvis Duran. Atria Books 2019. 288 pages
ISBN 9781982106331
Grades: Adult **B**
1. Duran, Elvis 2. Radio personalities 3. Radio programs 4. Gay men 5. Radio talk shows 6. Radio broadcasters 7. Radio industry and trade 8. Drug use 9. Autobiographies and memoirs 10. Life stories — Arts and culture — Performing arts — Entertainers and celebrities 11. Arts and Entertainment — Radio

The host of one of the nation's top morning shows, and the voice millions of Americans wake up to, shares his wildest stories and hardest-learned lessons, all with his trademark heart, honesty and humor.

Dykstra, Lenny
House of Nails: A Memoir of Life on the Edge. Lenny Dykstra; with Peter Golenbock. William Morrow 2016. 352 p.
ISBN 9780062407368
Grades: Adult **B**
1. Dykstra, Lenny, 1963- 2. Professional baseball players 3. Professional baseball 4. Drug addiction 5. Redemption 6. Steroids 7. Businesspeople 8. Former convicts 9. California 10. Autobiographies and memoirs 11. Sports and Competition — Baseball 12. Sports and Competition — Individual Athlete 13. Life stories — Sports — Athletes
LC 2017304573

Nicknamed "Nails" for his hustle and grit, Dykstra was named to three All-Star teams and played in two of the most memorable World Series of the modern era. After retiring he became a business mogul and investment guru. Now he tells all about his tumultuous career, from battling through crippling pain to steroid use and drug addiction, to a life of indulgence and excess, then an epic plunge and the long road back to redemption.

"Dykstra makes no apologies, offering 'The real truth,' but readers' opinions of him will be harsh." —*Kirkus*

Dylan, Bob
Chronicles; Volume 1. Bob Dylan. Simon & Schuster 2004. 304 p. : Illustration
ISBN 9780743228152
Grades: Adult **B**
1. Dylan, Bob, 1941- 2. Folk musicians 3. Folk music 4. Singers 5. United States 6. Autobiographies and memoirs 7. Biographies 8. Life stories — Arts and culture — Performing arts — Musicians and composers 9. Arts and Entertainment — Music — Folk
LC 2004056454

New York Times Notable Book, 2004; National Book Critics Circle Award for Biography finalist, 2004.

Building on the success of Bob Dylan in His Own Words, an autobiographical portrait of the acclaimed musical performer recounts personal and professional experiences and features black-and-white photography.

"This book will stand as a record of a young man's self-education, as contagious in its frank excitement as the letters of John Keats and as sincere in its ramble as Jack Kerouacs on the Road, to which Dylan frequently refers. A person of Dylans stature could have gotten away with far less; that he has been so thoughtful in the creation of this book is a measure of his talents, and a gift to his fans." —*Publishers Weekly*

Dyson, Freeman J.
Maker of Patterns: An Autobiography Through Letters. Freeman Dyson. Liveright Publishing 2018. 320 p.
ISBN 9780871403865
Grades: Adult **B**
1. Dyson, Freeman J. 2. Physicists 3. Scientific discoveries 4. Quantum theory 5. Scientists 6. Theories 7. Modern history 8. 20th century 9. Letters 10. Autobiographies and memoirs 11. Life stories — Science, technology, and medicine — Scientists and inventors 12. History writing — Science, technology, and medicine
LC 2017055725

The nonagenarian theoretical physicist and author of Disturbing the Universe presents a collection of letters written over a 40-year period that trace his life and the work of leading intellectuals, including J. Robert Oppenheimer, Richard Feynman and Steven Hawking, against a backdrop of the 20th century's major scientific advances.

"Who but Dyson formulates revolutionary physics while riding on a Greyhound bus through Iowa cornfields? in other episodes in this remarkable epistolary autobiography, readers join Dyson as he assesses with Godel equations for a rotating version of Einsteins universe, as he defends Feynmans quantum theorems against Oppenheimers doubts, and as he explores with Bohr the prospects for a nuclear spaceship." —*Booklist*

Dyson, Michael Eric
Holler If You Hear Me: Searching for Tupac Shakur. Michael Eric Dyson. Basic Civitas Books 2006. 292 p. : Illustration
ISBN 9780465017287
Grades: 11 12 Adult **B**
1. Shakur, Tupac, 1971-1996 2. Rap musicians 3. United States 4. Biographies 5. Arts and Entertainment — Music — Rap and R&B
LC Bl2006028334

Explores the legacy of rap artist Tupac Shakur, arguing that his icon status as the "Black James Dean" is an enduring one.

"Dyson's discussion goes beyond slogans and poses to the actualities of thug life and the consequences of Shakur's passions and allegiances. Piquant and analytical." —*Booklist*

Includes bibliographical references (p. [272]-285) and index; Originally published: C2001. With a new pref. by the author.

Eade, Philip
Evelyn Waugh: *A Life Revisited.* Philip Eade. Henry Holt and Co. 2016. 432 p.

ISBN 9780805097603

Grades: Adult   **B**

1. Waugh, Evelyn, 1903-1966 2. Homosexuality 3. Family relationships 4. Nervous breakdown 5. Authors, English 6. 20th century 7. Biographies 8. Life stories — Arts and culture — Writing — Authors

LC 2016019839

Marking a half-century since the English author's death, this biography sheds new light on his difficult relationship with his overly-sentimental father; his exploration of homosexuality at Oxford; and his disastrous first marriage, checkered military career and extreme nervous breakdown.

"Eade offers up a softer portrait of Waugh that might help bring him some new readers, which he deserves." —*Kirkus*

Includes bibliographical references and index.

Ebersol, Dick
From Saturday Night to Sunday Night: My Forty Years of Laughter, Tears, and Touchdowns in TV. Dick Ebersol. Simon & Schuster 2022. 288 p.

ISBN 9781982194468

Grades: Adult   **B**

1. Television producers and directors 2. Television industry and trade 3. Sports journalism 4. Olympic games 5. Television comedies 6. Autobiographies and memoirs 7. Life stories — Arts and culture — Performing arts — Directors and producers

A memoir by the legendary television executive detailing his pioneering work on Saturday Night Live, Sunday Night Football, the Olympics, the NBA, music videos, late night, and more.

"NBC sports producer Ebersol reminisces on an extraordinary career in his thoroughly entertaining debut....Told with grace and heart, this is an exhilarating outing for any sports fan." —*Publishers Weekly*

Ebert, Roger
Life Itself: *A Memoir.* Roger Ebert. Grand Central Pub. 2011. 352 p.

ISBN 9780446584975

Grades: Adult   **B**

1. Ebert, Roger 2. Critics 3. Celebrities 4. Journalism 5. Alcoholism 6. Friendship 7. Film history and criticism 8. Social life and customs 9. United States 10. 21st century 11. 20th century 12. Autobiographies and memoirs 13. Page to screen 14. Life stories — Arts and culture — Writing — Journalists

LC 2011022442

Roger Ebert has been reviewing films since 1967. The first film critic ever to win a Pulitzer Prize, he has been a fixture on television for over 30 years. Then, complications from thyroid-cancer treatment resulted in the loss of his ability to eat, drink, or speak. But with the loss of his voice, Ebert has only become a more prolific and influential writer. And now, for the first time, he tells the full, dramatic story of his life and career.

"Ebert illuminates and assesses his life with the same insight and clarity that mark his acclaimed movie reviews." —*Booklist*

This biography was made into a film under the same name in 2014, directed by Steve James.

Scorsese by Ebert. Roger Ebert; foreword by Martin Scorsese. University of Chicago Press 2010. 297 p.

ISBN 9780226182032

Grades: Adult   **B**

1. Scorsese, Martin, 1942- 2. Film industry and trade 3. Films, American 4. Film producers and directors 5. Film history and criticism 6. United States history 7. United States 8. 20th century 9. Biographies 10. Arts and Entertainment — Movies and Television

A first record of America's most respected film critic's engagement with the works of one of America's greatest living directors chronicles every single feature film in Martin Scorsese's considerable oeuvre and explores the different phases of his development and the abiding themes.

"This book is proof that the greatest criticism is simply careful and educated observation that connects a filmmaker with his subject, his audience, and his time. Ebert is one of the most acclaimed and perceptive critics of his time, and this unique book is an invaluable study in the canon of both film and criticism." —*Library Journal*

Eckert, Allan W.
A Sorrow in Our Heart: The Life of Tecumseh. Allan W. Eckert. Bantam Books 1993. xv, 1068 p. : Map

ISBN 9780553561746

Grades: Adult   **B**

1. Tecumseh, Shawnee chief, 1768-1813 2. Indigenous peoples of North America — Wars 3. Indigenous peoples of North America — History 4. Shawnee (North American people) 5. 18th century 6. 19th century 7. Biographies 8. History writing — Indigenous peoples — United States

LC BL 99752181

A biography of the Shawnee leader describes his vision to unite North American tribes into one Indian nation capable of forcing back the encroaching white settlers.

A biography of the Shawnee leader describes his vision to unite North American tribes into one powerful Indian nation capable of forcing back the encroaching white settlers and his attempts to do so.

Includes bibliographical references (p. [1010]-1051) and index; Reprint. Originally published: 1992.

Edmonds, Chris
No Surrender: A Father, a Son, and an Extraordinary Act of Heroism That Continues to Live on Today. Chris Edmonds, Douglas Century. HarperCollins 2019. 304 p.

ISBN 9780062905017

Grades: Adult   **B**

1. Edmonds, Roddie (Roderick Waring), 1919-1985 2. Righteous Gentiles in the Holocaust 3. World War II 4. War crimes 5. Prisoners of war 6. Prisons 7. Jewish people 8. Interethnic relations 9. Germany 10. Biographies 11. Life stories — Facing adversity — War and oppression — Holocaust 12. History writing — Wars and conflicts — Holocaust — World War II

LC 2019020974

The Piney Grove Baptist Church senior pastor documents the true story of his father, a devout Christian who risked his life to protect hundreds of Jewish-American GIs who were brutally targeted by the Nazis.

"A you-are-there portrait of the horrors of war and the incredible effect one selfless person can have on hundreds." —*Kirkus*

Includes bibliographical references.

Edmundson, Mark
Why Football Matters: My Education in the Game. Mark Edmundson. The Penguin Press 2014. 240 p.

ISBN 9781594205750

Grades: Adult   **B**

1. Edmundson, Mark, 1952- 2. Football 3. Character 4. Masculinity 5. Courage 6. Fathers and sons 7. Football players 8. United States 9. Autobiographies and memoirs 10. Biographies 11. Sports and competition — Football 12. Life stories — Sports 13. Life stories — Relationships — Growing up

LC 2014009726

An acclaimed essayist and author of Why Read? uses his own rite of passage as a high school football player to showcase larger truths about the ways America's game shapes its men.

"Beautifully written and impressively thought out, this smart memoir should appeal to a wide audience." —*Library Journal*

Edstrom, Erik
Un-american: A Soldier's Reckoning of Our Longest War. Erik Edstrom. Bloomsbury Publishing 2020. 304 p.

ISBN 9781635573749

Grades: Adult   **B**

1. Edstrom, Erik 2. Soldiers 3. Afghan War veterans 4. Conscientious objectors 5. Afghan War, 2001-2021 6. Infantry 7. Terrorism prevention 8. Military-industrial complex 9. War on Terrorism, 2001-2009 10. Military policy

ESSENTIAL AND RECOMMENDED TITLES
Biography

11. Asian history 12. United States 13. Afghanistan 14. Autobiographies and memoirs 15. Life stories — Law and order — Armed forces personnel 16. Life stories — Politics — Activists and reformers 17. Politics and global affairs — World politics — United States 18. Life stories — Facing adversity — War and oppression — War survivors 19. History writing — Wars and conflicts — War in Afghanistan

LC 2019055362

Before engaging in war, Erik Edstrom asks us to imagine three rarely imagined scenarios: First, imagine your own death. Second, imagine war from "the other side." Third: Imagine what might have been if the war had never been fought. Pursuing these realities through his own combat experience, Erik reaches the unavoidable conclusion about America at war. Un-American is a hybrid of social commentary and memoir that exposes how blind support for war exacerbates the problems it's intended to resolve, devastates the people allegedly being helped, and diverts assets from far larger threats like climate change. Un-American is a revolutionary act, offering a blueprint for redressing America's relationship with patriotism, the military, and military spending.

"An insider's you-are-there look at modern war. Veterans will love it or hate it, but there will be few in between." —*Kirkus*

Edwards, Anne
Matriarch: Queen Mary and the House of Windsor. Anne Edwards. W. Morrow 1984. 527 p, 32 p. of plates : Illustration
ISBN 9780688035112
Grades: Adult   B

1. Mary, Queen, consort of George V, King of Great Britain, 1867-1953 2. Windsor, House of 3. Royal houses 4. Women rulers 5. British history 6. Great Britain 7. 20th century 8. Biographies 9. History writing — Europe — United Kingdom 10. Life stories — Politics — Royalty 11. Life stories — Politics — Politicians 12. Life stories — People in history — Famous families

LC 84060447

The life of Princess May of Teck is one of the great Cinderella stories in history. From a family of impoverished nobility, she was chosen by Queen Victoria as the bride for her eldest grandson, the scandalous Duke of Clarence, heir to the throne, who died mysteriously before their marriage. Despite this setback, she became queen, mother of two kings, grandmother of the current queen, and a lasting symbol of the majesty of the British throne.

Chronicles the life of Princess May of Teck, from her selection as bride for the Duke of Clarence to her rise to queen and mother of two kings.

Includes bibliographical refernces (p.[495]-508) and index.

Edwards, Bob
Edward R. Murrow and the Birth of Broadcast Journalism. Bob Edwards. Wiley 2004. xiii, 174 p.
ISBN 9780471477532
Grades: 11 12 Adult   B

1. Murrow, Edward R, 1908-1965 2. War correspondents 3. Broadcasting 4. Journalism 5. Journalists 6. Social life and customs 7. United States 8. Second World War era (1939-1945) 9. 20th century 10. Biographies 11. Arts and Entertainment — Movies and Television 12. Life stories — Arts and culture — Writing — Journalists

LC 2003021223

An account of one of the most important names in twentieth-century journalism examines Murrow's role in pioneering broadcast media, the famous stories that he covered, and his influential career, as well as evaluating the decline of broadcast news since the 1980s.

"Edwards brings to life the early days of radio and television and the innovations that Murrow sparked.... Readers interested in journalism will enjoy this slim book." —*Booklist*

Includes bibliographical references (p. 167-168) and index.

Egan, Timothy
★ *The Immortal Irishman: The Irish Revolutionary Who Became an American Hero.* Timothy Egan. Houghton Mifflin Harcourt 2016. 384 p.
ISBN 9780544272880
Grades: Adult   B

1. Meagher, Thomas Francis, 1823-1867 2. Irish Americans 3. Governors 4. Heroes and heroines, American 5. Exiles 6. Prisoners 7. United States Civil War, 1861-1865 8. Revolutionaries 9. Generals 10. United States history 11. Irish history 12. Ireland 13. United States 14. American Civil War era (1861-1865) 15. Irish Potato Famine (1845-1852) 16. Biographies 17. Life stories — Politics — Activists and reformers 18. History writing — Wars and conflicts — American Civil War

LC 2015037256

Montana Book Award, 2016.

Places the improbable life of revolutionary hero Thomas Francis Meagher against a backdrop of Irish-American history, detailing his leadership during Irish uprisings, service with the Irish Brigade in the Civil War, and achievements as the territorial governor of Montana.

Includes bib and index.

Eger, Edith Eva
The Choice: Embrace the Possible. Edith Eva Eger. Scribner 2017. 288 p.
ISBN 9781501130786
Grades: Adult   B

1. Holocaust survivors 2. Psychic trauma 3. Coping 4. Psychologists 5. Survival 6. Post-traumatic stress disorder 7. Self-acceptance 8. Autobiographies and memoirs 9. Biographies 10. Life stories — Facing adversity — War and oppression — Holocaust 11. Life stories — Facing adversity

LC BI2017029926

National Jewish Book Award, 2017.

A dual memoir and practical guide to healing by an eminent psychologist and Holocaust survivor counsels patients on how to escape the prisons of their own minds, describing her harrowing experiences in Auschwitz and how it gave her particular insights into the challenges of PTSD.

"A searing, astute study of intensive healing and self-acceptance through the absolution of suffering and atrocity." —*Kirkus*

Eggers, Dave
The Monk of Mokha. by Dave Eggers. Alfred A. Knopf 2018. 368 p.
ISBN 9781101947319
Grades: Adult   B

1. Alkhanshali, Mokhtar 2. Coffee industry and trade 3. Businesspeople 4. Determination 5. Biographies 6. Life stories — Business 7. Business and economics — Industries — Agriculture and food

LC 2017032893

Traces the story of Mokhtar Alkhanshali, a Yemeni-American in San Francisco, and his dream of resurrecting the ancient art of cultivating, roasting, and importing Yemeni coffee, an endeavor that is challenged by the brutal realities of Yemen's 2015 civil war.

"Eggerss book works as both a heartwarming success story with a winning central character and an account of real-life adventures that read with the vividness of fiction." —*Publishers Weekly*

Ehrenreich, Barbara
★ *Nickel and Dimed: On (not) Getting by in America.* Barbara Ehrenreich. Metropolitan Books 2001. 221 p.
ISBN 9780805063882
Grades: 11 12 Adult   B

1. Poor people 2. Minimum wage 3. Low-wage workers 4. Blue collar workers 5. Rent and renting 6. Intersectionality 7. Poverty 8. Economics 9. United States 10. 20th century 11. Society and culture — Wealth and class — Poverty 12. Adult books for young adults 13. Nonfiction that reads like fiction

LC 00052514

Alex Award, 2002; Los Angeles Times Book Prize for Current Interest, 2001; New York Times Notable Book, 2001; School Library Journal Best Books: Best Adult Books 4 Teens, 2002.

Nickel and Dimed is a modern classic that deftly portrays the plight of America's working-class poor. Author Barbara Ehrenreich decides to see if she can scratch out a comfortable living in blue-collar America. What she discovers is a culture of desperation, where workers often take multiple low-paying jobs just to keep a roof overhead.

PUBLIC LIBRARY CORE COLLECTION: NONFICTION
Twentieth Edition

"No real answers to the problem but a compelling sketch of its reality and pervasiveness." —*Library Journal*

Ehrlich, Gretel
Unsoclaced: Along the Way to All That Is. Gretel Ehrlich. Pantheon Books 2021. 256 p.
ISBN 9780307911797
Grades: Adult **B**
1. Ehrlich, Gretel 2. Effect of environment on humans 3. Authors, American 4. Environmental degradation 5. Nature 6. Home (Concept) 7. Climate change 8. Women poets 9. Memory 10. Voyages and travels 11. Greenland 12. Africa 13. The West (United States) 14. Arctic regions 15. 20th century 16. Autobiographies and memoirs 17. Nature Writing — Personal responses 18. Travel Writing — General 19. Life stories — Nature and outdoors 20. Nature Writing — Environmental issues
LC 2020013919

Ehrlich shows us how these forces have shaped her experience and her understanding as she recalls the split-end strands of friendships spliced to new loves, houses built and lived in, conversations that shifted outlooks, as she tries to catch a glimpse of herself and the places she has sought as an anchor for her spirit. Ehrlich's quest is not for the comfort of permanence, but for transience, the need to be unsettled—to find stillness in the disquiet of engagement, to find in the landscapes of earth, ice, climate, genetic mayhem, and shifting canvas of memory—the possibility of longing. From the author of the enduring classic, the Solace of Open Spaces, here is a wondrous meditation on how water, light, wind, mountain, bird, and horse has shaped her life and understanding of a world besieged by a climate crisis.

"Writing with fire and ice of beauty, risk, and devastation, Ehrlich shares wonder, wisdom, candor, and concern to soul-ringing effect." —*Booklist*

Eichenwald, Kurt
A Mind Unraveled: A Memoir. Kurt Eichenwald. Ballantine Books 2018. 416 p.
ISBN 9780399593628
Grades: Adult **B**
1. Eichenwald, Kurt, 1961- 2. People with epilepsy 3. Journalists 4. Epilepsy 5. Sick people 6. Amnesia 7. Medical care 8. Medical care services 9. Incompetence 10. Discrimination 11. Neurologists 12. Survival 13. Autobiographies and memoirs 14. Life stories — Facing adversity — Medical issues — Physical illness 15. Life stories — Arts and culture — Writing — Journalists 16. Science Writing — Medicine and health — Illness and disease
LC 2018018965

The author of the Informant traces the decades he spent fighting and hiding the symptoms of epilepsy, a battle involving severe depression and medical mistakes before a dedicated neurologist helped him to survive and thrive.

"Eichenwald has created a universal tale of resilience wrapped in a primal scream against the far-too-savage world. Book clubs will clamor for this tale of survival and call for compassion." —*Booklist*

Eig, Jonathan
★ *Ali: A Life*. Jonathan Eig. Houghton Mifflin Harcourt 2017. 623 p.
ISBN 9780544435247
Grades: Adult **B**
1. Ali, Muhammad, 1942-2016 2. African American boxers 3. Boxers (Sports) 4. Black Muslims 5. Race relations 6. Sports and Competition — Boxing 7. Life stories — Sports — Athletes
LC Bl2017033332

New York Times Notable Book, 2018; Shortlisted for the James Tait Black Memorial Prize for Biography, 2017.

Presents an unauthorized portrait of the iconic champion fighter, arguing that race was a central theme in Muhammad Ali's career, faith, and advocacy work and that his political beliefs and neurological health shaped his complex character.

"Eig does a fine job of covering all the bases, and though the book is occasionally overwritten, it's only out of enthusiasm for his undeniably great subject, about whom the author is now working with Ken Burns to develop a documentary. An exemplary life of an exemplary man who, despite a few missteps, deserves to be remembered long in to the future." —*Kirkus*
Includes bibliographical references and index.

★ *King: A Life*. Jonathan Eig. Farrar, Straus and Giroux 2023. 688 p.
ISBN 9780374279295
Grades: Adult **B**
1. King, Martin Luther, Jr, 1929-1968 2. African American civil rights workers 3. Civil rights workers 4. African Americans 5. Civil Rights Movement 6. African American men 7. Clergy 8. African American Baptists 9. Race relations 10. United States history 11. 20th century 12. Biographies 13. Page to screen 14. Life stories — Politics — Activists and reformers — Civil Rights Leaders 15. History writing — African American — Civil rights — United States
LC 2022056721

Pulitzer Prize for Biography, 2024; National Book Critics Circle Award for Biography finalist, 2023.

The first full biography in decades, "King" mixes revelatory and exhaustive new research with brisk and accessible storytelling to forge the definitive life for our times.

"A must for readers interested in moving beyond clichéd catchphrases to see a more complete and complex King, the context of his charisma, and the creation and content of his character." —*Library Journal*

Adapted into a film in 2024; Includes bibliographical references and index.

Eire, Carlos M. N.
Learning to Die in Miami: Further Confessions of a Cuban Boy. Carlos Eire. Free Press 2010. 256 p.
ISBN 9781439181904
Grades: 11 12 Adult **B**
1. Eire, Carlos M. N. 2. Cuban Americans 3. Child refugees 4. Immigrants 5. Assimilation (Sociology) 6. Growing up 7. Foster children 8. Miami, Florida 9. 1960s 10. Autobiographies and memoirs 11. Family and Relationships — Growing up 12. History writing — Immigration — United States 13. Life stories — Relationships — Growing up
LC 2009052286

Presents the story of the author's exile in America, where his brother and he relocated as youths from their revolution-torn home in Cuba, struggled with the loss of their cultural identity, and acclimated to American culture.

Sequel to: Waiting for snow in Havana.

Eisler, Benita
★ *Chopin's Funeral*. Benita Eisler. Alfred A. Knopf 2003. 230 p. : Illustration
ISBN 9780375409455
Grades: Adult **B**
1. Chopin, Frederic, 1810-1849 2. Sand, George, 1804-1876 3. Composers 4. Pianists 5. Funerals 6. Death 7. 1840s 8. Biographies 9. Arts and Entertainment — Music — Classical 10. Life stories — Arts and culture — Performing arts — Musicians and composers
LC 2002073097

New York Times Notable Book, 2003.

An intimate portrait of the great composer provides a close-up look at his final years, his legendary affair with novelist George Sand, his life as an artist in exile, and his decline and destitute final days.

"Eisler is a compelling storyteller, sweeping the reader into the exhilarating milieu of Paris in the 1820s and 1830s." —*Library Journal*

Includes bibliographical references (p. 217-218) and index.

The Red Man's Bones: George Catlin, Artist and Showman. Benita Eisler. W.W. Norton & Company 2013. 384 p.
ISBN 9780393066166
Grades: Adult **B**
1. Catlin, George, 1796-1872 2. Painters 3. Indigenous peoples of North America in art 4. The West (United States) in art 5. Frontier and pioneer life 6. Artists 7. The West (United States) history 8. United States 9. 19th century 10. Biographies 11. Life stories — Arts and culture — Artists 12. History writing — Westward expansion — United States

ESSENTIAL AND RECOMMENDED TITLES
Biography

LC 2013013973

Highlights the life and work of the American painter, author, and traveler who specialized in images of Native Americans and who advocated for them before ultimately exploiting them in a live show that brought tragedy to both the artist and his performers.

"A welcome new evaluation of a significant American artist honed by the Wild West spirit and hucksterism of the age. Biographer of Byron, Chopin, George Sand and others (Naked in the Marketplace: The Lives of George Sand, 2007, etc.), Eisler now turns her considerable research talents to fleshing out the life and work of Pennsylvania-born artist George Catlin (1796-1892), whose sympathetic portraits of the Native Americans he sought out and lived among render an incalculable record of (and tribute to) a vanished people." —*Kirkus*

Includes bibliographical references and index.

Eizenstat, Stuart

★ *President Carter: The White House Years*. Stuart E. Eizenstat. Thomas Dunne Books, St. Martin's Press 2018. 528 p.

ISBN 9781250104557

Grades: Adult   **B**

1. Carter, Jimmy, 1924- 2. Political leadership 3. Cabinet officers 4. Presidents 5. Politics and government 6. United States 7. 20th century 8. 1970s 9. 1980s 10. Biographies 11. History writing — Presidency — 20th century — United States 12. Life stories — Politics — Politicians

LC 2017043521

The former U.S. Ambassador and author of Imperfect Justice presents an insider's history of the Carter Administration that shares insights into the 39th President's admirable character and the achievements that positively reshaped the country and the world long after Carter's single term.

"A compelling reassessment of an oft-maligned chief executive." —*Booklist*

Eliot, Marc

The Hag: The Life, Times, and Music of Merle Haggard. Marc Eliot. Hachette Books 2022. 304 p.

ISBN 9780306923210

Grades: Adult   **B**

1. Haggard, Merle 2. Country musicians 3. Country music 4. Biographies 5. Life stories — Arts and culture — Performing arts — Musicians and composers 6. Arts and Entertainment — Music — Country

An award-winning biographer tells, without compromise, the extraordinary life of country legend Merle Haggard, who lifted himself out of poverty, oppression, loss and wanderlust, to become one of the American artists admired around the world.

"Likely to become the definitive Merle Haggard biography and will sit nicely alongside Haggard's own two memoirs." —*Library Journal*

Includes bibliographical references and index.

Elledge, Scott

E.B. White: A Biography. Scott Elledge. Norton 1986. xvii, 400 p. : Illustration

ISBN 9780393303056

Grades: Adult   **B**

1. White, E. B. (Elwyn Brooks), 1899-1985 2. Children's literature writing 3. Authors, American 4. Social life and customs 5. United States 6. 20th century 7. Biographies 8. Arts and Entertainment — Writing and Publishing 9. Life stories — Arts and culture — Writing — Authors

LC 85029807

A biography of the popular American children's author recounts his childhood, his education at Cornell, and his long association with the New Yorker magazine.

"The author is fair, respectful, thorough, entertaining, skillful and unpedantic. He has performed a splendid exercise in scholarship and literary analysis, and the result is fun." —*New York Times Book Review*

Includes bibliographical references (p. 383-387) and index.

Ellis, Joseph J.

★ *His Excellency: George Washington*. Joseph J. Ellis. Alfred A. Knopf 2004. xiv, 320 p. : Illustration

ISBN 9781400040315

Grades: 11 12 Adult   **B**

1. Washington, George, 1732-1799 2. American Revolution, 1775-1783 3. Command of troops 4. Presidents 5. Revolutions 6. Politicians 7. Generals 8. Soldiers 9. French and Indian War, 1754-1763 10. Men-women relations 11. United States history 12. United States 13. 18th century 14. Colonial America (1600-1775) 15. Revolutionary America (1775-1783) 16. 1780s 17. Biographies 18. History writing — Presidency — 18th century — United States 19. Life stories — Politics — Politicians 20. History writing — Military — Military leadership 21. Life stories — Law and order — Military leaders 22. History writing — Early America — United States 23. History writing — Colonial America — United States 24. Adult books for young adults

LC 2004046576

Booklist Editors' Choice, 2004.

From the French and Indian War to Mount Vernon, from the American Revolution to the presidency, Ellis delivers what will stand the test of time as the definitive biography of an American icon.

"The author offers a magisterial account of the life and times of George Washington, celebrating the heroic image of the president whom peers like Jefferson and Madison recognized as their unquestioned superior while acknowledging his all-too-human qualities." —*Publishers Weekly*

Includes bibliographical references and index.

Ellmann, Richard

Oscar Wilde. Richard Ellmann. Knopf 1988. xvii, 680 p. [32] p. of plates : Illustration; Portrait

ISBN 9780394554846

Grades: Adult   **B**

1. Wilde, Oscar, 1854-1900 2. Authors, Irish 3. Poets, Irish 4. Playwrights, Irish 5. Sexuality 6. Ireland 7. 19th century 8. Biographies 9. Page to screen 10. Arts and Entertainment — Writing and Publishing 11. Life stories — Arts and culture — Writing — Authors

LC 88207185

National Book Critics Circle Award for Biography, 1988; Pulitzer Prize for Biography or Autobiography, 1989.

Presents an in-depth study of the complex and tragic life of Oscar Wilde and a tribute to his inimitable wit and brilliant writings.

"Wilde's life epitomizes the classic formula for a tragic history, the man who, by hubris, falls from greatness. In Mr. Ellmann's hands, the story becomes as compelling as fiction while never deviating from the facts. Humour and elegance illuminate the accounts of Wilde's family, his friends and the enemies he earned." —*The Economist*

Includes bibliographical references (p. 555-588) and index; Originally published: London : H. Hamilton, 1987.

Elnoury, Tamer

American Radical: Inside the World of an Undercover Muslim FBI Agent. Tamer Elnoury with Kevin Maurer. E. P. Dutton 2017. 368 p.

ISBN 9781101986158

Grades: Adult   **B**

1. Spies 2. Espionage 3. Antiterrorists 4. Terrorism prevention 5. Muslim men 6. FBI agents 7. International relations 8. United States 9. Southwest Asia and North Africa (Middle East) 10. Autobiographies and memoirs 11. Life stories — Law and order — Spies and secret agents

LC 2017029950

A Muslim American FBI agent shares how he brought down a terror cell in North America.

"Elnoury heightens the suspense in vividly described scenes, such as when he nearly gets run over by a train while scouting locations for the attack with two suspected terrorists, and provides insight into the worldview and intentions of al-Qaeda affiliates. There is never a dull moment in this intimate story of an American Muslim going to great lengths to serve and protect his country." —*Publishers Weekly*

PUBLIC LIBRARY CORE COLLECTION: NONFICTION
Twentieth Edition

Emezi, Akwaeke
★ *Dear Senthuran: A Black Spirit Memoir.* Akwaeke Emezi. Riverhead Books 2021. 240 p.
ISBN 9780593329191
Grades: Adult　　　　　B
1. Emezi, Akwaeke 2. Authors, Nigerian 3. Genderqueer people 4. LGBTQIA+ people 5. Intersectionality 6. Autobiographies and memoirs 7. Life stories — Arts and culture — Writing — Authors 8. Life stories — Identity — LGBTQIA+ 9. Life stories — Identity — Race and ethnicity 10. Arts and Entertainment — Writing and Publishing

Stonewall Book Awards: Israel Fishman Non-fiction Award, 2022.

A New York Times-best-selling author offers a provocative memoir in letters.

"With this first work of nonfiction, best-selling novelist Emezi writes an expressive memoir in letters, with an overlapping focus on spirit, divinity, and humanity." —*Library Journal*

Engle, Charlie
Running Man: A Memoir. Charlie Engle. Scribner 2016. 288 p.
ISBN 9781476785783
Grades: Adult　　　　　B
1. Engle, Charlie 2. Ultramarathon runners 3. Long-distance runners 4. Ultramarathon running 5. Long distance running 6. Runners 7. Running 8. Autobiographies and memoirs 9. Life stories — Sports — Athletes 10. Sports and Competition — Racing — Track and Field

LC Bl2016030356

A personal account by a world-class ultra-marathon runner chronicles his globe-spanning races, record-breaking run across the Sahara and struggles with drug addiction and wrongful imprisonment.

"Similar to the journey of self-discovery chronicled in Rich Rolls Finding Ultra (2012), this is a fast-paced, well-written account of a man who accepts pain, pushes beyond imagined limits, and ultimately finds redemption and peace." —*Booklist*

Enninful, Edward
A Visible Man: A Memoir. Edward Enninful. Penguin Group USA 2022. 272 p.
ISBN 9780593299487
Grades: Adult　　　　　B
1. Fashion periodicals 2. Fashion 3. Clothing industry and trade 4. Black people 5. Gay men 6. Immigrants 7. Great Britain 8. Autobiographies and memoirs 9. Life stories — Arts and culture — Fashion 10. Arts and entertainment — Fashion

One of fashion's most important changemakers, a Black, gay, working-class refugee discusses how he forged a career in fashion and rose to become the first Black editor in chief of British Vogue.

"Enninful, British Vogue's editor-in-chief, makes a dazzling debut with this chronicle of his remarkable path to becoming a world-renowned style visionary." —*Publishers Weekly*

Enss, Chris
Mochi's War: The Tragedy of Sand Creek. Chris Enss and Howard Kazanjian. TwoDot 2015. 192 p.
ISBN 9780762760770
Grades: Adult　　　　　B
1. Mochi, approximately 1841-1881 2. Sand Creek Massacre, November 29, 1864 3. Cheyenne (North American people) 4. European Americans 5. Race relations 6. Massacres 7. Revenge 8. Indigenous prisoners 9. Prisoners of war 10. Indigenous peoples of North America — Forced removal 11. Indigenous peoples of North America — Wars 12. Indigenous peoples of North America 13. Colorado 14. Biographies 15. Life stories — Facing adversity — War and oppression 16. History writing — Indigenous peoples — United States

LC 2015005372

As with many incidents in American history, the victors wrote the first version of history—turning the tragedy of the Sand Creek Massacre into a heroic feat by the Colorado militia tasked with moving the Cheyenne onto reservations. The truth of those events has made Colonel John Chivington's name infamous in Colorado and American history, and this dramatic and poignant reflection on the events leading to the tragic events of the massacre and the ensuing years of violence offers new perspectives with the hindsight of more than a century and a half of repercussions by telling the story of one of the women, a Cheyenne named Mochi, who became swept up in the cycle of war and vengeance that ensued.

"Highly recommended for adult readers of Western and Native American history, this biographical account provides a counterpoint to the many works that have mythologized such women as Pocahontas and Sacajawea." —*Library Journal*

Includes bibliographical references and index.

Ephron, Delia
Left on Tenth: A Second Chance at Life: A Memoir. Delia Ephron. Little Brown & Company 2022. 304 p.
ISBN 9780316267656
Grades: Adult　　　　　B
1. Ephron, Delia 2. Grief 3. Loss 4. Women cancer survivors 5. Cancer 6. Widows 7. Women authors 8. Love 9. Interpersonal relations 10. Men-women relations 11. Autobiographies and memoirs 12. Life stories — Arts and culture — Writing — Authors 13. Life stories — Facing adversity — Medical issues — Physical illness 14. Life stories — Relationships

The best-selling novelist and screenwriter of You've Got Mail shares how she got a second chance at love later in life with Peter, a Bay Area psychiatrist; her battle with AML with Peter and friends by her side, and her feelings about facing death.

"Ephron's harrowing account of coping with multiple, agonizing courses of treatment rivals that of any against-all-odds, true-adventure memoir." —*Booklist*

Epstein, Franci
Franci's War: A Woman's Story of Survival. Franci Rabinek Epstein; afterword by Helen Epstein. Penguin Books 2020. 256 pages
ISBN 9780143135579
Grades: Adult　　　　　B
1. Epstein, Franci 2. Holocaust (1933-1945) 3. Fashion designers 4. Holocaust survivors 5. European history 6. Prague, Czech Republic 7. Czechoslovakia 8. Second World War era (1939-1945) 9. Biographies 10. Life stories — Facing adversity — War and oppression — Holocaust 11. Adult books for young adults

LC 2019039140

One incredibly strong young woman—a glamorous Jewish fashion designer, who endured the horrors of the Holocaust along with the women prisoners in her tight-knit circle of friends offers powerful testimony in an intense, candid and sometimes funny account of those dark years.

"This devastating account documents a personal slice of Holocaust history." —*Booklist*

Erickson, Carolly
Great Catherine. Carolly Erickson. St. Martin's Griffin 1995. 392 p.
ISBN 9780312135034
Grades: 11 12 Adult　　　　　B
1. Catherine II, Empress of Russia, 1729-1796 2. Women 3. Russian history 4. Russia 5. Romanov Dynasty (1613-1917) 6. Biographies 7. History writing — Europe — Russia 8. Life stories — Politics — Politicians

LC 95022619

Presents a biography of the legendary Russian empress that emphasizes Catherine the Great's political ability, humanitarian inclinations, and other accomplishments.

"Erickson's fluid, captivating portrait of Catherine the Great reads like a first-rate historical novel." —*Booklist*

Includes index.

Ernaux, Annie
★ *The Years.* Annie Ernaux; translated by Alison L. Strayer. Seven Stories Press 2017. 237 pages

ESSENTIAL AND RECOMMENDED TITLES
Biography

ISBN 9781609807870
Grades: Adult **B**
1. Ernaux, Annie, 1940- 2. Authors, French 3. Personal diaries 4. Working class families 5. Popular culture 6. Memories 7. Time 8. Social history 9. Social change 10. Generations 11. French history 12. 20th century 13. Autobiographies and memoirs 14. Translations — French to English 15. History writing — Europe — France 16. History writing — Arts and culture 17. Life stories — Arts and culture — Writing — Authors
LC 2017003723

The author describes her life in France from 1941 to 2006, mixing personal history and memory with descriptions of the popular culture of each decade.

"A memoir that captures nostalgia's twinge while also documenting the many societal changes that shaped postwar France." —*Library Journal*

First published in French as Les Années (Paris : Gallimard, c2008).

Eruzione, Mike
The Making of a Miracle: The Untold Story of the Captain of the 1980 Gold Medal-winning U.S. Olympic Hockey Team. Mike Eruzione, with Neal Boudette. HarperCollins 2020. 288 p.
ISBN 9780062960955
Grades: Adult **B**
1. Eruzione, Mike 2. Hockey players 3. Hockey teams 4. Olympic medal winners 5. Hockey 6. Olympic athletes 7. Growing up 8. Winning and losing 9. Autobiographies and memoirs 10. Life stories — Sports — Athletes 11. Sports and Competition — Hockey 12. Sports and Competition — Individual Athlete
LC Bl2020005267

The captain of the 1980 U.S. Men's Olympic Hockey team traces his blue-collar upbringing in Massachusetts, minor-league achievements, and encounters with such individuals as AL Michaels, Herb Brooks, and an elite array of Russian Hall of Famers.

"Eruzione recalls what seemed to be a simpler time—when major news came through television, newspapers, or word of mouth, and when the U.S. Olympic team was comprised of scrappy amateurs. This heartwarming memoir will delight more than just hockey fans." —*Publishers Weekly*

Erwin, Jon
Beyond Valor: A World War II Story of Extraordinary Heroism, Sacrificial Love, and a Race Against Time. Jon Erwin and William Doyle. Thomas Nelson 2020. 240 pages
ISBN 9781400216833
Grades: Adult **B**
1. Erwin, Henry Eugene, 1921-2002 2. Airplane accidents 3. War wounds 4. B-29 bomber 5. Medal of Honor 6. Husband and wife 7. Faith 8. Burns and scalds 9. Aerial operations 10. Military history 11. People with disabilities 12. Veterans 13. World War II 14. Birmingham, Alabama 15. United States 16. Japan 17. Second World War era (1939-1945) 18. Biographies 19. History writing — Wars and conflicts — World War II — Pacific Theater 20. Life stories — Law and order — Armed forces personnel
LC 2020001894

Beyond Valor is one soldier's extraordinary tale of bravery, heroism, faith, and devotion.

"… this thrilling biography…. combines historical fact and anecdotal material to reveal Red's religious devotion and profound patriotism…. keen on historical data and delivery of technical, medical, and emotional detail…. This is a miraculous story of tenacity under pressure and the optimistic power of faith." —*Publishers Weekly*

Includes bibliographical references.

Essinger, James
Ada's Algorithm: How Lord Byron's Daughter Ada Lovelace Launched the Digital Age. James Essinger. Melville House 2014. 288 p.
ISBN 9781612194080
Grades: Adult **B**
1. Lovelace, Ada King, Countess of, 1815-1852 2. Babbage, Charles, 1791-1871 3. Women mathematicians 4. Computers 5. Algorithms 6. Mathematicians 7. Technology 8. British history 9. 19th century 10. Biographies 11. Life stories — Science, technology, and medicine — Scientists and inventors 12. Science Writing — Computing, the Internet, and Technology
LC 2014021837

Based on ten years of research and filled with fascinating characters and observations of the period, not to mention numerous illustrations, Essinger tells Ada's fascinating story in unprecedented detail to absorbing and inspiring effect.

"Essinger (Spellbound: The Surprising Origins and Astonishing Secrets of English Spelling, 2007, etc.) presents Ada's story with great enthusiasm and rich detail, painting her life as one that was rich with opportunity and access but stifled by sexism. Ada continues to inspire, and by using her own voice via letters and research, the author brings her to life for a new generation of intrepid female innovators. A robust, engaging and exciting biography." —*Kirkus*

Includes bibliographical references and index.

Eteraz, Ali
Children of Dust: A Memoir. Ali Eteraz. Harpercollins 2009. 288 p.
ISBN 9780061567087
Grades: Adult **B**
1. Muslims 2. Pakistani people in the United States 3. Fundamentalism 4. Immigrants 5. Immigration and emigration 6. Islam 7. Social life and customs 8. Self-awareness 9. Pakistan 10. Autobiographies and memoirs 11. Spirituality and Religion — Islam 12. Life stories — Religion and spirituality — Personal faith
LC 2009009666

A memoir reveals the inside of militant Islamic fundamentalism in Pakistan and the culture shock of moving to the United States, in a book that explores the author's search for his Islamic identity.

Etheridge, Melissa
Talking to My Angels. Melissa Etheridge. Harper Wave 2023. 304 p.
ISBN 9780063257450
Grades: Adult **B**
1. Etheridge, Melissa 2. Women rock musicians 3. Lesbians 4. LGBTQIA+ people 5. Growing up 6. Musical performance 7. Songwriting 8. Romantic love 9. Tragedy 10. Death of sons 11. Loss 12. Healing 13. North American people 14. American people 15. Autobiographies and memoirs 16. Life stories — Arts and culture — Performing arts — Musicians and composers 17. Life stories — Relationships 18. Life stories — Facing adversity — Coping with death 19. Arts and Entertainment — Music — Rock
LC 2023022334

The Grammy and Oscar award-winning rock star and trailblazing LGBTQAI icon shares how numerous, life-altering tragedies served as a catalyst for growth, and what the past two decades have taught her about the value of music, love, family and life in the face of death.

"A must for Etheridge fans, with plenty of lessons for striving musicians." —*Kirkus*

Evans, R. Tripp
Grant Wood: A Life. R. Tripp Evans. Alfred A. Knopf 2010. xii, 402 p, 8 p. of plates : Illustration; Color
ISBN 9780307266293
Grades: Adult **B**
1. Wood, Grant, 1891-1942 2. Painters 3. Homosexuality 4. Painting technique 5. United States history 6. Iowa 7. United States 8. 20th century 9. Biographies 10. Life stories — Arts and culture — Artists
LC 2010018019

Booklist Editors' Choice, 2010.

Wood was one of America's most famous regionalist painters. In his time he was an "almost mythical figure," recognized supremely for his hard-boiled farm scene, American Gothic, a painting that has come to reflect the essence of America's traditional values—a simple decent, home spun tribute to our lost agrarian age. America's most acclaimed, and misunderstood, regionalist painter, Grant Wood, is revealed to have been anything but plain, or simple.

"Evans transforms our view of painter Grant Wood and his all-American paintings, including American Gothic, in a revelatory and heartrending biography of an artist forced to conceal his homosexuality." —*Booklist*

Includes bibliographical references and index.

PUBLIC LIBRARY CORE COLLECTION: NONFICTION
Twentieth Edition

Evanzz, Karl
The Messenger: The Rise and Fall of Elijah Muhammad. Karl Evanzz. Pantheon Books 1999. xv, 667 p. : Illustration
ISBN 9780679442608
Grades: 11 12 Adult   **B**
1. Elijah Muhammad, 1897-1975 2. Black Muslims 3. African Americans 4. Biographies 5. History writing — African American — Civil rights — United States 6. Spirituality and Religion — Islam 7. Life stories — Religion and spirituality — Religious and spiritual leaders
LC 99011826

A definitive biography of the controversial founder and "prophet" of the Nation of Islam describes Elijah Muhammad's rise to power, his charismatic teachings, his role in the struggle for African-American equality, and the turbulent, contradictory personal life that led to his fall.

"A critical biography of one of America's leading Black nationalists of the 20th century. One of the founders of the Nation of Islam (NOI), Muhammad helped convert thousands of African Americans to the religion popularly known as the Black Muslims. Evanzz concludes that Muhammad was essentially a con man who used his considerable powers of persuasion to get rich and seduce women. Especially fascinating is Evanzz's extensive use of FBI files to make his case." —*Library Journal*

Includes bibliographical references (p. 589-633) and index.

Evaristo, Bernardine
Manifesto: On Never Giving up. Bernardine Evaristo. Grove Press 2022. 224 p.
ISBN 9780802158901
Grades: Adult   **B**
1. Evaristo, Bernardine, 1959- 2. Women authors, English 3. Multiracial women 4. Actors and actresses 5. Feminism 6. Racism 7. Social classes 8. Sexuality 9. Aging 10. Social advocates 11. Creativity 12. Resilience 13. Marginalized women 14. 20th century 15. Autobiographies and memoirs 16. Life stories — Identity — Race and ethnicity 17. Life stories — Arts and culture — Performing arts 18. Society and culture — Race
LC 2021052955

In Manifesto, Evaristo charts her theory of unstoppability, showing creative people how they too can visualize and find success in their work, ignoring the naysayers. Both unconventional memoir and inspirational text, Manifesto is a unique reminder to us all to persist in doing work we believe in, even when we might feel overlooked or discounted. Evaristo shows us how we too can follow in her footsteps, from first vision, to insistent perseverance, to eventual triumph.

"Novelist Evaristo (Girl, Woman, Other) charts her path from struggling in a working-class family to becoming the first Black British person to win the Booker Prize, in this sprawling memoir.... Readers will find much to ruminate over in this meditation on the power of art and persistence." —*Publishers Weekly*

Originally published in the UK by Hamish Hamilton, London, in 2021.

Everitt, Anthony
Alexander the Great: His Life and His Mysterious Death. Anthony Everitt. Random House 2019. 496 p.
ISBN 9780425286524
Grades: Adult   **B**
1. Alexander, the Great, 356-323 B.C.E 2. Leadership 3. Command of troops 4. Determination 5. Rulers 6. Ancient Greece 7. Macedonia, Ancient Greece 8. Ancient Greece (800 B.C.E.-640 C.E.) 9. Biographies 10. Life stories — Law and order — Military leaders 11. History writing — Ancient — Greece
LC 2018059885

A reconstruction of the life of the ancient Greek conqueror highlights his contradictory depictions throughout history, placing his achievements against a backdrop of his own historical time to discuss his growing empire, respect for regional traditions and mysterious death.

Includes bibliographical references and index.

Cicero: The Life and Times of Rome's Greatest Politician. Anthony Everitt. Random House 2001. xv, 359 p. : Illustration; Map
ISBN 9780375507465
Grades: 11 12 Adult   **B**
1. Cicero, Marcus Tullius 2. Consuls 3. Politicians 4. Rhetoric 5. Politics and government 6. Ancient Rome 7. Roman Republic (509-27 B.C.E.) 8. Biographies 9. History writing — Ancient — Rome 10. Life stories — Politics — Politicians 11. Adult books for young adults
LC 2001048531

Booklist Editors' Choice, 2002.

A portrait of the Roman politician describes the life and times of the ancient statesman, based on the witty and candid letters that Cicero wrote to his friend Atticus in which he described the events and personalities that shaped the final days of Republican Rome.

"This masterful biography draws on Cicero's letters to his friend Atticus to give a clear picture of the famous Roman orator, noting both his brilliance and his faults." —*Booklist*

Includes bibliographical references (p. [327]-346) and index; Originally published: John Murray Publishers, Great Britain, 2001.

Hadrian and the Triumph of Rome. Anthony Everitt. Random House 2009. 432 p.
ISBN 9781400066629
Grades: Adult   **B**
1. Hadrian, Emperor of Rome, 76-138 2. Roman emperors 3. Ancient history 4. Politics and government 5. Ancient Rome 6. Roman Empire (27 B.C.E.-476 C.E.) 7. Biographies 8. History writing — Ancient — Rome 9. Life stories — Politics — Politicians
LC 2009005683

A meticulously researched profile of the enigmatic Roman emperor places his formative years against a backdrop of first-century events and chronicles his successful efforts to end a century of disorder and warfare. By the best-selling author of Cicero.

"Emperor from 117 to 138 A.D, Hadrian styled himself princeps, or first among equals, and his reversal of his predecessors' expansionist policies contributed to an era of prosperity and relative calm. He was unapologetically Hellenic, a poet and a dabbler in magic, and he kept in his retinue a young male lover whom he later deified. If Hadrian is indeed an enigma, it's because so few accounts of his life have survived, and this is where Everitt—whose books rely heavily on primary sources—runs into difficulty. One gets a clear and compelling sense of Hadrian's times, but the Emperor himself remains tantalizingly unknowable." —*The New Yorker*

Eyman, Scott
Cary Grant: A Brilliant Disguise. Scott Eyman. Simon & Schuster 2020. xi, 556 p.
ISBN 9781501192111
Grades: Adult   **B**
1. Grant, Cary, 1904-1986 2. Men 3. Acting 4. Interpersonal relations 5. Insecurity 6. Films 7. Actors and actresses 8. United States 9. 20th century 10. Biographies 11. Life stories — Arts and culture — Performing arts — Actors and actresses 12. Arts and Entertainment — Movies and Television
LC 2020001234

A heavily researched portrait of the Hollywood legend that includes coverage of Grant's early start as a teen acrobat, his complicated relationships and his Golden Era performances.

"Combining existing research with voluminous new interviews and access to Grant's personal papers, this is an informative and entertaining biography of a legendary actor." —*Library Journal*

Charlie Chaplin vs. America: When Art, Sex, and Politics Collided. Scott Eyman. Simon & Schuster 2023. 432 p.
ISBN 9781982176358
Grades: Adult   **B**
1. Chaplin, Charlie, 1889-1977 2. Actors and actresses 3. Comedians 4. Film producers and directors 5. Celebrities 6. Postwar life 7. McCarthyism 8. Liberalism 9. Sexuality 10. Extramarital affairs 11. Relationships between young women and older men 12. Public opinion 13. Pariahs 14. Expatriates 15. Exile (Punishment) 16. British people 17. English people 18. North American people 19. American people 20. Biographies 21. Life stories — Arts and culture — Performing arts — Actors and actresses 22. Life stories — Arts and culture — Per-

ESSENTIAL AND RECOMMENDED TITLES
Biography

forming arts — Entertainers and celebrities 23. Arts and Entertainment — Movies and Television

LC 2023020977

Hollywood biographer and film historian Scott Eyman tells the story of Charlie Chaplin's fall from grace. In the aftermath of World War Two, Chaplin was criticized for being politically liberal and internationalist in outlook. He had never become a US citizen, something that would be held against him as xenophobia set in when the postwar Red Scare took hold. Politics aside, Chaplin had another problem: His sexual interest in young women. He had been married three times and had had numerous affairs. His sexuality became a convenient way for those who opposed his politics to condemn him.

"Eyman gives the history a sense of urgency by highlighting the danger that government interference poses to artistic speech, and his account of how 'Chaplin's forced exile destroyed him as an artist' is affecting." —*Publishers Weekly*

Includes bibliographical references and index.

Empire of Dreams: The Epic Life of Cecil B. Demille. Scott Eyman. Simon & Schuster 2010. 576 p.

ISBN 9780743289559

Grades: Adult **B**

1. DeMille, Cecil B, 1881-1959 2. Film producers and directors 3. Film industry and trade 4. Filmmakers 5. Silent film industry and trade 6. Hollywood, California 7. Biographies 8. Arts and Entertainment — Movies and Television 9. Life stories — Arts and culture — Performing arts — Directors and producers

LC 2010027710

The most authoritative biography ever of director Cecil B. DeMille, incorporating letters and personal papers made available for the first time.

"Eyman's evocative prose and exhaustive research makes this an engaging and authoritative biography." —*Publishers Weekly*

John Wayne: The Life and Legend. Scott Eyman. Simon & Schuster 2014. 512 pages

ISBN 9781439199589

Grades: Adult **B**

1. Wayne, John, 1907-1979 2. Western films 3. Popular culture 4. Films 5. Actors and actresses 6. United States 7. 20th century 8. Biographies 9. Life stories — Arts and culture — Performing arts — Actors and actresses 10. Arts and Entertainment — Movies and Television

LC 2013032604

A revelatory biography of the enduringly popular John Wayne that draws on more than 100 interviews as well as exclusive access to the files of Wayne's film production company to answer the question why he became and remains an iconic American figure.

"Insightful, exhaustive and engrossinga definitive portrait of the man and the legend." —*Kirkus*

Includes bibliographical references and index.

Fabes, Stephen

Signs of Life: A Doctor's Journey Around the Edges of the World. Stephen Fabes. Pegasus Books 2020. 416 pages

ISBN 9781643131955

Grades: Adult **B**

1. Fabes, Stephen 2. Physicians 3. Bicycle touring 4. Voyages and travels 5. Bicyclists 6. Rural health services 7. Trips around the world 8. Medical care 9. Weather 10. Wounds and injuries 11. Autobiographies and memoirs 12. Life stories — Science, technology, and medicine — Healthcare professionals 13. Travel Writing — Modes of Transportation — Cycling 14. Society and culture — Illness and disease

This inspiring narrative follows the author, a doctor and cyclist, on a six-year journey around the world by bicycle during which he visits remote medical clinics and health systems on the edge of society.

"Witty and wild, intrepid and inspirational, the book chronicles two parallel journeys: Fabes' physical cycling tour of many countries and his look at health across the globe.... An entertaining and epic chronicle of a journey of extremes." —*Booklist*

Fagan, Kate

All the Colors Came Out: A Father, a Daughter, and a Lifetime of Lessons. Kate Fagan. Little Brown & CO 2021. 208 pages

ISBN 9780316706919

Grades: Adult **B**

1. Fagan, Kate (Sports writer) 2. Fathers and daughters 3. Basketball 4. Basketball players 5. Lesbians 6. Death of fathers 7. Family relationships 8. People with terminal illnesses 9. Fathers 10. Autobiographies and memoirs 11. Life stories — Identity — LGBTQIA+ 12. Life stories — Relationships — Parent and child 13. Life stories — Sports — Athletes 14. Life stories — Facing adversity — Coping with death 15. Family and relationships — Aging and death 16. Sports and competition — Basketball 17. Book club best bets

From # 1 New York Times bestselling author Kate Fagan comes an unforgettable story about basketball and the enduring bonds between a father and daughter.

"When her father receives a devastating medical diagnosis, Fagan (What Made Maddy Run) leaves her job as an ESPN reporter and returns home to help care for him as he navigates life with ALS.... With strong appeal for book clubs, this heartbreaking, yet strongly inspirational memoir is very highly recommended for all public library collections, and deserving of a wide readership." —*Library Journal*

Fagone, Jason

The Woman Who Smashed Codes: A True Story of Love, Spies, and the Unlikely Heroine Who Outwitted America's Enemies. Jason Fagone. Dey Street Books 2017. 288 p.

ISBN 9780062430489

Grades: Adult **B**

1. Friedman, Elizabeth, 1892-1980 2. Cryptographers 3. Cryptography 4. Military intelligence 5. Codes (Communication) 6. Spies 7. Biographies 8. Life stories — Law and order 9. History writing — Spies and spying 10. Adult books for young adults

LC 2017470719

ALA Notable Book, 2018.

Describes the true story of Elizabeth Smith, a Shakespeare expert, who met and married a groundbreaking cryptologist and worked with him to discover and expose Nazi spy rings in South America by cracking multiple versions of the Enigma machine.

"Riveting, inspiring, and rich in colorful characters, Fagones extensively researched and utterly dazzling title is popular history at its very best and a book club natural." —*Booklist*

Fair, Eric

Consequence: A Memoir. Eric Fair. Henry Holt and Company 2016. 272 p.

ISBN 9781627795135

Grades: Adult **B**

1. Fair, Eric 2. Iraq War, 2003-2011 3. Military interrogation 4. Torture 5. Government contractors 6. Linguists 7. Guilt 8. Atrocities 9. Iraq 10. Autobiographies and memoirs 11. Life stories — Law and order — Armed forces personnel

LC 2015031396

In this harrowing and unprecedented memoir, a man questions everything—his faith, his morality, his country—as he recounts his experience with torture as an interrogator in Iraq.

A startling debut from a haunted individual who wishes he had left Iraq earlier 'With my soul intact.' —*Kirkus*

Fairweather, Jack

The Volunteer: One Man, an Underground Army, and the Secret Mission to Destroy Auschwitz. Jack Fairweather. Custom House 2019. xvi, 505 pages : Illustration; Map

ISBN 9780062561411

Grades: Adult **B**

1. Pilecki, Witold, 1901-1948 2. Prisoners 3. Espionage 4. Holocaust victims 5. Insurgency 6. Men 7. Soldiers 8. Military intelligence 9. Concentration camps 10. Holocaust (1933-1945) 11. Undercover operations 12. Infiltration (Military

science) 13. Concentration camp resistance and revolts 14. Biographies 15. History writing — Wars and conflicts — Holocaust — World War II

Costa Book of the Year Award, 2019; Costa Biography Award, 2019.

Documents the remarkable true story of an ill-fated Polish resistance fighter's infiltration of Auschwitz to sabotage the camp from within, chronicling his daring escape to smuggle evidence of murderous Nazi activities to Allied forces.

Faliveno, Melissa

Tomboyland. Melissa Faliveno. Little A/TOPPLE Books, 2020. 254 p.
ISBN 9781542014199
Grades: Adult   B

1. Faliveno, Melissa, 1983- 2. Gender role 3. Social classes and family 4. Desire 5. Identity 6. LGBTQIA+ people 7. Interpersonal relations 8. Genderqueer people 9. Sexuality 10. Families 11. Gender identity 12. United States 13. Essays 14. Autobiographies and memoirs 15. Life stories — Relationships — Growing up 16. Life stories — Identity — Gender 17. Life stories — Identity — LGBTQIA+ 18. Family and Relationships — Growing up

LC Bl2020046072

A fiercely personal and startlingly universal essay collection about the mysteries of gender and desire, of identity and class, of the stories we tell and the places we call home.

"Faliveno, a Sarah Lawrence creative writing instructor, explores identity in her winning debut collection. . . . Readers who prefer to answer their questions about gender and sexuality with more questions will appreciate this perceptive meditation." —*Publishers Weekly*

Faludi, Susan

In the Darkroom. Susan Faludi. Metropolitan Books 2016. 432 p.
ISBN 9780805089080
Grades: Adult   B

1. Faludi, Susan 2. Identity 3. Fathers and daughters 4. Transgender people 5. Transgender parents 6. Jewish people 7. Intersectionality 8. Eastern European people 9. Hungarian people 10. Autobiographies and memoirs 11. Life stories — Identity — LGBTQIA+ 12. Life stories — Relationships — Parent and child

LC 2016013605

ALA Notable Book, 2017; Kirkus Prize for Nonfiction, 2016; Library Journal Best Books, 2016; New York Times Notable Book, 2016; Pulitzer Prize for Biography or Autobiography finalist, 2017.

Pulitzer Prize-winning journalist Susan Faludi had barely heard from her father Steven for over 20 years when she received an email in which Steven came out as transgender. Now called Stefánie Faludi, she wanted to make her daughter's acquaintance all over again. In the Darkroom explores Stefánie's life, beginning in Budapest after World War I. Susan based this biography on recollections from her childhood, conversations and correspondence with Stefánie, as well as interviews with other family members and friends, Stefánie's surgeon, and other transgender women. In this fascinating account, Susan disentangles fact from fiction in Stefánie's recollections, painting a moving and insightful portrait.

"A moving and penetrating inquiry into manifold struggles for identity, community, a nd authenticity." —*Kirkus*

Farley, Audrey Clare

The Unfit Heiress: The Tragic Life and Scandalous Sterilization of Ann Cooper Hewitt. Audrey Clare Farley. Grand Central Publishing 2021. 304 p.
ISBN 9781538753354
Grades: Adult   B

1. Hewitt, Ann Cooper, 1914-1956 2. Heirs and heiresses 3. Socialites 4. Involuntary sterilization 5. Reproductive rights 6. Inheritance and succession 7. United States 8. 20th century 9. Biographies 10. Life stories — People in history 11. History writing — United States 12. History writing — Women's history

LC 2020053583

Documents the sobering 1934 court battle between Ann Cooper Hewitt and her socialite mother, citing the eugenics law that permitted the former to be declared unfit for promiscuity and sterilized without her knowledge.

"Historian Farley debuts with an intriguing account of socialite Ann Cooper Hewitt, who filed a." —*Publishers Weekly*

Includes bibliographical references.

Farrell, John A.

Clarence Darrow: Attorney for the Damned. John A. Farrell. Doubleday 2011. 576 p.
ISBN 9780385522588
Grades: Adult   B

1. Darrow, Clarence, 1857-1938 2. Lawyers 3. Progressivism (United States politics) 4. Defense attorneys 5. Social advocacy 6. Law and society 7. Politics and government 8. United States 9. 20th century 10. Biographies 11. History writing — Judicial branch — United States 12. Life stories — Law and order — Judges and lawyers

LC 2010046273

Los Angeles Times Book Prize for Biography, 2011; New York Times Notable Book, 2011.

A portrait of the legendary defense attorney and progressive covers his decision to leave a promising career to advocate on behalf of disadvantaged groups, his campaign against Jim Crow policies, and his achievements in headline-making trials.

"Farrell gleans from previously undisclosed material to offer a completely engaging portrait of a flawed man of noble ideals." —*Booklist*

Includes bibliographical references and index.

★ *Richard Nixon: The Life.* John A. Farrell. Doubleday 2017. 752 pages
ISBN 9780385537353
Grades: Adult   B

1. Nixon, Richard M. (Richard Milhous), 1913-1994 2. Politicians 3. Power 4. Watergate Scandal 5. Government cover-ups 6. Presidents 7. Politics and government 8. Ruthlessness 9. United States 10. 20th century 11. Biographies 12. Life stories — Politics — Politicians 13. History writing — Presidency — 20th century — United States

LC 2016049856

American History Book Prize, 2018; Longlisted for the Andrew Carnegie Medal for Excellence in Non-Fiction, 2018; Pulitzer Prize for Biography or Autobiography finalist, 2018.

An extensively researched portrait of the 37th president by the biographer of Clarence Darrow traces Nixon's early political ambitions in his post-military years, his early achievements as a senator and vice president and his forward-thinking ideas in health care, poverty, civil rights, the environment and foreign affairs.

Ted Kennedy: A Life. John A. Farrell. Penguin Press 2022. 592 p.
ISBN 9780525558071
Grades: Adult   B

1. Kennedy, Edward M. (Edward Moore), 1932-2009 2. Kennedy family 3. Legislators 4. Democrats 5. Politicians 6. Politics and government 7. United States 8. 20th century 9. 21st century 10. Biographies 11. Life stories — Politics — Politicians 12. Politics and global affairs — Political figures

LC 2021060432

Drawing on new sources, including segments of Kennedy's personal diary and his private confessions to members of his family, an award-winning biographer, who covered this fourth son of the Kennedy clan closely for years, reveals his famously epic and turbulent life of almost unimaginable tragedy and triumph.

"Biographer Farrell (Richard Nixon: The Life) untangles in this masterful account the complex blend of political dexterity, recklessness, and unflagging support of the less fortunate that defined Ted Kennedy's rise from overlooked youngest son of a political dynasty to 'Lion of the Senate.'…The result is the definitive one-volume biography of a consequential American lawmaker." —*Publishers Weekly*

Includes bibliographical references and index.

Fauber, L. S.

Heaven on Earth: How Copernicus, Brahe, Kepler, and Galileo Discovered the Modern World. L. S. Fauber. Pegasus Books 2019. 336 pages
ISBN 9781643132044

ESSENTIAL AND RECOMMENDED TITLES
Biography

Grades: Adult **B**
  1. Copernicus, Nicolaus, 1473-1543 2. Brahe, Tycho, 1546-1601 3. Kepler, Johannes, 1571-1630 4. Galilei, Galileo, 1564-1642 5. Renaissance science 6. Astronomy 7. Astronomers 8. Mathematicians 9. Planets 10. Science 11. European history 12. Solar system 13. Renaissance (1300-1600) 14. 16th century 15. Biographies 16. Life stories — Science, technology, and medicine — Scientists and inventors 17. History writing — Science, technology, and medicine 18. History writing — Renaissance — Europe 19. Science Writing — Space and Flight
LC Bl2019033971

A vivid narrative that connects the lives of four great astronomers as they discovered, refined, and popularized the first majorscientific discovery of the modern era: That the Earth moves around the Sun.

Faust, Drew Gilpin
Necessary Trouble: Growing up at Midcentury. Drew Gilpin Faust. Farrar, Straus and Giroux 2023. 320 p.
ISBN 9780374601805
Grades: Adult **B**
  1. Faust, Drew Gilpin 2. Gilpin family 3. Students 4. Civil Rights Movement 5. Race relations 6. Families 7. Civil rights 8. Gender role 9. Social life and customs 10. United States 11. Virginia 12. 20th century 13. 1950s 14. 1960s 15. Autobiographies and memoirs 16. Life stories — Relationships — Growing up 17. History Writing — United States
LC 2023008685

A memoir of coming of age in a conservative Southern family in postwar America. Index.

"The first memoir by Faust (This Republic of Suffering, 2008), a formidable historian and former Harvard president, is an origin story that traces her evolution from the child of a privileged Virginia family into an outraged young adult activist and protester and then into a respected scholar of slavery and the American Civil War." —*Booklist*

Includes bibliographical references and index.

Feaver, William
★ *The Lives of Lucian Freud: The Restless Years, 1922-1968.* by William Feaver. Knopf 2019. 704 pages
ISBN 9780525657521
Grades: Adult **B**
  1. Freud, Lucian 2. Painters 3. Artists 4. Portrait painters 5. Biographies 6. Arts and Entertainment — Painting, Drawing, and Sculpture 7. Life stories — Arts and culture — Artists
LC 2019016659

The first biography of the epic life of one of the most important, enigmatic and private artists of the 20th century. Drawn from almost 40 years of conversations with the artist, letters and papers, it is a major work written by a well-known British art critic.

Originally published in Great Britain by Bloomsbury Publishing Plc, London, in 2019; Includes bibliographical references and index.

Feige, David
Indefensible: One Lawyer's Journey into the Inferno of American Justice. David Feige. Little, Brown and Co. 2006. 276 p.
ISBN 9780316156233
Grades: Adult **B**
  1. Feige, David 2. Public defenders 3. Criminal justice system 4. Bronx, New York City 5. Autobiographies and memoirs 6. True Crime — Police and Lawyers 7. Life stories — Law and order — Judges and lawyers
LC 2006001283

A former Trial Chief of the Bronx Defenders recounts an ordinary day in the life of a South Bronx public defender, citing encounters with a range of factors, from dramatic courtroom battles and threatening defendants to unscrupulous lawyers and vindictive judges.

"The author takes us through a typically harrowing day as a public defender, dealing with arbitrary judges and clients who are often victims of the judicial system. Feige skillfully shares his wisdom and his humanity and sheds light on a justice system that too often works irrationally." —*Publishers Weekly*

Feinstein, Adam
Pablo Neruda: A Passion for Life. Adam Feinstein. Bloomsbury 2004. xii, 497 p. : Illustration
ISBN 9781582344102
Grades: Adult **B**
  1. Neruda, Pablo, 1904-1973 2. Authors 3. Chilean people 4. Social life and customs 5. Chile 6. 20th century 7. Biographies 8. Arts and Entertainment — Writing and Publishing 9. Life stories — Arts and culture — Writing — Authors
LC 2004000715

A biography of the Chilean author and poet traces his odyssey from a poverty-stricken youth, through his participation in the Spanish Civil War and exile from his own country, to his remarkable literary endeavors.

"Feinstein undoubtedly researched every existent source and found new ones, and the result is a detailed and accurate biography. This is a necessary book, with many beautiful photos." —*Publishers Weekly*

Includes bibliographical references (p. [451]-466) and index.

Feinstein, John
★ *The Legends Club: Dean Smith, Mike Krzyzewski, Jim Valvano, and an Epic College Basketball Rivalry.* John Feinstein. Doubleday 2016. 304 p.
ISBN 9780385539418
Grades: Adult **B**
  1. Basketball coaches 2. Basketball teams 3. Sports rivalry 4. College sports 5. Sports and Competition — Basketball 6. Sports and Competition — Coaches 7. Sports and Competition — Rivalry
LC 2015029890

In 1980, a legendary rivalry was heating up between three schools in NCAA basketball's Atlantic Coast Conference, all just a few miles apart. When this rousing history begins, two of the three coaches—now all household names—were just starting out: Duke's unknown new coach Mike Krzyzewski hadn't earned his moniker (Coach K), while Jim Valvano at NC State was, likewise, a brand-new hire. Only UNC-Chapel Hill's Dean Smith was well-established, but he still hadn't won a national championship. In this engaging book, longtime sportswriter John Feinstein uses extensive interviews to paint a picture of the rivalries and relationships—both on and off the court—between the three men over the ensuing years.

"A text that will delight college basketball fans but also raises tacit questions about the effects of big-time athletics on a university's academic mission." —*Kirkus*

Quarterback: Inside the Most Important Position in the National Football League. John Feinstein. Doubleday 2018. 352 p.
ISBN 9780385543033
Grades: Adult **B**
  1. Professional football 2. Quarterbacks (Football) 3. Professional football players 4. Professional athletes 5. Sports and Competition — Football
LC 2018031266

Dives deep into the most coveted and hallowed position in the NFL, exploring the stories of five top quarterbacks. By the #1 New York Times best-selling author of a Good Walk Spoiled.

Feldman, Deborah
Exodus. Deborah Feldman. Blue Rider Press 2014. 288 p.
ISBN 9780399162770
Grades: Adult **B**
  1. Feldman, Deborah, 1986- 2. Jewish women 3. Women authors 4. Single mothers 5. Jewish people 6. Survivor guilt 7. Identity 8. Independence 9. Autobiographies and memoirs 10. Spirituality and Religion — Judaism 11. Life stories — Religion and spirituality — Leaving religion
LC 2013046263

The author of the best-selling Unorthodox traces her new life as an independent young woman and single mother searching for an authentic and personal Jewish identity, describing how after leaving her Hasidic community she pursued healing in a circle of like-minded outcasts and misfits.

"The overall effect is captivating, entertaining and informative, providing readers with an honest assessment of the strength of one's convictions and the effect a strict religious background can have on a person. An enthralling account of how one Orthodox Jewish woman turned her back on her religion and found genuineness and validity in her new life." —*Kirkus*

Unorthodox: *The Scandalous Rejection of My Hasidic Roots.* Deborah Feldman. Simon & Schuster 2012. 272 p.
ISBN 9781439187005
Grades: Adult B
1. Feldman, Deborah, 1986- 2. Hasidim 3. Jewish women 4. Fundamentalists 5. Judaism 6. Oppression (Psychology) 7. Judaic doctrines 8. Women authors, American 9. Jewish people 10. Sexism 11. Self-discovery 12. Brooklyn, New York City 13. New York City 14. Autobiographies and memoirs 15. Page to screen 16. Biographies 17. Life stories — Arts and culture — Writing — Authors 18. Spirituality and Religion — Judaism
LC 2011001386

Traces the author's upbringing in a Hasidic community in Brooklyn, describing the strict rules that governed her life, arranged marriage at the age of seventeen, and the birth of her son, which led to her plan to leave and forge her own path in life.

"Born into the insular and exclusionary Hasidic community of Satmar in Brooklyn to a mentally disabled father and a mother who fled the sect, Feldman, as she recounts in this nicely written memoir, seemed doomed to be an outsider from the start. Raised by devout grandparents who forbade her to read in English, the ever-curious child craved books outside the synagogue teaching. Feldman's spark of rebellion started with sneaking off to the library and hiding paperback novels under her bed. She starts to experience panic attacks and the stirrings of her final break with being Hasidic. It's when she finally does get pregnant and wants something more for her child that the full force of her uprising takes hold and she plots her escape. Feldman, who now attends Sarah Lawrence College, offers this engaging and at times gripping insight into Brooklyn's Hasidic community." —*Publishers Weekly*

This memoir was adapted into a Netflix TV series in 2021 by the same name.

Feldman, Noah
The Three Lives of James Madison: Genius, Partisan, President. Noah Feldman. Random House 2017. 944 p.
ISBN 9780812992755
Grades: Adult B
1. Madison, James, 1751-1836 2. Founding fathers of the United States 3. Presidents 4. Politicians 5. Political leadership 6. Politics and government 7. United States 8. 18th century 9. Biographies 10. Life stories — Politics — Politicians 11. History writing — Presidency — 18th century — United States 12. History writing — Early America — United States
LC 2017000125

A controversial assessment of what the author identifies as the three distinct arcs of the fourth American President's career explores how he redefined the United States in each of his political roles through his design of the Constitution, co-founding of the Democratic-Republican Party and invention of wartime economic sanctions.

"With its lively prose and political acumen, this biography will be of interest to general-history readers and scholars alike." —*Publishers Weekly*

Includes bibliographical references and index.

Felix, Camonghne
Dyscalculia: *A Love Story of Epic Miscalculation.* Camonghne Felix. One World 2023. 240 p.
ISBN 9780593242179
Grades: Adult B
1. Healing 2. Childhood 3. Psychic trauma 4. Neurodivergent people 5. Dyscalculia 6. Mental health 7. Breaking up (Interpersonal relations) 8. Love 9. Interpersonal relations 10. African American women 11. Mathematics 12. Learning disabilities 13. Self-discovery 14. Autobiographies and memoirs 15. Life stories — Relationships 16. Family and relationships — General

The acclaimed author of Build Yourself a Boat examines a painful breakup and subsequent healing through the prism of her childhood "dyscalculia"—a disorder that makes it difficult to learn math.

"After a breakup so thornily horrendous that she ended up in the hospital, poet/Essayist Felix uses her childhood dyscalculia—a disorder that makes math hard to learn—as a means of understanding her missteps in love and in life." —*Library Journal*

Fellman, Michael
The Making of Robert E. Lee. Michael Fellman. Johns Hopkins University Press 2003. xx, 360 p. : Illustration
ISBN 9780801874116
Grades: Adult B
1. Lee, Robert E. (Robert Edward), 1807-1870 2. Generals 3. Gentry 4. Biographies 5. Life stories — Law and order — Military leaders 6. History writing — Wars and conflicts — American Civil War
LC 2002043290

With rigorous research and unprecedented insight into Robert E. Lee's personal and public lives, Michael Fellman here uncovers the intelligent, ambitious, and often troubled man behind the legend, exploring his life within the social, cultural, and political context of the nineteenth-century American South.

Includes bibliographical references and index; Originally published in hardcover by Random House, Inc, New York, 2000—T.P. verso.

Felton, Tom
★ **Beyond** *the Wand: The Magic and Mayhem of Growing up a Wizard.* Tom Felton. Grand Central Publishing 2022. 272 p.
ISBN 9781538741368
Grades: Adult B
1. Felton, Tom, 1987- 2. Actors and actresses 3. Fame 4. Growing up 5. Popular culture 6. Harry Potter films 7. Life change events 8. Acting 9. Films 10. Autobiographies and memoirs 11. Life stories — Arts and culture — Performing arts — Actors and actresses 12. Arts and Entertainment — Movies and television

The actor who played iconic role of the Draco Malfoy in the Harry Potter movies recalls his experiences growing up in the whirlwind of the pop culture phenomenon while navigating life as a normal teenager.

"Actor Felton, best known for his portrayal of bleached-blond antagonist Draco Malfoy in the Harry Potter films, recounts his career in his charming debut memoir." —*Publishers Weekly*

Fenn, Lisa
Carry On: A Story of Resilience, Redemption, and an Unlikely Family. Lisa Fenn. Harper Wave 2016. 320 p.
ISBN 9780062427830
Grades: Adult B
1. Fenn, Lisa 2. Crockett, Dartanyon 3. Sutton, Leroy 4. African Americans 5. People with disabilities 6. Friendship 7. Wrestlers 8. Inner city 9. Love 10. People who are blind 11. Teenagers 12. Cleveland, Ohio 13. Autobiographies and memoirs 14. Life stories — Relationships — Friendship 15. Life stories — Facing adversity — Personal transformation 16. Sports and recreation — Wrestling
LC 2016012130

An Emmy-winning ESPN producer describes how she developed a surprising, profound and lasting bond with two disabled African-American, inner-city high school wrestlers after filming a segment about them for television.

Fennelly, Beth Ann
Heating *& Cooling: 52 Micro-memoirs.* Beth Ann Fennelly. W W Norton & CO Inc 2017. 128 p.
ISBN 9780393609479
Grades: Adult B
1. Fennelly, Beth Ann, 1971- 2. Women poets 3. Everyday life 4. Mother and child 5. Men-women relations 6. Autobiographies and memoirs 7. Life stories — Relationships
LC 2017026664

The 52 micro-memoirs in genre-defying Heating & Cooling offer bright glimpses into a richly lived life, combining the compression of poetry with the truth-telling of nonfiction into one heartfelt, celebratory book. Ranging from childhood recollections to quirky cultural observations, these micro-memoirs build on one another to arrive at a portrait of Beth Ann Fennelly as a wife, mother, writer, and deeply original observer of life's challenges and joys.

ESSENTIAL AND RECOMMENDED TITLES
Biography

"A sleek, delightful collection." —*Kirkus*

Ferguson, Jane
No Ordinary Assignment: A Memoir. Jane Ferguson. Mariner Books 2023. 320 p.
ISBN 9780063272248
Grades: Adult B
1. Ferguson, Jane 2. Women war correspondents 3. War in the news media 4. Women journalists 5. War correspondents 6. Irish people 7. War 8. Ambition 9. Journalism 10. Autobiographies and memoirs 11. Life stories — Arts and culture — Writing — Journalists 12. Arts and Entertainment — Writing and Publishing
LC 2023009676

From award-winning journalist Jane Ferguson, an unflinching memoir of ambition and war—from the Troubles to the fall of Kabul.

"An award-winning war reporter recounts her remarkable career in some of the most dangerous places on the planet." —*Kirkus*

Fernandez-Armesto, Felipe
★ *Amerigo: The Man Who Gave His Name to America.* Felipe Fernandez-Armesto. Random House 2007. xxi, 231 p. : Illustration; Map
ISBN 9781400062812
Grades: 11 12 Adult B
1. Vespucci, Amerigo, 1451-1512 2. Explorers 3. Exploration 4. Spanish people 5. Western Hemisphere 6. Florence, Italy 7. Biographies 8. History writing — Exploration 9. Life stories — People in history — Explorers 10. Adult books for young adults
LC 2006051739

Booklist Editors' Choice, 2007.

In this groundbreaking work, leading historian Felipe Fernandez-Armesto tells the story of our hemisphere as a whole, showing why it is impossible to understand North, Central, and South America in isolation without turning to the intertwining forces that shape the region.

"Faced by unreliable sources, Fernandez-Armesto sticks to what can be said of Vespucci with confidence, and wisely opts to paint a rich portrait of the times rather than speculate about details that may never be known." —*Times Literary Supplement*

Includes bibliographical references (p. [205]-220) and index.

Field, Sally
In Pieces. Sally Field. Grand Central Publishing 2018. VIII, 404 p.
ISBN 9781538763025
Grades: Adult B
1. Field, Sally 2. Actors and actresses 3. Celebrities 4. Fame 5. Mothers and daughters 6. Motherhood 7. Family relationships 8. Autobiographies and memoirs 9. Life stories — Arts and culture — Performing arts — Actors and actresses 10. Arts and Entertainment — Movies and Television 11. Life stories — Relationships — Family
LC Bl2018134673

Library Journal Best Books, 2018; New York Times Notable Book, 2018.

The Academy Award-winning actress shares insights into her difficult childhood, the artistic pursuits that helped her find her voice and the powerful emotional legacy that shaped her journey as a daughter and mother.

Fiennes, Ranulph
Shackleton: The Biography. Ranulph Fiennes. Pegasus Books 2022. 452 p.
ISBN 9781643138794
Grades: Adult B
1. Shackleton, Ernest Henry, Sir, 1874-1922 2. Explorers 3. Exploration 4. Antarctica 5. Biographies 6. Life stories — People in history — Explorers 7. Adventure Writing — Exploration

In 1915, Sir Ernest Shackleton's attempt to traverse the Antarctic was cut short when his ship, Endurance, became trapped in ice. The disaster left Shackleton and his men alone at the frozen South Pole, fighting for their lives. Their survival and escape is the most famous adventure in history. Shackleton is an enthralling new account of the adventurer, his life and his incredible leadership under the most extreme of circumstances. Written by polar adventurer and 'The world's greatest living explorer' Sir Ranulph Fiennes, who brings his own unique insights to bear on the expedition, Shackleton is both re-appraisal and a valediction, separating the man from the myth he has become.

"A world-renowned explorer and prolific writer turns his attention to Ernest Shackleton (1874-1922), a giant of the heroic age of polar exploration, with entirely satisfying results." —*Kirkus*

Originally published in the UK by Michael Joseph, London, in 2021.

Fifield, Anna
The Great Successor: The Divinely Perfect Destiny of Brilliant Comrade Kim Jong Un. Anna Fifield. PublicAffairs 2019. 288 p.
ISBN 9781541742482
Grades: Adult B
1. Kim, Chong-un, 1984- 2. Dictators 3. Fascism 4. Isolationism 5. Communist countries 6. Dictatorship 7. Politics and government 8. North Korea 9. Politics and global affairs — World politics — Asia 10. History writing — Asia — North and South Korea
LC 2019004479

A Washington Post journalist with exclusive access to the dictator's inner circle, including an aunt and uncle and a Japanese sushi chef he befriended, paints a fascinating portrait of the most isolated regime in the world.

"A compelling mix of biography, cultural history, and political intrigue." —*Kirkus*

Includes bibliographical references and index.

Fincham-Gray, Suzanne
My Patients and Other Animals: A Veterinarian's Stories of Love, Loss, and Hope. by Suzanne Fincham-Gray. Spiegel & Grau 2018. 288 p.
ISBN 9780812998184
Grades: Adult B
1. Fincham-Gray, Suzanne 2. Veterinarians 3. Animals 4. Human-animal relationships 5. Autobiographies and memoirs 6. Life stories — Relationships — Pets and owners
LC 2017025329

A memoir of the author's life spent in the company of animals illuminates the universal experiences of loving, healing and losing beloved pets, describing some of the remarkable cases that shaped her career while sharing a veterinarian's perspectives into the many ways that animals change our lives.

Finkel, Michael
The Stranger in the Woods: The Extraordinary Story of the North Pond Hermit. by Michael Finkel. Alfred A. Knopf 2017. 240 p.
ISBN 9781101875681
Grades: Adult B
1. Knight, Christopher Thomas, 1965- 2. Solitude 3. Eccentrics and eccentricities 4. Wilderness survival 5. Hermits 6. Recluses 7. Stealing 8. Maine 9. Biographies 10. Life stories — General 11. Adventure writing — Survival 12. Adult books for young adults 13. Nonfiction that reads like fiction
LC 2016029910

LibraryReads Favorites, 2017.

Documents the true story of a man who endured a hardscrabble, isolated existence in a tent in the Maine woods, never speaking with others and surviving by stealing supplies from nearby cabins, for 27 years, in a portrait that illuminates the survival means he developed and the reasons behind his solitary life.

"With inevitable comparisons to Jon Krakauer's into the Wild, this book will appeal to recreational readers interested in outdoor adventure, survival stories, or escaping the mainstream." —*Library Journal*

This is a Borzoi book—Title page verso.

Finkelman, Paul
Millard Fillmore: The 13th President, 1850-1853. Paul Finkelman. Times Books 2011. 192 p. (American presidents series (Times Books))
ISBN 9780805087154
Grades: 11 12 Adult B

PUBLIC LIBRARY CORE COLLECTION: NONFICTION
Twentieth Edition

1. Fillmore, Millard, 1800-1874 2. Politicians 3. Civil war 4. United States Civil War, 1861-1865 5. Presidents 6. Vice-presidents 7. Causes of war 8. Politics and government 9. United States history 10. United States 11. 19th century 12. American Civil War era (1861-1865) 13. Biographies 14. History writing — Presidency — 19th century — United States 15. History writing — Antebellum America — United States 16. Life stories — Politics — Politicians

LC 2010047174

A portrait of the 13th President traces his rise from virtual obscurity after the sudden death of Zachary Taylor, evaluating his roles in promoting Southern agendas, dividing the Whig party and setting the groundwork for the American Civil War.

"The author describes Millard Fillmore's nearly forgotten presidency by rigidly contrasting him with Abraham Lincoln, another self-made man who wrestled with racial and regional tensions as president. . . . This book is an enlightening view into the often overlooked beginnings of the Civil War, which history buffs and students alike will find enjoyable." —*Publishers Weekly*

Includes bibliographical references and index.

Finn, Adharanand
The Rise of the Ultra Runners: A Journey to the Edge of Human Endurance. Adharanand Finn. Pegasus Books 2019. 320 p.

ISBN 9781643131351

Grades: Adult B

1. Finn, Adharanand 2. Running 3. Ultramarathon running 4. Long-distance running 5. Endurance sports 6. Ultramarathon runners 7. Cross-country running 8. Long-distance runners 9. Runners 10. Training 11. Autobiographies and memoirs 12. Sports and Competition — Racing — Track and Field 13. Life stories — Sports — Athletes

Investigates the rise in popularity of extreme distance running from the deserts of Oman to the Rocky Mountains and provides fascinating profiles of the ultrarunners who test the boundaries of human endurance and endeavor.

"Finn's race descriptions are so riveting, readers are running alongside him feeling all his pain and pleasure as he accomplishes each incredible distance." —*Library Journal*

Finnegan, William
Barbarian Days: A Surfing Life. William Finnegan. Penguin Press 2014. 384 p.

ISBN 9781594203473

Grades: Adult B

1. Surfing 2. Surfers 3. Obsession 4. Voyages and travels 5. Autobiographies and memoirs 6. Life stories — Sports — Athletes 7. Sports and Competition — General 8. Adventure writing — Adventure travel 9. Book club best bets

LC 2015472507

New York Times Notable Book, 2015; Pulitzer Prize for Biography or Autobiography, 2016.

Surfers ahoy! If you can't get enough surfing memoirs or detailed examinations of surfing's subcultures or history, you won't want to miss this richly detailed story of William Finnegan's experiences as a lifelong surfer. Whether you're reading this on the beach or the couch, surfers will recognize Finnegan's search for the perfect wave in some of the most beautiful places on Earth.

"The constants flowing through this part coming-of-age story and part travelog are the ocean and the waves that the author tries to better understand. The result is an up-close and personal homage to the surfing lifestyle through the author's journey as a lifelong surfer." —*Library Journal*

Fischer, David Hackett
Champlain's Dream. David Hackett Fischer. Simon & Schuster 2008. 608 p.

ISBN 9781416593324

Grades: 11 12 Adult B

1. Champlain, Samuel de, 1567-1635 2. Explorers 3. Colonialism 4. Diplomacy 5. Exploration 6. Canadian history 7. Canada 8. United States 9. Quebec (Province) 10. 17th century 11. New France (1534-1763) 12. Biographies 13. Life stories — People in history — Explorers 14. History writing — Exploration 15. Adult books for young adults 16. History writing — Early Canada to Confederation (1867) — Canada

LC 2008016286

Booklist Editors' Choice, 2008; New York Times Notable Book, 2008; Cundill Prize in Historical Literature finalist.

Traces the story of Quebec's founder while explaining his influential perspectives about peaceful colonialism, in a profile that also evaluates his contributions as a soldier, mariner, and cultural diplomat.

Includes bibliographical references and index.

Fisher, Todd
My Girls: A Lifetime with Carrie and Debbie. Todd Fisher. William Morrow 2018. x, 388 pages, 32 unnumbered pages of plates : Illustration; Color

ISBN 9780062792310

Grades: Adult B

1. Fisher, Todd, 1958- 2. Reynolds, Debbie 3. Fisher, Carrie 4. Film producers and directors 5. Family relationships 6. Siblings 7. Mother and child 8. Celebrities 9. Memories 10. Growing up 11. Entertainment industry and trade 12. Films 13. Actors and actresses 14. Hollywood, California 15. Autobiographies and memoirs 16. Life stories — Relationships — Family 17. Arts and Entertainment — Movies and Television 18. Life stories — Arts and culture — Performing arts — Actors and actresses 19. Life stories — Arts and culture — Performing arts — Directors and producers

a personal tribute to the lives of Carrie Fisher and Debbie Reynolds shares poignant stories of the author's experiences growing up with his sister and their mother among Hollywood royalty.

Fishman, Boris
Savage Feast: Three Generations, Two Continents, and a Dinner Table, a Memoir with Recipes. Boris Fishman. HarperCollins 2019. 320 p.

ISBN 9780062867896

Grades: Adult B

1. Fishman, Boris, 1979- 2. Immigrant families 3. Jewish people 4. Food 5. Intergenerational relations 6. Belarusian people 7. Family relationships 8. Immigrants, Jewish 9. Recipes 10. Eastern European people 11. European people 12. Autobiographies and memoirs 13. Life stories — Identity — Immigrants 14. Food writing — Memoirs and biographies

LC 2018277185

The acclaimed author of A Replacement Life shifts between heartbreak and humor in a recipe-filled memoir that is all-at-once a family story, an immigrant story, a love story and an epic meal.

Fitzgerald, Isaac
Dirtbag, Massachusetts: A Confessional. Isaac Fitzgerald. Bloomsbury Publishing Place USA 2022. 304 p.

ISBN 9781635573978

Grades: Adult B

1. Masculinity 2. Identity 3. Gender role 4. Forgiveness 5. Psychic trauma 6. Dysfunctional families 7. Poverty 8. Self-acceptance 9. Essays 10. Autobiographies and memoirs 11. Life stories — Identity — Gender 12. Life stories — Relationships — Growing up

The founding editor of BuzzFeed Books searches for a more expansive vision of masculinity in a collection of personal essays—with "life mistakes are my copilot" as his motto.

"Journalist Fitzgerald (How to Be a Pirate) weaves a raucous mosaic of a rough-and-ready New England rarely seen with a transfixing story of his path to finding himself….The result is a marvelous coming-of-age story that's as wily and raunchy as it is heartfelt." —*Publishers Weekly*

Fitzharris, Lindsey
The Butchering Art: Joseph Lister's Quest to Transform the Grisly World of Victorian Medicine. Lindsey Fitzharris. Scientific American / Farrar, Straus and Giroux 2017. 288 p.

ISBN 9780374117290

Grades: Adult B

1. Lister, Joseph, Baron, 1827-1912 2. Surgeons 3. Surgery 4. Medicine 5. Physicians 6. 19th century 7. Biographies 8. Life stories — Science, technology, and medicine — Healthcare professionals 9. History writing — Science, tech-

ESSENTIAL AND RECOMMENDED TITLES
Biography

nology, and medicine 10. Science Writing — Medicine and health — Doctors and nurses

LC 2016059275

ALA Notable Book, 2018.

A dramatic account of how 19th-century Quaker surgeon Joseph Lister developed an antiseptic method that indelibly changed medicine, describes the practices and risks of early operating theaters as well as the belief systems of Lister's contemporaries.

Includes bibliographical references and index.

Fleming, Brandon P.
Miseducated: A Memoir. Brandon P. Fleming. Hachette Books 2021. 254 p.
ISBN 9780306925139
Grades: Adult   **B**
1. Fleming, Brandon P. 2. College teachers 3. Transformations, Personal 4. African American men 5. Personal conduct 6. Growing up 7. Adult child abuse victims 8. Self-destructive behavior 9. Drugs 10. Psychic trauma 11. College dropouts 12. United States 13. Autobiographies and memoirs 14. Life stories — Facing adversity 15. Life stories — Education — Scholars and educators

LC 2020054279

In this inspiring memoir, readers will witness the author's transformation from a delinquent, drug-dealing dropout to an award-winning Harvard educator through literature and debate and how he takes what he learns about words and power to help others like himself.

"Fleming gives us an intimate look at his transformation from a troubled youth to an esteemed scholar and educator in this intimate memoir." —*Library Journal*

Fleshman, Lauren
★ *Good for a Girl: A Woman Running in a Man's World.* Lauren Fleshman. Penguin Books 2023. 352 p.
ISBN 9780593296783
Grades: Adult   **B**
1. Fleshman, Lauren 2. Women runners 3. Women athletic coaches 4. Mentors 5. Sex discrimination against women 6. Sex discrimination in sports 7. Women's sports 8. North American people 9. American people 10. United States 11. Autobiographies and memoirs 12. Life stories — Sports 13. Society and culture — Gender — Women 14. Sports and Competition — Individual Athlete 15. Sports and Competition — Coaches

LC 2022028016

Lauren Fleshman has grown up in the world of running: One of the most decorated collegiate athletes of all time and a national champion as a pro, she was a major face of women's running for Nike before leaving to shake up the industry with feminist running brand Oiselle and now coaches elite young female runners. Every step of the way, she has seen the way that our sports systems-originally designed by men, for men and boys-fail young women and girls as much as empower them. Part memoir, part manifesto, Good for a Girl is Fleshman's story of falling in love with running as a girl and daring to fight for a better way for female athletes.

"As the author lays bare the price women pay for success in an athletic system that still favors males, she offers a thoughtful, much-needed plea for a more humane, gender-neutral sporting system." —*Kirkus*

Includes bibliographical references.

Flexner, James Thomas
George Washington: Anguish and Farewell 1793-1799. James Thomas Flexner. Little, Brown 1972. xii, 554 p. : Illustration
ISBN 9780316286022
Grades: Adult   **B**
1. Washington, George, 1732-1799 2. Presidents 3. Generals 4. Politics and government 5. United States history 6. United States 7. 18th century 8. Early America (1784-1819) 9. Biographies 10. History writing — Presidency — 18th century — United States 11. History writing — Presidency — United States 12. History writing — Early America — United States 13. Life stories — Politics — Politicians

LC 72006875

Profiles Washington from his second term as president to his death, focusing on his struggles to unite the new republic.

Includes bibliographyical references (p. 509-516).

Foer, Esther Safran
I Want You to Know We're Still Here: A Post-holocaust Memoir. Esther Safran Foer. Tim Duggan Books 2020. 288 p.
ISBN 9780525575986
Grades: Adult   **B**
1. Foer, Esther Safran 2. Children of Holocaust survivors 3. Family history 4. Jewish families 5. Loss 6. Family secrets 7. Immigrants, Jewish 8. Voyages and travels 9. Holocaust survivors 10. Jewish women 11. United States 12. Poland 13. Ukraine 14. Autobiographies and memoirs 15. Life stories — Relationships — Family 16. Family and relationships — Families

LC 2019025860

A Jewish-American community leader and founding CEO of Sixth & I describes her parents' silence on their Holocaust experiences and her visit to the Ukraine in search of her family's stories.

"Foer explores her family with context and detail. Her story will interest readers of historical and personal narratives, especially memoirs and genealogy." —*Library Journal*

Fogerty, John
Fortunate Son: My Life, My Music. John Fogerty. Little Brown & CO 2015. 320 p.
ISBN 9780316244572
Grades: Adult   **B**
1. Fogerty, John, 1945- 2. Rock musicians 3. United States 4. Autobiographies and memoirs 5. Biographies 6. Arts and Entertainment — Music — Rock 7. Life stories — Arts and culture — Performing arts — Musicians and composers

LC Bl2015033619

The legendary singer-songwriter and creative force behind Creedence Clearwater Revival, as well as a Grammy-winning solo artist in his own right, presents his long-awaited memoir.

"This isn't just an account of one musician's ups and downs with art and life; Fogerty has created a solid study of popular music over the past 50 years." —*Publishers Weekly*

Foles, Nick
Believe It: My Journey of Success, Failure, and Overcoming the Odds. Nick Foles, with Joshua Cooley. The nonfiction imprint of Tyndale House Publishers, Inc. 2018. 288 p.
ISBN 9781496436498
Grades: Adult   **B**
1. Foles, Nick 2. Quarterbacks (Football) 3. Football players 4. Determination 5. Faith (Christianity) 6. Autobiographies and memoirs 7. Sports and Competition — Football 8. Life stories — Sports — Athletes

LC 2018021881

The author describes how he separates himself from his football career and how his past mistakes have shaped him into the man he is today.

Foo, Stephanie
★ *What My Bones Know: A Memoir of Healing from Complex Trauma.* Stephanie Foo. Ballantine Group 2022. 320 p.
ISBN 9780593238103
Grades: Adult   **B**
1. Foo, Stephanie 2. Post-traumatic stress disorder 3. Family secrets 4. Families 5. Mind and body 6. Family violence 7. Healing 8. Intergenerational trauma 9. Psychic trauma 10. Autobiographies and memoirs 11. Life stories — Facing adversity — Medical issues — Mental illness 12. Science writing — Medicine and health — Mental health 13. Life stories — Relationships 14. Family and relationships — General

LC 2021042024

By age thirty, Stephanie Foo was successful on paper: She had her dream job as a radio producer at This American Life and had won an Emmy. But behind her office door she was having panic attacks and sobbing at her desk. After years of questioning what was wrong with her, she was diagnosed with Complex PTSD-a condition that occurs when trauma happens continuously, over the course of years. Both of Stephanie's parents had abandoned her as a teenager after years of physical and verbal abuse and neglect. She thought she'd overcome her trauma, but her diagnosis illuminated the ways in which her past continued to threaten her health, her relationships, and her career. Finding few resources to help her heal, Stephanie set out to map her experience onto the scarce scientific research on C-PTSD.

"What takes this brilliant work from a personal story to a cultural touch point is the way Foo situates her experiences into a larger conversation about intergenerational trauma, immigration, and the mind-body connection." —Publishers Weekly

Forbes, Nancy
Faraday, Maxwell, and the Electromagnetic Field: How Two Men Revolutionized Physics. Nancy Forbes, Basil Mahon. Prometheus Books 2014. 300 p.
ISBN 9781616149420
Grades: Adult   B
1. Faraday, Michael, 1791-1867 2. Maxwell, James Clark, 1831-1879 3. Physicists 4. Electromagnetism 5. Electricity 6. Magnetism 7. Scientists 8. Research 9. Biographies 10. Science Writing — Physics 11. Life stories — Science, technology, and medicine — Scientists and inventors

Describes how Faraday and Maxwell discovered the electromagnetic field and devised a radical new theory which overturned the strictly mechanical view of the world that had prevailed since Newton's time.

Forche, Carolyn
What You Have Heard Is True: A Memoir of Witness and Resistance. Carolyn Forche. Penguin Group 2019. 400 pages
ISBN 9780525560371
Grades: Adult   B
1. Poets 2. Resistance to government 3. State-sponsored terrorism 4. Options, alternatives, choices 5. Poverty 6. Political activists 7. War 8. Death squads 9. Civil war 10. Politics and government 11. El Salvador 12. Autobiographies and memoirs 13. Life stories — People in history — Witness to history 14. History writing — Regimes and political violence — Latin America 15. Life stories — Arts and culture — Writing — Poets
LC 2018289788

New York Times Notable Book, 2019; National Book Award for Nonfiction finalist, 2019.

The prize-winning author of Blue Hour describes her deep friendship with a mysterious intellectual who introduced her to the culture and people of El Salvador, inspiring her work as an unlikely activist.

"Episode by episode, dodging death squads, Forch builds a story filled with violence and intrigue worthy of Graham Greene around which a river of blood flowsdoing so, unstanched, with the avid support of America's leaders. A valuable firsthand report of a time of terror." —Kirkus

Ford, Ashley C.
★ *Somebody's Daughter: A Memoir.* Ashley C. Ford. Flatiron Books 2021. 304 p.
ISBN 9781250305978
Grades: Adult   B
1. Ford, Ashley C. 2. African American families 3. Children of prisoners 4. Family secrets 5. Prisoners' families 6. Growing up 7. African American teenagers 8. Single-parent families 9. Rape victims 10. Abandonment (Psychology) 11. Self-acceptance 12. Familial love 13. African American women 14. Indiana 15. Autobiographies and memoirs 16. Biographies 17. Life stories — Facing adversity — Abuse survivors 18. Life stories — Relationships — Growing up 19. Life stories — Identity — Race and ethnicity 20. Family and Relationships — Families 21. Family and Relationships — Growing up 22. Book club best bets
LC 2021002077

Rise: A Feminist Book Project List, 2022; National Book Critics Circle Award: John Leonard Prize finalist, 2021.

One of the prominent voices of her generation, the author presents this coming-of-age recollection of a childhood defined by the ever looming absence of her incarcerated father and a traumatic event, revealing the threads between who you are and what you are born into.

"Journalist Ford debuts with a blistering yet tender account of growing up with an incarcerated father. . . . This remarkable, heart-wrenching story of loss, hardship, and self-acceptance astounds." —Publishers Weekly

Ford, Christine Blasey
One Way Back: A Memoir. Christine Blasey Ford. St Martins Press 2024. 320 p.
ISBN 9781250289650
Grades: Adult   B
1. Kavanaugh, Brett, 1965- 2. Sexual violence victims 3. Whistle blowers 4. Whistle blowing 5. Sex crimes 6. American people 7. Autobiographies and memoirs 8. Life stories — Politics 9. Life stories — Facing adversity — Victims of crime

On September 27, 2018, Christine Blasey Ford testified before the Senate Judiciary Committee which was considering the nomination of Judge Brett Kavanaugh to the United States Supreme Court; this is the true behind-the-scenes story of that testimony.

"A hero of the #MeToo movement tells her full life story in her own words in this revealing, confident memoir." —Kirkus

Ford, Elizabeth
Sometimes Amazing Things Happen: Heartbreak and Hope on the Bellevue Hospital Psychiatric Prison Ward. Elizabeth Ford. Regan Arts 2017. 272 p.
ISBN 9781941393437
Grades: Adult   B
1. Ford, Elizabeth (Elizabeth B.) 2. Women forensic psychiatrists 3. Medical care services 4. People with mental illnesses 5. Criminals 6. Forensic psychiatry 7. Prison industry and trade 8. Prison-industrial complex 9. Prisoners 10. Autobiographies and memoirs 11. Life stories — Science, technology, and medicine 12. Society and culture — Violence and crime — Criminal justice system

The Chief of Psychiatry for Correctional Health Services in New York City presents a revelatory and compassionate memoir of her work inside Bellevue Hospital's forensic psychiatry unit to share insights into the cases, colleagues and system that have shaped her views about survival and humanity.

Ford, Richard
Between Them: Remembering My Parents. Richard Ford. Ecco Press 2017. 192 p.
ISBN 9780062661883
Grades: Adult   B
1. Ford, Richard, 1944- 2. Parent and child 3. Traveling sales personnel 4. Growing up 5. Arkansas 6. Autobiographies and memoirs 7. Life stories — Relationships — Growing up 8. Family and Relationships — Families
LC 2017478573

The Pulitzer Prize-winning author of the Bascombe novels presents a memoir in two parts on the lives of his parents in the Depression-era South that explores their motivations and dreams, his traveling salesman father's early death and the family's transient lives in a series of hotels.

"Illustrated with family photographs, Fords remembrance of his parents is a masterful distillation of sensuous description, psychological intricacy, social insights, and a keen sense of place." —Booklist

Ford, Tanisha C.
Our Secret Society: Mollie Moon and the Glamour, Money, and Power Behind the Civil Rights Movement. Tanisha C. Ford. Amistad Press 2023. 353 p.
ISBN 9780063115712
Grades: Adult   B
1. Moon, Mollie 2. African American women 3. Socialites 4. Women political activists 5. Progressivism (United States politics) 6. Civil Rights Movement 7. Fund raising 8. Philanthropy 9. Social justice 10. African American history 11. North American people 12. American people 13. Biographies 14. Life stories — Politics — Activists and Reformers — Civil Rights Leaders 15. History writing — African American — Civil rights — United States

ESSENTIAL AND RECOMMENDED TITLES
Biography

Our Secret Society illuminates a little known yet highly significant aspect of the civil rights movement that has been long overlooked—the powerhouse fundraising effort that supported the movement. No one knew this world better or ruled over it with more authority than Mollie Moon. Historian and cultural critic Tanisha C. Ford brings Mollie into focus as never before, charting her rise from Jim Crow Mississippi to doyenne of Manhattan and Harlem, where she became one of the most influential philanthropists of her time—a woman feared, resented, yet widely respected.

Historian Ford (Liberated Threads) sets forth a riveting portrait of the 'Doyenne of Harlem society,' Mollie Lewis Moon (1907?1990), charting her rise from 'Leftist social worker to famed African American fundraiser.' —*Publishers Weekly*

Foreman, Amanda
Georgiana, Duchess of Devonshire. Amanda Foreman. Modern Library 2001. xx, 456 p. : Illustration
ISBN 9780375753831
Grades: Adult **B**
1. Cavendish, Georgiana Spencer, Duchess of Devonshire, 1757-1806 2. Devonshire, William Cavendish, Duke of, 1748-1811 3. Women politicians 4. Nobility 5. Social life and customs 6. British history 7. Great Britain 8. 18th century 9. Georgian era (1714-1837) 10. Biographies 11. Page to screen 12. History writing — Europe — United Kingdom 13. History writing — Women's history 14. Life stories — Politics — Royalty
LC 00064579
Booklist Editors' Choice, 2000; New York Times Notable Book, 2000; Whitbread Book Award for Biography, 1998.

Amanda Foreman, a Londoner, freelance journalist, and Oxford graduate, presents the captivating story of Lady Georgiana Spencer, the Duchess of Devonshire. In 1774, Georgiana married wealthy aristocrat and fifth duke of Devonshire, William Cavendish. The marriage spoiled immediately, and Georgiana, noted for her style and political involvement, yet limited as a woman by law, dealt with her adulterous and cold husband through secret substance and gambling addictions as well as illicit romances.

"Georgiana was the society leader of her day. Daughter of the fabulously wealthy Earl Spencer (and ancestor of the late princess of Wales) and married to the even more wealthy duke of Devonshire, Georgiana was watched, adored, and imitated. But she evolved herself into more than just a fashionable hostess; she got involved in Whig politics, to an extent unprecedented for women. The tenor of the subject's time and placein this instance, aristocratic Britain in the late 1700s and early 1800sis both colorfully and meaningfully realized." —*Booklist*

Book made into a movie called the Duchess; Includes bibliographical references (p. [423]-432) and index; Originally published as Duchess: London : HarperCollins, 1998.

Foreman, Tom
My Year of Running Dangerously: A Dad, a Daughter, and a Ridiculous Plan. Tom Foreman. Blue Rider Press, an imprint of Penguin Random House 2015. 224 p.
ISBN 9780399175473
Grades: Adult **B**
1. Foreman, Tom 2. Marathon running 3. Fathers and daughters 4. Aging 5. Long distance runners 6. Journalists 7. Endurance sports 8. Autobiographies and memoirs 9. Life stories — Personal growth
LC 2015017237

As a journalist whose career spans three decades, CNN correspondent Tom Foreman has reported from the heart of war zones, riots, and natural disasters. He has interviewed serial killers and been in the line of fire. But the most terrifying moment of his life didn't occur on the job—it occurred at home, when his 18-year old daughter asked, 'How would you feel about running a marathon with me?' at the time, Foreman was approaching 51 years old, and his last marathon was almost 30 years behind him. The race was just sixteen weeks away, but Foreman reluctantly agreed. Training with his daughter, who had just started college, would be a great bonding experience, albeit a long and painful one. My Year of Running Dangerously is Foreman's journey through four half-marathons, three marathons, and one 55-mile race.

"Even the author's long-suffering family had to admit at the end of the season that he was happier, and readers will enjoy running alongside him." —*Kirkus*

Forgosh, Linda B.
Louis Bamberger: Department Store Innovator and Philanthropist. Linda B. Forgosh. Brandeis University Press 2016. 296 p.
ISBN 9781611689815
Grades: Adult **B**
1. Bamberger, Louis, 1855-1944 2. Jewish people 3. Businesspeople 4. Philanthropists 5. Department stores 6. Biographies
LC 2016004971

"This biography is the first comprehensive examination of Bamberger's life, and it is long overdue." —*Library Journal*
Includes bibliographical references and index.

Foster, Sutton
Hooked: How Crafting Saved My Life. Sutton Foster. Grand Central 2021. 224 p.
ISBN 9781538734285
Grades: Adult **B**
1. Foster, Sutton 2. Actors and actresses 3. Handicraft 4. Divorce 5. Mental health 6. Marriage 7. Fertility 8. Family relationships 9. Autobiographies and memoirs 10. Life stories — Arts and culture — Performing arts — Actors and actresses 11. Life stories — Relationships 12. Family and relationships — General 13. Arts and Entertainment — Movies and television

The Broadway and television actress discusses how cross-stitching, crocheting, painting and other craft projects kept her sane while dealing with an agoraphobic mother, a painful public divorce and struggles with fertility.

"Foster's fans will delight in this inspiring story of the multitalented actor's heights and pitfalls, while crafters will discover newfound purpose, embedded meaning, and shared serendipity in their universal pastime. An intimate, moving mosaic of art and memoir." —*Kirkus*
Also published in large print format.

Fox, Amaryllis
Life Undercover: Coming of Age in the CIA. Amaryllis Fox. Alfred A. Knopf 2019. 336 p.
ISBN 9780525654971
Grades: Adult **B**
1. Fox, Amaryllis 2. Women intelligence officers 3. Women spies 4. Terrorism prevention 5. Antiterrorists 6. Intelligence service 7. Undercover operations 8. Autobiographies and memoirs 9. Life stories — Law and order — Spies and secret agents 10. Adult books for young adults 11. Nonfiction that reads like fiction
LC 2019009838

A chronicle of an extraordinary life, and of one woman's courage and passion, follows the author as she spends 10 years in the most elite clandestine ops unit of the CIA, hunting down the world's most dangerous terrorist while marrying and becoming a mother.

"Fans of Showtime's Homeland and espionage novels will devour this highly recommended memoir, as will readers interested in counterterrorism, nonprofileration, and peacemaking." —*Library Journal*

Fox, Julia
Down the Drain. Julia Fox. Simon & Schuster 2023. 320 p.
ISBN 9781668011508
Grades: Adult **B**
1. Fox, Julia, 1990- 2. Actors and actresses 3. Fashion models 4. Women celebrities 5. Growing up 6. Fame 7. North American people 8. American people 9. Autobiographies and memoirs 10. Life stories — Arts and culture — Performing arts — Entertainers and celebrities 11. Arts and Entertainment — Movies and Television 12. Arts and Entertainment — Fashion

Capturing her improbable evolution from grade-school outcast to fashion-world icon as well as her transition from girlhood to womanhood to motherhood, the multidisciplinary—and unapologetic—artist chronicles her shocking life and her unrelenting determination to not only survive but to achieve her dreams.

"Actor and model Fox debuts with an unvarnished account of her tumultuous childhood, struggles with drug use, complicated friendships, and volatile romances." —*Publishers Weekly*

Fox, Michael J.
No Time Like the Future: An Optimist Considers Mortality. Michael J. Fox. Flatiron Books 2020. VIII, 238 p.
 ISBN 9781250265616
Grades: Adult   B
 1. Fox, Michael J, 1961- 2. Actors and actresses 3. People with Parkinson's disease 4. Spinal cord 5. Hope 6. Optimism 7. Medical care 8. Patient advocacy 9. Mortality 10. Loss 11. Resilience 12. Friendship 13. Family relationships 14. Wounds and injuries 15. Autobiographies and memoirs 16. Canadian literature 17. Life stories — Arts and culture — Performing arts — Actors and actresses 18. Life stories — Facing adversity — Medical issues — Physical illness

Actor Michael J. Fox shares personal stories and observations about illness and health, aging, the strength of family and friends, and how our perceptions about time affect the way we approach mortality. Thoughtful and moving, but with Fox's trademark sense of humor, his book provides a vehicle for reflection about our lives, our loves, and our losses.

"Back to the Future Fox focuses on issues of hope, fear, toughness, and being realistic as he explains his struggles with Parkinson's and spinal-cord surgery that led to his learning to walk again." —*Library Journal*

Foxx, Jamie
Act Like You Got Some Sense: And Other Things My Daughters Taught Me. Jamie Foxx. Grand Central Publishing 2021. 288 p.
 ISBN 9781538703281
Grades: Adult   B
 1. Foxx, Jamie 2. African American comedians 3. Fathers and daughters 4. Childhood 5. Parenting 6. Fatherhood 7. Grandmothers 8. Daughters 9. Comedians 10. Actors and actresses 11. African Americans 12. United States 13. Autobiographies and memoirs 14. Life stories — Arts and culture — Performing arts — Actors and actresses 15. Life stories — Relationships — Parent and child 16. Family and relationships — Parenting 17. Humor Writing — Family and relationship humor

The award-winning actor, singer and comedian takes a hilarious and candid look at the lessons he has learned from his teenage daughters, and how life on the A-list doesn't help him with his parenting challenges.

"Oscar-winning actor Foxx takes readers on a rollicking ride through his childhood, rise to stardom, and parenting adventures that are still in progress with two daughters: Anelise in her teens and Corinne in her mid-twenties. . . . Foxx's fans will be eager to read his upbeat blend of memoir and in-the-thick-of-it guide to parenting." —*Booklist*

Francis
Life: My Story Through History. Pope Francis with Fabio Marchese Ragona; translated by Aubrey Botsford. HarperOne 2024. 208 p.
 ISBN 9780063387522
Grades: Adult   B
 1. Francis, Pope, 1936- 2. Popes 3. Clergy 4. Christianity 5. Religions 6. War 7. History 8. Ecology 9. Social change 10. Social forecasting 11. South American people 12. Argentine people 13. 20th century 14. 21st century 15. Translations — Italian to English 16. Life stories — Religion and spirituality — Religious and spiritual leaders 17. History writing — General 18. Spirituality and Religion — Christianity — Political Aspects

An extraordinary personal and historical journey, Life is the story of a man and a world in dramatic change. Pope Francis recalls his life through memories and observations of the most significant occurrences of the past eight decades. The "pope callejero" recounts these world-changing moments with the candor and compassion that distinguishes him, and offers important messages on major crises confronting us now, including social inequalities, climate change, international war, atomic weapons, racial discrimination, and the battles over social and cultural issues.

"Pope Francis (A Good Life) provides a plainspoken overview of how some of the most significant events of the 20th and early 21st centuries shaped his life and morals." —*Publishers Weekly*

Frank, Anne
The Diary of Anne Frank: The Critical Edition. Prepared by the Netherlands State Institute forWar Documentation; introduced by Harry Paape,Gerrold van der Stroom, and David Barnouw; with asummary of the report by the Netherlands ForensicInstitute; compiled by H.J.J. Hardy; edited byDavi. Doubleday 2003. IX, 851 p. : Illustration
 ISBN 9780385508476
Grades: 11 12 Adult   B
 1. Frank, Anne, 1929-1945 2. Jewish people 3. Holocaust (1933-1945) 4. Amsterdam, Netherlands 5. Diaries 6. Autobiographies and memoirs 7. History writing — Wars and conflicts — Holocaust — World War II
 LC 2003269527

A complete collection of Anne Frank writings includes five recently discovered diary pages; her short stories, fables, and personal reminiscences; and her unfinished novel, Cady's Life.

"This volume brings together the three known versions of Frank's diary: the original, a self-edited version… [and] another edited by her father. It also contains … handwriting and paper analyses, new documentation regarding the Frank family's arrest, and … information about the diary's troubled publication history." —*Library Journal. {review of 1989 edition*

Translation of: Achterhuis; Includes bibliographical references.

Frank, Barney
Frank: A Life in Politics from the Great Society to Same-sex Marriage. Barney Frank. Farrar, Straus and Giroux 2015. 320 p.
 ISBN 9780374280307
Grades: Adult   B
 1. Frank, Barney, 1940- 2. Gay politicians 3. Coming out (Sexual or gender identity) 4. Right and left (Political science) 5. Social change 6. Democrats 7. Political culture 8. Politicians 9. Legislators 10. Politics and government 11. United States 12. Massachusetts 13. 20th century 14. Autobiographies and memoirs 15. Biographies 16. Liberal writing 17. Life stories — Politics — Politicians 18. Life stories — Identity — LGBTQIA+
 LC 2014040383

The candid political memoir of Barney Frank, former House Representative from Massachusetts (Democrat) and a pioneering, openly gay politician.

"Anyone interested in contemporary history or politics will definitely want to read this highly accessible memoir." —*Library Journal*

Includes index.

Frank, Joseph
★ *Dostoevsky: A Writer in His Time.* Joseph Frank. Princeton University Press 2009. 984 p.
 ISBN 9780691128191
Grades: Adult   B
 1. Dostoyevsky, Fyodor, 1821-1881 2. Authors, Russian 3. Writing 4. Intellectual life 5. Russian history 6. Russia 7. 19th century 8. Biographies 9. Arts and Entertainment — Writing and Publishing 10. Life stories — Arts and culture — Writing — Authors 11. Arts and Entertainment — Writing and Publishing — Literary criticism
 LC 2009001418

An account of the Russian writer's life is a combination of biography, intellectual history, and literary criticism.

"Frank displays a brilliant command of Dostoyevsky's heroic endeavors, and his biography reads readily, especially for such a scholarly work." —*Library Journal*

Frank, Michael
★ *One Hundred Saturdays: Stella Levi and the Search for a Lost World.* Michael Frank; artwork by Maira Kalman. Avid Reader Press 2022. 224 p.
 ISBN 9781982167226
Grades: Adult   B

ESSENTIAL AND RECOMMENDED TITLES
Biography

1. Nonagenarians 2. Jewish women 3. Memories 4. Growing up 5. Island life 6. Deportation 7. Antisemitism 8. Holocaust (1933-1945) 9. Concentration camp survivors 10. Holocaust survivors 11. Self-discovery 12. Intergenerational friendship 13. 20th century 14. Life stories — Relationships — Growing up 15. Life stories — Facing adversity — War and oppression — Holocaust 16. History writing — Jewish history 17. History writing — Europe

Sophie Brody Medal, 2023.

With nearly a century of life behind her, Stella Levi had never before spoken in detail about her past. Then she met Michael Frank. He came to her Greenwich Village apartment one Saturday afternoon to ask her a question about the Juderia, the neighborhood in Rhodes where she'd grown up in a Jewish community that had thrived there for half a millennium. Neither of them could know this was the first of one hundred Saturdays that they would spend in each other's company as Stella traveled back in time to conjure what it felt like to come of age on this luminous, legendary island in the eastern Aegean.

"Accompanied by illustrations from Maira Kalman, Frank writes Stella's harrowing journey with care, and the result is this beautifully crafted true story of friendship, love, survival, and redemption." —*Booklist*

Frankl, Viktor E.

★ *Man's Search for Meaning.* Viktor E. Frankl; part one translated by Ilse Lasch; foreword by Harold S. Kushner; afterword by William J. Winslade. Beacon Press 2006. xvi, 165 p.

ISBN 9780807014264

Grades: Adult **B**

1. Frankl, Viktor E. (Viktor Emil), 1905-1997 2. Holocaust (1933-1945) 3. Psychologists 4. Concentration camp survivors 5. Translations — German to English 6. Spirituality and Religion — General 7. History writing — Wars and conflicts — Holocaust — World War II

LC 2006287144

Internationally renowned psychiatrist, Viktor E. Frankl, endured years of unspeakable horror in Nazi death camps. During, and partly because of his suffering, Dr. Frankl developed a revolutionary approach to psychotherapy known as logotherapy. At the core of his theory is the belief that man's primary motivational force is his search for meaning.

Originally published as Psycholog erlebt das Konzentrationslager, 1962; Translated from the German.

Franklin, Benjamin

★ *The Autobiography of Benjamin Franklin.* Introduction by Lewis Leary. Simon & Schuster 2004. xiv, 143 p.

ISBN 9780743255066

Grades: Adult **B**

1. Franklin, Benjamin, 1706-1790 2. Scientists 3. Printers 4. Education 5. Politicians 6. Inventors 7. United States 8. Autobiographies and memoirs 9. Biographies 10. History writing — Colonial America — United States 11. History writing — Early America — United States 12. Life stories — Politics — Politicians 13. Life stories — Science, technology, and medicine — Scientists and inventors

LC 2003054477

Considered to be one of the best autobiographies written in colonial America, Franklin portrays a fascinating picture of life in pre-revolutionary Philadelphia. In his own words he describes his life as a printer, inventor, scientist, and politician.

A Touchstone book.

The Compleated Autobiography. by Benjamin Franklin; compiled and edited by Mark Skousen. Regnery Pub. 2006. xxvi, 484 p. : Illustration; Color

ISBN 9780895260338

Grades: Adult **B**

1. Franklin, Benjamin, 1706-1790 2. Politicians 3. Politics and government 4. United States 5. Colonial America (1600-1775) 6. 18th century 7. 19th century 8. Biographies 9. History writing — Colonial America — United States 10. History writing — Early America — United States 11. Life stories — Politics — Politicians 12. Adult books for young adults

A lifelong scholar of Benjamin Franklin's life completes the unfinished "Autobiography" with information on Franklin's attitudes about such topics as the Constitutional Convention, slavery, and Thomas Jefferson.

Includes bibliographical references and index.

Franklin, Jonathan

A Wild Idea: The True Story of Douglas Tompkins - the Greatest Conservationist You've Never Heard of. Jonathan Franklin. HarperOne 2021. 304 p.

ISBN 9780062964120

Grades: Adult **B**

1. Tompkins, Douglas 2. Environmentalists 3. Entrepreneurs 4. Environmental protection 5. Businesspeople 6. Land use 7. Environmentalism 8. Biographies 9. Life stories — Nature and outdoors 10. Nature Writing — General

The true story of the founder of the company the North Face, who sold his stake in the company and used his fortunes to protect over 25 million acres of land in South America from development.

"Investigative reporter Franklin recounts the life of the free-spirited millionaire entrepreneur who used his fabulous wealth in the fight to save nature." —*Kirkus*

Franklin, Missy

Relentless Spirit: The Unconventional Raising of a Champion. Missy Franklin with D. A. and Dick Franklin. E. P. Dutton 2016. 320 p.

ISBN 9781101984925

Grades: Adult **B**

1. Franklin, Missy, 1995- 2. Olympic athletes 3. Families 4. Christian life 5. Parent and child 6. Women Olympic athletes 7. Faith (Christianity) 8. Women Olympic medal winners 9. Everyday life 10. Women swimmers 11. Autobiographies and memoirs 12. Life stories — Sports — Athletes 13. Sports and Competition — Individual Athlete 14. Family and Relationships — Families 15. Life stories — Religion and spirituality — Personal faith 16. Adult books for young adults

LC 2016046031

The four-time Olympic Gold medalist and her parents trace the inspirational story of how she became both a legendary athlete and a happy and confident woman, achievements that were accomplished by doing things their own way and making the right choices for their family.

"A consistently sunny, family-oriented story of persistence and achievement." —*Kirkus*

Franklin, Ruth

Shirley Jackson: A Rather Haunted Life. Ruth Franklin. Liveright Publishing Corporation 2016. 656 p.

ISBN 9780871403131

Grades: Adult **B**

1. Jackson, Shirley, 1916-1965 2. Women's role 3. Motherhood 4. Married women 5. Addiction 6. Marital conflict 7. Authors, American 8. Women authors, American 9. Anxiety 10. Vermont 11. 20th century 12. Biographies 13. Arts and Entertainment — Writing and Publishing 14. Life stories — Arts and culture — Writing — Authors

LC 2016014711

ALA Notable Book, 2017; Anthony Award for Best Critical/Nonfiction, 2017; Booklist Editors' Choice, 2016; Bram Stoker Award for Best Nonfiction, 2016; Edgar Allan Poe Award for Best Critical/Biographical, 2017; National Book Critics Circle Award for Biography, 2016.

Reveals the tumultuous life and inner darkness of the American author, demonstrating how her unique contribution to the Gothic genre came from a focus on domestic horror drawn from an era hostile to women.

"A consistently interesting biography that deftly captures the many selves and multiple struggles of a true American original." —*Kirkus*

Includes bibliographical references and index.

Franklin, Sara B.

★ *The Editor: How Publishing Legend Judith Jones Shaped Culture in America.* Sara B. Franklin. Atria Books 2024. 320 p.

ISBN 9781982134341

PUBLIC LIBRARY CORE COLLECTION: NONFICTION
Twentieth Edition

Grades: Adult **B**
1. Editors 2. Women editors 3. Publishers and publishing 4. American literature 5. 20th century 6. Biographies 7. Arts and Entertainment — Writing and Publishing 8. Life stories — Arts and culture — Writing
LC 2023057173

Based on exclusive interviews, never-before-seen personal papers and years of research, this tribute to legendary editor reveals the audacious woman behind some of the most important authors of the 20th century, including Sylvia Plath, John Updike, Anne Frank and Julie Child, changing culture mores and expectations along the way.

"The result is an exceptional feast for bibliophiles and foodies alike."—*Publishers Weekly*

Includes bibliographical references and index.

Fraser, Antonia
Love and Louis XIV: The Women in the Life of the Sun King. Antonia Fraser. Nan A. Talese, Doubleday 2006. xxviii, 388 p. : Illustration; Color
ISBN 9780385509848
Grades: Adult **B**
1. Louis XIV, King of France, 1638-1715 2. Louis XIV King of France 1638-1715 3. Monarchy, French 4. Paramours 5. Mothers and sons 6. Favorites, Royal 7. Sexuality 8. Rulers 9. Men-women relations 10. French history 11. France 12. 17th century 13. 18th century 14. Biographies 15. History writing — Europe — France 16. Family and Relationships — Dating and Marriage 17. Life stories — Politics — Royalty
LC 2006044674

Booklist Editors' Choice, 2006.

A study of the life and reign of the Sun King looks at the world of King Louis XIV from the perspective of his intimate relationships with the women in his life, from his mother, Anne of Austria, and his official queen, Marie-Therese, to his many mistresses—including Louise de la Valliere, Athenais, marquise de Montespan, and Francoise de Maintenon.

"One of the most enveloping popular histories of the current publishing season."—*Booklist*

Includes bibliographical references (p. 344-355) and index.

Marie Antoinette: The Journey. Antonia Fraser. Nan A. Talese, Doubleday 2001. xxii, 512 p. : Illustration; Color; Map
ISBN 9780385489485
Grades: 11 12 Adult **B**
1. Marie Antoinette, Queen, consort of Louis XVI, King of France, 1755-1793 2. Monarchy, French 3. Women rulers 4. Rulers 5. French history 6. France 7. 18th century 8. Biographies 9. History writing — Europe — France 10. History writing — Women's history 11. Life stories — Politics — Royalty
LC 2001023493

Booklist Editors' Choice, 2001; New York Times Notable Book, 2001.

Describes the life of Marie Antoinette from her betrothal as a fourteen-year-old girl to the future King Louis XVI, through her life in the French court, to her courage in the face of revolutionaries who sent her to the guillotine.

"A well-researched biography that may cause one to rethink the role in which history has cast Marie Antoinette."—*Library Journal*

Illustrated with unpaged color plates; Includes bibliographical references (p. 479-490) and index.

Mary, Queen of Scots. by Antonia Fraser. Delta Trade Paperbacks 2001. xv, 613 p. : Illustration
ISBN 9780385311298
Grades: Adult **B**
1. Mary, Queen of Scots, 1542-1587 2. Women rulers 3. Catholic women 4. Monarchy 5. Scottish history 6. British history 7. Great Britain 8. 16th century 9. Tudor period (1485-1603) 10. Renaissance (1300-1600) 11. Elizabethan era (1558-1603) 12. Scottish Stewart period (1371-1603) 13. Biographies 14. History writing — Renaissance — Europe 15. History writing — Europe — United Kingdom 16. Life stories — Politics — Royalty
LC 2001278458

James Tait Black Memorial Prize for Biography, 1969.

A biography of Mary Queen of Scots captures the essence of the impulsive and beautiful Scottish queen who lost a throne for love and whose power struggle with Elizabeth I of England ended with her beheading.

Includes bibliographical references (p. [593]-613) and index; Originally published: New York : Delta, 1993.

Fraser, Caroline
★ *Prairie Fires: The American Dreams of Laura Ingalls Wilder.* Caroline Fraser. Metropolitan Books 2017. 480 p.
ISBN 9781627792769
Grades: Adult **B**
1. Wilder, Laura Ingalls, 1867-1957 2. Frontier and pioneer life 3. Authors, American 4. Pioneer women 5. United States 6. 20th century 7. Biographies 8. Life stories — Arts and culture — Writing — Authors 9. Adult books for young adults 10. Arts and Entertainment — Writing and Publishing — Literary criticism
LC 2017028870

LibraryReads Favorites, 2017; National Book Critics Circle Award for Biography, 2017; New York Times Notable Book, 2017; Pulitzer Prize for Biography or Autobiography, 2018.

A comprehensive historical portrait of Laura Ingalls Wilder draws on unpublished manuscripts, letters, diaries and official records to fill in the gaps in Wilder's official story, sharing lesser-known details about her pioneer experiences while challenging popular misconceptions about how her books were ghostwritten.

"A vivid portrait of frontier life and one of its most ardent celebrants."—*Kirkus*

Includes index.

Fredriksen, Paula
Jesus of Nazareth, King of the Jews: A Jewish Life and the Emergence of Christianity. Paula Fredriksen. Knopf 1999. xxi, 327 p. : Illustration; Map
ISBN 9780679446750
Grades: Adult **B**
1. Jesus Christ 2. Christianity 3. Biographies 4. Spirituality and Religion — Christianity — History 5. Spirituality and Religion — Religious Leaders
LC 99031054

The author of from Jesus to Christ presents a richly textured portrait of the historical Jesus that draws on biblical narratives, the Dead Sea Scrolls, early rabbinic writings, and other sources to create a study of of a man living in the world of late Second Temple Judaism.

Includes bibliographical references (p. 303-310) and indexes.

Freeberg, Ernest
A Traitor to His Species: Henry Bergh and the Birth of the Animal Rights Movement. Ernest Freeberg. Basic Books 2020. 336 p.
ISBN 9780465093861
Grades: Adult **B**
1. Bergh, Henry, 1811-1888 2. Animal rights advocates 3. Animal welfare 4. Animal rights 5. Legislation 6. Human-animal relationships 7. 19th century 8. Gilded Age (1865-1898) 9. Society and culture — Social activism and philanthropy 10. History writing — Gilded Age — United States
LC Bl2020052174

An award-winning historian, in the revelatory social history, tells the story of an extraordinary man who gave voice to the voiceless and shaped our modern relationship with animals.

"Freeberg marshals a wealth of detail in tracking Bergh's campaigns and paints a vivid picture of Gilded Age America. Animal lovers and history buffs will savor this immersive account."—*Publishers Weekly*

Includes bibliographical references and index.

Freeman, Douglas Southall
Lee: An Abridgement in One Volume of the Four-volume R.E. Lee. by Douglas Southall Freeman; Richard Harwell; with a new foreword by James M. McPherson. Collier Books; 1993. xxiii, 601 p. : Illustration
ISBN 9780684829531

ESSENTIAL AND RECOMMENDED TITLES
Biography

Grades: Adult **B**
1. Lee, Robert E. (Robert Edward), 1807-1870 2. Command of troops 3. Generals 4. United States 5. 19th century 6. Biographies 7. History writing — Military — Military leadership 8. Life stories — Law and order — Military leaders 9. History writing — Wars and conflicts — American Civil War
LC 93006528

A condensation of Freeman's definitive biography of the Confederate hero.

"Students of history will continue to want and to use the original four-volume work but most general readers will find this abridgment more convenient and adequate to their interest. All footnotes and all of the appendix have been omitted as well as details of Civil War action that are not necessary to show the main course of Lee's life and action." —*Booklist*

Originally published: New York : Scribner, 1961; Includes index.

Freeman, Hadley
House of Glass: The Story and Secrets of a Twentieth-century Jewish Family. Hadley Freeman. Simon & Schuster 2020. 256 pages
ISBN 9781501199158
Grades: Adult **B**
1. Glass family 2. Jewish families 3. Refugees, Jewish 4. Holocaust survivors 5. Hiding 6. Family secrets 7. Antisemitism 8. Holocaust (1933-1945) 9. France 10. Biographies 11. Life stories — Facing adversity — War and oppression — Holocaust
LC 2019049707

Investigating her own family's secret history after a shocking discovery, a writer for the Guardian newspaper in the UK reveals a broad range of experiences of Eastern European Jews during the Holocaust as she uncovers a story that spans a century, two World Wars and three generations.

"A timely exploration of family secrets, immigration, and anti-Semitism, this work will appeal to readers of World War II-era history." —*Library Journal*

Includes bibliographical references.

Fremont, Helen
The Escape Artist: A Memoir. Helen Fremont. Simon & Schuster 2020. 352 p.
ISBN 9781982113605
Grades: Adult **B**
1. Fremont, Helen 2. Children of Holocaust survivors 3. Dysfunctional families 4. Jewish families 5. Lesbians 6. Gender identity 7. Family secrets 8. Dishonesty 9. Mental illness 10. Conflict in families 11. Psychic trauma 12. United States 13. Autobiographies and memoirs 14. Life stories — Relationships — Family 15. Family and Relationships — Families 16. Life stories — Personal growth
LC 2019022576

Helen Fremont's bestselling memoir, After Long Silence, vividly recounts her discovery in adulthood that her parents were not Catholics, as she thought (having herself been raised in that faith), but Jewish Holocaust survivors living invented lives. Not even their names were their own. In her frank, moving, and often surprisingly funny new memoir, Fremont delves even deeper into the family dynamic that produced such a startling devotion to secret-keeping. She begins her story with the discovery that she has been disinherited in her mother's will, her existence as a member of the family erased, and she writes with unflinching candor about growing up in a household whose members were devoted to hiding the truth.

"The discrepancies may not bother readers seeking psychological insights rather than factual accuracy, but others will wonder if this book should have been labeled a fictionalized autobiography rather than a memoir. A vivid sequel that strains credulity." —*Kirkus*

French, Patrick
The World Is What It Is: The Authorized Biography of V.S. Naipaul. by Patrick French. Knopf 2008. 480 p.
ISBN 9781400044054
Grades: Adult **B**
1. Naipaul, V. S. (Vidiadhar Surajprasad), 1932-2018 2. Authors, Trinidadian 3. Nobel Prize winners 4. Brahmins 5. Writing 6. Trinidad and Tobago 7. 20th century 8. Biographies 9. Arts and Entertainment — Writing and Publishing 10. Life stories — Arts and culture — Writing — Authors 11. Adult books for young adults
LC 2008006988

Hawthornden Prize, 2009; National Book Critics Circle Award for Biography, 2008; New York Times Notable Book, 2008.

This authorized study of Nobel laureate V.S. Naipaul examines his difficult early life as a child of Indian parents in colonial Trinidad, his Oxford education, the depression that marked his life in England, his complex personal life and romantic relationships, and his pursuit of becoming a great writer.

"This book is a prodigious achievement, a wonderful biography, a justification for the art of biography itself." —*Times Literary Supplement*

Includes bibliographical references and index.

Frenkel, Francoise
A Bookshop in Berlin: The Rediscovered Memoir of One Woman's Harrowing Escape from the Nazis. Francoise Frenkel; foreword by Patrick Modiano. Atria Books 2019. 304 pages
ISBN 9781501199844
Grades: Adult **B**
1. Frenkel, Francoise, 1889-1975 2. Holocaust (1933-1945) 3. Jewish women 4. Women booksellers 5. Refugees, Jewish 6. Bookstores 7. Kristallnacht, 1938 8. Survival 9. Hiding 10. Escapes 11. Resilience 12. Berlin, Germany 13. France 14. Autobiographies and memoirs 15. Translations — French to English 16. Biographies 17. Life stories — Facing adversity — War and oppression — War survivors 18. History writing — Wars and conflicts — Holocaust — World War II 19. History writing — Jewish history 20. Adult books for young adults
LC Bl2019037959

Published quietly in 1945, then rediscovered nearly sixty years later in an attic, a Bookshop in Berlin is a remarkable story of survival and resilience, of human cruelty and human spirit. In the tradition of Suite Française, this book is the tale of a fearless woman whose lust for life and literature refuses to leave her, even in her darkest hours.

"A compelling account of crushing oppression, those who sought to flee it, and those who, at great risk, offered help." —*Kirkus*

First published in France as Rien où poser sa tête by L'Arbalète Gallimard in 2015; Originally published: Geneva : Jeheber, 1945; Translated from the French.

Frey, Julia Bloch
Toulouse-lautrec: A Life. Julia Frey. Phoenix Giants 1995. xxii, 597 p. : Illustration; Color
ISBN 9781857993639
Grades: Adult **B**
1. Toulouse-Lautrec, Henri de, 1864-1901 2. Artists 3. Social life and customs 4. France 5. 19th century 6. Biographies 7. Arts and Entertainment — Painting, Drawing, and Sculpture 8. Life stories — Arts and culture — Artists
LC BL 00006387

National Book Critics Circle Award for Biography finalist, 1994.

A chronicle of the life of one of the world's great artists draws from previously unavailable family letters to capture the essence of Toulouse-Lautrec's life and times.

"The author chronicles Toulouse-Lautrec's transformation from a pampered invalid into one of the most radical of the fin de siecle artists. Her sensitive, eloquent, and richly illustrated biography has brought the real Toulouse-Lautrec out from behind the scrim of myth." —*Booklist*

Includes bibliographical references (p. [494]-576) and index; Originally published: London : Weidenfeld and Nicolson, 1994.

Fried, Stephen
Rush: Revolution, Madness, and Benjamin Rush, the Visionary Doctor Who Became a Founding Father. Stephen Fried. Crown Publishing 2018. 416 p.
ISBN 9780804140065
Grades: Adult **B**
1. Rush, Benjamin, 1746-1813 2. Founding fathers of the United States 3. Physicians 4. Revolutionaries 5. Social advocacy 6. Biographies 7. Life stories — Science, technology, and medicine — Healthcare professionals 8. Life stories

— Politics 9. History writing — Wars and conflicts — Revolutionary War (America) 10. History writing — Early America — United States

ALA Notable Book, 2019.

The remarkable story of Benjamin Rush, medical pioneer and one of our nation's most provocative and unsung Founding Fathers. In the summer of 1776, fifty-six men put their quills to a dangerous document they called the Declaration of Independence. Among them was a thirty-year-old doctor named Benjamin Rush. One of the youngest signatories, he was also, among stiff competition, one of the most visionary.

Friedman, Matti

Pumpkinflowers: A Soldier's Story of a Forgotten War. Matti Friedman. Algonquin Books of Chapel Hill 2016. 288 p.

ISBN 9781616204587

Grades: Adult **B**

1. Friedman, Matti 2. Soldiers 3. Arab-Israeli conflict 4. War 5. Lebanon 6. 1990s 7. Autobiographies and memoirs 8. Life stories — Law and order — Armed forces personnel

LC 2015031466

Canadian Jewish Book Award, 2017; New York Times Notable Book, 2016; Booklist Editors' Choice, 2016; Shortlisted for the Charles Taylor Prize for Literary Non-Fiction, 2017; Hilary Weston Writers' Trust Prize for Nonfiction finalist, 2016.

Describes the author's harrowing experiences manning a remote Israeli outpost with a regiment of other young soldiers, during a small, unnamed war in the late 1990s that foreshadowed other unwinnable conflicts in the Middle East.

"A haunting yet wry tale of young people at war, cursed by political forces beyond their control, that can stand alongside the best narrative nonfiction coming out of Afghanistan and Iraq." —*Kirkus*

Friedman, Maurice S.

Encounter on the Narrow Ridge: A Life of Martin Buber. Maurice Friedman. Paragon House 1991. xi, 496 p. : Illustration

ISBN 9781557784537

Grades: Adult **B**

1. Buber, Martin, 1878-1965 2. Zionists 3. Biographies 4. Spirituality and Religion — General

LC 90044502

Traces the life of the renowned Jewish religious philosopher, discussing his youth, his education in turn-of-the-century Vienna, his Zionism, and the impact of world politics on his life and thought.

Includes bibliographical references (p. 461-471) and index.

Friedman, Tova

★ *The Daughter of Auschwitz: My Story of Resilience, Survival and Hope.* Tova Friedman and Malcolm Brabant, forward by Sir Ben Kingsley. Hanover Square Press 2022. 320 p.

ISBN 9781335449306

Grades: Adult **B**

1. Holocaust survivors 2. Survival (in concentration camps, prisons, etc.) 3. Antisemitism 4. Autobiographies and memoirs 5. Life stories — Facing adversity — War and oppression — Holocaust

A powerful memoir by one of the youngest survivors of Auschwitz, Tova Friedman, following her childhood growing up during the Holocaust and surviving a string of near-death experiences in a Jewish ghetto, a Nazi labor camp, and Auschwitz.

"Holocaust survivor Friedman recalls her experiences in Auschwitz-Birkenau as a young child in this heartrending memoir….Enriched by Friedman's earnest reckonings with her trauma and hard-won sense of optimism, this is a poignant testament to survival and faith." —*Publishers Weekly*

Fritz, Ian

What the Taliban Told Me. Ian Fritz. Simon & Schuster 2023. 288 p.

ISBN 9781668010693

Grades: Adult **B**

1. War 2. Military intelligence 3. Military life 4. Afghanistan 5. Autobiographies and memoirs 6. Life stories — Law and order — Armed forces personnel 7. History writing — Wars and conflicts — War in Afghanistan

A memoir of a young Air Force linguist coming-of-age in Afghanistan in a war that is lost.

"Fritz holds nothing back in this raw and engrossing debut memoir about his experiences in Afghanistan as a cryptologic linguist for the U.S. Air Force." —*Publishers Weekly*

Fuhrmann, Joseph T.

Rasputin: The Untold Story. Joseph T. Fuhrmann. John Wiley & Sons 2012. 304 p.

ISBN 9781118172766

Grades: Adult **B**

1. Rasputin, Grigori Efimovich, 1869-1916 2. Mystics 3. Courts and courtiers 4. Murder 5. Healers 6. Russian history 7. Romanov Dynasty (1613-1917) 8. Biographies 9. History writing — Europe — Russia 10. Life stories — Religion and spirituality — Religious and spiritual leaders

Shares new stories and drawn from archival sources such as published documents, memoirs and other studies, corrects misconceptions and errors about the life and death of the Siberian mystic and healer.

Published simultaneously in Canada—T.P. verso; Includes bibliographical references and index.

Fuller, Alexandra

Don't Let's Go to the Dogs Tonight: An African Childhood. Alexandra Fuller. Random House 2001. 301 p. : Illustration; Map

ISBN 9780375507502

Grades: Adult **B**

1. Fuller, Alexandra, 1969- 2. Girls 3. British people in Africa 4. Family relationships 5. Segregation 6. Growing up 7. Childhood 8. Racism 9. Race relations 10. African history 11. Zimbabwe 12. 1970s 13. Autobiographies and memoirs 14. Biographies 15. Life stories — Relationships — Growing up 16. Adult books for young adults 17. History writing — Colonization — Africa

LC 2001041752

Book Sense Book of the Year Nonfiction, 2003; New York Times Notable Book, 2002.

Alexandra Fuller tells the idiosyncratic story of her life growing up white in rural Rhodesia as it was becoming Zimbabwe. The daughter of hardworking, yet strikingly unconventional English-bred immigrants, Alexandra arrives in Africa at the tender age of two. She moves through life with a hardy resilience, even as a bloody war approaches.

"Fuller grew up in Rhodesia (now Zimbabwe) during the civil war, and she watched her parents fight against the local Africans to keep their farm. In a memoir powerful in its frank straightforwardness, she neither apologizes for nor champions her family's views and actions. Instead she gives us an honest, moving portrait of one family struggling to survive tumultuous times." —*Booklist*

Sequel: Cocktail hour under the tree of forgetfulness.

Leaving Before the Rains Come. Alexandra Fuller. Penguin Group USA 2015. 256 p.

ISBN 9781594205866

Grades: Adult **B**

1. Fuller, Alexandra, 1969- 2. Marriage 3. Self-discovery 4. Self-fulfillment 5. Divorce 6. Zimbabwe 7. Autobiographies and memoirs 8. Life stories — Relationships — Couples 9. Adult books for young adults

LC Bl2014055302

A child of the Rhodesian wars and daughter of two deeply complicated parents, Alexandra Fuller is no stranger to pain. But the disintegration of Fuller's own marriage leaves her shattered. Looking to pick up the pieces of her life, she finally confronts the tough questions about her past, about the American man she married, and about the family she left behind in Africa.

"Although her batty and unhinged relatives emerge more vividly than her taciturn husband, Fuller's talent as a storyteller makes this memoir sing." —*Kirkus*

Travel Light, Move Fast. Alexandra Fuller. Penguin Press 2019. 272 p.

ESSENTIAL AND RECOMMENDED TITLES
Biography

ISBN 9781594206740
Grades: Adult **B**
1. Fuller, Alexandra, 1969- 2. Fuller, Tim (Timothy Donald), 1940-2015 3. British people in Africa 4. Death of fathers 5. Nonconformists 6. Eccentrics and eccentricities 7. Family relationships 8. Grief 9. Coping 10. Life stories — Relationships — Parent and child 11. Life stories — Facing adversity — Coping with death

LC 2019000116

The best-selling author of Don't Let's Go to the Dogs Tonight explores how her late father's service during the Rhodesian War, work as a banana farmer in Zambia and preference of unpredictability over security inspired her life.

Funder, Anna
Wifedom: Mrs. Orwell's Invisible Life. Anna Funder. Alfred A. Knopf 2023. 320 p.
ISBN 9780593320686
Grades: Adult **B**
1. Blair, Eileen, 1905-1945 2. Orwell, George, 1903-1950 3. Authors' spouses 4. Married women 5. Marriage 6. Women authors 7. Gender role 8. England 9. Life stories — Arts and culture — Writing 10. History Writing — Women's history 11. Arts and Entertainment — Writing and publishing 12. Nonfiction that reads like fiction

LC 2023002866

Australian Book Industry Awards, Biography of the Year, 2024.

Drawing on newly discovered letters from George Orwell's wife, Eileen O'Shaughnessy, to her best friend, an award-winning author recreates the marriage behind some of the most famous literary works of the 20th century, pondering the question of what it takes to be a writer—and what it is to be a wife.

"An electrifying biography of George Orwell's first wife…A sharp, captivating look at a complicated relationship and a resurrection of a vital figure in Orwell's life." —*Kirkus*

This is a Borzoi Book published by Alfred A. Knopf; Includes bibliographical references.

Gabbard, Krin
Better Git It in Your Soul: An Interpretive Biography of Charles Mingus. Krin Gabbard. University of California Press 2016. 323 p.
ISBN 9780520260375
Grades: Adult **B**
1. Mingus, Charles, 1922-1979 2. Composers 3. Jazz musicians 4. Bass players 5. Biographies 6. Essays 7. Life stories — Arts and culture — Performing arts — Musicians and composers 8. Arts and Entertainment — Music — Jazz and the Blues

LC 2015031907

This biography traces the output of jazz master Charles Mingus—his recordings, his compositions, and his writings—highlighting key moments in his life and musicians who influenced him and were influenced by him.

"A solid addition to the literature of jazz." —*Booklist*

Includes bibliographical references and index.

Gabler, Neal
★ *Against* the Wind: Edward Kennedy and the Rise of Conservatism, 1976-2009. Neal Gabler. Crown 2022. 944 p.
ISBN 9780593238622
Grades: Adult **B**
1. Kennedy, Edward M, (Edward Moore), 1932-2009 2. Democrats 3. Politicians 4. Conservatism 5. Legislators 6. Politics and government 7. United States 8. 20th century 9. Biographies 10. History writing — Politicians — United States 11. Life stories — Politics — Politicians

LC 2022016140

Against the Wind completes Neal Gabler's magisterial biography of Ted Kennedy, but it also unfolds the epic, tragic story of the fall of liberalism and the destruction of political morality in America. With Richard Nixon having stilled the liberal wind that once propelled Kennedy's—and his fallen brothers'—political crusades, Ted Kennedy faced a lonely battle. As Republicans pressed Reaganite dogmas of individual freedom and responsibility and Democratic centrists fell into line, Kennedy was left as the most powerful voice legislating on behalf of those society would neglect or punish: the poor, the working class, and African Americans.

"Ted Kennedy (1932-2009) spent the second half of his life fighting for liberalism against a gale of conservative politics, according to the magisterial conclusion (after Catching the Wind) to Gabler's two-volume biography of the Massachusetts senator….This smart, illuminating, and stirring portrait of a liberal champion fascinates." —*Publishers Weekly*

Includes bibliographical references and index.

Catching the Wind: Edward Kennedy and the Liberal Hour, 1932-1975. Neal Gabler. Crown 2020. 928 p.
ISBN 9780307405449
Grades: Adult **B**
1. Kennedy, Edward M. (Edward Moore), 1932-2009 2. Kennedy family 3. Legislators 4. Liberals 5. Politicians 6. Liberalism 7. Political ethics 8. Politics and government 9. United States 10. 20th century 11. 21st century 12. Biographies 13. Life stories — Politics — Politicians 14. History writing — Politicians — United States

LC 2020019328

The epic, definitive biography of Ted Kennedy—an immersive journey through the life of a complicated man and a sweeping history of the fall of liberalism and the collapse of political morality. Edward M. Kennedy was never expected to succeed. The youngest of nine, he lacked his brothers' natural gifts and easy grace. Yet after winning election to the Senate at the tender age of thirty, he became the most consequential legislator of his lifetime, perhaps even American history. A landmark study of legislative genius and a powerful exploration of the man who spent his career upholding his mandate in service of a better America.

Offers an immersive journey through the life of a complicated man and a sweeping history of the fall of liberalism and the collapse of political morality.

"The result of staggering research and expert analysis, Gabler's discerning evaluation of the totality of influences upon one of the twentieth century's most persuasive and popular statesmen is a triumphant achievement and essential reading for everyone fascinated by the Kennedys, politics, and governance." —*Booklist*

Includes bibliographical references and index.

Walt Disney: The Triumph of the American Imagination. Neal Gabler. Knopf 2006. xx, 851 p, 32 p. of plates : Illustration
ISBN 9780679438229
Grades: Adult **B**
1. Disney, Walt, 1901-1966 2. Animators 3. Biographies 4. Arts and Entertainment — Comics, Cartoons, and Animation 5. Life stories — Arts and culture — Artists 6. Life stories — Business — Business leaders

LC 2006045257

Los Angeles Times Book Prize for Biography, 2006.

A portrait of the private life and public career of Walt Disney ranges from his deprived youth, to his contributions to the art of animation, to his visionary creation of the first synergistic entertainment empire, to his reclusive and lonely private world.

"Although Gabler focuses on corporate matters at the expense of critical treatment of the films, he presents a balanced treatment of the man and his achievements, realistically assessing Disney's considerable impact and offering insight into the hidden, restless soul who constantly challenged himself, risking the financial stability of his empire more than once in his unceasing pursuit of his dreams." —*Booklist*

Includes bibliographical references (p. [805]-815) and index.

Gabriel, Mary
Madonna: A Rebel Life. Mary Gabriel. Little, Brown & Company 2023. 840 p.
ISBN 9780316456470
Grades: Adult **B**
1. Madonna, 1958- 2. Women singers 3. Women celebrities 4. Popular music 5. Fashion 6. Creativity 7. Ambition 8. Feminism 9. Social advocacy 10. Family relationships 11. North American people 12. American people 13. Biographies 14. Life stories — Arts and culture — Performing arts — Musicians and composers 15. Life stories — Arts and culture — Performing arts — Entertainers and celebrities 16. Arts and Entertainment — Music — Pop

With her arrival on the music scene in the early 1980s, Madonna generated nothing short of an explosion, taking the nation by storm with her liberated politics and breathtaking talent. But Madonna was more than just a pop star. Everywhere, fans gravitated to her as an emblem of a new age, one in which feminism could shed the buttoned-down demeanor of the 1970s and feel relevant to a new generation. Deftly tracing Madonna's story from her Michigan roots to her rise to super-stardom, biographer Mary Gabriel captures the dramatic life and achievements of one of the greatest artists of our time.

"Pulitzer Prize finalist Gabriel's (Ninth Street Women) massive biography of singer Madonna follows her life from her Michigan childhood to the conclusion of her Madame X tour of 2019-20." —*Library Journal*

Includes bibliographical references and index.

Gadsby, Hannah
★ *Ten Steps to Nanette: A Memoir Situation*. Hannah Gadsby. Ballantine Books 2022. 368 p.

ISBN 9781984819789

Grades: Adult   B

1. Women comedians 2. LGBTQIA+ people 3. Lesbians 4. Autistic women 5. Fat women 6. Attention-deficit hyperactivity disorder 7. Neurodivergent people 8. Autobiographies and memoirs 9. Life stories — Identity

A multi-award-winning comedian takes readers through the defining moments in her life that led to the creation of Nanette and her powerful decision to tell the truth—no matter the cost.

"In this memoir/Humorous collection of essays, award-winning stand-up comic Gadsby reflects on pop culture, feminism, and her sudden rise to stardom, all via the irreverent yet thought-provoking musings she's known for." —*Library Journal*

Gaffigan, Jeannie
When Life Gives You Pears: The Healing Power of Family, Faith, and Funny People. Jeannie Gaffigan. Grand Central Publishing 2019. 305 p.

ISBN 9781538751046

Grades: Adult   B

1. Gaffigan, Jeannie, 1970- 2. People with brain tumors 3. Faith (Christianity) 4. Mothers 5. Determination 6. Catholic women 7. Autobiographies and memoirs 8. Life stories — Facing adversity — Medical issues — Physical illness 9. Life stories — Religion and spirituality — Personal faith

The wife of acclaimed comic Jim Gaffigan shares an uplifting account of her fight to survive a brain tumor, the toll its treatment took on her family and the lessons she learned along the way. 100,000 first printing. Media tie-in.

Gaffney, Ginger
Half Broke: A Memoir. Ginger Gaffney. W W Norton & Company 2020. 256 pages

ISBN 9781324003076

Grades: Adult   B

1. Gaffney, Ginger 2. Horse trainers 3. Equestrian therapy 4. Women horse trainers 5. Horse training 6. Prisoners 7. Criminals 8. Lesbians 9. Healing 10. Rehabilitation 11. Human-animal communication 12. Human-animal relationships 13. New Mexico 14. Autobiographies and memoirs 15. Life stories — Facing adversity 16. Life stories — Relationships — Pets and owners 17. Life stories — Identity — LGBTQIA+ 18. Nature Writing — Animal Studies

LC 2019030052

A top-ranked horse trainer at an alternative prison ranch in New Mexico describes how her work rehabilitating abandoned horses and traumatized inmates helped her form profound bonds and overcome difficult personal challenges.

"Gaffney's story will delight horse lovers, and her anxieties as an introvert will broaden the appeal of this passionate memoir." —*Publishers Weekly*

Gage, Beverly
G-man: J. Edgar Hoover and the Making of the American Century. Beverly Gage. Viking 2022. xix, 837 p.

ISBN 9780670025374

Grades: Adult   B

1. Hoover, J. Edgar, 1895-1972 2. Government executives 3. National security 4. Anti-Communism 5. Racism 6. Xenophobia 7. Power 8. Interpersonal relations 9. North American people 10. American people 11. Politics and government 12. United States history 13. United States 14. 20th century 15. Biographies 16. Life stories — Law and order 17. Life stories — Politics 18. History writing — United States

LC 2022021309

Los Angeles Times Book Prize for Biography, 2022; National Book Critics Circle Award for Biography, 2022; Pulitzer Prize for Biography, 2023; American History Book Prize, 2024.

This major new biography of the man who served for almost 50 years as FBI director looks at the full sweep of his life and career and how he planted the seeds for the today's conservative political landscape.

Includes bibliographical references and index.

Gagne, Patric
Sociopath. Patric Gagne. Simon & Schuster 2024. 352 p.

ISBN 9781668003183

Grades: Adult   B

1. Gagne, Patric 2. Psychopaths 3. Antisocial personality disorders 4. Mental illness 5. Life stories — Facing adversity — Medical issues — Mental illness 6. Science Writing — Medicine and health — Mental health 7. Nonfiction that reads like fiction

LibraryReads Favorites, 2024.

A fascinating, revelatory memoir revealing the author's struggle to come to terms with her own sociopathy and shed light on the often maligned and misunderstood mental disorder.

"Courageously candid and sometimes shocking, this no-holds-barred self-portrait offers an illuminating glimpse at a mental health disorder long shrouded by shame." —*Publishers Weekly*

Gaines, James R.
For Liberty and Glory: Washington, Lafayette, and Their Revolutions. James R. Gaines. W.W. Norton & Co. 2007. 512 p.

ISBN 9780393061383

Grades: Adult   B

1. Washington, George, 1732-1799 2. Lafayette, Marie Joseph Paul Yves Roch Gilbert Du Motier, marquis de, 1757-1834 3. Politicians 4. American Revolution, 1775-1783 5. Presidents 6. Revolutions 7. French history 8. United States history 9. United States 10. Revolutionary France (1789-1799) 11. Revolutionary America (1775-1783) 12. History writing — Wars and conflicts — Revolutionary War (America) 13. History writing — Wars and conflicts — French Revolution

LC 2007022449

A narrative account of the "sister revolutions" of France and America reveals the lesser-known agendas that intertwined the conflicts, discussing the close but complex relationship between Washington and the Marquis de Lafayette.

"This is a fresh and engaging new look at the pair. Gaines has a dry sense of humor and an appreciation for human foibles. The American founding fathers, in particular, come across as extraordinary men with ordinary obsessions and surprise! senses of humor." —*Christian Science Monitor*

Includes bibliographical references and index.

Gaines, Joanna
The Stories We Tell: Every Piece of Your Story Matters. Joanna Gaines. Harper Select 2022. VII, 247 p.

ISBN 9781400333875

Grades: Adult   B

1. Gaines, Joanna, 1978- 2. Women television personalities 3. Interior decorators 4. Korean Americans 5. Marginalized women 6. Marriage 7. Motherhood 8. Family relationships 9. Perfectionism 10. Vulnerability 11. Healing 12. Empathy 13. Self-fulfillment 14. North American people 15. American people 16. East Asian people 17. Korean people 18. Autobiographies and memoirs 19. Life stories — Arts and culture — Performing arts — Entertainers and celebrities 20. Life stories — Personal growth

LC 2022037086

ESSENTIAL AND RECOMMENDED TITLES
Biography

In her first solo memoir, Joanna Gaines invites us on an authentic and deeply vulnerable journey into her story, and helps shine a light on the beauty of our own, guiding us to release the weights that hold us back so we may live and share our story in truth.

"In this touching memoir, designer and Magnolia Network cofounder Gaines (Magnolia Table, Vol. 2: A Collection of Recipes for Gathering) details how she learned self-acceptance." —*Publishers Weekly*

Gandhi
*An **Autobiography**: The Story of My Experiments with Truth.* Mohandas K. Gandhi; translated from the original in Gujarati by Mahadev Desai; with a foreword by Sissela Bok. Beacon Press 1993. xxix, 528 p.
ISBN 9780807059098
Grades: Adult **B**
1. Gandhi, Mahatma, 1869-1948 2. Politicians 3. Nationalists 4. Peace activists 5. Politics and government 6. India 7. Autobiographies and memoirs 8. Biographies 9. Life stories — Politics — Activists and reformers 10. History writing — Asia — South Asia — India
LC 93019758

Portrays the life of Gandhi, describes the development of his nonviolent political protest movement, and discusses his religious beliefs.

Includes index; Originally published: Washington : Public Affairs Press, 1948.

Garcia Marquez, Gabriel
***Living** to Tell the Tale.* Gabriel Garcia Marquez; translated by Edith Grossman. A.A. Knopf 2003. 483 p. : Map
ISBN 9781400041343
Grades: Adult **B**
1. Garcia Marquez, Gabriel, 1928-2014 2. Authors, Colombian 3. Memories 4. Small towns 5. South American history 6. Colombia 7. 20th century 8. Autobiographies and memoirs 9. Arts and Entertainment — Writing and Publishing 10. Life stories — Arts and culture — Writing — Authors 11. Adult books for young adults
LC 2003058924

Booklist Editors' Choice, 2003; Library Journal Best Books, 2003.

The author traces his life from his birth in 1927 to his 1950 proposal to his wife, discussing such topics as his love for Colombia, the impact of literature and music on his life, and how his written works reflect his life.

"Garcia Mrquez tells the entrancing story of his remarkable family, chronicles the turbulence of his troubled country, Colombia, and offers a piquant portrait of himself as a struggling young writer. A resplendent memoir written with compassion and artistry." —*Booklist*

Originally published in Spanish as Vivir para contarla: Barcelona, Spain : Mondadori, 2002.

Garcia, Amanda Yates
***Initiated**: Memoir of a Witch.* Amanda Yates Garcia. Grand Central Publishing 2019. 304 p.
ISBN 9781538763056
Grades: Adult **B**
1. Garcia, Amanda Yates 2. Witches 3. Wiccans 4. Witchcraft 5. Feminism 6. Empowerment 7. Patriarchy 8. Feminist spirituality 9. Goddess worship 10. Magic 11. Rites and ceremonies 12. Occultism 13. Self-discovery 14. Media tie-ins 15. Spirituality and Religion — General 16. Society and culture — Gender — Women 17. Life stories — Personal growth
LC 2019011190

A writer, artist, professional witch and Oracle of Los Angeles presents this haunting, lyrical memoir in which she describes her journey to return to her body, harness her power and create the magical world she longed for through witchcraft.

Based on a podcast.

Garcia, Rodrigo
*A **Farewell** to Gabo and Mercedes: A Son's Memoir.* Rodrigo Garcia. HarperVia 2021. 176 p.
ISBN 9780063158337
Grades: Adult **B**
1. Garcia Marquez, Gabriel, 1928-2014 2. Barcha, Mercedes 3. Garcia, Rodrigo, 1959- 4. Authors, Colombian 5. Grief 6. Death 7. People with Alzheimer's disease 8. Family relationships 9. Death of parents 10. Loss 11. Autobiographies and memoirs 12. Life stories — Relationships — Parent and child 13. Life stories — Facing adversity — Coping with death 14. Family and Relationships — Aging and death 15. Life stories — Arts and culture — Writing — Authors 16. Book club best bets
LC 2021010396

National Book Critics Circle Award for Autobiography/Memoir finalist, 2021.

Both an illuminating memoir and a heartbreaking work of reportage, a Farewell to Gabo and Mercedes transforms this towering genius from literary creator to protagonist, and paints a rich and revelatory portrait of a family coping with loss. At its center is a man at his most vulnerable, whose wry humor shines even as his lucidity wanes. Gabo savors affection and attention from those in his orbit, but wrestles with what he will lose—and what is already lost. Throughout his final journey is the charismatic Mercedes, his constant companion and the creative muse who was one of the foremost influences on Gabo's life and his art.

"An intensely personal reflection on his father's legacy and his family bonds, tender in its treatment and stirring in its brevity. . . . An intimate portrait of immense loss." —*Booklist*

Gardiner, John Eliot
Bach: Music in the Castle of Heaven. by John Eliot Gardiner. Alfred A. Knopf 2013. 640 p.
ISBN 9780375415296
Grades: Adult **B**
1. Bach, Johann Sebastian, 1685-1750 2. Composers 3. Classical music 4. Classical musicians 5. Biographies 6. Life stories — Arts and culture — Performing arts — Musicians and composers 7. Arts and Entertainment — Music — Classical
LC 2013030398

National Book Critics Circle Award for Biography finalist, 2013.

A revisionist assessment of the life and achievements of the 18th-century master composer, written by one of the modern world's leading conductors and interpreters, shares scholarly insights into how Bach worked, how his effects are achieved and how his music reflects the man.

"Although Gardiner celebrates Bach's accomplishments through this dense, demanding but rewarding work, he reminds readers continually that the composer was no saint. [T]he author's focus is not so much on the man but on the music." —*Kirkus*

Includes bibliographical references and index.

Garelick, Rhonda K.
__Mademoiselle__: Coco Chanel and the Pulse of History. Rhonda Garelick. Random House 2014. 608 p.
ISBN 9781400069521
Grades: Adult **B**
1. Chanel, Coco, 1883-1971 2. Fashion designers 3. Women fashion designers 4. Fashion design 5. Social life and customs 6. France 7. 20th century 8. Biographies 9. Arts and Entertainment — Fashion 10. Life stories — Arts and culture — Fashion
LC 2014006844

Little black dresses. Fake pearls. Jersey knit. Blazers. Ballet flats. Today—and for nearly the last hundred years—we all see some version of Gabrielle "Coco" Chanel every time we pass a woman on the street. But few among us realize that Chanel's role in the events of the twentieth century was as pervasive as her influence on fashion, or how deeply she absorbed and then brilliantly reimagined the historical currents around her. Here, with unprecedented detail and ambition—and through fascinating, thoroughly researched portraits of Chanel's lovers and friends—Rhonda Garelick shows us the Chanel who conquered the world. .. a woman who thirsted to create others in her image, who ruthlessly and innovatively borrowed from her famous (and infamous) intimates, who understood the idea of branding and image well ahead of her time, who created "wearable personality." This is Chanel at the nexus of history: a woman of

PUBLIC LIBRARY CORE COLLECTION: NONFICTION
Twentieth Edition

daring, passion, and legendary vision, in a wonderful biography that gives her long-awaited due.

Garelick pursues the catalog of Chanel's subsequent ill-fated lovers, her work with the Ballets Russes, her vast earnings from Chanel No. 5 and her fraught partnership with the Wertheimer brothers while frankly discussing her relentless, social-climbing attraction to right-wing, reactionary and racist elements. Certainly a definitive portrait, especially considering Garelicks intriguing venture into modern 'Branding.' —*Kirkus*

Includes bibliographical references and index.

Garner, Dwight
The **Upstairs** *Delicatessen: On Eating, Reading, Reading About Eating, and Eating While Reading.* Dwight Garner. Farrar, Straus and Giroux 2023. 240 p.
ISBN 9780374603427
Grades: Adult   **B**
1. Food habits 2. Food writing 3. Food writers 4. Books and reading 5. Food consumption 6. Gastronomy 7. Restaurant critics 8. American people 9. North American people 10. United States 11. Autobiographies and memoirs 12. Life stories — Arts and culture — Writing — Journalists 13. Food writing — General 14. Arts and Entertainment — Writing and Publishing

LC 2023014918

The New York Times book critic gathers his literary chorus to capture the pure pleasure of reading and eating in this comic, soulful, semi-autobiographic treasure.

"New York Times book critic Garner (Read Me) meanders through a lifetime of eating—from boyhood mayo-and-cheese sandwiches to the French bouillabaisses of middle age—and summons wordsmiths from Thackeray to Houellebecq in this amusing mix of memoir, criticism, and cultural history." —*Publishers Weekly*

Includes index.

Garrison, Jessica
The **Devil's** *Harvest: A Ruthless Killer, a Terrorized Community, and the Search for Justice in California's Central Valley.* Jessica Garrison. Hachette Books 2020. 336 p.
ISBN 9780316455688
Grades: Adult   **B**
1. Martinez, Jose Manuel, 1962- 2. Drug dealers 3. Murderers 4. Serial murders 5. Crimes against immigrants 6. Assassins 7. California 8. True Crime — Murder 9. Life stories — Law and order — Criminals and law-breakers

LC 2019055804

Jose Martinez, a ruthless drug cartel hitman, ravaged California's Central Valley with murder after murder while their police forces did nothing. Widely known as a loving father and devoted son, he was also a merciless murderer and responsible for numerous kidnappings and illegal shipments of drugs and weapons. The Devil's Harvest presses upon moral questions haunting our politically divided country: Why do some deaths-and some lives-matter more than others?

"Garrison, former Los Angeles Times reporter and Buzzfeed News West Coast investigations editor, delivers in her debut an expertly researched account of the life and alleged crimes of Jose Manuel Martinez, one of America's most prolific hit men. . . . This is essential reading for true crime buffs." —*Publishers Weekly*

Includes bibliographical references.

Garrow, David J.
Rising Star: The Making of Barack Obama. David Garrow. William Morrow 2017. 960 p.
ISBN 9780062641830
Grades: Adult   **B**
1. Obama, Barack 2. Politicians' families 3. Presidents 4. African Americans 5. Politics and government 6. Hawaii 7. Chicago, Illinois 8. United States 9. Biographies 10. Life stories — Politics — Politicians 11. History writing — Presidency — United States

LC 2017033946

The Pulitzer Prize-winning author of Bearing the Cross presents a definitive account of Barack Obama's life before his presidency, sharing insights into his formative years in Honolulu and Jakarta, his influential associates and his community work in Chicago.

"An exhaustive epic of Barack Obama's trajectory to the presidency." —*Kirkus*

Gaskell, Elizabeth Cleghorn
The Life of Charlotte Bronte. Elizabeth Gaskell; edited with an introduction by Angus Easson. Oxford University Press 1996. xxxvi, 587 p.
ISBN 9781108020527
Grades: Adult   **B**
1. Bronte, Charlotte, 1816-1855 2. Authors, English 3. Social life and customs 4. England 5. 19th century 6. 20th century 7. Biographies 8. Arts and Entertainment — Writing and Publishing 9. Life stories — Arts and culture — Writing — Authors

LC 95000491

Includes bibliographical references (p. [xxxi]-xxxii) and index; Originally published: London: Smith, Elder & Co, 1857.

Gates, Henry Louis
Colored People: A Memoir. Henry Louis Gates, Jr. Knopf 1994. xvi, 216 p.
ISBN 9780679421795
Grades: 11 12 Adult   **B**
1. Gates, Henry Louis, 1950- 2. African Americans 3. African American scholars 4. Critics 5. Growing up 6. Racism 7. Segregation 8. West Virginia 9. United States 10. 1960s 11. 1950s 12. Autobiographies and memoirs 13. Biographies 14. Life stories — Relationships — Growing up 15. Life stories — Relationships — Family 16. Life stories — Education — Scholars and educators 17. Society and culture — Race 18. History writing — African American — Civil rights — United States

LC 93012256

ALA Notable Book, 1995; Booklist Editors' Choice, 1994.

Presents a portrait of Henry Louis Gates, growing up in a West Virginia hill town, presenting a study of his family, his childhood icons, and the social institutions and mores of the time.

"As Gates traces his evolution from Negro to Afro-wearing 'Black,' he also traces the evolution of Piedmont (and, by extension, of much of America) at a time when the relationship between the races was being redefined." —*Newsweek*

Gawande, Atul
Complications: A Surgeon's Notes on an Imperfect Science. Atul Gawande. Metropolitan Books 2002. x, 269 p.
ISBN 9780805063196
Grades: Adult   **B**
1. Gawande, Atul 2. Hospital patients 3. Medical errors 4. Decision-making 5. Medicine 6. Medical ethics 7. Surgeons 8. Coping 9. Surgery 10. Death 11. United States 12. Essays 13. Science Writing — Medicine and health — Doctors and nurses

LC 2001055884

ALA Notable Book, 2003; New York Times Notable Book, 2002; National Book Award for Nonfiction finalist, 2002.

Drawing from compelling true accounts of patients and doctors, a provocative examination of the power and limits of modern medicine reveals a world where science is uncertain, information is limited, and deadly mistakes occur. 60,000 first printing.

"The author describes the work of a trainee surgeon. The pieces range from edgy accounts of medical traumas to sobering analyses of doctors' anxieties and burnout. These exquisitely crafted essays, in which medical subjects segue into explorations of much larger themes, place Gawande among the best in the field." —*Publishers Weekly*

Several of these pieces have appeared, in slightly different form, in the New Yorker and Slate—T.P. verso; Also published with the title Complications: Notes from the life of a young surgeon; Includes bibliographical references (p. 253-264) and index.

ESSENTIAL AND RECOMMENDED TITLES
Biography

Gay, Peter
Freud: A Life for Our Time. Peter Gay. Norton 2006. xx, 810 p, 32 p. of plates : Illustration
ISBN 9780393328615
Grades: 11 12 Adult **B**
1. Freud, Sigmund, 1856-1939 2. Psychoanalysts 3. Jewish men 4. Psychoanalysis 5. Biographies 6. Science Writing — Medicine and health — Mental health 7. Life stories — Science, technology, and medicine — Healthcare professionals
National Book Award for Nonfiction finalist, 1988; Pulitzer Prize for Biography or Autobiography finalist.
A thorough biographical portrait of the pivotal thinker and practitioner probes many aspects of Freud's life, including his family, his city, his professional challenges, and his innovative and controversial theories.
"This biography provides an updating of our knowledge of the life of the founder of psychoanalysis . and it also delineates the continuing impact of Freud's thought on modern endeavors in a number of fields."—*Science Books & Films*
Includes bibliographical references (p. 741-779) and index; Originally published: New York : Norton, 1988. With a new foreword.

Gaye, Jan
After the Dance: My Life with Marvin Gaye. by Jan Gaye with David Ritz. HarperCollins 2015. 224 p.
ISBN 9780062135513
Grades: Adult **B**
1. Gaye, Marvin 2. Gaye, Jan 3. Singers 4. Musicians' spouses 5. Soul musicians 6. African American singers 7. Abused women 8. Marriage 9. Drug use 10. Men-women relations 11. Autobiographies and memoirs 12. Biographies 13. Life stories — Arts and culture — Performing arts — Musicians and composers 14. Life stories — Relationships — Couples
LC 2016560527
The second wife of the late, legendary R&B star, describes how she met the Motown superstar when she was 17 and began a torrid love affair and marriage that was eventually shattered by drugs, family dysfunction and the burdens of fame.
"Gaye's explicitly confessional account of her doomed uphill struggle to stay with Marvin is a prime example of how obsessive celebrity worship can so easily (and dangerously) masquerade as enduring love. A fascinating, unsentimental account of a be-careful-what-you-wish-for romance."—*Kirkus*

Gefter, Philip
What Becomes a Legend Most: A Biography of Richard Avedon. Philip Gefter. HarperCollins 2020. xv, 644 p. Illustration
ISBN 9780062442710
Grades: Adult **B**
1. Avedon, Richard 2. Photographers 3. Photography 4. Fashion photographers 5. Jewish men 6. Gay men 7. Artists 8. Social life and customs 9. United States 10. 20th century 11. Biographies 12. Life stories — Arts and culture — Artists 13. Arts and entertainment — Photography
A portrait of the twentieth-century photographer examines how Avedon endured intense personal and professional discrimination to join an influential group of artists who transformed women's culture.
"Gefter does a remarkable job of situating Avedon within the broader art scene, though the level of detail he goes into may overwhelm readers with a more casual interest in the subject. Nonetheless, this work serves as a definitive and insightful look into one of the titans of 20th century photography."—*Publishers Weekly*
Includes bibliographical references and index.

Gehrig, Lou
The Lost Memoir. Lou Gehrig, Alan D. Gaff. Simon & Schuster 2020. 224 p.
ISBN 9781982132392
Grades: Adult **B**
1. Gehrig, Lou, 1903-1941 2. Baseball players 3. Professional sports 4. Baseball 5. New York City 6. 20th century 7. Autobiographies and memoirs 8. Life stories — Sports — Athletes 9. Sports and Competition — Baseball 10. Sports and Competition — Sports History
LC 2019033015
The lost memoir from baseball icon Lou Gehrig-a major historical discovery, published for the first time as a book, with "color commentary" from historian Alan Gaff. In 1927, the legendary Lou Gehrig sat down to write the remarkable story of his life and career. He was at his peak, fresh off a record-breaking season with the fabled '27 World Series champion Yankees. It was an era unlike any other. Gehrig's personal remembrances were published that year as popular weekly columns in the Oakland Tribune. Until now, those pages were lost to history. Lou comes alive in his captivating memoir. It is a heartfelt rags-to-riches tale about a poor kid from New York who grew up to become one of the greatest. He takes us to his childhood home, to Columbia University where he flashed as a prospect, all the way to the dugout at Yankee Stadium where he recounts his first major league hit and bonding with Babe Ruth. There is a real poignancy to this tale. Built like a heavyweight boxer, "Iron Horse" Lou was one of the most powerful men to play the game. Off the field he was a shy, gentle soul. He would die prematurely from ALS, a degenerative neuromuscular disease now known as Lou Gehrig's Disease. Here is Lou back at bat-Hall of Famer, All Star, and MVP. Lou Gehrig is a monument and tribute to a singular life and career.
"A baseball icon's rediscovered memoir, enhanced with biographical material by the independent scholar who found it. . . . A simple gem for baseball fans."—*Kirkus*
Portions of this text were previously published in 1927 by the Oakland Tribune as Following the Babe; Includes bibliographical references and index.

Gehring, Wes D.
James Dean: Rebel with a Cause. Wes D. Gehring. Indiana Historical Society Press 2005. xix, 303 p. : Illustration
ISBN 9780871951816
Grades: 11 12 Adult **B**
1. Dean, James, 1931-1955 2. Bisexual men 3. Fatal traffic accidents 4. Entertainers 5. Films 6. Actors and actresses 7. Gay men 8. Social life and customs 9. United States 10. 20th century 11. Biographies 12. Arts and Entertainment — Movies and Television 13. Life stories — Arts and culture — Performing arts — Actors and actresses 14. Life stories — Identity — LGBTQIA+ 15. Adult books for young adults
LC 2005041440
Aided by the cooperation of Dean's family members and friends, chronicles the life of the actor who died in a car accident at the age of twenty-four and is known for his roles in "East of Eden" and "Rebel without a Cause."
"This is a study of Dean's entire life and an appreciation of his rightful place in film history. Gehring makes the point that audiences have confused the actor with his troubled-teenager roles, and he counters that misimpression with a fuller portrait."—*Booklist*
Filmography (p. 269-270); Includes bibliographical references (p. [295]-303).

Geller, Danielle
Dog Flowers: A Memoir. Danielle Geller. One World 2021. 272 p. : Illustration
ISBN 9781984820396
Grades: Adult **B**
1. Geller, Danielle 2. Navajo (Diné) (North American people) 3. Loss 4. Alcoholic mothers 5. Childhood 6. Self-discovery 7. Family relationships 8. Grief 9. Death of mothers 10. Women teachers 11. Mothers and daughters 12. Identity 13. Autobiographies and memoirs 14. Life stories — Relationships — Family 15. Family and Relationships — Families 16. Life stories — Identity
LC 2020006990
An award-winning essayist draws on archival documents in a narrative account that explores how her family's troubled past and the death of her mother, a homeless alcoholic, reflected the traditions and tragic history of her Navajo heritage.
"Geller's mix of archival research and personal memoir allows readers to see a refreshing variety of perspectives and layers, resulting in an eye-opening, moving narrative."—*Kirkus*

PUBLIC LIBRARY CORE COLLECTION: NONFICTION
Twentieth Edition

Gellman, Barton
★ *Dark* Mirror: Edward Snowden and the American Surveillance State. Barton Gellman. Penguin Press 2020. 400 p.
ISBN 9781594206016
Grades: Adult   B
1. Snowden, Edward J, 1983- 2. Gellman, Barton, 1960- 3. Investigative journalists 4. Secrecy in government 5. Electronic surveillance 6. Government information 7. Privacy 8. Politics and government 9. United States 10. Politics and global affairs — National security 11. Politics and global affairs — World politics — United States
LC 2019049573
An inside account of the surveillance-industrial revolution and its discontents, fighting back against state and corporate intrusions into our most private spheres.
"A riveting, timely book sure to be one of the most significant of the year." —*Kirkus*

George-Warren, Holly
★ *Janis:* Her Life and Music. Holly George-Warren. Simon & Schuster 2019. xv, 377 pages, 32 unnumbered pages : Illustration; Color
ISBN 9781476793108
Grades: Adult   B
1. Joplin, Janis, 1943-1970 2. Women singers 3. Rock musicians 4. Social acceptance 5. Blues (Music) 6. Women rock musicians 7. Drug addiction 8. 1960s 9. 1950s 10. Biographies 11. Life stories — Arts and culture — Performing arts — Musicians and composers 12. Arts and Entertainment — Music — Rock
LC 2018055881
The Grammy nominee and award-winning co-author of the Road to Woodstock presents an intimate portrait of the counterculture music artist that includes coverage of her conservative upbringing, her extraordinary voice and her boundary-breaking legacy.
"This poignant and ultimately tragic account of an iconic performer is a must for Joplin fans, but anyone who enjoys a good biography will appreciate this exceptional work." —*Library Journal*
Includes bibliographical references (pages [323]-352) and index.

Gerald, Casey
There Will Be No Miracles Here: A Memoir. Casey Gerald. Riverhead Books 2018. 352 p.
ISBN 9780735214200
Grades: Adult   B
1. Gerald, Casey 2. African American gay men 3. American dream 4. Success (Concept) 5. Identity 6. College graduates 7. Growing up 8. Poverty 9. Social classes 10. Elitism 11. Intersectionality 12. Inequality 13. Social marginality 14. Autobiographies and memoirs 15. Life stories — Facing adversity 16. Life stories — Identity 17. Society and culture — Wealth and class 18. Adult books for young adults
LC 2018377393
New York Times Notable Book, 2018.
The co-founder of MBAs Across America describes his upbringing in a Black evangelical family, his football recruitment into Yale and the brutal wealth gap that is forcing increasingly large numbers of marginalized groups to redefine the American Dream.
"Hardly a by-the-numbers memoir, this is a powerful book marked by the author's refreshingly complicated and insightful storytelling." —*Kirkus*

Gerber, Robin
Barbie and Ruth: The Story of the World's Most Famous Doll and the Woman Who Created Her. Robin Gerber. Collins Business 2009. 288 p.
ISBN 9780061341311
Grades: 11 12 Adult   B
1. Handler, Ruth 2. Dollmakers 3. Barbie dolls 4. Toys 5. Businesspeople 6. Doll industry and trade 7. Popular culture 8. History writing — Microhistory 9. Arts and Entertainment — General 10. Business and economics — Industries — Retail products and services
LC 2008029838
Draws on previously unavailable material to trace the parallel lives of the Barbie doll and its creator, Ruth Handler, discussing the latter's origins as a tenth child of Polish-Jewish immigrants and a competitive business pioneer who drew on the lessons of her fight with breast cancer to become a respected humanitarian and entrepreneur.
Includes bibliographical references and index.

Gerwarth, Robert
Hitler's Hangman: The Life and Death of Reinhard Heydrich. Robert Gerwarth. Yale University Press 2011. 336 p.
ISBN 9780300115758
Grades: Adult   B
1. Heydrich, Reinhard, 1904-1942 2. Nazis 3. World War II 4. Holocaust (1933-1945) 5. Third Reich, 1933-1945 6. Politics and government 7. Germany 8. Czechoslovakia 9. Biographies 10. History writing — Wars and conflicts — World War II — European Theater 11. History writing — Europe — Germany 12. Life stories — Law and order — Armed forces personnel
LC 2011013535
Examines Heydrich's progression from a privileged middle-class youth to a mass murderer, offering insight into his character, motivations, consequences of his efforts to alter the ethnic makeup of Europe.

Gevisser, Mark
A Legacy of Liberation: Thabo Mbeki and the Future of the South African Dream. by Mark Gevisser. Palgrave Macmillan 2009. 400 p.
ISBN 9780230611009
Grades: Adult   B
1. Mbeki, Thabo 2. Political leadership 3. Presidents 4. South African people 5. Race relations 6. Politics and government 7. South Africa 8. History writing — Africa — South Africa
LC 2008050763
Follows the family of former South African President Thabo Mbeki to demystify the legacy of liberation struggle and understand the future of the country under new President Jacob Zuma.
"This is a biography of South Africa's second president. Gevisser traces Mbeki's family back several generations, from colonial dispossession through the struggle for liberation. Mbeki's life story has the makings of a gripping tale. Gevisser writes well, particularly when he is witness to an event, when his narrative leaps off the page." —*New York Times Book Review*
Includes bibliographical references and index.

Gewen, Barry
★ *The* Inevitability of Tragedy: Henry Kissinger and His World. Barry Gewen. W.W. Norton & Company 2020. 448 p.
ISBN 9781324004059
Grades: Adult   B
1. Kissinger, Henry, 1923-2023 2. Cabinet officers 3. International relations 4. Diplomacy 5. Vietnam War, 1961-1975 6. World War II 7. Intellectuals 8. Power 9. Philosophy 10. Politicians 11. Refugees 12. United States 13. Biographies 14. Life stories — Politics — Politicians 15. History writing — Wars and conflicts — Vietnam War 16. Politics and global affairs — Political philosophy
LC 2019050503
New York Times Notable Book, 2020.
A revisionist portrait of the diplomatic advisor under the Nixon and Ford administrations illuminates the controversies and fundamental ideas behind his policies, discussing how Kissinger's views were partly shaped by his experiences as a Jewish-German refugee.
"Masterly work on the making of Henry Kissinger—and what American foreign policy can learn from his dark experience and pessimistic outlook." —*Kirkus*

Ghafari, Zarifa
Zarifa: A Woman's Battle in a Man's World. Zarifa Ghafari with Hannah Lucinda Smith. Perseus Books Group 2022. 288 p.
ISBN 9781541702639
Grades: Adult   B

ESSENTIAL AND RECOMMENDED TITLES
Biography

1. Human rights activists 2. Political activists 3. Afghan people 4. Afghanistan 5. Autobiographies and memoirs 6. Life stories — Facing adversity — War and oppression — War survivors

Afghanistan's youngest female mayor of Maidan Wardak, Kabul, and campaigner for human rights describes what she accomplished, the women she still tries to help as they live under the Taliban and her vision for how grassroots activism can change their lives and the lives of women everywhere.

"A politician and activist recounts the personal and political effects of the rise and fall of the Taliban in her native country of Afghanistan....A searingly honest, profoundly courageous memoir of one fearless woman's fight for her homeland." —*Kirkus*

Ghostface Killah
Rise of a Killah. Ghostface Killer. St. Martin's Press 2024. 256 p.
ISBN 9781250274274
Grades: Adult   B

1. Ghostface Killah (Rapper) 2. African American rap musicians 3. Rap musicians 4. Hip-hop culture 5. Mental health 6. Rap music 7. Rap music industry and trade 8. United States 9. Autobiographies and memoirs 10. Life stories — Arts and culture — Performing arts — Musicians and composers 11. Arts and Entertainment — Music — Rap and R&B

LC 2023045832

The co-founder of the Wu-Tang Clan, a legendary hip-hop group who broke all the rules, focuses on the people, places and events that mean the most to him, sharing his defining personal moments as well as exclusive photos and memorabilia, in this one-of-a-kind holy grail for Wu-Tang and Ghost fans alike.

"Rapper Ghostface Killah...portrays in his heartfelt memoir the 'Sharper than cleats' youth he drew on for his rhymes." —*Publishers Weekly*

Gibson, Larry S.
Young Thurgood: The Making of a Supreme Court Justice. by Larry S. Gibson. Prometheus Books 2012. 390 p.
ISBN 9781616145712
Grades: Adult   B

1. Marshall, Thurgood, 1908-1993 2. Judges 3. African American civil rights 4. Civil rights 5. African American judges 6. Social life and customs 7. United States history 8. United States 9. 20th century 10. Biographies 11. History writing — Judicial branch — United States 12. Life stories — Law and order — Judges and lawyers 13. History writing — African American — Civil rights — United States

LC 2012027517

The only biography of Thurgood Marshall endorsed by his immediate family covers his whole life, from his upbringing to his landmark work with the NAACP and his appointment as the first African-American justice of the Supreme Court.

Includes bibliographical references and index.

Giddings, Paula
Ida: A Sword Among Lions : Ida B. Wells and the Campaign Against Lynching. Paula J. Giddings. Amistad 2008. xii, 800 p, 16 p. of plates : Illustration
ISBN 9780060519216
Grades: 11 12 Adult   B

1. Wells, Ida B, 1862-1931 2. African American women civil rights workers 3. African American women social reformers 4. Civil rights 5. Lynching 6. African American women 7. Race relations 8. United States history 9. United States 10. 20th century 11. Biographies 12. History writing — Women's history 13. Life stories — Politics — Activists and reformers 14. Adult books for young adults 15. History writing — African American — Civil rights — United States

LC Bl2008005797

BCALA Literary Award for Nonfiction, 2009; Los Angeles Times Book Prize for Biography, 2008; National Book Critics Circle Award for Biography finalist, 2008.

Traces the life and legacy of the nineteenth-century activist and pioneer, documenting her birth into slavery and upbringing in the Victorian-era South, where she became a journalist and pioneer for civil rights and suffrage, in an account that also describes her determination to counter lynching activities.

"An iconic figure in American history, Wells was not always celebrated by her contemporaries for her groundbreaking activism because of her assertive politics and difficult personality.... Giddings offers a look at how Wells' own self-assertion affected her relationships with family, friends, colleagues, and the broader American public as she evolved as a woman and an activist.... With meticulous research, including Wells' own diary, Giddings brings to life one of the most fascinating women in American history, giving readers a real feel for the texture and context of Wells' life." —*Booklist*

Giddins, Gary
Bing Crosby: A Pocketful of Dreams: The Early Years, 1903-1940. Gary Giddins. Little, Brown 2001. 736 p. : Illustration (Bing Crosby (Gary Giddins), 1)
ISBN 9780316881883
Grades: 11 12 Adult   B

1. Crosby, Bing, 1904-1977 2. Crooning 3. Singers 4. Actors and actresses 5. Radio programs 6. Popular culture 7. Social life and customs 8. United States history 9. Hollywood, California 10. United States 11. 20th century 12. Biographies 13. Arts and Entertainment — Music — Jazz and the Blues 14. Life stories — Arts and culture — Performing arts — Musicians and composers

LC 00044403

Booklist Editors' Choice, 2001; Library Journal Best Books, 2001; New York Times Notable Book, 2001.

Traces the rise of Bing Crosby from his early successes as a radio star to his initial foray into Hollywood.

"Giddins has contributed a landmark study of popular singing in the first half of the twentieth century." —*Booklist*

Discography: V. [1], p. [593]-606; Filmography (complete): V. [1], p. [607]-621; Includes bibliographical references (v. [1], p. [[671]-686) and index.

Bing Crosby: Swinging on a Star: The War Years, 1940-1946. Gary Giddins. Little Brown & CO 2018. 736 p. (Bing Crosby (Gary Giddins), 2)
ISBN 9780316887922
Grades: Adult   B

1. Crosby, Bing, 1904-1977 2. Crooning 3. World War II 4. Singers 5. Actors and actresses 6. Radio programs 7. Popular culture 8. Social life and customs 9. United States history 10. Hollywood, California 11. United States 12. 20th century 13. Biographies 14. Arts and Entertainment — Music — Jazz and the Blues 15. Life stories — Arts and culture — Performing arts — Musicians and composers

LC Bl2018190537

In a much-anticipated follow-up to the universally acclaimed first volume of a comprehensive Bing Crosby biography, an NBCC Winner and preeminent cultural critic focuses on Crosby's most memorable period, the war years and the origin story of White Christmas.

"For a twenty-first-century audience, the idea of Bing Crosby as both a swoonworthy movie idol and an inspiration to battle-hardened soldiers may seem difficult to comprehend, but that is the brilliance of Giddins work: He makes us see how, in a very different time, Crosby's easygoing, waggish style was just what the country craved, on records and radio, at the movies, and in person." —*Booklist*

Gienapp, William E.
Abraham Lincoln and Civil War America: A Biography. William E. Gienapp. Oxford University Press 2002. xiii, 239 p. : Illustration; Map
ISBN 9780195150995
Grades: 11 12 Adult   B

1. Lincoln, Abraham, 1809-1865 2. Presidents 3. Politics and government 4. United States 5. 19th century 6. American Civil War era (1861-1865) 7. Biographies 8. History writing — Presidency — United States 9. History writing — Wars and conflicts — American Civil War 10. Life stories — Law and order — Armed forces personnel 11. Adult books for young adults 12. History writing — Presidency — 19th century — United States

LC 2001050056

Chronicles Abraham Lincoln's life during the Civil War, revealing the president as a quick study in military tactics and political manipulation.

"In spite of the book's size, its discriminating history of Lincoln's life is surprisingly rich, and the narrative of his presidency and the unfolding of the war is crisp and coherent." —Bookmarks

Includes bibliographical references (p. [228]-232) and index.

Gies, Miep

★ *Anne Frank Remembered: The Story of the Woman Who Helped to Hide the Frank Family.* Miep Gies and Alison Leslie Gold. Simon and Schuster Paperbacks 2009. 264 p, 24 p. of plates : Illustration

ISBN 9781416598855

Grades: 11 12 Adult **B**

1. Gies, Miep, 1909-2010 2. Frank, Anne, 1929-1945 3. Righteous Gentiles in the Holocaust 4. World War II 5. Resistance to government 6. Hidden children (Holocaust) 7. Jewish people 8. Holocaust (1933-1945) 9. Religious persecution 10. Teenage girls 11. Jewish teenagers 12. Interethnic relations 13. Courage 14. Amsterdam, Netherlands 15. Netherlands 16. Autobiographies and memoirs 17. History writing — Wars and conflicts — Homefront — World War II 18. Life stories — Facing adversity — War and oppression — War survivors

LC 2009294295

The reminiscences of Miep Gies, the woman who hid the Frank family in Amsterdam during the Second World War, presents a vivid story of life under Nazi occupation.

"These vignettes and the description of what was happening in Amsterdam provide insight into how the Nazi occupation affected the lives of innocent people, and into the heroism of a remarkable woman, Miep Gies." —School Library Journal

Includes index.

Gilbert, Elizabeth

Eat, Pray, Love: One Woman's Search for Everything Across Italy, India and Indonesia. Elizabeth Gilbert. Viking 2006. 334 p.

ISBN 9780670034710

Grades: Adult **B**

1. Gilbert, Elizabeth, 1969- 2. Divorced women 3. Happiness 4. Travel writers 5. Cooking, Italian 6. Ashrams 7. Voyages and travels 8. Self-discovery 9. India 10. Italy 11. Indonesia 12. Bali (Island) 13. Autobiographies and memoirs 14. Page to screen 15. Biographies 16. Travel Writing — General 17. Food Writing — Food and Culture 18. Life stories — Personal growth 19. Nonfiction that reads like fiction

LC 2005042435

New York Times Notable Book, 2006.

Traces the author's decision to quit her job and travel the world for a year after suffering a midlife crisis and divorce, a journey that took her to three places in her quest to explore her own nature and learn the art of spiritual balance.

"A probing, thoughtful title with a free and easy style, this work seamlessly blends history and travel for a very enjoyable read." —Library Journal

Gildea, William

The Longest Fight: In the Ring with Joe Gans, Boxing's First African American Champion. William Gildea. Farrar, Straus and Giroux 2012. 224 p.

ISBN 9780374280970

Grades: 9 10 11 12 Adult **B**

1. Gans, Joe 2. Boxing matches 3. Boxers (Sports) 4. African American boxers 5. Boxing 6. Race relations 7. United States 8. 1910s 9. Biographies 10. Sports and Competition — Boxing

LC 2011040170

An account of the lesser-known story of early sports hero Jon Gans centers on his epic 1906 boxing match against Oscar "Battling" Nelson, discussing how the competition reflected period racial tensions and the realities endured by African-American athletes.

Includes bibliographical references and index.

Gill, Anton

Art Lover: A Biography of Peggy Guggenheim. Anton Gill. Harper Collins 2003. xvi, 480 p.

ISBN 9780060196974

Grades: Adult **B**

1. Guggenheim, Peggy, 1898-1979 2. Art collectors and collecting 3. Art patrons 4. Rich women 5. Sexuality 6. Art patronage 7. Antisemitism 8. Women's role 9. Social life and customs 10. Self-perception 11. Insecurity 12. United States 13. Europe 14. 20th century 15. Biographies 16. Arts and Entertainment — Museums and Collections 17. Life stories — Arts and culture

LC 2001051731

An account of one of the twentieth-century's most controversial and influential art collectors retraces Guggenheim's steps through Europe, where she met some of the most important artists and writers of her time.

"Guggenheim was known as much for her sexual exploits as for her championing of modern art, a fact Gill . examines with candor, sensitivity, and mellifluous grace." —Booklist

Includes bibliographical references (p. [447]-451) and index.

Gillette, Michael L.

Lady Bird Johnson: An Oral History. Michael L. Gillette. Oxford University Press 2012. 400 p.

ISBN 9780199908080

Grades: Adult **B**

1. Johnson, Lady Bird, 1912-2007 2. Johnson, Lyndon B, 1908-1973 3. Women and politics 4. Women 5. Campaigning 6. Women and war 7. Presidents' spouses 8. Political participation 9. Politics and government 10. Determination 11. United States 12. 1940s 13. 1950s 14. 20th century 15. Biographies 16. Interviews 17. History writing — Presidency — 20th century — United States 18. Life stories — Politics — Politicians 19. History writing — Post World War II - 1959 — United States

LC 2012011580

A fascinating look at the life of Lady Bird Johnson draws largely on 47 recorded oral history interviews, conducted by the author and his colleagues over a span of 18 years.

Includes bibliographical references and index.

Gilliam, Dorothy Butler

Trailblazer: A Pioneering Journalist's Fight to Make the Media Look More Like America. Dorothy Butler Gilliam. Center Street 2019. 360 p.

ISBN 9781546083443

Grades: Adult **B**

1. Gilliam, Dorothy Butler, 1936- 2. African American women journalists 3. Women civil rights workers 4. African American women 5. African American civil rights workers 6. Gender equity 7. Journalists 8. Race relations 9. Washington D.C. 10. United States 11. 20th century 12. Autobiographies and memoirs 13. Biographies 14. Life stories — Arts and culture — Writing — Journalists 15. Life stories — Identity — Race and ethnicity 16. Life stories — Identity — Gender 17. Society and culture — Race 18. Society and culture — Gender — Women

LC 2018034533

The barrier-breaking civil-rights journalist presents a comprehensive view of racial relations and the media in the U.S. that draws on her personal and professional experiences to celebrate the behind-the-scenes victories that have shaped decades of struggle.

"In her compelling memoir, she recounts her trailblazing career during the turbulence of the Vietnam War, the civil rights and womens movements, and Watergate and looks beyond her personal journey to examine efforts to diversify the staffs of news organizations and other challenges currently facing the press." —Booklist

Includes bibliographical references and index.

Gillon, Steven M.

America's Reluctant Prince: The Life of John F. Kennedy Jr. Steven M. Gillon. Dutton, an imprint of Penguin Random House LLC 2019. 464 p.

ISBN 9781524742386

Grades: Adult **B**

1. Kennedy, John F. Jr, 1960-1999 2. Children of presidents 3. Periodical publishers and publishing 4. Celebrities 5. United States 6. Biographies 7. Life stories — People in history — Famous families

LC 2019014938

ESSENTIAL AND RECOMMENDED TITLES
Biography

Through the lens of their decades-long friendship and including exclusive interviews and details from previously classified documents, noted historian and New York Times bestselling author Steven M. Gillon examines John F. Kennedy Jr.'s life and legacy from before his birth to the day he died. Gillon covers the highs, the lows, and the surprising incidents, viewpoints, and relationships that John never discussed publicly, revealing the full story behind JFK Jr.'s complicated and rich life. In the end, Gillon proves that John's life was far more than another tragedy—rather, it's the true key to understanding both the Kennedy legacy and how America's First Family continues to shape the world we live in today.
Includes bibliographical references and index.

Ginzberg, Lori D.
Elizabeth Cady Stanton: An American Life. Lori D. Ginzberg. Hill and Wang 2009. 272 p.
ISBN 9780809094936
Grades: 11 12 Adult   B
1. Stanton, Elizabeth Cady, 1815-1902 2. Feminists 3. Women's rights 4. Suffrage 5. Suffragist Movement 6. Feminism 7. Intellectual life 8. Women 9. United States history 10. United States 11. 19th century 12. Biographies 13. History writing — Women's history 14. History writing — United States 15. Life stories — Politics — Activists and reformers
LC 2008054395

Historian Lori D. Ginzberg narrates the life of a woman of great charm, enormous appetite, and extraordinary intellectual gifts who turned the limitations placed on women like herself into a universal philosophy of equal rights.

"Ginzberg has produced a readable and realistic account of the life of one of the most important feminists and intellectuals of the 19th century, a woman who was at once an abolitionist who could sound like a racist and an advocate of civil rights for women whose language often reeked of elitism." —*Library Journal*
Includes bibliographical references and index.

Girma, Haben
Haben: The Deafblind Woman Who Conquered Harvard Law. by Haben Girma. Twelve 2019. 256 p.
ISBN 9781538728727
Grades: Adult   B
1. Girma, Haben, 1988- 2. Women with disabilities 3. Determination 4. Refugees 5. Eritrean people 6. Women lawyers 7. Disability rights advocates 8. People who are blind and deaf 9. Women 10. Courage 11. Autobiographies and memoirs 12. Life stories — Facing adversity — Medical issues — Living with disabilities 13. Adult books for young adults
LC 2018050294

Documents the story of the first deaf and blind graduate of Harvard Law School, tracing her refugee parents' harrowing experiences in the Eritrea-Ethiopian war and her development of innovations that enabled her remarkable achievements.

"Articulated in elegant prose, lawyer and activist Girma's struggles navigating an ableist world as a person with disabilities are motivating, heartbreaking, and real." —*Booklist*

Glaser, Gabrielle
American Baby: A Mother, a Child, and the Shadow History of Adoption. Gabrielle Glaser. Viking 2020. 352 p.
ISBN 9780735224681
Grades: Adult   B
1. Rosenberg, David, 1961-2014 2. Katz, Margaret Erle 3. Adopted children 4. Adoption 5. Adoption agencies 6. Corruption 7. Jewish families 8. Birthparents 9. Teenage mothers 10. Stigma (Social psychology) 11. Identity 12. Mother-separated children 13. Child-separated mothers 14. Identification 15. New York City 16. Family and Relationships — Parenting — Adoption 17. Life stories — Facing adversity 18. Life stories — Relationships — Parent and child
LC 2020005338

A history of adoption in postwar America explores the impact of "Baby Boom" values and limited birth control on the life of a pregnant teen who was forced by the institutions of the 1960s to give up her rights.

"A searing narrative that combines the detailed saga of one unwed teenage mother with deep research on all aspects of a scandalous adoption industry." —*Kirkus*
Includes bibliographical references and index.

Glass, Philip
Words Without Music: A Memoir. Philip Glass. Liveright Publishing Co. 2015. 288 p.
ISBN 9780871404381
Grades: Adult   B
1. Glass, Philip, 1937- 2. Composers 3. Music 4. Composition (Music) 5. Autobiographies and memoirs 6. Life stories — Arts and culture — Performing arts — Musicians and composers 7. Arts and entertainment — Music — Classical 8. Adult books for young adults
LC 2015000421

While striving to achieve recognition for his musical works, award-winning composer Philip Glass installed drywall, moved furniture, drove a New York City cab, and even taught himself plumbing. Glass eventually became known for his innovative approach to composition, which incorporates multicultural musical, literary, and philosophical influences. He reveals himself in Words Without Music as an engaging storyteller, creating a colloquial, vivid, and unpretentious self-portrait that will appeal to any reader—not just classical music fans.

"Aspiring musicians and artists will learn much from Glass, as will general readers, musical or not, who will discover an artistic life exceptionally well lived." —*Booklist*

Glass, Sara
Kissing Girls on Shabbat. Sara Glass. Signal Press 2024. 288 p.
ISBN 9781668031216
Grades: Adult   B
1. Glass, Sara 2. Self-acceptance 3. Psychotherapists 4. LGBTQIA+ people 5. Identity 6. Protectiveness 7. Families 8. Lesbians 9. Mothers 10. Assault and battery 11. Orthodox Judaism 12. Jewish people 13. Loss 14. Communities 15. Autobiographies and memoirs 16. Life stories — Religion and spirituality — Leaving religion 17. Life stories — Identity — LGBTQIA+

No longer able to conform to her controlling Hasidic community, the author walked away from the world she knew and onto a path of self-acceptance as she, after a divorce, custody battle, remarriage and a shocking sexual assault, decided to finally be true to herself and embrace her queer identity.

"Searching and provocative, this book chronicles a woman's struggle with faith and freedom while also celebrating the necessity of personal choice. A courageously candid memoir." —*Kirkus*

Gleiberman, Owen
Movie Freak: My Life Watching Movies. Owen Gleiberman. Hachette Books 2016. 304 p.
ISBN 9780316382960
Grades: Adult   B
1. Gleiberman, Owen 2. Films 3. Film critics 4. Autobiographies and memoirs 5. Arts and Entertainment — Movies and Television 6. Life stories — Arts and culture — Writing — Journalists
LC 2015039430

From a personal obsession with film, to an unorthodox mentorship with the legendary Pauline Kael, to establishing himself with the upstart Entertainment Weekly, Movie Freak is the memoir by veteran film critic Owen Gleiberman that will speak to anyone whose life has been changed by a great film.

"A story of societal change, rich in cultural as well as personal history." —*Kirkus*
Includes index.

Glenconner, Anne
★ *Lady in Waiting: My Extraordinary Life in the Shadow of the Crown.* Anne Glenconner. Hachette Books 2020. 256 pages
ISBN 9780306846366
Grades: Adult   B

PUBLIC LIBRARY CORE COLLECTION: NONFICTION
Twentieth Edition

1. Glenconner, Anne 2. Margaret, Princess, Countess of Snowdon, 1930-2002 3. Elizabeth II, Queen of Great Britain, 1926-2022 4. Ladies-in-waiting 5. Courts and courtiers 6. Motherhood 7. Married people 8. Sexism 9. Classism 10. Men-women relations 11. Great Britain 12. 20th century 13. Autobiographies and memoirs 14. Life stories — Politics — Royalty 15. History writing — Europe — United Kingdom

LC Bl2020007748

The daughter of the 5th Earl of Leicester, unable to inherit her father's estate, describes growing up with royalty, having served as Maid of Honor at Queen Elizabeth's coronation and as lady in waiting to Princess Margaret.

"An insider's look at the world of palaces, princesses, and the pressure of public life . . . A must-have for loyal royal fans." —*Kirkus*

Originally published: London : Hodder & Stoughton, 2019.

Glendinning, Victoria

Leonard Woolf: A Biography. Victoria Glendinning. Free Press 2006. 498 p. : Illustration

ISBN 9780743246538

Grades: Adult   B

1. Woolf, Leonard, 1880-1969 2. Political scientists 3. Publishers and publishing 4. Socialists 5. Authors, English 6. British history 7. 20th century 8. Biographies 9. Life stories — Education — Scholars and educators 10. History writing — Europe — United Kingdom

LC 2006049784

New York Times Notable Book, 2007.

An account of the life and career of the Bloomsbury political intellectual and husband of Virginia Woolf covers his comfortable Jewish childhood, role in inspiring the League of Nations, and relationships with such figures as E.M. Forster and T.S. Eliot.

"Glendinning's generous biography does not ignore that Woolf could be grumpy and was too often cheeseparing, but her account does justice to his range of passions, his literary and political contributions and, above all, his human goodness; he was a man who knew how to live." —*New Statesman*

Includes bibliographical references (p. [475]-477) and index.

Gless, Sharon

Apparently There Were Complaints: A Memoir. Sharon Gless. Simon & Schuster 2021. 304 p.

ISBN 9781501125959

Grades: Adult   B

1. Gless, Sharon 2. Acting 3. Alcoholism 4. Interpersonal relations 5. Mental health 6. Families 7. Fame 8. Actors and actresses 9. Autobiographies and memoirs 10. Life stories — Arts and culture — Performing arts — Actors and actresses 11. Arts and Entertainment — Movies and Television

LC 2021013758

A deeply personal story about Gless's complicated family and her struggles with alcoholism and fear of romantic commitment and a juicy, hilarious tell-all about Hollywood and Sharon's encounters with some of the industry's biggest stars. Gless puts it all out on the page in the same way she has lived—never with moderation.

"Emmy Award-winning actor Gless debuts with a no-holds-barred look at her long and storied career. . . . Written by a masterful storyteller, this smart account boldly reveals both the grit and the glamour of Gless's life, candidly contending with her substance abuse, various affairs, and the fact that writing her memoir took almost seven years." —*Publishers Weekly*

Godwin, Gail

Getting to Know Death: A Meditation. Gail Godwin. Bloomsbury Publishing Place USA 2024. 176 p.

ISBN 9781639734443

Grades: Adult   B

1. Godwin, Gail 2. Wounds and injuries 3. Women authors 4. Senior women 5. Healing 6. Purpose in life 7. Memories 8. Life 9. Death 10. Autobiographies and memoirs 11. Life stories — Facing adversity — Coping with death 12. Family and relationships — Aging and death

The three-time National Book Award finalist recounts her long path to recovery after a major injury at age 86 and discusses the lessons she has learned as she enters the twilight of her life.

"The veteran novelist looks with a clear eye at her declining health and the loss of many of those she has loved." —*Kirkus*

Goessel, Tracey

The First King of Hollywood: The Life of Douglas Fairbanks. Tracey Goessel. Chicago Review Press 2015. 560 p.

ISBN 9781613734049

Grades: Adult   B

1. Fairbanks, Douglas, 1883-1939 2. Silent films 3. Films 4. Actors and actresses 5. Biographies 6. Life stories — Arts and culture — Performing arts — Actors and actresses

LC 2015018526

The first truly definitive biography of Douglas Fairbanks, the greatest leading man of the silent film era.

"The author draws on the actor's voluminous speeches and public statements, as well as a cache of love letters between Doug and Mary. Sadly, many Fairbanks films have been lost, but this highly recommended book illuminates a vanished era of American film." —*Library Journal*

Includes bibliographical references and index.

Goetsch, Diana

This Body I Wore: A Memoir. Diana Goetsch. Farrar, Straus and Giroux 2022. 320 p.

ISBN 9780374115098

Grades: Adult   B

1. Goetsch, Diana 2. Trans women 3. Poets, American 4. Transitioning (Gender identity) 5. LGBTQIA+ people 6. Identity 7. Childhood 8. Gender identity 9. Transgender people 10. Autobiographies and memoirs 11. Life stories — Identity — LGBTQIA+

LC 2021059968

A memoir of one woman's long journey to late transition, in an era before real community or appropriate language was available to help her understand herself.

"A valuable memoir enriched by years of personal and societal insight into the fraught subject of gender identity." —*Kirkus*

Golay, Michael

America 1933: The Great Depression, Lorena Hickok, Eleanor Roosevelt, and the Shaping of the New Deal. by Michael Golay. Free Press 2013. 320 p.

ISBN 9781439196014

Grades: Adult   B

1. Hickok, Lorena Alice, 1893-1968 2. Investigative journalism 3. Depressions, 1929-1941 4. Poverty 5. Journalists 6. Women journalists 7. Economics 8. United States history 9. United States 10. 1930s 11. Depression era (1929-1941) 12. History writing — Great Depression — United States

LC 2012041139

Documents the 18-month journey of woman journalist Lorena Hickok during the height of the Great Depression, recounting her experiences and influence in some of the nation's worst-hit regions as documented in almost daily letters written to close friend Eleanor Roosevelt.

Goldberg, Whoopi

Bits and Pieces: My Mother, My Brother, and Me. Whoopi Goldberg. Blackstone Publishing 2024. 258 p.

ISBN 9798200920235

Grades: Adult   B

1. Goldberg, Whoopi, 1955- 2. Families 3. Influence (Literary, artistic, etc.) 4. Childhood 5. Growing up 6. African American families 7. Loss 8. Actors and actresses 9. African American women 10. Mothers 11. Brothers 12. Autobiographies and memoirs 13. Life stories — Relationships — Family 14. Life stories — Arts and culture — Performing arts — Actors and actresses 15. Family and Relationships — Families

"Generous, candid, and uplifting." —*Booklist*

ESSENTIAL AND RECOMMENDED TITLES
Biography

Goldberger, Paul
Building Art: The Life and Work of Frank Gehry. by Paul Goldberger. Alfred A. Knopf 2015. 528 pages
ISBN 9780307701534
Grades: Adult B
1. Gehry, Frank O, 1929- 2. Architecture, American 3. Buildings 4. United States 5. 20th century 6. Biographies 7. Life stories — Arts and culture — Architects 8. Arts and Entertainment — Architecture
LC 2015026562
A biography of the Canadian-born architect Frank Gehry.
"With avid precision and invaluable insight, Goldberger charts the complicated, punishing battles Gehry waged to construct his ambitious, dreamworld buildings, from private homes to Guggenheim Bilbao, the Walt Disney Concert Hall, Facebook headquarters, and beyond. The result is an involving work of significant architectural history and a discerning and affecting portrait of a daring and original master builder." —*Booklist*

Goldblatt, Duchess
Becoming Duchess Goldblatt: A Memoir. Anonymous. Houghton Mifflin Harcourt 2020. 240 p.
ISBN 9780358216773
Grades: Adult B
1. Goldblatt, Duchess 2. Anonymous people 3. Social media 4. Humorous writing 5. Anonyms and pseudonyms 6. Personal conduct 7. Compassion 8. Virtual community 9. Autobiographies and memoirs 10. Life stories — Arts and culture — Writing 11. Life stories — Facing adversity 12. Society and culture — Media and technology
LC 2019027260
Becoming Duchess Goldblatt is two stories: That of the reclusive real-life writer who created a fictional character out of loneliness and thin air, and that of the magical Duchess Goldblatt herself, a bright light in the darkness of social media. Fans around the world are drawn to Her Grace's voice, her wit, her life-affirming love for all humanity, and the fun and friendship of the community that's sprung up around her.
"How does a fictional character write a real memoir? Very, very well. . . . She's created a long-term fever dream of humor, compassion, wordplay, and dog photos. A fascinating memoir by a 21st-century original." —*Kirkus*

Goldfarb, Bruce
★ *18 Tiny Deaths: The Untold Story of Frances Glessner Lee and the Invention of Modern Forensics.* Bruce Goldfarb. Sourcebooks Inc 2020. 336 pages
ISBN 9781492680475
Grades: Adult B
1. Lee, Frances Glessner, 1878-1962 2. Women forensic scientists 3. Forensic scientists 4. Forensic sciences 5. Crime scenes 6. Criminal investigation 7. Murder investigation 8. Dioramas 9. Training 10. Coroners 11. United States 12. Biographies 13. True Crime — Forensic Sciences 14. Life stories — Law and order 15. Life stories — Politics — Activists and reformers
LC 2019031080
An account of the life of the woman best known for creating the Nutshell Studies of Unexplained Death dioramas describes her transition from a wealthy socialite to a leader in modern forensics whose methods are still used today.
"A stand-out addition to any library's true-crime collection." —*Booklist*
Includes bibliographical references and index.

Goldsmith, Martin
The Inextinguishable Symphony: A True Story of Music and Love in Nazi Germany. Martin Goldsmith. Wiley 2000. VI, 346 p. : Illustration
ISBN 9780471350972
Grades: 11 12 Adult B
1. Goldsmith, George, 1913-2009 2. Goldsmith, Rosemary, 1917-1984 3. Musicians 4. Jewish people 5. Holocaust (1933-1945) 6. German history 7. 20th century 8. Biographies 9. History writing — Wars and conflicts — Holocaust — World War II 10. Family and Relationships — Dating and Marriage 11. Life stories — Arts and culture — Performing arts — Musicians and composers
LC 00025955
An account of two Jewish musicians who fell in love while playing for Frankfort's Kulturbund orchestra, which served as a haven for persecuted Jews and as a Nazi propoganda tool, describes how love maintained through the horrors of the Third Reich.
"Goldsmith's weaving together of cultural and personal history constitutes a gripping tale of persecution, intrigue, and love and an insider'sor two insiders' view of a dark time." —*Booklist*
Includes bibliographical references (p. 337-338).

Goldstein, Meredith
Can't Help Myself: Lessons & Confessions from a Modern Advice Columnist. Meredith Goldstein. Grand Central Publishing 2018. 256 p.
ISBN 9781455543779
Grades: Adult B
1. Goldstein, Meredith 2. Love 3. Interpersonal relations 4. Advice columnists 5. Self-fulfillment 6. Autobiographies and memoirs 7. Life stories — Relationships 8. Life stories — Arts and culture — Writing — Journalists
LC 2017041731
Every day, Boston Globe advice columnist Meredith Goldstein takes on the relationship problems of thousands of dedicated readers. They look to her for wisdom on all matters of the heart- how to cope with dating fatigue and infidelity, work romances, tired marriages, true love, and true loss. In her column, she has it all figured out, but in her real life she is a lot less certain. Whether it's her own reservations about the traditional path of marriage and family, her difficulty finding someone she truly connects with, or the evolution of her friendships as her friends start to have their own families, Meredith finds herself looking for insight, just like her readers.
"The book will appeal to loyal readers of advice columns—particularly Goldsteins—but be forewarned, this book is a tearjerker." —*Publishers Weekly*

Goldstein, Nancy
Jackie Ormes: The First African American Woman Cartoonist. Nancy Goldstein. University of Michigan Press 2008. IX, 225 p. : Illustration; Color
ISBN 9780472116249
Grades: 10 11 12 Adult B
1. Ormes, Jackie, 1911-1985 2. Cartoonists 3. African American cartoonists 4. African Americans 5. United States 6. Biographies 7. Arts and Entertainment — Comics, Cartoons, and Animation 8. Life stories — Arts and culture — Artists 9. Adult books for young adults
LC 2007035395
Looks at the life and career of the first African American woman cartoonist.
"In the first book devoted to Ormes, Goldstein not only recounts with enthusiasm the trailblazing cartoonist's remarkable story from her birth in Pittsburgh to her celebrity-filled life in Chicago but also keenly analyzes Ormes' influential cartoons and the role Black newspapers played in the struggle for racial equality. With a generous selection of Ormes' 'Forward-looking' cartoons resurrected for the first time, this is one exciting and significant book." —*Booklist*
Includes bibliographical references (p. 205-213) and index.

Goldsworthy, Adrian Keith
Augustus: First Emperor of Rome. Adrian Goldsworthy. Yale University Press 2014. 624 p.
ISBN 9780300178722
Grades: Adult B
1. Augustus, Emperor of Rome, 63 B.C.E.-14 C.E 2. Roman emperors 3. Ancient history 4. Politics and government 5. Ancient Rome 6. Roman Empire (27 B.C.E.-476 C.E.) 7. Biographies 8. Life stories — Politics — Royalty 9. History writing — Ancient — Rome
LC 2014940657
In this highly anticipated biography Goldsworthy puts his deep knowledge of ancient sources to full use, recounting the events of Augustus' long life in greater detail than ever before. Goldsworthy pins down the man behind the myths: a consummate manipulator, propagandist, and showman, both generous and ruthless. Under Augustus' rule the empire prospered, yet his success was never assured and the events of his life unfolded with exciting unpredictability.

Goldsworthy captures the passion and savagery, the public image and private struggles of the real man whose epic life continues to influence western history.

"Goldsworthy tells the story well. A commendable book. Summing Up: Highly recommended. General and undergraduate readers." —*Choice*

Includes bibliographical references and index.

★ *Caesar: Life of a Colossus.* Adrian Goldsworthy. Yale University Press 2006. 583 p. : Illustration; Map

ISBN 9780300120486

Grades: Adult   B

1. Caesar, Julius, 100-44 B.C.E 2. Heads of state 3. Politicians 4. Generals 5. Politics and government 6. Ancient Rome 7. Roman Republic (509-27 B.C.E.) 8. Biographies 9. History writing — Ancient — Rome 10. Life stories — Politics — Politicians 11. Life stories — Law and order — Military leaders

LC 2006922060

The first major biography in decades examines the full complexity of Julius Caesar's character in an incisive portrait that shows why his political and military leadership continues to resonate two thousand years following his death.

"This biography draws together Julius Caesar's personal, political, and military history into a single volume. This is an engaging and well-drawn resource for those who wish to be introduced to the man who was Caesar." —*Library Journal*

Includes bibliographical references (p. 529-533) and index.

Golinkin, Lev

A Backpack, a Bear, and Eight Crates of Vodka: A Memoir. Lev Golinkin. Doubleday 2014. 288 p.

ISBN 9780385537773

Grades: Adult   B

1. Golinkin, Lev 2. Jewish people 3. Refugees, Jewish 4. Defectors 5. Defection 6. Russian people 7. Identity 8. Soviet Union 9. Austria 10. Eastern Europe 11. 1980s 12. Autobiographies and memoirs 13. Life stories — Facing adversity — War and oppression — Refugees 14. History writing — Europe — Eastern Europe

LC 2014005408

A compelling story of two intertwined journeys: a Jewish refugee family fleeing persecution and a young man seeking to reclaim a shattered past. In the twilight of the Cold War (the late 1980s), nine-year old Lev Golinkin and his family cross the Soviet border with only ten suitcases, $600, and the vague promise of help awaiting in Vienna. Years later, Lev, now an American adult, sets out to retrace his family's long trek, locate the strangers who fought for his freedom, and in the process, gain a future by understanding his past.

Gomez, Edgar

High-risk Homosexual: A Memoir. Edgar Gomez. Soft Skull Press 2022. 304 p.

ISBN 9781593767051

Grades: Adult   B

1. Gomez, Edgar 2. Gay men 3. Authors 4. Men 5. Machismo 6. Identity 7. Sexuality 8. LGBTQIA+ people 9. Gender role 10. Interpersonal relations 11. Florida 12. Autobiographies and memoirs 13. Life stories — Identity — LGBTQIA+ 14. Life stories — Identity — Race and Ethnicity 15. Life stories — Arts and Culture — Writing — Authors

Lambda Literary Award for Gay Memoir/Biography, 2023.

The Florida-born writer presents a memoir tracing his hard-won path to taking pride in himself as a gay Latinx man despite the culture of machismo surrounding him, including his uncle's cockfighting ring in Nicaragua.

"In this crackling debut, Gomez recounts his coming-of-age as a queer man, passionately exploring what it means to celebrate one's identities and to make space for joy in the most unlikely places.... The result transcends a simple coming-out story to instead offer a brilliant and provocative interrogation of sex, gender, race, and love." —*Publishers Weekly*

Gonell, Aquilino

American Shield: The Immigrant Sergeant Who Defended Democracy. Aquilino Gonell, and Susan Shapiro; preface by Congressman Jamie Raskin. Counterpoint 2023. 336 p.

ISBN 9781640096288

Grades: Adult   B

1. Capitol Riot, Washington, D.C, 2021 2. Political violence 3. Riots 4. Veterans 5. Post-traumatic stress disorder 6. Dominican Americans 7. North American people 8. Autobiographies and memoirs 9. Life stories — Law and order — Armed forces personnel

LC 2023018980

The story of a Dominican immigrant who fought in Iraq, became a member of the United States Capitol Police force and sustained grievous injuries while facing down the January 6, 2021 mob that tried to subvert democracy.

"Gonell describes the calamity in goosebump-inducing detail and is refreshingly candid in his disparagement of the attackers who attempted to overturn the results of the 2020 election." —*Publishers Weekly*

Gooch, Brad

★ *Flannery: A Life of Flannery O'Connor.* Brad Gooch. Little, Brown and Co. 2008. 464 p.

ISBN 9780316000666

Grades: 11 12 Adult   B

1. O'Connor, Flannery 2. Medical genetics 3. Personal letters 4. Short story writing 5. Lupus 6. Women authors, American 7. Diagnosis 8. Social life and customs 9. United States 10. Georgia 11. 20th century 12. Biographies 13. Arts and Entertainment — Writing and Publishing 14. Life stories — Arts and culture — Writing — Authors 15. Adult books for young adults

LC 2008028504

Booklist Editors' Choice, 2009; New York Times Notable Book, 2009; National Book Critics Circle Award for Biography finalist, 2009.

Evaluates the ways in which the mid-twentieth-century novelist reflected American culture and influenced literature, in a portrait that includes coverage of her relationships with such contemporaries as Robert Lowell, Elizabeth Hardwick, and James Dickey.

Includes bibliographical references and index.

Radiant: The Life and Line of Keith Haring. Brad Gooch. HarperCollins 2024. 448 p.

ISBN 9780062698261

Grades: Adult   B

1. Haring, Keith, 1958-1990 2. Artists 3. Chalk drawing 4. Popular culture 5. Gay men 6. People with HIV 7. Gay culture 8. LGBTQIA+ people 9. American people 10. New York City 11. 1980s 12. Interviews 13. Biographies 14. Life stories — Arts and culture — Artists

LC 2023027845

Chronicles the life of an artist known for his NYC chalk drawings in the 1980s as well as other works that provoked and called for radical change.

"This new biography of artist Keith Haring is a thorough and thoughtful look at his childhood through his death in 1990 at age 31." —*Library Journal*

Includes index.

Goodall, Jane

★ *Beyond Innocence: An Autobiography in Letters : The Later Years.* Jane Goodall; edited by Dale Peterson. Houghton Mifflin 2001. xiii, 418 p. : Illustration

ISBN 9780618125203

Grades: 11 12 Adult   B

1. Goodall, Jane, 1934- 2. Primatologists 3. Zoologists 4. Women primatologists 5. Chimpanzees 6. Women scientists 7. Environmentalism 8. Autobiographies and memoirs 9. Biographies 10. Nature Writing — Animal Studies — Primates 11. Life stories — Science, technology, and medicine — Scientists and inventors 12. Adult books for young adults

LC 00054124

A second volume of Jane Goodall's autobiography in letters covers the years during which she made many of her most important discoveries on chimpanzee behavior, gave birth to her son, and became an environmental activist.

"In this volume of Goodall's letters, a lively portrait is formed through her missives as the young woman rose to the height of her scientific contributions and fame. She became a mother, divorced her first husband, married her second, and lost him to cancer. She was also the first to observe cannibalism in chimps,

ESSENTIAL AND RECOMMENDED TITLES
Biography

lost many of her study troop during a polio epidemic, and weathered the kidnapping of a group of her students. This illuminating glimpse into the mind, emotions, and philosophy of an important scientist who also happens to be a celebrated figure will be requested in all libraries." —*Booklist*

Goodwin, Doris Kearns
★ *Team of Rivals: The Political Genius of Abraham Lincoln.* Doris Kearns Goodwin. Simon & Schuster 2005. xix, 916 p. : Illustration; Map
ISBN 9780684824901
Grades: Adult   B
1. Lincoln, Abraham, 1809-1865 2. Seward, William Henry, 1801-1872 3. Chase, Salmon Portland, 1808-1873 4. Political consultants 5. Genius 6. Political leadership 7. Presidents 8. Politics and government 9. Leadership 10. United States 11. 1860s 12. American Civil War era (1861-1865) 13. 19th century 14. Page to screen 15. History writing — Antebellum America — United States 16. History writing — Wars and conflicts — American Civil War
LC 2005044615
American History Book Prize, 2005; Booklist Editors' Choice, 2005; Library Journal Best Books, 2005; New York Times Notable Book, 2005; National Book Critics Circle Award for Biography finalist, 2005.

An analysis of Abraham Lincoln's political talents identifies the character strengths and abilities that enabled his successful election, in an account that also describes how he used the same abilities to rally former opponents in winning the Civil War.

"The knowledge gained here about these three significant figures who well attended Lincoln gain for the reader an even keener appreciation of the rare individual that he was." —*Booklist*

Team of rivals was the inspiration for the film Lincoln (2012); Includes bibliographical references and index.

★ *An Unfinished Love Story: A Personal History of the 1960s.* Doris Kearns Goodwin. Simon & Schuster 2024. 496 p.
ISBN 9781982108663
Grades: Adult   B
1. United States history 2. Married people 3. Politicians 4. Archives 5. Death of married men 6. 1960s 7. Autobiographies and memoirs 8. Life stories — Politics 9. History writing — Politicians — United States

Weaves together biography, memoir and history and takes readers along on the emotional journey she and her husband embarked upon in the last years of his life.

"A heartfelt tribute to the author's late husband and a captivating reflection on this pivotal era in American politics." —*Kirkus*

Goodyear, C. W.
President Garfield: From Radical to Unifier. C. W. Goodyear. Simon & Schuster 2023. 544 p.
ISBN 9781982146917
Grades: Adult   B
1. Garfield, James Abram, 1831-1881 2. Politicians 3. Presidents 4. United States 5. Biographies 6. History writing — Presidency — 19th century — United States 7. Politics and global affairs — Political figures 8. Life stories — Politics — Politicians

A prominent historian presents this magisterial biography chronicling the extraordinary, tragic life and times of our 20th president—an impoverished boy working his way from the frontier to the presidency, trying to raise a more righteous, peaceful republic out of the ashes of civil war.

"A masterful portrait of a man of great intellect, patience, and ability who should not be overlooked by history." —*Kirkus*

Gopnik, Blake
★ *Warhol.* Blake Gopnik. Ecco Press 2020. 864 p.
ISBN 9780062298393
Grades: Adult   B
1. Warhol, Andy, 1928-1987 2. Artists 3. Pop artists 4. Nonconformists 5. Homosexuality 6. Social change 7. Pop art 8. Social life and customs 9. Creativity 10. United States 11. 20th century 12. Biographies 13. Arts and Entertainment — Painting, Drawing, and Sculpture 14. Life stories — Arts and culture — Artists
LC BI2020012640
From his impoverished childhood as the son of Slovak immigrants in 1930s Pittsburgh, to finding commercial success as an advertising illustrator, to his painstaking pivot into fine art to becoming one of the first people to bring a queer aesthetic out into the open; Warhol shows us how deliberately Andy Warhol reflected the changing winds of commercialism, capitalism and celebrity in the 1960s that still underpin our world today.

"Warhol fans and pop art enthusiasts alike will find this an endlessly engrossing portrait." —*Publishers Weekly*

Gordon, Edmund
The Invention of Angela Carter: A Biography. Edmund Gordon. Oxford University Press 2017. 504 pages
ISBN 9780190626846
Grades: Adult   B
1. Carter, Angela, 1940-1992 2. Women authors 3. Authors, English 4. 20th century 5. Biographies 6. Life stories — Arts and culture — Writing — Authors 7. Arts and Entertainment — Writing and Publishing 8. Arts and Entertainment — Writing and Publishing — Literary criticism
LC 2016042329
New York Times Notable Book, 2017; Somerset Maugham Award, 2017; National Book Critics Circle Award for Biography finalist, 2017.

Angela Carter is widely considered one of the best loved and most highly acclaimed English writers of the last hundred years. Dozens of books have been written about Carter's work, but only a few have considered the author's life. Gordon takes readers through Carter's childhood in England, her struggling years as an apprentice writer, her breakthroughs in fiction, as well as insights into her private life.

"Written with grace and assurance, this volume will long stand as the definitive biography of Carter." —*Choice*

Includes bibliographical references (p. 427-496) and index.

Gordon, Kim
Girl in a Band. by Kim Gordon. Dey Street Books 2015. 288 p.
ISBN 9780062295897
Grades: Adult   B
1. Gordon, Kim, 1953- 2. Women rock musicians 3. Marital conflict 4. Alternative rock music 5. Alternative rock musicians 6. Rock groups 7. New wave music 8. Rock music 9. Intersectionality 10. 1980s 11. Autobiographies and memoirs 12. Life stories — Arts and culture — Performing arts — Musicians and composers 13. Arts and Entertainment — Music — Rock
LC 2014038070
A founding member of Sonic Youth, fashion icon and role model for a generation of women, now tells her story—a memoir of life as an artist, of music, marriage, motherhood, independence and as one of the first women of rock and roll.

Gordon, Linda
Dorothea Lange: A Life Beyond Limits. Linda Gordon. W.W. Norton 2009. 560 p.
ISBN 9780393057300
Grades: Adult   B
1. Lange, Dorothea, 1895-1965 2. Photographers 3. Documentary photography 4. Photography 5. Photographs 6. Social life and customs 7. United States 8. 20th century 9. Biographies 10. Arts and Entertainment — Photography 11. Life stories — Arts and culture — Artists
LC 2009019639
Los Angeles Times Book Prize for Biography, 2009; WILLA Literary Awards: Scholarly Nonfiction, 2010; New York Times Notable Book, 2009.

Charts the iconic photographer's life from her struggles with polio and family experiences to her early career in San Francisco and rise to a chronicler of the Great Depression and World War II, exploring her growing radicalization while showcasing rare and previously suppressed images.

"Gordon's elegant biography is testament to Lange's gift for challenging her country to open its eyes." —*New York Times Book Review*

Includes bibliographical references and index.

Gordon, Lyndall
★ *T.S. Eliot: An Imperfect Life.* Lyndall Gordon. Norton 1999. xv, 721 p, 16 p. of plates : Illustration
ISBN 9780393047288
Grades: Adult   B
1. Eliot, T. S, (Thomas Stearns), 1888-1965 2. Critics 3. Poets, American 4. 20th century 5. Biographies 6. Arts and Entertainment — Writing and Publishing 7. Life stories — Arts and culture — Writing — Poets
LC 98046864

Explores Eliot's poetry, drama, and literary criticism in relation to his life in America and England, his relationship with his first wife, his anti-Semitism, and his misogyny.

"Gordon's book is the most authoritative life of Eliot thus far, and is certain to spark new controversies." —*Publishers Weekly*

Includes bibliographical references (p. 677-698) and index; Originally published: London : Vintage, 1998.

Gordon, Meryl
Bunny Mellon: The Life of an American Style Legend. Meryl Gordon. Grand Central Publishing 2017. 400 p.
ISBN 9781455588749
Grades: Adult   B
1. Mellon, Paul, Mrs 2. Gardeners 3. Philanthropists 4. Upper class 5. Upper class women 6. White privilege 7. United States history 8. 20th century 9. Biographies 10. Life stories — People in history
LC 2017016493

Drawing on Bunny Mellon's letters, diaries, and appointment books, as well as extensive interviews, the author chronicles the life of the style icon and aristocrat who designed the White House Rose Garden and was a living witness to twentieth-century U.S. history.

"Readers interested in gardening, art, and interior design will drool over Bunnys fine tastes, and her ease at fulfilling every one of them, but all lovers of biographies will marvel at Gordons portrayal of Bunnys long life, and the significant figures who buzzed in and out of it." —*Booklist*

Includes bibliographical references and index.

Gordon-Reed, Annette
Andrew Johnson: The 17th President, 1865-1869. Annette Gordon-Reed. Times Books 2008. 192 p. (American presidents series (Times Books))
ISBN 9780805069488
Grades: 11 12 Adult   B
1. Johnson, Andrew, 1808-1875 2. African Americans 3. Presidents 4. Politicians 5. Race relations 6. Politics and government 7. United States 8. 19th century 9. Biographies 10. History writing — Presidency — 19th century — United States 11. History writing — Reconstruction — United States 12. Life stories — Politics — Politicians
LC Bl2007025255

A portrait of America's seventeenth president describes Andrew Johnson's failed efforts to bring about reconciliation following the Civil War, the antagonism of congressional leaders who sought his impeachment, and his legacy for the present.

Gorrindo, Simone
★ *The Wives.* Simone Gorrindo. Gallery Books 2024. 416 p.
ISBN 9781982178499
Grades: Adult   B
1. Army spouses 2. Military spouses 3. Military life 4. Communities 5. Marriage 6. Female friendship 7. American people 8. United States 9. Autobiographies and memoirs 10. Life stories — Relationships — Friendship

Tells the story of one woman's experience of joining a community of army wives after leaving her New York City job—a profoundly intimate look at marriage, friendship and today's America.

"Journalist Gorrindo meditates in her powerfully candid debut on the good, bad, and ugly of military marriage…It's a haunting, beautifully written celebration of found sisterhood." —*Publishers Weekly*

Gortemaker, Heike B.
Eva Braun: Life with Hitler. by Heike B. Görtemaker; translated from the German by Damion Searls. Alfred A. Knopf 2011. 320 p.
ISBN 9780307595829
Grades: 11 12 Adult   B
1. Braun, Eva 2. Hitler, Adolf, 1889-1945 3. Mistresses 4. Women and politics 5. Paramours 6. Third Reich, 1933-1945 7. Biographies 8. History writing — Wars and conflicts — World War II 9. History writing — Women's history 10. History writing — Europe — Germany 11. Life stories — People in history — Witness to history
LC 2011009551

A comprehensive portrait of Hitler's long-time mistress challenges popular depictions while profiling the bourgeois existence she shared with the F?hrer out of the public eye, drawing on newly discovered documents and anecdotal accounts to discuss such topics as her role as his trusted confidante, her position in his entourage and their double suicide two days after their marriage.

This is a Borzoi book—T.P. verso; Includes bibliographical references; Originally published in Germany as Eva Braun : Leben mit Hitler, by Verlag C.H. Beck, Munich, in 2010.

Gotch, Jen
The Upside of Being Down: How Mental Health Struggles Led to My Greatest Successes in Work and Life. Jen Gotch. Gallery Books 2020. 288 pages
ISBN 9781982108816
Grades: Adult   B
1. Gotch, Jen, 1971- 2. People with bipolar disorder 3. Creativity 4. Bipolar disorder 5. New businesses 6. Work-life balance 7. Businesspeople 8. Women 9. Self-awareness 10. United States 11. Autobiographies and memoirs 12. Biographies 13. Life stories — Facing adversity — Medical issues — Mental illness 14. Life stories — Business — Business leaders
LC 2019045250

The founder of the multimillion-dollar lifestyle brand ban.Do discusses her history of mental illness and how once it was properly diagnosed, helped to lead her towards a new life of self-awareness, success and joy.

"Anyone who's ever dealt with mental illness will appreciate this forthcoming and empathetic volume." —*Publishers Weekly*

Gottlieb, Lori
★ *Maybe You Should Talk to Someone: A Therapist, Her Therapist, and Our Lives Revealed.* Lori Gottlieb. Houghton Mifflin Harcourt 2019. 320 p.
ISBN 9781328662057
Grades: Adult   B
1. Gottlieb, Lori 2. Psychotherapists 3. Purpose in life 4. Psychotherapist and patient 5. Psychic trauma 6. Belonging 7. Alienation 8. Self-discovery 9. Autobiographies and memoirs 10. Society and culture — Psychology and human behavior 11. Family and Relationships — Dating and Marriage 12. Life stories — Science, technology, and medicine — Healthcare professionals
LC 2018042562

The national advice columnist presents a behind-the-scenes tour of a therapist's world from the perspective of both a patient and a psychotherapist who found answers in her client's journeys.

"Saturated with self-awareness and compassion, this is an irresistibly addictive tour of the human condition." —*Kirkus*

Gottlieb, Robert
George Balanchine: The Ballet Maker. Robert Gottlieb. Harper Collins Atlas Books 2004. 216 p. : Illustration (Eminent lives)
ISBN 9780060750701
Grades: 11 12 Adult   B
1. Balanchine, George 2. Choreographers 3. Ballet dancers 4. Social life and customs 5. United States 6. 20th century 7. Biographies 8. Arts and Entertainment — Dance 9. Life stories — Arts and culture — Performing arts — Dancers and choreographers
LC 2004048856

ESSENTIAL AND RECOMMENDED TITLES
Biography

Documents the life and achievements of the foremost contemporary ballet choreographer, discussing how he founded what would become the New York City Ballet and choreographed major stage and movie productions.

"This loving tribute captures Balanchine's legacy: His energy, confidence, lack of pretension and, most important, his joy in creation." —*Publishers Weekly*

Includes bibliographical references (p. 209-214).

Goudsouzian, Aram
Sidney Poitier: Man, Actor, Icon. Aram Goudsouzian. University of North Carolina Press 2004. xii, 480 p. : Illustration
ISBN 9780807828434
Grades: Adult   B
1. Poitier, Sidney 2. Actors and actresses 3. African Americans 4. United States 5. Biographies 6. Arts and Entertainment — Movies and Television 7. Life stories — Arts and culture — Performing arts — Actors and actresses
LC 2003019372

Traces the life and career of Sidney Poitier, highlighting his work as the only Black leading man during the civil rights era and the honors he has received for his work for racial equality in Hollywood.

"The author traces Poitier's journey from life as the son of a poor Bahamian farmer to celebrity status in the States as a trailblazing actor who has received as much criticism as praise for his portrayal of dignified and stoical Black men." —*Booklist*

Includes bibliographical references (p. [447]-465) and index.

Gracie, Rickson
Breathe: A Life in Flow. Rickson Gracie and Peter Maguire; foreword by Jocko Willink. Dey Street Books 2021. 304 p.
ISBN 9780063018952
Grades: Adult   B
1. Gracie, Rickson 2. Jiu-jitsu 3. Martial artists 4. Families 5. Family relationships 6. Judo 7. Men 8. Martial arts 9. Death of sons 10. Mixed martial arts 11. Loss 12. Brazilian people 13. Purpose in life 14. Sports 15. Autobiographies and memoirs 16. Life stories — Sports — Athletes 17. Sports and Competition — Martial arts

The legendary MMA master tells the story of his own career and the legacy of his family, who created Brazilian Jiu-Jii and founded the Ultimate Fighting Championship empire.

"Fans of Gracie's fights, practitioners or fans of martial arts, and those interested in the evolution of Gracie Jiu-Jitsu will find excellent insight here." —*Library Journal*

Graff, Henry F.
Grover Cleveland: The American Presidents. Henry F. Graff. Times Books 2002. xviii, 154 p. : Portrait
ISBN 9780805069235
Grades: Adult   B
1. Cleveland, Grover, 1837-1908 2. Presidents 3. United States 4. Biographies 5. Life stories — People in history 6. Life stories — Politics — Politicians
LC 2002020315

An examination of the political contributions of the nineteenth-century president traces his rags-to-riches personal story and his efforts to restore stature to the office in the wake of several weak administrations.

"This volume is a valuable addition to the literature on the Presidency and is a compelling argument for taking Cleveland seriously as a President." —*Library Journal*

Includes bibliographical references (p. [143]-144) and index.

Graham, Ashley
A New Model: What Confidence, Beauty, and Power Really Look Like. Ashley Graham with Rebecca Paley. HarperCollins 2017. 304 p.
ISBN 9780062667946
Grades: Adult   B
1. Graham, Ashley 2. Body image 3. Fashion models 4. Self-acceptance 5. Fat women 6. Fashion modeling 7. Self-confidence 8. Self-perception 9. Autobiographies and memoirs 10. Life stories — Arts and culture — Performing arts — Entertainers and celebrities 11. Society and culture — Pop culture 12. Adult books for young adults
LC BI2017011778

The outspoken plus-sized model and body image activist presents a collection of provocative essays that chronicle her life in fashion and offer insight into how ideas around body image are and are not evolving in today's culture.

"Positive, understanding, and uplifting." —*Booklist*

Graham-Dixon, Andrew
Caravaggio: A Life Sacred and Profane. Andrew Graham-Dixon. W.W. Norton 2011. xxviii, 514 p, [40] p. of plates : Illustration; Color; Map
ISBN 9780393081497
Grades: Adult   B
1. Caravaggio, Michelangelo Merisi da, 1573-1610 2. Artists 3. Painters 4. Painting 5. 16th century 6. 17th century 7. Biographies 8. Life stories — Arts and culture — Artists 9. Arts and Entertainment — Painting, Drawing, and Sculpture
LC 2010497954

New York Times Notable Book, 2011.

A British art critic and historian describes the painter's artistic achievements and volatile life during the Counter-Reformation in Italy which included public brawls, murder, sexual escapades, and imprisonment in Malta.

Includes bibliographical references and index; Originally published: London : Allen Lane, 2010.

Granata, Vince
Everything Is Fine: A Memoir. Vince Granata. Atria Books 2021. 304 p.
ISBN 9781982133443
Grades: Adult   B
1. Granata, Vince 2. Parricide 3. People with schizophrenia 4. Death of mothers 5. Grief 6. Loss 7. Schizophrenia 8. Forgiveness 9. Family and schizophrenia 10. Mental illness 11. Family relationships 12. United States 13. Autobiographies and memoirs 14. Life stories — Relationships — Family 15. Life stories — Facing adversity — Coping with death 16. Family and Relationships — Illness and the family 17. Science writing — Medicine and health — Illness and disease
LC 2020039378

A Pushcart Prize-nominated writer describes the circumstances of his mother's death at the hands of his younger brother, a patient with uncontrolled schizophrenia, whose disease the author painstakingly researched throughout a devastating murder trial.

"Granata's poignant debut delves into loss and pain and living in the aftermath of tragedy.... He not only brings a personal perspective to living alongside a family member with mental illness, but also shows that there isn't a right way to grieve." —*Library Journal*

Grandin, Greg
Kissinger's Shadow: The Long Reach of America's Most Controversial Statesman. Greg Grandin. Metropolitan Books 2015. 224 p.
ISBN 9781627794497
Grades: Adult   B
1. Kissinger, Henry, 1923-2023 2. Diplomats 3. International relations 4. United States 5. Biographies 6. History writing — Politicians — United States 7. Life stories — Politics — Politicians

A new account of America's most controversial diplomat moves beyond simple praise or condemnation to reveal Henry Kissinger as the architect of America's current imperial stance.

"Grandin will win no friends among Kissinger supporters, yet this book will find its audience among political scientists, historians, and informed readers attempting to assess the statesman's complex legacy." —*Library Journal*

Grandmaster Flash
The Adventures of Grandmaster Flash: My Life, My Beats. Grandmaster Flash with David Ritz. Harlem Moon 2008. 272 p.
ISBN 9780767924757
Grades: 11 12 Adult   B

1319

1. Grandmaster Flash 2. Rap musicians 3. African American rap musicians 4. African-American disc jockeys 5. African American men 6. Hip-hop culture 7. Drug addiction 8. Record industry and trade 9. South Bronx, New York City 10. United States 11. 21st century 12. 20th century 13. Autobiographies and memoirs 14. Biographies 15. Arts and Entertainment — Music — Rap and R&B 16. Life stories — Arts and culture — Performing arts — Musicians and composers 17. Adult books for young adults

LC 2007048224

A luminary in the world of hip hop music and a revered musical icon offers a firsthand look at the early days of the hip hop revolution and documents his own musical journey from the mean streets of the South Bronx, detailing his rise to musical stardom, financial disaster and cocaine addiction, and ultimate redemption with the love of family and friends.

"Grandmaster Flash is best known in conjunction with the Furious Five, the first hip-hop artists inducted into the Rock and Roll Hall of Fame. But before the fame, Joseph Robert Saddler was born into an abusive family in the Bronx. His evolution from a kid spinning records in the streets to hip-hop stardom is an inspiring story filled with heartbreak, determination, and perseverance." —*Library Journal*

Grann, David

The White Darkness. David Grann. Doubleday 2018. 144 p.
ISBN 9780385544573
Grades: Adult   **B**

1. Worsley, Henry 2. Shackleton, Ernest Henry, Sir, 1874-1922 3. Explorers 4. Obsession 5. Adventurers 6. Walking 7. Solitude 8. Exploration 9. Voyages and travels 10. Antarctica 11. Travel writing — Retracing historic journeys 12. Travel writing — Modes of transportation — on foot

LC 2018023450

Traces the South Pole expedition of a decorated British special forces officer, an admirer of Ernest Shackleton's expedition and descendant of one of Shackleton's crew, who in 2015 risked his life to walk across Antarctica alone.

"A modern-day hero dedicated to a goal is much needed in today's society." —*Library Journal*

Grant, Colin

The Natural Mystics: Marley, Tosh & Wailer. Colin Grant. W W Norton & CO Inc 2011. 320 p.
ISBN 9780393081176
Grades: Adult   **B**

1. Reggae musicians 2. Reggae music 3. Rastafarians 4. Social life and customs 5. Jamaica 6. Biographies 7. Arts and Entertainment — Music 8. Life stories — Arts and culture — Performing arts — Musicians and composers

LC 2011012323

Describes the history of the Wailers from their upbringing in the brutal slums of Kingston to their first recordings and super stardom through the lens of Jamaican politics, heritage, race, religion and the cultural revolution taking place in the 1970s.

Grant, Gail Milissa

At the Elbows of My Elders: One Family's Journey Toward Civil Rights. Gail Milissa Grant. Missouri History Museum : 2008. xix, 251 p. : Illustration
ISBN 9781883982669
Grades: Adult   **B**

1. Grant, Gail Milissa, 1949- 2. African American families 3. Civil Rights Movement 4. Institutional racism 5. African Americans 6. Middle class African American families 7. Segregation 8. African American history 9. Civil rights 10. Race relations 11. United States history 12. United States 13. St. Louis, Missouri 14. 20th century 15. Autobiographies and memoirs 16. Biographies 17. History writing — African American — Civil rights — United States 18. History writing — 1960s — United States 19. Family and Relationships — Families 20. Life stories — Relationships — Growing up 21. Adult books for young adults

LC 2008024219

An African-American family history focuses on the everyday life of a middle class Black family living in Saint Louis, Missouri in the first half of the 20th century.

"This is a fascinating look at the struggles of one Black family that mirrored the national struggle for civil rights." —*Booklist*

Includes bibliographical references (p. 245-247) and index.

Grant, James

★ *John Adams: Party of One.* James Grant. Farrar, Straus and Giroux 2005. 530 p, 16 p. of plates : Illustration
ISBN 9780374113148
Grades: Adult   **B**

1. Adams, John, 1735-1826 2. Social reformers 3. Founding Fathers of the United States 4. Presidents 5. United States history 6. United States 7. 18th century 8. 19th century 9. Biographies 10. History writing — Presidency — 18th century — United States 11. History writing — Early America — United States 12. Life stories — Politics — Politicians

LC 2004010863

A biography of the revolutionary, founding father, and second president of the United States explores his origins as a son of Massachusetts who crafted himself into an uncompromisingly ethical politician and social reformer.

"The author is excellent at developing Adams' devotion to liberty, honed by British policies that affronted him and turned him into a revolutionary. In Grant's fine synthesis, Adams on the page is the pious, ambitious, and loving man he was in life." —*Booklist*

Includes bibliographical references (p. 451-507) and index.

Grant, Ulysses S.

★ *The Annotated Memoirs of Ulysses S. Grant.* Edited with an Introduction by Elizabeth D. Samet. Liveright Publishing Corporation, a division of W. W. Norton & Company 2018. 1024 p.
ISBN 9781631492440
Grades: Adult   **B**

1. Grant, Ulysses S, 1822-1885 2. Presidents 3. Generals 4. Military campaigns 5. United States history 6. United States 7. 19th century 8. American Civil War era (1861-1865) 9. Autobiographies and memoirs 10. Biographies 11. Life stories — Politics — Politicians 12. Life stories — Law and order — Military leaders 13. History writing — Presidency — 19th century — United States

LC 2018029962

Originally published in 1885 by Mark Twain, this newly annotated edition of General Grant's biography provides detailed historical and cultural contexts to create a more vivid picture of the Civil War era.

"The end result is a very rich reading experience that highlights unexpected connections between events in the text, its historical moment, and its connections to larger cultural themes." —*Publishers Weekly*

Includes bibliographical references.

Memoirs and Selected Letters: Personal Memoirs of U.S. Grant, Selected Letters 1839-1865. Ulysses S. Grant. Library of America : 1990. P. Illustration
ISBN 9780940450585
Grades: 11 12 Adult   **B**

1. Grant, Ulysses S, 1822-1885 2. Generals 3. Presidents 4. United States 5. Biographies 6. Life stories — Law and order — Armed forces personnel 7. Arts and Entertainment — Writing and Publishing

LC 90060013

Letters from Grant to his wife, fellow officers, and government officials accompany his account of his life as a soldier, from West Point to the end of the Civil War.

Includes bibliographical references and index.

Gray, Michael

Hand Me My Travelin' Shoes: In Search of Blind Willie McTell. Michael Gray. Bloomsbury 2009. 448 p.
ISBN 9781556529757
Grades: Adult   **B**

1. McTell, Blind Willie, 1901-1959 2. Blues musicians 3. People who are blind 4. African American musicians 5. Blues (Music) 6. Guitarists 7. Street music 8. Street musicians 9. Social life and customs 10. Georgia 11. Biographies 12. Arts and Entertainment — Music — Jazz and the Blues 13. Life stories —

ESSENTIAL AND RECOMMENDED TITLES
Biography

Arts and culture — Performing arts — Musicians and composers 14. Adult books for young adults

LC 2009022329

Shortlisted for the James Tait Black Memorial Prize for Biography, 2007.

Biography of a blind man who made light of his disability, who exploded every stereotype about blues musicians.

"Less a conventional biography than a mixture of history, travelogue and detective story, Gray paints an evocative portrait of an artist who defied blues stereotypes." —*Kirkus*

Includes bibliographical references and index.

Greenberg, Amy S.

Lady First: The World of First Lady Sarah Polk. by Amy S. Greenberg. Alfred A. Knopf 2019. 400 p.

ISBN 9780385354134

Grades: Adult   B

1. Polk, Sarah Childress, 1803-1891 2. Polk, James K. (James Knox), 1795-1849 3. Political intrigue 4. Women's rights 5. Power 6. Social history 7. Rich women 8. Businesspeople 9. Slaveholders 10. Governors' spouses 11. Presidents' spouses 12. Politics and government 13. Ambition 14. United States 15. 19th century 16. Biographies 17. Life stories — Politics — Politicians 18. History writing — Women's history 19. History writing — Presidency — 19th century — United States

LC 2018010748

An exploration of Sarah Polk's political savvy and contributions to American feminism details the contradictions attributed to her character, her wartime achievements, and her influence in Washington politics during her husband's presidency.

"This is an in-depth, telling account of a largely overlooked woman who was able to effect profound influence while working within the constraints of her time and place." —*Booklist*

Includes bibliographical references and index.

Greenblatt, Stephen

★ *Will in the World: How Shakespeare Became Shakespeare.* Stephen Greenblatt. W. W. Norton 2004. 430 p. : Illustration; Color

ISBN 9780393050578

Grades: 11 12 Adult   B

1. Shakespeare, William, 1564-1616 2. Playwrights, English 3. Poets, English 4. Intellectual life 5. English language 6. Theater 7. English history 8. England 9. Renaissance (1300-1600) 10. 16th century 11. Biographies 12. Arts and Entertainment — Theater 13. Arts and Entertainment — Writing and Publishing 14. History writing — Europe — United Kingdom 15. History writing — Renaissance — Europe 16. Life stories — Arts and culture — Writing — Authors

LC 2004011512

Library Journal Best Books, 2004; New York Times Notable Book, 2004; National Book Award for Nonfiction finalist, 2004; National Book Critics Circle Award for Biography finalist, 2004; Pulitzer Prize for Biography or Autobiography finalist, 2005.

A portrait of Elizabethan England and how it contributed to the making of William Shakespeare discusses how he moved to London lacking money, connections, and a formal education and rose to became his age's foremost playwright.

"Greenblatt is at his best when he merges his gifts as a literary critic and scholar with his instincts as a biographer. He writes with real subtlety and skill about the sonnets. He also writes very well about the climate of fear and the use of public punishment and torture in Elizabethan and early Jacobean England, and how this enters into the very spirit of Shakespeare's work." —*New York Times Book Review*

Includes bibliographical references (p. [391]-407) and index.

Greene, Joshua

Unstoppable: Siggi B. Wilzig's Astonishing Journey from Auschwitz Survivor and Penniless Immigrant to Wall Street Legend. Joshua M. Greene; foreword by Deborah E. Lipstadt. Insight Editions 2021. xvii, 315 pages : Illustration; Color

ISBN 9781647222154

Grades: Adult   B

1. Wilzig, Siegbert B. 2. Holocaust survivors 3. Businesspeople 4. United States 5. Biographies 6. Life stories — Business — Business leaders 7. Life stories — Facing adversity — War and oppression — Holocaust

LC Bl2021008962

Unstoppable is the ultimate immigrant story and an epic David-and-Goliath adventure. While American teens were socializing in ice cream parlors, Siggi was suffering beatings by Nazi hoodlums for being a Jew and was soon deported along with his family to the darkest place the world has ever known: Auschwitz. Siggi used his wits to stay alive, pretending to have trade skills the Nazis could exploit to run the camp. After two death marches and near starvation, he was liberated from camp Mauthausen and went to work for the US Army hunting Nazis, a service that earned him a visa to America. On arrival, he made three vows: to never go hungry again, to support the Jewish people, and to speak out against injustice. He earned his first dollar shoveling snow after a fierce blizzard. His next job was laboring in toxic sweatshops. From these humble beginnings, he became President, Chairman and CEO of a New York Stock Exchange-listed oil company and grew a full-service commercial bank to more than $4 billion in assets.

"Greene lets Wilzig's effervescent spirit shine through, and his story will appear to a wide variety of readers." —*Library Journal*

Includes bibliographical references (pages 295-315).

Greenfield, Martin

★ *Measure of a Man: A Memoir : From Auschwitz Survivor to Presidents' Tailor.* Martin Greenfield with Wynton Hall. Regnery Publishing, a Salem Communications Company 2014. 234 p.

ISBN 9781621572664

Grades: Adult   B

1. Greenfield, Martin, 1928-2024 2. Tailors 3. Jewish people 4. Concentration camp survivors 5. Holocaust survivors 6. Fashion designers 7. Jewish American men 8. Fashion design 9. Tailoring 10. Holocaust (1933-1945) 11. Businesspeople 12. Czech people 13. Eastern European people 14. Poland 15. United States 16. Autobiographies and memoirs 17. Biographies 18. Life stories — Facing adversity — War and oppression — Holocaust 19. Business and economics — Business leaders and entrepreneurs 20. Arts and Entertainment — Fashion 21. Life stories — Facing adversity — Personal transformation

LC 2014035566

The owner of New York's prestigious Martin Greenfield Clothiers in Brooklyn shares his inspiring story as a Holocaust survivor who learned tailoring skills during his incarceration before building a fashion empire in America.

Greenfield, Robert

True West: Sam Shepard's Life, Work, and Times. Robert Greenfield. Crown 2023. 352 p.

ISBN 9780525575955

Grades: Adult   B

1. Shepard, Sam, 1943-2017 2. Authors 3. Authors, American 4. Playwrights 5. Actors and actresses 6. Biographies 7. Life stories — Arts and culture — Performing arts — Actors and actresses 8. Arts and Entertainment — Theater

LC 2022041266

This revelatory biography of the world-famous playwright and actor delves deeply into his life as well as the ways in which his work illuminates it, making the case for Shepard not just as a great American writer but a unique figure who first brought the sensibility of rock 'N' roll to theater.

"Greenfield (Mother American Night), a former Rolling Stone editor, delivers a riveting account of the life of playwright and actor Sam Shepard (1943?2017)." —*Publishers Weekly*

Includes bibliographical references and index.

Greenhouse, Linda

Becoming Justice Blackmun: Harry Blackmun's Supreme Court Journey. Linda Greenhouse. Times Books 2005. xiii, 268 p. : Illustration

ISBN 9780805077919

Grades: Adult   B

1. Blackmun, Harry A, 1908-1999 2. Judges 3. Constitutional history 4. United States 5. Biographies 6. History writing — Judicial branch — United States 7. Life stories — Law and order — Judges and lawyers

PUBLIC LIBRARY CORE COLLECTION: NONFICTION
Twentieth Edition

LC 2004063772

New York Times Notable Book, 2005.

Reveals the workings of the U.S. Supreme Court, as seen through the eyes and writings of Justice Harry A. Blackmun, as he reflects on issues including the death penalty, abortion, and sex discrimination.

"The author's achievement in her meticulous narrative history is to provide new ammunition for Justice Blackmun's critics as well as his admirers. And readers who are unfamiliar with the inner workings of the court could not hope for a more engrossing introduction." —*New York Times*

Includes index.

Greenidge, Kerri

Black Radical: The Life and Times of William Monroe Trotter. Kerri K. Greenidge. Liveright Publishing Corporation, a division of W.W. Norton & Co. 2020. xxii, 408 p.

ISBN 9781631495342

Grades: Adult　　B

1. Trotter, William Monroe, 1872-1934 2. African American radicals 3. African American civil rights workers 4. African American journalists 5. Journalists 6. Social justice 7. African Americans 8. African American history 9. Political participation 10. Race relations 11. United States history 12. 19th century 13. 20th century 14. Biographies 15. Life stories — Politics — Activists and Reformers — Civil Rights Leaders 16. History writing — African American — Civil rights — United States 17. History writing — Early 20th century — United States 18. Life stories — Arts and culture — Writing — Journalists

LC 2019037416

Mark Lynton History Prize, 2020.

A portrait of the lesser-known, turn-of-the-20th-century civil rights activist explores how he used his influence as an emancipator and the editor of the Guardian to promote gradualist politics and rally Black working-class Americans throughout the post-Reconstruction era. This long-overdue biography reestablishes William Monroe Trotter's essential place next to Douglass, Du Bois, and King in the pantheon of American civil rights heroes.

"A must-read for both scholars and general readers interested in the civil rights movement." —*Library Journal*

Includes bibliographical references and index.

Greenman, Ben

Dig If You Will the Picture: Funk, Sex, God and Genius in the Music of Prince. Ben Greenman. Henry Holt and Company 2017. 304 p.

ISBN 9781250128379

Grades: Adult　　B

1. Prince 2. Popular music composers 3. Popular music 4. African American musicians 5. African American rock musicians 6. Rock musicians 7. Musicians 8. Popular culture 9. United States 10. 20th century 11. 1980s 12. Biographies 13. Life stories — Arts and culture — Performing arts — Musicians and composers 14. Arts and Entertainment — Music — Pop 15. Arts and Entertainment — Music — Rock

LC 2016054759

Presents a unique and kaleidoscopic look into the life, legacy and electricity of the pop legend Prince and his wide-ranging impact on our culture.

"As much a fan boy as an authority, rock journalist Greenman . investigates Princes development as an artist, his career trajectory, his massive creative output, and his numerous side projects." —*Booklist*

Includes bibliographical references.

Gregory, Rebekah

Taking My Life Back: My Story of Faith, Determination, and Surviving the Boston Marathon Bombing. Rebekah Gregory, with Anthony Flacco. Revell 2017. 320 p.

ISBN 9780800728212

Grades: Adult　　B

1. Gregory, Rebekah 2. Boston Marathon Bombing, Boston, Mass, 2013 3. Boston Marathon 4. People who have had amputations 5. Convalescence 6. Bombings 7. Terrorism 8. Faith (Christianity) 9. Autobiographies and memoirs 10. Life stories — Facing adversity — Medical issues 11. Life stories — Facing adversity — Victims of crime — Terrorism

LC 2016048311

A spectator at the 2013 Boston Marathon bombing who suffered the loss of her leg and incurred other debilitating injuries while protecting her son explores how her lengthy journey to recovery has compelled her to explore her faith in unique ways and advanced her resolve to live a meaningful life.

"This is a truly feel-good book that doesnt stint on the challenges that life throws at us." —*Publishers Weekly*

Gretzky, Wayne

99: Stories of the Game. Wayne Gretzky. G. P. Putnam's Sons 2016. 320 p.

ISBN 9780399575471

Grades: Adult　　B

1. Gretzky, Wayne, 1961- 2. Hockey players 3. Hockey 4. Professional hockey 5. Professional hockey players 6. Hockey teams 7. Autobiographies and memoirs 8. Sports and Competition — Hockey 9. Life stories — Sports — Athletes

LC 2016036048

One of the greatest sports figures of all time offers candid reflections on the mentors, teammates, and rivals who inspired him and discusses famous moments in hockey history from the viewpoint of one who created many of those moments.

Grey, Jennifer

Out of the Corner: A Memoir. Jennifer Grey. Ballantine Books 2022. 304 p.

ISBN 9780593356708

Grades: Adult　　B

1. Grey, Jennifer, 1960- 2. Growing up 3. Fame 4. Resilience 5. Films 6. Actors and actresses 7. Autobiographies and memoirs 8. Life stories — Arts and culture — Performing arts — Actors and actresses 9. Life stories — Facing adversity — Medical issues 10. Arts and Entertainment — Movies and Television

LC 2021054442

The star of the iconic movie Dirty Dancing richly evokes the places and times that defined a nation, looks back on her unbridled romantic adventures in Hollywood, shares the fallout from a plastic surgery procedure that negatively impacted her career and reveals how she took her life back.

In a gossipy, lively memoir, Grey (b. 1960) chronicles her evolving sense of identity—as a woman, actor, wife, and, most satisfyingly, mother—in what she calls an 'Ongoing coming-of-age story.' —*Kirkus*

Grey, Joel

Master of Ceremonies: A Memoir. Joel Grey. Flatiron Books 2016. 320 p.

ISBN 9781250057235

Grades: Adult　　B

1. Grey, Joel, 1932- 2. Theater 3. Jewish-Americans 4. Photographers 5. Actors and actresses 6. New York City 7. Autobiographies and memoirs 8. Biographies 9. Arts and Entertainment — Theater 10. Life stories — Arts and culture — Performing arts — Actors and actresses

LC 2015040157

The Broadway star and Academy Award-winning performer best known for his iconic role as the irascible emcee in Cabaret traces his remarkable life story, documenting his Jewish-American upbringing in 1930s Cleveland, childhood roles, rise to fame and challenging losse.

"The diminutive, unforgettable creator of the emcee in Cabaret both on stage and on screen writes frankly of his diverse career, exacting mother, and public embrace of his homosexuality." —*Kirkus*

Grossi, Craig

Craig & Fred: A Marine, a Stray Dog, and How They Rescued Each Other. Craig Grossi. William Morrow & Company 2017. 224 p.

ISBN 9780062693389

Grades: Adult　　B

1. Grossi, Craig 2. Dogs 3. Marines 4. Humans and dogs 5. Men and dogs 6. Post traumatic stress disorder 7. Human-animal relationships 8. Afghanistan 9. Autobiographies and memoirs 10. Life stories — Relationships — Pets and owners 11. Family and relationships — Pets and owners 12. Life stories — Law and order — Armed forces personnel

ESSENTIAL AND RECOMMENDED TITLES
Biography

LC Bl2017033341

A Marine Corps veteran and Purple Heart recipient shares the story of his friendship with a stray dog he met on an Afghan battlefield and how, against military regulations, he worked to bring the dog home, where the pair battled PTSD and began touring America to work with veteran programs.

"Death, violence, and fear are a constant in the battlefield, but Grossi manages to find humor in the midst of horror and life after loss…Positive, encouraging, and inspirational." —*Kirkus*

Grue, Jan

I Live a Life Like Yours: A Memoir. Jan Grue; translated from the Norwegian by B.L. Crook. FSG Originals/Farrar, Straus and Giroux 2021. 224 p.

ISBN 9780374600785

Grades: Adult **B**

1. Grue, Jan, 1981- 2. Authors, Norwegian 3. People with disabilities 4. Loss 5. Interpersonal relations 6. Spinal muscular atrophy 7. Disabilities 8. Neuromuscular diseases 9. Human body 10. College teachers 11. Identity 12. Norway 13. Autobiographies and memoirs 14. Translations — Norwegian to English 15. Life stories — Facing adversity — Medical issues — Living with disabilities 16. Family and Relationships — Disabled family members

LC 2021011635

In this essayistic autobiography, Jan Grue reflects on social structures, disability, loss, relationships, and the body: in short, on what it means to be human.

"Norwegian novelist Grue (The Best of All Possible Worlds) elegantly flows between memoir, essay, and intellectual discourse in this magnificent story about living with a disability." —*Publishers Weekly*

Translated from the Norwegian.

Gruen, Bob

Right Place, Right Time: The Life of a Rock & Roll Photographer. Bob Gruen. Abrams Press 2020. xiv, 380 pages : Illustration; Color

ISBN 9781419742132

Grades: Adult **B**

1. Gruen, Bob 2. Photographers 3. Rock music industry and trade 4. Photographs 5. Rock musicians 6. Celebrities 7. Rock music 8. United States 9. Autobiographies and memoirs 10. Life stories — Arts and culture — Artists 11. Arts and Entertainment — Photography

For more than fifty years Gruen has documented the music scene in pictures that have captured the world's attention. Here he tells of his winding, adventure-filled journey in a series of wildly entertaining stories. Gruen offers a unique window into the evolution of American music culture over the last five decades.

"Rock fans will devour this narrative and find its 'You are there' style eminently palpable." —*Library Journal*

Grylls, Bear

Never Give Up: My Life in the Wild. Bear Grylls. National Geographic 2022. 336 p.

ISBN 9781426222627

Grades: Adult **B**

1. Grylls, Bear 2. Television personalities 3. Survivalists 4. Nature 5. Wilderness survival 6. Adventure 7. Television programs 8. Autobiographies and memoirs 9. Life stories — Nature and outdoors 10. Adventure writing — Survival 11. Nature Writing — Personal Responses 12. Arts and Entertainment — Movies and Television

In Never Give Up, global adventurer and TV presenter Bear Grylls chronicles his life and career since stepping onto screen, taking readers along with him on his most famous adventures, sharing personal stories from his favourite expeditions, and capturing his hairiest survival challenges. The follow up to the internationally bestselling Mud, Sweat and Tears, in this new autobiography Bear takes readers behind the scenes on infamous 'Man vs. Wild' shoots and provides an insight into what it's really like to go 'Running Wild' with guests including President Obama, Roger Federer and Julia Roberts. Along the way, Bear explores the valuable lessons he's learned in the wild, opens up about his most personal challenges and achievements, and celebrates the true value of adventure and the enduring importance of courage, kindness and resilience.

"Grylls (Mud, Sweat and Tears), star of Man vs. Wild, looks back at the 'Greatest hits' of his career as a professional adventurer in this exhilarating autobiography." —*Publishers Weekly*

Originally published in the UK by Bantam, London, in 2021.

Guarnere, William

Brothers in Battle, Best of Friends: Two Wwii Paratroopers from the Original Band of Brothers Tell Their Story. William. Berkley Caliber 2007. xxiii, 296 p, 16 p. of plates : Illustration

ISBN 9780425217283

Grades: Adult **B**

1. Guarnere, William 2. Heffron, Edward 3. World War II 4. Military campaigns 5. Western Front (World War II) 6. Male friendship 7. Soldiers 8. European history 9. United States history 10. United States 11. 20th century 12. Biographies 13. History writing — Wars and conflicts — World War II — European Theater 14. Family and Relationships — Friendship

LC 2007021056

The story of two inseparable friends and soldiers portrayed in the HBO miniseries Band of Brothers. William "Wild Bill" Guarnere and Edward "Babe" Heffron were among the first paratroopers of the U.S. Army—members of an elite unit of the 101st Airborne Division called Easy Company. Arguably the bravest, most efficient, physically fit, and tight-knit group of soldiers the Army has ever produced, the unit was called upon for every high-risk operation of the war, including D-Day, Operation Market Garden inHolland, the Battle of the Bulge, and the capture of Hitler's Eagle's Nest in Berchtesgaden. They fought side by side, until Guarnere lost his leg in the Battle of the Bulge. The two reconnected at the war's end and have been the best of friends ever since. Their story is a tribute to the lasting bond forged between comrades in arms.

Includes index.

Gucci, Patricia

In the Name of Gucci: A Memoir. Patricia Gucci. Crown Archetype 2016. 320 p.

ISBN 9780804138932

Grades: Adult **B**

1. Gucci family 2. Gucci, Patricia 3. Fashion designers 4. Family secrets 5. Heirs and heiresses 6. Illegitimacy 7. Clothing industry and trade 8. Family history 9. Autobiographies and memoirs 10. Life stories — Arts and culture — Fashion 11. Life stories — Relationships — Family

LC 2015037677

Aldo Gucci's daughter chronicles the gripping family drama—and never-before-told love story—surrounding the rise and fall of her late father, the man responsible for making the legendary fashion label the powerhouse it is today.

Guelzo, Allen C.

Robert E. Lee: A Life. Allen C. Guelzo. Alfred A. Knopf 2021. 576 p.

ISBN 9781101946220

Grades: Adult **B**

1. Lee, Robert E. (Robert Edward), 1807-1870 2. Generals 3. United States Civil War, 1861-1865 4. Command of troops 5. Leadership 6. Ambition 7. Biographies 8. Impartial writing 9. Life stories — Law and order — Military leaders 10. History writing — Confederacy — United States 11. History writing — Military — Military leadership

An award-winning historian presents this definitive biography of one of the most confounding figures in American history, following him from his refined upbringing all the way up to his leadership during the Civil War, capturing his hypocrisy, courage, honor and disloyalty.

Historian Guelzo (Reconstruction: A Very Short Introduction) demystifies Robert E. Lee in this evenhanded and insightful biography. . . . Deeply researched and elegantly written, this nuanced portrait captures Lee's 'Ambiguous place in American history.' —*Publishers Weekly*

Includes bibliographical references and index.

Guerrero, Jean

Hatemonger: Stephen Miller, Donald Trump, and the White Nationalist Agenda. Jean Guerrero. William Morrow & Company 2020. 336 p.

ISBN 9780062986719
Grades: Adult   B
1. Miller, Stephen (Political advisor) 2. Political consultants 3. Speechwriters 4. Immigration policy 5. Immigration and emigration law 6. Separated friends, relatives, etc. 7. White supremacy movements 8. Racism 9. Multiculturalism 10. Presidential staff 11. Politics and government 12. Immigration and emigration 13. United States 14. Biographies 15. Life stories — Politics 16. Politics and global affairs — Political figures 17. Politics and global affairs — Immigration
LC Bl2020015865

Stephen Miller is one of the most influential advisors in the White House. He has crafted Donald Trump's speeches, designed immigration policies that ban Muslims and separate families, and outlasted such Trump stalwarts as Steve Bannon and Jeff Sessions. But he's remained an enigma. Until now. Investigative journalist and author Jean Guerrero charts the thirty-four-year-old's astonishing rise to power, drawing from more than one hundred interviews with his family, friends, adversaries and government officials. Hatemonger unveils the man driving some of the most divisive confrontations over what it means to be American—and what America will become.

"An unsparing portrait of the young architect of Trumpian nationalism. . . . A readable study in the banality of evil, even if it comes clothed in bespoke suits." —*Kirkus*

Guha, Ramachandra
Gandhi Before India. Ramachandra Guha. Alfred a Knopf 2014. 656 p.
ISBN 9780385532297
Grades: Adult   B
1. Gandhi, Mahatma, 1869-1948 2. Social advocates 3. Indian people in Africa 4. Lawyers 5. Social reformers 6. Men 7. Vegetarianism 8. Religious life 9. Pacifism 10. Indian people 11. Indian people in Great Britain 12. African history 13. South Africa 14. London, England 15. India 16. 20th century 17. Biographies 18. Life stories — Politics — Activists and reformers
LC 2013025014
New York Times Notable Book, 2014.

A first volume of a series detailing the life and work of the influential political advocate draws on private papers and other untapped sources to cover his birth in 1869 through his upbringing in Gujarat, discussing his London education and decades as a lawyer in South Africa.

"This first volume in a two-part biography of Gandhi from Guha . proves itself an essential work for its bold purpose, extensive research, and engaging prose." —*Publishers Weekly*

Gandhi: The Years That Changed the World: 1914-1948. Ramachandra Guha. Alfred A. Knopf 2018. 688 p.
ISBN 9780385532310
Grades: Adult   B
1. Gandhi, Mahatma, 1869-1948 2. Social reformers 3. Social advocates 4. Lawyers 5. Social change 6. Colonialism 7. Caste 8. Passive resistance 9. Indian history 10. India 11. 20th century 12. Biographies 13. Life stories — Politics — Activists and reformers 14. History writing — Asia — South Asia — India
LC 2018953456
New York Times Notable Book, 2018.

A conclusion to the wide-reaching profile that began with Gandhi Before India covers in scholarly detail Gandhi's arrival in 1915 Bombay and his role in addressing such issues as colonialism, the caste system, religious conflict and the emancipation of women.

Guinn, Jeff
Go Down Together: The True, Untold Story of Bonnie and Clyde. Jeff Guinn. Simon & Schuster 2009. 480 p.
ISBN 9781416557067
Grades: Adult   B
1. Parker, Bonnie, 1910-1934 2. Barrow, Clyde, 1909-1934 3. Crime in the news media 4. Criminals 5. Thieves 6. Fame 7. Biographies 8. True Crime — Heists and Robbery 9. Life stories — Law and order — Criminals and law-breakers
LC 2008053342

An account of the exploits of Bonnie and Clyde explores the ways in which they captured the imaginations of people during and after their time, reveals the role of youth and luck in their two-year crime spree, and recounts the events that led to their deaths.

"As Guinn relates, Bonnie and Clyde didn't commit many of the acts—particularly the murders—they were accused of. Their crime spree only lasted from spring 1932 to May 1934. But in the worst of the Depression, Americans ate up accounts of the Barrow exploits as a form of entertainment. The gang fed the newspapers terrific stuff, including the staged photo of Bonnie holding a gun and smoking a cigar. For folks living hardscrabble lives, the fact that the gang robbed the same bankers who were foreclosing on their farms made the exploits of Bonnie and Clyde even sweeter. Guinn succeeds marvelously in recreating the spirit of the times, the desperation of unemployment and financial ruin." —*PopMatters*

Includes bibliographical references and index.

★ *Manson: The Life and Times of Charles Manson.* Jeff Guinn. Simon & Schuster 2013. 352 p.
ISBN 9781451645163
Grades: Adult   B
1. Manson, Charles, 1934-2017 2. Mass murderers 3. Criminals 4. Prisoners 5. Murder 6. Social life and customs 7. United States 8. California 9. 20th century 10. Biographies 11. True Crime — Murder 12. Life stories — Law and order — Criminals and law-breakers
LC 2012050176
New York Times Notable Book, 2013.

Guinn's biography answers lingering questions about the Manson Family murders, while delivering stunning revelations about the life of America's most notorious psychopath.

Includes bibliographical references and index.

Gulman, Gary
Misfit: Growing up Awkward in the '80s. Gary Gulman. Flatiron Books 2023. 288 p.
ISBN 9781250777065
Grades: Adult   B
1. Gulman, Gary 2. Stand-up comedians 3. Memories 4. Growing up 5. Childhood 6. Schools 7. People with depression 8. Belonging 9. Healing 10. North American people 11. American people 12. 1980s 13. Autobiographies and memoirs 14. Life stories — Arts and culture — Performing arts — Entertainers and celebrities 15. Life stories — Relationships — Growing up 16. Life stories — Facing adversity — Medical issues — Mental illness

For years, Gary Gulman had been the comedian's comedian, acclaimed for his delight in language and his bracing honesty. But after two stints in a psych ward, he found himself back in his mother's house in Boston—living in his childhood bedroom at age forty-six, as he struggled to regain his mental health. That's where Misfit begins. Then it goes way back. Gulman has an astonishing memory and takes the reader through every year of his childhood education, with obsessively detailed stories that are in turn alarming and riotously funny.

"A good-natured, hilarious memoir from a gifted comedian." —*Kirkus*

Guo, XIaolu
Nine Continents: A Memoir in and Out of China. XIaolu Guo. Grove Press 2017. 366 pages
ISBN 9780802127136
Grades: Adult   B
1. Guo, XIaolu, 1973- 2. Authors, Chinese 3. Growing up 4. Moving to a new city 5. Personal conduct 6. Self-discovery 7. China 8. Autobiographies and memoirs 9. Life stories — Relationships — Growing up 10. Life stories — Arts and culture — Writing — Authors 11. Nonfiction that reads like fiction
LC 2017032639
National Book Critics Circle Award for Autobiography, 2017.

An acclaimed, Chinese-born, modern writer describes how she became a citizen of the world after being raised in a fishing village shack by her grandparents, moving into a thriving underground art scene in Beijing and finally winding up in Europe.

ESSENTIAL AND RECOMMENDED TITLES
Biography

"A rich and insightful coming-of-age story of not only a woman, but an artist and the country in which she was born." —*Kirkus*

Gupta, Prachi
★ *They Called Us Exceptional: And Other Lies That Raised Us*. Prachi Gupta. Crown 2023. 273 p.
ISBN 9780593442982
Grades: Adult   B
1. Gupta, Prachi (Journalist) 2. Families 3. Indian Americans 4. Children of immigrants 5. Asian American women 6. Women journalists 7. Upward mobility 8. High achievement 9. Belonging 10. Alienation 11. Expectation 12. Dysfunctional families 13. Sexism 14. Abusive men 15. Death of brothers 16. Love 17. South Asian people 18. Indian people 19. North American people 20. American people 21. Intergenerational trauma 22. Independence 23. Autobiographies and memoirs 24. Life stories — Identity — Immigrants 25. Life stories — Relationships — Family 26. Life stories — Facing adversity — Coping with death 27. Family and Relationships — Abuse
LC 2023011957

Prachi Gupta's family embodied the American Dream: a doctor father and a nurturing mother who raised two high-achieving children with one foot in the Indian American community, the other in Pennsylvania's white suburbia. But their belonging was predicated on a powerful myth: That Asian Americans have perfected the alchemy of middle-class life, raising tight-knit, ambitious families that are immune to hardship. Molding oneself to fit this perfect image often comes at a steep but hidden cost. In They Called Us Exceptional, Gupta articulates the dissonance, shame, and isolation of being upheld as an American success story while privately navigating traumas invisible to the outside world.

"[Gupta's] startling candor and willingness to confront painful truths make this sing." —*Publishers Weekly*

Includes bibliographical references.

Guralnick, Peter
★ *Sam Phillips: The Man Who Invented Rock 'N' Roll*. Peter Guralnick. Little, Brown and Company 2015. 752 p.
ISBN 9780316042741
Grades: Adult   B
1. Phillips, Sam, 1923-2003 2. Sound recording executives and producers 3. Sound recording industry and trade 4. Music industry and trade 5. Music 6. Biographies 7. Arts and Entertainment — Music 8. Life stories — Arts and culture
LC 2015024690

Draws on interviews and firsthand personal observations extending throughout a twenty-five-year period with both Phillips and legendary Sun Records artists to explain the label's unique and influential integration of new music styles.

"The author emphasizes Phillips's contributions to rock and roll's 1950s emergence in the racially charged South and his personal and professional relationships with not only the many famous singers and musicians who benefited commercially and artistically from his vision, encouragement, and technical skills but also the obscure rockabilly, blues, country, and pop artists who were given an opportunity to express themselves on vinyl. This long but consistently engaging book offers a more detailed and intimate account than Kevin and Tanja Crouch's Sun King and is recommended to fans of early American popular music." —*Library Journal*

Includes bibliographical references and index.

Gutman, Robert W.
Mozart: A Cultural Biography. Robert W. Gutman. Harcourt Brace 1999. xxii, 839 p. : Illustration
ISBN 9780151004829
Grades: Adult   B
1. Mozart, Wolfgang Amadeus, 1756-1791 2. Composers 3. Biographies 4. Arts and Entertainment — Music — Classical 5. Life stories — Arts and culture — Performing arts — Musicians and composers
LC 99031953

An exhaustively researched account of a great composer's life offers new perspectives and interpretations, placing him within the context of his times, discussing the musical genres he worked in, and giving a clear picture of the man behind the legends.

Includes bibliographical references (p. 758-773) and indexes.

Guy, John
Hunting the Falcon: Henry VIII, Anne Boleyn, and the Marriage That Shook Europe. John Guy, Julia Fox. HarperCollins 2023. 464 p.
ISBN 9780063073449
Grades: Adult   B
1. Anne Boleyn, Queen, consort of Henry VIII, King of England, 1507-1536 2. Henry VIII, King of England, 1491-1547 3. Executions and executioners 4. Death of married women 5. Courtship 6. Marriage 7. British history 8. 16th century 9. Renaissance (1300-1600) 10. Biographies 11. History writing — Women's history 12. Life stories — Politics — Royalty 13. History writing — Europe — United Kingdom 14. History writing — Renaissance — Europe

A groundbreaking, freshly-researched examination of one of the most dramatic and consequential marriages in history: Henry VIII's long courtship, short union and brutal execution of Anne Boleyn.

"An intriguing, thought-provoking, extensively researched look at the marriage that impacted and changed history." —*Kirkus*

Gwynne, S. C.
Empire of the Summer Moon: Quanah Parker and the Rise and Fall of the Comanches, the Most Powerful Indian Tribe in American History. S.C. Gwynne. Scribner 2010. 336 p.
ISBN 9781416591054
Grades: Adult   B
1. Parker, Quanah, Comanche chief, 1847-1911 2. Comanche (North American people) 3. Indigenous peoples of North America — Wars 4. Battles 5. War 6. Chiefs (Political anthropology) 7. Race relations 8. Frontier and pioneer life 9. Indigenous peoples of North America 10. The West (United States) 11. The West (United States) 12. 19th century 13. Biographies 14. Impartial writing 15. History writing — Wars and conflicts — American Indigenous Wars 16. History writing — Westward expansion — United States 17. Nonfiction that reads like fiction
LC 2009049747

Oklahoma Book Award for Nonfiction, 2011; New York Times Notable Book, 2010; National Book Critics Circle Award for Nonfiction finalist, 2010; Pulitzer Prize for General Nonfiction finalist, 2011.

"A welcome contribution to the history of Texas, Westward expansion and Native America." —*Kirkus*

Rebel Yell: The Violence, Passion, and Redemption of Stonewall Jackson. S.C. Gwynne. Scribner 2014. 688 pages
ISBN 9781451673289
Grades: Adult   B
1. Jackson, Stonewall, 1824-1863 2. Generals 3. Civil war 4. Confederate soldiers 5. United States Civil War, 1861-1865 6. United States history 7. American Civil War era (1861-1865) 8. Biographies 9. History writing — Confederacy — United States 10. Life stories — Law and order — Military leaders
LC 2014010046

National Book Critics Circle Award for Biography finalist, 2014.

In this insightful character study of Confederate General Thomas "Stonewall" Jackson, author S.C. Gwynne weaves incidents from Jackson's life into the chronologically presented account of his Civil War actions. A reserved and deeply religious man, Jackson seemed to be stern, stubborn, and even arbitrary in his military leadership. Yet he was so bold and effective in battle that he was considered the greatest of the Confederacy's leaders. Gwynne's compelling biography is essential reading matter for Civil War and general military history buffs, as well as for anyone who enjoys life stories.

"Gwynne presents Jackson's eccentric personality in biographical episodes that he injects into the arc of Jackson's Civil War campaigns and battles. [The] technique succeeds, thanks to his spry prose and cogent insight, in revealing Jackson's character." —*Booklist*

Includes bibliographical references.

PUBLIC LIBRARY CORE COLLECTION: NONFICTION
Twentieth Edition

H, Lamya
★ *Hijab* Butch Blues. Lamya H.. Dial Press 2023. 272 p.
ISBN 9780593448762
Grades: Adult   B
1. H, Lamya 2. Immigrants 3. Muslims 4. LGBTQIA+ people 5. Faith 6. Growing up 7. Safety 8. Belonging 9. Identity 10. South Asian people 11. Autobiographies and memoirs 12. Book club best bets 13. Life stories — Identity — LGBTQIA+ 14. Family and relationships — Growing up 15. Debut title 16. Life stories — Relationships — Growing up

Stonewall Book Awards: Israel Fishman Non-fiction Award, 2024.

A queer Muslim immigrant recalls her coming of age and how she drew inspiration from the stories in the Quran throughout her lifetime search for safety and belonging.

"A queer Muslim writer and organizer chronicles a life navigating between religion and culture….As the author examines her evolving relationship to her religion, she also vibrantly explores what it means to live with an open-minded, open-hearted activist seeking to change the world for the better." —*Kirkus*

Haddish, Tiffany
The *Last Black Unicorn.* Tiffany Haddish. Gallery Books 2017. 278 p.
ISBN 9781501181825
Grades: Adult   B
1. Haddish, Tiffany, 1979- 2. Women comedians 3. African Americans 4. Entertainment industry and trade 5. Gender role 6. Social classes 7. Race (Social sciences) 8. Intersectionality 9. Foster care 10. African American women 11. African American comedians 12. Actors and actresses 13. Teenage girls 14. Mother-separated teenagers 15. Autobiographies and memoirs 16. Arts and Entertainment — Comedy 17. Life stories — Facing adversity — Personal transformation 18. Life stories — Arts and culture — Performing arts 19. Arts and Entertainment — Movies and Television

LC 2017038059

Goodreads Choice Award, 2018.

The stand-up comedienne presents an uproarious and poignant collection of autobiographical essays that reflect her disadvantaged youth as a foster child in South Central Los Angeles; her discovery of her talent for comedy; and her struggles with gender, race and class boundaries in the entertainment industry.

Hadlow, Janice
A *Royal* Experiment: The Private Life of King George III. Janice Hadlow. Henry Holt and Company 2014. 512 pages
ISBN 9780805096569
Grades: Adult   B
1. George III, King of Great Britain, 1738-1820 2. Royal houses 3. Home (Social sciences) 4. Fatherhood 5. Families 6. Biographies 7. Life stories — Politics — Royalty 8. History writing — Europe — United Kingdom 9. Family and relationships — Families

LC 2014024707

Booklist Editors' Choice, 2014.

Documents the American Revolution-era king's radical pursuit of happiness in his private life with Queen Charlotte and their 15 children, describing his resolve to avoid the cruelties of his progenitors, his determined faithfulness and his approaches to parenting.

"Extended forays into the king's periods of madness, which began in 1788 and finally incapacitated him for good in 1811, also diffuse the narrative focus. Unconvincing as revisionist history but enjoyable for its vivid depiction of several varieties of royal lifestyles - and plenty of royal gossip." —*Kirkus*

Hagan, Joe
Sticky Fingers: The Life and Times of Jann Wenner and Rolling Stone Magazine. Joe Hagan. Alfred A. Knopf 2017. 560 p.
ISBN 9781101874370
Grades: Adult   B
1. Wenner, Jann 2. Editors 3. Publishers and publishing 4. Rock music 5. Celebrities 6. Popular culture 7. Biographies 8. Arts and Entertainment — Music — Rock 9. Life stories — Arts and culture — Performing arts — Entertainers and celebrities

LC 2017018102

The biography of founder, editor, and publisher of Rolling stone magazine Jann Wenner.

"This biographical chronicle of the cultural evolution from the 1960s to the present is a must-read for counterculture enthusiasts and historians." —*Library Journal*

Hager, Jenna Bush
Sisters First: Stories from Our Wild and Wonderful Life. Jenna Bush Hager and Barbara Pierce Bush, with a foreword by Laura Bush. Grand Central 2017. 256 p.
ISBN 9781538711415
Grades: Adult   B
1. Hager, Jenna Bush, 1981- 2. Bush, Barbara Pierce 3. Bush family 4. Twin sisters 5. Families 6. Presidents 7. Growing up 8. 20th century 9. History writing — Presidency — 20th century — United States 10. Life stories — Relationships — Growing up 11. Life stories — Politics — Politicians

LC 2017471187

The fraternal twin daughters of the 43rd U.S. president share lighthearted and poignant personal stories and reflections from their lives within a powerhouse political dynasty, from their witness to their grandfather's presidency through their subsequent upbringing and work under the eyes of the Secret Service, public and paparazzi.

"The two first daughters emerge as surprisingly well-adjusted, intelligent young women with strong family bonds in this insightful look at life inside the White House." —*Booklist*

Halberstam, David
The *Amateurs.* David Halberstam. Fawcett Columbine 1996. 221 p. : Illustration
ISBN 9780449910030
Grades: Adult   B
1. Rowers 2. Olympic games 3. Rowing 4. Athletes 5. United States 6. 1980s 7. Biographies 8. Sports and Competition — Olympic Sports 9. Sports and Competition — Racing — Boats

LC BL 99791675

The Pulitzer Prize-winning journalist profiles the struggles of four unknown young men who compete to represent the U.S. as its lone single sculler in the 1984 Olympics.

Originally published: New York : Morrow, c1985.

The *Teammates:* A Portrait of Friendship. David Halberstam. Hyperion 2003. 217 p. : Illustration
ISBN 9781401300579
Grades: 11 12 Adult   B
1. Williams, Ted, 1918-2002 2. Doerr, Bobby, 1918-2017 3. DiMaggio, Dom 4. Pesky, Johnny, 1919-2012 5. Friendship 6. Baseball 7. Professional baseball players 8. Professional baseball 9. Male friendship 10. Baseball players 11. United States 12. 1940s 13. Biographies 14. Sports and Competition — Baseball 15. Sports and Competition — Teams 16. Family and Relationships — Friendship 17. Nonfiction that reads like fiction

LC 2003042334

New York Times Notable Book, 2003.

Follows the friendship of Boston Red Sox teammates Ted Williams, Bobby Doerr, Dom DiMaggio, and Johnny Pesky from their playing days in the 1940s to Ted Williams' death in 2002.

"This account of good people living full lives and appreciating the experience will move readers." —*Booklist*

Hale, Sheila
Titian: His Life. Sheila Hale. HarperCollins 2012. 704 p.
ISBN 9780060598761
Grades: Adult   B
1. Titian, 1477-1576 2. Painters 3. Painting, Renaissance (Europe) 4. Painting, Italian 5. Art, Renaissance (Europe) 6. Art, Italian 7. Artists 8. Italian history 9. Venice, Italy 10. 16th century 11. Biographies 12. Arts and Entertainment — Painting, Drawing, and Sculpture 13. Life stories — Arts and culture — Artists

ESSENTIAL AND RECOMMENDED TITLES
Biography

LC Bl2012044871

A full-length biography of a leading painter of the Italian High Renaissance takes into account recent historical art research and scholarship and examines all contemporary accounts of Titian's life and work, attempting to explain the evolution of his complex methods.

Hales, Dianne R.
Mona Lisa: A Life Discovered. Dianne Hales. Simon & Schuster 2014. 336 pages
ISBN 9781451658965
Grades: Adult B
1. Leonardo, da Vinci, 1452-1519 2. Del Giocondo, Lisa, 1479- 3. Mona Lisa (Painting) 4. Art, Renaissance (Europe) 5. Artists' models 6. Italian history 7. Florence, Italy 8. Biographies 9. Life stories — People in history 10. History writing — Europe — Italy

LC 2013042086

A genius immortalized her. A French king paid a fortune for her. An emperor coveted her. No face has ever captivated so many for so long. Every year more than nine million visitors trek to her portrait in the Louvre. Yet while everyone recognizes her smile, hardly anyone knows her story. This book rests on the premise that the woman in the Mona Lisa is indeed the person identified in its earliest description: Lisa Gherardini (1479-1542), wife of the Florence merchant Francesco del Giocondo. Dianne Haleshas followed facts wherever she could find them—from the Florence State Archives, to the squalid street where she was born, to the ruins of the convent where she died. Lisa Gherardini was a quintessential woman of her times, caught in a whirl of political upheavals, family dramas, and public scandals. Descended from ancient nobles, she gave birth to six children and died at age sixty-three. Her life spanned the most tumultuous chapters in the history of Florence, decades of war, rebellion, invasion, siege, and conquest—and of the greatest artistic outpouring the world has ever seen. Her story creates an extraordinary tapestry of Renaissance Florence, inhabited by larger-than-legend figures such as Leonardo, Michelangelo, and Machiavelli. Mona Lisa: A Life Discovered takes readers beyond the frame of Leonardo's masterpiece and introduces them to a fully dimensional human being.

"This engaging account of a Renaissance woman will appeal to a general audience." —*Library Journal*

Based on research by Giuseppe Pallanti, author of La Vera Identità della Gioconda, Milan: Skira Editore, 2006.

Hall, Sands
★ *Flunk, Start: Reclaiming My Decade Lost in Scientology.* Sands Hall. Counterpoint Press 2018. 368 p.
ISBN 9781619021785
Grades: Adult B
1. Hall, Sands 2. Scientologists 3. Autobiographies and memoirs 4. Life stories — Facing adversity 5. Life stories — Religion and spirituality — Personal faith

LC 2017038728

The compelling story of what drew the author, actress, and musician to Scientology, why she stayed as long as she did, and how she has come to embrace a decade that for years she thought of as lost.

"An early candidate for memoir of the year, this is a thrilling story of one woman's search for truth and her place in the world." —*Library Journal*

Hallberg, David
A Body of Work: Dancing to the Edge and Back. David Hallberg. Touchstone 2017. 400 p.
ISBN 9781476771151
Grades: Adult B
1. Hallberg, David 2. Ballet dancers 3. Ballet 4. Dancing 5. Men ballet dancers 6. Dancers 7. Dance companies 8. Autobiographies and memoirs 9. Life stories — Arts and culture — Performing arts — Dancers and choreographers 10. Arts and Entertainment — Dance

LC Bl2017036576

The first American to join the Bolshoi Ballet as a principal dancer traces his struggles with bullying in childhood, the roles of self-doubt and perfectionism on his performances, and his return from a career-threatening injury.

"Balletomanes and anyone interested in the creative process will appreciate this thoughtful account of the life of an accomplished artist." —*Booklist*

Halpern, Sue
A Dog Walks into a Nursing Home: Lessons in the Good Life from an Unlikely Teacher. Sue Halpern. Riverhead Books 2013. 304 p.
ISBN 9781594487200
Grades: Adult B
1. Nursing homes 2. Happiness 3. Dogs 4. Women and dogs 5. Seniors 6. Humans and dogs 7. Women dog owners 8. Pet therapy 9. Human-animal relationships 10. Vermont 11. Autobiographies and memoirs 12. Family and Relationships — Pets and Owners 13. Life stories — Relationships — Pets and Owners

As an outlet to break up the tedium after her daughter leaves for college, author Sue Halpern signed up for a therapy dog course with her Labradoodle, Pransky. Despite Halpern's anxieties about being around old people, she volunteers for a regular visitation with Pransky at a local nursing home. Pransky had no such reservations, showing a remarkable ability to relate to people—regardless of age or physical condition. Halpern recounts heartwarming (but not overly sentimentalized) experiences with the residents, and shares what she learned from Pransky's example: Restraint, prudence, faith, fortitude, hope, love, and charity.

Hamill, Kirkland
Filthy Beasts: A Memoir. Kirkland Hamill. Avid Reader Press 2020. 311 p.
ISBN 9781982122768
Grades: Adult B
1. Hamill, Kirkland 2. Rich families 3. Poverty 4. Mothers and sons 5. Family fortunes 6. Brothers 7. Alcoholic women 8. Family and addiction 9. Child neglect 10. Dysfunctional families 11. Growing up 12. Survival 13. Coming out (Sexual or gender identity) 14. Gay men 15. Familial love 16. Family secrets 17. Family relationships 18. Bermuda Islands 19. New York City 20. Autobiographies and memoirs 21. Life stories — Relationships — Family 22. Family and Relationships — Abuse 23. Life stories — Identity — LGBTQIA+ 24. Life stories — Relationships — Growing up 25. Life stories — Facing adversity

LC Bl2020014792

Following a rancorous split from New York's upper-class society, newly divorced Wendy Hamill and her three sons are exiled from the East Coast elite circle. Wendy's middle son, Kirk, is eight when she moves the family to her native Bermuda, leaving the three young boys to fend for themselves as she chases after the highs of her old life: Alcohol, a wealthy new suitor, and other indulgences. A fascinating window into the life of extreme privilege and a powerful story of self-acceptance, Filthy Beasts recounts Kirk's unforgettable journey as he confronts his family's many imperfections, accepts his unconventional childhood, and finally comes to terms with his own hidden secrets.

"A stunning, deeply satisfying story about how we outlive our upbringings." —*Kirkus*

Hamilton, Duncan
For the Glory: Eric Liddell's Journey from Olympic Champion to Modern Martyr. Duncan Hamilton. Penguin Group USA 2016. 320 p.
ISBN 9781594206207
Grades: Adult B
1. Liddell, Eric, 1902-1945 2. Runners 3. Missionaries 4. Prisoners of war 5. Christian missionaries 6. Christian missions 7. Running races 8. Olympic athletes 9. Biographies 10. Sports and Competition — Racing — Track and Field 11. Life stories — Sports — Athletes

LC 2016449372

In the 1924 Olympics, devout Scottish sprinter Eric Liddell refused to run in his race—the 100 meter—because it fell on a Sunday. Instead, he spent the months leading up to the Olympics training for the 400, which no one expected him to win. But win he did, and his victory was later immortalized in the 1981 film Chariots of Fire. But this was only the beginning of his sacrifices and his principled stance—at the peak of his career, Liddell went on to dedicate his life to missionary work in China, where he ultimately died in a Japanese work camp.

PUBLIC LIBRARY CORE COLLECTION: NONFICTION
Twentieth Edition

Hamilton, Gabrielle
Blood, Bones, and Butter: The Inadvertent Education of a Reluctant Chef. Gabrielle Hamilton. Random House 2011. 304 p.
ISBN 9781400068722
Grades: Adult   B
1. Hamilton, Gabrielle 2. Cooks 3. Restaurateurs 4. Cooking 5. Food habits 6. New York City 7. Autobiographies and memoirs 8. Food writing — Memoirs and biographies 9. Life stories — Arts and culture — Culinary arts 10. Adult books for young adults
LC 2010017518
Indies' Choice Book Awards, Adult Nonfiction, 2012; James Beard Foundation Book Awards, Writing and Literature, 2012; New York Times Notable Book, 2011.

The chef of New York's East Village Prune restaurant presents an account of her search for meaning and purpose in the central rural New Jersey home of her youth, marked by a first chicken kill, an international backpacking tour, and the opening of a first restaurant.

"Though this book is rhapsodic about foodin every variety, from the humble egg-on-a-roll sandwich served by Greek delis in New York to more esoteric things like fried zucchini agrodolce with fresh mint and hot chili flakesthe book is hardly just for foodies. Ms. Hamilton . Is as evocative writing about people and places as she is at writing about cooking." —*New York Times*

Hamilton, Lisa M.
The Hungry Season: A Journey of War, Love, and Survival. Lisa M. Hamilton. Little, Brown & Compnay 2023. 368 p.
ISBN 9780316415897
Grades: Adult   B
1. Moua, IA 2. Women farmers 3. Hmong (Southeast Asian people) 4. Rice farmers 5. Arranged marriage 6. War 7. Tragedy 8. Abandonment (Psychology) 9. Male domination (Social structure) 10. Refugees 11. Refugee camps 12. Immigration and emigration 13. Survival 14. Family relationships 15. Women entrepreneurs 16. Agriculture 17. Southeast Asian people 18. Laotian people 19. North American people 20. American people 21. Laos 22. Thailand 23. California 24. Biographies 25. Life stories — Nature and outdoors — Farmers and ranchers 26. Life stories — Facing adversity — War and oppression — Refugees 27. Life stories — Identity

An unforgettable portrait of resilience: a nonfiction drama ranging from the mist-covered mountains of Laos to the sunbaked flatlands of Fresno, California, tracing one woman's journey to overcome the wounds inflicted by war and family alike?

"Award-winning journalist Hamilton crafts a radiant work of compelling portraiture in this deep exploration of one woman's lifelong passion for farming despite the most trying of circumstances." —*Booklist*

Hamlin, Kimberly A
Free Thinker: Helen Hamilton Gardener's Audacious Pursuit of Equality and the Vote. Kimberly A. Hamlin. W.W. Norton & Company 2020. 352 pages
ISBN 9781324004974
Grades: Adult   B
1. Gardener, Helen H. (Helen Hamilton), 1853-1925 2. Suffragists 3. Women intellectuals 4. Women's rights 5. Women authors, American 6. Social advocates 7. Sex customs 8. United States 9. 19th century 10. 20th century 11. History writing — Women's history 12. Life stories — Politics — Activists and reformers 13. Life stories — Arts and culture — Writing — Authors
LC 2019044543

Describes the life of the author, suffragist and civil servant who pretended to be married to her lover, openly opposed sexist piety, debunked "science" that claimed women's brains were inferior and worked tirelessly for the Nineteenth Amendment.

"Based on archival sources and Gardener's own voluminous writings, this highly readable book should provide plenty of new insight into the period and Gardener's fascinating life for general readers, scholars, and aspiring political activists alike." —*Library Journal*

Includes bibliographical references and index.

Hammer, Langdon
James Merrill: Life and Art. Langdon Hammer. Knopf 2015. 512 p.
ISBN 9780375413339
Grades: Adult   B
1. Merrill, James Ingram 2. Gay poets 3. Gay men 4. Poets, American 5. 20th century 6. Biographies 7. Life stories — Arts and culture — Writing — Poets 8. Life stories — Identity — LGBTQIA+
LC 2014029325
Lambda Literary Award for Gay Memoir/Biography, 2016.

The first biography of one of the most important poets in the second half of the twentieth century, whose life story is unparalleled in its narrative interest. The story of James Merrill (1926-1995) is that of a young man escaping, but inevitably reproducing, the energies and obsessions of glamorous, powerful parents (his father founded Merrill Lynch); of a gay man inventing his identity against a shifting social and sexual backdrop; and of a brilliantly gifted poet testing the redemptive potential of his art.

"While certainly organized for readers who adore biographies and life dramas, this will strongly appeal to those who love to discover where art springs from life." —*Library Journal*

A Borzoi book.

Hanna, Kathleen
Rebel Girl: My Life as a Feminist Punk. Kathleen Hanna. Ecco 2024. 256 p.
ISBN 9780062825230
Grades: Adult   B
1. Hanna, Kathleen, 1968- 2. Women rock musicians 3. Women singers 4. Growing up 5. Punk rock music 6. Riot grrrl movement 7. Feminism 8. Punk culture 9. Interpersonal relations 10. American people 11. Autobiographies and memoirs 12. Life stories — Arts and culture — Performing arts — Musicians and composers 13. Life stories — Relationships 14. Arts and Entertainment — Music — Rock
LC 2023049603

In Rebel Girl, Hanna's raw and insightful new memoir, she takes us from her tumul tuous childhood to her formative college years and her first shows. As Hanna makes clear, being in a punk "girl band" in those years was not a simple or safe prospect. Male violence and antagonism threatened at every turn, and surviving as a singer who was a lightning rod for controversy took limitless amounts of determination. But the relationships she developed during those years buoyed her, and her friendships with her bandmates and with musicians like Kurt Cobain, Ian MacKaye, and Kim Gordon reminded her that, despite the odds, the punk world could still nurture and care for its own.

"An impressively perspicacious memoir from one of feminism's most influential artists." —*Kirkus*

Harden, Blaine
The Great Leader and the Fighter Pilot: The True Story of the Tyrant Who Created North Korea and the Young Lieutenant Who Stole His Way to Freedom. Blaine Harden. Penguin Group USA 2015. 288 p.
ISBN 9780670016570
Grades: Adult   B
1. Kim, Il-song, 1912-1994 2. No, Kum-Sok 3. Totalitarianism 4. Defectors 5. Communism 6. Fighter pilots 7. Fighter planes 8. Dictators 9. Military history 10. International relations 11. North Korea 12. United States 13. Biographies 14. Life stories — Facing adversity — War and oppression 15. History writing — Asia — North and South Korea
LC 2014038542

Documents the rise of Kim IL Sung, the origins of North Korea's anti-American stance and the daring theft of a Soviet MiG-15 warplane to benefit the United States by fighter pilot No Kum Sok. By the New York Times best-selling author of Escape from Camp 14. Map(s).

Harden, Marcia Gay
The Seasons of My Mother: A Memoir of Love, Family, and Flowers. Marcia Gay Harden. Pocket Books 2018. 288 p.
ISBN 9781501135705
Grades: Adult   B

ESSENTIAL AND RECOMMENDED TITLES
Biography

1. Mothers and daughters 2. Alzheimer's disease 3. Coping 4. Actors and actresses 5. People with Alzheimer's disease 6. Women 7. Autobiographies and memoirs 8. Biographies 9. Life stories — Relationships — Parent and child 10. Life stories — Arts and culture — Performing arts — Actors and actresses

LC 2017049024

A lyrical, uplifting memoir by the Academy- and Tony Award-winning actress traces the story of her childhood and career while using the imagery of flowers and the art of Ikebana as metaphors to represent the unique creative bond she shares with her mother, who has been succumbing in recent years to Alzheimer's.

"Praise, love, and honor all play roles in this respectful, highly affectionate memoir about a spirited mother-daughter relationship." —*Kirkus*

Hardin, Lara Love

★ *The Many Lives of Mama Love: A Memoir of Lying, Stealing, Writing, and Healing.* Lara Love Hardin. Simon & Schuster 2023. 320 p.

ISBN 9781668069608

Grades: Adult **B**

1. Hardin, Lara Love 2. Shame 3. Dishonesty 4. Stealing 5. Addiction 6. Imprisonment 7. Writing 8. Drug abuse 9. Healing 10. Ghostwriters 11. Compassion 12. Criminal justice system 13. Redemption 14. Autobiographies and memoirs 15. Book club best bets 16. Life stories — Facing adversity — Medical issues — Addiction 17. Life stories — Arts and culture — Writing

A writer and literary agent tells the story of how she overcame addiction, a criminal record, and social ostracism to lovingly embrace her 'Beautiful mess of a life.' —*Kirkus*

Hardman, Robert

Queen of Our Times: The Life of Queen Elizabeth II. Robert Hardman. Pegasus Books 2022. x, 694 p.

ISBN 9781643139098

Grades: Adult **B**

1. Elizabeth II, Queen of Great Britain, 1926-2022 2. Windsor, House of 3. Women rulers 4. Royal houses 5. Matriarchs 6. Family relationships 7. Marriage 8. Social change 9. Monarchy 10. British people 11. English people 12. British history 13. Great Britain 14. 20th century 15. 21st century 16. Biographies 17. Life stories — Politics — Royalty 18. History writing — Europe — United Kingdom

On February 6th, 2022, she marks 70 years on the Throne. Robert Hardman, the acclaimed and respected author of Her Majesty and Queen of the World has already examined the Queen as a modern monarch and her role as a stateswoman abroad. Now, he wraps up the full story of one of the undisputed greats in a thousand years of monarchy. With peerless access to members of the Royal Family, staff, friends and royal records, Queen of Our Times will bring fresh insights and scholarship on the modern royal story.

"Hardman (Queen of the World) commemorates Queen Elizabeth II's Platinum Jubilee with an engaging, in-depth biography covering key events in the 95-year-old monarch's life." —*Library Journal*

Includes bibliographical references.

Queen of the World: Elizabeth II, Sovereign and Stateswoman. Robert Hardman. Pegasus Books 2019. 368 p.

ISBN 9781643130026

Grades: Adult **B**

1. Elizabeth II, Queen of Great Britain, 1926-2022 2. Windsor, House of 3. Royal houses 4. Nobility 5. Monarchy 6. Women rulers 7. Rulers 8. British history 9. Great Britain 10. 20th century 11. 21st century 12. Biographies 13. Life stories — Politics — Royalty

LC BI2018191949

Written by the renowned royal biographer, Robert Hardman, and with privileged access to the Royal Family and the Royal Household, a brilliant new portrait of the most famous woman in the world and her place in it.

"Throughout, Hardman's analysis is discerning, knowledgeable, and fascinating." —*Booklist*

Includes bibliographical references and index; Originally published by Century, 2018.

Hargrove, Brantley

The Man Who Caught the Storm: The Life of Legendary Tornado Chaser Tim Samaras. Brantley Hargrove. Simon & Schuster 2018. 320 p.

ISBN 9781476796093

Grades: Adult **B**

1. Samaras, Tim 2. Tornadoes 3. Storm chasers 4. Weather forecasting 5. Disasters 6. Meteorology 7. Biographies 8. Life stories — Nature and outdoors 9. Science Writing — Weather

LC 2018014605

Documents the life and achievements of late engineer and storm chaser Tim Samaras, describing his development of innovative new tools and his life-risking efforts in pursuit of scientific information that has transformed the field of meteorology.

"An exemplar of narrative nonfiction; readers from all across the spectrum will enjoy this title." —*Library Journal*

Hari, Daoud

The Translator: A Tribesman's Memoir of Darfur. Daoud Hari. Random House 2008. 224 p.

ISBN 9781400067442

Grades: 7 8 9 10 11 12 Adult **B**

1. Hari, Daoud 2. Torture 3. Genocide 4. Translators 5. Life change events 6. Southwest Asia and North Africa (Middle East) history 7. Sudan 8. Autobiographies and memoirs 9. Adult books for young adults 10. History writing — Wars and conflicts — Civil Wars 11. Life stories — Facing adversity — War and oppression — War survivors

LC 2007042308

A young Zaghawa tribesman from the Darfur region of the Sudan describes his escape from the attack that destroyed his village, his struggle for survival, his role as a translator and the dangers he confronted, his ultimate capture, and his new life.

Harjo, Joy

Crazy Brave: A Memoir. Joy Harjo. W. W. Norton 2012. 208 p.

ISBN 9780393073461

Grades: Adult **B**

1. Harjo, Joy, 1951- 2. Indigenous women poets 3. Identity 4. Teenage pregnancy 5. Adult child abuse victims 6. Spirituality 7. Women poets 8. Indigenous authors 9. Self-discovery 10. Imagination 11. Autobiographies and memoirs 12. Arts and Entertainment — Writing and Publishing 13. Life stories — Arts and culture — Writing — Poets 14. Life stories — Facing adversity — Personal transformation 15. Life stories — Facing adversity — Abuse survivors 16. Adult books for young adults

LC 2012011198

This memoir from the Native American poet and author of She Had Some Horses describes her youth with an abusive stepfather, becoming a single teen mom and how she struggled to finally find inner peace and her creative voice.

★ *Poet Warrior: A Memoir.* Joy Harjo. W.W. Norton & Company 2021. 240 p.

ISBN 9780393248524

Grades: Adult **B**

1. Harjo, Joy, 1951- 2. Indigenous women poets 3. Adult child abuse victims 4. Justice 5. Loss 6. Families 7. Family violence 8. Women poets 9. Indigenous authors 10. Autobiographies and memoirs 11. Poetry 12. Life stories — Arts and culture — Writing — Poets 13. Arts and Entertainment — Writing and Publishing 14. Life stories — Facing adversity — Abuse survivors

LC 2021025215

Poet Laureate Joy Harjo offers a vivid, lyrical, and inspiring call for love and justice in this contemplation of her trailblazing life. In the second memoir from the first Native American to serve as US poet laureate, Joy Harjo invites us to travel along the heartaches, losses, and humble realizations of her "poet-warrior" road.

"Musician, visual artist, and U.S. Poet Laureate Harjo continues her personal story in her second memoir, following the award-winning Crazy Brave (2013), in a genre-bending approach that interweaves poetry and anecdotes, memories, and familial and ancestral history." —*Booklist*

PUBLIC LIBRARY CORE COLLECTION: NONFICTION
Twentieth Edition

Harlan, Elizabeth
George Sand. Elizabeth Harlan. Yale University Press 2004. xx, 376 p.
ISBN 9780300104172
Grades: Adult **B**
1. Sand, George, 1804-1876 2. Authors, French 3. Social life and customs 4. France 5. 19th century 6. Biographies 7. Arts and Entertainment — Writing and Publishing 8. Life stories — Arts and culture — Writing — Authors
LC 2004010315

"Sand, nee, Aurore Dupin, left her husband and two children in provincial France and successfully launched herself as a self-supporting writer in Paris, donning men's clothing to ease passage into the professional world and taking a pseudonym to protect her aristocratic family's name. Sand took on many lovers, among them poet Alfred de Musset and composer Frederic Chopin. Yet despite Sand's outward daring, as Harlan shows, she obsessed over her identity, as both a woman and an aristocrat. Harlan sensitively analyzes the gaps and idiosyncrasies in her subject's heavily self-edited correspondence, autobiography and novels to uncover a fresh portrait of this volatile, imaginative woman of letters." —*Publishers Weekly*

Includes bibliographical references (p. 353-359) and index.

Harlan, Louis R.
Booker T. Washington: The Making of a Black Leader, 1856-1901. Louis R. Harlan. Oxford University Press 1972. xi, 379 p. : Illustration
ISBN 9780195019155
Grades: Adult **B**
1. Washington, Booker T, 1856-1915 2. African American men 3. African American educators 4. Intellectual life 5. African Americans 6. 19th century 7. Biographies 8. Life stories — Education — Scholars and educators 9. History writing — African American — United States
LC 72077499

Examines the Black educator's life, paying special attention to his role in party politics, presidential legislation, and the freedman's struggle for equality.

Bibliography: P. 325-369.

Booker T. Washington: The Wizard of Tuskegee, 1901-1915. Louis R. Harlan. Oxford University Press 1983. xiv, 548 p. : Portrait
ISBN 9780195042290
Grades: 11 12 Adult **B**
1. Washington, Booker T, 1856-1915 2. Educators 3. Middle class African Americans 4. African Americans 5. Leadership 6. United States history 7. 19th century 8. 20th century 9. Biographies 10. Life stories — Education — Scholars and educators 11. Life stories — Politics — Activists and reformers 12. History writing — African American — Civil rights — United States
LC 82014547

Pulitzer Prize for Biography or Autobiography, 1984.

A chronicle of Washington's last fifteen years reviews his accomplishments and explains how he gained strong political influence.

"Having avoided the pitfalls of white guilt and Black rage and the temptation to judge the past by standards of the present, Mr. Harlan deserves honors for his remarkable achievement." —*New York Times Book Review*

Includes bibliographical references and index.

Harman, Claire
Charlotte Bronte: A Fiery Heart. Claire Harman. Alfred A. Knopf 2016. 384 p.
ISBN 9780307962089
Grades: Adult **B**
1. Bronte, Charlotte, 1816-1855 2. Women authors, English 3. Authors, English 4. 19th century 5. Biographies 6. Life stories — Arts and culture — Writing — Authors 7. Arts and Entertainment — Writing and Publishing — Literary criticism
LC 2015028359

Charlotte Brontë wrote one of the most enduring novels of her era, Jane Eyre. More often portrayed jointly with her sisters Anne and Emily, her individual life story receives a thorough review in this biography by writer and literary critic Claire Harman, whose chronicle traces Charlotte's love life, connecting it with the romantic passion she depicts in her novels. This account brings Charlotte to life, offering a thoughtful consideration of her character both for her novels' fans and for readers generally interested in British literature.

This is a Borzoi book.

Harper, Michele
The Beauty in Breaking: A Memoir. Michele Harper. Riverhead Books 2020. xiv, 284 pages
ISBN 9780525537380
Grades: Adult **B**
1. Harper, Michele 2. Emergency physicians 3. Self-care 4. Psychic healing 5. Medical care 6. African American women physicians 7. Divorced women 8. Physician and patient 9. Family violence 10. Microaggressions 11. Racism 12. Autobiographies and memoirs 13. Life stories — Science, technology, and medicine — Healthcare professionals 14. Science Writing — Medicine and health — Doctors and nurses
LC 2019022440

New York Times Notable Book, 2020.

A female, African American ER physician describes how her own life and encounters with her patients led her to realize that every human is broken and recognizing that and moving towards a place of healing can bring peace and happiness.

"Poignant, helpful, and encouraging, Harper's lessons from life in and outside of the emergency room ultimately teach readers how to trust the healing process." —*Library Journal*

Includes bibliographical references.

Harpham, Heather Elise
Happiness: The Crooked Little Road to Semi-ever After: A Memoir. Heather Harpham. Henry Holt & Company 2017. 320 pages
ISBN 9781250131560
Grades: Adult **B**
1. Harpham, Heather Elise, 1967- 2. Newborn babies 3. Blood diseases 4. Parent and child 5. Blood transfusion 6. Separated couples 7. Unconditional love 8. Autobiographies and memoirs 9. Life stories — Facing adversity — Medical issues — Physical illness 10. Life stories — Relationships — Parent and child 11. Family and Relationships — Illness and the Family
LC 2016040488

A California girl with wanderlust whose opposites-attract relationship with a homebody writer was significantly compromised by an unplanned pregnancy describes how their baby's serious health disorder prompted the couple to reevaluate their views of family and what they were willing to risk for their child's health.

"Harpham has written a heartfelt exploration of familial bonds and the sometimes incredibly bumpy journey one must take to get to contentment." —*Publishers Weekly*

Published in the UK by Oneworld Publications, 2018.

Harrington, Joel F.
Dangerous Mystic: Meister Eckhart's Path to the God Within. Joel F. Harrington. Penguin Press 2018. 368 p.
ISBN 9781101981566
Grades: Adult **B**
1. Eckhart, Meister, -1327 2. Theologians 3. Mystics 4. Spirituality 5. Heresy 6. Clergy 7. Mysticism 8. Religions 9. 14th century 10. Biographies 11. Life stories — Religion and spirituality — Religious and spiritual leaders 12. Spirituality and Religion — Christianity 13. Spirituality and Religion — General
LC Bl2018000973

Looks at the life, times, and thought of Meister Eckhart, the fourteenth-century Christian spiritual leader, and how his thought has become relevant to the modern world.

The Faithful Executioner: Life and Death, Honor and Shame in the Turbulent Sixteenth Century. Joel F. Harrington. Farrar, Straus and Giroux 2013. 368 p.
ISBN 9780809049929
Grades: Adult **B**
1. Schmidt, Franz, d. 1634 2. Executions and executioners 3. Criminal justice system 4. Criminal procedure 5. Capital punishment 6. Occupations 7. Torturers

ESSENTIAL AND RECOMMENDED TITLES
Biography

8. Corporal punishment 9. Crime 10. Men 11. Torture 12. Personal diaries 13. Social life and customs 14. Shame 15. Nuremberg, Germany 16. 16th century 17. Diaries 18. Biographies 19. History writing — Europe 20. Life stories — People in history

LC 2012029017

A work of nonfiction that explores the thoughts and experiences of one early modern executioner, Nuremberg's Frantz Schmidt (1555-1634), through his own words—a rare personal journal, in which he recorded and described all the executions and corporal punishments he administered between 1573 and his retirement in 1617.

Includes index.

Harris, David
The Genius: How Bill Walsh Reinvented Football and Created an NFL Dynasty. David Harris. Random House 2008. 400 p.
ISBN 9781400066650
Grades: Adult   B
1. Walsh, Bill, 1931-2007 2. Football coaches 3. Professional football 4. Football teams 5. Biographies 6. Sports and Competition — Football 7. Sports and Competition — Coaches 8. Life stories — Sports — Athletes 9. Adult books for young adults 10. Life stories — Sports — Coaches, managers, and owners

LC 2008016566

Offers a portrait of football coach Bill Walsh, who transformed the San Francisco 49ers, the NFL's worst team in 1979, into a football powerhouse through a combination of organization innovation, player management, and determination.

"Walsh was one of the NFL's greatest coaches, and Harris' book does him justice." —*Booklist*

Harris, Ellen T.
George Frideric Handel: A Life with Friends. Ellen T. Harris. W. W. Norton & Company 2014. 496 p.
ISBN 9780393088953
Grades: Adult   B
1. Handel, Georg Friedrich, 1685-1759 2. Classical music 3. Composers 4. England 5. 18th century 6. Biographies 7. Life stories — Arts and culture — Performing arts — Musicians and composers 8. Arts and entertainment — Music — Classical 9. History writing — Europe — United Kingdom

LC 2014008148

During his lifetime, the sounds of Handel's music reached from court to theater, echoed in cathedrals, and filled crowded taverns, but the man himself—known to most as the composer of Messiah—is a bit of a mystery. Though he took meticulous care of his musical manuscripts and even provided for their preservation on his death, very little of an intimate nature survives. One document—Handel's will—offers us a narrow window into his personal life. In it, he remembers not only family and close colleagues but also neighborhood friends. In search of the private man behind the public figure, Ellen T. Harris has spent years tracking down the letters, diaries, personal accounts, legal cases, and other documents connected to these bequests.

"A readable tale of one of the world's most enigmatic musicians and composers." —*Publishers Weekly*

Includes bibliographical references and index.

Harris, J. William
The Hanging of Thomas Jeremiah: A Free Black Man's Encounter with Liberty. J. William Harris. Yale University Press 2009. 223 p. : Illustration; Map; Portrait
ISBN 9780300152142
Grades: 11 12 Adult   B
1. Jeremiah, Thomas, d. 1775 2. Laurens, Henry, 1724-1792 3. Campbell, William, 1745-1781 4. Free African Americans 5. Freedom 6. Slavery 7. Race relations 8. United States history 9. Charleston, South Carolina 10. 18th century 11. 19th century 12. Biographies 13. History writing — African American — Enslavement — United States 14. Life stories — Facing adversity — War and oppression — Enslaved people

Library Journal Best Books, 2009.

Describes the trial and execution of Thomas Jeremiah, a freeman falsely accused by whites of supporting insurrection among slaves, and reflects upon the political and social implications of his trial in pre-Revolutionary America.

Includes bibliographical references (p. [167]-210) and index.

Harris, Mark
Mike Nichols: A Life. Mark Harris. Penguin Books 2021. 688 p.
ISBN 9780399562242
Grades: Adult   B
1. Nichols, Mike 2. Film producers and directors 3. Theatrical producers and directors 4. Filmmakers 5. Actors and actresses 6. Celebrities 7. Immigrants 8. Ambition 9. Fame 10. Biographies 11. Impartial writing 12. Life stories — Arts and culture — Performing arts — Directors and producers 13. Arts and Entertainment — Movies and Television 14. Nonfiction that reads like fiction

National Book Critics Circle Award for Biography finalist, 2021.

The author of Pictures at a Revolution draws on interviews with such notables as Meryl Streep, Emma Thompson and Tom Hanks to document the remarkable creative achievements and private struggles of entertainment wunderkind Mike Nichols.

"Likely to become the definitive book about Nichols, Harris's exhaustive take should have widespread appeal, especially given the dearth of currently available literature about this important and influential entertainment icon." —*Library Journal*

Harris, Neil Patrick
Neil Patrick Harris: Choose Your Own Autobiography. Neil Patrick Harris. Crown Archetype 2014. 256 p.
ISBN 9780385346993
Grades: Adult   B
1. Harris, Neil Patrick, 1973- 2. Child actors and actresses 3. Actors and actresses 4. Singers 5. Drama 6. United States 7. Autobiographies and memoirs 8. Biographies 9. Life stories — Arts and culture — Performing arts — Actors and actresses

LC 2014016637

The Emmy Award-winning star of How I Met Your Mother shares his experiences as a child star, Broadway performer and father in an over-the-top, humorous account creatively designed in the style of the popular interactive adventure series.

Harris, Taylor
This Boy We Made: A Memoir of Motherhood, Genetics, and Facing the Unknown. Taylor Harris. Catapult 2022. 272 p.
ISBN 9781948226844
Grades: Adult   B
1. Harris, Taylor 2. Motherhood 3. African American women 4. Mother and child 5. Sick children 6. Uncertainty 7. Faith (Christianity) 8. Medical care 9. Anxiety 10. Parenting 11. African American families 12. Boys 13. Autobiographies and memoirs 14. Life stories — Relationships — Parent and child 15. Life stories — Facing adversity — Medical issues 16. Family and Relationships — Illness and the Family

Finalist for the Hurston/Wright Legacy Awards for Nonfiction, 2023.

In this moving examination of the bond between mother and child, the author, a Black mother, questions everything she thought she believed about science and medicine, about motherhood and about her faith as she searches for the cause of her son's illness.

"A Black woman with an anxiety disorder chronicles the process of caring for her son, whose undiagnosed illness thrust the family into uncertainty. . . . A compelling, insightful memoir about parenting through the unknown." —*Kirkus*

Harrison, Scott
Thirst: A Story of Redemption, Compassion, and a Mission to Bring Clean Water to the World. Scott Harrison; contributed by Lisa Sweetingham. Currency 2018. 272 p.
ISBN 9781524762841
Grades: Adult   B

PUBLIC LIBRARY CORE COLLECTION: NONFICTION
Twentieth Edition

1. Harrison, Scott 2. Charities 3. Nonprofit organizations 4. Water 5. Entrepreneurship 6. Entrepreneurs 7. Social advocates 8. Autobiographies and memoirs 9. Life stories — Business — Business leaders 10. Business and economics — Industries 11. Life stories — Politics — Activists and reformers

The founder of "charity:water" describes the unlikely establishment of his nonprofit and the renowned transparency, marketing and model that have helped it take a leading role in addressing the world's water crisis.

Harry

★ *Spare*. Prince Harry. Random House 2023. 410 p.
ISBN 9780593593806
Grades: Adult B

1. Harry, Prince, Duke of Sussex, 1984- 2. Princes 3. Royal houses 4. Family relationships 5. Growing up 6. Death of mothers 7. Life change events 8. Marriage 9. Fatherhood 10. British people 11. English people 12. North American people 13. American people 14. Independence 15. Autobiographies and memoirs 16. Book club best bets 17. Life stories — Politics — Royalty 18. Life stories — Relationships — Family

LC Bl2022036973

Loan Stars Favourites, 2023.

It was one of the most searing images of the twentieth century: Two young boys, two princes, walking behind their mother's coffin as the world watched in sorrow—and horror. As Diana, Princess of Wales, was laid to rest, billions wondered what the princes must be thinking and feeling—and how their lives would play out from that point on. For Harry, this is that story at last. With its raw, unflinching honesty, Spare is a landmark publication full of insight, revelation, self-examination, and hard-won wisdom about the eternal power of love over grief.

The book readers are waiting for, the story told with raw, unflinching honesty, by Prince Harry, Duke of Sussex, about the death of his mother Princess Diana. Recommended by a NoveList advisor.

"Sibling rivalry, fatherly neglect, and the crushing weight of public opinion haunt this anguished, searching, and occasionally vindictive memoir from Prince Harry….This royal family tell-all delivers." —*Publishers Weekly*

Harry, Debbie

Face It. Debbie Harry. Dey Street Books 2019. 304 p.
ISBN 9780060749583
Grades: Adult B

1. Harry, Debbie 2. Sexual violence victims 3. New wave musicians 4. Women rock musicians 5. New wave music 6. Punk rock music 7. Drug use 8. Fame 9. Sex crimes 10. Women 11. Counterculture 12. Identity 13. New York City 14. 1970s 15. Autobiographies and memoirs 16. Life stories — Arts and culture — Performing arts — Musicians and composers 17. Arts and Entertainment — Music — Rock

LC Bl2019022982

Complemented by rare photos, a memoir by the iconic performance artist traces seven decades in the entertainment industry while discussing her professional collaborations, struggles with addiction, near-escape from Ted Bundy and Blondie alter-ego.

Harss, Marina

The Boy from Kyiv: Alexei Ratmansky's Life in Ballet. Marina Harss. Farrar, Straus and Giroux 2023. VIII, 482 p.
ISBN 9780374102616
Grades: Adult B

1. Ratmanskii, Aleksei, 1968- 2. Choreographers 3. Ballet dancers 4. Ballet 5. Ambition 6. Creation (Literary, artistic, etc.) 7. Eastern European people 8. Ukrainian people 9. Russian people 10. North American people 11. American people 12. Biographies 13. Life stories — Arts and culture — Performing arts — Dancers and choreographers 14. Arts and Entertainment — Dance 15. Debut title

LC 2023012592

Alexei Ratmansky is transforming ballet for the twenty-first century. An artist of daring imagination, the choreographer has created breathtakingly original works for the world's most revered companies. He has fashioned a singular approach to balletic storytelling that bridges the space between narrative and abstraction and heightens ambiguity and surprise on the stage. In The Boy from Kyiv, the first biography of this groundbreaking artist, the celebrated dance writer Marina Harss takes us behind the curtain to reveal Ratmansky's fascinating life, from his Soviet boyhood through his globe-spanning career.

"Dance aficionados will delight in this vibrant portrait." —*Publishers Weekly*

Chronology of works by Alexei Ratmansky on page 413; Includes bibliographical references and index.

Hart, Hannah

Buffering: Unshared Tales of a Life Fully Loaded. Hannah Hart. HarperCollins 2016. 240 p.
ISBN 9780062457516
Grades: Adult B

1. Hart, Hannah, 1986- 2. YouTubers 3. Personal conduct 4. Essays 5. Autobiographies and memoirs 6. Life stories — Arts and culture — Performing arts — Entertainers and celebrities 7. Adult books for young adults

LC Bl2016034866

Alex Award, 2017.

The popular YouTube personality and author of the best-selling My Drunk Kitchen presents a collection of personal narrative essays on faith, family, love, sexuality, self-worth and friendship.

Hart, Kevin

I Can't Make This Up: Life Lessons. Kevin Hart, with Neil Strauss. Simon & Schuster 2017. 256 p.
ISBN 9781501155567
Grades: Adult B

1. Hart, Kevin, 1979- 2. Comedians 3. African American men 4. Men and success 5. Stand-up comedy 6. Determination 7. Autobiographies and memoirs 8. Arts and Entertainment — Comedy 9. Life stories — Arts and culture — Performing arts — Entertainers and celebrities 10. Adult books for young adults

LC 2016478508

The award-winning actor and comedian presents an inspirational memoir on the importance of believing in oneself, sharing stories about the addiction and abuse that marked his childhood and how his unique way of looking at the world enabled his survival and successful career.

"A truthful, self-deprecating, and funny look at the hard work behind Harts success." —*Booklist*

Hartigan, Patti

August Wilson: A Life. Patti Hartigan. Simon & Schuster 2023. 592 p.
ISBN 9781501180668
Grades: Adult B

1. Wilson, August 2. African American playwrights 3. African American poets 4. Playwrights, American 5. Poets, American 6. Childhood 7. Playwrights 8. African Americans 9. Biographies 10. Life stories — Arts and culture — Performing arts 11. Life stories — Arts and culture — Writing 12. Arts and Entertainment — Theater

This first authoritative biography of the most important and successful American playwright of the late 20th century traces his life from his childhood in Pittsburgh to his work chronicling the trials and triumphs of the African American experience.

"Drawing on original interviews with the playwright, Hartigan meticulously renders Wilson's often contentious relationships with collaborators and actors; his painstaking "rewrite and refine" process; and the complexities and limitations of his legacy." —*Publishers Weekly*

Harvey, Samantha

The Shapeless Unease: A Year of Not Sleeping. Samantha Harvey. Grove Press 2020. 192 pages
ISBN 9780802148827
Grades: Adult B

1. Harvey, Samantha, 1975- 2. Insomnia 3. Insomniacs 4. Sleep 5. Health 6. Writing 7. Memory 8. Sleep deprivation 9. Mental illness 10. Anxiety 11. Creativity 12. Mental health 13. Autobiographies and memoirs 14. Life stories — Facing adversity — Medical issues — Mental illness 15. Life stories — Arts and

ESSENTIAL AND RECOMMENDED TITLES
Biography

culture — Writing — Authors 16. Science Writing — Medicine and health — Mental health

LC 2020010114

The author of the Wilderness describes her year-long bout with insomnia, which was not helped with medication, therapy nor changes in diet or sleeping arrangements in an immersive exploration of memory, writing, influence, the will to survive and death.

"Sleeplessness gets the Susan Sontag illness-as-metaphor treatment in this pensive, compact, lyrical inquiry into the author's nighttime demons.... An exquisitely rendered voyage." —*Kirkus*

First published in 2020 in the United Kingdom by Jonathan Cape, an imprint of Vintage.

Haskell, Molly
Steven Spielberg: A Life in Films. Molly Haskell. Yale University Press 2017. 224 pages
ISBN 9780300186932
Grades: Adult   B
1. Spielberg, Steven, 1947- 2. Film producers and directors 3. Filmmaking 4. Jewish way of life 5. Films 6. Biographies 7. Life stories — Arts and culture — Performing arts — Directors and producers 8. Arts and Entertainment — Movies and Television 9. Life stories — Religion and spirituality — Personal faith

LC Bl2016052714

A biography of the popular and talented film director describes how his unique and evocative gift for storytelling evolved from experiences in his own life, including his parents' traumatic divorce and his return to Judaism after his son was born.

"Compact, incisive, and witty—a great starting point for those interested in Spielberg's life and art." —*Kirkus*

Hastings, Selina
The Secret Lives of Somerset Maugham: A Biography. Selina Hastings. Random House 2010. 672 p.
ISBN 9781400061419
Grades: Adult   B
1. Maugham, W. Somerset (William Somerset), 1874-1965 2. Gay men 3. Gay husbands 4. Homosexuality and literature 5. Authors, English 6. Social life and customs 7. England 8. 20th century 9. Biographies 10. Arts and Entertainment — Writing and Publishing 11. Life stories — Arts and culture — Writing — Authors

LC 2009035797

National Book Critics Circle Award for Biography finalist, 2010.

Draws on exclusive access to the literary master's private papers and interviews with his daughter to share insights into such topics as his work as a British spy and private homosexuality, in a profile that is complemented by previously unpublished photographs.

"This steady-eyed biography of an extraordinary, extravagant, generous and bitter artist will not only fascinate its readers but encourage some to go to his work for the first time." —*Times Literary Supplement*

Includes bibliographical references and index.

Haupt, Lyanda Lynn
Mozart's Starling. Lyanda Lynn Haupt. Little Brown & Co. 2017. 256 p.
ISBN 9780316370899
Grades: Adult   B
1. Haupt, Lyanda Lynn 2. Mozart, Wolfgang Amadeus, 1756-1791 3. Starlings 4. Birds as pets 5. Naturalists 6. Composers 7. Musicians 8. Pianists 9. Autobiographies and memoirs 10. Life stories — Relationships — Pets and owners 11. Family and Relationships — Pets and Owners 12. Nature Writing — Animal Studies — Birds and Birding 13. Arts and Entertainment — Music — Classical

LC Bl2017011192

A naturalist describes how Wolfgang Amadeus Mozart was enchanted by the intelligence and playful spirit of a starling in a Viennese shop and took it home for a family pet and discusses a natural history of the frequently reviled bird.

"This hard-to-put-down, charming blend of science, biography, and memoir illuminating the little-known story of the composer and his beloved bird is enlivened by the immediacy of Haupts tales of Carmen, and brimming with startling information, travelogues, and historical details about Mozarts Vienna." —*Booklist*

Includes bibliography.

Hauser, CJ
The Crane Wife: A Memoir in Essays. CJ Hauser. Doubleday 2022. 288 p.
ISBN 9780385547079
Grades: Adult   B
1. Hauser, CJ 2. Women authors 3. Interpersonal relations 4. Romantic love 5. LGBTQIA+ people 6. Self-discovery 7. Essays 8. Autobiographies and memoirs 9. Life stories — Arts and culture — Writing — Authors 10. Life stories — Relationships 11. Book club best bets

LC 2021043397

Ten days after calling off her wedding, CJ Hauser went on an expedition to Texas to study the whooping crane. After a week wading through the gulf, she realized she'd almost signed up to live someone else's life. In this intimate, frank, and funny memoir-in-essays, Hauser releases herself from traditional narratives of happiness and goes looking for ways of living that leave room for the unexpected, making plenty of mistakes along the way. Told with the late-night barstool directness of your wisest, most bighearted friend, the Crane Wife is a book for everyone whose life doesn't look the way they thought it would; for everyone learning to find joy in the not-knowing; for everyone trying, if sometimes failing, to build a new sort of life story, a new sort of family, a new sort of home, to live in.

"No matter her focus, Hauser's deductions about human nature are always arresting, delving, fresh, and exhilarating." —*Booklist*

Hawking, Stephen
My Brief History. Stephen Hawking. Bantam Books 2013. 127 pages : Illustration
ISBN 9780345535283
Grades: Adult   B
1. Hawking, Stephen, 1942-2018 2. Physicists 3. Cosmology 4. People with disabilities 5. Physics 6. Black holes (Astronomy) 7. Amyotrophic lateral sclerosis 8. People with amyotrophic lateral sclerosis 9. Autobiographies and memoirs 10. Life stories — Science, technology, and medicine — Scientists and inventors 11. Life stories — Facing adversity — Medical issues — Physical illness 12. Science Writing — Physics 13. Science Writing — Medicine and health — Disabilities and disorders

LC 2013027938

The famous physicist details the events of his life and career, including attending Oxford and Cambridge, his ALS diagnosis, his study of black holes, and his penning of the bestselling "A Brief History of Time."

"Hawking says it all with charm, intermingling his personal life with abstruse theoretical physics in nontechnical language. Revealing the power of mind over body, this is an enjoyable, entertaining, and inspiring work." —*Choice*

Hawksley, Lucinda
Queen Victoria's Mysterious Daughter: A Biography of Princess Louise. Lucinda Hawksley. Thomas Dunne Books 2015. 384 p.
ISBN 9781250059321
Grades: Adult   B
1. Louise, Princess of Great Britain, 1848-1939 2. Victoria, Queen of Great Britain, 1819-1901 3. Royal houses 4. Nobility 5. Sculptors 6. Illegitimate children of royalty 7. Princesses 8. British history 9. Great Britain 10. Victorian era (1837-1901) 11. Biographies 12. Life stories — Politics — Royalty 13. History writing — Europe — United Kingdom

LC 2015025030

Intrigue, scandal, and secrets abound in this lush royal biography penned by the great-great-great granddaughter of Charles Dickens.

Originally published: The mystery of Princess Louise. London : Chatto & Windus, 2013.

PUBLIC LIBRARY CORE COLLECTION: NONFICTION
Twentieth Edition

Hay, Matt
Soundtrack of Silence: Love, Loss, and a Playlist for Life. Matt Hay with Steve Eubanks. St. Martin's Press 2024. 272 p.
ISBN 9781250280220
Grades: Adult **B**
1. Hay, Matt, 1973- 2. People with disabilities 3. Deafness 4. Love 5. Interpersonal relations 6. Music 7. Popular music 8. Memory 9. Hearing disorders 10. People who are deaf 11. United States 12. Autobiographies and memoirs 13. Life stories — Facing adversity — Medical issues — Living with disabilities 14. Arts and Entertainment — Music — Pop
LC 2023033043
Made vivid with references to instantly recognizable songs, the author, going completely deaf just as he had fallen in love for the first time, shows how he found a way to create a mental playbook of the bands he loved to tap his most resonant memories, and asks us to do the same.
"A medical odyssey told sensitively but unsentimentally." —*Kirkus*

Hayes, Elaine M.
★ *Queen* of Bebop: The Musical Lives of Sarah Vaughan. Elaine M. Hayes. Ecco Press 2017. 320 p.
ISBN 9780062364685
Grades: Adult **B**
1. Vaughan, Sarah, 1924-1990 2. Women jazz musicians 3. Bebop music 4. Popular music 5. Jazz musicians 6. African American civil rights workers 7. Racism 8. Biographies 9. Life stories — Arts and culture — Performing arts — Musicians and composers
LC Bl2017020231
Booklist Editors' Choice, 2017.
Sarah Vaughan dropped out of school to become a jazz singer; her win at Amateur Night at the Apollo Theater landed her a gig singing with Earl Hines' band, where she performed with Dizzy Gillespie, Charlie Parker, and Billy Eckstine at the dawn of bebop. A champion of civil rights, with a voice like honey and a mouth that earned her the nickname "Sailor," Vaughan was a rare woman in a male-oriented business, a strong and successful performer despite mismanagement by the men in her life. Queen of Bebop provides an insightful look at her life and career—and the legacy she left behind.
"A deeply illuminating and unforgettable biography of a true American master." —*Booklist*

Haygood, Wil
Showdown: Thurgood Marshall and the Supreme Court Nomination That Changed America. Wil Haygood. Alfred A. Knopf 2015. 480 p.
ISBN 9780307957191
Grades: Adult **B**
1. Marshall, Thurgood, 1908-1993 2. African American judges 3. Judges 4. Civil rights 5. Politics and government 6. United States 7. 20th century 8. Biographies 9. History writing — Judicial branch — United States 10. Life stories — Law and order — Judges and lawyers 11. History writing — African American — Civil rights — United States
LC 2014044440
Booklist Editors' Choice, 2015.
The author of the Butler presents a revelatory biography of the first African-American Supreme Court justice—one of the giants of the civil rights movement, and one of the most transforming Supreme Court justices of the 20th century.
"The behind-the-scenes look at the hard-fought battle that Lyndon Johnson and his supporters waged on Marshalls behalf creates suspense, even though readers will already know of their ultimate success." —*Publishers Weekly*

★ *Sweet* Thunder: The Life and Times of Sugar Ray Robinson. by Wil Haygood. Alfred A. Knopf 2009. 416 p.
ISBN 9781400044979
Grades: Adult **B**
1. Robinson, Sugar Ray, 1920-1989 2. Boxers (Sports) 3. Boxing 4. African American athletes 5. United States 6. Biographies 7. Sports and Competition — Boxing 8. Sports and Competition — Individual Athlete 9. Life stories — Sports — Athletes
LC 2009005534
Documents the rise of the iconic boxer against a backdrop of the mid-twentieth century, describing his Harlem youth and emergence as a symbol of Black America while offering insight into his athletic talents and his relationships with such figures as Langston Hughes, Lena Horne, and Miles Davis.
A Borzoi book; Includes bibliographical references and index.

Hazleton, Lesley
The First Muslim: The Story of Muhammad. Lesley Hazleton. Riverhead Books 2012. 320 p.
ISBN 9781594487286
Grades: Adult **B**
1. Muhammad, Prophet, d. 632 2. Prophets 3. Religious leaders 4. Islam 5. Biographies 6. Spirituality and Religion — Islam — History 7. Life stories — Religion and spirituality — Religion and spiritual leaders 8. Spirituality and Religion — Religious Leaders
LC 2012038501
Biographer Lesley Hazleton offers an engaging, well-researched historical portrait of the Prophet Muhammad. The First Muslim offers a welcome introduction to the character and personality of this famous spiritual leader, while vividly portraying his life's major events—including his abandonment as an infant, his marriage to a much older widow, the mystical revelation he experienced (later transcribed as the Quran), and the political challenges he faced during the early development of Islam.

Mary: A Flesh-and-blood Biography of the Virgin Mother. Lesley Hazleton. Bloomsbury 2004. VII, 246 p.
ISBN 9781582342368
Grades: Adult **B**
1. Mary, Blessed Virgin, Saint 2. Motherhood 3. Biographies 4. Spirituality and Religion — Christianity — History 5. Life stories — Religion and spirituality — Religious and spiritual leaders
LC 2003017403
A portrait of the human side of Mary, the mother of Jesus, draws on Judaic and Christian history, theology, and anthropology, to reconstruct the life of a young peasant girl, through her diverse roles as mother, teacher, wise woman and healer, activist, and more, exploring her grief over the death of her son and how she transformed that pain into renewal and wisdom.
"Hazleton takes readers through an impressive array of historical, cultural, literary, and spiritual topics. This book is an easy read, and Hazleton's stream-of-consciousness style is intriguing." —*Library Journal*
Includes bibliographical references (p. 227-238) and index.

Hazzard, Kevin
A Thousand Naked Strangers: A Paramedic's Wild Ride to the Edge and Back. Kevin Hazzard. Scribner 2016. 288 p.
ISBN 9781501110832
Grades: Adult **B**
1. Hazzard, Kevin 2. Paramedics 3. Personal conduct 4. Life change events 5. Autobiographies and memoirs 6. Life stories — Science, technology, and medicine — Healthcare professionals
A former paramedic's poignant and mordantly whimsical account of a decade spent as an EMT in the urban regions of Atlanta describes his post-9/11 resolve to make a difference and his nightly encounters with violence and personal tragedy.

Heaney, Christopher
Cradle of Gold: The Story of Hiram Bingham, a Real-life Indiana Jones, and the Search for Machu Picchu. by Christopher Heaney. Palgrave Macmillan 2010. 304 p.
ISBN 9780230611696
Grades: Adult **B**
1. Bingham, Hiram, 1875-1956 2. Inca (South American people) 3. Indigenous peoples of South America 4. Cultural property 5. Indigenous peoples of South America — Antiquities 6. Indigenous peoples of South America — History 7. South American history 8. Machu Picchu, Peru 9. Peru 10. 1910s 11. 16th

ESSENTIAL AND RECOMMENDED TITLES
Biography

century 12. Biographies 13. History writing — Exploration 14. Life stories — People in history — Explorers 15. History writing — Indigenous peoples — Latin America
LC 2009038535

In 1911, a young Peruvian boy led an American explorer and Yale historian named Hiram Bingham into the ancient Incan citadel of Machu Picchu. Hidden amidst the breathtaking heights of the Andes, this settlement of temples, tombs and palaces was the Incas' greatest achievement. Tall, handsome, and sure of his destiny, Bingham believed that Machu Picchu was the Incas' final refuge, where they fled the Spanish Conquistadors. Bingham made Machu Picchu famous, and his dispatches from the jungle cast him as the swashbuckling hero romanticized today as a true Indiana Jones-like character. But his excavation of the site raised old specters of conquest and plunder, and met with an indigenous nationalism that changed the course of Peruvian history.

"On an archaeological trip to Peru on July 24, 1911, Hiram Bingham, an American explorer and history professor at Yale, happened upon the ruins of the Inca city of Machu Picchu. Although the site was already known to the local native people, Bingham made the Machu Picchu ruins famous and received acclaim as their discoverer. Heaney presents a well-researched and very readable biography of Bingham from his childhood in Hawaii as the son of missionaries, through his education and careers as historian, educator, explorer, and finally politician. He probes the depths of Bingham's work and character, examining setbacks, scandals, and achievements and skillfully unraveling Bingham's role in the controversy that still exists today between the government of Peru and Yale University over the ownership of the Machu Picchu burials and artifacts." —*Library Journal*

Includes bibliographical references and index.

Hecimovich, Gregg A.
★ *The Life and Times of Hannah Crafts: The True Story of the Bondwoman's Narrative.* Gregg Hecimovich. Ecco 2023. 304 p.
ISBN 9780062334732
Grades: Adult   **B**
1. Crafts, Hannah 2. African American women authors 3. Enslaved women 4. Freedom seekers 5. Fiction writing 6. Manuscripts 7. African American women 8. Biographies 9. Life stories — People in history 10. History Writing — African American — United States 11. Life stories — Arts and culture — Writing — Authors 12. Life stories — Facing adversity — War and oppression — Enslaved people
LC 2023010774

Los Angeles Times Book Prize for Biography, 2023; National Book Critics Circle Award for Biography finalist, 2023.

A groundbreaking study of the first Black female novelist and her life as an enslaved woman, from the biographer who solved the mystery of her identity, with a preface by Henry Louis Gates Jr.

"Interspersed with photos, descriptions of pertinent historical events, drawings, and digitized archival documents, this excellent biography will appeal to many readers, especially those interested in genealogy, literature, and African American history." —*Library Journal*

Includes bibliographical references and index.

Hegar, Mary Jennings
Shoot Like a Girl: One Woman's Dramatic Fight in Afghanistan and on the Home Front. Mary Jennings Hegar. New American Library 2016. 368 p.
ISBN 9781101988435
Grades: Adult   **B**
1. Hegar, Mary Jennings 2. Women soldiers 3. Helicopter pilots 4. Afghan War, 2001-2021 5. Women's rights 6. Sexism in the military 7. Women military helicopter pilots 8. Women in combat 9. Sex discrimination against women 10. Sexual harassment in the military 11. United States 12. Autobiographies and memoirs 13. Biographies 14. Life stories — Law and order — Armed forces personnel 15. Life stories — Identity — Gender 16. Adult books for young adults
LC 2015047084

An Air National Guard Major describes her experiences after being shot down on a Medevac mission in Afghanistan, recounting the courageous acts that saved lives and earned prestigious decorations before she began efforts to convince the U.S. government to allow women to serve openly on the front lines.

"Hegars inspirational memoir reflects the strength and grace with which she approached her service to her country, whether she was venturing behind enemy lines to rescue wounded soldiers or standing up for womens right to be on the front line." —*Booklist*

Heilbroner, Robert L.
★ *The Worldly Philosophers: The Lives, Times, and Ideas of the Great Economic Thinkers.* Robert L. Heilbroner. Simon & Schuster 1999. 365 p.
ISBN 9780684862149
Grades: 11 12 Adult   **B**
1. Economists 2. Economics 3. Business and economics — Economics — History
LC 99014050

Defines the world's greatest economic thinkers and explores the philosophies that motivate them.

A Touchstone book; Includes bibliographical references (p. 331-343) and index.

Helm, Sarah
A Life in Secrets: Vera Atkins and the Missing Agents of Wwii. Sarah Helm. Nan A. Talese 2006. xxviii, 493 p, 16 p. of plates : Map
ISBN 9780385508452
Grades: 11 12 Adult   **B**
1. Atkins, Vera, 1908-2000 2. French Resistance (World War II) 3. World War II 4. Missing in action 5. Intelligence officers 6. Women intelligence officers 7. Secret service 8. French history 9. Great Britain 10. 20th century 11. Biographies 12. History writing — Wars and conflicts — World War II — European Theater 13. History writing — Spies and spying 14. Life stories — Law and order — Spies and secret agents 15. Adult books for young adults 16. History writing — Wars and conflicts — Resistance — World War II
LC 2005056870

Library Journal Best Books, 2006.

Describes the life and espionage career of Vera Atkins, a talented agent who rose to the top of the Special Operations Executive (SOE), a British secret service dedicated to aiding resistance efforts throughout Nazi-occupied Europe.

"Helm has produced a memorable portrait of a woman who knowingly sent other women to their deaths and a searing history of female courage and suffering during WWII." —*Publishers Weekly*

Includes bibliographical references (p. [477]-480) and index; Originally published: London : Little, Brown, 2005.

Heminsley, Alexandra
Running Like a Girl: Notes on Learning to Run. Alexandra Heminsley. Scribner 2013. 224 p.
ISBN 9781451697124
Grades: Adult   **B**
1. Heminsley, Alexandra, 1976- 2. Running 3. Transformations (Personal) 4. Women runners 5. Runners 6. Determination 7. Running races 8. Running for women 9. Autobiographies and memoirs 10. Life stories — Personal growth 11. Life stories — Sports 12. Sports and Competition — Racing — Track and Field
LC 2013018909

A journalist and broadcaster shares her hilarious and inspirational personal journey from a self-proclaimed non-athlete to someone who, after many stumbling, painful efforts, has become a runner, which has transformed her relationships, her body and her life.

Hempel, Jessi
The Family Outing: A Memoir. Jessi Hempel. Harperone 2022. 304 p.
ISBN 9780063079014
Grades: Adult   **B**
1. Hempel, Jessi 2. Families 3. Secrets 4. Identity 5. Lesbians 6. LGBTQIA+ people 7. Family secrets 8. Transformations, personal 9. Psychic trauma 10. Self-discovery 11. Forgiveness 12. Love 13. Family relationships 14. Intergenerational trauma 15. Autobiographies and memoirs 16. Life stories — Relationships — Family 17. Life stories — Personal growth 18. Life stories — Identity — LGBTQIA+ 19. Family and Relationships — Families

When her family comes out—some embracing queer identities and another revealing a traumatic experience with a serial killer, other personal revelations and reckonings come to light, causing each of them to question their place in the world in new and liberating ways.

"Hempel, host of the Hello Monday podcast, shares the story of her family's personal and collective coming out journeys in this magnetic memoir." —*Library Journal*

Hemphill, Paul
Lovesick Blues: The Life of Hank Williams. Paul Hemphill. Viking 2005. 207 p.

ISBN 9780670034147

Grades: Adult   B

1. Williams, Hank, Sr, 1923-1953 2. Country musicians 3. United States 4. Biographies 5. Arts and Entertainment — Music — Country 6. Life stories — Arts and culture — Performing arts — Musicians and composers

LC 2004065113

Traces the life and career of the mid-twentieth-century country music star, from his sickly and fatherless childhood and musical education by an African-American street singer, to his early gigs in Depression-era rural honky-tonks and rise to Grand Ole Opry star, in an account that also discusses his struggles with alcoholism and early death.

"This is the finest work of literature about Williams yet written." —*Booklist*

Hendershot, Heather
Open to Debate: How William F. Buckley Put Liberal America on the Firing Line. Heather Hendershot. Broadside 2016. xxii, 357 p.

ISBN 9780062430458

Grades: Adult   B

1. Buckley, William F. (William Frank), 1925-2008 2. Journalists 3. Right and left (Political science) 4. Conservatives 5. Conservatism 6. United States 7. Biographies 8. Impartial writing 9. Politics and global affairs — Political parties 10. Life stories — Arts and culture — Performing arts — Entertainers and celebrities

LC 2016015903

Offers a portrait of William F. Buckley as the champion of conservative ideas in an age of liberal dominance, taking on the smartest adversaries he could find while singlehandedly reinventing the role of public intellectual in the network-TV era.

Henderson, Artis
Unremarried Widow: A Memoir. Artis Henderson. Simon & Schuster 2013. 272 p.

ISBN 9781451649284

Grades: Adult   B

1. Henderson, Artis 2. Widows 3. Military spouses 4. Iraq War, 2003-2011 5. Husband and wife 6. Grief 7. Loss 8. Helicopter pilots 9. Guilt 10. Loneliness 11. Autobiographies and memoirs 12. Life stories — Facing adversity — Coping with death 13. Family and Relationships — Aging and Death

LC 2013008799

Library Journal Best Books, 2013.

A journalist and essayist traces the difficult process of picking up the pieces of her life after it was shattered by the death of her husband, a Texan solider whose Apache helicopter crashed in Iraq.

"[Henderson's] willingness to reveal the complexities of her marriage as well as the raw emotion of her loss makes for a compelling page-turner." —*Booklist*

Includes bibliographical references and index.

Henderson, Danielle
★ *The Ugly Cry.* Danielle Henderson. Viking 2021. 304 p.

ISBN 9780525559351

Grades: Adult   B

1. Henderson, Danielle 2. African American women authors 3. Women television writers 4. Humorists 5. Growing up 6. Small towns 7. Grandmother and granddaughter 8. Family relationships 9. Girls 10. Mother-separated children 11. Autobiographies and memoirs 12. Life stories — Relationships — Growing up 13. Life stories — Relationships — Parent and child 14. Life stories — Identity — Race and ethnicity

An humorous, moving memoir about a grandmother's ferocious love and redefining what it means to be family.

"A redemptive memoir about a Black woman's victory over childhood abuse, racism, and mental illness." —*Kirkus*

Henderson, Rob Kim
Troubled: A Memoir of Foster Care, Family, and Social Class. Rob Henderson. Gallery Books 2024. 336 p.

ISBN 9781982168537

Grades: Adult   B

1. Henderson, Rob Kim 2. Abandoned children 3. Foster children 4. Growing up 5. Foster home care 6. Child neglect 7. Poverty 8. Military service 9. Higher education 10. Social classes 11. Privilege (Social psychology) 12. North American people 13. American people 14. Autobiographies and memoirs 15. Life stories — Facing adversity 16. Society and culture — Wealth and class 17. Debut title

The author vividly recounts growing up in foster care, enlisting in the U.S. Air Force, attending elite universities and pioneering the concept of "luxury beliefs"—ideas and opinions that confer status upon the upper class while inflicting costs on the less fortunate.

"A memoir of hardscrabble living, from foster care to the Air Force to Yale, that doubles as the education narrative of a young conservative." —*Kirkus*

Hendrickson, John
Life on Delay: Making Peace with a Stutter. John Hendrickson. Alfred A. Knopf 2023. 272 p.

ISBN 9780593319130

Grades: Adult   B

1. Hendrickson, John (Atlantic senior editor) 2. Stutterers 3. Speech disorders 4. Stuttering 5. Language disorders 6. Maryland 7. Autobiographies and memoirs 8. Book club best bets 9. Life stories — Facing adversity — Medical issues — Living with disabilities

LC 2021054996

A senior editor at the Atlantic, taking us deep inside the mind and heart of a stutterer, writes candidly about the issues stutterers like him face daily, leading us through the evolution of speech therapy and sharing portraits of fellow stutterers who have changed his life.

"A senior editor at the Atlantic reflects on how his lifelong stutter has shaped his life and relationships….This appealing and perceptive memoir takes an unsentimental look at life with a speech disorder." —*Kirkus*

Hendrix, Scott H.
Martin Luther: Visionary Reformer. Scott H. Hendrix. Yale University Press 2015. xxi, 341 pages, 16 unnumbered pages of plates : Illustration; Map

ISBN 9780300166699

Grades: Adult   B

1. Luther, Martin, 1483-1546 2. Reformation 3. Germany 4. Biographies 5. Life stories — Religion and spirituality 6. Spirituality and Religion — Christianity — History

LC 2015017636

Chronicles the life of the sixteenth century German friar whose public conflict with the Catholic Church triggered the Protestant Reformation.

"This carefully documented, fast-paced telling will delight readers of biography, history, and fiction; historians, theologians, and psychologists may gain deeper insights into how flaws in personality and the zeitgeist itself often prejudice the pursuit of truth." —*Library Journal*

Includes bibliographical references (pages 319-326) and index.

Henig, Robin Marantz
The Monk in the Garden: The Lost and Found Genius of Gregor Mendel, the Father of Genetics. Robin Marantz Henig. Houghton Mifflin 2000. VIII, 292 p. : Illustration

ISBN 9780395977651

Grades: 11 12 Adult   B

ESSENTIAL AND RECOMMENDED TITLES
Biography

1. Mendel, Gregor, 1822-1884 2. Geneticists 3. Scientists 4. Genetics 5. Research 6. Biology 7. Biographies 8. Science Writing — Biology 9. Life stories — Science, technology, and medicine — Scientists and inventors 10. Adult books for young adults

LC 00024341

National Book Critics Circle Award for Biography finalist, 2000.

A study of the groundbreaking work in genetics conducted by Gregor Mendel, acclaimed as the father of modern genetics, argues that the Moravian monk was far ahead of his time.

"The author explores Mendel's personality and experiments. The latter lasted but a few years in the 1850s and 1860s, ending when Mendel became the abbot of his monastery in what is now Brno in the Czech Republic. Henig crisply conveys how the laws of inheritance that Mendel derived from his statistical analysis remained unnoticed until several botanists who discovered them independently in 1900 also learned that Mendel found them first. This biography itself rediscovers a scientist often mentioned but insufficiently known." —*Booklist*

Includes bibliographical references (p. 278-279) and index; expanded bibliography and footnotes found only on the World Wide Web.

Hennessey, Patrick
The Junior Officers' Reading Club: Killing Time and Fighting Wars. Patrick Hennessey. Riverhead Books 2010. 336 p.

ISBN 9781594484797

Grades: Adult **B**

1. Hennessey, Patrick, 1982- 2. Soldiers 3. Iraq War, 2003-2011 4. Afghan War, 2001-2021 5. War 6. Autobiographies and memoirs 7. History writing — Military — Military Today 8. Life stories — Law and order — Armed forces personnel

LC 2010017134

Booklist Editors' Choice, 2010.

A revelatory first-hand account of a young enlistee's profound coming of age and how boys grow into men amid the frenetic, sometimes exhilarating violence, frequent boredom, and almost overwhelming responsibilities that frame a soldier's experience and the way we fight today.

Originally published: London : Allen Lane, 2009.

Hennessy, Kate
Dorothy Day: The World Will Be Saved by Beauty : an Intimate Portrait of My Grandmother. Kate Hennessy. Scribner 2017. 352 p.

ISBN 9781501133961

Grades: Adult **B**

1. Day, Dorothy, 1897-1980 2. Social reformers 3. Catholic women 4. Catholic Worker Movement 5. Catholics 6. Social advocacy 7. Biographies 8. Spirituality and Religion — Christianity — Catholicism 9. Life stories — Politics — Activists and reformers

LC Bl2016052573

The youngest grandchild of controversial Catholic and social activist Dorothy Day shares personal insights into her life and work that describe Day's experiences before and after conversion, her prolific writings and her sometimes radical perspectives.

"Hennessy has created an amazing tapestry of Day's life and the memories she left with her loved ones." —*Publishers Weekly*

Hensley, William L. Iggiagruk
Fifty Miles from Tomorrow: A Memoir of Alaska and the Real People. by William L. Iggiagruk Hensley. Farrar, Straus and Giroux 2008. 272 p.

ISBN 9780374154844

Grades: 11 12 Adult **B**

1. Hensley, William L. Iggiagruk 2. Iñupiat (North American people) 3. Childhood 4. Indigenous peoples of North America — Civil rights 5. Indigenous authors 6. Civil rights 7. Social life and customs 8. Alaska 9. Biographies 10. Autobiographies and memoirs 11. History writing — Indigenous peoples — United States 12. Life stories — Arts and culture — Writing — Authors 13. Adult books for young adults 14. Life stories — People in history — Indigenous peoples

LC 2008031409

Documents the author's traditional childhood north of the Arctic Circle, his education in the continental U.S, and his lobbying efforts that convinced the government to allocate resources to Alaska's natives in compensation for incursions on their way of life.

Includes index.

Henson, Taraji P.
Around the Way Girl: A Memoir. Taraji P. Henson. 37 Ink 2016. 320 p.

ISBN 9781501125997

Grades: Adult **B**

1. Henson, Taraji P. 2. Actors and actresses 3. Academy Award film nominees 4. Single mothers 5. African American women 6. Autobiographies and memoirs 7. Arts and Entertainment — Movies and Television 8. Life stories — Arts and culture — Performing arts — Actors and actresses 9. Adult books for young adults

LC 2016028253

The Academy Award nominee, Golden Globe winner and star of the hit show Empire recalls her beloved screen characters while tracing the story of her life and career, sharing coverage of such topics as her father's Vietnam service, her rise from the violence of the streets of Washington D.C. and her experiences as a single mother.

"Recommended for fans and aspiring actors alike." —*Library Journal*

Hepworth, David
Uncommon People: The Rise and Fall of the Rock Stars. David Hepworth. Henry Holt & Company 2017. 288 p.

ISBN 9781250124128

Grades: Adult **B**

1. Rock musicians 2. Rock music 3. Music history and criticism 4. 20th century 5. Biographies 6. Arts and entertainment — Music — Rock 7. History writing — Arts and culture

LC 2017036561

Presents an elegy to the age of the rock star that explores the defining moments and turning points in the lives of forty rock stars from 1955 to 1995, including Chuck Berry, Elvis, Madonna, David Bowie, and Prince.

"Hepworth perceptively shows how our notion of a rock star evolved over the years, as did the music itself. Despite its death-of-an-era theme, the book is really an enthusiastic, even passionate, celebration of rock stars and their music." —*Booklist*

Includes bibliographical references.

Herbert, Brian
Dreamer of Dune: The Biography of Frank Herbert. Brian Herbert. Tor 2003. 576 p. : Illustration

ISBN 9780765306463

Grades: Adult **B**

1. Herbert, Frank 2. Science fiction writing 3. Fathers and sons 4. Eccentric men 5. Authors, American 6. Dune (Imaginary place) 7. 20th century 8. Biographies 9. Arts and Entertainment — Writing and Publishing 10. Life stories — Arts and culture — Writing — Authors 11. Adult books for young adults

LC 2002042951

A chronicle of the life of the award-winning science-fiction writer, presented by his son, describes Herbert's childhood in Tacoma, Washington, his early years as a reporter and editor, his military service, his struggles to become published, and his creation of numerous works including Dune, the Green Brain, and the Santaroga Barrier.

"This moving, sometimes painfully obsessive biography is an impressive testament of family loyalty and love. A must-read for Herbert fans (both senior and junior), it includes family photos and a bibliography." —*Publishers Weekly*

A Tom Doherty Associates book; Includes bibliographical references (p. 537-562) and index.

Herlihy, David V.
The Lost Cyclist: The Epic Tale of an American Adventurer and His Mysterious Disappearance. David V. Herlihy. Houghton Mifflin Harcourt 2010. 320 p.

ISBN 9780547195575

Grades: Adult **B**
1. Lenz, Frank G. 2. Bicyclists 3. Bicycling 4. Missing persons 5. 1890s 6. 19th century 7. Travel Writing — Modes of Transportation — Cycling 8. Travel Writing — Historic Journeys

LC 2009028857

A cycling historian traces the epic journey of 1880s high-wheel racer Frank Lenz to cycle around the world as a correspondent for Outing magazine, an effort during which his murder sparked an international outcry and an ensuing investigation by fellow cyclist William Sachtleben.

Includes index.

Herman, Arthur
★ *Douglas* Macarthur: American Warrior. Arthur Herman. Random House 2016. 880 p.
ISBN 9780812994889
Grades: Adult **B**
1. MacArthur, Douglas, 1880-1964 2. Generals 3. Military history 4. United States 5. 20th century 6. Biographies 7. Impartial writing 8. Life stories — Law and order — Military leaders 9. History writing — Wars and conflicts — World War II

LC 2015039817

The Pulitzer Prize finalist and author of Gandhi & Churchill goes beyond the mythologies of the World War II general to illuminate his strengths and weaknesses, placing his career against a backdrop of history while discussing how he shaped his character to meet national needs.

"Herman presents a superb reexamination of MacArthur and his role in American history." —*Booklist*

Includes bibliographical references and index.

Hermes, Will
Lou Reed: The King of New York. Will Hermes. Farrar, Straus and Giroux 2023. xxvi, 529 p.
ISBN 9780374193393
Grades: Adult **B**
1. Reed, Lou 1942-2013 2. Rock musicians 3. Rock music 4. Singers 5. Songwriters 6. Influence (Psychology) 7. Interpersonal relations 8. LGBTQIA+ people 9. North American people 10. American people 11. New York City 12. Long Island, New York 13. Biographies 14. Impartial writing 15. Life stories — Arts and culture — Performing arts — Musicians and composers 16. Arts and Entertainment — Music — Rock

LC 2023012589

Since his death ten years ago, Lou Reed's living presence has only grown. The great rock-poet presided over the marriage of Brill Building pop and the European avant-garde, and left American culture transfigured. In Lou Reed: The King of New York, Will Hermes offers the definitive narrative of Reed's life and legacy, dramatizing his long, brilliant, and contentious dialogue with fans, critics, fellow artists, and assorted habitués of the demimonde.

"Rolling Stone contributor Hermes draws on recent interviews, previously unheard recordings, and the New York Public Library's Lou Reed Papers to create a study of Reed's life and outsize influence." —*Library Journal*

Includes bibliographical references and index.

Hernandez Castillo, Marcelo
Children of the Land: A Memoir. Marcelo Hernandez Castillo. Harper 2020. 362 pages
ISBN 9780062825599
Grades: Adult **B**
1. Hernandez Castillo, Marcelo, 1988- 2. Immigrant families 3. Child immigrants 4. Father-separated children 5. Mexican Americans 6. Deportation 7. Border patrols 8. Psychic trauma 9. Separated friends, relatives, etc. 10. Undocumented immigrants 11. Immigration policy 12. Intergenerational trauma 13. Immigration and emigration 14. United States 15. Mexico 16. Autobiographies and memoirs 17. Life stories — Identity — Immigrants 18. Life stories — Facing adversity 19. Society and culture — Immigration

LC Bl2020002598

ALA Notable Book, 2021.

An award-winning poet chronicles his experiences of growing up undocumented in the United States, describing how his family and his attempt to establish an adult life were heartbreakingly complicated by racist policies.

"Castillo lays bare the inherent unfairness and high psychological toll of the current immigration system on people in both the U.S. and Mexico." —*Booklist*

Includes bibliographical references (pages 361-362).

Hernandez, Daisy
A Cup of Water Under My Bed: A Memoir. by Daisy Hernández. Beacon Press 2014. 200 p.
ISBN 9780807014486
Grades: Adult **B**
1. Hernandez, Daisy 2. Hispanic American women 3. Bisexual women 4. Identity 5. Young women 6. Cuban Americans 7. Women journalists 8. Family relationships 9. Colombian Americans 10. New York City 11. United States 12. Autobiographies and memoirs 13. Biographies 14. Life stories — Identity — Race and ethnicity 15. Life stories — Identity — LGBTQIA+ 16. Adult books for young adults

LC 2014000820

It's 1980. Ronald Reagan has been elected president, John Lennon has been shot, and a little girl in New Jersey has been hauled off to English classes. Her teachers and parents and tias are expecting her to become white—like the Italians. This is the opening to a cup of water under my bed, the memoir of one Colombian-Cuban daughter's rebellions and negotiations with the women who raised her and the world that wanted to fit her into a cubbyhole. From language acquisition to coming out as bisexual to arriving as a reporting intern at the New York Times as the paper is rocked by its biggest plagiarism scandal, Daisy Hernandez chronicles what the women in her community taught her about race, sex, money, and love. This is a memoir about the private nexus of sexuality, immigration, race and class issues, but it is ultimately a daughter's cuento of how to take the lessons from home and shape them into a new, queer life.

Hernandez, Keith
I'm Keith Hernandez: A Memoir. Keith Hernandez. Little, Brown 2018. 320 p.
ISBN 9780316395731
Grades: Adult **B**
1. Hernandez, Keith 2. Baseball players 3. Professional athletes 4. Baseball 5. Professional baseball players 6. Autobiographies and memoirs 7. Life stories — Sports — Athletes 8. Sports and Competition — Baseball

LC 2017963935

The legendary first baseman best known for his World Series win with the New York Mets tells all.

"Often candid and even self-deprecating memories by an athlete who once stood at the summit o f his profession." —*Kirkus*

Herrera, Hayden
Frida: A Biography of Frida Kahlo. Hayden Herrera. Perennial 2002. xiii, 507 p. : Illustration; Color
ISBN 9780060911270
Grades: Adult **B**
1. Kahlo, Frida 2. Painters 3. Social life and customs 4. Mexico 5. Biographies 6. Page to screen 7. Arts and Entertainment — Painting, Drawing, and Sculpture 8. Life stories — Arts and culture — Artists

LC 80008688

An in-depth biography of Mexican artist Frida Kahlo details her haunting and original painting style, her turbulent marriage to muralist Diego Rivera, her association with communism, and her love of Mexican culture and folklore.

Includes bibliographical references (p. 445-448) and index; Originally published: New York : Harper & Row, c1983.

Listening to Stone: The Art and Life of Isamu Noguchi. Hayden Herrera. Farrar, Straus and Giroux 2015. 512 p.
ISBN 9780374281168
Grades: Adult **B**
1. Noguchi, Isamu, 1904-1988 2. Modern art 3. Sculptors 4. Japanese Americans 5. Artists 6. East Asian Americans 7. Sculpture 8. 20th century 9. Biogra-

ESSENTIAL AND RECOMMENDED TITLES
Biography

phies 10. Arts and Entertainment — Painting, Drawing, and Sculpture 11. Life stories — Arts and culture — Artists

LC 2014031274

Booklist Editors' Choice, 2015; Los Angeles Times Book Prize for Biography, 2015; New York Times Notable Book, 2015.

From the author of Arshile Gorky, a major biography of the great American sculptor that redefines his legacy.

"Herrera adroitly shows that Noguchi was more than just a sculptor—he was a skilled craftsman, a heartbreaker, and a philosopher of design." —*Publishers Weekly*

Includes bibliographical references and index.

Herriot, James

★ *All Creatures Great and Small.* James Herriot. St. Martin's Press 1992. 442 p; (All creatures great and small, 1)

ISBN 9781250766342

Grades: 11 12 Adult   **B**

1. Herriot, James 1916-1995 2. Veterinarians 3. Animals 4. Human-animal relationships 5. Social life and customs 6. Yorkshire, England 7. Autobiographies and memoirs 8. Page to screen 9. Biographies 10. Family and Relationships — Pets and Owners 11. Life stories — Relationships — Pets and Owners 12. Life stories — Nature and outdoors 13. Nature writing — Animal Studies

LC 92018975

A country veterinary surgeon in Yorkshire describes the joys and trials of his profession and recalls his early career and experiences with his unique clientele.

Made into a TV series of the same name on PBS beginning in 2020.

All Things Wise and Wonderful. James Herriot. St. Martin's Paperbacks 1998. 440 p; (All creatures great and small, 3)

ISBN 9780312966553

Grades: 11 12 Adult   **B**

1. Herriot, James 1916-1995 2. Husband and wife 3. Pregnant women 4. World War II 5. Veterinarians 6. Animals 7. Human-animal relationships 8. Social life and customs 9. England 10. Yorkshire, England 11. 20th century 12. Autobiographies and memoirs 13. Page to screen 14. Biographies 15. Nature Writing — Animal Studies 16. Life stories — Relationships — Pets and Owners 17. Life stories — Nature and outdoors

LC BL 99011426

In the midst of World War II, the Yorkshire veterinarian muses on past adventures through the Yorkshire dales, visiting with old friends and introducing scores of new characters—both human and animal.

Sequel to: All Things Bright and Beautiful; Made into the TV series All Creatures Great and Small on PBS beginning in 2020; Previously published: New York : St. Martin's Press, 1977.

Every Living Thing. James Herriot. St. Martin's Press 1992. 342 p; (All creatures great and small, 5)

ISBN 9780312081881

Grades: 11 12 Adult   **B**

1. Herriot, James 1916-1995 2. Veterinarians 3. Animals 4. Human-animal relationships 5. Yorkshire, England 6. Autobiographies and memoirs 7. Biographies 8. Nature Writing — Animal Studies 9. Family and Relationships — Pets and Owners 10. Life stories — Relationships — Pets and Owners 11. Adult books for young adults 12. Life stories — Nature and outdoors

LC 92018526

The author offers readers a new collection of memoirs, describing the family and friends who share his life on the Yorkshire dales.

"Herriot regales us with additional tales of his veterinary practice in Yorkshire. He picks up his story after World War II, when medicines and treatment have improved, his children are growing up and the family moves to a new house. There are no surprises here, just the expected mix of gentle humor and compassion for animals and people alike. Herriot's many fans will not be disappointed." —*Publishers Weekly*

James Herriot's Animal Stories. with an introduction by Jim Wright; and illustrations by Lesley Holmes. St. Martin's Press 1997. xii, 142 p. : Color illustration

ISBN 9780312168742

Grades: 11 12 Adult   **B**

1. Herriot, James 1916-1995 2. Veterinarians 3. Animals 4. Domestic animals 5. Human-animal relationships 6. Yorkshire, England 7. Autobiographies and memoirs 8. Nature Writing — Animal Studies 9. Family and Relationships — Pets and Owners 10. Life stories — Relationships — Pets and Owners 11. Life stories — Nature and outdoors

LC 97013863

Ten classic tales of cats, dogs, lambs, horses, cows, and their human counterparts are presented in a collection of the late Yorkshire veterinarian's true-life stories.

Herrmann, Dorothy

Helen Keller: A Life. Dorothy Herrmann. A. Knopf 1998. xvi, 394 p. : Illustration

ISBN 9780679443544

Grades: 11 12 Adult   **B**

1. Keller, Helen, 1880-1968 2. People who are blind and deaf 3. Women 4. Biographies 5. Science Writing — Medicine and health — Disabilities and disorders 6. Life stories — Facing adversity — Medical issues — Living with disabilities

LC 98014556

A full-scale biography draws on the massive archives of Helen Keller's estate and the unpublished memoirs of Keller's teacher, Annie Sullivan, to trace Keller's transformation from a furious girl to a world-renowned figure.

"The author takes us beyond the image of Helen Keller portrayed in the Miracle Worker to unearth a passionate, politically radical woman whose inspiration and teacher, Annie Sullivan, is equally fiery and brilliant. Herrmann brings us into the every day lives of the famous pair, but the story is hardly mundane.... Herrmann gives us fascinating details via archives and unpublished memoirs to show how society's view of disabled people was greatly shaped by Keller and Sullivan." —*Library Journal*

Includes bibliographical references (p. 375-378) and index.

Hersh, Seymour M.

Reporter: A Memoir. Seymour M. Hersh. Alfred A. Knopf 2018. 355 p.

ISBN 9780307263957

Grades: Adult   **B**

1. Hersh, Seymour M, 1937- 2. Journalists 3. Investigative journalism 4. Investigative journalists 5. Journalism 6. Freedom of the press 7. Autobiographies and memoirs 8. Life stories — Arts and culture — Writing — Journalists 9. Arts and Entertainment — Writing and Publishing 10. Nonfiction that reads like fiction

LC 2017051856

The Pulitzer Prize-winning journalist and National Book Critics Circle Award-winning author presents an account of his decades-long career scooping some of the most high-impact stories of the last half century.

"Rarely has a journalist's memoir come together so well, with admirable measures of self-deprecation, transparent pride, readable prose style, and honesty." —*Kirkus*

Herzog, Werner

★ *Every Man for Himself and God Against All: A Memoir.* Werner Herzog; translated by Michael Hofmann. Penguin Press 2023. 448 p.

ISBN 9780593490297

Grades: Adult   **B**

1. Herzog, Werner, 1942- 2. Film producers and directors 3. Authors 4. Creativity 5. Influence (Literary, artistic, etc.) 6. German people 7. Western European people 8. Autobiographies and memoirs 9. Life stories — Arts and culture — Performing arts — Directors and producers 10. Arts and entertainment — Movies and television

LC 2022060530

Spanning the seven continents and encompassing both documentary and fiction, the legendary filmmaker and celebrated author reflects on his epic artistic career as he unravels and relives his most important experiences and inspirations, telling his story for the first and only time.

"Herzog in all his extravagant, perspicacious glory...Fans and neophytes alike will relish the opportunity to delve deeply into Herzog's fascinating mind." —*Kirkus*

Originally published in German as Jeder für sich und Gott gegen alle by Carl Hanser Verlag GmbH & Co. KG, München.

Hesse, Maria
★ *Frida Kahlo: An Illustrated Life.* María Hesse; translated by Achy Obejas. University of Texas Press 2018. 149 p.
ISBN 9781477317280
Grades: Adult B
1. Kahlo, Frida 2. Women artists 3. Loss 4. Suffering 5. Men-women relations 6. Creativity 7. Biographical comics 8. Biographies 9. Translations — Spanish to English 10. Life stories — Arts and culture — Artists 11. Arts and entertainment — Painting, drawing, and sculpture

Frida Kahlo by Maria Hesse offers a highly unique way of getting to know the artist by presenting her life in graphic novel form, with striking illustrations that reimagine many of Kahlo's famous paintings.

Heughan, Sam
Waypoints: My Scottish Journey. Sam Heughan. Voracious 2022. 320 p.
ISBN 9780316495530
Grades: Adult B
1. Heughan, Sam, 1980- 2. Authors 3. Actors and actresses 4. Place (Philosophy) 5. Self-discovery 6. Families 7. Friendship 8. Love 9. Life 10. Ambition 11. Scottish people 12. Britain 13. Scotland 14. Autobiographies and memoirs 15. Life stories — Arts and culture — Writing — Authors 16. Life stories — Arts and culture — Performing arts — Actors and actresses 17. Arts and Entertainment — Writing and publishing 18. Arts and Entertainment — Movies and television

Journey deep into the Highlands in the first memoir by a #1 New York Times best-selling author and star of Outlander, exploring his life and reflecting on the waypoints that define him.

"The male lead of the TV series Outlander takes us on a long Scottish hike while recounting the travails of stage and screen." —*Kirkus*

Heumann, Judith E.
Being Heumann: An Unrepentant Memoir of a Disability Rights Activist. Judith Heumann, with Kristen Joiner. Beacon Press 2019. 232 p.
ISBN 9780807019290
Grades: Adult B
1. Heumann, Judith E. 2. People with disabilities 3. Ableism 4. People with poliomyelitis 5. Physical disabilities 6. Determination 7. Women with disabilities 8. Disability rights movement 9. Social movements 10. Human rights activists 11. Teachers 12. Social advocates 13. Independence 14. Autobiographies and memoirs 15. Biographies 16. Life stories — Facing adversity — Medical issues — Living with disabilities 17. Life stories — Politics — Activists and reformers 18. Society and culture — Illness and disease 19. Society and culture — Social activism and philanthropy

LC 2019026271

An influential disability-rights activist recounts her lifelong battles for education, employment and societal inclusion, in a personal account that includes coverage of her role in advising the Carter administration to help create the Americans with Disabilities Act.

"A driving force in the passage of the Americans with Disabilities Act looks back on a long career of activism.... A welcome account of politics in action, and for the best of causes." —*Kirkus*

Includes bibliographical references and index.

Hewitt, Catherine
Renoir's Dancer: The Secret Life of Suzanne Valadon. Catherine Hewitt. St. Martin's Press 2018. 368 p.
ISBN 9781250157652
Grades: Adult B
1. Valadon, Suzanne, 1865-1938 2. Women painters 3. Artists' models 4. Illegitimacy 5. Painters 6. Biographies 7. Life stories — People in history 8. History writing — Arts and culture 9. Adult books for young adults

LC 2017041095

Describes how the illegitimate daughter of an impoverished linen maid in rural France became a famous model for Renoir and other impressionists of the era and was also a talented artist herself who refused to be confined by gender or tradition.

"A well-researched tribute to and resurrection of a master of fin de sicle art." —*Kirkus*

Includes bibliographical references and index.

Hewitt, Sean
All Down Darkness Wide: A Memoir. Sean Hewitt. Penguin Press 2022. 224 p.
ISBN 9780593300084
Grades: Adult B
1. Hewitt, Sean 2. Gay men 3. Growing up 4. Couples 5. LGBTQIA+ people 6. Self-acceptance 7. Identity 8. Homophobia 9. Mental illness 10. Depression 11. Men-men relations 12. Autobiographies and memoirs 13. Life stories — Identity — LGBTQIA+ 14. Family and Relationships — LGBTQIA+

This memoir from the acclaimed Irish poet looks at his struggles growing up gay in Catholic church and the crisis he faced when his partner develops severe mental illness and deep depression.

"A poet recounts his relationship with a man suffering from paralyzing depression....A profoundly moving meditation on queer identity, mental illness, and the fragility of life." —*Kirkus*

Heyman, Stephen
The Planter of Modern Life: Louis Bromfield and the Seeds of a Food Revolution. Stephen Heyman. W.W. Norton & Company 2020. 340 p. : Illustration
ISBN 9781324001898
Grades: Adult B
1. Bromfield, Louis, 1896-1956 2. Agriculture 3. Farm life 4. Farmers 5. Authors, American 6. Literary landmarks 7. Ohio 8. 20th century 9. Biographies 10. Life stories — Nature and outdoors 11. Science writing — General 12. Life stories — Arts and culture — Writing

LC 2019044443

IACP Cookbook Awards, Literary Food Writing, 2021.

How a literary idol of the Lost Generation launched America's organic and sustainable food movement. In interwar France, Louis Bromfield was equally famous as a writer and as a gardener. He pruned dahlias with Edith Wharton, weeded Gertrude Stein's vegetable patch, and fed the starving artists who flocked to his farmhouse outside Paris. His best-selling novels earned him a Pulitzer-and the jealousy of friends like Ernest Hemingway. But his radical approach to the soil has aged better than his books, inspiring a wave of farmers, foodies, and chefs to rethink how they should grow and consume their food. In 1938, Bromfield returned to his native Ohio, an expat novelist now reinvented as the squire of 1,000-acre Malabar Farm. Transplanting ideas from India and Europe, he created a mecca for forward- thinking agriculturalists and a rural retreat for celebrities like Humphrey Bogart and Lauren Bacall (who were married there in 1945). Bromfield's untold story is a fascinating history of people and places-and of deep-rooted concerns about the environment and its ability to sustain our most basic needs and pleasures.

Includes bibliographical references (pages 291-328) and index.

Hiaasen, Carl
The Downhill Lie: A Hacker's Return to a Ruinous Sport. Carl Hiaasen. Alfred A. Knopf 2008. 207 p.
ISBN 9780307266538
Grades: Adult B
1. Hiaasen, Carl 2. Golfers 3. Golf 4. Journalists 5. Tournaments 6. Social life and customs 7. United States 8. 21st century 9. 20th century 10. Autobiographies and memoirs 11. Biographies 12. Sports and Competition — Golf 13. Humor writing — General 14. Life stories — Sports — Athletes

A hilarious golf memoir recounts the author's return to the fairways after quitting the game in college and waiting more than thirty years and into middle

ESSENTIAL AND RECOMMENDED TITLES
Biography

age before returning to the sport, describing how he purchased a set of clubs, joined a country club, practiced for eighteen long months, and agreed to compete in a tournament against much more talented players.

Hibbert, Christopher
Edward VII: The Last Victorian King. Christopher Hibbert. Palgrave Macmillan 2007. 348 p.
ISBN 9781403983770
Grades: Adult **B**
1. Edward VII, King of Great Britain, 1841-1910 2. Monarchy 3. Rulers 4. British history 5. Great Britain 6. Edwardian era (1901-1914) 7. Biographies 8. History writing — Europe — United Kingdom 9. Life stories — Politics — Royalty 10. Life stories — Politics — Politicians

To his mother, Queen Victoria, he was 'Poor Bertie,' to his wife he was 'My dear little man,' while the President of France called him 'A great English king,' and the German Kaiser condemned him as 'An old peacock.' King Edward VII was all these things and more, as Hibbert reveals in this captivating biography. Shedding new light on the scandals that peppered his life, Hibbert reveals Edward's dismal early years under Victoria's iron rule, his terror of boredom that led to a lively social life at home and abroad, and his eventual ascent to the throne at age 59. Edward is best remembered as the last Victorian king, the monarch who installed the office of Prime Minister.

Includes bibliographical references and index; First published by J.B. Lippincott Company, 1976—T.P verso.

Hickam, Homer H.
★ *Rocket Boys: A Memoir.* Homer H. Hickam, Jr. Delacorte Press 1998. xii, 368 p.
ISBN 9780385333207
Grades: 7 8 9 10 11 12 Adult **B**
1. Hickam, Homer H, 1943- 2. Coal mining towns 3. Small town life 4. Aerospace engineers 5. Childhood 6. High school students 7. Teenage boys 8. Social life and customs 9. United States 10. 20th century 11. Autobiographies and memoirs 12. Page to screen 13. Science Writing — Space and Flight 14. Science Writing — Physics 15. Life stories — Science, technology, and medicine — Scientists and inventors

LC 98019304
Booklist Editors' Choice: Adult Books for Young Adults, 1998; New York Times Notable Book, 1998; YALSA Best Books for Young Adults, 2000; National Book Critics Circle Award for Biography finalist, 1998.

The author traces the boyhood enthusiasm for rockets that eventually led to a career at NASA, describing how he built model rockets in the family garage in West Virginia, inspired by the launch of the Soviet satellite "Sputnik."

"Even if Hickam stretched the strict truth to metamorphose his memories into Stand by Me-like material for Hollywood . . . the embellishing only converts what is a good story into an absorbing, rapidly readable one that is unsentimental but artful about adolescence, high school, and family life." —*Booklist*

Book adapted into the 1999 film October sky.

Hilburn, Robert
★ *Johnny Cash: The Life.* Robert Hilburn. Little Brown & CO 2013. 608 p.
ISBN 9780316194754
Grades: Adult **B**
1. Cash, Johnny, 1932-2003 2. Country musicians 3. Country music 4. Music history and criticism 5. United States 6. Biographies 7. Arts and Entertainment — Music — Country 8. Life stories — Arts and culture — Performing arts — Musicians and composers

LC 2013941828
ALA Notable Book, 2014.

In cooperation with the Johnny Cash estate, a noted music critic who knew the icon tells the unvarnished truth about Cash, whose personal life was far more troubled and his artistry much more profound than even his most devoted fans have realized.

"The personal knowledge aided by extensive archival research and always compelling, accessible writing make this an instant-classic music biography with something to offer all generations of listeners." —*Kirkus*

Hilfiger, Tommy
American Dreamer: My Life in Fashion & Business. Tommy Hilfiger with Peter Knobler. Ballantine Books 2016. 352 pages
ISBN 9781101886212
Grades: Adult **B**
1. Hilfiger, Tommy 2. Fashion designers 3. Fashion 4. Fashion design 5. Businesspeople 6. Success in business 7. Dysfunctional families 8. Fathers and sons 9. Marriage 10. Social life and customs 11. United States 12. 20th century 13. Autobiographies and memoirs 14. Biographies 15. Arts and Entertainment — Fashion 16. Life stories — Arts and culture — Fashion 17. Adult books for young adults

LC 2016023113
A business and pop culture icon traces the story of his life and career, discussing his working-class childhood with eight siblings, the dyslexia that challenged his education, his novel approaches to commerce, and his enduring influence on American style.

"An honest, straightforward, mostly entertaining autobiography of the man who created a classic yet hip line of clothing." —*Kirkus*

Includes index.

Hill, Clint
Five Presidents: My Extraordinary Journey with Eisenhower, Kennedy, Johnson, Nixon, and Ford. Clint Hill with Lisa McCubbin. Gallery Books 2016. 400 p.
ISBN 9781476794136
Grades: Adult **B**
1. Hill, Clint 2. Secret service 3. National security 4. Safety 5. Presidents 6. Politics and government 7. United States 8. 20th century 9. Autobiographies and memoirs 10. History writing — Presidency — 20th century — United States 11. Life stories — Politics 12. Life stories — Law and order

LC 2015050618
A former Secret Service agent reveals his experiences throughout five presidential administrations, sharing anecdotes from some of the twentieth century's most significant historical events.

"An eloquently written travelog through midcentury America from the periphery of political power." —*Library Journal*

My Travels with Mrs. Kennedy. Clint Hill and Lisa McCubbin Hill. Gallery Books 2022. 288 p.
ISBN 9781982181116
Grades: Adult **B**
1. Hill, Clint 2. Onassis, Jacqueline Kennedy, 1929-1994 3. Presidents' spouses 4. Secret service 5. Bodyguards 6. Friendship 7. Voyages and travels 8. Autobiographies and memoirs 9. Life stories — Relationships 10. Life stories — People in history 11. Life stories — Law and order

LC 2022020892
The #1 New York Times best-selling authors of Mrs. Kennedy and Me reveal never-before-told stories of Secret Service Agent Clint Hill's travels with Jacqueline Kennedy through Europe, Asia, and South America.

"Yale historian Gage (The Day Wall Street Exploded) meticulously tracks the highs and lows of Hoover's career….Nuanced, incisive, and exhaustive, this is the definitive portrait of one of 20th-century America's most consequential figures." —*Publishers Weekly*

Hill, Jemele
Uphill: A Memoir. Jemele Hill. Henry Holt & Company 2022. 240 p.
ISBN 9781250624376
Grades: Adult **B**
1. Hill, Jemele 2. African American women 3. Women journalists 4. Family relationships 5. Work 6. Success (Concept) 7. Childhood 8. Resilience 9. Ambition 10. Racism 11. Faith (Christianity) 12. Sportswriters 13. Intergenerational trauma 14. Autobiographies and memoirs 15. Life stories — Arts and culture — Writing 16. Life stories — Identity 17. Arts and Entertainment — Writing and publishing

Loan Stars Favourites, 2022.
The Emmy Award-winning former cohost of ESPN's SportsCenter, who was fired for calling President Trump "a white supremacist," shares the whole story

of her work, the women of her family and her complicated relationship with God as she forges a new path, no matter how uphill life's battles might be.

"Atlantic contributing writer Hill, who rose to fame partly due to her online conflicts with Donald Trump, recounts the ups and downs of her early life as well as her successful career at ESPN and beyond." —*Kirkus*

Hillenbrand, Laura

★ *Unbroken: A World War II Story of Survival, Resilience, and Redemption.* Laura Hillenbrand. Random House 2010. xviii, 473 p. : Illustration; Map
ISBN 9781400064168
Grades: Adult　　　　　　　　　　　　　　　　　　　　　　　B
1. Zamperini, Louis, 1917- 2. World War II 3. Prisoners of war, American 4. Post-traumatic stress disorder 5. Air warfare 6. Alcoholic men 7. World War II veterans 8. Life change events 9. Prisoners of war, Japanese 10. Military campaigns 11. Prisons 12. Military history 13. Courage 14. Pacific Area 15. California 16. Japan 17. 20th century 18. Biographies 19. Page to screen 20. Life stories — Law and order — Armed forces personnel 21. Life stories — Facing adversity — War and oppression — Hostages and POWs 22. History writing — Wars and conflicts — World War II — Pacific Theater 23. Adult books for young adults 24. Nonfiction that reads like fiction

LC 2010017517

ALA Notable Book, 2012; Indies' Choice Book Awards, Adult Nonfiction, 2011; Los Angeles Times Book Prize for Biography, 2010.

Relates the story of a U.S. airman who survived when his bomber crashed into the sea during World War II, spent forty-seven days adrift in the ocean before being rescued by the Japanese Navy, and was held as a prisoner until the end of the war.

"Hillenbrand's triumph is that in telling Louie's story . she tells the stories of thousands whose suffering has been mostly forgotten. She restores to our collective memory this tale of heroism, cruelty, life, death, joy, suffering, remorselessness, and redemption." —*Publishers Weekly*

Includes bibliographical references and index.

Hilsum, Lindsey

In Extremis: The Life and Death of the War Correspondent Marie Colvin. Lindsey Hilsum. Farrar, Straus and Giroux 2018. 400 p.
ISBN 9780374175597
Grades: Adult　　　　　　　　　　　　　　　　　　　　　　　B
1. Colvin, Marie 2. War correspondents 3. Foreign correspondents 4. Journalists 5. Women war correspondents 6. Women journalists 7. Biographies 8. Life stories — Arts and culture — Writing — Journalists 9. Adult books for young adults

LC 2018022908

Booklist Editors' Choice, 2018; James Tait Black Memorial Prize for Biography, 2018.

Describes the life and tragic death of the accomplished war correspondent, who lost an eye reporting in Sri Lanka during its civil war, interviewed Gaddafi twice, and covered conflicts in Chechnya, Kosovo and Zimbabwe in her fearless and iconoclastic style.

"Hilsum has created something truly worthy of her subject, a biography that reads like high adventure, a masterwork that will draw well-deserved attention to a heroic witness." —*Booklist*

Includes index; Originally published in 2018 by Chatto & Windus, Great Britain.

Hilton, Paris

Paris: The Memoir. Paris Hilton. Dey Street Books 2023. 416 p.
ISBN 9780063224629
Grades: Adult　　　　　　　　　　　　　　　　　　　　　　　B
1. Hilton, Paris, 1981- 2. Celebrities 3. Socialites 4. Actors and actresses 5. Secrets 6. Child abuse 7. Healing 8. Purpose in life 9. United States 10. Autobiographies and memoirs 11. Biographies 12. Life stories — Arts and culture — Performing arts — Entertainers and celebrities

In this deeply personal memoir, the ultimate It Girl shares, for the first time, the hidden history that traumatized and defined her and how she rose above a series of heart-wrenching challenges to find healing, lasting love and a life of meaning and purpose.

"One of the world's most recognizable personalities delivers a memoir with surprising depth and purpose....Delivering a master class in owning your story, Hilton shows how to live with purpose, compassion, and beauty." —*Kirkus*

Hinojosa, Maria

Once I Was You: A Memoir of Love and Hate in a Torn America. Maria Hinojosa. Atria Books 2020. 343 p.
ISBN 9781982128654
Grades: Adult　　　　　　　　　　　　　　　　　　　　　　　B
1. Hinojosa, Maria, 1961- 2. Women journalists 3. Immigrants 4. Mexican Americans 5. American dream 6. Immigration policy 7. Racism 8. Immigration prisons 9. Mass media bias 10. Immigration and emigration 11. United States 12. Autobiographies and memoirs 13. Life stories — Identity — Immigrants 14. Politics and global affairs — Immigration 15. Society and culture — Immigration 16. Life stories — Arts and culture — Writing — Journalists

Maria Hinojosa is an award-winning journalist who has collaborated with the most respected networks and is known for bringing humanity to her reporting. In this beautifully-rendered memoir, she relates the history of US immigration policy that has brought us to where we are today, as she shares her deeply personal story. Once I Was You is an urgent call to fellow Americans to open their eyes to the immigration crisis and understand that it affects us all.

"A powerful memoir that doubles as an essential immigration primer." —*Publishers Weekly*

Hinton, Anthony Ray

The Sun Does Shine: How I Found Life and Freedom on Death Row. Anthony Ray Hinton, with Lara Love Hardin; and a foreword by Bryan Stevenson. St. Martin's Press 2018. 255 pages
ISBN 9781250124715
Grades: Adult　　　　　　　　　　　　　　　　　　　　　　　B
1. Hinton, Anthony Ray 2. Judicial error 3. Death row 4. Death row prisoners 5. Trials (Murder) 6. Mistaken identity 7. Capital punishment 8. Compensation for judicial error 9. Alabama 10. Autobiographies and memoirs 11. Life stories — Facing adversity 12. Life stories — Law and order — Prisoners and inmates

LC 2017044467

Booklist Editors' Choice, 2018.

A man who spent thirty years on death row for a crime he did not commit describes how he became a victim of a flawed legal system, recounting the years he shared with fellow inmates who were eventually executed before his exoneration.

Hirono, Mazie

Heart of Fire: An Immigrant Daughter's Story. Mazie K. Hirono. Viking 2021. 416 p.
ISBN 9781984881601
Grades: Adult　　　　　　　　　　　　　　　　　　　　　　　B
1. Japanese American women 2. Lieutenant governors 3. Legislators 4. Women immigrants 5. Women legislators 6. Politics and government 7. United States 8. Hawaii 9. 20th century 10. 21st century 11. Autobiographies and memoirs 12. Life stories — Politics — Politicians 13. History writing — United States 14. History writing — Women's history

LC 2020053648

An intimate biography of the first Asian-American woman and only immigrant serving in the U.S. Senate describes her upbringing in rural Japan and Hawaii, firsthand experiences with economic insecurity and dedicated advocacy of progressive change.

"This inspiring memoir follows Hirono's personal and political life, from her childhood as an immigrant living in Hawaii to becoming the first Asian-American woman to serve in the U.S. Senate.... Hirono's story of struggles and triumph satisfies and enlightens in equal measure." —*Publishers Weekly*

Includes bibliographical references.

Hirsch, James S.

Willie Mays: The Life, the Legend. James S. Hirsch, authorized by Willie Mays. Scribner 2010. 416 p.
ISBN 9781416547907

ESSENTIAL AND RECOMMENDED TITLES
Biography

Grades: Adult **B**
1. Mays, Willie, 1931-2024 2. Professional baseball 3. African American baseball players 4. Professional baseball players 5. Baseball 6. Baseball players 7. United States 8. Biographies 9. Sports and Competition — Baseball 10. Sports and Competition — Individual Athlete 11. Life stories — Sports — Athletes
LC 2009049214
New York Times Notable Book, 2010.

A biography authorized by the baseball great offers a gripping account of Willie Mays's life, drawn from interviews with the icon, as well as friends, family members and teammates.

"This is a superb baseball book, but it's also a riveting narrative of Mays' life and times, ranging from his penchant for fancy suits to urban development in New York City to the giddy cult of celebrity. In the mid-1950s, Willie Mays was as famous as anyone in the country, gracing the cover of Time and other magazines and appearing on numerous television shows. More impressive and what distinguishes this book from the run-of-the-mill sports biography is Hirsch's extensive and cogent take on race relations and the civil-rights movement both within and outside of baseball." —*Seattle Times*

Hirsch, Paul
A Long Time Ago in a Cutting Room Far, Far Away: My Fifty Years Editing Hollywood Hits; Star Wars, Carrie, Ferris Bueller's Day Off, Mission: Impossible, and More. Paul Hirsch. Chicago Review Press Incorporated 2019. 384 pages
ISBN 9781641602556
Grades: Adult **B**
1. Hirsch, Paul, 1945- 2. Film editors 3. Film editing 4. Filmmaking 5. Films, American 6. Academy Awards (Films) 7. Film industry and trade 8. Film history and criticism 9. United States 10. Autobiographies and memoirs 11. Arts and Entertainment — Movies and Television 12. Life stories — Arts and culture — Performing arts — Directors and producers
LC 2019014536

A behind-the-scenes look at some of the most influential films of the last 50 years by Paul Hirsch, a film editor who worked on more than 40 features. Starting with his work on Carrie, Hirsch gives insight into the production process, touching upon casting, directing, cutting, and scoring. Part film-school primer, part paean to legendary directors and professionals, the funny yet insightful writing will entertain and inform aficionados and casual moviegoers alike.

Includes index.

Hirshey, Gerri
Not Pretty Enough: The Unlikely Triumph of Helen Gurley Brown. Gerri Hirshey. Sarah Crichton Books; Farrar, Straus and Giroux 2016. 336 p.
ISBN 9780374169176
Grades: Adult **B**
1. Brown, Helen Gurley 2. Periodical editors 3. Editors 4. Feminism 5. Death of fathers 6. Independence 7. Biographies 8. Life stories — Identity — Gender 9. Life stories — Arts and culture — Writing
LC 2016007143

A portrait of the famed author of "Sex and the Single Girl" examines her role in advancing civil-rights feminism and traces her rags-to-riches story, transformation of "Cosmopolitan," and relationships with such figures as Liz Smith, Gloria Vanderbilt, and Barbara Walters.

Includes bibliographical references and index.

Hirsi Ali, Ayaan
★ *Infidel*. Ayaan Hirsi Ali. Free Press 2007. xii, 353 p, 8 p. of plates : Illustration
ISBN 9780743289689
Grades: 11 12 Adult **B**
1. Hirsi Ali, Ayaan, 1969- 2. Muslim women's rights 3. Women refugees 4. Muslim women 5. Politicians 6. Women politicians 7. Muslims 8. Refugees, Somali 9. Women social advocates 10. Somalia 11. Netherlands 12. Autobiographies and memoirs 13. Life stories — Facing adversity — War and oppression — Refugees 14. Life stories — Identity — Gender 15. Society and culture — Gender — Women 16. Adult books for young adults
LC 2006049762
Amelia Bloomer List, 2008.

Ultimately a celebration of triumph over adversity, Hirsi Ali's story tells how a bright little girl evolved out of dutiful obedience to become an outspoken, pioneering freedom fighter. As Western governments struggle to balance democratic ideals with religious pressures, no story could be timelier or more significant.

"The circuitous, violence-filled path that led Ms. Hirsi Ali from Somalia to the Netherlands is the subject of Infidel, her brave, inspiring and beautifully written memoir." —*New York Times*

Hirst, Michael
Michelangelo.: The Achievement of Fame, 1475-1534. Michael Hirst. Yale University Press 2012. x, 438 p. : Illustration; Color
ISBN 9780300118612
Grades: Adult **B**
1. Michelangelo Buonarroti, 1475-1564 2. Artists 3. Art, Italian 4. Biographies 5. Life stories — Arts and culture — Artists
LC 2011042294

This first book in a two-volume history of the great artist covers his rise to prominence, an era during which her created the statue Pietà, the giant marble David, the Sistine Ceiling frescoes, the new sacristy and library for the Medici family at San Lorenzo, and the monumental tomb for Pope Julius II in Rome.

Includes bibliographical references (p. [378]-415) and index.

Hitchens, Christopher
Hitch-22: A Political Memoir. Christopher Hitchens. Twelve 2010. 256 p.
ISBN 9780446540339
Grades: Adult **920**
1. Hitchens, Christopher, 1949-2011 2. Intellectuals 3. Authors, American 4. Political journalists 5. British people in the United States 6. Immigrants 7. Political activists 8. Journalists 9. Social life and customs 10. United States 11. 21st century 12. Autobiographies and memoirs 13. Biographies 14. Arts and Entertainment — Writing and Publishing 15. Life stories — Arts and culture — Writing — Journalists
LC 2009051959
Booklist Editors' Choice, 2010; New York Times Notable Book, 2010; National Book Critics Circle Award for Autobiography/Memoir finalist.

The controversial intellectual and author shares his own life story, explaining his contradictory stances on a variety of issues.

"Few authors can rile as easily as Hitchens does, but even his detractors might find it difficult to put down a book so witty, so piercing, so spoiling for a fight. He makes you want to be as good a reader as he is a writer." —*Booklist*

Thomas Jefferson: Author of America. Christopher Hitchens. Atlas Books 2005. xiv, 188 p; (Eminent lives)
ISBN 9780060598969
Grades: 11 12 Adult **B**
1. Jefferson, Thomas, 1743-1826 2. Politicians 3. Political leadership 4. Presidents 5. Politics and government 6. United States 7. 19th century 8. Biographies 9. History writing — Presidency — 19th century — United States 10. History writing — Early America — United States 11. History writing — Colonial America — United States 12. Life stories — Politics — Politicians 13. Adult books for young adults
LC 2005296593

An analysis of the third president's politics and contributions in light of the events that were shaping the development of the United States during his time discusses the impact of the Enlightenment era, the French Revolution, and Jefferson's versatility as a public speaker and writer.

"This opinionated, lively narrative sheds light not only on Jefferson's complex personality but on the politics of his time, making it both a fascinating character study and an excellent review of early American history." —*Publishers Weekly*

Hitler, Adolf
Mein Kampf. Adolf Hitler; translated from the German by Ralph Manheim. Houghton Mifflin 2001. xxii, 694 p.
ISBN 9780395951057
Grades: 11 12 Adult **B**

1. Hitler, Adolf, 1889-1945 2. Nazis 3. Right-wing extremists 4. Nazism 5. Politics and government 6. Germany 7. 20th century 8. Autobiographies and memoirs 9. Translations — German to English 10. Life stories — Politics — Politicians 11. History writing — Europe — Germany

LC 2001051609

A compilation of Hitler's most famous prison writings of 1923—the bible of National Socialism and the blueprint for the Third Reich.

A Mariner book; Originally published: Boston : Houghton Mifflin, 1943. With new introd.

Hoban, Phoebe

Alice Neel: The Art of Not Sitting Pretty. Phoebe Hoban. St. Martin's Press 2010. 416 p.

ISBN 9780312607487

Grades: 11 12 Adult **B**

1. Neel, Alice, 1900-1984 2. Women artists 3. Gender role 4. Portrait painting 5. Portrait painters 6. Artists 7. Biographies 8. Arts and Entertainment — Painting, Drawing, and Sculpture 9. Life stories — Arts and culture — Artists

LC 2010035781

Booklist Editors' Choice, 2010.

Documents the life of the leading 20th-century artist from her turn-of-the-century upbringing and education at the Philadelphia School of Design for Women to the development of her controversial political views and the role of the feminist movement in enabling her recognition.

Hobbs, Jeff

★ *The Short and Tragic Life of Robert Peace: A Brilliant Young Man Who Left Newark for the Ivy League but Did Not Survive.* Jeff Hobbs. Scribner 2014. 384 pages

ISBN 9781476731902

Grades: Adult **B**

1. Peace, Robert, 1980-2010 2. Hobbs, Jeff, 1980- 3. Street life 4. Working class African Americans 5. African American college students 6. College students 7. African American men 8. Communities 9. Violence 10. Newark, New Jersey 11. New Haven, Connecticut 12. Biographies 13. Life stories — Facing adversity — Personal transformation 14. Society and culture — Race 15. Society and culture — Urban and regional studies 16. Adult books for young adults

LC 2014001213

Booklist Editors' Choice, 2014; Booklist Editors' Choice: Adult Books for Young Adults, 2014; Los Angeles Times Book Prize for Current Interest, 2014; New York Times Notable Book, 2014.

Presents the life of Robert Peace, an African American who became a brilliant biochemistry student at Yale University, but after graduation lived as drug dealer and was brutally murdered at the age of thirty.

"Writing with novelistic detail and deep insight, Hobbs, who was Peace's roommate at Yale, registers the disadvantages his friend faced while avoiding hackneyed fatalism and sociology. Hobbs reveals a man whose singular experience and charisma made him simultaneously an outsider and a leader in both New Haven and Newark." —*Publishers Weekly*

Hochschild, Adam

Rebel Cinderella: From Rags to Riches to Radical, the Epic Journey of Rose Pastor Stokes. Adam Hochschild. Houghton Mifflin Harcourt 2020. 304 p.

ISBN 9781328866745

Grades: Adult **B**

1. Stokes, Rose Pastor, 1879-1933 2. Feminists 3. Women socialists 4. Women political activists 5. Protests, demonstrations, vigils, etc. 6. Refugees, Jewish 7. Women immigrants 8. Progressivism (United States politics) 9. Politics and government 10. United States history 11. New York City 12. United States 13. 20th century 14. Biographies 15. Life stories — Politics — Activists and reformers 16. History writing — Presidency — 20th century — United States 17. History writing — Women's history

LC 2019027932

From the bestselling author of King Leopold's Ghost and Spain in Our Hearts comes the astonishing but forgotten story of an immigrant sweatshop worker who married an heir to a great American fortune and became one of the most charismatic radical leadersof her time.

"Hochschild's captivating and fast-paced biography is a true delight and an excellent addition to women's history shelves." —*Booklist*

Includes bibliographical references and index.

Hodgman, John

Medallion Status: True Stories from Secret Rooms. John Hodgman. Viking 2019. 304 p.

ISBN 9780525561101

Grades: Adult **B**

1. Hodgman, John 2. Fame 3. Authors, American 4. Podcasters 5. Fathers and sons 6. Television personalities 7. Air travel 8. Essays 9. Autobiographies and memoirs 10. Life stories — Arts and culture — Writing

LC 2019024340

The "Judge John Hodgman" podcaster and best-selling author of Vacationland reflects on his unlikely career, the surreal dynamics of moderate fame, the cancellation of his television job and his relationship with his young son.

Vacationland: True Stories from Painful Beaches. John Hodgman. Viking Press 2017. 288 p.

ISBN 9780735224803

Grades: Adult **B**

1. Hodgman, John 2. Voyages and travels 3. Personal conduct 4. Essays 5. Autobiographies and memoirs 6. Life stories — Arts and culture — Writing

LC 2017031760

A memoir of the author's cursed travels through the woods of Massachusetts and coastal Maine, describing his midlife transformation from an idealistic youth to an eccentric family man and his observations on such subjects as the horror of freshwater clams and the evolutionary purpose of the mustache.

"Hodgman is a disarmingly witty storyteller, at once waggish and incisive, droll and tender. Indeed, deep feelings flow beneath the mirth." —*Booklist*

Hoffman, Adina

★ *My Happiness Bears No Relation to Happiness: A Poet's Life in the Palestinian Century.* Adina Hoffman. Yale University Press 2009. VII, 454 p. : Illustration; Map

ISBN 9780300141504

Grades: Adult **B**

1. Ali, Taha Muhammad 2. Poetry writing 3. Israeli-Palestinian relations 4. Arab people 5. Social life and customs 6. Israel 7. Palestine 8. Biographies 9. Arts and Entertainment — Writing and Publishing 10. Life stories — Arts and culture — Writing — Authors 11. Life stories — Arts and culture — Writing — Poets 12. Arts and Entertainment — Writing and Publishing — Literary criticism

LC 2008037298

From the Publisher: Beautifully written, and composed with a novelist's eye for detail, this book tells the story of an exceptional man and the culture from which he emerged. Taha Muhammad Ali was born in 1931 in the Galilee village of Saffuriyya and was forced to flee during the war in 1948. He traveled on foot to Lebanon and returned a year later to find his village destroyed. An autodidact, he has since run a souvenir shop in Nazareth, at the same time evolving into what National Book Critics Circle Award-winner Eliot Weinberger has dubbed "perhaps the most accessible and delightful poet alive today." as it places Muhammad Ali's life in the context of the lives of his predecessors and peers, My Happiness offers a sweeping depiction of a charged and fateful epoch. It is a work that Arabic scholar Michael Sells describes as "among the five 'Must read' books on the Israel-Palestine tragedy." in an era when talk of the "Clash of Civilizations" dominates, this biography offers something else entirely: a view of the people and culture of the Middle East that is rich, nuanced, and, above all else, deeply human.

"An exceptional introduction to a literary world that has, until now, been little known to English-language readers, this is highly recommended for all libraries." —*Library Journal*

Includes bibliographical references (p. 409-441) and index.

Hoffman, David E.

Give Me Liberty: The True Story of Oswaldo Paya and His Daring Quest for a Free Cuba. David E. Hoffman. Simon & Schuster 2022. 544 p.

ESSENTIAL AND RECOMMENDED TITLES
Biography

ISBN 9781982191191
Grades: Adult   B
1. Paya, Oswaldo, 1952-2012 2. Democracy 3. Communism 4. Freedom 5. Social advocates 6. Protests, demonstrations, vigils, etc. 7. Catholics 8. National liberation movements 9. Politics and government 10. Cuba 11. 20th century 12. Biographies 13. Life stories — Politics 14. History writing — Latin America — Cuba 15. Nonfiction that reads like fiction

A Pulitzer Prize-winning Washington Post reporter looks at the life of Oswaldo Payâa, a dissident Cuban who defied Fidel Castro, formed a pro-democracy movement and inspired thousands of Cubans to resist Communist rule.

"Hoffman profiles a lesser-known but fascinating figure from the Castro era, Oswaldo Payá, who grew up under Castro's rule but devoted his life to working within Cuba for freedom and human rights." —*Booklist*

Hogan, Linda
The Woman Who Watches Over the World: A Native Memoir. Linda Hogan. W.W. Norton 2001. 207 p.
ISBN 9780393050189
Grades: Adult   B
1. Hogan, Linda 2. Chickasaw (North American people) 3. Indigenous authors 4. Indigenous women 5. Indigenous peoples of North America 6. Authors, American 7. Family relationships 8. Self-acceptance 9. 20th century 10. Biographies 11. Arts and Entertainment — Writing and Publishing 12. Life stories — Arts and culture — Writing — Authors 13. Adult books for young adults
LC 00049005

Booklist Editors' Choice, 2001; Booklist Editors' Choice: Adult Books for Young Adults, 2001.

A Chickasaw woman blends her personal history of struggle with the stories of native women who participated in key events during the Indian Wars more than a century ago.

"In this memoir the author ... expresses a lacerating yet crucial vision of the tragic legacies of the U.S. government's brutal war on Native Americans." —*Booklist*

Hoja, Gulchehra
A Stone Is Most Precious Where It Belongs: A Memoir of Uyghur Exile, Hope, and Survival. Gulchehra Hoja. Hachette Books 2023. 336 p.
ISBN 9780306828843
Grades: Adult   B
1. Hoja, Gulchehra 2. Uighur (Turkic people) 3. Women journalists 4. Muslim families 5. Communities 6. Expatriates 7. Marginalized people 8. Disappeared people 9. Injustice 10. Social control 11. Political persecution 12. Social advocacy 13. East Asian people 14. Chinese people 15. North American people 16. American people 17. XInjiang, China 18. China 19. Autobiographies and memoirs 20. Life stories — Facing adversity — War and oppression 21. Life stories — Identity — Race and ethnicity 22. Society and culture — Ethnic studies

In February 2018, twenty-four members of Gulchehra Hoja's family disappeared overnight. In one evening, all those she had left behind in Ürümchi when she fled to a new life in the United States were arrested because of her. Her crime ? and thus that of her family ? was her award-winning investigations for Radio Free Asia on the plight of the Uyghur people. Revealing the beauty of East Turkistan and its people ? its music, its culture, its heritage, and above all its emphasis on community and family, a Stone is Most Precious Where it Belongs gives us a glimpse beyond what the Chinese state wants us to see.

In this moving, deeply personal account of a family's collective anguish, Hoja, a reporter for Radio Free Asia, re-creates in intimate detail her life story within the tight Uyghur community and their ultimate persecution and imprisonment in 'Reeducation camps.' —*Kirkus*

Holloway, Kris
Monique and the Mango Rains: Two Years with a Midwife in Mali. Kris Holloway; John Bidwell, consulting editor. Waveland Press 2007. xiii, 212 p, 8 p. of plates : Illustration; Map; Portrait
ISBN 9781577664352
Grades: Adult   B
1. Dembele, Monique 2. Midwives 3. Midwifery 4. Maternal health services 5. Mali 6. Autobiographies and memoirs 7. Life stories — Science, technology, and medicine — Healthcare professionals 8. Life stories — Relationships — Friendship 9. Family and Relationships — Friendship 10. Politics and global affairs — World politics — Africa

"This memoir recalls the two years Holloway spent as an impressionable Peace Corps volunteer in the remote village of Nampossela in Mali, West Africa. It centers on her close friendship with Monique [Dembele], the village's overburdened midwife. Holloway's moving account vividly presents the tragic consequences of inadequate prenatal and infant health care in the developing world and will interest all those concerned about the realities of women's lives outside the industrialized world." —*Publishers Weekly*

Includes bibliographical references (p. [209]-212).

Holton, Woody
Abigail Adams: A Life. Woody Holton. Free Press 2009. 512 p.
ISBN 9781416546801
Grades: 10 11 12 Adult   B
1. Adams, Abigail, 1744-1818 2. Adams, John, 1735-1826 3. Women and politics 4. Husband and wife 5. Presidents' spouses 6. Independence 7. United States history 8. United States 9. 18th century 10. Biographies 11. Life stories — Politics — Politicians 12. History writing — Early America — United States 13. History writing — Women's history
LC 2009016288

A narrative based on previously un-mined documents reveals that the popular "Founding Mother" was willing to disagree with her husband, shrewd when investing the family fortune, and eager to correspond about men's subjugation of women.

Includes bibliographical references and index.

Holzer, Harold
Monument Man: The Life and Art of Daniel Chester French. Harold Holzer. Princeton Architectural Press 2019. 268 p.
ISBN 9781616897536
Grades: Adult   B
1. French, Daniel Chester, 1850-1931 2. Artists 3. Sculptors 4. Memorials 5. Lincoln Memorial, Washington, D.C. 6. National characteristics, American 7. Buildings 8. Washington, D.C. 9. United States 10. 19th century 11. Biographies 12. Life stories — Arts and culture — Artists 13. History writing — United States 14. Arts and Entertainment — Architecture 15. Arts and Entertainment — Painting, Drawing, and Sculpture
LC 2018007925

The first comprehensive biography of Daniel Chester French, the preeminent artist who created the statue for the Lincoln Memorial among other renowned works, is filled with rich detail and archival photos and coincides with the 50th anniversary of the opening of his country home/Studio to the public and a major renovation of the Lincoln Memorial.

"This beautifully written, impeccably researched biography does much to resuscitate French's substantial contributions to American art." —*Kirkus*

Honnold, Alex
Alone on the Wall. Alex Honnold, with David Roberts. W. W. Norton & Company 2015. VIII, 248 pages, 16 unnumbered pages of plates : Color; Illustration
ISBN 9780393247626
Grades: Adult   B
1. Honnold, Alex 2. Rock climbing 3. Rock climbers 4. Autobiographies and memoirs 5. Life stories — Sports — Athletes 6. Sports and competition — Mountaineering

The extreme climber famed for his solo ascents without ropes, partners or gear describes his seven most significant achievements, including a free-solo climb up Mexico's Sendero Luminoso and the Fitz Traverse ascent in Patagonia.

hooks, bell
Wounds of Passion: A Writing Life. Bell hooks. H. Holt 1997. xxiii, 260 p.
ISBN 9780805041460
Grades: 11 12 Adult   B

PUBLIC LIBRARY CORE COLLECTION: NONFICTION
Twentieth Edition

1. hooks, bell, 1952-2021 2. Women authors, American 3. Feminism 4. Writing 5. African Americans 6. African American women 7. Feminists 8. Self-acceptance 9. Autobiographies and memoirs 10. Arts and Entertainment — Writing and Publishing 11. Life stories — Arts and culture — Writing — Authors.

LC 97023506

A powerful memoir tells how one woman writer found her own voice while creating a personal love relationship based on feminist thinking and reflects on the impact of birth control and the women's movement on society.

"In this continuation of the author's autobiography, Hooks chronicles her rigorous education, both in a long, complicated relationship with a fellow writer and as a college and graduate student, experiences that led her away from poetry (her first literary love) to groundbreaking prose that expressed her feminist convictions and views on the status of Black women in America." —*Booklist*

Sequel to: Bone Black.

Hope, Bradley
Blood and Oil: Mohammed Bin Salman's Ruthless Quest for Global Power. Bradley Hope and Justin Scheck. Hachette Books 2020. xvii, 346 p.

ISBN 9780306846663

Grades: Adult   **B**

1. AL Sa'ud, Muhammad bin Salman bin Abd al-Aziz, Crown Prince of Saudi Arabia, 1985- 2. AL Sa'ud, House of 3. Princes 4. Royal houses 5. Wealth 6. Ambition 7. Corruption 8. Social control 9. Oil industry and trade 10. International relations 11. Politics and government 12. Saudi Arabia 13. 21st century 14. Biographies 15. Life stories — Politics — Royalty 16. Politics and global affairs — Political figures 17. Politics and global affairs — World politics — Southwest Asia and North Africa (Middle East)

LC 2020015477

A revelatory look at the inner workings of the world's most powerful ruling family, the royal family of Saudi Arabia, revealing how a rift within that family produced Crown Prince Mohammed bin Salman, aka MBS, a charismatic leader with charm, ambition, and a ruthless streak.

"A thorough delineation of the rapacious, ambitious new economic plan for Saudi Arabia by the heir apparent to the throne, Mohammed bin Salman.... An excellent work of impressive research on a dangerous world leader." —*Kirkus*

Includes bibliographical references.

Hopkins, Jerry
No One Here Gets Out Alive. by Jerry Hopkins and Danny Sugerman. Warner Books 2006. xvi, 365 p. : Illustration

ISBN 9780446697330

Grades: Adult   **B**

1. Morrison, Jim, 1943-1971 2. Rock musicians 3. United States 4. Biographies 5. Arts and Entertainment — Music — Rock 6. Life stories — Arts and culture — Performing arts — Musicians and composers

LC 2005932572

A portrait of Jim Morrison is based on seven years of research and tells the story behind his musical genius, worship of darkness, rejection of all forms of authority, and tragic death when his life spun out of control, in a new edition of the compelling biography honoring the thirty-fifth anniversary of the singer's death. Reprint.

Discography: P. [361]-364; Filmography: P. 364; Includes bibliographical references (p. 365).

Hopwood, Shon
Law Man: My Story of Robbing Banks, Winning Supreme Court Cases, and Finding Redemption. Shon Hopwood with Dennis Burke. Crown Trade 2012. 320 p.

ISBN 9780307887832

Grades: Adult   **B**

1. Lawyers 2. Redemption 3. Prison libraries 4. Former convicts 5. Bank robberies 6. Nebraska 7. Autobiographies and memoirs 8. Life stories — Law and order — Criminals and law-breakers

LC 2011035313

Traces how the author, a local basketball star and son of church organizers, returned from the Navy with few prospects before committing five bank robberies and being sentenced to years in prison, describing how he rallied with the support of family and friends and learned savvy legal skills before building a promising life as a free man.

"Hopwood's prison memoir and long journey back into society are told with brutal and riveting honesty." —*Library Journal*

Horace, Matthew
The Black and the Blue: A Cop Reveals the Crimes, Racism, and Injustice in America's Law Enforcement. Matthew Horace, Ron Harris. Hachette Books 2018. 256 p.

ISBN 9780316440080

Grades: Adult   **B**

1. Police 2. Racism 3. Racism in law enforcement 4. Prejudice 5. Police brutality 6. Law enforcement 7. African American police 8. Racism in the judicial system 9. Race relations 10. United States 11. Autobiographies and memoirs 12. Life stories — Law and order — Police and law officers 13. Society and culture — Violence and crime — Criminal justice system 14. Society and culture — Race 15. Antiracist literature

LC Bl2018108105

A CNN contributor, and former law-enforcement himself, offers a personal account of the racism, crimes and color lines that challenge America's law enforcement, sharing insights into high-profile cases, the Black Lives Matter movement and what is needed for change.

"An astute, unvarnished account that should stand out from the crowd of pro- and anti-law enforcement books." —*Kirkus*

Horn, Jonathan
Washington's End: The Final Years and Forgotten Struggle. Jonathan Horn. Scribner 2020. 384 p.

ISBN 9781501154232

Grades: Adult   **B**

1. Washington, George, 1732-1799 2. Retirement 3. Command of troops 4. Diplomacy 5. Debt 6. Political parties 7. Presidents 8. Politics and government 9. United States 10. 18th century 11. Early America (1784-1819) 12. Biographies 13. Impartial writing 14. History writing — Presidency — 18th century — United States 15. History writing — Early America — United States 16. Life stories — Politics — Politicians

LC Bl2020000195

Historian and former White House speechwriter Jonathan Horn tells the astonishing true story of George Washington's forgotten last years—the personalities, plotting, and private torment that unraveled America's first post-presidency. Horn reveals that the quest to surrender power proved more difficult than Washington imagined and brought his life to an end he never expected. The statesman who had staked his legacy on withdrawing from public life would feud with his successors and find himself drawn back into military command. The patriarch who had dedicated his life to uniting his country would leave his name to a new capital city destined to become synonymous with political divisions.

"An outstanding biographical work on one of America's most prominent leaders. Highly recommended for those who want to better understand the early republic." —*Library Journal*

Includes bibliographical references and index.

Horn, Miriam
Rancher, Farmer, Fisherman: Conservation Heroes of the American Heartland. Miriam Horn. W W Norton & Co. 2016. 384 p.

ISBN 9780393247343

Grades: Adult   **B**

1. Environmental protection 2. Environmentalists 3. Ranchers 4. Farmers 5. Fishers 6. Nature writing — Environmental issues

LC 2016018263

Green Prize for Sustainable Literature: Adult Nonfiction, 2017.

Traces the lesser-known, large-scale conservation movement by ranchers, farmers, river workers and fishermen who in spite of separating themselves from political environmentalism are helping to restore and protect America's grasslands, wildlife, wetlands and oceans.

ESSENTIAL AND RECOMMENDED TITLES
Biography

Hornbacher, Marya
Wasted: A Memoir of Anorexia and Bulimia. Marya Hornbacher. Harper Perennial 2014. 298 p.
ISBN 9780062327031
Grades: 11 12 Adult **B**
1. Hornbacher, Marya, 1974- 2. People with anorexia 3. Anorexia nervosa 4. Eating disorders 5. Bulimia 6. Social life and customs 7. OCD 8. United States 9. 20th century 10. Autobiographies and memoirs 11. Science Writing — Medicine and health — Addiction 12. Life stories — Facing adversity — Medical issues — Addiction 13. Adult books for young adults
LC BL 99000897

The author shares her lifelong battle with bulimia and anorexia, chronicling her secret life of bingeing and purging and her obsession with food and body image, substance abuse, and sex.

"This is a gritty, unflinching look at eating disorders. Hornbacher is at her best when she zeroes in on the specifics of eating disorders and their origins." —*New York Times Book Review*

Includes bibliographical references (p. [291]-296); Originally published: New York : HarperCollins, 1998.

Horton, Michelle
Dear Sister: A Memoir of Secrets, Survival, and Unbreakable Bonds. Michelle Horton. Grand Central Publishing 2024. 320 p.
ISBN 9781538757154
Grades: Adult **B**
1. Addimando, Nikki 2. Horton, Michelle 3. Sisters 4. Abused women 5. Family violence 6. Secrets 7. Murder 8. Women prisoners 9. Parent-separated children 10. Criminal justice system 11. Familial love 12. North American people 13. American people 14. Autobiographies and memoirs 15. Life stories — Facing adversity — Abuse survivors 16. Life stories — Relationships — Family 17. Family and Relationships — Abuse 18. Society and culture — Gender — Women 19. Society and culture — Violence and crime — Criminal justice system 20. Debut title
LC 2023036406

A breathtaking memoir about two sisters and a high-profile case: Nikki Addimando, incarcerated for killing her abuser; and the author, Michelle Horton, left in the devastating fall-out to raise Nikki's young children and to battle the criminal justice system.

"Horton pulls back the curtain on domestic abuse in a shocking, true story of her sister Nikki Addimando, who shot her partner after enduring years of cruelty at his hands." —*Booklist*

Hough, Lauren
Leaving Isn't the Hardest Thing: Essays. Lauren Hough. Vintage Books 2021. 320 p.
ISBN 9780593080764
Grades: Adult **B**
1. Hough, Lauren, 1977- 2. LGBTQIA+ people 3. Cult members 4. Survival 5. Childhood 6. Identity 7. Cults 8. Essays 9. Autobiographies and memoirs 10. Life stories — Identity — LGBTQIA+ 11. Life stories — Facing adversity
LC 2020055114

The author, who has had many identities—an airman in the U.S. Air Force, a cable guy, a bouncer at a gay club—recounts her childhood growing up in the infamous cult the Children of God, in this searing and extremely personal collection of essays.

"In a series of personal essays, Hough details her life's traumatic experiences, addressing subjects such as poverty, mental illness, class, and sexism.... A page-turning account of belonging and not belonging, and what it means to start over." —*Library Journal*

Howard, Johnette
The Rivals: Chris Evert vs. Martina Navratilova : Their Epic Duels and Extraordinary Friendship. Johnette Howard. Broadway Books 2005. 296 p. : Illustration
ISBN 9780767918848
Grades: 11 12 Adult **B**
1. Evert, Chris, 1955- 2. Navratilova, Martina, 1956- 3. Sports rivalry 4. Women tennis players 5. Women 6. Lesbian athletes 7. Tennis players 8. Sexuality 9. Social life and customs 10. Competition 11. United States 12. 20th century 13. Biographies 14. Sports and Competition — Tennis 15. Sports and Competition — Rivalry 16. Adult books for young adults
LC 2004061918

Follows the careers of tennis greats Chris Evert and Martina Navratilova, from their first match in 1973 through the dramatic changes that occurred in the world of sports and society.

"This work makes a fine contribution to the history of women in sports." —*Publishers Weekly*

Howard, Ron
★ *The Boys: A Memoir of Hollywood and Family.* Ron Howard and Clint Howard. HarperCollins 2021. 320 p.
ISBN 9780063065246
Grades: Adult **B**
1. Howard, Ron, 1954- 2. Howard, Clint, 1959- 3. Growing up 4. Brothers 5. Former child actors and actresses 6. Fame 7. Filmmakers 8. Actors and actresses 9. Collective autobiographies and memoirs 10. Life stories — Arts and culture — Performing arts — Actors and actresses 11. Arts and Entertainment — Movies and Television 12. Family and Relationships — Siblings 13. Life stories — Relationships — Growing up

By turns confessional, nostalgic, heartwarming and harrowing, the award-winning filmmaker and his brother, an audience-favorite actor, share their unusual family story of navigating and surviving life as sibling child actors.

"Actors and brothers Ron and Clint Howard reflect on growing up in Hollywood in this fascinating dual autobiography.... Candid, humorous, and entertaining, this intimate account will be a hit with the brothers' fans." —*Publishers Weekly*

Howe, Ben Ryder
My Korean Deli: Risking It All for a Convenience Store. Ben Ryder Howe. Henry Holt and Co. 2010. 320 p.
ISBN 9780805093438
Grades: Adult **B**
1. Howe, Ben Ryder 2. Editors 3. Supplementary employment 4. Delicatessens 5. Culture conflict 6. Family businesses 7. Entrepreneurs 8. Convenience stores 9. Korean Americans 10. Businesspeople 11. East Asian Americans 12. Social life and customs 13. New York City 14. Brooklyn, New York City 15. Autobiographies and memoirs 16. Life stories — Business — Working life 17. Life stories — Relationships — Family 18. Family and Relationships — Families
LC 2010024962

A former senior editor of "The Paris Review" recounts his participation in a family effort to buy and run a Korean convenience store for his in-laws, a pursuit that raised issues about work and family while he shuttled between two divergent cultural arenas.

"The author's wife Gab bought (with the money the couple had saved for a down payment on their first house) her hardworking Korean parents a deli in Brooklyn as a gesture of thanks for all their self-sacrifice. What follows is a series of both comic and tragic vignettes that will leave the reader as surprised as the author about how emotionally invested you can get in a deli. [Howe] delivers a smartly written narrative about love, literature, and the lengths one goes to for family, which turns out to be epically far." —*Maclean's*

Howell, Georgina
Gertrude Bell: Queen of the Desert, Shaper of Nations. Georgina Howell. Farrar, Straus and Giroux 2007. xix, 481 p, 16 p. of plates : Illustration; Map
ISBN 9780374161620
Grades: 11 12 Adult **B**
1. Bell, Gertrude Lowthian, 1868-1926 2. Women travelers 3. Women archaeologists 4. Colonial administrators 5. Southwest Asia and North Africa (Middle East) history 6. 20th century 7. Biographies 8. History writing — Women's history 9. Life stories — People in history 10. History writing — Southwest Asia and North Africa (Middle East)
LC 2006029994

ALA Notable Book, 2008.

An account of the adventure-filled life of Gertrude Bell describes how a woman transcended the restrictions of her gender, class, and era to become a renowned world traveler, archaeologist, spy, Arabist, linguist, author, poet, photographer, and mountaineer, and played a key role in the history of the Middle East.

"Bell's role in the creation of Iraq and the placement of Faisal upon the throne, is fully detailed.... But the strength and delight of Howell's superb biography is in the fullness with which Bell's character is drawn." —*Publishers Weekly*

Originally published in 2006 by Macmillan, Great Britain, as Daugher of the desert—T.P. verso; Includes bibliographical references (p. [453]-460) and index.

Hsu, Hua

★ *Stay True: A Memoir.* Hua Hsu. Doubleday 2022. 204 p.
ISBN 9780385547772
Grades: Adult   B

1. Hsu, Hua, 1977- 2. Ishida, Kenneth N, 1977-1998 3. Taiwanese Americans 4. Japanese Americans 5. Male friendship 6. College students 7. Children of immigrants 8. Assimilation (Sociology) 9. Growing up 10. Popular culture 11. Murder victims 12. Loss 13. East Asian Americans 14. San Francisco Bay Area 15. 1990s 16. Autobiographies and memoirs 17. Life stories — Relationships — Friendship 18. Life stories — Identity — Race and ethnicity 19. Life stories — Facing adversity — Victims of crime 20. Life stories — Facing adversity — Coping with death

LC 2021055618

National Book Critics Circle Award for Autobiography, 2022; Pulitzer Prize for Memoir or Autobiography, 2023.

A New Yorker staff writer, in this gripping memoir on friendship, grief, the search for self and the solace that can be found through art, recounts his close friendship with Ken, with whom he endured the successes and humiliations of everyday college life until Ken was violently, senselessly taken away from him.

"This memoir is masterfully structured and exquisitely written. Hsu's voice shimmers with tenderness and vulnerability as he meticulously reconstructs his memories of a nurturing, compassionate friendship. The protagonists' Asian American identities are nuanced, never serving as the defining element of the story, and the author creates a cast of gorgeously balanced characters." —*Kirkus*

Huang, Eddie

Fresh off the Boat: A Memoir. Eddie Huang. Spiegel & Grau 2013. 240 p.
ISBN 9780679644880
Grades: Adult   B

1. Huang, Eddie, 1982- 2. Restaurateurs 3. Taiwanese Americans 4. Ethnic identity 5. Race relations 6. Cooking 7. East Asian Americans 8. Autobiographies and memoirs 9. Page to screen 10. Food writing — Memoirs and biographies 11. Life stories — Arts and culture — Culinary arts 12. Life stories — Identity — Immigrants 13. Adult books for young adults

LC 2012025704

A Taiwanese-American rebel restauranteur chronicles his rise to success from his difficult childhood in the American South to his turn as a drug dealer who embraced rap culture and more.

Huang, Yunte

Daughter of the Dragon: Anna May Wong's Rendezvous with American History. Yunte Huang. Liveright Publishing Corporation 2023. 384 p.
ISBN 9781631495809
Grades: Adult   B

1. Wong, Anna May, 1905-1961 2. Chinese Americans 3. Actors and actresses 4. Xenophobia 5. East Asian Americans 6. Films 7. Sexism 8. United States 9. 20th century 10. Biographies 11. Life stories — Identity — Race and ethnicity 12. Life stories — Arts and culture — Performing arts — Actors and actresses 13. Arts and Entertainment — Movies and television 14. History Writing — Women's history 15. History Writing — United States

National Book Critics Circle Award for Biography finalist, 2023.

The story of Anna May Wong, who fought virulent anti-Chinese xenophobia, unabashed sexism, cinematic exploitation and ageism that defined American culture in the 20th century to became Hollywood's first Chinese American film star.

"Huang's lively, surprising, and all-encompassing biography of Anna May Wong should be on everyone's...reading list. A must for libraries with strong film and pop culture collections." —*Library Journal*

Hubbard, Ben (Journalist)

Mbs: The Rise to Power of Mohammed Bin Salman. Ben Hubbard. Tim Duggan Books 2020. 359 p.
ISBN 9781984823823
Grades: Adult   B

1. Mohammed Bin Salman, Crown Prince of Saudi Arabia, 1985- 2. AL Sa'ud, House of 3. Princes 4. Assassination 5. Inheritance and succession 6. Authoritarianism 7. Geopolitics 8. Dictators 9. Dictatorship 10. Power 11. Politics and government 12. Ambition 13. Saudi Arabia 14. 21st century 15. Biographies 16. History writing — Nationalism — Southwest Asia and North Africa (Middle East) 17. Life stories — Politics — Royalty

LC Bl2020006712

Examines the effect Mohammed bin Salman has had since his father King Salman took the throne in Saudia Arabia, using his influence to restructure the economy, confront enemies, and ease the strict Islamic social codes within the kingdom.

"This account is, by far, the best characterization of this mercurial leader, along with his varied alliances and how he came to develop them ... an important and keen assessment of the Saudi Crown Prince that should be on every bookshelf." —*Library Journal*

Hudes, Quiara Alegria

★ *My Broken Language: A Memoir.* Quiara Alegria Hudes. One World 2021. 320 p.
ISBN 9780399590047
Grades: Adult   B

1. Hudes, Quiara Alegria 2. Hispanic American women 3. Multiracial women 4. Language and culture 5. Women playwrights 6. Home (concept) 7. Memory 8. Belonging 9. Families 10. Identity 11. Childhood 12. Playwrights 13. Communities 14. United States 15. Philadelphia, Pennsylvania 16. Autobiographies and memoirs 17. Life stories — Identity — Race and ethnicity 18. Life stories — Arts and culture — Performing arts 19. Life stories — Arts and culture — Writing 20. Arts and Entertainment — Theater 21. Book club best bets

LC 2020037277

A Pulitzer Prize-winning playwright shares her lyrical coming-of-age story against a backdrop of her devastated barrio home and the idiosyncratic, troubled and fiercely loving Puerto Rican family that inspired her literary voice.

"Pulitzer Prize-winning playwright Hudes (Water by the Spoonful) delivers a love letter to her Puerto Rican heritage in her astonishing debut memoir.... This heartfelt, glorious exploration of identity and authorship will be a welcome addition to the literature of Latinx lives." —*Publishers Weekly*

Huffman, Alan

Here I Am: The Story of Tim Hetherington, War Photographer. Alan Huffman. Grove Press 2013. 256 p.
ISBN 9780802120908
Grades: Adult   B

1. Hetherington, Tim 2. Photographers 3. Photojournalists 4. War correspondents 5. Civil war 6. Southwest Asia and North Africa (Middle East) history 7. African history 8. Libya 9. Liberia 10. 21st century 11. 20th century 12. Biographies 13. Arts and Entertainment — Photography 14. Life stories — Arts and culture — Writing — Journalists

LC Bl2012046677

Traces the life and career of the award-winning photojournalist whose life was ended in 2011 by a mortar blast while he was covering the Libyan Civil War, honoring his advocacy on behalf of countless war victims while tracing how his achievements reflected the realities of 21st-century war reporting.

ESSENTIAL AND RECOMMENDED TITLES
Biography

Hughes, Bettany
★ *The Hemlock Cup: Socrates, Athens, and the Search for the Good Life.* by Bettany Hughes. A.A. Knopf 2011. 384 p.
ISBN 9781400041794
Grades: 11 12 Adult   **B**
1. Socrates, 469-399 B.C.E 2. Philosophers 3. Ancient philosophers 4. Intellectual life 5. Athens, Greece 6. Ancient Greece 7. Biographies 8. History writing — Ancient — Greece 9. Life stories — Education — Philosophers
LC 2010045486

A dual portrait of the classical philosopher and fifth-century B.C. Athens draws on the latest sources to offer insight into the period's daily realities and elements ranging from the gymnasia and the red-light district to the battlefields and the teeming Agora where Socrates frequently spoke and was condemned to death. By the author of Helen of Troy.

"For decades, while his city underwent war and hardship and defeat and civil war and political restructuring, Socrates settled himself in the agora and talked of inner things, the essence of things. Some of his words were taken down by acolytes such as Plato and Xenophon; some of his mannerisms were mocked by playwrights such as Aristophanes; the master himself, a man Hughes claims we can all benefit from getting to know a little better, wrote nothing, but his recorded dialogues, his Socratic method of relentless questioning, have become indispensable pieces of our Western mental furniture. Hughes revisits all of this with the panache of a born explainer, enthusiastically filling out the world of ancient Athens. She takes readers through the torturous birth and early crises of Athenian democracy, and she's refreshingly evenhanded about the resentment such a democracy might feel toward somebody like Socrates." —*Washington Post*

Includes bibliographical references.

Hughes, Langston
★ *I Wonder as I Wander: An Autobiographical Journey.* by Langston Hughes; introd. by Arnold Rampersad. Hill and Wang 1993. xxii, 405 p.
ISBN 9780809015504
Grades: Adult   **B**
1. Hughes, Langston, 1902-1967 2. African American authors 3. African American poets 4. Authors, American 5. Writing 6. Voyages and travels 7. Poets, American 8. United States history 9. 1930s 10. 20th century 11. Depression era (1929-1941) 12. Autobiographies and memoirs 13. Biographies 14. Arts and Entertainment — Writing and Publishing 15. Life stories — Arts and culture — Writing — Poets
LC 92039307

The American author recalls and reflects on the people and places he encountered in his world travels during the 1930's.

"A book concerned with the individual, with social issues and with art as it is a part of these things will bring its rewards as a documentary and an important diary." —*Kirkus*

Originally published: New York : Rinehart, 1956.

Hughes, Robert
Goya. Robert Hughes. Alfred A. Knopf 2003. x, 429 p. : Illustration; Color
ISBN 9780394580289
Grades: Adult   **B**
1. Goya, Francisco, 1746-1828 2. Artists 3. People who are deaf 4. Men 5. Spanish history 6. 18th century 7. 19th century 8. Biographies 9. Arts and Entertainment — Painting, Drawing, and Sculpture 10. Life stories — Arts and culture — Artists
LC 2002043281

ALA Notable Book, 2005; Booklist Editors' Choice, 2003; Library Journal Best Books, 2003; New York Times Notable Book, 2003.

A portrait of the legendary Spanish artist provides a study of his life and varied works from the context of the turbulent world of eighteenth- and early nineteenth-century Spain.

"This is a remarkably vital, delectably discursive, and deeply affecting study." —*Booklist*

Includes bibliographical references (p. [409]-413) and index.

Humbert, Agnes
Resistance: A Woman's Journal of Struggle and Defiance in Occupied France. Agnes Humbert; translated by Barbara Mellor. Bloomsbury 2008. 208 p.
ISBN 9781596915596
Grades: 11 12 Adult   **B**
1. Humbert, Agnes 2. Prisoners of war, French 3. Forced labor 4. French Resistance (World War II) 5. World War II 6. Prisons 7. German occupation, World War II 8. French history 9. 1940s 10. History writing — Wars and conflicts — Homefront — World War II 11. Adult books for young adults 12. History writing — Wars and conflicts — Resistance — World War II
LC 2008016603

A diary by a key member of the French Resistance during the German occupation of 1940 recounts her group's betrayal to the Gestapo, her imprisonment and deportation to Germany, and the brutal treatment she and her friends endured in labor camps.

Translation of : Notre guerre.

Humez, Jean McMahon
Harriet Tubman: The Life and the Life Stories. Jean M. Humez. University of Wisconsin Press 2003. xii, 471 p. : Illustration
ISBN 9780299191207
Grades: 11 12 Adult   **B**
1. Tubman, Harriet, 1820?-1913 2. Enslaved people 3. Underground Railroad 4. Intellectual life 5. Women and literature 6. African American women 7. United States history 8. United States 9. 19th century 10. Biographies 11. History writing — African American — Enslavement — United States 12. History writing — Women's history 13. Life stories — Facing adversity — War and oppression — Enslaved people 14. Life stories — Politics — Activists and reformers
LC 2003005676

Harriet Tubman's name is known world-wide and her exploits as a self-liberated Underground Railroad heroine are celebrated in children's literature, film, and history books, yet no major biography of Tubman has appeared since 1943. Jean M. Humez's comprehensive Harriet Tubman is both an important biographical overview based on extensive new research and a complete collection of the stories Tubman told about her life—a virtual autobiography culled by Humez from rare early publications and manuscript sources.

Includes bibliographical references (p. 409-441) and index.

Humphreys, Richard
Under Pressure: Living Life and Avoiding Death on a Nuclear Submarine. Richard Humphreys. Hanover Square Press 2020. 267 p.
ISBN 9781335996244
Grades: Adult   **B**
1. Humphreys, Richard, 1967- 2. Sailors 3. Submarines 4. Nuclear submarines 5. Seafaring life 6. Cold War 7. 20th century 8. Life stories — Law and order — Armed forces personnel 9. History writing — Military — Naval history
LC Bl2020013351

A former Royal Navy nuclear submariner describes the daily experiences of his military life during the Cold War, a service marked by claustrophobia, disorientation, body odors, cramped conditions and constant fear.

"An amusing addition to the rare genre of submariner memoirs." —*Kirkus*

Hunt, Patrick
Hannibal. Patrick N. Hunt. Simon & Schuster 2017. 384 pages
ISBN 9781439102176
Grades: Adult   **B**
1. Hannibal, 247-182 B.C.E 2. Generals 3. Command of troops 4. Punic Wars, 264-146 B.C.E 5. Military campaigns 6. Politics and government 7. Carthage (Extinct city) 8. Ancient Rome 9. Roman Republic (509-27 B.C.E.) 10. Biographies 11. Life stories — Law and order — Military leaders 12. History writing — Military — Military leadership 13. History writing — Ancient — Rome
LC 2016051474

A portrait of the ancient-world commander includes discussions of his childhood under a master strategist father, his leadership during the Second Punic War and his famed crossing of the Alps with his army and war elephants in an epic battle against Rome.

"This easily digestible and engrossing biography is ideal for general readers with an interest in ancient history." —*Booklist*

Includes bibliographical references and index.

Hurston, Zora Neale

★ *Barracoon: The Story of the Last 'Black Cargo'.* Zora Neale Hurston, edited and with an introduction by Deborah G. Plant. Amistad Press 2018. 208 p.
ISBN 9780062748201
Grades: Adult   B
1. Lewis, Cudjo 2. Slave trade 3. Enslaved people 4. Slavery 5. Slaveholders 6. Freed people 7. Exploitation 8. African American history 9. History writing — African American — Enslavement — United States 10. Antiracist literature 11. Book club best bets

LC 2018466206

Presents a never-before-published work from the author of the American classic Their Eyes Were Watching God that illuminates the horror and injustices of slavery as it tells the true story of one of the last known survivors of the Atlantic slave trade—abducted from Africa on the last "Black Cargo" ship to arrive in the United States.

"This is a fascinating look at the journey of one man, reflective of the African American experience. It also attests to Hurston's development as an author and ethnographer, and stands as a work of profound relevance, its illumination of slavery, freedom, and race as timely as ever." —*Booklist*

Dust Tracks on a Road: The Restored Text Established by the Library of America. Zora Neale Hurston; with a foreword by Maya Angelou. Harper Perennial Modern Classics 2006. xii, 308, 16 p. : Illustration
ISBN 9780060854089
Grades: 11 12 Adult   B
1. Hurston, Zora Neale 2. African American women 3. Harlem Renaissance 4. Folklorists 5. African American authors 6. African Americans 7. Intellectual life 8. Authors, American 9. Social life and customs 10. Southern States 11. 20th century 12. Autobiographies and memoirs 13. Biographies 14. Arts and Entertainment — Writing and Publishing 15. Life stories — Arts and culture — Writing — Authors

LC 2005052616

Presents the story of an African American woman who rose from poverty to become an author who held a prominent place among the artists and intellectuals of the Harlem Renaissance.

Originally published in 1942 by J.B. Lippincott, Inc. The restored text was published in 1995 by the Library of America as part of Folklore, memoirs & other writings—T.P. verso; First Harper Perennial edition published 1996—T.P. verso; Includes bibliographical references (p. 299-302).

Zora Neale Hurston: A Life in Letters. Zora Neale Hurston; collected and edited by Carla Kaplan. Doubleday 2002. IX, 880 p, 8 p. of plates : Illustration
ISBN 9780385490351
Grades: Adult   B
1. Hurston, Zora Neale 2. Authors, American 3. Folklorists, American 4. African American authors 5. African American women authors 6. 20th century 7. Letters 8. Arts and Entertainment — Writing and Publishing

LC 00065671

New York Times Notable Book, 2003.

A collection of more than five hundred letters, written to such people as Langston Hughes, Dorothy West, and many others, paints a portrait of the enigmatic woman who became one of the greatest literary figures in American history.

"These letters reveal a gifted yet complex personality at once humorous, cynical, and analytical." —*Library Journal*

Includes bibliographical references (p. [817]-832) and index.

Hussey, Olivia

The Girl on the Balcony: Olivia Hussey Finds Life After Romeo and Juliet. Olivia Hussey with Alexander Martin; foreword by Franco Zeffirelli. Kensington Publishing 2018. 320 p.
ISBN 9781496717078
Grades: Adult   B
1. Hussey, Olivia 2. Actors and actresses 3. Fame 4. Film industry and trade 5. Teenage celebrities 6. Autobiographies and memoirs 7. Life stories — Arts and culture — Performing arts — Actors and actresses 8. Arts and Entertainment — Movies and Television

The woman who, at only the age of 16, portrayed Juliet in the 1968 Franco Zeffirelli film Romeo & Juliet shares the ups and downs of her life and career, including all the Hollywood elite she met along the way.

Huston, Anjelica

Watch Me: A Memoir. by Anjelica Huston. Scribner 2014. 400 p.
ISBN 9781476760346
Grades: Adult   B
1. Huston, Anjelica 2. Nicholson, Jack, 1937- 3. Academy Award film nominees 4. Women theatrical producers and directors 5. Films 6. Actors and actresses 7. Autobiographies and memoirs 8. Life stories — Arts and culture — Performing arts — Actors and actresses 9. Arts and Entertainment — Movies and Television

LC 2014029235

The Academy Award-winning actress and author of the best-selling a Story Lately Told discusses her long-time relationship with Jack Nicholson, her most memorable film appearances and her collaborations with a range of forefront directors.

"This memoir with both substance and flair is a must-read for Huston fans, those who enjoy film, and anyone who wishes to be inspired by a richly textured life well presented. For all entertainment collections." —*Library Journal*

Includes bibliographical references and index.

Hutchinson, Cassidy

Enough. Cassidy Hutchinson. Simon & Schuster 2023. 320 p.
ISBN 9781668028285
Grades: Adult   B
1. Hutchinson, Cassidy 2. Trump, Donald, 1946- 3. Democracy 4. Truth 5. Capitol Riot, Washington, D.C, 2021 6. Presidents 7. Politics and government 8. Washington, D.C. 9. United States 10. Autobiographies and memoirs 11. Life stories — Politics 12. Politics and global affairs — General

A former Trump White House staffer provides an account of her extraordinary experiences as an idealistic young woman thrust into the middle of a national crisis, where she risked everything to tell the truth about some of the most powerful people in Washington.

Huxley, Elspeth Joscelin Grant

The Flame Trees of Thika: Memories of an African Childhood. Elspeth Huxley. Penguin Books 2000. 280 p.
ISBN 9780141183787
Grades: Adult   B
1. Huxley, Elspeth, 1907-1997 2. Rural life 3. Authors, English 4. Social life and customs 5. Kenya 6. 20th century 7. 19th century 8. Autobiographies and memoirs 9. Page to screen 10. Biographies 11. Life stories — Arts and culture — Writing — Authors 12. History writing — Colonization — Africa

LC 99047965

Originally published in 1959, Huxley's autobiography recalls her extraordinary adventures as a child in Africa.

Book adapted into a British television mini-series in seven parts in 1981.

Huxtable, Ada Louise

★ *Frank Lloyd Wright.* Ada Louise Huxtable. Lipper/Viking 2004. xvii, 251 p. : Illustration
ISBN 9780670033423
Grades: Adult   B

ESSENTIAL AND RECOMMENDED TITLES
Biography

1. Wright, Frank Lloyd, 1867-1959 2. Architects 3. Biographies 4. Arts and Entertainment — Architecture 5. Life stories — Arts and culture — Architects
LC 2004046477

Provides a portrait of the American architect, describing his personal life, his career as a builder and craftsman, his architectural achievements, and his influence on the world of art and architecture.

"The eventfulness of the extraordinary life and the refreshing intelligence and craft of the author make this book a pleasure to read. That I found myself on occasion arguing with the text only proves the provocative quality of Huxtable's exploration." —*New York Times Book Review*

Hyland, William G.
George Gershwin: *A New Biography*. William G. Hyland. Praeger 2003. xv, 279 p. : Illustration
ISBN 9780275981112
Grades: Adult B

1. Gershwin, George, 1898-1937 2. Composers 3. United States 4. Biographies 5. Arts and Entertainment — Music 6. Life stories — Arts and culture — Performing arts — Musicians and composers
LC 2003046303

Traces the life and career of the noted composer, examines his most important works, and discusses his personal life and his influence on the development of American music and on the relationship between jazz and classical music.

"This fresh and well-researched biography of one of America's great composers is highly recommended for all libraries." —*Library Journal*

Includes bibliographical references (p. [257]-261) and index.

Hytner, Nicholas
Balancing Acts: *Behind the Scenes at London's National Theatre*. Nicholas Hytner. Alfred A. Knopf 2017. 320 p.
ISBN 9780451493408
Grades: Adult B

1. Hytner, Nicholas 2. Theatrical producers and directors 3. Theater 4. Theater companies 5. Autobiographies and memoirs 6. Arts and Entertainment — Theater 7. Life stories — Arts and culture — Performing arts
LC 2017016630

The former director of London's National Theatre presents a candid, behind-the-scenes memoir about his career directing theater, producing films and opera, and working closely with some of the world's most celebrated actors.

"Arts leaders in general will have something to gain from Hytners endless energy for developing new work and navigating the challenges facing todays cultural sector." —*Booklist*

Iandoli, Kathy
Baby Girl: Better Known as Aaliyah. by Kathy Iandoli. Atria Books 2021. 272 p.
ISBN 9781982156848
Grades: Adult B

1. Aaliyah, 1979-2001 2. Rhythm and blues musicians 3. Women singers 4. African American musicians 5. African American women 6. Films 7. Actors and actresses 8. Popular culture 9. United States history 10. 20th century 11. Biographies 12. Arts and Entertainment — Music — Rap and R&B 13. Life stories — Arts and culture — Performing arts — Musicians and composers
LC 2020055985

This definitive biography of the late R&B artist looks at her career in both music and acting which was cut short by a tragic plan crash at age 22 just as she was crossing into superstardom.

"Iandoli (God Save the Queens, 2019) is not only a journalist and author, but also a true Aaliyah fan, as she reveals in this in-depth journey through the life and career of a magnetic artist and icon." —*Booklist*

Includes bibliographical references.

Iguodala, Andre
The Sixth Man: A Memoir. Andre Iguodala with Carvell Wallace. Blue Rider Press 2019. 256 pages
ISBN 9780525533986

Grades: Adult B

1. Iguodala, Andre, 1984- 2. African American basketball players 3. Professional basketball players 4. Olympic athletes 5. Basketball 6. Basketball teams 7. Work ethic 8. Race relations in sports 9. African Americans and sports 10. Toleration 11. Interpersonal relations 12. Autobiographies and memoirs 13. Biographies 14. Life stories — Sports — Athletes 15. Sports and Competition — Basketball 16. Life stories — Identity — Race and ethnicity 17. Society and culture — Race
LC 2018047034

The NBA swingman and All-Star shares insights into his remarkable career, discussing such topics as his 2012 Men's Basketball Olympics gold-medal win, his 2015 NBA championship with the Warriors, and his off-court successes as a Silicon Valley insider.

"Theres plenty here about basketball, but the authors move well beyond the scores, hoops, and on-court drama that fill nearly all the pages of similar books. Iguodala is always focused on the relationships and motivations of his teammates and opponents. That insight, he shows, helps him bond with his teammates and defeat his opponents." —*Booklist*

Includes bibliographical references and index.

Inskeep, Steve
Imperfect Union: *How Jessie and John Frémont Mapped the West, Invented Celebrity, and Helped Cause the Civil War*. Steve Inskeep. Penguin Press 2020. 480 p.
ISBN 9780735224353
Grades: Adult B

1. Fremont, Jessie Benton, 1824-1902 2. Fremont, John Charles, 1813-1890 3. Explorers 4. Pioneer women 5. Pioneers 6. Politicians 7. Politicians' spouses 8. Women's rights 9. Anti-slavery movements 10. Husband and wife 11. United States history 12. 19th century 13. American Westward Expansion (1803-1899) 14. Biographies 15. Life stories — People in history — Pioneers 16. Life stories — Politics — Politicians 17. History writing — Westward expansion — United States
LC 2019030462

Steve Inskeep tells the riveting story of John and Jessie Fremont, the husband and wife team who in the 1800s were instrumental in the westward expansion of the United States, and thus became America's first great political couple.

"An insightful and welcome biography of consequential Americans." —*Booklist*

Includes bibliographical references and index.

Irving, Apricot Anderson
The Gospel of Trees: A Memoir. Apricot Irving. Simon & Schuster 2018. 384 p.
ISBN 9781451690453
Grades: Adult B

1. Irving, Apricot Anderson 2. Missionaries 3. Expatriates 4. Growing up 5. Expatriate women 6. Generation gap 7. Conflict in families 8. Fathers and daughters 9. Forest conservation 10. Humanitarianism 11. Children of missionaries 12. Faith (Christianity) 13. Deforestation 14. Idealism 15. Haiti 16. Caribbean Area 17. Autobiographies and memoirs 18. Life stories — Religion and spirituality — Spiritual journeys 19. Family and Relationships — Families 20. Travel Writing — Living Abroad
LC 2017049492

Oregon Book Awards, Sarah Winnemucca Award for Creative Nonfiction, 2019.

A first book by an award-winning writer recounts her childhood as a missionary's daughter in Haiti during a time of complicated and tumultuous foreign intervention, describing how her perspectives on the region transformed as she came of age and how her family struggled with disparate views about her father's absolute approaches to his work.

"With insight and admirable even-handedness, Irving shows the complex forces at play in both the story of Haitis cycle of poverty and the more personal dynamics at play in her family as they struggle mightily to do Gods work." —*Booklist*

PUBLIC LIBRARY CORE COLLECTION: NONFICTION
Twentieth Edition

Isaacson, Walter

★ *Benjamin Franklin: An American Life.* Walter Isaacson. Simon & Schuster 2003. x, 590 p, 16 p. of plates : Illustration; Color
ISBN 9780684807614
Grades: Adult   B
1. Franklin, Benjamin, 1706-1790 2. Scientists 3. Printers 4. Politicians 5. Inventors 6. Politics and government 7. United States 8. 18th century 9. Early America (1784-1819) 10. 19th century 11. 1780s 12. Biographies 13. History writing — Colonial America — United States 14. Science Writing — General 15. Life stories — Politics — Politicians

LC 2003050463

New York Times Notable Book, 2003.

Traces the life of Benjamin Franklin, from his days as a runaway printer to his triumphs as a statesman, inventor, and founding father. Chronicles his tumultuous relationship with his illegitimate son and grandson, his practical marriage, and his flirtations with the ladies of Paris.

"This is a thoroughly researched, crisply written, convincingly argued chronicle that is also studded with little nuggets of fresh information." —*New York Times Book Review*

Includes bibliographical references and index.

★ *Elon Musk.* Walter Isaacson. Simon & Schuster 2023. 608 p.
ISBN 9781982181284
Grades: Adult   B
1. Musk, Elon 2. Entrepreneurs 3. Inventors 4. Billionaires 5. Technological innovations 6. Electric vehicles 7. Space exploration 8. Creativity in business 9. Interpersonal relations 10. Southern African people 11. South African people 12. North American people 13. American people 14. Biographies 15. Impartial writing 16. Life stories — Business — Business leaders 17. Life stories — Science, technology, and medicine — Scientists and inventors 18. Business and economics — Business leaders and entrepreneurs

Loan Stars Favourites, 2023.

From the author of Steve Jobs and other best-selling biographies comes an intimate story of a controversial businessman who helped to lead the world into the era of electric vehicles, private space exploration and artificial intelligence.

"Reckless ambition, ruthless drive, and psychic demons swaddle the soul of a wounded child in this sweeping biography of the celebrated industrialist...Isaacson shadowed Musk for two years and conjures a richly detailed, evocative portrait that nails his impulsive personality." —*Publishers Weekly*

★ *The Innovators: How a Group of Inventors, Hackers, Geniuses, and Geeks Created the Digital Revolution.* Walter Isaacson. Simon & Schuster 2014. 528 p.
ISBN 9781476708690
Grades: Adult   B
1. Computers 2. Inventors 3. Technological innovations 4. Technology 5. Computer science 6. Science Writing — Computing, the Internet, and Technology

LC 2014021391

Booklist Editors' Choice, 2014.

A revelatory history of the people who created the computer and the internet discusses the process through which innovation happens in the modern world, citing the pivotal contributions of such figures as programming pioneer Ada Lovelace.

"Although full biographies of the individuals profiled here have been written in spades, Isaacson manages to bring together the entire universe of computing, from the first digitized loom to the web, presented in a very accessible manner that often reads like a thriller." —*Booklist*

★ *Leonardo Da Vinci.* Walter Isaacson. Simon & Schuster 2017. 576 p.
ISBN 9781501139154
Grades: Adult   B
1. Leonardo, da Vinci, 1452-1519 2. Gifted people 3. Scientists 4. Artists 5. Renaissance (1300-1600) 6. Biographies 7. Life stories — Arts and culture — Artists 8. Life stories — Science, technology, and medicine — Scientists and inventors 9. History writing — Renaissance — Europe 10. Arts and Entertainment — Painting, Drawing, and Sculpture

LC 2017020817

Longlisted for the Andrew Carnegie Medal for Excellence in Non-Fiction, 2018.

The best-selling author of Benjamin Franklin draws on da Vinci's remarkable notebooks as well as new discoveries about his life and work in a narrative portrait that connects the master's art to his science, demonstrating how da Vinci's genius was based on the skills and qualities of everyday people, from curiosity and observation to imagination and fantasy.

"Encompassing in its coverage, robust in its artistic explanations, yet written in a smart, conversational tone, this is both a solid introduction to the man and a sweeping saga of his genius." —*Booklist*

Includes bibliographical references and index.

★ *Steve Jobs: A Biography.* Walter Isaacson. Simon & Schuster 2011. 656 p.
ISBN 9781451648539
Grades: Adult   B
1. Jobs, Steve, 1955-2011 2. Chief executive officers 3. Millionaires 4. Computer industry and trade 5. Businesspeople 6. Social life and customs 7. United States 8. 20th century 9. Biographies 10. Interviews 11. Business and economics — Business leaders and entrepreneurs 12. Life stories — Business — Business leaders 13. Business and economics — Industries — Technology

LC 2011045006

Goodreads Choice Award, 2011.

Draws on more than forty interviews with Steve Jobs, as well as interviews with family members, friends, competitors, and colleagues, to offer a look at the co-founder and leading creative force behind the Apple computer company.

"This is an encyclopedic survey of all that Mr. Jobs accomplished, replete with the passion and excitement that it deserves." —*New York Times Book Review*

Ishikawa, Masaji

★ *A River in Darkness: One Man's Escape from North Korea.* Masaji Ishikawa; translated by Risa Kobayashi and Martin Brown. AmazonCrossing 2018. 172 pages
ISBN 9781503936904
Grades: Adult   B
1. Ishikawa, Masaji 2. Men 3. Defectors 4. Political persecution 5. Classism 6. Suffering 7. Immigration and emigration 8. Repatriation 9. Politics and government 10. North Korea 11. Autobiographies and memoirs 12. Translations — Japanese to English 13. Life stories — Facing adversity — War and oppression — Refugees 14. History writing — Asia — North and South Korea

LC B12018000903

In this memoir translated from the original Japanese, Ishikawa candidly recounts his tumultuous upbringing and the brutal thirty-six years he spent living under a crushing totalitarian regime, as well as the challenges he faced repatriating to Japan after barely escaping North Korea with his life.

"Ishikawa relates his painful story with sardonic humor and unwavering familial love even in the depths of despair, making human the often impersonal news coverage of mysterious and threatening North Korea." —*Booklist*

Translated from the Japanese.

Itzkoff, Dave

★ *Robin.* Dave Itzkoff. Henry Holt and Company 2018. 400 p.
ISBN 9781627794244
Grades: Adult   B
1. Williams, Robin, 1951-2014 2. Comedians 3. Suicide 4. Actors and actresses 5. People with depression 6. Men 7. Biographies 8. Life stories — Arts and culture — Performing arts — Actors and actresses 9. Arts and Entertainment — Comedy

LC 2017050678

The New York Times culture reporter and author of Mad as Hell presents a compelling portrait of Robin Williams that illuminates his comic brilliance, conflicting emotions and often misunderstood character, sharing insights into the gift for improvisation that shaped his wide range of characters, his struggles with addiction and depression and his relationships with friends and family members.

"The book has some nifty trivia (first choices to play Mork from Ork were John Byner and Dom DeLuise), but this isnt one of those skimming-the-surface

ESSENTIAL AND RECOMMENDED TITLES
Biography

Hollywood bios. Its a meaty, well-researched, moving story of a man who could never quite come to terms with his own brilliance." —*Booklist*
Includes bibliographical references and index.

Iyer, Pico
The Open Road: The Global Journey of the Fourteenth Dalai Lama. Pico Iyer. Alfred A. Knopf 2008. 288 p.
ISBN 9780307267603
Grades: 11 12 Adult   **B**
1. Dalai Lama XIV, 1935- 2. Buddhism 3. Religious leaders 4. Buddhists 5. Spirituality and Religion — Buddhism 6. Spirituality and Religion — Religious Leaders 7. Travel Writing — General 8. Adult books for young adults
LC 2007043991

An illuminating account of the Dalai Lama explores his diverse roles as a politician, scientist, philosopher, and religious leader; discusses his ideas about religion, Tibet, peace, and world events; and examines his hidden life, often pragmatic messages, and the daily challenges he confronts.

"The combination of Iyer's exacting observations, incisive analysis, and frank respect for the unknowable results in a uniquely internalized, even empathic portrait of one of the world's most embraced and least understood guiding lights." —*Booklist*
Includes bibliographical references.

Izgil, Tahir Hamut
Waiting to Be Arrested at Night: A Uyghur Poet's Memoir of China's Genocide. Tahir Hamut Izgil; translation and introduction by Joshua L. Freeman. Penguin Press 2023. 256 p.
ISBN 9780593491799
Grades: Adult   **B**
1. Izgil, Tahir Hamut, 1969- 2. Uighur (Turkic people) 3. Political activists 4. Genocide 5. Poets 6. Interethnic relations 7. Families 8. Surveillance 9. Resilience 10. Oppression (Psychology) 11. Escapes 12. Marginalized people 13. XInjiang, China 14. China 15. Autobiographies and memoirs 16. Life stories — Facing adversity — War and oppression 17. History Writing — Asia — China 18. Life stories — Arts and culture — Writing — Poets 19. Debut title
LC 2023009751

National Book Critics Circle Award: John Leonard Prize, 2023.

In this story of the political, social and cultural destruction of his homeland, a prominent poet and intellectual calls our attention to one of the world's most urgent humanitarian crises: the persecution of the Uyghur people—a predominantly Muslim minority group in western China.

"This is a spellbinding account of personal resilience and an eye-opening exposé on the humanitarian crisis in XInjiang." —*Publishers Weekly*

Izzard, Eddie
Believe Me: A Memoir of Love, Death, and Jazz Chickens. Eddie Izzard, with Laura Zigman. Blue Rider Press 2017. 400 p.
ISBN 9780399175831
Grades: Adult   **B**
1. Izzard, Eddie 2. Entertainers 3. Comedians 4. Autobiographies and memoirs 5. Life stories — Arts and culture — Performing arts — Entertainers and celebrities
LC 2017008493

A wide-ranging memoir by the critically acclaimed British comedian that details a childhood in multiple countries, Izzard's first performances on the streets of London, and the achievements that have marked international success.

"For Izzard's followers, this is definitely worth the read. Well written and sometimes laugh-out-loud funny, it's recommended for fans of comedy and theater and those who appreciate wicked and honest repartee." —*Library Journal*

Jackson, Angela
A Surprised Queenhood in the New Black Sun: The Life & Legacy of Gwendolyn Brooks. Angela Jackson. Beacon Press 2017. 204 p.
ISBN 9780807025048
Grades: Adult   **B**
1. Brooks, Gwendolyn, 1917-2000 2. Black Aesthetic Movement 3. Writing 4. African American poets 5. African American women poets 6. African American women 7. Poets, American 8. 20th century 9. Biographies 10. Arts and Entertainment — Writing and Publishing 11. Life stories — Arts and culture — Writing — Poets
LC 2017001533

A look back at the cultural and political force of Pulitzer Prize-winning poet Gwendolyn Brooks, in celebration of her hundredth birthday.

"Jackson presents an incisive portrait of poet Gwendolyn Brooks (19172000), sharing with her subject the experiences of an African American woman poet in Chicago." —*Booklist*
Includes bibliographical references.

Jackson, Bruce
Never Far from Home: My Journey from Brooklyn to Hip Hop, Microsoft, and the Law. Bruce Jackson. Atria Books 2023. 272 p.
ISBN 9781982191153
Grades: Adult   **B**
1. Jackson, Bruce (Lawyer) 2. Corporate lawyers 3. Childhood 4. Lawyers 5. Criminal justice system 6. Drug industry and trade 7. African American lawyers 8. United States 9. Autobiographies and memoirs 10. Life stories — Law and order — Judges and lawyers 11. Life stories — Facing adversity
LC 2022037019

In this incredible and inspirational memoir, Microsoft's associate general counsel, who has kept his past a secret until now, reveals an impoverished childhood in the criminal justice system and drug trade, and how he was saved by an offer that set him on a better path.

"In this earnest debut, lawyer Jackson recounts his rise from living in public housing to becoming associate general counsel for Microsoft….He pulls no punches when discussing the racism he's experienced throughout his life, but he remains determined to rise above the 'Unfairness in the DNA of our society'." —*Publishers Weekly*

Jackson, Curtis
Hustle Harder, Hustle Smarter. Curtis. Amistad 2020. xviii, 271 p.
ISBN 9780062953803
Grades: Adult   **B**
1. Jackson, Curtis, 1975- 2. 50 Cent (Musician) 3. Rap musicians 4. Television producers and directors 5. African American businesspeople 6. Success in business 7. United States 8. Autobiographies and memoirs 9. Biographies 10. Life stories — Business — Business leaders 11. Business and economics — Business leaders and entrepreneurs 12. Debut title
LC Bl2020010066

Curtis |50 Cent| Jackson opens up about his amazing comeback|from tragic personal loss to thriving businessman and cable|s highest-paid executive|in a unique self-help guide. By the New York Times best-selling author of the 50th Law.

"Savor the celebrity gossip and push through to the lessons of one of hip-hop's most successful businessmen ever." —*Kirkus*

Jackson, Julian
De Gaulle. Julian Jackson. The Belknap Press of Harvard University Press 2018. 928 p.
ISBN 9780674987210
Grades: Adult   **B**
1. Gaulle, Charles de, 1890-1970 2. Generals 3. World War II 4. French Resistance (World War II) 5. Presidents 6. Politics and government 7. Europe 8. France 9. 20th century 10. Biographies 11. Life stories — Politics — Politicians 12. Life stories — Law and order — Military leaders 13. History writing — Europe — France 14. History writing — Wars and conflicts — World War II — European Theater
LC 2018015618

Elizabeth Longford Prize for Historical Biography, 2019.

In a definitive biography of the mythic general who refused to accept Nazi domination of France, Julian Jackson captures this titanic figure as never before. Drawing on unpublished letters, memoirs, and resources of the recently opened de Gaulle archive, he shows how this volatile visionary put a broken France back at the center of world affairs.

"A long but excellent, highly useful addition to the library of modern European history as well as the political history of World War II and the Cold War." —*Kirkus*

Simultaneously published in the United Kingdom as a Certain Idea of France: The Life of Charles de Gaulle; Includes bibliographical references and index.

Jackson, Lawrence Patrick
Chester B. Himes: A Biography. Lawrence P. Jackson. Norton & Co. 2017. 448 p.
ISBN 9780393063899
Grades: Adult   B
1. Himes, Chester B, 1909-1984 2. African American authors 3. Authors 4. Former convicts 5. Social advocates 6. Racism 7. Race relations 8. United States 9. 20th century 10. Biographies 11. Life stories — Arts and culture — Writing — Authors 12. History writing — African American — United States

BCALA Literary Award for Nonfiction, 2018; Edgar Allan Poe Award for Best Critical/Biographical, 2018.

An account of the improbable life of the controversial writer explores Himes' middle-class origins, imprisonment, creative experiences during World War II and eventual escape to Europe, where he became famous for his Harlem detective series and its themes of sexuality, racism and social injustice.

"While two other Himes biographies exist…Jackson succeeds in his bid to offer a definitive life treatment." —*Booklist*

Jackson, Mitchell S.
Survival Math: Notes on an All-american Family. Mitchell S. Jackson. Scribner 2019. 304 p.
ISBN 9781501131707
Grades: Adult   B
1. Jackson, Mitchell S. 2. African Americans 3. African American neighborhoods 4. Growing up 5. Authors 6. African American families 7. Drug traffic 8. Drug addiction 9. Imprisonment 10. Survival 11. Marginalized people 12. Ghettoes, African American 13. Race relations 14. Portland, Oregon 15. Pacific Northwest 16. United States 17. Autobiographies and memoirs 18. Society and culture — Race 19. Society and culture — Wealth and class — Poverty 20. Society and culture — Urban and regional studies

LC Bl2019000943

With a poet's gifted ear, a novelist's sense of narrative, and a journalist's unsentimental eye, Mitchell S. Jackson candidly explores his tumultuous youth in the other America. Survival Math takes its name from the calculations Mitchell and his family made to keep safe—to stay alive—in their community, a small Black neighborhood in Portland, Oregon blighted by drugs, violence, poverty, and governmental neglect.

"Thanks to Jackson's fresh voice, this powerful autobiography shines an important light on the generational problems of America's oft-forgotten urban communities." —*Publishers Weekly*

Includes bibliographical references.

Jackson, Ted
★ *You Ought to Do a Story About Me: Addiction, an Unlikely Friendship, and the Endless Quest for Redemption.* Ted Jackson. Dey Street Books 2020. 332 p.
ISBN 9780062935670
Grades: Adult   B
1. Wallace, Jackie 2. Jackson, Ted 3. Former professional football players 4. Homeless men 5. African American men 6. Racism 7. Male friendship 8. Poverty 9. Drug addiction 10. Homelessness 11. Institutional racism 12. New Orleans, Louisiana 13. Louisiana 14. Biographies 15. Life stories — Sports — Athletes 16. Life stories — Facing adversity 17. Sports and Competition — Individual Athlete

LC Bl2020015853

Documents the photojournalist author's 30-year friendship with former NFL star Jackie Wallace, describing the losses and addiction that led the three-time Super Bowl star to homelessness on the streets of New Orleans.

"This story of a unique bond between two friends deserves wide readership in public libraries and is an ideal choice for book groups and discussions." —*Library Journal*

Jackson, Troy
Becoming King: Martin Luther King, Jr. And The Making of a National Leader. Troy Jackson; introduction by Clayborne Carson. University Press of Kentucky 2008. xx, 248 p.
ISBN 9780813125206
Grades: Adult   B
1. King, Martin Luther, Jr, 1929-1968 2. African American civil rights workers 3. Baptists 4. Segregation in transportation 5. Civil Rights Movement 6. Equality 7. African American history 8. Civil rights 9. Clergy 10. Race relations 11. United States history 12. Montgomery, Alabama 13. United States 14. Alabama 15. 20th century 16. Biographies 17. History writing — African American — Civil rights — United States 18. Life stories — Politics — Activists and Reformers — Civil Rights Leaders

LC 2008025041

"The author's comprehensive analysis of King's sermons before, during and after the boycott artfully depicts a man in transition, from naive do-gooder to world-changer. Jackson's treatment of Montgomery in the post-boycott era offers new insight into the void in leadership and the fractious infighting among the movement's luminaries after King departed the scene. An informed investigation of the struggles that defined a time and place-and the man who gave them a voice." —*Kirkus*

Includes bibliographical references (p. 229-239) and index.

Jacobs, Alexandra
Still Here: The Madcap, Nervy, Singular Life of Elaine Stritch. Alexandra Jacobs. Farrar, Straus and Giroux 2019. 352 p.
ISBN 9780374268091
Grades: Adult   B
1. Stritch, Elaine 2. Alcoholic women 3. Women entertainers 4. Theater 5. Actors and actresses 6. Social life and customs 7. New York City 8. United States 9. 20th century 10. Biographies 11. Arts and Entertainment — Theater 12. Life stories — Arts and culture — Performing arts — Actors and actresses 13. Life stories — Arts and culture — Performing arts — Entertainers and celebrities

LC 2019020220

A full chronicle of the Tony Award-winning star's life and career includes coverage of her upbringing in Depression-era Detroit, her psychologically fraught creative collaborations, her struggles with addiction and her Tony Award-winning performances.

Includes bibliographical references and index.

Jacobs, Harriet
★ *Incidents in the Life of a Slave Girl.* Harriet Jacobs, Farah Jasmine Griffin; edited by George Stade. Barnes & Noble Classics 2005. 272 p.
ISBN 9781593082833
Grades: Adult   B
1. Jacobs, Harriet, 1818-1896 2. Enslaved people 3. Slavery 4. Escapes 5. Freedom seekers 6. Intersectionality 7. African American women 8. United States history 9. North Carolina 10. 19th century 11. Autobiographies and memoirs 12. Biographies 13. History writing — African American — Enslavement — United States 14. Life stories — Facing adversity — War and oppression — Enslaved people

LC 2004112698

Incidents in the Life of a Slave Girl is a genuine story of a woman's struggle for self-identity, self-preservation, and liberation. It is one of the few remaining slave narratives written by a woman.

Jacobs, Sally H.
Althea: The Life of Tennis Champion Althea Gibson. Sally H. Jacobs. St. Martin's Press 2023. 304 p.
ISBN 9781250246554
Grades: Adult   B

ESSENTIAL AND RECOMMENDED TITLES
Biography

1. Gibson, Althea, 1927-2003 2. African American women 3. Women tennis players 4. Women athletes 5. Racism in sports 6. Prejudice 7. Exploitation 8. Civil Rights Movement 9. North American people 10. American people 11. Biographies 12. Life stories — Sports — Athletes 13. Life stories — Identity — Race and ethnicity 14. Sports and Competition — Tennis 15. Sports and Competition — Individual Athlete 16. History writing — African American — United States 17. History writing — Women's history

LC 2023015096

In 1950, three years after Jackie Robinson first walked onto the diamond at Ebbets Field, the all-white, upper-crust US Lawn Tennis Association opened its door just a crack to receive a powerhouse player who would integrate "the game of royalty." the player was a street-savvy young Black woman from Harlem named Althea Gibson who was about as out-of-place in that rarefied and intolerant world as any aspiring tennis champion could be, but her astonishing performance on the court soon eclipsed the negative feelings being cast her way as she eventually became one of the greatest American tennis champions.

"This important book honors the legacy of Althea Gibson, a tennis superstar who shattered racial, gender, and class barriers." —*Booklist*

Includes bibliographical references and index.

Jacoby, Karl
The Strange Career of William Ellis: The Texas Slave Who Became a Mexican Millionaire. Karl Jacoby. W.W. Norton & Company 2016. 352 p.
ISBN 9780393239256
Grades: Adult **B**

1. Ellis, William Henry, 1864-1923 2. Passing (Identity) 3. Reconstruction (United States history) 4. Enslaved people 5. Businesspeople 6. Millionaires 7. African Americans 8. Race relations 9. United States history 10. Mexican-American Border Region 11. Gilded Age (1865-1898) 12. Biographies 13. Life stories — Identity — Race and ethnicity 14. Life stories — People in history 15. History writing — Gilded Age — United States

LC 2016007019

To his contemporaries in Gilded Age Manhattan, Guillermo Eliseo was a fantastically wealthy Mexican, the proud owner of a luxury apartment overlooking Central Park, a busy Wall Street office, and scores of mines and haciendas in Mexico. But for all his obvious riches and his elegant appearance, Eliseo was also the possessor of a devastating secret: He was not, in fact, from Mexico at all. Rather, he had begun life as a slave named William Ellis, born on a cotton plantation in southern Texas during the waning years of King Cotton. After emancipation, Ellis, capitalizing on the Spanish he learned during his childhood along the Mexican border and his ambivalent appearance, engaged in a virtuoso act of reinvention. He crafted an alter ego, the Mexican Guillermo Eliseo, who was able to access many of the privileges denied to African Americans at the time: Traveling in first-class train berths, staying in upscale hotels, and eating in the finest restaurants.

"Jacoby's masterly writing places race and its meaning at the center of this essential work. Readers will gain fresh insight into life during Reconstruction as well as the riddle of racial identities." —*Library Journal*

Includes bibliographical references and index.

Jaher, David
The Witch of Lime Street: Seance, Seduction, and Houdini in the Spirit World. David Jaher. Crown Publishers 2015. 432 p.
ISBN 9780307451064
Grades: Adult **B**

1. Margery, 1888-1941 2. Houdini, Harry, 1874-1926 3. Doyle, Arthur Conan, Sir, 1859-1930 4. Spiritualists 5. Spiritualism 6. Women mediums 7. Competition 8. Skeptics 9. Life after death 10. Women psychics 11. United States 12. 1920s 13. 20th century 14. History writing — Roaring 20s — United States

LC 2015009392

Recounts how the wife of a Boston surgeon came to embody the national debate over Spiritualism and the rivalry that came from Harry Houdini's quest to unmask charlatans.

"Through a combination of feminine seduction and illusionist skill that even Houdini admired, Crandon became the one psychic to almost win the respect of the scientific community and outshine Houdini as an entertainer. Jaher's narrative style is as engaging as his character portraits are colorful. Together, they bring a bygone age and its defining spiritual obsessions roaring to life. Fascinating, sometimes thrilling, reading." —*Kirkus*

Includes bibliographical references and index.

Jahren, Hope
★ *Lab Girl*. Hope Jahren. Alfred A. Knopf 2016. 320 p.
ISBN 9781101874936
Grades: 10 11 12 Adult **B**

1. Jahren, Hope 2. Plants 3. Women scientists 4. Biologists 5. Geobiology 6. Friendship 7. Ambition 8. Autobiographies and memoirs 9. Life stories — Science, technology, and medicine — Scientists and inventors 10. Science Writing — Biology 11. Adult books for young adults

LC 2015024305

National Book Critics Circle Award for Autobiography, 2016; New York Times Notable Book, 2016; Science Books and Films Prize for Excellence in Science Books, Young Adult Science Book, 2017.

Hope Jahren, the geobiologist, presents her autobiography.

"Jahren's forthright, beautifully expressed, and galvanizing chronicle deserves the widest possible readership." —*Booklist*

A Borzoi Book; Includes bibliographical references.

Jaku, Eddie
★ *The Happiest Man on Earth: The Beautiful Life of an Auschwitz Survivor*. Eddie Jaku. Harper 2021. 208 p.
ISBN 9780063097681
Grades: Adult **B**

1. Jaku, Eddie 2. Jewish men 3. Holocaust survivors 4. Centenarians 5. Concentration camps 6. Forced labor 7. Escapes 8. Fugitives 9. Survival 10. Gratitude 11. Immigrants 12. World War II 13. Europe 14. Autobiographies and memoirs 15. Life stories — Facing adversity — War and oppression — Holocaust 16. History writing — Wars and conflicts — Holocaust — World War II

Australian Book Industry Awards, Biography of the Year, 2021.

Born in Leipzig, Germany, into a Jewish family, Eddie Jaku was a teenager when his world was turned upside-down. On November 9, 1938, during the terrifying violence of Kristallnacht, Eddie was beaten by SS thugs, arrested, and sent to a concentration camp with thousands of other Jews across Germany. Every day of the next seven years, Eddie faced unimaginable horrors in Buchenwald, Auschwitz, and finally on a forced death march during the Third Reich's final days. Against unbelievable odds, Eddie found the will to survive. Overwhelmingly grateful, he made a promise: He would smile every day in thanks for the precious gift he was given and to honor the six million Jews murdered by Hitler. Today, at 100 years of age, despite all he suffered, Eddie calls himself the "happiest man on earth."

"'My dear new friend.' These four words open a captivating memoir by centenarian Jaku. He tells his story of living through one of history's darkest periods and maintaining his sense of gratitude and hope." —*Library Journal*

Includes bibliographical references and index; Originally published: Sydney : Macmillan, 2020.

James, Laura E.
Odd Girl Out: My Extraordinary Autistic Life. Laura James. Seal Press 2018. 272 p.
ISBN 9781580057806
Grades: Adult **B**

1. James, Laura E. 2. Autistic women 3. Autistic people 4. Autism spectrum disorders 5. Neurodivergent people 6. Autobiographies and memoirs 7. Life stories — Facing adversity — Medical issues — Living with disabilities

From childhood, Laura James knew she was different. She struggled to cope in a world that often made no sense to her, as though her brain had its own operating system. It wasn't until she reached her forties that she found out why: Suddenly and surprisingly, she was diagnosed with autism.

James, Victoria
Wine Girl: The Obstacles, Humiliations, and Triumphs of America's Youngest Sommelier. Victoria James. Ecco Press 2020. 256 pages

ISBN 9780062961679
Grades: Adult — B

1. James, Victoria 2. Women restaurateurs 3. Resilience 4. Abused women 5. Interpersonal relations 6. Families 7. Friendship 8. Growing up 9. Sexism 10. Rape victims 11. Wine and wine making 12. Wine tasting 13. Hospitality industry and trade 14. Lifestyle change 15. Ambition 16. Autobiographies and memoirs 17. Life stories — Arts and culture — Culinary arts 18. Life stories — Facing adversity — Abuse survivors 19. Food writing — Memoirs and biographies

LC Bl2020007411

The country's youngest sommelier describes her experiences recommending and selling thousands of dollars of wine at a Michelin-starred restaurant where she still contended with groping patrons and abusive bosses in the fast-paced, but toxic restaurant world.

Jamison, Leslie

★ *The Recovering: Intoxication and Its Aftermath.* Leslie Jamison. Little Brown & CO 2018. 544 p.
ISBN 9780316259613
Grades: Adult — B

1. Jamison, Leslie, 1983- 2. Sobriety 3. Recovering alcoholics 4. Addiction and creativity 5. Addiction 6. Alcoholism 7. Alcoholic authors 8. Autobiographies and memoirs 9. Life stories — Facing adversity — Medical issues — Addiction

LC 2017946582

The best-selling author of the Empathy Exams presents an exploration of addiction that blends memoir, cultural history, literary criticism and journalistic reportage to analyze the role of stories in conveying the addiction experience, sharing insights based on the lives of genius artists whose achievements were shaped by addiction.

"The bracing, unflinching, and beautifully resonant history of a writer's addiction and hard-won reclamation." —*Kirkus*

Jang, Jin-sung

Dear Leader: Poet, Spy, Escapee - a Look Inside North Korea. Jang Jin-sung; translated by Shirley Lee. 37 Ink 2014. 368 pages
ISBN 9781476766553
Grades: Adult — B

1. Jang, Jin-sung 2. Kim, Chong-il, 1942-2011 3. Propaganda 4. Political refugees 5. Defectors 6. Poets 7. Politics and government 8. North Korea 9. Translations — Korean to English 10. Autobiographies and memoirs 11. Politics and global affairs — World politics — Asia 12. Life stories — Arts and culture — Writing — Poets 13. Life stories — Facing adversity — War and oppression — Refugees 14. Nonfiction that reads like fiction

LC 2014010236

In this rare insider's view into contemporary North Korea, a high-ranking counterintelligence agent describes his life as a former poet laureate to Kim Jong-il and his breathtaking escape to freedom. As North Korea's State Poet Laureate, Jang Jin-sung led a charmed life. With food provisions (even as the country suffered through its great famine), a travel pass, access to strictly censored information, and audiences with Kim Jong-il himself, his life in Pyongyang seemed safe and secure. But this privileged existence was about to be shattered. When a strictly forbidden magazine he lent to a friend goes missing, Jang Jin-sung must flee for his life. Never before has a member of the elite described the inner workings of this totalitarian state and its propaganda machine. An astonishing expose; told through the heart-stopping story of Jang Jin-sung's escape to South Korea, Dear Leader is a rare and unprecedented insight into the world's most secretive and repressive regime.

"A defector of Kim Jong-il's rarefied inner circle reveals the desperate, despicable machinations of North Korea's police state." —*Kirkus*

Jaouad, Suleika

★ *Between Two Kingdoms: A Memoir of a Life Interrupted.* Suleika Jaouad. Random House 2021. 368 p.
ISBN 9780399588587
Grades: Adult — B

1. Jaouad, Suleika 2. Women journalists 3. Twenties (Age) 4. Women cancer survivors 5. Diagnosis 6. Leukemia 7. People with cancer 8. Bone cancer 9. Cancer 10. Healing 11. Strangers 12. Letter writing 13. Friendship 14. Women and dogs 15. Voyages and travels 16. Cross-country automobile trips 17. Treatment 18. Autobiographies and memoirs 19. Page to screen 20. Life stories — Facing adversity — Medical issues — Physical illness 21. Life stories — Relationships — Friendship 22. Travel Writing — United States

A writer and activist describes the harrowing years she spent in early adulthood fighting leukemia and how she learned to live again while forging connections with other survivors of profound illness and suffering.

"New York Times columnist Jaouad (Life, Interrupted) makes a phenomenal debut with this big-hearted account of her devastating five-year battle with cancer. . . . This is a stunning memoir, well-crafted and hard to put down." —*Publishers Weekly*

Adapted into a documentary on Netflix in 2023.

Jarnow, Jesse

Big Day Coming: Yo La Tengo and the Rise of Indie Rock. Jesse Jarnow. Gotham Books 2012. 362 p. : Illustration
ISBN 9781592407156
Grades: Adult — B

1. Rock musicians 2. Rock music 3. Bands (Music) 4. Arts and Entertainment — Music — Rock

LC 2011053088

Recounts the career of the indie rock group, detailing how the group's underground following allowed them to reach fame and popularity without hitting the common pitfalls of the music industry.

Includes bibliographical references (p. [345]-350), discography (p. [351]-354), and index.

Jarrett, Valerie

Finding My Voice: My Journey to the West Wing and the Path Forward. Valerie Jarrett. Viking Press 2019. 320 p.
ISBN 9780525558132
Grades: Adult — B

1. Jarrett, Valerie, 1956- 2. Obama, Barack 3. Presidents 4. Social advocacy 5. Political consultants 6. Growing up 7. Women lawyers 8. African American women lawyers 9. Social philosophy 10. Businesspeople 11. African American women 12. 21st century 13. Autobiographies and memoirs 14. Biographies 15. Life stories — Politics — Politicians 16. History writing — Presidency — 21st century — United States

LC 2019002213

When Valerie Jarrett interviewed a promising young lawyer named Michelle Robinson in July 1991 for a job in Chicago city government, neither knew that it was the first step on a path that would end in the White House. Jarrett soon became Michelle and Barack Obama's trusted personal adviser and family confidante; in the White House, she was known as the one who "got" him and helped him engage his public life. Jarrett joined the White House team on January 20, 2009 and departed with the First Family on January 20, 2017, and she was in the room—in the Oval Office, on Air Force One, and everywhere else—when it all happened. No one has as intimate a view of the Obama Years, nor one that reaches back as many decades, as Jarrett shares in Finding My Voice.

"A modest and insightful addition to a growing shelf of books by insiders from the Obama administration." —*Kirkus*

Jawando, Will

★ *My Seven Black Fathers: A Young Activist's Memoir of Race, Family, and the Mentors Who Made Him Whole.* Will Jawando. Farrar, Straus and Giroux 2022. 224 p.
ISBN 9780374604875
Grades: Adult — B

1. Jawando, Will, 1983- 2. African American men 3. African Americans 4. Mentors 5. Role models 6. Nigerian Americans 7. Fathers and sons 8. Father figures 9. Racism 10. Prejudice 11. Family relationships 12. Multiracial men 13. Maryland 14. Autobiographies and memoirs 15. Life stories — Identity — Race and ethnicity 16. Life stories — Relationships — Growing up 17. Family and relationships — Growing up

ESSENTIAL AND RECOMMENDED TITLES
Biography

LC 2021057147

A narrative call to action runs counter to every racist stereotype that thwarts the lives of men of color today.

"A biracial Nigerian American lawyer, community leader, and activist tells his life story through the lens of his most important relationships with other Black men....A beautifully written and innovatively structured memoir of a biracial Black man's life journey." —*Kirkus*

Jayapal, Pramila
Use the Power You Have: A Brown Woman's Guide to Politics and Political Change. Pramila Jayapal. The New Press 2020. 240 p.
ISBN 9781620971437
Grades: Adult   B
1. Jayapal, Pramila, 1965- 2. Women legislators 3. Legislators 4. Women immigrants 5. Progressivism (United States politics) 6. Indian Americans 7. Politics and government 8. United States 9. 20th century 10. 21st century 11. Autobiographies and memoirs 12. Life stories — Identity — Immigrants 13. Life stories — Politics — Politicians 14. Politics and global affairs — World politics — United States

LC 2020010661

The first Indian American woman to serve in the House of Representatives and co-chair of the Congressional Progressive Caucus discusses how to achieve a progressive and more inclusive legislative agenda that serves all Americans.

"Passionate and unapologetically leftist, this hopeful book not only chronicles an immigrant's political successes, but, more significantly, the enduring faith in American democracy that inspired them. A passionately articulate memoir and political manifesto." —*Kirkus*

Includes bibliographical references and index.

Jebara, Mohamad
Muhammad, the World-changer: An Intimate Portrait. Mohamed Jebara. St. Martin's Essentials 2021. 352 p.
ISBN 9781250239648
Grades: Adult   B
1. Muhammad, Prophet, d. 632 2. Prophets 3. Religious leaders 4. Islam 5. Devotedness 6. Leadership 7. Biographies 8. Life stories — Religion and spirituality — Religious and spiritual leaders 9. Spirituality and Religion — Islam — History

LC 2021016104

A six-year-old cries in his mother's arms as she draws her last breaths to urge him: "Muhammad, be a world-changer!" the boy, suddenly orphaned in a tribal society that fears any change, must overcome enormous obstacles to unleash his own potential and inspire others to do the same. Fusing details long known to Muslim scholars but inaccessible to popular audiences, Mohamad Jebara brings to life the gripping personal story of Islam's founding prophet. From his dramatic birth to nearly being abducted into slavery to escaping assassination, Muhammad emerges as an unrelenting man on a mission. Jebara places Muhammad's life in a broader historical context, vividly evoking the Meccan society he was born into and arguing that his innovative vision helped shape our modern world.

"In this accessible debut, Islamic scholar Jebara delivers an intimate portrait of Muhammad as a spiritual figure and leader.... Those looking for an introduction to the life of the Islamic prophet would do well to start here." —*Publishers Weekly*

Includes bibliographical references and index.

Jefferson, Margo
On Michael Jackson. Margo Jefferson. Pantheon Books 2006. 146 p.
ISBN 9780375423260
Grades: Adult   B
1. Jackson, Michael, 1958-2009 2. Popular music 3. Popular culture 4. Mental health 5. Fame 6. Child celebrities 7. Arts and Entertainment — Music — Pop

LC 2005053489

Presents the cultural and social significance of Michael Jackson, exploring the ways in which the spectacle of Jackson's life and musical talents have shaped American social and popular culture.

"The author considers entertainer Jackson from many angles: with regard to his family, within the Black and the larger entertainment arena, as an artist, and as an entertainer in postslavery America. Raising the specter of Jackson's possible mental illness, the book loosely tracks his life from childhood through the 2004 child molestation trial." —*Library Journal*

Includes bibliographical references.

Jenkins, Jedidiah
To Shake the Sleeping Self: A Journey from Oregon to Patagonia, and a Quest for a Life with No Regret. Jedidiah Jenkins. Convergent Books 2018. VIII, 323 p.
ISBN 9781524761387
Grades: Adult   B
1. Jenkins, Jedidiah 2. Voyages and travels 3. Bicycling 4. Gay men 5. Adulthood 6. Faith (Christianity) 7. Bicycle touring 8. Identity 9. Self-discovery 10. United States 11. Central America 12. South America 13. Autobiographies and memoirs 14. Life stories — Personal growth 15. Life stories — Identity — LGBTQIA+ 16. Travel Writing — Modes of Transportation — Cycling 17. Travel Writing — United States 18. Travel Writing — Central and South America

On the eve of turning thirty, terrified of being funneled into a life he didn't choose, Jedidiah Jenkins quit his dream job and spent the next sixteen months cycling from Oregon to Patagonia. He chronicled the trip on Instagram, where his photos and profound reflections on life soon attracted hundreds of thousands of followers.

Includes bibliographical references and index.

Jeter, Derek
Jeter Unfiltered. Derek Jeter with Anthony Bozza; photographs by Christopher Anderson. Gallery Books 2014. 252 pages : Illustration; Color
ISBN 9781476783666
Grades: Adult   B
1. Jeter, Derek, 1974- 2. Baseball 3. Baseball players 4. United States 5. Autobiographies and memoirs 6. Biographies 7. Sports and Competition — Baseball 8. Life stories — Sports — Athletes

LC 2014033440

A biography of baseball player Derek Jeter.
Jeter Publishing.

Jobrani, Maziyar
I'm Not a Terrorist, but I've Played One on Tv: Memoirs of a Middle Eastern Funny Man. Maz Jobrani. Simon & Schuster 2014. 208 p.
ISBN 9781476749983
Grades: Adult   B
1. Jobrani, Maziyar, 1972- 2. Stereotypes 3. Iranian-Americans 4. Actors and actresses 5. Comedians 6. United States 7. Autobiographies and memoirs 8. Biographies 9. Life stories — Arts and culture — Performing arts — Entertainers and celebrities 10. Humor writing — Social humor 11. Society and culture — Ethnic studies

LC 2014015012

A founding member of the Axis of Evil Comedy Tour and regular on Better off Ted recounts his experiences as an Iranian growing up in America, his efforts to assimilate both cultures and his regular castings as a villain on TV and in movies.

John, Elton
★ *Me: Elton John Official Autobiography.* Elton John. Henry Holt & Company 2019. 320 p.
ISBN 9781250147608
Grades: Adult   B
1. John, Elton 2. Furnish, David 3. Fame 4. Pop musicians 5. Gay men 6. Recovering addicts 7. Addiction 8. Gay parents 9. Popular music 10. Rock music 11. Rock musicians 12. England 13. Autobiographies and memoirs 14. Biographies 15. Life stories — Arts and culture — Performing arts — Musicians and composers 16. Arts and Entertainment — Music — Pop

LC 2019947895

1357

An official autobiography by the influential music artist, published to coincide with the release of Rocketman, includes coverage of John's complicated upbringing in a London suburb, his celebrity collaborations, his struggles with addiction and the establishment of his AIDS Foundation.

"Intimate, with brushes of gossip and hard-won wisdom, this compelling work joins the ranks of other masterly rock memoirs. A must-read for John's many devotees, it will also make fans out of those new to his music." —*Library Journal*

Johnson, Brian
The Lives of Brian: A Memoir. Brian Johnson. Dey Street Books 2022. 320 p.
ISBN 9780063046382
Grades: Adult **B**
1. Johnson, Brian, 1947 October 5- 2. Rock musicians 3. Growing up 4. Poverty 5. Rock groups 6. Heavy metal music 7. Fame 8. British people 9. English people 10. Autobiographies and memoirs 11. Life stories — Arts and culture — Performing arts — Musicians and composers 12. Arts and Entertainment — Music — Rock

Brian Johnson's memoir from growing up in a small town to starting his own band to ultimately replacing Bon Scott, the lead singer of one of the world biggest rock acts, AC/DC.

"In his briskly told and forthright memoir, Johnson recounts his good fortune in becoming the voice on one of rock's highest-selling albums, AC/DC's Back in Black….Johnson's animated prose captures the ups and downs of his life and music with one of the world's most popular bands." —*Publishers Weekly*

Originally published in the UK by Michael Thomas, an imprint of Penguin Random House UK; Includes index.

Johnson, Graham
Poulenc: The Life in the Songs. Graham Johnson; translations of the song texts by Jeremy Sams. Liveright Publishing 2020. 672 p.
ISBN 9781631495236
Grades: Adult **B**
1. Poulenc, Francis, 1899-1963 2. Composers 3. Orchestral music 4. Classical music 5. Gay men 6. Interpersonal relations 7. Composition (Music) 8. Music history and criticism 9. 20th century 10. Biographies 11. Life stories — Arts and culture — Performing arts — Musicians and composers 12. Arts and Entertainment — Music — Classical

LC 2020010683

Francis Poulenc (1899?1963) is widely acknowledged as one of the twentieth century's most significant masters of vocal music—solo, choral, and operatic—quite apart from his achievements in instrumental spheres. But what it cost him, and the determined bravery it took for his unusual talent to thrive, has always been underestimated. In this seminal biography, which will serve as the definitive guide to the songs, acclaimed collaborative pianist Graham Johnson shows that it is in Poulenc's extraordinary songs, and seeing how they fit into his life—which included crippling guilt on account of his sexuality—that we discover Poulenc heart and soul. With the insight that comes from a lifetime of performing this music, Johnson provides an essential volume for singers, pianists, listeners, and readers interested in the artistic milieu of modernism in the first half of the twentieth century.

"This astute biography will be a boon to Poulenc fans and classical music buffs alike." —*Publishers Weekly*

Includes bibliographical references and index.

Johnson, Joyce
The Voice Is All: The Lonely Victory of Jack Kerouac. Joyce Johnson. Viking 2012. 512 p.
ISBN 9780670025107
Grades: Adult **B**
1. Kerouac, Jack, 1922-1969 2. Beat culture 3. Beat authors 4. Beat poets 5. Counterculture 6. Authors, American 7. Social life and customs 8. United States 9. 20th century 10. Biographies 11. Life stories — Arts and culture — Writing — Authors 12. Life stories — Arts and culture — Writing — Poets

LC 2012000603

The National Book Critics Circle Award-winning author of Minor Characters presents a profile of the iconic artist's early years that offers insight into his efforts to bridge his dual cultural heritage while exploring how his French Canadian background enriched his prose, discussing the breakthroughs that inspired such works as on the Road and Visions of Cody.

"Her book is essential reading for anyone interested in a deeper understanding of Kerouac's life and work." —*Library Journal*

Includes bibliographical references.

Johnson, Katherine G.
My Remarkable Journey. Katherine Johnson with Joylette Hylick and Katherine Moore. Amistad Press 2021. 288 p.
ISBN 9780062897664
Grades: Adult **B**
1. Johnson, Katherine G, 1918-2020 2. Women mathematicians 3. African American women 4. Mathematicians 5. Growing up 6. Childhood 7. Racism 8. African Americans 9. Sexism 10. Race relations 11. Social life and customs 12. Determination 13. United States 14. Autobiographies and memoirs 15. Life stories — Science, technology, and medicine — Scientists and inventors 16. History writing — African American — United States 17. Science Writing — Mathematics

In this memoir, Katherine shares her personal journey from child prodigy in the Allegheny Mountains of West Virginia to NASA human computer. In her life after retirement, she served as a beacon of light for her family and community alike. Her story is centered around the basic tenets of her life; no one is better than you, education is paramount, and asking questions can break barriers. The memoir captures the many facets of this unique woman: the curious "daddy's girl"; pioneering professional, and sage elder.

"Readers will enjoy Johnson's personal accounts of the space race and the roles of Black women in STEM. This wonderful, insightful memoir is the perfect companion piece to Margot Lee Shetterly's best-selling Hidden Figures." —*Library Journal*

"Johnson is a warm and compassionate author, filling her pages with the most personal of stories while also illuminating the times she lived through with an appreciation for all the dramatic changes occurring around her. Truly a lovely read." —*Booklist*

Johnson, Mindy
Ink & Paint: The Women of Walt Disney's Animation. Mindy Johnson; foreword by June Foray. Disney Editions 2017. 384 pages : Illustration; Color; Map; Portrait; Charts; Facsimile
ISBN 9781484727812
Grades: Adult **B**
1. Women cartoonists 2. Women animators 3. Animated films 4. Animation (Cinematography) 5. Women employees 6. Film history and criticism 7. Arts and Entertainment — Comics, Cartoons, and Animation 8. Adult books for young adults

LC Bl2017042093

From the earliest black-and-white Alice Comedies to the advent of CAPS and digital animation, meet the pioneering women who brought handrendered animated stories to vibrant, multicolored life at Walt Disney Studios and beyond.

Johnson, Paul
Churchill. by Paul Johnson. Viking 2009. 192 p.
ISBN 9780670021055
Grades: Adult **B**
1. Churchill, Winston, 1874-1965 2. Politicians 3. Prime ministers 4. Politics and government 5. Leadership 6. Great Britain 7. 20th century 8. Biographies 9. History writing — Europe — United Kingdom 10. History writing — Wars and conflicts — World War II 11. Life stories — Politics — Politicians

LC 2009008326

Shares unconventional and revelatory analyses of key moments in the twentieth-century prime minister's career, exploring his early achievements and subsequent leadership while providing anecdotal insights into the experiences and qualities that enabled his successes.

Includes bibliographical references and index.

Eisenhower: A Life. Paul Johnson. Viking 2014. 144 pages
ISBN 9780670016822

ESSENTIAL AND RECOMMENDED TITLES
Biography

Grades: Adult **B**
1. Eisenhower, Dwight D. (Dwight David), 1890-1969 2. Presidents 3. Generals 4. Politics and government 5. United States 6. 20th century 7. 1950s 8. 1960s 9. Biographies 10. Conservative writing 11. History writing — Presidency — 20th century — United States 12. Life stories — Politics — Politicians
LC 2014005313

A portrait of the 34th president places particular emphasis on his years as a five-star general and his two presidential terms, sharing additional coverage of such subjects as his Kansas childhood, West Point education and volatile relationship with Richard Nixon. By the best-selling author of Churchill.

Includes bibliographical references and index.

George Washington: The Founding Father. Paul Johnson. Atlas Books; Harper Collins 2005. 126 p. (Eminent lives)
ISBN 9780060753658
Grades: 11 12 Adult **B**
1. Washington, George, 1732-1799 2. Founding Fathers of the United States 3. American Revolution, 1775-1783 4. Command of troops 5. Presidents 6. Revolutions 7. Generals 8. Politics and government 9. Leadership 10. United States history 11. United States 12. 18th century 13. Revolutionary America (1775-1783) 14. Biographies 15. History writing — Presidency — 18th century — United States 16. History writing — Military — Military leadership 17. Life stories — Law and order — Military leaders
LC 2004052907

A portrait of the first American president examines how his character reflected eighteenth-century values, citing his pivotal contributions to the creation of the Constitution and his leadership during the Revolutionary War.

"The author submits a beautifully cogent, enthrallingly perceptive, and . . . startlingly fresh take on the ultimate American icon."—*Booklist*

Includes bibliographical references (p. 125-126).

Napoleon. Paul Johnson. Viking 2002. xii, 190 p.
ISBN 9780670030781
Grades: 11 12 Adult **B**
1. Napoleon I, Emperor of the French, 1769-1821 2. Generals 3. Politicians 4. Command of troops 5. Rulers 6. Politics and government 7. French history 8. France 9. 19th century 10. 18th century 11. Biographies 12. History writing — Military — Military leadership 13. Life stories — Law and order — Military leaders 14. History writing — Wars and conflicts — Napoleonic Wars 15. Life stories — Politics — Politicians
LC 2001045605

A historian turns his sights on Napoleon, casting his life in a new light, from his early displays of military genius through his lust for power and his eventual defeat at Waterloo and exile on St. Helena.

"Johnson presents a concise appraisal of Napoleon's career and a precise understanding of his enigmatic character. The author views Napoleon, not as an idea man whose ideology was the ladder by which he propelled himself to heights of power, but as an opportunist who took advantage of a series of events and situations he could manipulate into achieving supreme control."—*Booklist*

A Penguin life; a Lipper/Viking book; Includes bibliographical references.

Johnson, Stephanie
Tanqueray. Stephanie Johnson, Brandon Stanton. St. Martin's Press 2022. 304 p.
ISBN 9781250278272
Grades: Adult **B**
1. Johnson, Stephanie (Dancer) 2. Stripteasers 3. Women dancers 4. African American women 5. Burlesque 6. New York City 7. Autobiographies and memoirs 8. Life stories — Arts and culture — Performing arts — Dancers and choreographers 9. Life stories — Arts and culture — Performing arts — Entertainers and celebrities 10. Arts and Entertainment — General
LC 2022010197

In 2019, Humans of New York featured a photo of a woman in an outrageous fur coat and hat she made herself. She instantly captured the attention of millions. Her name is Stephanie Johnson, but she's better known to HONY followers as "Tanqueray," a born performer who was once one of the best-known burlesque dancers in New York City. Reeling from a brutal childhood, immersed in a world of go-go dancers and hustlers, dirty cops and gangsters, Stephanie was determined to become the fiercest thing the city had ever seen. And she succeeded. Real, raw, and unapologetically honest, this is the full story of Tanqueray as told by Brandon Stanton—a book filled with stories of Tanqueray's struggles and triumphs through good times and bad.

"Two years after Johnson shared her story on Stanton's popular Instagram account Humans of New York, she commands the spotlight again in this hypnotizing account of her past as a Black burlesque dancer."—*Publishers Weekly*

Jollett, Mikel
★ *Hollywood* Park: A Memoir. Mikel Jollett. Celadon Books 2020. 384 p.
ISBN 9781250621566
Grades: Adult **B**
1. Jollett, Mikel 2. Cults 3. Growing up 4. Self-discovery 5. Addiction 6. Parent and child 7. Dysfunctional families 8. Poverty 9. Rock music 10. Rock musicians 11. United States 12. Autobiographies and memoirs 13. Biographies 14. Life stories — Arts and culture — Performing arts — Musicians and composers 15. Life stories — Relationships — Growing up 16. Arts and entertainment — Music — Rock
LC 2020002685

The frontman of indie band the Airborne Toxic Event reveals his upbringing in the infamous Church of Synanon cult, where he endured poverty, addiction and emotional abuse before slowly working his way toward college and a music career.

"In this arresting debut memoir, Jollett, frontman of the indie band Airborne Toxic Event, writes of escaping a California cult named Synanon—where he lived in the 1970s until age five—with his mentally unstable mother and older brother. . . . All this results in a shocking but contemplative memoir about the aftermath of an unhealthy upbringing."—*Publishers Weekly*

Jones, Booker T.
Time Is Tight: My Life, Note by Note. Booker T. Jones. Little, Brown & Co. 2019. 320 p.
ISBN 9780316485609
Grades: Adult **B**
1. Soul musicians 2. Soul music 3. Musicians 4. Memphis, Tennessee 5. Autobiographies and memoirs 6. Biographies 7. Arts and Entertainment — Music — Jazz and the Blues 8. Life stories — Arts and culture — Performing arts — Musicians and composers

The leader of the famed Stax Records house band, architect of the Memphis soul sound and one of the most legendary figures in music presents his much anticipated memoir in which he shares his remarkable life story.

"A thoughtful autobiography that takes in not just the tunes, but the times that produced them—a delight for fans."—*Kirkus*

Jones, Brenda
Alexandria Ocasio-cortez: The Life, Times, and Rise Of. Brenda Jones and Krishan Trotman. Plume 2020. xviii, 186 p.
ISBN 9780593189856
Grades: 9 10 11 12 Adult **B**
1. Ocasio-Cortez, Alexandria, 1989- 2. Hispanic American women 3. Women legislators 4. Women politicians 5. Feminists 6. Social justice 7. Progressivism (United States politics) 8. Legislators 9. Politics and government 10. United States 11. New York City 12. 21st century 13. Biographies 14. Liberal writing 15. Life stories — Politics — Politicians 16. Politics and global affairs — Political figures 17. Life stories — Identity — Gender 18. Life stories — Identity — Race and ethnicity 19. Life stories — Politics — Activists and reformers
LC 2020012468

Not long ago, no one could even imagine a twenty-eight-year-old Latina upstart running for Congress representing Queens and the Bronx: It required facing the city's nearly all-white, all-male political machine. But since Alexandria Ocasio-Cortez graced the scene in all her bartending, tweet-talking, mold-breaking glory, the face of politics in the twenty-first century has changed. Today, Ocasio-Cortez is a foremost advocate for progress, whipping up support among her colleagues and gaining the secret admiration of her foes. She's jousting with

PUBLIC LIBRARY CORE COLLECTION: NONFICTION
Twentieth Edition

an outrageous president and a conservative media sphere that place her under relentless attack. Why? Because they fear her gift for speaking truth to power.
Includes bibliographical references.

Maxine Waters: The Life, Times and Rise Of. Brenda Jones and Krishan Trotman. Plume 2020. 208 pages
ISBN 9780593189870
Grades: Adult   **B**
1. Waters, Maxine 2. African American women legislators 3. Women legislators 4. African American women politicians 5. Women politicians 6. Feminists 7. Social justice 8. Voting 9. Legislators 10. African American women 11. Politics and government 12. United States 13. Los Angeles, California 14. 21st century 15. Biographies 16. Liberal writing 17. Life stories — Politics — Politicians 18. Politics and global affairs — Political figures 19. Life stories — Identity — Gender 20. Life stories — Identity — Race and ethnicity 21. Life stories — Politics — Activists and reformers

LC 2020012467

Part of a four-book series celebrating women in congress, this biography of the representative for California's 43rd congressional district describes growing up with a single mother in Missouri to forging a new political path for young people of color.

"A spirited tribute to an impressive woman." —*Kirkus*
Includes bibliographical references.

Jones, Brian Jay

★ *Becoming Dr. Seuss: Theodor Geisel and the Making of an American Imagination.* Brian Jay Jones. Dutton 2019. 448 p.
ISBN 9781524742782
Grades: Adult   **B**
1. Seuss, Dr 2. Illustrators 3. Children's literature authors 4. Children's book illustrators 5. Children's literature writing 6. Personal conduct 7. Authors, American 8. 20th century 9. Biographies 10. Life stories — Arts and culture — Writing — Authors 11. Arts and entertainment — Writing and publishing

LC 2018059288

A full-scale portrait of Theodor Geisel, best known as American icon Dr. Seuss, shares insights into his successful early career as a radical political cartoonist and the complicated genius that informed his beliefs on such subjects as empathy and environmentalism.

"This attractive biography should be on the bedside reading table of thousands of Dr. Seuss lovers, and deservedly so." —*Library Journal*
Includes bibliographical references.

George Lucas: A Life. Brian Jay Jones. Little Brown & Co. 2016. VIII, 550 pages, 16 unnumbered pages of plates : Illustration; Color
ISBN 9780316257442
Grades: Adult   **B**
1. Lucas, George, 1944- 2. Film industry and trade 3. Filmmaking 4. Star Wars films 5. Film producers and directors 6. United States 7. Biographies 8. Life stories — Arts and culture — Performing arts — Directors and producers 9. Adult books for young adults
Booklist Editors' Choice, 2016.

Traces the story of the man behind such blockbuster franchises as Star Wars and Indiana Jones, offering insight into the challenges he overcame and his influential legacy.

Includes bibliographical references (pages 527-529), filmography (pages 529-530), and index.

Jim Henson: The Biography. Brian Jay Jones. Ballantine Books 2013. 672 p.
ISBN 9780345526113
Grades: Adult   **B**
1. Henson, Jim 2. Puppeteers 3. Television producers and directors 4. Television 5. United States 6. Biographies 7. Life stories — Arts and culture — Performing arts — Entertainers and celebrities

LC 2013024039

Booklist Editors' Choice, 2013; Goodreads Choice Award, 2013.

Fans of the Muppets—or TV history at large—won't want to miss this compelling and informative behind-the-scenes story of "Muppets" inventor, Jim Henson. Henson began work in television in 1955. Joining forces with artist Jane Nebel, whom he later married, Henson enthusiastically developed the signature puppeteering style that landed him on Sesame Street—and brought the now-famous Muppet Kermit the Frog and many others to the world. Biographer Brian Jay Jones offers the first complete biography of Henson, detailing his personal life, the nature of his creative genius, his collaborations with Frank Oz and other industry stars.

Includes bibliographical references and index.

Jones, Chloe Cooper

★ *Easy Beauty: A Memoir.* Chloe Cooper Jones. Avid Reader Presss 2022. 288 p.
ISBN 9781982151997
Grades: Adult   **B**
1. Jones, Chloe Cooper 2. Women college teachers 3. Motherhood 4. Medical genetics 5. Women with disabilities 6. Physical disabilities 7. Beauty 8. Body image 9. Identity 10. Feminine beauty (Aesthetics) 11. Women journalists 12. Autobiographies and memoirs 13. Life stories — Facing adversity — Medical issues 14. Science Writing — Medicine and health — Disabilities and disorders

Pulitzer Prize for Memoir or Autobiography finalist, 2023.

A philosophy professor and freelance journalist born with a rare congenital which affects both her stature and gait discusses how she has navigated a world that both judges and pities her for her appearance.

"Cooper Jones (finalist for a 2020 Pulitzer Prize for feature writing) presents, with unflinching honesty, this memoir about living with disability....Readers will appreciate the book's portrayal of self and of living with disability, and the author's honest confrontation of beauty standards and motherhood." —*Library Journal*

Jones, Dylan

David Bowie: A Life. Dylan Jones. Crown Archetype 2017. 400 p.
ISBN 9780451497833
Grades: Adult   **B**
1. Bowie, David, 1947-2016 2. Rock music 3. Popular culture 4. Creativity 5. Songwriting 6. Overdoing things 7. Rock musicians 8. Celebrities 9. England 10. Biographies 11. Interviews 12. Oral histories 13. Arts and Entertainment — Music — Rock 14. Life stories — Arts and culture — Performing arts — Musicians and composers

LC 2017010571

Dylan Jones's engrossing, magisterial biography of David Bowie is unlike any Bowie story ever written. Drawn from over 180 interviews with friends, rivals, lovers, and collaborators, some of whom have never before spoken about their relationship with Bowie, this oral history weaves a hypnotic spell as it unfolds the story of a remarkable rise to stardom and an unparalleled artistic path.

"In this comprehensive oral history, GQ editor Jones delves deeply into the details of rock icon David Bowies fame, financial problems, drug use, sexuality, Buddhist practices, and romantic entanglements." —*Publishers Weekly*

Jones, Faith

Sex Cult Nun: Breaking Away from the Children of God, a Wild, Radical Religious Cult. Faith Jones. William Morrow & Company 2021. 384 p.
ISBN 9780062952455
Grades: Adult   **B**
1. Jones, Faith 2. Cults 3. Cult members 4. Christian sects 5. Growing up 6. Grandfather and granddaughter 7. Cult leaders 8. Polygamy 9. Child sexual abuse 10. Radicalism 11. Brainwashing 12. Patriarchy 13. Manipulation (Social sciences) 14. Freedom 15. Family relationships 16. Sexually abused children 17. Girls 18. Autobiographies and memoirs 19. Life stories — Facing adversity — Abuse survivors 20. Life stories — Religion and spirituality — Leaving religion 21. Spirituality and Religion — General 22. Debut title

In this story of liberation and self-empowerment, the author shares her hauntingly intimate coming-of-age narrative of growing up in and escaping from the Children of God, an oppressive, extremist religious cult.

"Complex and richly detailed, the book provides fascinating insights into a secretive religious organization while offering often heartbreaking details about the nature and repercussions of growing up indoctrinated in a cult." —*Kirkus*

ESSENTIAL AND RECOMMENDED TITLES
Biography

Jones, Michael K.
The Black Prince: England's Greatest Medieval Warrior. Michael K. Jones. Pegasus Books 2018. 488 p.
ISBN 9781681777412
Grades: Adult **B**
1. Edward, Prince of Wales, 1330-1376 2. Princes 3. Warriors 4. Knights and knighthood 5. Command of troops 6. British history 7. 14th century 8. Biographies 9. History writing — Europe — United Kingdom 10. History writing — Medieval — Europe 11. Life stories — Politics — Royalty 12. Life stories — Law and order — Military leaders
LC Bl2018056219

The remarkable and inspiring story of one of the greatest warrior-princes of the Middle Ages—and an unforgettably vivid portrait of warfare and chivalry in the fourteenth century.

Jones, Nathaniel R.
Answering the Call: An Autobiography of the Modern Struggle to End Racial Discrimination in America. Judge Nathaniel R. Jones; foreword by Evelyn Brooks Higginbotham. The New Press 2016. 352 p.
ISBN 9781620970751
Grades: Adult **B**
1. Jones, Nathaniel R, 1926-2020 2. Judges 3. Civil rights 4. United States 5. Autobiographies and memoirs 6. Life stories — Law and order — Judges and lawyers 7. History writing — African American — Civil rights — United States
LC 2015043150

Judge Nathaniel R. Jones's pathbreaking career was forged in the 1960s: as the first African American assistant U.S. attorney in Ohio; as assistant general counsel of the Kerner Commission; and, beginning in 1969, as general counsel of the NAACP. In that latter role, Jones coordinated attacks against Northern school segregation-a vital, divisive, and poorly understood chapter in the movement for equality-twice arguing in the pivotal U.S. Supreme Court case Bradley v. Milliken, which addressed school desegregation in Detroit. He also led the national response to the attacks against affirmative action, spearheading and arguing many of the signal legal cases of that effort.

"A forthright testimony by a witness to history." —*Kirkus*
Includes bibliographical references and index.

Jones, Saeed
How We Fight for Our Lives: A Memoir. Saeed Jones. Simon & Schuster 2019. 208 p.
ISBN 9781501132735
Grades: Adult **B**
1. Jones, Saeed 2. African American authors 3. Gay authors 4. Growing up 5. Identity 6. Intersectionality 7. Mothers and sons 8. Family relationships 9. Gay men 10. African Americans 11. Southern states 12. Autobiographies and memoirs 13. Life stories — Identity — Race and ethnicity 14. Life stories — Identity — LGBTQIA+ 15. Life stories — Relationships — Growing up 16. Adult books for young adults 17. Antiracist literature
LC 2019002515

Kirkus Prize for Nonfiction, 2019; Lambda Literary Award for Gay Memoir/Biography, 2020; Library Journal Best Books, 2019; New York Times Notable Book, 2019; Stonewall Book Awards: Israel Fishman Non-fiction Award, 2020.

The co-host of BuzzFeed's AM to DM, award-winning poet and author of Prelude to Bruise documents his coming-of-age as a young, gay, Black man in an American South at a crossroads of sex, race and power.

"A memoir of coming to terms that's written with masterful control of both style and material." —*Kirkus*
Includes bibliographical references and index.

Jordan, Mary
The Art of Her Deal: The Untold Story of Melania Trump. Mary Jordan. Simon & Schuster 2020. VII, 341 pages : Illustration; Color
ISBN 9781982113407
Grades: Adult **B**
1. Trump, Melania, 1970- 2. Trump, Donald, 1946- 3. Presidents' spouses 4. Decision-making 5. Loyalty 6. Immigrants 7. Married people 8. Political science 9. Ambition 10. Independence 11. 21st century 12. Biographies 13. Life stories — Politics — Politicians 14. Politics and global affairs — Political figures 15. History writing — Presidency — 21st century — United States 16. Life stories — Relationships — Couples

Traces Melania's journey from Slovenia, where her family stood out for their nonconformity, to her days as a fledgling model known for steering clear of the industry's hard-partying scene, to a tiny living space in Manhattan she shared platonically with a male photographer, to the long, complicated dating dance that finally resulted in her marriage to Trump.

"Interesting and fair . . . meticulously researched . . . as complete a portrait as we can expect of the current first lady." —*Kirkus*
Includes bibliographical references (pages 287-324) and index.

Joseph, Peniel E.
The Sword and the Shield: The Revolutionary Lives of Malcolm X and Martin Luther King Jr. Peniel E. Joseph. Basic Books 2020. 368 p.
ISBN 9781541617865
Grades: Adult **B**
1. King, Martin Luther, Jr, 1929-1968 2. Malcolm X, 1925-1965 3. Civil Rights Movement 4. Social advocates 5. Identity 6. African Americans 7. Racism 8. Political activists 9. Race relations 10. United States history 11. United States 12. 1960s 13. 1950s 14. 20th century 15. Life stories — Politics — Activists and reformers — Civil Rights leaders 16. History writing — African American — Civil rights — United States 17. History writing — 1960s — United States 18. Society and culture — Race
LC 2019051608

The Sword and the Shield is a dual biography of Malcolm X and Martin Luther King that transforms our understanding of the twentieth century's most iconic African American leaders. Peniel E. Joseph reveals a nuanced portrait of two men who, despite markedly different backgrounds, inspired and pushed each other throughout their adult lives. This is a strikingly revisionist biography, not only of Malcolm and Martin, but also of the movement and era they came to define.

"An authoritative dual biography from a leading scholar of African American history." —*Kirkus*
Includes bibliographical references and index.

Kahlo, Frida
The Diary of Frida Kahlo: An Intimate Self-portrait. Introduction by Carlos Fuentes; essay and commentaries by Sarah M. Lowe. H.N. Abrams; 2005. 295 p. : Illustration; Color
ISBN 9780810959545
Grades: Adult **B**
1. Kahlo, Frida 2. Painters 3. Surrealism 4. Diaries 5. Arts and Entertainment — Painting, Drawing, and Sculpture 6. Life stories — Arts and culture
LC Bl2005021601

A facsimile of the diary of the twentieth-century Mexican artist, which is accompanied by an English transcription and commentary and more than three hundred illustrations.

"Sprinkled with irony, black humor, even gaiety . this volume is a testament to Kahlo's resilience and courage." —*Publishers Weekly*
Includes bibliographical references (p. 293) and index; Reprint. Originally published: 1995.

Kaiser, Charles
The Cost of Courage. by Charles Kaiser. Other Press 2015. 300 p.
ISBN 9781590516140
Grades: Adult **B**
1. Audibert-Boulloche, Christiane 2. Katlama, Jacqueline Boulloche, 1918-1994 3. Boulloche, Andre 4. French Resistance (World War II) 5. Guerrillas 6. Military occupation 7. Spies 8. Concentration camps 9. Families 10. German occupation, World War II 11. French history 12. History writing — Wars and conflicts — World War II 13. History writing — Wars and conflicts — Resistance — World War II
LC 2015008560

PUBLIC LIBRARY CORE COLLECTION: NONFICTION
Twentieth Edition

Describes how the heroism of three siblings, who took over and lead the French Resistance during World War II after their older brother was betrayed, wounded and arrested by the Gestapo surviving three concentration camps.

"Kaiser's account of a family's devotion and resilience in the face of horrific tyranny tells a highly recommended story of resolve and bravery that can't help but feel romantic in its selfless and profound obligation, but this is not gloss nor ungrounded canonization." —*Library Journal*

Kalanithi, Paul
★ *When* Breath Becomes Air. Paul Kalanithi. Random House 2016. 240 p.
ISBN 9780812988406
Grades: Adult   B
1. Kalanithi, Paul 2. People with cancer 3. Personal conduct 4. Purpose in life 5. Thirties (Age) 6. Ethics 7. Lung cancer 8. Death 9. Grief 10. Fathers 11. Life change events 12. Neurosurgeons 13. Autobiographies and memoirs 14. Life stories — Facing adversity — Medical issues — Physical illness
LC 2015023815

Goodreads Choice Award, 2016; New York Times Notable Book, 2016; Library Journal Best Books, 2016; Pulitzer Prize for Biography or Autobiography finalist, 2017.

A young neurosurgeon faced with a terminal diagnosis describes his examination into what truly makes a meaningful life.

"This eloquent, heartfelt meditation on the choices that make life worth living, even as death looms, will prompt readers to contemplate their own values and mortality." —*Booklist*

Kaling, Mindy
Why Not Me? Mindy Kaling. Crown 2015. 240 p.
ISBN 9780804138147
Grades: Adult   B
1. Kaling, Mindy 2. Celebrities 3. Television writers 4. Women comedians 5. Women television personalities 6. Actors and actresses 7. Autobiographies and memoirs 8. Biographies 9. Life stories — Arts and culture — Performing arts — Actors and actresses 10. Arts and Entertainment — Comedy 11. Humor writing — Family and relationship humor
LC 2015020444

The star of the Mindy Project and author of the best-selling Is Everyone Hanging Out Without Me? presents a second collection of uproarious essays, observations, fears and advice on everything from prisoner fan mail to celebrity interactions.

Kamkwamba, William
★ The *Boy* Who Harnessed the Wind: Creating Currents of Electricity and Hope. William Kamkwamba and Bryan Mealer. William Morrow 2009. 347 p.
ISBN 9780061730320
Grades: 11 12 Adult   B
1. Kamkwamba, William, 1987- 2. Inventors 3. Windmills 4. Wind power 5. Electric power production 6. Famines 7. Teenage boys 8. Malawi 9. Africa 10. Autobiographies and memoirs 11. Page to screen 12. Life stories — Science, technology, and medicine — Scientists and inventors 13. History writing — Africa 14. Family and Relationships — Families 15. Adult books for young adults
LC Bl2009020076

Alex Award, 2010.

One of the coauthors tells his engaging and inspiring true story of hope, tenacity, and imagination, in which as an African teenager he built a windmill from scraps, creating electricity for his village—and a better life for himself and his family.

"This exquisite tale strips life down to its barest essentials, and once there finds reason for hopes and dreams, and is especially resonant for Americans given the economy and increasingly heated debates over health care and energy policy." —*Publishers Weekly*

This memoir is the inspiration for the 2019 film of the same name, starring, adapted and directed by Chiwetel Ejiofor.

Kan, Karoline
Under Red Skies: Three Generations of Life, Loss, and Hope in China. Karoline Kan. Hachette Books 2019. 320 p.
ISBN 9780316412049
Grades: Adult   B
1. Kan, Karoline, 1989- 2. Chinese women 3. Intergenerational relations 4. Social change 5. Family relationships 6. Journalists 7. Family secrets 8. Social life and customs 9. China 10. 20th century 11. Autobiographies and memoirs 12. Life stories — Relationships — Family 13. Life stories — People in history — Witness to history 14. History writing — Communist China — Asia — China
LC 2018036323

Using stories of her own family's history, a former New York Times author offers a personal look at how China is trying to reconcile its impoverished and troubled past with its new role as a world superpower.

"Kan presents an engaging debut memoir that would make an excellent book club choice and has strong YA crossover appeal." —*Library Journal*

Includes index.

Kandel, Eric R.
In Search of Memory: The Emergence of a New Science of Mind. Eric R. Kandel. W. W. Norton & Company 2006. xv, 510 p. : Illustration
ISBN 9780393058635
Grades: Adult   B
1. Kandel, Eric R. 2. Neurologists 3. Medical scientists 4. Nobel Prizes 5. Memory 6. Neurobiology 7. Neuroscience 8. Nobel Prize winners 9. United States history 10. 20th century 11. Autobiographies and memoirs 12. Science Writing — Biology 13. Life stories — Science, technology, and medicine — Scientists and inventors

Los Angeles Times Book Prize for Science and Technology, 2006; National Academies Communication Award, 2007.

Traces a five-decade convergence of four distinct disciplines including behaviorist psychology, cognitive psychology, neuroscience, and molecular biology; describing how it enabled the development of a new science in the field of memory that has a promising potential for more effective healing.

Includes bibliographical references (p. 453-484) and index.

Kander, Jason
Invisible Storm: A Soldier's Memoir of Politics and PTSD. Jason Kander. Mariner Books 2022. 320 p.
ISBN 9780358658962
Grades: Adult   B
1. Kander, Jason 2. Afghan War veterans 3. Politicians 4. People with post-traumatic stress disorder 5. Suicidal behavior 6. Married men 7. Families 8. Mental illness 9. Psychotherapy 10. Healing 11. Post-traumatic stress disorder 12. Treatment 13. People with depression 14. Men 15. Autobiographies and memoirs 16. Life stories — Law and order — Armed forces personnel 17. Life stories — Facing adversity — Medical issues — Mental illness 18. Family and Relationships — Illness and the Family

In 2017, President Obama, in his final Oval Office interview, was asked who gave him hope for the future of the country, and Jason Kander was the first name he mentioned. Suddenly, Jason was a national figure. As observers assumed he was preparing a run for the presidency, Jason announced a bid for mayor of Kansas City instead and was headed for a landslide victory. But after eleven years battling PTSD from his service in Afghanistan, Jason was seized by depression and suicidal thoughts. He dropped out of the mayor's race and out of public life. And finally, he sought help. In this brutally honest second memoir, following his New York Times best-selling debut Outside the Wire, Jason Kander has written the book he himself needed in the most painful moments of his PTSD.

"In this powerful memoir, Missouri politician Kander (Outside the Wire) recounts withdrawing from the 2019 Kansas City mayoral race to seek treatment for PTSD." —*Publishers Weekly*

Kanfer, Stefan
Tough Without a Gun: The Life and Extraordinary Afterlife of Humphrey Bogart. by Stefan Kanfer. New York 2011. 320 p.
ISBN 9780307271006

ESSENTIAL AND RECOMMENDED TITLES
Biography

Grades: Adult **B**
1. Bogart, Humphrey, 1899-1957 2. Film industry and trade 3. Actors and actresses 4. Films 5. United States 6. Biographies 7. Arts and Entertainment — Movies and Television 8. Life stories — Arts and culture — Performing arts — Actors and actresses

LC 2010022524

A comprehensive profile of the actor includes childhood and friendships to his four marriages and working relationships with directors and actors, evaluating his achievements against a backdrop of historical and cultural events.

Kang, Mia
Knockout: A Memoir. Mia Kang. Abrams Press 2020. 281 pages : Illustration
ISBN 9781419743320
Grades: 9 10 11 12 Adult **B**
1. Kang, Mia 2. Fashion models 3. Women martial artists 4. Television personalities 5. Multiracial women 6. Children of alcoholic mothers 7. Body image 8. Body dysmorphic disorder 9. Obsession 10. Eating disorders 11. Drug addiction 12. Self-acceptance 13. Self-esteem 14. Fat children 15. Resilience 16. Autobiographies and memoirs 17. Life stories — Arts and culture — Fashion 18. Life stories — Arts and culture — Performing arts — Entertainers and celebrities 19. Life stories — Facing adversity — Medical issues

LC 2020932370

Mia Kang is many things: a sought-after model, an immigrant, an eating disorder survivor, and a Muay Thai fighter. Knockout is the story of how she eschewed normative body standards and learned to use martial arts to redefine her sense of self-worth. After dealing with bullying, addiction, body dysmorphia, anxiety, depression, and even suicidal thoughts, Mia acknowledges that she is lucky to still be alive to tell readers what she's learned: to not let anyone else dictate who you are supposed to be.

"Knockout is a must-read memoir for the #MeToo era about a resilient young woman who kayos the myth of perfectionism." —*Booklist*

Kanigel, Robert
Eyes on the Street: The Life of Jane Jacobs. Robert Kanigel. Alfred A. Knopf 2016. 416 p.
ISBN 9780307961907
Grades: Adult **B**
1. Jacobs, Jane, 1916-2006 2. City life 3. Urban planning 4. Urban sociology 5. Urban renewal 6. Urban planners 7. Community activists 8. Neighborhoods 9. Urbanization 10. New York City 11. 1970s 12. 20th century 13. Biographies

LC 2015050758

Chronicles the life of a noted activist who wrote seven groundbreaking books, including her most famous, the Death and Life of Great American Cities; saved neighborhoods; stopped expressways; was arrested twice; and engaged at home and on the streets in thousands of debates?ll of which she won.

Includes bibliographical references and index.

The Man Who Knew Infinity: A Life of the Genius, Ramanujan. Robert Kanigel. C. Scribner's 1991. IX, 438 p. : Illustration; Map
ISBN 9780684192598
Grades: 11 12 Adult **B**
1. Ramanujan Aiyangar, Srinivasa, 1887-1920 2. Hardy, G. H. (Godfrey Harold), 1877-1947 3. Mathematicians 4. Genius 5. Social life and customs 6. India 7. Great Britain 8. 20th century 9. Biographies 10. Life stories — Science, technology, and medicine 11. Science Writing — Mathematics

LC 90049788

National Book Critics Circle Award for Biography finalist, 1991.

A biography of one of the most innovative mathematicians of all time traces the rise of Srinivasa Ramanujan from his days as a clerk to his collaboration with one of England's greatest mathematicians.

"Kanigel deserves high praise for a work of arduous research and rare insight." —*Booklist*

Includes bibliographical references (p. 375-423) and index.

Kaplan, Alice Yaeger
Looking for the Stranger: Albert Camus and the Life of a Literary Classic. Alice Kaplan. The University of Chicago Press 2016. 288 p.
ISBN 9780226241678
Grades: Adult **B**
1. Camus, Albert, 1913-1960 2. Authors, French 3. Philosophers 4. Biographies 5. Arts and Entertainment — Writing and Publishing 6. Life stories — Arts and culture — Writing — Authors 7. Arts and Entertainment — Writing and Publishing — Literary criticism

LC 2016008498

New York Times Notable Book, 2017.

An exploration of Albert Camus' work "The Stranger," draws on his diaries and letters to trace how the author's origins in colonial Algeria and work as a journalist in the criminal courts heavily influenced his writing.

"A compelling companion to a novel that has stayed strange." —*Kirkus*

Includes bibliographical references and index.

Kaplan, Fred
John Quincy Adams: American Visionary. Fred Kaplan. HarperCollins Publishers 2014. 672 pages
ISBN 9780061915413
Grades: Adult **B**
1. Adams, John Quincy, 1767-1848 2. Monroe Doctrine 3. Presidents 4. United States 5. 19th century 6. Biographies 7. History writing — Presidency — 19th century — United States 8. Life stories — Politics — Politicians 9. History writing — Early America — United States

LC 2013035334

Booklist Editors' Choice, 2014.

A brilliant combination of literary analysis and historical detail, this masterfully written biography of the much misunderstood sixth president of the United States reveals the many sides of this forward-thinking man whose progressive vision helped shape the course of America.

"Kaplan sees not an inadequate man in a position he could not manage. He sees instead a visionary, who stood for a united American republic free of the divisiveness of slavery." —*Booklist*

Includes bibliographical references and index.

Kariko, Katalin
Breaking Through: My Life in Science. by Dr. Katalin Karikó.. Crown 2023. 256 p.
ISBN 9780593443163
Grades: Adult **B**
1. Kariko, Katalin 2. Women biochemists 3. Biochemists 4. Vaccines 5. COVID-19 (Disease) 6. Women immigrants 7. Immigrants 8. Hungarian Americans 9. Hungarian people 10. Autobiographies and memoirs 11. Science Writing — Medicine and health — Medical breakthroughs 12. Life stories — Science, technology, and medicine — Healthcare professionals

LC 2023020863

In this gripping testament to perseverance and the power of conviction, the pioneering Hungarian American biochemist recounts her 30-year investigation into messenger RNA (mRNA), which nearly cost her everything, that led to the creation of vaccines that protected millions of people from the direst consequences of COVID-19.

"In Breaking Through, biochemist Karikó explains how her research (and longtime perseverance as both a scientist and an immigrant from postwar Hungary) led to the COVID vaccine." —*Library Journal*

Karr, Mary
The Art of Memoir. Mary Karr. HarperCollins 2015. 288 p.
ISBN 9780062223067
Grades: Adult **B**
1. Autobiography 2. Writing 3. Authors 4. Memory 5. Storytelling 6. Arts and entertainment — Writing and publishing

LC 2015373180

The best-selling author of the Liar's Club and renowned Syracuse University professor builds on her memoirs and literary anecdotes to outline her personal writing process while identifying the elements of a successful memoir.

PUBLIC LIBRARY CORE COLLECTION: NONFICTION
Twentieth Edition

Kashner, Sam
Furious Love: Elizabeth Taylor, Richard Burton, and the Marriage of the Century. Sam Kashner & Nancy Schoenberger. Harpercollins 2010. 512 p.
ISBN 9780061562846
Grades: Adult B
1. Taylor, Elizabeth, 1932-2011 2. Burton, Richard, 1925-1984 3. Actors and actresses 4. Marriages of celebrities 5. Entertainers 6. Films 7. Social life and customs 8. United States 9. 20th century 10. Biographies 11. Life stories — Arts and culture — Performing arts — Actors and actresses
LC 2010006732

The definitive, larger-than-life account of the greatest Hollywood love story ever—the romance of Elizabeth Taylor and Richard Burton.

"In this dual biography of the two legendary film stars, the authors draw upon new information, including interviews with Elizabeth Taylor and with the Burton family, to capture the famously passionate and tumultuous relationship between the legendary couple. It's a mesmerizing tale, but it's also sad, and sometimes ugly, as the two stars engaged in vicious fights, nursed their jealousies and insecurities, and descended into alcoholism while outwardly living a life of glamour and sophistication." —*Booklist*

Katz, David
Barack Before Obama: Life Before the Presidency. David Katz; foreword by Barack Obama. Ecco Press 2020. 303 pages : Illustration; Color
ISBN 9780063028746
Grades: Adult B
1. Obama, Barack 2. Legislators 3. African American legislators 4. Presidential candidates 5. African American presidential candidates 6. Politicians 7. Visual nonfiction 8. Life stories — Politics — Politicians
LC 2020047820

A personal, intimate, photographic celebration of President Barack Obama in the years prior to his presidency, from friend and former aide David Katz.

"This historic collection captures the transformation of Barack Obama from hopeful candidate to 44th president of the United States." —*Publishers Weekly*

Kavanagh, Julie
Nureyev: The Life. Julie Kavanagh. Pantheon Books 2007. 782 p.
ISBN 9780375405136
Grades: Adult B
1. Nureyev, Rudolf, 1938-1993 2. Ballet dancers 3. Ballet 4. Defectors 5. Gay men 6. Immigrants 7. Celebrities 8. Popular culture 9. Russia 10. United States 11. 20th century 12. Biographies 13. Page to screen 14. Arts and Entertainment — Dance 15. Life stories — Arts and culture — Performing arts — Dancers and choreographers
LC 2006038137

Booklist Editors' Choice, 2007; New York Times Notable Book, 2008.

A definitive portrait of the iconic ballet dancer describes Nureyev's Soviet youth, his dramatic 1961 defection to the West, the extraordinary performances that transformed him into an international celebrity, his flamboyant lifestyle, his major influence on the modern history of dance, his notorious sexual escapades, and the AIDS that claimed his life in 1993.

"In this biography of the Russian ballet dancer, the author chronicles Nureyev's many tempestuous relationships, including his legendary work with Margot Fonteyn and his formative affair with the outstanding Danish dancer Erik Bruhn. Kavanagh's consummate biography will stand as a pillar in dance history." —*Booklist*

This biography was adapted into the 2019 film the White Crow, directed by Ralph Fiennes and starring Oleg Ivenko; Includes bibliographical references and index.

Keaton, Diane
★ *Brother & Sister.* Diane Keaton. Alfred A. Knopf 2020. 192 pages
ISBN 9780451494504
Grades: Adult B
1. Keaton, Diane 2. Siblings 3. Alcoholics 4. Recluses 5. Mental illness 6. Family relationships 7. Families 8. Regret 9. Films 10. Actors and actresses 11. United States 12. Autobiographies and memoirs 13. Biographies 14. Life stories — Relationships — Family 15. Life stories — Arts and culture — Performing arts — Actors and actresses 16. Family and relationships — Siblings 17. Life stories — Facing adversity — Medical issues — Mental illness
LC 2019024947

From the beloved film star and best-selling author of Then Again—a heartfelt memoir about Diane Keaton's relationship with her younger brother, and a poignant exploration of the divergent paths siblings' lives can take.

"Immersive and haunting, this is a must for Keaton's fans and for those seeking to comprehend the nuances of sibling and family relationships." —*Library Journal*

Keeling, Ida
Can't Nothing Bring Me Down: Chasing Myself in the Race Against Time. Ida Keeling with Anita Diggs. Zondervan 2018. 199 pages : Illustration; Color
ISBN 9780310349891
Grades: Adult B
1. Keeling, Ida, 1915-2021 2. Runners 3. Personal conduct 4. Faith (Christianity) 5. Life change events 6. Running 7. Endurance sports 8. Women runners 9. Autobiographies and memoirs 10. Life stories — Sports — Athletes 11. Life stories — Religion and spirituality — Personal faith
LC 2017041065

The 101-year-old runner describes the obstacles she has faced in her life, from growing up the child of immigrants during the Depression to the murder of her sons, which inspired her to start running at sixty-seven.

Keflezighi, Meb
26 Marathons: What I Learned About Faith, Identity, Running, and Life from My Marathon Career. Meb Keflezighi, Scott Douglas. Rodale Books 2019. 256 p.
ISBN 9781635652888
Grades: Adult B
1. Keflezighi, Meb 2. Determination 3. Runners 4. Marathon runners 5. Olympic medal winners 6. Marathons 7. Faith 8. Marathon running 9. Autobiographies and memoirs 10. Life stories — Sports — Athletes 11. Sports and Competition — Racing — Track and Field
LC 2018055140

A four-time Olympian marathoner, through a focused narrative, reflects on each of the 26 marathons he's run during his career and shares the lessons on life, family, faith and running he learned along the way.

"26 Marathons is a swift read, guaranteed to be popular with student athletes plus hard-core and recreational runners, who will undoubtedly agree that Meb is an American treasure and running ambassador who never fails to inspire." —*Booklist*

Keiler, Allan
Marian Anderson: A Singer's Journey. Allan Keiler. Scribner 2000. 447 p. : Illustration
ISBN 9780684807119
Grades: 11 12 Adult B
1. Anderson, Marian, 1897-1993 2. African American women singers 3. African American singers 4. Racism 5. Women singers 6. United States 7. Biographies 8. Life stories — Arts and culture — Performing arts — Musicians and composers 9. Arts and Entertainment — Music — Opera
LC 99043319

New York Times Notable Book, 2000.

A definitive biography of one of America's greatest singers and a seminal figure in the American civil rights movement uncovers the life of the first African American soloist at the Met and the first African American singer to perform at the White House.

"The author's clear, succinct prose, initially lacking narrative coherence, gains strength and momentum as his subject matures from a young and struggling artist into one of the enduring voices of our century."—*Publishers Weekly*

A Lisa Drew book; Includes discography, bibliographical references, and index.

ESSENTIAL AND RECOMMENDED TITLES
Biography

Keith, Philip A.
All Blood Runs Red: The Legendary Life of Eugene Bullard-boxer, Pilot, Soldier, Spy. Phil Keith and Tom Clavin. Hanover Square 2019. 352 p.
ISBN 9781335005564
Grades: Adult **B**
1. Bullard, Eugene Jacques, 1895-1961 2. African American men 3. Military pilots 4. Civil rights 5. Social advocates 6. Boxers (Sports) 7. African American pilots 8. Heroes and heroines 9. World War II 10. Spies 11. European history 12. United States history 13. 20th century 14. Biographies 15. History writing — African American — Civil rights — United States 16. History writing — Wars and conflicts — World War II — European Theater 17. Life stories — Facing adversity — War and oppression 18. Nonfiction that reads like fiction
LC Bl2019032891

A biography of the first African American fighter pilot to fly in combat, Eugene Bullard, who served France in World War One and World War Two.

Keller, Helen
★ *The Story of My Life.* Helen Keller. Modern Library 2003. xlvi, 343 p. : Illustration
ISBN 9780679642879
Grades: 8 9 10 11 12 Adult **B**
1. Keller, Helen, 1880-1968 2. Sullivan, Annie, 1866-1936 3. Women with disabilities 4. Women 5. People who are blind 6. People who are blind and deaf 7. People who are deaf 8. Autobiographies and memoirs 9. Biographies 10. Biographies — Coping with challenges — Disability
LC 2002040971

A serious illness destroyed Helen Keller's sight and hearing at the age of two. At seven, she was helped by Anne Sullivan, her beloved teacher and friend. Through sheer determination and resolve, she learned to speak and prepared herself for entry into prep school by age sixteen. Later she enrolled at Radcliffe and graduated with honors. Her motto: "There are no handicaps, only challenges."

With her letters (1887-1901) and a supplementary account of her education, including passages from the reports and letters of her teacher, Anne Mansfield Sullivan, by John Albert Macy; Includes bibliographical references (p. [339]-343).

Kelly, Minka
★ *Tell Me Everything: A Memoir.* Minka Kelly. Henry Holt and Company 2023. 288 p.
ISBN 9781250852069
Grades: Adult **B**
1. Actors and actresses 2. Family relationships 3. Mothers and daughters 4. Single mothers 5. Addiction 6. Stripteasers 7. Resilience 8. United States 9. Autobiographies and memoirs 10. Life stories — Arts and culture — Performing arts — Actors and actresses 11. Life stories — Facing adversity 12. Life stories — Relationships — Parent and child
LC 2023005527

Fans know her as Lyla Garrity on Friday Night Lights or as the mysterious Samantha on HBO's Euphoria. But Minka Kelly's life has been anything but easy. Raised by a single mother who worked as a stripper and struggled with addiction, Minka and her mom bounced around the country, relying on friends and relatives to take them in. She reconnected with her father, Aerosmith's Rick Dufay, and eventually made her way to Los Angeles, where she landed the role of a lifetime on Friday Night Lights. Now she has poured her soul into the pages of this book, which ultimately tells a story of triumph over adversity, and how resilience and love are all we have in the end.

"Actor Kelly recalls her far-from-privileged upbringing and reflects on the skills that helped her survive it in this heart-stopping debut….It's an immensely moving story of one woman's unconquerable spirit."—*Publishers Weekly*

Kelly, Scott
★ *Endurance: A Year in Space, a Lifetime of Discovery.* Scott Kelly with Margaret Lazarus Dean. Alfred A. Knopf 2017. 400 pages.
ISBN 9781524731595
Grades: Adult **B**
1. Kelly, Scott, 1964- 2. Astronauts 3. Space flight 4. Autobiographies and memoirs 5. Life stories — Science, technology, and medicine — Astronauts and pilots
LC 2017024799

Booklist Editors' Choice, 2017.

A memoir by the astronaut who spent a record-breaking year aboard the International Space Station shares candid reminiscences of his voyage, his colorful formative years, and the off-planet journeys that shaped his early career.

"It's fascinating stuff, a tale of aches and pains, of boredom punctuated by terror and worries about what's happening in the dark and back down on Earth." —*Kirkus*

Kemper, Ellie
My Squirrel Days. Ellie Kemper. Scribner 2018. 288 p.
ISBN 9781501163340
Grades: Adult **B**
1. Kemper, Ellie, 1980- 2. Actors and actresses 3. Celebrities 4. Fame 5. Growing up 6. Autobiographies and memoirs 7. Life stories — Arts and culture — Performing arts — Actors and actresses 8. Arts and entertainment — Movies and television
LC 2018038665

The comedian and star of the Office and Unbreakable Kimmy Schmidt delivers a hilarious and uplifting collection of essays about one pale woman's journey from Midwestern naïf to Hollywood semi-celebrity to outrageously reasonable New Yorker.

Kennedy, Kostya
True: The Four Seasons of Jackie Robinson. Kostya Kennedy. St. Martin's Press 2022. 304 p.
ISBN 9781250274045
Grades: Adult **B**
1. Robinson, Jackie, 1919-1972 2. Baseball players 3. African American baseball players 4. African Americans 5. Baseball history 6. Race relations in sports 7. African American history 8. Civil rights 9. Race relations 10. United States history 11. 20th century 12. Biographies 13. Life stories — Sports — Athletes 14. Life stories — Politics — Activists and Reformers — Civil Rights Leaders 15. Sports and Competition — Baseball 16. Sports and Competition — Individual Athlete 17. History writing — African American — Civil rights — United States
LC 2021057160

For players, fans, managers, and executives, Jackie Robinson remains baseball's singular figure, the person who most profoundly extended, and continues to extend, the reach of the game. But Robinson's impact extended far beyond baseball: He opened the door for Black Americans to participate in other sports, and was a national figure who spoke and wrote eloquently about inequality. True: The Four Seasons of Jackie Robinson by Kostya Kennedy is an unconventional biography, focusing on four transformative years in Robinson's athletic and public life. Through it all, Robinson remained true to the effort and the mission, true to his convictions and contradictions.

"Journalist Kennedy (Lasting Impact), a former Sports Illustrated editor, takes an idiosyncratic and heartfelt look at the enduring legacy of sports pioneer Jackie Robinson through four seminal chapters of his life." —*Publishers Weekly*

Includes bibliographical references and index.

Kennedy, Michael
Richard Strauss. Michael Kennedy. Clarendon Press 1995. 250 p.
ISBN 9780198165811
Grades: Adult **B**
1. Strauss, Richard, 1864-1949 2. Composers 3. Social life and customs 4. Germany 5. 19th century 6. Biographies 7. Arts and Entertainment — Music — Classical 8. Life stories — Arts and culture — Performing arts — Musicians and composers
LC 95021613

Extensively revised, this well-received account of Richard Strauss's life and music enters its second edition. The life was rich in controversy, from the 'Outrage' caused by operas Salome and Elektra to the years under the Nazi regime. In his survey of the music, rejecting the generally accepted view that Strauss's ge-

PUBLIC LIBRARY CORE COLLECTION: NONFICTION
Twentieth Edition

nius declined in his middle years, Michael Kennedy traces refinements of style from the early 1920s to Strauss's late works.
Includes bibliographical references.

Kenner, Rob
The Marathon Don't Stop: The Life and Times of Nipsey Hussle. Rob Kenner. Atria Books 2020. 288 p.
ISBN 9781982140298
Grades: Adult   B
1. Hussle, Nipsey 2. Rap musicians 3. Hip-hop culture 4. Entrepreneurs 5. African American entrepreneurs 6. United States 7. Biographies 8. Arts and Entertainment — Music — Rap and R&B

LC 2020031307

The first in-depth biography of Nipsey Hussle, the hip hop mogul, artist, and activist whose transformative legacy inspired a generation with his motivational lyrics and visionary business savvy—before he was tragically shot down in the very neighborhood he was dedicated to building up.

Kennicott, Philip
Counterpoint: A Memoir of Bach and Mourning. Philip Kennicott. W. W. Norton & Company 2020. 224 pages
ISBN 9780393635362
Grades: Adult   B
1. Bach, Johann Sebastian, 1685-1750 2. Kennicott, Philip 3. Classical music 4. Grief 5. Pianists 6. Music theory 7. Composition (Music) 8. Interpersonal relations 9. Composers 10. Music history and criticism 11. Autobiographies and memoirs 12. Biographies 13. Arts and Entertainment — Music — Classical 14. Life stories — Facing adversity — Coping with death 15. Life stories — Arts and culture — Performing arts — Musicians and composers

LC 2019027075

The Pulitzer Prize-winning Washington Post critic and pianist describes how he navigated loss and a complicated childhood through the masterpieces of Bach, sharing insights into how Bach's genius compositions combine unique counterpoints to evoke transcendent emotion.
Includes bibliographical references.

Kerry, John
Every Day Is Extra. John Kerry. Simon & Schuster 2018. 608 p.
ISBN 9781501178955
Grades: Adult   B
1. Kerry, John, 1943- 2. Politicians 3. Cabinet officers 4. Presidential candidates 5. Legislators 6. Vietnam veterans 7. Politics and government 8. United States 9. Autobiographies and memoirs 10. Life stories — Politics — Politicians

LC 2018021806

John Kerry tells the story of his life—from son of a diplomat to decorated Vietnam veteran, five-term United States senator, 2004 Democratic presidential nominee and secretary of state for four years.
Includes index.

Kershaw, Ian
Hitler: 1936-1945, Nemesis. Ian Kershaw. W.W. Norton 2000. xxx, 1115 p, 48 p. of plates : Illustration; Map; Portrait
ISBN 9780393049947
Grades: 11 12 Adult   B
1. Hitler, Adolf, 1889-1945 2. Heads of state 3. Antisemitism 4. Nazis 5. Nazism 6. Third Reich, 1933-1945 7. Politics and government 8. German history 9. Germany 10. Between the Wars (1918-1939) 11. Biographies 12. History writing — Europe — Germany 13. History writing — Wars and conflicts — World War II — European Theater 14. Adult books for young adults 15. Life stories — Politics — Politicians
New York Times Notable Book, 2001; Shortlisted for the James Tait Black Memorial Prize for Biography, 2001.

Draws on previously unused sources, including Joseph Goebbel's diaries, to encompass the the period beginning with the Nazi dictator's attaining absolute power within Germany, through the second World War, to Hitler's suicide.

"Kershaw's two volumes will probably be the standard source for many years." —*Library Journal*
Includes bibliographical references (p. [1041]-1077) and index.

Hitler: A Biography. Ian Kershaw. W.W. Norton & Co. 2008. xli, 1029 p, 80 p. of plates : Illustration; Map; Plan
ISBN 9780393067576
Grades: Adult   B
1. Hitler, Adolf, 1889-1945 2. Nazis 3. Heads of state 4. Dictators 5. Politicians 6. Antisemitism 7. Nazism 8. Third Reich, 1933-1945 9. Politics and government 10. German history 11. Germany 12. Between the Wars (1918-1939) 13. Biographies 14. Life stories — Politics — Politicians 15. History writing — Europe — Germany

LC 2008037294

A single-volume edition of a classic biographical work traces Hitler's life and addresses key questions about the nature of Nazi radicalism, the Holocaust, and the factors that enabled European society to permit his atrocities.

"This abridgment of the author's two-volume biography on Hitler retains two themes of Kershaw's full-scale original: Analyzing the political support the demagogue mustered from the populace and key institutional centers of Germany on his ascent to and exercise of power; and the decisive personal role of Hitler in instigating World War II and genocide. The narrative Kershaw constructs on this foundation is a superb organization and expression of Hitlers chronological arc that plummeted the world into catastrophe and moral trauma, a trajectory informed by Kershaws attention to rationalizations by which people in and outside Germany, whether leaders or led, buried doubts about Hitler until his power was unrestrained, impossible to stop but by war or assassination. Manifestly, Kershaw constitutes core-collection material." —*Booklist*

An abridgement of Hitler, originally published in two volumes in 1998 (American ed. 1999) and 2000; Includes bibliographical references (p. 971-974) and index.

Khalaf, Farida
The Girl Who Escaped Isis: This Is My Story. Farida Khalaf, Andrea C. Hoffmann. Atria Books 2016. 224 p.
ISBN 9781501131714
Grades: Adult   B
1. Khalaf, Farida 2. Former captives 3. Captivity 4. Torture 5. Autobiographies and memoirs 6. Life stories — Facing adversity — War and oppression — Hostages and POWS

LC 2016022449

Presents a rare and riveting first-hand account of the terror and torture inflicted by ISIS on young Iraqi Yazidi women, and an inspiring personal story of bravery and resilience in the face of unspeakable horrors.

Khar, Erin
Strung Out: One Last Hit and Other Lies That Nearly Killed Me: A Memoir. Erin Khar. Park Row Books 2020. 304 p.
ISBN 9780778309734
Grades: Adult   B
1. Khar, Erin 2. Drug addicts 3. Heroin addiction 4. Sobriety 5. Denial (Psychology) 6. Growing up 7. Young women 8. Motherhood 9. Teenage drug abusers 10. Opioid abuse 11. United States 12. Autobiographies and memoirs 13. Life stories — Facing adversity — Medical issues — Addiction 14. Society and culture — Illness and disease — Addiction

LC Bl2020000168

The author shares her story of battling her addiction to heroin and how motherhood helped in her road to recovery. She also discusses the psychology of addiction and why people start taking opioids in the first place.

"This heartbreaking yet heartwarming memoir puts a human face on the drug crisis and the factors that lead to addiction." —*Publishers Weekly*

Khlevniuk, Oleg V.
Stalin: New Biography of a Dictator. Oleg V. Khlevniuk; translated by Nora S. Favorov. Yale University Press 2015. 384 p.
ISBN 9780300163889
Grades: Adult   B

ESSENTIAL AND RECOMMENDED TITLES
Biography

1. Stalin, Joseph, 1879-1953 2. Heads of state 3. Dictators 4. Political leadership 5. Politics and government 6. Soviet Union 7. 20th century 8. Biographies 9. Translations — Russian to English 10. Life stories — Politics — Politicians 11. History writing — Europe — Russia

LC 2014039237

Blends unpublished memos, reports, and diaries to resolve previous controversies and highlight major themes of the dictator's life while dissolving the mythology of Stalin as a benevolent or evil genius.

"Readers with an interest in Soviet history, and those who can't wait for the next two volumes of Kotkin's Stalin, will appreciate this well-documented portrayal of a man whose despotic rule reverberates in Russia to this day." —*Library Journal*

Includes bibliographical references and index.

Kidder, Tracy
A Truck Full of Money. Tracy Kidder. Random House 2016. 256 p.
ISBN 9780812995244
Grades: Adult B

1. English, Paul M, 1963- 2. Internet industry and trade 3. Entrepreneurs 4. Computer programmers 5. Information technology 6. Philanthropists 7. Businesspeople 8. People with bipolar disorder 9. Men 10. Biographies 11. Life stories — Business — Business leaders

LC 2015050454

The Pulitzer Prize- and National Book Award-winning author of Mountains Beyond Mountains presents the inspiring story of Kayak.Com founder Paul English, discussing his struggles with bipolar disorder and rebellious nature while tracing his achievements as an unconventional inventor and entrepreneur.

"While eminently readable as a biography, Kidders book is also a trenchant study of the new American economy and the technological world that built it. More engrossing work from a gifted practitioner of narrative nonfiction." —*Kirkus*

Kildea, Paul Francis
Chopin's Piano: In Search of the Instrument That Transformed Music. Paul Kildea. W W Norton & CO Inc 2018. 288 p.
ISBN 9780393652222
Grades: Adult B

1. Chopin, Frederic, 1810-1849 2. Pianos 3. Romanticism 4. Composers 5. Classical music 6. Paris, France 7. 19th century 8. Biographies 9. Arts and Entertainment — Music — Classical 10. Life stories — Arts and culture — Performing arts — Musicians and composers

LC 2018027829

The captivating story of Frederic Chopin and the fate of both his Mallorquin piano and musical Romanticism from the earlynineteenth to the mid-twentieth century.

"Densely written and packed with details, this title will appeal not only to readers who enjoy Chopin but also those interested in piano history." —*Library Journal*

Kim, Suki
Without You, There Is No US: My Time with the Sons of North Korea's Elite. Suki Kim. Crown Publishing 2014. 272 p.
ISBN 9780307720658
Grades: Adult B

1. Kim, Suki, 1970- 2. Women college teachers 3. Students 4. Totalitarianism 5. Paranoia 6. Young men 7. Teaching 8. North Korea 9. Autobiographies and memoirs 10. Life stories — Education — Scholars and educators 11. Travel Writing — Living Abroad 12. Travel Writing — Asia and the South Pacific

LC 2014012730

Traces the author's experiences as an English teacher to the sons of North Korea's elite during the last six months of Kim Jong Il's reign, an effort complicated by oppressive regime enforcers, propaganda, and evangelical missionaries.

"The result is a touching portrayal of the student experience in North Korea, which provides readers with a rare glimpse of life in the enigmatic country." —*Library Journal*

Kimball, George
Four Kings: Leonard, Hagler, Hearns, Duran, and the Last Great Era of Boxing. by George Kimball. McBooks Press 2008. 275 p.
ISBN 9781590131626
Grades: Adult B

1. Leonard, Sugar Ray, 1956- 2. Hearns, Thomas 3. Hagler, Marvelous Marvin, 1954- 4. Duran, Roberto, 1951- 5. Boxers (Sports) 6. Boxing matches 7. Boxing 8. Social life and customs 9. United States 10. Biographies 11. Sports and Competition — Boxing

LC 2008013825

The veteran sports journalists uses his eye-witness coverage and recent interviews with each of the boxers to profile the careers of four great middleweight champions: Sugar Ray Leonard, Marvelous Marvin Hagler, Thomas "Hit Man" Hearns, and Roberto Duran.

"The author resurrects Sugar Ray Leonard, Marvin Hagler, Thomas Hearns, and Roberto Duran from the mists of memory, re-creating the nine bouts the middleweights fought against one another in the 1980s. A great boxing book." —*Booklist*

Kimberley, Hannah
A Woman's Place Is at the Top: A Biography of Annie Smith Peck, Queen of the Climbers. Hannah Kimberley. St. Martin's Press 2017. 320 p.
ISBN 9781250084002
Grades: Adult B

1. Peck, Annie S. (Annie Smith), 1850-1935 2. Women mountaineers 3. Women explorers 4. Gender role 5. Mountaineering 6. Speakers 7. Mountaineers 8. Feminists 9. Gender equity 10. Political activists 11. Biographies 12. Life stories — People in history 13. History writing — Women's history 14. Sports and Competition — Mountaineering 15. Life stories — Nature and outdoors

LC 2017010843

Presents the life of the little-known early feminist, independent thinker and accomplished adventurer who became a political speaker and writer for women's suffrage and was the first person to conquer Mount Huascaran and raced Hiram Bingham to climb Mount Coropuna in 1911.

"Peck was a dynamic and compelling woman, and her story will be hard to resist for armchair travelers and fans of hidden history." —*Booklist*

Includes bibliographical references and index.

King, B. B.
★ *Blues All Around Me: The Autobiography of B.B. King.* B.B. King with David Ritz. Spike 1999. xii, 336 p. : Illustration
ISBN 9780380807604
Grades: 11 12 Adult B

1. King, B. B. 2. Blues musicians 3. Autobiographies and memoirs 4. Biographies 5. Arts and Entertainment — Music — Jazz and the Blues 6. Life stories — Arts and culture — Performing arts — Musicians and composers

LC BI2007011853

The fabled blues guitarist chronicles his youth on a Mississippi cotton farm, years as a disk jockey, experiences with racism and the civil rights movement, romantic relationships, and forty-five years on the road.

"This is one of the best recent pop-music bios. King speaks straight from the soul, it seems, just like he plays the guitar." —*Booklist*

Originally published: New York : Avon Books, 1996; Includes discography (p. 315-317) and index.

King, Billie Jean
★ *All In: An Autobiography.* Billie Jean King; with Johnette Howard and Maryanne Vollers. Alfred A. Knopf 2021. 384 p.
ISBN 9781101947333
Grades: Adult B

1. King, Billie Jean, 1943- 2. Women tennis players 3. Professional tennis players 4. Women social advocates 5. Lesbians 6. Feminists 7. Gender equity 8. LGBTQIA+ people 9. Social justice 10. Tennis 11. Sexuality 12. Love 13. Sexism in sports 14. Sports 15. Autobiographies and memoirs 16. Biographies 17. Sports and Competition — Tennis 18. Sports and Competition — Indi-

PUBLIC LIBRARY CORE COLLECTION: NONFICTION
Twentieth Edition

vidual Athlete 19. Life stories — Sports — Athletes 20. Life stories — Identity — LGBTQIA+

LC 2020055683

This autobiography from the tennis legend discusses not only her historic accomplishments on the court, but also her activism as a feminist and social justice fighter in the wake of her coming out as a gay at age 51.

"An absorbing story, richly told by one of the 20th century's pioneering sports figures and social activists. An essential memoir that will inspire and stay with readers of all ages." —*Library Journal*

Includes index.

King, Coretta Scott

★ *My Life, My Love, My Legacy.* by Coretta Scott King; as told to the Rev. Dr. Barbara Reynolds. Henry Holt and Company 2017. 368 pages

ISBN 9781627795982

Grades: Adult   B

1. King, Coretta Scott, 1927-2006 2. King, Martin Luther, Jr, 1929-1968 3. Civil rights workers 4. Social reformers 5. Spouses of clergy 6. Widows 7. Baptists 8. Christian women 9. Civil Rights Movement 10. Race relations 11. Women civil rights workers 12. Women political activists 13. African American women 14. African American history 15. Civil rights 16. United States history 17. 20th century 18. Autobiographies and memoirs 19. Biographies 20. History writing — African American — Civil rights — United States 21. Life stories — Politics — Activists and reformers 22. History writing — Women's history 23. History writing — United States 24. Adult books for young adults

LC 2016039557

Over the course of many years, Coretta Scott King's close friend, the Rev. Dr. Barbara Reynolds, recorded interviews with King about her experiences. In My Life, My Love, My Legacy, Reynolds assembles these accounts into an authorized biography. From her childhood in segregated Heiberger, Alabama through her college days in Ohio and her classical music studies in Boston, Coretta aspired to be a professional musician. That changed after Martin Luther King Jr persuaded her to marry him, build a family together, and return South to combat Jim Crow. This up-close, graceful narrative offers a vivid depiction of the Kings' lives, especially Coretta's, and the Civil Rights movement.

"King was undoubtedly a singular woman, and readers will be struck by just how strongly her exceedingly compelling story resonates today. She was much more than just the woman behind the man, and now, in the most eloquent of language, she proves that truth once and for all to generations of readers who will embrace her all over again." —*Booklist*

King, Gilbert

Beneath a Ruthless Sun: A True Story of Violence, Race, and Justice Lost and Found. Gilbert King. Riverhead Books 2018. 416 p.

ISBN 9780399183386

Grades: Adult   B

1. Daniels, Jesse Delbert, 1938-2018 2. Malicious accusation 3. People with developmental disabilities 4. Police misconduct 5. Frameups 6. Rape 7. False imprisonment 8. Legal malpractice 9. Florida 10. 1950s 11. True Crime — Sex Crimes 12. True Crime — Historical Crime 13. Society and culture — Violence and crime — Criminal justice system

LC 2017053110

ALA Notable Book, 2019.

The author of the Pulitzer Prize-winning Devil in the Grove documents the mid-20th-century case of a gentle, developmentally challenged youth who was falsely accused of raping a wealthy woman, in an account that traces the efforts of a crusading journalist to uncover the virulent racism and class corruption that led to his incarceration without a trial.

"From the opening pages, King's narrative barrels forward, leaving readers wondering what it will take for justice to prevail. By turns sobering, frightening, and thrilling, this meticulous account of the power and tenacity of officially sanctioned racism recalls a dark era that America is still struggling to leave behind." —*Kirkus*

Includes bibliographical references.

King, Greg

The Assassination of the Archduke: Sarajevo 1914 and the Romance That Changed the World. Greg King and Sue Woolmans. St. Martin's Press 2013. 432 p.

ISBN 9781250000163

Grades: Adult   B

1. Franz Ferdinand, Archduke of Austria, 1863-1914 2. Sophie, Archduchess of Austria, 1866-1914 3. Princes 4. Scandals 5. Assassination 6. Princesses 7. World War I 8. Causes of war 9. Men-women relations 10. European history 11. Austria 12. 1910s 13. History writing — Europe

LC 2013013949

Traces the story of the tragic romance and brutal assassination that led to World War I, exploring rumors of Serbian complicity, conspiracy, and official negligence that doomed the Archduke and his family.

King, Martin Luther

The Autobiography of Martin Luther King, Jr. Edited by Clayborne Carson. Intellectual Properties Management in association with Warner Books 1998. xi, 400 p. : Illustration

ISBN 9780446524124

Grades: 11 12 Adult   B

1. King, Martin Luther, Jr, 1929-1968 2. African American civil rights workers 3. Civil rights workers 4. Baptists 5. African Americans 6. African American history 7. Civil rights 8. Clergy 9. 20th century 10. Autobiographies and memoirs 11. Biographies 12. History writing — African American — Civil rights — United States 13. Life stories — Politics — Activists and Reformers — Civil Rights Leaders 14. Society and culture — Race

LC 98035704

Drawing on King's unpublished writings and other materials, a civil rights scholar assembles a first-person narrative of King's life.

"Carson, director of Martin Luther King Jr. Papers Project, brings together selections from King's writings, speeches, and recordings to create this fascinating 'Autobiography' of the famed civil rights leader and Nobel Peace Prize winner. The writings trace King's struggles with religion, philosophy, and the racial politics of the U.S." —*Booklist*

Includes bibliographical references (p. [371]-390) and index.

King, Maxwell

The Good Neighbor: The Life and Work of Fred Rogers. Maxwell King. Abrams Press 2018. 320 p.

ISBN 9781419727726

Grades: Adult   B

1. Rogers, Fred 2. Television personalities 3. Children's television personalities 4. Television programs for children 5. Values 6. Presbyterian Church 7. Personal conduct 8. Interpersonal relations 9. Clergy 10. Biographies 11. Life stories — Arts and culture — Performing arts — Entertainers and celebrities 12. Arts and Entertainment — Movies and Television

LC Bl2018134511

Goodreads Choice Award, 2018; Library Journal Best Books, 2018.

Drawing on original interviews, oral histories and archival documents, the author traces the iconic children's program host's personal, professional, and artistic life through decades of work.

"Grown-up fans, pop culture enthusiasts, and anyone interested in the history of educational television and child development will be inspired. An excellent and timely addition to most collections." —*Library Journal*

King, Stephen

On Writing: A Memoir of the Craft. by Stephen King. Scribner 2000. 288 p.

ISBN 9780684853529

Grades: 11 12 Adult   B

1. King, Stephen, 1947- 2. Horror writing 3. Writing 4. Authors, American 5. 20th century 6. Autobiographies and memoirs 7. Biographies 8. Arts and Entertainment — Writing and Publishing 9. Life stories — Arts and culture — Writing — Authors 10. Adult books for young adults

LC 00030105

ESSENTIAL AND RECOMMENDED TITLES
Biography

Bram Stoker Award for Best Nonfiction, 2000; Locus Award for Best Nonfiction/Related/Reference Book, 2001.

The author shares his insights into the craft of writing and offers a humorous perspective on his own experience as a writer.

"The author recounts his life from early childhood through the aftermath of the 1999 accident that nearly killed him. Along the way, King touts the writing philosophies of William Strunk and Ernest Hemingway, advocates a healthy appetite for reading, expounds upon the subject of grammar, critiques a number of popular writers, and offers the reader a chance to try out his theories.... Recommended for anyone who wants to write and everyone who loves to read." —*Library Journal*

Includes bibliographical references.

Kingston, Genevieve
Did I Ever Tell You?: A Memoir. Genevieve Kingston. Marysue Rucci Books, Scribner 2024. 256 p.

ISBN 9781668006290

Grades: Adult   B

1. Kingston, Genevieve 2. Mothers and daughters 3. Love 4. Gifts 5. Letter writing 6. Terminal illness 7. Family relationships 8. Cancer 9. Death of mothers 10. Autobiographies and memoirs 11. Life stories — Relationships — Parent and child 12. Family and Relationships — Aging and Death 13. Family and relationships — Parenting 14. Debut title

Based on the author's "Modern Love" essay in the New Yorker, this life-affirming memoir tells the story of the gifts and letters left behind by her mother who was diagnosed with terminal cancer during her childhood.

"Kingston's story captures the distinct way that a child experiences grief, even anticipatory grief, and the struggle of a child's mind to envision a future without a parent. As the shape of her grief changes with age, Kingston teaches us something essential about how to collect, hold, and savor memories of loved ones over a lifetime. A heart-tugging memoir." —*Kirkus*

"As the shape of her grief changes with age, Kingston teaches us something essential about how to collect, hold, and savor memories of loved ones over a lifetime." —*Kirkus*

Kingston, Maxine Hong
The Woman Warrior: China Men. Maxine Hong Kingston; with an introduction by Mary Gordon. Everyman's Library 2005. xxix, 541 p.

ISBN 9781400043842

Grades: 11 12 Adult   B

1. Kingston, Maxine Hong 2. Authors, American 3. Chinese Americans 4. East Asian Americans 5. California 6. 20th century 7. Autobiographies and memoirs 8. Biographies 9. History writing — Immigration — United States

LC 2004061143

Collects two works by the author that focus on the lives of Chinese Americans, the first of which reccounts her childhood in a tradition-bound Chinese family.

Originally published: The woman warrior. New York : Knopf, 1976. China men. New York : Knopf, 1980.

Kinzer, Stephen
Poisoner in Chief: Sidney Gottlieb and the CIA Search for Mind Control. Stephen Kinzer. Henry Holt & Company 2019. 352 p.

ISBN 9781250140432

Grades: Adult   B

1. Gottlieb, Sidney, 1918-1999 2. Brainwashing 3. Hallucinogenic drugs 4. Human experimentation in medicine 5. Scientists 6. Medical ethics 7. Mind control 8. LSD (Drug) 9. Brain 10. Poisoning 11. Research 12. Biographies 13. History writing — Science, technology, and medicine 14. Life stories — Science, technology, and medicine — Scientists and inventors 15. Science Writing — Medicine and health — Doctors and nurses 16. History writing — 1960s — United States 17. History writing — 1970s — United States

LC 2019007076

The award-winning foreign correspondent and author of All the Shah's Men documents the remarkable story of the brilliant but controversial chemist who oversaw the CIA's secret drug and mind-control experiments of the mid-20th century.

Includes bibliographical references and index.

Kirschbaum, Erik
Soccer Without Borders: Jurgen Klinsmann, Coaching the U.S. Men's National Soccer Team and the Quest for the World Cup. Erik Kirschbaum, Jurgen Klinsmann. Picador USA 2016. 224 p.

ISBN 9781250098313

Grades: Adult   B

1. Klinsmann, Jurgen 2. Soccer coaches 3. Soccer 4. Autobiographies and memoirs 5. Life stories — Sports — Coaches, managers, and owners 6. Sports and competition — Soccer

LC 2016002387

A controversial U.S men's soccer coach reveals his thoughts on building a winning soccer team.

"Kirschbaum provides a welcome sketch of Klinsmann, a thoughtful man of the world who has for years lived in California and who cannot be pigeonholed as merely a European trying to remake American soccer in the Old World image." —*Kirkus*

Includes index.

Kirtzman, Andrew
Giuliani: The Rise and Tragic Fall of America's Mayor. Andrew Kirtzman. Simon & Schuster 2022. 480 p.

ISBN 9781982153298

Grades: Adult   B

1. Giuliani, Rudolph W. 2. Lawyers 3. Mayors 4. Interpersonal relations 5. Scandals 6. Politics and government 7. New York City 8. United States 9. Biographies 10. Life stories — Politics — Politicians 11. Life stories — Law and order — Judges and lawyers 12. Politics and global affairs — Political figures

Rudy Giuliani was hailed after 9/11 as "America's Mayor," a singular figure who at the time was more widely admired than the pope. He was brilliant, accomplished—and complicated. He conflated politics with morality and caused his own downfall with a series of disastrous decisions and cynical compromises. He made reckless personal choices and engaged in self-destructive behavior. His need for power, money, and attention gradually ruined his reputation, cost him friendships, and ultimately damaged the country. This is the remarkable story of how it all began and how it came crashing down.

"The same 'Fanatical sense of righteousness' that propelled Rudy Giuliani's rise set him on the road to ruin, according to this richly detailed biography....This is a comprehensive and alarming portrait of Giuliani's downfall." —*Publishers Weekly*

Kiser, Joy M.
America's Other Audubon. Joy M. Kiser. Princeton Architectural Press 2012. 192 p.

ISBN 9781616890599

Grades: Adult   B

1. Jones, Genevieve (Genevieve Estelle), 1847-1879 2. Ornithologists 3. Birds 4. Birds in art 5. Painting 6. North America 7. Biographies 8. Visual nonfiction 9. Life stories — Nature and outdoors

LC 2011039605

America's Other Audubon chronicles the story of Genevieve Jones, her family, and the making of an extraordinary nineteenth-century book, Illustrations of the Nests and Eggs of Birds of Ohio.

Kizzia, Tom
Pilgrim's Wilderness: A True Story of Faith and Madness on the Alaska Frontier. by Tom Kizzia; edited by Kevin Doughten. Crown 2013. 336 p.

ISBN 9780307587824

Grades: Adult   B

1. Hale, Robert (Robert Allen), 1941-2008 2. Criminals 3. Abusive men 4. Dysfunctional families 5. Incest 6. Cults 7. Alaska 8. True Crime — Domestic Crime 9. Nonfiction that reads like fiction

LC 2012016502

Documents the story of Robert "Papa Pilgrim" Hale and the antiestablishment family settlement in remote Alaska that was exposed as a cult-like prison where Hale brutalized and isolated his wife and fifteen children.

"The horror at the heart of this story about religious extremism on the fringes of the last American frontier is slow to reveal itself, but when that horror fully emerges, it will swallow most readers. Provocative and disturbing." —*Kirkus*

Includes bibliographical references.

Klagsbrun, Francine
Lioness: Golda Meir and the Nation of Israel. Francine Klagsbrun. Schocken Books 2017. 864 p.

ISBN 9780805242379

Grades: Adult   B

1. Meir, Golda, 1898-1978 2. Women prime ministers 3. Zionists 4. Women politicians 5. Zionism 6. Jewish women 7. Politics and government 8. Israel 9. Autobiographies and memoirs 10. Impartial writing 11. History writing — Arab-Israeli relations — Southwest Asia and North Africa (Middle East) 12. Life stories — Politics — Politicians

LC 2017004908

A biography of the fourth prime minister of Israel, an iron-willed, chain-smoking grandmother, follows her childhood in Milwaukee to joining a kibbutz in Palestine and ending up in a series of public-service positions before her political career took off.

"With hundreds of books on Meir available, this one stands out with its depth of resources and research, building a convincing case that Meir's achievements are still relevant." —*Library Journal*

Klein, Jessi
I'll Show Myself Out: Essays on Midlife and Motherhood. Jessi Klein. HarperCollins 2022. 384 p.

ISBN 9780062981592

Grades: Adult   B

1. Klein, Jessi, 1975- 2. Motherhood 3. Middle-age 4. Aging 5. Expectation 6. Parenthood 7. Self 8. Identity 9. Body image 10. Marriage 11. Autobiographies and memoirs 12. Life stories — Relationships — Parent and child 13. Family and relationships — Parenting

The New York Times best-selling author and Emmy Award-winning writer and producer hilariously destroys the cultural myths and impossible expectations of modern-day motherhood and explores the humiliations, poignancies and possibilities of midlife.

"Comedian Klein (You'll Grow Out of It) takes a moving look at motherhood in this bold and irreverent collection." —*Publishers Weekly*

Klemperer, Victor
I Will Bear Witness: A Diary of the Nazi Years, 1942-1945. Victor Klemperer; translated from the German by Martin Chalmers. Random House 2000. 556 p. (The Diaries of Victor Klemperer, 2)

ISBN 9780375502408

Grades: Adult   B

1. Klemperer, Victor, 1881-1960 2. Holocaust (1933-1945) 3. Jewish people 4. College teachers 5. Philologists 6. Personal diaries 7. Western European people 8. German people 9. Third Reich, 1933-1945 10. Germany 11. Dresden, Germany 12. 1930s 13. 1940s 14. History writing — Wars and conflicts — Holocaust — World War II

LC 98015429

ALA Notable Book, 2000; Library Journal Best Books, 2000; New York Times Notable Book, 2000; National Book Critics Circle Award for Biography finalist, 2000.

A second volume of the author's firsthand account of life in Nazi Germany chronicles the worst years of the war, including the bombing of Dresden and his escape from deportation to a Jewish concentration camp by advancing American troops.

"Never has the isolation of living in a world that wishes one's people dead been rendered with greater pathos. Every act of cruelty as well as every gesture of kindness is scrupulously recorded." —*The Nation*

Originally published as Ich will Zeugnis ablegen bis zum letzten: Berlin : Aufbau-Verlag, 1995.

Kluger, Richard
Indelible Ink: The Trials of John Peter Zenger and the Birth of America's Free Press. Richard Kluger. W.W. Norton & Company 2016. xxi, 346 pages

ISBN 9780393245462

Grades: Adult   B

1. Zenger, John Peter, 1697-1746 2. Journalism 3. Trials (Libel) 4. Freedom of speech 5. Printing 6. Freedom of the press 7. Colonies 8. New York City history 9. North American history 10. United States 11. Great Britain 12. Colonial America (1600-1775) 13. 18th century 14. Biographies 15. History writing — Colonial America — United States 16. Life stories — Arts and Culture — Writing — Journalists 17. Politics and global affairs — Civil and human rights

LC 2016011040

The story of the battle to legalize free expression in America describes the strict censorship throughout colonization and the efforts of New York printer John Peter Zenger to avoid imprisonment for criticizing a corrupt politician.

"Event by compelling event, readers follow Zenger through the drama that eventually landed him in jail on libel chargesbefore a liberty-loving jury freed him with a 1735 verdict signaling a clear American commitment to the unfettered reporting that can check abuse of power." —*Booklist*

Includes bibliographical references (p. 329-332) and index.

Knausgaard, Karl Ove
Spring. Karl Ove Knausgaard, with illustrations by Anna Bjerger; translated from the Norwegian by Ingvild Burkey. Penguin Press 2018. 182 p. (Four seasons encyclopedia, 3)

ISBN 9780399563362

Grades: Adult   B

1. Knausgaard, Karl Ove, 1968- 2. Authors 3. Fathers and daughters 4. Fatherhood 5. Babies 6. Everyday life 7. Spring 8. Personal conduct 9. Autobiographies and memoirs 10. Letters 11. Translations — Norwegian to English 12. Life stories — Arts and culture — Writing — Authors

A Swedish father describes life with his newborn daughter, discussing the lightness and joy of the beginning of a new life, but also the creeping darkness and struggles in this new work from the author of Out of the World.

"This is a remarkably honest take on the strange linkages between love, loss, laughter, and self-destruction, a perfect distillation of Knausgaard's unique gifts." —*Publishers Weekly*

Translation of: Om varen; Originally published: Norway : Oktober, 2016; Translated from the Norwegian.

Knight, Philip H.
Shoe Dog: A Memoir by the Creator of Nike. Phil Knight. Simon & Schuster 2016. 384 p.

ISBN 9781501135910

Grades: Adult   B

1. Knight, Philip H, 1938- 2. Entrepreneurship 3. Entrepreneurs 4. Shoes 5. Business 6. Sneakers 7. Athletic shoes 8. Import export business 9. Shoe industry and trade 10. Businesspeople 11. Autobiographies and memoirs 12. Biographies 13. Life stories — Business — Business leaders 14. Business and economics — Industries — Retail products and services 15. Business and economics — Business leaders and entrepreneurs

LC 2016010080

The influential founder and CEO of Nike shares the inside story of the company's early days as an intrepid startup and its evolution to one of the world's most iconic and profitable brands, offering insights into his own experiences as a young man who envisioned a company that would be run in atypical ways.

"Has anyone else ever written as evocatively about selling shoes? Well, George Pelecanos wrote a crime novel called Shoedog, and theres a character in it who sells shoes with a definite flair, but thats really something very different. And, yet, maybe not. Pelecanos brings his street characters to vivid life and makes us care about them. Remarkably, Knight does the same thing for a giant corporationcertainly an even more formidable task." —*Booklist*

Kolker, Robert Phillip
Kubrick: An Odyssey. Robert P. Kolker and Nathan Abrams. Pegasus Books 2024. 752 p.

ESSENTIAL AND RECOMMENDED TITLES
Biography

ISBN 9781639366248
Grades: Adult **B**
1. Kubrick, Stanley, 1928-1999 2. Jewish men 3. Film producers and directors 4. Filmmakers 5. Films, American 6. Films 7. United States 8. Biographies 9. Life stories — Arts and culture — Performing arts — Directors and producers 10. Arts and Entertainment — Movies and Television

This definitive book is based on access to the latest research, especially Kubrick's archive at the University of the Arts, London, as well as other private papers plus new interviews with family members and those who worked with him. It offers comprehensive and in-depth coverage of Kubrick's personal, private, public, and working life. Stanley Kubrick: An Odyssey investigates not only the making of Kubrick's films, but also about those he wanted (but failed) to make like Burning Secret, Napoleon, Aryan Papers, and A.I.

"Though Stanley Kubrick and his body of work have been well documented, this book adds considerably to our knowledge of both the man and his masterpieces." —*Kirkus*

Korda, Michael
Clouds of Glory: The Life and Legend of Robert E. Lee. Michael Korda. HarperCollins 2014. 640 p.
ISBN 9780062116291
Grades: Adult **B**
1. Lee, Robert E. (Robert Edward), 1807-1870 2. Military history 3. Civil war 4. Command of troops 5. United States Civil War, 1861-1865 6. Confederate soldiers 7. Generals 8. Politics and government 9. United States history 10. United States 11. American Civil War era (1861-1865) 12. 19th century 13. 18th century 14. Biographies 15. History writing — Wars and conflicts — American Civil War 16. Life stories — Law and order — Military leaders 17. History writing — Military — Military leadership
LC 2014415636

Accompanied by stunning illustrations and in-text battle maps, this unrivaled biography of the brilliant general analyzes Lee's command during the Civil War, exploring his responsibility for the fatal stalemate at Antietam, his defeat at Gettysburg and his failed strategy for winning the war.

"Korda examines the life of Robert E. Lee from start to finish, illuminating not just the man, but his extended family and the society which produced him." —*Publishers Weekly*

Kot, Greg
I'll Take You There: Mavis Staples, the Staple Singers, and the March up Freedom's Highway. Greg Kot. Scribner 2014. 320 pages
ISBN 9781451647853
Grades: Adult **B**
1. Staples, Mavis 2. Gospel musicians 3. Women gospel singers 4. Civil Rights Movement 5. 1960s 6. Biographies 7. Life stories — Arts and culture — Performing arts — Musicians and composers 8. Arts and Entertainment — Music — Christian and Gospel
LC 2013032633

Though Mavis Staples has recently enjoyed a career resurgence as a solo artist, she's probably best known for singing with her family on the church circuit in Chicago before they made their way up the charts with songs like "I'll Take You There." in addition to describing their movements though gospel, R&B, and even disco, author Greg Kot also details friendships with other artists, like Bob Dylan and Aretha Franklin, and their involvement with the civil rights movement. Check out I'll Take You There for full immersion in the Mavis Staples sound.

"Kot's effort remains clear and respectful and takes us deep into the golden age of Mavis and her marvelously talented group." —*Publishers Weekly*

Includes bibliographical references.

Kotkin, Stephen
Stalin: Paradoxes of Power, 1878-1928. Stephen Kotkin. Penguin Press 2014. 512 p.
ISBN 9781594203794
Grades: Adult **B**
1. Stalin, Joseph, 1879-1953 2. Heads of state 3. Communism 4. Socialism 5. Russian history 6. European history 7. Soviet Union history 8. 1920s 9. 20th century 10. Russian Revolution and Civil War (1917-1921) 11. Biographies 12. History writing — Communism — Europe — Russia 13. Life stories — Politics — Politicians

Pulitzer Prize for Biography or Autobiography finalist, 2015.

A first volume in an extensively researched portrait of the Soviet dictator provides intimate coverage of such topics as his rise from humble origins, the inner geography of the Bolshevik regime and the early formation of Stalin's fabricated trial process.

Includes bibliographical references and index.

Stalin: Waiting for Hitler 1929-1941. Stephen Kotkin. Penguin Press 2017. 1154 p.
ISBN 9781594203800
Grades: Adult **B**
1. Stalin, Joseph, 1879-1953 2. Heads of state 3. Communism 4. Socialism 5. Famines 6. Russian history 7. European history 8. Soviet Union history 9. 1930s 10. 20th century 11. Biographies 12. History writing — Communism — Europe — Russia 13. Life stories — Politics — Politicians
LC Bl2017044852

Mark Lynton History Prize, 2018.

History of the world during the build-up to World War II from the vantage point of Joseph Stalin's sea of power, exploring how in the aftermath of achieving dictatorial power over the Soviet Empire, Stalin formally ordered the systematic collectivization of the world's largest peasant economy.

"The John P. Birkelund Professor in History and International Affairs at Princeton University, Kotkin offers his second in a magisterial three-volume biography of Soviet leader Joseph Stalin, following Pulitzer Prize finalist Stalin. Vol. 1: Paradoxes of Power, 1878-1928." —*Library Journal*

Kouchner, Camille
The Familia Grande: A Memoir. Camille Kouchner; translated from the French by Adriana Hunter. Other Press 2022. 208 p.
ISBN 9781635422122
Grades: Adult **B**
1. Kouchner, Camille, 1975- 2. Duhamel, Olivier, 1950- 3. Child sexual abuse 4. Incest 5. Women lawyers 6. Twins 7. Brothers 8. Family relationships 9. Elite (Social sciences) 10. Lawyers 11. Shame 12. Guilt 13. Family secrets 14. France 15. Autobiographies and memoirs 16. Translations — French to English 17. Family and relationships — Abuse 18. Life stories — Facing adversity 19. Life stories — Relationships — Family
LC 2021053102

In February 2017, Camille Kouchner gathered with family in Sanary-sur-Mer to bury her mother, who died with none of her five children present. Her passing would stir up old emotions, ultimately leading Camille to publicly confront a long-held and corrosive secret: Her stepfather sexually abused her twin brother when they were adolescents. This violation of the parent-child relationship was compounded by the complicity of their mother, who learned of her husband's actions and stood by him, shifting blame to Camille and her twin. The Familia Grande poignantly explores the family dynamics of abuse, and the questions of guilt and shame surrounding it. Camille grapples with her own sense of responsibility-for not having stopped her stepfather at the time, and for agreeing to keep silent as her brother asked-and also considers the wider societal forces that have allowed influential men to commit such crimes and avoid the consequences for so long.

"A Frenchwoman reflects on the familial abuse she witnessed and suppressed for years....A cathartic, blisteringly candid family portrait of abuse, dysfunction, and eventual epiphany." —*Kirkus*

Originally published in French as La familia grande in 2021 by Editions du Seuil, Paris—Title page verso.

Kozinn, Allan
The McCartney Legacy: Volume 1, 1969-73. Allan Kozinn, Adrian Sinclair. Dey Street Books 2022. 592 p.
ISBN 9780063000704
Grades: Adult **B**
1. McCartney, Paul 2. Rock musicians 3. Rock music 4. Songwriting 5. Interpersonal relations 6. Sound recordings 7. British people 8. English people 9. Bi-

ographies 10. Life stories — Arts and culture — Performing arts — Musicians and composers 11. Arts and Entertainment — Music — Rock

In this first of a multivolume set, THE MCCARTNEY LEGACY, VOL 1: 1969-73 captures the life of Paul McCartney in the years immediately following the dissolution of the Beatles, a period in which McCartney recreated himself as both a man and a musician.

"Meticulously researching the topic and writing in a lively, conversational style, the coauthors have delivered the definitive work about the immediate post-Beatles times of Paul McCartney." —*Library Journal*

Kozol, Jonathan

*The **Theft** of Memory: Losing My Father One Day at a Time.* Jonathan Kozol. Crown Publishers 2015. 352 p.
ISBN 9780804140973
Grades: Adult   B

1. Kozol, Jonathan 2. Kozol, Harry L, 1906-2008 3. People with Alzheimer's disease 4. Alzheimer's disease 5. Neurologists 6. Adult children of people with Alzheimer's disease 7. Fathers and sons 8. Autobiographies and memoirs 9. Life stories — Facing adversity — Medical issues — Mental illness 10. Life stories — Relationships — Parent and child 11. Family and Relationships — Families
LC 2014041699

Library Journal Best Books, 2015.

A deeply personal account of the life of the author's father—a nationally renowned neurologist who, after a life of helping to establish emerging fields in mental health, succumbed to Alzheimer's disease.

"The author's approach is shrewd yet warmly empathetic; he is curious about how the mind's gradual breakdown exposes its machinery, and raptly attuned to the emotional effects of these changes on his parents and himself. The result is a clear-eyed and deeply felt meditation on the aspects of family that age does not ravage." —*Publishers Weekly*

Kram, Mark

*Smokin' **Joe**: The Life of Joe Frazier.* Mark Kram, Jr. Ecco Press 2019. 376 pages : Illustration
ISBN 9780062654465
Grades: Adult   B

1. Frazier, Joe, 1944-2011 2. Boxers (Sports) 3. African American boxers 4. African American athletes 5. Boxing matches 6. Sports rivalry 7. Family relationships 8. Racism 9. Biographies 10. Life stories — Sports — Athletes 11. Sports and Competition — Boxing 12. Life stories — Identity — Race and ethnicity

An all-access portrait of the iconic American fighter that discusses his upbringing in the Jim Crow South, his barrier-breaking achievements and his famous rivalry with Muhammad Ali.

Includes bibliographical references (pages 353-361) and index.

Kramer, Clara

*Clara's **War**: One Girl's Story of Survival.* Clara Kramer with Stephen Glantz. Ecco 2009. xii, 339 p, [8] p. of plates : Illustration
ISBN 9780061728600
Grades: 11 12 Adult   B

1. Kramer, Clara 2. Antisemitism 3. Holocaust survivors 4. Jewish people 5. Holocaust (1933-1945) 6. World War II 7. Polish people 8. Religious persecution 9. European history 10. Poland 11. Autobiographies and memoirs 12. History writing — Wars and conflicts — Holocaust — World War II 13. History writing — Wars and conflicts — World War II 14. Adult books for young adults 15. Life stories — Facing adversity — War and oppression — Holocaust

Booklist Editors' Choice: Adult Books for Young Adults, 2009.

An account based on the subject's personal record of the months during which she hid from Nazis in an underground bunker with seventeen others includes coverage of such topics as the characteristics of their unlikely protector Mr. Beck, the house fire that threatened everyone's survival, and Beck's affair with Clara's cousin.

"Based on her wartime diary, which she kept while hiding in a basement in Poland, Kramer's book vividly recalls the tensions within her hidden community after the Nazis overtook the town of Zolkiew in 1942. Of particular interest are revelations about the family who hid the Kramers, particularly how an anti-Semitic Polish householder demonstrated great courage in shielding Jews in his basement." —*Library Journal*

Originally published in Great Britain in 2008 by Ebury Press, an imprint of Ebury Publishing, a Random House Company—T.P. verso.

Kranish, Michael

Trump Revealed: An American Journey of Ambition, Ego, Money, and Power. Michael Kranish and Marc Fisher. Scribner 2016. 384 p.
ISBN 9781501155772
Grades: Adult   B

1. Trump, Donald, 1946- 2. Presidential candidates 3. Businesspeople 4. Presidential election, 2016 5. Politics and government 6. United States 7. 2000s (Decade) 8. 2010s 9. Biographies 10. Impartial writing 11. Life stories — Politics — Politicians 12. Politics and global affairs — Political figures 13. Life stories — Business — Business leaders
LC 2016032645

A biography of Donald Trump is reported by a team of award-winning Washington Post journalists and co-authored by investigative political reporter Michael Kranish and senior editor Marc Fisher.

"The most definitive book about Trump to date." —*Booklist*

*The **World's** Fastest Man: The Extraordinary Life of Cyclist Major Taylor, America's First Black Sports Hero.* Michael Kranish. Scribner 2019. 388 p.
ISBN 9781501192593
Grades: Adult   B

1. Taylor, Major, 1878-1932 2. Bicyclists 3. African Americans 4. Racism in sports 5. Bicycle racing 6. Racism 7. Biographies 8. Life stories — Sports — Athletes 9. Life stories — Identity — Race and ethnicity 10. Sports and Competition — Racing — Cycling 11. Sports and Competition — Sports History
LC 2019006827

The author traces the lesser-known story of Major Taylor, who broke racial barriers at the height of the Jim Crow era by becoming the world's fastest and most famous bicyclist.

"Both inspiring and heartbreaking, this is an essential contribution to sports history and an excellent companion to Todd Balf's equally strong Major (2008)." —*Booklist*

Includes bibliographical references and index.

Krass, Peter

Carnegie. Peter Krass. John Wiley & Sons 2002. xi, 612 p. : Illustration
ISBN 9780471386308
Grades: Adult   B

1. Carnegie, Andrew, 1835-1919 2. Industrialists 3. Philanthropists 4. Steel industry and trade 5. United States 6. Biographies 7. Business and economics — Business leaders and entrepreneurs 8. Life stories — Business — Business leaders
LC 2002010162

An account of the legendary industrialist and philanthropist discusses his rise from a life of poverty, uncanny sense of destiny, work for literacy and world peace, public persona as a ruthless empire builder, and struggles with internal conflict.

"From bobbin boy in a cotton mill to one of American history's most famous characters, Carnegie's life was one of contradictions. In his lifetime, Carnegie gave away a staggering 350 million, setting a standard for social conscience. Krass used original sources such as letters, diaries, and other writings by primary and peripheral characters in Carnegie's life to penetrate the public persona and show the man who crusaded for universal literacy and world peace." —*Booklist*

Includes bibliographical references (p. 583-586) and index.

Kraus, Dita

*A **Delayed** Life: The True Story of the Librarian of Auschwitz.* Dita Kraus. Feiwel and Friends 2020. 339 p.
ISBN 9781250760890
Grades: Adult   B

1. Kraus, Dita, 1929- 2. Holocaust survivors 3. Jewish people 4. Women librarians 5. Concentration camps 6. Postwar life 7. Political persecution 8. Holocaust (1933-1945) 9. Czech people 10. Eastern European people 11. Children

ESSENTIAL AND RECOMMENDED TITLES
Biography

12. European history 13. Czechoslovakia 14. 20th century 15. Autobiographies and memoirs 16. Biographies 17. Life stories — Facing adversity — War and oppression — Holocaust 18. Life stories — Education — Scholars and educators 19. History writing — Wars and conflicts — Holocaust — World War II 20. History writing — Europe — Eastern Europe

LC B12020004040

A Delayed Life is the breathtaking memoir that tells the story of Dita Kraus, the real-life Librarian of Auschwitz. Dita Kraus grew up in Prague in an intellectual, middle-class Jewish family. She went to school, played with her friends, and never thought of herself as being different—until the advent of the Holocaust. Torn from her home, Dita was sent to Auschwitz with her family. From her time in the children's block of Auschwitz to her liberation from the camps and on into her adulthood, Dita's powerful memoir sheds light on an incredible life—one that is delayed no longer.

"Kraus, whose life inspired the critically acclaimed novel the Librarian of Auschwitz (2017), by Antonio Iturbe, here recalls the true story of her life. . . . Her memoir is a valuable addition to the literature of the Holocaust." —*Booklist*

Originally published by Ebury Publishing UK in 2020—Title page verso.

Kriegel, Mark

Pistol: The Life of Pete Maravich. Mark Kriegel. Free Press 2007. VIII, 381 p, 16 p. of plates : Illustration

ISBN 9780743284974

Grades: 11 12 Adult **B**

1. Maravich, Pete, 1947-1988 2. Professional basketball players 3. Professional basketball 4. Basketball players 5. Basketball 6. Faith (Christianity) 7. Social life and customs 8. United States 9. 20th century 10. Biographies 11. Sports and Competition — Basketball 12. Sports and Competition — Individual Athlete 13. Life stories — Sports — Athletes

LC 2006051526

Recounts the life and achievements of the troubled 1970s basketball star, from his relationship with his obsessive father and unbroken college scoring record to the personal demons that challenged his life and his evangelical Christian faith.

Includes bibliographical references and index.

Kristof, Nicholas D.

★ *Chasing Hope: A Reporter's Life.* Nicholas D. Kristof. Alfred A. Knopf 2024. 480 p.

ISBN 9780593536568

Grades: Adult **B**

1. Kristof, Nicholas D, 1959- 2. Journalists 3. Journalism 4. American people 5. Current events 6. Autobiographies and memoirs 7. Life stories — Arts and culture — Writing — Journalists 8. Arts and Entertainment — Writing and Publishing

LC 2023012344

The New York Times columnist, Pulitzer Prize winner and best-selling author discusses his life in journalism and the great members of his profession and the less-known extraordinary people he has met during his career.

One of the most consequential journalists of our time recounts his life and storied career, showing how 'Journalism is an act of hope.' —*Kirkus*

This is a Borzoi Book published by Alfred A. Knopf.

Kroeber, Theodora

Ishi in Two Worlds: A Biography of the Last Wild Indian in North America. Theodora Kroeber; with a new foreword by Karl Kroeber. University of California Press 2002. xxiii, 254 p, 14 p. of plates : Illustration

ISBN 9780520229402

Grades: Adult **B**

1. Ishi, d.1916 2. Yana (North American people) 3. Biographies 4. Life stories — People in history

LC 2005532000

An account of the life and culture of Ishi, the last survivor of a "lost" California Indian tribe.

Includes bibliographical references (p. [245]-254).

Kruzan, Sara

I Cried to Dream Again: Trafficking, Murder, and Deliverance : A Memoir. Sara Kruzan with Cori Thomas. Pantheon Books 2022. 224 p.

ISBN 9780593315880

Grades: Adult **B**

1. Kruzan, Sara, 1978- 2. Human trafficking victims 3. Abused women 4. Women prisoners 5. Survival 6. Social advocates 7. Autobiographies and memoirs 8. Life stories — Facing adversity — Abuse survivors 9. Society and culture — Violence and crime

LC 2021042731

A powerful memoir from a survivor of sex trafficking who killed her trafficker after five years of abuse, only to be sentenced as a juvenile to life in prison without parole.

"Kruzan powerfully chronicles the story of how she killed the man who abused and trafficked her during her teen years....A must-read for parents, civil servants, and activists." —*Kirkus*

Kugler, Rob

A Dog Named Beautiful: A Marine, a Dog, and a Long Road Trip Home. Rob Kugler. Flatiron Books 2019. 288 p.

ISBN 9781250164254

Grades: Adult **B**

1. Kugler, Rob 2. Marines 3. Iraq War veterans 4. Dogs 5. Animals with disabilities 6. Voyages and travels 7. Labrador retrievers 8. Dog owners 9. Iraq War, 2003-2011 10. Loss 11. War casualties 12. Human-animal relationships 13. Grief 14. Autobiographies and memoirs 15. Life stories — Relationships — Pets and Owners 16. Family and Relationships — Pets and Owners

LC 2019002979

A medically retired Marine describes the role of his beloved chocolate lab in his recovery from war injuries and the loss of his brother, recounting the poignant road journey they shared in the final months of his dog's life.

Kuo, Michelle

Reading with Patrick: A Teacher, a Student, and a Life-changing Friendship. Michelle Kuo. Random House 2017. 304 p.

ISBN 9780812997316

Grades: Adult **B**

1. Kuo, Michelle 2. Prisoners 3. Alternative schools 4. Books and reading 5. Literacy 6. Racism 7. Murder suspects 8. Teacher-student relationships 9. Education 10. Race relations 11. United States 12. Autobiographies and memoirs 13. Life stories — Education — Scholars and educators 14. Society and culture — General

LC 2016036759

Loan Stars Favourites, 2017.

A former alternative school teacher and Harvard Law School fellow shares the story of her work with a gifted student who was imprisoned for murder in the Mississippi Delta and whose education she continued through classic works of literature.

"Honest, thoughtful, and humane, Kuo's book is not only a testament to a remarkable friendship, but a must-read for anyone interested in social justice and race in America. Thoughtfully provocative reading." —*Kirkus*

Kurlansky, Mark

Birdseye: The Adventures of a Curious Man. Mark Kurlansky. Doubleday 2012. 304 p.

ISBN 9780385527057

Grades: Adult **B**

1. Birdseye, Clarence, 1886-1956 2. Inventors 3. Businesspeople 4. United States 5. Biographies 6. Life stories — Business — Business leaders 7. Business and economics — Business leaders and entrepreneurs 8. Business and economics — Industries — Agriculture and food

LC 2011044891

A profile of eccentric genius inventor Clarence Birdseye chronicles how his innovative fast-freezing process revolutionized the food industry and American agriculture.

Includes bibliographical references and index.

PUBLIC LIBRARY CORE COLLECTION: NONFICTION
Twentieth Edition

Kurosawa, Akira
Something Like an Autobiography. Akira Kurosawa; translated by Audie E. Bock. Vintage Books 1983. xiii, 205 p, 8 p. of plates : Illustration
ISBN 9780394714394
Grades: Adult   B
1. Kurosawa, Akira, 1910-1998 2. Film producers and directors 3. Autobiographies and memoirs 4. Arts and Entertainment — Movies and Television 5. Life stories — Arts and culture — Performing arts — Directors and producers
LC 82048900

The distinguished filmmaker chronicles his life from his birth in 1910 to the worldwide success in 1951 of his film "Rashomon" and provides a provocative account of the Japanese film industry.

"This is a fascinating, moving record of one man's pursuit of excellence in a single art." —*New York Times Book Review*

Translation of: Gama no abura; Includes index.

Kweli, Talib
Vibrate Higher: A Rap Story. Talib Kweli. MCD/Farrar, Straus and Giroux 2021. 336 p.
ISBN 9780374283407
Grades: Adult   B
1. Kweli, Talib 2. Rap musicians 3. African American men 4. Rap music industry and trade 5. Rap music 6. Growing up 7. Hip-hop culture 8. Autobiographies and memoirs 9. Life stories — Arts and culture — Performing arts — Musicians and composers 10. Arts and Entertainment — Music — Rap and R&B 11. Life stories — Identity — Race and ethnicity
LC 2018044014

Before Talib Kweli became a world-renowned hip hop artist, he was a Brooklyn kid who liked to cut class, spit rhymes, and wander the streets of Greenwich Village with a motley crew of artists, rappers, and DJs who found hip hop more inspiring than their textbooks. Eventually, childhood friendships turned into collaborations and Kweli gained notoriety as a rapper in his own right, ultimately leaving his record label and taking control of his own recording career. Kweli tells the winding, always compelling story of the people and events that shaped his own life as well as the culture of hip hop which informs American culture at large.

"Celebrated hip-hop artist Kweli, who founded the music-film-and-books juggernaut Javotti Media in 2011, here delivers not just a memoir but the story of hip-hop as a political force." —*Library Journal*

Includes index.

Kyle, Taya
American Spirit: Profiles in Resilience, Courage, and Faith. Taya Kyle, Jim DeFelice. HarperCollins 2019. 304 p.
ISBN 9780062683717
Grades: Adult   B
1. Kyle, Taya, 1974- 2. Resilience 3. Purpose in life 4. Despair 5. Courage 6. Faith 7. Survival 8. Communities 9. Biographies 10. Life stories — Facing adversity
LC Bl2019006330

The best-selling author of American Wife and widow of "American Sniper" Chris Kyle presents an inspiring collection of stories from history and the author's personal life that showcase the resilience of the American spirit.

"Kyle follows up American Wife, about her Navy SEAL husband Chris Kyle (author of American Sniper), with this moving and passionate collection of essays in which she shares her experiences with people she has met as a public speaker…Once again, Kyle and DeFelice inspire with touching stories of compassion." —*Publishers Weekly*

Lahiri, Jhumpa
In Other Words. Jhumpa Lahiri; translated from the Italian by Ann Goldstein. Alfred A. Knopf 2016. 240 p.
ISBN 9781101875551
Grades: Adult   B
1. Lahiri, Jhumpa 2. Italian language 3. Language and culture 4. Language and languages 5. Voyages and travels 6. Italy 7. Autobiographies and memoirs 8. Translations — Italian to English 9. Bilingual materials — English/Italian 10. Travel writing — Living abroad 11. Travel writing — Europe
LC 2015020998

The author traces her enduring love affair with the Italian language that prompted her family's move to Rome, where her efforts to master the language as a writer shaped her feelings of belonging and exile.

"Lahiri's unexpected metamorphosis provides a captivating and insightful lesson in the power of language to transform." —*Publishers Weekly*

Translated from the Italian of: In altre parole; Originally published: Parma : Guanda, 2015.

Lahti, Christine
True Stories from an Unreliable Eyewitness: A Feminist Coming of Age. Christine Lahti. HarperCollins 2018. 224 p.
ISBN 9780062663672
Grades: Adult   B
1. Lahti, Christine 2. Actors and actresses 3. Growing up 4. Aging 5. Acting 6. Feminists 7. Feminism 8. Hollywood, California 9. Autobiographies and memoirs 10. Life stories — Arts and culture — Performing arts — Actors and actresses 11. Society and culture — Gender — Women
LC Bl2018003905

A collection of interrelated personal stories by the actress best known for her work on such productions as "Chicago Hope" and "The Blacklist" focuses on the milestones of her childhood, early career, and midlife while reflecting on the realities of being a woman in Hollywood.

"Her style is irreverent, bawdy, and laugh-out-loud funny, but she doesnt shirk from painful subjects, including family mental illness. Lahti is one of those rare celebrities who not only has a fascinating life but who can also tell a relatable story with humility and humor." —*Booklist*

Lal, Ruby
Empress: The Astonishing Reign of Nur Jahan. Ruby Lal. W.W. Norton & Company 2018. 320 p.
ISBN 9780393239348
Grades: Adult   B
1. Nur Jahan, Empress, consort of Jahangir, Emperor of Hindustan, d. 1645 2. Women rulers 3. Civilization, Islamic 4. Muslim women 5. Indian history 6. Biographies 7. Life stories — Politics — Royalty 8. History writing — Asia — South Asia — India
LC 2018003419

Presents a deeply researched portrait of the seventeenth-century Mughal Empire ruler that illuminates her genius as a designer, architect, politician, hunter, and partner.

"A page-turning, eye-opening biography that shatters our impressions of India as established by the British Raj." —*Kirkus*

Includes bibliographical references and index.

Lambert, Raymond
Every Man a Hero: A Memoir of D-Day, the First Wave at Omaha Beach, and a World at War. Raymond Lambert, Jim DeFelice. HarperCollins 2019. 320 p.
ISBN 9780062937483
Grades: Adult   B
1. Lambert, Raymond, 1921- 2. World War II 3. Normandy Invasion, June 6, 1944 4. Military campaigns 5. Soldiers 6. Paramedics 7. Heroes and heroines 8. Brothers 9. Operation Neptune 10. Veterans 11. Courage 12. French history 13. Normandy 14. 1940s 15. Second World War era (1939-1945) 16. 20th century 17. Autobiographies and memoirs 18. History writing — Wars and conflicts — World War II — European Theater 19. History writing — Wars and conflicts — Battles 20. Life stories — Law and order — Armed forces personnel

A first-hand account of D-Day by a decorated U.S. Army medic describes how he landed with the first wave on June 6, 1944, and saved dozens of his fellow American soldiers on Omaha Beach.

ESSENTIAL AND RECOMMENDED TITLES
Biography

Lamott, Anne
★ *Dusk, Night, Dawn: On Revival and Courage.* Anne Lamott. Riverhead Books 2021. 224 p.
ISBN 9780593189696
Grades: Adult   B
1. Lamott, Anne 2. Authors, American 3. Christian life 4. Faith (Christianity) 5. Self-acceptance 6. Coping 7. Hope 8. United States 9. 20th century 10. Essays 11. Autobiographies and memoirs 12. Spirituality and Religion — Christianity 13. Life stories — Religion and spirituality — Personal faith
LC 2020014324

Anne Lamott explores the tough questions that many of us grapple with. How can we recapture the confidence we once had as we stumble through the dark times that seem increasingly bleak? as bad news piles up, from climate crises to daily assaults on civility, how can we cope? Where, she asks, do we start to our world and joy and hope and our faith in life back... with our sore feet, hearing loss, stiff fingers, poor digestion, stunned minds, broken hearts. We begin, Lamott says, by accepting our flaws and embracing our humanity. Drawing from her own experiences, Lamott shows us the intimate and human ways we can adopt to move through life's dark places and toward the light of hope that still burns ahead for all of us.

"By turns wise, funny, tragic, mystical, visionary, and imaginative, Lamott's latest book will appeal to a wide range of readers who have previously enjoyed her relatable writing." —*Library Journal*

Land, Stephanie
Maid: Hard Work, Low Pay, and a Mother's Will to Survive. Stephanie Land; foreword by Barbara Ehrenreich. Hachette Books 2019. 288 p.
ISBN 9780316505116
Grades: Adult   B
1. Land, Stephanie 2. Household employees 3. Low-wage workers 4. Poverty 5. Working class 6. Underclass 7. Single mothers 8. Class conflict 9. Welfare recipients 10. United States 11. Autobiographies and memoirs 12. Page to screen 13. Life stories — Business — Working life 14. Society and culture — Wealth and class — Poverty
LC 2018954908
New York Times Notable Book, 2019.

An economic hardship journalist describes the years she worked in low-pay domestic work under wealthy employers, contrasting the privileges of the upper-middle class to the realities of the overworked laborers supporting them.

"Writer Land's vivid and visceral yet nearly unrelenting memoir covers three dark years in the life of a single mother raising her young daughter, Mia, on the unlivable wages that come with the physically and emotionally grueling work of contract housekeeping." —*Library Journal*

Lane, Charles
Freedom's Detective: The Secret Service, the Ku Klux Klan and the Man Who Masterminded America's First War on Terror. Charles Lane. Hanover Square Press 2019. 352 p.
ISBN 9781335006851
Grades: Adult   B
1. Whitley, Hiram C, 1834-1875 2. Intelligence service 3. Undercover operations 4. Terrorism investigation 5. African Americans 6. Prejudice 7. Assassination 8. Conspiracies 9. Voter suppression 10. Reconstruction (United States history) 11. Suffrage 12. United States history 13. 19th century 14. Biographies 15. History writing — Reconstruction — United States 16. Life stories — Law and order — Police and law officers
LC Bl2019003970

Chronicles the story of the Reconstruction-era Secret Service and its battle against the KKK's effort to suppress the emancipated African-American vote, sharing particular insights into the career of controversial Secret Service chief, Hiram C. Whitley.

"A detail laden, arduously researched chronicle that delineates an important early era of the Secret Service." —*Kirkus*

Lane, Christina
Phantom Lady: Hollywood Producer Joan Harrison, the Forgotten Woman Behind Hitchcock. Christina Lane. Independent Pub Group 2020. 400 pages
ISBN 9781613733844
Grades: Adult   B
1. Harrison, Joan, 1907-1994 2. Hitchcock, Alfred, 1899-1980 3. Women film producers and directors 4. Women screenwriters 5. Women television producers and directors 6. Censorship 7. Hollywood Blacklist 8. Film noir 9. Films 10. Actors and actresses 11. England 12. Hollywood, California 13. Biographies 14. Life stories — Arts and culture — Performing arts — Directors and producers 15. Arts and Entertainment — Movies and Television
LC 2019041981
Agatha Award for Best Nonfiction, 2020; Edgar Allan Poe Award for Best Critical/Biographical, 2021.

Phantom Lady chronicles the untold story of Joan Harrison, Hollywood's most powerful female writer-producer of the 1940's. Alfred Hitchcock's confidante and the Oscar-nominated screenwriter of his first American film, Rebecca, she was one of his closest collaborators, critically shaping his brand as the "master of suspense." Forging an image as "the female Hitchcock," Harrison went on to produce numerous Hollywood features before becoming a television pioneer as the producer of Alfred Hitchcock Presents.

"Harrison's story is a compelling one. This superbly written, absorbing biography of a woman succeeding on her own terms will resonate with fans of Hollywood stories, as well as those who appreciate celebrations of previously unsung women." —*Library Journal*
Includes bibliographical references and index.

Lanegan, Mark
Sing Backwards and Weep: A Memoir. Mark Lanegan. Da Capo Press 2020. 352 pages
ISBN 9780306922800
Grades: Adult   B
1. Lanegan, Mark 2. Singers 3. Grunge groups 4. Drug addicts 5. Rock musicians 6. Addiction 7. Popular music 8. United States 9. Seattle, Washington 10. 1980s 11. 1990s 12. Autobiographies and memoirs 13. Biographies 14. Arts and Entertainment — Music — Rock 15. Life stories — Facing adversity — Medical issues — Addiction 16. Life stories — Arts and culture — Performing arts — Musicians and composers

A gritty, gripping memoir by the singer Mark Lanegan (Screaming Trees, Queens of the Stone Age, Soulsavers), chronicling his years as a singer and drug addict in Seattle in the '80s and '90s.

"Told in a distinctively heavy voice, this warts-and-all account of addiction's effect on one's body and self-worth comes with heft and hits like a ton of bricks." —*Library Journal*

Lang, Maya
What We Carry: A Memoir. Maya Shanbhag Lang. The Dial Press 2020. 288 pages
ISBN 9780525512394
Grades: Adult   B
1. Lang, Maya 2. Mothers and daughters 3. People with Alzheimer's disease 4. Postpartum depression 5. Mother and adult daughter 6. Family secrets 7. Children of immigrants 8. Family relationships 9. Women caregivers 10. Women authors 11. Indian Americans 12. Autobiographies and memoirs 13. Family and Relationships — Parenting 14. Life stories — Relationships — Parent and child 15. Family and Relationships — Illness and the Family 16. Family and Relationships — Aging and Death
LC 2019018845

The author of the Sixteenth of June offers a memoir about immigrants and their native-born children, the complicated love between mothers and daughters, and the surprising discovery of strength.

"Readers interested in examining their own family stories, or those who experienced the struggles of new parenthood or reversed parenting roles, will connect deeply with Lang's beautiful memoir." —*Library Journal*

PUBLIC LIBRARY CORE COLLECTION: NONFICTION
Twentieth Edition

Lanzmann, Claude
The Patagonian Hare: A Memoir. Claude Lanzmann; translated from the French by Frank Wynne. Farrar, Straus and Giroux 2012. 496 p.
ISBN 9780374230043
Grades: Adult B
1. Lanzmann, Claude 2. Film producers and directors 3. Journalists 4. Memories 5. Autobiographies and memoirs 6. Arts and Entertainment — General 7. Life stories — Arts and culture — Performing arts
LC 2011048058

The author traces his life in film and journalism, describing his early experiences as an underground soldier in occupied Paris, his affair with Simone de Beauvoir, and the making of his seminal documentary Shoah.

LaPointe, Sasha taqwseblu
Red Paint: An Ancestral Autobiography of a Coast Salish Punk. Sasha taqwsablu LaPointe. Counterpoint Press 2022. 208 p.
ISBN 9781640094147
Grades: Adult B
1. LaPointe, Sasha taqwseblu 2. Coast Salish (North American people) 3. Salishan women 4. Punk culture 5. Psychic trauma 6. Interpersonal relations 7. Families 8. Subcultures 9. Indigenous peoples of North America — Social life and customs 10. Indigenous peoples of North America — History 11. Resilience 12. Identity 13. Washington State 14. Life stories — Identity — Race and ethnicity 15. Society and culture — Ethnic studies 16. History writing — Indigenous peoples — United States
LC 2021029010

Sasha taqwéseblu LaPointe, a Coast Salish indigenous woman, has always longed for a sense of home. As a child her family moved around frequently, often staying in barely habitable church attics and trailers, dangerous places for young Sasha. As an adolescent determined to escape the poverty and abuse of her childhood in order to build a better future for herself and her people, Sasha throws herself headlong into the world, with little more to guide her than a passion for the thriving punk scene of the Pacific Northwest and a desire to live up to the responsibility of being the namesake of her beloved great-grandmother, a linguist who helped preserve her indiginous language of Lushootseed and one in a long line of powerful ancestors. Exploring what it means to be vulnerable in love and in art while offering an unblinking reckoning with personal traumas as well as the collective historical traumas of colonialism and genocide that continue to haunt native peoples, Red Paint is an intersectional autobiography of lineage, resilience and above all the ability to heal that chronicles Sasha's struggles navigating a collapsing marriage while answering the call to greater purpose. Set against a backdrop of tour vans and the breathtaking beauty of Coast Salish ancestral land and imbued with the universal spirit of punk-an ethos that challenges us to reclaim what's rightfully ours: Our histories, our power, our traditions, and our truths-Red Paint is ultimately a story of the ways we learn to heal while fighting for our right to a place to call home.

"LaPointe, a Coast Salish poet and artist, sifts through her family's lineage to reckon with the meaning of home in this stirring debut.... LaPointe's fresh and urgent perspective on Indigenous culture is enthralling." —*Publishers Weekly*

Author's name is spelled: Sasha taqws[schwa]blu, the e in her Coast Salish name in all instances the e should be a schwa, an upside down e and the w is written in superscript.—Publisher's email.

Larson, Edward J.
The Return of George Washington: 1783-1789. Edward Larson. William Morrow & Company 2014. 400 p.
ISBN 9780062248671
Grades: Adult B
1. Washington, George, 1732-1799 2. Founding Fathers of the United States 3. Presidents 4. Politics and government 5. United States 6. 18th century 7. Early America (1784-1819) 8. 1780s 9. Biographies 10. History writing — Presidency — 18th century — United States 11. Life stories — Politics — Politicians 12. History writing — Early America — United States
LC 2013497765

Documents Washington's lesser-known decision to come out of retirement to lead the Constitutional Convention and become America's first president, discussing his vital role in addressing key financial and policy challenges.

"Larson identifies Washington's three goals'respect abroad, prosperity at home, and development westward'and includes an account of an inaugural dish that makes turducken seem unambitious. Profound, even affectionate, scholarship infuses every graceful sentence." —*Kirkus*

Larson, Erik
In the Garden of Beasts: Love, Terror, and an American Family in Hitler's Berlin. Erik Larson. Crown Trade 2011. 464 p.
ISBN 9780307408846
Grades: Adult B
1. Dodd, William, 1869-1940 2. Diplomats 3. Historians 4. American people in Europe 5. Nazism 6. Politicians 7. Third Reich, 1933-1945 8. Germany 9. United States 10. 1930s 11. Biographies 12. Life stories — Politics — Politicians 13. History writing — Europe — Germany 14. History writing — Politicians — United States 15. Nonfiction that reads like fiction

New York Times Notable Book, 2011.

Documents the efforts of the first American ambassador to Hitler's Germany, William E. Dodd, to acclimate to a residence in an increasingly violent city where he is forced to associate with the Nazis while his daughter pursues a relationship with Gestapo chief Rudolf Diels.

Also published in large print format.

Larson, Kate Clifford
Bound for the Promised Land: Harriet Tubman, Portrait of an American Hero. Kate Clifford Larson. Ballantine 2004. 402 p.
ISBN 9780345456274
Grades: 11 12 Adult B
1. Tubman, Harriet, 1820?-1913 2. Underground Railroad 3. Freedom seekers 4. Enslaved people 5. History of anti-slavery movements 6. African American women 7. United States history 8. 19th century 9. Biographies 10. History writing — Women's history 11. History writing — African American — Enslavement — United States 12. Life stories — Facing adversity — War and oppression — Enslaved people 13. Life stories — Politics — Activists and reformers 14. Life stories — People in history 15. Adult books for young adults

Draws on extensive genealogical resources and new archives and materials to capture Harriet Tubman's complex life and personality, revealing her personal life, accomplishments, and influence.

"Using a clear writing style, Larson does an excellent job of placing Tubman in the context of her times." —*School Library Journal*

Rosemary: The Hidden Kennedy Daughter. Kate Clifford Larson. Houghton Mifflin Harcourt 2015. 288 p.
ISBN 9780547250250
Grades: Adult B
1. Kennedy, Rosemary, 1918-2005 2. Kennedy family 3. People with developmental disabilities 4. Institutionalized people 5. Psychosurgery 6. Frontal lobotomy 7. Biographies 8. Life stories — People in history — Famous families
LC 2015028793

Massachusetts Book Awards, Nonfiction Award, 2016.

Based on information contained in Rose Kennedy's diaries and correspondence, as well as exclusive family interviews, the author describes the plight of a woman forgotten to history, who was intellectually disabled and kept hidden by the family after she received a lobotomy at age 23.

Includes bibliographical references and index.

Walk with Me: A Biography of Fannie Lou Hamer. Kate Clifford Larson. Oxford University Press 2021. 384 p.
ISBN 9780190096847
Grades: Adult B
1. Hamer, Fannie Lou, 1917-1977 2. Civil rights 3. African American women social reformers 4. Social advocates 5. Women social advocates 6. Biographies 7. History writing — Women's history 8. History writing — African American — Civil rights — United States 9. Life stories — Politics — Activists

ESSENTIAL AND RECOMMENDED TITLES
Biography

and Reformers — Civil Rights Leaders 10. History writing — 1960s — United States

Presents the first full portrait of Fannie Lou Hamer and her galvanic part in the greatest social movement of our era.

"An inspiring read for activists fighting for voting rights and against racism." —*Library Journal*

Laughlin, James
The Luck of Friendship: The Letters of Tennessee Williams and James Laughlin. James Laughlin and Tennessee Williams, edited by Peggy Fox and Thomas Keith. W. W. Norton & Company 2018. 352 p.
ISBN 9780393246209
Grades: Adult B
1. Laughlin, James, 1914-1997 2. Williams, Tennessee, 1911-1983 3. Male friendship 4. Authors 5. Publishers and publishing 6. Interpersonal relations 7. Letters 8. Autobiographies and memoirs 9. Life stories — Relationships — Friendship

The chronicle of Tennessee Williams and James Laughlin's unlikely yet enduring literary and personal relationship.

"The rivers of mutual affection, admiration, and artistry form a powerful confluence in these deeply affecting exchanges." —*Kirkus*

Includes bibliographical references and index.

Lauterbach, Preston
Bluff City: The Secret Life of Photographer Ernest Withers. Preston Lauterbach. W. W. Norton & Company 2019. 288 p.
ISBN 9780393247923
Grades: Adult B
1. Withers, Ernest C, 1922-2007 2. African American photographers 3. African American civil rights workers 4. FBI informants 5. Civil Rights Movement 6. Informers 7. Photojournalists 8. 1950s 9. 1960s 10. Biographies 11. Life stories — Law and order — Spies and secret agents 12. Life stories — Arts and culture 13. History writing — African American — Civil rights — United States
LC 2018032872

Tells the little-known story of iconic photographer Ernest Withers, whose work both captured and influenced the 1950s and 1960s civil rights movement, while he also acted as an informant for the FBI.

Includes bibliographical references and index.

Lawson, Jenny
★ *Broken: (in the Best Possible Way).* Jenny Lawson. Henry Holt and Company 2021. 352 p.
ISBN 9781250077035
Grades: Adult B
1. Lawson, Jenny, 1973- 2. Journalists 3. Comedians 4. Depression 5. Health 6. Anxiety 7. Mental illness 8. People with depression 9. Treatment 10. Women 11. Autobiographies and memoirs 12. Life stories — Facing adversity — Medical issues — Mental illness 13. Science writing — Medicine and health — Mental health
LC 2020013954
LibraryReads Favorites, 2021; Loan Stars Favourites, 2021.

The award-winning humorist and author of Let's Pretend This Never Happened shares candid reflections on such topics as her experimental treatment for depression, her escape from three bears and her business ideas for Shark Tank.

"Lawson (You Are Here) returns with a wry and entertaining take on her battle with depression, anxiety, and rheumatoid arthritis. As always, the author is unrivaled in her ability to use piercing humor and insight to take on heavy subjects." —*Publishers Weekly*

Furiously Happy: A Funny Book About Horrible Things. Jenny Lawson. Flatiron Books 2015. 352 p.
ISBN 9781250077004
Grades: Adult B
1. Lawson, Jenny, 1973- 2. Self-acceptance 3. Anxiety 4. Depression 5. People with depression 6. Family relationships 7. Phobias 8. Identity 9. Mental illness 10. Women 11. People with mental illnesses 12. Autobiographies and memoirs 13. Science Writing — Medicine and health — Mental health 14. Life stories — Facing adversity — Medical issues — Mental illness
LC 2015022196
LibraryReads Favorites, 2015; Library Journal Best Books, 2015.

The popular blogger presents a humorous and candid memoir about her life-long battle with severe depression and anxiety, discussing how embracing both the flawed and the beautiful parts of life have enabled her to find joy in outrageous ways.

"Lawson's goal is not to offend, although that might happen to some readers, but to lay bare the truth about her struggles in life so that others can benefit. She does a solid job exposing the hidden nature of mental illness by putting a direct spotlight on her own issues, thereby illuminating an often taboo subject. Her amusing essays open up a not-so-funny topic: Mental illness in its many guises. Kudos to Lawson for being a flagrant and witty spokesperson for this dark subject matter." —*Kirkus*

Lawton, Georgina
Raceless: In Search of Family, Identity, and the Truth About Where I Belong. Georgina Lawton. HarperPerennial 2021. 304 p.
ISBN 9780063009486
Grades: Adult B
1. Lawton, Georgina 2. Identity 3. Family secrets 4. Racism 5. Growing up 6. Women journalists 7. Belonging 8. Multiracial women 9. Family relationships 10. Race (Social sciences) 11. Families 12. Autobiographies and memoirs 13. Life stories — Identity — Race and ethnicity

A former columnist for the Guardian explains how growing up in a color-blind household with white parents didn't equip her for dealing with prejudice and describes her personal journey for racial identity.

"In her debut memoir, Guardian columnist Lawton offers a unique perspective on identity and family in an era of racial awakening.... A timely, engaging exploration of family and racial belonging featuring many valuable lessons." —*Kirkus*

Laymon, Kiese
★ *Heavy: An American Memoir.* Kiese Laymon. Scribner 2018. 288 p.
ISBN 9781501125652
Grades: Adult B
1. African Americans 2. Mothers and sons 3. Obesity 4. Children of single parents 5. Prejudice 6. Racism 7. White privilege 8. Discrimination 9. Race relations 10. Mississippi 11. United States 12. Autobiographies and memoirs 13. Book club best bets 14. Life stories — Identity — Race and ethnicity 15. Adult books for young adults 16. Antiracist literature
LC 2018002915
Andrew Carnegie Medal for Excellence in Non-Fiction, 2019; Los Angeles Times Book Prizes, Christopher Isherwood Prize for Autobiographical Prose, 2018; New York Times Notable Book, 2018; Library Journal Best Books, 2018; ALA Notable Book, 2019; Kirkus Prize for Nonfiction finalist, 2018.

An essayist and novelist explores what the weight of a lifetime of secrets, lies and deception does to a Black body, a Black family and a nation teetering on the brink of moral collapse.

"Laymon applies his book's title to his body and his memories; to his inheritance as a student, a teacher, a writer, an activist, a Black man, and his mother's son—but also to the weight of truth, and writing it." —*Booklist*

Le Carre, John
The Pigeon Tunnel: Stories from My Life. John Le Carre. Viking 2016. 400 p.
ISBN 9780735220775
Grades: Adult B
1. Le Carre, John, 1931-2020 2. Spies in literature 3. Authors, English 4. Autobiographies and memoirs 5. Life stories — Arts and culture — Writing — Authors
LC 2016299972

The author of such best-selling suspense novels as a Delicate Truth shares personal anecdotes from his life, discussing subjects ranging from his Cold War-era service in British intelligence to his work as a writer in Russia before and after the collapse of the Berlin Wall.

"The author's self-deprecating humor and wit are never far away, and he proves a most elegant and genial host on this tour of his life and work." —*Publishers Weekly*

Le Guin, Ursula K.
Ursula K. Le Guin: Conversations on Writing. Ursula K. Le Guin with David Naimon. Tin House Books 2018. 150 p.
ISBN 9781941040997
Grades: Adult   B
1. Le Guin, Ursula K, 1929-2018 2. Women authors, American 3. Authors, American 4. Writing 5. Literary criticism 6. Civilization 7. United States 8. Interviews 9. Arts and Entertainment — Writing and Publishing 10. Society and culture — General 11. Arts and Entertainment — Writing and Publishing — Literary criticism

LC 2018003429

Locus Award for Best Nonfiction/Related/Reference Book, 2019.

In a series of interviews with David Naimon, Le Guin discusses craft, aesthetics, and philosophy in her fiction, poetry, and nonfiction respectively. The discussions provide ample advice and guidance for writers of every level, but also give Le Guin a chance to sound off on some of her favorite subjects: the genre wars, the patriarchy, the natural world, and what, in her opinion, makes for great writing.

"Readers and writers who have enjoyed Le Guin in her many forms throughout the years will likely relish the intimate insights the novelist shares. That said, the interviews are freely available online for those interested in listening to Le Guin's words in her own voice." —*Library Journal*

Leader, Zachary
The Life of Saul Bellow: Love and Strife, 1965-2005. by Zachary Leader. Alfred A. Knopf 2018. 784 p.
ISBN 9781101875162
Grades: Adult   B
1. Bellow, Saul 2. Literature and society 3. Literary prizes 4. Senior men 5. Perfectionism 6. Fathers and sons 7. Fathers and daughters 8. Literature 9. Authors, American 10. 20th century 11. Biographies 12. Life stories — Arts and culture — Writing — Authors 13. Arts and Entertainment — Writing and Publishing 14. Arts and Entertainment — Writing and Publishing — Literary criticism

LC 2017053381

The second volume of the biography of the storied author describes how he expanded his collection of awards in his later years and continued to lead a dramatic, volatile love life, fathering his fourth child in his eighties.

"This is biography at its best and will appeal widely." —*Library Journal*
Includes bibliographical references and index.

Leal, Brigitte
The Ultimate Picasso. Brigitte Leal, Christine Piot, Marie-Laure Bernadac; preface by Jean Leymarie. Harry N. Abrams 2003. 551 p. : Illustration; Color
ISBN 9780810991149
Grades: Adult   B
1. Picasso, Pablo, 1881-1973 2. Artists 3. Arts and Entertainment — Painting, Drawing, and Sculpture

LC 2003007773

Presents a concise version of a retrospective of Picasso's work, presenting more than 1,200 reproductions that include paintings, drawings, lithographs, ceramics, and sculpture, covering every major period in the artist's life.
Includes bibliographical references (p. 541-545) and index; Translated from the French original.

Leaming, Barbara
Jacqueline Bouvier Kennedy Onassis: The Life of Jacqueline Kennedy Onassis. by Barbara Leaming. Thomas Dunne Books 2014. 352 p. : Illustration
ISBN 9781250017642
Grades: Adult   B
1. Onassis, Jacqueline Kennedy, 1929-1994 2. Celebrities 3. People with post-traumatic stress disorder 4. Families of murder victims 5. Presidents' spouses 6. United States 7. 20th century 8. Biographies 9. History writing — Presidency — 20th century — United States 10. History writing — 1960s — United States 11. Life stories — Politics — Politicians 12. Life stories — Facing adversity — Medical issues — Mental illness

LC 2014026768

Traces the pattern of Jacqueline Onassis' life from her youth to her transformation into a deft political wife and unique First Lady, and examines her thirty-year struggle with PTSD after the assassination of her husband, John F. Kennedy.

"Leaming tells a heart-wrenching story of a woman who not only endured a horrific event but also struggled to recover and was often misunderstood as she eventually carved out a life of her own making." —*Booklist*
Includes bibliographical references and index.

Kick Kennedy: The Charmed Life and Tragic Death of the Favorite Kennedy Daughter. Barbara Leaming. Thomas Dunne Books 2016. 368 p.
ISBN 9781250071316
Grades: Adult   B
1. Kennedy, Kathleen, 1920-1948 2. Kennedy family 3. Socialites 4. American people in England 5. Young women 6. Catholics 7. Aristocracy 8. Families 9. Presidents 10. Social life and customs 11. United States 12. Great Britain 13. 20th century 14. Biographies 15. Life stories — People in history — Famous families

LC 2016007364

Kathleen "Kick" Kennedy was the incandescent life-force of the fabled Kennedy family, her father's acknowledged "favorite of all the children" and her brother Jack's "psychological twin." She was the Kennedy of Kennedys, sure of her privilege, magnetically charming and somehow not quite like anyone else on whatever stage she happened to grace.

"Leaming candidly demystifies the life of one of the least-known Kennedys and vividly illuminates the complex world of British aristocracy." —*Booklist*

Mrs. Kennedy: The Missing History of the Kennedy Years. Barbara Leaming. Simon & Schuster 2002. x, 406 p. : Illustration
ISBN 9780743227490
Grades: Adult   B
1. Onassis, Jacqueline Kennedy, 1929-1994 2. Presidents' spouses 3. Men-women relations 4. Politics and government 5. United States 6. 1960s 7. 20th century 8. Biographies 9. History writing — Presidency — 20th century — United States 10. History writing — 1960s — United States 11. Life stories — Politics — Politicians

LC BL2002012436

A portrait of Jacqueline Kennedy during the thousand days of JFK's administration sheds new light on her life as both a woman and as First Lady, revealing struggles for herself, her marriage, and her husband's presidency.

"Asserting that Jacqueline Kennedy's role in shaping her husband's presidency has been under-examined, Leaming . offers a corrective in this intimate look at a very private woman. Initially inclined to keep herself as much in the background as possible, says Leaming, Jacqueline Kennedy became an increasingly visible and vocal first lady as she realized how effective she could be as an image maker. It's in this capacity that Leaming convincingly depicts her as being instrumental in shaping the course of her husband's administration." —*Publishers Weekly*

A Touchstone book; Includes bibliographical references (p. [365]-392) and index; Originally published: New York : Free Press, 2001.

Lear, Linda J.
Beatrix Potter: A Life in Nature. Linda Lear. St. Martin's Press 2007. xix, 583 p. 32 p. of plates : Illustration; Color; Map
ISBN 9780312369347
Grades: Adult   B
1. Potter, Beatrix, 1866-1943 2. Authors 3. Illustrators 4. Children's literature authors 5. Children's literature writing 6. Authors, English 7. Lake District (England) 8. 20th century 9. Biographies 10. Arts and Entertainment — Writing and Publishing 11. Life stories — Arts and culture — Writing — Authors

LC 2006051245

Details the life of the children's author and illustrator who created such memorable characters as Peter Rabbit, Jemima Puddle-Duck, and Tom Kitten.

ESSENTIAL AND RECOMMENDED TITLES
Biography

"This is a meticulously researched and brilliantly recreated life that . Is endlessly fascinating and often illuminating. It is altogether a remarkable achievement." —*Booklist*

Includes bibliographical references (p. 541-554) and index.

Lear, Norman
Even This I Get to Experience. Norman Lear. Penguin Books 2014. 464 p.
ISBN 9781594205729
Grades: Adult **B**

1. Lear, Norman 2. Television programs 3. Television producers and directors 4. Television 5. Autobiographies and memoirs 6. Life stories — Arts and culture — Performing arts — Directors and producers 7. Arts and entertainment — Movies and television

LC 2014032903

The legendary creator of iconic television programs All in the Family, Sanford and Son, Maude, Good Times, the Jeffersons, and Mary Hartman, Mary Hartman, Norman Lear remade our television culture, while leading a life of unparalleled political, civic, and social involvement. Sharing the wealth of Lear's ninety years, Even This I Get to Experience is a memoir as touching and remarkable as the life he has led.

"A big-hearted, richly detailed chronicle of comedy, commitment and a long life lived fully." —*Kirkus*

Leavitt, David
The Man Who Knew Too Much: Alan Turing and the Invention of the Computer. David Leavitt. W. W. Norton 2006. 319 p. : Illustration
ISBN 9780393052367
Grades: Adult **B**

1. Turing, Alan Mathison, 1912-1954 2. Mathematicians 3. Gay men 4. Artificial intelligence 5. Computers 6. Legislation 7. British history 8. 20th century 9. Science Writing — Computing, the Internet, and Technology 10. Adult books for young adults

LC 2005018034

Outlines the English mathematician's efforts in devising a programmable calculating machine, his work in cracking the Nazi Enigma code, and how the revelation of his homosexuality led to his tragic imprisonment and suicide.

"The author succeeds in drawing a wonderfully vivid picture of his shy, dry, brilliant hero." —*National Review*

Atlas books; Includes bibliographical references and index.

Leavy, Jane
The Big Fella: Babe Ruth and the World He Created. Jane Leavy. Harper 2018. 320 p.
ISBN 9780062380227
Grades: Adult **B**

1. Ruth, Babe, 1895-1948 2. Professional baseball 3. Celebrities 4. Fame 5. Baseball history 6. Baseball Hall of Fame members 7. Baseball players 8. United States 9. 20th century 10. Biographies 11. Sports and Competition — Baseball 12. Sports and Competition — Individual Athlete 13. Life stories — Sports — Athletes

LC BI2018167865

National Book Critics Circle Award for Biography finalist, 2018.

A portrait of Babe Ruth and his partnership with business manager Christy Walsh traces how their strategies, achievements and notoriety established a blueprint for modern athletic stardom.

"A skilled strategist and nearly peerless player, Ruth proves himself worthy of, yes, yet another biography, this one warts-and-all but still admiring. Sparkling, exemplary sports biography, shedding new light on a storied figure in baseball history." —*Kirkus*

The Last Boy: Mickey Mantle and the End of America's Childhood. Jane Leavy. Harper 2010. xxiv, 456 p, [16] p. of plates : Illustration; Color
ISBN 9780060883522
Grades: Adult **B**

1. Mantle, Mickey, 1931-1995 2. Baseball Hall of Fame members 3. Outfielders (Baseball) 4. Baseball history 5. Baseball players 6. Social life and customs 7. United States 8. 20th century 9. Biographies 10. Sports and Competition — Baseball 11. Sports and Competition — Individual Athlete 12. Life stories — Sports — Athletes

LC 2010525670

New York Times Notable Book, 2010.

Drawing on more than five hundred interviews with loved ones and fellow baseball players, the author crafts a deeply personal biography of the Yankee great, weaving her own memories of the major league slugger with an authoritative account of his life onand off the field.

"This is unlike any biography on the sports shelf. Leavy, in exploring her own ambivalent feelings toward Mantle, permits readers to experience the same confusing emotions that many of those around him felt: Proud to bask in his reflected glory but too intimidated to confront him. A masterpiece of sports biography." —*Booklist*

Includes bibliographical references (p. [421]-438), filmography (p. 436-437), and index.

Sandy Koufax: A Lefty's Legacy. Jane Leavy. Harper Collins 2002. xxii, 282 p. : Illustration
ISBN 9780060195335
Grades: Adult **B**

1. Koufax, Sandy, 1935- 2. Jewish Americans 3. Jewish American men 4. Pitchers (Baseball) 5. Baseball players 6. Social life and customs 7. United States 8. 20th century 9. Biographies 10. Interviews 11. Sports and Competition — Baseball 12. Sports and Competition — Individual Athlete 13. Life stories — Sports — Athletes

LC 2002068722

Draws on more than four hundred interviews with friends, teammates, and opponents to present a portrait of the distinguished baseball pitcher.

"The author delivers an honest and exquisitely detailed examination of a complex man." —*Publishers Weekly*

Includes index.

Lecrae
★ *I Am Restored: How I Lost My Religion but Found My Faith.* Lecrae. Zondervan 2020. 170 p.
ISBN 9780310358039
Grades: Adult **B**

1. Lecrae (Musician) 2. Rap musicians 3. Christian men 4. African Americans 5. Depression 6. Addiction 7. Adult child sexual abuse victims 8. Psychic trauma 9. Healing 10. Faith (Christianity) 11. Autobiographies and memoirs 12. Life stories — Arts and culture — Performing arts — Musicians and composers 13. Life stories — Religion and spirituality — Spiritual journeys 14. Life stories — Personal growth 15. Spirituality and Religion — Christianity

LC BI2020021912

The award winning hip-hop artist discusses how he overcame his battles against sexual abuse, physical trauma, addiction, and depression to find healing and a new-found freedom in his relationship with God.

"This personal story of faith lost and found is especially recommended to Christians who are struggling to comprehend God's complex ways." —*Library Journal*

Lee, Helie
In the Absence of Sun: A Korean American Woman's Promise to Reunite Three Lost Generations of Her Family. Helie Lee. Harmony Books 2002. 342 p, [8] p. of plates : Illustration; Map
ISBN 9780609609347
Grades: Adult **B**

1. Lee family 2. Yi family 3. Baek, Hongyong, 1912-2012 4. Korean Americans 5. Families 6. East Asian Americans 7. Genealogy 8. California 9. North Korea 10. Family and Relationships — Families

LC 2002001680

Describes the attempt of Helie Lee to reunite her grandmother with her uncle who was lost decades ago during an escape from North Korea.

"Lee's Still Life with Rice (1996) was a novelized account of her grandmother's life and escape from what would become North Korea. As she now recounts her and her father's struggles to get other people out of the North, she

PUBLIC LIBRARY CORE COLLECTION: NONFICTION
Twentieth Edition

continues to wrestle with her own Korean heritage in particular, the paternalistic and patronizing attitudes toward women." —*Booklist*

Lee, Julia Sun-Joo
Biting the Hand: Growing up Asian in Black and White America. Julia Lee. Henry Holt Books and Company 2023. 256 p.
ISBN 9781250824677
Grades: Adult   B
1. Lee, Julia Sun-Joo, 1976- 2. Asian Americans 3. Asian American women 4. Racism 5. Identity 6. Self-discovery 7. Race (Social sciences) 8. Race relations 9. Social change 10. Influence (Psychology) 11. Children of immigrants 12. Autobiographies and memoirs 13. Life stories — Identity — Race and ethnicity

When Julia was fifteen, her hometown went up in smoke during the 1992 Los Angeles riots. The events forced Julia to question her racial identity and complicity. She was neither Black nor white. So who was she? This question would follow Julia for years to come, but it was only when she began a PhD in English that she found answers in the prose of writers like James Baldwin and Toni Morrison. Their works gave Julia the vocabulary and, more important, the permission to critically examine her own tortured position as an Asian American, setting off a powerful journey of racial reckoning, atonement, and self-discovery.

"A lively, wise, and immensely insightful memoir about Asian America's relationship with Whiteness." —*Kirkus*

Leerhsen, Charles
★ *Butch* Cassidy: The True Story of an American Outlaw. Charles Leerhsen. Simon & Schuster 2020. 304 p.
ISBN 9781501117480
Grades: Adult   B
1. Cassidy, Butch, 1866-1908 2. Thieves 3. Outlaws 4. Bank robberies 5. Train robberies 6. Ranchers 7. Crime 8. Criminals 9. The West (United States) 10. 19th century 11. Biographies 12. True Crime — Heists and Robbery 13. Life stories — Law and order — Criminals and law-breakers 14. History writing — Westward expansion — United States
LC 2019034980

A portrait of the notorious Wild West outlaw separates facts from folklore to discuss Robert Leroy Parker's impoverished early life, humane approaches to crime, partnership with Harry "The Sundance Kid" Longabaugh and flight from the Pinkerton Agency.

"Perhaps the most successful of the frontier outlaws, Cassidy receives an entertaining and likely definitive account." —*Kirkus*

Includes bibliographical references and index.

Lees, Gene
You Can't Steal a Gift: Dizzy, Clark, Milt, and Nat. Gene Lees; foreword by Nat Hentoff. Yale University Press 2001. xvii, 269 p. : Illustration
ISBN 9780300089653
Grades: Adult   B
1. Gillespie, Dizzy, 1917-1993 2. Terry, Clark 3. Hinton, Milt, 1910-2000 4. Cole, Nat 5. Jazz musicians 6. Race relations 7. United States history 8. Biographies 9. Arts and Entertainment — Music — Jazz and the Blues
LC 2001003444

"The author has a natural ease with words and a graceful prose style that captures the reader's attention." —*Booklist*

Includes index.

Legler, Casey
★ *Godspeed: A Memoir.* Casey Legler. Atria Books 2018. 192 p.
ISBN 9781501135750
Grades: Adult   B
1. Legler, Casey 2. Autistic women 3. Olympic athletes 4. Teenagers with depression 5. Teenagers 6. Growing up 7. Drug abuse 8. Loneliness in teenagers 9. Drug use 10. Neurodivergent people 11. Autobiographies and memoirs 12. Life stories — Facing adversity — Medical issues — Addiction 13. Life stories — Facing adversity — Medical issues — Mental illness 14. Life stories — Relationships — Growing up
LC 2018022193

A coming-of-age memoir by a former Olympic swimmer describes the crippling loneliness that marked her athletic childhood and her struggles with addiction and self-destructiveness prior to her diagnosis with autism.

"A coming-of-age drama captured through poetic prose and convincing honesty." —*Kirkus*

Lehrer, Riva
Golem Girl: A Memoir. Riva Lehrer. One World 2020. 448 p.
ISBN 9781984820303
Grades: 11 12 Adult   B
1. Lehrer, Riva, 1958- 2. People with disabilities 3. Intersectionality 4. Empowerment 5. Sexuality 6. Women painters 7. Ableism 8. Spina bifida 9. Women artists 10. Life stories — Arts and culture — Artists 11. Life stories — Identity — LGBTQIA+ 12. Society and culture — Illness and disease 13. Life stories — Facing adversity — Medical issues — Living with disabilities
LC 2020012800

National Book Critics Circle Award for Autobiography/Memoir finalist, 2020.

Memoir of an artist born with disabilities who searches for freedom and connection in a society afraid of strange bodies.

"Painter Lehrer applies the same unflinching gaze for which her portraits are known to a lifetime with spina bifida in this trenchant debut memoir of disability and queer culture." —*Publishers Weekly*

Leland, Andrew
★ *The Country of the Blind: A Memoir at the End of Sight.* Andrew Leland. Penguin 2023. 368 p.
ISBN 9781984881427
Grades: Adult   B
1. Leland, Andrew 2. Journalists 3. People who are blind 4. Married men 5. Fathers 6. Blindness 7. Diseases 8. Degeneration (Pathology) 9. People with disabilities 10. Identity 11. Curiosity 12. Ableism 13. Culture 14. Autobiographies and memoirs 15. Life stories — Facing adversity — Medical issues — Living with disabilities 16. Science Writing — Medicine and health — Disabilities and disorders 17. Society and culture — General 18. Debut title

Pulitzer Prize for Memoir or Autobiography finalist, 2024.

Part memoir, part historical and cultural investigation, the author, midway through his life with retinitis pigmentosa, explores the state of being that awaits him, not only the physical experience of blindness but also its language, politics and customs so he can not only survive this transition but grow from it.

"This informative and engaging memoir will appeal to readers who like to be entertained as they broaden their awareness of disability and others' lives." —*Library Journal*

Lemmon, Gayle Tzemach
Ashley's War: The Untold Story of a Team of Women Soldiers on the Special Ops Battlefield. Gayle Tzemach Lemmon. HarperCollins 2015. 320 p.
ISBN 9780062333810
Grades: Adult   B
1. Women and war 2. Afghan War, 2001-2021 3. Special operations (Military science) 4. Interpersonal relations 5. Women soldiers 6. Biographies 7. History writing — Military — Special Forces 8. Life stories — Law and order — Armed forces personnel 9. History writing — Wars and conflicts — War in Afghanistan
LC 2015460337

From the author of the New York Times best-seller the Dressmaker of Khair Khana comes the story of First Lieutenant Ashley White and a groundbreaking team of female American warriors who served alongside Special Operations soldiers on the battlefield in Afghanistan.

"This compassionate and intimate expos addressing the female battlefield experience will resonate with readers interested in the woman warriors of today's military." —*Library Journal*

The **Dressmaker** *of Khair Khana: Five Sisters, One Remarkable Family, and the Woman Who Risked Everything to Keep Them Safe.* Gayle Tzemach Lemmon. HarperCollins 2011. xxvi, 256 p. : Portrait
ISBN 9780061732379
Grades: 11 12 Adult   B

ESSENTIAL AND RECOMMENDED TITLES
Biography

1. Muslim women 2. Dressmakers 3. Women entrepreneurs 4. Women and war 5. Kabul, Afghanistan 6. Biographies 7. Adult books for young adults 8. Life stories — Facing adversity — War and oppression — War survivors 9. History writing — Wars and conflicts — War in Afghanistan 10. Society and culture — Gender — Women 11. Nonfiction that reads like fiction

Amelia Bloomer List, 2012.

The incredible true account of Kamila Sidiqi who, when her father and brother were forced to flee Kabul, became the sole breadwinner for her five siblings. Armed only with grit and determination, she picked up a needle and thread and created a thriving business of her own and held her family together.

Leng'ete, Nice
The Girls in the Wild Fig Tree: How I Fought to Save Myself, My Sister, and Thousands of Girls Worldwide. Nice Leng'ete. Little, Brown & Company 2021. 208 p.

ISBN 9780316463355

Grades: Adult   **B**

1. Leng'ete, Nice 2. Maasai (African people) 3. Women's rights 4. Human rights activists 5. Women human rights activists 6. Women 7. Social life and customs 8. Kenya 9. Autobiographies and memoirs 10. Life stories — Politics — Activists and reformers 11. Society and culture — Gender — Women

An inspirational story of one girl who changed the minds of her elders, reformed traditions from the inside, and is creating a better future for girls and women throughout Africa Born in a remote village in Kenya, Nice Leng'ete saw the young girls she grew up with receive the cut, the rite of passage into female adulthood in Masai culture. Every girl got the cut, and once you did, you'd be married off to a man triple your age. You might be his second or third wife. You'd have children in your teens. This is exactly what happened to Nice's sister. To resist the cut meant becoming an outcast in Masai culture. Yet Nice managed to avoid it and stay in school. It was not an easy time. She was shunned. At the age of 21, Nice moved to Nairobi to work for Amref Health Africa, an organization spearheading the campaign against Female Genital Mutilation. Though she was still considered an outcast in her village—even an entapai (someone who brought shame to her family)—young girls began to look up to Nice. They saw the life they could have, not the one chosen for them. Eventually, thanks to a combination of incredible instincts, excellent training and leading by example, Nice Leng'ete developed a platform for convincing women across Africa to forego the cut. First, she won over her village elders. It spread from there. Kenya outlawed the cut in 2011, and the Masai people abandoned it in 2014. To date, Nice and Amref Health Africa have collaborated to help more than 16,000 girls avoid FGM in Kenya and Tanzania.

"An inspirational memoir from a human rights activist who has devoted her life to fighting female genital mutilation." —*Kirkus*

Lepore, Jill
Book of Ages: The Life and Opinions of Jane Franklin. Jill Lepore. Alfred A. Knopf 2013. 480 p.

ISBN 9780307958341

Grades: Adult   **B**

1. Mecom, Jane, 1712-1794 2. Franklin, Benjamin, 1706-1790 3. Women 4. Siblings 5. Letter writing 6. United States history 7. Boston, Massachusetts 8. 18th century 9. Biographies 10. Life stories — People in history 11. History writing — Women's history

LC 2013001012

Booklist Editors' Choice, 2013; Mark Lynton History Prize, 2014; New York Times Notable Book, 2013; National Book Award for Nonfiction finalist, 2013.

A revelatory portrait of the founding father's youngest sister, Jane, draws on correspondences, artifacts and recently discovered portraits to reveal how in spite of obscurity and poverty she was, like her brother, a passionate reader, gifted writer and shrewd political commentator who made insightful observations about an early America.

Includes bibliographical references.

Lester, Toby
Da Vinci's Ghost: Genius, Obsession, and How Leonardo Created the World in His Own Image. Toby Lester. Free Press 2012. 304 p.

ISBN 9781439189238

Grades: Adult   **B**

1. Leonardo, da Vinci, 1452-1519 2. Intellectual life 3. Drawing 4. Anatomy 5. Architecture 6. Renaissance (1300-1600) 7. History writing — Renaissance — Europe

LC 2011027966

Citing the ubiquitous presence of the Renaissance master's meticulous rendering of an outstretched human form in a circle and square, an account of the epic intellectual journeys that inspired the Vitruvian Man's creation shares lesser-known aspects of da Vinci's life and how he served to bridge the Middle Ages to a monumental period of art, science and philosophy.

Includes bibliographical references.

Letts, Elizabeth
★ *The Ride of Her Life: The True Story of a Woman, Her Horse, and Their Last-chance Journey Across America.* Elizabeth Letts. Ballantine Books 2021. 272 p.

ISBN 9780525619321

Grades: Adult   **B**

1. Wilkins, Mesannie 2. Women equestrians 3. Senior women 4. Equestrianism 5. Transcontinental journeys 6. Women travelers 7. Women and horses 8. Horses 9. Dogs 10. Overland journeys to the Pacific 11. Fame 12. 1950s 13. Biographies 14. Life stories — People in history 15. Travel Writing — Women Travelers 16. Travel Writing — Modes of Transportation 17. History writing — Post World War II - 1959 — United States 18. Travel Writing — United States

LC 2020048732

In 1954, Annie Wilkins, a sixty-three-year-old farmer from Maine, embarked on an impossible journey. She had no relatives left, she'd lost her family farm to back taxes, and her doctor had just given her two years to live—but only if she "lived restfully." Instead, she decided she wanted to see the Pacific Ocean just once before she died. She bought a cast-off brown gelding named Tarzan, donned men's dungarees, loaded up her horse, and headed out from Maine in mid-November, hoping to beat the snow. She had no map, no GPS, no phone. But she had her ex-racehorse, her faithful mutt, and her own unfailing belief that Americans would treat a stranger with kindness. At a time when small towns were being bypassed by Eisenhower's brand-new interstate highway system, and the reach and impact of television was just beginning to be understood, Annie and her four-footed companions inspired an outpouring of neighborliness in a rapidly changing world.

The #1 New York Times best-selling author of the Perfect Horse and the Eighty-Dollar Champion presents the triumphant true story of 63-year-old Maine farmer Annie Wilkins who, in 1954, rode her horse across America, fulfilling her dying wish to see the Pacific Ocean.

"Letts (The Perfect Horse) inspires in this miraculous true story of one woman's trek from Maine to California on horseback. This story has it all: Bravery, determination, and a whole lot of heart." —*Publishers Weekly*

Includes bibliographical references and index.

Lever, Evelyne
Marie Antoinette: The Last Queen of France. by Evelyne Lever; translated from the French by Catherine Temerson. Farrar, Straus and Giroux 2000. VIII, 357 p. : Illustration

ISBN 9780374199388

Grades: 11 12 Adult   **B**

1. Marie Antoinette, Queen, consort of Louis XVI, King of France, 1755-1793 2. Women rulers 3. French history 4. 18th century 5. Revolutionary France (1789-1799) 6. Biographies 7. Translations — French to English 8. History writing — Europe — France 9. History writing — Wars and conflicts — French Revolution 10. Life stories — Politics — Politicians

LC 00028763

Booklist Editors' Choice, 2000.

A biography of the French queen explores the intrigue surrounding her life from her birth, through her unhappy marriage, her lavish life at Versailles, to the events leading up to her death by beheading during the French Revolution.

"The author examines the opulent Versailles subculture and the queen whose royal excesses served as a major catalyst for the revolutionary upheaval of 1789."

Through the skillful use of memoirs and other primary documents, Lever creates an empathic picture of Louis XVI's headstrong wife." —*Library Journal*

Includes bibliographical references (p. [331]-344) and index; Originally published in French as Marie-Antoinette: Paris : Fayard, 1991.

Levi, Primo
The Reawakening. Primo Levi; translated from the Italian by Stuart Woolf. Macmillan; 1993. 231 p. : Map
ISBN 9780020223696
Grades: 11 12 Adult   B
1. Levi, Primo 2. Holocaust survivors 3. Authors, Italian 4. Jewish people 5. Holocaust (1933-1945) 6. Western European people 7. Italian people 8. 20th century 9. Autobiographies and memoirs 10. Translations — Italian to English 11. History writing — Wars and conflicts — Holocaust — World War II 12. Life stories — Facing adversity — War and oppression — Holocaust
LC 92045264

Companion vol. to: Survival in Auschwitz; Translation originally published: London : Bodley Head, 1965.

★ *Survival in Auschwitz: The Nazi Assault on Humanity*. Primo Levi; translated from the Italian by Stuart Woolf; including. Simon & Schuster 1996. 187 p.
ISBN 9780684826806
Grades: 11 12 Adult   B
1. Levi, Primo 2. World War II 3. Holocaust (1933-1945) 4. Italy 5. Germany 6. History writing — Wars and conflicts — Holocaust — World War II
LC Bl2005012360

The author describes his twenty month ordeal in the Nazi death camp.

A Touchstone book; Translation of : Se questo e un uomo; Originally published: New York : Collier Books, 1993; Also published with the title If this is a man.

Levin, Daniel Barban
Slonim Woods 9: A Memoir. Daniel Barban Levin. Crown 2020. 288 p.
ISBN 9780593138854
Grades: Adult   B
1. Ray, Larry (Lawrence), 1960- 2. Levin, Daniel Barban 3. Cults 4. Criminals 5. Manipulation by men 6. Swindlers and swindling 7. Extortion 8. New York (State) 9. Autobiographies and memoirs 10. Page to screen 11. Life stories — Facing adversity — Abuse survivors 12. True Crime — General
LC 2020047466

A firsthand account of the creation of a modern cult under conman Larry Ray and the horrifying costs paid by his young victims: His daughter's college roommates.

Poet Levin debuts with a chilling account of the two years he spent living as part of a cult. Writing in eloquent prose, he describes how such a thing can happen, and why, as he puts it, 'The alarms kept screaming, and we ignored them.' —*Publishers Weekly*

Made into a television show on Hulu in 2023.

Levine, Bruce C.
Thaddeus Stevens: Civil War Revolutionary, Fighter for Racial Justice. Bruce Levine. Simon & Schuster 2021. 320 p.
ISBN 9781476793375
Grades: Adult   B
1. Stevens, Thaddeus, 1792-1868 2. United States Civil War, 1861-1865 3. Abolitionists 4. Reconstruction (United States history) 5. Equality 6. Civil war 7. African American history 8. Civil rights 9. Politics and government 10. United States history 11. United States 12. 1860s 13. 1870s 14. American Civil War era (1861-1865) 15. 19th century 16. Biographies 17. Life stories — Politics — Politicians 18. History writing — Reconstruction — United States

The best-selling author of Confederate Emancipation presents a portrait of the 19th-century statesman that includes discussions of Stevens's decades-long fight against slavery, key role in the Union war effort and postwar legislation for American racial justice.

"This is an accessible and well-researched introduction to one of the most consequential lawmakers in U.S. history." —*Publishers Weekly*

Levinsohn, Florence Hamlish
Looking for Farrakhan. Florence Hamlish Levinsohn. Ivan R. Dee 1997. xiii, 305 p.
ISBN 9781566631570
Grades: Adult   B
1. Farrakhan, Louis 2. Black Muslims 3. African Americans 4. Biographies 5. Spirituality and Religion — Islam 6. Life stories — Religion and spirituality — Religious and spiritual leaders 7. History writing — African American — United States
LC 97011335

Looks at the Black experience that transformed Eugene Walcott into Louis Farrakhan, the circumstances that brought him to power in the Nation of Islam, and the goals and prospects of the man himself.

"Levinsohn's biography, which reflects on the Black experience and how it changed young Eugene Walcott into Louis Farrakhan, leader of the Nation of Islam, attempts to make sense of this prominent figure in American politics." —*Library Journal*

Includes index.

Levy, Aidan
Saxophone Colossus: The Life and Music of Sonny Rollins. Aidan Levy. Hachette Books 2022. 640 p.
ISBN 9780306902796
Grades: Adult   B
1. Rollins, Sonny, 1930- 2. Jazz musicians 3. Musicians 4. Jazz music 5. African Americans 6. Saxophonists 7. Biographies 8. Life stories — Arts and culture — Performing arts — Musicians and composers 9. Arts and Entertainment — Music — Jazz and the blues 10. History Writing — African American — United States

"Levy…documents a 65-year career through conversations drawn from nearly everyone who interacted with Rollins….A definitive account of a jazz icon." —*Kirkus*

Levy, Deborah
The Cost of Living: A Working Autobiography. Deborah Levy. Bloomsbury 2018. 128 p.
ISBN 9781635571912
Grades: Adult   B
1. Levy, Deborah 2. Middle-aged women 3. Gender role 4. Lifestyles 5. Divorce 6. Life change events 7. Personal conduct 8. Femininity 9. Women 10. Autobiographies and memoirs 11. Life stories — Arts and culture — Writing Authors 12. Life stories — Personal growth 13. Life stories — Identity — Gender
LC 2018276218

New York Times Notable Book, 2018.

Drawing on her own experience of attempting to live with pleasure, value and meaning, the two-time Booker Prize finalist, in a "living autobiography," critiques the roles that society assigns to us and reflects on the politics of breaking with the usual gendered rituals.

"This timely look at how women are viewed (and often dismissed) by society will resonate with many readers, but particularly with those who have felt marginalized or undervalued." —*Publishers Weekly*

★ *Real Estate: A Living Autobiography*. Deborah Levy. Bloomsbury Publishing 2021. 209 p.
ISBN 9781635572216
Grades: Adult   B
1. Levy, Deborah 2. Women authors 3. Writing 4. Femininity 5. Divorce 6. Gender role 7. Aging 8. Identity 9. Houses 10. Home (Concept) 11. Autobiographies and memoirs 12. Life stories — Arts and culture — Writing — Authors 13. Society and culture — Gender — Women 14. Arts and Entertainment — Writing and Publishing

Los Angeles Times Book Prizes, Christopher Isherwood Prize for Autobiographical Prose, 2021.

Virginia Woolf wrote that in order to be a writer, a woman needs a room of one's own. Now, in Real Estate, acclaimed author Deborah Levy concludes her ground-breaking trilogy of living autobiographies with an exhilarating, boldly

ESSENTIAL AND RECOMMENDED TITLES
Biography

intimate meditation on home and the specters that haunt it. In this vibrant memoir, Levy employs her characteristic indelible writing, sharp wit, and acute insights to craft a searing examination of womanhood and ownership. Her inventory of possessions, real and imagined, pushes readers to question our cultural understanding of belonging and belongings and to consider the value of a woman's intellectual and personal life.

"Levy (The Cost of Living) brings her trilogy of autobiographies home in this incandescent meditation on writing, womanhood, and the places that nurture both.... Eloquent and unapologetically frank, Levy's astute narrative is a place worth lingering in." —*Publishers Weekly*

★ *Things I Don't Want to Know: On Writing.* Deborah Levy. Bloomsbury Pub 2014. 120 p.
ISBN 9781620405659
Grades: Adult   B
1. Writing 2. Women authors 3. Femininity 4. Motherhood 5. Immigrants 6. Memory 7. Autobiographies and memoirs 8. Life stories — Arts and culture — Writing — Authors

The author offers her own reflections of the writing life by using George Orwell's essay Why I write as a starting off point.

Lewis, Damien
Agent Josephine: American Beauty, French Hero, British Spy. Damien Lewis. Public Affairs 2022. 320 p.
ISBN 9781541700666
Grades: Adult   B
1. Baker, Josephine, 1906-1975 2. African American women dancers 3. Women dancers 4. World War II 5. Secret service 6. Spies 7. Women spies 8. African American entertainers 9. African American women 10. Biographies 11. History writing — Spies and spying 12. History writing — Women's history 13. History writing — Wars and conflicts — World War II 14. Life stories — Law and order — Spies and secret agents 15. Life stories — Arts and culture — Performing arts

This story of the world's richest and most glamorous entertainer looks at her heroic stint during World War II as an Allied spy in occupied France and her efforts to combat Nazism.

"Lewis provides a rollicking, energetic commentary on Baker's adventures." —*Booklist*

Originally published in London by Quercus in 2022 with the title the Flame of Resistance.

Lewis, David L.
★ *W.E.B. Du Bois: A Biography.* David Levering Lewis. Henry Holt and Co. 2009. xiv, 893 p.
ISBN 9780805088052
Grades: 11 12 Adult   B
1. Du Bois, W. E. B. (William Edward Burghardt), 1868-1963 2. African American intellectuals 3. African American civil rights workers 4. Civil Rights Movement 5. African American history 6. African Americans 7. Civil rights 8. United States history 9. 19th century 10. 20th century 11. Biographies 12. History writing — African American — Civil rights — United States 13. Life stories — Politics — Activists and Reformers — Civil Rights Leaders
LC 2008000696

The two-time Pulitzer Prize-winning biography of the civil-rights pioneer—now in one condensed, updated volume—chronicles Du Bois's long and storied career, detailing the momentous contributions to our national character that still echo today and offering over thirty archival photos.

A John Macrae/Holt paperback; Condensed and updated ed. of: 2 vol. set, originally published 1993-2000; Includes bibliographical references and index.

Lewis, Jenifer
Walking in My Joy: In These Streets. Jenifer Lewis. [Amistad, an imprint of HarperCollins Publishers] 2022. 320 p.
ISBN 9780063079656
Grades: Adult   B
1. Lewis, Jenifer, 1957- 2. Bipolar disorder 3. Fame 4. Social justice 5. Racism 6. Childhood 7. African Americans 8. Actors and actresses 9. People with bipolar disorder 10. Women 11. Essays 12. Autobiographies and memoirs 13. Life stories — Arts and culture — Performing arts — Actors and actresses 14. Arts and Entertainment — Movies and television
LC 2022006606

In this entertaining essay collection, the author of the Mother of Black Hollywood and the costar of ABC's hit sitcom Black-ish looks back on some of her memorable adventures and experiences, showing us how to be present in the moment and reject being a victim of circumstance.

"Lewis, the outspoken, hilariously profane, and wildly entertaining actress and activist, follows up her no-holds-barred memoir Mother of Black Hollywood with a new and equally entertaining collection of autobiographical essays....The latest memoir by fierce and fabulous Lewis easily switches between moving confessionals and fiery calls to eradicate oppression." —*Library Journal*

Lewis, John
Walking with the Wind: A Memoir of the Movement. John Lewis with Michael D'Orso. Simon & Schuster 1998. 496 p. : Illustration
ISBN 9780684810652
Grades: 11 12 Adult   B
1. Lewis, John, 1940-2020 2. Civil Rights Movement 3. Civil rights workers 4. African American civil rights workers 5. African American legislators 6. African American civil rights 7. Legislators 8. United States 9. 1950s 10. 1960s 11. Biographies 12. History writing — African American — Civil rights — United States 13. Life stories — Politics — Activists and Reformers — Civil Rights Leaders 14. Life stories — Politics — Politicians 15. Adult books for young adults 16. Antiracist literature
LC 98003040

Booklist Editors' Choice, 1998; New York Times Notable Book, 1998; Robert F. Kennedy Book Award, 1999.

The highest Black elected official in America, the congressman looks back on his life from his childhood on a Alabama cotton farm to his fight for civil rights, to his enduring commitment to the ideals of Martin Luther King, Jr.

"A classic, invaluable blockbuster history of the civil-rights movement." —*Kirkus*

Includes index.

Lewis, Michael
The Blind Side: Evolution of a Game. Michael Lewis. W. W. Norton 2006. 299 p.
ISBN 9780393061239
Grades: 11 12 Adult   B
1. Oher, Michael 2. Football 3. Football players 4. College football 5. College sports 6. United States 7. Page to screen 8. Biographies 9. Sports and Competition — Football 10. Sports and Competition — Sports History 11. Life stories — Sports — Athletes 12. Life stories — Facing adversity — Personal transformation 13. Adult books for young adults

Alex Award, 2007; New York Times Notable Book, 2006.

Follows one young man from his impoverished childhood with a crack-addicted mother, through his discovery of the sport of football, to his rise to become one of the most successful, highly-paid players in the NFL.

"The author describes the NFL's ever-growing obsession with left tackles as a means to counter defenders who seem to grow bigger, stronger, and more vicious each season. He juxtaposes that narrative with the unlikely story of [football player] Michael Oher.... The book works on three levels. First as a shrewd analysis of the NFL; second, as an expose of the insanity of big-time college football recruiting; and, third, as a moving portrait of the positive effect that love, family, and education can have in reversing the path of a life that was destined to be lived unhappily and, most likely, end badly." —*Booklist*

LI, Fei Fei
The Worlds I See: Curiosity, Exploration, and Discovery at the Dawn of Ai. Dr. Fei-Fei Li. Moment of Lift Books; 2023. 336 p.
ISBN 9781250897930
Grades: Adult   B
1. LI, Fei Fei, 1976- 2. Women computer scientists 3. Chinese American women 4. Asian American women 5. Growing up 6. Immigrant families 7. Teenage immigrants 8. Curiosity 9. Computers 10. Physics 11. Neuroscience 12.

PUBLIC LIBRARY CORE COLLECTION: NONFICTION
Twentieth Edition

Technological innovations 13. Artificial intelligence 14. High technology industry and trade 15. Technological forecasting 16. East Asian people 17. Chinese people 18. North American people 19. American people 20. Autobiographies and memoirs 21. Life stories — Science, technology, and medicine — Scientists and inventors 22. Life stories — Identity — Immigrants 23. Science Writing — Computing, the Internet, and Technology 24. Science Writing — Great Engineering Feats

LC 2023024261

The moving memoir of a girl coming of age as an immigrant in America who finds her calling as a scientist at the forefront of the AI revolution.

"Readers looking for a portal into a science that is not often illuminated or connected back to the human experience may especially enjoy this memoir." —*Booklist*

LI, Yiyun
Dear Friend, from My Life I Write to You in Your Life. Yiyun Li. Random House 2017. 224 p.
ISBN 9780399589096
Grades: Adult B
1. LI, Yiyun, 1972- 2. Authors, American 3. People with depression 4. Books and reading 5. Writing 6. Asian American women 7. Suicidal behavior 8. Women 9. 21st century 10. Essays 11. Autobiographies and memoirs 12. Life stories — Facing adversity — Medical issues — Mental illness

LC 2016017675

A memoir of the author's struggle with depression and suicidal thoughts includes reflections on the life-affirming solace she found in the journals, diaries, and fiction of other writers, including William Tervor, Katherine Mansfield, and Philip Larkin.

Lichtblau, Eric
Return to the Reich: A Holocaust Refugee's Secret Mission to Defeat the Nazis. Eric Lichtblau. Houghton Mifflin Harcourt 2019. 304 p.
ISBN 9781328528537
Grades: Adult B
1. Mayer, Frederick, 1921-2016 2. Spies 3. World War II 4. Jewish people 5. Immigrants 6. Refugees 7. Prisoners of war 8. Torture victims 9. Courage 10. Espionage 11. Western European people 12. German people 13. Resistance to military occupation 14. Germany 15. Austria 16. Biographies 17. Life stories — Law and order — Spies and secret agents 18. History writing — Wars and conflicts — World War II — European Theater 19. History writing — Spies and spying 20. History writing — Jewish history 21. Nonfiction that reads like fiction

LC 2019009834

The remarkable story of Fred Mayer, a German-born Jew who escaped Nazi Germany only to return as an American commando on a secret mission behind enemy lines. Growing up in Germany, Freddy Mayer witnessed the Nazis' rise to power. When he was sixteen, his family made the decision to flee to the United States—they were among the last German Jews to escape, in 1938. In America, Freddy tried enlisting the day after Pearl Harbor, only to be rejected as an "enemy alien" because he was German. He was soon recruited to the OSS, the country's first spy outfit before the CIA. Freddy, joined by Dutch Jewish refugee Hans Wynberg and Nazi defector Franz Weber, parachuted into Austria as the leader of Operation Greenup, meant to deter Hitler's last stand.

Includes bibliographical references and index.

Liedman, Sven-Eric
A World to Win: The Life and Works of Karl Marx. by Sven-Eric Liedman. Verso 2018. 832 p.
ISBN 9781786635044
Grades: Adult B
1. Marx, Karl, 1818-1883 2. Marxism 3. Communists 4. Communism 5. Philosophers 6. Political science 7. Philosophy 8. Biographies 9. Translations — Swedish to English 10. Life stories — Education — Philosophers 11. Politics and global affairs — Political philosophy

LC 2018003399

In this essential new biography—the first to give equal weight to both the work and life of Karl Marx—Sven-Eric Liedman expertly navigates the imposing, complex personality of his subject through the turbulent passages of global history. A World to Win follows Marx through childhood and student days, a difficult and sometimes tragic family life, his far-sighted journalism, and his enduring friendship and intellectual partnership with Friedrich Engels.

"Outstanding. Not the book for a budding Marxist to start w i th, but certainly one to turn to for reference and deeper insight." —*Kirkus*

Originally published as Karl Marx: En Biografi by Albert Bonniers Förlag, 2015; Translated from the Swedish.

Lieu, Susan
★ *The Manicurist's Daughter: A Memoir.* Susan Lieu. Celadon Books 2024. 288 p.
ISBN 9781250835048
Grades: Adult B
1. Death of mothers 2. Family relationships 3. Grief 4. Plastic surgery 5. Body image 6. Vietnamese Americans 7. Refugees, Vietnamese 8. Children of immigrants 9. Feminine beauty (Aesthetics) 10. Medical cover-ups 11. California 12. Autobiographies and memoirs 13. Life stories — Facing adversity — Coping with death 14. Life stories — Facing adversity — War and oppression — Refugees

LC 2023032071

The author faces her family's harrowing story: Vietnamese refugees who open two nail salons, well on their way to the American Dream, only to lose their inimitable matriarch after a routine plastic surgery operation goes horribly awry.

"Lieu delivers a stirring debut memoir focused on the fallout from her mother's untimely death in 1996." —*Publishers Weekly*

Lima, Jamie Kern
Believe It: How to Go from Underestimated to Unstoppable. Jamie Kern Lima. Gallery Books 2021. 288 p.
ISBN 9781982157807
Grades: Adult B
1. Lima, Jamie Kern 2. Women chief executive officers 3. New businesses 4. Cosmetics industry and trade 5. Success in business 6. Body image 7. Self-perception 8. Self-confidence 9. Faith (Christianity) 10. Advice 11. Self-doubt 12. Autobiographies and memoirs 13. Life stories — Business 14. Life stories — Personal growth 15. Business and economics — Business Advice

In Believe IT, Jamie Kern Lima, founder of IT Cosmetics, shares the wild but true story of how a once struggling waitress turned her against-the-grain idea into an international bestselling sensation, eventually selling the company for over a billion dollars and becoming the first female CEO of a brand in L'Oreal's 100+ year history. Faced with self-doubt, body-doubt, God-doubt, down to her last few dollars and told "No one is going to buy makeup from someone who has your body," Jamie reveals for the first time what really went down, how she almost didn't make it, how she learned to trust herself, and the powerful lessons you, too, can use to go from underestimated to unstoppable.

"Lima's empathy and cheer shine throughout.... This will particularly resonate with entrepreneurs struggling with self-doubt." —*Publishers Weekly*

Lin, Amy
Here After: A Memoir. Amy Lin. Zibby Books 2024. 272 p.
ISBN 9781958506325
Grades: Adult B
1. Lin, Amy 2. Loss 3. Grief 4. Widows 5. Death of married men 6. Love 7. Life change events 8. Autobiographies and memoirs 9. Canadian literature 10. Life stories — Facing adversity — Coping with death 11. Family and relationships — Aging and death

Here After is a poetic, raw depiction of an unlikely love followed by a dizzying loss. A stunning, taut memoir from debut Canadian author Amy Lin that will resonate deeply with anyone who has been in grief's grasp.

"A beautifully visceral and emotionally intimate depiction of young widowhood." —*Kirkus*

Lin, Jami Nakamura
The Night Parade: A Speculative Memoir. Jami Nakamura Lin. Mariner Books 2023. 272 p.

ESSENTIAL AND RECOMMENDED TITLES
Biography

ISBN 9780063213234
Grades: Adult   **B**
1. Lin, Jami Nakamura 2. People with bipolar disorder 3. Bipolar disorder 4. Mental illness 5. Family relationships 6. Grief 7. Loss 8. Mythology, Japanese 9. Mythology 10. Communities 11. Interpersonal relations 12. Autobiographies and memoirs 13. Life stories — Facing adversity — Medical issues — Mental illness 14. Life stories — Facing adversity — Coping with death 15. Family and relationships — Illness and the family 16. Science Writing — Medicine and health — Mental health

"In this gorgeous and unique debut memoir, Lin draws on the Japanese myth of the Hyakki Yagyo (the 'Night Parade of One Hundred Demons,' in which demons and spirits march through the streets at night) to document her struggles with bipolar disorder and her father's fatal illness." —*Publishers Weekly*

Lindwer, Willy
The Last Seven Months of Anne Frank. Willy Lindwer; translated from Dutch by Alison Meersschaert. Anchor Books 1992. xiii, 204 p. : Illustration
ISBN 9780385423601
Grades: 11 12 Adult   **B**
1. Frank, Anne, 1929-1945 2. Holocaust (1933-1945) 3. Concentration camps 4. Holocaust survivors 5. Interethnic relations 6. Netherlands 7. Biographies 8. History writing — Wars and conflicts — Holocaust — World War II 9. Life stories — Facing adversity — War and oppression — Holocaust
LC 92005407

Based on the testimony of six Jewish women who survived the concentration camps, this chronicle of the last seven months of Anne Frank's life picks up from the end of her diary to follow her from her family's arrest to her death.

Translation of: De laatste zeven maanden; Originally published: New York : Pantheon Books, 1991.

Lineberry, Cate
Be Free or Die: The Amazing Story of Robert Smalls' Escape from Slavery to Union Hero. Cate Lineberry. St. Martin's Press 2017. 288 pages
ISBN 9781250101860
Grades: Adult   **B**
1. Smalls, Robert, 1839-1915 2. Ship captains 3. Freedom seekers 4. Slavery 5. Union Soldiers 6. African American legislators 7. African American men 8. African Americans 9. Courage 10. United States history 11. South Carolina 12. American Civil War era (1861-1865) 13. 19th century 14. Biographies 15. Life stories — Facing adversity — War and oppression — Enslaved people 16. History writing — African American — Enslavement — United States 17. History writing — Wars and conflicts — American Civil War
LC 2017004245

Describes the amazing hijacking of a Confederate steamer in 1862 by a 23-year-old slave who avoided the heavily armed troops stationed in Charleston Harbor and delivered the vessel to Union forces, earning his freedom.

"This is unquestionably a remarkable story, and journalist Lineberry ably tells it as a microcosm of the war." —*Kirkus*

Includes bibliographical references and index.

Lippman, Laura
My Life as a Villainess: Essays. Laura Lippman. William Morrow 2020. x, 270 pages
ISBN 9780063007154
Grades: Adult   **B**
1. Women authors 2. Families 3. Aging 4. Motherhood 5. Writing 6. United States 7. Essays 8. Autobiographies and memoirs 9. Life stories — Arts and culture — Writing — Authors 10. Life stories — Relationships 11. Life stories — Arts and culture — Writing — Journalists

Collects the author's recent essays exploring motherhood as an older mom, her life as a reader, her relationships with her parents, her newspaper career, and her experiences as a novelist.

"Candid and quirky, this book will have special appeal to fans of her crime fiction. A wryly observed collection from a reliably good writer." —*Kirkus*

Lipska, Barbara K.
The Neuroscientist Who Lost Her Mind: My Tale of Madness and Recovery. Barbara K. Lipska with Elaine McArdle. Houghton Mifflin Harcourt 2018. 224 p.
ISBN 9781328787309
Grades: Adult   **B**
1. Lipska, Barbara K. 2. Cancer 3. Neuroscientists 4. Mental illness 5. Autobiographies and memoirs 6. Life stories — Facing adversity — Medical issues 7. Science Writing — Medicine and health — Illness and disease
LC 2017046211

Describes how the author, a leading expert on the neuroscience of mental illness, endured months of terrifying symptoms related to a brain melanoma before immunotherapy enabled a cure, recounting in vivid detail her recollection of the experience and what it revealed about the role of mental illness, brain injury and age on behavior, personality and memory.

Includes bibliographical references and index.

Litt, David
Thanks, Obama: My Hopey Changey White House Years. David Litt. Ecco 2017. 256 p.
ISBN 9780062568458
Grades: Adult   **B**
1. Litt, David, 1986- 2. Speechwriters 3. Humorists 4. Presidential staff 5. Social life and customs 6. Politics and government 7. Washington, D.C. 8. United States 9. 21st century 10. 2000s (Decade) 11. 2010s 12. Autobiographies and memoirs 13. Life stories — Politics 14. History writing — Presidency — 21st century — United States
LC 2017019330

The senior comic speechwriter and presidential advisor presents an account of his college education through his years working with Barack Obama, sharing behind-the-scenes anecdotes and his reflections on Obama's legacy in the age of Trump.

Liu, Simu
★ *We Were Dreamers: An Immigrant Superhero Origin Story.* Simu Liu. William Morrow & Company 2022. 320 p.
ISBN 9780063046498
Grades: Adult   **B**
1. Liu, Simu, 1989- 2. Actors and actresses 3. Immigrants, Chinese 4. Identity 5. Film industry and trade 6. Stereotypes 7. Acting 8. Family violence 9. Family relationships 10. Culture 11. American dream 12. Superheroes 13. Autobiographies and memoirs 14. Life stories — Arts and culture — Performing arts — Actors and actresses 15. Life stories — Identity 16. Arts and Entertainment — Movies and Television

The star of Marvel's first Asian superhero film, Shang-Chi and the Legend of the Ten Rings, tells his own origin story of being a Chinese immigrant, his battles with cultural stereotypes and his own identity, becoming a TV star, and landing the role of a lifetime.

"The star of Shang-Chi and the Legend of the Ten Rings recounts how he overcame his tortured relationship with his immigrant Chinese parents to pursue his dream of becoming an actor." —*Kirkus*

Lively, Penelope
Life in the Garden. Penelope Lively. Viking 2018. 208 p.
ISBN 9780525558378
Grades: Adult   **B**
1. Lively, Penelope, 1933- 2. Gardening 3. Thought and thinking 4. Aging 5. Authors, English 6. Women authors 7. 20th century 8. Autobiographies and memoirs 9. Biographies 10. Life stories — Arts and culture — Writing — Authors 11. Nature Writing — Gardens
LC 2018013220

Penelope Lively takes up her key themes of time and memory, and her lifelong passions for art, literature, and gardening in this philosophical and poetic memoir.

Lloyd Webber, Andrew
Unmasked: A Memoir. Andrew Lloyd Webber. HarperCollins 2018. 272 p.
ISBN 9780062424204
Grades: Adult   B
1. Lloyd Webber, Andrew, 1948- 2. Composers 3. Musicals 4. Theater 5. Autobiographies and memoirs 6. Life stories — Arts and culture — Performing arts — Musicians and composers 7. Arts and entertainment — Theater
LC 2017568260
Published to coincide with his 70th birthday, a memoir by the award-winning composer, producer and impresario of some of the most recognized musicals in theater history traces his half-century career, sharing insights into his eccentric, diverse family; his Oxford education; his creative process; and the events that shaped his characters and productions.

Lloyd, Carli
When Nobody Was Watching: My Hard-fought Journey to the Top of the Soccer World. Carli Lloyd, with Wayne Coffey. Houghton Mifflin Harcourt 2016. 256 p.
ISBN 9780544814622
Grades: Adult   B
1. Lloyd, Carli, 1982- 2. Women soccer players 3. Soccer players 4. Soccer 5. Professional athletes 6. Soccer teams 7. Autobiographies and memoirs 8. Life stories — Sports — Athletes 9. Sports and competition — Soccer
LC 2016036411
The celebrated star of the U.S. women's national soccer team chronicles her amazing journey to the top.
"This book is a remarkable portrait of the relentless drive and sacrifice required to truly be the best." —*Booklist*

Locke, Tembi
★ *From Scratch: A Memoir of Love, Sicily, and Finding Home.* Tembi Locke. Simon & Schuster 2019. x, 339 pages
ISBN 9781501187650
Grades: Adult   B
1. Locke, Tembi, 1970- 2. Interracial marriage 3. Family traditions 4. Widows 5. Food habits 6. Cooking, Italian 7. Family recipes 8. Romantic love 9. Familial love 10. Loss 11. Family relationships 12. Rural life 13. Grief 14. Sicily, Italy 15. Autobiographies and memoirs 16. Page to screen 17. Life stories — Facing adversity — Coping with death 18. Family and relationships — Aging and death 19. Life stories — Identity — Race and ethnicity 20. Food writing — Memoirs and biographies 21. Book club best bets
LC 2019002516
A poignant and transporting cross-cultural love story set against the lush backdrop of the Sicilian countryside, where one woman discovers the healing powers of food, family, and unexpected grace in her darkest hour.
Made into a TV show on Netflix, 2022.

Lockley, Thomas
African Samurai: The True Story of Yasuke, a Legendary Black Warrior in Feudal Japan. Thomas Lockley and Geoffrey Girard. Hanover Square Press 2019. 368 p.
ISBN 9781335141026
Grades: Adult   B
1. Yasuke (Black Samuraï) 2. Oda, Nobunaga, 1534-1582 3. Samurai 4. Warriors 5. War 6. Enslaved people 7. Warlords 8. Jesuit missionaries 9. Voyages and travels 10. Feudalism 11. African people in foreign countries 12. Child soldiers 13. Boys 14. Civil war 15. Japanese history 16. Japan 17. 16th century 18. Age of exploration (1419-1610) 19. Biographies 20. History writing — Asia — Japan 21. Life stories — People in history 22. Adult books for young adults
LC Bl2019004187
Traces the remarkable life story of history's first foreign-born samurai, detailing his near-mythical journey from a boy soldier in late-16th-century Northern Africa to the heights of Japanese society, where his presence triggered cultural riots.

"The title may seem rather implausible, but Lockley and Girard dispel any doubts as they tell the remarkable story of this legendary, world-traveling African warrior in the war-torn islands of sixteenth-century Japan." —*Booklist*
Published in the UK under the title Yasuke: the true story of the legendary African samurai.

Lockwood, Lewis
Beethoven: The Music and the Life. Lewis Lockwood. W.W. Norton 2003. xix, 604 p. : Illustration
ISBN 9780393050813
Grades: Adult   B
1. Beethoven, Ludwig van, 1770-1827 2. Composers 3. Biographies 4. Arts and Entertainment — Music — Classical 5. Life stories — Arts and culture — Performing arts — Musicians and composers
LC 2002075397
Library Journal Best Books, 2002; Pulitzer Prize for Biography or Autobiography finalist.
A portrait of the life, career, and milieu of the master composer describes the special challenges he faced as a gifted artist in the face of personal, historical, political, and cultural factors, in a volume that shares insight into his compositional methods through recreations of his sketchbooks and autograph manuscripts.
"Lockwood's study offers a new and authoritative interpretation of a prodigiously gifted and complex man and artist." —*Library Journal*
Includes bibliographical references (p. [559]-578) and indexes.

Lockwood, Patricia
Priestdaddy: A Memoir. Patricia Lockwood. Riverhead Books 2017. 352 p.
ISBN 9781594633737
Grades: Adult   B
1. Lockwood, Patricia 2. Homecomings 3. Nonconformists 4. Catholics 5. Father and adult daughter 6. Women poets 7. Identity 8. Priests 9. Parent and adult child 10. Growing up 11. Married people 12. Family relationships 13. Autobiographies and memoirs 14. Life stories — Relationships — Family 15. Family and relationships — Families
LC 2016029241
New York Times Notable Book, 2017; Thurber Prize for American Humor, 2018; Kirkus Prize for Nonfiction finalist, 2017.
The author of Motherland Fatherland Homelandsexuals presents a darkly comic memoir about her relationship with her unconventional married Catholic priest father, describing emblematic moments from her youth and the crisis that led the author and her non-religious husband to briefly live in her parents' rectory.
"Lockwood magically combines laugh-aloud moments with frank discussions of social issues and shows off her poets skills with lovely, metaphor-filled descriptions that make this memoir shine." —*Booklist*

Loftis, Larry
Code Name: Lise : The True Story of World War II's Most Highly Decorated Woman. Larry Loftis. Gallery Books, an imprint of Simon & Schuster, Inc. 2019. 320 p.
ISBN 9781501198656
Grades: Adult   B
1. Odette, 1912-1995 2. Women spies 3. World War II 4. Secret service 5. Spies 6. French Resistance (World War II) 7. Nazis 8. Espionage 9. 20th century 10. Biographies 11. Life stories — Law and order — Spies and secret agents 12. History writing — Spies and spying 13. History writing — Wars and conflicts — World War II 14. Nonfiction that reads like fiction
LC 2018028438
The extraordinary true story of Odette Sansom, the British spy who operated in occupied France and fell in love with her commanding officer during World War II—perfect for fans of Unbroken, the Boys in the Boat, and Code Girls.
"Reading like a thrilling spy novel and the most exciting sort of nonfictionwell researched, well written, and fast paced enough to keep the pages turningthis will interest fans of the history of espionage, World War II history, military history, women's history, and biography." —*Library Journal*
Includes bibliographical references and index.

ESSENTIAL AND RECOMMENDED TITLES
Biography

Logevall, Fredrik
★ *JFK: Coming of Age in the American Century, 1917-1956.* Fredrik Logevall. Random House 2020. 816 p.
ISBN 9780812997132
Grades: Adult   **B**
1. Kennedy, John F. (John Fitzgerald), 1917-1963 2. Kennedy family 3. Legislators 4. Presidents 5. Politics and government 6. Massachusetts 7. United States 8. 20th century 9. Biographies 10. Life stories — Politics — Politicians 11. Life stories — People in history — Famous families
LC 2020003488

Elizabeth Longford Prize for Historical Biography, 2021.

Beginning with the three generations of Kennedy men and women who transformed the clan from working-class Irish immigrants to members of Boston's political elite, Volume One spans the first thirty-nine years of JFK's life, from sickly second son to restless Harvard undergraduate and World War II hero, through his ascendance on Capitol Hill and, finally, his decision to run for president.

"This richly detailed portrait sometimes feels romanticized in its evocations of Kennedy's charisma, but Logevall helpfully reminds readers of the considerable substance beneath the glamour. Political history buffs will be enthralled." —*Publishers Weekly*

Includes bibliographical references and index.

Loh, Sandra Tsing
The Madwoman and the Roomba: My Year of Domestic Mayhem. Sandra Tsing Loh. W W Norton & CO Inc 2020. xv, 276 p.
ISBN 9780393249200
Grades: Adult   **B**
1. Loh, Sandra Tsing 2. Women authors, American 3. Middle-aged women 4. Aging 5. Femininity 6. Mothers and daughters 7. Family relationships 8. Housekeeping 9. Personal conduct 10. Expectation 11. Self-fulfillment 12. Autobiographies and memoirs 13. Life stories — Personal growth 14. Family and Relationships — Aging and Death 15. Humor writing — Family and relationship humor
LC 2019052108

Middle age, for Sandra Tsing Loh, feels more like living a disorganized 25-year-old's life in an 85-year-old's malfunctioning body. With raucous wit and carefree candor, Loh recounts the struggles of leaning in, staying lean, and keeping her family well-fed and financially afloat—all those burdens of running a household that still, all-too-often, fall to women.

"Loh's voice is laugh-out-loud hilarious, and her fun house perspective on the foibles of middle age are intelligent and effervescent. Fans of her previous memoir and her NPR program the Loh Down on Science will delight in this outing." —*Publishers Weekly*

Longerich, Peter
Goebbels: A Biography. Peter Longerich; translated by Alan Bance, Jeremy Noakes, Lesley Sharpe. Random House Inc 2014. 512 p.
ISBN 9781400067510
Grades: Adult   **B**
1. Goebbels, Joseph, 1897-1945 2. Nazis 3. Antisemitism 4. Nazism 5. Nazi propaganda 6. World War II 7. Holocaust (1933-1945) 8. Third Reich, 1933-1945 9. Politics and government 10. Germany 11. Biographies 12. Translations — German to English 13. Life stories — Politics — Politicians 14. History writing — Wars and conflicts — Holocaust — World War II 15. History writing — Wars and conflicts — World War II
LC 2014004828

Joseph Goebbels served as Adolf Hitler's Minister of Propaganda, not only crafting the public façade of the Third Reich but micromanaging government approval (or banning) of writers and other artists. In this detailed biography of the second most powerful man in Nazi Germany, historian Peter Longerich examines Goebbels' psychological profile, mines his diaries for descriptions of those around him, and explores his generally unsuccessful efforts to influence Hitler. This thoroughly researched study provides an important contribution to the history of the Third Reich and a fascinating account for biography fans.

"As Longerich acknowledges, his reliance on Goebbels diaries as a primary source is problematic, since Goebbels accounts of events and personalities seem designed to impress himself. Still Longerichs efforts to glean the truth from exaggerations and distortions are credible, and this is an outstanding contribution to our understanding of the Nazi regime." —*Booklist*

Translation from the German; Originally published: Munich : Siedler Verlag, 2010.

Hitler: A Life. Peter Longerich; translated by Jeremy Noakes and Lesley Sharpe. Oxford University Press 2019. 912 p.
ISBN 9780190056735
Grades: Adult   **B**
1. Hitler, Adolf, 1889-1945 2. Heads of state 3. Nazism 4. Holocaust (1933-1945) 5. Antisemitism 6. World War II 7. Third Reich, 1933-1945 8. Politics and government 9. Germany 10. Biographies 11. History writing — Wars and conflicts — World War II 12. Life stories — Law and order — Armed forces personnel 13. History writing — Europe — Germany
LC 2019015905

Booklist Editors' Choice, 2019.

Acclaimed historian Peter Longerich, author of Goebbels and Heinrich Himmler now turns his attention to Adolf Hitler in this new biography. While many previous portraits have speculated about Hitler's formative years, Longerich focuses on his central role as the driving force of Nazism itself. You cannot separate the man from the monstrous movement he came to embody.

Includes bibliographical references and index.

Longworth, Karina
Seduction: Sex, Lies, and Stardom in Howard Hughes's Hollywood. Karina Longworth. Custom House 2018. 416 p.
ISBN 9780062440518
Grades: Adult   **B**
1. Hughes, Howard, 1905-1976 2. Film industry and trade 3. Film producers and directors 4. Sexual harassment 5. Sexuality and power (Social sciences) 6. Films 7. Actors and actresses 8. United States history 9. Hollywood, California 10. 20th century 11. Media tie-ins 12. Arts and Entertainment — Movies and Television 13. Society and culture — Gender
LC 2018029872

The You Must Remember This podcaster and author of Hollywood Frame by Frame draws on the stories of iconic actresses to reveal how Howard Hughes' obsessions with sex, power and publicity made and destroyed Hollywood careers.

"Author Longworth adopts a conversational tone—this isn't a treatise on the subject of wealth and power in the first half of the twentieth century as much as it is a story about a man who traded in seduction, mystique, and money." —*Booklist*

Based on a podcast; Includes bibliographical references; Includes filmography.

Lopez, Barry Holstun
Horizon. Barry Lopez. Alfred A. Knopf 2019. xiv, 572 p.
ISBN 9780394585826
Grades: Adult   **B**
1. Lopez, Barry Holstun, 1945-2020 2. Authors, American 3. Travel writers 4. Travelers 5. Voyages and travels 6. Natural history 7. Anthropology 8. Environmental degradation 9. Travel Writing — General 10. Life stories — Nature and outdoors 11. Nature Writing — Environmental Issues
LC 2018033323

New York Times Notable Book, 2019.

The National Book Award-winning author of Arctic Dreams presents a lyrical, intellectual account of his world travels and the extraordinary encounters with people, animals and natural elements that shaped his life.

Includes bibliographical references and index.

Louvish, Simon
Monkey Business: The Lives and Legends of the Marx Brothers. Simon Louvish. Thomas Dunne Books 2000. VII, 471 p. : Illustration; Portrait
ISBN 9780312252922

PUBLIC LIBRARY CORE COLLECTION: NONFICTION
Twentieth Edition

Grades: 11 12 Adult **B**
1. Jewish American men 2. Brothers 3. Family relationships 4. Jewish American families 5. Comedians 6. Actors and actresses 7. Films 8. Social life and customs 9. New York City 10. United States 11. 20th century 12. Biographies 13. Arts and Entertainment — Comedy 14. Family and Relationships — Siblings 15. Life stories — Arts and culture — Performing arts — Actors and actresses

LC 2001270712

A biography of all five Marx Brothers chronicles their childhood, theatrical roots, twenty-four years on the stage, Broadway successes, films, personal lives, and legacies.

"In addition to Groucho, the author expands the canvas to appraise the contributions of the other brothers, plus Margaret Dumont, a regular target of the brothers' mayhem. Louvish does a solid job of separating fact from fiction and includes a family tree and a discussion of the FBI's file on the group." —*Library Journal*

Includes bibliographical references (p. 452-455), filmography (p. 426-434) and index; Originally published: London : Faber and Faber, 1999.

Lovato, Roberto
Unforgetting: A Memoir of Family, Migration, Gangs, and Revolution in the Americas. Roberto Lovato. HarperCollins 2020. 304 p.
ISBN 9780062938473
Grades: Adult **B**
1. Lovato, Roberto 2. Journalists 3. Families 4. Immigration and emigration 5. Violence in gangs 6. Fathers and sons 7. Poverty 8. Guerrilla warfare 9. Scholars and academics 10. Violence 11. Psychic trauma 12. San Francisco, California 13. El Salvador 14. Autobiographies and memoirs 15. Life stories — Facing adversity 16. Life stories — identity — Immigrants 17. History writing — Immigration — United States 18. Society and culture — Violence and crime

LC Bl2020018268

A journalistic memoir detailing the author's firsthand experiences with immigration, gang life and guerilla warfare explores the violence that shaped generations of his impoverished Salvadoran family to connect today's immigration crisis to the realities of everyday families.

"In a memoir that is at once profoundly personal and historically significant, accomplished journalist and scholar Lovato digs deep into his own troubled past to embark on the superhuman task of unforgetting the tortured history entwining his family, El Salvador, and the United States of América. . . . This mix of memoir and history is an essential chronicle, solidly researched and carefully sourced, and enriched with some poetry and plenty of hard-won wisdom." —*Booklist*

Lovell, Mary S.
Bess of Hardwick: Empire Builder. Mary S. Lovell. Norton 2006. xx, 555 p, 16 p. of plates : Illustration; Color; Portrait
ISBN 9780393062212
Grades: Adult **B**
1. Shrewsbury, Elizabeth Hardwick Talbot, Countess of, 1527?-1608 2. Counts and countesses 3. Women landowners 4. Nobility 5. British history 6. Great Britain 7. Tudor period (1485-1603) 8. Renaissance (1300-1600) 9. Elizabethan era (1558-1603) 10. Biographies 11. History writing — Women's history 12. History writing — Europe — United Kingdom 13. History writing — Renaissance — Europe 14. Life stories — Politics — Royalty

LC 2005030490

Chronicles the life of a sixteenth-century impoverished nobleman's daughter who rose to become one of England's most wealthy and powerful women, in an account that describes her four marriages, witness to four monarchies, and building of the great house at Chatsworth.

Includes bibliographical references (p. [529]-535) and index; Originally published as Bess of Hardwick : First lady of Chatsworth, 1527-1608, London : Little, Brown, 2005.

Lowman, Margaret
Life in the Treetops: Adventures of a Woman in Field Biology. Margaret D. Lowman. Yale University Press 1999. xvi, 219 p. : Illustration; Map
ISBN 9780300078183
Grades: 11 12 Adult **B**
1. Lowman, Margaret 2. Ecologists 3. Women ecologists 4. Women biologists 5. Biologists 6. Rain forest ecology 7. Forest canopy ecology 8. Motherhood 9. Research 10. Autobiographies and memoirs 11. Life stories — Science, technology, and medicine — Scientists and inventors 12. Science Writing — Biology

LC 98048691

Library Journal Best Books, 1999; New York Times Notable Book, 1999.

The tropical botanist shares the story of her advetues doing pioneering ecological research in forest canopies of Australia, Africa, Belize, and the United States.

"Lowman gives a funny, unassuming and deeply idiosyncratic chronicle of her trials and triumphs as a field biologist of tree canopies and other ecosystems in Australia, New England, Belize, Panama and elsewhere." —*New York Times Book Review*

Map of canopy sites on end papers; Includes index.

Lubow, Arthur
Diane Arbus: Portrait of a Photographer. Arthur Lubow. Ecco Press 2016. 320 p.
ISBN 9780062234322
Grades: Adult **B**
1. Arbus, Diane, 1923-1971 2. Photographers 3. Women photographers 4. Biographies 5. Arts and Entertainment — Photography 6. Life stories — Arts and culture — Artists

LC Bl2016015617

The definitive biography of the beguiling Diane Arbus, one of the most influential and important photographers of the twentieth century, a brilliant and absorbing exposition that links the extraordinary arc of her life to her iconic photographs.

"Lubows portrait is the most sharply focused, encompassing, and incisive to date." —*Booklist*

Lucas, Jack
Indestructible: The Unforgettable Story of a Marine Hero at Iwo Jima. Jack Lucas with D.K. Drum. Da Capo Press 2006. xi, 212 p. : Illustration
ISBN 9780306814709
Grades: 11 12 Adult **B**
1. Lucas, Jack, 1928-2008 2. Iwo Jima, Battle of, 1945 3. Marines 4. World War II 5. Military history 6. Japan 7. Second World War era (1939-1945) 8. History writing — Wars and conflicts — World War II — Pacific Theater 9. History writing — Wars and conflicts — Battles 10. Adult books for young adults

LC Bl2006011958

A candid combat memoir recalls the battlefield exploits of a seventeen-year-old Marine Corps private, whose selfless actions at the height of the Battle of Iwo Jima not only saved his companions, but also led to him becoming the youngest Marine in history to receive the Congressional Medal of Honor.

Includes index.

Lundquist, Verne
Play by Play: Calling the Wildest Games in Sports — from SEC Football to College Basketball, the Masters and More. Verne Lundquist. HarperCollins 2018. 320 p.
ISBN 9780062684448
Grades: Adult **B**
1. Lundquist, Verne 2. Sportscasters 3. Sports 4. Sportscasting 5. Professional sports 6. Autobiographies and memoirs 7. Sports and Competition — General 8. Life stories — Sports

LC Bl2018134709

An award-winning sportscaster chronicles his life and career, touching on such iconic sports moments as Jack Nicklaus' 1986 Masters victory, the attack on Nancy Kerrigan and the Dallas Cowboy victories of the 1970s.

Lynch, David
Room to Dream: A Life in Art. David Lynch and Kristina McKenna. Random House 2018. xii, 577 pages : Illustration
ISBN 9780399589195

ESSENTIAL AND RECOMMENDED TITLES
Biography

Grades: Adult **B**
1. Lynch, David, 1946- 2. Film producers and directors 3. Filmmaking 4. Creation (Literary, artistic, etc.) 5. Creativity 6. Experimental films 7. Avant-garde (Aesthetics) 8. Autobiographies and memoirs 9. Arts and Entertainment — Movies and Television 10. Life stories — Arts and culture — Performing arts — Directors and producers
LC 2017058580

The extraordinary and highly anticipated memoir from visionary filmmaker David Lynch. In this memoir, David Lynch opens up about a lifetime of extraordinary creativity, the friendships he has made along the way and the struggles he has faced, sometimes successful, sometimes not, to bring his projects to fruition. Part memoir, part biography, Room to Dream interweaves Lynch's own reflections on his life with the story of those times, as told by Kristine McKenna, drawing from extensive & explosive interviews with ninety of Lynch's friends, family members, actors, agents, musicians and collaborators. Lynch responds to each recollection and reveals the inner story of the life behind the art.

An incandescently detailed and complexly enlightening chronicle of a fervent, uncompromising life devoted to 'Pure creativity.' —*Booklist*

Includes bibliographical references (pages [537]-545) and index; Includes filmography.

Lynn, Loretta

★ *Me & Patsy Kickin' up Dust: My Friendship with Patsy Cline*. Loretta Lynn, with Patsy Lynn Russell; foreword by Dolly Parton. Grand Central Publishing 2020. xiii, 222 p.
ISBN 9781538701669
Grades: Adult **B**
1. Lynn, Loretta 2. Cline, Patsy, 1932-1963 3. Women country musicians 4. Country music 5. Female friendship 6. Death of friends 7. Women songwriters 8. Women singers 9. Memories 10. Fame 11. Loss 12. Sexism 13. Country music industry and trade 14. Autobiographies and memoirs 15. Life stories — Arts and culture — Performing arts — Musicians and composers 16. Life stories — Relationships — Friendship 17. Arts and Entertainment — Music — Country
LC Bl2020007341

Loretta Lynn and the late Patsy Cline are legends—country icons and sisters of the heart. For the first time ever Loretta tells their story: a celebration of their music and their relationship up until Patsy's tragic and untimely death. Full of laughter and tears, this eye-opening, heartwarming memoir paints a picture of two stubborn, spirited country gals who'd be damned if they'd let men or convention tell them how to be. Tender and fierce, Me & Patsy Kickin' up Dust is an up-close-and-personal portrait of a friendship that defined a generation and changed country music indelibly—and a meditation on love, loss and legacy.

"Fans will pounce on beloved country superstar Lynn's memoir about her bond with sister icon Patsy Cline." —*Booklist*

Includes index.

Still Woman Enough: A Memoir. Loretta Lynn with Patsy Bale Cox. Hyperion 2002. xix, 244 p. : Illustration
ISBN 9780786866502
Grades: Adult **B**
1. Lynn, Loretta 2. Country musicians 3. Social life and customs 4. United States 5. 20th century 6. Autobiographies and memoirs 7. Biographies 8. Arts and Entertainment — Music — Country 9. Life stories — Arts and culture — Performing arts — Musicians and composers
LC BL2002000807

The celebrated country singer discusses her turbulent relationship with Doo, the man she married at the age of thirteen, revealing a woman whose loyalty, spirit, and determination allowed her to triumph in the face of adversity.

"In this sequel to Coal miner's daughter, Lynn mostly focuses on her marriage and the trials and pleasures of Nashville stardom, including fond recollections of friends like Conway Twitty and Tammy Wynette. Though her grammar may make purists flinch . Lynn's literary voice is as natural and endearing as her songs." —*Publishers Weekly*

At head of title: Loretta Lynn; Includes discography (p. 236-244).

Maathai, Wangari

Unbowed: A Memoir. Wangari Muta Maathai. Alfred A. Knopf 2006. xvii, 314 p. : Illustration
ISBN 9780307263483
Grades: 11 12 Adult **B**
1. Maathai, Wangari 2. Kikuyu (African people) 3. Women environmentalists 4. Women politicians 5. Nobel Prize winners 6. Women political prisoners 7. Women biologists 8. Restoration ecology 9. Tree planting 10. Kenya 11. Autobiographies and memoirs 12. Biographies 13. Life stories — Politics — Activists and reformers 14. Adult books for young adults 15. History writing — Africa

Booklist Editors' Choice, 2006; Hurston/Wright Legacy Award: Nonfiction, 2007.

The recipient of the 2004 Nobel Peace Prize describes her life as a feminist, political activist, and environmentalist in Kenya, detailing her determination to receive an education despite the odds, her confrontations with the brutal Moi government, the 1977 establishment of the Green Belt Movement, her role in the transformation of Kenya's government, and her hope for the future.

Includes index.

MacCulloch, Diarmaid

Thomas Cromwell: A Revolutionary Life. Diarmaid MacCulloch. Viking 2018. 640 p.
ISBN 9780670025572
Grades: Adult **B**
1. Cromwell, Thomas, Earl of Essex, 1485?-1540 2. Henry VII, King of England, 1491-1547 3. Politicians 4. Rulers 5. Courts and courtiers 6. British history 7. Biographies 8. Life stories — Politics — Politicians 9. History writing — Europe — United Kingdom
LC Bl2018167915

Examines the life of Henry VII's right-hand man, who did everything he could to secure the future of a son he loved dearly, but who ultimately could not control the unpredictable monarch.

"A must-read biography of a man whose role in shaping English and Protestant history has long been misunderstood." —*Library Journal*

Machado, Carmen Maria

★ *In the Dream House: A Memoir*. Carmen Maria Machado. Graywolf Press 2019. 247 pages
ISBN 9781644450031
Grades: Adult **B**
1. Family violence 2. Dysfunctional families 3. Psychic trauma 4. Lesbians 5. Women-women relations 6. Autobiographies and memoirs 7. Family and Relationships — Dating and marriage 8. Life stories — Facing adversity — Abuse survivors 9. Life stories — Relationships — Couples

Booklist Editors' Choice, 2019; Lambda Literary Award for LGBTQ Nonfiction, 2020; Library Journal Best Books, 2019.

Shares the story of the author's relationship with an abusive partner and how it was shaped by her religious upbringing, her sexual orientation and inaccurate cultural beliefs about psychological trauma.

Includes bibliographical references.

Macintyre, Ben

★ *Agent Sonya: The Spy Next Door*. Ben Macintyre. Crown 2020. 400 p.
ISBN 9780593136324
Grades: Adult **B**
1. Werner, Ruth, 1907-2000 2. Women spies 3. Nuclear weapons 4. Cold War 5. Spies 6. Women and war 7. 20th century 8. Biographies 9. Life stories — Law and order — Spies and secret agents 10. History writing — Spies and spying 11. History writing — Cold War 12. History writing — Women's history
LC 2020019326

Reveals the story of the female spy hidden in plain sight who set the stage for the Cold War—one of the last great intelligence secrets of the 20th century.

"[MacIntyre's] fast-paced historical account reads like a novel, with surprising twists and turns, and will thrill readers until the very last page. Readers who enjoy the writings of Neal Bascomb or Candice Millard, and fans of historical fiction will relish this book." —*Library Journal*

Includes bibliographical references and index; Originally published as Agent Sonya : Moscow's most daring wartime spy, Crown, 2020.

Agent *Zigzag: A True Story of Nazi Espionage, Love, and Betrayal.* Ben MacIntyre. Harmony Books 2007. 364 p.
ISBN 9780307353405
Grades: Adult   **B**
1. Chapman, Eddie 2. World War II 3. Secret service 4. Spies 5. Intelligence service 6. German history 7. British history 8. 1940s 9. 20th century 10. Biographies 11. History writing — Spies and spying 12. History writing — Wars and conflicts — World War II 13. Life stories — Law and order — Spies and secret agents 14. Nonfiction that reads like fiction

New York Times Notable Book, 2007.

Eddie Chapman was a charming criminal, a con man, and a philanderer. He was also one of the most remarkable double agents Britain has ever produced. In 1941, after training as a German spy in occupied France, Chapman was parachuted into Britain with orders to blow up an airplane factory. Instead, he contacted MI5, the British Secret Service. For the next four years, he worked as a double agent, a British spy at the heart of the German Secret Service. Crisscrossing Europe under different names, weaving plans, spreading disinformation, and miraculously keeping his stories straight under intense interrogation, he even managed to gain some profit and seduce beautiful women along the way. MI5 has now declassified all of Chapman's files, allowing the full story to be told, a unique glimpse into the psychology of espionage, with its thin and shifting line between fidelity and betrayal.

"Meticulously researchedrelying extensively on recently released wartime files of Britain's Secret Intelligence ServiceMacintyre's biography often reads like a spy thriller." —*Publishers Weekly*

A **Spy** *Among Friends: Kim Philby's Great Betrayal.* Ben Macintyre. Crown 2014. 384 p.
ISBN 9780804136631
Grades: Adult   **B**
1. Philby, Kim, 1912-1988 2. Elliott, Nicholas, 1916-1994 3. Angleton, James, 1917-1987 4. Double agents 5. Betrayal 6. Spies 7. Secret service 8. Soviet Union history 9. British history 10. Great Britain 11. 20th century 12. Biographies 13. Page to screen 14. History writing — Spies and spying 15. Life stories — Law and order — Spies and secret agents

LC 2014003296

Elizabeth Longford Prize for Historical Biography, 2015; New York Times Notable Book, 2014.

The revelation in 1963 that British MI6 agent Kim Philby had betrayed Britain to the Soviets for decades rocked the Western intelligence community. In A Spy Among Friends, acclaimed journalist Ben Macintyre portrays Philby's extensive career and analyzes both his motives for selling out his country and why his treason went undetected for so long. This fascinating account delves into the gentlemen's club that was MI6 at the time Philby worked there—upper-crust acceptance of a man who was "one of us" protected Philby from exposure. Anyone interested in Cold War history or the annals of spycraft will find Macintyre's account both riveting and chilling.

"A tale of espionage, alcoholism, bad manners and the chivalrous code of spies—the real world of James Bond, that is, as played out by clerks and not superheroes." —*Kirkus*

Made into a TV series in 2023.

★ *The* **Spy** *and the Traitor: The Greatest Espionage Story of the Cold War.* Ben Macintyre. Crown Publishing 2018. VIII, 358 pages : Illustration; Color; Map
ISBN 9781101904190
Grades: Adult   **B**
1. Gordievsky, Oleg 2. Ames, Aldrich Hazen, 1941- 3. Cold War 4. Double agents 5. Spies 6. KGB agents 7. Intelligence service 8. Soviet Union 9. Biographies 10. Life stories — Law and order — Spies and secret agents 11. History writing — Spies and spying 12. History writing — Cold War 13. Nonfiction that reads like fiction

LC 2018024662

Gold Dagger Award for Best Nonfiction of the Year, 2019.

Traces the story of Russian intelligence operative Oleg Gordievsky, revealing how his secret work as an undercover MI6 informant helped hasten the end of the Cold War.

"In a feat of real authorial dexterity, Macintyre accurately portrays the long-game banality of spycraft—the lead time and persistence in planning—with such clarity and propulsive verve that the book often feels like a thriller." —*Publishers Weekly*

Includes bibliographical references (pages 335-343) and index.

MacPherson, Myra

All *Governments Lie: The Life and Times of Rebel Journalist I.F. Stone.* Myra MacPherson. Scribner 2006. xxvi, 564 p, 8 p. of plates : Illustration
ISBN 9780684807133
Grades: Adult   **B**
1. Stone, I. F, 1907-1989 2. Journalists 3. United States 4. Biographies 5. Life stories — Arts and culture — Writing — Journalists

LC 2006042389

A portrait of the twentieth-century independent journalist offers insight into his outspoken, five-decade pursuit of truthful, anti-establishment journalism, in an account that includes coverage of his denouncements of Cold War policies, McCarthyism, and the Vietnam Gulf of Tonkin incident.

"This biography interweaves his life and journalism within the context of the social and political era, providing an engaging overview of a complex man who challenged his contemporaries. Many of the political issues Stone confronted will resonate with today's readers." —*Library Journal*

Includes bibliographical references (p. [535]-545) and index.

Macy, Beth

★ **Truevine:** *Two Brothers, a Kidnapping, and a Mother's Quest: A True Story of the Jim Crow South.* Beth Macy. Little Brown & Company 2016. 416 p.
ISBN 9780316337540
Grades: Adult   **B**
1. Kidnapping 2. Racism 3. Injustice 4. Humiliation 5. Exploitation 6. Circus 7. Race relations 8. Albinism 9. Boys 10. African American children 11. Sideshows 12. Sideshow performers 13. Virginia 14. 1890s 15. True crime — Historical crime 16. History writing — African American — Civil rights — United States

LC BI2016036013

New York Times Notable Book, 2016; Booklist Editors' Choice, 2016; Kirkus Prize for Nonfiction finalist, 2016.

Tells the true story of two African-American brothers who were kidnapped and displayed as circus freaks, and whose mother endured a 28-year struggle to get them back.

"A rambling, colorful, and thought-provoking medley of human stories intersecting with one another in carnival tents and Virginia backlands, this solid popular history has much to offer regarding issues of race, family, disability, and spectacle." —*Library Journal*

Maddow, Rachel

Bag *Man: The Wild Crimes, Audacious Cover-up, and Spectacular Downfall of a Brazen Crook in the White House.* Rachel Maddow and Michael Yarvitz. Crown Publishing 2020. 240 p.
ISBN 9780593136683
Grades: Adult   **B**
1. Agnew, Spiro T, 1918-1996 2. Nixon, Richard M. (Richard Milhous), 1913-1994 3. Political corruption 4. Bribery 5. Extortion 6. Conspiracies 7. Vice-presidents 8. Politics and government 9. United States 10. 1960s 11. 1970s 12. Media tie-ins 13. Life stories — Politics — Politicians 14. Life stories — Law and order — Criminals and law-breakers 15. History writing — Scandals 16. History writing — Politicians — United States

LC 2019055625

The knockdown, drag-out, untold story of the other scandal that rocked Nixon's White House, and reset the rules for crooked presidents to come-with new reporting that expands on Rachel Maddow's podcast. Is it possible for a sitting vice president to direct a vast criminal enterprise within the halls of the White House? to have one of the most brazen corruption scandals in American

ESSENTIAL AND RECOMMENDED TITLES
Biography

history play out while nobody's paying attention? Rachel Maddow and Michael Yarvitz detail the investigation that exposed Sprio T. Agnew's crimes, the attempts at a cover-up—which involved future president George H. W. Bush—and the backroom bargain that forced Agnew's resignation but also spared him years in federal prison.

"Based on Maddow and Yarvitz's popular podcast of the same name, this book-length treatment of Agnew covers his rise from Maryland governor to Nixon's running mate in 1968." —*Library Journal*

Based on a podcast; Includes bibliographical references.

Maddox, Brenda
Rosalind Franklin: The Dark Lady of DNA. Brenda Maddox. Harper Collins 2002. xix, 380 p, 16 p. of plates : Illustration; Portrait
ISBN 9780060184070
Grades: Adult **B**
1. Franklin, Rosalind, 1920-1958 2. Molecular biologists 3. Women biologists 4. DNA research 5. Physical chemistry 6. Scientific discoveries 7. Deception 8. London, England 9. 1950s 10. Biographies 11. Science Writing — Biology 12. Life stories — Science, technology, and medicine — Scientists and inventors 13. Adult books for young adults
LC 2002068898

Los Angeles Times Book Prize for Science and Technology, 2002.

Presents the frequently overlooked story of the woman who helped discover the double helix structure of DNA, detailing the contributions of scientist Rosalind Franklin to the work of Watson, Crick, and Wilkins.

"The author does an excellent job of revisiting Franklin's scientific contributions ... while revealing Franklin's complicated personality." —*Library Journal*

Includes bibliographical references (p. 353-367) and index.

Maguire, James
Impresario: The Life and Times of Ed Sullivan. James Maguire. Billboard Books 2006. VII, 344 p. : Illustration
ISBN 9780823079629
Grades: Adult **B**
1. Sullivan, Ed, 1901-1974 2. Television personalities 3. United States 4. Biographies 5. Arts and Entertainment — Movies and Television 6. Life stories — Arts and culture — Performing arts — Entertainers and celebrities
LC 2005933953

An illustrated portrait of the cultural icon looks at the private life of the ambitious pop-culture figure who transformed the face of American entertainment with the Ed Sullivan Show, the legendary series that broke new ground for more than twenty years and introduced many notable entertainers and celebrities to the public.

"Well written and highly detailed, Sullivan's biography, like his career, has it all, really-big-show-wise. A must-have for collections emphasizing show-biz history." —*Booklist*

Includes bibliographical references (p. 309-317) and index.

Maiklem, Lara
Mudlark: In Search of London's Past Along the River Thames. Lara Maiklem. Liveright Publishing Corporation, a division of W.W. Norton & Company 2019. 336 pages
ISBN 9781631494963
Grades: Adult **B**
1. Maiklem, Lara, 1971- 2. Mud 3. Antiquities 4. Lost articles 5. Rivers 6. Scavenging 7. Tides 8. London, England 9. Thames River 10. Autobiographies and memoirs 11. History writing — Europe — United Kingdom 12. Nature Writing — Natural Landscapes 13. Life stories — Arts and culture — Writing

A quixotic journey through London's past, Mudlark plumbs the banks of the Thames to reveal the stories hidden behind the archaeological remnants of an ancient city. Tirelessly trekking across miles of the Thames' muddy shores, where others only see the detritus of city life, Maiklem unearths evidence of England's captivating, if sometimes murky, history—with some objects dating back to 43 AD, when London was but an outpost of the Roman Empire.

First published in Great Britain in 2019 under the title MUDLARKING: Lost and Found on the Thames River—Title page verso; Includes bibliographical references and index.

Mailhot, Terese Marie
Heart Berries: A Memoir. Terese Marie Mailhot. Counterpoint Press 2018. 160 p.
ISBN 9781619023345
Grades: Adult **B**
1. Mailhot, Terese Marie 2. Indigenous women 3. First Nations (Canada) 4. Indigenous reservations 5. Mothers and daughters 6. People with bipolar disorder 7. Post-traumatic stress disorder 8. People with post-traumatic stress disorder 9. Bipolar disorder 10. Autobiographies and memoirs 11. Life stories — Identity — Race and ethnicity 12. Life stories — Facing adversity — Medical issues — Mental illness 13. Book club best bets
LC 2017051069

Library Journal Best Books, 2018; Loan Stars Favourites, 2018.

Terese Mailhot's debut memoir chronicles her struggle to balance the beauty of her Native heritage with the often desperate and chaotic reality of life on the reservation.

Maisel, Ivan
I Keep Trying to Catch His Eye: A Memoir of Loss, Grief, and Love. Ivan Maisel. Hachette Books 2021. 288 p.
ISBN 9780306925740
Grades: Adult **B**
1. Maisel, Ivan, 1960- 2. Grief in parents 3. Teenagers 4. Loss 5. Grief 6. Suicide 7. Family and suicide 8. Love 9. Suicidal behavior 10. Autobiographies and memoirs 11. Life stories — Facing adversity — Coping with death 12. Life stories — Relationships — Parent and child 13. Family and Relationships — General
LC 2021022739

In February 2015, Ivan Maisel received a call that would alter his life forever: His son Max's car was found abandoned in a parking next to Lake Ontario. Two months later, Max's body would be found in the lake. I Keep Trying to Catch His Eye is the story of Maisel's love for a son who was so different from him, but who he loved so deeply, and how he came to learn that grief for Max was nothing more than a last, ultimate expression of love. Navigating the moments of their complicated relationship, as well as their love each other, Maisel explores the bridges he tried to build to his son and the grief that engulfed him and his family after Max's death by suicide. Taking its title from Max's love of photography—and his tendency to only love the camera when he was behind it, looking away whenever his picture was taken—I Keep Trying to Catch His Eye delves into the tragically transformative reality of losing a child, all with grace, depth, and refinement. But by humanizing Max and humanizing his grief, Maisel evokes understanding instead of sorrow, appreciation instead of anxiety—and love instead of fear.

"Maisel (The Maisel Report), a former senior writer for ESPN, reflects on the tragedy of losing his 21-year-old son, Max, to suicide in this beautiful and heart-wrenching work. . . . The result yields a deeply affecting testament to the fragility of life, and the human capacity for resilience." —*Publishers Weekly*

Makos, Adam
Spearhead: An American Tank Gunner, His Enemy, and a Collision of Lives in World War II. Adam Makos. Ballantine Books 2019. xiii, 393 pages, 32 unnumbered pages of plates : Illustration; Map
ISBN 9780804176729
Grades: Adult **B**
1. Smoyer, Clarence, 1923-2022 2. World War II 3. Military history 4. Tank warfare 5. Military campaigns 6. United States 7. Biographies 8. History writing — Wars and conflicts — World War II 9. Life stories — Law and order — Armed forces personnel
LC 2018039460

Clarence Smoyer began the war as a gentle giant, a factory worker from Pennsylvania coal country reluctant to unleash the power of the Sherman tank he crewed. But as his tank platoon fought its way from Normandy to the Rhine and beyond, and he watched his friends cut down one by one, he learned to kill with deadly accuracy and efficiency. His fight would climax in Cologne, in the shadow of the great cathedral, where he took a shot immortalized by a chance photograph—and where he would later forge a friendship with the German tanker he tragically dueled soon after.

The best-selling author of a Higher Call documents the lesser-known story of a World War II tank platoon and the gentle soldier behind the immortalized film footage of history's iconic duel at the great cathedral in Cologne.

Includes bibliographical references (pages [349]-381) and index.

Malcolm X

★ *The Autobiography of Malcolm X.* with the assistance of Alex Haley; introduction by M.S. Handler; epilogue by Alex Haley. Ballantine Books 1992. xv, 527 p.

ISBN 9780345376718

Grades: 11 12 Adult   **B**

1. Malcolm X, 1925-1965 2. Black Muslims 3. African Americans 4. Autobiographies and memoirs 5. Page to screen 6. Biographies 7. History writing — African American — Civil rights — United States 8. Life stories — Politics — Activists and Reformers — Civil Rights Leaders

LC 91093124

The Black leader discusses his political philosophy and reveals details of his life, shedding light on the ideas that enabled him to gain the allegiance of a still growing percentage of the Black population.

"Alex Haley did his job with sensitivity and with devotion. {The book will have a permanent place in the literature of the Afro-American struggle." —*New York Review of Books*

Book made into a movie called Malcolm X; Originally published: New York : Grove Press, 1965.

Malek, Alia

The Home That Was Our Country: A Memoir of Syria. Alia Malek. Nation Books 2017. 304 p.

ISBN 9781568585321

Grades: Adult   **B**

1. Malek, Alia, 1974- 2. City life 3. Arab Spring, 2010-2012 4. Home (Concept) 5. Exile (Punishment) 6. Southwest Asia and North Africa (Middle East) history 7. Damascus, Syria 8. Syria 9. 2010s 10. 2020s 11. Autobiographies and memoirs 12. Life stories — Facing adversity — War and oppression 13. Politics and global affairs — World politics — Southwest Asia and North Africa (Middle East) 14. History writing — Southwest Asia and North Africa (Middle East) 15. Adult books for young adults

LC 2016037114

Booklist Editors' Choice, 2017.

In The Home that Was My Country, Syrian-American journalist Alia Malek chronicles her return to her family home in Damascus and the history of the Jabban apartment building. Here, generations of Christians, Jews, Muslims, and Armenians lived, worked, loved, and suffered in close quarters. In telling the story of her family over the course of the last century, Alia brings to light the triumphs and failures that have led Syria to where it is today.

"Moving and insightful, Malek's memoir combines sharp-eyed observations of Syrian politics, only occasionally overdone, with elegiac commentary on home, exile, and a bygone era. Provocative, richly detailed reading." —*Kirkus*

Mallaby, Sebastian

The Man Who Knew: The Life and Times of Alan Greenspan. Sebastian Mallaby. Penguin Press 2016. 704 p.

ISBN 9781594204845

Grades: Adult   **B**

1. Greenspan, Alan, 1926- 2. Government economists 3. Economists 4. Monetary policy 5. Biographies 6. Life stories — Business — Business leaders 7. Business and economics — Economics — Contemporary U.S. economy

LC 2016017300

New York Times Notable Book, 2016.

Traces the life and career of one of the most important economic statesmen of the modern era, describing the array of business and government positions that led to his chairmanship of the Federal Reserve and how the financial crisis of 2008 damaged his reputation.

"He has written a masterful, detailed portrait of one of the leading economic figures of our time." —*Publishers Weekly*

A Council on Foreign Relations Book.

Malone, Jo

Jo Malone: My Story. Jo Malone. Simon & Schust,er 2016. 416 pages

ISBN 9781501110597

Grades: Adult   **B**

1. Malone, Jo 2. Businesspeople 3. Perfumes industry and trade 4. Beauty 5. Luxury 6. Growing up 7. People with dyslexia 8. People with breast cancer 9. Cancer survivors 10. Neurodivergent people 11. Autobiographies and memoirs 12. Life stories — Business — Business leaders 13. Life stories — Facing adversity

The creator of the internationally acclaimed Jo Malone London brand traces her upbringing in government-subsidized housing in Kent, her teen efforts to provide care for her stroke-victim mother, the dyslexia that shaped her experience of the world through scent and her survival of breast cancer.

Manchester, William

Goodbye, Darkness: A Memoir of the Pacific War. William Manchester. Back Bay Books/Little, Brown and Company 2002. 401 pages : Illustration

ISBN 9780316501118

Grades: Adult   **B**

1. Manchester, William, 1922-2004 2. World War II 3. Marines 4. Authors, American 5. Soldiers 6. Pacific Ocean 7. United States 8. 20th century 9. Autobiographies and memoirs 10. Biographies 11. History writing — Wars and conflicts — World War II — Pacific Theater 12. Life stories — Law and order — Armed forces personnel

LC Bl 99780144

Pulitzer Prize for General Nonfiction finalist.

The author relates his experiences as a Marine Corps sergeant in World War II, recalling the horrors of Guadalcanal and Okinawa.

"This memoir arises from a 1978 trip the author made to Pacific battlefields, seeking to exorcise three decades of nightmares dating to wartime days as a Marine Corps sergeant. First tracing his family background, youth, enlistment, training, and embarkation from San Diego, Manchester unravels a memoir featuring historical reconstruction, disjointed flash-forwards, shocking vignettes, {and redoubtable vocabulary." —*Choice*

Originally published: Boston : Little, Brown, 1980.

The Last Lion, Winston Spencer Churchill. by William Manchester. Little, Brown 1983. 992 p. (Last lion (William Manchester), 1)

ISBN 9780316545037

Grades: Adult   **B**

1. Churchill, Winston, 1874-1965 2. Aristocracy 3. Soldiers 4. Politicians 5. Prime ministers 6. Politics and government 7. English history 8. Great Britain 9. 20th century 10. Biographies 11. History writing — Europe — United Kingdom 12. Life stories — Politics — Politicians

LC 82024972

Describes the early life and political career of the British prime minister Winston Churchill.

Includes bibliographies and indexes.

The Last Lion, Winston Spencer Churchill. by William Manchester. Little, Brown 1988. 816 p. (Last lion (William Manchester), 2)

ISBN 9780316545129

Grades: Adult   **B**

1. Churchill, Winston, 1874-1965 2. Politicians 3. Prime ministers 4. Politics and government 5. Ambition 6. English history 7. Great Britain 8. 20th century 9. Biographies 10. History writing — Europe — United Kingdom 11. Life stories — Politics — Politicians

Details the life and times of one of the world's most powerful leaders.

The Last Lion, Winston Spencer Churchill. William Manchester and Paul Reid. Little, Brown, and Company 2012. 1232 p. (Last lion (William Manchester), 3)

ISBN 9780316547703

Grades: Adult   **B**

ESSENTIAL AND RECOMMENDED TITLES
Biography

1. Churchill, Winston, 1874-1965 2. Politicians 3. World War II 4. International relations 5. Prime ministers 6. Politics and government 7. English history 8. Great Britain 9. 20th century 10. Biographies 11. History writing — Europe — United Kingdom 12. Life stories — Politics — Politicians

Booklist Editors' Choice, 2012.

Details the life and times of Winston Churchill, one of the world's most powerful leaders.

Mandel, David
Who's Who in the Jewish Bible. David Mandel. Jewish Publication Society 2007. xx, 422 p.
ISBN 9780827608634
Grades: Adult **B**
1. Spirituality and Religion — Judaism — History 2. Reference books — Religion
LC 2007027288

An encyclopedic A-to-Z reference shares comprehensive profiles of approximately 3,000 characters in the Hebrew Bible complemented by informative facts, relevant stories, their locations in the Bible and the meanings of character names.

Includes bibliographical references (p. 421-422).

Mandel, Sarah
Little Earthquakes. Sarah Mandel. HarperCollins 2023. 208 p.
ISBN 9780063270916
Grades: Adult **B**
1. Cancer survivors 2. Cognitive therapy 3. Psychotherapy 4. Healing 5. Psychic trauma 6. Dissociative disorders 7. Breast cancer 8. Women psychotherapists 9. Pregnant women 10. Depression 11. Autobiographies and memoirs 12. Life stories — Facing adversity — Medical issues — Physical illness 13. Life stories — Facing adversity — Medical issues — Mental illness

Discovering she had Stage Four breast cancer while pregnant with her second baby, a clinical psychologist who specializes in trauma, after receiving good news, was unable to celebrate due to being frozen in a dissociated state and used the "narrative therapy" she used with her patients to navigate her own trauma.

"Couples dealing with cancer, or any other major setback, will find comfort in Mandel's beautifully written, moving memoir." —*Booklist*

Mandela, Nelson
Conversations with Myself. Nelson Mandela. Farrar Straus & Giroux 2010. 288 p.
ISBN 9780374128951
Grades: Adult **B**
1. Mandela, Nelson, 1918-2013 2. Politicians 3. Social advocates 4. Anti-apartheid activists 5. Leadership 6. History writing — Africa — South Africa
LC 2010933174

Draws on the author's personal archive of never-before-seen papers to offer unique access to the private world of the incomparable world leader, who worked from prison to end apartheid in South Africa.

"This volume of personal papers . adds much that has never been said before about Nelson Mandela, including diary entries from his time in the underground, debates about passive resistance and guerrilla warfare, letters from prison, and recorded reminiscences with former fellow prisoners." —*Booklist*

Dare Not Linger: The Presidential Years. Nelson Mandela with Mandla Langa; prologue by Graca Machel. Farrar Straus & Giroux 2017. 320 p.
ISBN 9780374134716
Grades: Adult **B**
1. Mandela, Nelson, 1918-2013 2. Anti-apartheid activists 3. Politicians 4. Social advocates 5. Equality 6. Racism 7. Presidents 8. Politics and government 9. South Africa 10. 20th century 11. Autobiographies and memoirs 12. Life stories — Politics — Politicians 13. Life stories — Politics — Activists and reformers 14. History writing — Africa — South Africa
LC 2017036979

A sequel to the best-selling Long Walk to Freedom completes the Nobel Prize Laureate's unfinished memoirs and is complemented by notes and speeches written by Mandela during his historic presidency.

"Essential to students of Mandela's political career as well as of modern African history." —*Kirkus*

In His Own Words. Nelson Mandela; edited by Kader Asmal, David Chidester, Wilmot James. Little, Brown and Co. 2003. xlii, 558 p. : Illustration
ISBN 9780316110198
Grades: 11 12 Adult **B**
1. Mandela, Nelson, 1918-2013 2. Nobel Prize winners 3. Political prisoners 4. Politicians 5. Presidents 6. Race relations 7. Politics and government 8. South Africa 9. 20th century 10. Autobiographies and memoirs 11. Speeches, addresses, etc. 12. Essays 13. Adult books for young adults 14. Life stories — Politics — Political prisoners 15. History writing — Africa — South Africa
LC 2004107807

A collection of speeches by the South African leader includes pieces that marked such moments in his life as his imprisonment and release, his acceptance of the Nobel Peace Prize, and his election as South Africa's first Black president.

"This collection of Mandela's speeches shows why he remains a universal hero. This volume will be in great demand for the personal drama, the history, and, yes, for the inspiring moral values." —*Booklist*

Includes index.

★ *Long Walk to Freedom: The Autobiography of Nelson Mandela.* Nelson Mandela. Little, Brown 1994. 558 p, 24 p. of plates : Portrait
ISBN 9780316545853
Grades: 11 12 Adult **B**
1. Mandela, Nelson, 1918-2013 2. Anti-apartheid activists 3. Politicians 4. Social advocates 5. Presidents 6. Politics and government 7. South Africa 8. 20th century 9. Page to screen 10. Autobiographies and memoirs 11. Life stories — Politics — Politicians 12. Life stories — Politics — Activists and reformers 13. History writing — Africa — South Africa 14. Antiracist literature
LC 94079980

Booklist Editors' Choice: Adult Books for Young Adults, 1994.

The leader of South Africa's antiapartheid movement chronicles his life, including his tribal years, his time spent in prison, and his return to lead his people.

"This book provides important new evidence to the forty-year story of apartheid, as seen by its most formidable opponent. And there is enough candour to provide insights into the nature of leadership." —*Times Literary Supplement*

Includes index; Film adaptation entitled Mandela: Long walk to freedom (2013).

Mandela: An Illustrated Autobiography. Nelson Mandela. Little, Brown 1996. 208 p. : Illustration; Color; Map; Portrait
ISBN 9780316550383
Grades: 11 12 Adult **B**
1. Mandela, Nelson, 1918-2013 2. Politicians 3. Social advocates 4. Anti-apartheid activists 5. Presidents 6. Politics and government 7. South Africa 8. 20th century 9. Autobiographies and memoirs 10. Life stories — Politics — Politicians 11. Life stories — Politics — Activists and reformers 12. History writing — Africa — South Africa

Booklist Editors' Choice: Adult Books for Young Adults, 1996.

Photographs from Mandela's childhood, career, imprisonment, and presidency are accompanied by text from his memoir "Long walk to freedom."

"The photos, from a variety of archives and journalistic sources, ably illustrate Mandela and, even more so, the South Africa around him." —*Library Journal*

This is an illustrated and abridged edition of Long walk to freedom: the autobiography of Nelson Mandela ...—T.P. verso; Includes index.

Mankell, Henning
Quicksand: What It Means to Be a Human Being. Henning Mankell. Vintage Books 2017. 320 pages
ISBN 9780525432159
Grades: Adult **B**

1. Mankell, Henning, 1948-2015 2. Authors, Swedish 3. Death 4. People with cancer 5. Coping 6. Personal conduct 7. Autobiographies and memoirs 8. Essays 9. Life stories — Facing adversity — Coping with death

LC Bl2016057757

The late activist and best-selling author of the Kurt Wallander mysteries explores in a sequence of intimate vignettes the myriad experiences of a life richly lived through his relationships and writings as evaluated after his 2014 lung cancer diagnosis.

"This book is a compelling attempt to leave behind something for future civilizations to stumble upon, to piece together what it meant to be a human in the 21st century." —*Library Journal*

Mann, Sally

★ *Hold* Still: *A Memoir with Photographs.* Sally Mann. Little, Brown and Company 2015. xiv, 482 pages : Illustration; Color

ISBN 9780316247764

Grades: Adult   B

1. Mann, Sally, 1951- 2. Photographers 3. Photography 4. Families 5. Family secrets 6. Virginia 7. Autobiographies and memoirs 8. Life stories — Arts and culture 9. Adult books for young adults

LC Bl2015017753

Andrew Carnegie Medal for Excellence in Non-Fiction, 2016; Booklist Editors' Choice, 2015; National Book Award for Nonfiction finalist, 2015.

The author tells her family's history in photographs and words, after sorting through a box of old papers that revealed scandals, alcohol and domestic abuse, affairs, family land ownership, and racial complications.

"Here photographer Mann chronicles her rich and eccentric family history, told through the exploration of old documents and images stored away in her attic. Raw and darkly humorous, Mann's writing is consistently honest and poignant as she depicts her beloved Virginia farm, her childhood, her parents, and her children." —*Library Journal*

Mann, William J.

The **Contender:** *The Story of Marlon Brando.* William J. Mann. Harper360 2019. 718 p.

ISBN 9780062427649

Grades: Adult   B

1. Brando, Marlon, 1924-2004 2. Acting 3. Actors and actresses 4. Social life and customs 5. United States 6. 20th century 7. Biographies 8. Life stories — Arts and culture — Performing arts — Actors and actresses 9. Arts and Entertainment — Movies and Television

LC 2019022978

Booklist Editors' Choice, 2019.

Based on new and revelatory material from Brando's own private archives, an award-winning film biographer presents a deeply-textured, ambitious, and definitive portrait of the greatest movie actor of the twentieth century, the elusive Marlon Brando, bringing his extraordinarily complex life into view as never before.

Hello, *Gorgeous: Becoming Barbra Streisand.* William J. Mann. Houghton Mifflin Harcourt 2012. 496 p.

ISBN 9780547368924

Grades: Adult   B

1. Streisand, Barbra 2. Jewish American women 3. Women entertainers 4. Women and success 5. Family relationships 6. Women celebrities 7. Fame 8. Women singers 9. Films 10. Actors and actresses 11. Social life and customs 12. United States 13. 20th century 14. Biographies 15. Arts and Entertainment — General 16. Life stories — Arts and culture — Performing arts — Actors and actresses 17. Life stories — Arts and culture — Performing arts — Entertainers and celebrities 18. Nonfiction that reads like fiction

LC 2012016364

Traces the formative years of the Academy Award-winning actress and platinum album music artist, providing coverage of such topics as her relationship with her mother, her marriage to Elliott Gould and the making of Funny Girl against a backdrop of the birth of off-off-Broadway.

Kate: *The Woman Who Was Hepburn.* William J. Mann. H. Holt 2006. xxviii, 621 p, 16 p. of plates : Illustration

ISBN 9780805076257

Grades: Adult   B

1. Hepburn, Katharine, 1907-2003 2. Sexuality 3. Alcoholic women 4. Films 5. Actors and actresses 6. Men-women relations 7. United States 8. Biographies 9. Arts and Entertainment — Movies and Television 10. Life stories — Arts and culture — Performing arts — Actors and actresses 11. Life stories — Identity — LGBTQIA+

LC 2006043367

New York Times Notable Book, 2006.

A biography of Katharine Hepburn draws on new interviews with friends and family and previously unavailable materials to offer a study of the complex, intelligent, sophisticated woman behind the mythic Hollywood image.

"This will surely be the definitive version of Hepburn's life for decades to come, as it is an outstanding example of painstaking research matched with splendid writing." —*Publishers Weekly*

Includes bibliographical references (p. [533]-589) and index.

The **Wars** *of the Roosevelts: The Ruthless Rise of America's Greatest Political Family.* William J. Mann. HarperCollins 2016. 624 p.

ISBN 9780062383334

Grades: Adult   B

1. Roosevelt family 2. Roosevelt, Franklin D. (Franklin Delano), 1882-1945 3. Roosevelt, Eleanor, 1884-1962 4. Roosevelt, Theodore, 1858-1919 5. Sibling rivalry 6. Ambition 7. Power 8. Jealousy 9. Family relationships 10. Family secrets 11. Families 12. Interpersonal relations 13. Scandals 14. Dysfunctional families 15. Elite (Social sciences) 16. Rich families 17. Ruthlessness 18. 20th century 19. Autobiographies and memoirs 20. Life stories — People in history — Famous families 21. History writing — Early 20th century — United States

LC Bl2016046398

A provocative group biography of the Roosevelt family draws on lesser-known family secrets and complex rivalries to argue that the Roosevelts' rise to power was driven by a series of inside competitions that were witnessed firsthand by an increasingly begrudging Eleanor Roosevelt.

"Perhaps best known for his popular film biographies and histories, and thus no stranger to tales of scandal and coverup, feuds and intrigue, Mann writes sympathetically about all the Roosevelts but particularly the black sheep, the nonconformists whose births into this powerful family imposed special burdens." —*Kirkus*

Manning, Chelsea

Readme.Txt: *A Memoir.* Chelsea Manning. Farrar, Straus and Giroux 2022. 224 p.

ISBN 9780374279271

Grades: Adult   B

1. Manning, Chelsea, 1987- 2. Military intelligence 3. Systems analysts 4. Trans women 5. Soldiers 6. Iraq War, 2003-2011 7. Intelligence service 8. Leaks (Disclosure of information) 9. Military secrets 10. National security 11. Trials (Treason) 12. Prison sentences 13. Pardon 14. Gender identity 15. Government accountability 16. Autobiographies and memoirs 17. Life stories — Law and order — Criminals and law-breakers 18. Life stories — Identity — LGBTQIA+ 19. Politics and global affairs — Civil and human rights 20. Politics and global affairs — National security 21. Society and culture — LGBTQIA+

When her sentence for disclosing classified and diplomatic records from Iraq is commuted by President Barack Obama, a former U.S. Army intelligence analyst recounts how her pleas for increased institutional transparency and government accountability took place alongside a fight to defend her rights as a trans woman.

"The trans Army analyst who served seven years in prison for disclosing documents tells her story….Manning demonstrates her integrity in this meticulous account of a person constitutionally opposed to secrets and lies." —*Kirkus*

Manseau, Peter

The **Apparitionists:** *A Tale of Phantoms, Fraud, Photography, and the Man Who Captured Lincoln's Ghost.* Peter Manseau. Houghton Mifflin Harcourt 2017. 352 pages

ESSENTIAL AND RECOMMENDED TITLES
Biography

ISBN 9780544745971
Grades: Adult **B**
1. Mumler, William H. 2. Photographers 3. Psychics 4. Paranormal phenomena 5. Spiritualism 6. Photography 7. Apparitions 8. Life after death 9. Faith (Christianity) 10. Skepticism 11. Trials (Fraud) 12. Gilded Age (1865-1898) 13. Biographies 14. Life stories — Arts and culture — Artists 15. Arts and Entertainment — Photography 16. History writing — Gilded Age — United States 17. History writing — Arts and culture 18. Nonfiction that reads like fiction
LC 2017018074

The story of "spirit photographer" William Mumler documents how his images of the ghosts of loved ones were highly sought and infamously denounced, tracing the story of his successful defense against charges of fraud, the yet-unsolved mystery behind his photography and what his successes reveal about period culture.

Includes bibliographical references and index.

Mansel, Philip
King of the World: The Life of Louis XIV. Philip Mansel. University of Chicago Press 2020. 608 pages
ISBN 9780226690896
Grades: Adult **B**
1. Louis XIV, King of France, 1638-1715 2. Louis XIV King of France 1638-1715 3. Rulers 4. Courts and courtiers 5. Monarchy, French 6. Power 7. War 8. Colonialism 9. Extramarital affairs 10. Interpersonal relations 11. Aristocracy 12. Men-women relations 13. French history 14. France 15. 17th century 16. Biographies 17. Life stories — Politics — Royalty 18. History writing — Europe — France

Philip Mansel's book is poised to become the new standard English-language biography of Louis XIV, one that takes into account the revolution in the last fifty years in knowledge about every aspect of the king's reign: the army; Catholicism; diplomacy; the arts; music; medicine; homosexuality at his court; the role of women and the publication of the entire correspondence of his second wife, Madame de Maintenon. This is a global biography of a global king, whose power on the French monarchy and state was large but also limited by laws and circumstances, and whose interests and ambitions stretched from the eastern frontiers of his territory, which he enlarged to what is essentially France's shape today, to the territories along the Mississippi and Mekongrivers. Through it all, we watch Louis XIV progressively turning from a dazzling, attractive monarch to a belligerent reactionary who sets France on the path to 1789.

"An impressive, comprehensive biography of the Sun King—a must-add to any Francophile's library." —*Kirkus*

Includes bibliographical references and index; Originally published: London : Allen Lane, 2019.

Manuel, Ian
My Time Will Come: A Memoir of Crime, Punishment, Hope, and Redemption. Ian Manuel; foreword by Bryan Stevenson. Pantheon Books 2021. 192 p.
ISBN 9781524748524
Grades: Adult **B**
1. African American men 2. Former convicts 3. Restorative justice 4. Racism in the criminal justice system 5. Imprisonment 6. Criminal justice system 7. Redemption 8. Juvenile delinquents 9. Boys 10. United States 11. Autobiographies and memoirs 12. Life stories — Law and order — Prisoners and inmates 13. Society and culture — Violence and crime — Criminal justice system 14. Life stories — Facing adversity — Personal transformation
LC 2020045133

Full of unexpected twists and turns as it describes a struggle to attain the glory of redemption, this at once wrenching and inspiring story shows how the author endured the savagery of the U.S. prison system and how his victim forgave him and advocated for his freedom.

"An unsparing memoir about the cruel, long-unexamined policy of sentencing juveniles to life in prison. Manuel's account is both heart-wrenching and uplifting." —*Kirkus*

Manzione, Gianmarc
Pin Action: Small-time Gangsters, High-stakes Gambling, and the Teenage Hustler Who Became a Bowling Champion. Gianmarc Manzione. Pegasus Books 2014. 336 p.
ISBN 9781605986456
Grades: Adult **B**
1. Schlegle, Ernie 2. Bowling 3. Gambling 4. Organized crime 5. Swindlers and swindling 6. New York City 7. 1960s 8. 1970s 9. Biographies 10. Life stories — Sports 11. Sports and Competition — General
LC 2015410656

Traces the rise of con artist-turned-bowling champion Ernie Schlegel against a backdrop of gritty 1960s and 1970s New York, profiling the sport of action bowling and the contributors who shaped his achievements.

"This well-researched account is for those who remember the glory days of bowling. Others will be fascinated by the gritty side of the sport, which few knew existed." —*Library Journal*

Marable, Manning
★ *Malcolm X: A Life of Reinvention.* Manning Marable. Viking 2011. 594 p, 16 p. of plates : Illustration
ISBN 9780670022205
Grades: Adult **B**
1. Malcolm X, 1925-1965 2. Black Muslims 3. Black nationalism 4. African American civil rights workers 5. Muslims 6. Radicalism 7. African Americans 8. United States history 9. United States 10. 20th century 11. Biographies 12. Life stories — Politics — Activists and Reformers — Civil Rights Leaders
LC 2010025768

ALA Notable Book, 2012; New York Times Notable Book, 2011; Pulitzer Prize for History, 2012; Andrew Carnegie Medal for Excellence in Non-Fiction finalist, 2012; National Book Critics Circle Award for Biography finalist, 2011; Pulitzer Prize for Biography or Autobiography finalist, 2012; Shortlisted for the James Tait Black Memorial Prize for Biography, 2011; National Book Award for Nonfiction finalist, 2011.

An authoritative biography of Malcolm X draws on new research to trace his life from his troubled youth through his involvement in the Nation of Islam, his activism in the world of Black Nationalism, and his assassination.

"This is an account of the lives of Malcolm X (192565), including his years as a street hustler in Boston and Harlem, his time in prison where voracious reading led to his transformation into a the devout follower of Elijah Muhammad's Nation of Islam (NOI), his rise as the NOI's chief minister, and, finally, his split from Elijah Muhammad and his acceptance of all people who would work for African American human and economic rights." —*Library Journal*

Includes bibliographical references (p. 563-576) and index.

Maraniss, Andrew
Strong Inside: Perry Wallace and the Collision of Race and Sports in the South. Andrew Maraniss. Vanderbilt University Press 2014. x, 467 p.
ISBN 9780826520234
Grades: Adult **B**
1. Wallace, Perry (Law professor) 2. African American basketball players 3. Racism in sports 4. College basketball 5. Basketball 6. Civil rights 7. Race relations 8. Social life and customs 9. United States 10. Southern States 11. 20th century 12. Biographies 13. Adult books for young adults 14. Life stories — Sports — Athletes 15. Sports and competition — Basketball 16. Society and culture — Race
LC 2014015257

Strong Inside is the dramatic, untold story of Perry Wallace, a brilliant student and talented athlete who became the first African-American basketball player in the SEC at Vanderbilt University during the tumultuous late 1960s. The fast-paced, richly detailed biography places Wallace's struggles and ultimate success into the larger contexts of civil rights and race relations in the South.

"Nuanced and complex, Strong Inside is an invaluable resource for studying the state of race relations in the US, both past and present." —*Choice*

Includes bibliographical references and index.

Maraniss, David

★ **Barack Obama:** *The Story.* by David Maraniss. Simon & Schuster 2012. 448 p.

ISBN 9781439160404

Grades: Adult   B

1. Obama, Barack 2. Politicians' families 3. Presidents 4. African Americans 5. Politics and government 6. Hawaii 7. United States 8. Biographies 9. Life stories — Politics — Politicians

LC 2011052983

Booklist Editors' Choice, 2012; New York Times Notable Book, 2012.

Based on interviews with the President himself and a wealth of letters, journals, and other documents, Maraniss' account spans Obama's childhood and political beginnings. Offering startling new insights, Maraniss reveals a man who struggled with his race and identity at a young age, but later embraced his strong character and ambition to rise to America's highest seat of power.

Includes bibliographical references and index.

Clemente: *The Passion and Grace of Baseball's Last Hero.* David Maraniss. Simon & Schuster 2006. 401 p, 16 p. of plates : Illustration; Map

ISBN 9780743217811

Grades: 11 12 Adult   B

1. Clemente, Roberto, 1934-1972 2. Baseball players 3. Athletes 4. Professional baseball players 5. Puerto Rican people in the United States 6. Right fielders (Baseball) 7. Baseball 8. Social life and customs 9. United States 10. 20th century 11. Biographies 12. Sports and Competition — Baseball 13. Sports and Competition — Individual Athlete 14. Life stories — Sports — Athletes 15. Adult books for young adults

New York Times Notable Book, 2006.

On New Year's Eve 1972, following eighteen magnificent seasons in the major leagues, Roberto Clemente died a hero's death, killed in a plane crash as he attempted to deliver food and medical supplies to Nicaragua after a devastating earthquake.

"The author has produced a baseball-savvy book sensitive to the social context that made Clemente, a Black Puerto Rican, a leading indicator of baseball's future." —*New York Times Book Review*

Includes bibliographical references (p. 385-387) and index.

★ **Path Lit by Lightning:** *The Life of Jim Thorpe.* David Maraniss. Simon & Schuster 2022. 512 p.

ISBN 9781476748412

Grades: Adult   B

1. Thorpe, Jim, 1887-1953 2. Athletes 3. Football players 4. Indigenous peoples of North America 5. Football 6. Indigenous athletes 7. Biographies 8. Life stories — People in history — Indigenous peoples 9. Sports and Competition — Individual Athlete 10. Life stories — Sports — Athletes

A Pulitzer Prize-winning journalist presents this riveting new biography of America's greatest all-around athlete and gold medal winner who survived racism, alcohol addiction, broken marriages and financial distress to become a myth and a legend.

"This essential work restores a legendary figure to his rightful place in history." —*Publishers Weekly*

Marcum, Diana

The **Fallen Stones:** *Chasing Butterflies, Discovering Mayan Secrets, and Looking for Hope Along the Way.* Diana Marcum. Little a 2022. 220 p.

ISBN 9781542022859

Grades: Adult   B

1. Marcum, Diana 2. Butterflies 3. Wildlife refuges 4. Epidemics 5. Farms 6. Nature 7. Interpersonal relations 8. Environmentalism 9. Belize 10. Central America 11. Autobiographies and memoirs 12. Life stories — Nature and outdoors 13. Nature Writing — Personal responses

Atop a hill in the rainforest of Belize, next to the ruins of a fallen civilization, a butterfly farm raises the brilliant blue morpho. What starts out as the worst vacation ever turns into a quest to learn more about the first-of-its-kind farm when journalist Diana Marcum inadvertently discovers this wildlife sanctuary, which is supported by an international live-butterfly trade. She quickly becomes acquainted with Clive, the whimsical British millionaire whose childhood passion created an industry, and Sebastian, the Maya farm manager whose stern expression belies a soft heart. Before long Diana and her partner, Jack Moody—new to being a couple—have moved into a long-empty jungle house, cohabitating with bats, scorpions, toucans, iguanas, and the vulnerable but resilient butterflies. Just ahead, although they don't know it, are a hurricane and a global pandemic. This warm, funny tale of finding a way forward when the world seems to be falling apart is filled with the beauty of the natural world and a heartfelt cry to protect it—beginning with butterflies.

"Pulitzer Prize winner Marcum (The Tenth Island) combines memoir, vivid nature writing, and sharp humor in this moving look at a Belizean butterfly farm. . . . This is a deeply human story, and one filled with plenty of hope." —*Publishers Weekly*

Mardini, Yusra

Butterfly: *From Refugee to Olympian, My Story of Rescue, Hope, and Triumph.* Yusra Mardini. St. Martin's Press 2018. 256 p.

ISBN 9781250184405

Grades: Adult   B

1. Mardini, Yusra 2. Women swimmers 3. Olympic athletes 4. Refugees 5. Resilience 6. Autobiographies and memoirs 7. Life stories — Sports — Athletes 8. Life stories — Facing adversity — War and oppression — Refugees 9. Adult books for young adults

LC 2017061098

Traces the author's life-changing rescue of a boatload of fellow refugees and how it inspired her to compete on the 2016 Refugee Olympic Team in Rio de Janeiro, tracing her subsequent work with the UN as a Goodwill Ambassador and her advocacy on behalf of people who have been forced from their homes by war.

First published in the United Kingdom by Bluebird, an imprint of Pan Macmillan—T.P. verso.

Margulies, Julianna

Sunshine *Girl: An Unexpected Life.* Julianna Margulies. Ballantine Books 2021. 272 p.

ISBN 9780525480259

Grades: Adult   B

1. Margulies, Julianna, 1966- 2. Family relationships 3. Growing up 4. Divorced mothers 5. Dysfunctional families 6. Acting 7. Families 8. Mothers and daughters 9. Actors and actresses 10. Men-women relations 11. Life stories — Arts and culture — Performing arts — Actors and actresses 12. Arts and Entertainment — Movies and Television

LC 2020037123

Filled with intimate stories and revelatory moments, this deeply powerful memoir from the award-winning actress is a riveting self-portrait of a woman whose resilience in the face of turmoil will leave readers intrigued and inspired.

"In her thought-provoking and revelatory memoir, Margulies, star of the popular TV shows the Good Wife and ER, reminisces about her life across time and continents." —*Library Journal*

Markham, Beryl

West with the Night. Beryl Markham. North Point Press 2013. xv, 293 pages

ISBN 9780865477636

Grades: Adult   B

1. Markham, Beryl, 1902-1986 2. Women pilots 3. Horse breeders 4. British people in Africa 5. Horse breeding 6. Race horse trainers 7. Hunting 8. Race relations 9. Pilots 10. Voyages and travels 11. East Africa 12. Autobiographies and memoirs 13. History writing — Women's history 14. Life stories — Science, technology, and medicine — Astronauts and pilots 15. History writing — Colonization — Africa

LC 2013498448

The author describes growing up in an Africa that no longer exists, training and breeding race horses, flying mail to Sudan, and being the first woman to fly the Atlantic from east to west.

Originally published: Boston : Houghton, Mifflin, 1942.

ESSENTIAL AND RECOMMENDED TITLES
Biography

Marnham, Patrick
Dreaming with His Eyes Open: A Life of Diego Rivera. Patrick Marnham. Knopf 1998. 350 p. : Illustration; Color
ISBN 9780679430421
Grades: Adult   B
1. Rivera, Diego, 1886-1957 2. Painters 3. Murals 4. Men-women relations 5. Mexican history 6. Mexico 7. Mexico City, Mexico 8. 20th century 9. Biographies 10. Arts and Entertainment — Painting, Drawing, and Sculpture 11. Life stories — Arts and culture — Artists
LC 98006145
New York Times Notable Book, 1999.
Explores the the life and work of the controversial Diego Rivera, his education, the influence of his native Mexico, his relationship with Frida Kahlo, and his creative artistry.
"For the browsing public as well as specialists in European, Latin American, and American modern art, this book is not to be overlooked." —*Library Journal*
Includes bibliographical references (p. [331]-334) and index.

Marsh, Charles
Strange Glory: A Life of Dietrich Bonhoeffer. Charles Marsh. Alfred a Knopf 2014. 528 p.
ISBN 9780307269812
Grades: Adult   B
1. Bonhoeffer, Dietrich, 1906-1945 2. Thought and thinking 3. German people in the United States 4. Christian martyrs 5. Righteous Gentiles in the Holocaust 6. Theology 7. Theologians 8. Anti-Nazi movement 9. German people in foreign countries 10. Faith 11. Germany 12. Biographies 13. Spirituality and Religion — Christianity 14. History writing — Wars and conflicts — World War II 15. Life stories — Religion and spirituality — Religious and spiritual leaders 16. History writing — Wars and conflicts — Resistance — World War II
LC 2013045873
A portrait of the German pastor-theologian draws on new research to cover the 1930 visit to America that shaped his perspectives on faith and moral responsibility, his achievements as an anti-Nazi activist and the plot against Hitler that would result in his execution.
"Marsh's portrait is of a spoiled, materialistic, and selfish young man who develops, over time, into a German hero. The writing is clear and concise, the endnotes extensive, and the index generous." —*Library Journal*

Marsh, Henry
Admissions: Life as a Brain Surgeon. Henry Marsh. Thomas Dunne Books 2017. 288 p.
ISBN 9781250127266
Grades: Adult   B
1. Marsh, Henry 2. Neurosurgeons 3. Medical care 4. Brain 5. Surgery 6. Surgeons 7. Autobiographies and memoirs 8. Life stories — Science, technology, and medicine — Healthcare professionals 9. Science Writing — Medicine and health — Doctors and nurses
LC 2017023778
National Book Critics Circle Award for Autobiography/Memoir finalist, 2017.
Traces the author's post-retirement work as a surgeon and teacher in such remote areas as NEPAL and Ukraine, illuminating the challenges of working in difficult regions and finding purposeful work after a career.
"Another thoughtful, painful, utterly fascinating mixture of nut-and-bolts brain surgery with a compassionate, workaholic surgeon's view of medicine around the world and his own limitations." —*Kirkus*

★ *Do No Harm: Stories of Life, Death and Brain Surgery.* Henry Marsh. Thomas Dunne Books 2015. 304 p.
ISBN 9781250065810
Grades: Adult   B
1. Marsh, Henry 2. Neurosurgeons 3. Brain 4. Physician and patient 5. Surgery 6. Surgeons 7. Autobiographies and memoirs 8. Life stories — Science, technology, and medicine — Healthcare professionals 9. Science Writing — Medicine and health — Doctors and nurses
LC 2015002573

Booklist Editors' Choice, 2015; New York Times Notable Book, 2015.
A leading neurosurgeon offers a revealing look into his life and work, discussing the triumphs, disasters, and regrets of a medical practice that carries grave risks and often requires agonizing decisions.
"One of the best books ever about a life in medicine, Do No Harm boldly and gracefully exposes the vulnerability and painful privilege of being a physician." —*Booklist*
Also published in large print format; Originally published: London : Weidenfeld & Nicolson, 2014.

Marshall, Cynthia
You've Been Chosen: Thriving Through the Unexpected. Cynt Marshall. Ballantine Books 2022. 240 p.
ISBN 9780593359419
Grades: Adult   B
1. Marshall, Cynthia, 1959- 2. African American women 3. Women executives 4. Cancer survivors 5. Success (Concept) 6. Faith (Christianity) 7. Empowerment 8. Persistence 9. Autobiographies and memoirs 10. Life stories — Business — Business leaders 11. Life stories — Identity — Race and ethnicity 12. Life stories — Facing adversity — Medical issues — Physical illness 13. Business and economics — Business leaders and entrepreneurs
LC 2022000427
One of the most influential Black business leaders in America today shares "the good, the great, the bad, and the ugly" of her journey through both cancer and everything that led up to it, offering hope and practical guidance for navigating life's most difficult challenges.
"Marshall debuts with a heartwarming spiritual memoir about her battle with cancer and navigating the corporate world as a Black woman." —*Publishers Weekly*

Marshall, Greg
Leg: The Story of a Limb and the Boy Who Grew from It: A Memoir. Greg Marshall. Abrams Press 2023. 304 p.
ISBN 9781419763601
Grades: Adult   B
1. Marshall, Greg (Essayist) 2. Authors 3. Growing up 4. Identity 5. Family relationships 6. Gay men 7. People with cerebral palsy 8. Family secrets 9. Coming out (Sexual or gender identity) 10. Familial love 11. Belonging 12. Resilience 13. North American people 14. American people 15. Utah 16. 1990s 17. Autobiographies and memoirs 18. Life stories — Facing adversity — Medical issues — Living with disabilities 19. Life stories — Identity — LGBTQIA+ 20. Life stories — Relationships — Growing up
In this hilarious and heartfelt memoir, the author shares outrageous stories of a singular childhood and his coming out of two closets—as a gay man and as a man living with cerebral palsy—and examines what it means to transform when there are parts of yourself you can't change.
"A sparkling portrait of personal discovery and a celebration of family, forgiveness, and thriving with a disability." —*Kirkus*

Marshall, Thurgood
Thurgood Marshall: His Speeches, Writings, Arguments, Opinions, and Reminiscences. Edited by Mark V. Tushnet; foreword by Randall Kennedy. Lawrence Hill Books 2001. xxvi, 548 p. (The library of Black America)
ISBN 9781556523861
Grades: 11 12 Adult   B
1. Marshall, Thurgood, 1908-1993 2. Judges 3. Racism 4. Legislation 5. Law — General
LC 2001016793
A collection of the first African American Supreme Court justice includes his arguments for school desegregation cases, reports on racism and race riots in the Army, notes on the history of civil rights, and opinions on several issues.
"In a career ranging from his trial and appellate work for the NAACP to his tenure as an associate justice of the Court, Marshall wrought revolutionary changes in U.S. law and politics, and this collection of his legal briefs, writings, speeches, and judicial opinions, plus a never-before-published oral interview,

gives us a superior analysis of the advocate, the democrat, the dissenter, and the unflagging fighter for equality." —*Library Journal*
Includes bibliographical references (p. 515-516) and index.

Martin, Gerald
★ *Gabriel Garcia Marquez: A Life.* Gerald Martin. Alfred A. Knopf 2009. xxiii, 642 p, [16] p. of plates : Illustration; Map
ISBN 9780307271778
Grades: 11 12 Adult   B
1. Garcia Marquez, Gabriel, 1928-2014 2. Authors, Colombian 3. Latin American people 4. Nobel prize winners 5. Authors 6. 20th century 7. Biographies 8. Arts and Entertainment — Writing and Publishing 9. Life stories — Arts and culture — Writing — Authors

Booklist Editors' Choice, 2009; Shortlisted for the James Tait Black Memorial Prize for Biography, 2008.

Describes the life and accomplishments of the Columbian novelist, from his childhood and early career to his Nobel Prize in Literature and his exploits as a political and social activist.

"This superbly researched biography is nothing short of a tour de force.... This work not only details the life of a great writer but also provides considerable insight into life in Latin America." —*Library Journal*
Includes bibliographical references (p. 609-620) and index; Originally published: London : Bloomsbury, 2008.

Martin, Manjula
The Last Fire Season: A Personal and Pyronatural History. Manjula Martin. Pantheon Books 2024. 272 p.
ISBN 9780593317150
Grades: Adult   B
1. Wildfires 2. Natural disasters 3. Climate change 4. Global warming 5. Effect of humans on nature 6. Effect of environment on humans 7. Forest management 8. Forest fires 9. Fire fighting 10. Fire prevention 11. Wildfire fighters 12. Fire ecology 13. California 14. Autobiographies and memoirs 15. Life stories — Nature and outdoors 16. Nature Writing — Environmental Issues 17. Nature Writing — Natural Disaster

In this part memoir, part natural history, part literary inquiry, the author recounts her experiences in Northern California during the worst fire season on record, which causes her to question her own assumptions about nature and the complicated connections between people and the land on which we live.

"Insightful and alarming, hopeful and consistently engaging." —*Kirkus*

Martin, Steve
Number One Is Walking: My Life in the Movies and Other Diversions. Steve Martin; drawings by Harry Bliss. Celadon Books 2022. 272 p. : Illustration
ISBN 9781250815293
Grades: Adult   B
1. Martin, Steve, 1945- 2. Comedians 3. Acting 4. Stand-up comedians 5. Stand-up comedy 6. Films 7. Fame 8. Celebrities 9. Entertainers 10. Actors and actresses 11. United States 12. Autobiographies and memoirs 13. Biographies 14. Autobiographical comics 15. Comics and Graphic novels 16. Arts and Entertainment — Movies and Television 17. Humor writing — General 18. Life stories — Arts and culture — Performing arts — Entertainers and celebrities
LC 2022015471

In this illustrated memoir of his forty years in the movie biz, the Academy Award-winning actor, using his unparalleled wit, shares anecdotes from the sets of his beloved films, bringing readers directly into his world, capturing the everyday moments that make up a movie star's life.

"Film buffs, comedy fans, and legion admirers of both the actor and artist will find themselves smiling from cover to cover." —*Publishers Weekly*

Martin, Valerie
Salvation: Scenes from the Life of St. Francis. Valerie Martin. Knopf 2001. xii, 268 p.
ISBN 9780375409837
Grades: Adult   B

1. Francis, of Assisi, Saint, 1182-1226 2. Christian saints 3. Assisi, Italy 4. Biographies 5. Spirituality and Religion — Christianity 6. Life stories — Religion and spirituality — Religious and spiritual leaders
LC 00044361

A moving biography of the great saint inspired by a fresco in Italy offers readers a window into the late-medieval world that influenced the teachings and mission of St. Francis of Assisi. By the author of Mary Reilly.

"This portrait will be most interesting to readers who are already familiar with the basic facts of Francis's life and remain open to exploring a new, gritty interpretation of them." —*Publishers Weekly*
Includes bibliographical references (p. [265]-268).

Martinez Wood, Jamie
Latino Writers and Journalists. Jamie Martinez Wood. Facts on File 2007. x, 294 p. : Illustration
ISBN 9780816064229
Grades: 11 12 Adult   B
1. Journalism 2. American literature 3. United States 4. History writing — Latin America 5. Life stories — Arts and culture — Writing 6. Reference — Biographical dictionaries
LC 2006017394

Each volume in this invaluable resource contains more than 150 biographical profiles of Latinos who have influenced and continue to impact the Latino community, the United States, and the world in a variety of fields and professions.

Presents alphabetically arranged biographical profiles of Latino authors and journalists who have influenced and continue to impact the Latino community, the United States, and the world.

"This book brings together 150 writers identified as Latino Americans. Approximately one-third of the profiles are accompanied by photographs." —*Booklist*
Includes bibliographical references (p. 269-271) and index.

Martini, Adrienne
Somebody's Gotta Do It: Why Cursing at the News Won't Save the Nation, but Your Name on a Local Ballot Can. Adrienne Martini. Henry Holt and Company 2020. 240 pages
ISBN 9781250247636
Grades: Adult   B
1. Martini, Adrienne, 1971- 2. Women politicians 3. Politicians 4. Local elections 5. Campaign management 6. Political campaigns 7. Women journalists 8. Politics and government 9. United States 10. New York (State) 11. 2010s 12. 2020s 13. Autobiographies and memoirs 14. Life stories — Politics — Politicians 15. Politics and global affairs — Elections
LC 2019039991

Both funny and instructive, this memoir is about a progressive woman—a knitter, runner, mom and resident of rural Otsego County in upstate New York—who ran for office and won, and then realized the critical importance of the job.

"Using humor and anecdotes, Martini shows the importance of running for local office and helps provide a broader understanding of local government. Readers interested in learning about government organization and policy, and those who might want to run for office one day will enjoy the insights and lessons offered throughout." —*Library Journal*

Marton, Kati
★ *The Chancellor: The Remarkable Odyssey of Angela Merkel.* Kati Marton. Simon & Schuster 2021. 400 p.
ISBN 9781501192623
Grades: Adult   B
1. Merkel, Angela, 1954- 2. Women prime ministers 3. World leaders 4. Political leadership 5. Politics and government 6. Leadership 7. Germany 8. Europe 9. 21st century 10. Biographies 11. Impartial writing 12. Life stories — Politics — Politicians 13. Politics and global affairs — Political figures 14. Politics and global affairs — World politics — Europe
LC 2021018287

The Chancellor is at once a riveting political biography and an intimate human story of a complete outsider—a research chemist and pastor's daughter

ESSENTIAL AND RECOMMENDED TITLES
Biography

raised in Soviet-controlled East Germany—who rose to become the unofficial leader of the West. Acclaimed biographer Kati Marton set out to pierce the mystery of how Angela Merkel achieved all this. Famously private, the Angela Merkel who emerges in the Chancellor is a role model for anyone interested in gaining and keeping power while holding onto one's moral convictions—and for anyone looking to understand how to successfully bridge huge divisions within society.

Journalist Marton (True Believer) largely succeeds in this meticulous and even-handed biography at her stated goal of creating 'A human rather than a political portrait' of German chancellor Angela Merkel.... This is a lucid and accessible introduction to 'The most powerful woman in the world.' —*Publishers Weekly*

Includes bibliographical references and index.

Hidden Power: Presidential Marriages That Shaped Our Recent History. Kati Marton. Pantheon Books 2001. 418 p. : Illustration
ISBN 9780375401060
Grades: 11 12 Adult **B**
1. Women 2. Husband and wife 3. Presidents' spouses 4. Presidents 5. Power 6. Political participation 7. Politics and government 8. United States 9. 20th century 10. Biographies 11. History writing — Presidency — 20th century — United States 12. Family and Relationships — Dating and Marriage 13. History writing — Women's history
LC BL2002008447

Drawing on private White House documents and interviews with participants and eyewitnesses, the author explores the personal dynamics and historical events that were shaped by White House marriages over the course of twelve administrations, from Edith and Woodrow Wilson to George W. and Laura Bush.

This book provides a survey of a dozen First Couples, from Edith and Woodrow Wilson to Laura and George Bush. Marton mixes some good history with a lot of pop marriage psychology to show the part that patience, tolerance, insight, determination, sex and occasionally even love have played in the pursuit and exercise of presidential power.Time.

Also published in large print format; Includes bibliographical references (p. [365]-392) and index.

Marvel, William
Lincoln's Autocrat: The Life of Edwin Stanton. William Marvel. The University of North Carolina Press 2015. 624 p.
ISBN 9781469622491
Grades: Adult **B**
1. Stanton, Edwin M. (Edwin McMasters), 1814-1869 2. Lincoln, Abraham, 1809-1865 3. Cabinet officers 4. Reconstruction (United States history) 5. United States Civil War, 1861-1865 6. Politicians 7. United States history 8. United States 9. American Civil War era (1861-1865) 10. Biographies 11. Life stories — Politics — Politicians 12. History writing — Wars and conflicts — American Civil War
LC 2014032690

Edwin M. Stanton (1814-1869), one of the nineteenth century's most impressive legal and political minds, wielded enormous influence and power as Lincoln's Secretary of War during most of the Civil War and under Johnson during the early years of Reconstruction. In the first full biography of Stanton in more than fifty years, William Marvel offers a detailed reexamination of Stanton's life, career, and legacy.

"A complex work that will appeal to Civil War scholars and general readers who want a deeper treatment of Stanton than found in Doris Kearns Goodwin's Team of Rivals." —*Library Journal*

Includes bibliographical references and index.

Marwell, David G.
Mengele: Unmasking The. David G. Marwell. W. W. Norton & Company 2020. 496 pages
ISBN 9780393609530
Grades: Adult **B**
1. Mengele, Josef, 1911-1979 2. War criminals 3. World War II 4. Physicians 5. Nazi hunters 6. Nazi fugitives 7. Death 8. Atrocities 9. Poland 10. Biographies 11. Life stories — Law and order — Criminals and law-breakers 12. History writing — Wars and conflicts — Holocaust — World War II
LC 2019033220

A gripping portrait of the infamous Nazi doctor, written by the former Justice Department official who proved his death, draws on victim interviews and visits to crime scenes to detail Mengele's university studies and brutal wartime experiments.

"With a distinctive blend of history and political intrigue, Marwell creates a thorough account of one of the most well-known war criminals in history and the efforts to bring him to justice. A worthy addition to Holocaust scholarship." —*Library Journal*

Includes bibliographical references and index.

Mason, Nick
Inside Out: A Personal History of Pink Floyd. Nick Mason; edited by Philip Dodd. Chronicle Books 2005. 359 p. : Illustration; Color
ISBN 9780811848244
Grades: Adult **B**
1. Mason, Nick 2. Rock musicians 3. Biographies 4. Arts and Entertainment — Music 5. Life stories — Arts and culture — Performing arts — Musicians and composers
LC 2005299905

Three hundred color and black-and-white photographs enliven an insider's history of the rock group, chronicling the evolution of Pink Floyd through its entire forty-year history, from its earliest origins in the 1960s to the present day.

Three hundred color and black-and-white photographs, many never before published, enliven a rich, insider's history of the seminal rock group, chronicling the evolution of Pink Floyd through its entire forty-year history, from its earliest origins in the 1960s to the present day.

Originally published: London : Weidenfeld & Nicolson, c2004.

Massie, Robert K.
Catherine the Great: Portrait of a Woman. by Robert K. Massie. Random House 2011. 544 p.
ISBN 9780679456728
Grades: 11 12 Adult **B**
1. Catherine II, Empress of Russia, 1729-1796 2. Women rulers 3. Nobility 4. Intellectual life 5. Rulers 6. Russian history 7. Leadership 8. Russia 9. 18th century 10. Romanov Dynasty (1613-1917) 11. Biographies 12. History writing — Europe — Russia 13. History writing — Women's history 14. Life stories — Politics — Royalty 15. Nonfiction that reads like fiction
LC 2011015279

Andrew Carnegie Medal for Excellence in Non-Fiction, 2012; Booklist Editors' Choice, 2011; New York Times Notable Book, 2011.

Presents a reconstruction of the eighteenth-century empress's life that covers her efforts to engage Russia in the cultural life of Europe, her creation of the Hermitage, and her numerous scandal-free romantic affairs.

"Massie delivers a fascinating account of dog-eat-dog politics in 18th-century Europe and the larger-than-life Russian empress who gave as good as she got." —*Kirkus*

Nicholas and Alexandra. Robert K. Massie. Ballantine Books 2000. 613 p. : Illustration; Map
ISBN 9780345438317
Grades: Adult **B**
1. Nicholas II, Emperor of Russia, 1868-1918 2. Alexandra, Empress, consort of Nicholas II, Emperor of Russia, 1872-1918 3. Romanov, House of 4. Royal houses 5. Rulers 6. Nobility 7. Russian history 8. Romanov Dynasty (1613-1917) 9. History writing — Europe — Russia
LC 99091507

An incisive account of the last of the Romanov dynasty details the love affair of Tsar Nicholas II and his wife, Alexandra, their family, their involvement with Rasputin, and the revolution that transformed imperial Russia.

"This book, solid with research, reads as lightly as a novel, as authoritatively as a textbook. Dialogue and lively description lend a sense of immediacy, but his notes, discreetly relegated to the back of the book, show how carefully he has avoided slipping into fiction." —*Christian Science Monitor*

This book was adapted to film in 1971, starring Michael Jayston and Janet Suzman and directed by Franklin J. Schaffner. The film won Academy Awards for Best Art Direction-Set Decoration and Best Costume Design, and was nominated for Best Actress in a Leading Role, Best Cinematography, Best Music, Original Dramatic Score and Best Picture; Includes bibliographical references (p. [589]-594) and index.

Masters, Oksana
The **Hard** *Parts: A Memoir of Courage and Triumph.* Oksana Masters. Scribner 2023. 288 p.
ISBN 9781982185503
Grades: Adult   **B**
1. Masters, Oksana 2. Women athletes 3. Olympic athletes 4. Olympic medal winners 5. Women with disabilities 6. Birth defects 7. Adoptees 8. Determination 9. Courage 10. Competition 11. North American people 12. American people 13. Eastern European people 14. Ukrainian people 15. Autobiographies and memoirs 16. Adult books for young adults 17. Life stories — Sports — Athletes 18. Life stories — Facing adversity — Medical issues — Living with disabilities 19. Sports and Competition — Olympic Sports

Alex Awards, 2024.

The United States' most decorated winter Paralympic or Olympic athlete tells how she overcame Chernobyl disaster-caused physical challenges through sheer determination and a drive to succeed to win world's best in elite rowing, biathlon, cross-country skiing and road cycling competitions.

"An inspirational, empowering chronicle of athletic strength and personal resiliency." —*Kirkus*

Matar, Hisham
The **Return**: *Fathers, Sons, and the Land in Between.* Hisham Matar. Random House 2016. 256 p.
ISBN 9780812994827
Grades: Adult   **B**
1. Matar, Hisham, 1970- 2. Authors, American 3. Missing persons 4. Kidnapping victims 5. Loss 6. Exiles 7. Political prisoners 8. Dissenters 9. Fathers and sons 10. Cairo, Egypt 11. Libya 12. Autobiographies and memoirs 13. Life stories — Politics — Political prisoners 14. Life stories — Relationships — Parent and child

LC 2015047925

New York Times Notable Book, 2016; Pulitzer Prize for Biography or Autobiography, 2017; National Book Critics Circle Award for Autobiography/Memoir finalist, 2016.

The award-winning author of Anatomy of a Disappearance describes his journey home to Libya after a 30-year absence due to his family's political exile and his father's kidnapping in Cairo, and his inextinguishable hopes that his father will be found alive.

"A beautifully written, harrowing story of a son's search for his father and how the impact of inexplicable loss can be unrelenting while the strength of family and cultural ties can ultimately sustain." —*Kirkus*

Matthews, Christopher
Bobby *Kennedy: A Raging Spirit.* Chris Matthews. Simon & Schuster 2017. 352 p.
ISBN 9781501111860
Grades: Adult   **B**
1. Kennedy, Robert Francis, 1925-1968 2. Legislators 3. Cabinet officers 4. Politicians 5. Politics and government 6. United States 7. 20th century 8. Biographies 9. Life stories — Politics — Politicians

LC Bl2017036574

A portrait of Robert F. Kennedy depicts him as a perpetual family underdog, sharing insights into his decision to join the Navy as a common sailor, his ability to connect with voters from all walks of life, and his assassination during his 1968 campaign.

"A child of that era himself, best-selling Matthews, host of MSNBCs Hardball, regards RFKS legacy through personal recollections and cogently illustrates leadership qualities Kennedy possessed that are sorely lacking in todays divisive culture." —*Booklist*

Matzen, Robert
Dutch *Girl: Audrey Hepburn and World War II.* Robert Matzen; foreword by Luca Dotti. Goodknight Books 2019. 373 p.
ISBN 9781732273535
Grades: Adult   **B**
1. Hepburn, Audrey, 1929-1993 2. Teenage girls 3. Anti-Nazi movement 4. Ballet dancers 5. Nazis 6. Nazi collaborators 7. World War II 8. German occupation, World War II 9. European history 10. Netherlands 11. Biographies 12. Life stories — Arts and culture — Performing arts — Actors and actresses 13. History writing — Wars and conflicts — World War II 14. Life stories — People in history — Witness to history

LC 2018966886

Twenty-five years after her passing, Audrey Hepburn remains the most beloved of all Hollywood stars, known as much for her role as UNICEF ambassador as for films like Roman Holiday and Breakfast at Tiffany's. Several biographies have chronicled her stardom, but none has covered her intense experiences through five years of Nazi occupation in the Netherlands. According to her son, Luca Dotti, "The war made my mother who she was."

"A meticulously detailed and researched look at the formative years of an iconic performer; for fans of Hepburn as well as anyone seeking a social history of the Dutch experience of World War II." —*Library Journal*

Includes bibliographical references and index.

Maupin, Armistead
Logical *Family: A Memoir.* Armistead Maupin. HarperCollins 2017. 400 p.
ISBN 9780062391223
Grades: Adult   **B**
1. Maupin, Armistead 2. Gay men 3. Transformations, Personal 4. Interpersonal conflict 5. Belonging 6. Families 7. Conflict in families 8. Social groups 9. Identity 10. Autobiographies and memoirs 11. Life stories — Identity — LGBTQIA+ 12. Life stories — Relationships 13. Life stories — Arts and culture — Writing — Authors

LC 2017276332

The best-selling author of the Tales of the City series chronicles his odyssey from the old South to freewheeling San Francisco, a personal journey that shaped his evolution from a curious youth to a ground-breaking writer and gay rights pioneer.

"Engaging reminiscences from an ebullient storyteller." —*Kirkus*

May, Gary
John *Tyler.* Gary May. Times Books/Henry Holt and Co. 2008. xviii, 183 p.
ISBN 9780805082388
Grades: 11 12 Adult   **B**
1. Tyler, John, 1790-1862 2. Governors 3. Legislators 4. Presidents 5. Vice-presidents 6. Politics and government 7. United States 8. Virginia 9. 19th century 10. Biographies 11. Life stories — People in history 12. Life stories — Politics 13. Life stories — Politics — Politicians

LC 2008018131

Traces the events of the tenth executive leader's presidency from his unexpected ascent after the premature death of William Henry Harrison and unpopular veto of a proposed Bank of the United States to his indirect role in promoting secession.

Traces the events of the tenth executive leader's presidency from his unexpected ascent after the premature death of William Henry Harrison and unpopular veto of a proposed Bank of the United States to his secret efforts to bring Texas into the Union and indirect role in promoting secession.

Includes bibliographical references (p. [167]-171) and index.

May, Meredith
The **Honey** *Bus: A Memoir of Loss, Courage and a Girl Saved by Bees.* Meredith May. Park Row 2019. 352 p.
ISBN 9780778307785
Grades: Adult   **B**

ESSENTIAL AND RECOMMENDED TITLES
Biography

1. May, Meredith 2. Growing up 3. Beekeeping 4. Grandfather and granddaughter 5. Family relationships 6. Bees 7. Children of divorced parents 8. Children of people with mental illnesses 9. Healing 10. Girls 11. Self-discovery in children 12. Autobiographies and memoirs 13. Life stories — Nature and outdoors 14. Nature Writing — Animal Studies 15. Life stories — Facing adversity

LC Bl2019009438

Meredith May recalls the first time a honeybee crawled on her arm. She was five years old, her parents had recently split and suddenly she found herself in the care of her grandfather, an eccentric beekeeper who made honey in a rusty old military bus in the yard. That first close encounter was at once terrifying and exhilarating for May, and in that moment she discovered that everything she needed to know about life and family was right before her eyes, in the secret world of bees.

"Journalist May mines her deeply upsetting personal history in this sharply visceral memoir." —*Booklist*

Mayes, Frances

A Year in the World: Journeys of a Passionate Traveller. Frances Mayes. Broadway Books 2006. xx, 420 p. : Map

ISBN 9780767910057

Grades: Adult **B**

1. Mayes, Frances 2. Travel writers 3. Voyages and travels 4. Travelers 5. Women travelers 6. Travel Writing — General

LC 2005050831

Celebrating the wonders, benefits, and experiences of travel, the best-selling author of Under the Tuscan Sun shares a collection of narrative essays in which she details her travels to Spain, Portugal, France, Britain, Turkey, Greece, southern Italy, and North Africa, interweaving personal insights with commentary on art, history, landscape, culture, and tradition.

"Befitting her gifts as a poet, Mayes' prose shines with evocative imagery, bringing life to every subject she encounters across her peripatetic year." —*Booklist*

Map on endpapers; Includes bibliographical references (p. [419]-420).

Mays, Willie

24: Life Stories and Lessons from the Say Hey Kid. Willie Mays and John Shea. St. Martin's Press 2020. 272 p.

ISBN 9781250230423

Grades: Adult **B**

1. Mays, Willie, 1931-2024 2. Professional baseball players 3. Personal conduct 4. Racism 5. Professional baseball 6. Baseball 7. Baseball players 8. United States 9. 20th century 10. Autobiographies and memoirs 11. Biographies 12. Life stories — Identity — Race and ethnicity 13. Life stories — Sports — Athletes 14. Sports and competition — Baseball

LC 2019058386

A man widely regarded as one the greatest all-around players in baseball history reflects on his lifetime of experience meeting challenges with positivity, integrity and triumph.

"This definitive work about a living legend is a must-buy for baseball fans." —*Publishers Weekly*

Includes index.

Mazzeo, Tilar J.

★ *Eliza Hamilton: The Extraordinary Life and Times of the Wife of Alexander Hamilton.* Tilar J. Mazzeo. Gallery Books, an imprint of Simon & Schuster, Inc. 2018. 320 p.

ISBN 9781501166303

Grades: Adult **B**

1. Hamilton, Elizabeth Schuyler, 1757-1854 2. Hamilton, Alexander, 1757-1804 3. Politicians' spouses 4. Women philanthropists 5. Women and politics 6. Sex scandals 7. Widows 8. Extramarital affairs 9. Biographies 10. Life stories — Politics 11. History writing — Early America — United States

LC 2018008245

A comprehensive biography of Eliza Hamilton, wife of founding father Alexander Hamilton, chronicles her early years in New York, her married life with Alexander and his tragic death, and her later years as a generous philanthropist.

"Mazzeo (Irenas Children) centers love and devotion in this satisfying cradle-to-grave biography, the first written about the wife of the first U.S. secretary of the treasury." —*Publishers Weekly*

Includes bibliographical references.

Irena's Children: The Extraordinary Story of the Woman Who Saved 2,500 Children from the Warsaw Ghetto. Tilar J. Mazzeo. Gallery Books 2016. 320 p.

ISBN 9781476778501

Grades: Adult **B**

1. Sendlerowa, Irena, 1910-2008 2. Righteous Gentiles in the Holocaust 3. Ghettoes, Jewish 4. Holocaust (1933-1945) 5. Jewish people 6. Rescues 7. World War II 8. Polish people 9. Children 10. German occupation, World War II 11. European history 12. Warsaw, Poland 13. Poland 14. 20th century 15. Biographies 16. History writing — Wars and conflicts — Holocaust — World War II 17. Life stories — Facing adversity — War and oppression — Holocaust

LC 2015051244

The best-selling author of the Widow Cliquot presents the story of a Holocaust rescuer to reveal the formidable risks she took to her own safety to save some 2,500 children from death and deportation in Nazi-occupied Poland during World War II.

"Mazzeo chronicles a ray of hope in desperate times in this compelling biography of a brave woman who refused to give up." —*Kirkus*

McBride, James

The Color of Water: A Black Man's Tribute to His White Mother. James McBride. Riverhead Books 1996. xiii, 228 p. : Illustration

ISBN 9781573220224

Grades: Adult **B**

1. McBride-Jordan, Ruth, 1921-2010 2. McBride, James, 1957- 3. Multiracial people 4. Interracial marriage 5. Jewish women 6. Mothers 7. African American men 8. Ethnic identity 9. Mothers and sons 10. New York City 11. Biographies 12. Family and Relationships — Families 13. Life stories — Identity — Race and ethnicity 14. Book club best bets

LC 95037243

ALA Notable Book, 1997.

A young African American man describes growing up as one of twelve children of a white mother and Black father, and discusses his mother's contributions to his life and his confusion over his own identity.

"Told with humor and clear-eyed grace, McBride's memoir is not only a terrific story, it's a subtle contribution to the current debates on race and identity. The sheer strength of spirit, pain and humor of McBride and his mother as they wrestled with different aspects of race and identity is vividly told." —*The Nation*

Kill 'Em and Leave: Searching for the Real James Brown. James McBride. Spiegel & Grau 2016. 256 pages

ISBN 9780812993509

Grades: Adult **B**

1. Brown, James, 1933-2006 2. Soul musicians 3. Soul music 4. African American musicians 5. Entertainers 6. Musicians 7. Social life and customs 8. United States 9. 20th century 10. Biographies 11. Arts and Entertainment — Music — Jazz and the Blues 12. Life stories — Arts and culture — Performing arts — Musicians and composers

LC 2015026358

Booklist Editors' Choice, 2016.

Prompted by a comment from James Brown's grandson, author James McBride decided to look into the complex life and legacy of the Godfather of Soul. With input from Brown's friends, family members, and colleagues, McBride paints a picture not just of the founder of funk but of the world that made him; musings on race, identity, influence, and the American South abound. While there are other, more traditional biographies of James Brown available, this one is unique as it adds cultural history, context, and a personal perspective.

"An unconventional and fascinating portrait of Soul Brother No. 1 and the significance of his rise and fall i n American culture." —*Kirkus*

McBrien, Richard P.

Lives of the Popes: The Pontiffs from St. Peter to Benedict XVI. Richard P. McBrien. HarperSanFrancisco 2006. 522 p, 16 p. of plates : Illustration

PUBLIC LIBRARY CORE COLLECTION: NONFICTION
Twentieth Edition

ISBN 9780060878078
Grades: Adult B
1. Papacy 2. Popes 3. Reference books — Religion 4. Spirituality and Religion — Christianity — Catholicism
LC 97021897

Arranged chronologically, a detailed look into the history of the papacy spans the centuries and includes vital information on the lives of each pontiff, major writings, controversies, and feats, both divine and immoral.

"McBrien offers plenty of historical facts and sobering, valuable judgments." —*New York Times Book Review*

Recently updated to include Benedict XVI—Cover; Includes bibliographical references (p. 491-493) and indexes.

McBrien, William
Cole Porter: A Biography. by William McBrien. Alfred A. Knopf 1998. xiii, 459 p. : Illustration
ISBN 9780394582351
Grades: Adult B
1. Porter, Cole, 1891-1964 2. Composers 3. Gay men 4. Songwriters 5. Marriage 6. Husband and wife 7. Men-women relations 8. United States 9. Biographies 10. Life stories — Arts and culture — Performing arts — Musicians and composers 11. Life stories — Identity — LGBTQIA+ 12. Arts and Entertainment — Music — Jazz and the Blues
LC 97046116

New York Times Notable Book, 1998.

Examines Porter's complex life, homosexuality, twenty-plus-year marriage, and Broadway and Hollywood successes.

"In this biography of the American songwriter, the author weaves a complex and groundbreaking portrait of Porter, interspersed with lyrics and 72 illustrations, recounting his affluent upbringing in Peru, Ind, and his emergence in the 1930s as the musical theater's reigning sophisticate. This astute biography will help to create a standard-setting portrait of Porter as a homosexual artist in a heterosexual world." —*Publishers Weekly*

Includes index.

McCabe, John
Cagney. John McCabe. Knopf 1997. xvi, 439 p. : Illustration
ISBN 9780679446071
Grades: Adult B
1. Cagney, James, 1899-1986 2. Films 3. Actors and actresses 4. United States 5. Biographies 6. Arts and Entertainment — Movies and Television 7. Life stories — Arts and culture — Performing arts — Actors and actresses
LC 97005067

New York Times Notable Book, 1998.

Draws on many hours of interviews with the film star that were not used in his autobiography to profile the quiet, private, artistic man behind Hollywood's greatest tough guy.

"The author traces Cagney's life from his poor beginnings with an alcoholic father but fiercely determined mother through his unexpected drift into vaudeville and the theater to his slow but inevitable rise to film stardom." —*Library Journal*

Includes bibliographical references (p. 425-429) and index; Filmography: P. 397-422.

McCaulley, Esau
How Far to the Promised Land: One Black Family's Story of Hope and Survival in the American South. by Esau McCaulley. Convergent Books 2023. 224 p.
ISBN 9780593241080
Grades: Adult B
1. McCaulley, Esau 2. African American families 3. African Americans 4. Poor people 5. Racism 6. Poverty 7. Psychic trauma 8. Faith 9. Communities 10. Huntsville, Alabama 11. Alabama 12. Southern states 13. Autobiographies and memoirs 14. Life stories — Identity — Race and ethnicity 15. Family and relationships — Families 16. Life stories — Relationships — Family
LC 2023011990

The New York Times contributing opinion writer and author of Reading While Black discusses his family's search for meaning in the American South and the struggles to find a path to prosperity as a Black person born into poverty.

"Theologian McCaulley recounts a hardscrabble life in the South and the rise of faith in the face of childhood trauma." —*Kirkus*

McClelland, Mac
Irritable Hearts: A PTSD Love Story. Mac McClelland. Flatiron Books 2015. 320 p.
ISBN 9781250052896
Grades: Adult B
1. McClelland, Mac 2. Post-traumatic stress disorder 3. Earthquakes 4. Haiti Earthquake, Haiti, 2010 5. Journalists 6. Men-women relations 7. United States 8. Autobiographies and memoirs 9. Biographies 10. Life stories — Facing adversity — Medical issues — Mental illness 11. Life stories — Relationships — Couples 12. Family and relationships — Dating and marriage
LC 2014034163

In 2010, human rights reporter Mac McClelland left Haiti after covering the devastation of the earthquake. Back home, she finds herself imagining vivid scenes of violence and can't sleep or stop crying. It becomes clear that she is suffering from Post Traumatic Stress Disorder, triggered by her trip and seemingly exacerbated by her experiences in the other charged places she'd reported from. The bewilderment about this sudden loss of self-control is magnified by her feelings for Nico, a French soldier she met in Haiti who despite their brief connection seems to have found a place in her confused heart. While we most often connect it to veterans, PTSD is more often caused by other manner of trauma, and can even be contagious—close proximity to those afflicted can trigger it in those around them.

McCloskey, Jim
When Truth Is All You Have: A Memoir of Faith, Justice, and Freedom for the Wrongly Convicted. Jim McCloskey with Philip Lerman; foreword by John Grisham. Doubleday 2020. 304 p.
ISBN 9780385545037
Grades: Adult B
1. McCloskey, Jim (Minister) 2. Social advocates 3. Judicial error 4. Faith (Christianity) 5. Christian church work with prisoners 6. Innocence (Law) 7. Clergy 8. Social justice 9. Life change events 10. Autobiographies and memoirs 11. Life stories — Politics — Activists and reformers 12. Society and culture — Violence and crime — Criminal justice system 13. Life stories — Religion and spirituality — Spiritual journeys 14. Society and culture — Social activism and philanthropy
LC 2019054453

The founder of the Centurion Ministries, the first American organization dedicated to freeing the wrongly imprisoned, describes his life-changing advocacy of an innocent convict and his establishment of a movement that has freed dozens of victims.

"This will be essential for collections focused on social justice, the wrongly convicted, and spiritual transformation." —*Library Journal*

McColl, Sarah
Joy Enough. Sarah McColl. Liveright Pub. Corp. 2019. 160 p.
ISBN 9781631494703
Grades: Adult B
1. McColl, Sarah 2. Mothers and daughters 3. Grief 4. Loss 5. Enjoyment 6. Death of mothers 7. Marital conflict 8. Coping 9. Autobiographies and memoirs 10. Life stories — Facing adversity — Coping with death 11. Family and relationships — Aging and death 12. Book club best bets
LC 2018026979

An editor-in-chief of Yahoo Food presents a life-affirming memoir of her experiences with dual loss, recounting how she endured the end of her marriage and her mother's cancer diagnosis by reconnecting with her childhood home and preparing elaborate, nourishing meals.

"McColl's resonant first book is resplendent with love, and the hope she finds in discovering that her unfathomable grief also carved a space for more profound joy." —*Booklist*

ESSENTIAL AND RECOMMENDED TITLES
Biography

McConaughey, Matthew
Greenlights. Matthew McConaughey. Crown 2020. 288 p.
ISBN 9780593139134
Grades: Adult **B**
1. McConaughey, Matthew, 1969- 2. Personal conduct 3. Self-fulfillment 4. Films 5. Actors and actresses 6. Autobiographies and memoirs 7. Life stories — Arts and culture — Performing arts — Actors and actresses 8. Arts and Entertainment — Movies and Television
LC 2020019330

From the Academy Award winning actor, an unconventional memoir filled with raucous stories, outlaw wisdom, and lessons learned the hard way about living with greater satisfaction.

"A conversational, pleasurable look into McConaughey's life and thought." —*Kirkus*

McCormick, Ty
Beyond the Sand and Sea: One Family's Quest for a Country to Call Home. Ty McCormick. St. Martin's Press 2021. 288 p.
ISBN 9781250240606
Grades: Adult **B**
1. Hussein, Asad, 1995- 2. Refugees 3. Somali Americans 4. Refugee camps 5. Home (Concept) 6. Immigration and emigration law 7. Families 8. Race relations 9. Immigration and emigration 10. United States 11. Kenya 12. Somalia 13. Collective biographies 14. Life stories — Facing adversity — War and oppression — Refugees 15. Life stories — Identity — Immigrants
LC 2020047433

An award-winning journalist documents the story of a writer who grew up in a Kenyan refugee camp, describing the daily hardships his family faced while waiting for more than a decade to join a sister in America.

"Foreign Affairs editor McCormick debuts with a moving and meticulously researched portrait of Asad Hussein, a Somali refugee born in the Dadaab Refugee Complex in Kenya, who won a full scholarship to Princeton." —*Publishers Weekly*

McCourt, Frank
Teacher Man: A Memoir. Frank McCourt. Scribner 2005. 258 p.
ISBN 9780743243773
Grades: Adult **B**
1. McCourt, Frank 2. High school teachers 3. Teaching 4. Self-acceptance 5. Education 6. Irish Americans 7. Social life and customs 8. New York City 9. Autobiographies and memoirs 10. Life stories — Education — Scholars and educators 11. Adult books for young adults
LC 2005054113

The author describes his coming of age as a teacher, storyteller, and writer, a personal journey during which he spent fifteen years finding his voice in the classroom, and came to terms with the undervalued importance of teaching.

"Full of gritty specifics, never preachy, often hilarious, McCourt's book thrusts you right into the hormones-and-catcalls chaos of the classroom—where learning is not just a mystery but a flat-out miracle." —*Newsweek*

'Tis: A Memoir. Frank McCourt. Scribner 1999. 367 p.
ISBN 9780684848785
Grades: 11 12 Adult **B**
1. McCourt, Frank 2. McCourt family 3. High school teachers 4. Immigrants, Irish 5. Self-acceptance 6. Irish Americans 7. Creative writing teachers 8. Authors 9. Family relationships 10. Immigration and emigration 11. New York City 12. 20th century 13. Autobiographies and memoirs 14. Biographies 15. Arts and Entertainment — Writing and Publishing 16. Life stories — Arts and culture — Writing — Authors
LC 99031280

New York Times Notable Book, 1999.

A sequel to Angela's Ashes picks up the sometimes harrowing tale of McCourt's youth as he immigrates from Ireland to America, joins the Army, goes to college, and begins building a life.

"This volume takes McCourt from his arrival in America and subsequent service in the Korean War through the mid-1980s. This memoir features a mesmerizing narrative fraught with sufferings. It triumphs by effecting a genuinely comic meditation upon human frailty, grace and possibility." —*Publishers Weekly*

Sequel to: Angela's ashes.

McCourt, Malachy
A Monk Swimming: A Memoir. Malachy McCourt. Hyperion 1998. 290 p.
ISBN 9780786863983
Grades: Adult **B**
1. McCourt, Malachy, 1931-2024 2. Irish Americans 3. Alcoholism 4. Immigrants, Irish 5. Voyages and travels 6. Divorce 7. Poverty 8. Actors and actresses 9. New York City 10. Autobiographies and memoirs 11. Biographies 12. Family and Relationships — Families 13. Life stories — General
LC 97046720

The actor-brother of Frank McCourt offers an entertaining, witty memoir of life in New York City during the freewheeling 1960s, detailing his quest for fame and fortune, family life, battle with alcoholism, and reunion with his long-estranged father.

"The memoir, which covers ground through 1963, will have readers smiling and laughing constantly." —*Publishers Weekly*

Singing My Him Song. Malachy McCourt. Harper Collins Publishers 2000. 242 p.
ISBN 9780060195939
Grades: Adult **B**
1. McCourt, Malachy, 1931-2024 2. Irish Americans 3. Alcoholism 4. Immigrants, Irish 5. Cancer 6. Politicians 7. Actors and actresses 8. Diagnosis 9. Social life and customs 10. New York (State) 11. Los Angeles, California 12. Limerick, Ireland 13. 20th century 14. Autobiographies and memoirs 15. Biographies 16. History writing — Immigration — United States 17. Family and Relationships — Families 18. Life stories — Arts and culture — Writing — Authors
LC 00059774

The author continues his life story beginning in 1963, discussing his careers in show business and politics, his battle with alcoholism, finding true love, and a cancer diagnosis.

McCubbin, Lisa
Betty Ford: First Lady, Women's Advocate, Survivor, Trailblazer. Lisa McCubbin; foreword by Susan Ford Bales. Gallery Books 2018. 336 p.
ISBN 9781501164682
Grades: Adult **B**
1. Ford, Betty, 1918-2011 2. Cancer survivors 3. Women social advocates 4. Women's rights 5. Presidents' spouses 6. United States 7. 20th century 8. Biographies 9. Life stories — Politics — Activists and reformers 10. History writing — 1970s — United States
LC 2018009239

Library Journal Best Books, 2018.

Drawing on interviews with family, friends, and colleagues, a biography of the groundbreaking, candid, and resilient First Lady discusses her marriage, her determination to speak out on controversial issues, and her founding of the Betty Ford Center.

"This timely biography of Betty Ford will introduce her to millennials and remind others of her importance in championing equal rights for women and speaking out on breast cancer, abortion, depression, and addiction at a time when women, especially a first lady, did not discuss these issues in public." —*Booklist*

McCullough, David G.
★ *John Adams.* David McCullough. Simon & Schuster 2001. 751 p, 40 p. of plates : Illustration; Color; Map
ISBN 9780684813639
Grades: 11 12 Adult **B**
1. Adams, John, 1735-1826 2. Lawyers 3. Politicians 4. Founding Fathers of the United States 5. Presidents 6. Politics and government 7. United States history 8. Massachusetts 9. Washington, D.C. 10. United States 11. 18th century 12. 19th century 13. Early America (1784-1819) 14. Biographies 15. Page to screen 16. History writing — Presidency — 18th century — United States 17. History

PUBLIC LIBRARY CORE COLLECTION: NONFICTION
Twentieth Edition

writing — Early America — United States 18. Life stories — Politics — Politicians 19. Nonfiction that reads like fiction

LC 2001027010

ALA Notable Book, 2002; Booklist Editors' Choice, 2001; Library Journal Best Books, 2001; Pulitzer Prize for Biography or Autobiography, 2002.

Chronicles the life of America's second president, including his youth, his career as a Massachusetts farmer and lawyer, his marriage to Abigail, his rivalry with Thomas Jefferson, and his influence on the birth of the United States.

"This is a wonderfully stirring biography; to read it is to feel as if you are witnessing the birth of a country firsthand." —*Booklist*

Includes bibliographical references (p. 703-726) and index.

Mornings *on Horseback*. David McCullough. Simon & Schuster 1982. 445 p, 32 p. of plates : Illustration; Portrait
ISBN 9780671447540
Grades: Adult   B
1. Roosevelt, Theodore, 1858-1919 2. Presidents 3. United States 4. Biographies 5. Life stories — Politics — Politicians

LC BL 99925995

Examines the life of Theodore Roosevelt from age ten to twenty-seven, focusing on the influence of his family relationships and experiences on his growth to manhood.

"Based on diligent and thorough research, with emphasis on family, physical ailments, and friends, and written with verve and color, this is a stimulating book that will appeal to the general reader." —*Library Journal*

Reprint. Originally published: 1981; Includes index; Bibliography: P. 413-424.

Truman. David McCullough. Simon & Schuster 1992. 1117 p. : Illustration
ISBN 9780671456542
Grades: 11 12 Adult   B
1. Truman, Harry S, 1884-1972 2. Politicians 3. Marshall Plan, 1948-1952 4. Anti-Communism 5. Presidential election, 1948 6. Presidents 7. Politics and government 8. United States history 9. United States 10. 1940s 11. 1950s 12. 20th century 13. Biographies 14. History writing — Presidency — 20th century — United States 15. History writing — Post World War II - 1959 — United States 16. Life stories — Politics — Politicians

LC 92005245

ALA Notable Book, 1993; Lionel Gelber Prize (Canada), 1992; Pulitzer Prize for Biography or Autobiography, 1993; National Book Award for Nonfiction finalist, 1992; National Book Critics Circle Award for Autobiography/Memoir finalist, 1992.

A biography of the thirty-third U.S. president explores Truman's brutal frontier childhood, his education, his dogged optimism, and his rise through the ranks of the Pendergast machine that controlled Missouri politics.

"This biography of the 33rd president not only conveys in rich detail Truman's accomplishments as a politician and statesman, but also reveals the character and personality of this constantly-surprising manas schoolboy, farmer, soldier, merchant, county judge, senator, vice president and chief executive. The book relates how Truman overcame the stigma of business failure and debt . . . and acquired a reputation for honesty, reliability and common sense." —*Publishers Weekly*

Includes bibliographical references (p. 1058-1082) and index.

★ *The **Wright** Brothers*. David McCullough. Simon & Schuster 2015. 650 p.
ISBN 9781476728742
Grades: Adult   B
1. Wright, Orville, 1871-1948 2. Wright, Wilbur, 1867-1912 3. Flight 4. Wright Flyer (Airplane) 5. Airplanes 6. Aviation history 7. Aviation 8. 20th century 9. Biographies 10. Life stories — Science, technology, and medicine — Astronauts and pilots 11. History writing — Technological innovations 12. Science Writing — Space and Flight

LC 2014046049

ALA Notable Book, 2016; Booklist Editors' Choice, 2015.

Chronicles the dramatic story-behind-the-story about the Wright brothers, sharing insights into the disadvantages that challenged their lives and their mechanical ingenuity.

"McCullough's usual warm, evocative prose makes for an absorbing narrative; he conveys both the drama of the birth of flight and the homespun genius of America's golden age of innovation." —*Publishers Weekly*

McCumber, David

Playing off *the Rail: A Pool Hustler's Journey.* David McCumber. Random House 1996. 367 p.
ISBN 9780380729234
Grades: Adult   B
1. Annigoni, Tony 2. Billiard players 3. Swindlers and swindling 4. Pool players 5. Pool (Game) 6. Sports and Competition — Games

LC 95006955

A journalist chronicles his cross-country journey with ace pool player Tony Annigoni, documenting their zany odyssey from New York to Seattle, his role as a "stakehorse," the fascinating places they visited, and the colorful characters they encountered.

McCurdy, Jennette

★ *I'm Glad My Mom Died*. Jennette McCurdy. Simon & Schuster 2022. 320 p.
ISBN 9781982185824
Grades: Adult   B
1. McCurdy, Jennette, 1992- 2. Addiction 3. Interpersonal relations 4. Eating disorders 5. Death of mothers 6. Healing 7. Emotional abuse 8. Psychotherapy 9. Self-fulfillment 10. Autobiographies and memoirs 11. Life stories — Relationships — Growing up 12. Family and relationships — Abuse 13. Life stories — Relationships — Parent and child 14. Adult books for young adults

Alex Awards, 2023.

The iCarly and Sam & Cat star, after her controlling mother dies, gets the help she needs to overcome eating disorders, addiction and unhealthy relationships—and finally decides what she really wants for the first time in her life.

"The heartbreaking story of an emotionally battered child delivered with captivating candor and grace." —*Kirkus*

McDonald, Michael

★ *What a Fool Believes*. Michael McDonald, with Paul Reiser. Dey Street Books 2024. 320 p.
ISBN 9780063357563
Grades: Adult   B
1. Rock musicians 2. Rock music 3. Insecurity 4. Drug addiction 5. Self-discovery 6. American people 7. Autobiographies and memoirs 8. Life stories — Arts and culture — Performing arts — Musicians and composers 9. Arts and Entertainment — Music — Rock

In his candid, laidback memoir, written with his friend, Emmy Award-nominated actor and comedian Paul Reiser, the Rock & Roll Hall of Famer, Grammy Award-winning and platinum-selling icon tells the story of his life and music, relaying the lessons he's learned along the way.

"McDonald's down-to-earth approach gives this rock and roll tell-all more weight than others of its kind." —*Publishers Weekly*

McDonough, James L.

William Tecumseh Sherman: In the Service of My Country : A Life. James Lee McDonough. W. W. Norton & Co. 2016. 832 p. : Illustration
ISBN 9780393241570
Grades: Adult   B
1. Sherman, William Tecumseh, 1820-1891 2. Personal conduct 3. Command of troops 4. Generals 5. Military campaigns 6. United States history 7. United States 8. American Civil War era (1861-1865) 9. Biographies 10. Life stories — Law and order — Military leaders 11. History writing — Wars and conflicts — American Civil War

LC 2016007023

A biography of the lauded general explores his involvement in the Civil War's most decisive battles, his good friendship with Ulysses S. Grant, his strained marriage, the loss of his young son and his plague of personal debts.

Includes bibliographical references and index.

ESSENTIAL AND RECOMMENDED TITLES
Biography

McDonough, Jimmy
Tammy Wynette: *Tragic Country Queen.* Jimmy McDonough. Viking 2010. 448 p.
ISBN 9780670021536
Grades: Adult **B**
1. Wynette, Tammy, 1942-1998 2. Country musicians 3. Country music 4. Women musicians 5. Women country musicians 6. United States 7. Biographies 8. Arts and Entertainment — Music — Country 9. Life stories — Arts and culture — Performing arts — Musicians and composers
LC 2009042565

A full-scale profile of the iconic country-music performer documents her small-town upbringing, struggles with addiction and high-profile divorce in a rapidly evolving Nashville."

"Mr. McDonough is crazy about Wynette but also detached enough to see her clearly, writing with obvious respect for both her life and art. You bookish types, as Mr. McDonough describes his readers, will surely want to listen to her sing on the basis of this book's recommendations. With an emphatic sense of her place in country musicat the top of the heap, casting a shadow big enough to obscure today's woefully synthetic assembly-line singershe combines a love of her overlooked and minor classics with a compelling big-picture life story. His opinions are often corroborated by the colorfully authentic voices of those who knew her well and marveled at her moxie." —*New York Times*

Includes bibliographical references and index.

McGilligan, Patrick
Funny Man: *Mel Brooks.* Patrick McGilligan. HarperCollins 2019. 832 p.
ISBN 9780062560995
Grades: Adult **B**
1. Brooks, Mel, 1926- 2. Filmmaking 3. Comedians 4. Film producers and directors 5. Films 6. Actors and actresses 7. Social life and customs 8. Obstinacy 9. United States 10. 20th century 11. Biographies 12. Arts and Entertainment — Movies and Television 13. Life stories — Arts and culture — Performing arts
LC Bl2019007786

A biography of a comic legend traces his life and career—from his childhood in Williamsburg tenements to becoming an actor, writer, and director responsible for such comedy classics as the Producers, Blazing Saddles, and Young Frankenstein.

"McGilligans exhaustive biography will be essential reading for anyone interested in Brooks or, more broadly, how Hollywood functioned during the second half of the 20th century." —*Publishers Weekly*

Oscar Micheaux: *The Great and Only : The Life of America's First Black Filmmaker.* Patrick McGilligan. HarperCollins 2007. VII, 402 p, [16] p. of plates : Illustration
ISBN 9780060731397
Grades: Adult **B**
1. Micheaux, Oscar, 1884-1951 2. African American film producers and directors 3. Race relations 4. African Americans in the performing arts 5. Independent films 6. African American authors 7. Film history and criticism 8. Social life and customs 9. United States 10. 20th century 11. Biographies 12. Arts and Entertainment — Movies and Television 13. Life stories — Arts and culture — Performing arts — Directors and producers
LC 2007060735

Traces the life and career of a pioneering director from the genre of African-American cinema, discussing his childhood in the homesteading communities of South Dakota, his direction of numerous silent and sound films at a time before Black-produced movies could be shown in white theaters, and his lesser-known influence on American Black culture.

"McGilligan's prose style may be pedestrian, but he organizes his biographical materials into a lively, readable tale." —*New York Times Book Review*

Includes bibliographical references (p. [375]-390) and index.

Young Orson: *The Years of Luck and Genius on the Path to Citizen Kane.* Patrick McGilligan. HarperCollins; 2015. 352 p.
ISBN 9780062112484
Grades: Adult **B**
1. Welles, Orson, 1915-1985 2. Film producers and directors 3. Men and success 4. Radio producers and directors 5. Theatrical producers and directors 6. Ambition 7. Biographies 8. Life stories — Arts and culture — Performing arts — Directors and producers 9. Arts and Entertainment — Movies and Television
LC 2016297780

In the history of American popular culture, there is no more dramatic story—no swifter or loftier ascent to the pinnacle of success and no more tragic downfall—than that of Orson Welles. In this magisterial biography, Patrick McGilligan brings young Orson into focus as never before. He chronicles Welles's early life growing up in Wisconsin and Illinois as the son of an alcoholic industrialist and a radical suffragist and classical musician, and the magical early years of his career, including his marriage and affairs, his influential friendships, and his artistic collaborations.

"Exhaustively researched but well-paced and stuffed with beguiling detail, this is a vivid, sympathetic portrait of Welless youthful promise and achievement, before the misfires and compromises of his later years." —*Publishers Weekly*

McGinniss, Joe
Fatal Vision. Joe McGinniss. G. P. Putnam's Sons 1983. 663 p.
ISBN 9780451165664
Grades: Adult **B**
1. MacDonald, Jeffrey R, 1943- 2. Murderers 3. Murder 4. Wife-killing 5. Child murders 6. North Carolina 7. True Crime — Domestic Crime 8. True Crime — Murder
LC 82024127

A study of a brutal multiple murder and its bizarre aftermath focuses on Jeffrey MacDonald, who was convicted, in 1979, of the murders of his pregnant wife and two small daughters nine years earlier.

Includes bibliographical references (p. [665]).

McGowan, Rose
Brave. Rose McGowan. HarperOnes 2018. 288 p.
ISBN 9780062655981
Grades: Adult **B**
1. McGowan, Rose, 1973- 2. Actors and actresses 3. Feminism 4. Sexual harassment 5. Social advocacy 6. Autobiographies and memoirs 7. Life stories — Arts and culture — Performing arts — Actors and actresses
LC Bl2017049932

The actress and award-winning director traces her childhood escape from an Italian cult and her rise in Hollywood, describing how she endured nightmarish exposure and sexualization before committing herself to feminist causes.

"Frank and bold, this memoir is a resounding wakeup call to the entertainment industry and to society as a whole." —*Publishers Weekly*

McGrath, Tim
James Monroe: *A Life.* Tim McGrath. Dutton 2020. 480 pages
ISBN 9780451477262
Grades: Adult **B**
1. Monroe, James, 1758-1831 2. Founding Fathers of the United States 3. Diplomats 4. Politicians 5. Presidents 6. Politics and government 7. United States 8. 19th century 9. 18th century 10. Biographies 11. History writing — Presidency — 19th century — United States 12. Life stories — Politics — Politicians
LC 2019056757

Describes the extraordinary life of Founding Father, statesman, diplomat and 5th president of the United States who sought to bridge divisions and sow unity despite never backing down from a fight, whether it be with Alexander Hamilton or George Washington.

"An excellent, exhaustively researched, thoughtful biography with appeal to armchair historians and academics alike." —*Library Journal*

Includes bibliographical references and index.

McKean, David
Suspected of Independence: *The Life of Thomas McKean, America's First Power Broker.* David McKean. PublicAffairs 2016. 320 p.

ISBN 9781610392211
Grades: Adult **B**
1. McKean, Thomas, 1734-1817 2. Founding Fathers of the United States 3. Politicians 4. Governors 5. American Revolution, 1775-1783 6. United States history 7. Revolutionary America (1775-1783) 8. Biographies 9. Life stories — Politics — Politicians 10. History writing — Politicians — United States

LC 2016005686

Thomas McKean was America's first political operator—a man who installed himself at the center of every major political event of his time. In an extraordinary career that spanned almost half a century, McKean represented Pennsylvania and Delaware to the Stamp Act Congress and both Continental Congresses, and was instrumental in the creation of both the Articles of Confederation and the Constitution. He was one of the first to lobby for independence from British rule, the last to sign the Declaration of Independence, and was briefly the second President of Congress while George Washington was away.

"His story has been long in coming and worth the wait. For students of the Revolutionary era, the author delivers a useful biography of a significant player in the birth pangs of the new nation." —*Kirkus*

Includes bibliographical references and index.

McKeon, Kathy

Jackie's Girl: My Life with the Kennedy Family. Kathy McKeon. Simon & Schuster 2017. 320 p.

ISBN 9781501158940
Grades: Adult **B**
1. McKeon, Kathy 2. Kennedy family 3. Onassis, Jacqueline Kennedy, 1929-1994 4. Personal assistants 5. Immigrants, Irish 6. Nannies 7. Mentors 8. Female friendship 9. Presidents' spouses 10. United States 11. 1960s 12. Autobiographies and memoirs 13. Life stories — People in history — Witness to history

LC 2017003981

A coming-of-age memoir by a young woman who was Jackie Kennedy's personal assistant and sometime nanny for 13 years describes her witness to several historical events and the lessons about life and love she learned from the beloved First Lady.

"Celebrity watchers who covet an insiders role will find McKeons frank yet benevolent memoir to be both a sobering reality check and an engaging foray into the ever-fascinating world of the Kennedy dynasty." —*Booklist*

McMurtry, Larry

Crazy Horse. Larry McMurtry. Viking 1999. 148 p.
ISBN 9780670882342
Grades: 11 12 Adult **B**
1. Crazy Horse, approximately 1842-1877 2. Oglala (North American people) 3. Warriors 4. Indigenous peoples of North America 5. Forced relocations 6. Betrayal 7. Race relations 8. United States history 9. South Dakota 10. 19th century 11. Biographies 12. History writing — Indigenous peoples — United States 13. Life stories — Politics — Politicians 14. Life stories — People in history — Indigenous peoples

LC 98026644

Strips away the tall tales of legend to reveal the essence of Crazy Horse, profiling him as a brilliant and ascetic warrior-hero whose life exemplified Native American tragedy and the end of the untamed West.

"Though essentially a loner and devoid of political ambition, Crazy Horse was a respected military tactician, equally feared and admired for the strength and the intensity of his convictions. Rather than merely attempting to sort out fact from fiction, McMurtry incorporates conjecture and legend into this philosophical portrait of both the man and the myth." —*Booklist*

A Lipper/Viking book; Includes bibliographical references (p. 143-148).

Custer. Larry McMurtry. Simon & Schuster 2012. 256 p.
ISBN 9781451626209
Grades: Adult **B**
1. Custer, George A. (George Armstrong), 1839-1876 2. Little Bighorn, Battle of the, 1876 3. Indigenous peoples of North America 4. United States Civil War, 1861-1865 5. Command of troops 6. Indigenous peoples of North America — Wars 7. Generals 8. United States history 9. United States 10. American Civil War era (1861-1865) 11. Biographies 12. History writing — Wars and conflicts — American Civil War 13. Life stories — Law and order — Military leaders

LC 2012012374

A lavishly illustrated portrait of the 19th-century cavalry commander traces his rise from an unpromising West Point graduate to a distinguished military leader, providing coverage of such topics as his complicated marriage, mythologized defeat at Little Big Horn and enduring legacy.

McNamara, Eileen

★ *Eunice: The Kennedy Who Changed the World*. Eileen McNamara. Simon & Schuster 2018. 320 p.

ISBN 9781451642261
Grades: Adult **B**
1. Shriver, Eunice Kennedy 2. Kennedy family 3. Women philanthropists 4. Philanthropists 5. Biographies 6. Life stories — Politics — Activists and reformers

LC 2017046517

Examines the life of Eunice Kennedy Shriver, covering her Stanford education, her inspirational relationship with her sister Rosemary, her advocacy on behalf of disabled citizens, and her role as founder of the Special Olympics.

"Along with providing insights into Eunices roles as wife, mother, sister, and daughter, McNamara uses her journalistic prowess to produce a complete and detailed portrait of this spirited and magnetic activist." —*Booklist*

Includes bibliographical references and index.

McPhee, Peter

Robespierre: A Revolutionary Life. Peter McPhee. Yale University Press 2012. 299 p.

ISBN 9780300118117
Grades: Adult **B**
1. Robespierre, Maximilien, 1758-1794 2. Revolutionaries 3. Politicians 4. Lawyers 5. Power 6. Politics and government 7. Ruthlessness 8. French history 9. France 10. Revolutionary France (1789-1799) 11. Biographies 12. History writing — Europe — France 13. History writing — Wars and conflicts — French Revolution 14. Life stories — Politics — Politicians

LC 2011027640

Chronicles the life and times of the French Revolutionary figure, looking at little known aspects, including his nervousness, lust for power, and role in "the Terror."

Includes bibliographical references.

McPherson, James M.

★ *Abraham Lincoln: A Presidential Life*. James M. McPherson. Oxford University Press 2009. xi, 79 p.

ISBN 9780195374520
Grades: 11 12 Adult **B**
1. Lincoln, Abraham, 1809-1865 2. Political leadership 3. Presidents 4. Politicians 5. United States 6. 19th century 7. Biographies 8. History writing — Presidency — 19th century — United States 9. History writing — Wars and conflicts — American Civil War 10. Life stories — Politics — Politicians 11. Adult books for young adults

LC 2008035623

McPherson follows Abraham Lincoln from his early frontier days to his turbulent years in the White House.

"McPherson, America's leading authority on Lincoln and his times, demonstrates his complete command of his subject in this concise but remarkably rich and perceptive biography.... This little book is bigger than its pages and should be in every library, schoolhouse, and home." —*Library Journal*

Includes bibliographical references (p. 73-77).

McRaven, William H.

Sea Stories: My Life in Special Operations. Admiral William H. McRaven, U.S. Navy Retired. Grand Central Publishing 2019. 352 p.

ISBN 9781538729748
Grades: Adult **B**

ESSENTIAL AND RECOMMENDED TITLES
Biography

1. McRaven, William H. (William Harry), 1955- 2. Admirals 3. Special operations (Military science) 4. Raids (Military science) 5. Commando troops 6. Autobiographies and memoirs 7. Life stories — Law and order — Military leaders 8. History writing — Military — Military leadership

LC 2019931174

A memoir from an accomplished military leader recounts stories of bravery and heroism from his career as a Navy SEAL and commander of America's Special Operations Forces.

"McRaven, a retired U.S. Navy admiral, follows his self-help guide, Make Your Bed, in which he shared principles for success learned during his more than 30 years as a Navy SEAL, with this collection of fascinating stories from his time as commander of the Special Operations Forces. McRavens war stories deliver remarkable insight into the life of a wartime leader." —*Publishers Weekly*

Meacham, Jon

★ *American Lion: Andrew Jackson in the White House.* Jon Meacham. Random House 2008. 512 p.

ISBN 9781400063253

Grades: Adult **B**

1. Jackson, Andrew, 1767-1845 2. Political leadership 3. Families 4. Political culture 5. Presidents 6. Generals 7. Politics and government 8. United States 9. 19th century 10. Biographies 11. History writing — Presidency — 19th century — United States 12. History writing — Antebellum America — United States 13. Life stories — Politics — Politicians 14. Adult books for young adults

LC 2008023466

Pulitzer Prize for Biography or Autobiography, 2009; New York Times Notable Book, 2008.

Chronicles the life and career of Andrew Jackson, a self-made man who went on to become a military hero and seventh president of the United States, analyzing Jackson's seminal role during a turbulent era in history.

Includes bibliographical references.

★ *And There Was Light: Abraham Lincoln and the American Struggle.* Jon Meacham. Random House 2022. 720 p.

ISBN 9780553393965

Grades: Adult **B**

1. Lincoln, Abraham, 1809-1865 2. Presidents 3. Slavery 4. Ethics 5. Values 6. United States Civil War, 1861-1865 7. Freed people 8. Race relations 9. Politics and government 10. United States history 11. United States 12. 19th century 13. Biographies 14. Life stories — Politics — Politicians 15. History writing — African American — Enslavement — United States 16. History writing — Presidency — 19th century — United States

LC 2022023164

A president who governed a divided country has much to teach us in a twenty-first-century moment of polarization and political crisis. Hated and hailed, excoriated and revered, Abraham Lincoln was at the pinnacle of American power when implacable secessionists gave no quarter in a clash of visions bound up with money, race, identity, and faith. In him we can see the possibilities of the presidency as well as its limitations.

Pulitzer winner Meacham (His Truth Is Marching On) more than justifies yet another Lincoln biography in this nuanced and captivating look at the president's 'Struggle to do right as he defined it within the political universe he and his country inhabited.'…Richly detailed and gracefully written, this is an essential reminder that 'Progress can be made by fallible and fallen presidents and peoples.' —*Publishers Weekly*

Includes bibliographical references and index.

★ *Destiny and Power: The American Odyssey of George Herbert Walker Bush.* Jon Meacham. Random House 2015. 848 p.

ISBN 9781400067657

Grades: Adult **B**

1. Bush, George, 1924-2018 2. Presidents 3. Politicians 4. Politics and government 5. United States 6. 20th century 7. Biographies 8. Impartial writing 9. History writing — Presidency — 20th century — United States 10. Life stories — Politics — Politicians 11. History writing — 1990s — United States

LC 2015016550

New York Times Notable Book, 2015.

Based on rigorous research, hours of private interviews, and extraordinary access to Bush's diaries and to his family, Destiny and Power paints a vivid and affecting portrait of the distinctive American life of a man from the Greatest Generation: His childhood in Connecticut, his heroic service in World War II, his entry into the Texas oil business, and his storied rise in politics from congressman to U.N. ambassador to head of the CIA to forty-first president of the United States.

"In Zelig-like fashion, George H. W. Bush was present at many of the most important events of the last 65-plus years, and the remarkable story of his life and times comes vividly alive in the words of this highly skilled writer." —*Booklist*

His Truth Is Marching On: John Lewis and the Power of Hope. Jon Meacham; afterword by John Lewis. Random House 2020. xii, 354 pages : Illustration

ISBN 9781984855022

Grades: Adult **B**

1. Lewis, John, 1940-2020 2. African American politicians 3. African American civil rights workers 4. Civil Rights Movement 5. African American civil rights 6. Civil rights demonstrations 7. Social movements 8. Equality 9. Social justice 10. Biographies 11. Life stories — Politics — Activists and Reformers — Civil Rights Leaders 12. History writing — African American — Civil rights — United States 13. Life stories — Identity — Race and ethnicity 14. Life stories — Politics — Politicians

LC 2020024320

John Lewis, who at age twenty-five marched in Selma, Alabama, and was beaten on the Edmund Pettus Bridge, was a visionary and a man of faith. Drawing on decades of wide-ranging interviews with Lewis, Jon Meacham writes of how this great-grandson of a slave and son of an Alabama tenant farmer was inspired by the Bible and his teachers in nonviolence, Reverend James Lawson and Martin Luther King, Jr, to put his life on the line in the service of what Abraham Lincoln called "the better angels of our nature." Integral to Lewis's commitment to bettering the nation was his faith in humanity and in God—and an unshakable belief in the power of hope.

"A well-crafted testament to a tumultuous time in American history and to one of the brave men who helped shape the world we know today." —*Library Journal*

Includes bibliographical references and index.

★ *Thomas Jefferson: The Art of Power.* Jon Meacham. Random House 2012. 448 p.

ISBN 9781400067664

Grades: Adult **B**

1. Jefferson, Thomas, 1743-1826 2. Diplomats 3. Power 4. Presidents 5. Politicians 6. Politics and government 7. Ambition 8. United States 9. Early America (1784-1819) 10. 19th century 11. Biographies 12. History writing — Presidency — 19th century — United States 13. History writing — Colonial America — United States 14. History writing — Early America — United States 15. Life stories — Politics — Politicians

LC 2012013700

Booklist Editors' Choice, 2012; New York Times Notable Book, 2012.

Presents a portrait of the third president that considers his early life, role as a Founding Father, and considerable achievements as a master politician.

Includes bibliographical references and index.

Mealer, Bryan

The Kings of Big Spring: God, Oil, and One Family's Search for the American Dream. Bryan Mealer. Flatiron Books 2018. 384 p.

ISBN 9781250058911

Grades: Adult **B**

1. Mealer, Bryan 2. Oil industry and trade 3. Rich people 4. Family fortunes 5. Drug addiction 6. Greed 7. Texas 8. 1980s 9. Biographies 10. Life stories — People in history 11. History writing — 1980s — United States 12. Life stories — Relationships — Family

LC Bl2017050135

Traces the story of the author's family, whose fortunes and prospects became subject to the Texas oil boom of the 1980s and its related glamour, corruption, drug affiliations, and risks.

"As tribute to the grit of the rural poor, as social history of dirt-and-oil Texas, and as rambunctious family saga, this work triumphs." —*Library Journal*

Means, Brittany
Hell If We Don't Change Our Ways: A Memoir. Brittany Means. Zibby Books 2023. 352 p.
ISBN 9798985282894
Grades: Adult   B
1. Means, Brittany 2. Growing up 3. Mothers and daughters 4. Voyages and travels 5. Escapes 6. Abused women 7. Partner abuse 8. Grandparents 9. Extended families 10. Dysfunctional families 11. Pentecostals 12. Faith (Christianity) 13. Psychic trauma 14. Adulthood 15. Healing 16. Resilience 17. North American people 18. American people 19. Autobiographies and memoirs 20. Life stories — Relationships — Growing up 21. Life stories — Relationships — Family 22. Life stories — Facing adversity — Abuse survivors 23. Family and Relationships — Families 24. Debut title

Brittany Means's childhood was a blur of highways and traumas that collapsed any effort to track time. Riding shotgun as her mother struggled to escape abusive relationships, Brittany didn't care where they were going—to a roadside midwestern motel, a shelter, or the Barn in Indiana, the cluttered mansion her Pentecostal grandparents called home—as long as they were together. But every so often, her mom would surprise her—and leave. As Brittany grew older and questioned her own complicated relationships, she began to recognize that hell wasn't only the place she read about in the Bible; it was the cycle of violence that entrapped her family.

"A potent reflection on emerging from a nomadic youth marked by trauma into an adulthood containing stability and tenderness." —*Kirkus*

Melvin, Leland
Chasing Space: An Astronaut's Story of Grit, Grace, and Second Chances. Leland Melvin. HarperCollins 2017. 256 p.
ISBN 9780062496720
Grades: 11 12 Adult   B
1. Melvin, Leland 2. Astronauts 3. Football players 4. African American astronauts 5. African American football players 6. Deafness 7. People who are deaf 8. Men 9. Autobiographies and memoirs 10. Life stories — Science, technology, and medicine — Astronauts and pilots 11. Life stories — Facing adversity — Medical issues — Living with disabilities 12. Adult books for young adults
LC Bl2017011674

Grand Canyon Reader Award (Arizona), Tween Nonfiction Book Category, 2019.

An uplifting memoir by the former NASA astronaut and NFL wide receiver traces his personal journey from the gridiron to the stars, examining the intersecting roles of community, perseverance and grace that create opportunities for success.

"The author makes his seemingly larger-than-life experiences relatable to readers, emphasizing how his hard work and confidence were crucial to his success." —*School Library Journal*

Merridale, Catherine
Lenin on the Train. Catherine Merridale. Metropolitan Books/Henry Holt and Company 2017. 224 p.
ISBN 9781627793018
Grades: Adult   B
1. Lenin, Vladimir Il'ich, 1870-1924 2. Exiles 3. Train rides 4. Espionage 5. Political stability 6. Revolutions 7. Revolutionaries 8. International relations 9. Soviet Union history 10. Soviet Union 11. Russia 12. Germany 13. Russian Revolution and Civil War (1917-1921) 14. History writing — Wars and conflicts — Russian Revolution
LC 2016043803

The author of Red Fortress presents a gripping, meticulously researched account of Lenin's fateful 1917 rail journey from Zurich to Petrograd, where he ignited the Russian Revolution and forever changed the world.

Published simultaneously in the UK by Allen Lane, London—Title page verso; Includes bibliographical references and index.

Merry, Robert W.
A Country of Vast Designs: James K. Polk and the Conquest of the American Continent. Robert Merry. Simon & Schuster 2009. 592 p.
ISBN 9780743297431
Grades: Adult   B
1. Polk, James K. (James Knox), 1795-1849 2. Presidents 3. Politicians 4. Politics and government 5. Territorial expansion 6. United States 7. 19th century 8. Biographies 9. History writing — Presidency — 19th century — United States 10. History writing — Antebellum America — United States 11. Life stories — Politics — Politicians
LC 2009024131

New York Times Notable Book, 2009.

Explores the one-term presidency of James K. Polk, during which the United States extended its territory across the continent by threatening England and manufacturing a controversial war with Mexico that Abraham Lincoln opposed.

"Merry's chronicle is filled with excellent insights into the critical events and fine portrayals of a cast of statesmen, warriors, and scheming rogues. [This is] an outstanding addition to American history collections." —*Booklist*

President McKinley: Architect of the American Century. Robert W. Merry. Simon & Schuster 2017. 448 p.
ISBN 9781451625448
Grades: Adult   B
1. McKinley, William, 1843-1901 2. Presidents 3. Politics and government 4. United States 5. 19th century 6. Biographies 7. History writing — Presidency — 19th century — United States 8. History writing — Gilded Age — United States 9. Life stories — Politics — Politicians
LC 2016050943

In this great American story, acclaimed historian Robert Merry resurrects the presidential reputation of William McKinley, which loses out to the brilliant and flamboyant Theodore Roosevelt who succeeded him after his assassination. He portrays McKinley as a chief executive of consequence whose low place in the presidential rankings does not reflect his enduring accomplishments and the stamp he put on the country's future role in the world.

"Critics or admirers of McKinleys presidency will agree it was a momentous one and that Merrys is a fair-minded profile of its central actor." —*Booklist*

Includes bibliographical references and index.

Merton, Thomas
The Intimate Merton: His Life from His Journals. Edited by Patrick Hart and Jonathan Montaldo. HarperSanFrancisco 1999. xvii, 374 p. : Illustration
ISBN 9780062516299
Grades: Adult   B
1. Merton, Thomas, 1915-1968 2. Personal diaries 3. Spirituality and Religion — Christianity 4. Spirituality and Religion — Christianity — Catholicism 5. Spirituality and Religion — General 6. Life stories — Religion and spirituality — Spiritual journeys
LC 99033239

Culling the beloved Trappist monk's journals for evidence of spiritual transformation, the author finds evidence aplenty, revealing Merton's passionate explorations of spirituality and the contemplative life, his relationship with Buddhism, his role in the 1960s anti-war movement, and much more.

Reveals Merton's passionate explorations of spirituality and the contemplative life, his relationship with Buddhism, and his role in the 1960s anti-war movement.

Includes index.

★ *The Seven Storey Mountain.* Thomas Merton. Harcourt Brace 1998. xxiii, 467 p.
ISBN 9780151004133
Grades: Adult   B
1. Merton, Thomas, 1915-1968 2. Faith (Christianity) 3. Authors, American 4. Christian writing 5. Faith 6. Autobiographies and memoirs 7. Spirituality and Religion — Christianity — Catholicism 8. Life stories — Religion and spirituality — Religious and spiritual leaders
LC 98198169

ESSENTIAL AND RECOMMENDED TITLES
Biography

The Seven Storey Mountain is the extraordinary spiritual testament of Thomas Merton (1915-1968), a man who experienced life to its fullest in the world before entering a Trappist monastery. By the end of his life, he had become one of the twentieth century's best known and loved Christian voices. This autobiography deals not with what happens to a man, but what happens inside his soul.

"The autobiography of a poet who became a convert to Catholicism and at the age of 26 after a full and traveled world career as student and teacher, entered a Trappist monastery." —*Publishers Weekly*

Includes index; Originally published: New York : Harcourt, Brace, 1948.

Messenger, Alex
The Twenty-ninth Day: Surviving a Grizzly Attack in the Canadian Tundra. Alex Messenger. Blackstone Publishing 2019. 272 pages

ISBN 9781982583330

Grades: Adult   **B**

1. Messenger, Alex 2. Young men 3. Animal attacks 4. Survival 5. Grizzly bear 6. Wounds and injuries 7. Canoeing 8. Wilderness survival 9. Canada 10. Autobiographies and memoirs 11. Adventure writing — Survival 12. Life stories — Facing adversity 13. Travel Writing — Canada

This true-life wilderness survival epic recounts seventeen-year-old Alex Messenger's near-lethal encounter with a grizzly bear during a canoe trip in the Canadian tundra.

Messud, Claire
Kant's Little Prussian Head and Other Reasons Why I Write: An Autobiography in Essays. Claire Messud. W. W. Norton & Company 2020. xxi, 306 p.

ISBN 9781324006756

Grades: Adult   **B**

1. Messud, Claire, 1966- 2. Authors, American 3. Family relationships 4. Influence (Literary, Artistic, etc.) 5. Art 6. Childhood 7. Families 8. Literature 9. 21st century 10. 20th century 11. Essays 12. Autobiographies and memoirs 13. Life stories — Arts and culture — Writing — Authors 14. Arts and Entertainment — Writing and Publishing

LC 2020018802

The award-winning author celebrates family, art and literature in essays that explore such subjects as her childhood relocation to Australia, her father's death in Beirut and her favorite paintings at Boston's Museum of Fine Arts.

"Powerful and inspirational: Messud is as fine a critic as she is a novelist." —*Kirkus*

Metatawabin, Edmund
Up Ghost River: A Chief's Journey Through the Turbulent Waters of Native History. Edmund Metatawabin, Alexandra Shimo. Knopf Canada 2014. 224 p.

ISBN 9780307399878

Grades: Adult   **B**

1. Metatawabin, Edmund, 1947- 2. First Nations (Canada) 3. Indigenous residential schools 4. Child abuse victims 5. Cree (Eeyou) (North American people) 6. Alcoholic men 7. Post-traumatic stress disorder 8. Indigenous authors 9. Indigenous peoples of North America 10. Ontario 11. Autobiographies and memoirs 12. Canadian literature 13. Biographies 14. Life stories — Facing adversity — Abuse survivors 15. Life stories — Facing adversity — Medical issues — Addiction

Governor General's Literary Awards, English-language Non-fiction finalist.

The autobiography of residential school survivor and former First Nations chief Edmund Metatawabin who was placed in the residential school St. Anne's in northern Ontario in the 1950's.

Metaxas, Eric
Martin Luther: The Man Who Rediscovered God and Changed the World. Eric Metaxas. Viking 2017. 416 p.

ISBN 9781101980019

Grades: Adult   **B**

1. Luther, Martin, 1483-1546 2. Reformation 3. Religious reformers 4. Lutheran Church 5. Protestantism 6. Religious leaders 7. Clergy 8. Church history 9. Germany 10. Renaissance (1300-1600) 11. 16th century 12. Biographies 13. Life stories — Religion and spirituality — Religious and spiritual leaders 14. Spirituality and Religion — Christianity — History 15. Spirituality and Religion — Religious leaders 16. History writing — Renaissance — Europe

LC 2017025388

Published to coincide with the 500th anniversary of the Reformation, a portrait of the influential religious figure shares insight into the purpose and influence of Martin Luther's famous 95 Theses while exploring his specific role in inspiring modern ideas about faith, virtue and freedom.

"A masterful portrait of a seminal figure." —*Booklist*

Includes bibliographical references and index.

Michaelis, David
Schulz and Peanuts. David Michaelis. Harper Collins 2007. 672 p.

ISBN 9780066213934

Grades: 11 12 Adult   **B**

1. Schulz, Charles M. (Charles Monroe), 1922-2000 2. Cartoonists 3. Peanuts (Comic strip) 4. Social life and customs 5. United States 6. Biographies 7. Arts and Entertainment — Comics, Cartoons, and Animation 8. Life stories — Arts and culture — Artists

LC Bl2007016508

New York Times Notable Book, 2007.

A portrait of the late creator of the "Peanuts" comic strip evaluates how his career was shaped by his midwestern working-class origins, family losses, and wartime experiences, offering insight into how familiar storylines closely reflected Schulz's private life.

"It is Mr. Michaelis's achievement in these pages that he leaves us with both a shrewd appreciation of Schulz's minimalist art and a sympathetic understanding of Schulz the man." —*New York Times*

Mikhail, Alan
God's Shadow: Sultan Selim, His Ottoman Empire, and the Making of the Modern World. Alan Mikhail. Liveright Publishing Corporation 2020. 496 p.

ISBN 9781631492396

Grades: Adult   **B**

1. Selim I, Sultan of the Turks, 1470-1520 2. Ayse Gulbahar Hatun, consort of Bayezid II, Sultan of the Turks, -1505 3. Southwest Asia and North Africa (Middle East) history 4. Turkey 5. 15th century 6. 16th century 7. Ottoman Empire (1299-1922) 8. History writing — Southwest Asia and North Africa (Middle East)

LC 2020010516

The Ottoman Empire was a hub of flourishing intellectual fervor, geopolitical power, and enlightened pluralistic rule. At the helm of its ascent was the omnipotent Sultan Selim I (1470-1520), who, with the aid of his extraordinarily gifted mother, Gülbahar, hugely expanded the empire, propelling it onto the world stage. Alan Mikhail centers Selim's Ottoman Empire and Islam as the very pivots of global history, redefining world-changing events.

"A wonderful, exciting, engaging, scholarly yet accessible work for all readers of world history, a book that addresses a critical but often overlooked axis of global history." —*Library Journal*

Includes bibliographical references and index.

Milch, David
Life's Work: A Memoir. David Milch. Random House 2022. 304 p.

ISBN 9780525510741

Grades: Adult   **B**

1. Milch, David, 1945- 2. Television writers 3. Television producers and directors 4. People with Alzheimer's disease 5. Writing 6. Drug addiction 7. Self-destructive behavior 8. Marriage 9. Parenthood 10. Sobriety 11. Autobiographies and memoirs 12. Life stories — Arts and culture — Writing 13. Life stories — Facing adversity — Medical issues — Physical illness 14. Life stories — Facing adversity — Medical issues — Addiction 15. Arts and Entertainment — Movies and Television

LC 2022004572

"I'm on a boat sailing to some island where I don't know anybody. A boat someone is operating and we aren't in touch." so begins David Milch's urgent accounting of his increasingly strange present and often painful past. From the start, Milch's life seems destined to echo that of his father, a successful if drug-addicted surgeon. Almost every achievement is accompanied by an act of self-immolation, but the deepest sadnesses also contain moments of grace. Like Milch's best screenwriting, Life's Work explores how chance encounters, self-deception, and luck shape the people we become, and how you keep living.

"A brilliant memoir from the writer who brought us Deadwood, NYPD Blue, and many other great TV shows....A master class for writers and a backstage bonanza for TV fans rolled into one unforgettable package." —*Kirkus*

Miles, Tiya
★ *Night* Flyer: Harriet Tubman and the Faith Dreams of a Free People. Tiya Miles. Penguin Press 2024. 240 p.
ISBN 9780593491164
Grades: Adult **B**
1. Tubman, Harriet, 1820?-1913 2. African American women 3. Enslaved people 4. Freedom seekers 5. Anti-slavery movements 6. African Americans 7. Interpersonal relations 8. Abolitionists 9. Women radicals 10. Underground Railroad 11. United States history 12. 19th century 13. Biographies 14. Biographies — Identity — Africans and African Americans 15. History books — African Americans — Slavery — Abolitionist movements and the Underground Railroad 16. Biographies — Politics — Activists and reformers — African American rights
LC 2023048092

Written with her characteristic tenderness and imaginative genius, a National Book Award-winning author weaves Tubman's life into the fabric of her world, probing the ecological reality of Tubman's surroundings and examining her kindship with other enslaved women, revealing a story of powerful inspiration for our own time of troubles.

"Miles chronicles and contextualizes Tubman's work to lead enslaved people to freedom in the North, spotlighting her subject's spiritual conviction and naturalistic know-how." —*Kirkus*

Includes bibliographical references and index.

Milford, Nancy
Savage Beauty: The Life of Edna St. Vincent Millay. Nancy Milford. Random House 2001. xviii, 550 p, 32 p. of plates : Illustration
ISBN 9780394575896
Grades: Adult **B**
1. Millay, Edna St. Vincent, 1892-1950 2. Bohemianism 3. Mothers and daughters 4. Sisters 5. Morphine addiction 6. Sexuality 7. Women and literature 8. Poets, American 9. Women poets 10. Social life and customs 11. Greenwich Village, New York City 12. United States 13. 20th century 14. Biographies 15. Arts and Entertainment — Writing and Publishing 16. Life stories — Arts and culture — Writing — Poets
LC 2001018598

Booklist Editors' Choice, 2001; Library Journal Best Books, 2001; New York Times Notable Book, 2001.

An authorized portrait of the Pulitzer Prize-winning poet draws on Millay's intimate diary, letters, and other papers to capture her flamboyant and turbulent life.

"In 1923, Edna St. Vincent Millay became the first woman to win the Pulitzer Prize for poetry. To write her biography, Milford . persuaded Millay's younger sister and sole heir, Norma, to give her access to hundreds of Millay's personal papers, letters, and notebooks. Selecting from this extraordinary collection, Milford meticulously integrates Millay's major poems, letters received and sent, reactions of friends, and comments from extensive interviews with Norma into an orderly and affecting narrative." —*Library Journal*

Includes bibliographical references and index.

Miller, Chanel
Know My Name: A Memoir. Chanel Miller. Viking 2019. VIII, 357 pages
ISBN 9780735223707
Grades: Adult **B**
1. Miller, Chanel 2. Injustice 3. Rape victims 4. Rape in universities and colleges 5. Crimes against women 6. Rapists 7. Sexual violence victims 8. Empowerment 9. College student rape victims 10. Courage 11. Autobiographies and memoirs 12. Society and culture — Violence and crime — Criminal justice system 13. Life stories — Facing adversity — Abuse survivors 14. True Crime — Sex Crimes
LC Bl2019028329

Library Journal Best Books, 2019; New York Times Notable Book, 2019; National Book Critics Circle Award for Autobiography, 2019; Rise: A Feminist Book Project List, 2021.

Miller (previously known as Emily Doe) reclaims her identity to tell her story of trauma, transcendence, and the power of words. She tells of her struggles with isolation and shame during the aftermath and the trial, reveals the oppression victims face in even the best-case scenarios, and illuminates a culture biased to protect perpetrators.

"A much-needed memoir giving voice to those who must be heard. Miller's writing stands apart." —*Library Journal*

Miller, Char
Gifford Pinchot and the Making of Modern Environmentalism. Char Miller. Island Press; Shearwater Books 2001. 458 p. : Illustration
ISBN 9781559638227
Grades: Adult **B**
1. Pinchot, Gifford, 1865-1946 2. Environmentalists 3. Conservation of natural resources 4. Forestry 5. Pollution control 6. Renewable energy sources 7. Politicians 8. Environmentalism 9. United States 10. 19th century 11. 20th century 12. Biographies 13. Life stories — Politics — Activists and reformers 14. Nature Writing — Environmental Issues 15. Adult books for young adults
LC 2001005665

National Outdoor Book Award for History/Biography, 2002.

Presents a biography of Gifford Pinchot, an avid outdoorsman from his youth, who became the architect of the conservation movement of the early twentieth century.

"Charismatic, progressive, and controversial, Gifford Pinchot (1865-1946) established and directed the Forest Service under Theodore Roosevelt, lobbied hard for responsible logging practices, expressed prescient warnings about pollution, and called for sustainable energy. Miller's animated biography portrays Pinchot in all his fervor, and environmentalism in all its complexity." —*Booklist*

Includes bibliographical references and index.

Miller, Jim
Examined Lives: From Socrates to Nietzsche. James Miller. Farrar, Straus and Giroux 2011. 432 p.
ISBN 9780374150853
Grades: Adult **B**
1. Philosophers 2. Philosophy 3. Intellectuals 4. Biographies 5. Life stories — Education — Philosophers
LC 2010014385

New York Times Notable Book, 2011.

An energetic introduction to the potential role of philosophy in a satisfying life shares anecdotal biographies of twelve famous philosophers including Plato, Aristotle and Kant to reveal how their views and examples can be applied to modern situations.

Includes bibliographical references and index.

Miller, Lulu
Why Fish Don't Exist: A Story of Loss, Love, and the Hidden Order of Life. Lulu Miller. Simon & Schuster 2020. 192 pages
ISBN 9781501160271
Grades: Adult **B**
1. Jordan, David Starrr, 1851-1931 2. Miller, Lulu 3. Naturalists 4. Ichthyologists 5. San Francisco Earthquake and Fire, Calif, 1906 6. Biology 7. Zoology 8. Persistence 9. College teachers 10. College presidents 11. Biological systems 12. United States 13. Biographies 14. Autobiographies and memoirs 15. Life stories — Science, technology, and medicine — Scientists and inventors 16. Life stories — Education — Scholars and educators 17. Life stories — Arts and culture — Writing — Journalists
LC Bl2020012647

The cofounder of NPR's Invisibilia tells the story of a scientist who started over after losing his life's work in the 1906 San Francisco earthquake and discusses whether he is a role model or a cautionary tale.

ESSENTIAL AND RECOMMENDED TITLES
Biography

"Part biography, part science report, and part meditation on how the chaos that caused Miller's existential misery could also bring self-acceptance and a loving wife, this unique book is an ingenious celebration of diversity and the mysterious order that underlies all existence. A quirky wonder of a book." —*Kirkus*

Miller, Marla
Betsy Ross and the Making of America. Marla R. Miller. Henry Holt 2010. 480 p.
ISBN 9780805082975
Grades: 11 12 Adult **B**
1. Ross, Elizabeth Griscom, 1752-1836 2. Patriotism 3. Women revolutionaries 4. Seamstresses 5. Artisans 6. American Revolution, 1775-1783 7. Flags 8. Revolutions 9. Revolutionaries 10. United States history 11. United States 12. Pennsylvania 13. 18th century 14. Revolutionary America (1775-1783) 15. Biographies 16. History writing — Wars and conflicts — Revolutionary War (America) 17. History writing — Women's history 18. Life stories — People in history — Witness to history 19. Adult books for young adults
LC 2009035385
Cundill Prize in Historical Literature finalist.
A comprehensively researched portrait of the iconic Revolutionary War figure draws on new sources to describe the fabled creation of the first flag while reconstructing her true life behind her seamstress legend and offering insight into the roles of period artisan families.
Includes bibliographical references.

Miller, Michelle
Belonging: A Daughter's Search for Identity Through Loss and Love. Michelle Miller. HarperCollins 2023. 320 p.
ISBN 9780063220430
Grades: Adult **B**
1. Identity 2. Mothers and daughters 3. Abandonment (Psychology) 4. Multiracial women 5. Belonging 6. Loss 7. Love 8. Autobiographies and memoirs 9. Life stories — Relationships — Parent and child 10. Family and relationships — Growing up 11. Life stories — Identity 12. Family and relationships — Families
The award-winning journalist and co-host of CBS Saturday Morning tells the candid, and deeply personal story of her mother's abandonment and how the search for answers forced her to reckon with her own identity and the secrets that shaped her family for five decades.
"Readers will be transfixed by Miller's thought-provoking queries about race and family, and inspired by her candor." —*Publishers Weekly*

Mills, Hayley
Forever Young. Hayley Mills. Grand Central Publishing 2021. 336 p.
ISBN 9781538704196
Grades: Adult **B**
1. Mills, Hayley, 1946- 2. Actors and actresses 3. Childhood 4. Acting 5. Child actors and actresses 6. Fame 7. Families 8. Growing up 9. Autobiographies and memoirs 10. Life stories — Arts and culture — Performing arts — Actors and actresses 11. Arts and Entertainment — Movies and television
Iconic actress Hayley Mills shares personal memories from her storied childhood, growing up in a famous acting family and becoming a Disney child star, trying to grow up in a world that wanted her to stay forever young.
"The iconic star of Pollyanna and the Parent Trap recalls her rise to stardom, her experiences on set, and her friendship with Walt Disney in this endearing memoir. . . . A warmhearted peek behind the curtain at youthful fame and filmmaking in the 1960s." —*Booklist*

Mills, Stephen Tukel
Chosen: A Memoir of Stolen Boyhood. Stephen Mills. Metropolitan Books 2021. 336 p.
ISBN 9781250823212
Grades: Adult **B**
1. Mills, Stephen Tukel 2. Adult child sexual abuse victims 3. Sexually abused children 4. Child sexual abuse 5. Justice 6. United States 7. Autobiographies and memoirs 8. Life stories — Facing adversity — Abuse survivors 9. True Crime — Sex Crimes 10. True Crime — Investigations and Trials
LC 2021060762
National Jewish Book Award, 2022.
At thirteen years old, Stephen Mills is chosen for special attention by the director of his Jewish summer camp, a charismatic social worker, who then grooms and molests him for two years. The boy tells no one, but the aftershocks rip through his life: Self-loathing, drugs, petty crime, and horrific nightmares, all made worse by the discovery that his abuser is moving from camp to camp, state to state, molesting countless other boys. Only physical and mental collapse bring Stephen to confront the truth of his boyhood and begin the painful path to recovery-as well as a decades-long crusade to stop a serial predator and find justice. .
"Mills (Next of Kin) lays bare in this unflinching account the irrevocable impact of the sexual abuse he suffered as a teen….This is a searing testament to human resilience." —*Publishers Weekly*

Min, Anchee
Red Azalea. Anchee Min. Anchor Books 2006. xiv, 306 p.
ISBN 9781400096985
Grades: Adult **B**
1. Min, Anchee, 1957- 2. Growing up 3. Actors and actresses 4. Women authors 5. Communism 6. Revolutions 7. Chinese history 8. China 9. Chinese Cultural Revolution (1966-1976) 10. Autobiographies and memoirs 11. History writing — Women's history 12. Life stories — People in history — Witness to history 13. Life stories — Facing adversity — War and oppression 14. Life stories — Arts and culture — Writing — Authors 15. History writing — Communist China — Asia — China
LC 2006271433
A woman who grew up in China during its Cultural Revolution describes the grueling physical labor she endured on Red Fire Farm, her forced segregation from men, her sexual relationship with her platoon leader, and her introduction to acting.
"In this memoir of growing up in China during the Cultural Revolution, sexual freedom becomes a powerful political as well as literary statement." —*New York Times Book Review*
With a new preface—Cover; Originally published in hardcover in a slightly different form in the United States by Pantheon Books … New York, in 1994—T.P. verso.

Minutaglio, Bill
The Most Dangerous Man in America: Timothy Leary, Richard Nixon & The Hunt for the Fugitive King of Lsd. Bill Minutaglio and Steven L. Davis. Twelve 2018. 400 p.
ISBN 9781455563586
Grades: Adult **B**
1. Leary, Timothy, 1920-1996 2. Fugitives 3. Escapes 4. Psychologists 5. Radicalism 6. Counterculture 7. LSD (Drug) 8. Politics and government 9. United States 10. 1960s 11. 1970s 12. Biographies 13. Life stories — Science, technology, and medicine — Healthcare professionals 14. History writing — 1960s — United States 15. History writing — 1970s — United States
LC 2017032575
Presents an account of Timothy Leary's 1970 prison escape and run from the law, detailing the events that led to his incarceration, his support by the terrorist group Weather Underground and his targeting by Richard Nixon.
"Minutaglio and Davis are superb storytellers, and throughout the narrative, they nimbly move between their two converging subjects. Their account is expertly detailed and blessedly fat-free." —*Kirkus*

Miraldi, Robert
Seymour Hersh: Scoop Artist. Robert Miraldi. Potomac Books, an Imprint of the University of Nebraska Press 2013. xvii, 415 pages
ISBN 9781612344751
Grades: Adult **B**
1. Hersh, Seymour M. 2. Journalists 3. Journalism 4. Investigative journalists 5. International relations 6. Politics and government 7. United States 8. Biographies 9. Life stories — Arts and culture — Writing — Journalists 10. Arts and Entertainment — Writing and Publishing

PUBLIC LIBRARY CORE COLLECTION: NONFICTION
Twentieth Edition

LC 2013023619

"A deep biographical treatment of the Pulitzer Prizewinning journalist who is the scourge of those in power. Hersh comes across as a good guy of limited patience when approached by fellow journalists and as a bulldog with sharp teeth when in his reporter mode." —*Kirkus*

Includes bibliographical references (pages 353-402) and index.

Mitchell, Wendy
Somebody I Used to Know: A Memoir. Wendy Mitchell. Random House 2018. 320 p.
ISBN 9781524797911
Grades: Adult   B
1. Mitchell, Wendy, 1969- 2. Nurses 3. People with dementia 4. People with Alzheimer's disease 5. Alzheimer's disease 6. Bloggers 7. Dementia 8. Memory disorders 9. Life change events 10. Women 11. Autobiographies and memoirs 12. Life stories — Facing adversity — Medical issues — Physical illness
Librarians' Choice (Australia), 2018.

A memoir by a former British National Heath Service employee and single parent describes her battles with early onset Alzheimer's, the management techniques she has developed to maintain her independence, and her efforts to make sense of her shifting world.

Originally published: London : Bloomsbury Publishing, 2018.

Mitnick, Kevin D.
Ghost in the Wires: My Adventures as the World's Most Wanted Hacker. Kevin Mitnick with William L. Simon. Little, Brown and Company 2011. 368 p.
ISBN 9780316037709
Grades: Adult   B
1. Mitnick, Kevin D. (Kevin David), 1963- 2. Hackers 3. Computer crimes 4. Computer security 5. Information superhighway 6. White collar crime 7. True Crime — General 8. Science Writing — Computing, the Internet, and Technology

LC 2010043461

Kevin Mitnick is one of the world's foremost computer hackers. He infiltrated some of the most complicated and advanced computer systems before the law finally caught up with him. Here, Mitnick chronicles his three years on the run from the FBI, during which he worked odd jobs, kept tabs on his pursuers, and continued to hack into systems throughout the world.

Includes bibliographical references and index.

Mizrahi, Isaac
I.M.: A Memoir. Isaac Mizrahi. Flatiron Books 2019. 384 pages
ISBN 9781250074089
Grades: Adult   B
1. Mizrahi, Isaac 2. Fashion designers 3. Popular culture 4. Gay men 5. Syrian Americans 6. Orthodox Jewish men 7. Insomnia 8. Depression 9. People with depression 10. Mothers and sons 11. Clothing industry and trade 12. Men-men relations 13. Autobiographies and memoirs 14. Arts and Entertainment — Fashion 15. Life stories — Arts and culture — Fashion 16. Life stories — Facing adversity 17. Adult books for young adults

LC 2018029257

A memoir by the multifaceted pop culture icon discusses his experiences as a gay youth in a Syrian Jewish Orthodox family, his education at LaGuardia High School for Performing Arts, and the making of his documentary, "Unzipped."

"There isn't a phony note in this memoir from fashion designer Mizrahi, who comes to us as he is, no holds barred, with a forthrightness that should appeal to readers of all stripes." —*Library Journal*

Mlodinow, Leonard
Stephen Hawking: A Memoir of Friendship and Physics. Leonard Mlodinow. Pantheon Books 2020. 240 pages
ISBN 9781524748685
Grades: Adult   B
1. Hawking, Stephen, 1942-2018 2. Mlodinow, Leonard, 1954- 3. Scientists 4. Physicists 5. People with disabilities 6. Friendship 7. Collaboration 8. Astrophysicists 9. Physics 10. People with amyotrophic lateral sclerosis 11. Biographies 12. Autobiographies and memoirs 13. Life stories — Science, technology, and medicine — Scientists and inventors 14. Life stories — Relationships — Friendship 15. Life stories — Facing adversity — Medical issues — Physical illness

LC 2019049362

The award-winning theoretical physicist and best-selling co-author of a Briefer History of Time presents an intimate account of his personal and professional relationship with the late Stephen Hawking throughout nearly two decades of collaborative work.

"This stirring portrait shines a well-deserved spotlight on a little-known victory in the fight for civil rights." —*Publishers Weekly*

Moby
Porcelain: A Memoir. Moby. Penguin 2016. 416 p.
ISBN 9781594206429
Grades: Adult   B
1. Moby 2. Dance music 3. Disc jockeys 4. Vegans 5. Christian men 6. Musicians 7. New York City 8. 1990s 9. Autobiographies and memoirs 10. Life stories — Arts and culture — Performing arts — Musicians and composers 11. Arts and Entertainment — Music

The DJ and musician chronicles his life and career through the New York city club scene of the late 1980s and early 1990s, where his white, Christian, vegan and teetotaling ways were a sharp contrast to the vice-fueled hedonism of the time.

Then It Fell Apart. Faber & Faber, Limited. 2019. 416 p.
ISBN 9780571339402
Grades: Adult   B
1. Moby 2. Rock musicians 3. Drug abuse 4. Fame 5. Disc jockeys 6. People with depression 7. Men 8. Self-destructive behavior 9. New York City 10. Autobiographies and memoirs 11. Life stories — Arts and culture — Performing arts — Musicians and composers 12. Life stories — Facing adversity — Medical issues — Addiction 13. Arts and Entertainment — Music

The soul-searching and humorous second volume in the memoir of the alternative musician describes how superstardom and hanging out with celebrities resulted in his taking ecstasy for breakfast and drinking bottles of vodka daily.

Mock, Janet
Surpassing Certainty: What My Twenties Taught Me. Janet Mock. Atria Books 2017. 288 pages
ISBN 9781501145797
Grades: Adult   B
1. Mock, Janet, 1983- 2. Transgender people 3. Multiracial people 4. Self-discovery 5. Women college students 6. Intimacy 7. First loves 8. Campus life 9. LGBTQIA+ people 10. African American women 11. Men-women relations 12. Courage 13. Autobiographies and memoirs 14. Life stories — Identity — LGBTQIA+ 15. Life stories — Identity — Race and ethnicity 16. Family and Relationships — LGBTQIA+ 17. Life stories — Arts and culture — Writing — Journalists 18. Adult books for young adults

The transgender activist and author of Redefining Realness presents a memoir of her search for purpose, love and self-realization in an early adulthood marked by her education at the University of Hawaii, a defining relationship and her entry into journalism.

"A defining chronicle of strength and spirit particularly remarkable for younger readers, both in transition or questioning." —*Kirkus*

Moghul, Haroon
How to Be a Muslim: An American Story. Haroon Moghul. Beacon Press 2017. 256 p.
ISBN 9780807020746
Grades: Adult   B
1. Moghul, Haroon 2. Islam 3. Identity 4. Faith (Islam) 5. Muslims 6. Muslim men 7. People with bipolar disorder 8. Men 9. Muslim Americans 10. Autobiographies and memoirs 11. Life stories — Identity 12. Spirituality and Religion — Islam

LC 2016041078

ESSENTIAL AND RECOMMENDED TITLES
Biography

A young Muslim leader shares his quest to forge a unique American Muslim identity that reflected his beliefs and personality in a post-9/11 world where he, in a society that fears Muslims, struggled with his faith and searching for intellectual forebears, as well as suffered with the onset of bipolar disorder.

"Highly recommended for its candor and relatability, this book will invite readers to fathom what it means to grasp Islam and religion and spirituality in general." —*Publishers Weekly*

Momus
Niche: A Memoir in Pastiche. Momus. Farrar, Straus and Giroux 2020. 320 p.
ISBN 9780374144081
Grades: Adult   B
1. Momus, 1960- 2. Musicians 3. Songwriters 4. Bloggers 5. Popular culture 6. Voyages and travels 7. Autobiographies and memoirs 8. Life stories — Arts and culture — Performing arts — Musicians and composers 9. Arts and Entertainment — Music
LC 2020012290

Rather than one avuncular tell-all relayed in his own voice, Momus has structured the narrative of his life as a typically atypical mockery of the rock-bio oral history. Instead of using living witnesses, Momus assumes the voices of 217 dead authors and artists and forces them to speak for and about him. From these dramatic monologues—sometimes unreliable, often comical—there gradually emerges a picture of one eccentric star's life across three continents and in his own, remarkable, niche.

"This is that rare show-biz memoir that's both entertaining and a literary triumph." —*Publishers Weekly*

Montillo, Roseanne
Fire on the Track: Betty Robinson and the Triumph of the Early Olympic Women. Roseanne Montillo. Crown 2017. 304 p.
ISBN 9781101906156
Grades: Adult   B
1. Robinson, Betty, 1911-1999 2. Women Olympic athletes 3. Women runners 4. Running 5. Sexism in sports 6. 1920s 7. Biographies 8. Life stories — Sports — Athletes 9. Sports and competition — Racing — Track and field 10. Adult books for young adults
LC 2017008783

Describes the life of the pioneering women's track star, who won gold at the 1928 Olympic Games in Amsterdam, only to nearly die in a plane crash and then miraculously rehab her way back onto the 1936 Olympic team.

"Robinson's life story and important role in breaking down barriers for women has already been optioned for film; this well-balanced biography and history of a groundbreaking female track star recalls a time and an athlete worth celebrating." —*Library Journal*

Montville, Leigh
Sting Like a Bee: Muhammad Ali vs. the United States of America, 1966-1971. Leigh Montville. Doubleday 2017. 320 p.
ISBN 9780385536059
Grades: Adult   B
1. Ali, Muhammad, 1942-2016 2. African American boxers 3. Boxers (Sports) 4. Black Muslims 5. Vietnam War, 1961-1975 6. Civil Rights Movement 7. Conscientious objectors 8. United States 9. Biographies 10. Sports and Competition — Boxing 11. Life stories — Sports — Athletes
LC 2016056528

The best-selling author of at the Altar of Speed presents an insightful portrait of the iconic heavyweight champion and activist that examines the cultural and political implications of Ali's refusal to serve in the military after converting to Islam.

Moody, Anthony David
Ezra Pound: Poet : A Portrait of the Man and His Work, 1885-1920. A. David Moody. Oxford University Press 2007. xv, 507 p.
ISBN 9780199215577
Grades: Adult   B
1. Pound, Ezra, 1885-1972 2. Poets, American 3. 20th century 4. Biographies 5. Arts and Entertainment — Writing and Publishing 6. Life stories — Arts and culture — Writing — Poets 7. Arts and Entertainment — Writing and Publishing — Literary criticism
LC 2007021413

Discusses the life of the poet, including his youthful ambition, his education in America, and his years in the London literary scene.
Includes index.

Mooney, Jonathan
Normal Sucks: How to Live, Learn, and Thrive Outside the Lines. Jonathan Mooney. Henry Holt & Company 2019. 245 p.
ISBN 9781250190161
Grades: Adult   B
1. Mooney, Jonathan 2. Children with learning disabilities 3. Normality (Psychology) 4. Teaching 5. Education 6. People with disabilities 7. Neuropsychology 8. Life stories — Facing adversity — Medical issues — Living with disabilities 9. Society and culture — Psychology and human behavior 10. Society and culture — Education
LC 2018053025

A writer diagnosed with dyslexia and ADHD as a child explores the toll the system takes on kids who are not "normal" and advocates for a revolution in the way we think about diversity, abilities and disabilities.

"In this engaging, eye-opening read, popular speaker and author Mooney (The Short Bus, 2007) shares his memories of navigating life with ADD and dyslexia, combined with his unique upbringing, and provides an invaluable history of and perspective on neurodiversity." —*Booklist*
Includes bibliographical references.

Moore, Beth
All My Knotted-up Life. Beth Moore. Tyndale House 2023. 304 p.
ISBN 9781496472670
Grades: Adult   B
1. Moore, Beth, 1957- 2. Christian women 3. Clergywomen 4. Growing up 5. Self-discovery 6. Faith (Christianity) 7. North American people 8. American people 9. Autobiographies and memoirs 10. Life stories — Religion and spirituality — Religious and spiritual leaders 11. Life stories — Religion and spirituality — Personal faith 12. Spirituality and Religion — Christianity
ECPA Christian Book Awards, Christian Book of the Year, 2024.

An incredibly thoughtful, disarmingly funny, and intensely vulnerable glimpse into the life and ministry of a woman familiar to many but known by few. All My Knotted-Up Life is a beautifully crafted portrait of resilience and survival, a poignant reminder of God's enduring faithfulness, and proof positive that if we ever truly took the time to hear people's full stories, we'd all walk around slack-jawed.

"Highly recommended for those interested in Christian studies, gender issues, and social history." —*Library Journal*

Moore, Colten
Catching the Sky. Colten Moore, Keith O'Brien. 37 Ink 2016. 256 p.
ISBN 9781501117244
Grades: Adult   B
1. Moore, Colten 2. Extreme sports 3. Snowmobiles 4. Death of brothers 5. Athletes 6. Autobiographies and memoirs 7. Life stories — Sports — Athletes 8. Sports and competition — Extreme sports 9. Sports and competition — Individual athlete
LC Bl2016000903

Family bonds and brotherly love shine in a poignant and exciting memoir as richly layered and emotionally complex as into Thin Air and Friday Night Lights when, in the wake of the devastating freestyle snowmobile accident that killed his older brother Caleb at Aspen's Winter X Games, Colten Moore returns to win gold.

"Moore's well-written memoir will enthrall fans of extreme sports, the X Games, and those trying to find their way after losing a loved one." —*Library Journal*

PUBLIC LIBRARY CORE COLLECTION: NONFICTION
Twentieth Edition

Moore, Kate

★ *The Woman They Could Not Silence: One Woman, Her Incredible Fight for Freedom, and the Men Who Tried to Make Her Disappear.* Kate Moore. Sourcebooks 2021. 496 p.

ISBN 9781492696728

Grades: Adult   B

1. Packard, E. P. W. (Elizabeth Parsons Ware), 1816-1897 2. Married women 3. Psychiatric hospitals 4. Involuntary treatment 5. Women prisoners 6. Social control 7. Patriarchy 8. Insanity (Law) 9. Mental health laws 10. Women's rights 11. Medical care reform 12. United States history 13. Illinois 14. 19th century 15. Biographies 16. Life stories — Facing adversity 17. Life stories — Politics — Activists and reformers 18. History writing — Women's history 19. Science Writing — Medicine and health — Mental health

LC 2020057492

LibraryReads Favorites, 2021.

1860: As the clash between the states rolls slowly to a boil, Elizabeth Packard, housewife and mother of six, is facing her own battle. The enemy sits across the table and sleeps in the next room. Her husband of twenty-one years is plotting against her because he feels increasingly threatened—by Elizabeth's intellect, independence, and unwillingness to stifle her own thoughts. So Theophilus makes a plan to put his wife back in her place. One summer morning, he has her committed to an insane asylum.

"A must-read for anybody interested in women's history or the history of reform in the United States. Like Radium Girls, this volume is a page-turner." —*Library Journal*

Moore, Marcus J.

The Butterfly Effect: How Kendrick Lamar Ignited the Soul of Black America. Marcus J. Moore. Atria Books 2020. 278 p.

ISBN 9781982107581

Grades: 9 10 11 12 Adult   B

1. Lamar, Kendrick, 1987- 2. Rap musicians 3. African American men 4. Fame 5. Influence (Literary, artistic, etc.) 6. Rap music 7. Songwriting 8. African American musicians 9. Celebrities 10. African Americans 11. United States 12. Biographies 13. Life stories — Arts and culture — Performing arts — Musicians and composers 14. Arts and Entertainment — Music — Rap and R&B 15. Adult books for young adults

A cultural portrait of the 13-time Grammy Award- and Pulitzer Prize-winning rap superstar documents his coming-of-age as an artist, his genius as a lyricist and his profound impact on today's racially fraught America.

"Fans will likely devour this title despite its problems, and the work has crossover appeal to young adult readers, who will be stirred by Lamar's professional and personal journey." —*Library Journal*

Includes bibliographical references.

Moore, Marianne

The Selected Letters of Marianne Moore. Marianne Moore; Bonnie Costello, general editor; Celeste Goodridge and Cristanne Miller, associate editors. Knopf 1997. xv, 597 p. : Illustration

ISBN 9780679439097

Grades: Adult   B

1. Moore, Marianne, 1887-1972 2. Poets, American 3. Women poets 4. Single women 5. 20th century 6. Letters 7. Arts and Entertainment — Writing and Publishing

LC 96052200

New York Times Notable Book, 1997.

Letters to Moore's family, friends, and fellow writers depict her views on life and poetry.

Includes index.

Moore, Thurston

Sonic Life: A Memoir. Thurston Moore. Doubleday 2023. 576 p.

ISBN 9780385548656

Grades: Adult   B

1. Moore, Thurston 2. Guitarists 3. Rock musicians 4. Music 5. Creativity 6. Rock music 7. Alternative rock music 8. Alternative rock musicians 9. Rock groups 10. American people 11. New wave music 12. North American people 13. Autobiographies and memoirs 14. Life stories — Arts and culture — Performing arts — Musicians and composers 15. Arts and Entertainment — Music — Rock

LC 2023005398

The founding member of Sonic Youth, a band that became a fixture in New York's burgeoning No Wave scene, recounts how they become commercial heavyweights, helping introduce listeners to such artists as Nirvana and Hole, and shows how the right song at the right moment can change the course of a life.

"The Sonic Youth guitarist and songwriter delivers a literate, absorbing account of life in the New York of CBGB, No Wave, and affordable spaces for artists." —*Kirkus*

Moore, Wayetu

The Dragons, the Giant, the Women: A Memoir. Wayetu Moore. Graywolf Press 2020. 272 p.

ISBN 9781644450314

Grades: Adult   B

1. Moore, Wayetu 2. Civil war 3. Refugees 4. Families 5. Race (Social sciences) 6. African people in the United States 7. African diaspora 8. War 9. Violence 10. Mothers 11. Voyages and travels 12. Women authors 13. African people in foreign countries 14. Liberia 15. United States 16. Autobiographies and memoirs 17. Life stories — Identity — Race and ethnicity 18. Life stories — Facing adversity — War and oppression — Refugees 19. Life stories — Arts and culture — Writing — Authors 20. Nonfiction that reads like fiction 21. Book club best bets

LC Bl2020013303

William Saroyan International Prize for Writing, Nonfiction category, 2022; New York Times Notable Book, 2020; National Book Critics Circle Award for Autobiography/Memoir finalist, 2020.

The author shares her experiences of escaping the First Liberian Civil War and building a life in the United States, shining the light on the great political and personal forces that continue to affect many migrants around the world.

"Readers will be both enraptured and heartbroken by Moore's intimate yet epic story of love for family and home." —*Publishers Weekly*

Moore, Wes

The Other Wes Moore: The Story of One Name and Two Fates. Wes Moore; afterword by Tavis Smiley. Spiegel & Grau 2010. 256 p.

ISBN 9780385528191

Grades: 11 12 Adult   B

1. Moore, Wes, 1978- 2. Moore, Wes, 1975- 3. Teenagers 4. Violence 5. Prisoners 6. Race relations 7. African American prisoners 8. Personal conduct 9. Teenage boys 10. African American teenagers 11. Boys 12. Father-separated children 13. Baltimore, Maryland 14. 20th century 15. Autobiographies and memoirs 16. Family and Relationships — Growing up 17. Life stories — Facing adversity — Personal transformation 18. Life stories — Law and order — Prisoners and inmates

LC 2009041663

BCALA Literary Award for Nonfiction, 2011.

Traces the parallel lives of two youths with the same name in the same community, describing how the author grew up to be a Rhodes Scholar and promising business leader while his counterpart suffered a life of violence and imprisonment.

The Work: My Search for a Life That Matters. Wes Moore. Spiegel & Grau 2014. 208 p.

ISBN 9780812993578

Grades: Adult   B

1. Moore, Wes, 1978- 2. Community activists 3. African American men 4. Purpose in life 5. Altruism 6. Veterans 7. Bankers 8. Determination 9. Autobiographies and memoirs 10. Biographies 11. Life stories — Facing adversity — Personal transformation

LC 2013038679

The delinquent-turned-Oxford scholar picks up after the events of his best-selling The Other Wes Moore to trace his search for purpose in Afghanistan,

ESSENTIAL AND RECOMMENDED TITLES
Biography

on Wall Street and in the White House, sharing inspirational stories by others who found meaning in a life in service.

"This is a beautifully philosophical look at the expectation that work should bring meaning to our lives through service to others." —*Booklist*

Moran, Caitlin
How to Be a Woman. Caitlin Moran. Harper Perennial 2012. 305 p.
ISBN 9780062124296
Grades: Adult   B
1. Moran, Caitlin, 1975- 2. Women 3. Femininity 4. Feminine beauty (Aesthetics) 5. Feminism 6. Intersectionality 7. 21st century 8. Autobiographies and memoirs 9. Life stories — Identity — Gender 10. Humor writing — Social humor 11. Society and culture — Gender — Women
LC 2012372347
British Book Award for Book of the Year, 2011.

Piecing together common-sense observations with scenes from her own life, the author sheds new light on feminism, discussing the reasons why female rights and empowerment are essential issues for both women and society itself.

"In her brilliant, original voice, Moran successfully entertains and enlightens her audience with hard-won wisdom and wit." —*Publishers Weekly*

Originally published: London : Ebury Press, 2011.

More Than a Woman. Caitlin Moran. Harper 2020. 255 p.
ISBN 9780062893710
Grades: Adult   B
1. Moran, Caitlin, 1975- 2. Women 3. Femininity 4. Feminism 5. Aging 6. Parenting 7. Sexuality 8. Marriage 9. Housekeeping 10. Body image 11. 21st century 12. Autobiographies and memoirs 13. Essays 14. Life stories — Identity — Gender 15. Society and culture — Gender — Women
LC 2020018256

As timely as it is hysterically funny, this memoir/Manifesto will have readers laughing out loud, blinking back tears, and redefining their views on feminism and the patriarchy. More Than a Woman is a brutally honest, scathingly funny, and absolutely necessary take on the life of the modern woman, and one that only Caitlin Moran can provide.

"Moran handles weighty topics with lightness and a welcoming spirit, delivering straight talk with empathy, humor, and hope." —*Booklist*

Mordden, Ethan
Ziegfeld: The Man Who Invented Show Business. Ethan Mordden. St. Martin's Press 2008. 352 p.
ISBN 9780312375430
Grades: 11 12 Adult   B
1. Ziegfeld, Florenz, 1869-1932 2. Theatrical producers and directors 3. Performing arts 4. Impresarios 5. Theater 6. Men-women relations 7. Social life and customs 8. United States 9. 19th century 10. 20th century 11. Biographies 12. Arts and Entertainment — Theater 13. Life stories — Arts and culture — Artists 14. Life stories — Business — Business leaders 15. Adult books for young adults
LC 2008028746
Booklist Editors' Choice, 2008.

An account of the life and legacy of the creator of the Follies covers such topics as his vision of the Ziegfeld Girl, development of landmark productions including Showboat, and role in the careers of numerous stars, from Marilyn Miller and Will Rogers to Eddie Cantor and Fanny Brice.

"In his witty, well-researched biography of the great producer Florenz Ziegfeld, Mordden discusses Ziegfeld's extraordinary eye for talent and transforming approach to staging musicals." —*Booklist*

Includes bibliographical references and index.

Morgan, Abi
This Is Not a Pity Memoir. Abi Morgan. Harper 2022. 352 p.
ISBN 9780358682950
Grades: Adult   B
1. Morgan, Abi 2. Women playwrights 3. Couples 4. Families 5. Sick men 6. Coma 7. Memory disorders 8. Convalescence 9. Intimacy 10. Caregivers 11. Psychic trauma 12. Loss 13. Despair 14. Love 15. Hope 16. People with cancer 17. Women 18. Great Britain 19. Autobiographies and memoirs 20. Life stories — Relationships — Couples 21. Life stories — Facing adversity — Medical issues — Physical illness 22. Family and Relationships — Illness and the Family

A moving memoir from the award-winning screenwriter and playwright Abi Morgan about what happens when the person you love most no longer recognizes you.

"In this raw and incandescent debut, screenwriter Morgan reflects on the emotional turmoil and growth of rebuilding a life with her partner after he was diagnosed with Capgras syndrome, a rare psychological illness that made him believe she was an imposter." —*Publishers Weekly*

Morgan, Robert
Boone: A Biography. by Robert Morgan. Algonquin Books of Chapel Hill 2007. 576 p.
ISBN 9781565124554
Grades: 11 12 Adult   B
1. Boone, Daniel, 1734-1820 2. Pioneers 3. Explorers 4. Frontier and pioneer life 5. Social life and customs 6. Kentucky 7. Biographies 8. History writing — Westward expansion — United States 9. Life stories — People in history — Pioneers
LC 2007014204

Often obscured by myth and folklore, Daniel Boone is as fascinating a character as any other American son. Here, Robert Morgan chronicles the life life of the frontier legend.

"This is an absorbing and stirring chronicle of the great frontiersman." —*Booklist*

Includes bibliographical references.

Morgan-Owens, Jessie
Girl in Black and White: The Story of Mary Mildred Williams and the Abolition Movement. Jessie Morgan-Owens. W.W. Norton & Company 2019. 272 p.
ISBN 9780393609240
Grades: Adult   B
1. Williams, Mary Mildred, 1847-1921 2. Enslaved children 3. Freed people 4. Photographs 5. Color of African Americans 6. Passing (Identity) 7. Slavery 8. Abolitionists 9. Anti-slavery movements 10. Racism 11. Multiracial children 12. Race relations 13. United States history 14. United States 15. 19th century 16. Biographies 17. Life stories — Facing adversity — War and oppression — Enslaved people 18. History writing — African American — Enslavement — United States 19. Life stories — Identity — Race and ethnicity
LC 2018053655

Presents the lesser-known story of slave Mary Mildred Williams, whose fair-skinned appearance rendered her the poster child of the American abolitionist movement and influenced the line where white sympathy was drawn and recognized. Illustrations.

Includes bibliographical references and index.

Morison, Samuel Eliot
John Paul Jones: A Sailor's Biography. Samuel Eliot Morison; with an introduction by James C. Bradford; charts and diagrams by Erwin Raisz. Naval Institute Press 1999. xxvi, 534 p. : Illustration; Map
ISBN 9781557504104
Grades: 11 12 Adult   B
1. Jones, John Paul, 1747-1792 2. Admirals 3. American Revolution, 1775-1783 4. Command of troops 5. Revolutions 6. Naval operations 7. United States history 8. United States 9. 18th century 10. Revolutionary America (1775-1783) 11. Biographies 12. History writing — Military — Naval history 13. Life stories — Law and order — Military leaders 14. History writing — Military — Military leadership 15. History writing — Wars and conflicts — Revolutionary War (America)
LC 00503558
Pulitzer Prize for Biography or Autobiography, 1960.

This book vividly portrays the illustrious career of John Paul Jones, from his early training at sea in the British West Indian merchant trade to his exploits in the newly independent American navy and his appointment as an admiral in the Russian navy and command of a squadron in the Black Sea.

Includes bibliographical references (p. [505]-522) and index; Originally published: Boston, MA : Little, Brown, 1959.

Morley, Paul
The Age of Bowie: How David Bowie Made a World of Difference. Paul Morley. Gallery Books 2016. 304 p.
ISBN 9781501151156
Grades: Adult   B
1. Bowie, David 1947-2016 2. Influence (Literary, artistic, etc.) 3. Music 4. Rock music 5. Rock musicians 6. Celebrities 7. Sound recordings 8. England 9. Biographies 10. Arts and Entertainment — Music — Rock 11. Life stories — Arts and culture — Performing arts — Musicians and composers

LC 2017561198

An author and cultural critic describes the greatest moments of the life of pioneering musician David Bowie and explores how he worked, played, aged, structured his ideas, influenced others, invented the future and became someone who will never be forgotten.

"There is a great deal of cultural history to enjoy in this personal, engaged and slyly scholarly biography. Morley's triumph is to know there is no such thing as the definitive story: New generations of fans will continue to make it up as they go along." —*New Statesman*

Morris, Desmond
The Lives of the Surrealists. Desmond Morris. Thames & Hudson 2018. 272 p.
ISBN 9780500021361
Grades: Adult   B
1. Modern arts 2. Arts 3. Surrealism 4. 20th century 5. Arts and Entertainment — Painting, drawing, and sculpture

LC Bl2018080005

Looks at the lives of surrealist artists, exploring their life histories, idiosyncrasies, personalities, characters, and love lives, with photographs of the artists and reproductions of their work.

Morris, Edmund
Beethoven: The Universal Composer. Edmund Morris. Atlas Books Harper Collins 2005. 243 p. : Portrait
ISBN 9780060759742
Grades: 11 12 Adult   B
1. Beethoven, Ludwig van, 1770-1827 2. Composers 3. Classical music 4. Classical musicians 5. Musicians 6. People who are deaf 7. Men 8. Biographies 9. Arts and Entertainment — Music — Classical 10. Life stories — Arts and culture — Performing arts — Musicians and composers 11. Adult books for young adults

LC 2006274925

Bashful with women and a stranger to romance, Beethoven was an abrasive, egotistical, and unsightly little man. Yet he was also a musical genius whose greatest works flowed from his deepest woes. His raging alcoholism and brooding psychosis seemed to stimulate not stifle his muse. But it wasn't until he lost the precious gift of hearing that he composed masterpieces whose grandeur and beauty tower above all others.

"The author clearly admires his subject not only for the work but also for his constant fight against the odds, and he has written an ideal biography for the general reader." —*Publishers Weekly*

Includes bibliographical references (p. 241-243).

★ *Colonel Roosevelt.* Edmund Morris. Random House 2010. 976 p.
ISBN 9780375504877
Grades: 11 12 Adult   B
1. Roosevelt, Theodore, 1858-1919 2. Progressivism (United States politics) 3. Presidents 4. Politicians 5. Politics and government 6. United States 7. 1910s 8. 20th century 9. 1920s 10. Biographies 11. History writing — Presidency — 20th century — United States 12. History writing — Early 20th century — United States 13. Life stories — Politics — Politicians

LC 2010005890

Booklist Editors' Choice, 2010; New York Times Notable Book, 2010.

Presents a chronicle of the last ten years of Theodore Roosevelt's life to cover his African safaris, return to public life, involvement with the Progressive movement, campaign for president in 1912, and various brushes with death.

Sequel to: Theodore Rex; Includes bibliographical references and index.

★ *Edison.* Edmund Morris. Random House 2019. 783 pages : Illustration
ISBN 9780812993110
Grades: Adult   B
1. Edison, Thomas A. (Thomas Alva), 1847-1931 2. Inventors 3. Determination 4. Electrical engineers 5. Workaholics 6. Biographies 7. Science writing — Great engineering feats 8. Life stories — Science, technology, and medicine — Scientists and inventors

LC 2019005173

A Pulitzer Prize-winning author presents a new biography of the prolific American inventor-genius, exploring his many roles, including botanist, naval strategist, iron miner, chemist, telegrapher and audio producer, created by virtue of his remarkable inventions.

"Writing in amusing, literate prose that's briskly paced despite a mountain of fascinating detail, Morris sets Edison's achievements against a colorful portrait of his splendid eccentricity—mostly deaf, he was given to biting phonographs and pianos to divine their acoustics—whose visionary obsessions drove his businesses near to bankruptcy. The result is an engrossing study of a larger-than-life figure who embodied a heroic age of technology." —*Publishers Weekly*

Includes bibliographical references and index.

★ *The Rise of Theodore Roosevelt.* Edmund Morris. Modern Library 2001. xxxiv, 920 p. : Illustration
ISBN 9780375756788
Grades: Adult   B
1. Roosevelt, Theodore, 1858-1919 2. Nobel Prize winners 3. Wildlife conservationists 4. Environmentalists 5. Presidents 6. Politicians 7. Politics and government 8. Governors 9. New York (State) 10. United States 11. 19th century 12. 20th century 13. 1900s (Decade) 14. Biographies 15. History writing — Presidency — 20th century — United States 16. History writing — Early 20th century — United States 17. Life stories — Politics — Politicians 18. Life stories — Politics — Activists and reformers

LC 2001030520

Pulitzer Prize for Biography or Autobiography, 1980.

Focuses on Roosevelt's pre-presidential career, covering the period between 1858 to 1901, during which time Roosevelt built himself up from a frail asthmatic youth to a robust man with varied interests.

"This first volume of a three volume study of the life and times of Theodore Roosevelt covers Roosevelt's life up to the age of 42, when an assassin's bullet elected him the youngest president in the nation's history." —*Booklist*

Sequel: Theodore Rex; Revised and updated—Cover; Includes bibliographical references and index; Originally published: New York : Coward, McCann & Geoghegan, 1979.

Morris, James McGrath
Eye on the Struggle: Ethel Payne, the First Lady of the Black Press. James McGrath Morris. Amistad 2015. 272 p.
ISBN 9780062198853
Grades: Adult   B
1. Payne, Ethel L. 2. Women journalists 3. African American women 4. Civil rights workers 5. Biographies 6. Life stories — Arts and culture — Writing — Journalists 7. History writing — African American — United States

LC 2015296496

Describes the life and career of the journalist and network news commentator who publicly asked President Eisenhower to support desegregation and covered such important civil rights events as the Montgomery Bus Boycott and the desegregation crisis in Little Rock.

"Morris straight-ahead chronicle of Paynes extraordinary front-line life reveals how invincible and incisive she was as she forthrightly combined journalism with advocacy and made the most of the box seat on history she fought so ardently and courageously to occupy." —*Booklist*

ESSENTIAL AND RECOMMENDED TITLES
Biography

Pulitzer: *A Life in Politics, Print, and Power.* James McGrath Morris. Harper 2010. 576 p.
ISBN 9780060798697
Grades: 11 12 Adult **B**
1. Pulitzer, Joseph, 1847-1911 2. Mass media 3. Newspaper publishers and publishing 4. Journalism 5. Journalistic ethics 6. Businesspeople 7. Journalists 8. Ownership 9. United States 10. Biographies 11. Arts and Entertainment — Writing and Publishing 12. History writing — Gilded Age — United States 13. Life stories — Arts and culture — Writing — Journalists
LC 2009027501
Comprehensive biography of media mogul Joseph Pulitzer.

Morris, Marc
*A **Great** and Terrible King: Edward I and the Forging of Britain.* Marc Morris. Pegasus Books 2015. 480 p.
ISBN 9781605986845
Grades: Adult **B**
1. Edward I, King of England, 1239-1307 2. Political leadership 3. Military strategy 4. Antisemitism 5. Sovereignty 6. Conquerors 7. Religious persecution 8. Rulers 9. British history 10. 13th century 11. Plantagenet period (1154-1485) 12. Biographies 13. History writing — Europe — United Kingdom 14. Life stories — Politics — Royalty
LC 2016303223
Describes the later part of the life of England's King Edward I, who travelled to the Holy Land, conquered Wales, raised one of the greatest armies of the Middle Ages, fathered 15 children and expelled the Jews from his kingdom. By the national best-selling author of the Norman Conquest.
"Highly recommended for scholars and generalists alike interested in the Middle Ages." —*Library Journal*

Morris, Mark
***Out* Loud:** *A Memoir.* Mark Morris and Wesley Stace. Penguin Books 2019. 384 p.
ISBN 9780735223073
Grades: Adult **B**
1. Morris, Mark, 1956- 2. Dancers 3. Choreographers 4. Dance companies 5. Gay men 6. Interpersonal relations 7. Dancing 8. Choreography 9. New York City 10. Autobiographies and memoirs 11. Life stories — Arts and culture — Performing arts — Dancers and choreographers 12. Arts and Entertainment — Dance
LC 2019947748
The acclaimed choreographer traces his rise from humble origins to the pinnacle of the performing-arts world, discussing his formation of the Mark Morris Dance Group and his celebrated collaborations with such artists as Mikhail Baryshnikov and Yo-Yo Ma.

Mortimer, Frank
Bee *People and the Bugs They Love.* Frank Mortimer. Citadel Press 2021. 304 p.
ISBN 9780806540832
Grades: Adult **B**
1. Mortimer, Frank 2. Beekeeping 3. Obsession 4. Beekeepers 5. Friendship 6. Bees 7. Human-animal relationships 8. New Jersey 9. Autobiographies and memoirs 10. Life stories — Nature and outdoors 11. Nature Writing — Animal Studies
A fascinating foray into the obsessions, friendships, scientific curiosity, misfortunes and rewards of suburban beekeeping -through the eyes of a Master Beekeeper.
"New or prospective beekeepers will find a useful how-to guide as well as an affectionate ode to nature's pollinators and honey makers, while any readers who have had their lives reshaped by a single overriding passion will enjoy learning how Mortimer found his." —*Publishers Weekly*
Includes bibliographical references.

Mortimer, Gavin
*The **Great** Swim.* Gavin Mortimer. Walker & Company 2008. 325 p. : Illustration; Map
ISBN 9780802715951
Grades: 11 12 Adult **B**
1. Women swimmers 2. Swimmers 3. Marathon swimming 4. Extreme sports 5. Endurance sports 6. United States history 7. 1920s 8. 1930s 9. Sports and Competition — Swimming and Diving 10. Sports and Competition — Extreme Sports 11. Adult books for young adults
LC 2008000256
Amelia Bloomer List, 2009.
Draws on primary sources, diaries, and family interviews to document the story of four American athletes who in 1926 became the first women to swim the English Channel, in an account that also cites the media frenzy that surrounded their achievement.
Includes bibliographical references (p. 291-313) and index.

Morton, Andrew
Diana: *Her True Story—in Her Own Words.* Andrew Morton. Simon & Schuster Paperbacks 1998. 448 pages, 16 unnumbered pages of plates : Illustration; Color; Portrait
ISBN 9781501169731
Grades: Adult **B**
1. Diana, Princess of Wales, 1961-1997 2. Celebrities 3. Fame 4. Princesses 5. British history 6. Great Britain 7. Biographies 8. Life stories — Politics — Royalty
LC 2017302299
An intimate portrait of the Princess of Wales describes her public and private life, reveals details about her marital problems, and discusses her attitudes toward motherhood and public service.
Includes index.

Wallis *in Love: The Untold Life of the Duchess of Windsor, the Woman Who Changed the Monarchy.* Andrew Morton. Grand Central Publishing 2018. 368 p.
ISBN 9781455566976
Grades: Adult **B**
1. Windsor, Wallis Warfield, Duchess of, 1896-1986 2. Windsor, Edward, Duke of, 1894-1972 3. Nobility 4. Marriages of royalty and nobility 5. British history 6. 1920s 7. 20th century 8. Biographies 9. Life stories — Politics — Royalty 10. History writing — Europe — United Kingdom
LC 2017034572
A portrait of the woman for whom Edward VIII infamously abdicated the British throne draws on journal entries, letters, and other previously unseen records to analyze her complex personality against the backdrop of Jazz Age London.

Morton, Brian
Tasha: *A Son's Memoir.* Brian Morton. Avid Reader Press 2022. 224 p.
ISBN 9781982178932
Grades: Adult **B**
1. Morton, Brian, 1955- 2. Mothers and sons 3. Parent and child 4. Aging 5. People with dementia 6. Jewish women 7. Teachers 8. Eccentrics and eccentricities 9. Family relationships 10. Autobiographies and memoirs 11. Life stories — Relationships — Parent and child 12. Family and relationships — Aging and death 13. Family and relationships — Families
In this surprising portrait of an unforgettable woman, her son explores the lessons he learned from his mother, presents a stark look at caring for an elderly parent and offers a meditation on the business of trying to honor ourselves without forsaking our parents.
"In his latest work, a son's loving and hard reflection on his mother, novelist Morton (Starting Out in the Evening) does his best to piece together the complex woman his mother was—from the progressive elementary school teacher, to the scatterbrained woman he remembered, to a woman in mental decline after the death of her husband….This is a charming and sad memoir." —*Kirkus*

PUBLIC LIBRARY CORE COLLECTION: NONFICTION
Twentieth Edition

Morton, Michael
Getting Life: An Innocent Man's 25-year Journey from Prison to Peace. Michael Morton. Simon & Schuster 2014. 256 p.
ISBN 9781476756820
Grades: Adult   B
1. Prisoners 2. Judicial error 3. Innocence (Law) 4. Criminal justice system 5. Forgiveness (Christianity) 6. Faith (Christianity) 7. Autobiographies and memoirs 8. Life stories — General 9. True Crime — Murder 10. Spirituality and Religion — Christianity 11. Life stories — Law and order — Prisoners and inmates

Draws on personal recollections, court transcripts and extensive journal entries to recount the author's wrongful conviction and imprisonment for the murder of his wife, sharing for the first time his views on the conviction of the actual killer and the legal malpractice charges against his prosecutor.

Moser, Benjamin
★ *Sontag:* Her Life and Work. Benjamin Moser. Ecco Press 2019. 832 p.
ISBN 9780062896391
Grades: Adult   B
1. Sontag, Susan, 1933-2004 2. Women authors 3. Women intellectuals 4. Feminists 5. Radicalism 6. Counterculture 7. Lesbians 8. Fame 9. Biographies 10. Life stories — Arts and culture — Writing — Authors 11. Arts and Entertainment — Writing and Publishing
LC 2018044760
Pulitzer Prize for Biography or Autobiography, 2020.

The author of Why This World chronicles the life story of the 20th-century activist and intellectual, sharing insights into Sontag's private life and indelible influence on modern politics, feminism and gender diversity.

"A nuanced, authoritative portrait of a legendary artist." —*Kirkus*
Includes bibliographical references and index.

Why This World: A Biography of Clarice Lispector. Benjamin Moser. Oxford University Press 2009. VIII, 479 p, 16 p of plates : Illustration
ISBN 9780195385564
Grades: Adult   B
1. Lispector, Clarice 2. Authors, Brazilian 3. Women authors 4. South American history 5. Brazil 6. 20th century 7. Biographies 8. Arts and Entertainment — Writing and Publishing 9. Life stories — Arts and culture — Writing — Authors
LC 2008055639
Booklist Editors' Choice, 2009; New York Times Notable Book, 2009; National Book Critics Circle Award for Biography finalist, 2009.

Uses previously unknown manuscripts and numerous interviews to explore the life and work of the Brazilian author.

Includes bibliographical references and index.

Moss, Jeremiah
Feral City: On Finding Liberation in Lockdown New York. Jeremiah Moss. W.W. Norton & Company 2022. 256 p.
ISBN 9780393868470
Grades: Adult   B
1. Moss, Jeremiah, 1971- 2. Cities and towns 3. Poets 4. Trans men 5. COVID-19 Pandemic, 2020- 6. Gentrification of cities 7. Income inequality 8. Marginalized people 9. Freedom 10. LGBTQIA+ people 11. Public spaces 12. Protests, demonstrations, vigils, etc. 13. Parties 14. Strangers 15. Social change 16. City life 17. New York City 18. Manhattan, New York City 19. Essays 20. Life stories — Identity — LGBTQIA+ 21. Society and culture — Illness and disease — Epidemics 22. Society and culture — Urban and regional studies 23. History writing — Regional history — United States

What happens when an entire social class abandons a metropolis? This genre-bending journey through lockdown New York offers an exhilarating, intimate look at a city returned to its rebellious spirit.

"Highly recommended, not just for queer readers or scholars of LGBTQIA+ culture but for anyone who has felt inexorably gutted and remade during the COVID pandemic." —*Library Journal*

Mouton, Deborah D. E. E. P.
Black Chameleon: Memory, Womanhood, and Myth. Deborah D.E.E.P. Mouton. Holt 2023. 272 p.
ISBN 9781250827852
Grades: Adult   B
1. Mouton, Deborah D. E. E. P. 2. African American women 3. African Americans 4. Childhood 5. Femininity 6. Growing up 7. African American poets 8. Women poets 9. Identity 10. Mythology 11. United States 12. Autobiographies and memoirs 13. Life stories — Identity — Race and ethnicity 14. Life stories — Relationships — Growing up 15. Family and relationships — Growing up 16. Family and relationships — Families
LC 2022036204

An internationally known African American poet reflects on her childhood as the daughter of a preacher and a harsh but loving mother and the challenges of living in the world as a Black woman.

"Houston's first Black poet laureate weaves mythology and magic into a genre-bending memoir….A formally inventive celebration of Black womanhood." —*Kirkus*

Mowat, Farley
Born Naked. Farley Mowat. Houghton Mifflin 1994. 256 p. : Illustration; Map
ISBN 9780395735282
Grades: 7 8 9 10   B
1. Mowat, Farley 2. Childhood 3. Families 4. Authors, Canadian 5. Canada 6. 20th century 7. Autobiographies and memoirs 8. Canadian literature 9. Biographies 10. Family and Relationships — Growing up 11. Life stories — Relationships — Growing up

The author highlights a period of his idyllic youth, revealing the mischievous, inquisitive boy whose fascination with wildlife brought him great joy and his family plenty of tolerant embarrassment.

"There are no dull pages here; every man, woman, child, and animal mentioned even casually makes an impression. Highly recommended to all those who like good writing." —*Library Journal*

Originally published: Toronto : Key Porter Books, 1993.

Moyle, Franny
Turner: The Extraordinary Life and Momentous Times of J.M.W. Turner. Franny Moyle. Penguin Group USA 2016. 400 p.
ISBN 9780735220928
Grades: Adult   B
1. Turner, J. M. W, 1775-1851 2. Landscape painters 3. Painters 4. Artists 5. Landscape painting 6. Impressionism (Art) 7. Travelers 8. Biographies 9. Life stories — Arts and culture — Artists 10. Arts and Entertainment — Painting, Drawing, and Sculpture
LC 2016043479

Chronicles the life of one of Western art's most admired, misunderstood and celebrated painters.

"This excellent biography shows the benefits, and the pitfalls, of such single-minded obsession." —*Kirkus*

Mueller, Melissa
Alice's Piano: The Life of Alice Herz-Sommer. Melissa Mueller, Reinhard Piechocki; foreword by Alice Herz-Sommer. St Martins Press 2012. 368 p.
ISBN 9781250007414
Grades: Adult   B
1. Herz-Sommer, Alice, 1903-2014 2. Women pianists 3. Holocaust survivors 4. Jewish women 5. Pianists 6. Holocaust (1933-1945) 7. Concentration camp survivors 8. Biographies 9. History writing — Wars and conflicts — Holocaust — World War II 10. Arts and Entertainment — Music — Classical 11. Life stories — Arts and culture — Performing arts — Musicians and composers

Chronicles the life of the oldest living Holocaust survivor, a classically trained pianist who used her love of music to provide hope to her fellow sufferers at the Theresienstadt concentration camp.

Muhammad, Ibtihaj
Proud: My Fight for an Unlikely American Dream. Ibtihaj Muhammad, with Lori L. Tharps. Hachette Books 2018. xiii, 270 pages : Illustration; Color
ISBN 9780316518963

ESSENTIAL AND RECOMMENDED TITLES
Biography

Grades: Adult **B**
1. Muhammad, Ibtihaj, 1985- 2. Fencers 3. Women fencers 4. African American women 5. Muslim women 6. Women Olympic athletes 7. Muslims 8. Racism 9. Sexism 10. Religious discrimination 11. Hijab (Islamic clothing) 12. Intersectionality 13. Autobiographies and memoirs 14. Life stories — Sports — Athletes 15. Sports and Competition — Olympic Sports 16. Life stories — Identity — Race and ethnicity 17. Life stories — Identity — Gender 18. Sports and Competition — Individual Athlete
LC Bl2018135206
Amelia Bloomer List, 2019.

Shares the life story of the Olympic fencer, including how she overcame feeling out of place in her sport and how she became the first American woman to compete in the Olympics wearing a hijab. As the only woman of color and the only religious minority on Team USA's saber fencing squad, Ibtihaj had to chart her own path to success and Olympic glory.

Muir, John
Nature Writings: The Story of My Boyhood and Youth, My First Summer in the Sierra, the Mountains of California, Stickeen, Selected Essays. John Muir. Library of America : 1997. 888 p. : Illustration
ISBN 9781883011246
Grades: Adult **B**
1. Muir, John, 1838-1914 2. Naturalists 3. Environmentalists 4. Natural history 5. United States 6. Autobiographies and memoirs 7. Essays 8. Nature Writing — General 9. Life stories — Relationships — Growing up 10. Life stories — Politics — Activists and reformers
LC 96009664

A collection of Muir's definitive writings is brought together in a volume that includes the Story of My Boyhood and Youth, My First Summer in the Sierra, the Mountains of California, and various other essays on his attempts to preserve the wilderness.

"This compilation of Muir's writings combines the Story of My Boyhood and Youth, My First Summer in the Sierra, the Mountains of California, Stickeen, and a number of his essays along with illustrations, a chronology of his life, and scholarly notes." —*Library Journal*
Includes index.

The Story of My Boyhood and Youth. John Muir. Sierra Club Books 1988. xii, 162 p.
ISBN 9780871567499
Grades: Adult **B**
1. Muir, John, 1838-1914 2. Naturalists 3. Wildlife conservationists 4. Environmentalists 5. Wildlife conservation 6. Biographies 7. Life stories — Nature and outdoors
LC 88023988

The American naturalist relates incidents from his boyhood in Scotland and the central Wisconsin wilderness.

Includes index; Originally published: Madison, University of Wisconsin Press, 1965.

Mullen, Bill
★ *James Baldwin: Living in Fire.* Bill V. Mullen. Pluto Press 2019. 256 p.
ISBN 9780745338545
Grades: Adult **B**
1. Baldwin, James, 1924-1987 2. Political participation 3. Authors, American 4. Gay men 5. African American authors 6. Civil rights 7. Social justice 8. LGBTQIA+ rights 9. African American gay men 10. Racism 11. Biographies 12. Arts and Entertainment — Writing and Publishing 13. Life stories — Arts and culture — Writing — Authors

In the first biography of James Baldwin in over a decade, Bill Mullen celebrates the personal and political life of the great American writer who refused to shy away from the fire. As a lifelong radical, anti-imperialist, Black queer advocate, feminist and pro-Palestinian, the life and writing of James Baldwin (1924-1987) has been an inspiration to generations and his words continue to resonate through our culture at large. Mullen explores how Baldwin's life and work channel the long history of the African-American. Fighting towards what he hoped would be a post-racial society, Baldwin's philosophy was tragically ahead of its time. As racist and reactionary forces rise across the world, this is an essential guide to the life and legacy of one of America's most important radical voices.

"A fresh, incisive, and uplifting biography/Social history." —*Kirkus*

Muller, Melissa
Anne Frank: The Biography. Melissa Muller; translated from the German by Rita and Robert Kimber. Metropolitan Books/Henry Holt and Company 2003. 458 p.
ISBN 9780805087314
Grades: 7 8 9 10 11 12 Adult **B**
1. Frank, Anne, 1929-1945 2. Jewish children 3. Jewish people 4. Girls 5. Holocaust (1933-1945) 6. Netherlands 7. Biographies 8. Translations — German to English 9. Biographies — Identity — Jewish 10. History books — Wars — Holocaust — World War II 11. Biographies — Identity — Children and teenagers 12. Biographies — People in history — Holocaust
LC 00266940

Moves beyond the girl's internationally beloved biography of life in hiding during the Holocaust to fill in the gaps—where did Anne come from, what was her relationship with her mother, and who betrayed the family to the Nazis.

Updated and expanded with new material; Includes index; Originally published in Germany in 1998 under the title DAS Madchen Anne Frank by Paul List Verlag, Munich; first published in the United States in 1998 by Metropolitan Books; second edition published in Germany in 2012 by S. Fischer Verlag, Frankfurt—Title page verso.

Mulley, Clare
The Spy Who Loved: The Secrets and Lives of Christine Granville. Clare Mulley. St. Martin's Press 2013. 432 p.
ISBN 9781250030320
Grades: Adult **B**
1. Skarbek, Krystyna, 1908-1952 2. Spies 3. Women spies 4. World War II 5. Secret service 6. Murder victims 7. Courage 8. Great Britain 9. Biographies 10. History writing — Spies and spying 11. History writing — Wars and conflicts — World War II 12. Life stories — Law and order — Spies and secret agents
LC 2013010210

Documents the story of a first British female agent in World War II, providing coverage of her mixed heritage, daring missions in numerous countries, significant intelligence contributions and subsequent murder by an obsessive colleague.

"A biography of the UK's first female secret agent. The author meticulously mined private archives, conducted personal interviews, and consulted previously published and unpublished sources in order to give the reader a balanced account of the woman behind the legend." —*Library Journal*

First published in the UK by Macmillan—Title page verso; Includes bibliographical references and index.

Munson, Richard
Tesla: Inventor of the Modern. Richard Munson. W.W. Norton & Company 2018. 320 p.
ISBN 9780393635447
Grades: Adult **B**
1. Tesla, Nikola, 1856-1943 2. Inventors 3. Electrical engineers 4. Electrical engineering 5. Serbian Americans 6. Biographies 7. Life stories — Science, technology, and medicine — Scientists and inventors 8. History writing — Science, technology, and medicine 9. History writing — Technological innovations
LC 2017055596

Describes how the formerly unappreciated scientist and inventor with the bizarre personal life and enigmatic behavior contributed so much to our modern world, including plans for cell phones, the internet, death-ray weapons and interstellar communications in the early 1900s.

"A lucid, expertly researched biography of the brilliant Nikola Tesla (1856-1943), a contemporary and competitor of Thomas Edison who was equally celebrated during his life." —*Kirkus*

Includes bibliographical references and index.

PUBLIC LIBRARY CORE COLLECTION: NONFICTION
Twentieth Edition

Murad, Nadia
★ *The Last Girl: My Story of Captivity, and My Fight Against the Islamic State.* Nadia Murad; foreword by Amal Clooney. Tim Duggan Books/Crown Publishing 2017. 320 pages
ISBN 9781524760434
Grades: Adult B
1. Murad, Nadia 2. Women refugees 3. Human trafficking 4. Survival 5. Social advocacy 6. Sexual slavery 7. Yezidis 8. Genocide 9. Human rights advocacy 10. Iraq War, 2003-2011 11. Iraq 12. Autobiographies and memoirs 13. Life stories — Facing adversity — War and oppression — Refugees 14. Life stories — Identity — Race and ethnicity 15. Politics and global affairs — Civil and human rights 16. Politics and global affairs — World politics — Southwest Asia and North Africa (Middle East)
LC 2017028775

A human rights activist and Nobel Peace Prize nominee traces the harrowing and ultimately inspiring story of her captivity by the Islamic State, describing how militants massacred the people of her Iraqi farming village, killing most of her family members and forcing her into prostitution before she escaped and became an advocate for human rights.

"Murad provides a rare glimpse into the rich culture of the Yazidi. Her memoir is powerful and heart-breaking and will inspire the world to action." —*Library Journal*

Murakami, Haruki
What I Talk About When I Talk About Running: A Memoir. by Haruki Murakami; translated from the Japanese by Philip Gabriel. Alfred A. Knopf 2008. 192 p.
ISBN 9780307269195
Grades: Adult B
1. Murakami, Haruki, 1949- 2. Authors, Japanese 3. Marathon runners 4. Marathon running 5. Distance running 6. Writing 7. Endurance sports 8. Training 9. Social life and customs 10. Japan 11. 21st century 12. Autobiographies and memoirs 13. Life stories — Arts and culture — Writing — Authors 14. Sports and Competition — Racing — Track and Field 15. Adult books for young adults
LC 2008017774

The Japanese writer recalls his four-month preparation for the 2005 New York City marathon, interweaving his reflections on the meaning of running in his life, his thoughts on the writing process and his career, and his experiences as an author and as an athlete.

Originally published in Japan ... by Bungeishunju, Ltd, Tokyo, in 2007—T.P. verso; Title is a translation of Hashiru koto ni tsuite kataru toki ni boku no kataru koto.

Murphy, Andrew R.
William Penn: A Life. Andrew R. Murphy. Oxford University Press 2019. 460 p.
ISBN 9780190234249
Grades: Adult B
1. Penn, William, 1644-1718 2. Pioneers 3. Quakers 4. Colonies 5. Colonialism 6. Religious persecution 7. Politics and government 8. United States history 9. Pennsylvania 10. Great Britain 11. Colonial America (1600-1775) 12. 17th century 13. Biographies 14. Life stories — People in history — Pioneers 15. History writing — Europe — United Kingdom 16. History writing — Colonial America — United States
LC 2018016591

The first major biography of William Penn in more than 40 years, and the first to make full use of Penn's private papers, presents a complex portrait of a man who, despite his importance, has remained an elusive figure.

"Well crafted and thoroughly researched, the writing style here is more academic than narrative. Yet, for anyone desiring comprehensive knowledge of Penn's life, this is the book to read." —*Library Journal*
Includes bibliographical references and index.

Murphy, Bruce Allen
Scalia: A Court of One. Bruce Allen Murphy. Simon & Schuster 2014. 592 p.
ISBN 9780743296496
Grades: Adult B
1. Scalia, Antonin, 1936-2016 2. Judges 3. Constitutional law 4. Law 5. Politics and government 6. United States 7. Biographies 8. Life stories — Law and order — Judges and lawyers
LC 2013042971

A deeply researched portrait of the controversial Supreme Court justice includes coverage of his impressive career achievements, his appointment in 1986 and his party-dividing resolve to support agendas from an ethical, rather than political, perspective.

"Murphy details Scalia's behind-the-scenes angling to push himself as the leading advocate for originalism and to get on the Supreme Court. But his scathing critiques set him at odds with conservatives, most notably Sandra Day O'Connor, pushing many to the center. Murphy offers a highly engaged, well-researched analysis of a brash justice whose single-mindedness may ultimately reduce his legacy." —*Booklist*
Includes bibliographical references and index.

Murray, Charles Shaar
Crosstown Traffic: Jimi Hendrix and the Post-war Rock'n'roll Revolution. Charles Shaar Murray. St. Martin's Press 1989. VIII, 247 p. : Illustration; Color
ISBN 9780312042882
Grades: 11 12 Adult B
1. Hendrix, Jimi, 1942-1970 2. African-American rock musicians 3. African American musicians 4. Rock musicians 5. United States 6. Biographies 7. Arts and Entertainment — Music — Rock 8. Life stories — Arts and culture — Performing arts — Musicians and composers
LC 89077681

Traces the history and music of Jimi Hendrix and discusses the influence and impact of one of rock music's most innovative guitarists on a generation.

"This informed, textured account will be irresistible to devotees of Hendrix and psychedelic rock as well as fans of blues, funk, jazz and rock 'N' roll." —*Booklist*
Includes bibliographical references (p. 235-238) and index; Discography: P. 218-231.

Murray, Liz
Breaking Night: My Journey from Homeless to Harvard. Liz Murray. Hyperion 2010. 352 p.
ISBN 9780786868919
Grades: 11 12 Adult B
1. Murray, Liz, 1980- 2. Children of drug abusers 3. Life change events 4. Homeless people 5. Runaway children 6. Girls 7. Determination 8. New York City 9. Autobiographies and memoirs 10. Family and Relationships — General 11. Life stories — Facing adversity — Personal transformation 12. Adult books for young adults
LC 2010013679

Alex Award, 2011.
The author offers an emotional account of her amazing journey from a 15-year-old living on the streets and eating garbage to her acceptance into Harvard, a feat that prompted a Lifetime movie and a successful motivational-speaking career.

Myers, Gary
Brady vs. Manning: The Untold Story of the Rivalry That Transformed the NFL. Gary Myers. Crown/Archetype 2015. 272 p.
ISBN 9780804139373
Grades: Adult B
1. Manning, Peyton 2. Brady, Tom, 1977- 3. Football players 4. Quarterbacks (Football) 5. Professional football 6. Sports rivalry 7. Football 8. Professional football players 9. Sports and Competition — Football
LC 2015027579

An insider's account of the contrasting characters of Tom Brady and Peyton Manning explores how their rivalry has shaped their careers and the NFL overall, sharing insights into their actual opinions about each other and the factors that shaped them as men and athletes.

ESSENTIAL AND RECOMMENDED TITLES
Biography

"Myers is a thorough professional with impeccable contacts to successfully tell this account, which will be of interest to all football fans."—*Library Journal*

Myers, Leah
Thinning Blood: A Memoir of Family, Myth, and Identity. Leah Myers. W.W. Norton & Company 2023. 176 p.
ISBN 9781324036708
Grades: Adult   B
1. Myers, Leah 2. Indigenous women 3. Indigenous peoples of North America 4. Klallam (North American people) 5. Multiracial people 6. Family history 7. Genealogy 8. Mothers and daughters 9. Totems 10. Identity 11. Culture 12. Language and languages 13. Genocide 14. Culture conflict 15. Survival 16. North American people 17. American people 18. Autobiographies and memoirs 19. Life stories — Identity — Race and ethnicity 20. Life stories — People in history — Indigenous peoples 21. Life stories — Relationships — Family 22. History writing — Indigenous peoples — United States 23. Debut title

Leah Myers may be the last member of the Jamestown S'Klallam Tribe in her family line, due to her tribe's strict blood quantum laws. Myers excavates the stories of four generations of women in order to leave a record of her family. Beginning with her great-grandmother, the last full-blooded Native member in their lineage, she connects each woman with her totem to construct her family's totem pole. As she pieces together their stories, Myers weaves in tribal folktales, the history of the Native genocide, and Native mythology. Throughout, she tells the larger story of how her "culture is being bleached out," offering sharp vignettes of her own life between White and Native worlds.

"In this searing debut, Myers—the last member of the Jamestown S'Klallam Tribe in her family line—explores what it means to be 'A Native woman at the end of a culture.'...Myers's fierce testimony is both record and reclamation of that history, told simply and beautifully." —*Publishers Weekly*

Myers, Steven Lee
The New Tsar: The Rise and Reign of Vladimir Putin. Steven Lee Myers. Alfred A. Knopf 2015. 416 p.
ISBN 9780307961617
Grades: Adult   B
1. Putin, Vladimir Vladimirovich, 1952- 2. Political leadership 3. Power 4. Presidents 5. Politics and government 6. Russia 7. Biographies 8. Impartial writing 9. History writing — Europe — Russia 10. Politics and global affairs — World politics — Europe 11. Life stories — Politics — Politicians
LC 2015010720

Tells the epic tale of the rise to power of Russia's current president—of his emergence from shrouded obscurity and deprivation to become one of the most consequential and complicated leaders in modern history.

A Borzoi book—Title page verso; Includes bibliographical references.

Nadella, Satya
Hit Refresh: The Quest to Rediscover Microsoft's Soul and Imagine a Better Future for Everyone. Satya Nadella with Greg Shaw and Jill Tracie Nichols; foreword by Bill Gates. HarperBusiness 2017. 320 p.
ISBN 9780062652508
Grades: Adult   B
1. Computer industry and trade 2. Success in business 3. Entrepreneurship 4. Leadership in business 5. Autobiographies and memoirs 6. Life stories — Science, technology, and medicine 7. Science Writing — Computing, the Internet, and Technology 8. Business and economics — Industries — Technology
LC Bl2017030064

Microsoft's CEO tells the inside story of the company's continuing transformation, tracing his own personal journey from a childhood in India to leading some of the most significant technological changes in the digital era.

Nafisi, Azar
★ *Reading Lolita in Tehran: A Memoir in Books.* Azar Nafisi. Random House 2003. 347 p.
ISBN 9780375504907
Grades: Adult   B
1. Nafisi, Azar 2. Khomeini, Ruhollah, 1902-1989 3. State-sponsored terrorism 4. Books and reading 5. English language teachers 6. Women 7. Book clubs 8. Banned books 9. Female friendship 10. Iranian revolution, 1979-1997 11. Social life and customs 12. Self-discovery 13. Deception 14. Southwest Asia and North Africa (Middle East) history 15. Iran 16. Tehran, Iran 17. Arts and Entertainment — Writing and Publishing 18. Adult books for young adults 19. History writing — Nationalism — Southwest Asia and North Africa (Middle East)
LC 2002036724

Book Sense Book of the Year Nonfiction, 2004; Library Journal Best Books, 2003.

From 1995-97 in Iran, Azar Nafisi gathered with seven of her former students, all young women, to read and discuss forbidden works of Western literature. Reserved at first, the women soon learned to speak their minds and share their repressed dreams.

"A spirited tribute both to the classics of world literature and to resistance against oppression." —*Kirkus*

The Republic of Imagination: A Portrait of America in Three Books. Azar Nafisi. Penguin Group USA. 2014. 368 p.
ISBN 9780670026067
Grades: Adult   B
1. Twain, Mark, 1835-1910 2. Lewis, Sinclair, 1885-1951 3. McCullers, Carson, 1917-1967 4. Literature and society 5. National characteristics, American 6. Fiction and culture 7. Books and reading 8. Democracy 9. Fiction writing 10. Social life and customs 11. United States 12. Autobiographies and memoirs 13. Arts and Entertainment — Writing and Publishing 14. Life stories — Education — Scholars and educators
LC 2014022287

The best-selling author of Reading Lolita in Tehran presents an impassioned tribute to the importance of fiction to democracy that blends memoir with close readings of the Adventures of Huckleberry Finn, Babbitt and the Heart Is a Lonely Hunter.

"The author's literary exegesis lightly moves through her own experiences as a student, teacher, friend and new citizen. Touching on myriad literary examples, from L.Frank Baum to James Baldwin, her work is both poignant and informative." —*Kirkus*

Things I've Been Silent About: A Memoir in Moments. Azar Nafisi. Random House 2008. 368 p.
ISBN 9781400063611
Grades: 11 12 Adult   B
1. Nafisi, Azar 2. Family relationships 3. Muslim women 4. Immigrants 5. Women 6. Growing up 7. Iran 8. Autobiographies and memoirs 9. Family and Relationships — Growing up 10. Life stories — Relationships — Growing up 11. Adult books for young adults 12. Book club best bets
LC Bl2008026872

Booklist Editors' Choice: Adult Books for Young Adults, 2009.

A memoir offers a portrait of the author's family and childhood in Iran, centered around her powerful mother and her manipulative fictions about herself, as she reflects on women's choices and her own struggle to free herself from her mother's influence.

Naifeh, Steven W.
Van Gogh: The Life. Steven Naifeh and Gregory White Smith. Random House 2011. 800 p.
ISBN 9780375507489
Grades: Adult   B
1. Gogh, Vincent van, 1853-1890 2. Painters 3. Impressionism (Art) 4. Modern art 5. Artists 6. Psychology 7. 19th century 8. Biographies 9. Life stories — Arts and culture — Artists
LC 2010053005

New York Times Notable Book, 2011.

The Pulitzer Prize-winning team presents an in-depth, accessible profile that has already been praised by Amsterdam's Van Gogh Museum as a "definitive biography," drawing on newly available primary sources to provide revisionist assessments of the influential artist's turbulent life and genius works.

PUBLIC LIBRARY CORE COLLECTION: NONFICTION
Twentieth Edition

Namath, Joe Willie
★ *All the Way: Football, Fame, and Redemption.* Joe Namath with Don Yaeger. Little, Brown and Company 2018. 320 p.
ISBN 9780316421102
Grades: Adult   B
1. Namath, Joe Willie, 1943- 2. Quarterbacks (Football) 3. Men 4. Recovering alcoholics 5. Christian life 6. Football players 7. Religious life 8. United States 9. Autobiographies and memoirs 10. Biographies 11. Sports and Competition — Football 12. Sports and Competition — Individual Athlete 13. Life stories — Sports — Athletes

LC Bl2018167851

The NFL icon who first brought show business to sports relates the story of his spectacular rise and reign as "Broadway Joe" and discusses his struggles with alcoholism and the redemption he found in God later in life.

"In time for the 50th anniversary of Namath's leading the New York Jets to a huge upset victory in the Super Bowl, here's a memoir recounting the football player's rise to stardom, glamorous social life, and post-retirement struggles with injuries and alcoholism." —*Library Journal*

Nasaw, David
Andrew Carnegie. David Nasaw. Penguin Press 2006. xiv, 878 p. : Illustration
ISBN 9781594201042
Grades: Adult   B
1. Carnegie, Andrew, 1835-1919 2. Industrialists 3. Philanthropists 4. Rich men 5. Men-women relations 6. Biographies 7. Life stories — Business — Business leaders 8. Business and economics — Business leaders and entrepreneurs

LC 2006044840

American History Book Prize, 2006; Library Journal Best Books, 2006; New York Times Notable Book, 2006; Pulitzer Prize for Biography or Autobiography finalist.

Chronicles the life of the iconic business titan from his modest upbringing in mid-1800s Scotland through his rise to one of the world's richest men, offering insight into his work as a peace advocate and his motivations for giving away most of his fortune.

"Highly readable despite it's length, Andrew Carnegie shows signs of prodigious original research on almost every page." —*New York Times*

Includes bibliographical references (p. [842]-850) and index.

The Chief: The Life of William Randolph Hearst. David Nasaw. Houghton Mifflin 2000. xv, 687 p. : Illustration
ISBN 9780395827598
Grades: Adult   B
1. Hearst, William Randolph, 1863-1951 2. Davies, Marion, 1897-1961 3. Hearst, Millicent Willson 4. Publishers and publishing 5. Newspaper publishers and publishing 6. Marriage 7. Businesspeople 8. Men-women relations 9. New York City history 10. United States history 11. San Francisco, California 12. 19th century 13. 20th century 14. Biographies 15. Business and economics — Business leaders and entrepreneurs 16. History writing — Gilded Age — United States 17. Life stories — Business — Business leaders

LC 99462122

J. Anthony Lukas Book Prize, 2001; Library Journal Best Books, 2000; New York Times Notable Book, 2000; National Book Critics Circle Award for Biography finalist, 2000.

Celebrates the life and work of the powerful newspaper publisher, and includes information on his relations with Hitler, Mussolini, Churchill, and Roosevelt, as well as on his turbulent private life.

"Few publishers have loomed as large in their lifetimes, or cast as long a shadow after death, as William Randolph Hearst. Nasaw's judicious and comprehensive biography sensibly seeks to understand its subject, not to judge him." —*The New Yorker*

Includes bibliographical references (p. [609]-656) and index.

★ *The Patriarch: The Remarkable Life and Turbulent Times of Joseph P. Kennedy.* David Nasaw. Penguin Press 2012. 832 p.
ISBN 9781594203763
Grades: Adult   B
1. Kennedy, Joseph P. (Joseph Patrick), 1888-1969 2. Kennedy family 3. Ambassadors 4. Politicians 5. Businesspeople 6. United States 7. Biographies 8. History writing — Politicians — United States 9. Life stories — Politics — Politicians

LC 2012027315

New York Times Notable Book, 2012; Pulitzer Prize for Biography or Autobiography finalist, 2013.

Draws on exclusive access to the subject's records to offer insight into his shrewd financial talents and considerable ambition for his family, discussing the controversies surrounding his character and his role in several mainstream political events.

Includes bibliographical references and index.

Nathan, Debbie
Sybil Exposed: The Extraordinary Story Behind the Famous Multiple Personality Case. Debbie Nathan. Free Press 2011. xxi, 297 p. : Illustration
ISBN 9781439168271
Grades: 11 12 Adult   B
1. Sybil, 1923-1998 2. Mason, Shirley, 1923-1998 3. People with dissociative identity disorder 4. Dissociative disorders 5. Personality disorders 6. Dissociative identity disorder 7. People with mental illnesses 8. Women 9. Biographies 10. Life stories — Facing adversity — Medical issues — Mental illness 11. Science Writing — Medicine and health — Mental health

LC 2011009164

Documents the stories of the three women behind the famous multiple-personality-disorder case, contending that a large portion of the story was fabricated by a willing patient, her psychiatrist and an ambitious journalist who took advantage of a public that was psychologically primed to believe their claims.

Includes bibliographical references (p. 247-282) and index.

Nathans, Sydney
To Free a Family: The Journey of Mary Walker. Sydney Nathans. Harvard University Press 2011. 360 p.
ISBN 9780674062122
Grades: Adult   B
1. Walker, Mary, d. 1872 2. Freedom seekers 3. Enslaved women 4. Family reunions 5. African American women 6. Enslaved people 7. Cambridge, Massachusetts 8. North Carolina 9. 19th century 10. History writing — African American — Enslavement — United States

LC 2011023122

Recounts the story of Mary Walker, who fled slavery in 1848 then spent the next 17 years trying to recover her family from the North.

Includes bibliographical references and index.

Navarro, Joe
Three Minutes to Doomsday: An Agent, a Traitor, and the Worst Espionage Breach in U.S. History. Joe Navarro. Scribner 2017. 288 p.
ISBN 9781501128271
Grades: Adult   B
1. Navarro, Joe, 1953- 2. Spies 3. Espionage 4. Military intelligence 5. Cold War 6. Soldiers 7. 1980s 8. Autobiographies and memoirs 9. Life stories — Law and order — Police and law officers 10. History writing — Cold War

In a real-life cat-and-mouse game between two brilliant men in the last days of the Cold War, one of the youngest agents ever hired by the FBI and an expert at reading body language, engages in a two-year long battle of wits with a former American solider whom he believed handed the Soviets the ability to utterly destroy the U.S.

"A fascinating account of counterintelligence in the pre-cyber era." —*Kirkus*

Ndopu, Eddie
Sipping Dom Pérignon Through a Straw: Reimagining Success as a Disabled Achiever. Eddie Ndopu (written entirely using my one good finger).. Legacy Lit 2023. 228 p.
ISBN 9780306829062
Grades: Adult   B

ESSENTIAL AND RECOMMENDED TITLES
Biography

1. Ndopu, Eddie 2. People with disabilities 3. Spinal muscular atrophy 4. Scholars and academics 5. Disability rights advocates 6. Human rights 7. Ableism 8. Intersectionality 9. LGBTQIA+ people 10. Success (Concept) 11. Southern African people 12. South African people 13. Autobiographies and memoirs 14. Life stories — Facing adversity — Medical issues — Living with disabilities 15. Life stories — Identity 16. Society and culture — Social activism and philanthropy

LC 2023008692

A global humanitarian born with spinal muscular atrophy—and the first-ever disabled African awarded a full scholarship at Oxford University—shows how he broke through every barrier put in front of him—a queer, Black wheelchair user—challenging the bias at the highest echelons of power and prestige.

"In his sharp, illuminating debut memoir, South African disability rights advocate Ndopu chronicles his trials and triumphs as a disabled gay Black man enrolled at Oxford University." —*Publishers Weekly*

Nelson, Maggie

★ *The Argonauts*. Maggie Nelson. Graywolf Press 2015. 160 p.
ISBN 9781555977078
Grades: Adult   B

1. Nelson, Maggie, 1973- 2. Interpersonal relations 3. Gender identity 4. Pregnancy 5. Love 6. Families 7. Intersectionality 8. Autobiographies and memoirs 9. Life stories — Identity — LGBTQIA+ 10. Life stories — Relationships — Family

LC Bl2015017696

New York Times Notable Book, 2015.

The Argonauts is a genre-bending memoir, a work of "autotheory" offering fresh, fierce, and timely thinking about desire, identity, and the limitations and possibilities of love and language. At its center is a romance: the story of the author's relationship with the artist Harry Dodge. This story, which includes Nelson's account of falling in love with Dodge, who is fluidly gendered, as well as her journey to and through a pregnancy, offers a firsthand account of the complexities and joys of (queer) family-making.

Nelson, Willie

It's a Long Story: My Life. Wille Nelson, David Ritz. Little, Brown and Co. 2015. 400 pages
ISBN 9780316403559
Grades: Adult   B

1. Nelson, Willie, 1933- 2. Country musicians 3. Country music industry and trade 4. Songwriting 5. Interpersonal relations 6. Bankruptcy 7. Fund raising 8. Men-women relations 9. Social life and customs 10. United States 11. 20th century 12. Autobiographies and memoirs 13. Biographies 14. Arts and Entertainment — Music — Country 15. Life stories — Arts and culture — Performing arts — Musicians and composers

LC 2015930343

The iconic Country Music Hall of Fame artist shares the story of his life and career, from his early ambitions and relationships through his bankruptcy and founding of Farm Aid.

Nemat, Marina

Prisoner of Tehran: A Memoir. Marina Nemat. Free Press 2007. IX, 306 p.
ISBN 9781416537427
Grades: 11 12 Adult

1. Nemat, Marina 2. Women political prisoners 3. Political prisoners 4. Politics and government 5. Iran 6. 20th century 7. Autobiographies and memoirs 8. Life stories — Politics — Political prisoners 9. History writing — Women's history 10. Life stories — Facing adversity — War and oppression — Hostages and POWs 11. History writing — Nationalism — Southwest Asia and North Africa (Middle East)

LC 2006050191

An autobiography of Marina Nemat, who was arrested at the age of 16 on false charges by Iranian Revolutionary Guards, tortured in Tehran's notorious Evin prison, and sentenced to death for "political crimes." LSC.

"The author's story is not so much a political history lesson than it is a memoir of faith and love, a protest against violence that cannot be silenced. . . . Her persistence in standing for goodness is a lesson for us all." —*Christian Science Monitor*

Nemiroff, Robert

To Be Young, Gifted, and Black: Lorraine Hansberry in Her Own Words. Adapted by Robert Nemiroff; with original drawings and art by Miss Hansberry; and an introduction by James Baldwin. Signet Classics 2011. 271 p. : Illustration
ISBN 9780451531780
Grades: Adult   B

1. Hansberry, Lorraine, 1930-1965 2. Women playwrights, American 3. African American playwrights 4. African Americans 5. 20th century 6. Arts and Entertainment — Theater — Plays

LC Bl2012007490

Detailing the Black experience in mid-twentieth-century America, this candid biography features selections from the works of the late African-American playwright, including play excerpts, autobiographical sketches, poetry, and drawings.

Originally published: Englewood Cliffs, N.J. : Prentice-Hall, 1969.

Nesmith, Michael

Infinite Tuesday: An Autobiographical Riff. Michael Nesmith. Random House Inc. 2017. 352 p.
ISBN 9781101907504
Grades: Adult   B

1. Nesmith, Michael 2. Musicians 3. Songwriters 4. Christian scientists 5. Spiritual life 6. Music videos 7. Christian science 8. Autobiographies and memoirs 9. Life stories — Arts and culture — Performing arts — Musicians and composers

LC 2016058926

An idiosyncratic memoir by the Monkees icon, songwriter and music-video innovator traces his experiences as a wild youth and celebrity before finding peace and creative wholeness through the teachings of Christian Science and his collaborations with like-minded fellow artists.

"This selectively revealing, insightful memoir casts the cerebral Monkee as a spiritual seeker and self-deprecating visionary." —*Kirkus*

Neu, Charles E.

Colonel House: A Biography of Woodrow Wilson's Silent Partner. Charles E. Neu. Oxford University Press 2015. 624 p.
ISBN 9780195045505
Grades: Adult   B

1. House, Edward Mandell, 1858-1938 2. Wilson, Woodrow, 1856-1924 3. Politicians 4. World War I 5. Male friendship 6. International relations 7. Politics and government 8. United States 9. 20th century 10. 1910s 11. 1920s 12. Biographies 13. Life stories — Politics — Politicians 14. History writing — Early 20th century — United States

LC 2014015227

Traces the life of the wealthy Texan who served as President Wilson's closest adviser and envoy to Europe in World War I, as well as the bitter split that ended his and Wilson's decades-long friendship.

"Neu deems House a 'Patient, crafty, and sometimes cynical' infighter and 'A shrewd observer of human foibles,' widely admired but faulted by some at the height of his fame for developing an exaggerated sense of his own importance. A significant, brightly written American story." —*Kirkus*

Includes bibliographical references and index.

Neumann, Ariana

When Time Stopped: A Memoir of My Father's War and What Remains. Ariana Neumann. Scribner 2020. 352 pages
ISBN 9781982106379
Grades: Adult   B

1. Neumann, Hanus Stanislav, 1921-2001 2. Newman family 3. Neumann, Ariana 4. Jewish people 5. Holocaust (1933-1945) 6. Holocaust survivors 7. Families 8. Fathers and daughters 9. Secrecy 10. Czech people 11. Eastern European people 12. Berlin, Germany 13. Czechoslovakia 14. Venezuela 15. Autobiographies and memoirs 16. Biographies 17. Life stories — Facing adversity —

War and oppression — Holocaust 18. History writing — Wars and conflicts — Holocaust — World War II 19. History writing — Jewish history

LC 2019045041

National Jewish Book Award, 2020.

A Venezuelan foreign correspondent describes the harrowing early experiences of her father, an only survivor of their Jewish-Czechoslovakian family, who hid from the Gestapo in plain sight before starting over in South America.

"Neumann's eloquent, skillfully researched book will appeal to many, especially those interested in family histories and the lives of Holocaust survivors." —*Library Journal*

Includes bibliographical references.

Neville, Aaron

Tell It Like It Is: My Story. Aaron Neville. Hachette Books 2023. 320 p.

ISBN 9780306832536

Grades: Adult   B

1. Neville, Aaron, 1941- 2. Singers 3. African American singers 4. Indigenous peoples of North America 5. Rhythm and blues music 6. Soul music 7. Soul musicians 8. Singing 9. Success (Concept) 10. Heroin addiction 11. Faith (Christianity) 12. Music 13. Racism 14. Autobiographies and memoirs 15. Life stories — Arts and culture — Performing arts — Musicians and composers 16. Arts and Entertainment — Music — Rap and R&B

"In his first memoir, iconic New Orleanian, platinum-record singer and songwriter Aaron Neville, a Grammy Hall of Famer for his unique voice, gorgeous solo work, and key part in the popular Neville Brothers, candidly reveals his little-known personal and professional struggles." —*Booklist*

Nevins, Sheila

You Don't Look Your Age: And Other Fairy Tales. Sheila Nevins. Flatiron Books 2017. 272 p.

ISBN 9781250111302

Grades: Adult   B

1. Nevins, Sheila 2. Career development 3. Personal conduct 4. Aging 5. Women 6. Essays 7. Autobiographies and memoirs 8. Life stories — General 9. Society and culture — Gender — Women

LC 2017003050

A famed television producer and president of HBO Documentary Films shares frank but lighthearted advice for today's women on how to navigate the challenges of pursuing a career in a man's world, balancing the responsibilities of a working parent, aging in a youth-obsessed culture and thriving as a feminist in a dynamic marriage.

Newkey-Burden, Chas

Taylor Swift: The Whole Story. by Chas Newkey-Burden. 2024. 300 pages

ISBN 9780008680718

Grades: Adult   B

1. Swift, Taylor, 1989- 2. Singers 3. Women singers 4. Sound recording industry and trade 5. Music 6. Popular music 7. Life stories — Arts and Culture — Performing Arts — Musicians and composers 8. Arts and Entertainment — Music

A biography of Taylor Swift that focuses on her singing career.

Fully updated unauthorized biography; First published by HarperCollinsPublishers in 2014—Copyright page; Includes bibliographical references (page 300).

Newman, Paul

The Extraordinary Life of an Ordinary Man: A Memoir. Paul Newman; interviews and oral histories conducted by Stewart Stern; compiled and edited by David Rosenthal. Alfred A. Knopf 2022. 320 p.

ISBN 9780593534502

Grades: Adult   B

1. Newman, Paul, 1925-2008 2. Philanthropists 3. Growing up 4. Acting 5. Fame 6. Marriage 7. Family relationships 8. Interpersonal relations 9. Films 10. Actors and actresses 11. Interviews 12. Life stories — Arts and culture — Performing arts — Actors and actresses 13. Arts and Entertainment — Movies and Television

LC 2022008087

Culled from thousands of pages of transcripts, this raw, candid, unvarnished memoir of the greatest movie star of the past 75 years, told with searing honesty, covers everything: His traumatic childhood, his career, his drinking, his intimate life with Joanne Woodward and his innermost fears and passions and joys.

"The much-anticipated, posthumously published, reflective ruminations of Paul Newman (1925?2008) proves worth the wait….Readers will want to savor the stories in this oral history-turned-autobiography and undoubtedly be motivated to watch or rewatch Newman's many films." —*Library Journal*

Includes index.

Newman, Richard S.

Freedom's Prophet: Bishop Richard Allen, the Amr Church, and the Black Founding Fathers. Richard S. Newman. New York University Press 2008. 368 p.

ISBN 9780814758267

Grades: Adult   B

1. Allen, Richard, 1760-1831 2. Bishops 3. African American clergy 4. United States 5. Biographies 6. Spirituality and Religion — Christianity 7. Life stories — Religion and spirituality — Religious and spiritual leaders

LC 2007043259

Looks at the life of the first Black pamphleteer, abolitionist, and founder of the African Methodist Episcopal Church.

Includes bibliographical references and index.

Nez, Chester

Code Talker: The First and Only Memoir by One of the Original Navajo Code Talkers of Wwii. Chester Nez, with Judith Schiess Avila. Berkley Caliber 2011. 320 p.

ISBN 9780425244234

Grades: 11 12 Adult   B

1. Nez, Chester 2. Navajo (Diné) code talkers 3. Indigenous code talkers 4. Cryptography 5. Codes (Communication) 6. World War II 7. Indigenous soldiers 8. Marines 9. Navajo (Diné) (North American people) 10. Indigenous peoples of North America 11. Postwar life 12. Military history 13. United States 14. 20th century 15. History writing — Wars and conflicts — World War II

LC 2011023701

A retired Marine and Navajo Indian describes his experiences as one of 29 top-secret code talkers during World War II and how his life growing up on the Checkerboard Area of the Navajo Reservation prepared him for his service.

"Accessible and compelling, this is recommended for general readers as well as World War II history buffs." —*Library Journal*

Includes bibliographical references and index.

Ng, Fae Myenne

Orphan Bachelors: A Memoir on Being a Confession Baby, Chinatown Daughter, Baa-bai Sister, Caretaker of Exotics, Literary Balloon Peddler, and Grand Historian of a Doomed American Family: A Memoir. Fae Myenne Ng. Grove Press 2023. 256 p.

ISBN 9780802162212

Grades: Adult   B

1. Ng, Fae Myenne, 1956- 2. Women authors 3. Chinese American families 4. Immigration and emigration 5. Growing up 6. Adulthood 7. Racism 8. Identity 9. Belonging 10. Family history 11. Fathers and daughters 12. Confession 13. Deception 14. Death of parents 15. Death of brothers 16. Loss 17. Memories 18. East Asian people 19. Chinese people 20. North American people 21. American people 22. Chinatown, San Francisco, California 23. San Francisco, California 24. Autobiographies and memoirs 25. Life stories — Identity — Race and ethnicity 26. Life stories — Facing adversity — Coping with death 27. Society and culture — Race 28. Society and culture — Immigration 29. History writing — Immigration — United States

LC 2022058847

Raised by a seafaring father and a seamstress mother, by San Francisco's Chinatown and its legendary Orphan Bachelors—men without wives or children—the author recounts how her family built a life in a country bent on exclusion and how she absorbed the Orphan Bachelor's suspicious, lonely, barren nature.

ESSENTIAL AND RECOMMENDED TITLES
Biography

"In this 'Book of living memory,' novelist Ng (Bone) examines the cascading effects of U.S. immigration laws on her Chinese family....The author's straightforward prose and the work's staggering scope bring home the myriad ways misguided policies damaged generations of immigrant families." —*Publishers Weekly*

Ngugi wa Thiong'o
In the House of the Interpreter: A Memoir. Ngugi wa'Thiong'o. Pantheon Books 2012. 272 p.
ISBN 9780307907691
Grades: 10 11 12 Adult   B
1. Ngugi wa Thiong'o, 1938- 2. Authors 3. Kenyan people 4. Imperialism, British 5. Resistance to government 6. Kikuyu (African people) 7. Revolutionaries 8. African history 9. Kenya 10. 1950s 11. 20th century 12. Autobiographies and memoirs 13. Life stories — Relationships — Growing up 14. Adult books for young adults 15. History writing — Colonization — Africa

LC 2012013986

Library Journal Best Books, 2012; National Book Critics Circle Award for Autobiography/Memoir finalist.

The second volume of memoirs from the renowned Kenyan novelist, poet and playwright covers his high school years at the end of British colonial rule in Africa, during the Mau Mau Uprising.

Follows: Dreams in a time of war (2010).

Nguyen, Bich Minh
Owner of a Lonely Heart: A Memoir. Beth Nguyen. Scribner 2023. 320 p.
ISBN 9781982196349
Grades: Adult   B
1. Nguyen, Bich Minh 2. Women immigrants 3. Refugees 4. Vietnamese Americans 5. Pregnant women 6. Motherhood 7. Mothers and daughters 8. Mother-separated children 9. Separated friends, relatives, etc. 10. Reunions 11. Belonging 12. Family relationships 13. Southeast Asian people 14. Vietnamese people 15. North American people 16. American people 17. Life stories — Facing adversity — War and oppression — Refugees 18. Life stories — Relationships — Parent and child 19. Family and Relationships — Families 20. Family and Relationships — Parenting

LC 2023011380

In this memoir about parenthood, absence and the condition of being a refugee, the author, who fled Saigon for America at the end of the Vietnam War, while her mother stayed behind, tells a coming-of-age story spanning her Midwestern childhood, her first meeting with her mother and becoming a parent herself.

"Nguyen's honesty and vulnerability will captivate readers instantly." —*Library Journal*

Nguyen, Viet Thanh
★ *A Man of Two Faces: A Memoir, a History, a Memorial*. Viet Thanh Nguyen. Grove Press 2023. 400 p.
ISBN 9780802160508
Grades: Adult   B
1. Nguyen, Viet Thanh, 1971- 2. Vietnamese Americans 3. Immigrants 4. Refugees 5. Vietnam War, 1961-1975 6. Colonialism 7. Ethnic identity 8. Marginalized people 9. Suffering 10. Family relationships 11. Southeast Asian people 12. Vietnamese people 13. North American people 14. American people 15. Intergenerational trauma 16. Vietnam 17. San Jose, California 18. Autobiographies and memoirs 19. Life stories — Facing adversity — War and oppression — Refugees 20. Life stories — Identity — Race and ethnicity 21. Life stories — Relationships — Family

LC 2023022993

Exploring the necessity of both forgetting and of memory, the Pulitzer Prize-winning author expands the genre of personal memoir by acknowledging larger stories of refugeehood, colonization and ideas about Vietnam and America as well as a deep emotional openness about his life as a father and a son.

"With his highly awarded first novel, the Sympathizer, adapted for a forthcoming streaming series, Nguyen's unflinching blend of memoir and social critique will garner avid attention." —*Booklist*

Includes bibliographical references.

Nicholl, Charles
The Reckoning: The Murder of Christopher Marlowe. Charles Nicholl. University of Chicago Press 1995. 413 p. : Illustration
ISBN 9780226580241
Grades: Adult   B
1. Marlowe, Christopher, 1564-1593 2. Playwrights, English 3. Murder 4. Murder victims 5. Spies 6. London, England history 7. 16th century 8. History writing — Spies and spying 9. History writing — Historical mysteries 10. True Crime — Historical Crime 11. True Crime — Murder

LC 95003004

Gold Dagger Award for Best Nonfiction of the Year, 1992; James Tait Black Memorial Prize for Biography, 1992.

An investigation into the death of Christopher Marlowe, the sixteenth-century author tragically stabbed to death in a lodging house, reveals the secrets behind the enigmatic literary legend.

"A remarkable piece of scholarship, this work carefully reconstructs the events leading up to the murder with all the excitement and suspense of a modern mystery novel; at the same time it vividly conveys the energy and color of Elizabethan England." —*Library Journal*

Originally published: London : J. Cape, 1992; Includes bibliographical references (p. [393]-399) and index.

Nietfeld, Emi
Acceptance: A Memoir. Emi Nietfeld. Penguin Press 2022. 352 p.
ISBN 9780593489475
Grades: Adult   B
1. Nietfeld, Emi 2. Foster children 3. Social mobility 4. Homelessness 5. Resilience 6. Addiction 7. Mental health 8. American dream 9. Dysfunctional families 10. United States 11. Autobiographies and memoirs 12. Life stories — Facing adversity 13. Life stories — Relationships — Growing up

LC 2021046322

The writer and software engineer looks back her dysfunctional childhood, years as a homeless teenager and eventual graduation from Harvard and how society's fixation on resilience comes with a terrible cost.

"An account of growing up in institutions and foster care by a Harvard graduate and former Google employee....A powerful memoir of overcoming adversity that also effectively interrogates the concept of meritocracy." —*Kirkus*

Nir, Sarah Maslin
Horse Crazy: The Story of a Woman and a World in Love with an Animal. Sarah Maslin Nir. Simon and Schuster 2020. 384 p.
ISBN 9781501196232
Grades: Adult   B
1. Nir, Sarah Maslin, 1983- 2. Equestrians 3. Horses 4. Horse owners 5. Women journalists 6. Equestrianism 7. Humans and horses 8. Human-animal relationships 9. United States 10. Autobiographies and memoirs 11. Life stories — Relationships — Pets and owners 12. Family and Relationships — Pets and Owners

LC 2019058615

Horse Crazy is a fascinating, funny, and moving love letter to these graceful animals and the people who-like her-are obsessed with them. It is also a coming-of-age story of Nir growing up an outsider within the world's most elite inner circles, and finding her true north in horses. Nir takes us into the lesser-known corners of the riding world and profiles some of its most captivating figures.

"This thoughtful, well-researched book offers a charming portrait of horses in America as well as of a woman who found self-acceptance in their graceful company. A bighearted debut book sure to please horse lovers." —*Kirkus*

Includes index.

Niven, Jennifer
Ada Blackjack: A True Story of Survival in the Arctic. by Jennifer Niven. Hyperion 2003. 431 p. : Illustration; Map
ISBN 9780786868636
Grades: Adult   B
1. Women explorers 2. Inuit women 3. Explorers 4. Expeditions 5. Survival 6. Wilderness survival 7. Exploration 8. Arctic regions 9. 1920s 10. Biographies

PUBLIC LIBRARY CORE COLLECTION: NONFICTION
Twentieth Edition

11. Adventure writing — Survival 12. History writing — Exploration 13. Life stories — People in history — Explorers 14. Adult books for young adults 15. Life stories — Facing adversity — Disasters and tragedies

LC 2003050826

Recounts the efforts of a young Inuit woman named Ada Blackjack and her four male companions to colonize a remote, desolate Arctic island, the deaths of her associates, her struggle to survive, and her return to civilization.

Includes bibliographical references and index.

Niven, Penelope
Thornton Wilder: A Life. Penelope Niven. HarperCollins 2012. 800 p.
ISBN 9780060831363
Grades: Adult   B

1. Wilder, Thornton, 1897-1975 2. Authors, American 3. Playwrights, American 4. Family relationships 5. Creativity 6. 20th century 7. Biographies 8. Arts and Entertainment — Writing and Publishing 9. Arts and Entertainment — Theater 10. Life stories — Arts and culture — Writing — Authors

LC 2012532027

Booklist Editors' Choice, 2012.

Drawn from thousands of pages of letters, journals, manuscripts and other documents, this brilliant biography of the three-time Pulitzer Prize-winning playwright and novelist explores his public persona, his private relationships and his complicated family.

Noah, Trevor
Born a Crime: Stories from a South African Childhood. by Trevor Noah. Spiegel & Grau 2016. 224 p.
ISBN 9780399588174
Grades: Adult   B

1. Noah, Trevor, 1984- 2. Comedians 3. Television personalities 4. Race relations 5. Growing up 6. Mothers and sons 7. Poverty 8. South Africa 9. Essays 10. Autobiographies and memoirs 11. Biographies 12. Life stories — Identity — Race and ethnicity 13. Humor writing — Family and relationship humor 14. Family and Relationships — Growing up 15. Adult books for young adults 16. Antiracist literature 17. Book club best bets

LC 2016031399

Booklist Editors' Choice, 2016; Booklist Editors' Choice: Adult Books for Young Adults, 2016; Children's Africana Book Awards, New Adult, 2019; New York Times Notable Book, 2017; Thurber Prize for American Humor, 2017.

Trevor Noah, host of The Daily Show, shares his remarkable story of growing up in South Africa, with a Black South African mother and a white European father at a time when it was against the law for a mixed-race child like him to exist. In a country where racism barred Blacks from social, educational, and economic opportunity, Trevor surmounted staggering obstacles and created a promising future for himself, thanks to his mother's unwavering love and indomitable will.

Also published in large print format.

Nolte, Nick
Rebel: My Life Outside the Lines. Nick Nolte. HarperCollins 2015. 320 p.
ISBN 9780062219572
Grades: Adult   B

1. Nolte, Nick 2. Film industry and trade 3. Actors and actresses 4. Films 5. Autobiographies and memoirs 6. Biographies 7. Life stories — Arts and culture — Performing arts — Actors and actresses

LC 2017278529

The three-time Academy Award nominee traces his half century in Hollywood, describing his extreme character-creation efforts as a method actor, the substance abuse issues that have overshadowed his life and his experiences as a father.

"Long since on the wagon and an obviously thoughtful man, Nolte seems to share the reader's surprise that he lived long enough to take that role. Better than the usual run of actor memoirs and plenty of fun to boot." —*Kirkus*

Noor
Leap of Faith: Memoirs of an Unexpected Life. Queen Noor. Miramax Books 2003. xi, 467 p, 16 p. of plates : Illustration; Color
ISBN 9780786867172
Grades: Adult   B

1. Noor, Queen, consort of Hussein, King of Jordan, 1951- 2. Hussein, King of Jordan, 1935-1999 3. Women rulers 4. Arab-Israeli conflict 5. Women's role 6. Rulers 7. Husband and wife 8. Men-women relations 9. Jordan 10. 20th century 11. Autobiographies and memoirs 12. History writing — Nationalism — Southwest Asia and North Africa (Middle East) 13. History writing — Women's history 14. Life stories — Politics — Royalty

LC 2004270644

Sharing a personal perspective on the past three decades of world history, Queen Noor talks frankly of the many challenges of her life as wife and partner to the monarch, providing both an intimate portrait of the late King Hussein and a moving account of their public role.

"The American-born widow of the late king Hussein of Jordan brings a unique perspective to Middle East politics." —*Booklist*

Includes index.

Nooyi, Indra
★ *My Life in Full: Work, Family, and Our Future.* Indra Nooyi. Portfolio 2021. 304 p.
ISBN 9780593191798
Grades: Adult   B

1. Nooyi, Indra, 1955- 2. Women executives 3. Women chief executive officers 4. Women immigrants 5. Marriage 6. Motherhood 7. Family and work 8. Leadership in business 9. Organizational change 10. Business 11. Social responsibility 12. Environmentalism 13. Indian Americans 14. Independence 15. Autobiographies and memoirs 16. Life stories — Business — Business leaders 17. Life stories — Identity 18. Business and economics — Business leaders and entrepreneurs

LC 2021011930

The first woman of color and immigrant to run a Fortune 500 company, the author, in this candid memoir, offers an inside look at PepsiCO and lays bare the difficulties that came with managing her demanding job with a growing family, and what she learned along the way.

"An autobiography of a female, immigrant CEO that is full of heart." —*Kirkus*

Nordland, Rod
Waiting for the Monsoon. Rod Nordland. Mariner Books 2024. 272 p.
ISBN 9780063096226
Grades: Adult   B

1. Nordland, Rod 2. Brain tumors 3. Conflict (Psychology) 4. Uncertainty 5. Self 6. Life change events 7. War correspondents 8. Interpersonal relations 9. Autobiographies and memoirs 10. Life stories — Facing adversity — Medical issues — Physical illness

In 2019, a Pulitzer Prize-winning war correspondent who reported in over 150 countries, many in violent upheaval, was diagnosed with a fatal brain tumor, which gave him the strength to face more personal conflicts, in this unforgettable final dispatch that reveals how facing the unknown can change our relationship to the world around us.

"Nordland writes with palpable gratitude for whatever time he has remaining and provides a stirringly clear-eyed perspective on his own mortality." —*Publishers Weekly*

Norgren, Jill
Belva Lockwood: The Woman Who Would Be President. Jill Norgren. New York University Press 2007. xviii, 311 p. : Illustration
ISBN 9780814758342
Grades: 11 12 Adult   B

1. Lockwood, Belva Ann Bennett, 1830-1917 2. Lawyers 3. Women lawyers 4. Ambition 5. 19th century 6. Biographies 7. Life stories — Politics — Activists and reformers 8. History writing — Women's history 9. Life stories — People in

ESSENTIAL AND RECOMMENDED TITLES
Biography

history 10. History writing — Gilded Age — United States 11. Adult books for young adults

LC 2006034486

Retells the life and career of Belva Lockwood, a women's rights advocate in the nineteenth century, who became the first woman to practice law before the United States Supreme Court and run for president.

"Those with interests in women's, political, social, and cultural history will enjoy Lockwood." —*Choice*

Includes bibliographical references (p. 233-290) and index.

Norman, Jesse

Adam Smith: Father of Economics. Jesse Norman. Basic Books 2018. 432 p.
ISBN 9780465061976
Grades: Adult **B**
1. Smith, Adam, 1723-1790 2. Economists 3. Economics 4. Capitalism 5. Capitalism and democracy 6. Philosophy 7. Biographies 8. Life stories — Education — Philosophers 9. Business and economics — Economics — History

LC 2018015933

Adam Smith (1723-1790) is now widely regarded as the greatest economist of all time. But what he really thought, and the implications of his ideas, remain fiercely contested. Was he an eloquent advocate of capitalism and individual freedom? a prime mover of "market fundamentalism"? an apologist for human selfishness? or something else entirely? Political philosopher Jesse Norman dispels the myths and caricatures, and provides a far more complex portrait of the man.

"It's hard to imagine an American politician writing with the same depth and grasp of an inordinately complex subject, but Norman pulls it off quite capably. A worthy addition to the literature surrounding Smith and that of modern conservative thought." —*Kirkus*

Previously published in the UK as Adam Smith: What he thought, and why it matters by Penguin Random House; Includes bibliographical references and index.

Norman, Philip

George Harrison: The Reluctant Beatle. Philip Norman. 2023. 352 p.
ISBN 9781982195861
Grades: Adult **B**
1. Harrison, George, 1943-2001 2. Rock musicians 3. Rock music 4. Songwriters 5. Composers 6. Spirituality 7. Music history and criticism 8. Popular culture 9. Musicians 10. English people 11. Great Britain 12. 20th century 13. Biographies 14. Arts and Entertainment — Music — Rock 15. Life stories — Arts and culture — Performing arts — Musicians and composers 16. Society and culture — Pop culture

Based on exhaustive research and access to inside sources, the longtime Beatles biographer returns with a revealing portrait of George Harrison, long known as the most mysterious and misunderstood member of the group.

"A well-informed, serviceably written biography of an enigmatic musician." —*Kirkus*

John Lennon: The Life. Philip Norman. Ecco 2008. 864 p.
ISBN 9780060754013
Grades: Adult **B**
1. Lennon, John, 1940-1980 2. Rock musicians 3. Rock music 4. Celebrities 5. Social life and customs 6. England 7. 20th century 8. Biographies 9. Arts and Entertainment — Music — Rock 10. Life stories — Arts and culture — Performing arts — Musicians and composers

LC 2008004684

Library Journal Best Books, 2008.

A comprehensive portrait of the rock icon covers topics ranging from Lennon's traumatic childhood in the care of his aunt and the Beatles' unprecedented rise to the in-fighting during the Yoko years and his early death in 1980.

"This work's ambitious range proves to be its strength, enveloping you in ways that a quicker read could not. [This] is a gift of a book, heartfelt and heart-rending." —*Christian Science Monitor*

★ *Wild Thing: The Short, Spellbinding Life of Jimi Hendrix.* Philip Norman. Liveright Publishing 2020. 400 p.
ISBN 9781631495892
Grades: Adult **B**
1. Hendrix, Jimi, 1942-1970 2. Guitarists 3. Rock music 4. Psychedelic rock music 5. African American musicians 6. Electric guitar 7. Fame 8. Death 9. Rock musicians 10. United States 11. Biographies 12. Life stories — Arts and culture — Performing arts — Musicians and composers 13. Arts and Entertainment — Music — Rock

LC 2020023464

Published to mark the 50th anniversary of Hendrix's death, a commemorative portrait by the best-selling author of Shout! draws on interviews with friends, lovers, bandmates and family members to include coverage of Hendrix's segregated early performances and historic appearances.

"Essential for music collections and anyone interested in Hendrix or music of the 1960s." —*Library Journal*

Includes bibliographical references and index.

Norrell, Robert J.

Up from History: The Life of Booker T. Washington. Robert J. Norrell. Belknap Press of Harvard University Press 2009. xi, 508 p. : Illustration
ISBN 9780674032118
Grades: 11 12 Adult **B**
1. Washington, Booker T, 1856-1915 2. African American men 3. African American educators 4. Intellectual life 5. African Americans 6. Education 7. United States history 8. 19th century 9. 20th century 10. Biographies 11. History writing — United States 12. Life stories — Education — Scholars and educators 13. Adult books for young adults 14. History writing — African American — Civil rights — United States

LC 2008032599

Library Journal Best Books, 2009.

A definitive biography of Booker T. Washington focuses on his efforts to support the cause of Black people in the segregated South by promoting an economic independence and development of moral character in order to integrate Blacks into American life and to overcome exploitation and discrimination.

Includes bibliographical references and index.

Norris, Robert S.

Racing for the Bomb: General Leslie R. Groves, the Manhattan Project's Indispensable Man. Robert S. Norris. Steerforth Press 2002. xxi, 722 p. : Illustration
ISBN 9781586420390
Grades: Adult **B**
1. Groves, Leslie Richard, 1896-1970 2. Nuclear weapons 3. Generals 4. Military engineering 5. Military history 6. United States 7. 20th century 8. Biographies 9. History writing — Wars and conflicts — Atomic Bomb — World War II 10. Science Writing — Physics 11. Life stories — Law and order — Military leaders

LC 2001057629

Follows the World War II race to build the atomic bomb while profiling its top commander, documenting how Colonel Groves drove countless individuals to collecting the necessary funds and materials as well as orchestrated solutions to thousands of technical problems.

"This work will not only serve scholars and general readers equally well but also take its place among the handful of best books about the birth of the atomic age." —*Booklist*

Includes bibliographical references (p. 559-683) and index.

Northup, Solomon

Twelve Years a Slave. Solomon Northup; introduction by Ira Berlin; general editor Henry Louis Gates, Jr. Penguin Books 2012. xxxvi, 240 p. : Illustration
ISBN 9780143106708
Grades: Adult **B**
1. Northup, Solomon, 1808-1863? 2. Enslaved people 3. Slavery 4. Plantation life 5. African Americans 6. United States history 7. Louisiana 8. 19th century 9. Autobiographies and memoirs 10. Page to screen 11. Biographies 12. Life stories — Facing adversity — War and oppression — Enslaved people 13. History writing — African American — Enslavement — United States

LC 2012012550

Describes the life of Solomon Northup, a free Black man from Saratoga, N.Y, who was kidnapped in 1841 and forced into slavery in Louisiana for twelve years.

Title adapted into a film entitled: 12 years a slave (2013); Twelve Years a Slave inspired the 1984 film Solomon Northup's Odyssey; Includes bibliographical references and index; Originally published: 1853.

Notaro, Laurie
Excuse Me While I Disappear: Tales of Midlife Mayhem. Laurie Notaro. Little a 2022. 256 p.
ISBN 9781542033510
Grades: Adult   B
1. Notaro, Laurie 2. Middle-age 3. Aging 4. Life 5. Middle-aged people 6. Middle-aged women 7. Personal conduct 8. Autobiographies and memoirs 9. Life stories — General 10. Family and relationships — Aging and death 11. Humor Writing — Social humor

The author and humorist returns with a candid and empowering memoir of the realities, perks, and opportunities facing those living life on the other side of fifty.

"Notaro (The Idiot Girls' Action-Adventure Club) riffs on her unpreparedness for navigating life after turning 50 and the surprising benefits of getting older in this tongue-in-cheek memoir." —*Publishers Weekly*

Nuland, Sherwin B.
Leonardo Da Vinci. Sherwin B. Nuland. Viking 2000. 170 p. : Illustration
ISBN 9780670893911
Grades: Adult   B
1. Leonardo, da Vinci, 1452-1519 2. Artists 3. Scientists 4. Intellectual life 5. Science 6. Art 7. Italian history 8. Renaissance (1300-1600) 9. Age of exploration (1419-1610) 10. Biographies 11. Science Writing — General 12. History writing — Renaissance — Europe 13. Life stories — Arts and culture — Artists 14. Life stories — Science, technology, and medicine — Scientists and inventors
LC 00032061

Attempts to unlock the secret of the great Renaissance man's love of art and science.

A Lipper/Viking book; Includes bibliographical references (p. 167-170).

Nusseibeh, Sari
Once Upon a Country: A Palestinian Life. Sari Nusseibeh; with Anthony David. Farrar, Straus and Giroux 2007. VIII, 542 p, 8 p. of plates : Illustration
ISBN 9780374299507
Grades: Adult   B
1. Nusseibeh, Sari 2. Palestinian people 3. Arab-Israeli conflict 4. Nationalism 5. Politics and government 6. Palestine 7. 20th century 8. History writing — Arab-Israeli relations — Southwest Asia and North Africa (Middle East) 9. Politics and global affairs — World politics — Southwest Asia and North Africa (Middle East) — Israel and Palestine
LC 2006013272

A Palestinian scholar and leader offers a look at the troubling recent history of his country and the Middle East from a Palestinian perspective, sharing his rationale for promoting a two-state solution to the problems affecting the region.

Includes bibliographical references (p. [537]-542).

Nyad, Diana
Find a Way. Diana Nyad. Knopf 2015. 304 p.
ISBN 9780385353618
Grades: Adult   B
1. Nyad, Diana 2. Women swimmers 3. Swimmers 4. Marathon swimming 5. Swimming 6. Endurance sports 7. Autobiographies and memoirs 8. Page to screen 9. Life stories — Sports — Athletes 10. Sports and Competition — Swimming and Diving
LC 2015009932

On September 2, 2013, at the age of 64, Diana Nyad emerged onto the shores of Key West after completing a 110 mile, 53 hour, record-breaking swim through shark-infested waters from Cuba to Florida. Her memoir shows why, at 64 she was able to achieve what she couldn't at 30 and how her repeated failures contributed to her success.

"Particularly effective in its ability to portray the complex psychology of an extreme endurance athlete, Nyad's moving account is well suited for readers interested in open-water swimming, endurance sports, athletes' memoirs, or age-defying adventures." —*Library Journal*

Made into a movie with the title Nyad on Netflix, fall 2023; a Borzoi book.

Nyamayaro, Elizabeth
I Am a Girl from Africa. Elizabeth Nyamayaro. Scribner 2021. 320 p.
ISBN 9781982113018
Grades: Adult   B
1. Nyamayaro, Elizabeth 2. Women social advocates 3. Women 4. Poverty 5. Starvation 6. Women immigrants 7. Gender equity 8. Humanitarian assistance 9. Social advocacy 10. Determination 11. Zimbabwe 12. Great Britain 13. United States 14. Autobiographies and memoirs 15. Life stories — Politics — Activists and reformers 16. Life stories — Facing adversity 17. Society and culture — Social activism and philanthropy

The award-winning humanitarian and former United Nations Senior Advisor on Gender Equality describes how an aid volunteer saved her life and inspired her work as an advocate for positive change in communities throughout the world.

"Nyamayaro's determined debut memoir chronicles the fearlessness that took her from a desperately underprivileged childhood in Zimbabwe to founder of the HeForShe gender equality movement, an effort begun under the auspices of UN Women." —*Publishers Weekly*

O'Brien, Jack
Jack Be Nimble: The Accidental Education of an Unintentional Director. Jack O'Brien. Farrar, Straus and Giroux 2013. 368 p.
ISBN 9780865478985
Grades: Adult   B
1. O'Brien, Jack, 1939- 2. Television producers and directors 3. Theater 4. Theatrical producers and directors 5. United States 6. Autobiographies and memoirs 7. Life stories — Arts and culture — Performing arts — Directors and producers 8. Arts and entertainment — Theater
LC 2012048077

A memoir from Jack O'Brien, one of America's best-loved theater directors and winner of three Tonys.

"Highly recommended for lovers of the theater and those interested in acting and directing." —*Library Journal*

Includes index.

O'Brien, Phillips Payson
The Second Most Powerful Man in the World: The Life of Admiral William D. Leahy, Roosevelt's Chief of Staff. Phillips Payson O'Brien. E.P. Dutton 2019. VIII, 531 p.
ISBN 9780399584800
Grades: Adult   B
1. Leahy, William D. 2. Admirals 3. White House chiefs of staff 4. Presidential staff 5. United States 6. 20th century 7. Biographies 8. Life stories — Politics — Politicians 9. History writing — Presidency — 20th century — United States 10. History writing — Wars and conflicts — World War II
LC 2018016899

A portrait of the influential presidential advisor explores his less-recognized but pivotal role in shaping administrative and military decisions during World War II, revealing his evolving leadership throughout the critical transition to the Truman White House.

"A lucid, opinionated life of a man who exerted far greater influence than historians give him credit forand a book sure to invite spirited argument from historians who disagree." —*Kirkus*

Includes bibliographical references and index.

ESSENTIAL AND RECOMMENDED TITLES
Biography

O'Brien, Vanessa
To the Greatest Heights: Facing Danger, Finding Humility, and Climbing a Mountain of Truth : A Memoir. Vanessa O'Brien. Emily Bestler Books/Atria 2020. 240 p.
ISBN 9781982123789
Grades: Adult   B
1. O'Brien, Vanessa, 1964- 2. Life change events 3. Mountaineering 4. Women mountaineers 5. Women chief executive officers 6. Determination 7. Autobiographies and memoirs 8. Sports and Competition — Mountaineering 9. Life stories — Sports — Athletes 10. Adventure writing — Adventure travel
LC 2020011973

An acclaimed mountaineer, explorer, public speaker and former business executive describes how after the 2008 economic meltdown sent her career careening, she decided to take on climbing Mount Everest and explains how it changed her whole perspective.

"British American mountaineer O'Brien pens a thrilling debut memoir about her mountain-climbing adventures and what they've taught her about life." —*Publishers Weekly*

O'Connell, Robert L.
Revolutionary: George Washington at War. Robert L. O'Connell. Random House Inc 2019. 400 p.
ISBN 9780812996999
Grades: Adult   B
1. Washington, George, 1732-1799 2. Generals 3. Command of troops 4. American Revolution, 1775-1783 5. Soldiers 6. Men 7. Military ethics 8. Psychology 9. Personal conduct 10. United States history 11. Revolutionary America (1775-1783) 12. Biographies 13. History writing — Wars and conflicts — Revolutionary War (America) 14. Life stories — Law and order — Military leaders
LC 2018013009

The military historian and author of Fierce Patriot presents a bold reappraisal of George Washington as a young soldier of destiny whose Revolutionary War leadership came to define the American character.

O'Connor, Garry
Ian McKellen: A Biography. Garry O'Connor. St. Martin's Press 2019. 352 pages
ISBN 9781250223883
Grades: Adult   B
1. McKellen, Ian 2. Actors and actresses 3. Gay men 4. LGBTQIA+ rights 5. Films 6. United States 7. Biographies 8. Life stories — Arts and culture — Performing arts — Actors and actresses 9. Life stories — Politics — Activists and reformers 10. Life stories — Identity — LGBTQIA+ 11. Arts and Entertainment — Movies and Television 12. Arts and Entertainment — Theater
LC 2019032544

A biography of the esteemed actor follows his career, which includes roles in over 400 plays and films, from his debut in London's West End in 1964 to playing Gandalf in the Lord of the Rings film adaptations.

Universal Father: A Life of Pope John Paul II. Garry O'Connor. Bloomsbury : 2005. xii, 436 p. : Illustration; Map
ISBN 9781596910966
Grades: Adult   B
1. John Paul II, Pope, 1920-2005 2. Popes 3. Communism and religion 4. 20th century 5. 21st century 6. Biographies 7. Spirituality and Religion — Christianity — Catholicism 8. Spirituality and Religion — Religious Leaders 9. Life stories — Religion and spirituality — Religious and spiritual leaders
LC BI2005008332

Chronicles the life of Pope John Paul II from his childhood and early years as a priest through his twenty-six year papacy, highlighting his opposition to communism, his travels, and changes within the Catholic Church during his reign.

"The text is divided into four distinct phases of Pope John Paul II's life: 1920-1946, 1946-1978, 1978-1990, and 1990-2005. Each phase balances fact with anecdotal evidence, which lends the biography both credibility and charm.

This timely and remarkable biography will be sought after by serious readers." —*Library Journal*
Includes bibliographical references (p. [411]-415) and index.

O'Connor, Ian
Belichick: The Making of the Greatest Football Coach of All Time. Ian O'Connor. Houghton Mifflin Harcourt 2018. 416 p.
ISBN 9780544785748
Grades: Adult   B
1. Belichick, Bill 2. Football coaches 3. Football teams 4. Coaching (Athletics) 5. Football 6. Social life and customs 7. United States 8. Biographies 9. Sports and Competition — Football 10. Sports and Competition — Coaches 11. Life stories — Sports — Athletes 12. Life stories — Sports — Coaches, managers, and owners
LC 2018017251

A biography of the NFL's most enigmatic, controversial, and yet successful coach follows his life in football, from watching Naval Academy games with his father to his success as head coach of the New England Patriots.

"...detailed look at Belichick's successful and controversial life." —*Library Journal*
Includes bibliographical references and index.

Coach K: The Rise and Reign of Mike Krzyzewski. Ian O'Connor. Mariner Books 2022. 320 p.
ISBN 9780358345404
Grades: Adult   B
1. Krzyzewski, Mike 2. Athletic coaches 3. Basketball 4. College sports 5. College basketball 6. United States 7. Biographies 8. Life stories — Sports — Coaches, managers, and owners 9. Sports and Competition — Basketball

This definitive biography of college basketball's all-time winningest coach looks at how he built a basketball empire at Duke and led Team USA to three Olympic basketball gold medals.

"New York Post sports columnist O'Connor (Belichick) delivers a standout definitive biography of Mike Krzyzewski, who led the Duke Blue Devils to five NCAA titles during his decades-long tenure as coach." —*Publishers Weekly*

O'Connor, Sinead
★ *Rememberings: Scenes from My Complicated Life.* Sinead O'Connor. Houghton Mifflin Harcourt 2021. 256 p.
ISBN 9780358423881
Grades: Adult   B
1. O'Connor, Sinead. 1966-2023 2. Singers 3. Rock musicians 4. Women radicals 5. Childhood 6. Rock music 7. Mental illness 8. Dysfunctional families 9. Autobiographies and memoirs 10. Life stories — Arts and culture — Performing arts — Musicians and composers 11. Arts and Entertainment — Music — Rock
LC 2020057679

From the acclaimed, controversial singer-songwriter Sinead O'Connor comes a revelatory memoir of her fraught childhood, musical triumphs, struggles with illness, and of the enduring power of song.

Complete with anecdotes told in singular form, the acclaimed, controversial singer-songwriter recounts her troubled childhood and musical triumphs, revealing the enduring power of song.

"The Grammy-winning Irish singer/Songwriter looks back on her eventful life.... A self-aware confessional from a successful and controversial musician." —*Kirkus*

O'Farrell, Maggie
I Am, I Am, I Am: Seventeen Brushes with Death. Maggie O'Farrell. Alfred A. Knopf 2018. 224 p.
ISBN 9780525520221
Grades: Adult   B
1. O'Farrell, Maggie, 1972- 2. Near-death experience 3. Accidents 4. Sick people 5. Vulnerability 6. Authors, Irish 7. Essays 8. Autobiographies and memoirs 9. Life stories — Facing adversity
LC 2017028597
Library Journal Best Books, 2018.

PUBLIC LIBRARY CORE COLLECTION: NONFICTION
Twentieth Edition

Presents a memoir told entirely in seventeen near-death experiences stemming from a dangerous childhood illness, accidents, an encounter with a disturbed person, and the author's daily efforts to protect her daughter from the vulnerabilities of a high-risk condition.

"O'Farrell's intrepidness and determination are awe-inspiring, her experiences overwhelming, and her writing impeccable. This is a memoiristic tour de force." —*Booklist*

O'Hara, Maryanne
Little Matches: A Memoir of Grief and Light. Maryanne O'Hara. HarperCollins 2021. 368 p.
ISBN 9780063027763
Grades: Adult — B
1. O'Hara, Maryanne 2. Authors, American 3. Mothers and daughters 4. Death of daughters 5. Grief 6. People with cystic fibrosis 7. Loss 8. Uncertainty 9. Motherhood 10. Hope 11. 20th century 12. Autobiographies and memoirs 13. Life stories — Facing adversity — Coping with death 14. Life stories — Relationships — Parent and child 15. Family and Relationships — Illness and the family 16. Family and Relationships — Aging and death

LC Bl2021002080

An emotionally raw and inspiring memoir that illuminates a mother's grief over the loss of her adult child and considers the hope of soulful connections that transcend the boundary of life and death.

"In this vividly written memoir featuring text messages, blog posts, and emails, novelist O'Hara (Cascade) shares a painful but ultimately beautiful account of her daughter Caitlin's life with cystic fibrosis." —*Library Journal*

O'Neill, Robert
The Operator: *Firing the Shots That Killed Osama Bin Laden and My Years as a Seal Team Warrior.* Robert O'Neill. Scribner 2017. 320 p.
ISBN 9781501145032
Grades: Adult — B
1. O'Neill, Robert, 1976- 2. Bin Laden, Osama, 1957-2011 3. Special forces 4. Afghan War, 2001-2021 5. Commando operations 6. War on Terrorism, 2001-2009 7. Special operations (Military science) 8. Navy SEALs 9. Afghanistan 10. Autobiographies and memoirs 11. History writing — Military — Special Forces 12. Life stories — Law and order — Armed forces personnel 13. History writing — Wars and conflicts — War in Afghanistan

LC 2017007867

One of America's most elite soldiers discusses his 400-mission career.

O'Reilly, Seamas
★ *Did* Ye Hear Mammy Died?: A Memoir. Seamas O'Reilly. Little Brown & Company 2022. 304 p.
ISBN 9780316424257
Grades: Adult — B
1. Growing up 2. Siblings 3. Families 4. Family relationships 5. Single-parent families 6. Grief 7. Death of mothers 8. Loss 9. Autobiographies and memoirs 10. Family and relationships — Siblings 11. Life stories — Relationships — Growing up 12. Family and relationships — Families 13. Life stories — Relationships — Family

This memoir from one of eleven siblings raised by a single dad in Northern Ireland at the end of the Troubles follows the family as they struggle to keep the household running.

"O'Reilly's recollection is a splendid paradox, both cheery and heartbreaking." —*Booklist*

O'Sullivan, Emer
The Fall *of the House of Wilde: Oscar Wilde and His Family.* Emer O'Sullivan. Bloomsbury 2016. 416 p.
ISBN 9781608199877
Grades: Adult — B
1. Wilde, Oscar, 1854-1900 2. Authors, Irish 3. Family relationships 4. Eccentrics and eccentricities 5. Homosexuality 6. Gay men 7. Self-destructive behavior 8. Public opinion 9. Trials (Libel) 10. Legislation 11. British history 12. London, England 13. 19th century 14. Victorian era (1837-1901) 15. Biographies 16. Life stories — Arts and culture — Writing — Authors 17. Life stories — Relationships — Family 18. History writing — Europe — United Kingdom

LC Bl2016044570

A first-ever biography of Oscar Wilde that places him within the context of his family and social and historical milieu finally tells the whole story of one of the most prominent characters of the late 19th century whose trial for indecency heralded decadence's demise—and his own.

"OSullivans impressively comprehensive biography is equal parts political history, literary criticism, and Shakespearean tragedy." —*Publishers Weekly*

O'Toole, Jennifer Cook
Autism in Heels: The Untold Story of a Female Life on the Spectrum. Jennifer O'Toole. Skyhorse 2018. 240 p.
ISBN 9781510732841
Grades: Adult — B
1. O'Toole, Jennifer Cook 2. Autistic women 3. Autistic people 4. Belonging 5. Coping 6. Autism spectrum disorders 7. Neurodivergent people 8. Autobiographies and memoirs 9. Life stories — Facing adversity — Medical issues — Living with disabilities 10. Adult books for young adults

Autism in Heels, an intimate memoir, reveals the woman inside one of autism's most prominent figures, Jennifer O'Toole. At the age of thirty-five, Jennifer was diagnosed with Asperger's syndrome, and for the first time in her life, things made sense. Now, Jennifer exposes the constant struggle between carefully crafted persona and authentic existence, editing the autism script with wit, candor, passion, and power. Her journey is one of reverse-self-discovery not only as an Aspie but—more importantly—as a thoroughly modern woman.

O'Toole, Patricia
The Moralist: *Woodrow Wilson and the World He Made.* Patricia O'Toole. Simon & Schuster 2018. 512 p.
ISBN 9780743298094
Grades: Adult — B
1. Wilson, Woodrow, 1856-1924 2. Political leadership 3. Presidents 4. International relations 5. United States 6. 20th century 7. Biographies 8. Impartial writing 9. History writing — Presidency — 20th century — United States 10. Life stories — Politics — Politicians

LC 2018006628

An in-depth portrait of the 28th President argues that controversial decisions by the Wilson administration established unprecedented levels of American overreach in foreign affairs, examining the challenges, leadership, failures and health setbacks that shaped the Paris Peace Conference of 1919 and founded the League of Nations.

Oakley, Charles
The Last *Enforcer: Outrageous Stories from the Life and Times of One of the Nba's Fiercest Competitors.* Charles Oakley with Frank Isola. Gallery Books 2022. 288 p.
ISBN 9781982175641
Grades: Adult — B
1. Oakley, Charles, 1963- 2. African American basketball players 3. Basketball players 4. Basketball 5. Professional basketball players 6. Interpersonal relations 7. Autobiographies and memoirs 8. Life stories — Sports — Athletes 9. Sports and Competition — Basketball 10. Sports and Competition — Individual Athlete

LC 2021035847

A memoir from Charles Oakley-one of the toughest and most loyal players in NBA history-featuring unfiltered stories about the journey that basketball has taken him on and his relationships with Michael Jordan, LeBron James, Charles Barkley, Patrick Ewing, Phil Jackson, Pat Riley, James Dolan, Donald Trump, George Floyd, and so many others.

"The hard-nosed former professional basketball star shares his bold outlook on life as well as wild tales on and off the court. . . . Basketball fans will enjoy Oakley's stories about the game's biggest stars and his opinions about them." —*Kirkus*

Includes index.

ESSENTIAL AND RECOMMENDED TITLES
Biography

Obama, Barack
★ *The Audacity of Hope: Thoughts on Reclaiming the American Dream.* Barack Obama. Crown Publishers 2006. 375 p.
ISBN 9780307237699
Grades: Adult   B
1. Obama, Barack 2. National characteristics, American 3. Political science 4. Legislators 5. African American legislators 6. Emotions 7. Values 8. Politics and government 9. Philosophy 10. United States 11. 2000s (Decade) 12. Liberal writing 13. Politics and global affairs — World politics — United States 14. Politics and global affairs — Political figures
LC 2006028967
BCALA Literary Award for Nonfiction, 2007.
The junior senator from Illinois discusses how to transform U.S. politics, calling for a return to America's original ideals and revealing how they can address such issues as globalization and the function of religion in public life.
Includes index.

★ *Dreams from My Father: A Story of Race and Inheritance.* Barack Obama. Crown Publishers 2007. xvii, 442 p.
ISBN 9780307383419
Grades: 7 8 9 10 11 12 Adult   B
1. Obama, Barack 2. African American legislators 3. Multiracial people 4. Community organizers 5. Racism 6. African Americans 7. Legislators 8. Race relations 9. Illinois 10. Chicago, Illinois 11. Kenya 12. United States 13. Autobiographies and memoirs 14. Biographies 15. Life stories — Politics — Politicians 16. Society and culture — Race 17. Antiracist literature
LC 2007271892
Booklist Editors' Choice: Adult Books for Young Adults, 1995; British Book Award for Biography of the Year, 2009.
The son of an African father and white American mother discusses his childhood in Hawaii, his struggle to find his identity as an African American, and his life accomplishments.
"The author offers an account of his life's journey that reflects brilliantly on the power of race consciousness in America. . . , Obama writes well; his account is sensitive, probing, and compelling." —*Choice.* [review of 1995 edition]
Originally published: New York : Times Books, c1995. With new introd.

★ *A Promised Land.* Barack Obama. Crown Publishers 2020. 784 p.
ISBN 9781524763169
Grades: Adult   B
1. Obama, Barack 2. Hope 3. African American politicians 4. Community organizers 5. Multiracial people 6. Presidents 7. Politics and government 8. Determination 9. United States 10. 21st century 11. 2000s (Decade) 12. 2010s 13. Autobiographies and memoirs 14. Life stories — Politics — Politicians 15. Politics and global affairs — World politics — United States 16. History writing — Presidency — 21st century — United States
LC Bl2020046605
New York Times Notable Book, 2020.
A deeply personal account of history in the making—from the president who inspired us to believe in the power of democracy.
"An eloquently written, enjoyable, and important memoir that will have a wide readership." —*Library Journal*

Obama, Michelle
★ *Becoming.* Michelle Obama. Crown 2018. 400 p.
ISBN 9781524763138
Grades: Adult   B
1. Obama, Michelle, 1964- 2. African American women lawyers 3. African American lawyers 4. Work-life balance 5. Women's role 6. Women's rights 7. Presidents' spouses 8. African American women 9. Politics and government 10. United States 11. 21st century 12. 2000s (Decade) 13. 2010s 14. Autobiographies and memoirs 15. History writing — Presidency — 21st century — United States 16. Life stories — Politics — Politicians 17. Life stories — Law and order — Judges and lawyers 18. Book club best bets
LC Bl2018183323
British Book Award for Narrative Nonfiction of the Year, 2019; New York Times Notable Book, 2019.

An intimate memoir by the former First Lady chronicles the experiences that have shaped her remarkable life, from her childhood on the South Side of Chicago through her setbacks and achievements in the White House.
"There are no dramatic revelations and not much overt politics here, but fans of the Obamas will find an interesting, inspiring saga of quiet social revolutions." —*Publishers Weekly*
Also published in large print format.

★ *The Light We Carry: Overcoming in Uncertain Times.* Michelle Obama. Crown 2022. xii, 318 pages
ISBN 9780593237465
Grades: Adult   B
1. Obama, Michelle, 1964- 2. Presidents' spouses 3. Women lawyers 4. African American women 5. Mothers 6. Role models 7. Influence (Psychology) 8. Friendship 9. Compassion 10. Resilience 11. Hope 12. North American people 13. American people 14. Life stories — Politics 15. Life stories — Relationships 16. Life stories — Personal growth 17. Book club best bets
Mrs. Obama offers readers a series of fresh stories and insightful reflections on change, challenge, and power, including her belief that when we light up for others, we can illuminate the richness and potential of the world around us, discovering deeper truths and new pathways for progress. Drawing from her experiences as a mother, daughter, spouse, friend, and First Lady, she shares the habits and principles she has developed to successfully adapt to change and overcome various obstacles—the earned wisdom that helps her continue to "become."
"Michelle Obama follows her best-selling Becoming (2018) with a self-help memoir full of inspiring stories and insightful reflections on her public and personal lives and how she has overcome challenges as a spouse, mother, and friend." —*Booklist*

Oberman, Heiko Augustinus
Luther: Man Between God and the Devil. Heiko A. Oberman; translated from the German by Eileen Walliser-Schwarzbart. Yale University Press 2006. xx, 380 p. : Illustration
ISBN 9780300103137
Grades: 11 12 Adult   B
1. Luther, Martin, 1483-1546 2. Reformation 3. Church history 4. Germany 5. 16th century 6. Biographies 7. Life stories — People in history 8. Life stories — Religion and spirituality
LC 2007039341
"The author posits that to understand Luther the reformer is to first realize he was a medieval man for whom Satan was as real as God and human. By placing Luther back into the context of his own age, Oberman strips away any simplistic, post-Enlightenment notions of Luther as the savior of humanity from the darkest obscurantism of the Catholic Church. A triumph of scholarship that brings Luther to life in all of his furious, outspoken, and violent passion." —*Booklist*
Translation of: Luther : Mensch zwischen Gott und Teufel; Includes bibliographical references (p. 331-354) and index.

Odell, Amy
Anna: The Biography. Amy Odell. Gallery Books 2022. 256 p.
ISBN 9781982122638
Grades: Adult   B
1. Wintour, Anna, 1949- 2. Women editors 3. Power 4. Publishers and publishing 5. Fashion periodicals 6. Women journalists 7. Influencers 8. Biographies 9. Life stories — Arts and culture — Writing 10. Arts and entertainment — Writing and publishing
This definitive biography of the legendary fashion journalist and media mogul follows her journey from the trendy fashion scene of swinging 1960s London to becoming the editor-in-chief of Vogue magazine.
"In this biography of Vogue editor-in-chief and Condé Nast executive Anna Wintour, fashion journalist Odell (Tales from the Back Row, 2015) lifts a couture curtain to reveal the woman behind the famous sunglasses and glossy bob." —*Booklist*

Odenkirk, Bob
Comedy Comedy Comedy Drama: A Memoir. Bob Odenkirk. Random House 2022. 304 p.

PUBLIC LIBRARY CORE COLLECTION: NONFICTION
Twentieth Edition

ISBN 9780399180514
Grades: Adult **B**
1. Odenkirk, Bob, 1962- 2. Comedians 3. Television comedy writers 4. Television producers and directors 5. Determination 6. Fame 7. Success (Concept) 8. Advice 9. Actors and actresses 10. Autobiographies and memoirs 11. Biographies 12. Life stories — Arts and culture — Performing arts — Actors and actresses 13. Life stories — Arts and culture — Performing arts — Directors and producers 14. Arts and Entertainment — Comedy 15. Arts and Entertainment — Movies and Television

LC 2021020154

The Emmy-winning star of Mr. Show, Breaking Bad and Better Call Saul discusses his early career as a cult comedy writer, as well as his reinvention as an action star at age 50.

"Writing from an insider's view on the industry, Odenkirk tells us what it is really like to work in and learn your way through the comedy business and beyond.... All readers who enjoy truth telling and satire will find Odenkirk's memoir engaging." —*Booklist*

Oelhafen, Ingrid von
Hitler's Stolen Children: The Shocking True Story of the Nazi Kidnapping Conspiracy. Ingrid von Oelhafen & Tim Tate with Dr. Dorothee Schmitz-Koster. Collins 2020. IX, 275 p. : Illustration
ISBN 9781443460637
Grades: Adult **B**
1. Oelhafen, Ingrid von 2. Eugenics 3. Kidnapping 4. Nazism 5. Adopted children 6. Birthparents 7. Identity 8. Family secrets 9. World War II 10. Children 11. Third Reich, 1933-1945 12. Germany 13. 20th century 14. Autobiographies and memoirs 15. Canadian literature 16. Life stories — People in history 17. History writing — Wars and conflicts — Homefront — World War II 18. History writing — Europe — Germany 19. Life stories — Identity

The author shares her story of being taken from her family in St. Sauerbrunn in what was then Yugoslavia and brought to Germany to be "Germanized" in the Lebensborn program.

"This riveting, raw, and heart-wrenching story of misplaced identity and one woman's quest to find peace and hope in the darkest of times will intrigue a variety of readers interested in a mix of history nestled among personal memoir." —*Library Journal*

Includes bibliographical references; Originally published under the title: Hitler's forgotten children. London : Elliott and Thompson, 2015; Also published: New York : Berkley Caliber, 2016.

Offerman, Nick
The **Greatest** *Love Story Ever Told: An Oral History.* Nick Offerman and Megan Mullally. Penguin Group USA 2018. 320 p.
ISBN 9781101986677
Grades: Adult **B**
1. Mullally, Megan 2. Offerman, Nick, 1970- 3. Couples 4. Actors and actresses 5. Dating 6. Interclass romance 7. Interpersonal attraction 8. Men-women relations 9. Los Angeles, California 10. Autobiographies and memoirs 11. Life stories — Relationships — Couples 12. Life stories — Arts and culture — Performing arts — Actors and actresses 13. Family and Relationships — Dating and Marriage

LC 2018410359

The popular comedic couple trace the story of their relationship, sharing anecdotes, family photos and secrets that reveal how they overcame considerable social differences through their shared values and mutual love of music and laughter.

Okporo, Edafe
Asylum: A Memoir & Manifesto. Edafe Okporo. Simon & Schuster 2022. 244 p.
ISBN 9781982183745
Grades: Adult **B**
1. Immigration and emigration 2. Immigration policy 3. Immigration and emigration law 4. Human rights activists 5. Gay activists 6. LGBTQIA+ people 7. Gay men 8. Nigeria 9. United States 10. Autobiographies and memoirs 11. Life stories — Politics — Activists and reformers 12. Life stories — Identity — LGBTQIA+

A poignant, moving memoir and urgent call to action for immigration justice by a Nigerian asylee and global gay rights and immigration activist Edafe Okporo.

"A moving story from an inspiring activist for social justice." —*Kirkus*

Oller, John
American Queen: The Rise and Fall of Kate Chase Sprague, Civil War. John Oller. Da Capo Press, a Member of the Perseus Books Group 2014. 288 p.
ISBN 9780306822803
Grades: Adult **B**
1. Sprague, Kate Chase, 1840-1899 2. Chase, Salmon P. (Salmon Portland), 1808-1873 3. Sprague, William, 1830-1915 4. Socialites 5. Scandals 6. Extramarital affairs 7. Politicians 8. Power 9. Social life and customs 10. Politics and government 11. Ambition 12. Washington (D.C.) 13. United States 14. 19th century 15. Biographies 16. History writing — Women's history 17. Life stories — People in history 18. History writing — Gilded Age — United States

LC 2014012054

Kate Chase, the charismatic daughter of Abraham Lincoln's treasury secretary, enjoyed unprecedented political power for a woman. As her widowed father's hostess, she set up a rival "court" against Mary Lincoln in hopes of making her father president and herself his First Lady. To facilitate that goal, she married one of the richest men in the country, the handsome "boy governor" of Rhode Island, in the social event of the Civil War. But when William Sprague turned out to be less of a prince as a husband, she found comfort in the arms of a powerful married senator. The ensuing scandal ended her virtual royalty, leaving her a social outcast who died in poverty. Yet in her final years she would find both greater authenticity and the inner peace that had always eluded her.

Oller's work is less the story of a woman's political rise and fall and more one that reveals how the social limitations of the past created tragic outcomes for talented females. A well-researched, thoughtful biography of a woman who 'Became entirely her own person, a rare feat for women of her day.' —*Kirkus*

Includes bibliographical references and index.

Ollestad, Norman
Crazy for the Storm: A Memoir of Survival. Norman Ollestad. Ecco 2009. 288 p.
ISBN 9780061766725
Grades: Adult **B**
1. Ollestad, Norman 2. Ollestad, Norman, 1935-1979 3. Airplane accident victims 4. Airplane accidents 5. Surfers 6. Skiing 7. Airplane accident survivors 8. Fathers and sons 9. Death of fathers 10. Survival 11. Competition 12. Adventure writing — Survival 13. Adult books for young adults

LC 2008053675

On February 19th, 1979, blinded by a blizzard, a small chartered plane crashed into the side of a massive mountain. Eleven-year-old Norman Ollestad, his father, his father's girlfriend, and the pilot were in the crash. After a nine-hour nightmare, only little Norman remained alive. Here, Norman Ollestad chronicles his harrowing experience and epic fight for survival.

"In the winter of 1979, the 11-year-old Ollestad survived a plane crash in which his father and his father's girlfriend were killed. Alternating with young Norman's nine-hour trek to safety are scenes from the year preceding the crash, when the boy took a surfing trip with his father through the jungle along Mexico's Pacific coast. The flashbacks sections are the most fascinating parts of the book, and Ollestad ably captures the contrast between his charismatically cool father, Norman Sr, and his bullying stepfather-to-be, Nick. [He] presents a captivating account of high-altitude disaster that nicely dovetails with his coming-of-age story in '70s California. Deep and resonant." —*Kirkus*

Ollivier, Bernard
Out of Istanbul: A Journey of Discovery Along the Silk Road. Bernard Ollivier; translated by Dan Golembeski. Skyhorse Publishing 2019. 320 pages
ISBN 9781510743755
Grades: Adult **B**
1. Ollivier, Bernard 2. Authors, French 3. Trade routes 4. Silk industry and trade 5. Walking 6. Travel writers 7. Voyages and travels 8. Asia 9. Silk Road 10.

ESSENTIAL AND RECOMMENDED TITLES
Biography

20th century 11. Autobiographies and memoirs 12. Translations — French to English 13. Travel Writing — Retracing Historic Journeys 14. History writing — Asia 15. Travel Writing — Modes of Transportation — on Foot 16. Travel Writing — Asia and the South Pacific

Ollivier's journey, far from bragging about some tremendous achievement, humbly takes the reader on a colossal adventure of human proportions, one in which walking itself, through a kind of alchemy, fosters friendships and fellowship.

Translation of: Longue marche: A pied de la Mediterranée jusqu'en Chine par la route de la Soie; Originally published: Paris : Editions Phebus, 2001; Translated from the French.

Olson, Lynne

★ *Empress of the Nile: The Daredevil Archaeologist Who Saved Egypt's Ancient Temples from Destruction.* Lynne Olson. Random House 2022. 448 pages
ISBN 9780525509479
Grades: Adult   B

1. Desroches-Noblecourt, Christiane, 1913-2011 2. Egyptologists 3. Archaeologists 4. French people 5. Antiquities 6. Material culture 7. Historic preservation 8. Southwest Asia and North Africa (Middle East) history 9. Egypt 10. 1960s 11. History writing — Archaeology 12. Life stories — Science, technology, and medicine — Scientists and inventors

LC 2022012856

Tells the story of Christiane Desroches-Noblecourt, a French archaeologist who led the international effort to save ancient Egyptian temples from the floodwaters of the Aswan Dam as well as her activities during the French Resistance in World War II.

"Enriched by fascinating digressions into Egyptian history, museum rivalries, the plundering of archaeological sites, the 1956 Suez Crisis, and more, this is a captivating portrait of a pathbreaking woman." —*Publishers Weekly*

Includes bibliographical references and index.

★ *Madame Fourcade's Secret War: The Daring Young Woman Who Led France's Largest Spy Network Against Hitler.* Lynne Olson. Random House 2019. 384 p.
ISBN 9780812994766
Grades: Adult   B

1. Fourcade, Marie-Madeleine, 1909-1989 2. Women spies 3. Secret service 4. Espionage 5. French Resistance (World War II) 6. World War II 7. German occupation, World War II 8. French history 9. France 10. Biographies 11. Life stories — Law and order — Spies and secret agents 12. History writing — Spies and spying 13. History writing — Wars and conflicts — World War II

LC 2018049180

The New York Times best-selling author of Citizens of London and Last Hope Island tells the true story of the woman who headed the largest spy network in occupied France during World War II.

"This masterfully told true story reads like fiction and will appeal to readers who devour WWII thrillers la Kristen Hannah's the Nightingale (2015)." —*Booklist*

Includes bibliographical references and index.

Oluseyi, Hakeem M.

A Quantum Life: My Unlikely Journey from the Street to the Stars. Hakeem Oluseyi and Joshua Horwitz. Ballantine Books 2021. 304 p.
ISBN 9781984819093
Grades: Adult   B

1. Oluseyi, Hakeem M. (Hakeem Muata) 2. Astrophysicists 3. African American men 4. Racism 5. Addiction 6. Poverty 7. Astrophysics 8. Childhood 9. Physicists 10. Hope 11. Crime 12. United States 13. Autobiographies and memoirs 14. Life stories — Science, technology, and medicine — Scientists and inventors 15. Life stories — Facing adversity 16. Science Writing — Physics 17. Science Writing — Space and flight

This memoir of the renowned astrophysicist tells the story of how he overcame his personal demons, including an impoverished childhood and life of crime as well as an addiction to crack cocaine and entrenched racism.

"This warts-and-all chronicle reveals how an African American kid from a poor and broken family who lived in the Deep South managed to overcome severe racial biases as well as a crippling crack cocaine addiction to achieve a successful and esteemed career that includes a PhD in physics from Stanford, studying solar atmospheres, and working with NASA." —*Publishers Weekly*

Onassis, Jacqueline Kennedy

Historic Conversations on Life with John F. Kennedy. Jacqueline Kennedy; interviews with Arthur M. Schlesinger, Jr, 1964; foreword by Caroline Kennedy; introduction and annotations by Michael Beschloss. Hyperion 2011. xxxii, 368 p. : Illustration
ISBN 9781401324254
Grades: Adult   B

1. Onassis, Jacqueline Kennedy, 1929-1994 2. Kennedy, John F. (John Fitzgerald), 1917-1963 3. Presidents' spouses 4. Presidents 5. United States 6. 20th century 7. Autobiographies and memoirs 8. Biographies 9. History writing — Presidency — 20th century — United States 10. Life stories — Politics — Politicians

LC Bl2011025216

Presents the annotated transcription and original audio for the 1964 interviews with Jacqueline Kennedy on her experiences and impressions as the wife of John F. Kennedy, offering an intimate and detailed account of the man and his times.

Issued in slipcase; Includes bibliographical references (p. 354-356) and index.

Oppedisano, Tony

Sinatra and Me: In the Wee Small Hours. by Tony Oppedisano with Mary Jane Ross. Scribner 2021. 320 p.
ISBN 9781982151782
Grades: Adult   B

1. Sinatra, Frank, 1915-1998 2. Oppedisano, Tony 3. Singers 4. Musicians 5. Friendship 6. Interpersonal relations 7. Celebrities 8. Male friendship 9. United States 10. Biographies 11. Life stories — Arts and culture — Performing arts — Musicians and composers 12. Arts and Entertainment — Music — Jazz and the Blues

LC 2021004411

Featuring never-before-seen photos and offering startlingly fresh anecdotes and new revelations that center on some of the most famous people of the past 50 years, this revealing portrait pulls back the curtain to reveal a man whom history has, in many ways, gotten wrong.

"A revealing memoir from the legendary singer's road manager. . . . A must-read for Sinatra fans, this lovingly written, sweetly devoted account may even help solve some pop-culture mysteries." —*Kirkus*

Includes index.

Orenstein, Peggy

Unraveling: What I Learned About Life While Shearing Sheep, Dyeing Wool, and Making the World's Ugliest Sweater. Peggy Orenstein. HarperCollins 2023. 320 p.
ISBN 9780063081727
Grades: Adult   B

1. Orenstein, Peggy 2. Handicraft 3. Knitting 4. Self-discovery 5. COVID-19 Pandemic, 2020- 6. Knitters 7. Grief 8. Aging 9. Life change events 10. Families 11. Sweaters 12. Autobiographies and memoirs 13. Arts and Entertainment — Crafts and hobbies 14. Life stories — Personal growth

The author sets out to make a sweater from scratch—shearing, spinning, dyeing wool—and in the process discovers how we find our deepest selves through craft.

"Journalist Orenstein...recounts her yearlong endeavor to make a sweater from scratch in this insightful memoir....This snapshot of creative self-discovery will enlighten readers." —*Publishers Weekly*

Orji, Yvonne

Bamboozled by Jesus: How God Tricked Me into the Life of My Dreams. Yvonne Orji. Worthy 2021. 256 p.
ISBN 9781546012672
Grades: Adult   B

PUBLIC LIBRARY CORE COLLECTION: NONFICTION
Twentieth Edition

1. Orji, Yvonne 2. Actors and actresses 3. African American comedians 4. Christian women 5. Faith (Christianity) 6. Christian life 7. Success (Concept) 8. Women comedians 9. Autobiographies and memoirs 10. Life stories — Arts and culture — Performing arts — Actors and actresses 11. Life stories — Religion and spirituality — Personal faith 12. Arts and Entertainment — Movies and television 13. Life stories — Arts and culture — Performing arts — Entertainers and celebrities 14. Spirituality and Religion — Christianity 15. Arts and Entertainment — Comedy

Orji takes readers on a journey through twenty-five life lessons, gleaned from her own experiences and her favorite source of inspiration: the Bible. But this ain't your mama's Bible study. Yvonne infuses wit and heart in sharing pointers like why the way up is sometimes down, and how fear is synonymous to food poisoning. Her joyful, confident approach to God will inspire everyone to catapult themselves out of the mundane and into the magnificent.

"Although Orji doesn't shy from portraying Christianity as her guiding light, her cultural colloquialisms and honesty leave room for all readers to relate, no matter their religious beliefs. . . . Inspiration practically leaps off the pages and into the hearts of readers—a feeling Orji demands be followed up with action." —*Booklist*

Ortiz, David
Papi: My Story. David Ortiz, with Michael Holley. Houghton Mifflin Harcourt 2017. 320 p.
ISBN 9780544814615
Grades: Adult   B
1. Ortiz, David, 1975- 2. African American baseball players 3. Batters (Baseball) 4. Baseball players 5. Baseball 6. Professional athletes 7. Autobiographies and memoirs 8. Life stories — Sports — Athletes 9. Sports and Competition — Baseball 10. Sports and Competition — Individual Athlete

An entertaining, unfiltered memoir by one of the game's greatest, most clutch sluggers at the end of his career, written with best-selling sports writer and talk show host Michael Holley.

"The ups and downs of a legendary baseball career." —*Kirkus*

Osborne, Richard
Herbert Von Karajan: A Life in Music. Richard Osborne. Northeastern University Press 2000. x, 851 p. : Illustration
ISBN 9781555534257
Grades: Adult   B
1. Karajan, Herbert von 2. Conductors (Music) 3. Biographies 4. Life stories — Arts and culture — Performing arts
LC 99059108

"Because Karajan's career developed in Nazi Germany, Osborne dwells at length . on Karajan's involvement with the regime and his postwar exoneration. Drawing on a vast variety of source materials and quoting some in full, Osborne takes us on the enthralling musical journey that was the life of one of the greatest of conductors." —*Booklist*

Includes bibliographical references (p. 760-824) and indexes; Originally published: London : Chatto & Windus, 1998.

Osbourne, Ozzy
I Am Ozzy. Ozzy Osbourne; Chris Ayres, contributor. Grand Central Pub. 2010. 320 p.
ISBN 9780446569897
Grades: 11 12 Adult   B
1. Osbourne, Ozzy, 1948- 2. Heavy metal music 3. Men 4. Rock music 5. Heavy metal musicians 6. Drug use 7. Rock musicians 8. Personal conduct 9. England 10. Autobiographies and memoirs 11. Biographies 12. Arts and Entertainment — Music — Rock 13. Life stories — Arts and culture — Performing arts — Musicians and composers
LC 2009937230

The Black Sabbath front man and reality TV star discusses his working class upbringing, his decision to quit a factory job for a life in music, his alcohol and substance excesses, his brushes with death and STDs, and the surreal experience of becoming a grandfather.

Osnos, Evan
Joe Biden: The Life, the Run, and What Matters Now. Evan Osnos. Scribner 2020. 177 p.
ISBN 9781982174026
Grades: Adult   B
1. Biden, Joseph R. 1942- 2. Presidential candidates 3. Family relationships 4. Resilience 5. Vice-presidents 6. Legislators 7. Politics and government 8. United States 9. Biographies 10. Impartial writing 11. Life stories — Politics — Politicians 12. Life stories — Facing adversity 13. Politics and global affairs — Political figures

Former vice president Joseph R. Biden Jr. has been called both the luckiest man and the unluckiest—fortunate to have sustained a fifty-year political career that reached the White House, but also marked by deep personal losses and disappointments that he has suffered. Yet even as Biden's life has been shaped by drama, it has also been powered by a willingness, rare at the top ranks of politics, to confront his shortcomings, errors, and reversals of fortune. Blending up-close journalism and broader context, Evan Osnos draws on his work for the New Yorker to capture the characters and meaning of an extraordinary presidential election.

Includes bibliographical references.

Owen, Mark
No Easy Day: The Firsthand Account of the Mission That Killed Osama Bin Laden : The Autobiography of a Navy SEAL. Mark Owen with Kevin Maurer. Dutton 2012. xiii, 316 p. : Illustration; Color; Map
ISBN 9780525953722
Grades: Adult   B
1. Owen, Mark 2. Bin Laden, Osama, 1957-2011 3. Afghan War, 2001-2021 4. Commando operations 5. War on Terrorism, 2001-2009 6. Special operations (Military science) 7. Special forces 8. Navy SEALs 9. Afghanistan 10. Autobiographies and memoirs 11. Life stories — Law and order — Armed forces personnel 12. History writing — Wars and conflicts — War in Afghanistan
LC Bl2012031043

Examines the mission that killed Osama Bin Laden, details the selection and training process for one of the most elite units in the military, and describes previously unreported missions that illustrate the life and work of a SEAL and the evolution of the team after the events of September 11.

Includes bibliographical references (p. 311-313).

No Hero: The Evolution of a Navy SEAL. Mark Owen, Kevin Maurer. Dutton 2014. 336 p.
ISBN 9780525954521
Grades: Adult   B
1. Owen, Mark 2. Former Navy SEALs 3. Combat 4. Military missions 5. War 6. Navy SEALs 7. Autobiographies and memoirs 8. Life stories — Law and order — Armed forces personnel 9. History writing — Military — Special Forces
LC 2015300011

Recounts definitive moments from the author's career as a Navy SEAL, discussing the missions that had the greatest personal meaning for him and explaining the lessons and values he hopes to pass on to the next generation.

Owusu, Nadia
Aftershocks: A Memoir. Nadia Owusu. Simon & Schuster 2020. 320 p.
ISBN 9781982111229
Grades: Adult   B
1. Owusu, Nadia, 1981- 2. Multiracial women 3. Multiracial people 4. Family secrets 5. Abandonment (Psychology) 6. Identity 7. Psychic trauma 8. Family relationships 9. Childhood 10. Interpersonal relations 11. United States 12. Autobiographies and memoirs 13. Life stories — Identity 14. Life stories — Relationships — Family 15. Family and Relationships — Families
LC 2019051473

An award-winning essayist combines literary memoir and cultural history to examine her personal struggles with her mixed-heritage identity and the emotional trauma of her mother's abandonment and father's dark secrets.

ESSENTIAL AND RECOMMENDED TITLES
Biography

"Owusu's yearning for a maternal figure and acceptance of her identity surround this moving memoir. Recommended for readers who enjoy stories of identity and multiculturalism." —*Library Journal*

Oz, Amos
A Tale of Love and Darkness. Amos Oz; translated from the Hebrew by Nicholas de Lange. Harcourt 2004. 538 p.
ISBN 9780151008780
Grades: Adult B
1. Oz, Amos 2. Authors, Israeli 3. Antisemitism 4. Zionism 5. Family relationships 6. Growing up 7. Jerusalem, Israel 8. 1940s 9. 1950s 10. Autobiographies and memoirs 11. Page to screen 12. Biographies 13. Arts and Entertainment — Writing and Publishing 14. History writing — Arab-Israeli relations — Southwest Asia and North Africa (Middle East) 15. Life stories — Relationships — Growing up
LC 2004007302
New York Times Notable Book, 2005.

The award-winning author recounts his boyhood in war-torn Jerusalem of the 1940s and 1950s, his mother's tragic suicide when he was twelve, his decision to join a kibbutz and change his name, and his participation in Israel's political upheavals.

Adapted into a film in 2015; Originally published in Hebrew as Sipur al ahavah ve-hoshekh: Jerusalem : Keter, 2002.

Pablo Cruz, Rosayra
The Book of Rosy: A Mother's Story of Separation at the Border. Rosayra Pablo Cruz and Julie Schwietert Collazo. HarperCollins 2020. 240 p.
ISBN 9780062941923
Grades: Adult B
1. Pablo Cruz, Rosayra 2. Collazo, Julie Schwietert 3. Undocumented immigrants 4. Refugees 5. Separated friends, relatives, etc. 6. Mother and child 7. Single mothers 8. Faith (Christianity) 9. Widows 10. Guatemalan people in the United States 11. Social justice 12. Prejudice 13. Immigration and emigration 14. Helpfulness 15. United States 16. 21st century 17. Collective autobiographies and memoirs 18. LIfe stories — Facing adversity — War and oppression — Refugees 19. LIfe stories — Identity — Immigrants 20. Life stories — Identity — Race and ethnicity 21. Life stories — Politics — Activists and reformers
LC 2019050658
A searing critique of the Trump administration-induced immigration crisis, written by a mother who was separated from her children and the American who helped reunite the family, shares timely insights into the injustices of today's migrant experience.

"This wrenching story brings to vivid life the plight of the many families separated at the U.S.-Mexico border. . . . Disturbing and unforgettable." —*Publishers Weekly*

Pace, Kristin Knight
This Much Country. Kristin Knight Pace. Grand Central Pub. 2019. 320 p.
ISBN 9781538762400
Grades: Adult B
1. Pace, Kristin Knight 2. Dogsledding 3. Women athletes 4. Transformations, Personal 5. Sled dogs 6. Sled dog racing 7. Divorced women 8. Endurance sports 9. Iditarod Trail Sled Dog Race, Alaska 10. Alaska 11. Yukon 12. Autobiographies and memoirs 13. Life stories — Facing adversity — Personal transformation 14. Sports and Competition — Racing — Dogs
LC BL2019005337
A memoir from one of the few women to have completed both the Yukon Quest and the Iditarod chronicles how she learned how to run sled dogs in one of the most remote places on earth.

"An honest, heartfelt, and exciting memoir and a must-read for all nature lovers seeking a glimpse into a truly Alaskan adventure." —*Booklist*

Packer, George
Our Man: Richard Holbrooke and the End of the American Century. by George Packer. Alfred A. Knopf 2019. 480 p.
ISBN 9780307958020
Grades: Adult B
1. Holbrooke, Richard C, 1941-2010 2. Diplomats 3. Ambassadors 4. Politicians 5. Power 6. Politics and government 7. Ambition 8. United States 9. 20th century 10. Biographies 11. Life stories — Politics — Politicians
LC 2018030382
Library Journal Best Books, 2019; Los Angeles Times Book Prize for Biography, 2019; New York Times Notable Book, 2019; Pulitzer Prize for Biography or Autobiography finalist, 2020; National Book Critics Circle Award for Biography finalist, 2019.

The National Book Award-winning author of The Unwinding draws on first-hand writings in a narrative portrait of the influential American diplomat that explores how his achievements over half a century of history were complicated by his political ambitions.

"An insightful and indispensable rendering of an intriguing and accomplished figure who persisted in the pursuit of peace." —*Library Journal*

A Borzoi book; Includes bibliographical references.

Page, Elliot
Pageboy: A Memoir. Elliot Page. Flatiron Books 2023. 272 p.
ISBN 9781250878359
Grades: Adult B
1. Page, Elliot, 1987- 2. Actors and actresses 3. Trans men 4. Transgender people 5. Fame 6. Marginalized people 7. Sexual violence victims 8. Coming out (Sexual or gender identity) 9. Transitioning (Gender identity) 10. Mental health 11. Self-discovery 12. Social advocacy 13. North American people 14. American people 15. Canadian people 16. Autobiographies and memoirs 17. Canadian literature 18. Life stories — Arts and culture — Performing arts — Actors and actresses 19. Life stories — Identity — LGBTQIA+ 20. Society and culture — LGBTQIA+ 21. Arts and Entertainment — Movies and Television 22. Debut title
LC 2022061625
Loan Stars Favourites, 2023.

Canadian actor/director/producer Elliot Page tells his story of untangling himself from the expectations of others on his journey to being his true self as a transgender man.

"Currently starring in the hit series the Umbrella Academy, Page is not just an Academy Award-nominated actor but a notable trans advocate. His much-anticipated memoir shares his thoughts on love, gender, mental health, relationships, and life in Hollywood." —*Library Journal*

Page, Susan
★ *The Matriarch: Barbara Bush and the Making of an American Dynasty*. Susan Page. Twelve 2019. VIII, 418 pages, 16 unnumbered pages of plates : Illustration; Color; Portrait
ISBN 9781538713648
Grades: Adult B
1. Bush, Barbara, 1925-2018 2. Bush family 3. Matriarchs 4. Families 5. Social advocacy 6. Presidents' spouses 7. Presidents 8. Politics and government 9. United States 10. 20th century 11. 21st century 12. Biographies 13. Life stories — Politics 14. History writing — Presidency — United States

Drawing on diary access and more than 100 interviews, a vibrant portrait of the former first lady by the Washington bureau chief of USA Today includes coverage of Barbara Bush's private struggles and remarkable political achievements.

"While the work is not officially authorized, Page interviewed Bush many times before her death in 2018 and had access to her voluminous diaries that no other historian has seen." —*Library Journal*

Includes bibliographical references (pages 391-400) and index.

★ *The Rulebreaker: The Life and Times of Barbara Walters*. Susan Page. Simon & Schuster 2024. 480 p.
ISBN 9781982197926
Grades: Adult B
1. Walters, Barbara, 1931-2022 2. Women journalists 3. Television personalities 4. Women television personalities 5. Women 6. Ambition 7. Journalists 8. United States 9. Biographies 10. Impartial writing 11. Biographies — Arts —

PUBLIC LIBRARY CORE COLLECTION: NONFICTION
Twentieth Edition

Writing — Journalists and publishers 12. Art and music — Television and radio 13. Biographies — Arts — Performing arts — Film and television

The definitive biography of one of the most successful female broadcasters of all time—Barbara Walters—a woman whose personal demons fueled an ambition that broke all the rules and finally gave women a permanent place on the air.

"A definitive and deeply researched biography, likely to be in high demand at all libraries, especially those with book clubs. Perfect for future journalists and young people who may not know what women went through to break into careers that were traditionally unwelcoming to them." —*Library Journal*

Pagels, Elaine H.
★ *Why Religion?: A Personal Story.* Elaine Pagels. Ecco, an imprint of HarperCollinsPublishers 2018. 256 p.
ISBN 9780062368539
Grades: Adult   B
1. Pagels, Elaine H, 1943- 2. Faith (Christianity) 3. Loss 4. Grief 5. Death of children 6. Death of married men 7. Death of sons 8. Widows 9. Coping 10. Autobiographies and memoirs 11. Spirituality and Religion — Christianity 12. Life stories — Facing adversity — Coping with death 13. Life stories — Religion and spirituality — Personal faith 14. Family and Relationships — Aging and Death
LC Bl2018183665

The author of "The Gnostic Gospels" draws on personal experiences and the perspectives of neurologists, anthropologists, and historians to illuminate the enduring capacity of faith in explaining and meeting the challenges of the twenty-first century.

"Pagels treats readers to the examined life behind her intellectual feats with extreme grace and depth. This luminous memoir strips religion to its elementary particles: Love, suffering, and mystery." —*Publishers Weekly*

Painter, Nell Irvin
Old in Art School: A Memoir of Starting Over. Nell Painter. Counterpoint Press 2018. 320 p.
ISBN 9781640090613
Grades: Adult   B
1. Painter, Nell Irvin 2. Artists 3. Senior artists 4. Adult learners 5. African American women artists 6. African American intellectuals 7. Women intellectuals 8. Career changes 9. Art students 10. Art schools 11. Ageism 12. Racism 13. Autobiographies and memoirs 14. Life stories — Arts and culture — Artists 15. Arts and Entertainment — Painting, Drawing, and Sculpture
LC 2017055407

National Book Critics Circle Award for Autobiography/Memoir finalist, 2018.

A Princeton University historian describes her post-retirement decision to study art, a venture that compelled her to find relevance in the undervalued masters she loves, the obstacles faced by women artists and the challenges of balancing art and life.

★ *Sojourner Truth: A Life, a Symbol.* Nell Irvin Painter. W.W. Norton 1996. xii, 370 p. : Illustration
ISBN 9780393027396
Grades: 11 12 Adult   B
1. Truth, Sojourner, d. 1883 2. African American abolitionists 3. Freedom seekers 4. Interracial friendship 5. Feminists 6. African American women political activists 7. Abolitionists 8. Women abolitionists 9. Social reformers 10. Women social reformers 11. Illiterate women 12. Anti-slavery movements 13. Women 14. United States history 15. 19th century 16. Gilded Age (1865-1898) 17. Biographies 18. History writing — African American — Enslavement — United States 19. History writing — Women's history 20. Life stories — Politics — Activists and reformers
LC 95047595

ALA Notable Book, 1997; BCALA Literary Award for Nonfiction, 1997; Booklist Editors' Choice, 1996.

"Painter persuasively offers us the real woman behind the myth." —*Publishers Weekly*

Includes bibliographical references (p. 293-343) and index.

Pak, Jung H.
Becoming Kim Jong Un: A Former CIA Officer's Insights into North Korea's Enigmatic Young Dictator. Jung H. Pak. Ballantine Books 2020. 288 pages : Illustration
ISBN 9781984819727
Grades: Adult   B
1. Kim, Chong-un, 1984- 2. Dictatorship 3. Power 4. Nuclear weapons 5. Ambition 6. Political leadership 7. Dictators 8. International relations 9. Politics and government 10. Asian history 11. North Korea 12. Biographies 13. Life stories — Politics — Politicians 14. History writing — Asia — North and South Korea
LC 2019048665

A CIA analyst's account of the rise of North Korean dictator Kim Jong Un looks at everything from his nuclear ambitions to his summits with President Donald J. Trump.

"An insightful analysis of perhaps the world's most dangerous dystopia." —*Kirkus*

Includes bibliographical references and index.

Pakula, Hannah
The Last Empress: Madame Chiang Kai-shek and the Birth of Modern China. Hannah Pakula. Simon & Schuster 2009. xix, 787 p, 32 p. of plates : Illustration
ISBN 9781439148938
Grades: Adult   B
1. Chiang, May-ling Soong, 1897-2003 2. Chiang, Kai-shek, 1887-1975 3. Monarchy 4. Royal houses 5. Political leadership 6. Presidents' spouses 7. Chinese history 8. Asian history 9. Taiwan 10. 20th century 11. Biographies 12. Life stories — Politics — Politicians 13. History writing — Communist China — Asia — China
LC 2009017576

New York Times Notable Book, 2009.

With the powerful Madame Chiang Kai-Shek at the center of one of the great dramas of the 20th century, the story of the founding of modern China ranges from the revolution that swept away the monarchy to the eventual loss to the communists and exile in Taiwan.

"A winning combination of measured, balanced research and critical evaluationthe definitive account of an important figure in 20th-century Chinese politics." —*Kirkus*

Includes bibliographical references (p. 751-761) and index.

Palahniuk, Chuck
Consider This: Moments in My Writing Life After Which Everything Was Different. Chuck Palahniuk. Grand Central Publishing 2020. 288 pages
ISBN 9781538717950
Grades: Adult   B
1. Palahniuk, Chuck 2. Writing 3. Creative writing 4. Advice 5. Fiction writing 6. Book industry and trade 7. Authors, American 8. Authors 9. 20th century 10. Autobiographies and memoirs 11. Biographies 12. Life stories — Arts and culture — Writing — Authors 13. Arts and Entertainment — Writing and Publishing
LC 2019036414

With advice grounded in years of careful study and a keenly observed life, Palahniuk combines practical advice and concrete examples from beloved classics, his own books, and a "kitchen-table MFA" culled from an evolving circle of beloved authors and artists, with anecdotes, postcards from the road, and much more.

"Fans will appreciate the insight into his own work, ... his tributes to friends and forebears, and how he delivers gracious and encouraging wisdom in his characteristically conversational style." —*Booklist*

Palmer, Arnold
A Golfer's Life. Arnold Palmer, with James Dodson. Ballantine Books 1999. xi, 420 p. : Illustration
ISBN 9780345414816
Grades: Adult   B

ESSENTIAL AND RECOMMENDED TITLES
Biography

1. Palmer, Arnold, 1929-2016 2. Golfers 3. Golf 4. Husband and wife 5. Male friendship 6. Men-women relations 7. Autobiographies and memoirs 8. Life stories — Sports — Athletes 9. Sports and Competition — Golf 10. Sports and Competition — Individual Athlete

LC 98051681

New York Times Notable Book, 1999.

The respected golfer recounts his life on and off the course, from his upbringing as the son of a country club groundskeeper to his battle with cancer at the age of sixty-eight.

"Palmer's immense popularity is widely credited with rescuing professional golf in the late 1950s and 1960s. Written with humor and candor, the book recounts Palmer's friendships and rivalries with the greats of the game, his enduring marriage to Winnie Palmer, his legendary triumphs and disasters, and his battle against cancer." —*Library Journal*

Includes index; Also published in large print format.

Panagore, Peter Baldwin
Heaven Is Beautiful: How Dying Taught Me That Death Is Just the Beginning. Peter Baldwin Panagore. Hampton Roads Pub. Co. : Distributed by Red Wheel-Weiser 2015. 256 p.
ISBN 9781571747341
Grades: Adult   B

1. Panagore, Peter Baldwin 2. Near-death experience 3. Spiritual journeys 4. Snow and ice climbing 5. Hypothermia 6. Autobiographies and memoirs 7. Life stories — Religion and spirituality — Spiritual journeys 8. Spirituality and religion — General

LC Bl2015042483

In 1980, Peter Panagore had a near-death experience when he became trapped on a mountain while ice climbing in Alberta. In Heaven is beautiful, he describes that experience, the minutes he spent on the other side, and how it changed his life.

"Readers who have a fascination with near-death experiences and mysticism will be drawn into Panagores remembrances of dying on the side of that mountain and the unexplainable feelings he encountered, and may find comfort in his assurance that death is not to be feared." —*Publishers Weekly*

Pantsov, Alexander
Mao: The Real Story. Alexander V. Pantsov with Steven I. Levine. Simon & Schuster 2012. 736 p.
ISBN 9781451654479
Grades: Adult   B

1. Mao, Zedong, 1893-1976 2. Heads of state 3. Communists 4. Politicians 5. Communism 6. Political leadership 7. Revolutions 8. Politics and government 9. China 10. 20th century 11. Biographies 12. Life stories — Politics — Politicians 13. History writing — Communist China — Asia — China

LC 2011053113

Draws on extensive, previously unavailable Russian documents to reveal surprising details about Mao Zedong's rise to power and leadership in China, providing coverage of such topics as his health, alleged affairs and controversial political decisions. Co-written by the author of the Bolsheviks and the Chinese Revolution 1919-1927.

"The Great Helmsman fully fleshed, still complicated and ever provocative." —*Kirkus*

Includes bibliographical references and index; Originally published in Russian: Moskva : Molodaia Gvardiia, 2007, under title Mao Tzedun.

Papenfuss, Mary
American Huckster: How Chuck Blazer Got Rich From-and Sold Out-the Most Powerful Fiefdom in World Sports. Mary Papenfuss and Teresa Thompson. HarperCollins Publishers 2016. 272 p.
ISBN 9780062449672
Grades: Adult   B

1. Blazer, Chuck, 1945-2017 2. White collar crime 3. Corruption 4. Sports corruption 5. Soccer 6. Sports and Competition — Soccer 7. True Crime — General

LC 2015050617

In a gripping true account of white-collar crime and betrayal at the highest levels of international business, two investigative reporters, drawing on sources in U.S. law enforcement, recount how Chuck Blazer, a stay-at-home New York soccer dad, illegally made millions from FIFA and became an unlikely FBI whistleblower.

"This grim, always entertaining cautionary tale of greed and runaway ego is a worthy addition to any reader's collection of business fantasies gone awry." —*Publishers Weekly*

Parcells, Bill
Parcells: A Football Life. Bill Parcells, Nunyo Demasio. Crown Publishing 2014. 400 p.
ISBN 9780385346351
Grades: Adult   B

1. Parcells, Bill, 1941- 2. Professional football coaches 3. Professional football teams 4. Football 5. Autobiographies and memoirs 6. Sports and competition — Football 7. Life stories — Sports — Coaches, managers, and owners

LC 2014027830

Bill Parcells may be the most iconic football coach of our time. During his decades-long tenure as an NFL coach, he turned failing franchises into contenders. He led the ailing New York Giants to two Super Bowl victories, turned the New England Patriots into an NFL powerhouse, reinvigorated the New York Jets, brought the Dallas Cowboys back to life, and was most recently enshrined in the Pro Football Hall of Fame. Taking readers behind the scenes with one of the most influential and fascinating coaches the NFL has ever known, PARCELLS will take a look back at this coach's long, storied and influential career, offer a nuanced portrayal of the complex man behind the coach, and examine the inner workings of the NFL.

Pardlo, Gregory
Air Traffic: A Memoir of Ambition and Manhood in America. Gregory Pardlo. Alfred A. Knopf 2018. 256 p.
ISBN 9781524731762
Grades: Adult   B

1. Pardlo, Gregory 2. Fathers and sons 3. African American families 4. Growing up 5. Personal conduct 6. Fatherhood 7. Autobiographies and memoirs 8. Life stories — Relationships — Growing up

LC 2017047413

From the Pulitzer Prize-winning poet, his first work of prose: a deeply felt memoir of a family's bonds and a meditation on race, addiction, fatherhood, ambition, and American culture the Pardlos were an average, middle-class African American family living in a New Jersey Levittown: Charismatic Gregory Sr, an air traffic controller, his wife, and their two sons, bookish Greg Jr. and musical-talent Robbie. But when "Big Greg" loses his job after participating in the Professional Air Traffic Controllers Strike of 1981, he becomes a disillusioned, toxic, looming presence in the household—and a powerful rival for young Greg. While Big Greg succumbs to addiction and exhausts the family's money, Greg Jr. rebels—he joins a boot camp for prospective Marines,follows a woman to Denmark, drops out of college again and again, and yields to alcoholism. Years later, he falls for a beautiful, no-nonsense woman named Ginger and becomes a parent himself. Then, he finally grapples with the irresistible yet ruinous legacy of masculinity he inherited from his father. In chronicling his path to recovery and adulthood—Gregory Pardlo gives us a compassionate, loving ode to his father, to fatherhood, and to the frustrating-yet-redemptive ties of family, as well as a scrupulous, searing examination of how African American manhood is shaped by contemporary American life.

"Endlessly introspective, wide-ranging, and lucid, Pardlos fearless inventory stuns with beautifully written, fully saturated snapshots of rich and complicated familial love." —*Booklist*

Parini, Jay
Robert Frost: A Life. Jay Parini. Henry Holt 2000. xii, 514 p.
ISBN 9780805063417
Grades: 11 12 Adult   B

1. Frost, Robert, 1874-1963 2. Poets, American 3. Social life and customs 4. United States 5. 20th century 6. Biographies 7. Arts and Entertainment — Writing and Publishing 8. Life stories — Arts and culture — Writing — Poets

PUBLIC LIBRARY CORE COLLECTION: NONFICTION
Twentieth Edition

LC BL2003013912

Based on interviews with Frost's friends and drawing from his personal archives, an account of the poet's life examines his varied literary career, tracing his rise to world fame and offering close readings of his works.

"Rarely has Frost's story been told this dexterously, or with a better understanding of the relation of Frost's personal crises to his accomplishment as a poet." —*Publishers Weekly*

Reprint. Originally published: 1999; an Owl book; Includes bibliographical references(p. [485]-487) and index.

Parks, Casey

Diary of a Misfit: A Memoir and a Mystery. Casey Parks. Alfred A. Knopf 2022. 336 p.

ISBN 9780525658535

Grades: Adult   B

1. Parks, Casey 2. Lesbians 3. Gender identity 4. Sex (Psychology) 5. Identity 6. Psychic trauma 7. Love 8. Self-fulfillment 9. Poverty 10. Addiction 11. Small towns 12. Rural life 13. Investigative journalism 14. Southern States 15. Autobiographies and memoirs 16. Life stories — Identity — LGBTQIA+ 17. Life stories — Relationships

LC 2021049946

Oregon Book Awards, Sarah Winnemucca Award for Creative Nonfiction, 2023.

Part memoir, part investigative reporting, a sweeping journalistic saga explores sexuality and gender, family trauma and the redemptive force of love.

"In this tantalizing blend of personal history and reportage, Washington Post reporter Parks seeks out the story of an enigmatic small-town country singer to reckon with her own fraught past….Out of this comes a brilliantly rendered and complex portrait of Southern life alongside a tender exploration of queer belonging." —*Publishers Weekly*

Parton, Dolly

★ *Behind the Seams: My Life in Rhinestones*. by Dolly Parton; with Holly George-Warren; currated by Rebecca Seaver. Ten Speed Press 2023. 327 pages : Illustration; Color

ISBN 9781984862129

Grades: Adult   B

1. Parton, Dolly, 1946- 2. Country musicians 3. Women country musicians 4. Clothing 5. Singers 6. Fashion design 7. Fashion photography 8. United States history 9. United States 10. 20th century 11. 21st century 12. Autobiographies and memoirs 13. Visual nonfiction 14. Arts and Entertainment — Music — Country 15. Life stories — Arts and culture — Performing arts — Musicians and composers

LC Bl2023115583

Showcasing the music legend's most unforgettable looks from the 1960s until now, this stunningly photographed book displays Dolly Parton's iconic sense of style along with entertaining personal anecdotes that, for the first time, reveal the full story behind her lifelong passion for fashion.

"[This] is both a lush visual feast and a testament to the originality and self-possession that made Parton a force to be reckoned with: an entertainer who refused to accede to trends, was firmly in control of her own sexuality, and expanded the stylistic possibilities available to female performers." —*Publishers Weekly*

★ *Dolly Parton, Songteller: My Life in Lyrics*. Dolly Parton; with Robert K. Oermann. Chronicle Books 2020. 380 p.

ISBN 9781797205090

Grades: Adult   B

1. Parton, Dolly, 1946- 2. Country music 3. Women country musicians 4. Women singers 5. Country musicians 6. Singers 7. Songwriting 8. Songwriters 9. Autobiographies and memoirs 10. Illustrated books 11. Life stories — Arts and culture — Performing arts — Musicians and composers 12. Arts and Entertainment — Music — Country

LC 2020031352

For the first time ever, legendary singer-songwriter Dolly Parton brings you behind the lyrics of 175 of her songs to reveal the personal stories and vibrant memories that have inspired sixty years of songwriting. Lushly illustrated and told in Dolly's inimitable voice, this rich collection offers an intimate, exclusive look at the colorful life, prolific career, and rags-to-rhinestones journey of one of the most revered entertainers of our time.

Includes index.

Passarlay, Gulwali

The Lightless Sky: A Twelve-year-old Refugee's Harrowing Escape from Afghanistan and His Extraordinary Journey Across Half the World. Gulwali Passarlay. HarperCollins 2016. 256 p.

ISBN 9780062443878

Grades: Adult   B

1. Passarlay, Gulwali 2. Refugees 3. Violence 4. Survival 5. Refugees, Afghan 6. Immigration and emigration 7. Child refugees 8. Death of fathers 9. Escapes 10. Afghanistan 11. Autobiographies and memoirs 12. Life stories — Facing adversity — War and oppression — Refugees 13. History writing — Wars and conflicts — War in Afghanistan 14. Adult books for young adults

LC 2015042841

Documents the author's traumatic flight from Afghanistan to the West at the age of 12, describing how he escaped from Taliban recruiters that killed his father, his journey over mountains through eight countries and his endurance against hunger, brutality and imprisonment.

"A vivid, timely story of survival. If spies live in boredom punctuated by flashes of terrifying action, then refugees on the run live in constant high anxiety punctuated by flashes of horror and panic." —*Kirkus*

Pataki, Allison

Beauty in the Broken Places: A Memoir of Love, Faith, and Resilience. by Allison Pataki. Random House 2018. 272 p.

ISBN 9780399591655

Grades: Adult   B

1. Pataki, Allison 2. People who have had strokes 3. Husband and wife 4. Convalescence 5. Caregivers 6. Memories 7. Strokes 8. Self-discovery 9. Autobiographies and memoirs 10. Life stories — Facing adversity — Medical issues — Physical illness

LC 2017058576

The best-selling author of the Accidental Empress describes how, while on a vacation during her pregnancy, her healthy 35-year-old surgical resident husband suffered a rare and life-threatening stroke that placed everything they had worked for in jeopardy, a struggle she navigated by writing daily letters to her husband that helped her make sense of challenges and fall in love with him all over again. Illustrations.

"In this powerful and immersive memoir, Pataki relives the harrowing year that followed her husbands stroke in June 2015." —*Publishers Weekly*

Patchett, Ann

This Is the Story of a Happy Marriage. Ann Patchett. HarperCollins 2013. 320 p.

ISBN 9780062236678

Grades: Adult   B

1. Patchett, Ann 2. Authors, American 3. Women authors 4. Childhood 5. Growing up 6. Marriage 7. Marital conflict 8. Remarriage 9. Divorce 10. Essays 11. Autobiographies and memoirs 12. Life stories — Relationships — Couples 13. Family and Relationships — Growing up 14. Family and relationships — Dating and Marriage

LC Bl2013040463

Inviting readers into her personal life, the New York Times best-selling author of State of Wonder and Bel Canto shares the stories of the people, places, ideals and art to which she has remained indelibly committed.

Truth & Beauty: A Friendship. Ann Patchett. Harper Collins 2004. 257 p.

ISBN 9780060572143

Grades: 11 12 Adult   B

1. Patchett, Ann 2. Grealy, Lucy 3. Friendship 4. People with disfigurements 5. Bone cancer 6. Women authors 7. Female friendship 8. People with cancer 9. Women 10. Autobiographies and memoirs 11. Family and Relationships — Friendship 12. Life stories — Relationships — Friendship 13. Adult books for young adults

ESSENTIAL AND RECOMMENDED TITLES
Biography

LC 2003067586

Alex Award, 2005.

The author describes her intimate twenty-year friendship with the late Lucy Grealy, tracing their introduction at a writer's workshop, the integral part their friendship played in their writing careers, and her witness to Grealy's medical deterioration.

"As young writers. Patchett and Lucy Grealy began an intense friendship that lasted until Grealy's tragic death. With intimacy, grace, and humor, Patchett's memoir captures Lucy's exuberance and her roller-coaster struggles with disfigurement and depression."—*Booklist*

Also published in large print format.

Patrick, James
Robert Johnson: Legend of the Delta Blues. James Patrick. Gareth Stevens Pub. 2010. 32 p. (Inspiring lives)

ISBN 9781433936197

Grades: Adult   B

1. Johnson, Robert, 1911-1938 2. Blues musicians 3. Songwriters 4. Blues music 5. Guitarists 6. Biographies 7. Biographies — Arts — Performing arts — Music 8. Art and music — Music

Introduces the noted early twentieth-century blues musician Robert Johnson, recounts his life, and explains why he was famous.

Includes bibliographical references and index.

Patterson, James
James Patterson by James Patterson: The Stories of My Life. James Patterson. Little Brown & Company 2022. 400 p.

ISBN 9780316397537

Grades: Adult   B

1. Patterson, James, 1947- 2. Authors, American 3. Growing up 4. Writing 5. Autobiographies and memoirs 6. Life stories — Arts and culture — Writing — Authors 7. Arts and Entertainment — Writing and publishing

A #1 best-selling author shows how a boy from small-town New York made it to literary stardom.

"This is a book of true stories the way I remember them. I'm sure I'll get a few things wrong,' suggests the mega-bestselling novelist in this blithe blend of personal asides, fan trivia, and hot takes."—*Publishers Weekly*

Patterson, Pat
Accepted: How the First Gay Superstar Changed Wwe. Pat Patterson with Bertrand Hebert, foreword by Vince McMahon. ECW Press 2016. 320 p.

ISBN 9781770412934

Grades: Adult   B

1. Patterson, Pat 2. Professional wrestlers 3. Professional wrestling 4. Entertainers 5. Entertainment industry and trade 6. Autobiographies and memoirs 7. Life stories — Arts and culture — Performing arts — Entertainers and celebrities 8. Life stories — Identity — LGBTQIA+ 9. Sports and Competition — Wrestling

LC Bl2016032588

The WWE Hall of Famer describes how he was rejected by his family for his sexual orientation and moved to the United States in the 1960s, where, in spite of language and discriminatory challenges, he applied his creative and athletic talents to climb to the upper ranks of sports entertainment.

"Patterson is a very good storyteller, and his tales from the road about well-known personalities such as the fun-seeking Andre the Giant and the forever-young-at-heart Ray Stevens are wonderfully told, and many of the wrestlers time-killing pranks are laugh-out-loud funny."—*Publishers Weekly*

Patton, George S.
War as I Knew It. George S. Patton, Jr; annotated by Paul D. Harkins; with a new introduction by Rick Atkinson. Houghton Mifflin Co. 1995. xxii, 425 p. : Illustration; Map

ISBN 9780395735299

Grades: Adult   B

1. Patton, George S, 1885-1945 2. Western Front (World War II) 3. Battles 4. World War II 5. Military campaigns 6. Military history 7. Military strategy 8. Command of troops 9. Generals 10. Southwest Asia and North Africa (Middle East) history 11. European history 12. United States 13. 20th century 14. Autobiographies and memoirs 15. Biographies 16. History writing — Military — Military leadership 17. History writing — Wars and conflicts — World War II 18. Life stories — Law and order — Armed forces personnel

LC 95196167

Transcripts from General Patten's war diary covering his campaigns in Sicily, France, and Germany.

Originally published: Boston, MA : Houghton Mifflin, 1947.

Paul, Joel R
★ *Without Precedent: Chief Justice John Marshall and His Times.* Joel Richard Paul. Riverhead Books 2018. 448 p.

ISBN 9781594488238

Grades: Adult   B

1. Marshall, John, 1755-1835 2. Judges 3. Early America (1784-1819) 4. Biographies 5. Life stories — Law and order — Judges and lawyers 6. History writing — Early America — United States

LC 2017016049

A portrait of the influential chief justice, statesman, and diplomat illuminates his pivotal role in the establishment of the Constitution and Supreme Court and recounts his work as an advisor to multiple presidents.

"This masterly work elucidates the indelible imprint that Marshall made on the U.S. Constitution and its subsequent interpretation."—*Library Journal*

Includes bibliographical references and index.

Paulsen, Gary
Winterdance: The Fine Madness of Running the Iditarod. Gary Paulsen. Harcourt Brace 1994. 256 p; Color illustration

ISBN 9780151262274

Grades: 6 7 8 9 10   B

1. Paulsen, Gary, 1939-2021 2. Iditarod Trail Sled Dog Race, Alaska 3. Mushers 4. Endurance sports 5. Autobiographies and memoirs 6. Sports and Competition — Racing — Dogs 7. Sports and Competition — Extreme Sports 8. Life stories — Sports — Athletes

LC 93042096

Paulsen and his team of dogs endured snowstorms, frostbite, dogfights, moose attacks, sleeplessness, and hallucinations in the relentless push to go on.

"This book is primarily an account of Paulsen's first Iditarod and its frequent life-threatening disasters. However, the book is more than a tabulation of tribulations; it is a meditation on the extraordinary attraction this race holds for some men and women." —*Library Journal*

Pavlychenko, Liudmyla Mykhailivna
Lady Death: The Memoirs of Stalin's Sniper. Lyudmila Pavlichenko; foreword by Martin Pegler; translated by David Foreman; edited by Alla Igorevna Begunova. Greenhill Books 2018. 252 p.

ISBN 9781784382704

Grades: Adult   B

1. Pavlychenko, Liudmyla Mykhailivna, 1916-1974 2. Snipers 3. Women soldiers 4. World War II 5. Ukraine 6. Soviet Union 7. Autobiographies and memoirs 8. Translations — Russian to English 9. History writing — Wars and conflicts — World War II — European Theater 10. Life stories — Law and order — Armed forces personnel 11. Adult books for young adults

LC Bl2018184916

The wartime memoir of Lyudmila Pavlichenko is a remarkable document: the publication of an English language edition is a significant coup. Pavlichenko was World War II's best scoring sniper and had a varied wartime career that included trips to England and America.In June 1941, when Hitler launched Operation Barbarossa, she left her university studies, ignored the offer of a position as a nurse, to become one of Soviet Russia's 2000 female snipers.Less than a year later she had 309 recorded kills, including 29 enemy sniper kills. She was withdrawn from active duty after being injured. She was also regarded as a key heroic figure for the war effort.

"Lady Death reads like a novel, and it is a rare war story by a patriot whose determination to fight for her country is inspiring and should firmly put to rest any doubts about women in combat. There is no question that this is a significant historical document, but it is also a gripping narrative (which includes her memories of travel in the U.S.) that devotees of history, especially WWII, should absolutely not miss." —*Booklist*

First published by Veche Publishers (Moscow) in 2015 as 'I - sniper : in battles for Sevastopol and Odessa'—Title page verso; Translated from the Russian.

Pawel, Miriam
The **Crusades** *of Cesar Chavez: A Biography.* Miriam Pawel. Bloomsbury 2014. 548 pages : Illustration; Color; Map
ISBN 9781608197101
Grades: Adult   B
1. Chavez, Cesar, 1927-1993 2. Human rights activists 3. Labor leaders 4. Labor movement 5. Labor unions 6. Race relations 7. United States history 8. California 9. United States 10. 20th century 11. Biographies 12. History writing — Immigration — United States 13. Life stories — Politics — Activists and reformers 14. Life stories — Nature and outdoors — Farmers and ranchers

Booklist Editors' Choice, 2014; Robert F. Kennedy Book Award, 2015; National Book Critics Circle Award for Biography finalist, 2014.

The Pulitzer Prize-winning author draws on thousands of documents and interviews to examine the myths and achievements marking the life of the iconic labor leader and civil rights activist, portraying him as a flawed but brilliant strategist who was often at odds with himself.

"Pawel's clear, accessible prose befits a subject famous for his plain rhetoric, ensuring a broad readership can appreciate this valuable exploration of Chavez's unique legacy." —*Publishers Weekly*

Includes bibliographical references (pages 487-548) and index.

Payne, Les
★ *The* **Dead** *Are Arising: The Life of Malcolm X.* Les Payne and Tamara Payne. Liveright Publishing Corporation 2020. 640 p.
ISBN 9781631491665
Grades: Adult   B
1. Malcolm X, 1925-1965 2. Black Muslims 3. Black nationalism 4. African American civil rights workers 5. African Americans 6. Civil Rights Movement 7. African American civil rights 8. Political activists 9. Identity 10. Race relations 11. United States history 12. United States 13. 20th century 14. Biographies 15. Life stories — Identity — Race and ethnicity 16. Life stories — Politics — Activists and reformers — Civil Rights leaders 17. History writing — African American — Civil rights — United States
LC 2020029637

Pulitzer Prize for Biography or Autobiography, 2021; National Book Award for Nonfiction, 2020; New York Times Notable Book, 2020; National Book Critics Circle Award for Biography finalist, 2020.

A revisionary portrait of the iconic civil rights leader draws on hundreds of hours of interviews with surviving family members, intelligence officers and political leaders to offer new insights into Malcolm X's Depression-era youth, religious conversion and 1965 assassination.

"This gripping read delivers penetrating explanations and fresh insights into previously unexamined dimensions of Malcolm X and his becoming and being El-hajj Malik El Shabazz within the context of Black life." —*Library Journal*

Includes bibliographical references and index.

Pearlman, Jeff
Gunslinger: *The Remarkable, Improbable, Iconic Life of Brett Favre.* Jeff Pearlman. Houghton Mifflin Harcourt 2016. 352 p.
ISBN 9780544454378
Grades: Adult   B
1. Favre, Brett 2. Football players 3. Professional football players 4. Quarterbacks (Football) 5. Biographies 6. Sports and Competition — Football 7. Life stories — Sports — Athletes
LC 2016287244

Tells the complete story of NFL quarterback Brett Favre's life, drawing on more than 500 interviews, including many from the people closest to Favre.

The **Last** *Folk Hero: The Life and Myth of Bo Jackson.* Jeff Pearlman. Mariner Books 2022. 352 p.
ISBN 9780358437673
Grades: Adult   B
1. Jackson, Bo, 1962- 2. Baseball players 3. Football players 4. United States 5. Biographies 6. Sports and Competition — Individual Athlete 7. Sports and Competition — Football 8. Sports and Competition — Baseball 9. Life stories — Sports — Athletes

Drawing on 720 original interviews, a New York Times best-selling sportswriter captures as never before the elusive truth about the greatest athlete of all time who took the world by storm from the mid-1980s into the early 1990s?—?and then, almost overnight, disappeared.

"Veteran sportswriter Pearlman delivers a captivating, copiously researched portrait of once-in-a-century supernova Bo Jackson, who excelled at the highest levels in football (1985 Heisman winner), baseball (1989 All-Star Game MVP), and even track (qualifying for the NCAA nationals in the 100-meter dash—twice)." —*Booklist*

Sweetness: *The Enigmatic Life of Walter Payton.* Jeff Pearlman. Gotham 2011. xvi, 480 p, 16 p. of plates : Illustration
ISBN 9781592406531
Grades: Adult   B
1. Payton, Walter, 1954-1999 2. African American football players 3. People with cancer 4. Football players 5. United States 6. Biographies 7. Life stories — Sports — Athletes 8. Sports and Competition — Football
LC 2011011466

Traces the life and career of the late Chicago Bears star, from his early athletic triumphs that helped bridge racial gaps in his segregated Mississippi childhood community through the tragic illness that ended his life.

"A highly readable warts-and-all portrait of an athletic giant, but those who prefer their idols unblemished may want to steer clear." —*Kirkus*

Includes index.

Pearson, Roger
Voltaire *Almighty: A Life in Pursuit of Freedom.* Roger Pearson. Bloomsbury 2005. xxxii, 447 p. : Illustration; Color
ISBN 9781582346304
Grades: Adult   B
1. Voltaire, 1694-1778 2. Authors, French 3. Social life and customs 4. France 5. 18th century 6. Biographies 7. Spirituality and Religion — General 8. Life stories — Education — Philosophers 9. Adult books for young adults
LC 2005053027

Shortlisted for the James Tait Black Memorial Prize for Biography, 2005.

Presents the life of the French philosopher, discussing his literary and philosophical writings, his tumultuous relationships with some of the rulers and thinkers of his day, and his lasting influence on French culture.

"The author has composed a lively and thorough account of the illustrious philosophe's chaotic life." —*Choice*

Includes bibliographical references (p. [433]-436) and index.

Peer, Basharat
Curfewed *Night: One Kashmiri Journalist's Frontline Account of Life, Love, and War in His Homeland.* Basharat Peer. Scribner 2010. 256 p.
ISBN 9781439109106
Grades: 11 12 Adult   B
1. Peer, Basharat, 1977- 2. Interethnic conflict 3. Journalists 4. Interethnic relations 5. India 6. Jammu and Kashmir (India) 7. Autobiographies and memoirs 8. Biographies 9. Life stories — Facing adversity — War and oppression — War survivors 10. Life stories — Arts and culture — Writing — Journalists 11. History writing — Asia — South Asia — India
LC 2009040416

A native to the war-torn region of Kashmir offers a portrait of the disputed area between India and Pakistan, featuring personal stories behind one of the modern world's most brutal conflicts.

Includes bibliographical references and index.

Pellegrino, Danny
How *Do I Un-remember This?: Unfortunately True Stories.* Danny Pellegrino. Sourcebooks 2022. 280 p.
ISBN 9781728247984

ESSENTIAL AND RECOMMENDED TITLES
Biography

Grades: Adult **B**
1. Pellegrino, Danny 2. Comedians 3. Podcasters 4. Gay men 5. Growing up 6. Coming out (Sexual or gender identity) 7. Self-discovery 8. Autobiographies and memoirs 9. Book club best bets 10. Life stories — Arts and culture — Performing arts — Entertainers and celebrities 11. Life stories — Identity — LGBTQIA+ 12. Life stories — Relationships — Growing up 13. Arts and Entertainment — Comedy
LC 2021052687

Growing up as a closeted gay kid in small-town Ohio wasn't easy, and Danny Pellegrino has the stories to prove it. But coming of age in the 90s still meant something magical to Danny. The music, film, and celebrity moments of his youth were truly iconic, and his love for all things pop culture connected him to a world larger than the one he knew in the suburban Midwest. With refreshing honesty and jaw-dropping absurdity, Danny invites readers to experience his most formative moments in life—from his hometown in Ohio to his hit podcast and career in entertainment today. Although he wouldn't change them for the world, these stories are—unfortunately—true.

"Podcaster and comedian Pellegrino (Fancy AF Cocktails) takes a humorous and heartfelt trip down memory lane in this candid account of the moments that shaped him." —*Publishers Weekly*

Penn, Kal
You Can't Be Serious. by Kal Penn. Gallery Books 2021. 304 p.
ISBN 9781982171384
Grades: Adult **B**
1. Penn, Kal, 1977- 2. Actors and actresses 3. Indian Americans 4. Entertainment industry and trade 5. Racism in the performing arts 6. Autobiographies and memoirs 7. Life stories — Arts and culture — Performing arts — Actors and actresses 8. Arts and Entertainment — Movies and television
LC 2021006581

In this series of funny, consequential, awkward and ridiculous stories from the actor and White House aide's idiosyncratic life, he reflects on the most exasperating and rewarding moments of his journey so far, showing that everyone can have more than one life story.

"Penn has a pleasing ability to be serious and funny at the same time. A story well worth hearing." —*Kirkus*

"How the ambitious, idealistic son of Indian immigrants became a force for change as both a beloved comic actor and an accidental public servant.... Penn has a pleasing ability to be serious and funny at the same time. A story well worth hearing." —*Kirkus*

Pennington, Bill
Billy Martin: Baseball's Flawed Genius. Bill Pennington. Houghton Mifflin Harcourt 2015. 496 p.
ISBN 9780544022096
Grades: Adult **B**
1. Martin, Billy, 1928-1989 2. Professional baseball managers 3. Baseball players 4. Professional baseball teams 5. Baseball history 6. Sports history 7. Biographies 8. Sports and Competition — Baseball 9. Life stories — Sports
LC 2014039677

A portrait of the 1950s New York Yankees second baseman explores the athletic and leadership genius behind his mercurial personality and controversial antics, tracing his shantytown upbringing and conflict-marked relationships.

"Pennington analyzes the ongoing conflict that was Billy Martin—including his relationships with equally complex individuals such as George Steinbrenner and Reggie Jackson—from all sides (Billys varied career is covered chronologically, but it's the Yankee years, however sporadic, that matter) and with balance and impressive depth." —*Booklist*

Pennington, Emily
Feral: Losing Myself and Finding My Way in America's National Parks. Emily Pennington. Little a 2023. 270 p.
ISBN 9781542039710
Grades: Adult **B**
1. National parks and reserves 2. Self-discovery 3. Adventure 4. Life change events 5. Resilience 6. Solitude 7. Self-reliance 8. Landscape 9. United States 10. Autobiographies and memoirs 11. Life stories — Personal growth 12. Life stories — Nature and outdoors

A bracing memoir about self-discovery, liberating escape, and moving forward across an adventurous and volatile American landscape. One year. One national park at a time.

"In this visceral memoir, travel writer Pennington depicts a year devoted to visiting 62 U.S. national parks....Pennington's story of personal growth is told with unflinching insight and immense awe at the natural wonders she encounters." —*Booklist*

Pentland, Jenny
This Will Be Funny Later: A Memoir. Jenny Pentland. Harper 2022. 256 p.
ISBN 9780062962928
Grades: Adult **B**
1. Pentland, Jenny 2. Growing up 3. Children of celebrities 4. Anxiety in children 5. Dysfunctional families 6. Independence 7. Autobiographies and memoirs 8. Life stories — Relationships — Family 9. Life stories — Relationships — Growing up 10. Life stories — Facing adversity — Medical issues — Mental illness

Growing up, Jenny Pentland's life was a literal sitcom. Many of the storylines for her mother's smash hit series, Roseanne, were drawn from Pentland's early family life in working-class Denver. But that was only the beginning of the drama. Roseanne Barr's success as a comedian catapulted the family from the Rockies to star-studded Hollywood—with its toxic culture of money, celebrity, and prying tabloids that was destabilizing for a child in grade school. In this scathingly funny and moving memoir, Pentland reveals what it's like to grow up as the daughter of a television star and how she navigated the turmoil, eventually finding her own path. This Will Be Funny Later is a darkly funny and frank chronicle of transition, from childhood to adulthood and motherhood—one woman's journey to define herself and create the life she always wanted.

"The daughter of comedian Roseanne Barr recounts her unusual childhood with humor and self-deprecation.... This offers plenty of heart and laughs, especially for children of the 1980s and 1990s." —*Booklist*

Pepin, Jacques
The Apprentice: My Life in the Kitchen. Jacques Pépin. Houghton Mifflin 2003. VIII, 318 p. : Illustration
ISBN 9780618197378
Grades: Adult **B**
1. Pepin, Jacques, 1935- 2. Cooking 3. Cooks 4. Family relationships 5. Food habits 6. France 7. Autobiographies and memoirs 8. Biographies 9. Life stories — Arts and culture — Culinary arts 10. Food writing — Memoirs and biographies
LC 2002192158

Library Journal Best Books, 2003; New York Times Notable Book, 2003.

The popular television cooking show host traces his rise from an intimidated thirteen-year-old apprentice to a famous chef, recounting his work under prestigious teachers, his journey to America, and his experiences with contemporaries.

"Pepin relates how his interest in food and culinary techniques developed into passions for cooking and teaching. He does this deftly, neatly capturing personalities and events with clear, concise writing." —*Library Journal*

Includes index.

Pepys, Samuel
The Diary of Samuel Pepys. Edited and with a preface by Richard Le Gallienne; introduction by Robert Louis Stevenson. Modern Library 2001. xxxv, 310 p.
ISBN 9780679642213
Grades: Adult **B**
1. Pepys, Samuel, 1633-1703 2. Cabinet officers 3. Social life and customs 4. British history 5. Great Britain 6. 17th century 7. Diaries 8. Arts and Entertainment — Writing and Publishing — Literary criticism 9. Life stories — Arts and culture — Writing
LC 00054817

Diary entries by the tailor's son who rose up through the royal ranks describe his experiences in London from 1660 to 1669, and explore the political and cultural scene during the Restoration, the Plague, and the Great Fire of London.

PUBLIC LIBRARY CORE COLLECTION: NONFICTION
Twentieth Edition

Peres, Shimon
No Room for Small Dreams: Courage, Imagination, and the Making of Modern Israel. Shimon Peres. CutsomHouse 2017. 384 p.
ISBN 9780062561442
Grades: Adult   B
1. Nation building 2. Israeli-Palestinian relations 3. Presidents 4. Political science 5. Politics and government 6. Southwest Asia and North Africa (Middle East) history 7. Israel 8. History writing — Southwest Asia and North Africa (Middle East)

LC 2017042669

The late Israeli Prime Minister who won the Nobel Prize for his role in the Oslo Accords presents an intimate and personal account of the building and potential future of modern Israel.

"A look back at Israeli history and forward to what it will take to establish peace in the Middle East." —*Library Journal*

Perkins, Kendrick
The Education of Kendrick Perkins: A Memoir. Kendrick Perkins with Seth Rogoff. St. Martin's Press 2023. 304 p.
ISBN 9781250280343
Grades: Adult   B
1. Perkins, Kendrick, 1984- 2. African American basketball players 3. Basketball players 4. Basketball 5. Identity 6. Fatherhood 7. African American athletes 8. Social justice 9. Political participation 10. Racism in sports 11. Racism 12. United States 13. Autobiographies and memoirs 14. Life stories — Sports — Athletes 15. Life stories — Identity — Race and ethnicity 16. Sports and competition — Basketball

LC 2022039369

An intimate memoir about race, fatherhood, and basketball, from former NBA player and outspoken cultural critic.

"A former NBA player reflects on lessons learned as a player, many centering on racism in professional sports and society in general….A well-balanced blend of activism and memoir that looks far beyond the court and locker room." —*Kirkus*

Perkins, Nichole
Sometimes I Trip on How Happy We Could Be: Essays. Nichole Perkins. Grand Central Publishing 2021. 256 p.
ISBN 9781538702741
Grades: Adult   B
1. Perkins, Nichole 2. African American women authors 3. Popular culture 4. Social media 5. Podcasters 6. Desire 7. Sexuality 8. Mental illness 9. Internet 10. African American women 11. United States 12. Essays 13. Autobiographies and memoirs 14. Life stories — Identity — Gender 15. Society and culture — Pop culture 16. Life stories — Identity — Race and ethnicity 17. Life stories — Arts and culture 18. Book club best bets

LC 2021010633

Combining her sharp wit, stellar pop culture sensibility and trademark spirited storytelling, the writer and podcast host takes readers on a rollicking ride through the last 20 years of music, media and the internet from the perspective of a Southern Black woman.

"Perkins (Lilith, but Dark), a poet and former cohost of the Thirst Aid Kit podcast, examines religion, Black womanhood, desire, and sexuality in this powerful work of cultural criticism." —*Publishers Weekly*

Perl, Jed
Calder: The Conquest of Space : The Later Years : 1940-1976. Jed Perl. Alfred A. Knopf 2020. VI, 669 p. : Illustration; Color
ISBN 9780451494115
Grades: Adult   B
1. Calder, Alexander, 1898-1976 2. Sculptors 3. Artists 4. Modernism (Aesthetics) 5. Biographies 6. Life stories — Arts and culture — Artists 7. Arts and Entertainment — Painting, Drawing, and Sculpture

LC 2019025621

The concluding volume of the first authorized biography of one of the most important, influential, and beloved of 20th century sculptors, and one of the greatest artists in the cultural history of America—a vividly written, illuminating account of his triumphant later years. The concluding volume of this magnificent biography begins during World War II, when Calder—known to all as Sandy—and his wife, Louisa, opened their home to the stream of artists and writers in exile from Europe. In the postwar decades, they divided their time between the United States and France, as Sandy made his first monumental public sculptures and received blockbuster commissions that included Expo '67 in Montreal, and the 1968 Olympics in Mexico City. Jed Perl makes clear how Sandy's radical sculptural imagination shaped the minimalist and kinetic art movements that emerged in the 1960s. And we see, as well, that through everything—their ever-expanding friendships with artists and writers of all stripes; working to end the war in Viet Nam; hosting riotous dance parties at their Connecticut home; seeing "mobile," Sandy's essential artistic invention, find its way into Webster's' dictionary—Sandy and Louisa remained the risk-taking, singularly bohemian couple they had beensince first meeting at the end of the Roaring Twenties. The biography ends with Sandy's death in 1976 at the age of seventy-eight—only weeks after an encyclopedic retrospective of his work opened at the Whitney Museum in New York—but leaves us with a new, clearer understanding of both the artist and the man.

Includes bibliographical references (pages 587-631) and index.

★ *Calder: The Conquest of Time: The Early Years 1898-1940.* Jed Perl. Alfred A. Knopf 2017. 768 p.
ISBN 9780307272720
Grades: Adult   B
1. Calder, Alexander, 1898-1976 2. Sculptors 3. Artists 4. Modernism (Aesthetics) 5. Biographies 6. Life stories — Arts and culture — Artists 7. Arts and entertainment — Painting, drawing, and sculpture

LC 2016054731

The first biography of America's greatest twentieth-century sculptor, Alexander Calder: an authoritative and revelatory achievement, based on a wealth of letters and papers never before available, and written by one of our most renowned art critics.

"Not only an essential record of the first 40 years of Calder's life, but an exceptional chronicle of the genesis of modernism." —*Kirkus*

Perry, Bruce
Malcolm: The Life of a Man Who Changed Black America. Bruce Perry. Station Hill 1991. xv, 542 p. : Illustration
ISBN 9780882681030
Grades: 11 12 Adult   B
1. Malcolm X, 1925-1965 2. Black Muslims 3. African Americans 4. Race relations 5. United States 6. Biographies 7. Life stories — Politics — Activists and Reformers — Civil Rights Leaders 8. History writing — African American — Civil rights — United States

LC 90023350

Traces the life of the influential Black leader, describes the people who helped shape his philosophy, and looks at the circumstances that led to his murder.

"Perry traces Malcolm X's footsteps from birth in 1925 to death in 1965, using several hundred interviews to fill in detail and correct the autobiography Alex Haley edited. Probing what he labels as the deep-seated and hidden causes that made Malcolm who and what he was, Perry produces a portrait of an emotionally abused and abandoned boy who grew to manipulate his fearful helplessness into emotional and political power." —*Library Journal*

Includes bibliographical references (p. [510]-520) and index.

Perry, Imani
Looking for Lorraine: The Radiant and Radical Life of Lorraine Hansberry. Imani Perry. Beacon Press 2018. 256 p.
ISBN 9780807064498
Grades: Adult   B
1. Hansberry, Lorraine, 1930-1965 2. Playwrights, American 3. African American playwrights 4. African American women civil rights workers 5. African American women 6. Biographies 7. Arts and entertainment — Theater 8. Life stories — Politics — Activists and reformers

LC 2017055552

ESSENTIAL AND RECOMMENDED TITLES
Biography

Lambda Literary Award for LGBTQ Nonfiction, 2019; New York Times Notable Book, 2018.

The Hughes-Rogers Professor of African American Studies at Princeton University provides powerful insight into the extraordinary life of the author of a Raisin in the Sun.

"Perrys ardent, expert, and redefining work of biographical discovery brings light, warmth, scope, and enlightening complexity to the spine-straightening story of a brilliant, courageous, seminal, and essential American writer." —*Booklist*

Perry, Joe
Rocks: My Life in and Out of Aerosmith. Joe Perry, with David Ritz. Simon & Schuster 2014. 416 p.
ISBN 9781476714547
Grades: Adult **B**
1. Perry, Joe 2. Guitarists 3. Rock musicians 4. Fame 5. Autobiographies and memoirs 6. Life stories — Arts and culture — Performing arts — Musicians and composers 7. Arts and entertainment — Music — Rock

The lead guitarist of Aerosmith shares behind-the-scenes perspectives into the Rock and Roll Hall of Fame-inducted band, discussing such topics as his teen decision to drop out of school, enduring relationship with Steve Tyler and experiences with fame and recovery.

Perry, Mark
The Most Dangerous Man in America: The Making of Douglas Macarthur. Mark Perry. Basic Books 2014. 384 p.
ISBN 9780465013289
Grades: Adult **B**
1. MacArthur, Douglas, 1880-1964 2. Leadership 3. World War II 4. Military campaigns 5. Command of troops 6. Generals 7. Pride and vanity 8. United States history 9. Japan 10. United States 11. 20th century 12. Biographies 13. History writing — Military — Military leadership 14. Life stories — Law and order — Military leaders
LC 2014004629

This biography of the brilliant, but egotistical and rebellious military commander describes the secrets to his success on the Pacific stage of World War II as well as the personal and professional challenges he faced to get there.

"While much has been written on the general topic, Perry is strong on discussing MacArthur's relationship with FDR as well as his fellow officers in the Pacific." —*Library Journal*

Perry, Matthew
Friends, Lovers, and the Big Terrible Thing: A Memoir. Matthew Perry. Flatiron Books 2022. 256 p.
ISBN 9781250866448
Grades: Adult **B**
1. Perry, Matthew, 1969-2023 2. Actors and actresses 3. Addicts 4. Addiction 5. Acting 6. Television programs 7. Drug abuse 8. Autobiographies and memoirs 9. Life stories — Arts and culture — Performing arts — Actors and actresses 10. Life stories — Facing adversity — Medical issues — Addiction 11. Arts and entertainment — Movies and television
LC 2022028340

The beloved Friends star shares candid behind the scenes stories from the legendary sitcom, as well as detailing his own struggles with addiction that threatened to derail his career.

"Friends star Perry goes all out to discuss his struggle with addiction while offering backstage anecdotes about the mega-hit sitcom." —*Library Journal*

Person, Charles
Buses Are a Comin': Memoir of a Freedom Rider. Charles Person, with Richard Rooker. St. Martin's Griffin 2022. 304 p.
ISBN 9781250274199
Grades: Adult **B**
1. Person, Charles 2. Freedom Riders (Civil rights movement) 3. Freedom Rides (Civil rights movement) 4. African American civil rights workers 5. Segregation 6. Violence against African Americans 7. African American history 8. Civil rights 9. Race relations 10. United States history 11. 20th century 12. Autobiographies and memoirs 13. Biographies 14. Life stories — Politics — Activists and Reformers — Civil Rights Leaders 15. History writing — African American — Civil rights — United States 16. History writing — 1960s — United States 17. Antiracist literature
LC 2020048562

A surviving original Freedom Rider recounts his firsthand experiences with the South's historical and ongoing resistance to racial equality, sharing insights into what is required for progressive change to become possible in America.

"Civil rights activist Person debuts with a striking personal history of the 1961 Freedom Rides in protest of the nonenforcement of Supreme Court rulings banning racial segregation on interstate transportation. . . . Shot through with vivid details of beatdowns, arrests, and awe-inspiring bravery, this inspirational account captures the magnitude of what the early civil rights movement was up against." —*Publishers Weekly*

Originally published in 2021 by St. Martin's Press; Includes bibliographical references and index.

Pessah, Jon
Yogi: A Life Behind the Mask. Jon Pessah. Little, Brown, & Company 2020. VIII, 566 pages : Illustration; Color
ISBN 9780316310994
Grades: Adult **B**
1. Berra, Yogi, 1925-2015 2. Baseball players 3. United States 4. Biographies 5. Life stories — Sports 6. Sports and Competition — Baseball
LC Bl2020046716

A portrait of the 13-time World Series champion traces his rise to one of baseball's most accomplished athletes, discussing such topics as his experiences as an impoverished first-generation immigrant, his heroic war service and his paradoxical quotes.

Includes bibliographical references (pages 513-550) and index.

Peters, Charles
Lyndon B. Johnson: The 36th President, 1963-1969. Charles Peters; Arthur M. Schlesinger, Jr, and Sean Wilentz, general editors. Times Books 2010. 192 p.
ISBN 9780805082395
Grades: 11 12 Adult **B**
1. Johnson, Lyndon B, 1908-1973 2. Politicians 3. Liberals 4. Liberalism 5. Presidents 6. Politics and government 7. United States 8. 20th century 9. Biographies 10. History writing — Presidency — 20th century — United States 11. History writing — Presidency — United States 12. History writing — 1960s — United States 13. Life stories — Politics — Politicians
LC 2009045612

Documents the 36th president's time in office and the legacy of his achievements, revealing the insights he gained while serving in the Senate and throughout the Kennedy-Johnson administration and discussing how factors including the Vietnam war drove him from office.

Includes bibliographical references and index.

Peterson, Marlon
Bird Uncaged: An Abolitionist's Freedom Song. Marlon Peterson. Bold Type Books 2021. 256 p.
ISBN 9781645036517
Grades: Adult **B**
1. Peterson, Marlon 2. Prison reform 3. Social advocates 4. Social justice 5. Growing up 6. Poverty 7. Children of immigrants 8. Criminal justice reform 9. Masculinity 10. Imprisonment 11. Violence 12. Brooklyn, New York City 13. New York city 14. Autobiographies and memoirs 15. Life stories — Politics — Activists and reformers 16. Society and culture — Violence and crime — Criminal justice system

Finalist for the Hurston/Wright Legacy Awards for Nonfiction, 2022.

A leading advocate for prison abolition and transformative justice shares insights from the author's firsthand experiences of growing up in a violent neighborhood and surviving a brutal incarceration.

"Peterson offers a valuable, hard-won perspective on seizing maturity from disastrous beginnings via a haunting prose lyricism that is only occasionally

PUBLIC LIBRARY CORE COLLECTION: NONFICTION
Twentieth Edition

maudlin or redundant. A worthwhile contribution to evolving conversations on race and criminal justice." —*Kirkus*

Petrushevskaia, Liudmila
The Girl from the Metropol Hotel: Growing up in Communist Russia. Ludmilla Petrushevskaya; translated with an introduction by Anna Summers. Penguin Books 2017. 176 p.

ISBN 9780143129974

Grades: Adult   B

1. Petrushevskaia, Liudmila 2. Authors, Russian 3. Communism 4. Growing up 5. Soviet Union history 6. Moscow, Russia 7. 20th century 8. Translations — Russian to English 9. Autobiographies and memoirs 10. Life stories — Relationships — Growing up 11. History writing — Communism — Europe — Russia 12. Adult books for young adults 13. Nonfiction that reads like fiction

LC 2016031256

National Book Critics Circle Award for Autobiography/Memoir finalist, 2017.

A memoir from the best-selling and award-winning Russian author, describes waiting in bread lines with her Bolshevik family who once lived across the street from the Kremlin and being raised by her aunt and grandmother after her mother left.

Translation of: Malen?kaia devochka iz Metropolia; Original Russian edition: 2006; Translated from the Russian.

Peyser, Marc N.
Hissing Cousins: The Untold Story of Eleanor Roosevelt and Alice Roosevelt Longworth. Marc Peyser and Timothy Dwyer. Nan A. Talese / Doubleday 2015. 336 p.

ISBN 9780385536011

Grades: Adult   B

1. Roosevelt family 2. Roosevelt, Eleanor, 1884-1962 3. Longworth, Alice Roosevelt, 1884-1980 4. Power 5. Jealousy 6. Cousins 7. Betrayal 8. Loss 9. Regret 10. Children of presidents 11. Women and politics 12. Extramarital affairs 13. Presidents' spouses 14. United States 15. 20th century 16. Biographies 17. History writing — Early 20th century — United States 18. Life stories — People in history — Famous families 19. Life stories — Politics — Politicians

LC 2014026766

A provocative dual portrait of first cousins Eleanor Roosevelt and Alice Roosevelt Longworth discusses how their tangled lives were shaped by 20th-century history and politics, sharing insights into their childhoods, respective beliefs and adversarial relationship.

"Peyser and Dwyers detailed and witty double biography is hard to put down, a fascinating look at an era and two exceptionally strong, intelligent women." —*Booklist*

Pfeffer, Anshel
Bibi: The Turbulent Life and Times of Benjamin Netanyahu. Anshel Pfeffer. Basic Books 2018. 400 p.

ISBN 9780465097821

Grades: Adult   B

1. Netanyahu, Binyamin 2. Politicians 3. Prime ministers 4. Heads of state 5. Zionists 6. Politics and government 7. Israel 8. Southwest Asia and North Africa (Middle East) 9. Biographies 10. Life stories — Politics — Politicians 11. Politics and global affairs — Political figures 12. Politics and global affairs — World politics — Southwest Asia and North Africa (Middle East) — Israel and Palestine

For many in Israel and elsewhere, Benjamin Netanyahu is anathema, an embarrassment, even a precursor to Donald Trump. But he continues to dominate Israeli public life. How can we explain his rise, his hold on Israeli politics, and his outsized role on the world's stage?

Phair, Liz
Horror Stories: A Memoir. Liz Phair. Random House 2019. 262 p.

ISBN 9780525511984

Grades: Adult   B

1. Phair, Liz 2. Women musicians 3. Women songwriters 4. Rock musicians 5. Rock music 6. Singers 7. Autobiographies and memoirs 8. Arts and Entertainment — Music — Rock 9. Life stories — Arts and culture — Performing arts — Musicians and composers

LC 2019022839

When Liz Phair shook things up with her musical debut, Exile in Guyville—making her as much a cultural figure as a feminist pioneer and rock star—her raw candor, uncompromising authenticity, and deft storytelling inspired a legion of critics, songwriters, musicians, and fans alike. Now, like a Gen X Patti Smith, Liz Phair reflects on the path she has taken in these piercing essays that reveal the indelible memories that have stayed with her.

Pham, Andrew X.
★ *The Eaves of Heaven: A Life in Three Wars*. by Andrew X. Pham on the behalf of my father Thong Van Pham. Harmony Books 2008. 320 p.

ISBN 9780307381200

Grades: 11 12 Adult   B

1. Pham, Thong Van 2. Vietnamese Americans 3. Refugees 4. Vietnam War, 1961-1975 5. Immigration and emigration 6. Southeast Asian Americans 7. Southeast Asian people 8. Asian history 9. Vietnam 10. 20th century 11. Biographies 12. History writing — Wars and conflicts — Vietnam War 13. History writing — Immigration — United States 14. Life stories — Identity — Immigrants 15. Life stories — Law and order — Armed forces personnel

LC 2007033894

National Book Critics Circle Award for Autobiography/Memoir finalist.

A memoir by the award-winning author offers a portrait of his father's experiences over the course of three wars—the French occupation of Indochina, the World War II Japanese invasion, and the Vietnam War—as he captures the trials of everyday life in Vietnam amid the tragedy, violence, and turbulence of war.

Phelan, Tom
We Were Rich and We Didn't Know It: A Memoir of My Irish Boyhood. Tom Phelan. Gallery Books 2019. 224 pages

ISBN 9781501197093

Grades: Adult   B

1. Growing up 2. Poor families 3. Farm life 4. Authors, Irish 5. Rural life 6. Rural families 7. Catholics 8. Life change events 9. Priesthood 10. Children of farmers 11. Fathers and sons 12. Poverty 13. Ireland 14. Autobiographies and memoirs 15. Life stories — Relationships — Growing up 16. Family and Relationships — Growing up 17. Spirituality and Religion — Christianity — Catholicism

An author recalls his formative years growing up in the Irish midlands in the 1940s, working on his family farm in an isolated rural community without electricity, telephones or indoor plumbing.

Philbrick, Nathaniel
★ *Valiant Ambition: George Washington, Benedict Arnold, and the Fate of the American Revolution*. by Nathaniel Philbrick. Viking Press 2016. 416 p.

ISBN 9780525426783

Grades: Adult   B

1. Washington, George, 1732-1799 2. Arnold, Benedict, 1741-1801 3. Command of troops 4. Military history 5. Politicians 6. American Revolution, 1775-1783 7. Generals 8. United States history 9. United States 10. 18th century 11. Revolutionary America (1775-1783) 12. Biographies 13. History writing — Wars and conflicts — Revolutionary War (America)

LC 2016303785

ALA Notable Book, 2017.

The National Book Award-winning author of in the Heart of the Sea presents an account of the complicated middle years of the American Revolution that shares lesser-known insights into the tragic relationship between George Washington and Benedict Arnold.

"Philbrick weaves exciting accounts of Arnold's impulsive battlefield exploits with the activities of self-interested military and civil associates into the demythified story of the circumstances of a tragic betrayal." —*Library Journal*

ESSENTIAL AND RECOMMENDED TITLES
Biography

Philipps, Busy
This Will Only Hurt a Little. Busy Philipps. Touchstone 2018. 288 p.
ISBN 9781501184710
Grades: Adult   B
1. Philipps, Busy, 1979- 2. Acting 3. Fame 4. Celebrities 5. Actors and actresses 6. United States 7. Autobiographies and memoirs 8. Biographies 9. Life stories — Arts and culture — Performing arts — Entertainers and celebrities 10. Arts and Entertainment — Movies and Television
LC Bl2018167913
Presents a memoir by the comedic actress known for her roles on "Freaks and Geeks," "Dawsons Creek," and "Cougar Town," who has become a breakout star on Instagram.
"… actress Philipps presents a candid look at her life in and out of the spotlight, all told through her unflinchingly authentic, no-filter voice." —*Library Journal*

Philipps, Roland
A Spy Named Orphan: The Enigma of Donald Maclean. Roland Philipps. W W Norton & Company 2018. 416 p.
ISBN 9780393608571
Grades: Adult   B
1. Maclean, Donald Duart, 1913-1983 2. Spies 3. Secret service 4. Great Britain 5. Biographies 6. Life stories — Law and order — Spies and secret agents 7. History writing — Spies and spying 8. History writing — Cold War
LC 2017060974
Drawing on a wealth of previously classified files and unseen family papers, the author meticulously documents the extraordinary story of one of the most treacherous spies of the Cold War era and a key member of the infamous "Cambridge Five" spy ring.

Phillips, Julie
James Tiptree, Jr.: The Double Life of Alice B. Sheldon. Julie Phillips. St. Martin's Press 2006. VI, 469 p, 16 p. of plates : Illustration
ISBN 9780312203856
Grades: Adult   B
1. Tiptree, James Jr, 1915-1987 2. Women science fiction authors 3. Authors, American 4. 20th century 5. Biographies 6. Arts and Entertainment — Writing and Publishing 7. Life stories — Arts and culture — Writing — Authors
LC 2006040095
Hugo Award for Best Related Non-Fiction Book, 2007; Locus Award for Best Nonfiction/Related/Reference Book, 2007; National Book Critics Circle Award for Biography, 2006; ALA Notable Book, 2007; New York Times Notable Book, 2006.
A profile of the successful woman author who hid behind the male pen name of James Tiptree, Jr, to publish popular short works of science fiction in the 1970s describes her childhood explorations of Africa with her mother, work as an intelligence officer during World War II, and shocking suicide.
Includes bibliographical references (p. 449-451) and index.

Philpott, Mary Laura
Bomb Shelter: Love, Time, and Other Explosives. Mary Laura Philpott. Atria Books 2022. 288 p.
ISBN 9781982160784
Grades: Adult   B
1. Philpott, Mary Laura 2. Middle-aged women 3. Purpose in life 4. Mother and child 5. Parenthood 6. Women authors, American 7. Optimism 8. Anxiety 9. Essays 10. Autobiographies and memoirs 11. Biographies 12. Life stories — Arts and culture — Writing — Authors 13. Life stories — Relationships 14. Family and Relationships — General
LC 2021060262
A poignant and powerful new memoir-in-essays that tackles the big questions of life, death, and existential fear with humor and hope.
"Philpott (I Miss You When I Blink) explores life's pleasures and uncertainties in this wry if meandering collection of essays." —*Publishers Weekly*

Pick-Goslar, Hannah Elizabeth
★ *My Friend Anne Frank: The Inspiring and Heartbreaking True Story of Best Friends Torn Apart and Reunited Against All Odds.* Hannah Pick-goslar, with Dina Kraft. Little, Brown Spark 2023. 320 p.
ISBN 9780316564403
Grades: Adult   B
1. Pick-Goslar, Hannah Elizabeth, 1928-2022 2. Frank, Anne, 1929-1945 3. Jewish children 4. Girls 5. Best friends 6. Neighbors 7. Refugees, Jewish 8. Holocaust (1933-1945) 9. Antisemitism 10. Atrocities 11. Internment camp inmates 12. Separated friends, relatives, etc. 13. Reunions 14. Western European people 15. German people 16. Dutch people 17. Southwest Asian (Middle Eastern) people 18. Israeli people 19. Amsterdam, Netherlands 20. Germany 21. Autobiographies and memoirs 22. Life stories — Facing adversity — War and oppression — Holocaust 23. Life stories — Relationships — Friendship 24. History writing — Wars and conflicts — Holocaust — World War II
In 1933, Hannah Pick-Goslar and her family fled Nazi Germany to live in Amsterdam, where she struck up a close friendship with her next-door neighbor, an outspoken and fun-loving young girl named Anne Frank. For several years, the inseparable pair enjoyed a carefree childhood of games, sleepovers, and treats with the other children in their neighborhood. But in 1942, Hannah and Anne's lives abruptly changed forever. As Hannah chronicles the experiences of her own life during and after the war, she provides a searing look at what countless children endured at the hands of the Nazi regime, as well as an intimate, never‑before‑seen portrait of the most recognizable victim of the Holocaust.
"Painful history but a good choice for readers interested in Anne Frank or Holocaust-era memoirs." —*Kirkus*

Pinckney, Darryl
Come Back in September: A Literary Education on West Sixty-seventh Street, Manhattan. Darryl Pinckney. Farrar, Straus and Giroux 2022. 464 p.
ISBN 9780374126650
Grades: Adult   B
1. Pinckney, Darryl, 1953- 2. Hardwick, Elizabeth 3. Epstein, Barbara, 1928-2006 4. Authors, American 5. Intellectual life 6. Friendship 7. Apprenticeship 8. New York City 9. 20th century 10. Autobiographies and memoirs 11. Life stories — Arts and culture — Writing — Authors 12. Arts and Entertainment — Writing and publishing 13. Life stories — Relationships — Friendship
LC 2022023644
James Tait Black Memorial Prize for Biography, 2022; National Book Critics Circle Award for Autobiography/Memoir finalist, 2022.
A critic and writer recalls his experiences as a friend and mentee of Elizabeth Hardwick and Barbara Epstein in the early 1970s and how they helped introduce him to the New York Literary world of the time.
"In this sparkling memoir, novelist and playwright Pinckney (High Cotton) recollects his salad days in the 1970s and '80s in the vibrant circle surrounding the New York Review of Books." —*Publishers Weekly*

Pipher, Mary Bray
A Life in Light: Meditations on Impermanence. Mary Pipher. Bloomsbury Publishing Place USA 2022. 256 p.
ISBN 9781635577587
Grades: Adult   B
1. Pipher, Mary Bray 2. Women psychologists 3. Women 4. Psychic trauma 5. Mental health 6. Culture 7. Resilience 8. Joy and sorrow 9. Change 10. Memories 11. Growing up 12. Autobiographies and memoirs 13. Essays 14. Life stories — Relationships — Growing up 15. Life stories — Science, technology, and medicine — Healthcare professionals 16. Family and relationships — General
The best-selling author of Women Rowing North and Reviving Ophelia returns with a series of essays drawing on her experiences as psychologist specializing in women, trauma and the effect of our culture on our mental health.
"Psychologist Pipher, author of Reviving Ophelia and Women Rowing North, reflects on aging, loneliness, and happiness in a serene, gently told memoir." —*Kirkus*

Pippen, Scottie
Unguarded. Scottie Pippen with Michael Arkush. Atria Books 2021. 288 p.

PUBLIC LIBRARY CORE COLLECTION: NONFICTION
Twentieth Edition

ISBN 9781982165192
Grades: Adult   B

1. Pippen, Scottie 2. Basketball 3. Professional basketball players 4. African American basketball players 5. Olympic medal winners 6. Professional basketball 7. Sports 8. Autobiographies and memoirs 9. Life stories — Sports — Athletes 10. Sports and Competition — Basketball 11. Sports and Competition — Individual Athlete

On the 30th anniversary of the Bulls' first championship, the six-time NBA Champion, two-time Olympic gold medalist and Hall of Famer is finally giving fans a raw, matter-of-fact look into his life, and role within one of the greatest, most popular teams of all time.

"In this autobiography, former Chicago Bulls star Scottie Pippen telegraphs his pass—in this case a takedown of Michael Jordan, he of the carefully cultivated perfect image and the man in whose shadow Pippen played during the Bulls' dynasty. . . . Basketball fans might disagree with Pippen's aggrieved tone but will want to give reading time to this story of a small-town hero and a big-time team." —*Library Journal*

Pittard, Hannah
We Are Too Many: A Memoir [kind Of]. Hannah Pittard. Henry Holt and Company 2023. 224 p.
ISBN 9781250869043
Grades: Adult   B

1. Pittard, Hannah 2. Women authors 3. Married women 4. Married men 5. Best friends 6. Cheating (Interpersonal relations) 7. Extramarital affairs 8. Divorce 9. Former friends 10. Memory 11. Betrayal 12. Loss 13. Healing 14. North American people 15. American people 16. Men-women relations 17. Autobiographies and memoirs 18. Life stories — Relationships — Couples 19. Life stories — Relationships — Friendship 20. Life stories — Personal growth

In this wryly humorous and innovative look at a marriage gone wrong, Hannah Pittard recalls a decade's worth of unforgettable conversations, beginning with the one in which she discovers her husband has been having sex with her charismatic best friend, Trish. These time-jumping exchanges are fast-paced, intimate, and often jaw-dropping in their willingness to reveal the vulnerabilities inherent in any friendship or marriage. Blending fact and fiction, Pittard takes stock not only of her own past and future but also of the larger, more universal experiences they connect with.

"Novelist Pittard (Visible Empire) recounts the marriage-ending affair between her husband and best friend in this bold and inventive memoir." —*Publishers Weekly*

Plummer, Christopher
In Spite of Myself: A Memoir. by Christopher Plummer. Knopf 2008. 608 p.
ISBN 9780679421627
Grades: Adult   B

1. Plummer, Christopher. 1929-2021 2. Actors and actresses 3. Social classes 4. Rich families 5. Social life and customs 6. Canada 7. Autobiographies and memoirs 8. Canadian literature 9. Arts and Entertainment — Movies and Television 10. Life stories — Arts and culture — Performing arts — Actors and actresses 11. Adult books for young adults

LC 2008031229

An entertaining self-portrait by one of today's most acclaimed actors details his privileged Canadian upbringing, his early acting days, his roles with the Royal Shakespeare Company, his film career, the legendary performers with whom he has worked, and more.

"The author is an enchanting observer of the showbiz cavalcade, drawing vivid thumbnails of everyone from Laurence Olivier to Lenny Bruce and tossing off witty anecdotes . like the most effortless ad libs. The result is a sparkling star turn from a born raconteur for whom all the world is indeed a stage." —*Publishers Weekly*

Poehler, Amy
Yes Please. Amy Poehler. It Books 2014. 288 p.
ISBN 9780062268341
Grades: Adult   B

1. Poehler, Amy, 1971- 2. Women comedians 3. Comedians 4. Actors and actresses 5. Friendship 6. Female friendship 7. Parenthood 8. Love 9. Interpersonal relations 10. United States 11. Autobiographies and memoirs 12. Biographies 13. Life stories — Arts and culture — Performing arts — Entertainers and celebrities 14. Arts and entertainment — Movies and television

LC 2014469870

Goodreads Choice Award, 2014.

The actress best known for her work on "Parks and Recreation" and "Saturday Night Live" reveals personal stories and offers her humorous take on such topics as love, friendship, parenthood, and her relationship with Tina Fey.

Poitier, Sidney
The Measure of a Man: A Spiritual Autobiography. Sidney Poitier. Harper San Francisco 2000. xiii, 255 p, 8 p. of plates : Illustration
ISBN 9780062516077
Grades: Adult   B

1. Poitier, Sidney 2. Spirituality 3. Actors and actresses 4. Family relationships 5. African Americans 6. Faith 7. Autobiographies and memoirs 8. Arts and Entertainment — Movies and Television 9. Life stories — Arts and culture — Performing arts — Actors and actresses 10. Spirituality and Religion — Christianity 11. Life stories — Religion and spirituality — Personal faith

LC 99088322

New York Times Notable Book, 2000.

The acclaimed actor reveals the depth, passion, and intellectual fervor that have driven his life and career, citing the elements of his childhood that gave him his sense of worth, family, and ethics and how these qualities are essential to spiritual development.

"Poitier attempts to unravel for himself his own remarkable life story, looking at early life experiences, his family, and various themes that he believes have contributed to his success. Measure is not a chronological autobiography; the book emphasizes themes that have shaped his life. Poitier's tale is an affirmation of the value of morality and personal integrity in leading a successful, fulfilling life." —*Booklist*

Includes index.

Pollack, Howard
★ *George Gershwin: His Life and Work*. Howard Pollack. University of California Press 2006. xvii, 884 p. : Illustration
ISBN 9780520248649
Grades: Adult   B

1. Gershwin, George, 1898-1937 2. Composers 3. Composition (Music) 4. Music 5. Pianists 6. United States 7. Biographies 8. Arts and Entertainment — Music — Classical 9. Life stories — Arts and culture — Performing arts — Musicians and composers

LC 2006017926

Traces the life and career of the noted composer, examines his most important works, and discusses his personal life and his influence on the development of American music and on the relationship between jazz and classical music.

"This engaging biography is also a tour de force of scholarship." —*Booklist*
Includes bibliographical references (p. 817-824) and index.

Polly, Matthew
★ *Bruce Lee: A Life*. Matthew Polly. Simon & Schuster 2018. 672 p.
ISBN 9781501187629
Grades: Adult   B

1. Lee, Bruce, 1940-1973 2. Martial artists 3. Actors and actresses 4. Martial arts 5. Films 6. Athletes 7. Training 8. Biographies 9. Life stories — Arts and culture — Performing arts — Actors and actresses 10. Life stories — Sports — Athletes 11. Arts and Entertainment — Movies and Television 12. Sports and Competition — Martial Arts

LC 2018013592

Featuring rarely seen photos, a first authoritative biography of the martial arts film legend traces his early years in Hong Kong cinema, his work as a celebrity trainer and his stereotype-breaking achievements.

"A fascinating story of a remarkable figure in popular culture, this is the biography Bruce Lees legion of fans have been waiting for." —*Booklist*

ESSENTIAL AND RECOMMENDED TITLES
Biography

Poole, W. Scott
Vampira: Dark Goddess of Horror. W. Scott Poole. Soft Skull Press 2014. 320 p.
ISBN 9781593765439
Grades: Adult   B
1. Vampira, 1921-2008 2. Women's role 3. Horror films 4. Entertainers 5. United States 6. 1950s 7. Biographies 8. History writing — Arts and culture 9. Life stories — Arts and culture — Performing arts — Entertainers and celebrities 10. History writing — United States
LC 2014014147

The new book from award-winning historian W. Scott Poole is a whip-smart piece of pop culture detailing the story of cult horror figure Vampira that actually tells the much wider story of 1950s America and its treatment of women and sex, as well as capturing a fascinating swath of Los Angeles history. In Vampire, Poole gives us the eclectic life of the dancer, stripper, actress, and artist Maila Nurmi, who would reinvent herself as Vampira during the backdrop of 1950s America.

"Before there was Dr. Morgus, Svengoolie, and Elvira, there was the titular Vampira. This stone-cold winner belongs in every American studies collection." —*Library Journal*

Popoff, Alexandra
Vasily Grossman and the Soviet Century. Alexandra Popoff. Yale University Press 2019. 384 p.
ISBN 9780300222784
Grades: Adult   B
1. Grossman, Vasilii Semenovich 2. Authors, Russian 3. Totalitarianism 4. Journalists 5. Dissenters 6. Russian history 7. 20th century 8. Biographies 9. History writing — Europe — Russia 10. Life stories — Arts and culture — Writing 11. Arts and Entertainment — Writing and Publishing
Canadian Jewish Book Award, 2019; Saskatchewan Book Awards, Non-Fiction Award, 2020.

If Vasily Grossman's 1961 masterpiece, Life and Fate, had been published during his lifetime, it would have reached the world together with Pasternak's Doctor Zhivago and before Solzhenitsyn's Gulag. But Life and Fate was seized by the KGB. When it emerged posthumously, decades later, it was recognized as the War and Peace of the twentieth century. Always at the epicenter of events, Grossman (1905?1964) was among the first to describe the Holocaust and the Ukrainian famine. His 1944 article "The Hell of Treblinka" became evidence at Nuremberg. Grossman's powerful anti?totalitarian works liken the Nazis' crimes against humanity with those of Stalin. His compassionate prose has the everlasting quality of great art. Because Grossman's major works appeared after much delay we are only now able to examine them properly. Alexandra Popoff's authoritative biography illuminates Grossman's life and legacy.

"This well-researched portrait should introduce many new readers to a significant writer whose stand against totalitarian ideology, as Popoff's epilogue on Putin's veneration of Stalin demonstrates, has taken on new relevance and urgency today." —*Publishers Weekly*

Porizkova, Paulina
No Filter: The Good, the Bad, and the Beautiful. Paulina Porizkova. The Open Field/Penguin Life 2022. 256 p.
ISBN 9780593493526
Grades: Adult   B
1. Porizkova, Paulina 2. Fashion models 3. Widows 4. Femininity 5. Women authors 6. Marriage 7. Motherhood 8. Loss 9. Grief 10. Aging 11. Essays 12. Autobiographies and memoirs 13. Life stories — Identity — Gender 14. Life stories — Relationships
LC 2022031683

Writer and former model Paulina Porizkova pens a series of intimate, introspective, and enlightening essays about the complexities of womanhood at every age, pulling back the glossy magazine cover and writing from the heart.

"Model, actor, and writer Porizkova (A Model Summer) shares her thoughts on beauty culture, the end of her marriage, and honesty online in this solid collection of memoir-driven essays." —*Publishers Weekly*

Porter, Billy
★ *Unprotected: A Memoir.* Billy Porter. Abrams Press 2021. 288 p.
ISBN 9781419746192
Grades: Adult   B
1. Porter, Billy 2. African American gay men 3. Singers 4. Actors and actresses 5. African American celebrities 6. Growing up 7. Misfits (People) 8. Gay teenagers 9. Intersectionality 10. Ostracism 11. Racism 12. Child sexual abuse 13. Ambition 14. Self-discovery 15. Determination 16. African American children 17. Boys 18. Autobiographies and memoirs 19. Life stories — Arts and culture — Performing arts 20. Life stories — Facing adversity 21. Life stories — Identity — LGBTQIA+ 22. Life stories — Identity — Race and ethnicity 23. Arts and Entertainment — General

Before Billy Porter was an acclaimed recording artist, actor, playwright, and director, he was a young boy in Pittsburgh who was seen as different, who didn't fit in. At five years old, Porter was sent to therapy to "fix" his effeminacy. He was endlessly bullied at school, sexually abused by his stepfather, and criticized at his church. Porter came of age in a world where simply being himself was a constant struggle. This is the story of a young man whose unbreakable determination led him through countless hard times to where he is now: a proud icon who refuses to back down or hide.

"Broadway and television star Porter lays bare his traumatic upbringing and path toward healing in his revelatory debut.... Haunting and inspirational, this is both a powerful indictment of the lasting harms of bigotry and an immensely moving account of moving forward." —*Publishers Weekly*

Porter, Cecelia Hopkins
Five Lives in Music: Women Performers, Composers, and Impresarios from the Baroque to the Present. Cecelia Hopkins Porter. University of Ill. Press 2012. xiv, 244 p. : Illustration
ISBN 9780252037016
Grades: Adult   B
1. Sophie Elisabeth, Duchess, consort of August, Duke of Braunschweig-Luneburg, 1613-1676 2. Bach, Maria, 1896-1978 3. Jacquet de La Guerre, Elisabeth-Claude, 1665-1729 4. Lang, Josephine, 1815-1880 5. Schein, Ann, 1939- 6. Composers 7. Musicians 8. Women composers 9. Women musicians 10. Biographies 11. Arts and Entertainment — Music 12. Life stories — Arts and culture — Performing arts
LC 2011051102

Examines the lives of five women musicians from the seventeenth century to the twentieth century, discussing the personal experiences of each to provide insight into each woman's general and musical culture.
Includes bibliographical references (p. [229]-237) and index.

Porter, Linda
Katherine the Queen: The Remarkable Life of Katherine Parr, the Last Wife of Henry VIII. Linda Porter. St. Martin's Press 2010. 464 p.
ISBN 9780312384388
Grades: Adult   B
1. Catharine Parr, Queen, consort of Henry VIII, King of England, 1512-1548 2. Henry VIII, King of England, 1491-1547 3. Henry VII, King of England, 1491-1547 4. Husband and wife 5. Rulers 6. Royal houses 7. British history 8. 16th century 9. Tudor period (1485-1603) 10. Renaissance (1300-1600) 11. Biographies 12. History writing — Europe — United Kingdom 13. Life stories — Politics — Royalty 14. History writing — Renaissance — Europe
LC 2010035251

Porter (The Myth of "Bloody Mary") claims Elizabeth I's education, religious beliefs, and consciousness of personal image owed much to her loving stepmother. Rich, perceptive, nuanced and creative, this first full-scale biography gives one of Britain's best but least-known queens her due.

"Although often depicted by the Victorians as a matronly nurse to an elderly king, Katherine Parr (1512-1548), according to Porter, was a stylish trendsetter of 30, sensual, confident, dynamic, exceptionally educated and cultured, and able to perform with aplomb on both an English and international stage. Rich, perceptive, nuanced and creative, this first full-scale biography gives one of Britain's best but least-known queens her due." —*Publishers Weekly*

Includes bibliographical references and index; Originally published: London : Macmillan, 2010.

Posey, Parker
You're on an Airplane: A Self-mythologizing Memoir. Parker Posey. Blue Rider Press 2018. 256 p.

ISBN 9780735218192

Grades: Adult   B

1. Posey, Parker, 1968- 2. Actors and actresses 3. Fame 4. Advice 5. Acting 6. Autobiographies and memoirs 7. Life stories — Arts and culture — Performing arts — Actors and actresses 8. Arts and Entertainment — Movies and Television 9. Humor writing — Social humor

LC 2018288327

Loan Stars Favourites, 2018.

The "Queen of the Indies" star of such productions as Waiting for Guffman shares insider perspectives on a life in entertainment, exploring the therapeutic activities that enrich her life and her relationships with forefront directors.

"Resilient and fiercely observant, Posey is an unflinchingly honest and entertaining interpreter of her many stories." —*Kirkus*

Possanza, Amelia
Lesbian Love Story: A Memoir in Archives. Amelia Possanza. Catapult 2023. 288 p.

ISBN 9781646221059

Grades: Adult   B

1. Possanza, Amelia 2. Lesbians 3. Love 4. LGBTQIA+ people 5. Lesbian culture 6. Families 7. Women-women relations 8. Autobiographies and memoirs 9. Debut title 10. Life stories — Identity — LGBTQIA+ 11. History writing — LGBTQIA+

Lambda Literary Award for Lesbian Memoir/Biography, 2024.

Sharing her journey to recover the personal histories of lesbians in the 20th century: Who they were, how they loved, why their stories were destroyed and where their memories echo and live on, the author, along the way, discovers her own love and adds her record to the archive.

"In her impressive debut, Possanza stitches together personal memoir, painstaking research, and fictional imaginings with a fluid style and a sure hand....This is an outstanding work of literary scholarship that also delivers a vulnerable, intimate portrait of its author." —*Publishers Weekly*

Potts, Monica
The Forgotten Girls: A Memoir of Friendship and Lost Promise in Rural America. Monica Potts. Random House 2023. 272 p.

ISBN 9780593730898

Grades: Adult   B

1. Childhood friends 2. Journalists 3. Options, alternatives, choices 4. Rural life 5. Poverty 6. Poor people 7. Working class 8. Intergenerational trauma 9. United States 10. Ozark Mountain region 11. Autobiographies and memoirs 12. Life stories — Identity — Gender 13. Life stories — Relationships — Friendship 14. Life stories — Facing adversity

While working as a journalist covering poverty, the author returns to her hometown in the Ozarks where she connects with her childhood best friend, who, once talented and ambitious, has become a statistic, and retraces the moments of decision and chance that led them toward two such different destinies.

"A hauntingly cleareyed and poignant memoir with strong, illustrative reportage." —*Kirkus*

Power, Carla
If the Oceans Were Ink: An Unlikely Friendship and a Journey to the Heart of the Qur'an. Carla Power. Henry Holt and Company 2015. 320 p.

ISBN 9780805098198

Grades: Adult   B

1. Power, Carla 2. Muslim women 3. Converts to Islam 4. Islam 5. Islamophobia 6. Friendship 7. Religions 8. Autobiographies and memoirs 9. Life stories — Religion and spirituality — Spiritual journeys 10. Spirituality and Religion — Islam 11. Life stories — Relationships — Friendship

LC 2014017543

Pulitzer Prize for General Nonfiction finalist, 2016; National Book Award for Nonfiction finalist, 2015.

If the Oceans Were Ink is Carla Power's eye-opening story of how she and her longtime friend Sheikh Mohammad Akram Nadwi found a way to confront ugly stereotypes and persistent misperceptions that were cleaving their communities. Their friendship—between a secular American and a madrasa-trained sheikh—had always seemed unlikely, but now they were frustrated and bewildered by the battles being fought in their names. Both knew that a close look at the Quran would reveal a faith that preached peace and not mass murder; respect for women and not oppression. And so they embarked on a year long journey through the controversial text.

"Powers narrative offers an accessible and enlightening route into a topic fraught with misunderstanding." —*Publishers Weekly*

Includes bibliographical references and index.

Powers, Ann
★ *Traveling: On the Path of Joni Mitchell.* Ann Powers. Dey Street Books 2024. 480 p.

ISBN 9780062463722

Grades: Adult   B

1. Mitchell, Joni, 1943- 2. Singers 3. Women singers 4. Folk musicians 5. Folk music 6. Women musicians 7. Creativity 8. Music appreciation 9. Music 10. Musicians 11. Music industry and trade 12. Music history and criticism 13. Biographies 14. Arts and Entertainment — Music — Folk 15. Life stories — Arts and culture — Performing arts — Musicians and composers

Kaleidoscopic in scope, and intimate in its detail, a celebrated music critic, through extensive interviews with Joni Mitchell's peers and deep archival research, charts the course of her musical evolution, ranging from early folk to jazz fusion to experimentation with pop synthetics.

"NPR music critic Powers (Good Booty) paints a dazzling portrait of a legendary musician whose restless creativity fueled her multifaceted career in the folk, jazz, rock, and soul genres." —*Publishers Weekly*

Powers, Thomas
The Killing of Crazy Horse. by Thomas Powers. Alfred A. Knopf 2010. 576 p.

ISBN 9780375414466

Grades: Adult   B

1. Crazy Horse, approximately 1842-1877 2. Oglala (North American people) 3. Indigenous peoples of North America 4. Death 5. Rulers 6. 19th century 7. History writing — Indigenous peoples — United States

LC 2010016842

Los Angeles Times Book Prize for History, 2010; Spur Award for Historical Nonfiction, 2011; National Book Critics Circle Award for Biography finalist, 2010.

Investigates the enigmatic Native American figure, assessing critical battles attributed to his leadership within a context of the Great Sioux Wars, exploring the relationships between the Lakota Sioux and other tribes and analyzing the subjugation of North Plains Native Americans.

"Despite the title, this beautifully written and absorbing work is less about the death of Crazy Horse and more about the personality and life of the Native American icon. It is also an insightful and scrupulously fair examination of the culture of Plains Indian bands and their interaction with advancing white civilization in the nineteenth century." —*Booklist*

Includes bibliographical references and index.

Prejean, Helen
River of Fire: My Spiritual Journey. Sister Helen Prejean, C.S.J... Random House 2019. 320 p.

ISBN 9781400067305

Grades: Adult   B

1. Prejean, Helen 2. Nuns 3. Faith (Christianity) 4. Social advocacy 5. Social justice 6. Belief and doubt 7. Autobiographies and memoirs 8. Life stories — Re-

ESSENTIAL AND RECOMMENDED TITLES
Biography

ligion and spirituality — Spiritual journeys 9. Society and culture — Social activism and philanthropy

LC 2018051678

In this revelatory, intimate memoir from the author of Dead Man Walking, the nation's foremost leader in efforts to abolish the death penalty shares the story of her growth as a spiritual leader, speaks out about the challenges of the Catholic Church, and shows that joy and religion are not mutually exclusive.

"Informing and entertaining, Prejeans exceptional memoir will be of special interest to Catholics and social justice advocates." —*Publishers Weekly*

Prescod, Danielle
Token Black Girl: A Memoir. Danielle Prescod. Little a 2022. 256 p.
ISBN 9781542035163
Grades: Adult B

1. Prescod, Danielle 2. African American women 3. Fashion 4. Periodical editors 5. Ethnic identity 6. Racism 7. Institutional racism 8. Interpersonal relations 9. Psychic trauma 10. Self-perception 11. Healing 12. Perfectionism 13. Autobiographies and memoirs 14. Life stories — Arts and culture 15. Life stories — Identity — Race and ethnicity 16. Life stories — Personal growth 17. Society and culture — Race 18. Debut title 19. Antiracist literature

A fashion and beauty insider, in this revealing and candid memoir, unpacks the adverse effects of insidious white supremacy in the media to tell a personal story about recovery from damaging concepts of perfection, celebrating identity and demolishing social conditioning.

"A Black fashion reporter describes how White supremacy led to her crippling perfectionism and subsequent eating disorder....A trenchant, honest, and unique memoir about body image, fashion, and Blackness." —*Kirkus*

Preston, Katherine
Out with It: How Stuttering Helped Me Find My Voice. Katherine Preston. Atria Books 2013. 272 p.
ISBN 9781451676587
Grades: Adult B

1. Preston, Katherine, 1984- 2. Young women 3. Self-perception 4. Stuttering 5. Stutterers 6. Perfection 7. Self-esteem 8. Voyages and travels 9. Language disorders 10. Autobiographies and memoirs 11. Life stories — Facing adversity — Medical issues 12. Science Writing — Medicine and health

LC 2012048984

A fresh, engaging account of a young woman's journey, first to find a cure for a lifelong struggle with stuttering, and ultimately to embrace the voice that has defined her character.

Preszler, Trent
Little and Often: A Memoir. Trent Preszler. William Morrow & Company 2021. 240 p.
ISBN 9780062976642
Grades: Adult B

1. Preszler, Trent 2. Father and adult son 3. Vietnam veterans 4. Death of fathers 5. Gay men 6. Masculinity 7. Conflict in families 8. Rejection 9. Inheritance and succession 10. Tools 11. Grief 12. Learning 13. Woodworking 14. Canoes 15. Canoe building 16. Healing 17. Reconciliation 18. People with terminal illnesses 19. Men 20. Autobiographies and memoirs 21. Life stories — Facing adversity — Coping with death 22. Family and Relationships — Aging and Death 23. Arts and Entertainment — Crafts and hobbies 24. Life stories — Personal growth 25. Debut title

Trent Preszler thought he was living the life he always wanted, with a job at a winery and a seaside Long Island home, when he was called back to the life he left behind. After years of estrangement, his cancer-stricken father had invited him to South Dakota for Thanksgiving. It would be the last time he saw his father alive. Preszler's only inheritance was a beat-up wooden toolbox that had belonged to his father, who was a cattle rancher, rodeo champion, and Vietnam War Bronze Star Medal recipient. Little and Often is an unflinching account of bereavement and a stirring reflection on the complexities of inheritance. Between his past and his present, and between America's heartland and its coasts, Preszler shows how one can achieve reconciliation through the healing power of creativity.

"For debut author Preszler, his father's battered toolbox, full of farming tools and other items, helped him make sense of their relationship. . . . A thoughtful and well-written memoir, this book will appeal to readers who have difficult relationships with family and those who find craftwork healing." —*Library Journal*

Price, Margo
Maybe We'll Make It: A Memoir. Margo Price. University of Texas Press 2022. 256 p.
ISBN 9781477323502
Grades: Adult B

1. Price, Margo, 1983- 2. Women country musicians 3. Women songwriters 4. Music industry and trade 5. Ambition 6. Sexism 7. Addiction 8. Poverty 9. Survival 10. Persistence 11. Autobiographies and memoirs 12. Life stories — Arts and culture — Performing arts — Musicians and composers 13. Life stories — Facing adversity 14. Arts and Entertainment — Music — Country 15. Debut title

When Margo Price was nineteen years old, she dropped out of college and moved to Nashville to become a musician. She busked on the street, played open mics, and even threw out her TV so that she would do nothing but write songs. She met Jeremy Ivey, a fellow musician who would become her closest collaborator and her husband. But after working on their craft for more than a decade, Price and Ivey had no label, no band, and plenty of heartache. Price, though, refused to break, and turned her lowest moments into the classic country songs that eventually comprised the debut album that launched her career.

"Grammy-nominated musician Price chronicles in her dazzling debut her hardscrabble path through addiction, poverty, and loss on the way to becoming a successful recording artist." —*Publishers Weekly*

Prideaux, Sue
Edvard Munch: Behind the Scream. Sue Prideaux. Yale University Press 2005. xiii, 391 p, [112] p. of plates : Illustration; Color; Map; Portrait
ISBN 9780300110241
Grades: Adult B

1. Munch, Edvard, 1863-1944 2. Artists 3. Painters 4. Painting 5. Art 6. Biographies 7. Arts and Entertainment — Painting, Drawing, and Sculpture 8. Life stories — Arts and culture — Artists

LC 2005012040

James Tait Black Memorial Prize for Biography, 2005.

A comprehensive biography of Edvard Munch explores the events of his turbulent life and places his experiences in their intellectual, emotional, and spiritual contexts.

"Prideaux's treatment is very effective and her writing, cohesive, clear, and often compelling." —*Library Journal*

Includes bibliographical references (p. [366]-370) and index.

I Am Dynamite!: A Life of Nietzsche. Sue Prideaux. Tim Duggan Books 2018. 480 p.
ISBN 9781524760823
Grades: Adult B

1. Nietzsche, Friedrich Wilhelm, 1844-1900 2. Philosophers 3. Intellectuals 4. Ethics 5. Philosophy 6. Family relationships 7. Eccentrics and eccentricities 8. People with mental illnesses 9. Men 10. Biographies 11. Life stories — Education — Philosophers 12. Society and culture — Philosophy

LC Bl2018167887

Hawthornden Prize, 2019.

Illuminates the life of the famous philosopher and the events and people—including his family members, composer Richard Wagner and former lover Lou Salomé—that helped shape his brilliant, eccentric, but also deeply troubled mind.

Prince
The Beautiful Ones. Prince. Spiegel & Grau 2019. 288 p.
ISBN 9780399589652
Grades: Adult B

1. Prince 2. Musicians 3. Songwriters 4. Growing up 5. Fame 6. Rock music 7. Funk music 8. Dance music 9. Autobiographies and memoirs 10. Life stories — Arts and culture — Performing arts — Musicians and composers 11. Arts and

Entertainment — Music — Rock 12. Arts and Entertainment — Music — Rap and R&B

The brilliant coming-of-age-and-into-superstardom story of one of the greatest artists of all time, in his own words—featuring never-before-seen photos, original scrapbooks and lyric sheets, and the exquisite memoir he began writing before his tragic death.

"A work at turns affecting and raw, given that Piepenbring was not allowed to take notes or record conversations, this is, ultimately, an altar candle lit in the wake of an icon's passing." —*Booklist*

Pritchett, Georgia
My Mess Is a Bit of a Life: Adventures in Anxiety. Georgia Pritchett. HarperOne, an imprint of HarperCollinsPublishers 2022. 224 p.
ISBN 9780063206373
Grades: Adult   B
1. Pritchett, Georgia 2. Women television writers 3. Television writers 4. Anxiety 5. Psychological growth 6. Mothers 7. Child rearing 8. Great Britain 9. Autobiographies and memoirs 10. Life stories — Facing adversity — Medical issues — Mental illness

LC 2021045382

A joyful memoir-in-vignettes discusses a life of living—and thriving—with anxiety.

"British comedy writer Pritchett debuts with a collection of zippy and poignant anecdotes that describe living at the crossroads of imagination and anxiety. . . . The delivery's delightful and as finely tuned as poetry or a tight stand-up routine. Her torment, as well as her joys, are readers' gain." —*Publishers Weekly*

Originally published in the UK by Faber & Faber, London, in 2021.

Prose, Francine
1974: A Personal History. Francine Prose. HarperCollins 2024. 256 p.
ISBN 9780063314092
Grades: Adult   B
1. Prose, Francine, 1947- 2. Russo, Anthony J. (Anthony Joseph) 3. Social advocates 4. Social change 5. Interpersonal relations 6. Political activists 7. Authors 8. Pentagon Papers Case 9. Identity 10. United States 11. 1970s 12. Autobiographies and memoirs 13. Life stories — Politics 14. Life stories — Arts and culture — Writing — Authors

This memoir from the renowned author delves into her connection with activist Anthony Russo, a key figure in the Pentagon Papers leak and explores the transformative year that helped reshape our nation.

"Bestselling novelist Prose (The Vixen) documents a single, pivotal year of her life in her visceral debut memoir." —*Publishers Weekly*

Proulx, Annie
Bird Cloud: A Memoir. by Annie Proulx. Simon & Schuster 2011. 320 p.
ISBN 9780743288804
Grades: 11 12 Adult   B
1. Proulx, Annie 2. Natural areas 3. House construction 4. Women authors 5. Wyoming 6. Autobiographies and memoirs 7. Biographies 8. Travel Writing — United States 9. Arts and Entertainment — Writing and Publishing 10. Life stories — Personal growth

LC 2011389064

The author describes her purchase of six hundred wilderness acres in Wyoming and construction of a library-centric home where she contemplated her rich family history, including a river boat captain ancestor who met historical figures.

"Proulx bought a 640-acre nature preserve by the North Platte River in Wyoming and started building her dream house, a project that took years and went hundreds of thousands of dollars over budget. In her bustling account, Proulx salivates over the prospect of a Japanese soak tub, polished concrete floor, solar panels, and luxe furnishings that often turn into pricey engineering fiascoes. [This] is a fine evocation of place that becomes a meditation on the importance of a home, however harsh and evanescent." —*Publishers Weekly*

Prud'homme, Alex
The French Chef in America: Julia Child's Second Act. Alex Prud'homme. Alfred A. Knopf 2016. 320 p.

ISBN 9780385351751
Grades: Adult   B
1. Child, Julia 2. Women cooks 3. Television programs 4. Cooking, French 5. Television cooking shows 6. Fame 7. Social life and customs 8. Massachusetts 9. United States 10. 20th century 11. Food writing — Memoirs and biographies 12. Life stories — Arts and culture — Culinary arts

LC 2015043441

Alex Prud'homme recounts Julia Child's life during the late sixties to the early eighties when, after the success of her book Mastering the art of French cooking brought her fame, she struggled to re-find herself and create her legacy in America.

"Kelsey provides as much information as possible about all of the participants in these journeys and manages to keep it interesting." —*Publishers Weekly*

Includes bibliographical references and index.

Psaki, Jen
Say More: Lessons from Work, the White House, and the World. Jen Psaki. Scribner 2024. 256 p.
ISBN 9781668019856
Grades: Adult   B
1. Psaki, Jen 2. White House press secretaries 3. Women political consultants 4. Presidential staff 5. Women television journalists 6. Motherhood 7. Interpersonal communication 8. Personal conduct 9. Advice 10. Politics and government 11. American people 12. Autobiographies and memoirs 13. Life stories — Politics 14. Life stories — Relationships 15. Politics and global affairs — Political figures 16. Debut title

Sharing her journey to the Briefing Room and beyond, a former White House Press Secretary, current MSNBC host and one of the most prominent voices in American politics today explains her straightforward approach to communication and offers unique yet universal advice about how to be a more effective communicator in any situation.

"Former White House Press Secretary and current MSNBC host Psaki shares entertaining, essential lessons in communication—managing difficult conversations, giving and receiving feedback, connecting with an audience, and more—as she recounts her time working at the White House under two presidents and now hosting a TV show while parenting two kids." —*Library Journal*

Purdum, Todd S.
Something Wonderful: Rodgers and Hammerstein's Broadway Revolution. Todd S. Purdum. Henry Holt 2018. 352 p.
ISBN 9781627798341
Grades: Adult   B
1. Rodgers, Richard, 1902-1979 2. Hammerstein, Oscar, II, 1895-1960 3. Musicals 4. Composers 5. Playwrights 6. Songwriting 7. Songwriters 8. Composition (Music) 9. Theater 10. Broadway, New York City 11. New York City 12. 20th century 13. Biographies 14. Life stories — Arts and culture — Performing arts 15. Arts and Entertainment — Theater

LC 2017044836

A revelatory portrait of the creative partnership that transformed musical theater and provided the soundtrack to the American Century.

"Purdums anecdote-filled account is a sterling primer on the influential duo, both for newcomers to their work and to those looking to rekindle an old flame." —*Publishers Weekly*

Purnell, Sonia
Clementine: The Life of Mrs. Winston Churchill. Sonia Purnell. Viking Press 2015. 448 p.
ISBN 9780525429777
Grades: Adult   B
1. Churchill, Winston, 1874-1965 2. Churchill, Clementine, 1885-1977 3. Prime ministers' spouses 4. World War II 5. British history 6. Great Britain 7. 1940s 8. 20th century 9. Biographies 10. Life stories — Politics — Politicians 11. History writing — Wars and conflicts — World War II

LC 2015373202

A portrait of Winston Churchill's extraordinary wife and her lesser-known role in World War II discusses her relationship with political mentor Eleanor

ESSENTIAL AND RECOMMENDED TITLES
Biography

Roosevelt, her role in safeguarding Churchill's health throughout key historical events and her controversial family priorities.

★ *A Woman of No Importance: The Untold Story of the American Spy Who Helped Win Wwii*. Sonia Purnell. Viking 2019. 352 pages : Illustration; Map
ISBN 9780735225299
Grades: Adult **B**
1. Hall, Virginia, 1906-1982 2. Women spies 3. Intelligence officers 4. French Resistance (World War II) 5. Women's role 6. Intelligence service 7. Espionage 8. Women with disabilities 9. Undercover operations 10. World War II 11. German occupation, World War II 12. French history 13. Second World War era (1939-1945) 14. Biographies 15. Life stories — Law and order — Spies and secret agents 16. History writing — Wars and conflicts — Resistance — World War II 17. History writing — Spies and spying 18. Life stories — Identity — Gender

LC 2018060359

Booklist Editors' Choice, 2019; National Book Critics Circle Award for Biography finalist, 2019.

Traces the story of mid-twentieth-century spy Virginia Hall, detailing her pivotal role in coordinating Resistance activities in Europe that helped change the course of World War II.

"Meticulous research results in a significant biography of a trailblazer who now has a CIA building named after her." —*Kirkus*

Includes bibliographical references and index.

Qaderi, Homeira

Dancing in the Mosque: An Afghan Mother's Letter to Her Son. Homeira Qaderi. HarperCollins 2020. 304 p.
ISBN 9780062970312
Grades: Adult **B**
1. Qaderi, Homeira 2. Motherhood 3. Women 4. Mothers and sons 5. Survival 6. Grief 7. Love 8. Misogyny 9. Mothers 10. Families 11. Divorced women 12. Self-sacrifice 13. Afghanistan 14. Autobiographies and memoirs 15. Life stories — Facing adversity 16. Life stories — Identity — Gender

Devastating in its power, Dancing in the Mosque is a mother's searing letter to a son she was forced to leave behind. In telling her story, and that of Afghan women, Homeira challenges you to reconsider the meaning of motherhood, sacrifice, and survival. Her story asks you to consider the lengths you would go to protect yourself, your family, and your dignity.

Qu, Anna

Made in China: A Memoir of Love and Labor. Anna Qu. Catapult 2021. 224 p.
ISBN 9781646220342
Grades: Adult **B**
1. Qu, Anna 2. Chinese American women 3. Growing up 4. Child immigrants 5. Mothers and daughters 6. Stepfathers 7. Forced labor 8. Child abuse victims 9. Child protective services 10. Family relationships 11. Intergenerational relations 12. Chinese people in the United States 13. Chinese people 14. New York City 15. Autobiographies and memoirs 16. Life stories — Identity — Immigrants 17. Life stories — Facing adversity — Abuse survivors 18. Life stories — Relationships — Parent and child

Taking us on a journey from Wenzhou to Xi'an to New York, a Chinese American writer presents this powerful debut memoir in which she, forced to work in a Queens sweatshop, calls child services on her mother—an act with consequences that impact the rest of her life.

"Qu rewrites the bootstrap narrative of immigrants building a better life for their children in her grim and entrancing debut. Her 'path to the American dream' amounts to a devastating story of abuse and abandonment." —*Publishers Weekly*

Quin, Tegan

★ *High School*. Tegan and Sara. Farrar, Straus and Giroux 2019. 384 p.
ISBN 9780374169947
Grades: Adult **B**
1. Quin, Tegan, 1980- 2. Quin, Sara, 1980- 3. Twin sisters 4. Singers 5. Musicians 6. Autobiographies and memoirs 7. Page to screen 8. Life stories — Identity — LGBTQIA+ 9. Life stories — Relationships — Growing up 10. Life stories — Arts and culture — Performing arts — Musicians and composers 11. Adult books for young adults

LC 2019014934

Loan Stars Favourites, 2019; Alex Award, 2020.

Award-winning identical twin music artists Tegan and Sara share the coming-of-age story of their high school years, detailing how their early relationships, family tragedies and high expectations shaped their rise to celebrated musicians and global LGBTQ icons.

Made into a TV show on Freevee, 2022.

Quindlen, Anna

★ *Nanaville: Adventures in Grandparenting*. Anna Quindlen. Random House 2019. 160 p.
ISBN 9780812996104
Grades: Adult **B**
1. Quindlen, Anna 2. Grandmothers 3. Grandparent and child 4. Grandmother and grandchild 5. Happiness 6. Autobiographies and memoirs 7. Life stories — Arts and culture — Writing — Authors 8. Life stories — Relationships 9. Family and Relationships — Parenting

LC 2018052184

Before mommy blogs were even invented, Anna Quindlen became a go-to writer on the joys and challenges of motherhood in her nationally syndicated column. Now she's taking the next step and going full Nana in the pages of this lively and moving book abouther grandchildren, her children, and her new and remarkable role.

"The author imparts sensible advice with self-deprecating humor and sincere gratitude for the bounty of her life. A warmhearted memoir sure to appeal to other new grandmothersand Quindlen's many fans." —*Kirkus*

Quinn, Susan

Eleanor and Hick: The Love Affair That Shaped a First Lady. Susan Quinn. Penguin Press 2016. 448 p.
ISBN 9781594205408
Grades: Adult **B**
1. Roosevelt, Eleanor, 1884-1962 2. Hickok, Lorena Alice, 1893-1968 3. Presidents' spouses 4. Female friendship 5. Women journalists 6. Women-women relations 7. 1930s 8. Collective autobiographies and memoirs 9. Life stories — Relationships — Friendship 10. Life stories — Politics — Politicians 11. Life stories — Arts and culture — Writing — Journalists 12. History writing — Great Depression — United States

LC 2016303873

An intimate account of the close relationship between First Lady Eleanor Roosevelt and reporter Lorena Hickok shares compassionate insights into how their more than three-decade friendship transformed their lives and empowered them to play significant roles in one of the most tumultuous periods in American history.

"A relentlessly captivating study of two remarkable individuals who helped extend the roles of American women in the public policy realm." —*Kirkus*

Quinn, Tallu Schuyler

What We Wish Were True: Reflections on Nurturing Life and Facing Death. Tallu Schuyler Quinn. Convergent 2022. 208 p.
ISBN 9780593442906
Grades: Adult **B**
1. Quinn, Tallu Schuyler 2. Women social reformers 3. Clergywomen 4. Families 5. Identity 6. Vocation 7. Communities 8. Personal conduct 9. Brain cancer 10. People with cancer 11. People with terminal illnesses 12. Women 13. Essays 14. Autobiographies and memoirs 15. Life stories — Facing adversity — Medical issues — Physical illness 16. Life stories — Religion and spirituality — Personal faith 17. Family and relationships — Illness and the family 18. Spirituality and religion — Christianity

LC 2021060338

A non-profit leader, humanitarian and minister, after being diagnosed with an aggressive form of terminal brain cancer, pens profound essays on what it means to live with a terminal diagnoses and still find meaning and how to discover beauty in life's ordinary moments.

PUBLIC LIBRARY CORE COLLECTION: NONFICTION
Twentieth Edition

"In this devastating debut memoir, food justice activist Quinn recounts life with an incurable brain cancer." —*Publishers Weekly*

Many of the essays in this work originally appeared in slightly different form on Tallu Schuyler Quinn's blog at www.Caringbridge.Org/Visit/Talluquinn, in 2020 and 2021.

Raban, Jonathan
Father and Son: A Memoir. Jonathan Raban. Alfred A. Knopf 2023. 336 p.
ISBN 9780375422454
Grades: Adult   B
1. Raban, Jonathan 2. Raban, Peter, 1918-1996 3. Authors 4. People who have had strokes 5. Fathers and sons 6. Paralysis 7. Rehabilitation 8. Life change events 9. World War II 10. Soldiers 11. Husband and wife 12. Letter writing 13. Combat 14. Family relationships 15. Resilience 16. British people 17. English people 18. North American people 19. American people 20. Second World War era (1939-1945) 21. Autobiographies and memoirs 22. Life stories — Facing adversity — Medical issues — Physical illness 23. Life stories — Facing adversity — War and oppression — War survivors 24. Life stories — Relationships — Family 25. History writing — Wars and conflicts — World War II — European Theater
LC 2022054048

In June 2011, Jonathan Raban was sitting down to dinner with his daughter when he found he couldn't move his knife to his plate. Later that night, at the hospital, doctors confirmed what all had suspected: That he had suffered a massive hemorrhagic stroke, paralyzing the right side of his body. During his long rehabilitation, Raban became acquainted with, and struggled to accept, the limitations of his new body. Woven into these pages is an account of a second battle, one that his own father faced in the trenches during World War II. Moving between narratives, Raban artfully explores the human capacity to adapt to trauma, as well as the warmth, strength, and humor that persist despite it.

"The late travel writer and playwright interweaves a tale of recovery from a stroke with wartime reminiscences of his father." —*Kirkus*

Raddatz, Martha
The Long Road Home: A Story of War and Family. Martha Raddatz. G. P. Putnam's Sons 2007. 310 p. : Illustration; Map
ISBN 9780399153822
Grades: 11 12 Adult   B
1. Iraq War, 2003-2011 2. Soldiers 3. American people in Southwest Asia and North Africa (Middle East) 4. Iraq 5. 21st century 6. History writing — Wars and conflicts — Iraq War 7. Adult books for young adults
LC 2006037332
YALSA Best Books for Young Adults, 2008.

Documents the two-day firefight in Sadr City that began the Iraqi insurgency, during which eight 1st Cavalry Division soldiers were killed and numerous others wounded, an engagement that was vigilantly monitored by their loved ones back home.

"This account has grit and high drama.... Sometimes the level of detail is astonishing." —*New York Times*

Rademacher, Tom
It Won't Be Easy: An Exceedingly Honest and Slightly Unprofessional Love Letter to Teaching. Tom Rademacher. University of Minnesota Press 2017. xiii, 189 p.
ISBN 9781517901127
Grades: Adult   B
1. Rademacher, Tom, 1981- 2. Teachers 3. Education 4. Teaching 5. Learning 6. First year teachers 7. Essays 8. Autobiographies and memoirs 9. Life stories — Education — Scholars and educators 10. Society and culture — Education

Tom Rademacher wishes someone had handed him this sort of book along with his teaching degree: a clear-eyed, frank, boots-on-the ground account of what he was getting into. But first he had to write it. And as 2014's Minnesota Teacher of the Year, Rademacher knows what he's talking about. Less a how-to manual than a tribute to an impossible and impossibly rewarding profession, It Won't Be Easy captures the experience of teaching in all its messy glory.

Raffel, Dawn
The Strange Case of Dr. Couney: How a Mysterious European Showman Saved Thousands of American Babies. Dawn Raffel. Blue Rider Press 2018. 304 p.
ISBN 9780399175749
Grades: Adult   B
1. Couney, Martin A. 2. Sideshows 3. Premature babies 4. Neonatal intensive care 5. Exhibitions 6. 20th century 7. Life stories — Science, technology, and medicine 8. Science Writing — Medicine and health 9. History writing — Early 20th century — United States 10. Adult books for young adults

Drawing on historical documents, original reportage, and interviews with surviving patients, acclaimed journalist and magazine editor Dawn Raffel tells the marvelously eccentric story of Couney's mysterious carnival career, his larger-than-life personality, and his unprecedented success as the savior of tiny babies.

Rahmani, Niloofar
Open Skies: My Life as Afghanistan's First Female Pilot. Niloofar Rahmani with Adam Sikes. Chicago Review Press 2021. 320 p. : Illustration
ISBN 9781641603348
Grades: Adult   B
1. Rahmani, Niloofar 2. Women pilots 3. Determination 4. Pilots 5. Gender role 6. Women 7. Sexism 8. Leadership 9. Afghanistan 10. Autobiographies and memoirs 11. Life stories — Science, technology, and medicine — Astronauts and pilots 12. Life stories — Law and order — Armed forces personnel 13. Life stories — Identity — Gender 14. History writing — Women's history

The first female fixed-wing pilot for the Afghan Air Force in 2013, who received the International women of Courage Award, shares how she had to break through social barriers to demonstrate confidence, leadership and decisiveness to realize her dreams.

"In this timely, compelling, and important title, Afghanistan's first female fixed-wing pilot details her struggle to serve her country.... Not simply an inspiring title, this is a memoir of devastation and determination that brings the country's trials into sharp focus." —*Booklist*

Rainbow, Randy
Playing with Myself. Randy Rainbow. St. Martin's Press 2022. 256 p.
ISBN 9781250276254
Grades: Adult   B
1. Rainbow, Randy, 1981- 2. Comedians 3. Singers 4. Internet personalities 5. Childhood 6. Growing up 7. Performance 8. Autobiographies and memoirs 9. Life stories — Arts and culture — Performing arts — Entertainers and celebrities 10. Arts and Entertainment — Comedy
LC 2021057158

Setting the record straight, the man who conquered YouTube with a stylish pair of pink glasses shares the journey that led to Randy Rainbow, from his childhood as an often-misunderstood little boy to the creation of his trademark comedy character.

"Rainbow (yes, that is his real name) rose to viral video fame through roasting the Trump administration via parody songs and skits, and in his first memoir, he drops names, sprinkling his signature wit throughout." —*Booklist*

Rakoff, Joanna Smith
My Salinger Year. Joanna Rakoff. Alfred A. Knopf 2014. 272 p.
ISBN 9780307958006
Grades: Adult   B
1. Rakoff, Joanna Smith, 1972- 2. Salinger, J. D. (Jerome David), 1919-2010 3. Literature 4. Authors, American 5. Literary agents 6. Fan mail 7. Life change events 8. Change (Psychology) 9. College graduates 10. Publishers and publishing 11. Men-women relations 12. New York City 13. 1990s 14. 21st century 15. Autobiographies and memoirs 16. Page to screen 17. Life stories — Arts and culture — Writing 18. Arts and Entertainment — Writing and Publishing 19. Adult books for young adults 20. Nonfiction that reads like fiction
LC 2013026931
School Library Journal Best Books: Best Adult Books 4 Teens, 2014.

ESSENTIAL AND RECOMMENDED TITLES
Biography

Traces the author's experiences in 1990s New York as the assistant to the agent of J. D. Salinger, a job that contrasted with her threadbare personal life and was enriched by the famous writer's fan letters. By the award-winning author of a Fortunate Age.

"As Rakoff recounts her funny and wrenching personal predicaments, she also charts the quiet battle of attrition between the values of the old publishing world, personal and impassioned, and the aggressively invasive corporate imperative. An intriguing look at the ever-fascinating Salinger and a gracefully incisive tale of love and literature, creativity and survival." —*Booklist*

Ramey, Sarah
*The **Lady's** Handbook for Her Mysterious Illness: A Memoir.* Sarah Ramey. Doubleday 2020. 304 p.
ISBN 9780385534079
Grades: Adult   B
1. Ramey, Sarah 2. Chronic diseases 3. Sexism in medicine 4. Women 5. Chronic pain 6. Pain 7. Medical care 8. Chronic pain syndrome 9. People with disabilities 10. Diagnostic errors 11. Health 12. Autobiographies and memoirs 13. Society and culture — Gender — Women 14. Society and culture — Illness and disease 15. Life stories — Facing adversity — Medical issues
LC 2019018299

The funny, defiant memoir of Sarah Ramey's years-long battle with a mysterious illness that doctors thought was all in her head—but wasn't. A revelation and an inspiration for millions of women whose legitimate health complaints are ignored.

"A visceral, scathing, erudite read that digs deep into how modern medicine continues to fail women and what can be done about it." —*Booklist*

Rampersad, Arnold
★ *The **Life** of Langston Hughes: Volume II, 1941-1967: I Dream a World.* Arnold Rampersad. Oxford University Press 2002. 522 p. : Illustration
ISBN 9780195151619
Grades: Adult   B
1. Hughes, Langston, 1902-1967 2. African American poets 3. Poets, American 4. 20th century 5. Biographies 6. Arts and Entertainment — Writing and Publishing 7. Life stories — Arts and culture — Writing — Poets
LC 2001058766

Pulitzer Prize for Biography or Autobiography finalist.

A biography of the Harlem poet whose works gave voice to the joy and pain of the Black experience in America.

Includes bibliographical references and indexes.

*The **Life** of Langston Hughes: Volume I, 1902-1941: I, Too, Sing America.* Arnold Rampersad. Oxford University Press 2002. 478 p. : Illustration; Portrait
ISBN 9780195151602
Grades: Adult   B
1. Hughes, Langston, 1902-1967 2. African American poets 3. Poets, American 4. 20th century 5. Biographies 6. Arts and Entertainment — Writing and Publishing 7. Life stories — Arts and culture — Writing — Poets
LC 2001058766

National Book Critics Circle Award for Biography, 1986.

A biography of the Harlem poet whose works gave voice to the joy and pain of the Black experience in America.

Includes bibliographical references (407-448) and index.

★ *Ralph Ellison: A Biography.* Arnold Rampersad. Alfred A. Knopf 2007. 657 p, 24 p. of plates : Illustration
ISBN 9780375408274
Grades: Adult   B
1. Ellison, Ralph 2. African American authors 3. Authors, American 4. Social life and customs 5. United States 6. 20th century 7. Biographies 8. Arts and Entertainment — Writing and Publishing 9. Life stories — Arts and culture — Writing — Authors
LC 2006026464

BCALA Literary Award for Nonfiction, 2008; New York Times Notable Book, 2007; National Book Award for Nonfiction finalist, 2007; National Book Critics Circle Award for Biography finalist, 2007.

A critical biography of the author of Invisible Man draws on access to Ellison's personal papers to offer a definitive study of the life, work, and influence of Ralph Ellison, detailing his poverty-stricken Oklahoma youth, his education and involvement in New York's liberal intellectual circles, his personal relationships, and the influence of racism on his life.

Includes bibliographical references (p. [569]-624) and index.

Ramsey, Franchesca
Well, That Escalated Quickly: Memoirs and Mistakes of an Accidental Activist. Franchesca Ramsey. Grand Central Publishing 2018. 288 p.
ISBN 9781538761038
Grades: Adult   B
1. Ramsey, Franchesca, 1983- 2. Bloggers 3. Social media 4. Television personalities 5. Communication and technology 6. Race relations 7. Social justice 8. Mass media 9. Comedians 10. YouTubers 11. Autobiographies and memoirs 12. Society and culture — Media and technology 13. Life stories — Arts and culture — Performing arts — Entertainers and celebrities
LC 2017055221

In this sharp, funny, and incredibly timely collection of personal essays, veteran video blogger and star of MTV's Decoded, Franchesca Ramsey explores race, identity, online activism, and the downfall of real communication in the age of Twitter rants and call-out wars.

Randall, David K.
*The **King** and Queen of Malibu: The True Story of the Battle for Paradise.* David K. Randall. W.W. Norton & Co. 2016. 256 p.
ISBN 9780393240993
Grades: Adult   B
1. Malibu, California 2. 1900s (Decade) 3. History writing — Regional history — United States
LC 2015038696

Describes the early 1900s fight between the widow of a wealthy businessman and the most powerful men in the country to determine who should ultimately have ownership of Malibu in California and the resulting creation of the Pacific Coast Highway.

"An engaging story about wealth, entitlement, property rights, change, loss, and pain." —*Kirkus*

Randall, Willard Sterne
George Washington: A Life. Willard Sterne Randall. Henry Holt & Co. 1997. IX, 548 p. : Map
ISBN 9780805027792
Grades: 11 12 Adult   B
1. Washington, George, 1732-1799 2. Founding Fathers of the United States 3. Command of troops 4. Presidents 5. Generals 6. Leadership 7. United States 8. 18th century 9. Biographies 10. History writing — Presidency — 18th century — United States 11. History writing — Early America — United States 12. History writing — Military — Military leadership 13. Life stories — Law and order — Military leaders
LC 97019125

Explores Washington's life from a personal rather than political perspective, sharing the story of his life as a man rather than a leader.

"Chronicling less the adaptive leader of the struggling rebellion or the persuasive conciliator of the infant republic, Randall. portrays instead the vain, restless, ambitious provincial who got tremendously lucky. Altogether human, Randall's demythologized Washington comes vividly to life." —*Publishers Weekly*

A John Macrae book; Includes bibliographical references (p. 516-531) and index.

Rannells, Andrew
Uncle of the Year: & Other Debatable Triumphs. Andrew Rannells. Crown 2023. 256 p.
ISBN 9780593443439
Grades: Adult   B

PUBLIC LIBRARY CORE COLLECTION: NONFICTION
Twentieth Edition

1. Rannells, Andrew 2. Actors and actresses 3. Adulthood 4. Singers 5. Anxiety 6. Ambition 7. Fame 8. Purpose in life 9. Gay men 10. Families 11. Essays 12. Autobiographies and memoirs 13. Life stories — Arts and culture — Performing arts — Actors and actresses 14. Life stories — Identity — LGBTQIA+ 15. Humor writing — General 16. Arts and Entertainment — Theater 17. Life stories — Relationships

LC 2022057099

In essays drawn from his life and career, the star of the Book of Mormon, Girls and Big Mouth reflects on anxiety, ambition and the uncertain path to adulthood, challenging us to take a long look at who we're pretending to be, who we know we are and who we want to become.

"Give this to the reader who is anxiously awaiting this year's Tony nominations or to fans of celebrity memoirs in general." —*Booklist*

Ransby, Barbara
Eslanda: The Large and Unconventional Life of Mrs. Paul Robeson. Barbara Ransby. Yale University Press 2013. 448 p.
ISBN 9780300124347
Grades: Adult   B

1. Robeson, Eslanda Goode, 1896-1965 2. Robeson, Paul, 1898-1976 3. Women social advocates 4. Women anthropologists 5. Intellectuals 6. Intellectual life 7. Women journalists 8. Independence 9. Biographies 10. History writing — Women's history 11. Life stories — Politics — Activists and reformers 12. History writing — African American — United States

LC 2012022359

Chronicles the eventful life of the anthropologist, journalist, and women's rights advocate, exploring her world travels, friendships with notables and world leaders, and defiant McCarthy committee testimony.

Includes bibliographical references and index.

Rao, Cheeni
In Hanuman's Hands: A Memoir of Recovery and Redemption. Cheeni Rao. HarperOne 2008. 416 p.
ISBN 9780060736620
Grades: Adult   B

1. Rao, Cheeni 2. Young men 3. Indian Americans 4. Hindus 5. Drug addicts 6. Homeless people 7. Redemption 8. Hanuman (Hindu deity) 9. Rehabilitation 10. Autobiographies and memoirs 11. Life stories — Facing adversity — Medical issues — Addiction 12. Spirituality and Religion — Hinduism 13. Life stories — Religion and spirituality — Personal faith

LC 2008055421

A descendant of Brahmin priests combines his own story of encountering western culture with the mythic tales of his Hindu ancestors to describe how he fell subject to the temptations of sex, crime, and drugs while attending an elite New England college before hitting bottom and finding the inspiration to recover through visions of the mischievous monkey god Hanuman.

Rapinoe, Megan
One Life. Megan Rapinoe. Penguin 2020. 224 p.
ISBN 9781984881168
Grades: 9 10 11 12 Adult   B

1. Rapinoe, Megan, 1985- 2. Women soccer players 3. Professional athletes 4. Women Olympic medal winners 5. Soccer 6. Lesbians 7. Sexism 8. Sex discrimination in sports 9. Social advocates 10. Human rights 11. Sports 12. Social justice 13. Autobiographies and memoirs 14. Life stories — Sports — Athletes 15. Life stories — Identity — LGBTQIA+ 16. Sports and Competition — Soccer 17. Society and culture — Social activism and philanthropy 18. Sports and Competition — Individual Athlete

Rainbow List, 2023.

The Olympic gold medalist and two-time Women's World Cup champion describes her childhood in a conservative California town, her athletic achievements and her public advocacy of civil rights and urgently needed social change.

"A compelling testimony for equality in sports with a resounding message of hope." —*Booklist*

Rapoport, Ron
Let's Play Two: The Legend of Mr. Cub, the Life of Ernie Banks. Ron Rapoport. Hachette Books 2019. 384 p.
ISBN 9780316318631
Grades: Adult   B

1. Banks, Ernie, 1931-2015 2. Baseball players 3. African American baseball players 4. Baseball 5. Racism in sports 6. Segregation 7. People with depression 8. Men 9. Race relations 10. Chicago, Illinois 11. Biographies 12. Interviews 13. Sports and Competition — Baseball 14. Life stories — Sports — Athletes 15. Sports and Competition — Individual Athlete

LC 2018044409

This biography of the baseball Hall of Famer examines his early years battling poverty and racism, his career with the Chicago Cubs and who, despite facing depression and loneliness, was known for his enthusiasm for the game.

"Regardless if readers are interested in Banks's psychological makeup, those who grew up baseball fans in the 1950s and 1960s will not want to miss this account of him and his midcentury Cubs." —*Kirkus*

Includes bibliographical references and index.

Rappleye, Charles
Herbert Hoover in the White House: The Ordeal of the Presidency. Charles Rappleye. Simon & Schuster 2016. 560 p.
ISBN 9781451648676
Grades: Adult   B

1. Hoover, Herbert, 1874-1964 2. Political leadership 3. Depressions, 1929-1941 4. Presidents 5. Politics and government 6. United States 7. 20th century 8. Depression era (1929-1941) 9. Biographies 10. History writing — Presidency — 20th century — United States 11. History writing — Great Depression — United States

LC 2015027333

Describes the uphill battle faced by the 31st president, who served his single term during the Great Depression, portraying the man as bright, well-meaning and energetic but ultimately lacking in the tools of leadership.

"A fair, fresh, and fantastic reappraisal of a forgotten figure." —*Library Journal*

Includes bibliographical references and index.

Rasenberger, Jim
Revolver: Sam Colt and the Six-shooter That Changed America. Jim Rasenberger. Scribner 2020. x, 436 p. : Illustration
ISBN 9781501166389
Grades: Adult   B

1. Colt, Samuel, 1814-1862 2. Colt revolver 3. Guns 4. Gunsmiths 5. Industrialists 6. Inventors 7. Revolvers 8. 19th century 9. Biographies 10. Life stories — Science, technology, and medicine — Scientists and inventors 11. History writing — Antebellum America — United States

LC Bl2020013073

A sweeping portrait of the inventor of the legendary Colt revolver shares engaging insights into the role of the six-shooter in triggering the industrial revolution and the resettlement of the American West.

"This rollicking and informative account will delight American history buffs." —*Publishers Weekly*

Includes bibliographical references and index.

Ratajkowski, Emily
★ *My Body.* Emily Ratajkowski. Metropolitan Books 2021. 256 p.
ISBN 9781250817860
Grades: Adult   B

1. Ratajkowski, Emily, 1991- 2. Fashion models 3. Actors and actresses 4. Femininity 5. Feminine beauty (Aesthetics) 6. Objectification (Social psychology) 7. Misogyny 8. Sex crimes 9. Identity 10. Women in mass media 11. Entertainment industry and trade 12. Essays 13. Life stories — Arts and culture — Performing arts 14. Life stories — Identity — Gender 15. Society and culture — Gender — Women 16. Life stories — Arts and culture — Fashion

In this personal exploration of feminism, sexuality and power, of men's treatment of women and women's rationalizations for accepting that treatment, the

ESSENTIAL AND RECOMMENDED TITLES
Biography

acclaimed model and actress presents essays that chronicle moments of her life while investigating culture's fetishization of girls and female beauty.

"A refreshingly candid, fearless look into a model's body of work and its impact on her identity and politics." —*Publishers Weekly*

Rathbone, John Paul
The Sugar King of Havana: The Rise and Fall of Julio Lobo, Cuba's Last Tycoon. John Paul Rathbone. Penguin Press 2010. 336 p.
ISBN 9781594202582
Grades: Adult   B
1. Lobo, Julio, 1898-1983 2. Sugar industry and trade 3. Businesspeople 4. Rich men 5. Exiles 6. Caribbean history 7. Cuba 8. 19th century 9. Biographies 10. Business and economics — Business leaders and entrepreneurs 11. Life stories — Business — Business leaders 12. History writing — Latin America — Cuba
LC 2010013790

Documents the career of an influential Cuban sugar magnate whose life mirrored the turbulent course of post-independence Cuba's republic, discussing his celebrity affairs, brushes with death, and strained relationship with Che Guevara.

Includes bibliographical references and index.

Ratliff, Evan
The Mastermind: Drugs, Empire, Murder, Betrayal. Evan Ratliff. Random House 2019. xxxi, 446 p.
ISBN 9780399590412
Grades: Adult   B
1. Le Roux, Paul Calder 2. Criminals 3. Drug traffic 4. Computer crimes 5. Crime bosses 6. Cartels 7. Computer programmers 8. Internet fraud 9. Narcotics investigation 10. Murder investigation 11. Biographies 12. Life stories — Law and order — Criminals and law-breakers 13. True Crime — Drugs
LC 2018035751

New York Times Notable Book, 2019.

It all started as an online prescription drug network, supplying hundreds of millions of dollars' worth of painkillers to American customers. It would not stop there. Before long, the business had turned into a sprawling multinational conglomerate engaged in almost every conceivable aspect of criminal mayhem. The man behind it all, pulling the strings from a laptop in Manila, was Paul Calder Le Roux—a reclusive programmer turned criminal genius who could only exist in the networked world of the twenty-first century, and the kind of self-made crime boss that American law enforcement had never imagined.

"Sifting through detail after nefarious detail, Ratliff serves up a taut narrative that limns a portrait of a sociopath whose powers were most definitely used to evil ends. A wholly engrossing story that joins the worlds of El Chapo and Edward Snowden; both disturbing and memorable." —*Kirkus*

Includes bibliographical references and index.

Reagan, Ronald
The Reagan Diaries. Ronald Reagan; edited by Douglas Brinkley. Harper Collins 2007. xiv, 767 p. : Illustration; Color
ISBN 9780060876005
Grades: 11 12 Adult   B
1. Reagan, Ronald 2. Presidents 3. Personal diaries 4. Politicians 5. Republicans 6. Cold War 7. Politics and government 8. United States 9. 1980s 10. 20th century 11. Diaries 12. History writing — Presidency — 20th century — United States 13. History writing — 1980s — United States
LC B12007006078

Culled from his handwritten daily diaries, an account of the fortieth president's eight years in the oval office offers insight into his character as well as the behind-the-scenes factors that contributed to such events as his first inauguration and the end of the Cold War.

"There is a kind of touching banality to many of the entries, as though Reagan were just another CEO writing about corporate life at the top, albeit corporate life that revolved around nuclear and hostage negotiations. Edited by Douglas Brinkley , the book shows a Reagan almost sweetly amazed by small trappings of office. Reading these diaries, Americans will find it easier to understand how Reagan did what he did for so long: by steady work, and a steadfast commitment to the job at hand." —*Newsweek*

Includes index.

Reagan: *A Life in Letters.* Edited, with an introduction and commentary by Kiron K. Skinner, Annelise Anderson, Martin Anderson; with a foreword by George P. Shultz. Free Press 2004. xx, 935 p.
ISBN 9780743219679
Grades: Adult   B
1. Reagan, Ronald 2. Presidents 3. Letter writing 4. Politics and government 5. United States 6. 20th century 7. Life stories — Politics — Politicians
LC B12004115990

A collection of letters from the former president's extensive correspondence library offers insight into his public and private life of more than seventy years, from his early financial struggles and Hollywood achievements to his political career and personal relationships.

"This volume consists of a sampling of the former president's copious outpouring of personal letters, from his childhood to the onset of Alzheimer's after the presidency. The editors . arrange the letters thematically, introduce each chapter with a brief commentary, and introduce each letter with a sentence or two of explanation. The editors have done an admirable job in compiling these documents. Their commentary is exactly as it might have been had Ronald Reagan been able to produce this volume himself." —*Choice*

Includes bibliographical references and indexes; Reprint. Originally published: 2003.

Reang, Putsata
Ma and Me: A Memoir. Putsata Reang. MCD, Farrar, Straus and Giroux 2022. 304 p.
ISBN 9780374279264
Grades: Adult   B
1. Reang, Putsata 2. Lesbians 3. Cambodian Americans 4. Mothers and daughters 5. Family relationships 6. Psychic trauma 7. Identity 8. Hope 9. Resilience 10. Southeast Asian Americans 11. Southeast Asian people 12. United States 13. Autobiographies and memoirs 14. Life stories — Identity — LGBTQIA+ 15. Life stories — Relationships — Parent and child 16. Family and relationships — Families
LC 2021059702

The memoir of a woman caught between her identity as a gay woman and the love and life debt she owes her mother.

"Reminiscent of Memoirs of a Geisha with its lyricism, parables, and honest nature, Reang's writing tracks the interconnected lives of a mother and daughter who escape the Cambodian genocide but live with guilt for having survived." —*Library Journal*

Reed, Julia
Dispatches from the Gilded Age: A Few More Thoughts on Interesting People, Far-flung Places, and the Joys of Southern Comforts. Julia Reed; edited by Everett Bexley; foreword by Roy Bount Jr. St. Martin's Press 2022. 304 p.
ISBN 9781250279439
Grades: Adult   B
1. Reed, Julia 2. Editors 3. Columnists 4. Women editors 5. Voyages and travels 6. Social life and customs 7. Civilization 8. United States 9. 20th century 10. Essays 11. Arts and Entertainment — Writing and publishing 12. Life stories — Arts and culture — Writing — Journalists
LC 2022007362

An essay collection by the former contributing editor at Garden & Gun and one of America's greatest chroniclers details her coverage of the murder of the Scarsdale Diet doctor by her former headmistress and her world travels.

"There is life after death—at least for an essayist with this much verve on the page." —*Kirkus*

Includes index.

Regan, Iliana
Fieldwork: A Forager's Memoir. by Iliana Regan. Agate 2023. 250 p.
ISBN 9781572843189
Grades: Adult   B

PUBLIC LIBRARY CORE COLLECTION: NONFICTION
Twentieth Edition

1. Cooks 2. Restaurateurs 3. Farm life 4. Lesbians 5. Infertility 6. Family relationships 7. Forest plants 8. Forests 9. LGBTQIA+ people 10. Mushrooms 11. American people 12. North American people 13. Michigan 14. Indiana 15. Autobiographies and memoirs 16. Life stories — Identity — Gender 17. Life stories — Identity — LGBTQIA+ 18. Life stories — Nature and outdoors

LC 2022019146

The National Book Award nominee presents a memoir of her life and heritage as a forager, her life in the forests of Michigan's Upper Peninsula and how her complex gender identity informs her work as a chef.

"Michelin-star chef Regan…connects stories from her childhood at a farmhouse in Indiana to the Milkweed Inn that she and her wife, Anna, run in Michigan….Her honesty is captivating, and her writing creates a tangible experience that is remarkable and unforgettable." —*Library Journal*

A Midway book; Sequel to Burn the Place, published in July of 2019.

Rehm, Diane

On My Own. Diane Rehm. Alfred A. Knopf 2016. 128 p.
ISBN 9781101875285
Grades: Adult   **B**

1. Rehm, Diane 2. Rehm, John B. 3. Radio broadcasters 4. Widows 5. Grief 6. Loss 7. Adjustment 8. People with Parkinson's disease 9. Husband and wife 10. Family relationships 11. Autobiographies and memoirs 12. Life stories — Facing adversity — Coping with death 13. Family and relationships — Aging and death

LC 2015023006

The NPR radio host recounts her late husband's long battle with Parkinson's and her efforts to reconstruct a life without him, describing how she found inspiration in the examples of widowed colleagues and her advocacy of the Right to Die movement.

"Rehm's forthright memoir, which probes the process of loss, grief, and renewal, will find a wide audience with fans of her show as well as many others facing this profound passage." —*Publishers Weekly*

Reichl, Ruth

Comfort Me with Apples: More Adventures at the Table. Ruth Reichl. Random House 2001. 302 p.
ISBN 9780375501951
Grades: Adult   **B**

1. Reichl, Ruth 2. Women food writers 3. Cooking 4. Divorce 5. Remarriage 6. Motherhood 7. Recipes 8. Food habits 9. United States 10. Autobiographies and memoirs 11. Life stories — Arts and culture — Culinary arts 12. Food writing — Memoirs and biographies 13. Life stories — Relationships — Couples

LC 00053355

New York Times Notable Book, 2001.

The noted food critic describes her odyssey from chef to food writer, traces her journey through restaurants from Bangkok to Paris to Los Angeles, and offers colorful anecdotes about her life and encounters with great food.

"In this second installment of her memoirs, {Reichl retraces her route from married life on a commune in late-seventies Berkeley to her first job as a food critic, dining at expensive restaurants in Los Angeles with her glamorous editor. Reichl writes with gusto, and her story has all the ingredients of a modern fairy tale: Hard work, weird food, and endless curiosity." —*The New Yorker*

Sequel to: Tender at the bone.

Garlic and Sapphires: The Secret Life of a Critic in Disguise. Ruth Reichl. Penguin Press 2005. 333 p.
ISBN 9781594200311
Grades: Adult   **B**

1. Reichl, Ruth 2. Restaurant critics 3. Food writers 4. Cooking 5. Food 6. Autobiographies and memoirs 7. Food writing — Memoirs and biographies 8. Life stories — Arts and culture — Culinary arts

LC 2004051362

The editor-in-chief of "Gourmet" recounts her visits to some of the world's most acclaimed restaurants, both as herself and as an anonymous diner in disguise, to offer insight into the differences in her dining experiences.

"Reichl's ability to experience meals in such a dramatic way brings an infectious passion to her memoir. Reading this work . ensures that the next time readers sit down in a restaurant, they'll notice things they've never noticed before." —*Publishers Weekly*

Includes index.

★ *Save Me the Plums: My Gourmet Memoir.* Ruth Reichl. Random House 2019. 266 p.
ISBN 9781400069996
Grades: Adult   **B**

1. Reichl, Ruth 2. Restaurant critics 3. Food writers 4. Cooking 5. Food 6. Autobiographies and memoirs 7. Food writing — Memoirs and biographies 8. Life stories — Arts and culture — Culinary arts

LC 2018025584

LibraryReads Favorites, 2019.

The six-time James Beard Award-winning journalist and best-selling author of My Kitchen Year chronicles her groundbreaking tenure as editor-in-chief of Gourmet magazine and her work with legendary fellow epicureans to transform how America thinks about food.

"This look back in time will appeal to Reichl's many fans, foodies, as well as general readers. It's part elegy, part picaresque for a recent history that already feels like another era after the Great Recession and the evolution of digital publishing." —*Library Journal*

Reiss, Tom

The Black Count: Glory, Revolution, Betrayal, and the Real Count of Monte Cristo. Tom Reiss. Crown Trade 2012. IX, 414 p. : Map
ISBN 9780307382467
Grades: 11 12 Adult   **B**

1. Dumas, Thomas Alexandre, 1762-1806 2. Dumas, Alexandre, 1802-1870 3. Characters and characteristics in literature 4. Soldiers 5. Multiracial men 6. Fathers and sons 7. Multiculturalism 8. Aristocracy 9. French history 10. France 11. 18th century 12. Biographies 13. History writing — Europe — France 14. Life stories — Law and order — Armed forces personnel 15. Nonfiction that reads like fiction

LC 2012017633

New York Times Notable Book, 2012; Pulitzer Prize for Biography or Autobiography, 2013; National Book Critics Circle Award for Biography finalist, 2012.

Traces the story of the mixed-race swordsman and father of novelist Alexandre Dumas, discussing his rise to the French aristocracy, his military triumphs,and the adventures that inspired such classics as "The Three Musketeers" and "The Count of Monte Cristo."

Includes bibliographical references (p. [341]-403) and index.

Rembert, Winfred

Chasing Me to My Grave: An Artist's Memoir of the Jim Crow South. Winfred Rembert, as told to Erin I. Kelly; foreword by Bryan Stevenson. Bloomsbury Publishing 2021. 256 p.
ISBN 9781635576597
Grades: Adult   **B**

1. Rembert, Winfred 2. African American artists 3. African American painters 4. Outsider art 5. Memories 6. Racism 7. Lynching 8. African American prisoners 9. Violence against African Americans 10. African American civil rights 11. Civil Rights Movement 12. Race relations 13. United States history 14. Georgia 15. United States 16. Southern States 17. 20th century 18. Autobiographies and memoirs 19. Oral histories 20. Life stories — Identity — Race and ethnicity 21. Life stories — Arts and culture — Artists 22. History writing — African American — United States 23. Life stories — Facing adversity

LC 2020047749

Pulitzer Prize for Biography or Autobiography, 2022.

Winfred Rembert grew up as a field hand on a Georgia plantation. He embraced the Civil Rights Movement, endured political violence, survived a lynching, and spent seven years in prison on a chain gang. Years later, seeking a fresh start at the age of 52, he discovered his gift and vision as an artist, and using leather tooling skills he learned in prison, started etching and painting scenes from his youth. Rembert's work has been exhibited at museums and galleries across the country, profiled in the New York Times and more, and honored by Bryan Stevenson's Equal Justice Initiative. In Chasing Me to My Grave, he re-

ESSENTIAL AND RECOMMENDED TITLES
Biography

lates his life in prose and paintings—vivid, confrontational, revelatory, complex scenes from the cotton fields and chain gangs of the segregated south to the churches and night clubs of the urban north. This is also the story of finding epic love, and with it the courage to revisit a past that begs to remain buried.

"In this posthumous work, artist Rembert (1945-2021) offers a powerful, unfiltered look at life growing up in Jim Crow Georgia. . . . This is a stunning portrait of hope in the face of evil, barbarity, and racism." —*Publishers Weekly*

Remnick, David
The Bridge: The Life and Rise of Barack Obama. David Remnick. Alfred A. Knopf 2010. x, 656 p, [16] p. of plates : Illustration; Color
ISBN 9781400043606
Grades: 11 12 Adult   B
1. Obama, Barack 2. Democrats 3. African American politicians 4. Community organizers 5. Multiracial people 6. Presidents 7. Politicians 8. Politics and government 9. Self-discovery 10. United States 11. 2000s (Decade) 12. Biographies 13. Life stories — Politics — Politicians 14. Politics and global affairs — Political figures
LC 2010922697

New York Times Notable Book, 2010.

Examines the experiences of Barack Obama's life and explores the ambition behind his rise to the presidency, from his relationship with his parents to how social and racial tensions influenced his philosophy.

"Writing with emotional precision and a sure knowledge of politics, Mr. Remnick situates Mr. Obama's career firmly within a historical context. He puts Mr. Obama's life and political philosophy in perspective with the civil rights movement that shaped his imagination, as well as the power politics of Chicago, and the politics of race as it has been played out, often nastily, on the state and national stages." —*New York Times*

Includes bibliographical references (p. [617]-623) and index.

Rempel, William C.
The Gambler: How Penniless Dropout Kirk Kerkorian Became the Greatest Deal Maker in Capitalist History. William C. Rempel. Dey Street Books 2018. 416 pages
ISBN 9780062456779
Grades: Adult   B
1. Kerkorian, Kirk, 1917-2015 2. Capitalists and financiers 3. Billionaires 4. Casinos 5. Gambling 6. Film industry and trade 7. Risk-taking 8. Malicious accusation 9. Scandals 10. Los Angeles, California 11. Las Vegas, Nevada 12. Biographies 13. Life stories — Business 14. Life stories — Arts and culture
LC Bl2017045465

The rags-to-riches story of the self-made billionaire, aviator, and recluse traces his World War II service, his talent for poker, his genius business acumen, and the scandals that overshadowed his later years.

Renehan, Edward
Commodore: The Life of Cornelius Vanderbilt. Edward J. Renehan, Jr. Basic Books 2007. xx, 364 p, 16 p. of plates : Illustration; Portrait
ISBN 9780465002559
Grades: Adult   B
1. Vanderbilt, Cornelius, 1794-1877 2. Railroads 3. Businesspeople 4. United States 5. 20th century 6. Biographies 7. History writing — Early 20th century — United States 8. Business and economics — Business leaders and entrepreneurs 9. Life stories — Business — Business leaders
LC 2007022392

Presents the life and accomplishments of the steamship and railroad entrepreneur, focusing on his success in building the first integrated railroad system in the Northeast and in establishing New York City as a financial capital.

"A warts and more warts portrait of a brilliantly successful, genuinely despicable man." —*Kirkus*

Includes bibliographical references (p. 325-346) and index.

Retta
So Close to Being the Sh*t, Y'all Don't Even Know. Retta. St. Martin's Press 2018. 224 p.
ISBN 9781250109347
Grades: Adult   B
1. Retta 2. Actors and actresses 3. Comedians 4. Personal conduct 5. Growing up 6. Essays 7. Autobiographies and memoirs 8. Life stories — Arts and culture — Performing arts — Actors and actresses
LC 2017056742

The Hollywood star of hit series as Parks and Recreation and Girlfriends' Guide to Divorce presents an uproarious collection of essays that trace her upbringing by hardworking Liberian parents, the events that shifted her career focus from medicine to comedy and the ways that her successes have been shaped by fear and circumstance.

Reynolds, David S.
★ *Abe: Abraham Lincoln in His Times.* David S. Reynolds. Penguin Press 2020. xx, 1066 pages : Illustration; Map
ISBN 9781594206047
Grades: Adult   B
1. Lincoln, Abraham, 1809-1865 2. Ideology 3. Growing up 4. Influence (Literary, artistic, etc.) 5. Political leadership 6. Integrity 7. Presidents 8. Social life and customs 9. Politics and government 10. United States 11. 19th century 12. Antebellum America (1820-1861) 13. American Civil War era (1861-1865) 14. Biographies 15. Life stories — Politics — Politicians 16. History writing — Presidency — 19th century — United States
LC 2019047287

The award-winning author of Walt Whitman's America presents an immersive portrait of the 16th President, from his younger life in the decades before the Civil War through his emergence as a progressive political leader and advocate for human justice.

"Reynolds' biography moves Lincoln's life ever forward, inserting digressions without slowing the narrative pace. Even readers who think they know Lincoln's life deeply will find new insights here. This is sure to win a wide audience." —*Booklist*

Includes bibliographical references (pages [939]-1030) and index.

John Brown, Abolitionist: The Man Who Killed Slavery, Sparked the Civil War, and Seeded Civil Rights. David S. Reynolds. Alfred A. Knopf 2005. x, 578 p. : Illustration
ISBN 9780375411885
Grades: 11 12 Adult   B
1. Brown, John, 1800-1859 2. Abolitionists 3. Anti-slavery movements 4. Militants 5. Harpers Ferry, Battle of, Harpers Ferry, W. Va, 1862 6. United States history 7. West Virginia 8. 19th century 9. 1860s 10. Biographies 11. History writing — Antebellum America — United States 12. History writing — African American — Enslavement — United States 13. Life stories — Politics — Activists and reformers
LC 2004048864

ALA Notable Book, 2006.

A new biography by the award-winning author of Walt Whitman's America captures the turbulent life of John Brown, shedding new light on the controversial abolitionist who was responsible for the massacre of unarmed citizens in Kansas, liberation of slaves in Missouri, and raid on the federal arsenal in Harpers Ferry, Virginia, in his anti-slavery campaign. Reprint. 17,500 first printing.

"Almost every page forces you to think hard, and in new ways, about American violence, American history, and what used to be called the American character." —*The New Yorker*

Includes bibliographical references and index.

Reynolds, Debbie
Make 'Em Laugh: Short-term Memories of Longtime Friends. Debbie Reynolds, with Dorian Hannaway. William Morrow & Co. 2015. 272 p.
ISBN 9780062416636
Grades: Adult   B
1. Reynolds, Debbie 2. Celebrities 3. Women celebrities 4. Motherhood 5. Friendship 6. Divorce 7. Autobiographies and memoirs 8. Life stories — Arts and culture — Performing arts — Entertainers and celebrities
LC Bl2015040779

PUBLIC LIBRARY CORE COLLECTION: NONFICTION
Twentieth Edition

A collection of anecdotes, stories, jokes, and random musings by the Hollywood star shares insights into her celebrity friendships, headline-making divorce from Eddie Fisher, and experiences as a mother.

"Reynolds, who refers to herself as a comic (hence the books title), has done some outstanding film workwith Singin in the Rain at the forefrontbut whats most impressive here is her (almost always) upbeat outlook and her fond regard for the deep friendships she has forged throughout her life. This isnt exactly a showbiz memoir; its more of a memory book by a woman who has lived a rich life that happened to involve Hollywood." —*Booklist*

Rezaian, Jason
Prisoner: My 544 Days in an Iranian Prison—solitary Confinement, a Sham Trial, High-stakes Diplomacy, and the Extraordinary Efforts It Took to Get Me Out. Jason Rezaian. HarperCollins 2019. 320 p.

ISBN 9780062691576

Grades: Adult   B

1. Rezaian, Jason 2. Hostages 3. Journalists 4. Political prisoners 5. Diplomatic negotiations in international disputes 6. Malicious accusation 7. Iranian Americans 8. Trials (Espionage) 9. Imprisonment 10. Prisons 11. Politics and government 12. Iran 13. 2010s 14. Autobiographies and memoirs 15. Life stories — Facing adversity — War and oppression — Hostages and POWs

LC Bl2018191914

The former Tehran bureau chief describes how he was kept hostage for 18 months on trumped-up charges of espionage and rendered a pawn in high-stakes diplomatic talks that became a part of the Iran nuclear deal.

"At a time when journalists find themselves increasingly under fire, both abroad and at home, Rezaians dedication to his craft is an inspiring homage to the fearlessness of these intrepid purveyors of truth." —*Booklist*

Rhodes, James
Instrumental: A Memoir of Madness, Medication, and Music. James Rhodes. Bloomsbury USA 2017. 304 p.

ISBN 9781632866967

Grades: Adult   B

1. Rhodes, James, 1975- 2. Psychic trauma 3. Music 4. Mental illness 5. Sexual violence victims 6. Rape 7. Rape victims 8. Pianists 9. Life change events 10. Personal conduct 11. Healing 12. Autobiographies and memoirs 13. Life stories — Facing adversity — Medical issues — Mental illness 14. Life stories — Arts and culture — Performing arts — Musicians and composers

An evocative memoir of trauma, recovery and the redemptive power of music by a famed classical piano prodigy describes the wrenching experiences of the author's youth that compelled him to walk away from the piano for 10 years, sharing insights into how the lives of some of history's greatest composers inspired his return to music.

Rhodes, Richard
Hedy's Folly: The Life and Breakthrough Inventions of Hedy Lamarr, the Most Beautiful Woman in the World. Richard Rhodes. Doubleday 2011. 336 p.

ISBN 9780385534383

Grades: Adult   B

1. Lamarr, Hedy, 1913-2000 2. Actors and actresses 3. Spread spectrum communications 4. Inventors 5. Inventions 6. Films 7. Arts and Entertainment — Movies and Television

LC 2011021746

Describes the lesser-known technological talents of actress Hedy Lamarr and the collaborative work with avant-garde composer George Antheil that eventually led to the development of spread-spectrum radio, cell phones, and GPS systems.

"Here's a recipe that might surprise you: Take a silver-screen sex goddess (Hedy Lamarr), an avant-garde composer (George Antheil), a Hollywood friendship, and mutual technological curiosity, and mix well. What results is a patent for spread-spectrum radio, which has impacted the development of everything from torpedoes to cell phones and GPS technologies. This surprising and long-forgotten story is brought to life . [by Rhodes,] who deftly moves between Nazi secrets, scandalous films, engineering breakthroughs, and musical flops to weave a taut story that straddles two very different worldsthe entertainment industry and wartime weaponryand yet somehow manages to remain a delectable read." —*Library Journal*

Includes bibliographical references and index.

Scientist: E. O. Wilson: A Life in Nature. Richard Rhodes. Doubleday 2021. 368 p.

ISBN 9780385545556

Grades: Adult   B

1. Wilson, Edward O. 2. Naturalists 3. College teachers 4. Biologists 5. Biodiversity 6. Biogeography 7. 20th century 8. Biographies 9. Nature Writing — General 10. Life stories — Education — Scholars and educators 11. Life stories — Science, technology, and medicine — Scientists and inventors 12. Science Writing — Biology

A Pulitzer Prize-winning author presents this fully authorized—and timely—biography of the Harvard biologist and naturalist who has become a leading voice on the crucial importance to all life of biodiversity and has worked tirelessly to synthesize the fields of science and the humanities in a fruitful way.

"An admiring biography of biologist E. O. Wilson, sometimes called 'the father of biodiversity' or 'the father of sociobiology,' based on in-depth research, interviews with Wilson and his colleagues, and Wilson's own writing. . . . A comprehensive account, by an impressive science writer, of one of the world's most influential biologists and his profound contributions." —*Library Journal*

Ribowsky, Mark
Dreams to Remember: Otis Redding, Stax Records, and the Transformation of Southern Soul. Mark Ribowsky. Liveright Publishing Corporation 2015. 336 p.

ISBN 9780871408730

Grades: Adult   B

1. Redding, Otis, 1941-1967 2. Soul musicians 3. Soul music 4. Musicians 5. Biographies 6. Arts and Entertainment — Music — Jazz and the Blues 7. Life stories — Arts and culture — Performing arts — Musicians and composers

LC 2015009097

The author of the Supremes: A Saga of Motown Dreams discusses soul icon Otis Redding and the southern music he helped popularize.

"Unlike other performers who died far too young, Reddings death did not come out of abuse, and though he suffered, it was a universal human suffering—a pain in the heart that, partnered with unerring musical instinct, personal strength, and a little tenderness, he transformed into art. Ribowsky goes into the seamy side of the record business but also the sheer beauty and magic of the sixties soul music that Redding epitomized." —*Booklist*

Includes bibliographical references and index.

Shula: The Coach of the NFL's Greatest Generation. Mark Ribowsky. Liveright Publishing Corporation, a division of W.W. Norton & Company 2019. 400 pages

ISBN 9781631494604

Grades: Adult   B

1. Shula, Don, 1930-2020 2. Football coaches 3. Professional football coaches 4. Children of immigrants 5. Professional football players 6. Biographies 7. Life stories — Sports — Coaches, managers, and owners 8. Sports and Competition — Coaches 9. Sports and Competition — Football

LC 2019014727

Spanning seven decades, the notorious loss of Super Bowl III, and an historic undefeated season with the Dolphins, Shula is the definitive biography of a coaching legend.

"Ribowsky's excellent biography will thrill football fans of all allegiances." —*Publishers Weekly*

Includes bibliographical references and index.

Signed, Sealed, and Delivered: The Innovations, Innervisions, and Higher Ground of Stevie Wonder. Mark Ribowsky. John Wiley & Sons 2010. 352 p.

ISBN 9780470481509

Grades: Adult   B

1. Wonder, Stevie 2. African American singers 3. Rhythm and blues musicians 4. Popular culture 5. Popular music 6. Soul musicians 7. Rhythm and blues music 8. Music history and criticism 9. Social life and customs 10. United States 11. 20th century 12. 21st century 13. Biographies 14. Arts and Entertainment —

ESSENTIAL AND RECOMMENDED TITLES
Biography

Music — Rap and R&B 15. Life stories — Arts and culture — Performing arts — Musicians and composers

LC 2009037587

The first definitive biography of music legend Stevie Wonder, "Signed, Sealed, and Delivered" takes an in-depth look at Stevie Wonder's life and his evolution from kid-soul pop star into a mature artist whose music helped lay the groundwork for the evolution of hip hop and rap.

Includes index.

The Supremes: The Saga of Motown, Dreams, Success, and Betrayal. Mark Ribowsky. Da Capo Press 2009. 416 p.
ISBN 9780306815867
Grades: Adult   **B**

1. African American women singers 2. Soul music 3. Music 4. Betrayal 5. African American music 6. Popular music 7. Women singers 8. African Americans 9. Music history and criticism 10. United States history 11. United States 12. 20th century 13. Biographies 14. Arts and Entertainment — Music — Rap and R&B 15. Adult books for young adults 16. History writing — African American — United States

LC 2008051422

Explores the rise and fall of this popular trio based on recollections from friends, family, and Motown contemporaries who were there when their songs were made, their hits climbed the charts, and the group faded away into history due to personal issues and professional strife.

Includes bibliographical references, discography, and index.

Ricanati, Elizabeth

Braided: A Journey of a Thousand Challahs. Beth Ricanati, MD.. She Writes Press 2018. 184 p.
ISBN 9781631524417
Grades: Adult   **B**

1. Ricanati, Elizabeth 2. Women physicians 3. Cooking, Jewish 4. Judaism 5. Baking 6. Challah 7. Kosher food 8. Motherhood 9. Husband and wife 10. Jewish way of life 11. Jewish women 12. Rites and ceremonies 13. Autobiographies and memoirs 14. Biographies 15. Spirituality and Religion — Judaism 16. Food writing — Cooking and cookbooks — Narrative cookbooks 17. Life stories — Science, technology, and medicine — Healthcare professionals

LC 2018937854

Written for all the women who are carrying a myriad of responsibilities and not taking even a few minutes to stop and smell the rising yeast, this beautifully written memoir is a physician and mother's recipe for how to be in the moment, make the bread, and take the time you need to take to be truly well.

Rice, Condoleezza

Extraordinary, Ordinary People: A Memoir of Family. Condoleezza Rice. Crown 2010. 352 p.
ISBN 9780307587879
Grades: Adult   **B**

1. Rice, Condoleezza, 1954- 2. African American families 3. African American women politicians 4. Families 5. Racism 6. African American women cabinet officers 7. Women 8. African Americans 9. African American women 10. Race relations 11. Birmingham, Alabama 12. Autobiographies and memoirs 13. Biographies 14. History writing — Politicians — United States 15. Life stories — Politics — Politicians

LC 2010021645

The personal story of the former Secretary of State traces her childhood in segregated Alabama, describes the influence of people who shaped her life, and pays tribute to her parents' characters and sacrifices.

No Higher Honor: A Memoir of My Years in Washington. Condoleeza Rice. Crown Pub. 2011. 384 p.
ISBN 9780307587862
Grades: Adult   **B**

1. Rice, Condoleezza, 1954- 2. African American women politicians 3. African American women cabinet officers 4. Presidential staff 5. African American women 6. Politics and government 7. United States 8. 2000s (Decade) 9. Autobiographies and memoirs 10. Biographies 11. History writing — Politicians — United States 12. Life stories — Politics — Politicians

LC 2011534059

A former national security advisor and Secretary of State offers the story of her eight years serving at the highest levels of government, including the difficult job she faced in the wake of 9/11.

Richards, Cecile

Make Trouble: Standing Up, Speaking Out, and Finding the Courage to Lead—My Life Story. Cecile Richards with Lauren Peterson. Touchstone 2018. 288 p.
ISBN 9781501187599
Grades: Adult   **B**

1. Richards, Cecile 2. Women political activists 3. Women's rights 4. Social justice 5. Leadership 6. Autobiographies and memoirs 7. Life stories — Politics — Activists and reformers 8. History writing — Women's history 9. Society and culture — Gender — Women 10. Adult books for young adults

LC 2017061243

Amelia Bloomer List, 2019.

The president of Planned Parenthood and daughter of the late Texas Governor Ann Richards shares the story of her lifetime spent fighting for women's rights and social justice, offering insight into her work as a labor organizer, the challenges of balancing her career with her family responsibilities and her views about the importance of taking risks, making mistakes and standing up for what is right.

Richards, Keith

Life. Keith Richards; contributions by James Fox. Little Brown & Co 2010. 564 p, 32 p. of plates : Illustration; Color
ISBN 9780316034388
Grades: Adult   **B**

1. Richards, Keith, 1943- 2. Rock musicians 3. Rock music 4. Rock groups 5. Bands (Music) 6. Autobiographies and memoirs 7. Arts and Entertainment — Music — Rock 8. Life stories — Arts and culture — Performing arts — Musicians and composers

LC 2010934918

New York Times Notable Book, 2010.

The lead guitarist for the Rolling Stones recounts his life, from a youth obsessed with Chuck Berry to the formation of the Stones and their subsequent stardom, and discusses his problems with drugs, the death of Brian Jones, and his relationship with Mick Jagger.

"This autobiography of the Rolling Stones guitarist is way more than a revealing showbiz memoir. It is also a high-def, high-velocity portrait of the era when rock 'N' roll came of age, a raw report from deep inside the counterculture maelstrom of how that music swept like a tsunami over Britain and the United States. It's an eye-opening all-nighter in the studio with a master craftsman disclosing the alchemical secrets of his art. And it's the intimate and moving story of one man's long strange trip over the decades, told in dead-on, visceral prose without any of the pretense, caution or self-consciousness that usually attend great artists sitting for their self-portraits." —*New York Times Book Review*

Includes index.

Richardson, Lance

House of Nutter: The Rebel Tailor of Savile Row. Lance Richardson. Crown Archetype 2018. 336 p.
ISBN 9780451496461
Grades: Adult   **B**

1. Nutter, Tommy, 1943-1992 2. Fashion designers 3. Fashion 4. Popular culture 5. Photographers 6. Brothers 7. Gay men 8. 1960s 9. Biographies 10. Australian literature 11. Life stories — Arts and culture — Fashion 12. Life stories — Identity — LGBTQIA+ 13. Arts and Entertainment — Fashion

LC 2017045881

Describes the life and career of the Savile Row tailor and his photographer brother who influenced the fashion of the swinging cultural revolution that took place in the late 60s and early 70s, influencing everyone from Bianca Jagger to the Beatles.

Includes bibliographical references.

PUBLIC LIBRARY CORE COLLECTION: NONFICTION
Twentieth Edition

Richardson, Robert D.
William James: In the Maelstrom of American Modernism : A Biography. Robert D. Richardson. Houghton Mifflin 2006. xvi, 622 p, 16 p. of plates : Illustration; Map
ISBN 9780618433254
Grades: Adult **B**
1. James, William, 1842-1910 2. Philosophers 3. Social life and customs 4. United States 5. 19th century 6. Biographies 7. Spirituality and Religion — General 8. Life stories — Education — Philosophers
LC 2005037776

Biographer Richardson has written a moving portrait of James—pivotal member of the Metaphysical Club and author of the Varieties of Religious Experience. The biography, ten years in the making, draws on unpublished letters, journals, and family records. Richardson paints extraordinary scenes from what James himself called the "buzzing blooming confusion" of his life, beginning with childhood, as he struggled to achieve amid the domestic chaos and intellectual brilliance of Father, brother Henry, and sister Alice. James was a beloved teacher who taught courage and risk-taking, and served as mentor to W.E.B. Du Bois, Gertrude Stein, and many other Harvard outsiders. Richardson also illuminates James's hugely influential works. One of the great figures in mysticism here brought richly to life, James is a man "whose leading ideas are still so fresh and challenging that they are not yet fully assimilated by the modern world they helped to bring about.

"The author's enthusiasm for what he calls the matchless incandescent spirit of William James is contagious." —*Publishers Weekly*

Maps on lining papers; Includes bibliographical references (p. 530-589) and index.

Ricks, Thomas E.
★ *The Generals: American Military Command from World War II to Today.* Thomas E. Ricks. Penguin Press 2012. 576 p.
ISBN 9781594204043
Grades: Adult **B**
1. Generals 2. Command of troops 3. Leadership 4. Military history 5. United States 6. 20th century 7. History writing — Military
LC 2012015110

Describes the values, strategic thinking, and leadership qualities of military leaders from World War II to the present day and how the widening separation between performance and accountability has not resulted in any recent Marshalls, Eisenhowers, or Pattons.

Includes bibliographical references and index.

Ridley, Jane
George V: Never a Dull Moment. Jane Ridley. Harper 2022. 752 p.
ISBN 9780062567499
Grades: Adult **B**
1. George V, King of Great Britain, 1865-1936 2. Mary, Queen, consort of George V, King of Great Britain, 1867-1953 3. Windsor, House of 4. Leadership 5. World War I 6. Revolutions 7. Social change 8. Husband and wife 9. Royal houses 10. Monarchy 11. Rulers 12. Great Britain 13. Biographies 14. Life stories — Politics — Royalty 15. History writing — Europe — United Kingdom

The grandfather of Queen Elizabeth II, King George V. reigned over the British Empire from 1910 to 1936, a period of unprecedented international turbulence. Yet no one could deny that as a young man, George seemed uninspired. However, though it lasted only a quarter-century, George's reign was immensely consequential. He faced a constitutional crisis, the First World War, the fall of thirteen European monarchies and the rise of Bolshevism. How this supposedly limited man managed to steer the crown through so many perils and adapt an essentially Victorian institution to the twentieth century is a great story in itself. But this book is also a riveting portrait of a royal marriage and family life. Queen Mary played a pivotal role in the reign as well as being an important figure in her own right. Under the couple's stewardship, the crown emerged stronger than ever.

"Drawing on prodigious research, historian Ridley brings astute sensitivity to her brisk, authoritative biography of George V. (1865-1936), an 'Unpromising prince' who evolved 'Into a statesman king and the founder of the modern monarchy.' . . . An engrossing history of an eventful reign." —*Kirkus*

The Heir Apparent: A Life of Edward VII, the Playboy Prince. Jane Ridley. Random House 2013. 752 pages
ISBN 9781400062553
Grades: Adult **B**
1. Edward VII, King of Great Britain, 1841-1910 2. Victoria, Queen of Great Britain, 1819-1901 3. Womanizers 4. Gamblers 5. Monarchy 6. Rulers 7. British history 8. Great Britain 9. Edwardian era (1901-1914) 10. Biographies 11. History writing — Europe — United Kingdom 12. Life stories — Politics — Royalty 13. Life stories — Politics — Politicians
LC 2013002597

Booklist Editors' Choice, 2013; New York Times Notable Book, 2013.

A profile of the early-20th-century British king discusses how he disappointed his mother, Queen Victoria, with his notorious gambling, gluttony and womanizing before his nine-year reign, during which he became an effective leader and diplomat who founded England's modern monarchy.

"Readers who enjoy British history and biographies, royal and otherwise, will enjoy this brilliant biography, as informative as it is absorbing." —*Library Journal*

Riggs, Nina
The Bright Hour: A Memoir of Living and Dying. Nina Riggs. Simon & Schuster 2017. 310 pages
ISBN 9781501169359
Grades: Adult **B**
1. Riggs, Nina 2. People with breast cancer 3. People with terminal illnesses 4. Death 5. Family and death 6. Mothers 7. Personal conduct 8. Purpose in life 9. Autobiographies and memoirs 10. Life stories — Facing adversity — Medical issues — Physical Illness 11. Life stories — Facing adversity — Coping with death 12. Family and Relationships — Illness and the Family 13. Family and Relationships — Aging and Death
LC 2017007161

Discussing motherhood, marriage, friendship, and the legacy of her great-great-great grandfather, Ralph Waldo Emerson, the author, who has been diagnosed with terminal breast cancer, explores what makes a meaningful life when one has limited time.

In this tender memoir Riggs displays a keen awareness of and reverence for all the moments of lifeboth the light, and the dark, 'The cruel, and the beautiful.' —*Publishers Weekly*

Rigsby, Cody
★ *XOXO, Cody: An Opinionated Homosexual's Guide to Self-love, Relationships, and Tactful Pettiness.* Cody Rigsby. Ballantine Books 2023. 224 p.
ISBN 9780593722534
Grades: Adult **B**
1. Rigsby, Cody 2. Personal trainers 3. Gay men 4. Self-acceptance 5. Men dancers 6. Interpersonal relations 7. United States 8. Autobiographies and memoirs 9. Life stories — Identity — LGBTQIA+ 10. Life stories — Arts and culture — Performing arts — Entertainers and celebrities
LC 2023010922

With candid and empowering stories about learning how to handle the scary sh*t, the beloved Peloton instructor opens up about his journey to accepting himself, from growing up gay and poor in the South to becoming a fitness icon, reminding us that sometimes laughing at ourselves is the best medicine.

"Peloton instructor Rigsby charts his journey from closeted Southern teen to fitness superstar in his endearing debut memoir." —*Publishers Weekly*

Riley, Kathleen
The Astaires: Fred & Adele. Kathleen Riley. Oxford University Press 2012. 272 p.
ISBN 9780199738410
Grades: Adult **B**
1. Astaire, Fred, 1899-1987 2. Astaire, Adele 3. Dancers 4. Dancing 5. Siblings 6. Actors and actresses 7. United States 8. Biographies 9. Arts and Entertainment — Dance 10. Arts and Entertainment — Movies and Television

ESSENTIAL AND RECOMMENDED TITLES
Biography

11. Life stories — Arts and culture — Performing arts — Dancers and choreographers 12. Life stories — Arts and culture — Performing arts — Actors and actresses

LC 2011018462

Traces siblings Fred and Adele Astaire's rise to fame, from humble Midwestern origins and early days as child performers on small-time vaudeville stages, to their 1917 debut on Broadway, to star billings on both sides of the Atlantic.

Includes bibliographical references and index.

Rinder, Mike
★ *A Billion Years: My Escape from a Life in the Highest Ranks of Scientology*. Mike Rinder. Gallery Books 2022. 320 p.

ISBN 9781982185763

Grades: Adult **B**

1. Rinder, Mike 2. Scientologists 3. Dianetics 4. Former cult members 5. Coercion 6. Escapes 7. Resilience 8. Autobiographies and memoirs 9. Life stories — Religion and spirituality — Leaving religion 10. Life stories — Facing adversity 11. Spirituality and Religion — General

One of the highest-ranking defectors from Scientology exposes the secret inner workings of the powerful organization in this remarkable memoir. Author Mike Rinder offers insights into the religion that only someone of his former high rank could provide and tells a harrowing but fulfilling story of personal resilience.

"In this riveting, meticulously detailed memoir, Rinder describes his life as a Scientologist, from when his family 'Preordained' him as a child in Australia through his departure in 2007, at age 52….An intensely personal, cathartic memoir of blind allegiance, betrayal, and liberation." —*Kirkus*

Rinehart, Lorissa
First to the Front: The Untold Story of Dickey Chapelle, Trailblazing Female War Correspondent. Lorissa Rinehart. St. Martin's Press 2023. 400 p.

ISBN 9781250276575

Grades: Adult **B**

1. Chapelle, Dickey, 1919-1965 2. War correspondents 3. Photojournalists 4. Women photographers 5. World War II 6. Vietnam War, 1961-1975 7. Women war correspondents 8. Journalists 9. War photography 10. Photojournalism 11. Photography 12. United States 13. 20th century 14. Biographies 15. Life stories — Arts and culture — Writing — Journalists 16. History Writing — Women's history 17. History Writing — Wars and conflicts 18. Arts and Entertainment — Photography 19. Debut title

LC 2022058083

This biography of photojournalist Dickey Chapelle chronicles her trailblazing and heroic career from World War II through the early days of Vietnam, including her radical style of reporting that focused on the humanity of the oppressed.

"Jam-packed with colorful details and incisive character sketches, this is a vivid reappraisal of a pioneering journalist." —*Publishers Weekly*

Includes bibliographical references and index.

Rinella, Steven
Meat Eater: Adventures from the Life of an American Hunter. Steven Rinella. Spiegel & Grau 2012. 272 p.

ISBN 9780385529815

Grades: Adult **B**

1. Rinella, Steven 2. Hunters 3. Hunting 4. Nature 5. United States 6. Sports and Competition — Hunting

LC 2012018129

The author of American Buffalo and host of the Sportsman Channel's MeatEater presents a treasury of engaging facts about the natural world and history of hunting that also chronicles his evolution as a sportsman, exploring such topics as Manifest Destiny, the ethics of killing and humanity's responsibility toward prey.

Ripa, Kelly
Live Wire: Long-winded Short Stories. Kelly Ripa. Dey Street Books 2022. 304 p.

ISBN 9780063073302

Grades: Adult **B**

1. Ripa, Kelly 2. Actors and actresses 3. Women television talk show hosts and guests 4. Women celebrities 5. Fame 6. Family relationships 7. Marriage 8. Entertainment industry and trade 9. Autobiographies and memoirs 10. Life stories — Arts and culture — Performing arts — Entertainers and celebrities 11. Life stories — Arts and culture — Performing arts — Actors and actresses 12. Arts and Entertainment — Movies and Television

The beloved daytime talk show host shares sharp-witted and insightful stories about her life as a professional, wife, daughter and mother, bringing hard-earned wisdom and an eye for the absurdity of life to every minute of the day. Surprising, at times savage, a little shameless and always with humor? Live Wire shows Kelly as she really is offscreen—a very wise woman who has something to say.

"Actor and talk show host Ripa offers a no-holds-barred glimpse of her personal and professional life in her self-deprecating debut….This banter-filled collection will delight daytime television devotees." —*Publishers Weekly*

Ripert, Eric
32 Yolks: From My Mother's Table to Working the Line. Eric Ripert, with Veronica Chambers. Random House 2016. 304 p.

ISBN 9780812992984

Grades: Adult **B**

1. Ripert, Eric 2. Cooks 3. Restaurateurs 4. Cooking, French 5. Cooking 6. Paris, France 7. Autobiographies and memoirs 8. Food writing — Memoirs and biographies 9. Life stories — Arts and culture — Culinary arts

LC 2015050280

The chef and co-owner of the New York restaurant Le Bernardin and a regular guest judge on Bravo's Top Chef shares how the events from his childhood prompted him to learn to cook and find happiness as he was finally able to share his lifelong love of food with other people.

"Readers may know Ripert as the meditative host of the PBS series Avec Eric; a fan-favorite judge on Bravo's Top Chef; and the owner of Le Bernardin, a French seafood restaurant in New York. His roots, however, are far from that calm and thoughtful adult. This memoir tells of Ripert's tumultuous childhood in France where a love of excellent food was instilled in him early on. Although the loving descriptions of flavors and cooking techniques will make some long for recipes, this narrative sheds light on the carefully controlled chaos behind the scenes at several top restaurants in the 1970s and 1980s." —*Library Journal*

Rippon, Adam
Beautiful on the Outside: A Memoir. Adam Rippon. Grand Central Publishing 2019. 245 pages, 16 unnumbered pages of plates : Color; Portrait

ISBN 9781538732403

Grades: Adult **B**

1. Rippon, Adam, 1989- 2. Figure skaters 3. Olympic medal winners 4. Figure skating 5. Gay men 6. Competition 7. Growing up 8. Autobiographies and memoirs 9. Life stories — Sports — Athletes 10. Sports and Competition — Olympic Sports 11. Life stories — Identity — LGBTQIA+ 12. Sports and Competition — Individual Athlete 13. Adult books for young adults

LC Bl2019022961

The medal-winning Olympics figure skater reveals the early poverty and discrimination that challenged his career as an openly gay athlete, describing his homeschooled childhood in Pennsylvania and the setbacks and successes that shaped his achievements.

Risner, Vaneetha Rendall
Walking Through Fire: A Memoir of Loss and Redemption. Vaneetha Rendall Risner. Nelson Books 2020. 256 p.

ISBN 9781400218110

Grades: Adult **B**

1. Risner, Vaneetha Rendall, 1964- 2. Conversion to Christianity 3. Christian life 4. Faith (Christianity) 5. Loss 6. Suffering 7. Redemption 8. Marriage 9. Joy and sorrow 10. People with poliomyelitis 11. Autobiographies and memoirs 12. Life stories — Religion and spirituality — Spiritual journeys 13. Spirituality and Religion — Christianity 14. Life stories — Facing adversity — Medical issues

LC 2020015645

The astonishing, Job-like story of how an existence filled with loss, suffering, questioning, and anger became a life filled with shocking and incomprehensible peace and joy.

"This beautifully redemptive memoir illustrates the staying power of true faith." —*Publishers Weekly*

Includes bibliographical references.

Rivera, Mariano

The Closer: My Story. Mariano Rivera with Wayne Coffey. Little Brown & Co 2014. 288 p.
ISBN 9780316400732
Grades: Adult   B
1. Rivera, Mariano, 1969- 2. Baseball players 3. Christian life 4. Baseball 5. Pitchers (Baseball) 6. Relief pitchers (Baseball) 7. Athletes 8. Christian men 9. Autobiographies and memoirs 10. Sports and Competition — Baseball 11. Life stories — Sports — Athletes

LC 2014934754

The nineteen-year veteran pitcher for the New York Yankees describes his life, discussing the difficulties in being a Latino baseball player in the U.S, how he keeps his Christian values in professional sports, and his championships and rivalries.

"[I]n this entertaining, admirably subdued autobiography, the glory is God's: Rivera's story brims with examples of his faith." —*Publishers Weekly*

Roberts, Andrew

★ *Churchill: Walking with Destiny.* Andrew Roberts. Viking 2018. 704 p.
ISBN 9781101980996
Grades: Adult   B
1. Churchill, Winston, 1874-1965 2. Leadership 3. Politicians 4. Prime ministers 5. World War II 6. Politics and government 7. Great Britain 8. 20th century 9. Biographies 10. Life stories — Politics — Politicians 11. History writing — Wars and conflicts — World War II

LC Bl2018183334

New York Times Notable Book, 2018.

Draws on extensive new materials, from private letters to transcripts of war cabinet meetings, to present a portrait of the iconic war leader that discusses Churchill's motivations and unwavering faith in the British Empire.

"This biography is exhaustively researched, beautifully written and paced, deeply admiring but not hagiographic, and empathic and balanced in its judgmentsa magnificent achievement." —*Publishers Weekly*

The Last King of America: The Misunderstood Reign of George III. Andrew Roberts. Viking Press 2021. 560 p.
ISBN 9781984879264
Grades: Adult   B
1. George III, King of Great Britain, 1738-1820 2. Rulers 3. Politics and government 4. Colonies 5. United States history 6. Great Britain 7. Revolutionary America (1775-1783) 8. Georgian era (1714-1837) 9. Biographies 10. History writing — Europe — United Kingdom 11. Life stories — Politics — Royalty

The last king of America, George III, has been ridiculed as a complete disaster who frittered away the colonies and went mad in his old age. The truth is much more nuanced and fascinating—and will completely change the way readers and historians view his reign and legacy. Maps.

"English historian and biographer Roberts, winner of the Wolfson History Prize and many other honors, draws on abundant archival sources to create a deeply textured portrait of George III (1738-1820), whom he calls 'The most unfairly traduced sovereign in the long history of the British monarchy.' . . . A capacious, prodigiously researched biography from a top-shelf historian." —*Kirkus*

★ *Napoleon: A Life.* Andrew Roberts. Viking Press 2014. 976 pages
ISBN 9780670025329
Grades: Adult   B
1. Napoleon I, Emperor of the French, 1769-1821 2. Rulers 3. Generals 4. Courts and courtiers 5. Political leadership 6. Command of troops 7. Politics and government 8. French history 9. France 10. 19th century 11. 18th century 12. Biographies 13. Life stories — Law and order — Military leaders 14. History writing — Military — Military leadership 15. History writing — Wars and conflicts — Napoleonic Wars 16. Life stories — Politics — Politicians

LC 2013497791

Los Angeles Times Book Prize for Biography, 2014; New York Times Notable Book, 2014.

In this voluminous biography of Napoleon Bonaparte, historian Andrew Roberts relates the Corsican general's early life and traces the details of his military campaigns. Arguing that Napoleon was an effective statesman and an intellectual as well as a brilliant commander, Roberts strives to refute the conclusions of less admiring biographers. He also highlights Napoleon's influence on later military strategists. Though this is a long work, Napoleon will appeal to a wide range of readers.

"Other opinionated observers . consider Napoleon a self-absorbed opportunist plagued by his incompetent economics, pugnacious foreign policy, totalitarian government and massive propaganda, but Roberts offers a solid reconsideration." —*Kirkus*

Originally published under the title Napoleon the Great: London : Allen Lane 2014.

Roberts, David

Limits of the Known. David Roberts. W W Norton & Company 2018. 336 p.
ISBN 9780393609868
Grades: Adult   B
1. Roberts, David, 1943- 2. Mountaineering 3. Adventurers 4. Purpose in life 5. People with cancer 6. Extreme sports 7. Autobiographies and memoirs 8. Life stories — Sports — Athletes 9. Life stories — Facing adversity — Medical issues — Physical illness 10. Sports and Competition — Mountaineering 11. Sports and Competition — Extreme Sports

LC 2017048507

The mountaineer and award-winning author of Alone on the Ice and the Lost World of the Old Ones recounts his search for meaning in the quests of history's famed explorers, drawing partially on his own relationship with extreme-risk adventure and serious illness to share insights into what may have motivated landmark expeditions and ascents.

"Roberts conveys the exhilaration and vitality of adventuring as well as the agony and anger of a cancer diagnosis with equal aplomb, making for a moving narrative that speaks to the glories of the human spirit and the limitations of the human body." —*Publishers Weekly*

Once They Moved Like the Wind: Cochise, Geronimo, and the Apache Wars. David Roberts. Simon & Schuster 1993. 368 p. : Illustration
ISBN 9780671702212
Grades: 11 12 Adult   B
1. Cochise, Apache chief, died 1874 2. Geronimo, Apache chief, 1829-1909 3. Apache (North American people) 4. Indigenous peoples of North America — History 5. Frontier and pioneer life 6. Interethnic relations 7. Indigenous peoples of North America — Wars 8. Indigenous peoples of North America 9. United States history 10. 19th century 11. Biographies 12. History writing — Wars and conflicts — American Indigenous Wars

LC 93007112

Recounts the days of the Indian wars when the U.S. Cavalry repeatedly tried to subdue the great warriors led by Cochise and, later, Geronimo.

"The book is history at its most engrossing." —*Publishers Weekly*

Includes bibliographical references (p. [349]-355) and index.

Roberts, Jason

A Sense of the World: How a Blind Man Became History's Greatest Traveler. Jason Roberts. HarperCollins 2006. xiv, 382 p. : Illustration
ISBN 9780007161065
Grades: 11 12 Adult   B
1. Holman, James, 1786-1857 2. Travelers 3. Voyages and travels 4. Blindness 5. Ocean travel 6. Sailors 7. Seafaring life 8. 19th century 9. Biographies 10. Travel Writing — Historic Journeys 11. Life stories — People in history 12. Life stories — Facing adversity — Medical issues — Living with disabilities 13. Adventure writing — Adventure travel 14. Adult books for young adults 15. Nonfiction that reads like fiction

LC 2005058166

ESSENTIAL AND RECOMMENDED TITLES
Biography

School Library Journal Best Books: Best Adult Books 4 Teens, 2006; National Book Critics Circle Award for Biography finalist, 2006.

Offers a portrait of James Holman, a nineteenth-century adventurer renowned for his solo journey around the world, despite a blindness brought on by a mysterious shipboard illness during the Napoleonic Wars.

"Roberts does Holman justice, evoking with grace and wit the tale of this man once lionized as the Blind Traveler." —*Publishers Weekly*

Includes bibliographical references.

Roberts, Randy
Joe Louis: Hard Times Man. Randy Roberts. Yale University Press 2010. 352 p.
ISBN 9780300122220
Grades: Adult   B
1. Louis, Joe, 1914-1981 2. Boxers (Sports) 3. African American boxers 4. Boxing 5. United States 6. Biographies 7. Sports and Competition — Boxing 8. Sports and Competition — Individual Athlete 9. Life stories — Sports — Athletes
LC 2010015422

Through meticulous research and first-hand interviews, the author presents Joe Louis's impact on boxing and the U.S, revealing an athlete who carefully managed his public image and who actually had complex relationships with both the Black and white communities, including mobsters.

"In this biography of the American boxer, Roberts handles the boxing action with professional aplomb, and he knows when to cut away to tell us something of consequence and when to return to the ring. The author ably chronicles Louis's rise from Alabama cotton fields to the cavernous Yankee Stadium, where celebrities glittered in the ringside seats for his big fights; the development of the mass media (boxing was enormously popular on radio); Louis's career in the U.S. Army; and his sad decline, amid unpayable debts and mental illness. All legendary athletes should hope for treatment by such capable, compassionate hands." —*Kirkus*

Includes bibliographical references and index.

Roberts, Steven V.
Cokie: A Life Well Lived. Steven V. Roberts. HarperCollins 2021. 272 p.
ISBN 9780062851475
Grades: Adult   B
1. Roberts, Cokie, 1943-2019 2. Women journalists 3. Journalism 4. Journalists 5. Biographies 6. Life stories — Arts and culture — Writing — Journalists 7. Arts and Entertainment — Writing and publishing

The husband of the late legendary journalist reflects on her career as a trailblazer for women as well as her private life, tenacious devotion to helping others and roles as wife, mother, advocate and historian.

"In this adoring tribute to award-winning journalist, analyst, and writer Cokie Roberts, his multitalented, multifaceted wife of 53 years, veteran journalist Steven Roberts extols the skills and exposes the strengths she developed throughout her personal life and career." —*Booklist*

Robertson, James I.
Stonewall Jackson: The Man, the Soldier, the Legend. James I. Robertson, Jr. Macmillan Pub. USA; 1997. xxiii, 950 p. : Illustration; Map
ISBN 9780028646855
Grades: Adult   B
1. Jackson, Stonewall, 1824-1863 2. Generals 3. United States Civil War, 1861-1865 4. Confederate soldiers 5. Command of troops 6. Biographies 7. History writing — Military — Military leadership 8. History writing — Wars and conflicts — American Civil War 9. Life stories — Law and order — Military leaders
LC 96017042

A portrait of Confederate General "Stonewall" Jackson traces his life from his humble beginnings through his military career, to his untimely death in 1863.

"Robertson's bibliography, which runs to 25 pages of fine print, reveals the solid bedrock on which this work is built; his documentation is a model of thoroughness. The book is illustrated with rare photographs. A highly readable, remarkably interesting study of Jackson as both man and military leader." —*Choice*

Includes bibliographical references (p. 793-787) and index.

Robertson, Robbie
★ *Testimony*. Robbie Robertson. Crown Archetype 2016. 336 p.
ISBN 9780307889782
Grades: Adult   B
1. Robertson, Robbie 2. Rock musicians 3. Rock groups 4. Rock music 5. Multiracial men 6. Social life and customs 7. United States 8. Canada 9. 20th century 10. Autobiographies and memoirs 11. Canadian literature 12. Arts and Entertainment — Music — Rock 13. Life stories — Arts and culture — Performing arts — Musicians and composers
LC 2016031782

Loan Stars Favourites, 2016.

A memoir by the influential rock artist traces his half-Jewish, half-Mohawk upbringing in Toronto, his early years with rockabilly legend Ronnie Hawkins, the rise of the Band, the stories behind his iconic songs and the Band's famous farewell concert, the Last Waltz.

"This book will enrich and delight any rock fan." —*Library Journal*

Robeson, Paul
Here I Stand. Paul Robeson; with a preface by Lloyd L. Brown and a new introduction by Sterling Stuckey. Beacon Press 1988. xxxvi, 121 p. : Portrait
ISBN 9780807064450
Grades: Adult   B
1. Robeson, Paul, 1898-1976 2. African Americans 3. Biographies 4. Society and culture — Ethnic studies
LC 87047882

The much beleaguered Black singer's 1958 statement on the Negro culture in America is introduced by a short background history.

The Undiscovered Paul Robeson: An Artist's Journey, 1898-1939. Paul Robeson, Jr. Wiley 2001. 400 p; Illustration
ISBN 9780471242659
Grades: Adult   B
1. Robeson, Paul, 1898-1976 2. Political activists 3. African American singers 4. African American political activists 5. African Americans 6. Actors and actresses 7. Singers 8. United States 9. Biographies 10. Life stories — Arts and culture — Performing arts — Entertainers and celebrities 11. History writing — African American — Civil rights — United States
LC 2001017656

A biography of Paul Robeson, who overcame racial discrimination to become a world-famous African-American athlete, actor, singer, and civil rights activist.

"Extensively illustrated with personal photographs, this is a unique account of a brilliant but troubled man." —*Library Journal*

Includes bibliographical references and index.

Robinson, Jackie
I Never Had It Made. by Jackie Robinson as told to Alfred Duckett. G. P. Putnam's Sons 1972. 287 p.
ISBN 9780060555979
Grades: 11 12 Adult   B
1. Robinson, Jackie, 1919-1972 2. Racism in sports 3. Racism in baseball 4. Baseball players 5. Professional baseball players 6. African American baseball players 7. African Americans 8. Autobiographies and memoirs 9. Biographies 10. Biographies — Identity — Africans and African Americans 11. Sports and recreation — Baseball 12. Biographies — Athletes 13. Sports and recreation — Athletes
LC 75175272

Coretta Scott King Award, Author Category, 1973.

In relating his life, Robinson reveals the struggles of a Black athlete in the white-dominated world of American sports.

"The hard nut of this moving book, however, is the young Jackie Robinson digging in against the profanity of prejudice in that public arena we had the temerity to call the national game before he arrived." —*Kirkus*

PUBLIC LIBRARY CORE COLLECTION: NONFICTION
Twentieth Edition

Robinson, Ray
Iron Horse: Lou Gehrig in His Time. Ray Robinson. W.W. Norton 1990. 300 p. : Illustration
ISBN 9780393028577
Grades: 11 12 Adult   B
1. Gehrig, Lou, 1903-1941 2. First base players (Baseball) 3. People with amyotrophic lateral sclerosis 4. Baseball Hall of Fame members 5. Marriage 6. Baseball players 7. Social life and customs 8. United States 9. 20th century 10. Biographies 11. Sports and Competition — Baseball 12. Sports and Competition — Individual Athlete 13. Life stories — Sports — Athletes
LC 89029272

Chronicles Gehrig's rise from poverty to fame in professional baseball, his remarkable record-breaking career, his happy marriage, and his courage in facing an untimely death from ALS.

"Playing in the considerable shadow of Babe Ruth, Lou Gehrig's accomplishments as baseball's Iron Horse include a legendary record of 2,." —*School Library Journal*

Includes bibliographical references (p. [285]-287) and index.

Robinson, Roxana
Georgia O'Keeffe: A Life. Roxana Robinson. Harper & Row 1989. x, 639 p. : Illustration
ISBN 9780060159658
Grades: Adult   B
1. O'Keeffe, Georgia, 1887-1986 2. Artists 3. Women artists 4. United States 5. Biographies 6. Arts and Entertainment — Painting, Drawing, and Sculpture 7. Life stories — Arts and culture — Artists
LC 89045061

The first biography written with the full cooperation of the O'Keeffe family examines the artist's long and distinguished career, her personal relationships, and her significance in terms of American art and the women's movement.

"This biography, the first to draw on sources unavailable during O'Keeffe's lifetimeand the first to be granted her family's cooperationoffers a persuasive feminist analysis of the life and work of an iconic figure in American art. [The author's] detailed, sensitive critique of O'Keeffe's work . alternates with an absorbing, intimate narrative of O'Keeffe's personal life." —*Publishers Weekly*

An Edward Burlingame book; Includes index; Bibliography: P. 609-615.

Robinson, Staci
★ *Tupac Shakur: The Authorized Biography.* by Staci Robinson. Crown 2023. 464 p.
ISBN 9781524761042
Grades: Adult   B
1. Shakur, Tupac, 1971-1996 2. Rap musicians 3. Rap music 4. Hip-hop culture 5. Popular culture 6. Actors and actresses 7. Poets 8. Mothers and sons 9. African Americans 10. African American musicians 11. American people 12. United States 13. Biographies 14. Arts and Entertainment — Music — Rap and R&B 15. Life stories — Arts and culture — Performing arts — Musicians and composers
LC 2023012070

More than a quarter of a century after his tragic death in 1996, this first-and-only Estate-authorized biography tells the powerful story of the one of the greatest and most controversial artists of all time whose unapologetic lyrics continue to inspire his fans around the world.

"Robinson (Interceptions), a screenwriter and longtime friend of Tupac Shakur, traces the hip-hop star's trials and triumphs in this riveting account." —*Publishers Weekly*

Includes index.

Robison, John Elder
Look Me in the Eye: My Life with Asperger's. John Elder Robison. Crown Publishers 2007. 304 p.
ISBN 9780307395986
Grades: 11 12 Adult   B
1. Robison, John Elder 2. Autistic people 3. Family relationships 4. Autism spectrum disorders 5. Neurodivergent people 6. Social life and customs 7. United States 8. Autobiographies and memoirs 9. Science Writing — Medicine and health — Disabilities and disorders 10. Family and Relationships — Abuse 11. Life stories — Facing adversity — Abuse survivors
LC 2007013139

The author describes life growing up different in an odd family, his unusual talents, his struggle to live a "normal" life, his diagnosis at the age of forty with Asperger's syndrome, and the dramatic changes that have occurred since that diagnosis.

"Robison's memoir is must reading for its unblinking (as only an Aspergian can) glimpse into the life of a person who had to wait decades for the medical community to catch up with him." —*Booklist*

Rodgers, Mary
Shy: The Alarmingly Outspoken Memoirs of Mary Rodgers. Mary Rodgers and Jesse Green. Farrar, Straus and Giroux 2022. 320 p.
ISBN 9780374298623
Grades: Adult   B
1. Rodgers, Mary, 1931-2014 2. Composers 3. Songwriters 4. Musicals 5. Jewish women 6. Motherhood 7. Women songwriters 8. Sexism 9. Self-fulfillment 10. Autobiographies and memoirs 11. Life stories — Arts and culture — Performing arts — Musicians and composers 12. Arts and entertainment — Music 13. Arts and entertainment — Theater
LC 2022018292

The memoirs of Mary Rodgers-writer, composer, Broadway royalty, and "a woman who tried everything."

"In this rollicking posthumous memoir, composer and writer Rodgers (1931?2014) revisits the highs and lows of her life and career." —*Publishers Weekly*

Roffman, Karin
The Songs We Know Best: John Ashbery's Early Life. Karin Roffman. Farrar, Straus and Giroux 2017. 496 p.
ISBN 9780374293840
Grades: Adult   B
1. Ashbery, John, 1927-2017 2. Poets, American 3. Biographies 4. Life stories — Arts and culture — Writing — Poets
LC 2016045038

New York Times Notable Book, 2017.

Drawing on unpublished correspondence, juvenilia and childhood diaries as well as more than 100 hours of conversation with the poet, a first comprehensive biography of the early life of the winner of nearly every major American literary award reveals how he drew on the details of his youth to populate the poems that made him an unpredictable literary force.

"This tender, youth-focused biography will be most enjoyed by Ashberys fans and readers interested in a remarkable gay artists midcentury coming-of-age story." —*Booklist*

Rogen, Seth
★ *Yearbook: Essays.* Seth Rogen. Crown 2021. 272 p.
ISBN 9781984825407
Grades: Adult   B
1. Rogen, Seth, 1982- 2. Film producers and directors 3. Screenwriters 4. Family relationships 5. Growing up 6. Actors and actresses 7. Films 8. Essays 9. Autobiographies and memoirs 10. Life stories — Arts and culture — Performing arts — Actors and actresses 11. Arts and Entertainment — Movies and television 12. Life stories — Arts and culture — Performing arts — Directors and producers
LC 2021004346

A collection of funny personal essays from one of the writers of Superbad and Pineapple Express and one of the producers of the Disaster Artist.

"Entertaining and funny, this work will delight fans of Rogen and his cohort." —*Library Journal*

Rogers, Robbie
Coming Out to Play. Robbie Rogers with Eric Marcus. Penguin Books 2014. 256 p.

ESSENTIAL AND RECOMMENDED TITLES
Biography

ISBN 9780143126614
Grades: Adult **B**
1. Rogers, Robbie 2. Gay athletes 3. Coming out (Sexual or gender identity) 4. Soccer players 5. Gay men 6. Toleration 7. Professional athletes 8. Homophobia 9. Autobiographies and memoirs 10. Biographies 11. Life stories — Identity — LGBTQIA+ 12. Life stories — Sports — Athletes 13. Sports and Competition — Soccer

LC 2014011229

Robbie Rogers knows better than most that keeping secrets can crush you. But for much of his life Robbie lived in paralyzing fear that sharing his big secret would cost him the love of his family and his career as a professional soccer player. So he never told anyone what was destroying his soul, both on and off the field. In Coming Out to Play, Robbie takes readers on his incredible journey from terrified teenager to a trailblazing out and proud professional soccer player for the L.A. Galaxy, who has embraced his new identity as a role model and champion for those still struggling with the secrets that keep them from living their dreams.

"Rogers's debut is great inspiration for people of all ages struggling with shame and grappling with identity issues with regard to sexuality or otherwise. Those who enjoy memoir and stories of people who overcome difficulty will embrace this account." —*Library Journal*

Rojas Contreras, Ingrid
★ *The Man Who Could Move Clouds: A Memoir.* Ingrid Rojas Contreras. Doubleday 2022. 320 p.
ISBN 9780385546669
Grades: Adult **B**
1. Rojas Contreras, Ingrid 2. Women authors 3. Hispanic American women 4. Colombian Americans 5. Mothers and daughters 6. Indigenous peoples of South America 7. Memories 8. Grandfathers 9. People with amnesia 10. Psychic ability 11. Occultism 12. Spiritualism 13. Curanderismo 14. Healers 15. Colonialism 16. Resilience 17. Family history 18. Intergenerational trauma 19. Colombia 20. United States 21. Autobiographies and memoirs 22. Life stories — Relationships — Family 23. Life stories — Identity — Race and ethnicity 24. Society and culture — Ethnic studies 25. History writing — Latin America — South America

LC 2021035817

National Book Critics Circle Award for Autobiography/Memoir finalist, 2022; Pulitzer Prize for Memoir or Autobiography finalist, 2023; National Book Award for Nonfiction finalist, 2022.

Interweaving spellbinding family stories, resurrected Colombian history and her own deeply personal reckonings with the bounds of reality, the author shares her inheritance of "the secrets"—the power to talk to the dead, tell the future, treat the sick and move the clouds.

"Novelist Rojas Contreras (Fruit of the Drunken Tree) returns with a lyrical meditation on her family's history and the legacy of colonialism in Colombia." —*Publishers Weekly*

Roll, David L.
George Marshall: Defender of the Republic. David L. Roll, Dutton Caliber 2019. 704 p.
ISBN 9781101990971
Grades: Adult **B**
1. Marshall, George C. (George Catlett), 1880-1959 2. World War II 3. Marshall Plan, 1948-1952 4. World War I 5. Korean War, 1950-1953 6. Political leadership 7. Politicians 8. Generals 9. International relations 10. Military history 11. Politics and government 12. United States 13. 20th century 14. Biographies 15. Life stories — Law and order — Military leaders 16. History writing — Wars and conflicts — World War II 17. History writing — Presidency — 20th century — United States

LC 2018055675

Traces the story of the distinguished U.S. soldier and statesman, examining his role in influencing two world wars and America's emergence as a global superpower.

"This well-written and captivating book will stand as the definitive biography of Marshall." —*Publishers Weekly*

Ronald, Susan
A **Dangerous** *Woman: American Beauty, Noted Philanthropist, Nazi Collaborator— the Life of Florence Gould.* Susan Ronald. St. Martin's Press 2018. 416 p.
ISBN 9781250092212
Grades: Adult **B**
1. Gould, Florence, 1895-1983 2. Nazi collaborators 3. Socialites 4. Philanthropists 5. American people in France 6. World War II 7. Paris, France 8. Biographies 9. Life stories — People in history 10. History writing — Wars and conflicts — World War II

LC B12017049997

A portrait of the wealthy socialite and patron of the arts details her marriage to railroad heir Frank Jay Gould and her role in creating a luxury hotel and casino empire before becoming a Nazi collaborator in World War II Paris.

"Although Florence's letters and photographs were inaccessible to the author, Ronald compensates with layers of research into the period and surrounding players. While the dense historical detail may deter lay readers, history lovers will welcome this impressive book about a captivating, flawed woman." —*Publishers Weekly*

The **Pirate** *Queen: Queen Elizabeth I, Her Pirate Adventures, and the Dawn of Empire.* Susan Ronald. Harper Collins Publishers 2007. xxiv, 471 p. : Illustration; Map
ISBN 9780060820664
Grades: Adult **B**
1. Elizabeth I, Queen of England, 1533-1603 2. Women rulers 3. Merchants 4. Privateers 5. Piracy 6. Naval history 7. British history 8. Great Britain 9. Renaissance (1300-1600) 10. 16th century 11. Elizabethan era (1558-1603) 12. Tudor period (1485-1603) 13. History writing — Europe — United Kingdom 14. History writing — Renaissance — Europe

LC 2006053171

An analysis of Elizabeth I's use of piracy to promote her financial security offers insight into the personal beliefs and vision that motivated her choices, in an account that also traces the contributions of her merchants, philosophers, and councilors.

Includes bibliographical references and index.

Ronstadt, Linda
Feels Like Home: A Song for the Sonoran Borderlands. Linda Ronstadt and Lawrence Downes; photographs by Bill Steen. Heyday Books 2022. 256 p.
ISBN 9781597145794
Grades: Adult **B**
1. Ronstadt, Linda, 1946- 2. Women rock musicians 3. Growing up 4. Immigrant families 5. Mexican Americans 6. Deserts 7. Borderlands 8. Memories 9. Cooking, Mexican 10. Music 11. Multiculturalism 12. Sonoran desert 13. Arizona 14. Mexican-American Border Region 15. Autobiographies and memoirs 16. Life stories — Arts and culture — Performing arts — Musicians and composers 17. Life stories — Relationships — Growing up 18. Life stories — Identity — Race and ethnicity 19. Society and culture — Urban and regional studies

The Rock and Roll Hall of Famer presents an illustrated memoir that focuses on the Sonoran Desert where she came of age as the granddaughter of Mexican immigrants.

"The renowned musician digs deep for her roots—familial, cultural, musical, and culinary….A lively, lovely exaltation of the dry, cactus-studded, indelible Sonoran Desert." —*Kirkus*

Rosen, Charles
Sugar: Micheal Ray Richardson, Eighties Excess, and the NBA. Charley Rosen. University of Nebraska Press 2018. 183 p.
ISBN 9781496202161
Grades: Adult **B**
1. Richardson, Micheal Ray 2. Basketball players 3. Professional athletes 4. Fame 5. Money 6. Drug abuse 7. Sports corruption 8. Basketball history 9. 1980s 10. Biographies 11. Life stories — Sports — Athletes 12. Sports and Competition — Basketball 13. Sports and Competition — Sports History

LC 2017038778

By constructing his various lines of narration around the polarizing figure of Richardson—equal parts basketball savant, drug addict, and pariah—Rosen illuminates some of the more unseemly aspects of the NBA during the 1980s, going behind the scenes to provide an account of what the league's darker side was like during its celebrated golden age.

Rosen, Jeffrey
Conversations with Rbg: Ruth Bader Ginsburg on Life, Love, Liberty, and Law. Jeffrey Rosen. Henry Holt & Company 2019. 259 p.
ISBN 9781250235169
Grades: Adult   B
1. Ginsburg, Ruth Bader, 1933-2020 2. Judges 3. Women judges 4. Women Supreme Court justices 5. Biographies 6. Life stories — Law and order — Judges and lawyers 7. Politics and global affairs — Judicial policy
LC 2019020971

Offers an intimate look at the life and career of Justice Ruth Bader Ginsburg, in her own words, through an extraordinary series of conversations.

"Libraries with patrons keenly interested in the Supreme Court, especially those serving law, political science, and American history students, will find this a compelling addition. For those eager to add a new resource on the Justice, this book provides a solid introduction to her life and thoughts on the American legal system." —*Library Journal*

Includes bibliographical references and index.

Rosen, Richard A.
Julius Chambers: A Life in the Legal Struggle for Civil Rights. Richard A. Rosen and Joseph Mosnier. The University of North Carolina Press 2016. 400 p.
ISBN 9781469628547
Grades: Adult   B
1. Chambers, Julius L. (Julius LeVonne), 1936-2013 2. Civil rights lawyers 3. African American lawyers 4. African Americans 5. Civil Rights Movement 6. Race relations 7. Race (Social sciences) 8. North Carolina 9. Biographies 10. Life stories — Law and order — Judges and lawyers 11. Life stories — People in history 12. History writing — African American — Civil rights — United States
LC 2016020980

A powerful biography of the nation's leading African American civil rights attorney in the 1960s and 1970s connects the details of his life to the wider struggle to secure racial equality through the development of modern civil rights law.

"Essential reading for those interested in African American history; the civil rights movement; and legal history, especially relating to North Carolina." —*Library Journal*

Includes bibliographical references and index.

Rosenberg, Justus
The Art of Resistance: My Four Years in the French Underground: A Memoir. Justus Rosenberg. William Morrow 2020. 320 pages
ISBN 9780062742193
Grades: Adult   B
1. Rosenberg, Justus, 1921- 2. Fry, Varian, 1908-1967 3. French Resistance (World War II) 4. Anti-Nazi movement 5. World War II 6. Jewish men 7. Jewish people 8. Language and languages 9. College teachers 10. Holocaust (1933-1945) 11. Polish people 12. Resistance to military occupation 13. German occupation, World War II 14. French history 15. France 16. Autobiographies and memoirs 17. Life stories — Facing adversity — War and oppression 18. History writing — Wars and conflicts — Resistance — World War II 19. Life stories — People in history 20. Life stories — Education — Scholars and educators
LC Bl2019037347

In this World War II memoir set in Nazi-occupied France—a story of bravery, daring, adventure, survival and romance—a former Eastern European Jew remembers his flight from the Holocaust and his extraordinary four years in the French underground.

Includes index.

Rosenberg, Rosalind
★ *Jane Crow: The Life of Pauli Murray.* Rosalind Rosenberg. Oxford Univ Pr 2017. 512 p.
ISBN 9780190656454
Grades: Adult   B
1. Murray, Pauli, 1910-1985 2. Social reformers 3. Civil Rights Movement 4. Women's movement 5. Social justice 6. Intersectionality 7. Clergywomen 8. Feminists 9. African American lawyers 10. Intellectuals 11. African American civil rights workers 12. Transgender people 13. African Americans 14. United States history 15. United States 16. 20th century 17. Biographies 18. History writing — Women's history 19. Life stories — Politics — Activists and reformers 20. History writing — African American — United States
LC 2017000717

This comprehensive and accessible biography of 20th-century lawyer and African American activist Pauli Murray is a detailed chronicle of her life and achievements, along with a history of the civil rights and feminist movements and early views of intersectionality.

"Rosenberg shows how Murray pursued an intersectional activism, repeatedly identifying the ways in which race, class, and gender worked together to constrain opportunity. The biography also deftly explores Murray's relationships and private struggles with identity. From childhood, Murray understood herself to be male, repeatedly seeking (unsuccessfully) medical treatment for gender dysphoria; she was also attracted to, and formed lasting relationships with, women during an era when both same-sex attraction and transgender identity were suspect categories. Placing Murray in historical context with practiced ease, Rosenberg weaves these many threads together into an authoritative narrative that will introduce Murray to many future generations." —*Publishers Weekly*

Includes bibliographical references and index.

Rosenblitt, J. Alison
The Beauty of Living: E. E. Cummings in the Great War. J. Alison Rosenblitt. W.W. Norton & Company 2020. 320 p.
ISBN 9780393246964
Grades: Adult   B
1. Cummings, E. E. (Edward Estlin), 1894-1962 2. Poets, American 3. World War I 4. Authors, American 5. Literature and history 6. 20th century 7. Biographies 8. Life stories — Arts and culture — Writing — Poets 9. Arts and Entertainment — Writing and Publishing
LC 2019058084

Using letters, journal entries, sketches and analyses of his work, describes the period of time the poet known for his intentionally fractured and fun prose was unjustly imprisoned in France during World War I.

"Rosenblitt breathes new life back into poems too often anthologized and too little read. Highly recommended." —*Library Journal*

Includes bibliographical references and index.

Rosenbloom, Joseph
Redemption: Martin Luther King Jr.'s Last 31 Hours. Joseph Rosenbloom. Beacon Press 2018. 289 p.
ISBN 9780807083383
Grades: Adult   B
1. King, Martin Luther, Jr, 1929-1968 2. African American civil rights workers 3. Civil Rights Movement 4. Civil rights 5. Biographies 6. Life stories — Politics — Activists and reformers 7. History writing — African American — Civil rights — United States 8. History writing — 1960s — United States 9. Adult books for young adults
LC 2017024226

A deeply intimate chronicle of the last 31 hours of Martin Luther King Jr.'s life draws on dozens of interviews with Memphis insiders and recently released archival materials to share insights into his personal and political activities as well as his marital difficulties at the same time James Earl Ray orchestrated his assassination.

Includes bibliographical references and index.

ESSENTIAL AND RECOMMENDED TITLES
Biography

Rosenthal, Jason
My Wife Said You May Want to Marry Me: A Memoir. Jason B. Rosenthal. HarperCollins 2020. 228 p.
ISBN 9780062940599
Grades: Adult **B**
1. Rosenthal, Jason 2. Rosenthal, Amy Krouse 3. Widowers 4. Loss 5. Family and death 6. Women authors 7. Single fathers 8. Life change events 9. Healing 10. Death of married women 11. Autobiographies and memoirs 12. Life stories — Facing adversity — Coping with death 13. Life stories — Relationships — Couples 14. Family and Relationships — Aging and Death
LC Bl2020007400

The "Journey Through Loss and Grief" TED Talk presenter and co-author of Dear Boy, traces the death of his wife, "Modern Love" columnist Amy Krouse Rosenthal, and his subsequent efforts to cope and honor Amy's final wish. Surveying his life before, with, and after Amy, Jason ruminates on love, the pain of watching a loved one suffer, and what it means to heal—how he and their three children, despite their profound sorrow, went on. Jason's emotional journey offers insights on dying and death and the excruciating pain of losing a soulmate, and illuminates the lessons he learned.

"Rosenthal's gut-wrenching, honest, and uplifting memoir offers reassurance and connection to readers experiencing their own losses." —*Booklist*

Rosnay, Tatiana de
Manderley Forever: A Biography of Daphne Du Maurier. Tatiana de Rosnay. St Martins Pr. 2017. 448 p.
ISBN 9781250099136
Grades: Adult **B**
1. Du Maurier, Daphne, 1907-1989 2. Authors, British 3. Women authors, British 4. Writing 5. Marriage 6. Married women 7. Thriller and suspense authors 8. Women authors 9. Authors 10. Independence 11. 20th century 12. Biographies 13. Translations — French to English 14. Life stories — Arts and culture — Writing — Authors 15. Arts and Entertainment — Writing and Publishing 16. Nonfiction that reads like fiction
LC 2016049032

A nonfiction debut by the best-selling author of Sarah's Key traces the life and achievements of classic novelist Daphne du Maurier, sharing creative insights into the master writer's life at different ages and her enduring influence in literature.

"Through De Rosnay's novel-like narrative, exhaustive research, and unbridled admiration, du Maurier's spirit comes alive on the page, endearing her to a new generation of fans." —*Publishers Weekly*

Originally published as Manderley for ever in 2015 by Albin Michel; Translated from the French by Sam Taylor.

Ross, Alex
Wagnerism: Art and Politics in the Shadow of Music. Alex Ross. Farrar, Straus and Giroux 2020. 784 p.
ISBN 9780374285937
Grades: Adult **B**
1. Wagner, Richard, 1813-1883 2. Influence (Literary, artistic, etc.) 3. Composers 4. Operas 5. Music and literature 6. Music 7. Art and music 8. Music history and criticism 9. Life stories — Arts and culture — Performing arts — Musicians and composers 10. Arts and Entertainment — Music — Opera 11. History writing — Arts and Culture
LC 2020012449

New York Times Notable Book, 2020.

A large-canvas narrative history, charting the impact of the cultural titan Wagner on art and politics. Ross will show how various artists-composers, novelists, poets, filmmakers-wrestled with the legacy of Wagner in the twentieth century.

"With this multifaceted jewel of a book, Ross has produced a monumental study of Wagner's legacy." —*Library Journal*

Includes bibliographical references and index.

Ross, Steve
From Broken Glass: My Story of Finding Hope in Hitler's Death Camps to Inspire a New Generation. Steve Ross, with Brian Wallace and Glenn Frank. Hachette Books 2018. 288 p.
ISBN 9780316513043
Grades: Adult **B**
1. Ross, Steve, (Graphic novelist) 2. Holocaust (1933-1945) 3. Holocaust survivors 4. Social advocates 5. World War II 6. Concentration camps 7. Jewish men 8. Second World War era (1939-1945) 9. Life stories — Facing adversity — War and oppression — Holocaust
LC 2017963705

A survivor of the Holocaust describes how—by observing and enduring inconceivable cruelty as well as by receiving compassion from caring fellow prisoners—he learned of the human capacity to rise above even the bleakest circumstances, and later used that knowledge to help underprivileged youth in Boston for more than 40 years.

Rothenberg, Ben
Naomi Osaka: Her Journey to Finding Her Power and Her Voice. Ben Rothenberg. Dutton 2024. 352 p.
ISBN 9780593472439
Grades: Adult **B**
1. Osaka, Naomi, 1997- 2. Women tennis players 3. Tennis players 4. Social advocates 5. Multiracial people 6. Tennis 7. Japanese people 8. Social justice 9. Mental health 10. Depression 11. Haitian Americans 12. Life stories — Sports — Athletes 13. Sports and competition — Individual Athlete 14. Sports and competition — Tennis
LC 2023041150

Published to coincide with her return to tennis, this deeply reported, revealing biography of the Haitian-American/Japanese phenomenon and activist chronicles her rise to fame and the incredible impact she's had on the game and on social justice as she advocates for racial justice and mental health.

"A comprehensive look at the career of a young tennis star." —*Kirkus*

Includes bibliographical references and index.

Roudinesco, Elisabeth
★ *Freud: In His Time and Ours.* Elisabeth Roudinesco; translated by Catherine Porter. Harvard University Press 2016. 530 p.
ISBN 9780674659568
Grades: Adult **B**
1. Freud, Sigmund, 1856-1939 2. Psychoanalysts 3. Jewish men 4. Biographies 5. Translations — French to English 6. Life stories — Science, technology, and medicine — Healthcare professionals
LC 2016013065

Elisabeth Roudinesco's bold reinterpretation of Sigmund Freud is a biography for the twenty-first century—a sympathetic yet impartial appraisal of a genius admired but misunderstood in his time and ours. Alert to tensions in his character and thought, she views Freud less as a scientific thinker than as an interpreter of civilization and culture.

First published as Sigmund Freud en son temps et dans le notre—Title page verso; Includes bibliographical references and index; Originally published: Paris : Ed. du Seuil, 2014; Translation from the French.

Roundtree, Dovey Johnson
★ *Mighty Justice: My Life in Civil Rights.* Dovey Johnson Roundtree and Katie McCabe; foreword by Tayari Jones. Algonquin Books of Chapel Hill 2019. xii, 273 pages, 8 unnumbered pages of plates : Illustration
ISBN 9781604731323
Grades: Adult **B**
1. Roundtree, Dovey Johnson, 1914-2018 2. Social advocates 3. Civil rights 4. Women lawyers 5. Civil Rights Movement 6. African American women 7. Segregation 8. Racism 9. United States 10. 20th century 11. Autobiographies and memoirs 12. Life stories — Politics — Activists and reformers — Civil Rights leaders 13. History writing — African American — Civil rights — United States

PUBLIC LIBRARY CORE COLLECTION: NONFICTION
Twentieth Edition

Legendary African American civil rights attorney Dovey Johnson Roundtree recounts her trailblazing life in this inspiring, beautifully told story that shows how one remarkable woman changed history, and how urgent it is to continue her work today.

"This eye-opening, accessible book documents the life of a trailblazing human rights advocate." —*Publishers Weekly*

Originally published in 2009 by the University Press of Mississippi under title: Justice older than the law : the life of Dovey Johnson Roundtree; Includes discussion questions (pages [267]-269); Includes bibliographical references (pages [233]-245) and index.

Rousseau, Jean-Jacques

Confessions. Jean-Jacques Rousseau; edited and introduced by P.N. Furbank. Knopf 1992. xli, 320, 306 p.
ISBN 9780679409984
Grades: Adult   B
1. Rousseau, Jean-Jacques, 1712-1778 2. Authors, French 3. 18th century 4. Biographies 5. Life stories — People in history

LC 91053194

Rousseau's ideas have influenced almost every major political development of the last two hundred years, and are crucial to an understanding of phenomena as diverse as the French Revolution, modern educational theory, and the contemporary environmental movement. This is reason enough to draw attention to his startlingly alive autobiography. But the Confessions is also among the greatest self-portraits in world literature -which suggests, even more than the impact of Rousseau's thought, the extent to which the very high opinion he had of himself was ultimately justified.

Includes bibliographical references (p. xxxiii).

Rowe, Mickey

Fearlessly Different: An Autistic Actor's Journey to Broadway's Biggest Stage. Mickey Rowe. Rowman & Littlefield 2022. 192 p.
ISBN 9781538163122
Grades: Adult   B
1. Rowe, Mickey, 1988- 2. Autistic people 3. Dysfunctional families 4. Growing up 5. Discrimination 6. Acting 7. Marriage 8. Parenthood 9. Persistence 10. Actors and actresses 11. Autistic children 12. Boys 13. Neurodivergent people 14. Autobiographies and memoirs 15. Biographies 16. Life stories — Arts and culture — Performing arts — Actors and actresses 17. Life stories — Facing adversity — Medical issues — Living with disabilities 18. Arts and Entertainment — General

LC 2021029539

An autistic actor opens up the world of autism to readers, while also helping those with autism to feel seen and understood, as he shares how he pushed beyond the stereotypes and obstacles that many disabled individuals face to shine on stage.

In this immensely inspiring debut, Rowe recounts how he achieved his acting dreams 'Because of and not in spite of my autism.' —*Publishers Weekly*

Includes index.

Rowe, Peggy

About My Mother: True Stories of a Horse-crazy Daughter and Her Baseball-obsessed Mother: A Memoir. Peggy Rowe. Forefront Books 2018. 172 p.
ISBN 9781948677165
Grades: Adult   B
1. Rowe, Peggy 2. Rowe, Thelma 3. Mothers and daughters 4. Growing up 5. Parental love 6. Parent and child 7. Women 8. Autobiographies and memoirs 9. Life stories — Relationships — Parent and child 10. Family and Relationships — Parenting

A love letter to mothers everywhere, About My Mother will make you laugh and cry—and see yourself in its reflection. Peggy Rowe's story of growing up as the daughter of Thelma Knobel is filled with warmth and humor.

Rowland, Ingrid D.

The Collector of Lives: Giorgio Vasari and the Invention of Art. Ingrid Rowland and Noah Charney. W.W. Norton & Company 2017. 400 p.
ISBN 9780393241310
Grades: Adult   B
1. Vasari, Giorgio, 1511-1574 2. Artists 3. Biographers 4. Art history 5. Aesthetics 6. European Renaissance 7. Italy 8. Biographies 9. Life stories — Arts and culture — Artists

LC 2017026667

Giorgio Vasari (1511-1574) was a man of many talents-a sculptor, painter, architect, writer, and scholar-but he is best known for Lives of the Artists, which singlehandedly established the canon of Italian Renaissance art. Before Vasari's extraordinary book, art was considered a technical skill, and artists were mere decorators and craftsmen. It was through Vasari's visionary writings that Raphael, Leonardo, and Michelangelo came to be regarded as great masters of life as well as art, their creative genius celebrated as a divine gift.Lauded by Sarah Bakewell as "insightful, gripping, and thoroughly enjoyable," the Collector of Lives reveals how one Renaissance scholar completely redefined how we look at art.

"Rowland and Charney do more than deliver a richly detailed life of this singular Renaissance figure. They raise intriguing questions about how tastes and standards develop." —*Kirkus*

Includes bibliographical references and index.

Royster, Francesca T.

Choosing Family: A Memoir of Queer Motherhood and Black Resistance. Francesca T. Royster. Harry N Abrams Inc 2023. 272 p.
ISBN 9781419756177
Grades: Adult   B
1. Ethnic identity 2. Gender identity 3. Interracial adoption 4. Interracial marriage 5. Black people 6. LGBTQIA+ people 7. Feminists 8. Intergenerational relations 9. Race relations 10. American people 11. North American people 12. Chicago, Illinois 13. Autobiographies and memoirs 14. Life stories — Identity — Race and ethnicity 15. Life stories — Identity — LGBTQIA+

A professor of English literature presents a memoir of family, identity and acceptance that examines the messiness and complexity of adoption and parenthood from a Black, queer and feminist perspective.

"Insightful and reflective, this is a moving tribute to the power of chosen family." —*Publishers Weekly*

Ruhl, Sarah

Smile: The Story of a Face. Sarah Ruhl. Simon & Schuster 2021. 256 p.
ISBN 9781982150945
Grades: Adult   B
1. Ruhl, Sarah, 1974- 2. Playwrights, American 3. Face 4. Facial paralysis 5. Married women 6. Mothers 7. Chronic diseases 8. Facial expression 9. Objectification (Social psychology) 10. Interpersonal relations 11. Self-perception 12. Self-acceptance 13. Nervous system 14. Diseases 15. Autobiographies and memoirs 16. Life stories — Arts and culture — Performing arts 17. Life stories — Facing adversity — Medical issues — Physical illness 18. Life stories — Personal growth

LC 2021031063

With a play opening on Broadway, and every reason to smile, Sarah Ruhl has just survived a high-risk pregnancy when she discovers the left side of her face is completely paralyzed. She is assured that 90 percent of Bell's palsy patients see spontaneous improvement and experience a full recovery. Like Ruhl's own mother. But Sarah is in the unlucky ten percent. And for a woman, wife, mother, and artist working in theater, the paralysis and the disconnect between the interior and exterior brings significant and specific challenges. So Ruhl begins an intense decade-long search for a cure while simultaneously grappling with the reality of her new face—one that, while recognizably her own, is incapable of accurately communicating feelings or intentions.

"Pulitzer Prize and Tony-nominated playwright Ruhl (The Clean House) takes readers behind the scenes in this intimate memoir about developing Bell's palsy, which partially paralyzed her face, after pregnancy complications. . . . A moving, insightful account that will appeal to many readers, especially those who like memoir." —*Library Journal*

Includes bibliographical references.

ESSENTIAL AND RECOMMENDED TITLES
Biography

Rule, Ann
The Stranger Beside Me. Ann Rule. Norton 2000. 456 p. : Illustration
ISBN 9780393050295
Grades: Adult **B**
1. Bundy, Ted, 1946-1989 2. Criminals 3. Serial murderers 4. Serial murders 5. Murder 6. Murderers 7. Deception 8. Page to screen 9. True Crime — Murder
LC 00040224

From the perspective of the former policewoman, crime writer, and unknowing personal friend, tells the story of Ted Bundy, a brilliant law student executed for killing three women, who confessed to killing thirty-five others.

Rundell, Katherine
★ *Super-infinite: The Transformations of John Donne.* Katherine Rundell. Farrar, Straus and Giroux 2022. 352 p.
ISBN 9780374607401
Grades: Adult **B**
1. Donne, John, 1572-1631 2. Poets, English 3. Marriage 4. Priests 5. Scholars and academics 6. Biographies 7. Life stories — Arts and culture — Writing — Poets
LC 2022022699

Baillie Gifford Prize for Non-Fiction, 2022; British Book Award for Narrative Nonfiction of the Year, 2023.

A very modern biography of John Donne-the poet of love, sex, and death-by bestselling children's book author and superstar academic Katherine Rundell.—

"Scholar Rundell (The Wolf Wilder) explores in this thoughtful biography the life and art of poet and priest John Donne (1572?1631), positioning him as an imaginative, witty, and sensual figure....This comprehensive study is poetic in its own right." —*Publishers Weekly*

Includes bibliographical references and index.

RuPaul
★ *The House of Hidden Meanings: A Memoir.* RuPaul. Dey Street Books 2024. 304 p.
ISBN 9780063263901
Grades: Adult **B**
1. RuPaul, 1960- 2. Drag queens 3. Television personalities 4. Family relationships 5. Families 6. Entertainers 7. Growing up 8. Childhood 9. Performing arts 10. LGBTQIA+ people 11. African Americans 12. Gay men 13. Autobiographies and memoirs 14. Life stories — Arts and culture — Performing arts — Entertainers and celebrities 15. Life stories — Identity — LGBTQIA+ 16. Arts and Entertainment — Movies and Television

From an international drag superstar and pop culture icon comes his most revealing and personal work to date—a deeply intimate memoir of growing up Black, poor and queer in a broken home to discovering the power of performance, found family and self-acceptance.

"The multi-hyphenate superstar's many fans will delight in these stories of the artist's beginnings." —*Booklist*

Rusbridger, Alan
★ *Play It Again: An Amateur Against the Impossible.* Alan Rusbridger. Farrar, Straus & Giroux 2013. 416 p.
ISBN 9780374232917
Grades: Adult **B**
1. Rusbridger, Alan 2. Chopin, Frederic, 1810-1849 3. Newspaper editors 4. Amateur musicians 5. Determination 6. Journalists 7. Change (Psychology) 8. Piano 9. Persistence 10. Character 11. Pianists 12. Arab Spring, 2010-2012 13. Diaries 14. Autobiographies and memoirs 15. Life stories — Personal growth 16. Life stories — Arts and culture 17. Arts and Entertainment — Music — Classical
LC 2013014884

Details the author's quest to learn, in the course of a year, Chopin's Ballade No. 1 in G minor, and the advice he received from legendary pianists, historians, and others to reach his goal.

Includes bibliographical references and index.

Rush, Chris
The Light Years: A Memoir. Chris Rush. Farrar, Straus and Giroux 2019. 352 p.
ISBN 9780374294410
Grades: Adult **B**
1. Rush, Chris, 1956- 2. Drug use 3. Growing up 4. Artists 5. Counterculture 6. LSD (Drug) 7. Communes 8. Change (Psychology) 9. Teenage boys 10. Moving to a new state 11. United States 12. 1970s 13. Autobiographies and memoirs 14. Biographies 15. Life stories — Relationships — Growing up
LC 2018020669

A coming-of-age memoir documents the author's descent into the counterculture of the 1970s, relating his preadolescent exposure to LSD, his teenage pursuit of kinship in the communes of the American West, and the factors that nearly ended his life.

Rushdie, Salman
Joseph Anton: A Memoir. Salman Rushdie. Random House 2012. 656 p.
ISBN 9780812992786
Grades: Adult **B**
1. Rushdie, Salman 2. Hiding 3. Ayatollahs 4. Death threats 5. Islam 6. Police 7. Secrecy 8. Freedom of speech 9. Interpersonal relations 10. Censorship 11. Freedom of the press 12. Authors, British 13. Autobiographies and memoirs 14. Life stories — Arts and culture — Writing — Authors 15. Life stories — Facing adversity — War and oppression 16. Spirituality and Religion — Islam — Political Aspects
LC 2012372283

Booklist Editors' Choice, 2012; Shortlisted for the James Tait Black Memorial Prize for Biography, 2012.

For the first time, author Salman Rushdie tells the story of his nine years spent underground, moving from house to house, an armed police protection team living with him at all times, and of how he regained his freedom.

★ *Knife: Meditations After an Attempted Murder.* Salman Rushdie. Random House 2024. 256 p.
ISBN 9780593730249
Grades: Adult **B**
1. Rushdie, Salman 2. Violence 3. Attempted murder 4. Art 5. Authors 6. Loss 7. Love 8. Life change events 9. Resilience 10. Writing 11. Autobiographies and memoirs 12. Life stories — Facing adversity — Victims of crime 13. Life stories — Arts and culture — Writing — Authors

The internationally renowned writer and Booker Prize winner speaks out for the first time about the traumatic events of August 12, 2022, when an attempt was made on his life, in this deeply personal meditation on violence, art, loss, love and finding the strength to stand up again.

"Booker Prize-winning novelist Rushdie (author of Victory City, Joseph Anton, the Satanic Verses, and over a dozen additional titles) turns to nonfiction once more to explore the shocking attempt to kill him, its repercussions, and the role of art in his life and the world." —*Library Journal*

Russell, Gareth
Young and Damned and Fair: The Life of Catherine Howard, Fifth Wife of King Henry VIII. Gareth Russell. Simon & Schuster 2017. 352 p.
ISBN 9781501108631
Grades: Adult **B**
1. Catherine Howard, Queen, consort of Henry VIII, King of England, d. 1542 2. Henry VIII, King of England, 1491-1547 3. Marriages of royalty and nobility 4. Monarchy 5. Women rulers 6. British history 7. Great Britain 8. 16th century 9. Renaissance (1300-1600) 10. Biographies 11. Life stories — Politics — Royalty 12. History writing — Europe — United Kingdom 13. History writing — Renaissance — Europe
LC 2016016842

Traces the tragic life of Henry VIII's doomed fifth wife against a backdrop of unprecedented social and political tensions and offers insight into her ambitious family and the errors in judgment that led to her execution.

"Catherine was the least politically consequential of Henry's wives, yet her story is important for what it reveals about the brutality and chauvinism of Henrician England." —*Library Journal*

PUBLIC LIBRARY CORE COLLECTION: NONFICTION
Twentieth Edition

Russell, Tony
Country Music Originals: The Legends and the Lost. Tony Russell. Oxford University Press 2010. 272 p.
ISBN 9780199732661
Grades: Adult **B**
1. Country musicians 2. Country music 3. Bluegrass music 4. Popular music 5. Music history and criticism 6. Arts and Entertainment — Music — Country
LC 2010561925
Presents profiles of more than one hundred country music singers, including Jimmie Rodgers, Charlie Poole, and Gene Autry.

Russert, Luke
Look for Me There: Grieving My Father, Finding Myself. Luke Russert. HarperHorizon 2023. 224 p.
ISBN 9780785291817
Grades: Adult **B**
1. Russert, Luke 2. Journalists 3. Grief 4. Self 5. Identity 6. Voyages and travels 7. Death of fathers 8. Loss 9. Fathers and sons 10. Self-discovery 11. Options, alternatives, choices 12. Autobiographies and memoirs 13. Life stories — Relationships — Parent and child 14. Family and relationships — Parenting
After his news legend father died unexpectedly, the Emmy Award-winning journalist embarked on a three-plus-year odyssey across six continents to discover the world and, ultimately, find himself, in this poignant reflection offering encouragement to examine our choices, take risks and discover our truest selves.
"Readers will sympathize with Luke as he mourns, feeling both self-doubt and gratitude." —*Booklist*

Ryckman, Pamela
Candace Pert: Genius, Greed, and Madness in the World of Science. Pamela Ryckman. Hachette Books 2023. 320 p.
ISBN 9780306831461
Grades: Adult **B**
1. Pert, Candace B, 1946-2013 2. Pharmacologists 3. Medicine 4. Neuroscientists 5. Feminists 6. Women scientists 7. Alternative medicine 8. Scientific discoveries 9. Sexism in medicine 10. Life stories — Science, technology, and medicine — Scientists and inventors 11. History Writing — Women's history 12. Science writing — Medicine and health
LC 2023017584
This biography of the maverick scientist Candace Pert who discovered the opiate receptor, the cellular binding site for endorphins in the brain, also examines her years as an advocate of alternative medicine.
"Pert, a neuroscientist and pharmacologist who pioneered research on opioid receptors, pushed boundaries…Ryckman provides a well-reported deep dive into the life of a radical and complicated genius." —*Booklist*
Includes bibliographical references.

Rynecki, Elizabeth
Chasing Portraits: A Great-granddaughter's Quest for Her Lost Art Legacy. Elizabeth Rynecki. NAL, New American Library 2016. 304 p.
ISBN 9781101987667
Grades: Adult **B**
1. Rynecki, Moshe, 1881-1943 2. Stolen property recovery 3. Art 4. Jewish people 5. 20th century 6. Biographies 7. Life stories — Arts and culture — Artists 8. Life stories — Facing adversity — War and oppression — Holocaust 9. History writing — Wars and conflicts — Holocaust — World War II 10. History writing — Jewish history 11. Nonfiction that reads like fiction
LC 2016012588
The memoir of one woman's emotional quest to find the art of her Polish-Jewish great-grandfather, lost during World War II. Moshe Rynecki's body of work reached close to eight hundred paintings and sculptures before his life came to a tragic end. It was his great-granddaughter Elizabeth who sought to rediscover his legacy, setting upon a journey to seek out what had been lost but never forgotten.
"A wonderful story beautifully told. Rynecki's yearslong search, successes, frustrations, and failures are a study in perseverance." —*Kirkus*

Sabar, Ariel
My Father's Paradise: A Son's Search for His Jewish Past in Kurdish Iraq. Ariel Sabar. Algonquin Books of Chapel Hill 2008. 348 p.
ISBN 9781565124905
Grades: Adult **B**
1. Sabar, Yona 2. Sabar, Ariel 3. Father and adult son 4. Family relationships 5. Islam 6. Jewish people 7. Kurds 8. Judaism 9. Voyages and travels 10. Iraq 11. History writing — Jewish history 12. History writing — Nationalism — Southwest Asia and North Africa (Middle East) 13. Family and Relationships — Families
LC 2008024811
National Book Critics Circle Award for Autobiography, 2008.
My Father's Paradise is Ariel Sabar's quest to reconcile present and past. As Ariel's father, Yona, travels with him to today's postwar Iraq to find what's left of Yona's birthplace, Ariel brings to life the ancient town of Zakho, telling his family's story and discovering his own role in this sweeping saga. What he finds in the Sephardic Jews' millennia-long survival in Islamic lands is an improbable story of tolerance and hope.
"This is an engaging account of a wonderful, enlightening journey, a voyage with the power to move readers deeply even as it stretches across differences of culture, family, and memory." —*Christian Science Monitor*
Includes bibliographical references.

Sacks, Oliver
★ *Everything* in Its Place: First Loves and Last Tales. by Oliver Sacks. Alfred A. Knopf 2019. 320 p.
ISBN 9780451492890
Grades: Adult **B**
1. Sacks, Oliver, 1933-2015 2. Neurologists 3. Science 4. Human behavior 5. Essays 6. Biographies 7. Life stories — Science, technology, and medicine — Scientists and inventors 8. Science Writing — General
LC 2018022660
From the best-selling author of Gratitude and on the Move, a final volume of essays that showcases Sacks's broad range of interests—from his passions for ferns, swimming, and horsetails, to his final case histories exploring schizophrenia, dementia, and Alzheimer's. Oliver Sacks, scientist and storyteller, is beloved by readers for his neurological case histories, his fascination and familiarity with human behavior at its most unexpected and unfamiliar. Everything in Its Place is a celebration of Sacks's myriad interests, all told with his characteristic compassion, erudition, and luminous prose.
"The essays in this final volume from late, great neurologist Sacks move from his love of ferns, swimming, and horsetails to his final case histories investigating schizophrenia, dementia, and Alzheimer's." —*Library Journal*
This is a Borzoi book.

On the Move: A Memoir. by Oliver Sacks. Alfred A. Knopf 2015. 416 p.
ISBN 9780385352543
Grades: Adult **B**
1. Sacks, Oliver, 1933-2015 2. Neurologists 3. Physicians 4. Drug addiction 5. Autobiographies and memoirs 6. Life stories — Science, technology, and medicine — Healthcare professionals
LC 2015001870
New York Times Notable Book, 2015.
An autobiography of the British neurologist Oliver Sacks.
"An engaging and candid introduction to a man who transcended the life of a clinical practitioner to become a medical storyteller and humanitarian." —*Choice*
This is a Borzoi book.

Safranski, Rudiger
Goethe: Life as a Work of Art. Rudiger Safranski; translated by David Dollenmayer. Liveright Publishing Corporation 2017. 704 p.
ISBN 9780871404909
Grades: Adult **B**
1. Goethe, Johann Wolfgang von, 1749-1832 2. Authors, German 3. German history 4. 18th century 5. 19th century 6. Biographies 7. History writing — Europe — Germany 8. Life stories — Arts and culture — Writing — Authors

ESSENTIAL AND RECOMMENDED TITLES
Biography

LC 2017008798

A philosopher and popular biographer highlights the life of the man considered to be the Shakespeare of German literature, relying on his published works, primary sources, and the author|s correspondence with contemporaries to create an illuminating portrait.

"Scholars will welcome this intellectual biography, richly embellished by primary sources and aided by the strong Dollenmayer translation." —*Publishers Weekly*

Includes bibliographical references and index.

Saint John, Bozoma
The Urgent Life: My Story of Love, Loss, and Survival. Bozoma Saint John. Viking Press 2023. 288 p.
ISBN 9780593300176
Grades: Adult   B
1. Saint John, Bozoma 2. Businesspeople 3. African American businesspeople 4. Love 5. Loss 6. Survival 7. Death of married men 8. Grief 9. United States 10. Autobiographies and memoirs 11. Life stories — Facing adversity — Coping with death 12. Family and relationships — Aging and death

LC 2022022454

Taking readers through the dizzying, numbing days of multiple griefs, the iconic shares her journey forward through the highs and lows as she negotiates life as a woman determined to learn from tragedies to build a remarkable life worth living even in her brokenness.

"Tender and fierce, this book explores loss, interracial love, and the complexity of human emotion with humility, candor, and grace." —*Kirkus*

Salaam, Yusef
Better, Not Bitter: Living on Purpose in the Pursuit of Racial Justice. Yusef Salaam. Grand Central Publishing 2021. 304 p.
ISBN 9781538705001
Grades: Adult   B
1. Salaam, Yusef, 1974- 2. Prisoners 3. False imprisonment 4. Judicial error 5. Racism in the criminal justice system 6. Mass incarceration 7. Prison reform 8. Social justice 9. Criminal justice system 10. New York City 11. Autobiographies and memoirs 12. Life stories — Politics — Activists and reformers 13. Society and culture — Violence and crime — Criminal justice system 14. Society and culture — Race

LC 2020054033

An inspirational memoir serves as a call to action from prison reform activist Yusef Salaam, of the Exonerated Five, that will inspire us all to turn our stories into tools for change in the pursuit of racial justice.

"One of the wrongly accused and imprisoned Central Park Five recounts his experiences with an unjust system of justice. . . . Warm, generous, and inspirational: a book for everyone." —*Kirkus*

Salisbury, Katie Gee
★ *Not Your China Doll: The Wild and Shimmering Life of Anna May Wong.* Katie Gee Salisbury. E.P. Dutton 2024. 464 p.
ISBN 9780593183984
Grades: Adult   B
1. Wong, Anna May, 1905-1961 2. Chinese Americans 3. Actors and actresses 4. East Asian Americans 5. Films 6. Racism 7. Acting 8. United States 9. 20th century 10. Biographies 11. Life stories — Identity — Race and ethnicity 12. Life stories — Arts and culture — Performing arts — Actors and actresses 13. Arts and Entertainment — Movies and television 14. History Writing — Women's history

Set against the glittering backdrop of the Jazz Age and the rise of Hollywood, this celebration of the first Asian American movie star who graced Oscar-winning films shows how she moved away from being typecast as a China doll or dragon lady and worked towards reshaping Asian American representation in film.

"Salisbury brings the life and career of this legendary film actor into sharp, immediate focus in a vibrant biography that celebrates Wong's tenacity and commitment to her race and culture." —*Booklist*

Samatar, Sofia
The White Mosque. Sofia Samatar. Catapult 2022. 336 p.
ISBN 9781646220977
Grades: Adult   B
1. Samatar, Sofia 2. Identity 3. Mennonites 4. Christianity 5. Villages 6. Faith 7. Communities 8. Voyages and travels 9. Silk Road 10. Asia 11. Uzbekistan 12. Autobiographies and memoirs 13. Life stories — Religion and spirituality 14. Travel Writing — Retracing historic journeys 15. Life stories — Identity 16. Spirituality and Religion — Christianity 17. History Writing — Asia

In the late nineteenth century, a group of German-speaking Mennonites traveled from Russia into Central Asia, where their charismatic leader predicted Christ would return. Over a century later, Sofia Samatar joins a tour following their path, fascinatednot by the hardships of their journey, but by its aftermath: the establishment of a small Christian village in the Muslim Khanate of Khiva. Named AK Metchet, "The White Mosque," after the Mennonites' whitewashed church, the village lasted for fifty years.

"Sci-fi writer Samatar (The Winged Histories) strays from her imagined worlds to excavate a very real past in this fascinating look at her religious heritage....This riveting meditation on the 'Great tides of history' yields a wondrous take on the ways the past and present intertwine." —*Publishers Weekly*

Sampson, Fiona
In Search of Mary Shelley: The Girl Who Wrote Frankenstein. Fiona Sampson. Pegasus Books 2018. 368 p.
ISBN 9781681777528
Grades: Adult   B
1. Shelley, Mary Wollstonecraft, 1797-1851 2. Women authors 3. Literary criticism 4. Young women 5. Poets 6. Husband and wife 7. 19th century 8. Biographies 9. Life stories — Arts and culture — Writing — Authors 10. History writing — Arts and culture 11. Arts and Entertainment — Writing and Publishing — Literary criticism

LC Bl2018087125

Published to coincide with the 200th anniversary of Frankenstein, a major new biography of Mary Shelley, written by an award-winning poet, shares literary insight into Shelley's firsthand experiences throughout her infamously turbulent life.

Includes bibliographical references and index.

Samuels, Robert
★ *His Name Is George Floyd: One Man's Life and the Struggle for Racial Justice.* Robert Samuels and Toluse Olorunnipa. Viking 2022. 320 p.
ISBN 9780593490617
Grades: Adult   B
1. Floyd, George, 1974-2020 2. African American men 3. Murder victims 4. Police brutality 5. Trials (Police misconduct) 6. Black Lives Matter movement 7. Racism 8. Racism in the criminal justice system 9. African American families 10. African American civil rights 11. Social justice 12. Race relations 13. United States history 14. 21st century 15. Life stories — Facing adversity — Victims of crime 16. Life stories — Identity — Race and ethnicity 17. Society and culture — Race 18. Society and culture — Violence and crime — Criminal justice system

LC 2021062302

Pulitzer Prize for General Nonfiction, 2023; Pulitzer Prize for Biography finalist, 2023; National Book Award for Nonfiction finalist, 2022.

The events of that day are now tragically familiar: on May 25, 2020, George Floyd became the latest Black person to die at the hands of the police, murdered outside of a Minneapolis convenience store by white officer Derek Chauvin. The video recording of his death set off a series of protests in the United States and around the world, awakening millions to the dire need for reimagining this country's broken systems of policing. But behind a face that would be graffitied onto countless murals, and a name that has become synonymous with civil rights, there is the reality of one man's stolen life: a life beset by suffocating systemic pressures that ultimately proved inescapable. This biography of George Floyd shows the athletic young boy raised in the projects of Houston's Third Ward who would become a father, a partner, a friend, and a man constantly in search of a better life.

PUBLIC LIBRARY CORE COLLECTION: NONFICTION
Twentieth Edition

"This multifaceted and exceptionally informative account is both a moving testament to Floyd and a devastating indictment of America's racial inequities." —*Publishers Weekly*

Includes bibliographical references.

Samuelsson, Marcus

Yes, Chef. Marcus Samuelsson. Random House 2012. 336 p.
ISBN 9780385342605
Grades: Adult   B

1. Samuelsson, Marcus 2. Swedish Americans 3. Interracial adoption 4. Cooks 5. Cooking 6. Autobiographies and memoirs 7. Food writing — Memoirs and biographies 8. Life stories — Arts and culture — Culinary arts 9. Adult books for young adults

LC 2011042220

IACP Cookbook Awards, Literary Food Writing, 2013; James Beard Foundation Book Awards, Writing and Literature, 2013.

The "Top Chef: Masters" winner and James Beard Award-winning proprietor of Harlem's Red Rooster traces his Ethiopian birth, upbringing by an adoptive family in Sweden and rise to a famous New York chef, sharing personal insights into his challenges as a Black man in a deeply prejudiced industry.

"This distinctive and compelling memoir has all the elements of a good story: Humor, travel, and a young individual overcoming obstacles via a passionate calling." —*Library Journal*

Sanchez, Erika L.

Crying in the Bathroom: A Memoir. Erika L. Sánchez. Viking 2022. 256 p.
ISBN 9780593296936
Grades: Adult   B

1. Sanchez, Erika L. 2. Mexican American women 3. Women authors 4. Hispanic Americans 5. Children of immigrants 6. Social marginality 7. Growing up 8. Adulthood 9. Motherhood 10. Gratitude 11. People with depression 12. Women 13. Autobiographies and memoirs 14. Essays 15. Life stories — Arts and culture — Writing — Authors 16. Life stories — Identity — Race and ethnicity 17. Life stories — Facing adversity — Medical issues — Mental illness

LC 2021054801

Rise: A Feminist Book Project List, 2023.

Growing up as the daughter of Mexican immigrants in Chicago in the nineties, Erika Sánchez was a self-described pariah, misfit, and disappointment—a foul-mouthed, melancholy rabble-rouser who painted her nails black but also loved comedy, often laughing so hard with her friends that she had to leave her school classroom. Twenty-five years later, she's now an award-winning novelist, poet, and essayist, but she's still got an irrepressible laugh, an acerbic wit, and singular powers of perception about the world around her. In these essays, Sánchez reveals an interior life rich with ideas, self-awareness, and perception.

"An accomplished poet and novelist, Sánchez (I Am Not Your Perfect Mexican Daughter, 2017) expands her oeuvre with this refreshingly candid memoir….An engrossing, accessible, heart-opening recollection of a fascinating life." —*Booklist*

Includes bibliographical references.

Sancton, Thomas

*The **Bettencourt** Affair: The World's Richest Woman and the Scandal That Rocked Paris.* Tom Sancton. Dutton 2017. 400 p.
ISBN 9781101984475
Grades: Adult   B

1. Bettencourt, Liliane 2. Banier, Francois-Marie 3. Sarkozy, Nicolas, 1955- 4. Senior women 5. Scandals 6. Swindlers and swindling 7. Heirs and heiresses 8. Inheritance and succession 9. Greed 10. Rich people 11. Cosmetics 12. Paris, France 13. Biographies 14. Life stories — People in history — Famous families 15. Family and Relationships — General 16. Life stories — Business — Business leaders

LC 2016058788

Part courtroom drama, part upstairs-downstairs tale, and part character-driven story of a complex, fascinating family and the intruder who nearly tore it apart, the Bettencourt affair started as a family drama but quickly became a massive scandal in France. As L'Oreal's shadowy corporate history and buried World War II secrets were uncovered, all of Paris was shaken by the blockbuster case, the shocking reversals, and the surprising final victim.

"A well-researched, crisply written, and entertaining story of family, greed, wealth, and the complex relations among them." —*Kirkus*

Sandburg, Carl

Abraham Lincoln: The Prairie Years and the War Years. Carl Sandburg. Harcourt 2002. xiv, 762 p. : Illustration; Map
ISBN 9780156027526
Grades: Adult   B

1. Lincoln, Abraham, 1809-1865 2. Presidents 3. Civil war 4. United States Civil War, 1861-1865 5. United States history 6. Illinois 7. 1860s 8. 19th century 9. American Civil War era (1861-1865) 10. Biographies 11. History writing — Presidency — 19th century — United States 12. History writing — Antebellum America — United States 13. History writing — Presidency — United States 14. History writing — Wars and conflicts — American Civil War 15. Life stories — Politics — Politicians

LC BL2006010116

Originally published in six volumes, Pulitzer Prize-winning author Carl Sandburg's Abraham Lincoln was called "the greatest historical biography of our generation." Sandburg distilled this work into one volume that became the definitive life of Lincoln.

A Harvest book; Includes bibliographical references (p. 743-747) and index.

Sandler, Lauren

This Is All I Got: A New Mother's Search for Home. Lauren Sandler. Random House 2020. 224 p.
ISBN 9780399589959
Grades: Adult   B

1. Homeless women 2. Homelessness 3. Single mothers 4. Twenties (Age) 5. Welfare 6. Poverty 7. Income inequality 8. New York City 9. Society and culture — Wealth and class — Poverty

LC 2019045309

New York Times Notable Book, 2020.

Chronicles a year in the life of a young, homeless single mother and her quest to find stability and shelter in New York City.

"A closely observed chronicle of a year in the life of a homeless single mother as she negotiates the system of public assistance . . . An impressive blend of dispassionate reporting, pungent condemnation of public welfare, and gritty humanity." —*Kirkus*

Sands, Philippe

*The **Ratline**: The Exalted Life and Mysterious Death of a Nazi Fugitive.* Philippe Sands. Alfred A. Knopf 2021. 432 p.
ISBN 9780525520962
Grades: Adult   B

1. Wachter, Otto, 1901-1949 2. Wachter, Horst von, 1939- 3. Nazis 4. War criminals 5. Fugitives 6. World War II 7. Holocaust (1933-1945) 8. Atrocities 9. 20th century 10. Second World War era (1939-1945) 11. Biographies 12. Life stories — Law and order — Criminals and law-breakers 13. History writing — Wars and conflicts — Holocaust — World War II

LC 2020022095

Describes the rise and fall of Baron Otto von Wc?hter, a high-ranking Nazi official who set off on a post-war, four-year flight to escape justice via "the Ratline" from Rome to Argentina.

"Human rights attorney Sands (East West Street) offers a real-life thriller that is stranger than fiction." —*Library Journal*

A Borzoi Book; Includes bibliographical references and index; Originally published in Great Britain in 2020 by Weidenfeld & Nicolson, an imprint of the Orion Publishing Group Ltd, London.

Santana, Carlos

*The **Universal** Tone: My Life.* Carlos Santana. Little Brown & Co 2014. 320 p.
ISBN 9780316244923
Grades: Adult   B

ESSENTIAL AND RECOMMENDED TITLES
Biography

1. Santana, Carlos 2. Music, Latin American 3. Guitarists 4. Mexican Americans 5. Rock musicians 6. Popular culture 7. United States history 8. United States 9. 20th century 10. Autobiographies and memoirs 11. Biographies 12. Arts and Entertainment — Music — Rock 13. Life stories — Arts and culture — Performing arts — Musicians and composers

LC Bl2014043161

An intimate account by the rock music artist traces his hardscrabble youth in Mexico and early days as a promising guitarist through his influential collaborations with fellow Latin stars.

"An appreciative and unpretentious chronicle, this is required reading for Santana fans and devotees of classic rock legends." —*Kirkus*

Sante, Lucy
I Heard Her Call My Name: A Memoir of Transition. Lucy Sante. Penguin Press 2024. 240 p.
ISBN 9780593493762
Grades: Adult   B

1. Sante, Lucy, 1954- 2. Women authors 3. Transgender people 4. Trans women 5. Gender identity 6. Psychology 7. Transitioning (Gender identity) 8. Change 9. Self-fulfillment 10. LGBTQIA+ people 11. Autobiographies and memoirs 12. Life stories — Identity — LGBTQIA+ 13. Life stories — Identity — Gender 14. Arts and Entertainment — Writing and Publishing

LC 2023019672

Lucy Sante's memoir braids together two threads of personal narrative: the arc of her life, and her recent step-by-step transition to a place of inner and outer alignment. Sante brings a loving irony to her account of her unsteady first steps; there was much she found she still needed to learn about being a woman after some sixty years cloaked in a man's identity, in a man's world. A marvel of grace and empathy, I Heard Her Call My Name parses with great sensitivity many issues that touch our lives deeply, of gender identity and far beyond.

"An absorbing analysis of a long-standing search for identity in writing and life." —*Kirkus*

Sardy, Marin
The Edge of Every Day: Sketches of Schizophrenia. Marin Sardy. Pantheon Books 2019. 304 pages
ISBN 9781524746933
Grades: Adult   B

1. Sardy, Marin 2. Schizophrenia 3. People with schizophrenia 4. Family and mental illness 5. Mental health services 6. Mental illness 7. Loss 8. Family relationships 9. Mothers 10. People with mental illnesses 11. Alaska 12. Anchorage, Alaska 13. Autobiographies and memoirs 14. Life stories — Facing adversity — Medical issues — Mental illness 15. Life stories — Relationships — Family

LC 2018042987

Shares highly informed meditations into how the author's childhood in Anchorage, her literary career, and the lives of beloved family members have been impacted by hereditary schizophrenia.

Sarsour, Linda
We Are Not Here to Be Bystanders: A Memoir of Love and Resistance. Linda Sarsour; foreword by Harry Belafonte. 37 INK, Simon & Schuster 2020. xii, 253 p.
ISBN 9781982105167
Grades: Adult   B

1. Sarsour, Linda, 1980- 2. Muslim women 3. Civil rights workers 4. Women political activists 5. Palestinian Americans 6. Feminists 7. Multiculturalism 8. Children of immigrants 9. Autobiographies and memoirs 10. Life stories — Politics — Activists and reformers 11. Society and culture — Social activism and philanthropy 12. Adult books for young adults

LC 2019030321

On a chilly spring morning in Brooklyn, nineteen-year-old Linda Sarsour stared at her reflection, dressed in a hijab for the first time. She saw in the mirror the woman she was growing to be—a young Muslim American woman unapologetic in her faith and her activism, who would discover her innate sense of justice in the aftermath of 9/11. Now heralded for her award-winning leadership of the Women's March on Washington, in We Are Not Here to Be Bystanders Linda Sarsour offers a poignant story of community and family. From the Brooklyn bodega her father owned, where Linda learned the real meaning of intersectionality, to protests in the streets of Washington DC, Linda's experience as a daughter of Palestinian immigrants is a moving portrayal of what it means to find one's voice and use it for the good of others.

"An incredible, galvanizing story of the power of participation." —*Booklist*
Includes bibliographical references and index.

Sasakamoose, Fred
Call Me Indian: From the Trauma of Residential School to Becoming the Nhl's First Treaty Indigenous Player. Fred Sasakamoose. Viking Canada 2021. 288 pages
ISBN 9780735240018
Grades: Adult   B

1. Sasakamoose, Fred, 1933-2020 2. First Nations (Canada) 3. Cree (Eeyou) (North American people) 4. Hockey players 5. Success (Concept) 6. Indigenous residential schools 7. Psychic trauma 8. Decision-making 9. Racism 10. Resilience 11. Family relationships 12. Determination 13. Saskatchewan 14. Autobiographies and memoirs 15. Canadian literature 16. Sports and Competition — Hockey 17. Life stories — Facing adversity — Personal transformation 18. Life stories — Politics — Politicians 19. Life stories — Sports — Athletes 20. Life stories — Identity — Race and ethnicity 21. History writing — Indigenous peoples — Canada

Loan Stars Favourites, 2021.

Trailblazer. Residential school survivor. First Indigenous player in the NHL. Fred Sasakamoose made his debut with the 1954 Chicago Black Hawks; after twelve games, he returned home to the family and culture that the Canadian government had ripped away from him. Sasakamoose continued to play in leagues around Western Canada, became a band councillor, served as Chief, and formed athletic programs for kids. His groundbreaking memoir intersects Canadian history and Indigenous politics, and follows his journey to reclaim pride in an identity that had previously been used against him.

"Call Me Indian is not only an excellent memoir about the first Indian hockey player with treaty status in the National Hockey League.... Sasakamoose's graphic recollection of every imaginable form of abuse at St. Michael's will stand for decades to come as one of the most damning indictments of the residential school system." —*Winnipeg Free Press*

Saul, Scott
★ *Becoming Richard Pryor.* Scott Saul. HarperCollins 2014. 352 p.
ISBN 9780062123305
Grades: Adult   B

1. Pryor, Richard 2. African American comedians 3. Comedians 4. Films 5. Actors and actresses 6. African Americans 7. United States 8. Biographies 9. Life stories — Arts and culture — Performing arts — Entertainers and celebrities 10. Arts and entertainment — Comedy

LC 2014034682

Drawing upon interviews with family and friends, court transcripts, unpublished journals and screenplay drafts, the author traces Richard Pryor's journey from his rough childhood, his trials in the Army and his apprentice days in Greenwich Village to his ascent in the "New Hollywood" of the 1970s and his struggles with drugs and fame.

"In the end, Pryor emerges as a revolutionary stand-up comic who perfected the art of dramatizing his own imperfections, and the world's." —*Publishers Weekly*
Includes bibliographical references and index.

Saunders, John
Playing Hurt: My Journey from Despair to Hope. John Saunders, with John U. Bacon. Da Capo Press 2017. 320 p.
ISBN 9780306824739
Grades: Adult   B

1. Saunders, John, 1955-2016 2. Sportscasters 3. People with depression 4. Depression 5. Coping 6. Personal conduct 7. Autobiographies and memoirs 8. Life stories — Facing adversity — Medical issues — Mental illness 9. Life stories — Arts and culture — Performing arts — Entertainers and celebrities

LC 2017285301

An autobiography of sportscaster John Saunders who suffered from depression.

"A story that merits both sympathy and attention." —*Kirkus*

Savage, Jodi M.
*The **Death** of a Jaybird: Essays on Mothers and Daughters and the Things They Leave Behind.* Jodi M. Savage. HarperPerennial 2023. 256 p.
ISBN 9780063276086
Grades: Adult　　　　　　　　　　　　　　　　　　　　B
1. Savage, Jodi M, 1978- 2. African American women 3. Identity 4. Memory 5. African American families 6. Medical care 7. Breast cancer 8. Femininity 9. Race (Social sciences) 10. Faith 11. People with breast cancer 12. African Americans 13. Grief 14. Brooklyn, New York City 15. New York City 16. Autobiographies and memoirs 17. Essays 18. Family and relationships — Families 19. Life stories — Relationships — Family 20. Life stories — Identity — Race and ethnicity 21. Life stories — Facing adversity — Medical issues
LC 2023017893

Reminiscent of the Year of Magical Thinking and Somebody's Daughter, a deeply empathetic and often humorous collection of essays that explore the author's ever-changing relationships with her grandmother and mother, through sickness and health, as they experience the joys and challenges of Black American womanhood.

"Throughout, Savage writes as if speaking with a friend, relating her experiences, and that of others, with sincerity. Readers of all backgrounds are certain to appreciate her struggles and her ability to cope with the challenges she has faced." —*Kirkus*

Saxton, Martha
*The **Widow** Washington: The Life of Mary Washington.* Martha Saxton. Farrar, Straus and Giroux 2019. 379 pages
ISBN 9780809097012
Grades: Adult　　　　　　　　　　　　　　　　　　　　B
1. Washington, Mary Ball, 1708-1789 2. Washington, George, 1732-1799 3. Mothering 4. Mothers and sons 5. Orphans 6. Widows 7. Slaveholders 8. Faith (Christianity) 9. Saving and thrift 10. Families 11. Presidents 12. United States history 13. United States 14. Virginia 15. Colonial America (1600-1775) 16. Revolutionary America (1775-1783) 17. Biographies 18. Life stories — People in history — Famous families 19. History writing — Presidency — United States
LC 2018056295

Biography of Mary Ball Washington, George Washington's mother. Places her life as an orphan, a young wife in rural Virginia, a slaveholder, a widow, and mother to the first president in the context of the changing economic circumstances and cultural values of colonial Virginia and a young nation.

"All readers will value this vivid account that corrects Mary's record and reveals the dilemmas and distorted sensibility of Virginian slave-holding white women, along with the devastation caused by the Revolutionary War." —*Library Journal*

Includes bibliographical references and index.

Schaap, Jeremy
Cinderella Man: James J. Braddock, Max Baer, and the Greatest Upset in Boxing History. Jeremy Schaap. Houghton Mifflin 2005. xii, 324 p. : Illustration
ISBN 9780618551170
Grades: Adult　　　　　　　　　　　　　　　　　　　　B
1. Braddock, James J, 1906- 2. Baer, Max, 1909-1959 3. Boxers (Sports) 4. Irish American men 5. Sports rivalry 6. Depressions, 1929-1941 7. Boxing 8. Social life and customs 9. United States 10. 20th century 11. Biographies 12. Sports and Competition — Boxing 13. Sports and Competition — Individual Athlete 14. Life stories — Sports — Athletes
LC 2004066085

Offers a portrait of an American icon, boxer James J. Braddock, who staged a remarkable comeback during the Depression that captured the imagination of millions of working-class Americans.

"The author goes into detail on the brawny, reserved Braddock, who, at his lowest moments, was reduced to living off government relief and doing grueling work on the Hoboken, N.J. docks. But the story is as much about Max Baer, the lovably clownish and handsome heavyweight Braddock defeated as a 10-to-one underdog. Boxing enthusiasts will be more than satisfied by Schaap's meticulous account, which includes round-by-round details of the fight, as well as profiles of other fighters of the era." —*Publishers Weekly*

Includes bibliographical references and index.

Schechter, Harold
Hell's Princess: The Mystery of Belle Gunness, Butcher of Men. Harold Schechter. Little a 2018. xvi, 316 pages
ISBN 9781477808955
Grades: Adult　　　　　　　　　　　　　　　　　　　　B
1. Gunness, Belle, 1859-1908 2. Women serial murderers 3. Serial murders 4. Violence 5. Indiana 6. Biographies 7. Life stories — Law and order — Criminals and law-breakers 8. True Crime — Murder
LC 2018276362

Hell's Princess is a riveting account of one of the most sensational killing sprees in the annals of American crime: the shocking series of murders committed by the woman who came to be known as Lady Bluebeard.

"This biography of a prolific and brutal serial killer will be of interest to Midwestern regional history buffs as well as true crime fans." —*Library Journal*

Includes bibliographical references (pages 263-294) and index.

Scheer, Paul
Joyful Recollections of Trauma. Paul Scheer. HarperOne 2024. 256 p.
ISBN 9780063293717
Grades: Adult　　　　　　　　　　　　　　　　　　　　B
1. Scheer, Paul, 1976- 2. Comedians 3. Actors and actresses 4. Filmmakers 5. Family violence 6. Childhood 7. Self-acceptance 8. Fatherhood 9. Autobiographies and memoirs 10. Life stories — Arts and culture — Performing arts 11. Arts and Entertainment — Comedy

The award-winning comedian, actor, filmmaker and podcaster presents a hilarious and candid memoir-in-essays that confront his sometimes shocking and difficult childhood, journey towards self-acceptance and his own experiences as a father.

"Award-winning actor/Comedian/Podcaster Scheer's charming, disarming, candid, and warm collection of essays will appeal to readers who like their humor best when it's bittersweet." —*Library Journal*

Scheeres, Julia
Jesus Land: A Memoir. Julia Scheeres. Counterpoint 2005. 356 p.
ISBN 9781582433387
Grades: 11 12 Adult　　　　　　　　　　　　　　　　　B
1. Scheeres, Julia 2. African American brothers 3. Children who are hyperactive 4. Child abuse victims 5. Christian education 6. Siblings 7. Interracial adoption 8. Racism 9. Growing up 10. Education 11. Dominican Republic 12. Indiana 13. Autobiographies and memoirs 14. Family and Relationships — Parenting — Adoption 15. Life stories — Relationships — Family 16. Family and Relationships — Siblings 17. Adult books for young adults
LC 2005014816

Alex Award, 2006.

Tells the story of a white girl who was sent from the Midwest to a Christian reform school in the Dominican Republic after she and her Black adopted brother fought back against the racism and bullying that was directed toward them.

"Tinged with sadness yet pervaded by a sense of triumph, Scheeres's book is a crisply written and earnest examination of the meaning of family and Christian values." —*Publishers Weekly*

Scheier, Liz
Never Simple: A Memoir. Liz Scheier. Henry Holt and Company 2022. 288 p.
ISBN 9781250823137
Grades: Adult　　　　　　　　　　　　　　　　　　　　B
1. Scheier, Liz 2. Mental illness 3. People with mental illnesses 4. Mothers and daughters 5. Single mothers 6. Identity 7. Family secrets 8. Dysfunctional families 9. Deception 10. Dishonesty 11. Borderline Syndrome (Psychiatry) 12. Family relationships 13. Manhattan, New York City 14. Autobiographies and

ESSENTIAL AND RECOMMENDED TITLES
Biography

memoirs 15. Life stories — Relationships — Growing up 16. Life stories — Relationships — Parent and child 17. Family and relationships — Growing up
LC 2021019083

The author shares her experiences growing up in '90s Manhattan with a brilliant, manipulative and mentally ill mother who built a farcical, half-true life for the two of them as she dives deep into the cascading effects of decades of lies and deception.

"A former Random House editor and content developer recounts an improbably complicated life courtesy of an eccentric, mentally ill mother." —*Kirkus*

Schemel, Patty
Hit so Hard: A Memoir. Patty Schemel. Da Capo Press 2017. 288 pages
ISBN 9780306825071
Grades: Adult   B
1. Schemel, Patty, 1967- 2. Women rock musicians 3. Drummers 4. Drug addiction 5. Fame 6. Homosexuality 7. Alternative rock music 8. Alternative rock musicians 9. Rock groups 10. Heroin addiction 11. Homelessness 12. Transformations, Personal 13. Sobriety 14. Autobiographies and memoirs 15. Life stories — Arts and culture — Performing arts — Musicians and composers 16. Life stories — Facing adversity — Medical issues — Addiction 17. Arts and Entertainment — Music — Rock 18. Society and culture — Illness and disease — Addiction

LC Bl2017045182

The former drummer for Hole provides a front-seat view into the life of Courtney Love and Kurt Cobain, her one-time housemates, and describes her own addictions to heroin that resulted in being fired, homelessness, multiple stints in rehab and petty theft and prostitution.

Schiavi, Michael R.
Celluloid Activist: The Life and Times of Vito Russo. Michael Schiavi. The University of Wisconsin Press 2011. xiii, 361 p. : Illustration
ISBN 9780299282301
Grades: Adult   B
1. Russo, Vito 2. Gay men 3. Gay activists 4. Homosexuality in films 5. Gay authors 6. Journalists 7. People with AIDS 8. 20th century 9. Biographies 10. Life stories — Identity — LGBTQIA+ 11. Life stories — Politics — Activists and reformers 12. Society and culture — LGBTQIA+

LC 2010044627

"Conventionally academic but complex portrait of an undeservedly obscure gay author and activist." —*Kirkus*

Includes bibliographical references and index.

Schiff, Stacy
★ *Cleopatra.* by Stacy Schiff. Little, Brown and Co. 2010. 368 p, 16 p. of plates : Illustration
ISBN 9780316001922
Grades: Adult   B
1. Cleopatra, Queen of Egypt, 69-30 B.C.E 2. Civilization, Ancient 3. Inheritance and succession 4. Women and politics 5. Women rulers 6. Leadership 7. Ancient Egypt 8. Ancient Egypt (3100 B.C.E.-640 C.E.) 9. Biographies 10. History writing — Ancient — Egypt 11. History writing — Women's history 12. Life stories — Politics — Royalty

LC 2010006988

New York Times Notable Book, 2010.

Separates fact from fiction to reconstruct the life of the most influential woman of her era, revealing Cleopatra as a complex woman and shrewd monarch whose life and death reshaped the ancient world.

"It's dizzying to contemplate the thicket of prejudices, personalities and propaganda Schiff penetrated to reconstruct a woman whose style, ambition and audacity make her a subject worthy of her latest biographer. After all, Stacy Schiff's writing is distinguished by those very same virtues." —*New York Times Book Review*

Includes bibliographical references and index.

Schlender, Brent
Becoming Steve Jobs: The Evolution of a Reckless Upstart into a Visionary Leader. Brent Schlender and Rick Tetzeli. Crown Business 2015. 448 p.
ISBN 9780385347402
Grades: Adult   B
1. Jobs, Steve, 1955-2011 2. Computer engineers 3. Leadership 4. Computer industry and trade 5. Success in business 6. Businesspeople 7. United States 8. Biographies 9. Life stories — Business — Business leaders 10. Business and economics — Industries — Technology

LC 2014031660

An account of how Apple cofounder Steve Jobs became the most famous and visionary CEO in the United States.

"Schlender and Tetzeli's account is unusually intimate thanks to voluminous interviews and Schlender's many personal encounters with Jobs over decades of covering him, and a reverential tone sometimes surfaces—as when Jobs's lieutenant Tim Cook offered Jobs his own liver for a transplant—in this corrective to Walter Isaacson's more jaundiced biography. But the authors are clear-eyed about Jobs's flaws and give lucid, detailed analyses of his maneuverings and product initiatives; theirs is one of the most nuanced and revealing assessments of Jobs's controversial career." —*Publishers Weekly*

Schlesinger, Arthur M.
A Life in the Twentieth Century: Innocent Beginnings, 1917-1950. Arthur M. Schlesinger, Jr. Houghton Mifflin 2000. 576 p. : Illustration
ISBN 9780395707524
Grades: 11 12 Adult   B
1. Schlesinger, Arthur M. (Arthur Meier), 1917-2007 2. Historians 3. Growing up 4. Intellectual life 5. 20th century 6. Autobiographies and memoirs 7. History writing — Early 20th century — United States 8. Life stories — Relationships — Growing up

LC 00061322

Booklist Editors' Choice, 2000; New York Times Notable Book, 2000.

The author considers events that occurred during his lifetime and that contributed to America's rise to world power status, as told through his personal experiences in childhood, in college, and during war times.

"Schlesinger's autobiography, skillfully interweaving the personal and the historical, is elegantly simple and marvellously clear. Complex thoughts are set forth with a lucidity that conceals the depth of the intellectual analysis. Wit, humour and the resources of a natural storyteller sweep the reader along." —*The Economist*

Includes index.

Schneider, Amy
In the Form of a Question: The Joys and Rewards of a Curious Life. Amy Schneider. Avid Reader Press 2023. xii, 251 p.
ISBN 9781668013304
Grades: Adult   B
1. Schneider, Amy, 1979- 2. Television personalities 3. Television game show contestants 4. Trivia games 5. Trans women 6. Transgender people 7. LGBTQIA+ people 8. Curiosity 9. Identity 10. Self-confidence 11. North American people 12. American people 13. Essays 14. Autobiographies and memoirs 15. Life stories — Arts and culture — Performing arts — Entertainers and celebrities 16. Life stories — Identity — LGBTQIA+ 17. Arts and Entertainment — Movies and Television 18. Debut title

LC 2023023214

Armed with boundless curiosity and fearless questioning, the most successful woman ever to compete on Jeopardy! shares how she won an even greater prize—the joy of being herself on national television and blazing a trail for openly queer and transgender people around the world.

"Readers will appreciate this generous and approachable collection of essays celebrating intellectual curiosity and the joy that comes with being your true self." —*Booklist*

Schott, Philipp
The Accidental Veterinarian: Tales from a Pet Practice. Philipp Schott. Ecw Press 2019. 200 pages

PUBLIC LIBRARY CORE COLLECTION: NONFICTION
Twentieth Edition

ISBN 9781770414808
Grades: Adult   B
1. Schott, Philipp 2. Veterinarians 3. Pet care 4. Humans and pets 5. Animals 6. Human-animal relationships 7. Autobiographies and memoirs 8. Nature Writing — Animal Studies 9. Family and Relationships — Pets and Owners 10. Life stories — Science, technology, and medicine — Healthcare professionals

With insight and humor, Dr. Philipp Schott shares tales from the unlikely path he took into his career of veterinary science and anecdotes from his successful small-animal clinic.

Schroeder, Alice
The Snowball: Warren Buffett and the Business of Life. Alice Schroeder. Bantam Books 2008. 864 p.
ISBN 9780553805093
Grades: Adult   B
1. Buffett, Warren 2. Capitalists and financiers 3. Brokers 4. Investment banking 5. Stock market 6. Investment bankers 7. Investors 8. Biographies 9. Business and economics — Business leaders and entrepreneurs 10. Life stories — Business — Business leaders
LC Bl2008002450

A portrait of the life and career of investment guru Warren Buffett sheds new light on the man, as well as on the work, ideas, business principles, strategies, and no-nonsense insights that have guided his phenomenally successful business endeavors.

"In a book that is dominated by unstinting descriptions of Buffett's appetitesfor profit, women (particularly nurturing maternal types), food (Buffett maintained his and his family's weight by dangling money)it is refreshing that Schroeder keeps her tone free of judgment or awe; Buffett's plain-speaking suffuses the book and renders his public and private successes and failures wonderfully human and universal. Inspiring managerial advice abounds and competes with gossipy tidbits . in this rich, surprisingly affecting biography." —*Publishers Weekly*

Schultz, Howard
From the Ground Up: A Journey to Reimagine the Promise of America. Howard Schultz. Random House 2019. 352 p.
ISBN 9780525509448
Grades: Adult   B
1. Schultz, Howard 2. Personal conduct 3. Corporate culture 4. Success (Concept) 5. Chief executive officers 6. Social responsibility 7. Corporate accountability 8. Life stories — Facing adversity — Personal transformation 9. Business and economics — Industries

The founder of Starbucks shares his dramatic, untold personal story—from his childhood in Brooklyn's housing projects to his rise as a business icon—and lays out his vision for how companies can improve their social impact.

Schulz, Kathryn
★ *Lost & Found: A Memoir.* Kathryn Schulz. Random House 2022. 256 p.
ISBN 9780525512462
Grades: Adult   B
1. Schulz, Kathryn 2. Love 3. Loss 4. Fathers and daughters 5. Death 6. Marriage 7. Married women 8. Grief 9. Gratitude 10. Family relationships 11. Self-discovery 12. Everyday life 13. Autobiographies and memoirs 14. Life stories — Relationships 15. Life stories — Facing adversity — Coping with death 16. Family and Relationships — General 17. Book club best bets

Lambda Literary Award for Lesbian Memoir/Biography, 2023.

Eighteen months before Kathryn Schulz's beloved father died, she met the woman she would marry. In Lost & Found, she weaves the stories of those relationships into a brilliant exploration of how all our lives are shaped by loss and discovery—from the maddening disappearance of everyday objects to the sweeping devastations of war, pandemic, and natural disaster; from finding new planets to falling in love. The resulting book is part memoir, part guidebook to living in a world that is simultaneously full of wonder and joy and wretchedness and suffering—a world that always demands both our gratitude and our grief.

"Journalist Schulz (Being Wrong) presents a charming and relatable portrait of her late father, in a memoir about processing grief and recognizing and learning from loss by finding new relationships and experiences. . . . It's full of curiosity and a great deal of love and compassion that readers will relish." —*Library Journal*

Schumer, Amy
The Girl with the Lower Back Tattoo. Amy Schumer. Gllery Books 2016. 352 p.
ISBN 9781501139888
Grades: Adult   B
1. Schumer, Amy 2. Celebrities 3. Gender role 4. Women comedians 5. Women 6. Comedians 7. Essays 8. Humor writing — Social humor
LC 2016299978

Goodreads Choice Award, 2016.

An uproarious collection of no-holds-barred personal essays by the Emmy Award-winning comedian reflects on her raucous childhood antics, her hard-won rise in the entertainment industry and her struggles to maintain the courage to approach the world in unstintingly honest ways.

"A hilarious and effective memoir from a woman with zero inhibitions." —*Kirkus*

Schwalbe, Will
★ *The End of Your Life Book Club.* Will Schwalbe. Alfred A. Knopf 2012. 336 p.
ISBN 9780307594037
Grades: Adult   B
1. Books and reading 2. People with cancer 3. Mother and adult son 4. Grief in families 5. Family relationships 6. Pancreatic cancer 7. People with terminal illnesses 8. Women 9. Autobiographies and memoirs 10. Life stories — Facing adversity — Coping with death 11. Family and Relationships — Illness and the Family 12. Science Writing — Medicine and health — Illness and disease 13. Arts and Entertainment — Writing and Publishing — Literary criticism
LC 2012018989

Recounts how the author and his mother read and discussed books during her chemotherapy treatments, describing how the activity involved a wide range of literary genres, furthered their appreciation for literature, and strengthened their bond.

"This book will bring tears to readers' eyes—it is an essential title for lovers of memoir. Recommended for anyone who enjoys books about mothers and sons, books about the love of books, and books about the strength of families." —*Library Journal*

We Should Not Be Friends: The Story of a Friendship. Will Schwalbe. Alfred a Knopf 2023. 336 p.
ISBN 9780525654933
Grades: Adult   B
1. Male friendship 2. Friendship 3. Life change events 4. Secrets 5. Toleration 6. Interpersonal relations 7. Autobiographies and memoirs 8. Life stories — Relationships — Friendship 9. Family and relationships — Friendship

Tracing an extraordinary, life-changing college friendship over decades of challenge and change, this warm, funny and irresistible book follows the author as he, joining a little-known secret society at Yale, finds an unlikely friend in a physically imposing, loud, star wrestler determined to become a Navy SEAL.

"An affecting, rewarding story of an unlikely friendship that, against all seeming odds, has endured." —*Kirkus*

Schwartz, David N.
The Last Man Who Knew Everything: The Life and Times of Enrico Fermi, Father of the Nuclear Age. David N. Schwartz. Basic Books, an imprint of Perseus Books, LLC, a subsidiary of Hachette Book Group, Inc. 2017. 448 p.
ISBN 9780465072927
Grades: Adult   B
1. Fermi, Enrico, 1901-1954 2. Physicists 3. Quantum theory 4. Nobel Prize winners 5. Nuclear physicists 6. Italian Americans 7. Physics 8. Intellectual life 9. Experiments 10. Immigrants 11. Interpersonal relations 12. Biographies 13. Life stories — Science, technology, and medicine — Scientists and inventors
LC 2017020558

A portrait of physicist and innovator Enrico Fermi assesses his pivotal role in achieving a nuclear chain reaction and shares insights into his complex personal-

ESSENTIAL AND RECOMMENDED TITLES
Biography

ity, family ties, and relationships with the Italian Fascist Party and the Manhattan Project.

"Though comparable to Segr and Hoerlins the Pope of Physics (2016) as an account of Fermis groundbreaking science, Schwartzs biography delivers a much fuller personal portrait, illuminating how this generous friend to scientific colleagues, this inspiring mentor to students, often proved a difficult husband and negligent father. A sophisticated portrayal of a complex man." —*Booklist*

Includes bibliographical references and index.

Scovell, Nell
Just the Funny Parts: And a Few Hard Truths About Sneaking into the Hollywood Boys' Club. Nell Scovell. Dey Street Books 2018. 288 p.
ISBN 9780062473486
Grades: Adult **B**
1. Scovell, Nell 2. Television writers 3. Sex discrimination against women 4. Entertainment industry and trade 5. Popular culture 6. Sexism 7. Hollywood, California 8. Autobiographies and memoirs 9. Life stories — Arts and culture — Writing — Authors 10. Society and culture — Gender — Women
LC Bl2018000687

The veteran television writer and creator of Sabrina the Teenage Witch shares insights into Hollywood's sexual politics throughout the past 30 years through anecdotes involving some of the industry's biggest names, including Mark Harmon, Bette Midler, David Letterman, Candice Bergen and Conan O'Brien.

"Scovell comes across as a smart, energetic, determined woman, someone who is always shooting for greater success and who really hates it when she fails at something. A revealing and timely portrait of a professional writer and the industry in which she works." —*Booklist*

Scurr, Ruth
Fatal Purity: Robespierre and the French Revolution. Ruth Scurr. Metropolitan Books 2006. xvii, 408 p. : Illustration; Map
ISBN 9780805079876
Grades: Adult **B**
1. Robespierre, Maximilien, 1758-1794 2. Revolutionaries 3. French history 4. France 5. Revolutionary France (1789-1799) 6. History writing — Wars and conflicts — French Revolution
LC 2005057694

Library Journal Best Books, 2006.

A biography of a key figure of the French Revolution captures the paradoxical life of Maximilien Robespierre, from his beginnings as a provincial lawyer, to his rise to power as a revolutionary leader, to his eventual end on the guillotine that had takenthe lives of so many during the Terror that he had orchestrated.

"This is quite the calmest and least abusive history of the Revolution you will ever read. It works well as a general history of the years 1789-94, besides being a succinct guide to one of its dominant figures." —*London Review of Books*

Includes bibliographical references (p. [379]-391) and index.

Seager, Sara
The Smallest Lights in the Universe: A Memoir. Sara Seager. Crown 2020. 304 p.
ISBN 9780525576259
Grades: Adult **B**
1. Seager, Sara 2. Women astrophysicists 3. Widows 4. Extrasolar planets 5. Astrophysicists 6. Autistic women 7. Loss 8. Death of married men 9. Space exploration 10. Neurodivergent people 11. Autobiographies and memoirs 12. Life stories — Facing adversity — Coping with death 13. Life stories — Facing adversity — Medical issues — Living with disabilities 14. Life stories — Science, technology and medicine — Scientists and inventors 15. Family and Relationships — Aging and Death 16. Science Writing — Space and Flight
LC 2020007803

Los Angeles Times Book Prize for Science and Technology, 2020.

In this luminous memoir, an MIT astrophysicist must reinvent herself in the wake of tragedy and discovers the power of connection on this planet, even as she searches our galaxy for another Earth.

"This thoughtful and affecting memoir of navigating life after loss reads like a comforting novel, inspiring others to follow their dreams and never give up on the possibilities of discovery and self-reflection. Readers seeking women's biographies and studies in planetary science will relish this heartfelt story." —*Library Journal*

Searcey, Dionne
In Pursuit of Disobedient Women: A Memoir of Love, Rebellion, and Family, Far Away. Dionne Searcey. Ballantine Books 2020. 288 pages : Map
ISBN 9780399179853
Grades: Adult **B**
1. Searcey, Dionne 2. Journalists 3. Family and work 4. Women 5. Political participation 6. Politics and government 7. Senegal 8. West Africa 9. Autobiographies and memoirs 10. Politics and global affairs — World politics — Africa 11. Life stories — Arts and culture — Writing — Journalists 12. Society and culture — Gender — Women 13. Politics and global affairs — Civil and human rights 14. Adult books for young adults
LC 2019038588

An award-winning West Africa bureau chief for the New York Times describes her family's four-year relocation to Senegal, where she witnessed the extraordinary lives and struggles of women shaped by war, globalization and an outdated patriarchy.

"Well-written and illuminating, Searcey's memoir introduces readers to life in contemporary West Africa and the work of overseas reporting." —*Booklist*

Sebag-Montefiore, Simon
Stalin: The Court of the Red Tsar. Simon Sebag Montefiore. Knopf 2004. xxvii, 785 p. : Illustration; Map
ISBN 9781400042302
Grades: Adult **B**
1. Stalin, Joseph, 1879-1953 2. Heads of state 3. Stalinism 4. Communism 5. Nazi-Soviet Pact, 1939 6. Soviet Union history 7. 20th century 8. Biographies 9. History writing — Communism — Europe — Russia 10. Life stories — Politics — Politicians
LC 2003027390

British Book Award for History Book of the Year, 2004; Library Journal Best Books, 2004; New York Times Notable Book, 2004.

A biography of the Soviet dictator and the men and women who surrounded him focuses on the foundation of human, psychological, and physical supports that encouraged him through the early days of Communism, World War II, and the Great Terror.

"In the relentless detail, the mood-setting descriptions of the leader's surroundings, the sketches of the people around him and in Stalin's own words, pranks and tempers, Montefiore gives us not only the most intimate view of the general secretary that we have to date but a rounded and complex portrait of a man who could go from charming to lethal in the space of a few seconds." —*The Nation*

Includes bibliographical references (p. [743]-755) and index; Originally published: London : Weidenfeld & Nicolson, 2003.

Young Stalin. Simon Sebag Montefiore. Alfred A. Knopf 2007. xxxii, 460 p, 32 p. of plates : Illustration; Map
ISBN 9781400044658
Grades: Adult **B**
1. Stalin, Joseph, 1879-1953 2. Heads of state 3. Dictators 4. Russian history 5. 20th century 6. Biographies 7. History writing — Communism — Europe — Russia 8. Life stories — Politics — Politicians
LC 2007029220

Costa Biography Award, 2007; Library Journal Best Books, 2007; Los Angeles Times Book Prize for Biography, 2007; Shortlisted for the James Tait Black Memorial Prize for Biography, 2007.

Examines the turbulent early years of a man who would become the personification of twentieth-century evil, detailing his poverty-stricken youth, religious training, role as a fanatical revolutionary, many love affairs, and evolution into a murderous tyrant.

Includes bibliographical references (p. [429]-438) and index.

PUBLIC LIBRARY CORE COLLECTION: NONFICTION
Twentieth Edition

Sebba, Anne
Ethel Rosenberg: An American Tragedy. Anne Sebba. St. Martin's Press 2021. 320 p.
ISBN 9781250198631
Grades: Adult — B
1. Rosenberg, Ethel, 1915-1953 2. Communists 3. Spies 4. Married women 5. Imprisonment 6. Crime 7. Executions and executioners 8. 20th century 9. Biographies 10. Life stories — Law and order — Criminals and law-breakers 11. History writing — Early 20th century — United States 12. History writing — Spies and spying

LC 2020057526

This biography of the wife and mother executed for espionage-related crimes tells how despite the flimsy evidence against her, refused to incriminate her husband and faced the death penalty for a crime she didn't commit.

"In this biography of Ethel Rosenberg (1915-53), author Sebba (Les Parisiennes) seeks to understand Ethel in her own right. . . . A deft, chilling, and long overdue biography of an American woman singled out by dark political and cultural forces that were bent on keeping women at home and 'Foreign' ideas out of American minds." —*Library Journal*

Includes bibliographical references and index; Originally published in Great Britain by Weidenfield & Nicolson.

Sebestyen, Victor
Lenin: The Man, the Dictator, and the Master of Terror. Victor Sebestyen. Pantheon 2017. 592 p.
ISBN 9781101871638
Grades: Adult — B
1. Lenin, Vladimir Il'ich, 1870-1924 2. Dictators 3. Torture 4. Communism 5. Communists 6. Totalitarianism 7. Revolutionaries 8. Politics and government 9. Soviet Union 10. Russia 11. Biographies 12. History writing — Communism — Europe — Russia 13. Life stories — Politics — Politicians

LC 2017008076

New York Times Notable Book, 2017.

Draws on diaries, memoirs, and private letters written by both the controversial dictator and his friends to explore how Vladimir Lenin's personal life, including key relationships with women, shaped his politics and role in launching the Russian Revolution.

"Sebestyen is to be commended for bringing the true Lenin to life for historians to consider. His study will rank with those of Richard Pipes and Robert Service in modern historiography." —*Choice*

Includes bibliographical references and index.

Secrest, Meryle
Frank Lloyd Wright. by Meryle Secrest. Harper Perennial 1993. xviii, 634 p. : Illustration
ISBN 9780060975678
Grades: Adult — B
1. Wright, Frank Lloyd, 1867-1959 2. Architects 3. Architecture, American 4. Biographies 5. Arts and Entertainment — Architecture 6. Life stories — Arts and culture — Architects

LC 92056269

A biography of the acclaimed architect describes Wright's Midwest boyhood, his apprenticeship with Louis Sullivan, his travels to Europe and subsequent success there, his three marriages, his work, and more.

"A portrait of a complex, often contradictory architect. Secrest writes with authority and compassion about Wright's long and turbulent career. Her exhaustive scholarship provides fresh insights into Wright's personality." —*Library Journal*

Includes bibliographical references (p. [605]-609) and index; Originally published: 1st ed. New York : Knopf, 1992.

Modigliani: A Life. by Meryle Secrest. Alfred A. Knopf 2011. 384 p.
ISBN 9780307263681
Grades: 11 12 Adult — B
1. Modigliani, Amedeo, 1884-1920 2. Painters 3. Modernism (Art) 4. Tuberculosis 5. People with tuberculosis 6. Paris, France 7. Biographies 8. Arts and Entertainment — Painting, Drawing, and Sculpture 9. Life stories — Arts and culture — Artists

LC 2010045357

A full-scale profile of the celebrated modernist artist includes coverage of his upbringing as a Sephardic Jewish youth by a impoverished Italian family, his considerable training and the ways in which his private battles with tuberculosis shaped his achievements.

A Borzoi book; Includes bibliographical references and index.

Sedaris, David
Theft by Finding: Diaries 1977-2002. David Sedaris. Little, Brown & Co. 2017. 528 p.
ISBN 9780316154727
Grades: Adult — B
1. Sedaris, David 2. Personal conduct 3. Family relationships 4. Diaries 5. Anthologies 6. Life stories — Arts and culture — Writing — Authors 7. Humor writing — General

LC 2016959026

Longlisted for the Andrew Carnegie Medal for Excellence in Non-Fiction, 2018.

An anthology of personal favorite diary entries by the best-selling author of Let's Explore Diabetes with Owls features excerpts that have inspired his famed autobiographical essays and shares insights into the intimate arenas of his life.

"A candid, socially incisive, and sharply amusing chronicle of the evolution of an arresting comedic artist." —*Booklist*

Segura, Tom
★ *I'd* Like to Play Alone, Please: Essays. Tom Segura. Grand Central Publishing 2022. 272 p.
ISBN 9781538704639
Grades: Adult — B
1. Segura, Tom 2. Comedians 3. Celebrities 4. Performance 5. Solitude 6. Autobiographies and memoirs 7. Life stories — Arts and culture — Performing arts — Entertainers and celebrities 8. Humor writing — Social humor

The stand-up comedian and podcast hosts shares stories of his crazy life on the road and punishing schedule, including bizarre celebrity encounters and his philosophy that an increasingly insane world, sometimes you just need to be alone. 100,000 printing.

"Inside every smart-ass is the person they're publicly scared to be,' muses comedian Segura in this irreverent collection of personal stories, his debut." —*Publishers Weekly*

Sehee, Baek
I Want to Die but I Want to Eat Tteokbokki. Baek Sehee; translated by Anton Hur. Bloomsury Publishing Place USA 2022. 176 p.
ISBN 9781635579383
Grades: Adult — B
1. Sehee, Baek 2. Mental illness 3. People with depression 4. Korean people 5. Stigma (Social psychology) 6. Mental health 7. Depression 8. Self esteem 9. Anxiety 10. South Korean people 11. East Asian people 12. Women 13. Autobiographies and memoirs 14. Translations — Korean to English 15. Life stories — Facing adversity — Medical issues — Mental illness 16. Science Writing — Medicine and health — Mental health 17. Life stories — Identity — Gender

Baek Sehee is a successful young social media director at a publishing house when she begins seeing a psychiatrist about her—what to call it?—depression? She feels persistently low, anxious, endlessly self-doubting, but also highly judgmental of others. She hides her feelings well at work and with friends, performing the calmness her lifestyle demands. The effort is exhausting, overwhelming, and keeps her from forming deep relationships. This can't be normal. But if she's so hopeless, why can she always summon a yen for her favorite street food: the hot, spicy rice cake, tteokbokki? Is this just what life is like?

"A South Korean author recounts her long journey through anxiety and depression....At once personal and universal, this book is about finding a path to awareness, understanding, and wisdom." —*Kirkus*

ESSENTIAL AND RECOMMENDED TITLES
Biography

Seidelman, Susan
Desperately Seeking Something: A Memoir About Movies, Mothers, and Material Girls. Susan Seidelman. St. Martin's Press 2024. 304 p.
ISBN 9781250328212
Grades: Adult   **B**
1. Seidelman, Susan 2. Film producers and directors 3. Filmmaking 4. Film 5. Women film producers and directors 6. Independent films 7. Growing up 8. Influence (Literary, artistic, etc.) 9. Creativity 10. Popular culture 11. 20th century 12. Autobiographies and memoirs 13. Life stories — Arts and culture — Performing arts — Directors and producers 14. Arts and Entertainment — Movies and television

The funny and insightful first-person story of the trailblazing movie director of the 80s and 90s whose fearless punk drama, "Smithereens," became the first American indie film to compete at Cannes, and smash hit "Desperately Seeking Susan" led to a four-decade career in film.

"A quick and easy read about the life and career of a trailblazing filmmaker. Will appeal to many audiences, including those unfamiliar with Seidelman's career." —*Library Journal*

Seiple, Samantha
Louisa on the Front Lines: Louisa May Alcott in the Civil War. Samantha Seiple. Seal Press 2019. 320 p.
ISBN 9781580058049
Grades: Adult   **B**
1. Alcott, Louisa May, 1832-1888 2. Military nurses 3. United States Civil War, 1861-1865 4. Women authors, American 5. Women authors 6. Women and war 7. Military nursing 8. United States history 9. American Civil War era (1861-1865) 10. 19th century 11. Biographies 12. Life stories — Arts and culture — Writing — Authors 13. History writing — Wars and conflicts — American Civil War 14. Adult books for young adults 15. Nonfiction that reads like fiction
LC 2018032967

An examination of Little Women author Louisa May Alcott's service as a Civil War nurse reveals how her experiences shaped her writing and activism, from her commitment to abolitionism to the creation of her book, Hospital Sketches.

"While other biographies may provide a more complete picture of Alcotts life, Seiples version is laser-focused on this particular period, convincingly making the unique argument that Alcotts difficult trials forged her personality and informed virtually every facet of her work." —*Publishers Weekly*

Includes bibliographical references and index.

Selleck, Tom
You Never Know: A Memoir. Tom Selleck. Dey Street Books 2024. 320 p.
ISBN 9780062945761
Grades: Adult   **B**
1. Selleck, Tom, 1945- 2. Actors and actresses 3. Celebrities 4. Television personalities 5. Fame 6. Sex symbolism 7. Interpersonal relations 8. American people 9. Autobiographies and memoirs 10. Life stories — Arts and culture — Performing arts — Actors and actresses 11. Arts and Entertainment — Movies and Television

An American icon and famed actor brings us on his uncharted but serendipitous journey to the top in Hollywood, clearing up misconceptions; sharing dozens of never-before-told stories from both his personal and professional lives; and offering a truly fresh perspective on a changing industry and a changing world.

"Magnum, PI actor Selleck delivers a breezy autobiography that covers his path from college basketball player to Hollywood heartthrob." —*Publishers Weekly*

Sellers, Bakari
My Vanishing Country: A Memoir. Bakari Sellers. Amistad 2020. 224 p.
ISBN 9780062917454
Grades: Adult   **B**
1. Sellers, Bakari, 1984- 2. African American legislators 3. Racism 4. Legislators 5. Rural African Americans 6. Rural life 7. Political participation 8. South Carolina 9. Autobiographies and memoirs 10. Life stories — Politics — Politicians
LC 2019040021

The CNN analyst and record-setting South Carolina State Representative chronicles the past, present and likely future of the American South, discussing his father's civil rights heroism and the ignored harsh realities of the Black working class.

"A strong voice for social justice emerges in an engaging memoir." —*Kirkus*

Selvaratnam, Tanya
Assume Nothing: A Story of Intimate Violence. Tanya Selvaratnam. Harper 2021. xii, 256 p.
ISBN 9780063059900
Grades: Adult   **B**
1. Selvaratnam, Tanya 2. Schneiderman, Eric T, 1954- 3. Abused women 4. Abusive men 5. Partner abuse 6. Family violence 7. Dysfunctional families 8. Misogyny 9. Women authors 10. Women filmmakers 11. Attorneys general 12. Control 13. Manipulation (Social sciences) 14. United States 15. Autobiographies and memoirs 16. Life stories — Facing adversity — Abuse survivors 17. Family and Relationships — Abuse 18. Society and culture — Violence and crime

The author shares her harrowing experiences with abuse at the hands of a top law enforcer to expose the realities of partner violence while counseling readers on how to recognize, expose and end domestic abuse.

"Selvaratnam (The Big Lie) deftly combines memoir and research to deliver a timely, must-read analysis of domestic violence.... A critical and timely piece in the era of the #metoo movement, this work will appear to a wide audience." —*Library Journal*

Semenya, Caster
The Race to Be Myself. Caster Semenya. W W Norton & Co Inc 2023. 320 p.
ISBN 9781324035770
Grades: Adult   **B**
1. Semenya, Caster, 1991- 2. Intersex people 3. Gender identity 4. Gender equity 5. Women Olympic athletes 6. Women Olympic medal winners 7. Human rights 8. Intersexuality 9. Genetic screening 10. Hormones, Sex 11. Testosterone 12. Gender nonconformity 13. Body image 14. Women runners 15. Women track and field athletes 16. South African people 17. Resilience 18. Autobiographies and memoirs 19. Society and culture — Gender — Women 20. Life stories — Identity — Gender

Olympian and World Champion Caster Semenya is finally ready to share the vivid and heartbreaking story of how the world came to know her name. Thrust into the spotlight at just eighteen years old after winning the Berlin World Championships in 2009, Semenya's win was quickly overshadowed by criticism and speculation about her body, and she became the center of a still-raging firestorm about how gender plays out in sports, our expectations of female athletes, and the right to compete as you are.

A furiously proud memoir by 'The most recognizable intersex person in the world.'...Moving, inspiring testimony by a woman facing hardship merely 'Because of a biological condition I was born with.' —*Kirkus*

Sen, Amartya
Home in the World: A Memoir. Amartya Sen. Liveright Publishing 2022. 464 p.
ISBN 9781324091615
Grades: Adult   **B**
1. Sen, Amartya 2. Economists 3. Political activists 4. Intellectuals 5. Social advocates 6. Poverty 7. Inequality 8. Social justice 9. Autobiographies and memoirs 10. Life stories — Education — Scholars and educators 11. Life stories — Politics — Activists and reformers 12. Business and economics — Economics
LC 2021048968

Amartya Sen reflects on the cataclysmic events that soon tore his world asunder, from the Bengal famine of 1943 to the struggle for Indian independence against colonial tyranny—and the outbreak of political violence that accompanied the end of British rule. Witnessing these lacerating tragedies only amplified Sen's sense of social purpose. He went on to study famine and inequality, wholly reconstructing theories of social choice and development. In 1998, he was awarded the Nobel Prize for his contributions to welfare economics, which included a fuller understanding of poverty as the deprivation of human capability.

"Nobel Prize-winning economist Sen (Harvard Univ; Collective Choice and Social Welfare) shares in this memoir the rich and varied professional life that has allowed him to work across the globe and interact with some of the greatest intellectuals of the 20th and 21st centuries.... A vivid memoir, recommended for those interested in the intersection of economics and social science." —*Library Journal*

Originally published in the UK by Allen Lane, London, in 2021; Includes bibliographical references.

Senik, Troy
A Man of Iron: The Turbulent Life and Improbable Presidency of Grover Cleveland. Troy Senik. Threshold Editions 2022. 368 p.

ISBN 9781982140748

Grades: Adult   B

1. Cleveland, Grover, 1837-1908 2. Presidents 3. Labor policy 4. Monetary policy 5. Scandals 6. Independence 7. Gilded Age (1865-1898) 8. 19th century 9. Biographies 10. Life stories — Politics — Politicians 11. History writing — Presidency — 19th century — United States

Featuring a wealth of in-depth research and newly uncovered details, a Man of Iron explores the remarkable life and extraordinary career of Grover Cleveland—one of America's most unusual presidents and the only one to serve two non-consecutive terms. A headstrong executive who alienated Congress, political bosses, and even his own party, his stubbornness nevertheless became the key to his political appeal.

"Robust biography of an overlooked president....A capably written introduction to a political leader who, though no rock star, deserves to be better known." —*Kirkus*

Sentilles, Sarah
Stranger Care: A Memoir of Loving What Isn't Ours. Sarah Sentilles. Random House 2021. xv, 404 p.

ISBN 9780593230039

Grades: Adult   B

1. Sentilles, Sarah 2. Foster parents 3. Foster children 4. Foster care 5. Babies 6. Injustice 7. Errors 8. Birthmothers 9. Grief 10. Parenting 11. Families 12. United States 13. Autobiographies and memoirs 14. Life stories — Relationships — Parent and child 15. Family and Relationships — Families 16. Family and Relationships — Parenting — Adoption

LC 2020032793

In a moving story, the author shares what she learned from fostering a newborn—about injustice, about mistakes, and about how to better love and protect people outside of our immediate families.

"Sentilles (Draw Your Weapons) describes her experience of adoption and foster care in this memoir of grief and beauty." —*Library Journal*

Includes bibliographical references.

Servadio, Gaia
Rossini. Gaia Servadio. Carroll & Graf Publishers 2003. xii, 244 p. : Illustration

ISBN 9780786711956

Grades: Adult   B

1. Rossini, Gioacchino, 1792-1868 2. Composers 3. Operas 4. Classical music 5. Chamber music 6. Music history and criticism 7. Music 8. People with depression 9. Men 10. Italian history 11. 19th century 12. Biographies 13. Arts and Entertainment — Music — Classical 14. Life stories — Arts and culture — Performing arts — Musicians and composers

LC 2003043563

Recounts the life of the nineteenth century Italian composer of such works as "The Barber of Seville" and "William Tell."

"This is a deeply rewarding book, written with real personality and much scholarship." —*Publishers Weekly*

Includes bibliographical references and index.

Service, Robert
Lenin—a Biography. Robert Service. Harvard University Press 2000. xxv, 561 p. : Illustration; Map

ISBN 9780674003309

Grades: Adult   B

1. Lenin, Vladimir Il'ich, 1870-1924 2. Heads of state 3. Revolutionaries 4. Communism 5. Communists 6. Politics and government 7. Russia 8. Soviet Union 9. Biographies 10. History writing — Communism — Europe — Russia 11. Life stories — Politics — Politicians

LC 00021394

A biography of the first Soviet leader delves into his heavily mythologized life to show why he was so feared, respected, and loved in Russia.

Includes bibliographical references and index.

Shafrir, Doree
Thanks for Waiting: The Unexpected Joy (& Weirdness) of Being a Late Bloomer. Doree Shafrir. Ballantine Books 2021. 240 p.

ISBN 9780593156742

Grades: Adult   B

1. Shafrir, Doree 2. Women authors, American 3. Editors 4. Podcasters 5. Social norms 6. Self-discovery 7. Interpersonal relations 8. Women's role 9. Growing up 10. Friendship 11. Self-fulfillment 12. 20th century 13. Autobiographies and memoirs 14. Life stories — Arts and culture — Writing — Authors 15. Life stories — Relationships — Growing up

LC 2021005264

In her debut memoir, the co-host of the podcast Forever 35 explores the enormous pressures women feel to hit certain milestones at certain times and how we can redefine what it means to be a late bloomer.

"Shafrir (Startup), a former BuzzFeed editor and cohost of the Forever35 podcast, delivers a heartwarming and witty account of how she figured it out—'whatever "It" is'—on her own terms.... This coming-of-age story raises the bar." —*Publishers Weekly*

Shahani, Aarti Namdev
Here We Are: American Dreams, American Nightmares. Aarti Namdev Shahani. Celadon Books 2019. 320 p.

ISBN 9781250204752

Grades: Adult   B

1. Shahani, Aarti Namdev 2. Racism 3. Immigrants 4. American dream 5. Drug cartels 6. Imprisonment 7. Immigrants, Indian 8. Indian Americans 9. Prisoners' families 10. Racism in the criminal justice system 11. Criminal justice system 12. Radio journalists 13. Fathers and daughters 14. New York City 15. Autobiographies and memoirs 16. Life stories — Identity — Immigrants 17. Life stories — Facing adversity 18. Society and culture — Immigration 19. Society and culture — Violence and crime — Criminal justice system 20. Adult books for young adults

LC Bl2019023083

An award-winning NPR correspondent presents a heartfelt memoir about the immigrant experience in modern America, detailing her education as a scholarship student at an elite Manhattan prep school and her father's victimization by a notorious drug cartel.

Shahidi, Afshin
Prince: A Private View. Afshin Shahidi; foreword by Beyonce Knowles-Carter. St. Martin's Press 2017. xvi, 235 pages : Color; Illustration

ISBN 9781250134431

Grades: Adult   B

1. Prince 2. Photographers 3. Rock musicians 4. United States 5. Illustrated books 6. Biographies 7. Arts and Entertainment — Photography 8. Life stories — Arts and culture — Performing arts — Musicians and composers

LC 2017032068

The photographer who was a trusted friend to and long-time collaborator with Prince presents 250 photos of the late artist, taken between 2001 and 2010, that provide never-before-seen glimpses into his personal and professional life.

ESSENTIAL AND RECOMMENDED TITLES
Biography

Shakespeare, Nicholas
Ian Fleming: The Complete Man. Nicholas Shakespeare. HarperCollins 2024. 864 p.
ISBN 9780063012240
Grades: Adult B
1. Fleming, Ian, 1908-1964 2. James Bond (Fictitious character) 3. Authors, English 4. Journalists 5. Intelligence service 6. Biographies 7. Life stories — Arts and culture — Writing — Authors 8. Arts and Entertainment — Writing and Publishing
ALCS Gold Dagger for Best Non-fiction of the Year, 2024.
A fresh portrait of the man behind James Bond, and his enduring impact, by an award-winning biographer with unprecedented access to the Fleming Archive.
"This richly detailed, well-documented, and exquisitely written biography is highly recommendable to fans of Fleming, Bond, or both." —*Booklist*
Originally published in the UK by Harvill Secker, London, in 2023.

Shakur, Prince
When They Tell You to Be Good: A Memoir. Prince Shakur. Tin House 2022. 296 p.
ISBN 9781953534422
Grades: Adult B
1. Family relationships 2. Voyages and travels 3. Homophobia 4. Race relations 5. Family secrets 6. Jamaican Americans 7. African American gay men 8. African American political activists 9. African American authors 10. Intergenerational trauma 11. Self-discovery 12. United States 13. Autobiographies and memoirs 14. Life stories — Identity — Race and ethnicity 15. Life stories — Identity — LGBTQIA+ 16. Life stories — Identity — Immigrants
LC 2022020914
After immigrating from Jamaica to the United States, Prince Shakur's family is rocked by the murder of Prince's biological father in 1995. Behind the murder is a sordid family truth, scripted in the lines of a diary by an outlawed uncle hell-bent on avenging the murder of Prince's father. As Shakur begins to unravel his family's secrets, he must navigate the strenuous terrain of coming to terms with one's inner self while confronting the steeped complexities of the Afro-diaspora.
"In this electric debut, essayist and organizer Shakur turns an unflinching eye to the realities of growing up queer and Black amid the racialized violence and political backlash of recent decades….The result is a searing account of self-discovery in the face of structural oppression." —*Publishers Weekly*

Shannon, Molly
★ *Hello, Molly!: A Memoir.* Molly Shannon. Ecco Press 2022. 304 p.
ISBN 9780063056237
Grades: Adult B
1. Shannon, Molly, 1964- 2. Actors and actresses 3. Resilience 4. Family relationships 5. Comedians 6. Women comedians 7. Growing up 8. Loss 9. Redemption 10. Autobiographies and memoirs 11. Life stories — Arts and culture — Performing arts — Actors and actresses 12. Life stories — Arts and culture — Performing arts — Entertainers and celebrities 13. Arts and entertainment — Comedy
A candid, humorous, and heartbreaking memoir of resilience and redemption by a noted alum of Saturday Night Live.
"Actor and comedian Shannon (Tilly the Trickster) revisits a life colored by grief in this surprisingly raw and personal account….Supremely inspiring, this will leave fans astonished." —*Publishers Weekly*

Shapiro, Ari
★ *The Best Strangers in the World: Stories from a Life Spent Listening.* Ari Shapiro. HarperOne, an imprint of HarperCollinsPublishers 2023. 272 p.
ISBN 9780063221345
Grades: Adult B
1. Shapiro, Ari, 1978- 2. Radio journalists 3. Journalists 4. Jewish men 5. Gay men 6. LGBTQIA+ people 7. Radio journalism 8. Radio talk shows 9. Journalism 10. Identity 11. American people 12. North American people 13. Autobiographies and memoirs 14. Essays 15. Life stories — Arts and Culture — Writing — Journalists 16. Arts and Entertainment — Writing and Publishing 17. Life stories — Identity — LGBTQIA+
LC 2022037630
From the host of NPR's All Things Considered comes a stirring memoir-in-essays that is also a love letter to journalism.
"In this genial debut memoir-in-essays, NPR host and occasional Pink Martini singer Shapiro mixes reported vignettes with reflections on his own life." —*Publishers Weekly*

Shapiro, Dani
★ *Inheritance: A Memoir of Genealogy, Paternity, and Love.* Dani Shapiro. Alfred A. Knopf 2019. 256 p.
ISBN 9781524732714
Grades: Adult B
1. Shapiro, Dani 2. Fathers and daughters 3. Paternity 4. Jewish women 5. Genealogy 6. Birthfathers 7. Children of sperm donors 8. Women authors, American 9. Family secrets 10. Identity 11. Autobiographies and memoirs 12. Life stories — Identity 13. Life stories — Relationships — Family 14. Family and relationships — Families 15. Book club best bets
LC 2018024082
National Jewish Book Award, 2019.
The acclaimed and beloved author of Hourglass now gives us a new memoir about identity, paternity, and family secrets—a real-time exploration of the staggering discovery she made last year about her father, and her struggle to piece together the hidden story of her own life.
"This beautifully written, thought-provoking genealogical mystery will captivate readers from the very first pages." —*Publishers Weekly*

Shapland, Jenn
My Autobiography of Carson McCullers: A Memoir. Jenn Shapland. Tin House Books 2020. xv, 266 pages
ISBN 9781947793286
Grades: Adult B
1. Shapland, Jenn, 1987- 2. McCullers, Carson, 1917-1967 3. Bisexual women 4. Letter writing 5. Lesbians 6. Authors, American 7. Women authors 8. Women-women relations 9. 20th century 10. Autobiographies and memoirs 11. Biographies 12. Life stories — Arts and culture — Writing — Authors 13. Life stories — Identity — LGBTQIA+ 14. Society and culture — LGBTQIA+
LC 2019031475
Lambda Literary Award for Lesbian Memoir/Biography, 2021; National Book Award for Nonfiction finalist, 2020.
A Pushcart Prize-winning writer draws on an intimate correspondence between McCullers and a woman named Annemarie to share previously unknown insights into the 20th-century novelist's private life, her approaches to queer fiction and the influence of her time at Yaddo.
"Celebrating McCullers, love, and the idea that every story told includes something of its teller, Shapland writes an involving literary journey of the self." —*Booklist*
Includes bibliographical references (pages 259-266).

Sharapova, Maria
Unstoppable: My Life so Far. Maria Sharapova. Sarah Crichton Books, Farrar, Straus and Giroux 2017. 304 p.
ISBN 9780374279790
Grades: Adult B
1. Sharapova, Maria, 1987- 2. Tennis players 3. Women tennis players 4. Tennis 5. Autobiographies and memoirs 6. Life stories — Sports — Athletes 7. Sports and competition — Tennis 8. Adult books for young adults
LC 2017017149
The five-time Grand Slam winner presents the remarkable story of how her father relocated her at the age of 7 from their native Russia to America to develop her tennis talents before she embarked on a record-setting career shaped by astonishing competitions, her provocative beliefs and her recent fight to return to the court.
"Unstoppable is an inspiring memoir about coming-of-age within the elite tennis community and a tribute to the unconditional support from families and coaches who make success possible." —*Booklist*

PUBLIC LIBRARY CORE COLLECTION: NONFICTION
Twentieth Edition

Sharma, Nina
The Way You Make Me Feel: Love in Black and Brown. Nina Sharma. Penguin Press 2024. 336 p.
ISBN 9780593492826
Grades: Adult — B
1. Interracial marriage 2. Love 3. Caste 4. Race (Social sciences) 5. Colorism 6. Mental health 7. South Asian Americans 8. African Americans 9. Indian Americans 10. Popular culture 11. Interracial couples 12. Race relations 13. United States 14. Essays 15. Autobiographies and memoirs 16. Life stories — Relationships — Couples 17. Life stories — Identity — Race and ethnicity 18. Society and culture — Race

LC 2023026570

Told through one Asian and Black interracial relationship, this author, in this funny and moving memoir in essays, chronicles her own sweeping romance while reckoning with caste, race, colorism and mental health and seamlessly weaving in history, pop culture and politics to reaffirm the idea that allyship is an act of true love.

"Sharma debuts with a memoir in essays as she talks about her love story with a Black man and the racism they encounter due to their interracial marriage." —*Library Journal*

Includes bibliographical references.

Shatner, William
Boldly Go: Reflections on a Life of Awe and Wonder. William Shatner with Joshua Brandon. Atria Books 2022. 320 p.
ISBN 9781668007327
Grades: Adult — B
1. Shatner, William 2. Nature 3. Exploration 4. Acting 5. Interpersonal relations 6. Actors and actresses 7. Autobiographies and memoirs 8. Canadian literature 9. Life stories — Arts and culture — Performing arts — Actors and actresses 10. Arts and Entertainment — Movies and Television

The beloved star of Star Trek and recent space traveler reflects on the interconnectivity of all things, our fragile bond with nature and the joy that comes from exploration.

"Acting legend Shatner, now a vibrant 91, looks back at his adventures, including a recent trip into space on Jeff Bezos' Blue Origin, and ahead to what's still to come in this collection of essays penned with Brandon." —*Booklist*

Live Long And—: What I Learned Along the Way. William Shatner; with David Fisher. Thomas Dunne Books 2018. 224 p.
ISBN 9781250166692
Grades: Adult — B
1. Shatner, William 2. Actors and actresses 3. Quality of life 4. Personal conduct 5. Men and success 6. Acting 7. Health 8. Childhood 9. Autobiographies and memoirs 10. Canadian literature 11. Life stories — Arts and culture — Performing arts — Actors and actresses 12. Arts and Entertainment — Movies and Television

LC 2018012331

The "Star Trek" legend reflects on his career and the health scare that informed and reinforced his beliefs about living a good life, sharing engaging stories about his childhood, personal setbacks, and iconic successes.

"Anyone who has read a Shatner book or seen him speak in person is familiar with his anecdotal, conversational style, and although there aren't a lot of Star Trek memories referenced here, fans will enjoy Shatner's musings on his passions and adventures." —*Booklist*

Includes bibliographical references and index.

Shattuck, Ben
Six Walks: In the Footsteps of Henry David Thoreau. Ben Shattuck. Tin House 2022. 175 pages
ISBN 9781953534040
Grades: Adult — B
1. Shattuck, Ben, 1984- 2. Thoreau, Henry David, 1817-1862 3. Walking 4. Nature 5. Walks 6. Men and nature 7. Loss 8. Voyages and travels 9. New England 10. Autobiographies and memoirs 11. Nature Writing — Personal Responses 12. Nature Writing — Natural Landscapes 13. Travel Writing — United States 14. Life stories — Nature and outdoors

LC 2021050923

On an autumn morning in 1849, Henry David Thoreau stepped out his front door to walk the beaches of Cape Cod. Over a century and a half later, Ben Shattuck does the same. Over years of following Thoreau, Shattuck finds himself uncovering new insights about family, love, friendship, and fatherhood, and understanding more deeply the lessons walking can offer through life's changing seasons. Intimate, entertaining, and beautifully crafted, Six Walks is a resounding tribute to the ways walking in nature can inspire us all.

"In this resplendent debut, Pushcart Prize winner Shattuck traipses from quiet elegy to compassionate celebration through a series of jaunts patterned after Henry David Thoreau's rambles....Echoing Thoreau's brilliant reflections with his own, Shattuck distills the healing power of nature into a narrative that's a pure pleasure to wander through." —*Publishers Weekly*

Includes bibliographical references.

Shawcross, William
The Queen Mother: The Official Biography. William Shawcross. Alfred A. Knopf 2009. 1120 p.
ISBN 9781400043040
Grades: Adult — B
1. Elizabeth, Queen, consort of George VI, King of Great Britain, 1900-2002 2. Women and politics 3. Monarchy 4. Women rulers 5. British history 6. Great Britain 7. 20th century 8. Biographies 9. History writing — Europe — United Kingdom 10. Life stories — Politics — Royalty

The official and definitive biography of Queen Elizabeth the Queen Mother: Consort of King George VI, mother of Queen Elizabeth II, grandmother of Prince Charles—and the most beloved British monarch of the twentieth century. A revelatory royal biography that is, as well, a singular history of Britain in the twentieth century.

Shearer, Stephen Michael
Beautiful: The Life of Hedy Lamarr. Stephen Michael Shearer. Thomas Dunne Books 2010. 432 p.
ISBN 9780312550981
Grades: Adult — B
1. Lamarr, Hedy, 1913-2000 2. Spread spectrum communications 3. Women inventors 4. Films 5. Actors and actresses 6. Biographies 7. Life stories — Arts and culture — Performing arts — Actors and actresses 8. Arts and Entertainment — Movies and Television

LC 2010013058

Providing probing and detailed coverage of Hedy Lamarr's five marriages, children, various lawsuits, radio roles and shoplifting headlines, Shearer has combined extensive archival research with insightful interview quotes. The result is a fascinating biography that recreates Hollywood's Golden Age of Glamour.

"This biography chronicles the life of Hollywood legend Hedy Lamarr, from her cosseted childhood in an assimilated Jewish family in Austria to her early breaks in Max Reinhardt's internationally famous theater company; her scandalous, career-launching nude scene in the Czech film Ecstasy; her tortured first marriage to Jewish Nazi arms manufacturer Friedrich Mandl (dubbed an honorary Aryan by the Third Reich); and her daring escape from the sadistic Mandl and Nazi Germany to Los Angeles and MGM. One finishes the book feeling that one has read a complete portrait of Hedy Lamarr, actor and inventor, a biography that reveals, with drama and wit, how much more there was to this complex, brilliant woman than her ethereal natural beauty." —*Booklist*

Sheehan, Jason
Cooking Dirty: A Story of Life, Sex, Love and Death in the Kitchen. Jason Sheehan. Farrar, Straus and Giroux 2009. 368 p.
ISBN 9780374289218
Grades: Adult — B
1. Sheehan, Jason 2. Cooks 3. Food writers 4. Cooking 5. Kitchens 6. Restaurants 7. Autobiographies and memoirs 8. Biographies 9. Food writing — Memoirs and biographies 10. Life stories — Business — Working life

LC 2008047158

Library Journal Best Books, 2009.

ESSENTIAL AND RECOMMENDED TITLES
Biography

Describes the James Beard Award-winning author's experiences in a series of kitchens from a pizzeria and a French colonial to an all-night diner and a crab shack, jobs during which he fraternized with cooking staffs throughout numerous professional and personal challenges.

"Sheehan's memoir is emphatically not about the glam end of cooking or celebrity chefs, but about a straight blue-collar gig, where the kitchens are staffed by the kind of guys who get off on the fact that the work is insanely grueling. The war stories are as profane and outrageous as you'd expect, and Sheehan finds just the right balance between bravado and humility." —*Publishers Weekly*

Sheehan, Neil
A Fiery Peace in a Cold War: Bernard Schriever and the Ultimate Weapon. Neil Sheehan. Random House 2009. 560 p.
ISBN 9780679422846
Grades: Adult **B**
1. Schriever, Bernard A. 2. Cold War 3. Intercontinental ballistic missiles 4. Nuclear weapons 5. Military aviation 6. Astronautics 7. Generals 8. Aviation history 9. Military engineering 10. United States 11. Biographies 12. History writing — Cold War 13. History writing — Military — Weapons
LC 2009002247
New York Times Notable Book, 2009.

The Pulitzer- and National Book Award-winning author of a Bright Shining Lie chronicles the mid-twentieth-century effort to prevent the Soviet Union from acquiring nuclear superiority, in an account that describes the pivotal contributions of Bernard Schriever, Eisenhower, and Stalin.

Includes bibliographical references and index.

Sheff, David
The Buddhist on Death Row: How One Man Found Light in the Darkest Place. David Sheff. Simon & Schuster 2020. 320 pages
ISBN 9781982128456
Grades: Adult **B**
1. Masters, Jarvis Jay, 1962- 2. Buddhists 3. Death row prisoners 4. Meditation 5. Buddhist meditation 6. Psychological growth 7. Prisoners 8. African American men 9. United States 10. Biographies 11. Life stories — Law and order — Prisoners and inmates 12. Life stories — Religion and spirituality — Spiritual journeys 13. Spirituality and Religion — Buddhism
LC 2019040344

The #1 New York Times bestselling author of Beautiful Boy explores the transformation of Jarvis Jay Masters who became one of America's most respected Buddhist practitioners during his two decades in solitary confinement in San Quentin.

"An indelible portrait of an incarcerated man finding new life and purpose behind bars." —*Kirkus*

Shehadeh, Raja
★ *We Could Have Been Friends, My Father and I: A Palestinian Memoir.* Raja Shehadeh. Other Press 2023. 160 p.
ISBN 9781635423648
Grades: Adult **B**
1. Shehadeh, Raja, 1951- 2. Shehadeh, Aziz 3. Lawyers 4. Political activists 5. Human rights 6. Palestinian men 7. Arab-Israeli conflict 8. Fathers and sons 9. Death of fathers 10. Children of murder victims 11. Love 12. Regret 13. Family relationships 14. Ethnic Identity 15. Social advocacy 16. Southwest Asian (Middle Eastern) people 17. Palestinian people 18. Autobiographies and memoirs 19. Life stories — Facing adversity — War and oppression 20. Life stories — Relationships — Parent and child 21. History writing — Arab-Israeli relations — Southwest Asia and North Africa (Middle East) 22. History writing — Wars and conflicts — Arab-Israeli conflict
LC 2022027365
National Book Award for Nonfiction finalist, 2023.

A subtle psychological portrait of the author's relationship with his father during the twentieth-century battle for Palestinian human rights. Aziz Shehadeh was many things: Lawyer, activist, and political detainee, he was also the father of bestsellingauthor and activist Raja. In this new and searingly personal memoir, Raja Shehadeh unpicks the snags and complexities of their relationship. This is not only the story of the battle against the various oppressors of the Palestinians, but a moving portrait of a particular father and son relationship.

"A well-established Palestinian voice fashions a loving portrayal of the unsung achievements of his activist father." —*Kirkus*

First published in Great Britain in 2022 by Profile Books.

Shelden, Michael
Mark Twain: Man in White : The Grand Adventure of His Final Years. Michael Shelden. Random House 2010. 528 p.
ISBN 9780679448006
Grades: 11 12 Adult **B**
1. Twain, Mark, 1835-1910 2. Authors, American 3. Humorists 4. Writing 5. United States history 6. 19th century 7. Biographies 8. Arts and Entertainment — Writing and Publishing 9. Life stories — Arts and culture — Writing — Authors
LC 2009019719
Library Journal Best Books, 2010.

Drawing heavily on Twain's own letters and journals, Shelden illuminates Mark Twain's twilight years in this account of the legendary author's life, recounting both Twain's private family experiences and his larger-than-life public image.

Includes bibliographical references.

Sherman, Casey
Hunting Whitey: The Inside Story of the Capture & Killing of America's Most Wanted Crime Boss. Casey Sherman and Dave Wedge. William Morrow 2020. 340 p.
ISBN 9780062972545
Grades: Adult **B**
1. Bulger, Whitey, 1929-2018 2. Crime bosses 3. Organized crime 4. Fugitives 5. Assassins 6. Murder victims 7. Informers 8. Women FBI agents 9. Criminal investigation 10. Trials 11. Violent crimes 12. Boston, Massachusetts 13. Biographies 14. Life stories — Law and order — Criminals and law-breakers 15. True Crime — Organized Crime, Mafia, and Gangs 16. True Crime — Investigations and Trials
LC BI2020012645

For the first time, Boston reporters Casey Sherman and Dave Wedge draw on exclusive interviews and exhaustive investigative reportage to tell the complete story of Whitey Bulger, one of the most notorious crime bosses in American history, and a longtime FBI informant. The leader of Boston's Winter Hill Gang and #1 on the FBI's Most Wanted list, Bulger was indicted for nineteen counts of murder, racketeering, narcotics distribution, and extortion. But it was his sixteen-year flight from justice on the eve of his arrest that made him a legend and exposed deep corruption within the FBI. Granted access to exclusive prison letters and interviews with dozens of people connected to the case on both sides, Sherman and Wedge offer a trove of fascinating new stories and create an incomparable portrait of one of the most infamous criminals in American history.

"A deeply unpleasant but highly readable story of crime and punishment." —*Kirkus*

Sherr, Lynn
Sally Ride: America's First Woman in Space. Lynn Sherr. Simon & Schuster 2014. 320 p.
ISBN 9781476725765
Grades: 11 12 Adult **B**
1. Ride, Sally 2. Space programs 3. Sexism 4. Women physicists 5. Lesbians 6. Astronauts 7. Women astronauts 8. International competition 9. United States 10. Biographies 11. Life stories — Science, technology, and medicine — Astronauts and pilots 12. Science Writing — Space and Flight 13. History writing — Women's history 14. Adult books for young adults
LC 2013039647
Amelia Bloomer List, 2015; Booklist Editors' Choice, 2014.

Sally Ride, the first American woman to go into space, competed successfully in the male-dominated profession of physics and became an inspiration to girls who dreamed of science careers. Journalist Lynn Sherr, drawing on materials provided by Ride's family and friends as well as official records and Sherr's own friendship with Ride, offers a moving and sensitive portrait of this pioneer who guarded her private life—her long-term lesbian relationship only became known through her obituary.

Includes bibliographical references and index.

Shields, Aomawa L.

Life on Other Planets: A Memoir of Finding My Place in the Universe. Aomawa Shields. Viking, an imprint of Penguin Random House LLC 2023. 288 p.

ISBN 9780593299180

Grades: Adult   **B**

1. Shields, Aomawa L. 2. Women astronomers 3. Astronomers 4. Belonging 5. African American women 6. Cosmobiology 7. Actors and actresses 8. Purpose in life 9. Astronomy 10. Marginalized women 11. Identity 12. Motherhood 13. Autobiographies and memoirs 14. Life stories — Science, technology, and medicine 15. Science Writing — Space and flight

LC 2022043791

The pioneering Black astronomer and astrobiologist recalls her journey from a professional acting career to scaling to the top of her scientific field studying the universe outside our solar system.

"In her first book, Shields unpacks her experiences as a rare Black woman in the STEM disciplines and how she was inspired to begin widening the opportunities for others…A lyrical, image-rich investigation of an unconventional blueprint for authentic living." —*Kirkus*

Includes bibliographical references.

Shields, Charles J.

Lorraine Hansberry: The Life Behind a Raisin in the Sun. Charles J. Shields. Henry Holt and Company 2022. 352 p.

ISBN 9781250205537

Grades: Adult   **B**

1. Hansberry, Lorraine, 1930-1965 2. Playwrights, American 3. African American playwrights 4. African American women civil rights workers 5. African American women 6. Playwrights 7. Civil rights workers 8. Biographies 9. Arts and entertainment — Theater 10. Life stories — Politics — Activists and reformers 11. Life stories — Arts and culture — Performing arts

LC 2021047382

The moving story of the life of the woman behind a Raisin in the Sun, the most widely anthologized, read, and performed play of the American stage.

"This biography substantiates Hansberry's accomplishments, despite her short life." —*Library Journal*

Includes bibliographical references and index.

Shih, David

Chinese Prodigal: A Memoir in Eight Arguments. David Shih. Atlantic Monthly Press 2023. 304 p.

ISBN 9780802158994

Grades: Adult   **B**

1. Shih, David, 1970- 2. Chinese Americans 3. Identity 4. Fathers and sons 5. Race relations 6. Children of immigrants 7. American dream 8. Racism 9. United States 10. Wisconsin 11. Dallas, Texas 12. Autobiographies and memoirs 13. Life stories — Identity — Race and ethnicity 14. Family and relationships — Families 15. Life stories — Relationships — Family

LC 2023011447

From an exciting and sharp-voiced new observer of American culture, a forthright and probing debut exploring Asian American identity in a racially codified country.

"University of Wisconsin-Eau Claire English professor Shih presents a raw, moving debut memoir about his complicated relationship with his father and his Asian American identity…It amounts to a thoughtful meditation on the gap between the promise the American dream dangles in front of minorities and the realities of their discriminatory treatment." —*Publishers Weekly*

Shipnuck, Alan

Phil: The Rip-roaring and Unauthorized! Biography of Golf's Most Colorful Superstar. Alan Shipnuck. Avid Reader Press 2022. 256 p.

ISBN 9781476797090

Grades: Adult   **B**

1. Mickelson, Phil, 1970- 2. Professional golfers 3. Professional golf 4. Personal conduct 5. Golf 6. Sports 7. Golfers 8. Biographies 9. Life stories — Sports — Athletes 10. Sports and competition — Golf 11. Sports and Competition — Individual Athlete

In this raw, uncensored and unauthorized biography of the legendary golf champion, a longtime Sports Illustrated writer and best-selling author delves deep into all the rumors and controversies that have forever dogged Phil Mickelson, while celebrating his random acts of kindness and generosity of spirit.

Sports Illustrated writer Shipnuck (Bud, Sweat, and Tees) delivers a rollicking look at the career of legendary golfer Phil Mickelson, a 'Subject of much fascination and more than a little scorn.' —*Publishers Weekly*

Shirley, Craig

Mary Ball Washington: The Untold Story of George Washington's Mother. Craig Shirley. Broadside 2019. 400 pages

ISBN 9780062456519

Grades: Adult   **B**

1. Washington, Mary Ball, 1708-1789 2. Washington, George, 1732-1799 3. Washington family 4. Mothering 5. Mothers and sons 6. Widows 7. Generation gap 8. Faith (Christianity) 9. Saving and thrift 10. Slaveholders 11. Families 12. Presidents 13. United States history 14. United States 15. Virginia 16. Colonial America (1600-1775) 17. Revolutionary America (1775-1783) 18. Biographies 19. Life stories — People in history — Famous families 20. History writing — Presidency — United States

LC 2019021060

In Mary Ball Washington, New York Times bestselling author Craig Shirley uncovers startling details about the inner workings of the Washington family. He vividly brings to life a resilient widow who singlehandedly raised six children and ran a large farm at a time when most women's duties were relegated to household matters. Throughout, Shirley compares and contrasts mother and son, illuminating the qualities they shared and the differences that divided them.

Includes bibliographical references and index.

Shlaes, Amity

Coolidge. Amity Shlaes. HarperCollins 2012. 480 p.

ISBN 9780061967559

Grades: Adult   **B**

1. Coolidge, Calvin, 1872-1933 2. Public opinion 3. Popularity 4. Prosperity 5. Republicans 6. Former lawyers 7. Government regulation 8. Economic policy 9. Economics 10. Presidents 11. New England history 12. United States history 13. Washington, D.C. 14. United States 15. 1920s 16. 20th century 17. Biographies 18. History writing — Presidency — 20th century — United States 19. Life stories — Politics — Politicians

LC 2012032098

Examines America's thirtieth president, revealing a man who restored national trust in government, lived by example, suffered great tragedy, emphasized the importance of presidential humility, and inspired optimism.

Short, Martin

I Must Say: My Life as a Humble Comedy Legend. Martin Short. HarperCollins 2014. 320 p.

ISBN 9780062309525

Grades: Adult   **B**

1. Short, Martin, 1950- 2. Comedians 3. Actors and actresses 4. Autobiographies and memoirs 5. Canadian literature 6. Life stories — Arts and culture — Performing arts — Entertainers and celebrities 7. Arts and entertainment — Movies and television

LC 2014028617

A memoir by Canadian comedian, Martin Short, known for his work on SCTV and Saturday night live, his roles in a number of great comedy films, and his memorable theatrical appearances.

"A true vaudevillian, Short is always on as he delivers funny anecdotes from a diffuse and storied career." —*Kirkus*

ESSENTIAL AND RECOMMENDED TITLES
Biography

Short, Philip
Putin. Philip Short. Henry Holt & Company 2022. 848 p.
ISBN 9781627793667
Grades: Adult B
1. Putin, Vladimir Vladimirovich, 1952- 2. Political leadership 3. Presidents 4. Politics and government 5. Economics 6. Russia 7. Biographies 8. Life stories — Politics — Politicians 9. History writing — Europe — Russia

The monumental biography of the most influential leader on the world stage in the last twenty years. Vladimir Putin is a pariah to the West. He has the power to reduce the United States and Europe to ashes in a nuclear firestorm and has threatened to do so. He invades his neighbours, most recently Ukraine, meddles in western elections and orders assassinations inside and outside Russia. The regime he heads is autocratic and corrupt. Yet many Russians continue to support him. By fair means or foul, under Putin's leadership, Russia has once again become a force to be reckoned with.

"Short's robustly researched biography of Vladimir Putin mines the Russian autocrat's past for perspective on his recent maneuvers." —*Booklist*

Shteyngart, Gary
★ *Little Failure: A Memoir.* Gary Shteyngart. Random House 2014. 369 pages
ISBN 9780679643753
Grades: Adult B
1. Shteyngart, Gary, 1972- 2. Growing up 3. Jewish people 4. Russian people in the United States 5. Immigrants, Russian 6. Authors, American 7. Russian people 8. Queens, New York City 9. 21st century 10. Autobiographies and memoirs 11. Life stories — Relationships — Growing up 12. Family and Relationships — Growing Up
LC 2013013217

LibraryReads Favorites, 2014; New York Times Notable Book, 2014; National Book Critics Circle Award for Autobiography/Memoir finalist.

Traces the author's uproarious experiences as a young bullied Jewish-Russian immigrant in Queens, his haphazard college pursuits and his initial forays into a literary career.

"An immigrant's memoir like few others, with as sharp an edge and as much stylistic audacity as the author's well-received novels." —*Kirkus*

Shuster, Simon
★ *The Showman: Inside the Invasion That Shook the World and Made a Leader of Volodymyr Zelensky.* Simon Shuster. William Morrow & Company 2024. 352 p.
ISBN 9780063307421
Grades: Adult B
1. Zelensky, Volodymyr, 1978- 2. War 3. International relations 4. World leaders 5. Politicians 6. Politics and government 7. Ukraine 8. 21st century 9. Biographies 10. Life stories — Politics — Politicians 11. History Writing — Europe

An acclaimed journalist gives readers the first inside account of the Russian invasion of Ukraine from the perspective of President Volodymyr Zelensky and his team, who granted him unprecedented access.

Time magazine correspondent Shuster debuts with an up-close account of Ukrainian president Volodymyr Zelensky's transformation from comedian and political satirist to steadfast wartime leader and world symbol of 'Fortitude.' —*Publishers Weekly*

Sielski, Mike
The Rise: Kobe Bryant and the Pursuit of Immortality. Mike Sielski. St. Martin's Press 2022. 352 p.
ISBN 9781250275721
Grades: Adult B
1. Bryant, Kobe, 1978-2020 2. Basketball players 3. African American basketball players 4. Basketball 5. Professional basketball players 6. Sports 7. United States 8. Biographies 9. Life stories — Sports — Athletes 10. Sports and competition — Basketball
LC 2021037759

The inside look at one of the most captivating and consequential figures in our culture with never-before-seen material. Kobe Bryant's death in January 2020 did more than rattle the worlds of sports and celebrity. The tragedy of that helicopter crash unveiled the full breadth and depth of his influence on our culture, and by tracing and telling the oft-forgotten and lesser-known story of his early life, the Rise promises to provide an insight into Kobe that no other analysis has. This will be more than a basketball book. This will be an exploration of the identity and making of an icon and the effect of his development on those around him-the essence of the man before he truly became a man.

"Philadelphia Inquirer columnist Sielski (Fading Echoes) presents a riveting chronicle of the life of basketball superstar Kobe Bryant (1978-2020) from his youth up to when 'Great things' were just beginning to happen.... Fans will relish this nuanced take on an oft-overlooked part of the legend's remarkable story." —*Publishers Weekly*

Includes bibliographical references and index.

Simmons, Ruth
★ *Up Home: One Girl's Journey.* Ruth J. Simmons. Random House 2023. 224 p.
ISBN 9780593446003
Grades: Adult B
1. Simmons, Ruth, 1945- 2. African American women 3. Women educators 4. College presidents 5. Universities and colleges 6. Growing up 7. African American sharecroppers 8. Rural life 9. Familial love 10. Education 11. Ambition 12. Identity 13. North American people 14. American people 15. Leadership 16. Texas 17. Southern States 18. Autobiographies and memoirs 19. Life stories — Education — Scholars and educators 20. Life stories — Identity — Race and ethnicity 21. Life stories — Relationships — Growing up
LC 2023010288

Both an origin story set in the segregated South and an uplifting story of girlhood, the first Black president of an Ivy League University who has inspired generations of students as she herself made history depicts an era long gone but whose legacies of inequality we still live with today.

"Simmons, who became the first Black president of an Ivy League institution in 2001 when she took that position at Brown University, chronicles the first 22 years of her life, in this poignant and inspiring memoir." —*Publishers Weekly*

Simmons, Sylvie
I'm Your Man: The Life of Leonard Cohen. Sylvie Simmons. Ecco Press 2012. 384 p.
ISBN 9780061994982
Grades: Adult B
1. Cohen, Leonard, 1934-2016 2. Songwriters 3. Musicians 4. Buddhism 5. Men-women relations 6. Biographies 7. Arts and Entertainment — Music 8. Life stories — Arts and culture — Performing arts — Musicians and composers
LC 2013560061

Booklist Editors' Choice, 2012.

Exploring the many facets of Cohen's life, this intimate portrait of one of the most important and influential songwriters of our time draws upon his private archives and a wealth of interviews with many of his closest associates, colleagues and other artists whose work he has inspired.

Simon, Marie
Underground in Berlin: A Young Woman's Extraordinary Tale of Survival in the Heart of Nazi Germany. Marie Simon, translated by Anthea Bell. Little Brown & Co. 2015. 368 p.
ISBN 9780316382090
Grades: Adult B
1. Simon, Marie, 1922-1998 2. Jewish people 3. Hiding 4. Deception 5. Holocaust (1933-1945) 6. Jewish women 7. World War II 8. Nazis 9. Impostors 10. Western European people 11. German people 12. Religious persecution 13. Berlin, Germany 14. 1940s 15. Translations — German to English 16. Autobiographies and memoirs 17. Life stories — Facing adversity — War and oppression — Holocaust 18. History writing — Wars and conflicts — Holocaust — World War II
LC 2015935821

In this absorbing memoir, author Marie Jalowicz Simon relates her experiences as a hidden Jew in Berlin during World War II. In 1941, when she realized that the SS was likely to round her up for deportation to a concentration camp, she disappeared into the city, relying on family and friends to help her survive to the end of the war. Simon's son Hermann transcribed his mother's unusual odyssey from her tape recordings. This emotionally touching but unsentimental account expresses hope for the future.

Also published: Toronto : Knopf Canada, 2015; Translation of: Untergetaucht, 2014.

Simpson, J. A.
The Word Detective: Searching for the Meaning of It All at the Oxford English Dictionary. John Simpson. Basic Books 2016. 336 p.
ISBN 9780465060696
Grades: Adult   B
1. Simpson, J. A, 1953- 2. Lexicographers 3. Lexicography 4. Dictionaries 5. Autobiographies and memoirs 6. Life stories — Arts and culture — Writing 7. Arts and entertainment — Writing and publishing
LC 2016025594

The Word Detective is John Simpson's memoir as the former Chief Editor of the Oxford English Dictionary (OED). Simpson takes us from his first encounter with the dictionary in the old-fashioned world of Oxford in 1976 through to his retirement as Chief Editor thirty-seven years later. Simpson introduces us to the dusty basement archives and the traditional OED afternoon tea ceremony, and recounts the personal adventures of a life well lived, from marriage, to the birth of his two daughters. Simpson presents lexicography as an examination of the links between our language and our history.

Includes index.

Sims, Michael
Arthur and Sherlock: Conan Doyle and the Creation of Holmes. Michael Sims. Bloomsbury USA 2017. 320 p.
ISBN 9781632860392
Grades: Adult   B
1. Doyle, Arthur Conan, Sir, 1859-1930 2. Mystery authors 3. Authors, Scottish 4. Holmes, Sherlock (Fictitious character) 5. Detectives in literature 6. 19th century 7. Biographies 8. Life stories — Arts and culture — Writing — Authors 9. Arts and entertainment — Writing and publishing
LC 2016033351

The author of The Story of Charlotte's Web explores the rich events behind the creation of young Arthur Conan Doyle's iconic detective, revealing the impact of his early poverty and medical experience on the development of his characters and stories.

"Sims's skill and deftness with narrative biography will lead Sherlockians to hope that he continues the story of Conan Doyle's life in a future volume." —*Publishers Weekly*

Sinclair, Safiya
★ *How to Say Babylon.* Safiya Sinclair. 37 Ink 2023. 448 p.
ISBN 9781982132330
Grades: Adult   B
1. Sinclair, Safiya 2. Women poets 3. Growing up 4. Patriarchy 5. Gender role 6. Rastafari movement 7. Rastafarians 8. Fathers and daughters 9. Family violence 10. Culture 11. Self 12. Childhood 13. Families 14. Identity 15. Autobiographies and memoirs 16. Book club best bets 17. Life stories — Identity — Gender 18. Life stories — Relationships — Growing up 19. Family and relationships — Growing up

National Book Critics Circle Award for Autobiography, 2023; Shortlisted for the Women's Prize for Non-Fiction, 2024.

This stunning story of the author's struggle to break free of her strict Rastafarian upbringing ruled by a father whose rigid beliefs, rage and paranoia led to violence shows how found her own power and provides a unique glimpse into a rarefied world we know little about.

"Sinclair's gorgeous prose is rife with glimmering details, and the narrative's ending lands as both inevitable and surprising. More than catharsis; this is memoir as liberation." —*Kirkus*

Singh, Julietta
The Breaks: An Essay. Julietta Singh. Coffee House Press 2021. 168 p.
ISBN 9781566896160
Grades: Adult   B
1. Singh, Julietta, 1976- 2. Indian people in the United States 3. Mother and child 4. Mothering 5. LGBTQIA+ people 6. Inheritance and succession 7. Parenting 8. Families 9. Family relationships 10. Interracial couples 11. Queer theory 12. Racism 13. United States 14. Autobiographies and memoirs 15. Life stories — Identity — LGBTQIA+ 16. Family and Relationships — Parenting 17. Life stories — Relationships — Family
LC 2021007841

An epistolary essay about race, inheritance, and mothering at the end of the world.

In a letter to her six-year-old daughter, Julietta Singh writes about such topics as race, queer mothering, and climate change.

"In this epistolary memoir, a queer, biracial scholar writes to her daughter about what it's like 'To mother at the end of the world.' . . . A well-argued book-length essay about queer, multiracial parenting." —*Kirkus*

Sinise, Gary
Grateful American: A Journey from Self to Service. Gary Sinise with Marcus Brotherton. Nelson Books 2019. 272 p.
ISBN 9781400208128
Grades: Adult   B
1. Sinise, Gary 2. Veterans 3. Actors and actresses 4. People with disabilities 5. Helpfulness 6. United States 7. Autobiographies and memoirs 8. Biographies 9. Life stories — Arts and culture — Performing arts — Actors and actresses 10. Debut title
LC 2018032657

Gary Sinise shares the never-before-told story of his journey from troublemaking Chicago kid to cofounder of the legendary Steppenwolf Theater Company, world-famous actor, and tireless advocate for America's active duty defenders, veterans, and first responders.

Sipress, David
What's so Funny?: A Cartoonist's Memoir. David Sipress. Mariner Books 2022. 240 p.
ISBN 9780358659099
Grades: Adult   B
1. Sipress, David 2. Cartoonists 3. Jewish families 4. Family relationships 5. Cartoons 6. Dysfunctional families 7. Growing up 8. New York City 9. Autobiographies and memoirs 10. Life stories — Arts and culture — Artists 11. Arts and Entertainment — Comics, Cartoons, and Animation 12. Life stories — Relationships — Family 13. Life stories — Relationships — Growing up 14. Family and Relationships — Families 15. Family and relationships — Growing up

From a longtime New Yorker staff cartoonist comes an evocative family memoir, a love letter to New York City, and a delightful exploration of the origins of creativity—richly interleaved with the author's witty, beloved cartoons.

"New Yorker cartoonist Sipress (It's a Cat's Life) draws on his gift for evoking the predicaments of human nature to tell beguiling stories about his life and career. . . . The result is a delightful jaunt through an inspiring artist's mind." —*Publishers Weekly*

Skaife, Christopher
The Ravenmaster: My Life with the Ravens at the Tower of London. Ravenmaster Christopher Skaife, Yeoman Warder of Her Majesty's Royal Palace and Fortress, the Tower of London. Farrar, Straus and Giroux 2018. 256 p.
ISBN 9780374113346
Grades: Adult   B
1. Skaife, Christopher, 1965- 2. Ravens 3. Men and birds 4. Animal intelligence 5. Animal behavior 6. Human-animal relationships 7. London, England 8. Autobiographies and memoirs 9. Life stories — Relationships
LC 2018016402

Yeoman Warder Christopher Skaife describes his years of service to the Queen, which include caring for the infamous ravens of the Tower of London,

ESSENTIAL AND RECOMMENDED TITLES
Biography

painting a vivid and intimate portrait of these intelligent, unusual and often misunderstood birds.
Includes index.

Skloot, Rebecca
★ *The Immortal Life of Henrietta Lacks.* Rebecca Skloot. Crown Publishers 2009. x, 369 p, 8 p. of plates : Illustration; Color
ISBN 9781400052172
Grades: 8 9 10 11 12 Adult B
1. Lacks, Henrietta, 1920-1951 2. People with cancer 3. Cell culture 4. Medical ethics 5. Scientific discoveries 6. Medical research 7. Human experimentation in medicine 8. Cancer research 9. Bioethics 10. African American women 11. Biographies 12. Page to screen 13. Life stories — Facing adversity — Medical issues 14. Science Writing — Biology 15. Nonfiction that reads like fiction 16. Book club best bets
LC 2009031785

ALA Notable Book, 2011; Booklist Editors' Choice, 2010; Goodreads Choice Award, 2010; Library Journal Best Books, 2010; National Academies Communication Award, 2011; New York Times Notable Book, 2010; Science Books and Films Prize for Excellence in Science Books, Science Book for High School Readers, 2011.

Documents the story of how scientists took cells from an unsuspecting descendant of freed slaves and created a human cell line that has been kept alive indefinitely, enabling discoveries in such areas as cancer research, in vitro fertilization and gene mapping.

Adapted into a film by HBO network and released in 2017; Includes bibliographical references and index.

Slate, Jenny
Little Weirds. Jenny Slate. Little, Brown 2019. 304 p.
ISBN 9780316485340
Grades: Adult B
1. Slate, Jenny 2. Loss 3. Growing up 4. Female friendship 5. Self-care 6. Creativity 7. Actors and actresses 8. Autobiographies and memoirs 9. Essays 10. Life stories — Arts and culture — Performing arts — Actors and actresses 11. Life stories — Relationships
LC 2019933749

LibraryReads Favorites, 2019.

The actress, stand-up comedian and best-selling children's book author explores her internal self, dreams and insecurities through bursts of writing on a wide range of subjects from heartbreak and divorce, to the smell of honeysuckle and a French-kissing rabbit.

"This volume mixes the oddball self-examination of Jenny Lawson with moments of poetic insight. Recommended for lovers of fizzy memoirs." —*Library Journal*

Slawenski, Kenneth
★ *Salinger: A Life.* Kenneth Slawenski. Random House 2010. 464 p.
ISBN 9781400069514
Grades: 10 11 12 Adult B
1. Salinger, J. D. (Jerome David), 1919-2010 2. Writing 3. Creativity 4. Authors, American 5. 20th century 6. Biographies 7. Arts and Entertainment — Writing and Publishing 8. Life stories — Arts and culture — Writing — Authors 9. Adult books for young adults
LC 2010008926

Examines the life of the reclusive author of "Catcher in the Rye," including his encounters with celebrities, his love life, his devotion to Eastern religion, and his conflicted relationship with his success.
Includes bibliographical references and index.

Slevin, Peter
Michelle Obama: A Life. Peter Slevin. Alfred A. Knopf 2015. 384 p.
ISBN 9780307958822
Grades: Adult B
1. Obama, Michelle, 1964- 2. African American women 3. Politicians' spouses 4. Presidential election, 2008 5. Presidents' spouses 6. United States 7. 21st century 8. Biographies 9. History writing — Presidency — 21st century — United States 10. Life stories — Politics — Politicians
LC 2014041100

Here is the first comprehensive account of the life and times of Michelle Obama, a woman of achievement and purpose—and the most unlikely first lady in modern American history.

"She is one of his greatest assets in public office and an important foil to criticism that he is not Black enough. Slevin delivers a somewhat fawning portrait, but when necessary, he is willing to criticize and reveal his subject's missteps." —*Kirkus*

Slouka, Mark
Nobody's Son: A Memoir. Mark Slouka. W. W. Norton & Company 2016. 304 p.
ISBN 9780393292305
Grades: Adult B
1. Slouka, Mark 2. Mothers and sons 3. Family secrets 4. Refugees 5. Czech Americans 6. Authors, American 7. Autobiographies and memoirs 8. Life stories — Facing adversity — War and oppression — Refugees 9. Life stories — Relationships — Parent and child
LC 2016018257

Library Journal Best Books, 2016.

The son of Czechoslovakian parents who were smuggled out of their country to escape the Nazis, only to endure postwar Communist purges traces the experiences of the war's refugees and the author's own efforts to reconnect with his mother through a labyrinth of trauma, displacement and denial.

Smarsh, Sarah
★ *Heartland: A Memoir of Working Hard and Being Broke in the Richest Country on Earth.* Sarah Smarsh. Simon & Schuster 2018. 304 p.
ISBN 9781501133091
Grades: Adult B
1. Smarsh, Sarah 2. Poverty 3. Working class 4. Income inequality 5. Classism 6. Inequality 7. Poor families 8. Class conflict 9. Family history 10. Kansas 11. Autobiographies and memoirs 12. Society and culture — Wealth and class — Poverty 13. Life stories — Facing adversity — Personal transformation 14. Business and economics — Economics — Socioeconomics
LC 2017301189

National Book Award for Nonfiction finalist, 2018; Kirkus Prize for Nonfiction finalist, 2018.

Reveals one woman's experience of working-class poverty with a startlingly observed, eye-opening and topical personal story.

"Will appeal to readers who enjoy memoirs and to sociologists. While Smarsh ends on a hopeful note, she offers a searing indictment of how the poor are viewed and treated in this country." —*Library Journal*

Smiley, Jane
Thirteen Ways of Looking at the Novel. Jane Smiley. Knopf 2005. x, 591 p.
ISBN 9781400040599
Grades: Adult B
1. Smiley, Jane 2. Authors, American 3. Fiction writing 4. Books and reading 5. United States 6. 20th century 7. Arts and Entertainment — Writing and Publishing
LC 2005045181

The author celebrates the art of fiction as she looks at one hundred very different examples of the novel, ranging from the classics to little-known gems, and discusses the evolution of the novel and the practice of novel-writing.

"The book is roughly divided into three sections: the first classifies the novel, beginning with the most simple of definitions (e.g., it's long, in prose, has a protagonist), and adds moral and aesthetic complexity as it moves along. The second section consists of a primer for fledgling novelists. The result is a thorough reflection on the art and craft of the novel from one of its best-known contemporary practitioners." —*Publishers Weekly*

PUBLIC LIBRARY CORE COLLECTION: NONFICTION
Twentieth Edition

Smith, Carol
Crossing the River: Seven Stories That Saved My Life: A Memoir. Carol Smith. Harry N Abrams 2021. 272 p.
ISBN 9781419750137
Grades: Adult   B
1. Mothers 2. Grief 3. Loss 4. Death of sons 5. Life change events 6. Survival 7. Psychological growth 8. Hope 9. Healing 10. Women journalists 11. Autobiographies and memoirs 12. Life stories — Facing adversity — Coping with death 13. Family and Relationships — Aging and Death

An award-winning journalist discusses her own journey of grief after the loss of her son through a series of profiles of others who have coped with intense personal challenges and how their stories helped her heal.

"A journalist dealing with the tragic death of her young son tells seven stories about people 'Reinventing, finding purpose, and discovering strength.' ... An uplifting group of moving stories." —*Kirkus*

Smith, David James
Young Mandela: The Revolutionary Years. David James Smith. Little, Brown 2010. 416 p.
ISBN 9780316035484
Grades: 11 12 Adult   B
1. Mandela, Nelson, 1918-2013 2. Apartheid 3. Anti-apartheid movements 4. Political prisoners 5. Civil rights workers 6. Politics and government 7. South Africa 8. 20th century 9. Biographies 10. Adult books for young adults 11. Life stories — Politics — Activists and reformers 12. History writing — Africa — South Africa

LC 2010031883

In the twilight of his life, Nelson Mandela is a national hero, a world leader, and a household name. While many people know the story of Mandela's imprisonment, release, and role in reuniting South Africa, few have studied his childhood and upbringing. Here, journalist David James Smith chronicles the childhood that shaped Nelson (born Rolihlahla) into a man and reveals several little-known facts about the great leader.

"Smith's focus is on Mandela's legal training and practice, his relationship with the multiracial ANC, and his early revolutionary years leading up to his arrest, trial, and conviction for sabotage and treason, followed by his sentencing to life in prison on Robben Island in 1964. Smith leaves Mandela there at age 46." —*Library Journal*

Includes bibliographical references.

Smith, Douglas
Rasputin: Faith, Power, and the Twilight of the Romanovs. Douglas Smith. Farrar, Straus and Giroux 2016. 544 p.
ISBN 9780374240844
Grades: Adult   B
1. Rasputin, Grigori Efimovich, 1869-1916 2. Romanov, House of 3. Mystics 4. Courts and courtiers 5. Aristocracy 6. Scandals 7. Politics and government 8. Russian history 9. Russia 10. Romanov Dynasty (1613-1917) 11. Biographies 12. History writing — Europe — Russia 13. Life stories — Religion and spirituality — Religious and spiritual leaders

LC 2016027558

Shortlisted for the James Tait Black Memorial Prize for Biography, 2016.

On the 100th anniversary of his murder, a biography of the mystical faith healer and close friend of the last Tsar of Russia describes his strange rise to power, his penchant for debauchery and his involvement in the end of the Romanov dynasty.

Includes bibliographical references and index.

Smith, Freda Love
I Quit Everything: How One Woman's Addiction to Quitting Helped Her Confront Bad Habits and Embrace Midlife. Freda Love Smith. Midway 2023. 223 p.
ISBN 9781572843271
Grades: Adult   B
1. Smith, Freda Love 2. Women college teachers 3. Women musicians 4. COVID-19 Pandemic, 2020- 5. Adjustment 6. Social isolation 7. Alcoholism 8. Drug abuse 9. Social media 10. Workaholism 11. Addiction 12. Sobriety 13. Self-improvement 14. Health 15. Mental health 16. North American people 17. American people 18. Autobiographies and memoirs 19. Life stories — Facing adversity — Medical issues — Addiction 20. Life stories — Personal growth 21. Society and culture — Illness and disease — Addiction

LC 2023007818

The musician, journalist and author chronicles her efforts to remove one destructive or addictive behavior such as alcohol, sugar, caffeine and social media from her life each month to see whether getting sober is all it's cracked up to be.

"A retired rock drummer and nonfiction writer explores how a personal challenge to quit bad habits led to an unexpected life reset." —*Kirkus*

Includes bibliographical references.

Smith, Jada Pinkett
Worthy. Jada Pinkett Smith. Dey Street Books 2023. 304 p.
ISBN 9780063320680
Grades: Adult   B
1. Smith, Jada Pinkett, 1971- 2. Actors and actresses 3. African American women 4. Growing up 5. Acting 6. Fame 7. Marriage 8. Family relationships 9. Self-fulfillment 10. North American people 11. American people 12. Autobiographies and memoirs 13. Life stories — Arts and culture — Performing arts — Actors and actresses 14. Arts and Entertainment — Movies and Television

From an unconventional upbringing in Baltimore, to an unconventional marriage to one of the most famous men in the world, adhering to the status quo has never been a familiar road for Jada Pinkett Smith. In Worthy, Smith strips herself of all the labels and stories crafted by others, and reclaims her narrative with radical self-love. Worthy teaches us who Jada is, and how to embrace our most authentic lovable souls. An impactful memoir that engages and educates, Worthy is a courageous love song to self, to family, to life, and to the world.

Smith, Jean Edward
FDR. Jean Edward Smith. Random House 2007. xx, 858 p. : Illustration
ISBN 9781400061211
Grades: Adult   B
1. Roosevelt, Franklin D. (Franklin Delano), 1882-1945 2. Presidents 3. United States history 4. United States 5. 20th century 6. Biographies 7. History writing — Presidency — United States 8. History writing — Presidency — 20th century — United States

LC 2006043087

Presents a multi-faceted study of the complex American president, detailing his diverse roles as commander-in-chief, leader of a social revolution, and statesman, and exploring his personal life and the physical disabilities that he hid from the general public.

"Smith's FDR is at once a careful, intelligent synopsis of the existing Roosevelt scholarship (the sheer bulk of which is huge) and a meticulous reinterpretation of the man and his record. Smith pays more attention to Roosevelt's personal life than have most previous biographers. He is openly sympathetic yet ready to criticize when that is warranted, and to do so in sharp terms; he conveys the full flavor and import of Roosevelt's career without ever bogging down in detail." —*Washington Post Book World.*

Includes bibliographical references (p. [791]-825) and index.

John Marshall: Definer of a Nation. Jean Edward Smith. H. Holt & Co. 1996. xi, 736 p. : Illustration
ISBN 9780805013894
Grades: Adult   B
1. Marshall, John, 1755-1835 2. Judges 3. United States history 4. United States 5. Biographies 6. History writing — Judicial branch — United States 7. Life stories — Law and order — Judges and lawyers

LC 96015072

Chronicles the life, career, and contributions of the man who sat on the United States Supreme Court for thirty-five years and who was instrumental in molding the court into the powerful body it is today.

"Mr. Smith's splendid biography deserves a large readership mostly because it has recovered Marshall the man." —*New York Times Book Review*

A Marian Wood book; Includes bibliographical references (p. 677-707) and index.

ESSENTIAL AND RECOMMENDED TITLES
Biography

Smith, Jeremy N.
Breaking and Entering: The Extraordinary Story of a Hacker Called. Jeremy N. Smith. Houghton Mifflin Harcourt 2019. 320 p.
ISBN 9780544903210
Grades: Adult B
1. Alien (Hacker) 2. Hackers 3. Computer security 4. Hacking 5. Women hackers 6. Computer criminals 7. Computer crimes 8. Biographies 9. Life stories — Science, technology, and medicine 10. Life stories — Law and order — Criminals and law-breakers 11. Nonfiction that reads like fiction
LC 2018024873
Portrays the career of an accomplished hacker—a woman known only as Alien—describing her experiences at MIT, cybersecurity firms, and with a boutique hacking outfit that caters to banks, retailers, and government agencies.
An Eamon Dolan Book.

Smith, Kenny
Talk of Champions: Stories of the People Who Made Me: A Memoir. Kenny Smith. Doubleday 2023. 304 p.
ISBN 9780385548052
Grades: Adult B
1. Smith, Kenny, 1965 March 8- 2. Basketball 3. Sportscasters 4. Sports 5. Former basketball players 6. African American men 7. Interpersonal relations 8. Mentoring 9. Autobiographies and memoirs 10. Life stories — Sports 11. Sports and competition — Basketball
The host of top-rated Inside the NBA and two-time NBA champion relates memorable stories about each of the extraordinary people who taught him valuable life lessons, including Michael Jordan, Shaquille O'Neal, Charles Barkley, Kobe Bryant and many others, while interweaving personal material about his upbringing and his family.
"Smith...delivers a smartly structured memoir that reinforces the significance of relationships, perspective, and social awareness in the making of a champion." —*Kirkus*

Smith, Maggie
★ *You Could Make This Place Beautiful: A Memoir.* Maggie Smith. Signal Press 2023. 320 p.
ISBN 9781982185855
Grades: Adult B
1. Smith, Maggie, 1977- 2. Middle-aged women 3. Marriage 4. Betrayal 5. Divorce 6. Parenting 7. Memory 8. Autobiographies and memoirs 9. Life stories — Relationships 10. Family and relationships — Divorce
The best-selling poet and author of Keep Moving offers a memoir that explores coming of age in the middle of life.
"In her memoir, award-winning poet Smith (Good Bones) uses poetic vignettes to dissect the ending of her marriage and her journey toward self-love." —*Library Journal*

Smith, Patti
★ *Just Kids.* Patti Smith. Ecco 2010. xii, 278 p. : Illustration; Portrait
ISBN 9780066211312
Grades: Adult B
1. Smith, Patti 2. Mapplethorpe, Robert, 1946-1989 3. Women rock musicians 4. Women poets 5. Musicians 6. Songwriters 7. Poets, American 8. Friendship 9. Photographers 10. Artists 11. Writing 12. Music 13. Brooklyn, New York City 14. New York City 15. 1960s 16. Autobiographies and memoirs 17. Life stories — Arts and culture — Writing — Poets 18. Life stories — Arts and culture — Performing arts — Musicians and composers 19. Arts and Entertainment — Music
LC 2010279646
ALA Notable Book, 2011; Library Journal Best Books, 2010; National Book Award for Nonfiction, 2010; National Book Critics Circle Award for Autobiography/Memoir finalist.
An artist and musician recounts her romance, lifetime friendship, and shared love of art with Robert Mapplethorpe, in a memoir that includes such influential artists as Bob Dylan, Allen Ginsberg, Andy Warhol, and William Burroughs.

"This is one of the best books ever written on becoming an artistnot the race for online celebrity and corporate sponsorship that often passes for artistic success these days, but the far more powerful, often difficult journey toward the ecstatic experience of capturing radiance of imagination on a page or stage or photographic paper." —*Washington Post*

★ *M Train.* Patti Smith. Alfred A. Knopf 2015. 272 p.
ISBN 9781101875100
Grades: Adult B
1. Smith, Patti 2. Women rock musicians 3. Loss 4. Authors 5. Dreams 6. Reality 7. Writing 8. Creativity in art 9. Memories 10. Widows 11. Grief 12. Creativity 13. Biographies 14. Arts and Entertainment — Music — Rock 15. Life stories — Arts and culture — Performing arts — Musicians and composers 16. Adult books for young adults 17. Arts and Entertainment — Writing and Publishing — Literary criticism
LC 2015012904
ALA Notable Book, 2016; Booklist Editors' Choice, 2015.
The Rock and Roll Hall of Fame inductee presents reflections on her inner life from the unique perspectives of the cafes and cultural haunts she has visited and worked in around the world.

★ *Year of the Monkey.* Patti Smith. Alfred A. Knopf 2019. 176 pages
ISBN 9780525657682
Grades: Adult B
1. Smith, Patti 2. Women rock musicians 3. Wanderers and wandering 4. Chinese zodiac 5. Life change events 6. Loss 7. Aging 8. Political culture 9. Poets, American 10. 20th century 11. Autobiographies and memoirs 12. Life stories — Arts and culture — Writing — Poets 13. Life stories — Arts and culture — Performing arts — Musicians and composers 14. Arts and Entertainment — Music 15. Arts and Entertainment — Writing and Publishing — Literary criticism
LC 2019009856
From the author of Just Kids and M Train comes a memoir in which dreams and reality are vividly woven into a tapestry of one transformative year.
"Fans of Smith's extensive body of work and those who enjoy well-crafted personal narratives will find much to love in this brief and vibrant book." —*Library Journal*

Smith, R. J.
American Witness: The Art and Life of Robert Frank. R. J. Smith. Da Capo Press 2017. 320 p.
ISBN 9780306823367
Grades: Adult B
1. Frank, Robert, 1924-2019 2. Photographers 3. Biographies 4. Arts and Entertainment — Photography 5. Life stories — Arts and culture — Artists
LC BI2017045742
Describes the cross-country family trip by photographer and friend to bohemians and beats, including Jack Kerouac and Allen Ginsberg, that led him to take 27,000 photos, of which 83 ended up in his best-known work, the Americans.

Smith, Richard Norton
An Ordinary Man: The Surprising Life and Historic Presidency of Gerald R. Ford. Richard Norton Smith. Harper 2023. 992 p.
ISBN 9780062684165
Grades: Adult B
1. Ford, Gerald R, 1913-2006 2. Presidents 3. Political leadership 4. North American people 5. American people 6. Politics and government 7. United States 8. 1970s 9. 20th century 10. Life stories — Politics — Politicians 11. History writing — Presidency — 20th century — United States 12. Politics and global affairs — Political figures
For many Americans, President Gerald Ford was the genial accident of history who controversially pardoned his Watergate-tarnished predecessor, presided over the fall of Saigon, and became a punching bag on Saturday Night Live. Yet as Richard Norton Smith reveals in a book full of surprises, Ford was an underrated leader whose tough decisions and personal decency look better with the passage of time.
"Historian Smith (On His Own Terms), the former director of the Gerald R. Ford Museum and Library, delivers an exhaustive account of Ford's life and

presidency....This is a solid and revealing biography of an underestimated president." —*Publishers Weekly*

Smith, Sally Bedell
Elizabeth the Queen: The Life of a Modern Monarch. Sally Bedell Smith. Random House 2011. 384 p.
ISBN 9781400067893
Grades: Adult   B
1. Elizabeth II, Queen of Great Britain, 1926-2022 2. Windsor, House of 3. Royal houses 4. Rulers 5. Monarchy 6. Women rulers 7. British history 8. Leadership 9. Great Britain 10. England 11. 20th century 12. 21st century 13. Biographies 14. Life stories — Politics — Royalty 15. Life stories — Politics — Politicians
LC 2011023661
Goodreads Choice Award, 2012.

A tribute to the life and enduring reign of Elizabeth II draws on numerous interviews and previously undisclosed documents to juxtapose the queen's public and private lives.

"A microscopically detailed portrait of the reigning Queen of England." —*Kirkus*

Includes bibliographical references and index.

Prince Charles: The Passions and Paradoxes of an Improbable Life. Sally Bedell Smith. Random House 2017. 528 p.
ISBN 9781400067909
Grades: Adult   B
1. Charles, III, King of Great Britain, 1948- 2. Windsor, House of 3. Princes 4. Marriages of royalty and nobility 5. British history 6. European history 7. Great Britain 8. 20th century 9. Biographies 10. History writing — Europe — United Kingdom 11. Life stories — Politics — Royalty
LC 2016031117

The best-selling author of Elizabeth the Queen presents a revelatory portrait of the crown royal that offers new insights into his lonely childhood, intellectual quests, entrepreneurial pursuits and marriages.

"In this biography, historian and frequent biographer Smith . presents a multidimensional portrait of a complex, sensitive, and often visionary man . who has carved out a dynamic public role as he waits his turn to govern." —*Library Journal*

Includes bibliographical references and index.

Smith, Starr
Jimmy Stewart: Bomber Pilot. Starr Smith; foreword by Walter Cronkite. Zenith Press 2005. 287 p. : Illustration; Map
ISBN 9780760321997
Grades: Adult   B
1. Stewart, James, 1908-1997 2. Air warfare 3. Western Front (World War II) 4. Bomber pilots 5. World War II 6. Military campaigns 7. Films 8. Actors and actresses 9. United States 10. Biographies 11. History writing — Wars and conflicts — World War II 12. Arts and Entertainment — Movies and Television 13. Life stories — Arts and culture — Performing arts — Actors and actresses 14. Life stories — Law and order — Armed forces personnel
LC 2005041450
Includes bibliographical references (p. 278-283) and index.

Smith, Will
★ *Will*. Will Smith, with Mark Manson. Penguin Books 2021. 352 p.
ISBN 9781984877925
Grades: Adult   B
1. Smith, Will, 1968- 2. Actors and actresses 3. Rap musicians 4. African American men 5. Growing up 6. Fame 7. Autobiographies and memoirs 8. Life stories — Arts and culture — Performing arts — Actors and actresses 9. Arts and Entertainment — Movies and Television

A product of a profound journey of self-knowledge, and a reckoning with all that your will can get you and all that it can leave behind, in this memoir, one of the most dynamic and globally recognized entertainment forces of our time opens up fully about his life.

"One of Hollywood's biggest stars delivers a memoir of success won through endless, relentless work and self-reckoning. . . . A refreshing celebrity memoir focused not strictly on the self but on a much larger horizon." —*Kirkus*

Smyth, Katharine
All the Lives We Ever Lived: Seeking Solace in Virginia Woolf. Katharine Smyth. Crown 2019. 308 pages : Illustration
ISBN 9781524760625
Grades: Adult   B
1. Smyth, Katharine, 1981- 2. Woolf, Virginia, 1882-1941 3. Fathers and daughters 4. Death of fathers 5. Grief 6. Autobiographies and memoirs 7. Arts and Entertainment — Writing and Publishing — Literary criticism
LC 2018289715

An intimate work of memoir and literary criticism describes how the author found literary solace and insights in Virginia Woolf's to the Lighthouse while mourning a beloved parent's death.

"A work of incisive observation and analysis, exquisite writing, and an attempt to determine if there is any revelation that could lessen loss, that could help to make the fact of death okay." —*Kirkus*

Includes bibliographical references (pages 299-302).

Snyder, Brad
A Well-paid Slave: Curt Flood's Fight for Free Agency in Professional Sports. Brad Snyder. Viking 2006. 472 p. : Illustration
ISBN 9780670037940
Grades: Adult   B
1. Flood, Curt, 1938-1997 2. Baseball players 3. African American baseball players 4. Free agents (Sports) 5. Biographies 6. Sports and Competition — Baseball
LC 2006046139

Traces the landmark Supreme Court case between All-Star center fielder Curt Flood and Major League Baseball, documenting how he fought to play for the team of his choice at the cost of his career and placement in the Hall of Fame but paved the way for future players to become free agents.

Includes bibliographical references (p. [437]-456) and index.

Snyder, Rachel Louise
Women We Buried, Women We Burned. Rachel Louise Snyder. Bloomsbury Publishing Place USA 2023. 352 p.
ISBN 9781635579123
Grades: Adult   B
1. Snyder, Rachel Louise 2. Survival 3. Resilience 4. Runaway teenagers 5. Journalists 6. Women journalists 7. Healing 8. Growing up 9. Family violence 10. Grief 11. Families 12. Violence against women 13. Autobiographies and memoirs 14. Life stories — Facing adversity 15. Family and Relationships — General 16. Life stories — Identity — Gender 17. Life stories — Arts and culture — Writing — Journalists

An award-winning journalist, in this necessary story of family struggle, female survival and the passionate drive to bear witness, relates her personal journey from teenage runaway to reporter on the global epidemic of violence against women.

"Exceptional writing, a harrowing coming-of-age story, and critical awareness combine to make a must-read memoir." —*Kirkus*

Snyder, Timothy
The Red Prince: The Secret Lives of a Habsburg Archduke. Timothy Snyder. Basic Books 2008. 324 p.
ISBN 9780465002375
Grades: Adult   B
1. Habsburg-Lothringen, Wilhelm, 1895-1949 2. Habsburg, House of 3. Princes 4. Nobility 5. Politicians 6. Nationalists 7. Nationalism 8. European history 9. Eastern Europe 10. Ukraine 11. Between the Wars (1918-1939) 12. Biographies 13. History writing — Europe 14. Life stories — Politics — Royalty 15. Life stories — People in history — Famous families
LC 2008002783

ESSENTIAL AND RECOMMENDED TITLES
Biography

A portrait of Wilhelm Von Habsburg sheds new light on an aristocrat whose life parallels the upheavals of the first half of the twentieth century and the violent birth of modern Europe, as it describes a man who played a seminal role in a world in which the old order was giving way to the future.

"Snyder portrays him as a restless spirit with dreams of grandeur who was attractive, even charismatic, without being particularly admirable." —*Booklist*

Includes bibliographical references and index.

Solnit, Rebecca

Orwell's Roses. Rebecca Solnit. Viking 2021. 308 pages

ISBN 9780593083369

Grades: Adult B

1. Orwell, George, 1903-1950 2. Roses 3. Gardening 4. Nature 5. Imperialism 6. Horticulture 7. Authors, English 8. 20th century 9. Biographies 10. Nature Writing — Gardens 11. Life stories — Arts and culture — Writing — Authors 12. Arts and Entertainment — Writing and Publishing

LC 2021003710

National Book Critics Circle Award for Nonfiction finalist, 2021.

This reflection on George Orwell's passion for gardening, particularly flowers, and his involvement with the natural world reveals his other commitments as a writer and antifascist, and the intertwined politics of power and nature.

"Solnit carefully charts the life of George Orwell (1903-1950) by focusing on his love of roses and all things natural in this brilliant survey." —*Publishers Weekly*

Includes bibliographical references and index.

★ *Recollections of My Nonexistence: A Memoir.* Rebecca Solnit. Viking 2020. 256 p.

ISBN 9780593083338

Grades: Adult B

1. Solnit, Rebecca 2. Women authors, American 3. Women intellectuals 4. Feminism 5. Writing 6. Violence against women 7. Misogyny 8. Gender identity 9. Social marginality 10. Self-fulfillment 11. San Francisco, California 12. Autobiographies and memoirs 13. Life stories — Arts and culture — Writing — Authors 14. Life stories — Identity — Gender 15. Society and culture — Gender — Women

LC 2019022497

Loan Stars Favourites, 2020; Shortlisted for the James Tait Black Memorial Prize for Biography, 2020.

In Recollections of My Nonexistence, Rebecca Solnit describes her formation as a writer and as a feminist in 1980s San Francisco, in an atmosphere of gender violence on the street and throughout society and the exclusion of women from cultural arenas. She tells of being poor, hopeful, and adrift in the city that became her great teacher, and of the small apartment that, when she was nineteen, became the home in which she transformed herself. Beyond being a memoir, Solnit's book is also a passionate argument: That women are not just impacted by personal experience, but by membership in a society where violence against women pervades.

"This is a thinking person's book about writing, female identity, and freedom by a powerful and motivating voice for change." —*Publishers Weekly*

Solomon, Deborah

American Mirror: The Life and Art of Norman Rockwell. Deborah Solomon. Farrar, Straus and Giroux 2013. 512 p.

ISBN 9780374113094

Grades: Adult B

1. Rockwell, Norman, 1894-1978 2. Painters 3. Illustrators 4. Depression 5. Mental illness 6. Americana 7. OCD 8. United States 9. Biographies 10. Life stories — Arts and culture — Artists 11. Arts and Entertainment — Painting, Drawing, and Sculpture

LC 2013021682

New York Times Notable Book, 2014.

The celebrated critic and author of Utopia Parkway presents a portrait of the classic 20th-century American artist that explores his achievements and influence as a long-time illustrator for the Saturday Evening Post, sharing additional insights into his unexpectedly complex private life.

"Praised for her biographies of Jackson Pollock and Joseph Cornell, noted art critic Solomon makes a surprise leap to rock-solid Americana artist Norman Rockwell. But as she says, Rockwell painted a history of the American people that had never happened, and she goes on to detail his not-so-apple-pie personality." —*Library Journal*

Includes index.

Jackson Pollock: A Biography. Deborah Solomon. Cooper Square Press 2001. 287 p. : Illustration

ISBN 9780815411826

Grades: Adult B

1. Pollock, Jackson, 1912-1956 2. Painters 3. Artists 4. Abstract expressionism 5. Abstract expressionists 6. Social life and customs 7. United States 8. 20th century 9. Biographies 10. Arts and Entertainment — Painting, Drawing, and Sculpture 11. Life stories — Arts and culture — Artists

LC 2001028915

"A concisely written biography; the footnotes indicate solid research." —*Library Journal*

Includes bibliographical references (p. 257-279) and index; Originally published: New York : Simon and Schuster, 1987.

Soloway, Jill

She Wants It: Desire, Power, and Toppling the Patriarchy. Jill Soloway, Crown Archetype 2018. 288 p.

ISBN 9781101904749

Grades: Adult B

1. Soloway, Jill 2. Gender identity 3. Coming out (Sexual or gender identity) 4. Women television producers and directors 5. Nonbinary people 6. Gender-nonconforming people 7. Transgenderism 8. Women theatrical producers and directors 9. Women television writers 10. Autobiographies and memoirs 11. Life stories — Identity — LGBTQIA+ 12. Life stories — Arts and culture — Performing arts — Directors and producers

LC 2018022379

The creator of "Transparent" shares the poignant story of how her parent came out as transgender, compelling the author to challenge the male-dominated landscape of Hollywood to create her Emmy- and Golden Globe-winning series.

"This is an honest look at Soloways mind-opening journey, which allowed for deeper understanding of Hollywoods patriarchy as well as of the authors own gender, art, and self." —*Booklist*

Soni, Jimmy

A Mind at Play: How Claude Shannon Invented the Information Age. Jimmy Soni and Rob Goodman. Simon & Schuster 2017. 384 pages

ISBN 9781476766683

Grades: Adult B

1. Shannon, Claude Elwood, 1916-2001 2. Mathematicians 3. Electrical engineers 4. Information theory 5. Technological innovations 6. Computer science 7. Biographies 8. Life stories — Science, technology, and medicine — Scientists and inventors 9. Science Writing — Computing, the Internet, and Technology 10. History writing — Science, technology, and medicine

LC 2016050944

Chronicles the life and times of the lesser-known Information Age intellect, revealing how his discoveries and innovations set the stage for the digital era, influencing the work of such collaborators and rivals as Alan Turing, John von Neumann and Vannevar Bush.

"A welcome and inspiring account of a largely unsung herounsung because, the authors suggest, he accomplished something so fundamental that it's difficult to imagine a world without it." —*Kirkus*

Includes bibliographical references and index.

Sorensen, Theodore C.

Counselor: A Life at the Edge of History. Ted Sorensen. Harper 2008. 576 p.

ISBN 9780060798710

Grades: Adult B

1. Sorensen, Theodore C. 2. Kennedy, John F. (John Fitzgerald), 1917-1963 3. Political consultants 4. Speechwriters 5. Lawyers 6. Bay of Pigs Invasion, 1961 7. Cuban Missile Crisis, 1962 8. Ballistic missiles 9. Missiles 10. Presi-

dents 11. Politicians 12. Politics and government 13. United States 14. 1960s 15. 20th century 16. Autobiographies and memoirs 17. Biographies 18. History writing — Presidency — 20th century — United States 19. History writing — 1960s — United States 20. Life stories — Law and order — Judges and lawyers 21. Life stories — People in history — Witness to history 22. Life stories — Politics

LC 2007047328

A prominent international lawyer and former advisor to JFK recounts their conversations during some of the most decisive moments of the thirty-fifth president's career, including the Bay of Pigs, the Cuban Missile Crisis, and the writing of "Profiles in Courage."

"This book is instantly essential for any student of the period. It fills gaps in the historical record; it vividly conveys life inside the administration; and it generously dishes anecdotes." —*Washington Post Book World.*

Sotomayor, Sonia

★ *My Beloved World: A Memoir.* Sonia Sotomayor. Knopf 2013. 320 p.
ISBN 9780307594884
Grades: 10 11 12 Adult   **B**
1. Sotomayor, Sonia, 1954- 2. Judges 3. Women judges 4. Hispanic American women 5. Hispanic Americans 6. United States 7. Autobiographies and memoirs 8. Biographies 9. Life stories — Law and order — Judges and lawyers 10. Adult books for young adults

LC 2012031797

Library Journal Best Books, 2013; New York Times Notable Book, 2013; School Library Journal Best Books: Best Adult Books 4 Teens, 2013.

Appointed to the Supreme Court in 2009, Sonia Sotomayor became the first Latina to achieve this high judicial office. My Beloved World offers a moving portrait of her gritty South Bronx neighborhood and her extended Puerto Rican family, as well as details of the many challenges she has faced during her formative years and early career. This open, eloquent memoir describes how she overcame poverty, her father's early death, and even the onset of her own early health issues to excel in school, attend Princeton and Yale Law School—while still remaining true to her heritage.

"Graceful, authoritative memoir from the country's first Hispanic Supreme Court justice.... The author's text forms a cultural patchwork of memories and reflections as she mines the nuances of her parents' tumultuous relationship, fondly recalls family visits in Puerto Rico and offers insight on a judicial career that's just beginning when the memoir ends.... Mature, life-affirmative musings from a venerable life shaped by tenacity and pride." —*Kirkus*

Souder, William

On a Farther Shore: The Life and Legacy of Rachel Carson. William Souder. Crown Publishing Group 2012. 496 p.
ISBN 9780307462206
Grades: Adult   **B**
1. Carson, Rachel, 1907-1964 2. Women naturalists 3. Women environmentalists 4. Marine biologists 5. Naturalists 6. Environmentalists 7. Science writers 8. Pesticides 9. Environmentalism 10. Environmental ethics 11. Biographies 12. Science Writing — Biology 13. Nature Writing — Environmental Issues 14. Life stories — Science, technology, and medicine — Scientists and inventors

LC 2012003077

New York Times Notable Book, 2012.

Published to commemorate the 50th anniversary of Silent Spring, an in-depth portrait of the biologist and reformer examines how she helped to raise awareness of the natural world, the importance of conservation and the dangers of synthetic pesticides.

Includes bibliographical references and index.

Southon, Emma

Agrippina: The Most Extraordinary Woman of the Roman World. Emma Southon. Pegasus Books 2019. 352 pages
ISBN 9781643130781
Grades: Adult   **B**
1. Agrippina, Minor, 15-59 2. Claudius I, Emperor of Rome, 10 B.C.E.-54 C.E 3. Nero Emperor of Rome 37-68 4. Women rulers 5. Ancient history 6. Political intrigue 7. Motherhood 8. Roman emperors 9. Power 10. Manipulation (Social sciences) 11. Assassination 12. Social life and customs 13. Politics and government 14. Ambition 15. Ancient Rome 16. Roman Empire (27 B.C.E.-476 C.E.) 17. Biographies 18. Life stories — Politics — Politicians 19. History writing — Ancient — Rome 20. Adult books for young adults

LC Bl2019021742

A portrait of the influential matriarch who played a major role throughout three generations of the Julio-Claudia dynasty includes coverage of her relationship with her brother, Caligula, her marriage to her uncle, Claudius, and her assassination by her son, Nero.

Spears, Britney

The Woman in Me. Britney Spears. Gallery Books 2023. 320 p.
ISBN 9781668009048
Grades: Adult   **B**
1. Spears, Britney, 1981- 2. Women singers 3. Women celebrities 4. Fame 5. Motherhood 6. Popular music 7. Interpersonal relations 8. North American people 9. American people 10. Autobiographies and memoirs 11. Life stories — Arts and culture — Performing arts — Musicians and composers 12. Life stories — Arts and culture — Performing arts — Entertainers and celebrities 13. Life stories — Personal growth 14. Arts and Entertainment — Music — Pop

Loan Stars Favourites, 2023.

The noted pop star offers a moving story about freedom, fame, motherhood, survival, faith, and hope.

"There's plenty of standard-issue celeb memoir name dropping—meetings with Madonna, parties with Lenny Kravitz—but the prevailing tone is more shell-shocked than glamorous." —*Publishers Weekly*

Speer, Albert

Inside the Third Reich: Memoirs. Albert Speer; translated from the German by Richard and Clara Winston; introduction by Eugene Davidson. Simon & Schuster 1997. xx, 596 p. : Illustration
ISBN 9780684829494
Grades: 11 12 Adult   **B**
1. Speer, Albert, 1905-1981 2. Hitler, Adolf, 1889-1945 3. Nazis 4. Architects 5. War criminals 6. Third Reich, 1933-1945 7. Politics and government 8. Germany 9. Autobiographies and memoirs 10. History books — Europe — Germany 11. Biographies — Law and order — Criminals and law-breakers 12. Biographies — Arts — Visual arts — Architects

LC BL 99791720

The author presents a detailed account of his fifteen-year association with the German Fuhrer.

A Touchstone book; Includes bibliographical references and index; Originally published: New York : Macmillan, 1970.

Spera, Keith

Groove Interrupted: Loss, Renewal, and the Music of New Orleans. Keith Spera. St. Martin's Press 2011. 272 p.
ISBN 9780312552251
Grades: 11 12 Adult   **B**
1. Musicians 2. Disaster victims 3. Hurricane Katrina, 2005 4. Music history and criticism 5. New Orleans, Louisiana 6. Collective autobiographies and memoirs 7. Arts and Entertainment — Music 8. Life stories — Arts and culture — Performing arts — Musicians and composers 9. History writing — Natural disasters and tragedies

LC 2011010122

Presents Hurricane Katrina stories from musicians, including Fats Domino's efforts to promote a tribute CD, Alex Chilton's decision to live out his life in a New Orleans cottage, and rapper Mystikal's release from prison where he rode out the storm.

"This look at the music community of New Orleans is a collection of profiles of individual musicians who all had their ability to make music threatened after Hurricane Katrina in 2005. many of the stories presented here had their origin in Spera's articles written before and after Katrina. All of them show how artists as varied as blues guitarist Clarence Gatemouth Brown, jazz trumpeter Terence Blanchard, heavy metal singer Phil Anselmo of Pantera, and New Orleans legends Fats Domino and Allen Toussaint tried to make sense of the storm through music, comforting themselves and uplifting those around them. Some of the fin-

ESSENTIAL AND RECOMMENDED TITLES
Biography

est profiles—and there is no weak one in the book—detail a combination of sadness and joy, such as Aaron Neville's triumphant return to the city after the death of his wife to close out the 2008 New Orleans Jazz & Heritage Festival." —*Publishers Weekly*

Sperber, Jonathan
Karl Marx: A Nineteenth-century Life. Jonathan Sperber. Liveright Pub. Corp. 2013. 512 p.
ISBN 9780871404671
Grades: Adult   **B**
1. Marx, Karl, 1818-1883 2. Communists 3. Philosophers 4. Intellectuals 5. Communism 6. Biographies 7. History writing — Europe — Germany 8. Life stories — Education — Philosophers
LC 2012044951
Pulitzer Prize for Biography or Autobiography finalist.
This biography of the philosopher and political revolutionary describes his childhood and family life along with his public life as an agitator and dissident and compares him to his contemporaries including Napoleon III, Bismarck, Adam Smith and Charles Darwin.
Includes bibliographical references and index.

Spiegel, Maura
Sidney Lumet: A Life. Maura Spiegel. St Martins Pr 2019. 384 pages
ISBN 9781250030153
Grades: Adult   **B**
1. Lumet, Sidney, 1924-2011 2. Television producers and directors 3. Filmmaking 4. Films 5. Work ethic 6. Creativity 7. Interpersonal relations 8. Film producers and directors 9. United States 10. Biographies 11. Life stories — Arts and culture — Performing arts — Directors and producers 12. Arts and Entertainment — Movies and Television
LC 2019031704
A portrait of the influential, five-time Oscar-nominated director shares insights into his use of gritty realism in his stage and television productions as well as his acclaimed work on such Hollywood films as 12 Angry Men and Serpico.
"A likely definitive exploration of the director's distinguished career—of great interest to budding filmmakers and film enthusiasts." —*Kirkus*
Includes bibliographical references and index.

Spiegel, Renia
Renia's Diary: A Holocaust Journal. Renia Spiegel, Elizabeth Bellak, Sarah Durand, Deborah Lipstadt; translated by Anna Blasiak, Marta Dziurosz. St. Martin's Press 2019. 176 p.
ISBN 9781250244024
Grades: Adult   **B**
1. Spiegel, Renia, 1924-1942 2. Holocaust victims 3. Antisemitism 4. Ghettoes, Jewish 5. Jewish people 6. Hidden children (Holocaust) 7. Holocaust (1933-1945) 8. Personal diaries 9. Polish people 10. German occupation, World War II 11. European history 12. Poland 13. Life stories — Facing adversity — War and oppression — Holocaust 14. History writing — Wars and conflicts — Holocaust — World War II
LC 2019024270
A first English-language translation of teen holocaust victim Renia Spiegel's secret journal chronicles her witness to the Nazi invasion of Poland, her Jewish family's forced relocation to the Przemysl ghetto and her attempt to go into hiding.
"This familys epic, layered story of survival serves as an important Holocaust document." —*Publishers Weekly*

Spiegelman, Art
Metamaus: A Look Inside a Modern Classic. Art Spiegelman. Pantheon Books 2011. 320 p.
ISBN 9780375423949
Grades: 11 12 Adult   **B**
1. Spiegelman, Art 2. Cartoonists 3. Modern literature 4. Comics and graphic novel writing 5. Jewish Americans 6. Literary criticism 7. 20th century 8. Autobiographies and memoirs 9. Biographies 10. Life stories — Arts and culture — Artists
LC 2010052045
National Jewish Book Award, 2011.
A New Yorker contributor and co-founder of RAW traces the creative process that went into his Pulitzer Prize-winning classic, revealing the inspirations for his work while providing on an accompanying DVD a reference copy of the Complete Maus and audio interviews with his father.
"Informative everything you may or may not have thought to ask about Maus and the Spiegelmans, this exhaustive purgative has been well organized and packaged and succeeds in being grimly entertaining, indeed almost addictive." —*Library Journal*

Spitz, Bob
★ *The Beatles: The Biography.* Bob Spitz. Little, Brown 2005. 983 p. : Illustration
ISBN 9780316803526
Grades: 11 12 Adult   **B**
1. Bands (Music) 2. Rock musicians 3. Popular culture 4. English history 5. United States history 6. England 7. 20th century 8. Biographies 9. Arts and Entertainment — Music — Rock 10. Life stories — Arts and culture — Performing arts — Musicians and composers
LC 2005003838
Library Journal Best Books, 2005; New York Times Notable Book, 2005.
Even before the Beatles hit the big time, a myth was created. This version of the Beatles legend smoothed the rough edges and filled in the fault lines, and for more than forty years this manicured version of the Beatles story has sustained as truth—until now.
"This beautifully written chronicle breathes new life into the familiar story of the Liverpool boys who conquered the world and became . the most influential entertainers of the past century. The author's passion for his subject, and for every nuance of every scene, electrifies even the most familiar moments in the legend." —*New York Times Book Review*
Includes bibliographical references (p. [948]-958, discography (p. [959]-961), and index.

★ *Dearie: The Remarkable Life of Julia Child.* Bob Spitz. Random House Inc 2012. 432 p.
ISBN 9780307272225
Grades: Adult   **B**
1. Child, Julia 2. Cooks 3. Cooking 4. Businesspeople 5. Family relationships 6. Cooking, French 7. Social life and customs 8. United States 9. Biographies 10. Life stories — Arts and culture — Performing arts — Entertainers and celebrities
LC 2012019632
Draws on the iconic culinary figure's personal diaries and letters to present a one-hundredth birthday commemoration that offers insight into her role in shaping women's views and influencing American approaches to cooking.
"An engrossing biography of a woman worthy of iconic status." —*Kirkus*

★ *Reagan: An American Journey.* Bob Spitz. Penguin Press 2018. 608 p.
ISBN 9781594205316
Grades: Adult   **B**
1. Reagan, Ronald 2. Conservatism 3. Presidents 4. Films 5. Actors and actresses 6. Politics and government 7. United States 8. 20th century 9. 1980s 10. Biographies 11. Impartial writing 12. History writing — Presidency — 20th century — United States 13. History writing — 1980s — United States 14. Life stories — Politics — Politicians 15. Nonfiction that reads like fiction
LC 2018019603
Draws on hundreds of interviews and previously unavailable documents to present a post-partisan biography of the fortieth president that offers insight into Reagan's universal appeal and transformative leadership.
"In visiting his final years, readers share the pathos of Reagans descent into dementia and feel the intense sorrow of the millions who mourn his passing. Candid, complete, compelling." —*Booklist*

PUBLIC LIBRARY CORE COLLECTION: NONFICTION
Twentieth Edition

Spoto, Donald
The Dark Side of Genius: The Life of Alfred Hitchcock. by Donald Spoto; with a new introduction by the author. Da Capo Press 1999. xiv, 594 p. : Illustration
ISBN 9780306809323
Grades: Adult   **B**
1. Hitchcock, Alfred, 1899-1980 2. Film producers and directors 3. Film noir 4. Film history and criticism 5. Biographies 6. Arts and Entertainment — Movies and Television 7. Life stories — Arts and culture — Performing arts — Directors and producers

LC 99037941

Edgar Allan Poe Award for Best Critical/Biographical, 1984.

Drawing on the author's personal relationship with the enigmatic director, interviews, and rich archival materials, this full biography traces the complex patterns of Hitchcock's art and apprenticeship in Germany.

"This is a vivid and perceptive portrait of a man whose character was as strange and shadowed as his films. Hitchcock's final obsession was secretiveness, but he has been well served by a knowledgeable and revealing biography." —*Time*

The films of Alfred Hitchcock: P. [569]-580; Includes bibliographical references (p. [565]-568) and index; Originally published: Boston, MA : Little, Brown, 1983.

High Society: The Life of Grace Kelly. Donald Spoto. Random House 2009. 356 p.
ISBN 9780307395610
Grades: Adult   **B**
1. Grace, Princess of Monaco, 1929-1982 2. Women entertainers 3. Princesses 4. Films 5. Actors and actresses 6. Social life and customs 7. Monaco 8. United States 9. 20th century 10. Biographies 11. Arts and Entertainment — Movies and Television 12. History writing — Europe 13. Life stories — Arts and culture — Performing arts — Actors and actresses 14. Life stories — Politics — Royalty

Based on never-before-published interviews with Grace Kelly and her friends and colleagues, from co-stars James Stewart and Cary Grant to director Alfred Hitchcock. Also includes documents disclosed by her children for the first time. Acclaimed biographer Donald Spoto explores the transformation of a convent schoolgirl to New York model, successful television actress, Oscar-winning movie star, and beloved royal.

Joan: The Mysterious Life of the Heretic Who Became a Saint. Donald Spoto. Harper San Francisco 2007. xviii, 222 p.
ISBN 9780060815172
Grades: 11 12 Adult   **B**
1. Joan of Arc, Saint, 1412-1431 2. Women saints 3. Hundred Years' War, 1339-1453 4. French history 5. Renaissance (1300-1600) 6. 15th century 7. Biographies 8. History writing — Renaissance — Europe 9. Spirituality and Religion — Christianity — History 10. Life stories — Religion and spirituality — Religious and spiritual leaders 11. Adult books for young adults

LC Bl2007004975

An account of the life of Joan of Arc draws on newly discovered transcripts of her trial to offer insight into the factors that contributed to her remarkable achievements, the plausibility of the role of divinity in her mission to serve her country, and the factors that contributed to her discrediting and execution.

Includes bibliographical references (p. [209]-222).

Springsteen, Bruce
★ *Born to Run.* Bruce Springsteen. Simon & Schuster 2016. 512 p.
ISBN 9781501141515
Grades: Adult   **B**
1. Springsteen, Bruce 2. Rock music 3. Men and success 4. Rock musicians 5. Celebrities 6. Popular culture 7. United States history 8. United States 9. 20th century 10. Autobiographies and memoirs 11. Biographies 12. Life stories — Arts and culture — Performing arts — Musicians and composers 13. Arts and Entertainment — Music — Rock

LC 2016016742

New York Times Notable Book, 2016.

In a personal account inspired by the remarkable 2009 Super Bowl halftime show, a Rock and Roll Hall of Famer traces his life from his childhood in a Catholic New Jersey family and the musical experiences that prompted his career to the rise of the E Street Band and the stories behind some of his most famous songs.

"A superb memoir by any standard, but one of the best to have been written by a rock star." —*Kirkus*

Spurling, Hilary
Anthony Powell: Dancing to the Music of Time. Hilary Spurling. Alfred A. Knopf 2018. 480 p.
ISBN 9780525521341
Grades: Adult   **B**
1. Powell, Anthony, 1905-2000 2. Authors, English 3. 20th century 4. Biographies 5. Arts and Entertainment — Writing and Publishing 6. Life stories — Arts and culture — Writing — Authors

LC 2017051875

Booklist Editors' Choice, 2018.

Examines the life of the English literary figure best known for his 12-volume comedic work that examines political, cultural and military life in the mid-20th century and who was friends with Evelyn Waugh, Henry Green and George Orwell.

Originally published: London : Penguin Books, 2017.

Matisse the Master: A Life of Henri Matisse, the Conquest of Colour, 1909-1954. Hilary Spurling. A.A. Knopf 2005. xxi, 512 p. : Illustration; Color
ISBN 9780679434290
Grades: Adult   **B**
1. Matisse, Henri, 1869-1954 2. Artists 3. Painters 4. Painting, French 5. Marriage 6. Men-women relations 7. Fear 8. 20th century 9. Biographies 10. Arts and Entertainment — Painting, Drawing, and Sculpture 11. Life stories — Arts and culture — Artists

LC 2004051074

Los Angeles Times Book Prize for Biography, 2005; Whitbread Book Award for Biography, 2005; Whitbread Book of the Year Award, 2005; New York Times Notable Book, 2005.

Chronicles the later years of the influential artist, interweaving analyses of his work with a study of Matisse's relationships with family and friends, trips around the world, the women in his life, and the continuing influences on the evolution of his art.

"Spurling's rich, flexible style is well attuned to the rigors and flights of Matisse's creative life." —*Publishers Weekly*

Sequel to: The unknown Matisse; Includes bibliographical references (p. 469-496) and index.

Spurrier, Steve
Head Ball Coach: My Life in Football, Doing It Differently—and Winning. Steve Spurrier with Buddy Martin. Blue Rider Press 2016. 416 p.
ISBN 9780399574665
Grades: Adult   **B**
1. Spurrier, Steve, 1945- 2. Football coaches 3. Football 4. Former professional football players 5. Autobiographies and memoirs 6. Life stories — Sports — Coaches, managers, and owners 7. Sports and Competition — Football

LC 2016029233

College football's most colorful, endearing, and successful pioneer, Steve Spurrier, shares his story of a life in football—from growing up in Tennessee to winning the Heisman Trophy to playing and coaching in the pros to leading the Florida Gators to six SEC Championships and a National Championship to elevating the South Carolina program to new heights—and coaching like nobody else.

St. John, Warren
Outcasts United: A Refugee Team, an American Town. Warren St. John. Spiegel & Grau 2009. 320 p.
ISBN 9780385522038
Grades: 11 12 Adult   **B**

ESSENTIAL AND RECOMMENDED TITLES
Biography

1. Mufleh, Luma 2. Soccer coaches 3. Child refugees 4. Social change 5. Refugees, African 6. Children 7. Recreation 8. Social life and customs 9. Georgia 10. Sports and Competition — Soccer 11. History writing — Immigration — United States 12. Adult books for young adults

LC 2008040697

Documents the lives of a wildly diverse group of young kids who unite as a team under the leadership of their American-educated Jordanian coach, against the backdrop of a fading American town struggling to make a haven for its new arrivals—refugees.

Stahl, Jerry
Nein, Nein, Nein!: One Man's Tale of Depression, Psychic Torment, and a Bus Tour of the Holocaust. Jerry Stahl. Akashic Books 2022. 264 p.

ISBN 9781636140254

Grades: Adult   B

1. Stahl, Jerry 2. Psychic trauma 3. Tourism 4. Holocaust (1933-1945) 5. Anxiety 6. Concentration camps 7. Bus travel 8. People with depression 9. Men 10. Voyages and travels 11. Poland 12. Germany 13. Travel Writing — Europe

A guided group tour to concentration camps in Poland and Germany allows Stahl to confront personal and historical demons with both deep despair and savage humor.

"Fusing provocative insights with razor-edged wit, this offers a captivating take on a haunting chapter of history." —*Publishers Weekly*

Stahr, Celia
Frida in America: The Creative Awakening of a Great Artist. Celia Stahr. St. Martin's Press 2020. 384 p.

ISBN 9781250113382

Grades: Adult   B

1. Kahlo, Frida 2. Rivera, Diego, 1886-1957 3. Women artists 4. Artists 5. Voyages and travels 6. Expatriate artists 7. Husband and wife 8. Women painters 9. Painting 10. Miscarriage 11. United States 12. San Francisco, California 13. New York City 14. Detroit, Michigan 15. 1930s 16. Biographies 17. Arts and Entertainment — Painting, Drawing, and Sculpture 18. Life stories — Arts and culture — Artists

LC 2019041724

Describes the years the Mexican artist spent in America beginning in 1930 with her new, older, and already world-famous husband, Diego Rivera, and the impact living in diverse cities of San Francisco, Detroit and New York had on her painting.

"Featuring meticulous research and elegant turns of phrase, Stahr's engrossing account provides scholarly though accessible analysis for both feminists and art lovers." —*Publishers Weekly*

Includes bibliographical references and index.

Stahr, Walter
Seward: Lincoln's Indispensable Man. by Walter Stahr. Simon & Schuster 2012. 608 p.

ISBN 9781439121160

Grades: Adult   B

1. Seward, William Henry, 1801-1872 2. Cabinet officers 3. Republicans 4. Politicians 5. International relations 6. Politics and government 7. Governors 8. New York (State) 9. United States 10. 1860s 11. American Civil War era (1861-1865) 12. 19th century 13. Biographies 14. History writing — Politicians — United States 15. Life stories — Politics — Politicians

LC 2011052984

A in-depth profile of the leader of the 16th President's "Team of Rivals" examines his considerable political roles including those of a progressive Governor of New York, Secretary of State and Lincoln's advisor during the Civil War, offering insight into his status as a polarizing figure and his pivotal contributions to keeping Britain and France from formally recognizing the Confederacy.

Includes bibliographical references and index.

★ *Stanton: Lincoln's War Secretary.* Walter Stahr. Simon & Schuster 2017. 480 p.

ISBN 9781476739304

Grades: Adult   B

1. Stanton, Edwin M. (Edwin McMasters), 1814-1869 2. Lincoln, Abraham, 1809-1865 3. Cabinet officers 4. Politicians 5. Reconstruction (United States history) 6. United States Civil War, 1861-1865 7. United States history 8. American Civil War era (1861-1865) 9. Biographies 10. Life stories — Politics — Politicians 11. History writing — Wars and conflicts — American Civil War

LC 2017022628

Walter Stahr, award-winning author of the New York Times bestseller Seward, tells the story of Abraham Lincoln's indispensable Secretary of War, Edwin Stanton, the man the president entrusted with raising the army that preserved the Union.

"A lively, lucid, and opinionated history, and his research supports his skepticism on some historical claims. The book should be Stanton's definitive biography for some time to come." —*Kirkus*

Staiti, Paul J.
Of Arms and Artists: The American Revolution Through Painters' Eyes. Paul Staiti. Bloomsbury Press 2016. 320 p.

ISBN 9781632864659

Grades: Adult   B

1. Peale, Charles Willson, 1741-1827 2. Copley, John Singleton, 1738-1815 3. Trumbull, John, 1756-1843 4. West, Benjamin, 1738-1820 5. Stuart, Gilbert, 1755-1828 6. American Revolution, 1775-1783 7. Painting 8. Art history 9. Art and history 10. Art and politics 11. Painters 12. United States history 13. United States 14. 18th century 15. Revolutionary America (1775-1783) 16. Biographies 17. Arts and Entertainment — Painting, Drawing, and Sculpture 18. History writing — Wars and conflicts — Revolutionary War (America)

LC 2016007703

Booklist Editors' Choice, 2016.

A vibrant and original perspective of the American Revolution through the stories of five great artists of the Revolutionary period who contributed greatly to America's founding spirit paints a new picture of this era, deepening our understanding of the whirlwind out of which the United States emerged.

Includes bibliographical references and index.

Stamos, John
If You Would Have Told Me: A Memoir. John Stamos. Henry Holt and Company 2023. 352 p.

ISBN 9781250890979

Grades: Adult   B

1. Stamos, John, 1963- 2. Actors and actresses 3. Celebrities 4. Television comedies 5. Fame 6. Grief 7. Sobriety 8. Self-fulfillment 9. North American people 10. American people 11. Autobiographies and memoirs 12. Life stories — Arts and culture — Performing arts — Actors and actresses 13. Arts and Entertainment — Movies and Television 14. Debut title

If you would have told a young John Stamos flipping burgers at his dad's fast-food joint that one day he'd be a household name and that, at the height of his success, he'd be living alone, divorced, with no kids, high on a cocktail of forgetting, he might've asked, "You want fries with that?" but Stamos beat the odds and over the past four decades has proved himself to be one of his generation's most successful and beloved actors. Whether showing off his comedic chops on Full House or his dramatic skills on ER, pushing the boundaries on Broadway or living out his youthful dreams as an honorary Beach Boy, John has surprised everyone, most of all himself.

"In this charming debut, Full House star Stamos reflects on fame and family." —*Publishers Weekly*

Standefer, Katherine E.
Lightning Flowers: My Journey to Uncover the Cost of Saving a Life. Katherine E. Standefer. Little, Brown Spark 2020. 288 p.

ISBN 9780316450362

Grades: Adult   B

1. Standefer, Katherine E, 1985- 2. Medical technology 3. Medical care 4. Identity 5. Pain 6. Social ethics 7. Effect of humans on nature 8. Grief 9. Diseases 10. California 11. Congo (Democratic Republic) 12. Autobiographies and memoirs 13. Life stories — Facing adversity — Medical issues — Physical illness 14. Science writing — Medicine and health

Kirkus Prize for Nonfiction finalist, 2021.

In this gripping, intimate memoir about health, illness, and the invisible reverberating effects of our medical system, Standefer recounts the astonishing true story of the rare diagnosis that upended her rugged life in the mountains of Wyoming and sent her tumbling into a fraught maze of cardiology units, dramatic surgeries, and slow, painful recoveries. As her life increasingly comes to revolve around the internal defibrillator freshly wired into her heart, she becomes consumed with questions about the supply chain that allows such an ostensibly miraculous device to exist. So she sets out to trace its materials back to their roots.

"An intensely personal and brave accounting of a medical battle and the countless hidden costs of health care." —*Kirkus*

Includes index.

Stangneth, Bettina
Eichmann Before Jerusalem: The Unexamined Life of a Mass Murderer. by Bettina Stangneth; translated from the German by Ruth Martin. Knopf 2014. 608 pages

ISBN 9780307959676

Grades: Adult B

1. Eichmann, Adolf, 1906-1962 2. Holocaust (1933-1945) 3. Nazis 4. War crime trials 5. World War II 6. Atrocities 7. Jerusalem, Israel 8. Biographies 9. Translations — German to English 10. History writing — Wars and conflicts — Holocaust — World War II 11. Life stories — Law and order — Military leaders

LC 2014001031

New York Times Notable Book, 2014; Cundill Prize in Historical Literature finalist.

A total re-assessment of the life of Adolf Eichmann that reveals his activities and notoriety amongst a global network of National Socialists following the collapse of the Third Reich, and permanently undermines Hannah Arendt's often-cited notion of the "banality of evil."

"Stangneth masterfully sifts through the information from these lively social gatherings conducted at journalist Sassens home three years before Eichmanns kidnapping by Israeli agents. A rigorously documented, essential work not only about Eichmanns masterly masquerade, but also about how we come to accept appearances as truth." —*Kirkus*

Originally published in German as Eichmann vor Jerusalem by Arche, 2011.

Staniforth, Nate
Here Is Real Magic: A Magician's Search for Wonder in the Modern World. Nate Staniforth. Bloomsbury 2018. 288 p.

ISBN 9781632864246

Grades: Adult B

1. Staniforth, Nate 2. Magicians 3. Sense of wonder 4. Magic tricks 5. Autobiographies and memoirs 6. Life stories — Arts and culture — Performing arts — Entertainers and celebrities

LC 2017016409

Chronicling his evolution from an obsessed young magician to a broken wanderer and back again, the former host of the Discovery Channel's international hit TV show Breaking Magic tells the story of his rediscovery of astonishment and the importance of wonder in everyday life.

"The result is a personal story that conjures up the wonder and magic of life without any trickery or deceit." —*Publishers Weekly*

Stanley, Amy
Stranger in the Shogun's City: A Japanese Woman and Her World. Amy Stanley. Scribner 2020. 352 p.

ISBN 9781501188527

Grades: Adult B

1. Tsuneno 1804-1853 2. Women 3. Women's role 4. Samurai 5. Culture 6. Social life and customs 7. Japanese history 8. Tokyo, Japan 9. Japan 10. 19th century 11. Biographies 12. Life stories — People in history 13. History writing — Asia — Japan 14. History writing — Women's history

National Book Critics Circle Award for Biography, 2020; Pulitzer Prize for Biography or Autobiography finalist, 2021.

This story of an unconventional Japanese woman in the early 19th century examines the cultural and political changes in the country as it stood on the brink of a momentous conflict with the West.

"Tsuneno belongs to a vanished world, but historian Stanley brings both her and the Japanese city of Edo back to life in this breathtaking work." —*Booklist*

Stanley, Paul
Backstage Pass: The Starchild's All-access Guide to the Good Life. Paul Stanley. Harperone 2019. 256 p.

ISBN 9780062820280

Grades: Adult B

1. Stanley, Paul 2. Rock musicians 3. Self improvement 4. Rock groups 5. Rock music 6. Happiness 7. Parenting 8. Interpersonal relations 9. Social life and customs 10. United States 11. 20th century 12. Autobiographies and memoirs 13. Life stories — Arts and culture — Performing arts — Musicians and composers 14. Arts and Entertainment — Music — Rock

LC 2019004755

The legendary front man and rhythm guitarist of KISS offers an anecdotal tour of his personal life and celebrity relationships, offering insights into the creative perspectives that have shaped his career and family dynamics.

Face the Music: A Life Exposed. Paul Stanley. Harperone 2014. 272 p.

ISBN 9780062114044

Grades: Adult B

1. Stanley, Paul 2. Rock musicians 3. Rock groups 4. Rock music 5. Birth defects 6. Social life and customs 7. Ambition 8. United States 9. 20th century 10. Autobiographies and memoirs 11. Life stories — Arts and culture — Performing arts — Musicians and composers 12. Arts and Entertainment — Music — Rock 13. Adult books for young adults

The co-founder and lead singer of the rock band Kiss discusses his childhood, the drama of his life on and off the stage, his personal relationships, and the turbulent dynamics with his bandmates over the past four decades.

Stanton, Mike
★ *Unbeaten:* Rocky Marciano's Fight for Perfection in a Crooked World. Mike Stanton. Henry Holt and Company 2018. 384 p.

ISBN 9781627799195

Grades: Adult B

1. Marciano, Rocky, 1923-1969 2. Boxers (Sports) 3. Boxing 4. Immigrants 5. Corruption 6. Biographies 7. Sports and Competition — Boxing 8. Sports and Competition — Individual Athlete 9. Life stories — Sports — Athletes

LC 2017057871

Library Journal Best Books, 2018.

Presents a revelatory portrait of the legendary heavyweight champion that covers his rise from an Italian immigrant family, his signature "Suzie Q" punch, and his struggles with the sport's corrupt elements.

"This meticulously documented and well-written work should stand for both fans and scholars as Marciano's definitive biography." —*Library Journal*

Includes bibliographical references and index.

Stark, Peter
Young Washington: How Wilderness and War Forged America's Founding Father. Peter Stark. Ecco 2018. 384 p.

ISBN 9780062416063

Grades: Adult B

1. Washington, George, 1732-1799 2. Generals 3. Presidents 4. Politicians 5. Military history 6. Command of troops 7. French and Indian War, 1754-1763 8. United States history 9. 18th century 10. Biographies 11. History writing — Presidency — 18th century — United States 12. Life stories — Politics — Politicians

LC 2017052000

A portrait of the first U.S. president's early years shares insights into how his service in the British military and his stationing in the brutal wilderness of the Ohio Valley shaped his nascent leadership and indirectly fed the conflict that led to the French and Indian War.

Includes bibliographical references and index.

ESSENTIAL AND RECOMMENDED TITLES
Biography

Starks, Glenn L.
Thurgood Marshall: A Biography. Glenn L. Starks, F. Erik Brooks. Greenwood 2012. 168 p. (Greenwood biographies)
ISBN 9780313349164
Grades: Adult B
1. Marshall, Thurgood, 1908-1993 2. African American judges 3. Judges 4. African Americans 5. United States 6. Biographies 7. Government and politics — Supreme Court and the judicial branch — Biographies — United States 8. Biographies — Law and order — Judges and lawyers 9. Biographies — Identity — Africans and African Americans
LC 2011051894

This book provides a detailed examination of the life and legal legacy of Supreme Court Justice Thurgood Marshall, including a discussion of the many legal cases in which he was involved.
Includes index.

Stauffer, John
Picturing Fredrick Douglass: An Illustrated Biography of the Nineteenth Century's Most Photographed American. John Stauffer, Zoe Trodd, and Celeste-Marie Bernier. Liveright Publishing Corporation 2015. 320 p.
ISBN 9780871404688
Grades: Adult B
1. Douglass, Frederick, 1818-1895 2. Abolitionists 3. African American abolitionists 4. Anti-slavery movements 5. United States history 6. 19th century 7. Biographies 8. History writing — African American — Enslavement — United States 9. Life stories — Politics — Activists and reformers
LC 2015020546

Picturing Frederick Douglass is a work that promises to revolutionize our knowledge of race and photography in nineteenth-century America. Teeming with historical detail, it is filled with surprises, chief among them the fact that neither George Custer nor Walt Whitman, and not even Abraham Lincoln, was the most photographed American of that century. In fact, it was Frederick Douglass (1818?1895), the ex-slave turned leading abolitionist, eloquent orator, and seminal writer whose fiery speeches transformed him into one of the most renowned and popular agitators of his age.

"The authors have pieced together an illuminating life portrait without extraneous biographical material, focusing intensely on their subject's belief in the strength of photographs." —*Kirkus*

Stein, Judith E.
Eye of the Sixties: Richard Bellamy and the Transformation of Modern Art. Judith Stein. Farrar, Straus and Giroux 2016. 320 p.
ISBN 9780374151324
Grades: Adult B
1. Bellamy, Richard 2. Art dealers 3. Art and society 4. 1960s 5. Biographies 6. Life stories — Arts and culture 7. Arts and entertainment — Painting, drawing, and sculpture
LC 2015036468

A portrait of the founder of the fabled Green Gallery explores such topics as his mixed heritage, advocacy of pop art and other less-represented forms and influential relationships with such figures as Norman Mailer, Yoko Ono and Diane Arbus.
Includes bibliographical references and index.

Steinbeck, John
Travels with Charley: In Search of America. John Steinbeck. Penguin Books 2002. 214 p. : Map
ISBN 9780142000700
Grades: 11 12 Adult B
1. Steinbeck, John, 1902-1968 2. Authors, American 3. Automobile travel 4. Men and dogs 5. Poodles 6. Dogs 7. Travelers 8. Men and pets 9. Voyages and travels 10. United States 11. 1960s 12. 20th century 13. Travel Writing — Modes of Transportation — Road Trips 14. Travel Writing — United States
LC 2001055444

Author John Steinbeck was 58 when he set out to rediscover the country he had been writing about for so many years. With his elderly French poodle, Charley, he embarked on a quest across America, from the northernmost tip of Maine to California's Monterey Peninsula. Traveling the interstates and the country roads, they stopped to smell America: Trucker and strangers, old friends and new acquaintances. Steinbeck's poignant, perceptive reflections reveal the American character: a blend of unexpected kindnesses and racial hostilities, loneliness and humor.

John Steinbeck centennial edition (1902-2002); Originally published: New York : Viking Press, 1962.

Steinberg, Jonathan
Bismarck: A Life. Jonathan Steinberg. Oxford University Press 2011. 544 p.
ISBN 9780199782529
Grades: Adult B
1. Bismarck, Otto, Furst von, 1815-1898 2. Politicians 3. Politics and government 4. Leadership 5. Germany 6. 19th century 7. Biographies 8. History writing — Europe — Germany 9. Life stories — Politics — Politicians
LC 2010045387

Examines the life of Otto von Bismarck, the statesman who unified Germany but who also embodied everything brutal and ruthless about Prussian culture.

"The author delves into Bismarck's life as both an individual and a statesman, drawing on observations from his friends, colleagues, and enemies to advance the idea that much of Bismarck's power came from his magnetic, larger-than-life personality." —*Library Journal*
Includes bibliographical references and index.

Steinberg, Jonny
A Man of Good Hope. by Jonny Steinberg. Alfred A. Knopf 2014. 336 p.
ISBN 9780385352727
Grades: Adult B
1. Abdullahi, Asad 2. Refugees, Somali 3. Interethnic conflict 4. Children of murder victims 5. Somali Americans 6. Violence against marginalized people 7. Orphans 8. Teenage refugees 9. Survival 10. Interethnic relations 11. Southwest Asia and North Africa (Middle East) history 12. Somalia 13. 20th century 14. Biographies 15. Life stories — Facing adversity — War and oppression — Refugees 16. History writing — Civil wars and genocide — Africa
LC 2013046388

Drawing on interviews with Asad Abdullahi himself and with people in Europe and the U.S. who knew his parents, one of South Africa's most distinguished journalists tells the story of Asad Abdullahi, a Somali man who, after witnessing his mother's murder by Somali militiamen, moved from place to place searching for peace and stability. Includes 6 maps.

"Steinberg's solid prose is perfect for the task of sharing Asad's history. He probes the darkest moments of his subject's life without ever becoming maudlin, telling the story starkly and bluntly." —*Kirkus*
This is a Borzoi book—T.P. verso.

Winnie and Nelson: Portrait of a Marriage. Jonny Steinberg. Alfred A. Knopf 2023. 576 p.
ISBN 9780525656852
Grades: Adult B
1. Mandela, Nelson, 1918-2013 2. Politicians 3. Women politicians 4. Presidents 5. Presidents' spouses 6. Marriage 7. Husband and wife 8. Apartheid 9. Anti-apartheid movements 10. Political prisoners 11. Separation 12. Marital conflict 13. Divorce 14. Psychic trauma 15. Social justice 16. Southern African people 17. South African people 18. Politics and government 19. South Africa 20. Collective biographies 21. Life stories — Politics — Activists and reformers 22. Life stories — Politics — Politicians 23. Life stories — Relationships — Couples 24. History writing — Africa — South Africa

National Book Critics Circle Award for Biography, 2023.

One of the most celebrated political leaders of a century, Nelson Mandela has been written about by many biographers and historians. But in one crucial area, his life remains largely untold: His marriage to Winnie Madikizela-Mandela. During his years in prison, Nelson grew ever more in love with an idealized version of his wife, courting her in his letters as if they were young lovers frozen in time. But Winnie, every bit his political equal, found herself increasingly estranged from her jailed husband's politics. Jonny Steinberg tells the tale of this unique marriage—its longings, its obsessions, its deceits—making South African history a page-turning political biography.

"Journalist Steinberg (A Man of Good Hope) vividly recreates the political and private lives of anti-apartheid activists Nelson and Winnie Mandela in this exceptional dual biography....Readers will be mesmerized by the thrumming tension and profound emotional complexity of this intimate portrait of two global icons." —Publishers Weekly

Steinem, Gloria
My Life on the Road. Gloria Steinem. Random House 2015. 304 p.
ISBN 9780679456209
Grades: Adult — B
1. Steinem, Gloria, 1934- 2. Feminists 3. Intersectionality 4. Feminism 5. Women 6. United States 7. Biographies 8. Life stories — Politics — Activists and reformers 9. Life stories — Arts and culture — Writing — Journalists
LC 2015010718

A feminist activist and co-founder of Ms. magazine presents a memoir comprised of reflections on definitive events in her career, from her time on the campaign trail and interactions with forefront political leaders to her visits to India and her encounters with "civilian" feminists.

"Illuminating and inspiring, this book presents a distinguished woman's exhilarating vision of what it means to live with openness, honesty, and a willingness to grow beyond the apparent confinement of seemingly irreconcilable polarities. An invigoratingly candid memoir from a giant of women's rights." —Kirkus

Stevens, John Paul
The Making of a Justice: Reflections on My First 94 Years. John Paul Stevens. Little Brown & Co 2019. 560 p.
ISBN 9780316489645
Grades: Adult — B
1. Stevens, John Paul, 1920-2019 2. Judges 3. Federal judges 4. Criminal justice system 5. Federal courts 6. Autobiographies and memoirs 7. History writing — Judicial branch — United States 8. Life stories — Law and order — Judges and lawyers
LC 2018962439

The former Supreme Court justice provides a personal account of his youth, his early days in private practice, and some of the most important Supreme Court decisions from his thirty-four-year tenure.

Stevens, Norma
Avedon: Something Personal. Norma Stevens and Steven M.L. Aronson. Spiegel & Grau 2017. 704 p.
ISBN 9780812994438
Grades: Adult — B
1. Avedon, Richard 2. Photographers 3. Photography 4. Artists 5. Biographies 6. Life stories — Arts and culture — Artists 7. Arts and entertainment — Photography
LC Bl2017036562

A candid portrait of the famed photographer, co-written by his longtime business partner and confidante, traces Avedon's life from his humble New York childhood to his death during a shoot in 2004.

Stevenson, Bryan
Just Mercy: A Story of Justice and Redemption. Bryan Stevenson. Spiegel & Grau 2014. x, 336 pages
ISBN 9780812994520
Grades: Adult — B
1. Stevenson, Bryan 2. Capital punishment 3. Criminal justice system 4. Justice 5. Redemption 6. Lawyers 7. Social advocates 8. Mercy 9. Poverty 10. Malicious accusation 11. Marginalized people 12. Intersectionality 13. Alabama 14. Autobiographies and memoirs 15. Page to screen 16. Life stories — Law and order — Judges and lawyers 17. Society and culture — Violence and crime — Criminal justice system 18. True Crime — Police and Lawyers 19. Antiracist literature

ALA Notable Book, 2015; Andrew Carnegie Medal for Excellence in Non-Fiction, 2015; Booklist Editors' Choice, 2014; in the Margins Book Awards: Advocacy and Social Justice, 2015; New York Times Notable Book, 2014; Kirkus Prize for Nonfiction finalist, 2014.

The founder of the Equal Justice Initiative in Montgomery, Alabama recounts his experiences as a lawyer working to assist those desperately in need, reflecting on his pursuit of the ideal of compassion in American justice.

"Stevenson details changes in victims rights, incarceration of juveniles, death penalty reforms, inflexible sentencing laws, and the continued practices of injustice that see too many juveniles, minorities, and mentally ill people imprisoned in a frenzy of mass incarceration in the U.S. A passionate account of the ways our nation thwarts justice and inhumanely punishes the poor and disadvantaged." —Booklist

Includes bibliographical references.

Stewart, David O.
Madison's Gift: Five Partnerships That Built America. David O. Stewart. Simon & Schuster 2015. 432 p.
ISBN 9781451688580
Grades: Adult — B
1. Madison, James, 1751-1836 2. Founding Fathers of the United States 3. Politicians 4. Presidents 5. United States history 6. United States 7. 18th century 8. Biographies 9. History writing — Presidency — 18th century — United States 10. Life stories — Politics — Politicians 11. History writing — Early America — United States
LC 2014021393

James Madison, one of the Founders of the U.S. and its fourth president, seems to fade into the background in comparison with his revolutionary comrades, who were physically taller and more extroverted. However, Madison was a brilliant writer and skilled collaborator, making him indispensable to the success of the new republic the Founders were designing. In Madison's Gift, acclaimed author David Stewart highlights Madison's abilities and details his work with five collaborators—four other Founders and his wife Dolley.

Includes bibliographical references and index.

Stewart, Patrick
★ *Making It So: A Memoir.* Patrick Stewart. Gallery Books 2023. 432 p.
ISBN 9781982167738
Grades: Adult — B
1. Stewart, Patrick, 1940- 2. Actors and actresses 3. Television 4. Films 5. Theater 6. Fame 7. British people 8. English people 9. Autobiographies and memoirs 10. Life stories — Arts and culture — Performing arts — Actors and actresses 11. Arts and Entertainment — Movies and Television

The distinguished stage and screen actor whose illustrious career spans six decades and who has captivated audiences around the world presents his long-awaited memoir in which he recounts his journey thus far, from his humble beginnings in Yorkshire, England, to the very heights of Hollywood.

Stiles, T. J.
Custer's Trials: A Life on the Frontier of a New America. T. J. Stiles. Alfred A. Knopf 2015. 352 p.
ISBN 9780307592644
Grades: Adult — B
1. Custer, George A. (George Armstrong), 1839-1876 2. Little Bighorn, Battle of the, 1876 3. Indigenous peoples of North America 4. Married men 5. Household employees 6. Freedom seekers 7. United States Civil War, 1861-1865 8. Command of troops 9. Frontier and pioneer life 10. Generals 11. United States history 12. The West (United States) history 13. The West (United States) 14. United States 15. 19th century 16. American Civil War era (1861-1865) 17. Biographies 18. Life stories — Law and order — Military leaders 19. History writing — Westward expansion — United States 20. History writing — Military — Military leadership
LC 2015002070

Pulitzer Prize for History, 2016; Spur Award for Biography, 2016; National Book Critics Circle Award for Biography finalist, 2015; Pulitzer Prize for Biography or Autobiography finalist, 2016.

ESSENTIAL AND RECOMMENDED TITLES
Biography

A biography of the iconic Civil War commander examines his contributions to politics and the Industrial Revolution, sharing insights into his turbulent relationships, perspectives on Native Americans, and conflicts with the military.

"Stiles ably points out [Custer's] many defining flaws: His heroic style didn't work in an era of tact and skill, and there is no doubt that he was self-serving, generally assuming that rules weren't made for him and never showing remorse. In addition to examining Custer's life, the author also introduces his cook, the fascinating Eliza Brown, an escaped slave who deserves a biography of her own." —*Kirkus*

Includes bibliographical references and index.

★ *The First Tycoon: The Epic Life of Cornelius Vanderbilt*. T.J. Stiles. Alfred A. Knopf 2009. 752 p.
ISBN 9780375415425
Grades: Adult   B
1. Vanderbilt, Cornelius, 1794-1877 2. Millionaires 3. Steamboats 4. Railroads 5. Businesspeople 6. United States history 7. United States 8. 19th century 9. Biographies 10. Business and economics — Business leaders and entrepreneurs 11. Life stories — Business — Business leaders
LC 2008047879

National Book Award for Nonfiction, 2009; Pulitzer Prize for Biography or Autobiography, 2010; New York Times Notable Book, 2009.

A biography of the combative man whose genius and force of will created modern capitalism, documenting how Vanderbilt helped launch the transportation revolution, propel the Gold Rush, reshape Manhattan, and invent the modern corporation.

"This is a mighty and mighty confident work, one that moves with force and conviction and imperious wit through Vanderbilt's noisy life and times. This is state-of-the-art biography, crisper and more piquant than a 600-page book has any right to be." —*New York Times*

Includes bibliographical references and index.

Jesse James: Last Rebel of the Civil War. T.J. Stiles. A.A. Knopf 2002. xiii, 510 p, 8 p. of plates : Illustration; Map
ISBN 9780375405839
Grades: Adult   B
1. James, Jesse, 1847-1882 2. Outlaws 3. Guerrillas 4. Civil war 5. United States Civil War, 1861-1865 6. Resistance to military occupation 7. United States history 8. The West (United States) 9. Missouri 10. 1860s 11. American Civil War era (1861-1865) 12. Biographies 13. History writing — Westward expansion — United States 14. History writing — Wars and conflicts — American Civil War
LC 2002025493

ALA Notable Book, 2003; Library Journal Best Books, 2002; New York Times Notable Book, 2002.

A reassessment of the legendary American outlaw chronicles the life of Jesse James, from his youth in Missouri, to his teenage years fighting alongside Confederate guerrillas, to his criminal career.

"This is a well-written and often surprising reinterpretation of the life of a legendary and enigmatic figure." —*Booklist*

Includes bibliographical references (p. 473-489) and index.

Stone, Alex
Fooling Houdini: Magicians, Mentalists, Math Geeks, and the Hidden Powers of the Mind. Alex Stone. Harper 2012. 320 p.
ISBN 9780061766213
Grades: Adult   B
1. Stone, Alex 2. Magicians 3. Magic tricks 4. Occultism 5. Autobiographies and memoirs 6. Life stories — Arts and culture — Performing arts — Entertainers and celebrities
LC 2011041927

A biography of magician Alex Stone, his quest to join the ranks of master magicians and the interesting characters he meets along the way.

Stone, Daniel
The Food Explorer: The True Adventures of the Globe-trotting Botanist Who Transformed the American Dinner Table. Daniel Stone. Dutton 2018. xvi, 397 pages, [8] unnumbered pages of plates : Illustration; Color; Map
ISBN 9781101990582
Grades: Adult   B
1. Fairchild, David, 1869-1954 2. Botanists 3. Plant introduction 4. Agriculture 5. Food habits 6. Alien plants 7. Plant geography 8. Voyages and travels 9. United States 10. Biographies 11. Business and economics — Industries — Agriculture and food 12. Life stories — Science, technology, and medicine — Scientists and inventors 13. History writing — Science, technology, and medicine
LC 2017009136

Documents the adventures and legacy of 19th-century botanist and food explorer David Fairchild to reveal the stories of how diverse crops ranging from avocadoes and mangoes to seedless grapes and pomegranates were introduced to America from faraway cultures.

"An erudite and entertaining historical biography of a food pioneer with particular interest for gastronomes and agriculture enthusiasts." —*Kirkus*

Includes bibliographical references and index.

Stone, Sharon
The Beauty of Living Twice. Sharon Stone. Alfred a Knopf 2021. 256 p.
ISBN 9780525656760
Grades: Adult   B
1. Stone, Sharon, 1958- 2. Actors and actresses 3. People who have had strokes 4. Celebrities 5. Psychic trauma 6. Family relationships 7. Life change events 8. Resilience 9. Humanitarianism 10. Love 11. Healing 12. Strokes 13. Autobiographies and memoirs 14. Life stories — Arts and culture — Performing arts — Actors and actresses 15. Life stories — Facing adversity 16. Arts and Entertainment — Movies and Television

The Nobel Peace Summit Award-winning actress, activist and humanitarian chronicles her efforts to recover and rebuild after a massive stroke, discussing how her health challenges were also shaped by industry standards, childhood traumas and family bonds.

"The celebrated actor reflects on a life of success, activism, and cleansing self-discovery. . . . Fans will blissfully revel in the intimate if restlessly delivered details in this perceptive memoir." —*Kirkus*

Stone, Sly
Thank You (falettinme Be Mice Elf Agin): A Memoir. Sly Stone, with Ben Greenman; foreword by Ahmir Khalib Thompson. AUWA Books / MCD / Farrar, Straus and Giroux 2023. 288 p.
ISBN 9780374606978
Grades: Adult   B
1. Stone, Sly 2. African American musicians 3. African American singers 4. Rhythm and blues musicians 5. Rock musicians 6. Funk music 7. Fame 8. Drug addiction 9. Sobriety 10. Gratitude 11. North American people 12. American people 13. Autobiographies and memoirs 14. Life stories — Arts and culture — Performing arts — Musicians and composers 15. Life stories — Facing adversity — Medical issues — Addiction 16. Arts and Entertainment — Music — Rap and R&B
LC 2023015269

One of the few indisputable geniuses of pop music, Sly Stone is a trailblazer and a legend. He created a new kind of music, mixing Black and white, male and female, funk and rock. As a songwriter, he penned some of the most iconic anthems of the 1960s and '70s. As a performer, he electrified audiences with a persona and stage presence that set a lasting standard for pop-culture performance. Yet his life has also been a cautionary tale, known as much for how he dropped out of the spotlight as for what put him there in the first place. In his much-anticipated memoir, he's finally ready to share his story—a story that many thought he'd never have the chance to tell.

"It's unadulterated, unapologetic Sly." —*Publishers Weekly*

Includes index.

PUBLIC LIBRARY CORE COLLECTION: NONFICTION
Twentieth Edition

Stourton, James
 Kenneth Clark: Life, Art and Civilisation. James Stourton. Alfred A. Knopf 2016. 304 p.
 ISBN 9780385351171
 Grades: Adult   B
 1. Clark, Kenneth, 1903-1983 2. Art historians 3. Museum curators 4. Biographies 5. Life stories — Arts and culture 6. Arts and entertainment — Museums and collections
 LC Bl2016047148
 The first and definitive biography of this brilliant polymath—director of the National Gallery, author, patron of the arts, social lion, and singular pioneer of television—that also tells the story of the arts in the twentieth century through his astonishing life.
 "A sparkling, thoroughly entertaining portrait of a brilliant popularizer who brought art to the masses." —*Kirkus*

Stratton, W. K.
 Floyd Patterson: The Fighting Life of Boxing's Invisible Champion. W. K. Stratton. Houghton Mifflin Harcourt 2012. 286 p.
 ISBN 9780151014309
 Grades: 9 10 11 12 Adult   B
 1. Patterson, Floyd 2. Boxers (Sports) 3. African American boxers 4. Boxing 5. United States 6. Biographies 7. Sports and Competition — Boxing 8. Life stories — Sports — Athletes
 LC 2012017319
 Oklahoma Book Award for Nonfiction, 2013.
 Documents the inspiring story of the civil rights activist, Olympic gold medalist, and history's youngest World Heavyweight Champion, placing his career against a backdrop of boxing's golden age while analyzing misunderstood aspects of his character.
 "Stratton's attention to detail is impressive, and he seems to have uncovered every little tidbit about Patterson's life both in and out of the ring, making this warm biography a must for boxing fanatics. An engaging, breezy portrait of an underappreciated boxing giant." —*Kirkus*

Strayed, Cheryl
 ★ *Wild: From Lost to Found on the Pacific Crest Trail.* Cheryl Strayed. Alfred A. Knopf 2012. 315 p. : Map
 ISBN 9780307592736
 Grades: Adult   B
 1. Strayed, Cheryl, 1968- 2. Authors, American 3. Hiking 4. Loss 5. Transformations, Personal 6. Death of mothers 7. Voyages and travels 8. Grief 9. Pacific Crest Trail 10. 21st century 11. Autobiographies and memoirs 12. Page to screen 13. Life stories — Facing adversity — Coping with death 14. Travel Writing — Women Travelers 15. Adult books for young adults
 LC 2011033752
 Amelia Bloomer List, 2013; Goodreads Choice Award, 2012; Indies' Choice Book Awards, Adult Nonfiction, 2013; Oregon Book Awards, Readers' Choice, 2013; School Library Journal Best Books: Best Adult Books 4 Teens, 2012.
 Ttraces the personal crisis the author endured after the death of her mother and a painful divorce, which prompted her ambition to undertake a dangerous 1,100-mile solo hike that both drove her to rock bottom and helped her to heal.
 Also published in large print format.

Streisand, Barbra
 ★ *My Name Is Barbra.* Barbra Streisand. Viking Press 2023. 1040 p.
 ISBN 9780525429524
 Grades: Adult   B
 1. Streisand, Barbra 2. Singers 3. Actors and actresses 4. Grammy award winners 5. Women film producers and directors 6. Women social advocates 7. Women and success 8. Jewish American women 9. Popular music 10. Jewish people 11. Jewish women 12. American people 13. North American people 14. Self-fulfillment 15. Brooklyn, New York City 16. New York City 17. Autobiographies and memoirs 18. Life stories — Arts and culture — Performing arts — Musicians and composers 19. Life stories — Arts and culture — Performing arts — Actors and actresses 20. Life stories — Arts and culture — Performing arts — Directors and producers
 LC 2023022687
 In her own words, the living legend tells the story of her life and extraordinary career, from growing up in Brooklyn to her first star-making appearances in NY nightclubs to her breakout performance in Funny Girl to the long string of successes in every medium in the years that followed.

Stuart, Amanda Mackenzie
 Empress of Fashion: A Life of Diana Vreeland. Amanda Mackenzie Stuart. HarperCollins 2012. 400 p.
 ISBN 9780061691744
 Grades: Adult   B
 1. Vreeland, Diana, 1903-1989 2. Fashion periodical editors 3. Fashion history 4. Women periodical editors 5. Fashion periodicals 6. Social life and customs 7. United States 8. 20th century 9. Autobiographies and memoirs 10. Biographies 11. Arts and Entertainment — Fashion 12. Life stories — Arts and culture — Writing — Journalists
 LC Bl2012038528
 This rare glimpse into the life of the innovative fashion editor of Harper's Bazaar and the legendary editor-in-chief of Vogue who, redefining women's sense of beauty and style, launched the careers of such timeless beauties Lauren Bacall and Lauren Hutton, explores her originality, her tenacity and her inimitable sensibility.

Stump, Al
 Cobb: A Biography. by AL Stump; with a foreword by Jimmie Reese. Algonquin Books of Chapel Hill 1994. xvii, 436 p. : Illustration
 ISBN 9780945575641
 Grades: 11 12 Adult   B
 1. Cobb, Ty, 1886-1961 2. Baseball players 3. People with cancer 4. Alcoholic men 5. Family relationships 6. Biographies 7. Sports and Competition — Baseball 8. Sports and Competition — Individual Athlete 9. Life stories — Sports — Athletes
 LC 94026122
 As a boy in the 1890s, he went looking for thrills in a rural Georgia that still burned with the humiliation of the Civil War. As an old man in the 1960s, he dared death, picked fights, refused to take his medicine, and drove off all his friends and admirers. He went to his deathbed alone, clutching a loaded pistol and a bag containing millions of dollars worth of cash and securities. During the years in between, he was, according to AL Stump, "the most shrewd, inventive, lurid, detested, mysterious, and superb of all baseball players." He was Ty Cobb. AL Stump tells how the dying Cobb hired him in 1960 to ghostwrite his autobiography, giving him a fascinating window into the life and times of the Georgia Peach.
 Includes bibliographical references (p. [423]) and index.

Sturgis, Matthew
 Oscar Wilde: A Life. Matthew Sturgis. Alfred A. Knopf 2021. 512 p.
 ISBN 9780525656364
 Grades: Adult   B
 1. Wilde, Oscar, 1854-1900 2. Gay men 3. Authors, Irish 4. Social life and customs 5. Ireland 6. Great Britain 7. United States 8. 19th century 9. Biographies 10. Arts and Entertainment — Writing and Publishing 11. Life stories — Arts and culture — Writing — Authors
 LC 2020054352
 Drawing on newly discovered letters, documents, first draft notebooks and the full transcript of the libel trial, this meticulously researched account of Oscar Wilde's life returns the man "to his times, and to the facts," giving us Wilde's own experience as he experienced it.
 "Historian Sturgis (Walter Sickert: A Life) delivers a comprehensive portrait of playwright and poet Oscar Wilde (1854-1900) in this extraordinary account." —*Publishers Weekly*
 Includes bibliographical references and index.

ESSENTIAL AND RECOMMENDED TITLES
Biography

Suchet, John
Beethoven: The Man Revealed. John Suchet. Atlantic Monthly Press 2013. xv, 389 pages : Illustration; Color
ISBN 9780802122063
Grades: Adult   B
1. Beethoven, Ludwig van, 1770-1827 2. Composers 3. Biographies 4. Life stories — Arts and culture — Performing arts
LC Bl2013043813

Drawing on the latest research as well as using source material, a leading authority on the life and works of Ludwig van Beethoven reveals the man behind the legend, painting a complete portrait of one of the greatest composers who ever lived.

Drawing on the latest research as well as using source material, a leading authority on the life and works of Ludwig van Beethoven reveals the man behind the legend, painting a complete portrait of the greatest composer who ever lived.

"For the many readers lacking the proper background in musical theory, British broadcaster and Beethoven authority Suchet's explanations of Beethoven's music sing to us almost as if we could hear it." —*Kirkus*

Includes index.

Mozart: The Man Revealed. John Suchet. Pegasus Books 2017. 288 pages : Illustration; Color
ISBN 9781681775098
Grades: Adult   B
1. Mozart, Wolfgang Amadeus, 1756-1791 2. Composers 3. Genius 4. Classical music 5. Musicians 6. Biographies 7. Life stories — Arts and culture — Performing arts — Musicians and composers 8. Arts and Entertainment — Music — Classical
LC Bl2017030785

The illustrated life-story of the world's most beloved composer, bringing vividly to life the man himself, his influences, achievements, and the glittering milieu of the Habsburg empire in eighteenth-century Europe.

"Rich with wit and warmth, this compact biography is thoroughly enchanting." —*Kirkus*

Includes bibliographical references and index.

Suetonius
★ *The Twelve Caesars.* by Gaius Suetonius Tranquillus; translated from the Latin by Robert Graves. Penguin 1979. 363 p. : Table; Map; Portrait
ISBN 9780140449211
Grades: Adult   B
1. Roman emperors 2. Rulers 3. Ancient history 4. Politics and government 5. Ancient Rome 6. Roman Empire (27 B.C.E.-476 C.E.) 7. History writing — Ancient — Rome
LC 80456493

First-century Roman life is portrayed in sketches of the family histories, public careers, physical traits, private lives, and vices of Roman rulers from Julius Caesar to Domitian.

Includes indexes.

Sullivan, Rosemary
Stalin's Daughter: The Extraordinary and Tumultuous Life of Svetlana Alliluyeva. Rosemary Sullivan. Harper 2015. 416 p.
ISBN 9780062206107
Grades: Adult   B
1. Allilueva, Svetlana, 1926-2011 2. Stalin, Joseph, 1879-1953 3. Children of heads of state 4. Freedom 5. Communism 6. Immigrants, Russian 7. Defectors 8. Adult children of suicide victims 9. Runaway mothers 10. Women artists 11. Soviet Union history 12. 20th century 13. Biographies 14. Life stories — Politics 15. History writing — Communism — Europe — Russia
LC 2014045982

ALA Notable Book, 2016; British Columbia Award for Canadian Non-Fiction, 2016; Charles Taylor Prize for Literary Non-Fiction (Canada), 2016; Hilary Weston Writers' Trust Prize, 2015; New York Times Notable Book, 2015; National Book Critics Circle Award for Biography finalist, 2015.

A painstakingly researched, revelatory portrait of the Soviet dictator's daughter traces her formative years in the Kremlin, the losses of numerous loved ones and her controversial defection to the United States.

"Svetlanas letters and family photographs enhance the portrait of a woman tortured by the secrets, lies, and intrigues at the center of her early life as a Kremlin princess and in later years as the object of fascination and scorn as the daughter of the feared Russian dictator." —*Booklist*

Includes biblliographical references.

Summitt, Pat Head
Sum It Up: 1,098 Victories, a Couple of Irrelevant Losses, and a Life in Perspective. Pat Summitt with Sally Jenkins. Crown 2013. 256 p.
ISBN 9780385346870
Grades: Adult   B
1. Summitt, Pat Head, 1952- 2. Women basketball coaches 3. College basketball 4. Basketball for women 5. People with Alzheimer's disease 6. Autobiographies and memoirs 7. Sports and Competition — Basketball 8. Sports and Competition — Coaches 9. Life stories — Sports — Athletes 10. Life stories — Sports — Coaches, managers, and owners
LC 2012050333

Describes how Summitt's upbringing helped her to develop a balanced coaching style that contributed to the Tennessee Vols record-breaking wins, recounting her recent personal battle against early onset Alzheimer's disease.

Sun, Carrie
Private Equity: A Memoir. Carrie Sun. Penguin 2024. 352 p.
ISBN 9780593654996
Grades: Adult   B
1. Sun, Carrie 2. Women executives 3. Chinese American women 4. Children of immigrants 5. Ambition 6. Hedge funds 7. Capitalists and financiers 8. Wealth 9. Workaholism 10. Corporate power 11. Corporate culture 12. Greed 13. Work-life balance 14. East Asian people 15. Chinese people 16. North American people 17. American people 18. Autobiographies and memoirs 19. Life stories — Business 20. Business and economics — Industries — Finance 21. Debut title

When we meet Carrie Sun, she can't shake the feeling that she's wasting her life. So when she gets the rare opportunity to work at one of the most prestigious hedge funds in the world, she knows she can't say no. Fourteen interviews later, she's in. A searing examination of our relationship to work, Carrie's story illuminates the struggle for balance in a world of extremes: Efficiency and excess, status and aspiration, power and fortune.

"Sun's memoir provides both a measured account of how soul-devouring the corporate world is and of how employees as well as bosses are complicit." —*Kirkus*

Sundberg, Kelly
Goodbye, Sweet Girl: A Story of Domestic Violence and Survival. Kelly Sundberg. HarperCollins 2018. 272 p.
ISBN 9780062497673
Grades: Adult   B
1. Sundberg, Kelly, 1977- 2. Family violence 3. Abusive men 4. Abused women 5. Violence against women 6. Married people 7. Marital conflict 8. Autobiographies and memoirs 9. Life stories — Facing adversity — Abuse survivors
LC Bl2018094994

The author describes her abusive marriage to a man who was funny, warm and supportive but also vengeful and violent and how she finally rejected the abuse, accepted responsibility for herself and decided that she deserved better.

Suny, Ronald Grigor
Stalin: Passage to Revolution. Ronald Grigor Suny. Princeton Univ Press 2020. 856 p.
ISBN 9780691182032
Grades: Adult   B
1. Stalin, Joseph, 1879-1953 2. Communists 3. Heads of state 4. Dictators 5. Soviet Union history 6. 20th century 7. Biographies 8. Life stories — Politics — Politicians 9. History writing — Communism — Europe — Russia

LC 2019034217

This is the definitive biography of Joseph Stalin from his birth to the October Revolution of 1917, a panoramic and often chilling account of how an impoverished, idealistic youth from the provinces of tsarist Russia was transformed into a cunning and fearsome outlaw who would one day become one of the twentieth century's most ruthless dictators.

"A comprehensive, deeply researched study of one of the world's most brutal dictators as he took the paths that would lead him to power." —*Kirkus*

Includes bibliographical references and index.

Suvari, Mena

The Great Peace: A Memoir. Mena Suvari. Hachette Books 2021. 256 p.
ISBN 9780306874529
Grades: Adult   B
1. Suvari, Mena, 1979- 2. Actors and actresses 3. Abused women 4. Psychological growth 5. Errors 6. Redemption 7. Women 8. Drugs 9. Sexuality 10. Fame 11. Interpersonal relations 12. Empowerment 13. Autobiographies and memoirs 14. Life stories — Arts and culture — Performing arts — Actors and actresses 15. Arts and Entertainment — Movies and Television

An award-winning actor, in this harrowing, heartbreaking coming-of-age story set in Hollywood, not only reveals her own mistakes, but also the lessons she learned and her efforts to understand and grow rather than casting blame, proving that there is always a light at the end.

"In this haunting debut, actor Suvari—best known for her roles in American Beauty, and American Pie—chronicles her life and rise in Hollywood, and opens up for the first time about being sexually abused.... While the experiences she details are devastating, her ability to weave them into a narrative of empowerment is what makes this so moving." —*Publishers Weekly*

Swafford, Jan

★ *Beethoven: Anguish and Triumph : A Biography*. Jan Swafford. Houghton Mifflin Harcourt 2014. xxi, 1077 pages : Illustration
ISBN 9780618054749
Grades: Adult   B
1. Beethoven, Ludwig van, 1770-1827 2. Composers 3. Music, German 4. Enlightenment (European intellectual movement) 5. Music history and criticism 6. Germany 7. Austria 8. Biographies 9. Life stories — Arts and culture — Performing arts — Musicians and composers 10. Arts and entertainment — Music — Classical

An esteemed music historian provides a rich, detailed overview of the life of Ludwig van Beethoven, traveling from Enlightenment-era Bonn to the musical capital of Europe, Vienna, to vividly describe the composer's career, ill health and romantic rejections.

"Rich in biographical detail, the volume contains revealing excerpts from many of Beethovens letters and from the written observations of his visitors and family; it also contains detailed analyses of many of his most notable works." —*Kirkus*

Includes bibliographical references (pages 946-955) and index.

Charles Ives: A Life with Music. Jan Swafford. W.W. Norton 1996. xv, 525 p. : Illustration
ISBN 9780393038934
Grades: Adult   B
1. Ives, Charles, 1874-1954 2. Composers 3. Insurance agents 4. Modern music 5. United States 6. Biographies 7. Arts and Entertainment — Music — Classical 8. Life stories — Arts and culture — Performing arts — Musicians and composers

LC 95022549

L. L. Winship/PEN New England Award, 1997; National Book Critics Circle Award for Biography finalist, 1996.

A biography of the American composer examines how his music was shaped by his Yankee background, the influence of his father, and his Yale education.

"Ives was a professional organist, a successful insurance executive, a political idealist, and an immensely prolific composer. The author believes that Ives's transcendentalism was central to his identity, ceaselessly inspiring him while also spurring him on to an inevitable physical collapse. Swafforda composer himselfintersperses his biography with valuable 'Entr'actes' of approachable musical analysis, and ends with a ringing endorsement of Ives as an ideal composer for a democratic society." —*The New Yorker*

Includes bibliographical references (p. [508]-512) and index.

Johannes Brahms: A Biography. Jan Swafford. Alfred A. Knopf 1997. xxii, 699 p. : Illustration
ISBN 9780679422617
Grades: Adult   B
1. Brahms, Johannes, 1833-1897 2. Composers 3. 19th century 4. Biographies 5. Life stories — Arts and culture — Performing arts — Musicians and composers 6. Arts and Entertainment — Music — Classical

LC 97029308

New York Times Notable Book, 1998.

A biography of the nineteenth-century German composer looks at his daily life, his associates—including his relationships with Robert Schumann, Clara Shumann, Richard Wagner, and Eduard Hanslick—and his achievements as a composer.

"Swafford's study, clearly a labor of profound affection, is a model biography: Eloquent, clear-sighted and often moving." —*Publishers Weekly*

Includes bibliographical references (p. [671]-678) and index.

Mozart: The Reign of Love. Jan Swafford. HarperCollins 2020. 592 p.
ISBN 9780062433572
Grades: Adult   B
1. Mozart, Wolfgang Amadeus, 1756-1791 2. Composers 3. Genius 4. Classical music 5. Musicians 6. 18th century 7. Biographies 8. Life stories — Arts and culture — Performing arts — Musicians and composers 9. Arts and Entertainment — Music — Classical

Mozart is the complete exhumation of a genius in his life and ours: a man who would enrich the world with his talent for centuries to come and who would immeasurably shape classical music. As Swafford reveals, it's nearly impossible to understand classical music's origins and indeed its evolutions, as well as the Baroque period, without studying the man himself.

Composer and biographer Swafford brings expertise and insight to bear on a comprehensive, animated life of Wolfgang Amadeus Mozart (1756-1791). Debunking a romanticized image of Mozart as a tormented artist, the author portrays a 'Jolly and informal' man with a 'Boundless appetite for pleasure.' —*Kirkus*

Swarns, Rachel L.

★ *American Tapestry: The Story of the Black, White, and Multiracial Ancestors of Michelle Obama*. Rachel L. Swarns. HarperCollins 2012. 400 p.
ISBN 9780061999864
Grades: Adult   B
1. Obama, Michelle, 1964- 2. Ancestors 3. Generations 4. Kinship 5. Presidents' spouses 6. Family history 7. United States 8. Biographies 9. History writing — General 10. Life stories — Politics — Politicians

LC 2012454035

Booklist Editors' Choice, 2012; New York Times Notable Book, 2012.

Illuminating the lives of the ordinary people who fought for freedom in the Revolutionary and Civil Wars, this intimate family history traces the compelling story of Michelle Obama's ancestors, taking readers on a journey from slavery to the White House in five generations that bears witness to our changing nation.

"The result is an engrossing book that demonstrates a lot of research, dedication, and care. Recommended to all readers interested in biographies that employ genealogical research, as well as readers in African American heritage and history." —*Library Journal*

Sweig, Julia

Lady Bird Johnson: Hiding in Plain Sight. Julia Sweig. Random House 2021. 560 p.
ISBN 9780812995909
Grades: Adult   B
1. Johnson, Lady Bird, 1912-2007 2. Johnson, Lyndon B, 1908-1973 3. Presidential election, 1964 4. Women and politics 5. Women 6. Presidents' spouses 7. Political participation 8. Politics and government 9. Determination 10. United States 11. 20th century 12. 1960s 13. Biographies 14. Page to screen 15. History

ESSENTIAL AND RECOMMENDED TITLES
Biography

writing — Presidency — 20th century — United States 16. Life stories — Politics — Politicians

LC 2020001666

A magisterial portrait of Lady Bird Johnson, and a major reevaluation of the profound yet underappreciated impact the First Lady's political instincts had on LBJ's presidency.

"An award-winning author/Journalist who is currently nonresident senior research fellow at the LBJ School of Public Affairs at the University of Texas-Austin, Sweig offers a thoroughgoing and revisionist view of the quiet Lady Bird Johnson, here presented as a true power behind the throne." —*Library Journal*

Made into a movie with the tilte the Lady Bird Diaries on Huly, fall 2023; Includes bibliographical references and index.

Sykes, Christopher Simon
David Hockney: The Biography. Christopher Simon Sykes. Nan A. Talese/Doubleday 2012. 384 p.
ISBN 9780385531443
Grades: Adult   B
1. Hockney, David, 1937- 2. Artists 3. Pop art 4. Gay men 5. Modern art 6. Biographies 7. Arts and Entertainment — Painting, Drawing, and Sculpture 8. Life stories — Arts and culture — Artists

LC 2011041629

A first half of an authorized account of the life and work of the influential British artist and leading proponent of the Pop art genre includes coverage of his education at the Royal College of Art, the role of the 1960s in shaping his vision and his relationship with Peter Schlesinger during the turbulent emergence of gay rights.

Includes bibliographical references and index; Originally published: Hockney: the biography. London : Century, the Random House Group, 2011.

David Hockney: The Biography. Christopher Simon Sykes. Nan A. Talese/Doubleday 2014. 430 p.
ISBN 9780385535908
Grades: Adult   B
1. Hockney, David, 1937- 2. Artists 3. Pop art 4. Gay men 5. Modern art 6. Biographies 7. Arts and Entertainment — Painting, Drawing, and Sculpture 8. Life stories — Arts and culture — Artists

Presents an authorized account of the life and work of the influential British artist.

"Recommended for anyone interested in the remarkable life of this highly regarded painter. Rich with archival detail and the insight of family, friends, and the artist himself, the book is an engaging read." —*Library Journal*

Symonds, Craig L.
Lincoln and His Admirals. Craig L. Symonds. Oxford University Press 2008. 448 p.
ISBN 9780195310221
Grades: Adult   B
1. Lincoln, Abraham, 1809-1865 2. Welles, Gideon, 1802-1878 3. Fox, Gustavus Vasa, 1821-1883 4. Naval battles 5. Command of troops 6. Military strategy 7. Civil war 8. United States Civil War, 1861-1865 9. Presidents 10. Naval operations 11. Naval history 12. United States history 13. United States 14. 19th century 15. American Civil War era (1861-1865) 16. Biographies 17. History writing — Presidency — 19th century — United States 18. History writing — Wars and conflicts — American Civil War 19. Adult books for young adults

LC 2008004251

A prize-winning historian reveals how Abraham Lincoln managed the men who ran the naval side of the Civil War and transformed himself into one of the greatest naval strategists of his age, in a unique and riveting account of the commander-in-chief during the Civil War.

Includes bibliographical references and index.

Szarkowski, John
Ansel Adams at 100. John Szarkowski. Little, Brown and Co. 2001. 191 p. : Illustration
ISBN 9780821225158

Grades: Adult   B
1. Adams, Ansel, 1902-1984 2. Artistic photography 3. Landscape photography 4. Art exhibitions 5. Picture books for adults 6. Arts and Entertainment — Photography

LC 00069941

Library Journal Best Books, 2001.

Commemorates the art of the late landscape photographer and accompanies an international exhibit by showcasing 114 photographic images complemented by a critical essay on Adams' contributions to modern art.

In association with the San Francisco Museum of Modern Art.

Szczeszak-Brewer, Agata
The Hunger Book: A Memoir from Communist Poland. Agata Izabela Brewer. Mad Creek Books, an imprint of the Ohio State University Press 2023. 240 p.
ISBN 9780814258781
Grades: Adult   B
1. Szczeszak-Brewer, Agata 2. Mothers and daughters 3. Adult children of alcoholics 4. Families 5. Childhood 6. Polish people 7. Motherhood 8. Resilience 9. Psychic trauma 10. Food security 11. Nature 12. Communism 13. Eastern European people 14. Poland 15. Autobiographies and memoirs 16. Life stories — Relationships — Growing up 17. Family and relationships — Families 18. History Writing — Europe

LC 2023011456

Personal essays exploring the author's experiences growing up in Communist Poland against a backdrop of food insecurity, parental mental illness and addiction, and the hardships of living under a totalitarian regime.

"A memorable meditation on hunger for food and love, childhood in a totalitarian regime, and resilience." —*Kirkus*

Szerlip, Barbara
The Man Who Designed the Future: Norman Bel Geddes and the Invention of Twentieth-century America. B. Alexandra Szerlip. Melville House 2017. xvii, 396 p.
ISBN 9781612195629
Grades: Adult   B
1. Geddes, Norman Bel, 1893-1958 2. Designers 3. Design 4. 1960s 5. Biographies 6. Life stories — Arts and culture 7. History writing — Arts and culture

LC 2016050576

A history of American innovation follows a polymath with humble origins who found himself at the center of the worlds of industry, advertising, theater and even gaming, designing everything from the first all-weather stadium to Manhattan's most exclusive nightclub to Futurama, the prescient 1939 exhibit that envisioned how America would look in the not-too-distant future.

"In this fascinating and minutely researched biography, Szerlip brings the brilliant, indefatigable industrial designers imagination to life so we can marvel once more." —*Booklist*

Includes bibliographical references.

Szwed, John F.
Cosmic Scholar: The Life and Times of Harry Smith. John Szwed. Farrar, Straus and Giroux 2023. 416 p.
ISBN 9780374282240
Grades: Adult   B
1. Smith, Harry Everett, 1923-1991 2. Artists 3. Beat generation 4. Film producers and directors 5. Anthropologists 6. United States 7. Biographies 8. Life stories — Arts and culture — Performing arts — Directors and producers 9. Arts and Entertainment — General

LC 2023008707

A biography of filmmaker, anthropologist, and mystic Harry Smith.

"In this vividly detailed biography, music scholar Szwed (Billie Holiday) brilliantly captures the life and legacy of the enigmatic filmmaker, folklorist, painter, producer, anthropologist, archivist, Kabbalist, and alchemist Harry Smith (1923?1991)…The result is a masterful ode to a 'Strange and singular character' in American arts." —*Publishers Weekly*

Includes bibliographical references and index.

PUBLIC LIBRARY CORE COLLECTION: NONFICTION
Twentieth Edition

Taffa, Deborah Jackson
★ *Whiskey Tender: A Memoir.* Deborah Jackson Taffa. Harper 2024. 320 p.
ISBN 9780063288515
Grades: Adult — B
1. Ethnic identity 2. Indigenous reservations 3. Family relationships 4. Assimilation (Sociology) 5. Culture conflict 6. Survival 7. Pueblo (North American people) 8. Quechan (North American people) 9. Indigenous peoples of North America 10. Arizona 11. California 12. New Mexico 13. 20th century 14. Life stories — Identity — Race and ethnicity
LC 2023020169
The author presents a memoir of family and survival, coming-of-age on and off the reservation, and of the frictions between mainstream American culture and Native inheritance; assimilation and reverence for tradition.
"With an emphasis on her youth and coming-of-age, Taffa offers readers a much-needed Indigenous perspective on American life." —*Booklist*

Taing, Mae Bunseng
Under the Naga Tail: A True Story of Survival, Bravery, and Escape from the Cambodian Genocide. Mae Bunseng Taing, with James Taing. Greenleaf Book Group 2023. 319 p.
ISBN 9798886450187
Grades: Adult — B
1. Taing, Mae Bunseng 2. Revolutions 3. Military government 4. Refugees 5. Teenage refugees 6. Cambodian genocide, 1975-1979 7. Atrocities 8. Authoritarianism 9. Families 10. Escapes 11. Survival 12. Southeast Asian people 13. Cambodian people 14. Asian history 15. Cambodia 16. 20th century 17. Autobiographies and memoirs 18. Life stories — Facing adversity — War and oppression — Refugees 19. History writing — Asia — Southeast Asia 20. History writing — Wars and conflicts
Forced from his home by the Khmer Rouge, teenager Mae Taing struggles to endure years of backbreaking work, constant starvation, and ruthless cruelty from his captors—supposed freedom fighters who turned against their own people. This gripping and inspiring memoir, written with Mae's son, James, is not merely an incredible story of survival, but a testament to the human spirit's capacity in us all to endure and prevail in spite of great adversity.
"A memorable story of war and seemingly miraculous escape." —*Kirkus*

Tallent, Elizabeth
Scratched: A Memoir of Perfectionism. Elizabeth Tallent. Harper360 2020. 256 pages
ISBN 9780062410375
Grades: Adult — B
1. Perfectionism 2. Women authors 3. Families 4. Women college teachers 5. Divorced mothers 6. Mental health 7. Women authors, American 8. Self-acceptance 9. 20th century 10. Autobiographies and memoirs 11. Biographies 12. Life stories — Arts and culture — Writing — Authors 13. Life stories — Facing adversity — Medical issues 14. Life stories — Relationships — Parent and child
LC Bl2020006474
The acclaimed author of Museum Pieces explores her ferocious need for perfection that caused a 22-year gap in writing after initially publishing five literary novels between the ages of 27 and 37.
"The author's prose is dense, precise, and often lyrical, but the relentless energy of her long sentences and pageslong paragraphs sometimes feels overwhelming. A candid, sharply etched self-portrait." —*Kirkus*

Talley, Andre Leon
The Chiffon Trenches: A Memoir. Andre Leon Talley. Ballantine Books 2020. xv, 284 pages : Illustration; Plate
ISBN 9780593129258
Grades: Adult — B
1. Talley, Andre Leon. 1948-2022 2. Clothing industry and trade 3. Fashion 4. Editors 5. Racism 6. Growing up 7. African Americans 8. Fashion periodical editors 9. Autobiographies and memoirs 10. Biographies 11. Life stories — Identity — Race and ethnicity 12. Arts and Entertainment — Fashion 13. Life stories — Arts and culture — Fashion
LC 2019055525
A revealing memoir by a noted style icon captures the fashion world from the inside out, in its most glamorous and most cutthroat moments.
"Though the text brims with gossipy anecdotes, Talley mixes the serious and the saucy with equal heft. Though his legacy speaks for itself, this balanced, entertaining memoir is dramatic proof in print. A heartfelt and often eyebrow-raising memoir perfect for armchair fashionistas or high-fashion insiders." —*Kirkus*

Tallis, Frank
★ *Mortal Secrets: Freud, Vienna, and the Discovery of the Modern Mind.* Frank Tallis. St. Martin's Press 2024. 352 p.
ISBN 9781250288950
Grades: Adult — B
1. Freud, Sigmund, 1856-1939 2. Intellectual life 3. Influence (Literary, artistic, etc.) 4. Psychoanalysts 5. Psychoanalysis 6. Civilization 7. Culture 8. European history 9. Jewish men 10. Vienna, Austria 11. 19th century 12. 20th century 13. Biographies 14. History Writing — Europe 15. Life stories — Science, technology, and medicine — Healthcare professionals 16. Science Writing — Medicine and health — Mental health 17. Society and culture — Psychology and human behavior
LC 2023051591
A clinical psychologist, whose mystery novels form the basis of PBS's Vienna Blood series, illuminates Sigmund Freud and his times, chronicling the evolution of psychoanalysis and opening up his life to embrace the Vienna he lived in and the lives of the people he associated with.
"Stunning in its breadth and depth, this is a magisterial treatment of a towering thinker." —*Publishers Weekly*
Includes bibliographical references.

Tallis, Nicola
Crown of Blood: The Deadly Inheritance of Lady Jane Grey. Nicola Tallis. Pegasus Books 2016. 384 p.
ISBN 9781681772448
Grades: Adult — B
1. Grey, Jane, Lady, 1537-1554 2. Tudor, House of 3. Women rulers 4. Inheritance and succession 5. Rulers 6. English history 7. British history 8. Great Britain 9. Tudor period (1485-1603) 10. Renaissance (1300-1600) 11. 16th century 12. Biographies 13. History writing — Renaissance — Europe 14. Life stories — Politics — Royalty 15. Life stories — People in history — Famous families
LC Bl2016047401
A history of Lady Jane Grey's often-misunderstood trial and execution places events against a backdrop of the dangerous plots and political intrigues of her time, examining her qualities as a charismatic advocate and martyr of the Protestant faith.
"Readers will share Tallis sympathy with the devout, passive Jane but also approve of her emphasis on the more powerful, ambitious, and unpleasant men and women that surrounded her." —*Kirkus*

Uncrowned Queen: The Life of Margaret Beaufort, Mother of the Tudors. Nicola Tallis. Basic Books 2020. 416 p.
ISBN 9781541617872
Grades: Adult — B
1. Beaufort, Margaret, Countess of Richmond and Derby, 1443-1509 2. Tudor, House of 3. Matriarchs 4. Women's power 5. Women and war 6. Nobility 7. Wars of the Roses, 1455-1485 8. British history 9. Great Britain 10. 15th century 11. Plantagenet period (1154-1485) 12. Tudor period (1485-1603) 13. Elizabethan era (1558-1603) 14. Biographies 15. History writing — Europe — United Kingdom 16. Life stories — People in history 17. Life stories — Politics — Royalty 18. History writing — Women's history
LC 2019054272
A portrait of Tudor matriarch Lady Margaret Beaufort details her critical role in the ending of the War of the Roses, the ascendancy of Henry VII and the political and ceremonial affairs of late-15th-century England.
"A highly sympathetic, spirited portrait of a major figure of the late Plantagenet and early Tudor reigns. Interested readers might also seek out Michael Jones and Malcolm Underwood's the King's Mother." —*Library Journal*
Includes bibliographical references and index.

ESSENTIAL AND RECOMMENDED TITLES
Biography

Tamblyn, Amber
★ *Era of Ignition: Coming of Age in a Time of Rage and Revolution.* Amber Tamblyn. Crown Archetype 2019. 272 p.
ISBN 9781984822987
Grades: Adult   **B**
1. Tamblyn, Amber 2. Feminists 3. Transformations, personal 4. Women's rights 5. Social advocacy 6. Intersectionality 7. Political culture 8. Actors and actresses 9. United States 10. Essays 11. Autobiographies and memoirs 12. Biographies 13. Liberal writing 14. Life stories — Arts and culture 15. Life stories — Identity — Gender 16. Society and culture — Gender — Women 17. Society and culture — Social activism and philanthropy 18. Adult books for young adults
LC 2018047443

The activist poet and Emmy-nominated actress presents a passionate, deeply personal exploration of feminism in today's divisive world that recalls a turning point in her life that helped her take control of her own destiny.

"A personal and passionate story about making a world 'that is nourished, healed, and flourishing.'" —*Kirkus*

Tamimi, Ahed
★ *They Called Me a Lioness: A Palestinian Girl's Fight for Freedom.* Ahed Tamimi and Dena Takruri. One World 2022. 224 p.
ISBN 9780593134580
Grades: Adult   **B**
1. Tamimi, Ahed, 2001- 2. Palestinian people 3. Arab-Israeli conflict 4. Women political activists 5. Teenagers 6. Military occupation 7. Marginalized people 8. Protests, demonstrations, vigils, etc. 9. Imprisonment 10. Resistance to government 11. Social justice 12. Political participation 13. West Bank (Jordan River) 14. Autobiographies and memoirs 15. Life stories — Facing adversity — War and oppression 16. Life stories — Politics — Activists and reformers 17. Politics and global affairs — World politics — Southwest Asia and North Africa (Middle East) — Israel and Palestine
LC 2022001373

Seen by some as a freedom-fighting hero and by others as a naive agitator, a Palestinian activist recounts her well-publicized interactions with Israeli solders and her unwavering commitment to family—and her fearless command of her own voice despite threats, intimidation and even incarceration.

"An expertly crafted, trenchant memoir from a formidable activist." —*Kirkus*

Includes bibliographical references.

Tammet, Daniel
Born on a Blue Day: Inside the Extraordinary Mind of an Autistic Savant : A Memoir. Daniel Tammet. Free Press 2007. IX, 226 p. : Illustration
ISBN 9781416535072
Grades: 11 12 Adult   **B**
1. Tammet, Daniel, 1979- 2. Autistic people 3. Savant syndrome 4. Autism spectrum disorders 5. Synesthesia 6. Social acceptance 7. Mathematical ability 8. Celebrities 9. Neurodivergent people 10. Social life and customs 11. Independence 12. Compulsive behavior 13. England 14. Autobiographies and memoirs 15. Science Writing — Medicine and health — Disabilities and disorders 16. Life stories — Facing adversity — Medical issues 17. Adult books for young adults
LC 2006041331

Booklist Editors' Choice, 2007; YALSA Best Books for Young Adults, 2008.

An autistic savant with genius-level mathematical talents describes how he was shunned by his classmates in spite of his super-human capacity for math and language and offers insight into how he experiences the world.

"This autobiography is as fascinating as Benjamin Franklin's and John Stuart Mill's, both of which are, like his, about the growth of a mind." —*Booklist*

Originally published: London : Hodder & Stoughton, 2006.

Tan, Amy
★ *Where the Past Begins: A Writer's Memoir.* Amy Tan. Ecco Press 2017. 224 p.
ISBN 9780062319296
Grades: Adult   **B**
1. Tan, Amy 2. Authors, American 3. Writing 4. Creativity 5. Women authors 6. Loss 7. Autobiographies and memoirs 8. Life stories — Arts and culture — Writing — Authors 9. Family and Relationships — Families
LC 2017036982

Longlisted for the Andrew Carnegie Medal for Excellence in Non-Fiction, 2018.

The best-selling author of such novels as the Joy Luck Club presents an intimate memoir on her life as a writer that explores formative experiences from her childhood and her evolving perspectives on the symbiotic relationship between fiction and emotional memory.

"In her ambushing and revealing memoir, beloved novelist Tan . chronicles with striking candor, sharp wit, and storytelling magic stranger-than-fiction traumas." —*Booklist*

Tanais
In Sensorium: Notes for My People. Tanais. HarperCollins 2022. 256 p.
ISBN 9780358381709
Grades: Adult   **B**
1. Tanais 2. Perfumes 3. Love 4. Violence 5. Healing 6. Bangladeshi Americans 7. Smell 8. Muslims 9. Material culture 10. Intergenerational relations 11. Sexual violence 12. Civilization 13. Spirituality 14. Identity 15. Odors 16. South Asian Americans 17. South Asian people 18. Intergenerational trauma 19. Autobiographies and memoirs 20. Life stories — Identity

Kirkus Prize for Nonfiction, 2022.

A writer and performer presents a memoir focused on the history of perfumes and how they have been used to mark the differences between the civilized and the barbaric and the pure and polluted.

"Readers will find more than just their olfactory senses heightened by this beautiful meditation." —*Publishers Weekly*

Taraborrelli, J. Randy
After Camelot: An Intimate History of the Kennedy Family, 1968 to the Present. J. Randy Taraborrelli. Grand Central Pub. 2012. 624 p.
ISBN 9780446553902
Grades: Adult   **B**
1. Kennedy family 2. Rich people 3. Family relationships 4. Biographies 5. History writing — United States 6. Life stories — People in history — Famous families
LC 2011029518

In this groundbreaking biography of the Kennedys, Taraborrelli brings this complex and dynamic family to life as he recounts the years following the murders of Jack and Bobby. He describes the challenges Bobby's children faced as they grew into adulthood; Eunice and Sargent Shriver's remarkable philanthropic work; the emotional turmoil Jackie faced after JFK's assassination and the complexities of her eventual marriage to Aristotle Onassis; the sudden death of JFK Jr. and the stoicism and grace of his sister, Caroline. He also brings into clear focus the complex and intriguing story of Ted Kennedy and shows how he influenced the sensibilities of the next generation and challenged them to uphold the Kennedy name.

Includes bibliographical references and index.

★ *Jackie: Public, Private, Secret.* J. Randy Taraborrelli. St. Martin's Press 2023. 528 p.
ISBN 9781250276216
Grades: Adult   **B**
1. Onassis, Jacqueline Kennedy, 1929-1994 2. Celebrities 3. Presidents' spouses 4. Fame 5. North American people 6. American people 7. United States 8. 20th century 9. Biographies 10. Life stories — Arts and culture — Performing arts — Entertainers and celebrities 11. History writing — Women's history 12. Life stories — Politics
LC 2023009379

Based on hundreds of new interviews, this often startling look at the life of the legendary former first lady explores the flaws and contradictions that only served to make her even more iconic.

"Stunning, scintillating, and, at times, a bit salacious, Kennedy expert Taraborrelli's latest biography of the legendary Jackie O shares intimate details about her most rewarding yet frequently vexing relationships." —*Booklist*

Includes index.

★ *The Secret Life of Marilyn Monroe*. J. Randy Taraborrelli. Grand Central Pub. 2009. 576 p.

ISBN 9780446580823

Grades: Adult   B

1. Monroe, Marilyn, 1926-1962 2. Mental illness 3. Mothers and daughters 4. Child-separated fathers 5. Celebrities 6. Medical genetics 7. Psychology 8. Films 9. Actors and actresses 10. People with emotional illnesses 11. Women 12. People with mental illnesses 13. Men-women relations 14. United States history 15. Hollywood, California 16. United States 17. 20th century 18. Biographies 19. Arts and Entertainment — Movies and Television 20. Life stories — Arts and culture — Performing arts — Actors and actresses 21. Science Writing — Medicine and health — Mental health

LC 2008044704

A profile of the iconic actress explores the roles of the influential women in her life, including her mentally ill mother, in an account that also discusses Monroe's own struggles with mental illness, her estranged father, and the Kennedys.

"For this biography, the author delves beneath the legend of Marilyn Monroe to uncover the stark facts of the life and times of a singularly vulnerable woman woefully unequipped to deal with the quotidian business of normal life, much less the pressures of a Hollywood career and international celebrity. A painful and engrossing account of the profoundly damaged personality at the heart of the world's greatest sex symbol." —*Kirkus*

Includes index.

Tate, Christie

B.F.F.: A Memoir of Friendship Lost and Found. Christie Tate. Avid Reader Press 2023. 288 p.

ISBN 9781668009420

Grades: Adult   B

1. Female friendship 2. Interpersonal relations 3. Social isolation 4. Self-evaluation 5. American people 6. North American people 7. Self-discovery 8. Self-esteem 9. Autobiographies and memoirs 10. Life stories — Relationships — Friendship 11. Family and Relationships — Friendship

The author of the New York Times bestseller Group, reflects on her lifelong struggles to sustain female friendship and how the return of an old friend helped her explore the reasons she has avoided attachment.

"In this intensive yet refreshing self-analysis, Tate...dissects the nature of her bonds with women....A meaningful, memorable journey from inner pain to honest, open, and enduring friendship." —*Kirkus*

★ *Group: How One Therapist and a Circle of Strangers Saved My Life*. Simon & Schuster 2020. 288 p.

ISBN 9781982154615

Grades: Adult   B

1. Tate, Christie 2. Group psychotherapy 3. Psychotherapists 4. Eating disorders 5. Compulsive behavior 6. Self-hate 7. Women lawyers 8. Dating 9. Bulimia 10. Men-women relations 11. Chicago, Illinois 12. Texas 13. Autobiographies and memoirs 14. Book club best bets

LC Bl2020022051

A top law school graduate struggling with suicidal thoughts and an eating disorder describes her reluctant participation in a therapeutic support group that taught her the meaning of human connection and intimacy. A first book.

"Tate delivers a no-holds-barred account of her five-plus years in group therapy in this dazzling debut memoir." —*Publishers Weekly*

Taubman, William

Gorbachev: His Life and Times. William Taubman. W.W. Norton & Company 2017. xxv, 852 pages

ISBN 9780393647013

Grades: Adult   B

1. Gorbachev, Mikhail, 1931-2022 2. Heads of state 3. Presidents 4. Cold War 5. Social change 6. Glasnost 7. Perestroika 8. Communism 9. Politics and government 10. Soviet Union 11. 1980s 12. 1990s 13. Biographies 14. Life stories — Politics — Politicians 15. History writing — Communism — Europe — Russia 16. History writing — Cold War

LC 2017015009

Longlisted for the Andrew Carnegie Medal for Excellence in Non-Fiction, 2018; National Book Critics Circle Award for Biography finalist, 2017.

An extensive portrait of the transformational world leader examines his liberal policies of perestroika and glasnost, his role in ending the Cold War and his unintentional oversight over the collapse of the Soviet Union.

"Taubman (political science, Amherst College) has written a monumental, groundbreaking study of Soviet President Mikhail Sergeyevich Gorbachev." —*Choice*

Includes bibliographical references and index.

Khrushchev: The Man and His Era. William Taubman. Norton 2003. xx, 876 p. : Illustration; Map

ISBN 9780393051445

Grades: Adult   B

1. Khrushchev, Nikita Sergeevich, 1894-1971 2. Stalin, Joseph, 1879-1953 3. Cold War 4. Heads of state 5. International relations 6. Politics and government 7. Soviet Union 8. 20th century 9. Biographies 10. History writing — Communism — Europe — Russia 11. History writing — Cold War 12. Life stories — Politics — Politicians

LC 2002026404

ALA Notable Book, 2004; Booklist Editors' Choice, 2003; National Book Critics Circle Award for Biography, 2003; Pulitzer Prize for Biography or Autobiography, 2004.

A portrait of the head of the Soviet Union whose rule followed Stalin's identifies his impact on the country and the rest of the world, citing how his career reflected of the Soviet experience and tracing his efforts to reform communism and ease the cold war.

Maps on lining papers; Includes bibliographical references (p. 793-824) and index.

Taupin, Bernie

Scattershot: Life, Music, Elton, and Me. Bernie Taupin. Hachette Books 2023. 384 p.

ISBN 9780306828676

Grades: Adult   B

1. Taupin, Bernie 2. John, Elton 3. Songwriting 4. Songwriters 5. Music 6. Autobiographies and memoirs 7. Arts and Entertainment — Music 8. Life stories — Arts and culture — Performing arts — Musicians and composers

In this much anticipated memoir, the man who wrote the lyrics for Elton John—and half of one of the greatest creative partnerships in popular music—shares, for the first time, his own account of their adventures, transporting readers across the decades and around the world.

"Award-winning Taupin, the lyricist behind Elton John's stardom, impressionistically recounts people, places, and events in his action-packed life." —*Library Journal*

Taussig, Rebekah

Sitting Pretty: The View from My Ordinary Resilient Disabled Body. Rebekah Taussig. HarperOne 2020. 224 p.

ISBN 9780062936790

Grades: Adult   B

1. Taussig, Rebekah 2. Disability rights advocates 3. Identity 4. Ableism 5. Barrier-free design 6. People with paraplegia 7. Women with disabilities 8. Disabilities 9. Women wheelchair users 10. People with disabilities 11. Autobiographies and memoirs 12. Essays 13. Life stories — Facing adversity — Medical issues — Living with disabilities 14. Science Writing — Medicine and health — Disabilities and disorders

LC 2019056133

From disability advocate with a PhD in disability studies and creative nonfiction, and creator of the Instagram account

@sitting pretty, an essay collection based on a lifetime of experiences in a paralyzed body, tackling themes of identity, accessibility, bodies, and representation.

ESSENTIAL AND RECOMMENDED TITLES
Biography

"An invaluable, eye-opening look at disability from a firsthand perspective." —*Booklist*

Taylor, Barbara Brown
 Holy Envy: Finding God in the Faith of Others. Barbara Brown Taylor. HarperOne 2019. 240 p.
  ISBN 9780062406569
 Grades: Adult B
  1. Taylor, Barbara Brown 2. Religions 3. Interfaith relations 4. Spirituality 5. Spiritual life 6. Clergywomen 7. Religious life 8. Faith 9. United States 10. 21st century 11. Autobiographies and memoirs 12. Life stories — Religion and spirituality — Personal faith 13. Spirituality and Religion — General
  LC 2018033141

The award-winning author recounts her inspirational discoveries of finding the sacred in unexpected places while teaching the world's religions to undergraduate students in Baptist rural Georgia.

"Taylor effectively reminds us that religion is more than beliefs, that it involves our deepest selves and is the fabric of our shared lives." —*Library Journal*

Taylor, Cory
 Dying: A Memoir. Cory Taylor. Tin House Books 2017. 141 pages
  ISBN 9781941040706
 Grades: Adult B
  1. Taylor, Cory, 1955-2016 2. People with terminal illnesses 3. Death 4. Autobiographies and memoirs 5. Australian literature 6. Life stories — Facing adversity — Coping with death

Shortlisted for the Stella Prize.

At the age of sixty, Cory Taylor is dying of melanoma-related brain cancer. Her illness is no longer treatable. As she tells us in her remarkable last book, she now weighs less than her neighbour's retriever. Written in the space of a few weeks, in a tremendous creative surge, this powerful and beautifully written book is a clear-eyed account of what dying has taught Cory: She describes the tangle of her feelings, she reflects on her life, and she remembers the lives and deaths of her parents. She tells us why she would like to be able to choose the circumstances of her own death.

"This slender volume brings a fresh point of view to end-of-life care, the concept of having a sense of control over the unknown, and the role of chance in life." —*Publishers Weekly*

Originally published: Melbourne, Vic. : Text Publishing Company, 2016.

Taylor, D. J.
 Orwell: The New Life. D. J. Taylor. Pegasus Books 2023. 464 p.
  ISBN 9781639364510
 Grades: Adult B
  1. Orwell, George, 1903-1950 2. Journalists 3. Authors, English 4. 20th century 5. Biographies 6. Arts and Entertainment — Writing and Publishing 7. Life stories — Arts and culture — Writing — Authors 8. Life stories — Arts and culture — Writing — Journalists

An award-winning Orwellian biographer and scholar, drawing on new sources available for the first time, shows how the way we look at a writer and his canon has changes even over the course of the last two decades, presenting a fresh and relevant biography seen through a post-millennial prism.

"This stands out in the crowded field of Orwell biographies." —*Publishers Weekly*

Taylor, Goldie
 The Love You Save. Goldie Taylor. Hanover Square Press 2022. 320 p.
  ISBN 9781335449375
 Grades: Adult B
  1. Taylor, Goldie 2. Childhood 3. Families 4. Family relationships 5. Family violence 6. African American women 7. Racism 8. Psychic trauma 9. Growing up 10. Faith 11. Books and reading 12. Rape 13. Autobiographies and memoirs 14. Nonfiction that reads like fiction 15. Life stories — Facing adversity 16. Life stories — Identity 17. Family and relationships — Abuse 18. Family and relationships — Growing up

An acclaimed journalist and human rights activist shares the harrowing yet deeply hopeful story of her troubled childhood in East St. Louis—a memoir of family, faith and the power of books.

"Journalist and human rights activist Taylor serves up a sometimes brutal, sometimes tender coming-of-age story….An affecting memoir of overcoming adversity when every deck is stacked against you." —*Kirkus*

Taylor, Jay
 The Generalissimo: Chiang Kai-shek and the Struggle for Modern China. Jay Taylor. Belknap Press of Harvard University Press 2009. 736 p.
  ISBN 9780674033382
 Grades: Adult B
  1. Chiang, Kai-shek, 1887-1975 2. Civil war 3. Nationalism 4. Presidents 5. Leadership 6. Chinese history 7. Asian history 8. Taiwan 9. 20th century 10. Biographies 11. Life stories — Politics — Politicians 12. History writing — Communist China — Asia — China
  LC 2008040492

Lionel Gelber Prize (Canada), 2010.

Chiang was a man of war who led the most ancient and populous country in the world through a quarter century of bloody revolutions, civil conflict, and wars of resistance against Japanese aggression. In 1949, when he was defeated by Mao Zedong, he fled to Taiwan, where he ruled for another twenty-five years. Playing a key role in the cold war with China, Chiang suppressed opposition with his "white terror," controlled inflation and corruption, carried out land reform, and raised personal income, health,and educational levels on the island.—from publisher description.

"Taylor's fact-based chronological presentation of Chiang should temper the preexisting opinions of him that history readers may take into reading the book. An important biography, essential to the Chinese history shelves." —*Booklist*

Includes bibliographical references and index.

Taylor, Justin
 Riding with the Ghost: A Memoir. Justin Taylor. Random House 2020. 240 p.
  ISBN 9780593129296
 Grades: Adult B
  1. Taylor, Justin, 1982- 2. Authors, American 3. Fathers and sons 4. Faith 5. People with depression 6. Fatherhood 7. Loss 8. Teachers 9. Family relationships 10. 21st century 11. Autobiographies and memoirs 12. Life stories — Relationships — Parent and child 13. Family and Relationships — Parenting 14. Family and Relationships — Aging and Death 15. Society and culture — Gender — Men
  LC 2019041738

The acclaimed author describes how his father's unsuccessful suicide attempt amidst struggles to keep his marriage together while fighting long-term illness and depression forced him to confront and reckon with troubles in his own life.

"A greater literary achievement than Taylor's impressive fiction." —*Kirkus*

Taylor, Stephen
 Commander: The Life and Exploits of Britain's Greatest Frigate Captain. Stephen Taylor. W.W. Norton 2012. 320 p.
  ISBN 9780393071641
 Grades: Adult B
  1. Exmouth, Edward Pellew, Viscount, 1757-1833 2. Frigates 3. Ship captains 4. Seafaring life 5. Naval battles 6. Naval history 7. Great Britain 8. 18th century 9. 19th century 10. Biographies 11. History writing — Military — Naval history 12. Life stories — Law and order — Armed forces personnel
  LC 2012027783

Depicts the adventurous and heroic life story of the British naval officer who started from the bottom and worked his way up to ultimately commanding the HMS Indefatigable during the Revolutionary War and also fought during the French Revolution and Napoleonic Wars.

Includes bibliographical references and index.

PUBLIC LIBRARY CORE COLLECTION: NONFICTION
Twentieth Edition

Tea, Michelle
Against Memoir: Complaints, Confessions & Criticism. Michelle Tea. Amethyst Editions/The Feminist Press at the City University of New York 2018. 300 p.
ISBN 9781936932184
Grades: Adult — B
1. Tea, Michelle 2. Authors, American 3. Lesbian authors 4. Gender identity 5. Gender role 6. Gender fluid 7. Essays 8. Life stories — Identity — LGBTQIA+ 9. Society and culture — Gender — Women 10. Society and culture — LGBTQIA+
LC 2017049287

A queer countercultural icon divulges on all things artistic, romantic, and neurotic in this collection of essays.

"Author and poet Tea (Without a Net) covers the gamut of her experience in this unputdownable antimemoir, which consists of previously published articles, talks, essays, and reviews but mostly recollections of her experience as a queer activist." —*Library Journal*

Teachout, Terry
★ *All in the Dances: A Brief Life of George Balanchine.* Terry Teachout. Harcourt 2004. xv, 185 p. : Illustration
ISBN 9780151010882
Grades: Adult — B
1. Balanchine, George 2. Choreographers 3. Dancers 4. Ballet dancers 5. Social life and customs 6. United States 7. 20th century 8. Biographies 9. Arts and Entertainment — Dance 10. Life stories — Arts and culture — Performing arts — Dancers and choreographers
LC 2004009226

Documents the late ballet magnate's Russian heritage, love for American culture, four marriages, and ongoing legacy that has caused his works to be danced by prestigious companies continuously since 1948.

"Balanchine's ballets are modern masterpieces, and Teachout, moving chronologically from work to work, uses them as stepping stones to tell Balanchine's own story. This is highly recommended as a first book on the life and art of George Balanchine for students and the general reader." —*Publishers Weekly*

Includes bibliographical references (p. [179]-185).

Duke: A Life of Duke Ellington. Terry Teachout. Gotham Books 2013. 496 p.
ISBN 9781592407491
Grades: Adult — B
1. Ellington, Duke, 1899-1974 2. African American jazz musicians 3. Composers 4. Jazz music 5. Extramarital affairs 6. Collaboration 7. Biographies 8. Life stories — Arts and culture — Performing arts — Musicians and composers 9. Arts and Entertainment — Music — Jazz and the Blues
LC 2013011138

An account of the public and private lives of the eminent jazz artist includes coverage of his slave heritage, the musical talent that inspired some 1,500 compositions and his relationships with numerous lovers. By the author of Pops: A Life of Louis Armstrong.

Pops: A Life of Louis Armstrong. Terry Teachout. Houghton Mifflin Harcourt 2009. 496 p.
ISBN 9780151010899
Grades: Adult — B
1. Armstrong, Louis, 1900-1971 2. African American jazz musicians 3. Jazz music 4. Jazz trumpeters 5. Trumpet music (Jazz) 6. Musicians 7. Jazz musicians 8. Biographies 9. Arts and Entertainment — Music — Jazz and the Blues 10. Life stories — Arts and culture — Performing arts — Musicians and composers
LC 2009006035

New York Times Notable Book, 2010.

Louis Armstrong was the greatest jazz musician of the twentieth century and a giant of modern American culture. Offstage he was witty, introspective and unexpectedly complex, a beloved colleague with an explosive temper whose larger-than-life personality was tougher and more sharp-edged than his worshipping fans ever knew. Wall Street Journal arts columnist Terry Teachout has drawn on new sources unavailable to previous biographers, including hundreds of private recordings of backstage and after-hours conversations, to craft a sweeping new narrative biography of this towering figure that shares, for the first time, full, accurate versions of such storied events as Armstrong's quarrel with President Eisenhower and his decision to break up his big band.

"The author makes an eloquent case for Armstrong's status as a pioneer, not just in jazz but in the broader context of 20th-century art. A rewarding jazz biography and a revealing look at a broad swath of American cultural history." —*Kirkus*

Includes bibliographical references and index.

Tefertiller, Casey
Wyatt Earp: The Life Behind the Legend. Casey Tefertiller; foreword by Angus Cameron. J. Wiley 1997. xii, 403 p. : Illustration; Map
ISBN 9780471189671
Grades: Adult — B
1. Earp, Wyatt, 1848-1929 2. Peace officers 3. United States marshals 4. United States history 5. Southwest (United States) 6. Tombstone, Arizona 7. Arizona 8. 19th century 9. Biographies 10. History writing — Westward expansion — United States 11. Life stories — Law and order — Police and law officers
LC 97002932

New York Times Notable Book, 1997.

Chronicles the life of the Western lawman, examining his legendary status in the Old West, and the question of whether he was a hero or a villian.

"An engrossing, satisfying inspection of a quintessential figure in American popular culture." —*Booklist*

Includes bibliographical references (p. 373-375) and index.

Teffi, N. A.
Memories: From Moscow to the Black Sea. by Teffi; translated by Robert and Elizabeth Chandler, Anne-Marie Jackson and Irina Steinberg; introduction by Edythe Haber. New York Review Books 2016. 240 p.
ISBN 9781590179512
Grades: Adult — B
1. Teffi, N. A. (Nadezhda Aleksandrovna), 1872-1952 2. Women 3. Women authors 4. Soviet Union history 5. Russian Revolution and Civil War (1917-1921) 6. Translations — Russian to english 7. Autobiographies and memoirs 8. Life stories — Arts and culture — Writing — Authors 9. Life stories — Facing adversity — War and oppression 10. History writing — Wars and conflicts — Russian revolution
LC 2015043142

Considered Teffi's single greatest work, Memories: From Moscow to the Black Sea is a deeply personal account of the author's last months in Russia and Ukraine, suffused with her acute awareness of the political currents churning around her, many of which have now resurfaced.

Originally published in Russian as Vospominaniia, 1980.

Tenzin Priyadarshi
Running Toward Mystery: The Adventure of an Unconventional Life. by the Venerable Tenzin Priyadarshi and Zara Houshmand. Spiegel & Grau 2019. 272 pages
ISBN 9781984819857
Grades: Adult — B
1. Tenzin Priyadarshi 2. Buddhist monks 3. Mentoring 4. Mentors 5. Scholars and academics 6. College teachers 7. Chief executive officers 8. Friendship 9. Conflict resolution 10. Ethics 11. India 12. United States 13. Autobiographies and memoirs 14. Life stories — Religion and spirituality — Religious and spiritual leaders 15. Spirituality and Religion — Buddhism 16. Spirituality and Religion — Religious Leaders
LC 2019021238

A revered monk and teacher as well as president and CEO of the Dalai Lama Center for Ethics and Transformative Values shares the spiritual journey that led him to where he is today.

"The purpose of this memoir, which is highly recommended for all spirituality collections, is not to impress but to inspire readers to find a thread connecting them to humanity and the courage to explore the many facets of oneself. A cross between Paramahansa Yogananda's Autobiography of a Yogi and Pema

ESSENTIAL AND RECOMMENDED TITLES
Biography

Chödrön's When Things Fall Apart, this more than succeeds." —*Library Journal*

Tester, Jon
Grounded: A Senator's Lessons on Winning Back Rural America. Jon Tester, US senator for Montana, with Aaron Murphy. Ecco Press 2020. 406 p.
ISBN 9780062977489
Grades: Adult — B
1. Tester, Jon, 1956- 2. Legislators 3. Farmers 4. Rural life 5. Responsibility 6. Politics and government 7. United States 8. Autobiographies and memoirs 9. Life stories — Politics — Politicians 10. Politics and global affairs — General
LC 2020033859

Senator Jon Tester is a rare voice in Congress. He is the only United States senator who manages a full-time job outside of the Senate—as a farmer. But what has really come to distinguish Tester in the Senate is his commitment to accountability, his ability to stand up to Donald Trump, and his success in, time and again, winning red state voters back to the Democratic Party. The media and Democrats too often discount rural people as Trump supporters; Tester knows better. His voice is vital to the public discourse as we seek to understand the issues that are important to rural and working-class America in not just the 2020 election but also for years to come.

"Montana senator Tester's candid and appealing debut interweaves autobiography and insights into the issues and values that resonate with rural voters.... This political memoir stands apart from the pack." —*Publishers Weekly*

Tetro, Tony
Con/Artist: The Life and Crimes of the World's Greatest Art Forger. Tony Tetro and Giampiero Ambrosi. Hachette Books 2022. 288 p.
ISBN 9780306826481
Grades: Adult — B
1. Tetro, Tony 2. Art forgers 3. Corruption 4. Secrets 5. Art 6. Art history 7. Art forgeries 8. Autobiographies and memoirs 9. Life stories — Law and order — Criminals and law-breakers 10. Arts and Entertainment — Painting, Drawing, and Sculpture 11. True Crime — General

A world-renowned art forger who has been duping the art world for 45 years and served time for a widely-publicized trial, describes the secrets and corruption of that universe while giving an art history lesson.

"Tetro tells his rollicking story well, and the result is a unique narrative. An entertaining account that shines a light onto a shady world as well as a personal story of hubris and redemption." —*Kirkus*

Theoharis, Jeanne
The Rebellious Life of Mrs. Rosa Parks. Jeanne Theoharis. Beacon Press 2012. 360 p.
ISBN 9780807050477
Grades: Adult — B
1. Parks, Rosa, 1913-2005 2. Civil Rights Movement 3. African American women civil rights workers 4. African American social advocates 5. Civil rights workers 6. African American civil rights 7. Segregation in transportation 8. Race relations 9. Montgomery, Alabama 10. 1960s 11. Biographies 12. History writing — African American — Civil rights — United States 13. History writing — 1960s — United States 14. Life stories — Politics — Activists and reformers
LC 2012031992

Examines the historical icon's six decades of activism, challenging perceptions of her as an accidental actor in the civil rights movement.
Includes bibliographical references and index.

Thi, Kim Phuc Phan
Fire Road: The Napalm Girl's Journey Through the Horrors of War to Faith, Forgiveness, and Peace. Kim Phuc Phan Thi, with Ashley Wiersma. Tyndale Momentum, the nonfiction imprint of Tyndale House Publishers 2017. 272 p.
ISBN 9781496424303
Grades: Adult — B
1. Thi, Kim Phuc Phan 2. Burn victims 3. Children and war 4. Converts to Christianity 5. Life change events 6. Vietnam War, 1961-1975 7. Faith (Christianity) 8. Determination 9. Autobiographies and memoirs 10. Life stories — Facing adversity — War and oppression — War survivors 11. Life stories — Religion and spirituality — Personal faith 12. Spirituality and religion — Christianity

Kim Phuc Phan Thi reveals the horror she experienced during the napalm bombing in the Vietnam War, which destroyed her world and almost took her life. This story tells of her journey from hellish fire to healing.

Thomas, Dylan
A Child's Christmas in Wales. Dylan Thomas; with woodcuts by Ellen Raskin. New Directions Pub. 2007. 51 p. : Color illustration
ISBN 9780811217316
Grades: 11 12 Adult — B
1. Thomas, Dylan, 1914-1953 2. Christmas 3. Poets 4. Welsh people 5. Social life and customs 6. Wales 7. 20th century 8. Autobiographies and memoirs
LC 2007024727

Captures a child's-eye view, and an adult's fond memories, of a magical time of presents, aunts and uncles, the frozen sea, and in the best of circumstances, newly fallen snow.

"For any season of the year the language is enchanting and the poetry shines with an unearthly radiance." —*New York Times Book Review*

Thomas, Evan
Being Nixon: A Man Divided. Evan Thomas. Random House 2015. 656 p.
ISBN 9780812995367
Grades: Adult — B
1. Nixon, Richard M. (Richard Milhous), 1913-1994 2. Political leadership 3. Presidents 4. Politicians 5. Politics and government 6. United States 7. 20th century 8. 1960s 9. 1970s 10. Biographies 11. History writing — Presidency — 20th century — United States 12. Life stories — Politics — Politicians
LC 2015009669

Reveals the personal and political lives of the American president, whose accomplishments during his presidency opened foreign relations with the Soviet Union and China but also led to his political downfall in the Watergate scandal.

"Thomas doesn't shy away from showing Nixon at his worst, acknowledging Nixon's penchant for the maudlin, his self-pity, his fear of confrontation, and his often poisonous rivalry with Henry Kissinger. Thomas is generous to his subject, contextualizing Nixon and often teasing out his well-concealed desire to do the right thing." —*Publishers Weekly*

Includes bibliographical references and index.

★ *First: Sandra Day O'Connor, an American Life.* Evan Thomas. Random House 2019. 416 p.
ISBN 9780399589287
Grades: Adult — B
1. O'Connor, Sandra Day, 1930-2023 2. Sexism 3. Women judges 4. Women and politics 5. Women Supreme Court Justices 6. Determination 7. United States 8. 20th century 9. Biographies 10. History writing — Judicial branch — United States 11. Life stories — Law and order — Judges and lawyers
LC 2018040502

Based on exclusive interviews and access to the Supreme Court archives, an authoritative portrait of America's first female Supreme Court justice covers her convention-breaking achievements and role in shaping decades of American law.

"This highly readable biography shows the underlying factors motivating O'Connor both on and off the Court. It will have considerable popular appeal to both political scientists and historians, as well as general readers interested in how America's government interacts with the public in resolving political issues related to the law." —*Library Journal*

Includes bibliographical references and index.

★ *John Paul Jones: Sailor, Hero, Father of the American Navy.* Evan Thomas. Simon & Schuster 2003. 383 p, 16 p. of plates : Illustration
ISBN 9780743205832
Grades: Adult — B
1. Jones, John Paul, 1747-1792 2. Admirals 3. Sailing 4. Command of troops 5. American Revolution, 1775-1783 6. Revolutions 7. Naval operations 8. United States history 9. United States 10. Revolutionary America (1775-1783)

11. Biographies 12. History writing — Military — Military leadership 13. Life stories — Law and order — Military leaders 14. History writing — Military — Naval history

LC 2003042411

New York Times Notable Book, 2003.

John Paul Jones, at sea and in the heat of battle, was the great American hero of the Age of Sail. He was to history what Patrick O'Brian's Jack Aubrey and C. S. Forester's Horatio Hornblower are to fiction. Ruthless, indomitable, clever; he vowed to sail, as he put it, 'In harm's way.'.

"The complex portrait is rendered with nautical precision—the author knows his topsail from his topgallant—and a lively eye for such details as the Enlightenment virtues espoused by Freemasonry or the proper way to kiss a French lady in the eighteenth century." —*Publishers Weekly*

Includes bibliographical references and index.

★ *Robert* Kennedy: His Life. Evan Thomas. Simon & Schuster 2000. 509 p, 16 p. of plates : Illustration

ISBN 9780684834801

Grades: 11 12 Adult   B

1. Kennedy, Robert Francis, 1925-1968 2. Family relationships 3. Politicians 4. Legislators 5. United States 6. Biographies 7. History writing — Politicians — United States 8. History writing — 1960s — United States 9. Life stories — Politics — Politicians 10. Adult books for young adults

LC 00041995

New York Times Notable Book, 2000.

Provides a detailed portrait of a man who was at once kind and cruel, devious and honest, fearful and brave, and one who was centrally engaged in most of the important issues of the postwar era, illuminates his failings as well as his strengths, and places Robert in the complex knot of relationships characteristic of the Kennedy family.

"A solid, judicious life of a politician whose tragic death inspired a generation of what-if history." —*Booklist*

Includes bibliographical references (p. [479]-487) and index.

Thomas, Franklin A.

An **Unplanned** *Life: A Memoir.* Franklin A. Thomas. The New Press 2022. 304 p.

ISBN 9781620977576

Grades: Adult   B

1. Thomas, Franklin A. 2. Philanthropists 3. African American men 4. African Americans 5. Race relations 6. United States 7. Autobiographies and memoirs 8. Life stories — Politics — Activists and reformers 9. History Writing — African American — United States

LC 2022020524

A major autobiography of a remarkable life that broke down racial barriers, transformed institutions, and energized the struggle for justice, by the former president of the Ford Foundation.

"Thomas's extraordinary life, lived in service to community, equality, and basic human rights, will inspire readers to accept the mantle of bettering society." —*Library Journal*

Includes index.

Thomas, Joseph Earl

Sink: *A Memoir.* Joseph Earl Thomas. Grand Central Publishing 2023. 256 p.

ISBN 9781538706176

Grades: Adult   B

1. Thomas, Joseph Earl 2. Children of drug abusers 3. Drug addicts 4. Parenting 5. Geeks (Computer enthusiasts) 6. Misfits (People) 7. Family violence 8. Belonging 9. Family relationships 10. Autobiographies and memoirs 11. Life stories — Relationships — Growing up 12. Family and relationships — Growing up 13. Family and relationships — Families 14. Life stories — Facing adversity

LC 2022004492

In a series of exacting and fierce vignettes, the author, who found salvation in geek culture, takes readers through the unceasing cruelty of his impoverished childhood toward an understanding of what it means to lose the desire to fit in and build community and love on your own terms.

"In his wrenching debut, Thomas recounts his foray into nerd culture while coming of age amid squalor and abuse in 1990s Philadelphia....The result is a lyrical exploration of identity and survival." —*Publishers Weekly*

Thomas, Louisa

Louisa: The Extraordinary Life of Mrs. Adams. Louisa Thomas. Penguin Press 2016. 480 p.

ISBN 9781594204630

Grades: Adult   B

1. Adams, Louisa Catherine, 1775-1852 2. Adams, John Quincy, 1767-1848 3. Women and politics 4. Role models 5. Culture conflict 6. Gender role 7. Marital conflict 8. Presidents' spouses 9. Determination 10. United States 11. Early America (1784-1819) 12. 19th century 13. Biographies 14. History writing — Presidency — 19th century — United States 15. Life stories — Politics — Politicians

LC 2015510022

ALA Notable Book, 2017.

An intimate portrait of the British-born wife of John Quincy Adams details her significantly different upbringing from her husband, their tempestuous marriage, their wide range of residences and her efforts to forge her own sense of self.

"Thomas has written an excellent account of the life of this woman, who certainly merits greater attention and praise." —*Booklist*

Thomas, R. Eric

★ **Congratulations,** *the Best Is Over!: Essays.* R. Eric Thomas. Ballantine Books 2023. 240 p.

ISBN 9780593496268

Grades: Adult   B

1. Thomas, R. Eric 2. Authors, American 3. African American gay men 4. Middle age 5. Home (Concept) 6. Identity 7. Purpose in life 8. Baltimore, Maryland 9. Essays 10. Life stories — Identity 11. Humor Writing — Social humor

LC 2023009188

The best-selling author of Here for It: Or, How to Save Your Soul in America presents a collection of relatable and humorous essays that explore his return to his hometown of Baltimore.

"In this hilariously candid memoir-in-essays, bestseller Thomas (Here for It) offers a glimpse at his experiences returning to his hometown of Baltimore from Philadelphia after decades away." —*Publishers Weekly*

Here *for It: Or, How to Save Your Soul in America; Essays.* R. Eric Thomas. Ballantine Books 2020. 272 pages

ISBN 9780525621034

Grades: Adult   B

1. Thomas, R. Eric 2. Authors, American 3. African American gay men 4. Christian gay men and lesbians 5. Religion and homosexuality 6. Men 7. Identity 8. Playwrights 9. Married men 10. Faith (Christianity) 11. Journalists 12. Men-men relations 13. United States 14. 21st century 15. Essays 16. Autobiographies and memoirs 17. Biographies 18. Life stories — Relationships — Growing up 19. Life stories — Identity — Race and ethnicity 20. Life stories — Identity — LGBTQIA+ 21. Life stories — Religion and spirituality — Personal faith 22. Life stories — Arts and culture — Writing — Journalists 23. Book club best bets

LC 2019037442

A humorist and playwright provides a heartfelt and humorous memoir-in-essays about growing up seeing the world differently, finding unexpected hope and every awkward, extraordinary stumble along the way.

"A laugh-out-loud memoir that is strongly recommended for everyone." —*Library Journal*

Thompson, Hunter S.

★ **Fear** *and Loathing in America: The Brutal Odyssey of an Outlaw Journalist, 1968-1976.* Hunter S. Thompson; foreword by David Halberstam; edited by Douglas Brinkley. Simon & Schuster 2000. xxv, 756 p. : Illustration

ISBN 9780684873152

Grades: Adult   B

ESSENTIAL AND RECOMMENDED TITLES
Biography

1. Thompson, Hunter S. 2. Journalists 3. Political journalism 4. Journalism 5. United States history 6. 1960s 7. 20th century 8. Letters 9. Page to screen 10. Arts and Entertainment — Writing and Publishing

LC 00047012

New York Times Notable Book, 2001.

Letters spanning the years between 1968 and 1976 highlight the author's biting wit, scary powers of observation, and encounters with such notables as Jimmy Carter, Tom Wolfe, and Kurt Vonnegut.

"During the period covered in this collection, Thompson was a vital, deliriously erratic force in journalism, covering the turbulent 1968 Democratic National Convention in Chicago, the 1968 election of Richard M. Nixon, the 1972 campaign, Watergate, the falls of Nixon and Saigon." —*New York Times Book Review*

Sequel to: The proud highway.

Thompson, J. M.
Running Is a Kind of Dreaming. by J. M. Thompson. Harper One 2021. x, 306 pages

ISBN 9780062947079

Grades: Adult   **B**

1. Thompson, J. M. (Clinical psychologist) 2. Clinical psychologists 3. Running 4. Depression 5. People with depression 6. Resilience 7. Runners 8. Psychic trauma 9. Autobiographies and memoirs 10. Life stories — Facing adversity — Medical issues — Mental illness 11. Life stories — Science, technology, and medicine — Healthcare professionals 12. Science Writing — Medicine and health — Mental health 13. Society and culture — Psychology and human behavior

Using his expert knowledge of the inner workings of the brain, illness and madness, a clinical psychologist and counselor shares his own descent into darkness and how physical movement saved him and helped him run toward his present.

"This will beam a ray of hope to those dealing with addiction, as well as their loved ones." —*Publishers Weekly*

Includes bibliographical resources (pages 305-306).

Thompson, Juan F.
Stories I Tell Myself: Growing up with Hunter S. Thompson. Juan F. Thompson. Alfred A. Knopf 2015. 320 p.

ISBN 9780307265357

Grades: Adult   **B**

1. Thompson, Hunter S. 2. Thompson, Juan F. 3. Fathers and sons 4. Drug abuse 5. Gonzo journalism 6. Authors, American 7. Journalists 8. United States 9. 20th century 10. Biographies 11. Life stories — Arts and culture — Writing — Journalists 12. Life stories — Arts and culture — Writing — Authors 13. Life stories — Relationships — Parent and child

LC 2015006934

A detailed and intimate description of the life of the manic, drug-fueled, charismatic and sensitive wildman of American journalism, known for his fearless style covering everything from biker gangs to presidential elections, as told by his only son.

"The son of the legendary gonzo journalist recalls his turbulent but exciting years swimming in the wake of a most mercurial creature." —*Kirkus*

Thompson, Kenan
When I Was Your Age: Life Lessons, Funny Stories & Questionable Parenting Advice from a Professional Clown. Kenan Thompson. HarperCollins 2023. 288 p.

ISBN 9780063348066

Grades: Adult   **B**

1. Thompson, Kenan 2. Comedians 3. African American comedians 4. Actors and actresses 5. African Americans 6. Parenting 7. Psychological growth 8. Personal conduct 9. Life stories — Arts and culture — Performing arts — Actors and Actresses 10. Life stories — Arts and culture — Performing arts — Entertainers and celebrities 11. Arts and Entertainment — Comedy

LC 2023023720

In this heartwarming and surprising ode to growing up, getting older and wiser and learning from your mistakes, SNL's longest-ever-serving cast member shares hilarious yet poignant essays that offer any reader valuable advice on parenting, focusing on positivity and having fun in life.

"Thompson has made a successful career with his avuncular charm and comforting brand of 'Clean comedy,' and his warmhearted memoir proves to be just as likable." —*Kirkus*

Thompson, Wright
The Cost of These Dreams: Sports Stories and Other Serious Business. Wright Thompson. Penguin Books 2019. 448 p.

ISBN 9780143133872

Grades: Adult   **B**

1. Athletes 2. Coach and athlete 3. Athletic coaches 4. Professional sports 5. Ambition 6. Fathers and sons 7. Sports 8. Essays 9. Biographies 10. Sports and Competition — Individual Athlete 11. Sports and Competition — Coaches 12. Life stories — Sports

LC 2018037816

An award-winning sports journalist and senior writer for ESPN the Magazine provides a collection of true stories along with his trademark insights and humor about the players who chased their dream of greatness and what it cost.

"A senior writer for ESPN the Magazine debuts with a collection of his explorations of sports-world notables who reachedor are reachingthe ends of their careers. Thompson's abundant strengths as a long-form journalist are evident on nearly every page." —*Kirkus*

Thomson, David
Bette Davis. David Thomson; photo research by Lucy Gray. Faber and Faber, Inc. 2010. 144 p.

ISBN 9780865479319

Grades: Adult   **B**

1. Davis, Bette, 1908-1989 2. Film industry and trade 3. Actors and actresses 4. Films 5. Hollywood, California 6. Biographies 7. Arts and Entertainment — Movies and Television 8. Life stories — Arts and culture — Performing arts — Actors and actresses

LC 2009041760

Presents the life and career of the motion picture actress, focusing on her legacy in the world of Hollywood and her storied personal life.

"Chronicling Davis' life and evolution in Hollywood, Thomson illustrates how changes in her often-disappointing private life (she had a habit of marrying the wrong men) influenced and often deepened her onscreen persona. Reading of how Davis bounced from one bad movie to the next in the early years of her career, it's hard not to share Thomson's enthusiasm for her talent, drive, and will. And it is hard not to feel Thomson's disappointment when Davis' major, artistic breakthroughs (The Little Foxes, All About Eve) are followed by lapses into forgettable mediocrity (The Man Who Came to Dinner, Payment on Demand)." —*Booklist*

Ingrid Bergman. David Thomson; photo research by Lucy Gray. Faber and Faber, Inc. 2010. 118 p.

ISBN 9780865479340

Grades: Adult   **B**

1. Bergman, Ingrid, 1915-1982 2. Actors and actresses 3. Film industry and trade 4. Films 5. United States history 6. Hollywood, California 7. Biographies 8. Arts and Entertainment — Movies and Television 9. Life stories — Arts and culture — Performing arts — Actors and actresses

LC 2009041757

Presents the life and career of the motion picture actresse, focusing on the contradictions between her image and her emotional life, her most important films, and how her tumultuous personal life affected her career.

"In this biography, the author describes Bergman's Hollywood-like rise, seemingly both unexpected and preordained, from talented Swedish actress to Hollywood goddess. He reserves his harshest criticism not for her increasingly chaotic private life but for how, after her brilliance in the 1940s—Casablanca, Gaslight, and the Hitchcock masterpieces Spellbound and Notorious, and more—she settled into a kind of unsatisfying mediocrity in the 1950s and 1960s. Thomson speculates that her fortunes faded with her legendary beauty." —*Booklist*

PUBLIC LIBRARY CORE COLLECTION: NONFICTION
Twentieth Edition

Thomson, Graeme
George Harrison: Behind the Locked Door. Graeme Thomson. Overlook Omnibus 2015. 464 p.
ISBN 9781468310658
Grades: Adult   B
1. Harrison, George, 1943-2001 2. Guitarists 3. Rock groups 4. Filmmakers 5. Career changes 6. Men 7. Rock music 8. Popular music 9. Rock musicians 10. Musicians 11. Spiritual life 12. Music history and criticism 13. Shyness 14. Great Britain 15. England 16. 20th century 17. 1960s 18. Biographies 19. Life stories — Arts and culture — Performing arts — Musicians and composers 20. Arts and Entertainment — Music — Rock

Draws on interviews to track the Beatle through his many changes and conflicts, from schoolboy guitarist to global superstar, and examines his struggle to walk a spiritual path while avoiding the temptations of fame.

"Thomson is especially compelling in his illumination of Harrison's inner life, his robust spirituality, and his deep love of Indian culture." —*Booklist*
Includes bibliographical references and index.

Thorp, Edward O.
A Man for All Markets: From Las Vegas to Wall Street, How I Beat the Dealer and the Market. Edward O. Thorp. Random House 2017. 256 p.
ISBN 9781400067961
Grades: Adult   B
1. Thorp, Edward O. 2. Investment advisers 3. Gambling 4. Statistics 5. Mathematicians 6. Gambling systems 7. Gamblers 8. Casinos 9. Probabilities 10. Games of chance 11. Investments 12. Finance 13. Autobiographies and memoirs 14. Life stories — Business 15. Business and economics — Industries — Finance 16. Sports and Competition — Gambling and Betting
LC 2016026545

The incredible real-life story of the card-counting mathematics professor who taught the world how to beat the dealer and helped start a revolution on Wall Street.

"Readers who like to read the life stories of ambitious, creative, and successful people with fascinating stories to tell should be steered in this books direction." —*Booklist*
Includes index.

Threadgill, Henry
Easily Slip into Another World: A Life in Music. Henry Threadgill and Brent Hayes Edwards. Alfred A. Knopf 2023. 368 p.
ISBN 9781524749071
Grades: Adult   B
1. Threadgill, Henry 2. Musicians 3. Growing up 4. Composers 5. Saxophonists 6. Family relationships 7. Music 8. Music, American 9. Autobiographies and memoirs 10. Life stories — Arts and culture — Performing arts — Musicians and composers 11. Arts and Entertainment — Music — Jazz and the Blues

This autobiography from one of the towering figures of contemporary American music recalls his childhood and upbringing in Chicago, his family life and education and his brilliant career in music.

"A vivid, vigorous memoir that every budding musician should read." —*Kirkus*

Thwaite, Ann
Goodbye Christopher Robin: A. A. Milne and the Making of Winnie-the-pooh. Ann Thwaite; with a preface by Frank Cottrell-Boyce. St. Martin's Griffin 2017. xxxi, 254 pages, 8 unnumbered pages of plates : Illustration
ISBN 9781250190901
Grades: Adult   B
1. Milne, A. A. (Alan Alexander), 1882-1956 2. Milne, Christopher, 1920-1996 3. Authors, English 4. Fathers and sons 5. 20th century 6. Biographies 7. Life stories — Arts and culture — Performing arts 8. Life stories — Arts and culture — Writing
LC 2017041098

Goodbye Christopher Robin: A.A. Milne and the Making of Winnie-the-Pooh is drawn from Ann Thwaite's Whitbread Award-winning biography of A. A. Milne, one of England's most successful writers. After serving in the First World War, Milne wrote a number of well-received plays, but his greatest triumph came when he created Winnie-the-Pooh, Piglet, Tigger, Eeyore and, of course, Christopher Robin, the adventurous little boy based on his own son. Goodbye Christopher Robin inspired the film directed by Simon Curtis and starring Domhnall Gleeson, Margot Robbie and Kelly Macdonald. It offers the reader a glimpse into the relationship between Milne and the real-life Christopher Robin, whose toys inspired the magical world of the Hundred Acre Wood. Goodbye Christopher Robin is a story of celebrity, a story of both the joys and pains of success and, ultimately, the story of how one man created a series of enchanting tales that brought hope and comfort to an England ravaged by the First World War.

First published in Great Britain under the title A.A. Milne : His life by Faber & Faber. Previously published in Great Britain as this abridged edition by Pan Books, an imprint of Pan Macmillan.

Tjipombo, Tupa
I Am Not Your Slave: A Memoir. Tupa Tjipombo, Chris Lockhart. Lawrence Hill Books 2020. 256 pages
ISBN 9781641602372
Grades: Adult   B
1. Tjipombo, Tupa 2. Human trafficking victims 3. Sexual slavery 4. Human trafficking 5. Rape 6. Women kidnapping victims 7. Rape victims 8. Sexual violence 9. Violence against marginalized women 10. Slavery 11. Girls 12. Young women 13. Escapes 14. Child kidnapping victims 15. Africa 16. Dubai 17. Autobiographies and memoirs 18. Life stories — Facing adversity — Abuse survivors 19. Life stories — Facing adversity — Victims of crime 20. Society and culture — Violence and crime 21. True Crime — Sex Crimes
LC 2019029549

I Am Not Your Slave is the true story of a young African girl who was abducted from southwestern Africa and funneled through an extensive yet almost completely unknown human-trafficking network spanning the entire African continent. As she is transported from the point of her abduction on a remote farm and channeled to her ultimate destination in Dubai, her three-year odyssey exposes the brutal horrors of a modern day middle passage.

"In this harrowing, unsparing memoir, the author documents unimaginable brutality against women with dignity and grace and provides readers with an urgent education about the devastating scope of human trafficking in the modern world. Difficult but necessary reading." —*Kirkus*

Tobin, James
Ernie Pyle's War: America's Eyewitness to World War II. James Tobin. Free Press 1997. 312 p. : Illustration
ISBN 9780684836423
Grades: Adult   B
1. Pyle, Ernie, 1900-1945 2. War correspondents 3. Journalists 4. World War II 5. Journalism 6. Objectivity 7. Pacific Ocean 8. 1940s 9. Biographies 10. Impartial writing 11. History writing — Wars and conflicts — World War II 12. Life stories — Law and order — Armed forces personnel
LC 97006165

National Book Critics Circle Award for Biography, 1997; New York Times Notable Book, 1997.

Presents a biography of the newsman who every day during World War II brought the voices of America's fighting men to the front page and who became a pioneer for today's war journalists.

"Living and working among the troops he so vividly chronicled, Pyle offered a unique insider's perspective of the harsh reality experienced by the common soldier during World War II. A respectful and insightful biography of a giant among journalists." —*Booklist*
Includes bibliographical references and index.

Todd, Olivier
Albert Camus: A Life. Olivier Todd; translated by Benjamin Ivry. Alfred A. Knopf 1997. x, 434 p. : Illustration
ISBN 9780679428558
Grades: Adult   B

ESSENTIAL AND RECOMMENDED TITLES
Biography

1. Camus, Albert, 1913-1960 2. Authors, French 3. Algerian people 4. Anti-Nazi Movement 5. France 6. Paris, France 7. 20th century 8. Biographies 9. Arts and Entertainment — Writing and Publishing 10. Life stories — Arts and culture — Writing — Authors

LC 97002991

New York Times Notable Book, 1998.

A biography of the novelist and philosopher draws on previously unused personal correspondence, public records and firsthand interviews to reveal Camus's private and public life.

"Todd's exhaustive biography, which aimsand succeedsin presenting the man and not just the writer, has been shortened for its English translation, which refers readers to the French edition for notes, sources and bibliography." —*Publishers Weekly*

Originally published in French with the same title: Paris : Gallimard, 1996; Includes index.

Tolan, Sandy
★ *The Lemon Tree: An Arab, a Jew, and the Heart of the Middle East.* Sandy Tolan. Bloomsbury USA 2006. xiv, 362 p. : Map
ISBN 9781582343433
Grades: Adult   B

1. Palestinian people 2. Friendship 3. Arab-Israeli conflict 4. Israeli-Palestinian relations 5. Israeli people 6. Biographies 7. Life stories — Relationships — Friendship 8. History writing — Arab-Israeli relations — Southwest Asia and North Africa (Middle East) 9. Family and Relationships — General 10. Adult books for young adults

LC 2005030360

Booklist Editors' Choice, 2006; National Book Critics Circle Award for Nonfiction finalist, 2006.

Describes how a simple act of faith and the relationship between two families—one Israeli, one Palestinian—represents a personal microcosm of decades of Israeli-Palestinian history and symbolizes the hope for peace in the Middle East.

Includes bibliographical references (p. [269]-282) and index.

Tolinski, Brad
Light and Shade: Conversations with Jimmy Page. Brad Tolinski. Crown 2012. 272 p.
ISBN 9780307985712
Grades: Adult   B

1. Page, Jimmy 2. Popular culture 3. English history 4. 20th century 5. Biographies 6. Arts and Entertainment — Music — Rock 7. Life stories — Arts and culture — Performing arts — Musicians and composers

For the first time and in his own words, iconic guitarist Jimmy Page opens up to journalist Brad Tolinski, exploring in-depth his remarkable life and musical journey.

Tomalin, Claire
Samuel Pepys: The Unequalled Self. Claire Tomalin. A.A. Knopf 2002. xxxiii, 470 p, 24 p. of plates : Illustration; Map
ISBN 9780375411434
Grades: Adult   B

1. Pepys, Samuel, 1633-1703 2. Cabinet officers 3. Authors, British 4. Social life and customs 5. British history 6. Great Britain 7. 17th century 8. Stuart period (1603-1714) 9. Restoration England (1660-1688) 10. Diaries 11. Biographies 12. Arts and Entertainment — Writing and Publishing 13. Life stories — Arts and culture — Writing — Authors

LC 2002075701

Whitbread Book Award for Biography, 2002; Whitbread Book of the Year Award, 2002.

A biography of the master diarist and chronicler of Restoration London draws on the famous diaries, as well as on other sources and period material, to furnish a candid chronicle of the life and times of Samuel Pepys.

"Tomalin mines the diary, and she also expands upon the characters and events, great and small, that affected Pepys' life and livelihood to bring the man and his milieu to lifepungently as well as vibrantly." —*Booklist*

Includes bibliographical references (p. [443]-450) and index.

***Thomas** Hardy.* Claire Tomalin. Penguin Press 2007. xxv, 486 p, 16 p. of plates : Illustration; Map
ISBN 9781594201189
Grades: Adult   B

1. Hardy, Thomas, 1840-1928 2. Authors, English 3. Social life and customs 4. London, England 5. 19th century 6. 20th century 7. Biographies 8. Arts and Entertainment — Writing and Publishing 9. Life stories — Arts and culture — Writing — Authors

LC 2007295886

New York Times Notable Book, 2007; National Book Critics Circle Award for Biography finalist, 2007.

A portrait of the enigmatic nineteenth-century novelist and poet discusses his humble origins, rise through the London literary scene, and efforts to challenge the sexual and religious conventions of his time.

Includes bibliographical references (p. [453]-461) and index.

Tometich, Annabelle
The Mango Tree: A Memoir of Fruit, Florida, and Felony. Annabelle Tometich. Little, Brown and Company 2024. 320 p.
ISBN 9780316540322
Grades: Adult   B

1. Tometich, Annabelle, 1980- 2. Growing up 3. Filipino Americans 4. Mothers 5. Dysfunctional families 6. Families 7. Mangoes 8. Identity 9. Family relationships 10. Florida 11. Autobiographies and memoirs 12. Family and relationships — Growing up 13. Family and relationships — Families 14. Life stories — Identity 15. Life stories — Relationships — Growing up

With clear-eyed compassion and piercing honesty, the Mango Tree is a family saga that navigates the tangled branches of Annabelle's life, from her childhood days in an overflowing house flooded by balikbayan boxes, vegetation, and juicy mangoes, to her winding path from medical school hopeful to restaurant critic. It is a love letter to her fellow Filipino Americans, her lost younger self, and the beloved fruit tree at the heart of her family. But above all, it is an ode to Annabelle's hot-blooded, whip-smart mother Josefina, a woman who made a life and a home of her own, and without whom Annabelle would not have herself.

"The Mango Tree is a candid account of half-Filipino, half-Yugoslavian Annabelle Tometich's coming-of-age in Fort Myers, Florida, and her love-hate relationship with her mother." —*Booklist*

Tomlinson, Janis A.
★ *Goya: A Portrait of the Artist.* Janis A. Tomlinson. Princeton University Press 2020. 388 p.
ISBN 9780691192048
Grades: Adult   B

1. Goya, Francisco, 1746-1828 2. Painters 3. Painting, Spanish 4. Painting, Modern 5. Modern art 6. Art criticism 7. Portrait painters 8. Art patronage 9. Interpersonal relations 10. Family relationships 11. Biographies 12. Life stories — Arts and culture — Artists 13. Arts and Entertainment — Painting, Drawing, and Sculpture

LC 2019041721

The life of Francisco Goya (1746?1828) coincided with an age of transformation in Spanish history that brought upheavals in the country's politics and at the court which Goya served, changes in society, the devastation of the Iberian Peninsula in the war against Napoleon, and an ensuing period of political instability. Janis Tomlinson draws on a wide range of documents—including letters, court papers, and a sketchbook used by Goya in the early years of his career—to provide a nuanced portrait of a complex and multifaceted painter and printmaker, whose art is synonymous with compelling images of the people, events, and social revolution that defined his life and era.

"Tomlinson's meticulous distillation of a voluminous number of parish records, drawings, notes, and letters is impressive, and her knowledge of and pas-

PUBLIC LIBRARY CORE COLLECTION: NONFICTION
Twentieth Edition

sion for Goya continually shine through in her writing, making for a fascinating and insightful reading experience. A top-notch biography." —*Kirkus*
Includes bibliographical references and index.

Tomlinson, Tommy
The Elephant in the Room: One Fat Man's Quest to Get Smaller in a Growing America. Tommy Tomlinson. Simon & Schuster 2019. 256 p.
ISBN 9781501111617
Grades: Adult   B
1. Tomlinson, Tommy 2. Fat men 3. Obesity 4. Food habits 5. Diet 6. Middle-aged men 7. United States 8. Essays 9. Autobiographies and memoirs 10. Life stories — Personal growth

An acclaimed journalist provides a candid exploration of what it's like to live as a fat man and how he decided he had to change his life as he neared the age of 50 weighing in at 460 pounds.

Toorpakai, Maria
A Different Kind of Daughter: The Girl Who Hid from the Taliban in Plain Sight. Maria Toorpakai with Katharine Holstein. Twelve 2016. 256 p.
ISBN 9781455591411
Grades: Adult   B
1. Toorpakai, Maria, 1990- 2. Passing (Identity) 3. Escapes 4. Women's rights 5. Women 6. Women athletes 7. Oppression (Psychology) 8. Pakistan 9. Autobiographies and memoirs 10. Politics and global affairs — Civil and human rights 11. Life stories — Sports — Athletes 12. Society and culture — Gender — Women 13. Life stories — Facing adversity
LC 2015050405

A woman from an oppressive Pakistani tribal region, where women playing sports is forbidden, discusses how she passed as a boy in order to play the sports she loved, thus becoming a lightning rod of freedom in her country's fierce battle over women's rights, as well as the subject of a forthcoming 2016 documentary.

"This astonishing and inspirational memoir chronicles more than Maria's life; it also relates the story of her parents, an incredible couple, who, despite the odds, fought for the betterment and education of themselves, their children, and the Pakistani people." —*Library Journal*

Torre, Joe
The Yankee Years. Joe Torre and Tom Verducci. Doubleday 2009. 512 p.
ISBN 9780385527408
Grades: Adult   B
1. Torre, Joe, 1940- 2. Baseball managers 3. Baseball 4. Baseball teams 5. Social life and customs 6. New York City 7. Autobiographies and memoirs 8. Sports and Competition — Baseball 9. Life stories — Sports — Coaches, managers, and owners
LC 2008052628

The former Yankees manager offers a study of the Yankees organization, detailing the challenges of working for a team in which executives and the media question every decision and the concerns of managing a clubhouse of superstars.

"This is an interesting and fast read and, for those who are not aficionados of baseball, the clash of powerful personalities and drama are more than sufficient to merit attention. Baseball enthusiasts, while undoubtedly familiar with the characters and events, will find the quick review of 12 years of Yankee history enjoyable for its details, particularly as the men's words flesh out the drama behind the sports pages." —*USA Today*

Totenberg, Nina
★ *Dinners with Ruth: A Memoir on the Power of Friendships.* Nina Totenberg. Simon & Schuster 2022. 256 p.
ISBN 9781982188085
Grades: Adult   B
1. Totenberg, Nina 2. Ginsburg, Ruth Bader 1933-2020 3. Women journalists 4. Female friendship 5. Judges 6. Women judges 7. Social change 8. Autobiographies and memoirs 9. Life stories — Relationships — Friendship 10. Life stories — Law and order — Judges and lawyers 11. Family and relationships — Friendship

In this moving story of the joy and true meaning of friendship, NPR's award-winning legal affairs correspondent recounts her nearly 50-year friendship with Supreme Court Justice Ruth Bader Ginsburg, presenting an extraordinary account of how they paved the way for future generations by tearing down professional and legal barriers.

"Longtime NPR legal affairs correspondent Nina Totenberg shares the engrossing and engaging story of her friendship with the late Supreme Court Justice Ruth Bader Ginsburg." —*Booklist*

Townsend, Alan R.
★ *This Ordinary Stardust: A Scientist's Path from Grief to Wonder.* Alan R. Townsend. Grand Central Publishing 2024. 256 p.
ISBN 9781538741184
Grades: Adult   B
1. Townsend, Alan R. 2. Families 3. People with cancer 4. Cancer 5. Brain cancer 6. Children with cancer 7. Religion and science 8. Biogeochemical cycles 9. Grief 10. Life stories — Facing adversity — Coping with death 11. Family and relationships — Illness and the family 12. Science Writing — General
LC 2023041436

After dealing with two unthinkable, catastrophic diagnoses: His 4-year-old daughter and his brilliant scientist wife developed life-threatening forms of brain cancer, and its aftermath, the author offers a moving perspective on the common ground between science and religion through the spiritual fulfillment he found in his work.

"An insightful exploration of loss and the role of intellectual curiosity and spiritual openness in addressing it." —*Kirkus*

Tran, Ly
House of Sticks: A Memoir. Ly Tran. Scribner 2021. 368 p.
ISBN 9781501118814
Grades: Adult   B
1. Tran, Ly, 1989- 2. Family relationships 3. Families 4. Childhood 5. Immigrant families 6. Growing up 7. Racism 8. Identity 9. Sexism 10. Immigrants, Vietnamese 11. Vietnamese Americans 12. Brooklyn, New York city 13. New York city 14. Autobiographies and memoirs 15. Life stories — Identity 16. Life stories — Relationships — Growing up 17. Family and Relationships — Growing up
LC 2020024046

A powerful memoir by 25-year-old Ly Tran about her immigrant experience and her recent family history in the aftermath of the war that spans from Vietnam to Brooklyn, and ultimately to the Ivy League.

"A moving coming-of-age memoir by a young Vietnamese American girl growing up in New York City.... A brutally honest, ultimately hopeful narrative of family, immigration, and resilience." —*Kirkus*

Tran, Phuc
★ *Sigh, Gone: A Misfit's Memoir of Great Books, Punk Rock, and the Fight to Fit in.* Phuc Tran. Flatiron Books 2020. 306 p.
ISBN 9781250194718
Grades: Adult   B
1. Tran, Phuc, 1974- 2. Vietnamese Americans 3. Teenage immigrants 4. Misfits (People) 5. Books and reading 6. Punk rock music 7. Teenage boys 8. Skateboarders 9. Growing up 10. Belonging 11. Assimilation (Sociology) 12. Racism 13. Fathers and sons 14. Abusive men 15. Family violence 16. Child abuse victims 17. Family relationships 18. Self-discovery 19. High school teachers 20. Immigrants, Vietnamese 21. Refugees, Vietnamese 22. Vietnam War, 1961-1975 23. Southeast Asian Americans 24. Southeast Asian people 25. Refugees 26. Pennsylvania 27. Autobiographies and memoirs 28. Adult books for young adults 29. Life stories — Identity — Immigrants 30. Life stories — Relationships — Growing up 31. Arts and Entertainment — Writing and Publishing 32. Life stories — Facing adversity — Abuse survivors 33. Antiracist literature
LC 2019047906

In 1975, during the fall of Saigon, Phuc Tran immigrates to America along with his family. By sheer chance they land in Carlisle, Pennsylvania, a small town where the Trans struggle to assimilate into their new life. In this coming-of-age memoir told through the themes of great books such as the Metamorphosis, the Scarlet Letter, the Iliad, and more, Tran navigates the push and pull of

ESSENTIAL AND RECOMMENDED TITLES
Biography

finding and accepting himself despite the challenges of immigration, feelings of isolation, and teenage rebellion, all while attempting to meet the rigid expectations set by his immigrant parents.

"This high-impact, emotional memoir about growing up in a Vietnamese immigrant family refracts the author's angry adolescence through a prism of classic literature." —*Publishers Weekly*

Traub, James
John Quincy Adams: Militant Spirit. James Traub. Basic Books, a member of the Perseus Books Group 2016. 560 p.
ISBN 9780465028276
Grades: Adult B
1. Adams, John Quincy, 1767-1848 2. Adams family 3. Political leadership 4. Presidents 5. Politicians 6. International relations 7. Politics and government 8. United States history 9. United States 10. 19th century 11. Biographies 12. History writing — Presidency — 19th century — United States 13. Life stories — Politics — Politicians
LC 2015030745

Drawing on Adams' diary, letters and writings, a scholar and journalist chronicles the diplomat and president's numerous achievements—and equally numerous failures—that both stand as testaments to his unwavering moral convictions, revealing a brilliant, flinty and unyielding man whose life exemplified political courage.

An impassioned biography of 'A coherent and consistent thinker who adhered to his core political convictions across his decades of public service.' —*Kirkus*

Includes bibliographical references and index.

Travis, Randy
Forever and Ever, Amen: A Memoir of Music, Faith, and Braving the Storms of Life. Randy Travis with Ken Abraham. Nelson Books 2019. 304 p.
ISBN 9781400207985
Grades: Adult B
1. Travis, Randy 2. Country musicians 3. Fame 4. Faith (Christianity) 5. People who have had strokes 6. Family violence 7. Divorced men 8. Country music 9. Autobiographies and memoirs 10. Arts and Entertainment — Music — Country 11. Life stories — Arts and culture — Performing arts — Musicians and composers 12. Life stories — Facing adversity — Personal transformation
LC 2018046406

The long-awaited, deeply personal story of one of American music's greatest icons, a remarkable tale of the utmost heights of fame and success, the deepest lows of life's sorrows, and a miraculous return from the brink of death—told as only Randy Travis can.

"Travis writes honestly about his ups and downs as well as his serious health problems and closes on a hopeful note. For Travis many fans and all who love country music." —*Booklist*

Includes bibliographical references.

Travisano, Thomas J.
Love Unknown: The Life and Worlds of Elizabeth Bishop. Thomas Travisano. Viking 2019. 432 p.
ISBN 9780525428817
Grades: Adult B
1. Bishop, Elizabeth, 1911-1979 2. Poets, American 3. Poetry writing 4. Women poets 5. Women authors 6. Psychic trauma in children 7. Voyages and travels 8. Lesbians 9. Lesbian poets 10. Literary criticism 11. 20th century 12. Biographies 13. Life stories — Arts and culture — Writing — Poets 14. Life stories — Identity — LGBTQIA+ 15. Arts and Entertainment — Writing and Publishing — Literary criticism
LC 2019016018

An illuminating new biography of one of the greatest American poets of the twentieth century, Elizabeth Bishop.

Trebincevic, Kenan
The Bosnia List: A Memoir of War, Exile, and Return. Kenan Trebincevic and Susan Shapiro. Penguin Books 2014. 320 pages

ISBN 9780143124573
Grades: Adult B
1. Trebincevic, Kenan, 1980- 2. Yugoslav War, 1991-1995 3. Muslims 4. Interethnic conflict 5. Refugees 6. Forced relocations 7. Interethnic relations 8. Death threats 9. Healing 10. Genocide 11. Bosnian Americans 12. Bosnia and Hercegovina 13. Autobiographies and memoirs 14. Life stories — Facing adversity — War and oppression — War survivors 15. History writing — Wars and conflicts — Civil Wars 16. History writing — Europe — Eastern Europe
LC 2013035345

This poignant, searing memoir chronicles Kenan's miraculous escape from the brutal ethnic cleansing campaign that swept the former Yugoslavia. After two decades in the United States, Kenan honors his father's wish to visit their homeland, making a list of what he wants to do there. Kenan decides to confront the former next door neighbor who stole from his mother, see the concentration camp where his Dad and brother were imprisoned and stand on the grave of his first betrayer to make sure he's really dead. Back in the land of his birth, Kenan finds something more powerful-and shocking-than revenge.

"An engaging memoir of war trauma and the redemption to be found in confronting it." —*Kirkus*

Includes bibliographical references and index.

Trejo, Danny
Trejo: My Life of Crime, Redemption, and Hollywood. Danny Trejo with Donal Logue. Atria Books 2021. 288 p.
ISBN 9781982150822
Grades: Adult B
1. Trejo, Danny, 1944- 2. Actors and actresses 3. Crime 4. Mexican American men 5. Redemption 6. Addiction 7. Loss 8. Fame 9. Acting 10. Imprisonment 11. Violence 12. California 13. Autobiographies and memoirs 14. Life stories — Arts and culture — Performing arts — Actors and actresses 15. Arts and Entertainment — Movies and television 16. Life stories — Facing adversity

For the first time, the full, fascinating, and inspirational true story of Danny Trejo's journey from crime, prison, addiction, and loss to unexpected fame as Hollywood's favorite bad guy with a heart of gold.

"In this inspiring, engaging memoir, actor Trejo chronicles his experiences with addiction, prison, violence, and loss, and his journey from construction worker at L.A.'s famous Cinerama Dome, to eventual star of the movies that played there." —*Library Journal*

Tresch, John
The Reason for the Darkness of the Night: Edgar Allan Poe and the Forging of American Science. John Tresch. Farrar, Straus and Giroux 2021. 352 p.
ISBN 9780374247850
Grades: Adult B
1. Poe, Edgar Allan, 1809-1849 2. Authors, American 3. Literature and science 4. Poets, American 5. Science 6. United States 7. 19th century 8. Biographies 9. Life stories — Arts and culture — Writing — Authors 10. Arts and Entertainment — Writing and Publishing 11. Science Writing — General
LC 2020058350

A biography of Edgar Allan Poe with an emphasis on his engagement with the scientists and scientific discoveries of his era.

"Historian Tresch (The Romantic Machine) sheds light on Edgar Allan Poe's engagement with science in this intriguing biography." —*Publishers Weekly*

Includes bibliographical references and index.

Trethewey, Natasha D.
★ *Memorial Drive: A Daughter's Memoir.* Natasha Trethewey. ECCO 2020. 224 p.
ISBN 9780062248572
Grades: Adult B
1. Families of murder victims 2. Death of mothers 3. Women poets 4. Life change events 5. Grief 6. Family violence 7. Family history 8. Children of abused women 9. Multiracial women 10. Mississippi 11. Atlanta, Georgia 12. Southern states 13. 20th century 14. Autobiographies and memoirs 15. Life stories — Facing adversity
LC BI2020014813

ALA Notable Book, 2021; LibraryReads Favorites, 2020; New York Times Notable Book, 2020.

The former U.S. poet laureate and Pulitzer Prize-winning author shares a chillingly personal memoir about the brutal murder of her mother at the hands of her former stepfather.

"In this beautifully composed, achingly sad memoir, U.S. poet laureate Trethewey (Monument) addresses the 1985 murder of her mother.... This profound story of the horrors of domestic abuse and a daughter's eternal love for her mother will linger long after the book's last page is turned." —*Publishers Weekly*

Trimborn, Jurgen
Leni Riefenstahl: A Life. Jurgen Trimborn; translated from the German by Edna McCown. Faber and Faber 2007. xii, 375 p. of plates : Illustration
ISBN 9780374184933
Grades: Adult   B
1. Riefenstahl, Leni 2. Propaganda 3. Film producers and directors 4. Women film producers and directors 5. Nazi propaganda 6. Nazi collaborators 7. Art 8. Nazism 9. Films 10. Third Reich, 1933-1945 11. Social life and customs 12. Germany 13. 20th century 14. Biographies 15. Life stories — Arts and culture — Performing arts — Directors and producers 16. Arts and Entertainment — Movies and Television 17. History writing — Wars and conflicts — World War II
LC 2006013263

A revealing portrait of the controversial filmmaker examines Riefenstahl's remarkable contributions to the cinematic art, her relationship with Adolf Hitler, the two monumental films she created for him—Triumph of the Will and Olympia—and her refusal to be held accountable for her role in the Holocaust and the atrocities of the Nazi regime.

"Trimborn interviewed Riefenstahl in 1997, when he was twenty-five, having already spent six years of 'Intensive labor' on the project, and he briefly entertained the quixotic hope of writing a definitive book with her blessing and collaboration. Unwilling to misrepresent himself as a hagiographer, he was doomed to fail, though his disappointment does not seem to have warped his fair-mindness. [The author's] aim was to correct the murky published record and the 'Attitudes' of his compatriots. One has to admire the sniperlike precision with which he takes out fugitive falsehoods that have lived under cover for a century." —*The New Yorker*

Includes bibliographical references (p. [317]-327) and index.

Trump, Mary L.
Too Much and Never Enough: How My Family Created the World's Most Dangerous Man. Mary Trump. Simon & Schuster 2020. 225 pages
ISBN 9781982141462
Grades: Adult   B
1. Trump, Donald, 1946- 2. Trump family 3. Presidents 4. Businesspeople 5. Dysfunctional families 6. Fathers and sons 7. Family relationships 8. Manipulation (Social sciences) 9. Politics and government 10. United States history 11. United States 12. 2010s 13. 2020s 14. 21st century 15. Biographies 16. Life stories — Politics — Politicians 17. History writing — Presidency — 21st century — United States 18. Politics and global affairs — World politics — United States 19. Life stories — People in history — Famous families
LC Bl2020015126

In this revelatory, authoritative portrait of Donald J. Trump and the toxic family that made him, Mary L. Trump, a trained clinical psychologist and Donald's only niece, shines a bright light on the dark history of their family in order to explain how her uncle became the man who now threatens the world's health, economic security, and social fabric.

"Trump, a trained clinical psychologist and the niece of President Donald Trump, delivers a concise and damning account of her family's dysfunctions and their role in shaping her uncle's toxic blend of cruelty, incompetence, and vainglory." —*Publishers Weekly*

Includes index.

Tubbs, Michael
The Deeper the Roots: A Memoir of Hope and Home. Michael Tubbs. Flatiron Books 2021. 288 p.
ISBN 9781250173447
Grades: Adult   B

1. Tubbs, Michael, 1990- 2. African American politicians 3. African American mayors 4. Children of single parents 5. Growing up 6. Poverty 7. Family relationships 8. Role models 9. Municipal government 10. Progressivism (United States politics) 11. Social justice 12. Autobiographies and memoirs 13. Biographies 14. Life stories — Politics — Politicians 15. Life stories — Identity — Race and ethnicity 16. Politics and global affairs — Political figures
LC 2021021941

Don't tell nobody our business," Michael Tubbs's mother often told him growing up. For Michael, that meant a lot of things: Don't tell anyone about the day-to-day struggle of being Black and broke in Stockton, CA. Don't tell anyone the pain of having a father incarcerated for 25 years to life. So for a long time Michael didn't tell anyone his story, but as he went on to a scholarship at Stanford and an internship in the Obama White House, he began to realize the power of his experience, the need for his perspective in the halls of power. By the time he returned to Stockton to become, in 2016 at age 26, its first Black mayor and the youngest-ever mayor of a major American city, he knew his story meant something.

"Tubbs, former mayor of Stockton, CA, writes about his impoverished childhood with an incarcerated father and becoming a Stanford graduate and political leader.... Part coming-of-age story and part political autobiography, Tubbs's book is an accessible and compelling account of his life." —*Library Journal*

Tucci, Stanley
★ *Taste: My Life Through Food.* Stanley Tucci. Gallery Books 2021. 320 p.
ISBN 9781982168018
Grades: Adult   B
1. Tucci, Stanley 2. Cooking, Italian 3. Food writers 4. Actors and actresses 5. United States 6. Autobiographies and memoirs 7. Biographies 8. Life stories — Arts and culture — Culinary arts 9. Food writing — Memoirs and biographies 10. Food Writing — Food and Culture
LC 2021007791

The food-obsessed, award-winning actor, reflecting on the intersection of food and life, presents a heartfelt and delicious memoir of life in and out of the kitchen that takes readers on a gastronomic journey through the good times and bad.

"The actor explores his 'Love of food and all that it encompasses,' a passion that 'Only continues to grow every year.'... The warmth and sincerity with which Tucci tells his stories will make you feel like part of the family." —*Kirkus*

Tuchman, Barbara W.
Stilwell and the American Experience in China, 1911-45. Barbara W. Tuchman. Grove Press 2001. xv, 621 p. : Map
ISBN 9780802138521
Grades: 11 12 Adult   B
1. Stilwell, Joseph Warren, 1883-1946 2. Military attaches 3. International relations 4. Revolutions 5. World War II 6. Politics and government 7. Chinese history 8. United States 9. China 10. 20th century 11. History writing — Communist China — Asia — China
LC 2001040154

Pulitzer Prize for General Nonfiction, 1972.

Joseph Stilwell was the military attache to China in 1935 to 1939, commander of United States forces, and allied chief of staff to Chiang Kai-shek in 1942-44. His story unfolds against the background of China's history, from the revolution of 1911 to the turmoil of World War II, when China's Nationalist government faced attack from Japanese invaders and Communist insurgents.

Includes bibliographical references (p. 541-552) and index; Originally published: New York : Macmillan, 1970.

Tumulty, Karen
The Triumph of Nancy Reagan. Karen Tumulty. Simon & Schuster 2021. 480 p.
ISBN 9781501165191
Grades: Adult   B
1. Reagan, Nancy, 1921-2016 2. Reagan, Ronald 3. Reagan family 4. Childhood 5. Marriage 6. Families 7. Presidents' spouses 8. Politics and government 9. Washington (D.C.) 10. California 11. United States 12. 1980s 13. Biographies

ESSENTIAL AND RECOMMENDED TITLES
Biography

14. Life stories — Politics 15. History writing — Women's history 16. History writing — United States

LC 2020031177

The definitive biography of the fiercely vigilant and politically astute First Lady who shaped one of the most consequential presidencies of the 20th century: Nancy Reagan.

"In a luminous and exhaustive biography, Washington Post political columnist Tumulty chronicles the private life and political influence of Ronald Reagan's wife. . . . The definitive biography of the woman who drove her husband's presidential ambitions." —*Kirkus*

Includes bibliographical references and index.

Tur, Katy
Rough Draft: A Memoir. Katy Tur. Signal Press 2022. 304 p.
ISBN 9781982118181
Grades: Adult **B**
1. Tur, Katy, 1983- 2. Women journalists 3. Broadcast journalism 4. Childhood 5. Growing up 6. Parents 7. Family relationships 8. Families 9. Burn out (Psychology) 10. Self-doubt 11. Autobiographies and memoirs 12. Life stories — Arts and culture — Writing — Journalists 13. Arts and Entertainment — Writing and publishing

In this deeply personal memoir about a life spent chasing the news, the MSNBC anchor and daughter of two pioneering helicopter journalists recounts her eccentric and volatile California childhood and charts her own journey to globe-trotting foreign correspondent as she tries to write her own story.

"A colorfully candid memoir from a dedicated journalist." —*Kirkus*

Turan, Kenneth
★ *Free for All: Joe Papp, the Public, and the Greatest Theater Story Ever Told.* Kenneth Turan and Joseph Papp. Broadway 2009. 648 p.
ISBN 9780767931687
Grades: Adult **B**
1. Papp, Joseph, 1921-1991 2. Theatrical producers and directors 3. Jewish Americans 4. Actors and actresses 5. Biographies 6. Interviews 7. Arts and Entertainment — Theater 8. Life stories — Arts and culture — Artists

LC 2008050887

An oral history of the New York Shakespeare Festival and the Public Theater draws on interviews with 160 celebrity contributors including Meryl Streep, James Earl Jones and Kevin Kline to trace the pivotal artistic contributions of producer and director Joe Papp.

"A wonderful book that clearly and powerfully shows that Papp's own story was the most enduring drama he ever produced." —*Kirkus*

Turner, John G.
Brigham Young, Pioneer Prophet. John G. Turner. The Belknap Press of Harvard University Press 2012. 490 p.
ISBN 9780674049673
Grades: Adult **B**
1. Young, Brigham, 1801-1877 2. Mormons 3. Faith 4. Biographies 5. Spirituality and Religion — Christianity — Mormonism 6. Spirituality and Religion — Religious Leaders 7. Life stories — Religion and spirituality — Religious and spiritual leaders

LC 2012015555

Provides a comprehensive portrait of the Mormon spiritual leader, viewed by followers as a protector and by opponents as a heretic, and describes how his faith has impacted the Mormon religion for over a century.

"There aren't enough superlatives for this book. It will remain the standard biography for a long time. Because of its thorough documentation, academics will take it seriously, while general readers will appreciate its clarity of prose and argument." —*Library Journal*

Includes bibliographical references and index.

Twain, Mark
★ *Autobiography of Mark Twain: Volume 3.* Mark Twain; Harriet Elinor Smith, editor; associate editors: Benjamin Griffin, Victor Fischer, Michael B. Frank. University of California Press 2015. 792 p.

ISBN 9780520279940
Grades: Adult **B**
1. Twain, Mark, 1835-1910 2. Authors 3. Humorists 4. Intellectual life 5. Storytelling 6. Literature and society 7. Authors, American 8. 19th century 9. Autobiographies and memoirs 10. Biographies 11. Arts and Entertainment — Writing and Publishing 12. Life stories — Arts and culture — Writing — Authors 13. Arts and Entertainment — Writing and Publishing — Literary criticism

LC Bl2015038084

A concluding volume of the literary master's uncensored collection of writings on his inner and outer life features his daily dictations from March 1907 to December 1909 and cover his honorary degrees from Oxford, critical assessments of Theodore Roosevelt and controversial "Ashcroft-Lyon Manuscript."

★ *Autobiography of Mark Twain: Volume 1.* Harriet Elinor Smith, editor; associate editors: Benjamin Griffin, Victor Fischer, Michael B. Frank, Sharon K. Goetz, Leslie Myrick. University of California Press 2010. 760 p.
ISBN 9780520267190
Grades: 11 12 Adult **B**
1. Twain, Mark, 1835-1910 2. Authors 3. Humorists 4. Intellectual life 5. Storytelling 6. Literature and society 7. Authors, American 8. 19th century 9. Autobiographies and memoirs 10. Biographies 11. Arts and Entertainment — Writing and Publishing 12. Life stories — Arts and culture — Writing — Authors

LC 2009047700

In the first complete and uncensored edition of his autobiography, one of America's foremost authors and humorists relates experiences lived, people encountered, places visited, and judgments rendered throughout his lifetime.

"Laced with Twain's unique blend of humor and vitriol, the haphazard narrative is engrossing, hugely funny, and deeply revealing of its author's mind." —*Publishers Weekly*

A publication of the Mark Twain Project of the Bancroft Library; Includes bibliographical references (p. 681-712) and index.

★ *Autobiography of Mark Twain: Volume 2.* Harriet Elinor Smith, editor; associate editors: Benjamin Griffin, Victor Fischer, Michael B. Frank, Sharon K. Goetz, Leslie Myrick. University of California Press 2013. xix, 733 p.
ISBN 9780520272781
Grades: 11 12 Adult **B**
1. Twain, Mark, 1835-1910 2. Authors 3. Humorists 4. Intellectual life 5. Storytelling 6. Literature and society 7. Authors, American 8. 19th century 9. Autobiographies and memoirs 10. Biographies 11. Arts and Entertainment — Writing and Publishing 12. Life stories — Arts and culture — Writing — Authors

LC Bl2013041739

The second volume of Mark Twain's uncensored autobiography continues to describe the events of the author's life in his own humorous and opinionated voice, including his preoccupation with money and his dislike of the politicians of his day.

"Twain traveled extensively and befriended many luminaries, and his colorful experiences give the book the same Dickensian scope as the first volume, and presents a vivid picture of America in the 19th century and Twain's indelible mark on it." —*Publishers Weekly*

Includes bibliographical references and index.

Tweedy, Jeff
Let's Go (so We Can Get Back): A Memoir of Recording and Discording with Wilco, Etc. Jeff Tweedy. Dutton 2018. 336 p.
ISBN 9781101985267
Grades: Adult **B**
1. Tweedy, Jeff, 1967- 2. Alternative rock musicians 3. Guitarists 4. Prescription drug abuse 5. Prescription drug abusers 6. Popular music 7. Anxiety 8. Autobiographies and memoirs 9. Life stories — Arts and culture — Performing arts — Musicians and composers 10. Arts and Entertainment — Music — Rock

The singer, guitarist, and songwriter, best known for this work with the bands Uncle Tupelo and Wilco, opens up about his past, his songs, the music and the people that have inspired him.

PUBLIC LIBRARY CORE COLLECTION: NONFICTION
Twentieth Edition

Tworkov, Helen
Lotus Girl: My Life at the Crossroads of Buddhism and America. Helen Tworkov. St. Martin's Essentials 2024. 320 p.
ISBN 9781250321558
Grades: Adult   B
1. Tworkov, Helen 2. Buddhist women 3. Converts to Buddhism 4. Home (Concept) 5. Buddhism 6. Spirituality 7. United States 8. Autobiographies and memoirs 9. Life stories — Religion and spirituality — Spiritual journeys 10. Spirituality and religion — Buddhism
LC 2023038225
Interweaving experience, research, and revelation, Helen Tworkov explores the relationship between Buddhist wisdom and American values, presenting a wholly unique look at the developing landscape of Buddhism in the West. Lotus Girl offers insight not only into Tworkov's own search for the truth, but into the ways each of us can better understand and transform ourselves.
"In this stimulating and elegant memoir, Tworkov (Zen in America), the founding editor of the nonsectarian Buddhist magazine Tricycle, chronicles the lifelong search for answers that drew her to Buddhism." —*Publishers Weekly*

Tye, Larry
★ *Bobby* Kennedy: The Making of a Liberal Icon. Larry Tye. Random House 2016. 608 pages
ISBN 9780812993349
Grades: Adult   B
1. Kennedy, Robert Francis, 1925-1968 2. Family relationships 3. Politicians 4. Legislators 5. United States 6. Biographies 7. Life stories — Politics — Politicians 8. History writing — Politicians — United States 9. History writing — 1960s — United States
LC 2016004991
Booklist Editors' Choice, 2016.
Draws on unpublished memoirs, unreleased government files, private papers, and interviews with Kennedy's close family and colleagues to chronicle his transformation from 1950s cold warrior to a liberal champion of the working class, the poor, and minorities.
"The author chides RFK for such things as slanting his account of the Bay of Pigs, his perhaps excessive pursuit of Jimmy Hoffa, and his early hawkishness on Vietnam. But the contrary image is clear: a good, if not great man; an unspeakable loss." —*Kirkus*
Includes bibliographical references and index.

★ *Demagogue:* The Life and Long Shadow of Senator Joe McCarthy. Larry Tye. Houghton Mifflin Harcourt 2020. 608 p.
ISBN 9781328959720
Grades: Adult   B
1. McCarthy, Joseph, 1908-1957 2. Subversive activities 3. Politicians 4. Demagoguism and demagogues 5. Antisemites 6. Anti-Communist movements 7. Legislators 8. Politics and government 9. United States 10. 20th century 11. Biographies 12. Impartial writing 13. Life stories — Politics — Politicians 14. History writing — Early 20th century — United States
LC 2019024932
The definitive biography of the most dangerous demagogue in American history, based on first-ever access to his personal and professional papers, medical and military records, and recently-unsealed transcripts of his closed-door Congressional hearings.
"A definitive biography that will stand the test of time." —*Library Journal*
Includes bibliographical references and index.

Satchel: The Life and Times of an American Legend. Larry Tye. Random House 2009. 416 p.
ISBN 9781400066513
Grades: Adult   B
1. Paige, Satchel, 1906-1982 2. African American baseball players 3. Pitchers (Baseball) 4. Race relations in sports 5. Negro leagues players 6. Baseball history 7. Baseball players 8. Negro Leagues 9. United States history 10. United States 11. 20th century 12. Autobiographies and memoirs 13. Biographies 14. Sports and Competition — Baseball 15. Sports and Competition — Individual Athlete 16. Life stories — Sports — Athletes
LC 2008044858
New York Times Notable Book, 2009.
A portrait of the Negro League pitcher and pioneer in the integration of baseball evaluates the role of discrimination in limiting his career, the Jim Crow biases that prevented his signing with the big leagues until he was in his forties, and his lasting legacy.
"This is a discerning, empathetic and hype-free [biography]. While Paige's life has become the stuff of legend, its particulars are not easily verified. Yet Satchel makes a cool, clear, tenacious effort to find the real Paige behind all [the] hyperbole." —*New York Times*

Tyson, Cicely
★ *Just* as I Am: A Memoir. Cicely Tyson. HarperCollins 2021. 432 p.
ISBN 9780062931061
Grades: Adult   B
1. Tyson, Cicely, 1924-2021 2. Actors and actresses 3. African American women 4. Acting 5. African Americans 6. Men-women relations 7. Intergenerational trauma 8. United States 9. Autobiographies and memoirs 10. Life stories — Arts and culture — Performing arts — Actors and actresses 11. Arts and Entertainment — Movies and Television
LC Bl2020071908
BCALA Literary Award for Nonfiction, 2022.
The Academy, Tony, and three-time Emmy Award-winning actor and trailblazer tells her stunning story, looking back at her six-decade career and life.
"Whether discussing the politics of natural hair or the racial violence that led to the Black Lives Matter movement, Tyson speaks with incisive clarity, humor, and moral authority." —*Booklist*

Tyson, Mike
Iron Ambition: My Life with Cus D'amato. Mike Tyson. Blue Rider Press 2017. 320 p.
ISBN 9780399177033
Grades: Adult   B
1. Tyson, Mike, 1966- 2. D'Amato, Cus 3. Boxers (Sports) 4. Boxing trainers 5. Mentors 6. Coach and athlete 7. African American athletes 8. African American boxers 9. United States 10. Autobiographies and memoirs 11. Biographies 12. Sports and Competition — Boxing 13. Sports and Competition — Individual Athlete 14. Life stories — Sports — Athletes 15. Life stories — Relationships
LC 2017007907
The former heavyweight champion and best-selling memoirist presents an intimate look at the life and leadership lessons of the legendary boxing trainer, exploring D'Amato's pivotal role in the careers of multiple World Champions and his legal adoption of Tyson in the aftermath of the latter's mother's death.
"A belated but welcome homage to a boxing legend who died shortly before Tyson's career took off." —*Kirkus*

Ulander, Perry A.
Walking Point: From the Ashes of the Vietnam War. Perry A. Ulander. North Atlantic Books 2016. 252 p.
ISBN 9781623170127
Grades: Adult   B
1. Ulander, Perry A, 1948-2023 2. Vietnam War, 1961-1975 3. Marijuana 4. Drug use 5. Soldiers 6. United States 7. Autobiographies and memoirs 8. Biographies 9. Life stories — Law and order — Armed forces personnel 10. History writing — Wars and conflicts — Vietnam War
LC 2015022372
This intimate memoir by an American GI who served in Vietnam offers a powerful narrative for readers with an interest in the effects of war and violence, American involvement in Vietnam and how trauma can be a catalyst for transformation.
"Ulanders fine memoir should take a place among the best works in the Vietnam War autobiographical canon." —*Publishers Weekly*

Ullman, Ellen
Life in Code: A Personal History of Technology. Ellen Ullman. MCD, Farrar, Straus and Giroux 2017. 320 pages

ESSENTIAL AND RECOMMENDED TITLES
Biography

ISBN 9780374534516
Grades: Adult **B**
1. Ullman, Ellen 2. Computer programmers 3. Computer programming 4. Internet 5. Technology and civilization 6. Computers and civilization 7. Autobiographies and memoirs 8. Life stories — Science, technology, and medicine 9. Science Writing — Computing, the Internet, and Technology 10. History writing — Science, technology, and medicine
LC 2017012764

The award-winning author of Close to the Machine shares insights into the past half century of online development to explore how digital technology has lost its innocence, changing life in unexpected and sometimes sinister ways.

"Neither technophilic nor technophobic, this collection creates a time-lapse view of the rapid development of technology in recent years and provides general readers with much-needed grounding for the sweeping changes of the revolution underway." —*Publishers Weekly*

Ullrich, Volker
Hitler: Ascent, 1889-1939. Volker Ullrich; translated from the German by Jefferson Chase. Alfred A. Knopf 2016. 880 p.
ISBN 9780385354387
Grades: Adult **B**
1. Hitler, Adolf, 1889-1945 2. Nazism 3. Dictators 4. Personality 5. Heads of state 6. Third Reich, 1933-1945 7. Biographies 8. Translations — German to English 9. Life stories — Politics — Politicians 10. History writing — Europe — Germany 11. History writing — Wars and conflicts — World War II — European Theater
LC 2015047202

Los Angeles Times Book Prize for Biography, 2016; New York Times Notable Book, 2016.

Draws on previously unseen papers and recent scholarly research to shed new light on the man behind the public persona—from Hitler's childhood and his failures as a young man in Vienna to his First World War experience and his rise as a far-right party leader.

"Above all, in this long but skillfully narrated study, Ullrich reveals Hitler to have been an eminently practical politician and frighteningly so… one of the best works on Hitler and the origins of the Third Reich to appear in recent years." —*Kirkus*

A Borzoi book—Title page verso; Originally published in Germany … copyright 2013, S. Fischer Verlag GmbH, Frankfurt am Main—Title page verso; Translation of : Adolf Hitler; Translated from the German.

Hitler: Downfall, 1939-1945. Volker Ullrich; translated from the German by Jefferson Chase. Alfred A. Knopf 2020. IX, 838 p.
ISBN 9781101874004
Grades: Adult **B**
1. Hitler, Adolf, 1889-1945 2. Nazism 3. Heads of state 4. Dictators 5. Power 6. World War II 7. Military campaigns 8. Third Reich, 1933-1945 9. Politics and government 10. Germany 11. Second World War era (1939-1945) 12. Biographies 13. Translations — German to English 14. Life stories — Politics — Politicians 15. History writing — Wars and conflicts — World War II — European Theater 16. History writing — Europe — Germany
LC 2019053386

In the summer of 1939 Hitler was at the zenith of his power. The Nazis had consolidated political control in Germany and a series of foreign-policy coups had restored Germany to the status of a major world power. He now embarked on realizing his lifelong ambition: to provide the German people with the resources they needed to flourish and to exterminate those who stood in the way. Yet despite a series of stunning initial triumphs, Hitler's decision to invade the Soviet Union in 1941 turned the tide for good. This is a masterful account of a spectacular downfall, and an essential addition to our understanding of Hitler and the Second World War.

"German historian Ullrich completes his comprehensive biography of the man who is perhaps history's most hated figure…. An endlessly revealing look at the Nazi regime that touches on large issues and small details alike." —*Kirkus*

Includes bibliographical references and index; Originally published: Frankfurt : S. Fischer, 2018; Translated from the German.

Umar, Ousman
North to Paradise: A Memoir. Ousman Umar; translated by Kevin Gerry Dunn. Amazon Pub 2022. 167 p.
ISBN 9781542030113
Grades: Adult **B**
1. Umar, Ousman 2. Entrepreneurs 3. Immigration and emigration 4. Racism 5. Human smuggling 6. Exploitation 7. Violence 8. Voyages and travels 9. Survival 10. Ghana 11. Africa 12. Europe 13. Autobiographies and memoirs 14. Translations — Spanish to English 15. Life stories — Identity — Immigrants 16. Life stories — Facing adversity

The inspiring true story of one man's treacherous boyhood journey from a rural village in Ghana to the streets of Barcelona—and the path that led him home.

"A Ghanaian social entrepreneur tells the story of his five-year journey across Africa to the 'Promised Land' of Europe…. Both sobering and inspiring, this story about a young African man's awakening to the realities of an often uncaring world offers a compelling portrait of humanity at its ignorant worst and enlightened best." —*Kirkus*

Originally published in Spanish under the title Viaje al pais de los blancos by Plaza & Janes in Spain in 2019.

Ung, Loung
Lucky Child: A Daughter of Cambodia Reunites with the Sister She Left Behind. Loung Ung. Harper Perennial 2006. xv, 268 p. : Illustration
ISBN 9780060733957
Grades: 11 12 Adult **B**
1. Ung, Loung 2. Ung, Chou 3. Cambodian Americans 4. Refugees 5. Sisters 6. Genocide 7. Atrocities 8. Southeast Asian Americans 9. Southeast Asian people 10. Cambodia 11. 20th century 12. Autobiographies and memoirs 13. Biographies 14. History writing — Immigration — United States 15. Family and Relationships — Siblings 16. Life stories — Identity — Immigrants 17. Life stories — Facing adversity — War and oppression — Refugees 18. Adult books for young adults
LC Bl2006030732

Describes the Ung family's experiences of relocation from war-torn Cambodia and assimilation in Vermont, a transition marked by leaving a sibling behind and the family's struggles to forge a new life in a very different society.

"This book is alternately heart-wrenching and heartwarming, as it follows the parallel lives of Loung Ung and her closest sister, Chou, during the 15 years it took for them to reunite." —*Publishers Weekly*

Sequel to: First they killed my father; Sequel: Lulu in the sky; Includes bibliographical references (p. 267-268); Originally published: New York : HarperCollins, 2005.

Unger, Debi
George Marshall: An Interpretive Biography. Debi Unger, Irwin Unger, Stanley Hirshson. HarperCollins 2014. 560 p.
ISBN 9780060577193
Grades: Adult **B**
1. Marshall, George C. (George Catlett), 1880-1959 2. Marshall Plan, 1948-1952 3. Command of troops 4. Politicians 5. Generals 6. United States 7. Biographies 8. History writing — Military — Military leadership 9. Life stories — Law and order — Military leaders
LC 2015413285

This interpretive biography of George C. Marshall follows his life from his childhood in Western Pennsylvania and his military training at the Virginia Military Institute to his role during and after World War II and his death in 1959 at the age of seventy-eight. It brings to light the virtuous historical role models who inspired him, including George Washington and Robert E. Lee, and his relationships with the Washington political establishment, military brass, and foreign leaders, from Harry Truman to Chiang Kai-shek. It explores Marshall's successes and failures during World War II, and his contributions through two critical years of the emerging Cold War—including the transformative Marshall Plan, which saved Western Europe from Soviet domination, and the failed attempt to unite China's nationalists and communists.

"The authors praise him [Marshall] for his management of the vast military expansion and his ability to cope with the difficulties inherent in controlling a gi-

PUBLIC LIBRARY CORE COLLECTION: NONFICTION
Twentieth Edition

ant military coalition. His decisions regarding the implementation of D-Day and the planned invasion of Japan are justifiably questioned, as are his choices as the Cold War commenced. This is an excellent reexamination of Marshall's career that is ideal for general readers." —*Booklist*

Unger, Harlow G.
First Founding Father: Richard Henry Lee and the Call to Independence. Harlow Giles Unger. Da Capo Press 2017. 320 p.
ISBN 9780306825613
Grades: Adult   B
1. Lee, Richard Henry, 1732-1794 2. Politicians 3. Founding fathers of the United States 4. American Revolution, 1775-1783 5. Revolutions 6. United States history 7. United States 8. Revolutionary America (1775-1783) 9. Biographies 10. Life stories — Politics — Politicians 11. History writing — Early America — United States

LC 2017040744

Before Washington, before Jefferson, before Franklin or John Adams, there was Lee—Richard Henry Lee, the First Founding Father. Richard Henry Lee was the first to call for independence, and the first to call for union. He was "father of our country" as much as George Washington, securing the necessary political and diplomatic victories in the Revolutionary War. Lee played a critical role in holding the colonial government together, declaring the nation's independence, and ensuring victory for the Continental Army by securing the first shipments of French arms to American troops. Next to Washington, Lee was arguably the most important American leader in the war against the British.

"Ungers thorough research, smooth narrative, and placement of Lee in the context of 18th-century America will inform both general readers and historians." —*Choice*

Includes bibliographical references and index.

The Last Founding Father: James Monroe and a Nation's Call to Greatness. Harlow Giles Unger. Da Capo Press 2009. xii, 388 p. : Illustration; Map; Plan
ISBN 9780306818080
Grades: Adult   B
1. Monroe, James, 1758-1831 2. Founding Fathers of the United States 3. Diplomats 4. Presidents 5. Politicians 6. Politics and government 7. United States 8. 19th century 9. 18th century 10. Biographies 11. History writing — Presidency — 18th century — United States 12. Life stories — Politics — Politicians

LC 2009026195

Recounts the life of the fifth president from his fierce participation in critical Revolutionary War battles through his political contributions, documenting his efforts toward securing the nation's durability and his mentorship under the first four presidents.

Includes bibliographical references (p. 353-376) and index.

Unger, Miles
★ *Michelangelo: A Life in Six Masterpieces.* Miles J. Unger. Simon & Schuster 2014. 448 pages
ISBN 9781451678741
Grades: Adult   B
1. Michelangelo Buonarroti, 1475-1564 2. Artists 3. European Renaissance 4. 16th century 5. Biographies 6. Life stories — Arts and culture — Artists 7. History writing — Europe — Italy

LC 2013045778

Booklist Editors' Choice, 2014.

The life of perhaps the most famous, most revolutionary artist in history, told through the stories of six of his magnificent masterpieces.

Includes bibliographical references and index.

Union, Gabrielle
We're Going to Need More Wine: Stories That Are Funny, Complicated, and True. Gabrielle Union. Dey Street Books 2017. 304 p.
ISBN 9780062693983
Grades: Adult   B
1. Union, Gabrielle 2. Actors and actresses 3. African American women 4. Women social advocates 5. Rape victims 6. Racism 7. Sexism 8. Feminism 9. Fame 10. Power 11. Essays 12. Autobiographies and memoirs 13. Life stories — Arts and culture — Performing arts — Actors and actresses 14. Society and culture — Gender — Women 15. Arts and entertainment — Movies and television

LC 2017277365

LibraryReads Favorites, 2017.

Union launched her career with roles in iconic '90s movies. When she revealed her own trauma as a victim of sexual assault, she urged compassion for victims of sexual violence. In this moving collection of essays, Union tells astonishingly personal and true stories about power, color, gender, feminism, and fame. She discusses her experiences with bullying, beauty standards, and competition between women in Hollywood; growing up in white California suburbia, and coping with the divorce of her parents. Throughout, she reminds us of the importance of confidence, self-awareness, and the power of sharing truth, laughter, and support.

"This sparkling book collects amusing and heartbreaking stories from the life of actress Union (Being Mary Jane)." —*Publishers Weekly*

You Got Anything Stronger?: Stories. Gabrielle Union. Dey Street Books 2021. xi, 242 p.
ISBN 9780062979933
Grades: Adult   B
1. Union, Gabrielle 2. Women celebrities 3. Political activists 4. Female infertility 5. Motherhood 6. Family relationships 7. Blended families 8. Film industry and trade 9. African Americans 10. Actors and actresses 11. Autobiographies and memoirs 12. Essays 13. Life stories — Arts and culture — Performing arts — Actors and actresses 14. Life stories — Relationships — Family 15. Life stories — Relationships — Parent and child 16. Arts and Entertainment — Movies and Television

LC 2021020916

Acclaimed activist, actress, and author Gabrielle Union is back with an even more intimate, revealing, and powerful collection of essays.

"Following the success of We're Going to Need More Wine (2017), actress Union returns with more wise, intimate personal stories, welcoming readers back into her life and family with all the candor and wit of her first memoir.... Always smart, inviting, and generous with emotion, Union's second exquisite memoir reads like a conversation with your most enlightened, thoughtful friend." —*Booklist*

Urofsky, Melvin I.
Louis D. Brandeis: A Life. Melvin I. Urofsky. Pantheon Books 2009. 976 p.
ISBN 9780375423666
Grades: Adult   B
1. Brandeis, Louis Dembitz, 1856-1941 2. Judges 3. Lawyers 4. Federal judges 5. Law reform 6. Jurisprudence 7. Practice of law 8. Politics and government 9. United States 10. 20th century 11. Biographies 12. History writing — Judicial branch — United States 13. Life stories — Law and order — Judges and lawyers

LC 2009003992

New York Times Notable Book, 2009.

A full-scale portrait of the early twentieth-century Supreme Court justice seeks to distinguish his personal life from his achievements as a reformer and jurist, offering additional insight into his role in the development of pro bono legal services, the creations of the Federal Reserve Act and other key legislations, and his contributions to American-Jewish affairs as a practicing Zionist.

"This is a monumental, authoritative and appreciative biography of the man Franklin D. Roosevelt called Isaiah." —*New York Times Book Review*

Includes bibliographical references and index.

Utley, Robert M.
★ *Geronimo.* Robert M. Utley. Yale University Press 2012. 384 p.
ISBN 9780300126389
Grades: Adult   B
1. Geronimo, Apache chief, 1829-1909 2. Apache (North American people) 3. Indigenous peoples of North America 4. Race relations 5. Battles 6. Indigenous peoples of North America — Wars 7. 19th century 8. Biographies 9. History writing — Indigenous peoples — United States 10. Life stories — People in

ESSENTIAL AND RECOMMENDED TITLES
Biography

history — Indigenous peoples 11. Life stories — Law and order — Military leaders

LC 2012019521

Spur Award for Biography, 2013; Western Heritage Award for Outstanding Nonfiction Book, 2013.

This biography of the famous Apache uncovers the truth behind the myths and rumors that enshroud his life, describing how the warrior escaped capture, what his training was like and explains why he was feared by both whites and other Apaches.

"Highly recommended for academic libraries in particular, it will be essential to many public libraries and private readers as well." —*Library Journal*

Includes bibliographical references and index.

Sitting Bull: The Life and Times of an American Patriot. Robert M. Utley. Henry Holt & Co 2008. 464 p.
ISBN 9780805088304
Grades: 11 12 Adult B
1. Sitting Bull, 1831-1890 2. Indigenous peoples of North America 3. Dakota (North American people) 4. Chiefs (Political anthropology) 5. Indigenous peoples of North America — History 6. The West (United States) history 7. North America 8. 19th century 9. Biographies 10. History writing — Indigenous peoples — United States 11. Life stories — People in history — Indigenous peoples

LC Bl2008012894

"This book is well written, strongly documented, and fairly reasoned to satisfy even specialists within the field. It surpasses all previous biographies of Sitting Bull." —*Choice*

Valleley, Paul
Pope Francis: The Struggle for the Soul of Catholicism. Paul Valleley. Bloomsbury USA 2015. xxv, 470 p.
ISBN 9781632861153
Grades: Adult B
1. Francis, Pope, 1936- 2. Popes 3. Church and the world 4. Church and social problems 5. Christian church work with poor people 6. Poverty 7. Biographies 8. Spirituality and Religion — Christianity — Catholicism 9. Spirituality and Religion — Religious Leaders 10. Life stories — Religion and spirituality — Religious and spiritual leaders

LC Bl2015026821

From his first appearance on a Vatican balcony Pope Francis proved himself a Pope of Surprises. With a series of potent gestures, history's first Jesuit pope declared a mission to restore authenticity and integrity to a Catholic Church bedevilled by sex abuse and secrecy, intrigue and in-fighting, ambition and arrogance. He declared it should be 'A poor Church, for the poor'. But there is a hidden past to this modest man with the winning smile. Jorge Mario Bergoglio was previously a bitterly divisive figure. His decade as leader of Argentina's Jesuits left the religious order deeply split. And his behaviour during Argentina's Dirty War, when military death squads snatched innocent people from the streets, raised serious questions—on which this book casts new light.

"A well-written, balanced portrait of a man leading the church in a new direction. This title will appeal to anyone who seeks a well-rounded study of the current Pope." —*Library Journal*

Previously published in 2013 under the title, Pope Francis: Untying the knots.

Van Es, Bart
The Cut Out Girl: A Story of War and Family, Lost and Found. Bart Van Es. Penguin Press 2018. 304 p.
ISBN 9780735222243
Grades: Adult B
1. De Jong, Hesseline 2. Van Es, Bart 3. Jewish people 4. Holocaust (1933-1945) 5. Child Holocaust survivors 6. Family secrets 7. Foster children 8. World War II 9. Dutch people 10. Western European people 11. Family history 12. Children 13. German occupation, World War II 14. European history 15. Netherlands 16. Autobiographies and memoirs 17. History writing — Wars and conflicts — Holocaust — World War II 18. Life stories — Facing adversity — War and oppression — Holocaust 19. Family and Relationships — General

LC 2018006209

Costa Biography Award, 2018; Costa Book of the Year Award, 2018.

The author describes his friendship with an 80-year-old woman in Amsterdam who was smuggled as a child into his grandfather's family during the Nazi occupation and together they confront the dark truth of the Dutch cooperation in rounding up the Jews.

Van Haaften, Julia
★ *Berenice Abbott: A Life in Photography.* Julia Van Haaften. W.W. Norton & Company 2018. 544 p.
ISBN 9780393292787
Grades: Adult B
1. Abbott, Berenice, 1898-1991 2. Photographers 3. Women photographers 4. Photography 5. Biographies 6. Life stories — Arts and culture — Artists 7. Arts and entertainment — Photography

LC 2017056400

Berenice Abbott is to American photography as Georgia O'Keeffe is to painting or Willa Cather to letters. She was a photographer of astounding innovation and artistry, a pioneer in both her personal and professional life. Abbott's sixty-year career established her not only as a master of American photography, but also as a teacher, writer, archivist, and inventor.

"Van Haaftens expert foundational biography brings Abbott into sharp focus as a photographer able to express deep feeling through technical mastery." —*Booklist*

Includes bibliographical references and index.

Van Zandt, Steve
Unrequited Infatuations. Stevie Van Zandt. Hachette Books 2021. 256 p.
ISBN 9780306925429
Grades: Adult B
1. Van Zandt, Steve 2. Rock musicians 3. Actors and actresses 4. Political activists 5. Social justice 6. Interpersonal relations 7. Music industry and trade 8. Film industry and trade 9. Autobiographies and memoirs 10. Life stories — Arts and culture — Performing arts — Musicians and composers 11. Life stories — Arts and culture — Performing arts — Actors and actresses 12. Life stories — Politics — Activists and reformers

Uncover never-before-told stories in this epic tale of self-discovery by a Rock n Roll disciple and member of the E Street Band. What story begins in a bedroom in suburban New Jersey in the early '60s, unfolds on some of the country's largest stages, and then ranges across the globe, demonstrating over and over again how Rock and Roll has the power to change the world for the better? This story. Unrequited Infatuations chronicles the twists and turns of Stevie Van Zandt's always surprising life.

"Guitarist, songwriter, producer, actor, and activist Van Zandt tells his fascinating life story in this compelling memoir. . . . By turns philosophical, earthy, metaphysical, humorous, and charmingly self-deprecating, Van Zandt chronicles a multifaceted life, charts his musical and political manifestos, and travels intriguing roads that will distinguish his book among music memoirs." —*Library Journal*

Vanasco, Jeannie
Things We Didn't Talk About When I Was a Girl: A Memoir. Jeannie Vanasco. Tin House Books 2019. 357 p.
ISBN 9781947793453
Grades: Adult B
1. Vanasco, Jeannie 2. Rape victims 3. Sexual violence 4. Sexual harassment of women 5. Sex crimes 6. Rape 7. Me Too movement 8. Acquaintance rape 9. Autobiographies and memoirs 10. Society and culture — Violence and crime 11. Life stories — Facing adversity — Victims of crime 12. True Crime — Sex Crimes 13. Society and culture — Gender — Women 14. Adult books for young adults

LC 2019013796

A part-memoir, part-true-crime account and testament to female friendship describes how the author navigated sexual trauma by contacting her former friend and rapist, who agreed to come forward and explore how biases shape sexual violence and its perceptions.

PUBLIC LIBRARY CORE COLLECTION: NONFICTION
Twentieth Edition

Vance, J. D.
Hillbilly Elegy: A Memoir of a Family and Culture in Crisis. J. D. Vance. HarperCollins 2016. 352 p.
ISBN 9780062300546
Grades: Adult   B
1. Vance, J. D. 2. Poor families 3. Working class 4. Communities 5. Upward mobility 6. Social mobility 7. Poverty 8. Consequences 9. Families 10. Autobiographies and memoirs 11. Page to screen 12. Life stories — Relationships — Family 13. Society and culture — Wealth and class — Poverty
LC 2016304613
Kirkus Prize for Nonfiction finalist, 2016.
Shares the poignant story of the author's family and upbringing, describing how they moved from poverty to an upwardly mobile clan that included the author, a Yale Law School graduate, while navigating the demands of middle-class life and the collective demons of the past.
"Both heartbreaking and heartwarming, this memoir is akin to investigative journalism." —*Library Journal*

Vargas, Jose Antonio
Dear America: Notes of an Undocumented Citizen. Jose Antonio Vargas. Dey Street Books 2018. 320 p.
ISBN 9780062851352
Grades: Adult   B
1. Vargas, Jose Antonio 2. Immigrants 3. Political activists 4. Human rights activists 5. Undocumented immigrants 6. Filipino Americans 7. Homelessness 8. Immigration and emigration 9. Journalists 10. Southeast Asian Americans 11. Southeast Asian people 12. United States 13. Autobiographies and memoirs 14. Biographies 15. Life stories — Politics — Activists and reformers 16. Society and culture — Immigration 17. Politics and global affairs — Immigration 18. Life stories — Arts and culture — Writing — Journalists 19. Adult books for young adults
LC Bl2018134469
The journalist and immigration-rights activist presents a memoir relating how he was sent from the Philippines to the U.S. as a child, his discovery of his undocumented status as a teenager, and his decision to reveal his immigration status publicly in 2011.

Varon, Elizabeth R.
Longstreet: The Confederate General Who Defied the South. Elizabeth R. Varon. Simon & Schuster 2023. 528 p.
ISBN 9781982148270
Grades: Adult   B
1. Longstreet, James, 1821-1904 2. Generals 3. Confederate soldiers 4. Reconstruction (United States history) 5. Civil war 6. Military campaigns 7. New Orleans, Louisiana 8. American Civil War era (1861-1865) 9. Biographies 10. Life stories — People in history 11. Life stories — Law and order — Military leaders 12. History Writing — Reconstruction — United States
LC 2023021160
This authoritative biography of the controversial Confederate general shows how he, after the Civil War, dramatically changed course by supporting Black voting and the integrated postwar government in Louisiana, for which he was branded a traitor.
"This biography offers a fresh and balanced appraisal of Longstreet's life and postwar career. Readers interested in American history, the Civil War, and biographies will enjoy this well-written treatment." —*Library Journal*
Includes bibliographical references and index.

Vasquez-Lavado, Silvia
In the Shadow of the Mountain: A Memoir of Courage. Silvia Vasquez-Lavado. Henry Holt and Company 2022. 320 p.
ISBN 9781250776747
Grades: Adult   B
1. Vasquez-Lavado, Silvia 2. Mountaineers 3. Hispanic American women 4. Sexuality 5. Alcoholism 6. Adult child sexual abuse victims 7. Resilience 8. Women in technology 9. Psychic trauma 10. Women 11. Faith 12. Interpersonal relations 13. Family relationships 14. Courage 15. Mount Everest 16. Autobiographies and memoirs 17. Life stories — Nature and outdoors 18. Life stories — Facing adversity — Abuse survivors 19. Sports and competition — Mountaineering 20. Book club best bets
LC 2021036935
When Silvia's mother called her home to Peru, she knew something finally had to give. A Latinx hero in the elite macho tech world of Silicon Valley, privately, she was hanging by a thread. She was deep in the throes of alcoholism, hiding her sexuality from her family, and repressing the abuse she'd suffered as a child. Her visit to Peru would become a turning point in her life. Silvia started climbing. Something about the brute force required for the ascent-the restricted oxygen at altitude, the vast expanse of emptiness around her, the risk and spirit and sheer size of the mountains, the nearness of death-woke her up. And then, she took her biggest pain to the biggest mountain: Everest. "The Mother of the World," as it's known in Nepal, allows few to reach her summit, but Silvia didn't go alone. She gathered a group of young female survivors and led them to base camp alongside her, their strength and community propelling her forward.
"A Peruvian-born mountaineer and humanitarian tells the story of how mountain-climbing helped her and a group of young sexual abuse survivors process old traumas.... An emotionally raw and courageous memoir." —*Kirkus*

Vaughan, Liam
Flash Crash: A Trading Savant, a Global Manhunt, and the Most Mysterious Market Crash in History. Liam Vaughan. Doubleday 2020. 336 pages
ISBN 9780385543651
Grades: Adult   B
1. Sarao, Navinder Singh 2. Stock market 3. Financial crises 4. White collar crime 5. Brokers 6. Stocks 7. Computer crimes 8. 21st century 9. True Crime — General
LC 2020005099
Describes the story of a trading prodigy who amassed millions playing the markets like a video game from his working-class West London childhood home until he unwittingly started the Flash Crash and the FBI showed up at his door.
"A cleareyed, smart account that merits high rank in the library of computer crime." —*Kirkus*

Vaughn, Ellen Santilli
★ *Becoming Elisabeth Elliot.* Ellen Vaughn; foreword by Joni Eareckson Tada. B & H Publishing 2020. 304 p.
ISBN 9781535910934
Grades: Adult   B
1. Elliot, Elisabeth 2. Women missionaries 3. Christian women 4. Widows 5. Self-sacrifice 6. Church work 7. Faith (Christianity) 8. Faith 9. Resilience 10. Biographies 11. Life stories — Religion and spirituality — Religious and spiritual leaders 12. Spirituality and Religion — Christianity
In this authorized biography, Becoming Elisabeth Elliot, bestselling author Ellen Vaughn uses Elisabeth's private, unpublished journals, and candid interviews with her family and friends, to paint the adventures and misadventures God used to shape one of the most influential women in modern church history.
"Even those well-acquainted with Elliot's works will find fresh perspective and revealing insights here." —*Publishers Weekly*
Includes bibliographical references.

Vella, Christina
George Washington Carver: A Life. Christina Vella. Louisiana State University Press 2015. 416 p. (Southern Biography Series)
ISBN 9780807160756
Grades: Adult   B
1. Carver, George Washington, 1864?-1943 2. Agriculturists 3. African American men 4. Agricultural research 5. Peanuts 6. African American agriculturists 7. African American scientists 8. Biographies 9. Life stories — Politics — Activists and reformers 10. Life stories — Science, technology, and medicine — Scientists and inventors 11. Adult books for young adults 12. History writing — African American — United States
Provides an in-depth look at the life of the famed botanist, including his relationship with his friends and his prolific career.

ESSENTIAL AND RECOMMENDED TITLES
Biography

Velshi, Ali
Small Acts of Courage: A Legacy of Endurance and the Fight for Democracy. Ali Velshi. St. Martin's Press 2024. 288 p.
ISBN 9781250288851
Grades: Adult   B
1. Immigrants 2. Family history 3. Social justice 4. Courage 5. Endurance 6. Democracy 7. Canadian people in the United States 8. South Asian people 9. Muslims 10. United States 11. Autobiographies and memoirs 12. Life stories — Identity — Immigrants
LC 2023058455

Tapping into 125 years of family history to advocate for social justice as a living, breathing experience, the Chief Correspondent for MSNBC relates the stories of regular people who made a lasting commitment to fight for change, even when success seemed impossible, and urges us to do the same.

"This family saga educates, entertains, and fascinates as a study of the Indian and Ismaili Muslim diasporas and of immigrants' countless contributions to their new homelands." —*Library Journal*

Includes index.

Verant, Samantha
Seven Letters from Paris: A Memoir. Samantha Verant. Sourcebooks 2014. xv, 254 pages
ISBN 9781402297229
Grades: Adult   B
1. Verant, Samantha 2. American people in France 3. Love letter writing 4. Reunions 5. Lost love 6. Paris, France 7. Autobiographies and memoirs 8. Life stories — Relationships — Couples 9. Family and Relationships — Dating and Marriage
LC 2014016020

At age 40, Samantha Verant's life is falling apart. Then one day she finds 7 old love letters written by Jean-Luc, the sexy French scientist she met in Paris when she was 19. She tracks him down online, and what starts out as flirty e-mails transforms into pure romance as Samantha visits France to see Jean-Luc for the first time in 20 years. Reunited with her lost love in Paris, Samantha realizes that she has finally found what she was looking for all along.

Verdelle, A. J.
Miss Chloe: A Memoir of a Literary Friendship with Toni Morrison. A.J. Verdelle. Amistad 2022. 160 p.
ISBN 9780063031661
Grades: Adult   B
1. Verdelle, A. J, 1960- 2. Morrison, Toni, 1931-2019 3. African American women authors 4. African American women 5. Publishers and publishing 6. Female friendship 7. Writing 8. Authors 9. Friendship 10. Autobiographies and memoirs 11. Life stories — Arts and culture — Writing — Authors 12. Life stories — Relationships — Friendship
LC 2021051660

The award-winning author of the Good Negress shares her own path to success that led to a friendship with enigmatic cultural icon Toni Morrison, painting an illuminating portrait of the legendary author and offering an honest assessment of what it means to be a writer.

"The joys, challenges, and lasting lessons of a friendship with Chloe Ardelia Wofford, aka Toni Morrison." —*Kirkus*

Viren, Sarah
To Name the Bigger Lie: A Memoir in Two Stories. Sarah Viren. Scribner 2023. 304 p.
ISBN 9781982166595
Grades: Adult   B
1. Viren, Sarah, 1979- 2. Truth 3. Dishonesty 4. Innocence (Law) 5. Honesty 6. Betrayal 7. Couples 8. Trust 9. Philosophy 10. Sex crimes 11. LGBTQIA+ people 12. Conspiracies 13. College teachers 14. Life stories — Education — Scholars and educators 15. Nonfiction that reads like fiction

Part coming-of-age story, part psychological thriller, part philosophical investigation, this unforgettable memoir traces the ramifications of a series of lies that threaten to derail the author's life—exploring the line between truth and deception, fact and fiction, and reality and conspiracy.

"Past and present collide in this propulsive, one-of-a-kind meditation on truth and conspiracy from Viren (Mine), based on her viral essay of the same name....The result is a mesmerizing page-turner pulled tight with psychological tension." —*Publishers Weekly*

Vitale, Tom
In the Weeds: Around the World and Behind the Scenes with Anthony Bourdain. Tom Vitale. Hachette Books 2021. 288 p.
ISBN 9780306924095
Grades: Adult   B
1. Vitale, Tom 2. Bourdain, Anthony, 1956-2018 3. Television cooking shows 4. Food habits 5. Television personalities 6. Celebrities 7. Loss 8. Interpersonal relations 9. Grief 10. Biographies 11. Oral histories 12. Life stories — Arts and culture — Culinary arts 13. Food writing — Food and culture 14. Travel writing — General 15. Life stories — Arts and culture — Performing arts — Entertainers and celebrities
LC 2021022682

The long-time director and producer of Anthony Bourdain's television series discusses his experiences filming the in some of the most volatile regions in the world and presents an unvarnished view of the late star.

"It will resonate with many readers as a travel and entertainment memoir, exploration of grief, and tribute to a beloved figure." —*Library Journal*

Vogel, Ezra F.
Deng XIaoping and the Transformation of China. Ezra F. Vogel. Belknap Press of Harvard University Press 2011. xxiv, 876 p, 22 p. of plates : Illustration
ISBN 9780674055445
Grades: Adult   B
1. Deng, XIaoping, 1904-1997 2. Heads of state 3. Communists 4. Communism 5. Politicians 6. Politics and government 7. China 8. 20th century 9. Biographies 10. Life stories — Politics — Politicians 11. History writing — Communist China — Asia — China
LC 2011006925

Lionel Gelber Prize (Canada), 2012; National Book Critics Circle Award for Biography finalist, 2011.

"This hefty work assesses Deng XIaoping's years (1978?92) as China's paramount leader." —*Booklist*

Includes bibliographical references and index.

Vogel, Joseph
Man in the Music: The Creative Life and Work of Michael Jackson. Joseph Vogel; with a foreword by contributing editor Anthony Decurtis. Sterling 2011. 384 p.
ISBN 9781402779381
Grades: Adult   B
1. Jackson, Michael, 1958-2009 2. Popular music 3. Musicians 4. Biographies 5. Arts and Entertainment — Music — Pop 6. Life stories — Arts and culture — Performing arts — Musicians and composers
LC 2010051263

Analyzes every song and album of Jackson's solo career, from 1979's groundbreaking "Off the Wall" to his yet-to-be released material, placing the music in its social, historical, and cultural context.

Includes bibliographical references and index.

Volpe, Joseph
The Toughest Show on Earth: My Rise and Reign at the Metropolitan Opera. Joseph Volpe with Charles Michener. Knopf 2006. x, 304 p. : Illustration
ISBN 9780307262851
Grades: Adult   B
1. Volpe, Joseph 2. Opera producers and directors 3. Social life and customs 4. New York City 5. 21st century 6. Autobiographies and memoirs 7. Arts and Entertainment — Theater 8. Life stories — Arts and culture — Artists
LC 2005057932

PUBLIC LIBRARY CORE COLLECTION: NONFICTION
Twentieth Edition

On the eve of his retirement as general manager of the Metropolitan Opera, the outspoken culture czar offers a behind-the-scenes glimpse of life at one of the world's great operatic houses, recalling the political and artistic intrigues in which he has played a part, the business of running a cultural institution, and his collaboration with noted musicians, singers, directors, and conductors.

Includes bibliographical references (p. 287) and index.

Von Drehle, David

★ *The Book of Charlie: Wisdom from the Remarkable American Life of a 109-year-old Man*. David Von Drehle. Simon & Schuster 2023. 208 p.
ISBN 9781476773926
Grades: Adult   B

1. Von Drehle, David 2. Journalists 3. New neighbors 4. Senior men 5. Centenarians 6. Former physicians 7. Friendship 8. Intergenerational friendship 9. Reminiscing in old age 10. Wisdom 11. Advice 12. Purpose in life 13. United States history 14. 20th century 15. Life stories — Relationships — Friendship 16. Life stories — Personal growth

When Washington journalist David Von Drehle moved to Kansas, he met a new neighbor who was more than a century old. Little did he know that he was beginning a long friendship—and a profound lesson in the meaning of life. When a shocking tragedy interrupted his idyllic boyhood, Charlie White mastered survival strategies that reflect thousands of years of human wisdom. Von Drehle came to understand that Charlie's resilience and willingness to grow made this remarkable neighbor a master in the art of thriving through times of dramatic change.

"The Book of Charlie looks at universal truths through the lens of one man's long life." —*Booklist*

Von Furstenberg, Diane

The Woman I Wanted to Be. Diane von Furstenberg. Simon & Schuster 2014. 416 p.
ISBN 9781451651546
Grades: Adult   B

1. Von Furstenberg, Diane 2. Women 3. Women fashion designers 4. Fashion designers 5. People with cancer 6. Businesspeople 7. Identity 8. United States 9. Autobiographies and memoirs 10. Biographies 11. Arts and Entertainment — Fashion 12. Life stories — Arts and culture — Fashion 13. Nonfiction that reads like fiction

LC 2014033232

The influential fashion designer and author of Diane: A Signature Life describes her pursuit of a creativity and independence, providing coverage of such topics as her childhood in Brussels, her struggles with cancer and her creation of a genre-defining dress design.

"This is a fascinating glimpse into the life of one of the fashion worlds most enduring stars that will fascinate fashionistas and fans of strong, creative women." —*Publishers Weekly*

Vowell, Sarah

Assassination Vacation. Sarah Vowell. Simon & Schuster 2005. 258 p. : Illustration
ISBN 9780743260039
Grades: 11 12 Adult   B

1. Vowell, Sarah, 1969- 2. Assassins 3. Historic sites 4. Assassination 5. Presidents 6. Local history 7. Voyages and travels 8. United States 9. Biographies 10. History writing — Presidency — United States 11. True Crime — Murder 12. Travel Writing — United States 13. Adult books for young adults

LC 2004059134

In this engaging and highly unusual travelogue, journalist Sarah Vowell explores the history of American presidential assassinations. From the Florida Keys all the way to Alaska, Vowell visits assassination sites, museums, prisons, monuments, and even a religious commune. Along the way she shares strange-but-true historical facts—for instance, did you know that Robert Todd Lincoln, "a.K.A. Jinxy McDeath," was present at several presidential assassinations?—and offers keen observations about history, politics, and the connection of the past to the present.

Wacker, Grant

America's Pastor: Billy Graham and the Shaping of a Nation. Grant Wacker. The Belknap Press of Harvard University Press 2014. 413 pages
ISBN 9780674052185
Grades: Adult   B

1. Graham, Billy, 1918-2018 2. Christianity and culture 3. Evangelistic work (Christianity) 4. Evangelists 5. Clergy 6. Evangelicalism 7. United States 8. Biographies 9. Life stories — Religion and spirituality — Religious and spiritual leaders 10. Spirituality and Religion — Religious Leaders 11. Spirituality and Religion — Christianity

LC 2014014155

Examines the life of Billy Graham and how he impacted American culture by successfully tapping into broader cultural trends.

"Wacker doesn't shrink, however, from showing how Graham's fascination with presidential politics led him astray repeatedly while allowing that he was a genuine spiritual counselor to the presidents—Lyndon Johnson, in particular. If a great subject deserves a great book, Billy Graham has one." —*Booklist*

Includes bibliographical references and index.

Wagamese, Richard

For Joshua. Richard Wagamese. Milkweed Editions 2023. 240 p.
ISBN 9781571313898
Grades: Adult   B

1. Wagamese, Richard, 1955-2017 2. Fathers and sons 3. Ojibwe (North American people) 4. First Nations (Canada) 5. Letter writing 6. Separated friends, relatives, etc. 7. Wisdom 8. Growing up 9. Foster home care 10. Addiction 11. Self-discovery 12. Belonging 13. Tradition (Philosophy) 14. Indigenous peoples of North America 15. North American people 16. Canadian people 17. Letters 18. Autobiographies and memoirs 19. Canadian literature 20. Life stories — Identity — Race and ethnicity 21. Life stories — Relationships — Parent and child 22. Family and Relationships — Parenting

LC 2019036387

Ojibwe tradition calls for fathers to walk their children through the world, sharing the ancient understanding "that we are all, animate and inanimate alike, living on the one pure breath with which the Creator gave life to the Universe." in this intimate series of letters to the six-year-old son from whom he was estranged, Richard Wagamese fulfills this traditional duty with grace and humility, describing his own path through life—separation from his family as a boy, substance abuse, incarceration, and ultimately the discovery of books and writing—and braiding this extraordinary story with the teachings of his people.

"Originally published in Canada in 2002, this harrowing memoir from Ojibwe novelist Wagamese (1955?2017) reflects on his turbulent childhood and struggle with alcoholism." —*Publishers Weekly*

One Native Life. Richard Wagamese. Douglas & McIntyre 2008. xi, 257 pages
ISBN 9781553653646
Grades: Adult   B

1. Wagamese, Richard, 1955-2017 2. Ojibwe (North American people) 3. Indigenous authors 4. First Nations (Canada) 5. Writing 6. Adult child abuse victims 7. Indigenous peoples of North America 8. Authors, Canadian 9. Social life and customs 10. Coping 11. Canada 12. 20th century 13. Autobiographies and memoirs 14. Canadian literature 15. Biographies 16. History writing — Indigenous peoples — Canada 17. Arts and Entertainment — Writing and Publishing 18. Life stories — Arts and culture — Writing — Authors 19. Life stories — People in history — Indigenous peoples

An autobiography of author Richard Wagamese's life, from his abuse-filled childhood to his adulthood struggling with alcoholism.

Wagner, Alex

Futureface: A Family Mystery, an Epic Quest, and the Secret to Belonging. Alex Wagner. One World 2018. xii, 338 pages : Illustration
ISBN 9780812997941
Grades: Adult   B

1. Wagner, Alex 2. Women journalists 3. Interethnic families 4. Women 5. Ethnic identity 6. Genealogy 7. Family lore 8. Cultural differences 9. Intercultural communication 10. Identity 11. Autobiographies and memoirs

ESSENTIAL AND RECOMMENDED TITLES
Biography

12. Life stories — Identity — Race and ethnicity 13. Society and culture — Ethnic studies

An Atlantic senior editor and former host of NOW with Alex Wagner documents her international travels in search of answers to the mystery of her ancestry and broader questions about the American experience of race and immigration, evaluating the cost of today's obsession with race and identity and whether or not it is possible for society to forge an all-inclusive future.

Includes bibliographical references (pages [333]-338).

Wainaina, Binyavanga
One Day I Will Write About This Place. Binyavanga Wainaina. Graywolf Press 2011. 272 p.
ISBN 9781555975913
Grades: Adult B
1. Authors 2. Kenyan people 3. Family relationships 4. Political violence 5. African history 6. Kenya 7. Autobiographies and memoirs 8. Life stories — Relationships — Growing up
LC 2011923190

New York Times Notable Book, 2011.

A founding editor of Kwani and winner of the Caine Prize traces the story of his middle-class youth in Kenya, marked by his mother's religious period, family trips and his love of reading before a writing award compelled his literary career.

Wald, Elijah
★ *Escaping the Delta: Robert Johnson and the Invention of the Blues*. Elijah Wald. Amistad 2004. xxvi, 342 p.
ISBN 9780060524234
Grades: 11 12 Adult B
1. Johnson, Robert, 1911-1938 2. Guitarists 3. Blues musicians 4. Blues (Music) 5. Music history and criticism 6. Delta region, Mississippi 7. Biographies 8. Arts and Entertainment — Music — Jazz and the Blues 9. Life stories — Arts and culture — Performing arts — Musicians and composers 10. Adult books for young adults
LC 2003052287

Booklist Editors' Choice, 2004.

A look at the life and music of Robert Johnson and his contributions to the blues describes his obscurity during his own life, his innovative influence on American popular music, and how the history of blues music was shaped by white fans.

"The author writes better than anyone else ever has about the blues. If you read only one book about blues—maybe ever—read this one." —*Booklist*

Includes bibliographical references (p. [317]-321) and index.

Walder, Tracy
The Unexpected Spy: From the CIA to the FBI, My Secret Life Taking Down Some of the World's Most Notorious Terrorists. Tracy Walder; with Jessica Anya Blau. St Martins Press 2020. 272 pages
ISBN 9781250230980
Grades: Adult B
1. Walder, Tracy 2. Women spies 3. Terrorism prevention 4. War on Terrorism, 2001-2009 5. Misogyny 6. Sexism 7. Intelligence service 8. United States 9. Autobiographies and memoirs 10. Life stories — Law and order — Spies and secret agents 11. Life stories — Identity — Gender 12. Adult books for young adults
LC 2019036365

Offers a riveting account of a young woman who went straight from her college sorority to the CIA, where she hunted terrorists and weapons of mass destruction.

"Walder's fast-paced and intense narrative opens a window into life in two of America's major intelligence agencies." —*Publishers Weekly*

Waldman, Ayelet
A Really Good Day. Ayelet Waldman. Alfred A. Knopf 2017. 256 pages
ISBN 9780451494092
Grades: Adult B

1. Waldman, Ayelet 2. People with bipolar disorder 3. Bipolar disorder 4. People with depression 5. Hallucinogenic drugs 6. Mental illness 7. Neuropsychology 8. Treatment 9. Alternative medicine 10. Autobiographies and memoirs 11. Science Writing — Medicine and health — Mental health 12. Life stories — Facing adversity — Medical issues — Mental illness
LC 2016023416

A lighthearted account of the author's experiment with microdoses of LSD in an effort to treat a debilitating mood disorder details what she has learned about the misunderstood drug and how she believes psychedelics can be appropriately used as therapeutic medicines.

"This great read will attract open-minded psychology buffs, contemporary biography readers, and those keen to hear a new voice discuss issues associated with so-called illicit drugs in America." —*Library Journal*

Waldstreicher, David
The Odyssey of Phillis Wheatley: A Poet's Journeys Through American Slavery and Independence. David Waldstreicher. Farrar, Straus and Giroux 2023. 352 p.
ISBN 9780809098248
Grades: Adult B
1. Wheatley, Phillis, 1753-1784 2. African American women poets 3. African American poets 4. Poets, American 5. Enslaved people 6. United States history 7. 18th century 8. Biographies 9. Life stories — Arts and culture — Writing — Poets 10. History writing — African American — United States 11. History Writing — Women's history 12. Arts and Entertainment — Writing and publishing 13. History writing — Colonial America — United States
LC 2022053331

In this new biography of Phillis Wheatley, whose poetry was at the heart of the American Revolution, a noted historian offers the deepest account to date of her life and works, correcting myths, reconstructing intimate friendships and deepening our understanding of the revolutionary era.

"Waldstreicher (Slavery's Constitution), a history professor at the City University of New York Graduate Center, delivers a magisterial biography of 18th-century poet Phillis Wheatley (1753?1784)....The result is an indispensable take on an essential early American poet." —*Publishers Weekly*

Includes bibliographical references and index.

Walker, Alice
Gathering Blossoms Under Fire: The Journals of Alice Walker 1965-2000. Edited by Valerie Boyd. Simon & Schuster 2022. 512 p.
ISBN 9781476773155
Grades: Adult B
1. Walker, Alice, 1944- 2. Authors, American 3. African American women authors 4. Social reformers 5. Intellectual life 6. Interpersonal relations 7. Personal diaries 8. Social life and customs 9. United States 10. 20th century 11. Diaries 12. Life stories — Arts and culture — Writing — Authors 13. Arts and Entertainment — Writing and Publishing
LC 2021047979

This collection of journals from the National Book Award and Pulitzer Prize—winning author combines her person life with political events and traces her development as an artist activist and intellectual.

"Legendary author and 'Womanist' Alice Walker connects her past and present in this revealing and frequently heart-wrenching 50-year collection of journal writings....Walker's journals add a new dimension to her profoundly influential oeuvre and will be of great interest to her ardent readers." —*Booklist*

Includes index.

Wall, Duncan
The Ordinary Acrobat : A Journey into the Wondrous World of the Circus, Past and Present. Duncan Wall. Alfred A. Knopf 2013. 320 p.
ISBN 9780307271723
Grades: Adult B
1. Wall, Duncan 2. Circus 3. Acrobats 4. Acrobatics 5. Circus performers 6. Entertainers 7. Autobiographies and memoirs 8. Life stories — Arts and culture — Performing arts — Entertainers and celebrities 9. Arts and Entertainment — General 10. Sports and Competition — General
LC 2012038250

PUBLIC LIBRARY CORE COLLECTION: NONFICTION
Twentieth Edition

Duncan Wall recounts his experience as a student at the Ecole Nationale des Arts du Cirque and looks at the evolution of the circus, including the innovative Cirque du Soleil.

Wallace, Carvell
Another Word for Love: A Memoir. Carvell Wallace. MCD/Farrar, Straus and Giroux 2024. 240 p.
ISBN 9780374237820
Grades: Adult   **B**
1. Journalists 2. Podcasters 3. African Americans 4. Healing 5. Homelessness 6. Parenting 7. Love 8. LGBTQIA+ people 9. American people 10. United States 11. Autobiographies and memoirs 12. Life stories — Arts and culture — Writing — Authors

LC 2023050756

A transformative memoir that reimagines the conventions of love and posits a radical vision for healing.

"The story of a poet and podcaster's journey to claim the fullness of his identity and power as a queer Black American." —*Kirkus*

Wallace, Christopher
Twentieth-Century Man: The Wild Life of Peter Beard. Christopher Wallace. Ecco Press 2023. 304 p.
ISBN 9780063066410
Grades: Adult   **B**
1. Beard, Peter Hill, 1938-2020 2. Photographers 3. Naturalists 4. Wildlife 5. Socialites 6. Nature 7. Interpersonal relations 8. Voyages and travels 9. East Africa 10. 20th century 11. Biographies 12. Life stories — Nature and outdoors 13. Life stories — Arts and culture — Artists

"Overall, Beard's life reads like the adventure it was. Recommended for both general interest readers and photography enthusiasts." —*Library Journal*

Wallach, Janet
Desert Queen: The Extraordinary Life of Gertrude Bell, Adventurer, Adviser to Kings, Ally of Lawrence of Arabia. Janet Wallach. Anchor Books 2005. xxii, 425 p. : Illustration; Map
ISBN 9781400096190
Grades: Adult   **B**
1. Bell, Gertrude Lowthian, 1868-1926 2. Colonial administrators 3. Women travelers 4. Women archaeologists 5. Southwest Asia and North Africa (Middle East) history 6. British history 7. 20th century 8. Biographies 9. History writing — Women's history 10. Life stories — People in history 11. History writing — Southwest Asia and North Africa (Middle East)

LC 2005277878

Turning her back on her privileged life in Victorian England, Gertrude Bell journeyed the world and became fascinated with all things Arab. Traveling the length and breadth of the Arab region, armed with a love for its language and its people, she not only produced several enormously popular books based on her experiences, but became instrumental to the British foreign office. Janet Wallach reveals a woman whose achievements and independent spirit were especially remarkable for her times.

"Wallach … brings the resolute Bell and her complex world vividly to life." —*Booklist*

Includes bibliographical references (p. [399]-407) and index.

Waller, Douglas C.
Wild Bill Donovan: The Spymaster Who Created the OSS and Modern American Espionage. Douglas C. Waller. Free Press 2011. 400 p.
ISBN 9781416567448
Grades: Adult   **B**
1. Donovan, William J. (William Joseph), 1883-1959 2. Intelligence officers 3. World War II 4. Secret service 5. Intelligence service 6. Spies 7. Biographies 8. History writing — Wars and conflicts — World War II 9. Life stories — Law and order — Spies and secret agents

LC 2010024986

Examines the controversial life of the father of the CIA and the man that many consider to be the father of modern espionage itself.
Includes bibliographical references and index.

Wallis, Michael
Billy the Kid: The Endless Ride. Michael Wallis. W.W. Norton & Co. 2007. xvii, 328 p, 16 p. of plates : Illustration; Map; Portrait
ISBN 9780393060683
Grades: 11 12 Adult   **B**
1. Billy, the Kid 2. Outlaws 3. Frontier and pioneer life 4. Southwest (United States) 5. Biographies 6. History writing — Westward expansion — United States 7. True Crime — Historical Crime 8. Life stories — Law and order — Criminals and law-breakers

LC 2006101364

Historian Wallis has spent several years re-creating the rich, anecdotal saga of Billy the Kid (1859-1881), a deeply mythologized young man who became a legend in his own time and yet remains an enigma to this day. With the Gilded Age in full swing and the Industrial Revolution reshaping the American landscape, "the Kid," who was gunned down by Sheriff Pat Garrett in the New Mexico Territory at the age of 21, became a new breed of celebrity outlaw. He arose amid the mystery and myth of the swiftly vanishing frontier and, sensationalized beyond recognition by the tabloids and dime-store romances of the day, emerged as one of the most enduring icons of the American West—not to mention one of Hollywood's most misrepresented characters. This new biography, filled with dozens of rare images and period photographs, separates myth from reality in its portrait of this brief and violent life.

"Drawing on archival sources and interviews as well as secondary works, Wallis digs beneath the surface, clearly identifying what is known or probable and presenting the reasonable alternatives for what is conjecture." —*Library Journal*

Includes bibliographical references (p. [297]-308) and index.

Walls, Jeannette
★ *The Glass Castle: A Memoir.* Jeannette Walls. Scribner 2005. 288 p.
ISBN 9780743247535
Grades: 11 12 Adult   **B**
1. Walls, Jeannette 2. Dysfunctional families 3. Eccentrics and eccentricities 4. Growing up 5. Children of alcoholics 6. Poor people 7. Child neglect victims 8. Homeless people 9. Family relationships 10. Autobiographies and memoirs 11. Page to screen 12. Biographies 13. Family and Relationships — Growing up 14. Life stories — Relationships — Growing up 15. Adult books for young adults 16. Nonfiction that reads like fiction

ALA Notable Book, 2006; Alex Award, 2006; Booklist Editors' Choice: Adult Books for Young Adults, 2005; Garden State Teen Book Award (New Jersey), Nonfiction, 2008; New York Times Notable Book, 2005; Virginia Readers' Choice Award for High School, 2009.

The child of an alcoholic father and an eccentric artist mother discusses her family's nomadic upbringing, during which she and her siblings fended for themselves while their parents outmaneuvered bill collectors and the authorities.

"Shocking, sad, and occasionally bitter, this gracefully written account speaks candidly, yet with surprising affection, about parents and about the strength of family ties—for both good and ill." —*Booklist*

Adapted into a film by the same name in 2017.

Walls, Laura Dassow
★ *Henry David Thoreau: A Life.* Laura Dassow Walls. The University of Chicago Press 2017. 640 p.
ISBN 9780226344690
Grades: Adult   **B**
1. Thoreau, Henry David, 1817-1862 2. Authors, American 3. Intellectuals 4. Naturalists 5. Social life and customs 6. United States 7. 19th century 8. Biographies 9. Life stories — Arts and culture — Writing — Authors 10. Arts and Entertainment — Writing and Publishing — Literary criticism

LC 2016053416

Los Angeles Times Book Prize for Biography, 2017; New York Times Notable Book, 2017; Kirkus Prize for Nonfiction finalist, 2017.

ESSENTIAL AND RECOMMENDED TITLES
Biography

Traces the life of the extraordinary poet, best known for his meditations on nature at Walden Pond, who also spent time with good friend and neighbor Ralph Waldo Emerson and worked as a manual laborer, an inventor and a radical political activist.

"A superbly researched and written literary portrait that broadens our understanding of the great American writer and pre-eminent naturalist who has too long been regarded as a self-righteous scold." —*Kirkus*

Includes bibliographical references and index.

Walsh, Stephen
★ *Debussy: A Painter in Sound*. Stephen Walsh. Random House Inc 2018. 336 p.
ISBN 9781524731922
Grades: Adult   **B**
1. Debussy, Claude, 1862-1918 2. Piano music 3. Composers 4. Classical music 5. Belle Epoque (1871-1914) 6. Biographies 7. Arts and Entertainment — Music — Classical 8. Life stories — Arts and culture — Performing arts — Musicians and composers
LC 2017058738

Claude Debussy (1862-1918) was that rare creature, a composer who reinvented the language of music without alienating the majority of music lovers. The creator of such classics as La Mer and Clair de Lune, of Pelleas et Melisande and his magnificent, delicate piano works, he is the modernist everybody loves, the man who drove French music into entirely new regions of beauty and excitement at a time when old traditions—and the overbearing influence of Wagner—threatened to stifle it. As a central figure at the birth of modernism, Debussy's influence on French culture was profound. Yet at the same time his own life was complicated and often troubled by struggles over money, women, and ill-health.

"Walsh uses the musical compositions of French composer Achille-Claude Debussy (1862-1918) as a framework to tell the story of his short life in this richly descriptive biography." —*Publishers Weekly*

Walton, Bill
Back from the Dead. Bill Walton. Simon & Schuster 2016. 288 p.
ISBN 9781476716862
Grades: Adult   **B**
1. Walton, Bill, 1952- 2. Basketball players 3. Sportscasters 4. People with spinal cord injuries 5. Autobiographies and memoirs 6. Life stories — Facing adversity — Medical issues 7. Life stories — Sports
LC 2015031712

An NBA sports star and cultural icon discusses his catastrophic spinal collapse in 2007, the excruciating pain he suffered and his slow recovery, as well as his childhood, sports career and the political and cultural upheaval of the 1960s.

"This memoir is defined by trials as much as successes and will appeal to readers who appreciated Walton as player and commentator." —*Library Journal*

Includes index.

Walton, Sam
Sam Walton, Made in America: My Story. by Sam Walton with John Huey. Bantam Books 1993. xiii, 346 p. : Illustration
ISBN 9780553562835
Grades: Adult   **B**
1. Walton, Sam, 1918- 2. Millionaires 3. Life stories — Business
LC BL 99738358

In an account of his rise to the top of the American retail business, the reminiscences of the billionaire retailer are combined with interviews with Walton's family and friends.

Includes index; Originally published: New York : Doubleday, 1992.

Wambach, Abby
Forward: A Memoir. Abby Wambach. Dey Street Books 2016. 240 pages
ISBN 9780062466983
Grades: Adult   **B**
1. Wambach, Abby, 1980- 2. Women soccer players 3. Soccer 4. Soccer players 5. Lesbians 6. Autobiographies and memoirs 7. Life stories — Sports — Athletes 8. Life stories — Identity — LGBTQIA+ 9. Sports and competition — Soccer
LC 2016037369

The U.S. Women's national team captain—winner of the 2015 World Cup and the highest international goal scorer of all time—shares her story, her struggles and her worldview in a memoir that is also a rousing call to arms to dream big and fight for a better world.

"A cut above the standard sports memoir." —*Booklist*

Wang, Connie
Oh My Mother!: A Memoir in Nine Adventures. Connie Wang. Viking 2023. 256 p.
ISBN 9780593490921
Grades: Adult   **B**
1. Wang, Connie 2. Women authors 3. Authors 4. Asian American women 5. Mothers and daughters 6. Family relationships 7. Children of immigrants 8. Voyages and travels 9. Belonging 10. Self-discovery 11. Asian Americans 12. Autobiographies and memoirs 13. Life stories — Identity — Race and ethnicity 14. Life stories — Relationships — Family 15. Family and relationships — Families 16. Travel Writing — General
LC 2022057609

Exploring her complicated relationship with her mother through the "oh my god" moments in their travels together around the world, a journalist relates their many adventures, revealing the true story of two women who became comfortable with the feeling of not belonging and experienced something almost like freedom.

"A creative and entertaining shared memoir of identity, place, and their indelible connection to each other." —*Kirkus*

Wang, Qian Julie
★ *Beautiful Country: A Memoir*. Qian Julie Wang. Doubleday 2021. 320 p.
ISBN 9780385547215
Grades: Adult   **B**
1. Wang, Qian Julie, 1987- 2. Chinese Americans 3. Immigrants 4. Undocumented immigrants 5. Growing up 6. Poverty 7. Racism 8. Resilience 9. Chinese American women 10. East Asian Americans 11. China 12. Brooklyn, New York City 13. Autobiographies and memoirs 14. Life stories — Identity — Immigrants 15. Life stories — Identity — Race and ethnicity 16. Life stories — Relationships — Growing up 17. Life stories — Facing adversity 18. Book club best bets
LC 2020053188

This memoir from a Chinese woman who arrived in New York City at age seven examines how her family lived in poverty out of fear of being discovered as undocumented immigrants and how she was able to find success.

"In this extraordinary debut, civil rights lawyer Wang recounts her years growing up as an undocumented immigrant living in 'The furtive shadows' of America. . . . Consider this remarkable memoir a new classic." —*Publishers Weekly*

Ward, Clarissa
On All Fronts: The Education of a Journalist. Clarissa Ward. Penguin Press 2020. 384 p.
ISBN 9780525561477
Grades: Adult   **B**
1. Ward, Clarissa, 1980- 2. Television journalists 3. War correspondents 4. Women journalists 5. Iraq War, 2003-2011 6. Southwest Asia and North Africa (Middle East) history 7. Syria 8. 2010s 9. 2020s 10. Autobiographies and memoirs 11. Life stories — Arts and culture — Writing — Journalists 12. History writing — Wars and conflicts
LC 2019049839

The five-time Emmy Award-winning CNN chief international correspondent draws on the wrenching stories of soldiers, civilians and rebels in war-torn Syria to illuminate the human cost of Bashar al Assad's reign of terror and its personal impact on her family.

"Ward's journalism skills shine, putting readers on the front lines. Readers interested in the life stories of intrepid women journalists and the nature of inves-

tigative, international journalism will be captivated by this engrossing account."
—*Library Journal*
Includes index.

Ward, Geoffrey C.

*A **Disposition** to Be Rich: How a Small-Town Pastor's Son Ruined an American President, Brought on a Wall Street Crash, and Made Himself the Best-Hated Man in the United States.* by Geoffrey C. Ward. Alfred A. Knopf 2012. 432 p.

ISBN 9780679445302

Grades: Adult **B**

1. Ward, Ferdinand De Wilton, 1851-1925 2. Grant, Ulysses S, 1822-1885 3. Capitalists and financiers 4. Ponzi schemes 5. Children of clergy 6. Financial crises 7. United States history 8. United States 9. 19th century 10. Gilded Age (1865-1898) 11. Biographies 12. Business and economics — Corruption and scandal 13. History writing — Scandals 14. History writing — Gilded Age — United States 15. Nonfiction that reads like fiction

LC 2011035140

New York Times Notable Book, 2012.

Documents the story of Gilded Age con artist Ferdinand Ward, recounting how his large-scale pyramid operation and other sensational schemes triggered one of the greatest financial scandals in American history.

This is a Borzoi book—T.P. verso; Includes bibliographical references.

★ *The **Roosevelts:** An Intimate History.* Geoffrey C. Ward; based on a documentary film by Ken Burns; with a preface by Ken Burns; picture research by Susanna Steisel; design by Maggie Hinders. Alfred A. Knopf 2014. 528 p.

ISBN 9780307700230

Grades: Adult **B**

1. Roosevelt, Theodore, 1858-1919 2. Roosevelt, Franklin D. (Franklin Delano), 1882-1945 3. Roosevelt, Eleanor, 1884-1962 4. Presidents' spouses 5. Presidents 6. Politics and government 7. United States 8. 20th century 9. Biographies 10. Media tie-ins 11. History writing — Presidency — 20th century — United States 12. Life stories — Politics — Politicians

LC 2014019251

An extraordinarily vivid and personal portrait of a great American political family and its impact on the United States serves as the tie-in volume to the PBS documentary to air in the fall of 2014.

"Starting with Teddy's asthma-plagued youth and ending with Eleanor's death in 1962, every aspect of their lives and legacies is touched upon. Hundreds of photos, newspaper clippings, and accompanying captions flesh out the story, which expands to cover their friends and family, enemies, and (alleged) lovers."
—*Publishers Weekly*
Includes bibliographical references and index.

Unforgivable Blackness: The Rise and Fall of Jack Johnson. by Geoffrey C. Ward. A. A. Knopf 2004. xi, 492 p. : Illustration

ISBN 9780375415326

Grades: Adult **B**

1. Johnson, Jack, 1878-1946 2. Boxers (Sports) 3. African American boxers 4. Interracial romance 5. Boxing 6. United States 7. Biographies 8. Sports and Competition — Boxing 9. Sports and Competition — Individual Athlete 10. Life stories — Sports — Athletes

LC 2004048524

New York Times Notable Book, 2004.

Presents the life of the first Black heavyweight boxing champion, whose flamboyant personality and defiance of racial stereotypes in the early twentieth century often made him the object of public outrage and a target of law enforcement officials.

"The author brings us back into Johnson's life and times with exquisitely rendered details, and the fight scenes themselves are gripping: Fights so bloody that referees have to change shirts midbout, for instance, and a manager who pulls a gun on his fighter to keep him from quitting. The authoritative biography of Johnson for sure, but also one of the best boxing books in recent memory."
—*Booklist*

Includes bibliographical references (p. [453]-478) and index.

Ward, Jesmyn

★ *Men We Reaped: A Memoir.* Jesmyn Ward. Bloomsbury 2013. 272 p.

ISBN 9781608195213

Grades: Adult **B**

1. Ward, Jesmyn 2. African American women authors 3. Rural poor people 4. Children of single parents 5. Death 6. African American men 7. African Americans 8. Mississippi 9. Autobiographies and memoirs 10. Biographies 11. Life stories — Identity — Race and ethnicity 12. Life stories — Facing adversity 13. Life stories — Relationships — Growing up

LC 2013013600

New York Times Notable Book, 2013; National Book Critics Circle Award for Autobiography/Memoir finalist.

A National Book Award winner recounts the loss of five young men in her life to drugs, accidents, suicide and the bad luck that can follow people who live in poverty, particularly Black men, sharing her experiences of living through the dying as she searches through answers in her community.

"Ward's candid account is full of sadness and hope that takes readers out of their comfort zone and proves that education and hard work are the way up for the young and downtrodden." —*Library Journal*

Includes bibliographical references and index.

Ward, Maitland

Rated X: How Porn Liberated Me from Hollywood. Maitland Ward. Atria Books 2022. 256 p.

ISBN 9781982195892

Grades: Adult **B**

1. Ward, Maitland, 1977- 2. Actors and actresses 3. Pornographic film industry and trade 4. Pornographic films 5. Desire 6. Ambition 7. Hollywood, California 8. Autobiographies and memoirs 9. Life stories — Arts and culture — Performing arts — Actors and actresses 10. Arts and entertainment — Movies and television

LC 2021057349

Maitland Ward joined the cast of the Bold and the Beautiful as a teenager and found fame as the loveable, sexy (but not too sexy) co-ed Rachel McGuire in the later seasons of the beloved ABC sitcom Boy Meets World. Forced into the "good girl" role time and again, she was denied the darker, meatier roles she truly wanted to sink her teeth into. And so she turned away from Disney gold, and eventually established herself as one of the most-respected actresses in porn today. Full of jaw-and panty-dropping anecdotes, as well personal stories from her time on one of the most beloved sitcoms of the '90s, RATED X won't be your run-of-the-mill celebrity memoir.

"The memoir of a former TV star who found freedom, success, and herself in the pornography industry." —*Kirkus*

Wariner, Ruth

*The **Sound** of Gravel: A Memoir.* Ruth Wariner. Flatiron Books 2016. 352 pages

ISBN 9781250077691

Grades: Adult **B**

1. Wariner, Ruth 2. Mormon women 3. Polygamy 4. Mormons 5. Cults 6. Childhood 7. Communities 8. Siblings 9. American people in Mexico 10. Farm life 11. Adult child sexual abuse victims 12. Welfare recipients 13. Mormon theology 14. Resilience 15. Mexico 16. California 17. Autobiographies and memoirs 18. Life stories — Facing adversity — Abuse survivors 19. Life stories — Relationships — Growing up 20. Spirituality and Religion — Christianity — Mormonism 21. Adult books for young adults

LC 2015037663

An account of the author's coming-of-age in a polygamist Mormon Doomsday cult describes her childhood on a Mexico hills farm as one of her father's more than 40 welfare-dependent children, the extreme religious beliefs that haunted her daily life and her escape in the aftermath of a devastating tragedy.

"With power and insight, Wariners tale shows a road to escape from the most confining circumstances." —*Booklist*

ESSENTIAL AND RECOMMENDED TITLES
Biography

Warren, Louis S.
Buffalo Bill's America: William Cody and the Wild West Show. Louis S. Warren. Alfred A. Knopf 2005. xvi, 652 p. : Illustration
ISBN 9780375412165
Grades: Adult B
1. Buffalo Bill, 1846-1917 2. Wild West shows 3. Pioneers 4. Frontier and pioneer life 5. Entertainers 6. The West (United States) 7. United States 8. Biographies 9. History writing — Westward expansion — United States 10. Arts and Entertainment — Theater 11. Life stories — Arts and culture — Performing arts — Actors and actresses 12. Life stories — Arts and culture — Performing arts — Entertainers and celebrities 13. Adult books for young adults
LC 2004063280
Spur Award for Historical Nonfiction, 2006.
Explores the life and times of the colorful Pony Express rider, trapper, Civil War soldier, professional buffalo hunter, Indian fighter, cavalry scout, actor, and dime-novel hero within the social and cultural context of his era.
"This book is well written and exhaustively researched, the weightiest and surely the most ambitious book ever published about Cody and his times."
—*New York Times Book Review*
Includes bibliographical references and index.

Warren, Rosanna
Max Jacob: A Life in Art and Letters. Rosanna Warren. W. W. Norton & Company 2020. 736 pages
ISBN 9780393078855
Grades: Adult B
1. Jacob, Max, 1876-1944 2. Cubism 3. Poets, French 4. Poetry writing 5. Modernism (Art) 6. Avant-garde (Aesthetics) 7. Faith 8. Art 9. Artists 10. Gay men 11. Intellectual life 12. Europe 13. Paris, France 14. 20th century 15. Biographies 16. Life stories — Arts and culture — Writing — Poets 17. Arts and Entertainment — Writing and Publishing 18. Arts and Entertainment — Painting, Drawing, and Sculpture 19. Life stories — Arts and culture — Artists
LC 2020017722
A comprehensive portrait of the early 20th-century poet explores how Max Jacob's complex relationships with art, faith and sexuality impacted his life in bohemian Paris and shaped the symbolic themes in his poetry.
"An exemplary work of biography and intellectual history; essential reading for students of literary and artistic modernism." —*Kirkus*
Includes bibliographical references and index.

Warren, W. Lee
No Place to Hide: A Brain Surgeon's Long Journey Home from the Iraq War. Major W. Lee Warren, MD U.S. Air Force (Ret.).. Zondervan 2014. 352 pages
ISBN 9780310338031
Grades: Adult B
1. Warren, W. Lee, 1969- 2. Iraq War, 2003-2011 3. Surgeons 4. War 5. Faith (Christianity) 6. Iraq 7. Autobiographies and memoirs 8. Life stories — Law and order — Armed forces personnel 9. Life stories — Facing adversity — War and oppression
LC 2013033127
A neurosurgeon stationed at the biggest Air Force theater hospital of the Iraq War recounts stories of life and death, revealing how he went to war and came out stronger spiritually, emotionally, and physically.

Washington, Booker T.
★ *Up from Slavery.* Booker T. Washington. Penguin Books 1986. LIII, 332 p.
ISBN 9780140390513
Grades: 7 8 9 10 11 12 Adult B
1. Washington, Booker T, 1856-1915 2. Educators 3. Social advocates 4. Race relations 5. Freed people 6. African American businesspeople 7. African Americans 8. 19th century 9. Autobiographies and memoirs 10. Biographies 11. Life stories — Education — Scholars and educators 12. History writing — African American — Civil rights — United States
LC 8516712

The African-American educator documents his struggle for freedom and self-respect and his fight to establish industrial training and educational programs for Black Americans.
Includes bibliographical references (p. xliv-lii) and index; Originally published: New York : Doubleday, Page, & Co. 1901.

Washington, Kerry
Thicker Than Water: A Memoir. Kerry Washington. Little, Brown Spark 2023. 304 p.
ISBN 9780316497398
Grades: Adult B
1. Washington, Kerry, 1977- 2. Actors and actresses 3. African American women 4. Multiracial women 5. Celebrities 6. Acting 7. Social advocacy 8. Identity 9. Self-discovery 10. North American people 11. American people 12. Autobiographies and memoirs 13. Life stories — Arts and culture — Performing arts — Actors and actresses 14. Life stories — Identity 15. Arts and Entertainment — Movies and Television
In this profoundly moving and beautifully written memoir, the award-winning actor and activist provides an intimate view into both her public and private worlds as she chronicles her life's journey thus far, sharing how she discovered her truest self and, with it, a deeper sense of belonging.

Wassef, Nadia
Shelf Life: Chronicles of a Cairo Bookseller. Nadia Wassef. Farrar, Straus & Giroux 2021. 240 p.
ISBN 9780374600181
Grades: Adult B
1. Wassef, Nadia 2. Women booksellers 3. Bookstores 4. Independent bookstores 5. Women business owners 6. Misogyny 7. Books and reading 8. Success in business 9. Cairo, Egypt 10. Autobiographies and memoirs 11. Life stories — Business — Working life 12. Business and economics — Industries — Retail products and services 13. Arts and Entertainment — Writing and Publishing 14. Life stories — Identity — Gender
LC 2021020108
In 2002, with her sister, Hind, and their friend, Nihal, Nadia Wassef founded Diwan, a fiercely independent bookstore. They were three young women with no business degrees, no formal training, and nothing to lose. At the time, nothing like Diwan existed in Egypt. Culture was languishing under government mismanagement, and books were considered a luxury, not a necessity. Ten years later, Diwan had become a rousing success, with ten locations, 150 employees, and a fervent fan base. Frank, fresh, and very funny, Nadia Wassef's memoir tells the story of this journey. Its eclectic cast of characters features Diwan's impassioned regulars, and the many people, mostly men, who said Diwan would never work.
"In this memoir, Wassef, the cofounder of the influential Cairo bookstore Diwan, recounts building her business and narrates her journey as a wife, working mother, and Egyptian. . . . The narrative combines memoir, a business success story, and literary criticism, and Wassef shares her love of fiction and the kinds of books she has gravitated to in times of need." —*Library Journal*

Waters, Alice
Coming to My Senses: The Making of a Counterculture Cook. Alice Waters. Clarkson Potter 2017. 304 pages
ISBN 9780307718280
Grades: Adult B
1. Waters, Alice 2. Women cooks 3. Restaurants 4. Restaurateurs 5. Food 6. Cooking, French 7. Seasonal cooking 8. Recipes 9. Interpersonal relations 10. Counterculture 11. Berkeley, California 12. California 13. 1960s 14. 1970s 15. Autobiographies and memoirs 16. Food writing — Memoirs and biographies 17. Life stories — Arts and culture — Culinary arts 18. Food writing — Cooking and cookbooks — Chefs and restaurants
LC BI2017029928
The executive chef of Chez Panisse in California presents the story of her tumultuous culinary journey, describing her efforts to promote distinctive flavors in a time of uniform convenience foods, her achievements within the bohemian 1960s cultural circuit and her ongoing reflections as the head of one of the world's most influential restaurants.

PUBLIC LIBRARY CORE COLLECTION: NONFICTION
Twentieth Edition

"Chef, restaurateur, activist, and author Waters writes about her childhood and formative years leading up to the opening of her iconic Berkeley, CA, restaurant Chez Panisse." —*Library Journal*

Waters, John
Role Models. John Waters. Farrar, Straus and Giroux 2010. 256 p.
ISBN 9780374251475
Grades: Adult B
1. Waters, John, 1946- 2. Influence (Literary, artistic, etc.) 3. Screenwriters 4. Artists 5. Film producers and directors 6. United States 7. Essays 8. Biographies 9. Arts and Entertainment — Movies and Television
LC 2009042211

The cult film director of such productions as Hairspray and Pink Flamingos presents irreverent literary profiles of the figures who influenced his life and work, from martyr Saint Catherine of Siena to English novelist Denton Welch."

"The famed cult-film director recalls the famous and not-so-famous people he has idolized over the years. In this consistently charming and witty collection of essays, he fondly remembers the many artists he has admired throughout his life, from stars, such as Little Richard, to such near-unknown figures as the 1960s Baltimore stripper Lady Zorro. An impressive, heartfelt collection by a true American iconoclast." —*Kirkus*

Watkins, D.
Black Boy Smile: A Memoir in Moments. D. Watkins. Legacy Lit, an imprint of Grand Central Publishing, Hachette Book Group 2022. 208 p.
ISBN 9780306924002
Grades: Adult B
1. Watkins, D. (Dwight) 2. Drug dealers 3. Child abuse 4. Fathers and sons 5. Male friendship 6. Masculinity 7. Growing up 8. Adulthood 9. Violence 10. Poor African Americans 11. African American authors 12. African American children 13. Boys 14. Baltimore, Maryland 15. Autobiographies and memoirs 16. Life stories — Facing adversity 17. Life stories — Arts and culture — Writing — Authors 18. Life stories — Identity
LC 2021053871

Finalist for the Hurston/Wright Legacy Awards for Nonfiction, 2023.

Black Boy Smile lays bare Watkins's relationship with his father and his brotherhood with the boys around him. He shares candid recollections of early assaults on his body and mind and reveals how he coped using stoic silence disguised as manhood. His harrowing pursuit of redemption, written in his signature street style, pinpoints how generational hardship, left raw and unnurtured, breeds toxic masculinity. Watkins discovers a love for books, is admitted to two graduate programs, meets with his future wife, an attorney—and finds true freedom in fatherhood.

"While depictions of violence and a scene featuring a graphic sexual assault of a minor should be noted, this book could have tremendous value to teens living in circumstances similar to the author's as well as to readers who may be unaware of those struggles." —*Booklist*

"In this memoir, author and prolific essayist Watkins (We Speak for Ourselves, 2019) delves into his boyhood through a series of personal stories that illustrate how Black boys are all too often forced into a facade of manhood as a method of self-preservation and protection." —*Booklist*

Watson, Richard A.
Cogito Ergo Sum: The Life of Rene Descartes. Richard A. Watson. David R. Godine 2002. VIII, 375 p. : Illustration
ISBN 9781567921847
Grades: Adult B
1. Descartes, Rene, 1596-1650 2. Philosophers 3. Mathematicians 4. Reason 5. Philosophy 6. Metaphysics 7. Biographies 8. Life stories — Education — Philosophers
LC 2001040858

"For all of his puckish delight in a juicy anecdote, Watson recognizes and carefully explicates the cultural centrality of Descartes' intellectual legacy. That legacy ensures numerous readers sure to praise a biographer who delivers both the philosopher's cerebral doctrines and his unmistakably human conduct." —*Booklist*

Includes bibliographical references (p. 331-345) and indexes.

Watts, Jill
Hattie McDaniel: Black Ambition, White Hollywood. Jill Watts. Amistad 2005. xi, 352 : Illustration
ISBN 9780060514907
Grades: 11 12 Adult B
1. McDaniel, Hattie, 1895-1952 2. Race relations 3. African American women 4. Films 5. Actors and actresses 6. African Americans 7. United States 8. Biographies 9. Arts and Entertainment — Movies and Television 10. Life stories — Arts and culture — Performing arts — Actors and actresses
LC 2005042126

An exploration of Hollywood racism as reflected in the life and career of the actress best known for her portrayal of "Mammy" in "Gone with the Wind" describes her denigration in spite of her Oscar-winning performance, her controversial decision to stick to stereotypical roles, and her successful efforts to integrate a Los Angeles neighborhood.

"Watts is both sympathetic and honest: We pity McDaniel and her unenviable position, but at the same time, see how her intense careerism drove her often to accommodate rather than challenge film industry racism. Watts' research is extensive, her writing clear and accessible, and her book a thorough, engaging, intelligent piece of historical scholarship." —*Women's Review of Books*

Filmography: P. [283]-286; Includes bibliographical references (p. [327]-341) and index.

Watts, Reggie
Great Falls, Mt: Fast Times, Post-punk Weirdos, and a Tale of Coming Home Again. Reggie Watts. Tiny Reparations 2023. 288 p.
ISBN 9780593472460
Grades: Adult B
1. Watts, Reggie 2. Musicians 3. Comedians 4. Television personalities 5. Multiracial men 6. Growing up 7. Small towns 8. Misfits (People) 9. Friendship 10. Identity 11. Belonging 12. Home (Concept) 13. North American people 14. American people 15. Montana 16. Autobiographies and memoirs 17. Life stories — Arts and culture — Performing arts — Entertainers and celebrities 18. Life stories — Identity — Race and ethnicity 19. Family and Relationships — Growing up 20. Arts and Entertainment — Comedy 21. Arts and Entertainment — Music 22. Debut title

Growing up as the only biracial kid in Great Falls, MT, the comedian, musician and band leader takes us through his story, hitting upon the culture shock he experienced after moving from Europe to Montana—a place he needed to leave, but is ultimately drawn back to.

Watts, a comedian and house bandleader for the Late Late Show with James Corden, writes of his boyhood and teenage years in Great Falls, an Air Force town along the Missouri River that helped shape his future life as 'A musician, comedian, and consummate weirdo.' —*Kirkus*

Watts, Steven
The People's Tycoon: Henry Ford and the American Century. Steven Watts. A.A. Knopf 2005. xv, 614 p. : Illustration
ISBN 9780375407352
Grades: Adult B
1. Ford, Henry, 1863-1947 2. Industrialists 3. Automobile designers 4. Mass production 5. Consumerism 6. Antisemites 7. Philanthropists 8. Automobile industry and trade 9. Businesspeople 10. United States 11. 20th century 12. Biographies 13. Business and economics — Business leaders and entrepreneurs 14. Life stories — Business — Business leaders 15. History writing — Early 20th century — United States 16. Business and economics — Industries — Transportation
LC 2004048594

A biography of the controversial entrepreneur who transformed the world of American business explores the contradictions of Henry Ford's life and assesses his accomplishments within the context of early tewntieth-century America.

"Steven Watts is intelligent, thorough and engaging . in telling the story of an American who not only was influential but remains unavoidable to this day." —*New York Times Book Review*

Includes bibliographical references (p. 539-592) and index.

ESSENTIAL AND RECOMMENDED TITLES
Biography

***Self-help** Messiah: Dale Carnegie and Success in Modern America.* by Steven Watts. Other Press 2013. 592 pages
ISBN 9781590515020
Grades: Adult **B**
1. Carnegie, Dale, 1888-1955 2. Writing 3. Success (Concept) 4. Authors, American 5. Vocational guidance 6. 20th century 7. Biographies 8. Life stories — Arts and culture — Writing — Authors 9. Arts and Entertainment — Writing and Publishing
LC 2013003227

A full-scale portrait of the famed author of How to Win Friends and Influence People traces his humble origins in rural Mississippi and the early failures that inspired his career, describing how he wrote his best-selling book to promote interpersonal relations, effective communication skills and psychological insights. By the author of Mr. Playboy.

"A fascinating portrait of the father of self-help and incisive analysis of the mercurial era that produced him." —*Kirkus*

Weatherford, J. McIver
★ *Genghis Khan and the Making of the Modern World.* Jack Weatherford. Crown 2004. xxxv, 312 p. : Illustration; Map
ISBN 9780609610626
Grades: 9 10 11 12 **B**
1. Genghis Khan, 1162-1227 2. Mongols 3. Rulers 4. Biographies 5. Life stories — Law and order — Armed forces personnel 6. Adult books for young adults 7. History writing — Asia
LC 2003020659
Minnesota Book Award for History, 2005.

A re-evaluation of Genghis Khan's rise to power examines the reforms the conqueror instituted throughout his empire and his uniting of East and West, which set the foundation for the nation-states and economic systems of the modern era.

Includes bibliographical references (p. 293-300) and index; Originally published: New York : Crown, 2004.

Webb, Kinari
Guardians of the Trees: A Journey of Hope Through Healing the Planet. Kinari Webb, M.D.. Flatiron Books 2021. 304 p.
ISBN 9781250751386
Grades: Adult **B**
1. Webb, Kinari 2. Women physicians 3. Environmentalists 4. Environmental health 5. Rain forests 6. Forestry 7. Deforestation 8. Indigenous peoples 9. Effect of environment on humans 10. Clinics 11. Nonprofit organizations 12. Biotic communities 13. Human ecology 14. Autobiographies and memoirs 15. Life stories — Science, technology, and medicine — Healthcare professionals 16. Nature Writing — Environmental Issues 17. Science Writing — Medicine and health 18. Science Writing — Biology
LC 2021024209

When Kinari Webb first traveled to Indonesian Borneo at 21 to study orangutans, she was both awestruck by the beauty of her surroundings and heartbroken by the rainforest destruction she witnessed. As she got to know the local communities, she realized that their need to pay for expensive healthcare led directly to the rampant logging, which in turn imperiled their health and safety even further. Webb realized her true calling was at the intersection of medicine and conservation. Full of hope and optimism, Webb takes us on an exhilarating, galvanizing journey across the world, sharing her passion for the natural world and for humanity. In our current moment of crisis, Guardians of the Trees is an essential roadmap for moving forward and the inspiring story of one woman's quest to heal the world.

"The inspiring story of the creation of an award-winning model for reversing rainforest loss and improving human well-being." —*Kirkus*

Weber, Thomas
Becoming Hitler: The Making of a Nazi. Thomas Weber. Basic Books 2017. 480 p.
ISBN 9780465032686
Grades: Adult **B**
1. Hitler, Adolf, 1889-1945 2. Nazis 3. Right-wing extremists 4. Heads of state 5. Nazism 6. Politics and government 7. Germany 8. Between the Wars (1918-1939) 9. Biographies 10. History writing — Europe — Germany 11. Life stories — Politics — Politicians
LC 2017022799

Examines Hitler's years in Munich after World War I and his radical transformation from a directionless loner into the leader of Munich's right-wing movement.

"Compelling research and original insights bring a fuller understanding to the mind and motives of the demagogue." —*Kirkus*

Includes bibliographical references and index.

Weigel, Alicia Roth
Inverse Cowgirl: A Memoir. Alicia Roth Weigel. HarperOne 2023. 256 p.
ISBN 9780063295285
Grades: Adult **B**
1. Weigel, Alicia Roth 2. Political activists 3. Intersex people 4. Growing up 5. Surgery 6. Secrets 7. Self-acceptance 8. Coming out (Sexual or gender identity) 9. Gender nonconformity 10. Social advocacy 11. LGBTQIA+ rights 12. North American people 13. American people 14. Autobiographies and memoirs 15. Life stories — Identity — LGBTQIA+ 16. Life stories — Politics — Activists and reformers 17. Society and culture — LGBTQIA+ 18. Debut title

Two percent of the world's population—the same percentage of humans who have naturally red hair—is born intersex. Yet many people aren't even familiar with the word. Intersex individuals are born with both male and female reproductive organs, yet many are stripped of their identity at birth when a parent designates M or F on a birth certificate. Alicia Weigel is an intersex activist fighting back against the hate and fearmongering to protect the rights and lives of everyone. In this book, Alicia boldly speaks out about how we can reclaim bodily autonomy, and encourages us to amplify our voices to be heard.

"Insightful, fierce, and candid, this book is a welcome addition to the growing body of personal accounts about living as a member of one of the most marginalized, silenced, and misunderstood of sexual minorities." —*Kirkus*

Weiner, Eric
Ben & Me: In Search of a Founder's Formula for a Long and Useful Life. Eric Weiner. Avid Reader Press 2024. 352 p.
ISBN 9781501129049
Grades: Adult **B**
1. Franklin, Benjamin, 1706-1790 2. Weiner, Eric, 1963- 3. Politicians 4. Authors 5. Ethics 6. Voyages and travels 7. Purpose in life 8. Identity 9. Influence (Literary, artistic, etc.) 10. Autobiographies and memoirs 11. Life stories — Personal growth 12. Travel Writing — General 13. Life stories — People in history
LC 2023058232

Drawing inspiration from the life of Benjamin Franklin, a New York Times best-selling author combines biography, travelogue and personal insight to offer a book filled with both practical lessons and inspiration.

"Benjamin Franklin for the 21st century….A warm combination of homage and introspective memoir." —*Kirkus*

Includes bibliographical references and index.

Weiner, Tim
One Man Against the World: The Tragedy of Richard Nixon. Tim Weiner. Henry Holt and Company 2015. 352 p.
ISBN 9781627790833
Grades: Adult **B**
1. Nixon, Richard M. (Richard Milhous), 1913-1994 2. Presidents 3. Politicians 4. Politics and government 5. United States 6. 1970s 7. 20th century 8. 1960s 9. Biographies 10. History writing — Presidency — 20th century — United States 11. History writing — 1970s — United States 12. Life stories — Politics — Politicians
LC 2015012381

A crucial new look at the greatest political suicide in history, One Man Against the World leaves us not only with new insight into this tumultuous period, but also into the motivations and demons of an American president who saw enemies everywhere, and, thinking the world was against him, undermined the foundations of the country he had hoped to lead.

PUBLIC LIBRARY CORE COLLECTION: NONFICTION
Twentieth Edition

"Those seeking to understand America in the second half of the twentieth century and, distressingly, beyond would do well to begin here. The tragedy was not Nixon's alone, but his role in it has never been portrayed more vividly." —*Booklist*

Weir, Alison

The Children of Henry VIII. Alison Weir. Ballantine Books 1997. xiv, 385 p. : Illustration
ISBN 9780345407863
Grades: 11 12 Adult   B
1. Henry VIII, King of England, 1491-1547 2. Edward VI, King of England, 1537-1553 3. Grey, Jane, Lady, 1537-1554 4. Mary I, Queen of England, 1516-1558 5. Elizabeth I, Queen of England, 1533-1603 6. Tudor, House of 7. Rulers 8. Royal houses 9. Inheritance and succession 10. Marriages of royalty and nobility 11. Women rulers 12. British history 13. Great Britain 14. Tudor period (1485-1603) 15. Renaissance (1300-1600) 16. Biographies 17. History writing — Europe — United Kingdom 18. History writing — Renaissance — Europe

LC BL 99790061

Booklist Editors' Choice: Adult Books for Young Adults, 1996.

Recounts the lives of Henry VIII's heirs and the intrigues that arose from their struggle to ascend their father's throne.

"This book covers the lives of Henry's children Mary Tudor and Edward VI, but it only takes Elizabeth up to her accession, and it also includes the entire short life of Jane Grey, the granddaughter of Henry's sister Mary. When Henry died in 1547, he left a country embroiled in several social problems brought about by the enclosure of common lands, the high cost of his European wars, and the closure of monasteries. How his heirs dealt with these problems, along with their relationships, makes interesting reading." —*Library Journal*

Reprint of Children of England: the heirs of King Henry VIII, 1547-1558; Includes bibliographical references (p. [367]-375) and index; Originally published: London : J. Cape, 1996.

Eleanor of Aquitaine: A Life. Alison Weir. Ballantine Books 2001. xxi, 441 p. : Illustration; Map
ISBN 9780345434876
Grades: 11 12 Adult   B
1. Eleanor, of Aquitaine, Queen, consort of Henry II, King of England, 1122?-1204 2. Women rulers 3. British history 4. French history 5. Great Britain 6. Plantagenet period (1154-1485) 7. Medieval period (476-1492) 8. Biographies 9. History writing — Medieval — Europe 10. History writing — Europe — France 11. History writing — Women's history 12. Life stories — Politics — Royalty

LC BL2001003353

A biography of one of the most influential women of the Middle Ages discusses her marriages to Louis VII of France and Henry II of England, and her later efforts to secure the throne of England for her sons.

"In approaching as complex a subject as feudalism, Weir wears her learning lightly and has a pleasant habit of anticipating all the questions of a curious reader." —*Publishers Weekly*

Includes bibliographical references (p. [355]-373) and index; Originally published: London : Jonathan Cape, 1999.

Henry VIII: The King and His Court. Alison Weir. Ballantine Books 2002. VIII, 632 p. : Illustration; Color
ISBN 9780345437082
Grades: Adult   B
1. Henry VIII, King of England, 1491-1547 2. Henry VII, King of England, 1491-1547 3. Rulers 4. Courts and courtiers 5. British history 6. Great Britain 7. Tudor period (1485-1603) 8. Renaissance (1300-1600) 9. 16th century 10. Biographies 11. History writing — Renaissance — Europe 12. Life stories — Politics — Royalty

LC BL2002013730

Examines the king's remarkable influence on the laws, customs, culture, and politics of his kingdom and profiles the diverse courtiers, artists, and scholars who surrounded Henry VIII.

"In this biography of the Tudor king, the author examines the minutiae of his daily life and gives prominence to the background players of his court. At times, the weighty detail and numerous characters will make the work inaccessible; however, as a scholarly study it is a significant achievement." —*Library Journal*

Includes bibliographical references (p. [500]-539) and index.

The Lady in the Tower: The Fall of Anne Boleyn. Alison Weir. Ballantine Books 2009. 384 p.
ISBN 9780345453211
Grades: 11 12 Adult   B
1. Anne Boleyn, Queen, consort of Henry VIII, King of England, 1507-1536 2. Henry VIII, King of England, 1491-1547 3. Political prisoners 4. Imprisonment 5. Death of married women 6. Rulers 7. Executions and executioners 8. English history 9. British history 10. 16th century 11. Renaissance (1300-1600) 12. Biographies 13. History writing — Women's history 14. Life stories — Politics — Royalty 15. History writing — Europe — United Kingdom 16. History writing — Renaissance — Europe

LC 2009042748

An account of Henry VIII's second wife's final days seeks to vindicate her from popular negative perceptions while offering insight into additional nuances that affected her character and marriage to the infamous monarch.

The Life of Elizabeth I. Alison Weir. Ballantine 1998. 532 p. : Illustration
ISBN 9780345405333
Grades: Adult   B
1. Elizabeth I, Queen of England, 1533-1603 2. Women rulers 3. British history 4. Great Britain 5. 16th century 6. Tudor period (1485-1603) 7. Renaissance (1300-1600) 8. Elizabethan era (1558-1603) 9. Biographies 10. History writing — Renaissance — Europe 11. History writing — Women's history 12. History writing — Europe — United Kingdom 13. Life stories — Politics — Royalty 14. Adult books for young adults

LC 98034917

Presents an exhaustively researched biography that reveals the personality, private life, and romantic intrigues of Elizabeth I.

"Weir brings a fine sense of selection and considerable zest to her portrait of the self-styled Virgin Queen." —*Publishers Weekly*

Includes bibliographical references (p. [491]-508) and index; Originally published: London : J. Cape, 1998.

The Lost Tudor Princess: The Life of Margaret Douglas of Scotland. Alison Weir. Ballantine Books 2016. 432 p.
ISBN 9780345521392
Grades: Adult   B
1. Lennox, Margaret Douglas, Countess of, 1515-1578 2. Henry VIII, King of England, 1491-1547 3. Mary, Queen of Scots, 1542-1587 4. Nobility 5. British history 6. Tudor period (1485-1603) 7. Renaissance (1300-1600) 8. 16th century 9. Biographies 10. Life stories — People in history — Famous families 11. History writing — Europe — United Kingdom 12. History writing — Renaissance — Europe

LC 2015037958

A profile of the niece of Henry VIII reveals her lesser-known contributions to period politics, covering her two affairs, arrangement of her son's marriage to Mary Queen of Scots and role in securing the throne for James VI.

"An abundantly detailed history from an author steeped in England's past." —*Kirkus*

Includes bibliographical references and index.

Weiss, Helga

Helga's Diary: A Young Girl's Account of Life in a Concentration Camp. Helga Weiss, Neil Bermel, Francine Prose. W W Norton & Co. Inc 2012. 208 p.
ISBN 9780393077971
Grades: Adult   B
1. Concentration camps 2. Holocaust (1933-1945) 3. Teenage girls 4. Prague, Czech Republic 5. Diaries 6. Autobiographies and memoirs 7. Translations — Czech to English 8. History writing — Wars and conflicts — Holocaust — World War II 9. Life stories — Facing adversity — War and oppression — War survivors

LC 2013003775

ESSENTIAL AND RECOMMENDED TITLES
Biography

Reconstructed from her original notebook diary that was hidden in a brick wall, documents the life of a young Jewish schoolgirl in Prague who survived the concentration camps of both Terezin and Auschwitz.

Weller, Sam
The Bradbury Chronicles: The Life of Ray Bradbury. Sam Weller. William Morrow 2005. x, 384 p. : Illustration
ISBN 9780060545819
Grades: 11 12 Adult **B**
1. Bradbury, Ray, 1920-2012 2. Science fiction writing 3. Authors, American 4. Literary criticism 5. Social life and customs 6. United States 7. 20th century 8. Biographies 9. Science fiction 10. Arts and Entertainment — Writing and Publishing 11. Life stories — Arts and culture — Writing — Authors 12. Adult books for young adults
LC 2004059491

An authorized portrait of the renowned science-fiction author's life draws on hundreds of hours of interviews with editors, family members, friends, and the writer himself, in an account that discusses his creative process and the inspirations for such works as the Martian Chronicles and Fahrenheit 451.

"Weller's research—based on interviews with Bradbury as well as family members and colleagues—is almost exhaustive in its detail, and he does a fine job of presenting the facts of his subject's unique life. The lively, conversational prose brings out the writer's winning personality and turns his struggles and successes into a highly readable story." —*School Library Journal*

Includes bibliographical references (p. [341]-370) and index.

Weller, Sheila
Carrie Fisher: A Life on the Edge. Sheila Weller. Sarah Crichton Books/Farrar, Straus and Giroux 2019. 416 pages
ISBN 9780374282233
Grades: Adult **B**
1. Fisher, Carrie 2. Families 3. Bipolar disorder 4. Drug addiction 5. Family relationships 6. Actors and actresses 7. Women authors 8. Biographies 9. Life stories — Arts and culture — Performing arts — Actors and actresses 10. Life stories — Arts and culture — Writing — Authors 11. Life stories — Facing adversity — Medical issues 12. Arts and Entertainment — Movies and Television
LC 2019021323

A candid portrait of the beloved Hollywood actress and writer discusses her complicated relationships with her famous parents, her Star Wars fame and her struggles with bipolar disorder and drug addiction.

Includes bibliographical references and index.

Welteroth, Elaine
More Than Enough: Claiming Space for Who You Are (no Matter What They Say). Elaine Welteroth. Viking 2019. 272 p.
ISBN 9780525561583
Grades: Adult **B**
1. Welteroth, Elaine, 1986- 2. African American women journalists 3. Personal conduct 4. Multiracial women 5. Periodical writing 6. Journalists 7. Determination 8. Self-acceptance 9. Autobiographies and memoirs 10. Biographies 11. Life stories — Arts and culture — Writing — Journalists 12. Adult books for young adults
LC 2019002372

In this part-manifesto, part-memoir, the revolutionary editor who infused social consciousness into the pages of Teen Vogue explores what it means to come into your own—on your own terms.

"Welteroth's inspiring debut follows her personal and professional trajectories as she unpacks her ascent to becoming editor-and-chief of Teen Vogue in 2017 and details her experience as a Black woman in media. From humble beginnings as a brown girl boss running a makeshift hair salon out of her Newark, Calif, cul-de-sac home, Welteroth built an illustrious editorial career as she worked her way up through increasingly substantial roles at Ebony and Glamour magazines." —*Publishers Weekly*

Welty, Eudora
One Writer's Beginnings. Eudora Welty. Simon & Schuster 2020. 128 p.
ISBN 9780674639270
Grades: 11 12 Adult **B**
1. Welty, Eudora, 1909-2001 2. Women authors 3. Writing 4. Creativity 5. Authors, American 6. Social life and customs 7. Mississippi 8. 20th century 9. Autobiographies and memoirs 10. Biographies 11. Arts and Entertainment — Writing and Publishing 12. Life stories — Arts and culture — Writing — Authors
LC 91019527

National Book Award for Nonfiction finalist, 1984; National Book Critics Circle Award for Biography finalist, 1984.

With a new introduction, this updated edition of the award-winning and best-selling author's classic book of guidance for aspiring writers is part memoir, offering a vivid glimpse into life in early 1900s Mississippi, and part an exploration of cultivating creativity.

"Less shapely or focused than Welty's stories, and a little too wispy in its self-portrait—but a welcome, often-eloquent arrival nonetheless, for Welty readers and writing students in about equal measure." —*Kirkus*

Originally published: Cambridge, Mass. : Harvard University Press, 1984.

Wenner, Jann
Like a Rolling Stone: A Memoir. Jann S. Wenner. Little Brown & Company 2022. 560 p.
ISBN 9780316415194
Grades: Adult **B**
1. Wenner, Jann 2. Journalists 3. Music 4. Money 5. Desire 6. Editors 7. Social life and customs 8. United States 9. Autobiographies and memoirs 10. Life stories — Arts and culture — Writing — Journalists 11. Arts and Entertainment — Writing and publishing 12. Arts and Entertainment — Music

The Rolling Stone magazine founder, co-editor and publisher offers a once-in-a-generation memoir from the beating heart of classic rock and roll.

"The Rolling Stone founder and publisher recounts a golden age of sex, drugs, rock 'N' roll, and cash flow….A frank, sharp memoir by a zeitgeist-savvy entrepreneur who ranks among the earliest of modern influencers." —*Kirkus*

Wert, Jeffry D.
Cavalryman of the Lost Cause: A Biography of J.E.B. Stuart. Jeffry D. Wert. Simon & Schuster 2008. 512 p.
ISBN 9780743278195
Grades: 11 12 Adult **B**
1. Stuart, Jeb, 1833-1864 2. Generals 3. Military history 4. Military strategy 5. Interpersonal relations 6. Civil war 7. United States Civil War, 1861-1865 8. Confederate soldiers 9. Command of troops 10. Cavalry 11. Military campaigns 12. United States history 13. 19th century 14. American Civil War era (1861-1865) 15. Biographies 16. History writing — Wars and conflicts — American Civil War 17. Life stories — Law and order — Military leaders 18. History writing — Military — Military leadership 19. Adult books for young adults
LC 2007051552

A balanced portrait of the controversial Confederate cavalryman describes his military contributions, contentious relationships with his staff and subordinates, and battlefield death at the age of thirty-one.

Includes bibliographical references and index.

Custer: The Controversial Life of George Armstrong Custer. Jeffry D. Wert. Simon & Schuster 1996. 462 p, [16] p. of plates : Illustration; Map
ISBN 9780684810430
Grades: 11 12 Adult **B**
1. Custer, George A. (George Armstrong), 1839-1876 2. Command of troops 3. Generals 4. United States history 5. United States 6. 19th century 7. Biographies 8. History writing — Military — Military leadership 9. Life stories — Law and order — Military leaders
LC 96007290

Draws on previously overlooked documents to probe the puzzles that have continued to mark the legendary general's life and career.

"Focusing on Custer's Civil War actions, Wert methodically examines a man often considered an enigma in American history. Clear writing and excellent use

PUBLIC LIBRARY CORE COLLECTION: NONFICTION
Twentieth Edition

of primary source materials demonstrate how history should be written." —*Booklist*

Includes bibliographical references (p. [417]-443) and index.

Weschler, Lawrence
And How Are You, Dr. Sacks?: A Biographical Memoir of Oliver Sacks. Lawrence Weschler. Farrar, Straus and Giroux 2019. 352 pages
ISBN 9780374236410
Grades: Adult   B
1. Sacks, Oliver, 1933-2015 2. Weschler, Lawrence 3. Neurologists 4. Scientists 5. Gay men 6. Biographies 7. Autobiographies and memoirs 8. Life stories — Science, technology, and medicine — Healthcare professionals
LC 2018060824

The New Yorker veteran and author of Mr. Wilson's Cabinet of Wonder draws on decades of friendship to trace the lesser-known early story of the brilliant neurologist and author of the Man Who Mistook His Wife for a Hat.

West, Cait
★ *Rift: A Memoir of Breaking Away from Christian Patriarchy.* Cait West. William B. Eerdmans Publishing Company 2024. 252 p.
ISBN 9780802883582
Grades: Adult   B
1. West, Cait, 1988- 2. Christian women 3. Abused women 4. Child abuse victims 5. Patriarchy 6. Psychic trauma 7. Oppression (Psychology) 8. Spiritual abuse 9. Emotional abuse 10. Christianity 11. Religious psychology 12. Autobiographies and memoirs 13. Life stories — Facing adversity — Abuse survivors 14. Life stories — Religion and spirituality 15. Family and Relationships — Abuse
LC 2023046459

Cait West's memoir shares her upbringing as a stay-at-home daughter and her eventual escape from Christian patriarchy.

"It's a powerful meditation on what it means to be trapped and what it takes to break free." —*Publishers Weekly*

West, Jerry
West by West: My Charmed, Tormented Life. Jerry West and Jonathan Coleman. Little, Brown and Co. 2011. 336 p.
ISBN 9780316053495
Grades: Adult   B
1. West, Jerry, 1938-2024 2. Professional basketball 3. Basketball players 4. Basketball coaches 5. Basketball 6. Autobiographies and memoirs 7. Sports and Competition — Basketball 8. Life stories — Sports — Athletes 9. Life stories — Sports — Coaches, managers, and owners
LC 2011019736

The coach responsible for the championship-winning success of the Lakers for the past 40 years describes his difficult childhood, being a star player at West Virginia University, his career and his relationships with sports legends from Wilt Chamberlain to Shaquille O'Neal.

Includes index.

Westheimer, Ruth
The Doctor Is In: Dr. Ruth on Love, Life, and Joie De Vivre. Ruth Westheimer, Pierre A. Lehu. Amazon Publishing 2015. 191 pages
ISBN 9781477828366
Grades: Adult   B
1. Westheimer, Ruth, 1928-2024 2. Sex counselors and therapists 3. Personal conduct 4. Optimism 5. Life skills 6. Love 7. Social values 8. Change (Psychology) 9. Quality of life 10. Autobiographies and memoirs 11. Life stories — Arts and culture — Performing arts — Entertainers and celebrities
LC Bl2015020100

Everyone knows Dr. Ruth as America's most famous and trusted sex therapist, but few people know she was raised in an orphanage in Switzerland, narrowly escaping death during the Holocaust—or that she was an ace sniper in the Israeli army. After years spent as a professor in Paris, Dr. Ruth came to America with big dreams and even bigger chutzpah. And, at the age of eighty-seven, she is as feisty as ever. Through intimate and funny stories, Dr. Ruth sheds light on how she's learned to live a life filled with joie de vivre.

"While Westheimer has covered some of this ground previously, her wit and brassy style breathe new life into familiar self-help material." —*Publishers Weekly*

Westover, Tara
★ *Educated: A Memoir.* Tara Westover. Random House 2018. 384 p.
ISBN 9780399590504
Grades: 11 12 Adult   B
1. Westover, Tara 2. Survivalism 3. Home schooling 4. Family violence victims 5. Women college students 6. Family violence 7. Subcultures 8. Rural life 9. Idaho 10. Autobiographies and memoirs 11. Adult books for young adults 12. Life stories — Facing adversity — Abuse survivors 13. Nonfiction that reads like fiction 14. Book club best bets
LC 2017037645

ALA Notable Book, 2019; Alex Award, 2019; Goodreads Choice Award, 2018; Indies' Choice Book Awards, Adult Nonfiction, 2019; LibraryReads Favorites, 2018; Library Journal Best Books, 2018; New York Times Notable Book, 2018; National Book Critics Circle Award for Autobiography/Memoir finalist, 2018.

Traces the author's experiences as a child born to survivalists in the mountains of Idaho, describing her participation in her family's paranoid stockpiling activities and her resolve to educate herself well enough to earn an acceptance into a prestigious university and the unfamiliar world beyond.

"In its keen exploration of family, history, and the narratives we create for ourselves, Educated becomes more than just a success story." —*Booklist*

Wetherall, Tyler
No Way Home: A Memoir of Life on the Run. Tyler Wetherall. St. Martin's Press 2018. 320 p.
ISBN 9781250112194
Grades: Adult   B
1. Wetherall, Tyler, 1983- 2. Children of criminals 3. Fathers and daughters 4. Fugitives 5. Hiding 6. Criminals 7. Growing up 8. Autobiographies and memoirs 9. Life stories — Facing adversity 10. Life stories — Relationships — Parent and child
LC 2017049579

A New York writer presents a memoir of her childhood spent on the run in a series of homes in five different countries under an assumed name, describing her discovery of her father's fugitive status and his half-billion-dollar marijuana smuggling operation, her self-destructive youth and her efforts to reconcile her family's past with her own realities.

Wheelan, Joseph
★ *Terrible Swift Sword: The Life of General Philip H. Sheridan.* Joseph Wheelan. Da Capo Press 2012. 352 p.
ISBN 9780306820274
Grades: Adult   B
1. Sheridan, Philip Henry, 1831-1888 2. Cavalry 3. Civil war 4. Leadership 5. Total war 6. Military strategy 7. Environmentalists 8. Union soldiers 9. Indigenous peoples of North America — Forced removal 10. United States Civil War, 1861-1865 11. United States history 12. American Civil War era (1861-1865) 13. Biographies 14. Life stories — Law and order — Armed forces personnel 15. History writing — Confederacy — United States 16. History writing — Wars and conflicts — American Civil War
LC 2012018587

Analyzes the leadership and tactics of the Civil War general, citing his role in introducing scorched-earth methods and the contributions of his Cavalry Corps in Lee's surrender and explaining the cavalry and total war strategies that became staples of warfare.

"A sympathetic portrait of "Grant's most dependable troubleshooter."" —*Kirkus*

Wheen, Francis
Karl Marx: A Life. Francis Wheen. Norton 2000. 431 p. : Illustration

ESSENTIAL AND RECOMMENDED TITLES
Biography

ISBN 9780393049237
Grades: Adult **B**
1. Marx, Karl, 1818-1883 2. Communists 3. Intellectuals 4. Communism 5. Biographies 6. History writing — Europe — Germany 7. Life stories — Education — Philosophers
LC 99087466

New York Times Notable Book, 2000.

Looks at the life of the father of Communism focusing primarily on the human side of the man rather than his works.

"Following Marx from his childhood in Trier, Germany, through his exile in London, Wheen takes readers from hovel to grand house, from the International Working Man's Association to Capital, from obscurity to notoriety and back again." —*Publishers Weekly*

Originally published: London : Fourth Estate, 1999; Includes bibliographical references (p. [393]-420) and index.

White, Charles
The Life and Times of Little Richard: The Quasar of Rock. Charles White. Da Capo 1994. xvi, 282 p. : Illustration
ISBN 9780306805523
Grades: Adult **B**
1. Little Richard, 1932-2020 2. Rock musicians 3. Biographies 4. Arts and Entertainment — Music — Rock 5. Life stories — Arts and culture — Performing arts
LC 93048054

Written largely in Richard's own words, but also including testimony from a star-studded cast of family, friends, and fellow musicians, this classic of rock literature tells all—his flamboyant stage antics; his blatant flaunting of racial taboos; his sexual experiences; his bewildering career that careened between show business and the church; and exactly how he created the music that would become a symbol of rebellion for kids all over the world.

Includes index; Previous ed.: New York : Harmony Books, 1984; Discography/Filmography: P. 257-269.

White, Gayle Jessup
Reclamation: Sally Hemings, Thomas Jefferson, and a Descendant's Search for Her Family's Lasting Legacy. Gayle Jessup White. Amistad Press 2021. 304 p.
ISBN 9780063028654
Grades: Adult **B**
1. White, Gayle Jessup, 1957- 2. Jefferson, Thomas, 1743-1826 3. Hemings, Sally, 1773-1835? 4. African American women 5. Genealogy 6. African American families 7. Slavery 8. Enslaved people 9. Race relations 10. Historical research 11. Historiography 12. Presidents 13. United States history 14. United States 15. 19th century 16. Autobiographies and memoirs 17. Life stories — Identity — Race and ethnicity 18. Life stories — People in history — Famous families 19. History writing — African American — Enslavement — United States 20. Society and culture — Race 21. History writing — Presidency — 19th century — United States

Gayle Jessup White had long heard the stories passed down from her father's family, that they were direct descendants of Thomas Jefferson—lore she firmly believed, though others did not. For four decades the acclaimed journalist and genealogy enthusiast researched her connection to Thomas Jefferson, to confirm its truth once and for all. After she was named a Jefferson Studies Fellow, Jessup White discovered her family lore was correct. In Reclamation she chronicles her remarkable journey to definitively understand her heritage and reclaim it, and offers a compelling portrait of what it means to be a Black woman in America, to pursue the American dream, to reconcile the legacy of racism, and to ensure the nation lives up to the ideals advocated by her legendary ancestor.

"White, a former journalist who now works in public relations at Monticello, debuts with a vivid account of her search for proof that she is related to Thomas Jefferson and two of the families he enslaved, the Hemingses and the Hubbards. . . . This spirited memoir charts a hopeful path for a more honest reckoning with the legacy of slavery." —*Publishers Weekly*

White, Neil
In the Sanctuary of Outcasts: A Memoir. Neil White. William Morrow 2009. xii, 316 p. : Illustration
ISBN 9780061351600
Grades: Adult **B**
1. White, Neil, 1960- 2. Fraud 3. White collar criminals 4. Prisoners 5. Leprosy 6. Convict labor 7. Life change events 8. Autobiographies and memoirs 9. True Crime — General 10. Life stories — Law and order — Prisoners and inmates

White tells his emotional, incredible true story of crime and redemption, vanity and spirituality, as he discovers happiness and fulfillment in an unlikely place—imprisonment in the Long Center, the last leper colony in the U.S.

"Following conviction for bank fraud, White spent a year in a minimum-security prison in Carville, La, housed in the last leper colony in mainland America. His fascinating memoir reflects on the sizable group of lepers living alongside the prisoners, social outcasts among the motley inmate crew of drug dealers, mob types and killers." —*Publishers Weekly*

Includes bibliographical references (p. [315]-316).

White, Richard Antoine
I'm Possible: A Story of Survival, a Tuba, and the Small Miracle of a Big Dream. Richard Antoine White. Flatiron Books 2021. 256 p.
ISBN 9781250269645
Grades: Adult **B**
1. White, Richard Antoine 2. African American musicians 3. Tuba players 4. Tuba 5. Classical musicians 6. Growing up 7. Homelessness 8. Marginalized children 9. Ability 10. Ambition 11. Autobiographies and memoirs 12. Life stories — Arts and culture — Performing arts — Musicians and composers 13. Life stories — Facing adversity 14. Arts and Entertainment — Music — Classical 15. Arts and Entertainment — Music — Instruments
LC 2021026488

From the streets of Baltimore to the halls of the New Mexico Philharmonic, a professor, mentor and motivational speaker shares the extraordinary story of how he unexpectedly discovered a talent for music and a sense of purpose that led him to where he is today.

"White, principal tubist at the New Mexico Philharmonic, salutes 'The people who saved my life' in a plucky debut that charts his rise from the streets to the classical concert hall. . . . The result is a vivid, inspiring saga of talent sprouting in unlikely places." —*Publishers Weekly*

White, Ronald C.
A. Lincoln: A Biography. Ronald C. White, Jr. Random House Pub. Group 2009. 816 p.
ISBN 9781400064991
Grades: Adult **B**
1. Lincoln, Abraham, 1809-1865 2. Political leadership 3. Presidents 4. Politicians 5. Politics and government 6. United States 7. 19th century 8. American Civil War era (1861-1865) 9. Biographies 10. History writing — Presidency — 19th century — United States 11. History writing — Wars and conflicts — American Civil War 12. Life stories — Law and order — Armed forces personnel 13. Adult books for young adults 14. Life stories — Politics — Politicians
LC 2008028840

A biography of America's sixteenth president portrays Lincoln as a man of integrity whose moral compass holds the key to understanding his life, examining his speeches, his ideas on slavery, his religious odyssey, and his role as Commander-in-Chief.

"In this biography, the author follows the familiar trajectory of the 16th President's life; what's unique is his insight into the moral and intellectual framework of Lincoln's thinking. An exceptional work that belongs in every public and academic library." —*Library Journal*

Includes bibliographical references and index.

★ *American Ulysses: A Life of Ulysses S. Grant.* Ronald C. White, Jr. Random House 2016. 816 p.
ISBN 9781400069026
Grades: Adult **B**

PUBLIC LIBRARY CORE COLLECTION: NONFICTION
Twentieth Edition

1. Grant, Ulysses S, 1822-1885 2. Presidents 3. Generals 4. United States Civil War, 1861-1865 5. Command of troops 6. Politics and government 7. United States history 8. United States 9. American Civil War era (1861-1865) 10. 19th century 11. Biographies 12. History writing — Presidency — 19th century — United States 13. Life stories — Law and order — Military leaders

LC 2015044513

A profile of the Civil War general and eighteenth U.S. president challenges his historical unpopularity, drawing on years of research with primary documents to explore Grant's character as one of generosity, curiosity, and introspection.

"The author portrays a humble, gentle, independent soul—a writer, in the end, who found his voice writing his extraordinary memoirs just before his death in 1885. An engaging resurrection of Grant featuring excellent maps and character sketches." —*Kirkus*

Includes bibliographical references and index.

Lincoln in Private: What His Most Personal Reflections Tell Us About Our Greatest President. Ronald C. White. Random House 2021. xx.328 p.
ISBN 9781984855091
Grades: Adult   B

1. Lincoln, Abraham, 1809-1865 2. Writing 3. Politics and government 4. United States 5. 19th century 6. Biographies 7. History writing — Presidency — 19th century — United States 8. Life stories — Politics — Politicians

The New York Times best-selling author of A. Lincoln and American Ulysses and renowned Lincoln historian walks us through 12 of Lincoln's most private notes, showcasing his brilliance, empathy, very human anxieties and ambitions.

"Abraham Lincoln's private jottings reveal his evolving outlook in this probing biographical study.... Lincoln fans will love these novel glimpses into his powerful mind." —*Publishers Weekly*

On Great Fields: The Life and Unlikely Heroism of Joshua Lawrence Chamberlain. Ronald C. White. Random House 2023. 400 p.
ISBN 9780525510086
Grades: Adult   B

1. Chamberlain, Joshua Lawrence, 1828-1914 2. Generals 3. United States Civil War, 1861-1865 4. Gettysburg, Battle of, 1863 5. Civil war veterans 6. Governors 7. Teachers 8. College presidents 9. North American people 10. American people 11. United States history 12. Biographies 13. Life stories — Law and order — Military leaders 14. Life stories — Politics — Politicians 15. History writing — Wars and conflicts — American Civil War

LC 2023008048

Before 1862, Joshua Lawrence Chamberlain had rarely left his home state of Maine, where he was a trained minister and mild-mannered professor at Bowdoin College. His colleagues were shocked when he volunteered for the Union army, but he was undeterred and later became known as one of the North's greatest heroes. In this book, Ronald C. White captures the complex and inspiring man behind the hero.

"Based on extensive primary research, this book gives fresh insight into Chamberlain's life." —*Library Journal*

Includes bibliographical references and index.

White, Shane
Prince of Darkness: The Untold Story of Jeremiah G. Hamilton, Wall Street's First Black Millionaire. Shane White. Palgrave Macmillan 2015. 320 p.
ISBN 9781250070562
Grades: Adult   B

1. Hamilton, Jeremiah G. -1875 2. African American millionaires 3. African American businesspeople 4. African Americans 5. Securities industry and trade 6. Race relations 7. United States history 8. Wall Street, New York City 9. 19th century 10. Australian literature 11. Biographies 12. Life stories — Business — Business leaders 13. History writing — African American — United States

LC 2015011416

A prominent historian brings to life the story of a man who defied every convention of his time by becoming Wall Street's first Black millionaire in pre-Civil War New York, marrying a white woman, owning railroad stock on trains he was not legally allowed to ride and outsmarting his contemporaries.

"Superb scholarship and a sprightly style recover an unaccountably overlooked life in our history." —*Kirkus*

Whitney, Emerson
Heaven. Emerson Whitney. McSweeney's Books 2020. 191 p.
ISBN 9781944211769
Grades: Adult   B

1. Whitney, Emerson 2. Gender identity 3. Gender fluid 4. Transgender people 5. Nonbinary people 6. Gender-nonconforming people 7. Growing up 8. Self-discovery 9. Mother and child 10. Grandmother and grandchild 11. Family relationships 12. Autobiographies and memoirs 13. Life stories — Identity — LGBTQIA+ 14. Life stories — Relationships — Growing up 15. Family and relationships — Growing up

Emerson Whitney writes, "Really, I can't explain myself without making a mess." What follows is that mess-electrifying, gorgeous, defiant. At Heaven's center, Whitney seeks to understand their relationship to their mother and grandmother, those first windows into womanhood and all its consequences. Whitney retraces a roving youth in deeply observant, psychedelic prose-all the while folding in the work of thinkers like Judith Butler, Donna Haraway, and C. Riley Snorton-to engage transness and the breathing, morphing nature of selfhood.

"An incisive, nuanced inquiry into gender and body." —*Kirkus*

Whyte, Kenneth
Hoover: An Extraordinary Life in Extraordinary Times. Kenneth Whyte. Alfred A. Knopf 2017. 752 pages
ISBN 9780307597960
Grades: Adult   B

1. Hoover, Herbert, 1874-1964 2. Businesspeople 3. Politicians 4. Depressions, 1929-1941 5. Humanitarian assistance 6. World War I 7. Presidents 8. Politics and government 9. United States 10. 20th century 11. Biographies 12. Canadian literature 13. Life stories — Politics — Politicians 14. History writing — Presidency — 20th century — United States 15. History writing — Early 20th century — United States

LC 2017015685

National Book Critics Circle Award for Biography finalist, 2017.

A portrait of the 31st president traces his difficult childhood and meteoric business career through his significant contributions during World War I and the Great Depression, sharing insights into his less-recognized economic and political achievements.

"With adept explanations of the Depressions complexities and a refreshing sense of objectivity regarding Hoovers approach to combatting it, Whyte portrays a figure to be neither pitied nor reviled, but better understood." —*Publishers Weekly*

A Borzoi Book; Includes bibliographical references and index.

The Uncrowned King: The Sensational Rise of William Randolph Hearst. Kenneth Whyte. Counterpoint 2009. 546 p, 16 p. of plates : Illustration; Portrait
ISBN 9781582434674
Grades: Adult   B

1. Hearst, William Randolph, 1863-1951 2. Publishers and publishing 3. Newspaper publishers and publishing 4. Newspapers 5. Sensationalism in journalism 6. Spanish-American War, 1898 7. Ownership 8. Presidential elections 9. New York City history 10. United States 11. 19th century 12. 20th century 13. Biographies 14. Canadian literature 15. Business and economics — Business leaders and entrepreneurs 16. Life stories — Arts and culture — Writing 17. Adult books for young adults

LC 2008047442

Traces the unique life of William Randolph Hearst as a successful and controversial figure and the impact his publications had on the world, and offers a detailed examination of his long-fought battle with his rival, Joseph Pulitzer.

"A very worthwhile reexamination of the rise of a flawed but accomplished man." —*Booklist*

Includes bibliographical references (p. 505-511) and index; Originally published: Toronto : Random House Canada, 2008.

ESSENTIAL AND RECOMMENDED TITLES
Biography

Widmer, Edward L.
Lincoln on the Verge: Thirteen Days to Washington. Ted Widmer. Simon & Schuster 2020. xii, 606 pages
ISBN 9781476739434
Grades: Adult **B**
1. Lincoln, Abraham, 1809-1865 2. Presidents 3. Attempted assassination 4. Railroad travel 5. Democracy 6. Secession 7. 1860s 8. 19th century 9. Biographies 10. Life stories — Politics — Politicians 11. History writing — Presidency — 19th century — United States

Draws on new research to profile Abraham Lincoln during 13 pivotal days of his president-elect period, during which he forged essential bonds with everyday people, foiled an assassination attempt and demonstrated early signs of legacy greatness.

"While general readers may lose interest during the journey, Lincoln buffs will undoubtedly devour the book. A colorful, richly detailed overture to Lincoln's odyssey." —*Kirkus*

Martin Van Buren. Ted Widmer. Times Books 2005. 189 p. (American presidents series (Times Books))
ISBN 9780805069228
Grades: 11 12 Adult **B**
1. Van Buren, Martin, 1782-1862 2. Presidents 3. Politics and government 4. United States 5. 19th century 6. Biographies 7. History writing — Presidency — United States 8. History writing — Antebellum America — United States 9. Life stories — Politics — Politicians 10. Adult books for young adults 11. History writing — Presidency — 19th century — United States
LC 2004053652

Examines the life and presidency of Martin Van Buren, describing his failed efforts to control such issues as slavery and the great banking panic of 1837.

"The author keenly evokes the environment that enabled Van Buren to thrive." —*New York Times Book Review*

Includes bibliographical references (p. [177]-179) and index.

Wiener, Anna
★ *Uncanny Valley: A Memoir.* Anna Wiener. 2020. 320 p.
ISBN 9780374278014
Grades: Adult **B**
1. Wiener, Anna, 1987- 2. High technology industry and trade 3. New businesses 4. Overdoing things 5. Computer industry and trade 6. Corporate culture 7. Entrepreneurship 8. Twenties (Age) 9. Silicon Valley, California 10. Autobiographies and memoirs 11. Life stories — Business — Working life
LC 2019021999
New York Times Notable Book, 2020.

The author chronicles her experience at a big-data startup in the heart of the Silicon Valley bubble: a world of surreal extravagance, dubious success and fresh-faced entrepreneurs hell-bent on domination, glory and, of course, progress.

"A funny, highly informative, and terrifying read." —*Kirkus*

Wiesel, Elie
All Rivers Run to the Sea: Memoirs. Elie Wiesel. Knopf 1995. 432 p, [8] p. of plates : Illustration
ISBN 9780679439165
Grades: 11 12 Adult **B**
1. Wiesel, Elie, 1928-2016 2. Authors, Jewish 3. Holocaust (1933-1945) 4. Holocaust survivors 5. Authors, French 6. 20th century 7. Autobiographies and memoirs 8. Translations — French to English 9. Biographies 10. History writing — Wars and conflicts — Holocaust — World War II 11. Arts and Entertainment — Writing and Publishing 12. Life stories — Facing adversity — War and oppression — Holocaust
LC 95017607

The memoirs of the Nobel Peace Laureate chronicle his prewar childhood, suffering in Auschwitz, adult struggles with faith, literary endeavors, and relationships with such figures as Golda Meir.

"Wiesel's immensely moving, unforgettable memoir has the searing intensity of his novels and autobiographical tales." —*Publishers Weekly*

Includes index; Translation of : Tous les fleuves vont a la mer.

And the Sea Is Never Full: Memoirs, 1969-. Elie Wiesel; translated from the French by Marion Wiesel. Schocken Books 2000. x, 429 p, [8] p. of plates : Illustration
ISBN 9780805210293
Grades: Adult **B**
1. Wiesel, Elie, 1928-2016 2. Authors, Jewish 3. Holocaust survivors 4. Holocaust (1933-1945) 5. Jewish history 6. Social advocates 7. Public opinion 8. Autobiographies and memoirs 9. Biographies 10. History writing — Jewish history 11. Arts and Entertainment — Writing and Publishing 12. Life stories — Arts and culture — Writing — Authors 13. Life stories — Facing adversity — War and oppression — Holocaust
LC 00030129

Continues the author's memoirs from 1968, when he was forty years old, and focuses on a wide range of topics, including divisions within Israel and Reagan's visit to the cemetery at Bitburg.

"This concluding volume begins when the author is age 40. He continues his travels . and he continues to write, his books including Souls on fire, Four Hasidic Masters, Twilight, and more. Wiesel is the most significant writer to have made the Holocaust the major theme of his work, just as it has been of major importance to his life. The horror of the Holocaust can be felt in this memoir with an intensity beyond words." —*Booklist*

Includes index.

★ *Night.* Elie Wiesel; foreword by Francois Mauriac; translated from the French by Stella Rodway. Hill and Wang 1960. 116 p.
ISBN 9780809073504
Grades: 9 10 11 12 Adult **B**
1. Wiesel, Elie, 1928-2016 2. God (Judaism) 3. Concentration camp survivors 4. Holocaust survivors 5. Separated friends, relatives, etc. 6. Jewish families 7. Loss 8. Belief and doubt 9. Growing up 10. Holocaust (1933-1945) 11. Teenage boys 12. Guilt in teenagers 13. Jewish teenagers 14. Third Reich, 1933-1945 15. Transylvania, Romania 16. Autobiographies and memoirs 17. History writing — Wars and conflicts — Holocaust — World War II 18. Life stories — Facing adversity — War and oppression — War survivors 19. Antiracist literature
LC 60014910

A terrifying account of the Nazi death camp horror that turns a young Jewish boy into an agonized witness to the death of his family.

Sequel: Dawn; Reprinted in 2017 with updated front and back matter to include speeches and essays commemorating his recent death; Originally published in Yiddish in a more expanded version, under title (transliterated: Un di velt hot geshvign).

Wilder, Laura Ingalls
Pioneer Girl: The Annotated Autobiography. Laura Ingalls Wilder; Pamela Smith Hill, editor. South Dakota Historical Society Press 2014. 400 pages
ISBN 9780984504176
Grades: Adult **B**
1. Wilder, Laura Ingalls, 1867-1957 2. Frontier and pioneer life 3. Women authors 4. Pioneer women 5. Authors, American 6. Children's literature writing 7. United States 8. Autobiographies and memoirs 9. Life stories — People in history — Pioneers 10. History writing — Westward expansion — United States 11. Life stories — Arts and culture — Writing — Authors 12. History writing — Women's history 13. Adult books for young adults
LC 2014027174

Laura Ingalls Wilder's unedited, and unpublished, draft of her autobiography that was written for an adult audience and eventually served as the foundation for her popular Little House on the Prairie series includes not-safe-for-children tales that feature stark scenes of domestic abuse, love triangles gone awry and a man who lit himself on fire while drunk off whiskey.

"Lengthy footnotes make the manuscript somewhat tricky to navigate, but Hills comments are cogent and her arguments strong, and this will be welcomed wherever there are Wilder fans. Illustrated with maps, photos, and artwork, and appended with additional manuscripts and an extensive bibliography." —*Booklist*

A publication of the Pioneer Girl Project; Includes bibliographical references and index.

*The **Selected** Letters of Laura Ingalls Wilder.* William Anderson. HarperCollins 2016. 320 p.

ISBN 9780062419682

Grades: Adult   B

1. Wilder, Laura Ingalls, 1867-1957 2. Authors 3. Writing 4. Letters 5. Arts and Entertainment — Writing and Publishing 6. Adult books for young adults 7. Arts and Entertainment — Writing and Publishing — Literary criticism

LC 2016591797

A single-volume collection of personal writings by the beloved American author spans 60 years of her life and shares deeply personal insights into her experiences, beliefs, family dynamics and career.

Wilder-Taylor, Stefanie

★ ***Drunk-ish:*** *A Memoir of Loving and Leaving Alcohol.* Stefanie Wilder-Taylor. Gallery Books 2024. 288 p.

ISBN 9781668019412

Grades: Adult   B

1. Alcoholism 2. Alcoholics 3. Alcoholic women 4. Recovering alcoholics 5. Sobriety 6. Self-help psychology 7. Dependency 8. Autobiographies and memoirs 9. Life stories — Facing adversity — Medical issues — Addiction

LC 2023031362

For Stefanie Wilder-Taylor, alcohol was the seasoning that could give almost any activity more flavor. A drink took the edge off and made even the most difficult adversary (a tough crowd in a comedy club or a judgmental PTA mom) not just bearable but fun. As the years go by, Stefanie wonders if her relationship with alcohol is different from other people's. Grappling with the question of whether or not she is a "real" alcoholic, one evening brings Stefanie close to losing it all, and she decides that she doesn't need to hit rock bottom before deciding to stop drinking; if sobriety will improve her life, that's reason to quit. A tender and funny farewell letter to a beloved but toxic friend.

"A mother drags herself kicking and screaming into sobriety in this raucous memoir from humorist Wilder-Taylor...The results are funny, neurotic, and woozily uplifting." —*Publishers Weekly*

Wilderson, Frank B.

Afropessimism. Frank B. Wilderson III.. Liveright Publishing Corporation 2020. 352 p.

ISBN 9781631496141

Grades: Adult   B

1. Wilderson, Frank B, III, 1956- 2. African American intellectuals 3. African Americans 4. Racism 5. Marginalized people 6. African American political activists 7. African American college teachers 8. College teachers 9. Institutional racism 10. Identity 11. Autobiographies and memoirs 12. Biographies 13. Life stories — Identity — Race and ethnicity 14. Society and culture — Race

LC 2019051446

The award-winning author of Incognegro offers an account of the non-analogous experience of being Black by theorizing the Black experiences through a lens of perpetual and incomparable slavery that flourishes in today's world.

"An essential contribution to any discussion of race and likely to be a standard text in cultural studies for years to come." —*Kirkus*

Includes bibliographical references.

Wilkinson, Alec

*The **Protest** Singer: An Intimate Portrait of Pete Seeger.* by Alec Wilkinson. Alfred A. Knopf 2009. 176 p.

ISBN 9780307269959

Grades: 11 12 Adult   B

1. Seeger, Pete, 1919-2014 2. Folk singers 3. Music 4. Folk music, American 5. Peace movements 6. Folk musicians 7. Social life and customs 8. United States 9. 21st century 10. 20th century 11. Biographies 12. Arts and Entertainment — Music — Folk 13. Life stories — Arts and culture — Performing arts — Musicians and composers

LC 2008054387

Presents a portrait of the folk singer, tracing his career and influence as a singer and surveying his political development.

Willetts, Paul

King Con: The Bizarre Adventures of the Jazz Age's Greatest Impostor. Paul Willetts. Random House Inc 2018. 304 p.

ISBN 9780451495815

Grades: Adult   B

1. Laplante, Edgar, 1888-1944 2. Fraud 3. Vaudeville performers 4. Swindlers and swindling 5. False personation 6. Deception 7. Impostors 8. 1920s 9. Biographies 10. Life stories — Law and order — Criminals and law-breakers

LC 2018014380

A portrait of charismatic vaudeville performer and 1920s con artist Edgar LaPlante describes how he amassed millions through a fraudulent charity, his seduction of a wealthy Austrian countess and his friendships with celebrities and powerful world leaders.

"With the rise of identity theft, celebrity worship, and manipulative s o cial media, this sprightly story of a legendary con artist's outrageous successes becomes a cautionary tale for the digital age." —*Kirkus*

Williams, Billy Dee

★ ***What*** *Have We Here: Portraits of a Life.* Billy Dee Williams. Alfred A. Knopf 2024. 320 p.

ISBN 9780593318607

Grades: Adult   B

1. Williams, Billy Dee, 1937- 2. African American men 3. Actors and actresses 4. Self-confidence 5. Success (Concept) 6. Film industry and trade 7. Television industry and trade 8. Racism 9. Discrimination 10. American people 11. North American people 12. Harlem, New York City 13. Autobiographies and memoirs 14. Arts and Entertainment — Movies and Television 15. Life stories — Arts and culture — Performing arts — Actors and actresses

LC 2023031857

Recalling his remarkable life of nearly eight decades, the film legend who has starred in 40 movies, seven Broadway plays and has made more than 40 TV shows and movies combined shows how he, as the first Black character in the Star Wars universe, became a true pop culture icon.

"Eighty-six-year-old Star Wars actor Williams provides a candid look back at his life and career in this genial debut memoir." —*Publishers Weekly*

Includes index.

Williams, Jay

Life Is Not an Accident: A Memoir of Reinvention. Jay Williams. HarperCollins 2015. 304 p.

ISBN 9780062327987

Grades: Adult   B

1. Williams, Jay 2. Basketball players 3. Accident victims 4. Motorcycle accidents 5. African American athletes 6. Professional basketball 7. Sports corruption 8. Determination 9. Autobiographies and memoirs 10. Biographies 11. Life stories — Sports — Athletes 12. Life stories — Facing adversity 13. Sports and Competition — Basketball 14. Sports and Competition — Individual Athlete

LC 2015050965

In a candid, no-holds-barred memoir, the former Chicago Bulls' top draft pick talks about the accident that ended his career and sent him down a new path, shares behind-the-scenes details of life as an All-American and speaks out about corruption in the NBA.

"Recommended for anyone interested in a behind-the-scenes look at the lives of college basketball and NBA players." —*Library Journal*

Williams, Juan

Thurgood Marshall: American Revolutionary. Juan Williams. Times Books 1998. xviii, 459 p. : Illustration

ISBN 9780812920284

Grades: 11 12 Adult   B

1. Marshall, Thurgood, 1908-1993 2. Judges 3. Civil rights workers 4. African American judges 5. School desegregation decision, 1954 6. United States

ESSENTIAL AND RECOMMENDED TITLES
Biography

7. Biographies 8. Life stories — Law and order — Judges and lawyers 9. Life stories — Politics — Activists and reformers 10. History writing — African American — Civil rights — United States

LC 98009735

Booklist Editors' Choice, 1998; New York Times Notable Book, 1998.

Presents a biography of the first African American appointed to the Supreme Court, from his crusade against segregation to his friendships with other famous Black figures.

"Williams presents Marshall as a revolutionary of grand vision, but this well-rounded portrait of the man also addresses his vanities and warts, from his ascension to his deflation and subsequent redemption. This is a must read for all Americans concerned with the struggle for civil and individual rights." —*Booklist*

Includes bibliographical references (p. 431-436) and index.

Williams, Kate
Ambition and Desire: The Dangerous Life of Josephine Bonaparte. Kate Williams. Ballantine Books 2014. 384 p.
ISBN 9780345522832
Grades: Adult   B
1. Josephine, Empress of the French, 1763-1814 2. Napoleon I, Emperor of the French, 1769-1821 3. Women rulers 4. Biographies 5. Life stories — Politics — Royalty 6. History writing — Europe — France 7. History writing — Women's history

LC 2014030438

Biographer Kate Williams, in Ambition and Desire, brings Josephine Bonaparte out from the aura surrounding her husband, Emperor Napoleon Bonaparte, to claim her place on the stage of history. Born to an ordinary but aspiring family on the tiny West Indian island of Martinique, Josephine made her way to Paris, survived the Revolution, became a star of the salons, and married the man who was her match in both brilliance and ambition. This compelling account offers up-close insight into Josephine's passion and achievements as well as her tumultuous relationship with Napoleon.

"Meeting her match in Napolon Bonaparte, Josephine and he embarked on a doomed marital odyssey characterized by personal jealousies and political obsessions. An in-depth portrait of the substantive woman behind the throne." —*Booklist*

Originally published under the title Josephine: Desire, ambition, Napoleon in the United Kingdom by Hutchinson, a member of the Random House Group Limited, London, in 2013; Includes bibliographical references and index.

Williams, Lucinda
Don't Tell Anybody the Secrets I Told You: A Memoir. by Lucinda Williams. Crown 2023. 304 p.
ISBN 9780593136492
Grades: Adult   B
1. Williams, Lucinda 2. Singers 3. Childhood 4. Psychic trauma 5. Music 6. Musicians 7. Music industry and trade 8. OCD 9. Southern states 10. United States 11. Autobiographies and memoirs 12. Life stories — Arts and culture — Performing arts — Musicians and composers 13. Arts and entertainment — Music — Country

LC 2022052271

The three-time Grammy winner discusses her traumatic childhood in the Deep South, how she fought through years of music industry anonymity and hostility, and the events that helped shaped her music.

"In a conversational style, Grammy Award winner Williams takes readers through the ups and downs of her family life and musical career....Williams's story will likely appeal to readers interested in music, poetry, literature, or mental health." —*Library Journal*

Williams, Mary
The Lost Daughter. Mary Williams. Blue Rider Press 2013. 320 p.
ISBN 9780399160868
Grades: Adult   B
1. Williams, Mary 1967- 2. Fonda, Jane, 1937- 3. Interracial adoption 4. Dysfunctional families 5. Child abuse victims 6. Life change events 7. Reconciliation 8. Growing up 9. Poverty 10. Teenage girls 11. Adopted teenagers 12. African American teenagers 13. Race relations 14. 1970s 15. Autobiographies and memoirs 16. Life stories — Relationships — Family 17. Family and Relationships — Growing up 18. Family and Relationships — Parenting — Adoption 19. Society and culture — Race

LC 2013001245

The adopted daughter of Jane Fonda describes her youth in politically charged 1970s Oakland, California, her daunting prospects in the face of her dysfunctional family and the ways in which a positive, structured home life enabled her world travels and eventual reconnection with her biological family.

Williams, Michael Kenneth
Scenes from My Life: A Memoir. Michael K. Williams with John Sternfeld. Crown 2022. 304 p.
ISBN 9780593240373
Grades: Adult   B
1. Williams, Michael Kenneth 2. African American dancers 3. Actors and actresses 4. Dancers 5. Addiction 6. African Americans 7. United States 8. Autobiographies and memoirs 9. Life stories — Arts and culture — Performing arts — Actors and actresses 10. Arts and Entertainment — Movies and television

LC 2022016149

Written by the late, iconic actor before his death, this candid and moving memoir of hard-won success, struggles with addiction and a lifelong mission to give back tells the story of his whole life in his own voice, in his own words, as only he could.

"The late Emmy-nominated actor recounts his endeavor to overcome poverty, abuse, and addiction in this immensely inspiring and candid debut." —*Publishers Weekly*

Williams, Michelle
Checking In: How Getting Real About Depression Saved My Life - and Can Save Yours. Michelle Williams. Nelson Books, an imprint of Thomas Nelson 2021. xviii, 215 p.
ISBN 9781400223336
Grades: Adult   B
1. Williams, Michelle (Tenitra Michelle) 2. African American women singers 3. Mental health 4. Mental illness 5. Social advocates 6. Faith (Christianity) 7. Treatment 8. People with depression 9. Women 10. Autobiographies and memoirs 11. Life stories — Arts and culture — Performing arts — Musicians and composers 12. Life stories — Facing adversity — Medical issues — Mental illness 13. Life stories — Religion and spirituality — Spiritual journeys

LC 2020042612

In her first book, an acclaimed musical artist courageously shares the hidden secrets that nearly ended her life; the importance of her faith, family, and friends; and the lessons she learned about prioritizing her mental health.

"Christians struggling with depression will relate to and find comfort in Williams's vulnerable reflections." —*Publishers Weekly*

Includes bibliographical references.

Williams, Patricia
Rabbit: The Autobiography of Ms. Pat. Patricia Williams with Jeannine Amber. Dey Street Books 2017. 256 pages
ISBN 9780062407306
Grades: Adult   B
1. Williams, Patricia (Comedian) 2. Children of alcoholic mothers 3. Growing up 4. Teenage mothers 5. Comedians 6. Poverty 7. Personal conduct 8. Self-discovery 9. Atlanta, Georgia 10. Autobiographies and memoirs 11. Life stories — Relationships — Growing up 12. Life stories — Arts and culture — Performing arts — Entertainers and celebrities

LC 2017486713

The popular comedian traces her youth in Atlanta's most troubled neighborhood at the height of the crack epidemic, discussing the experiences with an alcoholic mother, four siblings, petty crime and prostitution that led to her becoming a mother at age 13 before resolving to secure a better life for her children.

"Both savagely honest and often genuinely funny, this is the story of how a resilient woman survived a harrowing early life and found unexpected salvation through humor. Sassy, inspiring, and uplifting." —*Kirkus*

PUBLIC LIBRARY CORE COLLECTION: NONFICTION
Twentieth Edition

Williams, Richard
Black and White: The Way I See It. Richard Williams with Bart Davis. Atria Books 2014. 320 pages
ISBN 9781476704203
Grades: Adult B
1. Williams, Richard, 1942- 2. Williams, Serena, 1981- 3. Williams, Venus, 1980- 4. Tennis coaches 5. Tennis 6. Daughters 7. Families 8. Autobiographies and memoirs 9. Sports and Competition — Tennis 10. Family and Relationships — Families 11. Life stories — Sports — Coaches, managers, and owners
LC 2013033646

The gripping story of Richard Williams, the father who raised and trained two of the greatest women in sports, Venus and Serena. He achieved greatness in spite of hardship and disadvantages to become a successful businessman, family man and tennis coach.

Includes bibliographical references and index.

Williams, Zach
Rescue Story: Faith, Freedom, and Finding My Way Home. Zach Williams; with Robert Noland. Zondervan 2024. 272 p.
ISBN 9780310368465
Grades: Adult B
1. Williams, Zach 2. Childhood 3. Growing up 4. Musicians 5. Christian life 6. Faith (Christianity) 7. Drug abuse 8. Addiction 9. Autobiographies and memoirs 10. Life stories — Arts and culture — Performing arts — Musicians and composers 11. Life stories — Facing adversity — Medical issues — Addiction 12. Arts and Entertainment — Music

In this powerful memoir, two-time Grammy Award winner Zach Williams shares his personal Rescue Story as he reflects on his childhood and the prophecy that kept his parents from giving up hope, his descent into substance abuse which held him captive for so long, and ultimately the rescue he didn't think was possible but embraced with open arms.

"Grammy Award-winning vocalist Williams recounts in his candid debut memoir how he clawed his way out of addiction and built a redemptive relationship with God…This inspires." —*Publishers Weekly*

Williamson, Edwin
Borges: A Life. Edwin Williamson. Viking 2004. xviii, 574 p. : Illustration
ISBN 9780670885794
Grades: 11 12 Adult B
1. Borges, Jorge Luis, 1899-1986 2. Authors, Argentine 3. Social life and customs 4. Argentina 5. 20th century 6. Biographies 7. Arts and Entertainment — Writing and Publishing 8. Life stories — Arts and culture — Writing — Authors
LC 2004041290

A portrait of the Latin American writer and poet draws on interviews and previously unavailable sources to cover such topics as Borges' ancestry in Argentina, the challenges that marked his life, and the evolution of his political ideas.

"This is a richly psychological, dynamically intellectual, and deeply affecting portrait of an often anguished and inhibited man who, through heroic perserverance and spiritual conviction, found salvation in writing and transformed literature for all time." —*Booklist*

Includes bibliographical references (p. 537-549) and index.

Willis, Raquel
The Risk It Takes to Bloom: On Life and Liberation. Raquel Willis. St. Martin's Press 2023. 240 p.
ISBN 9781250275684
Grades: Adult B
1. Willis, Raquel 2. Trans women 3. Transgender people 4. LGBTQIA+ rights 5. Civil rights 6. African American women 7. Identity 8. African Americans 9. Marginalized people 10. Violence against marginalized people 11. United States 12. Autobiographies and memoirs 13. Life stories — Identity — LGBTQIA+ 14. Life stories — Politics — Activists and reformers
LC 2023025379

One of the most formidable Black trans activists in history, in this passionate and powerful memoir, recounts the possibility of transformation after tragedy, and how complex moments can push us all to take necessary risks and bloom toward collective liberation.

"This pleasantly conversational memoir mixes somber activism and youthful levity, combining glittering details of a buoyant social life with sorrowful reflections on violence against trans people. It's an inspiring account." —*Publishers Weekly*

Includes bibliographical references.

Willner, Nina
Forty Autumns: A Family's Story of Courage and Survival on Both Sides of the Berlin Wall. Nina Willner. William Morrow 2016. 384 p.
ISBN 9780062410313
Grades: Adult B
1. Willner, Nina, 1961- 2. Military intelligence officers 3. Separated friends, relatives, etc. 4. Cold War 5. Women intelligence officers 6. Families 7. Mothers 8. Communism 9. Resilience 10. Courage 11. Family reunions 12. German history 13. Berlin, Germany 14. East Germany 15. 20th century 16. Autobiographies and memoirs 17. Life stories — Facing adversity — War and oppression 18. Family and Relationships — Families 19. History writing — Europe — Germany 20. Adult books for young adults 21. Nonfiction that reads like fiction
LC 2016038924

Author Nina Willner, the first female U.S. Army intelligence officer to work in East Germany, had a whole family living behind the Iron Curtain. While her mother Hanna had escaped from East Berlin in 1948, marrying an American and raising her children there, all Hanna's relatives remained behind. In Forty Autumns, Willner relates their story: Both her grandfather's brutal "re-education" in a mental institution and the family's loving solidarity in the face of Communist oppression. The Berlin Wall's destruction in 1989 allowed Hanna's first reunion with her relatives in 40 years. Gripping, heartrending, and inspiring, this combined history and family memoir relates the history of the Cold War in personal terms.

"A poignant and engrossing, occasionally harrowing, family memoir." —*Kirkus*

Wills, Garry
James Madison. Garry Wills. Times Books 2002. xx, 184 p. (American presidents series (Times Books))
ISBN 9780805069051
Grades: 11 12 Adult B
1. Madison, James, 1751-1836 2. Political leadership 3. War of 1812 4. Presidents 5. Politicians 6. Politics and government 7. United States history 8. United States 9. 19th century 10. 1810s 11. Early America (1784-1819) 12. 18th century 13. Biographies 14. History writing — Presidency — 18th century — United States 15. History writing — Early America — United States 16. History writing — Wars and conflicts — War of 1812 17. Life stories — Law and order — Armed forces personnel 18. Life stories — Politics — Politicians 19. Adult books for young adults
LC 2002019692

New York Times Notable Book, 2002.

Chronicles the life and career of the fourth American president from his work constructing the U.S. Constitution, his years in the legislature, his two presidential terms, and his later role as elder statesman.

"The author maintains that Madison possessed qualities that served him well early in his career but proved to be a handicap during his Presidency.... Written with flair, this clear and balanced account is based on a sure handling of the material." —*Library Journal*

Includes bibliographical references (p. [173]-174) and index.

Saint Augustine. Garry Wills. Viking 1999. xx, 152 p.
ISBN 9780670886104
Grades: Adult B
1. Augustine, Saint, Bishop of Hippo 2. Christian saints 3. Bishops 4. 4th century 5. Biographies 6. Life stories — Religion and spirituality — Religious and spiritual leaders 7. Spirituality and Religion — Christianity — History 8. Spirituality and Religion — Religious Leaders
LC 98050317

New York Times Notable Book, 1999.

ESSENTIAL AND RECOMMENDED TITLES
Biography

A portrait of one of the founding fathers of Western religious philosophy, challenging misconceptions concerning his early hedonistic life and his influential interpretations of Christian doctrine.

"Wills begins by addressing centuries of misconceptions. Though his admiration for the saint is occasionally tainted by defensiveness, his account of Augustine's search for a faith and a philosophy engages our sympathy. He also conveys the turbulence of the era, when the Roman Empire was beleaguered by barbarians and the Catholic Church by heretics, and shows how Augustine's responses to the troubles of his time have shaped Christianity down to our own."
—*The New Yorker*

Includes bibliographical references (p. 147-149).

Wilson, A. N.
Victoria: A Life. A. N. Wilson. Penguin Press 2014. 624 p.
ISBN 9781594205996
Grades: Adult   B
1. Victoria, Queen of Great Britain, 1819-1901 2. Women rulers 3. British history 4. Great Britain 5. Victorian era (1837-1901) 6. Biographies 7. Life stories — Politics — Royalty 8. History writing — Europe — United Kingdom
LC 2014013973

Booklist Editors' Choice, 2014.

Queen Victoria reigned over Britain and its Empire for 64 years, becoming the namesake for a whole era and overseeing significant political developments in her government. Her children married important royalty throughout Europe, extending her influence well past her death in 1901. Victoria's life was darkened by the great sadness of Prince Consort Albert's premature demise, but also notable for her collaboration with a series of effective prime ministers. Biographer A.N. Wilson's fluid and balanced account brings Victoria's complex personality to life, portraying her as an interesting woman and successful monarch.

"[F]ew if any previous biographers have viewed her as incisively and absorbingly as Wilson does in his lengthy but smoothly flowing treatment of the queens long life. [He] sees Victoria as a woman who battled demons and emerged from her various darknesses victorious as a functioning woman and monarch." —*Booklist*

Includes bibliographical references and index.

Wilson, Brian
I Am Brian Wilson: A Memoir. Brian Wilson with Ben Greenman. Da Capo Press 2016. 320 p.
ISBN 9780306823060
Grades: Adult   B
1. Wilson, Brian, 1942- 2. Rock musicians 3. Music 4. Creativity 5. Psychologist and patient 6. People with mental illnesses 7. United States 8. Autobiographies and memoirs 9. Life stories — Arts and culture — Performing arts — Musicians and composers 10. Life stories — Facing adversity — Medical issues — Mental illness
LC 2016030071

The memoirs of the legendary co-founder of the Beach Boys offer insights into his difficult relationship with his father, the women in his life, his parenting experiences, and the events that inspired his music.

Includes bibliographical references and index.

Wilson, Chris
The Master Plan: My Journey from Life in Prison to a Life of Purpose. Chris Wilson; with Bret Witter. G.P. Putnam's Sons 2019. 416 p.
ISBN 9780735215580
Grades: Adult   B
1. Wilson, Chris, 1978- 2. Former convicts 3. Self-fulfillment 4. Personal conduct 5. Purpose in life 6. African American men 7. Goals and objectives 8. Determination 9. Criminals 10. Businesspeople 11. Rehabilitation 12. Maryland 13. United States 14. Autobiographies and memoirs 15. Biographies 16. Life stories — Law and order — Criminals and law-breakers 17. Life stories — Identity — Race and ethnicity
LC 2018041588

The inspiring, instructive, and ultimately triumphant memoir of a man who used hard work and a Master Plan to turn a life sentence into a second chance.

"Wilson engagingly tells his riveting story while also exposing corrupt justice practices and the ways that society consistently works against former convicts, especially Black men." —*Booklist*

Wilson, Derek
Out of the Storm: The Life and Legacy of Martin Luther. Derek Wilson. St. Martin's Press 2008. 416 p.
ISBN 9780312375881
Grades: 11 12 Adult
1. Luther, Martin, 1483-1546 2. Church history 3. Religious leaders 4. Religions 5. Renaissance (1300-1600) 6. 16th century 7. Biographies 8. Spirituality and Religion — Christianity — History 9. History writing — Renaissance — Europe 10. Life stories — Religion and spirituality — Religious and spiritual leaders 11. Spirituality and Religion — Religious leaders 12. History writing — Europe — Germany
LC 2007039331

A definitive portrait of the renegade monk whose activities helped ignite the Protestant Reformation and transformed the face of Europe provides a revealing study of the complex life, motivations, convictions, and religious, social, and cultural legacy of Martin Luther for both his own time and later eras.

"A nuanced portrait of a perplexing titan." —*Booklist*

Includes bibliographical references and index.

Wilson, Katherine
Only in Naples: Lessons in Food and Famiglia from My Italian Mother-in-law. Katherine Wilson. Random House 2016. 304 p.
ISBN 9780812998160
Grades: Adult   B
1. Wilson, Katherine, 1974- 2. American people in Italy 3. Cultural differences 4. Cooking 5. Daughters-in-law 6. Mothers-in-law 7. Families 8. Social life and customs 9. Naples, Italy 10. Autobiographies and memoirs 11. Travel Writing — Living Abroad 12. Life stories — Relationships — Family
LC 2015016098

After graduating from college, well-to-do Katherine Wilson left Washington, D.C. and headed to Naples, Italy for an unpaid internship at the American Consul. Though Naples was considered "dirty and dangerous" by her friends and family, she discovered that people either loved or hated the city, and she loved it. Not only did she learn to eat better (she'd been a binge eater), but she was embraced by an Italian family and their chic, well-connected matriarch, Raffaella, who taught Wilson about Neapolitan culture and how to cook delicious local foods—and eventually lessons about marriage and motherhood when Wilson married her son. This lighthearted, charming look at Italian life includes recipes.

"Each experience, each delicious meal is insightfully described as the reader follows Wilsons path toward carnale, becoming confident and comfortable in ones own skin." —*Booklist*

Wilson, Rebel
Rebel Rising: A Memoir. Rebel Wilson. Simon & Schuster 2024. 320 p.
ISBN 9781668007204
Grades: Adult   B
1. Actors and actresses 2. Self-discovery 3. Success (Concept) 4. Health 5. Gender identity 6. Fertility 7. Rejection 8. Autobiographies and memoirs 9. Life stories — Arts and culture — Performing arts — Actors and actresses 10. Arts and Entertainment — Movies and Television

From the scene-stealing star of Pitch Perfect and Bridesmaids comes a refreshingly candid, hilarious, and inspiring book about her unconventional journey to Hollywood success and loving herself.

"A lively and reflective celebrity memoir seasoned with comedy and sincerity." —*Kirkus*

Wilson, Robert
Barnum: An American Life. Robert Wilson. Simon & Schuster 2019. 384 pages
ISBN 9781501118623
Grades: Adult   B

PUBLIC LIBRARY CORE COLLECTION: NONFICTION
Twentieth Edition

1. Barnum, P. T. (Phineas Taylor), 1810-1891 2. Circus 3. Circus owners 4. Entrepreneurs 5. Businesspeople 6. Resilience 7. Popular culture 8. United States 9. 19th century 10. Biographies 11. Life stories — Business — Business leaders 12. Life stories — Arts and culture — Performing arts

LC 2019000245

A biography of P.T. Barnum, nearly 125 years after his death, captures the full genius, infamy and allure of the forefather of American entertainment, and makes the case for his place among the icons of American history.

Includes bibliographical references and index.

Mathew Brady: Portraits of a Nation. Robert Wilson. Bloomsbury 2013. 320 p.

ISBN 9781620402030

Grades: Adult   **B**

1. Brady, Mathew B, ca. 1823-1896 2. Photographers 3. Photography 4. War photography 5. Photojournalists 6. Photojournalism 7. United States Civil War, 1861-1865 8. United States history 9. 19th century 10. American Civil War era (1861-1865) 11. Biographies 12. Life stories — Arts and culture — Writing — Journalists 13. Arts and Entertainment — Photography 14. History writing — Wars and conflicts — American Civil War

LC 2013016928

A narrative portrait of the Civil War visual historian illuminates his pivotal role in establishing photography as a valued documenting tool, analyzing his portraits of period dignitaries and his self-sacrificing effort to capture images of the Civil War.

Wilson, Victoria

A Life of Barbara Stanwyck: Steel-true 1907-1940. Victoria Wilson. Simon and Schuster 2013. 1056 pages

ISBN 9780684831688

Grades: Adult   **B**

1. Stanwyck, Barbara, 1907-1990 2. Films 3. Actors and actresses 4. Social life and customs 5. United States 6. 20th century 7. Biographies 8. Arts and Entertainment — Movies and Television 9. Life stories — Arts and culture — Performing arts — Actors and actresses

LC 2013023244

A first volume of a full-scale portrait of the acclaimed screen actress includes coverage of her years as a dancer in New York, her fraught marriage to Broadway figure Frank Fay, her partnership with Zeppo Marx and her marriage to Robert Taylor.

Includes bibliographical references and index.

Wilson-Lee, Edward

★ *The Catalogue of Shipwrecked Books: Christopher Columbus, His Son, and the Quest to Build the World's Greatest Library.* Edward Wilson-Lee. Scribner 2019. 384 p.

ISBN 9781982111397

Grades: Adult   **B**

1. Colon, Fernando, 1488-1539 2. Columbus, Christopher, 1451-1506 3. Libraries 4. Books and reading 5. Archives 6. Intellectual life 7. Intellectuals 8. Civilization, Western 9. Explorers 10. Father and adult son 11. Exploration 12. Western Hemisphere 13. 15th century 14. Renaissance (1300-1600) 15. Biographies 16. Arts and Entertainment — Writing and Publishing 17. History writing — Exploration 18. Life stories — People in history — Explorers

LC 2019934427

Shortlisted for the James Tait Black Memorial Prize for Biography, 2018.

A vividly rendered account of the lesser-known quest by Christopher Columbus' illegitimate son, Hernando, to create a multicultural library details his world travels to collect thousands of books. 75,000 first printing. Illustrations.

"An elegantly written, absorbing portrait of a visionary man and his age." —*Kirkus*

Winchester, Simon

The Map That Changed the World: William Smith and the Birth of Modern Geology. Simon Winchester; illustrations by Soun Vannithone. Harper Collins 2001. xix, 329 p, 2 p. of plates : Illustration; Map; Color

ISBN 9780060193614

Grades: Adult   **B**

1. Smith, William, 1769-1839 2. Geologists 3. Cartographers 4. Cartography 5. Geology, Stratigraphic 6. British history 7. 19th century 8. Biographies 9. Science Writing — Geology 10. History writing — Microhistory 11. Life stories — Science, technology, and medicine — Scientists and inventors

LC 2001016603

New York Times Notable Book, 2001.

The world's coal and oil industry, its gold mining, its highway systems, and its railroad routes were all derived entirely from the creation of William Smith's first map. Simon Winchester unfolds the poignant sacrifice behind this world-changing discovery.

"In the early years of the nineteenth century, William Smith created the first geological map of Great Britain, a time-consuming, solitary project that helped establish geology as one of the fundamental fields of study. Winchester tells Smith's story, including the dramatic ups and downs of his personal life. This is just the kind of creative nonfiction that elevates a seemingly arcane topic into popular fare." —*Booklist*

Includes bibliographical references (p. [311]-316) and index.

Winder, Elizabeth

Pain, Parties, Work: Sylvia Plath in New York, Summer 1953. Elizabeth Winder. HarperCollins 2013. 272 p.

ISBN 9780062085498

Grades: Adult   **B**

1. Plath, Sylvia 2. Periodicals 3. Internship programs 4. Interns 5. Poets, American 6. Women poets 7. New York City 8. 1950s 9. 20th century 10. Biographies 11. Arts and Entertainment — Writing and Publishing 12. Life stories — Arts and culture — Writing — Poets

LC Bl2013008794

Marking the 50th anniversary of Sylvia Plath's death, this brilliant biography captures a moment in time—the month she spent in New York City in June of 1953 as a Guest Editor for Mademoiselle's prestigious annual College issue.

Windhorst, Brian

Lebron, Inc.: The Making of a Billion-dollar Athlete. Brian Windhorst. Grand Central Publishing 2019. 288 p.

ISBN 9781538730874

Grades: Adult   **B**

1. James, LeBron 2. Professional basketball players 3. Name-brand products 4. Marketing 5. Basketball players 6. Advertising 7. Basketball 8. Businesspeople 9. Ambition 10. Business and economics — Industries — Entertainment and media 11. Sports and Competition — Basketball

LC 2019286139

The best-selling author of Return of the King traces the story of LeBron James' professional journey to becoming a billion-dollar global brand and businessman who has influenced how professional athletes understand their value.

"In his fourth publication on the NBA superstar, sportswriter Windhorst (Return of the King) focuses on the aspirations LeBron James continues to craft off the court. Highly recommended for NBA fans and readers curious about the happenings behind the scenes." —*Library Journal*

Windsor, Edie

A Wild and Precious Life: A Memoir. Edie Windsor, with Joshua Lyon. St. Martin's Press 2019. xiii, 274 pages : Illustration; Color

ISBN 9781250195135

Grades: Adult   **B**

1. Windsor, Edie 2. Lesbians 3. Social advocates 4. LGBTQIA+ rights 5. Gay activists 6. Women computer programmers 7. Gay marriage 8. LGBTQIA+ people 9. Autobiographies and memoirs 10. Life stories — Identity — LGBTQIA+ 11. Life stories — Politics — Activists and reformers 12. History writing — LGBTQIA+ 13. Society and culture — LGBTQIA+

Edie Windsor became internationally famous when she sued the US government, seeking federal recognition for her marriage to Thea Spyer, her partner of more than four decades. The Supreme Court ruled in Edie's favor, a landmark victory that set the stage for full marriage equality in the US. Beloved by the LGBTQ community, Edie embraced her new role as an icon; she had already been living an extraordinary and groundbreaking life for decades.

ESSENTIAL AND RECOMMENDED TITLES
Biography

Winkler, Henry
★ *Being* Henry: The Fonz...and Beyond. Henry Winkler; written with James Kaplan. Celadon Books 2023. 320 p.
ISBN 9781250888099
Grades: Adult   B
1. Winkler, Henry, 1945- 2. Actors and actresses 3. Television producers and directors 4. Growing up 5. Children with dyslexia 6. Acting 7. Fame 8. Interpersonal relations 9. Wisdom 10. North American people 11. American people 12. Neurodivergent people 13. Autobiographies and memoirs 14. Life stories — Arts and culture — Performing arts — Actors and actresses 15. Life stories — Arts and culture — Performing arts — Directors and producers 16. Arts and Entertainment — Movies and Television
LC 2023025430

With profound heart, charm and self-deprecating humor, the Emmy award-winning actor, producer and director, who has endeared himself to a new generation, shares the disheartening truth of his childhood, the pressures of a role that takes on a life of its own and the path forward once your wildest dream seems behind you.

"With heartwarming honesty and self-deprecating humor, Emmy-winning actor, producer, and writer Winkler opens up about life after the role of a lifetime, his becoming a children's-book author, and his struggles with dyslexia in this charming memoir." —*Library Journal*

Winn, Raynor
★ *The Salt Path: A Memoir.* Raynor Winn. Penguin Books 2019. 272 p.
ISBN 9780143134114
Grades: Adult   B
1. Winn, Raynor 2. Homeless people 3. Husband and wife 4. Hikers 5. Rural life 6. Life change events 7. Wilderness survival 8. People with terminal illnesses 9. Great Britain 10. England 11. Autobiographies and memoirs 12. Life stories — Facing adversity — Personal transformation
LC 2018032887

Just days after Raynor learns that Moth, her husband of 32 years, is terminally ill, their home is taken away and they lose their livelihood. With nothing left and little time, they make the brave and impulsive decision to walk the 630 miles of the sea-swept South West Coast Path, from Somerset to Dorset, via Devon and Cornwall. The Salt Path is ultimately a portrayal of home—how it can be lost, rebuilt, and rediscovered in the most unexpected ways.

"Winn and her husband, Moth, worked hard to build a rural life in Wales. In a matter of weeks, it all unraveled....|A beautifully written and deeply satisfying read." —*Booklist*

First published in Great Britain by Michael Joseph, an imprint of Penguin Random House UK, 2018; Originally published in the UK, 2018.

The Wild Silence. Raynor Winn. Penguin Books 2021. 288 p.
ISBN 9780143136422
Grades: Adult   B
1. Winn, Raynor 2. Winn, Moth 3. Hikers 4. Terminal illness 5. People with terminal illnesses 6. Husband and wife 7. Adjustment 8. Voyages and travels 9. Cornwall, England 10. Iceland 11. Autobiographies and memoirs 12. Life stories — Relationships — Couples 13. Life stories — Facing adversity — Medical issues 14. Family and Relationships — Illness and the family
LC 2020045809

This follow-up to the Salt Path follows the difficulties faced by the author and her husband who is facing a terminal diagnosis after returning home from a 630 mile trek walking across the English coastline.

"British author Winn (The Salt Path) returns with a powerful memoir about overcoming life's obstacles.... This powerful narrative proves the resilience of the human spirit and stuns with its grace." —*Publishers Weekly*

Winter, Molly Roden
More: A Memoir of Open Marriage. Molly Roden Winter. Doubleday 2024. 304 p.
ISBN 9780385549455
Grades: Adult   B
1. Winter, Molly Roden 2. Love 3. Open marriage 4. Desire 5. Psychological growth 6. Sexuality 7. Motherhood 8. Self 9. Marriage 10. Sexual freedom 11. Autobiographies and memoirs 12. Society and culture — Sex and sexuality 13. Life stories — Relationships 14. Family and relationships — Dating and marriage 15. Nonfiction that reads like fiction

The author, in this unputdownable memoir of love, desire and personal growth, shares how she and her husband embarked on an unexpected open marriage, allowing her to explore her sexuality but causing her to grapple with her past and what it means to be both a mother and her truest self.

"Winter shares her and her husband's deeply personal, candid story about deciding to make their relationship non-monogamous...An honest look at how an open marriage can work, an excellent read for people interested in self-discovery or ethical non-monogamy." —*Library Journal*

Winters, Kathleen C.
Amelia Earhart: The Turbulent Life of an American Icon. Kathleen C. Winters. Palgrave Macmillan 2010. 256 p.
ISBN 9780230616691
Grades: 11 12 Adult   B
1. Earhart, Amelia, 1897-1937 2. Women pilots 3. Flight 4. Pilots 5. United States 6. Biographies 7. Science Writing — Space and Flight 8. Life stories — Science, technology, and medicine — Astronauts and pilots 9. Adult books for young adults
LC 2010020026

When Amelia Earhart disappeared over the Pacific in 1937, she was at the height of her fame. Fascination with Earhart remains just as strong today, as her mysterious disappearance continues to inspire speculation. In this nuanced and often surprising biography, acclaimed aviation historian Kathleen C. Winters moves beyond the caricature of the spunky, precocious pilot to offer a more complex portrait. Drawing on a wealth of contemporary accounts, airline records, and other original research, this book reveals a flawed heroine who was frequently reckless and lacked basic navigation skills, but who was also a canny manipulator of mass media. Winters details how Earhart and her husband, publisher George Putnam, worked to establish her as an international icon, even as other spectacular pilots went unnoticed. Sympathetic yet unsentimental, this biography helps us to see Amelia Earhart with fresh eyes.

Winters, Richard D.
Beyond Band of Brothers. Major Dick Winters with Colonel Cole C. Kingseed. Berkley Caliber 2006. xv, 304 p, 16 p. of plates : Illustration
ISBN 9780425208137
Grades: Adult   B
1. Winters, Richard D. 2. Western Front (World War II) 3. Leadership 4. Concentration camps 5. Courage 6. Military strategy 7. World War II 8. Military campaigns 9. Soldiers 10. Aerial operations 11. Europe 12. United States 13. Autobiographies and memoirs 14. Biographies 15. Life stories — Law and order — Armed forces personnel 16. History writing — Wars and conflicts — World War II — European Theater 17. Adult books for young adults
LC 2005048302

The commander of Easy Company provides a firsthand memoir of combat during World War II, describing the role of the "Band of Brothers" during the D-Day invasion, the march into Germany, and the liberation of an S.S. death camp.

Wizenberg, Molly
Fixed Stars. Molly Wizenberg. Abrams Books 2020. 256 pages
ISBN 9781419742996
Grades: Adult   B
1. Wizenberg, Molly 2. Questioning (Sexual or gender identity) 3. Coming out (Sexual or gender identity) 4. Married women 5. Women 6. Identity 7. Divorce 8. Life change events 9. Sexuality 10. Autobiographies and memoirs 11. Life stories — Identity — LGBTQIA+ 12. Family and Relationships — LGBTQIA+
LC Bl2020018888

A best-selling memoirist describes how, as a married woman with a toddler, she found herself drawn to a female attorney during jury duty and began to question her identity and desires and let go of ideals that no longer fit.

PUBLIC LIBRARY CORE COLLECTION: NONFICTION
Twentieth Edition

"An essential addition that will resonate with fans of Wizenberg's earlier memoirs and anyone probing the complicated ways that sexuality and traditional family life overlap or diverge." —*Library Journal*

Wojczuk, Tana
Lady Romeo: The Radical and Revolutionary Life of Charlotte Cushman, America's First Celebrity. Tana Wojczuk. Avid Reader Press, an imprint of Simon & Schuster, Inc. 2020. VIII, 226 pages : Illustration
ISBN 9781501199523
Grades: Adult   B
1. Cushman, Charlotte, 1816-1876 2. Gender role 3. Lesbians 4. Social norms 5. Theater 6. Actors and actresses 7. LGBTQIA+ people 8. United States 9. 19th century 10. Biographies 11. Life stories — Identity — LGBTQIA+ 12. Arts and Entertainment — Theater 13. Life stories — Arts and culture — Performing arts — Actors and actresses
LC Bl2020014811

A portrait of the less-remembered 19th-century queer actress draws on rare correspondence to trace the radical formative years, glittering performances and professional affiliations that shaped the cultural landscapes of 19th-century New York City.

"This enthralling history restores Cushman to her rightful place in the spotlight." —*Publishers Weekly*

Includes bibliographical references (pages 211-216) and index.

Wolf, Brandon J.
A Place for Us: a Memoir. Brandon J. Wolf. Little a 2023. 222 p.
ISBN 9781542036467
Grades: Adult   B
1. Wolf, Brandon J. 2. Self-discovery 3. Identity 4. LGBTQIA+ people 5. Loss 6. Social advocates 7. Love 8. Resilience 9. Multiracial people 10. Genderqueer people 11. Social justice 12. Communities 13. Autobiographies and memoirs 14. Life stories — Identity — LGBTQIA+ 15. Life stories — Facing adversity

"Public speaker/activist Wolf, who survived the 2016 horrific massacre at the Pulse nightclub in Orlando, FL, shares his coming-of-age story." —*Library Journal*

Wolfe, Charles K.
★ *The Life and Legend of Leadbelly.* Charles Wolfe and Kip Lornell. Harper Collins Publishers 1992. xv, 333 p. : Illustration
ISBN 9780060168629
Grades: Adult   B
1. Leadbelly, 1885-1949 2. Blues musicians 3. Biographies 4. Arts and Entertainment — Music — Jazz and the Blues 5. Life stories — Arts and culture — Performing arts — Musicians and composers
LC 92052606

A biography of the legendary folk and blues singer discusses his influences, his close relationships with folk greats Woody Guthrie and Pete Seeger, and his involvement in left-wing politics and the labor movement.

"Drawing on a variety of primary and secondary sources, including numerous interviews, Wolfe and Lornell attempt to separate fact from fiction. Photographs, informative notes, and a full discography are valuable additions." —*Choice*

Includes bibliographical references (p. 267-287) and index; Discography: P. 289-322.

Wolff, Christoph
Johann Sebastian Bach: The Learned Musician. Christoph Wolff. W.W. Norton 2001. xvii, 599 p. : Illustration; Map
ISBN 9780393322569
Grades: Adult   B
1. Bach, Johann Sebastian, 1685-1750 2. Composers 3. Biographies 4. Arts and Entertainment — Music — Classical 5. Life stories — Arts and culture — Performing arts — Musicians and composers
LC BL2001010688

Pulitzer Prize for Biography or Autobiography finalist.

Chronicles the life, work, and legacy of the inventive musician, composer, performer, scholar, and teacher.

"This work is likely to be the standard one-volume Bach biography for some time to come. It is a solid, richly informative treatment, presenting the copious details of Bach's life in a coherent, readable narrative." —*New York Review of Books*

Reprint. Originally published: 2000; Includes bibliographical references (p. [545]-554) and indexes.

Wolff, Tobias
This Boy's Life: A Memoir. Tobias Wolff. Atlantic Monthly Press 1989. 288 p.
ISBN 9780802136688
Grades: 11 12 Adult   B
1. Wolff, Tobias, 1945- 2. Growing up 3. Family violence 4. Stepfathers 5. Mothers and sons 6. Authors, American 7. Violence 8. Washington (State) 9. 20th century 10. Autobiographies and memoirs 11. Page to screen 12. Family and Relationships — Growing up 13. Family and Relationships — Abuse 14. Life stories — Facing adversity — Abuse survivors
LC 88017600

Los Angeles Times Book Prize for Biography, 1989; National Book Critics Circle Award for Biography finalist, 1989.

The author chronicles the tumultuous events of his early life, discussing his parents' divorce, the nomadic wanderings with his mother that followed, and the strange and eventful process of growing up.

"The novelist and short story writer offers an engrossing and candid look into his childhood and adolescence in his first book of nonfiction. In unaffected prose he recreates scenes from his life that sparkle with the immediacy of narrative fiction. The result is an intriguingly guileless book, distinct from the usual reflective commentary of autobiography." —*Library Journal*

Womack, John
Zapata and the Mexican Revolution. John Womack, Jr. Knopf 1969. xi, 435, xxi p. Illustration; Portrait
ISBN 9780394708539
Grades: Adult   B
1. Zapata, Emiliano, 1879-1919 2. Revolutionaries 3. Mexican history 4. Mexico 5. Life stories — People in history 6. History writing — Latin America — Mexico
LC 68023947

A biography of the Mexican patriot who organized and led his rural community in resistance to the central government.
Bibliography: P. 413-435.

Wong, Ali
★ *Dear Girls: Intimate Tales, Untold Secrets, and Advice for Living Your Best Life.* Ali Wong. Random House 2019. 224 p.
ISBN 9780525508830
Grades: Adult   B
1. Wong, Ali 2. Women comedians 3. Television writers 4. Mothers and daughters 5. Parent and child 6. Personal conduct 7. Asian American women 8. Actors and actresses 9. Comedians 10. United States 11. Letters 12. Autobiographies and memoirs 13. Biographies 14. Life stories — Arts and culture — Performing arts — Entertainers and celebrities 15. Life stories — Relationships — Parent and child 16. Family and Relationships — Parenting 17. Humor writing — Family and relationship humor 18. Adult books for young adults
LC 2019022835

Goodreads Choice Award, 2019.

In her hit Netflix comedy special Baby Cobra, an eight-month pregnant Ali Wong resonated so heavily that she became a popular Halloween costume. Wong told the world her remarkably unfiltered thoughts on marriage, sex, Asian culture, working women, and why you never see new mom comics on stage but you sure see plenty of new dads. The sharp insights and humor are even more personal in this completely original collection. She shares the wisdom she's learned from a life in comedy and reveals stories from her life off stage, including the brutal singles life in New York (i.e. the inevitable confrontation with erectile dysfunction), reconnecting with her roots (and drinking snake blood) in Viet-

ESSENTIAL AND RECOMMENDED TITLES
Biography

nam, tales of being a wild child growing up in San Francisco, and parenting war stories. Though addressed to her daughters, Ali Wong's letters are absurdly funny, surprisingly moving, and enlightening (and disgusting) for all.

"Wong brings the same dedication here, where mistakes inspire wisecracking wisdom. A down-to-earth collection that is raw but not irreverent." —*Kirkus*

Wong, Alice
★ *Year of the Tiger: An Activist's Life.* Alice Wong. Vintage Books 2022. 352 p.
ISBN 9780593315392
Grades: Adult   B
1. Wong, Alice, 1974- 2. Asian Americans 3. People with disabilities 4. Community organizers 5. Social advocates 6. Ableism 7. Asian American women 8. Disabilities 9. Muscular dystrophy 10. Essays 11. Autobiographies and memoirs 12. Life stories — Politics — Activists and reformers 13. Life stories — Facing adversity — Medical issues — Living with disabilities

Asian Pacific American Award for Literature: Adult Nonfiction, 2024.

Drawing on a collection of original essays, previously published work, conversations, graphics, photos, commissioned art by disabled and Asian American artists, and more, the author uses her unique talent to share an impressionistic scrapbook of her life as an Asian American disabled activist, community organizer, media maker, and dreamer.

"The prominent community organizer and founder of the Disability Visibility Project strikes again with an imaginative and insightful memoir about her journey as an activist and her continued fight to dismantle systemic ableism....An essential read for anyone with an interest in accessible futures, community building, and social justice." —*Library Journal*

Wong, Carmen Rita
Why Didn't You Tell Me?: A Memoir. Carmen Rita Wong. Crown 2022. 272 p.
ISBN 9780593240250
Grades: Adult   B
1. Wong, Carmen Rita 2. Authors, American 3. Women television personalities 4. Internet personalities 5. Identity 6. Multiracial women 7. Family secrets 8. Children of immigrants 9. Family relationships 10. Secrets 11. Race (Social sciences) 12. Belonging 13. 20th century 14. Autobiographies and memoirs 15. Life stories — Identity 16. Life stories — Relationships — Family 17. Family and Relationships — Families

LC 2021054234

When her immigrant mother's long-held secrets are revealed, bring clarity to so much of her life, the author, after her mother passes away, searches to understand who she really is, in this story of race and culture in America and how they shape who we think we are.

"In this propulsive account from former CNBC host Wong (Never Too Late), a life built on secrets unfolds to reveal a suspenseful story about race, family, and identity." —*Publishers Weekly*

Wong, Jane
★ *Meet Me Tonight in Atlantic City: A Memoir.* Jane Wong. Tin House 2023. 304 p.
ISBN 9781953534675
Grades: Adult   B
1. Wong, Jane 2. Chinese American women 3. Chinese Americans 4. Women poets 5. Childhood 6. Identity 7. Families 8. Poets 9. Atlantic City, New Jersey 10. Seattle, Washington 11. Autobiographies and memoirs 12. Life stories — Identity — Race and ethnicity 13. Life stories — Relationships — Family

LC 2022060779

Filled with beauty found in unexpected places, Meet Me Tonight in Atlantic City is a resounding love song of the Asian American working class, a portrait of how we become who we are, and a story of lyric wisdom to hold and to share.

"With a poet's ear for language and a satirist's eye for human foibles, Wong masterfully marries her personal story with larger questions about Chinese American identity." —*Publishers Weekly*

Includes bibliographical references.

Woodfox, Albert
Solitary: Unbroken by Four Decades in Solitary Confinement. My Story of Transformation and Hope. Albert Woodfox. Grove Press 2019. 320 p.
ISBN 9780802129086
Grades: Adult   B
1. Woodfox, Albert 2. Solitary confinement 3. False imprisonment 4. Judicial error 5. Racism 6. Criminal justice system 7. Innocence (Law) 8. African American prisoners 9. Prisoners 10. Louisiana 11. Autobiographies and memoirs 12. Society and culture — Violence and crime — Criminal justice system 13. Life stories — Law and order — Prisoners and inmates 14. True Crime — General

LC 2018045958

Hurston/Wright Legacy Award: Nonfiction, 2020; in the Margins Book Awards: Advocacy and Social Justice, 2020; New York Times Notable Book, 2019; Pulitzer Prize for General Nonfiction finalist, 2020; National Book Award for Nonfiction finalist, 2019.

Chronicles the author's extraordinary achievements as an activist during and after spending 40 years in solitary confinement for a crime he did not commit, describing how he has committed his post-exoneration life to prison reform.

"Woodfoxs shocking memoir of his years in prison, mostly under solitary confinement, is a testament to the human spirit and a scathing indictment of the justice system." —*Booklist*

Woodress, James Leslie
Willa Cather: A Literary Life. James Woodress. University of Nebraska Press 1989. xx, 583 p. : Illustration
ISBN 9780803297081
Grades: Adult   B
1. Cather, Willa, 1873-1947 2. Authors, American 3. 20th century 4. Arts and Entertainment — Writing and Publishing — Literary criticism

LC Bl2005010011

Drawing on letters, interviews, speeches, and reminiscences, looks at the life and career of the American novelist.

Reprint. Originally published: 1987; Bison books—Spine; Includes bibliographical references (p. [507]-562) and index.

Woods, Tiger
The 1997 Masters: My Story. Tiger Woods, with Lorne Rubenstein. Grand Central Pub. 2017. 256 p.
ISBN 9781455543588
Grades: Adult   B
1. Woods, Tiger 2. Professional golfers 3. Golf 4. Tournaments 5. Autobiographies and memoirs 6. Sports and Competition — Golf 7. Life stories — Sports — Athletes

LC Bl2017002359

Published to coincide with the 20th anniversary of Tiger Woods' historic win at the 1997 Masters, an account of the pro golfer's historic career shares previously unknown stories and the ways his record-setting win changed both the sport and his life on and off the course.

"An in-depth, inside look at the legendary golfer's historic 1997 Masters win." —*Kirkus*

Woodward, Bob
The Final Days. Bob Woodward, Carl Bernstein. Simon and Schuster Paperbacks 2005. 470 p. : Illustration
ISBN 9780743274067
Grades: 11 12 Adult   B
1. Nixon, Richard M. (Richard Milhous), 1913-1994 2. Political corruption 3. Watergate Scandal 4. Government cover-ups 5. Politicians 6. Presidents 7. Politics and government 8. United States history 9. United States 10. 1970s 11. 20th century 12. History writing — Presidency — 20th century — United States 13. History writing — Presidency — United States 14. History writing — 1970s — United States

LC 2005282821

The Washington Post reporters draw on interviews, leaks, and investigations to reconstruct the events and circumstances, in and outside the White House, during the unsettled and unsettling final weeks of the Nixon administration.
Includes index.

Woolever, Laurie
Bourdain: The Definitive Oral Biography. Laurie Woolever. Ecco Press 2021. 384 p.
ISBN 9780062909107
Grades: Adult **B**
1. Bourdain, Anthony 1956-2018 2. Television cooking shows 3. Cooks 4. Authors 5. Celebrities 6. Television personalities 7. Fame 8. Food habits 9. Interpersonal relations 10. Memories 11. Biographies 12. Oral histories 13. Life stories — Arts and culture — Culinary arts 14. Life stories — Arts and culture — Performing arts — Entertainers and celebrities 15. Food writing — Memoirs and biographies

When Anthony Bourdain died in June 2018, fans around the globe came together to celebrate the life of a man who dedicated his life to traveling nearly everywhere (and eating nearly everything), shedding light on the lives and stories of others. Laurie Woolever, Bourdain's longtime assistant and confidante, interviewed nearly a hundred of the people who shared Tony's orbit—from members of his kitchen crews to his writing, publishing, and television partners, to his daughter and his closest friends—in order to piece together a remarkably full, vivid, and nuanced vision of Tony's life and work.

"Celebrated chef and author Anthony Bourdain (1956-2018) cuts a charismatic yet enigmatic figure in this kaleidoscopic oral history.... This fascinating mosaic doesn't unearth Bourdain's inner demons, but it does capture the inimitable legacy he left behind." —*Publishers Weekly*

Woolf, Virginia
Moments of Being. Virginia Woolf; edited, with an introduction and notes, by Jeanne Schulkind. Grafton Books 1989. 249 p.
ISBN 9780586073261
Grades: Adult **B**
1. Woolf, Virginia, 1882-1941 2. Women authors, British 3. Authors, English 4. 20th century 5. Autobiographies and memoirs 6. Biographies 7. Arts and Entertainment — Writing and Publishing 8. Life stories — Arts and culture — Writing — Authors

LC 91111059

Six autobiographical pieces that span her entire career reveal the underlying unity of Woolf's art, thought, and sensibility and the unusual degree to which she integrated personal experiences within her fiction.
Includes bibliographical references and index; Originally published: London : Chatto and Windus, 1976.

Woolley, Benjamin
The King's Assassin: The Secret Plot to Murder King James I. Benjamin Woolley. St Martins Pr 2018. 368 p.
ISBN 9781250125033
Grades: Adult **B**
1. James I, King of England, 1566-1625 2. Assassination plots 3. Favorites, Royal 4. Death of rulers 5. Murder 6. Princes 7. Malaria 8. Poisoning 9. Assassination 10. British history 11. 17th century 12. Stuart period (1603-1714) 13. Page to screen 14. History writing — Europe — United Kingdom

LC 2018006541

The author of the Queen's Conjurer draws on new historical scholarship to validate centuries of theories that James I may have been murdered by his gentleman of the royal bedchamber and lover, George Villiers.

"Woolley presents an engrossing portrait of an ambitious man trusted by two kings that both casual readers and Stuart history fans can enjoy." —*Publishers Weekly*

Adapted into the miniseries Mary & George airing on STARZ in 2023.

Worsley, Lucy
★ *Agatha Christie: An Elusive Woman.* Lucy Worsley. Pegasus Crime 2022. 432 p.
ISBN 9781639362523
Grades: Adult **B**
1. Christie, Agatha, 1890-1976 2. Women authors 3. Authors 4. Mystery writing 5. Homemakers 6. 20th century 7. Biographies 8. Life stories — Arts and culture — Writing — Authors 9. Arts and Entertainment — Writing and publishing

A new, fascinating account of the life of Agatha Christie from celebrated literary and cultural historian Lucy Worsley.

"Drawing on personal letters and modern criticism, Worsley manages to make her subject feel fresh and new." —*Publishers Weekly*

Queen Victoria: Twenty-four Days That Changed Her Life. Lucy Worsley. St. Martin's Press 2019. 288 p.
ISBN 9781250201423
Grades: Adult **B**
1. Victoria, Queen of Great Britain, 1819-1901 2. Gender role 3. Monarchy 4. Rulers 5. Motherhood 6. Husband and wife 7. Family relationships 8. Women 9. Women rulers 10. British history 11. Great Britain 12. Victorian era (1837-1901) 13. Biographies 14. Life stories — Politics — Royalty 15. History writing — Europe — United Kingdom

LC 2018039820

The BBC historian presenter and best-selling author of Courtiers explores the life and myriad roles of Queen Victoria as they reflected her defiance of gender conventions and defining position in a time of extraordinary change and political resistance.

"Fans of biography and history, especially related to British history should find this fascinating reading. Those interested in Queen Victoria will find this to be a wonderful addition to the literature." —*Library Journal*

Includes bibliographical references and index.

Worster, Donald
A Passion for Nature; the Life of John Muir. Donald Worster. Oxford University Press 2008. 528 p.
ISBN 9780195166828
Grades: Adult **B**
1. Muir, John, 1838-1914 2. Naturalists 3. Environmentalists 4. Nature 5. Environmentalism 6. Biographies 7. Nature Writing — General 8. Life stories — Nature and outdoors 9. Life stories — Politics — Activists and reformers 10. Adult books for young adults

LC 2008001441

A definitive biography traces the life of John Muir from his boyhood in Scotland up to his death on the eve of World War I and offers important insights into the passionate nature of America's first great conservationist and founder of the Sierra Club.

"The author draws on John Muir's (1838-1914) correspondence and writings to offer an enlightening biography of the influential naturalist. Competently documented, this all-inclusive biography explains the life and times of a figure known to all who love nature and will appeal to general readers and anyone interested in the early roots of today's green movement and its founding fathers." —*Library Journal*

Includes bibliographical references.

Wright, Jennifer Ashley
★ *Madame Restell: The Life, Death, and Resurrection of Old New York's Most Fabulous, Fearless, and Infamous Abortionist.* by Jennifer Wright. Hachette Books 2023. 320 p.
ISBN 9780306826795
Grades: Adult **B**
1. Restell, Madame, 1811-1878 2. Abortion providers 3. Abortion 4. Immigrants 5. Women 6. Women medical personnel 7. Medical care 8. Birth control 9. Reproductive rights 10. Nonprescription drugs 11. Trials (Abortion) 12. New York city 13. New York state 14. 19th century 15. Gilded Age (1865-1898) 16. History Writing — Women's history 17. Life stories — Identity — Gender 18. Life stories — People in history

LC 2022032437

ESSENTIAL AND RECOMMENDED TITLES
Biography

The story of Madame Restell, a glamorous Manhattan socialite who used her vast resources to provide healthcare to women, despite the efforts of male doctors to reduce the role of women in medicine.

"A fresh contribution to women's history." —*Kirkus*

Includes bibliographical references and index.

Wright, Richard

★ *Black Boy: (American Hunger) : A Record of Childhood and Youth.* Richard Wright; foreword by Edward P. Jones. Harper Collins Publishers 2005. x, 419 p.

ISBN 9780060834005

Grades: 11 12 Adult   B

1. Wright, Richard, 1908-1960 2. African Americans 3. African American authors 4. Racism 5. Authors, American 6. Literary landmarks 7. Mississippi 8. 20th century 9. Autobiographies and memoirs 10. Biographies 11. Life stories — Arts and culture — Writing — Authors 12. Adult books for young adults 13. History writing — African American — Civil rights — United States

LC 2005052698

Traces the author's coming of age in the Jim Crow-era South, a period during which he struggled to survive while journeying from innocence to adulthood.

The restored text established by the Library of America; Includes bibliographical references (p. [409]-419); Originally published: New York : Harper & Brothers, 1945.

Wu, Constance

Making a Scene. Constance Wu. Scribner 2022. 320 p.

ISBN 9781982188542

Grades: Adult   B

1. Wu, Constance, 1982- 2. Actors and actresses 3. Asian American women 4. Growing up 5. Acting 6. Self-acceptance 7. Childhood 8. Sexual violence 9. Identity 10. Success (Concept) 11. Families 12. Autobiographies and memoirs 13. Life stories — Arts and culture — Performing arts — Actors and actresses 14. Arts and Entertainment — Movies and television

The star of Crazy Rich Asians delivers her memoir in a series of essays.

"Wu dazzles in this essay collection about love, family, and her hard-won path to Hollywood success...her determination radiates from every page." —*Publishers Weekly*

"Award-winning actress Wu (Crazy Rich Asians) is refreshingly honest in this look back at the most formative moments of her life, with each chapter acting as a stand-alone, deeply personal essay." —*Library Journal*

Wulf, Andrea

The Invention of Nature: Alexander Von Humboldt's New World. by Andrea Wulf. Alfred A. Knopf 2015. 480 p.

ISBN 9780385350662

Grades: Adult   B

1. Humboldt, Alexander von, 1769-1859 2. Scientists 3. Naturalists 4. Exploration 5. Nature 6. Conservation of natural resources 7. Biographies 8. Life stories — Science, technology, and medicine — Scientists and inventors 9. Nature Writing — General

LC 2015017505

Booklist Editors' Choice, 2015; Costa Biography Award, 2015; Los Angeles Times Book Prize for Science and Technology, 2015; New York Times Notable Book, 2015; Royal Society General Prizes for Science Books, 2016; Andrew Carnegie Medal for Excellence in Non-Fiction Finalist, 2016; Cundill Prize in Historical Literature finalist, 2016; Kirkus Prize for Nonfiction finalist, 2015.

A portrait of the lesser-known German naturalist reveals his ongoing influence on humanity's relationship with the natural world today, discussing such topics as his views on climate change, conservation and nature as a resource for all life. By the author of Founding Gardeners.

"Wulf presents with zest and eloquence the full story of Humboldt's adventurous life and extraordinary achievements, from making science 'Accessible and popular' to his early warnings about how deforestation, monoculture agriculture, and industrialization would engender disastrous climate change." —*Booklist*

THIS IS A BORZOI BOOK—T.P. verso; Includes bibliographical references and index.

Wullschlager, Jackie

★ *Chagall: A Biography.* by Jackie Wullschlager. Alfred A. Knopf 2008. 608 p.

ISBN 9780375414558

Grades: 11 12 Adult   B

1. Chagall, Marc, 1887-1985 2. Artists 3. Art 4. Painters 5. Painting 6. Social life and customs 7. Russia 8. Biographies 9. Arts and Entertainment — Painting, Drawing, and Sculpture 10. Life stories — Arts and culture — Artists 11. Adult books for young adults

LC 2008006162

Shortlisted for the James Tait Black Memorial Prize for Biography, 2008.

An insightful portrait of the Russian-born modernist artist describes his stunning studies of the lost world of Eastern European Jewry in his paintings of the shtetl life of his childhood, his pioneering role in twentieth-century art, his colorful personal life, and his lasting artistic legacy, in a study highlighted by more than forty reproductions of important paintings.

Wynn-Grant, Rae

Wild Life: Finding My Purpose in an Untamed World. Dr. Rae Wynn-Grant. Get Lifted Books 2024. 336 p.

ISBN 9781638930402

Grades: Adult   B

1. Wynn-Grant, Rae 2. Women ecologists 3. African American women 4. Nature 5. Ecology 6. Wildlife conservation 7. Effect of humans on nature 8. Environmental degradation 9. Human-animal relationships 10. Voyages and travels 11. American people 12. Autobiographies and memoirs 13. Life stories — Science, technology, and medicine — Scientists and inventors 14. Life stories — Nature and outdoors 15. Life stories — Identity 16. Nature Writing — General

In a vulnerable and urgent memoir, the author explores the ever-shifting relationship between humans, animals and the earth through her personal journey to becoming a wildlife ecologist.

"This isn't simply a nature book or memoir, but a memorable marriage of the two that will leave readers inspired." —*Kirkus*

Yancey, Philip

★ *Where the Light Fell: A Memoir.* Philip Yancey. Convergent 2021. 304 p.

ISBN 9780593238509

Grades: Adult   B

1. Yancey, Philip 2. Christians 3. Authors 4. Growing up 5. Postwar life 6. Poor families 7. Christian families 8. Fundamentalism 9. Extremism 10. Mothers and sons 11. Brothers 12. Family secrets 13. Racism 14. Psychic trauma 15. Social change 16. Christian life 17. Self-discovery 18. Autobiographies and memoirs 19. Life stories — Religion and spirituality — Spiritual journeys 20. Life stories — Relationships — Family 21. Spirituality and Religion — Christianity

LC 2021012926

One of today's most celebrated Christian writers recounts his strict fundamentalist upbringing and gives testament to the enduring power of our search for truth and the possibility of faith rooted in grace instead of fear.

"Christian writer Yancey (What's so Amazing About Grace?) excavates his roots in the fundamentalist South in the 1950s and '60s in this gripping memoir... Yancey's eloquent descriptions of coming to faith and his exacting self-examination make this a standout." —*Publishers Weekly*

Young, Damon

★ *What Doesn't Kill You Makes You Blacker: A Memoir in Essays.* Damon Young. Ecco Press. 2019. 320 p.

ISBN 9780062684301

Grades: Adult   B

1. Young, Damon, 1978- 2. African Americans 3. Identity 4. Growing up 5. Racism 6. Race relations 7. Pittsburgh, Pennsylvania 8. United States 9. Autobiographies and memoirs 10. Essays 11. Society and culture — Race 12. Life stories — Identity — Race and ethnicity 13. Antiracist literature

LC BI2019000961

Thurber Prize for American Humor, 2020.

The co-founder of VerySmartBrothas.Com presents a provocative and humorous memoir-in-essays that explores the direct impact of racism on his life, the shifting definition of Black male identity and the ongoing realities of white supremacy.

"Young uses pop culture references and personal stories to look at a life molded by structural racism, the joy of having a family that holds together in a crisis, and the thrill of succeeding against difficult odds. Youngs charm and wit make these essays a pleasure to read; his candid approach makes them memorable." —*Publishers Weekly*

Young, Daniella Mestyanek

Uncultured: A Memoir. Daniella Mestyanek Young, with Brandi Larsen. St. Martin's Press 2022. 352 p.

ISBN 9781250280114

Grades: Adult B

1. Mestyanek Young, Daniella 2. Cults 3. Cult members 4. Growing up 5. Escapes 6. Military recruiting and enlistment 7. Women intelligence officers 8. Social psychology 9. Group identity 10. Marginalized women 11. Autobiographies and memoirs 12. Life stories — Religion and spirituality — Leaving religion 13. Life stories — Facing adversity — Abuse survivors 14. Life stories — Personal growth 15. Debut title

LC 2022014463

In this unforgettable memoir, the author recounts her escape from the religious cult the Children of God, and how she worked her way up to become a military intelligence officer, soon discovering her new world is remarkably similar to the one she desperately tried to leave behind.

"Mestyanek Young's page-turning debut details her escape from the Children of God religious cult and her disillusionment after joining the U.S. Army." —*Publishers Weekly*

Young, Neil

Waging Heavy Peace: A Hippie Dream. Neil Young. Blue Rider Press 2012. 416 p.

ISBN 9780399159466

Grades: Adult B

1. Young, Neil, 1945- 2. Rock music 3. Musicians 4. Rock musicians 5. Autobiographies and memoirs 6. Canadian literature 7. Biographies 8. Arts and Entertainment — Music — Rock 9. Life stories — Arts and culture — Performing arts — Musicians and composers

LC 2012026138

The two-time Rock and Roll Hall of Fame inductee presents the story of his career against a backdrop of forty years of history, discussing such topics as his collaborations with fellow artists, his creative process, and his activist work with Farm Aid and the Bridge School.

Young, Steve

QB: My Life Behind the Spiral. Steve Young with Jeff Benedict. Houghton Mifflin Harcourt 2016. 416 p.

ISBN 9780544845763

Grades: Adult B

1. Young, Steve, 1961- 2. Football players 3. Quarterbacks (Football) 4. Football 5. Mormons 6. Autobiographies and memoirs 7. Life stories — Sports — Athletes 8. Sports and competition — Football

LC 2016024863

A memoir by the NFL Hall of Famer shares insights into what it takes to become an elite professional quarterback, describing his unlikely rise in sports as a devout Mormon and high-achieving student with an eidetic memory, the media pressure, his infamous confrontation with Joe Montana and the other factors that challenged his career.

Includes index.

Yousafzai, Malala

I Am Malala : The Story of the Girl Who Stood up for Education and Was Shot by the Taliban. Malala Yousafzai with Christina Lamb. Little, Brown, & Co. 2013. VIII, 327 pages, 16 unnumbered pages of plates

ISBN 9780316322409

Grades: 9 10 11 12 Adult B

1. Yousafzai, Malala, 1997- 2. Girls 3. Children's rights 4. Victims of crimes 5. Women's rights 6. Life change events 7. Teenage girls 8. Courage 9. Determination 10. Girls' schools 11. Education 12. Pakistan 13. Autobiographies and memoirs 14. Life stories — Facing adversity — Victims of crime — Terrorism 15. Society and culture — Education 16. Society and culture — Gender — Women

Amelia Bloomer List, 2014; Goodreads Choice Award, 2013; Library Journal Best Books, 2013.

Describes the life of a young Pakistani student who advocated for women's rights and education in the Taliban-controlled Swat Valley who survived an assassination attempt and became the youngest nominee for the Nobel Peace Prize.

Yousafzai, Ziauddin

Let Her Fly: A Father's Journey. Ziauddin Yousafzai with Louise Carpenter; foreword by Malala Yousafzai. Little, Brown and Company 2018. 144 p.

ISBN 9780316450508

Grades: Adult B

1. Yousafzai, Ziauddin 2. Yousafzai, Malala, 1997- 3. Political activists 4. Educators 5. Fathers and daughters 6. Social reformers 7. Gender role 8. Girls 9. Women's rights 10. Education 11. Autobiographies and memoirs 12. Society and culture — Gender 13. Life stories — Politics — Activists and reformers 14. Society and culture — Education 15. Life stories — Education — Scholars and educators 16. Family and Relationships — Families 17. Life stories — Facing adversity

LC Bl2018183646

The father of Malala Yousafzai traces his journey from an unconfident, stammering little boy living in a mud hut in Pakistan to a man who has broken with tradition and proven there are many faces of feminism.

"Yousafzai isn't just a Pakistani diplomat, educator, educational activist, and human rights campaigner; he's also the father of Nobel laureate Malala Yousafzai. Here he explains what he has learned from his daughter." —*Library Journal*

Ypi, Lea

★ *Free: A Child and a Country at the End of History.* Lea Ypi. W.W. Norton & Company 2022. 256 p.

ISBN 9780393867732

Grades: Adult B

1. Ypi, Lea, 1979- 2. Political scientists 3. Growing up 4. Communism 5. Post-communism 6. Socialism 7. Freedom 8. Political stability 9. Civil war 10. Social change 11. Political persecution 12. Family secrets 13. Disappeared people 14. Identity 15. Immigration and emigration 16. Albania 17. 20th century 18. Autobiographies and memoirs 19. Life stories — Relationships — Growing up 20. Life stories — Facing adversity — War and oppression 21. History writing — Europe — Eastern Europe 22. History writing — Cold War

LC 2021033437

RSL Ondaatje Prize, 2022.

Lea Ypi grew up in the last Stalinist country in Europe: Albania, a place of queuing and scarcity, of political executions and secret police. Then the statues of Stalin and Hoxha were toppled, people could vote and worship freely, and invest in hopes of striking it rich. But factories shut, jobs disappeared and thousands fled to Italy, only to be sent back. Pyramid schemes bankrupted the country, leading to violence. One generation's dreams became another's disillusionment. As her own family's secrets were revealed, Lea found herself questioning what "freedom" really means.

"In this vivid memoir, political commentator Lea Ypi recalls her adolescence during the complete social upheaval in Albania in the late 1980s and early 1990s. . . . Ypi's experiences and perspective are invaluable, especially for politically minded readers dreaming up the future." —*Booklist*

Originally published in the UK with the title Free: Coming of age at the end of history by Allen Lane, London, in 2021.

Zack, Ian

Odetta: A Life in Music and Protest. Ian Zack. Beacon Press 2020. 276 pages

ISBN 9780807035320

Grades: Adult B

ESSENTIAL AND RECOMMENDED TITLES
Biography

1. Odetta, 1930-2008 2. African American women singers 3. Civil Rights Movement 4. Folk singers 5. Racism 6. Sexism 7. African American women 8. Women singers 9. United States 10. Biographies 11. Life stories — Identity — Race and ethnicity 12. Life stories — Arts and culture — Performing arts — Musicians and composers 13. Life stories — Politics — Activists and reformers — Civil rights leaders 14. History writing — African American — Civil rights — United States 15. Arts and entertainment — Music — Folk

LC 2019056298

The untold story of the woman whose music and afro inspired a generation, whose voice provided a soundtrack for the unfolding civil rights movement of the 1950s and '60s.

"A much-needed biography of a crucial American artist and activist." —*Booklist*

Includes bibliographical references and index.

Zambone, Albert Louis
Daniel Morgan: A Revolutionary Life. Albert Louis Zambone. Westholme Publishing 2018. 376 p.
ISBN 9781594163159
Grades: Adult **B**

1. Morgan, Daniel, 1736-1802 2. Generals 3. Command of troops 4. American Revolution, 1775-1783 5. Military history 6. United States history 7. 18th century 8. Revolutionary America (1775-1783) 9. Biographies 10. Media tie-ins 11. History writing — Wars and conflicts — Revolutionary War (America) 12. Life stories — Law and order — Military leaders 13. History writing — Military — Military leadership

LC 2020275151

A Major New Biography of a Man of Humble Origins Who Became One of the Great Military Leaders of the American Revolution. In Daniel Morgan: A Revolutionary Life, the first biography of this iconic figure in forty years, historian Albert Louis Zambone presents Morgan as the quintessential American everyman, who rose through his own dogged determination from poverty and obscurity to become one of the great battlefield commanders in American history.

"Zambone is careful to avoid speculating on gaps in the record and diligently reviews primary documents, such as store ledgers listing quotidian purchases. The resulta look at a consequential but now-obscure figure who came from, as Zambone puts it, the often-silent ranks of the colonial poorwill fascinate readers." —*Publishers Weekly*

Based on a podcast; Includes bibliographical references and index.

Zambreno, Kate
The Light Room: On Art and Care. Kate Zambreno. Riverhead 2023. 272 p.
ISBN 9780593421062
Grades: Adult **B**

1. Zambreno, Kate 2. Motherhood 3. Epidemics 4. Caretakers 5. Happiness 6. Children 7. COVID-19 Pandemic, 2020- 8. Art 9. Social isolation 10. Fear 11. Loss 12. Uncertainty 13. Autobiographies and memoirs 14. Life stories — Facing adversity 15. Life stories — Relationships — Parent and child

LC 2023000937

Moving through the seasons, this profound and affecting account of caretaking in a time of uncertainty and loss captures the isolation and exhaustion of a mother being home with a baby and a small child, but also small and transcendent moments of beauty and joy.

"In this poignant memoir, novelist and critic Zambreno (How to Write as If Already Dead) reflects on caring for her two young children during the early days of the COVID-19 pandemic." —*Publishers Weekly*

Zamora, Javier
★ *Solito: A Memoir.* Javier Zamora. Hogarth Press 2022. 400 p.
ISBN 9780593498064
Grades: Adult **B**

1. Zamora, Javier 2. Salvadoran Americans 3. Refugees, Salvadoran 4. Civil war 5. Nine-year-old boys 6. Voyages and travels 7. Separated friends, relatives, etc. 8. Border security 9. Fear 10. Despair 11. Kindness 12. Unaccompanied immigrant children 13. Immigrant families 14. Immigration and emigration 15. El Salvador 16. United States 17. Autobiographies and memoirs 18. Life stories — Identity — Immigrants 19. Book club best bets 20. Life stories — Facing adversity — War and oppression — Refugees 21. Society and culture — Immigration 22. Adult books for young adults

Alex Awards, 2023; Los Angeles Times Book Prizes, Christopher Isherwood Prize for Autobiographical Prose, 2022.

A young poet reflects on his 3,000-mile journey from El Salvador to the United States when he was nine years old, during which he was faced with perilous boat trips, relentless desert treks, pointed guns, arrests and deceptions during two life-altering months alongside a group of strangers who became an unexpected family.

"Poet Zamora (Unaccompanied) presents an immensely moving story of desperation and hardship in this account of his childhood migration from El Salvador to the U.S….This sheds an urgent and compassionate light on the human lives caught in an ongoing humanitarian crisis." —*Publishers Weekly*

Zamoyski, Adam
Napoleon: A Life. Adam Zamoyski. Basic Books 2018. 800 p.
ISBN 9780465055937
Grades: Adult **B**

1. Napoleon I, Emperor of the French, 1769-1821 2. Napoleonic Wars, 1800-1815 3. Generals 4. Politicians 5. Command of troops 6. Rulers 7. Politics and government 8. French history 9. France 10. 19th century 11. 18th century 12. Biographies 13. Life stories — Politics — Politicians 14. Life stories — Law and order — Military leaders 15. History writing — Europe — France 16. History writing — Wars and conflicts — Napoleonic Wars

LC 2018015891

Describes the life of Napoleon, who was born poor, became an army general at 26 and let his love of an older woman transform him into a military commander who was crowned Emperor of France by age 35.

Includes bibliographical references and index.

Zanes, Warren
Petty: The Biography. Warren Zanes. Henry Holt and Company 2015. 336 pages
ISBN 9780805099683
Grades: Adult **B**

1. Petty, Tom 2. Rock groups 3. Rock music 4. Musicians 5. Rock musicians 7. United States 8. Biographies 9. Life stories — Arts and culture — Performing arts — Musicians and composers 10. Arts and Entertainment — Music — Rock

LC 2015019677

Zanes provides an honest and evocative examination of Petty's music, and the remarkable rock and roll history he and his band helped to write. Petty was a kid without a whole lot of promise; rock and roll made it otherwise. His story has all the drama ofa rock and roll epic. Dark and mysterious, Petty manages to come back, again and again, showing us what the music can do and where it can take us.

Zanglein, Jayne E.
The Girl Explorers: The Untold Story of the Globetrotting Women Who Trekked, Flew, and Fought Their Way Around the World. Jayne Zanglein. Sourcebooks Inc 2021. xxxvii, 376 pages : Illustration
ISBN 9781728215242
Grades: Adult **B**

1. Niles, Blair 2. Earhart, Amelia, 1897-1937 3. Women explorers 4. History writing — Women's history 5. History writing — Exploration

LC 2020053533

Don't take women when you go exploring!" in 1932, Roy Chapman Andrews, the president of the Explorers Club, told hundreds of female students at Barnard College that women and exploration could never mix. He obviously didn't know a thing about either… the Girl Explorers is the inspirational and untold story of the women who broke apart the stuffy men's club and founded the Society of Woman Geographers (SWG), and how some key members—including Blair Niles, Amelia Earhart, Gloria Hollister, and Anna Heyward Taylor-paved the way for women scientists by scaling mountains, exploring the seas, flying across the Atlantic, and recording the world through film, sculpture, and art.

"Historian Zanglein debuts with an entertaining look at the founders and early members of the International Society of Women Geographers." —*Publishers Weekly*

Includes bibliographical references (pages 333-373).

Zara, Christopher
Uneducated: A Memoir of Flunking Out, Falling Apart, and Finding My Worth. Christopher Zara. Little Brown & Company 2023. 272 p.
ISBN 9780316268974
Grades: Adult B
1. Zara, Christopher 2. Identity 3. Social classes 4. Journalism 5. Flunking 6. Journalists 7. Universities and colleges 8. Drug abuse 9. Education 10. Autobiographies and memoirs 11. Humor writing — Social humor 12. Life stories — Education

Boldly honest, wryly funny, and utterly open-hearted, Uneducated is one diploma-less journalist's map of our growing educational divide and, ultimately, a challenge: in our credential-obsessed world, what is the true value of a college degree?

"More than anything, Zara writes a necessary and inspiring story about how we are more than our educational histories." —*Booklist*

Zauner, Michelle
★ *Crying in H Mart: A Memoir.* Michelle Zauner. Alfred A. Knopf 2021. 320 p. : Illustration
ISBN 9780525657743
Grades: Adult B
1. Zauner, Michelle 2. Rock musicians 3. Korean Americans 4. Identity 5. Families 6. Grief 7. Loss 8. Mothers and daughters 9. Growing up 10. Death of mothers 11. Singers 12. East Asian Americans 13. People with terminal illnesses 14. Mothers 15. Autobiographies and memoirs 16. Life stories — Arts and culture — Performing arts — Musicians and composers 17. Life stories — Identity — Race and ethnicity 18. Life stories — Relationships — Family 19. Family and Relationships — General

LC 2020022470

The Japanese Breakfast indie pop star presents a full-length account of her viral New Yorker essay to share poignant reflections on her experiences of growing up Korean-American, becoming a professional musician and caring for her terminally ill mother.

"Based on the viral 2018 New Yorker essay of the same name, this debut by Zauner is an exceptionally vivid memoir that deftly explores the complex relationships between culture and family, mothers and daughters." —*Library Journal*

Zenith, Richard
Pessoa: A Biography. Richard Zenith. Liveright Publishing 2021. 992 p.
ISBN 9780871404718
Grades: Adult B
1. Pessoa, Fernando, 1888-1935 2. Poets 3. Men recluses 4. Eccentrics and eccentricities 5. Anonyms and pseudonyms 6. Intellectual life 7. Poetry writing 8. Literary criticism 9. Portuguese people 10. 20th century 11. Biographies 12. Life stories — Arts and culture — Writing — Poets 13. Arts and Entertainment — Writing and Publishing

LC 2021005140

Eighty-five years after his wrenching death in a cramped Lisbon apartment, where he left more than 25,000 manuscript sheets in a wooden trunk, Fernando Pessoa (1888-1935) remains one of the most enigmatic and underappreciated poets of the twentieth century. Celebrated for writing in dozens of different poetic voices, known as heteronyms, Pessoa has finally found his definitive biographer in renowned translator Richard Zenith. Setting the story of Pessoa's life against the nationalistic currents of early twentieth-century European history, Zenith charts the depths of Pessoa's explosive imagination and literary genius.

"Zenith delivers careful readings of Pessoa's works and examines with sensitivity his varied intellectual, spiritual, and aesthetic proclivities as well as his longing for posthumous fame, which he amply accrued." —*Kirkus*

Includes bibliographical references and index.

Zimmerman, Paul
Dr. Z: The Lost Memoirs of an Irreverent Football Writer. Paul Zimmerman; edited by Peter King. Triumph Books 2017. 280 p.
ISBN 9781629374642
Grades: Adult B
1. Zimmerman, Paul 2. Sportswriters 3. Athletes 4. Sports 5. Authors 6. Football 7. Social life and customs 8. United States 9. 20th century 10. Autobiographies and memoirs 11. Biographies 12. Life stories — Sports 13. Sports and competition — General

LC 2017009840

Dr. Z's memoir is a rich package of personalities, stories never shared about such characters as Vince Lombardi, Walter Payton, Lawrence Taylor, and Johnny Unitas. Even Joe Namath, with whom Zimmerman had a legendary and well-documented 23-year feud, saw fit to eventually unburden himself to the remarkable scribe.

Zoglin, Richard
Hope: Entertainer of the Century. Richard Zoglin. Simon & Schuster 2014. 384 p.
ISBN 9781439140277
Grades: Adult B
1. Hope, Bob, 1903-2003 2. Comedians 3. United States 4. Biographies 5. Arts and Entertainment — Comedy 6. Life stories — Arts and culture — Performing arts — Entertainers and celebrities

LC 2014014371

Draws on exclusive reporting to honor Bob Hope's top-rated successes while discussing such topics as his secret first marriage, stint in reform school and ambivalent relationships with fellow stars.

"Not just for Hope fans, Zoglins work will also appeal to readers interested in the colorful history of American entertainment, in which Hope played a prominent role." —*Booklist*

Includes bibliographical references and index.

Zuckerman, Gregory
The Frackers: The Outrageous Inside Story of the New Billionaire Wildcatters. Gregory Zuckerman. Portfolio Penguin 2013. 320 p.
ISBN 9781591846451
Grades: Adult B
1. Oil industry and trade 2. Entrepreneurs 3. Natural gas industry and trade 4. Energy industry and trade 5. Businesspeople 6. Hydraulic fracturing 7. Natural resources 8. Natural gas 9. Gas wells 10. Politics and global affairs — Environmental issues and policies 11. Nonfiction that reads like fiction

LC 2013037926

Documents the innovations pursued in response to the energy crisis that has rendered the United States the world's fastest-growing energy power, tracing the contributions of a group of ambitious individuals who tapped massive, long-overlooked oil deposits while making or losing their fortunes.

"[S]hows us the beneficial side of fracking and the potentially environmentally disastrous side, and lets us find our own ground to stand on. A lively, exciting, and definitely thought-provoking book." —*Booklist*

Zuckoff, Mitchell
Ponzi's Scheme: The True Story of a Financial Legend. Mitchell Zuckhoff. Random House 2005. xiii, 390 p. : Illustration
ISBN 9781400060399
Grades: Adult B
1. Ponzi, Charles 2. Swindlers and swindling 3. Ponzi schemes 4. White collar crime 5. True Crime — General

LC 2004046770

A look at the career of the man who developed the most famous scheme in American finance explains how, in 1920, Charles Ponzi raked in millions of dollars from investors by promising them he could double their investments in three months.

"The author chronicles Ponzi's mercurial rise and fall as he conjured up one get-rich-quick scheme after another. Zuckoff provides not only a definitive por-

ESSENTIAL AND RECOMMENDED TITLES
Biography

trait of Ponzi's life but also insights into immigrant life and the social world of early 20th-century Boston." —*Publishers Weekly*

Includes bibliographical references (p. [373]-375) and index.

Zweibel, Alan
Laugh Lines: My Life Helping Funny People Be Funnier : A Cultural Memoir. Alan Zweibel; foreword by Billy Crystal. Abrams Press 2020. 336 p.

ISBN 9781419735288

Grades: Adult   B

1. Zweibel, Alan 2. Comedians 3. Television writers 4. Humorous writing 5. Television comedies 6. Television comedy writers 7. Actors and actresses 8. Entertainment industry and trade 9. Autobiographies and memoirs 10. Life stories — Arts and culture — Writing 11. Arts and Entertainment — Comedy 12. Arts and Entertainment — Movies and Television

LC Bl2020046065

Alan Zweibel started his comedy career selling jokes for seven dollars apiece to the last of the Borscht Belt standups. Then one night, despite bombing on stage, he caught the attention of Lorne Michaels and became one of the first writers at Saturday Night Live, where he penned classic material for Gilda Radner, John Belushi, and all of the original Not Ready for Prime Time Players. From SNL, he went on to have a hand in a series of landmark shows—from It's Garry Shandling's Show to Curb Your Enthusiasm. Throughout the pages of Laugh Lines Zweibel weaves together his own stories and interviews with his friends and contemporaries, including Richard Lewis, Eric Idle, Bob Saget, Mike Birbiglia, Sarah Silverman, Judd Apatow, Dave Barry, Carl Reiner, and more.

"Comics and comedy fans alike will delight in this hilarious and self-deprecating memoir." —*Publishers Weekly*

Zwick, Edward
★ *Hits, Flops, and Other Illusions: My Fortysomething Years in Hollywood.* Ed Zwick. Gallery Books 2024. 288 p.

ISBN 9781668046999

Grades: Adult   B

1. Zwick, Edward 2. Film producers and directors 3. Television producers and directors 4. Memories 5. Actors and actresses 6. Filmmaking 7. Creation (Literary, artistic, etc.) 8. Entertainment industry and trade 9. North American people 10. American people 11. Autobiographies and memoirs 12. Life stories — Arts and culture — Performing arts — Directors and producers 13. Arts and Entertainment — Movies and Television 14. Debut title

"I'll be dropping a few names," Ed Zwick confesses in the introduction to his book. "Over the years I have worked with self-proclaimed masters-of-the-universe, unheralded geniuses, hacks, sociopaths, savants, and saints." Written mostly with love, sometimes with rue, this memoir is also a meditation on working, sprinkled throughout with tips for anyone who has ever imagined writing, directing, or producing for the screen. Fans with an appreciation for the beautiful mysteries—as well as the unsightly, often comic truths—of crafting film and television won't want to miss it.

"Director, producer, and writer Zwick shares the highs and lows of his storied career in this lively and intimate memoir." —*Booklist*